Black's Law Dictionary®

Tenth Edition

BOOKS WRITTEN OR EDITED BY BRYAN A. GARNER

Black's Law Dictionary
(all post-1995 editions)

Garner's Dictionary of Legal Usage

Garner's Modern American Usage

Reading Law: The Interpretation of Legal Texts
with Justice Antonin Scalia

Making Your Case: The Art of Persuading Judges
with Justice Antonin Scalia

The Winning Brief
100 Tips for Persuasive Briefing in Trial and Appellate Courts

The Redbook: A Manual on Legal Style

Garner on Language and Writing
(preface by Justice Ruth Bader Ginsburg)

Legal Writing in Plain English

The Elements of Legal Style
(preface by Charles Alan Wright)

The Winning Oral Argument

Ethical Communications for Lawyers

The Chicago Manual of Style, ch. 5, "Grammar and Usage"

HBR Guide to Better Business Writing

Securities Disclosure in Plain English

The Rules of Golf in Plain English
with Jeffrey Kuhn

Quack This Way:
David Foster Wallace and Bryan A. Garner Talk Language and Writing

A New Miscellany-at-Law
by Sir Robert Megarry

Texas, Our Texas: Remembrances of the University

Black's Law Dictionary®

Tenth Edition

Bryan A. Garner
Editor in Chief

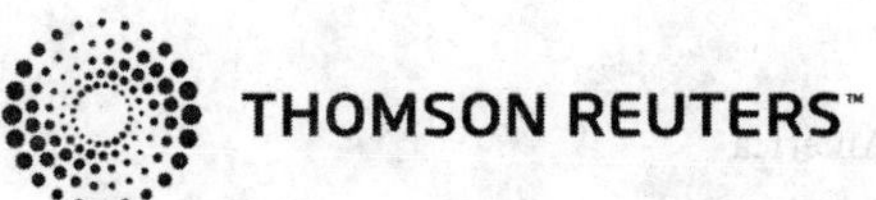

Mat # 41372510
Mat # 41513461—deluxe

Disclaimer

Although this publication was created to provide you with accurate and authoritative information about legal terminology, it was not necessarily prepared by persons licensed to practice law in a particular jurisdiction. The publisher is not engaged in rendering legal or other professional advice, and this publication is not a substitute for an attorney's advice. If you require legal or other expert advice, you should seek the services of a competent attorney or other professional.

Copyright Clearance Center

Copyright information

610 Opperman Drive
St. Paul, MN 55123
1-800-313-9378
Printed in the United States of America

ISBN: 978-0-314-61300-4
ISBN: 978-0-314-62130-6 (deluxe)

Black's Law Dictionary

Tenth Edition

EDITOR IN CHIEF

Bryan A. Garner, J.D., LL.D.
President, LawProse, Inc.
Distinguished Research Professor of Law
Southern Methodist University
Dallas, Texas

ASSOCIATE EDITORS

Karolyne H.C. Garner, J.D.
LawProse, Inc.
Dallas, Texas

Tiger Jackson, J.D., LL.M.
LawProse, Inc.
Dallas, Texas

Becky R. McDaniel, J.D.
LawProse, Inc.
Dallas, Texas

Jeff Newman, J.D.
LawProse, Inc.
Dallas, Texas

CONTRIBUTING LAWYER–EDITORS

Herbert J. Hammond
Dallas, Texas

Tony Honoré
Oxford, England

Brian Melendez
Minneapolis, Minnesota

Gary Muldoon
Rochester, New York

Ann Taylor Schwing
Sacramento, California

Fred Shapiro
New Haven, Connecticut

Joseph F. Spaniol Jr.
Bethesda, Maryland

PRONUNCIATION EDITOR

Charles Harrington Elster
San Diego, California

PANEL OF ACADEMIC CONTRIBUTORS
Page vi

PANEL OF PRACTITIONER CONTRIBUTORS
Page vii

Black's Law Dictionary

PANEL OF ACADEMIC CONTRIBUTORS

Hans W. Baade
University of Texas

Lynn A. Baker
University of Texas

Thomas E. Baker
Florida International University

Mitchell N. Berman
University of Texas

Barbara Aronstein Black
Columbia University

Hon. Thomas Buergenthal
George Washington University

Edward H. Cooper
University of Michigan

Daniel Robert Coquillette
Boston College

David Crump
University of Houston

Ross E. Davies
George Mason University

Deborah A. DeMott
Duke University

Deborah W. Denno
Fordham University

A. Darby Dickerson
Texas Tech University

Christopher R. Drahozal
University of Kansas

James Joseph Duane
Regent University

Meredith J. Duncan
University of Houston

David G. Epstein
University of Richmond

(the late) E. Allan Farnsworth
Columbia University

Ward Farnsworth
University of Texas

Martha A. Field
Harvard University

Monroe H. Freedman
Hofstra University

Richard D. Freer
Emory University

Mark A. Geistfeld
New York University

S. Elizabeth Gibson
University of North Carolina

Antonio Gidi
University of Houston

Alex Glashausser
Washburn University

(the late) Richard J. Graving
South Texas College of Law

Alan Gunn
University of Notre Dame

Egon Guttman
American University

Geoffrey C. Hazard Jr.
University of California–Hastings

R.H. Helmholz
University of Chicago

Tony Honoré
Oxford University

Heidi M. Hurd
University of Illinois

Julian C. Juergensmeyer
Georgia State University

Sanford H. Kadish
University of California at Berkeley

Gideon Kanner
Loyola Law School

Joseph Kimble
Thomas M. Cooley Law School

Edward J. Kionka
Southern Illinois University

Douglas Laycock
University of Virginia

(the late) Saúl Litvinoff
Louisiana State University

John S. Lowe
Southern Methodist University

(the late) Julius J. Marke
St. John's University

Mary Beth Matthews
University of Arkansas

Thomas William Mayo
Southern Methodist University

Lucy S. McGough
Appalachian School of Law

Joseph W. McKnight
Southern Methodist University

John K. McNulty
University of California at Berkeley

Ernest Metzger
University of Aberdeen

James E. Moliterno
Washington & Lee University

Jane Campbell Moriarty
Duquesne University

James A.R. Nafziger
Willamette University

John B. Oakley
University of California at Davis

John V. Orth
University of North Carolina

Mary F. Radford
Georgia State University

Alan N. Resnick
Hofstra University

O.F. Robinson
University of Glasgow

Hon. Jean Rosenbluth
University of Southern California

Paul Frederick Rothstein
Georgetown University

Ronald Daniel Rotunda
Chapman University

Stephen A. Saltzburg
George Washington University

Ronald J. Scalise Jr.
Tulane University

Frederic S. Schwartz
Oklahoma City University

Charles Silver
University of Texas

Lawrence M. Solan
Brooklyn Law School

John G. Sprankling
Pacific McGeorge School of Law

Marc I. Steinberg
Southern Methodist University

Michael F. Sturley
University of Texas

Symeon C. Symeonides
Willamette University

Peter Meijes Tiersma
Loyola Law School

Mark V. Tushnet
Harvard University

William D. Underwood
Mercer University

David M. Walker
University of Glasgow

Robert Weisberg
Stanford Law School

Mary Whisner
University of Washington

Peter Winship
Southern Methodist University

Charles W. Wolfram
Cornell Law School

Richard C. Wydick
University of California at Davis

A.N. Yiannopoulos
Tulane University

Kyu Ho Youm
University of Oregon

Judith T. Younger
University of Minnesota

Black's Law Dictionary

PANEL OF PRACTITIONER CONTRIBUTORS

Sherri K. Adelkoff
Pittsburgh, Pennsylvania

Daniel Alexander
Los Angeles, California

Suzanne Antley
San Diego, California

Leslie Karyn Arfine
Ridgefield, Connecticut

John R. Armstrong II
Irvine, California

Brad D. Bailey
Evergreen, Colorado

William P. Baker
Baltimore, Maryland

Judith M. Bambace
San Diego, California

Daniel P. Barer
Los Angeles, California

Ben A. Baring Jr.
Houston, Texas

Chad Baruch
Dallas, Texas

Isabel Barzun
New York, New York

Eric S. Basse
Bremerton, Washington

Laurie T. Baulig
Lancaster, Pennsylvania

Hugh C. Beck
Littleton, Ohio

Adron W. Beene
San Jose, California

Bill C. Berger
Denver, Colorado

Xanthe M. Berry
Oakland, California

Nathan V. Bishop
East Hills, New York

Michael R. Blum
San Francisco, California

Deborah L. Borman
Chicago, Illinois

Sara E. Bouley
Salt Lake City, Utah

Kevin J. Breer
Westwood, Kansas

Mark A. Bregman
Scottsdale, Arizona

Beth A. Brennan
Missoula, Montana

Joyce Murphy Brooks
Charlotte, North Carolina

Diana Brown
Houston, Texas

Lynne Thaxter Brown
Fresno, California

James Andrew Browne
San Francisco, California

Julie A. Buffington
Dallas, Texas

B. Chad Bungard
Fredericksburg, Virginia

Beverly Ray Burlingame
Dallas, Texas

Fritz Byers
Toledo, Ohio

H. Thomas Byron III
Washington, D.C.

Christopher A. Camardello
Minneapolis, Minnesota

David D. Cardone
San Diego, California

David L. Cargille
New York, New York

Robert J. Carty Jr.
Houston, Texas

Thomas L. Casey
Lansing, Michigan

Bradley Charles
Grand Rapids, Michigan

Li Chen
Dallas, Texas

Jordan B. Cherrick
St. Louis, Missouri

Peter Clapp
Richmond, California

Kristina A. Clark
Washington, D.C.

Randall B. Clark
Boston, Massachusetts

A. Craig Cleland
Atlanta, Georgia

Michael Scott Coffman
Salt Lake City, Utah

Elizabeth J. Cohen
Chicago, Illinois

Charles Dewey Cole Jr.
New York, New York

Samuel Scott Cornish
New York, New York

Emily Côté
San Jose, California

Jefferson Coulter
Seattle, Washington

Jim Covington
Springfield, Illinois

Bernadette S. Curry
Fairfield, California

Jonathan A. Darcy
Philadelphia, Pennsylvania

Elaine Maier Deering
Boca Raton, Florida

A. Charles Dell'Ario
Oakland, California

C. David Dietz
St. Paul, Minnesota

Michael J. Dimino
Washington, D.C.

Richard S. Dodd II
Reston, Virginia

Francis X. Doherty
San Rafael, California

Leah Domstead
Dallas, Texas

Preston Saul Draper
Norman, Oklahoma

John C. Duncan
Norman, Oklahoma

Gerald F. Dusing
Covington, Kentucky

Steve C. Eggimann
Minneapolis, Minnesota

Daniel P. Elms
Dallas, Texas

Ann Erickson Gault
Pontiac, Michigan

Michael T. Fackler
Jacksonville, Florida

Michael E. Faden
Rockville, Maryland

John D. Faucher
Thousand Oaks, California

Bruce Ellis Fein
Washington, D.C.

Janet Rosenblum Fipphen
Fairfield, Connecticut

Angela Fisher
Knoxville, Tennessee

Neil Fried
Arlington, Virginia

Elizabeth Klein Frumkin
Cambridge, Massachusetts

Mark W. Gaffney
Pelham Manor, New York

Duane H. Gall
Denver, Colorado

Nicole S. Gambrell
Dallas, Texas

Baldemar Garcia Jr.
Laredo, Texas

Kathryn Gardner
Topeka, Kansas

Black's Law Dictionary

PANEL OF PRACTITIONER CONTRIBUTORS

Caroline B. Garner
New York, New York

Anne W. Gill
Castle Rock, Colorado

Alexander C.D. Giza
Culver City, California

Kevin W. Grierson
Norfolk, Virginia

Ellen B. Gwynn
Tallahassee, Florida

Matthew C. Hans
St. Louis, Missouri

Yaakov Har-Oz
Beit Shemesh, Israel

William M. Hart
Minneapolis, Minnesota

Molly Hatchell
Austin, Texas

Scott M. Heenan
Cincinnati, Ohio

Marie Hejl
Austin, Texas

Susan Hoffman
San Luis Obispo, California

Jeffrey A. Hogge
Elk Grove, California

Brian John Hooper
Arlington, Virginia

Henry W. Huffnagle
Washington, D.C.

Hon. Lynn N. Hughes
Houston, Texas

Roger N. Hughes
Virginia Beach, Virginia

Maryanne Burnes Hutchinson
Braintree, Massachusetts

Amy B. Ikerd
Coldwater, Ohio

Peter O. Israel
Los Angeles, California

Dianne L. Izzo
Austin, Texas

Matthew A. Jacober
St. Louis, Missouri

Robert A. James
San Francisco, California

Eric K. Johnson
Murray, Utah

David R. Johnstone
Washington, D.C.

Richard B. Katskee
Washington, D.C.

Stuart B. Katz
Chappaqua, New York

Paul D. Keeper
Austin, Texas

Darlene Azevedo Kelly
Oakhurst, California

H. Dennis Kelly
Fort Worth, Texas

Paul Kiernan
Washington, D.C.

Clark D. Kimball
Rochester, New York

James A. King
Columbus, Ohio

Andrew D. Klein
Cherry Hill, New Jersey

Melissa Lin Klemens
Washington, D.C.

William M. Klimon
Washington, D.C.

Heléna Klumpp
Deerfield, Illinois

Jonathan H. Koenig
Wauwatosa, Wisconsin

Thomas J. Koffer
New York, New York

Christina M. Kotowski
San Francisco, California

Mike Kueber
San Antonio, Texas

Nanda P.B.A. Kumar
Philadelphia, Pennsylvania

Robert J. Lally
Cleveland, Ohio

Hon. Harriet Lansing
St. Paul, Minnesota

Geoffrey Larson
Minneapolis, Minnesota

James Hays Lawson
Louisville, Kentucky

Hon. Steve Leben
Topeka, Kansas

James V. Leito
Dallas, Texas

Michelle Thomas Leifeste
Boulder, Colorado

Andrew D. Levy
Baltimore, Maryland

Janet Li
Foster City, California

Dryden J. Liddle
Alameda, California

Raymond J. Liddy
San Diego, California

Jacob R. Lines
Tucson, Arizona

Morris D. Linton
Salt Lake City, Utah

David W. Long
Washington, D.C.

Thomas G. Lovett IV
Minneapolis, Minnesota

Margaret I. Lyle
Dallas, Texas

David P. Lyons
Chicago, Illinois

Robert N. Markle
Fairfax, Virginia

Anthony J. Marks
Los Angeles, California

Catherine M. Masters
Chicago, Illinois

Jeffrey Matloff
Bellevue, Washington

Michael J. Mauro
Stamford, Connecticut

Olga I. May
San Diego, California

Jeffrey T. McPherson
St. Louis, Missouri

John W. McReynolds
Dallas, Texas

Edward R. Mevec
Buchanan, New York

Andrew E. Miller
Los Angeles, California

Matthew C. Miller
Kansas City, Missouri

Daphna H. Mitchell
New York, New York

Michael S. Mitchell
New Orleans, Louisiana

Andrew W. Moeller
Amherst, New York

Thomas J. Moses
San Francisco, California

R. Eric Nielsen
Bethesda, Maryland

Siobhán Nurre
San Jose, California

Consuelo Marie Ohanesian
Phoenix, Arizona

Erin J. O'Leary
Orlando, Florida

Kymberly K. Oltrogge
Drippings Springs, Texas

William S. Osborn
Dallas, Texas

James C. Owens
Washington, D.C.

Black's Law Dictionary

PANEL OF PRACTITIONER CONTRIBUTORS

Christine C. Pagano
Oakland, California

Paul I. Perlman
Buffalo, New York

Arthur R. Petrie II
Newport Beach, California

Rebecca B. Phalen
Atlanta, Georgia

David Pickle
Washington, D.C.

Mark D. Plaisance
Baker, Louisiana

Matthew Eliot Pollack
Topsham, Maine

Jeffrey D. Polsky
San Francisco, California

Sam J. Polverino
San Jose, California

Christina E. Ponig
Houston, Texas

Steve Putman
Houston, Texas

Robert M. Redis
White Plains, New York

James M. Reiland
Chicago, Illinois

Tracy L. Reilly
Dallas, Texas

David E. Robbins
Broomall, Pennsylvania

Armando Rodriguez-Feo
Washington, D.C.

Susan L. Ronn
Kohimarama Auckland, New Zealand

Joseph E. Root
Montara, California

Hon. Janice M. Rosa
Erie County, New York

Glenn F. Rosenblum
Philadelphia, Pennsylvania

Joseph M. Russell
Chicago, Illinois

James B. Ryan
San Diego, California

Patrick M. Ryan
San Francisco, California

James F. Schaller II
Toledo, Ohio

Edward Schiffer
San Francisco, California

Daniel J. Schultz
Tempe, Arizona

David W. Schultz
Houston, Texas

Herbert R. Schulze
Truckee, California

Benjamin G. Shatz
Los Angeles, California

Denise Wimbiscus Shepherd
Solon, Ohio

Richard A. Sherburne Jr.
Baton Rouge, Louisiana

Anne M. Sherry
Riverswood, Illinois

Jordan M. Sickman
Southfield, Michigan

Marshall Simmons
Dallas, Texas

Fred A. Simpson
Houston, Texas

Adam Snyder
Wadsworth, Illinois

Randall J. Snyder
Bismarck, North Dakota

William C. Spence
Chicago, Illinois

Scott A. Stengel
Washington, D.C.

Heather E. Stern
Los Angeles, California

Scott Patrick Stolley
Dallas, Texas

Victor R. Stull
Redlands, California

Michelle Dimond Szambelan
Spokane, Washington

Tony Tanke
Davis, California

Craig D. Tindall
Phoenix, Arizona

Nick Tishler
Niskayuna, New York

Peter J. Toren
New York, New York

Renée Maria Tremblay
Ottawa, Ontario, Canada

Craig J. Trocino
Fort Lauderdale, Florida

R. Collins Vallée
Mandeville, Louisiana

Arthur A. Vingiello
Baton Rouge, Louisiana

M. Bruce Volbeda
Seattle, Washington

Mani S. Walia
Houston, Texas

Kristin P. Walinski
Richmond, Virginia

Richard S. Walinski
Toledo, Ohio

Alison Wallis
Harvey, Louisiana

Mark R. Wasem
Dallas, Texas

Christine E. Watchorn
Columbus, Ohio

M. John Way
Tumwater, Washington

Philip Weltner II
Atlanta, Georgia

Garner K. Weng
San Francisco, California

Eric R. Werner
Fort Worth, Texas

Donald C. Wheaton Jr.
St. Clair Shores, Michigan

Carla L. Wheeler
Chevy Chase, Maryland

Daniel R. White
Los Angeles, California

Malcolm E. Whittaker
Houston, Texas

Jamison Wilcox
Hamden, Connecticut

Hon. Bruce Donald Willis
Plymouth, Minnesota

Conrad R. Wolan
Elmira, New York

Craig M. Wolff
Yarmouth, Maine

Sara T.S. Wolff
Yarmouth, Maine

Albert J. Wollerman
Tallahassee, Florida

William C. Wright
West Palm Beach, Florida

STAFF COUNSEL

Heather C. Haines, J.D.
LawProse, Inc.
Dallas, Texas

STAFF PARALEGAL

Ryden McComas Anderson
LawProse, Inc.
Dallas, Texas

STAFF EDITOR

Hayden English
LawProse, Inc.
Dallas, Texas

STAFF PARALEGAL

Ashley E. Stroope
LawProse, Inc.
Dallas, Texas

GARNER LAW SCHOLARS – SMU SCHOOL OF LAW

Christina Gigliotti
Dallas, Texas

Ryan P. Graney
Dallas, Texas

Timothy D. Martin
The Colony, Texas

Barry A. McCain
Dallas, Texas

Arrissa K. Meyer
Dallas, Texas

Charles S. North
Dallas, Texas

Seth C. Rasmussen
Richardson, Texas

Jonathan Michael Thomas
Dallas, Texas

Peter R. Thompson
Dallas, Texas

Laurie M. Velasco
Dallas, Texas

Contents

Preface to the Tenth Edition

Most dictionary users do not read the front matter. They should but don't. You are among the cognoscenti.

After 33 years as a legal lexicographer, I can attest that marshaling, defining, arranging, and elucidating the whole of the legal vocabulary—as well as ascertaining the most classic and useful explications of terminology to be found in the literature—has never been more challenging. This tenth edition, my fourth as editor in chief, contains new material on every page: material that will be valuable to a range of dictionary users, from students to practicing lawyers to scholars and historians.

Several features of this new edition are noteworthy:

- The dating of terms is significantly more extensive. Fred Shapiro of the Yale Law Library has extended his research for this project by providing dates of earliest uses in English for nearly all the terms here recorded.
- Some 7,500 new entries have been added, after painstaking research over the past five years. Some of these new terms are colorful (e.g., *affluenza defense*, *legaldygook*), and some edgy (e.g., *judgitis*, *judicial diva*), but most are mainstream words that perhaps might have been included years ago (e.g., *rationale*, *reason*, *requisition*).
- The number of sources quoted and cited has more than doubled. Hence the bibliographic coverage has become radically more extensive—and mostly from classic works.

This last point merits elaboration. As I noted in an earlier preface (p. xxiv), I have developed a new method in this dictionary for providing illustrative quotations in which scholars comment usefully on a term, its history, its nuances and ambiguities, or the distinctions between it and its near allies. The quotations are longer than those found in the *Oxford English Dictionary* mostly because they are more than illustrative: they are substantive. With each quotation, I have tried to provide the seminal remark—the *locus classicus*—for an understanding of the term. Identifying and locating these passages was no small endeavor, yet it was a solo endeavor: this part of the work I undertook singlehandedly because it is hardly a delegable task, requiring as it does a fairly thorough grounding in Anglo-American legal literature.

Why did I not choose more quotations from caselaw? There's a simple answer and a more complex one. The simple answer is that courts, in their opinions, rarely discuss terminology in a way that elucidates anything other than the case currently being decided. They are eminently unquotable perhaps because, unlike leading scholars, they haven't spent years grappling with the subtleties of the one crucial word or phrase. Instead, they spent perhaps a day or a week writing an opinion that decides a particular case, in the course of which they may discuss a crucial word or phrase. But the discussion is typically context-specific, and often statute-specific, in a way that makes the comment of local interest only.

Contrast that approach with what my late friend Neil MacCormick, the Scottish legal philosopher, pithily wrote about the terms *lie* and *social democracy.* Or consider any of the hundreds of other examples you can readily find in these pages, for which I'll cite just a few representatives: Holdsworth (*arbitration*), Dhokalia (*codification*), G.W. Keeton (*family law*), Clapham (*human rights*), Black (*interpretation clauses*), Williams (*justification*), Plucknett (*murder*), Lieber (*nation*), Story (*promissory note*), and Paton (*vested*). A few are pleasingly fanciful, as with Palmer (*simplify*) and Pigott (*statute*). None should prove unilluminating to someone interested in the particular term.

The authors of these quotations lend the book a good deal of historical depth. Yet unlike the words of courts in their judicial opinions, the passages cited are not readily available to most lawyers and scholars, even through computer searches. They must be found the old-fashioned way: by consulting the books themselves.

Librarians and bibliographers have thanked me for the thorough bibliography in previous editions. Here it is twice the length and is set forth with greater detail in publishing history (pp. 1995–2016). Although these sources are not the only classics in legal literature, they are among the best on questions of terminological nuance. One curiosity I've noted over the years is that many legal scholars (perhaps half?) can write long books and articles without so much as a single noteworthy comment on words and phrases. As a lexicographer, I find these works dreadfully abstract and tedious. Other legal scholars are almost obsessed with words, how they are used, what they mean (or should mean), and their history. Glanville Williams comes to mind as the archetypal example. These scholars write not only with verbal astuteness but also, typically, with verve and flair. They contribute enormously to what is good in legal literature.

Black's Law Dictionary is commonly classified as a secondary resource, and that would be correct if it were merely a compilation of judicial statements—as it verged on being when I took on the editorship. If you are curious, look at the sixth edition's entry for *hotel*: not only is the definition substantively flawed, but it is also ungrammatical. It was taken nearly verbatim from the judicial opinion there cited. So were many other definitions in that edition.

I have always thought that a dictionary, properly written, should be considered a primary resource—that is, a primary lexicographic resource. The *Oxford English Dictionary* has achieved that distinction and, as the most widely cited lawbook in the English-speaking world, *Black's Law Dictionary* can certainly lay claim to it. When my colleagues and I prepare an entry, we may consult 5, 15, or perhaps 50 cases to write a definition. And we *write* them. We are not mere compilers. So no single citation to a case, or even two, would suffice to signal the authority on which the definition is based because not all the nuances would be captured in the source cited.

Citations to the West Key Number System have been eliminated from this tenth edition for a simple reason: they are constantly being altered, so that the book's citations would gradually become inaccurate. Unable to change this reality, I have simply removed them. The good news is that the extra space has proved invaluable for supplying all the new substantive material.

You might like a window into one aspect of how part of this book was produced. Let me illustrate how 900 new Latin maxims were collected and defined for Appendix B (pp. 1897–1969). Although the ninth edition of *Black's* already contained the most extensive and accurate listing of maxims in print (see page xix), I unearthed more. Consulting a 40-volume encyclopedia published between 1901 and 1913, I noticed that its coverage of legal maxims was particularly thorough. Several different editors of that set, beginning with a man named Howard P. Nash, were put in charge of maxims for that encyclopedia. I assigned two student assistants who had studied Latin to find all the maxims not included in the ninth edition. After 90 days of reviewing tens of thousands of pages in that encyclopedia, my assistants identified a thousand new maxims—or, rather, old maxims that had never been recorded in *Black's*. Then one of my lawyer–colleagues at LawProse, Heather Haines, meticulously verified the accuracy of their work against the early-20th-century encyclopedia. That was a painstaking process, and Heather made many corrections. Once all was in line with the encyclopedia, I edited the definitions in a nonsubstantive way so as to make the wordings more idiomatic and modern. Then I sent the thousand maxims off to two superb classicists in Missouri, Professor Edwin Carawan and his wife, Alison Parker, both of whom had served as consultants on maxims in the seventh through the ninth editions. They spent three months correcting the Latin, amending the translations, and supplying many citations to Roman-law classics such as Justinian's Digest, as well as to Coke. They identified 100 as being mere gibberish; these I rejected. In all, Carawan and Parker thoroughly revised about 85% of the newly discovered maxims. By all reports, it was an arduous process that showed the unreliability of the old encyclopedia.

Once all the Carawan and Parker corrections had been entered, I sent the remaining 900 maxims to Professor Tony Honoré of All Souls College, the emeritus regius professor of Roman law at Oxford University. He modified the translations of perhaps half the maxims, noting that a certain medieval concept might be better translated with a term other than the one used in the then-current draft.

It took Professor Honoré 60 days to do his work. Back in Dallas, all his corrections were entered and doubly verified.

The polished revision went back to Carawan and Parker, who found several remaining errors in the Latin. They were grateful to see Honoré's work, and they found several additional points of improvement.

Once the final corrections were entered and verified, the maxims went into Appendix B. It took a week for a LawProse staffer to verify the alphabetical ordering of all 4,000 maxims.

Having gone through this same process with all the Latin maxims over the seventh through ninth editions, we've uncovered and corrected hundreds of errors in the Latin that had appeared in the first six editions. Those errors might have occurred in the sources that Black and other lexicographers consulted in the 19th century, or they might simply have been transcription errors.

What I've just described is the typical process. We've put all the definitions in the book through a similar process of research, review, and revision by LawProse staff and by law professors, judges, and practitioners—among the best in their fields.

I would be remiss if I didn't profusely thank my dedicated colleagues at LawProse Inc. We're a small company of six lawyers, two paralegals, a staff editor, and an MBA. But that hardly tells the story. Jeff Newman has laid out every page of the last two editions—as well as most of my other recent books; he is also a superlative editor and researcher. Tiger Jackson, who joined the company in 2000, is likewise a prodigious editor and researcher, and I'm fortunate to have the benefit of her perceptive eyes. Becky McDaniel minutely verified all the thousands of edits that I and others made throughout the course of the project, and did much more besides. My wife, Karolyne H.C. Garner, reviewed many of the entries as I composed them and, as a member of the patent bar, contributed enormously to the IP terminology throughout. Heather Haines typed and proofed hundreds of quotations I selected for inclusion, almost all of them from books held in our LawProse library. (We like to own original copies of the books we cite.) Ryden Anderson and Hayden English edited with a keen eye and verified all the cross-references, among many other tasks. Ashley Stroope ably handled many logistical tasks during the final year of the project. Without the devotion of such a talented team, the qualities of this dictionary would be impossible to attain.

Over the years, I have been fortunate to acquire many friends and lexicographic allies. Not least are the contributing editors (p. v), all of whom added a great many terms within their specialties: criminal law (Muldoon), conservation and litigation (Schwing), federal agencies (Spaniol), Roman law and legal philosophy (Honoré), financial litigation (Melendez), intellectual property (Hammond), and lexicographic dating (Shapiro). I could never have imagined the degree of their assiduity and learning, nor indeed of their warm friendship. Similarly invaluable were the professors on our academic panel (p. vi) and the judges and lawyers on our practitioner panel (pp. vii–ix). Among others who merit special mention are my correspondents Marco Barreto, Josiah Daniel, Peter Kirchikov, Jordan Reilly, Sandro Tomasi, and Bruce Volbeda, all of whom have sent me useful materials.

During our collaboration on two books, Justice Antonin Scalia helped me on countless terms: I'd sneak in a lexicographic query during one of our marathon sessions in Washington as we took a short break from writing *Making Your Case* or *Reading Law*. Justice Scalia rightly insisted that the definitions in *Black's* must be utterly even-handed and must be written as much as possible from an omniscient perspective. That advice echoed extensive conversations I once had with Charles Alan Wright, my legal mentor, when I assumed the editorship in the mid-1990s. My colleagues and I have strived to make the entries as balanced, objective, and neutral as possible, whatever the subject.

I thank Thomson Reuters for all the cooperative work, especially in the electronic versions, which should be more helpful than ever. Jean Maess and John Wierzbicki have been strong supports and publishing allies. So have Heather Axtman, Andrea Delsing, Lisé Freking, Michelle Montana, Michael Marrs, Susan Martin, Michael Poccia, Chris Schultz, Lora Thody, and Sarah White.

Law librarians near and far have lent helping hands. My profound thanks go to Gail Daly and Gregory Ivy of Southern Methodist University's Underwood Law Library; Cattleya Concepcion, Melanie Knapp, and Debbie Shrager of the George Mason University Law Library; Scott B. Pagel of the George Washington University Law Library; Uwe Beltz of the Texas Tech Law Library; and Barbara A. Bintliff of the University of Texas's Tarlton Law Library. They all generously made their resources available to me whenever I was in the area, and I am grateful. The book would not have been as good as it is without them.

The incomparable Samuel Johnson once said: "Dictionaries are like watches: the worst is better than none, and the best cannot be expected to go quite true." He was right, of course. He also said, somewhat cynically, that a lexicographer cannot aspire to praise, but at most to escaping censure. Again, he was right, as almost any experienced lexicographer can attest.

Even as we go to press, I find things I'd like to supplement or alter. That's in the nature of all scholarship. Yet this edition must have an end. So I present it to the profession in hopes that it will prove to be a valuable resource.

Bryan A. Garner
Dallas, Texas
17 March 2014

Preface to the Ninth Edition

Since becoming editor in chief of *Black's Law Dictionary* in the mid-1990s, I've tried with each successive edition—the seventh, the eighth, and now the ninth—to make the book at once both more scholarly and more practical.

Anyone who cares to put this book alongside the sixth or earlier editions will discover that the book has been almost entirely rewritten, with an increase in precision and clarity. It's true that I've cut some definitions that appeared in the sixth and earlier editions. On a representative sample of two consecutive pages of the sixth can be found *botulism*, *bouche* (mouth), *bough of a tree*, *bought* (meaning "purchased"), *bouncer* (referring to a nightclub employee), *bourg* (a village), *boulevard*, *bourgeois*, *brabant* (an obscure kind of ancient coin also called a *crocard*), *brabanter* (a mercenary soldier in the Middle Ages), and *brachium maris* (an arm of the sea). These can hardly be counted as legal terms worthy of inclusion in a true law dictionary, and *Black's* had been properly criticized for including headwords such as these.*

Meanwhile, though, within the same span of terms, I've added entries for three types of boundaries (*agreed boundary*, *land boundary*, *lost boundary*), as well as for *bounty hunter*, *bounty land*, *bounty-land warrant*, *boutique* (a specialized law firm), *box day* (a day historically set aside for filing papers in Scotland's Court of Session), *box-top license* (also known as a *shrink-wrap license*), *Boykin Act* (an intellectual-property statute enacted after World War II), *Boyle defense* (also known as the *government-contractor defense*), *bracket system* (the tax term), *Bracton* (the title of one of the earliest, most important English lawbooks), and *Brady Act* (the federal law for background checks on handgun-purchasers). And all the other entries have been wholly revised—shortened here and amplified there to bring the book into better proportion.

Hence, in one brief span of entries, the sixth and the ninth editions appear to be entirely different books. That's true throughout the work.

But it's not as if I've revised the book with any hostility toward historical material. In fact, I've added hundreds of Roman-law terms that had been omitted from earlier editions and retranslated all the others on grounds that current users of the dictionary might need to look up the meanings of these historical terms. But whatever appears here, in my view, should be plausibly a law-related term—and *closely* related to the law.

Users ought to be reminded once again about the handy collection of legal maxims in Appendix B. It is, I believe, the most comprehensive and accurate set of translated maxims to be found anywhere in print—thanks to the erudite revisions of two civil-law experts of the first rank: Professor Tony Honoré of Oxford and Professor David Walker of Glasgow.

A lexicographer must do what is practicable to improve each new edition of a dictionary. One of the notable features of this new edition is the dating of the most common terms—that is, the parenthetical inclusion of a date to show the term's earliest known use in the English language. For researching these dates, I'm grateful to the distinguished and industrious lexicographer at the Yale Law Library, Fred R. Shapiro.

*See David Mellinkoff, *The Myth of Precision and the Law Dictionary*, 31 U.C.L.A. L. Rev. 423, 440 (1983).

PREFACE TO THE NINTH EDITION

As a lexicographer, I've learned a great deal from my friends and mentors in the field—especially the late Robert W. Burchfield, editor of the *Oxford English Dictionary Supplement* during the latter half of the 20th century. Like his 19th-century precursors at the *Oxford English Dictionary*, Burchfield had a battalion of lexicographic volunteers from around the globe to help him in his momentous work.

I have tried to do the same. Because I genuinely believe in a community of scholars—a community of learned people who understand the cultural and historical importance of having a first-rate dictionary, and are willing to play a role in producing it—I have called on volunteers to help in the production of this vast and complex dictionary. It has been rewarding to have so many lawyers, judges, and scholars answer the call. Take a moment, if you will, and scan the masthead on pages vi–ix. Consider that each of these contributors personally edited 30 to 50 pages of single-spaced manuscript—some more than that. They suggested improved wordings and solved editorial difficulties they encountered. Consider the geographical variety of the panelists, and ponder the years of specialist knowledge they brought to their work. Look at the panel of academic contributors (p. vi) and notice that they are distinguished scholars of the highest order, many of them household names among lawyers. They exerted themselves not just for the betterment of this book, but for the betterment of the law as a whole. For this is the law dictionary that the profession has relied on for over a century. Everyone who cares about the law owes our contributors a debt of thanks.

Bryan A. Garner
LawProse, Inc.
Dallas, Texas
April 2009

Preface to the Eighth Edition

This massive new edition of *Black's Law Dictionary* continues the undertaking begun by Henry Campbell Black in 1891: to marshal legal terms to the fullest possible extent and to define them accurately. But more than that, it continues the effort begun with the seventh edition: to follow established lexicographic principles in selecting headwords and in phrasing definitions, to provide easy-to-follow pronunciations, and to raise the level of scholarship through serious research and careful reassessment.*

The terminology in several fields of law now finds greater coverage in the book than ever before. Specialists generously improved our treatment of terms in admiralty (Michael F. Sturley), contracts (E. Allan Farnsworth), criminal law (Stephen A. Saltzburg, Robert Weisberg), ecclesiastical law (R.H. Helmholz), family law (Lucy S. McGough, Janice M. Rosa), federal agencies (Joseph F. Spaniol Jr.), international law (Thomas Buergenthal), Louisiana law (Saúl Litvinoff, Symeon Symeonides, A.N. Yiannopoulos), oil and gas (John S. Lowe), parliamentary law (Brian Melendez), Roman law (Tony Honoré, O.F. Robinson, Ernest Metzger), and Scots law (O.F. Robinson, David Walker).

Beyond those specialized reviews, however, a newly created panel of academicians reviewed the entire alphabetical span of the book. That way, the entire text received thorough scrutiny by many of the best legal minds in the world. Entries have been updated and expanded to reflect both contemporary and historical usage. I am much indebted to everyone on the panel (see p. vi).

Many intellectual-property lawyers reviewed and commented on the terms in their field: Ray Aust, David L. Cargille, Li Chin, Jonathan A. Darcy, Michael J. Dimino, Herbert J. Hammond, Karen G. Horowitz, Audrey E. Klein, Nanda P.B.A. Kumar, Eric Myers, Jeff Mode, Todd A. Norton, Michael A. Papalas, Tracy L. Reilly, and Eric Sofir. Special thanks go to Herbert J. Hammond, who expertly drafted many entries for intellectual property.

The first two appendixes have been greatly amplified. Kurt Adamson of the Underwood Law Library at Southern Methodist University skillfully prepared the table of abbreviations found in Appendix A. The legal maxims in Appendix B were scrutinized and corrected by Professors Honoré and Walker. The maxims have been amended and supplemented to such a degree that it can probably be called the most exhaustive and authoritative collection anywhere to be found.

For the first time, *Black's Law Dictionary* contains citations to key numbers and to *Corpus Juris Secundum* — a significant aid to research. My special thanks to Robin Gernandt, who spearheaded the effort, along with his many colleagues: Jill Bergquist, Kara Boucher, Barbara Bozonie, David Brueggemann, Kevin Callahan, Dan Dabney, Lynn Dale, Lisa Dittmann, Robert Dodd, Wayne Foster, Valerie Garber, Phil Geller, Gerald Gross, Craig Gustafson, Nancy Johnson, Charles Kloos, Nicholas Koster, Jana Kramer, Patricia Larson, Jeffrey Locke, Richard Mattson, Timothy Nornes, Joel Nurre, Frederick Steimann, James Vculek, and Linda Watts. Three who did an extraordinary

---

**See generally* Bryan A. Garner, *Legal Lexicography: A View from the Front Lines*, 6 Green Bag 2d 151 (2003).

amount of this highly skilled work merit double mention: Robin Gernandt, Phil Geller, and Lisa Dittmann.

Several splendid lawyers helped edit the manuscript in the final months, often working nights and weekends. My thanks to Julie Buffington, Beverly Ray Burlingame, Nicole Gambrell, and Ann Schwing. Others — namely, Jordan Cherrick, Charles Dewey Cole Jr., Margaret I. Lyle, Steve Putman, and Scott Patrick Stolley — generously took on the task of reviewing batches of new entries. They all made the book better than it otherwise would have been.

In the final stages of preparing the manuscript, Mayuca Salazar and Liliana Taboada, two learned lawyers from Monterrey, Mexico, helpfully reviewed the several Spanish-law terms that appear here.

In the last few days before the manuscript went to the printer, several Minneapolis-area lawyers volunteered to proofread batches of manuscript. My thanks to Catherine Berryman, Vanya S. Hogen, Seth J.S. Leventhal, Michael A. Stanchfield, and Edward T. Wahl. They all made valuable contributions.

As in the past, the business side of producing the dictionary ran smoothly. At West, Doug Powell, Pamela Siege Chandler, and Louis H. Higgins all provided important support. Timothy L. Payne of West painstakingly shepherded the book through production.

Many others have contributed to the book in one way or another: Angee Calvert, Edwin Carawan, Caroline B. Garner, Harris L. Hartz, Donald F. Hawbaker, Cynde L. Horne, Thomas B. Lemann, Karen Magnuson, R. Eric Nielsen, Alison Parker, Wanda Raiford, Patrick M. Ryan, David W. Schultz, Andre Stipanovic, and Christina E. Wilson. As in the seventh edition, we had the benefit of Charles Harrington Elster's excellent pronunciations.

Finally, I thank my two assistant editors, Tiger Jackson and Jeff Newman, who worked closely with me for several years to produce this much-amplified eighth edition.

Bryan A. Garner
Dallas, Texas
February 2004

Preface to the Seventh Edition

When Henry Campbell Black published the first edition of *Black's Law Dictionary* back in 1891, the *Oxford English Dictionary* had not yet been completed. Nor was the *OED* finished when Black prepared his second edition in 1910. By today's standards, the "gentle art of lexicography,"[1] as it has been called, was yet to experience the tremendous dictionary-making developments that the 20th century had in store, the highlights being the *OED* (1928), *Webster's Second* (1934), *Webster's Third* (1961), and the second edition of the *OED* (1989). Largely through the influence of these major works, dictionaries today are much better than they used to be.

Legal scholarship has also made tremendous strides — even in describing pre-19th-century law. The great legal historians Pollock, Maitland, and Holdsworth had not yet produced their monumental works when Black put out the first edition. Our understanding of Roman law is better today than it was a century ago. Our understanding of feudal law is much better. Meanwhile, our precedent-based system still has not entirely escaped the influence of Roman and feudal law.

At the same time, modern law hurtles headlong into decade after decade of new statutes, new doctrines, and new tripartite tests. The world — as well as the law that tries to govern it — is changing at a dizzying pace. If you want evidence of this change, look inside for the hundreds of new entries such as *cyberstalking, jurimetrics, parental kidnapping, quid pro quo sexual harassment, reproductive rights,* and *viatical settlement.*

Given all these developments—both in lexicography and in law—it is hardly surprising that, by the end of the 20th century, *Black's Law Dictionary* had come to need a major overhaul. This edition is the result of that effort.

New Features in the Seventh Edition

Significant strides have been made both in modernizing this edition and in improving its historical depth. The editors' goal was to make it at once the most scholarly and the most practical edition ever published. More than 4,500 entries in the book are entirely new. (Some of the new entries are surprising: previous editions had omitted some commonplace terms such as *act of Congress, circuit judge, motion for summary judgment, senatorial courtesy,* and *sidebar comment.*) Of the remaining 20,000 entries, all have been thoroughly revised: sharpened and tightened.

Aside from the thousands of new entries and subentries, the differences between earlier editions and this one are many. The headwords show whether a term should be uppercase or lowercase, roman or italic. The pronunciation symbols are easy to understand. For the first time ever, etymologies systematically appear. Senses of words are analytically broken down and given numbers — as never before. Definitions are clearer than ever (though the battle for clarity, when the subject is feudal law, can never be completely won). Bullets now appear within definitions to help differentiate definitional information (before the bullet) from encyclopedic information (after the bullet). More

1. Eric Partridge, *The Gentle Art of Lexicography, as Pursued and Experienced by an Addict* (1963).

than 2,000 newly added quotations from some 400 important works of Anglo-American legal scholarship appear throughout the text to help convey the nuances of the legal vocabulary. (More about these in a moment.) The 2,200 legal maxims (mostly Latin) are conveniently collected in an appendix, instead of cluttering the main lexicon. In addition, my colleagues and I have:

- Attempted a thorough marshaling of the language of the law from original sources.
- Examined the writings of specialist scholars rather than looking only at judicial decisions.
- Considered entries entirely anew rather than merely accepting what previous editions have said. We have often checked Westlaw and other sources when trying to decide which of two competing forms now predominates in legal usage.
- Imposed analytical rigor on entries by avoiding duplicative definitions and by cataloguing and numbering senses.
- Ensured that specialized vocabularies are included — from bankruptcy to securities law, from legal realism to critical legal studies.

This modern approach to legal lexicography is only a beginning. To its great credit, the West Group has now made the editing of *Black's Law Dictionary*, in its various editions, an ongoing project. This means that *Black's*, like all major dictionaries outside the law, will be a continuing work in progress. As the law continues its rapid evolution, *Black's Law Dictionary* will keep apace.

The Inclusion of Scholarly Quotations

In a novel feature, more than 2,000 quotations from scholarly works appear throughout the text to help round out the treatment of various terms. In selecting these quotations, my colleagues and I have sought a blend of characteristics: temporal and geographic range, aptness, and insight. Some scholars show great astuteness in discussing terminology — particularly Blackstone (English law), Glanville Williams (criminal law and jurisprudence), Rollin Perkins (criminal law), and Charles Alan Wright (federal procedure). Although Blackstone and Wright are well known to American lawyers, Williams and Perkins are not: their work deserves more widespread attention.

In the Bibliography of Works Cited (Appendix I) appear the 400-plus lawbooks cited in these pages. We have tried to locate the best scholarly discussions of legal terminology and to give snippets of them. In future editions, we intend to continue this practice, and we encourage readers to submit published quotations for this purpose.

The Challenge of Legal Lexicography

Law dictionaries have a centuries-old tradition of apologizing in advance for errors and omissions. Some of the apologies are moving — especially to one who understands the arduousness of lexicography — and a few border on the humorous:

1607: "[I]f I have either omitted any hard word within my circuit, or set it downe not expounded, I give you good leave to impute the one to my negligence, the other to mine ignorance: and so commend these my paines to your best profit, and you unto God."[2]

1670: "If I have sometimes committed a *Jeofaile*, or hunted Counter in any explication or Etymology, in so large a field of words, and stor'd with such variety of Game, it will be no wonder, and, I hope, will draw no censure upon me from the Ingenuous. . . . [I]f I leave some words with a *Quaere* . . . to be resolved or corrected by the more learned; it is but what Cowell frequently, and Spelman has sometimes done."[3]

1732: "[W]here there is such great Variety of Learning and abundant Quantity of Nice Matter, with the utmost Care, there must be some Faults and Failings to be Pardon'd by the Reader."[4]

1839: "To those who are aware of the difficulties of the task, the author deems it unnecessary to make any apology for the imperfections which may be found in the work. His object has been to be useful; if that has been accomplished in any degree, he will be amply rewarded for his labour; and he relies upon the generous liberality of the members of the profession to overlook the errors which may have been committed in his endeavours to serve them."[5]

1848: "It is not without very considerable diffidence, that this Lexicon is submitted to the indulgence of the Profession and the Public, for no man can be more conscious of the difficulties besetting such a subject — of the many requisites of the task — and above all, of the great discrepancy usually exhibited between what a book *ought to be*, and what it *is* — than the Author of the present undertaking."[6]

1859: "[T]he work is now submitted to the examination of the profession. That its execution has fallen far short of its design, is already but too apparent to the author's own observation. Of the defects that may be discovered in its pages, some seem to be inseparable from the task of first compiling any matter of the kind from sources so numerous, and scattered over so wide a field."[7]

1874: "[W]ithout craving the indulgence of the public, whose servant he is, and to whom, therefore, if he serve up anything he should in all conscience serve up a proper dish, [the Author] is reluctant to acknowledge that an unaccustomed feeling of diffidence has once or twice assailed him, lest his work should not prove so absolutely faultless or so generally useful as it has been his wish to make it."[8]

In the first edition of this book (1891), Henry Campbell Black broke the tradition, boldly asserting the exhaustiveness of his work:

"The dictionary now offered to the profession is the result of the author's endeavor to prepare a concise and yet comprehensive book of definitions of the terms, phrases, and maxims used in American and English law and necessary to be

---

2. John Cowell, *The Interpreter* 5 (1607).

3. Thomas Blount, *Nomo-Lexicon: A Law-Dictionary* [n.p.] (1670).

4. Giles Jacob, *A New Law-Dictionary* 4 (2d ed. 1732).

5. John Bouvier, *A Law Dictionary* viii (1839).

6. J.J.S. Wharton, *The Legal Lexicon, or Dictionary of Jurisprudence* iii (1st Am. ed. 1848).

7. Alexander M. Burrill, *A Law Dictionary and Glossary* xv (1859).

8. Archibald Brown, *A New Law Dictionary* vi (1874).

> understood by the working lawyer and judge, as well as those important to the student of legal history or comparative jurisprudence. . . . Of the most esteemed law dictionaries now in use, each will be found to contain a very considerable number of words not defined in any other. None is quite comprehensive in itself. The author has made it his aim to include *all* these terms and phrases here, together with some not elsewhere defined." Henry Campbell Black, *A Dictionary of Law* iii (1891).

There is no lack of confidence expressed anywhere in his preface.

Yet in putting forth this seventh edition, my feelings incline more to those of Black's predecessors than to those of Black himself.

A Lot of Help from Our Friends

Diffidence, though, can lead to safeguards. And so it has in this work. I engaged several distinguished scholars who thoroughly vetted the entire manuscript:

- Tony Honoré, former holder of the Regius Chair in Civil Law at Oxford University, and author of many important books, including *Causation in the Law* (with H.L.A. Hart).
- Joseph F. Spaniol Jr., former Clerk of the Supreme Court of the United States, whose wide-ranging experience includes decades of service in federal rulemaking as a consultant to the Standing Committee on Rules of Practice and Procedure.
- David M. Walker, former holder of the Regius Chair in Civil Law at Glasgow University, perhaps the most prolific legal writer in the British Isles, and author of the renowned *Oxford Companion to Law* (1980).

Additionally, in about a third of the manuscript, we had the help of Hans W. Baade, holder of the Hugh Lamar Stone Chair in Civil Law at the University of Texas. He is a comparativist of the first rank whose expertise ranges from domestic relations to international transactions to conflict of laws.

On the editorial side, several of my colleagues at LawProse, Inc. played crucial roles. David W. Schultz, a seasoned editor who joined the *Black's* team in 1995, was invaluable in producing both the pocket edition (which appeared in 1996) and this unabridged edition. His editorial judgments have improved every page. Lance A. Cooper, an aspiring legal historian, joined the team in 1997, working skillfully on thousands of entries for more than 18 months. Elizabeth C. Powell arrived in 1998, bringing with her a keen intellect, ten years of lawyerly experience, and an amazing capacity for hard work. All three — Schultz, Cooper, and Powell — are splendid lawyers who, not so long ago, never imagined they would one day be legal lexicographers. Yet they learned dictionary-making as the best lexicographers do: on the job. And they've become quite accomplished.

When it came to pronunciations, though, I knew we needed someone already expert in the art. This dictionary presents extraordinary challenges to a pronunciation editor, being full of Latin and French as well as Law Latin (the impure Latin of Renaissance lawyers) and Law French (the Norman French of medieval lawyers). Fortunately, Charles Harrington Elster of San Diego, an orthoepist with several excellent books to his credit, was willing to take on the task. He wisely guided us through the confusing mazes of Anglo-Latin, the only type of Latin with a continuous tradition in Anglo-American law. Even if some of the pronunciations strike you at first as odd, you can be sure that there is sound authority for them.

On translating Greek, Latin, and French, we had the benefit of many scholars' expertise. Professors Honoré and Walker supplied many of our etymologies. So did Edward Carawan and Alison Parker, both of whom hold Ph.D.s in Classics; they examined all the maxims listed in Appendix B and supplied new translations and annotations for them.

As the manuscript deadline approached, I asked 30 judges, lawyers, and academics — mostly practicing lawyers — to read and comment on a batch of 150 pages of manuscript each. All of them generously agreed. I am enormously grateful to each of these learned lawyers:

Paul H. Anderson
Beverly Ray Burlingame
Jordan B. Cherrick
Charles Dewey Cole Jr.
Dana Fabe
Stephen F. Fink
Neal Goldfarb
C. Kenneth Grosse
Harris L. Hartz
Molly H. Hatchell
Lynn N. Hughes
Susan L. Karamanian
Joseph Kimble
Edward J. Kionka
Harriet Lansing
Clyde D. Leland
James K. Logan
Margaret I. Lyle
Lann G. McIntyre
Paul G. McNamara
John W. McReynolds
Kent N. Mastores
Wayne Moore
James L. Nelson
R. Eric Nielsen
George C. Pratt
Carol Marie Stapleton
Scott Patrick Stolley
Randall M. Tietjen
Carla L. Wheeler
Richard C. Wydick

What I hadn't fully reckoned, when sending out batches of manuscript, was how challenging it would be to integrate more than 4,500 pages of lightly to heavily edited text. Evaluating and entering the edits into our database took three full-time lawyers the better part of six weeks. Fortunately, Beverly Ray Burlingame of Dallas, an immensely talented editor and prodigiously hard worker, took time off from her busy law practice to help complete the project. She made huge contributions during the final stage.

But hers was not the only extraordinary act of voluntarism. During the final months, Michael L. Atchley of Dallas, upon learning of our deadline, began sending us draft entries for several hundred terms that were missing from the sixth edition. His broad legal knowledge, as well as his natural aptitude for lexicography, showed in all his work. Then he generously read and commented on large stacks of manuscript.

Several lawyers made important contributions beyond those I've already described. Ann Taylor Schwing of Sacramento painstakingly culled through the 90 volumes of *Words and Phrases* for possible inclusions, and she read large portions of the manuscript. Elizabeth Sturdivant Kerr of Fort Worth contributed drafts of many entries for the letters E, H, and T, and she read much of the manuscript. Michelle D. Monse of Dallas contributed drafts of many L entries. Stephen W. Kotara of Dallas contributed to the letters F and G. Meanwhile, Terrence W. Kirk of Austin submitted many helpful drafts of criminal-law definitions.

As the work progressed, I occasionally ran queries by scholars in various legal specialties, and they all responded helpfully. Many thanks to J.H. Baker, Peter Butt, Robert W. Hamilton, Herbert J. Hammond, Geoffrey C. Hazard Jr., Gideon Kanner, Robert E. Keeton, John S. Lowe, Neil MacCormick, Joseph W. McKnight, Sir Robert Megarry, Richard A. Posner, William C. Powers Jr., Thomas M. Reavley, Christoph Schreuer, and Charles Alan Wright. In a specialized review, Marc I. Steinberg commented on the business-law terms throughout the book.

Several universities provided significant assistance. While working on the project, I was an adjunct professor at Southern Methodist University School of Law. Meanwhile, I had stints as a visiting scholar at the University of Glasgow (July 1996), under the sponsorship of Professor David M. Walker; at the University of Cambridge (July 1997), under the sponsorship of Vice-Chancellor Emeritus Sir David Williams; and at the University of Salzburg (July 1998), under the sponsorship of Professors Wolfram Karl and Christoph Schreuer. I used the libraries at each of those universities to good advantage. I also made good use of the renowned Tarlton Law Library at the University of Texas (thanks to Professor Roy M. Mersky and his colleagues). And the entire *Black's* team constantly used the Underwood Law Library at Southern Methodist University (thanks to Professor Gail Daly and her colleagues). Also, I was able to carry out some research at the Langdell Law Library at Harvard University. To all of these libraries and their staffs, I am grateful for the cordial help they unfailingly gave.

Professor Mersky helped in another notable way: he and several of his colleagues — Beth Youngdale, Marlyn Robinson, and Monika Szakasits — generously verified the accuracy of our List of Books Cited.

Five research assistants — extraordinarily talented law students at Southern Methodist University School of Law — verified citations throughout the book. The editors are much indebted to Daniel Alexander, Julie Buffington, Nicole Schauf Gambrell, Peggy Glenn-Summitt, and Kenneth E. Shore. I especially thank Julie Buffington for organizing this team and ensuring the timely completion of a complex task.

Karen Magnuson of Portland, who has worked on several of my other books, courageously proofread the entire 3,500-page single-spaced manuscript as we worked through the final draft. Her talents as a proofreader are, in my experience, unmatched.

Many others contributed to the book in various ways: the late Alexander Black of Rochester began a reading program to gather illustrative quotations for our files; Thomas G. Fleming of Rochester continued that program for most of its duration; Caroline B. Garner of Dallas located historical legal terms in early dictionaries; E.N. Genovese of San Diego helped supply some foreign pronunciations; Tanya Glenn of Dallas typed the initial list of maxims; Michael Greenwald of Philadelphia helped on terms relating to the American Law Institute; and Tinh T. Ngyuen of Dallas, with unusual enthusiasm, carried out the tedious but necessary task of checking cross-references and alphabetization.

At the West Group, David J. Oliveiri, Doug Powell, John Perovich, and Brendan Bauer had the imagination and the forcefulness to make the book a reality. Their logistical support, not to mention their moral support, helped everyone involved in the project. In the production department, Kathy Walters worked wonders to produce the book within a tight deadline.

Tremendous amounts of talent and toil have gone into the making of this book. Yet the worries of early lexicographers have a haunting ring: this work might not prove as absolutely faultless as it has been my wish to make it. If that turns out to be so, as it inevitably will, I can only hope that readers will recognize the genuine merits residing in these pages.

Bryan A. Garner
Dallas, Texas
June 1999

Guide to the Dictionary

1. Alphabetization

All headwords, including abbreviations, are alphabetized letter by letter, not word by word. Spaces, apostrophes, hyphens, virgules, and the like are ignored. An ampersand (&) is treated as if it were the word *and*. For example:

Pan-American Convention
P & L
***Panduit* test**
per annum
P/E ratio
per capita
percentage lease
per diem
peremptory

Numerals included in a headword precede the letter "a" and are arranged in ascending numerical order:

Rule 10b–5
Rule 11
rule absolute
rulemaking
rule of 72
rule of 78

A numeral at the beginning of a headword is alphabetized as if the numeral were spelled out:

Eighth Amendment
eight-hour law
8–K
ejection

Commas break the letter-by-letter alphabetization if they are backward-looking (e.g., *attorney, power of*), but not if they are forward-looking (e.g., *right, title, and interest*).

2. Pronunciations

Boldface syllables receive primary stress:

oligopoly (ol-ə-**gop**-ə-lee), *n.*

If a word has more than one acceptable pronunciation, the preferred pronunciation appears first and the variant form after *or*:

talesman (**taylz**-mən *or* **tay**-leez-mən).

A pronunciation of dubious standing is preceded by *also*:

condition precedent (prə-**seed**-ənt *also* **pres**-ə-dənt).

For variably pronounced syllables, often only the changed syllables are included.

ejusdem generis (ee-**jəs**-dəm **jen**-ə-ris *also* ee-**joos**- or ee-**yoos**-).

Brackets in pronunciations indicate an optional sound:

> **fiduciary** (fi-**d**[y]**oo**-shee-er-ee), *adj.*

For handy reference, the pronunciation guide is located inside the front cover.

3. Etymologies

The origins of most foreign words and phrases are given in brackets. By far the most frequent etymologies are "Latin" (i.e., classical Latin used during the Roman Empire) and "Law Latin" (i.e., the Anglicized Latin formerly used in legal documents and proceedings). Essentially, the *Law Latin* tag corresponds to what some dictionaries call *Late Latin* and others call *Medieval Latin*. Other languages of origin are listed as well, including French, Law French (i.e., medieval common-law French), Old English, Greek, German, and Dutch.

4. Dates

The parenthetical dates preceding many of the definitions show the earliest known use of the word or phrase in English. For some words, the date is merely a century (e.g., 14c), but for most of the recently emerging vocabulary a precise year is given. The editors hope to extend this feature to most or even all the entries in future editions. Interested researchers should know that we welcome certifiable ante-datings.

5. Tags

Two types of tags appear. First, there are usage tags:

> *Hist.* = historical; no longer current in law
> *Archaic* = old-fashioned and declining in use
> *Rare* = very infrequent in modern usage
> *Slang* = very informal

Second, there are many subject-matter tags that identify the field of law that a particular term or sense belongs to (e.g., *Antitrust*, *Commercial law*, *Insurance*, and *Wills & estates*). Two of these tags deserve special mention. *Roman law* indicates a term that can be traced back to the legal system of the ancient Romans. *Civil law* indicates a term that is used in modern civil-law systems, including much of the law in Louisiana.

6. Angle Brackets

Contextual illustrations of a headword are given in angle brackets:

> **avail,** *n.* **1.** Use or advantage <of little or no avail>. **2.** (*pl.*) Profits or proceeds, esp. from a sale of property <the avails of the trust fund>.

7. Bullets

Bullets are used to separate definitional information (before the bullet) from information that is not purely definitional (after the bullet), such as encyclopedic information or usage notes.

8. Cognate Forms

This dictionary lists corresponding parts of speech. For example, under the definition of *consultation*, the corresponding verb (*consult*) and adjectives (*consulting*, *consultative*) are listed.

If a cognate form applies to only one sense of a headword, that form is denoted as follows:

> **enjoin,** *vb.* **1.** To legally prohibit or restrain by injunction <the company was enjoined from selling its stock>. **2.** To prescribe, mandate, or strongly encourage <the graduating class was enjoined to uphold the highest professional standards>. — **enjoinment** (for sense 1), *n.* — **enjoinder** (for sense 2), *n.*

9. Cross-references

a. See

The signal *See* is used in three ways.

(1) To indicate that the definition is at another location in the dictionary:

> **call loan.** See LOAN.
>
> **perpetuities, rule against.** See RULE AGAINST PERPETUITIES.

(2) To refer to closely related terms:

> **nationalization,** *n.* **1.** The act of bringing an industry under governmental control or ownership. **2.** The act of giving a person the status of a citizen. See NATURALIZATION.
>
> **cognovit** (kog-**noh**-vit). [Latin "the person has conceded (a debt or an action)"] An acknowledgment of debt or liability in the form of a confessed judgment. See *confession of judgment* under JUDGMENT.

(3) To refer to a synonymous subentry:

> **binding instruction.** See *mandatory instruction* under JURY INSTRUCTION.

b. Cf.

Cf. is used to refer to related but contrastable terms:

> ***Gallagher* agreement.** A contract that gives one codefendant the right to settle with the plaintiff for a fixed sum at any time during trial and that guarantees payment of the sum regardless of the trial's outcome. *City of Tucson v. Gallagher*, 493 P.2d 1197 (Ariz. 1972). Cf. MARY CARTER AGREEMENT.
>
> **false imprisonment.** A restraint of a person in a bounded area without justification or consent. • False imprisonment is a common-law misdemeanor and a tort. It applies to private as well as governmental detention. Cf. *false arrest* under ARREST.

c. Also termed

The phrase also termed at the end of an entry signals a synonymous word or phrase. Variations include also spelled, also written, and often shortened to.

d. Terms with multiple senses

If the cross-referenced term has multiple senses, the particular sense referred to is indicated in parentheses:

> **light work.** See WORK (1).
> **rule day.** See *return day* (3) under DAY.

10. Quotations

The editors have selected quotations on the basis of aptness, insight, and clarity. Most quotations are included because they provide information or nuances that would not otherwise be available within the strict confines of a traditional definition. Quotations are set off in smaller, sans serif type:

> **discovery abuse. 1.** The misuse of the discovery process, esp. by making overbroad requests for information that is unnecessary or beyond the scope of permissible disclosure or by conducting discovery for an improper purpose.
>
> "The term 'discovery abuse' has been used as if it were a single concept, but it includes several different things. Thus, it is useful to subdivide 'abuse' into 'misuse' and 'overuse.' What is referred to as 'misuse' would include not only direct violation of the rules, as by failing to respond to a discovery request within the stated time limit, but also more subtle attempts to harass or obstruct an opponent, as by giving obviously inadequate answers or by requesting information that clearly is outside the scope of discovery. By 'overuse' is meant asking for more discovery than is necessary or appropriate to the particular case. 'Overuse,' in turn, can be subdivided into problems of 'depth' and of 'breadth,' with 'depth' referring to discovery that may be relevant but is simply excessive and 'breadth' referring to discovery requests that go into matters too far removed from the case." Charles Alan Wright, *The Law of Federal Courts* § 81, at 580 (5th ed. 1994).

Older quotations show what scholars have said about legal terminology at particular points in history. Although some of the older quotations may not fully reflect current law, all should help deepen the user's knowledge of how the term has been used or misused—or give an insight into its history.

11. Subentries

Many terms in this dictionary are collected by topic. For example, the different types of contracts, such as *bilateral contract* and *gratuitous contract*, are defined under the main term *contract*. (Cross-references in B and G will redirect the reader who looks up *bilateral contract* or *gratuitous contract* to *contract*.) If a term has more than one sense, then the corresponding subentries are placed under the appropriate sense of that term.

12. Typefaces

The typefaces used in this dictionary are mostly self-explanatory. For instance, all headwords and cognate forms are in boldface type, and all subentries are noted with triangular pointers. As for headwords of foreign origin, those that are fully naturalized are in boldface Roman type, while those that are not fully naturalized are in boldface italics. Generally, small caps are used with "See" and "Cf." cross-references to main entries. There are, however, three other uses of small caps deserving special mention.

a. Small caps refer to a synonymous headword. In the following example, the small caps suggest that you review the definition at *contiguous* for more information:

> **adjoining.** Touching; sharing a common boundary; CONTIGUOUS. — **adjoin,** *vb.*

b. Small caps also refer to the predominant form when it may be phrased or spelled in more than one way. For example, the following uses of small caps direct you to the entries at *perjury* and *payor*:

> **false swearing.** See PERJURY.
>
> **payer.** See PAYOR.

c. Small caps also refer to the spelled-out form of abbreviations (the term is defined at the spelled-out headword, not the abbreviated form). For example:

> **FDIC.** *abbr.* FEDERAL DEPOSIT INSURANCE CORPORATION.
>
> **Federal Deposit Insurance Corporation.** A federal corporation that protects bank and thrift deposits by insuring accounts up to $100,000, examining banks that are not members of the Federal Reserve System, and liquidating failed institutions. — Abbr. FDIC.

13. Abbreviations

For a list of abbreviations used within entries see the following page. For a list of abbreviations used within legal texts generally, see Appendix A.

14. Latin Maxims

The first six editions of *Black's Law Dictionary* interspersed hundreds of legal maxims (full Latin or Law French sentences) within the main body of the dictionary, somewhat cluttering the main text. For greater convenience, a much fuller set of maxims was collected into an appendix in the seventh edition. With new translations and nearly 1,000 new entries, that collection is found in Appendix B.

List of Abbreviations

abbr. = abbreviated as; abbreviation for
adj. = adjective
adv. = adverb
AmE = American English
bef. = before
BrE = British English
ca. = circa
cap. = capitalized
cf. = (*confer*) compare with
ch. = chapter
C.J.S. = *Corpus Juris Secundum*
conj. = conjunction
ed. = edition; editor
e.g. = (*exempli gratia*) for example
esp. = especially
et seq. = (*et sequentes*) and those (pages or sections) that follow
fr. = from; derived from
Hist. = historical; no longer in use
id. = (*idem*) in the same work
i.e. = (*id est*) that is
l.c. = lowercase
n. = noun; note
no. = number
occas. = occasionally
¶ = paragraph
pl. = plural
pp. = pages
p.pl. = past participle
prep. = preposition
pt. = part
repr. = reprinted
rev. = revised by; revision
§ = section
sing. = singular
specif. = specifically
usu. = usually
vb. = verb

a. **1.** (*usu. cap. & often ital.*) A hypothetical person <*A* deeds Blackacre to *B*>. **2.** [Latin] From; by; in; on; of; at. **3.** [Law Latin] With. **4.** [Law French] Of; at; to; for; in; with. **5.** *Securities.* A letter used in a newspaper stock-transaction table to indicate that an extra or irregular dividend was paid during the year in addition to regular dividends. **6.** *Securities.* A letter used in a newspaper mutual-fund transaction table to indicate a yield that may include capital gains and losses as well as current interest. **7.** (*cap.*) *Hist. Securities.* A letter used in a newspaper corporate earnings report to identify the American Stock Exchange as the primary market of a firm's common stock. • In 2008, the American Stock Exchange was merged into the New York Stock Exchange. **8.** (*cap.*) *Securities.* An above-average grade given to a debt obligation by a rating agency. • The grades, as ranked by Standard & Poor's, range from AAA (highest) down to D. The equivalent grades from Moody's are Aaa, Aa, A, Baa, and so on down to C. **9.** *Marine insurance.* A rating assigned in *Lloyd's Register of Shipping* to ships considered to be in first-class condition. Cf. A1. **10.** *abbr.* ADVERSUS. **11.** (*cap.*) *Hist.* A scarlet letter worn as punishment by someone convicted of adultery. **12.** *Roman law.* An abbreviation for *absolvo* written on a wooden tablet by a criminal-court judge to indicate a vote for acquittal. **13.** *Roman law.* An abbreviation for *antiquo* ("for the old law") written on a wooden tablet by a participant in a popular assembly to indicate a vote against a proposed bill. **14.** (*cap.*) *abbr.* ATLANTIC REPORTER.

A1, *adj.* (18c) First-rate; excellent in every way. • The term originated in the classification scheme used by *Lloyd's Register of British and Foreign Shipping* to describe a vessel considered to be in superb condition. Cf. A (9).

A.2d. *abbr. Atlantic Reporter Second Series.* See ATLANTIC REPORTER.

AAA. *abbr.* **1.** AMERICAN ARBITRATION ASSOCIATION. **2.** AMERICAN ACCOUNTING ASSOCIATION. **3.** AMERICAN ACADEMY OF ACTUARIES. **4.** AGRICULTURAL ADJUSTMENT ACT. **5.** See *accumulated-adjustments account* under ACCOUNT. **6.** ANTI-ASSIGNMENT ACT.

AAC. *abbr.* ANNO ANTE CHRISTUM.

AACN. *abbr.* ANNO ANTE CHRISTUM NATUM.

AACWA. *abbr.* ADOPTION ASSISTANCE AND CHILD WELFARE ACT.

AALL. *abbr.* American Association of Law Libraries, founded in 1906 to promote law libraries and scholarship in the field of law-library science.

AALS. *abbr.* ASSOCIATION OF AMERICAN LAW SCHOOLS.

AAMVA. *abbr.* AMERICAN ASSOCIATION OF MOTOR VEHICLE ADMINISTRATORS.

AARC. *abbr.* ALTERNATIVE AGRICULTURAL RESEARCH AND COMMERCIALIZATION CORPORATION.

AAS. *abbr.* **1.** Approved accounting standard. **2.** Australian Accounting Standards.

AAT. *abbr.* Administrative appeals tribunal.

AAU. *abbr.* See *amendment to allege use* under TRADEMARK-APPLICATION AMENDMENT.

a aver et tener (ay **ay**-vər [*or* ah **ah**-vər] et **ten**-ər). [Law French] To have and to hold. See HABENDUM CLAUSE.

AB. *abbr.* See *able-bodied seaman* under SEAMAN.

ab, *prep.* [Latin] From; by; of.

ABA. *abbr.* **1.** AMERICAN BAR ASSOCIATION. **2.** AMERICAN BANKERS ASSOCIATION.

abacinate (ə-**bas**-ə-nayt), *vb.* (1884) To blind (a person) by placing a red-hot iron or metal plate in front of the eyes.

abaction (ab-**ak**-shən). See ABIGEATUS.

ab actis (ab **ak**-tis), *n.* [Latin "in relation to proceedings"] *Roman law.* An officer responsible for public records (*acta*), registers, journals, or minutes; a court clerk; a notary.

abactor (ab-**ak**-tər *or* -tor). See ABIGEUS.

ab agendo (ab ə-**jen**-doh), *adj.* [Latin] (17c) Unable to act; incapacitated for business or transactions of any kind.

abalienation (ab-**ayl**-yə-nay-shən), *n.* [fr. Latin *abalienare* "to alienate"] (1828) *Civil law.* The transfer of an interest in or title to property; ALIENATION (1). • In Roman law, the term was *abalienatio* ("a perfect conveyance from one Roman citizen to another"), which was anglicized to *abalienation.* — **abalienate,** *vb.*

abamita (ə-**bam**-ə-tə). [Latin] (16c) *Civil law.* A great-great-great aunt.

abandon, *vb.* (14c) **1.** To leave (someone), esp. when doing so amounts to an abdication of responsibility. **2.** To relinquish or give up with the intention of never again reclaiming one's rights or interest in. **3.** To desert or go away from permanently. **4.** To stop (an activity) because there are too many problems and it is impractical or impossible to continue. **5.** To cease having (an idea, attitude, or belief); to give over or surrender utterly. **6.** To leave (a ship) because of sinking or the threat of sinking. **7.** *Insurance.* (Of an insured) to surrender to the underwriters the insured's interest in (the insured property) while claiming payment for the total loss.

abandoned and malignant heart. (1843) A reckless indifference to an unjustifiably high risk to human life; MALICE. — Sometimes shortened to *abandoned heart.* — Sometimes written *malignant and abandoned heart.*

abandoned application. (1853) *Patents & Trademarks.* An application removed from the U.S. Patent and Trademark Office docket of pending applications because the applicant (or the applicant's attorney or agent of record) filed an express notice of abandonment, failed to take appropriate or timely action at some stage in the prosecution of a nonprovisional application, or failed to pay the issue fee. • Abandonment of a patent or trademark application does not automatically result in abandonment of the invention or the mark because an abandoned application may be revived by petition. Cf. *abandoned invention* under INVENTION; *abandoned trademark* under TRADEMARK.

abandoned experiment. (1858) *Patents.* An unsuccessful attempt to reduce an invention to practice. • Unless it is publicly known, an abandoned experiment does not qualify as prior art under § 102 of the Patent Act, so it does not bar future patents.

abandoned heart. See ABANDONED AND MALIGNANT HEART.

abandoned invention. See INVENTION.

abandoned mark. See *abandoned trademark* under TRADEMARK.

abandoned-pleadings doctrine. (1989) *Evidence.* The rule that a party may introduce into evidence abandoned pleadings as evidentiary admissions against an opposing party. • The law governing the admissibility of abandoned pleadings differs from jurisdiction to jurisdiction. For example, some jurisdictions require the party to have an opportunity to explain why the pleadings were abandoned.

abandoned property. See PROPERTY.

abandoned, suppressed, or concealed, *adj.* (1939) *Patents.* Intentionally or accidentally hidden from public notice, not reduced to practice, or not patented. • Another person's earlier invention will not be considered prior art if the first inventor abandoned the field to others or is held to have lost the right to patent by suppressing or concealing the invention. But if the suppression or concealment occurred after the art was known to the public, then it still qualifies as prior art. *See* MPEP § 2138.03.

abandoned trademark. See TRADEMARK.

abandonee (ə-ban-də-**nee**), *n.* (1848) One to whom property rights are relinquished; one to whom something is formally or legally abandoned.

abandonment, *n.* (1809) **1.** The relinquishing of a right or interest with the intention of never reclaiming it. • In the context of contracts for the sale of land, courts sometimes use the term *abandonment* as if it were synonymous with *rescission*, but the two should be distinguished. An abandonment is merely one party's acceptance of the situation that a nonperforming party has caused. But a rescission due to a material breach is a termination or discharge of the contract for all purposes. **2.** The act of withdrawing or discontinuing one's help or support, esp. when a duty or responsibility exists.

▸ **medical abandonment.** (1962) A medical professional's discontinuation of an established doctor–patient relationship before the patient's necessary treatment has ended and without arranging for continuing treatment or care. • It is a form of medical malpractice. — Also termed *abandonment of a patient*. See *medical malpractice* under MALPRACTICE.

3. *Property.* The relinquishing of or departing from a homestead, etc., with the present, definite, and permanent intention of never returning or regaining possession. **4.** *Family law.* The act of leaving a spouse or child willfully and without an intent to return. • Child abandonment is grounds for termination of parental rights. Spousal abandonment is grounds for divorce. — Also termed (as to a child) *criminal abandonment*; (as to a spouse) *spousal abandonment*; *abandonment of spouse*. Cf. DESERTION.

> "The lines of distinction between abandonment and the many forms of child neglect are often not very clear so that failure to support or to care for a child may sometimes be characterized as abandonment and sometimes as neglect." Homer H. Clark Jr., *The Law of Domestic Relations in the United States* § 20.6, at 895 (1988).

▸ **abandonment of minor children.** See NONSUPPORT.

▸ **constructive abandonment.** See *constructive desertion* under DESERTION.

▸ **malicious abandonment.** (1865) **1.** The desertion of a spouse without just cause. See *criminal desertion* under DESERTION. **2.** See *voluntary abandonment.*

▸ **voluntary abandonment.** (1833) **1.** As a ground for divorce, a final departure without the consent of the other spouse, without sufficient reason, and without the intention to return. **2.** In the law of adoption, a natural parent's willful act or course of conduct that implies a conscious disregard of or indifference to a child, as if no parental obligation existed. — Also termed *malicious abandonment.*

5. *Criminal law.* RENUNCIATION (3). **6.** *Bankruptcy.* A trustee's court-approved release of property that is burdensome or of inconsequential value to the estate, or the trustee's release of nonadministered property to the debtor when the case is closed. **7.** *Contracts.* RESCISSION (2). **8.** *Insurance.* An insured's relinquishing of damaged or lost property to the insurer as a constructive total loss. Cf. SALVAGE (2). **9.** *Trademarks.* A mark owner's failure to maintain the mark's proper use in commerce or failure to maintain its distinctive character. • Abandonment is an affirmative defense to an action for trademark infringement. — Also termed *nonuse.* **10.** *Hist. Copyright.* An affirmative defense to a copyright-infringement claim governed by pre-1989 law, based on the author's general publication of the work without a copyright notice. • Before March 1989, authors who did not affix a copyright notice to their published works risked losing legal protection for those works. Congress eliminated the copyright-notice requirement when it ratified the Berne Convention. **11.** *Intellectual property.* The loss of an intellectual-property right, as by disuse, neglect of formalities, failure to pay a required fee, or (for a trade secret) failure to ensure concealment. — **abandon,** *vb.*

▸ **abandonment by operation of law.** See *constructive abandonment.*

▸ **actual abandonment.** (1823) **1.** *Patents.* Intentional relinquishment of the right to patent protection, evidenced, for example, by more than mere inactivity or delay in filing the application. • Actual abandonment may be express or implied, but every reasonable doubt about intent will be resolved in the inventor's favor. **2.** *Trademarks.* Intentional loss of trademark protection by discontinuing commercial use of the mark with the intention of not using it again.

▸ **constructive abandonment.** (1861) **1.** *Patents.* The closing of a patent-application prosecution by the U.S. Patent and Trademark Office when an applicant fails to respond to an office action within the time allowed, usu. six months, or fails to pay an issue fee. • If the delay was unintentional or unavoidable, the application may be revived. **2.** *Patents.* Abandonment of an invention by operation of law regardless of the inventor's intention, as when the inventor forfeits the right to patent by selling or offering to sell the invention or by describing it in a publication more than a year before seeking patent protection. 35 USCA § 102. **3.** *Trademarks.* An owner's loss of trademark protection, regardless of whether the mark is registered, by allowing the mark to lose its distinctiveness, such as by letting the name become a generic term for that type of goods, or by otherwise failing to maintain the mark's distinctive character. • For example, licensing the use of the mark without retaining control over how it is used may result in constructive abandonment. — Also termed *abandonment by operation of law.*

▸ **express abandonment.** (1910) *Patents.* An applicant's intentional and clear termination of a patent prosecution. • An express abandonment must be made in a signed writing and received by the U.S. Patent and Trademark Office in time for the Office to act before the patent issues. Once an application is expressly abandoned, it cannot be revived, and the applicant cannot preclude the public from freely availing itself of the invention's benefits. Unless there is an express abandonment filed, abandonment of a patent application does not result in abandonment of the invention. — Also termed *formal abandonment.*

▸ **formal abandonment.** See *express abandonment.*

▸ **implied abandonment.** (1871) *Patents.* An inventor's failure to take steps to protect an invention, such as by failing to claim the invention when disclosed in a patent application or by permitting an application to be abandoned, esp. by failing to file an answer to an office action within the time allowed.

abandonment defense. See WITHDRAWAL DEFENSE.

abandonment doctrine. (1957) *Criminal law.* The rule that one has no expectation of privacy (under the Fourth Amendment protection against unreasonable searches and seizures) in one's discarded or abandoned property. See FOURTH AMENDMENT.

abandonment of a patient. See *medical abandonment* under ABANDONMENT (2).

abandonment of contest. *Patents.* A party's withdrawal from an interference contest. • The abandonment of contest must be in writing. The contest is dissolved as to the abandoning party.

abandonment of spouse. See ABANDONMENT (4).

abandum (ə-**ban**-dəm), *n.* [Law Latin] (18c) *Hist.* A thing that has been forfeited. — Also spelled *abandun; abandonum.*

ab ante (ab **an**-tee), *adv.* [Latin] *Hist.* Before; beforehand; in advance. — Also termed *ab antecedente.*

ab antecedente. See AB ANTE.

ab antiquo (ab an-**tı**-kwoh), *adv.* [Law Latin] *Hist.* From ancient times; of old. — Also termed *ab antiqua.*

ab ardendo (ab ahr-**den**-doh), *adv.* [Latin] (17c) By burning; of burning; from burning.

abarnare (ab-ahr-**nair**-ee), *vb.* [Law Latin] *Hist.* To detect or disclose a secret crime; to bring to judgment.

abatable nuisance. See NUISANCE.

abatamentum (ə-bay-tə-**men**-təm), *n.* [Law Latin] *Hist.* See ABATEMENT (5).

abatare (ab-ə-**tair**-ee), *vb.* [Law Latin] *Hist.* To abate.

abatement (ə-**bayt**-mənt), *n.* (14c) **1.** The act of eliminating or nullifying <abatement of a nuisance> <abatement of a writ>. **2.** The suspension or defeat of a pending action for a reason unrelated to the merits of the claim <the defendant sought abatement of the suit because of misnomer>; esp., the discontinuation of criminal proceedings before they are concluded in the normal course of litigation, as when the defendant dies. See *plea in abatement* under PLEA.

> "Although the term 'abatement' is sometimes used loosely as a substitute for 'stay of proceedings,' the two may be distinguished on several grounds. For example, when grounds for abatement of an action exist, the abatement of the action is a matter of right, but a stay is granted in the court's discretion. And in proper circumstances a court may stay a proceeding pending the outcome of another proceeding although a strict plea in abatement could not be sustained." 1 Am. Jur. 2d *Abatement, Survival, and Revival* § 3 (1994).

▸ **abatement in equity.** *Hist.* The suspension of a suit for lack of the proper parties necessary for it to proceed. • Abatement in equity differed from abatement at law in that the action was entirely defeated in the latter case, whereas in the former the action was merely suspended and could be revived later (usu. when appropriate parties were substituted for the originals within a specified time).

3. The act of lessening or moderating; diminution in amount or degree <abatement of the debt>. **4.** *Wills & estates.* The reduction of a legacy, general or specific, as a result of the estate's being insufficient to pay all debts and legacies <the abatement of legacies resulted from the estate's insolvency>. Cf. ADEMPTION. **5.** *Archaic.* The act of tortiously entering real estate after the owner dies and before the legal heir enters <abatement of freehold>. — Also termed (in sense 5) *abatamentum.* — **abate,** *vb.* — **abatable,** *adj.*

abatement clause. (1890) A lease provision that releases the tenant from the rent obligation when an act of God or other specified reason precludes occupancy.

abater (ə-**bay**-tər *or* -tor), *n.* (17c) **1.** Someone who abates something. **2.** A plea in abatement. See *plea in abatement* under PLEA.

abator (ə-**bay**-tər *or* -tor), *n.* (16c) **1.** Someone who eliminates a nuisance. See ABATEMENT (1). **2.** *Hist.* Someone who tortiously intrudes on an heir's freehold before the heir takes possession. See ABATEMENT (5).

abatuda (ab-ə-**t[y]oo**-də), *n.* [fr. Law Latin *abatudus* "debased"] *Hist.* A thing diminished, such as money reduced in value by clipping (*moneta abatuda*).

abavia (ə-**bay**-vee-ə), *n.* [Latin] (16c) *Civil law.* A great-great-grandmother.

abavunculus (ab-ə-**vəng**-kyə-ləs), *n.* [Latin] (16c) *Civil law.* A great-great-great uncle. — Also termed *avunculus maximus.*

abavus (**ab**-ə-vəs), *n.* [Latin] (16c) *Civil law.* A great-great-grandfather.

abbacy (**ab**-ə-see), *n.* (16c) *Eccles. law.* An abbot's jurisdiction or term of tenure.

abbess (**ab**-is), *n.* (13c) *Eccles. law.* A female superior or governess of a convent. Cf. ABBOT.

abbey (**ab**-ee), *n.* (13c) *Eccles. law.* A monastery governed by an abbot, or a convent governed by an abbess.

abbey land. (*usu. pl.*) (17c) *Hist.* Real property held by an abbey in mortmain and therefore exempt from tithes. See MORTMAIN.

abbot (**ab**-ət), *n.* (bef. 12c) *Eccles. law.* A superior or governor of an abbey. Cf. ABBESS.

abbreviated term sheet. See TERM SHEET.

abbreviation. (15c) **1.** The act of shortening or abridging, esp. a word or phrase. **2.** The resulting shortened or abridged version of a word or phrase. • There are three types of abbreviations: a simple truncation or elision, which is usu. read or spoken as the full word <Co.: Company; Dr.: Doctor>; an acronym, which is read or spoken as one word <radar: radio detection and ranging>; and an initialism, which is sounded letter by letter. <ABA: American Bar Association>. **3.** A brief summary; an abridgment.

Abbreviatio Placitorum (ə-bree-vee-**ay**-shee-oh plas-i-**tor**-əm), *n.* [Law Latin "summary of the pleas"] *Hist.* An abstract of pleadings culled from the rolls of the *Curia Regis*, Parliament, and common-law courts from the 12th to 14th centuries, compiled in the 17th century, printed in 1811, and attributed variously to Arthur Agarde, Deputy Chamberlain of the Exchequer, and to other keepers of the records. Cf. YEAR BOOKS.

abbreviator, *n.* (16c) **1.** Someone who abbreviates, abridges, or shortens. **2.** *Eccles. law.* An officer in the court of Rome appointed as assistant to the vice-chancellor for drawing up the Pope's briefs and reducing petitions, when granted, into proper form to be converted into papal bulls.

abbroachment (ə-**brohch**-mənt), *n.* (17c) *Hist.* The act of forestalling the market by buying wholesale merchandise to sell at retail as the only vendor. — Also spelled *abbrochment*; *abbrochement.* — **abbroach,** *vb.*

ABC test. (1962) The rule that an employee is not entitled to unemployment-insurance benefits if the employee (A) is free from the control of the employer, (B) works away from the employer's place of business, and (C) is engaged in an established trade. • The name derives from the A, B, and C commonly used in designating the three parts of the test.

ABC transaction. (1955) *Oil & gas.* A sale of a working interest from an owner (A) to an operator (B) in return for a cash payment and the right to another (usu. larger) payment when the well produces, followed by A's sale of the right to the production payment to a corporation (C), which pays A in cash borrowed from a lender on C's pledge of the production payment. • Thus A receives cash taxed at capital-gains rates, and B pays part of the purchase price with nontaxable production income. The tax advantages of this transaction were eliminated by the Tax Reform Act of 1969.

abdication (ab-di-**kay**-shən), *n.* (16c) The act of renouncing or abandoning privileges or duties, usu. those connected with high office; esp., the stepping down from the position of a monarch <Edward VIII's abdication of the Crown in 1936> <the court's abdication of its judicial responsibility>. — **abdicate** (**ab**-di-kayt), *vb.* — **abdicable** (**ab**-di-kə-bəl), *adj.* — **abdicator** (**ab**-di-kay-tər), *n.*

abditory (**ab**-di-tor-ee), *n.* [Law Latin *abditorium* "box, receptacle"] (17c) A repository used to hide and preserve goods or money. — Also termed *abditorium* (ab-di-**tor**-ee-əm).

abduction (ab-**dək**-shən), *n.* (17c) *Criminal law.* **1.** The act of leading someone away by force or fraudulent persuasion. • Some jurisdictions have added various elements to this basic definition, such as that the abductor must have the intent to marry or defile the person, that the abductee must be a child, or that the abductor must intend to subject the abductee to concubinage or prostitution. **2.** *Archaic.* The crime of taking away a female person, esp. someone who is below a certain age (such as 16 or 18), without her effective consent by use of persuasion, fraud, or violence, for the purpose of marriage, prostitution, or illicit sex. **3.** Loosely, KIDNAPPING. See ENTICEMENT OF A CHILD. — **abduct,** *vb.* — **abductor,** *n.* — **abductee,** *n.*

> "Abduction seems not to have been a crime at early common law, but found its way thereinto through an old English statute which defined the crime substantially as the taking of a woman against her will for lucre, and afterwards marrying her, or causing her to be married to another, or defiling her, or causing her to be defiled." Justin Miller, *Handbook of Criminal Law* § 104, at 319 (1934).

▸ **child abduction.** (1963) The abduction of a minor, esp. a young one; specif., the wrongful taking or retention of one's child in violation of another's custody rights, esp. by one who has parental responsibility for the child.

abductive reasoning. See REASONING.

abearance (ə-**bair**-ənts), *n.* (16c) *Archaic.* Behavior; conduct.

> "The other species of recognizance, with sureties, is for the *good abearance*, or *good behaviour*. This includes security for the peace . . . ." 4 William Blackstone, *Commentaries on the Laws of England* 253 (1769).

ab epistolis (ab ee-**pis**-tə-lis), *n.* [Latin] (16c) *Hist.* An officer who maintained the correspondence (*epistolae*) for a superior; a secretary.

***Abercrombie* classification.** (1992) *Trademarks.* A characterization of a trade designation — whether by mark, name, or dress — as generic, descriptive, suggestive, and arbitrary or fanciful, in increasing order of distinctiveness. *Abercrombie & Fitch Co. v. Hunting World, Inc.*, 537 F.2d 4, 9 (2d Cir. 1976).

aberrance, *n.* (17c) The state or condition of wandering or departing from the right, normal, or standard way; atypicality. Cf. ABNORMALITY (2).

aberrant behavior (a-**ber**-ənt *or* **ab**-ər-ənt). (1924) A single act of unplanned or thoughtless criminal behavior. • Many courts have held that aberrant behavior justifies a downward departure — that is, a more lenient sentence — under the federal sentencing guidelines, based on a comment in the introduction to the *Guidelines Manual* to the effect that the guidelines do not deal with single acts of aberrant behavior. *U.S. Sentencing Guidelines Manual*, ch. 1, pt. A, ¶ 4.

abesse (ab-**es**-ee), *vb.* [Law Latin] *Roman & civil law.* To be absent; to be away from a place where one is supposed to be (as before a court). Cf. ADESSE.

abet (ə-**bet**), *vb.* (14c) **1.** To aid, encourage, or assist (someone), esp. in the commission of a crime <abet a known felon>. **2.** To support (a crime) by active assistance <abet a burglary>. See AID AND ABET. Cf. INCITE. — **abetment,** *n.*

abettor, *n.* (16c) Someone who instigates the commission of a crime or advises and encourages others to commit it. — Also spelled *abetter.* See *principal in the second degree* under PRINCIPAL.

ab extra (ab **ek**-strə), *adv.* [Latin] (17c) From outside; extra; beyond.

abeyance (ə-**bay**-ənts), *n.* (17c) **1.** Temporary inactivity; suspension. **2.** *Property.* A lapse in succession during which no person is vested with title. — **abeyant,** *adj.*

> "Abeyance, from the French *bayer,* to expect, is that which is in expectation, remembrance, and intendment of law. By a principle of law, in every land there is a fee simple in somebody, or else it is in *abeyance;* that is, though for the present it be in no man, yet it is in expectancy belonging to him that is next to enjoy the land." 1 Richard Burn, *A New Law Dictionary* 4 (1792).

abiaticus (ab-ee-**ay**-tə-kəs), *n.* [Law Latin "descended from a grandfather"] *Hist.* A grandson in the male line; a son's son. — Also spelled *aviaticus.*

abide, *vb.* (bef. 12c) **1.** To tolerate or withstand <the widow found it difficult to abide the pain of losing her husband>. **2.** To obey; (with *by*) to act in accordance with or in conformity to <try to abide the doctor's order to quit smoking> <abide by the rules>. **3.** To await <the death-row prisoners abide execution>. **4.** To perform or execute (an order or judgment) <the trial court abided the appellate court's order>. **5.** To stay or dwell <the right to abide in any of the 50 states>.

ab identitate rationis (ab I-den-ti-**tay**-tee ray-shee-**oh**-nis *or* rash-ee-**oh**-nis). [Law Latin] *Hist.* By identity of reason; for the same reason.

abiding conviction. See CONVICTION (4).

abigeatus (ə-bij-ee-**ay**-təs), *n.* [Latin] (16c) *Roman & civil law.* The act of stealing cattle by driving them away (*abigere*); cattle rustling. • In the later civil law, the usual term for this was *abaction.* — Also termed *abigeat.*

abigeus (ə-**bij**-ee-əs), *n.* [Latin] (16c) *Roman & civil law.* Someone who steals cattle, esp. in large numbers; a cattle rustler. • This was known in the later civil law as an *abactor.* Pl. ***abigei.***

> "The stealing of a single horse or ox might make a man an abigeus, but it seems that the crime could not be committed on less than four pigs or ten sheep. They need not however be taken all together. In such a state of the law one would expect thefts of three pigs or eight sheep to become abnormally common." 1 James Fitzjames Stephen, *A History of the Criminal Law of England* 27 (1883).

ability, *n.* (14c) The capacity to perform an act or service; esp., the power to carry out a legal act <ability to enter into a contract>.

▸ **financial ability.** A party's wherewithal to honor contractual commitments. See PRESUMPTION OF FINANCIAL ABILITY.

▸ **present ability.** (16c) The actual, immediate power to do something (esp. to commit a crime).

ab inconvenienti (ab in-kən-vee-nee-**en**-tI), *adv.* [Law Latin] (17c) From hardship or inconvenience. See *argumentum ab inconvenienti* under ARGUMENTUM.

ab initio (ab i-**nish**-ee-oh), *adv.* [Latin] (16c) From the beginning <the injunction was valid *ab initio*>. Cf. IN INITIO.

ab intestato (ab in-tes-**tay**-toh), *adv.* [Latin] (17c) By intestacy <succession *ab intestato* is often treated as being necessary because of the neglect or misfortune of the deceased proprietor>. Cf. EX TESTAMENTO.

ab invito (ab in-**vI**-toh), *adv.* [Latin] (1900) By or from an unwilling party; against one's will <a transfer *ab invito*>. Cf. IN INVITUM.

ab irato (ab I-**ray**-toh), *adv.* [Latin] (1941) By one who is angry. • This phrase usu. refers to a gift or devise made adversely to an heir's interests, out of anger. An action to set aside this type of conveyance was known at common law as an *action ab irato.*

abishering. See MISKERING.

abjudge (ab-**jəj**), *vb.* (17c) *Archaic.* To take away or remove (something) by judicial decision. Cf. ADJUDGE (2).

> "As a result of the trial a very solemn judgment is pronounced. The land is adjudged to the one party and his heirs, and abjudged (*abiudicata*) from the other party and his heirs for ever." 2 Frederick Pollock & Frederic W. Maitland, *The History of English Law Before the Time of Edward I* 63 (2d ed. 1899).

abjudicatio (ab-joo-di-**kay**-shee-oh), *n.* [Law Latin] (18c) The act of depriving a person of a thing by judicial decision.

abjuration (ab-juu-**ray**-shən), *n.* (15c) A renouncing by oath.

▸ **abjuration of the realm.** (18c) An oath taken to leave the realm forever.

> "If a malefactor took refuge [in sanctuary] . . . the coroner came and parleyed with the refugee, who had his choice between submitting to trial and abjuring the realm. If he chose the latter course, he hurried dressed in pilgrim's guise to the port that was assigned to him, and left England, being bound by his oath never to return. His lands escheated; his chattels were forfeited, and if he came back his fate was that of an outlaw." 2 Frederick Pollock & Frederic W. Maitland, *History of English Law Before the Time of Edward I* 590 (2d ed. 1899).

abjure (ab-**joor**), *vb.* (15c) **1.** To renounce formally or on oath <abjure one's citizenship>. **2.** To avoid or abstain from <abjure one's civic duties>. — **abjuratory** (ab-**joor**-ə-tor-ee), *adj.*

ablative fact. See *divestitive fact* under FACT.

able, *adj.* (15c) **1.** Capable of performing one or more relevant tasks or having skill at an acceptable level of facility <able to walk>. **2.** Showing great professional competence <an able lawyer>. **3.** Legally competent and qualified <able to transfer title>.

able-bodied seaman. See SEAMAN.

abled, *adj.* Having a specific degree of ability. • The term often appears in the phrase *differently abled* as a euphemism for *disabled.*

ablegate (**ab**-lə-gayt), *n.* (17c) A papal envoy on a special mission, such as carrying a newly appointed cardinal's insignia of office.

ableism (**ay**-bəl-iz-əm), *n.* (1981) Prejudice against or disregard of disabled people's needs and rights; discrimination that unreasonably favors able-bodied persons. See DISCRIMINATION (2), (3). — **ableist,** *adj.*

able seaman. See *able-bodied seaman* under SEAMAN.

able to work. (1939) *Labor law.* (Of a worker) released from medical care and capable of employment; esp., not qualified to receive unemployment benefits on grounds of illness or injury.

ablocation (ab-loh-**kay**-shən), *n.* (17c) *Archaic.* The leasing of property for money. Cf. LOCATIO.

abmatertera (ab-mə-**tər**-tər-ə), *n.* [Latin] (17c) *Civil law.* A great-great-great aunt. See MATERTERA MAXIMA.

abmatertera magna. See ATMATERTERA.

abnepos (ab-**nep**-ahs *or* -ohs), *n.* [Latin] (16c) *Civil law.* A great-great-grandson; the grandson of a grandson or granddaughter.

abneptis (ab-**nep**-tis), *n.* [Latin] (16c) *Civil law.* A great-great-granddaughter; the granddaughter of a grandson or granddaughter.

abnormal gain. See GAIN (1).

abnormality. (1847) **1.** Something that deviates from the standard or average; something that is irregular, unusual, or exceptional. **2.** The state or quality of deviating from the norm; the state or quality of being irregular, unusual, or exceptional. Cf. ABERRANCE.

abnormal law. (1880) The law as it applies to persons who are under legal disabilities such as infancy, alienage, insanity, criminality, and (formerly) coverture.

abnormally dangerous activity. (1957) An undertaking that necessarily carries with it a significant risk of serious harm even if reasonable care is used, and for which the actor may face strict liability for any harm caused; esp., an activity (such as dynamiting) for which the actor is held strictly liable because the activity (1) involves the risk of serious harm to persons or property, (2) cannot be performed without this risk, regardless of the precautions taken, and (3) does not ordinarily occur in the community. • Under the Restatement (Second) of Torts, determining whether an activity is abnormally dangerous includes analyzing whether there is a high degree of risk of harm, whether any harm caused will be substantial, whether the exercise of reasonable care will eliminate the risk, whether the activity is a matter of common usage, whether the activity is appropriate to the place in which it occurs, and whether the activity's value to society outweighs its dangerousness. Restatement (Second) of Torts § 520 (1977). — Abbr. ADA. — Also, esp. formerly, termed *abnormally hazardous activity; extrahazardous activity; ultrahazardous activity.* See *strict liability* under LIABILITY. Cf. ULTRAHAZARDOUS ACTIVITY.

abnormal plaintiff. See PLAINTIFF.

abnormal sensitivity. (1916) A highly receptive and delicate nervous system and psyche that make a person unusually susceptible to hurt feelings and physical injury that would probably not occur to a person with a normal nervous system and psyche.

abode, *n.* (13c) A home; a place of residence. See DOMICILE; PLACE OF ABODE.

▸ **fixed abode.** A permanent home or place of residence.

abogado (ah-boh-**gah**-doh), *n.* [Spanish] *Spanish law.* An advocate; a lawyer.

ab olim (ab **oh**-lim), *adj.* [Law Latin] Of old.

abolish, *vb.* (15c) To annul, eliminate, or destroy, esp. an ongoing practice or thing; specif., to officially end an established law, system, tradition, etc.

abolition, *n.* (16c) **1.** The act of abolishing. **2.** The quality, state, or condition of being annulled or abrogated. **3.** (*usu. cap.*) The legal termination of slavery in the United States. **4.** *Civil law.* Withdrawal of a criminal accusation; a sovereign's remission of punishment for a crime. **5.** *Hist.* Permission granted to the accuser in a criminal action to withdraw from its prosecution. See NOLLE PROSEQUI.

abominable and detestable crime against nature. See SODOMY.

a bon droit (ay *or* a bawn **drwah**), *adv.* [Law French] With good reason; justly; rightfully.

ab orco usque ad coelum. [Latin] From the ground to the sky. Cf. USQUE AD COELUM.

aboriginal cost. See COST (1).

aboriginal title. See TITLE (2).

aborigine, *n.* (16c) **1.** A descendant of the earliest-known indigenous inhabitants of a country. • Because in Latin the collective term *aborigines* ("original native inhabitants") has no singular, the English singular *aborigine* is actually a back-formation made by regarding the Latin term as an English plural. Originally viewed as a solecism, *aborigine* is now considered unobjectionable on linguistic grounds. The term is traditionally used in the phrase *Australian aborigines,* but in Australia itself the usual term has been *aborigines* or *aboriginals.* Today, however, all those terms are considered pejorative and racially insensitive in Australian usage because they are seen as promoting a stereotype and ignoring the diversity among aboriginal peoples. So the usual terms there today are *indigenous Australian peoples, aboriginal person* or *people,* or (when applicable) *Torres Strait Islander.* A little-used technical term is *autochthon* or *autochthonous person.* **2.** (*usu. pl.*) A specimen of the indigenous flora or fauna of a country or district.

abortee (ə-bor-**tee**), *n.* (1912) A woman who undergoes an abortion.

aborticide. See ABORTIFACIENT.

abortifacient (ə-bor-tə-**fay**-shənt), *n.* (1857) A drug, article, or other thing designed or intended to produce an abortion. — Also (rarely) termed *aborticide.* — **abortifacient,** *adj.*

abortion, *n.* (16c) **1.** An artificially induced termination of a pregnancy for the purpose of destroying an embryo or fetus. • In *Roe v. Wade,* the Supreme Court first recognized a woman's right to choose to end her pregnancy as a privacy right stemming from the Due Process Clause of the 14th Amendment. 410 U.S. 113, 93 S.Ct. 705 (1973). Sixteen years later, in *Webster v. Reproductive Health Services,* the Court permitted states to limit this right by allowing them to enact legislation that (1) prohibits public facilities or employees from performing abortions, (2) prohibits the use of public funds for family planning that includes information on abortion, or (3) severely limits the right to an abortion after a fetus becomes viable — that is, could live independently of its mother. 492 U.S. 490, 109 S.Ct. 3040 (1989). In 1992, the Court held that (1) before viability, a woman has a fundamental right to choose to terminate her pregnancy, (2) a law that imposes an undue burden on the woman's right to choose before viability is unconstitutional, and (3) after viability, the state, in promoting its interest in potential human life, may regulate or prohibit abortion unless it is necessary to preserve the life or health of the mother. *Planned Parenthood of Southeastern Pa. v. Casey,* 505 U.S. 833, 112 S.Ct. 2791 (1992). In 2000, the Court again considered abortion rights and reaffirmed *Casey* in holding the Nebraska law at issue unconstitutional because (1) it failed to provide an exception to preserve the health of the mother, and (2) it unduly burdened a woman's right to choose a late-term abortion, thereby unduly burdening her right to choose abortion itself. *Stenberg v. Carhart*, 530 U.S. 914, 120 S.Ct. 2597 (2000). — Formerly also termed *procuring an abortion*; *criminal operation*; *criminal miscarriage*; *procuring miscarriage*. **2.** The spontaneous expulsion of an embryo or fetus before viability; MISCARRIAGE. — **abort,** *vb.*

"The word 'abortion,' in the dictionary sense, means no more than the expulsion of a fetus before it is capable of living. In this sense it is a synonym of 'miscarriage.' With respect to human beings, however, it has long been used to refer to an intentionally induced miscarriage as distinguished from one resulting naturally or by accident. There has been some tendency to use the word to mean a criminal miscarriage, and there would be distinct advantages in assigning this meaning to it; but there are so many references to lawful abortion or justification for abortion that it is necessary to speak of 'criminal abortion' or the 'crime of abortion' to emphasize the element of culpability." Rollin M. Perkins & Ronald N. Boyce, *Criminal Law* 186–87 (3d ed. 1982).

"Modern legal historians dispute whether, and to what extent, abortion constituted a crime at English common law. One view finds that, at most, abortion was an ecclesiastical crime, and concludes that the common law allowed a woman and her abortionist to terminate a pregnancy at all stages of gestation without secular penalties. Another claims that all abortions are at least secular wrongs to the fetus and that only the problems of proving a causal relationship between some abortions and fetal death prevented the punishment of all abortions. Substantial authority exists, however, for a middle ground: although no penalties attached to abortions before the fetus had quickened, performing a postquickening abortion was a common-law crime, most likely a misdemeanor." Susan Frelich Appleton, "Abortion," in 1 *Encyclopedia of Crime and Justice* 1, 1 (Sanford H. Kadish ed., 1983).

▸ **aspiration abortion.** (1975) A type of in-clinic abortion performed by suctioning a women's uterus. • An aspiration abortion is the most common type of abortion performed in the first trimester of pregnancy. — Also termed *vacuum abortion*.

▸ **back-alley abortion.** An abortion performed esp. by an unqualified person in circumstances involving questionable sanitation, usu. at a time when all abortions are considered illegal, or perhaps when the type of abortion being performed is illegal.

▸ **criminal abortion.** An abortion committed in circumstances that make it a criminal act; esp., the formerly unlawful act of purposely terminating any pregnancy. — Also termed *illegal abortion*.

▸ **dilation-and-evacuation abortion.** (1983) A type of abortion that uses both suctioning and surgical instruments to empty a women's uterus, usu. performed in the second trimester of pregnancy. — Abbr. D&E. See DILATION AND CURETTAGE.

▸ **forced abortion.** (1924) An abortion performed without the mother's consent.

▸ **illegal abortion.** See *criminal abortion*.

▸ **in-clinic abortion.** (2009) An abortion performed in a public or private facility specializing in abortions. Cf. *medication abortion*.

▸ **induced abortion.** (1926) An abortion purposely and artificially caused either by the mother herself or by a third party. See ABORTIFACIENT.

▸ **late-term abortion.** (1975) An abortion performed during the latter stages of pregnancy, usu. after the middle of the second trimester.

▸ **medically necessary abortion.** An abortion performed to preserve the life or health of the mother. — Also termed *therapeutic abortion*.

▸ **medication abortion.** (2006) An abortion induced by taking an oral medication in the early stages of pregnancy, usu. within the first nine weeks. See ABORTION PILL; EMERGENCY CONTRACEPTIVE PILL. Cf. *in-clinic abortion*.

▸ **partial-birth abortion.** (1995) An abortion in which a fetus is partly extruded from the womb and then destroyed.

▸ **spontaneous abortion.** See MISCARRIAGE (1).

▸ **therapeutic abortion.** (1896) See *medically necessary abortion*.

"Until recently it was common to speak of 'therapeutic abortion.' The literal meaning of the term is an abortion induced for medical reasons, but it was commonly understood to mean one for the purpose of saving the mother's life . . . ." Rollin M. Perkins & Ronald N. Boyce, *Criminal Law* 193 (3d ed. 1982).

▸ **vacuum abortion.** See *aspiration abortion*.

abortion clinic. A facility at which medical staff terminate pregnancies. — Also (broadly) termed *reproductive-health clinic*; *family-planning clinic*.

abortionist, *n.* (1844) *Pejorative.* A person who performs abortions, esp. illegal ones.

abortion pill. (1858) A drug that is taken orally to end a pregnancy by blocking hormones and causing the uterus to empty. See *medication abortion* under ABORTION. Cf. EMERGENCY CONTRACEPTIVE PILL.

abortive child. See CHILD.

abortive trial. See MISTRIAL.

aboutissement (a-boo-tees-**mahn**), *n.* [Law French] An abuttal or abutment.

above, *adj.* & *adv.* (18c) (Of an appellate court) having the power to review the case at issue; having dealt with an appeal in the case at issue <the court above> <when the case was heard above, the issue was not raised>. Cf. BELOW (3).

above-mentioned, *adj.* See AFORESAID.

above-stated, *adj.* See AFORESAID.

above-the-line, *adj.* (1973) (Of a deduction) taken after calculating gross income and before calculating adjusted gross income. • Examples of above-the-line deductions are IRA contributions and moving expenses. Formerly, individual tax returns had a dark line above which these deductions were written. Cf. BELOW-THE-LINE.

above-the-line tax deduction. See DEDUCTION (2).

abpatruus (ab-**pa**-troo-əs), *n.* [Latin] (16c) *Roman & civil law.* A great-great-great uncle. — Also termed *patruus maximus*.

A-B-Q trust. See *bypass trust* under TRUST (3).

abridge, *vb.* (14c) **1.** To reduce or diminish <abridge one's civil liberties>. **2.** To condense (as a book or other writing) <the author abridged the treatise before final publication>.

abridgment, *n.* (15c) **1.** The reduction or diminution of something concrete (as a treatise) or abstract (as a legal right). **2.** A condensed version of a longer work **3.** *Archaic.* A legal digest or encyclopedia, esp. one with alphabetically arranged entries that attempt to set forth comprehensive essays on the major topics of a legal system. — Also spelled (BrE) *abridgement.*

abridgment of damages. (1985) The right of a court to reduce the damages in certain cases. See REMITTITUR.

abroad, *adv.* (15c) Outside a country; esp., other than in a forum country.

abrogare (ab-roh-**gair**-ee), *vb.* [Latin] *Roman law.* (16c) To remove something from an old law by a new law. — Also termed *exrogare.*

abrogate (**ab**-rə-gayt), *vb.* (16c) To abolish (a law or custom) by formal or authoritative action; to annul or repeal. Cf. OBROGATE.

abrogation. The abolition or repeal of a law, custom, institution, or the like.

▸ **express abrogation.** (1857) The repeal of a law or provision by a later one that refers directly to it; abrogation by express provision or enactment.

▸ **implied abrogation.** The unannounced or nonexplicit repeal of a legal doctrine, legal power, or other rule, esp. resulting from an old law's incompatibility with a new one; specif., the nullification of a law or provision by a later one that is inconsistent with or contradictory to the first, without an express repeal.

abrogation of adoption. (1900) *Family law.* An action brought by an adoptive parent to terminate the parent–child relationship by annulment of the decree of adoption. • An adoption may be nullified if it resulted from fraud, misrepresentation, or undue influence, or if nullification is in the child's best interests. — Also termed *annulment of adoption.* Cf. WRONGFUL ADOPTION.

ABS. *abbr.* **1.** AMERICAN BUREAU OF SHIPPING. **2.** AUTOMATED BOND SYSTEM. **3.** See *able-bodied seaman* under SEAMAN. **4.** See *asset-backed security* under SECURITY (4).

abscond (ab-**skond**), *vb.* (16c) **1.** To depart secretly or suddenly, esp. to avoid arrest, prosecution, or service of process. **2.** To leave a place, usu. hurriedly, with another's money or property. — **absconder,** *n.*

abscondence. See ABSCONDMENT.

absconding debtor. See DEBTOR.

abscondment, *n.* (1841) The act of secretly leaving one's usual place of abode or business, esp. to avoid arrest, prosecution, or service of process. — Also termed *abscondence* (ab-**skon**-dənts).

absence, *n.* (14c) **1.** The quality, state, or condition of being away from one's usual place of residence. **2.** A failure to appear, or to be available and reachable, when expected. **3.** *Louisiana law.* The quality, state, or condition of being an absent person. — Also termed (in sense 3) *absentia.*

absent debtor. See DEBTOR.

absent deponent. See DEPONENT.

absente (ab-**sen**-tee). [Latin] In the absence of. • This term formerly appeared in law reports to note the absence of a judge <the court, *absente* Ellis, J., was unanimous>.

absentee (ab-sən-**tee**), *adj.* (18c) Not present <absentee voter>.

absentee, *adv.* (1940) In the manner of one who is not present <Debby voted absentee>.

absentee, *n.* (17c) **1.** Someone who is away from his or her usual residence; one who is absent. **2.** Someone who is not present where expected, specif., one who should be at a place or event but is not there. **3.** Someone who either resides out of state or has departed from the state without having a representative there.

> "Generally, a person is an absentee when he is absent from his domicile or usual place of residence; but in light of pertinent statutes he is an absentee when he is without the state and has no representative therein." 1 C.J.S. *Absentee* § 2, at 339 (1985).

absentee ballot. 1. See BALLOT (2). **2.** See *absentee voting* under VOTING.

absenteeism. (1850) Repeated absence from work, school, etc. without good reason.

absentee landlord. See LANDLORD.

absentee management. See *absentee landlord* under LANDLORD.

absentee vote. See *absentee voting* under VOTING.

absentee voting. See VOTING.

absente reo (ab-**sen**-tee **ree**-oh). [Latin] The defendant being absent. • This phrase appears syntactically as what English language grammarians term a "nominative absolute."

absentia. See IN ABSENTIA.

absent parent. See *noncustodial parent* under PARENT (1).

absent person. See PERSON (1).

absent witness. See WITNESS.

absent-witness instruction. See MISSING-WITNESS INSTRUCTION.

absoile (ab-**soyl**), *vb.* See ASSOIL.

absolute, *adj.* (14c) **1.** Free from restriction, qualification, or condition <absolute ownership>. **2.** Conclusive and not liable to revision <absolute delivery>. **3.** Unrestrained in the exercise of governmental power <absolute monarchy>. — **absolute,** *n.*

absolute assignee. See ASSIGNEE.

absolute assignment. See ASSIGNMENT (2).

absolute auction. See *auction without reserve* under AUCTION.

absolute-bar rule. (1979) The principle that when a creditor sells collateral without giving reasonable notice to the debtor, the creditor may not obtain a deficiency judgment for any amount of the debt that is not satisfied by the sale. • The rule governs commercially unreasonable sales made in violation of the UCC.

absolute contraband. See CONTRABAND.

absolute conveyance. See CONVEYANCE (1).

absolute covenant. See COVENANT (1).

absolute deed. See DEED.

absolute defense. See *real defense* under DEFENSE (4).

absolute delivery. See DELIVERY.

absolute disability. See DISABILITY (2).

absolute discharge. See DISCHARGE (5).

absolute disparity. (1976) *Constitutional law.* The difference between the percentage of a group in the general population and the percentage of that group in the pool of prospective jurors on a venire. • For example, if African-Americans make up 12% of a county's population and 8% of the potential jurors on a venire, the absolute disparity of African-American veniremembers is 4%. The reason for calculating the disparity is to analyze a claim that the jury was not impartial because the venire from which it was chosen did not represent a fair cross-section of the jurisdiction's population. Some courts criticize the absolute-disparity analysis, favoring instead the comparative-disparity analysis, in the belief that the absolute-disparity analysis understates the deviation. See FAIR-CROSS-SECTION REQUIREMENT; DUREN TEST; STATISTICAL-DECISION THEORY. Cf. COMPARATIVE DISPARITY.

absolute divorce. See *divorce a vinculo matrimonii* under DIVORCE.

absolute duty. See DUTY (1).

absolute estate. See ESTATE (1).

absolute gift. See *inter vivos gift* under GIFT.

absolute guaranty. See GUARANTY (1).

absolute immunity. See IMMUNITY (1).

absolute interest. See INTEREST (2).

absolute law. (16c) A supposed law of nature thought to be unchanging in principle, although circumstances may vary the way in which it is applied. See NATURAL LAW.

absolute legacy. See LEGACY (1).

absolute liability. See LIABILITY.

absolutely privileged communication. See COMMUNICATION.

absolute majority. See MAJORITY.

absolute martial law. See MARTIAL LAW (2).

absolute novelty. See NOVELTY.

absolute nuisance. See NUISANCE.

absolute nullity. See NULLITY.

absolute obligation. See OBLIGATION.

absolute order. See *decree absolute* under DECREE.

absolute pardon. See PARDON (1).

absolute pollution exclusion. See *pollution exclusion* under EXCLUSION (3).

absolute presumption. See *conclusive presumption* under PRESUMPTION.

absolute-priority rule. (1928) *Bankruptcy.* The rule that a confirmable reorganization plan must provide for full payment to a class of dissenting unsecured creditors before a junior class of claimants will be allowed to receive or retain anything under the plan. • Some jurisdictions recognize an exception to this rule when a junior class member, usu. a partner or shareholder of the debtor, contributes new capital in exchange for an interest in the debtor. 11 USCA § 1129(b)(2)(B)(ii).

absolute privilege. See PRIVILEGE (1).

absolute property. See PROPERTY.

absolute responsibility. See *absolute liability* under LIABILITY.

absolute right. See RIGHT.

absolute rule. See *decree absolute* under DECREE.

absolute sale. See SALE.

absolute simulated contract. See CONTRACT.

absolute title. See TITLE (2).

absolute veto. See VETO.

absolute warrandice. See WARRANDICE.

absolutio (ab-sə-**loo**-shee-oh). See ABSOLUTION (2).

absolution (ab-sə-**loo**-shən), *n.* (bef. 12c) **1.** Release from a penalty; the act of absolving. **2.** *Civil law.* An acquittal of a criminal charge. — Also termed *absolutio.* **3.** *Eccles. law.* Official forgiveness of a sin or sins.

absolutism (**ab**-sə-loo-tiz-əm), *n.* (1824) **1.** A doctrine that is ironclad and unconditional. See MORAL ABSOLUTISM. **2.** A political system in which the ruler has unbridled power and authority; specif., the existence of unconditional power and political sovereignty vested esp. in a dictator or oligarchy; authoritarianism. **3.** The philosophy of governing that underpins such a system. **4.** Absoluteness; the quality of that which is immediate, downright, and exceptionless. — **absolutist** (**ab**-sə-loo-tist), *adj. & n.*

> "Revival of absolutism in the present generation is a manifest fact. One might use a fashionable phrase of the time and call it a brute fact, since to the self-styled realist of today brutality seems to be a measure of actuality and not a little brutality has gone with recrudescence of absolute government and of political and juristic ideas appropriate to that form of rule. Certainly a revival of absolute government is too manifest to need any elaborate specification to a generation which has seen three great European powers turn from representative parliamentary institutions to avowed dictatorships and the polity of more than one country which in form hews to parliamentary rule take on the substance of personal rule above and behind it. Nor need it be argued to the student of political theory. The books of the day are full of theories which when carried out lead to organization of society in an omni-competent state in which the individual man is submerged. Nor is the proposition less true in juristic theory. The most widely known teacher, with the largest following on the Continent while free to teach there, taught an absolutist theory of law on a basis of philosophical relativism. In England, where parliamentary government and the doctrine of the supremacy of the law had their origin, professors are now teaching the superseding of the law which knew of private rights and guaranteed individual liberties by a law which knows them not, or subordinates them to the claims of officials of whom it is postulated that they act for the general good. Even in the law itself, and Anglo-American law had been averse to recognizing absolute power anywhere in anyone, the absolutist thinking in politics and in jurisprudence has been having an effect, manifest especially in administrative adjudication and in the relation of administrative agencies to the courts." Roscoe Pound, *Contemporary Juristic Theory* 1–2 (1940).

absolve (ab- *or* əb-**zolv**), *vb.* (15c) **1.** To release from an obligation, debt, or responsibility. **2.** To free from the penalties for misconduct. — **absolver,** *n.*

absolvitor (ab-**sol**-vi-tər), *n.* (16c) *Scots law.* A decision in a civil action in favor of the defender; an acquittal. — **absolvitory,** *adj.*

absorbable risk. See RISK.

absorbed, *adj.* (Of an issue of bonds or a block of stock) having been entirely taken up or disposed of.

absorption, *n.* (18c) **1.** The act or process of including or incorporating a thing into something else; esp., the application of rights guaranteed by the U.S. Constitution to actions by the states. **2.** *Int'l law.* The merger of one country into another, whether voluntarily or by subjugation. **3.** *Labor law.* In a postmerger collective-bargaining agreement, a provision allowing seniority for union members in the resulting entity. **4.** *Real estate.* The rate at which property will be leased or sold on the market at a given time. **5.** *Commercial law.* A sales method by which a manufacturer pays the reseller's freight costs, which the manufacturer accounts for before quoting the reseller a price. — Also termed (in sense 5) *freight absorption.* — **absorb,** *vb.*

absque (**abs**-kwee), *adv.* [Latin] Without.

absque aliquo inde reddendo (**abs**-kwee **al**-ə-kwoh **in**-dee ri-**den**-doh), *adv.* [Law Latin] *Hist.* Without rendering anything therefrom. • This phrase appeared in royal grants in which no tenure was reserved.

absque consideratione curiae (**abs**-kwee kən-sid-ə-ray-shee-**oh**-nee **kyoor**-ee-ee), *adv.* [Law Latin] Without the consideration of the court; without judgment.

absque dubio (**abs**-kwee **d[y]oo**-bee-oh), *adv.* [Latin] Without doubt.

absque hoc (**abs**-kwee **hok**), *adv.* [Latin] *Archaic.* Without this. • The phrase was formerly used in common-law pleading to introduce the denial of allegations. — Also termed *sans ce que.* See TRAVERSE.

absque impetitione vasti (**abs**-kwee im-pə-tish-ee-**oh**-nee **vas**-tɪ), *adv.* [Law Latin] *Hist.* See WITHOUT IMPEACHMENT OF WASTE.

absque injuria damnum (**ab**-skwee in-**joor**-ee-ə **dam**-nəm). [Latin] *Civil law.* See DAMNUM ABSQUE INJURIA. — Often shortened to *absque injuria.*

absque ipsius regis speciali licentia (**abs**-kwee **ip**-see-əs **ree**-jis spesh-ee-**ay**-lɪ li-**sen**-shee-ə). [Law Latin] *Hist.* Without the special authority of the king himself. • The phrase was part of a law forbidding Crown vassals to transfer land without a special warrant.

absque tali causa (**abs**-kwee **tay**-lɪ **kaw**-zə), *adv.* [Law Latin] Without such cause. • In common-law pleading, this was part of the larger phrase *de injuria sua propria, absque tali causa* ("of his own wrong, without such cause") appearing in a reply that a trespass plaintiff made to counter a defendant's claim of excuse. In an assault case, for example, if a defendant pleaded that he had struck the plaintiff in self-defense, the plaintiff could reply that the defendant was guilty of his own wrong committed without such cause as alleged. See DE INJURIA.

ABS Rules. (1958) *Maritime law.* Industry standards for the construction, maintenance, and operation of seagoing vessels and stationary offshore facilities, as set and enforced by the American Bureau of Shipping. See AMERICAN BUREAU OF SHIPPING.

abstain, *vb.* (1885) **1.** To voluntarily refrain from doing or having something one enjoys, esp. something in which one has a history of overindulging. **2.** To choose not to vote for or against something, esp. in a formal parliamentary session. **3.** (Of a federal court) to refrain from exercising jurisdiction over a matter.

abstention. (16c) **1.** The act of not doing something, esp. something enjoyable. **2.** The act of not voting for or against something. **3.** A federal court's relinquishment of jurisdiction when necessary to avoid needless conflict with a state's administration of its own affairs. **4.** The legal principle underlying such a relinquishment of jurisdiction. Cf. COMITY (1); OUR FEDERALISM.

▸ **abstention in the interests of justice.** See *permissive abstention.*

▸ ***Brillhart* abstention.** A federal court's refusal to hear a declaratory-judgment action when a proceeding has already been brought in state court to resolve the same rights at issue as in the federal action. *Brillhart v. Excess Insurance Co.,* 316 U.S. 491, 62 S.Ct. 1173 (1942).

▸ ***Burford* abstention.** (1967) A federal court's refusal to review a state court's decision in cases involving a complex regulatory scheme and sensitive areas of state concern. *Burford v. Sun Oil Co.,* 319 U.S. 315, 63 S.Ct. 1098 (1943).

▸ ***Colorado River* abstention.** (1976) A federal court's decision to abstain while relevant and parallel state-court proceedings are under way. *Colorado River Water Conservation Dist. v. U.S.,* 424 U.S. 800, 96 S.Ct. 1236 (1976).

▸ **discretionary abstention.** See *permissive abstention.*

▸ **equitable abstention.** (1948) A federal court's refraining from interfering with a state administrative agency's decision on a local matter when the aggrieved party has adequate relief in the state courts.

▸ **mandatory abstention.** (1984) Abstention that a bankruptcy court must exercise in a related (noncore) proceeding that could not have been brought in federal court in the absence of the pending bankruptcy. 28 USCA § 1334(c)(2). Cf. *permissive abstention.*

▸ **permissive abstention.** (1985) *Bankruptcy.* Abstention that a bankruptcy court can, but need not, exercise in a dispute that relates to the bankruptcy estate but that can be litigated, or is being litigated, in another forum. • In deciding whether to abstain, the bankruptcy court must consider (1) the degree to which state law governs the case, (2) the appropriateness of the procedure to be followed in the other forum, (3) the remoteness of the dispute to the issues in the bankruptcy case, and (4) the presence of nondebtor parties in the dispute. 28 USCA § 1334(c)(1). — Also termed *abstention in the interests of justice; discretionary abstention.* Cf. *mandatory abstention.*

▸ ***Pullman* abstention.** (1963) A federal court's decision to abstain so that state courts will have an opportunity to settle an underlying state-law question whose resolution may avert the need to decide a federal constitutional question. *Railroad Comm'n v. Pullman Co.,* 312 U.S. 496, 61 S.Ct. 643 (1941).

▸ ***Thibodaux* abstention** (**tib**-ə-doh). (1974) A federal court's decision to abstain so that state courts can decide difficult issues of public importance that, if decided by the federal court, could result in unnecessary friction between state and federal authorities. *Louisiana Power & Light Co. v. City of Thibodaux,* 360 U.S. 25, 79 S.Ct. 1070 (1959).

▸ ***Younger* abstention.** (1972) **1.** A federal court's decision not to interfere with an ongoing state criminal proceeding by issuing an injunction or granting declaratory relief, unless the prosecution has been brought in bad faith or merely as harassment. *Younger v. Harris,* 401

U.S. 37, 91 S.Ct. 746 (1971). — Also termed *equitable-restraint doctrine.* **2.** By extension, a federal court's decision not to interfere with a state-court civil proceeding used to enforce the criminal law, as to abate an obscene nuisance. See OUR FEDERALISM.

abstention doctrine. (1943) The principle that federal courts should not hear cases better heard in state courts. — Also termed *doctrine of abstention.*

abstention in the interests of justice. See *permissive abstention* under ABSTENTION.

abstinence (**ab**-stə-nənts), *n.* (13c) The practice of refraining completely from indulgence in some act; esp., the practice of not having sex or of not consuming alcoholic beverages.

abstract (**ab**-strakt), *n.* (15c) **1.** A concise statement of a text, esp. of a legal document; a summary. See ABSTRACT OF DEED; ABSTRACT OF JUDGMENT; ABSTRACT OF TITLE. **2.** *Patents.* A one-paragraph summary of an invention's design and function, including its nature, structure, purpose, and novelty. • The abstract is a required part of a patent application, and also appears on the front page of the patent itself. It may not exceed 150 words. For the purpose of determining adequacy of disclosure, the abstract is considered to be part of the specification. *See* 35 USCA § 112. — Also termed *abstract of the disclosure*; *abstract of the specification.*

abstract compromis. See *general compromis* under COMPROMIS (1).

abstracter. See ABSTRACTOR.

abstract idea. (1847) *Intellectual property.* A concept or thought, removed from any tangible embodiment. • An abstract idea is one of the categories of unpatentable subject matter, along with natural phenomena and laws of nature. But a process that uses abstract ideas to produce a useful result can be patented. Copyright law likewise will not protect an abstract idea, but only its expression. The law of unfair competition, on the other hand, does protect abstract ideas that meet the other criteria of a trade secret. See *business-method patent* under PATENT (3).

abstraction (ab- *or* əb-**strak**-shən), *n.* (16c) **1.** The mental process of considering something without reference to a concrete instance <jurisprudence is largely the abstraction of many legal particulars>. **2.** A theoretical idea not applied to any particular instance <utopia in any form is an abstraction>. **3.** The summarizing and recording of a legal instrument in public records <abstraction of the judgment in Tarrant County>. **4.** The act of taking with the intent to injure or defraud <the abstraction of funds was made possible by the forged signature on the check>. **5.** The act of taking away or of separating, as apart from a whole; esp., taking water from a supply. — **abstract** (ab-**strakt** [in senses 1, 2, 4 & 5] *or* **ab**-strakt [in sense 3]), *vb.*

abstraction-filtration-comparison test. (1992) *Copyright.* A judicially created test for determining whether substantial similarity exists between two works in an action for infringement. • First, the court dissects the copyrighted work's structure and isolates each level of abstraction or generality (abstraction test). Second, the court examines each level of abstraction and separates out the unprotectable elements such as ideas, processes, facts, public-domain information, and merger material (filtration test). Finally, the court compares the resulting core of protectable expression with the accused work to determine whether substantial elements of the copyrighted work have been misappropriated (comparison test). This test was first applied in *Computer Associates Int'l, Inc. v. Altai, Inc.*, 982 F.2d 693 (2d Cir. 1992). Although the test is usu. applied in software-infringement cases, the test has also been applied to nonsoftware works. — Abbr. AFC test. — Also termed *abstraction-filtration test.* See SIMILARITY. Cf. ABSTRACTIONS TEST.

abstraction-filtration test. See ABSTRACTION-FILTRATION-COMPARISON TEST.

abstractions test. (1951) *Copyright.* A means of comparing copyrighted material with material that allegedly infringes the copyright by examining whether the actual substance has been copied or whether the two works merely share the same abstract ideas. • The primary authority for the abstractions test is Judge Learned Hand's opinion in *Nichols v. Universal Pictures Corp.*, 45 F.2d 119 (2d Cir. 1930). Although referred to as a "test," it is not a bright-line test, but an approach to discerning the boundaries of protectable expression by isolating and comparing each level of abstraction in the two works, from the lowest (most detailed) to the highest (most conceptual). Cf. ABSTRACTION-FILTRATION-COMPARISON TEST.

abstract juridical act. See ACT (2).

abstract of a fine. See NOTE OF A FINE.

abstract of conviction. (1955) A summary of the court's finding on an offense, esp. a traffic violation.

abstract of deed. A summary of a deed's contents and of any related contract of sale, usu. including any reservations and exclusions, and often the conditions and price of conveyance. — Also termed *deed abstract.* Cf. ABSTRACT OF TITLE.

abstract of judgment. (1812) A copy or summary of a judgment that, when filed with the appropriate public office, creates a lien on the judgment debtor's nonexempt property. See *judgment lien* under LIEN.

abstract of record. (18c) An abbreviated case history that is thorough enough to show an appellate court that the questions presented for review have been preserved.

abstract of the disclosure. See ABSTRACT (2).

abstract of the specification. See ABSTRACT (2).

abstract of title. (1858) A concise statement, usu. prepared for a mortgagee or purchaser of real property, summarizing the history of a piece of land, including all conveyances, interests, liens, and encumbrances that affect title to the property. — Also termed *title examination*; *examination of title*; *title abstract*; *title abstraction*; *brief*; *brief of title.* Cf. ABSTRACT OF DEED.

▸ **good and merchantable abstract of title.** (1910) An abstract of title showing clear, good, and marketable title, rather than showing only the history of the property. See *clear title*, *good title*, and *marketable title* under TITLE (2).

abstractor (ab- *or* əb-**strak**-tər), *n.* (1873) Someone who prepares abstracts of title. — Also spelled *abstracter.*

abstract question. See HYPOTHETICAL QUESTION.

absurdity, *n.* (16c) **1.** The quality, state, or condition of being grossly unreasonable. **2.** An interpretation that would lead to an unconscionable result, esp. one that the parties or (esp. for a statute) the drafters could not have intended. Cf. GOLDEN RULE.

absurdity canon. See ABSURDITY DOCTRINE.

absurdity doctrine. The principle that a provision in a legal instrument may be either disregarded or judicially corrected as an error (esp. when the correction is textually simple) if failing to do so would result in a disposition that no reasonable person could approve. — Also termed *absurdity canon*; *absurdity principle*; *absurd-result principle*; *presumption against absurdity.*

absurd-result principle. See ABSURDITY DOCTRINE.

A-B trust. See *bypass trust* under TRUST (3).

ab urbe condita (ab **ər**-bee **kon**-di-tə). [Latin] From the founding of the city (esp. Rome in 753 B.C.). • This term is sometimes used in abbreviated form in classical dates. For example, the date "23 A.U.C." means "23 years after the founding of Rome," or 730 B.C. — Abbr. A.U.C.

abuse (ə-**byoos**), *n.* (15c) **1.** A departure from legal or reasonable use; misuse. **2.** Cruel or violent treatment of someone; specif., physical or mental maltreatment, often resulting in mental, emotional, sexual, or physical injury. — Also termed *cruel and abusive treatment.* Cf. NEGLECT; CRUELTY.

▸ **abuse of the elderly.** (1971) Abuse of a senior citizen, generally someone at least 60–65 years old, esp. by a caregiver or relative. • Examples include deprivation of food or medication, beatings, oral assaults, and isolation. — Also termed *elder abuse.*

▸ **adult abuse.** Neglect or maltreatment by a caregiver, guardian, or conservator of an adult entrusted to the person's care. • Adult abuse is a crime in many jurisdictions. — Also termed *vulnerable-adult abuse.*

▸ **carnal abuse.** See *sexual abuse* (1).

▸ **child abuse.** (1891) **1.** Intentional or neglectful physical or emotional harm inflicted on a child, including sexual molestation; esp., a parent's or caregiver's act or failure to act that results in a child's exploitation, serious physical or emotional injury, sexual abuse, or death. **2.** An act or failure to act that presents an imminent risk of serious harm to a child. • Child abuse can be either intentional or negligent. The first case of child abuse actually prosecuted occurred in New York City in 1874. An eight-year-old girl named Mary Ellen was found to have been severely abused. Her abusers were prosecuted under the law for prevention of cruelty to animals, since no law protecting children then existed. Child abuse was first recognized as a medical concern in 1962, when Dr. C. Henry Kempe introduced the medical concept of battered-child syndrome. — Also termed *cruelty to a child*; *cruelty to children*; *child maltreatment.* See *abused child* under CHILD; *battered child* under CHILD; BATTERED-CHILD SYNDROME. Cf. *secondary abuse.*

▸ **domestic abuse.** See *domestic violence* under VIOLENCE.

▸ **elder abuse.** See *abuse of the elderly.*

▸ **emotional abuse.** (1963) Physical or verbal abuse that causes or could cause serious emotional injury. — Also termed *mental abuse*; *psychological abuse.*

▸ **medical abuse.** The unlawful treatment of a medical patient.

▸ **mental abuse.** See *emotional abuse.*

▸ **psychological abuse.** See *emotional abuse.*

▸ **secondary abuse.** (1997) Emotional harm suffered by children who, although they are not physically abused, witness domestic violence within their families. Cf. *child abuse.*

▸ **sexual abuse.** (1874) **1.** An illegal or wrongful sex act, esp. one performed against a minor by an adult. — Also termed *carnal abuse.* **2.** RAPE (2). — Also termed (in both senses) *sex abuse.*

▸ **spousal abuse.** (1978) Physical, sexual, or psychological abuse inflicted by one spouse on the other spouse; esp., wife-beating. See BATTERED-WOMAN SYNDROME.

▸ **verbal abuse.** (1811) Emotional abuse inflicted by one person on another by means of words, esp. spoken words, in a way that causes distress, fear, or similar emotions. • Verbal abuse may include name-calling, insults, threatening gestures, excessive and unfounded criticism, humiliation, and denigration. — Also sometimes termed *vulgar abuse.*

▸ **vulgar abuse.** See *verbal abuse.*

▸ **vulnerable-adult abuse.** See *adult abuse.*

abuse (ə-**byooz**), *vb.* (15c) **1.** To damage (a thing). **2.** To depart from legal or reasonable use in dealing with (a person or thing); to misuse. **3.** To injure (a person) physically or mentally. **4.** In the context of child welfare, to hurt or injure (a child) by maltreatment. • In most states, a finding of abuse is generally limited to maltreatment that causes or threatens to cause lasting harm to the child. Cf. MALTREAT; MISTREAT.

abused child. See CHILD.

abusee (ə-byoo-**zee**), *n.* (1836) Someone who is or has been abused.

abuse excuse. (1993) *Criminal law.* The defense that a defendant cannot tell right from wrong or control impulses because of physical or mental abuse suffered as a child. • Like the traditional excuse of insanity, the abuse excuse is asserted by a defendant in an effort to mitigate or avoid culpability for the crime charged. Cf. BATTERED-CHILD SYNDROME; BATTERED-WOMAN SYNDROME.

abuse of discovery. See DISCOVERY ABUSE.

abuse of discretion. (18c) **1.** An adjudicator's failure to exercise sound, reasonable, and legal decision-making. **2.** An appellate court's standard for reviewing a decision that is asserted to be grossly unsound, unreasonable, illegal, or unsupported by the evidence. See DISCRETION (4).

abuse of distress. (1809) *Hist.* The wrongful seizure and use of another's property as a means of collecting damages or coercing the property's owner to perform a duty.

abuse of legal process. See ABUSE OF PROCESS.

abuse of power. (16c) The misuse or improper exercise of one's authority; esp., the exercise of a statutorily or otherwise duly conferred authority in a way that is tortious, unlawful, or outside its proper scope.

abuse of process. (1809) The improper and tortious use of a legitimately issued court process to obtain a result that is either unlawful or beyond the process's scope. — Also termed *abuse of legal process*; *malicious abuse of process*; *malicious abuse of legal process*; *wrongful process*; *wrongful process of law.* Cf. MALICIOUS PROSECUTION.

"Distinction between a malicious use and a malicious abuse of process. — There is a distinction between a malicious use and a malicious abuse of legal process. An abuse of legal process is where the party employs it for some unlawful object, not for the purpose which it is intended by law to effect; in other words, it is a perversion of it. For example, if a man is arrested, or his property seized, in order to extort money from him, even though it be to pay a just claim, other than that in suit, or to compel him to give up possession of a deed or anything of value not the legal object of the process, it is settled there is an action for such malicious abuse of process. It is not necessary to prove that the action in which the process issued has been determined or to aver that it was sued out without probable cause." Martin L. Newell, *A Treatise on the Law of Malicious Prosecution, False Imprisonment, and the Abuse of Legal Process* 7 (1892).

"One who uses a legal process, whether criminal or civil, against another primarily to accomplish a purpose for which it is not designed is subject to liability to the other for harm caused by the abuse of process." Restatement (Second) of Torts § 682 (1977).

abuse of rights. **1.** *Int'l law.* A country's exercise of a right either in a way that impedes the enjoyment by other countries of their own rights or for a purpose different from that for which the right was created (e.g., to harm another country). **2.** *Louisiana law.* A person's exercise of a right in an unneighborly spirit that provides no benefit to the person but causes damage to the neighbor.

abuse-of-rights doctrine. (1933) *Civil law.* The principle that a person may be liable for harm caused by doing something the person has a right to do, if the right is exercised (1) for the purpose or primary motive of causing harm, (2) without a serious and legitimate interest that is deserving of judicial protection, (3) against morality, good faith, or elementary fairness, or (4) for a purpose other than its intended legal purpose.

abuse of the elderly. See ABUSE.

abuse-of-the-writ doctrine. (1973) *Criminal procedure.* The principle that a petition for a writ of habeas corpus may not raise claims that should have been, but were not, asserted in a previous petition. Cf. SUCCESSIVE-WRIT DOCTRINE.

abuser (ə-**byoo**-zər), *n.* (15c) **1.** Someone who abuses someone or something. **2.** *Hist.* ABUSE, *n.* (1). **3.** MISUSER.

abusive (ə-**byoo**-siv), *adj.* (16c) **1.** Characterized by wrongful or improper use <abusive discovery tactics>. **2.** (Of a person) habitually cruel, malicious, or violent; esp., using cruel words or physical violence <abusive parent>. — **abusively,** *adv.*

abusive discovery. See DISCOVERY ABUSE (1).

abusive tactics. Tactics in litigation or negotiation intended to vex, harass, or intimidate an adverse party, to drive up that party's costs, or to delay the proceedings rather than conclude a matter by agreement or adjudication.

abusus (ə-**byoo**-səs), *n.* (16c) *Civil law.* The right to dispose of one's property.

abut (ə-**bət**), *vb.* (15c) To join at a border or boundary; to share a common boundary with <the company's land in Arizona abuts the Navajo Indian reservation>.

abutment, (ə-**bət**-mənt), *n.* **1.** The act, process, or condition of abutting. **2.** Something that abuts. **3.** A place at which two or more things touch; the part that abuts or that is abutted.

abuttals (ə-**bət**-əlz). (17c) Land boundaries; the boundary lines of a piece of land in relation to other contiguous lands. — Also termed (archaically) *buttals.*

abutter (ə-**bət**-ər). (1874) **1.** The owner of adjoining land; one whose property abuts another's.

"The major right of [an abutter] is that of access to his property — a right of reasonable ingress and egress. He is entitled to compensation for any substantial impairment of this reasonable access. The right normally includes the right to have, at some point, a driveway onto his premises. An abutter does *not* have the right to the continued flow of traffic in the same amount or pattern past his premises." Osborne M. Reynolds Jr., *Handbook of Local Government Law* § 180, at 620 (1982).

2. Land that adjoins the land in question.

abutting foot. See FRONT FOOT.

a/c. *abbr.* ACCOUNT (4).

academic, *adj.* (16c) **1.** Of, relating to, or involving a school or a field of study, esp. one that is neither vocational nor commercial, such as the liberal arts <academic courses>. **2.** Theoretical; specif., not practical or immediately useful <academic question>.

academic degree. See DEGREE (5).

academic freedom. (1863) The right (esp. of a university teacher) to speak freely about political or ideological issues without fear of loss of position or other reprisal.

academic lawyer. (1913) A law professor, usu. one who maintains a law practice on the side.

Académie de Droit International de La Haye. See HAGUE ACADEMY OF INTERNATIONAL LAW.

academy. (15c) **1.** An institution of higher learning. **2.** An association dedicated to the advancement of knowledge in a particular field, such as the American Academy of Matrimonial Lawyers. **3.** A private high school. **4.** (*cap.*) A garden near Athens where Plato taught; hence, the school of philosophy that he led.

a cancellando (ay kan-sə-**lan**-doh). [Law Latin] From canceling.

"It has its name of chancery, *cancellaria,* from the judge who presides here, the lord chancellor or *cancellarius;* who, Sir Edward Coke tells us, is so termed *a cancellando,* from cancelling the king's letters patents when granted contrary to law . . . ." 3 William Blackstone, *Commentaries on the Laws of England* 46 (1768).

a cancellis (ay kan-**sel**-is), *n.* [Law Latin] *Hist.* A chancellor, so called because he performed the duties of office behind a *cancelli* ("lattice").

a cancellis curiae explodi (ay kan-**sel**-is **kyoor**-ee-ɪ ek-**sploh**-dɪ). [Law Latin] *Hist.* To be expelled from the bar of the court.

a cause de cy (ay **kaw**-zə də **see**), *adv.* [Law French] For this reason.

accedas ad curiam (ak-**see**-dəs ad **kyoor**-ee-əm), *n.* [Law Latin "you are to go to the court"] *Hist.* An original writ for removing a replevin action to a royal court from either of two feudal courts — a court baron or a hundred court. • It is a *recordare facias loquelam* for replevin actions. See RECORDARI FACIAS LOQUELAM.

accede (ak-**seed**), *vb.* (15c) **1.** To consent or agree; specif., to agree to (a demand, proposal, etc.), esp. after first disagreeing. **2.** To be added (to something else) through accession. **3.** To adopt. See ADOPTION (5). **4.** (Of a body politic) to accept unification with or annexation into another body politic. — **accession,** *n.* — **accedence** (ak-**see**-dənts), *n.*

Accelerated Cost Recovery System. (1981) An accounting method that is used to calculate asset depreciation and that allows for the faster recovery of costs by assigning the asset a shorter useful life than was previously permitted under the Internal Revenue Code. • This system applies to property put into service from 1981 to 1986. It was replaced in 1986 by the Modified Accelerated Cost Recovery System. — Abbr. ACRS.

accelerated depreciation. See DEPRECIATION.

accelerated depreciation method. See DEPRECIATION METHOD.

accelerated disclosure. See *accelerated discovery* under DISCOVERY.

accelerated discovery. See DISCOVERY.

accelerated-market damages. See *headstart damages* under DAMAGES.

accelerated-reentry theory. See POST-EXPIRATION-SALES THEORY.

accelerated remainder. See REMAINDER (1).

acceleration, *n.* (18c) **1.** The act or process of quickening or shortening the duration of something, such as payments or other functional activities <acceleration of rent>. **2.** The advancing of a loan agreement's maturity date so that payment of the entire debt is due immediately <acceleration of the date>. **3.** *Property.* The hastening of an owner's time for enjoyment of an estate because of the failure of a preceding estate; esp., the shortening of the time for vesting in possession of an expectant interest <the acceleration of the vesting for all remaindermen>. — Also termed *acceleration of remainder.* **4.** *Securities.* The SEC's expediting of a registration statement's effective date so that the registrant bypasses the required 20-day waiting period <acceleration of an SEC registration>. — **accelerate,** *vb.*

acceleration clause. (1905) A loan-agreement provision that requires the debtor to pay off the balance sooner than the due date if some specified event occurs, such as failure to pay an installment or to maintain insurance. Cf. DEMAND CLAUSE; INSECURITY CLAUSE.

acceleration of remainder. See ACCELERATION (3).

acceptable, *adj.* (14c) **1.** Good enough to be used for a particular purpose or to be considered satisfactory; capable, worthy, and sure of being favorably received. **2.** (Of behavior) morally or socially good enough; minimally accordant with standards of decency.

Acceptable Identification of Goods and Services Manual. *Trademarks.* A U.S. government publication that sets forth, for goods and services, known acceptable international class categorizations and descriptions that may be used in trademark applications submitted to the U.S. Patent and Trademark Office. • This manual is available from the U.S. Government Printing Office, Washington, D.C. 20402 and through the PTO's website at http://www.uspto.gov.

acceptance, *n.* (16c) **1.** An offeree's assent, either by express act or by implication from conduct, to the terms of an offer in a manner authorized or requested by the offeror, so that a binding contract is formed. • If an acceptance modifies the terms or adds new ones, it generally operates as a counteroffer. Cf. OFFER (1), (2).

▸ **acceptance at variance to an offer.** See *varying acceptance.*

▸ **acceptance by silence.** (1847) Acceptance of an offer not by explicit words but through the lack of an offeree's response in circumstances in which the relationship between the offeror and the offeree justifies both the offeror's expectation of a reply and the offeror's reasonable conclusion that the lack of one signals acceptance. • Ordinarily, silence does not give rise to an acceptance of an offer.

▸ **accommodation acceptance.** (1807) The acceptance of an offer to buy goods for current or prompt shipment by shipping nonconforming goods after notifying the buyer that the shipment is intended as an accommodation. • This type of "acceptance" is not truly an acceptance under contract law, but operates instead as a counteroffer if the buyer is duly notified.

▸ **constructive acceptance.** Acceptance by a buyer of goods that are not identified in the contract with the seller, the acceptance arising from an act by which the buyer manifests ownership of the goods, as by reselling them.

▸ **free acceptance.** (16c) In the law of restitution, the acceptance of an offered benefit after having an opportunity to reject the benefit and with the knowledge that the benefit was not offered as a gift.

▸ **general acceptance.** (17c) An unconditional acceptance of an offer's terms; esp., in a bill of exchange, an unqualified agreement to pay the bill in full.

▸ **partial acceptance.** (18c) See *varying acceptance.*

▸ **qualified acceptance.** (18c) See *varying acceptance.*

▸ **varying acceptance.** (1837) A conditional or partial acceptance that varies the original terms of an offer and operates as a counteroffer; esp., in negotiable instruments (bills of exchange), an acceptor's variation of the terms of the instrument, as by paying only part of the sum or paying at a different time or place. • A varying acceptance is ineffective if its material terms differ from those of the offer, but is effective under the knockout rule if the only terms at variance with the offer are nonmaterial. — Also termed *partial acceptance; qualified acceptance; acceptance at variance to an offer; acceptance au besoin.* See MIRROR-IMAGE RULE; KNOCKOUT RULE.

2. A buyer's assent that the goods are to be taken in performance of a contract for sale. • Under UCC § 2-606, a buyer's acceptance consists in (1) signifying to the seller that the goods are conforming ones or that the buyer will take them despite nonconformities, (2) not making an effective rejection, or (3) taking any action inconsistent with the seller's ownership. If the contract is for the sale of goods that are not identified when the contract is entered into, there is no acceptance until the buyer has had a reasonable time to examine the goods. But if the buyer deals with them as owner, as by reselling them, a court may find constructive acceptance.

> "Acceptance means communicated acceptance. . . . [It] must be something more than a mere mental assent." William R. Anson, *Principles of the Law of Contract* 34 (Arthur L. Corbin ed., 3d Am. ed. 1919). [But Corbin adds:]

"This use of the word 'communicated' is open to some objection. To very many persons the word means that knowledge has been *received*. Frequently a contract is made even though the offeror has no such knowledge. In such case the acceptance is not 'communicated' and yet it consummates the contract." *Id.* n.2.

"Acceptance of a conveyance or of a document containing a promise is a manifestation of assent to the terms thereof made, either before or after delivery, in accordance with any requirements imposed by the grantor or promisor. If the acceptance occurs before delivery and is not binding as an option contract, it is revocable until the moment of delivery." Restatement (Second) of Contracts § 106 (1979).

3. The formal receipt of and agreement to pay a negotiable instrument; specif., under Article 3 of the UCC, the drawer's signed engagement to honor a draft as presented. UCC § 3-409(a). • The acceptance becomes operative upon notification or delivery.

▸ **acceptance *au besoin*** (oh bə-**zwan**). [French "in case of need"] (1843) An acceptance by one who has agreed to pay the draft in case the drawee fails to do so.

▸ **acceptance for honor.** (18c) An acceptance or undertaking not by a party to the instrument, but by a third party, for the purpose of protecting the honor or credit of one of the parties, by which the third party agrees to pay the debt when it becomes due if the original drawee does not. • This type of acceptance inures to the benefit of all successors to the party for whose benefit it is made. — Also termed *acceptance supra protest*; *acceptance for honor supra protest*.

▸ **blank acceptance.** (1850) Acceptance by a bill-of-exchange drawee before the bill is made, as indicated by the drawee's signature on the instrument.

▸ **conditional acceptance.** (18c) An agreement to pay a draft on the occurrence or nonoccurrence of a particular event.

▸ **express acceptance.** (18c) A written or oral expression indicating that the drawee has seen the instrument and does not dispute its sufficiency. • While a written acceptance is typically signified by the stamped or written word "accepted" or "presented," usu. on the instrument itself, an oral acceptance must be made directly to a drawer or holder who has waived the right to a written acceptance.

▸ **implied acceptance.** (18c) An acceptance implied by a drawee whose actions indicate an intention to comply with the request of the drawer; conduct by the drawee from which the holder is justified in concluding that the drawee intends to accept the instrument.

▸ **special acceptance.** (18c) An acceptance that departs from either the terms of a bill or the terms added to but not otherwise expressed in a bill. • An example is an acceptance of a draft as payable in a particular place even though the draft contains no such limitation.

4. A negotiable instrument, esp. a bill of exchange, that has been accepted for payment.

"'Acceptance for honour *supra protest*' is an exception to the rule that only the drawee can accept a bill. A bill which has been dishonoured by non-acceptance and is not overdue may, with the consent of the holder, be accepted in this way for the honour of either the drawer or an indorser (i.e., to prevent the bill being sent back upon the drawer or indorser as unpaid) by a friend placing his own name upon it as acceptor for the whole, or part only, of the amount of the bill; after a protest has been drawn up declaratory of its dishonour by the drawee. Similarly, where a bill has been dishonoured by non-payment and protested any person may intervene and pay it *supra protest* for the honour of any person liable thereon; the effect being to discharge all parties subsequent to the party for whose honour it is paid." 2 *Stephen's Commentaries on the Laws of England* 202–03 (L. Crispin Warmington ed., 21st ed. 1950).

▸ **bank acceptance.** See *banker's acceptance*.

▸ **banker's acceptance.** (1841) A bill of exchange drawn on and accepted by a commercial bank; esp., a short-term credit instrument that an importer's bank issues to guarantee payment of an exporter's invoice. • Banker's acceptances are often issued to finance the sale of goods in international trade. — Abbr. BA. — Also termed *bank acceptance*.

▸ **trade acceptance.** (1919) A bill of exchange for the amount of a specific purchase, drawn on and accepted by the buyer for payment at a specified time.

5. An insurer's agreement to issue a policy of insurance.

"And in some instances, insurance companies have even specified in the application forms that acceptance of an applicant's offer will not occur until the insurance policy is literally delivered to the applicant — that is, the insurer chooses to structure the arrangement so that acceptance is to be manifested by the physical delivery of the insurance policy to the applicant." Robert E. Keeton & Alan I. Widiss, *Insurance Law: A Guide to Fundamental Principles, Legal Doctrines, and Commercial Practices* § 2.1, at 39–40 (1988).

6. An heir's agreement to take an inheritance. See TACIT ACCEPTANCE. **7.** See ADOPTION (5). — **accept**, *vb*.

acceptance at variance to an offer. See *varying acceptance* under ACCEPTANCE (1).

acceptance *au besoin*. See ACCEPTANCE (3).

acceptance by silence. See ACCEPTANCE (1).

acceptance company. See *sales finance company* under FINANCE COMPANY.

acceptance credit. See *time letter of credit* under LETTER OF CREDIT.

acceptance criteria. (1986) *Intellectual property.* Agreed-on performance standards that custom-made products such as computer software or hardware or a commercial website must meet before the customer is legally obligated to accept the product and pay for it.

acceptance doctrine. (1992) *Construction law.* The principle that, once a property owner accepts the work of a contractor, the contractor is not liable to third parties for an injury arising from the contractor's negligence in performing under the contract, unless the injury results from a hidden, imminently dangerous defect that the contractor knows about and the owner does not know about. — Also termed *accepted-work doctrine*.

acceptance for honor. See ACCEPTANCE (3).

acceptance for honor *supra protest*. See *acceptance for honor* under ACCEPTANCE (3).

acceptance-of-the-benefits rule. (1972) The doctrine that a party may not appeal a judgment after having voluntarily and intentionally received all or some part of the relief provided by it.

acceptance sampling. (1983) The practice of examining only a few items from a shipment to determine the acceptability of the whole shipment.

acceptance supra protest. See *acceptance for honor* under ACCEPTANCE (3).

acceptance testing. (1955) *Intellectual property.* Formal experiments conducted by or on behalf of the customer to determine whether computer software or hardware or a commercial website satisfies the customer's acceptance criteria. • Usu., an acceptance-testing provision in a sales contract or license agreement is accompanied by a termination provision allowing the customer to back out of the contract if the product is not acceptable. — Also termed *requirements testing.* See ACCEPTANCE CRITERIA.

acceptare (ak-sep-**tair**-ee), *vb.* [Latin] *Civil law.* To accept or assent to, as a promise made by another.

accepted-work doctrine. See ACCEPTANCE DOCTRINE.

acceptilatio. See ACCEPTILATION.

acceptilation (ak-sep-tə-**lay**-shən), *n.* [fr. Latin *acceptilatio* "release"] (16c) *Roman & civil law.* An oral release from an obligation even though payment has not been made in full; a complete discharge, esp. through a fictitious payment. — Also termed (in Roman law) *acceptilatio.* Cf. APOCHA.

acceptor, *n.* (18c) A person or entity that accepts a negotiable instrument and agrees to be primarily responsible for its payment or performance.

> "As the term 'maker' denotes the *promisor in a note,* and him only, so the term 'acceptor' in the terminology of the Law Merchant denotes the *drawee of a bill,* foreign or inland, who has bound himself in due form of law to pay the bill according to its tenor, to the payee or any subsequent holder in due course. There can therefore by no 'acceptance' of a promissory note, nor, commercially speaking, of a check. But the acceptance of the bill and the certification of the check are so closely related with respect to form and legal effect . . . ." Melville M. Bigelow, *The Law of Bills, Notes, and Checks* 115 (William Minor Lile ed., 3d ed. 1928).

acceptor supra protest. (18c) Someone who, to protect the honor of the drawer or an indorser of a note or bill, accepts a bill that has been protested. See *acceptance for honor* under ACCEPTANCE (3).

accept service. (18c) To agree that process has been properly served even when it has not been. — Also termed *accept service of process.*

accept service of process. See ACCEPT SERVICE.

access, *n.* (14c) **1.** A right, opportunity, or ability to enter, approach, pass to and from, or communicate with <access to the courts>.

▸ **disabled access.** See *handicapped access.*

▸ **handicapped access.** The way by which a person of impaired mobility can enter, use, and leave a building, including such accommodations as wheelchair ramps, automatic doors, and elevators. — Also termed *disabled access.*

2. *Family law.* The legal right to see and spend time with one's children, a prisoner, an official, etc.; esp., VISITATION (2). **3.** *Family law.* The opportunity to have, or feasibility of having, sexual intercourse; also, the occurrence of copulation. Cf. NONACCESS.

▸ **multiple access.** (1974) *Hist.* In a paternity suit, the defense that the mother had one or more sexual partners other than the defendant around the time of conception. • The basis for the defense is that because the mother bears the burden of proof, she must be able to prove that only the defendant could be the child's father. In some jurisdictions, this is still known by its common-law name, the *exceptio plurium concubentium* defense, or simply the *plurium* defense. Juries or judges who wished to dismiss the case because of the mother's promiscuity, rather than because of the improbability of the defendant's paternity, often accepted this defense. Most states have now abrogated the defense. In recent years the issue of multiple access has declined in importance with the rise of highly accurate paternity testing.

4. *Patents & Trademarks.* The right to obtain information about and to inspect and copy U.S. Patent and Trademark Office files of patents, patent applications, trademark applications, and *inter partes* proceedings pertaining to them. **5.** *Copyright.* An opportunity by one accused of infringement to see, hear, or copy a copyrighted work before the alleged infringement took place <the duplication of the error proved that the defendant had access to the work>. • Proof of access is required to prove copyright infringement unless the two works are strikingly similar.

> "Since direct evidence of copying is rarely available, a plaintiff can rely upon circumstantial evidence to prove this essential element; the most important component of such circumstantial evidence to support a copyright infringement claim is proof of access. Evidence of access and substantial similarity create an inference of copying and establish a prima facie case of copying." 18 Am. Jur. 2d *Copyright and Literary Property* § 206 (1985).

6. *Copyright.* The right to obtain information about and to inspect and copy U.S. Copyright Office files and deposited materials. See (for senses 4 & 6) POWER TO INSPECT. — **access,** *vb.*

access easement. See EASEMENT.

accessio (ak-**sesh**-ee-oh), *n.* [Latin] *Roman law.* **1.** The doctrine by which something of lesser size, value, or importance is integrated into something of greater size, value, or importance.

> "If the identity of one thing (the accessory) is merged and lost in the identity of the other (the principal), the owner of the principal is the owner of the thing. . . . There is said to be *accessio.* . . . The term is used by some commentators (and, following them, by the French Civil Code) in a much wider sense to include all cases in which there has been an addition to my right, i.e. in which the object of my ownership has increased. The owner of an animal therefore acquires ownership of the young of the animal at birth by *accessio,* though in physical terms there has been not an accession but a separation. In this sense *accessio* includes all the original natural modes except *occupatio* and *thesauri inventio.* And there are other, intermediate, meanings. Since *accessio* as an abstract word is not Roman and no clear classification emerges from the texts, no one meaning or classification can be said to be 'right,' but those adopted by the French Civil Code are so wide as to be almost meaningless." Barry Nicholas, *An Introduction to Roman Law* 133 & n.1 (1962).

2. ACCESSION (4). **3.** ACCESSION (5).

accession (ak-**sesh**-ən), *n.* (16c) **1.** The act of acceding or agreeing <the family's accession to the kidnapper's demands>. **2.** A coming into possession of a right or office <as promised, the state's budget was balanced within two years after the governor's accession>. **3.** *Int'l law.* A method by which a country that is not among a treaty's original signatories becomes a party to it. <Italy became a party to the nuclear-arms treaty by accession>. *See* Vienna Convention on the Law of Treaties, art. 15 (1155 U.N.T.S. 331, 8 I.L.M. 679 (1969)). — Also termed *adherence; adhesion.* See INSTRUMENT OF ACCESSION. **4.** The acquisition of title to personal property by one who in good faith bestows labor or materials on raw material owned by another to convert it to another thing, as where A inadvertently uses clay owned by B to create a valuable statue. — Also termed (in Roman law) *accessio*. See ADJUNCTION (2).

"*Accessio* is the combination of two chattels belonging to different persons into a single article: as when A's cloth is used to patch B's coat, or a vehicle let on hire-purchase has new accessories fitted to it." R.F.V. Heuston, *Salmond on the Law of Torts* 113 (17th ed. 1977).

5. A property owner's right to all that is added to the property (esp. land) naturally or by labor, including land left by floods and improvements made by others <the newly poured concrete driveway became the homeowner's property by accession>. • In Louisiana law, accession is the owner's right to whatever is produced by or united with something, either naturally or artificially. La. Civ. Code arts. 483, 490, 507. Cf. ANNEXATION.

"Accession . . . might happen from the gradual deposit of alluvial soil by a river suddenly leaving its channel, or it might happen from the act of man, such as from building or planting on the soil." John George Phillimore, *Private Law Among the Romans* 143 (1863).

6. An improvement to existing personal property, such as new shafts on golf clubs.

"The problem of accessions arises infrequently, judging from reported cases, but an obvious instance of the difficulty arises where a motor vehicle is being financed by a secured party and the debtor in possession of necessity acquires a new engine or new tires for the vehicle . . . . If the seller of the engine or tires reserved a security interest at the time the goods were installed, the seller should prevail over the vehicle's secured party, with a right to remove the accessions. Conversely, if the sale were on open credit with no security interest reserved, or if the seller acquired a security interest after installation of the goods, then the financer of the vehicle should prevail." Ray D. Henson, *Handbook on Secured Transactions Under the Uniform Commercial Code* § 4-22, at 93 (2d ed. 1979).

7. The physical uniting of goods with other goods in such a manner that the identity of the original goods is not lost. UCC § 9-102(a)(1). **8.** ACCESSORYSHIP.

accession council. (*often cap.*) (1901) *English law.* A group of Privy Councillors, Lords Spiritual and Temporal, the Lord Mayor and aldermen of London, and (in recent years) Commonwealth High Commissioners in London who, shortly after the monarch's death, convene to see the successor monarch take the oath for the security of the realm.

access order. See VISITATION ORDER.

accessorial (ak-sə-**sor**-ee-əl), *adj.* (18c) **1.** (Of a promise) made for the purpose of strengthening another's credit <an accessorial pledge by way of guaranty>. — Also termed *accessory.* **2.** *Criminal law.* Of, relating to, or involving an accessory to a crime <accessorial guilt>.

accessorial obligation. 1. See COLLATERAL OBLIGATION. **2.** See *secondary obligation* under OBLIGATION.

accessory, *adj.* See ACCESSORIAL (1).

accessory (ak-**ses**-ə-ree), *n.* (15c) **1.** Something of secondary or subordinate importance. **2.** *Criminal law.* Someone who aids or contributes in the commission or concealment of a crime. • An accessory is usu. liable only if the crime is a felony. Cf. ACCOMPLICE; PRINCIPAL, *n.* (2). — **accessory,** *adj.* — **accessoryship,** *n.*

"In most jurisdictions, the common-law distinctions between principals and accessories have largely been abolished, although the pertinent statutes vary in form and substance. Conceptually, the common-law pattern remains the same: The person who aids, abets, commands, counsels, or otherwise encourages another to commit a crime is still regarded as a party to the underlying crime as at common law, even though the labels principal in the first degree, principal in the second degree, and accessory before the fact are no longer used, and even though it usually does not matter whether the aider and abettor is or is not present at the scene of the crime." 1 Charles E. Torcia, *Wharton's Criminal Law* § 35, at 202–03 (15th ed. 1993).

▸ **accessory after the fact.** (17c) An accessory who was not at the scene of the crime but knows that a crime has been committed and who helps the offender try to escape arrest or punishment. 18 USCA § 3. • Most penal statutes establish the following four requirements: (1) someone else committed a felony before the accessory acted; (2) the accessory is not guilty as a principal; (3) the accessory personally helped the principal try to avoid the consequences of the felony; and (4) the accessory helped despite having actual or imputed knowledge about the principal's guilt. An accessory after the fact may be prosecuted for obstructing justice. — Sometimes shortened to *accessory after.*

"At common law, an accessory after the fact is one who, knowing that a felony has been committed by another, receives, relieves, comforts, or assists the felon, or in any manner aids him to escape arrest or punishment. To be guilty as an accessory after the fact one must have known that a completed felony was committed, and that the person aided was the guilty party. The mere presence of the defendant at the scene of the crime will not preclude a conviction as an accessory after the fact, where the evidence shows the defendant became involved in the crime after its commission." 21 Am. Jur. 2d *Criminal Law* § 209, at 275–76 (1998).

▸ **accessory at the fact.** See *principal in the second degree* under PRINCIPAL (2).

"A principal in the second degree is one by whom the actual perpetrator of the felony is aided and abetted at the very time when it is committed; for instance, a car-owner sitting beside the chauffeur who kills someone by over-fast driving, or a passenger on a clandestine joy-riding expedition which results in manslaughter; or a bigamist's second 'wife,' if she *knows* he is committing bigamy. (In early law he was not ranked as a principal at all, but only as a third kind of accessory — the accessory *at* the fact.)" J.W. Cecil Turner, *Kenny's Outlines of Criminal Law* 86 (16th ed. 1952).

▸ **accessory before the fact.** (17c) An accessory who assists or encourages another to commit a crime but who is not present when the offense is actually committed. • Most jurisdictions have abolished this category of accessory and instead treat such an offender as an accomplice. — Sometimes shortened to *accessory before.* See ACCOMPLICE.

"An accessory before the fact is a person who procures or advises one or more of the principals to commit the felony. This definition requires from him an instigation so active that a person who is merely shown to have acted as the stake-holder for a prize-fight, which ended fatally, would not be punishable as an accessory. The fact that a crime has been committed in a manner different from the mode which the accessory had advised will not excuse him from liability for it. Accordingly if *A* hires *B* to poison *C*, but *B* instead kills *C* by shooting him, *A* is none the less liable as accessory before the fact to *C*'s murder. But a man who has counselled a crime does not become liable as accessory if, instead of any form of the crime suggested, an entirely different offence is committed." J.W. Cecil Turner, *Kenny's Outlines of Criminal Law* 88 (16th ed. 1952).

accessory building. See BUILDING.

accessory contract. See CONTRACT.

accessory obligation. See OBLIGATION.

accessory right. See RIGHT.

accessoryship, *n.* (1895) The status or fact of being an accessory. — Also termed (loosely) *accession.*

accessory thing. See THING (1).

accessory use. See USE (1).

access to counsel. See RIGHT TO COUNSEL.

access to justice. (18c) The ability within a society to use courts and other legal institutions effectively to protect one's rights and pursue claims. — Also termed *access to the courts.*

access-to-justice commission. (1997) An agency of a state's judicial system designed to encourage the judicial, executive, and legislative branches of government, the bar, law schools, legal-aid providers, and others to work together to provide civil legal services to low-income citizens. — Abbr. AJC.

access to the courts. See ACCESS TO JUSTICE.

accident, *n.* (14c) **1.** An unintended and unforeseen injurious occurrence; something that does not occur in the usual course of events or that could not be reasonably anticipated; any unwanted or harmful event occurring suddenly, as a collision, spill, fall, or the like, irrespective of cause or blame <the accident was staged as part of an insurance scam>. **2.** *Equity practice.* An unforeseen and injurious occurrence not attributable to the victim's mistake, negligence, neglect, or misconduct; an unanticipated and untoward event that causes harm.

> "The word 'accident,' in accident policies, means an event which takes place without one's foresight or expectation. A result, though unexpected, is not an accident; the means or cause must be accidental. Death resulting from voluntary physical exertions or from intentional acts of the insured is not accidental, nor is disease or death caused by the vicissitudes of climate or atmosphere the result of an accident; but where, in the act which precedes an injury, something unforeseen or unusual occurs which produces the injury, the injury results through accident." 1A John Alan Appleman & Jean Appleman, *Insurance Law and Practice* § 360, at 455 (rev. vol. 1981).

▸ **automobile accident.** See *car accident.*

▸ **car accident.** An accident in which a motor vehicle collides with another vehicle or with a person, animal, or object, usu. causing damage or injury. — Also termed *automobile accident; motor-vehicle accident; vehicular accident; traffic accident; traffic collision.*

▸ **culpable accident.** (1926) An accident due to negligence. • A culpable accident, unlike an unavoidable accident, is no defense except in those few cases in which wrongful intent is the exclusive and necessary basis for liability.

▸ **fatal accident.** An accident that results in someone's death.

▸ **inevitable accident.** See *unavoidable accident.*

▸ **motor-vehicle accident.** See *car accident.*

▸ **pure accident.** See *unavoidable accident.*

▸ **traffic accident.** See *car accident.*

▸ **unavoidable accident.** (17c) An accident that cannot be avoided because it is produced by an irresistible physical cause that cannot be prevented by human skill or reasonable foresight. • Examples include accidents resulting from lightning or storms, perils of the sea, inundations or earthquakes, or sudden illness or death. Proving an unavoidable accident has been considered a means of avoiding both civil and criminal liability. — Also termed *inevitable accident; pure accident; unavoidable casualty.* Cf. ACT OF GOD.

> "Inevitable accident . . . does not mean a catastrophe which could not have been avoided by any precaution whatever, but such as could not have been avoided by a reasonable man at the moment at which it occurred, and it is common knowledge that a reasonable man is not credited with perfection of judgment." P.H. Winfield, *A Textbook of the Law of Tort* § 15, at 43 (5th ed. 1950).

> "An unavoidable accident is an occurrence which was not intended and which, under all the circumstances, could not have been foreseen or prevented by the exercise of reasonable precautions. That is, an accident is considered unavoidable or inevitable at law if it was not proximately caused by the negligence of any party to the action, or to the accident." W. Page Keeton et al., *Prosser and Keeton on the Law of Torts* § 29, at 162 (5th ed. 1984).

▸ **vehicular accident.** See *car accident.*

accidental, *adj.* (16c) **1.** Not having occurred as a result of anyone's purposeful act; esp., resulting from an event that could not have been prevented by human skill or reasonable foresight. **2.** Not having been caused by a tortious act.

accidental death. See DEATH.

accidental-death benefit. (1907) An insurance-policy provision that allows for an additional payment (often double the face amount of the policy) if the insured dies as a result of an accident, as defined in the policy, and not from natural causes. — Abbr. ADB.

accidental harm. See HARM.

accidentalia (ak-si-den-**tay**-lee-ə). [Law Latin "accidental things"] *Hist.* Incidents of a contract; nonessential contractual terms to which the parties expressly stipulate. Cf. ESSENTIALIA.

> "*Accidentalia* have their existence entirely by express stipulation, and are never presumed without it." William Bell, *Bell's Dictionary and Digest of the Law of Scotland* 406 (George Watson ed., 7th ed. 1890).

accidentalia feudi (ak-si-den-**tay**-lee-ə **fyoo**-dɪ). [Law Latin] (18c) *Hist.* All nonessential terms in a feudal contract; esp., those that are not essential to the fee (such as building restrictions). Cf. ESSENTIALIA FEUDI.

accidental injury. See INJURY.

accidental killing. (17c) Homicide resulting from a lawful act performed in a lawful manner under a reasonable belief that no harm could occur. — Also termed *death by misadventure; homicide by misadventure; killing by misadventure; homicide per infortunium.* See *justifiable homicide* under HOMICIDE; *involuntary manslaughter* under MANSLAUGHTER. Cf. MALICIOUS KILLING.

accidental stranding. See STRANDING.

accident and health insurance. See *health insurance* under INSURANCE.

accident-based insurance. See *occurrence-based liability insurance* under INSURANCE.

accident insurance. See INSURANCE.

accident policy. See INSURANCE POLICY.

accident reconstruction. (1956) The science of examining all evidence, including physical evidence, that exists as a result of an accident and analyzing it in line with established principles of mathematics and physics in order to re-create or otherwise reenact the event. • Accident reconstruction involves a detailed piecing together of possible events that could have contributed to the accident. *Beech Aircraft Corp. v. Rainey*, 488 U.S. 153, 157 (1988). Some accident reconstructions use computer-generated evidence to demonstrate how the accident could have occurred. See *computer-generated evidence* under EVIDENCE.

accidere (ak-**sid**-ər-ee), *vb.* [Latin] *Civil law.* **1.** To fall down. **2.** By extension, to befall or happen to.

accipe ecclesiam (**ak**-si-pee e-**klee**-z[h]ee-əm). [Law Latin] *Hist. Eccles. law.* Receive this church or living. • The phrase was used by Patrons in presenting an incumbent to a vacant parish. *Trado tibi ecclesiam* ("I deliver this church [or living] to you") was also used. Cf. TRADO TIBI ECCLESIAM.

accipere (ak-**sip**-ər-ee), *vb.* [Latin] *Civil law.* To receive; esp., to take under a will.

accipitare (ak-sip-ə-**tair**-ee), *vb.* [Law Latin] *Hist.* To pay (a lord) in order to become a vassal; esp., to pay relief upon succeeding to an estate.

acclamation, *n.* (1827) *Parliamentary law.* **1.** Approval or election by general consent, usu. demonstrated by applause or cheering. • Election by acclamation is common in large conventions where only one candidate has been nominated. **2.** Voting by applause or shouting.

accola (**ak**-ə-lə), *n.* [Latin "person living nearby"] **1.** *Roman law.* Someone who inhabits or occupies land near a certain place, such as one who dwells near a river. **2.** *Hist.* An agricultural tenant; a tenant of a manor.

accolade (**ak**-ə-layd), *n.* (16c) **1.** A sign or token of praise, commendation, or affection, esp. one accompanied by an embrace. **2.** *English law.* The traditional ceremony for conferring a knighthood, formerly by the monarch's tapping or even hitting the knight's neck or shoulder, but in more recent years by the monarch's touching him on the shoulder with the flat of a sword.

accomenda (ak-ə-**men**-də), *n. Hist. Maritime law.* A contract between a cargo owner and a shipmaster whereby the parties agree to sell the cargo and divide the profits (after deducting the owner's costs). • This contract actually consists of two agreements: a *mandatum*, by which the owner gives the shipmaster the power to dispose of the cargo, and a partnership contract, by which the parties divide any profits arising from the sale. — Also spelled *accommenda.* See MANDATE (5).

accommodated party. (1851) A party for whose benefit an accommodation party signs and incurs liability. Cf. ACCOMMODATION PARTY.

accommodation, *n.* (17c) **1.** A loan or other financial favor. **2.** The act of signing an accommodation paper as surety for another. See ACCOMMODATION PAPER. **3.** The act or an instance of making a change or provision for someone or something; an adaptation or adjustment. **4.** A convenience supplied by someone; esp., lodging and food.

▸ **business accommodation.** A commercial entity's action that is beneficial to another party but that is not legally required, such as a company's undertaking to become a gratuitous bailee.

▸ **disability accommodation.** **1.** An adaptation, adjustment, or allowance made for a handicapped person's needs. See *handicapped access* under ACCESS (1). **2.** See *reasonable accommodation.*

▸ **public accommodation.** (1859) A business that provides lodging, food, entertainment, or other services to the public; esp. (as defined by the Civil Rights Act of 1964), one that affects interstate commerce or is supported by state action.

▸ **reasonable accommodation.** (1976) An adaptation, adjustment, or allowance made for a disabled person's needs or an employee's religious beliefs or practices without imposing an undue hardship on the party taking the action. • Under the Americans with Disabilities Act, an employer must make reasonable accommodations for an employee's disability. Examples of reasonable accommodations that have been approved by the courts include providing additional unpaid leave, modifying the employee's work schedule, and reassigning the employee to a more appropriate, vacant position. — Also termed *disability accommodation.* See HARDSHIP (1).

accommodation acceptance. See ACCEPTANCE (1).

accommodation bill. See ACCOMMODATION PAPER.

accommodation director. See *dummy director* under DIRECTOR.

accommodation endorsement. See *accommodation indorsement* under INDORSEMENT.

accommodation indorsement. See INDORSEMENT.

accommodation indorser. See INDORSER.

accommodation land. See LAND.

accommodation line. (1934) *Insurance.* One or more policies that an insurer issues to retain the business of a valued agent, broker, or customer, even though the risk would not be accepted under the insurer's usual standards.

accommodation loan. See LOAN.

accommodation maker. See MAKER.

accommodation note. **1.** See NOTE (1). **2.** ACCOMMODATION PAPER.

accommodation paper. (18c) A negotiable instrument that one party cosigns, without receiving any consideration, as surety for another party who remains primarily liable. • An accommodation paper is typically used when the cosigner is more creditworthy than the principal debtor. — Also termed *accommodation bill; accommodation note; bill of accommodation.* See NOTE (1).

accommodation party. (1812) Someone who, without recompense or other benefit, signs a negotiable instrument for the purpose of being a surety for another party (called the *accommodated party*) to the instrument. • The accommodation party can sign in any capacity (i.e., as maker, drawer, acceptor, or indorser). An accommodation party is liable to all parties except the accommodated party, who impliedly agrees to pay the note or draft and to indemnify the accommodation party for all losses incurred in having to pay it. See SURETY. Cf. ACCOMMODATED PARTY.

accommodation road. (1823) A private road over land not adjoining a main road; a byway.

accommodation subpoena. See *friendly subpoena* under SUBPOENA.

accommodation surety. See *voluntary surety* under SURETY (1).

accommodation works. (1846) Bridgework, protective fencing, gates, culverts, hedging, and similar structures located alongside a highway, railroad, etc., for the convenience of adjoining landowners.

accommodatum (ə-kom-ə-**day**-təm), *n.* See COMMODATUM.

accompany, *vb.* (15c) To go along with (another); to attend. • In automobile-accident cases, an unlicensed driver is not considered accompanied by a licensed driver unless the latter is close enough to supervise and help the former.

accomplice (ə-**kom**-plis). (1854) *Criminal law.* **1.** Someone who is in any way involved with another in the commission of a crime, whether as a principal in the first or second degree or as an accessory. • Although the definition includes an accessory before the fact, not all authorities treat this term as including an accessory after the fact.

> "There is some authority for using the word 'accomplice' to include all principals and all accessories, but the preferred usage is to include all principals and accessories before the fact, but to exclude accessories after the fact. If this limitation is adopted, the word 'accomplice' will embrace all perpetrators, abettors and inciters." Rollin M. Perkins & Ronald N. Boyce, *Criminal Law* 727 (3d ed. 1982).

> "A person is an 'accomplice' of another in committing a crime if, with the intent to promote or facilitate the commission of the crime, he solicits, requests, or commands the other person to commit it, or aids the other person in planning or committing it." 1 Charles E. Torcia, *Wharton's Criminal Law* § 38, at 220 (15th ed. 1993).

2. Someone who knowingly, voluntarily, and intentionally unites with the principal offender in committing a crime and thereby becomes punishable for it. See ACCESSORY (2). Cf. PRINCIPAL, *n.* (2).

> "By definition an accomplice must be a person who acts with the purpose of promoting or facilitating the commission of the substantive offense for which he is charged as an accomplice. *State v. White*, N.J. 1984, 484 A.2d 691, 98 N.J. 122." Model Penal Code § 2.06 annot. (1997).

accomplice-corroboration rule. (1938) *Criminal law.* The doctrine, applicable in some states, that a jury must not rely solely on an accomplice's testimony to convict a criminal defendant but must require independent evidence connecting the defendant to the crime charged. • The rule is based on concern about the reliability of evidence obtained by the prosecution in exchange for some benefit received by the accomplice, such as a reduction of charges.

accomplice liability. See LIABILITY.

accomplice testimony. *Criminal law.* Personal evidence given by an accomplice witness. See WITNESS.

accomplice witness. See WITNESS.

accompt. See ACCOUNT (1).

accord, *n.* (14c) **1.** An amicable arrangement between parties, esp. between peoples or countries; COMPACT; TREATY. **2.** An offer to give or to accept a stipulated performance in the future to satisfy an obligor's existing duty, together with an acceptance of that offer. • The performance becomes what is known as a *satisfaction.* — Also termed *executory accord*; *accord executory.* See ACCORD AND SATISFACTION; SATISFACTION. Cf. COMPROMISE; NOVATION.

> "An accord is a contract under which an obligee promises to accept a stated performance in satisfaction of the obligor's existing duty. Performance of the accord discharges the original duty." Restatement (Second) of Contracts § 281(1) (1979).

> "The term *executory accord* is sometimes used to underscore the point that the accord itself does not discharge the duty. It also reflects an historical anachronism, now generally rejected, under which an unperformed accord was not a defense to an action on the underlying duty." E. Allan Farnsworth, *Contracts* § 4.24, at 289 n.10 (3d ed. 1999).

3. A signal used in a legal citation to introduce a case clearly supporting a proposition for which another case is being quoted directly or to indicate that the law of one jurisdiction is consistent with that of another.

accord, *vb.* (12c) **1.** To furnish or grant, esp. what is suitable or proper <accord the litigants a stay of costs pending appeal>. **2.** To agree <they accord in their opinions>.

accord and satisfaction. (18c) An agreement to substitute for an existing debt some alternative form of discharging that debt, coupled with the actual discharge of the debt by the substituted performance. • The new agreement is called the *accord*, and the discharge is called the *satisfaction.* Cf. COMPROMISE; NOVATION; SETTLEMENT (2), (3).

> "'Accord and satisfaction' means an agreement between the parties that something shall be given to, or done for, the person who has the right of action, in satisfaction of the cause of action. There must be not only agreement ('accord') but also consideration ('satisfaction'). Such an arrangement is really one of substituted performance." 1 E.W. Chance, *Principles of Mercantile Law* 101 (P.W. French ed., 13th ed. 1950).

accordant (ə-**kor**-dənt), *adj.* (14c) In agreement <accordant with these principles>.

accord executory. See ACCORD (2).

accost, *vb.* **1.** To assail or attack, esp. by words. **2.** Loosely, to assail or attack physically.

accouchement (ə-**koosh**-mənt *or* ak-oosh-***mawn***). [French] (1803) Childbirth.

account, *n.* (14c) **1.** ACCOUNTING (3) <the principal filed an action for account against his agent>. — Also spelled (archaically) *accompt.*

> "The action of account lies where one has received goods or money for another in a fiduciary capacity, to ascertain and recover the balance due. It can only be maintained where there is such a relationship between the parties, as to raise an obligation to account, and where the amount due is uncertain and unliquidated." Benjamin J. Shipman, *Handbook of Common-Law Pleading* § 56, at 144 (Henry Winthrop Ballantine ed., 3d ed. 1923).

2. ACCOUNTING (4) <the contractor filed an action for account against the nonpaying customer>. **3.** A statement by which someone seeks to describe or explain an event <Fred's account of the holdup differed significantly from Martha's>. **4.** A detailed statement of the debits and credits between parties to a contract or to a fiduciary relationship; a reckoning of monetary dealings <the trustee balanced the account at the end of each month>. • In wills and estates, an account is a brief financial statement of the manner in which an executor or administrator has performed the official duties of collecting the estate's assets and paying those who are entitled. An account charges the executor or administrator with the value of the estate as shown by the inventory, plus any increase, and credits the executor with expenses and costs, duly authorized disbursements, and the executor's commission. — Abbr. acct.; a/c. — Also termed *accounting.* See STATEMENT OF

ACCOUNT. 5. A course of business dealings or other relations for which records must be kept <open a brokerage account>.

▸ **account current.** See *current account.*

▸ **account in trust.** (18c) An account established by an individual to hold the account's assets in trust for someone else.

▸ **account payable.** (*usu. pl.*) (1936) An account reflecting a balance owed to a creditor; a debt owed by an enterprise in the normal course of business dealing. — Often shortened to *payable; payables; bill payable.* — Also termed *note payable.* Pl. **accounts payable.**

▸ **account receivable.** (*usu. pl.*) (1936) An account reflecting a balance owed by a debtor; a debt owed by a customer to an enterprise for goods or services. — Often shortened to *receivable; receivables.* — Also termed *note receivable; bill receivable.* Pl. **accounts receivable.**

▸ **account rendered.** (17c) An account produced by the creditor and presented for the debtor's examination and acceptance. — Also termed *bill rendered.*

▸ **account settled.** (18c) An account with a paid balance.

▸ **account stated.** (17c) **1.** A balance that parties to a transaction or settlement agree on, either expressly or by implication. • The phrase also refers to the agreement itself or to the assent giving rise to the agreement. **2.** A plaintiff's claim in a suit for such a balance. **3.** *Equity practice.* A defendant's plea in response to an action for an accounting. • The defendant states that the balance due on the statement of the account has been discharged and that the defendant holds the plaintiff's release. — Also termed *stated account.*

▸ **accumulated-adjustments account.** (1982) *Tax.* An item on the books of an S corporation (usu. an equity item on the corporation's balance sheet) to account for taxable-income items passed through to shareholders, such as accumulated earnings — earned before the corporation converted from a C corporation to an S corporation — that would have been distributed as a dividend to the shareholders if the corporation had remained a C corporation. • One of the theories underlying the accumulated-adjustments account is that the shareholders should not be permitted to avoid dividend-tax treatment on a corporation's accumulated earnings just because the corporation converts from C status to S status. IRC (26 USCA) § 1368(e)(1). — Abbr. AAA.

▸ **adjunct account.** (1998) An account that accumulates additions to another account.

▸ **annual account.** See *intermediate account.*

▸ **assigned account.** (1893) An account receivable that is pledged to a bank or factor as security for a loan.

▸ **bank account.** (18c) A deposit or credit account with a bank, such as a demand, time, savings, or passbook account. UCC § 4-104(a)(1). See *deposit account.*

▸ **blocked account.** (1937) An account at a bank or other financial institution, access to which has been restricted either by the government or by an authorized person. • An account may be blocked for a variety of reasons, as when hostilities erupt between two countries and each blocks access to the other's accounts. — Also termed *frozen account.*

▸ **book account.** (17c) A detailed statement of debits and credits giving a history of an enterprise's business transactions.

▸ **capital account.** (1849) An account on a partnership's balance sheet representing a partner's share of the partnership capital.

▸ **charge account.** See CHARGE ACCOUNT.

▸ **checking account.** (1923) A bank account from which one can take money at any time and for which one is given checks to direct payment to others.

▸ **client trust account.** See CLIENT TRUST ACCOUNT.

▸ **closed account.** (1831) An account that no further credits or debits may be added to but that remains open for adjustment or setoff.

▸ **collection account.** See *concentration account.*

▸ **community account.** (1855) An account consisting of community funds or commingled funds. See COMMUNITY PROPERTY.

▸ **concentration account.** (1981) A single centralized bank account that is established to aid the processing of bank-customer transactions, usu. on the same day. — Also termed *special-use account; omnibus account; suspense account; settlement account; intraday account; sweep account; collection account.*

▸ **contra account** (**kon**-trə). (1881) An account that serves to reduce the gross valuation of an asset.

▸ **convenience account.** (1934) An apparent joint account, but without right of survivorship, established by a creator to enable another person to withdraw funds at the creator's direction or for the creator's benefit. • Unlike a true joint account, only one person, the creator, has an ownership interest in the deposited funds. Convenience accounts are often established by those who need a financial manager's help and want to make it easy for the manager to pay bills. Although the manager's name is on the account, the manager does not contribute any personal funds to the account and can write checks or make withdrawals only at the direction of or on behalf of the creator.

▸ **credit account.** See CHARGE ACCOUNT.

▸ **current account.** (18c) **1.** A running or open account that is settled periodically, usu. monthly. **2.** A partner's account that reflects salary, withdrawals, contributions, and other transactions in a given period. **3.** *Banking.* A depositor's checking account. **4.** The portion of a country's balance of payments that represents its exports, imports, and transfer payments. — Also termed *account current.*

▸ **custodial account.** (1925) An account opened on behalf of someone else, such as one opened by a parent for a minor child, and usu. administered by a responsible third party. • Custodial accounts most often arise under the Uniform Transfers to Minors Act (1983). All states have enacted either that act or its earlier version, the Uniform Gifts to Minors Act. Property can be set aside by a donor or transferred to a third party as custodian for the benefit of a minor, usu. as an irrevocable gift. This is a much simpler mechanism than a trust. The custodian has powers and fiduciary duties similar to those of a trustee, except that the custodian is not under a court's supervision. The custodian must account for the property and turn it over to the beneficiary when he or she reaches majority. See UNIFORM TRANSFERS TO MINORS ACT.

▸ **deposit account.** (1811) A demand, time, savings, passbook, or similar account maintained with a bank, savings-and-loan association, credit union, or like organization, other than investment property or an account evidenced by an instrument. UCC § 9-102(a)(29). — Abbr. D.A.

▸ **discretionary account.** (1905) An account that allows a broker access to a customer's funds to purchase and sell securities or commodities for the customer based on the broker's judgment and without first having to obtain the customer's consent to the purchase or sale. See *securities broker* under BROKER.

▸ **drawing account.** (18c) A temporary owner's equity account used by a sole proprietorship or a partnership to record an owner's or partner's withdrawals of cash or other assets from the business for personal use.

▸ **escrow account.** (1911) **1.** A bank account, generally held in the name of the depositor and an escrow agent, that is returnable to the depositor or paid to a third person on the fulfillment of specified conditions. — Also termed *escrow deposit.* See ESCROW (2). **2.** See *impound account.*

▸ **expense account.** See EXPENSE ACCOUNT.

▸ **frozen account.** See *blocked account.*

▸ **impound account.** (1961) An account of accumulated funds held by a lender for payment of taxes, insurance, or other periodic debts against real property. — Also termed *escrow*; *escrow account*; *reserve account.* See ESCROW (2).

▸ **intermediate account.** (1818) An account filed by an executor, administrator, or guardian after the initial account and before the final account. • This account is usu. filed annually. — Also termed *annual account.*

▸ **intraday account.** See *concentration account.*

▸ **joint account.** (17c) A bank or brokerage account opened by two or more people, by which each party has a present right to withdraw all funds in the account and, upon the death of one party, the survivors become the owners of the account, with no right of the deceased party's heirs or devisees to share in it. • Typically, the account-holders are designated as "joint tenants with right of survivorship" or "joint-and-survivor account-holders." In some jurisdictions, they must be so designated to establish a right of survivorship. — Abbr. JA. — Also termed *joint-and-survivorship account.*

▸ **lien account.** (1858) A statement of claims that fairly informs the owner and public of the amount and nature of a lien.

▸ **liquidated account.** (18c) An account whose assets are clearly ascertained, either by agreement of the parties or by law.

▸ **long account.** (18c) An account involving numerous items or complex transactions in an equitable action, usu. referred to a master or commissioner.

▸ **margin account.** (1973) A brokerage account that allows an investor to buy or sell securities on credit, with the securities usu. serving as collateral for the broker's loan.

▸ **multiple-party account.** (1973) An account that has more than one owner with a current or future interest in the account. • Multiple-party accounts include joint accounts, payable-on-death (P.O.D.) accounts, and trust accounts. Unif. Probate Code § 6-201(5).

▸ **mutual account.** (18c) An account showing mutual transactions between parties, as by showing debits and credits on both sides of the account. — Also termed *mutual running account.*

> "[E]ach party to a mutual account occupies both a debtor and creditor relation with regard to the other party. A mutual account arises where there are mutual dealings, and the account is allowed to run with a view to an ultimate adjustment of the balance. In order to establish a mutual account, it is not enough that the parties to the account have cross demands or cross open accounts; there must be an actual mutual agreement, express or implied, that the claims are to be set off against each other." 1 Am. Jur. 2d *Accounts and Accounting* § 6, at 564 (1994).

▸ **mutual-fund wrap account.** (1993) An investment account that allocates an investor's assets only among mutual funds rather than stocks or other investments. See *wrap account.*

▸ **mutual running account.** See *mutual account.*

▸ **negotiable-order-of-withdrawal account.** See *NOW account.*

▸ **nominal account (nahm-ə-nəl).** (1904) An income-statement account that is closed into surplus at the end of the year when the books are balanced.

▸ **nominee account.** (1942) An account in which a named person or entity holds assets on behalf of a beneficiary; esp., in securities law, a brokerage account in which the securities are owned by an investor but registered in the name of the brokerage firm. • The certificate and the records of the issuing company show the brokerage as the holder of record. But the brokerage records show the investor as the beneficial owner of the securities in the nominee account. — Also termed *street-name security.*

▸ **nondiscretionary account.** (1936) A client's investment account, held by a broker who has no authority to trade without trade-specific consent from the client. See *securities broker* under BROKER.

▸ **NOW account** (now). (1977) An interest-bearing savings account on which the holder may write checks. — Also termed *negotiable-order-of-withdrawal account.*

▸ **offset account.** (1879) One of two accounts that balance against each other and cancel each other out when the books are closed.

▸ **omnibus account.** See *concentration account.*

▸ **open account.** (18c) **1.** An unpaid or unsettled account. **2.** An account that is left open for ongoing debit and credit entries by two parties and that has a fluctuating balance until either party finds it convenient to settle and close, at which time there is a single liability.

▸ **partial account.** (18c) A preliminary accounting of an executor's or administrator's dealings with an estate.

▸ **pay-on-death account.** (1987) A bank account whose owner instructs the bank to distribute the account's balance to a beneficiary upon the owner's death. • Unlike a joint-and-survivorship account, a pay-on-death account does not give the beneficiary access to the funds while the owner is alive. — Abbr. POD account. — Also termed *pay-on-death bank account.* Cf. TRANSFER-ON-DEATH REGISTRATION.

▸ **pledged account.** (1887) A mortgagor's account pledged to a lender in return for a loan bearing interest at a below-market rate.

▸ **profit-and-loss account.** (18c) A transfer account of all income and expense accounts, closed into the retained earnings of a corporation or the capital account of a partnership.

▸ **real account.** (1832) An account that records assets and liabilities rather than receipts and payments.

▸ **reserve account.** See *impound account.*

▸ **revolving charge account.** See *revolving credit* under CREDIT (4).

▸ **running account.** (18c) An open, unsettled account that exhibits the reciprocal demands between the parties.

▸ **savings account.** (1850) A savings-bank depositor's account usu. bearing interest or containing conditions (such as advance notice) to the right of withdrawal.

▸ **sequestered account.** (1988) An account (such as a joint bank account) that a court has ordered to be separated, frozen, and impounded.

▸ **settlement account.** See *concentration account.*

▸ **share account.** See *share-draft account.*

▸ **share-draft account.** (1978) An account that a member maintains at a credit union and that can be drawn on through the use of share drafts payable to third parties. • A share-draft account operates much like a checking account operates at a bank. — Also termed *share account.*

▸ **special-use account.** See *concentration account.*

▸ **stated account.** See *account stated.*

▸ **suspense account.** (1830) **1.** A temporary record used in bookkeeping to track receipts and disbursements of an uncertain nature until they are identified and posted in the appropriate ledgers and journals. • A suspense account does not appear in a final financial statement. It is a useful tool when, for example, a lump-sum receipt or expenditure must be broken down to match several transactions before posting. **2.** See *concentration account.*

▸ **sweep account.** See *concentration account.*

▸ **tax-deferred account.** (1979) An interest-bearing account whose earnings are not taxable as income to the account holder before the earnings are withdrawn. • Tax-deferred accounts include most types of IRAs, variable annuities, 401(k) plans, cash-value life insurance, and most other types of tax-deferred savings instruments.

▸ **trust account.** See CLIENT TRUST ACCOUNT.

▸ **wrap account.** (1989) An investment account for which the investor, helped by a stockbroker, selects an account manager and pays a fee based on a percentage of the total assets to be managed. • Most wrap accounts contain a portfolio of investments, including stocks, bonds, and cash. Investors generally provide a risk profile but do not select the investments or give instructions to buy or sell. — Also termed *wrap-fee account.* See *mutual-fund wrap account.*

▸ **wrap-fee account.** See *wrap account.*

accountable, *adj.* (14c) Responsible; answerable <the company was held accountable for the employee's negligence>. — **accountability,** *n.*

accountable receipt. See RECEIPT (2).

accountancy. (17c) The art or practice of an accountant; the work of someone who keeps, examines, or is skilled in accounts.

accountant. (16c) **1.** A person authorized under applicable law to practice public accounting; a person whose business is to keep books or accounts, to perform financial audits, to design and control accounting systems, and to give tax advice. • For some purposes, the term includes a professional accounting association, a corporation, and a partnership, if they are so authorized.

▸ **certified public accountant.** (1896) An accountant who has satisfied the statutory and administrative requirements to be registered or licensed as a public accountant. — Abbr. CPA.

2. A defendant in an action of account.

accountant–client privilege. See PRIVILEGE (3).

accountant general. (17c) **1.** *Hist. English law.* A chancery officer who received all funds lodged in court and deposited them with the Bank of England. **2.** The principal or responsible accountant in a public office or in a mercantile company or bank.

accountant of court. (1850) *Scots law.* An official of the Court of Session who exercises supervision over the accounts of court-appointed managers and receivers of estates, such as trustees in bankruptcy and guardians of incompetent persons.

accountantship. (17c) The employment or office of an accountant.

accountant's lien. See LIEN.

account book. (16c) **1.** A ruled book for entering details of receipts and expenditures. **2.** A book containing records of transactions, esp. sales, purchases, and payments. See SHOP BOOKS.

account current. See *current account* under ACCOUNT.

account day. (1815) A semimonthly day designated for the adjustments of differences between brokers on a stock exchange. — Also termed *settlement date.*

account debtor. See DEBTOR.

account duty. See DUTY (4).

account executive. See STOCKBROKER.

account for, *vb.* (17c) **1.** To furnish a good reason or convincing explanation for; to explain the cause of. **2.** To render a reckoning of (funds held, esp. in trust). **3.** To answer for (conduct).

accounting. (18c) **1.** The act or a system of establishing or settling financial accounts; esp., the process of recording transactions in the financial records of a business and periodically extracting, sorting, and summarizing the recorded transactions to produce a set of financial records. — Also termed *financial accounting.* Cf. BOOKKEEPING. **2.** A rendition of an account, either voluntarily or by court order; esp., the reckoning of the proceeds of a property's sale usu. to take place before the terms of any express or constructive trust are applied, as an alternative or in addition to the trust. • The term frequently refers to the report of all items of property, income, and expenses prepared by a personal representative, trustee, or guardian and given to heirs, beneficiaries, or the probate court. — Also termed *equitable accounting.* See ACCOUNT (4). **3.** A legal action to compel a defendant to account for and pay over money owed to the plaintiff but held by the defendant (often the plaintiff's agent); ACCOUNTING FOR PROFITS. — Also termed *account render*; *account*; *action of account.* See ACCOUNT (1).**4.** More broadly, an action for the recovery of money for services performed, property sold and delivered, money loaned, or damages for the nonperformance of simple contracts. • Such an action is available when the rights of parties will be adequately protected by the payment of money. — Also termed *action on account*; *account*; *action of book debt.* **5.** *Commercial law.* An equitable proceeding for a complete settlement of all partnership affairs, usu. in connection with partner misconduct or with a winding up. See WINDING UP. **6.** *Secured transactions.* A record that (1) is authenticated by a secured party, (2) indicates the aggregate unpaid secured obligation as of a date no more than 35 days before or after the date of the record, and (3) identifies the components of the obligations in reasonable detail. UCC § 9-102(a)(4).

accounting for fruits. (1879) *Civil law.* A claim for the return of natural or civil fruits (income) against an adverse possessor or other person obligated by law or contract to account for fruits (income). See FRUIT (2).

accounting for profits. (1871) An action for equitable relief against a person in a fiduciary relationship to recover profits taken in a breach of the relationship. — Often shortened to *accounting.* — Also termed *account of profits*; *equitable accounting.*

> "The term accounting, or accounting for profits, is used in several ways. In its most important meaning, it is a restitutionary remedy based upon avoiding unjust enrichment. In this sense it reaches monies owed by a fiduciary or other wrongdoer, including profits produced by property which in equity and good conscience belonged to the plaintiff. It resembles a constructive trust in that tracing may be used to reach profits. But even if tracing fails, the plaintiff may recover a judgment for the profits due from use of his property." 1 Dan B. Dobbs, *Law of Remedies* § 4.3(5), at 608 (2d ed. 1993).

accounting method. (1908) A system for determining income and expenses, profit and loss, asset value, appreciation and depreciation, and the like, esp. for tax purposes.

▸ **accrual accounting method** (ə-**kroo**-əl). (1942) An accounting method that records entries of debits and credits when the revenue or liability arises, rather than when the income is received or an expense is paid. — Also termed *accrual basis.* Cf. *cash-basis accounting method.*

▸ **capitalization accounting method.** (2005) A method of determining an asset's present value by discounting its stream of expected future benefits at an appropriate rate.

▸ **cash-basis accounting method.** (1954) An accounting method that considers only cash actually received as income and cash actually paid out as an expense. — Also termed *cash accounting*; *cash-accounting method.* Cf. *accrual accounting method.*

▸ **completed-contract accounting method.** (1957) A method of reporting profit or loss on certain long-term contracts by recognizing gross income and expenses in the tax year that the contract is completed.

▸ **cost-accounting method.** (1927) The practice of recording the value of assets in terms of their historical cost. — Also shortened to *cost accounting.*

▸ **direct charge-off accounting method.** A system of accounting by which a deduction for bad debts is allowed when an account has become partially or completely worthless.

▸ **equity accounting method.** (1976) A method of accounting for long-term investment in common stock based on acquisition cost, investor income, net losses, and dividends.

▸ **fair-value accounting method.** (1970) The valuation of assets at present actual or market value. • When this method is used to determine the value of a security or other financial instrument, it is also termed *mark-to-market accounting method.*

▸ **installment accounting method.** (1954) A method by which a taxpayer can spread the recognition of gains from a sale of property over the payment period by computing the gross-profit percentage from the sale and applying it to each payment.

▸ **mark-to-market accounting method.** See *fair-value accounting method.*

▸ **percentage-of-completion method.** (1931) An accounting method in which revenue is recognized gradually during the completion of the subject matter of the contract.

▸ **physical-inventory accounting method.** A method of counting a company's goods at the close of an accounting period.

▸ **purchase accounting method.** (1983) A method of accounting for mergers whereby the total value paid or exchanged for the acquired firm's assets is recorded on the acquiring firm's books, and any difference between the fair market value of the assets acquired and the purchase price is recorded as goodwill.

accounting period. (1903) A regular span of time used for accounting purposes; esp., a period used by a taxpayer in determining income and related tax liability.

Accounting Research Bulletin. A publication containing accounting practices recommended by the American Institute of Certified Public Accountants. — Abbr. ARB.

Accounting Series Release. A bulletin providing the Securities and Exchange Commission's requirements for accounting and auditing procedures to be followed in reports filed with that agency. — Abbr. ASR.

account in trust. See ACCOUNT.

account of profits. See ACCOUNTING FOR PROFITS.

account party. (1952) The customer in a letter-of-credit transaction. — Also termed *applicant.*

account payable. See ACCOUNT.

account receivable. See ACCOUNT.

account render. See ACCOUNTING (3).

account rendered. See ACCOUNT.

account representative. See STOCKBROKER.

account settled. See ACCOUNT.

accounts-receivable insurance. See *accounts-receivable insurance* and *credit insurance* under INSURANCE.

account stated. See ACCOUNT.

account statement. See STATEMENT OF ACCOUNT.

accouple, *vb.* (17c) *Archaic.* To unite; to marry.

accredit (ə-**kred**-it), *vb.* (18c) **1.** To give official authorization or status to. **2.** To recognize (a school) as having sufficient academic standards to qualify graduates for higher education or for professional practice. **3.** *Int'l law.* To send (a person) with credentials as an envoy. — **accreditation** (ə-kred-i-**tay**-shən), *n.*

accredited, *adj.* (18c) **1.** Having official approval to do something, esp. by reason of having reached an acceptable standard. **2.** (Of a governmental or diplomatic official) approved to act as an official representative for one's home country while serving in a foreign country.

accredited investor. See INVESTOR.

accredited law school. See LAW SCHOOL.

accredited representative. See REPRESENTATIVE (1).

accredulitare (ə-kred-yə-lə-**tair**-ee), *vb.* [Law Latin] *Hist.* To purge an offense by an oath.

accresce (ə-**kres**), *vb.* (17c) *Civil law.* To accrue or increase.

accretion (ə-**kree**-shən). (1830) **1.** A layer of substance that slowly forms on something; specif., a gradual process by which new things are added and something gradually changes or gets bigger. **2.** The gradual accumulation of land by natural forces, esp. as alluvium is added to land situated on the bank of a river or on the seashore. Cf. ALLUVION; AVULSION (2); DELICTION; EROSION. **3.** Any increase in trust property other than increases ordinarily considered as income. **4.** *Civil law.* The right of heirs or legatees to unite their shares of the estate with the portion of any coheirs or legatees who do not accept their portion, fail to comply with a condition, or die before the testator. **5.** A beneficiary's gain through the failure of a coheir or colegatee to take his or her share. **6.** *Scots law.* The perfection of an imperfect or defective title by some act of the person who conveyed title to the current holder. — **accretive, accretionary,** *adj.*

accroach (ə-**krohch**), *vb.* (16c) To exercise power without authority; to usurp. — **accroachment** (ə-**krohch**-mənt), *n.*

accrocher (a-kroh-**shay**), *vb.* [Law French] **1.** ACCROACH. **2.** To delay.

accrocher un procès (a-kroh-**shay** ən proh-**say**). [French] To stay the proceedings in a suit.

accrual, clause of. See CLAUSE OF ACCRUAL.

accrual accounting method. See ACCOUNTING METHOD.

accrual basis. See *accrual accounting method* under ACCOUNTING METHOD.

accrual bond. See BOND (3).

accrual rule. (1939) A doctrine delaying the existence of a claim until the plaintiff has discovered it. • The accrual rule arose in fraud cases as an exception to the general limitations rule that a claim comes into existence once a plaintiff knows, or with due diligence should know, facts to form the basis for a cause of action. *See Merck & Co. v. Reynolds*, 559 U.S. 633, 646–47, 130 S.Ct. 1784, 1794–95 (2010). See DISCOVERY RULE.

accrue (ə-**kroo**), *vb.* (15c) **1.** To come into existence as an enforceable claim or right; to arise <the plaintiff's cause of action for silicosis did not accrue until the plaintiff knew or had reason to know of the disease>.

> "The term 'accrue' in the context of a cause of action means to arrive, to commence, to come into existence, or to become a present enforceable demand or right. The time of accrual of a cause of action is a question of fact." 2 Ann Taylor Schwing, *California Affirmative Defenses* § 25:3, at 17–18 (2d ed. 1996).

2. To accumulate periodically; to increase over a period of time <the savings-account interest accrues monthly>. — **accrual,** *n.*

accrued asset. See ASSET.

accrued compensation. See COMPENSATION.

accrued depreciation. See *accumulated depreciation* under DEPRECIATION.

accrued dividend. See *accumulated dividend* under DIVIDEND.

accrued expense. See EXPENSE.

accrued income. See INCOME.

accrued interest. See INTEREST (3).

accrued liability. See LIABILITY.

accrued right. See RIGHT.

accrued salary. See SALARY.

accrued tax. See TAX.

accruer. See CLAUSE OF ACCRUAL.

accruing costs. See COST (3).

acct. *abbr.* ACCOUNT (4).

accumulando jura juribus (ə-kyoom-yə-**lan**-doh **joor**-ə **joor**-i-bəs). [Law Latin] *Hist.* By adding rights to rights.

> "[*Accumulando jura juribus*] will be found in deeds, as expressing the intention of the maker or granter of it that the right thereby conferred on the grantee is not to be regarded as coming in place of other rights which the grantee has or may acquire otherwise, but as an addition thereto: the rights conferred are not prejudicial to other rights existing or future." John Trayner, *Trayner's Latin Maxims* 10 (4th ed. 1894).

accumulated-adjustments account. See ACCOUNT.

accumulated deficit. (1917) A business's net losses that are carried over on the balance sheet from earlier periods. • The deficit is shown under owners' or stockholders' equity.

accumulated depreciation. See DEPRECIATION.

accumulated dividend. See DIVIDEND.

accumulated-earnings credit. See CREDIT (7).

accumulated-earnings tax. See TAX.

accumulated income. See INCOME.

accumulated legacy. See LEGACY (1).

accumulated profit. See PROFIT (1).

accumulated surplus. See SURPLUS.

accumulated taxable income. See INCOME.

accumulatio actionum (ə-kyoom-yə-**lay**-shee-oh ak-shee-**oh**-nəm). [Law Latin] (18c) *Scots law.* The accumulation of actions, which was permitted only in certain circumstances, as when a widow and her children jointly sued to recover damages for the husband's and father's death.

accumulation, *n.* (15c) **1.** The increase of a thing by repeated additions to it; esp., the increase of a fund by the repeated addition of the income that it creates. **2.** The concurrence of several titles to the same thing. **3.** The concurrence of several circumstances to the same proof. **4.** The retention of dividends for future distribution. **5.** *Insurance.* An increase in the principal sum insured for, effective upon renewal of a policy, without a change of premiums. — **accumulate,** *vb.*

accumulations, rule against. (1924) The rule that a direction to accumulate income from property — the income to be distributed later to certain beneficiaries — is valid only if confined to the perpetuity period. Cf. RULE AGAINST PERPETUITIES.

accumulation trust. See TRUST (3).

accumulative (ə-**kyoo**-myə-lay-tiv *or* -lə-tiv), *adj.* (17c) Increasing by successive addition; cumulative.

accumulative damages. See DAMAGES.

accumulative dividend. See *cumulative dividend* under DIVIDEND.

accumulative judgment. See JUDGMENT (2).

accumulative legacy. See LEGACY (1).

accumulative sentences. See *consecutive sentences* under SENTENCE.

accusation, *n.* (14c) **1.** A statement that a person has engaged in an illegal or immoral act; a statement saying that someone is guilty of a crime or of doing something wrong. **2.** A formal charge of criminal wrongdoing. • The accusation is usu. presented to a court or magistrate having jurisdiction to inquire into the alleged crime.

▸ **cross-accusation,** *n.* (1909) An accusation made against one who previously accused the new accuser. — **cross-accuse,** *vb.*

▸ **malicious accusation.** (16c) An accusation against another for an improper purpose and without probable cause. See MALICIOUS PROSECUTION.

accusatio suspecti tutoris (ak-yoo-**zay**-shee-oh sə-**spek**-tı t[y]oo-**tor**-is). [Latin "accusation against a suspected tutor"] *Roman law.* A civil action on behalf of a child under the age of puberty against a tutor for negligence or fraud in the performance of the tutor's duties.

accusator (ak-yoo-**zay**-tər), *n.* [Latin] (14c) *Roman law.* The person who brought charges in a criminal case. Pl. ***accusatores.***

accusatorial system. See ADVERSARY SYSTEM.

accusatory (ə-**kyoo**-zə-tor-ee), *adj.* (16c) Of, relating to, or involving an accusation; pertaining to an unmistakable remark or look showing that one thinks someone has done something wrong.

accusatory body. (1877) A body (such as a grand jury) that hears evidence and determines whether a person should be charged with a crime.

accusatory instrument. (1957) See CHARGING INSTRUMENT.

accusatory part. (1883) The section of an indictment in which the offense is named.

accusatory pleading. See PLEADING (1).

accusatory procedure. See ADVERSARY SYSTEM.

accusatory stage. (1954) *Criminal procedure.* The point in a criminal proceeding when the suspect's right to counsel attaches. • This occurs usu. after arrest and once interrogation begins. Cf. CRITICAL STAGE.

accusatory system. (1834) The Anglo-American system of criminal procedure in which someone levels an accusation of crime against a person whose conduct is then assessed by a judge and usu. a jury to determine whether the charge has been substantiated. See ADVERSARY SYSTEM. Cf. INQUISITORIAL SYSTEM.

accusatrix (ə-**kyoo**-zə-triks), *n.* (17c) *Hist.* A female accuser.

accuse, *vb.* (14c) To charge (a person) judicially or publicly with an offense; to make an accusation against <she accused him of the crime> <he was accused as an accomplice>.

accused, *adj.* (1876) **1.** Of, relating to, or involving someone or something implicated in wrongdoing <accused infringer>. **2.** *Intellectual property.* Of, relating to, or involving a product that allegedly infringes someone's intellectual-property rights <accused device> <accused work>.

accused, *n.* (16c) **1.** Someone who has been blamed for wrongdoing; esp., a person who has been arrested and brought before a magistrate or who has been formally charged with a crime (as by indictment or information). **2.** A person against whom legal proceedings have been initiated.

accuser. (14c) *Civil & Eccles. law.* Someone who accuses another of a crime. • In ecclesiastical courts, an accuser cannot be a person who has been convicted of a crime, has been excommunicated, or is otherwise disqualified.

accusing jury. See GRAND JURY.

a ce (a sə), *adv.* [Law French] For this purpose.

a cel jour (ə sel **zhoor**), *adv.* [Law French] At this day.

ac etiam (ak **ee**-shee-əm *or* **esh**-ee-əm). [Law Latin] *Common-law pleading.* **1.** And also. • These words introduced a genuine claim in a pleading in a common-law case in which a fictitious claim had to be alleged to give the court jurisdiction. In other words, the phrase *ac etiam* directed the court to the real cause of action. — Also spelled *acetiam.*

> "[T]o remedy this inconvenience, the officers of the king's bench devised a method of adding what is called a clause of *ac etiam* to the usual complaint of trespass; the bill of Middlesex commanding the defendant to be brought in to answer the plaintiff of a plea of trespass, *and also* to a bill of debt: the complaint of trespass giving cognizance to the court, and that of debt authorizing the arrest." 3 William Blackstone, *Commentaries on the Laws of England* 288 (1768).

> "[Once] it was established that the King's Bench was not exclusively a court for 'crown cases,' but could also be used for civil litigation, it was not difficult to extend the jurisdiction a step further by allowing the ordinary citizen to allege that the defendant had committed a trespass or other breach of the peace 'and also' that the defendant was under some obligation to the plaintiff, and to treat the allegation concerning breach of the peace as a mere fiction which need not be proved, and to allow the suit to be maintained solely on the basis of the civil obligation. The Latin words 'ac etiam' were the crucial ones in the old complaint that stated the fictitious breach of the peace 'and also' the actual civil obligation." Charles Herman Kinnane, *A First Book on Anglo-American Law* 269 (2d ed. 1952).

2. The clause that introduced the real allegation after a fictitious allegation of trespass. — Also termed (in sense 2) *ac etiam clause.*

ac etiam clause. See AC ETIAM (2).

ACF. *abbr.* ADMINISTRATION FOR CHILDREN AND FAMILIES.

achieve, *vb. Hist.* To do homage upon the taking of a fee or fief.

acid deposition. See ACID RAIN.

acid precipitation. See ACID RAIN.

acid rain. (1845) The depositing of wet precipitation (e.g., rain, snow, sleet, or fog) or dry materials (e.g., dust or smoke) that have unusually high levels of nitric and sulfuric acids. • Acid rain harmfully affects lakes, aquatic animals, and trees, and it can corrode or damage materials such as metal, paint, and stone. — Also termed *acid precipitation*; *acid deposition*.

acid-test ratio. See QUICK-ASSET RATIO.

acknowledge, *vb.* (15c) **1.** To recognize (something) as being factual or valid <acknowledge the federal court's jurisdiction>. **2.** To show that one accepts responsibility for <acknowledge paternity of the child>. **3.** To make known the receipt of <acknowledged the plaintiff's letter>. **4.** To confirm as genuine before an authorized officer <acknowledged before a notary public>. **5.** (Of a notary public or other officer) to certify as genuine <the notary acknowledged the signature as genuine>.

acknowledged father. See FATHER.

acknowledgment. (16c) **1.** A recognition of something as being factual. **2.** An acceptance of responsibility. **3.** The act of making it known that one has received something. **4.** A formal declaration made in the presence of an authorized officer, such as a notary public, by someone who signs a document and confirms that the signature is authentic. • In most states, the officer certifies that (1) he or she personally knows the document signer or has established the signer's identity through satisfactory evidence, (2) the signer appeared before the officer on the date and in the place (usu. the county) indicated, and (3) the signer acknowledged signing the document freely, being aware of its nature. Cf. VERIFICATION (1).

> "An acknowledgment is a verification of the fact of execution, but is not a verification of the contents of the instrument executed; in other words, an acknowledgment is the method of authenticating an instrument by showing it was the act of the person executing it, while a verification is a sworn statement as to the truth of the facts stated within an instrument." 1A C.J.S. *Acknowledgments* § 2 (1985).

5. The officer's certificate that is affixed to the document. — Also termed (in sense 5) *certificate of acknowledgment*; (loosely) *verification.* See PROOF OF ACKNOWLEDGMENT. **6.** A father's public recognition of a child as his own. — Also spelled (BrE) *acknowledgement.* — Also termed (in sense 6) *acknowledgment of paternity.*

▸ **formal acknowledgment.** (1816) **1.** A father's recognition of a child as his own by a formal, written declaration that meets a state's requirements for execution, typically by signing in the presence of two witnesses. • In Louisiana law, this recognition may also be made by a mother. La. Civ. Code art. 203. **2.** A father's recognition of a child as his own in the child's registry of birth or at the child's baptism. • In this sense, a formal acknowledgment typically occurs when a man signs the birth certificate or baptismal certificate as the father or announces at the baptismal service that he is the father. The fact that a man is named as the father on a certificate of birth or baptism is not a formal acknowledgment unless the father signs the document.

▸ **informal acknowledgment.** (1848) A father's recognition of a child as his own not by a written declaration but by receiving the child into his family or supporting the child and otherwise treating the child as his own offspring.

acknowledgment money. See LAUDEMIUM.

acknowledgment of debt. (18c) *Louisiana law.* Recognition by a debtor of the existence of a debt. • An acknowledgment of debt interrupts the running of prescription.

acknowledgment of paternity. See ACKNOWLEDGMENT (6).

ACLU. *abbr.* (1936) AMERICAN CIVIL LIBERTIES UNION.

a coelo usque ad centrum (ə **kı**-loh **əs**-kwee ad **sen**-trəm). [Latin] (1899) From the heavens to the center of the earth. See AD COELUM DOCTRINE. Cf. AD COELUM ET AD INFEROS.

a confectione (ay kən-fek-shee-**oh**-nee). [Law Latin] From the making.

a confectione praesentium (ay kən-fek-shee-**oh**-nee pri-**zen**-shee-əm). [Law Latin] From the making of the indentures.

a consiliis (ay kən-**sil**-ee-is), *n.* [Law Latin "of counsel"] See APOCRISARIUS.

a contrario sensu (ay kən-**trair**-ee-oh **sen**-s[y]oo), *adv.* [Law Latin] On the other hand; in the opposite sense.

ACP. *abbr.* **1.** ASSIGNED-COUNSEL PROGRAM. **2.** ADMINISTRATIVE DOMAIN-NAME CHALLENGE PANEL.

ACPA. *abbr.* **1.** ANTICYBERSQUATTING CONSUMER PROTECTION ACT. **2.** ANTICOUNTERFEITING CONSUMER PROTECTION ACT. **3.** ANTITRUST CIVIL PROCESS ACT.

ACP challenge. (1997) *Trademarks.* An administrative procedure to settle disputes over Internet domain names, conducted by an Administrative Domain-Name Challenge Panel (ACP) under the auspices of the World Intellectual Property Organization and in accordance with the WIPO (Revised) Substantive Guidelines.

acquaintance rape. See RAPE (2).

acquest (ə-**kwest**). See ACQUET.

acquet (a-**kay** *or* ə-**kwet** *or* ə-**ket**), *n.* (*usu. pl.*) [French *acquêt* "acquisition"] (1813) *Civil law.* **1.** Property acquired by purchase, gift, or any means other than inheritance. • The term is most commonly used to denote a marital acquisition that is presumed to be community property. — Also termed *acquets and conquets.* **2.** Property acquired by either spouse during the marriage. — Also termed *acquest.* See COMMUNITY PROPERTY; ACQUIST.

acquets and conquets. See ACQUET (1).

acquets and gains (ə-**kets**). (1817) *Louisiana law.* The assets comprising the community property of spouses who are subject to the Louisiana community-property laws. — Often shortened to *acquets.*

acquiesce (ak-wee-**es**), *vb.* (17c) To accept tacitly or passively; to give implied consent to (an act) <in the end, all the partners acquiesced in the settlement>. — **acquiescent,** *adj.*

acquiescence (ak-wee-**es**-ənts). (17c) **1.** A person's tacit or passive acceptance; implied consent to an act.

> "The requirements for acquiescence include: the notoriety of the facts and claims, their prolonged tolerance by the state(s) whose interests are specially affected, and general toleration by the international community. As to burden of proof, it has been said that the inference from the conduct amounting to acquiescence may be 'so probable as to [be] almost certain.' Acquiescence has so far been applied mostly to claims over territory. As tacit acceptance justifying an assumption of consent over time, however, it falls within the broader category of unilateral acts." James Crawford, *Brownlie's Principles of Public International Law* 419–20 (8th ed. 2012) (citation omitted).

▸ **commercial acquiescence.** (1970) *Patents.* Action or inaction by a patentee's competitor that reflects the competitor's belief that the patent is valid. • A patent owner may use another person's actions or inactions, such as taking a license or attempting to design around a patent, as circumstantial evidence of the nonobviousness of a patented invention or of a patent's validity or enforceability.

2. *Int'l law.* Passivity and inaction on foreign claims that, according to customary international law, usu. call for protest to assert, preserve, or safeguard rights. • The result is that binding legal effect is given to silence and inaction. Acquiescence, as a principle of substantive law, is grounded in the concepts of good faith and equity.

acquietandis plegiis (ə-kwI-ə-**tan**-dis **plee**-jee-is), *n.* [Law Latin "for acquitting sureties"] (17c) *Hist.* A writ to force a creditor to discharge a surety when the debt has been satisfied.

acquietatus (ə-kwI-ə-**tay**-təs), *p.pl.* [Law Latin] *Hist.* Pronounced not guilty by a jury; acquitted.

acquire, *vb.* (15c) **1.** To gain possession or control of; to get or obtain. **2.** To gain as an attribute of form <the statute acquired a judicial gloss>.

acquired allegiance. See ALLEGIANCE (1).

acquired corporation. See CORPORATION.

acquired distinctiveness. See DISTINCTIVENESS.

acquired federal land. See LAND.

acquired land. See LAND.

acquired right. See RIGHT.

acquired-rights doctrine. (1928) The principle that once a right has vested, it may not be reduced by later legislation. • The Universal Copyright Convention applies the doctrine to copyright protections, esp. terms that controlled before the Convention took effect. — Also termed *doctrine of acquired rights.*

acquired servitude. See SERVITUDE (3).

acquired surplus. See SURPLUS.

acquirenda, *n. pl.* [Latin] *Hist.* Things to be gained by purchase.

acquiring bank. See BANK.

acquisita et acquirenda (ə-**kwiz**-i-tə et ak-wə-**ren**-də). [Law Latin] (1861) *Scots law.* Things acquired and to be acquired. • Certain legal actions (such as inhibition) affected both acquired property and property to be acquired, while others (such as seizure) affected only property that had already been acquired.

acquisition, *n.* (14c) **1.** The process by which one gains knowledge or learns a skill <language acquisition>. **2.** The gaining of possession or control over something; esp., the act of getting land, power, money, etc. <the acquisition of new paintings for the museum> <acquisition of the target company's assets>. **3.** Something acquired; esp., something one has obtained by buying it or being given it <a valuable acquisition>.

▸ **creeping acquisition.** (1964) The gradual purchase of a corporation's stock at varying prices on the open market. • As a takeover method, a creeping acquisition does not involve a formal tender offer, although the SEC may classify it as such for regulatory purposes. — Also termed *creeping tender offer.*

▸ **derivative acquisition.** (18c) An acquisition obtained from another, as by sale or gift. Cf. *original acquisition,*

▸ **new acquisition.** (17c) An estate not originating from descent, devise, or gift from the paternal or maternal line of the owner. • For example, an estate acquired from a nonrelative is a new acquisition. See *nonancestral estate* under ESTATE (1).

▸ **original acquisition.** (17c) An acquisition that has never been the property of anyone else, such as a copyright owned by an author. Cf. *derivative acquisition*

acquisition cost. See COST (1).

acquisitive offense. See OFFENSE (2).

acquisitive prescription. See PRESCRIPTION.

acquist (ə-**kwist**), *n.* (17c) *Hist.* The act of obtaining (a thing); acquisition. • The idiomatic tendency is to use *acquist* for the action and *acquet* for the result. Cf. ACQUET.

acquit, *vb.* (13c) **1.** To clear (a person) of a criminal charge; specif., to give an official decision in a court of law that someone is not guilty of a crime <she was acquitted on all three counts>. **2.** To pay or discharge (a debt or claim) <he acquitted his student loans>. **3.** To do something well, esp. something difficult that one does for the first time before others <acquitted himself admirably on the pommel horse>.

acquit-first instruction. See JURY INSTRUCTION.

acquittal, *n.* (15c) **1.** The legal certification, usu. by jury verdict, that an accused person is not guilty of the charged offense; an official statement in a court of law that a criminal defendant is not guilty. — Also termed *not-guilty verdict.*

▸ **acquittal in fact.** (17c) An acquittal by a jury verdict of not guilty.

▸ **acquittal in law.** (17c) An acquittal by operation of law, as of someone who has been charged merely as an accessory after the principal has been acquitted.

▸ **implied acquittal.** (1858) An acquittal in which a jury convicts the defendant of a lesser included offense without commenting on the greater offense. • Double jeopardy bars the retrial of a defendant on the higher offense after an implied acquittal.

▸ **predicate acquittal.** *Criminal procedure.* A previous finding of not guilty or a similar dismissal of charges that might cause a prosecutor to consent to a plea bargain favorable to the defendant.

2. *Contracts.* A release or discharge from debt or other liability; ACQUITTANCE. **3.** *Hist.* The obligation of a middle lord to protect a tenant from a claim, entry, or molestation by a paramount lord arising out of service that the middle lord owes the paramount lord.

acquit-first instruction. See JURY INSTRUCTION.

acquittance, *n.* (14c) A document by which one is discharged from a debt or other obligation; a receipt or release indicating payment in full. — **acquit,** *vb.*

acquitted, *adj.* (17c) **1.** Judicially discharged from an accusation; absolved. **2.** Released from a debt.

acre. (bef. 12c) **1.** An area of land measuring 43,560 square feet. Cf. COMMERCIAL ACRE.

▸ **foot acre.** (1909) ACRE-FOOT.

2. *Hist.* The area of land that a man with two oxen could plow in one day. • Beginning in the mid-13th century, this was statutorily limited to an area of 14,520 square feet.

acreage-contribution agreement. (1961) *Oil & gas.* A support agreement under which one party promises to grant leases or interest in leases in the area of a test well to the party who drills the test well in exchange for drilling or geological information if the test well is drilled to a certain depth. See SUPPORT AGREEMENT.

acre-foot. (1909) A volume measurement, as of coal, water, or other material, equal to the amount that will cover one acre of land to a depth of one foot (approximately 325,850 gallons of liquid). • This measure is used in stating the volume and capacity of reservoirs and to value coal land for tax purposes. The number of acre-feet of a material in a given area is the number of acres in the area multiplied by the average depth (thickness), measured in feet, of the material. — Also termed *foot acre.*

acre right. *Hist.* In New England, a citizen's share in the common lands. • The value of the acre right varied among towns but was fixed in each town. A 10-acre lot in a certain town was equivalent to 113 acres of upland and 12 acres of meadow, and an exact proportion was maintained between the acre right and salable land.

across-the-board, *adj.* (1950) Applying to all classes, categories, or groups <an across-the-board tax cut>.

ACRS. *abbr.* ACCELERATED COST-RECOVERY SYSTEM.

ACT. *abbr.* ASSET-COVERAGE TEST.

act, *n.* (14c) **1.** Something done or performed, esp. voluntarily; a deed. — Also termed *action.*

> "'[A]ct' or 'action' means a bodily movement whether voluntary or involuntary . . . ." Model Penal Code § 1.13.

2. The process of doing or performing; an occurrence that results from a person's will being exerted on the external world; ACTION (1). — Also termed *positive act; act of commission.*

> "The term act is one of ambiguous import, being used in various senses of different degrees of generality. When it is said, however, that an act is one of the essential conditions of liability, we use the term in the widest sense of which it is capable. We mean by it any event which is subject to the control of the human will. Such a definition is, indeed, not ultimate, but it is sufficient for the purpose of the law." John Salmond, *Jurisprudence* 367 (Glanville L. Williams ed., 10th ed. 1947).

> "The word 'act' is used throughout the Restatement of this Subject to denote an external manifestation of the actor's will and does not include any of its results, even the most direct, immediate, and intended." Restatement (Second) of Torts § 2 (1965).

▸ **abstract juridical act.** (1994) *Civil law.* A juridical act whose validity may be independent of the existence or lawfulness of the underlying cause. • In some systems, examples include negotiable instruments, debt remission, debt acknowledgment, and the novation of an obligation. See *juridical act.*

▸ **act *in pais*** (in pay). [Law French] *Archaic.* An act performed out of court, such as a deed made between two parties on the land being transferred. See IN PAIS.

▸ **act in the law.** (1829) An act that is intended to create, transfer, or extinguish a right and that is effective in law for that purpose; the exercise of a legal power. — Also termed *juristic act; act of the party; legal act.*

▸ **act of bankruptcy.** (17c) An insolvent debtor's act that renders the debtor liable to involuntary bankruptcy proceedings, esp. for concealing, removing, or disposing of property to defraud creditors. • The 1978 Bankruptcy Reform Act abolished this requirement as a condition to an involuntary bankruptcy proceeding.

▸ **act of court.** See ACT OF COURT.

▸ **act of God.** See ACT OF GOD.

▸ **act of grace.** (16c) *Archaic.* An executive or legislative act pardoning one or more people who have offended against the law; esp., such a pardon performed at the beginning of a monarch's reign or at some other significant occasion.

▸ **act of honor.** See ACT OF HONOR.

▸ **act of hostility.** See ACT OF HOSTILITY.

▸ **act of law.** See *act of the law.*

▸ **act of nature.** **1.** ACT OF GOD. **2.** VIS MAJOR.

▸ **act of omission.** See *negative act.*

▸ **act of petition.** See ACT OF PETITION.

▸ **act of possession.** See ACT OF POSSESSION.

▸ **act of providence.** **1.** ACT OF GOD. **2.** VIS MAJOR.

▸ **act of the law.** (17c) The creation, extinction, or transfer of a right by the operation of the law itself, without any consent on the part of the persons concerned. — Also termed *legal act; act of law.* Cf. LEGAL ACT.

▸ **act of the party.** See *act in the law.*

▸ **act of war.** (17c) *Int'l law.* An act considered sufficient cause for hostilities; ACT OF HOSTILITY.

▸ **administrative act.** (1818) An act made in a management capacity; esp., an act made outside the actor's usual field (as when a judge supervises court personnel). • An administrative act is often subject to a greater risk of liability than an act within the actor's usual field. See IMMUNITY (1).

▸ **authorized act.** (1805) *Agency.* An undertaking sanctioned by a principal, esp. an employer, or necessarily involved in the performance of an agent's duties.

▸ **bilateral act.** (1895) An act that involves the consenting wills of two or more distinct parties, as with a contract, a conveyance, a mortgage, or a lease; AGREEMENT (1).

▸ **continuing act.** (17c) An act that one maintains or persists in over some duration, such as wrongful imprisonment.

▸ **conversionary act.** (1959) An act that, unless privileged, makes the actor liable for conversion.

▸ **criminal act.** A unlawful act that subjects the actor to prosecution under criminal law.

▸ **external act.** (16c) An act involving bodily activity, such as speaking.

▸ **intentional act.** (17c) An act resulting from the actor's will directed to that end. • An act is intentional when it is foreseen and desired by the doer, and this foresight and desire resulted in the act through the operation of the will.

▸ **internal act.** (16c) An act of the mind, such as thinking.

▸ **involuntary act.** (16c) An unwilled bodily movement; an act in which there is neither choice nor intention.

> "Involuntary action is action in which there is no choice or no intention. A man in a convulsion fit, a person walking in his sleep, a person whose face changes its expression and whose heart beats violently under the influence of passion supply cases of involuntary action. No involuntary action is a crime." James Fitzjames Stephen, *A General View of the Criminal Law of England* 69 (2d ed. 1890).

▸ **judicial act.** (16c) An act involving the exercise of judicial power. — Also termed *act of court*. Cf. *legislative act*; QUASI-JUDICIAL ACT.

> "The distinction between a judicial and a legislative act is well defined. The one determines what the law is, and what the rights of parties are, with reference to transactions already had; the other prescribes what the law shall be in future cases arising under it." *Union Pacific R.R. v. U.S.*, 99 U.S. 700, 721 (1878) (Field, J., dissenting).

▸ **jural act** (**joor**-əl). (1860) An act taken in the context of or in furtherance of a society's legal system. — Also termed *jural activity*.

> "In order to identify an act as a jural act, it must be the kind of act that would be engaged in by someone who is enforcing a law, determining an infraction of the law, making or changing a law, or settling a dispute." Martin P. Golding, *Philosophy of Law* 23 (1975).

▸ **juridical act.** (17c) *Civil law.* A lawful volitional act intended to have legal consequences. See *abstract juridical act*.

▸ **juristic act.** See *act in the law*.

▸ **legal act.** See LEGAL ACT.

▸ **legislative act.** (17c) See ACT (3). Cf. *judicial act*.

▸ **ministerial act.** (18c) An act performed without the independent exercise of discretion or judgment. • If the act is mandatory, it is also termed *ministerial duty*. See *ministerial duty* under DUTY (2).

▸ **negative act.** (17c) The failure to do something that is legally required; a nonoccurrence that involves the breach of a legal duty to take positive action. • This takes the form of either a forbearance or an omission. — Also termed *act of omission*. Cf. *positive act*.

▸ **negligent act.** (18c) An act that creates an unreasonable risk of harm to another.

▸ **overt act.** See OVERT ACT.

▸ **positive act.** **1.** An act of commission, as distinguished from an act of omission. Cf. *negative act*. **2.** OVERT ACT.

▸ **predicate act.** See PREDICATE ACT.

▸ **quasi-judicial act.** See QUASI-JUDICIAL ACT.

▸ **tortious act.** (17c) An act that subjects the actor to liability under the principles of tort law.

▸ **unilateral act.** (1861) An act in which there is only one party whose will operates, as in a testamentary disposition, the exercise of a power of appointment, or the voidance of a voidable contract.

▸ **unintentional act.** (1820) An act not resulting from the actor's will toward what actually takes place.

▸ **verbal act.** (18c) **1.** An act performed through the medium of words, either spoken or written. **2.** *Evidence.* A statement offered to prove the words themselves because of their legal effect (e.g., the terms of a will). • For this purpose, the statement is not considered hearsay.

▸ **voluntary act.** (16c) A willed bodily movement; esp., the type of act that is necessary for the imposition of criminal liability when such liability is not predicated on an omission. • Under both the common law and the Model Penal Code, a person cannot be held liable for a crime without engaging in a prohibited voluntary act or omission. A bodily movement that is a product of the effort or determination of the actor, either conscious or habitual, is a voluntary act. Reflexes, convulsions, and movements made while unconscious, asleep, or under the influence of hypnosis are not voluntary acts. Model Penal Code § 2.01. Cf. ACTUS REUS.

> "Voluntary and involuntary actions are contradictory, but voluntary action may be either compulsory or free. To walk to the gallows is a voluntary act done under the strongest compulsion. When a thirsty man drinks, he acts freely. It will thus be seen that in the case of voluntary actions freedom is the general rule, and compulsion the rare exception, for no one would be said to be compelled unless he was under the influence of motives at once terrible and powerful, which is rarely the case." James Fitzjames Stephen, *A General View of the Criminal Law of England* 69 (2d ed. 1890).

> "A person is not guilty of an offense unless his liability is based on conduct which includes a voluntary act or the omission to perform an act of which he is physically capable." Model Penal Code § 2.01(1).

▸ **wrongful act.** An act that harms another in the absence of any privilege or justification; esp., TORT (1). See *wrongful conduct* under CONDUCT.

3. The formal product of a legislature or other deliberative body exercising its powers; esp., STATUTE. • For the various types of acts, see the subentries under STATUTE.

▸ **act of adjournal.** See ACT OF ADJOURNAL.

▸ **act of assembly.** See ACT OF ASSEMBLY.

▸ **act of attainder.** See BILL OF ATTAINDER.

▸ **act of Congress.** See ACT OF CONGRESS.

▸ **act of indemnity.** See ACT OF INDEMNITY.

▸ **act of legislation.** See ACT OF LEGISLATION.

▸ **act of Parliament.** See ACT OF PARLIAMENT.

▸ **act of Parliament of Scotland.** See ACT OF PARLIAMENT OF SCOTLAND.

▸ **act of sedurunt.** See ACT OF SEDURUNT.

▸ **cognate act.** (1852) A statute whose subject-matter is related to that of another, esp. when the two statutes were enacted at about the same time. See IN PARI MATERIA.

▸ **general act.** See PUBLIC LAW (2).

▸ **public act.** See PUBLIC LAW (2).

▸ **special act.** See *special statute* under STATUTE.

4. A writing; esp., a legal instrument.

▸ **act under private signature.** (1814) *Civil law.* A legal instrument signed without the aid or supervision of a notary or other public authority. • Although the instrument need not be written by the parties, it must be signed by them. La. Civ. Code art. 1837.

▸ **act under private signature duly acknowledged.** (1900) *Civil law.* A signed legal instrument that is acknowledged by the signer, who recognizes the signature as his or her own before a court, or before a notary public or other officer authorized to perform that function, in the presence of two witnesses. La. Civ. Code art. 1836.

▸ **authentic act.** (17c) *Civil law.* **1.** A writing signed before a notary public or other public officer. • Under Louisiana law, the writing must not only be notarized but also be attested by two witnesses. La. Civ. Code art. 1833. **2.** A certified copy of a writing.

acta, *n. pl.* (1812) *Roman law.* The collective enactments of Roman emperors, embracing *edicta, decreta,* and rescripta. See EDICTUM (1); DECRETUM (1); RESCRIPT (3).

acta diurna (**ak**-tə dɪ-**ər**-nə). [Latin "daily proceedings"] (17c) *Roman law.* A public register of the daily proceedings of the senate, assemblies of the people, or the courts.

acta gestionis (**ak**-tə jes-chee-**oh**-nis), *n. pl.* [Latin "acts of business"] (1950) Commercial transactions, whether carried out by private citizens, companies, or governments. See GESTOR.

acta imperii (**ak**-tə im-**per**-ee-ɪ), *n. pl.* [Latin "acts of official authority"] (18c) *Int'l law.* Acts carried out by a sovereign state in its governmental role.

act and deed. (16c) **1.** A formally delivered written instrument that memorializes a bargain or transaction. **2.** *Hist.* Words in a traditional spoken formula used when signing a legal instrument. • Immediately after signing, the party would touch the seal and declare, "I deliver this as my act and deed."

act and warrant. (17c) *Scots law.* A sheriff's order appointing a trustee in bankruptcy, upon which the trustee assumes office and becomes vested with the bankruptcy estate.

acta publica (**ak**-tə **pəb**-li-kə), *n. pl.* [Latin] (17c) *Roman & civil law.* Things of general knowledge and concern; matters transacted before certain public officers.

acta senatus (**ak**-tə si-**nay**-təs), *n. pl.* (17c) *Roman law.* The recorded proceedings in the Roman senate under the Empire (753 B.C.–A.D. 476), made by a senator chosen by the emperor. — Also termed *commentarii senatus.* See SENATUS.

acte (akt), *n.* [French] *French law.* **1.** An instrument; a proof in writing, such as a deed, bill of sale, or birth certificate.

▸ ***acte authentique*** (**akt** oh-tawn-**teek**). A deed executed with certain prescribed formalities, in the presence of a notary or other official.

▸ ***acte de décès*** (**akt** də day-**say**). A death certificate.

▸ ***acte de francisation*** (**akt** də frangk-ə-za-**syawn**). A certificate confirming that a ship is of French nationality.

▸ ***acte de mariage*** (**akt** də mar-**yahzh**). A marriage certificate.

▸ ***acte de naissance*** (**akt** də **nay**-sənts). A birth certificate.

▸ ***acte de notoriété*** (**akt** də noh-tor-ee-ay-**tay**). A deposition made before a notary to record and preserve a claim, usu. to property. • Historically, most *actes de notoriété* were conducted to establish the identity and genealogy of a purported heir. The depositions were subject to exclusion as hearsay. But an *acte de notoriété* may also appear in a chain of title. *See U.S. v. Repentigny,* 72 U.S. 211 (1866).

▸ ***acte extrajudiciaire*** (**akt** eks-trə-zhuu-dee-**syair**). A document served by a *huissier* at the request of one party on another party without legal proceedings. See HUISSIER (1).

▸ ***l'acte de l'état civil*** (**lakt** də lay-**tah** see-**veel**). A public document relating to status (e.g., birth, divorce, death).

2. An act; conduct.

▸ ***acte d'héritier*** (**akt** day-ri-**tyay**). [French "act of an heir"] Conduct by an heir indicating an intent to accept the succession.

acting, *adj.* (18c) Holding an interim position; serving temporarily <an acting director>.

acting chargé d'affaires. See CHARGÉ D'AFFAIRES.

acting executor. See EXECUTOR (2).

acting in good faith. (1803) Behaving honestly and frankly, without any intent to defraud or to seek an unconscionable advantage. See GOOD FAITH.

acting officer. See OFFICER (1).

act *in pais.* See ACT (2).

act in the law. See ACT (2).

actio (**ak**-shee-oh *also* **ak**-tee-oh), *n.* [Latin] **1.** *Roman & civil law.* An action; a right or claim. **2.** A right of action. **3.** *Hist.* At common law, a lawsuit. Pl. ***actiones*** (ak-shee-**oh**-neez).

▸ ***actio ad exhibendum*** (**ak**-shee-oh ad ek-si-**ben**-dəm). *Roman law.* An action to compel a defendant to produce property so as to establish that it is in the defendant's possession. Pl. ***actiones ad exhibendum.***

> "*Actio ad exhibendum.* The object of this action was to compel the possessor of any moveable to produce it for the inspection of anyone who had a just and probable cause (of the existence of which the judge was to determine) for demanding to see it." John George Phillimore, *Private Law Among the Romans* 182 (1863).

▸ ***actio aestimatoria*** (**ak**-shee-oh es-ti-mə-**tor**-ee-ə). See DE AESTIMATO.

▸ ***actio arbitraria*** (**ak**-shee-oh ahr-bi-**trair**-ee-ə). *Roman law.* An action in which a judex issued an interlocutory decree ordering the defendant to do something (such as restoring property to the plaintiff) on pain of a monetary judgment payable to the plaintiff. • This action was so called because the judex could assess the damage at a high figure if the defendant failed to comply with the interlocutory order. Pl. ***actiones arbitrariae*** (ak-shee-**oh**-neez ahr-bi-**trair**-ee-ɪ).

▸ ***actio auctoritas*** (**ak**-shee-oh awk-**tor**-i-tas). *Roman law.* A seller's guarantee against eviction from mancipated land coupled with a promise to pay twice the sale price as damages if the buyer is evicted. • The guarantee was implicit in the mancipation process. See MANCIPATION.

▸ ***actio bonae fidei*** (**ak**-shee-oh **boh**-nee **fɪ**-dee-ɪ). *Roman law.* One of a class of actions in which a judge could take equitable considerations into account in rendering a decision. Pl. ***actiones bonae fidei.***

▸ ***actio calumniae*** (**ak**-shee-oh kə-**ləm**-nee-ee). *Roman law.* An action to restrain, or collect damages for, a malicious civil suit. • The victim could also pursue criminal charges. See CALUMNIA. Pl. ***actiones calumniae.***

▸ ***actio civilis*** (**ak**-shee-oh sə-**vɪ**-lis). [Latin "a civil action"] *Roman law.* An action founded on the traditional Roman law, rather than the innovations of magistrates. Cf. ACTIONES HONORARIAE. Pl. ***actiones civiles.***

▸ ***actio commodati*** (**ak**-shee-oh kom-ə-**day**-tɪ). [Latin "action on loan"] *Roman law.* An action for the recovery of a thing gratuitously lent but not returned to the lender. — Also termed *commodati actio.* See COMMODATUM. Pl. ***actiones commodati.***

▸ ***actio commodati contraria*** (**ak**-shee-oh kom-ə-**day**-tɪ kən-**trair**-ee-ə). *Roman law.* An action by a gratuitous borrower against a lender for extraordinary expenses or damage caused by the lender's default. Pl. ***actiones commodati contrariae.***

▸ ***actio commodati directa*** (**ak**-shee-oh kom-ə-**day**-tɪ di-**rek**-tə). *Roman law.* An action by a lender against a borrower for restitution for an item gratuitously lent. Pl. ***actiones commodati directae.***

▸ ***actio condictio indebiti*** (**ak**-shee-oh kən-**dik**-shee-oh in-**deb**-ə-tɪ). See *condictio indebiti* under CONDICTIO. • Strictly speaking, the headword is a solecism, since a *condictio* is a type of *actio,* but this phrase is occasionally found in legal literature. Pl. ***actiones condictio indebiti.***

▸ ***actio conducti*** (**ak**-shee-oh kən-**dək**-tɪ). [Latin "action for the thing hired"] An action by the lessee of a thing or the hirer of another's services to enforce the contract or claim damages for breach. — Also termed *actio ex conducto.* Cf. *actio locati.*

▸ ***actio confessoria*** (**ak**-shee-oh kon-fə-**sor**-ee-ə). [Latin "action based on an admission"] **1.** See *vindicatio servitutis* under VINDICATIO. **2.** An action in which the defendant admits liability but does not express it in a fixed sum. • A judge therefore assesses the damages.

▸ ***actio contraria*** (**ak**-shee-oh kən-**trair**-ee-ə). *Roman law.* A counterclaim. Cf. *actio directa.* Pl. ***actiones contrariae.***

▸ ***actio criminalis*** (**ak**-shee-oh kri-mə-**nay**-lis). *Roman law.* A criminal action. Pl. ***actiones criminales.***

▸ ***actio damni injuria*** (**ak**-shee-oh **dam**-nɪ in-**joor**-ee-ə). *Roman law.* An action for damages for tortiously causing pecuniary loss. See *actio legis Aquiliae.* Pl. ***actiones damni injuriae.***

▸ ***actio damni injuria dati.*** See *actio legis Aquiliae.*

▸ ***actio de communi dividundo*** (**ak**-shee-oh dee kə-**myoo**-nɪ di-vi-**dən**-doh). [Latin "for dividing a thing held in common"] *Roman & civil law.* An action to partition common property. — Sometimes shortened to *de communi dividundo.* See ADJUDICATIO. Pl. ***actiones de communi dividundo.***

▸ ***actio de dolo malo*** (**ak**-shee-oh dee **doh**-loh **mal**-oh). *Roman law.* An action of fraud. • This type of action was widely applied in cases involving deceitful conduct. — Also termed *actio doli; doli actio.* Pl. ***actiones de dolo malo.***

▸ ***actio de in rem verso*** (**ak**-shee-oh dee **in rem vər**-soh). See *action de in rem verso* under ACTION (4). Pl. ***actiones de in rem verso.***

▸ ***actio de pauperie*** (**ak**-shee-oh dee **paw**-pər-ee). *Roman law.* An action for harm done by a domestic four-legged animal. • The owner could either pay for the damage or surrender the animal to the injured party. Justinian extended this action to include wild animals in some circumstances. See PAUPERIES.

▸ ***actio de peculio*** (**ak**-shee-oh dee pə-**kyoo**-lee-oh). *Roman law.* An action against a paterfamilias or slave-owner concerning the value of the child's or slave's separate funds (*peculium*). Pl. ***actiones de peculio.***

▸ ***actio de pecunia constituta*** (**ak**-shee-oh dee pə-**kyoo**-nee-ə kon-sti-**t[y]oo**-tə). *Roman law.* An action on a promise to pay a preexisting debt. Pl. ***actiones de pecunia constituta.***

▸ ***actio depositi contraria*** (**ak**-shee-oh di-**poz**-ə-tɪ kən-**trair**-ee-ə). *Roman law.* An action that a depositary has against the depositor for unpaid expenses. Pl. ***actiones depositi contrariae.***

▸ ***actio depositi directa*** (**ak**-shee-oh di-**poz**-ə-tɪ di-**rek**-tə). *Roman law.* An action that a depositor has against a depositary for the return of the deposited item. Pl. ***actiones depositi directae.***

▸ ***actio de tigno juncto*** (**ak**-shee-oh dee **tig**-noh **jəngk**-toh). [Latin "action for joining timber"] *Roman law.* An action by the owner of material incorporated without payment into the defendant's building. • It was akin to a theft action. The plaintiff could recover up to twice the value of the material. Pl. ***actiones de tigno juncto.***

▸ ***actio directa*** (**ak**-shee-oh di-**rek**-tə). *Roman law.* **1.** An action founded on strict law and conducted according to fixed forms; an action based on clearly defined obligations actionable at law based on a statute or a praetor's edict. **2.** A direct action, as opposed to a counterclaim (*actio contraria*). Cf. *actio in factum; actio utilis.* Pl. ***actiones directae.***

▸ ***actio doli*** (**ak**-shee-oh **doh**-lɪ). See *actio de dolo malo.*

▸ ***actio empti*** (**ak**-shee-oh **emp**-tɪ). *Roman law.* An action by a buyer to compel a seller to deliver the item sold or for damages for breach of contract. — Also termed *actio ex empto.* Pl. ***actiones empti.***

▸ ***actio ex conducto*** (**ak**-shee-oh eks kən-**dək**-toh). See *actio conducti.* Pl. ***actiones ex conducto.***

▸ ***actio ex contractu*** (**ak**-shee-oh eks kən-**trak**-t[y]oo). *Roman law.* An action arising out of a contract. • This term had a similar meaning at common law. Pl. ***actiones ex contractu.***

▸ ***actio ex delicto*** (**ak**-shee-oh eks də-**lik**-toh). *Roman law.* An action founded on a tort. Pl. ***actiones ex delicto.***

▸ ***actio ex empto*** (**ak**-shee-oh eks **emp**-toh). See *actio empti.*

▸ ***actio exercitoria*** (**ak**-shee-oh eg-zər-si-**tor**-ee-ə). *Roman law.* An action against the owner or lessee (*exercitor*) of a vessel, esp. for contracts made by the master. Pl. ***actiones exercitoriae.***

▸ ***actio ex locato*** (**ak**-shee-oh eks loh-**kay**-toh). See *actio locati.*

▸ ***actio ex stipulatu*** (**ak**-shee-oh eks stip-yə-**lay**-t[y]oo). *Roman law.* An action brought to enforce a *stipulatio.* See STIPULATION (3).

▸ ***actio ex vendito*** (**ak**-shee-oh eks **ven**-də-toh). See *actio venditi.*

▸ ***actio familiae erciscundae*** (**ak**-shee-oh fə-**mil**-ee-ee ər-sis-**kən**-dee). [Latin "action to divide an estate"] An action for the partition of the inheritance among heirs. — Sometimes shortened to *familiae erciscundae.* See ADJUDICATIO.

▸ ***actio finium regundorum*** (**ak**-shee-oh **fɪ**-nee-əm ri-gən-**dor**-əm). [Latin "action for regulation of boundaries"] *Roman law.* An action among neighboring proprietors to fix or to preserve property boundaries. See ADJUDICATIO.

▸ ***actio furti*** (**ak**-shee-oh **fər**-tɪ). *Roman law.* An action by which the owner of stolen goods can, according to the circumstances, recover a multiple of their value from the thief by way of penalty, without prejudice to a further action to recover the goods themselves or their value. See *furtum manifestum* under FURTUM.

▸ ***actio honoraria*** (**ak**-shee-oh [h]on-ə-**rair**-ee-ə). See ACTIONES HONORARIAE. Pl. ***actiones honorariae.***

▸ ***actio hypothecaria*** (**ak**-shee-oh hɪ-poth-ə-**kair**-ee-ə). See HYPOTHECARIA ACTIO.

▸ ***actio in factum*** (**ak**-shee-oh in **fak**-təm). *Roman law.* An action granted by the praetor when no standard action was available. • The closest Anglo-American equivalent is *action on the case* or *trespass on the case.* See *trespass on the case* under TRESPASS. Cf. *actio directa; actio utilis.*

▸ ***actio injuriarum*** (**ak**-shee-oh in-joor-ee-**ahr**-əm). *Roman law.* An action that lay against anyone who had attacked the body, reputation, or dignity of any person. — Also spelled *actio iniuriarum.* Pl. ***actiones injuriarum*** (ak-shee-**oh**-neez in-joor-ee-**ahr**-əm).

▸ ***actio in personam*** (**ak**-shee-oh in pər-**soh**-nəm). See *action in personam* under ACTION (4).Pl. ***actiones in personam.***

▸ ***actio in rem*** (**ak**-shee-oh in **rem**). **1.** See *action in rem* UNDER ACTION (4). **2.** See *real action* under ACTION (4). Pl. ***actiones in rem.***

▸ ***actio institoria*** (**ak**-shee-oh in-sti-**tor**-ee-ə). [Latin] *Roman law.* An action against a principal by one who contracted with the principal's business agent, limited to matters arising out of the business. See INSTITOR.

▸ ***actio judicati*** (**ak**-shee-oh joo-di-**kay**-tɪ). *Roman law.* An action to enforce a judgment by execution on the defendant's property. Pl. ***actiones judicati.***

▸ ***actio legis*** (**ak**-shee-oh **lee**-jis). See LEGIS ACTIO.

▸ ***actio legis Aquiliae*** (**ak**-shee-oh **lee**-jis ə-**kwil**-ee-ee). *Roman law.* An action under the Aquilian law; specif., an action to recover for loss caused by intentional or negligent damage to another's property. — Also termed *actio damni injuria; actio damni injuria dati.* See LEX AQUILIA.

▸ ***actio locati*** (**ak**-shee-oh loh-**kay**-tɪ). [Latin "action for what has been hired out"] *Roman law.* An action that a lessor (the *locator*) of a thing might have against the hirer, or an employer against a contractor. — Also termed *actio ex locato* (**ak**-shee-oh eks loh-**kay**-toh). Cf. *actio conducti.*

▸ ***actio mandati*** (**ak**-shee-oh man-**day**-tɪ). **1.** *Civil law.* An action to enforce a contract for gratuitous services or remuneration. **2.** *Hist.* An action to enforce a contract for gratuitous services. See MANDATUM. Pl. ***actiones mandati.***

▸ ***actio mixta*** (**ak**-shee-oh **mik**-stə). *Roman law.* A mixed action; an action in which two or more features are combined, as an action for damages and for a penalty, or an action *in rem* and *in personam.* Pl. ***actiones mixta*** (ak-shee-**oh**-neez **mik**-stə).

▸ ***actio negativa.*** See *actio negatoria.*

▸ ***actio negatoria*** (**ak**-shee-oh neg-ə-**tor**-ee-ə). *Roman law.* An action brought by a landowner against anyone claiming to exercise a servitude over the landowner's property. — Also termed *actio negativa.* Pl. ***actiones negatoriae.***

▸ ***actio negotiorum gestorum*** (**ak**-shee-oh nə-goh-shee-**or**-əm jes-**tor**-əm). *Roman law.* An action against a *gestor* for the mismanagement of the principal's property, or for any acquisitions made in the course of management. • The *gestor* could bring a counter action to recover management-related expenses *(actio contraria negotiorum gestorum).* See NEGOTIORUM GESTOR. Pl. ***actiones negotiorum gestorum.***

▸ ***actio non accrevit infra sex annos*** (**ak**-shee-oh non ə-**kree**-vit seks **an**-ohs). [Latin "the action did not accrue within six years"] *Hist.* A plea to the statute of limitations by which the defendant asserts that the plaintiff's cause of action has not accrued within the last six years. Pl. ***actiones non accreverant infra sex annos.***

▸ ***actio non ulterius*** (**ak**-shee-oh non əl-**teer**-ee-əs). [Latin "an action no further"] *Hist.* The distinctive clause in a plea to abate further maintenance of the action. • This plea replaced the *puis darrein continuance.* Cf. *plea to further maintenance to the action, plea puis darrein continuance* under PLEA (3). Pl. ***actiones non ulterii.***

▸ ***actio notalis.*** See *notal action.*

▸ ***actio Pauliana*** (**ak**-shee-oh paw-lee-**ay**-nə). [Latin "action attributed to Paul" or "Paulian action"] An action to rescind a transaction (such as alienation of property) that an insolvent debtor made to deceive the debtor's creditors. • This action was brought against the debtor or the third party who benefited from the transaction. Pl. ***actiones Paulianae.***

> "[A]*ctio Pauliana*, a name which has been shewn to be inserted by a glossator, after the first publication of the Digest. It lay where the debtor had impoverished himself to the detriment of his creditors, e.g. by alienations, by incurring liabilities or allowing rights to lapse, but not for failing to acquire or for paying just debts . . . . It lay against the debtor, who might have since acquired property . . . . But its chief field was against acquirers privy to the fraud, or even innocent, if the acquisition was gratuitous." W.W. Buckland, *A Text-book of Roman Law from Augustus to Justinian* 596 (Peter Stein ed., 3d ed. 1963).

▸ ***actio perpetua*** (**ak**-shee-oh pər-**pech**-oo-ə). *Roman law.* An action that is not required to be brought within a specified time. Cf. *actio temporalis*. Pl. ***actiones perpetuae.***

▸ ***actio personalis*** (**ak**-shee-oh pər-sə-**nay**-lis). *Roman law.* A personal action. See *action in personam* under ACTION (4). Pl. ***actiones personales.***

▸ ***actio pigneratitia*** (**ak**-shee-oh pig-nə-rə-**tish**-ee-ə). *Roman law.* An action of pledge; an action founded on a contract of pledge. — Also spelled *actio pigneraticia*; *actio pignoratitia*. — Also termed *pigneratitia actio*. See PIGNUS. Pl. ***actiones pignoratitiae.***

▸ ***actio poenalis*** (**ak**-shee-oh pi-**nay**-lis). *Roman law.* An action in which the plaintiff sued for a penalty rather than compensation. Cf. *actio rei persecutoria*. Pl. ***actiones poenales*** (ak-shee-**oh**-neez pi-**nay**-leez).

▸ ***actio popularis*** (**ak**-shee-oh pop-yə-**lair**-is). [Latin "popular action"] *Roman law.* An action that a male member of the general public could bring in the interest of the public welfare. Pl. ***actiones populares*** (ak-shee-**oh**-neez pop-yə-**lair**-eez).

> "Actiones populares. Actions which can be brought by 'any one among the people.' . . . They are of praetorian origin and serve to protect public interest . . . . They are penal, and in case of condemnation of the offender the plaintiff receives the penalty paid . . . . There are instances, however, established in statutes or local ordinances, in which the penalty was paid to the state or municipal treasury, or divided between the *aerarium* and the accuser, as, e.g., provided in a decree of the Senate in the case of damage to aqueducts." Adolf Berger, *Encyclopedic Dictionary of Roman Law* 347 (1953).

▸ ***actio praejudicialis*** (**ak**-shee-oh pree-joo-dish-ee-**ay**-lis). *Roman law.* A preliminary action; an action begun to determine a preliminary matter on which other litigated matters depend. Pl. ***actiones praejudiciales.***

▸ ***actio praetoria*** (**ak**-shee-oh pri-**tor**-ee-ə). *Roman law.* A praetorian action; one introduced by a praetor rather than founded on a statute. Pl. ***actiones praetoriae*** (ak-shee-**oh**-neez pri-**tor**-ee-I).

▸ ***actio pro socio*** (**ak**-shee-oh proh **soh**-shee-oh). *Roman law.* An action brought by one partner against another. See SOCIETAS. Pl. ***actiones pro socio.***

▸ ***actio Publiciana*** (**ak**-shee-oh pə-blish-ee-**ay**-nə). *Roman law.* An action allowing a person who had acquired bonitary ownership of land to recover it from a third party, so that the person would in due course acquire full title by prescription. • This action is named for Publicius, who might have been the first praetor to grant the action. — Also termed *actio Publiciana in rem*. See *bonitary ownership* under OWNERSHIP.

▸ ***actio quanti minoris*** (**ak**-shee-oh **kwon**-tI mi-**nor**-is). [Latin "an action for the shortfall in value"] *Roman & civil law.* A purchaser's action to recover for his overpayment for a defective item. Cf. *actio redhibitoria*. Pl. ***actiones quanti minoris.***

> "If a defect appeared which had not been so declared the buyer, if he sued within six months, could claim rescission of the sale by the *actio redhibitoria*, and, if within twelve months, could claim the difference between the price paid and the actual value of the defective slave or animal by the *actio quanti minoris*. In both actions the knowledge or ignorance of the seller was irrelevant: liability was strict." Barry Nicholas, *An Introduction to Roman Law* 181 (1962).

▸ ***actio quod jussu*** (**ak**-shee-oh kwod **jəs**-[y]oo). *Roman law.* An action against a paterfamilias or a slaveowner for enforcement of a debt contracted on behalf of the paterfamilias or slaveowner by a son or a slave.

▸ ***actio quod metus causa*** (**ak**-shee-oh kwod **mee**-təs **kaw**-zə). *Roman law.* An action to penalize someone who wrongfully compelled the plaintiff to transfer property or to assume an obligation. • The plaintiff could obtain damages of four times the value of the loss suffered. Pl. ***actiones quod metus causa.***

▸ ***actio realis*** (**ak**-shee-oh ree-**ay**-lis). [Law Latin] *Hist.* A real action. See *real action* under ACTION (4). Pl. ***actiones reales.***

▸ ***actio redhibitoria*** (**ak**-shee-oh red-i-bi-**tor**-ee-ə). *Roman & civil law.* An action for restoration to cancel a sale because of defects in the thing sold. See REDHIBITION. Cf. *actio quanti minoris*. Pl. ***actiones redhibitoriae.***

▸ ***actio rei persecutoria*** (**ak**-shee-oh **ree**-I pər-si-kyoo-**tor**-ee-ə). [Law Latin "an action for pursuing a thing"] *Roman law.* An action to recover a specific thing or monetary compensation, rather than a penalty. Cf. *actio poenalis*. Pl. ***actiones rei persecutoriae*** (ak-shee-**oh**-neez **ree**-I pər-si-kyoo-**tor**-ee-I).

▸ ***actio rerum amotarum*** (**ak**-shee-oh **reer**-əm am-ə-**tair**-əm). *Roman law.* An action to recover items stolen by a spouse shortly before a divorce. Pl. ***actiones rerum amotarum.***

▸ ***actio rescissoria*** (**ak**-shee-oh re-si-**sor**-ee-ə). *Roman law.* An action to restore to the plaintiff property lost by prescription. • This action was available to minors and other persons exempt from prescriptive claims against their property. Pl. ***actiones rescissoriae.***

▸ ***actio sacramenti*** (**ak**-shee-oh sak-rə-**men**-tI). SACRAMENTO.

▸ ***actio serviana*** (**ak**-shee-oh sər-vee-**ay**-nə). *Roman law.* An action by which a lessor could seize, in satisfaction of unpaid rent, the lessee's personal property brought onto the leased premises. Pl. ***actiones servianae.***

▸ ***actio servi corrupti*** (**ak**-shee-oh sər-vI kə-**rəp**-tI). [Latin] *Roman law.* An action for corrupting a slave or servant. • Since the "corruption" could take the form of bribery to find out the master's confidential business information, one scholar suggested in a famous article that it could be the precursor of the modern law of trade secrets. A. Arthur Schiller, *Trade Secrets and the Roman Law: The Actio Servi Corrupti*, 30 Colum. L. Rev. 837 (1930). Other scholars strongly disagree (see Alan Watson's quotation).

> "*Actio servi corrupti.* This actio lay against the seducer or corrupter of a slave . . . or the labourer of one who had run away. . . . It applied to one who made a bad slave worse, as well as to one who made a good slave bad." John George Phillimore, *Private Law Among the Romans* 189–90 (1863).

> "The *actio servi corrupti* presumably or possibly could be used to protect trade secrets and other similar commercial interests. That was not its purpose and was, at most, an incidental spin-off. But there is not the slightest evidence that the action was ever so used." Alan Watson, *Trade Secrets and Roman Law: The Myth Exploded*, 11 Tul. Eur. & Civ. L.F. 19 (1996).

▸ ***actio spolii*** (**ak**-shee-oh **spoh**-li-ee). (1888) *Hist. Eccles. law.* An action for the recovery of things stolen. • Founded on the Roman-law interdict *unde vi*, this action was the precursor to the assize of novel disseisin. See UNDE VI; *assize of novel disseisin* under ASSIZE (8).

▸ ***actio stricti juris*** (**ak**-shee-oh **strik**-tI **joor**-is). *Roman law.* A class of personal actions enforceable exactly as stated in the *formula* without taking equitable considerations into account; an action of strict right. • This type of action was often used to recover a definite sum of money or a particular object that was the subject of a formal promise (*stipulatio*). See FORMULA (1). Pl. ***actiones stricti juris.***

▸ ***actio temporalis*** (**ak**-shee-oh tem-pə-**ray**-lis). *Roman & civil law.* An action that must be brought within a specified time. Cf. *actio perpetua.* Pl. ***actiones temporales.***

▸ ***actio tutelae*** (**ak**-shee-oh t[y]oo-**tee**-lee). *Roman law.* An action arising from a breach of the duty owed by a guardian (*tutor*) to the ward, such as mismanagement of the ward's property. Pl. ***actiones tutelae.***

▸ ***actio utilis*** (**ak**-shee-oh **yoo**-tə-lis). *Roman law.* An extension of a direct action, founded on utility rather than strict right, available esp. to persons having an interest in property less than ownership. • This type of action was modeled after the *actio directa.* Cf. *actio directa; actio in factum.* Pl. ***actiones utiles.***

▸ ***actio venditi*** (**ak**-shee-oh **ven**-də-tI). *Roman law.* An action by which a seller could obtain his price or enforce a contract of sale. — Also termed *actio ex vendito.* Pl. ***actiones venditi.***

▸ ***actio vi bonorum raptorum*** (**ak**-shee-oh **vI** bə-**nor**-əm rap-**tor**-əm). *Roman law.* A penal action to recover goods taken by force. • A successful plaintiff would also receive three times the value of the taken property. Cf. INTERDICTUM QUOD VI AUT CLAM.

▸ ***actio vulgaris*** (**ak**-shee-oh vəl-**gair**-is). *Hist.* An ordinary action, as opposed to one granted in special circumstances. Pl. ***actiones vulgares.***

▸ ***commodati actio.*** See *actio commodati.*

▸ ***legis actio.*** See LEGIS ACTIO.

action. (14c) **1.** The process of doing something; conduct or behavior. **2.** A thing done; ACT (1). **3.** *Patents.* OFFICE ACTION.

▸ **advisory action.** *Patents.* See *advisory office action* under OFFICE ACTION.

4. A civil or criminal judicial proceeding.

> "An action has been defined to be an ordinary proceeding in a court of justice, by which one party prosecutes another party for the enforcement or protection of a right, the redress or prevention of a wrong, or the punishment of a public offense. But in some sense this definition is equally applicable to special proceedings. More accurately, it is defined to be any judicial proceeding, which, if conducted to a determination, will result in a judgment or decree. The action is said to terminate at judgment." 1 Morris M. Estee, *Estee's Pleadings, Practice, and Forms* § 3, at 1 (Carter P. Pomeroy ed., 3d ed. 1885).

> "The terms 'action' and 'suit' are nearly if not quite synonymous. But lawyers usually speak of proceedings in courts of law as 'actions,' and of those in courts of equity as 'suits.' In olden time there was a more marked distinction, for an action was considered as terminating when judgment was rendered, the execution forming no part of it. A suit, on the other hand, included the execution. The word 'suit,' as used in the Judiciary Act of 1784 and later Federal statutes, applies to any proceeding in a court of justice in which the plaintiff pursues in such court the remedy which the law affords him." Edwin E. Bryant, *The Law of Pleading Under the Codes of Civil Procedure* 3 (2d ed. 1899).

> "'Action' in the sense of a judicial proceeding includes recoupment, counterclaim, set-off, suit in equity, and any other proceeding in which rights are determined." UCC § 1-201(b)(1).

▸ **action at law.** (17c) A civil suit stating a legal cause of action and seeking only a legal remedy. See *suit at law* and *suit in equity* under SUIT.

▸ **action *de die in diem*** (dee **dI**-ee in **dI**-em). [Law Latin "from day to day"] *Hist.* **1.** An action occurring from day to day; a continuing right of action. **2.** An action for trespass for each day that an injury continues.

> "That trespass by way of personal entry is a continuing injury, lasting as long as the personal presence of the wrongdoer, and giving rise to actions *de die in diem* so long as it lasts, is sufficiently obvious." R.F.V. Heuston, *Salmond on the Law of Torts* 42 (17th ed. 1977).

▸ **action *de in rem verso*** (dee **in rem vər**-soh). [Latin "action for money applied to (the defendant's) advantage"] (18c) **1.** *Roman & civil law.* An action for unjust enrichment, in which the plaintiff must show that an enrichment was bestowed, that the enrichment caused an impoverishment, that there is no justification for the enrichment and impoverishment, and that the plaintiff has no other adequate remedy at law, including no remedy under an express or implied contract. **2.** *Roman law.* An action brought against a paterfamilias or a slaveowner who benefited from the transaction of a child or slave. — Also termed (in both senses) *actio de in rem verso.*

▸ **action *en declaration de simulation.*** (1850) *Louisiana law.* An action to void a contract. See *simulated contract* under CONTRACT.

▸ **action *ex contractu*** (eks kən-**trak**-t[y]oo). (18c) A personal action arising out of a contract.

> "*Actions ex contractu* were somewhat illogically classified thus: *covenant, debt, assumpsit, detinue,* and *account.* The *action of covenant* lay where the party claimed damages for a breach of contract or promise under seal. The *writ of debt* lay for the recovery of a debt; that is, a liquidated or certain sum of money alleged to be due from defendant to plaintiff. The *writ of detinue* was the ancient remedy where the plaintiff claimed the specific recovery of goods, chattels, deeds, or writings detained from him. This remedy fell into disuse by reason of the unsatisfactory mode of trial of 'wager of law,' which the defendant could claim; and recourse was had to the action of replevin. In the American States an action of replevin founded upon statute provisions is almost universally the remedy for the recovery of specific personal property." Edwin E. Bryant, *The Law of Pleading Under the Codes of Civil Procedure* 5 (2d ed. 1899).

▸ **action *ex delicto*** (eks də-**lik**-toh). (1816) A personal action arising out of a tort.

> "The actions *ex delicto* were originally the action of *trespass* and the action of *replevin.*" Edwin E. Bryant, *The Law of Pleading Under the Codes of Civil Procedure* 5 (2d ed. 1899).

▸ **action for mesne profits.** See ACTION FOR MESNE PROFITS.

▸ **action for money had and received.** (18c) At common law, an action by which the plaintiff could recover money paid to the defendant, the money usu. being recoverable because (1) the money had been paid by mistake or under compulsion, or (2) the consideration was insufficient.

"The *action for money had and received* lay to recover money which the plaintiff had paid to the defendant, on the ground that it had been paid under a mistake or compulsion, or for a consideration which had wholly failed. By this action the plaintiff could also recover money which the defendant had received from a third party, as when he was accountable or had attorned to the plaintiff in respect of the money, or the money formed part of the fruits of an office of the plaintiff which the defendant had usurped." Robert Goff & Gareth Jones, *The Law of Restitution* 3 (3d ed. 1986).

▸ **action for money paid.** (18c) At common law, an action by which the plaintiff could recover money paid to a third party — not to the defendant — in circumstances in which the defendant had benefited.

"The *action for money paid* was the appropriate action when the plaintiff's claim was in respect of money paid, not to the defendant, but to a third party, from which the defendant had derived a benefit. Historically, the plaintiff had to show that the payment was made at the defendant's request; but we shall see that the law was prepared to 'imply' such a request on certain occasions, in particular where the payment was made under compulsion of law or, in limited circumstances, in the course of intervention in an emergency on the defendant's behalf, which in this book we shall call necessitous intervention." Robert Goff & Gareth Jones, *The Law of Restitution* 3 (3d ed. 1986).

▸ **action for poinding.** (17c) *Hist.* A creditor's action to obtain sequestration of the land rents and goods of the debtor to satisfy the debt or enforce a distress.

▸ **action for the loss of services.** (1809) *Hist.* **1.** A lawsuit by a master for the loss of his servant's services, filed against a third party who has (it is alleged) wrongfully prevented the provision of those services. **2.** A husband's lawsuit against one who has taken away, imprisoned, or physically harmed his wife in circumstances in which (1) the act is wrongful to the wife, and (2) the husband is deprived of her society or services.

▸ **action for the recovery of land.** See EJECTMENT.

▸ **action for the recovery of mesne profits.** See ACTION FOR MESNE PROFITS.

▸ **action in equity.** (18c) An action that seeks equitable relief, such as an injunction or specific performance, as opposed to damages. See *suit in equity* under SUIT.

▸ **action in personam** (in pər-**soh**-nəm). (1800) **1.** An action brought against a person rather than property. • An *in personam* judgment is binding on the judgment-debtor and can be enforced against all the property of the judgment-debtor. **2.** An action in which the named defendant is a natural or legal person. — Also termed *personal action*; (in Roman and civil law) *actio in personam*; *actio personalis.* See IN PERSONAM. Pl. ***actiones in personam***; ***actiones personales.***

▸ **action in rem** (in **rem**). (18c) **1.** An action to determine the title to property and the rights of the parties, not merely among themselves, but also against all persons at any time claiming an interest in that property; a real action. **2.** *Louisiana law.* An action brought to protect possession, ownership, or other real rights in immovable property. La. Civ. Code arts. 3651 et seq. **3.** *Louisiana law.* An action to recover possession of immovable property. La. Civ. Code art. 526. — Also termed (in Roman law) *actio in rem*; *actio realis*; *real action.* See IN REM. Pl. ***actiones in rem.*** **4.** An action in which the named defendant is property, either real or personal.

▸ **action of account.** See ACCOUNTING (3).

▸ **action of assize.** (1804) *Hist.* A real action by which the plaintiff proves title to land merely by showing an ancestor's possession. See ASSIZE.

▸ **action of book debt.** See ACCOUNTING (4).

▸ **action of covenant.** (16c) *Archaic.* A lawsuit seeking damages or the specific performance of a contract under seal; COVENANT (3). See *contract under seal* under CONTRACT.

▸ **action of debt.** See CONDICTIO.

▸ **action of declarator.** (17c) *Scots law.* An action brought in the Court of Session for the purpose of establishing a legal status or right. — Also termed *declarator*; *action for declaratory.*

▸ **action of ejectment.** See EJECTMENT (3).

▸ **action of reprobator.** See REPROBATOR.

▸ **action of trespass for mesne profits.** See ACTION FOR MESNE PROFITS.

▸ **action on account.** See ACCOUNTING (4).

▸ **action on expenditure.** (1833) An action to require the principal debt to be paid by a personal surety.

▸ **action on the case.** See *trespass on the case* under TRESPASS.

▸ **action *per quod servitium amisit*** (pər kwod sər-**vish**-ee-əm ə-**mɪ**-sit). [Latin] (18c) *Hist.* An action for the loss of a servant's services. See *action for the loss of services.*

▸ **action quasi in rem** (**kway**-sɪ in **rem** *or* **kway**-zɪ). (1883) An action brought against the defendant personally, with jurisdiction based on an interest in property, the objective being to deal with the particular property or to subject the property to the discharge of the claims asserted. See *quasi in rem* under IN REM.

▸ **action to quiet title.** (1837) A proceeding to establish a plaintiff's title to land by compelling the adverse claimant to establish a claim or be forever estopped from asserting it. — Also termed *quiet-title action.*

▸ **action to review judgment.** (1853) *Rare.* **1.** MOTION FOR NEW TRIAL. **2.** A request for judicial review of a nonjudicial body's decision, such as an administrative ruling on a workers'-compensation claim. • The grounds for review are usu. similar to those for a new trial, esp. patent errors of law and new evidence.

▸ **amicable action.** See *test case* (1) under CASE (1).

▸ **civil action.** (16c) An action brought to enforce, redress, or protect a private or civil right; a noncriminal litigation. — Also termed (if brought by a private person) *private action*; (if brought by a government) *public action.*

"The code of New York, as originally adopted, declared, 'the distinctions between actions at law and suits in equity, and the forms of all such actions and heretofore existing, are abolished; and there shall be in this State hereafter but one form of action for the enforcement or protection of private rights and the redress of private wrongs, which shall be denominated a civil action.' With slight verbal changes the above provision has been enacted in most of the States and Territories which have adopted the reformed procedure." Edwin E. Bryant, *The Law of Pleading Under the Codes of Civil Procedure* 106 (2d ed. 1899).

▸ **class action.** See CLASS ACTION.

▸ **collusive action.** (18c) An action between two parties who have no actual controversy, being merely for the purpose of determining a legal question or receiving a precedent that might prove favorable in related litigation. — Also termed *fictional action*.

▸ **common-law action.** (18c) An action governed by common law, rather than constitutional, statutory, equitable, or civil law.

▸ **criminal action.** (16c) An action instituted by the government to punish offenses against the public.

▸ **cross-action.** (18c) An action brought by the defendant against the plaintiff based on the same subject matter as the plaintiff's action. See CROSS-CLAIM.

▸ **derivative action.** See DERIVATIVE ACTION.

▸ **direct action.** See DIRECT ACTION.

▸ **fictional action.** See *collusive action*.

▸ **fictitious action.** (17c) An action, usu. unethical, brought solely to obtain a judicial opinion on an issue of fact or law, rather than for the disposition of a controversy.

▸ **Good Samaritan action.** See GOOD SAMARITAN ACTION.

▸ **guardianship action.** (1931) *Family law.* An action brought for the purpose of asking a court to appoint a temporary or permanent guardian to care for property or for a person who is underage or incapacitated. See *guardian of the estate* & *guardian of the person* under GUARDIAN (1).

▸ **hypothecary action** (hɪ-**poth**-ə-ker-ee). (1815) *Roman & civil law.* An action for the enforcement of a mortgage (*hypotheca*); a lawsuit to enforce a creditor's claims under a hypothec or hypothecation. — Also termed *actio hypothecaria*.

▸ **informal action.** (1963) *Administrative law.* An executive-branch action that does not fall under rulemaking or formal adjudication procedures in the Administrative Procedure Act. • Informal actions are not subject to specific notice and procedural requirements mandated by the APA for rulemaking and formal adjudications. See ADMINISTRATIVE PROCEDURE ACT.

▸ **innominate action** (i-**nom**-i-nət). (1903) An action that has no special name by which it is known. Cf. *nominate action*.

▸ **joint action.** (17c) **1.** An action brought by two or more plaintiffs. **2.** An action brought against two or more defendants.

▸ **local action.** (18c) An action that can be brought only in the jurisdiction where the cause of action arose, as when the action's subject matter is real property.

▸ **matrimonial action.** (1881) An action relating to the state of marriage, such as an action for separation, annulment, or divorce.

▸ **mixed action.** (15c) An action that has some characteristics of both a real action and a personal action.

> "In early times the only mixed actions were those for the partition of lands, for which a writ was provided in the common-law courts. The remedy was further enlarged by the statute of 31 Hen. VII c. 1, and 32 Hen. VIII c. 32, which gave compulsory partition, by writ at common law. These statutes formed the basis of partition in the American States; but in England and here courts of Chancery have been found most convenient, and their procedure most favorable for the division of estates in land. The statutes at the present time, in most of the States, prescribe a procedure which is quite similar to that in equity practice." Edwin E. Bryant, *The Law of Pleading Under the Codes of Civil Procedure* 10–11 (2d ed. 1899).

▸ **nominate action** (**nom**-i-nət). (1993) An action that is known by a name, such as a confessory action, a petitory action, or a possessory action. Cf. *innominate action*.

▸ **nonpersonal action.** (1971) An action that proceeds within some category of territorial jurisdiction other than in personam — that is, jurisdiction in rem, quasi in rem, or over status.

▸ **penal action.** (16c) **1.** A criminal prosecution. **2.** A civil proceeding in which either the state or a common informer sues to recover a penalty from a defendant who has violated a statute. • Although civil in nature, a penal action resembles a criminal proceeding because the result of a successful action is a monetary penalty intended, like a fine, to punish the defendant. See COMMON INFORMER.

> "At one time it was a frequent practice, when it was desired to repress some type of conduct thought to be harmful, to do so by the machinery of the civil rather than of the criminal law. The means so chosen was called a penal action, as being brought for the recovery of a penalty; and it might be brought, according to the wording of the particular statute creating the penal action, either by the Attorney-General on behalf of the state, or by a common informer on his own account. A common informer was anyone who should first sue the offender for the penalty. Penal actions are still possible in a few cases, and their existence renders invalid several suggested distinctions between civil wrongs and crimes." John Salmond, *Jurisprudence* 107 (Glanville L. Williams ed., 10th ed. 1947).

> "For in 'penal actions,' unless the statute expressly authorizes private persons to act as informers, the State alone can sue and recover the penalty; and yet there is full authority for ranking such suits by it as merely civil proceedings." J.W. Cecil Turner, *Kenny's Outlines of Criminal Law* 538 (16th ed. 1952).

3. A civil lawsuit by an aggrieved party seeking to recover a statutory fine or a penalty, such as punitive damages.

> "[T]here exists a well-known class of proceedings called 'penal actions,' by which pecuniary penalties can be recovered — in some cases by any person who will sue for them — from the doers of various prohibited acts; these acts being thus prohibited, and visited with penalties, solely on account of their tendency to cause evil to the community at large, 'considered as a community.' For example, a person who, in advertising a reward for the return of lost property, adds that 'no questions will be asked' incurs by the Larceny Act, 1861, a penalty of £50 recoverable by anyone who will sue for it." J.W. Cecil Turner, *Kenny's Outlines of Criminal Law* 533–34 (16th ed. 1952).

▸ **personal action.** (17c) **1.** An action brought to recover debts, personal property, or damages arising from any cause. — Also termed *remedial action*.

> "Personal actions are subdivided into those brought for the recovery of a debt or of damages for the breach of a contract, or for tort, for some injury to the person or to relative rights or to personal or real property. The most common of these actions are debt, covenant, assumpsit, detinue, trespass, trespass on the case, trover, and replevin." Benjamin J. Shipman, *Handbook of Common-Law Pleading* § 34, at 65 (Henry Winthrop Ballantine ed., 3d ed. 1923).

2. See *action in personam*.

▸ **petitory action** (**pet**-ə-tor-ee). (17c) **1.** *Roman & civil law.* An action to establish and enforce title to property independently of the right to possession. **2.** *Civil law.*

An action to recognize ownership or other real right in immovable (or sometimes movable) property. • In civil-law systems, the petitory action (revendication) is a much broader and more effective remedy than the *rei-vindicatio*, the Roman prototype. This action is based on, and tends to protect, real rights, that is, ownership and its dismemberments. It is therefore a real action, distinguishable from personal actions based on (and tending to protect) personal rights. Generally, the petitory action is available for the protection of the ownership of both movables and immovables. In Louisiana, however, the petitory action is for the recognition of ownership or other real right in immovable property, brought by a person who is not in possession of it. La. Code Civ. Proc. art. 3651. An action for the recognition of such a right in movable property is an innominate real action, known as a *revendicatory action*. — Also termed *petitory suit*; *petitorium*; *revendication*.

▸ **plenary action** (**plee**-nə-ree *or* **plen**-). (1837) A full hearing or trial on the merits, as opposed to a summary proceeding. Cf. *summary proceeding* under PROCEEDING.

▸ **possessory action** (pə-**zes**-ə-ree). (17c) **1.** An action to obtain, recover, or maintain possession of property but not title to it, such as an action to evict a nonpaying tenant. — Also termed *possessorium*.

"The possessory action is available for the protection of the *possession* of corporeal immovables as well as for the protection of the *quasi-possession* or real rights in immovable property. It is distinguished from the *petitory* action which is available for the recognition and enforcement of ownership or of real rights in another's immovable, such as a usufruct, limited personal servitudes, and predial servitudes." A.N. Yiannopoulos, *Property: The Law of Things — Real Rights — Real Actions* § 333, at 653 (4th ed. 2001).

2. *Maritime law.* An action brought to recover possession of a ship under a claim of title.

▸ **private action.** See *civil action*.

▸ **public action.** See *civil action*.

▸ **real action.** (16c) **1.** An action brought to recover land or other real property; specif., an action to recover the possession of a freehold estate in real property, or seisin. **2.** *Civil law.* An action based on, and tending to protect, a real right, namely, the right of ownership and its dismemberments. • It is distinguishable from a personal action, which is based on (and tends to protect) a personal right. **3.** *Louisiana law.* An action brought to protect possession, ownership, or other real rights in immovable property. La. Code Civ. Proc. arts. 3651 et seq. — Also termed *action in rem*; *actio in rem*; *actio realis*. See SEISIN.

"If the question be asked why it was that a large part of the really English law which Bracton undertook to expound is found in connection with the subject of real actions, while in Blackstone's treatise only the personal actions are deemed worthy of attention, the answer must be that the former were dying out. When Chitty wrote (1808) the old real actions were practically obsolete, and in the succeeding generation such vestiges of them as remained were abolished by statute." Hannis Taylor, *The Science of Jurisprudence* 574 (1908).

"The principal real actions formerly in use were (1) the writs of right; (2) the writs of entry; (3) the possessory assizes, such as novel disseisin and mort d'ancestor. Real actions are those in which the demandant seeks to recover seisin from one called a tenant, because he holds the land. They are real actions at common law because the judgment is in rem and awards the seisin or possession." Benjamin J. Shipman, *Handbook of Common-Law Pleading* § 32, at 63 (Henry Winthrop Ballantine ed., 3d ed. 1923).

▸ **redhibitory action.** (18c) *Civil law.* An action brought to void a sale of a thing having a defect that renders it either useless or so flawed that the buyer would not have bought it in the first place. See REDHIBITION.

▸ **remedial action. 1.** See REMEDIAL ACTION. **2.** See *personal action* (1).

▸ **representative action. 1.** CLASS ACTION. **2.** DERIVATIVE ACTION (1).

▸ **rescissory action.** (18c) *Scots law.* An action to set aside a deed.

▸ **revendicatory action** (ree-**ven**-di-kə-tor-ee). See *petitory action*.

▸ **sacramental action.** See SACRAMENTO.

▸ **separate action.** (18c) **1.** An action brought alone by each of several complainants who are all involved in the same transaction but either cannot legally join the suit or, not being required to join, choose not to join it. **2.** One of several distinct actions brought by a single plaintiff against each of two or more parties who are all liable to a plaintiff with respect to the same subject matter. — Also termed *several action*.

▸ **several action.** See *separate action*.

▸ **sham action.** (17c) An objectively baseless lawsuit the primary purpose of which is to hinder or interfere with a competitor's business relationships. *See Professional Real Estate Investors, Inc. v. Columbia Pictures Indus., Inc.*, 508 U.S. 49, 113 S.Ct. 1920 (1993). — Also termed *sham lawsuit*; *sham suit*. See SHAM EXCEPTION.

▸ **statutory action.** (18c) An action governed by statutory law rather than equitable, civil, or common law.

▸ **test action.** See *test case* (2) under CASE (1).

▸ **third-party action.** (1872) An action brought as part of a lawsuit already pending but distinct from the main claim, whereby a defendant sues an entity not sued by the plaintiff when that entity may be liable to the defendant for all or part of the plaintiff's claim. • A common example is an action for indemnity or contribution.

▸ **transitory action.** (17c) An action that can be brought in any venue where the defendant can be personally served with process.

"Transitory actions are universally founded on the supposed violation of rights which, in contemplation of law, have no locality. They are personal actions, that is, they are brought for the enforcement of purely personal rights or obligations. If the transaction on which the action is founded could have taken place anywhere, the action is generally regarded as transitory; but if the transaction could only have happened in a particular place . . . the action is local. Some authorities, considering the effect of the distinction, define transitory actions as actions which may be tried wherever defendant may be found and served." 92 C.J.S. *Venue* § 8, at 678–79 (1955).

Action. A former independent federal agency that administered various volunteer-services programs including Foster Grandparents, Retired Senior Volunteers, Senior Companions, Volunteers in Service to America, and Student Community Service Projects. • Its functions were transferred to the Corporation for National and Community Service in 1995. See CORPORATION FOR NATIONAL AND COMMUNITY SERVICE.

action, cause of. See CAUSE OF ACTION.

action, form of. See FORM OF ACTION.

action, right of. See RIGHT OF ACTION.

actionable, *adj.* (16c) **1.** Furnishing the legal ground for a lawsuit or other legal action <intentional interference with contractual relations is an actionable tort>.

▸ **actionable per quod** (pər **kwod**). (1916) (Of potentially defamatory words) not inherently defamatory and therefore requiring allegation and proof of special damages. • For example, if the defendant says, "The plaintiff is crazy," the utterance is actionable per quod. That is, the plaintiff must prove, in addition to the utterance, that the defendant intended the words to mean that the plaintiff was mentally impaired or deficient in business or professional capacity, and that these words caused the plaintiff to suffer special damages. See PER QUOD.

▸ **actionable per se** (pər **say**). (1808) (Of defamatory words) legally and conclusively presumed defamatory. • In the law of defamation, words actionable per se are inherently libelous or slanderous. For example, if a person says of a fiduciary, "That person embezzles client funds," the utterance is actionable per se. The plaintiff does not have to allege or prove special damages. See PER SE.

> "The terminology 'actionable per se' has proven treacherous, in that it has invited confusion with another doctrine which obtains in defamation cases. This is the doctrine which distinguishes between words (such as, 'You are a thief') which convey a defamatory meaning on their face, and, on the other hand, words of veiled detraction whose offense is apparent only when the context and circumstances are revealed. The former are sometimes said to be defamatory 'per se' or slanderous 'per se' or libelous 'per se,' whereas the latter, to be properly pleaded, must have an accompanying 'innuendo' or explanation. Clearly this requirement has no relationship to the other rule, that certain slanders are and others are not actionable without a showing of special damage, but the use of the phrase 'per se' in both connections has produced confusion, and we find many American courts adopting the practice of requiring, in cases where the defamation, whether slander or libel, must be explained by an 'innuendo' to reveal its defamatory meaning, that special damages be also pleaded." Charles T. McCormick, *Handbook on the Law of Damages* § 113, at 417 (1935).

2. Loosely, requiring prompt attention and decisive measures to be taken <actionable items on the agenda> • Sense 2 is business jargon to be avoided. It is a great shame that this sense has become widespread enough to be recorded here.

actionable negligence. See NEGLIGENCE (1).

actionable nuisance. See NUISANCE (3).

actionable per quod. See ACTIONABLE (1).

actionable per se. See ACTIONABLE (1).

actionable word. (18c) A term that is defamatory in itself. See *libel per se* under LIBEL.

action agenda. See *action calendar* under CALENDAR (4).

actionare (ak-shee-ə-**nair**-ee), *vb.* [Law Latin] To bring an action; to sue.

action at law. See ACTION (4).

action calendar. See CALENDAR (4).

action de die in diem. See ACTION (4).

action de in rem verso. See ACTION (4).

actio negativa. See *actio negatoria* under ACTIO.

actio negatoria. See ACTIO.

actio negotiorum gestorum. See ACTIO.

actionem non habere debet. See ACTIO NON.

action *en declaration de simulation.* See ACTION (4).

action *en desaveu* (**ak**-shən on des-ə-**vuu**). (1841) *Louisiana law.* A lawsuit to disavow paternity brought by a man who is legally presumed to be the father of the child.

actiones honorariae (ak-shee-**oh**-neez [h]on-ə-**rair**-ee-ɪ). (1869) A praetorian action; a class of equitable actions introduced by the praetors to prevent injustices.

actiones legis. See LEGIS ACTIO.

actiones nominatae (ak-shee-**oh**-neez nom-ə-**nay**-tee), *n. pl.* [Latin "named actions"] *Hist.* Actions for which the Chancery had well-established forms. See CASU CONSIMILI.

actiones poenales (ak-shee-**oh**-neez pee-**nay**-leez), *n. pl.* [Latin "penal actions"] See *actio poenalis* under ACTIO.

action ex contractu. See ACTION (4).

action ex delicto. See ACTION (4).

action for declaratory. See *action of declarator* under ACTION (4).

action for mesne profits. A lawsuit seeking damages suffered by a landowner who has succeeded in a common-law action of ejectment whereby the plaintiff may recover for both the use of the land during the wrongful occupation and the costs of ejectment. — Also termed *action of trespass for mesne profits*; *action for the recovery of mesne profits.*

> "[A]n action for the *mesne profits* is *consequential* to the recovery in ejectment. It may be brought by the lessor of the plaintiff in his *own* name or in the name of the *nominal lessee*; and in either shape it is equally *his* action. But, if the action is brought in the name of the nominal lessee in the ejectment suit, the mesne profits can be recovered only since the time of the demise laid in the declaration in the original action of ejectment. If the interest of the lessor of the plaintiff in the ejectment suit to the mesne profits has passed to an assignee, devisee, or personal representative of such lessor, the action for such mesne profits may be maintained by the successor of such lessor in his own name or in the name of the nominal lessor in the ejectment suit, under the same rule applicable to the original lessor." Ransom H. Tyler, *A Treatise on the Remedy by Ejectment and the Law of Adverse Enjoyment in the United States* 840 (1870) (citations omitted).

action for money had and received. See ACTION (4).

action for money paid. See ACTION (4).

action for poinding. See ACTION (4).

action for the loss of services. See ACTION (4).

action for the recovery of land. See EJECTMENT.

action for the recovery of mesne profits. See ACTION FOR MESNE PROFITS.

action in equity. 1. ACTION (4). **2.** See *suit in equity* under SUIT.

action in personam. See ACTION (4).

action in rem. See ACTION (4).

action of account. See ACCOUNTING (3).

action of assize. See ACTION (4).

action of book debt. See ACCOUNTING (4).

action of covenant. 1. See ACTION (4). **2.** COVENANT (3).

action of debt. 1. DEBT (4). **2.** CONDICTIO.

action of declarator. See ACTION (4).

action of ejectment. See EJECTMENT (3).

action of reprobator. See REPROBATOR.

action of trespass for mesne profits. See ACTION FOR MESNE PROFITS.

actio non (**ak**-shee-oh **non**). [Latin "an action not"] (1802) *Hist.* A declaration in a special plea denying the plaintiff's right to maintain the action. • The full phrase was *actionem non habere debet* (ought not to have or maintain the action). See *special plea* under PLEA.

action on account. See ACCOUNTING (4).

actio non accrevit infra sex annos. See ACTIO.

action on decision. (1940) A legal memorandum from attorneys in the Internal Revenue Service's litigation division to the Service's Chief Counsel, containing advice on whether the Service should acquiesce, appeal, or take some other action regarding a court's decision that is unfavorable to the Service. — Abbr. AOD.

action on expenditure. See ACTION (4).

action on the case. See *trespass on the case* under TRESPASS.

actio non ulterius. See ACTIO.

actio noxalis (**ak**-shee-oh nok-**say**-lis), *n.* See NOXAL ACTION.

action *per quod servitium amisit.* See ACTION (4).

action quasi in rem. See ACTION (4).

action to quiet title. See ACTION (4).

action to review judgment. See ACTION (4).

actio Pauliana. See ACTIO.

actio perpetua. See ACTIO.

actio personalis. See *action in personam* under ACTION (4).

actio pigneratitia. See ACTIO.

actio poenalis. See ACTIO.

actio popularis. See ACTIO.

actio praejudicialis. See ACTIO.

actio praetoria. See ACTIO.

actio pro socio. See ACTIO.

actio Publiciana. See ACTIO.

actio Publiciana in rem. See *actio Publiciana* under ACTIO.

actio quanti minoris. See ACTIO.

actio quod jussu. See ACTIO.

actio quod metus causa. See ACTIO.

actio realis. See ACTIO.

actio redhibitoria. See ACTIO.

actio rei persecutoria. See ACTIO.

actio rerum amotarum. See ACTIO.

actio rescissoria. See ACTIO.

actio serviana. See ACTIO.

actio servi corrupti. See ACTIO.

actio spolii. See ACTIO.

actio stricti juris. See ACTIO.

actio temporalis. See ACTIO.

actio tutelae. See ACTIO.

actio utilis. See ACTIO.

actio venditi. See ACTIO.

actio vi bonorum raptorum. See ACTIO.

actio vulgaris. See ACTIO.

active adoption-registry statute. See ADOPTION-REGISTRY STATUTE.

active breach of contract. See BREACH OF CONTRACT.

active case. See CASE (1).

active concealment. See CONCEALMENT.

active conduct. See CONDUCT.

active-control-of-vessel duty. See ACTIVE-OPERATIONS DUTY.

active covenant. See COVENANT (1).

active debt. See DEBT.

active duty. (1801) **1.** *Military law.* The full-time status of being in any of the U.S. armed forces. — Also termed *active service.* **2.** See *positive duty* under DUTY (1).

active euthanasia. See EUTHANASIA.

active income. See INCOME.

active inducement. See INDUCEMENT (1).

active mass. (1838) *Civil law.* The aggregate of a decedent's assets and debts in addition to the value of donations that the decedent made within three years before death. • Premiums paid for life insurance and contributions to certain deferred compensation and pension plans are excluded from the calculations. *See* La. Civ. Code art. 1505.

active misrepresentation. See *affirmative misrepresentation* under MISREPRESENTATION.

active negligence. See NEGLIGENCE.

active-operations duty. (1994) *Maritime law.* A shipowner's obligation to provide safe working conditions, in the work areas that it controls, for the longshoremen who are loading or unloading the ship. — Also termed *active-control-of-vessel duty.* Cf. TURNOVER DUTY; INTERVENTION DUTY.

active service. See ACTIVE DUTY.

active supervision. (1950) *Antitrust.* Under the test for determining whether a private entity may claim a state-action exemption from the antitrust laws, the right of the state to review the entity's anticompetitive acts and to disapprove those acts that do not promote state policy. See STATE-ACTION DOCTRINE; MIDCAL TEST.

> "The active supervision requirement stems from the recognition that where a private party is engaging in the anticompetitive activity, there is a real danger that he is acting to further his own interests, rather than the governmental interests of the State. The requirement is designed to ensure that the state-action doctrine will shelter only the particular anticompetitive acts that, in the judgment of the State, actually further state regulatory policies. To accomplish this purpose, the active supervision requirement mandates that the State exercise ultimate control over the challenged anticompetitive conduct." *Patrick v. Burget*, 486 U.S. 94, 100–01, 108 S.Ct. 1658, 1663 (1988).

active trust. See TRUST (3).

active use. See USE (4).

active waste. See *commissive waste* under WASTE (1).

activist lawyering. See CAUSE LAWYERING.

activity. (16c) **1.** The collective acts of one person or of two or more people engaged in a common enterprise.

▸ **commercial activity.** (18c) An activity, such as operating a business, conducted to make a profit.

2. See MARKET VOLUME.

activity incident to service. (1950) An act undertaken by a member of the armed forces as a part of a military operation or as a result of the actor's status as a member of the military. • For example, if a member of the military takes advantage of that status by flying home on a military aircraft, the flight is activity incident to service, and a claim against the government for any injuries received may be barred under the *Feres* doctrine. See FERES DOCTRINE.

acto (**ahk**-toh), *n. Spanish law.* **1.** ACT (1). **2.** ACT (2). **3.** An action or lawsuit.

Act of Adjournal. (17c) *Scots law.* A regulation issued by the High Court of Justiciary to regulate procedure both in that court and in the lower criminal courts.

Act of Assembly. (17c) *Scots law.* A piece of legislation passed by the General Assembly of the Church of Scotland for governing the affairs of that church and its members.

act of attainder. See BILL OF ATTAINDER.

act of bankruptcy. See ACT (2).

act of commission. See ACT (2).

act of Congress. (18c) A statute that is formally enacted in accordance with the legislative power granted to Congress by the U.S. Constitution. • To become a law, or an act of Congress, a bill or resolution must be passed by a majority of the members of both the House of Representatives and the Senate. Bills or resolutions may generally be introduced in either chamber, except that bills for generating revenue must be introduced in the House of Representatives. When a bill or resolution is introduced in a chamber, it is usu. assigned to a committee. If it is passed by the committee, it is reported to the full chamber. If it passes in the full chamber, it is reported to the other chamber, which then usu. assigns it to a committee in that chamber. If it passes by majority votes of the committee and full body in that chamber, it is reported back to the originating chamber. If its terms have changed in the second chamber, it is submitted to a conference committee, consisting of members from both chambers, to work out a compromise. When the bill or resolution is passed, with the same terms, by both chambers, it is signed by the Speaker of the House and the President of the Senate (usu. the president pro tempore), and is presented to the President of the United States for signature. If the President signs it or fails to return it to Congress within ten days, the bill or resolution becomes law. But if the President vetoes the bill or resolution, it must be passed by a two-thirds majority of the House of Representatives and the Senate to become law. U.S. Const. art. I, § 7.

act of court. (16c) **1.** See *judicial act* under ACT (2). **2.** *Scots law.* A memorandum setting forth the proceedings in a lawsuit. **3.** *Scots law.* A rule made by a sheriff regulating proceedings within the shrievalty.

Act of Elizabeth. *Hist. English law.* **1.** The 1558 statute that made Queen Elizabeth I head of the Church of England and, among other things, made parochial provision for the relief of the poor. **2.** STATUTE OF ELIZABETH.

act of God. (18c) An overwhelming, unpreventable event caused exclusively by forces of nature, such as an earthquake, flood, or tornado. • The definition has been statutorily broadened to include all natural phenomena that are exceptional, inevitable, and irresistible, the effects of which could not be prevented or avoided by the exercise of due care or foresight. 42 USCA § 9601(1). — Also termed *act of nature*; *act of providence*; *superior force*; *vis major*; *irresistible superhuman force*; *vis divina*. Cf. FORCE MAJEURE; *unavoidable accident* under ACCIDENT.

> "Act of God may be defined as *an operation of natural forces so unexpected that no human foresight or skill could reasonably be expected to anticipate it.* It has been suggested that it also has the wider meaning of 'any event which could not have been prevented by reasonable care on the part of anyone.' This nearly identifies it with inevitable accident, but, however desirable this may be for scientific arrangement of the law, there is no sufficient authority to back this view." P.H. Winfield, *A Textbook of the Law of Tort* § 16, at 45–46 (5th ed. 1950).

> "As a technical term, 'act of God' is untheological and infelicitous. It is an operation of 'natural forces' and this is apt to be confusing in that it might imply positive intervention of the deity. This (at any rate in common understanding) is apparent in exceptionally severe snowfalls, thunderstorms and gales. But a layman would hardly describe the gnawing of a rat as an act of God, and yet the lawyer may, in some circumstances, style it such. The fact is that in law the essence of an act of God is not so much a positive intervention of the deity as a process of nature not due to the act of man, and it is this negative side which needs emphasis." P.H. Winfield, *A Textbook of the Law of Tort* § 16, at 47 (5th ed. 1950).

> "[A]ll natural agencies, as opposed to human activities, constitute acts of God, and not merely those which attain an extraordinary degree of violence or are of very unusual occurrence. The distinction is one of kind and not one of degree. The violence or rarity of the event is relevant only in considering whether it could or could not have been prevented by reasonable care; if it could not, then it is an act of God which will relieve from liability, howsoever trivial or common its cause may have been. If this be correct, then the unpredictable nature of the occurrence will go only to show that the act of God in question was one which the defendant was under no duty to foresee or provide against. It is only in such a case that the act of God will provide a defence." R.F.V. Heuston, *Salmond on the Law of Torts* 330 (17th ed. 1977).

act of grace. See ACT (2).

act of honor. (18c) **1.** *Archaic. Commercial law.* A transaction, memorialized in an instrument prepared by a notary public, evidencing a third person's agreement to accept, for the credit of one or more of the parties, a bill that has been protested. • The UCC eliminated this type of transaction. **2.** The legal instrument setting forth the protest, acceptance, or payment.

act of hostility. (16c) An event that may be considered an adequate cause for war; CASUS BELLI. — Also termed *hostile act*. See *act of war* under ACT (2).

act of indemnity. (17c) **1.** A statute that relieves specified persons, esp. government officials, from some penalty to which they might be subject as a result of having exceeded their powers or having otherwise acted illegally. **2.** A statute that compensates persons for damage incurred as a result of either some public measure or government service.

act of law. 1. See ACT (2). **2.** See LEGAL ACT.

act of legislation. (17c) **1.** A formal change in the law that existed previously. **2.** A statute.

act of nature. See ACT (2).

act of omission. See *negative act* under ACT (2).

act of Parliament. (15c) A law made by the British sovereign, with the advice and consent of the Lords and the Commons; a British statute.

act of Parliament of Scotland. (18c) **1.** A statute passed by the Parliament of Scotland between its creation in the 14th century and 1707. **2.** ACT OF THE SCOTTISH PARLIAMENT.

act of petition. *Hist.* A summary proceeding in which litigants provide brief statements supported by affidavit. • This procedure was used in the English High Court of Admiralty.

act of possession. (16c) **1.** The exercise of physical control over a corporeal thing, movable or immovable, with the intent to own it. **2.** Conduct indicating an intent to claim property as one's own; esp., conduct that supports a claim of adverse possession.

act of providence. 1. See ACT OF GOD. **2.** See VIS MAJOR.

Act of Rescission. *Hist. Scots law.* A 1662 statute by which all laws made during the preceding 28 years were abrogated.

act of sale. (17c) An official record of a sale of property; esp., a document drawn up by a notary, signed by the parties, and attested by witnesses.

Act of Security. *Hist. Scots law.* A statute of 1703–1704 by which Queen Anne declared the independence of Scotland. • This assertion of independence was overcome by the English Parliament in 1705 with the passage of the Alien Act, which offered Scots the prospect of being designated aliens subject to the commercial restrictions over access to markets in England and the Colonies.

act of sederunt (sə-**deer**-ənt). (17c) *Scots law.* A regulation issued by the Court of Session to regulate procedure in that court or in the lower civil courts.

Act of Settlement. *Hist.* An act of Parliament (12 & 13 Will. 3, ch. 2, 1701) that resolved the question of royal succession unsettled after the Glorious Revolution of 1688. • The question was resolved by limiting the Crown to Protestant members of the House of Hanover. The Act also provided that the sovereign must be a member of the Church of England, and it established that judges would hold office during good behavior rather than at the will of the sovereign. — Also termed *Settlement of the Crown.*

act-of-state doctrine. (1910) *Int'l law.* The principle that no country can judge the legality of a foreign country's sovereign acts within its own territory. • As originally formulated by the U.S. Supreme Court in 1897, the doctrine provides that "the courts of one country will not sit in judgment on the acts of the government of another done within its own territory." *Underhill v. Hernandez,* 168 U.S. 250, 252, 18 S.Ct. 83, 84 (1897). The Supreme Court later declared that though the act-of-state doctrine is compelled by neither international law nor the Constitution, it has "institutional underpinnings." *Banco Nacional de Cuba v. Sabbatino,* 376 U.S. 398, 423, 84 S.Ct. 923, 937 (1964).

Act of Supremacy. *Hist. English law.* A 1534 statute that named the English sovereign as supreme head of the Church of England (26 Hen. 8, ch. 1). • The Act was passed during King Henry VIII's reign and confirmed in 1559 (1 Eliz., ch. 1) to counteract pro-Catholic legislation enacted during the reign of Mary Tudor. In addition to making the monarch both head of state and head of the church, the Act defined some of the monarch's powers as head of the church, such as the power to issue injunctions relating to ecclesiastical affairs.

act of the law. See ACT (2).

act of the party. See *act in the law* under ACT (2).

act of the Scottish Parliament. (1996) A statute passed by the Parliament of Scotland created by the Scotland Act of 1998. • It is typically cited by year, the letters ASP, and a serial number. The phrase *act of the Scottish Parliament,* denoting a statute enacted by an earlier parliament, dates back to the early 18th century. — Also termed *act of Parliament of Scotland.*

Act of Uniformity. *Hist. English law.* Any of several 16th- and 17th-century acts mandating uniform religious practices in England and Ireland; specif., an act requiring the use of the *Book of Common Prayer.*

Act of Union. *English law.* Any of several acts of Parliament uniting various parts of Great Britain. • The term applies most commonly to (1) the Laws in Wales Act (1535), which united Wales with England and made that principality subject to English law, and (2) the Union with Ireland Act (1800), which abolished the Irish Parliament and incorporated Ireland into the United Kingdom of Great Britain and Ireland. It is used loosely in reference to the Union with Scotland in 1707, which was made not by statute but by treaty, approved by separate acts of the parliaments of Scotland and England. The treaty dissolved each parliament and created the new state of Great Britain with one parliament, the Parliament of Great Britain.

act of war. See ACT (2).

actor. (14c) **1.** Someone who acts; a person whose conduct is in question.

▸ **bad actor.** (1901) An actor who is shown or perceived to have engaged in illegal, impermissible, or unconscionable conduct. • A presumption that a person is a bad actor may be created by an adverse-inference instruction.

2. *Archaic.* A male plaintiff. **3.** *Hist.* An advocate or pleader; one who acted for another in legal matters. Cf. REUS (1). **4.** *Roman law.* (*ital.*) Someone who sues; a claimant. — Also termed (in sense 4) *petitor.* Pl. (in sense 4) ***actores.***

actrix (**ak**-triks). (16c) *Archaic.* A female plaintiff.

acts of adjournal. (18c) *Scots law.* Rules of the High Court of Justiciary for regulating practice and procedure.

acts of assembly. See SESSION LAWS.

actual, *adj.* (14c) Existing in fact; real <actual malice>. Cf. CONSTRUCTIVE.

actual abandonment. See ABANDONMENT (11).

actual agency. See AGENCY (1).

actual allegiance. See ALLEGIANCE (1).

actual assent. See ASSENT.

actual authority. See AUTHORITY (1).

actual bailment. See BAILMENT (1).

actual bias. See BIAS.

actual capital. See CAPITAL.

actual cash value. See VALUE (2).

actual cause. See *but-for cause* under CAUSE (1).

actual change of possession. (18c) A real, rather than constructive, transfer of ownership. • A creditor of the transferor cannot reach property that has actually changed possession.

actual consumer confusion. See CONSUMER CONFUSION.

actual controversy. **1.** See CONTROVERSY (2). **2.** See CONTROVERSY (3).

actual damages. See DAMAGES.

actual delivery. See DELIVERY.

actual escape. See ESCAPE (2).

actual eviction. See EVICTION.

actual-evidence test. See BLOCKBURGER TEST.

actual force. See FORCE.

actual fraud. See FRAUD.

actual-injury trigger. (1993) *Insurance.* The point at which an insured suffers damage or injury (such as the time of an automobile accident), so that there is an occurrence invoking coverage under an insurance policy. — Also termed *injury-in-fact trigger.* Cf. EXPOSURE THEORY; MANIFESTATION THEORY; TRIPLE TRIGGER.

actual innocence. See INNOCENCE.

actuality. **1.** (*usu. pl.*) (16c) The realities or facts, as opposed to what people might believe or imagine. **2.** The quality, state, or condition of being real or truly existing.

actual knowledge. See KNOWLEDGE (1).

actual loss. See LOSS.

actually litigated. (1969) (Of a claim that might be barred by collateral estoppel) properly raised in an earlier lawsuit, submitted to the court for a determination, and determined. • A party is barred by the doctrine of collateral estoppel from relitigating an issue that was actually litigated — usu. including by summary judgment but not necessarily by default judgment — in an earlier suit involving the same parties, even if that suit involved different claims. Restatement (Second) of Judgments § 27 cmt. d (1980).

actual malice. See MALICE.

actual market value. See *fair market value* under VALUE (2).

actual notice. See NOTICE (3).

actual physical control. (1880) Direct bodily power over something, esp. a vehicle. • Many jurisdictions require a showing of "actual physical control" of a vehicle by a person charged with driving while intoxicated.

actual possession. See POSSESSION.

actual reduction to practice. See REDUCTION TO PRACTICE.

actual-risk test. (1964) The doctrine that, for an injured employee to be entitled to workers'-compensation benefits, the employee must prove that the injury arose from, and occurred in the course and scope of, employment.

actual seisin. See *seisin in deed* under SEISIN.

actual service. **1.** PERSONAL SERVICE (1). **2.** See SERVICE (7).

actual taking. See *physical taking* under TAKING (2).

actual total loss. See LOSS.

actual user confusion. See CONSUMER CONFUSION.

actual value. See *fair market value* under VALUE (2).

actuarial equivalent. (1920) The amount of accrued pension benefits to be paid monthly or at some other interval so that the total amount of benefits will be paid over the expected remaining lifetime of the recipient.

actuarially sound retirement system. (1947) A retirement plan that contains sufficient funds to pay future obligations, as by receiving contributions from employees and the employer to be invested in accounts to pay future benefits. Cf. NONACTUARIALLY SOUND RETIREMENT SYSTEM.

actuarial method. (1935) A means of determining the amount of interest on a loan by using the loan's annual percentage rate to separately calculate the finance charge for each payment period, after crediting each payment, which is credited first to interest and then to principal.

actuarial present value. (1939) The amount of money necessary to purchase an annuity that would generate a particular monthly payment, or whatever periodic payment the plan provides, for the expected remaining life span of the recipient.

actuarial surplus. (1976) An estimate of the amount by which a pension plan's assets exceed its expected current and future liabilities, including the amount expected to be needed to fund future benefit payments.

actuarial table. (1917) An organized chart of statistical data indicating life expectancies for people in various categories (such as age, family history, and chemical exposure). • Actuarial tables are usu. admissible in evidence. — Also termed *expectancy table*; *mortality table*; *mortuary table.* Cf. LIFE TABLE.

actuarial value. See VALUE (2).

actuarius (ak-choo-**air**-ee-əs *or* ak-tyoo-), *n.* [Latin] (16c) *Roman law.* **1.** A notary or clerk; a shorthand writer. **2.** A keeper of public records.

actuary (**ak**-choo-air-ee), *n.* (18c) A statistician who determines the present effects of future contingent events; esp., one who calculates insurance and pension rates on the basis of empirically based tables. — **actuarial** (ak-choo-**air**-ee-əl), *adj.*

actum (**ak**-təm), *n.* [Latin] A thing done; an act or deed.

actum et tractatum (**ak**-təm et trak-**tay**-təm). [Law Latin] *Hist.* (Of an instrument) done and transacted.

act under private signature. See ACT (4).

act under private signature duly acknowledged. See ACT (4).

actus (**ak**-təs), *n.* [Latin] **1.** An act or action; a thing done. **2.** *Hist.* An act of Parliament; esp., one passed by both houses but not yet approved by the monarch. Cf. STATUTUM (1). **3.** A road for passengers riding or driving; a public road or highway. **4.** *Roman law.* A servitude for driving cattle or a carriage across another's land. — Also termed (in sense 4) *jus actus*. Cf. ITER (1).

actus animi (**ak**-təs **an**-ə-mɪ). [Law Latin] (17c) *Hist.* An act of the mind; an intention. See ANIMUS.

> "Again, consent, which is essential to all contracts, is an *actus animi*, and is presumed in all cases where the contract is *ex facie* regular." John Trayner, *Trayner's Latin Maxims* 21–22 (4th ed. 1894).

actus jure imperii (**ak**-təs **joor**-ee im-**pair**-ee-ɪ) [Law Latin] (1974) *Hist.* An act done by right of authority.

actus legitimus (**ak**-təs lə-**jit**-ə-məs). [Law Latin] (1832) *Hist.* An act in the law; a juristic act; specif., an act the performance of which was accompanied by solemn rituals.

actus proximus (**ak**-təs **prok**-si-məs). [Law Latin] (17c) *Hist.* An immediate act, as distinguished from a preparatory act, esp. in the commission of a crime.

actus reus (**ak**-təs **ree**-əs *also* **ray**-əs). [Law Latin "guilty act"] (1902) **1.** The wrongful deed that comprises the physical components of a crime and that generally must be coupled with mens rea to establish criminal liability; a forbidden act <the actus reus for theft is the taking of or unlawful control over property without the owner's consent>. **2.** The voluntary act or omission, the attendant circumstances, and the social harm caused by a criminal act, all of which make up the physical components of a crime. — Also termed *deed of crime*; *overt act*. See CORPUS DELICTI; *voluntary act* under ACT (2). Cf. MENS REA; CULPABILITY.

> "One cannot formulate a test for the ingredients of an act, except the test of what is required by law for the external situation of a crime. Writers have often pointed out that there is generally no harm in a man's crooking his right forefinger, unless it is (for example) around the trigger of a loaded gun which is pointing at someone. The muscular contraction, regarded as an *actus reus*, cannot be separated from its circumstances. When the specification of a crime includes a number of circumstances, all of these are essential and all must be regarded as part of the *actus reus*. It will be shown later that any narrower view is undesirable because it creates greater uncertainty and also because it leads straight to haphazard strict responsibility in crime, enabling judges to pick and choose in different ways between elements of a crime for the purpose of the requirement of *mens rea*. The view that *actus reus* means *all* the external ingredients of the crime is not only the simplest and clearest but the one that gives the most satisfactory results." Glanville Williams, *Criminal Law: The General Part* 19 (2d ed. 1961).

> "The phrase 'deed of crime' [= *actus reus*] as so used does not indicate the crime itself but merely one of the ingredients of crime; and this ingredient may be present without any crime at all, just as hydrogen is one of the ingredients of water but may be present without water. The words 'deed of crime' are so suggesting of the crime itself, however, that perhaps the Latin phrase '*actus reus*' is less likely to cause confusion. The *actus reus* is essential to crime but is not sufficient for this purpose without the necessary mens rea, just as mens rea is essential to crime but is insufficient without the necessary *actus reus*." Rollin M. Perkins & Ronald N. Boyce, *Criminal Law* 831 (3d ed. 1982).

actus reus defense. See DEFENSE (1).

ACUS. *abbr.* ADMINISTRATIVE CONFERENCE OF THE UNITED STATES.

A.D. *abbr.* ANNO DOMINI.

ad (ad), *prep.* [Latin] At; by; for; near; on account of; to; until; upon; with relation to; concerning.

ADA. *abbr.* **1.** AMERICANS WITH DISABILITIES ACT. **2.** Assistant district attorney. **3.** ABNORMALLY DANGEROUS ACTIVITY. **4.** Anti-Dumping Agreement, esp. Art. VI of the General Agreement on Tariffs and Trade 1994.

ad abundantiorem cautelam (ad ab-ən-dan-shee-**or**-əm kaw-**tee**-ləm). [Law Latin] *Hist.* For more abundant caution. — Also termed *ad cautelam ex superabundanti* (ad kaw-**tee**-ləm eks s[y]oo-pər-ab-ən-**dan**-tɪ).

ad admittendum clericum (ad ad-mi-**ten**-dəm **kler**-ə-kəm). [Law Latin] See DE CLERICO ADMITTENDO.

adage (**ad**-ij), *n.* (16c) A pithy saying or sententious formulation; a familiar proverb or aphorism that neatly encapsulates a generalization about people or the world.

ad aliud examen (ad **ay**-lee-əd eg-**zay**-mən), *adv.* [Law Latin] To another tribunal. Cf. ALIUD EXAMEN.

ad alium diem (ad **ay**-lee-əm **dɪ**-əm), *adv.* [Law Latin] To another day.

adaptation, *n.* (16c) **1.** The act or process of fitting or suiting one thing or form to another; the process of adjusting oneself or some thing to new conditions <in his adaptation he changed the dialogue somewhat>. **2.** The quality, state, or condition of being suited or fitted <the perfect adaptation of means to ends>. **3.** The beneficial modification of a biological organism to changes in its environment <evolution is largely an accumulation of specific adaptations>. **4.** The gradual change in a sensory organ through prolonged or repeated stimulation. **5.** Loosely, a derivative work. See *derivative work* under WORK (2). — Also termed (erroneously in modern contexts) *adaption*.

adaptation right. (1965) *Copyright.* A copyright holder's exclusive right to prepare derivative works based on the protected work. 17 USCA § 106(2). • For example, before a movie studio can make a film version of a book, it must secure the author's adaptation right. See *derivative work* under WORK (2).

adaption. See ADAPTATION.

ad assisas capiendas (ad ə-**sɪz**-əs kap-ee-**en**-dəs). [Law Latin] To take assizes; to hold assizes.

a dato (ay **day**-toh), *adv.* [Law Latin] From the date. — Also termed *a datu*.

a datu. See A DATO.

ad auctoritatem praestandam (ad awk-tor-i-**tay**-təm pree-**stand**-dəm). [Law Latin] *Hist.* For interposing their authority. • The phrase typically referred to tutors or curators *ad litem* who provided authority but incurred no personal liability in exercising their office.

ad audiendam considerationem curiae (ad aw-dee-**en**-dəm kən-sid-ə-ray-shee-**oh**-nəm **kyoor**-ee-ɪ), *vb.* [Law Latin] To hear the judgment of the court.

ad audiendum et determinandum (ad aw-dee-**en**-dəm et di-tər-mi-**nan**-dəm), *vb.* [Law Latin] To hear and determine. See OYER AND TERMINER.

ad avisandum (ad a-vi-**zan**-dəm). [Law Latin] *Hist.* For deliberation; in order to deliberate.

ADB. *abbr.* ACCIDENTAL-DEATH BENEFIT.

ad barram (ad **bahr**-əm), *adv.* [Law Latin] To the bar; at the bar.

ad barram evocatus (ad **bahr**-əm ee-voh-**kay**-təs). [Law Latin] Called to the bar. See CALL TO THE BAR.

ad campi partem (ad **kam**-pɪ **pahr**-təm *or* -tem). [Law Latin] For a share of the field or land.

ad captandum lucrum (ad cap-**tan**-dəm **loo**-krəm). [Law Latin] *Hist.* For the purpose of making gain.

ad captum vulgi (ad **kap**-təm **vəl**-jɪ). [Law Latin] Adapted to the common understanding. • The phrase appeared in reference to statutes concerning matters that people usu. handled without legal assistance.

ad cautelam ex superabundanti. See AD ABUNDANTIOREM CAUTELAM.

ad civilem effectum (ad sə-**vɪ**-ləm e-**fek**-təm). [Law Latin] *Hist.* As to the civil effect. • The phrase appeared in reference to the effect of an act in a civil case, as distinguished from the effect of the same act in a criminal case.

***ad coelum* doctrine** (ad **kɪ**-ləm). (1919) The common-law rule that a landowner holds everything above and below the land, up to the sky and down to the earth's core, including all minerals. • This rule governs ownership of "hard" (immovable) minerals such as coal, but not "fugacious" (volatile) minerals such as oil and gas. Cf. RULE OF CAPTURE; A COELO USQUE AD CENTRUM; AD COELUM ET AD INFEROS.

ad coelum et ad inferos (ad **kɪ**-ləm et ad in-**fair**-ohs). [Law Latin] Up to the sky and down to the center of the earth <the ownership of land extends *ad coelum et ad inferos*>. Cf. A COELO USQUE AD CENTRUM.

ad colligenda bona. See AD COLLIGENDUM BONA DEFUNCTI.

ad colligendum (ad kol-i-**jen**-dəm). [Law Latin] For collecting <administrator *ad colligendum*>.

ad colligendum bona defuncti (ad kol-i-**jen**-dəm boh-nə di-**fəngk**-tɪ). [Law Latin "for collecting the goods of the deceased"] Special letters of administration authorizing a person to collect and preserve a decedent's property. — Often shortened to *ad colligendum bona.* — Also termed *ad colligenda bona (defuncti).*

ad communem legem (ad kə-**myoo**-nəm **lee**-jəm), *n.* [Law Latin "to common law"] *Hist.* A writ of entry available after the death of a life tenant to recover a reversionary interest in land alienated by the tenant. — Also termed *entry ad communem legem.*

ad commune nocumentum (ad kə-**myoo**-nee nok-yə-**men**-təm), *adv.* [Law Latin] To the common nuisance.

ad comparandum. See AD COMPARENDUM.

ad comparendum (ad kom-pə-**ren**-dəm), *vb.* [Law Latin] To appear. • This term is part of the larger phrase *ad comparendum, et ad standum juri* ("to appear and to stand to the law"). — Also termed (in standard Latin) *ad comparandum.*

ad computum reddendum (ad kəm-**pyoo**-təm ri-**den**-dəm), *vb.* [Law Latin] To render an account.

ad consimiles casus (ad kən-**sim**-ə-leez **kay**-səs). [Law Latin] *Hist.* To similar cases. See CASU CONSIMILI.

ad convincendam conscientiam judicis (ad kon-vin-**sen**-dəm kon-shee-**en**-shee-əm **joo**-di-sis). [Law Latin] *Scots law.* Sufficient to satisfy the moral conviction of the judge. • The phrase appeared in reference to circumstantial evidence that was admissible in paternity cases because direct proof was unavailable.

adcordabilis denarii (ad-kor-**day**-bə-lis di-**nair**-ee-ɪ), *n.* [Latin] *Hist.* Money paid by a vassal to the lord upon the sale or exchange of a feud.

ad culpam (ad **kəl**-pəm), *adv.* [Law Latin] Until misconduct.

ad curiam (ad **kyoor**-ee-əm), *adv.* [Law Latin] At a court; to court.

ad curiam vocare (ad **kyoor**-ee-əm voh-**kair**-ee), *vb.* [Law Latin] To summon to court.

ad custagia (ad kə-**stay**-jee-ə), *adv.* [Law Latin] At the costs.

ad custum (ad **kəs**-təm), *adv.* [Law Latin] At the cost.

add, *n. Parliamentary law.* A form of amendment that places new wording at the end of a motion or of a paragraph or other readily divisible part within a motion. See *amendment by adding* under AMENDMENT (3).

***ad damnum* clause** (ad **dam**-nəm). [Latin "to the damage"] (1840) A clause in a prayer for relief stating the amount of damages claimed. See PRAYER FOR RELIEF. Cf. DAMNUM.

> "Where the amount the plaintiff is entitled to recover appears from the statement of facts — as where the amount due the plaintiff is alleged on breach of a money demand, the demand of judgment may take the place of an *ad damnum* clause." Edwin E. Bryant, *The Law of Pleading Under the Codes of Civil Procedure* 209 (2d ed. 1899).

added damages. See *punitive damages* under DAMAGES.

ad defendendum (ad di-fen-**den**-dəm), *vb.* [Latin] To defend.

addendum (ə-**den**-dəm). (17c) Something to be added, usu. to a document; esp., a supplement to a speech, book, contract, or other document to alter its contents or give more information.

addicent (**ad**-i-sent), *adj.* (1880) *Roman law.* Someone who transfers something by official authority.

addicere (ə-**dis**-ər-ee), *vb.* [Latin] *Roman law.* To adjudge, allot, or condemn.

addict (**a**-dikt), *n.* (1899) Someone who is psychologically or physiologically dependent on a substance or activity; esp., one who cannot stop taking controlled substances. — **addict** (ə-**dikt**), *vb.* — **addictive,** *adj.* — **addiction,** *n.*

▸ **drug addict.** (1905) Someone who is psychologically or physiologically dependent on a narcotic drug.

addict, *vb.* (16c) *Roman law.* **1.** To adjudge (to); to deliver under court order. **2.** More broadly, to surrender a thing (to someone else).

addictio (ə-**dik**-shee-oh), *n.* [Latin] (17c) *Roman law.* The awarding by a magistrate of a person or thing to another, as the property of a debtor to a creditor, or as a form of conveyance. — Also termed *addiction.* Pl. ***addictiones*** (ə-dik-shee-**oh**-neez).

addictio in diem (ə-**dik**-shee-oh in **dɪ**-əm). [Latin "assignment for a fixed period" or "postponement to a date"] (17c) *Roman law.* A clause in a contract of sale in which the parties agree that the contract can be terminated if the seller receives a better offer within a specified period. — Also termed *in diem addictio.*

addiction. (17c) **1.** The habitual and intemperate use of a substance, esp. a potentially harmful one such as a narcotic drug; specif., the compulsive need to take a harmful substance — or a substance that becomes harmful in significant quantities — frequently and without the ability to stop on one's own. • The usual requisites are (1) an emotional dependence that leads to compulsiveness; (2) an enhanced tolerance of the substance, leading to more potent doses; and (3) physical dependence such that withdrawal symptoms result from deprivation. **2.** ADDICTIO.

addictive drug. See DRUG.

ad diem (ad **dI**-əm). [Latin] At a day; at the appointed day.

addition. (17c) **1.** A structure that is attached to or connected with another building that predates the structure; an extension or annex. • Although some courts have held that an addition is merely an appurtenant structure that might not actually be in physical contact with the other building, most courts hold that there must be physical contact. **2.** A title or appellation appended to a person's name to show rank, occupation, or place of residence. • In English law, there are traditionally four kinds of additions: (1) those of estate, such as yeoman, gentleman, or esquire; (2) those of degree (or dignity), such as knight, baron, earl, marquis, or duke; (3) those of trade or occupation, such as scrivener, painter, mason, or carpenter; and (4) those of place of residence, such as London, Bath, or Chester. It was formerly required by the statute of additions (1 Hen. 5, ch. 5) that original writs and indictments state a person's addition, but the practice has long since been abolished.

additional claims after allowance. (1967) *Patents.* Claims submitted for the first time by amendment after the U.S. Patent and Trademark Office has informed the applicant of the patent application's allowance. • Once a notice of allowance has been issued, the applicant may not by right submit additional claims. But in some circumstances, such as when the applicant seeks to add only dependent claims, the supervisory examiner has authority to enter an amendment containing additional claims after allowance but on or before the date when the issue fee is paid. See *amendment after allowance* under PATENT-APPLICATION AMENDMENT.

additional-consideration rule. (1951) *Employment law.* An exception to the employment-at-will principle, whereby an employee who does not have a written contract but who undertakes substantial hardship in addition to the normal job duties — as by relocating to a different city based on oral assurances of job security — can maintain a breach-of-contract claim if the employer does not fulfill its agreement.

additional damages. See DAMAGES.

additional direction. See *additional instruction* under JURY INSTRUCTION.

additional extended coverage. (1957) *Insurance.* A policy endorsement providing supplemental residential coverage for a variety of perils, including vandalism, damage from falling trees, and water damage from the plumbing system.

additional grand jury. See *special grand jury* under GRAND JURY.

additional instruction. See JURY INSTRUCTION.

additional insurance. See INSURANCE.

additional insured. See INSURED.

additional legacy. See LEGACY (1).

additional-perils clause. See INCHMAREE CLAUSE.

additional servitude. See SERVITUDE (3).

additional standard deduction. See DEDUCTION (2).

additional tax. See *stopgap tax* under TAX.

additional term. See TERM (5).

additional work. See WORK (1).

additur (**ad**-ə-tuur). [Latin "it is added to"] (1894) A trial court's order, issued usu. with the defendant's consent, that increases the jury's award of damages to avoid a new trial on grounds of inadequate damages. • The term may also refer to the increase itself, the procedure, or the court's power to make the order. — Also termed *increscitur.* Cf. REMITTITUR.

add-on clause. (1965) An installment-contract provision that converts earlier purchases into security for new purchases.

addone (ə-**doh**-nee), *p.pl.* [Law French] Given to. — Also spelled *addonne.*

add-on interest. See INTEREST (3).

add-on loan. See LOAN.

address, *n.* (17c) **1.** The place where mail or other communication is sent. **2.** In some states, a legislature's formal request to the executive to do a particular thing, such as to remove a judge from office. **3.** *Equity practice.* The part of a bill in which the court is identified. See DIRECTION (5).

addressee. (18c) A person to whom a letter, parcel, etc. is addressed.

addresser. (17c) *Hist. English law.* A petitioner.

address for service. (1841) The place where legal process can be served on a litigant or other person; esp., the place designated by a party or a corporation for the receipt of pleadings, other court papers, and notices. — Also termed (more fully) *address for service of process.*

address for service of process. See ADDRESS FOR SERVICE.

address to the court. (17c) A lawyer's speech made to a judge or panel of judges. • If in trial court, this speech might be an opening or closing statement to a judge and jury. Cf. ORAL ARGUMENT.

address to the Crown. Upon a reading of a royal speech in Parliament, the ceremonial resolution by Parliament expressing thanks to the sovereign for the gracious speech. • Formerly, two members were selected in each house for moving and seconding the address. With the commencement of the 1890–1891 session, a single resolution was adopted.

adduce (ə-**d[y]oos**), *vb.* (15c) To offer or put forward for consideration (something) as evidence or authority <adduce the engineer's expert testimony>. — **adduction** (ə-**dək**-shən), *n.* — **adducible** (ə-**d[y]oo**-sə-bəl), *adj.*

ADEA. *abbr.* AGE DISCRIMINATION IN EMPLOYMENT ACT.

adeem, *vb.* (1845) To revoke or satisfy (a willed gift) by some other gift.

ad effectum (ad i-**fek**-təm). [Law Latin] To the effect.

ad effectum sequentem (ad i-**fek**-təm si-**kwen**-təm). [Law Latin] To the effect following.

ademptio (ə-**demp**-shee-oh), *n.* [Latin] *Roman law.* ADEMPTION. • The term referred to the revocation of a legacy under certain circumstances, as when the item bequeathed no longer existed or when the testator no longer owned the item. The ablative form *ademptione* means "by ademption." Pl. ***ademptiones*** (ə-demp-shee-**oh**-neez).

ademption (ə-**demp**-shən), *n.* (16c) *Wills & estates.* The destruction or extinction of a testamentary gift by reason of a bequeathed asset's ceasing to be part of the estate at the time of the testator's death; a beneficiary's forfeiture of a legacy or bequest that is no longer operative. • There are two theories of ademption. Under the *identity theory of ademption,* a devise of a specific piece of property will fail if that property is not a part of the testator's estate upon his or her death. Under the *intent theory of ademption,* by contrast, when a specific devise is no longer in the testator's estate at the time of his or her death, the devisee will receive a gift of equal value if it can be proved that the testator did not intend the gift to be adeemed. The intent theory has been codified in § 2-606 of the 1990 Uniform Probate Code. — Also termed *extinguishment of legacy.* Cf. ABATEMENT (4); ADVANCEMENT (1); LAPSE (2). — **adeem** (ə-**deem**), *vb.* — **adeemed, adempted,** *adj.*

▸ **ademption by extinction.** (1847) An ademption that occurs because the unique property that is the subject of a specific bequest has been sold, given away, or destroyed, or is not otherwise in existence at the time of the testator's death.

▸ **ademption by satisfaction.** (1916) An ademption that occurs because the testator, while alive, has already given property to the beneficiary in lieu of the testamentary gift.

adeo (**ad**-ee-oh). [Latin] So; as.

adequacy of consideration. (1802) The fairness and reasonableness of the value given for the performance of an enforceable promise. See *adequate consideration* under CONSIDERATION (1).

adequacy of disclosure. (1918) *Patents.* Satisfaction of the statutory requirements that the specification in a patent application (1) gives enough detailed information to enable one skilled in the art to make and use the claimed invention (the enablement requirement), (2) discloses the best way the inventor knows to make and use the invention (the best-mode requirement), and (3) shows that the inventor was in full possession of the claimed invention on the application's filing date (the written-description requirement). • A patent that fails to meet any one of these requirements may be rejected under 35 USCA § 112. Any issued patent with an inadequate disclosure is invalid, although the challenger has to overcome the presumption of validity. — Also termed *sufficiency of disclosure.* See ENABLEMENT REQUIREMENT; BEST-MODE REQUIREMENT.

adequacy test. See IRREPARABLE-INJURY RULE.

adequate, *adj.* (17c) Legally sufficient <adequate notice>.

adequate assurance. See ASSURANCE.

adequate care. See *reasonable care* under CARE (2).

adequate cause. See *adequate provocation* under PROVOCATION.

adequate compensation. See *just compensation* under COMPENSATION.

adequate consideration. See CONSIDERATION (1).

adequate indicia of reliability, *n.* (1973) *Constitutional law.* Sufficient indicators of trustworthiness, the requirement being that statements introduced at trial by a declarant who is unavailable must either fall within a firmly rooted hearsay exception or be supported by a showing of specific guarantees of veracity and accuracy, which can be shown by the totality of the circumstances. *See Idaho v. Wright,* 497 U.S. 805, 814, 110 S.Ct. 3139, 3146 (1990).

adequate notice. See *due notice* under NOTICE (3).

adequate protection. (1981) *Bankruptcy.* Consideration that a debtor provides to secured creditors to protect them from the deteriorating condition or diminishing value of their collateral during the pendency of the bankruptcy. • The consideration, which can be in any form, is most commonly an additional payment, additional lien, or replacement lien.

> "Bankruptcy intends to safeguard secured creditors' encumbrances, but the stay threatens them by preventing the secured creditors from foreclosing or taking other actions to apply the property's value against the secured debt. Bankruptcy aims to guard against this threat by ordering relief . . . for lack of adequate protection of the secured interest." David G. Epstein et al., *Bankruptcy* § 3-27, at 140 (1993).

adequate provocation. See PROVOCATION.

adequate remedy at law. See REMEDY.

adequate representation. See REPRESENTATION (3).

adequate-state-grounds doctrine. (1962) A judge-made principle that prevents the U.S. Supreme Court from reviewing a state-court decision based partially on state law if a decision on a federal issue would not change the result.

adequate warning. See WARNING.

adesse (ad-**es**-ee), *vb. Civil law.* To be present. Cf. ABESSE.

adeu (ə-**dyoo**), *adv.* [Law French] Without day. • This is a common term in the Year Books, indicating a final dismissal from court (*alez adeu* "go hence without day"). See GO HENCE WITHOUT DAY; ALLER SANS JOUR.

ad eundem gradum (ad ee-**yən**-dəm **grad**-əm). [Latin] (17c) To the same degree. • This phrase is traditionally used in reference to the privileges of a university graduate. — Often shortened to *ad eundem.*

ad eversionem juris nostri (ad i-vər-shee-**oh**-nəm **joor**-is **nos**-trɪ). [Law Latin] To the overthrow of our right.

ad excambium (ad eks-**kam**-bee-əm). [Law Latin] For exchange; for compensation.

ad exhaeredationem (ad eks-heer-ə-day-shee-**oh**-nəm). [Law Latin] To the disinheritance; to the injury of the inheritance.

> "The writ of waste calls upon the tenant to appear and shew cause why he hath committed waste and destruction in the place named, *ad exhaeredationem,* to the disinherison of the plaintiff." 3 William Blackstone, *Commentaries on the Laws of England* 228 (1768).

ad exitum (ad **ek**-si-təm). [Law Latin] At issue; at the end (usu. of pleadings).

ADF. *abbr.* AFRICAN DEVELOPMENT FOUNDATION.

ad faciendam juratam illam (ad fay-shee-**en**-dəm jə-**ray**-təm **il**-əm). [Law Latin] To make up that jury.

ad faciendum (ad fay-shee-**en**-dəm). [Latin] To do; to make.

ad factum praestandum (ad **fak**-təm pree-**stand**-dəm). [Law Latin "for the performance of a particular act"] *Scots law.* An obligation to perform an act other than paying money; an obligation that must be strictly fulfilled (such as to hand over a vase sold).

> "In popular language almost all obligations may be said to be of this class, but there are obligations of a peculiar character which alone are denoted by the legal signification of this phrase. The obligation of a debtor is clearly one for the performance of a certain act, namely, the payment of his debt; but a decree at the instance of his creditor would not be termed a decree *ad factum praestandum*. An obligation *ad factum praestandum* is one for the performance of an act within the power of the obligant . . . ." John Trayner, *Trayner's Latin Maxims* 27 (4th ed. 1894).

ad feodi firmam (ad **fee**-ə-dɪ **fər**-məm). [Law Latin] To fee farm. See FEE FARM.

ad fidem (ad **fɪ**-dəm), *adv.* [Law Latin] In allegiance; under allegiance; owing allegiance. • This term appeared in a variety of phrases, including *ad fidem regis* ("under the king's allegiance") and *natus ad fidem regis* ("born in allegiance to the king").

ad filum aquae (ad **fɪ**-ləm **ak**-wee), *adv.* [Law Latin] To the thread of the water; to the central line or middle of a stream. • This refers to the ownership reach of a riparian proprietor. — Also termed *ad medium filum aquae.*

ad filum viae (ad **fɪ**-ləm **vɪ**-ee), *adv.* [Law Latin] To the middle of the way; to the central line of the road. — Also termed *ad medium filum viae.*

ad finem (ad **fɪ**-nəm), *adv.* [Latin] To the end. • This citation signal, abbreviated in text *ad fin.*, formerly provided only the first page of the section referred to, but now usu. directs the reader to a stated span of pages.

adfinis (ad-**fɪn**-is), *n.* [Latin] *Roman law.* A relative of one's spouse. Pl. ***adfines*** (ad-**fɪ**-neez).

adfinitas (ad-**fin**-i-tas), *n.* [Latin] *Roman law.* The connection between a husband or wife and relatives of his or her spouse.

ad firmam tradidi (ad **fər**-məm tray-də-dɪ), *n.* [Law Latin] See FARM LET.

ad fundandam jurisdictionem (ad fən-**dan**-dəm joor-is-dik-shee-**oh**-nəm). [Law Latin] *Hist.* For the purpose of founding jurisdiction. See ARRESTUM JURISDICTIONIS FUNDANDAE CAUSA.

ad gaolam deliberandam (ad **jay**-ləm di-lib-ə-**ran**-dəm), *vb.* [Law Latin] To deliver the jail; to make jail delivery. See COMMISSION OF GAOL DELIVERY; JAIL DELIVERY.

ad gravamen (ad grə-**vay**-mən), *adv.* [Latin] To the grievance, injury, or oppression of (another person).

adhere, *vb.* **1.** (Of one house in a bicameral legislature) to reject the other house's insistence on a difference in legislation that has passed both houses, without requesting a conference. Cf. INSIST.

> "When both houses have insisted [on differing views about an amendment] without a request for conference, it is also in order to move to adhere. Adoption of a motion to adhere represents an unyielding attitude of the adopting house. It is unparliamentary for an adhering house to request a conference; however, the other house may continue to insist and request a conference. It is in order for an adhering house to recede from its adherence and agree to a conference." National Conference of State Legislatures, *Mason's Manual of Legislative Procedure* § 768, at 556–57 (2000).

2. *Scots law.* To live together as husband and wife. **3.** *Scots law.* (Of an appellate court) to affirm a lower court's judgment. — **adherence,** *n.*

adherence. (17c) **1.** ACCESSION (3). **2.** *Scots law.* The duty of spouses to live together. **3.** Behavior that accords with a particular rule, belief, principle, etc. <adherence to democratic principles>.

adherent, *n.* (15c) **1.** Someone who is attached or devoted to a person, party, or principle; a devotee; someone who supports a particular belief, plan, principle, etc. **2.** *Rare.* An appendage.

adhesion. See ACCESSION (3).

adhesionary contract. See *adhesion contract* under CONTRACT.

adhesion contract. See CONTRACT.

adhesive contract. See *adhesion contract* under CONTRACT.

adhesory contract. See *adhesion contract* under CONTRACT.

adhibere (ad-hə-**bair**-ee), *vb.* [Latin] *Civil law.* To apply; to put (a thing) to use; to exercise.

adhibere diligentiam (ad-hə-**bair**-ee dil-ə-**jen**-shee-əm), *vb.* [Latin] *Civil law.* To use care.

ad hoc (ad **hok**), *adj.* [Latin "for this"] (17c) Formed for a particular purpose <the board created an ad hoc committee to discuss funding for the new arena>. — **ad hoc,** *adv.*

ad hoc arbitration. See ARBITRATION.

ad hoc committee. See *special committee* under COMMITTEE (1).

ad hoc compromis. See COMPROMIS (1).

ad hominem (ad **hom**-ə-nəm), *adj.* [Latin "to the person"] (16c) Appealing to personal prejudices rather than to reason; attacking an opponent's character, esp. in lieu of a rational response to the opponent's stand or statement <the brief was replete with ad hominem attacks against opposing counsel>. — **ad hominem,** *adv.*

ad hunc diem (ad **həngk dɪ**-əm), *adv.* [Law Latin] To this day.

adiate (**ad**-ee-ayt), *vb.* (1845) *Roman–Dutch law.* To accept as beneficiary under a will. — **adiation,** *n.*

ad idem (ad **ɪ**-dəm). [Latin] To the same point or matter; of the same mind <the parties reached a consensus *ad idem* and agreed to consummate a sale>.

a die confectionis (ay **dɪ**-ee kən-fek-shee-**oh**-nis), *adv.* [Law Latin] From the day of the making.

a die datus (ay **dɪ**-ee **day**-təs), *n.* [Latin "given from (such-and-such) a day"] A lease provision establishing the beginning of the rental period.

adieu (ə-**dyoo**). [Law French "to God"] (14c) Farewell. • This term, although etymologically distinct, appears sometimes in the Year Books in place of *adeu.* See ADEU; ALLER A DIEU.

ad ignorantiam. See *argumentum ad ignorantiam* under ARGUMENTUM.

ad inde (ad **in**-dee), *adv.* [Law Latin] To that or them; thereto.

ad inferos. [Law Latin] To the center of the earth. See AD COELUM ET AD INFEROS.

ad infinitum (ad in-fə-**nɪ**-təm). [Latin "without limit"] (17c) To an indefinite extent <a corporation has a duration *ad infinitum* unless the articles of incorporation specify a shorter period>.

ad informandum judicem (ad in-for-**man**-dəm **joo**-di-səm). [Law Latin] *Hist.* For the judge's information. — Also termed *ad informationem judicis.*

ad informationem judicis. See AD INFORMANDUM JUDICEM.

ad inquirendum (ad in-kwə-**ren**-dəm), *n.* [Law Latin "to inquire"] *Hist.* A writ instructing the recipient to investigate something at issue in a pending case.

ad instantiam partis (ad in-**stan**-shee-əm **pahr**-tis), *adv.* [Law Latin] *Hist.* At the instance of a party.

ad interim (ad **in**-tər-im), *adv.* [Latin] *Hist.* In the meantime; temporarily.

ad interim copyright. See COPYRIGHT.

adiratus (ad-ə-**ray**-təs), *adj.* [Law Latin] *Hist.* Lost; strayed; removed.

aditio (ə-**dish**-ee-oh), *n. Hist.* An outsider's informal acceptance of heirship.

aditio hereditatis (ə-**dish**-ee-oh hə-red-i-**tay**-tis). [Latin "entering on an inheritance"] *Roman law.* An heir's acceptance of an inheritance. — Also spelled *aditio haereditatis.* See CRETION.

adjacent, *adj.* (15c) Lying near or close to, but not necessarily touching. Cf. ADJOINING.

adject (a-**jekt**), *vb.* (15c) To annex or adjoin. — **adject,** *adj.*

adjectio dominii per continuationem possessionis (ə-**jek**-shee-oh də-**min**-ee-ɪ pər kən-tin-yoo-ay-shee-**oh**-nəm pə-zes[h]-ee-**oh**-nis). [Latin] *Roman law.* The acquisition of the right to property ownership by continued possession. • This acquisition is otherwise known as *usucapio* or *acquisitive prescription.* See USUCAPIO; *acquisitive prescription* under PRESCRIPTION.

adjectival law. See ADJECTIVE LAW.

adjective law (**aj**-ik-tiv). (1808) The body of rules governing procedure and practice; PROCEDURAL LAW. — Also termed *adjectival law.*

> "The body of law in a State consists of two parts, *substantive* and *adjective* law. The former prescribes those rules of civil conduct which declare the rights and duties of all who are subject to the law. The latter relates to the remedial agencies and procedure by which rights are maintained, their invasion redressed, and the methods by which such results are accomplished in judicial tribunals." Edwin E. Bryant, *The Law of Pleading Under the Codes of Civil Procedure* 1 (2d ed. 1899).

adjoiner. See *adjoining owner* under OWNER.

adjoining (ə-**joyn**-ing), *adj.* (15c) Touching; sharing a common boundary; CONTIGUOUS. Cf. ADJACENT. — **adjoin** (ə-**joyn**), *vb.*

adjoining owner. See OWNER.

adjourn (ə-**jərn**), *vb.* (15c) *Parliamentary law.* To end or postpone (a proceeding). Cf. RECESS (2).

> "A motion to recess *suspends* the current meeting until a later time; the unqualified motion to adjourn *terminates* the meeting. When an assembly reconvenes following a recess, it resumes the meeting at the point where it was interrupted by the motion to recess. When an assembly reconvenes following an adjournment, it begins an entirely new meeting, starting with the first step in the regular order of business." Alice Sturgis, *The Standard Code of Parliamentary Procedure* 76 (4th ed. 2001).

▸ **adjourn sine die** (**sɪ**-nee [or **sin**-ay] **dɪ**-ee). [Latin "without date"] (17c) To end a deliberative assembly's or court's session without setting a time to reconvene. — Also termed *adjourn without day.* See SINE DIE. Cf. RISE (4).

▸ **adjourn to a day certain.** (18c) To end a deliberative assembly's or court's session while fixing a time for the next meeting. — Also termed *adjourn to a day and time certain; fix a day to which to adjourn.*

> "When a meeting adjourns without ending the session, this necessarily means that the time for another meeting to continue the same business or order of business has already been set (or that provision has been made for such a meeting to be held 'at the call of the chair'). The time or provision for this next meeting of the session may have been established by one of the following methods . . . : (a) through a program adopted at the beginning of a convention; (b) by the adoption in the present meeting of a motion . . . to fix the time to which to adjourn; or (c) by a specification in the motion to adjourn . . . ." Henry M. Robert, *Robert's Rules of Order Newly Revised* § 8, at 85–86 (11th ed. 2011).

▸ **adjourn without day.** See *adjourn sine die.*

adjournatur (aj-ər-**nay**-tər). [Latin] (17c) It is adjourned. • This word formerly appeared at the end of reported decisions.

adjourned. See STAND ADJOURNED.

adjourned meeting. See MEETING.

adjourned summons. See SUMMONS.

adjourned term. See TERM (5).

adjournment (ə-**jərn**-mənt), *n.* (17c) **1.** The act of adjourning; specif., a putting off of a court session or other meeting or assembly until a later time or an ending of it altogether. See ADJOURN.

▸ **adjournment sine die** (ə-**jərn**-mənt **sɪ**-nee [or **sin**-ay] **dɪ**-ee). (17c) The ending of a deliberative assembly's or court's session without setting a time to reconvene. — Also termed *adjournment without day.*

> "The term *adjournment sine die* (or *adjournment without day*) usually refers to the close of a session of several meetings: (a) where the adjournment dissolves the assembly — as in a series of mass meetings or in an annual or biennial convention for which the delegates are separately chosen for each convention; or (b) where, unless called into special session, the body will not be convened again until a time prescribed by the bylaws or constitution — as in the case of a session of a legislature." Henry M. Robert, *Robert's Rules of Order Newly Revised* § 8, at 81 (10th ed. 2000).

▸ **adjournment without day.** See *adjournment sine die.*

▸ **conditional adjournment.** (18c) An adjournment that does not schedule another meeting, but provides for reconvening the assembly at an officer's or board's call or under other defined circumstances.

2. The period or interval between adjourning and reconvening. **3.** A meeting held as a continued part of the same session as the preceding meeting of the same body; an adjourned meeting. • The latter meeting is said to be an adjournment of the earlier one. — See *adjourned meeting, continued meeting* under MEETING; *adjourn to a day certain* under ADJOURN.

adjournment day. See DAY.

adjournment day in error. See DAY.

adjournment in contemplation of dismissal. (1970) *Criminal procedure.* A usu. probationary disposition of a case that the prosecution is willing to stop prosecuting, while the defendant is willing to forgo a trial, often with further orders in place, such as a restitution order, an order of protection, or mandatory community service. • If the terms of the probation are satisfied, the charge may be dismissed and the record sealed — no further court appearance being necessary.

adjournment sine die. See ADJOURNMENT (1).

adjournment without day. See *adjournment sine die* under ADJOURNMENT (1).

adjourn sine die. See ADJOURN.

adjourn to a day and time certain. See *adjourn to a day certain* under ADJOURN.

adjourn to a day certain. See ADJOURN.

adjourn without day. See *adjourn sine die* under ADJOURN.

adjudge (ə-**jəj**), *vb.* (14c) **1.** ADJUDICATE (1). **2.** To deem or pronounce to be. **3.** To award judicially. Cf. ABJUDGE. **4.** *Scots law.* (Of a creditor) to take a debtor's estate through adjudication. See ADJUDICATION (3). **5.** To award (some or all of a debtor's estate) to a creditor.

adjudger, *n.* (1833) **1.** Someone who adjudges. **2.** *Scots law.* An adjudging creditor.

adjudicataire (ə-joo-di-kə-**tair**), *n. Canadian law.* Someone who buys property at a judicial sale.

adjudicate (ə-**joo**-di-kayt), *vb.* (17c) **1.** To rule on judicially. **2.** ADJUDGE (2). **3.** ADJUDGE (3). — Also termed *judicate.*

adjudicatee (ə-joo-di-kə-**tee**). (1859) *Civil law.* A purchaser at a judicial sale.

adjudicated water right. See WATER RIGHT.

adjudicatio. *Roman law.* A part of a formula in a partition action by which the judge assigned the parties real rights in their shares; specif., a part of a formula (i.e., the praetor's statement of an issue for a judex) directing the judex to apportion property in a divisory action. • *Adjudicatio* was used to apportion property in divisory actions such as *actio de communi dividundo, actio familiae erciscundae,* and *actio finium regundorum.* It was not part of the formula in any other type of action. See FORMULA (1).

adjudication (ə-joo-di-**kay**-shən), *n.* (17c) **1.** The legal process of resolving a dispute; the process of judicially deciding a case. **2.** JUDGMENT (2).

> "Adjudication is the effort to identify the rights of the contending parties *now* by identifying what were, in law, the rights and wrongs, or validity or invalidity, of their actions and transactions *when entered upon and done.*" John Finnis, *Philosophy of Law* 399 (2011).

▸ **former adjudication.** See FORMER ADJUDICATION.

3. *Scots law.* The Court of Session's transfer of heritable property to a creditor as security for or in satisfaction of a debt, or its vesting title in an entitled claimant.

adjudication hearing. See HEARING.

adjudication withheld. See DEFERRED PROSECUTION.

adjudicative (ə-**joo**-di-kə-tiv), *adj.* (1848) **1.** Of, relating to, or involving adjudication. **2.** Having the ability to judge. — Also termed *adjudicatory; judicative.*

adjudicative-claims arbitration. See ARBITRATION.

adjudicative fact. See FACT.

adjudicative law. See CASELAW.

adjudicator (ə-**joo**-di-kay-tər). (1835) A person whose job is to render binding decisions; one who makes judicial pronouncements.

adjudicatory. See ADJUDICATIVE.

adjudicatory hearing. See *adjudication hearing* under HEARING.

adjudicatory jurisdiction. See JURISDICTION (2).

adjudicatory proceeding. See *adjudication hearing* under HEARING.

ad judicium provocare (ad joo-**dish**-ee-əm proh-və-**kair**-ee), *vb.* [Latin] To summon to court; to commence an action.

adjunct (**aj**-əngkt), *adj.* (16c) Added as an accompanying object or circumstance; attached in a subordinate or temporary capacity <an adjunct professor>. — **adjunct,** *n.*

adjunct account. See ACCOUNT.

adjunction (ə-**jəngk**-shən). (17c) **1.** The act of adding to. **2.** *Civil law.* The union of an item of personal property owned by one person with that owned by another. See ACCESSION (4).

adjunctum accessorium (ə-**jəngk**-təm ak-sə-**sor**-ee-əm), *n.* [Law Latin] An accessory or appurtenance.

ad jungendum auxilium (ad jən-**jen**-dəm awg-**zil**-ee-əm), *vb.* [Law Latin] To join in aid.

ad jura regis (ad **joor**-ə **ree**-jis), *n.* [Law Latin "for the rights of the king"] *Hist.* A writ brought against a person seeking to eject the holder of a royal benefice. • The writ was available to the holder of the benefice.

adjuration (aj-ə-**ray**-shən), *n.* (14c) **1.** The act of solemnly charging or entreating. **2.** A swearing; a solemn oath.

adjure (ə-**joor**), *vb.* (14c) To charge or entreat solemnly <the President adjured the foreign government to join the alliance>. — **adjuration** (aj-ə-**ray**-shən), *n.* — **adjuratory** (ə-**joor**-ə-tor-ee), *adj.* — **adjurer, adjuror** (ə-**joor**-ər), *n.*

adjust, *vb.* (18c) **1.** To determine the amount that an insurer will pay an insured to cover a loss. **2.** To arrive at a new agreement with a creditor for the payment of a debt.

adjustable-rate mortgage. See MORTGAGE.

adjustable-rate preferred stock. See STOCK.

adjusted basis. See BASIS.

adjusted book value. See BOOK VALUE.

adjusted cost basis. See BASIS.

adjusted gross estate. See ESTATE (3).

adjusted gross income. See INCOME.

adjusted interrogatory. See INTERROGATORY.

adjusted ordinary gross income. See INCOME.

adjusted present value. See PRESENT VALUE.

adjuster. (17c) One appointed to ascertain, arrange, or settle a matter; esp., an independent agent or employee of an insurance company who investigates claimed losses, and negotiates and settles claims against the insurer. — Also termed *claims adjuster; insurance adjuster;* (BrE) *loss adjuster.* Cf. LOSS ASSESSOR.

▸ **average adjuster.** (1846) *Maritime law.* An adjuster who determines the proportionate value of sacrificed cargo as a percentage of the total value of the ship, cargo, and freight, and who allocates contribution among the owners of the surviving properties. See CONTRIBUTION (8).

"The mutual contributions are settled by the 'statements' of persons called *average adjusters*, who are not truly arbitrators or umpires between the parties, but who can, by their impartiality, command so high a degree of respect for their 'statements,' that they are likely to be accepted by the parties; unless indeed there should arise an important question of principle calling for judicial determination." 2 *Stephen's Commentaries on the Laws of England* 247 (L. Crispin Warmington ed., 21st ed. 1950).

▸ **independent adjuster.** (1886) An adjuster who solicits business from more than one insurance company; one who is not employed by, and does not work exclusively for, one insurance company.

adjusting entry. (1922) An accounting entry made at the end of an accounting period to record previously unrecognized revenue and expenses, as well as changes in assets and liabilities.

adjustment, *n.* (17c) **1.** The act of adapting or conforming to a particular use; orderly regulation or arrangement. **2.** That which adapts one thing to another or to a particular use. **3.** The act of settling or arranging, as a dispute or other difference; SETTLEMENT (3). **4.** An amount added or deducted based on settlement. **5.** *Marine insurance.* The act of ascertaining the amount of indemnity that an insured is entitled to receive under an insurance policy after all proper allowances and deductions have been made, and the settling of the portion of indemnity for which each underwriter is liable. **6.** *Juvenile delinquency.* An informal consensual resolution of a case under the auspices of probation services.

adjustment board. (1925) An administrative agency charged with hearing and deciding zoning appeals. — Also termed *board of adjustment*; *board of zoning appeals.*

adjustment bond. See BOND (3).

adjustment of status. (1952) *Immigration law.* The changing of an alien's classification from nonimmigrant or parolee (temporary) resident to immigrant (permanent) resident. • This is a technical term used in United States immigration filings. Cf. 245(I) WAIVER.

adjustment security. See SECURITY (4).

adjutant general (**aj**-ə-tənt), *n.* (*usu. cap.*) (17c) **1.** The administrative head of a military unit having a general staff. **2.** An officer in charge of the National Guard of a state.

ad largum (ad **lahr**-gəm), *adj.* [Law Latin] At large; at liberty; unconfined.

adlegiare (ad-lee-jee-**air**-ee), *vb.* [Law Latin] To purge (oneself) of a crime by oath. See PURGATION.

ad levandam conscientiam (ad lə-**van**-dəm kon-shee-**en**-shee-əm). [Law Latin] *Scots law.* For the purpose of easing the conscience. • The phrase typically described certain confessions that a criminal suspect voluntarily made when apprehended and that could be used as evidence in the criminal trial. But an arrested suspect's responses to questions posed by the arresting officer were usu. not admissible because only a magistrate could ask such questions.

ad libellum rescribere (ad lə-**bel**-əm ri-**skrɪ**-bə-ree), *vb.* [Latin] *Roman law.* To write an answer to a petition, esp. one to the emperor. See RESCRIPT (3).

ad libitum (ad **lib**-i-təm), *adv.* [Law Latin] (17c) At pleasure. • The modern term *ad-lib* (adj. & vb.), borrowed from drama and music, is essentially the same; it means "at the performer's pleasure," and allows the performer discretion in innovating a part impromptu.

"[B]ut in actions where the damages are precarious, being to be assessed *ad libitum* by a jury, as in actions for words, ejectment, or trespass, it is very seldom possible for a plaintiff to swear to the amount of his cause of action; and therefore no special bail is taken thereon . . . ." 3 William Blackstone, *Commentaries on the Laws of England* 292 (1768).

ad litem (ad **lɪ**-tem *or* -təm). [Latin "for the suit"] (18c) For the purposes of the suit; pending the suit. See *guardian ad litem* under GUARDIAN (1); *attorney ad litem* under ATTORNEY.

ad longum (ad **long**-gəm). [Law Latin] *Hist.* At length.

ad lucrandum vel perdendum (ad loo-**kran**-dəm vel pər-**den**-dəm), *adv.* [Law Latin] For gain or loss. • These were emphatic words in a warrant of attorney. It is sometimes expressed "to lose and gain." See WARRANT OF ATTORNEY.

ad majorem cautelam (ad mə-**jor**-əm kaw-**tee**-ləm), *adv.* [Law Latin] For greater security.

admanuensis (ad-man-yoo-**en**-sis), *n.* [Law Latin fr. Latin *ad-* + *manus* "a hand"] (18c) *Hist.* An oath-taker who places a hand on the Bible. Cf. AMANUENSIS.

ad manum (ad **may**-nəm), *adj.* [Latin] At hand; ready for use.

admeasurement (ad-**mezh**-ər-mənt), *n.* (16c) **1.** Ascertainment, assignment, or apportionment by a fixed quantity or value, or by certain limits <the ship's admeasurement is based on its crew, engine, and capacity>. **2.** A writ obtained for purposes of ascertaining, assigning, or apportioning a fixed quantity or value or to establish limits; esp., a writ available against persons who usurp more than their rightful share of property. — **admeasure** (ad-**mezh**-ər), *vb.*

▸ **admeasurement of dower.** (17c) *Hist.* A writ available to an heir (or the heir's guardian if the heir is an infant) to reduce the dower of the ancestor's widow who, while the heir was an infant, was assigned more dower than she was entitled to. — Also termed *admensuratione dotis.*

"If the heir or his guardian do not assign her dower within the term of quarantine, or do assign it unfairly, she has her remedy at law, and the sheriff is appointed to assign it. Or if the heir (being under age) or his guardian assign more than she ought to have, it may be afterwards remedied by writ of *admeasurement* of dower." 2 William Blackstone, *Commentaries on the Laws of England* 136 (1766).

▸ **admeasurement of pasture.** (17c) *Hist.* A writ against a person whose cattle have overgrazed a common pasture.

ad medium filum aquae. See AD FILUM AQUAE.

ad medium filum viae. See AD FILUM VIAE.

ad melius inquirendum (ad **mee**-lee-əs in-kwə-**ren**-dəm), *n.* [Law Latin "for making better inquiry"] (16c) *Hist.* A writ commanding a coroner to hold a second inquest.

admensuratio (ad-men-shə-**ray**-shee-oh), *n.* [Law Latin] (17c) *Hist.* Admeasurement. See ADMEASUREMENT.

admensuratione dotis. See *admeasurement of dower* under ADMEASUREMENT.

adminicle (ad-**min**-i-kəl), *n.* (18c) **1.** Corroborative or explanatory proof. **2.** *Scots law.* A writing that tends to establish the existence or terms of an otherwise unavailable document, such as a lost will or deed. — Also termed *adminiculum.*

adminicular (ad-mə-**nik**-yə-lər), *adj.* (17c) Corroborative or auxiliary <adminicular evidence>.

adminicular evidence. See EVIDENCE.

adminiculate (ad-mə-**nik**-yə-layt), *vb.* (17c) *Scots law.* To give corroborating evidence.

adminiculum (ad-mə-**nik**-yə-ləm), *n.* [Latin "support"] (17c) *Roman law.* Legal or evidentiary means of supporting one's case; ADMINICLE.

administer, *vb.* (14c) **1.** To manage (work or money) for a business or organization <the money will be administered by the charitable foundation>. **2.** To provide or arrange (something) officially as part of one's job <courts administer justice>. **3.** To give (medicine or medical treatment) to someone <administer the probiotic each evening at bedtime>.

administration, *n.* (14c) **1.** The management or performance of the executive duties of a government, institution, or business; collectively, all the actions that are involved in managing the work of an organization. **2.** In public law, the practical management and direction of the executive department and its agencies. **3.** A judicial action in which a court undertakes the management and distribution of property. • Examples include the administration of a trust, the liquidation of a company, and the realization and distribution of a bankrupt estate. See JOINT ADMINISTRATION. **4.** The management and settlement of the estate of an intestate decedent, or of a testator who has no executor, by a person legally appointed and supervised by the court. • Administration of an estate involves realizing the movable assets and paying out of them any debts and other claims against the estate. It also involves the division and distribution of what remains.

▸ **administration *cum testamento annexo*** (kəm tes-tə-**men**-toh ə-**nek**-soh). [Latin "with the will annexed"] (17c) An administration granted when (1) a testator's will does not name any executor or when the executor named is incompetent to act, is deceased, or refuses to act, and (2) no successor executor has been named who is qualified to serve. — Abbr. c.t.a. — Also termed *administration with the will annexed.*

▸ **administration *de bonis non*** (dee **boh**-nis **non**). [Latin "of the goods not administered"] (17c) An administration granted for the purpose of settling the remainder of an intestate estate that was not administered by the former administrator. — Abbr. d.b.n.

▸ **administration *de bonis non cum testamento annexo*** (de **boh**-nis non kəm tes-tə-**men**-toh ə-**nek**-soh). (17c) An administration granted to settle the remainder of a testate estate not settled by a previous administrator or executor. • This type of administration arises when there is a valid will, as opposed to an *administration de bonis non*, which is granted when there is no will. — Abbr. d.b.n.c.t.a.

▸ **administration *durante absentia*** (d[y]uu-**ran**-tee ab-**sen**-shee-ə). (18c) An administration granted during the absence of either the executor or the person who has precedence as administrator.

▸ **administration *durante minore aetate*** (d[y]uu-**ran**-tee mi-**nor**-ee ee-**tay**-tee). (17c) An administration granted during the minority of either a child executor or the person who has precedence as administrator.

▸ **administration pendente lite** (pen-**den**-tee **lɪ**-tee). (18c) An administration granted during the pendency of a suit concerning a will's validity. — Also termed *pendente lite administration; special administration.* See PENDENTE LITE.

▸ **administration with the will annexed.** See *administration cum testamento annexo.*

▸ **ancillary administration** (**an**-sə-ler-ee). (1814) An administration that is auxiliary to the administration at the place of the decedent's domicile, such as one in another state. • The purpose of this process is to collect assets, to transfer and record changed title to real property located there, and to pay any debts in that locality. — Also termed *foreign administration.*

> "The object of ancillary administration is to collect assets of nonresident decedents found within the state and remit the proceeds to the domiciliary executor or administrator. . . . One of the principal purposes of ancillary administration is to protect local creditors of nonresident decedents by collecting and preserving local assets for their benefit." 31 Am. Jur. 2d *Executors and Administrators* §§ 1057–58, at 686 (2002).

▸ ***caeterorum* administration** (set-ə-**ror**-əm). [Latin "of the rest"] An administration granted when limited powers previously granted to an administrator are inadequate to settle the estate's residue.

▸ **domiciliary administration** (dom-ə-**sil**-ee-er-ee). (1850) The handling of an estate in the state where the decedent was domiciled at death.

▸ **foreign administration.** See *ancillary administration.*

▸ **general administration.** (18c) An administration with authority to deal with an entire estate. Cf. *special administration.*

▸ **limited administration.** (18c) An administration for a temporary period or for a special purpose.

▸ **original administration.** An administration that is not ancillary to a domiciliary administration.

▸ **pendente lite administration.** See *administration pendente lite.*

▸ **public administration.** (1893) In some jurisdictions, an administration by an officer appointed to administer an estate for an intestate who has left no person entitled to apply for letters of administration (or whose possible representatives refuse to serve).

▸ **special administration.** (18c) **1.** An administration with authority to deal with only some of a decedent's property, as opposed to administering the whole estate. **2.** See *administration pendente lite.* Cf. *general administration.*

▸ **temporary administration.** (18c) An administration in which the court appoints a fiduciary to administer the affairs of a decedent's estate for a short time before an administrator or executor can be appointed and qualified.

administration bill. See BILL (3).

administration expense. (1918) *Tax.* A necessary expenditure made by an administrator in managing and distributing an estate. • These expenses are tax-deductible even if not actually incurred by the time the return is filed.

Administration for Children and Families. A unit in the U.S. Department of Health and Human Services responsible for health, economic, and social well-being issues involving children and families, refugees, legalized aliens, and people with developmental disabilities. — Abbr. ACF.

administration letters. See LETTERS OF ADMINISTRATION.

administration of justice. (16c) The maintenance of right within a political community by means of the physical force of the state; the state's application of the sanction of force to the rule of right.

▸ **due administration of justice.** The proper functioning and integrity of a court or other tribunal and the proceedings before it in accordance with the rights guaranteed to the parties.

Administration on Aging. A unit in the U.S. Department of Health and Human Services responsible for promoting the welfare of the elderly, often in collaboration with governmental agencies that provide services to the elderly and to caregivers of the elderly.

administration pendente lite. See ADMINISTRATION.

administration with the will annexed. See *administration cum testamento annexo* under ADMINISTRATION.

administrative, *adj.* (17c) Of, relating to, or involving the work of managing a company or organization; executive.

administrative act. See ACT (2).

administrative action. (1857) A decision or an implementation relating to the government's executive function or a business's management.

administrative adjudication. (1909) The process used by an administrative agency to issue regulations through an adversary proceeding. Cf. RULEMAKING.

administrative agency. See AGENCY (3).

administrative closure. *Immigration law.* A federal authority's decision to indefinitely suspend pursuit of a removal proceeding against an illegal immigrant until either the authority or the immigrant asks for the proceeding to be docketed.

administrative collateral estoppel. See COLLATERAL ESTOPPEL.

Administrative Conference of the United States. An independent federal agency that provides a forum where agency heads, private attorneys, university professors, and others study ways to improve the procedures that agencies use in administering federal programs. • It was abolished in 1995 but reinstated in 2010. — Abbr. ACUS.

administrative-control rule. *Tax.* The rule making the grantor of a trust liable for tax if the grantor retains control that may be exercised primarily for the grantor's own benefit. IRC (26 USCA) § 675.

administrative-convenience exception. (1980) *Bankruptcy.* A provision permitting a bankruptcy plan to have a separate classification for small, unsecured claims, to the extent that the separate classification will assist in a more efficient disposition of the estate, as by paying or eliminating the small claims earlier than other claims. 11 USCA § 1122(b).

administrative crime. See CRIME.

administrative deviation. (1978) A trustee's unauthorized departure from the terms of the trust.

administrative discharge. See DISCHARGE (8).

administrative discovery. See DISCOVERY.

administrative discretion. See DISCRETION (4).

Administrative Domain-Name Challenge Panel. *Trademarks.* A board of experts convened under the auspices of the World Intellectual Property Organization to decide Internet domain-name disputes. — Abbr. ACP.

administrative expense. (1915) **1.** OVERHEAD. **2.** *Bankruptcy.* A cost incurred by the debtor, after filing a bankruptcy petition, that is necessary for the debtor to continue operating its business. • Administrative expenses are entitled to payment on a priority basis when the estate is distributed. 11 USCA § 503(b). See *general administrative expense* under EXPENSE.

administrative freeze. (1982) *Bankruptcy.* The refusal by a debtor's bank to permit withdrawals from the debtor's bank account after the bank learns that the debtor has filed bankruptcy, usu. because the debtor owes money to the bank in addition to maintaining funds on deposit.

administrative hearing. (1911) An administrative-agency proceeding in which evidence is offered for argument or trial.

administrative international law. See *international administrative law* under ADMINISTRATIVE LAW (1).

administrative interpretation. See INTERPRETATION (1).

administrative law. (1896) **1.** The law governing the organization and operation of administrative agencies (including executive and independent agencies) and the relations of administrative agencies with the legislature, the executive, the judiciary, and the public. • Administrative law is divided into three parts: (1) the statutes endowing agencies with powers and establishing rules of substantive law relating to those powers; (2) the body of agency-made law, consisting of administrative rules, regulations, reports, or opinions containing findings of fact, and orders; and (3) the legal principles governing the acts of public agents when those acts conflict with private rights.

> "Administrative law deals with the field of legal control exercised by law-administering agencies other than courts, and the field of control exercised by courts over such agencies." Felix Frankfurter, *The Task of Administrative Law*, 75 U. Pa. L. Rev. 614, 615 (1927).

> "[A]dministrative law is to labor law, securities regulation, and tax what civil procedure is to contracts, torts, and commercial law. Administrative law studies the way government institutions do things. It is therefore the procedural component to any practice that affects or is affected by government decisionmakers other than just the courts. Its study goes beyond traditional questions; it explores a variety of procedures and it develops ideas about decisionmaking and decisionmakers." 1 Charles H. Koch, *Administrative Law and Practice* § 1.2, at 2 (2d ed. 1997).

▸ **international administrative law.** (1887) **1.** The internal law and rules of international organizations. **2.** The substantive rules of international law that directly refer to the administrative matters of individual states. **3.** Domestic administrative law specifically concerned with international problems or situations. — Also termed *administrative international law.*

2. The part of public law delineating the nature of the activity of the executive department of the government in action. 3. The part of a country's legal system that determines the legal status and liabilities of all state officials, defines the rights and liabilities of private individuals who deal with public officials, and specifies the procedures by which those rights and liabilities are enforced.

administrative-law judge. (1972) An official who presides at an administrative hearing and who has the power to administer oaths, take testimony, rule on questions of evidence, and make factual and legal determinations. 5 USCA § 556(c). — Abbr. ALJ. — Also termed *hearing examiner*; *hearing officer*; *trial examiner*.

administrative offense. See *administrative crime* under CRIME.

Administrative Office of the United States Courts. An office in the judicial branch of the federal government responsible for administering the nonjudicial business of the federal courts (except the Supreme Court), disbursing funds, collecting statistics, fixing certain salaries, and purchasing supplies and equipment. • Created in 1939 the Office is supervised by the Judicial Conference of the United States. 28 USCA §§ 601 et seq. — Abbr. AOUSC; AO. See JUDICIAL CONFERENCE OF THE UNITED STATES.

administrative officer. See OFFICER (1).

administrative order. See ORDER (2).

administrative patent judge. See JUDGE.

Administrative Procedure Act. 1. A federal statute establishing practices and procedures to be followed in rulemaking and adjudication. • The Act was designed to give citizens basic due-process protections such as the right to present evidence and to be heard by an independent hearing officer. 5 USCA § 551. 2. A similar state statute. — Abbr. APA.

administrative proceeding. (1841) A hearing, inquiry, investigation, or trial before an administrative agency, usu. adjudicatory in nature but sometimes quasi-legislative. — Also termed *evidentiary hearing*; *full hearing*; *trial-type hearing*; *agency adjudication*.

administrative process. (1874) 1. The procedure used before administrative agencies. 2. The means of summoning witnesses to an agency hearing.

administrative remedy. See REMEDY.

administrative review. See REVIEW.

administrative rule. (1856) An officially promulgated agency regulation that has the force of law. • Administrative rules typically elaborate the requirements of a law or policy.

administrative rulemaking. See RULEMAKING.

administrative search. See SEARCH (1).

administrative search warrant. See *administrative warrant* under WARRANT (1).

administrative subpoena. See SUBPOENA.

administrative tribunal. See TRIBUNAL.

administrative warrant. See WARRANT (1).

administrator (ad-**min**-ə-stray-tər). (15c) 1. Someone who manages or heads a business, public office, agency, or other organization.

▸ **court administrator.** (1939) An official who supervises the nonjudicial functions of a court, esp. the court's calendar, judicial assignments, budget, and nonjudicial personnel.

▸ **local administrator.** (1923) *Conflict of laws.* An administrator appointed in the state where property is located or where an act is done.

2. A person appointed by the court to manage the assets and liabilities of an intestate decedent. • This term once referred to males only (as opposed to *administratrix*), but legal writers now generally use *administrator* to refer to someone of either sex. In the Restatement of Property, the term *administrator* includes the term *executor* unless specifically stated otherwise. Cf. EXECUTOR (2).

> "An administrator is a person authorized by a competent court to manage and distribute the estate of an intestate, or of a testate who has no executor." Simon Greenleaf Croswell, *Handbook on the Law of Executors and Administrators* § 2, at 5 (1897).

▸ **administrator *ad colligendum*** (ad kol-i-**jen**-dəm). (1830) An administrator appointed solely to collect and preserve the decedent's estate. — Also termed *administrator ad colligendum bona*.

▸ **administrator ad litem** (ad lɪ-tem *or* -təm). (1855) A special administrator appointed by the court to represent the estate's interest in an action usu. either because there is no administrator of the estate or because the current administrator has an interest in the action adverse to that of the estate.

▸ **administrator *ad prosequendum*** (ad prahs-ə-**kwen**-dəm). (1880) An administrator appointed to prosecute or defend a certain action or actions involving the estate.

▸ **administrator c.t.a.** See *administrator cum testamento annexo*.

▸ **administrator *cum testamento annexo*** (kəm tes-tə-**men**-toh ə-**nek**-soh). [Latin "with the will annexed"] (17c) An administrator appointed by the court to carry out the provisions of a will when the testator has named no executor, or the executors named refuse, are incompetent to act, or have died before performing their duties and no qualified successor has been named. — Also termed *administrator c.t.a.*; *administrator with the will annexed*.

▸ **administrator d.b.n.** See *administrator de bonis non*.

▸ **administrator *de bonis non*** (dee **boh**-nis **non**). [fr. Law Latin *de bonis non administratis* "of the goods not administered"] (17c) An administrator appointed by the court to settle the remainder of an intestate estate not settled by an earlier administrator or executor. • If there is no will, the administrator bears the name *administrator de bonis non* (abbr. *administrator d.b.n.*), but if there is a will, the full name is *administrator de bonis non cum testamento annexo* (abbr. *administrator d.b.n.c.t.a.*).

▸ **administrator *de bonis non cum testamento annexo*** (dee **boh**-nis non tes-tə-**men**-toh ə-**nek**-soh). (17c) An administrator appointed by the court to settle the remainder of a testate estate not settled by an earlier administrator or executor.

▸ **administrator *durante absentia*** (d[y]uu-**ran**-tee ab-**sen**-shee-ə). (18c) An administrator appointed to act while an estate's executor or an administrator with precedence is temporarily absent.

▸ **administrator *durante minore aetate*** (d[y]uu-**ran**-tee mi-**nor**-ee ee-**tay**-tee). (17c) An administrator who acts during the minority of a person who either is named by the testator as the estate's executor or would be appointed as the estate's administrator but for the person's youth.

▸ **administrator pendente lite** (pen-**den**-tee **lɪ**-tee). See *special administrator.*

▸ **administrator with the will annexed.** See *administrator cum testamento annexo.*

▸ **ancillary administrator** (**an**-sə-ler-ee). (1825) A court-appointed administrator who oversees the distribution of the part of a decedent's estate located in a jurisdiction other than where the decedent was domiciled (the place of the main administration). — Also termed *foreign administrator.* See *ancillary administration* under ADMINISTRATION.

▸ **domiciliary administrator.** (1838) A person appointed to administer an estate in the state where the decedent was domiciled at death.

▸ **foreign administrator.** (1806) An administrator appointed in another jurisdiction; an ancillary administrator.

▸ **general administrator.** (18c) A person appointed to administer an intestate decedent's entire estate. Cf. *special administrator.*

▸ **public administrator.** (1809) A state-appointed officer who administers intestate estates that are not administered by the decedent's relatives (because no one was entitled to apply for letters of administration, or the possible representatives refused to serve). • This officer's right to administer is usu. subordinate to the rights of creditors, but in a few jurisdictions the creditors' rights are subordinate.

▸ **special administrator.** (18c) **1.** A person appointed to administer only a specific part of an intestate decedent's estate. **2.** A person appointed to serve as administrator of an estate solely because of an emergency or an unusual situation, such as a will contest. — Also termed (in sense 2) *administrator pendente lite.* See PENDENTE LITE. Cf. *general administrator.*

administrator ad colligendum bona. See *administrator ad colligendum* under ADMINISTRATOR (2).

administrator's bond. See *fiduciary bond* under BOND (2).

administrator's deed. See DEED.

administratrix (ad-min-ə-**stray**-triks *or* ad-**min**-ə-strə-triks). *Archaic.* A female administrator. See ADMINISTRATOR (2). Pl. **administratrixes, administratrices.**

admiralitas (ad-mə-**ral**-ə-tas), *n.* [Law Latin] (18c) **1.** Admiralty; an admiralty court. **2.** SOCIETAS NAVALIS.

admiral's mast. See MAST (1).

admiralty (**ad**-mə-rəl-tee), *n.* (16c) **1.** A court that exercises jurisdiction over all maritime contracts, torts, injuries, or offenses. • The federal courts are so called when exercising their admiralty jurisdiction, which is conferred by the U.S. Constitution (art. III, § 2, cl. 1). — Also termed *admiralty court; maritime court.* **2.** The system of jurisprudence that has grown out of the practice of admiralty courts; MARITIME LAW. **3.** Narrowly, the rules governing contract, tort, and workers'-compensation claims arising out of commerce on or over navigable water. — Also termed (in senses 2 & 3) *admiralty law.* — **admiralty,** *adj.*

Admiralty, First Lord. See FIRST LORD OF THE ADMIRALTY.

admiralty and maritime jurisdiction. (18c) The exercise of authority over maritime cases by the U.S. district courts sitting in admiralty. *See* 28 USCA § 1333. — Often shortened to *admiralty jurisdiction; maritime jurisdiction.* See ADMIRALTY (1); SUPPLEMENTAL RULES FOR CERTAIN MARITIME AND ADMIRALTY CLAIMS.

Admiralty Clause. (1859) *Constitutional law.* The clause of the U.S. Constitution giving the federal government jurisdiction over admiralty and maritime cases. U.S. Const. art. III, § 2, cl. 1.

admiralty court. See ADMIRALTY (1).

Admiralty Extension Act. A 1948 statute extending admiralty-tort jurisdiction to include all cases in which damage or injury is caused by a vessel on navigable water, regardless of where the injury or damage occurred. 46 USCA app. § 740. • Specifically, the Act extended jurisdiction over damages and injuries that a vessel causes on land, such as to bridges and piers or to people on them. — Abbr. AEA.

admiralty jurisdiction. See ADMIRALTY AND MARITIME JURISDICTION.

admiralty law. 1. See ADMIRALTY (2). **2.** See ADMIRALTY (3).

ad misericordiam. See *argumentum ad misericordiam* under ARGUMENTUM.

admissibility (ad-mis-ə-**bil**-ə-tee), *n.* (18c) The quality, state, or condition of being allowed to be entered into evidence in a hearing, trial, or other official proceeding.

> "'Admissibility' can best be thought of as a concept consisting of two quite different aspects: disclosure to the trier of fact and express or implied permission to use as 'evidence.' If we think of admissibility as a question of disclosure or nondisclosure, it is usually easy to say whether or not an item of evidence has been admitted. When we consider the question of permissible use, the concept seems much more complex. In the first place, evidence may be 'admissible' for one purpose but not for another. . . . In the second place, questions of the permissible use of evidence do not arise only at the time of disclosure to the trier of fact. The court may have to consider admissibility in deciding whether to give the jury a limiting instruction, whether or not an opponent's rebuttal evidence is relevant, and whether or not counsel can argue to the jury that the evidence proves a particular point." 22 Charles Alan Wright & Kenneth W. Graham Jr., *Federal Practice and Procedure* § 5193, at 184 (1978).

▸ **conditional admissibility.** (1904) The evidentiary rule that when a piece of evidence is not itself admissible, but is admissible if certain other facts make it relevant, the evidence becomes admissible on condition that counsel later introduce the connecting facts. • If counsel does not satisfy this condition, the opponent is entitled to have the conditionally admitted piece of evidence struck from the record, and to have the judge instruct the jury to disregard it.

▸ **curative admissibility.** (1904) The rule that an inadmissible piece of evidence may be admitted if offered to cure or counteract the effect of some similar piece of the opponent's evidence that itself should not have been admitted. See CURATIVE-ADMISSIBILITY DOCTRINE.

> "It is sometimes said that, if irrelevant evidence is adduced by one party, his opponent may seek to dispel its effect by calling irrelevant evidence himself. Whichever the position may be in certain American jurisdictions, this principle (which Wigmore described as one of 'curative admissibility') is not recognized by the English courts." Rupert Cross, *Evidence* 19 (3d ed. 1967)

▸ **limited admissibility.** (1910) The principle that testimony or exhibits may be admitted into evidence for a restricted purpose. • Common examples are admitting prior contradictory testimony to impeach a witness but not to establish the truth, and admitting evidence against one party but not another. The trial court must, upon request, instruct the jury properly about the applicable limits when admitting the evidence. Fed. R. Evid. 105.

▸ **multiple admissibility.** (1904) The evidentiary rule that although a piece of evidence is inadmissible under one rule for the purpose given in offering it, it is nevertheless admissible if relevant and offered for some other purpose not forbidden by the rules of evidence.

admissible (ad-**mis**-ə-bəl), *adj.* (17c) **1.** Capable of being legally admitted; allowable; permissible <admissible evidence>. See ADMISSIBILITY. **2.** Worthy of gaining entry or being admitted <a person is admissible to the bar upon obtaining a law degree and passing the bar exam>.

admissible evidence. See EVIDENCE.

admission (ad-**mish**-ən), *n.* (15c) **1.** A statement in which someone admits that something is true or that he or she has done something wrong; esp., any statement or assertion made by a party to a case and offered against that party; an acknowledgment that facts are true. Cf. CONFESSION.

> "Admissions are not confessions. The distinction between a confession and an admission, as applied in criminal law, is not a technical refinement, but based upon the substantive differences of the character of the evidence educed from each. A confession is a direct acknowledgment of guilt on the part of the accused, and, by the very force of the definition, excludes an admission, which, of itself, as applied in criminal law, is a statement by the accused, direct or implied, of facts pertinent to the issue and tending, in connection with proof of other facts, to prove his guilt, but of itself is insufficient to authorize a conviction. The principle of confessions has no application to admissions. It is necessary to observe the distinction in every case. The loose phraseology of courts, stating that a certain fact may be construed as an admission or a confession, is misleading. Under the law, the court may instruct the jury as to the conclusive character of a confession; but, as to an admission, the instruction must be as to its weight as a circumstance in connection with other proof. Thus, silence under an accusation of crime may constitute conduct, or a circumstance from which guilt may be inferred. But such silence can never have the legal effect of a confession of a crime." 2 Francis Wharton, *A Treatise on the Law of Evidence in Criminal Issues* 1400–01 (O.N. Hilton ed., 10th ed. 1912) (citations omitted).

▸ **admission against interest.** (1828) A person's statement acknowledging a fact that is harmful to the person's position, esp. as a litigant. • An admission against interest must be made either by a litigant or by one in privity with or occupying the same legal position as the litigant; as an exception to the hearsay rule, it is admissible whether or not the person is available as a witness. Fed. R. Evid. 801(d)(2). A declaration against interest, by contrast, is made by a nonlitigant who is not in privity with a litigant; a declaration against interest is also admissible as an exception to the hearsay rule, but only when the declarant is unavailable as a witness. Fed. R. Evid. 804(b)(3). — Also termed *statement against interest.* See *declaration against interest* under DECLARATION (6).

▸ **admission by employee or agent.** (2003) An admission made by a party-opponent's agent during employment and concerning a matter either within the scope of the agency or authorized by the party-opponent.

▸ **admission by party-opponent.** (1959) A statement that is offered against an opposing party and that (1) is the party's own statement, made in an individual or a representative capacity; (2) the party has manifested an adoption of or a belief in the truth of; (3) was made by one whom the party authorized to make a statement on the subject; (4) was made by the party's agent or employee and concerned a matter within the scope of, and was made during the existence of, the agency or employment; or (5) was made by a coconspirator of the party during, and in furtherance of, the conspiracy. • Such an admission is not considered hearsay. Fed. R. Evid. 801(d)(2).

▸ **admission by silence.** (1867) *Criminal law.* An implication of agreement or disagreement, truth or falsity of a statement, or other reaction under circumstances in which a person would be expected to react, esp. to deny guilt upon someone else's making an incriminating statement about the person; the failure of a party to speak after another party's assertion of fact that, if untrue, would naturally compel a person to deny the statement. — Also termed *adoption by silence.*

▸ **admission *in judicio*.** See *judicial admission.*

▸ **adoptive admission.** (1933) *Criminal law.* An incriminating statement made by someone other than the defendant but which the defendant acknowledges and either assents to or acquiesces in, so that the statement effectively becomes the defendant's own admission; an act by one person that indicates approval of another person's statement, and thereby acceptance that the statement is true.

▸ **extrajudicial admission.** (1824) An admission made outside court proceedings. — Also termed *informal admission.*

▸ **formal admission.** (18c) A sworn admission by a party that a fact is true, thereby obviating any need to prove the fact at trial.

▸ **implied admission.** (18c) An admission reasonably inferable from a party's action or statement, or a party's failure to act or speak. — Also termed *tacit admission.* Cf. TACIT-ADMISSION DOCTRINE.

▸ **incidental admission.** (1829) An admission made in some other connection or involved in the admission of some other fact.

▸ **incriminating admission.** (1893) An admission of facts tending to establish guilt.

▸ **informal admission.** See *extrajudicial admission.*

▸ **judicial admission.** (18c) A formal waiver of proof that relieves an opposing party from having to prove the admitted fact and bars the party who made the admission from disputing it. — Also termed *solemn admission*; *admission in judicio*; *true admission.*

▸ **quasi-admission.** (1813) An act or utterance, usu. extrajudicial, that creates an inconsistency with and discredits, to a greater or lesser degree, a present claim or other evidence of the person creating the inconsistency.

▸ **solemn admission.** See *judicial admission.*

▸ **tacit admission.** See *implied admission.*

▸ **true admission.** See *judicial admission.*

2. Acceptance of a lawyer by the established licensing authority, such as a state bar association, as a member of the practicing bar, usu. after the lawyer passes a bar examination and supplies adequate character references <admission to the bar>; the entry of a lawyer on the rolls of an integrated bar, usu. after the fulfillment of two prerequisites: graduating from law school and passing a state bar examination. — Also termed *admission to practice law.*

▸ **admission on motion.** (1903) Permanent admission of a lawyer who is in good standing in the bar of a different state without the need for a full bar examination. — Also termed *admission by motion.*

▸ **admission *pro hac vice*** (proh hak **vɪ**-see *or* proh hak **vee**-chay). (1841) Temporary admission of an out-of-jurisdiction lawyer to practice before a court in a specified case or set of cases. See PRO HAC VICE.

3. *Patents.* A concession or representation by a patent applicant that an activity, knowledge, or a publication is prior art. • An admission requires the U.S. Patent and Trademark Office examiner to consider the relevant item as prior art, even if it does not technically qualify as prior art. — Also termed *admission of prior art.* **4.** Permission given to someone to enter a building or place, or to become a member of a school, club, etc. **5.** The process of accepting someone into a hospital for treatment, tests, or care. **6.** The cost of entrance to an event such as a theatrical performance, movie, or sports event. **7.** (*pl.*) The process of allowing people to enter a college, university, or other institution. **8.** (*pl.*) The number of people who can enter according to established criteria or rules, or the number who actually enter (if fewer). **9.** *Immigration law.* The entry into a country by an alien with apparent legal permission to do so, usu. as obtained with a visa.

admission against interest. See ADMISSION (1).

admission by employee or agent. See ADMISSION (1).

admission by party-opponent. See ADMISSION (1).

admission by silence. See ADMISSION (1).

admission *in judicio.* See *judicial admission* under ADMISSION (1).

admission of evidence. (18c) The allowance before a factfinder of testimony, documents, or other materials for consideration in determining the facts at issue in a trial or hearing.

admission of prior art. See ADMISSION (3).

admission on motion. See ADMISSION (2).

admission *pro hac vice.* See ADMISSION (2).

admission tax. See TAX.

admission to bail. (18c) An order to release an accused person from custody after payment of bail or receipt of an adequate surety for the person's appearance for trial. See BAIL (1).

admission to practice law. See ADMISSION (2).

admission to sufficient facts. See SUBMISSION TO A FINDING.

admittance. (16c) **1.** The act of entering a building, locality, or the like. **2.** Permission to enter a place. **3.** *Hist.* The act of giving seisin of a copyhold estate. • Admittance corresponded with livery of seisin of a freehold. Copyhold estates were abolished by the Law of Property Act of 1922. See COPYHOLD.

admitted asset. See ASSET.

admitted corporation. See CORPORATION.

admittendo clerico (ad-mi-**ten**-doh **kler**-ə-koh). See DE CLERICO ADMITTENDO.

admittendo in socium (ad-mi-**ten**-doh in **soh**-shee-əm). [Latin] (17c) *Hist.* A writ for associating certain persons, such as knights, to justices of assize on the circuit.

admixture (ad-**miks**-chər). (17c) **1.** The mixing of things. **2.** A substance formed by mixing.

admonishment. See ADMONITION.

admonition (ad-mə-**nish**-ən), *n.* (14c) **1.** A warning or expression of disapproval about someone's behavior. **2.** Any authoritative advice or caution from the court to the jury regarding their duty as jurors or the admissibility of evidence for consideration <the judge's admonition that the jurors not discuss the case until they are charged>. **3.** A reprimand or cautionary statement addressed to counsel by a judge <the judge's admonition that the lawyer stop speaking out of turn>. **4.** *Eccles. law.* An authoritatively issued warning or censure. — Also termed (in all senses) *admonishment.* — **admonish** (ad-**mon**-ish), *vb.* — **admonitory** (ad-**mon**-ə-tor-ee), *adj.*

admonitio trina (ad-mə-**nish**-ee-oh **trɪ**-nə), *n.* [Law Latin "triple warning"] *Hist.* A threefold warning advising a defendant charged with a capital crime that refusal to answer questions about the offense would in itself be considered a capital crime punishable by death. See PEINE FORTE ET DURE.

ad mordendum assuetus (ad mor-**den**-dəm ə-**swee**-təs), *adj.* [Law Latin] *Hist.* Accustomed to bite. • This phrase was a common charge in a declaration of damage done by a dog to a person or to another animal.

admortization (ad-mor-tə-**zay**-shən). (18c) *Hist.* The reduction of lands or tenements to mortmain.

adnepos (ad-**nep**-ohs), *n.* [Latin] (18c) *Hist.* A great-great grandson.

adneptis (ad-**nep**-tis), *n.* [Latin] (18c) *Hist.* A great-great-granddaughter.

adnihilare (ad-nɪ-hə-**lair**-ee), *vb.* [Law Latin] *Hist.* To annul; to make void.

ad nocumentum (ad nok-yoo-**men**-təm), *adv.* [Law Latin] (17c) *Hist.* To the nuisance; to the hurt or injury.

ad non executa (ad non ek-sə-**kyoo**-tə), *adv.* [Latin] (17c) *Hist.* For the things not done (as by an executor).

adnotatio (ad-noh-**tay**-shee-oh), *n.* [Latin] *Roman law.* A note written in the margin of a document; esp., the reply of the emperor in his own hand to a petition addressed to him. See RESCRIPT (3). Pl. ***adnotationes*** (ad-noh-tay-shee-**oh**-neez).

ad omissa vel male appretiata (ad oh-**mis**-ə vel **mal**-ee ə-pree-shee-**ay**-tə). [Law Latin] *Scots law.* Concerning things omitted or undervalued. • The phrase refers to an executor's duty to include in an estate's inventory previously omitted items or to reevaluate undervalued items in the estate's inventory.

adoptability, *n.* (1843) *Family law.* **1.** A child's availability to be adopted, esp. by reason of all legal impediments having been removed. **2.** The likelihood of a child's being adopted; a prospective adoptee's desirability from the prospective parents' point of view. — **adoptable,** *adj.*

adopted child. 1. See CHILD. **2.** ADOPTEE.

adoptee. (1892) Someone who has legally become the child of one or two nonbiological parents. — Also termed *adopted child.*

adoption, *n.* (14c) **1.** *Family law.* The creation by judicial order of a parent–child relationship between two parties who usu. are unrelated; the relation of parent and child created by law between persons who are not in fact parent and child. • This relationship is brought about only after a determination that the child is an orphan or has been abandoned, or that the parents' parental rights have been terminated by court order. Adoption creates a parent–child relationship between the adopted child and the adoptive parents with all the rights, privileges, and responsibilities that attach to that relationship, though there may be agreed exceptions. Adoption is distinguishable from legitimation and from fosterage. Adoption usu. refers to an act between persons unrelated by blood; legitimation refers to an act between persons related by blood. Universally, a decree of adoption confers legitimate status on the adopted child. Adoption is permanent; fosterage is a temporary arrangement for a child's care. See *adopted child, foster child* under CHILD. Cf. LEGITIMATION (2); FOSTER CARE (1). — **adopt,** *vb.*

> "Although adoption is found in many societies, ancient and modern, primitive and civilized, and is recognized by the civil law, it was unknown at common law. Accordingly, adoption is entirely a creature of statute . . . ." Elias Clark et al., *Gratuitous Transfers: Wills, Intestate Succession, Trusts, Gifts, Future Interests, and Estate and Gift Taxation Cases and Materials* 73–74 (4th ed. 1999).

▸ **adoption by estoppel.** (1933) **1.** An equitable adoption of a child by one who promises or acts in a way that precludes the person and his or her estate from denying adopted status to the child. **2.** An equitable decree of adoption treating as done that which ought to have been done. • Such a decree is entered when no final decree of adoption has been obtained, even though the principal has acted as if an adoption has been achieved. A petitioner must show an agreement of adoption, relinquishment of parental authority by the child's biological parents, assumption of parental responsibility by the foster parents, and a de facto relationship of parent and child over a substantial period. Such a claim typically occurs when an adoptive parent has died intestate, and the child tries to be named an heir. In a minority of states, adoption by estoppel may be a basis for allowing a child to participate in a wrongful-death action. — Also termed *equitable adoption*; *virtual adoption.* See ESTOPPEL (1). **3.** See *de facto adoption.*

▸ **adoption by will.** (1916) *Roman law.* A posthumous adoption effected by a testator's written statement declaring the intention to adopt and naming the person adopted. • The only legal effect of such an adoption was to entitle the adopted person to assume the testator's family name and be regarded as the testator's child. Because the adopted person was never subject to the testator's legal control (*patria potestas*), the person could not acquire agnatic rights or make a claim on the estate beyond any specific testamentary grants.

▸ **adult adoption.** (1889) The adoption of one adult by another. • Many jurisdictions do not allow adult adoptions. Those that do often impose restrictions, as by requiring consent of the person to be adopted, but may not look too closely at the purpose for which adoption is sought.

▸ **agency adoption.** (1951) An adoption in which parental rights are terminated and legal custody is relinquished to an agency that finds and approves the adoptive parents. • An agency adoption can be either public or private. In all states, adoption agencies must be licensed, and in most they are nonprofit entities. Parents who voluntarily place a child for adoption most commonly use a private agency. Cf. *private adoption.*

▸ **black-market adoption.** (1976) **1.** An illegal adoption in which an intermediary (a broker) receives payment for his or her services. **2.** Baby-selling.

▸ **closed adoption.** (1977) An adoption in which the biological parent relinquishes his or her parental rights and surrenders the child to an unknown person or persons; an adoption in which there is no disclosure of the identity of the birth parents, adopting parent or parents, or child. • Adoptions by stepparents, blood relatives, and foster parents are exceptions to the no-disclosure requirement. — Also termed *confidential adoption.* Cf. *open adoption*; *cooperative adoption.*

▸ **confidential adoption.** See *closed adoption.*

▸ **cooperative adoption.** (1987) A process in which the birth parents and adoptive parents negotiate to reach a voluntary agreement about the degree and type of continuing contact after adoption, including direct visitation or more limited arrangements such as communication by telephone or mail, the exchange of either identifying or nonidentifying information, and other forms of contact. Cf. *open adoption*; *closed adoption.*

▸ **de facto adoption.** (1943) An adoption that falls short of the statutory requirements in a particular state. • The adoption agreement may ripen to a de jure adoption when the statutory formalities have been met or if a court finds that the requirements for adoption by estoppel have been met. — Also termed *adoption by estoppel.* See *adoption by estoppel.*

▸ **de facto stepparent adoption.** See *second-parent adoption.*

▸ **direct adoption.** See *private adoption.*

▸ **direct-placement adoption.** See *private adoption.*

▸ **embryo adoption.** (1981) *Slang.* The receipt of a previously frozen embryo that is implanted into a recipient's womb. • Donors must waive all parental rights before the recipients of the embryo assume legal ownership or custody. The process is not considered to be a legal adoption because American law does not treat embryos as children.

▸ **equitable adoption.** See *adoption by estoppel.*

▸ **gray-market adoption.** See *private adoption.*

▸ **identified adoption.** See *private adoption.*

▸ **independent adoption.** See *private adoption.*

▸ **intercountry adoption.** See *international adoption.*

▸ **international adoption.** (1965) An adoption in which parents domiciled in one country travel to a foreign country to adopt a child there, usu. in accordance with the laws of the child's country. • International adoptions first became popular after World War II and escalated after the Korean Conflict because of the efforts of humanitarian programs working to find homes for children left orphaned by the wars. More recently, prospective parents have turned to international adoption as the number of healthy babies domestically available for adoption has steadily declined. — Also termed *transnational adoption*; *intercountry adoption*. See MULTIETHNIC PLACEMENT ACT OF 1994.

▸ **interracial adoption.** See *transracial adoption*.

▸ **interstate adoption.** (1961) An adoption in which the prospective parents live in one state and the child lives in another state. See INTERSTATE COMPACT ON THE PLACEMENT OF CHILDREN.

▸ **joint adoption.** (1922) An adoption in which the prospective parents apply as a couple and are approved or rejected as a couple, as opposed to filing separate and individual applications to adopt a child. • Although the term most often applies to adoption by a married couple, it also applies to an adoption petition by two unmarried partners who are adopting a child.

▸ **open adoption.** (1979) An adoption in which the biological mother (sometimes with the biological father) chooses the adoptive parents and in which the child often continues to have a post-adoption relationship with his or her biological family. • Typically the birth parents meet the adoptive parents and participate in the separation and placement process. The birth parents relinquish all legal, moral, and nurturing rights over the child, but usu. retain the right to continuing contact and to knowledge of the child's welfare and location. Cf. *closed adoption*; *cooperative adoption*.

▸ **posthumous adoption.** (1957) An adoption that becomes legally final after the death of either an adoptive parent or the adopted child. • Few states recognize posthumous adoptions.

▸ **private adoption.** (1865) The placement of a child for adoption by a parent, lawyer, doctor, or private agency rather than by a government agency; specif., an adoption that occurs independently between the biological mother (and sometimes the biological father) and the adoptive parents without the involvement of an agency. • A private adoption is usu. arranged by an intermediary such as a lawyer, doctor, or counselor. Legal custody — though sometimes not physical custody — remains with the biological parent or parents until the termination and adoption are complete. — Also termed *private-placement adoption*; *direct-placement adoption*; *direct adoption*; *gray-market adoption*; *identified adoption*; *independent adoption*; *private placement*; *direct placement*. Cf. *agency adoption*.

▸ **private-placement adoption.** See *private adoption*.

▸ **pseudo-stepparent adoption.** See *second-parent adoption*.

▸ **second-parent adoption.** (1986) An adoption by an unmarried cohabiting partner of a child's legal parent, not involving the termination of a legal parent's rights; esp., an adoption in which a lesbian, gay man, or unmarried heterosexual person adopts his or her partner's biological or adoptive child. *See* Restatement (Third) of Property: Wills and Other Donative Transfers § 2.5 cmt. i. (1999) • Although not all jurisdictions recognize second-parent adoption, the practice is becoming more widely accepted. *See In re Adoption of B.L.V.B.*, 628 A.2d 1271 (Vt. 1993); *In re Adoption of Tammy*, 619 N.E.2d 315 (Mass. 1993); *In re Adoption of Evan*, 583 N.Y.S.2d 997 (Sur. Ct. 1992). — Also termed *de facto stepparent adoption*; *pseudo-stepparent adoption*. Cf. *stepparent adoption*.

▸ **stepparent adoption.** (1954) The adoption of a child by a stepfather or stepmother. • Stepparent adoptions are the most common adoptions in the United States. Cf. *second-parent adoption*.

▸ **transnational adoption.** See *international adoption*.

▸ **transracial adoption.** (1970) An adoption in which at least one adoptive parent is of a race different from that of the adopted child. • Under federal law, child-placement agencies may not use race as a factor in approving adoptions. 42 USCA § 5115a. — Also termed *interracial adoption*. See MULTIETHNIC PLACEMENT ACT OF 1994.

▸ **virtual adoption.** See *adoption by estoppel*.

▸ **wrongful adoption.** See WRONGFUL ADOPTION.

2. *Roman law.* The legal process of creating a parent–child relationship with a young person who is still under the power of another father. • The adopted person became part of the new paterfamilias's agnatic family with exactly the same standing as children (or grandchildren) by blood. This was later modified by Justinian. Cf. ADROGATION. **3.** *Contracts.* The process by which a person agrees to assume a contract previously made for that person's benefit, such as a newly formed corporation's acceptance of a preincorporation contract. **4.** *Trademarks.* The mental act necessary to acquire legal rights in a trademark, consisting of knowledge and intention to use a trademark on or in connection with a product or service in commerce. **5.** *Parliamentary law.* A deliberative assembly's act of agreeing to a motion or the text of a resolution, order, rule, or other paper or proposal, or of endorsing as its own statement the complete contents of a report. — Also termed *acceptance*; *consent*; *passage*. Cf. RATIFICATION; REJECTION (3). — **adopt,** *vb.* — **adoptive,** *adj.*

> "As applied to an assembly's action with respect to board or committee reports or any of their contents, the expressions *adopt*, *accept*, and *agree to* are all equivalent — that is, the text adopted becomes in effect the act or statement of the assembly. It is usually best to use the word *adopt*, however, since it is the least likely to be misunderstood." Henry M. Robert III et al., *Robert's Rules of Order Newly Revised* § 51, at 508 (11th ed. 2011).

adoption agency. (1937) A licensed establishment where a biological parent can voluntarily surrender a child for adoption. See *agency adoption* under ADOPTION (1).

Adoption and Safe Families Act. A 1997 federal statute that requires states to provide safe and permanent homes for abused and neglected children within shorter periods than those required by earlier state and federal laws. • The primary focus is on the safety and well-being of the child, in contrast to the previously paramount rights of the parents. The ASFA signaled a dramatic shift in the philosophy of child-protection proceedings that had controlled since 1980 under the Adoption Assistance and Child Welfare Act. — Abbr. ASFA. See ADOPTION ASSISTANCE AND CHILD WELFARE ACT; FOSTER-CARE DRIFT.

Adoption Assistance and Child Welfare Act. A 1980 federal statute whose purpose was to force states to use reasonable efforts (1) to avoid removing children from their homes, (2) to reunite families when children had been removed because of abuse or neglect, and (3) when reunification failed, to terminate parental rights and place the children in permanent homes. 42 USCA §§ 620 et seq., §§ 670 et seq. • The Act provided funds for foster-care placement, Child Protective Services, family preservation and reunification, and foster-care reform to states complying with the Act. Its aim was to prevent the unnecessary removal of children from homes and to hasten the return of children in foster care to their families. It has now been essentially overruled in philosophy by the 1997 enactment of the Adoption and Safe Families Act. — Abbr. AACWA. See ADOPTION AND SAFE FAMILIES ACT.

adoption-assistance plan. (1988) An employer-sponsored program that provides financial assistance to employees for adoption-related expenses.

adoption by estoppel. See ADOPTION (1).

adoption by reference. See INCORPORATION BY REFERENCE (1).

adoption by silence. See *admission by silence* under ADMISSION (1).

adoption by will. See ADOPTION (1).

adoption leave. See LEAVE.

adoption-registry statute. (2001) A law that provides for the release of adoption information if the biological parent, the adoptive parent, and the adoptee (after he or she reaches a certain statutorily prescribed age) all officially record their desire for its release. • The statute may provide for an active registry, authorizing a state agency to seek out the other parties' desires to obtain or release their information when one party expresses a desire for it, or a passive registry, requiring a match between parties that have registered before any information is released or additional contact is made. — Also termed *voluntary-registry law.*

▸ **active adoption-registry statute.** A registry statute that authorizes a state authority to seek out parties' desires to obtain or release adoption information when one party expresses a desire for that information.

▸ **passive adoption-registry statute.** A registry statute allowing parties to register their desires for release of adoption information after an adopted child reaches a specified age.

adoptive admission. See ADMISSION (1).

adoptive-admissions rule. (1949) *Evidence.* The principle that a statement offered against an accused is not inadmissible hearsay if the accused is aware of the statement and has, by words or conduct, indicated acceptance that the statement is true. See *adoptive admission* under ADMISSION (1).

adoptive father. See *adoptive parent* under PARENT (1).

adoptive mother. See *adoptive parent* under PARENT (1).

adoptive parent. See PARENT (1).

ad opus (ad **oh**-pəs), *adv.* [Law Latin] For the benefit; for the use. • This term indicated an intent to create a use to benefit another. See USE, *n.* (4).

ad ostendendum (ad ah-sten-**den**-dəm), *vb.* [Law Latin] To show.

ad ostium ecclesiae (ad **ah**-stee-əm e-**klee**-z[h]ee-ee), *adv.* [Law Latin] At the church door. See *dower ad ostium ecclesiae* under DOWER.

ad paratam executionem (ad pə-**ray**-təm ek-si-kyoo-shee-**oh**-nəm). [Law Latin] *Hist.* For execution on completed diligence. • The phrase appeared in judgments.

ad pares casus (ad **par**-eez **kay**-səs). [Law Latin] *Hist.* To similar cases.

ad perpetuam rei memoriam (ad pər-**pech**-oo-əm **ree**-ɪ mə-**mor**-ee-əm). [Latin] *Hist.* For a perpetual record of the matter.

> "By the statute 1685, a register-book is appointed to be kept, in which entails are to be recorded, with the name of the maker, the heirs, the provisions and conditions of the entail, 'all to remain in the said register *ad perpetuam rei memoriam*.'" John Trayner, *Trayner's Latin Maxims* 29–30 (4th ed. 1894).

ad perpetuam remanentiam (ad pər-**pech**-oo-əm rem-ə-**nen**-shee-əm). [Law Latin] *Hist.* To remain forever. • When a vassal surrendered the right of property to the superior *ad perpetuam remanentiam*, the surrender was in favor of the superior, as distinguished from a transfer *in favorem*, in which the vassal transferred the property to the superior to be regranted in favor of a purchaser.

ad pios usus (ad **pɪ**-ohs **yoo**-səs *or* **yoo**-zəs), *adv.* [Law Latin] For pious (religious or charitable) uses or purposes. • This phrase was used in reference to gifts and bequests.

ad pristinum statum (ad **pris**-ti-nəm **stay**-təm). [Latin] *Hist.* To its pristine condition.

adpromissio. See ADPROMISSION.

adpromission (ad-prə-**mish**-ən). [fr. Latin *adpromissio*] *Roman law.* **1.** A suretyship contract in which the surety promises to be liable for no more than the debtor owes. • Roman law had three types of adpromission: (1) sponsion; (2) fidepromission; and (3) fidejussion. In addition, *mandatum* and *pactum de constitutio* could indirectly be used by way of guarantee. **2.** A suretyship relation. — Also termed *adpromissio.*

adpromissor (ad-**prom**-is-ər), *n.* [Latin] (1875) *Roman law.* A surety for a debtor under a promise by stipulation. See ADPROMISSION.

ad prosequendam (ad prahs-ə-**kwen**-dəm), *vb.* [Law Latin] To prosecute.

ad punctum temporis (ad **pəngk**-təm **tem**-pə-ris), *adv.* [Law Latin] At the point of time.

ad quaerimoniam (ad kweer-ə-**moh**-nee-əm), *adv.* [Law Latin] On complaint of.

ad quem (ad **kwem**), *adv.* [Latin] To which. • This term is used as a correlative to *a quo* in computation of time or distance. For example, the *terminus a quo* is the point of beginning or departure; the *terminus ad quem* is the end of the period or point of arrival.

ad quod curia concordavit (ad kwod **kyoor**-ee-ə kon-kor-**day**-vit). [Law Latin] To which the court agreed.

ad quod damnum (ad kwod **dam**-nəm). [Latin "to what damage"] *Hist.* A writ directing the sheriff to inquire of jurors under oath to what damage a grant (as of a fair, market, liberty, or other franchise) would be to various people if the king were to make the grant. • The writ was issuable from the court of chancery. — Also termed *writ of ad quod damnum.*

ad quod non fuit responsum (ad kwod non **fyoo**-it ri-**spon**-səm). [Law Latin] To which there was no answer. • This phrase was used in law reports to indicate an unresponded-to argument or objection.

ADR. *abbr.* **1.** ALTERNATIVE DISPUTE RESOLUTION. **2.** ASSET-DEPRECIATION RANGE. **3.** AMERICAN DEPOSITORY RECEIPT.

ad rationem ponere (ad ray-shee-**oh**-nəm **poh**-nə-ree), *vb.* [Law Latin "to give a reason"] To cite (a person) to appear. • The Exchequer summoned persons to appear and explain a charge with this phrase.

ad recognoscendum (ad ree-kog-nə-**sen**-dəm), *vb.* [Law Latin] To recognize. • These were formal words in writs.

adrectare (ad-rek-**tair**-ee), *vb.* [Law Latin] *Hist.* To do right; to satisfy.

ad rectum (ad **rek**-təm), *vb.* [Law Latin] To right; to meet an accusation.

ad rem. [Latin] (16c) To the point.

ad reparationem et sustentationem (ad rep-ə-ray-shee-**oh**-nəm et sə-sten-tay-shee-**oh**-nəm), *adv.* [Law Latin] For repairing and keeping in suitable condition.

ad reprimendam improbitatem huius generis hominum (ad rep-ri-**men**-dəm im-proh-bi-**tay**-təm **hɪ**-əs [or **hwɪ**-əs] **jen**-ə-ris **hom**-ə-nəm). [Latin] *Hist.* To repress the dishonesty of this class of men. • The phrase appeared in reference to obligations that the law imposed on certain persons (such as innkeepers) because they were in a unique position to receive and misappropriate valuables entrusted to them. Cf. NAUTAE, CAUPONES, STABULARII.

ad respondendum (ad ree-spon-**den**-dəm). [Latin] To answer. See *capias ad respondendum* under CAPIAS; *habeas corpus ad respondendum* under HABEAS CORPUS.

ad rimandam veritatem (ad ri-**man**-dəm ver-i-**tay**-təm). [Latin] *Hist.* For the investigation of the truth. • Parol testimony was sometimes allowed *ad rimandam veritatem.*

adrogate (**ad**-roh-gayt), *vb.* (17c) *Roman law.* (Of a man) to adopt a son or daughter who is not already under another father's power (*patria potestas*). • Daughters became eligible for adoption in the later Empire.

adrogation (ad-roh-**gay**-shən), *n.* [fr. Latin *arrogatio* (a-roh-**gay**-shee-oh)] (16c) *Roman law.* An adoption of a person of full capacity (*sui juris*) into another family. — Also termed *adrogatio* (ad-roh-**gay**-shee-oh). Cf. ADOPTION (2).

> "When the person to be adopted was *sui juris*, and not in the power of a *paterfamilias*, the ceremony of adoption was called *adrogatio*." Lord Mackenzie, *Studies in Roman Law* 132 (John Kirkpatrick ed., 7th ed. 1898).

ADS. *abbr.* AMERICAN DEPOSITARY SHARE.

ads. *abbr.* AD SECTAM.

ad satisfaciendum (ad sat-is-fay-shee-**en**-dəm). [Latin] To satisfy. See *capias ad satisfaciendum* under CAPIAS.

adscendentes (ad-sen-**den**-teez), *n. pl.* [Latin] *Civil law.* Ascendants.

adscriptitius (ad-skrip-**tish**-ee-əs), *n.* [Latin] *Roman law.* **1.** A supernumerary citizen or soldier. **2.** A tenant bound to the land. — Also spelled *adscripticius*; *ascripticius.*

adscriptus (ad-**skrip**-təs), *adj.* [Latin] *Roman law.* **1.** Added, annexed, or bound by or in writing; enrolled or registered. **2.** Bound, as in *servus colonae adscriptus* (a tenant bound to an estate as a cultivator) or *fundus adscriptus* (an estate bound to or burdened with a duty). — Also termed *ascriptus; ascriptitius.* See ADSCRIPTUS GLEBAE.

adscriptus glebae (ad-**skrip**-təs **glee**-bee), *n.* [Latin "(a tenant) tied to the soil"] *Roman law.* A tenant or serf bound to the land. • If the land was conveyed, the serfs were conveyed along with it, but in other respects they were free citizens. — Also termed *glebae ascriptitius.* Pl. ***adscripti glebae*** (ad-**skrip**-tɪ **glee**-bee), *n.*

ad sectam (ad **sek**-təm), *adj.* [Law Latin] At the suit of. • This term, in abbreviated form, was used in indexing the names of cases by defendant — for example, "B *ads.* A" if B is the defendant. — Abbr. *ads.*; *adsm.*

adsessor (ad-**ses**-ər), *n.* [Latin] (17c) **1.** *Roman law.* A legally qualified assistant or adviser to a judge. **2.** *Hist.* Assessor. • This was a title of a master in chancery. — Also spelled *assessor.*

ad similes casus (ad **sim**-ə-leez **kay**-səs). [Law Latin] *Hist.* To like cases. See CASU CONSIMILI.

adsm. *abbr.* AD SECTAM.

adstipulator (ad-**stip**-yə-lay-tər), *n.* [Latin] (1880) *Roman law.* An additional party to a contract who could enforce the contract along with the principal (i.e., the *stipulator*). • An *adstipulator* who enforced an agreement would have to, in turn, pay the *stipulator.* An *adstipulator* was brought in to avoid the rule that a person could not directly stipulate for payment after death.

adsum (**ad**-səm). [Latin] (16c) I am present; I am here.

ad summam. [Latin] (16c) In brief; in short.

ad sustinenda onera matrimonii (ad səs-ti-**nen**-də **on**-ər-ə ma-trə-**moh**-nee-ɪ). [Latin] *Scots law.* To bear the burdens or expenses of the married state. • The phrase appeared in reference to the purpose for which the dowry was used.

ad tentandas vires haereditatis (ad ten-**tan**-dəs **vɪ**-reez hə-red-i-**tay**-tis). [Latin] *Hist.* For the purpose of testing the strength of the inheritance.

ad terminum annorum (ad **tər**-mə-nəm ə-**nor**-əm), *adv.* [Law Latin] For a term of years.

ad terminum qui praeteriit (ad **tər**-mə-nəm kwɪ pri-**ter**-ee-it). [Law Latin "for a term which has passed"] A writ of entry to recover land leased out to a holdover tenant. — Also termed *entry ad terminum qui praeteriit.*

ad testificandum (ad tes-ti-fi-**kan**-dəm). [Latin] To testify. See *habeas corpus ad testificandum* under HABEAS CORPUS; *subpoena ad testificandum* under SUBPOENA.

ad tunc. [Latin] Then and there.

ad tunc et ibidem (ad **təngk** et i-**bɪ**-dəm *or* **ib**-i-dəm), *adv.* [Latin] *Hist.* Then and there being found. • This phrase was formerly used in indictments.

adult (ə-**dəlt** *or* **ad**-əlt), *n.* (17c) Someone who has attained the legal age of majority, generally 17 in criminal cases and 18 for other purposes. — Also termed *major.* Cf. MINOR (1). — **adult** (ə-**dəlt**), *adj.*

▸ **consenting adult.** An adult who, being capable of making decisions, decides to willingly participate in an activity; specif., someone who is considered old enough to decide whether to participate in sexual activity.

▸ **disabled adult.** A person of legal age who has a temporary or permanent physical or mental handicap. See DISABILITY (2).

▸ **vulnerable adult.** (1982) An adult who is physically or mentally disabled; esp., one dependent on institutional services.

adult abuse. See ABUSE.

adult adoption. See ADOPTION (1).

adult correctional institution. See PRISON.

adult disabled person. See PERSON (1).

adulter (ə-**dəl**-tər), *n.* [Latin] (16c) *Roman law.* An adulterer; a man guilty of adultery.

adultera (ə-**dəl**-tə-rə), *n.* [Latin] *Roman law.* An adulteress; a woman guilty of adultery.

adulterant, *n.* (18c) **1.** Any foreign material added to another substance to create impurity. **2.** *Criminal law.* A usu. inexpensive material used to dilute and increase the bulk or quantity of a controlled substance, regardless of its effect on the substance's chemical nature. • An example is flour added to cocaine. Some states include adulterants when calculating the weight of a controlled substance for prosecution of the possessor. — Also termed *dilutant; diluent; cutting agent.*

adulterate (ə-**dəl**-tə-rayt), *vb.* (16c) To debase or make impure by adding a foreign or inferior substance. — **adulteration,** *n.*

adulterated drug. See DRUG.

adulterator (ə-**dəl**-tə-ray-tər), *n.* [Latin fr. *adulterare* "to adulterate"] (17c) *Civil law.* A corrupter; a forger; a counterfeiter, as in *adulteratores monetae* ("counterfeiters of money").

adulterine (ə-**dəl**-tə-rin), *adj.* (16c) **1.** Characterized by adulteration. **2.** Illegal; unlicensed. **3.** Born of adultery. **4.** Of or involving adultery; adulterous.

adulterine, *n.* (18c) *Archaic.* An illegitimate child.

adulterine bastard. See BASTARD.

adulterine guild. (18c) *Hist.* A group of traders who act like a corporation without a charter and who pay an annual fine for permission to exercise their usurped privileges.

adulterini (ə-dəl-tə-**rɪ**-nɪ). [Law Latin] *Hist.* Children begotten adulterously. Cf. INCESTUOSI.

adulterium (ad-əl-**teer**-ee-əm), *n.* [Latin] *Roman & civil law.* **1.** The crime of adultery. **2.** A punishment imposed for the offense of adultery.

> "Adulterium. . . . [A]dultery . . . was considered a criminal offense only when committed by a married woman (*adultera*) . . . . [Before the *Lex Julia de adulteriis coercendis* of 18 B.C.], customary law admitted only immediate revenge of the husband . . . . Under the Julian statute, the father of the adulterous woman was permitted to kill her and her partner (*adulter*) if he surprised them in his or her husband's house. The husband's rights were rather limited; he was forced to divorce her, for otherwise he made himself guilty of matchmaking [pandering] . . . . Besides, he or his father had to accuse the adulteress of *adulterium* which now became a public crime prosecuted before a criminal court." Adolf Berger, *Encyclopedic Dictionary of Roman Law* 352 (1953).

adultery (ə-**dəl**-tə-ree), *n.* (15c) Voluntary sexual intercourse between a married person and someone other than the person's spouse. • In many jurisdictions, adultery is a crime, but it is rarely prosecuted. In states that still permit fault divorce, proof of adultery is a ground on which a divorce may be granted. A court may also use proof of adultery as a reason to reduce the offending spouse's marital-property award in a property division. Judges traditionally viewed adultery as a reason for denying the offending spouse primary custody of a child in a child-custody dispute. But today, only the deleterious effect of immoral behavior on the child is typically considered relevant. — Formerly also termed *spouse-breach; avowtry.* Cf. FORNICATION; INFIDELITY. — **adulterous,** *adj.* — **adulterer, adulteress,** *n.*

> "In those states which make adultery a criminal offense, without defining it, sexual intercourse between a married woman and a man other than her husband is held by all authorities to constitute the crime; and in some of the states this is held to be an exclusive definition of the offense, on the ground that the gist of the crime is the danger of introducing spurious heirs into the family. In other states, however, it is held that the offense is committed by sexual connection between a man and a woman, one of whom is lawfully married to a third person, and that whether the married person is a man or woman makes no difference." Martin L. Newell, *The Law of Defamation, Libel and Slander* 152 (1890).

> "Returning to the question of adultery, evidently this word cannot be interpreted today in precisely the meaning it bore for the Old Testament patriarchs. On Old Testament principles one may marry several wives, even two sisters; and a married man may and should beget children for his dead brother. When Sarah found herself childless, she advised her husband Abraham to go in unto her maid, so that she might obtain children by the maid. Such acts, though evidently not adulterous within the original meaning of the Decalogue, would be regarded as adulterous by the laws and customs of Western society at the present day." Glanville Williams, *The Sanctity of Life and the Criminal Law* 134 (1957).

> "If a statute provided for the punishment of adultery without definition of the term, this gave rise to a difficulty as to the meaning of the word. In England, (1) the common-law meaning of the word was sex with another's wife, but this was not a common-law offense; (2) as the name of an offense it referred to sex by a married person with one other than the spouse, but that was recognized only in the ecclesiastical court." Rollin M. Perkins & Ronald N. Boyce, *Criminal Law* 455 (3d ed. 1982).

> "In some states, sexual intercourse between two married persons, who are not married to each other, constitutes adultery on the part of both; sexual intercourse between a married person and an unmarried person likewise constitutes adultery on the part of both. In other states, adultery can be committed only by a married person. Thus, sexual intercourse between two married persons, who are not married to each other, constitutes adultery on the part of both; but if only one party to the sexual intercourse is married, the intercourse constitutes adultery on the part of the married person and fornication on the part of the unmarried person. In other states, sexual intercourse constitutes adultery only where the woman is the married party. Thus, sexual intercourse between a married woman and a married man other than her spouse or sexual intercourse between a married woman and an unmarried man constitutes adultery on the part of both; but if the woman is unmarried, neither party is guilty of adultery even if the man is married." 2 Charles E. Torcia, *Wharton's Criminal Law* § 211, at 531 (15th ed. 1994).

▸ **double adultery.** (15c) Adultery between persons who are both married to other persons.

▸ **incestuous adultery.** (16c) Adultery between relatives; adultery committed by persons who are closely related.

▸ **open and notorious adultery.** (18c) *Archaic.* Adultery in which the parties reside together publicly, as if married, and the community is generally aware of the living arrangement and the fact that the couple are not married.

▸ **single adultery.** (17c) Adultery in which only one of the persons is married.

adult offender. See OFFENDER.

Adult Protective Services. (1973) A governmental agency with responsibility for investigating allegations of elder abuse and neglect and for responding appropriately. • Every state has such an agency. — Abbr. APS. Cf. CHILD PROTECTIVE SERVICES.

ad usum et commodum (ad **yoo**-səm [*or* -zəm] et **kom**-ə-dəm), *adv.* [Law Latin] To the use and benefit.

ad valentiam (ad və-**len**-shee-əm), *adv.* [Law Latin] To the value.

ad valorem (ad və-**lor**-əm), *adj.* [Latin "according to the value"] (18c) (Of a tax) proportional to the value of the thing taxed. — **ad valorem,** *adv.*

ad valorem duty. See DUTY (4).

ad valorem tariff. See TARIFF (2).

ad valorem tax. See TAX.

advance, *n.* (17c) **1.** The furnishing of money or goods before any consideration is received in return. **2.** The money or goods furnished.

advance bill. See BILL (6).

advance cost. See COST (1).

advance-decline index. See INDEX (2).

advance directive. (1984) **1.** A document that takes effect upon one's incompetency and designates a surrogate decision-maker for healthcare matters. • The Uniform Health-Care Decisions Act (1993) states that the power of attorney for healthcare must be in writing and signed by the principal. Unless otherwise stated, the authority is effective only upon a determination that the principal lacks capacity, and it ceases to be effective once the principal regains his capacity. The agent must make decisions in accordance with the principal's relevant instructions, if there are any, or in the principal's best interests. — Also termed *power of attorney for healthcare*; *healthcare proxy.* See POWER OF ATTORNEY; UNIFORM HEALTH-CARE DECISIONS ACT. **2.** A legal document explaining one's wishes about medical treatment if one becomes incompetent or unable to communicate. — Often shortened to *directive.* — Also termed *medical directive*; *physician's directive*; *written directive.* See NATURAL-DEATH ACT; INSTRUCTION DIRECTIVE; PROXY DIRECTIVE. Cf. LIVING WILL. **3.** DO-NOT-RESUSCITATE ORDER.

advanced notice. See *advance notice* under NOTICE (3).

Advanced Television Enhancement Forum. A standard-setting organization that defines the protocols for HTML-based enhanced television. • The organization is an alliance of representatives from broadcast and cable networks, the consumer electronics and personal-computer industries, and television-transport companies. — Abbr. ATVEF.

advance-fee fraud. See FRAUD.

advancement, *n.* (15c) **1.** A payment to an heir (esp. a child) during one's lifetime as an advance share of one's estate, with the intention of reducing or extinguishing or diminishing the heir's claim to the estate under intestacy laws. • In some jurisdictions, the donor's intent is irrelevant if all the statutory elements of an advancement are present. A few jurisdictions define the relationship between the donor and donee to include inter vivos transfers between ancestors and descendants. — Also termed *preheritance.* See SATISFACTION (4). Cf. ADEMPTION.

> "It is sometimes difficult to know whether money which a parent has given to his child is an advancement or not, but, generally speaking, an advancement is money which is given either to start a child in life or to provide for him, and does not include casual payments, so that a child is not bound to account for every sum received from a parent." G.C. Cheshire, *Modern Law of Real Property* 784 (3d ed. 1933).

2. Progress or development in a person's job, skills, or level of knowledge. — **advance,** *vb.*

advance notice. See NOTICE (3).

advance payment. See PAYMENT (2).

advance premium. See PREMIUM (1).

advance pricing agreement. (1990) *Tax.* A usu. binding arrangement made between a multinational company and one or more national tax authorities about what method the company will use to calculate transfer prices. • The agreement's purpose is to reduce or eliminate double taxation. — Abbr. APA.

▸ **bilateral advance pricing agreement.** (1994) An advance pricing agreement made between a company and two tax authorities.

▸ **multilateral advance pricing agreement.** (1995) An advance pricing agreement made between a company and more than two tax authorities.

▸ **unilateral advance pricing agreement.** (2008) An advance pricing agreement made between a company and one tax authority. • This does not necessarily allow a company to avoid double taxation. A tax authority that is not a party to the agreement is not bound by the transfer-pricing method specified in the agreement.

advance sheets. (1868) A softcover pamphlet containing recently reported opinions by a court or set of courts. • Advance sheets are published during the interim between an opinion's announcement and its inclusion in a bound volume of law reports. Cf. *slip opinion* (1) under OPINION (1); REPORT (3).

> "As a bound volume of any series of reports is not published until sufficient matter has accumulated to fill it, it necessarily results in the holding of the first decisions rendered after the preceding volume has been issued, until there are enough more to justify the publication of the next volume. Even after enough material has been accumulated to fill a volume, there is necessarily considerable time consumed in its printing, indexing, and binding before the book is ready for delivery. Hence, it is customary, as soon as a part of the volume has come from the press, to issue such part in pamphlet form; and these paper-bound copies are known as 'advance sheets.' They are portions of the next volume issued in advance of final publication, being paged as they will appear in the bound volume. Advance sheets enable the enterprising lawyer to obtain the decisions right down almost to the date of his search for the law." Frank Hall Childs, *Where and How to Find the Law* 21 (1922).

advancing market. See *bull market* under MARKET.

advantage, *n.* (13c) **1.** A circumstance, ability, or condition that produces a superior position or state of being; superiority of state or position. **2.** Something that helps one to become more successful than others. **3.** The quality, state, or condition of possessing something that helps one to become more successful than others. **4.** A good or useful feature that something, such as a product, has. **5.** Any benefit or gain, esp. when derived from superiority of state or position. — **advantage,** *vb.* — **advantageous,** *adj.*

▸ **competitive advantage.** (1889) The potential benefit from information, ideas, or devices that, if kept secret by a business, might be economically exploited to improve the business's market share or to increase its income.

▸ **financial advantage.** The condition of being able to gain or of having more money than another. — Also termed *pecuniary advantage.*

▸ **pecuniary advantage.** See *financial advantage.*

advantaged, *adj.* (17c) Having more money, a better social position, etc. than someone else.

advantagium (ad-van-**tay**-jee-əm), *n.* [Law Latin] *Hist.* An advantage.

advena (**ad**-və-nə), *n.* [Latin] *Roman law.* Someone who has come from abroad, esp. for a temporary stay; a sojourner.

adventitia bona (ad-ven-**tish**-ee-ə **boh**-nə). See BONA ADVENTITIA.

adventitia dos (ad-ven-**tish**-ee-ə dohs), *n.* [Latin] *Civil law.* A dowry given by someone other than the wife's paterfamilias. Pl. ***adventitiae dotes.***

adventitious property. See PROPERTY.

ad ventrem inspiciendum (ad **ven**-trəm in-spish-ee-**en**-dəm), *n.* [Latin] See DE VENTRE INSPICIENDO.

adventura (ad-ven-**t[y]oor**-ə), *n.* [Law Latin] *Hist.* An adventure. • Flotsam, jetsam, and lagan were styled *adventurae maris* ("adventures of the sea").

adventure. (17c) **1.** A commercial undertaking that has an element of risk; a venture. Cf. JOINT VENTURE. **2.** *Marine insurance.* A voyage involving financial and insurable risk, as to a shipment of goods. — Often shortened to *venture.*

▸ **common adventure.** (17c) A maritime enterprise, characterized as an undertaking in which all participants, including the carrier, everyone with an interest in the cargo, and the insurers, share the risks of the perils of the sea. • The principle of shared risk is fundamental to maritime law. — Also termed *joint adventure; common venture.*

▸ **gross adventure.** (17c) A loan on bottomry, so called because the lender will be liable for the gross (or general) average. See BOTTOMRY.

▸ **joint adventure.** (17c) **1.** See *common adventure.* **2.** See JOINT VENTURE.

adventurer. (17c) Someone who undertakes a hazardous action or enterprise; one with a stake in a commercial adventure.

ad verecundiam. See *argumentum ad verecundiam* under ARGUMENTUM.

adversarial, *adj.* Involving or characterized by dispute or a clash of interests. — **adversary,** *n.*

adversarius (ad-vər-**sair**-ee-əs), *n.* [Latin] *Roman law.* An adversary in a lawsuit.

adversary (**ad**-vər-ser-ee), *n.* (14c) An opponent; esp., opposing counsel. — Also termed *opposition.* — **adversary,** *adj.*

adversary procedure. See ADVERSARY SYSTEM.

adversary proceeding. (1744) **1.** A hearing involving a dispute between opposing parties <Judge Adams presided over the adversary proceeding between the landlord and tenant>. **2.** *Bankruptcy.* A lawsuit that is brought within a bankruptcy proceeding, governed by special procedural rules, and based on conflicting claims usu. between the debtor (or the trustee) and a creditor or other interested party <the Chapter 7 trustee filed an adversary proceeding against the party who received $100,000 from the debtor one week before the bankruptcy filing>.

adversary system. (1936) A procedural system, such as the Anglo-American legal system, involving active and unhindered parties contesting with each other to put forth a case before an independent decision-maker. — Also termed *adversary procedure;* (in criminal cases) *accusatorial system; accusatory procedure.* Cf. INQUISITORIAL SYSTEM.

> "The term *adversary system* sometimes characterizes an entire legal process, and sometimes it refers only to criminal procedure. In the latter instance, it is often used interchangeably with an old expression of continental European origin, 'accusatorial procedure,' and is juxtaposed to the 'inquisitorial,' or 'nonadversary,' process. There is no precise understanding, however, of the institutions and arrangements denoted by these expressions." Mirjan Damaska, "Adversary Procedure," in 1 *Encyclopedia of Crime and Justice* 24, 24–25 (Sanford H. Kadish ed., 1983).

adverse, *adj.* (15c) **1.** Against; opposed (to). **2.** Having an opposing or contrary interest, concern, or position. **3.** Contrary (to) or in opposition (to). **4.** HOSTILE.

adverse action. (18c) A decision or event that unfavorably affects a person, entity, or association. • Common examples of adverse actions include a decrease in one's pay by an employer or a denial of credit by a lender.

adverse-agent doctrine. (1954) The rule that an agent's knowledge will not be imputed to the principal if the agent is engaged in fraudulent activities that are concealed as part of the fraud. See DOCTRINE OF IMPUTED KNOWLEDGE.

adverse authority. See AUTHORITY (4).

adverse-domination doctrine. (1989) The equitable principle that the statute of limitations on a breach-of-fiduciary-duty claim against officers and directors (esp. a corporation's action against its own officers and directors) is tolled as long as a corporate plaintiff is controlled by the alleged wrongdoers. • The statute is tolled until a majority of the disinterested directors discover or are put on notice of the claim against the wrongdoers. The purpose of this doctrine is to prevent a director or officer from successfully hiding wrongful or fraudulent conduct during the limitations period. *FDIC v. Shrader & York,* 991 F.2d 216, 227 (5th Cir. 1993). This doctrine is available only to benefit the corporation. — Also termed *adverse dominion; doctrine of adverse domination.*

adverse dominion. **1.** ADVERSE-DOMINATION DOCTRINE. **2.** *Rare. Torts.* The unlawful exercise of authority or control over goods so that the true owner is dispossessed. See CONVERSION (2). **3.** *Rare.* ADVERSE POSSESSION (1).

adverse easement. See *prescriptive easement* under EASEMENT.

adverse employment action. (1977) An employer's decision that substantially and negatively affects an employee's job, such as a termination, demotion, or pay cut. — Often shortened to *employment action*. — Also termed *adverse job action*; *job action*.

adverse enjoyment. See ENJOYMENT.

adverse impact. See DISPARATE IMPACT.

adverse inference. See INFERENCE (1).

adverse-inference charge. See *adverse-inference instruction* under JURY INSTRUCTION.

adverse-inference instruction. See JURY INSTRUCTION.

adverse-inference rule. See ADVERSE-INTEREST RULE.

adverse interest. (17c) An interest that is opposed or contrary to that of someone else.

adverse-interest rule. (1904) The principle that if a party fails to produce a witness who is within its power to produce and who should have been produced, the judge may instruct the jury to infer that the witness's evidence is unfavorable to the party's case. — Also termed *empty-chair doctrine*; *adverse-inference rule*.

adverse job action. See ADVERSE EMPLOYMENT ACTION.

adverse opinion. See OPINION (2).

adverse party. See PARTY (2).

adverse possession. (18c) **1.** The enjoyment of real property with a claim of right when that enjoyment is opposed to another person's claim and is continuous, exclusive, hostile, open, and notorious. • In Louisiana, it is the detention or enjoyment of a corporeal thing with the intent to hold it as one's own. La. Civ. Code art. 3421. — Also termed *adverse dominion*. Cf. PRESCRIPTION (5).

▸ **constructive adverse possession.** (1823) **1.** Adverse possession in which the claim arises from the claimant's payment of taxes under color of right rather than by actual possession of the land. **2.** *Louisiana law*. Adverse possession by operation of law. • When a possessor holds title to the property and corporeally possesses part of it, the possessor is deemed to have constructive possession of the rest of the property described in the title. La. Civ. Code art. 3426.

2. The doctrine by which title to real property is acquired as a result of such use or enjoyment over a specified period of time. See POSSESSION.

adverse presumption. See *adverse inference* under INFERENCE (1).

adverse title. See TITLE (2).

adverse use. See USE (1).

adverse witness. See *hostile witness* under WITNESS.

adversus (ad-**vər**-səs), *prep*. [Latin] Against. • The first letter of this term was formerly used in law reports in place of the more commonly used *v.* ("versus"). — Abbr. a.

adversus bonos mores. See CONTRA BONOS MORES.

advertent negligence. See NEGLIGENCE.

advertisement. A commercial solicitation; an item of published or transmitted matter made with the intention of attracting clients or customers. — **advertise,** *vb*.

advertising. (18c) **1.** The action of drawing the public's attention to something to promote its sale. **2.** The business of producing and circulating advertisements.

▸ **ambient advertising.** (1997) Advertising that is present on objects that are not traditionally expected to have it, such as pens, lampshades, train tickets, and floors.

▸ **comparative advertising.** (1936) Advertising that specifically compares the advertised brand with another brand of the same product.

▸ **competitive advertising.** (1954) Advertising that contains little information about the advertised product, and that is used only to help a producer maintain a share of the market for that product.

▸ **deceptive advertising.** See FALSE ADVERTISING.

▸ **false advertising.** See FALSE ADVERTISING.

▸ **informative advertising.** (1968) Advertising that gives information about the suitability and quality of a product.

advertising injury. See INJURY.

advertising substantiation. (1972) A doctrine of the Federal Trade Commission making it an unfair and deceptive act to put out an advertisement unless the advertiser first has a reasonable basis for believing that each claim in the advertisement is true.

advice (ad-**vɪs**). (14c) **1.** Guidance offered by one person, esp. a lawyer, to another; professional counsel. See ADVICE OF COUNSEL. **2.** Notice of the drawing of a draft for goods or services. See LETTER OF ADVICE; ADVICE OF CREDIT. — **advise** (ad-**vɪz**), *vb*.

▸ **legal advice.** See ADVICE OF COUNSEL (1).

▸ **remittance advice.** (1921) Notice that a sum of money has been sent for goods or services. See REMITTANCE.

advice and consent. (1787) **1.** *Constitutional law*. The power of the U.S. Senate to participate in making and ratifying treaties and appointing federal officers, provided by U.S. Const. art II, § 2. • For treaties, a two-thirds majority of the Senate is necessary for ratification. For federal officers, a simple majority is sufficient. **2.** *English law*. The power of Parliament to enact legislation nominally made by the sovereign. • A modern British Act of Parliament typically contains the following enacting clause: "Be it enacted by the Queen's most Excellent Majesty, by and with the advice and consent of the Lords Spiritual and Temporal, and Commons, in this Present Parliament assembled, and by the authority for the same, as follows. . . ."

Advice and Consent Clause. *Constitutional law*. The constitutional provision that the President of the United States may exercise certain powers only after the Senate has reviewed the proposed exercise and agreed to it. • The clause requires the Senate's advice on and consent to, among other things, making treaties, appointing ambassadors, and appointing United States Supreme Court Justices. U.S. Const. art. II, § 2, cl 2.

advice of counsel. (17c) **1.** The guidance given by lawyers to their clients. — Also termed *legal advice*. **2.** A defense in which a party seeks to avoid liability or punishment by claiming that he or she acted reasonably and in good faith on the attorney's advice. • Such a defense usu. requires waiver of the attorney–client privilege, and the attorney cannot have knowingly participated in implementing an illegal plan. — Also termed *advice-of-counsel defense*. **3.** In a malicious-prosecution lawsuit, a defense requiring both a complete presentation of facts by the defendant to his or her attorney and honest compliance with the attorney's advice. See MALICIOUS PROSECUTION.

> "Advice of counsel is a defense to a limited number of torts involving lack of probable cause, bad faith, or malice as an element of the cause of action. By far the most frequent cause of action against which the defense is asserted is malicious prosecution. The defense may also be asserted to avoid liability for punitive damages on the reasoning that good faith reliance on advice of counsel defeats the malice necessary to an award of punitive damages. In civil matters, the advice is typically obtained from the defendant's own attorney; when the underlying proceeding is criminal, the advice may be obtained from the district attorney's office or similar source and may take the form of action by that officer rather than advice followed by action by the defendant." 4 Ann Taylor Schwing, *California Affirmative Defenses* § 41:26, at 82 (2d ed. 1996).

advice-of-counsel defense. (1976) **1.** ADVICE OF COUNSEL (2). **2.** *Patents.* In an action for infringement, an assertion that after learning of the owner's rights, the defendant sought, obtained, and relied on an attorney's well-reasoned opinion before continuing the challenged act. • Courts treat the assertion as a factor in determining whether an act was willful (to support enhanced damages). It is not a true defense. Cf. *willful infringement* under INFRINGEMENT; LEGAL-ADVICE EXCEPTION.

advice of credit. (1885) Notice by an advising bank of the issuance of a letter of credit. See ADVICE (2).

ad vindictam publicam (ad vin-**dik**-təm **pəb**-li-kəm). [Latin] (17c) *Scots law.* For vindicating the public interest. • The phrase appeared in reference to the purpose for which government prosecuted crimes.

advisare (ad-vi-**zair**-ee), *vb.* [Law Latin] To consult, deliberate, or consider. See CURIA ADVISARI VULT.

advisement (ad-**vɪz**-mənt). (14c) Careful consideration; the activity or process of deliberation, esp. by a judge <the judge took the matter under advisement and promised a ruling by the next day>.

advising bank. See BANK.

advisory action. *Patents.* See *advisory office action* under OFFICE ACTION.

advisory committee. (1867) A committee formed to make suggestions to an executive or legislative body or to an official; esp., any one of five committees that propose to the Standing Committee on Rules of Practice and Procedure amendments to federal court rules, the five committees being responsible for appellate, bankruptcy, civil, criminal, and evidence rules.

advisory counsel. See COUNSEL.

advisory jury. See JURY.

advisory office action. See OFFICE ACTION.

advisory opinion. See OPINION (1).

ad vitam (ad **vɪ**-təm), *adj.* [Latin] For life.

ad vitam aut culpam (ad **vɪ**-təm awt **kəl**-pəm), *adj.* [Law Latin] For life or until misbehavior. • This phrase described a tenure of office.

ad vitandum perjurium (ad vɪ-**tan**-dəm pər-**joor**-ee-əm). [Latin] *Scots law.* For avoiding perjury. See OB METUM PERJURII.

advocacy. (15c) **1.** The work or profession of an advocate. **2.** The art of pleading for or actively supporting a cause or proposal.

advocare (ad-və-**kair**-ee), *vb.* [Law Latin] **1.** To advocate, defend, or protect. **2.** To acknowledge or admit openly, as to acknowledge paternity of a child (*advocare filium*).

advocassie (**ad**-və-kə-see), *n.* [Law French] Advocacy.

advocata (ad-və-**kay**-tə), *n.* [Law Latin] *Hist.* A patroness; a woman holding the right to present to a church.

advocate (**ad**-və-kit), *n.* (14c) **1.** Someone who assists, defends, pleads, or prosecutes for another. **2.** *Civil & Scots law.* A barrister; specif., a member of the Faculty of Advocates (the Scottish counterpart of a barrister) or of the Society of Advocates in Aberdeen (a society of solicitors). • A member of the Aberdeen society is designated "advocate in Aberdeen." Cf. BARRISTER. **3.** *Hist. Eccles. law.* Someone who is trained in both canon and secular law and can (1) appear in an ecclesiastical or admiralty court on another's behalf, and (2) give legal advice. • Members of the College of Advocates (also known as Doctors' Commons) bore the title of *advocate.* After the dissolution of the College in 1857, the term became indistinguishably associated with *barrister.* — **advocate** (**ad**-və-kayt), *vb.* — **advocacy** (**ad**-və-kə-see), *n.*

advocate-depute (di-**pyoot**). (18c) *Scots law.* One of a number of advocates appointed by the Lord Advocate to prosecute criminal cases in his or her name.

Advocate General. (1998) *Scots law.* An officer appointed under the Scotland Act of 1998 to advise the British government on Scotland and to represent it in court.

advocate of the faith. *Eccles. law.* Counsel for the prosecution in a heresy trial.

advocate's bias. See BIAS.

advocate–witness rule. (1972) See LAWYER–WITNESS RULE.

advocati ecclesiae (ad-və-**kay**-tɪ e-**klee**-z[h]ee-ee), *n. pl.* [Latin "church advocates"] *Hist. Eccles. law.* **1.** Church patrons who had a right to present a clerk to a benefice. See ADVOWSON. **2.** Legal advocates retained to argue cases relating to a church.

advocatio (ad-və-**kay**-shee-oh), *n.* [Law Latin] *Hist.* **1.** An inferior's management of a business for a superior. **2.** The defense of a religious establishment. **3.** ADVOWSON. **4.** *Civil law.* The quality, function, privilege, office, or service of an advocate; legal assistance.

advocation (ad-və-**kay**-shən), *n.* (16c) *Scots law.* The transfer of a criminal case from a lower court by the High Court of Justiciary to itself for verdict.

advocatione decimarum (ad-və-kay-shee-**oh**-nee des-ə-**mair**-əm), *n.* [Law Latin] (17c) *Hist.* A writ to collect a tithe belonging to the church.

advocator (ad-voh-**kay**-tər), *n.* [Law Latin] (15c) *Hist.* **1.** Someone who calls on another to warrant a title. **2.** A warrantor. **3.** The patron of a benefice.

advocatus (ad-voh-**kay**-təs). [Latin "advocate"] **1.** *Roman law.* A legal adviser; a person who assists clients with cases before judicial tribunals. Cf. CAUSIDICUS. **2.** *Hist.* The patron who has an advowson. — Also termed *advowee; avowee.* See ADVOWSON. **3.** *Hist.* A person called on by another to warrant a title.

advocatus diaboli (ad-voh-**kay**-təs dɪ-**ab**-ə-lɪ), *n.* [Latin "devil's advocate"] (1842) *Eccles. law.* An official who argues against a person's beatification or canonization.

advocatus ecclesiae (ad-və-**kay**-təs e-**klee**-z[h]ee-ee). [Law Latin] *Hist. Eccles. law.* The patron of a benefice.

advocatus fisci (ad-voh-**kay**-təs **fisk**-ɪ). [Latin] (17c) *Roman law.* An official responsible for representing the emperor in cases involving the public fisc.

ad voluntatem (ad vol-ən-**tay**-təm), *adv. & adj.* [Law Latin] At will.

advouter. See ADVOUTRER.

advouterer. See ADVOUTRER.

advoutrer (ad-**vow**-trər), *n.* [Law French] *Hist.* An adulterer. — Also termed *advouter; advouterer; advoutre.*

advoutry (ad-**vow**-tree), *n.* [Law French] *Hist.* Adultery between two married persons. — Also spelled *advowtry.*

advowee (ad-vow-**ee**). (17c) A patron who holds an advowson; ADVOCATUS (2). — Also spelled *avowee.*

▸ **advowee paramount.** (17c) The sovereign, or highest patron.

advowson (ad-**vow**-zən). (13c) *Eccles. law.* The right of presenting or nominating a person to a vacant benefice in the church. • The person enjoying this right is called the "patron" (*patronus*) of the church, and was formerly termed "advocatus," the advocate or defender, or in English, the "advowee." The patron presents the nominee to the bishop (or, occasionally, another church dignitary). If there is no patron, or if the patron neglects to exercise the right within six months, the right lapses and a title is given to the ordinary (usu. the bishop) to appoint a cleric to the church. Cf. PRESENTATION (2); INSTITUTION (5).

> "A right of presentation has always been regarded as a valuable object of a sale, a species of real property which can be transferred and dealt with generally in the same way as a fee simple estate in lands . . . . Thus an advowson may be conveyed away in fee simple, fee tail, for life or years, or the conveyance may be limited to the right of next presentation or of a specified number of future presentations." G.C. Cheshire, *Modern Law of Real Property* 110 (3d ed. 1933).

> "An advowson is the perpetual right of presentation to an ecclesiastical living. The owner of an advowson is known as the patron. When a living becomes vacant, as when a rector or vicar dies or retires, the patron of the living has a right to nominate the clergyman who shall next hold the living. Subject to a right of veto on certain specified grounds, the Bishop is bound to institute (formally appoint) any duly qualified person presented. This is a relic of the days when it was common for the lord of a manor to build and endow a church and in return have the right of patronage." Robert E. Megarry & P.V. Baker, *A Manual of the Law of Real Property* 414 (4th ed. 1969).

▸ **advowson appendant** (ə-**pen**-dənt). (17c) An advowson annexed to a manor, and passing as incident to it, whenever the manor is conveyed to another. • The advowson passes with the manor even if it is not mentioned in the grant.

▸ **advowson collative** (kə-**lay**-tiv). (18c) An advowson for which there is no separate presentation to the bishop because the bishop happens to be the patron as well. • In this case, the one act by which the benefice is conferred is called "collation."

▸ **advowson donative** (**don**-ə-tiv *or* **doh**-nə-tiv). (1803) An advowson in which the patron has the right to put a cleric in possession by a mere gift, or deed of donation, without any presentation to the bishop. • This type of advowson was converted into the *advowson presentative* by the Benefices Act of 1898. — Also termed *donative advowson.*

> "An advowson donative is when the king, or any subject by his licence, doth found a church or chapel, and ordains that it shall be merely in the gift or disposal of the patron; subject to his visitation only, and not to that of the ordinary; and vested absolutely in the clerk by the patron's deed of donation, without presentation, institution, or induction. This is said to have been anciently the only way of conferring ecclesiastical benefices in England; the method of institution by the bishop not being established more early than the time of archbishop Becket in the reign of Henry II." 2 William Blackstone, *Commentaries on the Laws of England* 23 (1766).

▸ **advowson in gross.** (17c) An advowson that is separated from the manor and annexed to a person. • All advowsons that have been separated from their original manors are advowsons in gross.

▸ **advowson presentative** (pri-**zen**-tə-tiv). (1802) The usual kind of advowson, in which the patron has the right to make the presentation to the bishop and to demand that the nominee be instituted, if the bishop finds the nominee canonically qualified. See *advowson donative.*

▸ **donative advowson.** See *advowson donative.*

AEA. *abbr.* ADMIRALTY EXTENSION ACT.

aedes (**ee**-deez), *n.* [Latin] *Roman law.* A building; esp., a temple (*aedes sacra*).

aedificare (ee-də-fi-**kair**-ee), *vb.* [Latin] *Roman law.* To erect a building.

aedile (**ee**-dɪl). (16c) *Roman law.* A magistrate charged with policing the city, managing public buildings and services, supervising markets, and arranging public games. — Also spelled *edile.*

aedilitium edictum (ee-də-**lish**-ee-əm ee-**dik**-təm). See *edictum aedilicium* under EDICTUM.

aegrotus (ee-**groh**-təs), *adj.* [Latin] Sick; indisposed by illness.

aemulationis causa (ee-myə-lay-shee-**oh**-nis **kaw**-zə). [Latin] *Hist.* For the purpose of rivaling or annoying.

aemulatio vicini (ee-myə-**lay**-shee-oh **vis**-i-nee). [Latin] *Scots law.* **1.** The use of land in a way injurious to a neighbor. **2.** The principle that one must not exercise what is otherwise a legitimate right for solely spiteful or malicious reasons.

aenum. See *ordeal by water* (2) under ORDEAL.

aequitas (**ek**-wə-tas *or* ee-kwə-tas), *n.* [Latin] *Roman law.* Equity, as opposed to *jus strictum* or *jus summum.*

aequus (**ee**-kwəs), *adj.* [Latin] Equal; even. • A provision in a will, for example, might divide the residuary estate *ex aequis* (the adverbial form) among the legatees.

aerarium (i-**rair**-ee-əm), *n.* [Latin fr. *aes* "money"] (16c) *Roman law.* The central treasury of the Roman Republic, housed in the Temple of Saturn. See FISCUS.

aes (eez), *n.* [Latin] *Roman law.* **1.** Copper. **2.** Money, of whatever metal.

aes alienum (**eez** ay-lee-**ee**-nəm *or* al-ee-), *n.* [Latin "another's money"] (16c) *Roman law.* Money owed to another; borrowed money.

aesnecia (ees-**neesh**-ee-ə). [Law Latin] See ESNECY.

aes suum (**eez** s[y]**oo**-əm), *n.* [Latin "one's own money"] (16c) *Roman law.* Money lent to a borrower.

aesthetic functionality. See FUNCTIONALITY.

aesthetic zoning. See ZONING.

aestimatio (es-tə-**may**-shee-oh), *n.* [Latin] *Roman law.* An agreement by which the owner of goods handed them over to another person with the understanding that the other would sell what he could for the most he could get, paying the owner an agreed price for whatever goods sold and returning the others. — Also termed *aestimaterian contract.* Pl. ***aestimationes*** (es-tə-may-shee-**oh**-neez).

aetas (**ee**-tas), *n.* [Latin] *Roman law.* Age.

aetas infantiae proxima (**ee**-tas in-**fan**-shee-ee **prok**-sə-mə), *n.* [Latin] (18c) *Roman law.* The first part of the period of childhood between infancy (up to 7 years) and puberty (12 to 14 years); esp., for males, the period between 7 and 10½ years of age. Cf. AETAS PUBERTATI PROXIMA; PUERITIA.

aetas legitima (**ee**-tas lə-**jit**-ə-mə), *n.* [Latin] (18c) *Roman law.* Lawful age.

aetas perfecta (**ee**-tas pər-**fek**-tə), *n.* [Latin] *Roman law.* Complete age; the age of majority.

aetas prima (**ee**-tas **prɪ**-mə), *n.* [Latin] (17c) *Roman law.* First age. See INFANTIA.

aetas pubertati proxima (**ee**-tas pyoo-bər-**tay**-tɪ **prok**-sə-mə), *n.* [Latin] (18c) *Roman law.* The second period of childhood, (for males) from 10½ to 14 years of age. Cf. AETAS INFANTIAE PROXIMA; PUERITIA.

aetate probanda (ee-**tay**-tee proh-**ban**-də). See DE AETATE PROBANDA.

AFC test. *abbr.* ABSTRACTION-FILTRATION-COMPARISON TEST.

AFDC. *abbr.* AID TO FAMILIES WITH DEPENDENT CHILDREN.

aff'd. *abbr.* Affirmed.

affect, *n.* (14c) Inner feelings, emotions, and desires, esp. as they are reflected in a person's facial expressions.

affect, *vb.* (15c) **1.** Most generally, to produce an effect on; to influence in some way. **2.** *Civil law.* To pledge (property or revenues) as security for a loan; HYPOTHECATE. **3.** *Scots law.* To seize (debtor's property, etc.).

affectation doctrine. See AFFECTS DOCTRINE.

affecting commerce. (1812) (Of an industry, activity, etc.) touching or concerning business, industry, or trade; esp., under the Labor–Management Relations Act, burdening or obstructing commerce, or having led or tending to lead to a labor dispute that burdens or obstructs the free flow of commerce. 29 USCA § 152(7).

affection. (14c) **1.** Fond attachment, devotion, or love <alienation of affections>. **2.** *Hist.* The pawning or mortgaging of a thing to ensure the payment of money or performance of some other obligation.

affects doctrine. (1996) *Constitutional law.* The principle allowing Congress, under the Commerce Clause, to regulate intrastate activities that have a substantial effect on interstate commerce. • The doctrine is so called because the test is whether a given activity "affects" interstate commerce. — Also termed *effects doctrine* or (erroneously) *affectation doctrine.*

affectus (ə-**fek**-təs), *n.* [Latin] *Hist.* Intent; disposition of mind.

affectus sine effectu (e-**fek**-təs **sɪ**-nee e-**fek**-t[y]oo). [Latin "an intention without effect"] *Hist.* An intention that is not carried out.

affeer (ə-**feer**), *vb.* [fr. Old French. *affeurer* "to tax"] (15c) *Hist.* To fix the amount of an amercement. — **affeerment,** *n.*

affeeror (ə-**feer**-ər), *n.* (15c) *Hist.* An official responsible for assessing amercements in cases in which no precise penalty is given by statute.

affermer (a-fər-**may**), *vb.* [Law French] **1.** To let to farm. **2.** To make sure; to confirm.

aff'g. *abbr.* Affirming.

affiance (ə-**fɪ**-ənts). (14c) **1.** *Archaic.* The act of confiding. **2.** The pledging of faith; specif., the act of promising to wed.

affiant (ə-**fɪ**-ənt). (1807) **1.** Someone who makes an affidavit or declaration under oath. — Also termed *deponent; declarant.* **2.** COMPLAINANT (2).

affidare (af-ə-**dair**-ee), *vb.* [Law Latin] To swear faith to; esp., a tenant's pledge of faith to a lord.

affidatio dominorum (af-ə-**day**-shee-oh dom-ə-**nor**-əm), *n.* [Law Latin] (18c) *Hist.* An oath taken by lords in Parliament.

affidatus (af-ə-**day**-təs), *n.* [Law Latin] (17c) *Hist.* A tenant by fealty.

affidavit (af-ə-**day**-vit). (16c) A voluntary declaration of facts written down and sworn to by a declarant, usu. before an officer authorized to administer oaths. • A great deal of evidence is submitted by affidavit, esp. in pretrial matters such as summary-judgment motions. Cf. DECLARATION (1), (8).

▸ **affidavit after appeal.** (1949) *Patents.* A sworn statement submitted to the U.S. Patent and Trademark Office after the filing of a notice of appeal from an adverse determination by an examiner. • An affidavit or declaration submitted after a case has been appealed will not be admitted without a showing of good and sufficient reasons why it was not presented earlier.

▸ **affidavit after final rejection.** (1939) *Patents.* A sworn statement submitted to the U.S. Patent and Trademark Office after an application's final rejection. — Also termed *declaration after final rejection.*

▸ **affidavit for the record.** An affidavit made by a surveyor or engineer to supplement, correct, update, or otherwise alter existing information in official real-estate records.

▸ **affidavit of claim.** (1850) An affidavit in which a plaintiff asserts that he or she has a meritorious cause of action.

▸ **affidavit of continued use.** See DECLARATION OF USE.

▸ **affidavit of defense.** See *affidavit of merits.*

▸ **affidavit of incontestability.** See DECLARATION OF INCONTESTABILITY.

▸ **affidavit of increase.** (1834) *Hist.* An affidavit that lists — and seeks reimbursement from the opposing party for — the additional costs (above the filing fee and other basic fees charged by the court clerk) incurred by a party in taking a matter through trial. • Attorney fees, witness payments, and the like were included in this affidavit. See COSTS OF INCREASE.

▸ **affidavit of inquiry.** (1925) An affidavit, required in certain states before substituted service of process on an absent defendant, in which the plaintiff's attorney or a person with knowledge of the facts indicates that the defendant cannot be served within the state.

▸ **affidavit of merit.** See *certificate of merit* (2) under CERTIFICATE.

▸ **affidavit of merits.** (18c) An affidavit in which a defendant asserts that he or she has a meritorious defense. — Also termed *affidavit of defense.*

▸ **affidavit of nonprosecution.** (1980) An affidavit in which a crime victim requests that the perpetrator not be prosecuted. • In many cases, if the victim files an affidavit of nonprosecution, the prosecutor will withdraw or not file criminal charges against the perpetrator on grounds that there is no victim. Sometimes, though, the prosecutor will go forward with the prosecution even if the victim files an affidavit of nonprosecution, as in some cases of domestic violence.

▸ **affidavit of notice.** (18c) An affidavit stating that the affiant has given proper notice of hearing to other parties to the action.

▸ **affidavit of service.** (18c) An affidavit certifying the service of a notice, summons, writ, or process.

▸ **affidavit of use.** See DECLARATION OF USE.

▸ **affidavit of verification.** See VERIFICATION (1).

▸ **affidavit under § 8.** See DECLARATION OF USE.

▸ **affidavit under § 15.** See DECLARATION OF INCONTESTABILITY.

▸ **argumentative affidavit.** (1859) An affidavit that improperly contains more than just factual statements, esp. opinion, reasoning, or attempts at persuasion. • An argumentative affidavit is subject to being struck by the court.

▸ ***Byrd* affidavit.** (1984) *Criminal procedure.* A defendant's affidavit in support of a motion to sever on the grounds that a codefendant will give exculpatory testimony for the defendant. • The affidavit must show (1) a bona fide need for the testimony, (2) the substance of the testimony, (3) its exculpatory nature, and (4) that the codefendant would actually testify if the cases were severed. See *Byrd v. Wainwright*, 428 F.2d 1017 (5th Cir. 1970).

▸ **counteraffidavit.** (18c) An affidavit made to contradict and oppose another affidavit, as with one filed in opposition to a motion for summary judgment.

▸ **IFP affidavit.** See *poverty affidavit.*

▸ **in forma pauperis affidavit.** See *poverty affidavit.*

▸ **pauper's affidavit.** See *poverty affidavit.*

▸ **plea affidavit.** See PLEA AFFIDAVIT.

▸ **poverty affidavit.** (1887) An affidavit made by an indigent person seeking public assistance, appointment of counsel, waiver of court fees, or other free public services. 28 USCA § 1915. — Also termed *pauper's affidavit; in forma pauperis affidavit; IFP affidavit.*

▸ **search-warrant affidavit.** (1929) An affidavit, usu. by a police officer or other law-enforcement agent, that sets forth facts and circumstances supporting the existence of probable cause and asks the judge to issue a search warrant.

▸ **self-proving affidavit.** (1964) An affidavit attached to a will and signed by the testator and witnesses certifying that the statutory requirements of due execution of the will have been complied with. • The affidavit, which recites the facts of the will's proper execution, permits the will to be probated without the necessity of having the witnesses appear and prove due execution by their testimony.

▸ **sham affidavit.** (1942) An affidavit that contradicts clear testimony given by the same witness, usu. used in an attempt to create an issue of fact in response to a motion for summary judgment. • All the federal circuit courts have adopted some form of the sham-affidavit rule, which precludes a litigant from creating an issue of material fact by contradicting earlier sworn testimony in the absence of persuasive reasons why the new testimony is more accurate than the earlier testimony.

▸ **supplemental affidavit.** (18c) An affidavit made in addition to a previous one, usu. to supply additional facts.

affidavit of continued use. See DECLARATION OF USE.

affidavit of defense. See *affidavit of merits* under AFFIDAVIT.

affidavit of engagement. (1916) A lawyer's sworn statement to a court requesting an adjournment because of another court appearance scheduled for the same time. — Also termed *affidavit of prior engagement.*

affidavit of errors. (1943) An appellant's written statement enumerating the grounds for appeal, usu. from a court not of record (that is, in which proceedings have not been transcribed by a court reporter).

affidavit of incontestability. See DECLARATION OF INCONTESTABILITY.

affidavit of increase. See AFFIDAVIT.

affidavit of inquiry. See AFFIDAVIT.

affidavit of merit. See *certificate of merit* (2) under CERTIFICATE.

affidavit of merits. See AFFIDAVIT.

affidavit of nonprosecution. See AFFIDAVIT.

affidavit of notice. See AFFIDAVIT.

affidavit of prior engagement. See AFFIDAVIT OF ENGAGEMENT.

affidavit of service. See AFFIDAVIT.

affidavit of use. See DECLARATION OF USE.

affidavit of verification. See VERIFICATION (1).

affidavit under § 8. See DECLARATION OF USE.

affidavit under § 15. See DECLARATION OF INCONTESTABILITY.

affile (ə-fīl), *vb.* [Law Latin *affiliare* "to put on record, to file"] (14c) *Archaic.* To file.

affiliate (ə-fil-ee-it), *n.* (1930) **1.** A corporation that is related to another corporation by shareholdings or other means of control; a subsidiary, parent, or sibling corporation. **2.** *Securities.* Someone who controls, is controlled by, or is under common control with an issuer of a security. SEC Rule 10b-18(a)(1) (17 CFR § 240.10b-18(a)(1)). See

CONTROL PERSON. Cf. ASSOCIATED PERSON (2). — **affiliate** (ə-**fil**-ee-ayt), *vb.*

affiliate click fraud. See FRAUD.

affiliated director. See *outside director* under DIRECTOR.

affiliated group. (1924) A chain of corporations that can elect to file a consolidated tax return because at least 80% of each corporation is owned by others in the group.

affiliated purchaser. See PURCHASER (1).

affiliation, *n.* (18c) **1.** The connection or involvement that someone or something has with a political, religious, etc. organization. **2.** The joining of a smaller group with a larger one.

affiliation order. See *filiation order* under ORDER (2).

affinal (ə-**fin**-əl), *adj.* (1843) Related by marriage <affinal siblings>.

affine (ə-**fin**), *n.* (16c) A relative by marriage.

affinitas (ə-**fin**-ə-tas), *n.* [Latin] *Roman law.* Relationship by marriage.

affinitas affinitatis (ə-**fin**-i-tas ə-fin-i-**tay**-tis), *n.* [Law Latin "affinity of affinity"] (17c) *Hist.* Relationship by two marriages, e.g., with one's stepmother's stepchild; a connection that arises from marriage but is neither consanguinity nor affinity. Cf. CONSANGUINITY; AFFINITY (2), (3); *relative by affinity* under RELATIVE.

> "There is no affinity between the blood relatives of one spouse and the blood relatives of the other. A husband is related by affinity to his wife's brother, but not to the wife of his wife's brother. There is no affinity between the husband's brother and the wife's sister; this is called affinitas affinitatis." 2 Charles E. Torcia, *Wharton's Criminal Law* § 242, at 573 (15th ed. 1994).

affinity (ə-**fin**-ə-tee). (14c) **1.** A close agreement. **2.** The relation that one spouse has to the blood relatives of the other spouse; relationship by marriage. **3.** Any familial relation resulting from a marriage. See *relative by affinity* under RELATIVE. Cf. AFFINITAS AFFINITATIS; CONSANGUINITY.

▸ **collateral affinity.** (16c) The relationship of a spouse's relatives to the other spouse's relatives. • An example is that between a woman's brother and her husband's sister.

▸ **direct affinity.** (1899) The relationship of a spouse to the other spouse's blood relatives. • An example that between a woman and her husband's brother.

▸ **quasi-affinity.** (1872) *Civil law.* The affinity existing between two persons, one of whom has been engaged to a relative of the other.

▸ **secondary affinity.** (17c) The relationship of a spouse to the other spouse's marital relatives. • An example that between a woman and her husband's sister-in-law.

affinity fraud. See FRAUD.

affirm, *vb.* (14c) **1.** To confirm, ratify, or approve (a lower court's judgment) on appeal. • Sometimes, the verb is used without a direct object <we affirm>. The equivalent expression in British English is *to deny the appeal.* **2.** To solemnly declare rather than swear under oath. **3.** To testify or declare by affirmation.

affirmance, *n.* (16c) **1.** A ratification, reacceptance, or confirmation. **2.** The formal confirmation by an appellate court of a lower court's judgment, order, or decree. **3.** The manifestation of a choice by someone with the power of avoidance to treat a voidable or unauthorized transaction as valid or authorized.

> "A party who has the power of avoidance may lose it by action that manifests a willingness to go on with the contract. Such action is known as 'affirmance' and has the effect of ratifying the contract. *See* Restatement of Restitution § 68. The rule stated in this Section is a special application of that stated in § 85, under which a promise to perform a voidable duty is binding. On ratification, the affirming party is bound as from the outset and the other party continues to be bound." Restatement (Second) of Contracts § 380 cmt. a (1979).

4. The manifestation of a choice, by one on whose behalf an unauthorized act has been performed, to treat the act as authorized. Restatement (Second) of Agency § 83 (1958). — **affirm,** *vb.*

affirmance day general. See DAY.

affirmant. (18c) Someone who testifies under affirmation and not under oath. See AFFIRM (2).

affirmation, *n.* (15c) A solemn pledge equivalent to an oath but without reference to a supreme being or to swearing; a solemn declaration made under penalty of perjury, but without an oath. Fed. R. Evid. 603; Fed. R. Civ. P. 43(b). • While an oath is "sworn to," an affirmation is merely "affirmed," but either type of pledge may subject the person making it to the penalties for perjury. Cf. OATH. — **affirm,** *vb.* — **affirmatory,** *adj.*

affirmative, *adj.* (15c) **1.** Supporting the existence of certain facts <affirmative evidence>. **2.** Involving or requiring effort <an affirmative duty>. **3.** Giving assent <an affirmative vote>.

affirmative, *n.* (15c) The side (in a debate or vote) that gives assent or support <she voted in the affirmative>.

affirmative action. (1961) **1.** The practice of selecting people for jobs, college spots, and other important posts in part because some of their characteristics are consistent with those of a group that has historically been treated unfairly by reason of race, sex, etc.; specif., a preference or decision-making advantage given to members of a racial minority that has historically been subjected to systemic discrimination. **2.** An action or set of actions intended to eliminate existing and continuing discrimination, to redress lingering effects of past discrimination, and to create systems and procedures to prevent future discrimination, all by taking into account individual membership in a minority group so as to achieve minority representation in a larger group. — Also termed (BrE) *positive discrimination.* See *reverse discrimination* under DISCRIMINATION (3).

> "Broadly defined, 'affirmative action' encompasses any measure that allocates goods — such as admission into selective universities or professional schools, jobs, promotions, public contracts, business loans, and rights to buy, sell, or use land and other natural resources — through a process that takes into account individual membership in designated groups, for the purpose of increasing the proportion of membership in designated groups, for the purpose of increasing the proportion of numbers of those groups in the relevant labor force, entrepreneurial class, or student population, where they are currently underrepresented as a result of past oppression by state authorities and/or present societal discrimination." Daniel Sabbagh, "Affirmative Action," in *The Oxford Handbook of Comparative Constitutional Law* 1124, 1124 (Michel Rosenfeld & András Sajó eds., 2012).

affirmative charge. See *affirmative instruction* under JURY INSTRUCTION.

affirmative condition. See *positive condition* under CONDITION (2).

affirmative-consent requirement. (1985) **1.** The principle that plain and clear consent must be obtained before certain acts or events, such as changes in policies that could impair an individual's rights or interests. **2.** A rule that sexual partners must have each other's positive, clear consent to each phase of sexual activity, esp. penetration. • Some argue that the failure to obtain affirmative consent before sexual relations can constitute rape. Some countries and a few jurisdictions, such as New Jersey, have adopted an affirmative-consent requirement that allows consent to be inferred from acts or statements in light of the surrounding circumstances.

> "Statutory definitions of consent, which can be used as a defense to a rape accusation, should not be construed as equivalent to an affirmative consent requirement. There is a difference between affirmative consent, where the yes has to be demonstrated (at each stage and/or to the penetration), and the defendant using the legal defense of consent to try to mitigate his culpability by arguing that it was not rape (forced sex) because she agreed to it. The difference between defining consent in statute and requiring the presence of an affirmative, positive yes is the difference between (his) ex post facto protestations and her (constant) indications that she is agreeable to the acts (lest the acts be deemed criminal ones). One is a far cry from the other." Susan Caringella, *Addressing Rape Reform in Law and Practice* 76–77 (2009).

affirmative converse instruction. See JURY INSTRUCTION.

affirmative covenant. 1. See COVENANT (1). **2.** See COVENANT (4).

affirmative defense. See DEFENSE (1).

affirmative direction. See *affirmative instruction* under JURY INSTRUCTION.

affirmative discrimination. See *reverse discrimination* under DISCRIMINATION (3).

affirmative duty. See DUTY (1).

affirmative easement. See EASEMENT.

affirmative injunction. See *mandatory injunction* under INJUNCTION.

affirmative instruction. See JURY INSTRUCTION.

affirmative misconduct. See MISCONDUCT (1).

affirmative misrepresentation. See MISREPRESENTATION (2).

affirmative plea. See *pure plea* under PLEA (3).

affirmative pregnant. (1807) A positive statement that ambiguously implies a negative; a statement that does not explicitly deny a charge, but instead answers an unasked question and thereby implies culpability, as when a person says "I returned your car yesterday" to the charge "You stole my car!" Cf. NEGATIVE PREGNANT.

affirmative proof. See PROOF.

affirmative relief. See RELIEF (3).

affirmative representation. See REPRESENTATION (1).

affirmative servitude. See *positive servitude* under SERVITUDE (3).

affirmative statute. See STATUTE.

affirmative testimony. See TESTIMONY.

affirmative warranty. See WARRANTY (3).

affirmative waste. See *commissive waste* under WASTE (1).

affix (ə-**fiks**), *vb.* (16c) **1.** To attach, add to, or fasten on permanently. See FIXTURE. **2.** *Trademarks.* To attach, physically or functionally, a trademark or servicemark to the goods or services it represents. • A mark must be affixed to show that it is used in trade. Where physical attachment is impossible or impracticable, the mark may be used on a container or tag, or (esp. with service marks) displayed prominently in advertising. — **affixation,** *n.* (af-ik-**say**-shən).

affixus (ə-**fik**-səs). [Latin] *Roman law.* Affixed or fastened to.

affluenza defense. (2013) A newfangled legal defense, generally not recognized, that a youthful offender cannot be held responsible for criminal acts because the wealthy environment in which he or she was reared precluded any learning about right vs. wrong. • The term, a portmanteau of *affluence* and *influenza*, achieved national prominence in December 2013, when attorneys for a 16-year-old boy in Texas successfully invoked the defense to obtain probation after the teenager killed four people while driving drunk.

afforare (af-ə-**rair**-ee), *vb.* [Law Latin] To set a price or value on a thing.

afforce (ə-**fors**), *vb.* (1818) To strengthen (a jury) by adding new members.

afforcement (ə-**fors**-mənt), *n.* [Law Latin] (1818) *Hist.* **1.** A reinforcement or fortification; esp., the reinforcing of a court on a solemn or extraordinary occasion. **2.** A fortress. — Also termed *afforciament* (ə-**for**-shə-mənt); *afforciamentum* (ə-for-shee-ə-**men**-təm).

afforciament. See AFFORCEMENT.

afforciamentum. See AFFORCEMENT .

afforcing the assize. *Hist.* A method of securing a jury verdict from a hung jury either by denying food and drink to the members until they reached a verdict or by bringing in new jurors until 12 would agree. Cf. ALLEN CHARGE.

Affordable Care Act. (2007) A 2010 federal healthcare law intended to decrease the number of American citizens who lack health insurance and reduce the overall costs of healthcare. • The proper name of the law is the Patient Protection and Affordable Care Act (PPACA or ACA). 124 Stat. 119. — Also termed (often pejoratively) *Obamacare.*

afforest, *vb.* (16c) To convert (land) into a forest, esp. by subjecting it to forest law. — **afforestation,** *n.*

affranchir (a-frah*n*-**sheer**). See AFFRANCHISE.

affranchise (ə-**fran**-chɪz), *vb.* (15c) *Archaic.* To set free; to liberate from servitude or an obligation. • The equivalent verb in Law French was *affranchir.*

affray (ə-**fray**). (14c) A noisy fight in a public place; specif., the fighting, by mutual consent, of two or more persons in some public place, to the terror of onlookers. • The fighting must be mutual. If one person unlawfully attacks another who resorts to self-defense, the first is guilty of assault and battery, but there is no affray. — Also termed *fray.* Cf. RIOT; *unlawful assembly* under ASSEMBLY (1); ROUT.

> "An affray differs from a riot, a rout, or an unlawful assembly in that an affray is not premeditated and in order

to constitute a riot, a rout, or an unlawful assembly at least three participants are essential, while . . . an affray may be committed by only two. Moreover, an affray is more of a private nature than a riot." 2A C.J.S. *Affray* § 3, at 519 (1972).

"The word 'affray' comes from the same source as the word 'afraid,' and the tendency to alarm the community is the very essence of this offense." Rollin M. Perkins & Ronald N. Boyce, *Criminal Law* 479 (3d ed. 1982).

▸ **casual affray.** See CHANCE-MEDLEY.

▸ **mutual affray.** See MUTUAL COMBAT.

affrectamentum (ə-frek-tə-**men**-təm). See AFFREIGHTMENT.

affreightment (ə-**frayt**-mənt). (18c) The contracting of a ship to carry cargo. — Also termed *charter of affreightment*; (in French law) *affretement*; (in Law Latin) *affrectamentum*. See CONTRACT OF AFFREIGHTMENT.

affretement. See AFFREIGHTMENT.

A file. *Immigration law. Slang.* An alien file, which contains information relating to a legal or illegal immigrant; a file maintained by the U.S. Immigration and Customs Enforcement on noncitizens. • The file may contain applications for permanent-resident status, documentation to support applications for citizenship, and the like.

a fine force (ay fɪn **fors**). [Law French] Of pure necessity.

AFIS. *abbr.* AMERICAN FORCES INFORMATION SERVICE.

AFL-CIO. *abbr.* AMERICAN FEDERATION OF LABOR AND CONGRESS OF INDUSTRIAL ORGANIZATIONS.

AF of M. *abbr.* AMERICAN FEDERATION OF MUSICIANS.

a force (ay **fors**). [Law French] Of necessity.

a force et armes (ay **fors** et **ahr**-mis). [Law French] With force and arms. — Also spelled *a force et armis*. See VI ET ARMIS.

aforementioned. See AFORESAID.

aforesaid (ə-**for**-sed), *adj.* (14c) Mentioned above; referred to previously. — Also termed *aforementioned*; *above-mentioned*; *above-stated*; *said*.

aforethought (ə-**for**-thawt), *adj.* (16c) Thought of in advance; deliberate; premeditated <libel aforethought>. For the term of art *malice aforethought*, which is commonly said to require neither malice nor forethought, see MALICE AFORETHOUGHT.

a fortiori (ay for-shee-**or**-ɪ *or* ah for-shee-**or**-ee), *adv.* [Latin] (16c) By even greater force of logic; even more so it follows <if a 14-year-old child cannot sign a binding contract, then, *a fortiori*, a 13-year-old cannot>. Cf. A MULTO FORTIORI.

afoul, *adv.* (1807) Against what is legal, allowable, or accordant with a set of rules or beliefs <to run afoul of the criminal law>.

African Development Foundation. A nonprofit federal foundation that supports the self-help efforts of poor people in African countries by making grants and by making and guaranteeing loans to any African entity engaged in peaceful activities that enable African people to develop more fully. • ADF was created by the African Development Foundation Act and began operating in 1984. 22 USCA § 290h. — Abbr. ADF.

AFS. *abbr.* ALTERNATIVE FINANCIAL SERVICES.

AFSP. *abbr.* AMERICAN FOUNDATION FOR SUICIDE PREVENTION.

after-acquired domicile. See DOMICILE.

after-acquired-evidence doctrine. (1993) *Employment law.* The rule that if an employer discharges an employee for an unlawful reason and later discovers misconduct sufficient to justify a lawful discharge, the employee cannot win reinstatement. • The doctrine either shields the employer from liability or limits the available relief when, after an employee has been terminated, the employer learns for the first time that the employee engaged in wrongdoing that would have resulted in a discharge anyway. *McKennon v. Nashville Banner Publ'g Co.*, 513 U.S. 352, 115 S.Ct. 879 (1995).

after-acquired property. (18c) **1.** *Secured transactions.* A debtor's property that is acquired after a security transaction and becomes additional security for payment of the debt. UCC § 9-204. — Also termed *future-acquired property*. **2.** *Bankruptcy.* Property that the bankruptcy estate acquires after commencement of the bankruptcy proceeding. 11 USCA § 541(a)(7). **3.** *Wills & estates.* Property acquired by a person after making a will. • The old rule was that a testamentary gift of personal property spoke at the time of the testator's death, whereas a gift of lands spoke from the date of the will's execution (so that after-acquired property was not disposed of), but this has been changed by legislation in most states.

after-acquired-property clause. (1888) A mortgage provision that makes any later-acquired real estate subject to the mortgage.

after-acquired title. See TITLE (2).

after-acquired-title clause. (1918) *Oil & gas.* A provision in an oil-and-gas lease extending the lease's coverage to include any interest in the property that the lessor may obtain after the lease is signed. • A common formulation is "This lease covers all the interest now owned by or hereafter vested in the lessor . . . ."

after-acquired-title doctrine. (1940) The principle that title to property automatically vests in a person who bought the property from a seller who acquired title only after purporting to sell the property to the buyer.

afterborn child. See CHILD.

afterborn heir. See HEIR.

aftercare. See *juvenile parole* under PAROLE.

after cost. See COST (1).

aftermarket. See *secondary market* under MARKET.

after the fact. (16c) Subsequent to an event of legal significance <accessory after the fact>.

AFTRA. *abbr.* AMERICAN FEDERATION OF TELEVISION AND RADIO ARTISTS.

AG. *abbr.* (1889) ATTORNEY GENERAL.

against the form of the statute. (16c) Contrary to the statutory requirements. • This formal phrase, which traditionally concludes an indictment, indicates that the conduct alleged contravenes the cited statute and therefore constitutes a criminal offense. In modern contexts, the full conclusion often reads: "against the form of the statute in such case made and provided." The phrase is a translation of the Law Latin *contra formam statuti*.

against the peace and dignity of the state. (18c) A concluding phrase in an indictment, used to condemn the offending conduct generally (as opposed to the specific charge of wrongdoing contained in the body of the instrument). • This phrase derives from the Law Latin *contra pacem domini regis* ("against the peace of the lord the king"), a charging phrase formerly used in indictments and in civil actions of trespass. Cf. KING'S PEACE.

against the weight of the evidence. (18c) (Of a verdict or judgment) contrary to the credible evidence; not sufficiently supported by the evidence in the record. See WEIGHT OF THE EVIDENCE.

against the will. (15c) Contrary to a person's wishes. • Indictments use this phrase to indicate that the defendant's conduct was without the victim's consent.

agalma (ə-**gal**-mə). [Greek] (18c) A figure or design on a seal.

agard (ə-**gahrd**). [Law French] An award. See NUL FAIT AGARD.

agarder (ah-gahr-**day**), *vb.* [Law French] To award, adjudge, or determine; to sentence or condemn.

age, *n.* (13c) A period of time; esp., a period of individual existence or the duration of a person's life. • In American usage, age is stated in full years completed (so that someone *15 years of age* might actually be 15 years and several months old). State statutes define various types of ages, as shown in the subentries.

▸ **age of capacity.** (1847) The age, usu. defined by statute as 18 years, at which a person is legally capable of agreeing to a contract, maintaining a lawsuit, or the like. • A person may be authorized to make certain critical personal decisions at an earlier age than the general age of capacity, such as the decision whether to bear a child, to donate blood, to obtain treatment for sexually transmitted diseases, to marry, or to write a will. The age of capacity to write a will is typically not 18, but 14. — Also termed *age of majority*; *legal age*; *lawful age*. See CAPACITY (2).

▸ **age of consent.** (16c) The age, usu. defined by statute as 16 years, at which a person is legally capable of agreeing to marriage (without parental consent) or to sexual intercourse. • If a person over the age of consent has sexual intercourse with a person under the age of consent, the older person may be prosecuted for statutory rape regardless of whether the younger person consented to the act. See *statutory rape* under RAPE (2); JAILBAIT.

▸ **age of criminal responsibility.** (1887) The age at which a child may be held responsible for a criminal act. • In American criminal law, some state statutes allow a child as young as 7 to be held responsible (as a juvenile) for some acts. *See, e.g.,* N.D. Cent. Code § 12.1-04-01. The minimum age for imposing adult liability is as low as 10. *See, e.g.,* Ind. Code Ann. § 31-30-3-4(3). But in some circumstances, at least one state allows an offender to be tried as an adult at any age. *See, e.g.,* Mich. Comp. Laws Ann. § 712A.2d.

▸ **age of discretion.** (14c) **1.** The age at which a person is considered responsible for certain acts and competent to exercise certain powers. • For example, a person must be a legal adult to be eligible to serve a summons. **2.** PUBERTY.

▸ **age of majority.** (16c) **1.** The age, usu. defined by statute as 18 years, at which a person attains full legal rights, esp. civil and political rights such as the right to vote. • The age of majority must be the same for men and women. In almost all states today, the age of majority is 18, but the age at which a person may legally purchase and consume alcohol is 21. — Also termed *lawful age*; *legal age*. **2.** See *age of capacity*. — Also termed (in both senses) *full age*.

▸ **age of reason.** (1884) The age at which a person becomes able to distinguish right from wrong and is thus legally capable of committing a crime or tort. • The age of reason varies from jurisdiction to jurisdiction, but 7 years is traditionally the age below which a child is conclusively presumed not to have committed a crime or tort, while 14 years is usu. the age below which a rebuttable presumption applies. A child of 14 or older has traditionally been considered legally competent to commit a crime and therefore held accountable. With the creation of juvenile courts and their investiture of delinquency jurisdiction over children from birth to age 18, these traditional distinctions have nearly vanished. They surface from time to time in murder cases when a juvenile court considers whether to certify or transfer a child under the age of 18 for trial in criminal court or when a prosecutor seeks to bypass the juvenile court by filing criminal charges against a child.

▸ **drinking age.** (1947) The age at which a person may legally buy and consume alcoholic beverages in a given jurisdiction.

▸ **fighting age.** (1917) The age at which a person becomes eligible to serve in (or liable to conscription into) a military unit.

▸ **full age.** See *age of majority*.

▸ **lawful age. 1.** See *age of capacity*. **2.** See *age of majority* (1).

▸ **legal age. 1.** See *age of capacity*. **2.** See *age of majority* (1).

▸ **marriageable age.** (17c) The age at which a person is allowed by law to marry. • At common law, marriageable age was 14 for males and 12 for females. Today, marriageable age is governed by local statutes, which generally specify 16 to 18 years of age. See MARRIAGEABLE.

age discrimination. See DISCRIMINATION (3).

Age Discrimination in Employment Act. A 1967 federal statute prohibiting job discrimination based on a person's age, esp. unfair and discriminatory employment decisions that negatively affect someone who is 40 years old or older. 29 USCA §§ 621–634. • The Act applies to businesses with 20 or more employees and to all state and local governmental entities. — Abbr. ADEA.

age group. (1876) Collectively, all the people within a continuous range of ages, considered as a cohort. Cf. AGE RANGE.

ageism, *n.* (1969) [on the analogy of *racism*, *sexism*, etc.] Unfair treatment of people based on their age, usu. because they are old. Cf. *age discrimination* under DISCRIMINATION. — **ageist,** *adj. & n.*

age limit. (1862) The youngest or oldest age at which someone is allowed to do something.

agency. (17c) **1.** A relationship that arises when one person (a principal) manifests assent to another (an agent) that the agent will act on the principal's behalf, subject to the principal's control, and the agent manifests assent or otherwise consents to do so. • An agent's actions have legal consequences for the principal when the agent acts within the scope of the agent's actual authority or with apparent authority, or the principal later ratifies the agent's action. — Also termed *common-law agency.* See AUTHORITY (1).

> "The basic theory of the agency device is to enable a person, through the services of another, to broaden the scope of his activities and receive the product of another's efforts, paying such other for what he does but retaining for himself any net benefit resulting from the work performed." Harold Gill Reuschlein & William A. Gregory, *The Law of Agency and Partnership* § 1, at 3 (2d ed. 1990).

▸ **actual agency.** (1835) An agency, whether created expressly or impliedly, in which the agent is in fact authorized to act on behalf of the principal.

▸ **agency by estoppel.** (1864) An agency created by operation of law when a person's actions have led a third party reasonably to believe that another actor was actually the person's agent. — Also termed *apparent agency*; *ostensible agency*; *agency by operation of law.*

▸ **agency by necessity.** (18c) A doctrine, esp. in English law, that confers authority to act for the benefit of another in an emergency without having obtained the latter's express consent; the relation between the person who so acts and the one to whom the benefit accrues. • This is a quasi-contractual relation formed by the operation of legal rules and not by the agreement of the parties. — Also termed *agency from necessity*; *agency of necessity.* See NEGOTIORUM GESTIO.

> "The two traditional cases from which the concept of agency by necessity derives are those of the shipmaster, who has wide powers to bind by contract his owner, and also sometimes the cargo owners, in situations of emergency; and the person who accepts a bill of exchange for honour and succeeds to the rights of the holder against the person for whom he accepts . . . . The dissimilarity between these two cases is enough to indicate immediately that a category comprising both of them is unlikely to be a satisfactory one." F.M.B. Reynolds, *Bowstead & Reynolds on Agency* 140 (18th ed. 2006).

▸ **agency by operation of law.** (1858) **1.** An agency that arises under circumstances specified by law without mutual consent between the principal and the agent having been manifested. • For example, in most states the secretary of state is designated as the agent for service of process for those carrying on specified activities within that state. See *statutory agent* under AGENT. **2.** See *agency by estoppel.* Cf. *common-law agency.*

▸ **agency coupled with an interest.** (1844) A relationship in which one party holds an irrevocable power to take action on behalf of another to protect a legal or equitable title or to secure performance of a duty apart from any duty owed to the holder by the grantor of the power. • An agency coupled with an interest is not an example of common-law agency because it is irrevocable by the grantor and because the relationship between holder and grantor is not a fiduciary relationship. See *irrevocable proxy* under PROXY; *power coupled with an interest* under POWER (3).

▸ **agency from necessity.** See *agency by necessity.*

▸ **agency in fact.** (1824) An agency created voluntarily, as by a contract. • Agency in fact is distinguishable from an agency relationship created by law, such as agency by estoppel.

▸ **agency of necessity.** See *agency by necessity.*

▸ **apparent agency.** See *agency by estoppel.*

▸ **clearing agency.** See *clearing agent* under AGENT.

▸ **common-law agency.** A fiduciary relationship of agency created by express or implied mutual consent manifested by both the principal and the agent, in which the agent is subject in some degree to the principal's control. Cf. *agency by operation of law.*

▸ **exclusive agency.** (1805) The right to represent a principal — esp. either to sell the principal's products or to act as the seller's real-estate agent — within a particular market free from competition. • Strictly speaking, an exclusive agency merely excludes all other brokers, but not the owner, from selling the products or property. — Also termed *exclusive agency to sell*; *exclusive franchise*; *sole selling agency.* Cf. EXCLUSIVE RIGHT OF SALE.

> "Contracts involving the element of exclusive agency generally fall into three classes: (1) where the contract does not prevent the principal from making direct sales but deprives him of the right to appoint other agents; (2) where the agent is the only one with any right to sell; and (3) where the exclusive agency is accompanied with a stipulated right to commissions on all sales whether made through the agent or not." 3 Am. Jur. 2d *Agency* § 268, at 768 (1986).

▸ **express agency.** (18c) An actual agency arising from the principal's written or oral authorization of a person to act as the principal's agent. Cf. *implied agency.*

▸ **financing agency.** (1927) A bank, finance company, or other entity that in the ordinary course of business (1) makes advances against goods or documents of title, or (2) by arrangement with either the seller or the buyer intervenes to make or collect payment due or claimed under a contract for sale, as by purchasing or paying the seller's draft, making advances against it, or taking it for collection, regardless of whether documents of title accompany the draft. UCC § 2-104(2).

▸ **general agency.** (18c) A principal's delegation to an agent, without restriction, to take any action connected with a particular trade, business, or employment. • The archetypal general agent manages a business, has authority to conduct a series of transactions, and serves the principal on an ongoing basis. — Also termed *universal agency.* Cf. *special agency.*

▸ **implied agency.** (18c) An actual agency arising from conduct by the principal that implies an intention to create an agency relationship. Cf. *express agency.*

▸ **ostensible agency.** See *agency by estoppel.*

▸ **special agency.** (1808) An agency in which the agent is authorized only to conduct a single transaction or a series of transactions not involving continuous service. Cf. *special agency.*

▸ **undisclosed agency.** (1871) An agency relationship in which an agent deals with a third party who has no knowledge that the agent is acting on a principal's behalf. • The fact that the agency is undisclosed does not prohibit the third party from seeking redress from the principal or the agent.

▸ **universal agency.** See *general agency.*

2. An agent's place of business. **3.** An official body, esp. within the government, with the authority to implement and administer particular legislation. — Also termed (in sense 3) *government agency*; *administrative agency*; *public agency*; *regulatory agency.*

▸ **commercial agency.** See CREDIT BUREAU.

▸ **federal agency.** (1859) A department or other instrumentality of the executive branch of the federal government, including a government corporation and the Government Printing Office. • The Administrative Procedure Act defines the term *agency* negatively as being any U.S. governmental authority that does not include Congress, the courts, the government of the District of Columbia, the government of any territory or possession, courts-martial, or military authority. 5 USCA § 551. The caselaw on this definition focuses on authority: generally, an entity is an agency if it has authority to take binding action. Other federal statutes define agency to include any executive department, government corporation, government-controlled corporation, or other establishment in the executive branch, or federal regulatory board.

▸ **independent agency.** (1902) A federal agency, commission, or board that is not under the direction of the executive, such as the Federal Trade Commission or the National Labor Relations Board. — Also termed *independent regulatory agency*; *independent regulatory commission.*

▸ **local agency.** (1842) A political subdivision of a state. • Local agencies include counties, cities, school districts, etc.

▸ **mercantile agency.** See CREDIT BUREAU.

▸ **quasi-governmental agency.** (1904) A government-sponsored enterprise or corporation (sometimes called a *government-controlled corporation*), such as the Federal National Mortgage Corporation.

▸ **state agency.** (1875) An executive or regulatory body of a state. • State agencies include state offices, departments, divisions, bureaus, boards, and commissions. — Also termed *state body.*

agency action, *n.* (1946) *Administrative law.* Under the Administrative Procedure Act, any conduct that includes the whole or a part of an agency rule, order, license, sanction, relief, or the equivalent, or else the denial of it or the agency's failure to act. 5 USCA § 551; *see Lujan v. Nat'l Wildlife Found.*, 497 U.S. 871, 890, 110 S.Ct. 3177, 3189 (1990).

agency adjudication. See ADMINISTRATIVE PROCEEDING.

agency adoption. See ADOPTION (1).

agency by estoppel. See AGENCY (1).

agency by necessity. See AGENCY (1).

agency by operation of law. See AGENCY (1).

agency coupled with an interest. See AGENCY (1).

Agency for Healthcare Research and Quality. An agency in the U.S. Department of Health and Human Services responsible for conducting research into improving the quality of healthcare, reducing its cost, and broadening access to essential healthcare services. — Abbr. AHRQ.

Agency for International Development. See UNITED STATES AGENCY FOR INTERNATIONAL DEVELOPMENT.

Agency for Toxic Substances and Disease Registry. An agency in the U.S. Department of Health and Human Services responsible for evaluating the impact on public health of the release of hazardous substances into the environment, for maintaining a registry of contaminated waste sites, and for conducting research on the effects of hazardous substances on human health. — Abbr. ATSDR.

agency from necessity. See *agency by necessity* under AGENCY (1).

agency head. (1901) The chief of a governmental department or of a public-service institution.

agency in fact. See AGENCY (1).

agency jurisdiction. See JURISDICTION.

agency of necessity. See *agency by necessity* under AGENCY (1).

agency records. (1966) Under the Freedom of Information Act, documents that are created or obtained by a government agency, and that are in the agency's control at the time the information request is made. 5 USCA § 552; *United States Dep't of Justice v. Tax Analysts*, 492 U.S. 136, 109 S.Ct. 2841 (1989).

agency regulation. See REGULATION (3).

agency security. See *government security* under SECURITY (4).

agency shop. See SHOP.

agency-shop membership. See FINANCIAL-CORE MEMBERSHIP.

agenda. (1907) A list of things to be done, as items to be considered at a meeting, usu. arranged in order of consideration. — Also termed *calendar*; *calendar of business*; *order of business.* Cf. PROGRAM (1).

▸ **action agenda.** See *action calendar* under CALENDAR (4).

▸ **consent agenda.** See *consent calendar* under CALENDAR (4).

▸ **debate agenda.** See *debate calendar* under CALENDAR (4).

▸ **final agenda.** (1918) An agenda that a deliberative assembly has adopted, or that has been adopted for a deliberative assembly by an officer or board charged with setting such an agenda.

▸ **proposed agenda.** (1919) An agenda offered, usu. with the notice calling the meeting that the agenda covers, for a deliberative assembly's consideration. — Also termed *tentative agenda.*

▸ **report agenda.** See *report calendar* under CALENDAR (4).

▸ **special-order agenda.** See *special-order calendar* under CALENDAR (4).

▸ **tentative agenda.** See *proposed agenda.*

▸ **unanimous-consent agenda.** See *consent calendar* under CALENDAR (4).

agens (ay-jenz), *n.* [Latin] **1.** Someone who acts or does an act; an agent. Cf. PATIENS. **2.** A plaintiff.

agent. (15c) **1.** Something that produces an effect <an intervening agent>. See CAUSE (1); ELECTRONIC AGENT. **2.** Someone who is authorized to act for or in place of another; a representative <a professional athlete's

agent>. — Also termed *commissionaire.* See AGENCY. Cf. PRINCIPAL, *n.* (1); EMPLOYEE.

> "Generally speaking, anyone can be an agent who is *in fact* capable of performing the functions involved. The agent normally binds not himself but his principal by the contracts he makes; it is therefore not essential that he be legally capable to contract (although his duties and liabilities to his principal might be affected by his status). Thus an infant or a lunatic may be an agent, though doubtless the court would disregard either's attempt to act if he were so young or so hopelessly devoid of reason as to be completely incapable of grasping the function he was attempting to perform." Floyd R. Mechem, *Outlines of the Law of Agency* 8–9 (Philip Mechem ed., 4th ed. 1952).

> "The etymology of the word agent or agency tells us much. The words are derived from the Latin verb, *ago, agere*; the noun *agens, agentis*. The word agent denotes one who acts, a doer, force or power that accomplishes things." Harold Gill Reuschlein & William A. Gregory, *The Law of Agency and Partnership* § 1, at 2–3 (2d ed. 1990).

▸ **agent by necessity.** (18c) An agent that the law empowers to act for the benefit of another in an emergency. — Also termed *agent of necessity.*

▸ **agent not recognized.** *Patents.* A patent applicant's appointed agent who is not registered to practice before the U.S. Patent and Trademark Office. • A power of attorney appointing an unregistered agent is void. See *patent agent.*

▸ **apparent agent.** (1823) Someone who reasonably appears to have authority to act for another, regardless of whether actual authority has been conferred. — Also termed *ostensible agent*; *implied agent.*

▸ **associate agent.** *Patents.* An agent who is registered to practice before the U.S. Patent and Trademark Office, has been appointed by a primary agent, and is authorized to prosecute a patent application through the filing of a power of attorney. • An associate agent is often used by outside counsel to assist in-house counsel. See *patent agent.*

▸ **bail-enforcement agent.** See BOUNTY HUNTER.

▸ **bargaining agent.** (1935) A labor union in its capacity of representing employees in collective bargaining.

▸ **broker-agent.** See BROKER.

▸ **business agent.** See BUSINESS AGENT.

▸ **clearing agent.** (1937) *Securities.* A person or company acting as an intermediary in a securities transaction or providing facilities for comparing data regarding securities transactions. • The term includes a custodian of securities in connection with the central handling of securities. Securities Exchange Act § 3(a)(23)(A) (15 USCA § 78c(a)(23)(A)). — Also termed *clearing agency.*

▸ **closing agent.** See *settlement agent.*

▸ **co-agent.** (16c) Someone who shares with another agent the authority to act for the principal. — Also termed *dual agent.* Cf. *common agent.*

▸ **commercial agent.** (18c) **1.** BROKER. **2.** A consular officer responsible for the commercial interests of his or her country at a foreign port. **3.** See *mercantile agent.* **4.** See *commission agent.*

▸ **commission agent.** (1812) An agent whose remuneration is based at least in part on commissions, or percentages of actual sales. • Commission agents typically work as middlemen between sellers and buyers. — Also termed *commercial agent.*

▸ **common agent.** (17c) An agent who acts on behalf of more than one principal in a transaction. Cf. *co-agent.*

▸ **corporate agent.** (1819) An agent authorized to act on behalf of a corporation; broadly, all employees and officers who have the power to bind the corporation.

▸ **county agent.** See *juvenile officer* under OFFICER (1).

▸ ***del credere* agent** (del **kred**-ə-ray *or* **kray**-də-ray). (1822) An agent who guarantees the solvency of the third party with whom the agent makes a contract for the principal. • A *del credere* agent receives possession of the principal's goods for purposes of sale and guarantees that anyone to whom the agent sells the goods on credit will pay promptly for them. For this guaranty, the agent receives a higher commission for sales. The promise of such an agent is almost universally held not to be within the statute of frauds. — Also termed *del credere factor.*

▸ **diplomatic agent.** (18c) A national representative in one of four categories: (1) ambassadors, (2) envoys and ministers plenipotentiary, (3) ministers resident accredited to the sovereign, or (4) chargés d'affaires accredited to the minister of foreign affairs.

▸ **double agent. 1.** A spy who finds out an enemy's secrets for his or her principal but who also gives secrets to the enemy. **2.** See *dual agent* (2).

▸ **dual agent.** (1881) **1.** See *co-agent.* **2.** An agent who represents both parties in a single transaction, esp. a buyer and a seller. — Also termed (in sense 2) *double agent.*

▸ **emigrant agent.** (1874) One engaged in the business of hiring laborers for work outside the country or state.

▸ **enrolled agent.** See ENROLLED AGENT.

▸ **escrow agent.** See ESCROW AGENT.

▸ **estate agent.** See *real-estate agent.*

▸ **fiscal agent.** (18c) A bank or other financial institution that collects and disburses money and services as a depository of private and public funds on another's behalf.

▸ **foreign agent.** (1938) Someone who registers with the federal government as a lobbyist representing the interests of a foreign country or corporation.

▸ **forwarding agent.** (1837) **1.** FREIGHT FORWARDER. **2.** A freight-forwarder who assembles less-than-carload shipments (small shipments) into carload shipments, thus taking advantage of lower freight rates.

▸ **general agent.** (17c) An agent authorized to transact all the principal's business of a particular kind or in a particular place. • Among the common types of general agents are factors, brokers, and partners. Cf. *special agent.*

▸ **government agent.** (1805) **1.** An employee or representative of a governmental body. **2.** A law-enforcement official, such as a police officer or an FBI agent. **3.** An informant, esp. an inmate, used by law enforcement to obtain incriminating statements from another inmate.

▸ **gratuitous agent.** An agent who acts without a right to compensation.

▸ **high-managerial agent.** (1957) **1.** An agent of a corporation or other business who has authority to formulate corporate policy or supervise employees. — Also termed *superior agent*. **2.** See *superior agent* (1).

▸ **implied agent.** See *apparent agent.*

▸ **independent agent.** (17c) An agent who exercises personal judgment and is subject to the principal only for the results of the work performed. Cf. *nonservant agent.*

▸ **innocent agent.** (1805) *Criminal law.* A person whose action on behalf of a principal is unlawful but does not merit prosecution because the agent had no knowledge of the principal's illegal purpose; a person who lacks the mens rea for an offense but who is tricked or coerced by the principal into committing a crime. • Although the agent's conduct was unlawful, the agent might not be prosecuted if the agent had no knowledge of the principal's illegal purpose. The principal is legally accountable for the innocent agent's actions. *See* Model Penal Code § 2.06(2)(a).

▸ **insurance agent.** See INSURANCE AGENT.

▸ **jural agent.** See JURAL AGENT.

▸ **land agent.** See LAND AGENT.

▸ **listing agent.** (1927) The real-estate broker's representative who obtains a listing agreement with the owner. Cf. *selling agent*; *showing agent.*

▸ **local agent.** (1804) **1.** An agent appointed to act as another's (esp. a company's) representative and to transact business within a specified district. **2.** See *special agent.*

▸ **managing agent.** (1812) A person with general power involving the exercise of judgment and discretion, as opposed to an ordinary agent who acts under the direction and control of the principal. — Also termed *business agent.*

▸ **mercantile agent.** (18c) An agent employed to sell goods or merchandise on behalf of the principal. — Also termed *commercial agent.*

▸ **nonservant agent.** (1920) An agent who agrees to act on the principal's behalf but is not subject to the principal's control over how the task is performed. • A principal is not liable for the physical torts of a nonservant agent. See INDEPENDENT CONTRACTOR. Cf. *independent agent*; SERVANT.

▸ **ostensible agent.** See *apparent agent.*

▸ **patent agent.** (1859) A specialized legal professional — not necessarily a lawyer — who has fulfilled the U.S. Patent and Trademark Office requirements as a representative and is registered to prepare and prosecute patent applications before the PTO. • To be registered to practice before the PTO, a candidate must establish mastery of the relevant technology (by holding a specified technical degree or equivalent training) in order to advise and assist patent applicants. The candidate must also pass a written examination (the "Patent Bar") that tests knowledge of patent law and PTO procedure. — Often shortened to *agent*. — Also termed *registered patent agent*; *patent solicitor.* Cf. PATENT ATTORNEY.

▸ **primary agent.** (18c) An agent who is directly authorized by a principal. • A primary agent generally may hire a subagent to perform all or part of the agency. Cf. *subagent* (1).

▸ **private agent.** (17c) An agent acting for an individual in that person's private affairs.

▸ **process agent.** (1886) A person authorized to accept service of process on behalf of another. See *registered agent.*

▸ **procuring agent.** (1954) Someone who obtains drugs on behalf of another person and delivers the drugs to that person. • In criminal-defense theory, the procuring agent does not sell, barter, exchange, or make a gift of the drugs to the other person because the drugs already belong to that person, who merely employs the agent to pick up and deliver them.

▸ **public agent.** (17c) A person appointed to act for the public in matters relating to governmental administration or public business.

▸ **real-estate agent.** (1844) An agent who represents a buyer or seller (or both, with proper disclosures) in the sale or lease of real property. • A real-estate agent can be either a broker (whose principal is a buyer or seller) or a salesperson (whose principal is a broker). — Also termed *estate agent.* Cf. REALTOR.

▸ **record agent.** See INSURANCE AGENT.

▸ **registered agent.** (1809) A person authorized to accept service of process for another person, esp. a foreign corporation, in a particular jurisdiction. — Also termed *resident agent.* See *process agent.*

▸ **registered patent agent.** See *patent agent.*

▸ **resident agent.** See *registered agent.*

▸ **secret agent.** See SECRET AGENT.

▸ **selling agent.** (1839) **1.** The real-estate broker's representative who sells the property, as opposed to the agent who lists the property for sale. **2.** See *showing agent.* Cf. *listing agent.*

▸ **settlement agent.** (1952) An agent who represents the purchaser or buyer in the negotiation and closing of a real-property transaction by handling financial calculations and transfers of documents. — Also termed *closing agent.* See also *settlement attorney* under ATTORNEY.

▸ **showing agent.** A real-estate broker's representative who markets property to a prospective purchaser. • A showing agent may be characterized as a subagent of the listing broker, as an agent who represents the purchaser, or as an intermediary who owes an agent's duties to neither seller nor buyer. — Also termed *selling agent.* Cf. *listing agent.*

▸ **soliciting agent.** (1855) **1.** *Insurance.* An agent with authority relating to the solicitation or submission of applications to an insurance company but usu. without authority to bind the insurer, as by accepting the applications on behalf of the company. **2.** An agent who solicits orders for goods or services for a principal. **3.** A managing agent of a corporation for purposes of service of process.

▸ **special agent.** (17c) **1.** An agent employed to conduct a particular transaction or to perform a specified act. Cf. *general agent.* **2.** See INSURANCE AGENT.

▸ **specially accredited agent.** (1888) An agent that the principal has specially invited a third party to deal with, in an implication that the third party will be notified if the agent's authority is altered or revoked.

▸ **statutory agent.** (1844) An agent designated by law to receive litigation documents and other legal notices for a nonresident corporation. • In most states, the secretary of state is the statutory agent for such corporations. Cf. *agency by operation of law* (1) under AGENCY (1).

▸ **stock-transfer agent.** (1873) See *transfer agent.*

▸ **subagent.** (18c) **1.** A person to whom an agent has delegated the performance of an act for the principal; a person designated by an agent to perform some duty relating to the agency. • If the principal consents to a primary agent's employment of a subagent, the subagent owes fiduciary duties to the principal, and the principal is liable for the subagent's acts. Cf. *primary agent*; *subordinate agent.* — Also termed *subservant.*

> "By delegation . . . the agent is permitted to use agents of his own in performing the function he is employed to perform for his principal, delegating to them the discretion which normally he would be expected to exercise personally. These agents are known as subagents to indicate that they are the agent's agents and not the agents of the principal. Normally (though of course not necessarily) they are paid by the agent. The agent is liable to the principal for any injury done him by the misbehavior of the agent's subagents." Floyd R. Mechem, *Outlines of the Law of Agency* § 79, at 51 (Philip Mechem ed., 4th ed. 1952).

2. See *buyer's broker* under BROKER.

▸ **subordinate agent.** (17c) An agent who acts subject to the direction of a superior agent. • Subordinate and superior agents are co-agents of a common principal. See *superior agent.* Cf. *subagent* (1).

▸ **successor agent.** (1934) An agent who is appointed by a principal to act in a primary agent's stead if the primary agent is unable or unwilling to perform.

▸ **superior agent.** (17c) **1.** An agent on whom a principal confers the right to direct a subordinate agent. See *subordinate agent.* **2.** See *high-managerial agent* (1).

▸ **transfer agent.** (1850) An organization (such as a bank or trust company) that handles transfers of shares for a publicly held corporation by issuing new certificates and overseeing the cancellation of old ones and that usu. also maintains the record of shareholders for the corporation and mails dividend checks. • Generally, a transfer agent ensures that certificates submitted for transfer are properly indorsed and that the transfer right is appropriately documented. — Also termed *stock-transfer agent.*

▸ **trustee-agent.** A trustee who is subject to the control of the settlor or one or more beneficiaries of a trust. See TRUSTEE (1).

▸ **undercover agent.** (1930) **1.** An agent who does not disclose his or her role as an agent. **2.** A police officer who gathers evidence of criminal activity without disclosing his or her identity to the suspect.

▸ **undisclosed agent.** An agent who deals with a third party who has no knowledge that the agent is acting on a principal's behalf. Cf. *undisclosed principal* under PRINCIPAL (1).

▸ **universal agent.** (18c) An agent authorized to perform all acts that the principal could personally perform.

▸ **vice-commercial agent.** (1800) *Hist.* In the consular service of the United States, a consular officer who was substituted temporarily to fill the place of a commercial agent who was absent or had been relieved from duty.

agent of necessity. See *agent by necessity* under AGENT.

agent provocateur (ay-jənt prə-vok-ə-**tər** *or* a-zhawn praw-vaw-kə-**tuur**), *n.* (1877) **1.** An undercover agent who instigates or participates in a crime, often by infiltrating a group suspected of illegal conduct, to expose and punish criminal activity. **2.** Someone who entraps another, or entices another to break the law, and then informs against the other as a lawbreaker; esp., someone who is hired to encourage people who are working against a government to do something illegal so that they will be caught.

agent's lien. See LIEN.

agent's power. See POWER (3).

age of capacity. See AGE.

age of consent. See AGE.

age of criminal responsibility. See AGE.

age of discretion. See AGE.

age of majority. See AGE.

age of reason. See AGE.

age out, *vb.* (1953) To become ineligible for a certain status by surpassing the maximum age limit, as by reaching the age (often 18) when foster care is no longer available or by turning 21 and thereby becoming ineligible for classification as a "child" under immigration laws. • In 2002, the Child Status Protection Act amended the Immigration and Nationality Act to allow certain people to retain their "child" status after turning 21. See CHILD STATUS PROTECTION ACT.

ager (**ay**-jər), *n.* [Latin] *Roman law.* Land or territory; esp., a portion of land enclosed by definite boundaries.

▸ ***ager arcifinius*** (**ay**-jər ahr-si-**fin**-ee-əs). [Latin "land having irregular boundaries; unsurveyed land"] (17c) *Roman law.* Land enclosed only as a means of identification, not as a limit. Cf. *ager limitatus.* Pl. ***agri arcifinii.***

▸ ***ager limitatus*** (**ay**-jər lim-i-**tay**-təs). [Latin "field limited" or "land enclosed by boundaries"] (18c) *Roman & civil law.* Land with settled boundaries; esp., land whose boundaries have been fixed by a surveyor. • The term applied to land belonging to the state by right of conquest, then granted and sold in individual plots. Cf. *ager arcifinius.* Pl. ***agri limitati*** (**ag**-rɪ lim-i-**tay**-tɪ).

> "The *agri limitati* of the Roman law were lands detached from the public domain, and converted into private property, by sale or grant, beyond the limits of which the owners could claim nothing." John Trayner, *Trayner's Latin Maxims* 36 (4th ed. 1894).

▸ ***ager publicus*** (**ay**-jər **pəb**-li-kəs). (1841) Land of the people; public land.

age range. (1897) A particular span of ages considered as a group <people in the 20–30 age range>. Cf. AGE GROUP.

aggravated, *adj.* (17c) **1.** (Of a crime) made worse or more serious by circumstances such as violence, the presence of a deadly weapon, or the intent to commit another crime <aggravated robbery>. Cf. SIMPLE (1). **2.** (Of a tort) made worse or more serious by circumstances such as intention to cause harm or reckless disregard for another's safety <the defendant's negligence was aggravated by malice>. **3.** (Of an injury) harmful to a part of the body previously injured or debilitated <an aggravated bone fracture>. See AGGRAVATION RULE.

aggravated arson. See ARSON.

aggravated assault. See ASSAULT.

aggravated battery. See BATTERY (1).

aggravated damages. See *punitive damages* under DAMAGES.

aggravated kidnapping. See KIDNAPPING.

aggravated larceny. See LARCENY.

aggravated misdemeanor. See *serious misdemeanor* under MISDEMEANOR.

aggravated robbery. See ROBBERY.

aggravated sodomy. See SODOMY.

aggravating circumstance. See CIRCUMSTANCE.

aggravating element. See *aggravating circumstance* under CIRCUMSTANCE.

aggravating factor. See *aggravating circumstance* under CIRCUMSTANCE.

aggravation. (17c) **1.** The fact of being increased in gravity or seriousness. **2.** *Eccles. law.* A censure threatening the recipient with an increase in the penalties associated with excommunication, usu. because the recipient disregarded an earlier sentence. • For example, a person who spurned a sentence of excommunication might be subjected to an anathema (a formal ban or curse). — **aggravate,** *vb.*

aggravation rule. (1968) *Workers' compensation.* The principle that when an on-the-job injury combines with a preexisting injury, resulting in a greater disability than that which would have resulted from the on-the-job injury alone, the entire disability is compensable as if it had occurred at work.

aggravator. (1985) **1.** Someone who commits a crime with an aggravating circumstance. **2.** See *aggravating circumstance* under CIRCUMSTANCE. Cf. MITIGATOR.

aggregate (**ag**-rə-git), *adj.* (15c) Formed by combining into a single whole or total <aggregate income>. — **aggregately,** *adv.*

aggregate (**ag**-rə-git), *n.* (17c) An assemblage of particulars; an agglomeration <aggregate of interests>.

aggregate (**ag**-rə-gayt), *vb.* (16c) To collect into a whole <aggregate the claims>.

aggregate concept. (1929) *Tax.* An approach to taxing business organizations whereby an organization is viewed as a collection of its individual owners, not as a separate taxable entity.

aggregate corporation. See *corporation aggregate* under CORPORATION.

aggregate demand. See DEMAND (4).

aggregate income. See INCOME.

aggregate sentence. See SENTENCE.

aggregate supply. See SUPPLY.

aggregate theory of partnership. (1913) The theory that a partnership does not have a separate legal existence (as does a corporation), but rather is only the totality of the partners who compose it. Cf. ENTITY THEORY OF PARTNERSHIP.

aggregate-weight rule. (1932) **1.** *Criminal law.* The doctrine that in a prosecution for possession of or trafficking in illicit drugs, the weight of the mixture containing the contraband — not the weight of the actual contraband when separated from the mixture — determines the degree of the crime. **2.** In transportation, a policy that allows a shipper to combine separate items or commodities into a single unit for handling to qualify for a lower rate.

aggregatio mentium (ag-rə-**gay**-shee-oh **men**-shee-əm). [Latin "gathering together of minds"] (17c) See MEETING OF THE MINDS.

aggregation. **1.** *Criminal procedure.* The prosecution's combining of charges such as larceny and possession of contraband so as to raise the seriousness of the offense being charged. **2.** *Patents.* A set of parts that do not cooperate in structure or function, and are therefore unpatentable as an invention; the opposite of a combination. Cf. COMBINATION (4), (6). **3.** *Hist.* A patent examiner's label for a claimed invention that may or may not be a patentable combination but whose claims do not clearly explain how the parts cooperate to produce a new or unexpected result. • As a term of art, *aggregation* lost its usefulness when it was replaced by a statutory test in § 103 of the Patent Act of 1952. — Also termed *juxtaposition.*

> "I think of a football team as a combination; one passes, one receives, another runs, and still others hold the line. Eleven men are doing different things, each in his own way, and not always simultaneously; yet they are working to a common end, to advance the ball; and they coact as a unit. I think of a track team as an aggregation; one runs, another hurdles, another jumps, another throws. They all work for a common general end, to amass points for their alma mater; but there is lacking the vital spark of cooperation or coordination. They work, not as one unit, but as several." *Skinner v. Oil,* 54 F.2d 896, 898–99 (10th Cir. 1931).

> "The mere combining of old machine parts, each operating in the old way and accomplishing the old result, is an aggregation, and hence unpatentable; whereas, if a new result be produced by the joint action of the elements, and if such a result be not the mere adding together of the contributions of the separate elements, then there exists a patentable combination." Roger Sherman Hoar, *Patent Tactics and Law* 38 (3d ed. 1950).

aggregation doctrine. (1942) **1.** The rule that precludes a party from totaling all claims for purposes of meeting the minimum amount necessary to give rise to federal diversity jurisdiction under the amount-in-controversy requirement. See *diversity jurisdiction* under JURISDICTION; AMOUNT IN CONTROVERSY. **2.** *Constitutional law.* A rule that allows Congress, under its Commerce Clause powers, to regulate purely private acts, such as growing wheat for one's own consumption, if the consequences of many such acts, taken together, would have an effect on interstate commerce. *See Wickard v. Filburn,* 317 U.S. 111, 63 S.Ct. 82 (1942).

aggregation of claims. (1972) *Patents.* In a patent application, an excessive number of claims that do not differ significantly in scope and are essentially duplicative. • Although a patent applicant may claim an invention and its various features in a reasonable number of ways, each claim must differ materially from the others. — Also termed *multiplicity of claims; undue multiplicity of claims.*

aggregation rejection. See REJECTION.

aggression. (18c) **1.** Angry or threatening behavior or statements that may well prompt or provoke fighting. **2.** *Int'l law.* The act of attacking a country, esp. in the absence of direct provocation, so that the attack is considered a grave breach of international law by a country. • The prohibition of aggression is a peremptory rule (*jus cogens*). Aggressors are guilty of an international crime. But there is no generally accepted definition of what constitutes aggression despite many attempts over the years to devise one.

In 1974, the United Nations General Assembly adopted a Resolution on the Definition of Aggression (Resolution 3314 (XXIX) of December 14, 1974). It defines aggression, in part, as "the use of armed force by a State against the sovereignty, territorial integrity, or political independence of another country, or in a manner inconsistent with the Charter of the United Nations. . . ." The definition does not extend to measures that, in certain circumstances, might constitute aggression, nor does it recognize exceptional circumstances that would make the enumerated acts defensive rather than offensive. The U.N. Security Council has never expressly relied on the resolution when determining whether a country's acts constitute a "threat to the peace, breach of the peace, or act of aggression." *See* U.N. Charter art. 39, 59 Stat. 1031. The difficulty of finding a generally accepted definition of *aggression* is reflected in Article 5 of the Statute of the International Criminal Court (37 I.L.M. 999). It confers jurisdiction on the Court over "the crime of aggression" but also requires the parties to the Statute to define the crime before the Court can exercise jurisdiction.

> "Although classical aggression has generally been thought to involve direct military operations by regular national forces under government control, today subjugation and control of peoples may well result from resort to non-military methods. Economic pressures on the other states; demands couched in traditional diplomatic terms but laden with implied threats to compel action or inaction; fifth column activities; the endless propaganda harangue urging another state's peoples to rise against their government; the aiding and abetting of rebel bands intent on overthrowing another government; and a wide range of other modern techniques must be included in the concept of aggression in so far as they are delicts at international law, for they are directed against the sovereign independence of a state." Ann Van Wynen Thomas & A.J. Thomas Jr., *The Concept of Aggression in International Law* 69 (1972).

▸ **direct aggression.** (18c) Aggression in which a state's regular armed forces participate.

▸ **indirect aggression.** (1939) Aggression carried out by some means other than through a state's regular armed forces.

> "[I]ndirect aggression would seem to have two prime meanings: (1) delictual acts armed or unarmed and conducted vicariously by the aggressor state through third parties which endanger the essential rights of a state, rights upon which its security depends, and (2) delictual acts taken directly by the governing authorities of a state against another state or vicariously through third-party groups which do not involve the use of armed force, but which do endanger the essential rights of a state upon which its security depends. No directly military operations by the regular armed forces of a state are involved in either case; therefore the aggression can be regarded as an indirect method of constraint carried on by the aggressor state." Ann Van Wynen Thomas & A.J. Thomas Jr., *The Concept of Aggression in International Law* 69 (1972).

aggressor, *n.* (16c) A person or country that initiates conflict with another person or country; an assailant.

aggressor corporation. See CORPORATION.

aggressor doctrine. (1947) The principle precluding tort recovery for a plaintiff who acts in a way that would provoke a reasonable person to use physical force for protection, unless the defendant in turn uses excessive force to repel the plaintiff.

aggrieved, *adj.* (16c) **1.** (Of a person or entity) having legal rights that are adversely affected; having been harmed by an infringement of legal rights. **2.** (Of a person) angry or sad on grounds of perceived unfair treatment.

aggrieved party. See PARTY (2).

AGI. *abbr.* See *adjusted gross income* under INCOME.

agillarius (aj-ə-**lair**-ee-əs), *n.* [Law Latin] (18c) *Hist.* A keeper of a herd of cattle in a common field; a hayward.

aging of accounts. (1959) A process of classifying accounts receivable by the time elapsed since the claim came into existence for the purpose of estimating the balance of uncollectible accounts as of a given date.

aging-out, *n.* (1980) A foster child's or minor ward's reaching the age at which any legal right to care expires. • Aging-out usu. occurs when the child reaches the age of majority and becomes ineligible for foster care. Some states allow an extension of eligibility up to age 21 if the child is still in school or cannot live independently, or if it is otherwise in the child's best interests to remain in foster care and the child consents. See INDEPENDENT-LIVING PROGRAM.

agio (**aj**-ee-oh *or* **ay**-jee-oh), *n.* (17c) The premium paid for the exchange of one kind of money for another, such as paper currency for coin or one country's currency for another's.

agiotage (**aj**-ee-ə-tij). (1828) **1.** The business of dealing in foreign exchange. **2.** The speculative buying and selling of securities.

agist (ə-**jist**), *vb.* (16c) To allow animals to graze on one's pasture for a fee.

agister (ə-**jis**-tər), *n.* (15c) Someone who takes and pastures grazing animals for a fee; a person engaged in the business of agistment. • An agister is a type of bailee for hire. — Also spelled *agistor.* — Also termed *gisetaker.*

agister's lien. See LIEN.

agistment (ə-**jist**-mənt). (16c) **1.** A type of bailment in which a person, for a fee, allows animals to graze on his or her pasture; the taking in of cattle or other livestock to feed at a per-animal rate. **2.** A charge levied on the owner or occupier of land. — Also termed *gisement.* See TITHE OF AGISTMENT.

▸ **agistment of sea-banks.** *Hist.* A charge on landowners for maintaining dikes that prevent encroachment by the sea.

agistor. See AGISTER.

agitprop (**aj**-it-prahp), *n.* (1925) Music, literature, or art that serves as political propaganda because it tries to persuade people to follow a particular set of political beliefs.

agnate (**ag**-nayt), *adj.* (1860) Related or akin through male descent or on the father's side.

agnate, *n.* (16c) **1.** A blood relative whose connection is through the male line. **2.** A relative on the father's side, whether or not traced exclusively through the male line. Cf. COGNATE.

agnatic (ag-**nat**-ik), *adj.* (18c) (Of a relationship) restricted to affiliations through the male line. — Also termed *agnatical* (ag-**nat**-i-kəl).

agnatical. See AGNATIC.

agnatio (ag-**nay**-shee-oh), *n.* [Latin] (17c) *Roman law.* Kinship through the male line, not necessarily involving blood ties; specif., an affiliation of free persons of either sex in the power (*patria potestas*) of the senior living male or of a male who would be in his power if he were living. • An agnatic relationship could be created either by adoption or by a blood relationship (*cognatio*) traced solely through the male side of a family. See COGNATIO; *patria potestas* under POTESTAS.

agnation (ag-**nay**-shən), *n.* (17c) The relationship of agnates.

agnatus (ag-**nay**-təs), *n.* [Latin] (17c) *Roman law.* A person related through the male line. Cf. COGNATUS.

"[*Agnati* were] all individuals subject for the time being to the same *patria potestas*, or who would be so subject were the common ancestor alive. Brothers and sisters, with their uncles, aunts, nephews, nieces, and other collaterals (not having been received into another family), if related through males, were agnates. The civil issue of the state was the Agnatic Family. Cognates were all persons who could trace their blood to a single ancestor or ancestress, and agnates were those cognates who traced their connection exclusively through males." John Bouvier, *Bouvier's Law Dictionary* (Francis Rawle ed., 8th ed. 1914).

agnomen (ag-**noh**-mən). [Latin] (18c) **1.** An additional name or title; a nickname. **2.** *Roman law.* An additional name, given in recognition of some achievement or to reflect adoption by a different *gens.* See NOMEN.

agnostic (ag-**nos**-tik), *n.* [fr. Greek *agnostos* "unknowable"] (1869) Someone who believes that knowledge about ultimate things, such as the origin of the universe or the existence of a deity, is not possible and therefore professes certainty or a strong probability of the unknowability of such matters. Cf. ATHEIST.

agrarian (ə-**grair**-ee-ən), *adj.* (17c) Of, relating to, or involving land, land tenure, or a division of landed property, esp. as regards farmers or farming. — **agrarian,** *n.*

agrarian law. (17c) *Roman & civil law.* The body of law governing the ownership, use, and distribution of rural land.

agrarium (ə-**grair**-ee-əm). [Law Latin] *Hist.* A tax on, or tribute payable out of, land.

a gratia (ay **gray**-shee-ə). [Law Latin] EX GRATIA.

agreamentum (ə-gree-ə-**men**-təm). [Law Latin] Agreement; an agreement.

agree, *vb.* (15c) **1.** To unite in thought; to concur in opinion or purpose. **2.** To exchange promises; to unite in an engagement to do or not do something. **3.** *Parliamentary law.* To adopt (usu. in the phrase *agree to*). See ADOPTION (5).

agreed-amount clause. (1965) An insurance-policy provision that the insured will carry a stated amount of coverage.

agreed boundary. See BOUNDARY (1).

agreed-boundary doctrine. (1941) The principle by which adjacent landowners resolve uncertainties over land boundaries by permanently fixing the boundaries by agreement; specif., the rule that owners of contiguous land may agree on the boundary between the parcels, as long as the actual boundary is uncertain, there is agreement between the two owners about the boundary line, there is acquiescence in the agreed line for a time exceeding the statute of limitations, and the agreed boundary is identifiable on the ground. — Also termed *doctrine of practical location.* See *agreed boundary* under BOUNDARY (1).

agreed case. See *agreed statement of facts* under STATEMENT OF FACTS.

agreed-damages clause. See LIQUIDATED-DAMAGES CLAUSE.

agreed decree. See DECREE.

agreed dismissal. See *dismissal agreed* under DISMISSAL (1).

agreed judgment. See JUDGMENT (2).

agreed price. See PRICE.

agreed statement of facts. See STATEMENT OF FACTS.

agreed statement on appeal. See *agreed statement of facts* under STATEMENT OF FACTS.

agreed value. See VALUE (2).

agreement. (15c) **1.** A mutual understanding between two or more persons about their relative rights and duties regarding past or future performances; a manifestation of mutual assent by two or more persons. **2.** The parties' actual bargain as found in their language or by implication from other circumstances, including course of dealing, usage of trade, and course of performance. UCC § 1-201(b)(3).

"The term 'agreement,' although frequently used as synonymous with the word 'contract,' is really an expression of greater breadth of meaning and less technicality. Every contract is an agreement; but not every agreement is a contract. In its colloquial sense, the term 'agreement' would include any arrangement between two or more persons intended to affect their relations (whether legal or otherwise) to each other. An accepted invitation to dinner, for example, would be an agreement in this sense; but it would not be a contract, because it would neither be intended to create, nor would it in fact create, any legal obligation between the parties to it. Further, even an agreement which is intended to affect the legal relations of the parties does not necessarily amount to a contract in the strict sense of the term. For instance, a conveyance of land or a gift of a chattel, though involving an agreement, is . . . not a contract; because its primary legal operation is to effect a transfer of property, and not to create an obligation." 2 *Stephen's Commentaries on the Laws of England* 5 (L. Crispin Warmington ed., 21st ed. 1950).

"An agreement, as the courts have said, 'is nothing more than a manifestation of mutual assent' by two or more parties legally competent persons to one another. Agreement is in some respects a broader term than contract, or even than bargain or promise. It covers executed sales, gifts, and other transfers of property." 1 Samuel Williston, *A Treatise on the Law of Contracts* § 2, at 6 (Walter H.E. Jaeger ed., 3d ed. 1957).

▸ **agreement incident to divorce.** See DIVORCE AGREEMENT.

▸ **agreement of imperfect obligation.** See *unenforceable contract* under CONTRACT.

▸ **agreement of rescission.** See RESCISSION (2).

▸ **agreement of sale.** (18c) An agreement that obligates someone to sell and that may include a corresponding obligation for someone else to buy.

▸ **agreement to agree.** (1876) **1.** An unenforceable agreement that purports to bind two parties to negotiate and enter into a contract; esp., a proposed agreement negotiated with the intent that the final agreement will be embodied in a formal written document and that neither party will be bound until the final agreement is executed. **2.** A fully enforceable agreement containing terms that are sufficiently definite as well as adequate consideration, but leaving some details to be worked out by the parties.

"Although the parties [to an agreement with open terms] expect that they will reach agreement on the missing terms, what they expect to happen if they fail to reach agreement is often unclear. They may understand that there will be no contract at all or they may understand that there will be a contract with the missing term supplied as a matter of law. If the latter is their understanding, a question arises whether the agreement is one with open terms sufficiently definite to be enforceable or whether it is a mere unenforceable 'agreement to agree.'" E. Allan Farnsworth, *Contracts* § 3.29, at 217 (3d ed. 1999).

▸ **agreement to marry.** See *marriage promise* under PROMISE.

▸ **agreement to sell.** (18c) An agreement that obligates someone to sell.

▸ **agreement under seal.** See *contract under seal* under CONTRACT.

▸ **antenuptial agreement.** See PRENUPTIAL AGREEMENT.

▸ **binding agreement.** (18c) An enforceable contract. See CONTRACT.

▸ **business-continuation agreement.** (1951) An agreement for the disposition of a business interest in the event of the owner's death, disability, retirement, or withdrawal from the business. • The agreement may be between the business and its individual owners, among the individual owners themselves, or between the individual owners and a key person, family member, or outsider. — Abbr. BCA. Cf. *cross-purchase agreement*; *third-party business-buyout agreement.*

▸ **certified agreement.** (1872) *Australian law.* An agreement between an employer and two or more employees or one or more unions detailing the terms and conditions of employment. — Also termed *collective agreement*; *enterprise bargaining agreement.*

▸ **closing agreement.** (1929) *Tax.* A written contract between a taxpayer and the Internal Revenue Service to resolve a tax dispute.

▸ **cohabitation agreement.** See COHABITATION AGREEMENT.

▸ **collective agreement.** See COLLECTIVE AGREEMENT.

▸ **criss-cross agreement.** See *cross-purchase agreement.*

▸ **cross-purchase agreement.** (1979) An agreement between a business's individual owners to purchase the interest of a withdrawing or deceased owner in order to continue operating the business. — Also termed *criss-cross agreement.* Cf. *business-continuation agreement*; *third-party business-buyout agreement.*

▸ **divorce agreement.** See DIVORCE AGREEMENT.

▸ **easement agreement.** See EASEMENT.

▸ **enterprise bargaining agreement.** See *certified agreement.*

▸ **exchange agreement.** (1910) An agreement to exchange real properties, usu. like-kind properties, often for tax purposes. See 1031 EXCHANGE; TAX-FREE EXCHANGE.

▸ **formal agreement.** (17c) An agreement for which the law requires not only the consent of the parties but also a manifestation of the agreement in some particular form (e.g., a signed writing), in default of which the agreement is unenforceable. Cf. *formal contract* under CONTRACT.

▸ **integrated agreement.** See INTEGRATED CONTRACT.

▸ **invalid agreement.** See *invalid contract* under CONTRACT.

▸ **joint agreement.** (16c) A contract under which the parties agree to combine their performances for a mutual purpose.

▸ **living-together agreement.** See COHABITATION AGREEMENT.

▸ **marital agreement.** See MARITAL AGREEMENT.

▸ **marital settlement agreement.** See DIVORCE AGREEMENT.

▸ **negotiated agreement.** See NEGOTIATED AGREEMENT.

▸ **noncircumvention agreement.** See NONCIRCUMVENTION AGREEMENT.

▸ **noncompetition agreement.** See *covenant not to compete* under COVENANT (1).

▸ **outsourcing agreement.** See OUTSOURCING AGREEMENT.

▸ **point-and-click agreement.** See POINT-AND-CLICK AGREEMENT.

▸ **postnuptial agreement.** See POSTNUPTIAL AGREEMENT.

▸ **prenuptial agreement.** See PRENUPTIAL AGREEMENT.

▸ **property settlement agreement.** See PROPERTY SETTLEMENT (2).

▸ **reconciliation agreement.** See RECONCILIATION AGREEMENT.

▸ **redemption agreement.** See STOCK-REDEMPTION AGREEMENT.

▸ **separation agreement.** See SEPARATION AGREEMENT.

▸ **shrinkwrap agreement.** See *shrinkwrap license* under LICENSE.

▸ **side agreement.** (1848) **1.** An agreement that is ancillary to another agreement. **2.** *Int'l law.* An international accord that is specifically negotiated to supplement a broader trade treaty. • For example, NAFTA contains no provisions about labor standards or environmental protection. But two side agreements about those areas were negotiated separately and designed to supplement NAFTA, making the treaty more attractive to the ratifying bodies. — Also termed *supplemental agreement.*

▸ **simple agreement.** (18c) An agreement for which the law requires nothing for its effective operation beyond some manifestation that the parties have consented.

▸ **stock-retirement agreement.** See STOCK-REDEMPTION AGREEMENT.

▸ **subordination agreement.** See SUBORDINATION AGREEMENT.

▸ **supplemental agreement.** See *side agreement.*

▸ **surrogate-parenting agreement.** See SURROGATE-PARENTING AGREEMENT.

▸ **takeover agreement.** An agreement under which a defaulting party's surety agrees to perform the original contract in the defaulting party's stead.

▸ **third-party business-buyout agreement.** An agreement by a business's owners to sell all or part of the business to an outside person who will continue to operate it. Cf. *business-continuation agreement*; *cross-purchase agreement.*

▸ **trust agreement.** See *declaration of trust* (2) under DECLARATION (1).

▸ **unconscionable agreement** (ən-**kon**-shə-nə-bəl). (1817) An agreement that no promisor with any sense, and not under a delusion, would make, and that no honest and fair promisee would accept. • For commercial contexts, see UCC § 2-302. — Also termed *unconscionable contract; unconscionable bargain.*

▸ **underwriting agreement.** (1898) An agreement between a corporation and an underwriter covering the terms and conditions of a new securities issue.

▸ **valid agreement.** See *valid contract* under CONTRACT.

▸ **voidable agreement.** See *voidable contract* under CONTRACT.

▸ **void agreement.** See *void contract* under CONTRACT.

agreement of sale. See AGREEMENT.

Agreement on Trade-Related Aspects of Intellectual Property Rights. See TRIPS.

Agreement Relating to Liability Limitation of the Warsaw Convention and The Hague Protocol. See MONTREAL AGREEMENT.

agreement under seal. See *contract under seal* under CONTRACT.

agri (**ag**-rɪ), *n. pl.* [Latin] Lands.

agribusiness. (1955) The pursuit of agriculture as an occupation or profit-making enterprise, including labor, land-use planning, and financing the cost of land, equipment, and other necessary expenses. • This term generally excludes smaller family-owned and -operated farms.

Agricultural Adjustment Act. A 1933 federal statute that paid farmers not to produce crops in an effort to raise crop prices. • The U.S. Supreme Court declared the Act unconstitutional in 1936 on grounds that Congress had overstepped its power to regulate commerce. A second, more limited Agricultural Adjustment Act was enacted in 1938. — Abbr. AAA.

Agricultural Cooperative Service. The federal agency within the U.S. Department of Agriculture responsible for helping farmers to organize farm cooperatives. • The Service also collects statistical information on co-ops and publishes *Farmer Cooperatives*, a monthly magazine.

agricultural-disparagement law. (1994) A statute designed to protect food producers from and provide remedies for pecuniary harm resulting from false and malicious reports of food contamination. • A typical statute applies to false and disparaging public statements implying or claiming that a perishable food product is unsafe for human consumption. It typically applies when the speaker or writer knows that the statements are false because the claim or implication has no basis in reliable scientific inquiry, facts, or data. — Also termed *veggie-libel law; perishable-food-disparagement act; agricultural-product-disparagement law; food-disparagement law.*

agricultural fixture. See FIXTURE.

agricultural labor. (18c) Work that is performed on a farm or ranch, or that pertains to the production of commodities, such as harvesting crops, raising livestock, or obtaining milk, honey, or other animal products. • Agricultural labor is often excluded from certain labor laws, such as unemployment insurance and workers' compensation.

agricultural lien. See LIEN.

Agricultural Marketing Service. An agency in the U.S. Department of Agriculture responsible for compiling and publishing marketing information, establishing and enforcing quality standards for agricultural products, testing those products, and making grants to states and farmers. • It was established by the Secretary of Agriculture in 1972. — Abbr. AMS.

agricultural-preservation easement. See *land-conservation easement* under EASEMENT.

agricultural-product-disparagement law. See AGRICULTURAL-DISPARAGEMENT LAW.

Agricultural Research Service. An agency in the U.S. Department of Agriculture responsible for conducting agricultural research to ensure the production of high-quality food and food products. — Abbr. ARS.

agriculture. (16c) The science or art of cultivating soil, harvesting crops, and raising livestock.

> "'Agriculture' is broader in meaning than 'farming'; and while it includes the preparation of soil, the planting of seeds, the raising and harvesting of crops, and all their incidents, it also includes gardening, horticulture, viticulture, dairying, poultry, bee raising, and ranching." 3 Am. Jur. 2d *Agriculture* § 1, at 934–35 (1986).

agri limitati (ag-rɪ lim-i-**tay**-tɪ). See *ager limitatus* under AGER.

agriterrorism. See TERRORISM.

agroterrorism. See *agriterrorism* under TERRORISM.

***Aguilar–Spinelli* test** (ah-gee-**lahr** spi-**nel**-ee *or* **ag**-wə-lahr). (1970) *Criminal procedure.* A standard for determining whether hearsay (such as an informant's tip) is sufficiently reliable to establish probable cause for a search or arrest, whereby officers must articulate (1) why they believe the information is truthful or reliable, and (2) the basis for the informant's knowledge. • The test was developed in two Supreme Court opinions: *Aguilar v. Texas*, 378 U.S. 108 (1964), and *Spinelli v. U.S.*, 393 U.S. 410 (1969). By 1983, the Supreme Court had moved to a different test — a totality-of-the-circumstances standard developed in *Illinois v. Gates*, 462 U.S. 213 (1983) — but some states, such as New York, continue to apply the *Aguilar–Spinelli* test. See TOTALITY-OF-THE-CIRCUMSTANCES TEST.

agunah (ah-**goo**-nah), *n.* [Hebrew] (1930) *Jewish law.* **1.** A woman whose husband has deserted her or otherwise disappeared. • She may not remarry until either proving his death or obtaining a Jewish divorce (*get*). See GET. **2.** A woman whose husband will not agree to such a divorce.

AGVA. *abbr.* AMERICAN GUILD OF VARIETY ARTISTS.

AHRQ. *abbr.* AGENCY FOR HEALTHCARE RESEARCH AND QUALITY.

ahupuaa (ah-hoo-poo-**ah**-ah). [Hawaiian] (1858) A variable measure of Hawaiian land, traditionally understood to stretch from the sea to the mountains, to allow the people to obtain the various materials needed for subsistence offered at different elevations. — Also spelled *ahupua'a.*

AI. *abbr.* (1945) ARTIFICIAL INSEMINATION.

AIA. *abbr.* AMERICA INVENTS ACT.

AICPA. *abbr.* AMERICAN INSTITUTE OF CERTIFIED PUBLIC ACCOUNTANTS.

AID. *abbr.* **1.** See *artificial insemination by donor* under ARTIFICIAL INSEMINATION. **2.** UNITED STATES AGENCY FOR INTERNATIONAL DEVELOPMENT.

aid, *n.* (17c) **1.** A contribution toward defense costs from a third party who has a joint interest in the defense but has not been sued. **2.** *Hist.* A subsidy or tax granted to the king for an extraordinary purpose. **3.** *Hist.* A benevolence or tribute (i.e., a sum of money) granted by the tenant to his lord in times of difficulty and distress. • Over time, these grants evolved from being discretionary to mandatory. The three principal aids were (1) to ransom the lord's person if he was taken prisoner; (2) to contribute toward the ceremony of knighting the lord's eldest son; and (3) to provide a suitable dowry for the lord's eldest daughter. — Also termed (in senses 2 & 3) *auxilium.* See AUXILIUM.

aid and abet, *vb.* (17c) To assist or facilitate the commission of a crime, or to promote its accomplishment. • Aiding and abetting is a crime in most jurisdictions. — Also termed *aid or abet; criminal facilitation; counsel and procure.* — **aider and abettor,** *n.*

> "The phrase 'aid and abet' and 'aider and abettor' seem unnecessarily verbose. . . . [A]ny aid given with mens rea is abetment; hence to add the word 'aid' to the word 'abet' is not necessary and is sometimes misleading." Rollin M. Perkins & Ronald N. Boyce, *Criminal Law* 724–25 (3d ed. 1982).

> "In connection with the principal in the second degree or accessory before the fact, the terms 'aid' and 'abet' are frequently used interchangeably, although they are not synonymous. To 'aid' is to assist or help another. To 'abet' means, literally, to bait or excite, as in the case of an animal. In its legal sense, it means to encourage, advise, or instigate the commission of a crime." 1 Charles E. Torcia, *Wharton's Criminal Law* § 29, at 181 (15th ed. 1993).

aid and comfort. (16c) Help given by someone to a national enemy in such a way that the help amounts to treason. • The phrase is a loan translation of the French *aide et confort,* which appears in the early 15th century in a French translation of the Bible. The first English-language use appears to have been in Grafton's *Chronicles* of 1568.

> "Aid and comfort may be given in various ways, such as buying a vessel and fitting it for service in aid of the enemy, delivering prisoners and deserters to the enemy, or selling critical materials with knowledge of the fact that the purchaser buys them to use in the manufacture of gunpowder for the enemy, or otherwise to aid him in his prosecution of the war. And the courts have given short shrift to the claim that such a sale was not intended to aid the enemy but only to make a profit." Rollin M. Perkins & Ronald N. Boyce, *Criminal Law* 502 (3d ed. 1982).

aided-awareness survey. (2004) *Trademarks.* A trademark survey in which interviewees are asked to choose from a spectrum of choices that prominently feature the desired response. • Aided-awareness surveys are often discounted or entirely disregarded by courts in trademark-infringement actions. — Also termed *aided-recall survey.*

aided-recall survey. See AIDED-AWARENESS SURVEY.

aide-mémoire (ayd-mem-**wahr**). [French] (1923) *Int'l law.* A diplomatic document that a diplomatic agent leaves with the receiving state's department of foreign affairs on the occasion of a *démarche.* • The *aide-mémoire* presents the receiving state with a precise record of the substance of the diplomatic agent's mission. It is typically written in an impersonal style, without mentioning either the addressee or the author. It appears on printed letterhead and is dated, but it is not signed, initialed, or embossed with a seal. See DÉMARCHE.

aider, *n.* (16c) **1.** An act of aiding; the curing of a defect. **2.** Someone who aids another.

aider by pleading over. (1860) The cure of a pleading defect by an adversary's answering the pleading without an objection, so that the objection is waived.

aider by subsequent pleading. (1909) The cure of a pleading defect by an adversary's answer that refers to or admits a material fact or allegation that was not mentioned in the pleading, or an answer that shows the correct basis for the plaintiff's pleading. — Also termed *express aider.*

aider by verdict. (1824) The cure of a pleading defect by a trial verdict, based on the presumption that the record contains adequate proof of the necessary facts even if those facts were not specifically alleged. — Also termed *cure by verdict.*

> "AIDER BY VERDICT. Wherever a pleading states the essential requisites of a cause of action or ground of defense, it will be held sufficient after a general verdict in favor of the party pleading, though the statement be informal or inaccurate; but a verdict will never aid the statement of a title or cause of action inherently defective." Benjamin J. Shipman, *Handbook of Common-Law Pleading* § 332, at 531 (Henry Winthrop Ballantine ed., 3d ed. 1923).

aiding-and-abetting liability. See LIABILITY.

aiding an escape. (18c) The crime of helping a prisoner escape custody.

aid of the king. *Hist.* A request of the king made by a tenant for relief from another's demand for rent.

aid or abet. See AID AND ABET.

aid or abet infringement. (1896) *Patents.* Through some affirmative act or conduct, to actively induce or assist with another person's infringement. • Aiding or abetting patent infringement is actionable under § 271(b) of the Patent Act. Cf. *infringement in the inducement* under INFRINGEMENT.

aid prayer. (17c) *Hist.* A plea by a life tenant or other holder of less than a fee simple to bring into the action another who holds an interest in the estate (such as a reversioner or remainderman) to help defend the title. — Also termed *prayer in aid.*

aids. See AID (2).

Aid to Families with Dependent Children. *Obsolete.* A federally funded, state-administered welfare program that provided financial assistance to needy families with dependent children. • Aid to Families with Dependent Children has been replaced by Temporary Assistance to Needy Families. — Abbr. AFDC. See TEMPORARY ASSISTANCE TO NEEDY FAMILIES.

aiel (**ay**-əl), *n.* [Law French] (14c) *Hist.* **1.** A grandfather. **2.** A writ by an heir of a grandfather for recovery of the grandfather's estate, which had been wrongfully possessed by a stranger. — Also spelled *aile; ayel; ayle.* — Also termed (in sense 2) *writ of aiel.* Cf. BESAYEL; COSINAGE.

AIH. *abbr.* See *artificial insemination by husband* under ARTIFICIAL INSEMINATION.

***Aiken* exemption.** (1983) *Copyright.* An exception in the law of infringement that permits retail establishments with less than 2,000 square feet of space to play radio and television broadcasts for employees and patrons without obtaining a license. *Twentieth Century Music Corp. v. Aiken,* 422 U.S. 151, 95 S.Ct. 2040 (1975). — Also termed *store-receiver exemption.*

ailment, *n.* (17c) An illness that is not very serious; a malady. Cf. ILLNESS; SICKNESS.

AIM. *abbr.* AIRMAN'S INFORMATION MANUAL.

AIP. *abbr.* AMERICAN INSTITUTE OF PARLIAMENTARIANS.

AIPA. *abbr.* AMERICAN INVENTORS PROTECTION ACT.

AIPLA. *abbr.* AMERICAN INTELLECTUAL PROPERTY LAW ASSOCIATION.

airbill. See *air waybill* under WAYBILL.

air-consignment bill. See *air waybill* under WAYBILL.

aircraft piracy. See *air piracy* under PIRACY (3).

air impurity. See AIR POLLUTION (1).

air law. (1920) The part of law, esp. international law, relating to civil aviation.

airman's certificate. (1944) A license that every aircraft pilot must have to operate an aircraft in U.S. airspace. 49 USCA §§ 44701–44711; 14 CFR § 61.3.

Airman's Information Manual. A publication of the Federal Aviation Administration, providing the fundamental requirements of any pilot who flies in national airspace. — Abbr. AIM.

air piracy. See PIRACY (3).

air police. See SECURITY POLICE (2).

air pollution. (1874) *Environmental law.* **1.** Any harmful substance or energy emitted directly or indirectly into the air, esp. if the harm is to the environment or to the public health or welfare; contaminants in the atmosphere. — Also termed *air impurity.* **2.** The artificial introduction of such substances or contaminants into the atmosphere; the emission of impurities into the air.

air-quality-control region. (1968) *Environmental law.* A federally designated area in which communities share an air-pollution problem, often involving several states; an interstate area or major intrastate area that the Environmental Protection Agency designates for monitoring and ameliorating ambient air quality. 42 USCA § 7407(c).

air-quality criteria. (1967) *Environmental law.* The legal limits that the Environmental Protection Agency sets for atmospheric or airborne pollutants in a defined area and at a specified time.

air right. (1922) The right to use all or a portion of the airspace above real property.

air-services agreement. See AIR-TRANSPORT AGREEMENT.

airspace. (1908) The space that extends upward from the surface of land, esp. so far as is necessary for the owner or possessor to have reasonable use and enjoyment of the incidents of its ownership or possession. Cf. OUTER SPACE (1).

▸ **national airspace.** (1932) *Int'l law.* The pillar of air above a country's territory — including internal waters and the territorial sea — over which it has complete and exclusive sovereignty and through which foreign aircraft have no right of innocent passage. • There is no agreement on the boundary between national airspace and outer space.

▸ **navigable airspace.** (1923) The area above the legally established minimum flight altitudes, including the area needed to ensure safe takeoffs and landings of aircraft. 49 USCA § 40102(a)(30).

air-traffic control. (1932) **1.** The job or activity of giving instructions to pilots by radio or the Internet. **2.** Collectively, the people whose job is to do this. — **air-traffic controller,** *n.*

air-transport agreement. (1939) A contract governing the operation of air services; esp., an agreement between governments regarding the operation of international air services between their territories. — Also termed *air-services agreement.* — Abbr. ATA.

air waybill. See WAYBILL.

airworthy, *adj.* (1829) (Of an aircraft) fit and safe to fly. Cf. SEAWORTHY.

aisiamentum (ay-shee-ə-**men**-təm). [Law Latin] An easement or privilege.

aisne. See EIGNE.

a issue (ah is[h]-**yoo**). [Law French] At issue.

AJC. *abbr.* ACCESS-TO-JUSTICE COMMISSION.

AJS. *abbr.* AMERICAN JUDICATURE SOCIETY.

a jure suo cadunt (ay **joor**-ee s[y]**oo**-oh **kay**-dənt). [Latin] *Scots law.* They fall from their right. • The phrase appeared in reference to those who lose a property right through loss of possession or through abandonment.

a.k.a. *abbr.* (1955) Also known as.

al (ahl), *prep.* [Law French] At.

a la grande grevaunce (ah lə **grawnd** grə-**vawns**). [Law French] To the great grievance.

a large (ah **lahrzh**). [Law French] Free; at large.

alarm, *n.* (14c) **1.** One or more loud noises, esp. shouts, intended to warn people that something bad is happening <when they smelled smoke, the neighbors raised an alarm throughout the neighborhood>. **2.** A piece of equipment that emits loud noises to warn people of danger; esp., a clock or other device that can be set to make a loud noise at a specified time <set the alarm for 6:15 a.m.> <burglar alarm>. **3.** A feeling of worry that something dangerous or bad might happen, esp. when the feeling is suddenly aroused <no cause for alarm>. **4.** Sudden apprehension by one or more soldiers of being attacked by surprise <alarm spread through the camp>.

▸ **false alarm.** (16c) **1.** The accidental or mistaken triggering of a device that warns of danger. **2.** A situation in which people mistakenly think that something bad is imminent.

Alaska trust. See *asset-protection trust* (1) under TRUST (3).

a latere (ay **lat**-ə-ree). [Latin] From the side; collaterally. • This term was formerly used to denote collateral succession rather than lineal succession.

albacea (ahl-bə-**thay**-ə), *n. Spanish law.* An executor; the person named by a testator to carry out the directions of a will.

alba firma (al-bə **fər**-mə). [Law Latin] See WHITE RENT.

albanus (al-**bay**-nəs), *n.* [Law Latin] See ADVENA.

al barre (ahl **bahr**). [Law French] At the bar.

album breve (**al**-bəm breev *or* bree-vee). See BREVE.

albus liber (**al**-bəs **lɪ**-bər). [Law Latin "white book"] (18c) *Hist.* An ancient book containing a compilation of the laws and customs of the city of London. — Also termed *White Book.*

alcalde (ahl-**kahl**-day *or* al-**kal**-dee). [fr. Arabic *al-qadi* "the Cadi" or "the judge"] (17c) *Spanish law.* **1.** *Hist.* A judicial officer. • The alcalde's functions typically resembled those of a justice of the peace. **2.** The mayor of a Spanish or Spanish-American town, usu. with a judicial element. • This is the modern sense.

▸ **alcalde ordinario.** *Spanish law.* A local judge.

alcohol. (18c) **1.** The intoxicating ingredient of wines, beers, and other fermented, distilled, or brewed beverages. **2.** Any liquid containing an appreciable amount of this ingredient.

Alcohol and Tobacco Tax and Trade Bureau. A bureau in the U.S. Department of the Treasury that administers the laws governing the production, use, and distribution of alcohol and tobacco products, and collects excise taxes on firearms and ammunition. • The Bureau has the tax-enforcement functions of the former Bureau of Alcohol, Tobacco, and Firearms. — Abbr. TTB.

alcoholic, *n.* (1852) Someone who habitually abuses alcohol and loses self-control, often to the extent of endangering the health, safety, or welfare of self or others. Cf. DRUNKARD.

alcohol impairment. See DRUNKENNESS.

alcoholometer. See BREATHALYZER.

Alco-Sensor. (1981) The tradename of a handheld device that police use as a preliminary breath test to determine whether a driver has consumed alcohol. Cf. BREATHALYZER.

alderman (**ahl**-dər-mən), *n.* [Anglo-Saxon *ealderman* "prince, ruler"] (13c) **1.** A member of a city council or other local governing body, often responsible for exercising certain judicial functions; BURGOMASTER (2). • In locales where the municipal legislative body consists of two chambers, the board of aldermen constitutes the upper branch. Although *alderwoman* and even *aldermaness* have been attested from the 16th century — mostly in the sense "the wife of an alderman" — the term *alderman* has been widely understood as a gender-neutral term since the 19th century. Yet some speakers and writers have pushed for *alderperson*, which remains a little-used alternative (except in Wisconsin). In many English-speaking jurisdictions, *alderman* has been updated to *councilor* (AmE) or *councillor* (BrE). **2.** *English law.* A member of the upper branch of a town council whose office corresponds to that of a Scottish bailie. **3.** *English law.* One of the lesser members of a county council. **4.** *Hist. English law.* In early Anglo-Saxon times, a chieftain, lord, or earl. **5.** *Hist. English law.* In later Anglo-Saxon times, the chief magistrate of a territorial district. **6.** *Hist. English law.* After the 7th century, the chief officer of a guild — that is, an association of persons engaged in kindred pursuits for mutual protection and aid. **7.** *Hist. Slang.* A turkey. Cf. ASSEMBLYMAN. Pl. **aldermen.**

aldermannus (al-dər-**man**-əs). [Law Latin] *Hist.* An alderman.

▸ ***aldermannus civitatis vel burgi*** (siv-i-**tay**-tis vel **bər**-jɪ). An alderman of a city or borough.

▸ ***aldermannus hundredi seu wapentachii*** (**hən**-dri-dɪ **syoo** wahp-ən-**tay**-kee-ɪ). An alderman of a hundred or wapentake.

▸ ***aldermannus regis*** (**ree**-jis). An alderman of the king, so called because he is appointed by the king or gives the king's judgment in the premises allotted to him.

▸ ***aldermannus totius Angliae*** (**toh**-shee-əs **ang**-glee-ee). An alderman of all England, similar to the chief justiciary of England in later times. See JUSTICIARY.

alderperson. See ALDERMAN.

alderwoman. (18c) A female member of a city council or other local governing body. See ALDERMAN. Pl. **alderwomen.**

alea (**ay**-lee-ə), *n.* [Latin] *Roman law.* **1.** A game of chance. **2.** The chance of gain or loss in a contract.

aleator (ay-lee-**ay**-tər). [Latin] *Roman law.* A gambler; dice player.

aleatoric. See ALEATORY.

aleatory (**ay**-lee-ə-tor-ee), *adj.* (17c) Dependent on uncertain contingencies. • The word *aleatory* derives from the Latin word *aleator*, meaning "a gambler," which itself comes from *alea* (a die used in gaming). — Also termed *aleatoric.*

aleatory contract. See CONTRACT.

aleatory promise. See PROMISE.

alegal, *adj.* (1991) Outside the sphere of law; not classifiable as being legal or illegal <the law often treats the promises of unmarried cohabitants as contractual words rather than alegal words of commitment>. — **alegality,** *n.*

aler a Dieu. See ALLER A DIEU.

aler sans jour. See ALLER SANS JOUR.

ale silver. (17c) *Hist.* A rent or tribute paid annually to the lord mayor of London by persons who sold ale within the city.

alevosia. *Spanish law.* See MALICE. *See Pico v. U.S.*, 228 U.S. 225, 33 S.Ct. 482 (1913).

alexander, *vb.* (17c) (Of a judge) to treat with harshness and severity; esp., to hang. • The term is an eponym of Sir Jerome Alexander, an Irish judge who in the 17th century became noted for his merciless decisions, esp. with regard to Presbyterians and other nonconformists.

alez adeu (ah-**lay** ah-**duu**). See ADEU.

alfet (**al**-fet). (bef. 12c) *Hist.* A cauldron filled with boiling water, used to scald the arm of a person undergoing an ordeal. See *ordeal by water* (2) under ORDEAL.

***Alford* plea.** (1972) A guilty plea that a defendant enters as part of a plea bargain without admitting guilt. • Similar to a plea of nolo contendere (allowed in some states), this plea is not considered compelled within the language of the Fifth Amendment if the plea represents a voluntary, knowing, and intelligent choice between the available options <the defendant — realizing the strength of the prosecution's evidence and not wanting to risk the death penalty — entered an *Alford* plea>. *North Carolina v. Alford*, 400 U.S. 25, 91 S.Ct. 160 (1970). — Also termed (in New York) *Serrano plea* (after *People v. Serrano*, 15 N.Y.2d 304 (1965)). Cf. NO CONTEST.

algorithm. (1938) *Patents.* A mathematical or logical process consisting of a series of steps, designed to solve a specific type of problem. • Algorithms were long considered abstract ideas and therefore unpatentable subject matter. But in 1998, the U.S. Court of Appeals for the

Federal Circuit found valid a patent on financial software as "a practical application of a mathematical algorithm [that] produces a useful, concrete and tangible result." *State St. Bank & Trust Co. v. Signature Fin. Grp.*, 149 F.3d 1368 (Fed. Cir. 1998). That precedent makes it easier to patent computer software, which consists almost entirely of algorithms.

> "An algorithm is a method or a process followed to solve a specific problem. In the simplest form, it is a means of getting from A to B. Consider the following non-technical example: The grass in your yard is very tall (Point A). The grass needs to be less tall given the community rules in your neighborhood (Point B). How you get from Point A to Point B can happen in a variety of ways. You can mow the grass yourself, you can pay someone to mow it, you can spray chemicals on the grass and kill it, or you can plant a garden so you no longer have any grass. Each of these solutions will take you from Point A to Pont B, but has its own idiosyncratic steps that are, in effect, an algorithm to solve the problem. While the above example demonstrates a problem can be solved by many different algorithms, note that a given algorithm solves only one problem (e.g., making the grass shorter). Similarly, programmers use algorithms to determine how software takes each step." Daniel B. Garrie & Francis M. Allegra, *Plugged In: Guidebook to Software and the Law* § 2.4, at 60–61 (2013).

algorithm exception. (1982) *Patents.* The traditional notion that although any new and useful process is patentable, an abstract mathematical function, such as an algorithm, cannot be patented. • The exception was first articulated by the U.S. Supreme Court in *Gottschalk v. Benson*, 409 U.S. 63, 93 S.Ct. 253 (1972). The rule was undermined by *State St. Bank & Trust Co. v. Signature Fin. Group*, 149 F.3d 1368 (Fed. Cir. 1998). In that case, the court decided that a machine's transformation of numerical data into a calculated share price was a sufficient and practical application of a mathematical algorithm, formula, or calculation, because the final share price was "a useful, concrete and tangible result." — Also termed *mathematical-algorithm exception.*

ALI. *abbr.* AMERICAN LAW INSTITUTE.

alia enormia (**ay**-lee-ə i-**nor**-mee-ə). [Law Latin "other serious wrongs"] *Hist.* A general allegation of injuries made at the conclusion of the declaration by a plaintiff in a trespass action.

aliamenta (al-ee-ə-**men**-tə). [Latin] A liberty of passage or open way, such as a path through another's hedge or drainage for a waterway.

alias (**ay**-lee-əs), *adj.* (17c) Issued after the first instrument has not been effective or resulted in action.

alias, *adv.* (16c) **1.** Otherwise called or named; also known as <William Grimsby, alias the Grim Reaper>. **2.** At another time.

alias, *n.* (17c) **1.** An assumed or additional name that a person has used or is known by. — Also termed *assumed name*; *fictitious name.* Cf. PSEUDONYM.

> "A name assumed without authority is simply an alias, and has precisely the same weight as the grandiloquent names which are assumed for the purpose of the theatre, or the haphazard *nommes des plumes* which are adopted by so many writers." Arthur Charles Fox-Davies & P.W.P. Carlyon-Britton, *A Treatise on the Law Concerning Names and Changes of Name* 55 (1906).

2. *Hist.* A second writ issued after the first has failed. See *alias writ* under WRIT. Pl. **aliases.**

▸ **corporate alias.** (1914) An assumed or additional name that a business uses. See D/B/A.

alias dictus (**ay**-lee-əs **dik**-təs), *adv.* [Latin] Otherwise called; ALIAS (1).

alias execution. See EXECUTION (4).

alias process. See PROCESS (2).

alias subpoena. See SUBPOENA.

alias summons. See SUMMONS.

alias writ. See WRIT.

a libellis (ay li-**bel**-is). [Law Latin] *Roman law.* **1.** An officer having charge of petitions (*libelli*) addressed to the emperor or sovereign. **2.** CHANCELLOR OF THE EXCHEQUER.

a libello ut libellatur (ay li-**bel**-oh ət lib-ə-**lay**-tər). [Law Latin] *Hist.* From the libel as laid. • The phrase appeared in a dismissal in favor of a defendant.

alibi (**al**-ə-bı), *n.* [Latin "elsewhere"] (18c) **1.** A defense based on the physical impossibility of a defendant's guilt by placing the defendant in a location other than the scene of the crime at the relevant time. Fed. R. Crim. P. 12.1. **2.** The quality, state, or condition of having been elsewhere when an offense was committed.

alibi, *vb.* (1909) To offer or provide an alibi for <the conspirators alibied for each other>.

alibi notice. (1928) *Criminal procedure.* The disclosure by a criminal defendant to the prosecution of an intent to raise a defense based in whole or in part on an alibi. • The notice may be required by law or may be triggered by the prosecutor's demand for the defense to disclose any such information — often with a deadline (e.g., eight days after the notice). See NOTICE-OF-ALIBI RULE.

alibi witness. See WITNESS.

alien (**ay**-lee-ən *or* **ayl**-yən), *n.* (14c) Someone who resides within the borders of a country but is not a citizen or subject of that country; a person not owing allegiance to a particular country. • In the United States, an alien is a person who was born outside the jurisdiction of the United States, who is subject to some foreign government, and who has not been naturalized under U.S. law.

▸ **alien ami.** See *alien friend.*

▸ **alien amy.** See *alien friend.*

▸ **alien enemy.** (17c) A citizen or subject of a country at war with the country in which the citizen or subject is living or traveling. — Also termed *enemy alien.*

> "In its natural meaning, the term 'alien enemy' indicates a subject of a State with which this country is at war; but in considering the enforcement of civil rights, the test is not nationality, but residence or place of business. Hence, if a person is voluntarily resident in or is carrying on business in an enemy country, then he is an alien enemy even though he be a British subject or the subject of a neutral State . . . ." 1 E.W. Chance, *Principles of Mercantile Law* 52–53 (P.W. French ed., 13th ed. 1950).

▸ **alien friend.** (17c) An alien who is a citizen or subject of a friendly power. — Also termed (in Law French) *alien amy*; *alien ami.*

▸ **alien immigrant.** See IMMIGRANT.

▸ **deportable alien.** (1927) A alien who has entered the United States but is subject to removal.

▸ **enemy alien.** See *alien enemy.*

▸ **excludable alien.** (1916) A alien ineligible for admission or entry into the United States.

▸ **illegal alien.** (1901) An alien who enters a country at the wrong time or place, eludes an examination by officials, obtains entry by fraud, or enters into a sham marriage to evade immigration laws. • Although the term was originally a clinical legalism, today it is often viewed as a snarl-phrase. Many writers therefore prefer *undocumented immigrant*, which others object to as a euphemism. The nomenclature has become a political battleground. — Also termed *undocumented alien; illegal immigrant; unauthorized alien; undocumented immigrant; unlawful noncitizen.*

▸ **inadmissible alien.** (1919) A deportable or excludable alien. *See* 8 USCA § 1182(a).

▸ **nonresident alien.** (1801) Someone who is neither a resident nor a citizen of the United States.

▸ **resident alien.** (18c) An alien who has a legally established domicile in the United States. See NATURALIZATION.

▸ **unauthorized alien.** See *illegal alien*.

▸ **undocumented alien.** See *illegal alien*.

alien, *vb.* See ALIENATE.

alienable (**ay**-lee-ə-nə-bəl *or* **ayl**-yə-), *adj.* (17c) Capable of being transferred to the ownership of another; transferable <an alienable property interest>. — **alienability,** *n.*

Alien Acts. See ALIEN AND SEDITION ACTS.

alienage (**ay**-lee-ə-nij *or* **ayl**-yə-nij), *n.* (1809) The condition or status of being an alien.

▸ **declaration of alienage.** See DECLARATION (1).

alien ami. See *alien friend* under ALIEN.

alien amy. See *alien friend* under ALIEN.

Alien and Sedition Acts. *Hist.* Four statutes passed in 1798 designed to silence critics of the Federalist party by tightening residency requirements for citizenship, granting to the President the power to jail aliens considered dangerous to the country, and restricting freedoms of the press and speech by criminalizing speech hostile to the government. • All the acts had expired or been repealed by 1802. — Often shortened to *Alien Acts.*

alienate (ay-lee-ə-nayt *or* **ayl**-yə-), *vb.* (16c) **1.** To transfer or convey (property or a property right) to another. **2.** To do something that makes (someone) unfriendly or unwilling to lend support. **3.** To make (someone) reluctant or unwilling to belong to a particular group or to feel comfortable with a particular person. — Also termed *alien.* — **alienator,** *n.*

alienated-premises clause. See ALIENATION CLAUSE.

alienatio feudi (ay-lee-ə-**nay**-shee-oh **fyoo**-dɪ). [Law Latin] *Hist.* Disposition of a feudal right.

alienatio feudifirmae feudifirmarum (ay-lee-ə-**nay**-shee-oh fyoo-di-**fər**-mee fyoo-di-fər-**mair**-əm). [Law Latin "disposition of a feuholding of feuholders"] *Hist.* A conveyance to avoid the prohibition on alienation of Crown lands. • It was nullified by statute in 1597.

alienation (ay-lee-ə-**nay**-shən *or* ayl-yə-**nay**-shən), *n.* (14c) **1.** Conveyance or transfer of property to another <alienation of one's estate>.

> "[A]ny transfer of real estate short of a conveyance of the title is not an alienation of the estate." 4A John Alan Appleman & Jean Appleman, *Insurance Law and Practice* § 2741, at 325 n.12 (rev. vol. 1969).

▸ **alienation in mortmain.** *Archaic.* The act of conveying land or tenements to a corporation, whether ecclesiastical or temporal. See MORTMAIN.

▸ **involuntary alienation.** (18c) Alienation against the wishes of the transferor, as by attachment. — Also termed *involuntary conveyance.*

2. Withdrawal from former attachment; the feeling of not being part of society or of some particular group. **3.** The feeling of becoming less friendly, less understanding, or less supportive because of something that has happened or been done; estrangement <alienation of affections>. — **alienative** (**ay**-lee-ə-nay-tiv *or* **ayl**-yə-), *adj.*

alienation clause. (1877) **1.** A deed provision that either permits or prohibits the further conveyance of the property. **2.** *Insurance.* A clause in an insurance policy voiding coverage if the policyholder alienates the insured property. — Also termed *alienated-premises clause.*

alienation of affections. (1867) A tort claim for willful or malicious interference with a marriage by a third party without justification or excuse. • Where the cause of action still exists, the elements are (1) some wrongful conduct by the defendant with the plaintiff's spouse, (2) the loss of affection or loss of consortium of the plaintiff's spouse, and (3) a causal relationship between the defendant's conduct and the loss of consortium. Only a few states allow this cause of action. But the doctrine thrives elsewhere. For example, a North Carolina court has upheld a $1 million award to an ex-wife who filed an alienation-of-affections action against her ex-husband's new wife. *Hutelmyer v. Cox*, 514 S.E.2d 554 (N.C. Ct. App. 1999). See CONSORTIUM; HEARTBALM STATUTE.

alienation office. *Hist. English law.* A London office where persons resorting to the judicial processes of fine and recovery for the conveyance of lands were required to present their writs and submit to the payment of fees called the *prefine* and the *postfine.* See PREFINE; POSTFINE.

alienative fact. See FACT.

alien corporation. See *foreign corporation* under CORPORATION.

alienee (ay-lee-ə-**nee** *or* ayl-yə-**nee**), *n.* (16c) Someone to whom property is transferred or conveyed. — Also termed *disponee.*

▸ **fraudulent alienee.** (1830) Someone who knowingly receives an asset by means of fraudulent alienation.

alien enemy. See ALIEN.

alien friend. See ALIEN.

alienigena (ay-lee-ə-**nij**-ə-nə). [Latin] *Hist.* An alien. Cf. INDIGENA.

alieni generis (ay-lee-**ee**-nɪ [*or* al-ee-] **jen**-ə-ris). [Latin] (18c) Of another kind; of a foreign kind.

alieni juris (ay-lee-**ee**-nɪ [*or* al-ee-] **joor**-is), *adj.* [Latin] (17c) *Roman law.* Subject to the power or authority of another. — Also spelled *alieni iuris.*

alien immigrant. See IMMIGRANT.

alienism. (18c) The state, condition, or character of an alien.

alienist. (1864) *Archaic.* A psychiatrist, esp. one who assesses a criminal defendant's sanity or capacity to stand trial.

alienor (**ay**-lee-ə-nər *or* -nor), *n.* (16c) Someone who transfers or conveys property to another. — Also termed *disponor.*

alien species. See SPECIES (1).

Alien Tort Claims Act. A section in the Judiciary Act of 1789 giving federal courts jurisdiction to hear tort claims brought by foreigners who allege a violation of international law or a treaty to which the United States is a party. 28 USCA § 1350. • The statute was largely dormant until the 1980s, when it was invoked in several cases involving torture, disappearances, or killings committed by non-Americans in foreign countries. *See, e.g., Filartiga v. Pena-Irala*, 630 F.2d 876 (2d Cir. 1980). Later, alien plaintiffs began using the law to sue large corporations and the United States government or those acting at the government's direction. *See, e.g., Sosa v. Alvarez-Machain*, 542 U.S. 692, 124 S.Ct. 2739 (2004); *Bano v. Union Carbide Corp.*, 273 F.3d 120 (2d Cir. 2001). — Abbr. ATCA. — Also termed *Alien Tort Statute.*

Alien Tort Statute. See ALIEN TORT CLAIMS ACT.

alienus (ay-lee- *or* al-ee-**ee**-nəs), *adj.* [Latin] *Roman law.* Belonging to another. • *Alienus homo* means "another's slave."

alii acta (**ay**-li-ee **ak**-tə). [Latin] *Hist.* The acts of another.

aliment. (17c) *Scots law.* The financial support that an indigent person is entitled to receive from a spouse or, if unmarried, from a relative or relatives in a prescribed order, beginning with the person's children. — Also termed (in English law) *alimony.*

alimenta (al-ə-**men**-tə). [Latin] *Roman law.* Things necessary to sustain life, such as food and clothing.

alimentary-canal smuggling. See SMUGGLING.

alimony (**al**-ə-moh-nee). (17c) **1.** A court-ordered allowance that one spouse pays to the other spouse for maintenance and support while they are separated, while they are involved in a matrimonial lawsuit, or after they are divorced; esp., money that a court orders someone to pay regularly to his or her former spouse after the marriage has ended. • Alimony is distinct from a property settlement. Alimony payments are taxable income to the receiving spouse and are deductible by the payor spouse; payments in settlement of property rights are not. The Supreme Court has held unconstitutional a statute that imposed alimony obligations on the husband only. *Orr v. Orr*, 440 U.S. 268, 99 S.Ct. 1102 (1979). — Also termed *spousal support*; *maintenance.* Cf. CHILD SUPPORT; DIVORCE AGREEMENT.

> "'Alimony,' which signifies literally nourishment or sustenance, means, in a general sense, the allowance required by law to be made to a spouse from the other spouse's estate for support or maintenance, either during a matrimonial suit or at its termination, where the fact of marriage is established and the right to a separate maintenance is proved. Similarly stated, alimony is the allowance which a party may be compelled to pay to his or her spouse for maintenance when they are living apart or after they have been divorced." 27B C.J.S. *Divorce* § 306, at 102–03 (1986).

▸ **alimony in gross.** (1871) Alimony in the form of a single and definite sum not subject to modification. — Also termed *lump-sum alimony.*

▸ **alimony pendente lite** (pen-**den**-tee **lɪ**-tee). [Latin *pendente lite* "pending litigation"] See *temporary alimony.*

▸ **final alimony.** See *permanent alimony.*

▸ **lump-sum alimony.** See *alimony in gross.*

▸ **periodic alimony.** See *permanent alimony.*

▸ **permanent alimony.** (1843) Alimony payable in usu. weekly or monthly installments either indefinitely or until a time specified by court order. • This kind of alimony may usu. be modified for changed circumstances of either party. It terminates upon the death of either spouse and usu. upon the remarriage of the obligee. — Also termed *final alimony*; *periodic alimony.*

▸ **provisional alimony.** See *temporary alimony.*

▸ **rehabilitative alimony.** (1972) Alimony found necessary to assist a divorced person in acquiring the education or training required to find employment outside the home or to reenter the labor force. • It usu. has time limitations, such as a maximum of one or two years. — Also termed *short-term alimony*; *transitional alimony.*

▸ **reimbursement alimony.** (1982) Alimony designed to repay a spouse who during the marriage made financial contributions that directly enhanced the future earning capacity of the other spouse. • An example is alimony for a wife who worked full-time supporting herself and her husband with separate-property earnings while he earned a medical degree.

▸ **short-term alimony.** See *rehabilitative alimony.*

▸ **temporary alimony.** (1838) Interim alimony ordered by the court pending an action for divorce or separation in which one party has made a claim for permanent alimony. — Also termed *provisional alimony*; *alimony pendente lite*; *allowance pendente lite.*

▸ **transitional alimony.** See *rehabilitative alimony.*

2. *Scots law.* ALIMENT.

alimony trust. See TRUST (3).

alio intuitu (**ay**-lee-oh in-**t[y]oo**-ə-t[y]oo), *adv.* [Latin "under a different aspect"] In a different view; with respect to another case or condition.

alioqui successurus (ay-lee-**oh**-kwɪ sək-**ses**-ə-rəs). [Latin] (17c) *Hist.* (Of an heir) otherwise entitled to succeed. • The phrase appeared in reference to an heir who would have succeeded to the property by law, even without a deed granting succession rights. — Also spelled *alioquin successurus.*

> "In the general case, an heir who succeeds to an estate, incurs by his succession liability for the debts and obligations of his ancestor . . . . But if the heir succeeding to the estate can take it up in a different character from that of heir of the last proprietor, if he be *alioqui successurus*, such liability is not incurred." John Trayner, *Trayner's Latin Maxims* 38 (4th ed. 1894).

aliqualis probatio (al-i-**kway**-lis proh-**bay**-shee-oh). [Law Latin] (18c) *Hist.* Proof of some sort. • The phrase referred to evidence that, although not meeting strict legal requirements, was the best available under the circumstances.

aliquot (**al**-ə-kwot), *adj.* (16c) Contained in a larger whole an exact number of times; fractional <5 is an aliquot part of 30>.

aliquot-part rule. (1947) The principle that a person must intend to acquire a fractional part of the ownership of property before a court can declare a resulting trust in the person's favor.

aliter (**al**-ə-tər), *adv.* [Latin] Otherwise; it would be otherwise.

> "If I trespass on another's land, and make an excavation there without leaving any rubbish on the land, the trespass ceases as soon as I leave the land, and does not continue until I have filled the excavation up again. Consequently only one action will lie, and in it full damages are recoverable for both the past and the future. *Aliter* if I have brought a heap of soil and left it on the plaintiff's land." R.F.V. Heuston, *Salmond on the Law of Torts* 42 (17th ed. 1977).

ALI test. See SUBSTANTIAL-CAPACITY TEST.

aliud (**ay**-lee-əd). [Latin] Something else; another thing.

aliud examen (**ay**-lee-əd ig-**zay**-mən). [Latin "another investigation" or "another trial"] (17c) A different or foreign mode of trial. Cf. AD ALIUD EXAMEN.

aliud simulatum, aliud actum (**ay**-lee-əd sim-yə-**lay**-təm, **ay**-lee-əd **ak**-təm). [Latin] *Hist.* One thing pretended, another thing done.

aliunde (ay-lee-**yən**-dee), *adj.* [Latin] (17c) From another source; from elsewhere <evidence aliunde>. See CORPUS DELICTI RULE; *extrinsic evidence* under EVIDENCE.

aliunde rule. (1943) *Evidence.* The doctrine that a verdict may not be impeached by a juror's testimony unless a foundation for the testimony is first made by competent evidence from another source. *See* Fed. R. Evid. 606(b).

ALJ. *abbr.* ADMINISTRATIVE-LAW JUDGE.

all and singular. (16c) Collectively and individually.

all-claims rule. (1987) *Patents.* The obsolete doctrine that a patent is invalid unless every inventor named in the patent made an inventive contribution to every claim in the patent. • Section 116 of the Patent Act now expressly provides that inventors may apply for a patent jointly even though each did not make a contribution to the subject matter of every claim.

allegata (al-ə-**gay**-tə). *pl.* [Latin] ALLEGATUM.

allegatio falsi (al-ə-**gay**-shee-oh **fal**-SI *or* **fawl**-SI). [Latin] *Hist.* An untrue allegation. Cf. EXPRESSIO FALSI.

allegation, *n.* (15c) **1.** A declaration that something is true; esp., a statement, not yet proved, that someone has done something wrong or illegal. **2.** Something declared or asserted as a matter of fact, esp. in a legal pleading; a party's formal statement of a factual matter as being true or provable, without its having yet been proved; AVERMENT. See PLEADING (quot.).

▸ **defensive allegation.** (18c) *Eccles. law.* A defendant's response in an ecclesiastical action; specif., a defendant's pleading of the facts relied on that require the plaintiff's response under oath. Cf. *primary allegation* (2).

> "The proceedings in the ecclesiastical courts are therefore regulated according to the practice of the civil and canon laws .... [T]heir ordinary course of proceeding is; first, by *citation,* to call the party injuring before them. Then . . . to set forth the complainant's ground of complaint. To this succeeds the *defendant's answer* upon oath; when, if he denies or extenuates the charge, they proceed to *proofs* by witnesses examined, and their depositions taken down in writing, by an officer of the court. If the defendant has any circumstances to offer in his defence, he must also propound them in what is called his *defensive allegation,* to which he is entitled in his turn to the *plaintiff's answer* upon oath, and may from thence proceed to *proofs* as well as his antagonist." 3 William Blackstone, *Commentaries on the Laws of England* 100 (1768).

▸ **disjunctive allegation.** (1814) A statement in a pleading or indictment that expresses something in the alternative, usu. with the conjunction "or" <a charge that the defendant murdered or caused to be murdered is a disjunctive allegation>.

▸ **material allegation.** (18c) In a pleading, an assertion that is essential to the claim, charge, or defense <a material allegation in a battery case is harmful or offensive contact with a person>.

▸ **primary allegation.** (1847) **1.** The principal charge made against an adversary in a legal proceeding. **2.** *Eccles. law.* The opening pleading in an action in ecclesiastical court. — Also termed *primary plea.* Cf. *defensive allegation.* **3.** *Eccles. law.* The entire statement of facts to be used in a contested suit.

allegation of faculties. (18c) *Archaic. Family law.* A statement detailing a husband's or wife's property, made by a spouse who seeks alimony. See FACULTIES.

allegation of use. See *amendment to allege use* under TRADEMARK-APPLICATION AMENDMENT.

allegations-of-the-complaint rule. See EIGHT-CORNERS RULE.

allegatum (al-ə-**gay**-təm), *n.* [Latin] A fact alleged in a pleading; ALLEGATION. Cf. PROBATUM. Pl. ***allegata.***

allege, *vb.* (13c) To assert as true, esp. that someone has done something wrong, though no occasion for definitive proof has yet occurred.

alleged (ə-**lejd**), *adj.* (15c) **1.** Asserted to be true as described <alleged offenses>. **2.** Accused but not yet tried <alleged murderer>.

allegedly (ə-**lej**-əd-lee), *adv.* (1823) **1.** According to reports; as related by one or more accusers <a golf shop allegedly used for money-laundering> <he was allegedly at the center of the conspiracy>. **2.** It is said or suspected that <Allegedly, she was held against her will>. • In sense 2, *allegedly* is commonly used as a sentence adverb.

allegiance. (15c) **1.** A citizen's or subject's obligation of fidelity and obedience to the government or sovereign in return for the benefits of the protection of the state. • Allegiance may be either an absolute and permanent obligation or a qualified and temporary one.

> "Allegiance implies submission to all properly authorized commands of the state, and acceptance of the tribunals of the state as a vehicle for determining and enforcing those commands. Protection and allegiance are indissolubly divided." G.W. Keeton, *The Elementary Principles of Jurisprudence* 39 (2d ed. 1949).

▸ **acquired allegiance.** (18c) The allegiance owed by a naturalized citizen or subject.

▸ **actual allegiance.** (17c) The obedience owed by one who resides temporarily in a foreign country to that country's government. • Foreign sovereigns, their representatives, and military personnel are typically excepted from this requirement. — Also termed *local allegiance.*

▸ **natural allegiance.** (16c) The allegiance that native-born citizens or subjects owe to their country.

▸ **permanent allegiance.** (18c) The lasting allegiance owed to a state by its citizens or subjects.

▸ **temporary allegiance.** (17c) The impermanent allegiance owed to a state by a resident alien during the period of residence.

2. *Hist.* A vassal's obligation to the liege lord. See LIEGE.

all-elements rule. (1976) *Patents.* The principle that under the doctrine of equivalents, there can be no patent infringement if even one element of a claim or its equivalent is not present in the accused device. • This rule limits the doctrine of equivalents and prevents that doctrine's application to an entire claim, rather than to the claim's constituent elements. — Also termed *all-limitations rule*; *rule against vitiation of a claim element.* Cf. ALL-STEPS RULE, INHERENCY DOCTRINE.

***Allen* charge.** (1940) *Criminal procedure.* A supplemental jury instruction given by the court to encourage a deadlocked jury, after prolonged deliberations, to reach a verdict. *Allen v. U.S.*, 164 U.S. 492, 17 S.Ct. 154 (1896). • For a historical antecedent, see AFFORCING THE ASSIZE. — Also termed *deadlock instruction*, esp. in response to a series of questions from the judge on whether the defendant understands the deal, the right to a trial, the consequences of a guilty plea, and the voluntary nature of the plea; *dynamite charge*; *dynamite instruction*; *nitroglycerine charge*; *shotgun instruction*; *third-degree instruction.*

aller a Dieu (a-**lay** ə **dyuu** *or* **dyoo**). [Law French] To go to God. • This phrase prays for the case to be dismissed from court. — Sometimes spelled *aler a Dieu.* Cf. ADIEU.

aller sans jour (a-**lay** san **zhoor**). [Law French] To go without day. • This phrase prays for a final dismissal of a case. — Also spelled *aler sans jour.* See GO HENCE WITHOUT DAY; ADEU.

all-estate clause. See ALL-THE-ESTATE CLAUSE.

all-events test. (1954) *Tax.* A requirement that all events fixing an accrual-method taxpayer's right to receive income or incur expense must occur before the taxpayer can report an item of income or expense.

alleviare (ə-lee-vee-**air**-ee), *vb.* [Law Latin] To levy or pay a fine or composition.

all faults, with. See AS IS.

all fours. See ON ALL FOURS.

all-holders rule. (1985) *Securities.* **1.** An SEC rule that prohibits a public offering by the issuer of shares to some, but not all, of the holders of a class of shares. **2.** An SEC rule requiring a tender offeror to make its offer to all the target company's shareholders.

alliance. (13c) **1.** A bond or union between persons, families, states, or other parties. Cf. STRATEGIC ALLIANCE. **2.** *Int'l law.* A union or association of two or more states or countries, usu. formed by league or treaty, esp. for jointly waging war or mutually protecting against and repelling hostile attacks. • An example is the North Atlantic Treaty Organization (NATO). Cf. DÉTENTE; ENTENTE.

allied offense. See OFFENSE (2).

all-inclusive mortgage. See *wraparound mortgage* under MORTGAGE.

allision (ə-**lizh**-ən), *n.* (1922) *Maritime law.* The contact of a vessel with a stationary object such as an anchored vessel or a pier. • In modern practice, the less specific term *collision* is often used where *allision* was once the preferred term. Cf. COLLISION. — **allide** (ə-**lɪd**), *vb.*

all-limitations rule. See ALL-ELEMENTS RULE.

allocable (**al**-ə-kə-bəl), *adj.* (1929) Capable of being allocated; assignable.

allocation, *n.* (16c) **1.** The amount or share of something that has been set aside or designated for a particular purpose. **2.** A designation or apportionment for a specific purpose; esp., the crediting of a receipt or the charging of a disbursement to an account <allocation of funds>. — **allocate,** *vb.* — **allocable,** *adj.* — **allocator,** *n.*

allocatione facienda (al-ə-kay-shee-**oh**-nee fay-shee-**en**-də), *n.* See DE ALLOCATIONE FACIENDA.

allocatur (al-ə-**kay**-tər). [Law Latin] It is allowed. • This word formerly indicated that a writ, bill, or other pleading was allowed. It is still used today in Pennsylvania to denote permission to appeal to the state supreme court. — Also termed *allogatur.*

▸ **special allocatur.** (1800) An allowance of a writ (such as a writ of error) that is legally required in certain cases.

allocute (**al**-ə-kyoot), *vb.* (1860) To deliver an allocution in court.

allocution (al-ə-**kyoo**-shən), *n.* (1858) *Criminal procedure.* **1.** A trial judge's formal address to a convicted defendant, asking whether the defendant wishes to make a statement or to present information in mitigation of the sentence to be imposed. • This address is required under Fed. R. Crim. P. 32(c)(3)(C). **2.** An unsworn statement from a convicted defendant to the sentencing judge or jury in which the defendant can ask for mercy, explain his or her conduct, apologize for the crime, or say anything else in an effort to lessen the impending sentence. • This statement is not subject to cross-examination. **3.** *Criminal procedure.* A defendant's admission of guilt made directly to a judge, esp. in response to a series of questions from the judge on whether the defendant understands the charges, the right to a trial, the consequences of a guilty plea, and the voluntary nature of the plea.

▸ **victim allocution.** See VICTIM ALLOCUTION.

allocutory (ə-**lok**-yə-tor-ee), *adj.* (1944) Of, relating to, or involving an allocution <allocutory pleas for mercy>.

allocutus. See ARREST OF JUDGMENT.

allod (**al**-əd), *n.* (17c) *Hist.* **1.** The domain of a household. — Also spelled *alod.* **2.** ALLODIUM.

allodial (ə-**loh**-dee-əl), *adj.* (17c) Held in absolute ownership; of, relating to, or involving an allodium. — Also spelled *alodial.* Cf. FEUDAL. — **allodially,** *adv.*

> "The term 'alodial' originally had no necessary reference to the mode in which the ownership of land had been conferred; it simply meant land held in absolute ownership, not in dependence upon any other body or person in whom the proprietary rights were supposed to reside, or to whom the possessor of land was bound to render service. It would thus properly apply to the land which in the original settlement had been allotted to individuals, while bookland was primarily applicable to land the title to which rested on a formal grant. Before long, however, the words appear to have been used synonymously to express land held in absolute ownership, the subject of free disposition *inter vivos* or by will." Kenelm E. Digby, *An Introduction to the History of the Law of Real Property* 11–12 (5th ed. 1897).

allodial, *n.* See ALLODIALIST.

allodialism (a-**lohd**-ee-ə-liz- əm), *n.* The allodial or freehold system.

allodialist (a-**lohd**-ee-ə-list), *n.* An allodial landowner. — Also termed *allodial,* n.

allodial title. See TITLE (2).

allodium (ə-**loh**-dee-əm), *n.* (17c) An estate held in fee simple absolute. — Also spelled *alodium.* — Also termed *alod; alode.*

> "In this country, one who has full ownership of land is said to own it allodially — that is, free of feudal services and incidents." Thomas F. Bergin & Paul G. Haskell, *Preface to Estates in Land and Future Interests* 18 (2d ed. 1984).

allogatur. See ALLOCATUR.

allograph (**al**-ə-graf). (1954) A writing or signature made on behalf of another. • This is the antonym of *autograph.*

allonge (a-**lawnzh**). [French *allonger* "to lengthen"] (1859) **1.** A slip of paper sometimes attached to a negotiable instrument for the purpose of receiving further indorsements when the original paper is filled with indorsements. • Former UCC § 3-202 required that indorsements be made on the instrument unless there was no space — and only then could an allonge be used. Current UCC § 3-204(a) eliminates that requirement and provides that "a paper affixed to the instrument is part of the instrument." The UCC comment makes it clear that the allonge is valid even if space is available on the instrument. **2.** A thrust or lunge, as in fencing.

all-or-none offering. See OFFERING.

all-or-none order. See ORDER (8).

all-or-nothing rule. (1954) **1.** A gloss on the rule against perpetuities holding that a class gift is invalid in its entirety if it is invalid in part. • The effect is to invalidate a class member's interest even if it vests within the period of the rule because it may be subject to partial divestment by the remote interest of another class member. **2.** A Federal Bureau of Prisons policy under which prison officials withhold an entire publication sent to an inmate by someone outside the prison if any part of the publication contains material that is excludable under federal regulations. **3.** A Federal Communications Commission rule under which if a competitive local-exchange carrier is interested in a service or network element provided by an incumbent local-exchange carrier, it may adopt in its entirety any approved agreement that includes that service or element to which the incumbent is already a party. 47 CFR § 51.809. *See New Edge Network, Inc. v. FCC,* 461 F.3d 1105 (9th Cir. 2006).

allotment, *n.* (16c) **1.** A share or portion of a thing that is given to someone or something, such as property previously held in common or shares in a corporation, or time assigned to speakers or sides in a deliberative assembly. **2.** The process of giving out such shares or portions. **3.** A small area of land that someone can rent for growing vegetables or crops. **4.** In American Indian law, the selection of specific land awarded to an individual tribal member from a common holding. — **allot,** *vb.*

allotment certificate. (1931) *Securities.* A document that records the essential elements of a subscription of shares, such as how many shares are to be purchased, the price to be paid, and the payment and delivery schedule.

allotment letter. See LETTER OF ALLOTMENT.

allotment note. (1917) *English law.* A seaman's written assignment of a portion of his wages to someone else, such as a wife, parent, grandparent, or sibling. • These notes are governed by the Merchant Shipping Act of 1970, § 13(1).

allotment system. (1834) *English law.* The practice of dividing land into small portions for cultivation by agricultural laborers and others.

allottee. (1846) One to whom an allotment is made; a recipient of an allotment.

allow, *vb.* **1.** To put no obstacle in the way of; to suffer to exist or occur; to tolerate <she allowed the neighbor's children to play on her lawn>. **2.** To give consent to; to approve <the appellate court allowed the writ of error>. **3.** To concede or admit; to acknowledge <will you allow that you were present on the evening of June 21?>. **4.** To recognize as a right or privilege; to accord as a legal entitlement <the law allows it> <they allowed their children $20 a week>. **5.** To permit to (oneself) by way of indulgence <allows herself no childish fripperies>. **6.** To assign (money, time, etc.) for a particular purpose <allow an extra hour for negotiating the heavy traffic>. **7.** To make allowance or provision for; to take into account <we should allow much on account of his lack of education>. **8.** To grant by addition or subtraction; esp., to abate or deduct <allow $150 off the rent for leaky plumbing>. **9.** To grant permission; to permit <to allow each student one absence>. **10.** To assert, declare, say, or opine; esp., by mental assertion, to mean, intend, or think <privately, he allowed that he might bear some of the blame>. **11.** In an intransitive sense, to make abatement or concession <allow for extra time spent>.

allowable, *adj.* (15c) **1.** Acceptable according to the rules; permissible <the maximum allowable award>. **2.** (Of costs that one may claim as a tax deduction) not subject to taxation <allowable receipts>.

allowable state. (1956) *Patents.* The quality or condition of a patent claim's containing patentable subject matter in an acceptable form. • The allowable state is recognized when the U.S. Patent and Trademark Office approves a patent claim.

allowance. (14c) **1.** A share or portion, esp. of money that is assigned or granted.

▸ **allowance pendente lite.** See *temporary alimony* under ALIMONY (1).

▸ **backhaul allowance.** (1980) A price discount given to customers who get their goods from a seller's warehouse as a reflection of the seller's freight-cost savings.

▸ **family allowance.** (1869) A portion of a decedent's estate set aside by statute for a surviving spouse, children, or parents, regardless of any testamentary disposition or competing claims. • Every state has a statute authorizing the probate court to award an amount for the temporary maintenance and support of the surviving spouse (and often for dependent children). The allowance may be limited for a fixed period (12 months under the Uniform Probate Code) or may continue until all contests are resolved and a decree of distribution is entered. This support, together with probate homesteads and personal-property allowances, is in addition to whatever interests pass by the will or by intestate succession. See *probate homestead* under HOMESTEAD (1). Cf. *spousal allowance.*

▸ **gratuitous allowance.** (1928) A pension voluntarily granted by a public entity. • The gratuitous (rather than contractual) nature of this type of allowance gives the pensioner no vested rights in the allowance.

▸ **spousal allowance.** (1985) A portion of a decedent's estate set aside by statute for a surviving spouse, regardless of any testamentary disposition or competing claims. • This allowance is superior to the claims of general creditors. In some states, it is even preferred to the expenses of administration, funeral, and last illness of the spouse. — Also termed *widow's allowance*; *widower's allowance.* See *probate homestead* under HOMESTEAD (1). Cf. *family allowance.*

▸ **widower's allowance.** See *spousal allowance.*

▸ **widow's allowance.** See *spousal allowance.*

2. The sum awarded by a court to a fiduciary as payment for services. **3.** A deduction.

▸ **depletion allowance.** (1920) A tax deduction for the owners of mines, oil and gas wells, other natural deposits, and timber resources corresponding to the reduced value of the property resulting from the removal of the resource or depreciation of improvements. 26 USCA § 611; 26 CFR 1.611-1(a).

4. *Archaic.* A special sum that a court awards to the prevailing party in addition to the usual costs of court, esp. in a difficult case. — Also termed *extra allowance*; *special allowance.* **5.** *Patents.* The U.S. Patent and Trademark Office's decision to issue a patent to an applicant; specif., the patent examiner's approval of at least one of an application's claims. • Within three months after a notice of allowance is sent, the inventor must pay an issue fee before the PTO issues the patent. 35 USCA § 151. **6.** *Trademarks.* The U.S. Patent and Trademark Office's decision to approve a trademark for which the application was made under § 1(b) of the Lanham Act. • If a trademark application made under § 1(b) is approved by the PTO, the Office publishes the mark and — unless it is successfully opposed — issues a certificate of registration and publishes notice of the registration in the Official Gazette. **7.** EMISSIONS PERMIT.

allowed application. See PATENT APPLICATION.

allow the appeal. See REVERSE.

alloynour (ə-**loy**-nər). [Law French] *Hist.* Someone who conceals, steals, or furtively carries off something.

all-persons-present search warrant. See SEARCH WARRANT.

all-purpose public figure. See PUBLIC FIGURE.

all rights reserved. (1874) *Copyright.* A phrase required as part of a valid copyright notice under the Buenos Aires Convention. • Because other international copyright treaties do not require the phrase, and all signatories to the Buenos Aires Convention are parties to other treaties, the phrase is now considered surplusage.

all-risk insurance. See INSURANCE.

all-steps rule. *Patents.* The doctrine that in order for a method or process claim to be literally infringed by an accused process, the accused process must have every step and limitation—or an equivalent—of the infringed claim. Cf. ALL-ELEMENTS RULE.

all substantial rights. (1926) *Patents.* Every right in a patent (whether or not held by the grantor) that is of value when the patent rights or an undivided interest in a patent is transferred. • A transfer is not a transfer of all substantial rights to a patent if (1) it is territorially restricted; (2) its term is less than the patent term; (3) it contains field-of-use limitations; or (4) it does not convey rights to all claims in the patent. 26 USCA § 1235; 26 CFR § 1.1235-2(b).

all-the-estate clause. (1830) *English law.* The provision in a conveyance transferring "all the estate, right, title, interest, claims, and demand" of the grantor in the property conveyed. — Also termed *all-estate clause.*

> "It was also usual before 1882 to add what was called an '*all estate clause*' with the object of ensuring that the entire interest of the grantor should be transferred. This was as a matter of fact quite ineffective to transfer anything that would not pass automatically, and it is now omitted in reliance on the enactment that, unless a contrary intention is expressed, every conveyance is effectual to pass all the estate, right, title, interest, claim, and demand which the conveying parties respectively have in, to, or on the property." G.C. Cheshire, *Modern Law of Real Property* 679–80 (3d ed. 1933).

allurement. (1873) *Archaic. Torts.* An attractive object that tempts a trespassing child to meddle when the child ought to abstain. See ATTRACTIVE-NUISANCE DOCTRINE. Cf. *attractive nuisance* under NUISANCE.

alluvial, *adj.* (18c) Of, relating to, or involving soil left by rivers, lakes, floods, etc.

alluvial mining. (1894) The practice of removing sand and gravel from a riverbed.

alluvio maris (ə-**loo**-vee-oh **mar**-is). [Latin "alluvion of the sea"] The formation of soil or land from the sea.

alluvion (ə-**loo**-vee-ən). [fr. Latin *alluvio* "flood"] (16c) *Roman & civil law.* **1.** Strictly, the flow or wash of water against a shore or riverbank. **2.** An accumulation of soil, clay, or other material deposited by water; esp., in land law, an addition of land caused by the buildup of deposits from running water, the added land then belonging to the owner of the property to which it is added. — Also termed *alluvium.* **3.** *Louisiana law.* An accumulation of soil, clay, or other material deposited on the bank of a river. • In Louisiana, lands formed on a seashore or the bank of a navigable lake are not alluvion. They belong to the state rather than the riparian owners. La. Rev. Stat. § 9:1101. Cf. ACCRETION (2); AVULSION (2); DELICTION; EROSION. — **alluvial,** *adj.* — **alluviate,** *vb.* — **alluviation,** *n.*

alluvium. See ALLUVION (2).

All Writs Act. A 1911 federal statute that gives the U.S. Supreme Court and all courts established by Congress the power to issue writs in aid of their jurisdiction and in conformity with the usages and principles of law. 28 USCA § 1651(a). — Abbr. AWA.

ally. (16c) *Int'l law.* **1.** A country tied to another by treaty or alliance; a country that has agreed to help or support another country, esp. in time of war. **2.** A citizen or subject of an allied country. **3.** Someone who helps or supports a person when others are opposing that person.

almaria (al-**mair**-ee-ə). [Latin "cupboard, bookcase"] The archives of a church or library. — Also termed *armaria.*

almoign (al-**moyn**). [Law French "alms"] (14c) **1.** Alms; a church treasury; an ecclesiastical possession. **2.** FRANKALMOIN.

almoin. See FRANKALMOIN.

almoner (**al**-mə-nər). (14c) A person charged with distributing the alms of a monarch, religious house, or other institution. • This office was first instituted in religious houses. Although formerly one of importance, it is now often a sinecure.

alms (ahmz *or* ahlmz). (bef. 12c) Charitable donations; any type of relief bestowed on the poor, esp. money and food.

alms fee. (bef. 12c) *Hist.* A fee held by frankalmoin. See FRANKALMOIN.

almshouse. (15c) *Archaic.* A dwelling for the poor publicly or privately supported within a city or county; a house where the poor can live without paying rent.

alms land. (1809) *Hist.* Land held in frankalmoin. See FRANKALMOIN.

alnager (**al**-nə-jər). [Law Latin] (16c) *Hist.* A royal official responsible for collecting taxes (the *alnage*) on woolen cloth. • The tax was abolished in 1699. — Also spelled *aulnager.*

alod. 1. ALLODIUM. **2.** ALLOD.

alode. See ALLODIUM.

alodial. See ALLODIAL.

alodium. See ALLODIUM.

a lour foy (ah loor **fwah**). [Law French "in their faith"] In their allegiance.

alpha subclass. *Patents.* In U.S. patent law, a patent classification that has an alphabetic suffix to facilitate searches within the arts under the jurisdiction of patent examiners. — Formerly also termed *unofficial subclass.*

alpha testing. (1982) *Intellectual property.* The first phase of operational experimenting with a software program before the program's production release, usu. at the developer's site. • Often, alpha testing involves only modular or component testing and not system testing. Alpha testing is usu. followed by beta testing, in which the entire system is tested at a customer's site before the product is released to the general public. Cf. BETA TESTING.

ALTA. *abbr.* American Land Title Association.

alta proditio (**al**-tə proh-**dish**-ee-oh). [Law Latin] See TREASON.

altarage (**awl**-tər-ij). (15c) *Eccles. law.* **1.** The offerings made on an altar or to a church. **2.** An endowment or honorarium received by a priest for services performed at the altar.

alta via (**al**-tə **vı**-ə). [Law Latin] A highway.

alteration. (1803) **1.** *Property.* A substantial change to real estate, esp. to a structure, usu. not involving an addition to or removal of the exterior dimensions of a building's structural parts. • Although any addition to or improvement of real estate is by its very nature an alteration, real-estate lawyers habitually use *alteration* in reference to a lesser change. Still, to constitute an alteration, the change must be substantial — not simply a trifling modification.

▸ **structural alteration.** (1905) A significant change to a building or other structure, essentially creating a different building or structure.

2. An act done to an instrument, after its execution, whereby its meaning or language is changed; esp., the changing of a term in a negotiable instrument without the consent of all parties to it. • Material alterations void an instrument, but immaterial ones do not. An alteration is material if it (1) changes the burden of a party (as by changing the date, time, place, amount, or rate of interest), (2) changes the liabilities or duties of any party (as by adding or removing the name of a maker, drawer, indorser, payee, or cosurety), or (3) changes the operation of the instrument or its effect in evidence (as by adding words or negotiability, changing the form of an indorsement, or changing the liability from joint to several).

> "With respect to written instruments, 'alteration' generally means a change in an instrument's sense of language caused by a party to the instrument, and does not include such changes by non-parties or 'strangers' to the instrument. Although the distinction is not always observed, technically an alteration by a non-party or stranger to the instrument is a 'spoliation,' not an alteration, which does not invalidate it or change the rights or liabilities of the parties in interest, so long as the original writing remains legible." 4 Am. Jur. 2d *Alteration of Instruments* § 1 (1995).

▸ **immaterial alteration.** (18c) A minor change in something; esp., a change in a legal instrument that does not alter the instrument's legal meaning or effect.

▸ **material alteration.** (17c) **1.** A significant change in something; esp., a change in a legal instrument sufficient to alter the instrument's legal meaning or effect. **2.** An unauthorized change in an instrument or an addition to an incomplete instrument resulting in the modification of a party's obligations. UCC § 3-407.

altercation. (15c) A vehement dispute; a noisy argument.

> "ALTERCATION. The traditional view is that this word refers to 'a noisy brawl or dispute,' not rising to the seriousness of physical violence. . . . But in AmE today, the word often denotes some type of scuffling or fighting, especially in police jargon." Bryan A. Garner, *Garner's Dictionary of Legal Usage* 48 (3d ed. 2011).

alter ego. (1879) A corporation used by an individual or a subservient corporation in conducting personal business, the result being that a court may impose liability on the individual or subservient corporation by piercing the corporate veil when someone dealing with the corporation is the victim of fraud, illegality, or injustice. See PIERCING THE CORPORATE VEIL.

alter-ego rule. (1939) **1.** *Corporations.* The doctrine that shareholders will be treated as the owners of a corporation's property, or as the real parties in interest, whenever it is necessary to do so to prevent fraud, illegality, or injustice. **2.** *Criminal law.* The principle that one who defends another against attack stands in the position of that other person and is allowed to use only the amount of force that the other person would be allowed to use under the circumstances.

altering or amending a judgment. (1978) A trial court's act of correcting a substantive mistake in a judgment, as by correcting a manifest error of law or fact. Fed. R. Civ. P. 59(e).

alternat (**awl**-tər-nit *or* al-ter-**nah**). [French] The rotation in precedence among states, diplomats, etc., esp. in the signing of treaties. • This practice gives each diplomat a copy of the treaty with the diplomat's signature appearing first.

alternate. (1812) *Parliamentary law.* A proxy for a delegate, usu. chosen in the same manner as the delegate rather than chosen by the delegate. See DELEGATE (2); PROXY (1).

alternate legacy. See LEGACY (1).

alternate valuation date. (1959) *Tax.* The date six months after a decedent's death. • Generally, the estate can elect to appraise the decedent's property either as of the date of the decedent's death or as of the alternate valuation date. 26 USCA § 2032. See BASIS.

alternatim (al-tər-**nay**-tim *or* awl-), *adv.* [Latin] Interchangeably; by turns.

Alternative Agricultural Research and Commercialization Corporation. A federally chartered corporation in the U.S. Department of Agriculture responsible for funding the development and marketing of new nonfood products made from farm and forestry materials. — Abbr. AARC; AARCC.

alternative constituency. See NONSHAREHOLDER CONSTITUENCY.

alternative contract. See CONTRACT.

alternative count. See COUNT (2).

alternative devise. See DEVISE.

alternative dispute resolution. (1978) Any procedure for settling a dispute by means other than litigation, as by arbitration or mediation. • See APPROPRIATE DISPUTE RESOLUTION for a discussion of the merits of one name as contrasted with the other. — Abbr. ADR. — Also termed *dispute resolution*; *appropriate dispute resolution*; *assisted dispute resolution*. See ARBITRATION; MEDIATION; *settlement counsel* under COUNSEL.

▸ **court-annexed ADR.** (1986) Any one of several methods of nonjudicial dispute resolution that take place in accordance with a court order.

> "ADR can be defined as encompassing all legally permitted processes of dispute resolution other than litigation. While this definition (or something like it) is widely used, ADR proponents may object to it on the ground that it privileges litigation by giving the impression that litigation is the normal or standard process of dispute resolution, while alternative processes are aberrant or deviant. That impression is false. Litigation is a relatively rarely used process of dispute resolution. Alternative processes, especially negotiation, are used far more frequently. Even disputes involving lawyers are resolved by negotiation far more often than litigation. So ADR is not defined as everything-but-litigation because litigation is the norm. Litigation is not the norm. ADR is defined as everything-but-litigation because litigation, as a matter of law, is the default process of dispute resolution." Stephen J. Ware, *Alternative Dispute Resolution* § 1.5, at 5–6 (2001).

alternative expression. (1891) *Patents.* In a patent claim, a recitation of two or more elements or limitations that perform the same function <iron, steel, or other magnetic material>. • Although once contrary to U.S. Patent and Trademark Office policy, alternative expressions are now permitted if they present no uncertainty or ambiguity about the scope or clarity of the claims. — Also termed *alternative language*. Cf. MARKUSH GROUP.

alternative financial services. (2001) Financial services performed by providers outside the traditional federal banking system. • These financial arrangements, such as rent-to-own, payday lending, auto-title lending, and pawning, are most commonly used by low-income households or people with poor credit ratings. — Abbr. AFS. See *payday loan* & *title loan* under LOAN.

alternative judgment. See JUDGMENT (2).

alternative language. See ALTERNATIVE EXPRESSION.

alternative liability. See LIABILITY.

alternative mandamus. See MANDAMUS.

alternative-means doctrine. (1968) *Criminal law.* The principle that when a crime might have been committed in more than one way, the jury must be unanimous on the defendant's guilt but need not be unanimous on the possible different methods of committing the crime, as long as each possible method is supported by substantial evidence.

alternative-methods-of-performance contract. See *alternative contract* under CONTRACT.

alternative minimum tax. See TAX.

alternativeness rejection. See REJECTION.

alternative obligation. See OBLIGATION.

alternative order. 1. ORDER (2). **2.** ORDER (8).

alternative pleading. See PLEADING (2).

alternative promise. See PROMISE.

alternative relief. See RELIEF (3).

alternative remainder. See REMAINDER (1).

alternative sentence. See SENTENCE.

alternative to incarceration. See ATI.

alternative verdict. See VERDICT (1).

alternative writ. See WRIT.

alternativity. 1. The moral ability to choose or reject. **2.** The situation in which more than one possibility is presented to a person's mind or will.

alternis vicibus (al-**tər**-nis **vis**-i-bəs). [Law Latin] *Hist. Eccles. law.* By turn; alternately. • The patrons of two united churches could exercise their right of presentation to a benefice *alternis vicibus*.

alterum non laedere (**al**-tər-əm [*or* awl-] non **lee**-də-ree). [Latin "not to injure another"] *Roman & civil law.* To hurt no one by word or deed. • This was one of the three general precepts in which Justinian expressed the requirements of the law (*Digest* 1.1.10.1; *Institutes* 1.1.3). Cf. HONESTE VIVERE; SUUM CUIQUE TRIBUERE.

alterum tantum (**al**-tər-əm **tan**-təm). [Latin] *Hist.* An equivalent amount.

alteruter (al-tər-**yoo**-tər *or* awl-). [Law Latin] One of two; either.

altius non tollendi (**al**-shee-əs non tə-**len**-dɪ). [Latin "of not raising higher"] (17c) *Roman & civil law.* A servitude prohibiting a landowner from building a house above a certain height.

altius tollendi (**al**-shee-əs tə-**len**-dɪ). [Latin "of raising higher"] (18c) *Roman & civil law.* A servitude that allows a landowner to build a house as high as desired.

alto et basso. See DE ALTO ET BASSO.

altum mare (**al**-təm **mair**-ee *or* **mahr**-ee), *n.* [Law Latin] (17c) *Hist.* The high seas; the deep seas.

a lui et a ses heritiers pour toujours (a **lwee** ay a **sayz** e-ree-**tyay** poor too-**zhoor**). [Law French] To him and his heirs forever. See AND HIS HEIRS.

alvei mutatio (**al**-vee-I myoo-**tay**-shee-oh). [Latin fr. *alveus* "the bed or channel of a stream"] *Hist.* A change in a stream's course.

alveus (**al**-vee-əs), *n.* [Law Latin] (17c) *Hist.* The bed or channel through which a stream flows in its ordinary course.

always-speaking statute. See *speaking statute* under STATUTE.

ALWD (**ahl**-wəd *or* **al**-wəd). *abbr.* ASSOCIATION OF LEGAL WRITING DIRECTORS.

ALWD Citation Manual. A guide to American legal citation written and edited by legal-writing professionals affiliated with the Association of Legal Writing Directors. • First published in 2000 as an alternative to *The Bluebook*, it contains one citation system for all legal documents and does not distinguish between citations in law-journal articles and those in other writings. The full name is the *ALWD Citation Manual: A Professional System of Citation*. — Often shortened to *ALWD Manual*. Cf. BLUEBOOK.

a.m. *abbr.* (18c) ANTE MERIDIEM.

AMA. *abbr.* (1911) **1.** American Medical Association. **2.** Against medical advice.

a ma intent (ah mah a*n*-**tawn**). [Law French] On my action.

amalgamation (ə-mal-gə-**may**-shən), *n.* (17c) The act of combining or uniting; consolidation <amalgamation of two small companies to form a new corporation>. See MERGER (1). — **amalgamate,** *vb.* — **amalgamator,** *n.*

Amalphitan Code (ə-**mal**-fə-tən). *Hist.* A compilation of maritime law made late in the 11th century at the port of Amalfi near Naples. • The Code was regarded as a primary source of maritime law throughout the Mediterranean to the end of the 16th century. — Also termed *Amalphitan Table*; *Laws of Amalfi*; *Tablets of Amalfi*.

Amalphitan Table. See AMALPHITAN CODE.

a manibus (ay **man**-ə-bəs), *n.* [Law Latin] *Hist.* A royal scribe.

amanuensis (ə-man-yoo-**en**-sis), *n.* [fr. Latin *ab-* "from" + *manus* "hand"] (17c) **1.** Someone who takes dictation; a scribe or secretary. **2.** An assistant, esp. one with scribal responsibilities. **3.** A protégé. See PROTÉGÉ (1).

a manu servus (ay **man**-yoo **sər**-vəs). [Latin] A handservant; scribe; secretary.

ambactus (am-**bak**-təs). [Latin] *Hist.* **1.** A messenger. **2.** A servant whose services are hired out by the master.

ambasciator (am-**bash**-ee-ay-tər). [Law Latin] *Hist.* A person sent about in the service of another; an ambassador.

ambassador. (14c) **1.** A diplomatic officer of the highest rank, usu. designated by a government as its resident representative in a foreign state. • Ambassadors represent the sovereign as well as the country and enjoy many privileges while abroad in their official capacity, including immunity. Ambassadors are distinguished from ministers and envoys, who represent only the state where they are from and not the sovereign. Ambassadors are also generally distinguished from certain legates who have only ecclesiastical authority. But the papal nuncio and some legates, such as the *legate a latere*, bear the rank of ambassador. See NUNCIO; LEGATE. **2.** A representative appointed by another. **3.** An unofficial or nonappointed representative. — Also spelled (archaically) *embassador*. — **ambassadorial,** *adj.* — **ambassadorship,** *n.*

▸ **ambassador extraordinary.** (17c) An ambassador who is employed for a particular purpose or occasion and has limited discretionary powers. Cf. *ambassador plenipotentiary*.

▸ **ambassador leger.** See *resident ambassador*.

▸ **ambassador ordinary.** See *resident ambassador*.

▸ **ambassador plenipotentiary.** (17c) An ambassador who has unlimited discretionary powers to act as a sovereign's or government's deputy, esp. to carry out a particular task, such as treaty negotiations. — Also termed *minister plenipotentiary*; *envoy plenipotentiary*. Cf. *ambassador extraordinary*.

▸ **ordinary ambassador.** See *resident ambassador*.

▸ **resident ambassador.** (16c) An ambassador who resides in a foreign land as the permanent representative of a sovereign or country. • A resident ambassador has the right to request a personal interview with the host country's head of state. — Also termed *ambassador leger*; *ordinary ambassador*; *ambassador ordinary*.

AMBER. *abbr.* See AMBER ALERT.

Amber Alert. (1998) A system by which the police can rapidly broadcast to the general public a report of a missing or endangered child by means of radio and television announcements, highway signs, and wireless devices. • The alert is named for Amber Hagerman of Texas, a nine-year-old who was abducted and murdered in 1996 by an unknown person. The system has been adopted by many communities in the U.S. and Canada. Local variations exist. In Arkansas, for example, the system is called the Morgan Nick Alert after a child who was abducted by a stranger in 1995. When the first word is in all capital letters, AMBER is an acronym meaning America's Missing: Broadcast Emergency Response. In 2003, the system was federalized by the Prosecutorial Remedies and Other Tools to End the Exploitation of Children Today Act (the so-called "Protect Act"). — Also termed *Amber Plan*. See AMBER'S LAW. Cf. CODE ADAM.

Amber Hagerman Act. See AMBER'S LAW.

Amber Plan. See AMBER ALERT.

Amber's law. A federal statute that requires, among other things, life in prison without parole for two-time sex offenders whose victims are children, and reports to Congress about judges whose sentences fall below federal guidelines. • The law was named for Amber Hagerman of Texas, a nine-year-old girl who was abducted and murdered by an unknown person in 1996. — Also termed *Amber Hagerman Act*. See AMBER ALERT.

A.M. Best Company. An investment-analysis and -advisory service that provides credit ratings for the insurance industry.

ambidexter. (16c) **1.** A judge or embracer who takes bribes from both sides in a dispute. **2.** A lawyer who takes money from both sides of a dispute; esp., a lawyer who abandons the party that he or she initially represented in a dispute to represent the opposing party in the same suit. **3.** Someone who engages in double-dealing; a double-dealer.

> "Ambidexter is he that, when a matter is in suit between men, takes money of the one side and of the other, either to labour the suit, or such like; or if he be of the jury, to give his verdict." William Rastell, *Termes de la Ley* 28 (1st. Am. ed. 1812).

ambient advertising. See ADVERTISING.

ambiguitas latens (am-bi-**gyoo**-ə-tas **lay**-tenz). See *latent ambiguity* under AMBIGUITY (1).

ambiguitas latens et ambiguitas patens (am-bi-**gyoo**-ə-tas **lay**-tenz et am-bi-**gyoo**-ə-tas **pay**-tenz). [Latin] *Hist.* Latent and patent ambiguity. See *latent ambiguity* and *patent ambiguity* under AMBIGUITY (1).

ambiguitas patens (am-bi-**gyoo**-ə-tas **pay**-tenz). See *patent ambiguity* under AMBIGUITY (1).

ambiguity (am-bi-**gyoo**-ə-tee), *n.* (15c) **1.** Doubtfulness or uncertainty of meaning or intention, as in a contractual term or statutory provision; indistinctness of signification, esp. by reason of doubleness of interpretation.

> "In the context of statutory interpretation the word most frequently used to indicate the doubt which a judge must entertain before he can search for and, if possible, apply a secondary meaning is 'ambiguity.' In ordinary language this term is often confined to situations in which the same word is capable of meaning two different things, but, in relation to statutory interpretation, judicial usage sanctions the application of the word 'ambiguity' to describe any kind of doubtful meaning of words, phrases or longer statutory provisions. *Hinchy's* case prompted the suggestion that if, in a particular context, words convey to different judges a different range of meanings 'derived from, not fanciful speculations or mistakes about linguistic usage, but from true knowledge about the use of words, they are ambiguous.'" Rupert Cross, *Statutory Interpretation* 76–77 (1976).

▸ **ambiguity on the factum.** (1832) An ambiguity relating to the foundation of an instrument, such as a question relating to whether a testator intended for a particular clause to be part of an agreement, whether a codicil was intended to republish a former will, or whether the residuary clause was accidentally omitted. — Also termed *ambiguity upon the factum.*

▸ **calculated ambiguity.** (1964) A purposeful use of unclear language, usu. when two negotiating parties cannot agree on clear, precise language and therefore leave a decision-maker to sort out the meaning in case of a dispute. • Strictly speaking, this is a misnomer: the more precise term is vagueness, not ambiguity. See VAGUENESS (1). — Also termed *deliberate ambiguity.*

▸ **deliberate ambiguity.** See *calculated ambiguity.*

▸ **extrinsic ambiguity.** See *latent ambiguity.*

▸ **intrinsic ambiguity.** See *patent ambiguity.*

▸ **latent ambiguity.** (18c) An ambiguity that does not readily appear in the language of a document, but instead arises from a collateral matter once the document's terms are applied or executed <the contract contained a latent ambiguity: the shipping terms stated that the goods would arrive on the *Peerless*, but two ships have that name>. — Also termed *extrinsic ambiguity*; *ambiguitas latens.*

> "In the case of a latent ambiguity and uncertainty, the actions of the parties previous to, and contemporaneous with, (but not subsequent to), the agreement are admissible to EXPLAIN it, by directing its application: As, if a bargain be made for wheat, without stating the quality, parol evidence of former dealings for a particular quality would perhaps be received. Where the agreement is clear, and there is no latent ambiguity, even prior letters of the parties cannot be received in evidence to restrain or alter the sense of the contract." Joseph Chitty Jr., *A Practical Treatise on the Law of Contracts* 24 (1827).

> "Instead of this word 'equivocation,' the phrase 'latent ambiguity' is sometimes used by courts, — 'latent' because it does not develop until we seek to apply it and then discover the equivocation. This phrase was invented by Lord Bacon, in one of his maxims, and it long held sway; but it has only served to confuse discussion, and his other word for the same thing, 'equivocation,' is more suitable, and has come into general use since Professor Thayer's masterly analysis of the subject some fifty years ago." John H. Wigmore, *A Students' Textbook of the Law of Evidence* 529 (1935). — In fact, the usual term today is *latent ambiguity.* — Eds.

▸ **patent ambiguity** (**pay**-tənt). (18c) An ambiguity that clearly appears on the face of a document, arising from the language itself <the nonperformance was excused because the two different prices expressed in the contract created a patent ambiguity>. — Also termed *intrinsic ambiguity*; *ambiguitas patens.*

> "[L]*atent* ambiguity . . . must be carefully distinguished from *patent* ambiguity, where words are omitted, or contradict one another; for in such cases explanatory evidence is not admissible. Where a bill of exchange was expressed in words to be drawn for 'two hundred pounds' but in figures for '£245,' evidence was not admitted to show that the figures expressed the intention of the parties." William R. Anson, *Principles of the Law of Contract* 401 (Arthur L. Corbin ed., 3d Am. ed. 1919).

2. An uncertainty of meaning based not on the scope of a word or phrase but on a semantic dichotomy that gives rise to any of two or more quite different but almost equally plausible interpretations. • How uncertain must wording be to have two meanings "almost equally plausible"? One commentator adopts the test of "consider[ing] a statute ambiguous if a lawyer would litigate the issue in court." Gregory E. Maggs, *Reducing the Costs of Statutory Ambiguity*, 29 Harv. J. Legis. 123, 125 (1992). **3.** Loosely, VAGUENESS. Cf. MEANING. — **ambiguous** (am-**big**-yoo-əs), *adj.*

ambiguity doctrine. See CONTRA PROFERENTEM.

ambiguity upon the factum. See *ambiguity on the factum* under AMBIGUITY (1).

ambit (**am**-bit). (14c) **1.** A boundary line or limit; esp., the scope of a statute or regulation, or the sphere of influence and authority of an agency, committee, department, or the like. **2.** A space surrounding a house or town. **3.** The range or limit of someone's power, authority, or influence.

ambitus (**am**-bi-təs), *n.* [Latin *ambitus* "deviousness, corruption"] *Hist.* The procuring of a public office by money or gifts; the unlawful buying and selling of a public office.

ambulance chaser. (1896) **1.** A lawyer who approaches victims of accidents in hopes of persuading them to hire the lawyer and sue for damages; esp., a lawyer who uses undue pressure to persuade an accident victim to sue with a contingent fee for the lawyer. **2.** A lawyer's agent who engages in this activity. — Also termed *chaser.* **3.** *Tendentious slang.* An attorney. — **ambulance-chasing,** *n.*

ambulance-chasing. (1897) A blatant form of solicitation in which a lawyer (either personally or through an agent) urges injured people to employ the lawyer to represent them.

ambulatory (**am**-byə-lə-tor-ee), *adj.* (16c) **1.** Able to walk <the accident victim is still ambulatory>. **2.** Capable of being altered or revised; not yet legally fixed <a will is ambulatory because it is revocable until the testator's death>.

ambulatory automatism. See AUTOMATISM.

ambulatory disposition. See DISPOSITION (2).

ambulatory will. See WILL.

a me (ay mee). [Latin] From me. • This phrase was used in feudal grants to denote tenure held directly of the chief lord. The phrase is short for *a me de superiore meo* (ay **mee** dee s[y]oo-peer-ee-**or**-ee **mee**-oh), meaning "from me of my superior." Cf. DE ME.

a me de superiore meo (ay **mee** dee s[y]oo-peer-ee-**or**-ee **mee**-oh). [Law Latin] *Hist.* From me, of my superior. • In a feudal land grant, this phrase provided that when feudal title was completed, the grantee would hold the land of the grantor's superior.

ameliorate (ə-**meel**-yə-rayt), *vb.* (18c) **1.** To make better <the charity tries to ameliorate the conditions of the homeless>. **2.** To become better <with time, the situation ameliorated>.

ameliorating waste. See WASTE (1).

amelioration, *n.* (17c) **1.** The act of improving something; the quality, state, or condition of being made better. **2.** An improvement. — **ameliorative,** *adj.*

amelioration doctrine. (1993) *Criminal law.* The rule that if a new statute reduces the penalty for a certain crime while a prosecution for that crime is pending, the defendant should gain the benefit of the reduction even though the crime was committed before the statute passed.

ameliorative waste. See *ameliorating waste* under WASTE (1).

amenable (ə-**mee**-nə-bəl *or* -**men**-), *adj.* (16c) Legally answerable; liable to being brought to judgment <amenable to process>. — **amenability,** *n.*

amend, *vb.* (13c) **1.** To correct or make usu. small changes to (something written or spoken); to rectify or make right <amend the order to fix a clerical error>. **2.** To change the wording of; specif., to formally alter (a statute, constitution, motion, etc.) by striking out, inserting, or substituting words <amend the legislative bill>. See AMENDMENT (3). — **amendable,** *adj.* — **amendability,** *n.*

▸ **amend a previous action.** See *amend something previously adopted.*

▸ **amend something previously adopted.** (1923) *Parliamentary law.* (Of a deliberative assembly) to change an otherwise final text. — Also termed *amend a previous action.*

amendatory (ə-**men**-də-tor-ee), *adj.* (1859) Designed or serving to amend; corrective <an amendatory rider to an insurance policy>.

amended complaint. See COMPLAINT.

amended pleading. See PLEADING (1).

amended return. See TAX RETURN.

amende honorable (ə-**mend on**-ə-rə-bəl *or* a-**mawnd** on-ə-**rah**-bəl). [French "honorable reparation"] (17c) *Hist.* A formal reparation for an offense or injury, done by making an open and usu. humiliating acknowledgment and apology so as to restore the victim's honor. • This apology could be accomplished, for example, by walking into church with a rope around the neck and a torch in hand, begging forgiveness from the injured party.

amende profitable (ə-**mend** proh-fee-**tahb**-lə), *n.* (1892) *Roman–Dutch law.* In a defamation action, reparations made by a defendant who pays a sum that the plaintiff has named under oath as being less than full satisfaction for the claim.

amender, *n.* (14c) Someone who amends (a document, etc.).

amending act. See *amending statute* under STATUTE.

Amending Article. *Constitutional law.* The constitutional provision giving Congress the power to propose amendments to the United States Constitution and setting forth the procedure. U.S. Const. art. V.

amending statute. See STATUTE.

amendment. (17c) **1.** A formal and usu. minor revision or addition proposed or made to a statute, constitution, pleading, order, or other instrument; specif., a change made by addition, deletion, or correction; esp., an alteration in wording. **2.** The process of making such a revision.

▸ **amendment as of course.** (1925) An amendment, usu. to pleadings, that a party has a statutory right to apply for without the court's permission. *See* Fed. R. Civ. P. 15(a).

▸ **amendment on court's own motion.** (1968) A change to a pleading or other document by the judge without a motion from a party.

▸ **nunc pro tunc amendment** (**nəngk** proh **təngk** *or* **nuungk** proh **tuungk**). (1937) An amendment that is given retroactive effect, usu. by court order to correct a clear mistake and prevent injustice, but not to alter the court's original purpose.

3. *Parliamentary law.* A motion that changes another motion's wording by striking out text, inserting or adding text, or substituting text. See AMEND (2). Cf. BLANK (2).

▸ **amendment by adding.** (1820) An amendment that places new wording at the end of a motion or of a paragraph or other readily divisible part within a motion. • Some authorities treat amendment by adding as a form of amendment by inserting. Cf. *amendment by inserting.*

▸ **amendment by inserting.** (18c) An amendment that places new wording within or around a motion's current wording. • Some authorities distinguish amendment by adding, which places new wording after the current wording, from amendment by inserting. Cf. *amendment by adding.*

▸ **amendment by striking out.** (1828) An amendment that removes wording from a motion's current wording.

▸ **amendment by striking out and inserting.** (1895) An amendment that removes wording and replaces it with alternative wording or, less often, puts the same wording in another place. • The motion can properly apply only to the placement or to the rewording of the wording being struck; it cannot strike out some wording and insert new wording in a different place. See *amendment by substituting*; CREATE A BLANK.

▸ **amendment by substituting.** (1821) **1.** A special type of amendment by striking out and inserting that replaces an entire main motion or a paragraph or other readily divisible part within a main motion; an amendment of greater scope than a perfecting amendment. Cf. *perfecting amendment.* **2.** See *amendment by striking out and inserting.* • Parliamentary writers differ on when an amendment by striking out and inserting qualifies as an amendment by substituting. Some manuals treat the two as equivalent and apply the same rules to them. Others maintain that an amendment is not a substitute unless it replaces the entire main motion — or at least a readily divisible part within the main motion — and apply different rules to an amendment by substituting than to a less drastic amendment. — Also termed *amendment in the nature of a substitute* (in sense 1); *substitute; substitution; substitute amendment.*

▸ **amendment from the floor.** See *floor amendment.*

▸ **amendment in the nature of a substitute.** See *amendment by substituting* (1).

▸ **amendment of the first degree.** See *primary amendment.*

▸ **amendment of the first rank.** See *primary amendment.*

▸ **amendment of the second degree.** See *secondary amendment.*

▸ **amendment of the second rank.** See *secondary amendment.*

▸ **amendment to the amendment.** See *secondary amendment.*

▸ **amendment to the main question.** See *primary amendment.*

▸ **amendment to the text.** See *primary amendment.*

▸ **committee amendment.** (1837) An amendment to a motion reported by a committee to which the motion was referred. Cf. *floor amendment.*

▸ **first-degree amendment.** See *primary amendment.*

▸ **floor amendment.** (1917) An amendment offered from the floor by an individual member, as distinguished from a committee amendment. — Also termed *amendment from the floor.* Cf. *committee amendment.*

▸ **friendly amendment.** (1853) An amendment that the mover of the motion being amended supports, and to which no other member objects.

"The term 'friendly amendment' is often used to describe an amendment offered by someone who is in sympathy with the purposes of the main motion, in the belief that the amendment will either improve the statement or effect of the main motion, presumably to the satisfaction of its maker, or will increase the chances of the main motion's adoption. Regardless of whether or not the maker of the main motion 'accepts' the amendment, it must be opened to debate and voted on formally (unless adopted by unanimous consent) and is handled under the same rules as amendments generally." Henry M. Robert III et al., *Robert's Rules of Order Newly Revised* § 12, at 162 (11th ed. 2011).

"Often, such an amendment is proposed as a 'friendly amendment,' simply indicating that the member proposing the amendment feels it will be acceptable to the maker of the main motion. If the maker of the original motion does not wish to accept the amendment, the amendment must then receive a second to come before the assembly, and will receive the usual consideration by the assembly. However, even the acceptance of the proposed amendment by the maker of the motion is simply a statement of support, and every member of the assembly retains the right to object to the amendment's adoption by general consent, and to debate and vote on the amendment." Alice Sturgis, *The Standard Code of Parliamentary Procedure* 53 (4th ed. 2001).

▸ **hostile amendment.** (1885) An amendment that is opposed by the supporters of the main motion.

▸ **killer amendment.** (1983) An amendment that has the effect, intended or not, of ensuring the defeat of the main motion.

▸ **nongermane amendment.** (1968) An amendment that adds an unrelated rider. • A nongermane amendment is out of order in most ordinary assemblies and many legislative bodies. But some legislative bodies, in jurisdictions where legislation may embrace more than one subject, allow nongermane amendments to a bill. See RIDER.

▸ **perfecting amendment.** (1926) An amendment that merely edits the form of a main motion or a primary amendment but does not substantially change its content; an amendment of lesser scope than an amendment by substituting. Cf. *amendment by substituting* (1).

▸ **poison-pill amendment.** (1969) A hostile amendment intended either to make the proposal unacceptable to its supporters or to render it ineffective or impractical to enforce if it is enacted.

▸ **primary amendment.** An amendment that directly amends the main motion or directly amends a pending motion other than an amendment. — Also termed *amendment of the first degree; amendment of the first rank; amendment to the main question; amendment to the text; first-degree amendment.* Cf. *secondary amendment.*

▸ **pro forma amendment.** (1945) An amendment moved solely for the purpose of obtaining the floor and treated as withdrawn once the mover has spoken. • The customary pro forma amendment in Congress is a motion "to strike the last word."

▸ **secondary amendment.** An amendment that makes a change in or presents an alternative to a pending primary amendment. — Also termed *amendment of the second degree; amendment of the second rank; amendment to the amendment; second-degree amendment.* Cf. *primary amendment.*

▸ **second-degree amendment.** See *secondary amendment.*

▸ **substitute amendment.** (1842) **1.** A secondary amendment that substantially replaces rather than edits a primary amendment. **2.** See *amendment by substituting.*

amendment after allowance. See PATENT-APPLICATION AMENDMENT.

amendment after appeal. See PATENT-APPLICATION AMENDMENT.

amendment after final action. See PATENT-APPLICATION AMENDMENT.

amendment after payment of issue fee. See PATENT-APPLICATION AMENDMENT.

amendment before first action. See *preliminary amendment* under PATENT-APPLICATION AMENDMENT.

amendment by implication. (1868) A rule of construction that allows a repugnant provision in a statute to be interpreted as an implicit modification or abrogation of a provision that appears before it. • Amendments by implication are disfavored. *See U.S. v. Welden*, 377 U.S. 95, 102 n.12, 84 S.Ct. 1082, 1087 n.12 (1964).

amendment from the floor. See *floor amendment* under AMENDMENT (3).

amendment in excess of filing fee. See PATENT-APPLICATION AMENDMENT.

amendment of indictment. (1828) The alteration of the charging terms of an indictment, either literally or in effect, after the grand jury has made a decision on it. • The indictment usu. cannot be amended at trial in a way that would prejudice the defendant by having a trial on matters that were not contained in the indictment. To do so would violate the defendant's Fifth Amendment right to be answerable only for those charges levied by a grand jury. — Also termed *amendment to the indictment.*

▸ **constructive amendment of indictment.** (1969) The improper admission of evidence that modifies the indictment by modifying the elements of a charged offense or by establishing an offense different from or in addition to those in the indictment. Cf. *fatal variance* under VARIANCE (1).

amendment of registration. See TRADEMARK-APPLICATION AMENDMENT.

amendment on court's own motion. See AMENDMENT (2).

amendment to allege use. See TRADEMARK-APPLICATION AMENDMENT.

amendment to different register. See TRADEMARK-APPLICATION AMENDMENT.

amendment to the indictment. See AMENDMENT OF INDICTMENT.

amends, *n. pl.* (14c) Compensation given for a loss or injury; reparation.

amenity. [fr. Latin *amoenitas* "pleasantness"] (1928) Something tangible or intangible that increases the enjoyment of real property, such as location, view, landscaping, security, or access to recreational facilities.

a mensa et thoro (ay **men**-sə et **thor**-oh). [Latin "from board and hearth"] (17c) (Of a divorce decree) effecting a separation of the parties rather than a dissolution of the marriage <a separation *a mensa et thoro* was the usual way for a couple to separate under English law up until 1857>. • Not all states provide for such a proceeding. See *divorce a mensa et thoro* under DIVORCE; SEPARATION; A VINCULO MATRIMONII.

amerce (ə-**mərs**), *vb.* (14c) **1.** To impose a fine or penalty that is not fixed but is left to the court's discretion; to punish by amercement. **2.** To fine or punish in any manner. — **amerceable** (ə-**mər**-sə-bəl), **amerciable** (ə-**mər**-see-ə-bəl), *adj.*

> "There were two more aspects to this financial scheme of permitting suitors to use the royal courts — for a consideration. The practice developed of 'amercing' or fining those who were 'in the mercy of the king' because they had put forward a false claim, or had made a false defense. In other words the loser of the suit had to pay a fine for his supposedly unjust effort to deny or resist the claim of his opponent." Charles Herman Kinnane, *A First Book on Anglo-American Law* 272 (2d ed. 1952).

amercement (ə-**mərs**-mənt), *n.* [fr. Law French *estre à merci* "to be at the mercy (of another)," fr. Latin *merces* "payment"] (14c) **1.** The imposition of a discretionary fine or penalty by a court, esp. on an official for misconduct <an amercement proceeding>. **2.** The fine or penalty so imposed <an amercement charged to the sheriff for failing to return the writ of execution>. — Also termed *cashlite*; (archaically) *amerciament*; *merciament*.

amerciament. See AMERCEMENT.

America Invents Act. *Patents.* A 2011 federal statute designed to harmonize U.S. patent law with that of other countries by changing the U.S. patent system from a first-to-invent to a first-to-file system. • Taking effect in March 2013, the statute also expanded the definition of prior art, abolished U.S. Patent and Trademark Office patent interferences, provided for opposition to patents after issuance, expanded inter partes reexaminations, and significantly restricted false-marking claims. — Abbr. AIA. See FIRST-TO-INVENT SYSTEM; FIRST-TO-FILE SYSTEM.

American Academy of Actuaries. A national organization of actuaries whose members must meet specified educational requirements and have at least three years of responsible actuarial experience. • Created in 1965, the Academy promotes public awareness of the actuarial profession, represents the profession before federal and state governments, and sponsors continuing-education conferences. — Abbr. AAA. See ACTUARY.

American Accounting Association. An organization of accounting practitioners, educators, and students, founded in 1916 to promote accounting as an academic discipline by sponsoring research projects and continuing-education seminars. — Abbr. AAA.

American Arbitration Association. A national nonprofit organization that promulgates standard-form procedural rules for arbitrations, maintains a roster of arbitrators for panels, and provides administrative services in support of arbitration proceedings. — Abbr. AAA.

American Association of Motor Vehicle Administrators. A private nonprofit organization that develops and provides guidelines for North American governmental agencies and private organizations responsible for administering and enforcing motor-vehicle laws and promoting highway safety. • Founded in 1933, the association is divided into four regions covering North America. — Abbr. AAMVA.

American Bankers Association. A voluntary trade association of banking institutions, including banks, trust companies, and savings banks and associations, whose members represent the vast majority of banking deposits in the United States. • The association was founded in 1875. — Abbr. ABA.

American Bar Association. A voluntary national organization of lawyers organized in 1878. • Among other things, it participates in law reform, law-school accreditation, and continuing legal education in an effort to improve legal services and the administration of justice. — Abbr. ABA.

American Bar Foundation. An outgrowth of the American Bar Association involved with sponsoring and funding projects in law-related research, education, and social studies. — Abbr. ABF.

American Bureau of Shipping. An organization of marine underwriters, shipbuilders, and marine carriers charged with conducting research, technological development, officer training, and standards of building, maintaining, and operating seagoing vessels and stationary offshore facilities. • The organization was founded in 1862 as the American Shipbuilders' Association. Its name was changed in 1898, and it was formally recognized in the Merchant Marine Act of 1920. Its core mission is to promulgate rules for evaluating the design of new vessels and structures and for maintaining all existing vessels and structures. — Abbr. ABS. See ABS RULES.

American Civil Liberties Union. A national organization whose primary purpose is to help enforce and preserve individual rights and liberties guaranteed by federal and state constitutions. — Abbr. ACLU.

American clause. (1835) *Marine insurance.* A policy provision that prevents an insurer from claiming contribution from a policy later purchased by the insured.

American common law. See COMMON LAW (2).

American depositary receipt. (1968) A negotiable instrument issued by an American bank as a substitute for stock shares in a foreign-based corporation. • ADRs are the most common method by which foreign companies secure American shareholders. Companies that offer ADRs maintain a stock listing in their domestic market in their domestic currency, while the ADRs are held in U.S. dollars and listed on a U.S. stock exchange, usu. the New York Stock Exchange. The holder of the receipt is entitled to receive the specified securities upon presentation of the ADR to the depositary institution — Abbr. ADR. — Also termed *American depository receipt.* Cf. AMERICAN DEPOSITARY SHARE.

American depositary share. (1978) A foreign security that is exempt from reporting requirements and deposited in an American bank to be held for private sale. • American depositary receipts are used to transfer the securities. — Abbr. ADS. Cf. AMERICAN DEPOSITARY RECEIPT.

American depository receipt. See AMERICAN DEPOSITARY RECEIPT.

American Experience Table of Mortality. *Insurance.* A chart developed by insurers in the 1860s to predict mortality rates and thereby more accurately set insurance rates. • The Table was widely used by insurers to establish rates until the 1950s.

American Federation of Labor and Congress of Industrial Organizations. A voluntary affiliation of more than 100 labor unions that operate autonomously yet benefit from the affiliation's political activities and its establishment of broad policies for the national labor movement. — Abbr. AFL-CIO.

American Federation of Musicians. A labor union composed of musicians, orchestra leaders, contractors, copyists, orchestrators, composers, and arrangers. • In the recording industry, artists hired by record companies that have agreements with the union must be paid according to the union's set scale. — Abbr. AF of M.

American Federation of Television and Radio Artists. A labor union composed of actors, announcers, narrators, and vocalists. • In the entertainment industry, performers hired by producers that have agreements with the union must be paid according to the union's set scale. It is affiliated with the AFL-CIO. — Abbr. AFTRA.

American Forces Information Service. An agency in the U.S. Department of Defense responsible for operating the Armed Forces Radio and Television Service, the Armed Forces Press and Publications Service, and a Broadcast Center. • Established in 1977, the Service publishes various periodicals and pamphlets and the *Stars and Stripes* newspapers. — Abbr. AFIS.

American Foundation for Suicide Prevention. A national nonprofit organization formed in 1987 to study and curb suicide through research, education, legislation, and providing help to those at risk and those affected by suicide. — Abbr. AFSP.

American Guild of Variety Artists. A labor union composed of performers in nightclubs, cabarets, theaters, and other areas of live entertainment. • The Guild regulates its members' contracts with agents through an agreement with the Artists' Representatives Association. — Abbr. AGVA.

American Indian law. See INDIAN LAW.

American Inns of Court Foundation. See INN OF COURT (2).

American Institute of Certified Public Accountants. A national organization formed in 1887 to support certified public accountants by providing programs, education, training, publications, and networking opportunities. — Abbr. AICPA.

American Institute of Parliamentarians. A national nonprofit educational organization founded in 1958 to improve and promote the rules of parliamentary procedure as a way of implementing sound democratic principles. — Abbr. AIP.

American Intellectual Property Law Association. A national bar association of lawyers who practice patent, trademark, copyright, trade-secret, and unfair-competition law. • The association was formerly known as the American Patent Law Association. Membership is also open to law students who are interested in intellectual-property law. — Abbr. AIPLA.

American Inventors Protection Act. *Patents.* A 1999 statute designed to (1) curb deceptive practices by invention-promotion companies, (2) reduce patent fees, (3) provide a defense against infringement for a party who in good faith reduced a patented invention to practice at least one year before a patent's effective filing date, (4) extend the patent term when the PTO is responsible for a delay in issuance, and (5) require publication of a patent application 18 months after its filing unless the applicant requests otherwise. Pub. L. No. 106-113, 113 Stat. 1537-544. — Abbr. AIPA.

American Judicature Society. A now-defunct organization of judges, lawyers, and lay people established to improve the administration of justice. • The AJS was founded in 1913. Its interests included ensuring the judiciary's independence, improving judicial selection and the performance of juries, and educating the public about the justice system. — Abbr. AJS.

American Law Institute. An organization of lawyers, judges, and legal scholars who promote consistency and simplification of American law by publishing the Restatements of the Law, and other model codes and treatises, as well as promoting continuing legal education. — Abbr. ALI.

American Law Institute test. See SUBSTANTIAL-CAPACITY TEST.

American Lloyd's. See LLOYD'S UNDERWRITERS.

American National Standards Institute. A private nonprofit organization, founded in 1918, that administers the U.S. standardization- and conformity-assessment system and coordinates voluntary participants in the system. — Abbr. ANSI.

American option. See OPTION (5).

American Patent Law Association. See AMERICAN INTELLECTUAL PROPERTY LAW ASSOCIATION.

American Printing House for the Blind. A federally aided institution that assists blind children by distributing Braille books, talking books, and educational aids without charge. • The printing house was incorporated in Kentucky in 1858. — Abbr. APH.

American Revolutionary War. See *revolutionary war* under WAR (1).

American rule. (1868) **1.** The general policy that all litigants, even the prevailing one, must bear their own attorney's fees. • The rule is subject to bad-faith and other statutory and contractual exceptions. Cf. ENGLISH RULE; TORT-OF-ANOTHER DOCTRINE. **2.** The doctrine that a witness cannot be questioned on cross-examination about any fact or circumstance not connected with the matters brought out in the direct examination.

American share. See SHARE (2).

American Society of Composers, Authors & Publishers. *Copyright.* One of the U.S. performing-rights societies that licenses and polices the public performance of nondramatic musical works on behalf of the copyright owners. — Abbr. ASCAP.

American Society of Legal Writers. The formal name for Scribes, an association of lawyers dedicated to the improvement of legal writing. • Founded in 1953, it sponsors annual writing competitions and publishes *The Scribes Journal of Legal Writing*, the first journal devoted exclusively to legal writing. It was originally called the American Society of Writers on Legal Subjects, but the name was shortened in 2006.

American Stock Exchange. An organized stock exchange and self-regulating organization under the Securities Exchange Act of 1934, located in New York City and engaged in national trading of corporate stocks. • It often trades in the securities of young or small companies because its listing requirements are less strict than those of the New York Stock Exchange. — Abbr. AMEX; ASE.

American-style option. See *American option* under OPTION (5).

Americans with Disabilities Act. A federal statute that prohibits discrimination in employment, public services, and public accommodations against any person because of the person's disability ("a physical or mental impairment that substantially limits one or more of the major life activities"). 42 USCA §§ 12101–12213. • Under the ADA and related regulations and caselaw, major life activities include those that an average person in the general population can perform with little or no difficulty, such as seeing, hearing, sleeping, eating, walking, traveling, and working. The statute applies to both private and governmental entities but not to a private employer having fewer than 15 employees. 42 USCA § 12111(5)(A). — Abbr. ADA. See DISABILITY (2); MAJOR LIFE ACTIVITY.

AMEX (am-eks). *abbr.* (1961) AMERICAN STOCK EXCHANGE.

ami (ə-**mee**), *n.* [Law French, fr. Latin *amicus*] A friend. • This term appears in several traditional legal phrases, such as *prochein ami* ("next friend"). — Also spelled *amy.* See NEXT FRIEND.

amiable compositeur. See AMIABLE COMPOSITOR.

amiable composition. (1930) An arbitration conducted by an amiable compositor. See AMIABLE COMPOSITOR. Cf. COMPOSITION (1).

amiable compositor. (1931) **1.** An arbitrator empowered, by agreement of the parties, to settle a dispute on the basis of what is equitable and good (*ex aequo et bono*), subject to procedural fairness and the terms of the arbitration agreement as opposed to the settled substantive rules of a given legal system. See EX AEQUO ET BONO. **2.** *Int'l law.* An unbiased third party, often a head of state or high government official, who suggests a solution that disputing countries might accept of their own volition. — Also termed *amiable compositeur* (ay-mee-**ah**-blə kon-poh-zee-**tuur**). See AMIABLE COMPOSITION.

amicable action. See *test case* (1) under CASE (1).

amicable compounder. See COMPOUNDER (1).

amicable scire facias to revive a judgment. See SCIRE FACIAS.

amicable suit. See *test case* (1) under CASE (1).

amicitia (am-i-**sit**-ee-ə). [Latin] *Roman law.* A treaty or convention of friendship, formal or informal, guaranteeing the safe sojourn of members of one country within another country's territory.

amicus. 1. AMICUS CURIAE. **2.** See *amicus brief* under BRIEF (1).

amicus brief. See BRIEF (1).

amicus counsel. See COUNSEL.

amicus curiae (ə-**mee**-kəs **kyoor**-ee-ɪ *or* ə-**mɪ**-kəs **kyoor**-ee-ee *also* **am**-i-kəs). [Latin "friend of the court"] (17c) Someone who is not a party to a lawsuit but who petitions the court or is requested by the court to file a brief in the action because that person has a strong interest in the subject matter. — Often shortened to *amicus.* — Also termed *friend of the court.* Pl. **amici curiae** (ə-**mee**-kee *or* ə-**mɪ**-sɪ *or* ə-**mɪ**-kɪ).

amicus publici (ə-**mee**-kəs **pəb**-lə-sɪ *or* ə-**mɪ**-kəs). [Latin] *Hist.* Friend of the public.

Amish exception. (1973) An exemption of the Amish from compulsory-school-attendance laws under the Free Exercise Clause of the First Amendment. • In *Wisconsin v. Yoder*, 406 U.S. 205, 92 S.Ct. 1526 (1972), the Supreme Court held that Amish children could not be compelled to attend high school even though they were within the age range of the state's compulsory-attendance law. The Court has very narrowly construed the Amish exception and has refused to extend it to non-Amish children. See COMPULSORY-ATTENDANCE LAW; FREE EXERCISE CLAUSE.

amita (**am**-ə-tə). [Latin] (16c) *Civil law.* The sister of one's father; an aunt on the father's side. Pl. ***amitae.***

amitina (am-ə-**tɪ**-nə). [Latin] *Civil law.* The daughter of a paternal aunt or maternal uncle; a female first cousin. Pl. ***amitinae.***

amitinus (am-ə-**tɪ**-nəs). [Latin] *Civil law.* The son of a paternal aunt or maternal uncle; a male first cousin. Pl. ***amitini.***

amittere curiam (ə-**mit**-ə-ree **kyoor**-ee-əm), *vb.* [Law Latin] *Hist.* To lose the privilege of attending court.

amittere legem terrae (ə-**mit**-ə-ree **lee**-jəm **ter**-ee). See LIBERAM LEGEM AMITTERE.

amittere liberam legem (ə-**mit**-ə-ree **lib**-ər-əm **lee**-jəm). See LIBERAM LEGEM AMITTERE.

amnesty, *n.* (16c) **1.** A pardon extended by the government to a group or class of persons, usu. for a political offense; the act of a sovereign power officially forgiving certain classes of persons who are subject to trial but have not yet been convicted <the 1986 Immigration Reform and Control Act provided amnesty for undocumented aliens already present in the country>. • Unlike an ordinary pardon, amnesty is usu. addressed to crimes against state sovereignty — that is, to political offenses with respect to which forgiveness is deemed more expedient for the public welfare than prosecution and punishment. Amnesty is usu. general, addressed to classes or even communities. — Also termed *general pardon.* See PARDON. — **amnesty,** *vb.*

> "*Amnesty* . . . derives from the Greek *amnestia* ('forgetting'), and has come to be used to describe measures of a more general nature, directed to offenses whose criminality is considered better forgotten." Leslie Sebba, "Amnesty and Pardon," in 1 *Encyclopedia of Crime and Justice* 59, 59 (Sanford H. Kadish ed., 1983).

▸ **express amnesty.** (1965) Amnesty granted in direct terms.

▸ **implied amnesty.** (1998) Amnesty indirectly resulting from a peace treaty executed between contending parties.

2. A period of time during which a person can admit having done something illegal without being punished <a three-year amnesty for illegal aliens>.

amnesty clause. (1895) A clause, esp. one found in a peace treaty, that wipes out past offenses such as treason, sedition, rebellion, and even war crimes. • A sovereign may grant amnesty to all guilty persons or only to certain categories of offenders.

Amnesty International. An international nongovernmental organization founded in the early 1960s to protect human rights throughout the world. • Its mission is to "secure throughout the world the observance of the Universal Declaration of Human Rights." Amnesty Int'l Statute, art. 1.

> "Founded in 1961 by the British lawyer Peter Benenson (1921–2005), Amnesty International is a nongovernmental organization (NGO) that works primarily for the release of prisoners of conscience, fair and prompt trials for political prisoners (defined as persons in prison for their beliefs who have not practiced or advocated violence), and the abolition of the death penalty, extrajudicial killings, and all forms of torture. The organization took root quickly in Europe and the United States, but it was not until the mid-1970s that its numerical and geographical growth became remarkable. It is the largest human rights NGO in the world and sets the standards for human rights monitoring, reporting, and campaigns. It was awarded the Nobel Peace Prize in 1977." J. Paul Martin, "Amnesty International," in 1 *The Oxford Companion to Comparative Politics* 42, 42 (Joel Krieger ed., 2013).

amorous-design evidence. (1999) *Criminal procedure.* Evidence about a defendant's prior sexual activities with the victim of an alleged sex crime. • It is generally considered inadmissible propensity evidence.

a morte testatoris (ay **mor**-tee tes-tə-**tor**-is). [Latin] *Hist.* From the death of the testator. • The phrase appeared in reference to the moment when a legacy vests in the beneficiary.

amortization (am-ər-tə-**zay**-shən), *n.* (1851) **1.** The act or result of gradually extinguishing a debt, such as a mortgage, usu. by contributing payments of principal each time a periodic interest payment is due. See MORTMAIN. Cf. AMORTIZE.

▸ **negative amortization.** (1978) An increase in a loan's principal balance caused by monthly payments insufficient to pay accruing interest.

2. The act or result of apportioning the initial cost of a usu. intangible asset, such as a patent, over the asset's useful life. Cf. DEPRECIATION. **3.** A method of terminating a nonconforming use by allowing it to continue only for a specified grace period, so that the owner may recover all or part of the investment. • After the grace period expires, the use must be ended. — Sometimes also termed *amortizement.*

amortization reserve. See RESERVE (1).

amortization schedule. (1930) A schedule of periodic payments of interest and principal owed on a debt obligation; specif., a loan schedule showing both the amount of principal and interest that is due at regular intervals over the loan term and the remaining unpaid principal balance after each scheduled payment is made.

amortize, *vb.* (1867) **1.** To extinguish (a debt) gradually, often by means of a sinking fund. **2.** To arrange to extinguish (a debt) by gradual increments. **3.** *Hist.* To alienate or convey lands to a corporation (that is, in mortmain). — Also spelled *amortise.* See MORTMAIN.

amortized loan. See LOAN.

amortized mortgage. See MORTGAGE.

amortizement. See AMORTIZATION.

amotion. (17c) **1.** A turning out, as the eviction of a tenant or the removal of a person from office. **2.** The common-law procedure available to shareholders to remove a corporate director for cause.

> "The cases do not distinguish clearly between disfranchisement and amotion. The former applies to members, and the latter only to officers; and if an officer be removed for good cause, he may still continue to be a member of the corporation. Disfranchisement is the greater power, and more formidable in its application; and in joint stock or moneyed corporations no stockholder can be disfranchised, and thereby deprived of his property or interest in the general fund, by any act of the corporation, without at least an express authority for that purpose." 2 James Kent, *Commentaries on American Law* *298 (George Comstock ed., 11th ed. 1866).

3. The wrongful moving or carrying away of another's personal property.

amount in controversy. (1809) The damages claimed or relief demanded by the injured party in a lawsuit. • For a federal court to have diversity jurisdiction, the amount in controversy must exceed $75,000. 28 USCA § 1332(a). — Also termed *jurisdictional amount; matter in controversy.* See DIVERSITY OF CITIZENSHIP; AGGREGATION DOCTRINE.

amount realized. (18c) *Tax.* The amount received by a taxpayer for the sale or exchange of an asset, such as cash, property, services received, or debts assumed by a buyer. Cf. GAIN (3); LOSS (2).

amove, *vb.* (16c) To remove (a person) from an office or position. — **amoval,** *n.*

amoveas manus (ay-**moh**-vee-əs **man**-əs). [Law Latin "that you remove your hands"] (17c) *Hist.* **1.** A judgment ordering the Crown to relinquish possession of land to the complainant. • The judgment is so called from the emphatic words *quod manus domini regis amoveantur* ("that the hands of the king be removed"). **2.** The writ issued on the judgment.

amparo. *Mexican law.* A summary proceeding intended to vindicate an individual's or company's rights without necessarily establishing a precedent for similarly situated parties. — Also termed *judicio de amparo.*

ampliatio (am-plee-**ay**-shee-oh), *n.* [Latin] (16c) *Roman law.* **1.** The act of deferring or reserving judgment. **2.** In a criminal trial before a *comitia,* the repeating of evidence at the jury's request. Pl. ***ampliationes*** (am-plee-ay-shee-**oh**-neez).

ampliation (am-plee-**ay**-shən). (17c) *Civil law.* An extending; a postponement of the decision in a case.

amplius (**am**-plee-əs), *adj.* & *adv.* [Latin] *Hist.* More; further.

AMS. *abbr.* AGRICULTURAL MARKETING SERVICE.

AMT. *abbr.* See *alternative minimum tax* under TAX.

Amtrak. See NATIONAL RAILROAD PASSENGER CORPORATION.

a multo fortiori (ay **məl**-toh for-shee-**or**-I). [Latin] By far the stronger reason. Cf. A FORTIORI.

amusement tax. See TAX.

amy (ə-**mee**), *n.* [Law French] A friend. • This is an alternative spelling of *ami.* See AMI.

anaconda clause. See MOTHER HUBBARD CLAUSE (1).

anacrisis (an-ə-**krI**-sis). (17c) *Civil law.* An investigation or inquiry, esp. one conducted by torture.

analog. (1837) *Patents.* A different material, usu. a chemical or DNA sequence, that produces the same result as the specified material when used in a certain way. • To prevent others from free-riding on their innovation without technically infringing their exclusive rights, patent applicants often include analogs in their claims. — Also spelled *analogue.* — Also termed *functional analog; equivalent.*

analogia proportionis (an-ə-**loh**-jee-ə prə-por-shee-**oh**-nis). [Latin] *Hist.* An analogy of proportion.

analogous art. See ART (3).

analogous use. (1886) **1.** *Patents.* The application of a process already known in one field of art to produce a similar result in another field. • Unless the fields are so unrelated or the outcomes so different as to produce a novel, useful, and nonobvious result, an analogous use is not patentable. **2.** *Trademarks.* The use of a mark in marketing and advertising a product or service before the actual sale of the product or service, in order to establish the mark's use in commerce. • For the owner to take advantage of the analogous-use doctrine, the marketing campaign must be substantial and the product or service must be available soon after the campaign. An owner who files an intent-to-use application may tack on the period of analogous use for purposes of priority and incontestability.

analytical, *adj.* (16c) **1.** Of, relating to, or involving detailed and intelligent thought about something so that one can understand and explain it clearly. **2.** Of, relating to, or involving the use of the scientific method to examine something. **3.** Of, relating to, or involving the use of sound legal methods to examine a problem; engaging in legal analysis.

analytical jurisprudence. See JURISPRUDENCE.

analytical memorandum. See *research memorandum* under MEMORANDUM (2).

analyze, *vb.* (16c) **1.** To examine or think about carefully for the purpose of understanding, esp. by breaking down into constituent parts; to study the factors of (an issue, problem, situation, etc.) in some detail so as to find a solution, recommendation, outcome, etc. **2.** To examine the mental makeup of (a person), esp. as part of a psychological evaluation. **3.** To examine or test (a substance, device, etc.) to see what it consists of or how it was made.

anarchism. 1. See ANARCHIST. **2.** See ANARCHY (2).

anarchist, *n.* (17c) Someone who believes that governments, laws, and rules are not necessary; specif., someone who advocates the overthrow of organized government by force or who believes in the absence of government as a political ideal. — **anarchism** (the philosophy), *n.*

anarchy, *n.* (16c) **1.** Absence of government; lawlessness. **2.** The political belief that there should be no government and that instead ordinary people should work together to improve society; specif., a sociopolitical theory holding that the only legitimate form of government is one under which individuals govern themselves voluntarily, free from any collective power structure enforcing compliance with social order. — Also termed (in sense 2) *anarchism.* — **anarchic,** *adj.*

▸ **criminal anarchy.** (1831) A doctrine advocating the overthrow of organized government by force or violence, by assassinating a head of government, or by some other unlawful act. • Most states have laws limiting speech that incites criminal anarchy. The laws do not apply to abstract philosophical expressions or predictions or like expressions protected by the First and Fourteenth Amendments. Criminal-anarchy statutes (e.g., 18 USCA § 2385) apply only to speech that is calculated to induce forceful and violent activity, such as attempts to incite people to riot, or that otherwise generates some "clear and present danger" that the advocated violent overthrow may be attempted or accomplished. *See Gitlow v. New York,* 268 U.S. 652, 666, 45 S.Ct. 625, 630 (1925).

anathema (ə-**nath**-ə-mə), *n.* (16c) An ecclesiastical curse that prohibits a person from receiving communion (as in excommunication) and bars the person from contact with members of the church. — **anathematize,** *vb.*

anatocism (ə-**nat**-ə-siz-əm), *n.* [fr. Greek *anatokismos* "to lend on interest again"] (17c) *Rare.* **1.** Compound interest. See *compound interest* under INTEREST (3). **2.** The practice of compounding interest.

anatomical gift. See GIFT.

ancestor, *n.* (17c) A person from whom an estate has passed; ASCENDANT. • This word is the correlative of *heir.* Cf. HEIR (1).

▸ **collateral ancestor.** See *collateral ascendant* under ASCENDENT.

▸ **common ancestor.** (17c) A person to whom the ancestry of two or more persons is traced.

ancestral debt. See DEBT.

ancestral estate. See ESTATE (3).

ancestral property. See PROPERTY.

ancestry. (14c) A line of descent; collectively, a person's forebears; lineage.

anchorage. (16c) *Maritime law.* **1.** An area where ships can anchor. **2.** A duty paid by shipowners for the use of a port; a toll for anchoring.

anchoring effect. The influence that a prior perception or judgment of a person, event, or object has on a future perception or judgments of another person, event, or object. — Often shortened to *anchoring.*

ancient, *adj. Evidence.* (14c) Having existed for a long time without interruption, usu. at least 20 to 30 years <ancient deed> <ancient map>. • Ancient items are usu. presumed to be authentic even if proof of authenticity cannot be made. Fed. R. Evid. 901(b)(8).

ancient, *n.* See ANCIENTS.

ancient demesne. See DEMESNE.

ancient document. See DOCUMENT (2).

ancient fact. See FACT.

ancient house. See HOUSE (1).

ancient law. (15c) The law of antiquity, considered esp. either from an anthropological standpoint or from the standpoint of tracing precursors to modern law.

> "Ancient law uniformly refuses to dispense with a single gesture, however grotesque; with a single syllable, however its meaning may have been forgotten; with a single witness, however superfluous may be his testimony. The entire solemnities must be scrupulously completed by persons legally entitled to take part in them, or else the conveyance is null, and the seller is re-established in the rights of which he had vainly attempted to divest himself." Henry S. Maine, *Ancient Law* 225–26 (17th ed. 1901).

ancient-lights doctrine. (1899) The common-law principle by which a landowner acquired, after 20 years of uninterrupted use, an easement preventing a neighbor from building an obstruction that blocks light from passing through the landowner's window. • The window (or other opening) is termed an *ancient light.* This doctrine has rarely been applied in the United States. — Also termed *ancient-windows doctrine; free-lights doctrine.*

> "[A] notice 'Ancient Lights,' which is often seen affixed to the wall of a building, only denotes a claim by or on behalf of the owner that he has acquired, by prescription or otherwise, a right to a reasonable amount of light, free from interruption, over adjoining land; but it must not be supposed that such a notice is necessary in order to protect a legal right." 2 *Stephen's Commentaries on the Laws of England* 347 (L. Crispin Warmington ed., 21st ed. 1950).

> "Under the English doctrine of ancient lights, which has been soundly repudiated in this country, if a landowner had received sunlight across adjoining property for a specified period of time, the landowner was entitled to continue to receive unobstructed access to sunlight across the adjoining property; the landowner acquired a negative prescriptive easement and could prevent the adjoining landowner from obstructing access to light." 1 Am. Jur. 2d *Adjoining Landowners* § 90, at 889 (1994).

ancient readings. (1812) *Hist.* Lectures on ancient English statutes, formerly having substantial legal authority.

ancient rent. (16c) *Hist.* The rent reserved at the time the lease is made, if the estate was not then under lease.

ancients. (16c) *Hist.* Certain members of seniority in the Inns of Court and Chancery. • In Gray's Inn, the society consisted of benchers, ancients, barristers, and students under the bar, with the ancients being the oldest barristers. In the Middle Temple, those who passed the readings were termed *ancients.* The Inns of Chancery consisted of both ancients and students or clerks. — Also termed (in singular) *ancient.*

ancient serjeant. (17c) *Hist. English law.* The eldest of the Crown's serjeants. • The last serjeant to hold this office died in 1866.

ancient wall. See WALL.

ancient watercourse. See WATERCOURSE.

ancient-windows doctrine. See ANCIENT-LIGHTS DOCTRINE.

ancient writing. See *ancient document* under DOCUMENT (2).

ancilla (an-**sil**-ə), *n.* [Latin] *Hist.* A female auxiliary or assistant.

ancillary (**an**-sə-ler-ee), *adj.* (17c) Supplementary; subordinate <ancillary claims>. — **ancillarity** (an-sə-**la[i]r**-ə-tee), *n.*

ancillary administration. See ADMINISTRATION.

ancillary administrator. See ADMINISTRATOR (2).

ancillary attachment. See ATTACHMENT (3).

ancillary bill. See *ancillary suit* under SUIT.

ancillary claim. See CLAIM (4).

ancillary guardianship. See GUARDIANSHIP.

ancillary jurisdiction. See JURISDICTION.

ancillary legislation. See LEGISLATION (3).

ancillary letters testamentary. See LETTERS TESTAMENTARY.

ancillary proceeding. See *ancillary suit* under SUIT.

ancillary process. See *ancillary suit* under SUIT.

ancillary receiver. See RECEIVER (1).

ancillary receivership. See RECEIVERSHIP.

ancillary suit. See SUIT.

ancillary to priority. (1932) *Patents.* (Of a legal issue) so logically related to the issue of priority of invention that it cannot be separated from the issue of priority. • The question whether an issue is ancillary to priority was once used to challenge the jurisdiction of the U.S. Patent and Trademark Office, but the Board of Patent Appeals and Interferences now has explicit jurisdiction over ancillary issues.

ancipitis usus. See *conditional contraband* under CONTRABAND.

Andean Community. A South American trade bloc comprising Bolivia, Colombia, Ecuador, and Peru, formed to encourage economic, environmental, political, and social cooperation. • Created in 1969 by the Cartagena Agreement and headquartered in Lima, Peru, it originally included Chile and at one time Venezuela, but both have since withdrawn.

***Anders* brief.** See BRIEF (1).

and his heirs. (15c) A term of art formerly required to transfer complete title (a fee simple absolute) to real estate <A conveys Blackacre to B and his heirs>. • This phrase originated in the translation of a Law French phrase used in medieval grants (*a lui et a ses heritiers pour toujours* "to him and his heirs forever"). See FEE SIMPLE.

"The development reached its culmination when the words 'and his heirs' in a transfer were thought to give full durational ownership to the immediate transferee and no ownership whatever to his heirs. This notion was expressed in the statement that the words 'and his heirs' are words of limitation and not words of purchase. They indicate the durational character of an estate, not its taker." Thomas F. Bergin & Paul G. Haskell, *Preface to Estates in Land and Future Interests* 93–94 (2d ed. 1984).

and other good and valuable consideration. See *other consideration* under CONSIDERATION (1).

androlepsia. See ANDROLEPSY.

androlepsy (**an**-drə-lep-see). [fr. Greek "seizure of men"] (18c) *Hist.* The taking by one country of citizens or subjects of another country either in reprisal or to enforce some claim (as to surrender or punish a fugitive). • Under this custom, the relatives of an Athenian citizen who was killed abroad, and whose killer was not extradited to Athens, were permitted to arrest up to three of the offending city's citizens to be held pending the killer's surrender or else tried in his stead. — Also termed (in Latin) *clarigatio.* — Also termed *androlepsia* (an-drə-**lep**-see-ə); (in Latin) *clarigatio.*

anecius (ə-**nee**-shee-əs), *n.* [Law Latin] *Hist.* The eldest; the firstborn; the senior, as contrasted with *puisne* ("the younger").

anew, *adj.* **1.** Over again; once more; afresh <let's start anew>. **2.** In a new and changed form <let's fashion this book anew>. • The word always implies some previous act or activity of the same kind.

angaria (ang-**gair**-ee-ə). [Greek] (16c) **1.** ANGARY. **2.** *Roman law. (ital.)* A compulsory service consisting in the transport of goods or persons for the imperial post; a public Pony Express rider. **3.** *Hist.* A service exacted by a lord beyond what is due. Pl. ***angariae.***

angary (**ang**-gə-ree). (1880) *Int'l law.* A country's right, in war or other urgent circumstances, to seize — for temporary use — neutral merchant ships in its inland or territorial waters as well as aircraft within its territory, with full indemnity by the country. — Also termed *right of angary; jus angariae; angaria.*

"In many respects the content and scope of the right of angary remain unclear and there is little evidence of State practice on several controversial questions. In practice, the right has been exercised mainly in wartime. Nevertheless, several writers consider it to be applicable in times of peace and in cases of absolute necessity, such as the evacuation of the population in the event of a national emergency." Rainer Lagoni, "Angary, Right of," in 1 *Encyclopedia of Public International Law* (1992).

angel. (1897) *Mergers & acquisitions.* An investor who infuses enough cash to close a deal or who comes in at the last minute to save a deal that otherwise would not close.

angel investor. See INVESTOR.

Anglicé (**ang**-glə-see), *adv.* [French] (16c) In English. • This term formerly appeared in pleadings to signal an English translation or restatement of a previous Latin word or phrase <*panis,* Anglicé, bread>.

Anglo-American common law. See *American common law* under COMMON LAW (2).

Anglo-Saxon law. (18c) The body of royal decrees and customary laws developed by the Germanic peoples who dominated England from the 5th century to 1066.

anhlote, *n.* (18c) *Hist.* A single tribute or tax paid according to custom, such as scot and lot. See SCOT AND LOT.

aniens. See ANIENTE.

aniente (**an**-ee-ənt *or* an-ee-**ent**), *adj.* [Law French] (Of a law, etc.) having no force or effect; void. — Also spelled *anient.* — Also termed *aniens.*

anilinctus. See ANILINGUS.

anilingus. The sexual act involving oral stimulation of another's anus. — Often misspelled *analingus.* — Also termed *anilinctus.*

animal. (14c) Any living creature (besides plants) other than a human being. — Also termed *creature.*

▸ **animal ferae naturae.** See *wild animal.*

▸ **animal mansuetae naturae.** See *domestic animal.*

▸ **dangerous animal.** (17c) An animal that has harmed or has threatened to harm a person or another animal.

▸ **domestic animal.** (17c) **1.** An animal that is customarily devoted to the service of humankind at the place where it normally lives, such as a dog or cat. See DOMITAE NATURAE; MANSUETAE NATURAE. **2.** Any animal that is statutorily so designated. — Also termed *animal mansuetae naturae.*

▸ **domesticated animal.** (18c) **1.** A wild animal that has been tamed. **2.** An animal that has customarily lived peaceably with people, such as farm animals and pets. See DOMITAE NATURAE.

▸ **feral animal.** (1877) A domestic animal that has returned to a wild state. • Feral animals, unlike others of their species, are usu. unsocialized to people.

▸ **game animal.** See GAME (1).

▸ **vicious animal.** (17c) **1.** An animal that has shown itself to be dangerous to humans. **2.** Loosely, one belonging to a breed or species that is known or reputed to be dangerous. • A vicious animal may be domestic, feral, or wild. See VICIOUS PROPENSITY.

▸ **wild animal.** (17c) **1.** An animal that is not customarily devoted to the service of humankind in the place where it normally lives, such as a bear or fox; esp., a type of animal that, as a matter of common knowledge, is naturally untamable, unpredictable, dangerous, or mischievous. See FERAE NATURAE. **2.** Any animal not statutorily designated as a domestic animal. — Also termed *wild creature; animal ferae naturae.*

"Wild creatures, such as game, are part of the land and pass with it, though it cannot be said that they are within the ownership of any particular person. Wild creatures which have been tamed belong to the person who has tamed them, and animals too young to escape belong to the owner of the land on which they are, but in each case the owner has only a qualified property in them, for the moment they gain or regain their natural liberty the ownership is lost." G.C. Cheshire, *Modern Law of Real Property* 118 (3d ed. 1933).

Animal and Plant Health Inspection Service. An agency in the U.S. Department of Agriculture responsible for controlling or eliminating pests and plant diseases by regulating the shipment of agricultural products within the United States. • Established in 1977, some of its functions were transferred to the U.S. Department of Homeland Security in 2003. — Abbr. APHIS.

animal cruelty. See CRUELTY.

animal enterprise. (1992) A commercial or academic undertaking or project that uses animals for research, testing, agriculture, or food and fiber production. • Because animal enterprises have sometimes been violently targeted by those who oppose the exploitation of animals, Congress enacted the Animal Enterprise Terrorism Act, 18 USCA § 43.

animal ferae naturae. See *wild animal* under ANIMAL.

animal law, *n.* (1902) The field of law dealing with vertebrates other than humans. • The field cuts across many traditional doctrinal areas (e.g., contracts, torts, administrative law) as well as jurisprudence. Topics include wildlife-management law, laws concerning treatment of laboratory animals, and laws relating to companion animals.

animal mansuetae naturae. See *domesticated animal* under ANIMAL.

animal research. (1910) Any test, study, experiment, procedure, or investigation in which one or more nonhuman creatures are subjected either to surgical, medical, biological, chemical, psychological, or physical treatment, or to abnormal environmental or dietary conditions.

animal rights, *n.* (1813) The idea or belief that people should treat animals well, esp. by not using them in tests to develop medicines or other products.

animo (**an**-ə-moh). [Latin] See ANIMUS (2).

animo et corpore (**an**-ə-moh et **kor**-pə-ree), *adv.* [Latin] By the mind and by the body; by the intention and by the physical act of control <possession is acquired *animo et corpore*>.

animo et facto (**an**-ə-moh et **fak**-toh), *adv.* [Latin] *Hist.* By act and intention.

> "Thus, for example, in acquiring a domicile, mere residence is not sufficient, if there be not the intention to acquire it, as domicile can only be acquired *animo et facto.*" John Trayner, *Trayner's Latin Maxims* 21 (4th ed. 1894).

animo felonico (**an**-ə-moh fə-**lon**-ə-koh), *adv.* [Latin] With felonious intent; with the intention to commit a felony.

animus (**an**-ə-məs). [Latin] (1816) **1.** Ill will; animosity.

▸ **class-based animus.** (1974) A prejudicial disposition toward a discernible, usu. constitutionally protected, group of persons. • A *class-based animus* is an essential element of a civil-rights conspiracy case.

2. Intention. • All the following Latin "animus" phrases have analogous adverbial forms beginning with "animo" (the definition merely needing "with" at the outset). For example, *animo furandi* means "with the intention to steal," *animo testandi* means "with testamentary intention," etc.

▸ ***animus adimendi*** (**an**-ə-məs ad-i-**men**-dɪ). [Latin] An intention to adeem.

▸ ***animus attestandi*** (**an**-i-məs a-tes-**tan**-dɪ). [Latin] (1903) An intention to bear witness. Cf. *animus testandi.*

▸ ***animus belligerendi*** (**an**-ə-məs bə-lij-ə-**ren**-dɪ). [Latin] An intention to wage war.

▸ ***animus cancellandi*** (**an**-ə-məs kan-sə-**lan**-dɪ). [Latin] An intention to cancel. • This phrase usu. refers to a will.

▸ ***animus capiendi*** (**an**-ə-məs kap-ee-**en**-dɪ). [Latin] An intention to take or capture.

▸ ***animus commerciandi*** (**an**-i-məs kə-mər-shee-**an**-dɪ). [Latin] *Hist.* An intention to trade.

▸ ***animus contrahentium*** (**an**-ə-məs kon-trə-**hen**-shee-əm). [Latin] The intention of the contracting parties.

▸ ***animus dedicandi*** (**an**-ə-məs ded-ə-**kan**-dɪ). [Latin] An intention to donate or dedicate.

▸ ***animus defamandi*** (**an**-ə-məs def-ə-**man**-dɪ). [Latin] An intention to defame.

▸ ***animus derelinquendi*** (**an**-ə-məs dee-rel-ing-**kwen**-dɪ). [Latin] An intention to abandon.

▸ ***animus deserendi*** (**an**-ə-məs des-ə-**ren**-dɪ). [Latin] An intention to desert (usu. a spouse, child, etc.).

▸ ***animus differendi*** (**an**-ə-məs dif-ə-**ren**-dɪ). [Latin] An intention to obtain a delay. • The phrase *animo differendi* ("with the intention to obtain a delay") appeared in reference to a presumption that certain actions of a defendant were designed to obtain a delay.

▸ ***animus disponendi*** (**an**-i-məs dis-pə-**nen**-dɪ). [Latin] *Hist.* Intention to dispose.

▸ ***animus domini*** (**an**-ə-məs **dom**-ə-nɪ). [Latin] *Roman law.* An intention to exercise dominion over a thing or to own it. Cf. *animus possidendi.*

> "All possession has two elements, a physical and a mental, which the Romans distinguish as corpus and animus. The first is the physical relation of the possessor to the object. The second is his sense of that relation. If he is minded to deal with the thing as his own (animus domini — animus sibi habendi), no matter whether rightfully or wrongfully, he possesses in the fullest sense." R.W. Lee, *The Elements of Roman Law* 179–80 (4th ed. 1956).

▸ ***animus donandi*** (**an**-ə-məs doh-**nan**-dɪ). [Latin] An intention of donating; the intention to give.

▸ ***animus et factum*** (**an**-ə-məs et **fak**-təm). [Latin "mind and deed"] The intention and the deed. • This phrase can refer to a person's intent to reside in a given country permanently or for an indefinite period.

▸ ***animus felonicus*** (**an**-ə-məs fe-**loh**-ni-kəs). [Latin] An intention to commit a felony.

▸ ***animus furandi*** (**an**-ə-məs fyuu-**ran**-dɪ). [Latin] An intention to steal. • In Roman law, the focus was on the unauthorized use of property rather than an intent to permanently deprive the owner of it.

> "[An] intent to deprive the owner of his property permanently, or an intent to deal with another's property unlawfully in such a manner as to create an obviously unreasonable risk of permanent deprivation, [is] all that is required to constitute the *animus furandi*—or intent to steal." Rollin M. Perkins & Ronald N. Boyce, *Criminal Law* 332–33 (3d ed. 1982).

▸ ***animus gerendi*** (**an**-ə-məs jə-**ren**-dɪ). [Latin] An intention to act as heir.

▸ ***animus immiscendi et adeundi hereditatem*** (**an**-ə-məs im-i-**sen**-dɪ et ad-ee-**ən**-dɪ hə-red-i-**tay**-təm). [Latin] An intention to meddle with and take up a succession.

▸ ***animus indorsandi*** (**an**-ə-məs in-dor-**san**-dɪ). [Law Latin] *Hist.* An intention to indorse. • One who indorsed a check *animo indorsandi* would be liable for the amount if the check was dishonored.

▸ ***animus injuriandi*** (**an**-ə-məs in-j[y]oor-ee-**an**-dɪ). [Latin] An intention to injure, esp. to insult.

▸ ***animus lucrandi*** (**an**-ə-məs loo-**kran**-dɪ). [Latin] An intention to make a gain or profit.

▸ ***animus malus*** (**an**-ə-məs **mal**-əs). [Latin] An evil intent.

▸ ***animus manendi*** (**an**-ə-məs mə-**nen**-dɪ). [Latin "will to remain"] An intention to remain; the intention to establish a permanent residence. — Also termed *animus remandendi.*

▸ ***animus morandi*** (**an**-ə-məs mə-**ran**-dɪ). [Latin "will to tarry"] An intention to remain. • Although *animus morandi* is broadly synonymous with *animus manendi, morandi* suggests less permanency.

▸ ***animus nocendi*** (**an**-ə-məs noh-**sen**-dɪ). [Latin] An intention to harm.

▸ ***animus obligandi*** (**an**-ə-məs ahb-li-**gan**-dɪ). [Latin] An intention to enter into an obligation.

▸ ***animus occidendi*** (**an**-ə-məs ahk-si-**den**-dɪ). [Latin] An intention to kill.

▸ ***animus occupandi*** (**an**-i-məs ok-yə-**pan**-dɪ). [Latin] *Hist.* Intention to occupy.

▸ ***animus possidendi*** (**an**-ə-məs pah-sə-**den**-dɪ). [Latin] *Roman law.* An intention to possess a thing. Cf. *animus domini.*

▸ ***animus quo*** (**an**-ə-məs **kwoh**). [Latin] An intention with which; motive.

▸ ***animus recipiendi*** (**an**-ə-məs ri-sip-ee-**en**-dɪ). [Latin] An intention to receive.

▸ ***animus recuperandi*** (**an**-ə-məs ri-k[y]oo-pə-**ran**-dɪ). [Latin] An intention to recover.

▸ ***animus remanendi*** (**an**-ə-məs rem-ə-**nen**-dɪ). [Latin] See *animus manendi.*

▸ ***animus republicandi*** (**an**-ə-məs ree-pub-lə-**kan**-dɪ). [Latin] An intention to republish.

▸ ***animus restituendi*** (**an**-ə-məs rə-sti-tyoo-**en**-dɪ). [Latin] An intention to restore.

▸ ***animus revertendi*** (**an**-ə-məs ree-vər-**ten**-dɪ). [Latin] (17c) An intention to return (to a place). • In Roman law, this intent was a factor in deciding whether animals, such as doves and bees, remained in a person's ownership.

▸ ***animus revocandi*** (**an**-ə-məs rev-oh-**kan**-dɪ). [Latin] An intention to revoke (a will) <her destruction of the will indicated that she had animus revocandi>.

▸ ***animus signandi*** (**an**-ə-məs sig-**nan**-dɪ). [Latin] An intention to sign.

▸ ***animus testandi*** (**an**-ə-məs tes-**tan**-dɪ). [Latin] Testamentary intention. Cf. *animus attestandi.*

▸ ***animus ulciscendi*** (**an**-ə-məs əl-si-**sen**-dɪ). [Latin] An intention to take revenge.

ankle bracelet. (1983) *Criminal law.* An electronic-monitoring device that alerts authorities if the wearer does any of various prohibited acts, such as violating restrictions on movement or consuming alcohol. • An ankle bracelet may be required as a condition of parole, probation, bail, or supervised release. See ELECTRONIC-MONITORING DEVICE; LOJACK (2).

annals, *n. pl.* [Latin pl. *annales* "chronicles" fr. *annus* "year"] (17c) The recorded history of something; specif., an account of events in chronological order, each event being recorded under the year in which it occurred <the worst outrage in the annals of crime>.

Annapolis. See UNITED STATES NAVAL ACADEMY.

annates (**an**-ayts *or* **an**-its), *n. pl.* [fr. Law Latin *annata*] See FIRST FRUITS (2).

annats (**an**-əts), *n. pl.* Annates. See FIRST FRUITS (2).

annex, *n.* (16c) Something that is attached to something else, such as a document to a report or an addition to a building. — Also spelled (esp. BrE) *annexe.*

annexable, *adj.* (17c) **1.** Capable of being attached to (something written) at the end; attachable. **2.** Capable of being joined into a larger unit or entity, often in a subordinate capacity; able to be incorporated.

annexation, *n.* (17c) **1.** The act of attaching; the quality, state, or condition of being attached. **2.** *Property.* The point at which a fixture becomes a part of the realty to which it is attached. **3.** A formal act by which a country, state, or municipality incorporates land within its dominion. • In international law, the usual formalities of announcing annexation involve having specially commissioned officers hoist the national flag and read a proclamation. **4.** The annexed land itself. Cf. ACCESSION (5). — **annex,** *vb.*

▸ **cherry-stem annexation.** (1995) **1.** Annexed land that resembles (on a map) a cherry because the annexed territory — the cherry — is not contiguous to the acquiring municipality, and the narrow corridor of annexed land leading to the targeted area resembles a stem. **2.** The process of annexing land with this configuration.

annexe. See ANNEX.

anniversary date. (1900) *Insurance.* The annually recurring date of the initial issuance of a policy. Cf. POLICY YEAR.

ann, jour, et wast (an, zhoor, ay wayst). [Law French] See YEAR, DAY, AND WASTE.

anno ante Christum (**an**-oh **an**-tee **kris**-təm), *adv.* [Latin] In the year before Christ. — Abbr. A.A.C.

anno ante Christum natum (**an**-oh **an**-tee **kris**-təm **nay**-təm), *adv.* [Latin] In the year before the birth of Christ. — Abbr. A.A.C.N.

Anno Domini (**an**-oh **dom**-ə-nɪ *or* -nee). [Latin "in the year of the Lord"] (16c) Since the supposed year in which Jesus Christ was born; of the current era <A.D. 1776>. — Abbr. A.D. — Also termed *in the year of Our Lord.*

annonae civiles (ə-**noh**-nee sə-**vɪ**-leez), *n.* [Latin] *Hist.* Yearly rents issuing out of particular lands and payable to certain monasteries.

anno orbis conditi (**an**-oh **or**-bis **kon**-di-tɪ), *n.* [Latin] The year of the creation of the world. — Abbr. AOC.

Anno Regni (**an**-oh **reg**-nɪ). [Latin] In the year of the reign. • A.R.V.R. 22, for example, is an abbreviated reference to *Anno Regni Victoriae Reginae vicesimo secundo* ("in the twenty-second year of the reign of Queen Victoria"). — Abbr. A.R.

annotatio (an-oh-**tay**-shee-oh). [Latin] RESCRIPT (3).

annotation (an-ə-**tay**-shən), *n.* (15c) **1.** A brief summary of the facts and decision in a case, esp. one involving statutory interpretation. **2.** A note that explains or criticizes a source of law, usu. a case. • Annotations appear, for example, in the *United States Code Annotated* (USCA). **3.** A volume containing such explanatory or critical notes. **4.** RESCRIPT (3). Cf. NOTE (2). — **annotate** (**an**-ə-tayt), *vb.* — **annotative** (**an**-ə-tay-tiv), *adj.* — **annotator** (**an**-ə-tay-tər), *n.*

> "One of the most important classes of Search Books is those included in the category of Annotations. They are important and valuable, in that they often purport to give, in very condensed form, some indication of the law, deduced from the cases or statutes, as well as to point out where similar cases can be found." William M. Lile et al., *Brief Making and the Use of Law Books* 84 (Roger W. Cooley & Charles Lesley Ames eds., 3d ed. 1914).

announce, *vb.* (15c) To make publicly known; to proclaim formally <the judge announced her decision in open court>.

announcement of readiness. (1922) **1.** Counsel's statement made to the court that his or her side is prepared to begin a proceeding, esp. trial. **2.** *Criminal law.* The prosecution's written statement, sent both to the court and to defense counsel, that the prosecution is prepared to proceed to trial — commonly required to comply with a speedy-trial statute.

annoyance. See NUISANCE (1).

annual, *adj.* (14c) **1.** Occurring once every year; yearly <annual meeting>. **2.** Of, relating to, or involving a period of one year <annual income>.

annual account. See *intermediate account* under ACCOUNT.

annual crops. See CROPS.

annual depreciation. See DEPRECIATION.

annual exclusion. See EXCLUSION (1).

annual gift-tax exclusion. See *annual exclusion* (1) under EXCLUSION (1).

annual leave. See VACATION (1).

annual meeting. See MEETING.

annual message. See MESSAGE.

annual percentage rate. See INTEREST RATE.

annual permit. (1902) A permit, required by some states, that must be renewed each year by a corporation that does business in the state. • In some states, the permit fee is set according to the corporation's capitalization.

annual report. (18c) A yearly corporate financial report for shareholders and other interested parties. • The Securities Exchange Act of 1934 requires registered corporations to file an annual report on the SEC's Form 10-K. An annual report includes a balance sheet, income statement, statement of changes in financial position, reconciliation of changes in owners' equity accounts, a summary of significant accounting principles, other explanatory notes, the auditor's report, and comments from management about prospects for the coming year. — Also termed *annual statement*; *financial report.*

annual statement. See ANNUAL REPORT.

annual value. See VALUE (2).

annua pensione. See DE ANNUA PENSIONE.

annuitant (ə-**n[y]oo**-ə-tənt), *n.* (18c) A beneficiary of an annuity.

annuity (ə-**n[y]oo**-ə-tee). (15c) **1.** An obligation to pay a stated sum, usu. monthly or annually, to a stated recipient. • These payments terminate upon the death of the designated beneficiary. **2.** A fixed sum of money payable periodically; specif., a particular amount of money that is paid each year to someone, usu. until death. **3.** A right, often acquired under a life-insurance contract, to receive fixed payments periodically for a specified duration. Cf. (for senses 1–3) PENSION (1), (3). **4.** *Patents.* MAINTENANCE FEE (4). **5.** A savings account with an insurance company or investment company, usu. established for retirement income. • Payments into the account accumulate tax-free, and the account is taxed only when the annuitant withdraws money in retirement.

▸ **annuity certain.** (18c) An annuity payable over a specified period, regardless of whether the annuitant dies before the period ends. — Also termed *term annuity.*

▸ **annuity due.** (18c) An annuity that makes payments at the beginning of each pay period. Cf. *ordinary annuity.*

▸ **cash-refund annuity.** (1941) See *refund annuity.*

▸ **constituted annuity.** (1858) *Louisiana law.* An annuity that has a maximum duration of 10 years and, under some circumstances, can be redeemed before the term's expiration. La. Civ. Code art. 2796.

▸ **contingent annuity.** (18c) **1.** An annuity that begins making payments when some future event occurs, such as the death of a person other than the annuitant. **2.** An annuity that makes an uncertain number of payments, depending on the outcome of a future event.

▸ **continuing annuity.** See *survivorship annuity.*

▸ **deferred annuity.** (1911) An annuity that begins making payments on a specified date if the annuitant is alive at that time. — Also termed *deferred-payment annuity.* Cf. *immediate annuity.*

▸ **fixed annuity.** (18c) An annuity that guarantees fixed payments, either for life or for a specified period.

▸ **group annuity.** (1939) An annuity payable to members of a group, esp. employees, who are covered by a single annuity contract, such as a group pension plan.

▸ **immediate annuity.** (1884) An annuity paid for with a single premium and that begins to pay benefits within the first payment interval. Cf. *deferred annuity.*

▸ **joint annuity.** (18c) An annuity payable to two annuitants until one of them dies, at which time the annuity terminates for the survivor (unless the annuity also provides for survivorship rights). See *survivorship annuity.*

▸ **life annuity.** (18c) An annuity payable only during the annuitant's lifetime, even if the annuitant dies prematurely.

▸ **life-income period-certain annuity.** An annuity that pays a specified number of payments even if the annuitant dies before the minimum amount has been paid.

▸ **nonrefund annuity.** (1939) An annuity with guaranteed payments during the annuitant's life, but with no refund to anyone at death. — Also termed *straight life annuity*; *pure annuity.* Cf. *refund annuity.*

▸ **ordinary annuity.** (1927) An annuity that makes payments at the end of each pay period. Cf. *annuity due.*

▸ **private annuity.** (18c) An annuity from a private source rather than from a public or life-insurance company.

▸ **pure annuity.** See *nonrefund annuity.*

▸ **refund annuity.** (1937) An annuity that, upon the annuitant's death, pays to the annuitant's estate the difference between the purchase price and the total payments received during the annuitant's lifetime. — Also termed *cash-refund annuity.* Cf. *nonrefund annuity.*

▸ **retirement annuity.** (1928) An annuity that begins making payments only after the annuitant's retirement. • If the annuitant dies before retirement, an agreed amount will usu. be refunded to the annuitant's estate.

▸ **single-premium deferred annuity.** (1943) An annuity for which a party pays a lump-sum premium in exchange for receiving a specified sum at a future date. • The income earned on the investment is tax-free until it is withdrawn. — Abbr. SPDA.

▸ **straight annuity.** (1932) An annuity that makes payments in fixed amounts at periodic intervals. Cf. *variable annuity.*

▸ **straight life annuity.** See *nonrefund annuity.*

▸ **survivorship annuity.** (1894) An annuity providing for continued payments to a survivor, usu. a spouse, after the original annuitant dies. — Also termed *continuing annuity.*

▸ **tax-deferred annuity.** See *403(b) plan* under EMPLOYEE BENEFIT PLAN.

▸ **tax-sheltered annuity.** See *403(b) plan* under EMPLOYEE BENEFIT PLAN.

▸ **term annuity.** See *annuity certain.*

▸ **variable annuity.** (1957) An annuity that makes payments in varying amounts depending on the success of the underlying investment strategy. See *variable annuity contract* under CONTRACT. Cf. *straight annuity.*

annuity bond. See BOND (3).

annuity depreciation method. See DEPRECIATION METHOD.

annuity insurance. See INSURANCE.

annuity policy. (1890) An insurance policy providing for monthly or periodic payments to the insured to begin at a fixed date and continue through the insured's life.

annuity trust. See TRUST (3).

annulment (ə-**nəl**-mənt), *n.* (15c) **1.** The act of nullifying or making void; VOIDANCE. **2.** A judicial or ecclesiastical declaration that a marriage is void. • An annulment establishes that the marital status never existed. So annulment and dissolution of marriage (or divorce) are fundamentally different: an annulment renders a marriage void from the beginning, while dissolution of marriage terminates the marriage as of the date of the judgment of dissolution. Although a marriage terminated by annulment is considered never to have occurred, under modern ecclesiastical law and in most states today a child born during the marriage is not considered illegitimate after the annulment. — Also termed *marital annulment*; *declaration of invalidity of marriage.* Cf. DIVORCE.

▸ **postmortem annulment.** An annulment of a deceased person's marriage at the request of a third party on grounds that made the marriage void from the beginning. • Who may seek a postmortem annulment and the grounds are prescribed by statute. Third parties may include executors and interested relatives of the deceased. Grounds may include bigamy, lack of capacity to consent to marry, or consent obtained by force, duress, or fraud.

3. A rescission. See RESCIND (3). — **annul** (ə-**nəl**), *vb.*

annulment of adoption. See ABROGATION OF ADOPTION.

annulment of judgment. (1832) A retroactive obliteration of a judicial decision, having the effect of restoring the parties to their pretrial positions. • Types of annulment include reversal and vacation. See REVERSE; VACATE (1).

annum luctus (**an**-əm **lək**-təs), *n.* [Latin "year of mourning"] (17c) *Roman law.* The year following the death of a married man during which his widow could not remarry, because of the confusion that would ensue in determining the parentage of a child born a few months after a second marriage within that year. — Also sometimes termed *year in mourning.*

annus (**an**-əs). [Latin] A year.

annus continuus (**an**-əs kən-**tin**-yoo-əs). [Latin "a continuous year"] *Roman law.* A straight 365-day period, without interruption. Cf. ANNUS UTILIS.

annus deliberandi (**an**-əs də-lib-ə-**ran**-dɪ). [Latin "the year for deliberating"] (17c) *Scots law.* The year during which an heir could determine whether to enter an inheritance and represent an ancestor. The period was later shortened to six months. See DAMNOSA AUT LUCROSA.

> "The entry of an heir infers serious responsibilities, and therefore the year is allowed for consideration. The *annus deliberandi* commences on the death of the ancestor, unless in the case of a posthumous heir, in which case the year runs from the heir's birth." William Bell, *Bell's Dictionary and Digest of the Law of Scotland* 47 (George Watson ed., 7th ed. 1890).

annus, dies, et vastum (**an**-əs, **dɪ**-eez, et **vas**-təm). [Law Latin] See YEAR, DAY, AND WASTE.

annus et dies (**an**-əs et **dɪ**-eez). [Law Latin] A year and a day. See YEAR-AND-A-DAY RULE.

annus utilis (**an**-əs **yoo**-tə-lis). [Latin "a year that can be used"] (18c) *Roman law.* A 365-day period during which legal rights could be exercised, not including days when the courts were closed or when a person could not otherwise pursue those rights; a year made up of the available days for conducting legal business. Cf. ANNUS CONTINUUS.

annuus reditus (**an**-əs **red**-ə-təs). [Law Latin] (17c) A yearly rent.

ANO. *abbr.* Affirmed, no opinion.

anomalous endorsement. See *irregular indorsement* under INDORSEMENT.

anomalous indorsement. See *irregular indorsement* under INDORSEMENT.

anomalous jurisdiction. See JURISDICTION.

anomalous-jurisdiction rule (ə-**nom**-ə-ləs). (1991) The principle that a court of appeals has provisional jurisdiction to review the denial of a motion to intervene in a case, and if the court of appeals finds that the denial was correct, then its jurisdiction disappears — and it must dismiss the appeal for want of jurisdiction — because an order denying a motion to intervene is not a final, appealable order. • This rule has been criticized by courts and commentators. Many appellate courts, upon finding that the trial court properly denied a motion to intervene, will affirm the denial instead of dismissing the appeal for want of jurisdiction. — Sometimes shortened to *anomalous rule*.

anomalous plea. See PLEA (3).

anomalous pleading. See PLEADING (1).

anomalous rule. See ANOMALOUS-JURISDICTION RULE.

a non domino (ay non **dom**-ə-noh). [Law Latin] *Hist.* From one who is not the proprietor.

a non habente potestatem (ay non ha-**ben**-tee poh-tes-**tay**-təm). [Latin] *Scots law.* From one not having power. • This phrase appeared most commonly in a conveyance in reference to a seller who was not the owner.

> "If A. disponed ground, which he held on a personal title, to B., he could not grant warrant for the infeftment of B., himself being uninfeft; but he could assign to B. the unexecuted precept of sasine in his (A.'s) own favour, and on it B. could complete his feudal title. If, instead of thus assigning a valid precept, A. himself granted a precept for the infeftment of B., such a precept was *a non habente potestatem*, and ineffectual. This was a defect, however, which was remedied by prescription." John Trayner, *Trayner's Latin Maxims* 5 (4th ed. 1894).

anonymous, *adj.* (17c) Not named or identified <the police arrested the defendant after a tip from an anonymous informant>. — **anonymity** (an-ə-**nim**-ə-tee), *n.*

anonymous case. (17c) A reported case in which the word "anonymous" is substituted for at least one party's name to conceal the party's identity. *See, e.g., Anonymous v. Anonymous*, 735 N.Y.S.2d 26 (App. Div. 2001).

anonymous jury. See JURY.

anonymous work. See WORK (2).

anoysance (ə-**noy**-zənts), *n.* [Law French] *Hist.* An annoyance or nuisance. See NUISANCE.

ANSI. *abbr.* AMERICAN NATIONAL STANDARDS INSTITUTE.

answer, *n.* (bef. 12c) **1.** A defendant's first pleading that addresses the merits of the case, usu. by denying the plaintiff's allegations. • An answer usu. sets forth the defendant's defenses and counterclaims.

▸ **false answer.** (18c) A sham answer in a pleading. See *sham pleading* under PLEADING (1).

2. A person's, esp. a witness's, response to a question posed.

▸ **evasive answer.** (17c) A response that neither directly admits nor denies a question. • In discovery, this is considered a failure to answer. Fed. R. Civ. P. 37(a)(3).

▸ **nonresponsive answer.** See *unresponsive answer.*

▸ **unresponsive answer.** (1891) *Evidence.* A response from a witness (usu. at a deposition or hearing) that is irrelevant to the question asked. — Also termed *nonresponsive answer.*

3. *Patents.* A patent applicant's response to an office action.

answer, *vb.* (12c) **1.** To respond to a question, a pleading, or a discovery request <the company failed to answer the interrogatories within 30 days>. **2.** To assume the liability of another <a guarantor answers for another person's debt>. **3.** To pay (a debt or other liability) <she promised to answer damages out of her own estate>.

answerable, *adj.* (16c) **1.** Required to explain one's actions to someone with more authority <the committee is answerable to the CEO>. **2.** Capable of being replied to accurately and intelligently; having a correct response <answerable questions>. **3.** Giving rise to enforceable liabilities; certain to incur legal responsibility <torts answerable in damages>.

answer date. See *answer day* under DAY.

answer day. See DAY.

answer in subsidium. (1840) *Hist.* In equity pleading, an answer supporting a plea.

antagonist (an-**tag**-ə-nist), *n.* (17c) One's opponent in a competition, battle, quarrel, litigation, etc.

antapocha (ant-**ap**-ə-kə). [Latin "counter-receipt"] (16c) *Roman & civil law.* A counterpart to a receipt (i.e., an *apocha*), signed by the debtor and delivered to the creditor as proof of payment. Cf. APOCHA.

ante (**an**-tee), *prep.* [Latin] Before. Cf. POST.

antea (**an**-tee-ə), *adv.* [Latin] Formerly; heretofore.

antebellum (an-tee-**bel**-əm), *adj.* (1862) Existing or occurring before a war, esp. the American Civil War (1861–1865) <the antebellum laws in the South>.

antecedent (an-tə-**see**-dənt), *adj.* (14c) Earlier; preexisting; previous. — **antecedent** (preceding thing), *n.* — **antecedence** (quality, state, or condition of going before), *n.*

antecedent basis. (1941) *Patents.* A general word or phrase in a patent claim or description to which a later specific word or phrase must refer. • Claims will be rejected as impermissibly vague or indefinite if the latter word is not clearly connected to its antecedent, because the wording becomes ambiguous. In general, a term is first introduced with an indefinite article and is later referred to with the definite article (or *said*).

antecedent character. (1817) *Criminal law.* A person's reputation as to honesty, reliability, and temperament before the commission or alleged commission of a criminal offense.

antecedent claim. (17c) A preexisting claim. • Under the UCC, a holder takes an instrument for value if it is taken for an antecedent claim. UCC § 3-303.

antecedent crime. See PRIOR CONVICTION.

antecedent debt. See DEBT.

antecedent offense. See PRIOR CONVICTION.

antecessor (an-tə-**ses**-ər *or* **an**-tə-ses-ər), *n.* [Latin] (15c) **1.** *Roman law.* A professor of law. **2.** *Hist.* An ancestor. **3.** *Hist.* A predecessor to an office.

antedate (**an**-ti-dayt), *vb.* (16c) **1.** To affix with a date earlier than the true date; BACKDATE (1) <antedate a check>. **2.** To precede in time; to occur, live, or be made earlier in history than something else <the doctrine antedates the *Smith* case by many years>. — Also termed *predate.* Cf. POSTDATE. — **antedate,** *n.*

antedating a reference. See ANTEDATING OF A PRIOR-ART REFERENCE.

antedating of a prior-art reference. (1990) *Patents.* The removal of a publication, a U.S. patent, or a foreign patent cited as prior art against the application by filing an affidavit or declaration establishing the applicant's completion of the invention in this country, or in another NAFTA or WTO member country, before the effective date of the cited reference. • The term applies only to U.S. patent applications. An issued patent may also antedate a prior-art reference if the conception predates the prior art and the inventor used due diligence in reducing the concept to practice. — Also termed *antedating a reference; swearing behind a prior-art reference; carrying back the date of invention.*

ante exhibitionem billae (**an**-tee ek-si-bish-ee-**oh**-nəm **bil**-ee). Before the exhibition of the bill; i.e., before a suit has begun.

ante factum. (17c) A thing done before; a previous act or fact. — Also spelled *ante-factum.*

ante hoc (an-tee **hok**). [Latin] Before this.

ante litem. [Latin] (18c) Before litigation.

ante litem motam (**an**-tee **lɪ**-tem **moh**-təm). [Law Latin "before the lawsuit was started"] (18c) *Hist.* Before an action has been raised; before a legal dispute arose — i.e., at a time when the declarant had no motive to lie. • This phrase was generally used in reference to the evidentiary requirement that the acts on which an action is based occur before the action is brought. In Scotland, the phrase also referred to the obligation of an estate intromitter to become confirmed as executor of the estate before a creditor could sue the estate. Otherwise, the intromitter could be held personally liable for the decedent's debts. — Sometimes shortened to *ante litem.*

ante meridiem (**an**-tee mə-**rid**-ee-əm). [Latin] (16c) Before noon. — Abbr. a.m.; A.M.

antemortem (**an**-tee **mor**-təm). [Latin] (17c) Before death.

antemortem interest. [Latin] (1961) An interest existing before (but not after) a transferor's death.

antemortem probate. See PROBATE (1).

antemortem statement. See *dying declaration* under DECLARATION (6).

antenatus (**an**-tee-**nay**-təs). [Law Latin] A person born before a certain political event that affected the person's political rights; esp., a person born before the signing of the Declaration of Independence. Cf. POSTNATUS. Pl. ***antenati.***

antenuptial (an-ti-**nəp**-shəl), *adj.* See PRENUPTIAL.

antenuptial agreement. See PRENUPTIAL AGREEMENT.

antenuptial contract. See PRENUPTIAL AGREEMENT.

antenuptial gift. See *prenuptial gift* under GIFT.

antenuptial will. See *prenuptial will* under WILL.

ante omnia (**an**-tee **ahm**-nee-ə). [Latin] *Hist.* **1.** Before anything else is done; first of all. • Objections that could bar the litigation were usu. discussed *ante omnia.* **2.** Above all other things.

ante redditas rationes (**an**-tee **red**-ə-tas ray-shee-**oh**-nis *or* rash-). [Law Latin] (17c) *Scots law.* Before accounts are rendered. • A tutor could not file an action against a minor to recover payments unless the tutor first provided an accounting of the ward's estate.

anthropometry (an-thrə-**pom**-ə-tree). (1839) A system of measuring the human body, esp. the size relationships among the different parts. • Before the advent of fingerprinting, minute measurements of the human body — taken and compared to other persons' measurements — were used to identify criminals and deceased persons. Cf. BERTILLON SYSTEM. — **anthropometric** (an-thrə-pə-**met**-trik), *adj.*

anti-antisuit injunction. See INJUNCTION.

Anti-Assignment Act. A federal statute prohibiting the assignment or transfer of claims against the United States. 31 USCA § 3727. — Abbr. AAA.

anti-assignment-in-gross rule. (1985) *Trademarks.* The doctrine that an assignment of a mark without the goodwill symbolized by the mark is invalid. • Although trademark rights are not destroyed when a mark is assigned in gross, the failure of the assignor to continue to use the mark, coupled with an ineffective transfer, may result in abandonment. See *assignment in gross* under ASSIGNMENT (2).

anti-bias rule. See BIAS RULE (1).

antibootleg, *adj.* (1994) *Copyright.* Of, relating to, or involving an effort to combat or discourage illegal recording, distribution, and sale of unauthorized reproductions of live and broadcast performances. • The federal antibootleg statute, 18 USCA § 2319A, and the antibootleg statutes of several states criminalize bootlegging activities. See ANTIBOOTLEG STATUTE. — **antibootlegging,** *adj.* & *n.*

antibootlegging statute. See ANTIBOOTLEG STATUTE.

antibootleg statute. (1994) *Copyright.* A law, esp. a state law, that prohibits making, distributing, or selling an unauthorized recording of a live performance. — Also termed *antibootlegging statute.*

antichoice, *adj.* See PRO-LIFE.

antichresis (an-ti-**kree**-sis). [Latin "in place of interest"] (16c) *Roman & civil law.* A mortgage in which the mortgagee retains possession of the mortgaged property and takes the fruits (such as rents) of the property in lieu of interest on the debt. La. Civ. Code art. 3176.

> "Under the Civil Code of Louisiana, taken from the Code Napoleon, there are two kinds of pledges: the pawn, when a movable is given as security, and the *antichresis,* when the security given consists in immovables or real estate. Under the latter the creditor acquires the right to take the rents and profits of the land, and to credit, annually, the same to the interest, and the surplus to the principal of the debt, and is bound to keep the estate in repair, and to pay the taxes. Upon default upon the part of the debtor, the creditor may prosecute the debtor, and obtain a decree for selling the land pledged." 3 James Kent, *Commentaries on American Law* *403–04 (George Comstock ed., 11th ed. 1866).

antichurning rule. (1977) *Tax.* A statutory or regulatory provision that denies certain tax advantages, esp. accelerated depreciation and amortization schedules, to taxpayers who acquire property in a transaction that does not result in a significant change in the property's ownership or use. See CHURNING (2).

anticipated, *adj. Patents.* (Of a patent claim) having all the same elements of a prior-art reference. • If a claim is anticipated by a previous invention or publication, that claim is not allowable; if a patent has already been issued it will be declared invalid. — Also termed *fully met.*

anticipated compromis. See *general compromis* under COMPROMIS (1).

anticipation. **1.** The distribution or receipt of trust income before it is due. **2.** *Patents.* The prior invention or disclosure of the claimed invention by another, or the inventor's own disclosure of the claimed invention by publication, sale, or offer to sell if that disclosure predates the date of the patent-application filing by more than one year. • By disproving the claim's novelty, anticipation bars the allowance of a claim and provides a defense to an action for infringement based on that claim. See NOVELTY; *prior art* under ART (3). — **anticipate,** *vb.*

> "Anticipation implies spoiling something for someone, by getting in ahead; obviously this can only be done *by* a device (or description of a device), and only *to* a patent." Roger Sherman Hoar, *Patent Tactics and Law* 51 (3d ed. 1950).

anticipatory breach. See BREACH OF CONTRACT.

anticipatory filing. (1975) The bringing of a lawsuit or regulatory action against another with the expectation that the other party is preparing an action of its own. • If properly brought, an anticipatory filing may determine procedural matters such as jurisdiction and venue. See FIRST-TO-FILE RULE; RACE TO THE COURTHOUSE.

anticipatory nuisance. See NUISANCE.

anticipatory offense. See *inchoate offense* under OFFENSE (2).

anticipatory refutation. See REFUTATION.

anticipatory replication. See REPLICATION.

anticipatory repudiation. See REPUDIATION.

anticipatory search warrant. See SEARCH WARRANT.

anticipatory self-defense. See *preemptive self-defense* under SELF-DEFENSE (2).

anticircumvention device. (1999) *Copyright.* An apparatus designed to prevent users from bypassing, avoiding, removing, deactivating, or impairing a technological measure that controls access to a work protected by copyright; an apparatus in a media player or receiver, such as a DVD or a TV satellite dish, designed to prevent unauthorized use or duplication of copyrighted material.

anticompetitive, *adj.* (1891) Having a tendency to reduce or eliminate competition. • This term describes the type of conduct or circumstances generally targeted by antitrust laws. Cf. PROCOMPETITIVE.

anticompetitive conduct. (1940) *Antitrust.* An act that harms or seeks to harm the market or the process of competition among businesses, and that has no legitimate business purpose.

anticontest clause. See NO-CONTEST CLAUSE.

Anticounterfeiting Consumer Protection Act. *Intellectual property.* A federal law to discourage counterfeiting of trademarks and copyrighted merchandise such as computer programs, phonorecords, and motion pictures. • The law imposes criminal liability for trafficking in counterfeit goods and services (18 USCA § 2318), provides for the seizure of counterfeit goods (15 USCA § 1116 (d) (9)), and provides enhanced statutory civil penalties (15 USCA § 1117(c)). — Abbr. ACPA.

Anticybersquatting Consumer Protection Act. *Trademarks.* A 1999 federal law authorizing a trademark owner to obtain a federal-court order transferring ownership of a domain name from a cybersquatter to the trademark owner. • A mark's owner must show that (1) the mark and the domain name are identical or confusingly similar, (2) the mark was distinctive when the domain name was first registered, (3) the trademark's owner used the mark commercially before the domain name was registered, and (4) the domain registrant acted in bad faith and intended to profit from the trademark's use. Registering a domain name with the intent to sell it to the trademark owner is presumptively an act of bad faith. But if a defendant can prove a legitimate reason for the domain-name registration, the defendant may be allowed to keep the name. — Abbr. ACPA. — Also termed *Trademark Cyberpiracy Prevention Act.*

antideficiency legislation. See LEGISLATION (3).

antideficiency statute. See *antideficiency legislation* under LEGISLATION (3).

antidestructibility statute. See DESTRUCTIBILITY OF CONTINGENT REMAINDERS.

antidestruction clause. (1985) A provision in a security protecting a shareholder's conversion rights, in the event of a merger, by granting the shareholder a right to convert the securities into the securities that will replace the company's stock when the merger is complete. See *convertible security* under SECURITY (4).

antidesuetude canon. See DESUETUDE CANON.

antidilution act. (1956) *Trademarks.* A statute prohibiting actions that are likely to lessen, diminish, or erode a famous mark's capacity to identify and distinguish goods and services, without regard to whether the action creates a likelihood of confusion, mistake, or deception. • The Federal Trademark Dilution Act provides relief against another's commercial use of a mark or tradename that dilutes the distinctive quality of a famous mark. More than half the states also have antidilution statutes, which are based on the International Trademark Association's 1964 Model State Trademark Bill. — Also termed *antidilution statute.*

antidilution provision. (1959) A convertible-security provision that safeguards the conversion privilege from share splits, share dividends, or other transactions that might affect the conversion ratio. See CONVERSION RATIO; DILUTION (2).

antidilution statute. See ANTIDILUTION ACT.

antidiscrimination convention. See CONVENTION (1).

antidiscrimination statute. (1901) A legislative enactment making specified forms of discrimination unlawful, esp. on the basis of sex, color, ethnic or national origin, disability, age, marital status, pregnancy, family responsibilities, sexual orientation, political opinion, or religion.

antidissection rule. (1987) *Trademarks.* A rule, applied in comparing potentially conflicting marks, that requires that the marks be compared as a whole or as they are viewed by consumers in the marketplace, not broken down into their component parts. • The antidissection rule does not preclude an analysis of the dominant and subordinate features of a mark to determine which features of the mark make the most significant impression on consumers, but the mark must still be considered in its entirety. See TOUT ENSEMBLE.

antidumping duty. See *antidumping tariff* under TARIFF (2).

antidumping law. (1917) A statute designed to protect domestic companies by preventing the sale of foreign goods at less than fair value, as defined in the statute (for example, at a price below that of the domestic market). See DUMPING.

antidumping tariff. See TARIFF (2).

anti-evolution statute. (1925) *Hist.* A law that forbids the teaching of the theory of evolution in schools. • Such statutes were held unconstitutional as violative of the Establishment Clause in *Epperson v. Arkansas*, 393 U.S. 97, 89 S.Ct. 266 (1968). — Also termed *evolution statute*. See CREATIONISM.

antifederalism. (18c) A political movement opposed to strengthening the federal government.

antifederalist. (1787) **1.** A person who opposes strengthening the federal goverment. **2.** (*usu. cap.*) *Hist.* A person who opposed the ratification of the United States Constitution. • The Antifederalists feared that a strong federal government would become a disguised monarchy, diminish the sovereignty of the states, and threaten newly gained liberties. **3.** (*cap.*) *Hist.* A member of the Antifederal Party, founded by Thomas Jefferson to oppose extension of the federal government's powers.

> "To the Antifederalists the Constitution represented a repudiation of everything that Americans had fought for. They could not have made a more severe or more accurate condemnation of the new government than to charge that it 'departed widely from the principles and political faith of '76.' In the context of conventional eighteenth-century political thought the Constitution obviously represented a reinforcement of '*energy*' at the expense of '*liberty*,' a startling strengthening of the rulers' power at the expense of the people's participation in the government. For the Antifederalists the same radical Whig terms that earlier had been used against the British monarchy were still applicable, terms that had been incorporated into America's Revolutionary constitutions. 'Poor little humble republican maxims have attracted the admiration, and engaged the attention, of the virtuous and wise in all nations, and have stood the shock of ages.' Now the Federalists were attempting to deny the validity of these principles that English Whigs had delighted in; they were deserting 'those maxims which alone can preserve liberty' in favor of newer, more refined maxims 'which tend to the prostration of republicanism.' Had the Constitution, the Antifederalists correctly pointed out time and again, 'been presented to our view ten years ago, . . . it would have been considered as containing principles incompatible with republican liberty, and therefore doomed to infamy.'" Gordon S. Wood, *The Creation of the American Republic, 1776-1787* 523 (1969) (citations omitted).

antiforensics. (2002) The use of tools or methods to erase or alter electronically stored data, usu. in an effort to frustrate examination. — Also written *anti-forensics*.

antiformalism. An interpretive method that permits, or even encourages, a judge to consider nontextual sources such as abstract purpose, legislative intent, and public policy when interpreting a statute, thereby giving the courts more discretion to make or create law. See REALISM. Cf. FORMALISM; PURPOSIVISM; CONSEQUENTIALISM (2). — **antiformalist,** *n.*

antifraud rule. See RULE 10B-5.

antigraph (**an**-ti-graf). (17c) *Archaic.* A copy, counterpart, or transcript of a written instrument, such as a deed.

antigraphus (an-**tig**-rə-fəs), *n.* [Law Latin] (17c) *Hist.* An officer who maintains tax revenues; a comptroller.

antiharassment order. See ORDER (2).

antihazing statute. (1988) A (usu. criminal) law that prohibits an organization, or members of an organization, from requiring a prospective member, as a condition of membership, to do or submit to any act that presents a substantial risk of physical or mental harm. • In 1874 Congress passed the first antihazing statute, directed at stopping hazing by midshipmen at the United States Naval Academy. Most states have passed their own antihazing statutes. — Also termed *hazing statute*.

anti-heartbalm statute. See HEARTBALM STATUTE.

Anti-Injunction Act. A federal statute providing that a federal court may not enjoin state-court proceedings unless an injunction is (1) expressly authorized by Congress, (2) necessary for the federal court's in rem jurisdiction, or (3) necessary to prevent relitigation of a judgment rendered by the federal court. 28 USCA § 2283. See NORRIS–LA GUARDIA ACT.

anti-irrepealability canon. See REPEALABILITY CANON.

antijohn law. (1979) A criminal-law statute punishing prostitutes' customers.

antilapse statute. (1937) *Wills & estates.* A statute that substitutes certain heirs of some types of testamentary beneficiaries when the beneficiary has predeceased the testator, allowing those heirs to take the gift that would otherwise fail and hence pass to the residuary beneficiary (if any) or to the intestate heirs. • Under the common law and the laws of all states, a testamentary beneficiary must survive a testator, or else the gift is said to lapse. The term *antilapse* is a misnomer because the statute does not prevent the devise from lapsing; rather, it makes a substitute gift for the testamentary gift when a lapse occurs. Although most states have enacted antilapse statutes, their terms vary from state to state. An antilapse statute usu. applies only when the deceased beneficiary is a relative of the testator. The statute's purpose is to effectuate the imputed intention of a testator who presumably would have wanted the devised property to pass to the beneficiary's relatives rather than to the testator's heirs or the residuary devisees. But the statute is inapplicable when there is evidence that the result would be contrary to the testator's intent. — Also termed *lapse statute*; *nonlapse statute*.

antilynching law. (1896) A statute that criminalizes any unjustified act of violence by two or more people against another, regardless of race. • Such laws were originally passed to stop all forms of extralegal violence aimed at black people. — Also termed *lynching law*.

antimanifesto. *Int'l law.* A proclamation in which a belligerent power asserts that a war is a defensive one for that power.

antimarital-facts privilege. See *marital privilege* (2) under PRIVILEGE (3).

antimiscegenation law. *Hist.* A statute that makes it unlawful for people of different races to marry one another.

antinomia (an-ti-**noh**-mee-ə). [Greek] *Roman law.* An ambiguity in the law. See ANTINOMY.

antinomy (an-**tin**-ə-mee), *n.* (16c) A contradiction in law or logic; esp., a conflict of authority, as between two decisions <antinomies in the caselaw>. — **antinomic** (an-ti-**nom**-ik), *adj.*

antipatent, *adj.* (1871) Of, relating to, or involving an effort to oppose or discourage patenting or patentability.

antipiracy, *adj.* (1940) *Intellectual property.* Of, relating to, or involving an effort to combat or discourage illegal reproduction, distribution, or use of copyrighted or trademarked products <an antipiracy group>.

antiqua custuma (an-tɪ-kwə **kəs**-t[y]oo-mə). [Law Latin "ancient customs"] *Hist.* A tax on wool, woolfells, and leather, under St. 3 Edw. • The distinction between *antiqua custuma* and *nova custuma* arose when the king imposed new taxes on the same articles in the 22nd year of his reign. Cf. NOVA CUSTUMA.

antiqua et nova (an-tɪ-kwə et **noh**-və). [Latin] *Hist.* Old and new (rights).

> "Antiqua et nova . . . . The technical terms in our law equivalent to these Latin terms are, heritage and conquest; heritage (*antiqua*) being that estate to which any one succeeds as heir; conquest (*nova*) that which he succeeds to or acquires by purchase, gift, or any singular title. The distinction between heritage and conquest is now abolished, 37 & 38 Vict. cap. 94, § 37." John Trayner, *Trayner's Latin Maxims* 50 (4th ed. 1894).

antiquare (an-ti-**kwair**-ee), *vb.* [Latin] *Roman law.* **1.** To reject a proposal for a new law. • Those who voted against a proposed law wrote on their ballots the letter "A" for *antiquo* ("I am for the old law"). **2.** To repeal a law.

antiqua statuta (an-tɪ-kwə stə-**t[y]oo**-tə). See VETERA STATUTA.

antiquum dominicum (an-tɪ-kwəm də-**min**-i-kəm). [Law Latin] (18c) Ancient demesne. See DEMESNE.

antiquus et novus extentus (an-**tɪ**-kwəs et **noh**-vəs ek-**sten**-təs). [Law Latin] *Scots law.* Old and new extent. • The phrase appeared in reference to the valuation of land for tax purposes, with old valuations assessed in the year 1280, and new valuations assessed several times after that date. Cf. QUANTUM NUNC VALENT; QUANTUM VALUERUNT TEMPORE PACIS.

anti-repugnance canon. See HARMONIOUS-READING CANON.

antishelving clause. *Patents.* A provision in a patent-licensing contract, usu. one in which payment is based on royalties, requiring the licensee to put the patented article into commercial use within a specified time and to notify the patentee if the licensee decides to stop selling or manufacturing it. • The licensee generally agrees to exploit the patent commercially or else risk losing the license or exclusivity. Antishelving clauses are also used in trademark licenses. — Also termed *antishelving provision; shelving clause; shelving provision.*

antishelving provision. See ANTISHELVING CLAUSE.

antisocial, *n.* See SOCIOPATH.

antisocial behavior order. (1998) *English law.* A judicial order prohibiting a person from certain types of conduct, potentially including conduct that is otherwise legal, where the conduct is likely to cause harm or distress to a nonoccupant of the individual's household • ASBOs were introduced in the United Kingdom by the Crime and Disorder Act 1998. — Abbr. ASBO.

antisocial personality disorder. See SOCIOPATH.

antispamming law. (2002) A statute enacted to combat or criminalize the sending of unsolicited commercial e-mail. • Many states have such a law. See SPAM.

antistructuring statute. (1988) A federal law that forbids structuring monetary transactions, such as by splitting a large deposit into several smaller ones, with the intent to evade federal reporting requirements. See SMURF (1).

antisubrogation rule (an-tee-səb-roh-**gay**-shən). (1993) *Insurance.* The principle that an insurance carrier has no right of subrogation — that is, no right to assert a claim on behalf of the insured or for payments made under the policy — against its own insured for the risk covered by the policy. See SUBROGATION.

antisuit, *adj.* (1961) Of, relating to, or involving a court order forbidding the defendant in a lawsuit, pending or resolved, from filing a similar action against the same party in another jurisdiction. • The purpose of an antisuit order is usu. to prevent forum-shopping. See RES JUDICATA; COLLATERAL ESTOPPEL.

antisuit injunction. See INJUNCTION.

antitakeover measure. (1978) A provision in a company's organizational documents intended to discourage unwanted takeover bids by setting forth the actions the company may take, as a target, to avoid an involuntary takeover. See TAKEOVER DEFENSE.

antitakeover statute. (1977) A state law designed to protect companies based in the state from hostile takeovers.

antithetarius (an-tith-ə-**tair**-ee-əs). [Law Latin] (18c) *Hist.* An accused person who asserts that his or her accuser is guilty of the crime. Cf. APPROVER (1).

antitrust. See ANTITRUST LAW.

Antitrust Civil Process Act. A federal law prescribing the procedures for an antitrust action by way of a petition in U.S. District Court. 15 USCA §§ 1311 et seq. — Abbr. ACPA.

Antitrust Guidelines for the Licensing of Intellectual Property. *Intellectual property.* A set of criteria, jointly issued by the Antitrust Division of the U.S. Department of Justice and the FTC, that those agencies apply in deciding whether to initiate an investigation or enforcement action as a result of restrictions in patent, copyright, trade-secret, and know-how licenses. 4 Trade Reg. Rep. (CCH) ¶ 13,132 (April 6, 1995).

antitrust injury. See INJURY.

antitrust law. (1890) **1.** The body of law designed to protect trade and commerce from restraints, monopolies, price-fixing, and price discrimination. • The principal federal antitrust laws are the Sherman Act (15 USCA §§ 1–7) and the Clayton Act (15 USCA §§ 12–27). — Often shortened to *antitrust.* — Also termed (BrE) *competition law.*

> "As legislative history and case law both disclose, the general objective of the antitrust laws is the maintenance of competition. Competition per se thus becomes a goal of the legal order. Yet, competition is not a concept which defines itself; notions about the desirability of competition may shape judgments about how the law should apply, at least at its indistinct edges." Lawrence A. Sullivan, *Handbook of the Law of Antitrust* § 5, at 20 (1977).

2. (*cap.*) SHERMAN ANTITRUST ACT.

antlike persistency. (1924) *Patents. Slang.* The steady tenacity of a patent practitioner or applicant who tries to wear down the U.S. Patent and Trademark Office by prosecuting patent claims in the hope that the Office will eventually relent. • Judge Learned Hand coined this pejorative expression in *Lyon v. Boh*, 1 F.2d 48, 49–50 (S.D.N.Y. 1924).

ANZUS Treaty (**an**-zəs *or* -zoos). A 1951 cooperative threeway security agreement between Australia, New Zealand, and the United States modeled on the North Atlantic Treaty Organization (NATO). • The name is an acronym from A (Australia) + NZ (New Zealand) + US (United States). See NORTH ATLANTIC TREATY ORGANIZATION.

AO. *abbr.* ADMINISTRATIVE OFFICE OF THE UNITED STATES COURTS.

AOC. *abbr.* **1.** ANNO ORBIS CONDITI. **2.** And other consideration. See *other consideration* under CONSIDERATION (1).

AOD. *abbr.* ACTION ON DECISION.

AOGI. *abbr.* See *adjusted ordinary gross income* under INCOME.

AOUSC. *abbr.* ADMINISTRATIVE OFFICE OF THE UNITED STATES COURTS.

APA. *abbr.* **1.** ADMINISTRATIVE PROCEDURE ACT. **2.** ADVANCE PRICING AGREEMENT.

a pais (ah **pay** *or* **pays**). [Law French] *Hist.* At or to the country; at issue.

a pari (ay **par**-ɪ). [Law Latin] *Hist.* Equally; in like manner.

apartheid (ə-**pahrt**-hayt *or* ə-**pahr**-tɪt). (1947) Racial segregation; specif., a comprehensive governmental policy of racial discrimination and segregation, as it was practiced in South Africa.

> "The term 'apartheid' derives from the Afrikaans word for 'apartness' or 'separateness.' Originally, it was used only to describe the distinctive South African system of racial segregation and classification along racial lines accompanied by a denial of basic human rights and political rights to the black and coloured population of South Africa between 1948 and 1994. Throughout the years, however, and particularly after apartheid rule ended in South Africa in 1994, the meaning of the term has broadened. Today, it is used as a synonym for any 'racial segregation and discrimination policies enacted by a government against a section of its own people.' . . . Apartheid was first labelled a crime against humanity in 1973 in Art. 1 International Convention on the Suppression and Punishment of the Crime of Apartheid ('Apartheid Convention' . . .). The definition set out in Art. 2 Apartheid Convention specifically refers to 'similar policies and practices of racial segregation and discrimination as practised in southern Africa,' but was not limited to the practice of apartheid in southern Africa, neither in geographical terms nor in terms of the acts prohibited. The crime of apartheid is also punishable under Art. 7 (1) (j) Rome Statute of the International Criminal Court (ICC)." Julia Gebhard, "Apartheid," in 1 *The Max Planck Encyclopedia of Public International Law* 461, 461–62 (Rüdiger Wolfrum ed., 2012).

apertum breve. See BREVE.

apertum factum (ə-**pər**-təm **fak**-təm). [Latin "open deed"] (17c) An overt act.

apertura testamenti (ap-ər-**t[y]oor**-ə tes-tə-**men**-tɪ). [Latin "opening of the testament"] (17c) *Roman law.* A procedure for proving a will by which the witnesses acknowledged their signatures and seal before a magistrate and the will was opened and publicly read.

apex deposition. See DEPOSITION (2).

apex juris (ay-peks **joor**-is). [Latin "summit of law"] (17c) An extreme point or subtlety of law, such as a merely technical objection in pleading or an extreme interpretation of a doctrine. Cf. APICES LITIGANDI.

apex rule. (1932) *Mining law.* The principle that a vein of ore may be mined if it extends beyond the vertical boundaries of the surface claim on which the vein apexes. — Also termed *extralateral right.* Cf. INTRALIMINAL RIGHT.

APH. *abbr.* AMERICAN PRINTING HOUSE FOR THE BLIND.

APHIS. *abbr.* ANIMAL AND PLANT HEALTH INSPECTION SERVICE.

apices litigandi (**ay**-pi-seez lit-i-**gan**-dɪ). [Law Latin] (18c) Extremely fine points (or subtleties) of litigation. Cf. APEX JURIS.

APJ. *abbr.* See *administrative patent judge* under JUDGE.

apocha (**ap**-ə-kə). (17c) *Roman & civil law.* A receipt acknowledging payment. • An apocha discharges only the obligation represented by the payment, in contrast to an acceptilation, which discharges an entire debt. — Also spelled *apoca.* Cf. ACCEPTILATION; ANTAPOCHA.

apochae oneratoriae (**ap**-ə-kee oh-nər-ay-**tor**-ee-ee). [Law Latin "cargo receipts"] *Hist.* Bills of lading.

apocha trium annorum (**ap**-ə-kə **trɪ**-əm ə-**nor**-əm). [Latin "receipt for three years"] (18c) *Hist. Scots law.* Receipts for three consecutive periodic payments, the production of which gave rise to a presumption that prior installments had been properly paid.

> "The production by the debtor of receipts for the last three consecutive instalments of a termly payment, such as feu-duty, rent, wages or interest, raises a presumption, the *apocha trium annorum*, rebuttable by parol evidence, that all prior instalments have been duly paid. The same inference is not justified by one receipt, even for three or more instalments. Nor do receipts for three instalments justify an inference that a bill, granted for earlier arrears, has been paid." 2 David M. Walker, *Principles of Scottish Private Law* 143 (4th ed. 1988).

apocrisarius (ə-pok-ri-**sair**-ee-əs), *n.* [Latin] (17c) *Hist. Eccles. law.* **1.** An ambassador; a messenger, such as a Pope's legate. **2.** Someone who answers for another; esp., an officer who presented church matters to the emperor and conveyed the answers to the petitioners. **3.** Someone who, upon consultation, gives advice in ecclesiastical matters. — Also termed *responsalis*; *a responsis*; *secretarius*; *consiliarius*; *referendarius*; *a consiliis.*

apographa (ə-**pog**-rə-fə), *n. pl.* [fr. Greek *apographein* "to copy"] (17c) **1.** *Civil law.* An examination and enumeration of things possessed; an inventory. **2.** Copies; transcripts. — **apographal,** *adj.*

apologia (ap-ə-**loh**-jee-ə), *n.* (18c) **1.** A formal justification for or defense of one's conduct or beliefs; esp., a personal history given in defense or justification of one's life. **2.** A formal statement in which one defends an idea or organization that one ardently believes in. — Also termed *apology.*

apology (ə-**pol**-ə-jee), *n.* (16c) **1.** A formal acknowledgment of a mistake or offense, usu. paired with regretful, palliative, or expiatory words. **2.** APOLOGIA. **3.** *Archaic.* An answer in a libel lawsuit, esp. one that states a defense or seeks to lessen the potential damages.

apostasy (ə-**pos**-tə-see). (14c) **1.** *Hist.* A crime against religion consisting in the total renunciation of Christianity by one who had previously embraced it. **2.** *Eccles. law.* Abandonment of religious vows without dispensation.

apostata capiendo. See DE APOSTATA CAPIENDO.

apostate (ə-**pos**-tayt). (14c) Someone who has forsaken religion or a particular religion. — Also termed (archaically) *apostata* (ap-ə-**stay**-tə).

a posteriori (ay pos-teer-ee-**or**-I *or* ah pos-teer-ee-**or**-ee), *adv.* [Latin "from what comes after"] (16c) Inductively; from the particular to the general, or from known effects to their inferred causes <as a legal analyst, she reasoned a posteriori — from countless individual cases to generalized rules that she finally applied>. Cf. A PRIORI. — **a posteriori,** *adj.*

apostille (ə-**pos**-til). [French "postscript, footnote"] (16c) **1.** A marginal note or comment, or a short addition to or comment on a document. **2.** *Int'l law.* A standard legal certificate attesting that the signatures, seals, or stamps are authentic on a public document used in a foreign country. • The certificate was created in the Hague Convention Abolishing the Requirement of Legalisation for Foreign Public Documents. — Also spelled *apostil.* — Sometimes termed *authentication.* See *certificate of authority* under CERTIFICATE. Cf. AUTHENTICATION (3).

apostle (ə-**pos**-əl), *n.* (18c) *Civil & maritime law.* **1.** A letter sent from a trial court to an appellate court, stating the case on appeal. **2.** The record or papers sent up on appeal. — Also termed *apostoli.* **3.** DIMISSORY LETTERS.

apostoli. See APOSTLE.

apostolus (ə-**pos**-tə-ləs), *n.* [fr. Greek *apostolos* "one sent from another"] (16c) *Hist.* A messenger, ambassador, legate, or nuncio. Pl. ***apostoli*** (ə-**pos**-tə-lI).

apotheca (ap-ə-**thee**-kə), *n.* [fr. Greek *apotheke* "store"] (17c) *Civil law.* A repository, as for wine or books. Pl. ***apothecae.***

apparatus. See MACHINE.

apparatus claim. See PATENT CLAIM.

apparatus limitation. (1937) *Patents.* The inclusion of a structure or physical apparatus in a method or process claim. • An apparatus limitation, while not objectionable, carries little weight toward establishing the patentability of a method or process claim.

apparent, *adj.* (14c) **1.** Visible; manifest; obvious. **2.** Ostensible; seeming.

apparent agency. See *agency by estoppel* under AGENCY (1).

apparent agent. See AGENT.

apparent assent. See ASSENT.

apparent authority. See AUTHORITY (1).

apparent danger. See DANGER.

apparent defect. See *patent defect* under DEFECT.

apparent easement. See EASEMENT.

apparent heir. See *heir apparent* under HEIR.

apparent principal. See PRINCIPAL (1).

apparent servitude. See SERVITUDE (3).

apparent title. See COLOR OF TITLE.

apparitor (ə-**par**-ə-tər *or* -tor). (16c) **1.** *Roman law. (ital.)* An officer who served a court, esp. as secretary, messenger (*viator*), or herald. — Also termed *viator.* **2.** *Civil law.* An officer who attends court to execute judicial orders. **3.** *Eccles. law.* An officer who executes orders and decrees, esp. by serving summonses.

apparlement (ə-**pahrl**-mənt), *n.* [Law French] *Hist.* Likelihood, as in the *apparlement* of war.

apparura (ap-ə-**ruur**-ə), *n.* [fr. Law Latin *apparare* "to furnish"] (18c) *Hist.* Furniture, apparel, implements, or tackle.

appeal, *n.* (13c) **1.** *Hist.* The charging of someone with a crime; specif., an accusation of a crime, esp. treason or a felony. **2.** A proceeding undertaken to have a decision reconsidered by a higher authority; esp., the submission of a lower court's or agency's decision to a higher court for review and possible reversal <the case is on appeal>. — Also termed *petition in error;* (in Scots law) *falsing of dooms.* See CERTIORARI.

▸ **appeal as of right.** See *appeal by right.*

▸ **appeal by application.** (1884) An appeal for which permission must first be obtained from the reviewing court. — Also termed *appeal by leave.* See APPLICATION FOR LEAVE TO APPEAL.

▸ **appeal by leave.** See *appeal by application.*

▸ **appeal by right.** (1932) An appeal to a higher court from which permission need not be first obtained. — Also termed *appeal as of right; appeal of right.* See APPLICATION FOR LEAVE TO APPEAL.

▸ **appeal de novo.** (18c) An appeal in which the appellate court uses the trial court's record but reviews the evidence and law without deference to the trial court's rulings. — Also termed *de novo review; de novo judicial review; merits review.*

▸ **appeal from the decision of the chair.** (1863) *Parliamentary law.* A motion by which a member invokes the assembly's right of reviewing its chair's decision on a point of order. • If the appeal is seconded, the chair must state what question was at issue and explain the reasons for the chair's decision, then allow the members present to vote in support of or against that decision.— Also termed *appeal from the ruling of the chair.*

▸ **appeal from the ruling of the chair.** See *appeal from the decision of the chair.*

▸ **appeal in forma pauperis** (in **for**-mə **paw**-pər-is). (1840) An appeal by an indigent party, for whom court costs are waived. Fed. R. App. P. 24. See IN FORMA PAUPERIS.

▸ **appeal of right.** See *appeal by right.*

▸ **consolidated appeal.** (1843) An appeal in which two or more parties, whose interests were similar enough to make a joinder practicable, proceed as a single appellant.

▸ **cross-appeal.** (18c) An appeal by the appellee, usu. heard at the same time as the appellant's appeal.

▸ **delayed appeal.** (1922) An appeal that takes place after the time for appealing has expired, but only when the reviewing court has granted permission because of special circumstances.

▸ **devolutive appeal** (di-**vol**-yə-tiv). (1819) An appeal that does not suspend the execution of the underlying judgment. Cf. *suspensive appeal.*

▸ **direct appeal.** (18c) An appeal from a trial court's decision directly to the jurisdiction's highest court, thus bypassing review by an intermediate appellate court. • Such an appeal may be authorized, for example, when the case involves the constitutionality of a state law.

▸ **duplicitous appeal.** (1912) An appeal from two separate judgments, from a judgment and an order, or from two orders.

▸ **federal appeal.** (1904) An appeal to a federal appellate court usu. from (1) a federal district court to a United States circuit court, (2) a United States circuit court to the Supreme Court of the United States, or (3) a state supreme court to the Supreme Court of the United States.

▸ **frivolous appeal.** (18c) An appeal having no legal basis, usu. filed for delay to induce a judgment creditor to settle or to avoid payment of a judgment. • Federal Rule of Appellate Procedure 38 provides for the award of damages and costs if the appellate court determines that an appeal is frivolous. Fed. R. App. P. 38.

▸ **interlocutory appeal.** (1847) An appeal that occurs before the trial court's final ruling on the entire case. 28 USCA § 1292(b). • Some interlocutory appeals involve legal points necessary to the determination of the case, while others involve collateral orders that are wholly separate from the merits of the action. See INTERLOCUTORY APPEALS ACT; FINAL-JUDGMENT RULE.

▸ **judgment-roll appeal.** (1944) An appeal based only on the pleadings, the findings of the court, and the judgment.

▸ **limited appeal.** (1860) An appeal from only certain portions of a decision, usu. only the adverse or unfavorable portions.

▸ **precautionary appeal.** See *protective appeal.*

▸ **protective appeal.** (1942) An appeal filed by counsel when the client might otherwise lose an effective right to appeal. • A protective appeal is typically filed when (1) a client's motion to intervene has been denied, and the trial court is entering other orders that the client wants to appeal, (2) counsel has doubts about where to appeal, (3) counsel has doubts about the length of the appeal period, or (4) the client must preserve uncertain or contingent rights. — Also termed *precautionary appeal.*

▸ **state appeal.** An appeal to a state appellate court, either from a court of first instance to any intermediate appellate court or from a lower court to the highest court in the state-court system.

▸ **suspensive appeal.** (18c) An appeal that stays the execution of the underlying judgment. Cf. *devolutive appeal.*

3. An urgent request for something important <a public appeal to locate the child>. **4.** An attempt to raise money for the benefit of someone who needs it. **5.** A quality that draws people to something or someone; attractiveness.

appeal, *vb.* (14c) **1.** To seek review (from a lower court's decision) by a higher court <petitioner appeals the conviction>. **2.** *Hist.* To charge with a crime; accuse. — **appealability,** *n.*

appealable, *adj.* (Of an order) meeting the standards required for consideration by an appellate court; capable of being appealed.

appealable decision. See DECISION (1).

appeal as of right. See *appeal by right* under APPEAL (2).

appeal bond. See BOND (2).

appeal brief. See BRIEF (1).

appeal by leave. See *appeal by application* under APPEAL (2).

appeal by right. See APPEAL (2).

appeal court. 1. See *appellate court* under COURT. **2.** (*cap.*) COURT OF APPEAL.

appeal de novo. See APPEAL (2).

appealer. *Archaic.* APPELLANT.

appeal from the decision of the chair. (1870) See APPEAL.

appeal in forma pauperis. See APPEAL (2).

appeal of felony. (16c) *Hist.* A procedure by which a person accused another of a crime, demanded proof of innocence by wager of battle, or informed against an accomplice. — Also termed *appellum de felonia.*

appeal of right. See *appeal by right* under APPEAL (2).

appeals council. (1942) A commission that hears appeals of rulings by administrative-law judges in social-security matters.

appeals court. See *appellate court* under COURT.

appearance, *n.* (14c) *Procedure.* A coming into court as a party or interested person, or as a lawyer on behalf of a party or interested person; esp., a defendant's act of taking part in a lawsuit, whether by formally participating in it or by an answer, demurrer, or motion, or by taking post-judgment steps in the lawsuit in either the trial court or an appellate court. — **appear,** *vb.*

> "The English courts did not, until modern times, claim jurisdiction over the person of the defendant merely by service of summons upon him. It was deemed necessary to resort to further process by attachment of his property and arrest of his person to compel 'appearance,' which is not mere presence in court, but some act by which a person who is sued submits himself to the authority and jurisdiction of the court. Any steps in the action, such as giving bail upon arrest, operated as an appearance or submission." Benjamin J. Shipman, *Handbook of Common-Law Pleading* § 5, at 24 (Henry Winthrop Ballantine ed., 3d ed. 1923).

> "The term 'appearance' is used particularly to signify or designate the overt act by which one against whom suit has been commenced submits himself to the court's jurisdiction, although in a broader sense it embraces the act of either plaintiff or defendant in coming into court . . . . An appearance may be expressly made by formal written or oral declaration, or record entry, or it may be implied from some act done with the intention of appearing and submitting to the court's jurisdiction." 4 Am. Jur. 2d *Appearance* § 1, at 620 (1995).

▸ **appearance *de bene esse.*** See *special appearance.*

▸ **appearance *pro hac vice*** (proh hak VI-see *or* proh hahk vee-chay). [Latin] (1923) An appearance made by an out-of-state lawyer for one particular case, usu. by leave of court. • For more on the pronunciation of this term, see PRO HAC VICE.

▸ **appearance under protest.** *English & Canadian law.* See *special appearance.*

▸ **compulsory appearance.** (1821) An appearance by one who is required to appear by having been served with process. Cf. *voluntary appearance.*

▸ **general appearance.** A general-purpose appearance that waives a party's ability later to dispute the court's authority to enter a binding judgment against him or her.

▸ **initial appearance.** A criminal defendant's first appearance in court to hear the charges read, to be advised of his or her rights, and to have bail determined. • The initial appearance is usu. required by statute to occur without undue delay. In a misdemeanor case, the initial appearance may be combined with the arraignment. See ARRAIGNMENT.

▸ **limited appearance.** See *special appearance.*

▸ **special appearance.** (18c) **1.** A defendant's pleading that either claims that the court lacks personal jurisdiction over the defendant or objects to improper service of process. **2.** A defendant's showing up in court for the sole purpose of contesting the court's assertion of personal jurisdiction over the defendant. • Special appearances have been abolished in federal court. Fed. R. Civ. P. 12(b). — Also termed *limited appearance*; *appearance de bene esse*; (in English & Canadian law) *appearance under protest.*

▸ **telephone appearance.** An appearance made by using an acceptable electronic means of communication, such as telephone, videoconference, or digital or audiovisual device. — Also termed *telephonic appearance.*

▸ **voluntary appearance.** (17c) An appearance entered by a party's own will, without the service of process. Cf. *compulsory appearance*

appearance bond. See *bail bond* under BOND (2).

appearance date. See *answer day* under DAY.

appearance day. See *answer day* under DAY.

appearance docket. See DOCKET (1).

appearance doctrine. (1972) In the law of self-defense, the rule that a defendant's use of force is justified if the defendant reasonably believed it to be justified.

appearance of impropriety. See IMPROPRIETY.

appearance term. See TERM (5).

appearance ticket. See CITATION (2).

appellant (ə-**pel**-ənt). (15c) A party who appeals a lower court's decision, usu. seeking reversal of that decision. — Also termed (archaically) *plaintiff in error*; (formerly) *appealer.* Cf. APPELLEE.

appellate (ə-**pel**-it), *adj.* (18c) Of, relating to, or involving an appeal or appeals generally.

appellate brief. See BRIEF (1).

appellate counsel. See COUNSEL.

appellate court. See COURT.

appellate division. (1879) A department of a superior court responsible for hearing appeals; an intermediate appellate court in some states, such as New York and New Jersey.

appellate jurisdiction. See JURISDICTION.

appellate record. See RECORD ON APPEAL.

appellate review. See REVIEW.

appellate rules. (1895) A body of rules governing appeals from lower courts.

Appellate Term. A division of the New York Supreme Court established to hear both appeals from decisions of the civil and criminal courts of New York City and appeals from district courts, town courts, and other lower courts. • The Appellate Term's decisions are often unpublished but are binding authority on the lower courts.

appellate triage. A method by which appeals courts treat certain types of cases, considered to be worthy of greater attention, with more care — according them oral argument, more lavishly detailed opinions, and heightened judicial attention — and other cases, considered to be simple or mundane, in a more perfunctory fashion (often with most of the work performed by staff). — Also termed *two-track system.*

> "Cases perceived to be more important continued to receive the traditional treatment, while cases of less perceived significance were consigned to an abbreviated appellate process. In those cases, oral argument was rare, the work was done mostly by the staff attorneys with little judicial input, and the decision was issued in an unpublished, nonprecedential opinion. We have called the set of new and abbreviated appellate procedures 'Track Two,' and we have attached the label of 'Appellate Triage' to the method by which cases are diverted from the traditional process and assigned to the new truncated pathway. Through the next several decades, the quantity and variety of cases consigned to Track Two treatment have increased steadily so that today less than 20 percent of the circuit courts' caseload receives the traditional appellate process. In other words, what started as a special set of shortcuts for dealing with a small and troublesome slice of the docket has morphed into the most common way for appeals to make their way through the federal appellate system." William M. Richman & William L. Reynolds, *Injustice on Appeal: The United States Courts of Appeals in Crisis* 225 (2013).

appellatio (ap-ə-**lay**-shee-oh), *n.* [Latin] (16c) *Roman law.* An appeal from a lower court. Pl. ***appellationes*** (ap-ə-lay-shee-**oh**-neez).

appellation of origin. (1992) *Trademarks.* Representation of a product's geographic origin by use of a mark — such as a symbol, word, phrase, or graphic element such as a map — whose use is regulated to ensure that the products so marked reflect some well-known feature peculiar to the region. • This term usu. applies to a product whose quality or other characteristic feature has been gained by natural means, such as by the nature of the local climate or soil, or by the nature of the way it is made, such as by local customs of production. For example, the appellation *burgundy* can be used only for wines made from certain types of varietal grapes from particular regions of France.

appellator (ap-ə-**lay**-tər), *n.* [Latin] (17c) *Roman & civil law.* An appellant.

appellee (ap-ə-**lee**). (16c) A party against whom an appeal is taken and whose role is to respond to that appeal, usu. seeking affirmance of the lower court's decision. See RESPONDENT (1). Cf. APPELLANT.

appello (ə-**pel**-oh), *vb.* [Latin] *Roman law.* I appeal. • This was the form of making an appeal *apud acta* (in the presence of the judge).

appellor (ə-**pel**-or *or* **ap**-ə-lor). (14c) *Hist. English law.* Someone who formally accuses another of a crime, challenges a jury, or informs against an accomplice.

appellum de felonia. See APPEAL OF FELONY.

appendant (ə-**pen**-dənt), *adj.* (15c) Attached or belonging to property as an additional but subsidiary right. — **appendant,** *n.*

appendant claim. See *dependent claim* under PATENT CLAIM.

appendant easement. See *easement appurtenant* under EASEMENT.

appendant power. See POWER (5).

appenditia (ap-en-**dish**-ee-ə), *n.* [Law Latin] *Hist.* The appendages or appurtenances of an estate.

appendix, *n.* (16c) **1.** A supplementary document attached to the end of a writing <the brief includes an appendix of exhibits>. • For the requirements of an appendix to a federal appellate brief, see Fed. R. App. P. 30. **2.** *English law.* A volume that contains material documents and other evidence presented in a lower court. • The volume is used by the House of Lords or Privy Council when functioning as an appellate tribunal. Pl. **appendixes, appendices.**

appensura (ap-en-**s[y]oor**-ə), *n.* [fr. Latin *appendere* "to weigh out"] (18c) *Hist.* The payment of money by weight rather than by count.

appertain, *vb.* (14c) To belong to or concern <membership and all the privileges appertaining thereto>. • This legalistic term is a heightened, formal synonym of *pertain.*

appliance, *n.* (16c) **1.** Anything through or by which something is achieved or accomplished; something essential to the course or operation of a particular thing <the appliances of war>; esp., an instrumental device used in the household <mixers, strainers, or other cooking appliances>. **2.** The act of putting to use or carrying into effect <appliance of this legal principle>.

applicable (**ap**-li-kə-bəl or [less good] ə-**plik**-ə-bəl). *adj.* (16c) **1.** Capable of being applied; fit and right to be applied. **2.** (Of a rule, regulation, law, etc.) affecting or relating to a particular person, group, or situation; having direct relevance.

applicable exclusion amount. (2002) *Tax.* The dollar amount of an estate's value that is exempt from federal estate and gift taxes. See *unified estate-and-gift-tax credit* under TAX CREDIT.

applicable exclusion credit. See *unified estate-and-gift-tax credit* under TAX CREDIT.

applicando singula singulis (ap-li-**kan**-doh **sing**-gyə-lə **sing**-gyə-lis). [Law Latin] (17c) *Hist.* By applying each to each; to apply each condition to. • The phrase was used in deed constructions in Scotland.

applicant. (18c) **1.** Someone who requests something; a petitioner, such as a person who applies for letters of administration. **2.** ACCOUNT PARTY.

application. (15c) **1.** A request or petition. See COPYRIGHT APPLICATION; PATENT APPLICATION; TRADEMARK APPLICATION. **2.** MOTION.

▸ **ex parte application.** See *ex parte motion* under MOTION (1).

▸ **interlocutory application.** (1811) A motion for equitable or legal relief sought before a final decision.

3. *Bankruptcy.* A request for an order not requiring advance notice and an opportunity for a hearing before the order is issued. **4.** The process by which a decisionmaker categorizes the legal facts at issue and hence ascertains the rule of law that is to govern them.

Application Division. *Patents.* The part of the U.S. Patent and Trademark Office that is responsible for accepting patent applications, assigning them serial numbers, checking them for completeness and formalities, placing them in file wrappers, and assigning them to an appropriate art group based on the invention's class and subclass of technology.

application for a reissue patent. See PATENT APPLICATION.

application for leave to appeal. (1882) A motion asking an appellate court to hear a party's appeal from a judgment when the party has no appeal by right or when the party's time limit for an appeal by right has expired. • The reviewing court has discretion whether to grant or reject such a motion. Cf. LEAVE TO APPEAL.

application for transfer. (1908) In some jurisdictions, a request to a state's highest court to hear an appeal from an intermediate court of appeal. • The appeal is heard as though it had been appealed to the highest court originally. The court may typically ignore the intermediate court's decision and may consider an error that was not raised in the intermediate court.

application number. (1895) *Patents & Trademarks.* The eight-digit sequential number assigned by the U.S. Patent and Trademark Office to a patent or trademark application. • Applications are typically referred to by an application number, which consists of a two-digit series code, a slash, and a six-digit serial number. References to patent applications also include the filing date <application no. 08/944,183, filed September 20, 1978>. — Also termed *serial number.*

application service provider. (1993) A business that hosts software on its computers and gives subscribers access as needed. • The subscriber does not need to purchase a license to use the software before the provider makes it available to the subscriber's computer, usu. over the Internet or a private electronic network. — Abbr. ASP.

applied-art doctrine. (2004) *Copyright.* The rule that a pictorial, graphic, or sculptural work that has an inherent use apart from its appearance, and is also an expressive work apart from its utility, may qualify for copyright protection. • Examples have included bookends, lamps, and sundials. In contrast to applied art, industrial designs are not copyrightable, although they may be protected by design patents instead. — Also termed *useful-article doctrine.*

applied cost. See COST (1).

apply, *vb.* (14c) **1.** To make a formal request or motion <apply for a loan> <apply for injunctive relief>. **2.** To employ for a limited purpose <apply payments to a reduction in interest>. **3.** To put to use with a particular subject matter <apply the law to the facts> <apply the law only to transactions in interstate commerce>.

appoint, *vb.* (14c) **1.** To fix by decree, order, command, decision, or mutual agreement; to constitute. **2.** To choose or designate (someone) for a position or job, esp. in government. **3.** To arrange or decide on (a time or place) for a particular purpose. **4.** To equip or fit out; to furnish with necessary equipment. **5.** To direct or determine the disposition of (an estate) by using a power of appointment to determine the person or persons in whom the estate will vest. **6.** To designate (a person) in whom an estate subject to a power of appointment will be vested.

appointed counsel. See *assigned counsel* under COUNSEL.

appointed day. See DAY.

appointee. (18c) **1.** Someone who is appointed. **2.** Someone who receives the benefit of a power of appointment. See POWER OF APPOINTMENT.

▸ **permissible appointee.** (1933) A person to whom appointive property may be assigned under a power of appointment. — Also termed *object of the power of appointment; object of the power; object of a power.*

appointing authority. (1873) *Arbitration.* A disinterested person or entity that selects an arbitrator when the arbitrating parties are unable to do, or that resolves a party's challenge to a chosen arbitrator.

> "The almost universal contractual mechanism for selecting an arbitrator is designation of a neutral 'appointing authority' to choose the arbitrator(s) if the parties [or] coarbitrators cannot agree. Failure to provide for an appointing authority in an arbitration can result in the process of constituting the tribunal becoming deadlocked or, more likely, a nation court . . . designating the arbitrator(s)." 1 Gary B. Born, *International Commercial Arbitration* 1408 (2009).

appointive asset. See ASSET.

appointive property. See PROPERTY.

appointment, *n.* (15c) **1.** The choice or designation of a person, such as a nonelected public official, for a job or duty; esp., the naming of someone to a nonelected public office <Article II of the U.S. Constitution grants the President the power of appointment for principal federal officials, subject to senatorial consent>.

▸ **at-pleasure appointment.** See *pleasure appointment.*

▸ **pleasure appointment.** (1936) The assignment of someone to employment that can be taken away at any time, with no requirement for cause, notice, or a hearing. — Also termed *at-pleasure appointment.*

▸ **public appointment.** (17c) An appointment to a public office.

▸ **recess appointment.** (1825) An appointment, including a judicial appointment, made by the President when the Senate is not in session, subject to the Senate's later ratification.

2. An office occupied by someone who has been appointed; a job or position involving some responsibility <a high appointment in the federal government>. **3.** *Parliamentary law.* The naming of an officer, the members of a committee, or the holder of any other title in an organization. **4.** The act of disposing of property, in exercise of a power granted for that purpose <the tenant's appointment of lands>. See POWER OF APPOINTMENT.

▸ **illusory appointment.** (18c) A nominal, unduly restrictive, or conditional transfer of property under a power of appointment.

> "Like many other theories which are very plausible in the abstract, experience has shown that the doctrine of illusory appointments is difficult in application, since the term 'illusory' is vague and indefinite. And, because of the difficulty of formulating rules for determining what is an illusory appointment and the evils resulting from attempts to substitute the judicial will for the intent of the donor and donee of the power, the doctrine has been condemned or rejected by many courts." 62 Am. Jur. 2d *Powers of Appointment* § 186 (1990).

5. An arrangement for a meeting at an agreed time and place, usu. for a particular purpose. — **appoint,** *vb.* — **appointer** (in senses 1–3), *n.* — **appointor** (in sense 4), *n.*

Appointments Clause. (1976) *Constitutional law.* The clause of the U.S. Constitution giving the President the power to nominate federal judges and various other officials. U.S. Const. art. II, § 2.

apport (ə-**port**), *n.* [Law French] (15c) *Hist.* A tax, expense, tribute, or payment.

apportionable claim. See CLAIM (4).

apportionment, *n.* (16c) **1.** Division into proportionate shares; esp., the division of rights and liabilities among two or more persons or entities. **2.** *Tax.* The act of allocating or attributing moneys or expenses in a given way, as when a taxpayer allocates part of profits to a particular tax year or part of the use of a personal asset to a business. **3.** Distribution of legislative seats among districts; esp., the allocation of congressional representatives among the states based on population, as required by the 14th Amendment. • The claim that a state is denying the right of representation to its citizens through improper apportionment presents a justiciable issue. — Also termed *legislative apportionment.* See REAPPORTIONMENT. **4.** The division (by statute or by the testator's instruction) of an estate-tax liability among persons interested in an estate. — **apportion,** *vb.*

apportionment clause. (1884) *Insurance.* A policy provision that distributes insurance proceeds in proportion to the total coverage.

apportionment of liability. (1855) *Torts.* The parceling out of liability for an injury among multiple tortfeasors, and possibly the plaintiff as well. • Apportionment of liability encompasses such legal doctrines as joint and several liability, comparative responsibility, indemnity, and settlements. *See* Restatement (Third) of Torts: Apportionment of Liability (1999).

apportionment rule. (1941) *Oil & gas.* The minority doctrine that royalties accrued under an oil-and-gas lease on land that was subdivided during the lease term must be shared by the landowners in proportion to their interests in the land. • For example, if Grey granted a lease to Simms, then sold one-half of the land to Metcalfe, Simms and Metcalfe would each be entitled to one-half of any royalty from the land, no matter where the newly producing well is located. Only California, Mississippi, and Pennsylvania follow this rule. Cf. NONAPPORTIONMENT RULE.

apportum (ə-**por**-təm), *n.* [Law Latin] *Hist.* The revenue, profit, or emolument that something brings to its owner. • This was often used in reference to a pension.

appose (ə-**pohz**), *vb.* (14c) *Hist.* **1.** To interrogate, esp. with difficult questions. **2.** To confront (someone) with objections to something. **3.** To examine the books and accounts of; audit.

apposer (ə-**pohz**-ər). (16c) *Hist.* **1.** A questioner; interrogator. **2.** An Exchequer officer who examined sheriffs' accounts; specif., an officer responsible for examining the sheriff's estreat (book of fines), comparing the entries with those in court records, and apposing (interrogating) the sheriff on each sum in the estreat. • This office was abolished in England in 1833. — Also termed *foreign apposer.*

apposite (**ap**-ə-zit), *adj.* (17c) Suitable; appropriate.

appraisal, *n.* (1817) **1.** The determination of what constitutes a fair price for something or how its condition can be fairly stated; the act of assessing the worth, value, or condition of something. **2.** The report of such a determination; specif., a statement or opinion judging the worth, value, or condition of something. — Also termed *appraisement.* Cf. ASSESSMENT (3). — **appraise,** *vb.*

▸ **USPAP appraisal.** *Real estate.* An appraisal performed and documented in a manner consistent with the Uniform Standards of Professional Appraisal Practice.

▸ **yellow-book appraisal.** *Real estate.* An appraisal conducted and documented in accordance with the Uniform Appraisal Standards for Federal Land Acquisitions and Supplemental Standards as issued by the Natural Resources Conservation Service.

appraisal clause. (1887) An insurance-policy provision allowing either the insurer or the insured to demand an independent estimation of a claimed loss.

appraisal contingency. *Real estate.* A standard provision in most real-estate purchase offers stipulating that if the property does not appraise for a minimum amount (typically the purchase price), then the buyer may cancel the offer and have any deposit refunded • This contingency must be satisfied before the buyer becomes obligated to buy.

appraisal remedy. (1949) The statutory right of corporate shareholders who oppose some extraordinary corporate action (such as a merger) to have their shares judicially appraised and to demand that the corporation buy back their shares at the appraised value. — Also termed *appraisal right; dissenters' right; right of dissent and appraisal.*

appraisal right. See APPRAISAL REMEDY.

appraisal trinity. (1968) The three most commonly accepted methods of appraising real property: the market approach, the cost approach, and the income approach. See MARKET APPROACH; COST APPROACH; INCOME APPROACH.

appraisement. (17c) **1.** APPRAISAL. **2.** An alternative-dispute-resolution method used for resolving the amount or extent of liability on a contract when the issue of liability itself is not in dispute. • Unlike arbitration, appraisement is not a quasi-judicial proceeding but instead an informal determination of the amount owed on a contract. See ALTERNATIVE DISPUTE RESOLUTION.

appraiser. (16c) An impartial person who estimates the value of something, such as real estate, jewelry, or rare books. — Also termed (esp. BrE) *valuer.*

▸ **business appraiser.** (1941) An appraiser who specializes in determining the value of commercial enterprises and property, including real estate and intellectual property.

▸ **merchant appraiser.** See MERCHANT APPRAISER.

appreciable, *adj.* (1818) Capable of being measured or perceived.

appreciate, *vb.* (18c) **1.** To understand the significance or meaning of. **2.** To increase in value.

appreciation, *n.* (18c) An increase in an asset's value, usu. because of inflation. Cf. DEPRECIATION. — **appreciate,** *vb.* — **appreciable,** *adj.*

appreciation surplus. See *revaluation surplus* under SURPLUS.

appreciation test. (1970) *Criminal law.* A test for the insanity defense requiring proof by clear and convincing evidence that at the time of the crime, the defendant suffered from a severe mental disease or defect preventing him or her from appreciating the wrongfulness of the conduct. • This test, along with the accompanying plea of *not guilty by reason of insanity,* was established by the Insanity Defense Reform Act of 1984. 18 USCA § 17. — Also termed *Insanity Defense Reform Act of 1984 test.* See INSANITY DEFENSE.

apprehensio (ap-ri-**hen**-see-oh). [Latin] **1.** APPREHENSION (1). **2.** *Civil law.* Seizure; a procedure for acquiring something that belongs to no one. • It is a type of *occupatio.*

apprehension, *n.* (14c) **1.** Seizure in the name of the law; arrest <apprehension of a criminal>. **2.** Perception; comprehension; belief <the tort of assault requires apprehension by the plaintiff of imminent contact>. **3.** Fear and anxiety about the future, esp. about dealing with an unpleasant person or a difficult situation <most people approach public speaking with some apprehension>. — **apprehend,** *vb.*

***Apprendi* rule.** (2000) *Criminal law.* The doctrine that if a fact other than prior convictions is to be relied on to increase the punishment for a crime beyond the statutory maximum, the fact-finder (usu. a jury) must find it to be proved beyond a reasonable doubt. *See Apprendi v. New Jersey,* 530 U.S. 466 (2000).

apprentice. (14c) **1.** *Hist.* A person bound by an indenture to work for an employer for a specified period to learn a craft, trade, or profession.

> "Apprentices, in the strict legal sense, are servants, usually but not necessarily infants, who agree to serve their masters with a view to learning some trade or business, and whose masters on their part agree to instruct them. The contract is usually for a term of years and is normally embodied in a deed, in which case the apprentice is said to be bound by an indenture of apprenticeship. It is customary for the father of the apprentice (or some person standing *in loco parentis*), as well as the apprentice himself to execute the deed or other instrument, and thus become liable for the due observance by the apprentice of his obligations thereunder. When an apprentice deliberately misconducts himself in such a way that, in the case of any other servant, his behaviour would amount to a repudiation of the agreement, and thereupon the master decides to accept the repudiation and dismisses him, the apprentice's repudiation is not effective, and the contract is not terminated, unless the Court find that such a course would be for the infant's benefit. Otherwise the infant could do indirectly what he could not do directly — namely, bring about a rescission of the contract." 2 *Stephen's Commentaries on the Laws of England* 133–34 (L. Crispin Warmington ed., 21st ed. 1950).

2. A learner in any field of employment or business, esp. one who learns by hands-on experience or technical on-the-job training by one experienced in the field; specif., someone who works for an employer for a fixed period in order to learn a particular skill or job.

apprentice en la ley. See APPRENTICE OF THE LAW.

apprentice of the law. (14c) *Hist.* **1.** A law student. **2.** A barrister of junior status. — Also termed *apprentice en la ley; apprenticius ad legem.*

apprenticius ad legem (a-pren-**tish**-ee-əs ad **lee**-jəm). [Law Latin] (18c) APPRENTICE OF THE LAW.

apprise, *vb.* (17c) To tell or give (someone) information about something; to give notice or inform <the President was apprised of all the relevant details>.

apprize, *vb.* (14c) To appraise; to assign a value to.

approach, right of. See RIGHT OF APPROACH.

approbate and reprobate. [fr. Latin *approbare et reprobare* "to approve and reprove"] (18c) *Scots law.* To (impermissibly) approve in one proceeding and then reject in a later proceeding (a contractual term, the interpretation of a legal instrument, etc.). • The principle is similar to that of equitable election and to estoppel.

approbation. (14c) **1.** The act of formally or authoritatively declaring something to be proper, commendable, or good; a solemn expression of favor or pleasure. **2.** A favorable pronouncement on the ethical soundness of conduct. **3.** *Hist.* A bishop's approval of a priest as confessor. **4.** *Hist.* The official approval of a book by a censor. — **approbate,** *vb.* — **approbation, approbatory,** *adj.* — **approbator,** *n.*

appropriate dispute resolution. (1976) ALTERNATIVE DISPUTE RESOLUTION. • This phrase originated as a supposedly superior synonym for *alternative dispute resolution.* Both terms are abbreviated *ADR,* but *appropriate* is sometimes viewed as a better choice because mediation and arbitration may supplement litigation without replacing it and because *alternative* seems to privilege litigation as the "normal" route.

appropriated retained earnings. See EARNINGS.

appropriated surplus. See SURPLUS.

appropriation, *n.* (14c) **1.** The exercise of control over property, esp. without permission; a taking of possession. Cf. EXPROPRIATION (1); MISAPPROPRIATION (1). **2.** *Torts.* An invasion of privacy whereby one person takes the name or likeness of another for commercial gain. **3.** A legislative body's or business's act of setting aside a sum of money for a specific purpose. • If the sum is earmarked for a precise or limited purpose, it is sometimes called a *specific appropriation.* **4.** The sum of money so voted. **5.** The transfer of a benefice, together with all its interests, to a spiritual corporation. See *spiritual corporation* under CORPORATION. Cf. IMPROPRIATION. **6.** The benefice so transferred. — **appropriate,** *vb.* — **appropriable,** *adj.* — **appropriator,** *n.*

appropriations bill. See BILL (3).

Appropriations Clause. *Constitutional law.* The constitutional provision mandating that federal funds may be spent only as Congress directs by law and requiring periodic publication of a statement and account of federal receipts and expenditures. U.S. Const. art. I, § 9, cl. 7

appropriative water right. See WATER RIGHT.

appropriator, *n.* (18c) *Hist. Eccles. law.* The corporate possessor of an appropriated benefice — that is, a benefice that has been perpetually annexed to a spiritual corporation, often a monastic house.

approval sale. See *sale on approval* under SALE.

approve, *vb.* (14c) **1.** To give formal sanction to; to confirm authoritatively. **2.** *Parliamentary law.* To adopt. See ADOPTION (5). — **approval,** *n.*

Approved Drug Products with Therapeutic Equivalence Evaluations. See ORANGE BOOK.

approved indorsed note. See NOTE (1).

approved list. See LEGAL LIST.

approvement. (15c) **1.** *English law.* The right of an owner of common lands to enclose them partially and receive income arising from them. • This right — originally granted by the Statute of Merton (1235) — is still available, but a landowner seeking to approve land must receive the government's consent to do so. **2.** *Hist.* The act of avoiding a capital conviction by accusing an accomplice; turning king's evidence.

approver (ə-**proo**-vər), *n.* (14c) *Hist.* **1.** Someone who offers proof; esp., a person charged with a felony who, in the hopes of leniency or a pardon, confesses and testifies against one or more accomplices. — Sometimes shortened to *prover.* See *relative confession* under CONFESSION (1). Cf. ANTITHETARIUS. **2.** An agent or bailiff; esp., one who manages a farm or estate for another.

approximation. (17c) **1.** A number, amount, weight, or quantity that is not exact but is nearly correct. **2.** Something that is similar to something else but not identical.

approximation, doctrine of. See DOCTRINE OF APPROXIMATION.

appruare (ap-roo-**air**-ee), *vb.* [Law Latin] *Hist.* To obtain a benefit from land by making improvements.

appurtenance (ə-**pərt**-[ə-]nənts), *n.* (14c) Something that belongs or is attached to something else; esp., something that is part of something else that is more important <the garden is an appurtenance to the land>.

> "The word 'appurtenances' which in former times at least was generally employed in deeds and leases is derived from the word *apparentir* which is Norman French and means to belong to. Speaking broadly, the word means anything corporeal or incorporeal which is an incident of, and belongs to some other thing as principal. At a time when the construction of conveyances was of a more technical character than it is at present the word was considered of much greater importance than it is now and it was considered that in its absence from a lease or other conveyance a very restricted meaning should attach to the words of the description of the premises conveyed." 1 H.C. Underhill, *A Treatise on the Law of Landlord and Tenant* § 291, at 442–43 (1909).

appurtenant, *adj.* (14c) Annexed to a more important thing. — Also termed (in Scots law) *part and pertinent.*

appurtenant covenant. See *covenant appurtenant* under COVENANT (4).

appurtenant easement. See *easement appurtenant* under EASEMENT.

APR. *abbr.* See *annual percentage rate* under INTEREST RATE.

à prendre (ah **prawn**-drə *or* -dər). [French] (17c) For taking; for seizure. See PROFIT À PRENDRE.

a priori (ay prɪ-**or**-ɪ *or* ah pree-**or**-ee), *adv.* [Latin "from what is before"] (17c) Deductively; from the general to the particular, or from previous experiences or facts to an inference of what the likely result or effect will be <as an analyst, he reasoned a priori — from seemingly self-evident propositions to particular conclusions>. Cf. A POSTERIORI. — **a priori,** *adj.*

a provisione viri (ay prə-vizh-ee-**oh**-nee vɪ-rɪ). [Latin] By the provision of a man (i.e., a husband).

APS. *abbr.* **1.** ADULT PROTECTIVE SERVICES. **2.** AUTOMATED PATENT SYSTEM.

APT. *abbr.* See *asset-protection trust* under TRUST (3).

apud acta (**ap**-əd **ak**-tə). [Latin] *Roman & civil law.* Among the acts; among the judicial proceedings recorded in writing. • This phrase refers to appeals taken orally in the presence of the judge.

apud judicem. See IN JUDICIO.

APV. *abbr.* See *adjusted present value* under PRESENT VALUE.

a qua (ay **kway** *or* **kwah**). [Latin] See A QUO.

aqua (**ak**-wə), *n.* [Latin] *Roman law.* (14c) **1.** Water. **2.** A watercourse. Pl. ***aquae*** (**ak**-wee).

▸ ***aqua aestiva*** (**ak**-wə es-**tɪ**-və). Summer water; water used only in the summer.

▸ ***aqua currens*** (**ak**-wə **kər**-enz). See *aqua profluens.*

▸ ***aqua dulcis*** (**ak**-wə **dəl**-sis). Fresh water. — Also termed *aqua frisca.*

▸ ***aqua fontanea*** (**ak**-wə fon-**tay**-nee-ə). Springwater.

▸ ***aqua frisca*** (**ak**-wə **fris**-kə). See *aqua dulcis.*

▸ ***aqua profluens*** (**ak**-wə **prof**-loo-enz). Flowing or running water. — Also termed *aqua currens.*

▸ ***aqua quotidiana*** (**ak**-wə kwoh-tid-ee-**ay**-nə). Daily water; water that can be drawn at all times of the year. — Also spelled *aqua cottidiane.*

▸ ***aqua salsa*** (**ak**-wə **sal**-sə). Salt water.

aquaeductus (ak-wee-**dək**-təs), *n.* [Latin "conveying of water"] See *servitus aquae ducendae* under SERVITUS.

aquae ferventis judicium. [Latin] *Eccles. law.* See *ordeal by water* (2) under ORDEAL.

aquae frigidae judicium. [Latin] *Eccles. law.* See *ordeal by water* (1) under ORDEAL.

aquaehaustus (ak-wee-**haws**-təs), *n.* [Latin "drawing of water"] A servitude granting the right to draw water from a well, pool, spring, or stream on another's land. — Also termed *jus aquaehaustus; servitus aquaehaustus; servitus aquae hauriendae.*

aquae immittendae (**ak**-wee im-ə-**ten**-dee). [Latin "waters to be discharged"] A servitude consisting in the right of one whose house is surrounded by other buildings to discharge wastewater on the neighboring roofs or yards. • This is similar to common-law drip rights. — Also termed *stillicidium.* Cf. *servitus stillicidii* under SERVITUS; DRIP RIGHTS.

aqua frisca. See *aqua dulcis* under AQUA (2).

aquagium (ə-**kway**-jee-əm), *n.* [Law Latin] *Hist.* **1.** A canal for draining water, esp. from marshy land. **2.** A payment for supplying water to a mill or carrying goods by water.

aquatic right. See WATER RIGHT.

Aquilian law. See LEX AQUILIA.

a quo (ah *or* ay **kwoh**), *adv.* [Latin] From which. — Also termed *a qua.* See AD QUEM; *court a quo* under COURT.

a quo invito aliquid exigi potest (ay kwoh in-**vɪ**-toh **al**-i-kwid **ek**-sə-jɪ **poh**-test). [Latin] (18c) *Scots law.* From whom something may be exacted against his will. • The phrase appeared in reference to the position of a debtor under a legal obligation, as distinguished from his position under a natural, voluntary obligation.

A.R. *abbr.* ANNO REGNI.

arabant (ə-**ray**-bənt). [Latin] They plowed. • This term was applied to those who held by the tenure of plowing and tilling the lord's lands within the manor.

arable land. See LAND.

aralia (ə-**ray**-lee-ə), *n.* See *arable land* under LAND.

aratia (ə-**ray**-shee-ə), *n.* See *arable land* under LAND.

arator (ə-**ray**-tər), *n.* [Law Latin] *Hist.* A farmer of arable land.

aratrum terrae (ə-**ray**-trəm **ter**-ee), *n.* [Law Latin] (18c) *Hist.* The amount of land that can be plowed with a single plow; plowland.

araturia (ar-ə-**t[y]oor**-ee-ə), *n.* [Law Latin] See *arable land* under LAND.

ARB. *abbr.* ACCOUNTING RESEARCH BULLETIN.

arbiter (**ahr**-bə-tər). (14c) One with the power to decide disputes, such as a judge <the Supreme Court is the final arbiter of legal disputes in the United States>. Cf. ARBITRATOR.

arbitrability. (1910) **1.** The status, under applicable law, of a dispute's being or not being resolvable by arbitrators because of the subject matter. • For example, in *Rodriguez de Quijas v. Shearson/American Express,* 490 U.S. 477 (1989), the Supreme Court addressed the arbitrability of claims under the 1933 Securities Act, holding that the Act permitted such claims to be resolved in arbitrations arising out of predispute arbitration agreements. **2.** The status of a dispute's being or not being within the jurisdiction of arbitrators to resolve, based on whether the parties entered into an enforceable agreement to arbitrate, whether the dispute is within the scope of the arbitration agreement, whether any procedural prerequisites to arbitration have been satisfied, and whether the applicable law permits the arbitrators to resolve the subject matter of the dispute.

> "Now 'arbitrability' is a word that might well be banned from our vocabulary entirely — or at least restricted, as in other legal systems, to the notion of what society will permit arbitrators to do." Alan Scott Rau, *The Arbitrability Question Itself,* 10 Am. Rev. Int'l Arb. 287, 308 (1999).

▸ **procedural arbitrability.** (1959) Arbitrability as determined by whether any procedural prerequisites to arbitration have been satisfied, such as whether the arbitration demand was timely filed.

▸ **substantive arbitrability.** (1959) Arbitrability as determined by whether a dispute is within the scope of the arbitration agreement. • Courts often distinguish "between substantive arbitrability, that is, whether the dispute falls within the scope of a valid arbitration agreement, and procedural arbitrability, that is, whether the procedural requirements for submitting the dispute to arbitration are met." 2 Ian R. Macneil et al., *Federal Arbitration Law* § 15.1.4.2 (1994).

arbitrable (**ahr**-bi-trə-bəl), *adj.* (16c) Subject to or suitable for arbitration.

arbitrable dispute. See DISPUTE.

arbitrage (**ahr**-bə-trahzh), *n.* (1875) The process of buying something, such as raw materials or a currency, in one place and selling it immediately elsewhere in order to profit from the difference in prices; esp., the simultaneous buying and selling of identical securities in different markets, with the hope of profiting from the price difference between those markets. — Also termed *space arbitrage.* — **arbitrager** (**ahr**-bə-trazh-ər), **arbitrageur** (ahr-bə-trah-**zhər**), *n.*

▸ **convertible arbitrage.** The purchase of a security that, having no restriction other than the payment of money, is exchangeable or convertible within a reasonable time to a second security, with a simultaneous offsetting sale of the second security. — Also termed *kind arbitrage.*

▸ **covered-interest arbitrage.** (1938) The simultaneous investment in a currency and execution of spot- and forward-rate foreign-exchange contracts to take advantage of exchange-rate and interest-rate differentials between currencies without assuming foreign-exchange risk.

▸ **currency arbitrage.** (1940) The simultaneous purchase of a currency in one market and sale of it in another to take advantage of differences or fluctuations in exchange rates.

▸ **kind arbitrage.** (1959) See *convertible arbitrage.*

▸ **risk arbitrage.** (1970) The arbitrage of assets that are probably, but not necessarily, equivalent; esp., arbitrage of corporate stock in a potential merger or takeover, whereby the target company's stock is bought and the acquiring company's stock is sold simultaneously.

▸ **time arbitrage.** (1938) The purchase of a commodity against a present sale of the identical commodity for a future delivery; esp., the simultaneous buying and selling of securities for immediate delivery and future delivery, with the hope of profiting from the difference in prices.

arbitrage bond. See BOND (3).

arbitral panel. See ARBITRATOR.

arbitral seat. See SEAT.

arbitral tribunal. See ARBITRATOR.

arbitrament (ahr-**bi**-trə-mənt). (15c) **1.** The power to decide finally and absolutely for oneself or others. **2.** The act of deciding or settling a dispute that has been referred to arbitration. **3.** ARBITRATION AWARD. — Also spelled (archaically) *arbitrement.*

arbitrament and award. (18c) A plea that the same matter has already been decided in arbitration.

arbitrary, *adj.* (15c) **1.** Depending on individual discretion; of, relating to, or involving a determination made without consideration of or regard for facts, circumstances, fixed rules, or procedures. **2.** (Of a judicial decision) founded on prejudice or preference rather than on reason or fact. • This type of decision is often termed *arbitrary and capricious.* Cf. CAPRICIOUS. — **arbitrariness,** *n.*

arbitrary arrest. See ARREST (2).

arbitrary detention. See DETENTION (1).

arbitrary mark. See *arbitrary trademark* under TRADEMARK.

arbitrary name. See *arbitrary trademark* under TRADEMARK.

arbitrary trademark. See TRADEMARK.

arbitration, *n.* (15c) A dispute-resolution process in which the disputing parties choose one or more neutral third parties to make a final and binding decision resolving the dispute. • The parties to the dispute may choose a third party directly by mutual agreement, or indirectly, such as by agreeing to have an arbitration organization select the third party. — Also termed (redundantly) *binding arbitration.* See ARBITRATOR; EXPERT DETERMINATION. Cf. MEDIATION (1). — **arbitrate,** *vb.* — **arbitral,** *adj.*

> "Arbitration may be defined as a method for the settlement of disputes and differences between two or more parties, whereby such disputes are submitted to the decision of one or more persons specially nominated for the purpose, either instead of having recourse to an action at law, or, by order of the Court, after such action has been commenced." John P.H. Soper, *A Treatise on the Law and Practice of Arbitrations and Awards* 1 (David M. Lawrence ed., 5th ed. 1935).

> "[A] recourse to arbitration was common in medieval England. But the courts did not look very favourably on a practice which tended to diminish their jurisdiction; and when they were asked to enforce the awards made by arbitrators against recalcitrant parties to an arbitration, they got many opportunities of laying down rules as to the conditions of the validity of these awards, as to the modes of entering them, and as to the conduct of arbitrators, which, at the end of the medieval period, were beginning to make the law as to arbitrators a very technical and not a very reasonable body of law. Its complexity was increased in the succeeding centuries; and, though some of the less reasonable medieval rules were eliminated, it became more elaborate and remained very technical, whilst the growing complexity in the law of pleading made it increasingly difficult to be sure that a disputed award would be enforced. In 1698 the Legislature made a salutary change in the law as to the method of entering awards, but it was not till the legislation of the 19th century that the manifold complexities and irrational technicalities of the common law as to arbitration were reformed, and the law assumed its modern form." 14 William Holdsworth, *A History of English Law* 187–88 (A.L. Goodhart & H.G. Hanbury eds., 1964).

▸ **ad hoc arbitration.** (1931) **1.** Arbitration of only one issue. **2.** An arbitration that does not involve an arbitration provider or institution to administer the proceeding.

▸ **adjudicative-claims arbitration.** (1968) Arbitration designed to resolve matters usu. handled by courts (such as a tort claim), in contrast to arbitration of labor issues, international trade, and other fields traditionally associated with arbitration.

▸ **class arbitration.** (1977) An arbitration conducted on a representative basis similar to that of a class action in court, with a single person or small group of people representing the interests of a larger group. — Also termed *classwide arbitration.*

▸ **compromissory arbitration.** (1983) An international arbitration grounded on a mutual promise to define the scope of the dispute and abide by the arbitrator's decision. See COMPROMIS.

▸ **compulsory arbitration.** (1813) See *mandatory arbitration.*

▸ **court-annexed arbitration.** (1978) An arbitration to which the judge in a pending case refers the parties, who present their arguments on the merits and receive the arbitrator's nonbinding decision. • This type of "arbitration" does not fit within the classical definition because it is nonbinding. — Also termed *court-ordered arbitration; judicial arbitration; mandatory arbitration.* Cf. *nonbinding arbitration.*

> "In court-annexed arbitration, one or more arbitrators issue a non-binding judgment on the merits, after an expedited, adversarial hearing. In some programs, unless one of the parties rejects the non-binding ruling within a certain time period and asks to proceed to trial, the arbitration decision becomes final. In other programs, the arbitration decision remains non-binding without any need for a party to object, and simply serves as a guide for the parties to aid them in

efforts to settle the case." Stephen C. Bennett, *Arbitration: Essential Concepts* 194 (2002).

▸ **court-ordered arbitration.** See *court-annexed arbitration.*

▸ **fast-track arbitration.** An arbitration with stringent deadlines for the steps in the proceedings so as to resolve the dispute speedily.

▸ **final-offer arbitration.** (1971) An arbitration in which each party submits a "final offer" to the arbitrator, who must choose one or the other party's final offer in making the award. • The theory behind the final-offer arbitration is that it gives each party the incentive to make its offer closer to the value of the case than the other party's offer, which may result in an award that better reflects the parties' expectations and which increases the likelihood that the parties will settle the dispute themselves.

"In the casual discussion of arbitration systems, it is often claimed that the final-offer arbitration system is more likely than the conventional arbitration system to lead the parties to present reasonable offers for the arbitrator's decision. . . . Of course, this discussion . . . depends entirely on the characterization of arbitrators as simply 'splitting the difference' in one way or another between the parties' offers in determining awards." Orley Ashenfelter, "Arbitration," in 1 *The New Palgrave Dictionary of Economics and the Law* 88, 91 (Peter Newman ed., 1998).

▸ **forced arbitration.** See *mandatory arbitration.*

▸ **grievance arbitration.** (1945) **1.** Arbitration that involves the violation or interpretation of an existing contract. • The arbitrator issues a final decision regarding the meaning of the contractual terms. **2.** *Labor law.* Arbitration of an employee's grievance, usu. relating to an alleged violation of the employee's rights under a collective-bargaining agreement. • The arbitration procedure is set out in the collective-bargaining agreement. Grievance arbitration is the final step in grievance procedure. — Also termed *rights arbitration.* See GRIEVANCE PROCEDURE.

▸ **interest arbitration.** (1959) Arbitration that involves settling the terms of a contract being negotiated between the parties; esp., in labor law, arbitration of a dispute concerning what provisions will be included in a new collective-bargaining agreement. • When the parties cannot agree on contractual terms, an arbitrator decides. This type of arbitration is most common in public-sector collective bargaining.

▸ **judicial arbitration.** (1912) See *court-annexed arbitration.*

▸ **mandatory arbitration.** (1927) **1.** Arbitration required by law or a contractual agreement. **2.** Arbitration required by a predispute arbitration clause included in a contract of adhesion. **3.** See *court-annexed arbitration.* — Also termed *compulsory arbitration; forced arbitration.* Cf. *voluntary arbitration.*

"[T]erms such as 'compulsory arbitration' or 'mandatory arbitration' . . . properly . . . describe arbitration imposed on the parties by law with no consent or manifestations of consent. Sometimes, however, they are used by judges or others respecting consensual arbitration such as FAA arbitration. This tends to happen when the person using the term is concerned about the circumstances that generated the consent, or about the genuineness of consent manifested, as in adhesion contracts. These concerns and their being raised are, of course, perfectly legitimate, as is a recognition of the coercive character of consenting to be bound by contracts. . . . To call the arbitration compulsory or mandatory[, however,] is to answer by label, not by attention to the facts and by analysis. It is far better to call these terms 'predispute' arbitration agreements." 2 Ian R. Macneil et al., *Federal Arbitration Law* § 17.1.2.2, at 17:8–17:9 (Supp. 1999).

▸ **nonbinding arbitration.** (1958) A dispute-resolution process that resembles arbitration except that the award is not binding on the parties. • The term may be considered a misnomer by some because arbitration is usu. intended to result in a final, binding award. Cf. *court-annexed arbitration.*

▸ **rights arbitration.** See *grievance arbitration.*

▸ **voluntary arbitration.** (18c) Arbitration by the agreement of the parties, esp. when the agreement to arbitrate occurred after the dispute arose. • This term is sometimes used to refer to postdispute agreements to arbitrate future consumer and employment disputes. Cf. *mandatory arbitration.*

arbitration act. (1807) A statute that makes arbitration agreements and awards legally enforceable. See FEDERAL ARBITRATION ACT; UNIFORM ARBITRATION ACT.

arbitration agreement. (18c) An agreement by which the parties consent to resolve one or more disputes by arbitration. • An arbitration agreement can consist of a clause in a contract or a stand-alone agreement and can be entered into either before a dispute has arisen between the parties (a *predispute arbitration agreement*) or after a dispute has arisen between the parties (a *postdispute arbitration agreement* or *submission agreement*).

arbitration and award. (1831) An affirmative defense asserting that the subject matter of the action has already been settled in arbitration.

arbitration award. (18c) A final decision by an arbitrator or panel of arbitrators. — Also termed *arbitrament.*

▸ **foreign arbitration award.** (1931) An arbitration award that is made in a country other than the country in which enforcement of the award is sought. • For example, if France is the arbitral seat, the award is made in France. When a party seeks to enforce the award in the United States, the award is considered a foreign award in the United States.

▸ **nondomestic arbitration award.** (2004) An arbitration award that is made in the United States but involves property located abroad, performance or enforcement abroad, or some other reasonable relationship with at least one foreign country. *See* 9 USCA § 202.

▸ **partial arbitration award.** (1987) An arbitration award in which the arbitrators finally resolve some but not all of the issues before them.

▸ **reasoned arbitration award.** (1979) An arbitration award in which the arbitrators explain the rationale for their decision.

arbitration board. (1886) A panel of arbitrators appointed to hear and decide a dispute according to the rules of arbitration.

arbitration bond. (17c) A performance bond executed by the parties in an arbitration. See PERFORMANCE BOND (1).

arbitration clause. (1828) A contractual provision mandating arbitration — and thereby avoiding litigation — of disputes about the contracting parties' rights, duties, and liabilities.

arbitration institution. See ARBITRATION PROVIDER.

arbitration of exchange. (1985) The simultaneous buying and selling of bills of exchange in different international markets, with the hope of profiting from the price difference of the currencies in those markets. See ARBITRAGE; DRAFT (1).

arbitration provider. (1993) An organization that provides administrative services to parties in arbitration. • The services provided typically include promulgating standard-form procedural rules, maintaining panels of arbitrators, providing administrative services in support of arbitral proceedings, and acting as appointing authority, if necessary. The term *arbitration provider* is most commonly used when discussing domestic arbitration, the more usual term for international arbitration being *arbitration institution.*

arbitrator, *n.* (15c) **1.** A neutral person who resolves disputes between parties, esp. by means of formal arbitration. **2.** A neutral decision-maker who is appointed directly or indirectly by the parties to an arbitration agreement to make a final and binding decision resolving the parties' dispute. • Parties usu. agree to have their dispute resolved by either a sole arbitrator or three arbitrators (referred to as an *arbitral panel* in domestic arbitration or an *arbitral tribunal* in international arbitration). — Also termed *impartial chair*; (in Latin) *compromissarius.* Cf. MEDIATOR; ARBITER. — **arbitratorship,** *n.*

▸ **party-appointed arbitrator.** (1948) An arbitrator appointed by one party to a dispute. • When appointing an arbitral panel or tribunal, each party usu. appoints one arbitrator and then the appointed arbitrators choose the last arbitrator. In international arbitration, party-appointed arbitrators are expected to be neutral and independent of the parties. In domestic arbitration, party-appointed arbitrators do not have to be neutral and independent of the parties, but they may have to reveal their lack of neutrality and independence.

▸ **presiding arbitrator.** (1903) The last arbitrator chosen for an arbitral panel or tribunal. • In both domestic and international arbitration, the presiding arbitrator must be neutral and independent of the parties. — Also termed *chair.*

arbitrement. *Archaic.* See ARBITRAMENT.

arbitrio boni judicis (ahr-**bi**-tree-oh **boh**-nɪ **joo**-di-sis). [Latin] *Hist.* In the opinion of a good judge.

arbitrium (ahr-**bi**-tree-əm). [Law Latin] An award; a decision of an arbitrator.

arbor civilis (**ahr**-bər **siv**-ə-lis). [Latin "civil tree"] (17c) A genealogical tree. — Also termed *arbor consanguinitatis.*

arbor consanguinitatis. See ARBOR CIVILIS.

arbor finalis (**ahr**-bər fi-**nay**-lis). [Latin] *Hist.* A boundary tree; a tree used for marking a boundary line.

arborum furtim caesarum (ahr-**bor**-əm **fər**-tim si-**sair**-əm *or* si-**zair**-). [Latin] *Roman law.* A civil action in tort for secretly cutting down trees on another's land.

arcana imperii (ahr-**kay**-nə im-**peer**-ee-ɪ). [Latin] (17c) State secrets.

arcarius (ahr-**kair**-ee-əs). [Latin] *Hist.* A treasurer; a keeper of public money.

Archaionomia (ahr-kee-ə-**noh**-mee-ə). A Latin translation of Saxon laws, published in 1568 by William Lambarde.

archbishop. (bef. 12c) *Eccles. law.* A church officer who has authority over all ecclesiastical matters within a province. • Within the Church of England, the Archbishop of Canterbury is superior in rank to but does not control the Archbishop of York, who has supreme authority in the province of York. Both are appointed for life by England's monarch (as head of the Church of England), on the advice of the Prime Minister, and are members of the House of Lords.

archbishopric. (bef. 12c) *Eccles. law.* An archbishop's jurisdiction or province.

archdeacon (ahrch-**dee**-kən), *n.* (bef. 12c) *Eccles. law.* A high official, traditionally the chief deacon, in the affairs of a diocese, often with jurisdiction to hold court periodically, his judicial acts being subject to appeal to the bishop. Cf. DEACON. — **archidiaconical** (ahr-ki-dɪ-**ak**-ə-nəl), *adj.*

archdeaconry (ahrch-**dee**-kən-ree), *n.* (16c) *Eccles. law.* **1.** An archdeacon's jurisdiction. **2.** The office or rank of an archdeacon.

Archdeacon's Court. See COURT OF ARCHDEACON.

Archdiaconal Court. See COURT OF ARCHDEACON.

Arches Court of Canterbury. See COURT OF ARCHES.

archicapellanus (ahr-kee-kap-ə-**lay**-nəs). [Law Latin] (18c) *Hist.* A chief or high chancellor. — Also termed *summus cancellarius.*

archipelago (ahr-ki-**pel**-ə-goh), *n.* (16c) *Int'l law.* **1.** Collectively, related islands that together stud a particular area within a large body of water, the islands forming (or historically having formed) a distinctive geographic, economic, and political entity. **2.** The waters in which those islands are located. — **archipelagic** (ahr-ki-pə-**laj**-ik), *adj.*

Architect of the Capitol. The officer in the legislative branch of the federal government responsible for maintaining the buildings and grounds of the U.S. Capitol, the Supreme Court, and the Library of Congress. • The Architect also plans and supervises new building construction. The office was established in 1876. 2 USCA §§ 1801, 1811.

architect's certificate. (1834) An architect's formal statement that a contractor has performed under a construction contract and is therefore entitled to payment.

architect's lien. See LIEN.

architectural review. See DESIGN REVIEW.

architectural work. See WORK (2).

archival copy. (1983) *Copyright.* A copy of an original piece of software, made by the consumer for backup. • An owner may make archival copies of software without infringing its copyright. But if the owner transfers the original software, all archival copies must also be transferred or else destroyed. 17 USCA § 117.

archive, *n.* (*usu. pl.*) (17c) **1.** A place where public, historical, or institutional records are systematically preserved. **2.** Collected and preserved public, historical, or institutional papers and records. **3.** Any systematic compilation of materials, esp. writings, in physical or electronic form. — **archive,** *vb.*

Archivist of the United States. The federal officer in charge of the National Archives and Records Administration.

arcifinious (ahr-sə-**fin**-ee-əs), *adj.* [fr. Latin *arcifinius* "having irregular boundaries"] (1859) *Civil law.* **1.** (Of a landed estate) having natural boundaries such as woods, mountains, or rivers. **2.** (Of a country) having a frontier that forms a natural defense.

arcta et salva custodia (**ahrk**-tə et **sal**-və kə-**stoh**-dee-ə). [Law Latin] *Hist.* In close and safe custody. • A defendant arrested under the writ of *capias ad satisfaciendum* was said to be kept *arcta et salva custodia.*

ardour. [Law French] *Hist.* An arsonist.

are. One hundred square meters.

area bargaining. (1961) Negotiation of collective-bargaining agreements by a union with several employers in a geographic area.

area-rate clause. (1974) *Oil & gas.* A price-escalation provision in a long-term gas contract permitting an automatic increase in the contract price if any regulatory agency prescribes or allows a higher price on gas sold in the area. — Also termed *FPC clause.*

area-standards picketing. (1967) *Labor law.* The practice that a union undertakes to protect its members in a particular region by picketing employers that may undercut the market through the potentially lower labor costs of a nonunion workforce.

area variance. See VARIANCE (2).

Areeda–Turner test. (1977) *Antitrust.* An economic test for predatory pricing whereby a price below average variable cost is presumed to be predatory and therefore illegal. • This test is widely accepted by federal courts. Its name derives from the coauthors of an influential law-review article: Phillip Areeda & Donald F. Turner, *Predatory Pricing and Practices Under Section 2 of the Sherman Act,* 88 Harv. L. Rev. 692 (1975). They reformulated their test in 3 Phillip Areeda & Donald F. Turner, *Antitrust Law* ¶¶ 710–722 (1978). See PREDATORY PRICING.

à rendre (ah **rawn**-drə *or* -dər). [Law French] To render; to yield.

arentare (ar-ən-**tair**-ee). [Law Latin] To rent out; to let out at a certain rent.

A reorganization. See REORGANIZATION (2).

arere (ə-**reer**), *adj.* [Law French] Behind in payment (as of rent); in arrears. See ARREAR (1).

a responsis (ay ri-**spon**-sis), *n.* [Law Latin] See APOCRISARIUS.

arg. *abbr.* ARGUENDO (2).

argentarius (ahr-jən-**tair**-ee-əs), *n.* [Latin] (14c) *Roman law.* A moneylender; a banker.

argentarius miles (ahr-jən-**tair**-ee-əs **mɪ**-leez), *n.* [Law Latin] (18c) *Hist.* A money porter who carries money from the lower to the upper Exchequer to be examined and tested.

argentum (ahr-**jen**-təm), *n.* [Latin] Silver; esp., silver coinage.

argentum dei (ahr-**jen**-təm **dee**-ɪ), *n.* [Law Latin] (17c) See DENARIUS DEI.

arguendo (ahr-gyoo-**en**-doh). [Latin "in arguing"] (1817) **1.** For the sake of argument <assuming arguendo that discovery procedures were correctly followed, the court still cannot grant the defendant's motion to dismiss>. **2.** During the course of argument <counsel mentioned arguendo that the case has been followed in three other decisions>. — Abbr. arg.

arguer. (14c) Someone who makes an oral argument; esp., an attorney, often one of several attorneys representing the same client, who presents an oral argument in court.

argument. (14c) **1.** A situation in which two or more persons expressly disagree and dispute one another's positions, often vehemently. **2.** A statement that attempts to persuade by setting forth reasons why something is true or untrue, right or wrong, better or worse, etc.; esp., the remarks of counsel in analyzing and pointing out or repudiating a desired inference, made for the assistance of a decision-maker. **3.** The act or process of attempting to persuade. See ORAL ARGUMENT; OPENING STATEMENT; CLOSING ARGUMENT.

> "[W]e may define . . . an argument as a course of reasoning which firmly establishes a matter about which there is some doubt." Cicero, *De Inventione; De Optimo Genere Oratorum; Topica* 387 (H.M. Hubbell trans. 1949) (repr. 2006).

argumentative, *adj.* (15c) **1.** Of, relating to, or involving argument or persuasion <an argumentative tone of voice>. **2.** Expressing not only facts, but also inferences and conclusions drawn from facts <the judge sustained the prosecutor's objection to the argumentative question>. **3.** Quarrelsome; disputatious.

argumentative affidavit. See AFFIDAVIT.

argumentative direction. See *argumentative instruction* under JURY INSTRUCTION.

argumentative instruction. See JURY INSTRUCTION.

argumentative pleading. See PLEADING (1).

argumentative question. (1878) A question in which the examiner interposes a viewpoint under the guise of asking a question. Cf. LEADING QUESTION.

argumentum (ahr-gyoo-**men**-təm), *n.* [Latin] An argument. Pl. ***argumenta.***

▸ ***argumentum ab auctoritate*** (ab awk-tor-ə-**tay**-tee). [Latin] An argument from authority (of a statute or case).

▸ ***argumentum ab impossibili*** (ab im-pah-**sib**-ə-lɪ). [Latin] An argument from impossibility.

▸ ***argumentum ab inconvenienti*** (ab in-kən-vee-nee-**en**-tɪ). [Latin] An argument from inconvenience; an argument that emphasizes the harmful consequences of failing to follow the position advocated.

▸ ***argumentum a contrario*** (ay kən-**trair**-ee-oh). [Latin] An argument for contrary treatment.

▸ ***argumentum ad baculum*** (ad **bak**-yə-ləm). [Latin] An argument depending on physical force to back it up.

▸ ***argumentum ad captandum*** (ad kap-**tan**-dəm). [Latin] An argument appealing to the emotions of a crowd.

▸ ***argumentum ad crumenam*** (ad kroo-**mee**-nəm). [fr. Latin *crumena* "purse"] An argument appealing to the purse (or one's desire to save money).

▸ ***argumentum ad hominem*** (ad **hom**-ə-nəm *or* -nem). [Latin "argument to the man"] (17c) An argument based on disparagement or praise of another in a way that obscures the real issue.

▸ ***argumentum ad ignorantiam*** (ad ig-nə-**ran**-shee-əm). [Latin] An argument based on an adversary's ignorance of the matter in dispute.

▸ ***argumentum ad invidiam*** (ad in-**vid**-ee-əm). [Latin] An argument appealing to one's hatreds or prejudices.

▸ ***argumentum ad judicium*** (ad joo-**dish**-ee-əm). [Latin] An argument addressed to the judgment; a proof based on knowledge or probability.

▸ ***argumentum ad misericordiam*** (ad miz-ə-ri-**kor**-dee-əm). [Latin] An argument appealing to pity.

▸ ***argumentum ad populum*** (ad **pop**-yə-ləm). [Latin] An argument appealing to the crowd.

▸ ***argumentum ad rem*** (ad **rem**). [Latin] An argument on the point at issue.

▸ ***argumentum ad verecundiam*** (ad ver-ə-**kən**-dee-əm). [Latin] An argument appealing to the listener's modesty; an argument based on the opinions of people who are considered authorities.

▸ ***argumentum a majore ad minorem*** (ay mə-**jor**-ee ad mi-**nor**-əm). [Latin] *Hist.* Argument from the larger scale to the smaller.

▸ ***argumentum a simili*** (ay **sim**-ə-lɪ). [Latin "argument from a like case"] An argument by analogy or similarity.

▸ ***argumentum baculinum*** (bak-yə-**lɪ**-nəm). [fr. Latin *baculus* "a rod or scepter"] An argument appealing to force.

▸ ***argumentum circulum*** (**sər**-kyə-ləm). [Latin] *Hist.* Circular argument. See PETITIO PRINCIPII.

▸ ***argumentum ex concesso*** (eks kən-**ses**-oh). [Latin] An argument based on an earlier admission by the adversary.

▸ ***argumentum ex silentio*** (eks si-**len**-shee-oh). [Latin] An argument from silence — i.e., based on the absence of express evidence to the contrary.

arise, *vb.* (bef. 12c) **1.** To originate; to stem (from) <a federal claim arising under the U.S. Constitution>. **2.** To result (from) <litigation routinely arises from such accidents>. **3.** To emerge in one's consciousness; to come to one's attention <the question of appealability then arose>. **4.** *Archaic.* (Of a court) to adjourn; to suspend sitting <the court arose for the day>.

arising-in jurisdiction. See JURISDICTION.

aristocracy (air-i-**stok**-rə-see). (16c) **1.** A privileged class of persons, esp. the hereditary nobility; specif., the people in the highest social class, who have traditionally possessed a great deal of land, money, and power. **2.** A government ruled by a privileged class. — **aristocratic,** *adj.* — **aristocrat,** *n.*

aristodemocracy. (17c) A government consisting of both democratic and aristocratic elements; a government in which power is divided between the nobility (or more powerful group) and the rest of the people.

Arizona method. See BLIND-STRIKE SYSTEM.

Arkansas rule. *Secured transactions.* The principle that the collateral securing a loan is presumed to be worth at least as much as the loan's balance, and that the creditor has the burden to prove that a sale of the collateral would not satisfy the loan amount. *Norton v. National Bank of Commerce,* 398 S.W.2d 538 (Ark. 1966).

ARM. *abbr.* See *adjustable-rate mortgage* under MORTGAGE.

arma (**ahr**-mə), *n. pl.* [Latin] *Roman law.* **1.** Arms; weapons. **2.** Military service.

▸ ***arma moluta*** (**ahr**-mə mə-**loo**-tə). [Law Latin] (17c) Sharp weapons that cut, as contrasted with blunt instruments that bruise or break.

▸ ***arma reversata*** (**ahr**-mə ree-vər-**say**-tə). [Law Latin] (18c) Reversed arms. • This was a punishment for a felon or traitor.

armaria. See ALMARIA.

armata vis (ahr-**may**-tə **vis**). See VIS ARMATA.

armed, *adj.* (13c) **1.** Equipped with a weapon <an armed robber>. **2.** Involving the use of a weapon <armed robbery>.

armed conflict. (1849) *Int'l law.* **1.** A state of open hostility between two countries, or between a country and an aggressive force. • A state of armed conflict may exist without a formal declaration of war by either side. **2.** A military action taken under Article 42 of the United Nations Charter. — Also termed *police action.*

armed neutrality. See NEUTRALITY.

armed peace. See PEACE.

armed robbery. See ROBBERY.

Armed Services Board of Contract Appeals. A quasi-judicial board that reviews appeals from final decisions of contracting officers involving disputes relating to contracts made by elements of the Department of Defense and designated civilian agencies. • Its decisions are subject to judicial review. — Abbr. ASBCA.

armiger (**ahr**-mə-jər), *n.* [Latin fr. *arma* "arms" + *gerere* "to bear"] (18c) *Hist.* **1.** Someone who bears arms; an armor-bearer; an esquire. **2.** A servant who carried the armor of a knight. **3.** A tenant by scutage; a valet.

arm-in-arm, *adj.* (2000) Of, relating to, or involving a transaction between parties whose personal interests are involved. Cf. ARM'S-LENGTH.

armiscara (ahr-mə-**skair**-ə), *n.* [Law Latin] *Hist.* **1.** A punishment consisting of carrying a saddle on one's back as a sign of subjection. **2.** A fine.

armistice. See TRUCE.

arm of the court. (1834) An officer of the court who performs tasks or duties related to the court's functions. • This term is sometimes applied to a governmental department, such as the probation department, that similarly serves the court.

arm of the sea. (16c) The portion of a river or bay in which the tide ebbs and flows. • It may extend as far into the interior as the water of the river is propelled backward by the tide.

arm of the state. (1953) An entity created by a state and operating as an alter ego or instrumentality of the state, such as a state university or a state department of transportation. • The 11th Amendment of the U.S. Constitution generally bars suits in federal court by individuals against states and has been interpreted as protecting arms of the state as well. Cities and local school districts have been held not to be arms of the state.

arms, law of. (15c) **1.** Rules concerning conditions of war, such as the treatment of prisoners. **2.** The law relating to the right to bear arms. **3.** The law relating to armorial bearings, i.e., coats of arms granted by the College of Heralds in England, Lord Lyon King of Arms in Scotland, and corresponding officers in some other countries.

arms, right to bear. See RIGHT TO BEAR ARMS.

arms control. (1961) *Int'l law.* A policy of minimizing instabilities in the military field by lessening the possibility of the outbreak of war while reducing in number a country's weapons of mass destruction; esp., the attempt by powerful countries to limit the number and kinds of weapons that exist. Cf. DISARMAMENT.

arm's-length, *adj.* (1858) Of, relating to, or involving dealings between two parties who are not related or not on close terms and who are presumed to have roughly equal bargaining power; not involving a confidential relationship <an arm's-length transaction does not create fiduciary duties between the parties>. Cf. ARM-IN-ARM.

arm's-length price. See PRICE.

arm's-length transaction. See TRANSACTION.

army. (14c) **1.** A military force, esp. of ground troops. **2.** Any substantial group of individuals armed for combat. **3.** A vast, organized group.

▸ **regular army.** (17c) The permanent military establishment, maintained during both war and peacetime.

Army Clause. *Constitutional law.* The constitutional provision granting Congress the power raise and support a federal army. U.S. Const. art. I, § 8, cl. 12 Cf. MILITIA CLAUSE.

ARPS. *abbr.* See *adjustable rate preferred stock* under STOCK.

arra (**ar**-ə), *n.* [Latin "earnest, deposit"] (16c) *Roman & civil law.* Earnest money; money given as evidence of a completed bargain. See DENARIUS DEI. Cf. GOD'S PENNY. — Also spelled *arrha.* Pl. ***arrae.***

arraignment (ə-**rayn**-mənt), *n.* (16c) The initial step in a criminal prosecution whereby the defendant is brought before the court to hear the charges and to enter a plea. Fed. R. Crim. P. 10. Cf. PRELIMINARY HEARING; *initial appearance* under APPEARANCE. — **arraign,** *vb.*

arranged marriage. See MARRIAGE (1).

arrangement, *n.* (17c) **1.** The putting of things into proper order; the disposition of things in a harmonious or suitable form <the arrangement of speeches>. **2.** The mode or system in which parts or elements have been put or disposed in accordance with some plan or design; the way in which something is organized <document-production arrangements>. **3.** A measure taken or plan made in advance of some occurrence, sometimes for a legal purpose; an agreement or settlement of details made in anticipation <travel arrangements>. **4.** The nonbinding settlement of a dispute or issue of mutual concern; a nonobligatory compromise reached between adversaries or potential adversaries <a legally nonbinding arrangement was concluded between the parties>. See FAMILY ARRANGEMENT. **5.** *English law.* An agreement between a debtor and his or her creditors to modify the obligations to them, esp. by composition <the debtor executed a deed of arrangement>. See COMPOSITION (1). **6.** *Int'l law.* A compact or similar instrument, less formal than a treaty, reflecting mutual accord on certain technical or practical matters <an arrangement between the two countries>. **7.** *Copyright.* A piece of music that has been specially adapted for a particular instrument or type of ensemble <a band arrangement of Wagner's *Tannhäuser* overture>.

arrangement in order of breadth. *Patents.* The placement of claims in a patent application in order of scope so that the first claim in the application or patent is the broadest and later claims are progressively narrower.

arrangements committee. See COMMITTEE (1).

arrangement with creditors. (1848) *Bankruptcy.* A debtor's agreement with creditors for the settlement, satisfaction, or extension of time for payment of debts. See BANKRUPTCY PLAN.

arranger for disposal. (1989) *Environmental law.* An entity that owns or possesses hazardous substances, and either disposes of them or has an obligation to control them. An arranger for disposal can be held liable for environmental cleanup costs under CERCLA.

array, *n.* (14c) **1.** A panel of potential jurors; VENIRE (1) <the array of mostly wealthy professionals seemed to favor the corporate defendant>. **2.** The jurors actually empaneled <the array hearing the case consisted of seven women and five men>. **3.** A list or roster of empaneled jurors <the plaintiff obtained a copy of the array to help prepare for voir dire>. **4.** Order; arrangement <the array of jurors from oldest to youngest>. **5.** A militia <the array organized antigovernment rallies>. **6.** A series of statistics or a group of elements <a mathematical array>. **7.** PHOTO ARRAY.

array, *vb.* (16c) **1.** To empanel a jury for trial. **2.** To call out the names of jurors, one by one, as they are empaneled.

arrear, *n.* (*usu. pl.*) (17c) **1.** The quality, state, or condition of being behind in the payment of a debt or the discharge of an obligation <the creditor filed a lawsuit against the debtor who was in arrears>. — Also termed *arrearage.* **2.** An unpaid or overdue debt <the creditor reached an agreement with the debtor on settling the arrears>. **3.** An unfinished duty <the arrears of work have accumulated>. See IN ARREARS.

arrearage. (14c) **1.** ARREAR (1). **2.** An unpaid dividend, from a past period, that is due to a holder of preferred stock. See *cumulative dividend* under DIVIDEND.

arrent (ə-**rent**), *vb.* (16c) *Hist.* To let at a fixed rent; specif., to give royal permission to enclose (a portion of public land) in exchange for annual rent.

arrest, *n.* (14c) **1.** A seizure or forcible restraint, esp. by legal authority. **2.** The taking or keeping of a person in custody by legal authority, esp. in response to a criminal charge; specif., the apprehension of someone for the purpose of securing the administration of the law, esp. of bringing that person before a court. — **arrest,** *vb.*

> "The question of what constitutes an arrest is a difficult one. On one end of the spectrum, it seems apparent that detention accompanied by handcuffing, drawn guns, or words to the effect that one is under arrest qualifies as an 'arrest' and thus requires probable cause. At the other end, a simple questioning on the street will often not rise to the level of an arrest. Somewhere in between lie investigative

detentions at the stationhouse . . . ." Charles H. Whitebread, *Criminal Procedure* § 3.02, at 61 (1980).

▸ **arbitrary arrest.** An arrest of a person without probable cause to believe the person permitted a crime.

▸ **arrest by warrant.** See *lawful arrest.*

▸ **arrest in execution.** See *arrest on final process.*

▸ **arrest in quarters.** (1942) *Military law.* A nonjudicial punishment that can be given to officers and warrant officers only by a general, a flag officer in command, or an officer exercising general court-martial jurisdiction. See BREACH OF ARREST.

▸ **arrest on final process.** (18c) *Hist.* Arrest in a civil case after the conclusion of a trial. — Also termed *arrest in execution.*

▸ **arrest on mesne process** (meen). (18c) *Hist.* Arrest in a civil case before trial takes place.

▸ **arrest without a warrant.** See *warrantless arrest.*

▸ **citizen's arrest.** (1941) An arrest of a private person by another private person on grounds that (1) a public offense was committed in the arrester's presence, or (2) the arrester has reasonable cause to believe that the arrestee has committed a felony.

▸ **civil arrest.** (18c) *Hist.* An arrest and detention of a civil-suit defendant until bail is posted or a judgment is paid. • Civil arrest is prohibited in most states.

▸ **criminal arrest.** (1818) An arrest made on suspicion, esp. on probable cause, that the person has committed a crime.

▸ **de facto arrest.** (1966) Police custody in which the defendant does not feel free to leave, despite having been explicitly told that he or she may leave.

▸ **dragnet arrest.** (1959) A sweeping arrest of people suspected of possible involvement in criminal activity or a civil disturbance. • This type of arrest is illegal in the United States because it is based not on probable cause but on unsupported suspicion or belief. — Also termed *round-up*; *wholesale arrest.*

▸ **false arrest.** (18c) An arrest made without proper legal authority. Cf. FALSE IMPRISONMENT.

▸ **gate arrest.** See *prison-gate arrest.*

▸ **house arrest.** See HOUSE ARREST.

▸ **lawful arrest.** (18c) The taking of a person into legal custody either under a valid warrant or on probable cause that the person has committed a crime. — Also termed *arrest by warrant*; *warrant arrest.* Cf. *unlawful arrest.*

▸ **malicious arrest.** (18c) An arrest made without probable cause and for an improper purpose; esp., an abuse of process by which a person procures the arrest (and often the imprisonment) of another by means of judicial process, without any reasonable cause. • Malicious arrest can be grounds for an action for abuse of process, false imprisonment, or malicious prosecution.

▸ **material-witness arrest.** (1968) An arrest and detention of a witness to a crime for the purpose of inducing the witness to provide material evidence to investigators or prosecutors. • This type of arrest requires a warrant based on probable cause.

▸ **mental-hygiene arrest.** (2004) The arrest of a person who appears to be mentally ill and is behaving in a manner likely to result in serious harm to self or others, the purpose of the arrest usu. being for immediate hospitalization.

▸ **parol arrest** (pə-**rohl** *or* **par**-əl). (1904) An arrest ordered by a judge or magistrate from the bench, without written complaint, and executed immediately, such as an arrest of a person who breaches the peace in open court. See CONTEMPT.

▸ **pretextual arrest.** (1968) An arrest of a person for a minor offense to create an opportunity to investigate the person's involvement in a more serious offense for which there is no lawful ground to make an arrest. — Also termed *pretext arrest.*

▸ **prison-gate arrest.** (1903) *English law.* An arrest made as soon as a person who has been released from incarceration steps outside a prison's walls or boundaries and is charged with other offenses committed before the person went to prison. — Also termed *gate arrest.*

▸ **rearrest.** (1852) A warrantless arrest of a person who has escaped from custody, violated parole or probation, or failed to appear in court as ordered.

▸ **subterfuge arrest.** (1971) An arrest of a suspect for the stated purpose of obtaining evidence of one crime but with the underlying intent to search the suspect for evidence of a different crime.

▸ **turnover arrest.** (1947) An arrest by a security guard who holds the suspect, usu. a shoplifter, until the police arrive and then turns the suspect over to them.

▸ **unlawful arrest.** (18c) The taking of a person into custody either without a valid warrant or without probable cause to believe that the person has committed a crime. Cf. *lawful arrest.*

▸ **warrant arrest.** See *lawful arrest.*

▸ **warranted arrest.** (1950) An arrest made under authority of a warrant.

▸ **warrantless arrest.** (1958) A legal arrest, without a warrant, based on probable cause of a felony, or for a misdemeanor committed in a police officer's presence. — Also termed *arrest without a warrant.* See WARRANT.

▸ **wholesale arrest.** See *dragnet arrest.*

3. *Maritime law.* The taking of a ship and sometimes its cargo into custody by virtue of a court's warrant.

arrestable offense. See OFFENSE (2).

arrestandis bonis ne dissipentur. See DE ARRESTANDIS BONIS NE DISSIPENTUR.

arrestando ipsum qui pecuniam recepit. See DE ARRESTANDO IPSUM QUI PECUNIAM RECEPIT.

arrestatio (ar-ə-**stay**-shee-oh), *n.* [Law Latin] *Hist.* An arrest.

arrest by warrant. See *lawful arrest* under ARREST (2).

arrestee. (1844) **1.** Someone who has been taken into custody by legal authority; a person who has been arrested. **2.** *Scots law.* Someone who holds property attached by arrestment. See ARRESTMENT (2).

arrester. (15c) Someone who arrests. — Also spelled *arrestor.*

arrest in execution. See *arrest on final process* under ARREST (2).

arrest in quarters. See ARREST (2).

arrestment. (15c) **1.** The arrest of a person or of personal effects. **2.** The taking or attachment of property belonging to another person but in the possession of a third party, either to obtain security or to found jurisdiction. • The process of attachment is similar to garnishment: the property holder is ordered to withhold the property from the debtor. The court may order that the property be transferred to the creditor.

▸ **arrestment in execution.** (1833) Postjudgment arrestment to preserve property on which to collect the judgment.

▸ **arrestment in security.** See *arrestment on the dependence.*

▸ **arrestment on the dependence.** (1829) Prejudgment arrestment to secure payment of a judgment against a debtor who is likely to leave the country to escape the creditor. • The arrestment may be ordered even though the creditor has not begun an action on the debt or an action is still pending. — Also termed *arrestment in security.*

▸ **arrestment to found jurisdiction.** (1835) Arrestment for the purpose of conferring legitimate legal authority on a court, esp. when the debtor is a foreigner who is not present in and does not own land in a given place.

3. The action of checking or stopping something.

arresto facto super bonis mercatorum alienigenorum (ə-**res**-toh **fak**-toh **s[y]oo**-pər **boh**-nis mər-kə-**tor**-əm ay-lee-**ee**-nɪ-jə-**nor**-əm *or* al-ee-). [Latin "seizure of the goods of foreign merchants"] *Hist.* A writ to seize the goods of an alien, taken in recompense of goods taken from an English subject living abroad.

arrest of inquest. (1923) A plea that a matter proposed for inquiry has already been investigated and should therefore not be reexamined.

arrest of judgment. (17c) The staying of a judgment after its entry; esp., a court's refusal to render or enforce a judgment because of a defect apparent from the record. • At common law, courts have the power to arrest judgment for intrinsic causes appearing on the record, as when the verdict differs materially from the pleadings or when the case alleged in the pleadings is legally insufficient. Today, this type of defect must typically be objected to before trial or before judgment is entered, so that the motion in arrest of judgment has been largely superseded. — Also termed *allocutus.*

> "An arrest of judgment [under common law] was the technical term describing the act of a trial judge refusing to enter judgment on the verdict because of an error appearing on the face of the record that rendered the judgment invalid." *U.S. v. Sisson*, 399 U.S. 267, 280–81, 90 S.Ct. 2117, 2125 (1970).

arrest on final process. See ARREST (2).

arrest on mesne process. See ARREST (2).

arrest record. (1930) **1.** A form completed by a police officer when a person is arrested. **2.** A cumulative list of the instances when a person has been arrested. — Also termed *police blotter*; (in sense 2) *bench blotter*; *blotter*; *log.*

arrestum jurisdictionis fundandae causa (ə-**res**-təm joor-is-dik-shee-**oh**-nis fun-**dan**-dee **kaw**-zə). [Law Latin "an arrestment for the purpose of founding jurisdiction"] *Scots law.* An arrestment to bring a foreigner under the jurisdiction of Scottish courts. • This type of arrestment originated in Dutch law. See JURISDICTIONIS FUNDANDAE.

arrest warrant. See WARRANT (1).

arrest without a warrant. See *warrantless arrest* under ARREST (2).

arrêt (ah-**ret** *or* -**ray**). [French] (17c) *Civil law.* **1.** A judgment, sentence, or decree of a court with competent jurisdiction. **2.** A sovereign's decree. Pl. ***arrêts.***

arrêt de règlement (ə-re də re-glə-**mahn**), *n.* [French] *Hist. Civil law.* A decision issued by Parliament to establish a rule of procedure, civil law, or custom.

arretted (ə-**ret**-id), *adj.* [Law French] (17c) (Of an accused) brought before a judge and charged with a crime.

arrha (**ar**-ə). See ARRA.

arrha sponsalitia (**ar**-ee spon-sə-**lish**-ee-ə). [Latin] *Roman law.* A payment made to guarantee fulfillment of a promise to marry.

arriage and carriage (**ar**-ij). (18c) *Hist.* Indefinite services formerly demandable from tenants, but prohibited by statute in the 18th century.

arrière-ban (ah-ree-air-**bahn** *or* **ar**-ee-air-**ban**), *n.* [French] (16c) *Hist.* **1.** A king's proclamation summoning vassals to military service. **2.** The group of vassals so summoned.

arriere fee. See *arriere fee* under FEE (2).

arriere fief. See *arriere fee* under FEE.

arriere vassal. See VASSAL.

arrogatio. See ADROGATION.

arrogation (ar-ə-**gay**-shən), *n.* (16c) **1.** The act of claiming or taking something without the right to do so; esp., the claim that one has a particular right, power, or position to which one has no legal right <some commentators argue that limited military actions unilaterally ordered by the President are an arrogation of Congress's power to declare war>. **2.** *Roman & civil law.* The adoption of an adult; specif., the adoption of a person sui juris, as a result of which the adoptee loses independence and comes within the paternal power (*patria potestas*) of the adopting father. — **arrogate,** *vb.*

ARS. *abbr.* AGRICULTURAL RESEARCH SERVICE.

arser in le main (ahr-**say** a*n* lə **man** *or* an lə **man**), *n.* [French "burning in the hand"] (18c) *Hist.* A punishment of burning or branding the left thumb of a lay offender who falsely claimed and was allowed the benefit of clergy, so that the offender would be distinguished if he tried to claim the benefit again. — Also termed *arsure en le main* (ahr-**soor** awn lə **man** *or* awn lə **man**).

arson, *n.* (17c) **1.** At common law, the malicious burning of someone else's dwelling house or outhouse that is either appurtenant to the dwelling house or within the curtilage.

> "Arson, *ab ardendo*, is the malicious and wilful burning of the house or outhouses of another man." 4 William Blackstone, *Commentaries on the Laws of England* 220 (4th ed. 1770).

> "The thing that is burnt must be a 'house,' but this word has a large meaning; already in 1220 we find the burning of a barn that was full of corn treated as a felony." 2 Frederick

Pollock & Frederic W. Maitland, *History of English Law Before the Time of Edward I* 492 (2d ed. 1899).

"The burning of one's own dwelling to collect insurance did not constitute common-law arson. It was generally assumed in early England that one had the legal right to destroy his own property in any manner he chose." Denis Binder, "Arson: Legal Aspects," in 1 *Encyclopedia of Crime and Justice* 80, 80 (Sanford H. Kadish ed., 1983).

"At common law, arson is the wilful and malicious burning of the dwelling house of another. It may occur during the nighttime or the daytime, and it is an offense against the security of habitation or occupancy, rather than against ownership or property." 3 Charles E. Torcia, *Wharton's Criminal Law* § 334, at 324–25 (15th ed. 1995).

2. Under modern statutes, the intentional and wrongful burning of someone else's property (as to destroy a building) or one's own property (as to fraudulently collect insurance). *See* Model Penal Code § 220.1(1). — Also termed (in Latin) *crimen incendii*; (in sense 2) *statutory arson*. Cf. HOUSEBURNING; CRIMINAL DAMAGE TO PROPERTY.

"The term 'statutory arson' is employed to designate the entire area of statutory proscription which is analogous to, but does not constitute, common-law arson. It is important to have mutually exclusive labels here not only for the reasons mentioned in the preceding section, but because some of the state statutes provide a penalty for arson without defining the word and hence adopt the common-law definition." Rollin M. Perkins & Ronald N. Boyce, *Criminal Law* 287 (3d ed. 1982).

"(1) Arson. A person is guilty of arson, a felony of the second degree, if he starts a fire or causes an explosion with the purpose of: (a) destroying a building or occupied structure of another; or (b) destroying or damaging any property, whether his own or another's, to collect insurance for such loss. It shall be an affirmative defense to prosecution under this paragraph that the actor's conduct did not recklessly endanger any building or occupied structure of another or place any other person in danger of death or bodily injury." Model Penal Code § 220.1 (1997).

▸ **aggravated arson.** (1833) Arson accompanied by some aggravating factor, as when the offender foresees or anticipates that one or more persons will be in or near the property being burned.

arsonable, *adj.* (1902) (Of property) of such a nature as to give rise to a charge of arson if maliciously burned <only real property, and not personal property, is arsonable>.

arson clause. (1983) *Insurance.* An insurance-policy provision that excludes coverage of a loss due to fire if the insured intentionally started the fire.

arson dog. See DOG (1).

arsonist. (1864) Someone who commits the crime of arson; INCENDIARY (1). See ARSON.

arsonous, *adj.* (1953) Of, relating to, or involving arson <an arsonous purpose>.

arsura (ahr-s[y]**oor**-ə), *n.* [Law Latin] *Hist.* **1.** The trial of money by heating it after it is coined. **2.** The loss in weight from this process.

arsure en le main (ahr-**soor** awn le **man**), *n.* [Law French] See ARSER IN LE MAIN.

ART. *abbr.* ASSISTED REPRODUCTIVE TECHNOLOGY.

art. (13c) **1.** Creative expression, or the product of creative expression. **2.** An occupation or business that requires skill; a craft. **3.** *Patents.* A field of useful endeavor; the methodical application of knowledge or skill in creating something new.

▸ **analogous art.** (1879) *Patents.* A technique, product, application, machine, or method that is reasonably related to the problem addressed by the invention, and with which the inventor is assumed to be familiar. — Also termed *pertinent art.* See NONOBVIOUSNESS.

▸ **nuisance prior art.** (1999) *Patents.* Information that appears to anticipate or obviate an invention, but does not actually do so because the earlier described invention was neither reduced to practice nor adequately disclosed in any documents. • Nuisance prior art does not bar a patent's issuance, but it may prolong the prosecution. The term does not apply to efforts that are not prior art at all, such as descriptions of unsuccessful attempts to reduce an invention to practice, or to writings that do not disclose real inventions or technology, such as science-fiction.

▸ **pertinent art. 1.** See *analogous art.* **2.** See *relevant art.*

▸ **prior art.** (1885) *Patents.* Knowledge that is publicly known, used by others, or available on the date of invention to a person of ordinary skill in an art, including what would be obvious from that knowledge. • Prior art includes (1) information in applications for previously patented inventions; (2) information that was published more than one year before a patent application is filed; and (3) information in other patent applications and inventor's certificates filed more than a year before the application is filed. The U.S. Patent and Trademark Office and courts analyze prior art before deciding the patentability of a comparable invention. 35 USCA § 102.

▸ **relevant art.** (1915) *Patents.* Art to which one can reasonably be expected to look for a solution to the problem that a patented device tries to solve. • The term includes not only knowledge about a problem in a particular industry, but also knowledge accumulated in scientific fields whose techniques have been commonly employed to solve similar problems. — Also termed *pertinent art.*

4. *Hist.* In a seduction case, the skillful and systematic coaxing of another to engage in sexual activity.

art and part, *adj. & adv. English & Scots law.* Aiding in or contributing to the commission of a crime <the lookout was involved in the burglary on an art-and-part basis> <the baker acted art and part in the prisoner's escape by producing a cake with a file in it>. See ACCESSORY (2).

art and part, *n.* (16c) *Scots law.* Participation in or encouragement of a crime; criminal guilt by assisting, advising, or participating in the crime. Cf. OPE ET CONSILIO.

"Scots law never distinguished between degrees of participation in a crime, between what English law distinguished as accession before the fact, concomitant accession, and accession after the fact. In treason all participants were treated as principal offenders and indictments in other cases charged the accused as 'actor or art and part.' The Criminal Procedure (Scotland) Act 1887 made this an unnecessary but implied charge in all indictments." 6 David M. Walker, *A Legal History of Scotland* 397 (2001).

artful interpretation. See INTERPRETATION (1).

artful pleading. See PLEADING (2).

art group. (1975) *Patents.* A collection of art units in the U.S. Patent and Trademark Office, led by a group director.

article, *n.* (13c) **1.** Generally, a particular item or thing <article of clothing>.

▸ **article of manufacture.** See MANUFACTURE.

▸ **article of merchandise.** **1.** See MERCHANDISE (1). **2.** See MERCHANDISE (2).

▸ **proprietary article.** (*often pl.*) (1871) A product manufactured under an exclusive right to sell it.

2. A separate and distinct part (as a clause or stipulation) of a writing, esp. in a contract, statute, or constitution <Article III>. **3.** (*pl.*) An instrument containing a set of rules or stipulations <articles of war> <articles of incorporation>. **4.** A nonfictional literary composition forming an independent part of a publication, such as a law review or journal <a well-researched, timely article>. **5.** *Patents.* A workpiece, product, or thing that is operated on, modified, or changed by a machine or process. **6.** *Patents.* An article of manufacture. See MANUFACTURE. **7.** *Eccles. law.* In an ecclesiastical court, one of a plaintiff's complaints or charges against the defendant. • The complaint or charge may be presented by oral declaration or by a written document.

article, *vb.* (15c) **1.** To bring charges against by an exhibition of articles. **2.** To be an articled clerk.

articled clerk. See CLERK (4).

article of manufacture. See ARTICLE (1).

article of merchandise. See ARTICLE (1).

Article I court. (1955) *Constitutional law.* **1.** See *legislative court* under COURT. **2.** A type of federal legislative court that is not bound by the requirements of or protected under U.S. Const. art. III, § 2, and that performs functions similar to those of an administrative agency, such as issuing advisory opinions. U.S. Const. art. I, § 8. Cf. ARTICLE III COURT.

> "Congress also has the power, within certain limits, to create what are called . . . Article I tribunals . . . . These Article I tribunals are really akin to administrative agencies; that is, the 'judges' do not have any constitutionally guaranteed lifetime tenure and protection from salary diminution; they are not governed by the case or controversy limitation of Article III . . . . At the present time, Article I courts include territorial courts, certain courts in the District of Columbia, courts martial, and legislative courts and administrative agencies that adjudicate 'public rights.'" John E. Nowak & Ronald D. Rotunda, *Constitutional Law* 22–23 (4th ed. 1991).

Article I judge. (1958) *Constitutional law.* **1.** A U.S. bankruptcy judge, magistrate judge, or administrative-law judge appointed for a term of years as authorized by Congress under Article I of the U.S. Constitution. 28 USCA §§ 151 et seq., §§ 631 et seq. **2.** A federal judge temporarily appointed by the President without prior Senate approval. • The appointment power derives from the recess-appointment clause, which allows the President to temporarily fill vacancies in government offices while Congress is not in session. U.S. Const. art. II, § 2, cl. **3.** See *recess appointment* under APPOINTMENT (1).

articles of agreement. (16c) A writing that records matters that the parties agreed on when forming a partnership or business or transferring real property. • Unlike a contract, articles of agreement usu. contain only agreements and not express promises of performance, e.g., "the parties agree that it isn't possible to guarantee delivery within 10 days." Articles of agreement often supplement a contract. They may be informal or detailed.

articles of amendment. (1891) A document filed to effectuate an amendment or change to a corporation's articles of incorporation.

articles of apprenticeship. (18c) *Hist.* A contract under which a minor agrees to work for a master for a specified time in exchange for learning a trade.

articles of association. (17c) **1.** ARTICLES OF INCORPORATION. **2.** A governing document — similar to articles of incorporation — that legally creates a nonstock or nonprofit organization. — Often shortened (informally) to *articles.* — Also termed *articles of organization.* See *governing document* under DOCUMENT (2).

Articles of Confederation. (1781) The instrument that governed the association of the 13 original states from March 1, 1781, until the adoption of the U.S. Constitution (September 17, 1787). • They were prepared by the Continental Congress, submitted to the states in 1777, and later ratified by representatives of the states empowered by their respective legislatures for that purpose.

> "The Articles of Confederation established the union of the original 13 states. The Second Continental Congress completed the Articles in the summer of 1777, submitted the document for ratification by the states in the fall of that year, and the Articles became the de jure form of government for the United States in 1781. The Articles served as the de facto form of government prior to the completion of the ratification process, which had stalled for several years over disputes about western lands. The Articles of Confederation created a very different form of government than that subsequently established by the U.S. Constitution, including with respect to the judicial power. The Articles failed to provide for a national judiciary, although Article IX did authorize Congress to create courts for 'the trial of piracies and felonies committed on the high seas' and 'courts for receiving and determining finally appeals in all cases of captures.' No member of Congress could serve as a judge." Scott Douglas Gerber, *A Distinct Judicial Power: The Origins of an Independent Judiciary, 1606–1787* 28–29 (2011).

articles of dissolution. (1802) A document that a dissolving corporation must file with the appropriate governmental agency, usu. the secretary of state, after the corporation has settled all its debts and distributed all its assets.

articles of impeachment. (17c) A formal document alleging the specific charges against a public official and the reasons for removing that official from office. • It is similar to an indictment in a criminal proceeding. See IMPEACHMENT (1).

articles of incorporation. (18c) A governing document that sets forth the basic terms of a corporation's existence, including the number and classes of shares and the purposes and duration of the corporation. • In most states, the articles of incorporation are filed with the secretary of state as part of the process of forming the corporation. In some states, the articles serve as a certificate of incorporation and are the official recognition of the corporation's existence. In other states, the government issues a certificate of incorporation after approving the articles and other required documents. — Often shortened (informally) to *articles.* — Also termed *articles of association*; *articles of organization*; *certificate of incorporation.* See *governing document* under DOCUMENT (2). Cf. BYLAW (1); CHARTER.

articles of organization. **1.** See ARTICLES OF INCORPORATION. **2.** An official document that sets forth the basic terms for a limited-liability corporation's operations. — Also termed *certificate of organization.* **3.** ARTICLES OF ASSOCIATION (2). See *governing document* under DOCUMENT (2).

articles of partnership. See PARTNERSHIP AGREEMENT.

Articles of the Clergy. *Hist.* A 1315 statute enacted to settle the jurisdictions of the ecclesiastical and temporal courts. — Also termed *Articuli Cleri.*

articles of the eyre (air). (17c) *Hist.* A series of questions put to the members of a community by the justices in eyre to discover what breaches of the law had occurred during the court's absence. • The inquiry enabled the justices to fine criminal behavior and to raise revenue for the Crown through the levying of penalties. — Also termed *capitula itineris.* See EYRE. Cf. CHAPITER.

articles of the peace. (16c) *English law.* A sworn complaint in which a person alleges that a named person poses a threat to the complainant's person, family, or property.

Articles of Union. *Hist.* The 25 articles agreed to by the English and Scottish parliaments in 1707 for the union of the two kingdoms.

articles of war. (17c) **1.** The rules and regulations that govern the activities of an army and navy. **2.** *(cap.)* The body of laws and procedures that governed the U.S. military until replaced in 1951 by the Uniform Code of Military Justice.

Article III court. (1949) *Constitutional law.* A federal court that, deriving its jurisdiction from U.S. Const. art. III, § 2, hears cases arising under the Constitution and the laws and treaties of the United States, cases in which the United States is a party, and cases between the states and between citizens of different states. — Also termed *constitutional court.* Cf. ARTICLE I COURT.

Article III judge. (1937) *Constitutional law.* A U.S. Supreme Court, Court of Appeals, or District Court judge appointed for life under Article III of the U.S. Constitution.

articulated pleading. See PLEADING (1).

articuli (ahr-**tik**-yə-lɪ), *n. pl.* [Latin] Articles; items. • This term was applied to several English statutes and treatises.

Articuli Cleri (ahr-**tik**-yə-lɪ **kleer**-ɪ). [Law Latin] See ARTICLES OF THE CLERGY.

articuli magnae chartae (ahr-**tik**-yə-lɪ **mag**-nee **kahr**-tee), *n.* [Latin] *Hist.* The 49 preliminary articles on which Magna Carta was founded.

Articuli super Cartas (ahr-**tik**-yə-lɪ s[y]**oo**-pər **kahr**-təs). [Law Latin "articles upon the charters"] *Hist.* A 1300 English statute enacted to confirm and enlarge many particulars of Magna Carta and the Forest Charter.

articulo mortis. See IN ARTICULO MORTIS.

artifice (**ahr**-tə-fis). (17c) A clever plan or idea, esp. one intended to deceive.

artificer. (14c) **1.** A skilled worker, such as a mechanic or craftsman; an artisan. **2.** Someone who builds or contrives; an inventor.

artificial, *adj.* (15c) **1.** Existing only by virtue of or in consideration of the law <artificial presumption>. • This term is often used in reference to a company or a corporation. See *artificial person* under PERSON (3). **2.** Made or produced by a human or human intervention rather than by nature <artificial condition>. **3.** Of, relating to, or involving artifice <an artificial demeanor>.

artificial conception. See CONCEPTION.

artificial condition. See CONDITION (5).

artificial day. See DAY.

artificial force. (1895) *Patents.* A natural force that is so transformed in character or energies by human power as to become something new.

artificial insemination. (1897) *Family law.* A process for achieving conception, whereby semen is inserted into a woman's vagina by some means other than intercourse. • If the woman is married when the artificial insemination and the birth occur, and her husband has consented to the insemination, and the insemination is performed by a licensed physician, the husband is considered the father of the child. If the woman is unmarried at the time of the insemination, several factors, varying from jurisdiction to jurisdiction, determine whether the donor is considered the father of the child. — Abbr. AI. Cf. GAMETE INTRAFALLOPIAN TRANSFER; IN VITRO FERTILIZATION; IN VIVO FERTILIZATION; ZYGOTE INTRAFALLOPIAN TRANSFER.

▸ **artificial insemination by donor.** (1955) Artificial insemination in which the semen donor is someone other than the recipient's husband. — Abbr. AID. — Also termed *heterologous artificial insemination*; *exogamous insemination.*

▸ **artificial insemination by husband.** (1949) Artificial insemination in which the semen donor is the recipient's husband. — Abbr. AIH. — Also termed *homologous insemination*; *endogenous insemination.*

▸ **endogenous insemination.** See *artificial insemination by husband.*

▸ **exogamous insemination.** See *artificial insemination by donor.*

▸ **heterologous artificial insemination.** See *artificial insemination by donor.*

▸ **homologous artificial insemination.** See *artificial insemination by husband.*

artificial person. See PERSON (3).

artificial-person canon. The doctrine that the word *person* in a legal instrument includes corporations and other entities, but not the sovereign.

artificial presumption. See *presumption of law* under PRESUMPTION.

artificial succession. See SUCCESSION (4).

artificial watercourse. See WATERCOURSE.

artisan. (16c) **1.** An artist; esp., a skilled crafter. **2.** *Patents.* A person of ordinary skill in an art, for purposes of determining whether a patent application meets the enablement requirement of 35 USCA § 112. • In patent-law terms, the disclosure in the application must teach the artisan how to practice the invention. — Also termed *skilled artisan.* See PERSON SKILLED IN THE ART.

artisan's lien. See *mechanic's lien* under LIEN.

artistic license. See LICENSE.

artistic work. See WORK (2).

art unit. (1965) *Patents.* A group of patent examiners in the U.S. Patent and Trademark Office specializing in a particular field of technology. • Each art unit is led by a senior patent examiner.

a rubro ad nigrum (ay **roo**-broh ad **nɪ**-grəm). [Latin] From the red to the black — i.e., from the title of a statute (formerly often printed in red letters) to its body (often printed in black letters).

as (as), *n.* [Latin] (17c) **1.** *Roman law.* A pound weight or a coin weighing a pound, divisible into 12 parts, called *unciae.* • *As* and the multiples of its *unciae* were used to denote interest rates. See UNCIA. **2.** *Roman & civil law.* A whole inheritance; the whole of an asset. Pl. ***asses.***

as-applied challenge. See CHALLENGE (1).

ASBCA. *abbr.* ARMED SERVICES BOARD OF CONTRACT APPEALS.

ASBO. *abbr.* See ANTISOCIAL BEHAVIOR ORDER.

ASCAP. *abbr.* AMERICAN SOCIETY OF COMPOSERS, AUTHORS AND PUBLISHERS.

ascendant (ə-**sen**-dənt), *n.* (17c) Someone who precedes in lineage, such as a parent or grandparent. — Also termed *ancestor.* Cf. DESCENDANT. — **ascendant,** *adj.*

▸ **collateral ascendant.** (1832) Loosely, an aunt, uncle, or other relative who is not strictly an ancestor. — Also termed *collateral ancestor.*

▸ **lineal ascendant.** (18c) A blood relative in the direct line of ascent; ancestor. • Parents, grandparents, and great-grandparents are lineal ascendants.

ascent. (17c) The passing of an estate upwards to an heir in the ascending line. Cf. DESCENT.

ascripticius. See ADSCRIPTITIUS.

ascriptitius (as-krip-**tish**-ee-əs), *n.* See ADSCRIPTITIUS.

ascriptus. See ADSCRIPTUS.

ASD. *abbr.* Anticipatory self-defense. See *preemptive self-defense* under SELF-DEFENSE (2).

ASE. *abbr.* AMERICAN STOCK EXCHANGE.

as effeirs. See EFFEIRS, AS.

as-extracted collateral. See COLLATERAL.

asexualization. See STERILIZATION.

asexually reproducing plant. (1981) *Patents.* A plant that reproduces other than by seeds. • Examples of asexual reproduction methods include cutting, grafting, and budding. Only new, distinctive, and nonobvious species of asexually reproducing plants may be protected under the Plant Patent Act. 35 USCA § 161.

ASFA. *abbr.* ADOPTION AND SAFE FAMILIES ACT.

ashore, *adj.* & *adv.* **1.** On or to the land adjoining water; on shore <they took the goods ashore>. **2.** On land; not on board a vessel — as opposed to *aboard* or *afloat* <the captain remained ashore>. **3.** (Of a ship) having the bottom lodged on the ground and therefore stranded; aground <the ship ran ashore>.

***Ashwander* rules.** (1953) A set of principles outlining the U.S. Supreme Court's policy of deciding constitutional questions only when necessary, and of avoiding a constitutional question if the case can be decided on the basis of another issue. • These rules were outlined in Justice Brandeis's concurring opinion in *Ashwander v. Tennessee Valley Authority,* 297 U.S. 288, 56 S.Ct. 466 (1936). They include the policy that the court should not decide a constitutional question in a friendly suit, should not anticipate a question of constitutional law, should not create a rule of constitutional law that is broader than that called for by the facts of the case, should not decide a constitutional issue if the case can be decided on another ground, should not rule on the constitutionality of a statute if the plaintiff is not harmed by the statute or if the plaintiff has accepted the benefits of the statute, and should not rule on the constitutionality of an act of Congress without first analyzing whether the act can be fairly construed in a way that would avoid the constitutional question. — Also termed *Brandeis rules.*

as is, *adv. & adj.* In the existing condition without modification <the customer bought the car as is>. • Under UCC § 2-316(3)(a), a seller can disclaim all implied warranties by stating that the goods are being sold "as is" or "with all faults." Generally, a sale of property "as is" means that the property is sold in its existing condition, and use of the phrase *as is* relieves the seller from liability for defects in that condition. — Also termed *with all faults.*

as-is warranty. See WARRANTY (2).

asked price. See PRICE.

asking price. See PRICE.

as of right. (17c) By virtue of a legal entitlement <the case is not one triable to a jury as of right>.

ASP. *abbr.* APPLICATION SERVICE PROVIDER.

as per. (18c) In accordance with; PER (3). • This phrase has traditionally been considered a barbarism, *per* being the preferred form in commercialese <per your request>. But even *per* can be improved on <as you requested>.

aspiration abortion. See ABORTION.

aspirational, *adj.* (1887) **1.** (Of a rule, mode of behavior, or ethic) desirable as being in line with high standards of conduct. **2.** (Of advertisements, marketing, etc.) appealing to what people want because they connect it with success, wealth, and happiness. **3.** (Of a person) having a strong desire to achieve. **4.** Of, relating to, or involving the use of a suction device.

aspirin wars. (1988) *Slang.* A series of false-advertising lawsuits between makers of over-the-counter pain relievers in the 1980s, all centering on the boundaries of comparative advertising.

asportation (as-pər-**tay**-shən), *n.* (18c) The act of carrying away or removing (property or a person). • Asportation is a necessary element of larceny. — Also termed *carrying away.* See LARCENY; CAPTION (4). — **asport,** *vb.* — **asportative,** *adj.*

> "There is no larceny unless the personal goods of another which have been taken by trespass are 'carried away,' but this technical requirement may be satisfied by a very slight movement. There must be 'asportation,' to use the word commonly found in the early cases, but the slightest start of the carrying-away movement constitutes asportation." Rollin M. Perkins & Ronald N. Boyce, *Criminal Law* 323 (3d ed. 1982).

> "To constitute larceny, there must be a taking or caption and carrying away or asportation of the property of another. There is a caption when the defendant takes possession. He takes possession when he exercises dominion and control over the property. There is an asportation when he carries away the property; any carrying away movement, however slight, is sufficient. An asportation presupposes a prior caption; therefore, there can be no asportation unless there has first been a caption." 3 Charles E. Torcia, *Wharton's Criminal Law* § 357, at 412–13 (15th ed. 1995).

asportavit (as-por-**tay**-vit). [Law Latin] He carried away.

ASR. *abbr.* ACCOUNTING SERIES RELEASE.

assailant. (16c) **1.** Someone who physically attacks another; one who commits an assault. See AGGRESSOR. **2.** Someone who attacks another using nonphysical means; esp., one who attacks another's position or feelings, as by criticism, argument, or abusive language.

assart. (16c) *Hist.* **1.** The act of pulling up trees and bushes in a forest to make the land arable. • This was a crime if done without a license. **2.** A piece of land made arable by clearing a forest.

assassination, *n.* (17c) The act of deliberately killing someone, esp. a public figure, usu. for hire or for political reasons; specif., the murder of an important person. — **assassinate,** *vb.* — **assassin,** *n.*

assault, *n.* (14c) **1.** *Criminal & tort law.* The threat or use of force on another that causes that person to have a reasonable apprehension of imminent harmful or offensive contact; the act of putting another person in reasonable fear or apprehension of an immediate battery by means of an act amounting to an attempt or threat to commit a battery. **2.** *Criminal law.* An attempt to commit battery, requiring the specific intent to cause physical injury. — Also termed (in senses 1 & 2) *simple assault*; *common assault.* **3.** Loosely, a battery. **4.** Popularly, any attack. Cf. BATTERY. — **assault,** *vb.* — **assaultive,** *adj.*

> "Ordinary usage creates a certain difficulty in pinning down the meaning of 'assault.' Etymologically, the word is compounded of the Latin *ad* + *saltare*, to jump at. In popular language, it has always connoted a physical attack. When we say that D assaults V, we have a mental picture of D attacking V, by striking or pushing or stabbing him. In the middle ages, however, the terms 'assault' and 'battery' were given technical meanings which they have retained ever since. It became settled that though an assault could be committed by physical contact, it did not require this, since a show of force raising an apprehension in the mind of the victim was sufficient. Also, a 'battery' did not require an actual beating; the use of any degree of force against the body would suffice. The acts of spitting on a person and kissing without consent are both batteries." Glanville Williams, *Textbook of Criminal Law* 135–36 (1978).

▸ **aggravated assault.** (18c) Criminal assault accompanied by circumstances that make it more severe, such as the intent to commit another crime or the intent to cause serious bodily injury, esp. by using a deadly weapon. *See* Model Penal Code § 211.1(2).

> "The common law did not include any offense known as 'aggravated assault.' However, it did make provision for certain situations in this field, under other names. If, for example, the intended application of force to the person would have resulted in murder, mayhem, rape or robbery, if successful, and the scheme proceeded far enough to constitute an attempt the prosecution was for an attempt to commit the intended felony." Rollin M. Perkins & Ronald N. Boyce, *Criminal Law* 180 (3d ed. 1982).

▸ **assault and battery.** See ASSAULT AND BATTERY.

▸ **assault by contact.** (1980) The offense of knowingly or intentionally touching another person when the actor knows or believes that the touch will offend or provoke the other person.

▸ **assault *purpensé*** (ə-**sawlt** poor-paw*n*-**say**). [French] *Hist.* Premeditated assault. — Also termed *assultus premeditatus* (ə-**səl**-təs pree-med-ə-**tay**-tis).

> "Even before the conquest, . . . deliberately planned assassinations came to be distinguished and put into the list of Crown pleas as *forsteal*. The original sense of this word was lying in wait to ambush the victim. After the conquest this is expressed in various terms in French and Latin, but frequently takes the form of *assault purpensé*, or *assultus premeditatus*. In time this yields before *malitia excogitata*, and so introduces us to the very troublesome word 'malice.'" Theodore F.T. Plucknett, *A Concise History of the Common Law* 444 (5th ed. 1956).

▸ **assault to rape.** See *assault with intent to commit rape.*

▸ **assault with a dangerous weapon.** See *assault with a deadly weapon.*

▸ **assault with a deadly weapon.** (1803) An aggravated assault in which the defendant, using a deadly weapon, threatens the victim with death or serious bodily injury. — Also termed *assault with a dangerous weapon.*

▸ **assault with intent.** (17c) Any of several assaults that are carried out with an additional criminal purpose in mind, such as assault with intent to murder, assault with intent to rob, assault with intent to rape, and assault with intent to inflict great bodily injury. • These are modern statutory inventions that are often found in state criminal codes.

▸ **assault with intent to commit rape.** (1837) An assault carried out with the additional criminal purpose of raping the victim. — Also termed *assault to rape.*

▸ **atrocious assault.** (18c) An assault that causes severe wounding or maiming.

▸ **attempted assault.** (1870) An attempt to commit an assault; an attempted battery that has not progressed far enough to be an assault, as when a person intends to harm someone physically but is captured while or after trying to locate the intended victim in his or her place of employment. • Traditionally, most commentators held that an attempted assault could not exist because assault was in itself an attempt to commit a crime. Many modern authorities, however, assert that an attempted assault can occur, and that it should be punishable. — Also termed *attempt to assault.* See ATTEMPT TO ATTEMPT.

> "[I]t is apparent that reference may be made to an 'attempt to assault' without logical absurdity. There is nothing absurd in referring to an attempt to frighten, which would constitute, if successful, a criminal assault in most jurisdictions. . . . It is not surprising, therefore, that there is a tendency to break away from the ancient view that there is no such offense known to the law as an attempt to commit an assault." Rollin M. Perkins & Ronald N. Boyce, *Criminal Law* 168 (3d ed. 1982).

▸ **civil assault.** (1892) An assault considered as a tort and not as a crime. • Although the same assaultive conduct can be both a tort and a crime, this term isolates the legal elements that give rise to civil liability.

▸ **common assault. 1.** ASSAULT (1). **1.** ASSAULT (2).

▸ **conditional assault.** (1971) An assault expressing a threat on condition, such as "your money or your life."

▸ **criminal assault.** (1835) An assault considered as a crime and not as a tort. • This term isolates the legal elements that give rise to criminal liability even though the act might also have been tortious.

▸ **excusable assault.** (1903) An assault committed by accident or while doing a lawful act by lawful means, with ordinary caution and without any unlawful intent.

▸ **felonious assault.** (18c) An assault that is of sufficient severity to be classified and punished as a felony. See *aggravated assault*; *assault with a deadly weapon.*

▸ **indecent assault.** See INDECENT ASSAULT.

▸ **indecent assault by contact.** See *sexual assault* (2).

▸ **indecent assault by exposure.** See INDECENT EXPOSURE.

▸ **intoxication assault.** (1993) An assault that occurs when an inebriated person causes bodily injury to another person.

▸ **malicious assault with a deadly weapon.** (1888) An aggravated assault in which the victim is threatened with death or serious bodily harm from the defendant's use of a deadly weapon. • Malice is inferred from both the nature of the assault and the weapon used.

▸ **sexual assault.** (1880) **1.** Sexual intercourse with another person who does not consent. • Several state statutes have abolished the crime of rape and replaced it with the offense of sexual assault. **2.** Offensive sexual contact with another person, exclusive of rape. • The Model Penal Code lists eight circumstances under which sexual contact results in an assault, as when the offender knows that the victim is mentally incapable of appreciating the nature of the conduct, either because of a mental disease or defect or because the offender has drugged the victim to prevent resistance. Model Penal Code § 213.4. — Also termed (in sense 2) *indecent assault*; *sexual assault by contact*; *indecent assault by contact*; *criminal sexual conduct*. Cf. RAPE (2); *sexual battery* under BATTERY (1).

▸ **sexual assault by contact.** See *sexual assault* (2).

▸ **simple assault. 1.** See ASSAULT (1). **2.** See ASSAULT (2).

> "(1) Simple Assault. A person is guilty of assault if he: (a) attempts to cause or purposely, knowingly or recklessly causes bodily injury to another; or (b) negligently causes bodily injury to another with a deadly weapon; or (c) attempts by physical menace to put another in fear of imminent serious bodily injury." Model Penal Code § 211.1 (1997).

assault and battery. (16c) Loosely, a criminal battery; esp., the act of threatening to attack someone physically and then actually doing it. See BATTERY.

> "Although the term *assault and battery* is frequently used when a battery has been committed, one who commits a battery cannot also be punished for committing an assault, since the lesser offense of assault blends into the actual battery." Paul Marcus, "Assault and Battery," in 1 *Encyclopedia of Crime and Justice* 88, 88 (Sanford H. Kadish ed., 1983).

assaultee. (1871) Someone who is assaulted.

assaulter. (16c) Someone who assaults another.

assault with a dangerous weapon. See *assault with a deadly weapon* under ASSAULT.

assault with a deadly weapon. See ASSAULT.

assay, *n.* (14c) **1.** A proof or trial, by chemical experiments, of the purity of metals, esp. gold and silver. **2.** An examination of weights and measures.

assayator regis. See ASSAYER OF THE KING.

assayer. (17c) Someone who makes assays of precious metals.

assayer of the king. (17c) *Hist.* An officer of the royal mint, appointed by the statute 2 Hen. 6, ch. 12, who received and tested bullion taken in for coining. — Also termed *assayator regis*.

assecurare (ə-sek-yə-**rair**-ee), *vb.* [Law Latin] *Hist.* To make secure, as by pledges.

assecuration (ə-sek-yə-**ray**-shən). (1815) *Marine insurance.* Insurance.

assecurator (ə-**sek**-yə-ray-tər). *Marine insurance.* An insurer.

assembly. (14c) **1.** A group of persons who are united and who meet for some common purpose.

▸ **delegate assembly.** See CONVENTION (4).

▸ **deliberative assembly.** (18c) *Parliamentary law.* A group of people meeting as a body, under such conditions that the rules of parliamentary law are generally applicable to the proceedings, to discuss and decide on actions to be taken on behalf of the entire group or by the authority vested in the body by a government, society, or organization. • A deliberative assembly typically has several distinguishing characteristics: (1) it is a group of people who meet to propose, discuss, and possibly vote on courses of action; (2) participants are free to use their own judgment; (3) enough people participate so that a certain degree of formality in the proceedings is desirable; (4) each participant has one vote and may dissent without fear of expulsion; and (5) when some members are absent, the members actually present have the authority to act for the entire group (subject to quorum and other requirements). *See* Henry M. Robert, *Robert's Rules of Order Newly Revised* § 1, at 2 (10th ed. 2000).

▸ **ordinary assembly.** (16c) *Parliamentary law.* A deliberative assembly other than a legislative body.

▸ **riotous assembly.** (16c) *Hist.* An unlawful assemblage of 12 or more persons causing a disturbance of the peace. See RIOT.

▸ **unlawful assembly.** (16c) A meeting of three or more persons who intend either to commit a violent crime or to carry out some act, lawful or unlawful, that will constitute a breach of the peace. Cf. RIOT.

> "When *three persons or more shall assemble themselves together, with an intent mutually to assist one another, against any who shall oppose them, in the execution of some enterprize of a private nature, with force or violence, against the peace, or to the manifest terror of the people, whether the act intended were of itself lawful or unlawful*; If they only meet to such a purpose or intent, although they shall after depart of their own accord, without doing any thing, this is an *unlawful assembly.*" Edward Bullingbrooke, *The Duty and Authority of Justices of the Peace and Parish Officers for Ireland* 695 (rev. ed. 1788).

> "In order that the assembly may be 'unlawful,' it is not necessary that the object of the meeting should itself be illegal. The test is, not the illegality of the purpose for which the persons are met, but the danger to the peace which their meeting involves. The mere fact, therefore, that the purpose is unlawful is not enough; it must be shown that it involves reasonable apprehension of a breach of the peace. Thus, if a number of persons meet to plan a fraud, they may be guilty of a conspiracy, but their meeting is not an unlawful assembly." 4 *Stephen's Commentaries on the Laws of England* 135–36 (L. Crispin Warmington ed., 21st ed. 1950).

> "An unlawful assembly differs from a riot in that if the parties assemble in a tumultuous manner, and actually execute their purpose with violence, it is a riot; but if they merely meet on a purpose, which, if executed, would make them rioters, and, having done nothing, they separate without carrying their purpose into effect, it is an unlawful assembly." 77 C.J.S. *Riot; Insurrection* § 2, at 565 (1994).

2. A group of people who are elected to make decisions and laws for a particular country, area, or organization; esp., in many states, the lower house of a legislature. 3. *Parliamentary law.* CONVENTION (4). 4. A meeting of all the teachers and students in a school. 5. The process of putting the parts of something together. 6. *Patents.* In a patent claim, a collection of parts used to form a structure.

assembly, right of. See RIGHT OF ASSEMBLY.

assemblyman (ə-**sem**-blee-mən). (17c) A member of a legislative assembly, often (but not always) a male one. • In some locales, *assemblyman* is the normal term for men and women alike. In others, *assemblywoman* is preferred for women. In still others, and sometimes also in locales where the other two norms prevail, *assemblyperson* occasionally appears as a gender-neutral alternative. Cf. ALDERMAN.

assensio mentium (ə-**sen**-see-oh **men**-shee-əm). [Latin] *Hist.* Agreement of the minds.

assent, *n.* (14c) Agreement, approval, or permission; esp., verbal or nonverbal conduct reasonably interpreted as willingness. See CONSENT. — **assent,** *vb.*

> "The requirement of 'assent,' which is fundamental to the formation of a binding contract, implies in a general way that both parties to an exchange shall have a reasonably clear conception of what they are getting and what they are giving up." Marvin A. Chirelstein, *Concepts and Case Analysis in the Law of Contracts* 66 (1990).

▸ **actual assent.** (17c) Assent given by words or conduct intended to express willingness.

▸ **apparent assent.** (17c) Assent given by language or conduct that, while not necessarily intended to express willingness, would be understood by a reasonable person to be so intended and is actually so understood.

▸ **constructive assent.** (1811) Assent imputed to someone based on conduct.

▸ **express assent.** (16c) Assent clearly and unmistakably communicated.

▸ **implied assent.** (18c) Assent inferred from one's conduct rather than from direct expression.

▸ **mutual assent.** (17c) Agreement by both parties to a contract, usu. in the form of offer and acceptance. • In modern contract law, mutual assent is determined by an objective standard — that is, by the apparent intention of the parties as manifested by their actions. Cf. MEETING OF THE MINDS.

assented stock. See STOCK.

assenting-silence doctrine. (1976) The principle that an accusation will be taken as true, despite silence by the accused, if the accusation was made under circumstances in which silence can be fairly said to be an agreement. • This doctrine is usu. held to be invalid as a measure of a criminal defendant's guilt.

assert, *vb.* (17c) 1. To state positively. 2. To invoke or enforce a legal right. — **assertory, assertive,** *adj.* — **assertor,** *n.*

assertion, *n.* (15c) 1. A declaration or allegation. 2. A person's speaking, writing, acting, or failing to act with the intent of expressing a fact or opinion; the act or an instance of engaging in communicative behavior. See *assertive conduct* under CONDUCT. — **assert,** *vb.* — **assertor,** *n.*

assertive-acts doctrine. (2012) *Evidence.* The doctrine that the hearsay rule applies to a person's nonverbal conduct if that conduct amounts to an assertion.

assertive conduct. See CONDUCT.

assertive question. (1968) *Civil law.* A question asked of a witness at a criminal trial, by which inadmissible evidence is sought, to provide the jury with details regarding another crime. Cf. INTERROGATIVE QUESTION.

assertory covenant. See COVENANT (1).

assertory oath. See OATH.

assessable income. See *taxable income* under INCOME.

assessable insurance. 1. See INSURANCE. 2. See *assessable policy* (1) under INSURANCE POLICY.

assessable policy. 1. See INSURANCE POLICY. 2. See *assessable insurance* (1) under INSURANCE.

assessable security. See SECURITY (4).

assessable stock. See STOCK.

assessed valuation. See VALUATION.

assessed value. See VALUE (2).

assessee (as-ə-see), *n.* (18c) A person against whom a payment is assessed.

assessment, *n.* (16c) 1. Determination of the rate or amount of something, such as a tax or damages <assessment of the losses covered by insurance>. 2. Imposition of something, such as a tax or fine, according to an established rate; the tax or fine so imposed <assessment of a luxury tax>.

> "There is a distinction between public improvements, which benefit the entire community, and local improvements, which benefit particular real estate or limited areas of land. The latter improvements are usually financed by means of special, or local, assessments. These assessments are, in a certain sense, taxes. But an assessment differs from a general tax in that an assessment is levied only on property in the immediate vicinity of some local municipal improvement and is valid only where the property assessed receives some special benefit differing from the benefit that the general public enjoys." Robert Kratovil, *Real Estate Law* 465 (6th ed. 1974).

▸ **assessment for benefits.** See *special assessment.*

▸ **deficiency assessment.** (1864) An assessment by the IRS — after administrative review and tax-court adjudication — of additional tax owed by a taxpayer who underpaid. See DEFICIENCY (2).

▸ **double assessment.** (18c) The act of requiring that tax be paid twice for the same property. See *double taxation* under TAXATION (1).

▸ **erroneous assessment.** (1825) An assessment that deviates from the law and creates a jurisdictional defect, and that is therefore invalid.

▸ **excessive assessment.** (1822) A tax assessment that is grossly disproportionate as compared with other assessments.

▸ **frontage assessment.** (1877) A municipal tax charged to a property owner for local improvements that abut a street or highway, such as sidewalks, pavements, or sewage lines.

▸ **jeopardy assessment.** (1924) An assessment by the IRS — without the usual review procedures — of additional tax owed by a taxpayer who underpaid, based on the IRS's belief that collection of the deficiency would be jeopardized by delay. IRC (26 USCA) §§ 6861–6862.

▸ **local assessment.** (1800) A tax to pay for improvements (such as sewers and sidewalks) in a designated area, levied on property owners who will benefit from the improvements. — Also termed *local-improvement assessment.*

"Since there is [an] important and fundamental distinction between the tax in the more limited sense and the local assessment, the question often arises whether provisions in constitutions and statutes which refer by name to taxes, include also local assessments. This is primarily a question of legislative intention. In the absence of anything to show the specific intention of the legislature, the general rule is that the local assessment possesses such marked peculiarities differentiating it from the tax in the more limited sense of the term, that the use of the term 'tax' does not *prima facie* show an intention to include local assessments." 1 William H. Page & Paul Jones, *A Treatise on the Law of Taxation by Local and Special Assessments* § 39, at 67 (1909).

▸ **local-improvement assessment.** See *local assessment.*

▸ **maintenance assessment.** See MAINTENANCE FEE (2).

▸ **political assessment.** (1882) *Hist.* A charge levied on officeholders and political candidates by a political party to defray the expenses for a political canvass.

▸ **reassessment.** (18c) **1.** A reappraisal, revaluation, or review; a recalculation of an amount payable or owed. **2.** *Tax.* An official revaluation of property, often repeated periodically, for the levying of a tax. **3.** *Insurance law.* A new determination of the benefits owed by an insurer to a policyholder, claimant, debtor, or other insurer. See ADJUSTMENT (3).

▸ **special assessment.** (1803) **1.** The assessment of a tax on property that benefits in some important way from a public improvement. — Also termed *assessment for benefits.* **2.** *Criminal law.* A mandatory financial penalty imposed at sentencing.

3. Official valuation of property for purposes of taxation <assessment of the beach house>. — Also termed *tax assessment.* Cf. APPRAISAL. **4.** An audit or review <internal financial assessment> <environmental site assessment>. — **assess,** *vb.*

assessment bond. See BOND (3).

assessment company. (1886) An association that offers its members life insurance, and then pays for death losses by levying an assessment on the surviving members of the association.

assessment contract. See CONTRACT.

assessment district. See DISTRICT.

assessment for benefits. See *special assessment* under ASSESSMENT (2).

assessment fund. (1857) The balance of the assessments of a mutual benefit association, minus expenses, from which beneficiaries are paid.

assessment insurance. See INSURANCE.

assessment list. See ASSESSMENT ROLL.

assessment period. (1884) A taxable period.

assessment ratio. (1889) For property tax purposes, the ratio of assessed value to fair market value.

assessment roll. (18c) A record of taxable persons and property, prepared by a tax assessor. — Also termed *assessment list*; (in some New England states) *grand list.*

assessment work. (1871) *Mining law.* The annual labor (such as improvements) that must be performed on an unpatented mining claim to continue to hold the claim.

assessor. (14c) **1.** An official who evaluates or makes assessments, esp. for purposes of taxation. — Also termed (specif.) *tax assessor.* **2.** Someone who advises a judge or magistrate about scientific or technical matters during a trial. See MASTER (2). **3.** ADSESSOR. **4.** Someone associated with another as an adviser or assistant; a sharer in rank or dignity. **5.** In some universities, a member of the supreme governing council. **6.** LOSS ASSESSOR. — **assessorial** (as-ə-**sor**-ee-əl), *adj.* — **assessorship,** *n.*

asset. (16c) **1.** An item that is owned and has value. **2.** (*pl.*) The entries on a balance sheet showing the items of property owned, including cash, inventory, equipment, real estate, accounts receivable, and goodwill. **3.** (*pl.*) All the property of a person (esp. a bankrupt or deceased person) available for paying debts or for distribution.

▸ **accrued asset.** (1929) An asset arising from revenues earned but not yet due.

▸ **admitted asset.** (1873) An asset that by law may be included in evaluating the financial condition of an insurance company. Cf. *nonadmitted asset.*

▸ **appointive asset.** (1950) An asset distributed under a power of appointment.

▸ **assets by descent.** (17c) The portion of an estate that passes to an heir and is sufficient to charge the heir with the decedent's specialty debts. — Also termed *assets per descent.*

▸ **assets entre main.** See *assets in hand.*

▸ **assets in hand.** (18c) The portion of an estate held by an executor or administrator for the payment of debts chargeable to the executor or administrator. — Also termed *assets entre main*; *assets entre mains.*

▸ **assets per descent.** See *assets by descent.*

▸ **asset under management.** (1980) A securities portfolio for which an investment adviser provides ongoing, regular supervisory or management services.

▸ **business asset.** (1872) Property or equipment bought and used primarily, if not exclusively, for business purposes.

▸ **capital asset.** (1908) **1.** A long-term asset used in the operation of a business or used to produce goods or services, such as equipment, land, or an industrial plant. — Also termed *fixed asset.* **2.** For income-tax purposes, any of most assets held by a taxpayer except those assets specifically excluded by the Internal Revenue Code. • Excluded from the definition are, among other things, stock in trade, inventory, and property held by the taxpayer primarily for sale to customers in the ordinary course of trade or business.

▸ **commercial assets.** (1833) The aggregate of available property, stock in trade, cash, and other assets belonging to a merchant.

▸ **current asset.** (1893) An asset that is readily convertible into cash, such as a marketable security, a note, or an account receivable. — Also termed *liquid asset*; *quick asset*; *near money*; *financial asset*. Cf. *illiquid asset*.

"*Current assets* are assets expected to be converted to cash, sold, or consumed during the next twelve months, or within the business's normal operating cycle if the cycle is longer than a year. The *operating cycle* is the period from the time that cash is used to acquire goods and services, these goods and services are sold to customers, and the accounts receivable from these customers are collected in cash. For a small retail store, the operating cycle may be only a few weeks or months. For a shipbuilding company, however, the normal operating cycle could run several years." Jay Alix & Elmer E. Heupel, *Financial Handbook for Bankruptcy Professionals* § 9.2, at 354 (1991).

▸ **dead asset.** (1920) A worthless asset; an asset that has no realizable value, such as an uncollectible account receivable.

▸ **earning asset.** (*usu. pl.*) (1916) An asset (esp. of a bank) on which interest is received. • Banks consider loans to be earning assets.

▸ **equitable asset.** (1868) An asset that is subject to payment only in a court of equity.

▸ **financial asset.** See *current asset*.

▸ **fixed asset.** (1886) See *capital asset* (1).

▸ **flawed asset.** An asset that is in the possession of a custodian and cannot be released until certain obligations are met.

▸ **frozen asset.** (1927) An asset that is difficult to convert into cash because of court order or other legal process.

▸ **hard asset.** See *real asset*.

▸ **hidden asset.** (1947) An asset carried on the books at a substantially reduced or understated value that is considerably less than market value.

▸ **illiquid asset.** (1961) An asset that is not readily convertible into cash, usu. because of (1) the lack of demand, (2) the absence of an established market, or (3) the substantial cost or time required for liquidation (such as for real property, even when it is desirable). Cf. *current asset*.

▸ **individual asset.** (*usu. pl.*) (1858) Property belonging to a member of a partnership as personal property, separate from the partnership's property.

▸ **intangible asset.** (1899) Any nonphysical asset or resource that can be amortized or converted to cash, such as patents, goodwill, and computer programs, or a right to something, such as services paid for in advance.

▸ **junk asset.** See *troubled asset*.

▸ **legal asset.** (1857) A decedent's asset that by law is subject to the claims of creditors or legacies. — Also termed *probate asset*.

▸ **liquid asset.** See *current asset*.

▸ **mass asset.** (1970) An intangible asset, such as a dominant market position, that is made up of several components but that is considered a single entity for purposes of depreciation, because the loss of any component of the asset is replaced by new components, so that the whole asset has little or no fluctuation in value. • An entity with a dominant market position might lose a vendor but, because of its dominant market position, still be able to replace the loss with a new vendor. The market position is therefore considered a mass asset.

▸ **net assets.** See *net worth* under WORTH (3).

▸ **net quick assets.** (1920) The excess of quick assets less current liabilities. See QUICK-ASSET RATIO.

▸ **new asset.** *Wills & estates*. In the administration of a decedent's estate, property that the administrator or executor receives after the time has expired to file claims against the estate.

▸ **nominal asset.** (1930) An asset whose value is difficult to assess, such as a judgment or claim.

▸ **nonadmitted asset.** (1966) An asset that by law may not be included in evaluating the financial condition of an insurance company because it cannot be converted quickly into cash without a financial loss. Cf. *admitted asset*.

▸ **nonprobate asset.** (1959) Property that passes to a named beneficiary upon the owner's death according to the terms of some contract or arrangement other than a will. • Such an asset is not a part of the probate estate and is not ordinarily subject to the probate court's jurisdiction (and fees), though it is part of the taxable estate. Examples include life-insurance contracts, joint property arrangements with right of survivorship, pay-on-death bank accounts, and inter vivos trusts. — Also termed *nonprobate property*. Cf. WILL SUBSTITUTE.

▸ **personal asset.** (1854) An asset in the form of money or chattels. Cf. *real asset*.

▸ **premarital asset.** (1986) Property that a spouse owned before marrying. • In most jurisdictions, this is part of the spouse's separate property. See SEPARATE PROPERTY. Cf. COMMUNITY PROPERTY.

▸ **probate asset.** See *legal asset*.

▸ **quick asset.** (1893) **1.** Cash and other current assets other than inventory. **2.** See *current asset*.

▸ **real asset.** (18c) **1.** An asset in the form of land. **2.** Loosely, any tangible asset. — Also termed *hard asset*. Cf. *personal asset*.

▸ **tangible asset.** (1891) An asset that has a physical existence and is capable of being assigned a value.

▸ **toxic asset.** See *troubled asset*.

▸ **troubled asset.** (1987) A debt-related asset, such as a mortgage loan, for which the debt has become or is likely to become uncollectible, resulting in a sudden, sharp decrease in the asset's value. — Also termed *toxic asset*; *junk asset*.

▸ **wasting asset.** (1903) An asset exhausted through use or the loss of value, such as an oil well or a coal deposit.

asset acquisition. (1946) Acquisition of a corporation by purchasing all its assets directly from the corporation itself, rather than by purchasing shares from its shareholders. — Also termed *asset purchase*. Cf. SHARE ACQUISITION.

asset allocation. (1958) The spreading of funds between different types of investments with the intention of decreasing risk and increasing return.

asset-backed security. See SECURITY (4).

asset-based financing. See FINANCING.

asset-coverage test. (1973) *Accounting*. A bond-indenture restriction that permits additional borrowing only if the ratio of assets (typically net tangible assets) to debt (typically long-term debt) does not fall below a specified minimum. — Abbr. ACT.

asset-depreciation range. (1971) *Tax.* The IRS's range of depreciation lifetimes allowed for assets placed in service between 1970 and 1980 and for assets depreciated under the Modified Accelerated Cost Recovery System under the Tax Reform Act of 1986. — Abbr. ADR. See ACCELERATED COST RECOVERY SYSTEM.

asset dividend. See DIVIDEND.

asset-protection trust. See TRUST.

asset purchase. See ASSET ACQUISITION.

asset sale and liquidation. (1978) *Mergers & acquisitions.* A merger in which a corporation's board and a majority of the stockholders approve a sale of most or all of the corporation's assets to another corporation in exchange for cash or debt.

assets by descent. See ASSET.

assets entre main. See *assets in hand* under ASSET.

assets in hand. See ASSET.

assets per descent. See *assets by descent* under ASSET.

asset-stripping, *n.* (1969) *Pejorative.* The practice of buying a company inexpensively and then selling what it owns for a profit, usu. within a short period; specif., the profitable divestiture by an undervalued company's new owners of some company holdings, often as a way of paying off the purchase price and usu. as a tactic of a corporate raider. — **asset-stripper,** *n.*

asset under management. See ASSET.

asset value. See NET ASSET VALUE.

asseverate (ə-**sev**-ə-rayt), *vb.* (1744) To state solemnly or positively; AVER. — **asseveration** (ə-sev-ə-**ray**-shən), *n.*

assideration (ə-sid-ər-**ray**-shən). (1851) The act of immersing a human being in ice-cold water to cause a death by undetectable means, esp. as a means of infanticide. See INFANTICIDE. — **assiderate,** *vb.*

assign, *n.* (*usu. pl.*) See ASSIGNEE.

assign, *vb.* (13c) **1.** To convey in full; to transfer (rights or property) <the bank assigned the note to a thrift institution>. **2.** To assert; to point out <the appellant assigned as errors two of the trial court's rulings>. See ASSIGNMENT OF ERROR.

assignable (ə-**sɪn**-ə-bəl), *adj.* (1809) Able to be assigned; transferable from one person to another, so that the transferee has the same rights as the transferor had <assignable right>. Cf. NEGOTIABLE. — **assignability,** *n.*

assignable lease. See LEASE.

assignation (as-ig-**nay**-shən), *n.* (17c) **1.** *Archaic.* An appointment of a time and place to meet secretly, esp. for engaging in illicit sex. **2.** *Eccles. law.* A specific allegation in a defendant's counterpleading. **3.** *French law.* A plaintiff's complaint; a writ of summons.

assignation house. See DISORDERLY HOUSE.

assign dower. To set out the legal description of a widow's share of her deceased husband's estate. See DOWER.

assigned account. See ACCOUNT.

assigned counsel. See COUNSEL.

assigned-counsel program. (1959) *Criminal law.* A locally funded and run program for lawyers to represent indigent litigants, esp. criminal defendants. — Abbr. ACP.

assigned error. See ERROR (2).

assigned risk. See RISK.

assigned servant. See SERVANT.

assignee (ə-sɪ-**nee** *or* as-ə-**nee**). (14c) **1.** Someone to whom property rights or powers are transferred by another. • Use of the term is so widespread that it is difficult to ascribe positive meaning to it with any specificity. Courts recognize the protean nature of the term and are therefore often forced to look to the intent of the assignor and assignee in making the assignment — rather than to the formality of the use of the term *assignee* — in defining rights and responsibilities. — Also termed *assign.*

▸ **absolute assignee.** (1809) Someone who is assigned an unqualified interest in property in a transfer of some or all of the incidents of ownership.

▸ **assignee ad interim.** An assignee appointed between the time of bankruptcy and the appointment of a regular assignee.

▸ **assignee for value.** (18c) An assignee who has paid for or otherwise given consideration for the assignment.

▸ **co-assignee.** (1856) Someone who, along with one or more others, is an assignee of the same subject matter.

▸ **collateral assignee.** (1889) A lender who is assigned an interest in property (usu. real property) as security for a loan.

▸ **gratuitous assignee.** (1928) An assignee under an assignment not given for value.

▸ **subassignee.** (1830) A person to whom a right is assigned by one who is a previous assignee of the right.

2. See *assigned servant* under SERVANT.

assignee clause. (1925) A provision of the Judiciary Act of 1789 that prevented a litigant without diversity of citizenship from assigning a claim to another who did have the required diversity. • In 1948 the assignee clause was replaced by 28 USCA § 1359, which denies federal jurisdiction when a party is improperly or collusively joined, by assignment or otherwise, merely to invoke jurisdiction.

assignee estoppel. See ESTOPPEL.

assigner. See ASSIGNOR.

assignment. (14c) **1.** The transfer of rights or property <assignment of stock options>. **2.** The rights or property so transferred <the aunt assigned those funds to her niece, who promptly invested the assignment in mutual funds>.

> "An *assignment* is a transfer or setting over of property, or of some right or interest therein, from one person to another; the term denoting not only the *act* of transfer, but also the instrument by which it is effected. In these senses the word is variously applied in law." Alexander M. Burrill, *A Treatise on the Law and Practice of Voluntary Assignments for the Benefit of Creditors* § 1, at 1 (James Avery Webb ed., 6th ed. 1894).

> "Negotiability differs from assignment, with which it has obvious affinities, in at least two respects. In the first place no notice need be given of the transfer of a negotiable instrument, and in the second place the transfer of such an instrument is not subject to equities. Thus whereas an assignor only transfers his rights subject to any defences which could be pleaded against him, a transfer of a negotiable instrument to someone in good faith passes a good

title, free from any such defences. For instance a person who receives a cheque in good faith obtains a good title, even though the cheque may have been stolen. It is not, of course, any document which has the attributes of negotiability. Only those documents recognized by the custom of trade to be transferable by delivery (or endorsement) are negotiable. Other documents can only be transferred by assignment." P.S. Atiyah, *An Introduction to the Law of Contract* 278–79 (3d ed. 1981).

▸ **absolute assignment.** (18c) An assignment that leaves the assignor no interest in the assigned property or right. Cf. *partial assignment.*

▸ **assignment by operation of law.** (18c) A transfer of a right or obligation as a necessary consequence of a change in legal status, regardless of the affected party's intent. • For example, a right and a corresponding obligation may disappear if they vest in the same person, as might happen in a merger or acquisition.

▸ **assignment for value.** (18c) An assignment given in exchange for consideration.

▸ **assignment in gross.** (1890) A transfer of a company's trademark separately from the goodwill of the business. • Courts often hold that such an assignment passes nothing of value to the transferee. — Also termed *naked assignment.* See ANTI-ASSIGNMENT-IN-GROSS RULE.

▸ **assignment of account.** (1808) An assignment that gives the assignee the right to funds in an account, usu. to satisfy a debt.

▸ **assignment of application.** (1896) **1.** *Patents.* The U.S. Patent and Trademark Office's formal routing of a patent or trademark application to the examining group to which it appears to belong based on subject matter. **2.** The transfer of the right to prosecute a patent or register a trademark. • The assignee must show ownership in the property to be patented or registered and, if less than absolute, the extent of ownership. *See* 37 CFR § 3.73.

▸ **assignment of dower** (**dow**-ər). (17c) The act of setting apart a widow's share of her deceased husband's real property.

▸ **assignment of income.** See *assignment of wages.*

▸ **assignment of lease.** (17c) An assignment in which a lessee transfers the entire unexpired remainder of the lease term, as distinguished from a sublease transferring only a portion of the remaining term.

▸ **assignment of mortgage.** (18c) An assignment in which a mortgage lender or borrower transfers the mortgage to a third party.

▸ **assignment of realty.** (1846) A transfer of a real-property interest that is less than a freehold. • The term includes debt-security interests in land.

▸ **assignment of wages.** (1836) A transfer of the right to collect wages from the wage earner to a creditor. — Also termed *assignment of income.*

▸ **assignment pro tanto.** (18c) An assignment that results when an order is drawn on a third party and made payable from a particular fund that belongs to the drawer. • The drawee becomes an assignee with respect to the drawer's interest in that fund.

▸ **bail assignment.** See BAIL ASSIGNMENT.

▸ **collateral assignment.** (18c) An assignment of property as collateral security for a loan.

▸ **common-law assignment.** (1824) An assignment for the benefit of creditors made under the common law, rather than by statute.

▸ **conditional assignment.** (18c) An assignment of income (such as rent payments or accounts receivable) to a lender, made to secure a loan. • The lender receives the assigned income only if the assignor defaults on the underlying loan.

▸ **effective assignment.** (1838) An assignment that terminates the assignor's interest in the property and transfers it to the assignee.

▸ **equitable assignment.** (18c) **1.** An assignment that, although not legally valid, will be recognized and enforced in equity — for example, an assignment of a chose in action or of future acquisitions of the assignor. • To accomplish an "equitable assignment," there must be an absolute appropriation by the assignor of the debt or fund sought to be assigned. **2.** An assignment that is valid and enforceable under the principles of fairness and justice.

▸ **fly-power assignment.** A blank written assignment that, when attached to a stock certificate, renders the stock transferable.

▸ **foreign assignment.** (18c) An assignment made in a foreign country or in another jurisdiction.

▸ **general assignment.** (18c) Assignment of a debtor's property for the benefit of all the assignor's creditors, instead of only a few. — Also termed *voluntary assignment.* See ASSIGNMENT FOR THE BENEFIT OF CREDITORS.

▸ **gratuitous assignment.** (18c) An assignment not given for value; esp., an assignment given or taken as security for — or in total or partial satisfaction of — a preexisting obligation.

▸ **legal assignment.** (17c) An assignment that meets all the statutory requirements and is enforceable by law.

▸ **mesne assignment** (meen). (18c) A middle or intermediate assignment; any assignment before the last one.

▸ **naked assignment.** See *assignment in gross.*

▸ **partial assignment.** (18c) The immediate transfer of part but not all of the assignor's right. Cf. *absolute assignment.*

▸ **preferential assignment.** See PREFERENTIAL TRANSFER.

▸ **total assignment.** (18c) An assignment empowering the assignee to enforce the entire right for the benefit of the assignor or others. • Examples are assignment to secure an obligation and assignment to a trustee.

▸ **voluntary assignment.** See *general assignment.*

▸ **wage assignment.** (1911) An assignment by an employee of a portion of the employee's pay to another (such as a creditor).

3. The instrument of transfer <the assignment was appended to the contract>. **4.** A welfare recipient's surrender of his or her rights to child support (both current and past due) in favor of the state as a condition of receiving governmental financial assistance <the assignment made economic sense to her because her child support amounted to $200 a month, while she received $400 a month in welfare>. **5.** A task, job, or appointment <the student's math assignment> <assignment as ambassador to a foreign country>.

▸ **intercircuit assignment.** (1956) The temporary appointment of a federal judge in one judicial circuit to serve in another circuit. • The Chief Justice of the United States has the statutory authority to assign judges temporarily to assist courts in other circuits that have excessive workloads. The Judicial Conference Committee on Intercircuit Assignments, consisting of three federal judges, maintains a roster of senior and active judges who have volunteered to accept assignments and advises the Chief Justice about which judges to appoint. Assignments are usu. brief, lasting from a few days to a few weeks.

▸ **intracircuit assignment.** (1961) The temporary appointment of a federal district judge to assist another district court within the same circuit. • The chief judge of the circuit authorizes temporary transfers among courts within the circuit.

6. The act of assigning a task, job, or appointment <the assignment of various duties>.

▸ **assignment of the floor.** *Parliamentary law.* The process by which the chair recognizes who is entitled to speak.

7. In litigation practice, a point that a litigant advances <the third assignment of error>.

▸ **assignment of error.** See ASSIGNMENT OF ERROR.

▸ **new assignment.** *Hist.* A plaintiff's restatement of a claim because the first complaint did not contain sufficient details. • The purpose was to allow a plaintiff to reply to a defendant's responsive plea that did not address the plaintiff's specific claim because the complaint was too general. New assignment has been replaced by amended pleadings. — Also termed *novel assignment.*

> "A new assignment is a restatement in the replication of the plaintiff's cause of action. Where the declaration in an action is ambiguous and the defendant pleads facts which are literally an answer to it, but not to the real claim set up by the plaintiff, the plaintiff's course is to reply by way of new assignment; that is, to allege that he brought his action, not for the cause supposed by the defendant, but for some other cause, to which the plea has no application." Benjamin J. Shipman, *Handbook of Common-Law Pleading* § 214, at 370 (Henry Winthrop Ballantine ed., 3d ed. 1923).

assignment clause. *Oil & gas.* See CHANGE-OF-OWNERSHIP CLAUSE.

Assignment Division. The section of the U.S. Patent and Trademark Office that is responsible for recording assignments and other documents affecting title to patent and trademark applications, patents, and registrations.

assignment for the benefit of creditors. (18c) Assignment of a debtor's property to another person in trust so as to consolidate and liquidate the debtor's assets for payment to creditors, any surplus being returned to the debtor. • This procedure serves as a state-law substitute for federal bankruptcy proceedings. The debtor is not discharged from unpaid debts by this procedure since creditors do not agree to any discharge.

assignment for value. See ASSIGNMENT (2).

assignment in gross. See ASSIGNMENT (2).

assignment of account. See ASSIGNMENT (2).

assignment of application. See ASSIGNMENT (2).

assignment of dower (**dow**-ər). See ASSIGNMENT (2).

assignment of error. (17c) A specification of the trial court's alleged errors on which the appellant relies in seeking an appellate court's reversal, vacation, or modification of an adverse judgment. See ERROR. Cf. WRIT OF ERROR. Pl. **assignments of error.**

assignment of income. See *assignment of wages* under ASSIGNMENT (2).

assignment-of-income doctrine. (1950) *Family law.* The common-law principle that the person who has earned income is the person taxed on it, regardless of who receives the proceeds. • Under this doctrine, future income assigned to another is taxable to the assignor. For example, in *Lucas v. Earl,* 281 U.S. 111, 50 S.Ct. 241 (1930), the Court held that a husband who was the sole wage-earner could not assign to his wife half his income and then pay the federal income tax on only the unassigned part.

assignment of lease. See ASSIGNMENT (2).

assignment of mortgage. See ASSIGNMENT (2).

assignment of property. See EQUITABLE DISTRIBUTION.

assignment of realty. See ASSIGNMENT (2).

assignment-of-rents clause. (1934) A mortgage provision or separate agreement that entitles the lender to collect rents from the mortgaged premises if the borrower defaults.

assignment of rights. (18c) *Contracts.* The transfer of rights, esp. contractual rights, from one party to another.

assignment of the floor. See ASSIGNMENT (6).

assignment of wages. See ASSIGNMENT (2).

assignment pro tanto. See ASSIGNMENT (2).

assignment system. *Hist.* A method of allotting convicts to settlers as unpaid farmhands or servants. See *assigned servant* under SERVANT.

assignor (as-ə-**nor** *or* ə-**sɪ**-nər *or* ə-sɪ-**nor**). (17c) Someone who transfers property rights or powers to another by assignment. — Also spelled *assigner.*

assignor estoppel. See ESTOPPEL.

assimilative crime. See CRIME.

Assimilative Crimes Act. A federal statute providing that state law applies to a crime committed within a federal enclave in that state (such as a reservation or military installation) if the crime is not punishable under federal law. 18 USCA § 13. • This statute uses local laws as gap-fillers for federal criminal law.

assisa armorum (ə-**sɪ**-zə ahr-**mor**-əm). [Law Latin "assize of arms"] (18c) *Hist.* A statute requiring the keeping of arms for the common defense. — Also termed *assize of arms.* See *Assize of Arms* under ASSIZE (2).

assisa cadere (ə-**sɪ**-zə **kad**-ə-ree), *vb.* [Law Latin] *Hist.* To fail in the assize, as by being nonsuited.

assisa continuanda (ə-**sɪ**-zə kən-tin-yoo-**an**-də) [Law Latin] (17c) *Hist.* A writ addressed to the justices of assize for the continuation of a case.

assisa de foresta (ə-**sɪ**-zə dee for-**es**-tə), *n.* [Law Latin "assize of the forest"] (17c) *Hist.* A statute concerning orders to be observed in the royal forest. — Also termed *ordinatio forestae; assisa forestae.*

assisa de mensuris (ə-sɪ-zə dee men-s[y]**oor**-is), *n.* [Law Latin "assize of measures"] *Hist.* A common rule for weights and measures, established by Richard I in the eighth year of his reign.

assisa de morte antecessoris. See *assize of mort d'ancestor* under ASSIZE (6).

assisa de nocumento (ə-**sɪ**-zə dee nok-yə-**men**-toh), *n.* [Law Latin "assize of nuisance"]. See *assize of nuisance* under ASSIZE (8).

assisa de utrum (ə-**sɪ**-zə dee **yoo**-trəm), *n.* [Law Latin "assize of utrum"] See ASSIZE UTRUM.

assisa forestae. See ASSISA DE FORESTAE.

assisa friscae fortiae. See *assize of fresh force* under ASSIZE (8).

assisa mortis d'ancestoris (ə-**sɪ**-zə **mor**-tis dan-ses-**tor**-is), *n.* [Law Latin] See *assize of mort d'ancestor* under ASSIZE (6).

assisa novae disseysinae (ə-**sɪ**-zə **noh**-vee di-**see**-zin-ee), *n.* [Law Latin] See *assize of novel disseisin* under ASSIZE (8).

assisa panis et cerevisiae (ə-**sɪ**-zə **pan**-is et ser-ə-**vish**-ee-ee), *n.* [Law Latin "assize of bread and ale"] *Hist.* A statute passed in the 51st year of the reign of Henry III, regulating the sale of bread and ale. — Also termed *statute of bread and ale.*

assisa proroganda. See DE ASSISA PROROGANDA.

assisa ultimae praesentationis (ə-**sɪ**-zə **əl**-ti-mee pree-zən-tay-shee-**oh**-nis *or* prez-ən-), *n.* [Law Latin] See *assize of darrein presentment* under ASSIZE (8).

assisa venalium (ə-**sɪ**-zə və-**nay**-lee-əm), *n.* [Law Latin] *Hist.* The assize of salable commodities.

assise. See ASSIZE.

assiser. See ASSIZER.

assistance. *Civil law.* Compensation for an effort to save a threatened vessel, cargo, or ship personnel at sea. Cf. NO CURE, NO PAY.

assistance, writ of. See WRIT OF ASSISTANCE.

assistance dog. See *service dog* under DOG (1).

assistance of counsel. (17c) *Constitutional law.* Representation by a lawyer, esp. in a criminal case. • The phrase in its modern uses derives from the Sixth Amendment: "In all criminal prosecutions, the accused shall enjoy the right . . . to have the assistance of counsel for his defense." U.S. Const. amend. VI. See RIGHT TO COUNSEL.

▸ **effective assistance of counsel.** (1937) A conscientious, meaningful legal representation, whereby the defendant is advised of all rights and the lawyer performs all required tasks reasonably according to the prevailing professional standards in criminal cases. *See* Fed. R. Crim. P. 44; 18 USCA § 3006A.

> "The law is in flux on precisely what constitutes the 'effective' assistance of counsel. The Supreme Court has yet to set forth a definitive standard, and lower courts have adopted differing ones. Prior to the 1970s the most common standard was the 'mockery of justice' standard, under which counsel's assistance was 'ineffective' only when it was so inadequate that it reduced the trial 'to a farce' or rendered it a 'mockery of justice.' Since that time, most courts have abandoned this formulation in favor of more stringent requirements, stipulating, for example, that 'counsel must exercise [the] normal skill and knowledge which normally prevails at the time and place' (*Moore v. United States*, 432 F.2d 730 (3d Cir. 1970)), that counsel must render the 'reasonably competent assistance of an attorney acting as his diligent advocate' (*United States v. Decoster*, 487 F.2d 1197 (D.C. Cir. 1973)), or that counsel's representation must be 'within the range of competence demanded of attorneys in criminal cases' (*Marzullo v. Maryland*, 561 F.2d 540 (4th Cir. 1977)). All of these new standards beg the questions of what traditional level of practice is to be regarded as 'customary,' 'diligent,' or 'reasonable.' Thus, little has been definitively resolved by the new, higher standards." Arval A. Morris, "Right to Counsel," in 1 *Encyclopedia of Crime and Justice* 278, 283 (Sanford H. Kadish ed., 1983).

▸ **inadequate assistance of counsel.** See *ineffective assistance of counsel.*

▸ **ineffective assistance of counsel.** (1957) A representation in which the defendant is deprived of a fair trial because the lawyer handles the case unreasonably, usu. either by performing incompetently or by not devoting full effort to the defendant, esp. because of a conflict of interest. • In determining whether a criminal defendant received ineffective assistance of counsel, courts generally consider several factors: (1) whether the lawyer had previously handled criminal cases; (2) whether strategic trial tactics were involved in the allegedly incompetent action; (3) whether, and to what extent, the defendant was prejudiced as a result of the lawyer's alleged ineffectiveness; and (4) whether the ineffectiveness was due to matters beyond the lawyer's control. — Abbr. IAC. — Also termed *inadequate assistance of counsel.*

> "The Sixth Amendment right to assistance of counsel has been held to imply the 'right to the effective assistance of counsel.' The Court has often said that the converse — ineffective assistance of counsel — is a constitutional denial of the Sixth Amendment right, even if the lawyer has been retained by rather than appointed for the defendant. 'Ineffective' does not necessarily mean incompetent or unprepared; it means an inability to perform as an independent lawyer devoted to the defendant. . . . However, counsel's assistance is not necessarily ineffective because the lawyer made mistakes. Only very serious errors, such as would likely have produced an entirely different outcome at trial, will suffice to require a new trial." Jethro K. Lieberman, *The Evolving Constitution* 263–64 (1992).

Assistant Commissioner for Patents. See *commissioner for patents* under COMMISSIONER.

Assistant Commissioner for Trademarks. See *commissioner for trademarks* under COMMISSIONER.

assistant jurisdiction. See JURISDICTION.

Assistant United States Attorney. See UNITED STATES ATTORNEY.

assisted conception. (1984) *Family law.* The fertilization of a woman's egg with a man's sperm by some means other than sexual intercourse. See ARTIFICIAL INSEMINATION; IN VITRO FERTILIZATION; GAMETE INTRAFALLOPIAN TRANSFER; ZYGOTE INTRAFALLOPIAN TRANSFER.

assisted dispute resolution. See ALTERNATIVE DISPUTE RESOLUTION.

assisted misrepresentation. See MISREPRESENTATION.

assisted reproductive technology. (1988) *Family law.* Any medical means of aiding human reproduction, esp. through laboratory procedures. — Abbr. ART. — Also termed *assisted reproduction; assisted-reproductive therapy.*

assisted self-determination. See *assisted suicide* under SUICIDE (1).

assisted suicide. See SUICIDE (1).

assize (ə-SIZ), *n.* (14c) **1.** (*often pl.*) A session of a court or council; esp., a meeting of a court presided over by a judge or judges who travel periodically from town to town.

> "Assise (*assessio*) anciently signified in general, a court where the judges or assessors heard and determined causes; and more particularly upon writs of *assize* brought before them, by such as were wrongfully put out of their possessions. Which writs heretofore were very frequent; but now mens possessions are more easily recovered by ejectments, and the like. Yet still the judges in their circuits have a commission of *assize*, directed to themselves and the clerk of assize, to take assizes, and to do right upon such writs." Edward Bullingbrooke, *The Duty and Authority of Justices of the Peace and Parish Officers for Ireland* 53 (rev. ed. 1788).

▸ **maiden assize.** (18c) *Hist.* **1.** An assize in which no prisoner is sentenced to death. **2.** An assize in which the sheriff presents the judges with white gloves because there are no prisoners to try. • This practice stemmed from a custom in which a prisoner who was convicted of murder but pardoned by the Crown presented gloves to the judges as a fee.

2. A law enacted by such a body, usu. one setting the measure, weight, or price of a thing.

▸ **Assize of Arms.** An 1181 statute requiring every man to keep arms suitable to his station in life. See ASSISA ARMORUM.

▸ **Assize of Clarendon (klair-ən-dən).** *Hist.* A decree issued in 1166 by Henry II to the justices in eyre and sheriffs concerning criminal procedure. • The Assize expanded the reach of the king's courts by asserting royal jurisdiction over serious crimes. See CONSTITUTIONS OF CLARENDON.

▸ **Assize of Northampton.** *Hist.* A decree issued in 1176 by Henry II as an expansion and reissue of the Assize of Clarendon, instructing judges esp. on questions of tenure, relief, and dower.

3. The procedure provided for by such an enactment. **4.** The court that hears cases involving that procedure. **5.** A jury.

▸ **grand assize.** (*often cap.*) (16c) A sworn panel summoned by judicial writ to resolve disputes concerning real property. • Henry II instituted the Grand Assize in the 12th century as an alternative to trial by battle. — Also termed *magna assisa.*

> "The word 'Assisa' means originally the sitting of a court or assembly. It then comes to denote the things done, the enactments passed, at such a court or assembly. Thus we speak of the Assize of Clarendon, or the Assize of Northampton. Certain of these enactments in Henry II's reign introduced a new procedure for the trial of questions as to the ownership or possession of lands held by free tenure. The Grand Assize introduced this new procedure for the determination of questions of ownership; the possessory assizes for the determination of question of possession." 1 William Holdsworth, *A History of English Law* 275 (7th ed. 1956).

▸ **petite assize.** A jury convened to decide questions of possession.

6. A jury trial.

▸ **assize of *mort d'ancestor*** (**mor**[t] **dan**-ses-tər). (17c) An action for the recovery of land belonging to the claimant's ancestor. • *Mort d'ancestor* was abolished in the early 19th century. — Also termed *assisa mortis d'ancestoris; assisa de morte antecessoris.*

▸ **judicial assize.** An assize begun by judicial writ and deriving from pleas of *gage, mort d'ancestor,* and *darrein presentment.*

▸ **petty assize.** (1889) An assize begun by an original writ. • Petty assizes were characterized by the form of the writ, which specified the questions to be put to the panel, and ordered that a panel be assembled. The petty assizes were *novel disseisin, mort d'ancestor, utrum,* and *darrein presentment.*

7. A jury's finding. **8.** A writ. — Also spelled *assise; assisa.*

▸ **assize *de ultima presentatione.*** See *assize of darrein presentment.*

▸ **assize *de utrum.*** See *assize utrum.*

▸ **assize of *darrein presentment*** (**dar**-ayn pri-**zent**-mənt), *n.* [fr. French *dernier présentation* "last presentment"] (18c) *Hist.* A writ allowing a person with a right of advowson that had been disturbed by another claimant to have a jury determine who had last presented a clerk to a benefice and then to allow that person to present again and to recover damages for interference. • This was abolished by the Real Property Limitation Act of 1833 and was replaced by the *quare impedit* action. — Also spelled *darreign.* — Also termed *darrein presentment; assize of last presentation; assisa ultimae praesentationis; assize de ultima presentatione.* See ADVOWSON; QUARE IMPEDIT.

> "An assise of *darrein presentment*, or last presentation, lies when a man, or his ancestors, under whom he claims, have presented a clerk to a benefice, who is instituted; and afterwards upon the next avoidance a stranger presents a clerk, and thereby disturbs him that is the real patron. In which case the patron shall have this writ, directed to the sheriff to summon an assise or jury, to enquire who was the last patron that presented to the church now vacant, of which the plaintiff complains that he is deforced by the defendant: and, according as the assise determines that question, a writ shall issue to the bishop; to institute the clerk of that patron, in whose favour the determination is made, and also to give damages . . . ." 3 William Blackstone, *Commentaries on the Laws of England* 245 (1768).

> "[A]t some time or another during his reign Henry gave a possessory action, the assize of darrein presentment . . . which stands to the writ of right of advowson in somewhat the same relation as that in which the novel disseisin stands to the writ of right for land. If the church is vacant and two persons are quarrelling about the advowson, it is very necessary that some provisional, some possessory judgment should be given . . . . The principle of the new assize is, simply stated, this: 'He who presented last time, let him present this time also; but this without prejudice to any question of right.' An inquest of neighbours is summoned to declare who it was that presented the last parson." 1 Frederick Pollock & Frederic W. Maitland, *The History of English Law Before the Time of Edward I* 148–49 (2d ed. 1898).

▸ **assize of fresh force.** (18c) *Hist.* A writ available in urban areas to disseise another's land. • This writ is so called because it was available only within the first 40 days after title accrued to the person seeking it. — Also termed *assisa friscae fortiae.*

▸ **assize of last presentation.** See *assize of darrein presentment.*

▸ **assize of novel disseisin.** (18c) *Hist.* A writ for a tenant who has been disseised of lands and tenements. • This institution of English law flourished for about 300 years — from the 12th century to the 15th. It had become wholly obsolete by the mid-17th century. — Also termed *assisa novae disseysinae*; *assisa novae disseisinae.*

"Perhaps the most important of his [Henry II's] procedural innovations is the *assisa novae disseisinae*, which seems to have been invented under the influence of the canon law *actio spolii*, and which granted to everyone who had been disseised the right to obtain a writ which directed the sheriff to form an *assisa* consisting of twelve men of the neighborhood (*duodecim liberos et legales homines de visneto*) who, as soon as the royal justices should arrive in the vicinage, should make answer to the justice whether or not a disseisin had taken place. This *assisa novae disseisinae* was followed at a later time by other assizes, the basic features of which were: summons by royal writ to appear before the justice and judgment based on a verdict of men of the neighborhood. In addition the king had granted to everyone who desired to assert a claim to the land the privilege of taking the matter out of the local communal court by means of a royal writ and of bringing it before the *curia regis*. These innovations offered many advantages to the parties, especially since the *curia regis* enjoyed a much greater measure of confidence than the local courts, employed a procedure that was much more expeditious and technically on a much higher plane than the clumsy ancient Germanic procedure, and had substituted for traditional, highly imperfect means of proof, such as trial by combat and oath with oath-helpers, the testimony of the men of the neighborhood." Eugen Ehrlich, *Fundamental Principles of the Sociology of Law* 272–73 (Walter L. Moll trans., 1962).

"[Up to the 15th century,] 'assize of novel disseisin' was a series of perfectly plain words, as plain as the words 'proceeding in recent ejectment,' which translate them into modern English, would be to us. Even to humble contemporaries whose linguistic horizons did not extend beyond English, the institution itself apart from its name was perfectly straightforward. It meant that if a freeholder of land was ejected from his property he could require the sheriff to set up a jury of twelve, have them go look at the land, and bring them before the king's justices when they next came to hold court in the county. The justices asked the jurors whether the freeholder had been illegally put out of his holding, as he complained, and if they said that he had then the court would restore the land to him at once." Donald W. Sutherland, *The Assize of Novel Disseisin* 1–2 (1973).

▸ **assize of nuisance.** (18c) *Hist.* A writ available to a landowner suffering from a nuisance on another's land; a writ to abate a nuisance. • This writ also entitled a successful plaintiff to damages. — Also termed *assisa de nocumento.*

"*The assize of nuisance.* — This was supplementary to the famous assize of novel disseisin which was limited to redressing any act of the defendant that interfered with the plaintiff's seisin of land. It was therefore useless if the injury to the plaintiff began wholly on the defendant's land (e.g., if he erected there a dam which diverted water from the plaintiff's land), for the injury was not a disseisin as there was no entry on the plaintiff's land. This gap was filled by the assize of nuisance as early as the thirteenth century. It extended both to injuries to servitudes *stricto sensu* and to common rights." P.H. Winfield, *A Textbook of the Law of Tort* § 130, at 443 (5th ed. 1950).

▸ **assize of *utrum*.** See ASSIZE UTRUM.

assize of last presentation. See *assize of darrein presentment* under ASSIZE (8).

Assize of Arms. See ASSIZE (2).

Assize of Clarendon. See ASSIZE (2).

Assize of Northampton. See ASSIZE (2).

assizer, *n.* (14c) *Hist.* **1.** A member of a grand assize. See *grand assize* under ASSIZE (5). **2.** *Scots law.* A juror. **3.** One having custody of the standards of weight and measure; esp., one who fixes the assize of bread, ale, and other items of general consumption. — Also spelled *assizor*; *assiser*; *assisor.*

Assizes de Jerusalem. (ə-**sɪz**-əz də jə-**roo**-sə-ləm). Two codes of feudal law intended to serve as the law of the lands conquered by the Crusaders. • Prepared in the 12th century after the 1099 conquest of Jerusalem, they were drawn up under the authority of Godfrey de Bouillon, the first crusading king of Jerusalem, and they were in force under Christian sovereignty in both Jerusalem and Cyprus. One code dealt with the nobility, and the other with common people. They were based on contemporary French law and customs. — Also termed *Assizes of Jerusalem*; *Letters of the Holy Sepulcher.*

assize utrum (**yoo**-trəm). [Latin] (1891) *Hist.* A writ to determine whether land claimed by a church was held by lay or spiritual tenure. • This writ is named after its emphatic word, which required the fact-finder to determine whether (*utrum*) the land belonged to the church. — Also termed (erroneously) *assize of utrum*; *assize de utrum.*

"In the assize utrum a jury was summoned to decide whether land was held by lay or spiritual tenure — a preliminary question to any litigation about it, for the Church claimed jurisdiction over spiritual land. Later the Church was to lose this jurisdiction, and the assize utrum became the parson's substitute for the writ of right. This curious development was brought about in this way. A parson could not use the writs of right, for, like a life tenant, he could not trace his title back to the seisin of an ancestor. The assize utrum could be made to serve the parson, however, for the question asked in the writ was whether certain land in a parish was 'the free alms of the Church of X.' If the answer was 'yes,' then it followed that it was the parson of the parish's land." A.W.B. Simpson, *An Introduction to the History of the Land Law* 30–31 (1961).

"[T]he 'assize utrum' . . . is important as being the first instance known to us of the general use of the royal procedure by way of inquest in a matter of private litigation. If the answer of the inquest was that this land was held in frankalmoign, then the case went to the ecclesiastical court; if that it was lay fee, then to the appropriate lay tribunal. In the course of the thirteenth century the ecclesiastical courts lost their jurisdiction over land held by spiritual tenure, and the 'assize utrum' came to be used not as a merely preliminary procedure but as a mode of deciding in royal courts a question of title to glebe land." Geoffrey Radcliffe & Geoffrey Cross, *The English Legal System* 33–34 (G.J. Hand & D.J. Bentley eds., 6th ed. 1977).

assizor. See ASSIZER.

associate, *n.* (16c) **1.** A colleague or companion. **2.** A junior member of an organization or profession; esp., a lawyer in a law firm, usu. with fewer than a certain number of years in practice, who may, upon achieving the requisite seniority, receive an offer to become a partner or shareholder. — Also termed *associate attorney.* **3.** *Hist. English law.* An officer of a common-law court responsible for maintaining the court's records, attending jury trials, and entering verdicts. • In 1894, associates' duties were taken over by the staff of the Central Office. See CLERK OF ASSIZE; CENTRAL OFFICE.

associate agent. See AGENT.

associate attorney. **1.** ASSOCIATE (2). **2.** See ATTORNEY (2).

associate director. See DIRECTOR.

associated person. *Securities.* **1.** A partner, officer, director, branch manager of a broker or dealer, or any person performing similar functions or occupying a similar status, any person directly or indirectly controlling, controlled by, or under common control with the broker or dealer, or any employee of the broker or dealer — with two exceptions: (1) those whose functions are solely clerical or ministerial, and (2) those required to register under state law as a broker or dealer solely because they are issuers of securities or associated with an issuer of securities. 15 USCA § 78c(a)(18), (21), (49). **2.** A natural person who is a partner, officer, director, or employee of (1) the issuer; (2) a general partner of a limited partnership issuer; or (3) a company or partnership that controls, is controlled by, or is under common control with the issuer. Cf. AFFILIATE (2).

associated-words canon. See NOSCITUR A SOCIIS.

associate judge. See JUDGE.

associate justice. See JUSTICE (5).

association. (16c) **1.** The process of mentally collecting ideas, memories, or sensations. **2.** A gathering of people for a common purpose; the persons so joined. **3.** An unincorporated organization that is not a legal entity separate from the persons who compose it. • If an association has sufficient corporate attributes, such as centralized management, continuity of existence, and limited liability, it may be classified and taxed as a corporation. — Also termed *unincorporated association*; *voluntary association*.

> "In the interval between the acceptance of the principle that a corporation in English law arises only as a result of state concession, and the passing of the first Companies Act in 1862, there were established many unincorporated associations, some of them of very great importance. Such an association enjoyed no legal existence distinct from that of its members. Its legal status was simply that of an association of persons, linked by contract, and the rights of members were determined by their contractual rights, in respect of the association." G.W. Keeton, *The Elementary Principles of Jurisprudence* 169 (2d ed. 1949).

▸ **beneficial association.** See *benevolent association*.

▸ **benefit association.** See *benevolent association*.

▸ **benevolent association.** (18c) An unincorporated, nonprofit organization that has a philanthropic or charitable purpose. — Also termed *beneficial association*; *benefit association*; *benevolent society*; *fraternal society*; *friendly society*.

▸ **homeowners' association.** (1900) **1.** An organization created to manage the property and affairs of a common-interest community, such as a housing tract or condominium project. • Regulated by statutes in many states, homeowners' associations are commonly created by a declaration or a similar instrument that is recorded by the developer. **2.** An association of people who own homes in a given area and have united to improve or maintain the area's quality. — Abbr. HOA. — Also written *homeowners association*. — Also termed *owners' association*.

▸ **nonprofit association.** (1899) A group organized for a purpose other than to generate income or profit, such as a scientific, religious, or educational organization.

▸ **owners' association. 1.** See *homeowners' association*. **2.** See OWNERS' ASSOCIATION.

▸ **professional association.** (1837) **1.** A group of professionals organized to practice their profession together, though not necessarily in corporate or partnership form. **2.** A group of professionals organized for education, social activity, or lobbying, such as a bar association. — Abbr. P.A.

▸ **trade association.** (1909) An association of business organizations having similar concerns and engaged in similar fields, formed for mutual protection, the interchange of ideas and statistics, and the establishment and maintenance of industry standards. • A trade association may be composed of members of a single industry (e.g., the Chemical Manufacturers Association) or members having a common interest or purpose (e.g., the Consumer Mortgage Coalition). Among the joint actions that a trade association often takes are collecting industry data, advertising, marketing, and engaging in public relations and government relations.

associational standing. See STANDING.

association-in-fact enterprise. (1970) Under RICO, a group of people or entities that have not formed a legal entity, but that have a common or shared purpose, and maintain an ongoing organizational structure through which the associates function as a continuing unit. • A RICO violation is not shown merely by proving that an enterprise, including an association-in-fact, exists. A pattern of racketeering activity must also be proved. 18 USCA § 1961(4); *U.S. v. Turkette*, 452 U.S. 576, 101 S.Ct. 2524 (1981).

Association of American Law Schools. An organization of U.S. law schools that have each graduated at least three annual classes of students. — Abbr. AALS.

Association of Legal Writing Directors. A nonprofit corporation composed of the directors and former directors of law-school legal-writing programs, mostly in the United States. • Created in 1996 to improve those programs, it supports research and scholarship; holds a biennial conference; conducts (with the Legal Writing Institute) an annual survey of the programs; maintains an e-mail list; represents writing teachers before the American Bar Association; and publishes various resources, including the *ALWD Citation Manual*. — Abbr. ALWD (**al**-wid). See ALWD CITATION MANUAL.

associative rights. (1962) The constitutional guarantees dealing with joint actions of individuals, esp. the rights to the freedom of petition, the freedom of assembly, and the freedom of association.

assoil (ə-**soyl**), *vb.* [Law French] *Hist.* To acquit or absolve; to deliver from excommunication. — Also spelled *assoile*. — Also termed *absoile*; *assoilyie*; *assoilzie*.

assultus premeditatus. See *assault purpensé* under ASSAULT.

assumed bond. See *guaranteed bond* (1) under BOND (3).

assumed name. See NAME.

assume or reject. (1910) *Bankruptcy.* (Of a debtor-in-possession or a trustee) to make an election under the Bankruptcy Code concerning an executory contract or an unexpired lease within a prescribed period, depending on the chapter of the Code under which the case is proceeding and the subject matter of the contract. • The timing, procedure, and consequences of the election are described in 11 USCA § 365.

assumpsit (ə-**səm**[**p**]-sit). [Law Latin "he undertook"] (16c) **1.** An express or implied promise, not under seal, by which one person undertakes to do some act or pay something to another <an assumpsit to pay a debt>. **2.** A common-law action for breach of such a promise or for breach of a contract <the creditor's assumpsit against the debtor>.

"It was early known as 'trespass on the case upon promises,' but in time came to be designated *assumpsit* (he assumed or promised), and lies for damages for breach of all contracts, parol or simple, whether written or verbal, express or implied." Edwin E. Bryant, *The Law of Pleading Under the Codes of Civil Procedure* 9–10 (2d ed. 1899).

"In its origin an action of tort, [assumpsit] was soon transformed into an action of contract, becoming afterwards a remedy where there was neither tort nor contract. Based at first only upon an express promise, it was afterwards supported upon an implied promise, and even upon a fictitious promise. Introduced as a special manifestation of the action on the case, it soon acquired the dignity of a distinct form of action, which superseded Debt, became concurrent with Account, with Case upon a bailment, a warranty, and bills of exchange, and competed with Equity in the case of the essentially equitable quasi-contracts growing out of the principle of unjust enrichment. Surely, it would be hard to find a better illustration of the flexibility and power of self-development of the Common Law." James Barr Ames, "The History of Assumpsit," in 3 *Select Essays in Anglo-American Legal History* 298 (1909).

▸ **assumpsit for nonfeasance.** (1871) *Archaic.* An action based on the defendant's failure to do what he or she was contractually obligated to do.

▸ **common assumpsit.** See *general assumpsit.*

▸ **express assumpsit.** See *special assumpsit.*

▸ **general assumpsit.** (18c) An action based on the defendant's breach of an implied promise to pay a debt to the plaintiff. — Also termed *common assumpsit*; *indebitatus assumpsit.*

"General assumpsit is brought for breach of a fictitious or implied promise raised by law from a debt founded upon an executed consideration. The basis of the action is the promise implied by law from the performance of the consideration, or from a debt or legal duty resting upon the defendant." Benjamin J. Shipman, *Handbook of Common-Law Pleading* § 59, at 153 (Henry Winthrop Ballantine ed., 3d ed. 1923).

"[T]he word 'assumpsit' suggest[s] the making of a promise. While that is true in the case of the action of special assumpsit, the promise alleged in the action of general assumpsit was only a fiction. Accordingly in the latter action, the word 'assumpsit' no more means that an obligation exists as the result of making a contract, than that a contract is involved because the obligation is described as quasi-contractual." Charles Herman Kinnane, *A First Book on Anglo-American Law* 633–34 (2d ed. 1952).

▸ ***indebitatus assumpsit*** (in-deb-i-**tay**-təs ə-**səm**[**p**]-sit). [Latin "being indebted, he undertook"] (17c) **1.** A form of action in which the plaintiff alleges that the defendant contracted a debt and, as consideration, had undertaken (i.e., promised) to pay. • The action was equivalent to the common-law action for debt (an action based on a sealed instrument), but could be used to enforce an oral debt. In England, *indebitatus assumpsit* was abolished in 1873 by the Judicature Act. But it is still used in several American states, such as California. See CONCESSIT SOLVERE. **2.** See *general assumpsit.*

"[I]f I verbally agree to pay a man a certain price for a certain parcel of goods, and fail in the performance, an action of debt lies against me; for this is a *determinate* contract: but if I agree for no settled price, I am not liable to an action of debt, but a special action on the case, according to the nature of my contract. And indeed actions of debt are now seldom brought but upon special contracts under seal . . . . [T]he plaintiff must recover the whole debt he claims, or nothing at all. For the debt is one single cause of action, fixed and determined; and which therefore, if the proof varies from the claim, cannot be looked upon as the same . . . action of debt . . . . But in an action on the case, on what is called an *indebitatus assumpsit*, which is not brought to compel a specific performance of the contract, but to recover damages for its non-performance, the implied *assumpsit*, and consequently the damages for the breach of it, are in their nature indeterminate; and will therefore adapt and proportion themselves to the truth of the case which shall be proved, without being confined to the precise demand stated in the declaration." 3 William Blackstone, *Commentaries on the Laws of England* 154 (1768).

▸ **special assumpsit.** (17c) An action based on the defendant's breach of an express contract. — Also termed *express assumpsit.*

"Special assumpsit lies for the recovery of damages for the breach of simple contract, either express or implied in fact. The term 'special contract' is often used to denote an express or explicit contract as contrasted with a promise implied in law." Benjamin J. Shipman, *Handbook of Common-Law Pleading* § 58, at 148 (Henry Winthrop Ballantine ed., 3d ed. 1923).

"From the allegations concerning the 'assumpsit,' a new action which split off from the action on the case came to be known as the action of assumpsit. Since, however, the plaintiff had to allege and prove a specific or special promise, in order to get a judgment, the action came to be known as the action of 'special assumpsit.' When the special promise came to be regarded as the basis of the action, the action came to be regarded as a contract action, rather than one based on unclassified 'wrongs.'" Charles Herman Kinnane, *A First Book on Anglo-American Law* 633–34 (2d ed. 1952).

assumption, *n.* (13c) **1.** A fact or statement taken as true or correct without definite proof; a supposition <a logical assumption>. **2.** The act of taking (esp. someone else's debt or other obligation) for or on oneself; the agreement to so take <assumption of a debt>. — **assume,** *vb.*

▸ **assumption of mortgage or trust deed.** The acquisition of real property coupled with the assumption of personal liability for debt secured by that property.

▸ **implied assumption.** (1852) The imposition of personal liability on a land purchaser who buys subject to a mortgage and who deducts the mortgage amount from the purchase price, so that the purchaser is treated as having assumed the debt.

assumption clause. (1878) **1.** A mortgage provision that prohibits another from assuming the mortgage without the permission of the mortgagee. **2.** A provision by which the transferee of an instrument agrees to assume an obligation of the transferor.

assumption fee. (1965) A lender's charge for processing records for a new buyer's assumption of an existing mortgage.

assumption of the risk. (1824) *Torts.* **1.** The act or an instance of a prospective plaintiff's taking on the risk of loss, injury, or damage <the skydiver's assumption of the risk>. — Also termed *assumption of risk.*

"[Assumption of risk] has been a subject of much controversy, and has been surrounded by much confusion, because 'assumption of risk' has been used by the courts in several different senses, which traditionally have been lumped together under the one name, often without realizing that any differences exist. There are even courts which have limited the use of the term 'assumption of risk' to cases in which the parties stand in the relation of master and servant, or at least some other contractual relation; but they have been compelled to invent other names for other cases, such as 'incurred risk,' or 'volenti non fit injuria.' This appears to be largely a distinction without a difference; and most courts have made general use of the one term. . . . In its most basic sense, assumption of risk means that the plaintiff, in advance, has given his express consent to relieve the defendant of an obligation of conduct toward him, and to take his chances of injury from a known risk arising from what the defendant is to do or leave undone." W. Page Keeton et al., *Prosser and Keeton on the Law of Torts* § 68, at 480–81 (5th ed. 1984).

2. The principle that one who takes on the risk of loss, injury, or damage cannot maintain an action against a party that causes the loss, injury, or damage <assumption of the risk was not a valid defense>. • Assumption of the risk was originally an affirmative defense, but in most jurisdictions it has now been wholly or largely subsumed by the doctrines of contributory or comparative negligence. The risk assumed by the person was often termed an *incurred risk*.

▸ **express assumption of the risk.** A plaintiff's express consent, usu. in a contract, to assume responsibility for a risk, thereby relieving the defendant of any duty with respect to that risk.

▸ **implied assumption of the risk.** (1895) Conduct by the plaintiff revealing an intent to assume a risk. • For such conduct to give rise to a defense, it must suggest (1) open consent to the risk, (2) voluntary participation in the activity despite the opportunity to avoid the risk by taking reasonable measures, and (3) full understanding of both the danger and the alternatives that might avoid it. See VOLENTI NON FIT INJURIA.

▸ **primary assumption of the risk.** (1973) A legal conclusion that the average or ordinary participant in an activity would reasonably assume the risks that are inherent in the activity, thereby relieving the defendant of any duty of care with respect to those risks. • The phrase appears most often in the context of recreational or sporting activities <a skydiver's primary assumption of the risk inherent in skydiving>.

"Primary assumption of risk occurs when the plaintiff voluntarily participates in an activity involving certain inherent risks and encounters one of the inherent risks; the defense is a complete bar to recovery because there is no duty of care to protect another from the risks inherent in a voluntary activity." 4 Ann Taylor Schwing, *California Affirmative Defenses* § 48:24, at 59 (2d ed. 1996).

"Primary assumption of risk is sometimes viewed as a misnomer. This concept is frequently described as a no-duty rule because the plaintiff, by engaging in a known and potentially risky activity, has relieved the defendant of the duty of care normally owed to the plaintiff. Under the primary-assumption-of-risk/no-duty doctrine, 'there [would be] no liability because the defendant did not breach a duty of care to the plaintiff.' [Kenneth S. Abraham, *The Forms and Functions of Tort Law* 155 (1997).] Traditionally, the no-duty rule completely bars a plaintiff's recovery. Courts limit the use of primary assumption of risk in comparative-negligence jurisdictions because of the harshness of this rule. Recently, some comparative-negligence jurisdictions have started to review primary assumption-of-risk claims within the framework of their comparative-fault system, refusing to automatically bar the plaintiff's entire recovery." Luke Ellis, Note, *Talking About My Generation: Assumption of Risk and the Rights of Injured Concert Fans in the Twenty-First Century*, 80 Texas L. Rev. 607, 618 (2002).

▸ **secondary assumption of risk.** (1971) **1.** The act or an instance of voluntarily encountering a known unreasonable risk that is out of proportion to any advantage gained. • With secondary assumption of the risk, the fact-finder considers the reasonableness of the plaintiff's conduct in the particular case, balancing the risks and utilities under the circumstances. **2.** An affirmative defense to an established breach of a duty, based on a claim that the plaintiff acted unreasonably in encountering a known risk. See *contributory negligence* under NEGLIGENCE.

▸ **voluntary assumption of the risk.** (1894) An intentional and unreasonable exposure of oneself to danger created by another's negligence, when one knows or has reason to know of the danger.

assurance, *n.* (14c) **1.** Something that gives confidence; the quality, state, or condition of being confident or secure <self-assurance>. **2.** *English law.* LIFE INSURANCE <she obtained assurance before traveling abroad, naming her husband as the beneficiary>. **3.** The act of transferring real property; the instrument by which it is transferred <the owner's assurance of the farm to his son>. **4.** A pledge or guarantee <adequate assurances of the borrower's solvency>. — **assure,** *vb.*

▸ **adequate assurance. 1.** *Contracts.* A circumstance or a contractual obligor's act that gives an obligee reason to be confident that the contract will be duly performed. • If the obligee has good reason to feel insecure and justifiably demands assurance, an obligor's failure to provide adequate assurance may constitute a repudiation of the contract. UCC § 2-609. **2.** *Bankruptcy.* Evidence that a debtor will probably be able to perform its obligations under a contract, such as the posting of a bond or a showing that the debtor will generate sufficient income to pay any arrearages and future payment obligations.

▸ **collateral assurance.** (17c) A pledge made in addition to the principal assurance of an agreement.

▸ **common assurance.** See MUNIMENT OF TITLE.

▸ **further assurance.** (17c) A covenant, usu. contained in a warranty deed, whereby the grantor promises to execute any document that might be needed in the future to perfect the title that the original instrument purported to transfer.

assured, *n.* (18c) *Insurance.* Someone who is indemnified against loss; INSURED.

assurer. See INSURER.

as their interests may appear. See ATIMA.

astipulation (as-tip-yə-**lay**-shən). (16c) *Archaic.* Agreement; assent.

astitution (as-tə-**t[y]oo**-shən). *Archaic.* See ARRAIGNMENT.

astrarius (as-**trair**-ee-əs), *n.* [Law Latin "hearth owner"] *Hist.* The owner or occupant of a house. — Also termed *astrer* (**as**-trər). See *heres astrarius* under HERES.

astronomical day. See *solar day* (2) under DAY.

astronomical tide. See TIDE.

asylee (ə-SI-**lee**). (1950) A refugee applying for asylum; an asylum-seeker.

asylum. (15c) **1.** A sanctuary or shelter. **2.** Protection of usu. political refugees from arrest by a foreign jurisdiction; a country or embassy that affords such protection. — Also termed *political asylum.* **3.** An institution for the protection and relief of the unfortunate, esp. the mentally ill. — Also termed (in sense 3, archaically) *insane asylum.*

asymmetric warfare. See WARFARE.

ATA. *abbr.* AIR-TRANSPORT AGREEMENT.

atamita (ə-**tam**-i-tə), *n.* [Latin] (18c) *Civil law.* A great-great-great-grandfather's sister.

at arm's length. See ARM'S-LENGTH.

atavia (ə-**tay**-vee-ə), *n.* [Latin] (17c) *Roman & civil law.* A great-great-great-grandmother.

atavunculus (at-ə-**vəngk**-yə-ləs), *n.* [Latin] *Civil law.* A great-great-great-grandfather's brother.

atavus (**at**-ə-vəs), *n.* [Latin] (16c) *Roman & civil law.* The male ascendant in the fifth degree; a great-grandfather's or great-grandmother's grandfather; a fourth grandfather.

at bar. (17c) Now before the court <the case at bar>. — Also termed *at bench*; *at the bar.*

at bench. See AT BAR.

ATCA. *abbr.* ALIEN TORT CLAIMS ACT.

at-call, *adj.* (1992) Of, relating to, or involving a short-term loan that does not have a set repayment schedule but is instead payable in full immediately upon demand <an at-call loan>. See CALL (2); *payable at call* under PAYABLE. — **at call,** *adv.*

ATDS. *abbr.* AUTOMATIC TELEPHONE DIALING SYSTEM.

a tempore cujus contrarii memoria non existet. See TIME IMMEMORIAL (1).

at equity. According to equity; by, for, or in equity.

a terme (a **tairm**). [Law French] For a term.

- ▸ ***a terme de sa vie*** (a **tairm** də sa **vee**). [Law French] For the term of his life.
- ▸ ***a terme que n'est mye encore passe*** (a **tairm** kə nay mee **awn**-kor **pahs**). [Law French] For a term that has not yet passed.
- ▸ ***a terme que passe est*** (a **tairm** kə **pahs ay**). [Law French] For a term that has passed.

atextual, *adj.* Having little or no regard for the words used in a writing, esp. a legal instrument <atextual interpretation>.

ATF. *abbr.* BUREAU OF ALCOHOL, TOBACCO, FIREARMS, AND EXPLOSIVES.

atheist (**ay**-thee-ist), *n.* [fr. Greek *atheos* "without god"] (16c) Someone who disbelieves the existence of all deities. — Also termed *nonbeliever.* Cf. AGNOSTIC.

ATI. *abbr. Criminal law. Slang.* Alternative to incarceration; a corrections program that does not include jail time, esp. for minor offenses, such as probation, house arrest, a fine, or community service. • In considering an ATI sentence, courts weigh risks such as the possible threat to the public, the likelihood of recidivism, and the hardship imposed on innocent third parties.

Atilian law. See LEX ATILIA.

ATIMA (ə-**tee**-mə). *abbr.* As their interests may appear. • The phrase is sometimes used in insurance policies to show that the named insured has an interest, usu. an unspecified one, in the property covered by the policy and is entitled to benefits to the extent of that interest. The phrase is also used in a policy's mortgage clause to protect the mortgagee's real-property interest. See *insurable interest* under INTEREST (2); MORTGAGE CLAUSE.

Atinian law. See LEX ATINIA.

at issue. (18c) Taking opposite sides; under dispute; in question <the federal appeals courts are at issue over a question of law>.

at-issue waiver. See WAIVER (1).

***Atkins* claim.** (2002) *Criminal law.* In a habeas corpus proceeding in a death penalty case, the assertion that the defendant is mentally retarded and is therefore exempt from execution. *Atkins v. Virginia*, 536 U.S. 304 (2002).

***Atkins* defense.** See DEFENSE (1).

Atlantic Reporter. A set of regional lawbooks, part of the West Group's National Reporter System, containing every published appellate decision from Connecticut, Delaware, Maine, Maryland, New Hampshire, New Jersey, Pennsylvania, Rhode Island, and Vermont, as well as the decisions of the District of Columbia Municipal Court of Appeals, from 1885 to date. • The first series ran from 1885 to 1938. The second series ran from 1938 to 2010. The third series is the current one. — Abbr. A.; A.2d; A.3d.

at large. (14c) **1.** Free; unrestrained; not under control <the suspect is still at large>. **2.** Not limited to any particular place, person, matter, or question <at-large election>. **3.** Chosen by the voters of an entire political entity, such as a state, county, or city, rather than from separate districts within the entity <councilmember at large>. **4.** Not ordered in a topical way; at random <statutes at large>. **5.** Fully; in detail; in an extended form <there wasn't time to discuss the issue at large>.

at-large election. See *election at large* under ELECTION.

at law. (16c) According to law; by, for, or in law.

atmatertera (at-may-**tər**-tər-ə), *n.* [Latin] *Civil law.* A great-great-great-grandmother's sister. — Also termed *abmatertera magna* (ab-may-**tər**-tər-ə **mag**-nə).

at maturity. See *date of maturity* under DATE.

ATM price. *abbr.* See *at-the-market price* under PRICE.

atort (a-**tor**), *adv.* [Law French] *Hist.* Wrongfully.

a tort et a travers (a **tor** ay a tra-**vair**). [Law French] Without consideration or discernment.

a tort ou a droit (a **tor** oo a **drwah**). [Law French] Right or wrong.

at par, *adj.* (1802) (Of a stock or bond) issued or selling at face value.

atpatruus (at-**pa**-troo-əs), *n.* [Latin] *Civil law.* A brother of a great-great-grandfather.

at-pleasure appointment. See *pleasure appointment* under APPOINTMENT (1).

ATR. *abbr.* See *average tax rate* under TAX RATE.

at-risk rules, *n. pl.* (1977) Statutory limitations of a taxpayer's deductible losses to the amount the taxpayer could actually lose, to prevent the taxpayer from sheltering income.

atrocious assault. See ASSAULT.

atrocious felony. See FELONY (1).

atrocity, *n.* (16c) **1.** An extremely cruel and violent act, esp. one committed in a war; an instance of extreme heinousness. **2.** The quality, state, or condition of extreme cruelty or criminality; enormous wickedness.

ATS. *abbr.* At the suit of.

ATSDR. *abbr.* AGENCY FOR TOXIC SUBSTANCES AND DISEASE REGISTRY.

at-sight, *adj.* (1854) Of, relating to, or involving a contractual clause requiring payment on demand, exercisable esp. when a buyer has missed payments in the past or generally has a higher risk of default <an at-sight draft>. — **at sight,** *adv.* <draft payable at sight>. See *payable at sight* under PAYABLE.

attach, *vb.* (14c) **1.** To annex, bind, or fasten <attach the exhibit to the pleading>. **2.** To take or seize under legal authority <attach the debtor's assets>. **3.** To become attributed; to adhere <jeopardy attaches when the jury is sworn>.

attaché (at-ə-**shay** *or* a-ta-**shay**), *n.* (1835) Someone who serves as a technical adviser to an embassy; specif., an embassy worker who specializes in a particular subject.

attachiamenta bonorum (ə-tach-ee-ə-**men**-tə bə-**nor**-əm), *n.* [Law Latin] (18c) *Hist.* A distress taken on goods and chattels by bailiffs, as security to answer an action for debt.

attachiamentum (ə-tach-ee-ə-**men**-təm), *n.* [Law Latin] (17c) An attachment. Pl. ***attachiamenta.***

attaching creditor. See CREDITOR.

attachment. (14c) **1.** The seizing of a person's property to secure a judgment or to be sold in satisfaction of a judgment. — Also termed (in civil law) *provisional seizure.* Cf. GARNISHMENT; SEQUESTRATION (4), (5).

▸ **attachment of wages.** (1857) The attachment by a plaintiff of a defendant's earnings as an employee. • In some jurisdictions, an attachment-of-earnings order requires the defendant's employer to deduct a specified sum or percentage of the defendant's wages or salary and to pay the money into court. The court then sends the money to the plaintiff. Federal law provides a garnishment statute for satisfaction of judgments for child support and alimony. Under this statute, up to 50% of a wage-earner's disposable income can be seized if the wage-earner has another family of dependents and up to 60% if there is only one family. If the obligor is more than three months in arrears, an additional 5% can be seized until the arrearage is paid. 15 USCA § 1673(b)(2). — Also termed *attachment of earnings; wage-withholding; automatic wage-withholding; wage assignment.* Cf. GARNISHMENT; INCOME-WITHHOLDING ORDER.

▸ **prejudgment attachment.** (1965) An attachment ordered before a case is decided. Cf. *provisional attachment.*

▸ **provisional attachment.** (1894) A prejudgment attachment in which the debtor's property is seized so that if the creditor ultimately prevails, the creditor will be assured of recovering on the judgment through the sale of the seized property. • Ordinarily, a hearing must be held before the attachment takes place, and most courts require the creditor to post a bond for any damages that result from the seizure (esp. if the creditor ultimately loses in the lawsuit). Cf. *prejudgment attachment.*

2. The arrest of a person who either is in contempt of court or is to be held as security for the payment of a judgment. **3.** A writ ordering legal seizure of property (esp. to satisfy a creditor's claim) or of a person. — Also termed *writ of attachment.*

▸ **ancillary attachment.** (1843) An attachment that results in seizure and holding of property pending a resolution of the plaintiff's claim. — Also termed *attachment on mesne process.*

4. The creation of a security interest in property, occurring when the debtor agrees to the security, receives value from the secured party, and obtains rights in the collateral. UCC § 9-203. Cf. PERFECTION. **5.** The act of affixing or connecting; something (as a document) that is affixed or connected to something else.

attachment bond. See BOND (2).

attachment lien. See LIEN.

attachment of earnings. See *attachment of wages* under ATTACHMENT (1).

attachment of risk. (1900) The point when the risk of loss of purchased goods passes from the seller to the buyer. UCC § 2-509.

attachment of wages. See ATTACHMENT (1).

attachment on mesne process. See *ancillary attachment* under ATTACHMENT (3).

attack dog. (1973) **1.** See *guard dog* under DOG (1). **2.** *Slang.* By extension, a person who aggressively criticizes another person or group with harsh, personal, and usu. public comments, esp. related to politics.

attainder (ə-**tayn**-dər), *n.* (15c) **1.** At common law, the act of extinguishing a person's civil rights when that person is sentenced to death or declared an outlaw for committing a felony or treason. **2.** *Hist.* A grand-jury proceeding to try whether a jury has given a false verdict. **3.** The conviction of a jury so tried. See BILL OF ATTAINDER. — **attaint** (ə-**taynt**), *vb.*

> "The word *attainder* is derived from the Latin term *attinctus,* signifying *stained* or *polluted,* and includes, in its meaning, all those disabilities which flow from a capital sentence. On the attainder, the defendant is disqualified to be a witness in any court; he can bring no action, nor perform any of the legal functions which before he was admitted to discharge; he is, in short, regarded as dead in law." 1 Joseph Chitty, *A Practical Treatise on the Criminal Law* 725 (2d ed. 1826).

attaint (ə-**taynt**), *adj.* (14c) Maligned or tarnished reputationally; under an attainder for crime.

attaint, *n.* (13c) *Hist.* A writ to inquire whether a 12-member jury gave a false verdict. • If it was so found (by a 24-member jury), the judgment based on the verdict was overturned. The writ was abolished in England in 1826.

attempt, *n.* (16c) **1.** The act or an instance of making an effort to accomplish something, esp. without success. **2.** *Criminal law.* An overt act that is done with the intent to commit a crime but that falls short of completing the crime. • Attempt is an inchoate offense distinct from the intended crime. Under the Model Penal Code, an attempt includes any act that is a substantial step toward commission of a crime, such as enticing, lying in wait for, or following the intended victim or unlawfully entering a building where a crime is expected to be committed. Model Penal Code § 5.01. — Also termed *criminal attempt; offer.* See DANGEROUS-PROXIMITY TEST; INDISPENSABLE-ELEMENT TEST; LAST-PROXIMATE-ACT TEST; PHYSICAL-PROXIMITY TEST; PREPARATION; PROBABLE-DESISTANCE TEST; RES IPSA LOQUITUR TEST;

SUBSTANTIAL-STEP TEST. Cf. CONSPIRACY; SOLICITATION (2). — **attempt,** *vb.*

"An attempt to commit an indictable offence is itself a crime. Every attempt is an act done with intent to commit the offence so attempted. The existence of this ulterior intent or motive is the essence of the attempt. . . . [Yet] [a]lthough every attempt is an act done with intent to commit a crime, the converse is not true. Every act done with this intent is not an attempt, for it may be too remote from the completed offence to give rise to criminal liability, notwithstanding the criminal purpose of the doer. I may buy matches with intent to burn a haystack, and yet be clear of attempted arson; but if I go to the stack and there light one of the matches, my intent has developed into a criminal attempt." John Salmond, *Jurisprudence* 387 (Glanville L. Williams ed., 10th ed. 1947).

"Attempt . . . is the most common of the preliminary crimes. It consists of steps taken in furtherance of an indictable offence which the person attempting intends to carry out if he can. As we have seen there can be a long chain of such steps and it is necessary to have some test by which to decide that the particular link in the chain has been reached at which the crime of attempt has been achieved; that link will represent the *actus reus* of attempt . . . ." J.W. Cecil Turner, *Kenny's Outlines of Criminal Law* 79 (16th ed. 1952).

attempted assault. See ASSAULT.

attempted marriage. See *void marriage* under MARRIAGE (1).

attempted monopolization. See MONOPOLIZATION.

attempted suicide. See SUICIDE (1).

attempting to pervert the course of justice. See PERVERTING THE COURSE OF JUSTICE.

attempt to assault. See *attempted assault* under ASSAULT.

attempt to attempt. (1903) A first step made toward a criminal attempt of some sort, such as a failed effort to mail someone a note inciting that person to engage in criminal conduct. • As a general rule, courts do not recognize an attempt to commit a crime that is itself an attempt. But some jurisdictions recognize this offense, esp. when the attempted crime is defined to be an independent substantive crime. For example, some jurisdictions recognize an attempted assault if assault is defined as placing a person in apprehension of bodily injury (as opposed to being defined merely as an attempted battery). In this situation, courts have been willing to punish conduct that falls short of the attempted crime but constitutes more than mere preparation to commit it. See *attempted assault* under ASSAULT.

attendance officer. See TRUANCY OFFICER.

attendant, *adj.* (15c) Accompanying; resulting <attendant circumstances>.

attendant circumstance. See CIRCUMSTANCE.

attendant term. See TERM (4).

attentate (ə-**ten**-tayt), *n.* (17c) *Hist.* **1.** A criminal attempt. **2.** An assault. **3.** An erroneous step taken by a lower-court judge after a case has been stayed or appealed.

attenuation doctrine (ə-ten-yə-**way**-shən). (1962) *Criminal procedure.* The rule providing that evidence obtained by illegal means may nonetheless be admissible if the connection between the evidence and the illegal means is sufficiently remote. • This is an exception to the fruit-of-the-poisonous-tree doctrine arising when the Fourth Amendment violation and the obtaining of the evidence are not causally related. See DUNAWAY HEARING; FRUIT-OF-THE-POISONOUS-TREE DOCTRINE.

atterminare (ə-tər-mi-**nair**-ee), *vb.* [Law Latin] **1.** To put off to a succeeding term; to adjourn. **2.** To prolong the time to pay a debt.

atterminement (ə-**tər**-min-mənt). (16c) **1.** The granting of a delay for some purpose; esp., the extension of time to pay a debt. **2.** The fixing of a time limit. — **attermine,** *vb.*

attermoiement (at-ər-**moy**-ə-mənt). [Law French] *Eccles. law.* COMPOSITION (2).

attest (ə-**test**), *vb.* (16c) **1.** To bear witness; testify <attest to the defendant's innocence>. **2.** To affirm to be true or genuine; to authenticate by signing as a witness <attest the will>. — **attestation** (a-te-**stay**-shən), *n.* — **attestative** (ə-**tes**-tə-tiv), *adj.*

attestant. See ATTESTER.

attestation clause. (18c) A provision at the end of an instrument (esp. a will) that is signed by the instrument's witnesses and that recites the formalities required by the jurisdiction in which the instrument might take effect (such as where the will might be probated). • The attestation strengthens the presumption that all the statutory requirements for executing the will have been satisfied. — Also termed *witnessing part.* Cf. TESTIMONIUM CLAUSE.

attestator. See ATTESTER.

attested copy. See *certified copy* under COPY (1).

attested will. See WILL.

attester (ə-**tes**-tər). (16c) Someone who attests or vouches for. — Also spelled *attestant*; *attestator*; *attestor.*

attesting witness. See WITNESS.

attestor. See ATTESTER.

at the bar. See AT BAR.

at the courthouse door. (Of the posting of a notice of judicial sale, etc.) on the courthouse door, or in direct proximity to the door, as on a bulletin board that is located just outside the door and that is regularly used for the posting of legal notices. • Some statutes may specify that the notice be actually posted on the door. See POSTING (5).

at-the-market price. See PRICE.

at-the-money option. See OPTION (5).

attorn (ə-**tərn**), *vb.* (15c) **1.** To agree to be the tenant of a new landlord. — Also termed *attorn tenant.* **2.** To transfer (money, goods, etc.) to another.

attornatus (at-ər-**nay**-təs). [Law Latin] Someone who is attorned, or put in the place of another; an attorney.

attorney. (14c) **1.** Strictly, one who is designated to transact business for another; a legal agent. — Also termed *attorney-in-fact*; *private attorney.* **2.** Someone who practices law; LAWYER. — Abbr. att'y. — Also termed (in sense 2) *attorney-at-law*; *public attorney.* Cf. COUNSEL (2). Pl. **attorneys.**

▸ **associate attorney.** (1913) **1.** ASSOCIATE (2). **2.** *Patents.* An attorney who is registered to practice before the U.S. Patent and Trademark Office, who has been appointed by a principal attorney, and who is authorized to prosecute a patent application through the filing of a power of attorney.

▸ **attorney ad litem** (ad lɪ-tem *or* -təm). (1819) A court-appointed lawyer who represents a child during the course of a legal action, such as a divorce, termination, or child-abuse case. • The attorney owes to the child the duties of loyalty, confidentiality, and competent representation. A child's right to legal representation in a juvenile proceeding was mandated in *In re Gault*, 387 U.S. 1, 87 S.Ct. 1428 (1967). The appointment of an attorney ad litem is a limited one — only for a specific lawsuit. — Also termed *child's attorney*; *attorney for the child*. Cf. *guardian ad litem* under GUARDIAN (1).

▸ **attorney not of record.** (1833) **1.** A lawyer who is not recognized as a party's legal representative. Cf. *attorney of record* (1). **2.** *Patents & Trademarks.* An attorney whose name is not included in a power of attorney on file with the U.S. Patent and Trademark Office for a patent or trademark application. • An attorney not of record may nevertheless prosecute a patent application if registered to practice before the U.S. Patent and Trademark Office and appointed by the principal attorney. 37 CFR 1.34(a). Cf. *attorney not recognized*.

▸ **attorney not recognized.** *Patents.* An attorney appointed by a patent applicant but not registered to practice before the U.S. Patent and Trademark Office. • A power of attorney appointing an unregistered attorney is void. Cf. *attorney not of record*.

▸ **attorney of record.** (18c) **1.** The lawyer who appears for a party in a lawsuit and who is entitled to receive, on the party's behalf, all pleadings and other formal documents from the court and from other parties. — Also termed *counsel of record*. See OF RECORD (1). Cf. *attorney not of record*. **2.** *Patents & Trademarks.* The attorney or agent whose name is included in the power of attorney filed by an applicant for a patent or a trademark registration. • For a patent application, the attorney of record must be a patent attorney or a patent agent.

▸ **briefing attorney.** (1942) **1.** An attorney who specializes in brief-writing, particularly appellate briefs and legal memoranda. **2.** CLERK (5).

▸ **panel attorney.** (1951) A private attorney who represents an indigent defendant at the government's expense. • A panel attorney is usu. a member of an affiliated list and assigned by a court to a particular client.

▸ **research attorney.** (1939) **1.** An attorney who specializes in providing legal support by researching, by writing memoranda, and by preparing drafts of documents. **2.** CLERK (5). • In some jurisdictions, a research attorney is a midlevel law clerk, above a briefing attorney but below a staff attorney.

▸ **settlement attorney.** (1937) An attorney who specializes in negotiating resolutions for disputes, such as pending lawsuits, or in finalizing negotiated transactions, such as real-property sales. — Sometimes also termed (in real-property sales) *settlement agent*.

▸ **special attorney.** See *special counsel* under COUNSEL.

▸ **staff attorney.** (1934) **1.** A lawyer who works for a court, usu. in a permanent position, on matters such as reviewing motions, screening docketing statements, preparing scheduling orders, and examining habeas corpus petitions. • Staff attorneys do not rule on motions or decide cases, but they review and research factual and legal points, and recommend proposed rulings to judges, as well as drafting the orders implementing those rulings. See CLERK (5). **2.** An in-house lawyer for an organization, esp. a nonprofit organization but sometimes for a corporation. Cf. *in-house counsel* under COUNSEL. **3.** A lawyer who works for a law firm and performs the functions of an associate but who is not on a partnership track.

attorney, power of. See POWER OF ATTORNEY.

attorney at law. See ATTORNEY (2).

attorney autonomy. See *lawyer autonomy* under AUTONOMY.

attorney–client privilege. See PRIVILEGE (3).

attorney–client relationship. See RELATIONSHIP.

attorney fees. See ATTORNEY'S FEE.

attorney for the child. See *attorney ad litem* under ATTORNEY.

attorney general. (16c) The chief law officer of a state or of the United States, responsible for advising the government on legal matters and representing it in litigation. • The term *general* in this phrase is a postpositive adjective, not an honorific, so the title should not, strictly speaking, be shortened. — Abbr. AG. Pl. **attorneys general.**

attorney general's opinion. (1808) **1.** An opinion furnished by the U.S. Attorney General to the President or another executive official on a request concerning a question of law. **2.** A written opinion by a state attorney general, usu. given at the request of a public official, interpreting a legal provision.

attorney in charge. See *lead counsel* (1) under COUNSEL.

attorney-in-fact. See ATTORNEY (1).

attorney malpractice. See *legal malpractice* under MALPRACTICE.

attorney not of record. See ATTORNEY.

attorney not recognized. See ATTORNEY.

attorney of record. See ATTORNEY.

Attorneys and Agents Registered to Practice Before the U.S. Patent and Trademark Office. A PTO publication listing all registered patent attorneys and agents by name and location.

attorney's certificate. See CERTIFICATE.

attorney's fee. (18c) (*usu. pl.*) The charge to a client for services performed for the client, such as an hourly fee, a flat fee, or a contingent fee. — Also spelled *attorneys' fees*. — Also termed *attorney fees*. Cf. RETAINER (4).

▸ **reasonable attorney's fee.** (1853) An attorney's compensation determined to be equitable or fair based on several factors, including the amount of time invested by the attorney; the level of attorney skill, experience, reputation, or ability required; the nature and length of the professional relationship with the client; the difficulty or novelty of questions involved; the dollar amount involved and the results obtained; whether the fee is fixed or contingent and the uncertainty of collection of the fee; and the prevailing market rate for similar services rendered. *See* Model Rule of Prof. Conduct 1.5 (2005).

attorney's lien. See LIEN.

attorney–witness rule. See LAWYER–WITNESS RULE.

attorney work product. See WORK PRODUCT.

attorney-work-product privilege. See WORK-PRODUCT RULE.

attornment (ə-tərn-mənt), *n.* (16c) **1.** A tenant's agreement to hold the land as the tenant of a new landlord. **2.** A constructive delivery involving the transfer of mediate possession while a third person has immediate possession; esp., a bailee's acknowledgment that he or she will hold the goods on behalf of someone other than the bailor. • For the other two types of constructive delivery, see CONSTITUTUM POSSESSORIUM; TRADITIO BREVI MANU. See also *bailment by attornment* under BAILMENT (1). — **attorn,** *vb.*

> "[Another] form of constructive delivery is that which is known to English lawyers as attornment. . . . The mediate possessor of a thing may deliver it by procuring the immediate possessor to agree with the transferee to hold it for the future on his account, instead of on account of the transferor. Thus if I have goods in the warehouse of A and sell them to B, I have effectually delivered them to B so soon as A has agreed with B to hold them for him, and no longer for me." John Salmond, *Jurisprudence* 306–07 (Glanville L. Williams ed., 10th ed. 1947).

attorn tenant. See ATTORN (1).

attractive nuisance. See NUISANCE.

attractive-nuisance doctrine. (1903) *Torts.* The rule that a person who owns property on which there is a dangerous thing or condition that will foreseeably lure children to trespass has a duty to protect those children from the danger <the attractive-nuisance doctrine imposed a duty on the school to protect the children from the shallow, polluted pond on school property>. — Also termed *turntable doctrine*; *torpedo doctrine.* See ALLUREMENT; DANGEROUS INSTRUMENTALITY.

attribute (at-tri-byoot), *n.* (14c) A quality or feature, usu. one considered to be good or useful.

attribution, *n.* (1960) **1.** The quality, state, or condition of being an attribute. **2.** The act or an instance of ascribing words, sentences, a passage, a work of art, a piece of music, etc. to a particular source. **3.** *Tax.* The process outlined in the Internal Revenue Code whereby — by which a person's or entity's stock ownership is assigned to a related family member or related entity for tax purposes. — Also termed *stock attribution.* — **attribute,** *vb.* — **attributive,** *adj.*

attribution right. (1994) *Copyright.* A person's right to be credited as a work's author, to have one's name appear in connection with a work, or to forbid the use of one's name in connection with a work that the person did not create. • Attribution rights constitute one aspect of the moral rights recognized primarily in civil-law countries. Under the Visual Artists Rights Act of 1990, the creators of a very limited class of works — called works of visual art — have certain statutory attribution rights. 17 USCA § 106A. Under the Berne Convention Implementation Act, attribution rights afforded foreign copyright owners may be enforceable in the United States. — Also termed *rights of attribution*; *paternity*; *maternity.* Cf. INTEGRITY RIGHT; MORAL RIGHT.

att'y. *abbr.* ATTORNEY.

ATVEF. *abbr.* ADVANCED TELEVISION ENHANCEMENT FORUM.

at will. (14c) Subject to one's discretion; as one wishes or chooses; esp., (of a legal relationship), able to be terminated or discharged by either party without cause <employment at will>.

at-will employment. See *employment at will* under EMPLOYMENT.

at-will tenancy. See *tenancy at will* under TENANCY.

***Atwood* doctrine.** (1996) The principle that, to the extent an ERISA plan and its summary plan description conflict regarding the circumstances under which benefits may be denied, the summary plan description controls. *Atwood v. Newmont Gold Co.*, 45 F.3d 1317 (9th Cir. 1995); 29 USCA § 1022. See SUMMARY PLAN DESCRIPTION.

au besoin (oh bə-zwan). [French "in case of need"] A designation in a bill of exchange stating who is responsible for payment if the drawee fails or refuses to pay. • For example, *au besoin* is part of the phrase *au besoin, chez Messrs. Garnier et DuCloux* (meaning "in case of need, apply to Messrs. Garnier and DuCloux").

A.U.C. *abbr.* AB URBE CONDITA.

auction, *n.* (16c) A public sale of property to the highest bidder; a sale by consecutive bidding, intended to reach the highest price of the article through competition for it. • Under UCC § 2-328(2), a sale by auction is ordinarily complete when the auctioneer so announces in a customary manner, as by pounding a hammer. — Also termed *auction sale.* — **auction,** *vb.*

▸ **absolute auction.** See *auction without reserve.*

▸ **auction without reserve.** (1963) An auction in which the property will be sold to the highest bidder, no minimum price will limit bidding, the owner may not withdraw property after the first bid is received, the owner may not reject any bids, and the owner may not nullify the bidding by outbidding all other bidders. • In an auction without reserve, the owner essentially becomes an offeror, and each successively higher bid creates a contingent acceptance, with the highest bid creating an enforceable contract. — Also termed *absolute auction.* See WITHOUT RESERVE.

▸ **auction with reserve.** (1963) An auction in which the property will not be sold unless the highest bid exceeds a minimum price. See WITH RESERVE.

▸ **Dutch auction.** (1834) **1.** An auction in which property is initially offered at an excessive price that is gradually lowered until the property is sold. **2.** An auction in which several identical items are offered simultaneously, one to a bidder, and sold to the highest bidders for the amount of the lowest winning bid. **3.** *Securities.* A method of tendering stock shares whereby a corporation provides a price range, shareholders indicate how many shares they will sell and at what price, and the corporation buys however many shares it wants at the lowest prices offered. — Also termed *Dutch-auction tender method.* **4.** *Securities.* An auction of securities, usu. other than stock, in which a security's price is gradually lowered until it meets an acceptable bid and is sold. — Also termed (in sense 4) *offer for sale by tender.* **5.** *Securities.* An auction of a new issue of stock in which there is a stated minimum price per share, but bidders may offer a higher price for any number of shares until the highest price offered becomes the final price at which all the shares issued will be sold.

▸ **knock-out auction.** (2003) An auction at which two or more bidders have agreed in advance not to bid against one another. • At common law, knock-out auctions were not forbidden, on grounds that a person could not be constrained to make an offer. But most jurisdictions now have statutes that (1) forbid dealers (those who buy at auctions with the intention of reselling to others) from giving or offering an inducement to abstain from bidding at an auction, and (2) penalize the person who seeks such an inducement from a dealer.

auction conditions. (1878) The terms on which an auction is conducted, esp. as regards the relationships between the auctioneer, the seller, and the bidders, esp. the highest bidder.

auctioneer, *n.* (18c) A person in charge of selling at an auction, with the responsibility of calling for bids, announcing how much money has already been offered for something, and gaveling down the hammer price; a person legally authorized to sell goods or lands of other persons at public auction for a commission or fee. • The auctioneer is the property owner's agent up to the moment when a purchaser's bid is accepted, when the auctioneer becomes the purchaser's agent. — Formerly also termed *vendue master.*

auctioneer's lien. See LIEN.

auction market. See MARKET.

auction sale. See AUCTION.

auctor (**ahk**-tor), *n.* [Latin "author"] (1875) **1.** The source of a right or title, such as a grantor; AUTHOR (2). **2.** A principal.

auctore praetore (awk-**tor**-ee pree-**tor**-ee). [Latin] **1.** *Roman law.* On the authority of the praetor. **2.** *Scots law.* With the sanction of a judge.

auctor in rem suam (**awk**-tor in **rem** s[y]**oo**-əm). [Latin] *Hist.* Someone who acts on one's own behalf; a principal in one's own affairs.

auctoritate judicis (awk-tor-ə-**tay**-tee **joo**-di-sis). [Latin] *Hist.* By judicial authority.

audibility hearing. See HEARING.

audience, *n.* (15c) A hearing before judges. See RIGHT OF AUDIENCE.

audience test. (1938) *Copyright.* A judicial analysis used to determine whether the lay observer or an ordinary, reasonable audience would conclude that the protectable expression in a copyrighted work is substantially similar to the expression in the accused work. — Also termed *ordinary-observer test; ordinary-lay-observer test.*

Audio Home Recording Act. *Copyright.* A 1992 federal law designed to prevent copyright-infringement suits based on the manufacture, importation, distribution, or sale of digital-audio technology. • Manufacturers of digital recording devices must pay royalties on sales of the devices and related media, and build security mechanisms into each device. The security mechanisms allow the owner of a digital-recording device to make a copy from the original medium, but not to make a copy from the copy. 17 USCA §§ 1001–1010. — Abbr. AHRA.

audiovisual work. See WORK (2).

audit, *n.* (15c) A formal examination of an individual's or organization's accounting records, financial situation, or compliance with some other set of standards. See GENERALLY ACCEPTED AUDITING STANDARDS. — **audit,** *vb.* — **auditor,** *n.*

▸ **audit of return.** See *tax audit.*

▸ **compliance audit.** (1974) An audit conducted by a regulatory agency, an organization, or a third party to assess compliance with one or more sets of laws and regulations.

▸ **correspondence audit.** (1952) An IRS audit of a taxpayer's return conducted by mail or telephone.

▸ **desk audit.** (1937) A review of a civil-service position to determine whether its duties and responsibilities fit the prescribed job classification and pay scale.

▸ **double audit.** (1859) An audit of the same subject performed separately by two independent auditors.

▸ **environmental audit.** (1973) A company's voluntary self-audit to evaluate its environmental-management programs and to determine whether it is in compliance with environmental regulations.

▸ **event-driven audit.** (1993) An audit that focuses on particular transactions or activities that may raise significant legal issues. • Unlike routine periodic audits, an event-driven audit can focus substantial auditing resources on analyzing a particular event.

▸ **field audit.** (1921) An IRS audit conducted at the taxpayer's business premises, accountant's offices, or lawyer's offices.

▸ **independent audit.** (1850) An audit conducted by an outside person or firm not connected with the person or organization being audited.

▸ **internal audit.** (1908) An audit performed by an organization's personnel to ensure that internal procedures, operations, and accounting practices are in proper order.

▸ **office audit.** (1921) An IRS audit of a taxpayer's return conducted in the IRS agent's office.

▸ **periodic audit.** (1918) An audit conducted at regular intervals to assess a company's current condition.

▸ **post audit.** (1912) An audit of funds spent on a completed capital project, the purpose being to assess the efficiency with which the funds were spent and to compare expected cash-flow estimates with actual cash flows.

▸ **tax audit.** (1924) The review of a taxpayer's return by the IRS, including an examination of the taxpayer's books, vouchers, and records supporting the return. — Also termed *audit of return.*

▸ **transactional audit.** (1985) An audit performed for due-diligence purposes to determine whether there are potentially significant problems with a transaction. • Transactional audits are often conducted in real-property transactions to identify any environmental problems. In that context, the audit is sometimes called a *site assessment.*

audita querela (aw-**dɪ**-tə kwə-**ree**-lə). [Law Latin "the complaint having been heard"] (16c) A writ available to a judgment debtor who seeks a rehearing of a matter on grounds of newly discovered evidence or newly existing legal defenses.

> "The writ of audita querela (= quarrel having been heard) . . . , introduced during the time of Edward III, was available to re-open a judgment in certain circumstances. It was issued as a remedy to defendant where an important matter concerning his case had arisen since the judgment. Its issue was based on equitable, rather than common law

principles." L.B. Curzon, *English Legal History* 103 (2d ed. 1979).

"Audita querela is distinguished from coram nobis in that coram nobis attacks the judgment itself, whereas audita querela may be directed against the enforcement, or further enforcement, of a judgment which when rendered was just and unimpeachable." 7A C.J.S. *Audita Querela* § 2, at 901 (1980).

audit certificate. See CERTIFICATE.

audit committee. See COMMITTEE (1).

audit letter. (1941) A written request for an attorney, banker, or someone else to give financial auditors information about a person or entity being audited, including information about pending or threatened litigation. • The recipient of an audit letter usu. sends the response (called an *audit-letter response*) directly to the financial auditors. See AUDIT RESPONSE.

audit-letter response. See AUDIT RESPONSE.

audit of return. See *tax audit* under AUDIT.

audit opinion. See OPINION (2).

auditor. (14c) A person or firm, usu. an accountant or an accounting firm, that formally examines an individual's or entity's financial records or status.

▸ **city auditor.** (18c) A municipal official responsible for examining a city's accounts and financial records.

▸ **county auditor.** (1826) An official who examines a county's accounts and financial records.

▸ **state auditor.** (18c) The appointed or elected official responsible for overseeing state fiscal transactions and auditing state-agency accounts. See AUDIT.

audit privilege. (1988) In an intellectual-property license agreement, the right of the licensor to inspect the licensee's books and records. — Also termed *audit rights.*

audit report. (1924) An independent auditor's written statement, usu. accompanying a company's financial statement, expressing the auditor's opinion of the accuracy of the company's financial condition as set forth in the financial statement.

audit response. (1980) A letter that an attorney provides to a client's financial auditors, usu. at the client's request, regarding matters such as pending or threatened litigation. • Audit responses should comply with the American Bar Association's Statement of Policy Regarding Lawyer's Responses to Auditors' Requests for Information, published in December 1975. — Also termed *audit-letter response.* See AUDIT LETTER.

audit rights. See AUDIT PRIVILEGE.

audit risk. (1967) **1.** The possibility that an internal auditor might not catch errors in financial statements that are based on materially misstated figures and might therefore render an inaccurate opinion. • Misstated figures may be due to negligence or fraud. **2.** The risk of being audited by the taxing authorities.

audit trail. (1954) The chain of evidence connecting account balances to original transactions and calculations.

augmented estate. See ESTATE (3).

aula regis (aw-lə **ree**-jis). [Latin "king's hall"] *Hist.* See CURIA REGIS (1).

aulnager. See ALNAGER.

***Aunt Jemima* doctrine.** (1949) *Trademarks.* The principle that a trademark is protected not only from use on a directly competing product, but also from use on a product so closely related in the marketplace that consumers would be confused into thinking that the products came from a single source. *Aunt Jemima Mills Co. v. Rigney & Co.*, 247 F. 407 (2d Cir. 1917); 15 USCA § 1114. • In the namesake case, the name used on pancake flour was later used on syrup. The issue was not whether a competitor was trying to pass off goods, but whether it was fair to let the name's second user jeopardize the goodwill built up by the first user. See COMPLEMENTARY GOODS.

aural acquisition. (1968) *Criminal law.* Under the Federal Wiretapping Act, hearing or tape-recording a communication, as opposed to tracing its origin or destination. 18 USCA § 2510(4).

AUSA. *abbr.* See *assistant United States attorney* under UNITED STATES ATTORNEY.

Australian ballot. See BALLOT (4).

aut dedere aut judicare. [Latin "extradite or prosecute"] (1972) *Int'l law.* The principle that a country where a fugitive from justice is found must, if the crime committed is recognized in both countries, either extradite the fugitive to the country from which the person has fled or to prosecute the person in its own courts. • This is an emerging principle, and not accepted as a customary rule in international law. Cf. AUT DEDERE AUT POENAM PERSEQUI; AUT DEDERE AUT JUDICARE AUT TRANSFERERE.

aut dedere aut judicare aut transferere. [Latin "extradite, prosecute, or transfer"] (2001) *Int'l law.* An emerging principle that a country may choose neither to extradite nor to prosecute a person accused of a crime but instead may "deliver" the person to a third country. • This is not a de facto extradition because the receiving state may also refuse to surrender the accused person to the requesting state. Cf. AUT DEDERE AUT JUDICARE; AUT DEDERE AUT POENAM PERSEQUI.

aut dedere aut poenam persequi. [Latin "extradite or enforce the sanction"] (1999) *Int'l law.* The rule that a sentence handed down by a court against a person who flees or has fled to another country should be enforced by that country if it chooses not to extradite the person. Cf. AUT DEDERE AUT JUDICARE; AUT DEDERE AUT JUDICARE AUT TRANSFERERE.

authentic act. See ACT (4).

Authenticae. See AUTHENTICUM (2).

authenticate, *vb.* (17c) **1.** To prove the genuineness of (a thing); to show (something) to be true or real. **2.** To render authoritative or authentic, as by attestation or other legal formality. *See* UCC § 9-102(a)(7).

authentication, *n.* (18c) **1.** Broadly, the act of proving that something (as a document) is true or genuine, esp. so that it may be admitted as evidence; the condition of being so proved <authentication of the handwriting>. **2.** Specif., the assent to or adoption of a writing as one's own.

"The concept of authentication, although continually used by the courts without apparent difficulty, seems almost to defy precise definition. Some writers have construed the term very broadly, as does Wigmore when he states that 'when a claim or offer involves impliedly or expressly any element of *personal connection with a corporeal object*, that connection must be made to appear . . . .' So defined, 'authentication' is not only a necessary preliminary to the introduction of most writings in evidence, but also to the introduction of various other sorts of tangibles." John W. Strong et al., *McCormick on Evidence* § 218, at 350 (5th ed. 1999) (italics in original).

▸ **self-authentication.** (1939) Authentication without extrinsic evidence of truth or genuineness. • In federal courts, certain writings, such as notarized documents and certified copies of public records, may be admitted into evidence by self-authentication. Fed. R. Evid. 902.

3. *Int'l law.* The process of having a document notarized and obtaining a Secretary of State's certification that the notary's signature and seal are genuine. Cf. APOSTILLE (2). **4.** APOSTILLE (2).

authentic interpretation. See INTERPRETATION (1).

authenticity (aw-then-**tis**-i-tee), *n.* (17c) **1.** The quality, state, or condition of being genuine, so that the origin or authorship is reliable as claimed. **2.** The quality, state, or condition of being true or in accordance with fact. **3.** The quality, state, or condition of being authoritative or entitled to acceptance.

authenticum (aw-**then**-tə-kəm). *Roman & civil law.* **1.** An original instrument. **2.** (*cap.*) A Latin version of 134 Novels promulgated by Justinian mostly in Greek between A.D. 535 and 556. — Also termed *Liber Authenticorum.*

author. (14c) **1.** *Copyright.* The person who creates an expressive work, or the person or business that hires another to create an expressive work. • In copyright law, "author" applies to a broad range of occupations, including writers, artists, programmers, choreographers, and translators. **2.** One from whom a right or title derives in some way other than by descent. See AUCTOR (1).

authoritative precedent. See *binding precedent* under PRECEDENT.

authority. (13c) **1.** The official right or permission to act, esp. to act legally on another's behalf; esp., the power of one person to affect another's legal relations by acts done in accordance with the other's manifestations of assent; the power delegated by a principal to an agent <authority to sign the contract>. — Also termed *power over other persons.* See AGENCY.

"The term 'authority,' like the term 'contract,' may easily be used in three senses, and is therefore a term to be avoided when accurate reasoning is desirable. It may be used to mean (1) the operative acts of the principal, (2) a physical document executed by the principal, or (3) the legal relations consequent upon the preceding operative facts (1) and (2), and especially the legal *power* conferred upon the agent to bring the principal into new legal relations without any further action by the principal. The operative facts may be spoken words, a document together with the acts necessary to execute it, or other conduct by the principal apparently expressing an intention to create a power. Hereafter, the word 'authority' will be used to denote these operative facts; in other cases the word *power* will usually be substituted. This latter word is not so likely to be taken in shifting senses, in spite of the fact that 'power of attorney' generally means a physical document under seal." William R. Anson, *Principles of the Law of Contract* 508 n.1 (Arthur L. Corbin ed., 3d Am. ed. 1919).

▸ **actual authority.** (18c) Authority that a principal intentionally confers on an agent or authority that the agent reasonably believes he or she has as a result of the agent's dealings with the principal. • Actual authority can be either express or implied. — Also termed *real authority.*

"Actual authority is such as a principal intentionally confers upon the agent, or intentionally, or by want of ordinary care, allows the agent to believe himself to possess." Cal. Civ. Code § 2316.

"Actual authority entitles an agent to act on behalf of a principal and to legally bind the principal. The source of actual authority rests in *manifestations* which may be in the form of 'written or spoken words or *other conduct*' from the principal to the agent. Based on the principal's manifestations to the agent, the agent must reasonably believe that he is acting in accordance with the principal's directive. An agent's actual authority may be express or implied." Marc I. Steinberg, *Developments in Business Law and Policy* 6 (2012) (citations omitted).

▸ **apparent authority.** (1808) Authority that a third party reasonably believes an agent has, based on the third party's dealings with the principal, even though the principal did not confer or intend to confer the authority. • Apparent authority can be created by law even when no actual authority has been conferred. — Also termed *ostensible authority; authority by estoppel.*

"The term 'apparent authority' means that a legal power is vested in the agent in the absence of any intention by the principle that it should exist, or even in spite of his intention that it should *not* exist. The operative facts causing this power to exist are acts of the principal which, considered along with surrounding facts, induce the third person with whom the agent deals to believe reasonably that the principal intended the power to exist. The power is real and not merely *apparent*. The agent is indeed a wrongdoer in exercising the power. He possesses the power but not the legal privilege of using it. Likewise, the *authority* (meaning the action of the principal creating the agent's power) is real. It is only the intention of the principal to create such a power that is merely apparent (i.e., *non-existent*)." William R. Anson, *Principles of the Law of Contract* 510 n.1 (Arthur L. Corbin ed., 3d Am. ed. 1919).

"'Apparent authority' of an insurance agent means such authority as an insurer knowingly permits the agent to assume, or which it holds him out as possessing, that is, such authority as he appears to have by reason of actual authority or such authority as a reasonably prudent man would suppose the agent to possess." John Alan Appleman & Jean Appleman, *Insurance Law and Practice* § 8674 (1981).

▸ **authority by estoppel.** See *apparent authority.*

▸ **authority coupled with an interest.** (17c) Authority given to an agent for valuable consideration. • This authority cannot be unilaterally terminated by the principal. Cf. *naked authority.*

▸ **binding authority.** See *imperative authority.*

▸ **constructive authority.** (1823) Authority that is inferred because of an earlier grant of authority.

▸ **derogable authority.** Authority that may be limited or reduced in some circumstances.

▸ **express authority.** (16c) Authority given to the agent by explicit agreement, either orally or in writing. — Also termed *stipulated authority.*

▸ **general authority.** (17c) A general agent's authority, intended to apply to all matters arising in the course of the principal's business.

▸ **implied authority.** (18c) Authority intentionally given by the principal to the agent as a result of the principal's conduct, such as the principal's earlier acquiescence to the agent's actions. — Also termed *presumptive authority; implied actual authority.*

▸ **incidental authority.** (18c) Authority needed to carry out actual or apparent authority. • For example, the actual authority to borrow money includes the incidental authority to sign commercial paper to bring about the loan. — Also termed *inferred authority.*

▸ **inherent authority.** (17c) Authority of an agent arising from the agency relationship.

▸ **legislative authority.** (17c) Authority conferred explicitly by statute.

▸ **naked authority.** (18c) Authority delegated to an agent solely for the principal's benefit, without a beneficial interest in the matter for the agent. • This authority can be revoked by the principal at any time. Cf. *authority coupled with an interest.*

▸ **ostensible authority.** See *apparent authority.*

▸ **presumptive authority.** See *implied authority.*

▸ **real authority.** See *actual authority.*

▸ **special authority.** (18c) Authority limited to an individual transaction.

▸ **stipulated authority.** See *express authority.*

▸ **supervisory authority.** See SUPERVISORY AUTHORITY.

2. The power a person has through an official position; governmental power or jurisdiction <within the court's authority>. **3.** An official organization or government department with particular responsibilities and decision-making powers; esp., a governmental agency or corporation that administers a public enterprise <transit authority>. — Also termed *public authority.*

▸ **constituted authority.** (*often pl.*) (18c) Each of the legislative, executive, and judicial departments officially and rightfully governing a country, people, municipality, or other governmental unit; an authority properly appointed or elected under organic law, such as a constitution or charter. — Also termed *duly constituted authority.*

▸ **examining authority.** (1988) A self-regulatory organization registered with the Securities and Exchange Commission and vested with the authority to examine, inspect, and otherwise oversee the activities of a registered broker or dealer.

▸ **local authority.** (18c) An administrative unit of a local government; a group of people responsible for the government of a particular area, town, or city.

4. A legal writing taken as definitive or decisive; esp., a judicial or administrative decision cited as a precedent <this case is good authority in Massachusetts>. • The term includes not only the decisions of tribunals but also statutes, ordinances, and administrative rulings.

▸ **adverse authority.** (18c) Authority that is unfavorable to an advocate's position. • Most ethical codes require counsel to disclose adverse authority in the controlling jurisdiction even if the opposing counsel has not cited it.

▸ **imperative authority.** (1809) Authority that is absolutely binding on a court. — Also termed *binding authority.* Cf. *binding precedent* under PRECEDENT.

▸ **persuasive authority.** (1842) Authority that carries some weight but is not binding on a court, often from a court in a different jurisdiction.

"It may be well to call attention to the fact that the word 'authority' is used by lawyers in at least two senses, one abstract and the other concrete. The word [in its concrete sense] refer[s] to the book or other repository to which one resorts to find propositions of law, and sometimes the word is used in an even narrower sense to mean reported cases. In its abstract sense, however, 'authority' is substantially equivalent to 'influence' or 'power,' and in this sense 'authority' may be divided into two grades, in that the force of a statement of law is either imperative (that is to say, absolutely binding upon the courts) or simply persuasive. The use of the terms 'primary' and 'secondary' authority, as applied in the concrete sense, must not be confused with the use of the terms 'imperative' and 'persuasive' authority, as used in the abstract sense. That is to say, a book of primary authority may be either imperative or persuasive, according to the circumstances . . . , or it may be of no force at all. Books of secondary authority are, in the nature of things, usually merely of persuasive authority." William M. Lile et al., *Brief Making and the Use of Law Books* 12 (Roger W. Cooley & Charles Lesley Ames eds., 3d ed. 1914).

▸ **primary authority.** (1826) Authority that issues directly from a law-making body; legislation and the reports of litigated cases.

▸ **secondary authority.** (1826) Authority that explains the law but does not itself establish it, such as a treatise, annotation, or law-review article. — Also termed *secondary source.*

5. A source, such as a statute, case, or treatise, cited in support of a legal argument <the brief's table of authorities>. **6.** Someone whose knowledge and opinions on a subject are respected because of proven scholarship and expertise.

authority by estoppel. See *apparent authority* under AUTHORITY (1).

authorization. (17c) **1.** Official permission to do something; sanction or warrant. **2.** The official document granting such permission.

authorization clause. (2003) *Patents.* A Patent Act provision directing that if a person uses or manufactures something protected by a valid U.S. patent, acts on behalf of the U.S. government, and acts with the government's authorization or consent, the U.S., not the person, is deemed the infringing user or manufacturer. • If an infringing act is done by a government contractor or subcontractor working for the U.S. and the act is covered by the authorization or consent clause, the patent owner's only recourse is a suit against the U.S. in the U.S. Claims Court for compensation. The authorization or consent clause is in the second paragraph of 28 USCA § 1498(a). — Also termed *consent clause.*

authorization to sell. See LISTING (1).

authorize, *vb.* (14c) **1.** To give legal authority; to empower <he authorized the employee to act for him>. **2.** To formally approve; to sanction <the city authorized the construction project>. — **authorization,** *n.*

authorized act. See ACT (2).

authorized capital. See *nominal capital* under CAPITAL.

authorized capital stock. See *capital stock* (1) under STOCK.

authorized committee. See SPECIAL LITIGATION COMMITTEE.

authorized officer. See OFFICER (1).

authorized shares. See *capital stock* (1) under STOCK.

authorized stock. See *capital stock* (1) under STOCK.

authorship. 1. The fact of having written a particular book or document. See *work of authorship* under WORK (2). **2.** The profession of writing books.

author's right. (1938) *Copyright.* The system of protecting the moral and economic rights of the creator of a work, esp. in civil-law countries. — Also termed (in French) *droit d'auteur*; (in German) *Urheberrecht*; (in Italian) *diritto d' autore*; (in Spanish) *derecho de autor.*

> "[O]n almost every point of consequence, the traditions of copyright and author's right are far more alike than they are unlike. One reason is that the Berne Convention bridges the two traditions, with the result that its extensive minimum standards have dictated substantively similar rules for countries in both camps." Paul Goldstein, *International Copyright: Principles, Law, and Practice* 4 (2001).

author's share. (1938) *Copyright.* An author's portion of royalties, as determined by an agreement with the publisher.

autocracy (aw-**tok**-rə-see), *n.* (17c) **1.** A system of government by one person with unlimited power and authority; unlimited monarchy. **2.** A country or organization that is completely controlled by one powerful person or group. — **autocratic** (aw-tə-**krat**-ik), *adj.* — **autocrat** (**aw**-tə-krat), *n.*

autograph, *n.* (17c) A person's own writing or signature; HOLOGRAPH. Cf. ALLOGRAPH.

autoist. See AUTOMOBILIST.

autolimitation, *n.* (1902) An authority's establishment of rules limiting its own power. — **autolimit,** *vb.*

> "The theory of Jellinek (*Allgemeine Staatslehre*), so far as the writer understands it, is not an explanation either. In his view something which he calls the State, not defined, but, as it seems, a group of persons, finds itself in possession of power, and establishes rules. These are the law. This process he calls 'autolimitation.' It is true that a body with supreme power does make law. An autocrat, man or group, without rules, may do justice, though it probably will not, but it does not make law — there is no *Rechtsstaat*. But autolimitation is, as Professor Brierly notes . . . , a contradiction in terms. If the State's power is limited, it must be by some superior power. But even accepting the analysis, we are no better off." W.W. Buckland, *Some Reflections on Jurisprudence* 24 (1945).

autolist. See AUTOMOBILIST.

Automated Bond System. The New York Stock Exchange's computerized network that enables subscribers to transmit quotations and execute orders for bond trades electronically. — Abbr. ABS.

Automated Patent System. A computerized database of patents, maintained by the U.S. Patent and Trademark Office database. — Abbr. APS. — Also termed *automated patent search system.*

automated transaction. (1977) A contract formed or performed, in whole or in part, by electronic means or by electronic messages whereby neither party's electronic actions or messages establishing the contract are intended to be reviewed by an individual in the ordinary course. UCITA §§ 2-102(a)(7), 102:10UC; UETA § 14.

automatic-adjustment clause. (1958) A provision in a utility-rate schedule allowing a public utility to increase or decrease its rates without a public hearing or state review, if certain operating costs, such as the price of fuel, change. *Federal Energy Regulatory Comm'n v. Mississippi*, 456 U.S. 742, 102 S.Ct. 2126 (1982).

automatic-assignment doctrine. *Trademarks.* The rule that, without evidence to the contrary, the sale of an entire business carries with it and transfers to the purchaser any common-law marks used by that business without the need for a written assignment. • For marks registered under the Lanham Act or under some state registration schemes, a written assignment is required to transfer an interest in a registered mark or in a pending application to register a mark.

automatic-crystallization clause. (1989) A contractual provision creating a floating charge but providing for the charge to become fixed (crystallized) either upon the occurrence of a specified event without the need for any further action on anyone's part or upon notice by the holder, depending on how the clause is drafted.

automatic discharge. See DISCHARGE (5).

automatic disclosure. See DISCLOSURE (2).

automatic perfection. See PERFECTION.

automatic reversion. See REVERSION.

automatic-revival rule. (2000) *Wills & estates.* The common-law doctrine that if a later will revoking an earlier will is itself revoked, the earlier will immediately becomes effective again. • When first developed by Lord Mansfield in *Goodright v. Glazier*, 98 Eng. Rep. 317 (K.B. 1770), the rule was not one of automatic revival but of "ambulatory revocation." Lord Mansfield's theory was that the later instrument did not take effect until the testator's death, either as an instrument to transfer property or as an instrument of revocation. Hence, if the testator revoked the revoking will, the earlier will had never been effectively revoked. See REVIVAL.

automatic stay. See STAY.

automatic suspension. See *automatic stay* under STAY.

automatic telephone-dialing system. Equipment that has the capacity to both store and produce telephone numbers to call by using a random- or sequential-number generator and to dial the numbers. 47 USCA § 227(a)(1). — Abbr. ATDS.

automatic-transfer statute. See TRANSFER STATUTE.

automatic wage-withholding. See *attachment of wages* under ATTACHMENT (1).

automatism (aw-**tom**-ə-tiz-əm), *n.* (1838) **1.** Action or conduct occurring without will, purpose, or reasoned intention, such as sleepwalking; behavior carried out in a state of unconsciousness or mental dissociation without full awareness. • Automatism may be asserted as a criminal defense to negate the requisite mental state of voluntariness. Cf. SOMNAMBULISM. **2.** The physical and mental state of a person who, though capable of action, is not conscious of his or her actions. — **automaton,** *n.*

> "How far is automatism a defence? It has been defined as involuntary action performed in a state of unconsciousness not amounting to insanity. Theoretically the defence is that no act in the legal sense took place at all — the plea is that there was no volition or psychic awareness." George Whitecross Paton, *A Textbook of Jurisprudence* 315 (G.W. Paton & David P. Derham eds., 4th ed. 1972).

▸ **ambulatory automatism.** (1946) Automatism that consists in involuntary, unknowing, or purposeless wanderings and actions.

▸ **insane automatism.** (1961) Automatism caused by an intrinsic physical condition that affects a person's brain and results in a temporary or permanent mental disorder.

▸ **sane automatism.** (1962) Automatism caused by an external factor that disorders a person's mind, such as anesthesia or a blow to the head.

automobile accident. See *car accident* under ACCIDENT (2).

automobile exception. (1970) The doctrine that when probable cause exists, a law-enforcement officer need not obtain a warrant before searching a movable vehicle (such as a car or boat) in which an individual has a lessened expectation of privacy. • This is an exception to the Fourth Amendment's warrant requirement for search and seizure; once probable cause exists, exigent circumstances are presumed to exist. Once the right to conduct a warrantless search arises, the actual search may take place at a later time. *Carroll v. U.S.*, 267 U.S. 132, 45 S.Ct. 280 (1925); *Cardwell v. Lewis*, 417 U.S. 583, 94 S.Ct. 2464 (1974); *California v. Acevedo*, 500 U.S. 565, 111 S.Ct. 1982 (1991). See *exigent circumstances* under CIRCUMSTANCE.

automobile exclusion. See EXCLUSION (3).

automobile-guest statute. See GUEST STATUTE.

automobile homicide. See *vehicular homicide* under HOMICIDE.

automobile insurance. See INSURANCE.

automobilist (ah-toh-moh-**beel**-ist), *n.* (1896) *Archaic.* One who owns, drives, or rides in a car or similar motor vehicle; DRIVER (1). — Also termed *autoist.* — **automobilism,** *n.*

autonomic law (aw-tə-**nom**-ik). (1832) An internal regulation that has its source in various forms of subordinate and restricted legislative authority possessed by private persons and groups of people. • Examples are corporate bylaws, university regulations, and the rules of the International Monetary Fund.

autonomous tariff. See TARIFF (2).

autonomy (aw-**tahn**-ə-mee), *n.* (17c) **1.** The right of self-government. **2.** A self-governing country. **3.** An individual's capacity for self-determination. — **autonomous** (aw-**tahn**-ə-məs), *adj.*

▸ **lawyer autonomy.** The right of a lawyer to choose where to practice. • The principle of lawyer autonomy has been used to bar or nullify noncompete agreements among lawyers. — Also termed *attorney autonomy.*

autonomy of the parties. See FREEDOM OF CONTRACT.

autonomy privacy. See PRIVACY.

autopsy (**aw**-top-see). [Greek "to see for oneself"] (1678) **1.** A medical examination of a corpse to determine the cause of death, esp. in a criminal investigation. — Also termed *postmortem examination; postmortem; necropsy.* **2.** The evidence of one's own senses.

> "To a rational man of perfect organization, . . . the best and highest proof of which any fact is susceptible is the evidence of his own senses. Hence *autopsy*, or the evidence of one's own senses, furnishes the strongest probability and indeed the only perfect and indubitable certainty of the existence of any sensible fact." *Gentry v. McMinnis*, 3 Dana 382 (1835) (as quoted in John H. Wigmore, *A Students' Textbook of the Law of Evidence* 214 (1935)).

autoptic evidence (aw-**top**-tik). See *demonstrative evidence* under EVIDENCE.

autoptic proference (proh-**fər**-ənts). (1899) **1.** The presentation of an item for inspection by the court. — See *real evidence* under EVIDENCE. **2.** See *demonstrative evidence* under EVIDENCE.

> "Yet another form of proof that may present difficulties in defining evidence is what Wigmore calls 'autoptic proference.' By this barbarism, the learned author was referring to those few cases in which it is possible to bring before the jury the material fact itself, rather than evidence of the fact." 22 Charles Alan Wright & Kenneth W. Graham Jr., *Federal Practice and Procedure* § 5163, at 33 (1978).

auto-title loan. See *title loan* under LOAN.

aut punire aut dedere (awt pyoo-**nɪ**-ree awt **ded**-ə-ree). [Latin] *Hist.* Either to punish or to deliver.

autre action pendant (**oh**-trə ak-see-**awn** pah*n*-**dahn**). [Law French "another action pending"] Another lawsuit that is pending on the same subject matter. • This phrase was formerly used in pleas of abatement.

autre droit (**oh**-trə **drwah**). [Law French] In right of another. • This phrase describes the manner in which a trustee, administrator, or executor holds property for a beneficiary.

autrefois (oh-trə-**fwah** *or* **oh**-tər-foyz). [Law French] On another occasion; formerly.

▸ ***autrefois acquit*** (ə-**kwit** *or* a-**kee**). [Law French "previously acquitted"] (18c) A common-law plea in bar of arraignment asserting that the defendant has been acquitted of the offense. — Also termed *former acquittal.* See DOUBLE JEOPARDY.

> "Suppose that a transgressor is charged and acquitted for lack of evidence, and evidence has now come to light showing beyond doubt that he committed the crime. Even so, he cannot be tried a second time. He has what is termed, in legal Frenglish, the defence of autrefois acquit. Similarly, if he is convicted, even though he is let off very lightly, he cannot afterwards be charged on fresh evidence, because he will have the defence of autrefois convict. These uncouth phrases have never been superseded, though they might well be called the defence of 'previous acquittal' and 'previous conviction'; and 'double jeopardy' makes an acceptable generic name for both." Glanville Williams, *Textbook of Criminal Law* 24 (1978).

▸ ***autrefois attaint*** (ə-**taynt**). [Law French "previously attainted"] (18c) *Hist.* A common-law plea in bar that the defendant has already been attainted for one felony and therefore cannot be prosecuted for another. • This plea was abolished in 1827.

▸ ***autrefois convict.*** [Law French "previously convicted"] (18c) A plea in bar of arraignment that the defendant has already been convicted of the offense. • This plea can be asserted in the alternative with a plea of not guilty. See DOUBLE JEOPARDY.

autre vie (**oh**-trə **vee**). [Law French "another's life"] **1.** See PUR AUTRE VIE. **2.** See VIE.

auxiliary (awg-**zil**-yə-ree), *adj.* (16c) **1.** Aiding or supporting. **2.** Subsidiary. **3.** Supplementary.

auxiliary covenant. See COVENANT (1).

auxiliary jurisdiction. See *assistant jurisdiction* under JURISDICTION.

auxiliator (awg-**zil**-ee-ay-tər), *n.* [Latin] (17c) *Hist.* A helper; an assistant.

auxilium (awg-**zil**-ee-əm), *n.* [Latin] *Hist.* Aid; esp., compulsory aid such as a tax or tribute to be paid by a vassal to a lord as an incident of the tenure by knight's service. See AID (2), (3). Pl. ***auxilia.***

> "In close connection with the *donum* we find the *auxilium*, also an extraordinary tax paid once a year, and distinguished from ordinary rent. It appears as a direct consequence of the political subjection of the tentry; it is, in fact, merely a right to tallage . . . . [T]he auxilium is in every respect like the *donum*. One very characteristic trait of both taxes is that they are laid primarily on the whole village, which is made to pay a certain round sum as a body." Paul Vinogradoff, *Villainage in England* 293–94 (1892; repr. 1968).

▸ ***auxilium ad filium militem faciendum et filiam maritandam*** (awg-**zil**-ee-əm ad **fil**-ee-əm **mil**-ə-tem fay-shee-**en**-dəm et **fil**-ee-am mar-ə-**tan**-dəm), *n.* [Law Latin] *Hist.* A writ ordering a sheriff to levy a tax toward the knighting of a son and the marrying of a daughter of tenants *in capite* of the Crown.

▸ ***auxilium curiae*** (awg-**zil**-ee-əm **kyoor**-ee-I *or* **kyoor**-ee-ee). [Latin] (18c) *Hist.* A court order summoning a party to appear and assist another party already before the court.

▸ ***auxilium regis*** (awg-**zil**-ee-əm **ree**-jis), *n.* [Latin] (18c) *Hist.* The Crown's tax levied for royal use and public service, such as a tax granted by Parliament.

▸ ***auxilium vice comiti*** (awg-**zil**-ee-əm **vI**-see **kom**-ə-tI), *n.* [Latin] *Hist.* An ancient tax paid to sheriffs.

avail, *n.* (15c) **1.** Use or advantage <of little or no avail>. **2.** (*pl.*) Profits or proceeds, esp. from a sale of property <the avails of the trust fund>.

available, *adj.* (15c) Legally valid or colorable <available claims> <available defenses>.

available for work, *adj.* (1884) (Of a person) ready, willing, and able to accept temporary or permanent employment when offered.

availment, *n.* (17c) **1.** The act of making use or taking advantage of something for oneself <availment of the benefits of public office>. See PURPOSEFUL-AVAILMENT DOCTRINE. **2.** *Archaic.* Profit, advantage, or benefit. — **avail,** *vb.*

avail of marriage. See VALOR MARITAGII.

aval (a-val), *n.* [French *aval* "to assist"] (1880) *Civil law.* A bank guaranty ensuring the payment of a note, bond, or draft; specif., a written undertaking by one who is not the drawer, indorser, or acceptor of a note or bill of exchange that it will be fully paid when mature. • An aval can be written on the note or bill itself, or on an allonge. It is typically expressed in the word *aval* or the phrase *good as aval*, accompanied by the guarantor's signature. — **avalize** (ə-**val**-Iz), *vb.*

avenge (ə-**venj**), *vb.* (14c) **1.** To seek vengeance on behalf of, esp. when the effort results in successful vindication or just retribution. **2.** To wreak vengeance on; to treat in a spitefully vindictive way.

aver (ə-**vər**), *vb.* (15c) To assert positively, esp. in a pleading; to allege.

average, *n.* (16c) **1.** A single value that represents the midpoint of a broad sample of subjects; esp., in mathematics, the mean of a series. **2.** The ordinary or typical level; the norm. **3.** *Maritime law.* Accidental partial loss or damage to an insured ship or its cargo during a voyage. — **average,** *vb.* & *adj.*

▸ **extraordinary average.** (18c) A contribution by all the parties concerned in a commercial voyage — whether for vessel or cargo — toward a loss sustained by some of the parties in interest for the benefit of all.

▸ **general average.** (17c) Average resulting from an intentional partial sacrifice of ship or cargo to avoid total loss. • The liability is shared proportionately by all parties who had an interest in the voyage. — Abbr. GA. — Also termed *gross average*; *general-average contribution*.

> "[G]eneral average refers to certain extraordinary sacrifices made or expenses incurred to avert a peril that threatens the entire voyage. In such a case the party sustaining the loss confers a common benefit on all the parties to the maritime venture. As a result the party suffering the loss has a right — apart from contract or tort — to claim contribution from all who participate in the venture. The doctrine of general average is thus an equitable principle derived from the general maritime law. General average is an exception to the principle of particular average that losses lie where they fall; rather the loss becomes 'general,' meaning that it is spread ratably among all the parties involved in the maritime adventure. The doctrine of general average is of ancient vintage, and can be traced back to remotest antiquity." Thomas J. Schoenbaum, *Admiralty and Maritime Law* § 16-1, at 522–23 (1987).

▸ **gross average.** See *general average.*

▸ **partial average.** See *particular average.*

▸ **particular average.** (18c) Average resulting from an accidental partial loss or damage. • Any average that is not general is termed particular. The liability is borne solely by the person who suffered the loss. — Also termed *simple average*; *partial average*; *petty average.*

▸ **petty average.** See *particular average.*

▸ **simple agent.** See *particular average.*

4. *Hist.* A service, esp. one of carriage, due from a feudal tenant to a lord. • The average is mentioned in the Domesday Book, but the exact nature of the service is unclear. Based on etymological studies, some authorities believe the term referred to the performance of work with or by beasts of burden. But because the term's origin is unclear, this theory is not universally accepted.

average adjuster. See ADJUSTER.

average bond. See *general-average bond* under BOND (2).

average clause. (18c) *Insurance.* An insurance-policy provision restricting the coverage for loss to a percentage of the actual loss equal to the full value of the thing insured divided by the amount covered by the policy. • For example, if a thing worth $10,000 is insured for $5,000, damage amounting to $1,000 would be covered only to $500. If the insured is underinsured, the average clause has the effect of reducing the amount recoverable (in the event of loss) in proportion to the amount of the underinsurance.

average cost. See COST (1).

average daily balance. See DAILY BALANCE.

average gross sales. See SALE.

average tax rate. See TAX RATE.

average variable cost. See COST (1).

averaging. See FAIR AVERAGING.

averaging down. (1962) An investment strategy in which shares in the same company are purchased at successively lower prices to achieve a lower average cost basis than that of the first purchase. • For example, if an investor buys an equal number of shares at $18, $15, $13, and $10, the average cost per share is $14. Yet an investor may buy any number of shares in each transaction, not necessarily the same number each time. Cf. AVERAGING UP.

averaging up. (1962) An investment strategy in a rising market whereby equal numbers of shares in the same company are purchased at successively higher prices to reduce the investment's average cost basis. • For example, if an investor buys an equal number of shares at $10, $13, $15, and $18, the average cost basis per share is $14.Yet an investor may buy any number of shares in each transaction, not necessarily the same number each time. Cf. AVERAGING DOWN.

averment (ə-**vər**-mənt), *n.* (15c) A positive declaration or affirmation of fact; esp., an assertion or allegation in a pleading <the plaintiff's averment that the defendant ran a red light>. Cf. ASSEVERATE.

▸ **immaterial averment.** (18c) An averment that alleges something in needless detail; a statement that goes far beyond what is at issue, as by mentioning irrelevancies. • This type of averment may be ordered struck from the pleading.

▸ **negative averment.** (18c) An averment that is negative in form but affirmative in substance and that must be proved by the alleging party. • An example is the statement "she was not old enough to enter into the contract," which is more than just a simple denial. Cf. TRAVERSE.

averment of notice. (18c) A statement in a pleading that someone else has been properly notified about some fact, esp. in special actions of assumpsit. See NOTICE.

aviation easement. See *avigational easement* under EASEMENT.

aviation insurance. See INSURANCE.

avigational easement. See EASEMENT.

avigation easement. See *avigational easement* under EASEMENT.

a vinculo matrimonii (ay **ving**-kyə-loh ma-trə-**moh**-nee-I). [Latin] (17c) From the bond of matrimony. — Often shortened to *a vinculo*. See *divorce a vinculo matrimonii* under DIVORCE.

avizandum (av-i-**zan**-dəm). [Law Latin] *Scots law.* Deliberation; advisement. • The judge is said later to "advise" the case — that is, to give an opinion.

> "To make avizandum with a process, or part of it, is to take it from the public court to the private consideration of the judge." William Bell, *Bell's Dictionary and Digest of the Law of Scotland* 82 (George Watson ed., 7th ed. 1890).

avoid, *vb.* (14c) To render void; VOID, *vb.* (1) <because the restrictive covenant was overbroad, the court avoided it>. • Because this legal use of *avoid* can be easily confused with the ordinary sense of the word, the verb *void* is preferable. See VOID, *vb.*

avoidable, *adj.* (17c) **1.** Not inevitable; preventable <an avoidable accident>.

▸ **practically avoidable.** (1884) (Of harm) capable of being eliminated in whole or substantial part without incurring prohibitive expense or hardship.

2. Capable of being refrained from; stoppable <avoidable habits>. **3.** VOIDABLE.

avoidable consequence. See CONSEQUENCE.

avoidable-consequences doctrine. See MITIGATION-OF-DAMAGES DOCTRINE.

avoidable cost. See COST (1).

avoidance, *n.* (14c) **1.** The act of evading or escaping <avoidance of tax liability>. See TAX AVOIDANCE. **2.** The act of refraining from (something) <avoidance of an argument>. **3.** RESCISSION (1) <avoidance of the agreement>. **4.** VOIDANCE <avoidance of a penalty>. **5.** ANNULMENT (1) <avoidance of the marriage>. **6.** CONFESSION AND AVOIDANCE <the defendant filed an avoidance in an attempt to avert liability>. — **avoid,** *vb.*

avoid-bias rule. See BIAS RULE (1).

avoiding power. See POWER (5).

avoision (ə-**voy**-zhən), *n.* (1979) An ambiguous act that falls between legal avoidance and illegal evasion of the law. • The term, coined by the economist Arthur Seldon, is a blend of *avoidance* and *evasion*. *Avoision* usu. refers to financial acts that are not clearly legal tax avoidance or illegal tax evasion, but it may appear in other contexts, such as the legalization of drugs.

> "The book is in three parts, divided into tiny chapterlets, forty-two in all. The first part takes up what Katz calls 'avoision': a fusion of 'avoidance' and 'evasion' that denotes cases in which it is unclear whether a person's conduct should be considered lawful avoidance of the law's prohibitions or illegal evasion. Two actresses are vying for the same part. Mildred knows that Abigail has been unfaithful to her husband. If she threatens to tell the husband unless Abigail forgoes the audition, that would be blackmail, and a crime. Instead she tells Abigail that she is mailing a letter addressed to the husband that reveals Abigail's infidelity and that has been timed to arrive the morning of the audition. Knowing that Abigail will stay home to intercept the letter, Mildred will have achieved the same end as she would have done by committing blackmail, yet her conduct is not criminal." Richard A. Posner, "The Immoralist," *New Republic*, 15 July 1996, at 38.

avoucher (ə-**vow**-chər). (16c) **1.** *Hist.* A tenant's calling on a warrantor of title to the land to help the tenant defend the title. **2.** Someone who declares a probable truth, corroborates, confirms, or confesses.

avoutry. See ADULTERY.

avowal (ə-**vow**-əl), *n.* (18c) **1.** An open declaration or public statement of a belief or conviction. **2.** OFFER OF PROOF. — **avow,** *vb.*

avowant (ə-**vow**-ənt), *n.* (16c) Someone who pleads avowry in an action of replevin.

avowee. See ADVOCATUS.

avowry (ə-**vow**-ree), *n.* (16c) *Common-law pleading.* In an answer to a replevin action, an acknowledgment that one has taken property, together with a justification for that taking <the defendant's avowry was based on alleged damage to the property by the plaintiff>. Cf. COGNIZANCE (4). — **avow,** *vb.*

avowter. *Hist.* An adulterer. • The crime was called *avowtry*. — Also spelled *advouterer*; *avowterer*; *avouter*; *advowter*.

avowtry. See ADULTERY.

avulsion (ə-**vəl**-shən), *n.* (17c) **1.** A forcible detachment or separation. **2.** A sudden removal of land caused by change in a river's course or by flood. • Land removed by avulsion remains the property of the original owner. Cf. ALLUVION; ACCRETION (2); DELICTION; EROSION. **3.** A tearing away of a body part surgically or accidentally. — **avulse,** *vb.*

avunculus (ə-**vəngk**-yə-ləs), *n.* [Latin] (16c) *Roman & civil law.* A maternal uncle; one's mother's brother.

avunculus maximus (**mak**-sə-məs). See ABAVUNCULUS.

avus (**av**-əs *or* **ay**-vəs), *n.* [Latin] (16c) *Roman & civil law.* A grandfather.

AWA. *abbr.* ALL WRITS ACT.

award, *n.* (14c) A final judgment or decision, esp. one by an arbitrator or by a jury assessing damages. — Also termed *arbitrament.* See ARBITRATION AWARD.

▸ **interim award.** (1833) An arbitral panel's decisions on the applicable law and its jurisdiction made before the panel decides the issues in an arbitration. — Also termed *partial award; preliminary award.*

award, *vb.* (14c) To grant by formal process or by judicial decree <the company awarded the contract to the low bidder> <the jury awarded punitive damages>.

award in interference. See PRIORITY AWARD.

away-going crops. See CROPS.

AWOL. *abbr.* (1921) *Military law.* Absent without leave; missing without notice or permission.

axiom (**ak**-see-əm), *n.* (15c) An established principle that is universally accepted within a given framework of reasoning or thinking; something that need not be proved because its truth is both self-evident and widely acknowledged <"innocent until proven guilty" is an age-old axiom of criminal law>. — **axiomatic** (ak-see-ə-**mat**-ik), *adj.*

ayant cause (**ay**-ənt). *Civil law.* **1.** One to whom a right has been assigned by will, gift, sale, or exchange; an assignee, legatee, or beneficiary. **2.** Someone who has a "cause" or standing in one's own right.

aye (I), *n.* (16c) *Parliamentary law.* An affirmative vote or voter.

ayel (**ay**-əl). See AIEL.

ayle (ayl). See AIEL.

B

B. *abbr.* BARON (3).

B2B. *abbr.* (1994) BUSINESS-TO-BUSINESS <a B2B transaction>.

B2C. *abbr.* (1998) BUSINESS-TO-CONSUMER <a B2C transaction>.

BA. *abbr.* **1.** See *banker's acceptance* under ACCEPTANCE (4). **2.** A bachelor of arts degree.

baby act, pleading the. (1898) *Slang.* The act of asserting a person's infancy as a defense to a contract claim.

baby bar examination. *Slang.* See FIRST-YEAR LAW STUDENTS' EXAMINATION.

baby-bartering. See BABY-SELLING.

baby bond. See BOND (3).

baby-brokering. See BABY-SELLING.

Baby Doe. (1974) A generic pseudonym for a very young child involved in litigation. • Today a gender designation is often added: *Baby Girl Doe* or *Baby Boy Doe.* The generic term shields the child's identity.

baby DWI. See DRIVING WHILE INTOXICATED.

Baby FTC Act. (1988) A state statute that, like the Federal Trade Commission Act, outlaws deceptive and unfair trade practices.

Baby Moses law. See SAFE-HAVEN LAW.

baby-selling. (1975) The exchange of money or something of value for a child. • All states have prohibitions against baby-selling. Yet it is not generally considered baby-selling for prospective adoptive parents to pay money to a birth mother for pregnancy-related expenses. — Also termed *baby-brokering; baby-bartering.*

baby-snatching. See *child-kidnapping* under KIDNAPPING.

BAC. *abbr.* BLOOD ALCOHOL CONTENT.

bacberende. see BACKBEREND.

bachelor, *n.* (14c) **1.** A man who has never been married. **2.** Traditionally, a first university degree in the arts or sciences. **3.** A person who has graduated from a college or university with a bachelor's degree. **4.** *English law.* A member of one of the orders of chivalry, such as the Order of the Bath. — Also termed (in sense 3) *knight bachelor.*

bachelor of laws. See LL.B.

back, *vb.* (18c) **1.** To indorse; to sign the back of (a negotiable instrument). **2.** To sign so as to show acceptance or approval. **3.** To sign so as to indicate financial responsibility for someone or something. **4.** *Hist.* (Of a magistrate) to sign (a warrant issued in another county) to permit execution in the signing magistrate's county.

> "[Although] the warrant of the judge of the Court of King's Bench extends over the whole realm, . . . that of a justice of the peace cannot be executed out of his county, unless it be *backed*, that is, indorsed by a justice of the county, in which it is to be carried into execution. It is said, that formerly there ought in strictness to have been a fresh warrant in every fresh county, but the practice of backing warrants has long been observed, and was at last sanctioned by the statute 23 Geo. 2. c. 26. s. 2, and 24 Geo. 2. c. 55." 1 Joseph Chitty, *A Practical Treatise on the Criminal Law* 45 (2d ed. 1826).

backadation. See BACKWARDATION.

back-alley abortion. See ABORTION.

backbearing. See BACKBEREND.

backberend (**bak**-ber-ənd), *n.* [Old English] (13c) *Hist.* **1.** The bearing of stolen goods on one's back or about one's person. • *Backberend* is sometimes modernized to *backbearing.* **2.** A person caught carrying stolen goods. — Also spelled *bacberende; backberinde.* Cf. HANDHABEND.

> "Backberinde signifieth bearing upon the Back, or about a Man. Bracton useth it for a Sign or Circumstance of Theft apparent, which the Civilians call Furtum manifestum . . . ." Giles Jacob, *A New Law-Dictionary* (8th ed. 1762).

back carry. *Hist.* The crime of carrying, on one's back, unlawfully killed game.

backdate, *vb.* (1944) **1.** To put a date earlier than the actual date on (something, as an instrument). • Under UCC § 3-113(a), backdating does not affect an instrument's negotiability. Cf. POSTDATE (1); ANTEDATE (1). **2.** To make (something) retroactively valid; to make (a payment, etc.) effective from an earlier date.

backdoor listing. (1957) A stock-exchange listing accomplished by buying the shell of an already-listed company and infusing it into the business of an unlisted company. — Also termed *reverse acquisition.*

back door to Berne. (1953) *Copyright.* A U.S. copyright owner's simultaneous publication of the copyrighted work in both the United States and in a Berne Convention country in order to obtain Berne Convention protection. • This backdoor method was used before March 1989, when the United States became a member of the Berne Convention. "Simultaneous" meant within 30 days.

back-end load. See *load fund* under MUTUAL FUND.

back freight. See FREIGHT.

background evidence. See EVIDENCE.

background of the invention. (1974) *Patents.* In a U.S. patent application and any resulting patent, the section that identifies the field of art to which the invention pertains, summarizes the state of the art, and describes the problem solved by the invention. • The Background of the Invention section usu. includes two subsections: "Field of the Invention" and "Description of the Related Art." A mistaken inclusion in this section of a reference that postdates the date of invention may be construed as an admission.

background right. See *implied right* under RIGHT.

backhaul allowance. See ALLOWANCE (1).

backing, *n.* Endorsement or support, esp. of a financial nature. • In law, the term often denotes a magistrate's approval or issuance of a warrant. See BACK (4).

back-in right. (1976) *Oil & gas.* A reversionary interest in an oil-and-gas lease entitling an assignor to a share of the working interest after the assignee has recovered specified costs from production.

back lands. (17c) Generally, lands lying away from — not next to — a highway or a watercourse.

back office. (1866) The department of a bank or other organization responsible for managing the work of the organization but not for dealing face-to-face with customers.

backpay, *n.* (1804) **1.** The wages or salary that an employee should have received but did not because of an employer's unlawful action in setting or paying the wages or salary. **2.** BACKPAY AWARD. — Also written *back pay.* Cf. FRONTPAY.

backpay award. (1940) A judicial or quasi-judicial body's decision that an employee or ex-employee is entitled to accrued but uncollected wages or benefits. — Sometimes shortened to *backpay.*

backspread, *n.* (1989) *Securities.* In arbitrage, a less-than-normal difference in the price of a currency or a commodity. See ARBITRAGE; SPREAD (3).

back taxes. See *back tax* under TAX.

back-title certificate. See BACK-TITLE LETTER.

back-title letter. (1968) An official letter from a title insurer advising about the condition of title to land as of a certain date. • With this information, the title can be examined from that date forward. — Also termed *back-title certificate.*

back-to-back loan. See LOAN.

back-to-back sentences. See *consecutive sentences* under SENTENCE.

back-to-work agreement. (1958) A contract between a union and an employer covering the terms under which the employees will return to work after a strike.

backwardation, *n.* (1993) *Securities.* **1.** A pricing structure in futures trading whereby deliveries in the near future have a higher price than those made later. • Backwardation occurs when demand is high for the near future. **2.** A fee paid by the seller of securities to allow for delivery after the delivery date originally agreed to. — Also termed *backadation; inverted market.* Cf. CONTANGO.

backward integration. See INTEGRATION (5).

backwater. See WATER.

baculus (**bak**-yə-ləs *or* **bak**-ə-ləs). *Hist.* A rod or staff used to symbolize the conveyance of unimproved land. See LIVERY OF SEISIN; FESTUCA.

bad, *adj.* (17c) Invalid or void; legally unsound <bad service of process> <bad law>.

bad actor. See ACTOR (1).

bad-boy disqualification. (1998) *Securities.* An issuer's disqualification from certain SEC-registration exemptions as a result of the issuer's securities-law violations.

bad-boy provision. (1979) *Securities.* A statutory or regulatory clause in a blue-sky law stating that certain persons, because of their past conduct, are not entitled to any type of exemption from registering their securities. • Such clauses typically prohibit issuers, officers, directors, control persons, or broker-dealers from being involved in a limited offering if they have been the subject of an adverse proceeding concerning securities, commodities, or postal fraud.

bad character. (17c) See CHARACTER.

bad check. See CHECK.

bad-conduct discharge. See DISCHARGE (8).

bad debt. See DEBT.

bad-debt loss ratio. (1959) The proportion of a business's uncollectible debt to its total receivables.

bad-debt reserve. See RESERVE (1).

bad faith, *n.* (17c) **1.** Dishonesty of belief, purpose, or motive <the lawyer filed the pleading in bad faith>. — Also termed *mala fides* (**mal**-ə-**fɪ**-deez).

> "A complete catalogue of types of bad faith is impossible, but the following types are among those which have been recognized in judicial decisions: evasion of the spirit of the bargain, lack of diligence and slacking off, willful rendering of imperfect performance, abuse of a power to specify terms, and interference with or failure to cooperate in the other party's performance." Restatement (Second) of Contracts § 205 cmt. d (1979).

2. *Insurance.* An insurance company's unreasonable and unfounded (though not necessarily fraudulent) refusal to provide coverage in violation of the duties of good faith and fair dealing owed to an insured. • Bad faith often involves an insurer's malicious failure to pay the insured's claim or a claim brought by a third party. **3.** *Insurance.* An insured's claim against an insurance company for an unreasonable and unfounded refusal to provide coverage. Cf. GOOD FAITH. — **bad-faith,** *adj.*

bad-faith denial. See DENIAL (4).

bad-faith enforcement. (1968) *Patents.* **1.** The filing of an infringement action by a patentee who knows that the accused product or process does not infringe or that the patent is invalid or unenforceable. **2.** In an infringement action, a counterclaim alleging that at the time of filing suit, the patentee knew that the accused product or process did not infringe or that the patent was invalid or unenforceable. • A counterclaim for bad-faith enforcement arises under § 2 of the Sherman Act and under the common law of unfair competition. Cf. PATENT-MISUSE DOCTRINE.

bad-faith filing, *n.* (1978) *Bankruptcy.* The act of submitting a bankruptcy petition that is inconsistent with the purposes of the Bankruptcy Code or is an abuse of the bankruptcy system (that is, by not being filed in good faith). • A court may dismiss a bankruptcy case with prejudice if it finds that the petition was filed in bad faith.

badge of fraud. (18c) A circumstance generally considered by courts as an indicator that a party to a transaction intended to hinder or defraud the other party, such as a transfer in anticipation of litigation, a transaction outside the usual course of business, or a false statement; an indication of fraudulent intent. See FRAUD; EARMARK, *n.* (3).

badge of slavery. (17c) **1.** Strictly, a legal disability suffered by a slave, such as the inability to vote or to own property. **2.** Broadly, any act of racial discrimination — public or private — that Congress can prohibit under the 13th Amendment.

badger game. (1858) A scheme to extort money or some other benefit by arranging to catch someone in a compromising position and then threatening to make that person's behavior public.

> "The 'badger game' is a blackmailing trick, usually in the form of enticing a man into a compromising position with a

woman whose real or pretended husband comes upon the scene and demands payment under threat of prosecution or exposure." Rollin M. Perkins & Ronald N. Boyce, *Criminal Law* 451 (3d ed. 1982).

bad judgment. See JUDGMENT (1).

bad-man theory. (1938) The jurisprudential doctrine or belief that a bad person's view of the law represents the best test of what the law actually is because that person will carefully calculate precisely what the rules allow and will operate up to the rules' limits. • This theory was first expounded by Oliver Wendell Holmes in his essay *The Path of the Law*, 10 Harv. L. Rev. 457 (1897). In the essay, Holmes maintained that a society's legal system is defined by predicting how the law will affect a person, as opposed to considering the ethics or morals supposedly underlying the law. Under Holmes's theory, the prediction is best made by viewing the law as would a "bad man" who is unconcerned with morals. Such a person is not concerned with acting morally or in accord with a grand philosophical scheme. Rather, that person is concerned with whether and to what degree certain acts will incur punishment by the public force of the law. See LEGAL REALISM. — Also termed *prediction theory*.

bad motive. See MOTIVE.

bad-mouth, *vb.* (1941) To denigrate or disparage (something or someone).

bads, *n. pl.* (1998) *Slang.* In economics, the counterpart of "goods," characterized by a negative correlation between the amount consumed and the consumer's wealth; specif., the kinds of products that tend to be bought only by poor people.

"Some products are termed 'bads' because consumption of the product tends to decrease with increasing wealth. Spam is one example of a bad, while beef tenderloin is generally thought to be a good." Donald S. Chisum et al., *Principles of Patent Law* 54 (1998).

bad title. See TITLE (2).

baga (**bag**-ə), *n.* [Law Latin] *Hist.* A bag or purse, esp. one in which original writs were kept by the Chancery.

bagman, *n.* (1928) *Slang.* Someone who collects and distributes illegally obtained money; esp., an intermediary who collects a bribe on behalf of a corrupt public official.

bail, *n.* (15c) **1.** A security such as cash, a bond, or property; esp., security required by a court for the release of a criminal defendant who must appear in court at a future time <bail is set at $500>. Cf. RECOGNIZANCE.

▸ **bail absolute.** (18c) A fiduciary bond conditioning a surety's liability on the failure of an estate administrator, executor, or guardian to properly account for estate funds. See *fiduciary bond* under BOND (2).

▸ **cash bail.** (1892) A sum of money (as opposed to a surety bond) posted to secure a criminal defendant's release from jail. — Also termed *stationhouse bail*.

▸ **civil bail.** (1869) **1.** A bond or deposit of money given to secure the release of a person arrested for failing to pay a court-ordered civil debt. • Release of the bail is conditioned on the payment of the debt. **2.** A bond or deposit of money intended to increase a creditor's chances of collecting a debt.

▸ **excessive bail.** (17c) Bail that is unreasonably high considering the risk that the accused will not appear for trial. • The Eighth Amendment prohibits excessive bail. See BAIL CLAUSE.

▸ **stationhouse bail.** See *cash bail*.

2. The process by which a person is released from custody either on the undertaking of a surety or on his or her own recognizance. **3.** Release of a criminal defendant on security for a future court appearance; esp., the delivery of a person in custody to a surety <the court refused bail for the accused serial killer>. **4.** One or more sureties for a criminal defendant <the attorney stood as bail for her client>. See BAILER (1).

"As a noun, and in its strict sense, bail is the person in whose custody the defendant is placed when released from jail, and who acts as surety for defendant's later appearance in court. . . . The term is also used to refer to the undertaking by the surety, into whose custody defendant is placed, that he will produce defendant in court at a stated time and place." 8 C.J.S. *Bail* § 2 (1988).

▸ **bail above.** See *bail to the action*.

▸ **bail below.** See *bail to the sheriff*.

▸ **bail common.** (18c) *Hist.* A fictitious surety filed by a defendant in a (usu. minor) civil action. — Also termed *common bail*; *straw bail*.

"[T]he Common Pleas made a distinction between common and special bail, allowing the former, in cases where the defendant voluntarily appeared to the process, or where the damage expressed in it appeared to be but of a trifling amount, and requiring the latter only, when the plaintiff's demand or the damage he had sustained appeared to be something considerable. In time therefore, in common cases, every defendant took the liberty of offering John Doe and Richard Roe, for his bail . . . ." 1 George Crompton, *Practice Common-Placed: Rules and Cases of Practice in the Courts of King's Bench and Common Pleas* lxi (3d ed. 1787).

▸ **bail in error.** See BAIL IN ERROR.

▸ **bail to the action.** (17c) *Hist.* A surety for a civil defendant arrested by a mesne process (i.e., a process issued during the lawsuit). • If the defendant lost the lawsuit, the *bail to the action* was bound either to pay the judgment or to surrender the defendant into custody. — Also termed *bail above*; *special bail*. Cf. *bail to the sheriff*.

▸ **bail to the sheriff.** (18c) *Hist.* Someone who pledged to the sheriff that a defendant served with process during a civil action would appear on the writ's return day. — Also termed *bail below*. Cf. *bail to the action*.

"This kind of bail is called bail *to the sheriff*, because given to that officer, and for his security; and bail *below*, because subordinate or preliminary to bail to the action or special bail, which is termed bail *above*." 1 Alexander M. Burrill, *A Law Dictionary and Glossary* 174 (2d ed. 1867).

▸ **common bail.** See *bail common*.

▸ **discretionary bail.** (18c) Bail set in an amount that is subject to judicial discretion.

▸ **special bail.** See *bail to the action*.

▸ **straw bail.** See *bail common*.

5. *Archaic.* Legal custody of a detainee or prisoner who obtains release by giving surety for a later appearance. **6.** *Canadian law.* A lease.

▸ ***bail-à-rente.*** (1832) A lease in perpetuity.

▸ ***bail emphytéotique.*** (1845) A renewable lease for a term of years that the lessee may prolong indefinitely. See EMPHYTEUSIS.

bail, *vb.* (16c) **1.** To obtain the release of (oneself or another) by providing security for a future appearance in court <his parents bailed him out of jail>. **2.** To release (a person) after receiving such security <the court bailed the prisoner>. **3.** To place (personal property) in someone else's charge or trust <bail the goods with the warehouse>.

bailable, *adj.* (16c) (Of an offense or person) eligible for bail.

bailable offense. See OFFENSE (2).

bailable process. See PROCESS (2).

bail application. (1917) *Criminal procedure.* A formal request filed by a criminal defendant asking the court to release the defendant on bail pending resolution of the proceedings.

bail-à-rente. See BAIL (6).

bail assignment. (1979) *Criminal law.* A legal instrument by which a person who has posted bail agrees to transfer the legal right to the money to another person named in the instrument. • When the case is over, the money that was posted is released to the assignee. Bail assignments are sometimes used as a means of retaining a criminal-defense lawyer.

bail bond. See BOND (2).

bail bondsman. See BAILER (1).

Bail Clause. (1951) *Constitutional law.* The provision in the Eighth Amendment to the U.S. Constitution prohibiting excessive bail. • This clause was derived from similar language in England's Bill of Rights (1689).

bail commissioner. (1870) **1.** An adjudicator or official empowered to hold an emergency hearing to set bail when a hearing cannot be held during regular court hours. • A bail commissioner does not review other judge's bail decisions. **2.** An officer appointed to take bail bonds. — Also termed *commissioner of bail.* **3.** *Hist.* A court-appointed officer who made a written acknowledgment of bail in civil cases.

bail condition. (1977) *Criminal procedure.* A limitation placed on the grant of a criminal defendant's bail.

Bail Court. *Hist.* An ancillary court of Queen's Bench responsible for ensuring that bail sureties were worth the sums pledged (i.e., hearing *justifications*) and for handling other procedural matters. • The court was established in 1830 and abolished in 1854. — Also termed *Practice Court.*

bail dock. (17c) A small compartment in a courtroom used to hold a criminal defendant during trial. — Often shortened to *dock.* — Also spelled *bale dock.* See DOCK (3).

bailee, *n.* (16c) **1.** Someone who receives personal property from another, and has possession of but not title to the property. • A bailee is responsible for keeping the property safe until it is returned to the owner. **2.** Someone who by warehouse receipt, bill of lading, or other document of title acknowledges possession of goods and contracts to deliver them. See BAILMENT.

bailee insurance. See INSURANCE.

bailee policy. See INSURANCE POLICY.

bailee's lien. (1879) A legal right or interest that a bailee acquires in the goods bailed, esp. when what has occurred is a bailment for mutual benefit. See *bailment for mutual benefit* under BAILMENT (1).

> "**Bailee's Lien.** It may perhaps be stated as a general rule, that *a bailee for reward* has a lien upon the thing bailed, until payment of his compensation. If this be not universally true, there are very few exceptions. Of tradesmen it may be said generally, that whenever an article is delivered to them to exercise their trade upon it, they may retain it until payment of their charges. Thus, if you incur charges at an inn, the innkeeper has a right to retain your baggage until you pay your bill. If you commit goods to a carrier for transportation, either by stage, wagon, boat, or ship, he may retain them until his freight be paid. If you send a horse to a farrier to be shod, he may retain the horse until you pay him for his work. If you land goods on a wharf, or send them to a warehouse for storage, the wharfinger or warehouseman may retain them until payment of his dues. If you send cloth to a tailor to be made into a garment, he may retain the garment until you pay him his charges. These examples sufficiently illustrate the general principle." Timothy Walker, *Introduction to American Law* 566–67 (10th ed. 1895).

bail emphytéotique. See BAIL (6).

bail-enforcement agent. See BOUNTY HUNTER.

bailer, *n.* (16c) **1.** Someone who provides bail as a surety for a criminal defendant's release. — Also spelled *bailor.* — Also termed *bail bondsman; bailsman.* **2.** BAILOR (1).

bailie (**bay**-lee), *n.* (13c) *Scots law.* **1.** A municipal officer with responsibilities and functions historically similar to those of an English alderman. **2.** *Hist.* A magistrate with responsibilities and functions historically similar to those of an English sheriff. **3.** *Hist.* A bailiff.

bailiff, *n.* (14c) **1.** A court officer who helps maintain order during court proceedings. • In many courts today, the bailiff also acts as crier, among other responsibilities. — Also termed (in England and Wales) *usher;* (in Scotland) *macer; camerarius.* See CRIER (1). **2.** A sheriff's officer who executes writs and serves processes.

▸ **bailiff-errant.** (16c) *Hist.* **1.** A bailiff appointed by the sheriff to deliver writs and other process within a county. Cf. *bailiff of a franchise.* **2.** A deputy to a bailiff; UNDERBAILIFF.

▸ **bailiff of a franchise.** (16c) *Hist.* A bailiff who executed writs and performed other duties in a privileged district that was outside the Crown's (and therefore the sheriff's) jurisdiction. Cf. *bailiff-errant.*

> "*Bailiffs of Franchises* are those who are appointed by every Lord within his Liberty, to do such Offices therein, as the *Bailiff Errant* does at large in the County." Thomas Blount, *Nomo-Lexicon: A Law-Dictionary* (1670).

▸ **bailiff of a hundred.** (16c) *Hist.* A bailiff appointed by a sheriff to collect fines, summon juries, attend court sessions, and execute writs and process in the county district known as a *hundred.* See HUNDRED.

▸ **bailiff of a manor.** (17c) *Hist.* A person appointed to superintend an estate of the nobility. • These bailiffs collected fines and rents, inspected buildings, and took account of waste, spoils, and misdemeanors in the forests and demesne lands.

▸ **bound bailiff.** (18c) *Hist.* A deputy sheriff placed under bond to ensure the faithful performance of assigned duties. — Also termed *bumbailiff.*

> "The sheriff being answerable for the misdemeanors of these bailiffs, they are therefore usually bound in a bond for the due execution of their office, and thence are called *bound-bailiffs;* which the common people have corrupted into a much more homely appellation [i.e., *bumbailiff*]." 1 William Blackstone, *Commentaries on the Laws of England* 334 (1765).

▸ **bumbailiff.** (17c) **1.** *BrE. Slang.* A bailiff of the lowest rank who performs the most menial tasks, such as arresting debtors and serving writs. • In British English, "bum" is slang for a person's buttocks. Some sources suggest that bumbailiffs are so called because they often approached debtors from behind before arresting them. **2.** See *bound bailiff.*

▸ **high bailiff.** (17c) *Hist.* A bailiff attached to a county court, responsible for attending court sessions, serving summonses, and executing orders, warrants, and writs.

▸ **special bailiff.** (17c) **1.** *Hist.* A deputy sheriff appointed at a litigant's request to serve or execute some writ or process related to the lawsuit. **2.** A sheriff with the authority to arrest a witness who has been duly subpoenaed but has failed to appear.

▸ **water bailiff.** See WATER BAILIFF.

3. *Hist.* A person who manages real property for the owner or tenant.

bail in error. (18c) Security given by a defendant who intends to bring a writ of error on a judgment and desires a stay of execution in the meantime. See *appeal bond, supersedeas bond* under BOND (2).

bailivia. See BAILIWICK (1).

bailiwick (**bay**-lə-wik), *n.* (15c) **1.** The office, jurisdiction, or district of a bailiff; esp., a bailiff's territorial jurisdiction. — Also termed *bailivia; baliva; balliva.* Cf. CONSTABLEWICK.

> "In the early days a village was called a 'wick.' Each village had a bailiff who was its peace officer. His authority was limited to the territory of the wick. A bailiff was popularly referred to as a 'bailie,' and before long a bailie's wick was expressed as his 'bailiwick.' And in time this word came to be used to indicate the special territory over which a peace officer exercises his authority as such. Although it may be changed by statute, the normal situation is that the bailiwick of a policeman is his city, the bailiwick of a sheriff is his county and the bailiwick of a state officer, such as a member of the Highway Patrol, is the state." Rollin M. Perkins & Ronald N. Boyce, *Criminal Law* 1096 (3d ed. 1982).

2. The range or limit of someone's power, authority, or influence; AMBIT (3).

bailiwick law. (2005) A statutorily established geographic limitation on a police officer's jurisdiction to make arrests.

bail-jumping, *n.* (1881) The criminal offense of failing to appear in court after being released on bail. *See* Model Penal Code § 242.8. See JUMP BAIL. — **bail-jumper,** *n.*

bailment, *n.* (16c) **1.** A delivery of personal property by one person (the *bailor*) to another (the *bailee*) who holds the property for a certain purpose, usu. under an express or implied-in-fact contract. • Unlike a sale or gift of personal property, a bailment involves a change in possession but not in title. Cf. PAWN.

> "The customary definition of a bailment considers the transaction as arising out of contract. Thus Justice Story defines a bailment as 'a delivery of a thing in trust for some special object or purpose, and upon a contract express or implied, to conform to the object or purpose of the trust' [Joseph Story, Bailments 5 (9th ed. 1878)]. There has, however, been a vigorous dissent to this insistence on the contractual element in bailments. Professor Williston . . . defines bailments broadly 'as the rightful possession of goods by one who is not the owner' [4 Samuel Williston, *Law of Contracts* 2888 (rev. ed. 1936)]. . . . It is obvious that the restricted definition of a bailment as a delivery of goods on a contract cannot stand the test of the actual cases. The broader definition of Professor Williston is preferable." Ray Andrews Brown, *The Law of Personal Property* § 73, at 252, 254 (2d ed. 1955).

> "Although a bailment is ordinarily created by the agreement of the parties, resulting in a consensual delivery and acceptance of the property, such a relationship may also result from the actions and conduct of the parties in dealing with the property in question. A bailment relationship can be implied by law whenever the personal property of one person is acquired by another and held under circumstances in which principles of justice require the recipient to keep the property safely and return it to the owner." 8A Am. Jur. 2d *Bailment* § 1 (1997).

▸ **actual bailment.** (1821) A bailment that arises from an actual or constructive delivery of property to the bailee.

▸ **bailment at will.** (1863) A bailment in which the bailer may retrieve the bailed goods at any time and thereby end or revoke the bailment altogether. — Also termed *revocable bailment.*

▸ **bailment by attornment.** (1980) A bailment that arises without any immediate physical transfer of goods, as when a seller accepts payment for goods and agrees, expressly or impliedly, that title has been transferred to the buyer, who will usu. take possession at some agreed-on time, as when the goods will be delivered in the regular course of business.

▸ **bailment by concealment.** (1983) A bailment that takes place without the bailee's knowledge, as when goods are secretly moved from a carriage onto another's land.

▸ **bailment for hire.** (1821) A bailment for which the bailee is compensated, as when one leaves a car with a parking attendant. — Also termed *lucrative bailment.* Cf. *bailment for mutual benefit.*

▸ **bailment for mutual benefit.** (1868) A bailment from which both the bailor and the bailee gain some tangible advantage or material profit; usu., a bailment for which the bailee is compensated and from which the bailor receives some additional benefit, as when one leaves a car with a parking attendant who will also wash the car during the time of bailment. See BAILEE'S LIEN. Cf. *bailment for hire.*

▸ **bailment for sale.** (1837) A bailment in which the bailee agrees to sell the goods on behalf of the bailor; a consignment.

▸ **bailment for sole benefit of bailor.** See *gratuitous bailment.*

▸ **constructive bailment.** (1843) A bailment that arises when the law imposes an obligation on a possessor of personal property to return the property to its rightful owner, as with an involuntary bailment. • For example, a police department becomes a constructive bailee for an impounded vehicle. Cf. *involuntary bailment.*

▸ **contractual bailment.** (1935) A bailment, usu. for hire, whose terms are specified in a contract.

▸ **gratuitous bailment.** (1811) A bailment for which the bailee receives no compensation, as when one borrows a friend's car. • A gratuitous bailee is liable for loss of the property only if the loss is caused by the bailee's gross negligence. — Also termed *naked bailment; depositum; naked deposit; gratuitous deposit; deposit; bailment for sole benefit of bailor.*

▸ **involuntary bailment.** (1840) A bailment that arises when a person accidentally, but without any negligence, leaves personal property in another's possession. • An involuntary bailee who refuses to return the property to the owner may be liable for conversion. — Also termed *involuntary deposit.* See *abandoned property, lost property, mislaid property* under PROPERTY. Cf. *constructive bailment.*

▸ **lucrative bailment.** See *bailment for hire.*

▸ **naked bailment.** See *gratuitous bailment.*

▸ **revocable bailment.** See *bailment at will.*

2. The personal property delivered by the bailor to the bailee. 3. The contract or legal relation resulting from such a delivery. 4. The act of posting bail for a criminal defendant. 5. The documentation for the posting of bail for a criminal defendant.

bailor (bay-**lor** *or* **bay**-lər), *n.* (17c) **1.** Someone who delivers personal property to another as a bailment. — Also spelled *bailer.* **2.** BAILER (1).

bailout, *n.* (1939) **1.** A rescue of an entity, usu. a corporation or an industry, from financial trouble. **2.** An attempt by a business to receive favorable tax treatment of its profits, as by withdrawing profits at capital-gain rates rather than distributing stock dividends that would be taxed at higher, ordinary-income rates.

bailout stock. See STOCK.

bailpiece, *n.* (18c) **1.** *Hist.* A document recording the nature of the bail granted to a defendant in a civil action; specif., a surety issued to attest the act of offering bail. Cf. EXONERETUR. **2.** More modernly, a warrant issued to a surety upon which the surety may arrest the person bailed. • The bailpiece was filed with the court and usu. was signed by the defendant's sureties. — Sometimes written *bail piece.* See BAIL (2); RECOGNIZANCE.

bail-point scale. (1999) A system for determining a criminal defendant's eligibility for bail, whereby the defendant either will be released on personal recognizance or will have a bail amount set according to the total number of points assessed in response to the defendant's background and behavior.

bail revocation. (1950) The court's cancellation of bail previously granted to a criminal defendant.

bailsman. See BAILER (1).

bail-source hearing. (1988) *Criminal procedure.* A proceeding in which the court examines the reliability of the person posting bail and considers whether the bail money derives from lawful activity. — Also termed *bail-sufficiency hearing; Nebbia hearing. See U.S. v. Nebbia,* 357 F.2d 303 (2d Cir. 1966).

bail-sufficiency hearing. See BAIL-SOURCE HEARING.

bail to the action. See BAIL (4).

bail to the sheriff. See BAIL (4).

bairn's part. See LEGITIM.

bait advertising. See BAIT AND SWITCH.

bait and switch. (1967) **1.** A sales practice whereby a merchant advertises a low-priced product to lure customers into the store only to induce them to buy a higher-priced product. • Most states prohibit the bait and switch when the original product is not actually available as advertised. Cf. LOSS LEADER. — Also termed *bait advertising.* **2.** The unethical practice of offering an attractive rate or premium to induce a person to apply for a loan or contract, with approval contingent on some condition, and then telling the person that the offered rate is not available but that a higher one can be substituted.

***Baker v. Selden* doctrine.** See MERGER DOCTRINE (1).

balance, *vb.* (16c) **1.** To compute the difference between the debits and credits of (an account) <the accountant balanced the company's books>. **2.** To equalize in number, force, or effect; to bring into proportion <the company tried to balance the ratio of mid-level managers to assembly-line workers>. **3.** To measure competing interests and offset them appropriately <the judge balanced the equities before granting the motion>. — **balance,** *n.*

balance billing. (1979) A healthcare provider's practice of requiring a patient or other responsible party to pay any charges remaining after insurance and other payments and allowances have been applied to the total amount due for the provider's services.

balanced budget. See BUDGET.

balanced economy. See ECONOMY.

balanced fund. See MUTUAL FUND.

balance of convenience. (1967) A balancing test that courts use to decide whether to issue a preliminary injunction stopping the defendant's allegedly infringing or unfair practices, weighing the benefit to the plaintiff and the public against the burden on the defendant. — Also termed *balance of hardship.*

balance of payments. (1844) The difference between what a country spends buying goods and services from abroad and what it earns selling goods and services abroad.

balance of power. (17c) **1.** A situation in which political or military strength is shared about evenly <the balance of power within Congress>. **2.** *Int'l law.* An equilibrium of political and military strength within the world or a part of it, esp. so as to prevent one country from overswaying others in setting policies, engaging in trade, etc.; specif., a relative equality of force between countries or groups of countries, as a result of which peace is encouraged because no country or group is in a position to predominate <the East–West balance of power during the Cold War>.

balance of probability. See PREPONDERANCE OF THE EVIDENCE.

balance of sentence suspended. (1942) A sentencing disposition in which a criminal defendant is sentenced to jail but is credited with the time already served before sentencing, resulting in a suspension of the remaining sentence and release of the defendant from custody. Cf. SENTENCED TO TIME SERVED.

balance of trade. (17c) The difference in value between a given country's imports and its exports. — Also termed *trade balance.* See *trade surplus* under SURPLUS; *trade deficit* under DEFICIT (1).

balance sheet. (18c) A statement of a financial position as of the statement's date, disclosing the value of assets, liabilities, and equity. — Also termed *statement of financial condition; statement of condition; statement of financial position; statement of financial performance.* Cf. INCOME STATEMENT.

balance-sheet insolvency. See INSOLVENCY.

balance-sheet risk. (1968) The potential risk at a given time to the financial condition of a company, other entity, or person resulting from volatile market conditions, such as interest rates, liquidity conditions, and foreign-exchange rates.

balance-sheet test. See *balance-sheet insolvency* under INSOLVENCY.

balancing test. (1951) A doctrine whereby an adjudicator measures competing interests and decides which interest should prevail. • In constitutional law, the interests weighed are typically those between individual rights and governmental powers, or between state authority and federal supremacy. See STRICT SCRUTINY; INTERMEDIATE SCRUTINY; RATIONAL-BASIS TEST.

baldfaced lie. See LIE, *n.*

bale, *n.* (14c) A package of goods wrapped in cloth and marked so as to be identifiable on a bill of lading.

bale dock. see BAIL DOCK.

baliva. See BAILIWICK (1).

ballistics, *n.* (18c) **1.** The science of the motion of projectiles such as bullets. **2.** The study of a weapon's firing characteristics, esp. as used in criminal cases to determine a gun's firing capacity and whether a particular gun fired a particular bullet. — **ballistic,** *adj.*

balliva. See BAILIWICK (1).

ballivo amovendo (bə-lɪ-voh ay-moh-**ven**-doh). [Latin "a bailiff to be removed"] (18c) *Hist.* A writ to remove from office a bailiff who does not have sufficient land in the bailiwick as required by the Statute of Westminster (1285).

balloon loan. See LOAN.

balloon note. See NOTE (1).

balloon payment. See PAYMENT (2).

balloon-payment mortgage. See MORTGAGE.

ballot, *n.* (16c) **1.** An instrument, such as a paper or ball, used for casting a vote. — Also termed (if in the form of paper) *ballot-paper.* **2.** The system of choosing officers or voting on a motion by recording individual votes, esp. in secret, by physical means such as marking slips of paper or electronically, and tallying the results when all votes have been cast. See VOTE.

▸ **absentee ballot.** (1917) A ballot that a voter submits, sometimes by mail, before an election. — Also termed *absentee vote.* See *absentee voting* under VOTING.

▸ **bullet ballot.** See *bullet vote* under VOTE (1).

▸ **butterfly ballot.** (2000) A punchcard ballot that opens like a book and usu. has arrows pointing to the punchhole beside a candidate's name. • The butterfly ballots used in Florida during the 2000 presidential elections produced widespread controversy because the layout of the candidates' names on the ballots allegedly confused voters and caused them to cast votes mistakenly for candidates for whom they did not intend to vote.

▸ **electronic ballot.** A ballot cast and counted electronically.

▸ **exhausted ballot.** See *exhausted vote* under VOTE (1).

▸ **joint ballot.** (1822) A vote by legislators of both houses sitting together as one body.

▸ **preferential ballot.** See *preferential vote* under VOTE (1).

▸ **secret ballot.** (17c) A vote in which individual voters' selections cannot be traced. Cf. *Australian ballot.*

> "The secret ballot, when used to protect citizens when choosing their representatives, is a hallmark of a democratic system of government; but, when it is used to conceal a public official's vote, it violates the fundamental tenet of an elected or appointed official's ultimate accountability to the electorate." Op. Tex. Att'y Gen. H-1163 (1978).

▸ **spoiled ballot.** (1886) A ballot reflecting a vote that cannot be counted because it was cast in a form or manner that does not comply with the applicable rules. See *illegal vote* under VOTE (1).

3. One vote in a series of votes that is not conclusive until one candidate attains the necessary majority or supermajority <the candidate was nominated on the 21st ballot>. **4.** A list of candidates running for office <four candidates are on the ballot>. — **ballot,** *vb.*

▸ **Australian ballot.** (1889) A uniform ballot printed by the government, listing all eligible candidates, and marked in secret. • Before Australian ballots became standard, parties or candidates often printed their own ballots with only their names, and watchers at polling places could see whose ballot a voter was casting. — Loosely termed *secret ballot.*

▸ **blanket ballot.** A ballot in which the names of all the candidates for each office are arranged alphabetically in one column, as opposed to being arranged in groups by the parties nominating them.

▸ **Massachusetts ballot.** (1888) A ballot listing the candidates' names and party designations in alphabetical order under the title of the office sought. • This is a type of Australian ballot.

▸ **office-block ballot.** (1965) A ballot listing the candidates' names under the title of the office sought without mentioning the candidates' party affiliations.

▸ **party-column ballot.** (1896) A ballot listing the candidates' names in separate columns by political party regardless of the offices sought in order to encourage straight-ticket voting.

▸ **Texas ballot.** (1944) A ballot that the voter marks for the candidates that he or she does not want elected. • The Texas ballot is particularly useful when the number of candidates only slightly exceeds a large number of representatives being elected.

Ballot Act. See REFORM BILL.

ballot box. (17c) **1.** A locked box into which ballots are deposited after voting. **2.** The system or process of voting in an election.

ballot-paper. See BALLOT (1).

ballot-rigging. (1908) The practice of cheating in an election by not counting the marked votes correctly.

Bamako Convention on the Ban of the Import into Africa and the Control of Transboundary Movement of Hazardous Wastes Within Africa. A 1991 treaty prohibiting the importation of hazardous wastes into Africa and restricting the transfer of wastes among African countries. • The treaty's objectives are to protect human health and the environment from the dangers posed by hazardous wastes by banning their importation, banning the dumping of waste in seas and internal waters, and reducing waste generation. Only a country that is a member of the Organization of African Unity (OAU) can become a party to the Bamako Convention. — Often shortened to *Bamako Convention.*

ban, *n.* (13c) **1.** A legal or otherwise official prohibition against something. **2.** BANNS OF MATRIMONY. **3.** *Hist.* A public proclamation or summons. • Bans dealt with a variety of matters, such as the calling to arms of a lord's vassals or the proclamation that an offender was henceforth to be considered an outlaw. **4.** *Eccles. law.* An authoritative ecclesiastical prohibition; an interdict or excommunication. — Also spelled (in senses 2, 3 & 4) *bann.*

ban, *vb.* (1816) To prohibit, esp. by legal means.

banality (bə-**nal**-i-tee), *n. Hist. French Canadian law.* A lord's right to make his vassals use his own wine press, olive-oil press, oven, mill, etc.

banc (bangk *or* bongk). [French] (18c) A bench; esp., the bench on which one or more judges sit. — Also spelled *bank.* — Also termed *bancus.* See EN BANC.

banc le common pleas. See COURT OF COMMON PLEAS (1).

banc le roy. See KING'S BENCH.

banco (**bang**-koh), *n.* (18c) **1.** A seat or bench of justice. See EN BANC. **2.** A tract of land cut off by the shifting of a river's course; esp., land that has become cut off in such a manner from the country to which it originally belonged. See AVULSION (2).

bancus (**bang**-kəs), *n.* [Law Latin "bench"] (17c) *Hist. English law.* A court or tribunal.

▸ ***bancus publicus*** (**bang**-kəs **puub**-li-kəs). See *bancus superior.*

▸ ***bancus reginae*** (**bang**-kəs rə-**jI**-nee). See QUEEN'S BENCH.

▸ ***bancus regis*** (**bang**-kəs **ree**-jəs). See KING'S BENCH.

▸ ***bancus superior*** (**bang**-kəs sə-**peer**-ee-ər). (17c) Upper bench. • The King's Bench was so called during the Protectorate (1653–1659). — Abbr. b.s. — Also termed *bancus publicus* ("public bench").

B and E. (1961) *abbr.* Breaking and entering. See BURGLARY (2).

bands, *n. pl.* (18c) Two strips of white cloth suspended from the front of a clerical-style collar, worn by advocates when appearing in the courts of the United Kingdom.

bane, *n.* (bef. 12c) *Hist.* A malefactor or murderer; someone whose criminal act called for the raising of the hue and cry.

banish, *vb.* See EXILE.

bank, *n.* (15c) **1.** A financial establishment for the deposit, loan, exchange, or issue of money and for the transmission of funds, organized in accordance with state or federal law; esp., a member of the Federal Reserve System. • Under securities law, a bank includes any financial institution if a substantial portion of the institution's business consists in receiving deposits or exercising fiduciary powers similar to those permitted to national banks and if the institution is supervised and examined by a state or federal banking authority; or a receiver, conservator, or other liquidating agent of any of the above institutions. 15 USCA § 78c(a)(6). **2.** The building or office in which such an establishment conducts transactions.

> "A bank is a quasi public institution, for the custody and loan of money, the exchange and transmission of the same by means of bills and drafts, and the issuance of its own promissory notes, payable to bearer, as currency, or for the exercise of one or more of these functions, not always necessarily chartered, but sometimes so, created to subserve public ends, or a financial institution regulated by law . . . . A bank is wholly a creature of statute doing business by legislative grace and the right to carry on a banking business through the agency of a corporation is a 'franchise' which is dependent on a grant of corporate powers by the state." 1A *Michie on Banks and Banking* § 2, at 5–6 (1993).

▸ **acquiring bank.** The bank that receives a merchant's transactions that are paid for by credit card.

▸ **advising bank.** (1921) A bank that gives notification of the issuance of credit by another bank.

▸ **bank for cooperatives.** (1934) A customer-owned bank that provides loans and other financial services to farmers' cooperatives and other eligible organizations. • It is regulated by the Farm Credit Administration.

▸ **bank of circulation.** (1838) A bank that issues banknotes, payable on demand to bearer. — Also termed *bank of issue.*

▸ **bank of deposit.** (1834) A bank that receives money on deposit. — Also termed *depositary bank.*

▸ **bank of discount.** (1822) A bank that lends money or collateral by means of discounting commercial paper.

▸ **bank of issue.** See *bank of circulation.*

▸ **bridge bank.** A national bank chartered to operate an insolvent bank for up to three years or until the bank is sold.

▸ **central bank.** (1901) A national bank that does business with the government and controls both the amount of money available and the general system of banks within the country; specif., an entity, such as the Federal Reserve Bank in the United States, responsible for overseeing the monetary system of a country or group of countries. • A central bank normally issues currency, functions as the government's bank, regulates the credit system, provides oversight for commercial banks, manages exchange reserves, and implements monetary policy.

▸ **collecting bank.** (1834) In the check-collection process, any bank handling an item for collection, except for the payor bank. UCC § 4-105(5). — Also termed *collecting institution.*

▸ **commercial bank.** (18c) A bank authorized to receive both demand and time deposits, to make loans, to engage in trust services, to issue letters of credit, to rent time-deposit boxes, and to provide similar services. • Once primarily used in antithesis to *investment bank,* the term *commercial bank* now commonly denotes a bank that serves mostly businesses.

▸ **confirming bank.** (1918) A bank that either undertakes to honor a credit already issued by another bank or provides assurance that such a credit will be honored by the issuer or a third bank.

▸ **correspondent bank.** (1887) A bank that acts as an agent for another bank in a geographical area to which the other bank does not have direct access, or that engages in an exchange of services with that bank.

▸ **custodian bank.** (1927) A bank or trust company that acts as custodian for a clearing corporation and that is supervised and audited by a state or federal authority.

▸ **depositary bank.** (1848) **1.** See *bank of deposit.* **2.** The first bank to which an item is transferred for collection, except when the holder presents the item for immediate payment over the counter. UCC § 4-105(2).

▸ **drawee bank.** See *payor bank.*

▸ **Federal Home Loan Bank.** See FEDERAL HOME LOAN BANK.

▸ **federal intermediate credit bank.** (1923) One of 12 regional banks created in 1923 to discount obligations of agricultural credit corporations and similar institutions making short-term loans to farmers and ranchers. • The banks were required by the Agricultural Credit Act of 1987 to merge with federal land banks to create the federal farm-credit system.

▸ **federal land bank.** See FEDERAL LAND BANK.

▸ **intermediary bank.** (1896) A bank to which an item is transferred in the course of collection, even though the bank is not the depositary or payor bank. UCC § 4-105(4).

▸ **investment bank.** (1826) A bank that buys and sells securities, stocks, or bonds; specif., a bank whose primary purpose is to acquire financing for businesses, esp. through the sale of securities. • Although investment banks do not accept deposits or provide loans, they often provide advisory services to the investing public. — Also termed UNDERWRITER. See INVESTMENT BANKER.

▸ **issuing bank.** The bank that issues a credit card and remits funds to cover the charges made by the cardholder.

▸ **member bank.** (1913) A bank that is a member of the Federal Reserve System. • If a member bank fails, the government insures the deposits up to a specified amount. — Also termed *reserve bank.* See FEDERAL RESERVE SYSTEM. Cf. *nonmember bank.*

▸ **merchant bank.** (18c) A bank that provides services for businesses; specif., a bank that specializes in international financial transactions and that underwrites or syndicates equity and bond issues.

▸ **mutual savings bank.** (1865) A bank that has no capital stock and in which the depositors are the owners. See SAVINGS-AND-LOAN ASSOCIATION.

▸ **national bank.** (1864) A bank incorporated under federal law and governed by a charter approved by the Comptroller of the Currency. • A national bank must use the term "national," "national bank," or "national association" as part of its name. 12 USCA §§ 21 et seq.

▸ **negotiating bank.** (1916) A financial institution that discounts or purchases drafts drawn under letters of credit issued by another bank.

▸ **nonbank bank.** (1978) A financial institution that either accepts demand deposits or makes commercial loans, but, unlike traditional banks, does not do both at the same time and therefore can avoid federal regulations on bank ownership. • Nonbank banks were esp. prolific in the 1980s, but amendments to the definition of a bank under federal law have essentially closed this loophole.

▸ **nonmember bank.** (1913) A bank that is not a member of the Federal Reserve System. • State-chartered banks that are not members of the Federal Reserve System are regulated primarily by the Federal Deposit Insurance Corporation. See FEDERAL RESERVE SYSTEM. Cf. *member bank.*

▸ **payor bank.** (1911) A bank that is asked to pay the amount of a negotiable instrument and, on the bank's acceptance, is obliged to pay that amount; a bank by which an item is payable as drawn or accepted. • Because the bank is the drawee of a draft, it is also termed *drawee bank*; *drawee institution.* UCC § 4-105(3).

▸ **presenting bank.** (1862) A nonpayor bank that presents a negotiable instrument for payment. UCC § 4-105(6).

▸ **private bank.** (17c) An unincorporated banking institution owned by an individual or a partnership and that may or may not, depending on state statutes, be subject to state regulation.

▸ **remitting bank.** (1864) A payor or intermediary bank that pays or transfers an item.

▸ **reserve bank.** See *member bank.*

▸ **respondent bank.** (1912) A bank, association, or other entity that exercises fiduciary powers, that holds securities on behalf of beneficial owners, and that deposits the securities for safekeeping with another bank, association, or other entity exercising fiduciary powers. SEC Rule 14a-1(k) (17 CFR § 240.14a-1(k)).

▸ **savings-and-loan bank.** See SAVINGS-AND-LOAN ASSOCIATION.

▸ **savings bank.** (1817) A bank that makes primarily home-mortgage loans and some other consumer loans, receives deposits and pays interest on them, and may offer checking accounts. • Historically, savings banks did not provide any checking services.

▸ **state bank.** (1820) A bank chartered by a state and supervised by the state banking department. • A state bank must have FDIC insurance on deposits but need not become a member of the Federal Reserve System to obtain the insurance. A state bank that is a member of the Federal Reserve is regulated by the state banking department and by the Federal Reserve. Nonmember state banks are regulated by both the state banking department and the FDIC.

bank, *vb.* (18c) **1.** To keep money at <he banks at the downtown branch>. **2.** To deposit (funds) in a bank <she banked the prize money yesterday>. **3.** *Slang.* To lend money to facilitate (a transaction) <who banked the deal?>.

bankable, *adj.* (1818) **1.** Acceptable to or at a bank; esp., (of a banknote, check, or other security) receivable as cash by a bank <a bankable bill of exchange>. **2.** Likely to be highly profitable <a bankable project>.

bankable paper. See PAPER.

bank acceptance. See *banker's acceptance* under ACCEPTANCE (4).

bank account. See ACCOUNT.

bank-account trust. See *Totten trust* under TRUST (3).

bank bill. See BANKNOTE.

bankbook. See PASSBOOK.

bank charter. See CHARTER (3).

bank check. See CHECK.

bank credit. See CREDIT (4).

bank deposit. See DEPOSIT (1).

bank discount. (1808) The interest that a bank deducts in advance of the maturation of a note. See DISCOUNT (2).

bank draft. See DRAFT (1).

banker, *n.* (16c) **1.** Someone who engages in the business of banking. **2.** An officer or owner of a bank; less commonly, anyone employed at a bank in a nonmenial position. **3.** INVESTMENT BANKER.

bankerout, *adj.* (16c) *Archaic.* Indebted beyond the means of payment; bankrupt. — Also spelled *bankrout.*

banker's acceptance. See ACCEPTANCE (4).

banker's bill. See *finance bill* under BILL (6).

banker's lien. See LIEN.

banker's note. See NOTE (1).

banker's opinion. (1924) An assessment of a bank customer's relative creditworthiness and financial reliability given confidentially by one bank to another, or to a commercial enterprise.

bank-examination privilege. See PRIVILEGE (3).

bank examiner. (1868) A federal or state official who audits banks with respect to their financial condition, management, and policies. — Sometimes shortened to *examiner.*

bank for cooperatives. See BANK.

bank fraud. See FRAUD.

bank holding company. (1921) A company that owns or controls one or more banks. • Ownership or control of 25% is usu. enough for this purpose. 12 USCA §1841. — Abbr. BHC.

banking, *n.* (18c) The business carried on by or with a bank or banker; the commercial activity of receiving and safeguarding others' money, paying and collecting checks, and lending out money to earn profits.

> "The business of banking consists primarily in the receiving by a corporation or a person engaged therein, called a bank or banker, of the money of others upon general deposit — that is, subject to repayment upon demand or order — and in the employment of such money by the bank or banker for its or his own benefit in making advances to others by way of loan and of discount of promissory notes and bills of exchange. To the functions of receiving deposits and of loaning and discounting may be added a third, that of issuing bank notes, or the promissory notes of the bank or banker, for use in general circulation as a substitute for money. The business of banking usually includes also the buying and selling of exchange, coin, and bullion, the remission of money, the collection of commercial paper, and the receiving of special deposits." Francis B. Tiffany, *Handbook of the Law of Banks and Banking* 1 (1912).

Banking Act of 1933. See GLASS–STEAGALL ACT.

banking day. (18c) **1.** The time during which a bank is open to the public for carrying on substantially all its banking functions. • Typically, if the bookkeeping and loan departments are closed by a certain hour, the remainder of that day is not part of that bank's banking day. **2.** A day on which banks are open for banking business.

> "'Banking day' is defined in [UCC §] 4-104(1)(c) [now 4-104(a)(3)]. The definition was designed to exclude from the 'banking day' all bank holidays (although some states added specifics on holidays) as well as the portions of a day on which one or more of the substantial departments of the bank closed off their services to the public, even though it remained open for accepting deposits and withdrawing funds as well as continuously processing items for payment or for dispatch. Clearly, when night depositaries came into vogue, their existence did not extend the 'banking day.' The present existence and growing use of so-called 24-hour teller machines also does not extend the banking day. The nature of the banking day is sufficiently tenuous that banks would do well to fix a definite cutoff hour under subsection 4-107(1) [now 4-108(a)]." William D. Hawkland, *Uniform Commercial Code Series* § 4-104:01, at 4-43 (1984).

banking game. (1843) A gambling arrangement in which the house (i.e., the bank) accepts bets from all players and then pays out winning bets and takes other bettors' losses.

bank night. (1935) A lottery in which a prize is awarded to a person (often a theater patron) whose name is drawn randomly from a hopper.

banknote, *n.* (17c) A bank-issued promissory note that is payable to bearer on demand and that may circulate as money. — Also written *bank note.* — Also termed *bank bill.*

> "A bank note is a promissory note issued by a bank and payable to bearer upon demand. Bank notes are designed to circulate as a substitute for money, but they are not a legal tender, although they are a good tender, unless objected to on that ground. By weight of authority (though there are decisions to the contrary) a bank note must be presented for payment in order to charge the bank, and until presentment the statute of limitations does not begin to run, but in states which have adopted the Negotiable Instruments Law such presentment is not necessary." Francis B. Tiffany, *Handbook of the Law of Banks and Banking* 256 (1912).

▸ **spurious banknote.** (1835) **1.** A banknote that is legitimately made from a genuine plate but that has forged signatures of the issuing officers, or the names of fictitious officers. **2.** A banknote that is not a legitimate impression from a genuine plate, or is made from a counterfeit plate, but that is signed by the persons shown on it as the issuing officers. — Also termed *spurious bank bill.*

bank of circulation. See BANK.

bank of deposit. See BANK.

bank of discount. See BANK.

bank of issue. See *bank of circulation* under BANK.

bank rate. See INTEREST RATE.

bankroll, *vb.* (1928) To provide money for (a person, business, venture, etc.).

bankrout. See BANKEROUT.

Bankr. Rep. *abbr.* Bankruptcy Reporter. — Also abbreviated B.R.

bankrupt, *adj.* (16c) Indebted beyond the means of payment; without enough money to pay back what one owes; insolvent. — Also spelled (archaically) *bankerout*; *bankrout.* — **bankrupt,** *vb.*

bankrupt, *n.* (16c) **1.** Someone who cannot meet current financial obligations; an insolvent person. • This term was used in bankruptcy statutes until 1979 and is still commonly used by nonbankruptcy courts. The Bankruptcy Code uses *debtor* instead of *bankrupt.* **2.** DEBTOR (2).

▸ **cessionary bankrupt.** (18c) *Archaic.* Someone who forfeits all property so that it may be divided among creditors. • For the modern near-equivalent, see CHAPTER 7.

bankruptcy, *n.* (18c) **1.** The quality, state, or condition of being without enough money to pay back what one owes; INSOLVENCY. — Also termed *failure to meet obligations*;

failing circumstances. **2.** A statutory procedure by which a (usu. insolvent) debtor obtains financial relief and undergoes a judicially supervised reorganization or liquidation of the debtor's assets for the benefit of creditors; a case under the Bankruptcy Code (Title 11 of the United States Code). • For various types of bankruptcy under federal law, see the entries at CHAPTER. — Also termed *bankruptcy proceeding; bankruptcy case.*

"In 1800 the Federalist majority in Congress enacted a bankruptcy law patterned after the existing English system. Although this law gave only large-scale creditors a remedy against merchant debtors, its sponsors believed it would preempt the field and counteract the fraudulent practices that occurred under state insolvency laws. A national system, moreover, would cure defects in the common law which favored local creditors over very distant ones. Under the common law, the first creditor to attach a debtor's property received a priority over later attachments. Under the bankruptcy system, all the creditors shared in the debtor's property on a *pro rata* basis.

"The statute gave any creditor claiming a debt greater than $1000 the authority to institute proceedings against a commercial debtor if the creditor feared the debtor had committed an 'act of bankruptcy' (i.e., fraudulent concealment or conveyance of goods, or an intention to flee the jurisdiction). In return for the surrender of the debtor's property, and with the concurrence of two thirds of the creditors, a U.S. district court judge could discharge the debtor from all his debts." Daniel Webster, "A Lawyer in Congress," in 2 *The Papers of Daniel Webster* 277 (Alfred F. Konefsky & Andrew J. King eds., 1983).

"There are two general forms of bankruptcy: (1) liquidation and (2) rehabilitation. Chapter 7 of the Code is entitled 'Liquidation.' The terms 'straight bankruptcy' and 'bankruptcy' often are used to describe liquidation cases under the bankruptcy laws because the vast majority of bankruptcy cases are liquidation cases. In a typical Chapter 7 liquidation case, the trustee collects the nonexempt property of the debtor, converts that property to cash, and distributes the cash to the creditors. The debtor gives up all the nonexempt property she owns at the time of the filing of the bankruptcy petition and hopes to obtain a discharge. Chapters 11, 12, and 13 of the Bankruptcy Code contemplate debtor rehabilitation. In a rehabilitation case, creditors look to future earnings of the debtor, not to the property of the debtor at the time of the initiation of the bankruptcy proceeding, to satisfy their claims. The debtor generally retains its assets and makes payments to creditors, usually from postpetition earnings, pursuant to a court-approved plan." David G. Epstein et al., *Bankruptcy* § 1-5, at 8–9 (1993).

▸ **family-farmer bankruptcy.** See CHAPTER 12 (2).

▸ **farmer bankruptcy.** See CHAPTER 12 (2).

▸ **involuntary bankruptcy.** (1842) A bankruptcy case commenced by the debtor's creditors (usu. three or more), or, if the debtor is a partnership, by some but not all of the general partners. 11 USCA § 303(b). — Also termed *involuntary proceeding.*

▸ **liquidation bankruptcy.** See CHAPTER 7 (2).

▸ **malicious bankruptcy.** (1920) An abuse of process by which a person wrongfully petitions to have another person adjudicated a bankrupt or to have a company wound up as insolvent.

▸ ***notour*** **bankruptcy.** See *notorious insolvency* under INSOLVENCY.

▸ **straight bankruptcy.** See CHAPTER 7 (2).

▸ **voluntary bankruptcy.** (18c) A bankruptcy case commenced by the debtor. 11 USCA § 301.

3. The field of law dealing with the rights of debtors who are financially unable to pay their debts and the rights of their creditors. — Also termed *bankruptcy law.* **4.** The status of a party who has declared bankruptcy under a bankruptcy statute. — Also termed *statutory insolvency.* • The roots of *bankruptcy* are the Latin *bancus* (table) and *ruptus* (broken). The English word *bankruptcy* derives from the Italian *banca rotta*, referring to the medieval Italian custom of breaking the counter of a financially failed merchant.

Bankruptcy Act. The Bankruptcy Act of 1898, which governed bankruptcy cases filed before October 1, 1979. — Also termed *Nelson Act.* Cf. BANKRUPTCY CODE.

bankruptcy case. (1835) A proceeding commenced by the filing of a voluntary or involuntary petition under a bankruptcy statute. See BANKRUPTCY (2).

bankruptcy clause. See IPSO FACTO CLAUSE.

Bankruptcy Code. Title I of the Bankruptcy Reform Act of 1978 (as amended and codified in 11 USCA), which governs bankruptcy cases filed on or after October 1, 1979. Cf. BANKRUPTCY ACT.

Bankruptcy Court. A U.S. district court subunit comprising the bankruptcy judges within the district and exclusively concerned with administering bankruptcy proceedings.

bankruptcy crime. (1930) A crime committed in connection with a bankruptcy case, such as a trustee's embezzling from the debtor's estate. 18 USCA §§ 152–157. See *bankruptcy fraud* under FRAUD.

bankruptcy estate. (1836) A debtor's legal and equitable interests in property at the beginning of a bankruptcy case where the property is subject to administration. *See* 11 USCA § 541.

bankruptcy fraud. See FRAUD.

bankruptcy judge. See JUDGE.

bankruptcy law. (18c) **1.** INSOLVENCY LAW. **2.** Traditionally, a statute that provides some relief and protection to an insolvent debtor or to the debtor's creditors. Cf. INSOLVENCY LAW. **3.** BANKRUPTCY (3).

bankruptcy notice. (1927) **1.** A letter or legal form alerting a creditor that bankruptcy proceedings have been instituted by or against a debtor; esp., NOTICE TO CREDITORS. **2.** A notice that a creditor serves on a debtor demanding the payment of a judgment debt, in default of which the creditor will institute involuntary bankruptcy proceedings against the debtor.

bankruptcy petition. See *voluntary petition* under PETITION (1).

bankruptcy plan. (1944) A detailed program of action formulated by a debtor, or its creditors in certain circumstances, to govern the debtor's rehabilitation, continued operation or liquidation, and payment of debts. • The bankruptcy court must approve the plan before it is implemented. — Often shortened to *plan.* — Also termed *plan of reorganization* (for Chapter 11); *plan of rehabilitation* (for Chapter 13). See ARRANGEMENT WITH CREDITORS.

bankruptcy proceeding. (1828) **1.** BANKRUPTCY (2). **2.** Any judicial or procedural action (such as a hearing) related to a bankruptcy.

bankruptcy-remote entity. (1993) A business entity formed in a manner designed to minimize the risk of becoming a debtor in a bankruptcy case. • The entity's organizational charter usu. requires at least one independent director to be appointed, as well as a unanimous vote by the entity's directors, before a bankruptcy petition may be filed. The business is usu. a special-purpose entity established to perform limited functions, such as to purchase and hold accounts receivable or other financial assets that generate revenue. It also has only one or a few primary creditors, thereby reducing the likelihood of an involuntary bankruptcy. A bankruptcy-remote entity will sometimes issue securities instead of receiving a loan from a financial institution. — Abbr. BRE. See SINGLE-PURPOSE PROJECT; SPECIAL-PURPOSE ENTITY; *project financing* under FINANCING.

Bankruptcy Rules. See FEDERAL RULES OF BANKRUPTCY PROCEDURE.

bankruptcy trustee. See TRUSTEE (2).

Bank Secrecy Act. A 1970 federal statute that requires banks and other financial institutions to maintain certain records of customers' transactions (as identified in Bank Secrecy Act regulations) and to report certain domestic and foreign transactions. • The statute is designed to help the federal government in criminal, tax, and other regulatory investigations. 12 USCA § 1829b; 31 USCA § 5311.

bank statement. See STATEMENT OF ACCOUNT (1).

bank-statement rule. (1974) *Commercial law.* The principle that if a bank customer fails to examine a bank statement and any items returned with it, and report to the bank within a reasonable time any unauthorized payments because of a material alteration or forgery, the customer may be precluded from complaining about the alteration or forgery. UCC § 4-406.

bann, *n.* [Law Latin] (13c) **1.** BAN. **2.** *Hist.* The power of a court to issue an edict, esp. one relating to the public peace. **3.** *Hist.* The edict itself. — Also termed *bannum.*

> "An essential attribute of judicial power in the later periods is the *bann*, the right to command and forbid. Etymologically, *bann* comes from a root signifying loud speech. It may have meant at first the order issued by the leader in war; later an administrative command or ordinance. Hence it covers the official proclamation of peace in the court, and then it comes to mean the peace itself. In the older Frank sources, *bann* appears in the Latin as *sermo*, and *sermo regis* is the king's peace. *Extra sermonem regis ponere* means to put out of the peace. Another Latin or rather Latinized German word is *forisbannire*, from which comes our word 'banish.'" Munroe Smith, *The Development of European Law* 35 (1928).

bannitio (bə-**nish**-ee-oh *or* ba-), *n.* [Law Latin] *Hist.* Expulsion by a ban or public proclamation; banishment. See EXILE; BAN (1).

bannitus (**ban**-ə-təs), *n.* [Law Latin] *Hist.* A person under a ban; an outlaw. See BAN (1).

banns of matrimony. (17c) *Family law.* Public notice of an intended marriage. • The notice is given to ensure that objections to the marriage would be voiced before the wedding. Banns are still common in many churches. — Also spelled *bans of matrimony.* — Also termed *banns of marriage.*

> "A minister is not obliged to publish banns of matrimony unless the persons to be married deliver to him, at least seven days before the intended first publication, a notice in writing stating the Christian name and surname and the place of residence of each of them and the period during which each has resided there. . . . Banns are to be published in an audible manner and in the form of words prescribed by the rubric prefixed to the office of matrimony in the *Book of Common Prayer* on three Sundays preceding the solemnisation of marriage during morning service or, if there be no morning service on a Sunday on which they are to be published, during evening service." Mark Hill, *Ecclesiastical Law* 136 (2d ed. 2001) (dealing with practice in the Church of England).

bannum. See BANN.

Banzhaf Index. (1965) A measurement that quantifies the political power of each member in a voting system by counting the potential winning coalitions in which each member's vote is decisive (critical to the win) and the total number of such decisive votes among all members. • The index is named after its inventor, John F. Banzhaf III. A Banzhaf Index would be calculation as in this example: Three parties (A, B, and C) are members of a voting body with a total of 100 votes, with A having 50 votes, B having 49 votes, and C having 1 vote. To reach a majority of 51 votes, the potential winning coalitions are AB, AC, and ABC. A's vote is decisive in all three coalitions; B's vote is decisive only in one (AB); and C's vote is decisive only in one (AC), for a total of five possible decisive votes among all members. Thus A has a Banzhaf power of 3/5; B a Banzhaf power of 1/5; and C a Banzhaf power of 1/5. — Also termed *Banzhaf power index. See Board of Estimate of City of N.Y. v. Morris,* 489 U.S. 688, 697–98, 109 S.Ct. 1433, 1440 (1989).

bar, *n.* (14c) **1.** In a courtroom, the railing that separates the front area, where court business is conducted, from the back area, which provides seats for observers; by extension, a similar railing in a legislative assembly <the spectator stood behind the bar>.

> "The *bar* of the old Courts at Westminster seems to have been guarded and kept with the same forms as in the more ancient *Curia Regis*. In the pictures and illuminations . . . we see the Judges on the different *Benches*, the officials at the tables below, and the litigants with their Counsel, the Serjeants of the Coif, *standing by them at the Bar*. The picture of the King's Bench, in addition to what we see in that of the Common Pleas, shows us the *Prisoner at the Bar* with his Counsel standing by him: and in other representations of the old Courts we have ample proof of the old use of *the bar* as the proper place for the pleader, the litigant, and the prisoner." Alexander Pulling, *The Order of the Coif* 178 (1834).

2. The whole body of lawyers qualified to practice in a given court or jurisdiction; the legal profession, or an organized subset of it; BAR ASSOCIATION <the attorney's outrageous misconduct disgraced the bar>.

▸ **integrated bar.** See *integrated bar association* under BAR ASSOCIATION.

▸ **local bar.** See *local bar association* under BAR ASSOCIATION.

▸ **specialty bar.** See *specialty bar association* under BAR ASSOCIATION.

▸ **state bar.** See *state bar association* under BAR ASSOCIATION.

▸ **unified bar.** See *integrated bar association* under BAR ASSOCIATION.

▸ **voluntary bar.** See *voluntary bar association* under BAR ASSOCIATION.

3. A particular court or system of courts <case at bar>. • Originally, *case at bar* referred to an important case tried "at bar" at the Royal Courts of Justice in London.

4. BAR EXAMINATION <Pendarvis passed the bar>. **5.** A barrier to or the destruction of a legal action or claim; the effect of a judgment for the defendant <a bar to any new lawsuit>. Cf. MERGER (6). **6.** A plea arresting a lawsuit or legal claim <the defendant filed a bar>. See PLEA IN BAR. **7.** *Patents.* Statutory preclusion from patentability, based on publication, use, sale, or other anticipatory activity that occurred before an invention's critical date and thereby negated the invention's novelty. • Under the Patent Act, 35 USCA § 102, a person is not entitled to a patent if (1) before the date of invention, the same invention was publicly known or used by others in this country or was patented or described in a printed publication anywhere in the world; (2) more than one year before the U.S. filing date, the invention was patented or described in a printed publication anywhere in the world or was in public use, on sale, or offered for sale in the U.S.; (3) the applicant has abandoned the invention; (4) the invention was first patented by the applicant or its representatives in a foreign country before the U.S. filing date, and the foreign application was filed more than 12 months before the U.S. filing; (5) before the date of invention, the invention was described in a patent granted on an application filed by someone else in the U.S.; (6) the inventor did not invent the subject matter of the application; or (7) the invention was previously made in this country by someone else who has not abandoned, suppressed, or concealed it. — Also termed *statutory bar.* **8.** *Trademarks.* Statutory preclusion of certain marks from listing on the Principal Register. • Under 15 USCA § 1052, a mark is not entitled to registration if (1) it consists of immoral, deceptive, or scandalous matter; (2) it falsely suggests a connection with, or brings into contempt or disrepute, a living or dead person, an institution, a belief, or a country's symbols; (3) it depicts or simulates the flag, coat of arms, or other insignia of the U.S., a state, a municipality, or a foreign country; (4) it consists of a geographic designation that, when used on wines or spirits, designates a place other than the goods' actual origin; (5) it consists of the name, signature, or portrait of a living person who has not consented to registration; (6) it is likely to deceive or to cause confusion or mistake because when applied to specific goods and services it resembles someone else's unabandoned mark registered in the U.S. Patent and Trademark Office, or an unabandoned mark or tradename previously used in the U.S.; (7) it is merely descriptive or deceptively misdescriptive of the goods or services; (8) it is primarily geographically descriptive or primarily geographically misdescriptive of the goods or services; (9) it is primarily a surname; or (10) it comprises matter that, as a whole, is functional.

bar, *vb.* (16c) To prevent or prohibit, esp. by legal objection <the statute of limitations barred the plaintiff's wrongful-death claim>.

bar association. (1856) An organization of members of the legal profession <several state bar associations sponsor superb CLE programs>. See BAR (2).

> "There is said to have been a 'bar association' formed in Essex County, Massachusetts, in 1770 and we know that the Essex County Bar had adopted a rule as to the members taking students into their offices and as to the time of study as far back as 1768. In the sketch of the history of the Essex Bar Association published by that Association in 1900 we are told that the first Essex Bar Association was formed in 1806. But the printed rules of 1806 show that there was not a bar association but an organized bar, comprising all the members of the bar. The title is: 'Rules and Regulations of the Bar in the County of Essex.' The first article begins: 'There shall be two stated meetings annually of the members of the bar.' There are records of bar meetings in 1812, but how much longer they were held is not known. There is a printed copy of rules under a new organization in 1831, but that organization lasted only a few years. The record of the organization of the present Essex Bar Association in 1856 is illuminating. It is headed: 'A record of the proceedings of the Essex Bar preliminary to the organization of the Essex Bar Association.' The record recites a meeting of the 'Essex Bar' on two days and the adoption of a 'Constitution of the Essex Bar Association,' and the first article tells how members of the Bar of Essex County may become members of the association." Roscoe Pound, *The Lawyer from Antiquity to Modern Times* 195–96 (1953).

▸ **integrated bar association.** (1918) A bar association in which membership is a statutory requirement for practicing law; a usu. statewide organization of lawyers in which membership is compulsory in order for a lawyer to have a law license. — Also termed *unified bar association.*

▸ **local bar association.** (1876) A bar association organized on a local level, such as an association within a county or city. • Local bar associations are voluntary in membership.

▸ **specialty bar association.** (1965) A voluntary bar association for lawyers with special interests, specific backgrounds, or common practices.

▸ **state bar association.** (1883) An association or group of attorneys that have been admitted to practice law in a given state; a bar association organized on a statewide level, often with compulsory membership. • State bar associations are usu. created by statute, and membership is often mandatory for those who practice law in the state. Unlike voluntary, professional-development bar associations such as the American Bar Association, state bar associations often have the authority to regulate the legal profession by undertaking such matters as disciplining attorneys and bringing lawsuits against those who engage in the unauthorized practice of law.

▸ **unified bar association.** See *integrated bar association.*

▸ **voluntary bar association.** (1894) A bar association that lawyers need not join to practice law. — Also termed *voluntary bar.*

barbarian laws. See LEGES BARBARORUM.

bar date. (1946) *Patents.* The date by which a U.S. patent application must be filed to avoid losing the right to receive a patent. • In the U.S., the bar date for a patent application is one year after the invention is disclosed in a publication or patented in another country, or put into public use, sold, or offered for sale in the U.S. <Since the invention was offered for domestic sale on January 1, 2000, the bar date for the U.S. patent application is January 1, 2001.> Cf. *absolute novelty* under NOVELTY.

bareboat charter. See CHARTER (8).

bareboat charterparty. See *bareboat charter* under CHARTER (8).

barebones indictment. See INDICTMENT.

barebones legislation. See *skeletal legislation* under LEGISLATION (3).

bare expectancy. See EXPECTANCY (2).

bare license. See LICENSE.

bare licensee. See LICENSEE.

bare ownership. See *trust ownership* under OWNERSHIP.

bare possibility. See *naked possibility* under POSSIBILITY.

bare promise. See *gratuitous promise* under PROMISE.

bare steerageway. (1888) *Maritime law.* The lowest speed necessary for a vessel to maintain course.

bare trustee. See TRUSTEE (1).

bar examination. (1875) A written test that a person must pass before being licensed to practice law. • The exam varies from state to state. — Often shortened to *bar.*

▸ **Multistate Bar Examination.** A nationally standardized part of a state bar examination given as a multiple-choice test covering broad legal subjects, including constitutional law, contracts, criminal law, evidence, property, and torts. — Abbr. MBE.

bar examiner. (1902) One appointed by the state to test applicants (usu. law-school graduates) by preparing, administering, and grading the bar examination.

bargain, *n.* (14c) An agreement between parties for the exchange of promises or performances. • A bargain is not necessarily a contract because the consideration may be insufficient or the transaction may be illegal. See BARGAIN AND SALE; *informal contract* under CONTRACT. — **bargain,** *vb.*

> "A bargain is an agreement of two or more persons to exchange promises, or to exchange a promise for a performance. Thus defined, 'bargain' is at once narrower than 'agreement' in that it is not applicable to all agreements, and broader than 'contract' since it includes a promise given in exchange for insufficient consideration. It also covers transactions which the law refuses to recognize as contracts because of illegality." 1 Samuel Williston, *A Treatise on the Law of Contracts* § 2A, at 7 (Walter H.E. Jaeger ed., 3d ed. 1957).

▸ **catching bargain.** (18c) An agreement on unconscionable terms to purchase real property from — or loan money secured by real property to — a person who has an expectant or reversionary interest in the property.

▸ **hard bargain.** (17c) An intensely negotiated bargain whose terms are favorable to one party or set of parties and disadvantageous to another <drive a hard bargain>.

▸ **illegal bargain.** (17c) A bargain whose formation or performance is criminal, tortious, or otherwise contrary to public policy.

▸ **plea bargain.** See PLEA BARGAIN.

▸ **time-bargain.** See FUTURES CONTRACT.

▸ **unconscionable bargain.** See *unconscionable agreement* under AGREEMENT.

bargain and sale. (16c) **1.** A negotiated transaction, usu. for goods, services, or real property. **2.** *Hist.* A written agreement for the sale of land whereby the buyer would give valuable consideration (recited in the agreement) without having to enter the land and perform livery of seisin, so that the parties equitably "raised a use" in the buyer. • The result of the transaction was to leave the legal estate in fee simple in the seller and to create an equitable estate in fee simple in the buyer until legal title was transferred to the buyer by delivery of a deed. In most jurisdictions, the bargain and sale has been replaced by the statutory deed of grant.

bargain-and-sale deed. See DEED.

bargained-for exchange. (1937) *Contracts.* A benefit or detriment that the parties to a contract agree to as the price of performance. • The Restatement of Contracts (Second) defines *consideration* exclusively in terms of bargain, but it does not mention benefit or detriment.

bargainee, *n.* (16c) The buyer in a bargained-for exchange.

bargaining agent. See AGENT.

bargaining position. (1921) **1.** The relative power that one party has vis-à-vis the other in negotiations; esp., the ability of a party to a transaction to achieve desirable results, esp. as a result of financial wherewithal, size, or status. — Also termed *bargaining power.* **2.** The latest offer or demand that a negotiator has made.

bargaining unit. (1934) A group of employees authorized to engage in collective bargaining on behalf of all the employees of a company or an industry sector.

bargain money. See EARNEST MONEY.

bargainor (bahr-gən-**or** *or* **bahr**-gə-nər), *n.* (17c) The seller in a bargained-for exchange.

bargain purchase. The acquisition of property or assets in exchange for something of value, but for less than fair market value. Cf. BARGAIN SALE.

bargain sale. (1898) A sale or exchange of property for less than its fair market value. • For tax purposes, the difference between the sale price and the fair market value must be taken into account. Bargain sales between family members may lead to gift-tax consequences. Cf. BARGAIN PURCHASE.

bargain theory of consideration. (1927) The theory that a promise or performance that is bargained for in exchange for a promise is consideration for the promise. • This theory underlies all bilateral contracts. See *bilateral contract* under CONTRACT.

> "[C]lassical contract theory tended to associate the doctrine of consideration with the concept of bargain. The emphasis of classical law shifted away from actual benefits and detriments to the mutual promises which constitute a wholly executory contract. American lawyers developed from this trend a 'bargain theory of consideration' and similarly in English law a more modern basis for the doctrine of consideration was found by some lawyers in the notion that a contract is a bargain in which the consideration is the price of the bargain. Allied to this is the supposed rule that nothing can be treated as a consideration unless it is seen by the parties as the 'price' of the bargain." P.S. Atiyah, *An Introduction to the Law of Contract* 119 (3d ed. 1981).

bark and hold. A police dog's act of finding a suspect and barking to summon a law-enforcement officer. • The dog is usu. trained not to bite the suspect as long as the suspect does not try to flee or actively resist. See *police dog* under DOG (1). Cf. BITE AND HOLD.

barometer stock. See STOCK.

baron, *n.* (12c) **1.** *Hist.* A man who held land directly from the Crown in exchange for military service. **2.** *Hist.* A husband. See BARON ET FEME. **3.** One of the judges of the former English or Scottish Courts of Exchequer. — Abbr. B. See BARONS OF THE EXCHEQUER. **4.** A noble rank; specif., the lowest rank in the British peerage. **5.** Generally, a lord or nobleman.

barones scaccarii. See BARONS OF THE EXCHEQUER.

baronet, *n.* (17c) *Hist.* A hereditary title of nobility that descends in the male line only. • Baronet is the lowest hereditary title, ranking below baron and above knight.

It originated in 1611 when James I began selling the title as a way to raise revenue.

baron et feme (**bar**-ən ay **fem**). [Law French] *Hist.* Husband and wife. See COVERTURE; *feme covert* under FEME.

baronial court. See COURT.

baron covert. See COVERT BARON.

Baron Parke's rule. See GOLDEN RULE (1).

Barons of the Exchequer. (15c) *Hist.* The six judges of the Court of Exchequer. • After the 1873 transfer of the Court's jurisdiction to the High Court of Justice, the judges were known as *justices of the High Court.* — Also termed *barones scaccarii.* See COURT OF EXCHEQUER.

barony (**bar**-ən-ee), *n.* **1.** The domain or territory of a baron. See BARON (1). **2.** The mode of tenure by which a baron held lands. See TENURE (2).

bar pilot. See *branch pilot* under PILOT.

barra (**bah**-rə), *n.* [Law French "bar"] *Hist.* **1.** PLEA IN BAR. **2.** BARRISTER. — Also spelled *barre.*

barrator (**bar**-ə-tər), *n.* (15c) **1.** Someone who commits barratry (in any sense). **2.** A fomenter of usu. meritless quarrels and lawsuits; one who stirs up dissension and litigation among people. — Also spelled *barretor.* Cf. CHAMPERTOR.

> "*Barrator* or *Barater* (Fr. *Barateur,* a Deceiver) Is a common mover or maintainer of Suits, Quarrels, or Parts, either in Courts or elsewhere in the Country, and is himself never quiet, but at variance with one or other." Thomas Blount, *Nomo-Lexicon: A Law-Dictionary* (1670).

barratry (**bar**-ə-tree *or* **bair**-), *n.* (15c) **1.** Vexatious incitement to litigation, esp. by soliciting potential legal clients. • There must typically be a showing that the resulting lawsuit was utterly baseless. Barratry is a crime in most jurisdictions. A person who is hired by a lawyer to solicit business is called a *capper.* See CAPPER (1). **2.** The bringing of a lawsuit or other legal proceeding without the permission or consent of the named plaintiff or complainant. **3.** *Maritime law.* Fraudulent or grossly negligent conduct (by a master or crew) that is prejudicial to a shipowner. • In the maritime sense, barratry is any fraudulent or illegal act of the master or crew whereby the shipowner suffers, such as sinking or deserting the ship with criminal intent.

> "[S]ailing out of port in violation of an embargo, or without paying the port duties, or to go out of the regular course upon a smuggling expedition, or to be engaged in smuggling against the consent of the owner, are all of them acts of barratry, equally with more palpable and direct acts of violence and fraud, for they are wilful breaches of duty by the master. It makes no difference in the reason of the thing, whether the injury the owner suffers be owing to an act of the master, induced by motives of advantage to himself, or of malice to the owner, or a disregard of those laws which it was the master's duty to obey, and which the owner relied upon him to observe. It is, in either case, equally barratry." 3 James Kent, *Commentaries on American Law* *305–06 (George Comstock ed., 11th ed. 1866).

4. The buying or selling of ecclesiastical or governmental positions. Cf. SIMONY. **5.** The crime committed by a judge who accepts a bribe in exchange for a favorable decision. Cf. BRIBE. — **barratrous** (**bar**-ə-trəs), *adj.*

barred, *adj.* (14c) **1.** Furnished or secured with bars <a barred gate>. **2.** Prevented; legally prohibited <he is barred from going within 100 feet of the plant for the next two years>. **3.** Admitted to practice law in a given jurisdiction <she is barred in three states>. • Sense 3 is nontraditional usage that seems to have arisen in the late 20th century. Although some will object to it, it cannot realistically be barred from the lexicon.

barretor. See BARRATOR.

barrier to entry. (1944) An economic factor that makes it difficult for a business to enter a market and compete with existing businesses.

> "Strictly speaking, a barrier to entry is a condition that makes the long-run costs of a new entrant into a market higher than the long-run costs of the existing firms in the market; a good example is a regulatory limitation on entry. The term is also used, more questionably, as a synonym for heavy start-up costs." Richard A. Posner, *Economic Analysis of Law* § 10.8, at 227 (2d ed. 1977).

barring of entail. (18c) The freeing of an estate from the limitations imposed by an entail and permitting its free disposition. • This was anciently done by means of a fine or common recovery, but later by a deed in which the tenant and next heir join. — Also termed *breaking of entail; disentailment.* See ENTAIL.

barrister (**bar**-is-tər), *n.* (15c) *English law.* In England or Northern Ireland, a lawyer who is admitted to plead at the bar and who may argue cases in superior courts. • In many other Commonwealth countries, the legal profession is similarly divided into barristers and solicitors. — Also termed *barra.* Cf. ADVOCATE (2); SOLICITOR (4). — **barristerial** (bar-ə-**steer**-ee-əl), *adj.*

▸ **inner barrister.** (17c) **1.** QUEEN'S COUNSEL. **2.** A student member of an Inn of Court.

▸ **outer barrister.** (18c) A barrister called to the bar, but not called to plead from within it, as a Queen's Counsel or (formerly) serjeant-at-law is permitted to do; a barrister belonging to the outer bar. — Also termed *utter barrister.* See CALL TO THE BAR; OUTER BAR.

▸ **paper barrister.** A barrister who has little if any experience in court.

> "The term is used as a convenient description of one who is a barrister but who lacks any experience of practice at the Bar. For very many years it has been common for those employed in government departments, by local authorities or in other salaried positions to join an Inn, eat their dinners, pass their examinations and then be called to the Bar. All this can be done in their spare time, without affecting their employment." R.E. Megarry, *Lawyer and Litigant in England* 105 (1962).

▸ **vacation barrister.** (17c) A barrister who, being newly called to the bar, for at least three years must attend inn-of-court functions that are held during the long vacation. See VACATION (3).

barter, *n.* (15c) The exchange of one commodity or service for another without the use of money. — **barter,** *adj.* & *vb.*

BAS. *abbr.* Business-activity statement.

base, *adj.* (16c) **1.** Inferior, mean, or debased in quality <base French>. **2.** *Hist.* Servile; (of a villein) holding land at the will of a lord and not upon fixed services <base tenures>. See *base estate* under ESTATE (1). **3.** Morally low; not having good moral principles; low-minded <base attitudes and desires>. **4.** Suitable to someone of inferior position; menial <a base, unskilled person>. **5.** Having little value <base metals>. **6.** Of, relating to, or involving a starting point; minimum <base pay>.

base, *n.* **1.** The lowest or supporting part of something; the foundation <the base of the tower>. **2.** A determining ingredient; a common element that is united with others to form a product <gin is the base for many cocktails>. **3.** The starting point or foundational part of something from which new ideas will develop <a sound research base>. **4.** A point, part, line, or quantity from which a reckoning or conclusion proceeds; a principle or datum <the base on which this argument proceeds>. **5.** A place or region that forms a military headquarters or center from which supplies or reinforcements are drawn <the military base at Wiesbaden>. **6.** The main place from which a company controls its activities; headquarters <the base of operations>. **7.** The people, money, groups, etc. that form the principal part of something <tax base>.

base, *vb.* **1.** To make, form, or serve as a foundation for <the left hand based her chin>. **2.** To establish (an agreement, conclusion, etc.); to place on a foundation; to ground <the claim is based in tort>. **3.** To use (something) as the thing from which something else is developed <their company is based on an abiding respect for the employees>. **4.** To take up or maintain one's headquarters; to have one's main place of work in a particular place <based in Dallas>.

base and meridian. (1856) *Property.* The east–west and north–south lines used by a surveyor to demarcate the position of the boundaries of real property. • A base line runs east and west; a meridian line runs north and south.

base court. See COURT.

based on. *Copyright.* Derived from, and therefore similar to, an earlier work. • If one work is "based on" an earlier work, it infringes the copyright in the earlier work. To be based on an earlier work, a later work must embody substantially similar expression, not just substantially similar ideas. See *derivative work* under WORK (2).

base estate. See ESTATE (1).

base fee. (1800) **1.** See FEE (2). **2.** See *fee simple determinable* under FEE SIMPLE.

Basel Convention on the Control of Transboundary Movements of Hazardous Waste and Their Disposal. A 1992 treaty establishing formal rules and procedures for the transportation and disposal of hazardous waste across national borders. • The United States had not ratified the treaty as of 2013. — Often shortened to *Basel Convention.*

baseless, *adj.* (17c) Having no basis in fact or sound reason; without any foundation or support; groundless.

baseline. (1952) *Int'l law.* The line, usu. the low-water line along the coast or the seaward limit of the internal waters of a coastal state, from which the breadth of the state's sovereignty over the bordering sea is measured.

baseline documentation. (1996) *Real estate.* A written report supplemented with maps, photographs, and other information describing the physical and biological condition of land subject to a conservation easement at the time when the easement is granted. • The report, signed by the landowner and a representative of the land trust, records the condition of the conservation values protected in the conservation easement and establishes photo points or other means for perpetually monitoring the restricted, expressed, permitted, and retained rights to protect these conservation values. 26 CFR §1.170A-14(g)(5)(i).

basement court. (1995) *Slang.* A low-level court of limited jurisdiction, such as a police court, traffic court, municipal court, or small-claims court.

base-point pricing. (1973) **1.** A pricing method that adds the price at the factory to the freight charges, which are calculated as the cost of shipping from a set location to the buyer's location, regardless of the actual cost of transportation. • The chosen shipping base-point may be the same for all customers, or it may be a specific, established location, such as a manufacturing plant nearest to the buyer. **2.** A uniform pricing policy in which the cost of transportation to all locations is presumed to be the same.

base rate. See INTEREST RATE.

base service. See SERVICE (6).

base tenure. See TENURE.

basic crops. See CROPS.

basic fact. See *intermediate fact* under FACT.

basic-form policy. See INSURANCE POLICY.

basic goods. See GOODS.

basic mistake. See MISTAKE.

basic norm. See NORM.

basic patent. See *pioneer patent* under PATENT (3).

basic wage. See *minimum wage* under WAGE.

basilica (bə-**sil**-i-kə), *n.* [Greek] (16c) *Hist.* **1.** (*cap.*) A 60-book Greek summary of Justinian's *Corpus Juris Civilis,* with comments (*scholia*). • The *Basilica* ("royal law") was begun by the Byzantine emperor Basil I, and it served as a major source of the law of the Eastern Empire from the early 10th century until Constantinople's fall in 1453. **2.** A colonnaded hall used as a law court or meeting place; specif., in ancient Rome, a public building usu. used as a court of justice. • A basilica typically featured a nave with two aisles and an apse. Architects adopted the basilica's layout for the design of early Christian churches.

basis, *n.* (14c) **1.** A fundamental principle; an underlying fact or condition; a foundation or starting point. **2.** *Tax.* The value assigned to a taxpayer's investment in property and used primarily for computing gain or loss from a transfer of the property. • Basis is usu. the total cost of acquiring the asset, including the purchase price plus commissions and other related expenses, less depreciation and other adjustments. When the assigned value represents the cost of acquiring the property, it is also called *cost basis.* — Also termed *tax basis.* Pl. **bases.**

▸ **adjusted basis.** (1932) Basis increased by capital improvements and decreased by depreciation deductions.

> "[I]t is well to consider the word 'adjusted' in the term 'adjusted basis.' Often, after property is acquired, certain adjustments (increases or decreases to the dollar amount of the original basis) must be made. After these adjustments, the property then has an 'adjusted basis.'" Michael D. Rose & John C. Chommie, *Federal Income Taxation* § 6.04, at 300 (3d ed. 1988).

▸ **adjusted cost basis.** (1934) Basis resulting from the original cost of an item plus capital additions minus depreciation deductions.

▸ **carryover basis.** (1952) The recipient's basis in property transferred by gift or in trust, equaling the transferor's basis. — Also termed *substituted basis.*

▸ **stepped-up basis.** (1951) The beneficiary's basis in property transferred by inheritance, equaling the fair market value of the property on the date of the decedent's death or on the alternate valuation date.

▸ **substituted basis.** (1932) **1.** The basis of property transferred in a tax-free exchange or other specified transaction. **2.** See *carryover basis*.

basis clause. (1975) *Insurance.* An insurance-policy clause that makes certain declarations by the insured, esp. the truth or existence of certain facts, the basis on which the insurer is willing to supply the insurance, and often a condition precedent to the policy's effectiveness.

basis point. (1951) One-hundredth of 1%; .01%. • Basis points are used in computing investment yields (esp. of bonds) and in apportioning costs and calculating interest rates in real-estate transactions. — Abbr. bp; bip.

Basket Clause. 1. NECESSARY AND PROPER CLAUSE. **2.** A contractual provision that generally allows an insurance company or a pension fund to invest a small percentage of its assets without regard to statutory restrictions.

basse justice (**bahs** zhoo-**stees**). [Law French "low justice"] (17c) *Hist.* A feudal lord's right to personally try a person charged with a minor offense.

bastard, *n.* (14c) *Archaic.* **1.** A person born out of wedlock. See *illegitimate child* under CHILD. **2.** A child born to a married woman whose husband could not be or is otherwise proved not to be the father. • Because the word is most commonly used as a slur, its use in family-law contexts is much in decline.

▸ **adulterine bastard.** (1826) A child born to a married woman whose husband is not the father of the child. • The rebuttable presumption is generally that a child born of the marriage is the husband's child. A child born to a woman by means of artificial insemination may be termed an *adulterine bastard*, but most jurisdictions prohibit a husband who has consented to the artificial insemination from denying paternity and responsibility for the child. Cf. ARTIFICIAL INSEMINATION.

bastard eigne. See EIGNE.

bastardy. See ILLEGITIMACY.

bastardy proceeding. See PATERNITY SUIT.

bastardy process. See PATERNITY SUIT.

bastardy statute. (1832) *Archaic.* A criminal statute that punishes an unwed father for failing to support his child. • These statutes have been found unconstitutional because they unfairly discriminate against fathers and do not punish unwed mothers. So they are unenforceable.

batable ground (**bay**-tə-bəl). (16c) Land of uncertain ownership. • *Batable* (or *debatable*) *ground* originally referred to certain lands on the border of England and Scotland before the 1603 union of the two kingdoms.

batch number. See SERIES CODE.

Bates number. See BATES-STAMP NUMBER.

Bates stamp, *n.* (1987) **1.** A self-advancing stamp machine used for affixing an identifying mark, usu. a number, to a document or to the individual pages of a document. **2.** BATES-STAMP NUMBER. — Sometimes (erroneously) written *Bate stamp.*

Bates-stamp, *vb.* (1988) To affix a mark, usu. a number, to a document or to the individual pages of a document for the purpose of identifying and distinguishing it in a series of documents <the paralegal is Bates-stamping the records described in the request for discovery>. — Sometimes (erroneously) written *Bate-stamp.*

Bates-stamp number. (1987) The identifying number or mark that is affixed to a document or to the individual pages of a document in sequence, usu. by numerals but sometimes by a combination of letters and numerals. • The term gets its name from a self-advancing stamp machine made by the Bates Manufacturing Company. The number is typically used to identify documents produced during discovery. — Often shortened to *Bates number; Bates stamp.*

bath. See IMMUNITY BATH.

bathtub conspiracy. See *intra-enterprise conspiracy* under CONSPIRACY.

BATNA. BEST ALTERNATIVE TO A NEGOTIATED AGREEMENT.

***Batson* challenge.** See CHALLENGE (1).

***Batson* rule.** (1986) *Criminal procedure.* The doctrine that neither the prosecution nor the defense may engage in the discriminatory exercise of peremptory challenges, esp. with regard to race but also with regard to religion or sex. • Under *Batson v. Kentucky*, the court may deny a peremptory challenge unless the court accepts a nondiscriminatory explanation. 476 U.S. 79, 106 S.Ct. 1712 (1986). See *Batson challenge* under CHALLENGE, *n.* (1).

battered child. See CHILD.

battered-child syndrome. (1962) *Family law.* A constellation of medical and psychological conditions of a child who has suffered continuing injuries that could not be accidental and are therefore presumed to have been inflicted by someone close to the child, usu. a caregiver. • The myriad issues include child abuse, physical neglect, emotional neglect, and sexual abuse. Diagnosis typically results from a radiological finding of distinct bone trauma and persistent tissue damage caused by intentional injury, such as twisting or hitting with violence. The phrase was first used by Dr. Henry Kempe and his colleagues in a 1962 article entitled "The Battered Child Syndrome," which appeared in the *Journal of the American Medical Association*. As a result of research on battered-child syndrome, the Children's Bureau of the United States Department of Health, Education, and Welfare drafted a model statute requiring physicians to report serious cases of suspected child abuse. — Abbr. BCS. See CHILD-ABUSE AND -NEGLECT REPORTING STATUTE.

battered-person syndrome. See BATTERED-WOMAN SYNDROME.

battered-spouse syndrome. See BATTERED-WOMAN SYNDROME.

battered-wife syndrome. See BATTERED-WOMAN SYNDROME.

battered woman. (1973) *Family law.* A woman who is the victim of domestic violence; a woman who has suffered physical, emotional, or sexual abuse at the hands of a spouse or partner. See *domestic violence* under VIOLENCE.

battered-woman syndrome. (1984) *Family law.* A constellation of medical and psychological symptoms of a woman who has suffered physical, sexual, or emotional abuse at the hands of a spouse or partner and who, as a result, cannot take action to escape the abuse. • Battered-woman syndrome was first recognized in the early 1970s by Dr. Lenore Walker, who described the syndrome as consisting of three stages: (1) the tension-building stage, which may include verbal and mild physical abuse; (2) the acute battering stage, which includes stronger verbal abuse, increased physical violence, and perhaps rape or other sexual abuse; and (3) the loving-contrition stage, which includes the abuser's apologies, attentiveness, kindness, and gift-giving. This syndrome is sometimes proposed as a defense to justify or mitigate a woman's killing of a man. — Abbr. BWS. — Sometimes (more specif.) termed *battered-wife syndrome*; (more broadly) *battered-spouse syndrome*; (broadly) *battered-person syndrome*. See *domestic violence* under VIOLENCE.

batterers' intervention program. (1995) *Criminal law.* An educational and therapeutic program for domestic abusers, usu. conducted by or coordinated with criminal-justice systems and community organizations. • The program may offer safety training for victims as well as rehabilitative services for abusers. — Abbr. BIP.

battery, *n.* (16c) **1.** *Criminal law.* The nonconsensual touching of, or use of force against, the body of another with the intent to cause harmful or offensive contact. — Also termed *criminal battery.*

> "Criminal battery, sometimes defined briefly as the unlawful application of force to the person of another, may be divided into its three basic elements: (1) the defendant's conduct (act or omission); (2) his 'mental state,' which may be an intent to kill or injure, or criminal negligence, or perhaps the doing of an unlawful act; and (3) the harmful result to the victim, which may be either a bodily injury or an offensive touching." Wayne R. LaFave & Austin W. Scott Jr., *Criminal Law* § 7.15, at 685 (2d ed. 1986).

▸ **aggravated battery.** (1811) A criminal battery accompanied by circumstances that make it more severe, such as the threatened or actual use of a deadly weapon or the fact that the battery resulted in serious bodily harm. • In most state statutes, aggravated battery is classified as a felony.

▸ **sexual battery.** (1974) The nonconsensual penetration of or contact with another's sexual organs or the perpetrator's sexual organs. • In most state statutes, sexual battery is classified as both a misdemeanor and a felony. — Also termed *criminal sexual battery* (CSG). Cf. RAPE; *sexual assault* under ASSAULT.

▸ **simple battery.** (1877) A criminal battery not accompanied by aggravating circumstances and not resulting in serious bodily harm. • Simple battery is usu. a misdemeanor but may rise to a felony if the victim is, for instance, a child or a senior citizen.

2. *Torts.* A nonconsensual, intentional, and offensive touching of another without lawful justification, but not necessarily with the intent to do harm or offense as required in a criminal battery. — Also termed *tortious battery.* Cf. ASSAULT. — **batter,** *vb.*

> "A *battery* is the actual application of force to the body of the prosecutor. It is, in other words, the assault brought to completion. Thus, if a man strikes at another with his cane and misses him, it is an assault; if he hits him, it is a battery. But the slightest degree of force is sufficient, provided that it be applied in a hostile manner; as by pushing a man or spitting in his face. Touching a man to attract his attention to some particular matter, or a friendly slap on the back is not battery, owing to the lack of hostile intention." 4 *Stephen's Commentaries on the Laws of England* 62–63 (L. Crispin Warmington ed., 21st ed. 1950).

battle of the forms. (1947) The conflict between the terms of standard forms exchanged between a buyer and a seller during contract negotiations. • UCC § 2-207 addresses battles of the forms by abandoning the common-law requirement of mirror-image acceptance and providing that a definite expression of acceptance may create a contract for the sale of goods even though it contains different or additional terms. — Also termed *UCC battle of the forms.* See MIRROR-IMAGE RULE.

> "The rules of offer and acceptance are difficult to apply in certain circumstances known as the 'battle of the forms' where parties want to enter into a contract, but jockey for position in an attempt to use the rules of law so as to ensure that the contract is on terms of their choosing." P.S. Atiyah, *An Introduction to the Law of Contract* 54 (3d ed. 1981).

batture (bə-**tyoor** *or* ba-**toor**), *n.* [French] (1856) The part of a riverbed that is not covered by water at the low-water mark but is covered at the high-water mark; specif., soil, stone, or other alluvial material that builds against a riverbank and occasionally, with fluctuations in water levels, breaks the surface of the water. • The term is especially common in Louisiana. See ALLUVION (2).

> "Since colonial days batture has been subject to a servitude of the State [of Louisiana] for use in the construction and maintenance of levees. It may be used for these purposes without the payment of compensation to the owner." *General Box Co. v. U.S.*, 351 U.S. 159, 160, 76 S.Ct. 728, 730 (1956).

Baumes Law. A statute that provides for stricter criminal prosecution and penalties up to life imprisonment for an offender who has four convictions for felonies or certain misdemeanors. • The first Baumes Law, named for New York state Senator Caleb H. Baumes, was passed by the New York legislature in 1926. Cf. THREE-STRIKES LAW.

bawd, *n.* (14c) *Archaic.* A person, usu. a woman, who solicits customers for a prostitute; a madam. See DISORDERLY HOUSE (2). Cf. PIMP.

bawdy house. See DISORDERLY HOUSE (2).

bay, *n.* (14c) *Int'l law.* An inlet of the sea, over which the coastal country exercises jurisdiction to enforce its environmental, immigration, and customs laws.

▸ **historic bay.** (1975) A bay that, because of its shape, would not be considered a bay subject to the coastal country's jurisdiction, except for that country's longstanding unilateral claim over it; a bay over which the coastal country has traditionally asserted and maintained dominion.

Bayh–Dole Act. *Patents.* A federal statute that permits the U.S. government to take title to or require licensing of nongovernmental inventions made by small businesses and nonprofit organizations while participating in federally funded programs. • Under the Act, an entity funded by the federal government must timely disclose any invention made in the course of a federally funded program. The entity may elect to retain title and to file and prosecute a patent application covering the invention. If the entity retains title to the invention, the government may still "march in" to force the entity to grant exclusive or nonexclusive licenses in appropriate circumstances. The Act is codified in 35 USCA §§ 200–212. — Also termed *Patent and Trademark Law Amendments Act.* See MARCH-IN RIGHTS.

BCA. *abbr.* See *business-continuation agreement* under AGREEMENT.

BCD. See *bad-conduct discharge* under DISCHARGE (8).

BCD special court-martial. See COURT-MARTIAL (2).

BCIA. *abbr.* BERNE CONVENTION IMPLEMENTATION ACT.

BCRA. *abbr.* BIPARTISAN CAMPAIGN REFORM ACT.

BCS. *abbr.* BATTERED-CHILD SYNDROME.

BEA. *abbr.* BUREAU OF ECONOMIC ANALYSIS.

beadle (**beed**-əl), *n.* (bef. 12c) **1.** *Hist.* A court crier with duties similar to those of a constable. See NUNTIUS (3). **2.** *Hist. Eccles. law.* A minor parish officer who serves the vestry's needs in various ways, including giving notice of the vestry's meetings, executing its orders, and attending its inquests. **3.** A macebearer at Oxford University or Cambridge University. — Also spelled *bedel.*

beak, *n.* (16c) *BrE Slang.* A magistrate or justice of the peace.

bear, *n. Securities.* A dealer, investor, or speculator who believes that the prices of securities or commodities will fall in the short term and therefore sells investments in hopes of building a portfolio later at a lower price. Cf. BULL (3).

bear, *vb.* (bef. 12c) **1.** To support or carry <bear a heavy load>. **2.** To produce as yield <bear interest>. **3.** To give as testimony <bear witness>.

bear drive. See BEAR RAID.

bearer, *n.* (13c) Someone who possesses a negotiable instrument marked "payable to bearer" or indorsed in blank.

bearer bill. See BILL (6).

bearer bill of lading. See BILL OF LADING.

bearer bond. See BOND (3).

bearer check. See CHECK.

bearer document. See *bearer paper* under PAPER.

bearer draft. See *bearer check* under CHECK.

bearer form. (1921) The condition of a security that runs to bearer according to its terms and not by reason of any indorsement.

bearer instrument. See *bearer paper* under PAPER.

bearer paper. See PAPER.

bearer security. See SECURITY (4).

bearer stock. See STOCK.

bear hug. (1977) *Slang.* A (usu. hostile) takeover strategy in which the acquiring entity offers the target firm a price per share that is significantly higher than market value, essentially forcing the target's board to accept because of its obligation to act in the best interests of its shareholders.

▸ **reverse bear hug.** (2001) A maneuver by which a takeover target responds to a bidder's offer by showing a willingness to negotiate but demanding a much higher price than that offered. • This is usu. an antitakeover tactic.

bear market. See MARKET.

bear raid. (1970) *Slang.* High-volume stock selling by a large trader in an effort to drive down a stock price in a short time. • Bear raids are prohibited by federal law. — Also termed *bear drive.*

beat, *n.* (18c) **1.** A law-enforcement officer's patrol territory. **2.** A colloquial term for the principal county subdivision in some southern states, such as Alabama, Mississippi, and South Carolina. **3.** A voting precinct.

be at the horn. *Scots law.* See PUT TO THE HORN.

beaupleader (boh-**plee**-dər), *n.* [Law French "fair pleading"] (13c) *Hist.* **1.** A fine imposed for bad or unfair pleading. **2.** A writ of prohibition that prevented a sheriff from taking a fine for bad pleading. • The Statute of Marlborough (1267) prohibited the taking of fines for this type of pleading. See PROHIBITION (2).

***Beauregard* claim.** (1998) *Patents.* A patent claim covering computer software that contains instructions for a computer to perform a particular process. • The term derives from *In re Beauregard,* 53 F.3d 1583 (Fed. Cir. 1995).

beauty contest. *Slang.* A meeting at which a major client interviews two or more law firms to decide which firm to hire.

bedel. See BEADLE.

bederepre. See BEDRIP.

bedrip. (13c) *Hist.* A copyhold tenant's service of reaping the landlord's grain. — Also spelled *bederepre; biderepe.*

bedside court. See COURT.

before-and-after theory. (1961) *Antitrust.* A method of determining antitrust damages for lost profits (and sometimes overcharges), whereby the plaintiff's profits are examined before, during, and after the violation to estimate the reduction in profits due to the defendant's violation. — Also termed *before-and-after method.* Cf. YARDSTICK THEORY; MARKET-SHARE THEORY (1).

> "In its simplest form, the [before-and-after] theory looks at the plaintiff's net profits before and after the injury period, discounts all dollars to their present value, and gives the plaintiff a sum that, before trebling, will bring its earnings during the injury period up to the same average level as its earnings during the noninjury periods." Herbert Hovenkamp, *Economics and Federal Antitrust Law* § 16.7, at 450 (1985).

before first action, *adv.* (1986) *Patents.* After the filing of a patent application but before the mailing of any office action by the U.S. Patent and Trademark Office examiner. • For example, an applicant typically files an information disclosure statement before first action, and often files preliminary amendments as well.

before the fact. (17c) In advance of an event of legal significance.

beg, *vb.* (13c) **1.** To request earnestly; to beseech. **2.** *Hist.* To request to be appointed as guardian for (a person). **3.** *Hist.* To request that someone be appointed as guardian for. **4.** To ask for charity, esp. habitually or pitiably.

beggar, *n.* (13c) Someone who communicates with people, often in public places, asking for money, food, or other necessities for personal use, often as a habitual means of making a living.

beggar-thy-neighbor policy. (1963) A government's protectionist course of action taken to discourage imports by raising tariffs and instituting nontariff barriers, usu. to reduce domestic unemployment and increase domestic output. • This term is sometimes applied to competitive currency devaluation.

beg the question. To engage in the fallacious assumption that a premise is true despite the lack of any warrant for so assuming; esp., to make an argument in which the point to be proved is implicitly taken for granted. See PETITIO PRINCIPII.

> "All of the tricks, pitfalls, irrelevancies, and fallacies we seek to prevent can be gathered under the heading of begging the question, which assumes as true that which must be proved. Laying a proper foundation represents the other pole. Begging the question is the extreme opposite of laying a foundation. 'Accept my argument because it is acceptable. Believe me because I am credible.' Well, saying does not make it so. You require adequate, relevant evidence in support of anyone's statement." Robert J. Dudley, *Think Like a Lawyer* 161 (1980).

behalf. [fr. Anglo-Saxon *healf* "unit, side"] Side, part, advantage, or interest. • The phrase *in behalf of* traditionally means "in the interest, support, or defense of"; *on behalf of* means "in the name of, on the part of, as the agent or representative of."

behavioral science. (1941) The body of disciplines (psychology, sociology, anthropology) that study human behavior.

behoof, *n.* (13c) *Archaic.* A use, profit, or advantage that is part of a conveyance <to his use and behoof>. — **behoove,** *vb.*

beige book. *Slang.* The popular name of the Federal Reserve's *Summary of Commentary on Current Economic Conditions by Federal Reserve District*, a publication that summarizes the economic conditions in each of the 12 Federal Reserve Bank regions. • Each Federal Reserve Bank gathers information from reports submitted by bank and branch directors; through interviews with economists, market experts, and key business contacts; and from other sources. The beige book is published eight times each year.

Bekanntmachung im Patentblatt. [German] *Patents.* The date on which a Gebrauchsmuster (German petty patent) is published and made available to the public.

belief, *n.* (12c) A state of mind that regards the existence or truth of something as likely or relatively certain; conviction about the truth of something.

▸ **conscientious belief.** (18c) A moral conviction so fundamental, and usu. so long-standing, that one feels duty-bound to obey it despite significant discomfort, suffering, or material loss. • A conscientious belief must be sincere and must be uninfluenced by any consideration of personal advantage or disadvantage, either to oneself or to others.

▸ **delusional belief.** (1938) A fake or bizarre belief that derives usu. from a psychological disturbance; DELUSION.

▸ **false belief.** (16c) A misconception deriving from either incorrect perceptions or faulty reasoning.

▸ **reasonable belief.** A sensible belief that accords with or results from using the faculty of reason.

belief–action distinction. (1966) *Constitutional law.* In First Amendment law, the Supreme Court's distinction between allowing a person to follow any chosen belief and allowing the state to intervene if necessary to protect others from the practices of that belief.

belief-cluster. (1962) In critical legal studies, a group of unconnected ideas or opinions that appear to be related when considered together in reference to a specific subject, such as racism, sexism, or religious intolerance.

believe, *vb.* (12c) **1.** To feel certain about the truth of; to accept as true. Cf. SUSPECT, *vb.*

▸ **reasonably believe.** (15c) To believe (a given fact or combination of facts) under circumstances in which a reasonable person would believe.

2. To think or suppose.

belligerency, *n.* (1863) *Int'l law.* **1.** The status assumed by a country that wages war against another country. • The rules of international law require that belligerency between countries be preceded by an absolute declaration of war or an ultimatum setting forth the terms on which the issuing power will refrain from war. **2.** The fact of being belligerent; the quality, state, or condition of waging war.

belligerent, *n.* (1811) A country involved in a war or other armed international conflict. Cf. NEUTRAL, *n.* (1). — **belligerent,** *adj.*

belligerent occupation. See OCCUPATION (3).

bellum (**bel**-əm). [Latin] See WAR (1).

bellum inter duos (**bel**-əm **in**-tər **d[y]oo**-ahs). [Law Latin] (18c) *Hist.* War between two persons; a duel.

bellum justum (**bel**-əm **jəs**-təm). [Latin] (1910) *Int'l law.* A just war; one that the proponent considers morally and legally justifiable, such as a war against an aggressive, totalitarian regime. • Under Roman law, before war could be declared, the *fetiales* (a group of priests who monitored international treaties) had to certify to the Senate that just cause for war existed. With the adoption of the U.N. Charter, the *bellum justum* concept has lost its legal significance. The Charter outlaws the use of force except in self-defense. U.N. Charter arts. 2(4), 51 (59 Stat. 1031). — Also termed *just war; justifiable war.*

bellum justum et pium (**bel**-əm **jes**-təm et **pɪ**-əm). [Latin] *Hist.* Just and pious war.

bellum omnium in omnes (**bel**-əm **om**-nee-əm in **om**-neez). [Latin] *Hist.* War of all against all.

bellwether stock. See *barometer stock* under STOCK.

bellwether trial. (1976) *Torts.* A nonbinding trial of a case, or set of cases, on issues representative of the common claims in a larger mass-tort proceeding, held to determine the merits of the claims and the strength of the parties' positions on the issues. • A bellwether trial is often used as a procedural device to encourage settlements.

belong, *vb.* (14c) **1.** To be the property of a person or thing <this book belongs to the judge>. See OWNERSHIP. **2.** To be connected with as a member <they belong to the state bar>.

belongings, *n. pl.* (1817) **1.** Personal property; EFFECTS. See *personal property* under PROPERTY. **2.** All property, including realty.

below, *prep., adv.* & *adj.* (14c) **1.** Beneath; under; underneath; at a lower level or position than. **2.** At a lower amount, at a lesser rank, or fewer in number than; less than. **3.** (Of a lower court) having heard or having the power to hear the case at issue in the first instance <court below>; at a lower level <the motion was heard below>. Cf. ABOVE.

below-market loan. See *interest-free loan* under LOAN.

below-the-line, *adj.* (1970) *Tax.* (Of a deduction) taken after calculating adjusted gross income and before calculating taxable income. • Examples of below-the-line deductions are medical payments and local taxes. Cf. ABOVE-THE-LINE.

below-the-line tax deduction. See DEDUCTION (2).

***Ben Avon* Doctrine.** (1930) The principle that due process entitles public utilities to judicial review of rates set by public-service commissions. *Ohio Valley Water Co. v. Ben Avon Borough*, 253 U.S. 287, 40 S.Ct. 527 (1920).

bench, *n.* (13c) **1.** The raised area occupied by the judge in a courtroom <approach the bench>. **2.** The court considered in its official capacity <remarks from the bench>. **3.** Judges collectively <bench and bar>. **4.** The judges of a particular court <the Fifth Circuit bench>.

▸ **cold bench.** (1966) A court, esp. an appellate court, in which the judges are largely unfamiliar with the facts and issues of a case, typically because they have not reviewed the briefs or the record before hearing oral arguments. Cf. *hot bench*; *lukewarm bench*.

> "Let's take the cold bench . . . The judges have read neither the briefs nor the record; they know nothing of the case, unless it is one of the few highly publicized cases that reach the newspapers — a Dr. Sheppard or a Texas Gulf Sulphur case — and represent less than 1 percent of all appellate cases. The judges have no preconceived notions as to how your case should be decided. They listen to your argument with an open mind." Samuel E. Gates, "Hot Bench or Cold Bench: When the Court Has Not Read the Brief before Oral Argument," in *Counsel on Appeal* 107, 115 (Arthur A. Charpentier ed., 1968).

▸ **hot bench.** (1966) A court, esp. an appellate court, in which, before oral argument, the judges thoroughly familiarize themselves with the facts and issues of the case, usu. by reading the briefs and the record, and often prepare questions for counsel. • In the United States today, courts are generally expected to be hot. Cf. *cold bench*; *lukewarm bench*.

> "[A] hot bench, in the narrow sense, is one on which all the judges have read the briefs and the salient parts of the record. The court, therefore, is generally familiar with the facts and the legal issues and has devoted some time to thinking about the case, perhaps even to the point of jotting down questions. Obviously, if the appellate tribunal reviewed your case at some prior stage in the proceedings, it must be considered hot. Likewise, if the court has had a good deal of experience in the area of law in which your case falls, I am inclined to classify that bench also as hot." Samuel E. Gates, "Hot Bench or Cold Bench: When the Court Has Not Read the Brief before Oral Argument," in *Counsel on Appeal* 107, 115–16 (Arthur A. Charpentier ed., 1968).

▸ **lukewarm bench.** (1966) A court, esp. an appellate court, in which only some of the judges, before oral argument, have familiarized themselves with the facts and issues of the case. — Also termed *tepid bench*. Cf. *hot bench*; *cold bench*.

> "I must digress, for a moment to discuss what I choose to call the 'tepid,' or 'lukewarm,' bench. That's the bench on which one or more of the panel try to read the briefs or are engaged in conversation with a colleague while the argument is being presented. The judges cannot concentrate on either the brief or the oral argument. You can only hope that the chandelier will fall and fix their attention on at least one thing and that their consciences will so prick them that later, in the quiet of their chambers, they will apply themselves to a study of the briefs without distraction." Samuel E. Gates, "Hot Bench or Cold Bench: When the Court Has Not Read the Brief before Oral Argument," in *Counsel on Appeal* 107, 121–22 (Arthur A. Charpentier ed., 1968).

▸ **tepid bench.** See *lukewarm bench*.

bench blotter. See ARREST RECORD (2).

bench brief. See BRIEF (1).

bench conference. See SIDEBAR CONFERENCE (1).

bench docket. See DOCKET (1).

bencher, *n.* (16c) A governing officer of an English Inn of Court; one of the Masters of the Bench. See INN OF COURT (1).

bench legislation. See JUDGE-MADE LAW (2).

benchmark, *n.* (1842) **1.** *Property.* A mark made on a permanent object by a surveyor to serve as a uniform reference point in making topographic surveys and tidal observations. — Formerly also written *bench mark*. **2.** A standard unit used as a basis for comparison.

bench memo. (1975) **1.** A short brief submitted by a lawyer to a trial judge, often at the judge's request. **2.** A legal memorandum prepared by an appellate judge's law clerk to help the judge in preparing for oral argument and perhaps in drafting an opinion. • A trial-court judge may similarly assign a bench memo to a law clerk for the judge's use in preparing for hearing or trial or in drafting an opinion. **3.** A memo that summarizes the facts and issues in a case, usu. prepared for a judge by a law clerk.

bench opinion. See OPINION (1).

bench parole. See *bench probation* under PROBATION (1).

bench probation. See PROBATION.

bench ruling. (1971) An oral ruling issued by a judge from the bench.

benchslap, *n.* (2005) *Slang.* A judge's sharp rebuke of counsel, a litigant, or perhaps another judge; esp., a scathing remark from a judge or magistrate to an attorney after an objection from opposing counsel has been sustained. • The term, an echo of the offensive and derogatory term *bitch-slap* (a slap delivered in order to humiliate its recipient), was coined in 2005 by David B. Lat, an Assistant U.S. Attorney and blogger. — Also written *bench-slap*. — **benchslap,** *vb.*

bench trial. See TRIAL.

bench warrant. See WARRANT (1).

bene decessit (**ben**-ay di-**ses**-it). [Late Latin "he has left well"] (1834) *Archaic.* **1.** A certificate given to a departing employee, pupil, or curate to assure third parties that he or she has left on good terms and not because of fault or misconduct. **2.** A statement, esp. in writing or in a ceremonious proceeding, that a decedent has died a natural death or has died well.

benefaction (ben-ə-**fak**-shən). (17c) **1.** An instance of doing good or of benefiting; esp., the act of giving something, esp. money, for charitable purposes. **2.** Something, esp. money, that someone gives to a person or organization in order to help the recipient do something good; a benefit conferred. — **benefactor,** *n.*

benefactor payment. See PAYMENT (2).

bene factum (**ben**-ay **fak**-təm). See BONUM FACTUM.

benefice (**ben**-ə-fis), *n.* (14c) **1.** *Hist.* A feudal estate in land, held during the life of the tenant. See BENEFICIUM (4).

> "[T]he vassal no longer owns the land, but 'holds' it 'of' the lord — the vassal has become a 'tenant' (from the Latin, 'tenere,' to hold). The vassal's interest in the land so

held, first called a 'benefice,' is now a 'feudum,' anglicised in modern law as 'fee.'" Peter Butt, *Land Law* 52 (3d ed. 1996).

2. *Hist. Eccles. law.* An estate held by the Catholic Church in feudal tenure. See BENEFICIUM (1), (2). **3.** An ecclesiastical office endowed with capital assets that provide a living to the officeholder; the position and pay of a Christian priest who is in charge of a parish; a preferment. **4.** The income provided to a priest by a bishopric or parish. **5.** BENEFICIUM (3).

bénéfice (bay-nay-**fees**), *n.* [French "benefit"] *French law.* A benefit or advantage; esp., a privilege given by law rather than by agreement of the parties.

beneficed, *adj.* (15c) Holding a benefice or church preferment <beneficed clergy>.

bénéfice de discussion. [French] BENEFIT OF DISCUSSION.

bénéfice de division. [French] BENEFIT OF DIVISION.

bénéfice d'inventaire. [French] BENEFIT OF INVENTORY.

beneficial, *adj.* (15c) **1.** Favorable; producing benefits; having a helpful, useful, or advantageous effect <beneficial ruling>. **2.** Consisting in a right that derives from something other than legal title <beneficial interest in a trust>.

beneficial association. See *benevolent association* under ASSOCIATION.

beneficial contract of service. See CONTRACT OF SERVICE (1).

beneficial enjoyment. See ENJOYMENT.

beneficial holder of securities. (1976) A holder of equitable title to corporate stock. • The stock is not registered under the holder's name in the corporation's records.

beneficial improvement. See *valuable improvement* under IMPROVEMENT.

beneficial interest. See INTEREST (2).

beneficial owner. See OWNER.

beneficial ownership. See OWNERSHIP.

beneficial power. See POWER (5).

beneficial statute. See *remedial statute* under STATUTE.

beneficial use. See USE (1).

beneficiary (ben-ə-**fish**-ee-er-ee *or* ben-ə-**fish**-ə-ree), *n.* (17c) **1.** Someone who is designated to receive the advantages from an action or change; esp., one designated to benefit from an appointment, disposition, or assignment (as in a will, insurance policy, etc.), or to receive something as a result of a legal arrangement or instrument. **2.** A person to whom another is in a fiduciary relation, whether the relation is one of agency, guardianship, or trust; esp., a person for whose benefit property is held in trust. **3.** Someone who is initially entitled to enforce a promise, whether that person is the promisee or a third party. **4.** Someone who is entitled under a letter of credit to draw or demand payment. **5.** Someone designated to receive money or property from a person who has died. — **beneficiary,** *adj.*

▸ **contingent beneficiary.** (1867) **1.** A person designated by the testator to receive a gift if the primary beneficiary is unable or unwilling to take the gift. — Also termed *contingency beneficiary.* **2.** A person designated in a life-insurance policy to receive the proceeds if the primary beneficiary is unable to do so. — Also termed *secondary beneficiary.*

▸ **creditor beneficiary.** (1894) A third-party beneficiary of a contract who is owed a debt that is to be satisfied by another party's performance under the contract.

"Where a promisee in a contract owes a debt or obligation to a third party and contracts for a performance to be rendered to the third party with the intention that such performance will discharge the debt thus owed by the promisee, the third party is a creditor beneficiary of the promise, entitled to enforce it in an action at law. Here it is plain that there is no intention to benefit the third party in the sense of conferring a gift upon him as in the case of the donee beneficiary. The promisee desires to secure the discharge of his own duty to the third party, and so to benefit himself. Yet 'intent to benefit' is very broadly asserted in the cases as the reason and test of giving the third party the right to enforce the promise. In the creditor beneficiary situation, then, intent to benefit is used in a different sense than in the donee case. Even though the promisee's motive or purpose in buying the promise was not to benefit his creditor but rather himself, yet it was clearly his expressed intent that the third person shall receive the benefit of performance. So intention to benefit in the creditor beneficiary case means an intention to create in the third party an enforceable right to the performance for which the promisee bargained and furnished the consideration." Laurence P. Simpson, *Handbook of the Law of Contracts* 303 (1954).

▸ **direct beneficiary.** See *intended beneficiary.*

▸ **donee beneficiary.** (1925) A third-party beneficiary who is intended to receive the benefit of the contract's performance as a gift from the promisee.

▸ **expectant beneficiary.** See *expectant distributee* under DISTRIBUTEE.

▸ **favored beneficiary.** (1866) A beneficiary of a will who receives disproportionate amounts of the testator's property as compared with others having equal claims to the property, raising the specter of the beneficiary's undue influence over the testator. See UNDUE INFLUENCE.

▸ **incidental beneficiary.** (1901) **1.** A third-party beneficiary who, though benefiting indirectly, is not intended to benefit from a contract and thus does not acquire rights under the contract. Cf. *intended beneficiary.* **2.** A person to whom a settlor of a trust does not manifest an intention to give a beneficial interest but who may benefit from the trust's performance.

▸ **income beneficiary.** (1945) A person entitled to income from property; esp., a person entitled to receive trust income.

▸ **intended beneficiary.** (1845) A third-party beneficiary who is intended to benefit from a contract and thus acquires rights under the contract as well as the ability to enforce the contract once those rights have vested. — Also termed *direct beneficiary.* Cf. *incidental beneficiary* (1).

▸ **life beneficiary.** (1953) Someone who receives payments or other benefits from a trust for life, but who does not own the trust property.

▸ **primary beneficiary.** (1850) The person designated in a life-insurance policy to receive the proceeds when the insured dies.

▸ **secondary beneficiary.** See *contingent beneficiary* (2).

▸ **third-party beneficiary.** (1894) Someone who, though not a party to a contract, stands to benefit from the contract's performance. • For example, if Ann and Bob agree to a contract under which Bob will render some performance to Chris, then Chris is a third-party beneficiary.

▸ **unborn beneficiary.** (1861) Someone who, though not yet born, is named in a general way as sharing in an estate or gift. • An example might be a grandchild not yet born when a grandparent specifies, in a will, that Blackacre is to go to "my grandchildren."

beneficiary deed. See DEED.

beneficiary heir. See HEIR.

beneficiary witness. See WITNESS.

beneficio primo ecclesiastico habendo (ben-ə-**fish**-ee-oh **prɪ**-moh ə-klee-z[h]ee-**as**-tə-koh hə-**ben**-doh). [Latin "having the first ecclesiastical benefice"] (17c) *Hist.* A writ from the king to the lord chancellor ordering the appointment of a named person to the first vacant benefice.

beneficium (ben-ə-**fish**-ee-əm), *n.* [Latin "benefit"] **1.** *Roman law.* A privilege, remedy, or benefit granted by law, such as the *beneficium abstinendi* ("privilege of abstaining"), whereby an heir could refuse to accept an inheritance (and thereby avoid the accompanying debt). **2.** *Hist.* A lease, generally for life, given by a ruler or lord to a freeman. • *Beneficium* in this sense arose on the continent among the German tribes after the collapse of the Roman Empire.

> "All those to whom the Frankish king had given land and to whom the Frankish emperor had granted political authority had received it on certain conditions. They were the recipients of royal favor — a *beneficium*. Their holding came to be so styled." Max Radin, *Handbook of Anglo-American Legal History* 126 (1936).

3. *Hist. English law.* An estate in land granted by the king or a lord in exchange for services. • Originally, a *beneficium* could not be passed to the holder's heirs, in contrast to *feuds*, which were heritable from an early date. Tenants, however, persisted in attempting to pass the property to their heirs, and over time the *beneficium* became a heritable estate. As this process occurred, the meaning of *beneficium* narrowed to a holding of an ecclesiastical nature. See BENEFICE (2).

> "Beneficia were formerly Portions of Land, etc. given by Lords to their Followers for their Maintenance; but afterwards as these Tenures became Perpetual and Hereditary, they left their Name of Beneficia to the Livings of the Clergy, and retained to themselves the Name of Feuds. And Beneficium was an estate in land at first granted for Life only, so called, because it was held ex mero Beneficio of the Donor . . . [b]ut at Length, by the Consent of the Donor, or his Heirs, they were continued for the Lives of the Sons of the Possessors, and by Degrees past into an Inheritance . . . ." Giles Jacob, *A New Law-Dictionary* (8th ed. 1762).

> "In England from almost, if not quite, the earliest moment of its appearance, the word feodum seems not merely to imply, but to denote, a heritable, though a dependent right. But if on the continent we trace back the use of this word, we find it becoming interchangeable with beneficium, and if we go back further we find beneficium interchangeable with precarium. A tenancy at will has, we may say, become a tenancy in fee . . . . The Norman conquest of England occurs at a particular moment in the history of this process. It has already gone far; the words feum, feudum, feodum are fast supplanting beneficium . . . ." 1 Frederick Pollock & Frederic W. Maitland, *The History of English Law Before the Time of Edward I* 67–68 (2d ed. 1898).

4. *Hist. Eccles. law.* A feudal tenure for life in church-owned land, esp. land held by a layperson. • Over time, this sense of *beneficium* faded, and it came to be restricted to that of an ecclesiastical living, i.e., a benefice. See BENEFICE (2), (3).

> "The pope became a feodal lord; and all ordinary patrons were to hold their right of patronage under this universal superior. Estates held by feodal tenure, being originally gratuitous donations, were at that time denominated *beneficia*: their very name as well as constitution was borrowed, and the care of the souls of a parish thence came to be denominated a *benefice*." 4 William Blackstone, *Commentaries on the Laws of England* 106 (1769).

5. *Hist.* A benefit or favor; any particular privilege, such as benefit of clergy (*beneficium clericale*). **6.** BENEFICE (3). — Also termed (in senses 3–5) *benefice*. Pl. ***beneficia***.

beneficium abstinendi (ben-ə-**fish**-ee-əm ab-sti-**nen**-dɪ). [Latin "privilege of abstaining"] *Roman law.* The right of an heir to refuse an inheritance and thus avoid liability for the testator's debts.

> "[T]hese heirs came also to be protected by the praetor, viz. by the *jus* or *beneficium abstinendi*. Provided they took care not to act as heir in any kind of way, then, whether they formally demanded the privilege or not, their own property could not be made liable for their ancestor's debts." R.W. Leage, *Roman Private Law* 220 (C.H. Ziegler ed., 2d ed. 1930).

beneficium cedendarum actionum (ben-ə-**fish**-ee-əm see-den-**day**-rəm ak-shee-**oh**-nəm). [Latin "privilege of having actions made over"] (18c) *Roman & Scots law.* The right of a cosurety who might or might not have paid the debt to compel the creditor to give over the right of action against the debtor and the other cosureties. • Under Scots law, a cosurety's (or *cocautioner's*) right of action against the nonpaying cosurety arises on payment, without the necessity of compelling the creditor to assign the action. But in Roman law, the right of action arose before the paying of the debt.

beneficium competentiae (ben-ə-**fish**-ee-əm kom-pə-**ten**-shi-ee). [Latin "privilege of competency"] (18c) *Roman & Scots law.* A debtor's right to be ordered to pay only as much as the debtor reasonably could, so that after assigning his or her estate to creditors, the debtor kept enough to live on. See ASSIGNMENT FOR THE BENEFIT OF CREDITORS; SALVO BENEFICIO COMPETENTIAE.

beneficium divisionis (ben-ə-**fish**-ee-əm di-vizh-ee-**oh**-nis). See BENEFIT OF DIVISION.

beneficium inventarii (ben-ə-**fish**-ee-əm in-ven-**tay**-ree-ɪ *or* in-ven-**tair**-ee-ɪ). [Latin "with the benefit of inventory"] (18c) *Roman law.* The right of an heir to take an inventory within a set time before deciding whether to accept an inheritance. • An heir could provisionally take the succession and disclaim responsibility for debts beyond the estate's value until the inventory was completed and the inheritance accepted or rejected. This right was introduced by Justinian. — Also termed *cum beneficio inventarii* (kəm ben-ə-**fish**-ee-oh in-ven-**tair**-ee-ɪ).

beneficium ordinis (ben-ə-**fish**-ee-əm **or**-də-nis). [Latin "privilege of order"] (18c) *Roman & Scots law.* A surety's right to require a creditor to seek payment from the principal debtor before seeking payment from the surety. See BENEFIT OF DISCUSSION.

> "Beneficium Ordinis . . . by the civil law and our own, a cautioner, simply bound as such, is entitled to insist that

the principal be first discussed by extreme diligence." Hugh Barclay, *A Digest of the Law of Scotland* 76 (3d ed. 1865).

beneficium separationis (ben-ə-**fish**-ee-əm sep-ə-ray-shee-**oh**-nis). [Latin "privilege of separation"] *Roman law.* The right of a creditor of the deceased to have the property of the deceased separated from an heir's property. • This separation protected the creditors by ensuring that the deceased's property was not used to pay the heir's creditors. — Also termed *separatio bonorum.*

benefit, *n.* (14c) **1.** The advantage or privilege something gives; the helpful or useful effect something has <the benefit of owning a car>. **2.** Profit or gain; esp., the consideration that moves to the promisee <a benefit received from the sale>. — Also termed *legal benefit; legal value.* Cf. DETRIMENT (2).

▸ **benefit officiously conferred.** (1948) A profit, gain, or advantage bestowed on another without the encouragement or even acquiescence of the person so enriched, the result being that there is no obligation to make restitution. • The person who so confers the benefit is known as a "mere volunteer" or (pejoratively) "officious intermeddler." See VOLUNTEER (4); OFFICIOUS INTERMEDDLER.

▸ **collateral benefit.** (18c) Any benefit incidental or in addition to a principal one.

▸ **death benefit.** (*usu. pl.*) (1873) A sum or sums paid to a beneficiary from a life-insurance policy on the death of an insured.

▸ **fringe benefit.** (1952) A benefit (other than direct salary or compensation) received by an employee from an employer, such as insurance, a company car, or a tuition allowance. — Often shortened (esp. in pl.) to *benefit.*

▸ **general benefit.** (1925) *Eminent domain.* The whole community's benefit as a result of a taking. • It cannot be considered to reduce the compensation that is due the condemnee.

▸ **peculiar benefit.** See *special benefit.*

▸ **pecuniary benefit.** (17c) A benefit capable of monetary valuation.

▸ **private benefit.** See PRIVATE BENEFIT.

▸ **special benefit.** (1857) *Eminent domain.* A benefit that accrues to the owner of the land in question and not to any others. • Any special benefits justify a reduction in the damages payable to the owner of land that is partially taken by the government during a public project. — Also termed *peculiar benefit.*

3. Financial assistance that is received from an employer, insurance, or a public program (such as social security) in time of sickness, disability, or unemployment <a benefit from the welfare office>. **4.** *Constitutional law.* A privilege or dispensation that the state is not constitutionally required to provide, esp. one offered in conditions that raise difficult constitutional questions under the unconstitutional-conditions doctrine. — Also termed *gratuitous benefit.* See UNCONSTITUTIONAL-CONDITIONS DOCTRINE. — **benefit,** *vb.*

benefit association. See *benevolent association* under ASSOCIATION.

benefit certificate. See CERTIFICATE.

benefit of an earlier filing date. (1930) *Patents & Trademarks.* For a patent or trademark applicant, the advantage of being assigned the filing date of a related, earlier-filed application. • Under 35 USCA § 119, a U.S. patent application is given the filing date of an earlier foreign application filed in accordance with the Paris Convention as long as the U.S. filing occurs not more than one year after the foreign filing. Meanwhile, a continuing application filed in accordance with 35 USCA § 120 is given the filing date of an earlier-filed U.S. application. Similarly, under 15 USCA § 1126(d), a U.S. trademark applicant receives the filing date of an earlier-filed foreign application if (1) the foreign application was filed in a Paris Convention country; and (2) the U.S. application is filed within six months after the foreign application. — Also termed *benefit of priority filing date; claim of priority.*

benefit-of-bargain rule. See BENEFIT-OF-THE-BARGAIN RULE.

benefit of cession. (16c) *Civil law.* A debtor's immunity from imprisonment for debt. • The immunity arises when the debtor's property is assigned to the debtor's creditors. See CESSIO BONORUM.

benefit of clergy. (15c) **1.** At common law, the privilege of a cleric not to be tried for a felony in the King's Court <in the Middle Ages, any man who could recite the "neck verse" was granted the benefit of clergy>. • Although *clergy* includes monks and nuns as well as priests, only in rare cases did women claim or receive benefit of clergy. Congress outlawed benefit of clergy in federal courts in April 1790. It was abolished in England in 1827 but survived even longer in some American states, such as South Carolina, where it was successfully claimed in 1855. *State v. Bosse,* 42 S.C.L. (8 Rich.) 276 (1855). — Also termed *clergy privilege; clericale privilegium.* See NECK VERSE.

"Benefit of clergy was a remarkable privilege which, although now obsolete, was for centuries of great importance in criminal law. Some knowledge of it is even now essential for a proper understanding of common law crimes. After William the Conqueror separated the ecclesiastical from the secular courts, the clergy put forward the claim that all persons in holy orders should be exempt from secular jurisdiction in all proceedings, civil or criminal. Eventually the rule was established that 'clerks' of all kinds, who committed any of the serious crimes termed felonies, could be tried only in an ecclesiastical court, and therefore were only amenable to such punishments as that court could inflict. Any clerk accused of such crime was accordingly passed over to the bishop's court. He was there tried before a jury of clerks by the oaths of twelve compurgators; a mode of trial which usually ensured him an acquittal." J.W. Cecil Turner, *Kenny's Outlines of Criminal Law* 75 (16th ed. 1952).

"'Benefit of clergy,' in its origin, was the right of a clergyman not to be tried for felony in the King's Court. In ancient times, when the Church was at the peak point of its power, it preempted jurisdiction over felony charges against clergymen. It demanded that in any case in which a clergyman was charged with felony, the case be transferred to the Ecclesiastical Court for trial. The benefit was extreme because conviction of felony in the King's Court resulted in the sentence of death, whereas the Ecclesiastical Court did not make use of capital punishment." Rollin M. Perkins & Ronald N. Boyce, *Criminal Law* 4 (3d ed. 1982).

2. Loosely, religious approval as solemnized by church ritual <the couple had several children without benefit of clergy>. • This common use of the phrase is premised on a misunderstanding of its original meaning (in sense 1).

benefit of counsel. See RIGHT TO COUNSEL (1).

benefit of discussion. (17c) *Civil law.* A guarantor's right to require a creditor to seek payment from the principal debtor before seeking payment from the guarantor. — Also termed (in French law) *bénéfice de discussion*; (in Scots law) *right of discussion*; *beneficium ordinis.*

> "*Benefit of Discussion.* By common law a cautioner, bound simply as such, had right to insist that the creditor should *discuss* the principal debtor, that is, exhaust his estate by diligence, before coming upon him for payment of the debt." William K. Morton & Dale A. Whitman, *Manual of the Law of Scotland* 299 (1896).

benefit of division. (17c) *Civil law.* A surety's right to be sued only for a part of the debt proportionate to the number of solvent cosureties. — Also termed (in Roman law) *beneficium divisionis*; (in French law) *bénéfice de division*; (in Scots law) *right of division.*

benefit officiously conferred. See BENEFIT (2).

benefit of inventory. (18c) *Civil law.* The principle that an heir's liability for estate debts is limited to the value of what is inherited, if the heir so elects and files an inventory of the estate's assets. — Also termed *bénéfice d'inventaire.*

benefit of priority filing date. See BENEFIT OF AN EARLIER FILING DATE.

benefit-of-the-bargain damages. See DAMAGES.

benefit-of-the-bargain rule. (1913) **1.** The principle that a party who breaches a contract must pay the aggrieved party an amount that puts that person in the same financial position that would have resulted if the contract had been fully performed. **2.** The principle that a defrauded buyer may recover from the seller as damages the difference between the value of the property as represented and the actual value received. — Also termed *benefit-of-bargain rule.* Cf. OUT-OF-POCKET RULE.

benefit seniority. See SENIORITY.

benevolent association. See ASSOCIATION.

benevolentia regis habenda (ben-ə-və-**len**-shee-ə **ree**-jis hə-**ben**-də). [Latin "the king's benevolence to be had"] (18c) *Hist.* A fine paid to receive the king's pardon and a restoration of place, title, or estate.

benevolent society. See *benevolent association* under ASSOCIATION.

benign discrimination. See *reverse discrimination* under DISCRIMINATION (3).

Benthamism. See *hedonistic utilitarianism* under UTILITARIANISM.

Benthamite, *adj.* (1829) Of, relating to, or involving the utilitarian theory or other theories of Jeremy Bentham. See *hedonistic utilitarianism* under UTILITARIANISM.

BEP. *abbr.* BUREAU OF ENGRAVING AND PRINTING.

BFPV. *abbr.* See *bona fide purchaser for value* under PURCHASER (1).

bequeath (bə-**kweeth**), *vb.* (12c) **1.** To officially arrange for someone to have (something that one owns) after one's death; esp., to give property (usu. personal property or money) by will. **2.** *Hist.* To assign or transfer real or personal property by formal declaration, either inter vivos or after death. **3.** By extension, to pass on (knowledge, customs, etc.) to people who outlive one or come after one).

bequeathal. See BEQUEST.

bequest (bə-**kwest**), *n.* (14c) **1.** The act of giving property (usu. personal property or money) by will. **2.** The money or other property that a person arranges to give to someone or an organization upon death; esp., property (usu. personal property or money) disposed of in a will. — Also termed *bequeathal* (bə-**kwee**-thəl). Cf. DEVISE; LEGACY.

▸ **charitable bequest.** (18c) A bequest given to a philanthropic organization. See CHARITABLE ORGANIZATION.

▸ **conditional bequest.** (18c) A bequest whose effectiveness or continuation depends on the occurrence or nonoccurrence of a particular event. • An example might be a testator's gift of "the income from the farm to my daughter, Betty, until she remarries." If a condition prohibits certain legal conduct, such as using tobacco or growing a beard, it is sometimes termed a *reformation condition* or *character-improvement condition.*

▸ **demonstrative bequest.** (1905) A bequest that, by its terms, must be paid out of a specific source, such as a stock fund.

▸ **executory bequest.** (18c) A bequest of a future, deferred, or contingent interest in personal property.

▸ **general bequest.** (18c) **1.** A bequest of a general benefit, rather than a particular asset, such as a gift of money or a gift of all the testator's stocks. **2.** A bequest payable out of the general assets of the estate.

▸ **monetary bequest.** See *pecuniary bequest.*

▸ **money bequest.** See *pecuniary bequest.*

▸ **pecuniary bequest.** (18c) A testamentary gift of money; a legacy. — Also termed *monetary bequest*; *money bequest.*

▸ **remainder bequest.** See *residuary bequest.*

▸ **residuary bequest.** (18c) A bequest of the remainder of the testator's estate after the payment of the debts, legacies, and specific bequests. — Also termed *remainder bequest.*

▸ **specific bequest.** (18c) A bequest of a specific or unique item of property, such as any real estate or a particular piece of furniture.

bereavement (bə-**reev**-mənt). (18c) The sense of loss one feels at the death of a relative or close friend.

bereavement leave. See LEAVE.

berewick (**beer**-wik), *n.* [Anglo-Saxon "barely land"] (bef. 12c) *Hist. Land law.* **1.** An outlying parcel of land treated as part of a manor for taxation purposes, even though it might have been located outside the manor. **2.** A village or hamlet inside a manor. — Also spelled *berewic.*

Berlin Act. *Copyright.* A 1908 revision of the Berne Convention prohibiting formalities as a requirement for copyright protection, recommending (but not requiring) a term of protection equal to the life of the author plus 50 years, and expanding the types of works eligible for copyright protection. • Motion pictures were included in copyright protection for the first time. — Also termed *Berlin Act of 1908*; *1908 Berlin Act.*

Berne Additional Protocol. *Copyright.* A 1914 amendment to the Berne Convention providing for reprisals against a foreign national who publishes simultaneously in both a member country and the author's own nonmember and nonreciprocating country. • The reprisal was aimed at the United States, which until 1989 refused to join the Berne Convention but whose citizens could enjoy Berne protection by first publishing in a member country. See BACK DOOR TO BERNE.

Berne Convention. *Copyright.* An international copyright treaty providing that works created by citizens of one signatory country will be fully protected in other signatory countries, without the need for local formalities. • The treaty was drafted in Berne in 1886 and has been revised many times since. It is now administered by the World Intellectual Property Organization and prescribes minimum levels and terms of copyright protection. The United States ratified the Berne Convention in 1989 and changed several aspects of U.S. copyright law to comply with the treaty's terms. — Also spelled *Bern Convention.* — Also termed *Berne Copyright Convention*; *Berne Convention for the Protection of Literary and Artistic Property.* See CONGRESS OF AUTHORS AND ARTISTS.

Berne Convention Implementation Act. *Copyright.* The 1988 federal law making the United States a signatory to the Berne Convention, 102 years after the convention was first opened for signatures. • The law ended rigid formalities for registration and marking, although registration is still required before United States-copyright owners can sue for infringement. Pub. L. No. 100-568, 102 Stat. 2853. — Abbr. BCIA.

Berne Copyright Convention. See BERNE CONVENTION.

Berne-minus, *adj.* (1997) *Copyright.* Of, relating to, or involving the second sentence of Art. 9(1) of the TRIPs Agreement, which provides that intellectual-property rights and duties under the Berne Convention will not be expressly enforced on noncomplying signators through the TRIPs Agreement. U.S. reluctance to expressly protect moral rights of authors and artists has been criticized as a "Berne-minus" attitude.

Berne Paris Act. *Copyright.* A 1971 revision of the Berne Convention reducing the obligations of countries that became members as colonies of signatories. — Also termed *1971 Paris Act of the Berne Convention.*

Berne-plus, *adj.* (1987) *Copyright.* Of, relating to, or involving a copyright-treaty provision that affords greater intellectual-property protection than the minimum required by the Berne Convention, either by granting stronger rights or by extending protection to new forms of subject matter. • The term arose during negotiations over the TRIPs Agreement, reflecting the principle that the treaty should incorporate and build on existing international law. The WIPO treaties are said to be "Berne-plus" treaties because they incorporate Berne protections and add additional protections of their own.

Berne Safeguard Clause. *Copyright.* A provision in the Universal Copyright Convention barring protection in Berne Union countries for the works of any country that withdraws from the Berne Union after January 1, 1951. • The purpose of the clause was to prevent countries from withdrawing from the Berne Union in favor of the more relaxed copyright-protection standards of the Convention. The clause was amended in 1971 to give developing countries the right to opt out of its mandate.

Berne Union. *Copyright.* The treaty alliance of Berne Convention member countries.

***Berry* rule.** (1956) *Criminal law.* The doctrine that a defendant seeking a new trial on grounds of newly discovered evidence must show that (1) the evidence is newly discovered and was unknown to the defendant at the time of trial; (2) the evidence is material rather than merely cumulative or impeaching; (3) the evidence will probably produce an acquittal; and (4) the failure to learn of the evidence was not due to the defendant's lack of diligence. *Berry v. State,* 10 Ga. 511 (1851).

berth charter. See *dock charter* under CHARTER (8).

berth charterparty. See CHARTERPARTY.

Bertillon system (**bər**-tə-lon *or* bair-tee-**yawn**). (1888) A system of anthropometry once used to identify criminals by measuring and describing them. • The Bertillon system is named for Alphonse Bertillon, the French anthropologist who developed the technique in the late 19th century. It has been largely replaced by fingerprinting. Cf. ANTHROPOMETRY.

> "The system of identification known as the Bertillon system is worked out on the assumption that an individual's physical measurements are constant after maturity is attained. Such measurements include height, span of arms, sitting height, length of head, width of right ear, length of left foot, length of left middle finger, length of left little finger, and length of left forearm. The Bertillon system also records photographs (front and profile), hair and eye color, complexion, scars, tattoo marks and any asymmetrical anomalies." *Encyclopedia of Criminology* 81–82 (Vernon C. Branham & Samuel B. Kutash eds., 1949), s.v. "Criminalistics."

bes (bes), *n.* [Latin] **1.** *Roman law.* Two-thirds of the Roman *as*, or pound, consisting of eight *unciae* (ounces) out of twelve. See AS; UNCIA. **2.** *Civil law.* Two-thirds of an inheritance.

besayel (bes-**ay**-əl), *n.* [Law French] (16c) *Hist.* **1.** A writ of right used by a great-grandfather's heirs to recover property held by the great-grandfather. See *assize of mort d'ancestor* under ASSIZE (6). **2.** A great-grandfather. — Also spelled *besaiel*; *besaile*; *bisaile*; *besayle.* Cf. AIEL; COSINAGE.

besluit (bi-**sloyt**), *n.* [Dutch "decision"] (1891) *Roman–Dutch law.* A legislative resolution or decree.

"besotted" test. A standard of intoxication that may defeat mens rea, and therefore provide a defense, if the defendant was so inebriated as to have been unable to form any mental intent. See *intoxication defense* under DEFENSE (1).

bespeaks-caution doctrine. (1993) *Securities.* The principle that if soft information in a prospectus is accompanied by cautionary language that adequately warns investors that actual results or events may affect performance, then the soft information may not be materially misleading to investors. • Soft information includes forecasts, estimates, opinions, and projections about future performance. The doctrine was codified in the Private Securities Litigation Reform Act of 1995.

best alternative to a negotiated agreement. (1981) A person's or party's optimal substitute course of action to take if a proposed agreement with another party does not materialize or proves unsatisfactory. — Abbr. BATNA.

best bid. See BID (1).

best edition. (1880) *Copyright.* A particular version of a copyrighted work that is published in the U.S. before the date of deposit and that is designated by the Library of Congress, in its discretion, as the most suitable for its purposes. • Two copies of a copyrighted work, in the selected best-edition form, must be deposited with the Library.

best efforts. (17c) Diligent attempts to carry out an obligation <the contractor must use best efforts to complete its work within the stated time>. • As a standard, a best-efforts obligation is stronger than a good-faith obligation. Best efforts are measured by the measures that a reasonable person in the same circumstances and of the same nature as the acting party would take. — Also termed *best endeavors.* Cf. *due diligence* (1) under DILIGENCE (2); GOOD FAITH.

> "The orthodox view is that a contractual provision requiring *best efforts* imposes extraordinary duties of assiduity: a very high standard of care, regardless of whether the required efforts might be commercially unreasonable. A provision requiring *reasonable efforts* is generally thought to impose a lesser standard of diligence. . . . In truth, both *best efforts* and *reasonable efforts* are vague phrases, and purposely so. The application of these requirements to the actual situation gives the decision-maker a good deal of latitude. As noted, the majority view is for courts to consider *best efforts* as imposing a higher standard than *reasonable efforts*. But others treat the two as synonymous. Perhaps the safest course is, when possible, to use a *best-efforts* provision when insisting on an opposite number's performance — and to use a *reasonable-efforts* provision for one's own client's performance. Yet the phrases are fuzzy, the judicial decisions irreconcilable, and the effects admittedly uncertain." Bryan A. Garner, *Garner's Dictionary of Legal Usage* 108 (3d ed. 2011).

best-efforts contract. See CONTRACT.

best-efforts underwriting. See UNDERWRITING.

best embodiment. See BEST MODE.

best endeavors. See BEST EFFORTS.

best evidence. See EVIDENCE.

best-evidence rule. (1894) The evidentiary rule providing that, to prove the contents of a writing (or a recording or photograph), a party must produce the original writing (or a mechanical, electronic, or other familiar duplicate, such as a photocopy) unless it is unavailable, in which case secondary evidence — the testimony of the drafter or a person who read the document — may be admitted. Fed. R. Evid. 1001–1004. — Also termed *documentary-originals rule*; *original-writing rule*; *original-document rule.*

> "Down to a century or more ago, the term 'best evidence' was a good deal used; 'the best evidence that the nature of the thing will afford' was said to be required. But this loose expression never represented a concrete rule. The only positive and concrete rules of the kind are those above named. And today, though the cant phrase is sometimes invoked, and though an inference may be made against a party who fails to produce what might be better evidence, yet no court will in general exclude relevant evidence because there might be better evidence available." John H. Wigmore, *A Students' Textbook of the Law of Evidence* 219 (1935).

bestiality (bes-chee-**al**-ə-tee), *n.* (14c) Sexual activity between a human and an animal. • Some authorities restrict the term to copulation between a human and an animal of the opposite sex. See SODOMY.

best interests of creditors. (1977) *Bankruptcy.* A test for confirmation of a reorganization plan whereby the court inquires into whether the plan ensures that the value of property to be distributed to each creditor is at least the amount that the creditor would receive if the debtor's estate were liquidated in a Chapter 7 case. • A court may not confirm a plan in a Chapter 9, Chapter 12, or Chapter 13 case unless it is in the best interests of the creditors. In a Chapter 11 case, a court may confirm a plan even though some creditors do not vote to accept it if the court finds that the plan is in the creditors' best interest. 11 USCA §§ 944, 1129(a)(7), 1225(a)(4), 1325(a)(4). — Often shortened to *best interests* or *best interest.* — Also written *best interest of creditors.*

best interests of the child. (1876) *Family law.* A standard by which a court determines what arrangements would be to a child's greatest benefit, often used in deciding child-custody and visitation matters and in deciding whether to approve an adoption or a guardianship. • A court may use many factors, including the emotional tie between the child and the parent or guardian, the ability of a parent or guardian to give the child love and guidance, the ability of a parent or guardian to provide necessaries, the established living arrangement between a parent or guardian and the child, the child's preference if the child is old enough that the court will consider that preference in making a custody award, and a parent's ability to foster a healthy relationship between the child and the other parent. — Abbr. BIC. — Often shortened to *best interests* or *best interest.* — Also termed *best interest of the child.* See BEST-INTERESTS-OF-THE-CHILD DOCTRINE. Cf. PARENTAL-PREFERENCE DOCTRINE.

best-interests-of-the-child doctrine. (1954) *Family law.* The principle that courts should make custody decisions based on whatever best advances the child's welfare, regardless of a claimant's particular status or relationship with the child. • One important factor entering into these decisions is the general belief that the child's best interests normally favor custody by parents, as opposed to grandparents or others less closely related. The doctrine is quite old, having been stated, for example, in the early 19th-century case of *Commonwealth v. Briggs*, 33 Mass. 203 (1834). — Sometimes shortened to *best-interests doctrine*; *best-interest doctrine.* See BEST INTERESTS OF THE CHILD. Cf. PARENTAL-PREFERENCE DOCTRINE.

best mode. *Patents.* The best way that the inventor knows to work the invention described and claimed in a patent or patent application. • A patent application must disclose the best mode known to the inventor at the time of the filing. Failure to disclose the best mode can render a patent invalid. 35 USCA § 112(a). — Also termed *best embodiment.* See BEST-MODE REQUIREMENT. Cf. ENABLEMENT REQUIREMENT.

best-mode requirement. (1967) *Patents.* The requirement that a patent application show the best physical method known to the inventor for using the invention. See BEST MODE. Cf. ENABLEMENT REQUIREMENT.

bestow, *vb.* (14c) To convey as a gift; to confer <bestow an honor on another>. See CONFER. — **bestowal,** *n.*

best practice. (*often pl.*) (1984) **1.** An optimally efficient and effective mode of proceeding or performing a particular activity, esp. in business. **2.** A description of such a mode of proceeding or performing prepared so that other people or companies may learn and follow it as a set of guidelines or rules.

best rent. See *open-market rent* under RENT.

best use. See *highest and best use* under USE (1).

bet, *n.* (16c) **1.** Something (esp. money) staked or pledged as a wager. — **bet,** *vb.* — **betting,** *n.* — **bettor,** *n.*

▸ **layoff bet.** (1925) A bet placed by a bookmaker to protect against excessive losses or to equalize the total amount placed on each side of the wager. See LAYOFF BETTOR.

2. WAGER (2).

beta, *n.* A statistical measure of a security's risk, based on how widely a particular security's return swings as compared to the overall return in the market for that security. • The market's beta is set at 1.0; a security with a beta lower than 1.0 is less risky than the general market, while a security with a beta higher than 1.0 is more so.

beta-test agreement. (1986) *Intellectual property.* A software license agreement, usu. between a software developer and a customer, permitting the customer to use the software program in a "live" environment before its release to the general public. • Beta-test agreements differ from more conventional software licenses in that they typically (1) have more significant limitations on liability; (2) contain few, if any, warranties; and (3) require user evaluation and feedback. — Also termed *software beta-test agreement.*

beta testing. (1982) *Intellectual property.* The process of testing products and services, esp. software, under real-life conditions. • Consumers often engage in beta testing at no cost in exchange for reporting to the developer how satisfied they are, any problems they encounter, and any suggested improvements. To protect a trade secret or to avoid a statutory bar, the developer may require the user to sign a nondisclosure agreement. Cf. ALPHA TESTING.

bet din. See BETH DIN.

beth din. (18c) [Hebrew "court of law"] A rabbinical tribunal empowered by Jewish law to decide and enforce matters of Jewish law and custom; esp., a tribunal consisting of three rabbis who decide questions of Jewish law. — Also spelled *bet din.*

betrothal, *n.* (1844) **1.** *Eccles. law.* A religious ceremony confirming an agreement to marry. • Historically, a betrothal was performed months or years before the parties wedded. It was in theory as legally binding as a marriage and created an impediment to marriage with any other person, but not an insurmountable impediment. In modern form, the betrothal is usu. part of the marriage ceremony. — Also termed *betrothment.* See ENGAGEMENT (2). Cf. *precontract* under CONTRACT; ESPOUSALS. **2.** *Slang.* A corporate merger agreement.

betrothment. See BETROTHAL (1).

betterment, *n.* (18c) **1.** An improvement that increases the value of real property; esp., an enhancement in the nature of an alteration or addition that goes beyond repair or restoration to a former condition. **2.** An improvement of a highway, railroad, or building that goes beyond repair or restoration. **3.** An increase in value, esp. real-estate value, attributable to improvements. See IMPROVEMENT.

betterment act. (1819) A statute requiring a landowner to compensate an occupant who improves the land under a mistaken belief that the occupant is the real owner. • The compensation usu. equals the increase in the land's value generated by the improvements. — Also termed *occupying-claimant act; occupant statute.*

betterment tax. (1876) A tax for the improvement of highways.

betting. See PARIMUTUEL BETTING.

beyond a reasonable doubt. See REASONABLE DOUBT.

beyond seas. (16c) *Hist.* **1.** (Of a person) being absent from a jurisdiction or country; out of the country, esp. across the ocean. • This term was used when a person could not be served with a summons, notice, etc. because the person was absent from the jurisdiction. Some jurisdictions toll the statute of limitations during a defendant's absence. **2.** Out-of-state. • Although originally *beyond seas* meant "out of the country," the U.S. Supreme Court declared that the term includes absence from a state. *Murray's Lessee v. Baker,* 16 U.S. 541, 545 (1818). — Also termed *beyond sea; beyond the seas; ultra mare.*

> "[I]t has been provided that if any person or persons *against* whom there shall be any cause of action shall at the time of its accrual be beyond seas, then the person or persons entitled to any such cause of action shall be at liberty to bring the same against such person or persons within such time as before limited, after his or their return from beyond seas." John Indermaur, *Principles of the Common Law* 240 (Edmund H. Bennett ed., 1st Am. ed. 1878).

b.f. *abbr.* BONUM FACTUM.

BFOQ. *abbr.* BONA FIDE OCCUPATIONAL QUALIFICATION.

BFP. See *bona fide purchaser* under PURCHASER (1).

BFWO. *abbr. Criminal procedure.* Bail forfeited, warrant ordered.

BHC. *abbr.* BANK HOLDING COMPANY.

BIA. *abbr.* **1.** BUREAU OF INDIAN AFFAIRS. **2.** BOARD OF IMMIGRATION APPEALS.

bias, *n.* (16c) A mental inclination or tendency; prejudice; predilection <the juror's bias prompted a challenge for cause>. — **bias,** *vb.* — **biased,** *adj.*

▸ **actual bias.** (1847) Genuine prejudice that a judge, juror, witness, or other person has against some person or relevant subject. Cf. *implied bias.*

▸ **advocate's bias.** (1971) The bias that attorneys often develop in favor of a client involved in a dispute and that may potentially cause such missteps as overlooking certain arguments or misjudging the way facts or legal precedents may appear to a dispassionate observer.

▸ **implied bias.** (1851) Bias, as of a juror, that the law conclusively presumes because of kinship or some other incurably close relationship; prejudice that is inferred from the experiences or relationships of a judge, juror, witness, or other person. — Also termed *presumed bias.* Cf. *actual bias.*

▸ **inferable bias.** (1997) A prospective juror's bias that does not rise to the level of an implied bias — because, for example, no blood relationship or other clear basis for an improper predilection exists — but that is known to exist because the prospective juror has disclosed a fact that bespeaks a possibility of partiality great enough to warrant a meritorious challenge for cause.

▸ **judicial bias.** (1876) A judge's bias toward one or more of the parties to a case over which the judge presides. • Judicial bias is usu. not enough to disqualify a judge from presiding over a case unless the judge's bias is personal or based on some extrajudicial reason.

▸ **presumed bias.** See *implied bias.*

bias rule. (1949) **1.** A principle of procedural fairness requiring a decision-maker not to be personally biased and not to appear to a reasonable, informed, detached observer to be prejudiced in any way in legal proceedings or in dealing with some matter in the course of making a decision. • A decision-maker's bias may arise from pecuniary or proprietary interest, from prior or existing associations, from extraneous information, from conduct, or from some other circumstance. — Also termed *anti-bias rule; avoid-bias rule.* **2.** The historian's principle that every historical source is biased in some way, and that even historians who strive to be objective are not entirely free from bias and selective accounts of the facts.

BIC. *abbr.* BEST INTERESTS OF THE CHILD.

bicameral, *adj.* (1832) (Of a legislature) having two legislative houses (usu. called the House of Representatives, or the Assembly, and the Senate). • The federal government and all states except Nebraska have bicameral legislatures.

Bicameral Clause. (1984) *Constitutional law.* The constitutional provision that creates the two legislative chambers of Congress. *See* U.S. Const. art. I, § 1.

bicameralism, *n.* A system of government with two legislative or parliamentary chambers. • Both chambers must pass a bill before it can be presented to the executive and enacted into law.

bid, *n.* (12c) **1.** A buyer's offer to pay a specified price for something that may or may not be for sale <a bid at an auction> <a takeover bid>.

▸ **best bid.** (1839) The highest auction bid; in the letting of a contract, the lowest bid by a qualified bidder.

▸ **bid in,** *n.* A bid made by the owner of auctioned property to ensure that the property is not sold below actual value; a bid better than the previous best offer, made by the property's owner in an effort to keep the property.

▸ **dummy bid.** A bid made in an auction by a person employed by the auctioneer or seller solely to stimulate bidding on the item up for sale. See *fictitious bid.*

▸ **fictitious bid.** A bid not made in good faith, usu. to drive up the price. — Also termed *rafter bid.*

▸ **full-credit bid.** A bid, made by the creditor-beneficiary at a foreclosure sale, equal to the complete unpaid principal and interest, plus costs, fees, and expenses of the sale. • This bid establishes that the value of the security for the debt was equal to the debt, so the debt is fully extinguished.

▸ **market bid.** See *bid price* under PRICE.

▸ **rafter bid.** See *fictitious bid.*

▸ **takeover bid.** See TAKEOVER BID.

▸ **underbid,** *n.* A bid that does not win; esp., the highest bid other than the winning bid.

▸ **upset bid.** (1845) A late bid in a judicial sale made for more than the purchaser's bid so that the sale will be set aside (i.e., upset) because the sale has not yet been confirmed.

2. A submitted price at which one will perform work or supply goods <the subcontractor's bid>. See BID-SHOPPING.

▸ **competitive bid.** (1870) A bid submitted in response to public notice of an intended sale or purchase.

▸ **firm bid.** (1907) A bid that, by its terms, remains open and binding until accepted or rejected. • A firm bid commonly contains no unusual conditions that might defeat acceptance.

▸ **open bid.** (1849) A bid that the bidder may alter after submission so as to meet competing bids.

▸ **sealed bid.** (1849) A bid that is not disclosed until all submitted bids are opened and considered simultaneously.

3. *Slang.* A prison sentence; jail term <state bid> <local bid>.

bid, *vb.* **1.** To ask, request, or invite <bid the guests in>. **2.** To wish earnestly or devoutly; to say by way of friendly greeting or parting <to bid good-day> <to bid farewell>. **3.** To command, order, or direct <do as you were bidden>. **4.** To offer to do work or provide services for a specific price, in competition with other offers <he bid on the job>. **5.** To offer to pay a given price for goods or services, esp. at an auction <she bid $400 on the royal moonflask and won the item>.

▸ **bid in,** *vb.* (Of an owner whose property is being sold at auction) to place a bid higher than the current highest bid in an effort to keep the property.

▸ **bid off,** *vb.* (18c) To purchase by bid at an auction or judicial sale.

▸ **bid out,** *vb.* To offer up work to contractors who may submit bids.

▸ **overbid,** *vb.* (17c) To offer too high a price for something, esp. at an auction.

▸ **underbid,** *vb.* (17c) To offer too low a price for something, esp. at an auction.

bid and asked. (1903) *Securities.* A notation describing the range of prices quoted for securities in an over-the-counter stock exchange. • *Bid* denotes the highest price the buyer is willing to pay, and *asked* denotes the lowest price the seller will accept. See SPREAD (2).

bid bond. See BOND (2).

bidder, *n.* (17c) **1.** Someone who makes a bid; esp., at an auction, one who signals a specific offer to buy the property being auctioned at an announced price. See BID, *n.* & *vb.* **2.** RESPONSIBLE BIDDER.

bidding up. (1823) The act or practice of raising the price for an auction item by making a series of progressively higher bids. • Bidding up is unlawful if the bids are made collusively by persons with an interest in raising the bids. Cf. BY-BIDDING; SHILLING (1).

biderepe. See BEDRIP.

bid in. 1. See BID, *n.* (1). **2.** See BID, *vb.*

bid peddling. See BID-SHOPPING.

bid price. See PRICE.

bid quote. (1972) *Securities.* The price a broker will pay for a security or commodity.

bid-shopping. (1964) A general contractor's effort, after being awarded a contract, to reduce its own costs by finding a subcontractor that will submit a lower bid than the one used in calculating the total contract price. • If a lower bid is obtained, the general contractor will receive a windfall profit because the savings are usu. not passed on to the property owner. The subcontractor whose bid is used in the initial proposal can seek to avoid bid-shopping by insisting that it be irrevocably named in the contract as the project's subcontractor. — Also termed *bid peddling.*

bid wanted. (1960) *Securities.* A dealer's notation that bids are being sought from anyone on a security for sale. • The notation appears in the pink sheets. — Abbr. BW. See PINK SHEET.

biennial session. See SESSION (1).

biennium (bɪ-**en**-ee-əm), *n.* (17c) **1.** A two-year period. **2.** The period for which many state legislatures make appropriations.

biens (beenz *or* byenz). [French] *Hist.* Goods; property. • *Biens* includes real property in most civil-law jurisdictions. Cf. BONA.

bifactoral obligation. See OBLIGATION.

bifurcate. To separate into two parts, esp. for convenience. • Multiple aspects of litigation, such as discovery, motions, defenses, trial, and jury deliberations, may be bifurcated to save time, reduce jury confusion, or achieve other benefits, with or without the same jury hearing both bifurcated parts.

bifurcated divorce. See *divisible divorce* under DIVORCE.

bifurcated hearing. See HEARING.

bifurcated trial. See TRIAL.

bigamous (**big**-ə-məs), *adj.* (17c) **1.** (Of a person) guilty of bigamy. **2.** (Of a marriage) involving bigamy.

bigamus (**big**-ə-məs), *n.* (16c) *Hist.* **1.** Someone who commits bigamy; a bigamist. **2.** A man who marries a widow, or who remarries. • Under ecclesiastical law, a bigamus could be denied benefit of clergy.

bigamy, *n.* (13c) **1.** The act of marrying one person while legally married to another. • Bigamy is distinct from adultery. It is a criminal offense if it is committed knowingly. In 1878, the U.S. Supreme Court held that the government was not constitutionally prohibited from banning Mormon polygamy. *Reynolds v. U.S.*, 98 U.S. (8 Otto) 145 (1878). **2.** *Eccles. law.* The act of marrying a widow or widower, or a divorced person. • Somewhat surprisingly, sense 2 is valid even under modern ecclesiastical law, but it is not an offense, only a bar to entering holy orders. — Also termed *sequential marriage.* See DEUTEROGAMY. Cf. POLYGAMY; MONOGAMY; ADULTERY. — **bigamist,** *n.*

big bath. (1998) *Slang.* A write-off of significant costs, taken to shed an unprofitable business line or to remove the necessity for future write-offs; esp., a business strategy by which a company's income statement is manipulated to make already poor earnings appear even worse so as to make earnings in the near future look better.

big business. (1812) **1.** Collectively, very large companies that form a powerful group with a great deal of economic and political influence <the sway that big business has in the legislature>. **2.** A product or type of activity on which people spend a lot of money <self-improvement has become big business>.

Big Board. (1929) **1.** The New York Stock Exchange. • This sense of *Big Board* may have derived from the former name of the NYSE — New York Stock and Exchange Board. **2.** A quotation display showing the current prices of securities listed on the New York Stock Exchange.

bigotry (**big**-ə-tree), *n.* (17c) **1.** Fiercely held closed-minded beliefs about a group of people one dislikes; such strongly held negative opinions about a group that one is unwilling to listen to others' opinions or contrary evidence. **2.** Obstinate and unreasonable actions ensuing from such beliefs or opinions. — **bigoted,** *adj.* — **bigot,** *n.*

big pot. See MAIN POT.

bilagines (bɪ-**lay**-jə-neez), *n. pl.* [Law Latin] (17c) *Hist.* Town bylaws; laws made by a town's inhabitants for their own government.

bilan (bee-**lahn**), *n.* [French "balance sheet"] *Civil law.* A book used by bankers and merchants to record all that they owe and all that is owed to them; a balance sheet.

bilanciis deferendis (bə-**lan**-shee-is def-ər-**en**-dis). (17c) *Hist.* An obsolete writ ordering a corporation to carry weights to a given place to weigh wool licensed for transportation.

bilateral, *adj.* (18c) Affecting or obligating both parties <a bilateral contract>.

bilateral act. See ACT (2).

bilateral advance pricing agreement. See ADVANCE PRICING AGREEMENT.

bilateral contract. See CONTRACT.

bilateral mistake. See *mutual mistake* (1) under MISTAKE.

bilateral monopoly. See MONOPOLY (2).

bilboes (**bil**-bohz), *n.* (16c) *Hist.* **1.** A device for punishment at sea consisting of a board with holes that secure an offender's hands and feet. Cf. STOCKS. **2.** An iron bar with sliding shackles for confining the ankles of prisoners, esp. on shipboard.

bill, *n.* (14c) **1.** A formal written complaint, such as a court paper requesting some specific action for reasons alleged. **2.** An equitable pleading by which a claimant brings a claim in a court of equity. • Before the merger of law and equity, the bill in equity was analogous to a declaration in law. The nine parts of every equitable bill are (1) the address to the person holding the great seal, (2) the introduction, which identifies the parties, (3) the premises, which state the plaintiff's case, (4) the confederating part, in which the defendants are charged with combination, (5) the charging part, in which the plaintiff may try to overcome defenses that the defendants may allege, (6) the jurisdictional clause, showing that the court has jurisdiction, (7) the interrogating part, inserted to try to compel a full and complete answer, (8) the prayer for relief, and (9) the prayer for process to compel the defendants to appear and answer. — Also termed *bill in chancery; bill of chancery; bill in equity; bill of equity; bill for foreclosure.* See DECLARATION (7).

> "The statement of the plaintiff's cause of action in equity is called the *bill*. To this bill the defendant (unless he could protect himself by a demurrer or a plea) was obliged to put in an *answer* under oath." George Tucker Bispham, *The Principles of Equity: A Treatise on the System of Justice*

Administered in Courts of Chancery § 9, at 12 (11th ed. 1931).

▸ **bill for a new trial.** (18c) A bill in equity to enjoin a judgment and to obtain a new trial because of some fact that would render enforcement of the judgment inequitable. • The fact must have been either unavailable or unknown to the party at trial through fraud or accident. Cf. MOTION FOR NEW TRIAL.

▸ **bill for redemption.** See *bill of redemption.*

▸ **bill in aid of execution.** (1847) A bill filed by a judgment creditor to set aside a fraudulent encumbrance or conveyance.

▸ **bill in perpetuam rei memoriam.** See *bill to perpetuate testimony.*

▸ **bill in the nature of a bill of review.** (18c) A postjudgment bill of review filed by someone who was neither a party to the original suit nor bound by the decree sought to be reversed. — Also termed *supplemental bill in the nature of a bill of review.*

▸ **bill in the nature of a bill of revivor.** (18c) A bill filed when a litigant dies or becomes incapacitated before the litigant's interest in property could be determined. • The purpose of the bill is to resolve who holds the right to revive the original litigation in the deceased's stead.

▸ **bill in the nature of a supplemental bill.** (18c) A bill bringing to court new parties and interests arising from events that occur after the suit is filed. • A *supplemental bill,* in contrast, involves parties or interests already before the court.

▸ **bill in the nature of interpleader.** (1831) A bill of interpleader filed by a person claiming an interest in interpleaded property.

▸ **bill of accommodation.** See ACCOMMODATION PAPER.

▸ **bill of certiorari.** (18c) A bill in equity seeking removal of an action to a higher court. See CERTIORARI.

▸ **bill of complaint.** (15c) An original bill that begins an action in a court of equity. See COMPLAINT (1).

▸ **bill of conformity.** (17c) A bill filed by an executor or administrator who seeks the court's guidance in administering an estate. • The bill is usu. filed to adjust creditors' claims.

▸ **bill of costs.** (16c) A certified, itemized statement of the amount of costs owed by one litigant to another, prepared so that the prevailing party may recover the costs from the losing party. — Also termed *cost bill.* See *review of costs* under REVIEW.

▸ **bill of discovery.** (17c) A bill in equity seeking disclosure of facts within the opposing party's knowledge. See DISCOVERY.

▸ **bill of evidence.** (18c) A transcript of testimony heard at trial.

▸ **bill of exceptions.** (17c) **1.** A formal written statement — signed by the trial judge and presented to the appellate court — of a party's objections or exceptions taken during trial and the grounds on which they are founded. • These bills have largely been replaced by straight appeals under the Federal Rules of Civil Procedure. See EXCEPTION (1). **2.** In some jurisdictions, a record made to preserve error after the judge has excluded evidence. — Abbr. BOE. — Also termed *bill of exception.*

▸ **bill of foreclosure.** (18c) A bill in equity filed by a lender to have mortgaged property sold to satisfy all or part of the secured, unpaid debt.

▸ **bill of interpleader.** (18c) An original bill filed by a party against two or more persons who claim from that party the same debt or duty. • The requesting party asks the court to compel the contenders to litigate and establish their rights to the debt or the duty. See INTERPLEADER.

"The common law offered the stakeholder no relief, in that if he paid in good faith to one claimant, he might nevertheless be sued by and required to pay another claimant. And a judgment at law in favor of one claimant against the stakeholder was no defense to an action against the stakeholder by another claimant. However, in equity the bill or suit of interpleader offers him a remedy in that he may interplead (bring) into one action all of the claimants, turn the money or property over to the court, be himself dismissed from the proceeding, and have the court decide which of the claimants is entitled to the fund or property . . . ." William Q. de Funiak, *Handbook of Modern Equity* § 108, at 241–42 (2d ed. 1956).

▸ **bill of peace.** (18c) An equitable bill filed by one who is threatened with multiple suits involving the same right, or with recurrent suits on the same right, asking the court to determine the question once and for all, and to enjoin the plaintiffs from proceeding with the threatened litigation. • One situation involves many persons having a common claim but threatening to bring separate suits; another involves one person bringing a second action on the same claim.

"By a bill of peace we are to understand a bill brought by a person to establish and perpetuate a right which he claims, and which, from its nature, may be controverted by different persons, at different times, and by different actions; or, where separate attempts have already been unsuccessfully made to overthrow the same right, and justice requires that the party should be quieted in the right, if it is already sufficiently established; or if it should be sufficiently established under the direction of the court. The obvious design of such a bill is to procure repose from perpetual litigation, and therefore, it is justly called a bill of peace." Joseph Story, *Commentaries on Equity Jurisprudence* § 853, at 567 (W.E. Grigsby ed., 1st English ed. 1884).

"If there was a dispute as to some right involving a multiplicity of persons (e.g., as to a man's right to take tolls, or to a right of way traversing many estates), a bill of peace could be brought in equity to establish the right and so secure repose from the prospect of incessant or multifarious litigation. Bills of peace have now in practice been superseded by modern procedural provisions for the joinder of parties and for representative actions." Robert E. Megarry & P.V. Baker, *Snell's Principles of Equity* 570 (27th ed. 1973).

▸ **bill of privilege.** (18c) *Hist.* The formal process for suing an attorney or officer of the court.

"Attorneys and all other persons attending the courts of justice (for attorneys, being officers of the court, are always supposed to be there attending) are not liable to be arrested by the ordinary processes of the court, but must be sued by a bill, called usually a bill of privilege, as being personally present in court." William Blackstone, 3 *Commentaries on the Laws of England* 289 (1768).

▸ **bill of redemption.** (18c) A bill in equity filed to enforce a right to redeem real property, usu. following a mortgage foreclosure or a delinquent-tax sale. — Also termed *bill for redemption.*

▸ **bill of review.** (17c) A bill in equity requesting that a court reverse or revise a prior decree.

▸ **bill of revivor.** (17c) A bill filed for the purpose of reviving and continuing a suit in equity when the suit has been abated before final consummation. • The most common cause of such an abatement is the death of either the plaintiff or the defendant.

▸ **bill of revivor and supplement.** (18c) A compound of a supplemental bill and a bill of revivor, joined for convenience. • Its distinct parts must be framed and proceeded on separately.

▸ **bill *quia timet.*** (18c) An equitable bill used to guard against possible or prospective injuries and to preserve the means by which existing rights are protected from future or contingent violations. • It differs from an injunction, which corrects past and present — or imminent and certain — injuries. One example is a bill to perpetuate testimony. See QUIA TIMET.

▸ **bill to carry a decree into execution.** (18c) A bill brought when a decree could not be enforced without further court order because of the parties' neglect or for some other reason. — Also termed *bill to enforce a decree.*

▸ **bill to perpetuate testimony.** (18c) An original bill to preserve the testimony of a material witness who may die or leave the jurisdiction before a suit is commenced, or to prevent or avoid future litigation. — Also termed *bill in perpetuam rei memoriam.*

▸ **bill to suspend a decree.** (1985) A bill brought to set aside a decree.

▸ **bill to take testimony *de bene esse*** (dee *or* də **bee**-nee **es**-ee *also* day **ben**-ay **es**-ay). (1856) A bill brought to take testimony pertinent to pending litigation from a witness who may be unavailable at the time of trial.

▸ **cost bill.** See *bill of costs.*

▸ **cross-bill.** (17c) A bill brought by the defendant against the plaintiff in the same suit, or against other defendants in the same suit, relating to the matters alleged in the original bill.

▸ **nonoriginal bill.** A bill relating to some matter already litigated by the same parties. • It is an addition to or a continuation of an original bill.

▸ **original bill.** (17c) A bill relating to some matter that has never before been litigated by the same parties with the same interests.

▸ **skeleton bill of exceptions.** (1877) A bill of exceptions that, in addition to the formal parts, contains only the court's directions to the clerk to copy or insert necessary documents into the record for appellate review, but does not contain the actual evidence or trial-court rulings. • For example, the statement "the clerk will insert the official transcript here" is typically a skeleton bill.

▸ **supplemental bill.** (18c) A bill filed for the purpose of adding something to an original bill. • This addition usu. results from the discovery of new facts or from a new understanding of facts after the defendant has put on a defense.

▸ **supplemental bill in the nature of a bill of review.** See *bill in the nature of a bill of review.*

3. A legislative proposal offered for debate before its enactment.

▸ **administration bill.** (1895) A bill drafted and submitted by the executive branch.

▸ **appropriations bill.** (18c) A bill that authorizes governmental expenditures. • The federal government cannot spend money unless Congress has appropriated the funds. U.S. Const. art. I, § 9, cl. 7. — Also termed *spending bill.* See APPROPRIATION (3), (4).

▸ **budget bill.** (18c) A bill designating how money will be allocated for the following fiscal year.

▸ **clean bill.** A bill that has been changed so much by a legislative committee that it is better to introduce a new bill (a "clean" one) than to explain the changes made. — Also termed *committee substitute.*

▸ **companion bill.** (1887) A bill introduced in the other house of a bicameral legislature in a substantially identical form.

▸ **deficiency bill.** (18c) An appropriations bill covering expenses omitted from the general appropriations bills, or for which insufficient appropriations were made. • An *urgent deficiency bill* covers immediate expenses usu. for one item, and a *general deficiency bill* covers a variety of items.

▸ **engrossed bill.** (18c) **1.** A bill in a form ready for final passage by a legislative chamber. **2.** A bill in the form passed by one house of the legislature. See ENGROSS (3); ENGROSSMENT (2).

> "An engrossment is a proofreading and verification in order to be certain that the bill before the house is identical with the original bill as introduced with all amendments that have been adopted correctly inserted." National Conference of State Legislatures, *Mason's Manual of Legislative Procedure* § 735-2, at 525 (2000).

▸ **enrolled bill.** (18c) A bill passed by both houses of the legislature and signed by their presiding officers. See ENROLL (2); ENROLLED-BILL RULE.

▸ **house bill.** (*often cap.*) (1871) A legislative bill being considered by a house of representatives. — Abbr. H; H.B.

▸ **money bill.** See *revenue bill.*

▸ **must-pass bill.** (1987) Legislation of vital importance, such as an appropriation without which the government will shut down. • A must-pass bill will often attract unrelated riders. See RIDER.

▸ **omnibus bill.** (1840) **1.** A single bill containing various distinct matters, usu. drafted in this way to force the executive either to accept all the unrelated minor provisions or to veto the major provision. **2.** A bill that deals with all proposals relating to a particular subject, such as an "omnibus judgeship bill" covering all proposals for new judgeships or an "omnibus crime bill" dealing with different subjects such as new crimes and grants to states for crime control.

▸ **prefiled bill.** A bill that has been drafted and submitted before a legislative session begins.

▸ **private bill.** (16c) A bill relating to a matter of personal or local interest only. Cf. *special law* under LAW.

> "A private Bill is a measure for the interest of some person or class of persons, whether an individual, a corporation, or the inhabitants of a county, town, parish, or other locality, and originates on the motion of some member of the [legislature] in which the Bill is introduced." Courtenay P. Ilbert, *Legislative Methods and Forms* 28 (1901).

▸ **private member's bill.** (1872) *English law.* A law introduced before the British Parliament by a member who is not a government minister.

▸ **public bill.** (18c) A bill relating to public policy in the whole community.

▸ **revenue bill.** (18c) A bill that levies or raises taxes. • Federal revenue bills must originate in the House of Representatives. U.S. Const. art. I, § 7, cl. 1. — Also termed *money bill.*

▸ **senate bill.** (*often cap.*) (1857) A legislative bill being considered by a senate. — Abbr. S.B.

▸ **spending bill.** See *appropriations bill.*

4. An enacted statute <the GI Bill>. **5.** An itemized list of charges; an invoice <hospital bill>. See FEE STATEMENT.

▸ **bill of parcels.** (16c) **1.** A seller's itemized list of goods and prices, intended to assist a buyer in detecting any mistakes or omissions in a shipment of goods. **2.** INVOICE.

▸ **bill payable.** See *account payable* under ACCOUNT.

▸ **bill receivable.** See *account receivable* under ACCOUNT.

▸ **bill rendered.** See *account rendered* under ACCOUNT.

6. BILL OF EXCHANGE; a draft <the bank would not honor the unsigned bill>. See DRAFT (1).

▸ **advance bill.** (1975) A bill of exchange drawn before the shipment of the goods.

▸ **banker's bill.** See *finance bill.*

▸ **bearer bill.** (1863) A bill of exchange that is either expressly or by law payable to the person who possesses it. See *payable to bearer* under PAYABLE. Cf. *bearer bill of lading* under BILL OF LADING.

▸ **bill payable at sight.** (18c) A bill of exchange requiring payment immediately upon its presentation. — Also termed *sight bill;* (in French) *billet à vue.* See *payable at sight* under PAYABLE.

▸ **blank bill.** (18c) A bill with the payee's name left blank. Cf. DRAFT (1).

▸ **domestic bill.** (1811) **1.** A bill of exchange that is payable in the state or country where it is drawn. **2.** A bill on which both the drawer and drawee reside within the same state or country. — Also termed (in sense 2) *inland bill of exchange.* Cf. *foreign bill.*

▸ **finance bill.** (18c) A bill of exchange drawn by a bank in one country on a bank in another country to raise short-term credit. • Finance bills are often issued in tight money periods, and usu. have maturity dates of more than 60 days. — Also termed *banker's bill; working capital acceptance.*

▸ **foreign bill.** (18c) A bill of exchange drawn in one state or country and payable in another. Cf. *domestic bill.*

▸ **inland bill of exchange.** See *domestic bill* (2).

▸ **investment bill.** A bill of exchange purchased at a discount and intended to be held to maturity as an investment.

▸ **sight bill.** See *bill payable at sight.*

7. A formal document or note; an instrument <bill of sale>.

▸ **bill obligatory.** (16c) A written promise to pay; a promissory note under seal. — Also termed *single bond.* See NOTE (1).

▸ **bill of debt.** (16c) A debt instrument, such as a bill obligatory or promissory note.

▸ **bill of lading.** See BILL OF LADING.

▸ **bill of sale.** See BILL OF SALE.

▸ **bill penal.** (18c) A written promise to pay that carries a penalty in excess of the underlying debt for failure to pay. Cf. *bill single.*

▸ **bill single.** (18c) A written promise to pay that is not under seal and has no penalty for failure to pay. — Also termed *single bill.* Cf. *bill penal.*

▸ **grand bill of sale.** See BILL OF SALE.

▸ **single bill.** See *bill single.*

▸ **skeleton bill.** (1864) A bill drawn, indorsed, or accepted in blank.

▸ **value bill.** (1869) A draft that is annexed to a bill of lading and requires payment before the goods are received.

8. A piece of paper money <a $10 bill>. **9.** A promissory note <the debtor signed a bill for $7,000>.

billable hour. (1968) A unit of time used by an attorney, law clerk, or paralegal to account for work performed and chargeable to a client. • Billable hours are usu. divided into quarters or tenths of an hour.

billable time. (1966) An attorney's, law clerk's, or paralegal's time that is chargeable to a client. Cf. NONBILLABLE TIME.

billa cassetur (**bil**-ə kə-**see**-tər). See CASSETUR BILLA.

billa excambii (**bil**-ə eks-**kam**-bee-ɪ). [Latin] Bill of exchange. See DRAFT (1).

billa exonerationis (**bil**-ə ig-zon-ə-ray-shee-**oh**-nis). [Latin] See BILL OF LADING.

billa vera (**bil**-ə **veer**-ə). [Latin] See TRUE BILL.

bill broker. (18c) A middleman who negotiates the purchase or sale of commercial paper.

Bill Chamber. *Hist. Scots law.* A division of the Court of Session in which some remedies could be granted. • The Lord Ordinary on the Bills presided over the court. It was abolished in 1933 and merged into the Court of Session.

billet (**bil**-et), *n.* (17c) **1.** The place where a soldier is lodged; military accommodations or quarters. **2.** A requisition on a household for a soldier's room and lodging. — **billet,** *vb.*

billeta (**bil**-ə-tə), *n. Hist.* A proposed statute or petition presented in Parliament.

billet à vue. See *bill payable at sight* under BILL (6).

bill for a new trial. See BILL (2).

bill for foreclosure. See BILL (2).

bill for redemption. See *bill of redemption* under BILL (2).

billhead, *n.* (1845) A printed invoice containing a business's name and address.

bill in aid of execution. See BILL (2).

bill in chancery. See BILL (2).

bill in equity. See BILL (2).

billing cycle. (1958) The period between billings for goods sold or services rendered.

billingsgate, *n.* Vulgar, vituperative language; coarse verbal abuse. • This term comes from the Billingsgate fish market in London, where the fishmongers were notorious for their scurrility.

bill *in perpetuam rei memoriam*. See *bill to perpetuate testimony* under BILL (2).

bill in the nature of a bill of review. See BILL (2).

bill in the nature of a bill of revivor. See BILL (2).

bill in the nature of a supplemental bill. See BILL (2).

bill in the nature of interpleader. See BILL (2).

bill number. (1903) The number assigned to a proposed piece of legislation, typically designating the house in which it was introduced (S for senate or HR for house of representatives) followed by a sequential number.

bill obligatory. See BILL (7).

bill of accommodation. See ACCOMMODATION PAPER.

bill of adventure. (17c) *Maritime law.* A shipper's written statement that the shipped property belongs to another and is conveyed at the owner's risk.

bill of attainder. (17c) *Constitutional law.* **1.** *Archaic.* A special legislative act that imposes a death sentence on a person without a trial. **2.** A special legislative act prescribing punishment, without a trial, for a specific person or group. • Bills of attainder are prohibited by the U.S. Constitution (art. I, § 9, cl. 3; art. I, § 10, cl. 1). — Also termed *act of attainder.* See ATTAINDER; BILL OF PAINS AND PENALTIES.

Bill of Attainder Clauses. *Constitutional law.* The constitutional provisions prohibiting the federal and state governments from either passing bills of attainder or ex post facto laws. U.S. Const. art. 1, § 9, cl. 3; art. 1, §10, cl. 1.

bill of certiorari. See BILL (2).

bill of chancery. See BILL (2).

bill of complaint. See BILL (2).

bill of conformity. See BILL (2).

bill of costs. See BILL (2).

bill of credit. (18c) **1.** Legal tender in the form of paper, issued by a state and involving the faith of the state, designed to circulate as money in the ordinary uses of business. U.S. Const. art. I, § 10. **2.** LETTER OF CREDIT.

bill of debt. See BILL (7).

bill of discovery. See BILL (2).

bill of entry. (17c) *Maritime law.* A written description of goods filed by an importer with customs officials to obtain permission to unload a ship's goods.

bill of equity. See BILL (2).

bill of evidence. See BILL (2).

bill of exceptions. See BILL (2).

bill of exchange. [loan translation of French *billet de change*] An unconditional written order by one person to another, signed by the maker, requiring the person addressed to pay to a third party a specified sum on demand or at a fixed or ascertainable future time; DRAFT (1).

> "A bill of exchange. . . may be defined, to be an open letter of request, addressed by one person to a second, desiring him to pay a sum of money to a third, or to any other to whom the third person shall order it to be paid: or it may be payable to bearer." Steward Kyd, *A Treatise on the Law of Bills of Exchange and Promissory Notes* 3 (2d ed. 1811).

> "A Bill of Exchange derives its name from a phrase, familiar in the language of Continental Europe, and most probably derived from that of France, in which it is called 'Billet de Change,' or 'Lettre de Change.' In the Middle Ages, the word *Concambium* was used to express the particular contract, known in our law by the name of exchange, that is to say, a transmutation of property, from one man to another, in consideration of some price or recompense in value, such as a commutation of goods for goods, or of money for money. Hence, among foreign Jurists, the phrase, *Cambium reale vel manuale,* is often used to express the latter contract whereas the contract by which one man, in consideration of a sum of money received in one place, entered into an engagement to pay him the like sum in another, was commonly called by the name of *Cambium locale, mercantile, trajectitium.*" Joseph Story, *Commentaries on the Law of Bills of Exchange* § 2, at 2 (Edmund Hatch Bennett ed., 4th ed. 1860).

> "A bill of exchange is usually called among business men a 'draft.' When duly accepted, it is called an 'acceptance.'
>
> "Anglo-American law classifies bills of exchange as either inland or foreign. According to English law an inland bill is one which is both drawn and payable within the British Islands (or both drawn and addressed to a drawee resident therein). Any other bill is a foreign bill. In the states of the United States similar definitions are accepted. Each state defines an inland bill as one both drawn and payable within *its* boundaries. For the purpose of the definition of a foreign bill, each state regards all other states of the Union, as well as foreign nations, as independent sovereignties. Accordingly, a bill which is both drawn and payable in one state is an inland bill by the law of that state, but a foreign bill by the law of every other state, notwithstanding its inland character in the state where it is drawn and payable. There is, therefore, no third class of 'foreign inland bills.'" Charles Phelps Norton, *Handbook of the Law of Bills and Notes* 31–32 (4th ed. 1914).

bill of foreclosure. See BILL (2).

bill of health. (17c) *Maritime law.* A statement certifying the healthy condition of a ship's cargo and crew. • The bill is issued by the port authority from which a vessel sails and is shown to the port authority at the ship's destination as proof that the ship's cargo and crew are disease-free. A "clean" bill states that no contagious or infectious diseases were present at the port; a "touched" or "foul" bill states that the named disease was suspected, anticipated, or actually present.

bill of indemnity. (17c) **1.** *Hist.* An act of Parliament passed annually to protect officeholders who unwittingly fail to take a required oath from liability for acts done in an official capacity. • A more general statute, the Promissory Oaths Act, replaced the bill of indemnity in 1868. **2.** A law protecting a public official from liability for official acts. **3.** An initial pleading by which a plaintiff seeks to require another (often an insurance company) to discharge the plaintiff's liability to a third person.

bill of indictment. (16c) An instrument presented to a grand jury and used by the jury to declare whether there is enough evidence to formally charge the accused with a crime. See INDICTMENT; NO BILL; TRUE BILL.

bill of information. (15c) **1.** INFORMATION. **2.** *Hist.* A civil suit begun by the Crown or by those under its protection, such as a charity.

bill of interpleader. See BILL (2).

bill of lading (**layd**-ing). (16c) A document acknowledging the receipt of goods by a carrier or by the shipper's agent and the contract for the transportation of those goods; a document that indicates the receipt of goods for shipment and that is issued by a person engaged in the business of transporting or forwarding goods. *See* UCC § 1-201(b)(6). • A negotiable bill of lading is a document of title. — Abbr. B/L. Cf. WAYBILL; *air waybill* under WAYBILL.

"A bill of lading may be regarded in three several aspects. (1) It is a receipt given by the master of a ship acknowledging that the goods specified in the bill have been put on board; (2) it is the document [that] contains the terms of the contract for the carriage of the goods agreed upon between the shipper of the goods and the shipowner (whose agent the master of the ship is); and (3) it is a 'document of title' to the goods, of which it is the symbol. It is by means of this document of title that the goods themselves may be dealt with by the owner of them while they are still on board ship and upon the high seas." William R. Anson, *Principles of the Law of Contract* 380 (Arthur L. Corbin ed., 3d Am. ed. 1919).

▸ **bearer bill of lading.** (1916) A negotiable bill of lading that authorizes the carrier or holder of freight to deliver it to the person who possesses the bill.

▸ **claused bill of lading.** See *unclean bill of lading.*

▸ **clean bill of lading.** (1835) A bill of lading containing no clause or notation qualifying the bill's terms. • Possible clauses or notations could include a provision for deck storage or a recording of cargo damage. Cf. *unclean bill of lading.*

▸ **destination bill of lading.** (1952) A bill procured to be issued at the destination point or any other place than the place of shipment. UCC § 7-305.

▸ **foul bill of lading.** See *unclean bill of lading.*

▸ **long-form bill of lading.** (1953) A bill of lading that expressly contains all the terms of the transportation contract. Cf. *short-form bill of lading.*

▸ **negotiable bill of lading.** (1889) A bill of lading calling for the delivery of goods to the bearer or to a named person's order. UCC § 7-104.

▸ **nonnegotiable bill of lading.** See *straight bill of lading.*

▸ **ocean bill of lading.** (1884) A negotiable bill of lading used in shipment by water. — Often shortened to *ocean bill.*

▸ **onboard bill of lading.** (1953) A bill of lading reflecting that goods have been loaded onto a ship. • In multimodal shipments, an onboard bill of lading may include goods loaded onto land vehicles also. — Often shortened to *onboard bill.*

▸ **order bill of lading.** (1902) A negotiable bill of lading stating that the goods are consigned to the order of the person named in the bill.

▸ **overseas bill of lading.** (1931) A bill of lading used for overseas shipment by water or air. UCC § 2-323. • In air freight, an overseas bill of lading is called an *air waybill.* — Often shortened to *overseas bill.*

▸ **short-form bill of lading.** (1950) A bill of lading that does not expressly contain all the terms of the transportation contract, but incorporates them by reference to another document, usu. one at the office of the carrier. Cf. *long-form bill of lading.*

▸ **spent bill of lading.** (1902) A negotiable bill of lading that is not produced, canceled, or surrendered after the carrier has delivered the goods. — Often shortened to *spent bill.*

▸ **straight bill of lading.** (1910) A nonnegotiable bill of lading that specifies a consignee to whom the carrier is contractually obligated to deliver the goods. • In some countries, including England, a document is not a bill of lading unless it is negotiable. — Also termed *nonnegotiable bill of lading.*

▸ **through bill of lading.** (1864) A bill of lading by which a carrier agrees to transport goods to a designated destination, even though the carrier will have to use a connecting carrier for part of the passage. UCC § 7-302. — Often shortened to *through bill.*

▸ **unclean bill of lading.** (1982) A bill of lading that shows on its face that the goods were damaged or that there was a shortage of goods at the time of shipment. — Also termed *claused bill of lading; foul bill of lading.* Cf. *clean bill of lading.*

billing error. See ERROR (1).

bill of Middlesex. (16c) *Hist.* A process by which the Court of the King's Bench in Middlesex obtains jurisdiction over a defendant who resides in a county outside the Court's jurisdiction, by alleging a fictitious trespass in a county over which the court has jurisdiction. • Once the sheriff returns the bill noting that the defendant is not in the county where the trespass occurred, a *latitat* is issued to the sheriff of the defendant's actual residence. See LATITAT.

"The bill of Middlesex is a kind of capias, directed to the sheriff of that county, and commanding him to take the defendant, and have him before our lord the king at Westminster on a day prefixed, to answer to the plaintiff of a plea of trespass. For this accusation of trespass it is, that gives the court of king's bench jurisdiction in other civil causes, as was formerly observed; since when once the defendant is taken into custody . . . , he, being then a prisoner of this court, may here be prosecuted for any other species of injury." 3 William Blackstone, *Commentaries on the Laws of England* 285 (1768).

bill of mortality. (17c) *Hist.* A record of the number of deaths occurring in a given district. • Bills of mortality were compiled — often week to week — in England from late in the 16th century to the 19th century as a way to keep track of the plague and other highly contagious diseases.

bill of pains and penalties. (18c) *Constitutional law.* A legislative act that, though similar to a bill of attainder, prescribes punishment less severe than capital punishment. • Bills of pains and penalties are included within the U.S. Constitution's ban on bills of attainder. U.S. Const. art I, § 9.

bill of parcels. See BILL (5).

bill of particulars. (1831) A formal, detailed statement of the claims or charges brought by a plaintiff or a prosecutor, usu. filed in response to the defendant's request for a more specific complaint. • The bill of particulars has been abolished in federal civil actions and replaced by the motion for a more definite statement. *See* Fed. R. Civ. P. 12(e). But it is still used in some states (such as California) and in federal criminal cases. *See* Fed. R. Crim. P. 7(f). — Also termed *statement of particulars.* See MOTION FOR MORE DEFINITE STATEMENT.

"Although it has been said that the bill of particulars is not a discovery device, it seems plain that it is a means of discovery, though of a limited nature. It is the one method open to a defendant in a criminal case to secure the details of the charge against him." 1 Charles Alan Wright, *Federal Practice and Procedure* § 129, at 646–47 (3d ed. 1999).

bill of peace. See BILL (2).

bill of privilege. See BILL (2).

bill of quantities. (1838) An itemized list used in the construction industry to detail the required materials, parts, and labor, together with their costs, for the purpose of eliciting bids from contractors or subcontractors. — Abbr. BOQ.

bill of redemption. See BILL (2).

bill of review. See BILL (2).

bill of revivor. See BILL (2).

bill of revivor and supplement. See BILL (2).

bill of rights. (18c) **1.** (*usu. cap.*) *Constitutional law.* A section or addendum, usu. in a constitution, defining the situations in which a politically organized society will permit free, spontaneous, and individual activity, and guaranteeing that governmental powers will not be used in certain ways; esp., the first ten amendments to the U.S. Constitution. **2.** (*cap.*) One of the four great charters of English liberty (1 W. & M. (1689)), embodying in statutory form all the principles of the other three charters, namely, Magna Carta, the Petition of Right (3 Car. I, 1628), and the Habeas Corpus Act (31 Car. 2, 1679).

> "Bills of rights give assurance to the individual of the preservation of his liberty. They do not define the liberty they promise. In the beginnings of constitutional government, the freedom that was uppermost in the minds of men was freedom of the body. The subject was not to be tortured or imprisoned at the mere pleasure of the ruler. There went along with this, or grew from it, a conception of a liberty that was broader than the physical. Liberty became identified with the reign of law. 'Freedom of men under government,' says Locke, 'is to have a standing rule to live by, common to every one of that society and made by the legislative power erected in it.' The individual may not be singled out from among his fellows, and made the victim of the shafts of malice." Benjamin N. Cardozo, *The Paradoxes of Legal Science* 97 (1928).

bill of sale. (16c) An instrument for conveying title to personal property, absolutely or by way of security. Cf. DEED.

> "The expression 'bill of sale' includes bills of sale, assignments, transfers, declarations of trust without transfer, inventories of goods with receipts thereto attached, or receipts for purchase-monies of goods, and other assurances of personal chattels, and also powers of attorney, authorities, or licences to take possession of personal chattels as security for any debt, and also any agreement, whether intended or not to be followed by the execution of any other instrument, by which a right in equity to any personal chattels, or to any charge or security thereon, shall be conferred . . . ." Joshua Williams, *Principles of the Law of Personal Property* 60 (11th ed. 1881) (tracking the definition in the [U.K.] Bills of Sale Act of 1878).

> "A transfer may be either an absolute assignment by way of gift or sale, or an assignment by way of mortgage or security only; but in either case when a written document of any sort is used to effect the transfer, the document is called technically a 'bill of sale.'" Albert Gibson, Arthur Weldon & H. Gibson Rivington, *Gibson's Conveyancing* 302 (14th ed. 1933).

▸ **grand bill of sale.** (18c) **1.** *Hist.* An instrument used to transfer title to a ship that is at sea. **2.** An instrument used to transfer title of a ship from the builder to the first purchaser.

bill of sight. (18c) *Maritime law.* A declaration made to a customs officer by an importer who is unsure about what is being shipped. • The bill of sight allows an importer to inspect the goods before paying duties.

bill of store. (17c) *Hist.* A license authorizing a merchant to carry necessary stores and provisions free of duty.

bill of sufferance. (17c) *Hist.* A license authorizing a merchant to trade between English ports without paying customs duties.

bill payable. See *account payable* under ACCOUNT.

bill payable at sight. See BILL (6).

bill penal. See BILL (7).

bill *quia timet*. See BILL (2).

bill receivable. See *account receivable* under ACCOUNT.

bill rendered. See *account rendered* under ACCOUNT.

bills and notes. **1.** See PAPER (1). **2.** See PAPER (2).

bills in a set. (1882) A bill of lading made up of a series of independent parts, each bearing a number and providing that goods delivered against any one part voids the other parts. • Traditionally, in overseas-goods shipments, the parts of this type of bill were sent under separate cover so that if one was lost, the buyer could take delivery of the goods with another one. UCC § 7-304.

bill single. See BILL (7).

bill status. (1970) The current state of a proposed law in the legislative process, such as its assignment to a committee, its schedule for a hearing or a vote, and its passage or defeat by one or both houses.

bill taken *pro confesso* (proh kən-fes-oh). [Latin "as if admitted"] (17c) *Hist.* An order issued by a court of equity when a defendant fails to file an answer.

bill to carry a decree into execution. See BILL (2).

bill to enforce a decree. See *bill to carry a decree into execution* under BILL (2).

bill to perpetuate testimony. See BILL (2).

bill to suspend a decree. See BILL (2).

bill to take testimony *de bene esse*. See BILL (2).

bimetallism, *n.* (1876) A monetary system in which currency is defined in terms of two metals (usu. gold and silver), both being legal tender and with a fixed rate of exchange between them. • The American money system was based on a bimetallic standard from 1792 to 1873.

bind, *vb.* (15c) **1.** To firmly tie, restrain, or confine with a cord, chain, or the like <to bind a prisoner>. **2.** To impose one or more legal duties on (a person or institution) <the contract binds the parties> <courts are bound by precedent>. **3.** To place (oneself) under constraint or duty to perform <he bound himself to deliver the goods on that day>. **4.** To make obligated by means of a binder. See BINDER. **5.** *Hist.* To indenture; to legally obligate to serve <to bind an apprentice>. — **binding,** *adj.* — **bindingness,** *n.*

bind day. See BOON DAY.

binder. (17c) **1.** A document in which the buyer and the seller of real property declare their common intention to bring about a transfer of ownership, usu. accompanied by the buyer's initial payment. **2.** Loosely, the buyer's initial payment in the sale of real property. Cf. EARNEST MONEY. **3.** An insurer's memorandum giving the insured temporary coverage while the application for an insurance policy is being processed or while the formal policy is being prepared. — Also termed *binding receipt*; *binding slip*.

binding, *adj.* (14c) **1.** (Of an agreement) having legal force to impose an obligation <a binding contract>. **2.** (Of an order) requiring obedience <the temporary injunction was binding on the parties>.

binding agreement. See AGREEMENT.

binding arbitration. See ARBITRATION.

binding authority. 1. See *binding precedent* under PRECEDENT. **2.** See *imperative authority* under AUTHORITY (4).

binding direction. See *mandatory instruction* under JURY INSTRUCTION.

binding instruction. See *mandatory instruction* under JURY INSTRUCTION.

binding precedent. See PRECEDENT (2).

binding receipt. See BINDER.

binding slip. See BINDER.

bind over, *vb.* (16c) **1.** To put (a person) under a bond or other legal obligation to do something, esp. to appear in court. **2.** To hold (a person) for trial; to turn (a defendant) over to a sheriff or warden for imprisonment pending further judicial action. • A court may bind over a defendant if it finds at a preliminary examination that there is enough evidence to require a trial on the charges against the defendant. — **binding over,** *n.* — **bindover,** *adj.*

bindover hearing. See PRELIMINARY HEARING.

binge drinking. (1964) The purposeful ingestion of large quantities of alcohol in a short period, esp. when the primary purpose is to become intoxicated, often to the point of losing volition or consciousness.

biochemical warfare. See WARFARE.

biolaw. The combined areas of law that pertain to the life sciences. • Biolaw is most commonly linked to medical and environmental law, but includes a wide array of fields such as agriculture, public health, food and drug regulations, medical ethics, and biotechnology.

biological, *adj.* (1847) **1.** Of, relating to, or involving biology or life <biological study>. **2.** Genetically related <biological parents>.

biological child. See *natural child* (1) under CHILD.

biological father. See FATHER.

biological material. (1965) *Patents.* Patentable microorganisms — such as bacteria, fungi, algae, protozoa, and viruses — that are capable of self-replication. • To satisfy the Patent Act's enablement requirement, biological material that is the subject of a U.S. patent application must be deposited in an appropriate cell depository before the patent is granted.

biological mother. See MOTHER.

biological parent. See PARENT (1).

biological terrorism. See *bioterrorism* under TERRORISM.

biological warfare. See WARFARE.

biotechnology, *n.* (1921) *Patents.* A branch of molecular biology dealing with the use of biological processes to produce useful medical and industrial materials. Cf. GENETIC ENGINEERING.

Biotechnology Patent Process Protection Act. *Patents.* A 1995 federal statute that made biotechnological processes per se patentable if either the process or the resulting material is novel and nonobvious. 35 USCA § 103(b). — Also termed *Biotechnology Act.*

bioterrorism. See TERRORISM.

bioweapon. See WEAPON.

bip. *abbr.* BASIS POINT.

BIP. *abbr. Criminal law.* BATTERERS' INTERVENTION PROGRAM.

Bipartisan Campaign Reform Act. A 2002 federal statute amending the Federal Election Campaign Act by (1) closing the FECA loophole that allowed corporations, unions, and private citizens to make unlimited contributions to national political parties; and (2) prohibiting national parties from raising or spending nonfederal funds. 116 Stat. 81 • In *Citizens United v. Federal Election Commission,* 558 U.S. 310, 130 S.Ct. 876 (2010), the Supreme Court struck down portions of BCRA § 203 banning the broadcast or transmission of "electioneering communications" paid for by corporations or unions within 30 days before a presidential primary and 60 days before a general election, holding that those provisions violated the First Amendment. — Abbr. BCRA. — Also termed *McCain–Feingold.* Cf. FEDERAL ELECTION CAMPAIGN ACT.

bipartite, *adj.* (16c) **1.** Consisting of two distinct parts. **2.** (Of an instrument) executed in two parts by both parties.

bird-dog fee. (1943) *Slang.* **1.** Money paid by a business to a person who directs consumers to the business. **2.** An illegal payment to a person who arranges a business deal; KICKBACK.

bird-nesting arrangement. (1993) *Family law.* A joint-custody scheme in which the children continue to reside full time in the family home while the parents take turns living in the home. • The family home is usu. not distributed as part of a final property award, and both parents must ordinarily contribute to maintaining it.

BIRPI. See INTERNATIONAL BUREAU FOR THE PROTECTION OF INTELLECTUAL PROPERTY.

birretum (bə-**ret**-əm), *n.* [Law Latin] (16c) A cap or coif formerly worn by British judges and serjeants-at-law.

birth, *n.* (12c) The complete emergence of a newborn baby from the mother's body. • The quotation below states the traditional legal view of birth. In a few jurisdictions, the state of the law may be changing. In South Carolina, for example, a child does not have to be born alive to be a victim of murder; a woman can be convicted of fetal murder if her baby is stillborn because of the mother's prenatal drug abuse.

> "For purposes of criminal law — and also for those of property law, e.g. to become a holder of property and so transmit it again to new heirs, or to enable the father to obtain curtesy of his wife's lands — *birth* consists in extrusion from the mother's body, i.e. in having 'come into the world.' If but a foot be unextricated, there can be no murder, the extrusion must be complete, the whole body of the infant must have been brought into the world. But it is not necessary that the umbilical cord should have been severed. And to be born alive the child must have been still in a living state after having wholly quitted the body of the mother." J.W. Cecil Turner, *Kenny's Outlines of Criminal Law* 104 (16th ed. 1952).

birth certificate. (1900) A formal document that records a person's birthdate, birthplace, and parentage. • In all

50 states, an adopted child receives a second birth certificate reflecting his or her adoptive parents. In such a case, the original birth certificate is usu. sealed and can be opened only by court order. Some states allow limited access, depending on the year when an adoptee was born and (sometimes) on whether the birth parents consent. The trend today is to open records if (1) both the child and the biological parent consent — for example, through an adoption registry, or (2) the child requests and, upon notification, the biological parent does not veto the request. Oregon enacted the first statute to permit access to birth records upon the unilateral demand of the adopted child, once the child reaches the age of majority. See ADOPTION-REGISTRY STATUTE.

birth control. (1914) **1.** Any means of preventing conception and pregnancy, usu. by mechanical or chemical means, but also by abstaining from intercourse. **2.** More narrowly, contraception.

birthday club. See GIFTING CLUB.

birth defect. (1905) A physical, chemical, or mental abnormality in a human newborn caused by genetic or environmental factors. • A birth defect may create a physical or mental disability, or it may cause death.

birth father. See *biological father* under FATHER.

birth injury. (1905) Harm that occurs to a fetus during the birth process, esp. during labor and delivery. Cf. PRENATAL INJURY.

birth mother. See MOTHER.

birth parent. See PARENT (1).

birth records. (1854) Statistical data kept by a governmental entity concerning people's birthdates, birthplaces, and parentage.

birthright. (16c) **1.** Something such as a right, property, estate, money, etc. that someone has as a personal entitlement to because of the family or country to which he or she belongs. **2.** Something that someone treats in such a way even though the entitlement is not legally recognized. **3.** Traditionally, PRIMOGENITURE (2).

BIS. *abbr.* BUREAU OF INDUSTRY AND SECURITY.

bisail, *n.* See BESAYEL.

bi-scot, *n.* (17c) *Hist. English law.* A fine imposed for not repairing banks, ditches, and causeways.

bisexual, *adj.* (1914) Of, relating to, or characterized by sexual desire for both males and females.

bishop, *n.* (bef. 12c) The chief superintendent and highest-ranking member of the clergy within a diocese. • The bishop is subject to the archbishop of a province.

> "[A] bishop . . . has several courts under him, and may visit at pleasure every part of his diocese. His chancellor is appointed to hold his courts for him, and to assist him in matters of ecclesiastical law . . . ." 1 William Blackstone, *Commentaries on the Laws of England* 370 (1765).

bishopric (**bish**-əp-rik), *n.* (bef. 12c) **1.** The area that a bishop is in charge of; DIOCESE. **2.** The office of bishop; the position of being a bishop.

bishop's court. (17c) **1.** An ecclesiastical court usu. held in the diocese cathedral and presided over by the bishop's chancellor. **2.** (*cap.*) *Hist. Eccles. law.* A court (usu.) held in the cathedral of a diocese, the judge being the bishop's chancellor, who applied civil canon law. • The jurisdiction included appeals from the Court of Archdeacon. In a large diocese, the bishop's chancellor would have commissaries in remote parts who held consistory courts. See CONSISTORY COURT.

bite and hold. A police dog's act of finding and biting a suspect, usu. on the arm, to restrain the person. See *police dog* under DOG (1). Cf. BARK AND HOLD.

bite-mark comparison. (1976) A method in forensic odontology seeking to match the tooth impressions found at a crime scene or on a crime victim with a person whose dentition is believed to be the source of those impressions. • Bite-mark comparison is relied on in criminal prosecutions and is among the most controversial aspects of forensic odontology: "[T]here is continuing dispute over the value and reliability of the collected [bite-mark] data for interpretation. . . . In numerous instances, experts diverge widely in their evaluation of the same bite-mark evidence, which has led to questioning of the value and scientific objectivity of such evidence." National Academy of Sciences, *Strengthening Forensic Science in the United States: A Path Forward* 176 (2009). See FORENSIC ODONTOLOGY.

biting rule. (1948) A rule of construction that once a deed or will grants a fee simple, a later provision attempting to cut down, modify, or qualify the grant will be held void.

***Bivens* action.** (1972) A lawsuit brought to redress a federal official's violation of a constitutional right. *Bivens v. Six Unknown Named Agents of the Federal Bureau of Narcotics*, 403 U.S. 388, 91 S.Ct. 1999 (1971). • A *Bivens* action allows federal officials to be sued in a manner similar to that set forth at 42 USCA § 1983 for state officials who violate a person's constitutional rights under color of state law.

.biz. (1995) *Trademarks.* A top-level Internet domain name assigned by ICANN for use by businesses as distinct from individual, personal, or noncommercial use. See DOMAIN NAME; INTERNET CORPORATION FOR ASSIGNED NAMES AND NUMBERS.

B/L. *abbr.* BILL OF LADING.

Blackacre. (17c) A fictitious tract of land used in legal discourse (esp. law-school hypotheticals) to discuss real-property issues. • When another tract of land is needed in a hypothetical, it is often termed "Whiteacre."

> "Blackacre is the most celebrated tract of land in the world of the law . . . . Blackacre is wholly mythical, yet totally real. It is a concept, living in the realm of the mind and doubly valuable since much of the law of property has the same type of reality." John E. Cribbet, *Principles of the Law of Property* 2 (2d ed. 1975).

Black Act. *Hist.* A 1722 English statute (9 Geo. ch. 22) establishing the death penalty for the unlawful killing or maiming of animals. • The statute was passed in the wake of crimes committed by persons with faces blackened or otherwise disguised. The statute was repealed in 1827. The classic study of this law is E.P. Thompson, *Whips and Hunters: The Origins of the Black Act* (1975).

Black Acts. *Scots law.* Statutes of the Scottish Parliament passed from 1535 to 1594 and recorded in a book printed in black letter.

blackball, *vb.* (18c) To vote against (someone) when there is a requirement of unanimity, esp. when doing so prevents the person from becoming a member of a club or social group; to exclude by vote of rejection. • Traditionally, blackballing was accomplished by placing one or more black balls in the ballot box. — **blackball, blackballing,** *n.*

Black Book of the Admiralty. *English law.* A medieval code of maritime law containing admiralty laws, ordinances, and proceedings, decisions, and acts of the monarch, the Lord High Admiral, and the Court of Admiralty. • The Black Book is considered a definitive source for customary English maritime law. It also contains a copy of the Rules of Oleron, an 11th-century compilation of common maritime law.

Black Book of the Exchequer. *Hist.* A record book containing treaties, conventions, charters, papal bulls, and other English state documents. • It dates from the 13th century. — Also termed *Liber Niger Parvus.*

black box. (1964) **1.** A computerized sensing device that records and stores data to be retrieved after the crash or accident of an aircraft, car, etc. for diagnosing how the incident happened • It is housed in a protective casing that is not black but is usually a bright color such as orange to make it easier to find. The name comes from the term *black box* in technology, science, and other fields, denoting any device, algorithm, function, or the like whose inner workings are not visible or obvious but opaque (i.e., black). **2.** *Slang.* A solitary-confinement cell in a prison or jail.

black cap. (1838) A square cap worn by English judges on certain state or solemn occasions. • The black cap was formerly worn by judges when handing down a death sentence.

black codes. (*usu. cap.*) (1814) *Hist.* **1.** Antebellum state laws enacted to regulate slavery. **2.** Laws enacted shortly after the Civil War in the ex-Confederate states to restrict the liberties of the newly freed slaves to ensure a supply of inexpensive agricultural labor and to maintain white supremacy.

> "Clearly, leaders of the old South who survived the war were in no mood for racial equality. It was a bitter enough pill that the slaves were legally free; there was no inclination to go beyond the formal status. The Black Codes of 1865, passed in almost all of the states of the old Confederacy, were meant to replace slavery with some kind of caste system and to preserve as much as possible of the prewar way of life." Lawrence M. Friedman, *A History of American Law* 504 (2d ed. 1985).

black economy. See SHADOW ECONOMY.

Black Hand. (1904) *Hist.* Any of several secret societies that were active in the late 19th and early 20th centuries. • Most of these organizations were composed of anarchists or separatists and engaged in terrorism. In the late 19th and early 20th centuries, a loosely knit Sicilian-Italian criminal organization called the Black Hand extorted money from Italian immigrants to the U.S. through threats and acts of violence. Chapters of the organization were established throughout the United States and Canada. The New York City Police Department created the country's first bomb squad to deal with the bombs used by the Black Hand. A band of Spanish anarchists in the late 19th century and a group of Serbian anarchists in the early 20th century were also called the Black Hand. The organizations were not related. — **blackhander,** *n.*

black-leg labor. See SCAB.

blackletter law. [fr. the Gothic "black letter" type used in early lawbooks] (18c) One or more legal principles that are old, fundamental, and well settled. • The term refers to the law printed in books set in Gothic type, which is very bold and black. — Also termed *hornbook law.*

blacklist, *n.* (17c) **1.** A list of people, products, countries, etc. that are disfavored and are therefore to be avoided or punished; esp., a roster of those considered objectionable by the makers or users of the roster, as for political or social misconduct. **2.** A list of defaulters; specif., an official list of insolvents, bankrupts, and other bad debtors. **3.** *Int'l law.* A list of firms and people of enemy nationality, living in neutral territory, with whom nationals of a belligerent country are forbidden by their government to trade.

blacklist, *vb.* (18c) To put the name of (a person) on a list of those who are disfavored and are therefore to be avoided or punished <the firm blacklisted the former employee>.

black-lung disease. See PNEUMOCONIOSIS.

blackmail, *n.* [fr. 16c Scottish *blak maill* "extorted payments"] (16c) **1.** The crime of making one or more threatening demands without justification; the offense of coercing someone by threats of public exposure or criminal prosecution; EXTORTION (2). Cf. FEEMAIL; GRAYMAIL; GREENMAIL (1), (2). — **blackmail,** *vb.*

> "[Blackmail is] a certain rate of Money, Corn, Cattle, or other consideration, paid to some inhabiting upon, or near the borders, being persons of name and power, allied with . . . known Robbers . . . to be thereby by them freed and protected from the danger of those Spoil-takers." Thomas Blount, *Nomo-Lexicon: A Law-Dictionary* (1670).

> "'Black-mail' (black rent) was anciently used to indicate 'rents reserved in work, grain or baser money' (i.e. baser than silver). It was also employed at one time to refer to 'a tribute formerly exacted in the north of England and in Scotland by freebooting chiefs for protection from pillage.' [Quoting *American College Dictionary* (1948).] Such practice was extortion, in the literal sense, and hence 'blackmail' is frequently used to indicate statutory extortion or sometimes an extorsive threat. And the federal statute forbidding the sending of an extorsive threat by mail has been referred to as the 'blackmail statute.'" Rollin M. Perkins & Ronald N. Boyce, *Criminal Law* 451 (3d ed. 1982).

2. *Hist.* A tax consisting of money, cattle, crops, or other consideration paid to freebooters or their allies to ensure immunity from pillage. • This form of blackmail was declared a felony in 1601. **3.** *Hist.* BLACK RENT.

blackmailer. Someone who tries to blackmail someone else, or who succeeds.

blackmail suit. See SUIT.

black maria. (1847) *Slang.* A locked van used by the police to transport prisoners to and from jail.

black market. 1. See MARKET. **2.** See SHADOW ECONOMY.

black-market adoption. 1. See ADOPTION (1). **2.** See SHADOW ECONOMY.

blackout period. (1991) *Trademarks.* The time between the examining attorney's approval of an intent-to-use application for publication in the Official Gazette and the issuance of a notice of allowance after publication, during which the applicant may not file a statement of use or make any other substantive amendment to the application.

blackout policy. (1999) *Securities.* A public company's voluntarily adopted position prohibiting directors and other officers from trading in the company's securities during periods when there is a heightened risk or perception of insider trading. See INSIDER TRADING.

blackout trading. (2002) *Securities.* The act or an instance of a corporate director's or officer's engaging in transactions of company securities during a blackout period.

black-rage insanity defense. See INSANITY DEFENSE.

black rent. (16c) *Hist.* Feudal rents paid in work, grain, or money baser than silver. — Also termed *blackmail.* Cf. WHITE RENT.

Black–Scholes formula. (1973) A mathematical model used to estimate the present value of stock options or warrants based on the exercise price, the length of the option's or warrant's exercise period, and the fair market value and volatility of the underlying security. • The term derives from Fischer Black and Myron Scholes, the names of the economists who presented the formula in *The Pricing of Options and Corporate Liabilities*, 81 J. Pol. Econ. 637 (1973).

Blackstone lawyer. (1814) *Slang.* **1.** A lawyer with a broad knowledge of blackletter principles. **2.** A self-educated lawyer (esp. in antebellum America) whose legal training consists primarily of reading Blackstone's *Commentaries.*

black ward. (18c) *Hist.* A subvassal; a vassal of the king's vassal.

Blaine amendment. (1947) *Constitutional law.* A provision in a state constitution for stricter separation of church and state than is required by the Establishment Clause. • In 1875, at the request of President Ulysses S. Grant, Senator James G. Blaine proposed an amendment to the U.S. Constitution, applying the Free Exercise and Establishment Clause to the states, and specifically prohibiting the use of any state funds to support any religious institutions, including private church-run schools (esp. Roman Catholic). The House of Representatives passed the amendment, but the Senate narrowly voted against it. Many states, however, amended their constitutions to include a "Blaine Amendment" strictly prohibiting the use of public money for the support of religious institutions.

blamable. See BLAMEWORTHY.

blame, *n.* (14c) **1.** Responsibility for a mistake or for something wrong; CULPABILITY <blame rested with all the defendants>. **2.** An attribution of fault; an expression of disapproval. — **blame,** *vb.*

blameless, *adj.* (14c) Free from guilt or any responsibility for something that has gone wrong; not deserving any reproof or censure.

blameworthy, *adj.* (14c) Deserving blame or disapproval for a mistake or for something that has gone wrong; culpable; censurable. — Also termed *blamable.*

blanc seign (blahnk **sayn**). [Law French] *Civil law.* A signed paper entrusted to someone with the power to bind the signer within the limits of the agreement between the signer and the grantee. See POWER OF ATTORNEY (1).

blandishment. (*usu. pl.*) (16c) Something pleasant that one says or offers in order to persuade or influence someone; esp., flattering endearment.

blank, *n.* (1817) *Parliamentary law.* **1.** A ballot cast without a vote, effectively an abstention. **2.** A name, number, time, or other term left open in a motion, to be filled in by vote after taking proposals from the floor. • An election is a common form of filling a blank: each nomination is effectively a proposal for filling the blank in the question, "*Resolved,* That ——— be elected." See CREATE A BLANK; FILL A BLANK. Cf. AMENDMENT (3).

blank acceptance. See ACCEPTANCE (3).

blank bar. (17c) *Hist.* A plea in bar interposed by a defendant in a trespass action. • This type of plea was filed to compel the plaintiff to state exactly where the alleged trespass occurred. — Also termed *common bar.*

blank bill. See BILL (6).

blank bond. See BOND (2).

blank check. See CHECK.

blank consent. (1947) A general authorization from a natural parent who voluntarily relinquishes a child for private adoption and allows adoption proceedings without the need for further consent. • Jurisdictions are divided over whether a blank consent is valid if the natural parents do not identify and approve the prospective adoptive parents. — Also termed *blanket consent*; *general consent.*

blank endorsement. See *blank indorsement* under INDORSEMENT.

blanket agreement. (1933) *Labor law.* A collective-bargaining agreement that applies to workers throughout an organization, industry, or geographical area.

blanket ballot. See BALLOT (4).

blanket bond. See BOND (2).

blanket clause. See CLAUSE.

blanket consent. See BLANK CONSENT.

blanket contract. See CONTRACT.

blanket license. See LICENSE.

blanket lien. See LIEN.

blanket mortgage. See MORTGAGE.

blanket order. (1903) **1.** A judicial order that covers a broad subject or class. — Also termed *umbrella order.* See ORDER (2). **2.** See *blanket protective order* under PROTECTIVE ORDER. **3.** An order negotiated by a customer with a supplier for multiple purchases and deliveries of specified goods over a stated period, as an alternative to placing a separate order for each transaction. — Also termed *blanket purchase agreement*; *blanket purchase order.* See PURCHASE AGREEMENT; PURCHASE ORDER.

blanket policy. See INSURANCE POLICY.

blanket protective order. See PROTECTIVE ORDER.

blanket purchase agreement. See BLANKET ORDER (3).

blanket purchase order. See BLANKET ORDER (3).

blanket search warrant. See SEARCH WARRANT.

blanket warrant. See *general warrant* (2) under WARRANT (1); *blanket search warrant* under SEARCH WARRANT.

blanket waybill. See WAYBILL.

blank form. (18c) *Copyright.* A form, usu. one for recordkeeping and business purposes, that does not convey information until it has been filled in. • Blank forms are not eligible for copyright protection. — Also termed *business form.* See BLANK-FORMS RULE.

blank-forms rule. (1990) *Copyright.* The principle that forms are not protectable by copyright if they are designed for recording information but do not themselves convey any information. • The rule, first promulgated by the U.S. Supreme Court in *Baker v. Selden*, 101 U.S. 99 (1880), is now a U.S. Copyright Office regulation, 37 CFR § 202.1(c). See MERGER DOCTRINE (1).

blank indorsement. See INDORSEMENT.

blank lineup. See LINEUP.

blank stock. See STOCK.

blank transfer. (1807) **1.** The sale or other conveyance of real property or securities without a record of the buyer's or transferee's name. • Whoever holds the certificate of sale or conveyance is legally presumed to be the new owner of the securities. **2.** The certificate or other legal instrument by which such a sale or conveyance is effected.

blasphemous libel. See LIBEL (2).

blasphemy (**blas**-fə-mee), *n.* (13c) Irreverence toward or contempt for God, religion, a religious icon, or something else considered sacred; language, behavior, or a work characterized by such irreverence or contempt. • Blasphemy was a crime at common law and remains so in some U.S. jurisdictions, but it is rarely if ever enforced because of its questionable constitutionality under the First Amendment. Cf. PROFANITY. — **blaspheme** (blas-**feem** *or* **blas**-feem), *vb.* — **blasphemous** (**blas**-fə-məs), *adj.* — **blasphemer** (blas-**fee**-mər), *n.*

> "Blasphemy is the malicious revilement of God and religion. In England blasphemy was the malicious revilement of the Christian religion. . . . Blasphemy has been held to be a common-law crime [in the United States] because of its tendency to stir up breaches of the peace. It is expressly made punishable by some of the statutes." Rollin M. Perkins & Ronald N. Boyce, *Criminal Law* 474, 475 (3d ed. 1982).

blastocyst. See ZYGOTE.

blended family. See FAMILY.

blended fund. See FUND (1).

blended sentence. See SENTENCE.

blended trust. See TRUST (3).

blending clause. (1947) A provision in a will disposing of both the testator's own property and the property over which the testator has a power of appointment, so that the two types of property are treated as a unit.

blind bidding. (1965) *Copyright.* In the licensing of movies for first-run engagements, the practice by film distributors of requiring theater owners to bid for and book movies without having seen them. • By statute, some states prohibit blind bidding.

blind entry. See ENTRY (2).

blind pig. See BLIND TIGER.

blind plea. See PLEA (1).

blind selling. (1946) The sale of goods without giving a buyer the opportunity to examine them.

blind-strike system. (1964) *Criminal procedure.* A method of jury selection in which both the prosecution and defense counsel must exercise peremptory challenges (or "strikes") at the same time, without knowing the other side's choices. — Also termed *Arizona method.*

blind tiger. (1857) *Slang.* A place where intoxicants are illegally sold. • This term was commonly used during Prohibition. — Also termed *blind pig.* See PROHIBITION (3).

blind trust. See TRUST (3).

BLM. *abbr.* BUREAU OF LAND MANAGEMENT.

bloc, *n.* (1903) A group of persons or political units aligned with a common interest or purpose, even if only temporarily <voting bloc>.

block, *n.* (18c) **1.** A municipal area enclosed by streets <three blocks away>. See LOT (1). **2.** A quantity of things bought or sold as a unit <a block of preferred shares>. **3.** SQUARE (1).

blockade, *n.* (17c) *Int'l law.* A belligerent's prevention of access to or egress from an enemy's ports by stationing ships to intercept vessels trying to enter or leave those ports. • To be binding, a blockade must be effective — that is, it must be maintained by a force sufficient to prevent access to ports. — Also termed *simple blockade; de facto blockade.*

> "A blockade must be existing in point of fact; and in order to constitute that existence, there must be a power present to enforce it. All decrees and orders, declaring extensive coasts and whole countries in a state of blockade, without the presence of an adequate naval force to support it, are manifestly illegal and void, and have no sanction in public law." 1 James Kent, *Commentaries on American Law* *144 (George Comstock ed., 11th ed. 1866).

> "The word blockade properly denotes obstructing the passage into or from a place on either element, but is more especially applied to naval forces preventing communication by water. Unlike siege it implies no intention to get possession of the blockaded place. With blockades by land or ordinary sieges neutrals have usually little to do." Theodore D. Woolsey, *Introduction to the Study of International Law* § 202, at 351 (5th ed. 1878).

▸ **pacific blockade.** (1887) *Int'l law.* A blockade that is established without a declaration of war.

▸ **public blockade.** (1865) *Int'l law.* An established blockade of which the blockading country gives formal notice to the governments of neutral countries.

blockage rule. (1937) *Tax.* The principle that a large block of stock shares may be valued at less than the total value of the individual shares because such a large block may be difficult to sell at full price. • The resulting reduction in price is called a blockage discount.

block booking, *n.* (1931) *Copyright.* In the licensing or use of movies, the practice by film distributors of conditioning the license or use on the acceptance of an entire package or block of films, which typically includes unwanted or inferior films. • In *U.S. v. Loew's Inc.*, 371 U.S. 38, 83 S.Ct. 97 (1962), the U.S. Supreme Court condemned block booking as an illegal tying arrangement that violates the Sherman Act.

***Blockburger* test.** (1954) *Criminal law.* A test, for double-jeopardy purposes, of whether a defendant can be punished separately for convictions on two charges or prosecuted later on a different charge after being convicted or acquitted on a charge involving the same incident; a comparison of two charges to see if each contains at least one element that the other does not. • Although the test is frequently called the *same-evidence test*, that term is misleading since the analysis involves the elements of the charged offenses rather than the facts of the incident. *Blockburger v. U.S.*, 284 U.S. 299, 304, 52 S.Ct. 180, 192 (1932). — Also termed *same-elements test;*

actual-evidence test. Cf. SAME-CONDUCT TEST; SAME-TRANSACTION TEST.

blockbusting, *n.* (1954) The act or practice, usu. by a real-estate broker, of persuading one or more property owners to sell their property quickly, and often at a loss, to avoid an imminent influx of minority groups. • Blockbusting is illegal in many states.

blocked account. See ACCOUNT.

blocked currency. See CURRENCY.

blocked income. See INCOME.

block grant. (1900) An unrestricted grant of federal funds.

blocking patent. See PATENT (3).

blocking statute. See STATUTE.

block interest. See *add-on interest* under INTEREST (3).

block policy. See INSURANCE POLICY.

block voting. (1978) A shareholders' agreement to cast their votes in a single block. See *voting trust* under TRUST (3).

***Blonder-Tongue* doctrine.** (1973) *Patents.* The rule that a patentee is barred by collateral estoppel from relitigating the validity of a patent that has been held invalid in an earlier proceeding in which the patentee had a full and fair opportunity to litigate the patent's validity. • The rule was adopted by the U.S. Supreme Court in *Blonder-Tongue Laboratories, Inc. v. University of Illinois Found.*, 402 U.S. 313, 91 S.Ct. 1434 (1971). — Also termed *Blonder-Tongue rule.*

blood, *n.* (13c) A relationship between persons arising by descent from a common ancestor. See RELATIVE.

▸ **entire blood.** See *full blood.*

▸ **full blood.** (1812) The relationship existing between persons having the same two parents; unmixed ancestry. — Also termed *whole blood; entire blood.*

▸ **half blood.** (17c) The relationship existing between persons having the same father or mother, but not both parents in common. — Sometimes written *half-blood.* See *relative of the half blood* under RELATIVE; DEMI-SANGUE.

> "At common law, in order that one might inherit as a collateral kinsman he, the claimant, must be a kinsman of the whole, not only of the half, blood. One could not inherit from his half brother, though the land had descended from their common parent, and though otherwise it would escheat. This rule has been changed in most, if not all, the states by divergent statutes. In a few states, kindred of the half blood succeed like those of the whole blood; and in others they inherit half shares only. In a number of states, the distinction between the whole and the half blood exists only as to ancestral land, and excludes from any share therein collateral kin not of the blood of the ancestor from whom the land was derived. In still other states the half blood does not take except in default of kindred of the whole blood in the same degree of relationship." Herbert Thorndike Tiffany, *A Treatise on the Modern Law of Real Property* § 734, at 769 (Carl Zollmann ed., abr. ed. 1940).

▸ **heritable blood.** (18c) *Hist.* A relationship between an ancestor and an heir that the law recognizes for purposes of passing good title to property. — Also termed *inheritable blood.*

▸ **mixed blood.** (1817) *Archaic.* The relationship between persons whose ancestors are of different races or nationalities.

> "The term 'mixed bloods,' as used in treaties and statutes, has been held to include persons of half, or more or less than half, Indian blood, derived either from the father or from the mother." 42 C.J.S. *Indians* § 3 (1991).

▸ **whole blood.** See *full blood.*

blood, corruption of the. See CORRUPTION OF BLOOD.

blood alcohol content. (1926) The concentration of alcohol in one's bloodstream, expressed as a percentage. • Blood alcohol content is used to determine whether a person is legally intoxicated, esp. under a driving-while-intoxicated law. In many states, a blood alcohol content of .08% is enough to charge a person with an offense. — Abbr. BAC. — Also termed *blood alcohol count; blood alcohol concentration.* See DRIVING UNDER THE INFLUENCE; DRIVING WHILE INTOXICATED.

blood border. (1985) *Slang.* The dividing line between adjoining states that have different minimum drinking ages. • The term derives from the fact that juveniles from the state with the higher minimum age drive to the state with a lower minimum age, purchase and consume alcohol, and drive home intoxicated.

blood brother. (1853) **1.** A brother by birth. **2.** A man who promises loyalty to another, as in a gang ritual in which the men's blood is ceremoniously mixed together.

blood diamond. See CONFLICT DIAMOND.

blood feud. See FEUD (4).

blood-grouping test. (1930) A test used in paternity and illegitimacy cases to determine whether a particular man could be the father of a child, examples being the genetic-marker test and the human-leukocyte antigen test. • The test does not establish paternity; rather, it eliminates men who could not be the father. See PATERNITY TEST; GENETIC-MARKER TEST; HUMAN-LEUKOCYTE ANTIGEN TEST.

blooding. See DNA DRAGNET.

blood letter. (1997) A letter given by an underwriter to the issuer in a public offering or by the initial purchasers in an unregistered offering under Rule 144A or Regulation S, whereby the underwriter or initial purchasers agree to indemnify the issuer for any losses resulting from the information supplied in the registration statement, prospectus, or offering memorandum.

> "The term 'blood letter' derives either from the fact that it represents the underwriters' acknowledged responsibility or from the phrase 'squeezing blood from a stone' because it is jokingly just as difficult to persuade the underwriters to put in writing their responsibility for parts of the contents of the registration statement and prospectus." Matt Swartz & Daniel Lee, *The Corporate, Securities, and M&A Lawyer's Job: A Survival Guide* 121 (2007).

blood money. (16c) **1.** Money paid to the family of someone who has been murdered; esp., a payment given by a murderer's family to the next of kin of the murder victim. — Also termed *wer.* **2.** Money paid to a hit man for murdering someone. **3.** A reward given for the apprehension of a person charged with a crime, esp. capital murder. **4.** Collectively, "charitable" donations that are made for or diverted to terrorist organizations. **5.** *Slang.* Damages paid by an individual defendant in a personal-injury case. **6.** *Slang.* Compensation paid to a blood donor.

blood relative. See RELATIVE.

blood-spatter evidence. (1978) *Criminal law.* An expert's analysis of the patterns of blood left on surfaces at the scene of a crime, including conclusions about the velocity, direction, and nature of an impact on a body. — Also termed *blood-splatter evidence.*

bloodsucker warrant. *Criminal law. Slang.* A judge's authorization to perform an involuntary blood test on a suspect, esp. one who might be charged with DWI after a serious traffic accident.

blood test. (1912) The medical analysis of blood, esp. to establish paternity or (as required in some states) to test for sexually transmitted diseases in marriage-license applicants. See SEROLOGICAL TEST.

bloodwite, *n.* (bef. 12c) *Hist.* **1.** EFFUSIO SANGUINIS (1). **2.** EFFUSIO SANGUINIS (2). **3.** The right to levy a fine involving the shedding of blood. **4.** The exemption from the payment of a fine involving the shedding of blood. **5.** *Scots law.* A penalty for a brawl or riot in which blood is shed.

blot on title. See CLOUD ON TITLE.

blotter, *n.* **1.** See ARREST RECORD. **2.** See WASTE BOOK.

BLS. *abbr.* BUREAU OF LABOR STATISTICS.

blue-blue-ribbon jury. See *blue-ribbon jury* under JURY.

Blue Book. 1. A compilation of session laws. See SESSION LAWS (2). **2.** A volume formerly published to give parallel citation tables for a volume in the National Reporter System. **3.** *English law.* A government publication, such as a Royal Commission report, issued in a blue paper cover.

Bluebook. A citation guide — formerly titled *A Uniform System of Citation* — that is generally considered an authoritative reference for American legal citations. • The book's complete title is *The Bluebook: A Uniform System of Citation.* Although it has been commonly called the *Bluebook* for decades, the editors officially included *Bluebook* in the title only in the mid-1990s. The book is compiled by the editors of the *Columbia Law Review,* the *Harvard Law Review,* the *University of Pennsylvania Law Review,* and *The Yale Law Journal.* Cf. ALWD CITATION MANUAL.

bluebook, *vb.* (1957) To ensure the conformity of citations with *The Bluebook: A Uniform System of Citation.*

blue books. See SESSION LAWS.

blue chip, *n.* (1927) A corporate stock that is considered a safe investment because the corporation has a history of stability, consistent growth, and reliable earnings. • The term is said to come from poker, in which the blue chips usu. have the highest value. — Also termed *blue-chip stock.* — **blue-chip,** *adj.*

blue law. (1762) A statute regulating or prohibiting commercial activity on Sundays. • Although blue laws were formerly common, they have declined since the 1980s, when many courts held them invalid because of their origin in religion (i.e., Sunday being the Christian Sabbath). Blue laws usu. pass constitutional challenge if they are enacted to support a nonreligious purpose, such as a day of rest for workers. — Also termed *Sunday law; Sunday-closing law; Sabbath law; Lord's Day Act.*

Blue List. *Securities.* A daily listing (on blue paper) of secondary-market offerings of municipal bonds.

> "Municipal bonds available for resale in the *secondary* market are listed by state in *The Blue List,* along with such information as the number of bonds offered, issuer, maturity date, coupon rate, price, and dealer making the offering. Ratings are *not* included. But there are sections on settlement dates of recent new offerings, prerefunded bonds, and miscellaneous offerings (some U.S. government and agency obligations, railroad equipment trust certificates, corporate bonds, and even preferred stocks). The dollar value of listings, referred to as the *floating supply,* gives an indication of the size and liquidity of the secondary municipal market." New York Institute of Finance, *How the Bond Market Works* 185 (1988).

blue note. See NOTE (1).

blue-on-blue, *adj.* (1982) Of, relating to, or involving an occasion during military hostilities when a soldier, sailor, or pilot is accidentally killed by his or her own side of the conflict. Cf. FRIENDLY FIRE (1).

blue-pencil test. (1921) A judicial standard for deciding whether to invalidate the whole contract or only the offending words. • Under this standard, only the offending words are invalidated if it would be possible to delete them simply by running a blue pencil through them, as opposed to changing, adding, or rearranging words.

blue-ribbon jury. See JURY.

blue-sky, *adj.* (1906) (Of a security) having little value. • The term was first used in reference to the assets at issue in *Lowell v. People,* 131 Ill. App. 137 (1907) ("hot air and blue sky").

blue-sky, *vb.* (1931) To approve (the sale of securities) in accordance with blue-sky laws <the company's IPO has not yet been blue-skyed>.

blue-sky law. (1912) A state statute establishing standards for offering and selling securities, the purpose being to protect citizens from investing in fraudulent schemes or unsuitable companies. • Such a statute typically includes provisions for licensing brokers, registering securities, and formal approvals of the offerings by the appropriate government agencies.

> "Although the public is probably more aware of the existence and operation of the several federal statutes administered by the Securities and Exchange Commission, most state legislation in this area is broader in scope. State securities laws, commonly referred to as 'blue sky' laws, were enacted long before the Securities Act of 1933, and Congress specifically preserved these laws instead of attempting to preempt the field for federal legislation." Louis Loss & Edward M. Cowett, *Blue Sky Law* 3 (1958).

> "The first legislative attempts to regulate securities transactions were effected on the state level, with the first general securities law being said to have been enacted by the State of Kansas in 1911, and with 48 jurisdictions having enacted such statutes by 1933. These statutes were said to be enacted to stop the sale of stock in fly-by-night concerns, visionary oil wells, distant gold mines, and other fraudulent exploitations. A similar description of the early legislative purpose is that such acts were aimed at 'speculative schemes which have no more basis than so many feet of blue sky,' and this description has had a lasting influence in that state securities acts are commonly referred to as 'blue sky laws.'" 69A Am. Jur. 2d *Securities Regulation — State* § 1 (1993).

> "The state legislatures entered the arena of securities regulation more than twenty years before Congress. . . . [T]he statutes, which vary widely in their terms and scope, are commonly referred to as 'blue sky' laws, an appellation with several suggested origins. It has been said, for example, that the Kansas legislature was spurred by the fear of fast-talking eastern industrialists selling everything including the blue sky." 1 Thomas Lee Hazen, *Treatise on the Law of Securities Regulation* § 8.1, at 490–92 (3d ed. 1995).

blue slip, *n.* **1.** In the House of Representatives, the formal rejection of Senate tax and spending bills that did not originate in the House by attaching a piece of blue paper to the legislation and returning it to the Senate. • Under the Original Clause of the Constitution, only the House has the power to initiate tax and spending legislation. **2.** A method by which a senator can approve or block a federal judicial appointment in the senator's state by stating an opinion about the nominee on a piece of blue paper or failing to return the paper at all. • The Senate Judiciary Committee takes the blue slip's return or withholding into account when deciding whether to recommend that the Senate approve or reject the nominee. — Also termed (in both senses) *blue-slipping.* — **blue-slip,** *vb.*

bluewater seaman. See *able-bodied seaman* under SEAMAN.

blurring, *n.* (1970) *Trademarks.* A form of dilution in which goodwill in a famous mark is eroded through the mark's unauthorized use by others on or in connection with dissimilar products or services. • Blurring is one type of dilution that is actionable under the Federal Trademark Dilution Act, 15 USCA § 1125(c). <The court found that Nabisco's use of a fish shape in its animal crackers diluted Pepperidge Farm's famous Goldfish trademark.> — Also termed *dilution by blurring; diminution.* Cf. TARNISHMENT.

> "Blurring is a lessening of the fame possessed by a famous mark. One might begin to think about blurring by recalling 'free association' exercises or games, in which one player says a word and the other player must respond instantly with the first word that pops into his or her head. By definition, a strong or famous mark is likely to produce both a prompt and a uniform 'free association' response when mentioned to most consumers. Thus when I say ROLEX, you—and almost everyone else—will likely say 'watches.' . . . On the other hand, a weak mark will produce no response at all, or a variety of responses from different consumers. . . . If the owners of the ROLEX mark had no way to prevent the use of that mark on pencils, or pianos, or pistachio nuts, because those products are so remote from watches that they could not prove any likelihood of confusion, eventually, the automatic free association of the ROLEX mark with watches, and watches alone, would be destroyed. The mark would be less famous than before. It would be blurred." Roger E. Schechter & John R. Thomas, *Intellectual Property* § 30.3, at 710–11 (2003).

BMI. *abbr.* BROADCAST MUSIC, INC.

BMP. *abbr.* See *business-method patent* under PATENT.

board, *n.* (14c) **1.** A group of persons having managerial, supervisory, or advisory powers <board of directors>. • In parliamentary law, a board is a form of deliberative assembly and is distinct from a committee — which is usu. subordinate to a board or other deliberative assembly — in having greater autonomy and authority. **2.** Daily meals furnished to a guest at an inn, boardinghouse, or other lodging <room and board>. **3.** BOARD OF DIRECTORS.

▸ **industrial board.** See INDUSTRIAL BOARD.

board-certified, *adj.* (1938) (Of a professional) recognized by an official body as a specialist in a given field of law or medicine <board-certified in civil litigation>. See BOARD OF LEGAL SPECIALIZATION.

boarder, *n.* (16c) **1.** Someone who lives in another's house and receives food and lodging in return either for regular payments or for services provided. **2.** A student, esp. of a primary or secondary school, who lives on campus during the school term, usu. receiving meals there, in return for payment. **3.** Someone who boards a vessel, train, or aircraft, esp. as part of an assault or hostile military action.

board lot. See *round lot* under LOT (3).

board of adjustment. See ADJUSTMENT BOARD.

board of aldermen. See CITY COUNCIL.

Board of Appeals. *Hist. Patents & Trademarks.* A quasi-judicial body within the U.S. Patent and Trademark Office that was empowered to hear appeals by applicants whose patent applications had been wholly or partially rejected by patent examiners. • Its work is now done by the Board of Patent Appeals and Interferences. See BOARD OF PATENT APPEALS AND INTERFERENCES.

board of directors. (18c) The governing body of a corporation, partnership, association, or other organization, elected by the shareholders or members to establish policy, elect or appoint officers and committees, and make other governing decisions. — Often shortened (informally) to *board.* — Also termed *board of governors; board of managers; board of trustees* (esp. in charitable and educational organizations); *executive board.* See DIRECTOR (2); DIRECTORATE (3).

▸ **classified board of directors.** See *staggered board of directors.*

▸ **staggered board of directors.** (1955) A board of directors whose members' terms of service overlap so that only part of the board's makeup is voted on in any single election. • Typically, members serve terms of two or more years, with some members' terms expiring at each annual election. *See* Del. Code Ann. tit. 8, § 141 (1991) (authorizing classified boards with two or three classes having two- or three-year terms). — Also termed *classified board of directors.*

board of education. (18c) A state or local agency that governs and manages public schools within a state or local district. Cf. SCHOOL BOARD.

board of equalization. See EQUALIZATION BOARD.

board of examiners. See EXAMINING BOARD.

board of fire underwriters. (1873) *Insurance.* An unincorporated voluntary association made up of fire insurers.

board of governors. 1. See BOARD OF DIRECTORS. **2.** (*cap.*) FEDERAL RESERVE BOARD OF GOVERNORS.

Board of Green Cloth. (16c) *Hist.* A group of persons responsible for governing the royal-household staff, esp. in financial matters such as accounting for expenses and paying servants' wages. • The Board consisted of the Lord Steward and inferior officers, and its name derived from the green cloth that covered the table used by the Board to conduct its duties. In more ancient times, it kept the peace and maintained courts of justice within the area around the royal household (i.e., the *verge*). — Also termed *Counting House of the King's Household; Green Cloth.*

board of health. (18c) A municipal or state agency charged with protecting the public health.

Board of Immigration Appeals. The highest administrative tribunal for interpreting and applying United States immigration law, esp. reviewing appeals from adverse decisions of immigration judges and district directors of the Department of Homeland Security. • The Board may have up to 15 permanent members appointed by the

Attorney General. — Abbr. BIA. — Also termed *Immigration Appeals Board.*

board of legal specialization. (1969) A body, usu. an arm of a state bar association, that certifies qualified lawyers as specialists within a given field. • Typically, to qualify as a specialist, a lawyer must meet a specified level of experience, pass an examination, and provide favorable recommendations from peers.

board of managers. See BOARD OF DIRECTORS.

Board of Medical Examiners. See EXAMINING BOARD.

board of pardons. (1872) A state agency, of which the governor is usu. a member, authorized to pardon persons convicted of crimes.

board of parole. See PAROLE BOARD.

Board of Patent Appeals and Interferences. *Patents & Trademarks.* The quasi-judicial body in the U.S. Patent and Trademark Office that hears (1) appeals from patent applicants whose claims have been rejected by a patent examiner, and (2) interference contests between two or more applicants trying to patent the same invention. • This tribunal assumed the work previously handled by the Board of Appeals and the Board of Patent Interferences. The U.S. Court of Appeals for the Federal Circuit hears appeals from this tribunal. — Abbr. BPAI. See INTERFERENCE (3).

board of police commissioners. (1826) An administrative tribunal vested with disciplinary powers over law-enforcement personnel.

board of regents. (18c) A panel of persons appointed to supervise an educational institution, esp. a university.

board of registration. (1866) A state agency authorized to license and discipline members of a trade or profession.

board of review. (1829) **1.** A body that reviews administrative-agency decisions. **2.** A body that reviews property-tax assessments. **3.** In some cities, a board that reviews allegations of police misconduct.

Board of Tax Appeals. See TAX COURT, U.S.

board of trade. (18c) **1.** A federation of business executives dedicated to advancing and protecting business interests. **2.** An organization that runs a commodities exchange. See CHICAGO BOARD OF TRADE. **3.** *Hist.* The Lords of the Committee of the Privy Council that had jurisdiction over trade and foreign plantations. • Today, the responsibilities once assigned to this committee are carried out by the Ministry for Trade and Industry.

board of trustees. See BOARD OF DIRECTORS.

Board of Veterans' Appeals. The agency in the U.S. Department of Veterans' Appeals responsible for reviewing decisions on entitlements to veterans' benefits. • The Board's decisions are subject to review by the U.S. Court of Appeals for Veterans Claims. — Abbr. BVA.

board of zoning appeals. See ADJUSTMENT BOARD.

boatable, *adj.* See NAVIGABLE.

boatable water. See NAVIGABLE WATER (1).

boc (bok), *n.* (bef. 12c) *Hist.* A written document, esp. one that conveys land. — Also spelled *bock.*

bockland. See BOOKLAND.

bocland. See BOOKLAND.

bodily harm. See HARM.

bodily heir. See *heir of the body* under HEIR.

bodily injury. See INJURY.

body, *n.* (15c) **1.** The main part of a written instrument, such as the central part of a statute (after the title and preamble) or the middle part of a complainant's bill in equity. **2.** A collection of laws. — Also termed *body of laws.* See CORPUS JURIS. **3.** An artificial person created by a legal authority. See CORPORATION. **4.** An aggregate of individuals or groups. See BODY POLITIC. **5.** A deliberative assembly <legislative body>. See *deliberative assembly* under ASSEMBLY (1). **6.** An aggregate of individuals or groups <student body>. **7.** BODY OF A CLAIM.

body corporate. See CORPORATION.

body execution. 1. See CAPIAS. **2.** See EXECUTION (4).

body of a claim. (1986) *Patents.* The portion of a patent claim that defines the elements or steps of the invention. • The body of the claim follows the preamble and transition phrase. In a combination claim, the body of a claim sets forth the elements of a patentable combination. — Sometimes shortened to *body.* Cf. PREAMBLE (2); TRANSITION PHRASE.

body of a county. (17c) A county as a whole.

body of laws. See BODY (2).

body order. (1947) *Criminal procedure.* A court order requiring that an inmate be brought into court.

body politic. (15c) A group of people regarded in a political (rather than private) sense and organized under a common governmental authority.

body-snatching, *n.* (1819) The unlawful removal of a corpse, esp. from a grave. — **body-snatcher,** *n.*

BOE. *abbr.* BILL OF EXCEPTIONS.

bogus (**boh**-gəs), *adj.* (1839) Not genuine; counterfeit; SPURIOUS (1) <bogus allegations>. Cf. GENUINE.

bogus check. See *bad check* under CHECK.

bogus document. See *false document* under DOCUMENT (2).

bogus will. See WILL.

boilerplate, *n.* (1893) **1.** Ready-made or all-purpose language that will fit in a variety of documents. • Originally, the term may have denoted a steel plate affixed to a boiler. But the modern sense comes from copy and artwork etched on metal plates (or molds made from a master plate) and distributed to newspapers and printers. The copy could not be edited. **2.** Fixed or standardized contractual language that the proposing party often views as relatively nonnegotiable. — **boilerplate,** *adj.*

boiler-room transaction. (1988) *Slang.* A high-pressure telephone sales pitch, often of a fraudulent nature. Cf. PHISHING; TELESCAM.

***Bolger* test.** (1987) The judicial test for determining whether a statement is commercial speech, by examining (1) whether it is an advertisement; (2) whether it refers to a specific product or service; and (3) whether the speaker has an economic motivation for making the statement. *Bolger v. Youngs Drug Prods. Corp.*, 463 U.S. 60, 66–67, 103 S.Ct. 2875, 2879–80 (1983). • An affirmative answer to all three questions is "strong support" that the speech is commercial, but it is not dispositive; rather, the decision should be based on common sense.

BOLO. *abbr.* (1972) *Criminal law. Slang.* Be on the lookout [for]. • Police sometimes use this expression for people or vehicles that they are trying to locate.

bolster, *vb.* (1915) To enhance (unimpeached evidence) with additional evidence. • This practice is often considered improper when lawyers seek to enhance the credibility of their own witnesses.

bolts, *n. pl.* (16c) *Hist.* Student-argued cases in the Inns of Court. • These practice cases were held privately, in contrast to the more formal and public *moots.* — Also termed *boltings.*

bomb, *n.* (17c) An explosive weapon that can be detonated by impact, trigger, fuse, proximity, timing device, or remote control.

- ▸ **cluster bomb.** (1967) A bomb that sends out smaller bombs when it explodes.
- ▸ **firebomb.** (1895) A bomb that starts a fire when it explodes.
- ▸ **letter bomb.** (1882) A small bomb hidden in a package and sent to someone to harm or kill that person; specif., a bomb that is put into a small box or special envelope wrapped in paper, sent by post, and rigged so that it will explode when opened. — Also termed *mail bomb; parcel bomb.*
- ▸ **petrol bomb.** (1913) See MOLOTOV COCKTAIL.
- ▸ **smoke bomb.** A device that emits clouds of smoke when detonated. • Smoke bombs are sometimes used by police to control crowds.
- ▸ **stink bomb.** (1915) A device, usu. a small container, that produces a foul stench when activated.
- ▸ **time bomb.** (1845) **1.** A bomb set to explode at a particular time. **2.** By extension, a situation that is likely to develop into an extremely serious problem.

bombardment, *n.* (18c) *Int'l law.* An attack from land, sea, or air with weapons that are capable of destroying enemy targets at a distance with bombs, missiles, or projectiles.

bomb scare. (1887) A situation in which people must be moved out of a building or area because of evidence that a bomb might have been planted there.

bona (**boh**-nə), *n.* [Latin "goods"] Chattels; personal property. Cf. BIENS.

- ▸ ***bona adventitia*** (**boh**-nə ad-ven-**tish**-ee-ə). [Latin] (17c) **1.** *Roman law.* Goods acquired by free persons in some way other than through their paterfamilias, or by slaves in a way other than through their owner. **2.** *Civil law.* Goods acquired fortuitously, but not by inheritance. — Also spelled *bona adventicia.* — Also termed *adventitia bona.*
- ▸ ***bona confiscata*** (**boh**-nə kon-fi-**skay**-tə). (17c) Goods confiscated by — or forfeited to — the Crown.
- ▸ ***bona felonum*** (**boh**-nə fə-**loh**-nəm). (17c) Personal property belonging to a convicted felon.
- ▸ ***bona forisfacta*** (**boh**-nə for-is-**fak**-tə). (17c) Forfeited goods.
- ▸ ***bona fugitivorum*** (**boh**-nə fyoo-jə-ti-**vor**-əm). (17c) Goods belonging to a fugitive. — Also termed *bona utlagatorum.*
- ▸ ***bona immobilia*** (**boh**-nə i-moh-**bil**-ee-ə). (17c) Immovable property.
- ▸ ***bona mobilia*** (**boh**-nə moh-**bil**-ee-ə). [Latin] (17c) Movable property. See MOVABLE.
- ▸ ***bona notabilia*** (**boh**-nə noh-tə-**bil**-ee-ə). (17c) Notable goods; property worth accounting for in a decedent's estate.
- ▸ ***bona paraphernalia*** (**boh**-nə par-ə-fər-**nay**-lee-ə). (17c) Clothes, jewelry, and ornaments not included in a married woman's dowry.
- ▸ ***bona peritura*** (**boh**-nə per-ə-**t[y]uur**-ə). (17c) Perishable goods; goods that an executor or trustee must diligently convert into money.
- ▸ ***bona utlagatorum*** (**boh**-nə ət-lay-gə-**tor**-əm). See *bona fugitivorum.*
- ▸ ***bona vacantia*** (**boh**-nə və-**kan**-shee-ə). [Latin "vacant goods"] (18c) **1.** Property not disposed of by a decedent's will and to which no relative is entitled under intestacy laws. See ESCHEAT. **2.** Ownerless property; goods without an owner. • *Bona vacantia* often resulted when a deceased person died without an heir willing and able to make a claim. The property either belonged to the finder or escheated to the Crown. — Sometimes shortened to *vacantia.* — Also termed *vacantia bona.*
- ▸ ***bona waviata*** (**boh**-nə way-vee-**ay**-tə). (18c) Stolen goods thrown away in flight by a thief. • The goods escheated to the Crown as a penalty to the owner for failing to pursue the thief and recover the goods.
- ▸ ***vacantia bona.*** See *bona vacantia.*

bona activa (**boh**-nə ak-**tɪ**-və). [Latin "active goods"] **1.** Assets. See ASSET (1). **2.** The claims that a person has against others. Cf. BONA PASSIVA.

bona castrensia et quasi castrensia (**boh**-nə ka-**stren**-shee-ə et **kway**-sɪ [*or* **kway**-zɪ] ka-**stren**-shee-ə). [Latin "goods acquired for military or quasi-military (i.e., public) service"] (17c) *Roman law.* The property that a son could dispose of, by testament or otherwise, without his paterfamilias's consent. See PATERFAMILIAS.

bonae fidei (**boh**-nee **fɪ**-dee-ɪ). [Latin] (18c) Of good faith; in good faith.

bonae fidei negotium (**boh**-nee **fi**-dee-ɪ ni-**goh**-shee-əm). [Latin] *Hist.* A negotiation in good faith.

***bonae fidei* possessor** (**boh**-nee **fɪ**-dee-ɪ pə-**zes**-ər). [Latin] (18c) *Roman law.* A good-faith possessor of property owned by another. • Unless the owner sued to recover the property, the possessor became the rightful owner after a specified time elapsed, unless the property had been stolen or taken by force. See USCAPIO.

bona et catalla (**boh**-nə et kə-**tal**-ə). [Law Latin] (17c) Goods and chattels.

bona fide (**boh**-nə fɪd *or* **boh**-nə **fɪ**-dee), *adj.* [Latin "in good faith"] (17c) **1.** Made in good faith; without fraud or deceit. **2.** Sincere; genuine. See GOOD FAITH. Cf. MALA FIDE; BONA FIDES. — **bona fide,** *adv.*

bona fide contract. See CONTRACT.

bona fide creditor. See CREDITOR.

bona fide emptor (**boh**-nə **fɪd**-ee **emp**-tər). [Latin] (18c) Good-faith purchaser. See *bona fide purchaser* under PURCHASER (1).

bona fide error. See ERROR (1).

bona fide holder for value. See HOLDER FOR VALUE.

bona fide intent to use. (1993) *Trademarks.* A specific, good-faith intention to use a mark in the ordinary course of trade in interstate commerce and not merely to reserve it for later use, as determined by objective circumstantial evidence. • A federal registration obtained under Lanham Act § 1(b) requires a bona fide intent to use the mark. If the required intent is later determined to be lacking, the registration may be invalidated.

bona fide judgment creditor. See JUDGMENT CREDITOR.

bona fide occupational qualification. (1945) An employment qualification that, although it may discriminate against a protected class (such as sex, religion, or national origin), relates to an essential job duty and is considered reasonably necessary to the operation of the particular business. • Such a qualification is not illegal under federal employment-discrimination laws. — Abbr. BFOQ.

> "The bona fide occupational qualification is a complete defense. It is invoked when the defendant makes a distinction expressly forbidden by Title VII, such as the refusal to hire women or women with preschool-age children, the reassignment of pregnant employees, or the exclusion of particular ethnic groups from particular jobs. . . . The employer's motivation for excluding the protected class is not significant in evaluating the BFOQ defense. The inquiry focuses on the necessity of using an expressly forbidden classification. The fact that the employer adopted the exclusion for invidious reasons, rather than for the business consideration on which the defense is based, is not material. Thus, if the exclusion, in fact, is proved to be necessary it may be used, even if invidiously motivated." Mack A. Player, *Employment Discrimination Law* § 5.29, at 282–83 (1988).

bona fide operation. (1899) A real, ongoing business.

bona fide payee. See *bona fide creditor* under CREDITOR.

bona fide perceptio et consumptio (**boh**-nə **fɪ**-dee pər-**sep**-shee-oh et kən-**sump**-shee-oh). [Latin] *Hist.* Gathering and consuming in good faith. • The phrase appeared in reference to the rights of a bona fide possessor to keep fruit that the possessor gathers in good faith and consumes in good faith.

bona fide possession. See POSSESSION.

bona fide purchaser. See PURCHASER (1).

bona fide purchaser for value. See *bona fide purchaser* under PURCHASER (1).

bona fides (**boh**-nə **fɪ**-deez), *n.* [Latin] (1845) **1.** GOOD FAITH. **2.** *Roman law.* The standard of conduct expected of a reasonable person, esp. in making contracts and similar actions; acting without fraudulent intent or malice.

bona fide sale. See SALE.

bona fiscalia (**boh**-nə- fis-**kay**-lee-ə), *n.* Public property.

bona forisfacta. See BONA.

bona fugitivorum. See BONA.

bona gratia (**boh**-nə **gray**-shee-ə). [Latin] (17c) *Roman law.* In goodwill; in a friendly way. • The phrase typically referred to a divorce by mutual consent.

bona gratia matrimonium dissolvitur (**boh**-nə **gray**-shee-ə ma-trə-**moh**-nee-əm di-**sol**-və-tər). [Law Latin "the marriage is dissolved in a friendly way"] *Hist.* A consensual divorce.

bona immobilia. See BONA.

bona memoria (**boh**-nə mə-**mor**-ee-ə). [Latin] (18c) Good memory. • *Bona memoria,* as used in the phrase *sanae mentis et bonae memoria* (of sound mind and good memory), refers to a testator's mental capacity. See MIND AND MEMORY.

bona mobilia. See BONA.

bona notabilia. See BONA.

bona paraphernalia. See BONA.

bona passiva (**boh**-nə pa-**sɪ**-və). *Roman law.* Liabilities. Cf. BONA ACTIVA.

bona peritura. See BONA.

bona utlagatorum. See *bona fugitivorum* under BONA.

bona vacantia. See BONA.

bona waviata. See BONA.

bond, *n.* (16c) **1.** An obligation; a promise.

> "[A]n obligation, or in English a 'bond,' is a document written and sealed containing a confession of a debt; in later times 'contract' is the genus, 'obligation' the species." 2 Frederick Pollock & Frederic W. Maitland, *The History of English Law* 207 (2d ed. 1899).

2. A written promise to pay money or do some act if certain circumstances occur or a certain time elapses; a promise that is defeasible upon a condition subsequent; esp., an instrument under seal by which (1) a public officer undertakes to pay a sum of money if he or she does not faithfully discharge the responsibilities of office, or (2) a surety undertakes that if the public officer does not do so, the surety will be liable in a penal sum.

> "The fact that an instrument is called a 'bond' is not conclusive as to its character. It is necessary to disregard nomenclature and look to the substance of the bond itself. The distinguishing feature of a bond is that it is an obligation to pay a fixed sum of money, at a definite time, with a stated interest, and it makes no difference whether a bond is designated by that name or by some other, if it possesses the characteristics of a bond. There is no distinction between bonds and certificates of indebtedness which conform to all the characteristics of bonds." 1 Silvester E. Quindry, *Bonds & Bondholders: Rights & Remedies* § 2, at 3–4 (1934).

▸ **administrator's bond.** See *fiduciary bond.*

▸ **appeal bond.** (18c) A bond that an appellate court may require from an appellant in a civil case to ensure payment of the costs of appeal; a bond required as a condition to bringing an appeal or staying execution of the judgment appealed from. Fed. R. App. P. 7. Cf. *supersedeas bond.*

▸ **appearance bond.** See *bail bond.*

▸ **arbitration bond.** See ARBITRATION BOND.

▸ **attachment bond.** (18c) A bond that a defendant gives to recover attached property. • The plaintiff then looks to the bond issuer to satisfy a judgment against the defendant.

▸ **average bond.** See *general-average bond.*

▸ **bail bond.** (17c) A bond given to a court by a criminal defendant's surety to guarantee that the defendant will duly appear in court in the future and, if the defendant is jailed, to obtain the defendant's release from confinement. • The effect of the release on bail bond is to transfer custody of the defendant from the officers of the law to the surety on the bail bond, whose undertaking is to redeliver the defendant to legal custody at the time and place appointed in the bond. — Also termed *appearance bond; personal bond; recognizance.* See BAIL. Cf. *unsecured bail bond.*

▸ **bid bond.** (1935) A bond filed in public construction projects to ensure that the bidding contractor will enter into the contract. • The *bid bond* is a type of performance bond. See PERFORMANCE BOND.

▸ **blank bond.** (17c) *Archaic.* A bond in which the space for the creditor's name is left blank.

▸ **blanket bond.** (1899) **1.** A bond covering several persons or projects that require performance bonds. **2.** See *fidelity bond.*

▸ **bond for land.** (1808) A bond given by the seller of land to a buyer, binding the seller to convey once the buyer tenders the agreed price. — Also termed *bond for a deed.* Cf. BINDER (1).

▸ **bond of corroboration.** (1933) An additional obligation undertaken to corroborate the debtor's original obligation.

▸ **bond to keep the peace.** See *peace bond.*

▸ **bottomry bond.** (18c) A contract for the loan of money on a ship, usu. at extraordinary interest, for maritime risks encountered during a certain period or for a certain voyage. • The loan can be enforced only if the vessel survives the voyage. — Also termed *bottomage bond.* See BOTTOMRY. Cf. *respondentia bond.*

> "A bottomry bond, strictly speaking, is a mortgage or pledge of a ship by the owner or agent, to secure the repayment of money lent for the use of the ship; and the conditions of it are, that if the ship is lost, the lender loses his money; but if it arrives, then, not only the ship itself is liable, but also the person of the borrower." John Indermaur, *Principles of the Common Law* 169 (Edmund H. Bennett ed., 1st Am. ed. 1878).

> "[T]he bottomry bond . . . is a sort of mortgage on a ship, entered into for the purpose of raising money in case of necessity in a foreign port. The advance of communications has caused bottomry and respondentia bonds to pass virtually out of use." Grant Gilmore & Charles L. Black Jr., *The Law of Admiralty* § 1-10, at 25 n.85 (2d ed. 1975).

▸ **claim-property bond.** See *replevin bond.*

▸ **common-defeasance bond.** See *penal bond.*

▸ **common-law bond.** (1833) A performance bond given by a construction contractor. • A common-law bond exceeds the requirements of a statutory performance bond because it provides additional coverage for construction projects. Cf. PERFORMANCE BOND.

▸ **common money bond.** (1828) A promise to pay money as a penalty for failing to perform a duty or obligation.

▸ **contract bond.** See PERFORMANCE BOND.

▸ **cost bond.** (1875) A bond given by a litigant to secure the payment of court costs.

▸ **counterbond.** (16c) A bond to indemnify a surety.

▸ **delivery bond.** See *forthcoming bond.*

▸ **depository bond.** (1896) A bond given by a bank to protect a public body's deposits should the bank become insolvent.

▸ **discharging bond.** (18c) A bond that both permits a defendant to regain possession of attached property and releases the property from the attachment lien. — Also termed *dissolution bond.* See *forthcoming bond.*

▸ **executor's bond.** (18c) A bond given to ensure the executor's faithful administration of the estate. See *fiduciary bond.*

> "The English law did not require an executor to give bond because he was appointed by the testator and his authority was derived from the will rather than court appointment. Some American jurisdictions do not require a bond of an executor. In the majority of our states a testator may by will dispense with the executor's bond, but in absence of such testamentary provision a bond will be required." Thomas E. Atkinson, *Handbook of the Law of Wills* § 113, at 621 (2d ed. 1953).

▸ **fidelity bond.** (1902) A bond to indemnify an employer or business for loss due to embezzlement, larceny, or gross negligence by an employee or other person holding a position of trust. — Also termed *blanket bond; fidelity guarantee; fidelity-guarantee insurance.*

▸ **fiduciary bond.** (1831) A type of performance bond required of a trustee, administrator, executor, guardian, conservator, or other fiduciary to ensure the proper performance of duties. — Also termed *administrator's bond.*

▸ **forthcoming bond.** (18c) **1.** A bond guaranteeing that something will be produced or forthcoming at a particular time, or when called for. **2.** A bond (usu. given to a sheriff) to permit a person to repossess attached property in exchange for that person's commitment to surrender the property in the event of an adverse judgment; specif., a bond required of a defendant as a condition of retaining or regaining possession of a chattel in an attachment or replevin action, whereby the surety agrees to surrender the chattel and to pay its value if the plaintiff wins the lawsuit. — Also termed *delivery bond.* Cf. *replevin bond.*

▸ **general-average bond.** (1867) *Maritime law.* A bond given to the captain of a ship by consignees of cargo subject to general average, guaranteeing payment of their contribution once it is ascertained. • When the contribution amounts are disputed, the carrier requires this bond before agreeing to unload the ship. It may also be required when the amounts are undisputed, as security for payment. — Also termed *average bond.* See *general average* under AVERAGE (3).

▸ **guaranty bond.** (1892) A bond combining the features of a fidelity bond and a performance bond, securing both payment and performance. — Also written *guarantee bond.*

▸ **heritable bond.** (17c) *Scots law.* A bond secured by land.

▸ **hypothecation bond.** (18c) *Maritime law.* A bond given in the contract of bottomry or respondentia.

▸ **indemnity bond.** (18c) A bond to reimburse the holder for any actual or claimed loss caused by the issuer's or some other person's conduct.

▸ **injunction bond.** (1850) A bond required of an injunction applicant to cover the costs incurred by a wrongfully enjoined party; a bond required as a condition of the issuance or continuance of an injunction. Fed. R. Civ. P. 65(c).

▸ **interim bond.** (1905) **1.** A bond set by a police officer when a person is arrested for a minor offense, such as a misdemeanor, without a warrant. • Although the bond allows the arrestee to be released, it requires that the person be available for arraignment. **2.** A bond set by a judge or magistrate and attached to a misdemeanor warrant.

▸ **joint bond.** (17c) A bond signed by two or more obligors. • In contrast to a joint and several bond, all the obligors must be joined if an action is brought on the bond. See *guaranteed bond* (1).

▸ **judicial bond.** (18c) A bond to indemnify an adverse party in a lawsuit against loss occasioned by delay or by deprivation of property resulting from the lawsuit. • Judicial bonds are usu. classified according to the nature of the action in which they are required, as with appeal bonds, injunction bonds, attachment bonds, replevin bonds, forthcoming or redelivery bonds, and bail bonds. A bond of a fiduciary — such as a receiver, administrator, executor, or guardian — is often required as a condition to appointment.

▸ **liability bond.** (1908) A bond intended to protect the assured from a loss arising from some event specified in the bond.

▸ **license bond.** (1850) A bond required of a person seeking a license to engage in a specified business or to receive a certain privilege. — Also termed *permit bond*.

▸ **maintenance bond.** (1855) A bond guaranteeing against construction defects for a period after the completion of the contracted-for work.

▸ **mortgage bond.** (1853) A bond secured by the issuer's real property. See *bond and mortgage*.

▸ **negotiable bond.** (1809) A bond that can be transferred from the original holder to another.

▸ **official bond.** (18c) **1.** A bond given by a public officer requiring the faithful performance of the duties of office. **2.** A bond filed by an executor, guardian, trustee, or other fiduciary. See *fiduciary bond*.

▸ **payment bond.** (1877) A bond given by a surety to cover any amounts that, because of the general contractor's default, are not paid to a subcontractor or materials supplier.

> "[T]he bond serves two purposes: it assures the owner a lien-free project, and it induces suppliers and subcontractors to accept work on the project, perhaps at a lower price, because of the assurance that they will be paid. Since no additional charge is generally made for a payment bond when a performance bond is being purchased, the two are usually issued simultaneously." Grant S. Nelson, *Real Estate Finance Law* § 12.2, at 881 (3d ed. 1994).

▸ **pay-when-paid bond.** A surety's bond according to which the surety must satisfy the claims of subcontractors, suppliers, or laborer's only to the extent that the contractor has been paid for the labor, services, or materials provided by those persons. • If a construction contract does not contain a pay-when-paid clause, the bond is considered an unconditional payment bond, and the surety must satisfy the claims of subcontractors, suppliers, or laborers regardless of whether the contractor has been paid.

▸ **peace bond.** (1846) A bond required by a court from a person who has breached or threatened to breach the peace. — Also termed *bond to keep the peace*. See BREACH OF THE PEACE.

▸ **penal bond.** (17c) A bond requiring the obligor to pay a specified sum as a penalty if the underlying obligation is not performed. — Also termed *penal bill*; *common-defeasance bond*.

▸ **performance bond.** See PERFORMANCE BOND.

▸ **permit bond.** See *license bond*.

▸ **personal bond.** (17c) **1.** See *bail bond*. **2.** A written document in which an obligor formally recognizes an obligation to pay money or to do a specified act. **3.** *Scots law.* A bond containing a promise without security.

▸ **probate bond.** (18c) A bond, such as that filed by an executor, required by law to be given during a probate proceeding to ensure faithful performance by the person under bond.

▸ **redelivery bond.** See *replevin bond*.

▸ **refunding bond.** (18c) A bond given to assure an executor that a legatee will return an estate distribution should the remaining estate assets be insufficient to pay the other legacies.

> "Refunding bonds taken by personal representatives afford a similar protection to them that indemnifying bonds do to sheriffs. The statute directs the bond to be filed in the clerk's office of the proper court; and, when so filed, it is a bar to an action against the personal representative who shall have paid a legacy or distributed the decedent's estate, by a creditor, the existence of whose debt shall not here been known to the personal representative before such payment or distribution, or within one year from his qualification. The creditor, however, may bring his suit upon the refunding bond in the name of the obligee, or his personal representative, for his own benefit." 1 R.T. Barton, *The Practice in the Courts of Law in Civil Cases* 162 (1891).

▸ **registered bond.** See REGISTERED BOND (1).

▸ **removal bond.** (1868) **1.** A bond to cover possible duties owed by a person who removes goods from a warehouse for export. **2.** A bond required in some states when a litigant seeks to remove an action to another court.

▸ **replevin bond** (ri-**plev**-in). (18c) **1.** A bond given by a plaintiff to replevy or attach property in the defendant's possession before judgment is rendered in a replevin action. • The bond protects the attaching officer and ensures the property's safekeeping until the court decides whether it should be returned to the defendant. **2.** A bond given by a defendant in a replevin action to regain attached property pending the outcome of litigation. • The bond does not discharge the attachment lien. — Also termed *replevy bond*; *claim-property bond*; *redelivery bond*. See REPLEVIN. Cf. *forthcoming bond*.

▸ **respondentia bond** (re-spon-**den**-shee-ə *or* ree-). (18c) A contract containing the pledge of a ship's cargo; a mortgage of a ship's cargo. Cf. *bottomry bond*.

> "A *respondentia bond* is a loan upon the pledge of the cargo, though an hypothecation of both ship and cargo may be made in one instrument; and generally, it is only a personal obligation on the borrower, and is not a specific lien on the goods, unless there be an express stipulation to that effect in the bond; and it amounts, at most, to an equitable lien on the salvage in case of loss." 3 James Kent, *Commentaries on American Law* *354–55 (George Comstock ed., 11th ed. 1866).

▸ **simple bond.** (17c) **1.** A bond without a penalty. **2.** A bond payable to a named obligee on demand or on a certain date.

▸ **statutory bond.** See STATUTORY BOND.

▸ **straw bond.** (1876) A bond, usu. a bail bond, that carries either a fictitious name or the name of a person who is unable to pay the sum guaranteed; a worthless or inadequate bond.

▸ **submission bond.** (18c) A bond given by a litigant who agrees to submit a lawsuit to arbitration and to be bound by an arbitrator's award.

▸ **supersedeas bond** (soo-pər-**see**-dee-əs). (18c) An appellant's bond to stay execution on a judgment during the pendency of the appeal. Fed. R. Civ. P. 62(d); Fed. R. App. P. 8(b). — Often shortened to *supersedeas.* See SUPERSEDE (2). Cf. *appeal bond.*

▸ **surety bond.** See PERFORMANCE BOND.

▸ **ten-percent bond.** (1968) A bail bond in the amount of 10% of the bond otherwise required for a defendant's release. • This type of bond usu. allows a defendant to arrange a bond without the services of a bondsman or other surety.

▸ **unsecured bail bond.** (1970) A bond that holds a defendant liable for a breach of the bond's conditions (such as failure to appear in court), but that is not secured by a deposit of or lien on property. See RECOGNIZANCE.

3. A long-term, interest-bearing debt instrument issued by a corporation or governmental entity, usu. to provide for a particular financial need; esp., such an instrument in which the debt is secured by a lien on the issuer's property. Cf. DEBENTURE.

▸ **accrual bond.** (1992) A bond — usu. the last collateralized-mortgage-obligation issue — from which no principal or interest payment will be made until any bonds issued earlier have been fully paid. — Also termed *Z-bond.*

▸ **adjustment bond.** (1917) A bond issued when a corporation is reorganized. — Also termed *reorganization bond.*

▸ **annuity bond.** (18c) A bond that lacks a maturity date and that perpetually pays interest. — Also termed *consol; perpetual bond; continued bond; irredeemable bond.*

▸ **arbitrage bond.** (1968) A municipal bond, the proceeds of which are invested in bonds paying a higher yield than that paid by the municipality on its own bonds. • Under the Internal Revenue Code, the tax-free aspect of municipal-bond income may be lost if the bonds are classified as arbitrage bonds. See ARBITRAGE.

▸ **assessment bond.** (1894) A municipal bond repaid from property assessment taxes.

▸ **assumed bond.** See *guaranteed bond* (1).

▸ **baby bond.** (1925) 1. A bond having a small face value, usu. less than $500 or $1,000. 2. *English law.* A voucher or contribution deposited on behalf of a child into a trust fund or individual savings account from which funds cannot be withdrawn until he or she becomes an adult.

▸ **bearer bond.** (1887) A bond payable to the person holding it. • The transfer of possession transfers the bond's ownership. Cf. *registered bond.*

▸ **bond and mortgage.** (1823) A bond that is backed by a mortgage on realty. — Also termed *mortgage bond.* Cf. DEBENTURE (3).

▸ **book-entry bond.** (1982) A bond for which no written certificate is issued to reflect ownership.

▸ **callable bond.** (1926) See *redeemable bond.*

▸ **chattel-mortgage bond.** (2005) A bond secured by a mortgage on personal property.

▸ **closed-end mortgage bond.** (1996) A mortgage bond with provisions prohibiting the debtor from issuing additional bonds against the bond's collateral.

▸ **collateral trust bond.** (1918) **1.** A bond representing a debt secured by the deposit of another security with a trustee. — Also termed *collateral trust certificate.* **2.** A long-term corporate bond that is secured by other companies' mortgage bonds held by the corporation, which pledges and deposits the mortgage bonds in trust. • The interest on these collateral trust bonds is typically lower than that received on the bonds pledged; the surplus is used to form a sinking fund to redeem the collateral trust bonds. A holding company often issues these bonds by pledging the stock of a subsidiary.

▸ **commodity-backed bond.** (1986) A bond with interest payments or principal repayment tied to the price of a specific commodity, such as gold. • This type of bond, which has a low interest rate but provides a hedge against inflation because the commodity price will usu. rise, is often issued by a firm with a stake in the commodity.

▸ **consolidated bond.** (1879) **1.** A railroad bond secured by a mortgage on the entire railroad line formed by several consolidated railroads. Cf. *divisional bond.* **2.** A single bond that replaces two or more outstanding issues.

▸ **construction bond.** (1880) A bond issued by a governmental entity for a building project.

▸ **continued bond.** See *annuity bond.*

▸ **convertible bond.** (1857) A bond that can be exchanged for stock shares in the corporation that issued the bond.

▸ **corporate bond.** (1842) **1.** An interest-bearing instrument containing a corporation's promise to pay a fixed sum of money at some future time. • A corporate bond may be secured or unsecured. **2.** A bond issued by a corporation, usu. having a maturity of ten years or longer.

▸ **county bond.** (1852) A county-issued bond paid through a levy on a special taxing district, whether or not the district is coextensive with the county.

▸ **coupon bond.** (1856) A bond with attached interest coupons that the holder may present to receive interest payments. See BOND COUPON.

▸ **cumulative-income bond.** See *income bond.*

▸ **cushion bond.** (1980) A bond paying an uncommonly high interest rate.

▸ **debenture bond.** See DEBENTURE (3).

▸ **deferred-interest bond.** (1959) A bond whose interest payments are postponed for a time.

▸ **discount bond.** (1918) A bond sold at its current market value, which is less than its face value. — Also termed *non-interest-bearing bond.*

▸ **divisional bond.** (1951) A railroad bond secured by a mortgage on a specific segment of a consolidated railroad system. Cf. *consolidated bond* (1).

▸ **endorsed bond.** See *guaranteed bond* (1).

▸ **equipment trust bond.** (1898) See EQUIPMENT TRUST CERTIFICATE.

▸ **ex coupon bond.** (1998) A bond sold without coupons attached.

▸ **ex legal municipal bond.** A municipal bond that does not have the legal opinion of a bond-law firm printed on it. Cf. *municipal bond.*

▸ **first-mortgage bond.** (1855) A long-term bond that has the first claim on specified assets.

▸ **flat bond.** (1916) A bond that trades without accrued interest.

▸ **floating-interest bond.** (1977) A bond with an interest rate that moves up and down with changing economic conditions.

▸ **flower bond.** (1974) A Treasury bond redeemable before maturity if used to settle federal estate taxes. • Flower bonds were issued before April 1971 and reached final maturity in 1998. Two etymological theories have been advanced to explain the term. The first, and more likely, is that the bonds had flowers engraved on their reverse side. The second is that they "blossomed" upon the death of their owner.

▸ **foreign bond.** (1830) A bond issued in a currency different from that used where the issuer is located, such as a Canadian-government bond that is denominated in U.S. dollars and issued in the United States.

▸ **full-faith-and-credit bond.** See *general-obligation bond.*

▸ **general-mortgage bond.** (1865) A corporate bond secured by a blanket mortgage on property. • The general-mortgage bond, however, is often less valuable because it is subordinate to prior mortgages.

▸ **general-obligation bond.** (1915) A municipal bond payable from general revenue rather than from a special fund. • Such a bond has no collateral to back it other than the issuer's taxing power. — Often shortened to *obligation bond.* — Also termed *full-faith-and-credit bond.*

> "There are two main types of bonds issued by local governments: general obligation bonds and revenue bonds. . . . Bonds will be assumed to be general obligation unless they themselves contain a clear promise to pay only out of a special fund." Osborne M. Reynolds Jr., *Handbook of Local Government Law* § 104, at 323 (1982).

▸ **gold bond.** (1868) **1.** *Hist.* A bond payable in gold coin or U.S. currency at the election of the bondholder. • This type of bond existed until 1933, when the U.S. monetary system abandoned the gold standard. **2.** A commodity-backed bond that is secured by gold and issued by a gold-mining company.

▸ **government bond. 1.** See *savings bond.* **2.** See *government security* under SECURITY (4).

▸ **guaranteed bond.** (1866) **1.** A bond issued by a corporation and guaranteed by a third party. • This type of bond is common among railroads. — Also termed *endorsed bond; assumed bond; joint bond.* **2.** A bond issued by a subsidiary corporation whose parent corporation guarantees the principal and interest payments.

▸ **high-yield bond.** (1906) A high-risk, high-yield subordinated bond issued by a company with a credit rating below investment grade. — Also termed *junk bond; high-yield debt obligation; high-yield security.*

▸ **improvement bond.** See *revenue bond.*

▸ **income bond.** (1882) A corporate bond secured by the corporation's net income, after the payment of interest on senior debt. • Sometimes this type of bond is a *cumulative-income bond,* in which case, if the income in any year is insufficient to pay the full interest, the deficit is carried forward as a lien on any future income. — Also termed *cumulative-income bond.*

▸ **indeterminate bond.** (1917) A callable bond with no set maturity date.

▸ **indexed bond.** (1957) A bond whose interest rate or maturity value is linked to an index such as the consumer price index.

▸ **industrial-development bond.** (1946) **1.** A type of revenue bond in which interest and principal payments are backed by a corporation rather than a municipality. • This type of bond usu. finances a private business facility. **2.** A tax-exempt municipal bond that finances a usu. local industry. — Also termed *industrial-revenue bond.*

▸ **inflation-indexed bond.** (1988) A bond whose interest rate is adjusted according to changes in the inflation rate so that the real rate of return is constant.

▸ **insurance bond.** (1983) A single-premium life-insurance policy designed to serve as an investment by accumulating a cash value that earns interest.

▸ **interchangeable bond.** (1906) A bond that can be exchanged for a different type of bond, such as a coupon bond that may be exchanged for a registered bond.

▸ **interest bond.** (1847) A bond paid in lieu of interest due on other bonds.

▸ **investment-grade bond.** (1901) A bond with a rating of BBB or better by the leading bond-rating services. See INVESTMENT-GRADE RATING.

▸ **irredeemable bond.** See *annuity bond.*

▸ **joint and several bond.** (18c) A bond in which the principal and interest are guaranteed by two or more obligors.

▸ **joint bond.** (17c) A bond signed by two or more obligors. • In contrast to a joint and several bond, all the obligors must be joined if an action is brought on the bond.

▸ **junior bond.** (1877) A bond subordinate in priority to another bond. — Also termed *subordinated bond.*

▸ **junk bond.** (1974) **1.** A bond that pays interest at a high rate because of significant risks — often issued to raise money quickly in order to buy the shares of another company. **2.** See *high-yield bond.*

▸ **leasehold-mortgage bond.** (1939) A bond issued by a lessee and secured by the lessee's leasehold interest.

▸ **Lloyd's bond.** *Hist. English law.* A corporate bond issued on work done or goods delivered. • A bond issued in this manner avoids any restriction on indebtedness existing either in law or in corporate bylaws. The term supposedly derives from an English lawyer named Lloyd, who is credited with devising the method.

▸ **mortgage bond.** (1853) A bond secured by the issuer's real property.

▸ **multimaturity bond.** See *put bond.*

▸ **municipal bond.** (1858) A bond issued by a nonfederal government or governmental unit, such as a state bond to finance local improvements. • The interest received from a municipal bond may be exempt from federal, state, and local taxes. — Often shortened (in plural) to *municipals*; *munies*. — Also termed *municipal security*. Cf. *ex legal municipal bond*.

▸ **noncallable bond.** See *noncallable security* under SECURITY (4).

▸ **non-interest-bearing bond.** See *discount bond*.

▸ **nonstatutory bond.** See *voluntary bond*.

▸ **obligation bond.** See *general obligation bond*.

▸ **open-end mortgage bond.** (1930) A mortgage bond that can be used as security for another bond issue.

▸ **optional bond.** (1930) A bond that the holder may redeem before its maturity date if the issuer agrees.

▸ **option tender bond.** See *put bond*.

▸ **participating bond.** (1928) A bond that entitles the holder to a share of corporate profits but does not have a fixed interest rate.

▸ **passive bond.** A bond bearing no interest. See *passive debt* under DEBT.

▸ **perpetual bond.** See *annuity bond*.

▸ **plain bond.** See DEBENTURE (3).

▸ **post-obit bond.** (18c) An agreement by which a borrower promises to pay to the lender a lump sum (exceeding the amount advanced) upon the death of a person whose property the borrower expects to inherit. • Equity traditionally enforces such bonds only if the terms are just and reasonable. — Also termed *post-obit agreement*.

▸ **premium bond.** (1871) A bond with a selling price above face or redemption value. See PREMIUM (3).

▸ **put bond.** A bond that gives the holder the right to redeem it for full value at specified times before maturity. — Also termed *multimaturity bond*; *option tender bond*. Cf. *put option* under OPTION (5).

▸ **railroad-aid bond.** (1873) A bond issued by a public body to fund railway construction.

▸ **redeemable bond.** (1902) A bond that the issuer may repurchase before the maturity date. — Also termed *callable bond*.

▸ **re-funding bond.** (1885) A bond that retires an outstanding bond.

▸ **registered bond.** See REGISTERED BOND (2).

▸ **reorganization bond.** See *adjustment bond*.

▸ **revenue bond.** (1853) A government bond repayable from public funds. — Also termed *improvement bond*.

▸ **savings bond.** (1948) A nontransferable bond issued by the U.S. government. — Also termed *government bond*.

▸ **school bond.** (1858) A bond issued by a city or school district to fund school construction.

▸ **secured bond.** (1849) A bond backed by some type of security. Cf. DEBENTURE (1), (3).

▸ **serial bond.** (1889) A bond issued concurrently with other bonds having different maturity dates.

▸ **series bonds.** (1920) A group of bonds issued under the authority of the same indenture, but offered publicly at different times and with different maturity dates and interest rates.

▸ **single bond.** See *bill obligatory* under BILL (7).

▸ **sinking-fund bond.** (1865) A bond backed by a sinking fund for bond redemption. See *sinking fund* under FUND (1).

▸ **special-tax bond.** (1872) A municipal bond secured by taxes levied for a specific governmental purpose, usu. improvements. — Also termed *special-assessment bond*.

▸ **state bond.** (1839) A bond issued by a state.

▸ **statutory bond.** See STATUTORY BOND.

▸ **subordinated bond.** See *junior bond*.

▸ **tax-exempt bond.** (1893) A bond that pays tax-free interest.

▸ **term bond.** A bond that matures concurrently with other bonds in that issue.

▸ **TIPS bond.** See TREASURY BOND.

▸ **Treasury bond.** See TREASURY BOND.

▸ **unsecured bond.** See DEBENTURE (3).

▸ **voluntary bond.** A bond not required by statute but given anyway. — Also termed *nonstatutory bond*.

▸ **Z-bond.** See *accrual bond*.

▸ **zero-coupon bond.** (1979) A bond paying no interest. • It is sold at a discount price and later redeemed at face value, the profit being the difference. — Also termed *passive bond*. See *zero-coupon security* under SECURITY (4).

bond, *vb.* (16c) **1.** To secure payment by providing a bond <at the creditor's insistence, Gabriel consolidated and bonded his various loans>. **2.** To provide a bond for (a person) <the company bonded its off-site workers>.

bondable, *adj.* (1922) Capable of obtaining a bond to protect another person; of, relating to, or involving a person whose record is sufficiently clear of criminal convictions or other evidence of questionable character that a bonding agency would be willing to guarantee the person's conduct. See BOND (2).

bondage (bahn-dij), *n.* (14c) **1.** *Hist.* Tenure of land by performing the meanest of services for a superior; VILLEINAGE (1). **2.** The state or condition of being a slave; involuntary servitude. **3.** By extension, the condition or state of having one's freedom limited or of being prevented from doing what one wants; subjection to some power or influence. **4.** The state or practice of being tied up for sexual pleasure.

bond and mortgage. See BOND (3).

bond conversion. (1879) The exchange of a convertible bond for another asset, usu. stock.

bond coupon. (1891) The part of a coupon bond that is clipped by the holder and surrendered to obtain an interest payment. See *coupon bond* under BOND (3).

bond covenant. A bond-indenture provision that protects bondholders by specifying what the issuer may or may not do, as by prohibiting the issuer from issuing more debt. See BOND INDENTURE (1).

bond creditor. See CREDITOR.

bond discount. See DISCOUNT (3).

bond dividend. See DIVIDEND.

bonded, *adj.* (1945) (Of a person or entity) acting under, or placed under, a bond <a bonded court official>.

bonded area. See FREEPORT.

bonded debt. See DEBT.

bonded warehouse. See WAREHOUSE.

bond for a deed. See *bond for land* under BOND (2).

bond for deed. 1. See CONVEYANCE (6). **2.** See BOND FOR TITLE.

bond for land. See BOND (2).

bond for title. (1834) *Real estate.* The seller's retention of legal title until the buyer pays the purchase price. — Also termed *bond for deed.* Cf. *installment land contract* under CONTRACT.

bond fund. See MUTUAL FUND.

bondholder. (1823) Someone who holds a government or business bond.

bond indenture. (1891) **1.** A contract between a bond issuer and a bondholder outlining a bond's face value, interest rate, maturity date, and other features. **2.** A mortgage held on specified corporate property to secure payment of the bond.

bonding company. See COMPANY.

bond issue. See ISSUE (2).

bondman. See BONDSMAN (2).

bond of corroboration. See BOND (2).

bond premium. See PREMIUM (3).

bond rating. (1852) A system of evaluating and appraising the investment value of a bond issue.

bond retirement. (1897) The cancellation of a bond that has been called or paid.

bondsman. (13c) **1.** Someone who guarantees a bond; a surety. **2.** *Hist.* A serf or peasant; VILLEIN. — Also termed (in sense 2) *bondman.*

bond table. (1867) A schedule used in determining a bond's current value by its coupon rate, its time to maturity, and its effective yield if held to maturity.

bond trust. See TRUST (3).

bones gents (bohn **jents**). [Law French "good men"] *Hist.* Qualified or competent persons; esp., men qualified to serve on a jury.

bonification (bahn-ə-fi-**kay**-shən). (18c) A tax remission, usu. on goods intended for export. • Bonification enables a commodity to be sold in a foreign market as if it had not been taxed.

boni homines (**boh**-nɪ **hom**-ə-neez). [Law Latin "good men"] *Hist.* Free tenants who judged each other in their lord's court.

> "[W]e may find traces of juries in the laws of all those nations which adopted the feodal system, as in Germany, France, and Italy; who had all of them a tribunal composed of twelve good men and true, 'boni homines' . . . ." 3 William Blackstone, *Commentaries on the Laws of England* 349 (1768).

boni mores (**boh**-nɪ **mor**-eez). [Latin] *Hist.* Good behavior.

bonis cedere (**boh**-nis **see**-də-ree). [Latin "to cede one's goods"] *Civil law.* A transfer or surrender of property, usu. from a debtor to a creditor.

bonis non amovendis. See DE BONIS NON AMOVENDIS.

bonitarian (bahn-ə-**tair**-ee-in), *adj.* (1861) *Roman law.* **1.** Equitable or beneficial. — Also termed *bonitary.* Cf. QUIRITARIAN. **2.** *Hist.* Of, relating to, or involving a property interest governed by praetorian edict rather than civil law. See *edictum praetoris* under EDICTUM.

bonitary (bahn-ə-**tair**-ee-in), *adj.* (1833) Equitable; BONITARIAN (1).

bonitary ownership. See OWNERSHIP.

bono et malo (**boh**-noh et **mal**-oh). See DE BONO ET MALO.

bonorum possessio contra tabulas (bə-**nor**-əm pə-**zes[h]**-ee-oh **kon**-trə **tab**-yə-ləs). [Latin "possession of goods contrary to the terms of the will"] *Roman law.* An order authorizing the applicant to take possession of an estate contrary to the testament. • Magistrates made such orders in certain cases, as where a testator passed over a daughter or an emancipated son who was not expressly disinherited. The legacies in the will remained valid, but if the testator passed over any male in the testator's power (*patria potestas*), the will was invalidated and intestacy resulted. — Also termed *contra tabulas.*

> "The Praetor could not affect the civil validity of a will; he could not make or unmake a heres. He could, however, give bonorum possessio to a person, heres or not at civil law, which gave him power to take possession of the goods by appropriate steps, bonorum possessio contra tabulas . . . ." W.W. Buckland, *A Text-book of Roman Law from Augustus to Justinian* 324 (Peter Stein ed., 3d ed. 1963).

bonum et aequum (**boh**-nəm et **ee**-kwəm). [Latin] *Hist.* The good and the equitable.

bonum factum (**boh**-nəm **fak**-təm). [Latin] (17c) A good or proper act or deed. — Abbr. *b.f.* — Also termed *bene factum.*

bonus. (18c) **1.** A premium paid in addition to what is due or expected; esp., a payment by way of division of a business's profits, given over and above normal compensation <year-end bonus>. • In the employment context, workers' bonuses are not a gift or gratuity; they are paid for services or on consideration in addition to or in excess of the compensation that would ordinarily be given. — Also termed *bonus payment.* **2.** BOUNTY (3). **3.** *Oil & gas.* A payment that is made in addition to royalties and rent as an incentive for a lessor to sign an oil-and-gas lease <the lessee received a large bonus at closing>.

> "The amount of bonus paid, usually referred to as a per acre amount, may fluctuate widely between properties. The amount paid depends upon the nature of the development activity in the vicinity. If the land is located in a semi-proven area, or in a logical extension of a proven field, the bonus paid may be substantial." Richard W. Hemingway, *The Law of Oil and Gas* § 2.5, at 57 (3d ed. 1991).

▸ **performance bonus.** (1905) A bonus given as a reward for outstanding productivity.

bonus fumus juris (**boh**-nəs **fyoo**-məs **joor**-is). [Latin] *Hist.* Good smoke of law. • The term was used in European courts to indicate the prima facie merit of an argument, petition, or plea.

bonus issue. (1892) *Securities.* A company's offer of free shares to existing shareholders, usu. in proportion to their holdings and esp. as an alternative to dividend payout. — Also termed *scrip issue*; *capitalization issue*.

bonus option. See OPTION (5).

bonus paterfamilias. See PATERFAMILIAS.

bonus payment. See BONUS (1).

bonus share. See *bonus stock* under STOCK.

bonus share dividend. See *bonus stock dividend* under DIVIDEND.

bonus stock. See STOCK.

bonus stock dividend. See DIVIDEND.

bonus stock issue. See *bonus stock issue* under ISSUE (2).

bonus zoning. See *incentive zoning* under ZONING.

boodle. (1883) *Slang.* Money paid as a bribe, usu. to a public official.

boodling. (1888) *Hist. Slang.* Bribery. — **boodle,** *vb.*

book, *vb.* (13c) **1.** To record in an accounting journal (as a sale or accounting item) <Jenkins booked three sales that day>. **2.** To record the name of (a person arrested) in a sequential list of police arrests, with details of the person's identity (usu. including a photograph and a fingerprint), particulars about the alleged offense, and the name of the arresting officer <the defendant was booked immediately after arrest>. **3.** To engage (someone) contractually as a performer or guest <although the group was booked for two full performances, the lead singer, Raven, canceled and this action ensued>. See BOOKING CONTRACT.

book account. See ACCOUNT.

book debt. See DEBT.

book entry. (18c) **1.** A notation made in an accounting journal. **2.** The method of reflecting ownership of publicly traded securities whereby a customer of a brokerage firm receives confirmations of transactions and monthly statements, but not stock certificates. See CENTRAL CLEARING SYSTEM.

book-entry bond. See BOND (3).

book equity. (1914) The percentage of a corporation's book value allocated to a particular class of stock. Cf. BOOK VALUE; MARKET EQUITY.

***Booker* error.** (2005) *Criminal law.* **1.** A sentencing judge's mistake of regarding the sentencing guidelines as mandatory, as opposed to merely advisory. See *U.S. v. Booker*, 543 U.S. 220, 125 S.Ct. 738 (2005). **2.** A sentencing judge's mistake of enhancing a sentence based not on facts found by a jury but instead on some other basis.

bookie. See BOOKMAKER.

booking contract. (1885) An agreement by which an actor or other performer is engaged.

bookkeeping, *n.* (17c) The mechanical recording of debits and credits or the summarizing of financial information, usu. about a business enterprise; esp., the job of recording the financial accounts of a business or other organization. Cf. ACCOUNTING.

▸ **double-entry bookkeeping.** (1839) A method of bookkeeping in which every transaction recorded by a business involves one or more "debit" entries and one or more "credit" entries. • The debit entries must equal the credit entries for each transaction recorded.

▸ **single-entry bookkeeping.** (1836) A method of bookkeeping in which each transaction is recorded in a single record, such as a record of cash or credit accounts.

bookland (**buuk**-land). (bef. 12c) *Hist.* Land held under royal charter or deed; freehold land. • This was a privileged form of ownership (usu. free of the customary burdens on land) generally reserved for churches and leaders. — Also spelled *bocland*; *bockland*. — Also termed *charter-land*. Cf. LOANLAND; FOLKLAND.

> "Charter-land is such as a man holds by charter, that is, by evidence in writing, which otherwise is called freehold. . . . [T]his land was held with more easy and commodious conditions, than folkland and copy-hold land held without writing; . . . it is a free and absolute inheritance; whereas land without writing is charged with payment and bondage; so that for the most part noblemen and persons of quality possess the former, and rustics the other. The first we call freehold and by charter: the other, land at the will of the lord." *Termes de la Ley 80* (1st. Am. ed. 1812).

> "From very early times it was common to make grants of land to religious bodies or to individuals. The grants were effected by the king as the chief of the community, with the consent of the great men, who in conjunction with the great ecclesiastics, after the introduction of Christianity, formed the Witenagemot, or Assembly of the Wise. The grant was made by means of a 'book' or charter. Land thus granted was said to be 'booked' to the grantee, and was called bocland or bookland. Thus bookland comes to mean land held under a written instrument by private persons or churches; who or whose predecessors are, or at least are supposed to have been, grantees of the community. The practice seems, after the introduction of Christianity, to have prevailed chiefly in favour of religious houses, and in this way the great ecclesiastical corporations acquired their property. . . . In process of time the conception of bookland seems to be coextensive with that of alodial land." Kenelm E. Digby, *An Introduction to the History of the Law of Real Property* 11–12 (5th ed. 1897).

> "Prior to the Conquest, property in land was divided into *bocland*, *folcland*, and *laenland*. The exact nature of these rights has been disputed, but probably *bocland* was held by owners of high station claiming under a charter of privileges originally granted by the King, while *folcland* was held by ordinary owners according to the custom of the district in which the land lay. *Laenland*, or loanland, appears to have represented something in the nature of a tenancy of a less enduring character. It derived its existence from the loan of land by one person to another, and hence emphasises the relation later known as that of feudal landlord and tenant. Furthermore, as *bocland* became more common, a tendency for *laenland* and *bocland* to coalesce appeared." A.K.R. Kiralfy, *Potter's Outlines of English Legal History* 195 (5th ed. 1958).

bookmaker. (1862) Someone who determines odds and receives bets on the outcome of events, esp. sports events, and pays out to winners. — Also termed *bookie*. See BOOKMAKING.

bookmaking. (1824) Gambling that entails the taking and recording of bets on an event, esp. a sporting event such as a horse race or football game.

book of business. (1959) **1.** A salesperson's list of accounts or clients. • Traditionally, the phrase is used in reference to financial advisers, insurance agents, private bankers, investment bankers, and financial planners. **2.** By extension, an experienced lawyer's roster of stable clients who are loyal enough to the lawyer to continue sending legal work to that lawyer regardless of which firm the lawyer might become affiliated with.

book of original entry. (1822) A day-to-day record in which a business's transactions are first recorded.

books of account. See SHOP BOOKS.

Books of Adjournal. *Scots law.* The records of the High Court of Justiciary.

Books of Sederunt. *Scots law.* The records of the Court of Session.

book value. (1894) **1.** The value at which an asset is carried on a balance sheet. Cf. BOOK EQUITY. — Also termed *carrying value.* **2.** See OWNERS' EQUITY.

▸ **adjusted book value.** (1909) The current actual value of an asset or liability as compared to the value when it was first acquired or incurred or when changes were previously updated.

▸ **net book value.** See OWNERS' EQUITY.

book-value stock. See STOCK.

boom. (1875) **1.** An artificial or fabricated enthusiasm or excitement, esp. in financial markets. • This Americanism originated as a metaphorical use of the term as denoting a swollen, torrential river that overflows its banks. **2.** A period during which sales or other business activities increase both substantially and rapidly. • The term is often used attributively <boom market> <boom town>. Cf. BUST (1).

boomage. (1862) **1.** A fee charged by a company for collecting and distributing logs that have accumulated in its boom (i.e., a line of sawed logs collected and stored on a stream's surface). **2.** A right to enter on riparian lands to fasten booms. **3.** An anchorage fee charged by a canal proprietor.

boon, *n.* (17c) *Hist.* Unpaid services, rendered in kind or labor, without being fixed in amount or time, that some tenants owed to the landowner as a condition of tenancy.

boon day. (*usu. pl.*) (17c) *Hist.* One of several days in the year when copyhold tenants were obliged to perform base services for the lord (such as reaping corn) without pay. — Also termed *due day.* — Sometimes (erroneously) termed *bind day.*

booster. (1908) **1.** Promoter; active supporter; fan. **2.** *Criminal law. Slang.* A professional or habitual shoplifter.

boot, *n.* **1.** *Tax.* Supplemental money or property subject to tax in an otherwise tax-free exchange. **2.** *Corporations.* In a corporate reorganization, anything received other than the stock or securities of a controlled corporation. **3.** *Commercial law.* Cash or other consideration used to balance an otherwise unequal exchange. **4.** *Hist.* ESTOVERS (1). **5.** BOTE (1).

boot camp. (1916) **1.** A camp for basic training of Navy or Marine Corps recruits. **2.** A military-like penal facility, esp. for juvenile offenders, characterized by rigorous discipline in stark barracks-style environments. • Boot camps are specialized programs for offenders who are generally nonviolent males from 17 to 25 years old. While proponents applaud the success of these programs, others find their long-term success limited at best. See *shock incarceration* under INCARCERATION. Cf. PRISON CAMP (2).

boothage (**boo**-thij). See BOTHAGIUM.

bootleg, *vb.* (1936) *Copyright.* To make, distribute, or traffic in unauthorized goods, esp. liquor or recordings of performances that have not been commercially released by the copyright owner. • For recordings, the term strictly applies only to unauthorized copies of commercially unreleased performances. *Dowling v. U.S.*, 473 U.S. 207, 209 n.2, 105 S.Ct. 3127, 3129 n.2 (1985). See PIRACY (4). — **bootleg; bootlegged,** *adj.*

bootleg copy. *Copyright.* See BOOTLEG RECORDING (1).

bootlegger, *n.* (1889) Someone who manufactures, transports, or sells something illegally, esp. liquor or unauthorized copies of commercially unreleased music or performances. See MOONSHINE.

bootleg recording, *n.* (1936) *Copyright.* **1.** An unauthorized fixation or copy of a live or broadcast performance in a tangible medium or digital duplication made available over the Internet. — Also termed *bootleg copy; underground recording; import recording.* **2.** See PIRATE RECORDING. **3.** COUNTERFEIT RECORDING.

bootstrap, *vb.* (1951) **1.** To succeed despite sparse resources. **2.** To reach an unsupported conclusion from questionable premises, esp. to use two legal presumptions, one based on the other. **3.** To overcharge a defendant by using a single felony charge twice to support an additional felony charge. — **bootstrapping,** *n.*

bootstrap doctrine. (1940) *Conflict of laws.* The doctrine that forecloses collateral attack on the jurisdiction of another state's court that has rendered final judgment. • The doctrine applies when a court in an earlier case has taken jurisdiction over a person, over status, or over land. It is based on the principle that under res judicata, the parties are bound by the judgment, whether the issue was the court's jurisdiction or something else. The bootstrap doctrine, however, cannot give effectiveness to a judgment by a court that had no subject-matter jurisdiction. For example, parties cannot, by appearing before a state court, "bootstrap" that court into having jurisdiction over a federal matter.

> "If the court which rendered the judgment has, with the parties before it, expressly passed upon the jurisdictional question in the case, or had opportunity to do so because the parties could have raised the question, that question is res judicata, and is therefore not subject to collateral attack in the state in which the judgment is sued on. This has been called the 'bootstrap doctrine,' the idea being that a court which initially had no jurisdiction can when the issue is litigated lift itself into jurisdiction by its own incorrect but conclusive finding that it does have jurisdiction." Robert A. Leflar, *American Conflicts Law* § 79, at 159 (3d ed. 1977).

bootstrap sale. See SALE.

booty. (15c) **1.** *Int'l law.* Movables taken from the enemy as spoils in the course of warlike operations. — Also termed *spoils of war.* **2.** Property taken by force or piracy; prize or loot.

BOP. *abbr.* **1.** BUREAU OF PRISONS. **2.** BURDEN OF PROOF.

BOQ. *abbr.* BILL OF QUANTITIES.

BOR. *abbr.* BUREAU OF RECLAMATION.

bordage (**bor**-dij). (17c) *Hist.* A type of tenure in which a tenant holds a cottage and a few acres in exchange for providing customary services to the lord. — Also termed *bordagium.*

bordar (**bor**-dər). (17c) *Hist.* A bordage tenant. • The status of such a tenant was less servile than that of a villein tenant. — Also termed *bordarius* (pl. *bordarii*). See BORDAGE; VILLEINAGE.

bordello. See BROTHEL.

border. (15c) **1.** The boundary between one country (or a political subdivision) and another. **2.** A frontier of a state or of the settled part of a country.

Border and Transportation Security Directorate. The division of the U.S. Department of Homeland Security responsible for maintaining the safety of the country's borders and transportation systems. • The Directorate includes the Transportation Security Administration, the U.S. Customs Service, the border security functions of the U.S. Citizenship and Immigration Service, the Animal & Plant Health Inspection Service, and the Federal Law Enforcement Training Center. It is the Department's largest division. — Abbr. BTS.

border control. (1917) *Int'l law.* A country's physical manifestation of its territorial sovereignty, by which it regulates which people and goods may enter and leave. • As a practical matter, border controls are often used to contain plant and animal diseases, fight terrorism, and detect the movement of criminals.

bordereau (bor-də-**roh**), *n.* (1897) **1.** A description of reinsured risks; esp., a periodic report provided by a cedent to a treaty reinsurer, consisting of basic information affecting the reinsurance treaty, such as the underlying insureds, the types of risks covered, policies, and dates of loss. See REINSURANCE TREATY. **2.** A detailed note of account. Pl. **bordereaux.** — **bordereau,** *vb.*

borderer. (16c) An inhabitant of an area near or adjacent to a border.

border land. (16c) Land on the frontiers of two contiguous countries, states, or regions. — **borderlander,** *n.*

border search. See SEARCH (1).

border security. (1948) The policing of the flow of people and goods across the boundaries of a country; esp., the protection of a country's outer boundaries from the illegal movement of weapons, drugs, contraband, and people, while allowing lawful entry and exit, so as to promote national sovereignty.

border state. (*often cap.*) (1842) In the pre-Civil War United States, any state bordering on a free state, the list usu. including Delaware, Maryland, Virginia, Kentucky, and Missouri.

border warrant. See WARRANT (1).

bord-halfpenny (bord-**hay**-pə-nee). See BOTHAGIUM.

bordlands. (17c) *Hist.* Land used by the nobility to produce food. • Bordlands remained under the nobility's direct control or were given to tenants who produced provisions for the landowner. Cf. BORDAGE.

borg (borg), *n. Hist. Scots law.* **1.** A thing deposited as a security, esp. for bail or a suretyship. **2.** A surety. — Also spelled *borgh; borh.*

borgh. 1. See BORG. **2.** See BORROW.

borh. 1. See BORG. **2.** See BORROW.

bork (bork), *vb.* (1987) *Slang.* **1.** (Of the U.S. Senate) to reject a nominee, esp. for the U.S. Supreme Court, on grounds of the nominee's political and legal philosophy. • The term derives from the name of Robert Bork (1927–2012), President Ronald Reagan's unsuccessful nominee for the Supreme Court in 1987. **2.** (Of political and legal activists) to embark on a media campaign to pressure U.S. Senators into rejecting a President's nominee. **3.** Generally, to smear a political opponent.

born-alive test. (1964) **1.** Under the common law, a showing that an infant was completely expelled from the mother's womb and possessed a separate and independent existence from the mother. **2.** A showing that an infant, at the time of birth, was capable of living a separate and independent existence (regardless of how long the infant actually lived). • This test was first announced in *Bonbrest v. Kotz,* 65 F. Supp. 138 (D.D.C. 1946).

born valid. (1985) *Patents.* Presumed to be good; entitled to the legal presumption that a patent was justified when issued and that challengers bear the burden of proving by clear and convincing evidence that the patent should not have been granted. • Defenses against infringement claims take three tacks: denying that the product infringes on the plaintiff's rights, challenging the validity of the patent itself, or challenging its enforceability. — Also termed *presumption of validity.*

> "The patent statute is unambiguous: 'A patent shall be presumed valid . . . . The burden of establishing invalidity of a patent or any claim thereof shall rest on the party asserting such invalidity.' A patent is born valid. It remains valid until a challenger proves it was stillborn or had birth defects, or is no longer viable as an enforceable right." *Roper Corp. v. Litton Sys., Inc.,* 757 F.2d 1266, 1270 (Fed. Cir. 1985) (quoting 35 USCA § 282).

borough (**bər**-oh *or* **bər**-ə), *n.* (bef. 12c) **1.** A town or township with a municipal charter, or one of the five principal political divisions of New York City. **2.** *Hist.* A fortified or important town. — Also spelled *burgh.* **3.** *English law.* A chartered town that originally sent a member to Parliament; specif., a town or part of a large city responsible for managing its own schools, hospitals, roads, etc.

▸ **burgage borough.** *Hist.* A borough whose charter gave the vote only to owners of specific parcels of property cited in them.

▸ **close borough.** See *pocket borough.*

▸ **corporation borough.** *Hist.* A borough in which the borough council (or corporation) selects those who may vote.

▸ **freeman borough.** *Hist.* A borough in which the voters were only those holding the formal status of borough freeman, often on a hereditary basis.

▸ **municipal borough.** (1838) *English law.* A municipal corporation, usu. not a city, endowed by royal charter with certain privileges.

▸ **nomination borough.** See *pocket borough.*

▸ **parliamentary borough.** (17c) *English law.* A town, whether incorporated or not, entitled to representation in Parliament — sometimes not coextensive with a municipal borough bearing the same name.

▸ **pocket borough.** (18c) *Hist. English law.* A parliamentary borough owned or controlled by a single person or family. — Also termed *close borough; nomination borough.*

> "The *pocket boroughs,* nomination or close boroughs, belonged to some patron as much as the watch he carried in his pocket; he owned the two seats of the borough and could dispose of them freely. The men he selected were to vote as he directed, and certainly never against his interests. Should they be unable to meet this obligations, they were bound in honor to vacate their seats. Obviously, the smaller a borough's electorate, the better chance the

borough had of falling into this category, where nomination by the patron was tantamount to election. In fact, most burgage boroughs were pocket boroughs in that patrons owned all or most of the property giving the franchise in them. The most famous such borough was Old Sarum, which for some time was the property of the Pitt family. It was, however, possible for a borough to have a wide franchise legally and yet to be a pocket borough in fact. Thus Gatton had the very generous qualification of mere residency, but such a paucity of residents that its electorate usually amounted to about six people, who as renters of Sir John Colebrooke did his bidding." Colin Rhys Lovell, *English Constitutional and Legal History* 428–29 (1962).

▸ **rotten borough.** (18c) A borough with such a small population as to have no real constituency, the individual voters being particularly susceptible to bribery.

borough council. (1879) The governing body of a borough.

borough court. (18c) *English law.* An inferior civil court of record, usu. presided over by the municipal recorder. • Most borough courts were abolished by Parliament in 1972. Cf. *borough session* under SESSION (1); RECORDER (1).

borough English. (16c) *Hist.* A common-law rule of descent whereby the youngest son (or sometimes the youngest daughter or collateral heir) inherited all his father's lands. • If the landowner had no issue, his youngest brother inherited the land. This practice applied to socage tenures in some parts of England. It was abolished by statute in 1925. — Also termed *postremogeniture; ultimogeniture.* — Also termed *burgh English; burgh Engloys.* See PRIMOGENITURE.

borough fund. (1835) *English law.* The revenue generated by a municipal borough.

borough-holder. See BORSHOLDER.

boroughmaster (**bər**-ə-mas-tər), *n.* (18c) **1.** The mayor of an English borough. — Also termed *burgomaster.* **2.** *Hist. English law.* Before 1832, a single person or family who controlled a parliamentary borough (known as a *close borough* or *pocket borough*).

borough reeve. See REEVE.

borough session. See SESSION (1).

borrow, *n.* (16c) A frankpledge. — Also spelled *borgh; borh.* See DECENARY; FRANKPLEDGE.

borrow, *vb.* (bef. 12c) **1.** To take something for temporary use. **2.** To receive money with the understanding or agreement that it must be repaid, usu. with interest. See LOAN.

borrowed capital. (18c) Funds lent to a corporation or other entity to finance its operations, such as cash dividends that are declared by a corporation but temporarily retained (with stockholder approval) to provide operating funds.

borrowed employee. See EMPLOYEE.

borrowed servant. See *borrowed employee* under EMPLOYEE.

borrowed-statutes doctrine. (1958) The proposition that if a legislature enacts a statute copied (borrowed) from another jurisdiction, the courts of the borrowing state are bound by any settled judicial construction of the statute in the lending state. *See Cathcart v. Robinson,* 30 U.S. (5 Pet.) 264, 264–65 (1831). — Also termed *borrowed-statute doctrine.* Cf. PRIOR-CONSTRUCTION CANON.

borrower. (15c) A person or entity to whom money or something else is lent.

borrowhead. See BORSHOLDER.

borrowing powers. (1847) *Corporations.* The limits on the amount of money that a company may borrow according to its own rules.

borrowing statute. (1934) A statute that specifies the circumstances in which a forum state will apply another state's statute of limitations. • Borrowing statutes constitute a legislative exception to the conflict-of-laws rule holding that a forum state must apply its own statute of limitations.

borsholder (**bors**-hohl-dər). (16c) *Hist.* **1.** The chief of a tithing or frankpledge. **2.** A petty constable. — Also termed *borough-holder; borrowhead; headborough.*

boscage (**bos**-kəj), *n.* (15c) *Hist. English law.* A tax on wood brought into a city. — Also spelled *boskage.*

Boston interest. See INTEREST (3).

Boston marriage. *Slang. Rare.* An arrangement in which two unrelated, unmarried women reside together, share expenses, and do not seek or entertain suitors. • The term, often used pejoratively, arose in New England and was popularized by Henry James in *The Bostonians* (1886), a novel in which two women have a long-term cohabiting relationship.

bote (boht). [Anglo-Saxon] (bef. 12c) *Hist.* **1.** A tax, assessment, or obligatory service exacted for the common good.

▸ **brigbote** (**brig**-boht), *n.* (17c) *Hist.* An obligation, often extracted as a tax or a charge on land, to contribute to the cost of maintaining castles, walls, and bridges. — Also spelled *bridgebote.* See TRINODA NECESSITAS.

▸ **burghbote.** A tax for the construction and repair of castles, walls, or other defenses of a burgh. See TRINODA NECESSITAS.

▸ **fyrdbote.** The obligation to serve in the national militia. — Often shortened to *fyrd.* See TRINODA NECESSITAS.

2. A privilege to use what is needed for subsistence or repair; esp., a tenant's right to use as much wood or other materials from the estate as necessary for fuel, fences, and other agricultural operations. • *Bote* in this sense is an earlier form of estovers. See ESTOVERS (1).

▸ **cartbote.** See *plowbote.*

▸ **firebote.** See *housebote.*

▸ **haybote** (**hay**-boht), *n.* [fr. French *haye* "a hedge" + Saxon *bote* "an allowance"] (12c) *Hist.* The right or privilege of a tenant for life or years to have material to repair the hedges or fences, or to make farming implements. — Also termed *hedgebote.*

▸ **hedgebote.** See *haybote.*

▸ **housebote.** (17c) An allowance of wood from the estate used to repair a house or to burn in the fireplace. — Also termed *firebote.*

▸ **plowbote.** (14c) An allowance of wood for the construction and repair of farm equipment. — Also termed *cartbote.*

▸ **wainbote.** (13c) An allowance of wood for the repair of wagons.

3. A compensatory payment for causing an injury. — Also spelled (in all three senses) *bot; boot.* Cf. BOTELESS.

"Bot (relief, remedy, compensation) was set at a certain number of shillings in case of wounding, a higher number if the wound injured not only flesh but also bone; indemnity had to be higher if the bone was broken. And so it went with other injuries." Charles Herman Kinnane, *A First Book on Anglo-American Law* 215 (2d ed. 1952).

▸ **Godbote.** (bef. 12c) A church fine paid for offenses against God. — Also termed *deedbote; dedbote.*

▸ **hadbote.** (bef. 12c) *Hist.* Amends for an affront to or violence against a person in holy orders. — Also spelled *had-bot.*

▸ **kinbote.** See *manbote.*

▸ **lowbote (loh-boht).** (18c) *Hist.* Compensation paid for the death of one killed in a disturbance.

▸ **maegbote (mag-boht).** (bef. 12c) Bote paid to the relatives of an injured person.

▸ **manbote.** (15c) Compensation for killing someone. — Also termed *kinbote.*

▸ **theftbote (theft-boht).** (15c) The acceptance of a payment from a thief in exchange for an agreement not to prosecute; COMPOUNDING A CRIME. • The payment might be either a bribe or a return of the stolen goods themselves. This was a form of compounding a felony.

"Another offence of this class is *theftbote* or composition with a thief by which the person robbed takes his goods again and by contract suppresses the robbery and defrauds justice. This crime is punishable by fine and imprisonment." 1 Robert Chambers, *A Course of Lectures on the English Law: 1767–1773* 448 (Thomas M. Curley ed., 1986).

boteless (boht-ləs), *adj.* (bef. 12c) *Hist.* **1.** Of, relating to, or involving an offense that cannot be expiated or otherwise remedied by the payment of a fine, the offender being required to suffer loss of liberty or life. • Boteless offenses appeared in Anglo-Saxon Britain about A.D. 700. They appear to have involved treason or violence against the king. **2.** Without relief or remedy; without the privilege of making satisfaction for a crime by pecuniary payment; NONCOMPENSABLE. • The modern word *bootless* is derived from this term. — Also spelled *botless.* Cf. BOTE (3).

"In the laws of Ine it appeared possible, in the discretion of the king, to put certain offenders to death, rather than let them save themselves by paying a money fine. This involved a step in the modern direction, as far as criminal law is concerned. The 'boteless' offense, that is, the offense which can not be fully expiated by the payment of a money fine so that the guilty person must suffer loss of liberty or life is so familiar to us that we take it as a matter of course; it seems, however, to have first appeared in Anglo-Saxon Britain about the year A.D. 700. In general, these 'boteless' offenses seem to have appeared in connection with matter that we would say now involved treason or violence offered to the king." Charles Herman Kinnane, *A First Book on Anglo-American Law* 216–17 (2d ed. 1952).

bothagium (bah-thay-jee-əm). (18c) *Hist.* Customary dues paid to a lord for placing a booth in a fair or market. — Also termed *bord-halfpenny; boothage.*

both-to-blame clause. (1938) *Marine insurance.* A bill-of-lading provision stipulating that if two or more ships collide and all are at fault, all the owners and shippers involved must share in the collective losses in proportion to the monetary value of their interests before the collision occurred. — Also termed *both-to-blame collision clause.*

both-to-blame collision clause. See BOTH-TO-BLAME CLAUSE.

botiler of the king. (17c) *Hist.* An officer who provided the king's wines. • By virtue of office, the *botiler* could choose two casks from every wine-laden ship. The modern word *butler* is derived from *botiler.*

bottomage bond. See *bottomry bond* under BOND (2).

bottom-hole agreement. (1937) *Oil & gas.* A support agreement in which the contributing party agrees to make a cash contribution to the drilling party in exchange for geological or drilling information if the well is drilled to the agreed depth. See SUPPORT AGREEMENT.

bottomland. (18c) Low-lying land, often located in a river's floodplain.

bottom line. (1967) **1.** The final line in a financial statement showing net income and loss. • The phrase originated in the physical placement of the net-income figure at the bottom of the page, all expenses having been subtracted from revenues. Revenues are considered "top line" figures. **2.** The decisive point or consideration. **3.** The end result; upshot.

bottomry. (17c) *Maritime law.* A contract by which a shipowner pledges the ship as security for a loan to finance a voyage (as to equip or repair the ship), the lender losing the money if the ship is lost during the voyage. • The term refers to the idea that the shipowner pledges the ship's bottom, or keel. Cf. RESPONDENTIA.

bottomry bond. See BOND (2).

bottomside brief. See BRIEF (1).

bottom-up reasoning. (1991) Rational thought that begins with judgments about particular instances and derives general principles or rules from them; INDUCTION (2). Cf. TOP-DOWN REASONING.

bought and sold notes. (1829) Two memoranda prepared by a broker to record the sale of a note. • The broker sends the *bought note* to the purchaser, and sends the *sold note* to the seller.

bought note. See NOTE (1).

boulevard rule. (1957) The principle that the driver of a vehicle approaching a highway from a smaller road must stop and yield the right-of-way to all highway traffic.

boulwarism. (1963) *Labor law.* A bargaining tactic in which an employer researches the probable outcome of collective bargaining and uses the information to make a firm settlement offer to a union on a take-it-or-leave-it basis, so that there is no real negotiation. • *Boulwarism* is now considered to be an unfair labor practice by the National Labor Relations Board. The practice takes its name from Lemuel Boulware, vice president for employee relations at General Electric Company, who used the technique during the mid-20th century.

bounced check. See *bad check* under CHECK.

bound, *adj.* (15c) **1.** Constrained by a contractual or other obligation <they are bound to make the payments by the first of each month>. **2.** (Of a court) constrained to follow a precedent <bound by a Supreme Court decision>.

bound, *n.* (*usu. pl.*) (13c) **1.** BOUNDARY <metes and bounds>. **2.** A limitation or restriction on action <within the bounds of the law>.

bound, *vb.* (14c) To delineate a property boundary <property bounded by the creek>. Cf. BIND.

boundary. (1598) **1.** A natural or artificial separation that delineates the confines of real property <the creek serves

as a boundary between the two properties>. See METES AND BOUNDS.

> "The object of all rules for the establishment of boundaries is to ascertain the actual location of the boundary as made at the time. The important and controlling consideration, where there is a conflict as to a boundary, is the parties' intention, whether express or shown by surrounding circumstances . . . ." 11 C.J.S. *Boundaries* § 3 (1995).

▸ **agreed boundary.** (1906) A negotiated boundary by which adjacent landowners resolve uncertainties over the extent of their land. — Also termed *boundary by agreement; boundary by acquiescence.* See AGREED-BOUNDARY DOCTRINE.

▸ **land boundary.** (18c) The limit of a landholding, usu. described by linear measurements of the borders, by points of the compass, or by stationary markers. See FORTY; LEGAL DESCRIPTION.

▸ **lost boundary.** (1828) A boundary whose markers have decayed, changed, or been removed or displaced in such a manner that the boundary's correct location can no longer be determined with confidence.

▸ **maritime boundary.** See *territorial waters* under WATER.

▸ **natural boundary.** (17c) Any nonartificial thing (such as a river or ocean) that forms a boundary of a country, a political subdivision, or a piece of property. — Also termed *natural object.* See *public boundary.*

▸ **private boundary.** (18c) An artificial boundary marker.

▸ **public boundary.** (1837) A natural formation that marks the beginning of a boundary line. — Also termed *natural boundary.*

2. *Int'l law.* A line marking the limit of the territorial jurisdiction of a state or other entity having an international status.

boundary by acquiescence. See *agreed boundary* under BOUNDARY (1).

boundary by agreement. See *agreed boundary* under BOUNDARY (1).

boundary traffic. (1912) The movement of persons or goods across an international boundary.

bound bailiff. See BAILIFF (2).

bounded tree. (18c) A tree that marks a corner of a property's boundary.

bounden, *adj.* (14c) *Archaic.* **1.** (Of a person) under obligation; beholden. **2.** (Of a duty) required as a matter of moral and ethical rectitude; enjoined by one's sense of morality.

bounder. (16c) **1.** A visible mark that indicates a territorial limit in a land survey. **2.** A dissolute man; a cad.

bounty. (13c) **1.** A premium or benefit offered or given, esp. by a government, to induce someone to take action or perform a service <a bounty for the killing of dangerous animals>. Cf. REWARD. **2.** A gift, esp. in a will; generosity in giving <the court will distribute the testator's bounty equally>. **3.** The portion of a salvage award exceeding what the salvor would be entitled to on the basis of quantum meruit. — Also termed *gratuity; bonus.*

bounty hunter. (1930) Someone who for a fee pursues someone charged with or suspected of a crime; esp., a person hired by a bail-bond company to find and arrest a criminal defendant who has breached the bond agreement by failing to appear in court as ordered. — Also termed *bail-enforcement agent.*

bounty land. See LAND.

bounty-land warrant. (1846) *Hist.* A state- or federal-government-issued certificate affirming a veteran's eligibility to apply for ownership of a certain amount of public land. • A veteran had to apply for a bounty-land warrant; it was not automatically granted. When the application was approved, the veteran received notice that the warrant had been issued in the veteran's name and was on file in the General Land Office. The veteran could then sell or otherwise transfer the bounty-land warrant to anyone, even a nonveteran. The warrant holder acquired the right to redeem the warrant and apply for a land patent. The last statute authorizing the issue of bounty-land warrants was enacted in 1894, and the last warrants were issued in 1906.

bourse (buurs). [French] (16c) *French law.* An exchange; a stock exchange. — Also termed *bourse de commerce.*

boutique (boo-**teek**). (1984) A small specialty business; esp., a small law firm specializing in one particular aspect of law practice <a tax boutique>.

boutique court. (2003) *Slang.* A court that hears only or primarily very specific types of cases, such as a drug court, domestic-violence court, mental-health court, or sex-offender court. — Also termed *problem-solving court.*

bovata terrae (boh-**vay**-tə **ter**-ee). [Law Latin "land of bovines"] *Hist.* See OXGANG.

bovate. See OXGANG.

bow-bearer. (16c) *Hist.* An officer responsible for apprehending trespassers and poachers in the king's forest.

box, *vb.* (1868) *Hist. English & Scots law.* To file a paper with a court of law.

box day. (1864) *Hist. Scots law.* (*often cap.*) One of the vacation days formerly appointed for filing papers in the Court of Session.

box-top license. See *shrinkwrap license* under LICENSE.

boycott, *n.* (1880) **1.** An action designed to achieve the social or economic isolation of an adversary, esp. by the concerted refusal to do business with it. • The term derives from Captain Charles C. Boycott, an English landowner in famine-plagued Ireland of the 1870s; because of his ruthless treatment of Irish tenant farmers, the Irish Land League ostracized him. **2.** A refusal to deal in one transaction in an effort to obtain favorable terms in a second transaction. • Under the Sherman Antitrust Act, even peaceful persuasion of a person to refrain from dealing with another can amount to a boycott. *See* 15 USCA §§ 1–7. Cf. PICKETING; STRIKE. **3.** The period during which the refusal to do business is in effect. — **boycott,** *vb.*

▸ **consumer boycott.** (1941) A boycott by consumers of products or services to show displeasure with the manufacturer, seller, or provider.

▸ **group boycott.** (1936) *Antitrust.* **1.** CONCERTED REFUSAL TO DEAL. **2.** A type of secondary boycott by two or more competitors who refuse to do business with one firm unless it refrains from doing business with an actual or potential competitor of the boycotters. • A group boycott can violate the Sherman Act and is analyzed under either the per se rule or the rule of reason, depending on the nature of the boycott. See PER SE RULE; RULE OF REASON.

▸ **primary boycott.** (1903) A boycott organized by union members and directed against an employer with whom they have a dispute.

▸ **secondary boycott.** (1903) A boycott of the customers or suppliers of a business so that they will withhold their patronage from that business. • For example, a group might boycott a manufacturer who advertises on a radio station that broadcasts messages considered objectionable by the group.

Boykin Act. *Hist. Patents.* A post-World War II statute that extended the U.S. patenting deadlines for citizens of former enemy countries. • A similar measure, the Nolan Act, was passed after World War I.

***Boyle* defense.** See GOVERNMENT-CONTRACTOR DEFENSE.

bp. *abbr.* BASIS POINT.

BPAI. *abbr.* BOARD OF PATENT APPEALS AND INTERFERENCES.

BPO. *abbr.* BUSINESS-PRODUCT OUTSOURCING.

B.R. *abbr.* **1.** Bankruptcy Reporter. — Also abbreviated *Bankr. Rep.* **2.** *Bancus Regis* [Latin "King's Bench"]. **3.** *Bancus Reginae* [Latin "Queen's Bench"]. • This abbreviation has been replaced by the English initials of these courts, K.B. and Q.B.

bracery. (16c) *Hist.* **1.** The offense of selling pretended rights or title to land. • This practice was outlawed by statute of 32 Hen. 8, ch. 9. **2.** EMBRACERY.

bracket creep. (1978) The process by which inflation or increased income pushes individuals into higher tax brackets.

bracket system. (1937) *Tax.* A system for collecting a sales tax based on an index providing for a graduated payment depending on the purchase price of the item, the purpose being fourfold: (1) to avoid having the seller collect a tax less than one cent; (2) to avoid requiring the state to figure the exact amount of tax on each sale; (3) to allow the seller to have a ready means for fixing the tax to be collected; and (4) to allow the state to collect about the right amount of tax. • This system may be provided for either by statute or by administrative regulation.

Bracton. The common title of one of the earliest books of English law, *De Legibus et Consuetudinibus Angliae* (ca. 1250). • Henry of Bratton (also known as *Bracton*), a judge of the Court of King's Bench and of Assize, is credited with writing the work. Cf. GLANVILL.

> "Bracton's book is the crown and flower of English medieval jurisprudence. . . . Romanesque in form, English in substance — this perhaps is the best brief phrase that we can find for the outcome of his labours; but yet it is not very good. He had at his command and had diligently studied . . . various parts of the Corpus Iuris Civilis, of the Decretum, and the Decretals, and he levied contributions from the canonist Tancred. . . . Bracton's debt — and therefore our debt — to the civilians is inestimably great. But for them, his book would have been impossible; but for them . . . we should have missed not only the splendid plan, the orderly arrangement, the keen dilemmas, but also the sacerdotal spirit of the work. On the other hand, the main matter of his treatise is genuine English law laboriously collected out of the plea rolls of the king's court. . . . [H]is endeavor is to state the practice, the best and most approved practice, of the king's court, and of any desire to romanize the law we must absolutely acquit him." 1 Frederick Pollock & Frederic W. Maitland, *The History of English Law Before the Time of Edward I* 206–09 (2d ed. 1898).

> "[T]he discovery of what is known as *Bracton's Notebook*, the raw materials on which his treatise is founded, and the use which Maitland has made of it, have shown beyond the possibility of refutation that Bracton was in reality giving an accurate picture of English law as it was applied in the courts in the time of Henry III." G.W. Keeton, *The Elementary Principles of Jurisprudence* 125 (2d ed. 1949).

Brady Act. A federal law establishing a national system for quickly checking the background of a prospective handgun purchaser. • The formal name of the law is the Brady Handgun Violence Prevention Act. The U.S. Supreme Court held unconstitutional the law's interim provision, which required chief state law-enforcement officers (usu. sheriffs) to conduct background checks until the national system was in place. The act is named for James Brady, who, as a member of President Ronald Reagan's staff, was wounded by gunfire during an attempted presidential assassination in 1981. 18 USCA §§ 921–930. — Also termed (informally) *Brady Bill.*

***Brady* material.** (1972) *Criminal procedure.* Information or evidence that is favorable to a criminal defendant's case and that the prosecution has a duty to disclose. • The prosecution's withholding of such information violates the defendant's due-process rights. *Brady v. Maryland*, 373 U.S. 83, 83 S.Ct. 1194 (1963). See *exculpatory evidence* under EVIDENCE. Cf. JENCKS MATERIAL.

***Brady* motion.** (1966) A criminal defendant's request that a court order the prosecution to turn over evidence favorable to the defendant when the evidence is relevant to the defendant's guilt or punishment. *Brady v. Maryland*, 373 U.S., 83 S.Ct. 1194 (1963). See BRADY MATERIAL.

brain death. See DEATH.

brain-stem death. See *whole-brain death* under DEATH.

brainwash, *vb.* (1951) To make (someone) believe something untrue by using coercion or force, engendering confusion, or continually repeating the untruth over a long period of time. — **brainwashing,** *n.*

brake. See DUKE OF EXETER'S DAUGHTER.

branch. (13c) **1.** An offshoot, lateral extension, or division of an institution <the executive, legislative, and judicial branches of government>. **2.** A line of familial descent stemming from a common ancestor <the Taylor branch of the Bradshaw family>. — Also termed *stock.* **3.** A license held by a ship's pilot. See *branch pilot* under PILOT.

branch pilot. See PILOT.

brand. (1854) *Trademarks.* A name or symbol used by a seller or manufacturer to identify goods or services and to distinguish them from competitors' goods or services; the term used colloquially in business and industry to refer to a corporate or product name, a business image, or a mark, regardless of whether it may legally qualify as a trademark. • Branding is an ancient practice, evidenced by individual names and marks found on bricks, pots, etc. In the Middle Ages, guilds granted their members the right to use a guild-identifying symbol as a mark of quality and for legal protection. — Also termed *brand name.* Cf. TRADEMARK; TRADENAME.

▸ **private brand.** (1867) An identification mark placed on goods made by someone else under license or other arrangement and marketed as one's own. • The seller of private-brand goods sponsors those goods in the market, becomes responsible for their quality, and has rights to prevent others from using the same mark.

brand architecture. (2005) *Trademarks.* The strategic analysis and development of optimal relationships among the multiple levels of a company and its brands, products, features, technology, or ingredient names.

Brandeis brief (bran-dis). (1930) A brief, usu. an appellate brief, that makes use of social and economic studies in addition to legal principles and citations. • The brief is named after Supreme Court Justice Louis D. Brandeis, who as an advocate filed the most famous such brief in *Muller v. Oregon*, 208 U.S. 412, 28 S.Ct. 324 (1908), in which he persuaded the Court to uphold a statute setting a maximum ten-hour workday for women.

Brandeis rules. See ASHWANDER RULES.

branding. (15c) **1.** The act of marking cattle with a hot iron to identify their owner. **2.** Formerly, the punishment of marking an offender with a hot iron.

brand name. 1. See BRAND. **2.** See TRADENAME.

branks (brangks). (16c) *Hist.* An instrument used to punish scolds, consisting of an iron framework that surrounded the head and entered the mouth to keep the offender's tongue depressed. — Also termed *scolding bridle.* See SCOLD. Cf. CASTIGATORY.

brassage (bras-ij). (1806) *Hist.* A government charge for the actual cost of coining metals. • Any profit is termed *seigniorage.* See SEIGNIORAGE (2).

brass knuckles, *n.* (1855) A piece of metal designed to fit over the fingers as a weapon for use in a fistfight. — Also termed (BrE) *knuckleduster.*

***Braswell* rule.** (1989) *Criminal procedure.* The doctrine that a corporate custodian cannot invoke the Fifth Amendment to avoid producing corporate records, even if the records might incriminate the custodian personally. *See Braswell v. U.S.*, 487 U.S. 99, 108 S.Ct. 2284 (1988).

brawl, *n.* (15c) **1.** A noisy quarrel or fight. **2.** The offense of engaging in such a quarrel or fight. • In most jurisdictions, the offense is a statutory civil misdemeanor. **3.** *Hist. Eccles. law.* The offense of disturbing the peace of a consecrated building or area; specif., a disturbance, such as arguing, within the churchyard or church. • Until 1860, offenders faced trial in ecclesiastical courts. — Also termed *brawling.* — **brawl,** *vb.*

BRE. *abbr.* BANKRUPTCY-REMOTE ENTITY.

breach, *n.* (15c) A violation or infraction of a law, obligation, or agreement, esp. of an official duty or a legal obligation, whether by neglect, refusal, resistance, or inaction <breach of warranty> <breach of duty>. — **breach,** *vb.*

breach by renunciation. See *anticipatory breach* under BREACH OF CONTRACT.

breach-date rule. (1922) The prima facie rule for breach-of-contract cases that damages are to be assessed at the date of breach.

breach of arrest. (1949) A military offense committed by an officer who, being under arrest in quarters, leaves those quarters without a superior officer's authorization. See *arrest in quarters* under ARREST (2).

breach of care. See BREACH OF DUTY OF CARE.

breach of close. (18c) The unlawful or unauthorized entry on another person's land; a common-law trespass. — Also termed *breaking a close.* See CLOSE (1).

breach of confidence. (17c) *Torts.* **1.** The disclosure of confidential information such as trade secrets or information that is privileged because of a relationship of trust, such as matters that a client shares in confidence with a legal representative. **2.** A claim or lawsuit against someone who has received confidential information and then used or disclosed it in a manner contrary to the purpose for which it was originally disclosed. • Any kind of secret information, including trade secrets and private confidences, can be subject to such a claim. The information must not be in the public domain, must have been disclosed to the recipient in circumstances implying confidence, and must have been misused.

breach of confidentiality. See BREACH OF CONFIDENCE.

breach of contract. (17c) Violation of a contractual obligation by failing to perform one's own promise, by repudiating it, or by interfering with another party's performance.

> "It is a rule, generally accepted, that when a promisor fails in any respect to carry out an existing duty calling for a present, immediate performance under a contract, he is guilty of a breach of contract which furnishes a basis for a cause of action of some sort. This is so, whether the present duty of performance which has been violated comprises the whole duty or only an infinitesimal part of what will ultimately be due, and whether or not any loss has been caused by such failure to perform as has occurred. As to these matters there is no cause for doubt. The questions of difficulty in this connection grow out of three related matters. These questions are: (1) whether a cause of action ever exists when, as yet, there has been no failure to carry out an immediate duty of present performance; (2) what kind of relief is available when a cause of action admittedly exists; and (3) whether, when the contract is one in which the performance called for by its terms is not to be rendered all at once, a partial though substantial breach is, for purposes of remedy, to be treated as the equivalent of a breach of the whole contract, thus giving the promisee, if he elects to sue for damages for breach of contract, the right to recover, in one action, prospective as well as actual losses; or whether each new failure to perform, as the later performances come due, is to be treated as the basis of a new and distinct cause of action." Grover C. Grismore, *Principles of the Law of Contracts* § 181, at 276 (John Edward Murray Jr. ed., 1965).

> "A breach may be one by non-performance, or by repudiation, or by both. Every breach gives rise to a claim for damages, and may give rise to other remedies. Even if the injured party sustains no pecuniary loss or is unable to show such loss with sufficient certainty, he has at least a claim for nominal damages. If a court chooses to ignore a trifling departure, there is no breach and no claim arises." *Restatement (Second) of Contracts* § 236 cmt. a (1979).

▸ **active breach of contract.** (1840) *Civil law.* The negligent performance of a contractual obligation, to the point of acting outside the contract's terms. • Under Louisiana law before 1984, active breach of contract was contrasted with passive breach of contract, which was a failure to perform the obligations created by the contract. Unlike a passive breach, an active breach of contract could give rise to a claim in contract and in tort. The distinction was abolished in 1984. Cf. *passive breach of contract.*

▸ **anticipatory breach.** (1889) A breach of contract caused by a party's anticipatory repudiation, i.e., unequivocally indicating that the party will not perform when performance is due. • Under these circumstances, the nonbreaching party may elect to treat the repudiation as an immediate breach and sue for damages. — Also termed *breach by anticipatory repudiation*; — Also termed *breach by renunciation*; *constructive breach*. See *anticipatory repudiation* under REPUDIATION.

> "A repudiation by one party may occur before the time for performance has arrived. Such a repudiation is called an anticipatory breach, and it gives the innocent party the option of treating the contract as terminated at once and suing for damages immediately if he chooses or, alternatively, of waiting until the time of performance has arrived, and then again calling on the other party to perform. Should he choose the latter course he runs the risk that the contract may possibly become frustrated in the interim, in which case he will have lost his right to damages." P.S. Atiyah, *An Introduction to the Law of Contract* 298 (3d ed. 1981).

▸ **constructive breach.** See *anticipatory breach*.

▸ **continuing breach.** (1817) A breach of contract that endures for a considerable time or is repeated at short intervals.

▸ **efficient breach.** (1977) An intentional breach of contract and payment of damages by a party who would incur greater economic loss by performing under the contract. See EFFICIENT-BREACH THEORY.

▸ **fundamental breach.** See *repudiatory breach*.

▸ **immediate breach.** (1820) A breach that entitles the nonbreaching party to sue for damages immediately.

▸ **material breach.** (1840) A breach of contract that is significant enough to permit the aggrieved party to elect to treat the breach as total (rather than partial), thus excusing that party from further performance and affording it the right to sue for damages.

> "In determining whether a failure to render or to offer performance is material, the following circumstances are significant: (a) the extent to which the injured party will be deprived of the benefit which he reasonably expected; (b) the extent to which the injured party can be adequately compensated for the part of that benefit of which he will be deprived; (c) the extent to which the party failing to perform or to offer to perform will suffer forfeiture; (d) the likelihood that the party failing to perform or to offer to perform will cure his failure, taking account of all the circumstances including any reasonable assurances; (e) the extent to which the behavior of the party failing to perform or to offer to perform comports with standards of good faith and fair dealing." Restatement (Second) of Contracts • § 241 (1979).

▸ **partial breach.** (18c) A breach of contract that is less significant than a material breach and that gives the aggrieved party a right to damages, but does not excuse that party from performance; specif., a breach for which the injured party may substitute the remedial rights provided by law for only part of the existing contract rights.

▸ **passive breach of contract.** (1832) *Civil law.* A failure to perform the requirements of a contract. • Under Louisiana law up to 1984, passive breach of contract was contrasted with active breach of contract, which was negligence in performing a contractual obligation. While an active breach of contract could give rise to claims in contract and in tort, a passive breach of contract usu. did not give rise to a tort claim. Cf. *active breach of contract*.

▸ **repudiatory breach.** (1967) A breach so fundamental that it permits the nonbreaching party to terminate without penalty any reciprocal performance or obligation. — Also termed *fundamental breach*.

▸ **total breach.** (18c) A breach of contract for which the remedial rights provided by law are substituted for all the existing contractual rights, or can be so substituted by the injured party; esp., a material breach that gives rise to a claim for damages based on the aggrieved party's remaining rights to performance under the contract.

breach of covenant. (16c) The violation of an express or implied promise, usu. in a contract, either to do or not to do an act. See COVENANT.

breach of duty. (16c) The violation of a legal or moral obligation; the failure to act as the law obligates one to act; esp., a fiduciary's violation of an obligation owed to another. See NEGLIGENCE.

breach of duty of care. (1925) Negligence that results in a foreseeable injury that would not have occurred but for the negligent person's actions; NEGLIGENCE (1). — Sometimes shortened to *breach of care*.

breach of injunction. (18c) A violation of the terms of a court's injunctive order. • A breach of injunction is often treated as a civil contempt of court.

breach of loyalty. (16c) An act that is detrimental to the interests of someone to whom a fiduciary duty is owed; esp., an act that furthers the actor's own interests or those of a competitor of the beneficiary.

breach of peace. See BREACH OF THE PEACE.

breach of prison. See PRISON BREACH.

breach of promise. (17c) The violation of one's word or undertaking, esp. a promise to marry. • Under English common law, an engagement to marry had the nature of a commercial contract, so if one party broke the engagement without justification, the innocent party was entitled to damages. See HEARTBALM STATUTE.

breach of statutory duty. (1844) The violation of an obligation imposed legislatively, esp. one for the protection or benefit of a particular class of persons; a failure to carry out or fulfill obligations imposed by legislation.

breach of the peace. (16c) The criminal offense of creating a public disturbance or engaging in disorderly conduct, particularly by making an unnecessary or distracting noise. — Also termed *breach of peace*; *disturbing the peace*; *disturbance of the peace*; *public disturbance*; *grithbreach*. See *disorderly conduct* under CONDUCT.

> "A breach of the peace takes place when either an assault is committed on an individual or public alarm and excitement is caused. Mere annoyance or insult is not enough: thus at common law a householder could not give a man into custody for violently and persistently ringing his door-bell. It is the particular duty of a magistrate or police officer to preserve the peace unbroken; hence if he has reasonable cause to believe that a breach of the peace is imminent he may be justified in committing an assault or effecting an arrest." R.F.V. Heuston, *Salmond on the Law of Torts* 131 (17th ed. 1977).

> "The beginning of our criminal justice . . . was concerned very largely with the problem of keeping the peace. Because of this fact all early indictments included some such phrase as 'against the peace of the King'; and until recent statutory provisions for simplification, indictments in this country were thought to be incomplete without some such conclusion as 'against the peace and dignity of the state.' As a result of this history all indictable offenses are sometimes regarded as deeds which violate the public

peace, and hence in a loose sense the term 'breach of the peace' is regarded as a synonym for crime." Rollin M. Perkins & Ronald N. Boyce, *Criminal Law* 477 (3d ed. 1982).

breach of trust. (17c) **1.** A trustee's violation of either the trust's terms or the trustee's general fiduciary obligations; the violation of a duty that equity imposes on a trustee, whether the violation was willful, fraudulent, negligent, or inadvertent. • A breach of trust subjects the trustee to removal and creates personal liability. **2.** See MALADMINISTRATION.

breach of warranty. (18c) **1.** A breach of an express or implied warranty relating to the title, quality, content, or condition of goods sold. UCC §§ 2-312 through 2-315. **2.** *Insurance.* A breach of the insured's pledge or stipulation that the facts relating to the insured person, thing, or risk are as stated. See WARRANTY (3).

bread acts. (1822) *Hist.* Laws providing for the sustenance of persons kept in prison for debt. • These laws were formerly on the books in both England and the United States.

bread-and-cheese ordeal. See *ordeal of the morsel* under ORDEAL.

breadth of a claim. (1902) *Patents.* The scope or extent to which a patent claim excludes others from infringing activity.

breadwinner, *n.* A family or household member who helps earn money that supports other members of the family or household; WAGE-EARNER (2).

break, *n.* See BUST (2).

break, *vb.* (bef. 12c) **1.** To violate or disobey (a law) <to break the law>. **2.** To nullify (a will or contract) by court proceeding <Samson, the disinherited son, successfully broke the will>. **3.** To escape from (a place of confinement) without permission <break out of prison>. **4.** To open (a door, gate, etc.) and step through illegally <break the close>.

breakable, *adj.* (1995) (Of a will, contract, or particular contractual provision) capable of being voided on grounds of public policy, as where a contract has been procured by fraud or deceit; worthy of being set aside. Cf. VOIDABLE.

breakage. (1848) **1.** An allowance given by a manufacturer to a buyer for goods damaged during transit or storage. **2.** Insignificant amounts of money retained by racetrack promoters from bets. • The retention of these small sums avoids the inconvenience of counting and paying out inconsequential winnings.

break a house. To violently and feloniously remove or sever any part of a house or its locks.

breakdown. (1832) **1.** A falling apart or collapse; esp., the failure of a system or relationship. **2.** A serious medical condition in which someone becomes mentally ill, often temporarily, and cannot work or handle the ordinary situations of life. **3.** An occasion when a machine stops working. **4.** A list of all the separate parts of something. **5.** The chemical metamorphosis of one substance into other substances.

breakdown of the marriage. See IRRETRIEVABLE BREAKDOWN OF THE MARRIAGE.

breaking, *n. Criminal law.* (17c) In the law of burglary, the act of entering a building without permission. • It does not require damage to the property.

"[T]o constitute a breaking at common law, there had to be the creation of a breach or opening; a mere trespass at law was insufficient. If the occupant of the dwelling had created the opening, it was felt that he had not entitled himself to the protection of the law, as he had not properly secured his dwelling. . . . In the modern American criminal codes, only seldom is there a requirement of a breaking. This is not to suggest, however, that elimination of this requirement has left the 'entry' element unadorned, so that any type of entry will suffice. Rather, at least some of what was encompassed within the common law 'breaking' element is reflected by other terms describing what kind of entry is necessary. The most common statutory term is 'unlawfully,' but some jurisdictions use other language, such as 'unauthorized,' by 'trespass,' 'without authority,' 'without consent,' or 'without privilege.'" Wayne R. LaFave & Austin W. Scott Jr., *Criminal Law* § 8.13, at 793–94 (2d ed. 1986).

breaking a case. (1950) **1.** The voicing by one appellate judge to another judge on the same panel of a tentative view on how a case should be decided. • These informal expressions assist the judges in ascertaining how close they are to agreement. **2.** The solving of a case by the police.

breaking a close. See BREACH OF CLOSE.

breaking and entering. See BURGLARY (2).

breaking a patent. (1985) The act of demonstrating that a patent is invalid or unenforceable because it was used unlawfully by the patentee (esp. in violation of antitrust laws), or improperly issued by the U.S. Patent and Trademark Office because of fraud, the existence of prior art, or any other barrier to proper issuance. • Defendants in patent-infringement actions may overcome the infringement allegations by showing that the patent should not have been allowed in the first place (so it is invalid), or that the patentee has misused the patent (so the patent is unenforceable).

breaking bulk, *n.* (18c) **1.** The act of dividing a large shipment into smaller units. **2.** Larceny by a bailee, esp. a carrier, who opens containers, removes items from them, and converts the items to personal use. — Also termed *breaking bale.* — **break bulk,** *vb.*

breaking-bulk doctrine. (1941) *Hist.* The rule that a bailee who had lawful possession of property delivered in bulk and wrongfully took the property committed larceny only if the bailee broke the container open and took part or all of the contents. • If the bailee wrongfully took the property without opening the container, the act was theft but not larceny. — Also termed *breaking-bale doctrine.*

breaking of entail. See BARRING OF ENTAIL.

breakup fee. See TERMINATION FEE; REVERSE BREAKUP FEE.

breast of the court. (17c) A judge's conscience, mind, or discretion. • This phrase is a loan translation (or calque) of the Latin phrase *in pectore judicis.* See IN PECTORE JUDICIS.

Breathalyzer. (1960) A device used to measure a person's blood alcohol content from a sample of the person's breath, esp. when the police suspect that the person was driving while intoxicated. • The term is a trademarked name. Breathalyzer test results are admissible as evidence if the test was properly administered. — Also termed *alcoholometer*; *drunkometer*; *intoxilyzer*; *intoximeter*. See BLOOD ALCOHOL CONTENT. — **breathalyze,** *vb.*

breathing room. (1967) *Slang.* The postbankruptcy period during which a debtor may formulate a debt-repayment plan without harassment or interference by creditors.

breath test. (1966) An analysis of a person's breath to measure the amount of alcohol that the person, esp. a driver, has consumed; specif., a police test in which a driver must breathe into a special bag to determine whether he or she has drunk too much alcohol. See *refusal hearing* under HEARING.

▸ **portable breath test.** (1973) **1.** A handheld device that measures the alcohol concentration in a breath sample. **2.** See *preliminary breath test.* — Abbr. PBT.

▸ **preliminary breath test.** (1969) A breath test done by a police officer using a portable breath-testing device to determine whether a person should be arrested for an intoxication-related offense. — Abbr. PBT. — Also termed *portable breath test*; *preliminary alcohol screening*; *point-of-arrest testing.*

bredwite (**bred**-wət). *Hist.* A penalty for not complying with regulations relating to the weight or quantity of bread.

breed-specific legislation. (1988) A statute that bans or imposes restrictions and conditions on ownership of a certain breed or breeds of dogs in a jurisdiction, usu. declaring that the breed is inherently dangerous or vicious. • Opponents assert that this is "canine profiling." — Abbr. BSL. — Also termed *breed-specific law.* See CANINE PROFILING. Cf. DANGEROUS-DOG LAW.

brehon (**bree**-hən). (16c) *Hist.* In Ireland, a judge.

Brehon law (**bree**-hən law). (16c) *Hist.* The ancient system of law in Ireland at the time of its conquest by Henry II. • This law was formally abolished in 1366. — Sometimes spelled *Brehon Law.*

> "[T]he Irish were governed by what they called the Brehon law, so stiled from the Irish name of judges, who were denominated Brehons. But king John in the twelfth year of his reign went into Ireland, and carried over with him many able sages of the law; and there by his letters patent, in right of the dominion of conquest, is said to have ordained and established that Ireland should be governed by the laws of England . . . . But to this ordinance many of the Irish were averse to conform, and still stuck to their Brehon law: so that both Henry the third and Edward the first were obliged to renew the injunction . . . . And yet, even in the reign of queen Elizabeth, the wild natives still kept and preserved their Brehon law . . . ." 1 William Blackstone, *Commentaries on the Laws of England* 100–01 (1765).

B reorganization. See REORGANIZATION (2).

brephotrophus (bre-**fah**-trə-fəs). [Latin fr. Greek] (18c) *Civil law.* Someone who manages institutions that receive and care for poor or abandoned children. • The word is Greek in origin (lit. meaning "one who feeds an infant") and was used in late Roman law, but it first appeared in English in the 18th century. Pl. ***brephotrophi.***

brethren (**breth**-rən), *n. pl.* (16c) Brothers, esp. those considered spiritual kin (such as male colleagues on a court) <my brethren argue in the dissent that my statutory interpretation is faulty>. • The use of this collegial term has naturally dwindled as more women have entered law and esp. into the judiciary. Cf. SISTREN.

Bretts and Scots, Laws of the. The customary laws used by the Celtic tribes of Scotland. • Edward I of England purported to abolish the laws in the early 14th century.

breve (breev *or* **bree**-vee), *n.* [Law Latin] (13c) *Hist.* Writ. • The word *brevis* meant "short," and *brevia* were short writs, unlike charters. Cf. BRIEVE. Pl. ***brevia*** (**bree**-vee-ə).

▸ ***album breve*** (**al**-bəm breev *or* **bree**-vee). (17c) A blank writ; a writ with a blank or omission in it.

▸ ***apertum breve*** (ə-**pər**-təm breev *or* **bree**-vee). [Latin "open writ"] An open, unsealed writ. See *patent writ* under WRIT. Cf. *close writ* under WRIT; CLAUSUM.

▸ ***breve de bono et malo*** (breev *or* **bree**-vee dee **boh**-noh et **mal**-oh). See DE ODIO ET ATIA.

▸ ***breve de conventione*** (breev *or* **bree**-vee dee kən-ven-shee-**oh**-nee). See WRIT OF COVENANT.

▸ ***breve de cursu.*** See WRIT OF COURSE.

▸ ***breve de recto*** (breev *or* **bree**-vee dee **rek**-toh). See DE RECTO.

▸ ***breve de transgressione super casum*** (breev *or* **bree**-vee dee trans-gres[h]-ee-**oh**-nee **s[y]oo**-pər **kay**-səm). See TRESPASS ON THE CASE.

▸ ***breve innominatum*** (breev *or* bree-vee i-nom-ə-**nay**-təm). [Latin "innominate writ"] (18c) A writ that recites a cause of action only in general terms.

▸ ***breve magnum de recto*** (breev *or* bree-vee **mag**-nəm dee **rek**-toh). See DE RECTO PATENS.

▸ ***breve nominatum.*** (18c) A writ in which the complaint particularly states the time, place, and demand.

▸ ***breve perquirere*** (breev *or* bree-vee pər-**kwɪ**-rə-ree). [Latin "to obtain a writ"] (18c) To purchase a writ or license of trial in the king's courts.

▸ ***breve rebellionis.*** See COMMISSION OF REBELLION.

▸ ***breve testatum*** (breev *or* **bree**-vee tes-**tay**-təm). [Latin "a witnessed writ"] (17c) A written memorandum used to memorialize the terms of a conveyance and investiture of land. • Witnesses to the conveyance did not sign the document, but their names were recorded. *Brevia testata* were introduced to reduce disputes concerning the terms of oral grants.

▸ ***brevia amicabilia*** (**bree**-vee-ə am-ə-kə-**bil**-ee-ə). [Latin "writs with agreement"] (18c) Writs obtained with the agreement or consent of the opposing party in an action.

▸ ***brevia anticipantia*** (**bree**-vee-ə an-tis-ə-**pan**-shee-ə). [Latin "anticipatory writs"] (18c) Anticipatory or preventive writs. • Six were included in this category: writs of *mesne*; *warrantia chartae*; *monstraverunt*; *audita querela*; *curia claudenda*; and *ne injuste vexes.* See QUIA TIMET.

▸ ***brevia formata*** (**bree**-vee-ə for-**may**-tə). [Latin "writs of approved form"] (18c) Writs of established and approved form, issued as a matter of course. Cf. *brevia magistralia.*

▸ ***brevia judicialia*** (**bree**-vee-ə joo-dish-ee-**ay**-lee-ə). [Latin "judicial writs"] (18c) Writs that issue during an action or afterward in aid of judgment; esp., writs issued in the course of proceedings. • A court issued such a writ after an original writ had issued out of Chancery. — Also termed *judicialia brevia.* Cf. *brevia originale.*

> "The issue of writs at the request of the plaintiff fell within the functions of the Chancellor, who sealed them with the

Great Seal. English writers, and Blackstone in particular, often compare Chancery, *officina justitiae*, to a store, or even to a factory or show, where writs were 'turned out' and 'sold'; the term *purchase a writ* is a traditional way of referring to the fee paid by the litigant for the writ. In exceptional circumstances, judges could issue a writ during the proceedings to facilitate the ordering of incidental matters. Thus arose the distinction between original writs (*originalia brevia*) which started proceedings and judicial writs (*judicialia brevia*) issued in the course of proceedings." Henri Lévy-Ullmann, *The English Legal Tradition: Its Sources and History* 63 (1935).

▸ ***brevia magistralia*** (**bree**-vee-ə maj-i-**stray**-lee-ə). [Latin "masters' writs"] (17c) Writs issued by the masters or clerks of Chancery according to the circumstances of particular cases. • These writs, unlike some others, might be varied in accordance with the complainant's particular situation. Cf. *brevia formata*.

▸ ***brevia originale*** (**bree**-vee-ə ə-rij-i-**nay**-lee). [Latin] Original writs. • Such writs began lawsuits, much as complaints do today. Cf. *brevia judicialia*.

▸ ***brevia selecta*** (**bree**-vee-ə sə-**lek**-tə). [Latin "selected writs"] (17c) Choice or selected writs or processes. — Abbr. *brev. sel.*

▸ ***judicialia brevia.*** See *brevia judicialia*.

brevet (brə-**vet** *or* **brev**-it). [French] (17c) **1.** *Military law.* A commission promoting an officer to a higher rank, esp. during wartime, but without a corresponding pay increase. **2.** *French law.* A privilege or warrant granted by the government to a private person, authorizing a special benefit or the exercise of an exclusive privilege. • For example, a *brevet d'invention* is a patent for an invention. **3.** *Patents.* A patent. — Also termed (in sense 3) *brevet d'invention*.

brevet officer. See OFFICER (2).

brevia amicabilia. See BREVE.

brevia anticipantia. See BREVE.

brevia formata. See BREVE.

brevia judicialia. See BREVE.

brevia magistralia. See BREVE.

brevia originale. See BREVE.

Breviarium Alaricianum (bree-vee-**air**-ee-əm al-ə-ri-**kay**-nəm). [Latin] An abridgment (or *breviary*) of Roman law compiled by order of the Visigoth king Alaric II, published for the use of his Roman subjects in the year 506. • Revised versions were known as the *Lex Romana Visigothorum*. It was also termed *Breviarium Aniani* after Alaric's chancellor, Anian, who edited and distributed the work. — Also termed *Breviary of Alaric* (**bree**-vee-er-ee əv **al**-ə-rik).

"Though the *Breviarium* was later replaced by the *Lex Visigothorum* in the Visigothic kingdom, it continued in use in southern France and Lombardy, which had meantime passed under the dominion of the Franks. Its qualities made the *Breviarium* a book of high authority throughout the whole of western Europe during the Middle Ages and it was one of the main channels through which Roman law entered western European law prior to the Reception." David M. Walker, *The Oxford Companion to Law* 151–52 (1980).

brevia selecta. See BREVE.

breviate (**bree**-vee-ət). [Latin] (16c) *Hist.* An abstract of a writing; esp., a short statement attached to a Parliamentary bill summarizing the contents of the bill.

brevia testata (**bree**-vee-ə tes-**tay**-tə). [Latin] *Hist.* See *breve testatum* under BREVE.

brevibus et rotulis liberandis (**bree**-və-bəs et **roch**-ə-ləs lib-ər-**an**-dis). [Latin "breves and rolls to be freed"] (18c) *Hist.* A writ ordering a sheriff to turn over to a successor all paraphernalia of office.

brevi manu (**bree**-vɪ **man**-yoo), *adv.* [Latin "with a short hand"] *Roman & civil law.* **1.** Directly; by the shortest route. **2.** Without a legal warrant; on one's own authority. • In Roman law, the term referred to the contractual transfer (*traditio*) of ownership of an item to one who already had physical control of the item. In Scotland, this phrase usu. signified the performance of an act without the necessity of resorting to the courts. See TRADITIO BREVI MANU; CONSTITUTUM POSSESSORIUM.

"Thus, for example, it was anciently the practice in Scotland for an heritable proprietor, on his own authority, to poind his tenant's moveables for payment of his rent, without applying to any other judge . . . . Brevi manu in the Roman law is usually applied to a kind of constructive delivery. A thing is said to be transferred by brevi manu tradition, when it has been previously in the buyer's possession on some other title, as pledge or loan." William Bell, Bell's *Dictionary and Digest of the Law of Scotland* 134 (George Watson ed., 7th ed. 1890).

brevitatis causa (brev-i-**tay**-tis **kaw**-zə). [Latin] (17c) *Scots law.* For the sake of brevity. • The phrase was inserted in legal documents to show that another document had been incorporated by reference but not fully quoted.

brev. sel. See *brevia selecta* under BREVE.

bribe, *n.* (15c) A price, reward, gift or favor given or promised with a view to pervert the judgment of or influence the action of a person in a position of trust. Cf. BARRATRY (5). — **bribe,** *vb.*

"The core concept of a bribe is an inducement improperly influencing the performance of a public function meant to be gratuitously exercised." John T. Noonan Jr., *Bribes* xi (1984).

bribee. (19c) Someone who receives a bribe. — Also termed *bribe-taker*.

bribe-giver. See BRIBER.

briber. (17c) Someone who offers a bribe. — Also termed *bribe-giver*.

bribery, *n.* (16c) The corrupt payment, receipt, or solicitation of a private favor for official action. • Bribery is a felony in most jurisdictions. *See* Model Penal Code § 240.1. Cf. KICKBACK. — **bribe,** *vb.*

"If money has been corruptly paid and corruptly received, for the purpose of influencing official action, do we have one crime of which two are guilty, or two different crimes? No uniform answer is possible under existing statutes. Under some of the provisions bribery is one offense and references to (1) giving or offering a bribe, or (2) to receiving or soliciting a bribe, are merely factual statements in regard to the guilt of one party or the other. Under another plan 'bribery' is employed as a generic term to cover two different offenses: (1) giving or offering a bribe, and (2) receiving or soliciting a bribe. A third plan uses the word 'bribery' to indicate the offense of the briber and 'receiving a bribe' for the other side of the transaction." Rollin M. Perkins & Ronald N. Boyce, *Criminal Law* 537 (3d ed. 1982).

▸ **commercial bribery.** (1927) **1.** The knowing solicitation or acceptance of a benefit in exchange for violating an oath of fidelity, such as that owed by an employee, partner, trustee, or attorney. Model Penal Code § 224.8(1). **2.** A supposedly disinterested appraiser's acceptance of a benefit that influences the appraisal of goods or services. Model Penal Code § 224.8(2). **3.** Corrupt dealing with the agents or employees of prospective buyers to secure an advantage over business competitors.

bribe-taker. See BRIBEE.

bribour (**brɪ**-bər). [fr. French *bribeur*] *Hist.* A thief.

brideprice. *Family law.* In some cultures, a gift of money or goods from a prospective groom or his family to the prospective bride or her family.

"*Brideprice* = in marriage customs of some cultures (mostly in Asia), the money or goods that pass from the prospective groom or his family to the bride or her family. *Dowry* = money or goods passing from the bride's side to the groom's. Neglected by many dictionaries, the term *brideprice* is established among anthropologists. It is an unfortunate label because it helps perpetuate the myth that in some cultures families sell their daughters into marriage. Some scholars have suggested *bridewealth* and *bridecost* as alternatives, but the misleading label appears, for the time being, to be entrenched." Bryan A. Garner, *Garner's Modern American Usage* 115–16 (3d ed. 2009).

bridge bank. See BANK.

bridgebote. See *brigbote* under BOTE (1).

bridge financing. See *bridge loan* under LOAN.

bridge loan. See LOAN.

bridge the gap. (1962) *Trademarks.* To capitalize on the goodwill associated with an existing trademark or tradename by using it or a similar mark on new lines of products or services, or on the same products or services in new marketing territories.

brief, *n.* (14c) **1.** A written statement setting out the legal contentions of a party in litigation, esp. on appeal; a document prepared by counsel as the basis for arguing a case, consisting of legal and factual arguments and the authorities in support of them. — Also termed *legal brief*; *brief of argument.*

▸ **amicus brief.** (1945) A brief, usu. at the appellate level, prepared and filed by an amicus curiae with the court's permission. — Sometimes shortened to *amicus.* — Also termed *friend-of-the-court brief.*

"There are many different types of amicus briefs that persons or organizations want to submit to a court of appeals. An amicus sometimes wants to file a brief because it lacks confidence in the party's ability to address the core issues in the case accurately and competently. In that circumstance, an amicus brief is similar to a party's brief, addressing the same issues as the party and advancing essentially the same points, although it may not include some of the required components of a party's brief (for example, a statement of the case and, in many instances, a statement of the facts). Another type of amicus brief is filed simply 'to enable the officers of trade associations to show their members that they are on the ball.' In that circumstance, as Justice Scalia has put it with characteristic bluntness, 'it really does not matter what the amicus brief says.' Ideally, however, an amicus will attempt to say something that is of use to the court and different from what the party says." *Federal Appellate Practice* 405–06 (Philip Allen Lacovara ed., 2008).

▸ ***Anders* brief.** (1969) *Criminal procedure.* A brief filed by a court-appointed defense attorney who wants to withdraw from the case on appeal based on a belief that the appeal is frivolous. • In an *Anders* brief, the attorney seeking to withdraw must identify anything in the record that might arguably support the appeal. The court then decides whether the appeal is frivolous and whether the attorney should be permitted to withdraw. *Anders v. California*, 386 U.S. 738, 87 S.Ct. 1396 (1967). — Also termed *no-merit brief.*

"*Anders* requires an attorney to assume two somewhat contradictory roles when filing a no-merit brief. The first, and most important, role is that of an advocate. *Anders* makes clear that the first duty of appellate counsel is to study the record and to consult with the defendant to ascertain whether there is anything in the record to support an appeal. Counsel should not consider the case with a view toward finding no merit or of acting as a neutral party. Only if counsel can find no issue of even arguable merit does he change hats and become an amicus curiae." Jonathan M. Purver & Lawrence E. Taylor, *Handling Criminal Appeals* § 138, at 285 (1980).

▸ **appeal brief.** (1912) **1.** See *appellate brief.* **2.** *Patents.* A patent applicant's brief to the Board of Patent Appeals and Interferences, arguing that the patent examiner was incorrect in rejecting the application. Cf. EXAMINER'S ANSWER.

▸ **appellate brief.** (1920) A brief submitted to an appeals court; specif., a brief filed by a party to an appeal pending in a court exercising appellate jurisdiction. • The brief may be filed for an individual party or on behalf of two or more parties. — Also termed *appeal brief.*

"An appellate brief is a written argument in support of or in opposition to the order, decree, or judgment below." Frederick Bernays Wiener, *Briefing and Arguing Federal Appeals* 37 (rev. ed. 1967).

▸ **bench brief.** (1974) An advocate's short brief, prepared for use by panelists in a moot-court competition or mock oral argument. • The brief summarizes the facts, law, and arguments for both sides on the issues.

"Bench briefs are superior to the appellate briefs in some cases, because people are more likely to read them. The bench brief should be more neutral than the briefs actually filed in the real proceeding, which will help your mock judges prepare questions to ask. By providing the mock-judges with these bench briefs, it is easier for them to become prepared, it is far less burdensome on the judges — and therefore easier to get them to agree to help — and you improve the quality of your presentation." Ronald J. Rychlak, *Effective Appellate Advocacy: Tips from the Teams*, 66 Miss. L.J. 527, 543 (1997).

▸ **bottomside brief.** [fr. the analogy of baseball innings — the "bottom" being the second side at bat.] An appellee's or respondent's brief.

▸ ***Brandeis* brief.** See BRANDEIS BRIEF.

▸ **brief on the merits.** (1906) A brief that sets out the issues to be decided, the party's position, and the arguments and authorities in support. — Also termed *points-and-authorities brief*; *merits brief.*

▸ **closed brief.** (1972) In law school, an appellate brief prepared by a student using only a stipulated factual outline and research materials provided in a package. • Closed briefs are usu. assigned in first-year legal-writing classes, sometimes in preparation for moot court. They may also be used to select among candidates for law review.

▸ **collective brief.** *English law.* An improper document by which a solicitor seeks to retain a barrister for more than one lawsuit with a single fee.

"A barrister may not take what is known as a 'collective brief.' This means that he must be paid a separate fee for every separate piece of work he does and every separate client he represents. He may not take a brief with

> a collective fee to represent a number of identical cases which are separately charged. He must be paid for each separate case, irrespective of the fact that having done the work for the first there may be little or none for the subsequent identical cases. The rules also provide that where in one action two QCs have been instructed to appear for two separate defendants the two defendants cannot have the same junior appearing on one brief. He must be separately instructed and paid a separate fee by each defendant." Michael Zander, *Lawyers and the Public Interest* 125 (1968).

▸ **friend-of-the-court brief.** See *amicus brief.*

▸ **merits brief.** See *brief on the merits.*

▸ **no-merit brief.** See *Anders brief.*

▸ **open brief.** (1973) In law school, an appellate brief prepared by a student using a stipulated factual outline and open-ended research that the student independently finds, as opposed to sources supplied by a professor.

▸ **opening brief.** (1887) A party's first brief at a given stage of a lawsuit. • Although this term is most often associated with a plaintiff or appellant, it is sometimes applied to a defendant or respondent. — Also termed *opening brief on the merits.*

▸ **points-and-authorities brief.** See *brief on the merits.*

▸ **proof brief.** (1997) A preliminary appellate brief to be reviewed by the clerk of the court for compliance with applicable rules. • Proof briefs are required by local rules of the U.S. Court of Appeals for the Sixth Circuit. A proof brief in full compliance will be accepted and filed. If not in compliance, it will be returned for corrections to be made, and a deadline will be set for refiling. After all proof briefs have been accepted in a case, a date is set for filing a final brief, which may be modified only to include joint-appendix references, repagination, or updated citations.

▸ **reply brief.** (1872) A brief that responds to issues and arguments raised in the brief previously filed by one's opponent; esp., a movant's or appellant's brief filed to rebut a brief in opposition. See REBUTTAL (3).

▸ **supplemental brief.** (1845) A pro se appellant's brief submitted in addition to the brief submitted by his or her appellate attorney.

▸ **topside brief.** [fr. the analogy of baseball innings — the "top" being the first side at bat.] An appellant's or petitioner's brief.

▸ **trial brief.** (1927) Counsel's written submission, usu. just before trial, outlining the legal issues before the court and arguing one side's position.

2. *English law.* A solicitor's document that abstracts the pleadings and facts to inform a barrister about the case. **3.** ABSTRACT OF TITLE. **4.** CASE NOTE. — **brief,** *vb.*

briefing attorney. See ATTORNEY.

brief-making. See BRIEF-WRITING.

briefmanship, *n.* (1963) The quality of the work done in producing a written legal argument.

> "Catering to the predilections of a judge is not toadyism; it is skillful briefmanship." Mortimer Levitan, "Effective Brief Writing," in *Lawyers Encyclopedia* 995, 998 (1963).

brief of argument. See BRIEF (1).

brief of title. See ABSTRACT OF TITLE.

brief on the merits. See BRIEF (1).

brief-writing. (1891) The art or practice of preparing legal briefs. — Also termed *brief-making.* — **brief-writer,** *n.*

brieve. (17c) *Hist. Scots law.* A chancery writ ordering that a trial be held on the matters specified in the writ. • By the late 20th century, brieves were rarely used except in proceedings to appoint a curator for an incompetent person. Cf. BREVE.

brieve of mortancestry. See MORT D'ANCESTOR.

brigandage (brig-ən-dij). (16c) *Archaic.* Plundering and banditry carried out by bands of robbers. • Piracy is sometimes called "maritime brigandage."

brigbote. See BOTE (1).

Briggs Law. *Archaic.* A 1921 Massachusetts statute that required all criminal defendants who had been repeatedly indicted, previously convicted of a felony, or charged with a capital offense to undergo psychiatric evaluation. • The purpose of the evaluation was "to determine [offenders'] mental condition and the existence of any mental disease or defect [that] would affect [their] criminal responsibility." Mass. Gen. Laws ch. 123, § 100A (1921). Although the term is no longer used in Massachusetts, an updated form of the law still exists, and every state has its own form of it.

bright-line rule. (1973) A legal rule of decision that tends to resolve issues, esp. ambiguities, simply and straightforwardly, sometimes sacrificing equity for certainty.

***Brignoni-Ponce* factors.** (1977) *Criminal law.* The eight factors affecting the reasonableness of a border-patrol stop of a vehicle: (1) characteristics of the area where the vehicle is found; (2) distance from the border; (3) traffic patterns on the road; (4) the agent's previous experiences with alien traffic; (5) information about recent alien border crossings; (6) the driver's demeanor, behavior, etc., esp. any attempt to avoid being stopped; (7) nature of the vehicle, esp. presence of concealed compartments; and (8) appearance that the vehicle is heavily loaded. *See U.S. v. Brignoni-Ponce,* 422 U.S. 873, 95 S.Ct. 2574 (1975).

***Brillhart* abstention.** See ABSTENTION.

bring an action. (16c) To sue; institute legal proceedings.

bring-down provision. (2003) *Contracts.* A contractual covenant that all of a party's representations and warranties were true when the contract was executed and will be true on the closing date.

bring to book. (1865) To arrest and try (an offender) <the fugitives were brought to book and convicted>.

brinkmanship. (1956) A method of gaining a negotiating advantage by suggesting a willingness to do something very dangerous or destructive. — Also termed (less correctly) *brinksmanship.*

British subject. (1981) The status conferred on a citizen of the United Kingdom and the Commonwealth countries such as Canada, Australia, New Zealand, and India by the British Nationality Act of 1981. • Although this is the current sense, the phrase *British subject* has had many different meanings over the years, under different statutes.

broadcasting license. See *broadcast license* under LICENSE.

broadcast license. See LICENSE.

Broadcast Music, Inc. *Copyright.* One of the U.S. performing-rights societies that, on behalf of copyright owners, licenses the public performance of nondramatic musical works. — Abbr. BMI.

broad construction. See *liberal interpretation* under INTERPRETATION (1).

broad constructionism. See *liberal constructionism* under CONSTRUCTIONISM.

broad constructionist. See *liberal constructionist* under CONSTRUCTIONIST.

broadened reissue patent. See PATENT (3).

broadening of a claim. (1909) *Patents.* The enlargement of the scope of a patent claim to expand its coverage without adding new matter. • The broader a patent claim, the greater the scope of protection because more methods or devices may potentially infringe the claim. But drafting a claim broadly increases the risk that an accused infringer may successfully invalidate the claim through prior art. See *prior art* under ART (3).

broadening statement. (1959) *Patents.* Wording in a claim to the effect that the invention includes forms other than the details shown in the application. • A broadening statement is usu. taken as boilerplate and given little or no effect. — Also termed *catch-all.*

broader than the invention, *adj.* (Of a patent claim) having a scope that exceeds the limits of the invention disclosed in the application or patent.

broad-form insurance. See INSURANCE.

broad-form policy. See INSURANCE POLICY.

broad interpretation. See *liberal interpretation* under INTERPRETATION (1).

broadside objection. See *general objection* under OBJECTION.

broad ultra vires. See ULTRA VIRES.

brocard (**brahk**-ərd *or* **broh**-kərd). (17c) An elementary legal principle or maxim, esp. one deriving from Roman law or ancient custom.

brocarius (broh-**kair**-ee-əs). [Law Latin] (18c) *Hist.* A broker; a middleman between buyer and seller.

broker, *n.* (14c) **1.** One who is engaged for another, usu. on a commission, to negotiate contracts relating to property in which he or she has no custodial or proprietary interest. **2.** An agent who acts as an intermediary or negotiator, esp. between prospective buyers and sellers; a person employed to make bargains and contracts between other persons in matters of trade, commerce, or navigation. • A broker differs from a factor because the broker usu. does not have possession of the property. Cf. FACTOR. **3.** *Securities.* A person engaged in the business of conducting securities transactions for the accounts of others.

> "The most important determining factor of what constitutes a 'broker' is whether the party is dealing for itself or for another. A broker may, by contract, have title to property pass through it (though usually it does not), and it may, by contract, collect from the consumer, but a broker does not deal on its account. Two preliminary requirements must be met for a finding that an individual is acting as a broker: (1) the person is acting for compensation; and (2) the person is acting on behalf of someone else." 12 Am. Jur. 2d *Brokers* § 1 (1997).

▸ **broker-agent.** (1850) **1.** Someone who acts as an intermediary between parties to a transaction, and as a representative of one of them. **2.** A person licensed both as a broker and as an agent.

▸ **broker-dealer.** (1934) A brokerage firm that engages in the business of trading securities for its own account (i.e., as a principal) before selling them to customers. • Such a firm is usu. registered with the SEC and with the state in which it does business. See DEALER (2).

▸ **broker for sale.** A broker retained to sell something, but having neither possession of the goods nor any right of action in the broker's own name on contracts that the broker enters into.

▸ **broker's broker.** A municipal securities broker or dealer who routinely effects transactions for the account of other brokers, dealers, and municipal securities dealers.

▸ **buyer's broker.** (1846) A real-estate broker who acts as the agent of a purchaser of property. • Statutes in many states permit prospective buyers to retain a licensed real-estate agent as their agent. In some states, a buyer's broker is treated as the subagent of the broker with whom the owner lists property for sale and not the agent of the buyer. See *real-estate broker; subagent* under AGENT.

▸ **commercial broker.** (1825) A broker who negotiates the sale of goods without having possession or control of the goods. Cf. FACTOR (3).

▸ **commission broker.** (1831) A member of a stock or commodity exchange who executes buy and sell orders.

▸ **commodity broker.** (17c) An individual or firm that deals in commodities and commodity futures. — Also termed *commodities broker.*

▸ **customhouse broker.** (1889) A broker who prepares paperwork for the entry or clearance of ships, and for the import or export of goods. — Also termed *customs broker.*

▸ **discount broker.** (1849) **1.** A broker who discounts bills of exchange and promissory notes, and advances money on securities. **2.** A broker who executes buy and sell orders at commission rates lower than those of full-service brokers.

▸ **government-securities interdealer broker.** A broker engaged exclusively in the business of transacting in government securities for parties who are themselves government brokers or dealers.

▸ **institutional broker.** (1970) A broker who trades securities for institutional clients such as banks, mutual funds, pension funds, and insurance companies.

▸ **insurance broker.** (18c) *Insurance.* Someone who, for compensation, brings about or negotiates contracts of insurance as an agent for someone else, but not as an officer, salaried employee, or licensed agent of an insurance company. • The broker is an agent for the buyer of the insurance policy and has certain fiduciary responsibilities as long as the relationship continues. Essentially, the broker acts as an intermediary between the insured and the insurer. — Also termed *producer.*

> "The term 'insurance broker' is often used to characterize an individual who is thought to act primarily on behalf of a purchaser in an insurance transaction. This delineation . . . is employed by some courts and writers even though almost all insurance brokers are actually compensated for their services through commissions that are paid by the insurers. Because brokers receive compensation from the insurer, it seems evident that a persuasive argument can be made for not treating a broker as an agent of the insurance purchaser." Robert E. Keeton & Alan I. Widiss, *Insurance Law:*

A Guide to Fundamental Principles, Legal Doctrines, and Commercial Practices § 2.5, at 83–84 (1988).

▸ **loan broker.** (1851) Someone who is in the business of lending money, usu. to an individual, and taking as security an assignment of wages or a security interest in the debtor's personal property.

▸ **merchandise broker.** (1830) Someone who negotiates the sale of merchandise without possessing it. • A merchandise broker is an agent with very limited powers.

▸ **money broker.** (17c) A broker who negotiates the lending or raising of money for others.

▸ **mortgage broker.** (1879) An individual or organization that markets mortgage loans and brings lenders and borrowers together. • A mortgage broker does not originate or service mortgage loans.

▸ **note broker.** (1856) A broker who negotiates the discount or sale of commercial paper.

▸ **real-estate broker.** (1835) A broker who negotiates contracts of sale and other agreements (such as mortgages or leases) between buyers and sellers of real property. • Real-estate brokers must be licensed in the states where they conduct business.

▸ **registered broker.** (1936) A broker registered or required to be registered under the Securities Exchange Act of 1934.

▸ **responsible broker-dealer.** (1959) A broker-dealer who communicates bids or offers on the floor of a stock exchange at the designated location for trading in a reported security or who, in an off-exchange transaction, communicates the bid or offer as either a principal or an agent, for its own or another's account. SEC Rule 11Acl–1(a)(21) (17 CFR § 240.11Acl–1(a)(21)).

▸ **securities broker.** (1938) A broker employed to buy or sell securities for a customer, as opposed to a securities dealer, who trades as a principal before selling the securities to a customer. See DEALER (2).

▸ **stockbroker.** See STOCKBROKER.

broker, *vb.* (17c) To arrange the terms of (a deal, etc.) so that all parties can agree to it.

brokerage. (15c) **1.** The business or office of a broker <a profitable stock brokerage>. **2.** A broker's fee; the amount of money that a broker charges <collect the brokerage after the house sells>.

brokerage contract. (1872) An agency agreement employing a broker to make contracts in the name of and on behalf of the principal and for which the broker receives a commission.

broker-agent. See BROKER.

brokerage-run dividend-reinvestment plan. See DIVIDEND-REINVESTMENT PLAN.

broker call loan. See *call loan* under LOAN.

broker-dealer. See BROKER.

broker for sale. See BROKER.

broker's broker. See BROKER.

broker's loan statement. (1973) *Property.* A document that details the costs of and deductions from a loan negotiated by a real-estate or mortgage broker on behalf of a borrower. • Deductions may be made for commissions and other costs. The borrower usu. signs the statement and retains a copy. The statement may be required by law. *See* Cal. Bus. & Prof. Code § 10240 (West 2008). Cf. CLOSING STATEMENT (2).

broker's note. See NOTE (3).

broker's placing slip. See LINE SLIP.

broker's slip. See LINE SLIP.

***Bronston* defense.** (1977) *Criminal law.* A defense to a perjury charge based on the literal truth of a defendant's sworn statement, even though it may have been unresponsive. • The responsibility lies with the questioner to recognize an evasive answer and to elicit a more specific answer. *Bronston v. U.S.*, 409 U.S. 352, 93 S.Ct. 595 (1973).

brothel. (16c) A house where men can pay to have sex; a building where prostitutes ply their trade. — Also termed *bordello; whorehouse; house of ill fame.* See DISORDERLY HOUSE (2).

brother. (bef. 12c) A male who has one parent or both parents in common with another person.

▸ **blood brother.** See BLOOD BROTHER.

▸ **brother-german.** (14c) A full brother; the son of both of one's parents. See GERMAN.

▸ **consanguine brother** (kon-**sang**-gwin *or* kən-**san**-gwin). (1812) *Civil law.* A brother who has the same father, but a different mother.

▸ **half brother.** (14c) A brother who has the same father or the same mother, but not both.

▸ **stepbrother.** (15c) The son of one's stepparent.

▸ **uterine brother** (**yoo**-tər-in). (15c) *Civil law.* A brother who has the same mother, but a different father.

brother-in-law. (14c) The brother of one's spouse or the husband of one's sister. • The husband of one's spouse's sister is also sometimes considered a brother-in-law. Pl. **brothers-in-law.**

brother-sister corporation. See *sister corporation* under CORPORATION.

Brougham's Act (**brooms** akt). *Hist. English law.* An 1850 statute that abolished the revival of repealed statutes upon the repeal of repealers and simplified legislative drafting by stipulating that the masculine gender includes the feminine (and vice versa) and the singular includes the plural (and vice versa) unless the context requires otherwise. 13 & 14 Vict. ch. 21. • The anti-revival provision states: "[W]here any Act repealing in whole or in part any former Act is itself repealed, such last repeal shall not revive the Act or provisions before repealed," unless words of explicit revival are included. Lord Brougham (1778–1868) sought to reform the law by eliminating cumbersome technicalities. Brougham's Act has been superseded by other interpretation acts that have incorporated the same ideas. — Also termed *Lord Brougham's Act; Interpretation Act of 1850.*

brownfield site. (1979) **1.** An abandoned, idled, or underused industrial or commercial site that is difficult to expand or redevelop because of environmental contamination. **2.** A place, esp. in a city, that was once used for industrial purposes and has been to some degree redeveloped through the building of new offices, homes, etc. • Sense 2 is especially prevalent in BrE. Cf. GREENFIELD SITE (1).

Brussels Act. *Copyright.* A 1948 revision of the Berne Convention mandating the life-plus-50-years copyright term as a minimum standard, extending the moral rights of attribution and integrity in most member countries to the full copyright term, extending the broadcast right to television, strengthening protection of several forms of copyright, and extending some protection to industrial designs.

Brussels Convention. See BRUSSELS SATELLITE CONVENTION.

Brussels Satellite Convention. *Copyright.* A 1974 treaty standardizing the regulation of broadcasting and cable retransmission using satellites. • Since the Convention addresses regulation of the signal rather than copyright or neighboring rights, what is transmitted is protected even if the content is not protected by any intellectual-property right. The U.S. ratified the Brussels Satellite Convention in 1984. — Also termed *Brussels Convention; Convention Relating to the Distribution of Program-Carrying Signals Transmitted by Satellite.*

***Bruton* error** (**broot**-ən). (1968) The violation of a criminal defendant's constitutional right of confrontation by admitting into evidence a nontestifying codefendant's confession that implicates both of them, where the statement is not admissible against the defendant under any exception to the hearsay rule. • The error is not cured by a limiting instruction to the jury to consider the confession only against the one who made it, because of the high risk that the jury will disregard the instruction. *Bruton v. U.S.*, 391 U.S. 123, 88 S.Ct. 1620 (1968).

brutum fulmen (**broo**-təm **fəl**-men *or* -mən). [Latin "inert thunder"] (17c) **1.** An empty noise; an empty threat; something ineffectual. **2.** A judgment void on its face; one that is, in legal effect, no judgment at all.

Bryan treaties. *Int'l law.* Any of 48 treaties designed to avert war by requiring the signatories to submit disputes of any kind to standing peace commissions. • The first of these treaties, named after Secretary of State William Jennings Bryan, was signed between the United States and Great Britain in 1914.

b.s. *abbr.* See *bancus superior* under BANCUS.

BSA. *abbr.* BUSINESS SOFTWARE ALLIANCE.

BSD license. See LICENSE.

BSD-style license. See *BSD license* under LICENSE.

BSL. *abbr.* BREED-SPECIFIC LEGISLATION.

BTA. *abbr.* Board of Tax Appeals. See TAX COURT, U.S.

BTO. *abbr.* Breath-test operator.

BTS. *abbr.* **1.** BORDER AND TRANSPORTATION SECURITY DIRECTORATE. **2.** BUREAU OF TRANSPORTATION STATISTICS.

bubble. (18c) *Slang.* **1.** A temporary market condition of inflated value created esp. in a particular segment of the economy by excessive speculation or buying, the result being artificial inflation of values. **2.** *Archaic.* A dishonest or insubstantial business project, generally founded on a fictitious or exaggerated prospectus, designed to ensnare unwary investors.

Bubble Act. A 1720 English statute enacted to prevent corporate fraud.

bucketing. (1905) *Securities.* The illegal practice of receiving an order to buy or sell stock but not immediately performing the order. • The perpetrator profits by executing the order when the stock market goes down or up, respectively, but confirming the order to the customer at the original price.

bucket shop. (1875) *Securities.* An establishment that is nominally engaged in stock-exchange transactions or some similar business, but in fact engages in registering bets or wagers, usu. for small amounts, on the rise or fall of the prices of stocks and commodities. • A bucket shop uses the terms and outward forms of the exchanges, but differs from exchanges because there is no delivery of — and no expectation or intention to deliver or receive — the securities or commodities nominally exchanged.

Buckley Amendment. See FAMILY EDUCATIONAL RIGHTS AND PRIVACY ACT.

Budapest Treaty on the International Recognition of the Deposit of Microorganisms for the Purpose of Patent Procedures. *Patents.* An international treaty promulgating standards and procedures for depositing microorganisms and requiring member countries to recognize a deposit of biological material made in any depository approved by the World Intellectual Property Organization. • The purpose of the Budapest Treaty is to allow inventors to satisfy the enablement requirement of national patent laws by depositing in a convenient depository a sample of a microorganism to be patented. The U.S. is a signatory to the Budapest Treaty.

budget. (15c) **1.** A statement of an organization's estimated revenues and expenses for a specified period, usu. a year. **2.** A sum of money allocated to a particular purpose or project.

▸ **balanced budget.** (1853) A budget in which a period's total projected income equals the total estimated expenses.

budget bill. See BILL (3).

Buenos Aires Convention. *Copyright.* A 1910 treaty regulating copyright reciprocity among Latin American countries and the United States. • Under this agreement, the phrase "all rights reserved" guaranteed copyright protection in member countries. Since all the Convention's signatories are now signatories to more recent and broader international-copyright treaties, this Convention now has little if any practical effect.

buffer zone. (1908) *Land-use planning.* An area of land separating two different zones or areas to help each blend more easily with the other, such as a strip of land between industrial and residential areas.

bug, *n.* (1876) **1.** The printed mark of a labor union. **2.** A computer program's flaw or mistake that results in an error or undesired result. **3.** *Slang.* See LISTENING DEVICE.

▸ **roving bug.** (1987) A listening device that can remotely activate a mobile phone's microphone and cause the phone to transmit without the possessor's knowledge.

buggery, *n.* (14c) Sodomy or bestiality. See SODOMY. — **bugger,** *vb.* — **bugger,** *n.*

bugging, *n.* (1955) A form of electronic surveillance by which conversations may be electronically intercepted, overheard, or recorded, usu. covertly; eavesdropping by electronic means. See EAVESDROPPING; WIRETAPPING.

building. (13c) A structure with walls and a roof, esp. a permanent structure. • For purposes of some criminal statutes, such as burglary and arson, the term *building* may include such things as motor vehicles and watercraft.

▸ **accessory building.** (1844) A building separate from but complementing the main structure on a lot, such as a garage. • The question whether a structure is an "accessory building" is often litigated in zoning disputes.

building-and-loan association. (1857) A quasi-public corporation that accumulates funds through member contributions and lends money to the members buying or building homes. Cf. SAVINGS-AND-LOAN ASSOCIATION.

building association. A society, often an incorporated joint-stock company, organized to aid some of its members in building houses or other edifices with money loaned or subscribed by the membership generally. — Also termed *building and loan association*.

> "In the year 1836, twenty-seven years after the Greenwich Union Building Society had been established, and in the same year which was distinguished in Great Britain by the passage of an Act of Parliament affording ample facilities for the formation of building associations in that country, the first association of this kind in America was organized in Brooklyn under the name of The Brooklyn Building and Mutual Loan Fund Association. After that date, they began to crop out plentifully throughout the eastern section of the country, partly as unincorporated, voluntary associations, partly under charters obtained by virtue of general acts of the several commonwealths, authorizing the incorporation of beneficial and such like associations. Their power and importance grew rapidly during the feverish era of our national development almost immediately preceding the civil war, and legislation became imperative. The decade between 1850 and 1860 comprises the period when most of the older States, already thickly strewn with building associations, made the first attempts at statutory regulation of the powers, formation and management of these societies. Since then, they have constituted a class of corporations distinct and different from every other, peculiar in their privileges as well as in their disabilities, the source of dispute and difference of opinion, about equally with reference to the application of legal principles, and in respect of their practical utility. In some States, they have proved a failure, and their formation has been either prohibited or abandoned. In others they have continued to prosper and multiply until their number and the amount of capital and property they control is at this day truly enormous." G.A. Endlich, *The Law of Building Associations* 5–6 (1886).

building code. (1903) A law or regulation setting forth standards for the construction, maintenance, occupancy, use, or appearance of buildings and dwelling units. — Also termed (for dwelling units) *housing code*. Cf. BUILDING RESTRICTIONS.

building lease. See LEASE.

building line. (1885) A boundary drawn along a curb or the edge of a municipality's sidewalks to establish how far a building must be set away from the street to maintain a uniform appearance. • This is often referred to as a *setback requirement*.

building loan. See LOAN.

building permit. (1868) A license granted by a government agency (esp. a municipality) for the construction of a new building or the substantial alteration of an existing structure.

building restrictions. (1859) Regulations governing the type of structures that can be constructed on certain property. • The restrictions are usu. listed in zoning ordinances or restrictive covenants in deeds. Cf. BUILDING CODE; *restrictive covenant* (1) under COVENANT (4).

building society. (1848) *English law.* A cooperative whose members pool resources to offer financial and lending services, such as mortgages. • Building societies evolved from friendly societies in the 19th century. They are similar to U.S. credit unions.

build-to-print contract. See CONTRACT.

built-in obsolescence. See *planned obsolescence* under OBSOLESCENCE.

bulk, *adj.* (17c) (Of goods) not divided into parts <a bulk shipment of grain>.

bulk discount. See *volume discount* under DISCOUNT.

bulk goods. See GOODS.

bulk mortgage. See MORTGAGE.

bulk sale. (1902) A sale of a large quantity of inventory outside the ordinary course of the seller's business. • Bulk sales are regulated by Article 6 of the UCC, which is designed to prevent sellers from defrauding unsecured creditors by making these sales and then dissipating the sale proceeds. — Also termed *bulk transfer*.

bulk-sales law. (1908) A statute regulating the transfer of business assets, usu. by requiring public notice of any sale to prevent business owners from disposing of assets to the detriment of creditors and suppliers. *See* UCC §§ 6-101 et seq. See BULK SALE.

bulk-supplier defense. See DEFENSE (1).

bulk transfer. See BULK SALE.

bulky goods. See GOODS.

bull, *n.* **1.** (13c) *Eccles. law.* A document issued by a pope, so called from the leaden seal (*bulla*) attached to it. **2.** *Eccles. law.* A seal attached to an official document, esp. a papal edict. **3.** *Securities.* A dealer, investor, or speculator who believes that the prices of securities or commodities will increase in the short term and therefore builds an investment portfolio on that assumption. See *bull market* under MARKET. Cf. BEAR, *n.*

bulla (**buul**-ə or **bəl**-ə). [Law Latin] A metal or wax papal seal or document.

bullet. *Criminal law. Slang.* An immutable prison sentence of one year; a 12-month jailhouse term.

bullet ballot. See *bullet vote* under VOTE (1).

bulletin des lois (buul-ə-**tan** day **lwah**). *French law.* The publication that provides official notice of the text and effective date of a law or decree.

bullet vote. See VOTE (1).

bullion (**buul**-yən). (15c) An uncoined solid mass of gold or silver.

bullion fund. (1875) Public money used by a mint to purchase precious metals for coinage and to pay bullion depositors.

bull market. See MARKET.

bullpen. (1809) *Slang.* **1.** An area in a prison where inmates are kept in close confinement. **2.** A detention cell where prisoners are held until they are brought into court.

bullpen therapy. (1992) *Criminal law. Slang.* An unscrupulous prosecutor's tactic of purposely and needlessly having an incarcerated defendant transported back and forth between the jail and court when nothing relating to the defendant's case has been calendared, esp. in an effort to coerce a guilty plea.

bully, *n.* (17c) **1.** A cruel person who uses physical strength or verbal intimidation, usu. involving insults, to frighten or hurt someone who is weaker. **2.** A blustering, quarrelsome, overbearing person who is more insolent than courageous.

bully, *vb.* (18c) **1.** To threaten, intimidate, embarrass, or pressure (a person) by force, taunt, or derision. **2.** To use abusive language or behavior against. See CYBERBULLYING.

bumbailiff. See BAILIFF (2).

bumbershoot insurance. See INSURANCE.

bum-marriage doctrine. (1999) *Evidence.* The principle that the marital-witness privilege may not be asserted by a partner in a marriage that is in fact moribund, though legally valid. See *marital privilege* (2) under PRIVILEGE (3).

bump, *n. Slang.* The elimination of a prospective juror, either for cause or by peremptory challenge.

bumping. (1937) **1.** Displacement of a junior employee's position by a senior employee. **2.** An airline-industry practice of denying seats to passengers because of overbooking.

bunco. (1872) A swindling game or scheme; any trick or ploy calculated to win a person's confidence in an attempt to deceive that person. — Also spelled *bunko.* — Also termed *bunco steering.* Cf. CONFIDENCE GAME.

bunco steerer. (1875) **1.** Someone who uses tricks, schemes, or other illegal devices to obtain money or property from others; a swindler. **2.** Someone who acts as a decoy in bunco. — Also termed *bunco operator; bunco man.* See CONFIDENCE MAN.

bundle, *n.* See RECORD, *n.* (4).

bundle, *vb.* (1975) To sell related products or services in one transaction at an all-inclusive price.

bundled software. (1982) Software that is sold together with hardware, other software, or services at a single price.

bundle of rights. See PROPERTY (1).

bundling, *n.* (1975) **1.** *Antitrust.* Anticompetitive tying esp. through vertical distribution agreements. See TYING ARRANGEMENT. **2.** In the computer industry, the practice of charging a single price for a combination of hardware, software, and services. • Personal computers are typically sold with bundled software, such as an operating system and applications software that are preinstalled on the hardware. **3.** The practice of gathering financial contributions from many individuals for submitting to a political campaign. • The person who solicits and submits the contributions is known as a *bundler.* **3.** The pooling of various debt or mortgage obligations into a salable instrument. See COLLATERALIZED MORTGAGE OBLIGATION.

bunkhouse rule. (1947) The principle that an employee's injury suffered while living in an employer's housing is compensable even if the injury occurs during off-duty hours.

burden, *n.* (bef. 12c) **1.** A duty or responsibility <the seller's burden to insure the shipped goods>. **2.** Something that hinders or oppresses <a burden on interstate commerce>. **3.** A restriction on the use or value of land; an encumbrance <the easement created a burden on the estate>. **4.** *Scots law.* An encumbrance, restriction, or obligation imposed on a person or on property <the burden of curatorship> <a servitude is a burden on land>. • When the burden is on real property, it is called a *real burden.* **5.** More generally, a difficult or worrisome responsibility or onus. — **burden,** *vb.*

▸ **undue burden.** A substantial and unjust obstacle to the performance of a duty or enjoyment of a right. • For example, excessive discovery requests place an undue burden on the person who must produce the data requested. And a state law requiring a particular kind of mud flap on trucks may place an undue burden on the flow of interstate commerce.

> "A finding of an undue burden is shorthand for the conclusion that a state regulation has the purpose or effect of placing a substantial obstacle in the path of a woman seeking an abortion of a nonviable fetus." *Planned Parenthood v. Casey,* 505 U.S. 833, 877 (1992) (joint opinion).

burden of allegation. (1862) A party's duty to plead a matter in order for that matter to be heard in the lawsuit. — Also termed *burden of pleading.*

burden of going forward with evidence. See BURDEN OF PRODUCTION.

burden of persuasion. (1923) A party's duty to convince the fact-finder to view the facts in a way that favors that party. • In civil cases, the plaintiff's burden is usu. "by a preponderance of the evidence," while in criminal cases the prosecution's burden is "beyond a reasonable doubt." — Also termed *persuasion burden; risk of nonpersuasion; risk of jury doubt;* (loosely) *burden of proof.* See STANDARD OF PROOF.

burden of pleading. See BURDEN OF ALLEGATION.

burden of production. (1893) A party's duty to introduce enough evidence on an issue to have the issue decided by the fact-finder, rather than decided against the party in a peremptory ruling such as a summary judgment or a directed verdict. — Also termed *burden of going forward with evidence; burden of producing evidence; production burden; degree of proof.*

burden of proof. (18c) **1.** A party's duty to prove a disputed assertion or charge; a proposition regarding which of two contending litigants loses when there is no evidence on a question or when the answer is simply too difficult to find. • The burden of proof includes both the *burden of persuasion* and the *burden of production.* — Also termed *evidentiary burden; evidential burden; onus probandi.* See SHIFTING THE BURDEN OF PROOF. Cf. STANDARD OF PROOF. **2.** Loosely, BURDEN OF PERSUASION. — Abbr. BOP.

> "In the past the term 'burden of proof' has been used in two different senses. (1) The burden of going forward with the evidence. The party having this burden must introduce some evidence if he wishes to get a certain issue into the case. If he introduces enough evidence to require consideration of this issue, this burden has been met. (2) Burden of proof in the sense of carrying the risk of nonpersuasion. The one who has this burden stands to lose if his evidence fails to convince the jury — or the judge in a nonjury trial. The present trend is to use the term 'burden of proof' only with this second meaning . . . ." Rollin M. Perkins & Ronald N. Boyce, *Criminal Law* 78 (3d ed. 1982).

> "The expression 'burden of proof' is tricky because it has been used by courts and writers to mean various things. Strictly speaking, burden of proof denotes the duty of establishing by a fair preponderance of the evidence the truth of the operative facts upon which the issue at hand is made to

turn by substantive law. Burden of proof is sometimes used in a secondary sense to mean the burden of going forward with the evidence. In this sense it is sometimes said that a party has the burden of countering with evidence a prima facie case made against that party." William D. Hawkland, *Uniform Commercial Code Series* § 2A-516:08 (1984).

▸ **middle burden of proof.** (1966) A party's duty to prove a fact by clear and convincing evidence. • This standard lies between the preponderance-of-the-evidence standard and the beyond-a-reasonable-doubt standard. See *clear and convincing evidence* under EVIDENCE.

burden-shifting analysis. (1980) A court's scrutiny of a complainant's evidence to determine whether it is sufficient to require the opposing party to present contrary evidence. • Burden-shifting is most commonly applied in discrimination cases. If the plaintiff presents sufficient evidence of discrimination, the burden shifts to the defendant to show a legitimate, nondiscriminatory basis for its actions. The precise components of the analysis vary according to the specifications of particular statutes. Cf. MCDONNELL DOUGLAS TEST.

burdensome, *adj.* (16c) Difficult to bear; seriously oppressive.

Bureau of Alcohol, Tobacco, and Firearms. 1. See ALCOHOL AND TOBACCO TAX AND TRADE BUREAU. **2.** See BUREAU OF ALCOHOL, TOBACCO, FIREARMS, AND EXPLOSIVES.

Bureau of Alcohol, Tobacco, Firearms, and Explosives. A unit in the U.S. Department of Homeland Security responsible for enforcing laws relating to firearms and explosives and laws relating to the production, taxation, and distribution of alcohol and tobacco products. • Formerly called the Bureau of Alcohol, Tobacco, and Firearms and a part of the Department of the Treasury, its law-enforcement functions were transferred in the Homeland Security Act of 2002. Pub. L. 107-296. — Abbr. ATF. Cf. ALCOHOL AND TOBACCO TAX AND TRADE BUREAU.

Bureau of Arms Control. A unit in the U.S. Department of State responsible for directing U.S. participation in multilateral arms-control negotiations and in the Organization for the Prohibition of Chemical Weapons. • It also monitors developments relating to arms control and weapons development.

Bureau of Consular Affairs. A unit in the U.S. Department of State responsible for protecting U.S. citizens and interests abroad. • Through its Office of Passport Services it issues over 7 million passports each year.

Bureau of Customs. See UNITED STATES CUSTOMS AND BORDER PROTECTION.

Bureau of Democracy, Human Rights, and Labor. A unit in the U.S. Department of State responsible for developing policy on human rights and freedoms and for preparing the annual *Country Reports on Human Rights Practices.* — Abbr. DRL.

Bureau of Diplomatic Security. A unit of the U.S. Department of State responsible for protecting the Secretary of State and domestic and foreign dignitaries, for investigating criminal activities such as identity-document fraud involving U.S. passports and visas, and for developing security programs protecting diplomats and American interests worldwide. • The Bureau employs special agents (members of the U.S. Foreign Service) who are located throughout the United States and in scores of embassies worldwide. It also operates the Diplomatic Courier Service and supervises the transportation of classified documents and materials. — Abbr. DS. — Also termed *Diplomatic Security Service.*

Bureau of Economic Analysis. A unit in the U.S. Department of Commerce responsible for compiling and analyzing data about the U.S. economy. • It is a part of the Department's Economics and Statistics Administration. — Abbr. BEA.

Bureau of Economic and Business Affairs. A unit in the U.S. Department of State responsible for developing policy on international matters relating to food, communications, energy, air transportation, and maritime affairs. — Abbr. EB.

Bureau of Engraving and Printing. A unit in the U.S. Department of the Treasury responsible for designing and printing the country's paper currency, postage stamps, Treasury securities, and other documents. — Abbr. BEP.

Bureau of Export Administration. The former name of a bureau in the U.S. Department of Commerce that issues export licenses and enforces export-control laws. • The unit's name was changed in 2002 to the Bureau of Industry and Security. — Abbr. BXA.

Bureau of Indian Affairs. A unit in the U.S. Department of the Interior responsible for helping Indian and Alaskan native people manage their affairs under the trust relationship with the U.S., and for promoting programs for their benefit. • Originally created as part of the War Department in 1824, the Bureau was transferred to the Interior Department in 1849. — Abbr. BIA.

Bureau of Industry and Security. A unit in the U.S. Department of Commerce responsible for issuing export licenses and enforcing export-control laws. • The Bureau is charged with furthering U.S. national-security, foreign-policy, and economic interests while furthering the growth of U.S. exports. It was named the Bureau of Export Administration until 2002. — Abbr. BIS.

Bureau of Intelligence and Research. A unit in the U.S. Department of State responsible for coordinating activities of U.S. intelligence agencies to ensure consistency with U.S. foreign policy. • The Bureau also monitors foreign public and media opinions. — Abbr. INR.

Bureau of International Labor Affairs. A unit in the U.S. Department of Labor responsible for helping formulate policy on international matters that affect American workers. • For example, the Bureau compiles and publishes worldwide data on child-labor practices and on foreign labor markets and programs. It also studies the labor consequences of immigration proposals and legislation.

Bureau of International Narcotics and Law Enforcement. A unit in the U.S. Department of State responsible for coordinating the narcotics and anticrime-assistance activities of the Department and for advising the President, the Secretary of State, and others on international narcotics matters. — Abbr. INL.

Bureau of International Organization Affairs. A unit in the U.S. Department of State responsible for coordinating U.S. diplomatic participation in the United Nations and other international organizations and conferences. — Abbr. IO.

Bureau of Labor Statistics. An independent agency in the U.S. Department of Labor responsible for compiling and analyzing statistical information on employment and the economy. • The Bureau reports on employment, unemployment, consumer and producer prices, consumer expenditures, import and export prices, wages and employee benefits, productivity and technological change, employment projections, and occupational illness and injury. — Abbr. BLS.

Bureau of Land Management. The unit within the U.S. Department of the Interior responsible for managing the national-resource lands (some 450 million acres) and their resources and for administering the mineral resources connected with acquired lands and the submerged lands of the Outer Continental Shelf (OCS). • The bureau was established on July 16, 1946, by consolidating the General Land Office (established in 1812) and the Grazing Service (established in 1934). *See* 43 USCA §§ 1731 et seq. — Abbr. BLM.

Bureau of Nonproliferation. A unit in the U.S. Department of State responsible for leading efforts to prevent the proliferation of weapons of mass destruction, delivery systems, and advanced conventional arms. — Also termed *Nonproliferation Bureau.*

Bureau of Oceans and International Environmental and Scientific Affairs. A unit in the U.S. Department of State responsible for coordinating U.S. ocean, environment, and health policies. — Abbr. OES.

Bureau of Political–Military Affairs. A unit in the U.S. Department of State responsible for analyzing defense-related policy issues, managing security-assistance funds, and coordinating peace-keeping and humanitarian operations. — Abbr. PM. — Also termed *Political–Military Affairs Bureau.*

Bureau of Population, Refugees, and Migration. A unit in the U.S. Department of State responsible for formulating policy and administering U.S. assistance and admissions programs for refugees and others. — Abbr. PRM.

Bureau of Prisons. The unit in the U.S. Department of Justice responsible for operating the federal prison system. • It oversees all federal penal and correctional facilities, assists states and local governments in improving their correctional facilities, and provides notice of prisoner releases. 18 USCA §§ 4041 et seq. See NATIONAL INSTITUTE OF CORRECTIONS. — Abbr. BOP.

Bureau of Reclamation. A unit in the U.S. Department of the Interior that built dams in 17 western states and is now responsible for selling hydroelectric power from those dams and water from the reservoirs. • Among the 600 dams constructed are Hoover Dam and Grand Coulee Dam. — Abbr. BOR.

Bureau of the Budget. See OFFICE OF MANAGEMENT AND BUDGET.

Bureau of the Census. A unit in the U.S. Department of Commerce responsible for conducting and publishing the census required by the U.S. Constitution to be taken every ten years. • Established in 1902, the Bureau also conducts other population surveys and estimates as required by law. It is a part of the Department's Economics and Statistics Administration. — Also termed *Census Bureau.*

Bureau of the Mint. See UNITED STATES MINT.

Bureau of the Public Debt. A unit in the U.S. Department of the Treasury responsible for issuing and redeeming Treasury bills, notes, and bonds, and for managing the U.S. Savings Bond Program.

Bureau of Transportation Statistics. A unit in the U.S. Department of Transportation responsible for compiling and publishing transportation statistics. — Abbr. BTS.

Bureau Veritas. See VERITAS.

Bureaux Internationaux Reunis pour la Protection de la Propriete Intellectuelle. See INTERNATIONAL BUREAU FOR THE PROTECTION OF INTELLECTUAL PROPERTY.

***Burford* abstention.** See ABSTENTION.

burgage (**bər**-gij). (14c) *Hist.* **1.** A type of socage tenure in which tenants paid annual rents to the lord of the borough. See SOCAGE. **2.** *Scots law.* The tenure by which a burgh held its land of the king, the service due being watching and warding. See WATCH AND WARD. — Also termed *burgage tenure.*

burgage borough. See BOROUGH.

burgator (bər-**gay**-tər). *Hist.* A burglar; a person who breaks into a house or an enclosed space.

burgess (**bər**-jis). (13c) *Hist.* **1.** An inhabitant or freeman of a borough or town. **2.** A magistrate of a borough. **3.** A person entitled to vote at elections. **4.** A representative of a borough or town in Parliament.

> "[Burgesses] are properly Men of Trade, or the Inhabitants of a Borow or Walled Town; yet we usually apply this name to the Magistrates of such a Town, as the Bailiff and *Burgesses of Leominster*. But we do now usually call those *Burgesses* who serve in Parliament, for any such Borow or Corporation." Thomas Blount, *Nomo-Lexicon: A Law-Dictionary* (1670).

burghalpenny (**bər**-gəl-pen-ee). *Hist.* A municipal tax in Anglo-Saxon times. • Monasteries were exempt.

burghbote. See BOTE (1).

burgh English (**bərg ing**-glish). See BOROUGH ENGLISH.

burgh Engloys (**bərg** ing-**gloiz**). See BOROUGH ENGLISH.

burglar, *n.* (16c) Someone who commits burglary.

burglarious (bər-**glair**-ee-əs), *adj.* (18c) Of, relating to, or involving burglary <burglarious intent>. — **burglariously,** *adv.*

burglarize, *vb.* (1871) To commit a burglary; esp., to go into (a building) with the purpose of stealing things <the defendant burglarized three houses>. — Also termed (esp. BrE) *burgle.*

burglary, *n.* (16c) **1.** The common-law offense of breaking and entering another's dwelling at night with the intent to commit a felony. See HOUSEBREAKING. **2.** The modern statutory offense of breaking and entering any building — not just a dwelling, and not only at night — with the intent to commit a felony. • Some statutes make petit larceny an alternative to a felony for purposes of proving burglarious intent. — Also termed (in sense 2) *breaking and entering; statutory burglary.* Cf. ROBBERY.

▸ **generic burglary.** (1990) An unlawful or unprivileged entry into, or remaining in, a building or structure with intent to commit a crime. *See Taylor v. U.S.*, 495 U.S. 575, 110 S.Ct. 2143 (1990).

burglary tool. (*often pl.*) (1903) An implement designed to help a person commit a burglary. • In many jurisdictions, it is illegal to possess such a tool if the possessor intends to commit a burglary. — Also termed *housebreaking implement*.

burgle. See BURGLARIZE.

burgomaster (**bər**-goh-mas-tər), *n.* (18c) **1.** BOROUGHMASTER (1). **2.** A member of a municipality's governing body; ALDERMAN (1).

burial insurance. See INSURANCE.

buried-facts doctrine. (1973) *Securities.* The rule that a proxy-statement disclosure is inadequate if a reasonable shareholder could fail to understand the risks presented by facts scattered throughout the proxy. • In applying this rule, a court will consider a securities disclosure to be false and misleading if its overall significance is obscured because material information is buried in footnotes, appendixes, and the like.

burking, *n.* (1827) The crime of murdering someone, usu. by smothering, for the purpose of selling the corpse. • This term arose from the Scottish murder team of Burke and Hare, whose practice in 1828 of suffocating their victims while leaving few visible marks made the corpses more salable to medical schools. — **burke,** *vb.*

burlaw. See BYRLAW.

burlaw court. See BYRLAW COURT.

burning the source. (1985) *Slang.* A journalist's voluntary disclosure of the identity of an anonymous source despite a promise of confidentiality. • In *Cohen v. Cowles Media Co.*, 501 U.S. 663, 111 S.Ct. 2513 (1991), the U.S. Supreme Court held that state contract law may apply to a journalist's breach of a confidentiality agreement with a source, and the First Amendment does not protect the journalist's disclosure. Cf. *journalist's privilege* (1) under PRIVILEGE (3).

burnt-records act. (1874) A statute that enables a property owner to quiet title if the public records for the property have been lost or destroyed in a disaster.

burrier. *Slang.* (1997) A drug smuggler; MULE. • The term is a portmanteau of *burro* and *courier.*

bursary (**bər**-sə-ree), *n.* (17c) **1.** The treasury of a public institution, religious order, or other similar entity. **2.** *English law.* A college scholarship granted esp. on the basis of need.

bursting-bubble theory. (1941) *Evidence.* The principle that a presumption disappears once the presumed facts have been contradicted by credible evidence.

Bush Doctrine. (2001) *Slang.* The policy announced by President George W. Bush after the September 11, 2001 attacks on the World Trade Center and the Pentagon, reserving the right to use preemptive military action to prevent the use of weapons of mass destruction against the United States, particularly by a terrorist organization and its harboring nation state. • Under this doctrine, countries harboring terrorists will be treated as terrorists themselves and may be subject to a first-strike strategy. Cf. SOVEREIGN EQUALITY.

business. (18c) **1.** A commercial enterprise carried on for profit; a particular occupation or employment habitually engaged in for livelihood or gain.

> "'Business' means 'that by which one earns a livelihood.' 'Occupation,' though sometimes used synonymously, is a broader term. A man is a lawyer by occupation. His business, i.e., 'that which busies him,' may be the arguing of cases, or it may be the preparation of briefs, or the care of trust property, or the drawing of deeds, or the searching of titles. . . . On the other hand, 'business' must not be confounded with 'labor.' A lawyer can writes letters; that is labor, but it is not a kind of business pertaining to his occupation. A typewriter, however, who can write letters, can pursue an important 'business pertaining to his occupation.'" Marland C. Hobbs, *Total Disability in Accident Insurance*, 4 Harv. L. Rev. 176, 180–81 (1891).

2. Commercial enterprises <business and academia often have congruent aims>. **3.** Commercial transactions <the company has never done business in Louisiana>. See DOING BUSINESS. **4.** By extension, transactions or matters of a noncommercial nature <the courts' criminal business occasionally overshadows its civil business>. **5.** *Parliamentary law.* The matters that come before a deliberative assembly for its consideration and action, or for its information with a view to possible action in the future. • In senses 2–4, the word is used in a collective meaning.

▸ **new business.** An item of business introduced from the floor or taken from the table without having been scheduled for consideration. See TAKE FROM THE TABLE.

▸ **old business.** See *unfinished business.*

▸ **unfinished business.** (18c) Business carried over from the previous session (or a previous meeting of the present session) because that session (or meeting) adjourned before or while considering it. • This class of business does not include unfinished special orders, which are included as a higher-priority subclass of special orders. The term "unfinished business" is preferred to "old business," which may incorrectly imply renewed consideration of business that has been finally disposed of. See *special order* under ORDER (4); SESSION (2).

▸ **unfinished business and general orders.** (18c) A common category on an agenda. See *unfinished business*; *general order* under ORDER (4).

business accommodation. See ACCOMMODATION.

business acquisition. See CORPORATE ACQUISITION.

business agent. (1849) **1.** See *managing agent* under AGENT. **2.** A labor-union representative selected to deal with employers.

business angel. See *angel investor* under INVESTOR.

business appraiser. See APPRAISER.

business asset. See ASSET.

business associations. See BUSINESS ENTERPRISES.

business combination. **1.** The consolidation, for accounting purposes, of a corporation and one or more incorporated or unincorporated businesses. **2.** The two entities considered as one entity for accounting purposes.

business compulsion. See *economic duress* under DURESS (3).

business-continuation agreement. See AGREEMENT.

business corporation. See CORPORATION.

business court. See COURT.

business cycle. (1897) The recurrent expansion and contraction of economic activity, including changes in employment, productivity, and interest rates.

business day. See DAY.

business efficacy. (1889) The capability of an enterprise to deliver products or services to its customers in the most cost-effective manner possible while still ensuring the high quality of its products, service, and support. — Also termed *operational efficiency.*

business enterprise. A for-profit company, business, or organization that provides financial, commercial, or industrial goods and services.

▸ **government-business enterprise.** (1940) A government-owned or -controlled entity that engages only in commercial activities.

business enterprises. The field of law dealing with various forms of business, such as corporations, limited-liability companies, and partnerships. — Also termed *business entities*; *business associations*; *enterprise organizations.*

business entities. See BUSINESS ENTERPRISES.

business entry. (1929) A writing admissible under the business-records exception to the hearsay rule. See BUSINESS-RECORDS EXCEPTION.

business-entry rule. See BUSINESS-RECORDS EXCEPTION.

business expense. See EXPENSE.

business form. See BLANK FORM.

business franchise. See *commercial franchise* under FRANCHISE (4).

business gain. **1.** See GAIN (2). **2.** See GAIN (3).

business guest. See BUSINESS VISITOR (1).

business homestead. See HOMESTEAD (1).

business income. See INCOME.

business-interruption insurance. See INSURANCE.

business invitee. **1.** See INVITEE. **2.** See BUSINESS VISITOR (1).

business-judgment rule. (1946) *Corporations.* The judicial presumption that in making business decisions not involving direct self-interest or self-dealing, corporate directors act on an informed basis, in good faith, and in the honest belief that their actions are in the corporation's best interest. • The rule shields directors and officers from liability for unprofitable or harmful corporate transactions if the transactions were made in good faith, with due care, and within the directors' or officers' authority.

> "The business judgment rule is a presumption protecting conduct by directors that can be attributed to any rational business purpose. In order to plead and prove a claim, a plaintiff must plead and prove facts overcoming this presumption. Where the presumption is overcome, directors bear the burden of proving the fairness of the challenged conduct. The difference between these two levels of judicial scrutiny — a presumption in favor of directors that protects conduct that is rational, versus a burden of proving fairness — frequently is outcome determinative." 1 Dennis J. Block et al., *The Business Judgment Rule* 18–19 (5th ed. 1998).

business loss. See *ordinary loss* under LOSS.

business meeting. See MEETING.

business method. *Patents.* A way or an aspect of a way in which a commercial enterprise is operated.

business-method exception. (1993) *Intellectual property.* The traditional doctrine that business methods are not protected by intellectual-property laws. • Early caselaw established that "pure methods of doing business" were unpatentable. But in 1998, the Federal Circuit held in *State St. Bank & Trust Co. v. Signature Fin. Group* (149 F.3d 1368) that business methods are not per se unpatentable if they otherwise meet the requirements for a valid patent. The European Patent Convention expressly excludes business methods from patent protection.

business-method patent. See PATENT (3).

Business Methods Patent Initiative. A U.S. Patent and Trademark Office program that added a second level to business-method-patent reviews for the purpose of reducing the number of business-method patents issued. • The PTO created the initiative in response to complaints that examiners improperly approved many business-method patents. After an examiner approves the application and before a business-method patent is granted, a second examiner must completely review the application and either reject the application or affirm the issuance of the patent.

business name. See NAME.

business opportunity. (1895) The chance to buy or lease either a going business, or a product, service, or equipment that will enable the buyer or lessee to profit.

business-partner insurance. See *partnership insurance* under INSURANCE.

business plan. (1890) A document that explains what a company wants to do in the future and how it plans to accomplish those goals; specif., a written proposal explaining a new business or business idea and usu. covering financial, marketing, and operational plans.

business-product outsourcing. (2001) The practice of asking people from outside a company to take charge of running a part of its activities. — Abbr. BPO. See OUTSOURCING.

business-purpose doctrine. (1939) *Tax.* The principle that a transaction must serve a bona fide business purpose (i.e., not just for tax avoidance) to qualify for beneficial tax treatment.

business record. (1897) A report, memorandum, or other record made usu. in the ordinary course of business. • It may be ordered produced as part of discovery in a lawsuit.

business-records exception. (1939) *Evidence.* A hearsay exception allowing business records (such as reports or memoranda) to be admitted into evidence if they were prepared in the ordinary course of business. • If there is good reason to doubt a record's reliability (e.g., the record was prepared in anticipation of litigation), the exception will not apply. Fed. R. Evid. 803(6). — Also termed *business-entry rule.*

business reputation. See REPUTATION (2).

business-risk exclusion. See EXCLUSION (3).

Business Software Alliance. *Copyright.* An international trade organization representing leading software and e-commerce developers, formed to educate governments and the public about software issues and to fight software piracy and Internet theft. — Abbr. BSA.

business-to-business, *adj.* Of, relating to, or involving commerce between businesses, as distinguished from commerce between a business and consumers. — Abbr. B2B. Cf. BUSINESS-TO-CONSUMER.

business-to-business e-commerce. (1996) Electronic commerce between businesses over the Internet.

business-to-consumer, *adj.* Of, relating to, or involving commerce between a business and consumers, as distinguished from commerce between businesses. — Abbr. B2C. Cf. BUSINESS-TO-BUSINESS.

business-to-consumer e-commerce. (1997) Electronic commerce between a business and consumers over the Internet.

business tort. See TORT.

business transaction. (1871) An action that affects the actor's financial or economic interests, including the making of a contract.

business trust. See TRUST (4).

business visitor. (1898) **1.** *Torts.* Someone who is invited or permitted to enter or remain on another's land for a purpose directly or indirectly connected with the landowner's or possessor's business dealings. — Also termed *business invitee; business guest.* See INVITEE. **2.** *Immigration law.* A non-U.S. citizen who has a B-1 visa, which allows the person to be employed while in the United States.

bust. (1842) **1.** A period during which sales or other business activities fall both substantially and rapidly. Cf. BOOM (2). **2.** *Securities.* The late cancellation of an order after a broker has already executed it. — Also termed (in sense 2) *break.*

bust-up merger. See MERGER (8).

busy-legislature model. The view that because most members of the legislature are content to endorse the views of the committees responsible for preparing certain bills, the intent of those involved in the drafting is properly regarded as that of the entire legislature. *See* Charles Tiefer, *The Reconceptualization of Legislative History in the Supreme Court,* 2000 Wis. L. Rev. 205, 209, 252–53.

but-for causation. See CAUSATION.

but-for cause. See CAUSE (1).

but-for materiality. (1974) *Patents.* In an analysis of allegedly inequitable conduct, a test for determining the materiality of withheld information by assessing whether the withheld information, if disclosed, would have resulted in a finding of unpatentability. • Under this test, the issue is whether the patent would have issued if not for the misconduct of the applicant. By contrast, under the subjective but-for test, the issue is whether the misrepresentation caused the examiner to issue the patent. Although both tests have been applied by the courts, the Federal Circuit has rejected the but-for materiality test in favor of the materiality test codified in 37 CFR 1.56. — Also termed *objective but-for test.*

but-for test. (1925) *Tort & criminal law.* The doctrine that causation exists only when the result would not have occurred without the party's conduct. — Also termed (in criminal law) *had-not test.* See *but-for cause* under CAUSE (1). Cf. SUBSTANTIAL-CAUSE TEST.

butlerage. (15c) *Hist.* A duty on wine imported into England, payable to the royal butler. Cf. PRISAGE.

but say. Yet let me extend to you instead a lower fee or price of. • This phrase, more typical on a fee statement or bill phrased in British English than American English, is the service-provider's or seller's way of extending a discount to a buyer who, it is hoped, might be grateful for the consideration <£10,000 but say £8,000>.

but see. See SED VIDE.

but so insane as not to be responsible. See GUILTY BUT MENTALLY ILL.

buttals (bət-əlz). *Archaic.* See ABUTTALS.

butterfly ballot. See BALLOT (2).

butts and bounds. See METES AND BOUNDS.

buy. See PURCHASE (1).

buy-and-sell agreement. See BUY–SELL AGREEMENT.

buyback, *n.* (1954) The act or an instance of repurchasing something; esp., a company's repurchase of outstanding shares on the market, usu. as a means to increase the value of those shares or to eliminate the threat of a corporate takeover by one who seeks a controlling share. — **buy back,** *vb.*

buyback clause. (1915) **1.** *Contracts.* A provision that requires a manufacturer or franchiser to buy back inventory and equipment if the distributor or franchisee's contract is terminated prematurely. **2.** *Contracts.* A clause allowing the seller of property the right or opportunity to repurchase the property under stated conditions. **3.** *Insurance.* An insurance-policy clause, typically in liability policies, providing for the reinstatement of coverage that the insurer excludes or cancels if the insured meets certain conditions. • For instance, buyback clauses are often used to reinstate some of the coverage taken away under pollution-exclusion clauses.

buy-bust, *n.* (1976) *Slang.* A police-arranged drug deal followed by an arrest, often with enough delay to protect a confidential informant's or undercover agent's identity.

buy-down, *n.* (1980) Money paid by the buyer of a house to reduce the mortgage-interest payments.

buyer. (12c) Someone who makes a purchase. See PURCHASER.

▸ **buyer in due course.** See *buyer in ordinary course of business.*

▸ **buyer in ordinary course of business.** (1915) A person who — in good faith and without knowledge that the sale violates a third party's ownership rights or security interest in the goods — buys from a person regularly engaged in the business of selling goods of that kind. • Pawnbrokers are excluded from the definition. UCC § 1-201(b)(9). — Also termed *buyer in due course.*

▸ **qualified institutional buyer.** (1993) *Securities.* An institution with more than $100 million in invested assets.

buyer in due course. See *buyer in ordinary course of business* under BUYER.

buyer's broker. See BROKER.

buyer's market. See MARKET.

buyer's option. See OPTION (5).

buying in, *n.* (17c) The purchase of property by the original owner or an interested party at an auction or foreclosure sale. — **buy in,** *vb.*

buying on margin. See MARGIN TRANSACTION.

buying syndicate. See SYNDICATE.

buy order. See ORDER (8).

buyout, *n.* (1976) The purchase of all or a controlling percentage of the assets or shares of a business; the acquisition of control of a company by buying all or most of its assets or shares. Cf. MERGER (8). — **buy out,** *vb.*

▸ **leveraged buyout.** (1975) The purchase of a publicly held corporation's outstanding stock by its management or outside investors, financed mainly with funds borrowed from investment bankers or brokers and usu. secured by the corporation's assets. — Abbr. LBO.

▸ **management buyout.** (1976) **1.** A buyout of a corporation by its own directors and officers. **2.** A leveraged buyout of a corporation by an outside entity in which the corporation's management has a material financial interest. — Abbr. MBO. See GOING PRIVATE.

buy–sell agreement. (1956) **1.** An arrangement between owners of a business by which the surviving owners agree to purchase the interest of a withdrawing or deceased owner. — Also termed *cross-purchase buy–sell agreement.* Cf. CONTINUATION AGREEMENT. **2.** *Corporations.* A share-transfer restriction that commits the shareholder to sell, and the corporation or other shareholders to buy, the shareholder's shares at a fixed price when a specified event occurs. — Also termed *buy-and-sell agreement.* Cf. OPTION AGREEMENT.

BVA. *abbr.* BOARD OF VETERANS' APPEALS.

BW. *abbr.* BID WANTED.

BWI. *abbr.* Boating while intoxicated. Cf. DRIVING WHILE INTOXICATED.

BWO. *abbr.* Bench warrant ordered.

BWS. *abbr.* BATTERED-WOMAN SYNDROME.

BXA. *abbr.* BUREAU OF EXPORT ADMINISTRATION.

by-bidder. (1863) At an auction, a person engaged by the seller to bid on property for the sole purpose of stimulating bidding by potential genuine buyers, thereby inflating the price while being secured from risk by a secret understanding with the seller that he or she need not make good on bids. — Also termed *puffer; shill; sham bidder; capper; decoy duck; white bonnet.*

by-bidding. (1880) The illegal practice of engaging a person to bid at an auction for the sole purpose of stimulating bidding on the seller's property. — Also termed *puffing.* Cf. BIDDING UP; SHILLING (1).

by-election. See ELECTION (3).

by God and my country. (17c) *Hist.* A customary reply for a criminal defendant when asked at arraignment, "Culprit, how wilt thou be tried?"

bylaw [fr. Danish *bye,* Old Norse *byr,* "town"] (14c) **1.** *Parliamentary law.* (*usu. pl.*) A rule or administrative provision adopted by an organization for its internal governance and its external dealings. • Although the bylaws may be an organization's most authoritative governing document, they are subordinate to a charter or articles of incorporation or association or to a constitution. The "constitution and bylaws" are sometimes a single document. See *governing document* under DOCUMENT (2); ARTICLES OF INCORPORATION. Cf. CONSTITUTION. **2.** A law made by a local government for people in that area to obey; esp., ORDINANCE. — Sometimes spelled *by-law; byelaw.*

> "*By-law* is now felt to be a compound of the preposition *by* and *law,* but originally *by* was the Danish *by* 'town, village' (found in Derby, Whitby, etc.), and the Danish genitive-ending is preserved in the other English form *byr-law.*" Otto Jespersen, *Growth and Structure of the English Language* 75 (9th ed. 1938).

bylaw man. *Hist.* One of the chief men of a town, usu. appointed for some purpose under the town's corporate bylaws.

by operation of law. See OPERATION OF LAW.

bypass trust. See TRUST (3).

byproduct. (1857) **1.** Something additional that is produced during a process, either natural or industrial; a secondary or additional product or material made in the course of manufacturing the principal product or material. **2.** An unplanned additional result of something that one does.

***Byrd* affidavit.** See AFFIDAVIT.

byrlaw (**bir**-lah), *n.* (14c) *Hist. English & Scots law.* **1.** The local custom of a township or district for resolving disputes over boundaries, trespasses, and the use of common lands, as well as farming issues. **2.** A particular custom established by the common consent of landholders in a township or district. **3.** The area over which a township or district court has jurisdiction. — Also spelled *burlaw.*

byrlaw court. (16c) *Hist. Scots law.* A community assembly that judged minor disputes arising in the community. • The assembly members were called *byrlawmen* or *birleymen.* — Also spelled *burlaw court.*

byrthynsak (**bər**-t̲h̲ən-sak), *n.* [Anglo-Saxon *byrthen* "burden" + *sacu* "lawsuit"] (15c) *Hist.* The theft of a calf or ram that is the most a man can carry on his back.

bystander. (16c) **1.** Someone who is present when an event takes place, but who does not become directly involved in it. **2.** Any party, other than a consumer, who might be entitled to recover under products liability for an injury caused by a defective product. See CONSUMER; PRODUCTS LIABILITY.

C

c. *abbr.* (1947) **1.** CIRCA. **2.** COPYRIGHT.

ca. *abbr.* CIRCA.

CA. *abbr.* **1.** CERTIFICATION AUTHORITY. **2.** COURT OF APPEAL. **3.** Chancery Appeals. **4.** Commercial agent.

CAA. *abbr.* CLEAN AIR ACT.

ca. ad re. *abbr.* See *capias ad respondendum* under CAPIAS.

cabal (kə-**bal** *or* kə-**bahl**). (17c) A small group of political schemers or conspirators. • The term is sometimes said to have originated as an acronym from a committee of five ministers of Charles II, whose surnames began with C, A, B, A, and L (Clifford, Arlington, Buckingham, Ashley, and Lauderdale). Though colorful, this etymology is false: the term came into English directly from the French *cabale* "intrigue," which derives ultimately from Hebrew *kabbalah* "received lore."

cabala (**kab**-ə-lə *or* kə-**bahl**-ə). (17c) An esoteric or obscure doctrine.

caballeria (kah-bah-ye-**ree**-ah). [Spanish] (1838) *Spanish law.* An allotment of land in regions formerly conquered by Spain, such as Mexico and the southwestern United States. • Originally a Spanish feudal tenure held by a soldier, a *caballeria* eventually came to refer to an area of land. It usu. measures 100 by 200 feet in the United States, and between 30 and 200 acres in Mexico and other former Spanish territories.

cabinet. (*often cap.*) (17c) The advisory council to an executive officer, esp. the President. • The President's cabinet is a creation of custom and tradition, dating back to the term of George Washington. The U.S. Constitution alludes to a group of presidential advisers — the President "may require the Opinion, in writing, of the principal Officer in each of the executive Departments, upon any Subject relating to the Duties of their respective Offices" (art. II, § 2, cl. 1) — but the term *cabinet* is not specifically mentioned. The cabinet today comprises the Vice President and the heads of the 15 executive departments: the Secretary of State, the Secretary of the Treasury, the Secretary of Defense, the Attorney General, the Secretary of the Interior, the Secretary of Agriculture, the Secretary of Commerce, the Secretary of Labor, the Secretary of Health and Human Services, the Secretary of Housing and Urban Development, the Secretary of Transportation, the Secretary of Energy, the Secretary of Education, the Secretary of Veterans Affairs, and the Secretary of Homeland Security. Other officials, such as the U.S. ambassador to the United Nations and the director of the Office of Management and Budget, have been accorded cabinet rank.

▸ **inner cabinet.** (1956) The heads of the departments of State, Treasury, Defense, and Justice. • This group is so called because in most administrations it tends to be closer to the executive and more influential than the rest of the cabinet (the *outer cabinet*).

▸ **kitchen cabinet.** (1832) An unofficial and informal body of noncabinet advisers who often have more sway with the executive than the real cabinet does. • This term was first used derisively in reference to some of President Andrew Jackson's advisers, who, because of their reputation for unpolished manners, were supposedly not important enough to meet in the formal rooms of the White House.

> "The term [*kitchen cabinet*] began to lose its sting after Jackson's time. But because most Presidents do have circles of personal friends, the idea remains. Theodore Roosevelt had his 'tennis cabinet.' Jonathan Daniels referred to Warren Harding's 'poker cabinet.' Herbert Hoover had an exercise-loving 'medicine ball cabinet.' Even governors can play the game. In writing of New York's Alfred Smith, Ed Flynn mentions the 'golfing cabinet.'" William Safire, *Safire's New Political Dictionary* 389 (1993).

Cable and Satellite Directive. See DIRECTIVE ON THE COORDINATION OF CERTAIN RULES CONCERNING COPYRIGHT AND NEIGHBOURING RIGHTS APPLICABLE TO SATELLITE BROADCASTING AND CABLE RETRANSMISSION.

cabotage (**kab**-ə-tij). (1831) *Int'l law.* **1.** The carrying on of trade along a country's coast; the transport of goods or passengers from one port or place to another in the same country. • The privilege to carry on this trade is usu. limited to vessels flying the flag of that country. **2.** The privilege of carrying traffic between two ports in the same country. **3.** The right of a foreign airline to carry passengers and cargo between airports in the same country.

> "Some writers maintain [that *cabotage*] should be applied only to maritime navigation; in this context one can distinguish between petit cabotage — transport between ports situated on the same sea (e.g. Bordeaux-Le Havre) — and grand cabotage — transport between ports situated on different seas (e.g. Bordeaux-Marseille). However, the term is also properly applied to transport between two inland points on an international river within one State, although the term grand cabotage is sometimes incorrectly applied to transnational transport between the inland ports of different riparian States on the same waterway. River cabotage properly so called is sometimes also referred to as local transport. Finally, the term has also been adopted to describe commercial air transport between airports situated in the same State." Robert C. Lane, "Cabotage," in 1 *Encyclopedia of Public International Law* 519–20 (1992).

cab-rank rule. (1962) *English law.* The rule that a barrister must accept all work assigned in a field in which the barrister professes competence, in a court at which he or she normally appears, at the usual fee, for every client assigned — even those unpopular or repugnant to the lawyer.

ca'canny strike. See *slowdown strike* under STRIKE (1).

cacicazgos (kah-see-**kahz**-gohs). Land held in entail by *caciques* (leaders of Indian villages) and their descendants in Spanish America.

cadastre (kə-**das**-tər). (18c) A survey and valuation of real estate in a county or region compiled for tax purposes. — Also spelled *cadaster.* — **cadastral,** *adj.*

cadaver. (15c) A dead body; a corpse.

cadaver dog. See DOG (1).

cadena (ka-**day**-nə). [Spanish "chain"] *Spanish law.* A period of imprisonment; formerly, confinement at hard labor while chained from waist to ankle.

▸ ***cadena perpetua*** (ka-**day**-nə pər-**pet**-wə). (1907) Life imprisonment.

▸ ***cadena temporal*** (ka-**day**-nə tem-por-**ahl**). (1907) Imprisonment for a term less than life.

cadere (**kad**-ə-ree). [Latin "to fail"] *Hist.* **1.** To end, cease, or fail. • This term usu. refers to the failure of a writ action. *Cadit breve,* for example, means "the writ fails." **2.** To be changed or turned into. • *Cadit assisa in juratum* means "the assise is changed into a jury."

cadit quaestio (**kay**-dit **kwes**-chee-oh). [Latin] *Hist.* The question falls to the ground; the dispute is over.

caduca (kə-**d[y]oo**-kə), *n. pl.* [Latin "fallen things"] **1.** *Civil law.* Heritable property; property descending to an heir. **2.** *Roman law.* Property forfeited for crime. See LAPSE. **3.** *Roman law.* Property that either was without an heir or could not be taken by the testamentary heir or legatee. • In many cases, the property would escheat to the state. See ESCHEAT.

caducary (kə-**d[y]oo**-kə-ree), *adj.* (18c) (Of a bequest or estate) subject to, relating to, or by way of escheat, lapse, or forfeiture of property <the statute was intended to waive the rights of the caducary heirs>.

caduce (kə-**d[y]oos**), *vb.* (17c) To take by escheat or lapse <the government caduced the unclaimed mineral royalties>.

caducity (kə-**d[y]oo**-sə-tee), *n.* (1875) The lapse of a testamentary gift <the testator failed to provide a contingency for the caducity of the legacy>.

caeteris paribus. See CETERIS PARIBUS.

caeteris tacentibus. See CETERIS TACENTIBUS.

caeterorum administration. See ADMINISTRATION.

c.a.f. Cost, assurance, and freight. • This term is synonymous with C.I.F.

> "[I]n a French contract the term 'C.A.F.' does not mean 'Cost and Freight' but has exactly the same meaning as the term 'C.I.F.,' since it is merely the French equivalent of that term. The 'A' does not stand for 'and' but for 'assurance,' which means insurance." William D. Hawkland, *Uniform Commercial Code Series* § 2-320 (1984).

CAFC. *abbr.* UNITED STATES COURT OF APPEALS FOR THE FEDERAL CIRCUIT.

cafeteria plan. (1984) An employee fringe-benefit plan allowing a choice of basic benefits up to a certain dollar amount.

***Cage* error.** (1992) *Criminal law.* The omission of a constitutionally required jury instruction — a mistake that mandates an automatic reversal. *See Cage v. Louisiana,* 498 U.S. 29 (1990).

cahoots (kə-**hoots**). (1862) *Slang.* Partnership, esp. in an illegal act; collusion <the lawyer was in cahoots with her client>.

Cairns's Act (**kairn**-zəz). *Hist. English law.* An 1858 statute that expanded the relief available in England's chancery courts to include monetary damages in addition to injunctive relief. • Cairns's Act was superseded by the Judicature Acts of 1873–1875. — Also spelled *Cairns' Act.* Cf. JUDICATURE ACTS.

CAJC. CENTRAL AMERICAN COURT OF JUSTICE.

***Calandra* rule** (kə-**lan**-drə). (1974) The doctrine that a grand-jury witness may be compelled to answer questions about certain items, even though the items were obtained by the police illegally. *U.S. v. Calandra,* 414 U.S. 338, 94 S.Ct. 613 (1974).

calculated, *adj.* (18c) **1.** Arrived at through mathematical computation <calculated projections of income>. **2.** Undertaken after close consideration of the probable outcome <calculated risks>. **3.** Planned so as to achieve a specific purpose; deliberate <a calculated move to replenish the fund>. **4.** Likely; apt <an action calculated to win approval>.

calculated ambiguity. See AMBIGUITY (1).

***Caldwell* error.** (1988) The constitutionally impermissible error of resting a death sentence on a determination made by a sentencer who has been led to believe that the responsibility for determining the appropriateness of the defendant's death sentence lies elsewhere. *Caldwell v. Mississippi,* 472 U.S. 320, 105 S.Ct. 2633 (1985). • The error most often occurs when the prosecutor or the judge tells the jury that the death sentence, if inappropriate, may be overturned on appeal.

calefagium (kal-i-**fay**-jee-əm), *n.* (18c) *Hist.* A feudal right to take wood from the King's forest or the lord's estate.

calendar, *n.* (15c) **1.** A systematized ordering of time into years, months, weeks, and days; esp., the Gregorian calendar established by Pope Gregory XIII in 1582 and adopted in Great Britain in 1752. • The Gregorian calendar is used throughout the Western world.

▸ **Gregorian calendar.** See NEW STYLE.

▸ **Julian calendar.** See OLD STYLE.

2. (18c) A court's list of civil or criminal cases. See DOCKET (2).

▸ **court calendar.** See COURT CALENDAR.

▸ **reserve calendar.** (1904) A "shadow" court calendar used for cases struck from the court's actual calendar, subject to restoration on motion of one of the litigants for good cause, such as a speedy-trial deadline.

▸ **short-cause calendar.** (1883) A trial calendar on which a short-cause trial may be scheduled for the 10th day after the opposing party is given notice. • The request for scheduling must include an affidavit that the trial will take no longer than a certain specified period (e.g., an hour).

▸ **special calendar.** (1894) A calendar marked with court cases that have been specially set for hearing or trial. See *special setting* under SETTING.

▸ **trial calendar.** See DOCKET (2).

3. A list of bills reported out of a legislative committee for consideration by the entire legislature. **4.** *Parliamentary law.* AGENDA. — Also termed *calendar of business.*

▸ **action calendar.** (1994) The list of business awaiting a deliberative assembly's vote. — Also termed *action agenda.*

▸ **consent calendar.** (1928) A list of unopposed business items awaiting a deliberative assembly's vote or automatic adoption. • The consent calendar is usu. approved without debate unless a member objects. — Also termed *consent agenda; unanimous-consent agenda; unanimous-consent calendar.*

"An assembly with a large number of routine or noncontroversial matters on its agenda may find it not only convenient but expeditious to consider these matters under unanimous consent procedure. This gives every member an opportunity to object. At the same time, it gives the presiding officer an opportunity to dispose of a great deal of the agenda confronting the assembly quickly and efficiently, particularly when it would be most helpful to the assembly to get its job done. This can even be done by taking en bloc action (that is, disposing of various items at the same time without taking separate consideration of them) when matters are not controversial or are of minor importance to the assembly, though every member has the right to object." Floyd M. Riddick & Miriam H. Butcher, *Riddick's Rules of Procedure* 56 (1985).

▸ **debate calendar.** (1982) The list of business that is awaiting a deliberative assembly's vote and that is not on the consent calendar. — Also termed *debate agenda.*

▸ **report calendar.** The list of business coming before a deliberative assembly for information only rather than for its vote. • An item on the report calendar may be the subject of a vote in the future. — Also termed *report agenda.*

▸ **special-order calendar.** (1934) The list of business scheduled as special orders. — Also termed *special-order agenda.* See *special order* under ORDER (4).

▸ **unanimous-consent calendar.** See *consent calendar.*

calendar, *vb.* (15c) **1.** To place an important event on a calendar, esp. so that the event will be remembered. **2.** To place a case on a calendar.

calendar call. (1918) A court session in which the judge calls each case awaiting trial, determines its status, and assigns a trial date.

calendar day. See DAY.

calendar month. See MONTH (1).

calendar motion. See MOTION (1).

calendar of business. See CALENDAR (4).

calendar of prisoners. (17c) *Hist.* A list kept by the sheriffs containing the names of all the prisoners in custody alongside notes about each prisoner's present and past convictions.

calendar year. See YEAR (1).

Calends (kal-əndz). *Roman law.* In the ancient Roman calendar, the first day of the month. — Also spelled *Kalends.* Cf. IDES; NONES.

CALI. *abbr.* Computer-assisted legal instruction.

call, *n.* (13c) **1.** A request, demand, or command, esp. to come or assemble; an invitation or summons.

▸ **call for the orders of the day.** (1827) *Parliamentary law.* A demand that the meeting proceed according to its order of business or scheduled orders of the day. — Also termed *call for the regular order.* See *order of business, order of the day* under ORDER (4).

▸ **call for the regular order.** See *call for the orders of the day.*

▸ **call of a meeting.** (18c) *Parliamentary law.* Formal written notice of a meeting's time and place, sometimes stating its business, sent to each member in advance.

▸ **call of the house.** (17c) A legislative body's order compelling each absent member's attendance, usu. instructing that the sergeant at arms arrest and present each absentee.

"In legislative bodies or other assemblies that have legal power to compel the attendance of their members, a procedure that can be used to obtain a quorum, if necessary, is the motion for a *Call of the House.* This is a motion that unexcused absent members be brought to the meeting under arrest. A *Call of the House* is not applicable in voluntary societies." Henry M. Robert, *Robert's Rules of Order Newly Revised* § 40, at 339 (10th ed. 2000).

▸ **call of the roll.** See *roll call.*

▸ **call to order.** (18c) *Parliamentary law.* **1.** The chair's declaration that a deliberative assembly has properly convened and is ready for business. — Also termed *convocation.* **2.** The chair's request that a member follow the applicable rules or observe appropriate decorum. See DECORUM.

▸ **quorum call.** (1926) A roll call to determine whether a quorum is present. See QUORUM.

▸ **roll call.** (18c) *Parliamentary law.* A calling of the roll to take attendance or a vote. See *roll-call vote* under VOTE (4). — Also termed *call of the roll.*

2. A demand for payment of money. See AT-CALL.

▸ **call on shares.** (18c) A company's demand of shareholders, at any time during the company's lifetime, that they pay all or part of the balance remaining unpaid on each share.

▸ **margin call.** (1888) A securities broker's demand that a customer put up money or stock as collateral when the broker finances a purchase of securities. • A margin call usu. occurs when the market prices of the securities are falling. — Also termed *maintenance call.*

3. See *call option* under OPTION (5). **4.** A demand for the presentation of a security (esp. a bond) for redemption before the maturity date. **5.** *Property.* A landmark designating a property boundary. • The landmarks are chosen by the surveyor and recorded in his field notes or in the accompanying deed. See DIRECTORY CALL; LOCATIVE CALL; METES AND BOUNDS. **6.** *Property.* In a metes-and-bounds legal description, an instruction for locating property lines, usu. expressed by bearing and distance from an established location.

▸ **flat call.** A call that does not include a reference to any adjoining, nearby, or terminal monument. See TIE (3).

call, *vb.* (bef. 12c) **1.** To summon. **2.** To demand payment of money. **3.** To redeem (a bond) before maturity.

callable, *adj.* (1892) (Of a security) redeemable by the issuing corporation before maturity. See REDEMPTION.

callable bond. See *redeemable bond* under BOND (3).

callable preferred stock. See STOCK.

callable security. See *redeemable security* under SECURITY (4).

called meeting. See *special meeting* under MEETING.

called party. Under the Telephone Consumer Protection Act, the person to whom a call is made. • Some courts have limited the meaning of *called party* to the call's intended recipient, while others have held that it means the person assigned to the called number when the call is made. 47 USCA § 227.

call equivalent position. (1997) *Securities.* A security position that increases in value as the value of the underlying equity increases. • It includes a long convertible security, a long call option, and a short put option. SEC Rule 16a-1(b) (17 CFR § 240.16a-1(b)).

call for the orders of the day. See CALL (1).

call for the regular order. See *call for the orders of the day* under CALL (1).

call frequency. See CALL VOLUME.

calling to the bar. See CALL TO THE BAR.

call-in pay. (1945) Compensation guaranteed by contract to workers who report to work when requested and are ready, but to whom no work is made available.

call loan. See LOAN.

call of a meeting. See CALL (1).

call of the house. See CALL (1).

call of the roll. See *roll call* under CALL (1).

call on shares. See CALL (2).

call option. See OPTION (5).

callover, *n.* A buyer's exercise of a call option — that is, of the right to buy the security underlying an option, as opposed to letting the option lapse. — **call over,** *vb.*

call patent. See PATENT (2).

call premium. See PREMIUM (3).

call price. See PRICE.

call-protection clause. (1992) A clause in a bond issue or a callable preferred stock issue prohibiting the issuer from recalling the security during a specified period.

call the question. (1840) *Parliamentary law.* **1.** (Of a member) to move to close debate. **2.** (Of a deliberative assembly) to adopt a motion to close debate. See CLOSE DEBATE.

call to order. See CALL (1).

call to the bar, *n.* (1844) The admission of a person to practice law. • This common phrase is a loan translation of the Latin *ad barram evocatus* ("called to the bar"). — Also termed *calling to the bar.* See AD BARRAM EVOCATUS.

call up, *vb. Parliamentary law.* To bring before a deliberative assembly business that is ready for consideration <call up the motion to reconsider>.

call volume. *Telecommunications.* The number, frequency, and pattern of telephone calls to or from a particular telephone number or set of numbers. • Courts can sometimes infer from the call volume whether calls to a debtor for the collection of a debt were made with the intent to harass. — Also termed (less precisely) *call frequency.*

CALR. *abbr.* Computer-assisted legal research.

calumnia (kə-**ləm**-nee-ə), *n. pl.* [Latin "vexatious proceedings"] *Roman law.* Vexatiously instituted civil proceedings or knowingly false criminal charges made against someone. • The victim had civil or criminal remedies depending on the circumstances.

calumniae judicium (kə-**ləm**-nee-ee joo-**dish**-ee-əm). [Latin "action for vexation"] *Roman law.* A countersuit that a defendant who was maliciously sued could bring after winning a judgment in the principal action.

calumniae jusjurandum (kə-**ləm**-nee-ee jəs-jə-**ran**-dəm). [Law Latin "oath of calumny"] *Roman law.* An oath given by a litigant that he is not suing or defending vexatiously.

calumniate (kə-**ləm**-nee-ayt), *vb.* (16c) To slander or make false charges against. See MALIGN. — **calumniator,** *n.*

calumny (**kal**-əm-nee), *n.* (16c) *Archaic.* **1.** The act of maliciously misrepresenting someone's words or actions in a way that is calculated to injure that person's reputation. See OBLOQUY (1). **2.** A defamatory charge or imputation; esp., an untrue and unfair statement about someone intended to besmirch the person's reputation. — **calumnious** (kə-**ləm**-nee-əs), *adj.* — **calumniator** (kə-**ləm**-nee-ay-tər), *n.*

Calvin's case. The decision establishing that persons born in Scotland after the 1603 accession of James I to the English throne were deemed natural-born subjects of the King of England and could inherit English land. *Calvin v. Smith*, 7 Eng. Rep. 1, 2 S.T. 559 (1608).

Calvo clause (**kahl**-voh). (1908) A contractual clause by which an alien waives the right to invoke diplomatic immunity. • Such a clause typically appears in a contract between a national government and an alien.

Calvo doctrine. (1903) *Int'l law.* The rule that resident aliens have the same rights to protection as citizens, but no more. • This doctrine, which sought to establish a minimum international standard for the treatment of aliens, was developed by the Argentinian jurist Carlos Calvo in his treatise *Le Droit International Théorique et Pratique* (5th ed. 1896). The doctrine was intended to prevent aliens from abusing their right of diplomatic protection. It was rejected by many states on the ground that the doctrine sought to deprive states of their right to protect their citizens in countries when the rights of the general population fell below the minimum international standards.

cambiale jus (kam-bee-**ay**-lee **jəs**). [Latin "law of exchange"] The law of commercial exchange.

cambiator (**kam**-bee-ay-tər). [Latin] *Hist.* An exchanger, usu. of money (*cambiatores monetae*). See CAMBIST.

cambist (**kam**-bist). [fr. Latin *cambiare* "to exchange"] (1809) A broker who trades promissory notes or bills of exchange. — Also termed *cambiator.*

cambium (**kam**-bee-əm). [Law Latin "exchange"] (18c) *Hist.* **1.** An exchange of money, debt, or land.

▸ ***cambium locale.*** A contract of exchange in which a person agrees to pay a sum of money at one location in consideration of money received at another location. — Also termed *cambium mercantile; cambium trajectitium.*

▸ ***cambium reale.*** An exchange of land. — Also termed *cambium manuale.*

2. A mercantile contract in which the parties agree to exchange money for money; a bill of exchange. — Also termed *escambium.* **3.** *Eccles. law.* An exchange of money that potentially allows one party to profit. • Historically, most forms of cambium were forbidden under laws against usury but were gradually allowed as a fair recompense for trouble and risk. Cf. (in sense 3) USURY.

camera (**kam**-ə-rə). [Latin] (17c) Chamber; room. See IN CAMERA.

camera regis (**kam**-ə-rə **ree**-jis). [Latin "chambers of the king"] (16c) *Hist.* A locale that the king takes a particular interest in, usu. expressed as a royal privilege benefiting a city.

camerarius (kam-ə-**rair**-ee-əs). [fr. Latin *camera* "chamber"] (18c) *Hist.* **1.** A chamberlain or other treasurer in charge of public money. **2.** BAILIFF (1).

Camera Scaccarii. See EXCHEQUER CHAMBER.

Camera Stellata (**kam**-ə-rə stə-**lay**-tə). [Law Latin] See STAR CHAMBER, COURT OF.

Campbell's Act. *Hist. English law.* Any one of several statutes passed during the tenure of Lord Campbell (1779–1861) as a member of Parliament in the 1840s and 1850s, esp. (1) an 1843 statute dealing with the punishment for defamatory libel, (2) an 1846 statute enabling the representatives of a wrongful-death victim to recover damages, or (3) an 1857 statute that made the sale of obscene material a statutory offense and empowered the courts to seize and destroy the offending material. — Also termed *Lord Campbell's Act.*

campers. *Hist.* The share of a lawsuit's proceeds payable to a champertor. See CHAMPERTY.

campipartia. See CHAMPERTY.

campiparticeps. See CHAMPERTOR.

campipartitio (kam-pə-pahr-**tish**-ee-oh). [Law Latin] See CHAMPERTY.

CAMs. *abbr.* See COMMON-AREA MAINTENANCE CHARGES.

can, *vb.* (bef. 12c) **1.** To be able to do something <you can lift 500 pounds>. **2.** To have permission (as often interpreted by courts); MAY <no appeal can be filed until the filing fee is paid>.

cancel, *vb.* (15c) **1.** To destroy a written instrument by defacing or obliterating it <she canceled her will by marking through it>. **2.** To terminate a promise, obligation, or right <the parties canceled the contract>.

canceled check. See CHECK.

cancellaria (kan-sə-**lair**-ee-ə). [Law Latin] See CHANCERY (1). — Also termed *curia cancellaria.*

cancellarius (kan-sə-**lair**-ee-əs). [Law Latin] **1.** A chancellor, scrivener, or notary. **2.** See LORD CHANCELLOR.

cancellation, *n.* (16c) **1.** The act of defacing or obliterating a writing (as by marking lines across it) with the intention of rendering it void. **2.** An annulment or termination of a promise or an obligation; specif., the purposeful ending of a contract because the other party has breached one or more of its terms. • The effect of cancellation is generally the same as that of termination, except that the canceling party retains remedies for breach of the whole contract or any unperformed balance.

▸ **flat cancellation.** (1913) The cancellation of an insurance policy without any charge to the insured.

3. An equitable remedy by which courts call in and annul outstanding void or rescinded instruments because they may either spawn vexatious litigation or cloud someone's title to property. **4.** *Trademarks.* The removal of a trademark from the Principal Register. • A trademark already on the Principal Register can be challenged by a person who claims to be damaged by the placement. For five years after a mark is allowed, it can be canceled for any reason that would have blocked allowance of the application. After that time, if the owner files a declaration under § 15, the grounds for cancellation are more restricted. See INCONTESTABILITY STATUS. Cf. OPPOSITION. **5.** Popularly, the decision that a planned event will not happen. — **cancel,** *vb.* — **cancelable,** *adj.*

cancellation clause. (1874) A contractual provision allowing one or both parties to annul their obligations under certain conditions. — Also termed *termination clause.*

cancellatura. *Hist.* See CANCELLATION.

cancelled check. See CHECK.

cancelli (kan-**sel**-ɪ). [Latin "lattice, grille"] (17c) *Archaic.* **1.** Lines drawn on a writing, esp. a will, indicating its revocation. See CANCELLATION (1). **2.** *Hist.* The rails or latticework enclosing the bar of a court.

cancerphobia claim. See FEAR-OF-CANCER CLAIM.

C&F. *abbr.* COST AND FREIGHT. — Also spelled *CandF.*

candidacy (**kan**-di-də-see), *n.* (1864) The state or condition of competing for an office or position, esp. in an election. — Also termed *candidature.*

candidate, *n.* [fr. Latin *candidatus,* "clothed in white"; fr. *candidus,* "white," from the white toga worn by a candidate for public office in ancient Rome as a symbol of clean government] (17c) **1.** An individual seeking election to an office, membership, award, or like title or status. **2.** Popularly, a person being considered for a job, nomination, or appointment. Cf. NOMINEE (1).

candidate species. See SPECIES (1).

candidature. See CANDIDACY.

Candlemas. See *quarter day* under DAY.

candor. The quality of being open, honest, and sincere; frankness; outspokenness. — **candid,** *adj.*

canfara (**kan**-fə-rə). [Law Latin] (18c) *Hist. English law.* A trial by hot iron, formerly used in England. See *ordeal by fire* under ORDEAL.

canine profiling. (2000) *Slang.* The practice of generally labeling an entire dog breed inherently dangerous or vicious, which in many states automatically creates legal restrictions and liabilities on a dog and its owner. See BREED-SPECIFIC LEGISLATION.

canon (kan-ən), *n.* (bef. 12c) **1.** A rule or principle, esp. a practical rule of guidance accepted as fundamental; a standard or test of judgment.

▸ **canon of construction.** (1831) A rule used in construing legal instruments, esp. contracts and statutes; a principle that guides the interpreter of a text. • Although a few states have codified the canons of construction — examples of which are *contra proferentem* and *ejusdem generis* — most jurisdictions treat the canons as mere customs not having the force of law. — Often shortened to *canon.* — Also termed *rule of construction; rule of interpretation; principle of interpretation; interpretive canon.*

> "The[] different ways of categorizing canons overlap. Most of the canons that state policy-neutral rules about vocabulary and syntax can be thought of as helping interpreters to grasp the intended meaning of statutory language, and at least some of the canons that put thumbs on the scale in favor of certain substantive policies can be thought of as telling courts how to proceed when their information about the enacting legislature's likely intent has run out.

But these correlations are not perfect. A few canons that are entirely policy-neutral (such as the so-called 'last-antecedent rule' . . .) are designed less to capture the likely intent behind particular formulations than to regularize the courts' approach to some recurring sources of ambiguity in English syntax. If these canons help courts ascertain the intended meaning of statutory language, it is only because legislators have come to know about the canons and to read bills against the backdrop that they provide. Conversely, many of the canons that favor particular substantive policies can be seen at least in part as tools for helping interpreters discern likely legislative intent, because the policies that they favor reflect norms that American legislatures have long tended to follow." Caleb Nelson, *Statutory Interpretation* 82 (2011).

▸ **canon of descent.** (*usu. pl.*) (18c) A common-law rule governing intestate succession. • In England, canons of descent tended to concentrate landholdings in the hands of a few people, an approach generally rejected in the United States. — Also termed *canon of inheritance.*

"The common-law canons of descent tended to prevent the diffusion of landed property, and to promote its accumulation in the hands of a few. The principles sprang from the martial genius of the feudal system. In the United States the English common law of descents, in its essential features, has been rejected; each State has established a law for itself." William C. Anderson, *A Dictionary of Law* 349 (1889).

▸ **canon of inheritance.** See *canon of descent.*

▸ **descriptive canon.** An interpretive principle that provides guidance about what the drafters of a legal instrument probably meant. Cf. *normative canon.*

▸ **interpretative canon.** See *canon of construction.*

▸ **normative canon.** An interpretive principle that directs courts to construe any doubtful provision in a way that furthers some policy objective. Cf. *descriptive canon.*

▸ **substantive canon.** An interpretive principle that reflects a policy drawn from the common law, a statute, or the Constitution. Cf. *textual canon.*

▸ **textual canon.** An interpretive principle that reflects accepted notions of diction, grammar, and syntax. Cf. *substantive canon.*

2. (*usu. cap.*) A maxim stating in general terms the standards of professional conduct expected of lawyers or judges. • The Model Code of Judicial Conduct (2011) contains four canons and dozens of specific rules. **3.** A rule of ecclesiastical law. **4.** A corpus of writings. **5.** A clergy member on the staff of a cathedral.

▸ **honorary canon.** (18c) A canon who serves without pay or other benefits.

6. A fixed regular payment or tribute made as a contribution payable to the church.

▸ **canon emphyteuticus** (**kan**-ən em-fi-**t[y]oo**-ti-kəs). [Latin fr. Greek] (18c) *Roman law.* The annual payment that an *emphyteuta* made under a contract of *emphyteusis.* See EMPHYTEUSIS; EMPHYTEUTA.

canonical (kə-**non**-ə-kəl), *adj.* (16c) **1.** (Of a rule or decree) prescribed by, in conformity with, or relating to canon law. See CANON LAW. **2.** Orthodox; conforming to accepted rules or conventions.

canonical disability. See DISABILITY (3).

canonical impediment. See IMPEDIMENT.

canonical law. See CANON LAW.

canonical purgation. See PURGATION.

canonist (**kan**-ən-ist), *n.* (16c) An expert in canon law; esp., a canon lawyer or professor of ecclesiastical law.

canon law. (14c) **1.** The laws of the Christian Church; esp., a body of western ecclesiastical law that was first compiled from the 12th to 14th centuries. • It has grown steadily since that time and is now codified in the *Codex Juris Canonici* of 1983, replacing that of 1918. — Also termed *corpus juris canonici; papal law; jus canonicum.* See CORPUS JURIS CANONICI. **2.** A body of law developed within a particular religious tradition. — Also termed *church law; canonical law.* Cf. ECCLESIASTICAL LAW.

"The indirect contributions of the canon law to the development of English law were as great as, and the direct contributions far greater than, those made by the civil law. Indirectly the canon lawyers gave much even to the purely secular law of England, because, during the early Middle Ages, most of the judges of the royal courts were ecclesiastics acquainted with the chief doctrines of canon law. . . . The direct influence of the canon law in England resulted from its being the law which was administered in the courts of the Church." W.J.V. Windeyer, *Lectures on Legal History* 41 (2d ed. 1949).

"Canon law has its roots in theology. But, so far as England is concerned, it may be defined as so much of the law of England as is concerned with the regulation of the affairs of the Church of England." E. Garth Moore & Timothy Briden, *Moore's Introduction to English Canon Law* 9 (2d ed. 1985).

canon of construction. See CANON (1).

canon of descent. See CANON (1).

canon of imputed common-law meaning. The doctrine that a statute using a common-law term, without defining it, adopts its common-law meaning.

canon of inheritance. See *canon of descent* under CANON (1).

cant (kant). (18c) *Civil law.* A method of dividing commonly held property by awarding it to the highest-bidding owner on condition that the successful bidder must buy out each coowner's interest. — Also termed *licitation.*

cantred (**kan**-tred). [fr. Welsh *cant* "hundred" + *tref* "village"] See HUNDRED.

CANT rule. The principle that a class action requires commonality, actionability, numerosity, and typicality.

canum (**kay**-nəm). [Law Latin] *Hist.* A duty or tribute payable from a tenant to a lord, usu. consisting of produce from the land.

canvass, *n.* (17c) **1.** The counting of votes and certifying of results. **2.** A survey of opinions. **3.** *Criminal law.* The scouring of a neighborhood or apartment building by law-enforcement officers, sometimes accompanied by the victim or witnesses, in search of more witnesses or of the perpetrator.

canvass, *vb.* (16c) **1.** To examine in detail; scrutinize <that issue has been repeatedly canvassed by our state's courts>. **2.** To formally count ballots and report the returns <canvass the votes>.

"When all the ballots have been collected, including those of the presiding officer, the secretary, and the tellers, the ballots are canvassed by the tellers. *Canvassing* the ballots means more than just counting. It includes evaluating ballots to identify those that are invalid, blank, cast for illegal nominees, illegible, abstaining, and the like, and reporting the total results to the presiding officer for his announcement of the results." Ray E. Keesey, *Modern Parliamentary Procedure* 113 (1994).

3. To solicit political support from voters or a voting district; to take stock of public opinion <the candidate is actively canvassing the Western states>. — **canvass,** *n.*

canvasser, *n.* (18c) Someone who has been officially appointed to count votes, esp. in a legislative assembly. — Also termed *vote counter*; *teller.*

cap, *n.* (1947) An upper limit, such as a statutory limit on the recovery in a tort action or on the interest a bank can charge. — **cap,** *vb.*

capacitate (kə-**pas**-ə-tayt), *vb.* (17c) To qualify; to make legally competent. — **capacitation** (kə-pas-ə-**tay**-shən), *n.*

capacity. (15c) **1.** The role in which one performs an act; esp., someone's job, position, or duty <in her corporate capacity>.

▸ **representative capacity.** (17c) The position of one standing or acting for another, esp. through delegated authority <an agent acting in a representative capacity for the principal>.

2. The power to create or enter into a legal relation under the same circumstances in which a normal person would have the power to create or enter into such a relation; specif., the satisfaction of a legal qualification, such as legal age or soundness of mind, that determines one's ability to sue or be sued, to enter into a binding contract, and the like <she had full capacity to bind the corporation with her signature>. • Unless necessary to show the court's jurisdiction, a plaintiff's pleadings need not assert the legal capacity of any party. A party wishing to raise the issue of capacity must do so by specific negative pleading. Fed. R. Civ. P. 9(a). — Also termed (specif.) *capacity to sue*; *power over oneself.* See STANDING. Cf. LACK OF CAPACITY.

▸ **corporate capacity.** (17c) The power of a corporation to enter into contracts, as well as to exercise other legal rights and assume other liabilities.

▸ **proprietary capacity.** (18c) The capacity of a city or town when it engages in a business-like venture rather than a governmental function. See PROPRIETARY FUNCTION.

3. The mental ability to understand the nature and effect of one's acts <his acute pain reduced his capacity to understand the hospital's admission form>. — Also termed *mental capacity*; *sane memory.* See COMPETENCY.

▸ **criminal capacity.** (1853) The mental ability that a person must possess to be held accountable for a crime; the ability to understand right from wrong. See INSANITY; INFANCY.

▸ **diminished capacity.** (1912) **1.** An impaired mental condition — short of insanity — that is caused by intoxication, trauma, or disease and that prevents a person from having the mental state necessary to be held responsible for a crime. • In some jurisdictions, a defendant's diminished capacity can be used to determine the degree of the offense or the severity of the punishment. **2.** A failure-of-proof defense or a partial-excuse defense based on the defendant's diminished capacity at the time of the offense. — Also termed *diminished responsibility*; *partial insanity*; *partial responsibility.* Cf. INSANITY.

> "*Diminished capacity* refers to two distinct doctrines: the use of evidence of mental abnormality to negate a mens rea required by the definition of the crime charged (the *mens rea variant*) and the use of mental abnormality evidence to establish some type of partial affirmative defense of excuse (the *partial excuse variant*). Courts have used various other terms, such as *diminished responsibility*, to refer to one or both of these distinct doctrines, but the term used is unimportant. Confusion arises, however, when the two types of doctrine are not clearly distinguished." Stephen J. Morse, "Diminished Capacity," in *Encyclopedia of Crime & Justice* 528, 528 (Joshua Dressler ed., 2d ed. 2002).

▸ **disposing capacity.** See *testamentary capacity.*

▸ **testamentary capacity.** (1819) The mental ability that a person must have to prepare a valid will. • This capacity is often described as the ability to recognize the natural objects of one's bounty, the nature and extent of one's estate, and the fact that one is making a plan to dispose of the estate after death. Traditionally, the phrase "of legal age and sound mind" refers to the testator's capacity. — Also termed *disposing capacity*; *disposing mind*; *sound mind*; *sound disposing mind.* See *age of capacity* under AGE.

4. Someone's ability to do a thing; the ability or power to do or experience something.

▸ **decreased capacity.** (1886) A diminution in a person's physical ability because of an illness, injury, or impairment.

5. The amount of something that a factory, company, machine, etc. can produce or deal with. **6.** The size or power of something, such as an engine.

capacity defense. See DEFENSE (1).

capacity to sue. See CAPACITY (2).

cap and trade. See EMISSIONS TRADING.

capax doli (**kay**-paks **doh**-lɪ). See DOLI CAPAX.

capax negotii (**kay**-paks ni-**goh**-shee-ɪ), *adj.* [Latin "capable of entering into a transaction"] (Of a person) having capacity to enter into a contract; capable of transacting business.

cape (**kay**-pee). [Latin "take"] (16c) *Hist.* A writ filed to recover possession of land.

▸ **cape magnum** (**kay**-pee **mag**-nəm). [Latin "grand" cape] (17c) A writ granting possession of land before a tenant's appearance in the action. — Also termed *magnum cape*; *grand cape.*

▸ **cape parvum** (**kay**-pee **pahr**-vəm). [Latin "little" cape] (17c) A writ for the recovery of land issuing after the appearance of the tenant in the action. — Also termed *petit cape.*

> "*Cape* is a writ judiciall touching plee of land or tenements, so tearmed (as most writs be) of that word in itselfe, which carieth the especiallest intention or end thereof. And this writ is divided in (*Cape magnum*, & *Cape parvum*:) both which . . . take hold of things immoveable, and seeme to differ betweene themselves in these points. First, because (*cape magnum*) or the (*grand Cape*) lyeth before appearance, and (*Cape parvum*) afterward. Secondly, the (*Cape magnum*) summoneth the tenent to aunswer to the default, and over to the demaundant: (*Cape parvum*) summoneth the tenent to aunswer to the default onely: and therefore is called (*Cape parvum*) or in French English (*petit Cape.*)" John Cowell, *The Interpreter* (1607).

capias (**kay**-pee-əs *or* **kap**-ee-əs). [Latin "that you take"] (15c) Any of various types of writs that require an officer to take a named defendant into custody. • A capias is often issued when a respondent fails to appear or when an obligor has failed to pay child support. — Also termed *writ of capias; body execution.*

▸ ***capias ad audiendum judicium*** (ad aw-dee-**en**-dəm joo-**dish**-ee-əm). [Latin "that you take to hear the judgment"] (18c) In a misdemeanor case, a writ issued to bring the defendant to hear the judgment to be imposed after having failed to appear.

▸ ***capias ad computandum*** (ad kom-pyoo-**tan**-dəm). [Latin "that you take for computation"] (17c) *Hist.* A writ issued when a debtor has failed to appear and make account after losing in an action of account render. See ACCOUNTING (3).

▸ ***capias ad faciendum.*** (ad fay-she-**en**-dəm) (17c) *Hist.* A writ used to enforce a creditor's judgment against a debtor by authorizing the debtor's arrest and imprisonment.

▸ ***capias ad respondendum*** (ad ree-spon-**den**-dəm). [Latin "that you take to answer"] (17c) A writ commanding the sheriff to take the defendant into custody to ensure that the defendant will appear in court. — Abbr. *ca. resp.*; *ca. re.*; *ca. res.*; *ca. ad re.*

▸ ***capias ad satisfaciendum*** (ad sat-is-fay-shee-**en**-dəm). [Latin "that you take to satisfy"] (16c) *Hist.* A postjudgment writ commanding the sheriff to imprison the defendant until the judgment is satisfied. — Abbr. *ca. sa.*

> "The *capias ad satisfaciendum* (termed for brevity the *ca. sa.*,) is a judicial writ, issuing out of the court in which the judgment was recovered, directed to the sheriff of the county into which it is issued, commanding him to *take* (*capias*) the party named in it, if he may be found in his county, or bailiwick, so that he may have his body before the justices of the court, at the return day, *to satisfy* (*ad satisfaciendum*) the party issuing the writ, of the amount of the judgment, &c.; concluding with the usual clause of attestation, or *teste*." 1 Alexander M. Burrill, *Treatise on the Practice of the Supreme Court of the State of New-York* 307–08 (2d ed. 1846).

▸ ***capias extendi facias*** (ek-**sten**-dɪ **fay**-shee-əs). [Latin "take for extending"] (18c) *Hist.* A writ of execution issued against one who is indebted to the Crown, commanding the sheriff to arrest the debtor.

▸ ***capias in withernam*** (**kay**-pee-əs in **wi<u>th</u>**-ər-nahm). [Law Latin "taking again"] (17c) A writ authorizing the sheriff to seize the goods or cattle of a wrongful distrainor. — Also termed *writ of withernam.* See WITHERNAM.

▸ ***capias pro fine*** (**kay**-pee-əs proh **fɪ**-nee). [Latin "that you take for the fine"] (17c) A writ for the arrest of a person who had not paid an imposed fine. — Also termed *capiatur pro fine.*

▸ ***capias utlagatum*** (**kay**-pee-əs ət-lə-**gay**-təm). [Latin "you take the outlaw"] (16c) A writ commanding the arrest of an outlawed person.

capias clause. (1844) The language in a writ authorizing an officer to arrest a person charged with a crime or to summon a person to answer a civil suit. • Formerly, the standard wording of the clause for an arrest was "and for want thereof to take the body of said defendant (if he may be found in your precinct) and him safely keep so that you may have him before our Justices." The language would be revised for a summons: "and to summon the defendant (if he may be found in your precinct) to appear before our Justices."

capiatur pro fine. See *capias pro fine* under CAPIAS.

capiendo securitatem pro duplicatione feudifirmae (kap-ee-**en**-doh si-kyuur-ə-**tay**-təm proh d[y]oo-pli-kay-shee-**oh**-nee fyoo-di-**fər**-mee). [Law Latin "by taking caution for the payment of a double of the feu-duty"] *Hist.* In a precept for entry of an heir, a clause that cautions against taking a double feu payment when the investiture did not expressly provide for it.

capita. See PER CAPITA.

capital, *adj.* (16c) **1.** Of, relating to, or involving economic or financial capital <capital market>. **2.** Punishable by execution; involving the death penalty <a capital offense>.

capital, *n.* (17c) **1.** Money or assets invested, or available for investment, in a business. **2.** The total assets of a business, esp. those that help generate profits. **3.** The total amount or value of a corporation's stock; corporate equity. See *capital stock* under STOCK.

▸ **actual capital.** Funds generated by the sale of stock. See *capital stock* (1) under STOCK.

▸ **authorized capital.** See *nominal capital.*

▸ **circulating capital.** See *floating capital.*

▸ **debt capital.** (1886) Funds raised by issuing bonds.

▸ **equity capital.** (1930) Funds provided by a company's owners in exchange for evidence of ownership, such as stock.

▸ **fixed capital.** (18c) **1.** The amount of money invested in fixed assets, such as land and machinery. **2.** Fixed assets.

▸ **floating capital.** (18c) **1.** Funds not allocated to a particular class of the corporation's capital stock. **2.** Funds not presently invested or committed; esp., money retained for the purpose of meeting current expenditures. — Also termed *circulating capital.*

▸ **impaired capital.** (1902) Corporate funds consisting of assets that are less than the sum of the corporation's legal capital and its liabilities.

▸ **issued capital.** See *subscribed capital.*

▸ **issued-share capital.** See *subscribed capital.*

▸ **legal capital.** (1811) An amount equal to the aggregate "par" or stated value of all outstanding shares of a corporation, or, in the case of stock without par value, an amount set by the board of directors. • A minority of states require this amount to remain in the corporation to protect creditors. — Also termed *stated capital.*

▸ **moneyed capital.** (18c) Money that is invested with the intent of making a profit.

▸ **nominal capital.** (18c) The minimum value of the shares that a company is authorized by its association documents to issue. — Also termed *authorized capital.*

▸ **paid-in capital.** (1863) The money paid for the capital stock of a corporation.

▸ **partnership capital.** See PARTNERSHIP CAPITAL.

▸ **proprietary capital.** Money that represents the initial investment in a sole proprietorship.

▸ **risk capital.** (1927) **1.** Money or property invested in a business venture, esp. one in which the investor has no managerial control. **2.** See *venture capital.*

▸ **stated capital.** (1892) **1.** See *legal capital*. **2.** The total equity of a corporation as it appears on the balance sheet.

▸ **subscribed capital.** (1818) The total value of stock for which there are subscriptions (contracts of purchase). — Also termed *subscribed-share capital*; *issued capital*; *issued-share capital*.

▸ **subscribed-share capital.** See *subscribed capital*.

▸ **venture capital.** (1928) Funds invested in a new enterprise that has high risk and the potential for a high return. — Abbr. VC. — Also termed *risk capital*. See SEED MONEY.

▸ **working capital.** (1912) Current assets (such as cash, inventory, and accounts receivable) less current liabilities. • Working capital measures liquidity and the ability to discharge short-term obligations.

capital account. See ACCOUNT.

capital asset. See ASSET.

capital contribution. (1913) **1.** Cash, property, or services contributed by partners to a partnership. **2.** Funds made available by a shareholder, usu. without an increase in stock holdings.

capital crime. See *capital offense* under OFFENSE (2).

capitale (kap-i-**tay**-lee). [Latin "a thing"] *Hist.* **1.** Movable property, esp. animals (such as 100 head of cattle). • Over time, *chattel* became the more common term. **2.** A stolen thing, or its equivalent value. Pl. ***capitalia***.

capital expenditure. (1898) An outlay of funds to acquire or improve a fixed asset. — Also termed *capital improvement*; *capital outlay*.

capital expense. See EXPENSE.

capital flight. (1922) The sending of large amounts of investment money out of a country, usu. as a result of panic caused by political turmoil or a severe recession.

capital gain. (1921) The profit realized when a capital asset is sold or exchanged. — Also termed *capital gains*. Cf. *ordinary gain* under GAIN (3); *capital loss* under LOSS.

▸ **long-term capital gain.** (1938) The profit realized from selling or exchanging a capital asset held for more than a specified period, usu. one year.

▸ **short-term capital gain.** (1938) The profit realized from selling or exchanging a capital asset held for less than a specified period, usu. one year. • It is treated as ordinary income under current federal tax law.

capital-gain distribution. See *capital-gain dividend* under DIVIDEND.

capital-gain dividend. See DIVIDEND.

capital gains. See CAPITAL GAIN.

capital-gains tax. See TAX.

capital goods. See GOODS.

capital impairment. (1926) The financial condition of a corporation whose assets are less than the sum of its legal capital and its liabilities.

capital improvement. See CAPITAL EXPENDITURE.

capital-intensive, *adj.* (1907) (Of a business, industry, etc.) requiring a great deal of money to function or operate properly.

capitalis (kap-i-**tay**-lis), *adj.* [Latin] **1.** *Roman law.* (Of a crime) punishable by death, loss of liberty, or loss of citizenship. See CAPUT. **2.** *Hist.* (Of a person or judicial proceeding) that is principal or chief.

capitalis, *n.* [Latin "chief"] *Hist.* A principal (or chief) person, object, or judicial proceeding.

capitalis baro (kap-i-**tay**-lis **bar**-oh). [Latin "chief baron"] (18c) *Hist.* The chief baron of the Court of Exchequer. See CHIEF BARON.

capitalis custos (kap-i-**tay**-lis **kəs**-tohs). [Latin "chief guardian"] *Hist.* **1.** A chief warden or magistrate. **2.** Loosely, a mayor.

capitalis dominus (kap-i-**tay**-lis **dom**-ə-nəs). [Latin "chief lord"] (16c) *Hist.* A tenant's immediate lord; CHIEF LORD.

capitalis justiciarius (kap-i-**tay**-lis jəs-tish-ee-**air**-ee-əs). [Latin "chief justiciary"] (17c) *Hist.* The principal minister of state who governed when the king traveled abroad. • By the 13th century the duties of office were more judicial than political. See JUSTICIARY (2).

capitalis justiciarius ad placita coram rege tenenda (kap-i-**tay**-lis jəs-tish-ee-**air**-ee-əs ad **plas**-ə-tə **kor**-əm **ree**-jee tə-**nen**-də). [Latin] *Hist.* Chief justice for holding pleas before the king. • This phrase — which dates from the 13th century — referred to the chief justice of the King's Bench.

capitalis justiciarius banci (kap-i-**tay**-lis jəs-tish-ee-**air**-ee-əs **ban**-sɪ). [Latin] Chief justice of the bench. • This phrase — which dates from the 13th century — referred to the chief justice of the Court of Common Pleas.

capitalis justiciarius totius Angliae (kap-i-**tay**-lis jəs-tish-ee-**air**-ee-əs **toh**-shee-əs **ang**-glee-ee). [Latin] (18c) *Hist.* Chief justice of all England. • This was the title of the presiding justice in the court of aula regis.

capitalism, *n.* (1849) An economic and political system in which businesses belong mostly to private owners and not to the government; esp., an economic system that depends on the private ownership of the means of production and on competitive forces to determine what is produced. Cf. COMMUNISM (1). — **capitalist,** *adj.* & *n.*

▸ **state capitalism.** (1886) An economic system in which capital is largely controlled or owned by the state.

capitalis plegius (kap-i-**tay**-lis **plee**-jee-əs). [Latin "chief pledge"] (18c) *Hist.* **1.** A chief pledge or surety. **2.** BORSHOLDER.

capitalis terra (kap-i-**tay**-lis **ter**-ə). [Latin "head-land"] *Hist.* A piece of land lying before, or at the head of, other land.

capitalization, *n.* (1860) **1.** The act or process of capitalizing or converting something into capital. **2.** The amount or sum resulting from this act or process. **3.** The total amount of long-term financing used by a business, including stocks, bonds, retained earnings, and other funds. **4.** The total par value or stated value of the authorized or outstanding stock of a corporation.

▸ **thin capitalization.** (1955) The financial condition of a firm that has a high ratio of liabilities to capital.

▸ **undercapitalization.** (1908) The financial condition of a firm that does not have enough capital to carry on its business.

capitalization accounting method. See ACCOUNTING METHOD.

capitalization issue. See BONUS ISSUE.

capitalization rate. (1914) The interest rate used in calculating the present value of future periodic payments. — Also termed *cap rate*; *income yield*.

capitalization ratio. (1935) The ratio between the amount of capital raised and the total capitalization of the firm. — Also termed *capital ratio*.

capitalize, *vb.* (1856) **1.** To convert (earnings) into capital. **2.** To treat (a cost) as a capital expenditure rather than an ordinary and necessary expense. **3.** To determine the present value of (long-term income). **4.** To supply capital for (a business).

capitalized expense. See EXPENSE.

capital lease. See LEASE-PURCHASE AGREEMENT.

capital leverage. (1940) The use of borrowed funds in a business to obtain a return greater than the interest rate. See LEVERAGE.

capital levy. See LEVY.

capital loss. See LOSS.

capital maintenance. See MAINTENANCE OF CAPITAL.

capital market. See MARKET.

capital offense. See OFFENSE (2).

capital outlay. (1857) **1.** CAPITAL EXPENDITURE. **2.** Money expended in acquiring, equipping, and promoting a business.

capital punishment. (16c) A criminal penalty that involves killing the perpetrator; the sentence of death for a serious crime. — Also termed *death penalty.* See DEATH PENALTY.

> "At Common Law capital punishment was imposed for a few very serious offences such as treason, murder, rape, and burning a dwelling-house. Even as late as 1688, despite the exceptionally rigorous laws which had been enacted during the reigns of the Tudors and Stuarts, no more than about fifty offences carried the death penalty. In the eighteenth century, however, their number began spectacularly to increase. . . . Broadly speaking, in the course of the hundred and sixty years from the Restoration to the death of George III, the number of capital offences had increased by about one hundred and ninety." 1 Leon Radzinowicz, *A History of English Criminal Law* § 1, at 4 (1948).

capital ratio. See CAPITALIZATION RATIO.

capital recovery. (1942) The collection of charged-off bad debt that has been previously written off against the allowance for doubtful accounts.

capital reserve. See RESERVE (1).

capital return. See RETURN.

capital–risk test. (1980) *Securities.* A method of determining whether a transaction constitutes an investment contract (subject to securities laws), whereby if a substantial portion of the capital used by a franchiser to start its operations is provided by a franchisee, then the transaction is treated as an investment contract. Cf. RISK–CAPITAL TEST.

capital stock. See STOCK.

capital-stock tax. See TAX.

capital structure. (1923) The mix of debt and equity by which a business finances its operations; the relative proportions of short-term debt, long-term debt, and capital stock.

capital surplus. See SURPLUS.

capital transaction. (1906) A purchase, sale, or exchange of a capital asset.

capitaneus (kap-i-**tay**-nee-əs). [Law Latin "tenant in chief"] **1.** *Hist.* A tenant *in capite*; one who holds title directly from the king. — Also termed *cataneus.* **2.** *Maritime law.* A ship captain or naval commander. **3.** A ruler or leader.

capitated, *adj.* (1986) *Insurance.* Of, relating to, or involving a healthcare system that gives a medical-care provider a fixed fee per patient regardless of the treatment required.

capitation. **1.** A tax or payment of the same amount for each person. See *poll tax* under TAX. **2.** A method of paying a healthcare provider based on the number of members in a health-benefit plan that the provider contracts to treat. • The health plan's sponsor agrees to pay a fixed amount per person each period, regardless of what services are provided.

capitation tax. See *poll tax* under TAX.

capitis aestimatio (**kap**-i-tis es-ti-**may**-shee-oh). [Latin "valuing of a head"] *Hist.* A monetary estimate of a person's life, made to assess a penalty for the person's slaying. See WERGILD.

capitis deminutio (**kap**-i-tis dem-i-**n[y]oo**-shee-oh). [Latin "reduction of status"] *Roman law.* A diminution or alteration of a person's legal status. — Also spelled *capitis diminutio.* See DE CAPITE MINUTIS.

> "Capitis deminutio is the destruction of the 'caput' or legal personality. Capitis deminutio, so to speak, wipes out the former individual and puts a new one in his place, and between the old and the new individual there is, legally speaking, nothing in common. A juristic personality may be thus destroyed in one of three ways: (1) by loss of the status libertatis. This is the capitis deminutio maxima; (2) by loss of the status civitatis. This is the capitis deminutio media (magna); (3) by severance from the agnatic family. This entails capitis deminutio minima." Rudolph Sohm, *The Institutes: A Textbook of the History and System of Roman Private Law* 178–79 (James Crawford Ledlie trans., 3d ed. 1907).

▸ ***capitis deminutio maxima*** (**kap**-i-tis dem-i-**n[y]oo**-shee-oh **mak**-si-mə). [Latin "maximum reduction of status"] (18c) *Roman law.* The diminution of a person's legal status as a result of being reduced to slavery.

▸ ***capitis deminutio media.*** See *capitis deminutio minor.*

▸ ***capitis deminutio minima*** (**kap**-i-tis dem-i-**n[y]oo**-shee-oh **min**-i-mə). [Latin "minimal reduction of status"] *Roman law.* The diminution of a person's legal status involving a change of family, while both citizenship and freedom were retained.

▸ ***capitis deminutio minor*** (**kap**-i-tis dem-i-**n[y]oo**-shee-oh **mɪ**-nər). [Latin "minor reduction of status"] *Roman law.* The diminution of a person's legal status involving a loss of citizenship but not of freedom. • Under the Empire, banishment for life to an island or other restricted area had this effect. — Also termed *capitis deminutio media.*

capitis deminutio media. See *capitis deminutio minor* under CAPITIS DEMINUTIO.

capitula (kə-**pich**-ə-lə). [Law Latin "chapters"] (17c) *Hist.* **1.** Collections of laws or ordinances organized under various headings. • The term is plural in form but usu.

singular in sense. — Also termed *capitulary.* **2.** Chapters or assemblies of ecclesiastical persons. Pl. **capitularia.**

▸ ***capitula coronae*** (kə-**roh**-nee). [Latin "chapters of the Crown"] (17c) *Hist.* A more detailed form of the articles of the eyre. See ARTICLES OF THE EYRE.

▸ ***capitula de judaeis*** (dee joo-**dee**-is). [Latin "chapters on the Jews"] (17c) *Hist.* **1.** Laws concerning the Jews. **2.** Questions posed by the justices in eyre to determine the amount a Jew would pay to receive the king's protection and a license to conduct business. • The *capitula de judaeis* reflected the pervasive anti-Semitism of medieval England. Cf. ARTICLES OF THE EYRE.

▸ ***capitula ecclesiastica*** (e-klee-z[h]ee-**as**-ti-kə). (1939) *Hist.* Salic law elaborated in councils of the bishops from A.D. 803–804 during the reign of Charlemagne (ca. A.D. 742–814). See CAPITULARY; SALIC LAW.

▸ ***capitula itineris*** (ɪ-**tin**-ə-ris). [Law Latin "chapters of the eyre"] See ARTICLES OF THE EYRE.

▸ ***capitula legibus addenda*** (**lee**-jə-bəs ə-**den**-də). (1907) *Hist.* Salic law consisting of additions made by the king of the Franks to the barbarian laws (see LEGES BARBARORUM). — Also termed *capitula pro lege habenda.*

▸ ***capitula missorum*** (mi-**sor**-əm). (1907) *Hist.* Salic law consisting of temporary instructions given by Charlemagne (ca. A.D. 742–814) and his successors to the *missi* sent into the various parts of the empire.

▸ ***capitula per se scribenda*** (pər say skrɪ-**ben**-də). (1907) *Hist.* Salic law consisting of political decrees that all subjects of the Frankish kingdom were bound to observe.

> "*Capitularia per se scribenda* were administrative regulations. As royal laws they were of territorial application. Although they did not require the *consensus populi*, they were sometimes submitted for approval to the king's council. Most of the administrative law of the period took the form of peace bans, but important innovations of law and procedure were also introduced in this way. By means of royal bans the king could put certain persons or classes of persons (cloisters, travelers, Jews, widows, orphans) or certain localities (forests, markets) under his special protection. A ban could be issued for an individual occasion; thus the king might place a specified fair under the king's peace. Among the more important *capitularia per se scribenda* may be mentioned: the *pactus pro tenore pacis* of Childebert I and Lotharius I of the second half of the sixth century, which was directed against organized robbery; the Edict of Chlothar II of 614, in which the king made important concessions to his noblemen, and which has been called the Magna Charta of the Frankish Empire; the *capitulare de villis* of Charlemagne of A.D. 800, which dealt with the administration of the royal estates; and the *capitulare de justitiis faciendis* of A.D. 820." H.R. Hahlo & Ellison Kahn, *The South African Legal System and its Background* 378–79 (1968).

▸ ***capitula pro lege habenda*** (proh **lee**-jee hə-**ben**-də). See *capitula legibus addenda.*

capitulare de villis. (1913) *Hist.* A 9th-century Salic law, enacted under Charlemagne (ca. A.D. 742–814), dealing with the management of royal estates.

capitulare saxonicum. (1880) *Hist.* An 8th-century Salic law, enacted under Charlemagne (ca. A.D. 742–814), establishing Frankish authority over the Saxon tribes and mandating Christianity. • The provisions were drafted at a council held in 797 in Aachen, part of Saxony (now Germany). The Saxons were allowed to participate in the legislative process as a step toward allowing them to participate in governing their own state.

capitulary (kə-**pich**-ə-ler-ee). [Latin "chapter *or* section (of a code)"] (17c) **1.** Any orderly and systematic collection or code of laws. See CAPITULA (1). **2.** *Hist.* (*often pl.*) A law or series of laws enacted by a Frankish king, esp. Charlemagne, dealing esp. with ecclesiastical affairs.

capitulation (kə-pich-ə-**lay**-shən), *n.* (16c) **1.** The act of surrendering or giving in. **2.** *Int'l law.* An agreement to surrender a fortified place or a military or naval force. • A commander in control may generally make such an agreement for the place or force.

> "CAPITULATION. Articles of agreement, by which besieged troops surrender at discretion, or with the honors of war. The terms granted depend upon circumstances of time, place, &c. Any surrender in the open field without fighting was stigmatized by Napoleon as dishonorable, as was also the surrender of a besieged place without the advice of a majority of a council of defence, before the enemy had been forced to resort to successive siege-works, and had been once repulsed from an assault through a practicable breach in the body of the place, and the besieged were without means to sustain a second assault; or else the besieged were without provisions or munitions of war." H.L. Scott, *Military Dictionary* 145 (1861).

3. *Hist.* An agreement between a Christian state and a non-Christian one (such as the Ottoman Empire) giving subjects of the former certain privileges in the territory of the latter. **4.** *Hist. Int'l law.* A special, usu. nonreciprocal, right established by a treaty through which one country could exercise jurisdiction over its citizens and their property within the territory of another country. • Capitulations were a common feature of trade treaties in particular because merchants often accumulated wealth in foreign countries. Capitulations became disfavored before World War I and were gradually abolished during the 20th century. — **capitulate,** *vb.* — **capitulatory,** *adj.*

capitulum. [Latin "small head"] (18c) A section or chapter of a Salic capitulary. See CAPITULARY. Pl. ***capitula.***

> "The *Capitula* are distinguishable from the *Leges*. They emanate directly from royal authority, they deal with less important matters, they have, probably, a less permanent effect." Edward Jenks, *Law and Politics in the Middle Ages* 18–19 (1898).

CAPJ. *abbr.* See *chief administrative patent judge* under JUDGE.

CAP law. Child-access-prevention law, requiring the safe storage of firearms.

capped interest. See INTEREST (3).

capper. (18c) **1.** Someone who solicits business for an attorney. See BARRATRY (1); RUNNER (2). **2.** *Slang.* Someone who acts as a lure for others (as in a gambling or confidence game). — Also termed (in sense 2) *stool pigeon.* **3.** BY-BIDDER.

cap plea, *n.* (1997) *Criminal procedure.* A plea entered upon a judge's assurance that the sentence imposed will be no greater than a certain term or specified range. • With a cap plea, the judge becomes involved in plea-bargaining — something allowed in some state courts but disallowed in federal court. — Also termed *sentence cap.*

cap rate. See CAPITALIZATION RATE.

caprice (kə-**prees**), *n.* (17c) **1.** Arbitrary or unfounded motivation. **2.** The disposition to change one's mind impulsively.

capricious (kə-**prish**-əs), *adj.* (17c) **1.** (Of a person) characterized by or guided by unpredictable or impulsive behavior; likely to change one's mind suddenly or to behave in unexpected ways. **2.** (Of a decree) contrary to the evidence or established rules of law. Cf. ARBITRARY.

CAPTA. *abbr.* CHILD ABUSE PREVENTION AND TREATMENT ACT.

captain-of-the-ship doctrine. (1962) In medical-malpractice law, the doctrine imposing liability on a surgeon for the actions of assistants who are under the surgeon's control but who are employees of the hospital, not the surgeon. — Also termed *doctrine of the captain of the ship.*

captain's mast. See MAST (1).

captation (kap-**tay**-shən). *Civil law.* Coercion of a testator resulting in the substitution of another person's desires for those of the testator. • The term formerly applied to the first stage of a hypnotic trance. Cf. UNDUE INFLUENCE.

captator (kap-**tay**-tər). (16c) *Civil law.* Someone who obtains or tries to obtain a gift or legacy through artifice. See UNDUE INFLUENCE.

captio (**kap**-shee-oh). *Hist.* **1.** An arrest of a person, or a seizure of a thing. **2.** The holding of court.

caption. (17c) **1.** The introductory part of a court paper stating the names of the parties, the name of the court, the docket or file number, and a description of the paper. Fed. R. Civ. P. 10(a). Cf. STYLE (1). **2.** The arrest or seizure of a person by legal process. **3.** See HEADING. **4.** A taking or seizure of property. • *Caption* sometimes refers to the taking element of common-law larceny. See (in sense 4) LARCENY; ASPORTATION.

captive, *n.* (14c) **1.** Someone who is unlawfully seized and held by another. Cf. PRISONER. **2.** Someone who is kept as a prisoner, esp. in a war; PRISONER OF WAR. **3.** An animal, esp. a wild one, that is caught and kept confined.

captive-audience doctrine. (1947) **1.** *Constitutional law.* The principle that when the listener cannot, as a practical matter, escape from intrusive speech, the speech can be restricted. **2.** *Labor law.* The rule that prohibits either party to a union election from making a speech on company time to a mass assembly of employees within 24 hours of an election. — Also termed *captive-audience rule.*

captive insurance. See INSURANCE.

captive insurance company. See INSURANCE COMPANY.

captive insurer. See *captive insurance company* under INSURANCE COMPANY.

captive law firm. See LAW FIRM.

captor (**kap**-tər). (17c) Someone who captures or takes a person or thing by force, stratagem, or surprise; esp., a person who has captured and is confining a person or wild animal.

capture. See RULE OF CAPTURE.

capture-and-hold rule. *Oil & gas.* For royalty-calculation purposes, the doctrine that "production" occurs when oil or gas is pumped to the surface and stored, whether at the wellhead or elsewhere on the leased property. Cf. MARKETABLE-PRODUCT RULE.

capture doctrine. See RULE OF CAPTURE (1).

caput (**kap**-ət), *n.* [Latin "head"] **1.** *Hist.* A head, chief, or principal person. **2.** *Roman law.* A person. **3.** *Roman law.* A person's condition or status.

> "A 'natural,' as opposed to an 'artificial,' person is such a human being as is regarded by the law as capable of rights or duties: in the language of Roman law as having a 'status.' . . . Besides possessing this general legal capacity, or status, a man may also possess various special capacities, such as the 'tria capita' of liberty, citizenship, and family rights. A slave having, as such, neither rights nor liabilities, had in Roman law, strictly speaking, no 'status,' 'caput,' or 'persona.' . . . It must however be remembered that the terms 'persona' and 'caput' were also used in popular language as nearly equivalent to 'homo,' and in this sense were applied to slaves as well as to freemen." Thomas E. Holland, *The Elements of Jurisprudence* 80–81 (4th ed. 1888).

caput comitatus (**kap**-ət kom-ə-**tay**-təs). [Latin "head of the county"] (18c) *Hist.* The head of a county; a sheriff.

caput gerat lupinum (**kap**-ət **jeer**-ət loo-**pI**-nəm). [Latin "let him bear the head of a wolf"] *Hist.* An outlawed felon considered a pariah — a lone wolf — open to attack by anyone. See OUTLAWRY.

> "He who breaks the law has gone to war with the community; the community goes to war with him. It is the right and duty of every man to pursue him, to ravage his land, to burn his house, to hunt him down like a wild beast and slay him; for a wild beast he is; not merely is he a 'friendless man,' he is a wolf. . . . *Caput gerat lupinum* — in these words the court decreed outlawry." 2 Frederick Pollock & Frederic W. Maitland, *The History of English Law Before the Time of Edward I* 449 (2d ed. 1899).

caput mortuum. (16c) *Archaic.* A matter or thing that is void as to all persons and for all purposes.

car accident. See ACCIDENT.

carbon credit. See EMISSIONS PERMIT.

carcanum (kahr-**kay**-nəm). [Latin "iron collar, pillory"] *Hist.* A prison or workhouse.

carcelage (**kahr**-sə-lij). [fr. Latin *carcer* "prison"] (17c) *Hist.* Prison fees.

carcer (**kahr**-sər), *n.* [Latin "jail, prison"] (16c) *Hist.* A prison or jail, esp. one used to detain rather than punish. • *Carcer,* as used in English law and Roman law, usu. referred to a jail used as a place of detention during trial or after sentence pending execution, rather than as a place of punishment. The modern term *incarceration* derives from this word.

cardinal-change doctrine. (1968) *Contracts.* The principle that if the government makes a fundamental, unilateral change to a contract beyond the scope of what was originally contemplated, the other party (usu. a contractor) will be released from the obligation to continue work under the contract. • A contractor's allegation of *cardinal change* is essentially an assertion that the government has breached the contract.

cardo controversiae (**kahr**-doh kon-trə-**vər**-shee-ee). [Law Latin] (17c) *Hist.* The hinge of the controversy; the main point of a controversy.

ca. re. See *capias ad respondendum* under CAPIAS.

care, *n.* (bef. 12c) **1.** Serious attention; heed <written with care>. **2.** Under the law of negligence or of obligations, the conduct demanded of a person in a given situation. • Typically, this involves a person's giving attention both to possible dangers, mistakes, and pitfalls and to ways of minimizing those risks <standard of care>. See DEGREE OF CARE; REASONABLE PERSON.

▸ **adequate care.** See *reasonable care.*

▸ **due care.** See *reasonable care.*

▸ **extraordinary care.** See *great care.*

▸ **great care.** (15c) **1.** The degree of care that a prudent person exercises in dealing with very important personal affairs. **2.** The degree of care exercised in a given situation by someone in the business or profession of dealing with the situation. — Also termed *extraordinary care; high degree of care; utmost care.*

▸ **high degree of care.** See *great care.*

▸ **highest degree of care.** (17c) **1.** The degree of care exercised commensurate with the danger involved. **2.** See *great care.*

▸ **ordinary care.** See *reasonable care.*

▸ **proper care.** See *reasonable care.*

▸ **reasonable care.** (17c) As a test of liability for negligence, the degree of care that a prudent and competent person engaged in the same line of business or endeavor would exercise under similar circumstances. • Generally, reasonable care is the application of whatever intelligence and attention one possesses for the satisfaction of one's needs. The term is always relative, depending on the particular circumstances. What is reasonable care in one case (for example, involving an adult) might be gross negligence in another (for example, involving an infant). — Also termed *due care; ordinary care; adequate care; proper care.* See REASONABLE PERSON.

▸ **slight care.** (17c) The degree of care a person gives to matters of minor importance; the degree of care given by a person of limited accountability.

▸ **utmost care.** See *great care.*

3. *Family law.* The provision of physical or psychological comfort to another, esp. an ailing spouse, child, or parent.

career criminal. See RECIDIVIST.

career judiciary. See JUDICIARY.

career offender. See OFFENDER.

career vice-consul. See VICE-CONSUL.

caregiver. (1966) *Family law.* A person, usu. not a parent, who has and exercises custodial responsibility for a child or for an elderly or disabled person. — Also termed *caretaker; custodian.* See RESIDENTIAL RESPONSIBILITY.

careless, *adj.* (bef. 12c) **1.** (Of a person) not exercising reasonable care. **2.** (Of an action or behavior) engaged in without reasonable care. See NEGLECTFUL. Cf. RECKLESS.

carelessness, *n.* (bef. 12c) **1.** The fact, condition, or instance of a person's either not having done what he or she ought to have done, or having done what he or she ought not to have done; heedless inattention. **2.** A person's general disposition not to do something that ought to be done.

> "The word 'carelessness' as a synonym for negligence is misleading unless we realise that legal carelessness can be committed by those who care deeply. A man may take all the care of which he is capable, and yet be accounted negligent for failing to reach the objective standard. He may honestly . . . believe that the facts are such that he is not imperilling anyone; but he may be held to have been negligent in arriving at that belief. An incompetent driver may be convicted of driving 'without due care and attention' even though he was doing his level best. The careless person is the person who does not *take* the care he ought to take: never mind whether he *felt* careful. He can be held to be negligent in making a perfectly honest mistake." Glanville Williams, *Textbook of Criminal Law* 44–45 (1978).

care proceedings. (1969) Judicial proceedings brought by a state or local government to safeguard the welfare of one or more children, usu. to take a child into state care because the child is not being looked after properly or is out of control.

ca. res. *abbr.* See *capias ad respondendum* under CAPIAS.

ca. resp. *abbr.* See *capias ad respondendum* under CAPIAS.

caretaker. See CAREGIVER.

caretaking functions. (1978) *Family law.* A parent's or caregiver's task that either involves interaction with a child or directs others' interaction with a child. • Some caretaking functions include feeding and bathing a child, guiding the child in language and motor-skills development, caring for a sick child, disciplining the child, being involved in the child's educational development, and giving the child moral instruction and guidance. *Principles of the Law of Family Dissolution: Analysis and Recommendations* § 2.03 (ALI, Tentative Draft No. 3, pt. I, 1998). Cf. PARENTING FUNCTION.

Carey Act. An 1894 federal statute giving any state containing desert land one million acres of that land, the donation being conditioned on the reclamation of the land by irrigation at the state's cost. • The act's sponsor was Senator Joseph M. Carey (1845–1924) of Wyoming. — Also termed *Carey Land Act; Desert Land Act; Desert Act.*

cargo. (17c) Goods transported by a vessel, airplane, or vehicle; FREIGHT (1).

▸ **dry cargo.** Cargo that, being solid and dry, does not require a controlled temperature.

▸ **general cargo.** (17c) Goods and materials of various types transported by carriers, often in a common load, with few or no restrictions.

▸ **hazardous cargo.** (1830) Dangerous goods or materials whose carriage is usu. subject to stringent regulatory and statutory restrictions.

cargo clause. (1933) A provision, usu. in an insurance policy or an employment agreement, specifying some aspect about the care, handling, or coverage of what is being shipped or transported.

▸ **hot-cargo clause.** (1950) A provision in a union contract allowing employees to refuse to handle or work on goods from a plant where workers are on strike or to provide services to a company that the union has designated as an unfair employer.

▸ **institute cargo clause.** (1933) One or more sets of terms for cargo insurance policies adopted as standard by many organizations, including the American Institute of Marine Underwriters, having variations from all-risk coverage to lesser levels of coverage.

cargo insurance. See INSURANCE.

carjacking. (1991) The forcible theft of a vehicle from a motorist; the unlawful commandeering of an automobile. 18 USCA § 2119. — **carjack,** *vb.*

carnal abuse. See *sexual abuse* (1) under ABUSE.

carnalis copula. See SEXUAL RELATIONS (1).

carnal knowledge. (15c) *Archaic.* Sexual intercourse, esp. with an underage female. — Sometimes shortened to *knowledge.*

"The ancient term for the act itself was 'carnal knowledge' and this is found in some of the recent cases and statutes. The phrase 'sexual intercourse,' more common today apart from legal literature, is also found in recent cases and statutes. Either term, when the reference is to rape, is sometimes coupled with the word 'ravish.' And unlawful intercourse with a girl under the age of consent is often characterized as 'carnal knowledge and abuse.'" Rollin M. Perkins & Ronald N. Boyce, *Criminal Law* 201 (3d ed. 1982).

carnet (kahr-**nay**). (1926) A customs document allowing an item (esp. an automobile) to be exported temporarily from one country into another country.

Caroline Doctrine. (1958) The principle that one seeking to invoke the right of self-defense must show that the necessity for the action taken was instant and overwhelming, leaving no choice of alternatives and no time for deliberation. • The doctrine originated in Daniel Webster's statement about the British seizure of the ship *Caroline* in 1837, while Webster was the U.S. Secretary of State. *See* Martin A. Rogoff & Edward Collins Jr., *The Caroline Incident and the Development of International Law,* 16 Brook. J. Int'l L. 493, 497 (1990).

Carolingian, *adj.* (1881) Of, relating to, or involving the dynasty of French kings founded by Charlemagne (ca. A.D. 742–814). — Sometimes spelled *Karolingian.*

Carolingian law. See SALIC LAW.

carriage. (15c) Transport of freight or passengers.

carriage and insurance paid to. (1981) A mercantile-contract term allocating the rights and duties of the buyer and the seller of goods with respect to delivery, payment, and risk of loss, whereby the seller must (1) clear the goods for export, (2) procure and pay for insurance against the buyer's risk of damage while the goods are in carriage, (3) deliver the goods to the buyer's chosen carrier, and (4) bear the costs of carriage (apart from import duties) to the named destination. • When the goods are delivered to the carrier, the seller's delivery is complete; the risk of loss then passes to the buyer. Any mode of transportation can be used to carry the goods. — Abbr. CIP. Cf. CARRIAGE PAID TO.

carriage by sea. (16c) The transportation of passengers or goods using ships. — Also termed *sea carriage.*

Carriage of Goods by Sea Act. *Maritime law.* A 1936 federal statute regulating a carrier's liability for the loss or damage, and sometimes the delay, of ocean cargo shipped under a bill of lading. 46 USCA §§ 30701 et seq. • The Act defines many of the rights and responsibilities of both the issuers and the holders of ocean bills of lading. — Abbr. COGSA.

"The Carriage of Goods by Sea Act (COGSA), the domestic enactment of the international convention popularly known as the Hague Rules, allocates the risk of loss for cargo damage that occurs during ocean transportation to or from the United States under contracts evidenced by bills of lading and similar documents of title. It is the central statute in commercial admiralty, governing over $200 billion worth of American foreign commerce annually. The other major maritime countries of the world have also adopted the Hague Rules to govern their international ocean commerce." Michael F. Sturley, *The Fair Opportunity Requirement Under COGSA Section 4(5): A Case Study in the Misinterpretation of the Carriage of Goods by Sea Act,* 19 J. Mar. L. & Com. 1, 1–2 (1988).

carriage paid to. (1849) A mercantile-contract term allocating the rights and duties of the buyer and the seller of goods with respect to delivery, payment, and risk of loss, whereby the seller must (1) clear the goods for export, (2) deliver them to the buyer's chosen carrier, and (3) pay the costs of carriage (apart from import duties) to the named destination. • When the goods are delivered to the carrier, the seller's delivery is complete; the risk of loss then passes to the buyer. Any mode of transportation can be used to carry the goods. — Abbr. CPT. Cf. CARRIAGE AND INSURANCE PAID TO.

carriageway. (18c) The part of a road designed, constructed, and normally used for vehicular traffic; HIGHWAY.

▸ **dual carriageway.** (1943) A divided or two-way road or highway.

▸ **single carriageway.** (1936) An undivided or one-way road or highway.

carried interest. See INTEREST (2).

carrier. (15c) **1.** An individual or organization (such as a shipowner, a railroad, or an airline) that contracts to transport passengers or goods for a fee. Cf. SHIPPER.

▸ **common carrier.** (15c) A commercial enterprise that holds itself out to the public as offering to transport freight or passengers for a fee. • A common carrier is generally required by law to transport freight or passengers without refusal if the approved fare or charge is paid. — Also termed *public carrier.*

"A common or public carrier is one who undertakes as a business, for hire or reward, to carry from one place to another, the goods of all persons who may apply for such carriage, provided the goods be of the kind which he professes to carry, and the person so applying will agree to have them carried upon the lawful terms prescribed by the carrier; and who, if he refuses to carry such goods for those who are willing to comply with his terms, becomes liable to an action by the aggrieved party for such refusal. To bring a person therefore within the description of a common carrier, he must be engaged in the business of carrying goods for others as a public employment, he must undertake to carry goods of the kind to which his business is confined, for persons generally, and he must hold himself out as ready to engage in the transportation of goods for hire as a business and not as a casual occupation. And this duty or obligation to the public by reason of the public nature of the employment and the increased responsibility imposed upon him by the law upon the grounds of public policy, mainly distinguish the common from the mere private carrier for hire." Robert Hutchinson, *A Treatise on the Law of Carriers* 30–31 (1882).

"[A] 'common carrier' is bound to take all goods of the kind which he usually carries, unless his conveyance is full, or the goods be specially dangerous; but may charge different rates to different customers." Thomas E. Holland, *The Elements of Jurisprudence* 299 (13th ed. 1924).

▸ **contract carrier.** See *private carrier.*

▸ **marine carrier.** (1847) A carrier operating on navigable waters subject to the jurisdiction of the United States.

▸ **non-vessel-operating common carrier.** (1972) *Maritime law.* A freight forwarder that does not own the means of transportation, but that contracts with a shipper to transport freight, and with a carrier to perform the transportation. • The non-vessel-operating common carrier becomes the carrier in the contract with the original shipper, and the shipper in the contract with the eventual carrier. — Abbr. NVOCC. See FREIGHT FORWARDER.

▸ **private carrier.** (18c) Any carrier that is not a common carrier by law. • A private carrier is not bound to accept business from the general public. — Also termed *contract carrier.*

▸ **public carrier**. See *common carrier.*

2. INSURER.

carrier's lien. See LIEN.

***Carroll* doctrine.** (1965) The principle that a broadcast licensee has standing to contest any grant of a competitive license by the Federal Communications Commission because the grant could lead to a diminution in broadcast service by causing economic injury to an existing licensee. *Carroll Broad. Co. v. FCC*, 258 F.2d 440 (D.C. Cir. 1958).

carry, *vb.* (14c) **1.** To sustain the weight or burden of; to hold or bear <more weight than a single person can carry>. **2.** To convey or transport <carrying the coal from one state to another>. **3.** To possess and convey (a firearm) in a vehicle, including the locked glove compartment or trunk of a car <he carried the guns in his trunk>. • The United States Supreme Court adopted this definition in interpreting the phrase *carries a firearm* as used in a statute imposing a mandatory prison term on a person who uses or carries a firearm while committing a drug-trafficking crime. *Muscarello v. U.S.*, 524 U.S. 125, 118 S.Ct. 1911 (1998). **4.** In a figurative sense, to possess or hold (insurance, etc.) <the decedent did not carry life insurance>. **5.** *Parliamentary law.* To adopt. • In this sense, the verb may be either intransitive <the motion carries> or transitive (in a passive construction) <the motion is carried>. See ADOPTION (5). **6.** To provide funds or credit for the payment of (stock, etc.), often as an advance, for an agreed-on period <the investor carried the stock purchases for eight months>. **7.** To absorb the cost of holding or having, usu. temporarily <the business will carry the debt for another quarter>.

carry away, *vb.* (16c) To take or move (stolen property, etc.). • The traditional count for larceny was that the defendant "did steal, take, and carry away" the property. A "carrying away" can be a slight movement of the property. See ASPORTATION.

carryback. (1942) *Tax.* An income-tax deduction (esp. for a net operating loss) that cannot be taken entirely in a given period but may be taken in an earlier period (usu. the previous three years). — Also termed *loss carryback*; *tax-loss carryback*. Cf. CARRYOVER.

carryforward. See CARRYOVER.

carrying away. See ASPORTATION.

carrying back the date of invention. See ANTEDATING OF A PRIOR-ART REFERENCE.

carrying charge. (1884) **1.** A cost, in addition to interest, paid to a creditor for carrying installment credit. **2.** Expenses incident to property ownership, such as taxes and upkeep.

carrying cost. See COST (1).

carrying value. See BOOK VALUE (1).

carryover. (1925) *Tax.* **1.** A sum transferred from one column, page, or book to another relating to the same account. **2.** An income-tax deduction (esp. for a net operating loss) that cannot be taken entirely in a given period but may be taken in a later period (usu. the next five years). — Also termed *loss carryover; tax-loss carryover; carryforward; loss carryforward; tax-loss carryforward; carryforward tax loss.* Cf. CARRYBACK.

carryover basis. See BASIS.

carta (**kahr**-tə). [Latin] *Hist.* A charter, deed, or other written instrument.

Carta de Foresta. See CHARTA DE FORESTA.

Carta Forestae. See CHARTA DE FORESTA.

Carta Mercatoria (**kahr**-tə mər-kə-**tor**-ee-ə). *Hist.* A 1303 English statute establishing various rules that favored certain foreign merchants. • In exchange for paying customs duties, merchants received extensive trading rights throughout England, the power to export their merchandise, the liberty to dwell where they pleased, and certain legal rights. — Also termed *Statutum de Nova Custuma.*

cartbote. See *plowbote* under BOTE (2).

carte blanche (kahrt **blahnsh**). [French "blank card"] (18c) **1.** A signed, blank instrument that is filled out at an agent's discretion. **2.** Full discretionary power; unlimited authority.

cartel (kahr-**tel**), *n.* (17c) **1.** A combination of producers or sellers that join together to control a product's production or price. **2.** An association of firms with common interests, seeking to prevent extreme or unfair competition, allocate markets, or share knowledge. **3.** *Int'l law.* An agreement between belligerents about the means of conducting whatever relations they allow during wartime; esp., such an agreement regarding the exchange of prisoners. — Also spelled *chartel.* — **cartelize** (**kahr**-tə-lɪz *or* kahr-**tel**-ɪz), *vb.* — **cartelistic** (kahr-tə-**liz**-tik), *adj.*

cartelism (kahr-**tel**-iz-əm), *n.* (1926) The act or practice of producers' or sellers' controlling production or prices.

cartelist (kahr-**tel**-ist), *n.* (1943) **1.** A member of a cartel. **2.** An advocate of cartelization.

cartelization (kahr-tə-li-**zay**-shən), *n.* (1923) The formation of a cartel. — **cartelize,** *vb.*

car-title loan. See *title loan* under LOAN.

cartman. (18c) **1.** Someone who drives or uses a cart; a teamster. **2.** Someone who transports goods or merchandise within the boundaries of a port. Cf. DRAYMAN (3).

cartulary (**kahr**-tyoo-lair-ee), *n.* (16c) A collection of legal documents, esp. charters and title deeds to property.

carucage (**kar**-ə-kij). [Law Latin] (16c) *Hist.* A tax imposed either on a carucate or on the plows used on the land. — Also termed *carvage.*

carucate (**kar**-ə-kayt). [Law Latin] (12c) *Hist.* A measure of land for assessment purposes, varying locally from 96 to 144 acres. • This amount was thought to be as much land as one plow with eight oxen could plow in a year. A *carucate* was used to assess taxes. — Also termed *carucata; carve; plowland.* Cf. HIDE (1); OXGANG.

carvage. See CARUCAGE.

carve (karv), *n.* See CARUCATE.

carve out, *vb.* (17c) **1.** To create an explicit exception to a broad rule. **2.** *Tax.* To separate from property the income derived from the property.

carveout, *n.* (1966) **1.** An explicit exception to a broad rule. **2.** *Tax.* For tax purposes, the separation from property of the income derived from the property.

ca. sa. See *capias ad satisfaciendum* under CAPIAS.

CASA. *abbr.* **1.** COURT-APPOINTED SPECIAL ADVOCATE. **2.** COURT APPOINTED SPECIAL ADVOCATES.

casata (kə-**say**-tə). (17c) *Hist.* A house with enough land to support one family.

casatus (kə-**zay**-təs). *Hist.* A vassal or feudal tenant possessing a casata.

CASA volunteer. (1982) *Family law.* A specially screened and trained child-welfare volunteer appointed by the court to conduct an independent investigation of both the state agency and the family and to submit a report with findings and recommendations. • In some jurisdictions such volunteers are provided for statutorily. They sometimes act as guardians ad litem. The CASA volunteer usu. (1) provides independent assessment of the child's needs, (2) acts as an advocate for the child, and (3) monitors agency decision-making and court proceedings. See COURT APPOINTED SPECIAL ADVOCATES.

case. (13c) **1.** A civil or criminal proceeding, action, suit, or controversy at law or in equity <the parties settled the case>.

▸ **active case.** (1949) A case that is still pending.

▸ **case agreed on.** See *case stated* (1).

▸ **case at bar.** (16c) A case under the immediate consideration of the court. — Also termed *case at bench*; *instant case*; *present case.* See BAR (3).

▸ **case at bench.** See *case at bar.*

▸ **case made.** See *case reserved* (1).

▸ **case of first impression.** (1806) A case that presents the court with an issue of law that has not previously been decided by any controlling legal authority in that jurisdiction.

> "If the case is the first of the kind, a case of first impression, the decision is not of great weight until supported by subsequent decisions. In a case of first impression, there is by definition a total lack of precedent; and there can also be only an imperfect foresight of the results to which the new decision may lead." Eugene Wambaugh, *The Study of Cases* § 60, at 56 (2d ed. 1894).

▸ **case reserved.** (18c) **1.** A written statement of the facts proved at trial and drawn up and stipulated to by the parties, so that certain legal issues can be decided by an appellate court. — Also termed *case made*; *special case.* **2.** *Hist.* An agreement between litigants to submit the case to a judge rather than to a jury.

> "It should have come as no surprise . . . that in most cases 'merchants were not fond of juries.' For one of the leading measures of the growing alliance between bench and bar on the one hand and commercial interests on the other is the swiftness with which the power of the jury is curtailed after 1790. . . . [D]uring the last years of the eighteenth century American lawyers vastly expanded the 'special case' or 'case reserved,' a device designed to submit points of law to the judges while avoiding the effective intervention of a jury. In England, Lord Mansfield had used a similar procedure to bring about an alliance between common lawyers and mercantile interests." Morton J. Horwitz, *The Transformation of American Law, 1780–1860* 141–42 (1977).

▸ **case stated.** (17c) **1.** A formal written statement of the facts in a case, submitted to the court jointly by the parties so that a decision may be rendered without trial. — Also termed *case agreed on.* **2.** *Hist.* A procedure used by the Court of Chancery to refer difficult legal questions to a common-law court. • This procedure was abolished in 1852. **3.** *English law.* An appeal from a Magistrates' Court to the Divisional Court of Queen's Bench on a point of criminal law. • After ruling, the magistrate states the facts for the appeal and the Queen's Bench rules on the question of law presented by the magistrate's ruling. — Also termed (in all three senses) *stated case.*

▸ **congressional-reference case.** (1914) A request by Congress for the United States Court of Claims to give an advisory opinion on the merits of a nonpension claim against the United States. *See* 28 USCA §§ 1492, 2509.

▸ **inactive case.** (1981) A pending case that is not proceeding toward resolution. • This may occur for several reasons, such as nonservice, want of prosecution, or (in a criminal case) the defendant's having absconded.

▸ **instant case.** See *case at bar.*

▸ **matrimonial case.** (18c) A case that arises out the relationship between spouses, such as domestic abuse, nonsupport, or divorce. — Also termed *matrimonial cause.*

▸ **present case.** See *case at bar.*

▸ **reference case.** (1915) *Canadian law.* An advisory opinion issued by the Supreme Court of Canada at the request of the executive or legislative branch of the federal government. • A reference is exceptional because the opinion interprets, and often resolves, a dispute even though no case or controversy is presented to the court. *See, e.g., Reference re Secession of Quebec,* [1998] 2 S.C.R. 217.

▸ **special case.** See *case reserved* (1).

▸ **stated case.** See *case stated.*

▸ **test case.** (1894) **1.** A lawsuit brought to establish an important legal principle or right. • Such an action is frequently brought by the parties' mutual consent on agreed facts — when that is so, a test case is also sometimes termed *amicable action* or *amicable suit.* The lawyer must have a good-faith basis for believing that the law or ruling challenged can be argued to be invalid on constitutional or other legal grounds.

> "The suit is spoken of, in the affidavits filed in support of it, as an amicable action, and the proceeding defended on that ground. But an amicable action, in the sense in which these words are used in courts of justice, presupposes that there is a real dispute between the parties concerning some matter of right. And in a case of that kind it sometimes happens, that, for the purpose of obtaining a decision of the controversy, without incurring needless expense and trouble, they agree to conduct the suit in an amicable manner, that is to say, that they will not embarrass each other with unnecessary forms or technicalities, and will mutually admit facts which they know to be true, and without requiring proof, and will bring the point in dispute before the court for decision, without subjecting each other to unnecessary expense or delay. But there must be an actual controversy, and adverse interests. The amity consists in the manner in which it is brought to issue before the court. And such amicable actions, so far from being objects of censure, are always approved and encouraged, because they facilitate greatly the administration of justice between the parties. The objection in the case before us is, not that the proceedings were amicable, but that there is no real conflict of interest between them; that the plaintiff and defendant have the same interest, and that interest adverse and in conflict with the interest of third persons, whose rights would be seriously affected if the question of

law was decided in the manner that both of the parties to this suit desire it to be." *Lord v. Veazie*, 49 U.S. 251, 255 (1850).

2. An action selected from several suits that are based on the same facts and evidence, raise the same question of law, and have a common plaintiff or a common defendant. • Sometimes, when all parties agree, the court orders a consolidation and all parties are bound by the decision in the test case. — Also termed *test action*.

2. A criminal investigation <the Manson case>. **3.** An individual suspect or convict in relation to any aspect of the criminal-justice system <the probation officer said he considers Mr. Jones a difficult case>. **4.** An argument <the debater made a compelling case for gun control>. **5.** An instance, occurrence, or situation <a case of mistaken identity> <a terminal case of cancer>. **6.** See *trespass on the case* under TRESPASS <the actions of trover and case are not entirely defunct>.

case abstract. See CASE NOTE.

case agent. *Criminal law.* The principal federal law-enforcement officer responsible for a particular criminal investigation. • The case agent may well testify, but he or she also frequently observes the entire trial as the government representative.

case agreed on. See *case stated* (1) under CASE (1).

Case and Controversy Clause. *Constitutional law.* The constitutional provision that limits Congress's power to confer jurisdiction on federal courts and distinguishes what lawsuits are within the federal judiciary's jurisdiction. U.S. Const. art. III, § 2, cl. 1. • This clause prevents courts from issuing advisory opinions or hearing cases that are moot or unripe.

case at bar. See CASE (1).

case at bench. See *case at bar* under CASE (1).

casebook. (18c) A compilation of extracts from instructive cases on a particular subject, usu. with commentary and questions about the cases, designed as a teaching aid. See SOCRATIC METHOD. Cf. HORNBOOK.

casebook method. (1915) An inductive system of teaching law in which students study specific cases to learn general legal principles. • Professor Christopher C. Langdell introduced the technique at Harvard Law School in 1869. The casebook method is now the most widely used form of instruction in American law schools. — Also termed *case method*; *case system*; *Langdell method*. Cf. SOCRATIC METHOD; HORNBOOK METHOD.

case brief. 1. CASE NOTE. **2.** CASE SUMMARY.

case evaluation. 1. Assessment of a case's strengths and weaknesses, along with the cost of litigation and the amount of potential liability or recovery, typically done to decide whether to accept a case or to advise a client or potential client about how to proceed. **2.** MEDIATION (1).

caseflow. (1957) **1.** The movement of cases through the judicial system, from the initial filing to the final appeal. **2.** An analysis of that movement.

case guardian. See *guardian ad litem* under GUARDIAN (1).

case-in-chief. (1853) **1.** The evidence presented at trial by a party between the time the party calls the first witness and the time the party rests. **2.** The part of a trial in which a party presents evidence to support the claim or defense. See EVIDENCE. Cf. REBUTTAL (1), (2).

caselaw. (1861) The law to be found in the collection of reported cases that form all or part of the body of law within a given jurisdiction. — Also written *case law*; *case-law*. — Also termed *decisional law*; *adjudicative law*; *jurisprudence*; *organic law*.

"It once bore the unhappily chosen name of unwritten law: modern writers call it after its source by the more convenient and accurate name of case-law. This system of case-law might be described in hostile popular language as a servile following of precedents tempered or supplemented by transparent fictions—a sort of hand-to-mouth scrambling work at best. It is true that the results are ill-arranged and difficult to get at. The state of English case-law as a whole might be not unfairly described as chaos tempered by Fisher's Digest." Frederick Pollock, "The Science of Case-Law," in *Essays in Jurisprudence and Ethics* 237, 237–38 (1882).

"Case law in some form and to some extent is found wherever there is law. A mere series of decisions of individual cases does not of course in itself constitute a system of law. But in any judicial system rules of law arise sooner or later out of the solution of practical problems, whether or not such formulations are desired, intended or consciously recognized. These generalizations contained in, or built upon, past decisions, when taken as normative for future disputes, create a legal system." Karl N. Llewellyn, "Case Law," in 3 *Ency. Soc. Sci.* 249 (1930).

case lawyer. (1938) An attorney whose knowledge is narrowly confined to a specific field of expertise.

"A working lawyer cannot expect to keep abreast of all this output of ideas, but he can at least study some portion so as to liberalize his views of law and to avoid the reproach of being a mere case lawyer." Lord Wright, *The Study of Law*, 54 Law Q. Rev. 185, 185 (1938).

caseload. (1938) **1.** The volume of cases assigned to a given court, agency, officer, judge, law firm, or lawyer. **2.** The number of people that a doctor, psychologist, social worker, etc. must deal with.

case made. See *case reserved* (1) under CASE (1).

case management. (1840) **1.** The handling over time of any project, transaction, service, or response that seeks to achieve resolution of a problem, claim, request, proposal, or other complex activity, often involving several persons and multiple communications. **2.** More specifically, a court's handling of a lawsuit or prosecution over the course of its pendency; specif., the court's control of litigation by assuming responsibility for it from pretrial phases through ultimate disposition so as to ensure that court resources are efficiently deployed and delays minimized. • Case-management devices include prehearing conferences, case plans, limits on discovery, rigorous scheduling, and mandatory alternative-dispute-resolution methods.

case-management order. (1979) A court order designed to control the procedure in a case on the court's docket, esp. by limiting pretrial discovery. — Abbr. CMO.

case method. See CASEBOOK METHOD.

case note. A short statement summarizing a case, esp. the relevant facts, the issues, the holding, and the court's reasoning. — Sometimes written *casenote*. — Also termed *brief*; *case brief*; *case statement*; *case abstract*; *case summary*.

case number. (1839) The number assigned to a lawsuit when it is filed with the clerk of the court. • Each case has a distinct number that distinguishes it from all other suits filed within the jurisdiction.

case of first impression. See CASE (1).

case-or-controversy requirement. (1937) The constitutional requirement that, for a federal court to hear a case, the case must involve an actual dispute. See CONTROVERSY (3); *advisory opinion* under OPINION (1).

> "The courts of the United States do not sit to decide questions of law presented in a vacuum, but only such questions as arise in a 'case or controversy.' The two terms can be used interchangeably, for, we are authoritatively told, a 'controversy,' if distinguishable at all from a 'case,' is distinguishable only in that it is a less comprehensive term, and includes only suits of a civil nature." Charles Alan Wright, *The Law of Federal Courts* 60 (5th ed. 1994).

case plan. A written procedure for the care and management of a child who has been removed from his or her home and placed in foster care or in an institution. • The case plan includes (1) a description of the place where the child has been placed, (2) a plan for providing the child with safe and proper care, and (3) a plan for services that will be provided to the child's parents. Each state must have a case-review system formulated to ensure that the child is placed in the least restrictive and most appropriate place and that the plan is in the best interests of the child; the plan must be reviewed every six months. See ADOPTION AND SAFE FAMILIES ACT.

case reserved. See CASE (1).

case stated. See CASE (1).

case statement. See CASE NOTE.

case summary. (1918) **1.** CASE NOTE. **2.** A written statement by an agency that has an interest in a proceeding, as when a board of examiners for sex offenders submits a statement in a proceeding relating to a sex offender's status and living arrangements.

case system. See CASEBOOK METHOD.

case theory. (1906) The particular line of reasoning of either party to a suit, the purpose being to bring together certain facts of the case in a logical sequence and to correlate them in a way that produces in the decision-maker's mind a definite result or conclusion favored by the advocate. — Also termed *theory of the case.* See CAUSE OF ACTION.

case-within-a-case rule. (1979) *Torts.* The requirement that a legal-malpractice-action plaintiff show that, but for the attorney's negligence, the plaintiff would have won the case underlying the malpractice action.

cas fortuit (**kah** for-**twee**). [French "fortuitous case"] (1806) *Insurance.* An unforeseeable event; an inevitable accident; FORTUITOUS EVENT.

cash, *n.* (16c) **1.** Money or its equivalent. **2.** Currency or coins, negotiable checks, and balances in bank accounts. — **cash,** *vb.*

- ▸ **petty cash.** (18c) Currency kept on hand for incidental expenditures.

cash accounting. See *cash-basis accounting method* under ACCOUNTING METHOD.

cash-accounting method. See *cash-basis accounting method* under ACCOUNTING METHOD.

cash-advance loan. See *payday loan* under LOAN.

cash-against-documents sale. See *documentary sale* under SALE.

cash-and-carry clause. (1938) *Int'l law.* A regulation that, before U.S. involvement in World War II, allowed belligerent countries to pay cash for goods whose export was prohibited. • Formally, this regulation was entirely neutral, but in practice it favored the United Kingdom.

cash bail. See BAIL (1).

cash-basis accounting method. See ACCOUNTING METHOD.

cash book. (17c) An account book of all cash received and paid out by a business.

cash budget. (1920) A period-by-period schedule of a business's opening cash on hand, estimated cash receipts, cash disbursements, and cash balance. • A cash budget is used to project a business's cash receipts and disbursements over some future period.

cash check. See CHECK.

cash collateral. See COLLATERAL.

cash cycle. (1935) The time it takes for cash to flow into and out of a business, such as the time between the purchase of raw materials for manufacture and the sale of the finished product.

cash discount. See DISCOUNT.

cash dividend. See DIVIDEND.

cash equivalent. (1859) A short-term security that is liquid enough to be considered equivalent to cash.

cash-equivalent doctrine. (1959) *Tax.* The doctrine requiring income to be reported even if it is not cash, as when the taxpayer barters to receive in-kind payments.

cash-expenditure method. (1953) *Tax.* A technique used by the IRS to reconstruct a taxpayer's unreported income by comparing the amount spent on goods and services during a given period with the income reported for that period. • If the expenditures exceed the reported revenue, the IRS treats the difference as taxable income.

cash flow. (1954) **1.** The movement of cash through a business, as a measure of profitability or liquidity. **2.** The cash generated from a business or transaction. **3.** Cash receipts minus cash disbursements for a given period. — Sometimes written *cashflow.*

- ▸ **cash flow per common share.** (1964) The cash flow from operations minus preferred stock dividends, divided by the number of outstanding common shares.
- ▸ **discounted cash flow.** (1953) A method of evaluating a capital investment by comparing its projected income and costs with its current value. • Discounted cash flow is used to determine the value of a company by calculating the present value of its future cash flows. In theory, the value of the corporation's assets equals the present value of the expected cash flow generated by those assets. — Abbr. DCF; DCF method. — Also termed *discounted-cash-flow method.*
- ▸ **incremental cash flow.** (1956) The net increase in cash flow attributable to a particular capital investment.
- ▸ **negative cash flow.** (1959) A financial situation in which cash outflow exceeds cash inflow. See INSOLVENCY.
- ▸ **net cash flow.** (1955) Cash inflow minus cash outflow. — Abbr. NCF.

cashier, *n.* (16c) **1.** Someone who receives and records payments at a business. **2.** A bank's or trust company's executive officer, who is responsible for banking transactions.

cashier, *vb.* (16c) To dismiss from service dishonorably, esp. of misconduct <after three such incidents, Jones was cashiered>.

cashier's check. See CHECK.

cash-in-hand, *adj.* (1981) (Of a payment) made in the form of currency and coins so that there is no record of the payment.

cashlite. See AMERCEMENT.

cash merger. See MERGER (8).

cash-option transaction. (1991) *Mergers & acquisitions.* A provision in a merger agreement giving the target company's stockholders a choice between receiving either a tax-free exchange of stock or a taxable cash buyout.

cash or deferred arrangement. (1978) A retirement-plan provision permitting an employee to have a certain amount of compensation paid in cash or contributed, on behalf of the employee, to a profit-sharing or stock-bonus plan. • A 401(k) plan is a type of cash or deferred arrangement. — Abbr. CODA.

cashout, *n.* (1971) An arrangement by a seller to receive the entire amount of equity in cash rather than retain an interest in the property. — **cash out,** *vb.*

cash-out merger. See *cash merger* under MERGER.

cash proceeds. See PROCEEDS (2).

cash-refund annuity. See *refund annuity* under ANNUITY.

cash sale. See SALE.

cash surrender value. See VALUE (2).

cash tender offer. See TENDER OFFER.

cash-transaction report. (1997) IRS Form 4789, which requires banks and other financial institutions to report cash transactions above a certain amount. — Abbr. CTR.

cash value. 1. See *fair market value* under VALUE (2). **2.** See *full cash value* under VALUE (2).

cash-value option. See OPTION (5).

casing. *Oil & gas.* The pipe in a wellbore hole, cemented into place to prevent pollution and to protect the hole.

▸ **intermediate casing.** Casing that protects deep formations against pollution from drilling and producing operations.

▸ **production casing.** Wellbore pipe through which oil and gas is produced. • Production casing is the last pipe set in the hole.

▸ **surface casing.** Casing that protects groundwater against pollution from drilling and producing operations. • Surface casing is the first pipe set in the hole.

casinghead gas. (1918) *Oil & gas.* Natural gas in a liquid solution with crude oil, produced at the casinghead (top) of an oil well. • Casinghead gas separates from the oil at the time of production or shortly afterward.

casing point. (1953) *Oil & gas.* The point at which a well has been drilled to the desired depth and the owners must decide whether to place production pipe ("casing") in the hole to complete and equip the well for production.

cassare (kə-**sair**-ee), *vb.* [Law Latin fr. Latin *cassus* "void"] *Hist.* To quash or nullify. • *Cassare* was usu. used in reference to voiding an agreement, law, or writ. See CASSETUR BILLA; CASSETUR BREVE.

cassation (ka-**say**-shən), *n.* (15c) A quashing. See COURT OF CASSATION.

cassetur billa (kə-**see**-tər **bil**-ə). [Latin "that the bill be quashed"] *Hist.* **1.** A judgment quashing a plea in abatement. **2.** A plaintiff's on-the-record admission that a defendant's plea in abatement cannot be avoided. • This statement discontinues the action. — Also termed *billa cassetur; quod billa cassetur.*

cassetur breve (kə-**see**-tər **bree**-vee). [Latin "that the writ be quashed"] *Hist.* A judgment quashing an action begun by writ.

CASSIS/BIB. *Patents.* A U.S. Patent and Trademark Office database of bibliographies relating to patents, sorted by their classification. • CASSIS stands for Classification and Search Support Information System. Cf. CASSIS/CLASS.

CASSIS/CLASS. *Patents.* A U.S. Patent and Trademark Office database of patents sorted by classification, available at any PTO Depository Library. Cf. CASSIS/BIB.

cast, *vb.* (1871) To formally deposit (a ballot) or signal one's choice (in a vote) <most voters cast their ballots for write-in candidates>.

cast a cloud on, *vb. Patents.* Create doubt about (a patent, esp. its validity).

castigatory (kas-ti-gə-tor-ee). (17c) *Hist.* A device for punishing scolds by repeatedly plunging them underwater. • This device is mentioned by the ancient Saxons (*scealfing stole*) and in Domesday Book (*cathedra stercoralis*). It was also used to punish bakers and brewers by ducking them into "stinking water" (*stercore*), possibly into a midden. — Also termed *ducking stool; cucking stool; trebucket.* See SCOLD. Cf. BRANKS.

> "[A] *common scold,* . . . if convicted, shall be sentenced to be placed in a certain engine of correction called the trebucket, castigatory, or *cucking* stool, which in the Saxon language signifies the scolding stool; though now it is frequently corrupted into *ducking* stool, because the residue of the judgment is, that, when she is so placed therein, she shall be plunged in the water for her punishment." 4 William Blackstone, *Commentaries on the Laws of England* 169 (1769).

casting vote. See VOTE (1).

cast-iron-pipe doctrine. See DIVIDEND-CREDIT RULE.

castle doctrine. (1892) *Criminal law.* An exception to the retreat rule allowing the use of deadly force by a person who is protecting his or her home and its inhabitants from attack, esp. from a trespasser who intends to commit a felony or inflict serious bodily harm. — Also termed *dwelling defense; defense of habitation.* See RETREAT RULE.

castle-guard, *n.* (16c) *Hist.* **1.** The protection of a castle. **2.** A form of knight-service in which a tenant must protect the lord's castle. **3.** The tenure giving rise to this knight-service. **4.** A tax once imposed in lieu of this knight-service. **5.** The territory that is chargeable with the tax imposed in lieu of the knight-service. — Also termed (in senses 2–5) *ward.*

> "Castleguard is an imposition upon such of the king's subjects as dwell within a certain compass of any castle, to the maintenance of such as watch and ward it. It is sometimes used for the circuit itself which is inhabited by such

as are subject to this service." William Rastell, *Termes de la Ley* 70 (1st Am. ed. 1812).

casual, *adj.* (14c) **1.** (Of employment) occurring without regularity; occasional <a casual employee>. See *casual employment* under EMPLOYMENT. **2.** (Of an event or occurrence) not expected, foreseen, or planned; fortuitous <a casual deficit>.

casual affray. See CHANCE-MEDLEY.

casual condition. See CONDITION (2).

casual deficit. (1846) An unforeseen shortfall of funds.

casual ejector. See EJECTOR.

casual employment. See EMPLOYMENT.

casualism, *n.* (1873) **1.** A situation or state of affairs in which chance rules. **2.** The doctrine that all things exist or are controlled by chance. **3.** A word or phrase that is notably informal and is traditionally unsuitable for formal prose.

casual negligence. See NEGLIGENCE.

casualty. (15c) **1.** A serious or fatal accident. **2.** A person or thing injured, lost, or destroyed.

casualty gain. (1974) *Insurance.* The profit realized by an insured when the benefits paid exceed the insured property's adjusted value.

casualty insurance. See INSURANCE.

casualty loss. See LOSS.

casualty pot. *Tax.* A step in evaluating tax liability in which casualty gains and losses are compared to determine whether a net loss or gain has occurred. Cf. MAIN POT.

casu consimili (**kay**-s[y]oo kən-**sim**-ə-lɪ), *n.* [Latin "in a like case"] (16c) *Hist.* A writ of entry allowing the holder of a reversionary interest in land to sue for the return of land alienated by a life tenant or a tenant by the curtesy. • This writ originated in the second Statute of Westminster (13 Edw. I) ch. 24 (1285), which expanded the writs available to litigants by requiring the Chancery to issue a writ for any situation that called for a writ similar to one that had previously issued *consimili casu* ("in a like case"). Specifically, the statute provided (in Latin) that "as often as it shall happen in chancery that in one case a writ is found, and in a like case [*in consimili casu*], falling under the same right, and requiring like remedy, no writ is to be found, the clerks of chancery shall agree in making a writ...." Many other writs were framed under Westminster 2, but this particular writ's close association with the statute led to its taking the generic name. — Also termed *consimili casu*; *entry in casu consimili.* See ACTIONES NOMINATAE.

casuistry (**kazh**-yə-wis-tree), *n.* [fr. Latin *casus* "case"] (18c) **1.** Reasoning used to resolve moral or legal issues by formulating inductive theoretical rules from particular instances and applying these rules to particular instances. **2.** Specious argumentation based on fallacious reasoning or the disingenuous use of subtly false principles, esp. on legal or moral questions; SOPHISTRY. — **casuist,** *n.* — **casuistical,** *adj.*

casu proviso (**kay**-s[y]oo prə-**vɪ**-zoh). [Latin "in the case provided"] (16c) *Hist.* A writ of entry to recover a reversion in land alienated by a tenant in dower, i.e., a widow with a life estate in the alienated land.

casu quo (**kay**-s[y]oo **kwoh**). [Latin] In this case; in a case in which.

casus (**kay**-səs). [Latin] **1.** A chance accident; an event without human intervention or fault. Cf. CULPA (1); DOLUS (1). **2.** A situation actually contemplated by the legislature in enacting a statute that applies to the situation. • In this sense, the term is opposed to *casus omissus.* Cf. CASUS OMISSUS.

casus amissionis (**kay**-səs ə-mis[h]-ee-**oh**-nis). [Latin "the occasion of the loss"] (17c) *Hist.* The circumstances under which a document is lost or destroyed. • In an action to prove the contents of a lost instrument, the circumstances under which a document was lost was required evidence. Lost documents are now covered by Federal Rule of Evidence 1004(1).

casus belli (**kay**-səs **bel**-ɪ). [Latin] (1849) An act or circumstance that provokes or justifies war.

casus foederis (**kay**-səs **fed**-ər-is). [Latin "the case of the treaty" *or* "the case of the agreement"] (18c) **1.** *Int'l law.* A provocative act by one country toward another, entitling the latter to call on an ally to fulfill the terms of an alliance. **2.** A clause within a treaty of alliance specifying such provocative acts. **3.** *Contracts.* A case or an event falling within the terms of a contract.

casus fortuitus (**kay**-səs for-**t[y]oo**-ə-təs). [Latin] (17c) *Roman & civil law.* **1.** A fortuitous event. **2.** A loss not attributable to human fault.

> "Casual loss (casus fortuitus) was that arising from causes which no human strength or foresight could avert. Unless by special compact, no person was responsible for it. The danger of such accidents was termed 'periculum.'" John George Phillimore, *Private Law Among the Romans* 105 (1863).

casus improvisus (**kay**-səs im-prə-**vɪ**-zəs). [Latin] *Hist.* An unforeseen case; a case not provided for.

> "*Casus improvisus* . . . . This phrase is of frequent occurrence, and admits of varied illustration. Thus, if an Act of Parliament has been passed for the removal of some inconvenience, or the suppression of some evil, and specifies the circumstances or cases in which it is to have application, and a case occurs which is not specified by the Act, in which, nevertheless, the application of the Statute would be beneficial, this is a *casus improvisus*, and neither the procedure nor the provisions of the Act can be applied to it. The Statute cannot be strained so as to be made applicable to a case for which it does not provide. Statutes, however, which are purely remedial are construed liberally, and are often extended to cases similar to those mentioned in the Act, although such cases do not fall within the letter of the enactment." John Trayner, *Trayner's Latin Maxims* 70 (4th ed. 1894).

casus incogitatus (**kay**-səs in-koj-i-**tah**-təs). [Law Latin] *Hist.* A circumstance unthought of; a situation that was not addressed by the author of a legal instrument. Cf. CASUS OMISSUS. Pl. ***casus incogitati*** (**kay**-səs in-koj-i-**tah**-tɪ).

casus insolitus (**kay**-səs in-**sol**-ə-təs). [Latin] (17c) *Hist.* An unusual circumstance; an unusual event.

casus major (**kay**-səs **may**-jər). [Latin] An extraordinary casualty.

casus male inclusus (**kay**-səs **mal**-ee in-**kloo**-səs). [Latin "case wrongly included"] A situation literally provided for by a statute or contract, but wrongly so because the provision's literal application has unintended or absurd consequences.

casus omissus (**kay**-səs ə-**mis**-əs). [Latin "case omitted"] (17c) A situation not provided for by a legal text such as a constitution, statute, or contract, and therefore governed either by common law or by new judge-made law. — Also termed *gap*. Cf. CASUS (2); CASUS INCOGITATUS. Pl. ***casus omissi.***

"At times a state of war appears to exist between the courts and the parliamentary draftsman. The courts decline to come to the rescue when a *casus omissus* is revealed, so words appropriate to cover the *casus omissus* are added to the statute. More frequently the draftsman gets in first and, anticipating a strict construction by the courts coupled with a total lack of sympathy if there should happen to be a *casus omissus,* he produces a statute which is nothing less than horrific in its detail." Rupert Cross, *Statutory Interpretation* 11–12 (1976).

***casus omissus* canon.** See OMITTED-CASE CANON.

casus rarior (**kay**-səs **rair**-ee-or). *Hist.* An exceptional case. Pl. ***casus rariores.***

catalla (kə-**tal**-ə). [Law Latin "chattels"] *Hist.* **1.** CHATTEL. — Also termed *catals.*

"*Catals (catalla) alias chatels,* cometh of the *Normans.* For . . . all movable goods . . . are called chatels: the contrary whereof is *(fief)* which we do call fee." John Cowell, *The Interpreter* (1607).

2. Cattle used for plowing.

catallactics (kat-ə-**lak**-tiks), *n.* (1831) **1.** The branch of political economy dealing with commercial exchanges of one thing for another. **2.** The principles operative in an economy in which exchange is the predominant factor.

catalla otiosa (kə-**tal**-ə oh-shee-**oh**-sə). [Law Latin "nonworking chattels"] *Hist.* **1.** Chattels that are not animals. **2.** Animals not used for plowing or pulling plows or carts (*averia carucae*).

catallis captis nomine districtionis (kə-**tal**-is **kap**-tis **nahm**-ə-nee di-strik-shee-**oh**-nis). [Latin "chattels taken in name of distress"] (17c) *Hist.* A writ permitting a landlord who is owed rent to distrain (i.e., seize) the doors, windows, and gates of the tenant's house.

catallis reddendis (kə-**tal**-is ri-**den**-dis). See DE CATALLIS REDDENDIS.

catals. See CATALLA.

cataneus. See CAPITANEUS (1).

catch-all, *adj.* (1875) Broad; widely encompassing <the catch-all factor allows the jury to consider all circumstances extenuating the gravity of the crime>.

catch-all, *n.* See BROADENING STATEMENT.

catchall exception. See EXCEPTION (1).

catching bargain. See BARGAIN.

catchpoll (**kach**-pohl). (14c) *Hist.* A sheriff's deputy or bailiff. — Also spelled *catchpol; catchpole.*

"Catchpol . . . (One that *catches* by the *Poll*) Though now taken as a word of Contempt, yet in ancient times, it was used, without reproach, for such as we now call *Sergeants of the Mace,* Bailiffs, or any other that use to Arrest Men upon any Action." Thomas Blount, *Nomo-Lexicon: A Law-Dictionary* (1670).

catch-time charter. See *time charter* under CHARTER (8).

categorical exclusion. See EXCLUSION (4).

categorical question. 1. QUESTION (1). **2.** LEADING QUESTION.

cater cousin (**kay**-tər). (16c) A distant relative. • The term derives from the French *quatrecousin,* meaning a cousin in the fourth degree.

cathedral. (16c) *Eccles. law.* The principal church of a diocese, in which the bishop's throne, or *cathedra,* is situated.

cathedral preferment. (18c) *Eccles. law.* In a cathedral church, a deanery, archdeaconry, canonry, or other office below the rank of bishop.

catholic creditor. See CREDITOR.

Catoniana regula (kə-toh-nee-**ay**-nə **reg**-yə-lə). See REGULA CATONIANA.

cat-out-of-the-bag theory. (1970) **1.** The view that once an objection to testimony has been forgone and the evidence has come before the fact-finder without objection, it is properly before the fact-finder for all purposes. **2.** *Criminal law.* The view that a defendant's later statement to police may be inadmissible if it was made only because of an earlier inadmissible statement.

cats and dogs. (1879) *Slang.* **1.** Nonperforming securities. **2.** Highly speculative securities.

"Wall Street disdainfully regards most penny stocks as *cats and dogs,* a popular phrase in use since 1879 to describe low-priced, often worthless, speculative securities. The single word *dog* also means a worthless security, and the related *pup* meant a low-priced, inactive stock during the 1940s and 1950s." Kathleen Odean, *High Steppers, Fallen Angels, and Lollipops: Wall Street Slang* 10 (1988).

cattle rustling. (1886) The stealing of cattle.

cattle-trespass. See TRESPASS.

caucus (**kaw**-kəs), *n.* (18c) **1.** A private meeting of representatives from a political party who assemble to nominate candidates and decide party policy. **2.** The collective representatives who participate in such a meeting. **3.** A meeting of a group, usu. within a deliberative assembly, of people aligned by party or interest to formulate a policy or strategy. **4.** Any similar meeting for similar purposes, as in a mediation. — **caucus,** *vb.*

"The term *caucus* is also sometimes applied to a similar meeting of all the known or admitted partisans of a particular position on an important issue — in a convention or any other deliberative assembly — who meet to plan strategy toward a desired result within the assembly. Such a meeting may be held on the presumed informal understanding that those who attend will follow the decisions of the caucus." Henry M. Robert III et al., *Robert's Rules of Order Newly Revised* § 59, at 606–07 (11th ed. 2011).

▸ **separate caucus.** (1970) A confidential mediation session that a mediator holds with one side of a dispute to elicit settlement offers and demands. • When separate caucuses are used, the mediator typically shuttles between the two (or more) sides of a dispute to communicate offers and demands. Formerly, ABA Model Rule of Professional Responsibility 2.2 (governing when a lawyer could act for more than one client or as an intermediary between parties) applied when a lawyer acted as a mediator. Although the rule was deleted from the Model in 2002, many states have similar rules in effect. The rule requires a lawyer acting as an intermediary to inform the parties about mediation and the mediator's role, to act impartially, and to have a good-faith belief that the matter can be resolved in all parties' best interests.

causa (**kaw**-zə), *n.* [Latin] (15c) **1.** CAUSE (1).

"One of the vaguest terms of the Roman juristic language. Starting from the basic meaning of cause, reason, inducement, the jurists use it in very different senses. . . . *Causa* is the reason for which some judicial measures (actions, exceptions, interdicts) were introduced by the praetor. . . . Sometimes *causa* is roughly identical with animus when it alludes to the subjective motive, intention, or purpose of a person." Adolf Berger, *Encyclopedic Dictionary of Roman Law* 382–83 (1953).

▸ ***causa causans*** (**kaw**-zə **kaw**-zanz). (17c) An immediate or effective cause. See *immediate cause* under CAUSE (1).

▸ ***causa jactitationis maritagii*** (**kaw**-zə jak-ti-tay-shee-**oh**-nis mar-ə-**tay**-jee-ɪ). [Latin "cause of assertion of marriage"] See JACTITATION OF MARRIAGE.

▸ ***causa matrimonii praelocuti*** (**kaw**-zə ma-trə-**moh**-nee-ɪ pree-lə-**kyoo**-tɪ). [Latin "cause of prearranged marriage"] (16c) *Hist.* A writ of entry available to a woman who had given land to a suitor who refused to marry her within a reasonable time. — Also termed *entry for marriage in speech.*

▸ ***causa proxima*** (**kaw**-zə **prok**-si-mə). (17c) The immediate or latest cause. See *proximate cause* under CAUSE (1).

▸ ***causa remota*** (**kaw**-zə ri-**moh**-tə). (17c) A remote or indirect cause. See *remote cause* under CAUSE (1).

▸ ***causa sine qua non*** (**kaw**-zə **sɪ**-nee kway **non** *also* **sin**-ay kwah **nohn**). (16c) A necessary cause; the cause without which the thing cannot be or the event would not have occurred. See *but-for cause* under CAUSE (1).

2. *Roman & civil law.* The partial execution of a contract by the act of one of the parties to it. *See* John George Phillimore, *Private Law Among Romans* 228 (1863). **3.** *Roman & civil law.* A consideration or inducement.

"The revolution of the ancient law of Contract was consummated when the Praetor of some one year announced in his Edict that he would grant equitable actions upon Pacts which had never been matured at all into Contracts, provided only that the Pacts in question had been founded on a consideration (*causa*)." Henry S. Maine, *Ancient Law* 28 (17th ed. 1901).

"Article 1131 of the French Civil Code provides that: 'L'obligation sans cause, ou sur une fausse cause, ou sur une cause illicite, ne peut avoir aucun effet.' This *cause* or *causa* is a synonym for consideration, and we find the terms used interchangeably in the earlier English authorities." John Salmond, *Jurisprudence* 361 (Glanville L. Williams ed., 10th ed. 1947).

▸ ***causa falsa*** (**kaw**-zə **fal**-sə [*or* **fawl**-sə]). See *falsa causa.*

▸ ***causa non secuta*** (**kaw**-zə non sə-**kyoo**-tə). [Latin "the (expected) consideration not having followed"] *Roman law.* A consideration that has failed; failure of consideration.

▸ ***falsa causa*** (**fal**-sə [*or* **fawl**-sə] **kaw**-zə). [Latin "mistaken reason or motive"] *Roman law.* Falsity of consideration. • This might result from several things, such as a mistaken reason for making a gift or bequest. — Also termed (esp. in civil law) *causa falsa.*

causa causae est causa causati (**kaw**-zə **kaw**-zee est **kaw**-zə kaw-**zay**-tɪ). [Latin "the cause of a cause is the cause of the thing caused"]. *Torts.* The principle that the cause of the cause (rather than only the immediate cause) should also be considered as the cause of the effect.

causa cognita (**kaw**-zə **kog**-ni-tə). [Latin] (17c) *Hist.* After investigation; the cause (or facts) having been ascertained. Cf. POST CAUSAM COGNITAM.

"Formerly, inhibitions were not granted except *causa cognita* (although a different rule now prevails), because they imposed a restraint on the full exercise of the rights of property; and in our own time decrees of divorce or judicial separation are not granted, except on inquiry into the facts, and cause shown warranting such orders." John Trayner, *Trayner's Latin Maxims* 71–72 (4th ed. 1894).

causa data causa non secuta (**kaw**-zə **day**-tə **kaw**-zə non si-**kyoo**-tə). [Latin] (17c) *Roman law.* The consideration having been given but the counterpart not having followed. • The phrase appeared in reference to consideration promised for an act that never took place — e.g., an advance payment for work not done, or a gift given in contemplation of marriage before the wedding was called off. See CONDICTIO.

causa debendi (**kaw**-zə di-**ben**-dɪ). [Latin] *Hist.* The grounds of debt.

causa et modus transferendi dominii (**kaw**-zə et **moh**-dəs trans-fər-**en**-dɪ də-**min**-ee-ɪ). [Law Latin] *Hist.* The title and the manner of transferring property. — Also (erroneously) spelled *causa et modus transferrendi dominii.*

causa falsa. See *falsa causa* under CAUSA (2).

causa impotentiae (**kaw**-zə im-pə-**ten**-shi-ee), *adv.* [Latin] *Hist.* By the cause of inability.

causa jactitationis maritagii (**kaw**-zə jak-ti-tay-shee-**oh**-nis mar-ə-**tay**-jee-ɪ). [Latin "cause of assertion of marriage"] See JACTITATION OF MARRIAGE.

causa justa. See JUSTA CAUSA.

causal (**kaw**-zəl), *adj.* (16c) **1.** Of, relating to, or involving causation <a causal link exists between the defendant's act and the plaintiff's injury>. **2.** Arising from a cause <a causal symptom>. Cf. CAUSATIVE.

causal challenge. See *challenge for cause* under CHALLENGE (2).

causality (kaw-**zal**-ə-tee), *n.* (17c) The principle of causal relationship; the relation between cause and effect <the foreseeability test is one of duty and of causality>. — Also termed *causation.* — **causal,** *adj.*

causa lucrativa. See LUCRATIVA CAUSA.

causa matrimonii praelocuti. See CAUSA (1).

causam nobis significes quare (**kaw**-zəm **noh**-bis sig-**nif**-ə-seez **kwair**-ee). [Latin "that you signify to us the cause why"] (16c) *Hist.* A writ ordering a town's mayor to give seisin of land to a grantee of the king.

causa mortis (**kaw**-zə **mor**-tis), *adj.* (17c) Done or made in contemplation of one's own death. See *gift causa mortis* under GIFT.

causa non secuta. See CAUSA (2).

causa petendi (**kaw**-zə pə-**ten**-dɪ). [Latin] *Hist.* The cause of the claim.

causa promissionis (**kaw**-zə prə-mish-ee-**oh**-nis). *Eccles. law.* The doctrine that an informal undertaking does not oblige if it lacks a good cause.

causa proxima. See CAUSA (1).

causare (kaw-**zair**-ee), *vb.* [Law Latin fr. Latin *causari* "to litigate"] To litigate; to show cause against.

causa remota. See CAUSA (1).

causa scientiae (**kaw**-zə **sɪ**-**en**-shee-ee). [Law Latin] (17c) *Scots law.* Cause of knowledge. • The phrase typically referred to a witness's basis for drawing a particular conclusion, esp. in a case involving scientific expertise.

causa sine qua non. See CAUSA (1).

causation (kaw-**zay**-shən). (17c) **1.** The causing or producing of an effect <the plaintiff must prove causation>. **2.** CAUSALITY.

> "Here is the key to the juridical treatment of the problems of causation. We pick out the cause which in our judgment ought to be treated as the dominant one with reference, not merely to the event itself, but to the jural consequences that ought to attach to the event." Benjamin Cardozo, *The Paradoxes of Legal Science* 83 (1928).

▸ **negative causation.** (1977) *Securities.* The defense that part of the plaintiff's damages were caused by factors other than the depreciation in value of the securities resulting from registration-statement defects. • If negative causation is proved, the plaintiff's damages should be reduced. 15 USCA § 77k(e).

▸ **overdetermined causation.** (1985) *Torts.* A situation in which two or more events or conditions each would have been sufficient to produce an injurious result, so that none of the events or conditions alone will emerge as a cause of the result through application of the but-for test for actual causation. • Overdetermined causation encompasses both duplicative causation and preemptive causation. In duplicative causation, two or more factors (such as two fires or two gunshot wounds) both operate to produce a result, yet either would have been sufficient in the absence of the other. In preemptive causation, only one factor is causally operative, yet had it not operated, an alternative factor would have produced the same result, as with a desert traveler who dies of thirst after his canteen is stolen, yet the water in the canteen had been poisoned before it was stolen and would have killed him anyway. Cf. *but-for cause*, *concurrent cause* under CAUSE (1); NECESSARY-AND-SUFFICIENT SET TEST.

▸ **transaction causation.** (1974) *Securities.* The fact that an investor would not have engaged in a given transaction if the other party had made truthful statements at the required time.

causative (**kaw**-zə-tiv), *adj.* (15c) **1.** Effective as a cause or producing a result <causative factor of the accident>. **2.** Expressive of causation <the causative relationship between drinking and assault>. Cf. CAUSAL.

causator (kaw-**zay**-tər), *n.* [Latin "promoter of litigation"] *Hist.* **1.** A litigant. **2.** Someone who manages or litigates a cause for another.

cause, *n.* (13c) **1.** Something that produces an effect or result <the cause of the accident>. Cf. AGENT (1).

> "It has been said that an act which in no degree contributed to the result in question cannot be a cause of it; but this, of course, does not mean that an event which *might* have happened in the same way though the defendant's act or omission had not occurred, is not a result of it. The question is not what would have happened, but what did happen." Joseph H. Beale, *The Proximate Consequences of an Act*, 33 Harv. L. Rev. 633, 638 (1920).

▸ **actual cause.** See *but-for cause.*

▸ **but-for cause.** (1924) The cause without which the event could not have occurred. — Also termed *actual cause*; *cause in fact*; *factual cause.* Cf. *overdetermined causation* under CAUSATION; NECESSARY-AND-SUFFICIENT SET TEST.

▸ **concurrent cause.** (17c) One of two or more causes that simultaneously produce a result. Cf. *overdetermined causation* under CAUSATION.

▸ **contributing cause.** (18c) A factor that — though not the primary cause — plays a part in producing a result.

▸ **cooperative cause.** (1879) *Archaic.* Someone who is contributorily or comparatively negligent.

▸ **direct and proximate cause.** See *proximate cause.*

▸ **direct cause.** See *proximate cause.*

▸ **effective cause.** See *immediate cause.*

▸ **efficient adequate cause.** See *proximate cause.*

▸ **efficient cause.** See *proximate cause.*

▸ **efficient intervening cause.** See *intervening cause.*

▸ **efficient proximate cause.** See *proximate cause.*

▸ **factual cause.** See *but-for cause.*

▸ **first cause.** See *proximate cause.*

▸ **immediate cause.** (16c) The last event in a chain of events, though not necessarily the proximate cause of what follows. — Also termed *effective cause.*

▸ **initial cause.** See *proximate cause.*

▸ **intervening cause.** (17c) An event that comes between the initial event in a sequence and the end result, thereby altering the natural course of events that might have connected a wrongful act to an injury; esp., an independent agency's act that destroys or severely weakens the causal connection between the defendant's negligent act and the wrongful injury, this independent act being the immediate cause, so that there typically can be no recovery from the defendant. • If the intervening cause is strong enough to relieve the wrongdoer of any liability, it becomes a *superseding cause.* A *dependent intervening cause* is one that is not an act and is never a superseding cause. An *independent intervening cause* is one that operates on a condition produced by an antecedent cause but in no way resulted from that cause. — Also termed *intervening act*; *intervening agency*; *intervening force*; *independent intervening cause*; *efficient intervening cause*; *supervening cause*; *novus actus interveniens*; *nova causa interveniens.* See *superseding cause.*

▸ **jural cause.** See *proximate cause.*

▸ **legal cause.** See *proximate cause.*

▸ **primary cause.** See *proximate cause.*

▸ **procuring cause. 1.** See *proximate cause* (2). **2.** *Real estate.* The efforts of the agent or broker who effects the sale of realty and who is therefore entitled to a commission.

▸ **proximate cause.** (17c) **1.** A cause that is legally sufficient to result in liability; an act or omission that is considered in law to result in a consequence, so that liability can be imposed on the actor. **2.** A cause that directly produces an event and without which the event would not have occurred. — Also termed (in both senses) *direct cause*; *direct and proximate cause*; *efficient proximate cause*; *efficient cause*; *efficient adequate cause*; *initial cause*; *first cause*; *legal cause*; *procuring cause*; *producing cause*; *primary cause*; *jural cause.* Cf. (in sense 2) *remote cause.*

> "The four 'tests' or 'clues' of proximate cause in a criminal case are (1) expediency, (2) isolation, (3) foreseeability and

(4) intention." Rollin M. Perkins & Ronald N. Boyce, *Criminal Law* 823 (3d ed. 1982).

"'Proximate cause' — in itself an unfortunate term — is merely the limitation which the courts have placed upon the actor's responsibility for the consequences of the actor's conduct. In a philosophical sense, the consequences of an act go forward to eternity, and the causes of an event go back to the dawn of human events, and beyond. But any attempt to impose responsibility upon such a basis would result in infinite liability for all wrongful acts, and would 'set society on edge and fill the courts with endless litigation.' [*North v. Johnson*, 58 Minn. 242, 59 N.W. 1012 (1894).] As a practical matter, legal responsibility must be limited to those causes which are so closely connected with the result and of such significance that the law is justified in imposing liability. Some boundary must be set to liability for the consequences of any act, upon the basis of some social idea of justice or policy." W. Page Keeton et al., *Prosser and Keeton on the Law of Torts* § 41, at 264 (5th ed. 1984).

▸ **remote cause.** (16c) A cause that does not necessarily or immediately produce an event or injury; specif., a wrongful cause that is too far removed to constitute the basis of a legal claim, as by reason of an independent intervening circumstance. Cf. *proximate cause* (2).

▸ **sole cause.** (16c) The only cause that, from a legal viewpoint, produces an event or injury. • If it comes between a defendant's action and the event or injury at issue, it is treated as a *superseding cause.*

"When this one dominant cause is found it is treated as the 'sole cause' for the purposes of the particular case, even if it might not be so treated in a different kind of cause of action. A 'sole cause' which intervenes between defendant's act and the result in question is spoken of as a 'superseding cause.' . . . The phrase 'sole cause,' meaning the only cause which will receive juridical recognition for the purposes of the particular case, is convenient to give emphasis to three points: (1) If defendant's act was the sole cause of the death or other socially-harmful occurrence, it is by definition a proximate cause thereof; (2) if something other than his act was the sole cause of the harm there need be no further inquiry so far as he is concerned; (3) it is not necessary that defendant's act should have been the sole cause of the harm, — which is merely another form of stating that a contributory cause is sufficient." Rollin M. Perkins & Ronald N. Boyce, *Criminal Law* 781–82 (3d ed. 1982).

▸ **superseding cause.** (1891) An intervening act or force that the law considers sufficient to override the cause for which the original tortfeasor was responsible, thereby exonerating that tortfeasor from liability. — Also termed *sole cause.* Cf. *intervening cause.*

▸ **supervening cause.** See *intervening cause.*

▸ **unavoidable cause.** (16c) A cause that a reasonably prudent person would not anticipate or be expected to avoid.

2. A ground for legal action <the plaintiff does not have cause to file suit>.

▸ **good cause.** (16c) A legally sufficient reason. • Good cause is often the burden placed on a litigant (usu. by court rule or order) to show why a request should be granted or an action excused. The term is often used in employment-termination cases. — Also termed *good cause shown; just cause; lawful cause; sufficient cause.*

"Issues of 'just cause,' or 'good cause,' or simply 'cause' arise when an employee claims breach of the terms of an employment contract providing that discharge will be only for just cause. Thus, just cause is a creature of contract. By operation of law, an employment contract for a definite term may not be terminated without cause before the expiration of the term, unless the contract provides otherwise." Mark A. Rothstein et al., *Employment Law* § 9.7, at 539 (1994).

▸ **just cause.** See *good cause.*

▸ **lawful cause.** See *good cause.*

▸ **probable cause.** See PROBABLE CAUSE.

▸ **sufficient cause. 1.** See *good cause.* **2.** PROBABLE CAUSE.

3. A lawsuit; a case <the court has 50 causes on the motion docket>.

▸ **preferred cause.** (1870) A case that a court may for good reason accelerate and try ahead of other cases. — Also termed *preference case; preference cause.*

▸ **short cause.** (17c) A case that requires little time to try, usu. half a day or less. — Also termed *short-cause trial.*

4. CAUSA (2). • In Romano-French jurisdictions, the concept of cause as legal consideration is used to determine which transactions are binding and which ones are not: "Cause is the reason why a party obligates himself." La. Civ. Code art. 1967.

cause, *vb.* (14c) To bring about or effect <dry conditions caused the fire>.

cause-and-prejudice rule. (1977) *Criminal law.* The doctrine that a state prisoner petitioning for a federal writ of habeas corpus on the basis of a claim not presented in state-court proceedings must show that the claim rests on either a rule of constitutional law newly announced by the Supreme Court of the United States (and thus previously unavailable) or a fact that could not have been uncovered earlier despite due diligence, and also show by clear and convincing evidence that the prisoner would not have been convicted but for the error. 28 USCA § 2254(e)(2). • This is an exception to the procedural-default doctrine. Before 1996, the cause-and-prejudice rule allowed federal courts to grant relief on the basis of a constitutional challenge that was not presented to the trial court if the prisoner showed good cause for failing to make the challenge at trial, and also showed that the trial court's error actually prejudiced the prisoner.

cause célèbre (kawz sə-leb *or* kawz say-leb-rə). [French "celebrated case"] (18c) A trial or decision in which the subject matter or the characters are unusual or sensational <the O.J. Simpson trial was a cause célèbre in the 1990s>.

cause in fact. See *but-for cause* under CAUSE (1).

cause lawyering. (1993) The practice of a lawyer who advocates for social justice by combining the activities of litigation, community organizing, public education, and lobbying to advance a cause past its current legal limitations and boundaries. — Also termed *activist lawyering; progressive lawyering; radical lawyering.* See *social justice* under JUSTICE (4). Cf. PUBLIC-INTEREST LAW.

cause list. See DOCKET (2).

cause of action. (15c) **1.** A group of operative facts giving rise to one or more bases for suing; a factual situation that entitles one person to obtain a remedy in court from another person; CLAIM (4) <after the crash, Aronson had a cause of action>.

"What is a cause of action? Jurists have found it difficult to give a proper definition. It may be defined generally to be a situation or state of facts that entitles a party to maintain an action in a judicial tribunal. This state of facts may be — (*a*) a primary right of the plaintiff actually violated

"... by the defendant; or (*b*) the threatened violation of such right, which violation the plaintiff is entitled to restrain or prevent, as in case of actions or suits for injunction; or (*c*) it may be that there are doubts as to some duty or right, or the right beclouded by some apparent adverse right or claim, which the plaintiff is entitled to have cleared up, that he may safely perform his duty, or enjoy his property." Edwin E. Bryant, *The Law of Pleading Under the Codes of Civil Procedure* 170 (2d ed. 1899).

2. A legal theory of a lawsuit <a malpractice cause of action>. — Also termed (in senses 1 & 2) *ground of action.* Cf. (in senses 1 & 2) RIGHT OF ACTION; CASE THEORY.

▸ **new cause of action.** (18c) A claim not arising out of, relating to, or involving the conduct, occurrence, or transaction contained in the original pleading. • An amended pleading often relates back to the date on which the original pleading was filed. Thus, a plaintiff may add claims to a suit without facing a statute-of-limitations bar, as long as the original pleading was timely filed. But if the amended pleading adds a claim that arises out of a different transaction or occurrence, or out of different alleged conduct, the amendment does not relate back to the date on which the original pleading was filed. Fed. R. Civ. P. 15(c).

3. Loosely, a lawsuit <there are four defendants in the pending cause of action>. — Abbr. COA.

cause-of-action estoppel. See COLLATERAL ESTOPPEL.

cause of death. (16c) The happening, occurrence, or condition that makes a person die; the injury, disease, or medical complication that results directly in someone's demise.

causer liability. See LIABILITY.

causidicus (kaw-**zid**-ə-kəs), *n.* [Latin "pleader"] (17c) *Roman law.* A speaker or pleader who pleaded cases orally for others; a barrister. Cf. ADVOCATUS (1). Pl. ***causidici.***

cautio (**kaw**-shee-oh), *n.* [Latin "security"] (16c) *Roman & civil law.* **1.** Security usu. given to ensure the performance of an obligation. See BAIL (1); BOND (2). **2.** A surety. Pl. ***cautiones*** (kaw-shee-**oh**-neez).

▸ ***cautio damni infecti*** (**kaw**-shee-oh **dam**-nI in-**fek**-shee). [Latin] Security against anticipated injury; specif., security that indemnifies a person who feels endangered or menaced by another's actions, as when a homeowner reasonably fears that a neighbor's house might collapse and fall on the homeowner's house.

▸ ***cautio fidejussoria*** (**kaw**-shee-oh fI-dee-yə-**sor**-ee-ə). [Latin] Security given by a third party in a contract of *fidejussio.* See FIDEJUSSION.

▸ ***cautio judicatum solvi*** (**kaw**-shee-oh joo-di-**kay**-təm **sol**-vI). [Latin] A plaintiff's security for court costs. — Also spelled *cautio judicatam solvi.*

▸ ***cautio Muciana*** (**kaw**-shee-oh myoo-shee-**ay**-nə). [Latin "security introduced by Mucius Scaevola"] (18c) Security given by an heir or legatee to obtain immediate possession of a conditional inheritance. • The condition in the will usu. required an heir to refrain from doing some act, such as marriage or overseas travel.

▸ ***cautio pigneratitia*** (**kaw**-shee-oh pig-nər-ə-**tish**-[ee]-ə). [Latin "security by pledge"] Security given by pledging goods. — Also spelled *cautio pigneraticia; cautio pignoratitia.* Cf. *actio pigneratitia* under ACTIO.

▸ ***cautio pro expensis*** (**kaw**-shee-oh proh ek-**spen**-sis). [Latin "security for costs"] Security for court costs.

▸ ***cautio usufructuaria*** (**kaw**-shee-oh yooz-yə-frək-choo-**air**-ee-ə). [Latin "tenant's security"] (17c) Security given by a usufructuary or tenant for life or a term of years against waste of the enjoyed property. See USUFRUCT.

caution (**kay**-shən). (13c) *Civil & Scots law.* **1.** Security given to ensure performance of some obligation. See JURATORY CAUTION (2). **2.** The person who gives the security; a cautioner. See BAIL (4).

cautionary direction. See *cautionary instruction* under JURY INSTRUCTION.

cautionary instruction. See JURY INSTRUCTION.

cautione admittenda. See DE CAUTIONE ADMITTENDA.

cautioner (**kaw**-shən-ər *or* [in senses 2 & 3] **kay**-shən-ər). (16c) **1.** Someone who cautions or warns. **2.** *Civil & Scots law.* Someone who puts up security to ensure the performance of some obligation. **3.** *Scots law.* A personal security.

caution money. See EARNEST MONEY.

cautionry (**kay**-shən-ree), *n.* (17c) *Scots law.* The obligation to act as surety for another.

c.a.v. *abbr.* CURIA ADVISARI VULT.

caveat (**kav**-ee-aht *or* **kay**-vee-at *or* **kav**-ee-at). [Latin "let him or her beware"] (16c) **1.** A warning or proviso <he sold the car to his friend with the caveat that the brakes might need repairs>.

▸ ***caveat actor*** (**ak**-tor). [Latin] (18c) Let the doer, or actor, beware.

▸ ***caveat emptor*** (**emp**-tor). [Latin "let the buyer beware"] (16c) A doctrine holding that a purchaser buys at his or her own risk. • Modern statutes and cases have greatly limited the importance of this doctrine.

"It [*caveat emptor*] is one of that tribe of anonymous Latin maxims that infest our law . . . they fill the ear and sound like sense, and to the eye look like learning; while their main use is to supply the place of either or both." Gulian C. Verplanck, *An Essay on the Doctrine of Contracts* 218 (1825).

"*Caveat emptor* is the ordinary rule in contract. A vendor is under no duty to communicate the existence even of latent defects in his wares unless by act or implication he represents such defects not to exist." William R. Anson, *Principles of the Law of Contract* 245 (Arthur L. Corbin ed., 3d Am. ed. 1919).

"This action of unfair competition is the embodiment in law of the rule of the playground — 'Play fair!' For generations the law has enforced justice. . . . The maxim *caveat emptor* is founded on justice; the more modern rule that compels the use of truth in selling goods is founded on fairness. It conflicts with the rule of *caveat emptor.*" Harry D. Nims, *The Law of Unfair Competition and Trade-Marks* 25 (1929).

▸ ***caveat subscriptor*** (səb-**skrip**-tor). [Latin "let the signer beware"] (1951) The doctrine that a signatory to an agreement is liable for his or her undertakings and for all the obligations and liabilities that ensue from the agreement.

▸ ***caveat venditor*** (**ven**-di-tor). [Latin] (17c) Let the seller beware.

▸ ***caveat viator*** (vI-**ay**-tor). [Latin "let the traveler beware"]. The duty of a traveler on a highway to use due care to detect and avoid defects in the way.

2. A formal notice or warning given by a party to a court or court officer requesting a suspension of proceedings <the decedent's daughter filed a caveat stating the facts on which her will contest is based>. **3.** Under the Torrens system of land titles, a formal notice of an unregistered interest in land. • Once lodged with the register of deeds, this notice prevents the register from recording any dealing affecting the estate or the interest claimed. See TORRENS SYSTEM. — **caveat,** *vb.*

caveatable (kay-vee-**at**-ə-bəl *or* kav-ee-**at**-ə-bəl), *adj.* (1932) Of, relating to, or involving a legal or equitable interest that is protectable by a caveat. See CAVEAT (2), (3).

caveatee (kay-vee-at-**ee**). (18c) One whose interest is challenged by a caveat.

caveator (**kay**-vee-ay-tər). (1881) Someone who files a caveat, esp. to challenge the validity of a will; CONTESTANT (1).

C.B. *abbr.* **1.** COMMON BENCH. **2.** *Hist.* Chief Baron of the Exchequer.

CBA. *abbr.* **1.** COLLECTIVE-BARGAINING AGREEMENT. **2.** COST-BENEFIT ANALYSIS.

CBO. *abbr.* CONGRESSIONAL BUDGET OFFICE.

c-board. See *c-level management* under MANAGEMENT (1).

CBOE. *abbr.* CHICAGO BOARD OPTIONS EXCHANGE.

CBOT. *abbr.* CHICAGO BOARD OF TRADE.

CBP. *abbr.* UNITED STATES CUSTOMS AND BORDER PROTECTION.

CBT. *abbr.* CHICAGO BOARD OF TRADE.

CC. *abbr.* **1.** Circuit, city, civil, or county court. **2.** Chancery, civil, criminal, or Crown cases. **3.** CIVIL CODE.

CCC. *abbr.* **1.** COMMODITY CREDIT CORPORATION. **2.** CUSTOMS COOPERATION COUNCIL.

CCE. *abbr.* Continuing criminal enterprise.

CCIPS (see-sips), *n. abbr.* The Computer Crime and Intellectual Property Section, a division of the U.S. Department of Justice.

C corporation. See CORPORATION.

CCPA. *abbr.* **1.** COURT OF CUSTOMS AND PATENT APPEALS. **2.** CONSUMER CREDIT PROTECTION ACT.

CCR. *abbr.* UNITED STATES COMMISSION ON CIVIL RIGHTS.

CD. *abbr.* CERTIFICATE OF DEPOSIT.

CDC. *abbr.* CENTERS FOR DISEASE CONTROL AND PREVENTION.

CDFI Fund. *abbr.* COMMUNITY DEVELOPMENT FINANCIAL INSTITUTION FUND.

CDO. *abbr.* CEASE-AND-DESIST ORDER.

CEA. *abbr.* **1.** COUNCIL OF ECONOMIC ADVISERS. **2.** COST-EFFECTIVENESS ANALYSIS.

ceap (cheep). (bef. 12c) *Hist.* Anything for sale; a chattel (usu. cattle) used as a medium for barter.

ceapgild (**cheep**-gild). (17c) *Hist.* A tax or fine paid with an animal rather than with money. — Also spelled *ceapgilde.*

cease, *vb.* (14c) **1.** To stop, forfeit, suspend, or bring to an end. **2.** To become extinct; to pass away. — **cessation** (se-**say**-shən), *n.*

cease-and-desist letter. (1959) A cautionary notice sent to an alleged wrongdoer, describing the offensive activity and the complainant's remedies and demanding that the activity stop. • A cease-and-desist letter is commonly used to stop or block the suspected or actual infringement of an intellectual-property right before litigation. Ignoring a cease-and-desist letter may be taken as evidence that the infringement was willful.

cease-and-desist order. (1918) **1.** A court's or agency's order prohibiting a person from continuing a particular course of conduct. See INJUNCTION; RESTRAINING ORDER. **2.** *Intellectual property.* An order issued by the U.S. International Trade Commission temporarily enjoining a party from further sale or distribution of allegedly infringing goods imported into the United States during the pendency of a § 337 investigation. See SECTION 337 INVESTIGATION. — Abbr. CDO.

ceasefire. An agreement to stop fighting for a period, esp. so that a more permanent agreement can be made. See TRUCE.

cedant. See REINSURED.

cede (seed), *vb.* (18c) **1.** To surrender or relinquish. **2.** To assign or grant. — **cession** (**sesh**-ən), *n.* — **cessionary** (**sesh**-ən-er-ee), *adj.*

ceded control. See CONTROL.

cedent. See REINSURED.

cédula (**say**-doo-lah). [Spanish] (18c) *Spanish law.* **1.** An official document used to identify someone; an identity card. **2.** A promissory note. **3.** A summons; specif., a citation requiring a fugitive to appear in court to face criminal charges. • The citation is usu. affixed to the fugitive's door. **4.** *Hist.* A decree of the Spanish Crown; esp., a royal enactment issued by the Council of Castile or of the Indies.

CEE. See *certificate of earned eligibility* under CERTIFICATE.

ceiling price. See PRICE.

ceiling rent. See RENT (1).

celibacy. (17c) The state or condition of abstaining from both sexual relations and marriage, esp. by lifelong vow; voluntary abstention from sex and marriage. Cf. CHASTITY.

cenegild (**kay**-nə-gild). (18c) *Hist.* An expiatory fine paid by a murderer to the victim's relatives.

censere (sen-**seer**-ee), *vb.* [Latin "to express an opinion"] *Roman law.* To decree or resolve.

censo (**sen**-soh). [Spanish] (16c) *Spanish law.* **1.** The census; specif., an official count of the people within a country, state, district, or other political subdivision. **2.** Ground rent. **3.** An annuity or payment for the use of land.

▸ ***censo al quitar*** (ahl kee-**tahr**). A redeemable annuity. — Also termed *censo redimible.*

▸ ***censo consignativo*** (kawn-seeg-nah-**tee**-voh). A transferable annuity backed by a lien on the debtor's real property. • The debtor retains full legal title to the real property. — Also termed *censo consignatorio.*

▸ ***censo enfiteutico*** (en-fee-**tay**-oo-tee-koh). A real property owner's annuity from a usufructuary tenant; an annuity paid from an emphyteusis (a long-term lease of land). See EMPHYTEUSIS.

- ▸ ***censo redimible.*** See *censo al quitar.*
- ▸ ***censo reservatio*** (ray-ser-vah-**tee**-oh). An annuity payable by a grantee of land to the grantor. • The annuity is reserved when the land is transferred to the grantee.

censor, *n.* (16c) **1.** *Roman law.* (*ital.*) A Roman officer who acted as a census taker, assessor, and reviewer of public morals. **2.** Someone who inspects publications, films, and the like for objectionable content. **3.** In the armed forces, someone who reads letters and other communications and deletes material considered a security threat. — **censorial,** *adj.* — **censorship,** *n.*

censor (**sen**-sər), *vb.* (1882) To officially inspect (esp. a book or film) and delete material considered offensive.

censorial jurisprudence. See LAW REFORM.

censumethidus (sen-sə-**meth**-ə-dəs). [Law Latin] See MORTMAIN. — Also spelled *censumorthidus.*

censure (**sen**-shər), *n.* (14c) An official reprimand or condemnation; an authoritative expression of disapproval or blame; reproach <the judge's careless statements subjected her to the judicial council's censure>. — **censorious,** *adj.*

censure, *vb.* (16c) To reprimand; to express official disapproval of <the Senate censured the senator for his inflammatory remarks>. — **censurable,** *adj.*

censure motion. (1934) An application calling for an official reprimand or condemnation of an official, esp. a government official.

census. (17c) An official count of people made for the purpose of compiling social and economic data for the political subdivision to which the people belong. Pl. **censuses.**

- ▸ **federal census.** (18c) A census of a state or territory, or a portion of either, taken by the Census Bureau of the United States. • The Constitution (art. I, § 2) requires only a simple count of persons for purposes of apportioning congressional representation among the states. Under Congress's direction, however, the census has evolved to include a wide variety of information that is useful to businesses, historians, and others not affiliated with the federal government.

Census Bureau. See BUREAU OF THE CENSUS.

centena (sen-**tee**-nə). [fr. Latin *centum* "hundred"] (17c) *Hist.* A district containing 100 freemen, established among the Germans, Franks, Goths, and Lombards. • The *centena* corresponds to the Saxon *hundred.*

centenarius (sen-tə-**nair**-ee-əs). [fr. Latin *centum* "hundred-man"] (17c) *Hist.* A petty judge or under-sheriff of a hundred. See HUNDRED.

Center for Minority Veterans. A unit in the U.S. Department of Veterans Affairs responsible for promoting the use of VA services, benefits, and programs by minority veterans.

Center for Nutrition Policy and Promotion. An agency in the U.S. Department of Agriculture that works to improve the health of Americans by researching and providing science-based dietary guidance and nutrition education. — Abbr. CNPP. See FOOD, NUTRITION, AND CONSUMER SERVICES.

Center for Women Veterans. A unit in the U.S. Department of Veterans Affairs responsible for advising female veterans about VA programs and for evaluating VA programs to ensure access by women.

center-of-gravity doctrine. (1957) *Conflict of laws.* The rule that, in choice-of-law questions, the law of the jurisdiction with the most significant relationship to the transaction or event applies. — Also termed *significant-relationship theory; grouping-of-contacts theory.*

Centers for Disease Control and Prevention. An agency in the U.S. Department of Health and Human Services responsible for conducting medical research, promoting measures to prevent disease and injury, and responding to public-health emergencies. • This agency was established in 1999 when the Department of Health and Human Services was reorganized. Its forerunner was the Communicable Diseases Center, established in 1964. — Abbr. CDC.

centesima (sen-**tes**-ə-mə), *n.* & *adj.* [Latin "one-hundredth"] (18c) *Roman law.* The hundredth part; 1%. See USURAE CENTESIMAE.

Central American Court of Justice. A court created in 1962 under the 1951 Charter of the Organization of Central American States between Costa Rica, El Salvador, Guatemala, Honduras, and Nicaragua, to guarantee the rights of the various republics to maintain peace and harmony in their relations and to prevent recourse to the use of force. • This court's predecessor of the same name was created by a 1908 convention between the same parties, and dissolved in 1918 when the convention expired. It was re-created in 1962 by the Organization of Central American States. — Abbr. CAJC. — Also termed *Corte de Justicia Centroamericana.*

central bank. See BANK.

central clearing system. (1969) A method of facilitating securities transactions in which an agent or subsidiary of an exchange acts as a clearinghouse for member brokerage firms by clearing their checks, settling their accounts, and delivering their payments. • Most transactions are reflected solely by computerized book entries, and clearinghouse statements are submitted showing the net balance to be paid to reconcile the member firm's accounts.

Central Criminal Court. *English law.* The Crown Court sitting in London, commonly known as the Old Bailey. • The Central Criminal Court, created in 1834, has jurisdiction to try all indictable offenses committed in London and, exceptionally, those committed elsewhere in England and in Wales. See CROWN COURT.

Central Criminal Court Act. See PALMER'S ACT.

central government. See *federal government* (1) under GOVERNMENT (3).

Central Intelligence Agency. An independent federal agency that compiles intelligence information, conducts counterintelligence activities outside the United States, and advises the President and the National Security Council on matters of foreign intelligence and national security. • It was created by the National Security Act of 1947. 50 USCA §§ 401 et seq. — Abbr. CIA. See NATIONAL SECURITY COUNCIL.

centralism. See CENTRALIZATION (1).

centralization. (1801) **1.** A concentration of powers in one central organization; esp., a method of governing in a country or controlling an organization in which one group with all the power dictates to people in other places what to do. — Also termed *centralism*. **2.** The act or process of gathering people or things into one system or of bringing them under one control.

Central Office. *English law.* The primary office for most of England's courts. • The Central Office was established in 1879 to consolidate the masters and associates of the common-law courts, and the clerical functions of the Crown Office of the Queen's Bench Division, the Report and Enrollment offices of the Chancery Division, and several other offices.

centumviri (sen-**təm**-və-rɪ), *n. pl.* [Latin "hundred men"] (17c) *Roman law.* A court with jurisdiction to hear important cases, esp. those relating to inheritances and disputed wills. • The court originally consisted of 105 judges — 3 from each of the 35 tribes.

CEO. *abbr.* (1975) CHIEF EXECUTIVE OFFICER.

ceorl (chorl). (bef. 12c) *Hist.* A Saxon freeman who either possessed no landed property or held land of a thane by paying rent or providing services. • After the Norman Conquest, ceorls were reduced to the status of unfree villeins. Under Norman rule, the variant form of the word, *churl*, became associated with a base peasant, and soon acquired the connotation of a surly, coarse person (hence the modern meaning). — Also termed *churl*; *cirliscus*.

cepi (**see**-pɪ). [Latin] *Hist.* I have taken. • *Cepi* was often used in a capias return by an arresting sheriff, as in *cepi corpus et est in custodia* ("I have taken the defendant [or body] and he is in custody").

> "But for injuries committed *with force* to the person, property, or possession, of the plaintiff, the law, to punish the breach of the peace, and prevent its disturbance in the future, provided also a process against the defendant's *person*. . . . This process was called a *capias ad respondendum*, which at once authorised the sheriff to take the defendant, and imprison him till the return-day, and then produce him in court. . . . If by this process the defendant was arrested, the sheriff returned it with *cepi corpus* indorsed. But notwithstanding this writ commanded the sheriff to take and secure him till the return-day, he might, at his own peril, have let the defendant continue at large; though he was liable, in case of his non appearance in court, to make amends to the plaintiff in an action for an escape, or to be amerced by the court for the contempt, in not producing the body pursuant to the return he had made on the writ." George Crompton, *Practice Common-Placed: Rules and Cases of Practice in the Courts of King's Bench and Common Pleas* xlii–xliii (3d ed. 1787).

▸ ***cepi corpus et bail*** (**see**-pɪ **kor**-pəs et **bayl**). I have arrested and then released the defendant on a bail bond.

▸ ***cepi corpus et committitur*** (**see**-pɪ **kor**-pəs et kə-**mit**-ə-tər). I have arrested and committed the defendant (to prison).

▸ ***cepi corpus et est languidus*** (**see**-pɪ **kor**-pəs et est **lang**-gwə-dəs). I have arrested the defendant and he is sick. • This notation in a sheriff's return indicated that the defendant was too sick to be moved safely from the place of arrest.

▸ ***cepi corpus et paratum habeo*** (**see**-pɪ **kor**-pəs et pə-**ray**-təm **hay**-bee-oh). I have made an arrest and am ready to produce the defendant.

cepit (**see**-pit). [Latin] *Hist.* He took. • This was the main verb in a declaration in an action for trespass or replevin. See *replevin in cepit* under REPLEVIN.

cepit et abduxit (**see**-pit et ab-**duk**-sit). [Latin] *Hist.* He took and led away. • This declaration appeared in either a writ of trespass or a larceny indictment for theft of an animal.

cepit et asportavit (**see**-pit et as-por-**tay**-vit). [Latin] *Hist.* He took and carried away. • This declaration appeared in either a writ of trespass or a larceny indictment for a defendant's wrongfully carrying away goods.

cepit in alio loco (**see**-pit in **ay**-lee-oh **loh**-koh). [Latin] *Hist.* He took in another place. • This phrase appeared in a replevin-action pleading in which a defendant asserted that the property had been taken at a place other than that named in the plaintiff's declaration.

CEQ. *abbr.* COUNCIL ON ENVIRONMENTAL QUALITY.

cerage (**seer**-ij). See WAX SCOT.

cera impressa (**seer**-ə im-**pres**-ə). [Latin "impressed wax"] *Hist.* An impressed seal. • *Cera impressa* originally referred only to wax seals, but later came to include any impressed seal, regardless of the substance impressed. See SEAL.

> "The courts have held that an impression made on wafers or other adhesive substance capable of receiving an impression comes within the definition of '*cera impressa.*' If then wax be construed to be merely a general term including any substance capable of receiving and retaining the impression of a seal, paper, if it has that quality, may well be included in the category. The machine now used to impress public seals does not require any substance to receive or retain the impression, which is as well defined, as durable — less likely to be defaced than that made on wax. It is the seal which authenticates, not the substance impressed." William C. Anderson, *A Dictionary of Law* 926 (1889).

ceratium (si-**ray**-shee-əm). See WAX SCOT.

CERC. *abbr.* Certified emission-reduction credit. See EMISSION-REDUCTION CREDIT.

CERCLA (**sər**-klə). *abbr.* Comprehensive Environmental Response, Compensation, and Liability Act of 1980. • This statute holds responsible parties liable for the cost of cleaning up hazardous-waste sites. 42 USCA §§ 9601 et seq. See SUPERFUND.

ceremonial marriage. See MARRIAGE (3).

cert. *abbr.* CERTIORARI.

certain contract. See CONTRACT.

certainty. (14c) **1.** The quality, state, or condition of being indubitable or certain, esp. upon a showing of hard evidence. **2.** Anything that is known or has been proved to be true. See MORAL CERTAINTY. Cf. UNCERTAINTY.

▸ **certainty of intention.** (1846) *Trusts.* The clear, unambiguous purpose on the part of the donor or testator to create a trust.

▸ **certainty of law.** See *legal certainty*.

▸ **certainty of object.** (1854) *Trusts.* The clear, unambiguous expression of who is to be the beneficiary of a trust.

▸ **certainty of subject-matter.** (1892) *Trusts.* The clear, unambiguous fact that specific property is part of a donor's or testator's trust.

▸ **certainty of term.** (1851) The unambiguous expression of the time of commencement of a legal instrument, esp. a lease, as well as its maximum duration.

▸ **legal certainty.** (17c) The clarity, unambiguity, and stability in a system of law allowing those within the system to regulate their conduct according to the law's dictates. — Also termed *certainty of law.*

▸ **moral certainty.** See MORAL CERTAINTY.

certainty of intention. See CERTAINTY.

certainty of law. See *legal certainty* under CERTAINTY.

certainty of object. See CERTAINTY.

certainty of subject-matter. See CERTAINTY.

certainty of term. See CERTAINTY.

certans de damno vitando (**sər**-tanz dee **dam**-noh vɪ-**tan**-doh). [Law Latin] (18c) *Hist.* Striving to avoid a loss.

certans de lucro captando (**sər**-tanz dee **loo**-kroh kap-**tan**-doh). [Law Latin] (18c) *Hist.* Striving to make a gain; attempting to obtain an advantage.

certifiable, *adj.* (1846) **1.** Good enough to be approved according to established standards <certifiable as sterling silver>. **2.** Undeniably of a particular kind or status <a certifiable sociopath>. **3.** *Slang.* Crazy, esp. in a nondangerous way <I'd say he's certifiable>.

certificando de recognitione stapulae (sər-ti-fi-**kan**-doh dee rek-əg-nish-ee-**oh**-nee **stay**-pyə-lee). [Law Latin "by certifying the recognition of the statute staple"] (17c) *Hist.* A writ commanding the holder of certain commercial debt instruments (i.e., the mayor of the staple) to certify to the lord chancellor the existence and terms of a statute staple (i.e., a bond for commercial debt) wrongfully detained by a party to the bond. See STATUTE STAPLE.

certificat d'utilite. *Patents.* [French] UTILITY MODEL.

certificate, *n.* (15c) **1.** A document certifying the bearer's status or authorization to act in a specified way; esp., an official paper stating that one has completed a course of study or passed an examination <nursing certificate>. **2.** A notice by one court to another court of the action it has taken <when issuing its opinion, the Seventh Circuit sent a certificate to the Illinois Supreme Court>. **3.** A transferable security consisting of an official voucher showing ownership of a share, as in a joint-stock company. **4.** A document in which a fact is formally attested <death certificate>. See STOCK CERTIFICATE.

▸ **airman's certificate.** See AIRMAN'S CERTIFICATE.

▸ **allotment certificate.** See ALLOTMENT CERTIFICATE.

▸ **architect's certificate.** See ARCHITECT'S CERTIFICATE.

▸ **attorney's certificate. 1.** A certificate issued by a court to a duly qualified lawyer permitting him or her to practice in that court or in all the courts of that court's jurisdiction. **2.** *English law.* An official document of the Inland Revenue Service that the named lawyer has paid the annual license duty.

▸ **audit certificate.** A certificate issued by an auditor about the accuracy of accounts.

▸ **back-title certificate.** See BACK-TITLE LETTER.

▸ **benefit certificate.** (1880) A written obligation to pay a named person a specified amount upon stipulated conditions. • Benefit certificates are traditionally issued by fraternal associations, beneficial societies, and the like. They are so named because the document specifies the precise benefit to be paid.

▸ **birth certificate.** See BIRTH CERTIFICATE.

▸ **certificate into chancery.** (18c) *English law.* The decision of a common-law court on a legal question submitted by the chancery court.

▸ **certificate of acknowledgment.** See ACKNOWLEDGMENT (5).

▸ **certificate of amendment.** (1822) A document filed with a state corporation authority, usu. the secretary of state, reflecting changes made to a corporation's articles of incorporation.

▸ **certificate of appealability.** (1961) **1.** A trial judge's written representation, usu. on a specific court form, that a case or an issue may properly be appealed. **2.** Permission granted to a habeas petitioner that his or her case is appealable from a lower court because the petitioner has made a substantial showing that a constitutional right has been denied; in an appeal from the denial of federal habeas corpus relief, a document issued by a United States circuit judge certifying that the prisoner showed that a constitutional right may have been denied. 28 USCA § 2253(c)(2). • The prisoner does not have to show that the case would succeed on the merits, only that reasonable jurists would find the claim at least debatable. *Miller-El v. Cockrell*, 537 U.S. 322, 377, 123 S.Ct. 1029, 1039 (2003). If the certificate is not issued, no appeal is possible. 28 USCA § 2253 (c)(1); Fed. R. App. P. 22(b). — Abbr. COA. — Also termed (before 1996) *certificate of probable cause* (CPC); *certificate of reasonable doubt*; *writ of probable cause.*

▸ **certificate of arrival.** (1816) *Hist.* A government-issued immigration document proving when and where an alien entered the country.

▸ **certificate of assize.** (17c) *Hist. English law.* In England, a writ granting a retrial. • The certificate of assize has been replaced by a court order granting a new trial.

▸ **certificate of authentication.** See *certificate of authority* (1).

▸ **certificate of authority.** (1808) **1.** A document authenticating a notarized document that is being sent to another jurisdiction. • The certificate assures the out-of-state or foreign recipient that the notary public has a valid commission. — Also termed *certificate of capacity*; *certificate of official character*; *certificate of authentication*; *certificate of prothonotary*; *certificate of magistracy*; *apostille*; *verification.* **2.** A document issued by a state agency, usu. the secretary of state, granting an out-of-state corporation the right to do business in the state. — Also termed (in some states) *certificate of qualification.*

▸ **certificate of bad faith.** (1943) In a case in which a party has been allowed to proceed in a United States District Court *in forma pauperis*, a court-issued document attesting that an appeal by that party would be frivolous and therefore should not be allowed unless the party pays the ordinary filing fees and costs. 28 USCA § 1915 (a)(3). Cf. *certificate of good faith.*

▸ **certificate of capacity.** See *certificate of authority* (1).

▸ **certificate of citizenship.** (18c) A government-issued document certifying that a person is a citizen of the country. • In the United States, certificates of citizenship are issued by the Department of Homeland Security. Cf. NATURALIZATION CERTIFICATE.

▸ **certificate of conference.** (1979) A section of a pleading or motion filed with the court, usu. contained separately on a page near the end of the document, whereby the party filing the pleading or motion certifies to the court that the parties have attempted to resolve the matter, but that a judicial determination is needed because an agreement could not be reached. • Courts require some motions to have a certificate of conference attached to them. This compels the parties to try to resolve the issue themselves, without burdening the court unless necessary. Fed. R. Civ. P. 26(c), 37.

▸ **certificate of convenience and necessity.** (1896) A certificate issued by an administrative agency granting operating authority to a utility or transportation company. — Also termed *certificate of public convenience and necessity.*

▸ **certificate of conviction.** (17c) A signed and certified warrant authorizing a person's imprisonment after an adjudication of guilt.

▸ **certificate of correction.** (1892) **1.** A document that corrects an error in an official document, such as a certificate of incorporation. **2.** *Patents.* A document issued by the U.S. Patent and Trademark Office after a patentee or assignee rectifies a minor error unrelated to either questions of ownership or defects in a patent application's specifications or drawings. • The certificate can correct only three types of errors: (1) mistakes made by the PTO, (2) minor clerical or typographical errors, and (3) the omission or misidentification of an inventor's name. 35 USCA §§ 254–256. Cf. *reissue patent* under PATENT (3).

▸ **certificate of deposit.** See CERTIFICATE OF DEPOSIT.

▸ **certificate of discharge.** See SATISFACTION PIECE.

▸ **certificate of dishonor.** See NOTICE OF DISHONOR.

▸ **certificate of dismissal.** (1843) In some jurisdictions, a judicially created document memorializing that a prosecution or civil lawsuit has terminated in dismissal by the court.

▸ **certificate of dissolution.** (1900) A document issued by a state authority (usu. the secretary of state) certifying that a corporation has been dissolved.

▸ **certificate of earned eligibility.** (1987) *Criminal law.* In some states, a document issued by a board within the correctional system stating that a prisoner is eligible for parole because of successful participation in prison programs — often as a means of easing overcrowding in state prisons and jails. — Abbr. CEE.

▸ **certificate of election.** (17c) A document issued by a governor, board of elections, or other competent authority certifying that the named person has been duly elected.

▸ **certificate of good conduct.** (1928) *Criminal law.* **1.** A document issued by a department of corrections attesting to a prisoner's exemplary behavior while incarcerated, given so that the prisoner may receive some advantage in consideration for early parole, a work-release program, or eligibility for employment after release. **2.** See *certificate of relief from disabilities.* — Abbr. CGC.

▸ **certificate of good faith.** (1952) In a case in which a party has been allowed to proceed in a United States District Court *in forma pauperis*, a document issued by the court attesting that an appeal by the party would not be frivolous, so the party should not be required to pay costs or security. • District judges occasionally issue certificates of good faith even though they are never required: a party is allowed to appeal *in forma pauperis* unless the court issues a certificate of bad faith. 28 USCA § 1915(a)(3). Cf. *certificate of bad faith.*

▸ **certificate of holder of attached property.** A certificate given by a person who holds — but does not own — property attached by a sheriff. • The certificate sets forth the holder's interest in the property.

▸ **certificate of incorporation.** (18c) **1.** A document issued by a state authority (usu. the secretary of state) granting a corporation its legal existence and the right to function as a corporation. — Also termed *charter*; *corporate charter.* **2.** ARTICLES OF INCORPORATION.

▸ **certificate of indebtedness. 1.** DEBENTURE (2). **2.** *Hist.* TREASURY BILL. **3.** CERTIFICATE OF DEPOSIT (1).

▸ **certificate of insurance.** (1852) A document acknowledging that an insurance policy has been written, and setting forth in general terms what the policy covers.

▸ **certificate of interest.** (1871) *Oil & gas.* A document evidencing a fractional or percentage ownership in oil-and-gas production.

▸ **certificate of magistracy.** See *certificate of authority* (1).

▸ **certificate of marriage.** See MARRIAGE CERTIFICATE.

▸ **certificate of merit.** (1874) **1.** *Archaic.* A certificate granted by the President of the United States to a soldier who has performed with distinction. • It traditionally entitles the recipient to extra pay. **2.** A certificate, signed by the plaintiff's attorney and filed with the complaint in a civil suit, declaring that the plaintiff's attorney has conferred with at least one competent expert and afterward concluded that the suit has merit. • Many states have a law mandating certificates of merit in certain types of cases, such as professional malpractice. The law's purpose is to weed out frivolous claims as early as possible. In those states, if a certificate is not filed with the complaint, the action is usu. dismissed. If the law requires the certificate to be signed under oath or penalty of perjury, it is sometimes called an *affidavit of merit.*

▸ **certificate of naturalization.** See NATURALIZATION CERTIFICATE.

▸ **certificate of occupancy.** (1880) A document indicating that a building complies with zoning and building ordinances, and is ready to be occupied. • A certificate of occupancy is often required before title can be transferred and the building occupied.

▸ **certificate of official character.** See *certificate of authority* (1).

▸ **certificate of organization.** See ARTICLES OF ORGANIZATION (2).

▸ **certificate of origin.** (1803) An official document required by some countries upon the entry of imported goods, listing the place of production and what goods are included, to be certified by a customs or consular officer.

▸ **certificate of probable cause.** See *certificate of appealability.*

▸ **certificate of proof.** See PROOF OF ACKNOWLEDGMENT.

▸ **certificate of protest.** See NOTICE OF DISHONOR.

▸ **certificate of prothonotary.** See *certificate of authority* (1).

▸ **certificate of public convenience and necessity.** See *certificate of convenience and necessity.*

▸ **certificate of purchase.** (1810) A document reflecting a successful bid for property at a judicial sale. • The bidder receives a property deed if the land is not redeemed or if the sale is confirmed by court order. — Also termed *certificate of sale.*

▸ **certificate of qualification.** See *certificate of authority* (2).

▸ **certificate of readiness.** See STATEMENT OF READINESS.

▸ **certificate of reasonable doubt. 1.** See *certificate of appealability.* **2.** *Hist. Criminal procedure.* In New York, a judge's certificate, issued to an appellate court, stating that there was reasonable doubt about whether a conviction should stand.

▸ **certificate of redemption.** (1834) A document issued by a sheriff or other statutorily designated officer to a debtor whose property has been foreclosed as evidence that the debtor paid the redemption price for the foreclosed property. See *statutory redemption* under REDEMPTION.

▸ **certificate of registration.** (1880) **1.** *Copyright.* A U.S. Copyright Office document approving a copyright application and stating the approved work's registration date and copyright registration number. **2.** *Trademarks.* A document affirming that the U.S. Patent and Trademark Office has allowed and recorded a trademark or servicemark. • The certificate identifies (1) the registered mark, (2) the date of first use, (3) the type of product or service the mark applies to, (4) the registration number and date, (5) the registration's term, (6) the original application date, and (7) any conditions or limitations on registration.

▸ **certificate of registry.** (18c) *Maritime law.* A document certifying that a ship has been registered as required by law. See REGISTRY (2).

▸ **certificate of rehabilitation.** (1948) **1.** A document issued in some states by a court or other authorized governmental agency, such as a parole board, as evidence that a convicted offender is entitled to recover at least some of the rights and privileges of citizenship. • The terms and conditions under which certificates of rehabilitation are issued vary widely among the states that use them. Some states, such as New York, issue different kinds of rehabilitation certificates based on the number or type of convictions. **2.** A document issued by a (usu. local) government on the renovation, restoration, preservation, or rehabilitation of a historic building. • The certificate usu. entitles the property owner to favorable tax treatment. **3.** A document attesting that substandard housing has been satisfactorily renovated and meets housing-code standards.

▸ **certificate of relief from civil disabilities.** See *certificate of relief from disabilities.*

▸ **certificate of relief from disabilities.** (1967) A document issued by a court or parole board as a matter of postconviction relief for a person who has committed one or more misdemeanors or one felony, to restore the person's civil rights and so that the person can prove to potential employers and licensing authorities that he or she has been rehabilitated. • A person who has such a certificate cannot be denied employment or a license on the grounds of the conviction. When a person receives such a document after committing two or more felonies, it is termed a *certificate of good conduct.* — Abbr. CRD. — Also termed *certificate of relief from civil disabilities.*

▸ **certificate of sale.** See *certificate of purchase.*

▸ **certificate of service.** (1819) **1.** A section of a pleading or motion filed with the court, usu. contained separately on the last page, in which the filing party certifies to the court that a copy has been mailed to or otherwise served on all other parties. • A certificate of service is usu. not included with the initial pleading that the plaintiff files to begin a suit, because that pleading is usu. filed before it is served (although the plaintiff may be required to file proof of service). Other pleadings and motions are usu. required to have a certificate of service. Fed. R. Civ. P. 5(d). — Also termed *proof of service.* **2.** A document issued by the Secretary of Defense in lieu of an original discharge that has been lost or destroyed.

▸ **certificate of stock.** See STOCK CERTIFICATE.

▸ **certificate of title.** (1831) A document indicating ownership of real or personal property. UCC § 9-102(a)(10). • This document usu. identifies any liens or other encumbrances.

▸ **certificate of transfer.** (1891) The contractually agreed transference of a patent application from one court to another.

▸ **clearinghouse certificate. 1.** A written guaranty by a clearinghouse; specif., a document traditionally used during a financial crisis to enable banks or trust companies to discharge their mutual obligations without a transfer of cash. **2.** *English law.* A document evidencing the balancing of accounts between banks.

▸ **collateral trust certificate.** See *collateral trust bond* (1) under BOND (3).

▸ **customhouse certificate.** A certificate issued to an importer by a customhouse when goods are accepted in bond, entitling the importer to recover duties paid if the goods are later exported.

▸ **death certificate.** See DEATH CERTIFICATE.

▸ **deposit certificate.** See CERTIFICATE OF DEPOSIT (1).

▸ **digital certificate.** See DIGITAL CERTIFICATE.

▸ **Employee's Withholding Allowance Certificate.** See W-4 FORM.

▸ **equipment trust certificate.** See EQUIPMENT TRUST CERTIFICATE.

▸ **estoppel certificate.** See ESTOPPEL CERTIFICATE.

▸ **face-amount certificate.** See STOCK CERTIFICATE.

▸ **facultative certificate.** See FACULTATIVE CERTIFICATE.

▸ **fully paid face-amount certificate.** See *face-amount certificate* under STOCK CERTIFICATE.

▸ **gold certificate.** See GOLD CERTIFICATE.

▸ **headright certificate.** See HEADRIGHT CERTIFICATE.

▸ **insurance certificate.** See INSURANCE CERTIFICATE.

▸ **interim certificate.** See INTERIM CERTIFICATE.

▸ **jumbo certificate.** See CERTIFICATE OF DEPOSIT.

▸ **land certificate.** See LAND CERTIFICATE.

▸ **land trust certificate.** See LAND TRUST CERTIFICATE.

▸ **loan certificate.** (1824) A certificate that a clearinghouse issues to a borrowing bank in an amount equal to a specified percentage of the value of the borrowing bank's collateral on deposit with the clearinghouse's loan committee.

▸ **marriage certificate.** See MARRIAGE CERTIFICATE.

▸ **mortgage certificate.** See MORTGAGE CERTIFICATE.

▸ **naturalization certificate.** See NATURALIZATION CERTIFICATE.

▸ **negotiable certificate of deposit.** See CERTIFICATE OF DEPOSIT.

▸ **no-setoff certificate.** See WAIVER OF DEFENSES.

▸ **notarial protest certificate.** See PROTEST CERTIFICATE.

▸ **notary's certificate.** See NOTARY'S CERTIFICATE.

▸ **partnership certificate.** See PARTNERSHIP CERTIFICATE.

▸ **periodic-payment-plan certificate.** See STOCK CERTIFICATE.

▸ **protest certificate.** See PROTEST CERTIFICATE.

▸ **receiver's certificate.** See RECEIVER'S CERTIFICATE.

▸ **reexamination certificate.** See REEXAMINATION CERTIFICATE.

▸ **share certificate.** See STOCK CERTIFICATE.

▸ **silver certificate.** See SILVER CERTIFICATE.

▸ **stock certificate.** See STOCK CERTIFICATE.

▸ **tax certificate.** See TAX CERTIFICATE.

▸ **treasury certificate.** See TREASURY CERTIFICATE.

▸ **trust certificate.** See EQUIPMENT TRUST CERTIFICATE.

▸ **voting-trust certificate.** See VOTING-TRUST CERTIFICATE.

certificate creditor. See CREDITOR.

certificated security. See SECURITY (4).

certificate into chancery. See CERTIFICATE.

certificate land. See LAND.

certificate of acknowledgment. See ACKNOWLEDGMENT (5).

certificate of amendment. See CERTIFICATE.

certificate of appealability. See CERTIFICATE.

certificate of arrival. See CERTIFICATE.

certificate of assize. See CERTIFICATE.

certificate of authentication. See *certificate of authority* (1) under CERTIFICATE.

certificate of authority. See CERTIFICATE.

certificate of bad faith. See CERTIFICATE.

certificate of capacity. See *certificate of authority* (1) under CERTIFICATE.

certificate of citizenship. See CERTIFICATE.

certificate of conference. See CERTIFICATE.

certificate of convenience and necessity. See CERTIFICATE.

certificate of conviction. See CERTIFICATE.

certificate of correction. See CERTIFICATE.

certificate of deposit. (1846) **1.** A banker's certificate acknowledging the receipt of money and promising to repay the depositor. — Also termed *certificate of indebtedness; deposit certificate.* **2.** A bank document showing the existence of a time deposit, usu. one that pays interest. — Abbr. CD.

▸ **jumbo certificate.** (1978) A certificate of deposit of $100,000 or more. — Also termed *jumbo.*

▸ **negotiable certificate of deposit.** (1845) A security issued by a financial institution as a short-term source of funds, usu. with a fixed interest rate and maturity of one year or less.

certificate of discharge. See SATISFACTION PIECE.

certificate of dishonor. See NOTICE OF DISHONOR.

certificate of dismissal. See CERTIFICATE.

certificate of dissolution. See CERTIFICATE.

certificate of earned eligibility. See CERTIFICATE.

certificate of election. See CERTIFICATE.

certificate of good conduct. See CERTIFICATE.

certificate of good faith. See CERTIFICATE.

certificate of holder of attached property. See CERTIFICATE.

certificate of incorporation. See CERTIFICATE.

certificate of indebtedness. **1.** DEBENTURE (2). **2.** *Hist.* TREASURY BILL. **3.** CERTIFICATE OF DEPOSIT (1).

certificate of insurance. See CERTIFICATE.

certificate of interest. See CERTIFICATE.

certificate of magistracy. See *certificate of authority* (1) under CERTIFICATE.

certificate of marriage. See MARRIAGE CERTIFICATE.

certificate of merit. See CERTIFICATE.

certificate of naturalization. See NATURALIZATION CERTIFICATE.

certificate of occupancy. See CERTIFICATE.

certificate of official character. See *certificate of authority* (1) under CERTIFICATE.

certificate of organization. See ARTICLES OF ORGANIZATION (2).

certificate of origin. See CERTIFICATE.

certificate of probable cause. See *certificate of appealability* under CERTIFICATE.

certificate of proof. See PROOF OF ACKNOWLEDGMENT.

certificate of protest. See NOTICE OF DISHONOR.

certificate of prothonotary. See *certificate of authority* (1) under CERTIFICATE.

certificate of public convenience and necessity. See *certificate of convenience and necessity* under CERTIFICATE.

certificate of purchase. See CERTIFICATE.

certificate of qualification. See *certificate of authority* (2) under CERTIFICATE.

certificate of readiness. See STATEMENT OF READINESS.

certificate of reasonable doubt. See CERTIFICATE.

certificate of redemption. See CERTIFICATE.

certificate of registration. See CERTIFICATE.

certificate of registry. See CERTIFICATE.

certificate of rehabilitation. See CERTIFICATE.

certificate of relief from civil disabilities. See *certificate of relief from disabilities* under CERTIFICATE.

certificate of relief from disabilities. See CERTIFICATE.

certificate of sale. See *certificate of purchase* under CERTIFICATE.

certificate of service. See CERTIFICATE.

certificate of stock. See STOCK CERTIFICATE.

certificate of title. See CERTIFICATE.

certificate of transfer. See CERTIFICATE.

certification, *n.* (15c) **1.** The act of attesting; esp., the process of giving someone or something an official document stating that a specified standard has been satisfied. **2.** The state of having been attested. **3.** An attested statement; esp., an official document stating that someone is allowed to do a certain job, that something is of good quality, etc. **4.** The writing on the face of a check by which it is certified. **5.** A procedure by which a federal appellate court asks the U.S. Supreme Court or the highest state court to review a question of law arising in a case pending before the appellate court and on which it needs guidance. • Certification is commonly used with state courts, but the U.S. Supreme Court has steadily restricted the number of cases it reviews by certification. *See* 28 USCA § 1254(2). Cf. CERTIORARI.

▸ **People's certification.** In New York practice, a prosecutor's written statement on appeal that the prosecution will be unable to proceed with the case without the admission of certain suppressed evidence. • In New York, such a certification is required when the prosecution seeks an appeal to overturn an order suppressing evidence.

▸ **union certification.** See UNION CERTIFICATION.

certification authority. (1996) An organization that issues digital certificates and maintains a database of certificates available on the Internet. • Many states have licensing laws for certification authorities. — Abbr. CA. — Also termed *certifying authority.*

certification hearing. See *transfer hearing* under HEARING.

certification mark. See *certification trademark* under TRADEMARK.

certification of bargaining agent. See UNION CERTIFICATION.

certification of labor union. See UNION CERTIFICATION.

certification to state court. (1980) The procedure by which a federal court of appeals defers deciding a novel question of state law by certifying the question to the highest court of the state. See CERTIFICATION (5).

certification trademark. See TRADEMARK.

certified agreement. See AGREEMENT.

certified check. See CHECK.

certified copy. See COPY (1).

certified emission-reduction credit. See EMISSION-REDUCTION CREDIT.

certified file history. (1963) *Patents.* A patent application together with records of all proceedings and correspondence related to its prosecution, as certified by the U.S. Patent and Trademark Office for appeals, arbitration, and other postprosecution proceedings. Cf. FILE WRAPPER.

certified financial planner. See FINANCIAL PLANNER.

certified financial statement. See FINANCIAL STATEMENT (1).

certified juvenile. See JUVENILE.

certified mail. See MAIL.

certified military lawyer. See LAWYER.

certified public accountant. See ACCOUNTANT (1).

certified question. (1835) A point of law on which a federal appellate court seeks guidance from either the U.S. Supreme Court or the highest state court by the procedure of certification.

certifier. (16c) A person whose job responsibilities include issuing a certificate for qualified candidates.

certify, *vb.* (14c) **1.** To authenticate or verify in writing. **2.** To attest as being true or as meeting certain criteria. **3.** (Of a court) to issue an order allowing a class of litigants to maintain a class action; to create (a class) for purposes of a class action. See CERTIFICATION. Cf. DECERTIFY. — **certified,** *adj.*

certifying authority. See CERTIFICATION AUTHORITY.

certiorari (sər-shee-ə-**rair**-I *or* -**rair**-ee *or* -**rah**-ree). [Law Latin "to be more fully informed"] (15c) An extraordinary writ issued by an appellate court, at its discretion, directing a lower court to deliver the record in the case for review. • The writ evolved from one of the prerogative writs of the English Court of King's Bench, and in the United States it became a general appellate remedy. The U.S. Supreme Court uses certiorari to review most of the cases that it decides to hear. — Abbr. cert. — Also termed *writ of certiorari.* Cf. CERTIFICATION (5).

> "The established method by which the Court of King's Bench from the earliest times exercised superintendence over the due observance of their limitations by inferior courts, checked the usurpation of jurisdiction, and maintained the supremacy of the royal courts, was by writs of prohibition and certiorari. A proceeding by writ of certiorari (cause to be certified) is a special proceeding by which a superior court requires some inferior tribunal, board, or judicial officer to transmit the record of its proceedings for review, for excess of jurisdiction. It is similar to a writ of error, in that it is a proceeding in a higher court to superintend and review judicial acts, but it only lies in cases not appealable by writ of error or otherwise." Benjamin J. Shipman, *Handbook of Common-Law Pleading* § 340, at 541 (Henry Winthrop Ballantine ed., 3d ed. 1923).

> "The discretionary writ of certiorari has come to control access to almost all branches of Supreme Court jurisdiction. Appeal jurisdiction has been narrowly limited, and certification of questions from federal courts of appeals has fallen into almost complete desuetude. Certiorari control over the cases that come before the Court enables the Court to define its own institutional role." Charles Alan Wright et al., *Federal Practice and Procedure* § 4004, at 22 (2d ed. 1996).

> "The writ of *certiorari* (from the Latin *certiorarie* 'in form') is used today in the United States as a general vehicle of discretionary appeal. Historically, however, the writ had a much narrower function. It lay only to inferior courts and

only to demand that the record be 'certified' and sent to the King's Bench to see if that [inferior] court had exceeded its power in particular cases. It was most frequently used to review criminal indictments and local administrative orders, and was often used to examine the statutory authority for acts of administrative bodies created by statute." Daniel R. Coquillette, *The Anglo-American Legal Heritage* 248 (1999).

▸ ***certiorari facias*** (**fay**-shee-əs). [Latin "a cause to be certified"] (18c) The command of a writ of certiorari, referring to certification of the court record for review.

▸ **limited certiorari.** See *narrow certiorari.*

▸ **narrow certiorari.** (1947) Certiorari limited to reviewing questions about jurisdiction, the regularity of the proceeding, the exercise of unauthorized powers, or constitutional rights. • Narrow certiorari is usu. applied to appeals from arbitrators' awards or the decisions of state agencies. It is most common in Pennsylvania. — Also termed *limited certiorari.*

certiorari petition. See PETITION (1).

cert pool. (1975) A group of clerks in the U.S. Supreme Court who read petitions for certiorari and write memorandums for the justices with a synopsis of the facts and issues and often a recommendation of whether a grant of certiorari is warranted.

"The cert pool is not without its critics. Some commentators have contended that inexperienced clerks in the cert pool give short shrift to cases of practical importance in favor of cases presenting esoteric legal questions. . . . Other critics have contended that the cert pool does little to advance its stated goal of efficiency. . . . Pool clerks frequently must take the time to formally summarize petitions that would occasion only a brief, candid recommendation to 'deny' from their own Justices." Robert L. Stern et al., *Supreme Court Practice* 291 (8th ed. 2002).

certum an et quantum debeatur? (**sər**-təm an et **kwon**-təm dee-bee-**ay**-tər). [Law Latin] *Hist.* Is it certain whether there is a debt due at all, and how much is owed? • These were the two questions that had to be resolved before a defendant could make a plea in compensation.

certus plegius (sər-təs **plee**-jee-əs). [Latin "sure pledge"] See SALVUS PLEGIUS.

certworthy, *adj.* (1965) *Slang.* (Of a case or issue) deserving of review by writ of certiorari. — **certworthiness,** *n.*

cess (ses), *n.* (16c) *Hist.* **1.** *English law.* An assessment or tax. **2.** *Scots law.* A land tax. — Also spelled *cesse; sess.*

cessate grant. See GRANT (4).

cessate probate. See *cessate grant* under GRANT (4).

cessation-of-production clause. (1965) *Oil & gas.* A lease provision that specifies what the lessee must do to maintain the lease if production stops. • The purpose of the clause is to avoid the uncertainties of the temporary-cessation-of-production doctrine. Cf. TEMPORARY-CESSATION-OF-PRODUCTION DOCTRINE.

cessavit per biennium (se-**say**-vit pər bɪ-**en**-ee-əm). [Latin "he ceased for two years"] (16c) *Hist.* A writ of right available to a landlord to recover land from a tenant who has failed to pay rent or provide prescribed services for a two-year period. • The writ could also be used to recover land donated to a religious order if the order has failed to perform certain spiritual services. — Also termed *cessavit.*

cesse. See CESS.

cesser (**ses**-ər). (16c) **1.** *Hist.* A tenant whose failure to pay rent or perform prescribed services gives the landowner the right to recover possession of the land. — Also spelled *cessor; cessure.* **2.** The termination of a right or interest.

"A proviso of *cesser* is usually annexed to long terms, raised by mortgage, marriage settlement, or annuity, whereby the term is declared to be determinable on the happening of a certain event; and until the event provided for in the declaration of *cesser* has occurred, the term continues." 4 James Kent, *Commentaries on American Law* *90 (George Comstock ed., 11th ed. 1866).

"The cesser of a term, annuity or the like takes place when it determines or comes to an end. The expression was formerly chiefly used with reference to long terms of years created by a settlement for the purpose of securing portions, etc., given to the objects of the settlement. In such cases, it was usual to introduce a proviso that the term should cease when the trusts thereof were satisfied (as, for example, on the death of the annuitant where the term was created to secure an annuity). This was called a proviso for cesser." *Jowitt's Dictionary of English Law* 308 (John Burke ed., 2d ed. 1977).

cesser clause. (1881) *Maritime law.* A clause in a charterparty by which the charterer, when the cargo is loaded, ceases to be liable for freight, the shipowner then relying on the shipowner's lien over the cargo. See CHARTERPARTY.

cesset executio (**ses**-ət ek-sə-**kyoo**-shee-oh). [Latin "let execution stay"] (17c) An order directing a stay of execution.

cesset processus (**ses**-ət proh-**ses**-əs). [Latin "let process stay"] (17c) An order entered on the record directing a stay of a legal proceeding.

cessio (**sesh**-ee-oh). [Latin "cession"] A relinquishment or assignment; CESSION.

cessio actionum (**sesh**-ee-oh ak-shee-**oh**-nəm). [Latin] *Roman law.* The assignment of an obligation by allowing a third party to (1) sue on the obligation in the name of the party entitled to it, and (2) retain the proceeds.

cessio bonorum (**sesh**-ee-oh bə-**nor**-əm). [Latin "cession of goods"] (16c) *Roman law.* An assignment of a debtor's property to creditors.

"It was the Roman equivalent of modern bankruptcy. . . . [O]ne who thus made *cessio bonorum* would not become *infamis*, was never liable in future beyond his means, for the old debts, and was not liable to personal seizure thereafter in respect of them." W.W. Buckland, *A Manual of Roman Private Law* 388 (2d ed. 1939).

cessio fori (**sesh**-ee-oh **for**-ɪ). [Latin] *Hist.* The giving up of business; the act of becoming bankrupt.

cessio in jure (**sesh**-ee-oh in **joor**-ee). [Latin "transfer in law"] (18c) *Roman law.* A fictitious action brought to convey property, whereby the claimant demanded certain property, the owner did not contest the claim, and a magistrate awarded the property to the claimant.

cession (**sesh**-ən). (15c) **1.** The act of relinquishing property rights. **2.** *Int'l law.* The relinquishment or transfer of land from one country to another, esp. after a war, as part of the price of peace. **3.** The land so relinquished or transferred.

cessionary bankrupt. See BANKRUPT.

cessment (**ses**-mənt). (16c) *Hist.* An assessment or tax.

cessor. See CESSER.

cessure. See CESSER.

cestui (**set**-ee *or* **ses**-twee). [French "he who"] (16c) *Archaic.* A beneficiary. — Also spelled *cestuy.*

cestui que trust (**set**-ee [*or* **ses**-twee] kee [*or* kə] **trəst**). [Law French "the one for whom [is] the trust"] (18c) *Archaic.* Someone who possesses equitable rights in property, usu. receiving the rents, issues, and profits from it; BENEFICIARY. — Also termed *fide-commissary; fidei-commissarius.* Pl. **cestuis que trust** or (erroneously) **cestuis que trustent.**

> "[A]n alternative name for the beneficiary is *'cestui que trust,'* an elliptical phrase meaning 'he [for] whose [benefit the] trust [was created].' In this phrase *cestui* is pronounced 'settee' (with the accent on the first syllable), *que* is pronounced 'kee,' and trust as in English. Grammatically the plural should be *cestuis que trust* (pronounced like the singular); but by an understandable mistake it is sometimes written *cestuis que trustent,* as if trust were a verb." Glanville Williams, *Learning the Law* 10 (11th ed. 1982).

cestui que use (**set**-ee [*or* **ses**-twee] kee [*or* kə] **yoos**). [Law French "the one for whom [is] the use"] (16c) *Archaic.* The person for whose use and benefit property is being held by another, who holds the legal title to the property. Pl. **cestuis que use** or (erroneously) **cestuis que usent.**

> "The basis of this institution was the transfer of property to a trusted friend, who was to hold it not for personal benefit but for the purpose of carrying out the transferor's instructions. The person to whom the land was conveyed for this purpose was the 'feoffee to uses'; the person for whose benefit the land was conveyed — the beneficiary — was the 'cestui que use' . . . , from the law French 'cestui a que use le feoffment fuit fait.'" Peter Butt, *Land Law* § 702, at 97 (3d ed. 1996).

cestui que vie (**set**-ee [*or* **ses**-twee] kee [*or* kə] **vee**). [Law French "the one for whose life"] (17c) *Archaic.* The person whose life measures the duration of a trust, gift, estate, or insurance contract. Cf. MEASURING LIFE.

> "[L]et us assume that A instead transfers 'to E *for the life of* A.' Since A has used his own life as the measuring life of E's estate, A has given away all that he had. Because E's estate is measured by the life of someone other than himself, his estate is called an estate *pur autre vie.* A, whose life is the measuring life, is called the *cestui que vie.*" Thomas F. Bergin & Paul G. Haskell, *Preface to Estates in Land and Future Interests* 36 (2d ed. 1984).

cestuy. See CESTUI.

ceteris paribus (**set**-ə-ris **par**-ə-bəs). [Latin] (16c) Other things being equal. — Also spelled *caeteris paribus.*

ceteris tacentibus (**set**-ə-ris ta-**sen**-tə-bəs). [Latin] *Hist.* The others being silent. • This phrase appeared in serially printed law reports after an opinion by one judge. It referred to the judges who did not vote or express an opinion. — Also spelled *caeteris tacentibus.* See SERIATIM.

cf. *abbr.* [Latin *confer*] (1850) Compare. • As a citation signal, *cf.* directs the reader's attention to another authority or section of the work in which contrasting, analogous, or explanatory statements may be found.

CF. *abbr.* COST AND FREIGHT.

CFC. See *controlled foreign corporation* under CORPORATION.

CFO. *abbr.* CHIEF FINANCIAL OFFICER.

CFP. *abbr.* Certified financial planner. See FINANCIAL PLANNER.

CFPB. *abbr.* CONSUMER FINANCIAL PROTECTION BUREAU.

CFR. *abbr.* **1.** CODE OF FEDERAL REGULATIONS. **2.** COST AND FREIGHT.

CFTC. *abbr.* COMMODITY FUTURES TRADING COMMISSION.

CGC. *abbr.* See *certificate of good conduct* under CERTIFICATE.

CGE. *abbr.* See *computer-generated evidence* under EVIDENCE.

CGL insurance. *abbr.* See *commercial general-liability insurance* under INSURANCE.

ch. *abbr.* **1.** Chapter. **2.** Chancellor. **3.** Chancery. **4.** Chief.

Chace Act. *Hist. Copyright.* An 1891 statute giving U.S. copyright protection to the citizens of other countries that in turn gave a similar degree of reciprocal protection to U.S. citizens. • The Act was invoked by presidential order or by treaty, primarily with European countries. Under the Act's manufacturing clause, English-language books and other printed matter had to be produced in the U.S. or Canada in order to qualify for domestic protection. — Also termed *1891 Copyright Amendment Act.*

chad. (1930) The small bit of precut paper that is attached to a punch-card ballot by several points and punched out by a voter to cast a vote. • Because most punch-card ballots are machine-read, the chad must be completely separated from the ballot for the vote to be counted. The results of the closely contested 2000 presidential election were delayed for several weeks because more than 40,000 ballots with partially attached chads had to be hand-counted.

▸ **dimpled chad.** (2000) A chad that is bulging but not pierced, with all its points attached to the ballot. — Sometimes termed *pregnant chad.*

▸ **hanging chad.** (2000) A chad that is attached to the ballot by a single point.

▸ **pregnant chad.** See *dimpled chad.*

▸ **swinging-door chad.** (2000) A chad that is attached to the ballot by two points.

▸ **tri-chad.** (2000) A chad that is attached to the ballot by three points.

chafewax (**chayf**-waks). (17c) *Hist.* A chancery officer who heated (or *chafed*) wax to seal writs, commissions, and other instruments. • The office was abolished in 1852. — Also spelled *chaffwax.*

chaffer (**chaf**-ər), *vb.* (18c) To bargain; negotiate; haggle; dicker. For *offer to chaffer,* see INVITATION TO NEGOTIATE.

chain. *Archaic. Property.* A unit of land measurement equal to 66 feet or 100 links. • This unit is sometimes found in deeds, esp. older ones. See LINK (2); ROD.

chain-certificate method. (1966) The procedure for authenticating a foreign official record by the party seeking to admit the record as evidence at trial. *See* Fed. R. Civ. P. 44.

chain conspiracy. See CONSPIRACY.

chain gang. (1833) A group of prisoners chained together to prevent their escape while they work outside a prison.

chain of causation. (18c) **1.** A series of events each caused by the previous one. **2.** The causal connection between a cause and its effects. Cf. CAUSATION.

chain-of-causation rule. (1981) *Workers' compensation.* The principle that an employee's suicide is compensable under workers'-compensation statutes if the employee suffered an earlier work-related injury that led to a mental disorder resulting in the suicide.

chain of custody. (1947) **1.** The movement and location of real evidence, and the history of those persons who had it in their custody, from the time it is obtained to the time it is presented in court. **2.** The history of a chattel's possession. — Also termed *chain of possession.*

chain of title. (18c) **1.** The ownership history of a piece of land, from its first owner to the present one. — Also termed *line of title; string of title.* **2.** The ownership history of commercial paper, traceable through the indorsements. • For the holder to have good title, every prior negotiation must have been proper. If a necessary indorsement is missing or forged, the chain of title is broken and no later transferee can become a holder.

chain-referral scheme. See PYRAMID SCHEME.

chair. (17c) *Parliamentary law.* **1.** A deliberative assembly's presiding officer <the chair calls for order>. See PRESIDE.

> "The term *the chair* refers to the person in a meeting who is actually presiding at the time, whether that person is the regular presiding officer or not. The same term also applies to the presiding officer's station in the hall from which he or she presides, which should not be permitted to be used by other members as a place from which to make reports or speak in debate during a meeting . . . ." Henry M. Robert, *Robert's Rules of Order Newly Revised* § 47, at 433 (10th ed. 2000).

▸ **chair by decree.** A chair appointed by an outside authority rather than elected by the deliberative assembly being presided over.

▸ **chair pro tempore.** (1835) A chair elected or appointed during or in anticipation of the regular presiding officer's (or officers') absence from the chair, and whose service ends when a regular presiding officer resumes the chair. — Often shortened to *chair pro tem.* See PRO TEMPORE.

2. The presiding officer's seat <take the chair>. **3.** The officer who heads an organization <the treasurer reports directly to the chair>. See CHAIR OF THE BOARD. **4.** See *presiding arbitrator* under ARBITRATOR. — Also termed *chairman* (in senses 1 & 3); *chairwoman* (of a female chair, in senses 1 & 3); *chairperson* (in senses 1 & 3); *moderator* (in sense 1); *president* (in senses 1 & 3); *presiding officer* (in sense 1); *speaker* (in sense 1). — **chair,** *vb.*

chairman. See CHAIR.

Chairman of Committee of the Whole House. The member of Parliament who presides over the House of Commons when it is sitting in committee.

chair of the board. (1839) The preeminent member of a board of directors, responsible for leading the firm's other officers and executives, presiding over board meetings, and ensuring that the firm's duties to shareholders are being fulfilled by acting as a link between the board and the upper management. — Abbr. COB. — Also termed *chairman of the board;* (of a female chair) *chairwoman of the board.*

chairperson. See CHAIR.

chairwoman. See CHAIR.

challenge, *n.* (14c) **1.** An act or instance of formally questioning the legality or legal qualifications of a person, action, or thing <a challenge to the opposing party's expert witness>.

▸ **as-applied challenge.** (1974) A claim that a law or governmental policy, though constitutional on its face, is unconstitutional as applied, usu. because of a discriminatory effect; a claim that a statute is unconstitutional on the facts of a particular case or in its application to a particular party. Cf. *facial challenge.*

▸ ***Batson* challenge.** (1987) *Procedure.* An objection that an opposing party has used a peremptory challenge to exclude a potential juror on the basis of race, ethnicity, or sex. • It is named for *Batson v. Kentucky,* 476 U.S. 79, 106 S.Ct. 1712 (1986), a criminal case in which the prosecution struck potential jurors on the basis of race. The principle of *Batson* was extended in later Supreme Court cases to civil litigants (*Edmonson v. Leesville Concrete Co.,* 500 U.S. 614, 111 S.Ct. 2077 (1991)) and to criminal-defense attorneys (*Georgia v. McCollum,* 505 U.S. 42, 112 S.Ct. 2348 (1992)). The Court also applied it to peremptory challenges based on a juror's sex (*J.E.B. v. Alabama,* 511 U.S. 127, 114 S.Ct. 1419 (1994)). *See* Fed. R. Civ. P. 47(b). See BATSON RULE.

▸ **constitutional challenge.** (1936) A claim that a law or governmental action is unconstitutional.

▸ **facial challenge.** (1973) A claim that a statute is unconstitutional on its face — that is, that it always operates unconstitutionally. Cf. *as-applied challenge.*

▸ **reverse *Batson* challenge.** (1992) A prosecution objection to the defense's attempted exercise of a peremptory challenge against a juror on grounds that the challenge may have been based on race or some other improper ground.

2. A party's request that a judge disqualify a potential juror or an entire jury panel <the personal-injury plaintiff used his last challenge to disqualify a neurosurgeon>. — Also termed *jury challenge.*

▸ **causal challenge.** See *challenge for cause.*

▸ **challenge for cause.** (17c) A party's challenge supported by a specified reason, such as bias or prejudice, that would disqualify that potential juror. — Also termed *for-cause challenge; for-cause; causal challenge; general challenge; challenge to the poll.*

▸ **challenge *propter affectum*** (**prop**-tər ə-**fek**-təm). (18c) A challenge based on a claim that some circumstance, such as kinship with a party, renders the potential juror incompetent to serve in the particular case.

▸ **challenge *propter defectum*** (**prop**-tər də-**fek**-təm). (1828) A challenge based on a claim that the juror is incompetent to serve on any jury for a reason such as alienage, infancy, or nonresidency.

▸ **challenge *propter delictum*** (**prop**-tər də-**lik**-təm). (1802) A challenge based on a claim that the potential juror has lost citizenship rights, as by being convicted of an infamous crime. See *civil death* (1) under DEATH.

▸ **challenge to the array.** (16c) A legal challenge to the manner in which the entire jury panel was selected, usu. for a failure to follow prescribed procedures designed to produce impartial juries drawn from a fair cross-section of the community. • Such a challenge is either a principal challenge (if some defect renders the jury prima facie incompetent, as where the officer selecting veniremembers is related to the prosecutor or defendant) or a challenge for favoritism (as where the defect does not amount to grounds for a principal challenge, but there is a probability of partiality). — Also termed *challenge to the jury array.*

▸ **challenge to the favor.** (1834) A challenge for cause that arises when facts and circumstances tend to show that a juror is biased but do not warrant the juror's automatic disqualification. See *challenge for cause*.

▸ **challenge to the poll.** See *challenge for cause*.

▸ **general challenge.** See *challenge for cause*.

▸ **peremptory challenge.** (16c) One of a party's limited number of challenges that do not need to be supported by a reason unless the opposing party makes a prima facie showing that the challenge was used to discriminate on the basis of race, ethnicity, or sex. • At one time, a peremptory challenge could not be attacked and did not have to be explained. But today if discrimination is charged, the party making the peremptory challenge must give a nondiscriminatory reason for striking the juror. The court must consider several factors in deciding whether the proffered reason is merely a screen for illegal discrimination. *Batson v. Kentucky*, 476 U.S. 79, 106 S.Ct. 1712 (1986). — Often shortened to *peremptory*. — Also termed *peremptory strike*; *sight strike*. See STRIKE (2); *Batson challenge* under CHALLENGE (1).

▸ **principal challenge.** (1830) A for-cause challenge that arises when facts and circumstances support a conclusive presumption of a juror's bias, resulting in automatic disqualification. See *challenge for cause*.

3. *Military law.* An objection to a member of the court serving in a court-martial case. • A military judge can be challenged only for cause.

challenge, *vb.* (13c) **1.** To dispute or call into question <the columnist challenged the wisdom of the court's ruling>.

▸ **challenge the vote.** See DIVIDE THE ASSEMBLY.

2. To formally object to the legality or legal qualifications of <the defendant challenged the person's eligibility for jury service>.

chamber, *n.* (13c) **1.** A room or compartment <gas chamber>. **2.** A legislative or judicial body or other deliberative assembly <chamber of commerce>. **3.** The hall or room where such a body conducts business <the senate chamber>. — **chamber,** *adj.*

▸ **judge's chamber.** (*usu. pl.*) (17c) **1.** The private room or office of a judge. **2.** Any place where a judge transacts official business when not holding a session of the court. See IN CAMERA.

▸ **lower chamber.** See LOWER HOUSE.

▸ **Star Chamber.** See STAR CHAMBER.

▸ **upper chamber.** See UPPER HOUSE.

chamber, *vb.* (18c) *Slang.* (Of a judge) to sit in one's chambers at a given location <Chief Judge Kaye chambers sometimes in New York City and sometimes in Albany>.

chamber business. (1805) Official judicial business conducted outside the courtroom.

chamberlain (**chaym**-bər-lin). (13c) *English law.* A treasurer; originally, the keeper of the royal treasure chamber. • The term has been used for several high offices in England, such as the Lord Great Chamberlain, Lord Chamberlain of the Household, and Chamberlain of the Exchequer.

chamberlaria (chaym-bər-**lair**-ee-ə). [Law Latin] (18c) Chamberlainship; the office of chamberlain.

chamber magistrate. See MAGISTRATE.

chamber of accounts. (1814) *French law.* A court responsible for adjudicating disputes concerning public-revenue collection. Cf. COURT OF EXCHEQUER.

chamber of commerce. (17c) An association of merchants and other business leaders who organize to promote the commercial interests in a given area and whose group is generally affiliated with the national organization of the same name.

champertor (**cham**-pər-tər), *n.* (16c) Someone who engages in champerty; one who supports and promotes another person's lawsuit for pecuniary gain. — Also termed (archaically) *campiparticeps*. Cf. BARRATOR.

champertous (**cham**-pər-təs), *adj.* (17c) Of, relating to, or characterized by champerty; constituting champerty <a champertous contract>.

champerty (**cham**-pər-tee), *n.* [fr. French *champs parti* "split field"] (15c) **1.** An agreement between an officious intermeddler in a lawsuit and a litigant by which the intermeddler helps pursue the litigant's claim as consideration for receiving part of any judgment proceeds; specif., an agreement to divide litigation proceeds between the owner of the litigated claim and a party unrelated to the lawsuit who supports or helps enforce the claim. — Also termed (archaically) *campipartia*. Cf. BARRATRY; MAINTENANCE (8).

> "There is disagreement in the American courts as to what constitutes champerty. (1) Some courts hold that an agreement to look to the proceeds of the suit for compensation is champerty. . . . (2) Some courts hold that in addition the attorney must prosecute the suit at his own cost and expense to constitute champerty. . . . (3) Some courts hold even in a case like (2) that there is no champerty. . . . (4) All authorities agree that a contract for a contingent fee is not champerty if it is not to be paid out of the proceeds of the suit. . . . (5) In some states it is declared that the common law doctrines of maintenance and champerty are unknown . . . ; in some the matter is regulated wholly by statute. . . . [A]nd in most there is a marked tendency to narrow the doctrines of champerty or to evade them." William R. Anson, *Principles of the Law of Contract* 294 n.2 (Arthur L. Corbin ed., 3d Am. ed. 1919).

> "The rule as to champerty has been generally relaxed under modern decisions and a majority of courts now recognize that an agreement by which the attorney is to receive a contingent fee, i.e., a certain part of the avails of a suit or an amount fixed with reference to the amount recovered, is valid as long as the attorney does not agree to pay the expenses and costs of the action." Walter Wheeler Cook, "Quasi-Contracts," in 1 *American Law and Procedure* 129 (1948).

2. *Hist.* A writ available to the party who is the target of a champertous action.

> "Champerty is a writ that lies where two men are impleading, and one gives the half or part of a thing in plea to a stranger, to maintain him against the other; then the party grieved shall have this writ against the stranger." William Rastell, *Termes de la Ley* 76 (1st Am. ed. 1812).

champion. (14c) *Hist.* A person chosen to represent a defendant in trial by combat. • If the champion lost, the defendant was adjudged guilty. A champion who survived was fined for intentionally or ignorantly defending an unjust cause; one who died was buried in unhallowed ground. See TRIAL BY COMBAT.

chance, *n.* (14c) **1.** A hazard or risk. **2.** The unforeseen, uncontrollable, or unintended consequences of an act. **3.** An accident. **4.** Opportunity; hope.

chance bargain. *Contracts.* A transaction in which the parties mutually agree to accept the risk that facts and circumstances assumed by the parties at the time of contracting may not actually be what the parties believe they are. • If no fraud or misrepresentation is involved, a court will uphold a chance bargain. For instance, in a chance bargain involving a land swap, each deed may describe a tract as containing a number of acres "more or less." If the tract is actually larger than described, the seller cannot demand more money for the excess. And if the tract is actually smaller, the disappointed buyer cannot ask for a reduced price to make up for the deficiency.

chancellor, *n.* (14c) **1.** A judge of a court of chancery. **2.** A university president or CEO of an institution of higher education. **3.** In the United States, a judge in some courts of chancery or equity. **4.** *Scots law.* The presiding juror; the foreperson of a jury. **5.** *Eccles. law.* A law officer who presides over the bishop's court. • The chancellor advises and assists the bishop in all matters of canon law, both juridical and administrative. — **chancellorship,** *n.*

Chancellor, Lord. See LORD CHANCELLOR.

Chancellor of the Exchequer. *English law.* The finance minister of the U.K. government, with responsibility for taxes and government spending. • Formerly, the Chancellor sat in the Court of Exchequer.

chancellor's foot. (17c) A symbol of the variability of equitable justice. • John Selden, the 17th-century jurist, is thought to have coined the phrase in this passage, from his best-known book: "Equity is a roguish thing. For law we have a measure, know what to trust to: equity is according to the conscience of him that is Chancellor, and as that is larger or narrower, so is equity. 'Tis all one as if they should make the standard for the measure the Chancellor's foot. What an uncertain measure would this be! One Chancellor has a long foot, another a short foot, a third an indifferent foot; 'tis the same thing in the Chancellor's conscience." *Table Talk* 18 (1689).

chance-medley. [fr. Anglo-Norman *chance medlee* "chance scuffle"] (16c) A spontaneous fight during which one participant kills another in self-defense. — Also termed *chaud-medley*; *casual affray.* Cf. MEDLEY.

> "But the self-defence, which we are now speaking of, is that whereby a man may protect himself from an assault, or the like, in the course of a sudden brawl or quarrel, by killing him who assaults him. And this is what the law expresses by the word *chance-medley*, or (as some rather choose to write it) *chaud-medley*; the former of which in its etymology signifies a *casual* affray, the latter an affray in the *heat* of blood or passion: both of them of pretty much the same import; but the former is in common speech too often erroneously applied to any manner of homicide by misadventure; whereas it appears . . . that it is properly applied to such killing, as happens in self-defence upon a sudden rencounter." 4 William Blackstone, *Commentaries on the Laws of England* 184 (1769).

chance-of-survival doctrine. (1991) The principle that a wrongful-death plaintiff need only prove that the defendant's conduct was a substantial factor in causing the death — that is, that the victim might have survived but for the defendant's conduct.

chancer (**chan**-sər), *vb.* (17c) To adjust according to equitable principles, as a court of chancery would. • The practice arose in parts of New England when the courts had no equity jurisdiction, and were compelled to act on equitable principles.

> "The practice of 'chancering' is a very old one. A forfeiture could be 'chancered' under a law of 1699 . . . . Adjudged cases in 1630–1692 may be found in the Records of the Court of Assistants of Massachusetts Bay Colony. The early laws of Massachusetts provided for 'chancering' the forfeiture of any penal bond . . . . In Rhode Island an act of 1746 provided for 'chancerizing' the forfeiture 'where any penalty is forfeited, or conditional estate recovered, or equity of redemption sued for, whether judgment is confessed or otherwise obtained.'" 1 John Bouvier, *Bouvier's Law Dictionary* 456–57 (Francis Rawle ed., 8th ed. 1914).

chancery (**chan**-sər-ee). (14c) **1.** A court of equity; collectively, the courts of equity. • The term is derived from the court of the Lord Chancellor, the original English court of equity. — Also termed *court of chancery*; *chancery court.*

> "Chancery's jurisdiction was complementary to that of the courts of common law — it sought to do justice in cases for which there was no adequate remedy at common law. It had originated in the petition, not the writ, of the party who felt aggrieved to the Lord Chancellor as 'keeper of the King's conscience.' In its origins, therefore, Chancery's flexible concern for justice complemented admirably the formalism of a medieval system of common law which had begun to adhere strictly, perhaps overstrictly on occasion, to prescribed forms. By 1800, however, Chancery's system was itself regarded as being both consistent and certain." A.H. Manchester, *Modern Legal History of England and Wales, 1750–1950* 135–36 (1980).

2. The system of jurisprudence administered in courts of equity. See EQUITY. **3.** *Int'l law.* The place where the head of a diplomatic mission and staff have their offices, as distinguished from the embassy (where the ambassador lives).

Chancery Court of York. *Eccles. law.* The ecclesiastical court of the Province of York, responsible for appeals from provincial diocesan courts. • This court corresponds to the Court of Arches in the Province of Canterbury. Cf. COURT OF ARCHES.

chancery deed. See *special master's deed* under DEED.

chancery guardian. See GUARDIAN (1).

chance verdict. See VERDICT (1).

change in circumstances. (1899) *Family law.* A modification in the physical, emotional, or financial condition of one or both parents, used to show the need to modify a custody or support order; esp., an involuntary occurrence that, if it had been known at the time of the divorce decree, would have resulted in the court's issuing a different decree, as when an involuntary job loss creates a need to modify the decree to provide for reduced child-support payments. — Also termed *change of circumstances*; *changed circumstances*; *material change in circumstances*; *substantial change in circumstances*; *change of condition.* See MODIFICATION ORDER.

change of condition. 1. *Workers' compensation.* A substantial worsening of an employee's physical health occurring after an award, as a result of which the employee merits an increase in benefits. **2.** *Family law.* CHANGE IN CIRCUMSTANCES.

change-of-ownership clause. (1978) *Oil & gas.* A provision in an oil-and-gas lease specifying what notice must be given to a lessee about a change in the leased land's ownership before the lessee is obliged to recognize the new owner. — Also termed *assignment clause.*

change of position. 1. One or more irrevocable steps taken in reliance on the words or acts of another. • The person who changes position may thereby have rights or defenses against the party on whom the reliance was made, as by the operation of equitable estoppel, promissory estoppel, or other doctrines. **2.** An affirmative defense to a claimed liability in restitution, the defendant professing to have acted in reasonable and innocent reliance on receipt of the plaintiff's property and that requiring a return of the property will thus leave the defendant worse off than before having received it. • The defense is most often asserted in cases of mistake, as when the plaintiff sends the defendant money in error and the defendant, without realizing this, spends the money on something that he or she would not otherwise have bought.

"The affirmative defense of change of position gives effect to inherent limitations of a liability based on unjust enrichment, and it is an important device by which the law of restitution justifies the imposition of liability independent of fault." Restatement (Third) of Restitution and Unjust Enrichment § 65 cmt. a (2011).

change-of-position defense. See DEFENSE (1).

change of venue. (18c) The transfer of a case from a court in one locale to another in the same judicial system to cure a defect in venue, either to minimize the prejudicial impact of local sentiment or to secure a more sensible location for trial. — Also termed *transfer of venue; transfer of proceedings.* See VENUE.

change order. 1. A modification of a previously ordered item or service. **2.** A directive issued by the federal government to a contractor to alter the specifications of an item the contractor is producing for the government.

changing fund. See FUND (1).

channel. (14c) **1.** The bed of a running stream of water; the groove through which a watercourse flows <digging a deeper channel was thought to help protect the river from flooding>.

▸ **main channel.** (16c) The bed over which the principal volume of water flows; the deepest and most navigable part of a channel.

▸ **natural channel.** (16c) The naturally formed bed and banks of a stream.

▸ **natural flood channel.** (1907) A channel through which floodwaters naturally accumulate and flow downstream.

2. The line of deep water that shipping vessels follow <a shipping channel>. **3.** A water route between two islands or an island and a continent <the English Channel>. **4.** A medium of transmission <the news channel>.

channel of distribution. See DISTRIBUTION CHANNEL.

channel of trade. See DISTRIBUTION CHANNEL.

chantry (**chan**-tree), *n.* (15c) *Hist. Eccles. law.* **1.** A benefice endowed for the saying of Mass by chantry priests for the soul of the founder or his designees. • This practice was abolished in England by the Chantry Acts of 1545 and 1547. **2.** A chapel or part of a church so endowed. — Also spelled *chauntry.*

chapiter (**chap**-ə-tər). [Law French] *Hist.* A list of matters drawn up by the king to be presented before the justices in eyre, justices of assise, or justices of the peace. — Also spelled *chapitre.* Cf. ARTICLES OF THE EYRE.

chapter. (17c) **1.** A section of a book; by analogy, any distinct part of a larger whole <the appointment opened a new chapter in her career>. **2.** A local part of a larger organization <the Philadelphia chapter of Big Brothers Big Sisters>. **3.** (*often cap.*) A major division within a statute, regulation, or other legal instrument <filed under Chapter 11>.

Chapter 7. 1. The chapter of the United States Bankruptcy Code allowing a trustee to collect and liquidate a debtor's nonexempt property, either voluntarily or by court order, to satisfy creditors. **2.** A bankruptcy case filed under this chapter. • An individual debtor who undergoes this type of liquidation usu. gets a fresh financial start by receiving a discharge of all debts. — Also termed (in sense 2) *straight bankruptcy; liquidation bankruptcy.*

"A Chapter 7 case has five stages: (1) getting the debtor into bankruptcy court; (2) collecting the debtor's property; (3) selling this property; (4) distributing the proceeds of the sale to creditors; and (5) determining whether the debtor is discharged from further liability to these creditors." David G. Epstein et al., *Bankruptcy* § 1-7, at 9 (1993).

Chapter 7 trustee. See TRUSTEE (2).

Chapter 9. 1. The chapter of the United States Bankruptcy Code governing the adjustment of a municipality's debts. **2.** A bankruptcy case filed under this chapter.

Chapter 11. (1970) **1.** The chapter of the United States Bankruptcy Code allowing an insolvent business, or one that is threatened with insolvency, to reorganize its capital structure under court supervision (and subject to creditor approval) while continuing its normal operations. • Although the Code permits individual nonbusiness debtors to use Chapter 11, the vast majority of Chapter 11 cases involve business debtors. **2.** A business reorganization conducted under this chapter; REORGANIZATION (1).

Chapter 12. 1. The chapter of the United States Bankruptcy Code providing for a court-approved debt-payment relief plan for family farmers with a regular income, allowing the farmer's net income to be collected by a trustee and paid to creditors. **2.** A bankruptcy case filed under this chapter. — Also termed (in sense 2) *family-farmer bankruptcy; farmer bankruptcy.*

Chapter 13. 1. The chapter of the United States Bankruptcy Code allowing a person's earnings to be collected by a trustee and paid to creditors by means of a court-approved debt-repayment plan if the person has a regular income. • A plan filed under Chapter 13 is sometimes called a *wage-earner's plan,* a *wage-earner plan,* or an *income-based plan.* Chapter 13 allows the debtor to propose a plan of rehabilitation to extend or reduce the balance of any obligations and to receive a discharge from unsecured debts upon completion of the payments under the plan. A plan made in good faith will be confirmed if the creditors receive what they would have received under Chapter 7, and if the plan pledges all of the debtor's disposable income for three years. **2.** A bankruptcy case filed under this chapter.

Chapter 13 trustee. See TRUSTEE (2).

Chapter 20. *Bankruptcy. Slang.* A debtor who files a Chapter 7 petition and receives a discharge, and then immediately files a Chapter 13 petition to deal with remaining nondischargeable or secured debts.

Chapter 22. *Bankruptcy. Slang.* A debtor, usu. a corporation, that files a second Chapter 11 petition shortly after a previous Chapter 11 petition has failed, because the debtor has become insolvent again or is again threatened with insolvency.

chapter surfing. *Slang.* A debtor's movement from a filing under one United States Bankruptcy Code chapter to a filing under another.

character, *n.* (17c) The qualities that combine to make an individual human being distinctive from others, esp. as regards morality and behavior; the disposition, reputation, or collective traits of a person as they might be gathered from close observation of that person's pattern of behavior. *See Franklin v. Lynaugh*, 487 U.S. 164, 174, 108 S.Ct. 2320, 2327 (1988). See *character evidence* under EVIDENCE; GOOD MORAL CHARACTER.

▸ **bad character.** (17c) A person's propensity for or tendency toward unlawful or immoral behavior. • In limited circumstances, proof of bad character may be introduced into evidence to discredit a witness. Fed. R. Evid. 608, 609. — Also termed *general bad character.* See *character evidence* under EVIDENCE.

▸ **good character.** (17c) A person's tendency to engage in lawful and moral behavior.

character and fitness. The mental suitability and high ability required of a lawyer.

character evidence. See EVIDENCE.

character-improvement condition. See *conditional bequest* under BEQUEST.

characterization. **1.** *Conflict of laws.* The classification, qualification, and interpretation of laws that apply to the case. — Also termed *qualification*; *classification*; *interpretation.*

> "In a conflict-of-laws situation, a court must determine at the outset whether the problem presented to it for solution relates to torts, contracts, property, or some other field, or to a matter of substance or procedure, in order to refer to the appropriate law. In other words, the court must initially, whether consciously or not, go through the process of determining the nature of the problem; otherwise, the court will not know which choice-of-law rule to apply to the case. This process is generally called 'characterization,' and sometimes 'classification,' 'qualification,' or 'interpretation.'" 16 Am. Jur. 2d *Conflict of Laws* § 3, at 12 (1998).

2. *Family law.* The process of classifying property accumulated by spouses as either separate or marital property (or community property). — **characterize,** *vb.*

character loan. See LOAN.

character merchandising. (1957) The adaptation or secondary exploitation of the name, likeness, or other essential features of a famous person or fictional character by the person, the creator of the character, or an authorizing third party, for use in the marketing of commercial products and services, as in logos and advertisements, usu. in return for a royalty.

character-reformation condition. See *conditional bequest* under BEQUEST.

character test. (1908) Any examination or moral-fitness standard that a person is required to pass before being admitted to some special privilege, such as the grant of a visa, membership in the ranks of a profession, or recognition as having a particular standing within a group.

character witness. See WITNESS.

charge, *n.* (13c) **1.** A formal accusation of an offense as a preliminary step to prosecution <a murder charge>. — Also termed *criminal charge.* **2.** An instruction or command <a mother's charge to her son>. **3.** JURY CHARGE <review the charge for appealable error>. **4.** An assigned duty or task; a responsibility <the manager's charge to open and close the office>. **5.** An encumbrance, lien, or claim <a charge on property>. **6.** A person or thing entrusted to another's care <a charge of the estate>. **7.** Price, cost, or expense <free of charge>.

▸ **delinquency charge.** (1898) A charge assessed against a borrower for failing to make a timely payment.

▸ **exceptional charge.** See *special charge.*

▸ **finance charge.** See FINANCE CHARGE.

▸ **fixed and floating charge.** A security interest for repayment of a loan effected by imposing a lien on a specified value of noncash assets and an adjustable amount of cash and stock. — Also termed *fixed and floating lien*; *fixed and floating debenture.* See *floating charge.*

▸ **floating charge.** (18c) **1.** A security interest in the fund of a company's or partnership's changing assets, the security interest possibly converting into a fixed interest at some point at which it attaches to specific assets. — Also termed *floating security.* **2.** See *floating lien* under LIEN.

▸ **late charge.** An additional fee assessed on a debt when a payment is not received by the due date.

▸ **noncash charge.** (1967) A cost (such as depreciation or amortization) that does not involve an outlay of cash.

▸ **one-time charge.** See *special charge.*

▸ **special charge.** An ordinary cost of business excluded from income calculations. • The term is meaningless under generally accepted accounting principles because "special charge" expenses do not meet the GAAP test for extraordinary items. — Also termed *one-time charge*; *unusual charge*; *exceptional charge.* See *extraordinary expense* under EXPENSE; *operating earnings* under EARNINGS.

▸ **unusual charge.** See *special charge.*

8. *Parliamentary law.* A deliberative assembly's mandate to a committee. — Also termed *committee jurisdiction.*

charge, *vb.* (13c) **1.** To accuse (a person) of an offense <the police charged him with murder>. **2.** To instruct or command <the dean charged the students to act ethically>. **3.** To instruct a jury on matters of law <the judge charged the jury on self-defense>. **4.** To impose a lien or claim; to encumber <charge the land with a tax lien>. **5.** To entrust with responsibilities or duties <charge the guardian with the ward's care>. **6.** To demand a fee; to bill <the clerk charged a small filing fee>.

chargeable, *adj.* (1863) **1.** (Of an act) capable of or liable to being charged as a criminal offense <taking that money for personal use would be chargeable>. **2.** (Of a person) capable of or liable to being charged for a criminal offense <you are chargeable with theft>. **3.** (Of a product or service) needing to be paid for <a chargeable service>. **4.** (Of a thing for which one pays) requiring tax to be paid; taxable <even interstate sales by Internet are now chargeable>.

charge account. (1903) A credit arrangement by which a customer purchases goods and services and pays for them periodically or within a specified time. — Also termed *credit account.* See CREDIT (4).

charge and discharge. *Equity practice.* Court-ordered account filings by a plaintiff and a defendant. • The plaintiff's account (*charge*) and the defendant's response (*discharge*) were filed with a master in chancery.

charge and specification. (1814) *Military law.* A written description of an alleged offense.

charge-back, *n.* (1952) **1.** A bank's deducting of sums it had provisionally credited to a customer's account, occurring usu. when a check deposited in the account has been dishonored. UCC § 4-214. **2.** The reversal of a credit-card transaction. • If a credit card is fraudulently used, the issuing bank is typically entitled to a charge-back of the dollar amount credited to the merchant bank, which would then typically charge back the dollar amount credited to the merchant.

charge bargain. See PLEA BARGAIN.

charge conference. (1972) A meeting between a trial judge and the parties' attorneys to develop a jury charge. — Also termed *prayer conference.*

chargé d'affaires (shahr-**zhay** də-**fair**). [French "one in charge of affairs"] (18c) **1.** A diplomat who is the second in command in a diplomatic mission (hence, subordinate to an ambassador or minister). **2.** An official who represents a particular government during the absence of an ambassador or in a country where the ambassadorship is vacant. — Also spelled *chargé des affaires.* Pl. **chargés d'affaires.**

▸ **acting chargé d'affaires.** (1864) A chargé d'affaires who performs mission functions when the leader of the mission is not available to do so or when the position is vacant. — Also termed *chargés d'affaires ad interim.*

▸ **permanent chargé d'affaires.** (1869) A chargé d'affaires with a high enough rank to head a mission (if there is no ambassador or minister). — Also termed *chargé d'affaires en pied; chargé d'affaires en titre.*

chargedown, *n.* (1942) *Criminal procedure.* A prosecutor's inclusion in the charging instrument of a lesser-included offense.

charged with notice. (1832) Imputed with knowledge or awareness that is legally binding <the defendant was charged with notice of the defect yet failed to act before the plaintiff was injured by it>. — Also termed *put on notice.*

chargee (chahr-**jee**). (1884) **1.** The holder of a charge on property or of a security on a loan; MORTGAGEE. **2.** One charged with a crime.

charge enhancement. (1983) *Criminal procedure.* The heightened classification of the seriousness of a criminal offense, as when prior DWI convictions make a fresh violation chargeable as felony DWI.

charge off, *vb.* To treat (an account receivable) as a loss or expense because payment is unlikely; to treat as a bad debt. See *bad debt* under DEBT.

charger (**chahr**-jər), *n.* (1869) **1.** *Archaic.* Someone who has a charge on a revenue or an estate. **2.** MORTGAGOR. **3.** Someone who charges; esp., a charging prosecutor. — Also spelled (esp. in sense 1) *chargor* (chahr-**jor**).

charge sheet. (1866) **1.** A police record showing the name of each person brought into custody, the nature of the accusations, and the identity of the accusers. **2.** A police record of the names and descriptions of people that the police have said may be guilty of a particular crime. **3.** *Military law.* A four-part charging instrument containing (1) information about the accused and the witnesses, (2) the charges and specifications, (3) the preferring of charges and their referral to a summary, special, or general court-martial for trial, and (4) for a summary court-martial, the trial record.

charging conference. (1978) *Criminal procedure.* A pre-summation meeting of the judge, the prosecution team, and the defense team at which the judge rules on the lawyers' requested jury instructions and on precisely what counts and lesser-included offenses will be considered by the jury.

charging instrument. (1951) *Criminal procedure.* Any of three formal legal documents by which a person can be officially charged with a crime: an indictment, information, or presentment. — Also termed *accusatory instrument.* See INDICTMENT; INFORMATION; PRESENTMENT (2).

charging lien. See LIEN.

charging order. (1904) *Partnership.* A statutory procedure whereby an individual partner's creditor can satisfy its claim from the partner's interest in the partnership.

charitable, *adj.* (14c) **1.** Dedicated to a general public purpose, usu. for the benefit of needy people who cannot pay for benefits received <charitable contribution>. **2.** Involved in or otherwise relating to charity <charitable foundation>.

charitable bequest. See BEQUEST.

charitable contribution. (17c) A gratuitous transfer of property to a charitable social-welfare, religious, scientific, educational, or other qualified organization. • Such a contribution has tax value because it may result in a current income-tax deduction, may reduce federal estate taxes, and may be free of any gift taxes.

charitable corporation. See CORPORATION.

charitable deduction. See DEDUCTION (2).

charitable gift. See GIFT.

charitable immunity. See IMMUNITY (2).

charitable lead trust. See TRUST (3).

charitable organization. (1897) *Tax.* A tax-exempt organization that (1) is organized and operated exclusively for religious, scientific, literary, educational, athletic, public-safety, or community-service purposes, (2) does not distribute earnings for the benefit of private individuals, and (3) does not participate in any way in political candidate campaigns, or engage in substantial lobbying. IRC (26 USCA) § 501(c)(3). — Also termed *charity; 501(c)(3) organization.*

charitable purpose. (1877) *Tax.* The purpose for which an organization must be formed so that it qualifies as a charitable organization under the Internal Revenue Code. — Also termed *charitable use.*

charitable remainder. See REMAINDER (1).

charitable-remainder annuity trust. See TRUST (3).

charitable-remainder trust. See TRUST (3).

charitable-remainder-trust retirement fund. See *charitable-remainder annuity trust* under TRUST (3).

charitable trust. See TRUST (3).

charitable use. 1. CHARITABLE PURPOSE. **2.** See *charitable trust* under TRUST (3).

charity, *n.* (12c) **1.** CHARITABLE ORGANIZATION. **2.** Aid given to the poor, the suffering, or the general community for religious, educational, economic, public-safety, or medical purposes.

> "'Charity,' in the laws of parliament, has been defined to mean any sum of money or other emolument arising from certain *specific funds,* appropriated to the assistance of persons in mean or poor circumstances." Arthur Male, *A Treatise on the Law and Practice of Elections* 167 (1818).

3. Goodwill.

charlatan (**shahr**-lə-tən), *n.* (17c) Someone who pretends to have more knowledge or skill than he or she actually has; a quack or faker. — **charlatanism, charlatanry,** *n.*

***Charming Betsy* doctrine.** (1989) The rule that when a federal law may be interpreted more than one way, one of which conflicts with international law, a court should try to interpret the law consistently with international law. • The doctrine originated in *Murray v. The Schooner Charming Betsy,* 6 U.S. (2 Cranch) 64 (1804). Writing for the Court, Chief Justice John Marshall observed that "an act of Congress ought never to be construed to violate the law of nations if any other possible construction remains, and consequently can never be construed to violate neutral rights, or to affect neutral commerce, further than is warranted by the law of nations as understood in this country." *Id.* at 118.

charta (**kahr**-tə). (17c) [Law Latin] *Hist.* **1.** A charter or deed. **2.** A token by which an estate is held. **3.** A royal grant of privileges or liberties.

Charta de Foresta. *Hist.* A charter that defined the extent of the crown's rights and privileges in the royal forests, granted the common people some rights to use the forests, and reduced the penalties for crimes such as poaching. • The charter was first promulgated in 1217 and revised in 1225. — Also termed *Carta de Foresta; Carta Forestae.*

chartae libertatum (**kahr**-tee lib-ər-**tay**-təm). [Latin] Charters of liberties. • This term refers to the two great sources of English liberties: *Magna Carta* and the *Charta de Foresta.*

chartel. See CARTEL.

charter, *n.* (13c) **1.** An instrument that establishes a body politic or other organization, or that grants rights, liberties, or powers to its citizens or members <Charter of the United Nations>. **2.** An instrument by which a municipality is incorporated, specifying its organizational structure and its highest laws; specif., a written document making the persons residing within a fixed boundary, along with their successors, a corporation and body politic for and within that boundary, and prescribing the powers, privileges, and duties of the corporation. • A city charter trumps all conflicting ordinances. — Also termed *municipal charter.*

> "Municipal Charters. — The charter issued to a municipality is in the nature of a constitution to it, being superior to all ordinances enacted by that municipality, though inferior in rank to all State laws of every kind." Frank Hall Childs, *Where and How to Find the Law* 8 (1922).

▸ **home-rule charter.** (1902) A local government's organizational plan or framework, analogous to a constitution, drawn by the municipality itself and adopted by popular vote of the citizenry. See HOME RULE.

3. A governmental act that creates a business or defines a corporate franchise; also, the document evidencing this act.

▸ **bank charter.** (18c) A document issued by a governmental authority permitting a bank to conduct business.

▸ **corporate charter.** (1828) **1.** CERTIFICATE OF INCORPORATION (1). **2.** A document that one files with the secretary of state upon incorporating a business. • The corporate charter is often the articles of incorporation.

▸ **special charter.** (16c) *Hist.* A legislative act creating a private corporation as opposed to a public, charitable, or educational corporation. • Special charters were common until the 19th century, when legislatures enacted general incorporation laws that allowed private corporations to be formed without legislative action.

4. The organic law of an organization; loosely, the highest law of any entity. Cf. ARTICLES OF INCORPORATION. **5.** A governing document granting authority or recognition from a parent organization to a subordinate or constituent organization, such as a local affiliate or chapter, organized under the parent organization's authority; or the instrument granting such authority or recognition. See *governing document* under DOCUMENT (2). **6.** *Hist.* The writing that accompanies a livery of seisin.

> "Among the documents of the Anglo-Norman period, the *charter* plays a prominent part; and a learned jurist has explained that the essential feature of a charter is that it is a 'dispositive' document, a document which transfers to B some right or interest which at present belongs to A." Edward Jenks, *Law and Politics in the Middle Ages* 40–41 (1898).

7. The leasing or hiring of an airplane, ship, or other vessel. **8.** CHARTERPARTY.

▸ **bareboat charter.** (1925) A charter under which the shipowner surrenders possession and control of the vessel to the charterer, who then succeeds to many of the shipowner's rights and obligations. • The charterer, who provides the personnel, insurance, and other materials necessary to operate the vessel, is known either as a *demise charterer* or as an *owner pro hac vice.* — Also termed *demise charter; demise charterparty; bareboat charterparty.*

> "The 'demise' or 'bareboat' charter is conceptually the easiest to understand. The charterer takes possession and operates the ship during the period of the charter as though the vessel belonged to the charterer. The bareboat charter is thus analogous to the driver who leases a car for a specified period or a tenant who rents a house for a term of years. The charterer provides the vessel's master and crew (much as the lessee-driver personally drives the car) and pays the operating expenses (much as the lessee-driver buys the gasoline." David W. Robertson, Steven F. Friedell & Michael F. Sturley, *Admiralty and Maritime Law in the United States* 371–72 (2002).

▸ **berth charter.** See *dock charter.*

▸ **catch-time charter.** See *time charter.*

▸ **demise charter.** See *bareboat charter.*

▸ **dock charter.** A charter under which the shipowner agrees to bring the vessel to a specified loading place in a port or at a dock. — Also termed *berth charter.*

▸ **gross charter.** (1889) A charter under which the shipowner provides all personnel and pays all expenses. — Also termed *gross charterparty.*

▸ **nondemise charter.** See *voyage charter.*

▸ **port charter.** A charter providing that the shipowner will make the vessel available in the commercial area of a port. • The shipowner need not bring the vessel to the loading place, but need only put the vessel at the charterer's disposal.

▸ **slot charter.** (1961) A charter for one or more slots on a container vessel. • Each slot accommodates a 20-foot container. A slot charter is a form of vessel-sharing agreement. — Also termed *slot charterparty.* Cf. *space charter.*

"Slot charters (and vessel-sharing agreements) have become increasingly popular in the container trades, as they enable two or more carriers to combine their capacities and offer more frequent service on their routes. If three carriers all serve the New York to Rotterdam route, for example, and each devotes one vessel to the route every three weeks, they can implicitly (with slot charters) join forces and each offer weekly service." David W. Robertson, Steven F. Friedell & Michael F. Sturley, *Admiralty and Maritime Law in the United States* 377 (2001).

▸ **space charter.** (1952) A charter for a part of a vessel's capacity, such as a specified hold or deck or a specified part of the vessel's carrying capacity. • A space charter is a form of vessel-sharing agreement. — Also termed *space charterparty.* Cf. *slot charter.*

▸ **time charter.** (1864) A charter for a specified period, rather than for a specific task or voyage; a charter under which the shipowner continues to manage and control the vessel, but the charterer designates the ports of call and the cargo carried. • Each party bears the expenses related to its functions and for any damage it causes. — Also termed *time charterparty; catch-time charter.* Cf. *voyage charter.*

▸ **voyage charter.** (1877) A charter under which the shipowner provides a ship and crew, and places them at the disposal of the charterer for the carriage of cargo to a designated port. • The voyage charterer may lease the entire vessel for a voyage or series of voyages — or may (by "space charter") lease only part of the vessel. — Also termed *voyage charterparty; nondemise charter; nondemise charterparty.* Cf. *time charter.*

"The fundamental difference between voyage and time charters is how the freight or 'charter hire' is calculated. A voyage charter party specifies the amount due for carrying a specified cargo on a specific voyage (or series of voyages), regardless of how long a particular voyage takes. A time charter party specifies the amount due for each day that the vessel is 'on hire,' regardless of how many voyages are completed." David W. Robertson, Steven F. Friedell & Michael F. Sturley, *Admiralty and Maritime Law in the United States* 377 (2001).

charter, *vb.* (15c) **1.** To establish or grant by charter <charter a bank>. **2.** To hire or rent for temporary use <charter a boat>.

charter agreement. See CHARTERPARTY.

chartered life underwriter. See UNDERWRITER.

chartered ship. See SHIP.

charterer (chahr-tər-rər), *n.* (1833) **1.** A person or company that contracts (by charterparty) with a shipowner for the transportation of passengers or cargo for a specified voyage or period of time.

"The landlord and tenant of the Admiralty are the owner and charterer, — his lease a charter-party, — its duration limited either by time or number of voyages; its terms the payment of a gross sum, or so much per ton, or a share of the profits. The tenant or charterer may hire the vessel equipped and manned as one might rent a suite of rooms in a boarding-house, or he may himself man and equip the vessel as one occupies an apartment. In any case he may so far obtain control and possession of the vessel as to become its owner *pro hac vice,* and subject it to liens for a tort, such as a collision, or for repairs and supplies furnished by contract. But there is no lien under maritime law or under a State statute for materials furnished on the order of the charterer, where the charterer agrees to provide them, if the material man knows of the charter, or is put on inquiry as to such agreement." William K. Townsend, "Admiralty," in *Two Centuries' Growth of American Law: 1701-1901* 448, 469 (1901).

2. Someone who reserves a boat, bus, or other mode of transportation for others' benefit. **3.** FREEHOLDER.

charter-land. *Hist.* See BOOKLAND.

charter member. See MEMBER (1).

charter of affreightment. See AFFREIGHTMENT.

charter of rights. (18c) A constitutional or statutory instrument that establishes fundamental legal rights, esp. civil liberties for the citizens in the country where it has effect.

Charter of the United Nations 1945. The constitutive document of the United Nations, signed on 26 June 1945 in San Francisco at the conclusion of the United Nations Conference on International Organization. • The Charter took effect on 24 October 1945. See STATUTE OF THE INTERNATIONAL COURT OF JUSTICE.

charterparty. [fr. Latin *charta partita* "divided charter," O.F. *chartre partie*] (16c) *Maritime law.* A contract by which a ship, or a principal part of it, is leased by the owner, esp. to a merchant for the conveyance of goods on a predetermined voyage to one or more ports or for a specified period of time; a special contract between the shipowner and charterer, esp. for the carriage of goods by sea. — Also written *charter-party; charter party.* — Often shortened to *charter.* — Also termed *charter agreement.* See CHARTER (8); CESSER CLAUSE.

"*Charter partie* (*charta partita*) is nothing but that which we call a paire of indentures, conteining the covenants and agreements made betweene merchants, or sea faring men touching their marine affaires." John Cowell, *The Interpreter* (1607).

▸ **bareboat charterparty.** See *bareboat charter* under CHARTER (8).

▸ **berth charterparty.** (1989) A charterparty that requires the chartered vessel to arrive at a specific berth.

▸ **demise charterparty.** See *bareboat charter* under CHARTER (8).

▸ **gross charterparty.** See *gross charter* under CHARTER (8).

▸ **nondemise charterparty.** See *voyage charter* under CHARTER (8).

▸ **slot charterparty.** See *slot charter* under CHARTER (8).

▸ **space charterparty.** See *space charter* under CHARTER (8).

▸ **time charterparty.** See *time charter* under CHARTER (8).

▸ **voyage charterparty.** See *voyage charter* under CHARTER (8).

chartis reddendis (**kahr**-tis ri-**den**-dis). [Latin "for returning charters"] (17c) *Hist.* A writ seeking the return of a charter of feoffment from a person who has been entrusted with the charter but who has refused to deliver it as instructed. See FEOFFMENT.

chartophylax (kahr-**tof**-ə-laks). (1879) *Hist.* A keeper of records or public instruments; a registrar.

chase, *n.* (15c) *Hist.* A franchise granted by the Crown empowering the grantee to keep, within a certain district, animals for hunting, i.e., the objects of the chase. • This franchise was also known as a *free chase* to contrast it with a *chase royal* — a chase held by the Crown.

▸ **common chase.** (17c) A chase in which everyone is entitled to hunt.

chaser. Someone who pursues potential legal claimants, esp. on behalf of a lawyer who engages the pursuer for purposes of illicit solicitation; AMBULANCE CHASER (2).

chasten, *vb.* (16c) To make (a person) realize that behavior was wrong or mistaken; to induce remorse, usu. over a slight infraction.

chastity. (13c) The condition, state, or principle of not having sex with anyone outside marriage; sexual purity. Cf. CELIBACY. — **chaste,** *adj.*

chattel (**chat**-əl). (*usu. pl.*) (14c) Movable or transferable property; personal property; esp., a physical object capable of manual delivery and not the subject matter of real property. See *chattel security* under SECURITY (1).

> "That Money is not to be accounted Goods or *Chattels*, because it is not of it self valuable . . . . *Chattels* are either *personal* or *real*. *Personal*, may be so called in two respects: One, because they belong immediately to the person of a Man, as a Bow, Horse, etc. The other, for that being any way injuriously withheld from us, we have no means to recover them, but Personal Actions. *Chattels real*, are such as either appertain not immediately to the person, but to some other thing, by way of dependency, as a Box with Charters of Land, Apples upon a Tree, or a Tree it self growing on the Ground. . . . [O]r else such as are issuing out of some immoveable thing to a person, as a Lease or Rent for the term of years." Thomas Blount, *Nomo-Lexicon: A Law-Dictionary* (1670).

▸ **chattel personal.** (16c) A tangible good or an intangible right (such as a patent). — Also termed *personal chattel.*

> "Chattels personal are the subjects of the present treatise. In ancient times they consisted entirely of movable goods, visible and tangible in their nature, and in the possession either of the owner or of some other person on his behalf. Nothing of an incorporeal nature was anciently comprehended within the class of chattels personal. In this respect the law of personal property strikingly differs from that of real property, in which, from the earliest times, incorporeal hereditaments occupied a conspicuous place. But, although there was formerly no such thing as an incorporeal chattel personal, there existed not unfrequently a right of action, or the liberty of proceeding in the courts of law, either to recover pecuniary damages for the infliction of a wrong or the non-performance of a contract, or else to procure the payment of money due. Such a right was called, in the Norman French of our early lawyers, a *chose* or thing *in action*, whilst movable goods were denominated *choses in possession*. Choses in action, though valuable rights, had not in early times the ordinary incident of property, namely, the capability of being transferred; for, to permit a transfer of such a right was, in the simplicity of the times, thought to be too great an encouragement to litigation; and the attempt to make such a transfer involved the guilt of *maintenance* or the maintaining of another person in his suit. It was impossible, however, that this simple state of things should long continue. Within the class of choses in action was comprised a right of growing importance, namely, that of suing for money due, which right is all that constitutes a *debt*. That a debt should be incapable of transfer was obviously highly inconvenient in commercial transactions; and in early times the custom of merchants rendered debts secured by bills of exchange assignable by endorsement and delivery of the bills. But choses in action, not so secured, could only be sued for by the original creditor, or the person who first had the right of action. In process of time, however, an indirect method of assignment was discovered, the assignee being empowered to sue in the name of the assignor; and in the reign of Henry VII, it was determined that a 'chose in action may be assigned over for lawful cause as a just debt, but not for maintenance, and that where a man is indebted to me in 20*l*., and another owes him 20*l*. by bond, he may assign this bond and debt to me in satisfaction, and I may justify for suing it *in the name of the other* at my own costs.' Choses in action, having now become assignable, became an important kind of personal property; and their importance was increased by an act of the following reign, whereby the taking of interest for money, which had previously been unlawful, was rendered legal to a limited extent. Loans and mortgages soon became common, forming a kind of incorporeal personal property unknown to the ancient law. In the reign of Queen Anne, promissory notes were rendered, by act of parliament, assignable by indorsement and delivery, in the same manner as inland bills of exchange. But other choses in action continue to this day assignable at law only by empowering the assignee to sue in the name of the assignor." Joseph J. Darlington, *A Treatise on the Law of Personal Property* 6–10 (1891) (citations omitted).

▸ **chattel real.** (16c) A real-property interest that is less than a freehold or fee, such as a leasehold estate. • The most important chattel real is an estate for years in land, which is considered a chattel because it lacks the indefiniteness of time essential to real property. — Also termed *real chattel.*

▸ **chattel vegetable.** A movable article of a vegetable origin, such as timber, undergrowth, corn, or fruit.

▸ **local chattel.** (1904) Personal property that is affixed to land; FIXTURE.

▸ **personal chattel.** See *chattel personal.*

▸ **real chattel.** See *chattel real.*

▸ **unique chattel.** (1886) A chattel that is absolutely irreplaceable because it is one of a kind.

chattel lien. See *mechanic's lien* under LIEN.

chattel mortgage. See MORTGAGE.

chattel-mortgage bond. See BOND (3).

chattel paper. (1935) A writing that shows both a monetary obligation and a security interest in or a lease of specific goods. UCC § 9-102(a)(11). • Chattel paper is generally used in a consumer transaction when the consumer buys goods on credit. The consumer typically promises to pay for the goods by executing a promissory note, and the seller retains a security interest in the goods. See SECURITY AGREEMENT.

> "'Chattel paper' means a record or records that evidence both a monetary obligation and a security interest in specific goods, a security interest in specific goods and software used in the goods, a security interest in specific goods and license of software used in the goods, a lease of specific goods, or a lease of specific goods and license of software used in the goods. . . . The term does not include (i) charters or other contracts involving the use or hire of a vessel or (ii) records that evidence a right to payment arising out of the use of a credit or charge card or information contained on or for use with the card. If a transaction is evidenced by records that include an instrument or series of instruments, the group of records taken together constitutes chattel paper." UCC § 9-102(a)(11).

▸ **electronic chattel paper.** (1998) Chattel paper evidenced by a record or records consisting of information stored in an electronic medium and retrievable in perceivable form. UCC § 9-102(a)(31).

▸ **tangible chattel paper.** (2003) Chattel paper evidenced by a record or records consisting of information inscribed on a tangible medium. UCC § 9-102(a)(79).

chattel personal. See CHATTEL.

chattel real. See CHATTEL.

chattel security. See SECURITY (1).

chattel vegetable. See CHATTEL.

chaud-medley (**showd**-med-lee). See CHANCE-MEDLEY.

chauntry (**chon**-tree), *n.* See CHANTRY.

chauvinism. (1851) **1.** A strong belief that one's country or race is better or more important than any other; exaggerated patriotism. **2.** A belief that one's own sex (esp. if male) is better or more important than the other sex; bigotry based on gender. — **chauvinistic,** *adj.*

cheapgild. *Hist.* See ORFGILD (1). — Also spelled *cheapegild.*

cheap stock. See STOCK.

cheat, *n.* (17c) **1.** CHEATING. **2.** Someone who habitually cheats; a swindler.

cheat, *vb.* (16c) To defraud; to practice deception.

cheater. (16c) **1.** Someone who cheats. **2.** ESCHEATOR.

cheating. (16c) The fraudulent obtaining of another's property by means of a false symbol or token, or by other illegal practices. — Also termed *cheating at common law; common-law cheat; cheat.* See FRAUD.

▸ **cheating by false pretenses.** (1827) The intentional obtaining of both the possession and ownership of money, goods, wares, or merchandise by means of misrepresentations, with the intent to defraud. See FALSE PRETENSES. Cf. *larceny by trick* under LARCENY.

check, *n.* (18c) A draft, other than a document draft, signed by the drawer, payable on demand, drawn on a bank, and unconditionally negotiable. • The term includes a cashier's check or teller's check. An instrument may be a check even though it is described on its face by another term, such as "money order." UCC § 3-104(f). — Also spelled *cheque.* See DRAFT (1).

> "A check is an unconditional order in writing, addressed to a bank or banker, signed by the person giving it, requiring the bank or banker to pay on demand a sum certain in money to a designated person, or to order, or to bearer. In other words, a check is an instrument in the form of a bill of exchange, drawn on a bank or banker, and payable on demand." Francis B. Tiffany, *Handbook of the Law of Banks and Banking* 96 (1912).

▸ **bad check.** (1856) A check that is not honored because the account either contains insufficient funds or does not exist. — Also termed *hot check; worthless check; rubber check; bounced check; cold check; bogus check; false check; dry check.*

▸ **bank check.** (18c) A check that a financial institution draws on itself, often as a way of providing cash or a cash equivalent in a commercial transaction.

▸ **bearer check.** (1875) A check that does not name a definite payee but instead is marked "cash," "the bearer," "X or bearer," so that the drawee institution is to pay anyone who presents it. — Also termed *bearer draft.*

▸ **blank check.** (1819) A check signed by the drawer but left blank as to the payee or the amount, or both.

▸ **bogus check.** See *bad check.*

▸ **bounced check.** See *bad check.*

▸ **canceled check.** (1839) A check bearing a notation that it has been paid by the bank on which it was drawn. • A canceled check is often used as evidence of payment. — Also spelled (BrE) *cancelled check.*

▸ **cash check.** (1857) A check that can be immediately either deposited for a cash transfer into an account or converted into cash, esp. because the drawer has written the words "pay cash" or "cash" in the space for the payee's name.

▸ **cashier's check.** (1846) A check drawn by a bank on itself, payable to another person, and evidencing the payee's authorization to receive from the bank the amount of money represented by the check; a draft for which the drawer and drawee are the same bank, or different branches of the same bank.

▸ **certified check.** (1841) **1.** A check drawn on a bank that guarantees, on the face of the check, the availability of funds for the check. UCC § 3-409(a), (d). • The guarantee may be by the drawee's signed agreement to pay the draft or by a notation on the check that it is certified. **2.** Under the UCC, a check that is accepted by the bank on which it is drawn, according to the drawee's signed agreement to pay the draft as presented. UCC § 3-409(a), (d).

> "A certified check is in all cases a promissory note of the bank, and has ceased to be a check at all. In other words, a certified check is a substituted obligation, the result of a novation, by which the maker is discharged. The holder or payee impliedly says, 'Give me the promise of the bank, and I will discharge you;' and the maker says to the bank, 'Promise the payee, and I will discharge you *pro tanto.*' The check is necessarily thereby extinguished. As has been said in numerous cases, a certified check is the same as a certificate of deposit, and it is nothing more." Francis R. Jones, *The Liability of the Maker of a Check After Certification,* 6 Harv. L. Rev. 138, 143 (1893).

▸ **cold check.** See *bad check.*

▸ **crossed check.** (1879) A check that has lines drawn across its face and writing that specifies the bank to which the check must be presented for payment. • The same effect is achieved by stamping the bank's name on the check. The check's negotiability at that bank is unaffected, but no other bank can honor it. Cf. *open check.*

▸ **depository-transfer check.** (1976) An unsigned, nonnegotiable check that is used by a bank to transfer funds from its branch to the collection bank.

▸ **dry check.** See *bad check.*

▸ **e-check.** (1997) An order for an electronic transfer of funds resulting from the conversion of a paper check, usu. by a merchant who has received the check from a consumer. • The payee electronically scans the check's magnetic-ink character-recognition coding to obtain the bank-routing, account, and serial numbers, then enters the amount of the check. This is usu., but not always, done at a point-of-sale terminal. — Also termed *electronic check.* See ELECTRONIC CHECK CONVERSION. Cf. *e-money* under MONEY.

▸ **electronic check.** See *e-check.*

▸ **false check.** See *bad check.*

▸ **hot check.** See *bad check.*

▸ **magnetic-ink-character-recognition check.** (1994) A check whose account number is printed with magnetic ink, which a bank's computer can read when processing the check for payment. — Abbr. MICR check.

▸ **memorandum check.** (1838) A check that a borrower gives to a lender for the amount of a short-term loan, with the understanding that it is not to be presented for payment but will be redeemed by the borrower when the loan falls due.

▸ **open check.** A check that may be cashed by any bank. Cf. *crossed check.*

▸ **order check.** (1875) A check that names a definite payee (X), as by being marked "X" or "X or order," the latter signifying that the payee may indorse it to someone else at will. — Also termed *order draft.*

▸ **personal check.** (1878) A check drawn on a person's own account.

▸ **postdated check.** (1838) A check that bears a date after the date of its issue and is payable on or after the stated date.

▸ **raised check.** (1867) A check whose face amount has been increased, usu. without the knowledge of the issuer — an act that under the UCC is considered an alteration. UCC § 3-407. See RAISING AN INSTRUMENT.

▸ **refund-anticipation check.** (1990) A check paid to a taxpayer for an income-tax refund after the tax preparer's fee and other fees have been deducted. • A tax preparer usu. charges a fee when the tax return is filed, but here the preparer waits and takes the fee out of the refund. Essentially, it is a short-term loan for the amount of the tax preparer's fee. The money is sometimes received by direct deposit or prepaid card rather than by "check." — Abbr. RAC.

▸ **registered check.** (1961) A check purchased at a bank and drawn on bank funds that have been set aside to pay that check.

▸ **rubber check.** See *bad check.*

▸ **stale check.** (1899) A check that has been outstanding for an unreasonable time — more than six months under the UCC. • Banks in jurisdictions adopting the UCC may choose not to honor such a check. UCC § 4-404. — Also termed *stale-dated check.*

▸ **substitute check.** (1910) In the check-collection process, a paper that shows images of the front and back of an original check, bears a computer-generated line containing all the information in the original check, and is suitable to serve as a legal equivalent when the original check is truncated. *See* 12 USCA § 5002(16). See CHECK TRUNCATION.

▸ **teller's check.** (1880) A draft drawn by a bank on another bank or payable at or through a bank.

▸ **traveler's check.** (1891) A cashier's check that must be signed by the purchaser at the time of purchase and countersigned when cashed; an instrument that (1) is payable on demand, (2) is drawn on or payable at or through a bank, (3) is designated by the term "traveler's check" or by a substantially similar term, and (4) requires, as a condition to payment, a countersignature by a person whose specimen signature appears on the instrument. UCC § 3-104(i). • Traveler's checks, which are available in various denominations, are typically purchased from a bank or financing company.

▸ **worthless check.** See *bad check.*

check, *vb.* (14c) **1.** To control or restrain <handcuffs checked the defendant's movement>. **2.** To verify or audit <an accountant checked the invoices>. **3.** To investigate <the police checked the suspect's story>. • In this sense, *check* is typically used with *up, on,* or *out.* **4.** To leave for safekeeping with an attendant <the diner checked her coat at the door>.

check-advance loan. See *payday loan* under LOAN.

check conversion. ELECTRONIC-CHECK CONVERSION. See *e-check* under CHECK.

check-flashing. See CHECK KITING.

checking account. See ACCOUNT.

check-kiting. (1892) The illegal practice of writing a check against a bank account with insufficient funds to cover the check, in the hope that the funds from a previously deposited check will reach the account before the bank debits the amount of the outstanding check. — Often shortened to *kiting.* — Also termed *check-flashing.*

> "Check kiting consists of drawing checks on an account in one bank and depositing them in an account in a second bank when neither account has sufficient funds to cover the amounts drawn. Just before the checks are returned for payment to the first bank, the kiter covers them by depositing checks drawn on the account in the second bank." *U.S. v. Stone,* 954 F.2d 1187, 1188 n.1 (6th Cir. 1992).

check-off system. (1919) The procedure by which an employer deducts union dues directly from the employees' wages and remits those dues to the union.

checkpoint. (18c) A roadblock or barrier used to check people and vehicles passing through, as for authorization to enter, security breaches, or law enforcement.

▸ **informational checkpoint.** (2004) A place where police randomly stop vehicles to seek investigative data that might help them locate and apprehend suspects who are not thought to be occupants in the vehicles stopped.

checkpoint search. See SEARCH (1).

checks and balances. (18c) The theory of governmental power and functions whereby each branch of government has the ability to counter the actions of any other branch, so that no single branch can control the entire government. • For example, the executive branch can check the legislature by exercising its veto power, but the legislature can, by a sufficient majority, override any veto. See SEPARATION OF POWERS.

check truncation. (1975) The removal of an original paper check from the check-collection or return process, and the sending to the recipient instead of that check a substitute check or, by agreement, information relating to that original check. • Check truncation speeds up the check-collection process. *See* 12 USCA § 5002(18). It has been implemented by federal legislation (12 USCA §§ 5001 et seq.).

chefe (chef). [Law French fr. French *chef* "head"] See WERGILD.

chemical test. (1932) *Criminal law.* Any type of test that a law-enforcement officer or a medical person administers or seeks to administer, esp. to determine whether a driver has been operating a motor vehicle under the influence of alcohol, drugs, etc. • Chemical tests include breath tests, blood tests, urine tests, and saliva tests.

chemical warfare. See WARFARE.

cheque. See CHECK.

cherry-stem annexation. See ANNEXATION.

chevage (**chee**-vij). [fr. French *chef* "head"] (15c) *Hist.* An annual tribute payment from a villein to a lord. • Chevage was commonly exacted from villeins for permission to marry or permission to work outside a lord's domain. — Also spelled *chivage*; *chiefage*.

> "Chevage, (*chevagium*) commeth of the French (*chef. i. caput*). It signifieth with us, a summe of money paid by villeins to their Lords, in acknowledgment of their slaverie. . . . It seemeth also to be used, for a summe of a mony, yearely given by a man to another of might & power, for his avowement, maintenance, and protection, as to their head or leader." John Cowell, *The Interpreter* (1607).

chevantia (chə-**van**-shee-ə). [Law French] *Hist.* A loan of money.

chevisance (**chev**-ə-zints). [Law French] (14c) *Hist.* **1.** A composition; an agreement between a creditor and a debtor. See COMPOSITION (2). **2.** An unlawful or usurious contract; esp., a contract intended to evade the statutes prohibiting usury.

***Chevron* deference.** (1986) A two-part test under which a court will uphold a federal agency's construction of a federal statute if (1) the statute is ambiguous or does not address the question at issue, and (2) the agency's interpretation of the statute is reasonable. • If the court finds that the legislature's intent is clearly expressed in the statute, then that intent is upheld. The U.S. Supreme Court enunciated the rule in *Chevron, U.S.A., Inc. v. Natural Res. Def. Council, Inc.*, 467 U.S. 837, 842–43, 104 S.Ct. 2778, 2781–82 (1984). — Also termed *Chevron rule*; *Chevron standard of review*.

***Chevron* standard of review.** See CHEVRON DEFERENCE.

cheze (shayz). [French *chez* "at the home of"] *Hist.* **1.** HOMESTEAD. **2.** A homestall; a farmyard.

Chicago Board of Trade. The commodities exchange where futures contracts in a large number of esp. agricultural products are made. — Abbr. CBT; CBOT.

Chicago Board Options Exchange. The predominant organized marketplace in the United States for trading options. — Abbr. CBOE.

chicanery (shi-**kay**-nər-ee), *n.* (17c) The use of clever plans or actions to deceive people; trickery; deception. — Also termed *chicane*. — **chicanerous,** *adj.*

chief, *n.* (13c) **1.** Someone who is put above the rest; the leader <chief of staff>. **2.** The principal or most important part or position <commander-in-chief>. — **chief,** *adj.*

chief administrative patent judge. See JUDGE.

chiefage. See CHEVAGE.

chief baron. (16c) *Hist.* The presiding judge of the English Court of Exchequer. • Upon the death of Chief Baron Kelly in 1880, the office was abolished. Through the Judicature Act of 1925, the Lord Chief Justice of England became the presiding judge. See BARONS OF THE EXCHEQUER.

chief executive. See EXECUTIVE (1).

chief executive officer. (1854) A corporation's highest-ranking administrator or manager, who reports to the board of directors. — Abbr. CEO.

chief financial officer. (1854) The executive in charge of making a company's accounting and fiscal decisions. — Abbr. CFO.

chief information officer. (1982) The executive who supervises a company's informational infrastructure, including the system for retaining and destroying records. — Abbr. CIO.

chief judge. See JUDGE.

chief justice. See JUSTICE (5).

Chief Justice of England. The former title of the Lord Chief Justice of England. See LORD CHIEF JUSTICE OF ENGLAND.

Chief Justice of the Common Pleas. *Hist.* Formerly, the presiding judge in the Court of Common Pleas. • The Judicature Act of 1875 reduced the Court of Common Pleas to the Common Pleas Division. In 1881 the last Chief Justice of the Common Pleas, Lord Coleridge, was appointed Lord Chief Justice of England, merging the Common Pleas Division and the Queen's Bench Division. The Lord Chief Justice of England now exercises the powers formerly belonging to the Chief Justice of the Common Pleas. Cf. LORD CHIEF JUSTICE OF ENGLAND.

Chief Justice of the United States. The formal title of the officer who is the Chief Justice of the Supreme Court of the United States. — Often shortened to *the Chief Justice*.

> "Popular interest naturally centers in the Chief Justice as the titular head of the Court. He is its executive officer; he presides at its sessions and at its conferences, and announces its orders. By virtue of the distinctive function of the Court he is the most important judicial officer in the world; he is the Chief Justice of the United States. In relation to the actual determinations of the Court, however, he is one of nine judges having no greater authority than any of his brethren in the decision of cases." Charles Evans Hughes, *The Supreme Court of the United States: Its Foundation, Methods and Achievements* 56 (1936).

chief justiciar. See JUSTICIARY (2).

chief lease. See HEADLEASE.

chief legal officer. (1878) The highest-ranking corporate officer responsible for a corporation's or agency's legal affairs. — Abbr. CLO.

> "We recognize that in-house legal departments vary widely in characteristics such as size, resources, culture, style, and the particular legal and business issues confronting their companies. Some in-house legal departments of large, multinational corporations rival the size of many large, global law firms. Moreover, they may employ lawyers with expertise as deep and varied as that which can be found in such firms. Other in-house law departments are smaller and rely more heavily on outside counsel. In short, there is no single, representative, or stereotypical chief legal officer. We describe a vision of the general counsel in the modern corporation that other general counsel or other constituents may wish to use to test their own understandings and visions of the general counsel's roles, responsibilities, and challenges." E. Norman Veasey & Christine T. Di Guglielmo, *Indispensable Counsel: The Chief Legal Officer in the New Reality* xxvii–xxviiii (2012).

chief lord. (14c) *Hist.* The immediate lord of a fee, to whom the tenants were directly and personally responsible.

chief magistrate. See MAGISTRATE (1).

Chief of Protocol. An officer in the U.S. Department of State responsible for managing the Office of Protocol and advising the President, Vice President, Secretary of State, and other U.S. officials on matters of diplomatic procedure governed by law or international custom and practice.

chief of staff. (18c) **1.** An official of high rank who advises the person in charge of an organization or government. **2.** A military officer of high rank who advises the officer in charge of a particular group or operation in the armed forces.

chief operating officer. (1919) A manager who supervises a company's day-to-day operations and who usu. reports to the chief executive officer. — Abbr. COO.

chief rents. (16c) *Hist.* A small, fixed, annual rent payable to the lord by a freeholder of a manor; annual quit rent. • Chief rents were abolished in 1922. See QUIT RENT.

chief risk officer. The corporate executive responsible for identifying, analyzing, and managing significant risks to a business's operations and investments, and ensuring compliance with government regulations. — Abbr. CRO. — Also termed *chief risk-management officer* (CRMO).

chiefry (**cheef**-ree). (16c) *Hist.* A small rent paid to the sovereign by a feudal landholder. — Also spelled *chiefrie*; *chiefery*.

chief use. A standard for determining a proper tariff classification in which a commodity's use is understood by examining the intended users as a whole, rather than individually.

child. (bef. 12c) **1.** An unemancipated person under the age of majority. **2.** *Hist.* At common law, a person who has not reached the age of 14. **3.** A boy or girl; a young person. **4.** A son or daughter.

> "The word 'children' is normally used to denote issue of the first generation only." Restatement of Property § 267, cmt. c (1940).

5. A baby or fetus. See JUVENILE; MINOR. Pl. **children.**

▸ **abortive child.** (16c) *Civil law.* A stillborn child or a child born so prematurely that it cannot and does not survive 24 hours.

▸ **abused child.** (17c) A child who has been subjected to physical or mental neglect or harm. See *child abuse* under ABUSE.

▸ **adopted child.** (16c) A child who has become the son or daughter of a parent or parents by virtue of legal or equitable adoption; ADOPTEE. See ADOPTION (1).

▸ **afterborn child.** (18c) A child born after execution of a will or after the time in which a class gift closes. — Also spelled *after-born child.* See *afterborn heir* under HEIR. Cf. *posthumous child.*

▸ **battered child.** (1962) A child on whom physical or sexual abuse has been inflicted, usu. by a relative, caregiver, or close family friend. See *child abuse* under ABUSE; *domestic violence* under VIOLENCE; BATTERED-CHILD SYNDROME.

▸ **biological child.** See *natural child* (1).

▸ **child in need of supervision.** (1955) A child who has committed an offense that only children can commit, such as being ungovernable and disobedient to parents, running away from home, violating a curfew, being habitually truant from school, violating age restrictions on the purchase or possession of liquor or tobacco, or the like. — Abbr. CHINS. — Also termed *person in need of supervision*; *minor in need of supervision.* Cf. *delinquent child.*

▸ **child out of wedlock.** See *illegitimate child.*

▸ **child prostitute.** See *prostituted child.*

▸ **child with disabilities.** (1983) Under the Individuals with Disabilities Education Act, a child who needs special-education or related services because of (1) mental retardation, (2) a hearing, language, or visual impairment, (3) a serious emotional disturbance, or (4) another health impairment or specific learning disability. See INDIVIDUALS WITH DISABILITIES EDUCATION ACT.

▸ **deadborn child.** (17c) A child that dies in utero before the birth process begins. — Also written *dead-born child.* Cf. *stillborn child.*

▸ **delinquent child.** (1902) A child who has committed an offense that would be a crime if committed by an adult. • A delinquent child may not be subject to the jurisdiction of the juvenile court if the child is under a statutory age. Cf. *child in need of supervision*; JUVENILE DELINQUENT.

▸ **dependent child.** (1896) A needy child who has been deprived of parental support or care because of the parent's or other responsible person's death, absence from the home, physical or mental incapacity, or (in some cases) unemployment. • This definition was formerly found in Aid to Families with Dependent Children (AFDC), 42 USCA § 606(a). When that program was replaced with Temporary Assistance to Needy Families (TANF), the definition was eliminated although sections of TANF refer to it (*see, e.g.*, 42 USCA § 672(h)).

▸ **deprived child.** (1941) A child who (1) lacks proper parental care or control, subsistence, education, or other care and control for his or her physical, mental, or emotional well-being, (2) has been placed for care or adoption in violation of the law, (3) has been abandoned, or (4) is without a parent, guardian, or legal custodian. Unif. Juvenile Delinquency Act, 18 USCA §§ 5031 et seq. Cf. *neglected child.*

▸ **disobedient child.** See *incorrigible child.*

▸ **foster child.** (12c) A child whose care and upbringing are entrusted to an adult other than the child's natural or adoptive parents, usu. by an agency. • A foster child may receive informal, voluntary care by someone (often a grandparent, other relative, or neighbor) who enters into an agreement with the parent or who simply substitutes for the parent as necessary to ensure the child's protection. More formally, the child may be part of the federal–state foster-care program that identifies, trains, and pays caregivers who will provide family care for children who lack parents or cannot safely remain with their biological or adoptive parents. — Also termed (archaically) *fosterling.* See *foster parent* under PARENT.

▸ **genetic child.** See *natural child* (1).

▸ **grandchild.** (16c) The child of one's son or daughter.

▸ **handicapped child.** (1915) A child who is mentally retarded, deaf or hearing-impaired, speech-impaired, blind or visually disabled, seriously emotionally disturbed, or orthopedically impaired, or who because of specific learning disabilities requires special education.

▸ **illegitimate child.** (17c) A child who was not conceived or born in lawful wedlock, nor later legitimated. • At common law, such a child was considered the child of nobody (*nullius filius*) and had no name except one that was gained by reputation. Being no one's child, an illegitimate child could not inherit, even from the mother, but all states now allow maternal inheritance. In cases such as *Levy v. Louisiana*, 391 U.S. 68, 88 S.Ct. 1509 (1968), and *Glona v. American Guar. & Liab. Ins. Co.*, 391 U.S. 73, 88 S.Ct. 1515 (1968), the Supreme Court held that limitations on a child's right to inherit from his or her mother were unconstitutional. As a result, states changed their laws to permit full maternal inheritance. Full paternal inheritance is permitted if the child can prove paternity in accordance with state law (the proof varies from state to state). This burden of proof, uniquely imposed on an illegitimate child, is constitutionally permissible. *Lalli v. Lalli*, 439 U.S. 259, 99 S.Ct. 518 (1978). — Also termed *bastard*; *child out of wedlock*; *nonmarital child*; (archaically) *natural child*. Cf. BASTARD.

▸ **incorrigible child.** (17c) A child who habitually refuses to obey his or her parents or guardians. — Also termed *disobedient child*.

▸ **intended child.** (1993) The child who is intended to result from a surrogacy contract. See *surrogate parent* under PARENT; *surrogate mother* under MOTHER; *intentional parent* under PARENT; *legal father* under FATHER; SURROGACY CONTRACT.

▸ **legitimate child.** (17c) **1.** At common law, a child conceived or born in lawful wedlock. **2.** Modernly, a child conceived or born in lawful wedlock, or legitimated either by the parents' later marriage or by a declaration or judgment of legitimation.

▸ **mantle child.** *Hist.* A child born out of wedlock and later legitimated when the parents are married, traditionally by standing under a cloak with the parents during the marriage ceremony.

"Our law . . . has no need to distinguish between various sorts of illegitimate children. A child is either a legitimate child or a bastard . . . . In the sharp controversy over this principle . . . the champion of what we may call the high-church party alleged that old English custom was in accord with the law of the church as defined by Alexander III. Probably there was some truth in this assertion. It is not unlikely that old custom, though it would not have held that the marriage in itself had any retroactive effect, allowed the parents on the occasion of their marriage to legitimate the already existing offspring of their union. The children were placed under the cloak which was spread over their parents during the marriage ceremony, and became 'mantle children.' We hear of this practice in Germany and France and Normandy; but we have here rather an act of adoption than a true legitimation . . . and it would not have fully satisfied the church." 2 Frederick Pollock & Frederic W. Maitland, *The History of English Law Before the Time of Edward I* 397–98 (2d ed. 1899).

▸ **natural child.** (16c) **1.** A child by birth, as distinguished from an adopted child. — Also termed *biological child*; *genetic child*. **2.** A child that is genetically related to the mother and father as opposed to a child conceived by donor insemination or by egg donation. **3.** *Archaic.* An illegitimate child, usu. one acknowledged by the father.

▸ **neglected child.** (17c) **1.** A child whose parents or legal custodians are unfit to care for him or her because of cruelty, immorality, or incapacity. **2.** A child whose parents or legal custodians refuse to provide the necessary care and medical services for the child. Cf. *deprived child*.

▸ **nonmarital child.** See *illegitimate child*.

▸ **posthumous child.** (17c) A child born after a parent's death. • Ordinarily, the phrase *posthumous child* suggests one born after the father's death. But in at least one case, a legally dead pregnant woman was kept on life-support machines until the child could be safely delivered; so it is possible for a mother's posthumous child to be born. Cf. *afterborn child*.

▸ **prostituted child.** (1966) A child who is offered or used for sex acts in exchange for money. • Some people object to the phrase *child prostitute* because it suggests a degree of voluntariness or choice on the child's part. *Prostituted child* avoids these often-inaccurate connotations. — Also termed *child prostitute*.

"Some victims of commercial sexual exploitation and sex trafficking are referred to as *child prostitutes, juvenile prostitutes*, and *adolescent prostitutes*. Prostitution is illegal in nearly all jurisdictions in the United States, and individuals who engage in prostitution are considered criminals. Therefore the terms *child prostitutes, juvenile prostitutes*, and *adolescent prostitutes* suggest that prostituted children are criminals; that is, victims and survivors of commercial sexual exploitation and sex trafficking may be viewed as willing participants in an illegal activity. As stated in its guiding principles, the committee firmly asserts that these young people should be recognized as victims, not criminals, and that commercial sexual exploitation and sex trafficking are forms of child abuse. Therefore, this report uses the terms *prostituted child (juvenile, adolescent)* and *prostitution of children (juveniles, adolescents)* as opposed to *child (juvenile, adolescent) prostitute* to describe victims of commercial sexual exploitation and sex trafficking. This usage is consistent with the committee's definition and understanding of commercial sexual exploitation and sex trafficking of minors." Institute of Medicine and National Research Council, *Confronting Commercial Sexual Exploitation and Sex Trafficking of Minors in the United States* 33–34 (2013).

▸ **quasi-posthumous child.** *Civil law.* A child who becomes a direct heir of a grandfather or other male ascendant because of the death of the child's father.

▸ **special-needs child.** (1977) **1.** A child with medical problems or with a physical, mental, or emotional handicap. **2.** A child that is likely to be unadoptable because of medical problems or physical, mental, or emotional handicaps, or by reason of age or ethnic background. See ADOPTION ASSISTANCE AND CHILD WELFARE ACT.

▸ **stepchild.** (14c) The child of one's spouse by a previous partner. • A stepchild is generally not entitled to the same legal rights as a natural or adopted child. For example, a stepchild has no right to a share of an intestate stepparent's property.

▸ **stillborn child.** (17c) A child that is alive in utero but dies during delivery and shows no signs of life after emerging from the mother's birth canal. Cf. *deadborn child*.

▸ **unborn child.** (bef. 12c) A child not yet born, esp. at the happening of some event.

child abduction. See ABDUCTION.

child abuse. See ABUSE.

child-abuse and -neglect reporting statute. (1975) *Family law.* A state law requiring certain persons, among them healthcare providers, teachers, and child-care workers, to report suspected child abuse. • By 1967, every state had adopted some form of reporting statute. In the

Child Abuse Prevention and Treatment Act (42 USCA §§ 5101–5157), Congress provided federal funding for all states that implement federal standards in their reporting statutes and defined child maltreatment broadly. See CHILD ABUSE PREVENTION AND TREATMENT ACT.

Child Abuse Prevention and Treatment Act. *Family law.* A 1974 federal statute that provides limited funding to states for preventing, identifying, and treating child abuse and neglect. • The Act was amended in 1996 to reinforce an emphasis on child safety. The Act established the National Center on Child Abuse and Neglect in the Department of Health and Human Services. Its function is to study child abuse, conduct research into its causes, and make grants to agencies for the study, prevention, and treatment of child abuse. 42 USCA §§ 5101–5157. — Abbr. CAPTA. See CHILD-ABUSE AND -NEGLECT REPORTING STATUTE.

child-access prevention statute. See SAFE-STORAGE STATUTE.

child agreement. See *parallel-parenting plan* under PARENTING PLAN.

child- and dependent-care tax credit. See TAX CREDIT.

child application. See PATENT APPLICATION.

child-assessment order. (1989) A court order to have a medical and psychological evaluation of a child, esp. one who may be in need of protection.

child-benefit theory. See STUDENT-BENEFIT THEORY.

childbirth-maintenance period. (1995) The period immediately preceding and following a child's birth, during which, in some jurisdictions, the mother may be entitled to compensation by the child's father.

child-care fund. (1971) *Family law.* State-government funds set aside to reimburse counties for part of the payments for children's foster care and expenses.

child-care rules. (1963) *Family law.* State administrative rules for the care of foster children. • In most states, departments concerned with social services establish and enforce the rules governing the welfare of foster children. A few states have created agencies expressly dedicated to services for children.

child custodian. See CUSTODIAN.

child custody. See CUSTODY (2).

child destruction. **1.** See FETICIDE. **2.** See INFANTICIDE (1).

child endangerment. (1981) The placing of a child in a place or position that exposes him or her to danger to life or health. — Also termed *endangering the welfare of a child.*

▸ **physical child endangerment.** Reckless behavior toward a child that has caused or could cause serious physical injury. — Sometimes shortened to *physical endangerment.*

child in need of supervision. See CHILD.

child-kidnapping. See KIDNAPPING.

child labor. (1878) The employment of workers under the age of majority. • This term typically focuses on abusive practices such as exploitative factory work; slavery, sale, and trafficking in children; forced or compulsory labor such as debt bondage and serfdom; and the use of children in prostitution, pornography, drug-trafficking, or anything else that might jeopardize their health, safety, or morals. Some writers restrict the term to activities forbidden by the International Labor Organization's minimum-age conventions. *See* ILO Minimum Age Convention ch. 138 (1973). See FAIR LABOR STANDARDS ACT. Cf. CHILD WORK.

▸ **oppressive child labor.** (1941) Under the Fair Labor Standards Act, the employment of workers under the age of 16 in any occupation, or the employment of those 16 to 18 years old in particularly hazardous occupations. 29 USCA § 203(*l*); 29 CFR § 570.1(b). The Secretary of Labor may assess civil penalties of up to $10,000 per violation. 29 USCA § 216(e). — Also termed *harmful child labor.*

child-labor law. (1904) A state or federal statute that protects children by prescribing the necessary working conditions for children in a workplace. See FAIR LABOR STANDARDS ACT.

child maintenance. See MAINTENANCE (5).

child maltreatment. See *child abuse* under ABUSE.

child molestation. See MOLESTATION.

child molester. (1939) Someone who interferes with, pesters, or persecutes a child in a sexual way, esp. when touching is involved.

childnapping. See *child-kidnapping* under KIDNAPPING.

child neglect. See NEGLECT.

Child Online Protection Act. A 1998 federal statute designed to control child pornography on the Internet by prohibiting Internet speech that is "harmful to minors." • Unlike the Communications Decency Act, COPA does not apply to e-mail or chat-room communications. Among other things, COPA applies to sexually explicit material that appears to depict minors, even if the people are actually over 18 or the images are computer-generated and do not depict living people. After several court challenges, COPA was held unconstitutional and never became effective. — Abbr. COPA.

child out of wedlock. See *illegitimate child* under CHILD.

child plan. See PARENTING PLAN.

child pornography. See PORNOGRAPHY.

child prostitute. See *prostituted child* under CHILD.

child prostitution. See PROSTITUTION (1).

Child Protective Services. (1961) A governmental agency responsible for investigating allegations of child abuse and neglect, providing family services to the parent or guardian of a child who has been abused or neglected, and administering the foster-care program. — Abbr. CPS. — Also termed (in some states) *Department of Social Services*; (esp. in Michigan) *family independence agency.* Cf. ADULT PROTECTIVE SERVICES.

child-rearing. (18c) *Family law.* The practices and customs followed in the upbringing of children, whether in a particular family or in society generally. — Sometimes written *childrearing.*

children's court. See *juvenile court* (1) under COURT.

children's rights. (17c) Protections accorded to minors as a matter of local, national, and international law. — Also termed *child rights.*

children's welfare. See CHILD WELFARE.

child rights. See CHILDREN'S RIGHTS.

child's attorney. See *attorney ad litem* under ATTORNEY.

child-sexual-abuse accommodation syndrome. (1983) A cluster of psychological phenomena said to deter an underage person who has been sexually molested from reporting the abuse. • Correlating behavior includes (1) secrecy about the abuse; (2) feelings of helplessness to change the abusive relationship; (3) accommodation, often in the form of self-abuse or mutilation; (4) delayed, conflicted, and unconvincing disclosure of the abuse; and (5) retraction of the disclosure in reaction to the chaos and retaliation it causes. The validity of the analysis has been repudiated by some experts in the field who say that it cannot be validated and thus cannot discriminate between abuse and nonabuse cases. — Abbr. CSAAS. — Also termed *child-sexual-abuse syndrome.*

child's income tax. See *kiddie tax* under TAX.

child-slaying. See INFANTICIDE.

child's part. (17c) An inheritance that, by statute in some states, a widow may claim in lieu of dower or what she would receive under her husband's will. • The amount is calculated by counting the widow as a child of the decedent, sharing equally any entitlement with any other child.

Child Status Protection Act. An act passed by Congress in 2002 to amend the Immigration and Nationality Act by changing the definition of *child* in immigration laws, if certain conditions are met, to protect a youth's benefits even though the child has turned 21. • The CSPA aims to protect a child's immigration classification from aging out because of governmental backlogs and long processing times. — Abbr. CPSA. See IMMIGRATION AND NATIONALITY ACT.

child-stealing. See *child-kidnapping* under KIDNAPPING.

child support. (1939) *Family law.* **1.** A parent's legal obligation to contribute to the economic maintenance and education of a child until the age of majority, the child's emancipation before reaching majority, or the child's completion of secondary education. • The obligation is enforceable both civilly and criminally. **2.** In a custody or divorce action, the money owed or paid by one parent to the other for the expenses incurred for children of the marriage. • The right to child support is the child's right and cannot be waived, and any divorce-decree provision waiving child support is void. See CHILD-SUPPORT AGREEMENT. Cf. ALIMONY.

▸ **decretal child support.** (1978) Child support provided for in a divorce decree or modification order.

child-support agreement. (1956) A written contract between parents or other responsible persons to provide child support. See CHILD SUPPORT.

child-support assessment. (1979) A court-ordered or administratively required independent evaluation of the amount of child support needed for a child in his or her particular circumstances.

child-support-enforcement agency. (1977) *Family law.* A governmental agency that helps custodial parents collect child support. • Under Title IV(D) of the Social Security Act (42 USCA § 654), states are required to establish child-support-enforcement agencies to collect support for obligee parents. Although the agencies are governed by a set of federal standards, each state has its own central registry. The CSE agency may operate through the state's Department of Human Services, its Department of Justice, its tax agency, or its Attorney General's office. The agency can help locate a missing parent and establish paternity. The agency works to establish and enforce support orders. — Abbr. CSE agency. — Also termed *IV-D agency.* See OFFICE OF CHILD-SUPPORT ENFORCEMENT.

child-support guidelines. (1977) *Family law.* Statutory provisions that govern the amount of child support that an obligor parent must pay. • Child-support guidelines have been developed in every state in response to the creation of the Temporary Assistance to Needy Families program. 42 USCA §§ 601–603a.

Child Support Recovery Act of 1994. A statute that made it a federal offense for a person to willfully fail to pay past-due child support for a child who lived in another state. • This Act has been replaced by the Deadbeat Parents Punishment Act. 18 USCA § 228. See DEADBEAT PARENTS PUNISHMENT ACT.

child welfare. (1908) The field of law dealing with protection services for minors, focusing esp. on the circumstances in which the government will intervene to provide care for minors who have been abused or neglected at home, or are at risk for abuse or neglect. — Also termed *children's welfare.*

childwit. (12c) *Hist.* A fine levied by a master on a servant who became pregnant without the master's consent.

child with disabilities. See CHILD.

child work. A minor's salutary employment, esp. within the family. • This term is sometimes used in contrast to *child labor,* the idea being that child work within the family unit can be a positive experience. Some scholars and courts note that child work can facilitate vocational skills and social adaptation, and is often viewed as an expression of family solidarity. Cf. CHILD LABOR.

chill, *vb.* (1952) To inhibit or discourage <chill one's free-speech rights>.

chilling a sale. (1881) The act of bidders or other potential buyers who combine or conspire to discourage others from attempting to buy an item so that they might buy the item themselves for a lower price.

chilling effect. (1952) **1.** *Constitutional law.* The result of a law or practice that seriously discourages the exercise of a constitutional right, such as the right to appeal or the right of free speech. **2.** Broadly, the result when any practice is discouraged. — Also termed *chilling bidding; chilling the bidding.*

chilling the bidding. **1.** See CHILLING EFFECT. **2.** See CHILLING A SALE.

***Chimel* search.** See *protective search* under SEARCH (1).

chimney money. See HEARTH MONEY (1).

Chinese Exclusion Act. An 1882 federal statute that suspended Chinese immigration for ten years and severely limited it after that. • The law, one of the most sweeping curtailments of legal immigration in U.S. history, was repealed in 1943 by the Magnuson Act. Cf. GEARY ACT.

Chinese Wall. See ETHICAL WALL.

CHINS. *abbr.* See *child in need of supervision* under CHILD.

chirograph (kI-rə-**graf**), *n.* (15c) **1.** *Civil law.* A handwritten instrument. **2.** A written deed, subscribed and witnessed. — Also termed *cyrographum.* **3.** Such a deed in two parts from a single original document separated by an indented line through the word "chirographum," each party retaining one part. **4.** *Hist.* FOOT OF THE FINE. — Also termed (in sense 4) *cyrographarius.* — **chirographic,** *adj.*

> "Formerly, when deeds were more concise than at present, it was usual to write both parts on the same piece of parchment, with some word or letters of the alphabet written between them; through which the parchment was cut, either in a straight or indented line, in such a manner as to leave half the word on one part and half on the other. Deeds thus made were denominated *syngrapha* by the canonists; and with us *chirographa,* or hand-writings." 2 William Blackstone, *Commentaries on the Laws of England* 295–96 (1766).

chirographer of fines (kɪ-**rahg**-rə-fər). (16c) *Hist.* A Court of Common Pleas officer who engrossed court-ordered fines and delivered indentures of the fines to the parties. See INDENTURE OF A FINE.

> "*Chirographer of fynes* . . . signifieth in our common lawe, him in the common bench office, that ingrosseth fines in that court acknowledged, into a perpetuall record, after they be acknowledged, and fully passed by those officers, by whome they are formerly examined; and that writeth and delivereth the indentures of them unto the party. This officer also maketh two indentures, one for the buier, another for the seller; and maketh one other indented peece, containing also the effect of the fine, which he delivereth over to the *custos brevium,* that is called the foote of the fine." John Cowell, *The Interpreter* (1607).

chirographum (kɪ-**rog**-rə-fəm). [Latin fr. Greek] (16c) *Roman law.* A handwritten document, usu. an undertaking or acknowledgment of debt written in the debtor's own hand. Cf. TYPOGRAPHUM. Pl. ***chirographa.***

chit. (18c) **1.** A signed voucher for money received or owed, usu. for food, drink, or the like. **2.** A slip of paper with writing on it.

chivage. See CHEVAGE.

chivalry (**shiv**-əl-ree). (14c) *Hist.* Tenure held by knight-service; tenure in which a person held land in exchange for military service of the highest order. See KNIGHT-SERVICE.

> "Chivalry is a tenure of land by knight's service: for the better understanding whereof it is to be known, that there is no land but is held mediately or immediately of the crown by some service or other; and therefore all our free-holds that are to us and our heirs are called fees, as proceeding from the bounty of the king for some small yearly rent, and the performance of such services as originally were imposed upon the land at the giving thereof . . . . And these services are all by Littleton divided into two sorts, chivalry and soccage: the one martial and military; the other clownish and rustical." *Termes de la Ley* 83–84 (1st Am. ed. 1812).

Ch.J. *abbr.* **1.** Chief Justice. **2.** Chief Judge.

choate (**koh**-it *or* -ayt), *adj.* (1878) **1.** Complete in and of itself. **2.** Having ripened or become perfected. Cf. INCHOATE. — **choateness,** *n.*

choate lien. See LIEN.

choice. See FREEDOM OF CHOICE.

choice of evils. See NECESSITY (1).

choice-of-evils defense. See *lesser-evils defense* under DEFENSE (1).

choice-of-exclusive-forum clause. See FORUM-SELECTION CLAUSE.

choice of jurisdiction. (1860) *Conflict of laws.* The choice of the state (or country) that should exercise jurisdiction over a case.

choice of law. (1900) The question of which jurisdiction's law should apply in a given case. Cf. CONFLICT OF LAWS.

choice-of-law clause. (1957) A contractual provision by which the parties designate the jurisdiction whose law will govern any disputes that may arise between the parties. Cf. FORUM-SELECTION CLAUSE.

choice voting. See *single transferable vote* under VOTE (1).

chop-shop, *n.* (1977) *Criminal law.* A garage where stolen automobiles are dismantled so that their parts can be sold separately.

chorepiscopi. See SUFFRAGAN.

chose (shohz), *n.* [French] (17c) A thing, whether tangible or intangible; a personal article; a chattel. See THING.

▸ **chose in action.** (17c) **1.** A proprietary right in personam, such as a debt owed by another person, a share in a joint-stock company, or a claim for damages in tort. **2.** The right to bring an action to recover a debt, money, or thing. **3.** Personal property that one person owns but another person possesses, the owner being able to regain possession through a lawsuit. — Also termed *thing in action; right in action.*

> "Chose, or, thing in action is, when a man hath cause, or may bring an action for some duty due to him; as an action of debt . . . and because they are things whereof a man is not possessed, but for recovery of them is driven to his action, they are called things in action." *Termes de la Ley* 85 (1st Am. ed. 1812).

> "The term *chose in action* has been in common use for a long time, but some doubts have been recently raised as to its precise meaning. (See *Law Quarterly Review* for 1893, 1894, 1895.) A Divisional Court, however, has now given us the following definition: '"chose in action" is a known legal expression used to describe all personal rights of property which can only be claimed or enforced by action, and not by taking physical possession.' Torkington v. Magee, [1902] 2 K.B. p. 430. The phrase 'rights *of property*' does not seem a very happy one, but it is quite clear that the court meant to include under the term *chose in action* rights under a contract and rights of action arising from breach of contract." William R. Anson, *Principles of the Law of Contract* 362 n.(b) (Arthur L. Corbin ed., 3d Am. ed. 1919).

▸ **chose in possession.** (18c) Personal property for which title and possession unite in the same person. — Also termed *thing in possession.*

▸ **chose local.** (17c) A fixed chattel.

▸ **chose transitory.** (17c) A movable chattel.

▸ **future chose in action.** (1826) The prospect of becoming entitled to an interest or right.

christianitatis curia (kris-tee-an-ə-**tay**-tis **kyoor**-ee-ə). [Latin "Christian court"] See *ecclesiastical court* (2) under COURT.

Christian name. See *personal name* under NAME.

church. (bef. 12c) **1.** A building dedicated to worship, esp. Christian worship; loosely, a building dedicated to any type of religious worship <a church erected in the 12th century>. **2.** An organization or assembly of worshipers, esp. Christian ones having a distinct history, liturgy, and ecumenical practice; a particular division or sect of Christian believers; a denomination <the Anglican Church>.

> "A church in law is a mere fraternal organization. It may or may not have a written constitution, but it must have some central doctrine as its foundation or constitution. Many of the Protestant denominations claim that the entire Bible is their constitution. The Jews may be said to consider the Old Testament as their constitution. All revealed truths may

be said to be the constitution of the Catholic Church, and when a doctrine concerning faith or morals is authoritatively declared by the Church to be a truth, it becomes a dogma. The Apostles' Creed is an example of several dogmatic truths. The code of the Church is the Ten Commandments. A few sects, by a majority vote, make and change their constitutions at will." Charles M. Scanlan, *The Law of Church and Grave* 23 (1909).

▸ **established church.** (17c) An official church or religion in a particular country; a governmentally sanctioned church of a nation. See ESTABLISHMENT OF RELIGION.

▸ **hierarchical church.** (17c) A church having stratified levels of authority, having congregations with a shared creed and set of doctrines, and being ruled by a common convocation or ecclesiastical head. *See Kedroff v. St. Nicholas Cathedral of Russ. Orthodox Church*, 344 U.S. 94, 110, 73 S.Ct. 143, 151 (1952).

3. The Christians within a particular geographic area, esp. those of a particular sect <the Eastern Church>. **4.** The entire body of Christian believers <the Christian church worldwide>. — Also termed *church catholic*; *universal church*. **5.** The clergy; the clerical profession <Sir Thomas More entered the church that year>. **6.** Ecclesiastical authority or power, as opposed to the powers of a civil government <the marriage was not recognized by the church, though it had been solemnized according to state law>.

church catholic. See CHURCH (4).

church court. See *ecclesiastical court* under COURT.

churchgrith, *n. Hist.* The sanctuary afforded by a church to one who seeks refuge there. See GRITH.

church law. See CANON LAW (2).

church rates. (18c) *Hist. Eccles. law.* A tax levied on parishioners by churchwardens and other representatives of the parish to raise funds for the repair and maintenance of the parish church. • The power to set and collect such taxes was abolished in England in 1868.

churl (chərl). See CEORL.

churn, burn, and bury, *vb.* (1988) (Of a stockbroker) to make numerous risky trades in (an account) and, as a result, squander the customer's money. • The term denotes the action involved in particularly reckless churning.

churning, *n.* (1953) **1.** *Securities.* A stockbroker's excessive trading of a customer's account to earn more commissions rather than to further the customer's interests; an abuse of a customer's confidence for personal gain by frequent and numerous transactions, disproportionate to the size and nature of the customer's account. • Under securities laws, the practice is illegal — a violation of § 10(b) of the Exchange Act (15 USCA § 78j(b)). But because the fraud is the activity as a whole and there is no communication between the broker and the customer about a specific sale of securities, there is not normally a right of action for fraud based on churning. **2.** *Tax.* A transfer of property that does not result in a significant change of ownership or use of the property, usu. to make the property eligible for amortization or a more favorable method of depreciation. See ANTICHURNING RULE; *reverse churning.* — **churn,** *vb.*

▸ **reverse churning.** (2008) *Securities.* A broker-dealer's practice of agreeing to a flat fee rather than a commission-based fee with a customer, then failing to make timely reviews and recommendations on the customer's investments.

CI. *abbr.* Confidential informant. — Also termed C/S (confidential source).

CIA. *abbr.* (1951) CENTRAL INTELLIGENCE AGENCY.

CID. *abbr.* CIVIL INVESTIGATIVE DEMAND.

CIF. *abbr.* COST, INSURANCE, AND FREIGHT.

CIF destination. See COST, INSURANCE, AND FREIGHT.

CIF place of destination. See *CIF destination* under COST, INSURANCE, AND FREIGHT.

Cinque Ports (singk ports). [French "five ports"] (17c) The five English ports — Hastings, Romney, Hythe, Dover, and Sandwich — that were important defenses against French invasion. • They received special privileges and were obliged to furnish a certain number of ships for use in war. See COURT OF SHEPWAY.

"Cinque ports . . . are those special havens that lie towards France, and therefore have been thought by our kings to be such as ought most vigilantly to be proserved [sic] against invasion. In which respect they have a special Governor or Keeper, called by his office, Lord Warden of the Cinque Ports." Thomas Blount, *Nomo-Lexicon* [n.p.] (1670).

"[M]ost of the seaport towns, or at least the more important ones, had local, as distinguished from national or centrally controlled, courts with jurisdiction over the administration of the local sea law. Among these ports was one group which was particularly notable, called the Cinque Ports, or Five Ports—'cinque' being the French word for five. These five ports were of particular importance as naval bases because of their nearness to the continent. In exchange for special naval assistance to the king in time of war, they were not only permitted to acquire but also to keep a position of special importance in the field of maritime law, and with it a considerable measure of local, independent jurisdiction, which served as a reminder in later centuries of the original local character of English admiralty jurisdiction." Charles Herman Kinnane, *A First Book on Anglo-American Law* 362 (2d ed. 1952).

CIO. *abbr.* **1.** The Congress of Industrial Organizations, which merged with the AFL in 1955. See AMERICAN FEDERATION OF LABOR AND CONGRESS OF INDUSTRIAL ORGANIZATIONS. **2.** CHIEF INFORMATION OFFICER.

CIP. *abbr.* **1.** CONTINUATION-IN-PART. **2.** CARRIAGE AND INSURANCE PAID TO.

cippi (sip-ɪ). [Law Latin] *Hist.* See STOCKS.

circa (sər-kə), *prep.* [Latin] (1861) About or around (a date, esp. an ancient one); approximately <the book was written circa 1938–1941>. — Abbr. ca.; c.

circle conspiracy. See *wheel conspiracy* under CONSPIRACY.

circuit, *n.* (15c) **1.** A judicial division in which hearings occur at several locations, as a result of which judges often travel to different locations. **2.** A judicial division of the United States — that is, one of the 13 circuits into which the U.S. courts of appeals are organized. 28 USCA § 41.

circuit court. See COURT.

circuit executive. (1970) The chief executive officer of a federal judicial circuit responsible for daily administration of the courts. • The circuit executive is the highest-ranking nonjudicial officer within a circuit.

circuit judge. See JUDGE.

circuit justice. See JUSTICE (5).

circuit mediator. (1991) An attorney–employee of a U.S. court of appeals who mediates civil cases, usu. before oral argument. — Also termed *preargument-conference attorney*; *settlement counsel*.

circuit-riding, *n.* (1890) *Hist.* The practice of a judge's traveling within a legislatively defined circuit to hear cases in one place for a time, then another, and so on. • The American practice of circuit-riding was based on the English eyre system, in which justices rode between the shire towns to hold assizes. See *circuit-riding justice* under JUSTICE (5).

> "The Judiciary Act of 1789 required that the justices of the Supreme Court serve also as judges of the circuit courts. The justices complained that circuit riding caused serious physical hardships and diverted them from more important duties in the nation's capital. . . . Congress in 1801 abolished circuit riding on grounds of efficiency, but a year later a new Jeffersonian Republican majority restored the practice, obliging each justice to hold circuit court along with a district judge. Gradually, however, improved communications, increasing business in the nation's capital, and the strengthening of American nationhood following the Civil War rendered circuit riding anachronistic. Congress in the Judiciary Act of 1869 established a separate circuit court judiciary, although the justices retained nominal circuit riding duties until the Circuit Court of Appeals Act of 1891. Congress officially ended the practice in 1911." *The Oxford Companion to the Supreme Court of the United States* 145 (Kermit L. Hall ed., 1992).

circuit-riding justice. See JUSTICE (5).

circuity of action. (17c) A procedure allowing duplicative lawsuits, leading to unnecessarily lengthy and indirect litigation, as when a defendant fails to bring a counterclaim, but later brings a separate action to recover what could have been awarded in the original lawsuit. • Civil-procedure rules have eliminated many problems associated with circuity of action.

> "Circuity of action is, when an action is rightfully brought for a duty, but yet about the bush, as it were, for that it might as well have been otherwise answered and determined, and the suit saved: and because the same action was more than needful, it is called circuity of action." *Termes de la Ley* 87 (1st Am. ed. 1812).

circular argument. See PETITIO PRINCIPII.

circular letter of credit. See LETTER OF CREDIT.

circular note. See LETTER OF CREDIT.

circulating capital. See *floating capital* under CAPITAL.

circumcision. [fr. Latin *circumcidere* "to cut around"] The act of cutting off the foreskin or prepuce on a male or of performing a similar (often more extensive) operation on the external genitalia of a female.

▸ **female circumcision.** See FEMALE GENITAL MUTILATION.

circumduction (sər-kəm-**dək**-shən). (17c) Annulment; cancellation.

circumduction of the term. (17c) *Scots law.* A judicial declaration that the time allowed for the parties to present evidence has expired.

circumlocution. Verbal indirection; a roundabout expression that avoids forthrightness. — **circumlocutory,** *adj.*

circum sacra (sər-kəm **say**-krə). [Law Latin] *Hist. Eccles. law.* Concerning sacred things. • The phrase appeared in reference to the church's supreme jurisdiction over questions of doctrine, as distinguished from a civil court's jurisdiction over other ecclesiastical matters.

Circumspecte agatis (sər-kəm-**spek**-tee ə-**gay**-tis). [Latin "that you act circumspectly"] *Hist.* A directive from the king to his justices detailing the boundaries of ecclesiastical jurisdiction. • The directive, issued circa 1285, was originally in the form of a writ, but over time it acquired statutory authority. The title *Circumspecte agatis* derives from the first few words of the writ: "*Rex talibus judicibus salutem; Circumspecte agatis* . . . ."

circumstance, *n.* (*often pl.*) (13c) An accompanying or accessory fact, event, or condition, such as a piece of evidence that indicates the probability of an event. — **circumstantial,** *adj.*

▸ **aggravating circumstance.** (17c) **1.** A fact or situation that increases the degree of liability or culpability for a criminal act. **2.** A fact or situation that relates to a criminal offense or defendant and that is considered by the court in imposing punishment (esp. a death sentence). • Aggravating circumstances in death-penalty cases are usu. prescribed by statute. For a list of aggravating circumstances in a capital-murder case, see Model Penal Code § 210.6(3). — Also termed *aggravating element*; *aggravating factor*; *aggravator*. Cf. *mitigating circumstance*; MITIGATOR.

▸ **attendant circumstance.** (18c) A fact that is situationally relevant to a particular event or occurrence. • A fact-finder often reviews the attendant circumstances of a crime to learn, for example, the perpetrator's motive or intent.

▸ **exigent circumstances.** (1906) **1.** A situation that demands unusual or immediate action and that may allow people to circumvent usual procedures, as when a neighbor breaks through a window of a burning house to save someone inside. **2.** A situation in which a police officer must take immediate action to effectively make an arrest, search, or seizure for which probable cause exists, and thus may do so without first obtaining a warrant. • Exigent circumstances may exist if (1) a person's life or safety is threatened, (2) a suspect's escape is imminent, or (3) evidence is about to be removed or destroyed. — Also termed *emergency circumstances*; *special circumstances*.

▸ **extenuating circumstance.** See *mitigating circumstance*.

▸ **extraordinary circumstances.** (17c) A highly unusual set of facts that are not commonly associated with a particular thing or event.

▸ **incriminating circumstance.** (1885) A fact or situation showing either that a crime was committed or that a particular person committed it.

▸ **mitigating circumstance.** (17c) **1.** A fact or situation that does not justify or excuse a wrongful act or offense but that reduces the degree of culpability and thus may reduce the damages (in a civil case) or the punishment (in a criminal case). **2.** A fact or situation that does not bear on the question of a defendant's guilt but that may bear on a court's possibly lessening the severity of its judgment. • A court's or jury's power to consider mitigating circumstances cannot be limited by statute. *See Lockett v. Ohio*, 438 U.S. 586, 606, 98 S.Ct. 2954, 2965 (1978). For a list of mitigating circumstances in a capital-murder case, see Model Penal Code § 210.6(4). **3.** *Contracts.* An unusual or unpredictable event that prevents performance, such as a labor strike. — Also termed *extenuating circumstance*. Cf. *aggravating circumstance*.

▸ **special circumstances.** See *exigent circumstances*.

circumstantial evidence. See EVIDENCE.

circumvent, *vb.* (16c) **1.** To avoid (a restrictive problem, rule, etc.), esp. by clever and sometimes dishonest means. **2.** To avoid (an obstacle, etc.) by changing route. **3.** To gain advantage over or get the better of by craft, deceit, or fraud; to outwit through artifice. **4.** To entrap or surround by stratagem or trickery.

circumvention. 1. *Copyright.* The act of bypassing, avoiding, removing, deactivating, or impairing a technological measure or device that controls access to a work protected by U.S. copyright law. • Circumvention of technology that effectively controls access to a work protected by a U.S. copyright is prohibited under 17 USCA § 1201. **2.** *Scots law.* FACILITY AND CIRCUMVENTION.

cirliscus (sər-**lis**-kəs). See CEORL.

CIT. *abbr.* Court of International Trade. See UNITED STATES COURT OF INTERNATIONAL TRADE.

citable, *adj.* (18c) Authorized by a court to be used as legal precedent. • In general, published opinions are citable, but unpublished ones are not. — Also spelled *citeable*. Cf. NONCITABLE.

citatio ad reassumendam causam (sɪ-**tay**-shee-oh ad ree-as-yoo-**men**-dəm **kaw**-zəm). [Latin "citation to take up a cause again"] *Civil law.* A citation issued to revive an action that was abated upon one party's death. • The citation issues against the deceased party's heir. Cf. *bill of revivor* under BILL (2).

citation, *n.* (13c) **1.** A court-issued writ that commands a person to appear at a certain time and place to do something demanded in the writ, or to show cause for not doing so. **2.** A police-issued order to appear before a judge on a given date to defend against a stated charge, such as a traffic violation. — Also termed *appearance ticket*. **3.** A reference to a legal precedent or authority, such as a case, statute, or treatise, that either substantiates or contradicts a given position. — Often shortened to (in sense 3) *cite*.

▸ **medium-neutral citation.** (1994) A citation that provides a case's decision number, the year it was decided, and the abbreviated title of the court but does not indicate a particular source for the case, such as a book or website. • Medium-neutral pinpoint citations refer to paragraph numbers rather than pages.

▸ **parallel citation.** (1911) An additional reference to a case that has been reported in more than one reporter. • For example, whereas a *Bluebook* citation reads "*Morgan v. U.S.*, 304 U.S. 1 (1938)," the same reference including parallel citations reads "*Morgan v. U.S.*, 304 U.S. 1, 58 S.Ct. 773, 82 L.Ed. 1129 (1938)," in which the main citation is to the *U.S. Reports* and the parallel citations are to the *Supreme Court Reporter* and to the *Lawyer's Edition*.

▸ **pinpoint citation.** (1961) The page on which a quotation or relevant passage appears, as opposed to the page on which a case or article begins. • For example, the number 217 is the pinpoint citation in *Baker v. Carr*, 369 U.S. 186, 217 (1962). — Also termed *jump citation*; *dictum page*; *pincite*.

▸ **publisher-neutral citation.** (2009) A citation that refers to the primary source of a case, identifying it as having been issued from a particular court rather than published in a commercial source, and is designed to facilitate electronic-database and Internet-cataloguing retrieval. — Also termed *public-domain citation*.

4. A reference to another document in support of an argument, as in a patent prosecution in which a party trying to defeat a claim of patentability refers to a previous patent or a publication to show that the invention lacks novelty or nonobviousness. See REFERENCE (4).

▸ **front-page citation.** *Patents.* A citation of prior art listed on the front page of a patent application and disclosing a patent or publication that is pertinent to the patentability of any of the application's claims.

▸ **textual citation.** (2006) *Patents.* A reference to a work containing prior art listed in a patent application's body.

5. A formal statement or document publicly praising someone's actions or achievements.

citational, *adj.* (1956) Of, relating to, or involving a citation (esp. a reference citation) <citational analysis>. Cf. CITATORY.

citation order. (1955) The appropriate ranking of the various authorities marshaled in support of a legal proposition.

Citations, Law of. *Roman law.* An A.D. 426 decree of Emperor Valentinian III listing Papinian, Paul, Gaius, Ulpian, and Modestinus as juristic writers who could be cited authoritatively in court. • If a majority of the writers agreed on an issue, the judge was bound to follow the majority view. The Law of Citations allowed the judge to use discretion only if the writers were equally divided and Papinian (whose view prevailed in a tie) was silent on the issue.

> "In 426 came the famous *lex de responsis prudentium* — the Law of Citations. . . . This law lessened the difficulties of the courts in dealing with juristic literature. It excluded a huge mass of conflicting doctrine, the relative value of which had not been determined, and which yet had to be used by the judges as a source of principle on which to base their decisions." W.W. Buckland, *A Text-book of Roman Law from Augustus to Justinian* 33 (Peter Stein ed., 3d ed. 1963).

citation signal. See SIGNAL (2).

citator (sɪ-tay-tər). (1899) A catalogued list of cases, statutes, and other legal sources showing the subsequent history and current precedential value of those sources. • Citators allow researchers to verify the authority of a precedent and to find additional sources relating to a given subject. Citators were originally printed on gummed paper and pasted next to the report of a cited case. Today, citators are published in volumes and are also available online; the two most popular are Shepard's and KeyCite.

> "A citator is a compilation showing where certain cases have been cited in other cases, and whether the provisions of constitutions and statutes have been repealed, amended, or otherwise affected, or have been judicially construed, or have been cited." Frank Hall Childs, *Where and How to Find the Law* 61 (1922).

citatory (sɪ-tə-tor-ee), *adj.* (17c) Of, relating to, or having the power of a citation or summons <letters citatory>. Cf. CITATIONAL.

cite, *n.* See CITATION (3).

cite, *vb.* (15c) **1.** To summon before a court of law <the witness was cited for contempt>. **2.** To refer to or adduce as precedent or authority <counsel then cited the appropriate statutory provision>. **3.** To commend or honor <the soldier was cited for bravery>.

citeable. See CITABLE.

CITES. *abbr.* Convention on the International Trade in Endangered Species.

citizen, *n.* (14c) **1.** Someone who, by either birth or naturalization, is a member of a political community, owing allegiance to the community and being entitled to enjoy all its civil rights and protections; a member of the civil state, entitled to all its privileges. Cf. RESIDENT, *n.*; DOMICILIARY, *n.*

▸ **citizen by naturalization.** See *naturalized citizen.*

▸ **federal citizen.** (1885) A citizen of the United States.

▸ **natural-born citizen.** (18c) A person born within the jurisdiction of a national government.

▸ **naturalized citizen.** (18c) A foreign-born person who attains citizenship by law. — Also termed *citizen by naturalization.*

2. For diversity-jurisdiction purposes, a corporation that was incorporated within a state or has its principal place of business there. 28 USCA § 1332(c)(1). **3.** Popularly, someone who lives in a particular town, county, or state.

citizen-informant. See INFORMANT.

citizenry. (1819) Collectively, all the citizens in a particular town, state, or country; the mass of citizens, as opposed to the soldiery or intelligentsia.

citizen's arrest. See ARREST (2).

citizenship, *n.* (17c) **1.** The status of being a citizen. **2.** The quality of a person's conduct as a member of a community.

▸ **corporate citizenship.** See CORPORATE CITIZENSHIP.

▸ **dual citizenship.** See DUAL CITIZENSHIP.

Citizenship Clause. (1896) *Constitutional law.* The clause of the U.S. Constitution providing that all persons born or naturalized in the United States are citizens of the United States and the state they reside in. U.S. Const. amend. XIV, § 1, cl. 1.

Citizenship Day. See CONSTITUTION DAY AND CITIZENSHIP DAY.

citizenship law. The field of law dealing with matters of citizenship and naturalization.

citizen suit. (1961) An action under a statute giving citizens the right to sue violators of the law (esp. environmental law) and to seek injunctive relief and penalties. • In the 1970s, during the heyday of antipollution statutes such as the Clean Water Act and the Clean Air Act, legislators believed that regulators sometimes become too close to the industries they oversee and, as a result, lack the aggressiveness that individual citizens bring to litigation. The statutes therefore authorize, among other things, "private attorneys general" (citizens) to protect the environment. This includes not only injunctions to stop pollution but also penalties to be paid to the U.S. Treasury. A federal plaintiff must sue under a statutory citizen-suit provision and also satisfy constitutional-standing requirements. See STANDING.

citology. See LEGAL CITOLOGY.

citra causae cognitionem (**sit**-rə **kaw**-zee kog-nish-ee-**oh**-nəm). [Latin] *Hist.* Without investigating the cause; absent a judicial investigation.

> "Citra causae cognitionem . . . . Formerly all interdiction was judicial, and proceeded upon an investigation of the facts and on its necessity or expediency being made out to the satisfaction of the Court. No other kind of interdiction was allowed, but voluntary interdiction, without such investigation, was afterwards admitted." John Trayner, *Trayner's Latin Maxims* 78 (4th ed. 1894).

city. (13c) **1.** A municipal corporation, usu. headed by a mayor and governed by a city council; a municipality of the highest grade. **2.** The territory within a city's corporate limits. **3.** Collectively, the people who live in this territory. Cf. TOWN.

city attorney. (1837) An attorney employed by a city to advise it and represent it in legal matters. — Also termed *municipal attorney*; *city counsel*; *corporation counsel*; *city solicitor.*

> "There may have been a time in this country when the function of the City Attorney of the average city consisted mainly of advising the Council, preparing an occasional ordinance or handling an infrequent lawsuit. The legal business of the average city is no longer so simple, so infrequent and so nonconsuming of the time of the City Attorney. Every action of the City must be justified by its legal powers, and the City Attorney is the municipal officer whose responsibility it is to decide whether any act or action is within the city's legal powers. The demands of citizens for augmented municipal services, and the resulting diversification of city operations have increased the volume of work to the point where the City Attorney, in many cities, has become a central consultant of the city officers and employees on a day-to-day, hour-to-hour basis." Allen Grimes, *The City Attorney: A Practice Manual* 6 (1978).

city auditor. See AUDITOR.

city clerk. See CLERK (1).

city council. (16c) The group of elected officials responsible for governing a city; specif., a city's legislative body, usu. responsible for passing ordinances, levying taxes, appropriating funds, and generally administering city government. — Also termed (in some states) *board of aldermen*; (for smaller municipalities) *town council.*

city counsel. See CITY ATTORNEY.

city court. See *municipal court* under COURT.

city hall. (17c) **1.** The building or buildings used by a city government for its administration. **2.** The government of a city, esp. municipal bureaucracy. Cf. TOWN HALL.

city manager. (1891) A local official appointed to manage and administer the executive affairs of a municipality in accordance with the policies established by the city council or other governing body.

city judge. See *municipal judge* under JUDGE.

city officer. See *municipal officer* under OFFICER (1).

city solicitor. See CITY ATTORNEY.

city-state, *n.* **1.** A country that is coterminous with a city in terms of both geography and sovereignty. **2.** A country in which the citizens of an independent city have sovereignty over the territories under the city's direct control, as in Athens and Rome in days of classical antiquity.

city treasurer. See TREASURER.

Civ. Ct. See *civil court* under COURT.

civic, *adj.* (1656) **1.** Of, relating to, or involving citizenship or a particular citizen <civic responsibilities>. **2.** Of, relating to, or involving a city <civic center>.

civil, *adj.* (14c) **1.** Of, relating to, or involving the state or its citizenry <civil rights>. **2.** Of, relating to, or involving private rights and remedies that are sought by action or suit, as distinct from criminal proceedings <civil litigation>. **3.** Of, relating to, or involving any of the modern legal systems derived from Roman law <Louisiana is a civil-law jurisdiction>.

civil action. See ACTION (4).

civil arrest. See ARREST (2).

civil assault. See ASSAULT.

civil-authority clause. (1973) *Insurance.* A clause, esp. in a fire-insurance policy, insuring against damages caused by firefighters, police, or other civil authority.

civil bail. See BAIL (1).

civil celebrant. See CIVIL-MARRIAGE CELEBRANT.

civil code. (18c) **1.** A comprehensive and systematic legislative pronouncement of the whole private, noncommercial law in a legal system of the continental civil-law tradition. **2.** (*caps.*) The code that embodies the law of France, from which a great part of the Louisiana civil code is derived. — Abbr. CC. — Also termed *Code Civil.* See NAPOLEONIC CODE. **3.** A codification of noncriminal statutes.

civil cognation. See COGNATION (2).

civil commitment. (1945) **1.** A court-ordered commitment of a person who is ill, incompetent, drug-addicted, or the like, as contrasted with a criminal sentence. • Unlike a criminal commitment, the length of a civil commitment is indefinite because it depends on the person's recovery. — Also termed *involuntary confinement.* **2.** A public demonstration by two people of their intent to be bound together in a marriage-like relationship. • The demonstration is usu. in the form of a ceremony, often identical to a wedding, but the relationship is usu. not legally recognized and can be dissolved without legal formalities. See CIVIL UNION. **3.** A residential program characterized by intense and strict supervision of sex offenders who have completed their prison sentences but whose recidivism is determined to be likely. **4.** The involuntary detention of a convicted felon beyond the specified release date, usu. because of a propensity to commit sex crimes. — Also termed (in senses 3 & 4) *civil management.*

civil-commitment statute. (1952) A law that provides for the confinement of a person who is mentally ill, incompetent, drug-addicted, or the like. • Unlike criminal incarceration, civil commitment is for an indefinite period.

civil commotion. (16c) A public uprising by a large number of people who, acting together, cause harm to people or property. • A civil commotion usu. involves many more people than a riot. — Sometimes shortened to *commotion.* Cf. RIOT.

civil conspiracy. See CONSPIRACY.

civil contempt. See CONTEMPT.

civil corporation. See CORPORATION.

civil court. See COURT.

civil-damage law. See DRAM-SHOP ACT.

civil day. See *artificial day* under DAY.

civil death. See DEATH.

civil defense. (18c) **1.** The practice of protecting civilians from dangers caused by hostilities or disasters and helping them recover from the immediate effects of such events. **2.** The policies that underlie this practice. **3.** The organization of ordinary as opposed to military people to help defend their country from military attack.

civil disability. See DISABILITY (3).

civil disobedience. (1866) A deliberate but nonviolent act of lawbreaking to call attention to a particular law or set of laws believed by the actor to be of questionable legitimacy or morality. Cf. NONVIOLENCE.

> "Social protest and even civil disobedience serve the law's need for growth. Ideally, reform would come according to reason and justice without self-help and disturbing, almost violent, forms of protest . . . . Still, candor compels one here again to acknowledge the gap between the ideal and the reality. Short of the millennium, sharp changes in the law depend partly upon the stimulus of protest." Archibald Cox, *Civil Rights, the Constitution, and the Courts,* 40 N.Y. State B.J. 161, 169 (1968).

> "Civil disobedience . . . is not just another form of political action, any more than Alexander's use of his sword to cut the rope of Gordius was just another way of untying knots. Civil disobedience asserts a claim much like John C. Calhoun's theory of interposition, the idea of the concurrent majority. But the advocate of civil disobedience, however high-minded he may be, is far more anti-democratic than Calhoun, because he interposes not his state's claim but his own between the majority will and its achievement. There is no majority, he contends, unless he and his fellows concur.
>
> "Thus, as has occurred so often in history, the political virtue of critical intelligence moves almost imperceptibly to the deadly sin of pride. That is the nature of tragedy — nobility of motivation destroyed, as Creon and Savonarola and Saint-Just were, by stiffnecked perfectionism and self-righteousness. All social life is an accommodation. We do not live alone. Legal obligation is not simply a gesture of courtesy to the state; it is the consideration we exchange with other citizens as the price of living together." Harry W. Jones, *The Efficacy of Law* 100–01 (1968).

civil disorder. (18c) A public disturbance involving three or more people who commit violent acts that cause immediate danger or injury to people or property. See RIOT; CIVIL COMMOTION.

civil embargo. See EMBARGO (2).

civil forfeiture. See FORFEITURE.

civil fraud. See FRAUD.

civil fruit. See FRUIT (2).

civilian, *n.* (15c) **1.** A person not serving in the military. **2.** A lawyer practicing in a civil-law jurisdiction. — Also termed *civilista.* **3.** A scholar in civil or Roman law. — **civilian,** *adj.*

civil impediment. See IMPEDIMENT.

civil imprisonment. *Hist.* See IMPRISONMENT FOR DEBT.

civil infraction. See INFRACTION.

civil injury. See INJURY.

civil investigative demand. (1963) **1.** A request for information served by the U.S. Attorney General on any person who may have documents or information relevant to a civil antitrust investigation or to an investigation authorized by section 3 of the International Antitrust Enforcement Assistance Act (15 USCA § 6202). • A civil investigative demand can be issued before a civil or criminal action is begun, and can be served on anyone — not just potential defendants — thought to possess information pertinent to the investigation. If the Attorney General begins a civil or criminal action, this demand may not be served on persons within the scope of the proceeding. **2.** A similar request for information served by a different governmental entity, esp. a state attorney general. — Abbr. CID.

civilis (sə-vɪ-lis), *adj.* [Latin] Of or according to civil law.

civilista (siv-ə-**lis**-tə). [Latin] *Hist.* See CIVILIAN (2).

civiliter (sə-**vil**-ə-tər), *adv.* [Latin "civilly"] **1.** By a civil, as distinguished from a criminal, proceeding <answerable *civiliter,* though not *criminaliter*>. Cf. CRIMINALITER. **2.** Civilly; as a citizen.

▸ ***civiliter mortuus*** (sə-**vil**-ə-tər **mor**-choo-əs). [Latin "civilly dead"] (17c) A person civilly dead, deprived of civil rights <the wife of a man *civiliter mortuus* had similar rights>. — Also termed *mortuus civiliter.* See *civil death* (1) under DEATH.

civility. Politely circumspect behavior in personal interaction; propriety and courtesy in conduct; the absence of rudeness.

civilization. (18c) The transformation of a criminal matter to a civil one by law or judgment. Cf. CRIMINALIZATION (1).

civil jurisprudence. See *municipal jurisprudence* under JURISPRUDENCE.

civil justice. (16c) The methods by which a society redresses civil wrongs. Cf. CRIMINAL JUSTICE (1).

civil law. (14c) **1.** (*usu. cap.*) One of the two prominent legal systems in the Western world, originally administered in the Roman Empire and still influential in continental Europe, Latin America, Scotland, and Louisiana, among other parts of the world; ROMAN LAW. • In reference to Romans, *civil law* (commonly referred to as *jus civile*) denotes the whole body of Roman law, from whatever source derived. But it is also used to denote that part of Roman law peculiar to the Romans, as opposed to the common law of all peoples (*jus gentium*). — Also termed *jus civile; Romanesque law.* Cf. COMMON LAW (2). **2.** The body of law imposed by the state, as opposed to moral law. **3.** The law of civil or private rights, as opposed to criminal law or administrative law. — Abbr. CL.

> "The difference between civil law . . . and criminal law turns on the difference between two different objects which the law seeks to pursue — redress or punishment. The object of civil law is the redress of wrongs by compelling compensation or restitution: the wrongdoer is not punished, he only suffers so much harm as is necessary to make good the wrong he has done. The person who has suffered gets a definite benefit from the law, or at least he avoids a loss. On the other hand, in the case of crimes, the main object of the law is to punish the wrongdoer; to give him and others a strong inducement not to commit the same or similar crimes, to reform him if possible, and perhaps to satisfy the public sense that wrongdoing ought to meet with retribution." William Geldart, *Introduction to English Law* 146 (D.C.M. Yardley ed., 9th ed. 1984).

civil liability. See LIABILITY.

civil-liability act. See DRAM-SHOP ACT.

civil liberty. (*usu. pl.*) (17c) Freedom from undue governmental interference or restraint; esp., the right of all citizens to be free to do as they please while respecting the rights of others. • This term usu. refers to freedom of speech, freedom of the press, freedom of religion, freedom of association, and other liberties associated with the Bill of Rights. In American law, early civil liberties were promulgated in the Lawes and Libertyes of Massachusetts (1648) and the Bill of Rights (1791). In English law, examples are found in Magna Carta (1215), the Petition of Right (1628), and the Bill of Rights (1689). — Also termed *civil right.*

> "I mean by civil liberty that liberty which plainly results from the application of the general idea of freedom to the civil state of man, that is, to his relations as a political being — a being obliged by his nature and destined by his Creator to live in society. Civil liberty is the result of man's twofold character, as an individual and social being, so soon as both are equally respected." Francis Lieber, *On Civil Liberty and Self-Government* 25 (Theodore D. Woolsey ed., 3d ed. rev. 1883).

civil list. (17c) An annual sum granted by Parliament for the expenses of the royal household.

civil management. See CIVIL COMMITMENT (3) & (4).

civil marriage. 1. See MARRIAGE (1). **2.** See MARRIAGE (3).

civil-marriage celebrant. (1992) Someone who, not being a minister, priest, or other religious official, is authorized to solemnize a marriage under local law. — Often shortened to *celebrant.* — Also termed *civil celebrant; marriage celebrant.*

civil month. See MONTH (1).

civil obligation. 1. See *conventional obligation* under OBLIGATION (3). **2.** See OBLIGATION (2).

civil offense. See *public tort* under TORT.

civil partnership. See CIVIL UNION.

civil penalty. See PENALTY (1).

civil-penalty order. (1981) A judicial decree imposing some type of punishment for violating a noncriminal statute.

civil possession. See POSSESSION.

civil power. See POLITICAL POWER.

civil procedure. (18c) **1.** The body of law — usu. rules enacted by the legislature or courts — governing the methods and practices used in civil litigation. • An example is the Federal Rules of Civil Procedure. **2.** A particular method or practice used in carrying on civil litigation in a particular jurisdiction.

civil proceeding. (*often pl.*) (17c) A judicial hearing, session, or lawsuit in which the purpose is to decide or delineate private rights and remedies, as in a dispute between litigants in a matter relating to torts, contracts, property, or family law.

civil process. See PROCESS (2).

civil-recovery statute. (1973) A law that allows store owners to sue a shoplifter for the value of stolen property. • Recovery does not require that the defendant first be convicted of any criminal charge resulting from the incident.

civil remedy. See REMEDY (1).

civil right. (*usu. pl.*) (17c) **1.** Any of the individual rights of personal liberty guaranteed by the Bill of Rights and by the 13th, 14th, 15th, and 19th Amendments, as well as by legislation such as the Voting Rights Act. • Civil rights include esp. the right to vote, the right of due process, and the right of equal protection under the law. 2. CIVIL LIBERTY.

"At common law a person convicted of a felony became an outlaw. He lost all of his civil rights and all of his property became forfeited. This harsh rule no longer prevails. Under modern jurisprudence the civil rights of a person convicted of a crime, be it a felony or misdemeanor, are in nowise affected or diminished except insofar as express statutory provisions so prescribe." Alexander Holtzoff, "Civil Rights of Criminals," in *Encyclopedia of Criminology* 55 (Vernon C. Branham & Samuel B. Kutash eds., 1949).

civil-rights act. (1867) One of several federal statutes enacted after the Civil War (1861–1865) and, much later, during and after the civil-rights movement of the 1950s and 1960s, for the purpose of implementing and giving further force to the basic rights guaranteed by the Constitution, and esp. prohibiting discrimination in employment and education on the basis of race, sex, religion, color, or age.

civil-rights removal. See REMOVAL (2).

civil salvage. See SALVAGE (1).

civil servant. (18c) Someone employed in a department responsible for conducting the affairs of a national or local government. — Also termed *public employee.*

civil service, *n.* (18c) **1.** The administrative branches of a government. **2.** The group of people employed by these branches. — **civil servant,** *n.*

Civil Service Commission. A former independent federal agency that supervised the government's personnel system. • The agency was created in 1883 and abolished by Reorganization Plan No. 2 of 1978. Its functions were transferred to the Merit Systems Protection Board and the Office of Personnel Management. — Abbr. CSC. See MERIT SYSTEMS PROTECTION BOARD; OFFICE OF PERSONNEL MANAGEMENT.

civil-service reform. (1869) The use of business principles and methods instead of the spoils system in the conduct of the civil service, esp. in awarding contracts and appointing officials.

civil society. See SOCIETY (1).

civil term. See TERM (5).

civil union. (1992) *Family law.* A marriage-like relationship, often between members of the same sex, recognized by civil authorities within a jurisdiction. • Vermont was the first state to recognize civil unions. In December 1999, the Vermont Supreme Court ruled that denying gay couples the benefits of marriage amounted to unconstitutional discrimination. *Baker v. State,* 744 A.2d 864 (Vt. 1999). Several months later the legislature passed a civil-unions law, which took effect on July 1, 2000. — Also termed *civil partnership.* Cf. DOMESTIC PARTNERSHIP; *same-sex marriage* under MARRIAGE (1).

civil war. See WAR (1).

civil wrong. (17c) **1.** See WRONG. **2.** See TORT (1). **3.** See DELICT (1).

civis (siv-is). [Latin] *Roman law.* A Roman citizen; a person entitled to the public and private rights associated with Roman citizenship. • Female citizens had only private rights. — Also termed *civis Romanus; civis Romana.*

civitas (siv-ə-tas), *n.* [Latin] *Roman law.* **1.** A state. **2.** An organized community; a territorial unit.

civitates esse immortales (siv-i-**tay**-teez **es**-ee im-or-**tay**-leez). [Latin] *Hist.* States are immortal.

civitatis amissio (siv-i-**tay**-tis ə-**mish**-ee-oh). [Latin] *Hist.* Loss of citizenship.

C.J. *abbr.* **1.** See *chief justice* under JUSTICE (5). **2.** See *chief judge* under JUDGE. **3.** See *circuit judge* under JUDGE. **4.** CORPUS JURIS.

CJC. *abbr.* CODE OF JUDICIAL CONDUCT.

CJE. *abbr.* CONTINUING JUDICIAL EDUCATION.

CJI. *abbr.* Criminal jury instructions — often pattern or form instructions issued by a state's court system.

C.J.S. *abbr. Corpus Juris Secundum.* — Also written CJS.

CL. *abbr.* CIVIL LAW.

***Claflin* trust.** See *indestructible trust* under TRUST (3).

***Claflin*-trust principle.** The doctrine that a trust cannot be terminated by the beneficiaries if the termination would defeat one of the settlor's material purposes in establishing the trust, even if all the beneficiaries seek its termination. • The *Claflin* principle, which derives from *Claflin v. Claflin,* 20 N.E. 454 (Mass. 1889), is often cited as the purest illustration of "deadhand control," in which the wishes of the now dead settlor prevail over the wishes and needs of living beneficiaries. If the settlor is alive and consents to the modification or termination of the trust, the trust may usu. be terminated, unless it is irrevocable. Trusts in the *Claflin* category are spendthrift trusts, support trusts, trusts in which the trustee has discretion to make distributions, and trusts in which the beneficiary is entitled to income until a certain age, at which point the beneficiary will receive the principal.

claim, *n.* (13c) **1.** A statement that something yet to be proved is true <claims of torture>. **2.** The assertion of an existing right; any right to payment or to an equitable remedy, even if contingent or provisional <the spouse's claim to half of the lottery winnings>. **3.** A demand for money, property, or a legal remedy to which one asserts a right; esp., the part of a complaint in a civil action specifying what relief the plaintiff asks for. — Also termed *claim for relief* (1808).

▸ **donation claim.** (18c) *Property.* A claim for ownership of land under a donation act or bounty-land warrant. See DONATION ACT; BOUNTY-LAND WARRANT.

▸ **honest claim.** (18c) A claim made by someone who believes, however unreasonably, that he or she has a right to something or that there is a chance that such a right exists.

▸ **liquidated claim.** (18c) **1.** A claim for an amount previously agreed on by the parties or that can be precisely determined by operation of law or by the terms of the parties' agreement. **2.** A claim that has been determined in a judicial proceeding. — Also termed *liquidated demand.*

▸ **maritime claim.** (1819) A claim related to a ship or a carriage of cargo by ship.

▸ **matured claim.** (1870) A claim based on a debt that is due for payment.

▸ **money claim.** See MONEY CLAIM.

▸ **small claim.** See SMALL CLAIM.

▸ **stale claim.** (18c) A claim that is barred by the statute of limitations or the defense of laches. — Also termed *stale demand.*

▸ **unliquidated claim.** (18c) A claim in which the amount owed has not been determined.

4. An interest or remedy recognized at law; the means by which a person can obtain a privilege, possession, or enjoyment of a right or thing; CAUSE OF ACTION (1) <claim against the employer for wrongful termination>.

▸ **ancillary claim.** (1906) A claim that is collateral to, dependent on, or auxiliary to another claim, such as a state-law claim that is sufficiently related to a federal claim to permit federal jurisdiction over it. • The concept of ancillary federal jurisdiction is now contained in the supplemental-jurisdiction statute, 28 USCA § 1367. See *ancillary jurisdiction* and *supplemental jurisdiction* under JURISDICTION.

▸ **antecedent claim.** See ANTECEDENT CLAIM.

▸ **apportionable claim.** (1994) A claim for economic loss or damage to property where more than one concurrent wrongdoer is responsible. • Each wrongdoer is liable in proportion to his or her responsibility for the harm done.

▸ **colorable claim.** (17c) **1.** A claim that is legitimate and that may reasonably be asserted, given the facts presented and the current law (or a reasonable and logical extension or modification of the current law). **2.** A claim in which the debtor and property holder are, as a matter of law, not adverse. • An example of a colorable claim is one made by a person holding property as an agent or bailee of the bankrupt.

▸ **commercial tort claim.** See COMMERCIAL TORT CLAIM.

▸ **consumer claim.** See CONSUMER CLAIM.

▸ **contingent claim.** (18c) A claim that has not yet accrued and is dependent on some future event that may never happen.

▸ **contribution claim.** See CONTRIBUTION CLAIM.

▸ **counterclaim.** See COUNTERCLAIM.

▸ **cross-claim.** See CROSS-CLAIM.

▸ **enhanced-injury claim.** See ENHANCED-INJURY CLAIM.

▸ **false-association claim.** See FALSE-ASSOCIATION CLAIM.

▸ **false claim.** See FALSE CLAIM.

▸ **fraudulent claim.** See FRAUDULENT CLAIM.

▸ **frivolous claim.** (18c) A claim that has no legal basis or merit, esp. one brought for an unreasonable purpose such as harassment. Fed. R. Civ. P. 11(b).

▸ **supplemental claim.** (1831) A claim for further relief based on events occurring after the original claim was made.

5. *Bankruptcy.* (1842) A right to payment or to an equitable remedy for breach of performance if the breach gives rise to a right to payment. • It does not matter whether the right has been reduced to judgment or whether it is liquidated or unliquidated, fixed or contingent, matured or unmatured, disputed or undisputed, or secured or unsecured.

▸ **creditor's claim.** (18c) A claim that a creditor has against a debtor.

▸ **involuntary gap claim.** (1985) A claim that accrues in the ordinary course of business after an involuntary bankruptcy petition has been filed but before the order for relief or the appointment of a trustee. • The Bankruptcy Code gives priority to creditors with claims of this type to encourage creditors to continue dealing with a debtor until the debtor has a chance to challenge the involuntary petition.

▸ **priority claim.** (1849) An unsecured claim that, under bankruptcy law, must be paid before other unsecured claims. • The Bankruptcy Code sets forth nine classes of claims, to be paid in order of priority: (1) administrative expenses of the bankruptcy estate, (2) involuntary gap claims, (3) wage claims, (4) contributions to employee benefit plans, (5) claims of grain farmers and fishermen, (6) consumer deposits, (7) alimony, maintenance, and child-support claims, (8) tax claims, and (9) capital requirements of an insured depository institution.

▸ **secured claim.** (1859) A claim held by a creditor who has a lien or a right of setoff against the debtor's property.

▸ **unsecured claim.** (1856) **1.** A claim by a creditor who does not have a lien or a right of setoff against the debtor's property. **2.** A claim by a creditor to the extent that its lien on or right of setoff against the debtor's property is worth less than the amount of the debt.

6. *Patents.* PATENT CLAIM. **7.** *Mining law.* See MINING CLAIM.

claim and delivery. (1842) A claim for the recovery of specific personal property wrongfully taken or detained, as well as for any damages caused by the taking or detention. • This claim derives from the common-law action of replevin. — Sometimes written *claim-and-delivery.* See REPLEVIN.

claimant, *n.* (15c) **1.** Someone who asserts a right or demand, esp. formally; esp., one who asserts a property interest in land, chattels, or tangible things. **2.** Someone who asserts a right against the government, esp. for money.

▸ **occupying claimant.** See OCCUPYING CLAIMANT.

claim check. (1913) A receipt obtained for bailed or checked property and surrendered by the holder when the bailee returns the property.

claim differentiation. (1913) *Patents.* A canon of construction presuming that each claim in a patent is different in scope and meaning from all other claims; the presumption that different terms in separate claims must have different meanings if one of the claims would otherwise be rendered superfluous. • The presumption cannot be used by the patentee to broaden claims, and a court will ignore it when convinced that its own interpretation of the claims is correct. The presumption is strongest when a different interpretation would be the only way to make a dependent claim more limiting than the independent claim it refers to. — Also termed *doctrine of claim differentiation.*

claim dilution. (1993) *Bankruptcy.* The reduction in the likelihood that a debtor's claimants will be fully repaid, including considerations of the time value of money.

claim for contribution. See CONTRIBUTION CLAIM.

claim for relief. (1808) See CLAIM (3).

claim in equity. *Hist. English law.* A summary proceeding created to eliminate protracted pleading procedure in simple cases. • The claim in equity was established in England in 1850 and abolished in 1860.

claim in recoupment. (1859) An obligor's counterclaim against the original payee of a negotiable instrument, arising from the transaction originally giving rise to the instrument. • *Claim in recoupment* is a UCC neologism denoting a particular kind of counterclaim that can be used against a transferee of an instrument, but only to reduce amounts owed rather than to create an affirmative net recovery. The drafters distinguished this type of offset (which reduces damages) from the term *defense* (which reduces liability). *See* UCC § 3-305(a)(3) and its official comments.

claim-jumping. (1846) **1.** The extension of the borders of a mining claim to infringe on other areas or claims. **2.** The filing of a duplicate claim to take advantage of a flaw in the original claim.

claim limitation. (1923) *Patents.* In a patent application, a statement that describes the means for performing a specified function without reciting the structure, materials, or acts that support that function. • Claim limitations define the invention by distinguishing it from prior art.

claim of appeal. See NOTICE OF APPEAL.

claim of cognizance. (18c) *Hist.* An intervention seeking the return of a case to the claimant's own court. • Cognizance may be claimed by a person, city, or public corporation granted the right to hold court. — Also termed *claim of conusance.* See COGNIZANCE; CONUSANCE.

claim of conusance. See CLAIM OF COGNIZANCE.

claim of individual right. (1953) *Tax.* A person's right to the separate use and benefit of corporate funds, distinct from the rights of a trustee under a constructive trust. *See Healy v. Commissioner,* 345 U.S. 278, 283, 73 S.Ct. 671, 674 (1953).

claim of liberty. (17c) *Hist.* A petition to the Crown, filed in the Court of Exchequer, seeking the Attorney General's confirmation of liberties and franchises.

claim of ownership. (1818) **1.** The possession of a piece of property with the intention of claiming it in hostility to the true owner. **2.** A party's manifest intention to take over land, regardless of title or right. — Also termed *claim of right; claim of title.*

claim of priority. See BENEFIT OF AN EARLIER FILING DATE.

claim of right. (16c) **1.** *Hist.* A criminal defendant's plea that the defendant committed the act in question under the mistaken but honest belief that it was legal. • Defendants accused of theft often raised this plea, asserting an honest belief in a superior right to the property taken. The claim of right could also be raised as a defense against bigamy if the defendant honestly believed that an earlier marriage had been legally dissolved. The usual phrase today is *honesty defense.* Cf. *honesty defense* under DEFENSE (1). **2.** *Hist.* An owner's action to recover unjustly taken land in fee simple by employing a writ of course. See WRIT OF COURSE. **3.** CLAIM OF OWNERSHIP.

claim-of-right defense. See DEFENSE (1).

claim-of-right doctrine. (1940) *Tax.* The rule that any income constructively received must be reported as income, whether or not the taxpayer has an unrestricted claim to it.

claim of title. See CLAIM OF OWNERSHIP.

claim preclusion. See RES JUDICATA.

> "[T]he principal distinction between claim preclusion and issue preclusion is . . . that the former forecloses litigation of matters that have never been litigated. This makes it important to know the dimensions of the 'claim' that is foreclosed by bringing the first action, but unfortunately no precise definition is possible." Charles Alan Wright, *The Law of Federal Courts* § 100A, at 723 (5th ed. 1994).

claim-property bond. See *replevin bond* under BOND (2).

claims adjuster. See ADJUSTER.

claims-consciousness, *n.* (1934) The quality characterizing a legal culture in which people have firm expectations of justice and are willing to take concrete steps to see that justice is done <claims-consciousness in the United States has resulted from certain social changes, not from any character deficiency>. — Also termed *rights-consciousness.* — **claims-conscious,** *adj.*

claims court. See *court of claims* under COURT.

Claims Court, U.S. See UNITED STATES COURT OF FEDERAL CLAIMS.

claims-made insurance. See INSURANCE.

claim the floor. (1840) *Parliamentary law.* To address the chair for the purpose of being recognized as entitled to speak. See FLOOR (1).

clam (klam), *adv.* [Latin] *Roman & civil law.* Secretly; covertly. • Under Roman law, an act (such as occupying or altering the condition of someone else's property) was committed *clam* when it was done with the intent to conceal it in an effort to avoid liability. See INTERDICTUM QUOD VI AUT CLAM.

clamea admittenda in itinere per attornatum (**klay**-mee-ə ad-mə-**ten**-də in ɪ-**tin**-ə-ree pər ə-tor-**nay**-təm). [Latin "claim to be admitted at the eyre by an attorney"] (17c) *Hist.* A writ from the king commanding the justices in eyre to permit by attorney the claim of a person employed in the king's service who cannot attend court in person.

clameur de haro (klah-**mər** dah-**roh**). [French] (18c) An outcry recognized in the Channel Islands as a protest against trespass to land. • The *clameur de haro* is a legal remnant of when the Duchy of Normandy held the islands before England took control in the 13th century. The victim's cry of *haro* (repeated 3 times) is popularly supposed to be an abbreviation of *Ha Rollo,* the first Duke of Normandy. The full cry, *Haro, Haro, Haro, a l'aide, mon prince, on me fait tort,* when registered at the local records office, enjoins the offender from possessing the land. See HARROW; HUE AND CRY; GRAND COUTUMIER DE PAYS ET DUCHÉ DE NORMANDIE.

clamor. (14c) **1.** *Hist.* A lawsuit; a claim. **2.** HUE AND CRY (1). **3.** *Civil law.* A claimant. **4.** *Civil law.* The thing claimed from another.

clan. (15c) A group of people having a common descent and sharing a strong interest and heritage in a particular geographic area.

clandestine (klan-**des**-tin), *adj.* (16c) Secret or concealed, esp. for illegal or unauthorized purposes.

clandestine marriage. See MARRIAGE (1).

clare constat (**klair**-ee **kon**-stat). [Law Latin] (17c) *Scots law.* It clearly appears. • The phrase referred to a precept, later a writ, for the grant of seisin to a vassal's heir, so called because the opening lines in the declaration stated that it clearly appeared that the grantee was the proper heir.

"A *Precept of Clare Constat* is a deed executed by a subject-superior, for the purpose of completing the title of his vassal's heir to the lands held by the deceased vassal, under the granter of the precept . . . . The precept of *clare constat* proceeded on any evidence, whether judicial or not, which satisfies the superior that the person claiming the entry is heir of the last vassal." William Bell, *Bell's Dictionary and Digest of the Law of Scotland* 185 (George Watson ed., 7th ed. 1890).

clarigatio. See ANDROLEPSY.

claris verbis (**kla**-ris **vər**-bis), *adv.* [Latin] *Hist.* In clear words.

Clarity. An international association of lawyers and other professionals who advocate plain language in legal and official documents. • Founded in 1983, it has members in more than 25 countries and a system of country representatives. It publishes a journal called *Clarity.*

class, *n.* (17c) **1.** A group of people, things, qualities, or activities that have common characteristics or attributes <a class of common-stock shares> <the upper-middle class>.

▸ **discrete and insular class.** (1938) *Constitutional law.* A group that is held to warrant special protection under equal-protection analysis, usu. because the class has suffered a history of discrimination. • This description of a suspect statutory classification was first used by Justice Harlan Fiske Stone in footnote 4 of *U.S. v. Carolene Prods. Co.*, 304 U.S. 144, 58 S.Ct. 778 (1938). — Also termed *discrete and insular minority.* See FOOTNOTE 4; SUSPECT CLASSIFICATION.

▸ **protected class.** (1906) A class of people who benefit from protection by statute, such as Title VII of the Civil Rights Act of 1964, which prohibits discrimination based on race, sex, national origin, or religion.

2. The order or rank in which people or things are arranged <she flew first class to Chicago>. **3.** A group of people, uncertain in number <a class of beneficiaries>.

▸ **testamentary class** (tes-tə-**men**-tə-ree *or* -tree). (1865) A group of beneficiaries who are uncertain in number but whose number will be ascertainable in the future, when each will take an equal or other proportionate share of the gift.

4. *Civil procedure.* A group of people who have a common legal position, so that all their claims can be efficiently adjudicated in a single proceeding <a class of asbestos plaintiffs>.

▸ **opt-out class.** (1978) A plaintiff class, certified under Federal Rule of Civil Procedure 23(b)(3), from which class members may choose to exclude themselves if they do not want to be bound by the decisions or settlements reached in the case. • Rule 23(e) permits courts to dismiss class members who request exclusion. Class members may wait until the settlement's terms are announced before choosing to opt out.

▸ **settlement class.** (1971) Numerous similarly situated people for whom a claimant's representative and an adversary propose a contract specifying the payment terms for the class members' claims in exchange for the release of all claims against the adversary. • During the 1980s and 1990s, mass-tort defendants began using settlement classes as a means of foreclosing claims by some unknown number of existing and future claimants. *See, e.g., Amchem Prods., Inc. v. Windsor,* 521 U.S. 591, 117 S.Ct. 2231 (1997).

class action. (1909) A lawsuit in which the court authorizes a single person or a small group of people to represent the interests of a larger group; specif., a lawsuit in which the convenience either of the public or of the interested parties requires that the case be settled through litigation by or against only a part of the group of similarly situated persons and in which a person whose interests are or may be affected does not have an opportunity to protect his or her interests by appearing personally or through a personally selected representative, or through a person specially appointed to act as a trustee or guardian. • Federal procedure has several prerequisites for maintaining a class action: (1) the class must be so large that individual suits would be impracticable, (2) there must be legal or factual questions common to the class, (3) the claims or defenses of the representative parties must be typical of those of the class, and (4) the representative parties must adequately protect the interests of the class. Fed. R. Civ. P. 23. — Also termed *class suit; representative action.*

"The class action was an invention of equity . . . mothered by the practical necessity of providing a procedural device so that mere numbers would not disable large groups of individuals, united in interest, from enforcing their equitable rights nor grant them immunity from their equitable wrongs. . . . By rule 23 the Supreme Court has extended the use of the class action device to the entire field of federal civil litigation by making it applicable to all civil actions." *Montgomery Ward & Co. v. Langer,* 168 F.2d 182, 187 (8th Cir. 1948).

▸ **hybrid class action.** (1937) *Hist.* A type of action in which the rights to be enforced were several and varied, but the object was to adjudicate claims that affected or might have affected the specific property in the action.

▸ **mandatory class action.** (1959) A class action in which the court does not allow class members to opt out. • Class actions under Fed. R. Civ. P. 23 (b)(1) and (b)(2) are sometimes certified as mandatory class actions, whereas class actions under subsection (b)(3) are not. *See Wal-Mart Stores, Inc. v. Dukes,* 131 S.Ct. 2541, 2558 (2011).

▸ **spurious class action.** (1937) *Hist.* A former category of class action in which the interests of class members are several, not interdependent, and joinder is allowed to avoid multiplicity of suits.

class-action waiver. (2000) A contractual provision by which a party explicitly forgoes the right to take part in a class action. Cf. CLASS-ARBITRATION WAIVER.

class arbitration. See ARBITRATION.

class-arbitration waiver. (2003) A contractual provision by which a party explicitly forgoes the right to take part in a class arbitration. Cf. CLASS-ACTION WAIVER.

class-based animus. See ANIMUS (1).

class-closing rules. (1954) The legal doctrines relating to who does and who does not become a member of a beneficiary class under the laws of descent and distribution. See DESCENT AND DISTRIBUTION.

class director. See DIRECTOR.

class fund. (1850) A sum of money or corpus of property to be distributed to a class or group of people, as opposed to one or more named individuals.

class gift. See GIFT.

classification. See CHARACTERIZATION (1).

classification of patents. *Patents.* **1.** The sorting of inventions by type into broad classes and narrow subclasses, as an aid in patent searches. **2.** Any one of the several classes into which the inventions are sorted. — Also termed (in both senses) *office classification*; (in sense 2) *field of invention*; (in sense 2) *field of search.*

classified board of directors. See *staggered board of directors* under BOARD OF DIRECTORS.

classified evidence. See EVIDENCE.

classified information. (1950) Data or material that, having been designated as secret or confidential, only a limited number of authorized persons may know about.

classified risk. See RISK.

classified tax. See TAX.

class legislation. See *local and special legislation* under LEGISLATION (3).

class lottery. See *Dutch lottery* under LOTTERY.

class of stock. A category of corporate shares used when more than one type of stock is issued. See *preferred stock* and *common stock* under STOCK.

class-one insured. See INSURED.

class rate. See RATE (2).

class representative. See REPRESENTATIVE (1).

class suit. See CLASS ACTION.

class-two insured. See INSURED.

class voting. See VOTING.

classwide arbitration. See *class arbitration* under ARBITRATION.

clausa rebus sic stantibus (**klawz**-ə **ree**-bəs sik **stan**-tə-bəs). [Law Latin] (1935) *Int'l law.* **1.** A treaty provision stating that the treaty is binding only as long as the circumstances in existence when the treaty was signed remain substantially the same. **2.** A doctrine by which the law supplies such a provision to a treaty that does not expressly contain one; REBUS SIC STANTIBUS. • The doctrine may be invoked when a fundamental change in circumstances (1) alters the essential basis for the parties' consent to be bound by the treaty, and (2) radically transforms the extent of the parties' performances under the treaty. But the doctrine does not apply to treaties establishing geographic boundaries. Vienna Convention on the Law of Treaties art. 62 (1155 U.N.T.S. 331, 8 I.L.M. 679 (1969)). — Often shortened to *clausa.* — Also termed *clausula rebus sic stantibus*; *clausula.*

clause, *n.* (13c) **1.** A distinct section or provision of a legal document or instrument. **2.** ITEM (3). — **clausal,** *adj.*

▸ **blanket clause.** A general or indefinite clause framed broadly to provide for any number of particulars.

▸ **confidentiality clause.** (1973) A clause prohibiting the parties to an agreement from disclosing to nonparties the terms of the agreement and, often, anything related to the formation of the agreement. — Also termed *nondisclosure clause*; *no-talk provision.*

▸ **enabling clause.** (18c) The part of a statute or constitution that gives governmental officials the power and authority to put the law into effect and to enforce it. Cf. *enacting clause.*

▸ **enacting clause.** (17c) The part of a statute stating the legislative authority by which it is made and often the date when it will take effect. • A typical enacting clause begins with the words "Be it enacted that . . . ." The enacting clause of a federal statute is, "Be it enacted by the Senate and House of Representatives of the United States of America in Congress assembled." Some state constitutions specify the enacting clause for legislation, without which the legislation is void. In codifications of statutes, enacting clauses generally appear not in the text of the statutes but in historical or legislative notes. Cf. *enabling clause.*

▸ **exordium clause.** See EXORDIUM.

▸ **introductory clause.** See INTRODUCTORY CLAUSE.

▸ **nondisclosure clause.** See *confidentiality clause.*

▸ **nondisparagement clause.** (1988) **1.** A contractual provision prohibiting the parties from publicly communicating anything negative about each other. **2.** *Family law.* A provision in a divorce decree, marital settlement agreement, parenting agreement, or similar document prohibiting either parent from criticizing the other parent in the presence of their child or children.

▸ **operative clause.** (18c) A provision under an enacting or resolving clause; a provision that is not a mere recital or preamble. See *resolving clause.*

▸ **partial-release clause.** (1895) A provision in a mortgage or trust deed allowing a certain property or portions of a property to be removed from the effect of a lien in exchange for an agreed payment. • This clause is often found in mortgages or trust deeds for properties covered by blanket liens, such as subdivisions or condominiums.

▸ **pay-if-paid clause.** (1991) In a construction contract, a provision that makes the general contractor's payment to the subcontractor for work performed contingent on whether the property owner pays the general contractor for the work. • The subcontractor must assume the risk of nonpayment if the owner fails to pay the general contractor. Courts in some states have held that this risk-shifting violates public policy. Cf. *pay-when-paid clause.*

▸ **pay-when-paid clause.** (1984) In a construction contract, a provision requiring a general contractor to pay a subcontractor within a specified period of time after the property owner pays the general contractor. • A minority of courts have held that the subcontractor bears the risk of nonpayment if the owner becomes insolvent. But because the general contractor normally bears the risk of nonpayment, most courts hold that a subcontractor is entitled to payment for work done despite the owner's insolvency. Cf. *pay-if-paid clause.*

▸ **resolving clause.** (1920) The clause that introduces a resolution's operative text, usu. beginning with "*Resolved,* That . . . ." • A resolving clause is comparable to a statute's enacting clause.— Also termed *operative clause.* See *enacting clause*; RESOLUTION (1). Cf. PREAMBLE (1).

▸ **satisfaction clause.** *Contracts.* A common provision in commercial contracts allowing a contracting party to refuse to pay the other party for services performed if the contracting party is not satisfied with the other party's performance. • If satisfaction is entirely subjective, then the contract may be illusory. The clause is typically construed to require satisfaction to be objectively reasonable or for payment not to be withheld without good-faith justification.

▸ **strong-arm clause.** (1935) A provision of the Bankruptcy Code allowing a bankruptcy trustee to avoid a security interest that is not perfected when the bankruptcy case is filed. 11 USCA § 544(a)(1).

▸ **title-object clause.** (1977) A provision in a state constitution rendering a statute unconstitutional if the contents of the statute are not reasonably reflected in the title or the statute has more than one object. • The purpose of the clause is to ensure that the public and legislature have notice of the content of legislation.

▸ **whereas clause. 1.** See RECITAL (2). **2.** See PREAMBLE (1).

claused bill of lading. See *unclean bill of lading* under BILL OF LADING.

clause of accrual. (1853) A provision, usu. found in a gift by will or in a deed between tenants in common, that grants a predeceasing beneficiary's shares to the surviving beneficiary. — Also termed *clause of accruer.*

clause paramount. (1922) *Maritime law.* A provision in a charterparty that specifies what jurisdiction's law will govern the agreement, typically incorporating the Carriage of Goods by Sea Act into the charter. See CHARTERPARTY; CARRIAGE OF GOODS BY SEA ACT.

clause potestative (**poh**-tes-tay-tiv). (1977) *French law.* A contractual provision in which one party reserves the right to annul the contract.

clause rolls. (17c) *Hist.* Sealed rolls containing royal writs (*close writs*) and other documents that the sovereign deemed inappropriate for the public record. — Also termed *close rolls.* See *close writ* (1) under WRIT.

clausula (**klawz**-yə-lə), *n.* [Latin] A clause; a sentence or part of a sentence in a written instrument or statute.

▸ ***clausula codicillaris*** (**klawz**-yə-lə kod-ə-si-**lair**-is). [Latin] *Roman law.* A codicillary clause; a codicil that, having been confirmed by a will (even in advance), operated as part of the will. • An unconfirmed codicil created directives that could be effective even in the absence or failure of a will. See FIDEICOMMISSUM.

▸ ***clausula derogativa*** (**klawz**-yə-lə də-rog-ə-**tɪ**-və). [Latin] See DEROGATORY CLAUSE.

▸ ***clausula derogatoria*** (**klawz**-yə-lə də-rog-ə-**tor**-ee-ə). See DEROGATORY CLAUSE.

▸ ***clausula rebus sic stantibus*** (**klawz**-yə-lə **ree**-bəs sik **stan**-tə-bəs). See CLAUSA REBUS SIC STANTIBUS.

▸ ***clausula tenoris*** (**klawz**-yə-lə te-**nor**-is). [Law Latin] *Hist.* The clause of tenure — that is, the clause in a charter describing the nature of a tenure.

clausum (**klawz**-əm). [Latin "close; closed"] *Hist.* **1.** CLOSE (1). — Also termed *clausura.* **2.** See *close writ* under WRIT.

clausum fregit (**klawz**-əm **free**-jit). [Latin "he broke the close"] See *trespass quare clausum fregit* under TRESPASS.

clausura (klaw-**zhuur**-ə). See CLAUSUM (1).

clawback, *n.* (1953) **1.** Money taken back. **2.** The retrieval or recovery of tax allowances by additional forms of taxation. — **claw back,** *vb.*

claw-back option. (2003) The right to require repayment of funds earmarked for a specific purpose if the funds are disbursed for another purpose or in a manner inconsistent with the document governing the specified purpose.

Clayton Act. A 1914 federal statute amending the Sherman Act to prohibit price discrimination, tying arrangements, and exclusive-dealing contracts, as well as mergers and interlocking directorates, if their effect might substantially lessen competition or create a monopoly in any line of commerce. 15 USCA §§ 12–27.

Cl. Ct. *abbr.* Claims Court. See UNITED STATES COURT OF FEDERAL CLAIMS.

CLE. *abbr.* CONTINUING LEGAL EDUCATION.

Clean Air Act. A 1963 federal statute designed to control air pollution through federal and state regulations. • The original statute created an air-pollution research program. It has been amended many times to expand regulatory controls and enforcement measures. The Environmental Protection Agency is responsible for developing and enforcing regulations under the Act. — Abbr. CAA.

> "The modern Clean Air Act (CAA) came into being in 1970, and although significant changes were made to it in 1977 and 1990, the basic structure of the Act has remained the same. Significant additions since 1970 include provisions addressing acid rain, chlorofluorocarbons (CFCs), indoor air, and chemical safety. In 2007, the Supreme Court confirmed the authority of the Environmental Protection Agency (EPA) to regulate greenhouse gases to mitigate climate disruption. The CAA regulates both stationary and mobile sources of pollution, taking into account the relative contributions of each to specific air pollution problems, and the relative capacity of different kinds of sources within each category to reduce their emissions." Nicholas A. Ashford & Charles C. Caldart, "Clean Air Act," in 1 *The Oxford Companion to American Politics* 190, 190 (David Coates ed., 2012).

clean bill. See BILL (3).

clean bill of lading. See BILL OF LADING.

clean-break principle. (1979) *Family law.* The doctrine that after a divorce or other breakup of a relationship other than a parent–child relationship, orders or arrangements should minimize the ongoing requirement of interaction and dependency except where it is appropriate for one ex-partner to provide continuing financial support to the other.

clean draft. See DRAFT (1).

clean-hands doctrine. (1914) The principle that a party cannot seek equitable relief or assert an equitable defense if that party has violated an equitable principle, such as good faith. • Such a party is described as having "unclean hands." For example, section 8 of the Uniform Child Custody Jurisdiction Act contains an unclean-hands provision that forbids a court from exercising jurisdiction in a child-custody suit in certain situations, as when one party has wrongfully removed a child from another state, has improperly retained custody of a child after visitation, or has wrongfully removed a child from the person with custody. The clean-hands doctrine evolved from the discretionary nature of equitable relief in English courts of equity, such as Chancery. — Also termed *unclean-hands doctrine.*

clean house, *vb. Slang.* **1.** To discharge a considerable number of employees, usu. in management, so that new employees may be brought in. **2.** To sell securities not meeting an investor's requirements.

clean letter of credit. See LETTER OF CREDIT.

clean-slate rule. (1984) *Criminal procedure.* The doctrine that the double-jeopardy prohibition does not apply to the retrial of a defendant who appealed and obtained a reversal of an earlier conviction.

cleanup action. (1968) *Environmental law.* **1.** Activities undertaken to remediate public or private land, water, or air that is contaminated or otherwise spoiled by natural disasters or man-made products such as oil, chemicals, and waste. **2.** A lawsuit to force a person or entity to remediate the plaintiff's property that has been contaminated or otherwise damaged.

cleanup clause. In a loan agreement, a clause that calls for the loan to be repaid in full within a given period, after which no further loans will be afforded to the debtor for a specified "cleanup" period.

cleanup doctrine. (1957) The jurisdictional principle that once an equity court has acquired jurisdiction over a case, it may decide both equitable and legal issues as long as the legal issues are ancillary to the equitable ones.

clear, *adj.* (13c) **1.** Free from encumbrances or claims. **2.** Free from doubt; sure. **3.** Unambiguous.

clear, *vb.* (15c) **1.** To acquit or exonerate <she was cleared of all wrongdoing>. **2.** (Of a drawee bank) to pay (a check or draft) out of funds held on behalf of the maker <the bank cleared the employee's check>. **3.** (Of a check or draft) to be paid by the drawee bank out of funds held on behalf of the maker <the check cleared yesterday>. **4.** *Maritime law.* To settle (customs, harbor dues, etc.) and obtain official permission to leave the port.

clearance. (18c) **1.** *Maritime law.* The right of a ship to leave port, or the certificate issued by the port collector evidencing the ship's right to leave port. **2.** The time that must elapse between runs of the same movie within a particular area; a theater's exclusive right of exhibition over competing theaters.

clearance card. (1886) A letter given by an employer to a departing employee, stating the duration and nature of the employment and the reasons for leaving. • The clearance card is not necessarily a recommendation.

clearance system. (1915) The established means and arrangements through which a stock exchange settles transactions.

clear and convincing evidence. See EVIDENCE.

clear and convincing proof. See *clear and convincing evidence* under EVIDENCE.

clear-and-present-danger test. (1939) *Constitutional law.* The doctrine allowing the government to restrict the First Amendment freedoms of speech and press if necessary to prevent immediate and severe danger to interests that the government may lawfully protect. • This test was formulated by Justice Oliver Wendell Holmes in *Schenck v. U.S.*, 249 U.S. 47, 39 S.Ct. 247 (1919). — Also termed *clear-and-present-danger doctrine.*

> "The 'clear and present danger' doctrine is concerned with distinguishing protected advocacy from unprotected incitement of violent or illegal conduct. . . . The conventional wisdom of the day was that speech was punishable as an attempt if the natural and reasonable tendency of what was said would be to bring about a forbidden effect. In addition, the criminal defendant must have used the words with an intent to bring about that effect, although such specific intent could be inferred from the tendency of the words on the presumption that one intends the consequences of one's speech. The formula announced by Justice Holmes easily fits within this framework. 'The question in every case is whether the words used are used in such circumstances and are of such a nature as to create a clear and present danger that they will bring about the substantive evils that Congress has a right to prevent.'" Laurence H. Tribe, *American Constitutional Law* 608 (1978) (quoting *Schenck v. U.S.*, 249 U.S. 47, 52, 39 S.Ct. 247, 249 (1919)).

clear and unmistakable error. See *clear error* under ERROR (2).

clear annual value. See VALUE (2).

clear chance. See LAST-CLEAR-CHANCE DOCTRINE.

clear day. See DAY.

clear error. See ERROR (2).

***Clearfield Trust* doctrine.** (1957) The doctrine describing the federal courts' power to make federal common law when there is both federal lawmaking power to do so and a strong federal interest in a nationally uniform rule. *Clearfield Trust Co. v. U.S.*, 318 U.S. 363, 63 S.Ct. 573 (1943). Cf. ERIE DOCTRINE.

clearing. (17c) **1.** *Banking.* The exchanging of checks and balancing of accounts. **2.** *Maritime law.* The departure of a ship from port, after complying with customs, health laws, and other local regulations. See CLEARANCE (1).

clearing account. (1895) *Banking.* An account (usu. a temporary one) containing amounts to be transferred to another account before the end of an accounting period.

clearing agency. See *clearing agent* under AGENT.

clearing agent. See AGENT.

clearing agreement. (1920) A contract designed to facilitate the collective settlement of monetary claims between creditors and debtors in different currency areas, without resort to foreign-exchange reserves.

clearing corporation. See CORPORATION.

clearinghouse. (18c) **1.** A place where banks exchange checks and drafts and settle their daily balances; an association of banks or other payors regularly clearing items. *See* UCC § 4-104(a)(4). **2.** A stock-and-commodity exchange where the daily transactions of the brokers are cleared. **3.** Any place for the exchange of specialized information. — Also written *clearing house.*

clearinghouse certificate. See CERTIFICATE.

clearing loan. See LOAN.

clearings. *Banking.* Checks or other items drawn on a local bank and presented for payment through a clearinghouse or directly to the drawee bank. See CLEARINGHOUSE (1).

clearly-erroneous standard. (1950) The standard of review that an appellate court usu. applies in judging a trial court's treatment of factual issues. • Under this standard, a judgment will be upheld unless the appellate court is left with the firm conviction that an error has been committed.

clear market value. See *fair market value* under VALUE (2).

clear-reflection-of-income standard. (1972) *Tax.* An income-accounting method that the IRS can force on a taxpayer if the method used does not clearly reflect income. IRC (26 USCA) § 446(b).

clear residue. (18c) The income deriving from funds used to pay a decedent's debts, administration expenses, and general legacies. — Also termed *true residue.*

clear-statement rule. A doctrine holding that a legal instrument, esp. a statute, will not impinge by mere implication on certain areas of jurisprudence, such as sovereign immunity, retroactivity, and federal-court abstention, but that the result sought must be unquestionably expressed in the text; specif., a doctrine requiring the legal drafter to use clarity of expression before some effect will follow, such as a judicial finding of infringement or the denial of an entitlement.

clear title. See TITLE (2).

clear-to-use search. See INFRINGEMENT SEARCH.

clear value. See VALUE (2).

clear-view doctrine. See PLAIN-VIEW DOCTRINE.

clemency (**klem**-ən-see), *n.* (15c) Mercy or leniency; esp., the power of the President or a governor to pardon a criminal or commute a criminal sentence. — Also termed *executive clemency.* See PARDON; COMMUTATION. — **clement** (**klem**-ənt), *adj.*

Clementines (**klem**-ən-tinz *or* -tɪnz *or* -teenz). *Eccles. law.* A collection of decretals of Pope Clement V, published in 1317 by his successor, Pope John XXII, and forming the fourth of the six parts of the *Corpus Juris Canonici,* completed in 1502. — Also termed *Clementine Constitutions.*

clergy, benefit of. See BENEFIT OF CLERGY.

clergyable, *adj.* (17c) *Archaic.* **1.** (Of an offense) not triable if benefit of clergy is claimed. **2.** (Of a person) eligible to claim benefit of clergy.

clergyman–penitent privilege. See *priest–penitent privilege* under PRIVILEGE (3).

clergy privilege. See BENEFIT OF CLERGY (1).

clericale privilegium (kler-ə-**kay**-lee priv-ə-**lee**-jee-əm). [Law Latin "clerical privilege"] See BENEFIT OF CLERGY (1).

clerical error. See ERROR (2).

clerical misprision. See MISPRISION (1).

clerici de cancellaria (**kler**-ə-sɪ dee kan-sə-**lair**-ee-ə). [Law Latin "clerks of the chancery"] (18c) Cursitors. — Also termed *clerici de cursu.* See CURSITOR.

clerici praenotarii (**kler**-ə-sɪ pree-nə-**tair**-ee-ɪ). [Law Latin "prenotary clerks"] See SIX CLERKS.

clerico capto per statutum mercatorium. See DE CLERICO CAPTO PER STATUTUM MERCATORIUM DELIBERANDO.

clerico convicto commisso gaolae in defectu ordinarii deliberando (**kler**-ə-koh kən-**vik**-toh kə-**mis**-oh **jay**-[ə]-lee in di-**fek**-t[y]oo di-lib-ə-**ran**-doh). [Law Latin "for delivering a cleric convicted and committed to gaol in defect of his ordinary"] (17c) *Hist.* A writ ordering the delivery of a clerk to the ordinary (i.e., a superior) after the clerk was convicted of a felony, and without the ordinary's questioning the clerk's right to claim benefit of clergy. — Also termed *de clerico convicto commisso gaolae in defectu ordinarii deliberando.* See ORDINARY (1); BENEFIT OF CLERGY (1).

clerico infra sacros ordines constituto, non eligendo in officium. See DE CLERICO INFRA SACROS ORDINES CONSTITUTO, NON ELIGENDO IN OFFICIUM.

clericus (**kler**-ə-kəs). [Law Latin "clergyman"] *Hist.* **1.** *Eccles. law.* A person in holy orders; a priest or deacon. **2.** A court clerk or officer of the royal household. **3.** AMANUENSIS.

clericus mercati (**kler**-ə-kəs mər-**kay**-tɪ). [Law Latin] See CLERK OF THE MARKET.

clerk, *n.* (bef. 12c) **1.** A public official whose duties include keeping records or accounts.

▸ **city clerk.** (17c) A public official who records a city's official proceedings and vital statistics.

▸ **town clerk.** (16c) An officer who keeps the records, issues calls for town meetings, and performs the duties of a secretary to the town's political organization.

2. A court officer responsible for filing papers, issuing process, and keeping records of court proceedings as generally specified by rule or statute. — Also termed *clerk of court.*

▸ **district clerk.** (1807) The clerk of a district court within a state or federal system. See *district court* under COURT.

3. An employee who performs general office work. **4.** A law student or recent law-school graduate who helps a lawyer or judge with legal research, writing, and other tasks. — Also termed *law clerk*; *extern*; or (depending on the time of year) *summer clerk*; *summer associate.* See INTERN.

▸ **articled clerk.** (18c) *English law.* A legal apprentice who, by written articles of agreement, serves under a supervising lawyer who provides practical training sufficient to entitle the apprentice to qualify for admission to practice law; esp., a clerk who works for a solicitor in exchange for learning the profession.

5. A lawyer who assists a judge with research, writing, and case management. — Also termed *briefing attorney*; *research attorney*; *staff attorney.*

> "[M]odern American judging in all courts of national significance — the federal courts and the more prominent state appellate courts — staggers along despite the burden of bloated caseloads and the shortcomings of distinctly human judges only by the delegation of a great deal of the labor of judging to law clerks: subordinate, anonymous, but often quite powerful lawyers who function as the noncommissioned officers in the army of the judiciary." John Bilyeu Oakley & Robert S. Thompson, *Law Clerks and the Judicial Process* 2 (1980).

▸ **elbow clerk.** (1975) An individual judge's personal clerk; esp., one who works closely with the judge. • The name derives from the metaphoric expectation that the clerk is always at the judge's elbow.

▸ **pool clerk.** (1976) A clerk who does not work for only one judge but performs a range of duties for several judges or for the entire court.

6. *Hist.* A cleric.

> "Eventually the rule was established that 'clerks' of all kinds, who committed any of the serious crimes termed felonies, could be tried only in an ecclesiastical court, and therefore were only amenable to such punishments as that court could inflict. Any clerk accused of such crime was accordingly passed over to the bishop's court. He was there tried before a jury of clerks by the oaths of twelve compurgators; a mode of trial which usually ensured him an

acquittal." J.W. Cecil Turner, *Kenny's Outlines of Criminal Law* 75 (16th ed. 1952).

7. SECRETARY (3).

▸ **reading clerk.** (1879) A legislative officer charged with reading bills to the body.

clerk, *vb.* (16c) To work as a clerk <she clerked for a Chicago law firm last summer>.

clerk and master's deed. See *special master's deed* under DEED.

clerk of arraigns (ə-raynz). (18c) *Hist. English law.* A deputy of the clerk of assize responsible for arraigning defendants and putting the formal questions to the jurors as they deliver their verdict. • The office was abolished in England in 1946.

clerk of assize (ə-sɪz). (17c) *Hist.* An assize associate responsible for record-keeping and other clerical and administrative functions. See ASSOCIATE (3).

clerk of court. See CLERK (2).

clerk of enrollments. (18c) *Hist. English law.* The former chief of the Enrollment Office, which the British Parliament abolished in 1879, reassigning its duties to the Central Office. See ENROLLMENT OFFICE; CENTRAL OFFICE.

clerk of indictment. (18c) *Hist. English law.* An officer of England's Central Criminal Court, responsible for preparing indictments and assisting the Clerk of Arraigns. • The office was abolished in 1946, when its duties were moved to the Central Office. See CENTRAL OFFICE.

Clerk of Nichils. See NICHIL.

clerk of records and writs. (1842) *Hist. English law.* An officer of the English Court of Chancery responsible for filing documents and sealing bills of complaint and writs of execution. • The office was abolished in 1879, when its duties were moved to the Central Office. See CENTRAL OFFICE.

clerk of the corporation. See SECRETARY (2).

Clerk of the Crown in Chancery. (17c) *English law.* The head of the permanent staff of the Crown Office in Chancery (of the Central Office), responsible for reading the title of Bills in the House of Lords, sending out writs of summons to peers, and issuing election writs.

Clerk of the House of Commons. (17c) *English law.* An officer of the House of Commons who keeps the House journal, signs orders, endorses bills sent to the House of Lords, and has custody of all records. • The Clerk is appointed for life by the Crown.

clerk of the market. (15c) *Hist. English law.* The overseer of a public market, responsible for witnessing oral contracts, inquiring into weights and measures, measuring land, and settling disputes between people dealing there. • The office has become obsolete as a result of various statutes regulating weights and measures.

Clerk of the Parliaments. (15c) *English law.* The principal permanent official of the House of Lords, responsible for the House's minutes and documents, and for advising the members on procedure.

Clerk of the Peace. (17c) *Hist. English law.* An officer of the Quarter Sessions responsible for maintaining the courts' records, preparing indictments, entering judgments, issuing process, and other clerical and administrative functions. • The office was abolished in England in 1971, when the Quarter Sessions' jurisdiction was transferred to the Crown Courts. See *quarter session* under SESSION (1).

Clerk of the Pells. (17c) *Hist. English law.* An Exchequer officer who entered tellers' bills on the parchment rolls (*pells*), one for receipts and the other for disbursements. — Also termed *Master of the Pells.*

Clerk of the Pipe. (15c) *Hist. English law.* An Exchequer officer responsible for the Pipe Rolls. • The office was abolished in 1833. — Also termed *Engrosser of the Great Roll.* See PIPE ROLLS.

Clerk of the Privy Seal (priv-ee seel). (16c) *Hist. English law.* An officer responsible for preparing documents for the Lord Privy Seal. • The use of the Privy Seal was abolished in 1884. See PRIVY SEAL.

Clerk of the Signet (sig-nit). (15c) *Hist. English law.* An officer who kept the privy signet and attended the sovereign's principal secretary. • The signet was used to seal royal letters and other documents not requiring the Great Seal of the Realm. The office was abolished in England in 1851. See *great seal* (3) under SEAL; PRIVY SIGNET.

clerkship. (1836) **1.** An internship in which a law student or recent law-school graduate assists a lawyer or judge with legal writing, research, and other tasks. • In many common-law jurisdictions, recent law-school graduates are required to complete clerkships as a condition of admission to the bar. **2.** *Hist.* A law student's employment as an attorney's apprentice before gaining admission to the bar. • Until shortly before World War II, a person could be admitted to the bar in many states without attending law school merely by passing the bar exam.

clerk's record. See RECORD (4).

c-level management. See MANAGEMENT (1).

clickfarming. Using a domain name that may or may not be legitimate but was selected at least in part to lure Internet users to a website primarily composed of click-through advertisements.

click fraud. See FRAUD.

clickwrap agreement. See POINT-AND-CLICK AGREEMENT.

clickwrap license. See POINT-AND-CLICK AGREEMENT.

cliens (klɪ-enz), *n.* [Latin "client"] *Roman law.* A dependent; a person who depended on another for defense in suits at law and other difficulties. • A *cliens* was often a freed slave or immigrant. Pl. ***clientes*** (klɪ-en-teez).

client, *n.* (14c) A person or entity that employs a professional for advice or help in that professional's line of work; esp., one in whose interest a lawyer acts, as by giving advice, appearing in court, or handling a matter. — **cliental,** *adj.*

client control. (1959) The influence that a lawyer may exercise over his or her client, esp. in relation to positions taken, decisions made, and general conduct with other parties and their attorneys. • Lawyers whose clients behave irrationally, as by acting vindictively or refusing even generous settlement offers, are said to have little or no client control.

clientela (klɪ-ən-tee-lə), *n.* [Latin] *Roman law.* **1.** Clientship; the relationship between a *cliens* and a patron. **2.** A person's dependents.

client-security fund. See FUND (1).

client's privilege. See *attorney–client privilege* under PRIVILEGE (3).

client state. See STATE (1).

client trust account. (1975) A bank account, usu. interest-bearing, in which a lawyer deposits money belonging to a client (e.g., money received from a client's debtor, from the settlement of a client's case, or from the client for later use in a business transaction). — Also termed *trust account.*

***Clifford* trust.** See TRUST (3).

climate refugee. See REFUGEE.

clinch, *vb. Parliamentary law.* To preclude further action on (an adopted motion or series of motions) by moving at once for reconsideration and then defeating that motion. • The clincher motion in a legislative body usu. takes the form of a motion to "reconsider and lay on the table [the motion to reconsider]." Since the motion has just been debated and passed, there are almost always enough votes to defeat a motion to reconsider. — **clincher,** *n.*

clinical diagnosis. See DIAGNOSIS.

clinical legal studies. (1972) Law-school training in which students participate in actual cases under the supervision of a practicing attorney or law professor. • This training was first introduced in the late 1960s under the leadership of Gary Bellow and others. It provided law students with a substitute for traditional apprenticeship programs. — Often shortened to *clinical studies.* Cf. CLERKSHIP (1).

clinical legal training. (1952) A form of legal education that involves law students' having practical and direct contact with indigent clients involved in civil disputes or facing criminal charges.

clinical pneumoconiosis. See PNEUMOCONIOSIS.

clitoridectomy. See FEMALE GENITAL MUTILATION (1).

CLO. *abbr.* CHIEF LEGAL OFFICER.

clog on the equity of redemption. (1908) An agreement or condition that prevents a defaulting mortgagor from getting back the property free from encumbrance upon paying the debt or performing the obligation for which the security was given. See EQUITY OF REDEMPTION.

cloister, *n.* (14c) A monastic establishment; esp., an area within a monastery or convent to which monks or nuns are restricted. — **cloister,** *vb.*

close, *n.* (14c) **1.** An enclosed portion of land. **2.** The interest of a person in a particular piece of land, enclosed or not. **3.** The final price of a stock at the end of the exchange's trading day; see *closing price* under PRICE.

close, *vb.* (13c) **1.** To conclude; to bring to an end <the case was closed>. **2.** To conclude discussion or negotiation about <close on a house>. See CLOSING.

close borough. See *pocket borough* under BOROUGH (3).

close-connectedness doctrine. (1970) A doctrine used by some courts to deny an assignee of a negotiable note holder-in-due-course status if the assignee is too closely connected to the original holder-mortgagee. — Also termed *close-connection doctrine.*

close corporation. See CORPORATION.

closed, *adj.* (13c) **1.** (Of a class or organization) confined to a limited number <a closed mass-tort class> <nonunion workers were excluded from the closed shop>. **2.** (Of a proceeding or gathering) conducted in secrecy <a closed hearing> <a closed shareholders' meeting>.

closed account. See ACCOUNT.

closed adoption. See ADOPTION (1).

closed brief. See BRIEF (1).

closed corporation. See *close corporation* under CORPORATION.

closed court. (1842) **1.** *Hist.* The English Court of Common Pleas, open only to serjeants-at-law. • The monopoly of the serjeants-at-law was abolished in 1845. **2.** See *closed session* (2) under SESSION (1). **3.** See *closed session* (3) under SESSION (1).

close debate. (1918) *Parliamentary law.* To pass a motion that ends debate and amendment of a pending question or series of questions. • The synonymous shorthand "previous question," a somewhat archaic and misleading term that several parliamentary manuals still use for this motion, has evolved over time. Two centuries ago, the motion was invented for suppressing an undesirable debate: if the original form — "Shall the main question be put?" — was voted down, then the body immediately stopped considering the pending question. The motion's form later became "Shall the main question be now put?," which if passed in the affirmative brought the pending question to an immediate vote. — Also termed *vote immediately.* See CLOTURE. Cf. EXTEND DEBATE; LIMIT DEBATE.

closed economy. See ECONOMY.

closed-ended claim. See PATENT CLAIM.

closed-end fund. See MUTUAL FUND.

closed-end mortgage. See MORTGAGE.

closed-end mortgage bond. See BOND (3).

closed insurance contract. See *closed policy* under INSURANCE POLICY.

closed memorandum. See MEMORANDUM (2).

closed mortgage. See *closed-end mortgage* under MORTGAGE.

closed nonunion shop. See SHOP.

closed policy. See INSURANCE POLICY.

closed session. See SESSION (1).

closed shop. See SHOP.

closed-shop contract. (1930) A labor agreement requiring an employer to hire and retain only union members and to discharge nonunion members. See *closed shop* under SHOP.

closed source, *adj.* (1998) Of or related to software that does not include the source code and cannot be modified without either damaging the program or violating the software developer's ownership rights. • Proprietary software is usu. closed source.

closed testament. See *mystic will* under WILL.

closed transaction. See TRANSACTION.

closed trial. See TRIAL.

closed union. See UNION.

closed union shop. See *closed shop* under SHOP.

closed-universe memo. See *closed memorandum* under MEMORANDUM (2).

closed will. See *mystic will* under WILL.

close interpretation. See *strict interpretation* under INTERPRETATION (1).

close-jail execution. See EXECUTION (4).

closely held corporation. See *close corporation* under CORPORATION.

close-nexus test. See NEXUS TEST.

close nominations. (1923) *Parliamentary law.* To end nominations from the floor by passage of a motion.

close rolls. See CLAUSE ROLLS.

close-security prison. See PRISON.

close writ. See WRIT.

closing. (1934) The final meeting between the parties to a transaction, at which the transaction is consummated; esp., in real estate, the final transaction between the buyer and seller, whereby the conveyancing documents are concluded and the money and property transferred. — Also termed *settlement.* Cf. *settlement date* (4) under DATE.

closing address. See CLOSING ARGUMENT.

closing agent. See *settlement agent* under AGENT.

closing agreement. See AGREEMENT.

closing argument. (1828) In a trial, a lawyer's final statement to the judge or jury before deliberation begins, in which the lawyer requests the judge or jury to consider the evidence and to apply the law in his or her client's favor. • After the closing arguments in a jury trial, the judge ordinarily instructs the jury on the law that governs the case. — Also termed *closing statement*; *final argument*; *jury summation*; *summing up*; *summation*; *closing address*; (in English law) *final submission*; (in English law) *final speech.*

closing costs. (1946) *Real estate.* The expenses that must be paid, usu. in a lump sum at closing, apart from the purchase price and interest. • These may include taxes, title insurance, and attorney's fees.

closing date. (1850) **1.** The last date on which it is possible to do something <the closing date for applications>. **2.** The date scheduled for the conclusion of a transaction, such as a real-estate sale <a memento from the closing date of our first house>.

closing of estate. (1843) *Wills & estates.* The completion of the administration of a decedent's estate, brought about by the administrator's distribution of estate assets, payment of taxes, and filing of necessary accounts with the probate court.

closing price. See PRICE.

closing statement. (1875) **1.** CLOSING ARGUMENT. **2.** A written breakdown of the costs involved in a particular real-estate transaction, usu. prepared by a lender or an escrow agent. — Also termed *settlement sheet*; *settlement statement.* Cf. BROKER'S LOAN STATEMENT.

closure. See CLOTURE.

cloture (kloh-chər), *n.* (1871) The procedure of ending debate in a legislative body and calling for an immediate vote. — Also spelled *closure.* — **cloture,** *vb.*

cloud computing. The practice of sharing computing resources via the Internet; esp., the practice of accessing, manipulating, processing, and storing data on a remote server. • Cloud computing is an elastic, measured service offering on-demand, self-service access to computational resource pooling through Internet-capable devices. Cloud computing services are typically divided into five categories: software as a service (SaaS), platform as a service (PaaS), infrastructure as a service (IaaS), hardware as a service (HaaS), and everything as a service (EaaS).

> "At its simplest, cloud computing is a way of delivering computing resources as a utility service via a network, typically the Internet, scalable up and down according to user requirements. As such, the cloud may prove to be as disruptive an innovation as was the emergence of cheap electricity on demand a century or so ago. Such computing resources may range from raw processing power and storage, such as servers or storage equipment, to full software applications. Users can 'rent' IT resources from third parties when needed, instead of purchasing their own, thus 'turning capex to opex' (capital expenditure into operating expenditure). . . . In slightly more technical terms, cloud computing is an arrangement whereby computing resources are provided on a flexible, location-independent basis that allows for rapid and seamless allocation of resources on demand. Typically, cloud resources are provided to specific users from a pool shared with other customers with pricing, if any, often proportional to the resources used. The delivery of cloud services often depends on complex, multilayered arrangements between various providers." W. Kuan Hon & Christopher Millard, "Cloud Technologies and Services," in *Cloud Computing Law* 3, 3–4 (Christopher Millard ed., 2013).

cloud on title. (1826) A defect or potential defect in the owner's title to a piece of land arising from some claim or encumbrance, such as a lien, an easement, or a court order. — Also termed *blot on title.* See *action to quiet title* under ACTION (4).

CLS. *abbr.* CRITICAL LEGAL STUDIES.

CLSer. See CRIT.

CLT. *abbr.* See *charitable lead trust* under TRUST (3).

CLU. *abbr.* See *chartered life underwriter* under UNDERWRITER.

Club Fed. (1987) *Slang.* A low-security federal prison, usu. for white-collar criminals, that has a comparatively informal, relaxed atmosphere and, reputedly, luxury facilities. • Some sources claim that "Club Fed" prisons offer weight-lifting equipment, tennis courts, cable television, computers, musical instruments, and even miniature golf.

club-law. Government by clubs (big sticks) or violence; the use of illegal force in place of law.

cluster bomb. See BOMB.

cluster zoning. See ZONING.

CMO. *abbr.* **1.** CASE-MANAGEMENT ORDER. **2.** COLLATERALIZED MORTGAGE OBLIGATION.

CMPPA. *abbr.* COMPUTER MATCHING AND PRIVACY PROTECTION ACT OF 1988.

CMR. *abbr.* **1.** Court of Military Review. See COURT OF CRIMINAL APPEALS (1). **2.** COURT-MARTIAL REPORTS.

CMV. *abbr.* **1.** Commercial motor vehicle. **2.** CURRENT MARKET VALUE.

CN. *abbr.* Code Napoléon. See NAPOLEONIC CODE (1).

CNCI. *abbr.* COMPREHENSIVE NATIONAL CYBERSECURITY INITIATIVE.

CNH. *abbr.* Criminally negligent homicide.

CNPP. *abbr.* CENTER FOR NUTRITION POLICY AND PROMOTION.

CNS. *abbr.* See *covenant not to sue* under COVENANT (1).

co-. *prefix.* (15c) Jointly or together with <coowner> <codefendant>.

co. *abbr.* (*usu. cap.*) (17c) **1.** COMPANY. **2.** COUNTY.

c/o. *abbr.* (1889) Care of.

CoA. *abbr.* CONTRACT OF AFFREIGHTMENT.

COA. *abbr.* **1.** CONTRACT OF AFFREIGHTMENT. **2.** Certificate of appealability. See CERTIFICATE. **3.** CAUSE OF ACTION.

co-accused. See CODEFENDANT.

coaching. 1. The training and drilling of someone to improve performance. **2.** The act or practice of working with a witness before testimony on what questions to expect. • Coaching becomes illegal tampering if it involves intimidation, the encouragement to lie, or the prompting of false answers.

coadjutor (koh-**aj**-ə-tər or koh-ə-**joo**-tər), *n.* (15c) **1.** Someone who works together with another; a helper or assistant. **2.** A bishop who helps a diocesan bishop, often with a right of succession. — **coadjutor,** *adj.*

co-administrator. (18c) *Wills & estates.* A person appointed to jointly administer an estate with one or more other administrators.

co-adventurer. See COVENTURER.

co-agent. See AGENT.

coal note. See NOTE (1).

coal notice. In Pennsylvania, a notice that must be included in deeds and other instruments relating to the sale of surface property (excepting mortgages or quitclaim deeds) detailing any severance of the ownership of coal under the land.

Coase Theorem (kohs). (1968) A proposition in economics describing the relationship between legal rules and economic efficiency. • The theorem, developed by Ronald Coase, holds that if there are no transaction costs — such as the costs of bargaining or acquiring information — then any legal rule will produce an efficient result. Whoever values an entitlement the most will either receive it from the legal system or buy it from the party who does. Coase's seminal article was *The Problem of Social Cost*, 3 J. L. & Econ. 1 (1960).

co-assignee. See ASSIGNEE.

coastal state. See STATE (1).

coastal-state control. (1939) *Maritime law.* The exercise of authority under international conventions for a state to stop, board, inspect, and when necessary detain vessels that are under foreign flags while they are navigating in the coastal state's territorial waters. • The purpose is to ensure the safety of the vessels and to enforce environmental regulations. Cf. FLAG-STATE CONTROL; PORT-STATE CONTROL.

coastal water. See WATER.

Coast Guard jurisdiction. (1945) The law-enforcement authority of the United States Coast Guard over the high seas and navigable waters over which the United States has jurisdiction, including the powers of stopping, searching, and seizing property, and arresting persons. See UNITED STATES COAST GUARD.

coasting license. (18c) *Maritime law.* A federal permit to operate a commercial vessel in coastal waters. • The Coasting Act of 1793, which originally created the licensing requirement, was intended to exclude foreign vessels from interstate trade and encourage the growth of American shipping.

coasting trade. (17c) *Maritime law.* Commerce among different coastal ports or navigable rivers of the United States, in contrast to commerce carried on between countries. — Also termed *coastwise trade.*

coast water. See *coastal water* under WATER.

coastwise trade. See COASTING TRADE.

COB. *abbr.* **1.** CHAIR OF THE BOARD. **2.** Chief of the boat.

COB clause. (1971) *Insurance.* A coordination-of-benefits clause, which provides that the total sums paid for medical and hospital care will not exceed the benefits receivable from all combined sources of insurance.

COBRA (**koh**-brə). *abbr.* (1986) CONSOLIDATED OMNIBUS BUDGET RECONCILIATION ACT OF 1985.

cockfighting. (15c) A traditional bloodsport in which specially bred and trained gamecocks are equipped with metal spurs and made to fight in a pen until at least one bird is killed or injured too seriously to continue fighting. • In the United States, cockfighting was once common in rural areas. Now considered a form of animal cruelty, it has been outlawed in every state.

coconspirator. (1836) Someone who engages in a criminal conspiracy with another; a fellow conspirator. — Also written *co-conspirator.* See CONSPIRATOR.

▸ **unindicted coconspirator.** (1936) Someone who has been identified by law enforcement as a member of a conspiracy, but who has not been named in the fellow conspirator's indictment. • Prosecutors typically name someone an unindicted coconspirator because any statement that the unindicted coconspirator has made in the course and furtherance of the conspiracy is admissible against the indicted defendants. — Also termed *unindicted conspirator.*

coconspirator's exception. (1954) An exception to the hearsay rule whereby one conspirator's acts and statements, if made during and in furtherance of the conspiracy, are admissible against a codefendant even if the statements are made in the codefendant's absence. *See* Fed. R. Evid. 801(d)(2)(E). — Also termed *coconspirator's rule.* See HEARSAY.

C.O.D. *abbr.* (1859) **1.** Cash on delivery; collect on delivery. • By consenting to this delivery term, the buyer agrees to pay simultaneously with delivery and appoints the carrier as the buyer's agent to receive and transmit the payment to the seller. With C.O.D. contracts, the practice of carriers has traditionally been to disallow inspection before payment. **2.** Costs on delivery. **3.** Cash on demand. — Sometimes written *c.o.d.*

CODA. *abbr.* CASH OR DEFERRED ARRANGEMENT.

code. (18c) **1.** A complete system of positive law, carefully arranged and officially promulgated; a systematic collection or revision of laws, rules, or regulations <the Uniform Commercial Code>. • Strictly, a code is a compilation not just of existing statutes, but also of much of the unwritten law on a subject, which is newly enacted as a complete system of law. — Also termed *consolidated laws.* See CODIFICATION

"A code is not only a collection of the existing statutory law, but also of much of the unwritten law on any subject, and is composed partly of such materials as might be at hand from all sources — from statutes, cases, and from customs — supplemented by such amendments, alterations, and additions as are deemed by the codifiers necessary to harmonize and perfect the existing system. In fact, in making a code, new laws may be added and old laws repealed in order to constitute a complete system." William M. Lile et al., *Brief Making and the Use of Law Books* 18–19 (Roger W. Cooley & Charles Lesley Ames eds., 3d ed. 1914).

2. (*usu. cap.*) The collection of laws and constitutions made by order of the Roman Emperor Justinian and first authoritatively published in A.D. 529 (with a second edition in 534). • Contained in 12 books, the Code is one of four works that make up what is now called the *Corpus Juris Civilis*. — Also termed (in sense 2) *Legal Code*. See CODEX; CORPUS JURIS CIVILIS.

Code Adam. (1994) A procedure used by offices, stores, and other places to alert people to look for a child who has become separated from a parent or guardian and has been reported as missing somewhere within the building. • Typically, a description of the missing child is broadcast over a paging system. All exits are locked or closely monitored. If the child is not found within a short time, the police are called. Many stores, museums, malls, and amusements parks have adopted some form of Code Adam. In 2003, Congress passed legislation requiring Code Adam programs in all federal office buildings. This term is a memorial to 6-year-old Adam Walsh of Florida, who in 1981 was abducted from a department store and murdered. Cf. AMBER ALERT.

Code Civil. The code embodying the civil law of France, dating from 1804. • It was first known as the *Code civil des français* to distinguish it from the other four codes promoted by Napoleon. From 1807 to 1816 it was called *Code Napoléon*, a title that was restored by a decree of Louis Napoleon. Since 1870, French statutes have consistently referred simply to the *code civil*. See CIVIL CODE (2). Cf. NAPOLEONIC CODE.

coded communications. (1930) Messages that are encoded or enciphered by some method of transposition or substitution so that they become unintelligible to anyone who does not have the key to the code or cipher.

Code de commerce (**kohd** də kaw-**mairs**). An 1807 codification of French commercial law enacted to deal with commercial transactions, bankruptcy, and the jurisdiction and procedure of the courts handling these subjects. • This code supplemented the *Code Napoléon*. See NAPOLEONIC CODE.

Code de procédure civil (**kohd** də praw-se-**door** see-**veel**). An 1806 French civil-procedure code that was appended to the *Code Napoléon*. See NAPOLEONIC CODE.

Code d'instruction criminelle (**kohd** dan-struuk-see-**awn** kri-mi-**nel**). An 1811 French criminal-procedure code that was appended to the *Code Napoléon*. See NAPOLEONIC CODE.

codefendant. (17c) One of two or more defendants sued in the same litigation or charged with the same crime. — Also termed *joint defendant*; *co-accused*. Cf. COPLAINTIFF.

Code Napoléon (**kohd** na-poh-lay-**awn**). See NAPOLEONIC CODE.

Code Noir (kohd **nwahr**). [French "black code"] *Hist.* A body of laws issued by Louis XIV and applied in French colonies. • The Code regulated slavery and banned Jews and non-Catholic religious practices from the Colonies.

code of conduct. (1919) A written set of rules governing the behavior of specified groups, such as lawyers, government employees, or corporate employees.

"Codes of conduct are regulatory instruments consisting of written sets of rules and principles which can deal with very specific or more general areas of regulatory concern, but always focus on a certain desirable conduct of the addressees. They are promulgated by and addressed to States, international or non-governmental organizations ('NGOs'), or private associations and persons, including corporations. . . . Codes of conduct tend to promulgate comparatively new and innovative norms which announce and reflect eras of change and are often harbingers of legal progression in areas where binding rules are non-existent or insufficiently developed. Although codes of conduct have so far been of a legally non-binding nature, they often also reflect legally binding rules, and thus often represent a mixture of voluntary and binding norms combined in an overall non-binding instrument. Finally, they often include or are accompanied by implementation procedures." Jürgen Friedrich, "Codes of Conduct," in 2 *The Max Planck Encyclopedia of Public International Law* 264, 264–65 (Rüdiger Wolfrum ed., 2012).

code of ethics. (18c) An officially adopted statement of the principles of acceptable conduct relevant to the activities of an occupational group, esp. a professional one. — Also termed *ethical code*.

Code of Federal Regulations. The annual collection of executive-agency regulations published in the daily Federal Register, combined with previously issued regulations that are still in effect. — Abbr. CFR.

Code of Hammurabi (hah-mə-**rah**-bee *or* ham-ə-). The oldest known written legal code, produced in Mesopotamia during the rule of Hammurabi (who reigned from 1792 to 1750 B.C.). • The code consisted of nearly 300 provisions, arranged under headings such as family, trade, real property, personal property, and labor.

Code of Judicial Conduct. The body of standards governing the professional ethics and behavior of judges. • The American Bar Association drafted a Model Code of Judicial Conduct and formally adopted it in 1972. In 1973, the U.S. Judicial Conference used the code as the basis for the Code of Conduct for United States Judges. Portions of the code are also found in federal law (*see, e.g.*, 28 USCA § 455). The 1972 ABA Code has been superseded by the 1990 ABA Model Code of Judicial Conduct. Each state has a code of judicial conduct, based on the 1972 or 1990 model codes or a blend of both. A state's highest court is responsible for drafting and enacting the code. A new rules-based Model Code of Judicial Conduct was adopted in 2007. — Abbr. CJC.

Code of Justinian. See JUSTINIAN CODE.

Code of Military Justice. The collection of substantive and procedural rules governing the discipline of members of the armed forces. 10 USCA §§ 801 et seq. — Also termed *Uniform Code of Military Justice* (UCMJ).

Code of Professional Responsibility. See MODEL CODE OF PROFESSIONAL RESPONSIBILITY.

Code of Theodosius. See THEODOSIAN CODE.

code of war. (1821) Legal rules that regulate international armed conflict. • A code of war may arise from many sources, including custom, treaties, scholarly writings, and domestic legislation. One of the earliest known treatises on rules governing the conduct of war was written by Sun Tzu in the 4th century B.C.

Code pénal (**kohd** pay-**nal**). The fourth of five codes promoted by Napoleon, enacted in 1810, setting forth the penal code of France. See NAPOLEONIC CODE.

code pleading. See PLEADING (2).

code state. (1867) *Hist.* A state that, at a given time, had already procedurally merged law and equity, so that equity was no longer administered as a separate system; a state in which there is only one form of civil action. • This term was current primarily in the early to mid-20th century. Cf. NONCODE STATE.

codex (**koh**-deks). [Latin] (16c) *Archaic.* **1.** A code, esp. the Justinian Code. See JUSTINIAN CODE. **2.** A book written on paper or parchment; esp., a volume of an ancient text.

Codex Gregorianus (**koh**-deks gri-gor-ee-**ay**-nəs). [Latin] *Roman law.* A collection of imperial constitutions compiled by the Roman jurist Gregorius and published in A.D. 291. — Also termed *Gregorian Code.*

> "The imperial enactments, rapidly increasing in number, covering, at hazard, the whole range of law, and, by reason of difficulties of communication and imperfect methods of promulgation, not always readily ascertainable, created a burden for the practitioner almost as great as that of the unmanageable juristic literature. Something was done to help him by two collections published privately about the end of the third century, the *Codex Gregorianus* and *Codex Hermogenianus*. These collections do not now exist: what is known of them is from citations in later literature . . . ." W.W. Buckland, *A Manual of Roman Private Law* 20–21 (2d ed. 1939).

Codex Hermogenianus (**koh**-deks hər-mə-jee-nee-**ay**-nəs). [Latin] *Roman law.* A collection of imperial constitutions compiled by the Roman jurist Hermogenianus and published A.D. 295. • The *Codex Hermogenianus* supplemented the *Codex Gregorianus.* — Also termed *Hermogenian Code.*

Codex Iustinianus Repetitae Praelectionis. See JUSTINIAN CODE.

codex juris canonici (**koh**-deks **joor**-is kə-**non**-ə-sɪ). [Latin] *Hist.* A code of canon laws.

Codex Justinianus. See JUSTINIAN CODE.

Codex Repetitae Praelectionis (**koh**-deks rep-ə-**tɪ**-tee pri-lek-shee-**oh**-nis). [Latin "code of the resumed reading"] *Roman law.* See JUSTINIAN CODE.

> "By the time when the *Digest* and *Institutes* had been completed it was obvious that the *Codex*, published little more than four years earlier, was incomplete, since in the interval Justinian . . . had promulgated other new constitutions. Tribonian, therefore, was appointed to revise the Code, so as to bring it fully up to date, and at the end of the year A.D. 534 this new Code, known as the *Codex Repetitae Praelectionis*, was promulgated, and is the only Code which survives to the present day. Justinian seems to have laboured under the erroneous impression that the system he had framed would be adequate for all time. But as there is nothing static about law, further legislative enactments, termed *Novellae Constitutiones*, were issued during his reign. . . . In modern times Justinian's various compilations came to be called collectively the *Corpus Juris Civilis*: the *Corpus* being regarded as a single work, made up of the *Institutes*, the *Digest*, the *Codex Repetitae Praelectionis*, and the *Novels*." R.W. Leage, *Roman Private Law* 44 (C.H. Ziegler ed., 2d ed. 1930).

Codex Theodosianus (**koh**-deks thee-ə-doh-shee-**ay**-nəs). [Latin] See THEODOSIAN CODE.

Codex Vetus. See JUSTINIAN CODE.

codicil (**kod**-ə-səl *or* -sil). (15c) A supplement or addition to a will, not necessarily disposing of the entire estate but modifying, explaining, or otherwise qualifying the will in some way. • When admitted to probate, the codicil becomes a part of the will.

> "A Schedule or supplement to a Will, or some other writing; some Writers, conferring a Testament, and a *Codicil* together, call a Testament a great Will, and a *Codicil* a little one; and compare a Testament to a Ship, and the *Codicil* to the Boat tied to the Ship." Thomas Blount, *Nomo-Lexicon: A Law-Dictionary* (1670).

> "A codicil, from *codicillus*, a small *codex*, a little book or writing, may be defined as a writing by the testator intended as a supplement or addition to his will, the effect of which may be either to enlarge or restrict it, or to annul or revoke it altogether. It may add to or subtract from provisions of the will, may explain or alter, confirm or revoke them wholly or in part; or, when the will itself is invalid, may by a valid re-execution and republication revive and renew the will." 1 H.C. Underhill, *A Treatise on the Law of Wills* § 7, at 11 (1900).

codicillary (kod-ə-**sil**-ə-ree), *adj.* (18c) Of, relating to, or involving a codicil.

codicillus (kod-ə-**sil**-əs), *n.* [Latin "little document"] *Roman law.* **1.** An informal document instructing an heir to carry out a certain performance, usu. the payment of money or the transfer of property to a third person. • During the reign of Augustus (27 B.C.–A.D. 14), directives (*fideicommissa*) contained in *codicilli* became legally binding. See FIDEICOMMISSUM. **2.** An imperially granted appointment or special privilege.

codification (kod-ə-fi-**kay**-shən), *n.* (1802) **1.** The process of compiling, arranging, and systematizing the laws of a given jurisdiction, or of a discrete branch of the law, into an ordered code. **2.** The code that results from this process. — **codify** (**kod**-ə-fɪ), *vb.* — **codifier** (**kod**-ə-fɪ-ər), *n.*

> "It was [Jeremy] Bentham who coined the word 'codification' and invented the term 'international law.' The meaning he attached to codification is found in his 'General View of a Complete Code of Laws,' published in 1802. According to him, the object of a code is that anyone may be able to consult the law as he stands in need, in the least possible time; he was convinced that 'to be without a code is to be without justice.' The code was conceived by him to be complete and self-sufficing, and in style to be characterized by force, harmony, and nobleness. Once prepared it was not to be developed, supplemented, or modified except by legislative enactment. It must remove the inconsistencies of law and the uncertainties and complexities of customary or judge-made law." R.P. Dhokalia, *The Codification of Public International Law* 39 (1970).

codifying statute. See STATUTE.

CODIS. *abbr.* COMBINED DNA INDEX SYSTEM.

CODIS hit. (2004) A match between a defendant's DNA and the DNA found at the scene of an unresolved crime.

Coefficient Clause. See NECESSARY AND PROPER CLAUSE.

coemptio (koh-**emp**-shee-oh), *n.* [Latin] (16c) *Roman law.* A form of civil marriage in which the husband "purchased" from a woman's father — by fictitious sale — the right to exercise marital power (*manus*) over the woman. • The father conveyed his daughter to her husband through the technical procedure of a sale of *res mancipi.* The imaginary sale took place in the presence of five adult Roman citizens and a balance-holder (*libripens*). The husband or fictitious purchaser was termed the *coemptionator* or *coemptioner.* The importance of *coemptio* as a method of civil marriage had faded by the end of the Republic period. Cf. CONFARREATIO; USUS (3). Pl. ***coemptiones*** (koh-emp-shee-**oh**-neez).

coemption (koh-**emp**-shən), *n.* (14c) **1.** The act of purchasing the entire quantity of any commodity. **2.** COEMPTIO. — **coemptional, coemptive,** *adj.*

coerce (koh-**ərs**), *vb.* (15c) To compel by force or threat <coerce a confession>.

coerced-compliant confession. See CONFESSION (1).

coerced-compliant false confession. See *coerced-compliant confession* under CONFESSION (1).

coerced confession. See CONFESSION (1).

coercion (koh-**ər**-zhən), *n.* (15c) **1.** Compulsion of a free agent by physical, moral, or economic force or threat of physical force. • An act that must be voluntary, such as signing a will, is not legally valid if done under coercion. And since a valid marriage requires voluntary consent, coercion or duress is grounds for invalidating a marriage.

▸ **criminal coercion.** (18c) Coercion intended to restrict another's freedom of action by (1) threatening to commit a criminal act against that person; (2) threatening to accuse that person of having committed a criminal act; (3) threatening to expose a secret that either would subject the victim to hatred, contempt, or ridicule or would impair the victim's credit or goodwill, or (4) taking or withholding official action or causing an official to take or withhold action.

▸ **implied coercion.** See UNDUE INFLUENCE (1).

▸ **moral coercion.** See UNDUE INFLUENCE (1).

2. Conduct that constitutes the improper use of economic power to compel another to submit to the wishes of one who wields it. — Also termed *economic coercion.* **3.** *Hist.* A husband's actual or supposed control or influence over his wife's actions. • Under the common-law doctrine of coercion, a wife who committed a crime in her husband's presence was presumed to have been coerced by him and thus had a complete defense. Courts have abolished this doctrine. — Also termed *doctrine of coercion*; (in sense 3) *marital coercion.* — **coercive,** *adj.* — **coercer,** *n.*

> "Although as an abstract statement any action or restraint imposed upon one by another may be spoken of as coercion, there has been a tendency in the criminal law to employ the word 'compulsion' for the general field and to reserve the word 'coercion' to indicate the exercise of such influence (actual or presumed) over a married woman by her husband. And since the latter is not merely a specific instance of the former, but is something which differs from it in kind so far as common-law consequences are concerned, there are important reasons for retaining this difference in the meaning to be assigned to these terms." Rollin M. Perkins & Ronald N. Boyce, *Criminal Law* 1018 (3d ed. 1982).

coercion test. *Constitutional law.* A court's examination of a government or government-sanctioned formal religious exercise, such as a public prayer, to determine to what extent it applies pressure on unwilling individuals to force or coerce them to participate. • The coercion test is drawn from *Lee v. Weisman*, 505 U.S. 577, 112 S.Ct. 2649 (1992).

coercion theory of law. (1999) The view that one fundamental facet of law is that all its commands are backed by sanctions for noncompliance.

coercive relief. See RELIEF (3).

coexecutor (koh-eg-**zek**-yə-tər). See *joint executor* under EXECUTOR (2).

coexistence. (1954) *Int'l law.* The peaceful continuation of countries, peoples, or other entities or groups within an effective political-military equilibrium.

coexisting motion. See MOTION (2).

cogent (**koh**-jənt), *adj.* (17c) Compelling or convincing <cogent reasoning>. — **cogency,** *n.*

cognate, *adj.* See COGNATIC.

cognate, *n.* (18c) Someone who is kin to another. • In Roman law, the term means a blood relationship and implies that the kinship derives from a lawful marriage. In Scots and later civil law, the term implies kinship from the mother's side. Cf. AGNATE.

cognate act. See ACT (3).

cognate nuisance. See NUISANCE.

cognate offense. See OFFENSE (2).

cognati. See COGNATUS.

cognatic (kog-**nat**-ik), *adj.* (18c) (Of a relationship) existing between cognates. — Also termed *cognate.*

cognatio (kog-**nay**-shee-oh), *n.* [Latin] *Roman law.* The relationship between people having a common ancestor; a blood relationship; cognates. Cf. AGNATIO.

cognation (kog-**nay**-shən), *n.* (14c) **1.** Relationship by blood rather than by marriage; relationship arising through common descent from the same man and woman, whether the descent is traced through males or females.

> "'Cognation' is . . . a relative term, and the degree of connexion in blood which it indicates depends on the particular marriage which is selected as the commencement of the calculation." Henry S. Maine, *Ancient Law* 122 (17th ed. 1901).

2. *Civil law.* A relationship existing between two people by blood, by family, or by both.

▸ **civil cognation.** A relationship arising by law, such as that created by adoption.

▸ **mixed cognation.** A relationship that combines the ties of blood and family, such as that existing between brothers who are born of the same marriage.

▸ **natural cognation.** (1949) A blood relationship, usu. arising from an illicit connection.

3. Relationship between persons or things of the same or similar nature; likeness.

cognatus (kog-**nay**-təs), *adj.* & *n.* [Latin] (16c) *Roman law.* A cognatic relative; a person related to another by a common ancestor. — Also termed *cognate.* Cf. AGNATUS. Pl. ***cognati.***

cognitio (kog-**nish**-ee-oh), *n.* [fr. Latin *cognoscere* "to know"] (16c) **1.** *Hist.* The acknowledgment of a fine, or the certificate of such an acknowledgment. **2.** *Roman law.* See COGNITIO EXTRAORDINARIA. Pl. ***cognitiones*** (kog-nish-ee-**oh**-neez).

cognitio extraordinaria (kog-**nish**-ee-oh ek-stror-di-**nair**-ee-ə *or* ek-strə-or-). [Latin] *Roman law.* A type of legal proceeding, arising at the beginning of the Empire, in which a government official controlled the conduct of a trial from beginning to end, as opposed to the earlier formulary system in which a magistrate shaped the issues and then turned the issues of fact and law over to a lay judge (a judex). — Sometimes shortened to *cognitio.* — Also termed *cognitio extra ordinem* (kog-**nish**-ee-oh **ek**-strə **or**-də-nəm).

> "The *cognitio extra ordinem* or *cognitio extraordinaria* is a collective name for all those legal procedures in which the trial consists of one stage only and in which judgment is given by the emperor or by an imperial official acting on behalf of the emperor. The disputes that were settled by means of the cognition procedure could be of very different kinds: not only could they be about matters concerning private law and criminal law, but they could also be disputes between citizens and government officials." Olga Tellegen-Couperus, *A Short History of Roman Law* 90 (1993).

cognitionibus mittendis (kog-nish-ee-**oh**-nə-bəs mi-**ten**-dis). [Latin "cognizance of pleas to be released"] (17c) *Hist.* A writ ordering a justice of the Common Pleas to certify a fine that the justice had imposed but refused to certify.

cognitionis causa tantum (kog-nish-ee-**oh**-nis **kaw**-zə **tan**-təm). [Latin "for the purpose of ascertaining a debt against the estate"] *Scots law.* A creditor's action against a deceased debtor's estate to ascertain the amount of the debt.

cognitive test. (1955) *Criminal law.* A test of the defendant's ability to know certain things, specifically the nature of his or her conduct and whether the conduct was right or wrong. • This test is used in assessing whether a defendant may rely on an insanity defense.

cognitor (**kog**-ni-tor), *n.* (16c) *Roman law.* A person formally appointed to represent another in a civil trial. Cf. PROCURATOR (1).

cognizable (**kog**-ni- *or* kog-**nɪ**-zə-bəl), *adj.* (17c) **1.** Capable of being known or recognized <for purposes of establishing standing, a plaintiff must allege a judicially cognizable injury>. **2.** Capable of being identified as a group because of a common characteristic or interest that cannot be represented by others <American Indians qualify as a cognizable group for jury-selection purposes>. **3.** Capable of being judicially tried or examined before a designated tribunal; within the court's jurisdiction <the tort claims are not cognizable under the consumer-protection statute>.

cognizance (**kog**-ni-zəns), *n.* (14c) **1.** A court's right and power to try and to determine cases; JURISDICTION. **2.** The taking of judicial or authoritative notice. **3.** Acknowledgment or admission of an alleged fact; esp. (*hist.*), acknowledgment of a fine. See FINE (1); FINE SUR COGNIZANCE DE DROIT. **4.** *Common-law pleading.* In a replevin action, a plea by the defendant that the goods are held in bailment for another. Cf. AVOWRY. — **cognizant,** *adj.*

cognizee (kog-ni-**zee**). (16c) *Hist.* The grantee of land in a conveyance by fine. — Also termed *conusee; conuzee.* See FINE (1).

cognizor (**kog**-ni-zər *or* -zor). (16c) *Hist.* The grantor of land in a conveyance by fine. — Also termed *conusor; conuzor.* See FINE (1).

> "Next comes the *concord,* or agreement itself, after leave obtained from the court; which is usually an acknowledgment . . . that the lands in question are the right of the complainant. And from this acknowledgment, or recognition of right, the party levying the fine is called the *cognizor,* and he to whom it is levied the *cognizee.*" 2 William Blackstone, *Commentaries on the Laws of England* 350–51 (1766).

cognovit (kog-**noh**-vit). [Latin "he has conceded (a debt or an action)"] (18c) An acknowledgment of debt or liability in the form of a confessed judgment. • Formerly, credit contracts often included a cognovit clause in which the consumer relinquished, in advance, any right to be notified of court hearings in any suit for nonpayment — but such clauses are now generally illegal. See CONFESSION OF JUDGMENT. Cf. WARRANT OF ATTORNEY (2).

> "A cognovit is an instrument signed by a defendant in an action actually commenced confessing the plaintiff's demand to be just, and empowering the plaintiff to sign judgment against him in default of his paying the plaintiff the sum due to him within the time mentioned in the cognovit." John Indermaur, *Principles of the Common Law* 8 (Edmund H. Bennett ed., 1st Am. ed. 1878).

cognovit actionem (kog-**noh**-vit ak-shee-**oh**-nəm). [Law Latin "he has confessed the action"] (17c) A defendant's written acknowledgment of the plaintiff's claim, authorizing the plaintiff to take a judgment for a named sum; a cognovit.

cognovit clause. (1925) A contractual provision by which a debtor agrees to jurisdiction in certain courts, waives notice requirements, and authorizes the entry of an adverse judgment in the event of a default or breach. • Cognovit clauses are outlawed or restricted in most states. See COGNOVIT.

cognovit judgment. See JUDGMENT (2).

cognovit note. (1878) A promissory note containing a cognovit clause. — Also termed *judgment note.*

COGSA. (1941) **1.** *abbr.* CARRIAGE OF GOODS BY SEA ACT. **2.** *Maritime law.* A country's enactment of the international convention popularly known as the Hague Rules. • The acronym is used even when the country's statute has a different title; for example, the Canadian Carriage of Goods by Water Act is referred to as the "Canadian COGSA."

coguarantor. See GUARANTOR.

cohabitation (koh-hab-ə-**tay**-shən), n. (15c) The fact, state, or condition of living together, esp. as partners in life, usu. with the suggestion of sexual relations. — **cohabit** (koh-**hab**-it), *vb.* — **cohabitative** (koh-**hab**-ə-tay-tiv), *adj.* — **cohabitant** (koh-**hab**-ə-tənt), *n.* — **cohabitor** (koh-**hab**-ə-tər), *n.*

> "Cohabitation is the name given to the arrangement by which a man and a woman live and have sex together without being married. This arrangement may be intended to last for a definite period, for example so long as they are both students, or until a certain event takes place, for instance until the woman becomes pregnant, or indefinitely. They may or may not make a formal agreement about sharing expenses, about their living accommodation and so forth." Tony Honoré, *Sex Law* 42–43 (1978).

▸ **illicit cohabitation.** (18c) *Archaic.* **1.** The offense committed by an unmarried man and woman who live together as husband and wife and engage in sexual intercourse. • This offense, where it still exists, is seldom prosecuted. **2.** The condition of a man and a woman who are not married to one another and live together in circumstances that make the arrangement questionable on grounds of social propriety, though not necessarily illegal. — Also termed *lascivious cohabitation; lewd and lascivious cohabitation.* Cf. FORNICATION.

▸ **lascivious cohabitation.** See *illicit cohabitation.*

▸ **matrimonial cohabitation.** (1843) The living together of husband and wife.

▸ **notorious cohabitation.** (18c) *Archaic.* Illicit cohabitation in which the parties make no attempt to hide their living arrangements. — Also termed *open and notorious cohabitation.* See *illicit cohabitation.*

cohabitation agreement. (1975) A contract outlining the property and financial arrangements between persons who live together. — Also termed *living-together agreement.* Cf. PRENUPTIAL AGREEMENT.

cohabiting unmarried person of the opposite sex. See CUPOS.

***Cohan* rule (koh-han).** (1948) *Tax.* A former rule that a taxpayer may approximate travel and entertainment expenses when no records exist if the taxpayer has taken all possible steps to provide documentation. • Since 1962, travel and entertainment expenses have been only partly deductible and must be carefully documented, but courts may apply the *Cohan* reasoning to other items. *Cohan v. Commissioner,* 39 F.2d 540 (2d Cir. 1930).

coheir (koh-**air**). See HEIR.

coheiress (koh-**air**-is). (17c) *Hist.* A female coheir.

***Cohen* doctrine (koh-ən).** See COLLATERAL-ORDER DOCTRINE.

coheres (koh-**heer**-eez), *n. Roman law.* A coheir. Pl. ***coheredes*** (koh-**heer**-ə-deez).

cohort analysis (koh-hort). (1954) A method of measuring discrimination in the workplace by comparing, at several points in time, the pay and promotions of employees of different cognizable groups. • Cohort analyses are often used in employment-discrimination cases.

COI. *abbr.* CONTINUITY OF INTEREST.

coif (koyf). (14c) *Hist.* **1.** A white linen headpiece formerly worn by serjeants at law (barristers of high standing) in common-law courts. **2.** The rank or order of serjeants at law. See ORDER OF THE COIF.

coinage (koy-nij), *n.* (14c) **1.** *Archaic.* The system or type of money used in a country <the coinage of the Macedonians>. **2.** The metal money used in one or more countries; coins collectively <a collector of coinage>. **3.** The making of coins; the minting of money <the U.S. Mint's coinage of nickels>. **4.** The invention of new words and phrases <the coinage of newfangled terminology is a common habit of legal theorists>. **5.** An invented word or phrase; a neologism <*affluenza* is a recent coinage>.

Coinage Clause. (1863) *Constitutional law.* The provision in the U.S. Constitution (art. I, § 8, cl. 5) granting to Congress the power to coin money.

coincide, *vb.* (17c) **1.** To correspond because of identity in parts, elements, or relations <the triangles coincide perfectly>. **2.** To happen at the same time as something else <our vacations coincided>. **3.** (Of ideas, beliefs, opinions, etc.) to be identical or very nearly the same <the interests of the two superpowers coincide on this point>. **4.** To meet or be in the same place or position <part of the tour coincides with the Appian Way>. **5.** (Of two persons, esp. authorities) to be of the same mind; to agree in opinion <Wright and Miller coincided on most points of federal procedure>.

coincident indicator. See INDICATOR.

coindictee. (1852) One of two or more persons who have been jointly indicted. See *joint indictment* under INDICTMENT.

coined mark. See *fanciful trademark* under TRADEMARK.

coined-name claim. See PATENT CLAIM.

coined term. See *fanciful trademark* under TRADEMARK.

coined trademark. See *fanciful trademark* under TRADEMARK.

coinsurance. See INSURANCE.

coinsurance clause. (1887) A provision in an insurance policy requiring a property owner to carry separate insurance up to an amount stated in the policy to qualify for full coverage. — Also termed *contribution clause.*

coinsurer. (18c) An insurer who shares losses sustained under an insurance policy. See *coinsurance* under INSURANCE.

cojudices. (18c) *Archaic. English law.* In England, associate judges.

COLA. *abbr.* COST-OF-LIVING ADJUSTMENT.

cold bench. See BENCH.

cold blood. (18c) A killer's state of mind when committing a willful and premeditated homicide <a shooting in cold blood>. See COOL BLOOD. Cf. HEAT OF PASSION.

cold check. See *bad check* under CHECK.

cold-comfort letter. See COMFORT LETTER (1).

cold-water ordeal. See *ordeal by water* (1) under ORDEAL.

colegatee (koh-le-gə-**tee**). (1809) A joint legatee; one of two or more persons who receive a legacy under a will. Cf. LEGATEE.

COLI. See *corporate-owned life insurance* under LIFE INSURANCE.

colibertus (kol-i-**bər**-təs). [Law Latin] *Hist.* A serf in free socage; that is, a serf who is nominally freed but is still subject to certain servile conditions. • A *colibertus* occupied a position in society between servile and free tenants. — Also spelled *collibertus.* See SOCAGE. Pl. ***coliberti.***

collaborative divorce. See DIVORCE.

collaborative law. (1993) A dispute-resolution method by which parties and their attorneys settle disputes using nonadversarial techniques to reach a binding agreement, with the understanding that if the parties cannot agree and choose to litigate instead, the attorneys involved in the negotiations will be disqualified from representing them any further. Cf. COOPERATIVE LAW; MEDIATION (1).

collapsible corporation. See CORPORATION.

collapsible partnership. See PARTNERSHIP.

collar, *n.* The minimum and maximum price or ratio for a transaction.

collate (kə-**layt**), *vb.* (1880) *Civil law.* To return (inherited property) to an estate for division <the grandchildren collated the property they had received>.

collateral (kə-**lat**-ər-əl), *adj.* (14c) **1.** Supplementary; accompanying, but secondary and subordinate to <whether the accident victim was wearing a seat belt is a collateral issue>. **2.** Not direct in line, but on a parallel or diverging line of descent; of, relating to, or involving a person who is related by blood but is neither an ancestor nor a descendant <an uncle is in a collateral, not a direct, line>. Cf. LINEAL. — **collaterality** (kə-lat-ər-**al**-ə-tee), *n.*

collateral (kə-**lat**-ər-əl), *n.* (17c) **1.** A person collaterally related to a decedent. **2.** Property that is pledged as security against a debt; the property subject to a security interest or agricultural lien. *See* UCC § 9-102(a)(12). — Also termed (in sense 2) *collateral security.*

> "'Collateral,' in the commercial sense of the word, is a security given in addition to a principal obligation, and subsidiary thereto; and is used as generally descriptive of all choses in action, as distinguished from tangible personal property, including the usual negotiable instruments of commerce; the quasi-negotiable securities, as certificates of stock, bills of lading, and warehouse or cotton receipts; and the divers non-negotiable choses in action and equitable assignments available as collateral." William Colebrooke, *A Treatise on the Law of Collateral Securities* 3 (1883).

▸ **as-extracted collateral.** (1999) **1.** Oil, gas, or other minerals that are subject to a security interest that is created by a debtor having an interest in the minerals before extraction and that attaches to the minerals as they are extracted. UCC § 9-102(a)(6)(A). **2.** An account arising out of the sale at the wellhead or minehead of oil, gas, or other minerals in which the debtor had an interest before extraction. UCC § 9-102(a)(6)(B).

▸ **cash collateral.** (1910) Collateral consisting of cash, negotiable instruments, documents of title, securities, deposit accounts, or other cash equivalents. 11 USCA § 363(a).

▸ **cross-collateral.** (1965) **1.** Security given by all parties to a contract. **2.** *Bankruptcy.* Bargained-for security that in addition to protecting a creditor's postpetition extension of credit protects the creditor's prepetition unsecured claims, which, as a result of such security, obtain priority over other creditors' prepetition unsecured claims. • Some courts allow this procedure, which is known as *cross-collateralization.*

collateral act. Any act (usu. excluding the payment of money) for which a bond or recognizance is given as security.

collateral advantage. (18c) A mortgage provision giving the lender some benefit in addition to the security, often an unfair or unconscionable one, such as an option to purchase the security. • A collateral advantage is often inconsistent with the mortgagor's right to extinguish the mortgage by paying off the secured debt.

collateral affinity. See AFFINITY.

collateral-agreement doctrine. See COLLATERAL-CONTRACT DOCTRINE.

collateral ancestor. See *collateral ascendant* under ASCENDANT.

collateral ascendant. See ASCENDANT.

collateral assignee. See ASSIGNEE.

collateral assignment. See ASSIGNMENT (2).

collateral assurance. See ASSURANCE.

collateral attack. (1833) An attack on a judgment in a proceeding other than a direct appeal; esp., an attempt to undermine a judgment through a judicial proceeding in which the ground of the proceeding (or a defense in the proceeding) is that the judgment is ineffective. • Typically a collateral attack is made against a point of procedure or another matter not necessarily apparent in the record, as opposed to a direct attack on the merits exclusively. A petition for a writ of habeas corpus is one type of collateral attack. — Also termed *indirect attack.* Cf. DIRECT ATTACK (1); *direct appeal* under APPEAL.

collateral benefit. See BENEFIT (2).

collateral-benefit rule. See COLLATERAL-SOURCE RULE.

collateral condition. See CONDITION (2).

collateral consanguinity. See CONSANGUINITY.

collateral consequence. See CONSEQUENCE.

collateral contract. See CONTRACT.

collateral-contract doctrine. (1947) The principle that in a dispute concerning a written contract, proof of a second (usu. oral) agreement will not be excluded under the parol-evidence rule if the oral agreement is independent of and not inconsistent with the written contract, and if the information in the oral agreement would not ordinarily be expected to be included in the written contract. — Also termed *collateral-agreement doctrine.*

collateral covenant. See COVENANT (1).

collateral defense. See DEFENSE (1).

collateral descendant. See DESCENDANT.

collateral descent. See DESCENT.

collateral estoppel (e-**stop**-əl). (1941) **1.** The binding effect of a judgment as to matters actually litigated and determined in one action on later controversies between the parties involving a different claim from that on which the original judgment was based. **2.** A doctrine barring a party from relitigating an issue determined against that party in an earlier action, even if the second action differs significantly from the first one. — Also termed *issue preclusion; issue estoppel; direct estoppel; estoppel by judgment; estoppel by record; estoppel by verdict; cause-of-action estoppel; technical estoppel; estoppel per rem judicatam.* Cf. RES JUDICATA.

▸ **administrative collateral estoppel.** (1977) Estoppel that arises from a decision made by an agency acting in a judicial capacity.

▸ **defensive collateral estoppel.** (1968) Estoppel asserted by a defendant to prevent a plaintiff from relitigating an issue previously decided against the plaintiff.

▸ **nonmutual collateral estoppel.** (1971) Estoppel asserted either offensively or defensively by a nonparty to an earlier action to prevent a party to that earlier action from relitigating an issue determined against it.

▸ **offensive collateral estoppel.** (1964) Estoppel asserted by a plaintiff to prevent a defendant from relitigating an issue previously decided against the defendant.

collateral fact. See FACT.

collateral fraud. See *extrinsic fraud* (1) under FRAUD.

collateral heir. See HEIR.

collateral-impeachment rule. (1972) The doctrine that extrinsic evidence about matters incidental to the fact at issue must not be used to impeach a witness. • The purpose of the rule is to expedite trials and prevent jury confusion about what facts are relevant. The judge has broad discretion in enforcing the rule.

collateral-inheritance tax. See TAX.

collateral issue. See ISSUE (1).

collateralize (kə-**lat**-ər-əl-IZ), *vb.* (1941) **1.** To serve as collateral for <the purchased property collateralized the loan agreement>. **2.** To make (a loan) secure with collateral <the creditor insisted that the loan be collateralized>. — **collateralization** (kə-lat-ər-əl-ə-**zay**-shən), *n.*

collateralized mortgage obligation. (1989) *Securities.* A bond secured by a group of mortgage obligations or pass-through securities and paid according to the payment schedule of its class (or *tranche*). • CMOs are issued by the Federal Home Loan Mortgage Corporation, and benefit from predictable payments of interest and principal. — Abbr. CMO. See *pass-through security* under SECURITY (4); TRANCHE.

collateral limitation. See LIMITATION (4).

collateral line. See LINE.

collateral loan. See *secured loan* under LOAN.

collateral matter. (17c) *Evidence.* Any matter on which evidence could not have been introduced for a relevant purpose. • If a witness has erred in testifying about a detail that is collateral to the relevant facts, then another party cannot call witnesses to contradict that point — cross-examination alone must suffice. Fed. R. Evid. 608(b).

collateral mistake. See *unessential mistake* under MISTAKE.

collateral mortgage. See MORTGAGE.

collateral negligence. See NEGLIGENCE.

collateral-negligence doctrine. (1941) The rule holding that one who engages an independent contractor is not liable for physical harm that the contractor causes if (1) the contractor's negligence consists solely of the improper manner in which the contractor's work is performed, (2) the risk of harm created is not normal to the work, and (3) the employer had no reason to contemplate the contractor's negligence when the contract was made.

collateral note. See *secured note* under NOTE (1).

collateral obligation. (17c) A liability undertaken by a person who becomes bound for another's debt. — Also termed *accessorial obligation.*

collateral order. See ORDER (2).

collateral-order doctrine. (1950) A doctrine allowing appeal from an interlocutory order that conclusively determines an issue wholly separate from the merits of the action and effectively unreviewable on appeal from a final judgment. — Also termed *Cohen doctrine* (fr. *Cohen v. Beneficial Indus. Loan Corp.*, 337 U.S. 541, 69 S.Ct. 1221 (1949)). See *appealable decision* under DECISION (1).

collateral power. See POWER (5).

collateral proceeding. See PROCEEDING.

collateral promise. See PROMISE.

collateral relative. See RELATIVE.

collateral security. See SECURITY (4).

collateral-source rule. (1951) *Torts.* The doctrine that if an injured party receives compensation for the injuries from a source independent of the tortfeasor, the payment should not be deducted from the damages that the tortfeasor must pay. • Insurance proceeds are the most common collateral source. — Also termed *collateral-benefit rule.*

collateral term. See *supplementary term* under TERM (2).

collateral trust bond. See BOND (3).

collateral trust certificate. See *collateral trust bond* (1) under BOND (3).

collateral use. See USE (1).

collateral warranty. See WARRANTY (1).

collatio bonorum (kə-**lay**-shee-oh bə-**nor**-əm). [Latin "collation of goods"] (17c) *Civil law.* The bringing into hotchpot of goods or money advanced by a parent to a child, so that the parent's personal estate will be equally distributed among the parent's children. See HOTCHPOT. Pl. ***collationes bonorum.***

> "[I]f the estates so given them, by way of advancement, are not quite equivalent to the other shares, the children so advanced shall now have so much as will make them equal. This just and equitable provision hath been also said to be derived from the *collatio bonorum* of the imperial law: which it certainly resembles in some points, though it differs widely in others. But it may not be amiss to observe, that, with regard to goods and chattels, this is part of . . . the common law of England, under the name of *hotchpot.*" 2 William Blackstone, *Commentaries on the Laws of England* 516–17 (1766).

collation (kə-**lay**-shən), *n.* (14c) **1.** The comparison of a copy with its original to ascertain its correctness; the report of the officer who made the comparison. **2.** The taking into account of the value of advancements made by an intestate to his or her children so that the estate may be divided in accordance with the intestacy statute. Cf. HOTCHPOT. **3.** *Eccles. law.* The act (by a bishop) of conferring a benefice in which the bishop holds the right of advowson, thus combining the acts of *presentation* and *institution.* — Also termed *collation to a benefice.* See *advowson collative* under ADVOWSON. — **collate** (kə-**layt**), *vb.* — **collator** (kə-**lay**-tər), *n.*

collatione facta uni post mortem alterius (kə-lay-shee-**oh**-nee **fak**-tə **yoo**-NI pohst **mor**-təm al-**teer**-ee-əs [*or* awl-]). [Law Latin "by collation to a benefice made to one after the death of the other"] (17c) *Hist.* A writ directed to the Court of Common Pleas, requesting that the court order a bishop to appoint a clerk in place of another who had died pending appointment.

collatione heremitagii (kə-lay-shee-**oh**-nee her-ə-mə-**tay**-jee-I). [Law Latin "by collation of hermitage"] (17c) *Hist.* A writ by which the Crown conferred the keeping of a hermitage on a clerk.

collation to a benefice. See COLLATION (3).

collatio signorum (kə-**lay**-shee-oh sig-**nor**-əm). [Law Latin "comparison of signs"] *Hist.* A method of testing a seal's genuineness by comparing it with another known to be genuine.

collative fact. See *investitive fact* under FACT.

collectability. (1848) The ability of a judgment creditor to make a judgment debtor pay the amount of the judgment; the degree to which a judgment can be satisfied through collection efforts against the judgment debtor.

collecting bank. See BANK.

collecting institution. See *collecting bank* under BANK.

collection. *Banking.* The process through which an item (such as a check) passes in a payor bank. See *payor bank* under BANK.

collection account. See *concentration account* under ACCOUNT.

collection endorsement. See *restrictive indorsement* under INDORSEMENT.

collection indorsement. See *restrictive indorsement* under INDORSEMENT.

collection item. (1897) An item (such as a documentary draft) taken by a bank for a customer's account, but not credited until payment for the item has actually been received. See *documentary draft* under DRAFT (1).

collective agreement. (1911) **1.** A contract between multiple parties, esp. where one side consists of many people or entities with a common interest, as when an association or other organization acts on behalf of its members. **2.** See COLLECTIVE-BARGAINING AGREEMENT. **3.** See *certified agreement* under AGREEMENT.

collective bargaining. (1891) Negotiations between an employer and the representatives of organized employees to determine the conditions of employment, such as wages, hours, discipline, and fringe benefits. See CONCESSION BARGAINING.

> "Collective bargaining means the joint determination by employees and employers of the problems of the employment relationship. Such problems include wage rates and wage systems, hours and overtime, vacations, discipline, work loads, classification of employees, layoffs, and worker retirement. The advent of collective bargaining does not give rise to these problems. Rather they are germane to the industrial relations environment, and exist with or without unionization." Benjamin J. Taylor & Fred Whitney, *Labor Relations Law* 3 (1971).

▸ **free collective bargaining.** (1917) Collective bargaining that is not controlled by legislation.

collective-bargaining agreement. (1922) *Labor law.* A contract between an employer and a labor union regulating employment conditions, wages, benefits, and grievances. — Abbr. CBA. — Also termed *labor agreement*; *labor contract*; *union contract*; *collective-labor agreement*; *collective agreement*; *trade agreement.*

collective brief. See BRIEF (2).

collective-knowledge rule. See FELLOW-OFFICER RULE.

collective-labor agreement. See COLLECTIVE-BARGAINING AGREEMENT.

collective mark. See *collective trademark* under TRADEMARK.

collective measure. *Int'l law.* An activity undertaken by more than one country to achieve an agreed-on end. • The countries involved may undertake a collective measure either in an ad hoc manner or through an institutionalized association.

collective punishment. (1872) A penalty inflicted on a group of persons without regard to individual responsibility for the conduct giving rise to the penalty. • Collective punishment was outlawed in 1949 by the Geneva Convention.

collective-security agreement. (1941) An international treaty between states by which all agree that if any one member state is attacked, the other member states will defend it.

collective trademark. See TRADEMARK.

collective work. See WORK (2).

collectivism. (1872) **1.** The belief that the people as a whole should own or control ownership of land, the means of production, the materials produced, and their distribution and exchange. **2.** A political system in which all businesses, farms, and other enterprises are owned by the state. — **collectivist,** *adj.* & *n.*

collector of decedent's estate. (1897) A person temporarily appointed by a probate court to collect assets and payments due to a decedent's estate, and to settle other financial matters requiring immediate attention. • A collector is often appointed to look after an estate when there is a will contest or a dispute about who should be appointed administrator. The collector's duties end when an executor or administrator is appointed.

collega (kə-**lee**-gə), *n.* [Latin] *Roman law.* A person invested with joint authority; a colleague or associate. • *Collega* usu. referred to a member of an association (*collegium*) or a coheir. See COLLEGIUM.

collegatarius (kə-leg-ə-**tair**-ee-əs), *n.* [Latin] *Roman law.* A colegatee.

collegatary (kə-**leg**-ə-ter-ee). (16c) *Civil law.* A person who shares a common legacy with one or more other persons; COLEGATEE.

college. (14c) **1.** An institution of learning that offers instruction in the liberal arts, humanities, and sciences, but not in the technical arts or in studies preparatory to admission to a profession. **2.** An assembly of people, established by law or private agreement to perform some special function or to promote some common purpose, usu. of an educational, political, ecclesiastical, or scientific nature.

College of Advocates and Doctors of Law. See DOCTORS' COMMONS.

College of Arms. See HERALDS' COLLEGE.

College of Civilians. See DOCTORS' COMMONS.

College of Justice. *Scots law.* The body of judges and lawyers created in 1532 to constitute the Court of Session, the superior civil court of Scotland.

collegium (kə-**lee**-jee-əm), *n.* [Latin] *Roman law.* An association of at least three people having the right to assemble and enact rules concerning membership, organization, and the rights and duties of members. • *Collegia* were formed for professional, cultural, charitable, and religious purposes. Pl. ***collegia.***

▸ ***collegium fetialium*** (kə-**lee**-jee-əm fee-shee-**ay**-lee-əm). [Latin] *Hist.* Fetial commission. See FETIAL LAW.

▸ ***collegium illicitum*** (kə-**lee**-jee-əm i-**lis**-ə-təm). A collegium that either is not sanctioned by law or assembles for some purpose other than that expressed in its charter.

▸ ***collegium licitum*** (kə-**lee**-jee-əm **lis**-ə-təm). An assemblage of people empowered to act as a juristic person in the pursuit of some useful purpose or business.

collibertus. See COLIBERTUS.

collision. (1848) *Maritime law.* **1.** The contact of two or more moving vessels. **2.** ALLISION.

collision insurance. See INSURANCE.

collisio obligationum (kə-**lizh**-ee-oh ob-li-gay-shee-**oh**-nəm). [Latin] *Hist.* Clash of obligations.

collisio officiorum (kə-**lizh**-ee-oh ə-fish-ee-**or**-əm). [Latin] *Hist.* Clash of duties.

colliterales et socii (kə-lit-ə-**ray**-leez et **soh**-shee-ɪ). [Law Latin "assistants and associates"] *Hist. English law.* In England, the former title of assistants to the Chancery judges (i.e., *masters in chancery*).

collobium (kə-**loh**-bee-əm). [Law Latin] (17c) *Hist.* A hood or covering for the shoulders, formerly worn by serjeants-at-law.

colloquium (kə-**loh**-kwee-əm). (17c) **1.** The offer of extrinsic evidence to show that an allegedly defamatory statement referred to the plaintiff even though it did not explicitly mention the plaintiff. **2.** The introductory averments in a plaintiff's pleading setting out all the special circumstances that make the challenged words defamatory. Cf. INDUCEMENT (4); INNUENDO (2). Pl. **colloquiums, colloquia.**

colloquy (**kol**-ə-kwee). (15c) Any formal discussion, such as an oral exchange between a judge, the prosecutor, the defense counsel, and a criminal defendant in which the judge ascertains the defendant's understanding of the proceedings and of the defendant's rights. • This discussion helps the court to determine the defendant's ability to continue in the proceedings (esp. important during a change-of-plea hearing).

collusion (kə-**loo**-zhən), *n.* (14c) **1.** An agreement to defraud another or to do or obtain something forbidden by law. **2.** As a defense to divorce, an agreement between a husband and wife to commit or to appear to commit an act that is grounds for divorce. • For example, before the advent of no-fault divorce, a husband and wife might agree to make it appear that one of them had committed adultery. Cf. CONNIVANCE (2); CONDONATION (2); RECRIMINATION (2). — **collude,** *vb.* — **collusive,** *adj.* — **colluder,** *n.*

▸ **tacit collusion.** *Antitrust.* See CONSCIOUS PARALLELISM.

collusive action. See ACTION (4).

collusive bidding agreement. (1960) The coordination of bids by auction bidders so as not to compete against each other, thereby keeping prices artificially low.

collusive joinder. See JOINDER.

***Collyer* doctrine** (**kol**-yər). (1972) *Labor law.* The principle under which the National Labor Relations Board will refer an issue brought before it to arbitration if the issue is arbitrable under the collective-bargaining agreement. *Collyer Insulated Wire*, 192 NLRB 837 (1971). Cf. SPIELBERG DOCTRINE.

colonialism. (1853) **1.** A policy advocating or based on a powerful country's ruling a weaker one, thereby establishing its own trade and society there.

▸ **neocolonialism.** (1961) Modernly, the economic and political policies by which a strong international power indirectly maintains or extends its influence or even control over other areas or people. — **neocolonialist,** *adj.* & *n.*

2. Something characteristic of a colony or colonist, including types of dress and modes of speech; a colonial peculiarity or idiom. **3.** The quality, state, or condition of being a member, inhabitant, or product of a colony. — **colonialist,** *adj.* & *n.*

colonial law. (18c) **1.** Law governing a colony or colonies. **2.** The body of law in force in the 13 original U.S. colonies before the Declaration of Independence.

colon-semicolon form. *Patents.* A style of writing patent claims that uses a colon after the preamble and semicolons between every two elements. Cf. OUTLINE FORM, SINGLE-PARAGRAPH FORM; SUBPARAGRAPH FORM.

colonus partiarius (kə-**loh**-nəs pahr-shee-**air**-ee-əs). [Latin "tenant farmer sharing produce" or "a sharing landholder"] (18c) *Roman law.* A farmer who gave a fixed portion of the farm's produce as payment (instead of money) to the landlord. Cf. SHARECROPPING.

colony, *n.* (16c) *Int'l law.* **1.** A dependent territorial entity subject to the sovereignty of an independent country, but considered part of that country for purposes of relations with third countries. **2.** A group of people who live in a new territory but retain ties with their parent country. **3.** The territory inhabited by such a group. See MOTHER COUNTRY. — **colonize,** *vb.* — **colonial,** *adj.*

color, *n.* (13c) **1.** Appearance, guise, or semblance; esp., the appearance of a legal claim to a right, authority, or office <color of title> <under color of state law>. **2.** *Common-law pleading.* An apparent, but legally insufficient, right or ground of action, admitted in a defendant's pleading to exist for the plaintiff; esp., a plaintiff's apparent (and usu. false) right or title to property, the existence of which is pleaded by the defendant and then attacked as defective, as part of a confession and avoidance to remove the case from the jury by turning the issue from one of fact to one of law. See GIVE COLOR.

> "It is a rule of pleading, that no man be allowed to plead specially such a plea as amounts only to the general issue, or a total denial of the charge; but in such case he shall be driven to plead the general issue in terms, whereby the whole question is referred to a jury. But if the defendant, in an assise or action of trespass, be desirous to refer the validity of his title to the court rather than the jury, he may state his title specially, and at the same time *give colour* to the plaintiff, or suppose him to have an appearance or colour of title, bad indeed in point of law, but of which the jury are not competent judges. As if his own true title be, that he claims by feoffment with livery from A, by force of which he entered on the lands in question, he cannot plead this by itself, as it amounts to no more than the general issue . . . *not guilty* in an action of trespass. But he may allege this specially, provided he goes farther and says, that the plaintiff claiming by *colour* of a prior deed of feoffment, without livery, entered; upon whom he entered; and may then refer himself to the judgment of the court which of these two titles is the best in point of law." 3 William Blackstone, *Commentaries on the Laws of England* 309 (1768).

▸ **express color.** (18c) *Hist.* A defendant's admission that the plaintiff has an apparent right to something coupled with an assertion that the plaintiff's right is legally inferior to the defendant's right to the same thing. • This pleading was typically used in cases of trespass to land by making fictitious allegations that put the plaintiff's ownership of the land in question. For instance, the defendant would admit that the plaintiff had shown apparent ownership of the land by possessing it but then claim that the plaintiff's title was somehow defective, so that the plaintiff did not actually own the land. This pleading was abolished by the Common-Law Procedure Act of 1852, 15 & 16 Vict., ch. 76, § 64.

"Express color is a fictitious allegation, not traversable, to give an appearance of right to the plaintiff, and thus enable the defendant to plead specially his own title, which would otherwise amount to the general issue. It is a licensed evasion of the rule against pleading contradictory matter specially." Benjamin J. Shipman, *Handbook of Common-Law Pleading* § 202, at 351 (Henry Winthrop Ballantine ed., 3d ed. 1923).

▸ **implied color.** (18c) **1.** A defendant's tacit admission of a plaintiff's prima facie case by failing to deny it. **2.** An apparent ground of action that arises from the nature of the defense, as when the defense consists of a confession and avoidance in which the defendant admits the facts but denies their legal sufficiency. • This is a quality inherent in all pleadings in confession and avoidance.

colorable, *adj.* (14c) **1.** (Of a claim or action) appearing to be true, valid, or right <the pleading did not state a colorable claim>. **2.** Intended to deceive; counterfeit <the court found the conveyance of exempt property to be a colorable transfer, and so set it aside>.

colorable alteration. (1814) *Intellectual property.* A modification that effects no real or substantial change, but is made only to distinguish an invention or work from an existing patent or copyright; a small change made in a product or process solely to avoid literal infringement of an earlier patent's claim. — Also termed *colorable deviation.*

colorable claim. See CLAIM (4).

colorable deviation. See COLORABLE ALTERATION.

colorable imitation. (1866) *Trademarks.* Any mark, whether or not created with an intent to deceive, whose resemblance to a registered mark is likely to cause confusion or mistake. See SIMILARITY.

colorable-imitation test. *Trademarks.* A test for a trademark violation in which a court determines whether an ordinary person who is not allowed to compare the two items side by side could recognize the difference between the two.

colorable transaction. See TRANSACTION.

colorable transfer. See TRANSFER.

Colorado Air Force School. See UNITED STATES AIR FORCE ACADEMY.

***Colorado River* abstention.** See ABSTENTION.

colorandi causa (kol-ə-**ran**-dɪ **kaw**-zə), *adv.* [Latin] *Hist.* For the purpose of decoration.

color book. *Archaic. Int'l law.* An official compilation of diplomatic documents and internal papers and reports of a government, the purpose of which is to inform the legislature and the public about foreign policy, esp. during foreign crises. • Color books reached their height of popularity in the late 19th and early 20th centuries. They are now little used in most countries.

colore officii (kə-**lor**-ee ə-**fish**-ee-ɪ). [Latin "by color of office"] See COLOR OF OFFICE.

colorism. (1983) *Slang.* Discrimination by people of a certain race against others of the same race based on skin tone.

color of apparent organization. (1888) The appearance of corporate authority, including the assumption and exercise of corporate functions in good faith, even though the corporation's organizers did not fully or substantially comply with the terms of the corporate charter or the statutory requirements for incorporation. See *de facto corporation* under CORPORATION.

color of authority. (16c) The appearance or presumption of authority sanctioning a public officer's actions. • The authority derives from the officer's apparent title to the office or from a writ or other apparently valid process the officer bears.

color of law. (17c) The appearance or semblance, without the substance, of a legal right. • The term usu. implies a misuse of power made possible because the wrongdoer is clothed with the authority of the state. *State action* is synonymous with *color of [state] law* in the context of federal civil-rights statutes or criminal law. See STATE ACTION.

color of office. (16c) The authority or power that is inherent in an office, esp. a public office. • Acts taken under the color of an office are vested with, or appear to be vested with, the authority entrusted to that office.

"The starting point in the law of bribery seems to have been when a judge, for doing his office or acting under color of his office, took a reward or fee from some person who had occasion to come before him, — and apparently guilt attached only to the judge himself and not to the bribe-giver." Rollin M. Perkins & Ronald N. Boyce, *Criminal Law* 527 (3d ed. 1982).

color of process. (16c) The appearance of validity and sufficiency surrounding a legal proceeding that is later found to be invalid.

color of right. The deliberately created false impression that title in property or goods is held by someone other than the actual owner.

color of title. (18c) A written instrument or other evidence that appears to establish title but does not in fact do so. — Also termed *apparent title.*

com. *abbr.* COMPANY.

comaker. (1846) Someone who participates jointly in borrowing money on a promissory note; esp., one who acts as surety under a note if the maker defaults. — Also termed *cosigner.* Cf. MAKER (2).

coma vigil. See VEGETATIVE STATE.

combatant (kəm-**bat**-ənt *or* **kom**-bə-tənt). (15c) *Int'l law.* Someone who participates directly in hostilities. • "Legitimate" combatants are members of the armed forces or uniformed members of a militia or volunteer corps, under military command and subject to the laws of war. Cf. NONCOMBATANT.

▸ **enemy combatant** (kəm-**bat**-ənt). (1942) Someone who belongs to or actively supports forces (such as al Qaeda) hostile to or in conflict with the United States or its allies. • In general, the separation-of-powers doctrine prevents a United States civilian court from interfering with the military's handling of enemy combatants, at least as long as the hostilities continue. An enemy combatant may be detained without charges but has the right to contest the detention. *Rasul v. Bush*, 542 U.S. 466, 124 S.Ct. 2686 (2004). United States citizenship does not prevent a person from being designated an enemy combatant, but the government must give a citizen-detainee notice of the factual basis for the classification and a fair opportunity to rebut the factual assertions before a neutral decision-maker. *Hamdi v.*

Rumsfeld, 542 U.S. 507, 124 S.Ct. 2633 (2004). See COMBATANT STATUS REVIEW TRIBUNAL.

Combatant Status Review Tribunal. A tribunal within the Department of Defense established in 2004 to determine the status of detainees at the Guantánamo Bay Detainment Camp. • The tribunals were established in response to the rulings in *Hamdi v. Rumsfeld*, 542 U.S. 507 (2004) and *Rasul v. Bush*, 542 U.S. 466 (2004). — Abbr. CSRT. See *enemy combatant* under COMBATANT.

combination. (16c) **1.** An alliance of individuals or corporations working together to accomplish a common (usu. economic) goal. See COMBINATION IN RESTRAINT OF TRADE. **2.** CONSPIRACY. **3.** STRADDLE. **4.** *Patents.* A union of old and new elements in an invention. • The term encompasses not only a combination of mechanical elements but also a combination of substances in a composition claim or steps in a process claim. Cf. AGGREGATION (2). **5.** *Patents.* An invention that uses two or more patented inventions to make a distinct and useful third product. • In the past, an inventor seeking a combination patent had to show "synergism," a surprising result from the combination. But the U.S. Court of Appeals for the Federal Circuit ruled that the term "combination" has no legal effect, because most inventions combine and build on existing technology. Today there are no special rules for combination patents. **6.** *Patents.* A union of elements in an invention that work together cooperatively to perform a useful function; the opposite of an aggregation. Cf. AGGREGATION (2).

▸ **exhausted combination.** See *old combination.*

▸ **old combination.** (1849) A combination in which an element works in a different way but performs the same function as the corresponding element in a previously patented combination. • The new element may be patentable but the combination may not be. — Also termed *exhausted combination.*

▸ **unlawful combination. 1.** An agreement by two or more people to engage in an illegal activity or to pursue an illegal end. **2.** *Obs.* A trade union.

combination in restraint of trade. (1859) *Antitrust.* An express or tacit agreement between two or more persons or entities designed to raise prices, reduce output, or create a monopoly. — Also termed *combine.*

combination patent. See PATENT (3).

combine (kom-bɪn), *n.* See COMBINATION IN RESTRAINT OF TRADE.

combined application. See TRADEMARK APPLICATION.

Combined DNA Index System. (2004) A database maintained by the FBI to support U.S. federal, state, and local crime labs and some international law-enforcement agencies investigating violent crimes.

combined § 8 and § 15 affidavit. *Trademarks.* A sworn statement that satisfies the requirements of both § 8 and § 15 of the Lanham Act. — Sometimes shortened to *§ 8 and § 15 affidavit.* — Also termed *combined § 8 and § 15 declaration.* See DECLARATION OF INCONTESTABILITY; DECLARATION OF USE.

combustio domorum (kəm-**bus**-tee-oh də-**mor**-əm). [Latin "houses burning"] *Hist.* See HOUSEBURNING.

comes (**koh**-meez). [Latin] *Hist.* **1.** A count or earl. **2.** Someone who is part of a high government official's retinue. See COMITATUS. Pl. ***comites.***

comes and defends. (17c) *Archaic.* Traditionally, the standard commencement of a defendant's plea or demurrer. • The phrase, now rarely used, announces the defendant's appearance in court and intent to defend against the action.

comes now. *Archaic.* Traditionally, the standard commencement in pleadings <Comes now the plaintiff, Gilbert Lewis, by and through his attorneys of record, and would show unto the court the following>. • For a plural subject, the phrase is *come now* <Come now the plaintiffs, Bob and Louise Smith>. — Sometimes shortened to *comes* <Comes the State of Tennessee>. — Also termed *now comes.*

comfort letter. (1962) **1.** *Securities.* A letter from a certified public accountant certifying that no false or misleading information has been used in preparing a financial statement accompanying a securities offering. • Such a letter usu. has limited effect because the CPA ordinarily attests to certain representations and warranties that the issuer has authorized the CPA to rely on. — Also termed *cold-comfort letter.* **2.** *Corporations.* A letter, esp. from a parent corporation on behalf of a subsidiary, stating its support (but short of a guarantee) for the activities and commitments of another corporation. **3.** *Criminal law.* A letter from a prosecuting or regulatory-enforcement authority that it has no present intention to commence proceedings against the recipient. — Also termed *letter of comfort.*

comfort opinion. See OPINION (2).

comfort person. (2004) A person such as a counselor, or possibly an animal, that sits nears a child, esp. the victim of a sexual offense, when he or she is testifying, so as to put the child at ease or impart a feeling of safety.

comingle, *vb.* See COMMINGLE.

comingling. See COMMINGLING.

coming-to-rest doctrine. (1946) *Insurance.* The principle that coverage of shipped goods ends when the goods are unloaded and any cables or other links to the transporting vehicle have been disconnected. • The coming-to-rest doctrine covers only the movement of goods from the shipping vehicle to a place of rest outside the vehicle, in contrast to the broader coverage of the complete-operation rule. Cf. COMPLETE-OPERATION RULE.

comitas (**kom**-ə-təs). [Latin "courtesy"] See COMITY.

comitas gentium. See COMITY.

comitas legum (**kom**-ə-təs **lee**-gəm). [Law Latin] *Hist.* Comity of laws. See COMITY.

comitatu commisso (kom-ə-**tay**-t[y]oo kə-**mis**-oh). [Latin "county commission"] (17c) *Hist.* A writ or commission authorizing a sheriff to take charge of a county.

comitatu et castro commisso (kom-ə-**tay**-t[y]oo et **kas**-troh kə-**mis**-oh). [Latin "county and castle commission"] *Hist.* A writ authorizing a sheriff to take charge of a county and a castle.

comitatus (kom-ə-**tay**-təs). [Latin] (1875) *Hist.* **1.** A county or shire. See POSSE COMITATUS. **2.** The territorial jurisdiction of a count or earl. **3.** A county court. **4.** The retinue accompanying a prince or high government official.

comites (**kom**-ə-teez). See COMES.

comites paleys (**kom**-ə-teez-pa-**lays**). [Law French] (17c) *Hist.* Counts or earls palatine; those who exercise royal privileges in a county palatine. See COUNTY PALATINE.

comitia (kə-**mish**-ee-ə), *n.* [Latin "assembly"] (17c) *Roman law.* An assembly of the Roman people, gathered together for legislative or judicial purposes. • Women were excluded from participation.

▸ ***comitia centuriata*** (kə-**mish**-ee-ə sen-tyoor-ee-**ay**-tə). (*often cap.*) (16c) An assembly of the entire populace, voting by centuries (that is, military units) empowered to elect magistrates and to act as a court of appeal in a capital matter.

"The *Comitia Centuriata,* said to have been originated by the sixth King, Servius Tullius, included the whole Roman people arranged in classes according to their wealth, so as to give the preponderating power to the richest. During the regal period it was a military organisation on the basis of property: under the Republic it became a legislative body, ousting the *Comitia Curiata.*" William A. Hunter, *Introduction to Roman Law* 16 (F.H. Lawson ed., 9th ed. 1934).

▸ ***comitia curiata*** (kə-**mish**-ee-ə kyoor-ee-**ay**-tə). (*often cap.*) (17c) An assembly of (originally) patricians whose chief function was to authorize private acts of citizens, such as declaring wills and adoptions. • The *comitia curiata* engaged in little legislative activity.

"The oldest [of the four assemblies of the Roman people] was the *Comitia Curiata.* In the regal period this assembly consisted of the *Populus Romanus* in its thirty curies (or family groups): it could meet only by summons of the King; it merely accepted or rejected the proposals submitted by him, without the right of discussion or amendment; nor was any decision by it valid without the authorisation of the Senate. Under the Republic it rapidly fell into the background, though it formally existed, represented by thirty lictors, down into Imperial times: for the private law its main importance lay in its meetings under pontifical presidency to deal with matters of religious significance, such as adrogations and wills." William A. Hunter, *Introduction to Roman Law* 15–16 (F.H. Lawson ed., 9th ed. 1934).

▸ ***comitia tributa*** (kə-**mish**-ee-ə tri-**byoo**-tə). (*often cap.*) (17c) An assembly of tribes convened to elect lower-ranking officials. • The *comitia tributa* undertook a great deal of legislative activity in the later Roman republic. Cf. CONCILIUM PLEBIS.

"The *Comitia Tributa* was the assembly of the whole Roman people in their tribes — a regional classification. In this assembly the influence of numbers predominated." William A. Hunter, *Introduction to Roman Law* 16 (F.H. Lawson ed., 9th ed. 1934).

comity (**kom**-ə-tee). (16c) **1.** A principle or practice among political entities (as countries, states, or courts of different jurisdictions) whereby legislative, executive, and judicial acts are mutually recognized. — Also termed *comitas gentium; courtoisie internationale.* See FEDERAL-COMITY DOCTRINE; JUDICIAL COMITY. Cf. ABSTENTION.

"'Comity,' in the legal sense, is neither a matter of absolute obligation, on the one hand, nor of mere courtesy and good will, upon the other. But it is the recognition which one nation allows within its territory to the legislative, executive, or judicial acts of another nation, having due regard both to international duty and convenience, and to the rights of its own citizens, or of other persons who are under the protection of its laws." *Hilton v. Guyot,* 159 U.S. 113, 163–64, 16 S.Ct. 139, 143 (1895).

2. INTERNATIONAL LAW. • This sense is considered a misusage: "[I]n Anglo-American jurisprudence, . . . the term is also misleadingly found to be used as a synonym for international law." Peter Macalister-Smith, "Comity," in 1 *Encyclopedia of Public International Law* 672 (1992). **3.** See *private international law* under INTERNATIONAL LAW.

Comity Clause. (1921) *Constitutional law.* The clause of the U.S. Constitution giving citizens of one state the right to all privileges and immunities enjoyed by citizens of the other states. U.S. Const. art. IV, § 2, cl. 1. See PRIVILEGES AND IMMUNITIES CLAUSE.

comm. *abbr.* **1.** COMMONWEALTH. **2.** Committee. **3.** *Archaic.* Commission.

command. (14c) **1.** An order; a directive. **2.** In legal positivism, the sovereign's express desire that a person act or refrain from acting a certain way, combined with the threat of punishment for failure to comply.

"Commands are orders backed by threats. It is in virtue of threatened evils, sanctions, that expressions of desire not only constitute commands but also impose an obligation or duty to act in the prescribed ways." Martin P. Golding, *Philosophy of Law* 26 (1975).

command, *vb.* (13c) To direct authoritatively; to order.

commander-in-chief. (17c) **1.** Someone who holds supreme or highest command of armed forces. **2.** (*cap.*) The title of the U.S. President when acting as the constitutionally designated leader of the country's military. U.S. Const. art. II, § 2.

Commander in Chief Clause. (1947) *Constitutional law.* The clause of the U.S. Constitution appointing the President as supreme commander of the military. U.S. Const. art. II, § 2, cl. 1.

commandment. (13c) *Hist.* **1.** An authoritative order of a judge or magisterial officer. **2.** The offense of inducing another to commit a crime.

command post. (1918) The place from which military leaders and their officers control activities.

command rape. See RAPE (2).

commencement. See INTRODUCTORY CLAUSE.

commencement date. See *effective date* under DATE.

commencement of an action. (18c) The time at which judicial or administrative proceedings begin, typically with the filing of a formal complaint. *See Unexcelled Chem. Corp. v. U.S.,* 345 U.S. 59, 66, 73 S.Ct. 580, 584 (1953).

commencement of infringement. (1878) *Copyright.* The first of a series of discrete copyright violations, such as the first of many separate sales of infringing items. See INFRINGEMENT.

commenda (kə-**men**-də). A business association in which one person has responsibility for managing all business property.

commendam (kə-**men**-dam *or* -dəm). (16c) **1.** *Hist. Eccles. law.* A vacant benefice held by a clerk until a regular pastor could be appointed. • Bishops and other dignitaries found commendams to be lucrative sources of income. Commendams were abolished in England in 1836. See BENEFICE. **2.** Partnership in commendam. See *limited partnership* under PARTNERSHIP.

commendation. (1818) *Hist.* The act of becoming a lord's feudal tenant to receive the lord's protection.

commendator (**kom**-ən-day-tər). (16c) *Eccles. law.* A person holding a commendam (a benefice) as a trustee. • Commendators are so called because benefices are commended to their supervision. See COMMENDAM.

commendatus (kom-ən-**day**-təs). (16c) *Hist.* Someone who, by voluntary oath of homage, was placed under a lord's protection.

comment, *n.* (14c) **1.** NOTE (2). **2.** An explanatory statement made by the drafters of a particular statute, code section, or rule. — **commentator,** *n.*

commentarii senatus. See ACTA SENATUS.

commentators. See POSTGLOSSATORS.

commenter. (14c) Someone who comments; esp., one who sends comments to an agency about a proposed administrative rule or regulation. See NOTICE-AND-COMMENT PERIOD.

comment letter. (1967) *Securities.* A letter prepared by an SEC examiner to request additional information or describe deficiencies in a filing, particularly a registration statement.

comment on the evidence. (18c) A statement made to the jury by the judge or by counsel on the probative value of certain evidence. Fed. R. Evid. 105. • Lawyers typically make such comments in closing argument, and judges may make such comments in federal court. But most state-court judges are not permitted to do so when examining a witness, instructing the jury, and the like (in which case the comment is sometimes termed an *impermissible comment on the evidence*).

comment on the failure to testify. (1903) A prosecutor's statement or implication to the jury, or a court's instruction to the jury, that a defendant's silence when he or she could have taken the stand is evidence of the defendant's guilt. • In *Griffin v. California*, 380 U.S. 609, 614–15 (1965), the Supreme Court explained that such a comment "solemnizes the silence of the accused into evidence against him" and violates the defendant's Fifth Amendment right to remain silent. — Also termed *comment on the refusal to testify.*

comment period. See NOTICE-AND-COMMENT PERIOD.

commerce. (16c) The exchange of goods and services, esp. on a large scale involving transportation between cities, states, and countries.

▸ **internal commerce.** See *intrastate commerce.*

▸ **international commerce.** (1819) Trade and other business activities between countries.

▸ **interstate commerce.** (1843) Trade and other business activities between those located in different states; esp., traffic in goods and travel of people between states. • For purposes of this phrase, most statutory definitions include a territory of the United States as a state. Some statutory definitions of *interstate commerce* include commerce between a foreign country and a state. — Also termed *interstate trade.*

▸ **intrastate commerce.** (1887) Commerce that begins and ends entirely within the borders of a single state. — Also termed *internal commerce.*

Commerce Clause. (1868) *Constitutional law.* U.S. Const. art. I, § 8, cl. 3, which gives Congress the exclusive power to regulate commerce among the states, with foreign countries, and with Indian tribes.

> "*The Commerce Clause*[.] One of the most important provisions of the American Constitution is one which has no counterpart in any aspect of the government of England, though the same general question does arise in other British countries, such as Canada and Australia. This provision is the Commerce Clause, Article I, section 8 of our Constitution, which provides that 'Congress shall have Power . . . to regulate Commerce with foreign Nations and among the several States, and with the Indian Tribes.' These are simple words, but they have had far-reaching effect. It is not too much to say, I think, that these words have had more to do with making us a Nation than any other provision of the Constitution." Erwin N. Griswold, *Law and Lawyers in the United States* 82 (1964).

▸ **Dormant Commerce Clause.** (1930) The constitutional principle that the Commerce Clause prevents state regulation of interstate commercial activity even when Congress has not acted under its Commerce Clause power to regulate that activity. — Also termed *Negative Commerce Clause.*

Commerce Court. See COURT.

commerce power. (1888) Congress's constitutionally conferred power to regulate trade between the states.

commercia belli (kə-**mər**-shee-ə **bel**-ɪ). [Latin "commerce of war"] (18c) Commercial dealings or contracts between countries at war, or between the subjects of countries at war, under which arrangements for nonhostile dealings are made.

commercial, *adj.* **1.** Of, relating to, or involving the buying and selling of goods; mercantile <commercial advertising>. **2.** Resulting or accruing from commerce or exchange <commercial gains>. **3.** Employed in trade; engaged in commerce <commercial travelers>. **4.** Manufactured for the markets; put up for trade <commercial products>. **5.** Of, relating to, or involving the ability of a product or business to make a profit <commercial potential>. **6.** Produced and sold in large quantities <commercial cosmetics>. **7.** *Pejorative.* More concerned with money than with quality <he sold out and became commercial>.

commercial acquiescence. See ACQUIESCENCE (1).

commercial acre. (1968) *Property.* The amount of land left in a subdivided acre after deducting the amount dedicated to streets, sidewalks, utilities, etc. • The area of a commercial acre is always less than an actual acre. Cf. ACRE.

commercial activity. See ACTIVITY (1).

commercial-activity exception. (1973) An exemption from the rule of sovereign immunity, permitting a claim against a foreign state to be adjudicated in the courts of another state if the claim arises from private acts undertaken by the foreign state, as opposed to the state's public acts. See RESTRICTIVE PRINCIPLE OF SOVEREIGN IMMUNITY; JURE GESTIONIS; JURE IMPERII.

commercial agency. See CREDIT BUREAU.

commercial agent. See AGENT.

commercial assets. See ASSET.

commercial bank. See BANK.

commercial bribery. See BRIBERY.

commercial broker. See BROKER.

commercial consignment. See CONSIGNMENT.

commercial court. See COURT.

commercial credit company. See *commercial finance company* under FINANCE COMPANY.

commercial crime. See CRIME.

commercial defamation. See *trade defamation* under DEFAMATION.

commercial disparagement. See TRADE DISPARAGEMENT.

commercial division. See *business court* under COURT.

commercial domicile. See DOMICILE.

commercial driver's license. See DRIVER'S LICENSE.

commercial finance company. See FINANCE COMPANY.

commercial franchise. See FRANCHISE (4).

commercial frustration. See FRUSTRATION (1).

commercial general-liability insurance. See INSURANCE.

commercial goodwill. See GOODWILL.

commercial impracticability. See IMPRACTICABILITY.

commercial insurance. See INSURANCE.

commercialized obscenity. See OBSCENITY.

commercial law. (18c) **1.** The substantive law dealing with the sale and distribution of goods, the financing of credit transactions on the security of the goods sold, and negotiable instruments. • Most American commercial law is governed by the Uniform Commercial Code. — Also termed *mercantile law.*

> "Although the term *commercial law* is not a term of art in American law it has become synonymous in recent years with the legal rules contained in the Uniform Commercial Code." Jonathan A. Eddy & Peter Winship, *Commercial Transactions* 1 (1985).

2. LAW MERCHANT.

commercial-law notice. See NOTICE (3).

commercial lease. See LEASE.

commercial letter of credit. See LETTER OF CREDIT.

commercial list. (1825) **1.** (*often cap.*) A branch of a general-jurisdiction court whose judges have experience and expertise in corporate and business matters, the judges often rotating in other areas of the law <Toronto judges sitting on the Commercial List>. **2.** A special docket of business-related cases that are heard by judges with experience and expertise in such matters. **3.** A roster of names, addresses, e-mail addresses, etc., sold for business uses.

commercial loan. See LOAN.

commercially reasonable, *adj.* (1922) (Of a property sale) conducted in good faith and in accordance with commonly accepted commercial practice. • Under the UCC, a sale of collateral by a secured party must be done in a commercially reasonable manner, or the obligor's liability for any deficiency may be reduced or eliminated. *See* UCC §§ 9-610(b), 9-626(a)(3).

commercially significant noninfringing use. (1984) *Intellectual property.* The routine use of a product in a way that does not infringe intellectual-property rights; the judicial test for determining whether the sale of a product amounts to contributory infringement. • If the product (such as a video recorder) can be used in a way that does not infringe those rights (such as recording a program in order to watch it at a later time), then its sale cannot be enjoined, nor its manufacturer subjected to a court-imposed royalty. *See Sony Corp. of Am. v. Universal City Studios, Inc.*, 464 U.S. 417, 442, 104 S.Ct. 774, 789 (1984). — Also termed *Sony doctrine*; *substantial noninfringing use.* Cf. PRIMARY PURPOSE OR EFFECT.

commercial morality. (18c) Collectively, fair practices among competitors. • Commercial espionage is often cited by courts as being below accepted standards of commercial morality.

commercial name. See TRADENAME.

commercial offense. See *commercial crime* under CRIME.

commercial paper. See PAPER.

commercial partnership. See *trading partnership* under PARTNERSHIP.

commercial set. 1. The primary documents covering shipment of goods, usu. including an invoice, bill of lading, bill of exchange, and certificate of insurance. **2.** The documents required under a letter of credit.

commercial sex act. (1977) Any sexual relations for which anything of value is given to or received by any person.

commercial sexual exploitation of a minor. (1978) Any one of a range of crimes committed against a child or adolescent as a subset of child abuse, including (1) the recruiting, enticing, harboring, transporting, providing, obtaining, or maintaining of a minor for sexual exploitation, (2) the exploitation of a minor through prostitution, (3) the exploitation of a minor by exchanging sexual acts for anything of value, such as food, shelter, or drugs, (4) the use of a minor in pornography, (5) the exploitation of a minor through sex tourism, mail-order-bride trade, or inappropriately early marriage, and (6) the exploitation of a minor through performances in sexual venues (such as peep shows and strip clubs). *See* National Institute of Medicine and National Research Council, *Confronting Commercial Sexual Exploitation and Sex Trafficking of Minors in the United States* 31 (Ellen Wright Clayton et al. eds., 2013). — Also termed *sex trafficking of minors*; *sex-trafficking in minors.*

commercial signature. (1878) *Trademarks.* A trademark (as commonly described).

commercial speech. See SPEECH (1).

commercial surety. See *compensated surety* under SURETY (1).

commercial tort claim. (1994) A claim arising in tort when the claimant is either (1) an organization, or (2) an individual whose claim arose in the course of the claimant's business or profession, and the claim does not include damages arising out of personal injury or death. UCC § 9-102(a)(13). • Typical commercial tort claims are fraud and conversion.

commercial transaction. (18c) A business deal or arrangement that alters legal rights.

commercial-traveler rule. (1963) *Workers' compensation.* The principle that an accident will be treated as occurring during the course of employment if it was caused by an employee whose job requires travel, and the employee was not on a personal errand. • The commercial-traveler rule is an exception to the going-and-coming rule. Cf. GOING-AND-COMING RULE.

commercial treaty. See TREATY (1).

commercial tribunal. See TRIBUNAL.

commercial unit. (1960) A unit of goods that by commercial usage is a single whole for purposes of sale and whose division materially impairs its character or value in the relevant market or in use. UCC § 2-105(6). • Under the UCC, "a commercial unit may be a single article (as a machine) or a set of articles (as a suite of furniture or an assortment of sizes) or a quantity (as a bale, gross, or carload) or any other unit treated in use or in the relevant market as a single whole." *Id.*

commercial use. See USE (1).

commercial value. See *exchange value* under VALUE (2).

commercium (kə-**mər**-see-əm). [Latin] *Roman law.* The capacity for acquiring or alienating property by civil methods unconnected with *conubium.* • Examples were mancipation, cession in court, and usucapion. Cf. CONUBIUM.

commettant (**kom**-ə-tənt), *n.* (1866) **1.** An employer. **2.** The principal in an agency relationship.

comminatorium (kə-min-ə-**tor**-ee-əm). [Latin *comminari* "threaten"] (17c) *Hist.* A clause often included at the end of a writ, admonishing the sheriff to be faithful in the writ's execution.

commingle (kə-**ming**-gəl), *vb.* (17c) **1.** To put together (as funds or property) into one mass, as by mixing together a spouse's separate property with marital or community property, or mixing together the separate property of both spouses. **2.** (Of a fiduciary) to mix personal funds with those of a beneficiary or client, usu. in an improper or illegal way. — Also spelled *comingle.* See COMMINGLING. Cf. TRACING (1).

commingled funds. See FUND, *n.* (2).

commingled goods. See GOODS.

commingling (kə-**ming**-gling), *n.* (1854) A mixing together; esp., a fiduciary's mixing of personal funds with those of a beneficiary or client. • Commingling is usu. considered a breach of the fiduciary relationship. Under the Model Rules of Professional Conduct, a lawyer is prohibited from commingling personal funds with those of a client. Commingling also occurs when a spouse has mixed his or her separate property with community property to such an extent that they cannot be separated. — Also spelled *comingling.*

commissary (**kom**-i-ser-ee), *n.* (14c) **1.** Someone who is delegated or commissioned to perform some duty, usu. as a representative of a superior. **2.** A general store, esp. on a military base. **3.** A lunchroom. — **commissary,** *adj.*

commissary court. See COURT.

commission, *n.* (14c) **1.** A warrant or authority, from the government or a court, that empowers the person named to execute official acts <the student received his commission to the U.S. Navy after graduation>. **2.** The authority under which a person transacts business for another <the client gave her attorney express commission to sign the contract>. **3.** A body of persons acting under lawful authority to perform certain public services <the Federal Communications Commission>.

▸ **public-service commission.** (1907) A commission created by a legislature to regulate public utilities or public-service corporations.

4. The act of doing or perpetrating (as a crime) <the perpetrator fled to Mexico after commission of the assault>. **5.** A fee paid to an agent or employee for a particular transaction, usu. as a percentage of the money received from the transaction <a real-estate agent's commission>.

▸ **double commission.** (17c) A commission obtained by a person acting in dual roles, each of which generates a commission, such as a person serving as both executor and trustee in an estate matter. • Double commissions paid without proper authority or disclosure may raise fiduciary-duty issues. See FIDUCIARY; *fiduciary duty* under DUTY (2).

commission agent. See AGENT.

commissionaire. See AGENT.

commission broker. See BROKER.

commission day. (17c) *English law.* The opening day of the assizes. • On this day the commission that authorizes the judge to act is publicly read. — Also written *commission-day.*

commission *del credere* (del **kred**-ər-ay). (18c) The commission received by the seller's agent for guaranteeing a buyer's debt.

commissioned officer. See OFFICER (2).

commissioner. (15c) **1.** Someone who directs a commission; a member of a commission. **2.** The administrative head of an organization, such as a government department or a professional sport. **3.** See *judicial officer* (3) under OFFICER.

▸ **bail commissioner.** See BAIL COMMISSIONER.

▸ **commissioner for oaths.** (1876) *English law.* A lawyer who may legally serve as a witness to particular legal documents.

▸ **Commissioner for Patents.** The chief operating officer of the patents section of the U.S. Patent and Trademark Office. • The commissioner is appointed by the Secretary of Commerce.

▸ **Commissioner for Trademarks.** The chief operating officer of the trademarks section of the U.S. Patent and Trademark Office. • The commissioner is appointed by the Secretary of Commerce.

▸ **commissioner in bankruptcy.** (1840) *English law.* A commissioner who is appointed by the Lord Chancellor and empowered to proceed in corporate-bankruptcy cases.

▸ **commissioner of bail.** See BAIL COMMISSIONER (2).

▸ **commissioner of circuit court.** A court-appointed officer who helps the circuit and district courts by performing judicial and ministerial functions.

▸ **commissioner of deeds.** (1834) An officer authorized by a state to take acknowledgments of deeds and other papers while residing in another state. • The acknowledgments are recognized in the state that licensed the commissioner. Cf. NOTARY PUBLIC.

▸ **commissioner of highways.** (1840) A public officer responsible for overseeing the construction, alteration, and repair of highways.

▸ **commissioner of partition.** (1854) An equity-court-appointed officer who is empowered to examine a request for partition and recommend an action to the court, or to make the partition and report the act to the court.

▸ **Commissioner of Patents and Trademarks.** See DIRECTOR OF THE UNITED STATES PATENT AND TRADEMARK OFFICE.

▸ **commissioner of police.** See *police commissioner.*

▸ **commissioner of woods and forests.** (1817) *Hist.* An officer who, by an 1817 Act of Parliament, assumed the jurisdiction of the Chief Justice of the Forest.

▸ **county commissioner.** (1819) A county officer charged usu. with the management of the county's financial affairs, its police regulations, and its corporate business. — Also termed *county supervisor.*

▸ **court commissioner.** (1868) An officer appointed by the court esp. to hear and report facts, or to conduct judicial sales.

▸ **high commissioner.** (16c) A top-ranked member or director of a commission.

▸ **jury commissioner.** (1877) An officer responsible for drawing and summoning the panels of potential jurors in a given county.

▸ **police commissioner.** (1819) A civil commissioner who supervises the policy, administration, and discipline of a police department, esp. that of a city. — Also termed *commissioner of police.*

▸ **public commissioner.** See PROSECUTOR (1).

▸ **town commissioner.** (1818) A member of the board of administrative officers charged with managing the town's business.

▸ **United States Commissioner.** *Hist.* A judicial officer appointed by a U.S. district court to hear a variety of pretrial matters in criminal cases. • Commissioners' duties have been transferred to U.S. Magistrate Judges. Cf. UNITED STATES MAGISTRATE JUDGE.

commissioner's court. See COURT.

commission government. (1901) A type of municipal government in which the legislative power is in the hands of a few people; COMMISSION PLAN.

commission merchant. See FACTOR (3).

commission of appraisement and sale. (18c) *Maritime law.* A court order requiring the sale of property in an in-rem admiralty action.

commission of assize. (18c) *Hist.* A royal authorization empowering a person to hold court and try cases arising while the justices in eyre held court elsewhere. Cf. EYRE.

> "[B]oth the presentment of crimes and the conduct of trials by assize or jury — which rapidly became a common feature of royal justice — required the presence of twelve or more men from the vicinity where the matter in question occurred. . . . The means of achieving this reconciliation was the frequent issue of commissions to perform judicial functions in the country. . . . [A]ssize commissioners had original jurisdiction to hear a case from beginning to end . . . . But the assizes, though moulded into a regular routine, never became a distinct 'court' in the permanent sense. The jurisdiction of the judges rested entirely on the commissions which issued for each circuit: the judges could therefore be regularly interchanged, and after 1340 it was quite normal for a Common Plea case to be tried at nisi prius by a King's Bench judge, and vice versa." J.H. Baker, *An Introduction to English Legal History* 67 (3d ed. 1990).

commission of charitable uses. (18c) *Hist.* An authorization issuing out of the Court of Chancery to a bishop or other person authorizing the appointee to investigate allegations of fraud or other disputed matters concerning charitable land grants.

commission of delegates. (17c) *Hist.* A commission appointing a person (usu. a lord, bishop, or judge) to sit with several other appointees to hear an appeal of an ecclesiastical judgment in the Court of Chancery. • This commission was abolished in 1832, and its functions transferred to the Judicial Committee of the Privy Council.

Commission of Fine Arts. An independent federal commission that advises the President, Congress, and governmental agencies on the design of public buildings, memorials, and parks in the country's capital so as to complement historic structures and districts. • The commission was created in 1910.

Commission of Gaol Delivery. *Hist.* A royal appointment authorizing a judge to go on the assize circuit and hear all criminal cases of those held in county jails. See JAIL DELIVERY. Cf. COMMISSION OF OYER AND TERMINER.

commission of lieutenancy. (17c) *Hist.* A commission issued to send officers into every county to establish military order over the inhabitants. • This commission superseded the former *commission of array,* which provided the same powers. The commissions became obsolete with the establishment of the militia system.

commission of lunacy. See DE LUNATICO INQUIRENDO.

Commission of Oyer and Terminer (oy-ər an[d] tər-mə-nər). [Law French *oyer et terminer* "to hear and determine"] (16c) *Hist.* A royal appointment authorizing a judge (often a serjeant-at-law) to go on the assize circuit and hear felony and treason cases. Cf. COMMISSION OF GAOL DELIVERY; COURT OF OYER AND TERMINER (1).

> "[U]nder the commission of *Oyer and Terminer,* as the judges are directed to *inquire* as well as to hear and determine the same, they can only proceed upon an indictment found at the same assize, and before themselves; for they must first *inquire* by means of the grand jury or inquest, before they are empowered to hear and determine by the intervention of the petit jury." 1 Joseph Chitty, *A Practical Treatise on the Criminal Law* 142 (2d ed. 1826).

commission of partition. (18c) An authorization appointing a person to sit with several other appointees for the purpose of dividing land held by tenants in common who desire a partition.

commission of rebellion. (16c) *Hist.* An attaching process that empowered a layperson to arrest and bring a defendant to Chancery to enforce obedience to a writ of subpoena or decree. • The commission of rebellion was abolished in 1841. — Also termed *writ of rebellion; commissio rebellionis; breve rebellionis.*

> "*Commission of rebellion* (*Commissio rebellionis*) is otherwise called a writte of rebellion, (*breve rebellionis*) and it hath use, when a man after proclamation made by the Shyreeve upon an order of the channcerie, or court of Starre chamber, under penaltie of his allegance, to present himselfe to the court by a certaine day, appeareth not. And this commission is directed by way of command to certain persons, to this end, that they . . . apprehend, or cause to be apprehended, the party as a rebell and contemner of the kings lawes." John Cowell, *The Interpreter* (1607).

commission of review. (17c) *Hist. English law.* In England, an authorization sometimes granted in an extraordinary case to review a judgment of the Court of Delegates. • The commission of review is no longer used because the Privy Council was substituted for the Court of Delegates as the appellate court in ecclesiastical cases in 1832. See COURT OF DELEGATES.

commission of the peace. (16c) *Hist.* An appointment of a person to keep the peace (i.e., provide police protection) on a local level. • Over time the recipients of these commissions began to acquire judicial responsibilities, and became known as justices of the peace.

commission of unlivery (ən-liv-ər-ee). (18c) *Hist.* A court order requiring the unloading of goods from a ship so that they may be appraised.

Commission on Civil Rights. See UNITED STATES COMMISSION ON CIVIL RIGHTS.

commission plan. (1919) A form of municipal government whereby both legislative and executive power is vested in a small group of elected officials. • Today, commission plans are used in only a few cities. — Also termed *commission government.*

commission to examine a witness. (18c) A judicial commission directing that a witness beyond the court's territorial jurisdiction be deposed. • The commission usu. identifies the person to be deposed, when and where the deposition will be taken, and any other information that will help the commissioner to perform. — Also termed *commission to take a deposition; commission to take testimony.* Cf. LETTER OF REQUEST (1).

commission to take a deposition. See COMMISSION TO EXAMINE A WITNESS.

commission to take testimony. See COMMISSION TO EXAMINE A WITNESS.

commissio rebellionis. See COMMISSION OF REBELLION.

commissive waste. See WASTE (1).

commissoria lex. See LEX COMMISSORIA.

commit, *vb.* (15c) **1.** To perpetrate (a crime). **2.** To send (a person) to prison or to a mental health facility, esp. by court order. **3.** *Parliamentary law.* REFER.

commitment, *n.* (14c) **1.** An agreement to do something in the future, esp. to assume a financial obligation <the shipper made a firm commitment to deliver the goods>. **2.** The act of entrusting or giving in charge; a consignment for safekeeping <commitment of money to the bank>. **3.** The referring of a bill, petition, motion, etc., as to a committee <commitment of the proposed legislation to Ways and Means>. **4.** A promise to do something or to behave in a particular way <our company's long-term commitment to customer service>. **5.** An obligation that one has undertaken and must perform as a matter of morals or ethics <family commitments>. **6.** The hard work and loyalty that someone gives to an organization <her commitment to her job is unquestioned>. **7.** An amount of money that one must pay regularly <financial commitments>. **8.** The use of money, time, people, etc. for a particular purpose <commitments of food and medical supplies of over $100 million>. **9.** The act of confining a person in a prison, mental hospital, or other institution; esp., the sending of a person to jail, by warrant or order, for crime, contempt, or contumacy <commitment of the felon to prison>. See COMMITTAL (1). **10.** The order directing an officer to take a person to a penal or mental institution; MITTIMUS (1) <the judge signed the commitment after ruling that it was in the best interest of the troubled teen>.

▸ **civil commitment.** See CIVIL COMMITMENT (1).

▸ **diagnostic commitment.** (1967) Pretrial or presentencing confinement of an individual, usu. to determine the individual's competency to stand trial or to determine the appropriate sentence to be rendered.

▸ **discretionary commitment.** (1962) A commitment that a judge may or may not grant, depending on whether the government has proved — usu. by clear and convincing evidence — that the commitment is necessary for the well-being of the defendant or society (as when the defendant is insane and dangerous). • Most states allow discretionary commitment.

▸ **mandatory commitment.** (1985) An automatically required commitment for a defendant found not guilty by reason of insanity. • This type of commitment is required under federal law, but in only a minority of states.

▸ **new court commitment.** (2007) The confinement in prison of a person who is being admitted on a new conviction — that is, someone who is not being returned to prison for a parole violation.

▸ **voluntary commitment.** (1916) A commitment of a person who is ill, incompetent, drug-addicted, or the like, upon the request or with the consent of the person being committed.

commitment document. (1965) **1.** An order remanding a defendant to prison in order to carry out a judgment and sentence. **2.** A binding contract, change order, purchase order, letter of intent, or other instrument relating to transactions for goods or services.

commitment fee. (1933) An amount paid to a lender by a potential borrower for the lender's promise to lend money at a stipulated rate and within a specified time. • Commitment fees are common in real-estate transactions. See LOAN COMMITMENT.

commitment letter. (1949) **1.** A lender's written offer to grant a mortgage loan. • The letter generally outlines the loan amount, the interest rate, and other terms. — Also termed *letter of commitment.* **2.** LETTER OF INTENT.

commitment warrant. See *warrant of commitment* under WARRANT (1).

committal. (18c) **1.** The process by which a court sends someone to a mental hospital or prison; COMMITMENT (9). **2.** The burial or cremation of a dead person; interment.

committee. (17c) **1.** (kə-**mit**-ee). A subordinate group to which a deliberative assembly or other organization refers business for consideration, investigation, oversight, or action <the bill was sent to legislative committee>.

> "One of the outstanding characteristics of membership organizations the world over is the powerful role played by committees in setting policy and in carrying out their objectives. The Congress, state legislatures, business associations, and countless clubs and societies have traditionally conducted their work through committees of their members." Lewis Deschler, *Deschler's Rules of Order* § 103, at 189 (1976).

▸ **ad hoc committee.** See *special committee.*

▸ **arrangements committee.** (1887) A committee charged with organizing the physical space in which a deliberative assembly meets.

▸ **audit committee.** (1847) A committee appointed by the board of an organization, esp. a corporation, to oversee the financial reporting process, select an independent auditor, and receive the audit. • Ideally, a committee member is financially literate and wholly independent, having no financial interest (direct or indirect) in the company, no executive position, and no familial relationship with any member of the company's management or a major shareholder.

▸ **committee of one.** A committee with only one member.

▸ **committee of the whole.** (1811) A committee that comprises all the deliberative assembly's members who are present. • A deliberative assembly may resolve itself into a committee of the whole so that it can take advantage of the greater procedural flexibility that a committee enjoys, usu. presided over by some chair other than the assembly's regular chair. Cf. *quasi committee of the whole.*

▸ **committee on conference.** See *conference committee.*

▸ **committee with full power.** See *committee with power.*

▸ **committee with power.** A committee to whom the referring body has delegated the necessary authority for acting on the business referred, usu. without need for a prior report to the referring body. — Also termed *committee with full power.*

▸ **conference committee.** (1879) A joint meeting of two legislative committees, one from each house of a bicameral legislature, usu. charged with adjusting differences in a bill passed by both houses in different versions. — Also termed *committee on conference.* See CONFERENCE (2).

> "A committee on conference from each of the two houses meeting together is not a joint committee but a joint meeting of two committees. The quorum of a committee on conference is a majority of the members of each committee. In voting in a conference committee, the committee of each house votes separately. The committee on conference from each house submits its report to the house from which it was appointed. The report, upon being received, may be treated like other reports, except that the report of a conference committee is usually given a higher precedence. Under no condition, including suspension of the rules, may the house alter or amend the report of the committee, but must adopt or refuse to adopt the report in the form submitted." National Conference of State Legislatures, *Mason's Manual of Legislative Procedure* § 770, at 558–59 (2000).

▸ **congressional committee.** (1855) A committee of the House of Representatives, a committee of the Senate, or a joint committee.

▸ **credentials committee.** (1901) A committee charged with preparing a roster of delegates entitled to be seated, examining contested claims to such entitlement, and preparing and issuing credentials to the delegates who appear so entitled. See CREDENTIAL.

▸ **executive committee.** (18c) The committee of principal officers and directors who directly manage an organization's affairs between board meetings.

▸ **joint committee.** (17c) A legislative committee composed of members of both houses of a legislature.

▸ **legislative committee.** (17c) A group of legislators appointed to help a legislature conduct its business, esp. by providing careful consideration of proposals for new legislation within a particular field so that the entire body can handle its work efficiently without wasting time and effort on unmeritorious submissions.

▸ **membership committee.** (1889) A committee charged with recruiting and keeping members and getting them involved.

▸ **nominating committee.** (1840) A committee charged with identifying (and perhaps recruiting) and recommending a suitable candidate or candidates for election by a deliberative assembly. — Also termed *screening committee.*

▸ **ordinary committee.** (18c) A committee other than a committee of the whole.

▸ **parent committee.** (1830) A committee that refers business to a subcommittee. • The parent committee is so called only when considered in relation to the subcommittee. See *subcommittee.*

▸ **permanent committee.** See *standing committee.*

▸ **platform committee.** (1896) A committee charged with developing a comprehensive statement of an organization's, usu. a political party's, public policies and principles.

▸ **program committee.** (1887) The committee that plans a convention's program, usu. including both its formal business and its educational and social events.

▸ **quasi committee of the whole.** (1849) The procedure of a deliberative assembly's acting "as if in committee of the whole." • The rules of debate and amendment, and for reporting amendments to the assembly to finally act upon under the regular rules, are the same as for a committee of the whole, but the body retains its powers as an assembly and is presided over by the regular chair. Cf. *committee of the whole.*

▸ **reference committee.** See *resolutions committee.*

▸ **resolutions committee.** (1896) A committee charged with screening the original main motions offered for a convention's consideration. — Also termed *reference committee; screening committee.*

▸ **rules committee.** (1884) A committee charged with drafting rules and an agenda for the orderly conduct of a deliberative assembly's business, particularly that of a legislative body or a convention.

▸ **screening committee. 1.** See *nominating committee.* **2.** See *resolutions committee.*

▸ **search committee.** (18c) A committee charged with finding a suitable choice from several options, such as candidates for employment or places for a meeting.

▸ **select committee.** See *special committee.*

▸ **special committee.** (17c) A committee established for a particular purpose or a limited time. • A legislature will ordinarily establish a special committee for a nonlegislative purpose, such as writing memorials, procuring chaplains, determining the qualifications of members, and settling election disputes. — Also termed *ad hoc committee; select committee; temporary committee.*

> "Select or special committees are, in principle, temporary committees without legislative authority. They may be used to study problems falling within the jurisdiction of several standing committees, to symbolize Congress's commitment to key constituency groups, or simply to reward

particular legislators. Select committees have been used for prominent investigations — the Senate's 1973 Watergate committee and the 1987 House and Senate select committees on the Iran-contra affair are examples. Major reforms of congressional rules and organization have originated in select committees. Unfortunately, committee nomenclature can be misleading. For example, without eliminating the word *select* from their names, the House and Senate have made their intelligence committees permanent and granted them the power to report legislation." Steven S. Smith, "The Congressional Committee System," in 2 *Encyclopedia of the American Legislative System* 641, 643 (Joel H. Silbey ed., 1994).

▸ **standing committee.** (17c) A committee that is established for ongoing business, that continues to exist from session to session, and that is usu. charged with considering business of a certain recurring kind. • A legislature will ordinarily establish a standing committee concerned with a specific field of legislation. A legislative standing committee usu. considers basic questions of legislative policy, holds hearings on legislation, eliminates unwanted bills, and prepares favored measures for passage. — Also termed *permanent committee.*

"Standing committees have legislative authority and permanent status. Their legislative jurisdiction is specified in chamber rules and precedents, and they may write and report legislation on any matter within their jurisdictions. In the case of the House, which must approve its rules at the start of each Congress, the jurisdictions of standing committees are routinely reapproved every two years. The rules articulating the jurisdictions and regulating the behavior of standing committees may be changed, of course, as they have been on occasion, but for the standing committees the burden is on proponents of change to gain support for amendments to the rules." Steven S. Smith, "The Congressional Committee System," in 2 *Encyclopedia of the American Legislative System* 641, 641–42 (Joel H. Silbey ed., 1994).

▸ **subcommittee.** (17c) A group within a committee to which the committee may refer business, standing in the same relation to its parent committee as the committee stands to the deliberative assembly. See *parent committee.*

▸ **tellers committee.** (1923) A committee that helps the chair administer an election or other vote by handing out and picking up ballots if necessary, counting the votes or canvassing the ballots, and reporting the result to the chair for announcement. See CANVASS (2).

▸ **temporary committee.** See *special committee.*

2. (kəm-i-**tee**) Someone who is civilly committed, esp. to a psychiatric hospital <the board determined that the committee was dangerous and should not be released>. **3.** (kəm-i-**tee**) The guardian for the person so committed <the patient's lawyer objected to the appointment of the committee>.

committee amendment. See AMENDMENT (3).

committee jurisdiction. See CHARGE (8).

committee of creditors. See CREDITORS' COMMITTEE.

committee report. See REPORT (1).

committee stage. (1870) The phase in the passage of a legislative bill in which each provision is considered and voted on by a legislative committee.

committee substitute. See *clean bill* under BILL (3).

committing magistrate. See MAGISTRATE.

committitur (kə-**mit**-ə-tər). [Latin "he is committed"] (18c) *Archaic.* An order or minute stating that the person named in it is to be committed to the custody of the sheriff.

▸ **interim committitur.** [Latin "in the meantime, let him be committed"] A court order directing that a defendant be incarcerated pending further action.

committitur piece. (18c) *Hist.* An instrument used to civilly charge a debtor already in prison, esp. by the plaintiff who had brought about the debtor's imprisonment. • The committitur piece was rendered obsolete by the 1869 Debtors Act, which abolished imprisonment for debt.

commixtio (kə-**miks**-tee-oh), *n.* [Latin "mixture"] *Roman law.* A mixture of separable (i.e. dry or solid) items belonging to different owners, the resulting mixture being held in common or divided in proportion to the shares contributed. See CONFUSION OF GOODS. Cf. CONFUSIO (1).

commodatary (kə-**mohd**-ə-tair-ee). [fr. Latin *commodatarius*] *Roman & civil law.* A bailee in a commodatum; borrower.

commodate (**kom**-ə-dayt), *n.* See COMMODATUM.

commodati actio (kom-ə-**day**-tɪ **ak**-shee-oh). See *actio commodati* under ACTIO.

commodator (**kom**-ə-day-tər), *n. Roman & civil law.* A lender or bailor.

commodatum (kom-ə-**day**-təm), *n.* [Latin *commodare* "to lend"] (17c) *Roman & civil law.* The gratuitous lending of goods to be used by the borrower and then returned undamaged to the lender. • This arrangement is for the sole benefit of the borrower. It is one of three types of contracts for permissive use, the other two being *locatio conductio* and *mutuum.* — Also termed *accommodatum; commodate.* Pl. ***commodata.***

"*Commodatum* was loan for use, the borrower being required to return the identical *res.* This contract was gratuitous, being usually for a limited time and a specific purpose. The borrower must use the greatest care in looking after the *res* but has not to answer for loss occasioned by fire or accident beyond his control, provided that there was no fault. If, however, the *res* was put to a use foreign to the terms of the agreement, strict liability might follow, e.g., if the *res* was wrongfully taken on a journey and lost through attack by enemies or shipwreck." G.W. Paton, *Bailment in the Common Law* 49–50 (1952).

commodities broker. See *commodity broker* under BROKER.

commodity. (14c) **1.** An article of trade or commerce. • The term embraces only tangible goods, such as products or merchandise, as distinguished from services. **2.** An economic good, esp. a raw material or an agricultural product.

▸ **hard commodity.** A commodity that is mined, such as aluminum, copper, lead, nickel, tin, and zinc.

▸ **soft commodity.** A perishable commodity, as with most foodstuffs.

commodity agreement. See INTERNATIONAL COMMODITY AGREEMENT.

commodity-backed bond. See BOND (3).

commodity broker. See BROKER.

Commodity Credit Corporation. A federally chartered corporation responsible for extending credit in order to stabilize farm income and prices. • Incorporated in Delaware in 1933 and operated in affiliation with the Reconstruction Finance Corporation, it was transferred to the U.S. Department of Agriculture in 1939 and chartered in 1948 as a federal corporation. 15 USCA § 714. — Abbr. CCC.

Commodity Futures Trading Commission. A five-member federal commission that regulates trading in futures and options contracts and monitors the activities of commodity-exchange members, brokerage houses, commission-registered salespeople, and others associated with the industry. • The commission began operating in April 1975. 7 USCA § 2(a)(2). — Abbr. CFTC.

commodity loan. See LOAN.

commodity option. See OPTION (5).

commodity paper. See PAPER.

common, *n.* (14c) **1.** A legal right to use another person's property, such as an easement. See PROFIT À PRENDRE.

▸ **common appendant** (ə-pen-dənt). (16c) *Hist.* A tenant's right to graze animals on the landowner's land as a result of longstanding practice. See *profit appendant* under PROFIT (2).

> "The . . . common appendant is founded on prescription, and is regularly annexed to arable land. . . . The tenant was limited to such beasts as were levant and couchant on his estate, because such cattle only were wanting to plough and manure his land. It was deemed an incident to a grant of land, as of common right, and to enable the tenant to use his plough land." 3 James Kent, *Commentaries on American Law* *404 (George Comstock ed., 11th ed. 1866).

▸ **common appurtenant** (ə-pər-tə-nənt). (16c) *Hist.* A landowner's right to graze animals on another's land as a result of a written grant relating to the ownership or occupancy of land. See *profit appurtenant* under PROFIT (2).

> "Common appurtenant may be affixed to any kind of land . . . . It allowed the owner to put in other beasts than such as plough or manure the land; and, not being founded on necessity, like the other rights, . . . was not favored in the law." 3 James Kent, *Commentaries on American Law* *404 (George Comstock ed., 11th ed. 1866).

▸ **common in gross.** (16c) *Hist.* A right to graze animals on another's land as a result of a written grant unrelated to ownership or occupancy of land. — Also termed *common at large.* See *profit in gross* under PROFIT (2).

▸ **common in the soil.** (17c) *Hist.* The right to dig and take away earth from another's land. — Also termed *common of digging.*

▸ **common of estovers** (e-stoh-vərz). (16c) *Hist.* A tenant's right to take necessary supplies, esp. wood, from the lord's estate; the right to estovers. See ESTOVERS (1).

▸ **common of fishery.** See *common of piscary.*

▸ **common of pasture.** (16c) *Hist.* A right to pasture one's cattle on another's land. • The common of pasture may be appendant, appurtenant, or in gross.

▸ **common of piscary** (pis-kə-ree). (18c) *Hist.* A right to fish in waters on another's land. — Often shortened to *piscary.* — Also termed *common of fishery.*

▸ **common of shack.** (18c) *Hist.* The right of people occupying land in a common field to release their cattle to graze after harvest.

▸ **common of turbary** (tər-bə-ree). (17c) *Hist.* The right to dig turf (for use as fuel in a house) from another's land.

▸ **common without stint.** (18c) *Hist.* A right to graze an unlimited number of cattle.

2. A tract of land set aside for the general public's use. — Also termed *common land.*

commonable, *adj.* (17c) **1.** (Of an animal) allowed to graze on common land. **2.** (Of land) capable of being held in common.

common adventure. See ADVENTURE.

common agent. See AGENT.

commonality test. (1974) The requirement that members of a group certified as a class in a class-action suit share at least one issue of law or fact whose resolution will affect all or a significant number of the putative class members. Cf. COMMON-CHARACTER REQUIREMENT.

common ancestor. See ANCESTOR.

common and notorious thief. See *common thief* under THIEF.

common appendant. See COMMON (1).

common appurtenant. See COMMON (1).

common area. (1905) *Property.* **1.** The realty that all tenants may use though the landlord retains control over and responsibility for it. **2.** An area owned and used in common by the residents of a condominium, subdivision, or planned-unit development. — Also termed *common elements.*

common-area maintenance charges. (1974) Fees paid by tenants, usu. on a pro rata basis, to compensate the landlord for the costs of operating, repairing, and maintaining common areas. • Such costs include those incurred for cleaning, lighting, and repairs. — Abbr. CAMs. — Also termed *common-area operating expenses.*

common-area operating expenses. See COMMON-AREA MAINTENANCE CHARGES.

common assault. **1.** See ASSAULT (1). **2.** See ASSAULT (2).

common assumpsit. See *general assumpsit* under ASSUMPSIT.

common assurance. See MUNIMENT OF TITLE.

common at large. See *common in gross* under COMMON (1).

common-authority rule. (1984) The principle that a person may consent to a police officer's search of another person's property if both persons use, control, or have access to the property. • Under this rule, the consenting person must have been legally able to permit the search in his or her own right, and the defendant must have assumed the risk that a fellow occupant might permit a search. *See U.S. v. Matlock,* 415 U.S. 164, 171 n.7, 94 S.Ct. 988, 993 n.7 (1974). See THIRD-PARTY CONSENT.

common bail. See *bail common* under BAIL (4).

common bar. See BLANK BAR.

Common Bench. *Hist.* The former name of the English Court of Common Pleas. • The court was so called because it was the forum for the common people, that is, for cases between two or more subjects when the Crown had no interest. — Abbr. C.B.

common-bond doctrine. (2004) The rule that prospective members of a credit union must share some connection (such as common employment) other than a desire to create a credit union.

common business purpose. (1882) Related activity by two or more associated businesses. • If one of the businesses comes within the jurisdiction of the Fair Labor Standards Act, then another business that shares a common business purpose will also.

common calling. (16c) **1.** An ordinary occupation that a citizen has a right to pursue under the Privileges and Immunities Clause. **2.** A commercial enterprise that offers services to the general public, with a legal duty to serve anyone who requests the services. • For example, an innkeeper or a common carrier engages in a common calling.

> "It was only in a very few cases indeed that a person was under a legal obligation to enter into a contract; virtually the only example of such an obligation in fact was the person exercising a 'common calling' such as the innkeeper and the common carrier who were (subject to certain safeguards) legally bound to contract with any member of the public who required their services." P.S. Atiyah, *An Introduction to the Law of Contract* 8 (3d ed. 1981).

common carrier. See CARRIER (1).

common cause. See *common plea* (1) under PLEA (3).

common-character requirement. (1997) The rule that for a group of persons to qualify as a class in a class-action lawsuit, the appointment of the class must achieve economies of time, effort, and expense, and must promote uniformity of decision for persons similarly situated, and the class members must share common questions of fact and law. Cf. COMMONALITY TEST.

common chase. See CHASE.

common cost. See *indirect cost* under COST (1).

common council. See COUNCIL (1).

common count. See COUNT (2).

common day. See DAY.

common debtor. See DEBTOR.

common-defeasance bond. See *penal bond* under BOND (2).

common descriptive name. See GENERIC NAME.

common design. (17c) **1.** The intention by two or more people to join in committing an unlawful act. **2.** An intention to commit more than one crime. **3.** The general design or layout of plots of land surrounding a particular tract. — Also termed *common scheme*; *common plan*. See ZONING.

common diligence. 1. See *due diligence* (1) under DILIGENCE (2). **2.** See *ordinary diligence* under DILIGENCE (2).

common disaster. (1878) An event that causes two or more persons (such as a testator and a devisee, or an insured and a beneficiary) to die at very nearly the same time, with no way of determining the order of their deaths, when the ownership of property depends on that order. See UNIFORM SIMULTANEOUS DEATH ACT; COMMORIENTES.

common-disaster clause. (1949) A provision in a dispositive instrument, such as an insurance policy or a will, covering the situation in which the transferor and transferee die in a common disaster.

common duty of care. (1887) A landowner's obligation to take reasonable care under the circumstances to see that a lawful visitor will be reasonably safe in using the premises for the purposes for which the visitor is permitted to be there.

common easement. See EASEMENT.

common elements. See COMMON AREA.

common-employment doctrine. See FELLOW-SERVANT RULE.

common-enemy doctrine. (1905) *Property.* The rule that a landowner may repel surface waters as necessary (as during a flood), without liability for the consequences to other landowners. • The doctrine takes its name from the idea that the floodwater is every landowner's common enemy.

common enterprise. See JOINT ENTERPRISE.

commoner. (17c) **1.** *BrE.* An ordinary citizen; one not a peer. **2.** *Archaic.* A member of the House of Commons. **3.** *Archaic.* A common-law lawyer. **4.** *Archaic.* A person having a right of common — that is, a right to pasture on a lord's land.

> "The term 'common' . . . as meaning a piece of land, is not a legal term. The distinguishing feature in law of that kind of land which is ordinarily referred to as a common, or as common land, is, that it is land subject to a right of common. What, then, is a right of common? A right of common is the right to take a profit out of the land of another man. The most usual and widely known right of common is that of common of pasture, i.e., the right to take grass and other eatable products of a common by the mouths of cattle turned out thereon. Another right is that of cutting and carrying away, generally for use in the house or land of the person taking it, furze or bushes growing on the common. Another right is that of digging sand, gravel, or loam on the common, and taking it away for similar uses. The persons who take these rights are called commoners." Robert Hunter, *The Preservation of Open Spaces, and of Footpaths, and Other Rights of Way* 1–2 (1896).

5. Someone who shares a right in common.

common error. (1897) *Copyright.* A mistake found both in a copyrighted work and in an allegedly infringing work, the mistake being persuasive evidence of unauthorized copying.

common external tariff. See TARIFF (2).

common fine. See FINE (4).

common fishery. See FISHERY (2).

common form. (18c) **1.** *Hist.* A common-law form of action in which the allegations were standardized in their general nature. **2.** The probate of an uncontested will that is proved by the executor's own oath.

common fund. (17c) A monetary amount recovered by a litigant or lawyer for the benefit of a group that includes others, the litigant or lawyer then being entitled to reasonable attorney's fees from the entire amount.

common-fund doctrine. (1969) The principle that a litigant who creates, discovers, increases, or preserves a fund to which others also have a claim is entitled to recover litigation costs and attorney's fees from that fund. — Also termed *equitable-fund doctrine*.

common gambler. (18c) **1.** Someone who owns or is employed by a gambling establishment; a bookmaker. **2.** A professional gambler. • A person who gambles but not customarily, habitually, or frequently, and who does not rely on gambling for a living, is considered a casual gambler, not a common gambler.

common heritage of mankind. (1916) *Int'l law.* The parts of the earth and cosmos that can be said to belong to all humanity, without regard for geographic location, and that should be protected and administered for its benefit. • The term embraces the ocean floor and its subsoil, and outer space. — Also termed *common heritage of humankind.*

common highway. See HIGHWAY.

common informant. See INFORMANT.

common informer. (18c) Someone who sues to recover a penalty in a penal action. • In some jurisdictions, such an action may be instituted either by the attorney general on behalf of the state or by a common informer. See INFORMER; *penal action* under ACTION (4).

common in gross. See COMMON (1).

common injunction. See INJUNCTION.

common intendment. See INTENDMENT (2).

common intercourse. See INTERCOURSE (1).

common-interest community. (1980) A real-estate development in which individually owned lots or units are burdened with private land-use restrictions administered by a homeowners' association, as in a housing tract or condominium project.

common-interest doctrine. See *joint-defense privilege* under PRIVILEGE (3).

common-interest exception. See *joint-defense privilege* under PRIVILEGE (3).

common-interest privilege. See *joint-defense privilege* under PRIVILEGE (3).

common in the soil. See COMMON (1).

common jury. See *petit jury* under JURY.

common knowledge. (17c) A fact that is so widely known that a court may accept it as true without proof. See JUDICIAL NOTICE.

common-knowledge exception. (1929) The principle that lay testimony concerning routine or simple medical procedures is admissible to establish negligence in a medical-malpractice action. • This is a narrow exception in some jurisdictions to the rule that a medical-malpractice plaintiff must present expert testimony to establish negligence.

common land. See COMMON (2).

common-law, *adj.* (1848) Of, relating to, involving, or according to the common law <common-law doctrine>.

common law, *n.* [fr. Law French *commen ley* "common law"] (14c) **1.** The body of law derived from judicial decisions, rather than from statutes or constitutions; CASELAW <federal common law>. Cf. STATUTORY LAW.

> "Historically, [the common law] is made quite differently from the Continental code. The code precedes judgments; the common law follows them. The code articulates in chapters, sections, and paragraphs the rules in accordance with which judgments are given. The common law on the other hand is inarticulate until it is expressed in a judgment. Where the code governs, it is the judge's duty to ascertain the law from the words which the code uses. Where the common law governs, the judge, in what is now the forgotten past, decided the case in accordance with morality and custom and later judges followed his decision. They did not do so by construing the words of his judgment. They looked for the reason which had made him decide the case the way he did, the *ratio decidendi* as it came to be called. Thus it was the principle of the case, not the words, which went into the common law. So historically the common law is much less fettering than a code." Patrick Devlin, *The Judge* 177 (1979).

▸ **federal common law.** (1855) The body of decisional law derived from federal courts when adjudicating federal questions and other matters of federal concern, such as disputes between the states and foreign relations, but excluding all cases governed by state law. • An example is the nonstatutory law applying to interstate streams of commerce.

▸ **general federal common law.** (1890) *Hist.* In the period before *Erie v. Tompkins* (304 U.S. 64, 58 S.Ct. 817 (1938)), the judge-made law developed by federal courts in deciding disputes in diversity-of-citizenship cases. • Since *Erie*, a federal court has been bound to apply the substantive law of the state in which it sits. So even though there is a "federal common law," there is no longer a *general* federal common law applicable to all disputes heard in federal court.

2. The body of law based on the English legal system, as distinct from a civil-law system; the general Anglo-American system of legal concepts, together with the techniques of applying them, that form the basis of the law in jurisdictions where the system applies <all states except Louisiana have the common law as their legal system>. Cf. CIVIL LAW (1).

▸ **American common law.** (1824) **1.** The body of English law that was adopted as the law of the American colonies and supplemented with local enactments and judgments. **2.** The body of judge-made law that developed during and after the United States' colonial period, esp. since independence. — Also termed *Anglo-American common law.*

> "Every country has its common law. Ours is composed partly of the common law of England and partly of our own usages. When our ancestors emigrated from England, they took with them such of the English principles as were convenient for the situation in which they were about to place themselves. It required time and experience to ascertain how much of the English law would be suitable to this country. By degrees, as circumstances demanded, we adopted the English usages, or substituted others better suited to our wants, until at length, before the time of the Revolution, we had formed a system of our own, founded in general on the English Constitution, but not without considerable variations." *Guardians of the Poor v. Greene*, 5 Binn. 554, 557 (Pa. 1813).

3. General law common to a country as a whole, as opposed to special law that has only local application <the issue is whether the common law trumps our jurisdiction's local rules>. — Also termed *jus commune.*

> "In its historical origin the term common law (*jus commune*) was identical in meaning with the term general law . . . . The *jus commune* was the general law of the land — the *lex terrae* — as opposed to *jus speciale*. By a process of historical development, however, the common law has now become, not the entire general law, but only the residue of that law after deducting equity and statute law. It is no longer possible, therefore, to use the expressions common law and general law as synonymous." John Salmond, *Jurisprudence* 97 (Glanville L. Williams ed., 10th ed. 1947).

> "[I]t is necessary to dispose briefly of a problem of nomenclature. European equivalents of the expression 'common law' have been used, especially in Germany, to describe an emergent system of national law, based on the Roman model, that came into existence before national parliaments undertook to enact laws for the nation as a whole. In this use, 'the common law' (*gemeines Recht*) was used to distinguish the commonly shared tradition of Roman law from local statutes and customs." Lon L. Fuller, *Anatomy of the Law* 133 (1968).

4. The body of law deriving from law courts as opposed to those sitting in equity <a mortgage founded in common law>. • The common law of England was one of the three main historical sources of English law. The other two were legislation and equity. The common law evolved from custom and was the body of law created by and administered by the king's courts. Equity developed to overcome the occasional rigidity and unfairness of the common law. Originally the king himself granted or denied petitions in equity; later the task fell to the chancellor, and later still to the Court of Chancery.

common-law action. See ACTION (4).

common-law agency. See AGENCY (1).

common-law assignment. See ASSIGNMENT (2).

common-law bond. See BOND (2).

common-law cheat. See CHEATING.

common-law contempt. See *criminal contempt* under CONTEMPT.

common-law copyright. See COPYRIGHT.

common-law corporation. See *corporation by prescription* under CORPORATION.

common-law crime. See CRIME.

common-law damages. See DAMAGES.

common-law dedication. See DEDICATION.

common-law DWI. See DRIVING WHILE INTOXICATED.

common-law extortion. See EXTORTION (1).

common-law fraud. See *promissory fraud* under FRAUD.

common-law husband. See HUSBAND.

common-law jurisdiction. See JURISDICTION.

common-law lawyer. (19c) A lawyer who is versed in or practices under a common-law system. — Also termed *common lawyer* (16c).

common-law lien. See LIEN.

common-law malice. See *actual malice* (2) under MALICE.

common-law marriage. See MARRIAGE (1).

common-law mortgage. See *deed of trust* under DEED.

common-law offense. See *common-law crime* under CRIME.

common-law pleading. See PLEADING (2).

common-law-property state. See COMMON-LAW STATE (2).

common-law rule. (17c) **1.** A judge-made rule as opposed to a statutory one. **2.** A legal rule as opposed to an equitable one. **3.** A general rule as opposed to one deriving from special law (such as a local custom or a rule of foreign law that, based on choice-of-law principles, is applied in place of domestic law). **4.** An old rule of English law.

common-law seal. See SEAL (1).

common-law specialty. 1. See *contract under seal* under CONTRACT. **2.** See SPECIALTY (1).

common-law state. (1848) **1.** NONCODE STATE. **2.** Any state that has not adopted a community-property regime. • The chief difference today between a community-property state and a common-law state is that in a common-law state, a spouse has no vested interest in property held by the other spouse until (1) the filing of a divorce action, or (2) the death of the other spouse. Cf. COMMUNITY-PROPERTY STATE.

common-law trust. See *business trust* under TRUST (4).

common-law wife. See WIFE.

common lawyer. See COMMON-LAW LAWYER.

common market. See MARKET.

Common Market. The European Economic Community. • *Common Market* is a colloquial term, not a formal designation. See EUROPEAN UNION.

common mistake. See *mutual mistake* (2) under MISTAKE.

common money bond. See BOND (2).

common-nucleus-of-operative-fact test. (1966) The doctrine that a federal court will have pendent jurisdiction over state-law claims that arise from the same facts as the federal claims providing a basis for subject-matter jurisdiction. • One purpose of this test is to promote judicial economy.

common nuisance. See *public nuisance* under NUISANCE.

common occupant. See *general occupant* under OCCUPANT.

common of digging. See *common in the soil* under COMMON (1).

common of estovers. See COMMON (1).

common of fishery. See *common of piscary* under COMMON (1).

common of pasture. See COMMON (1).

common of piscary. See COMMON (1).

common of shack. See COMMON (1).

common of turbary. See COMMON (1).

common order. See *conditional judgment* under JUDGMENT (2).

common ownership. See OWNERSHIP.

common parliamentary law. See PARLIAMENTARY LAW.

commonplacing, *n.* The activity or practice of extracting choice quotations from books and other sources for use in future research, essays, arguments, etc.; the habit of collecting striking or notable passages in books for future reference. • A notebook in which such passages are collected is traditionally called a *commonplace book* or *book of common places.* Commonplacing was once a widely recommended method of pursuing legal studies and law practice.

> "The merits and demerits of the system of *commonplacing* have occasioned much contrariety of opinions. 'Commonplacing,' says Fulbeck, 'is a profitable course under titles to digest the cases of the lawe, into which they may transfer such things as they have either heard or read; neither is it safe to trust to other men's abridgments, which are little available to such as have read a little: but that which we, by our owne sweat and labour do gaine, we do firmly retain, and in it we do principally delight; and I am persuaded that there hath never been any learned in the law and judicial, who hath not made a collection of his own, though he hath not neglected the abridgment of others.'" Samuel Warren, *A Popular and Practical Introduction to Law Studies* 388–89 (Isaac Grant Thompson ed., 1870) (spelling idiosyncrasies and inconsistencies in the original).

common plan. See COMMON DESIGN.

common plea. See PLEA (3).

Common Pleas, Court of. See COURT OF COMMON PLEAS.

common pleas court. See COURT OF COMMON PLEAS.

common property. See PROPERTY.

common recovery. (17c) *Hist.* An elaborate proceeding, full of legal fictions, by which a tenant in tail disentailed a fee-tail estate. • The action facilitated land transfer by allowing a potential transferee who was barred by law from receiving land to "recover" the land by suing the actual owner. Common recoveries, which were abolished early in the 19th century, had their origin in a method used by the clergy to avoid the land-conveyance restrictions imposed by mortmain acts. — Also termed *feigned recovery.* See MORTMAIN STATUTE. Cf. CESSIO IN JURE; *praecipe quod reddat* under PRAECIPE.

> "Here's how [the common recovery] worked. B, with the connivance of A [the tenant in tail], would bring a real action against A claiming falsely that he, B, owned the land and demanding recovery of it. A responded by claiming, just as falsely, that he had acquired the land from C and that C had warranted title to the land. When A demanded of C, also an accomplice of A, that he defend the title, C admitted falsely that he had, indeed, warranted the title. C allowed B to take a default judgment against A for the recovery of the land, and allowed A to obtain a default judgment against himself, C, for the recovery of land of equal value. The result of this fancy feudal footwork was to leave B with title to the land in fee simple and to leave A with his judgment against C. The judgment against C was viewed by the court as an adequate substitute for the entailed land. But when it came time for O [the reversioner] or A's lineal heirs to enforce the judgment, it would transpire that C had been selected by A because he had no land at all! (Why else would C have played along?) Did the court have any suspicion that A, B, and C were colluding? Of course they did — but how else, in the face of *De Donis*, could they unshackle land from the chains of the fee tail?" Thomas F. Bergin & Paul G. Haskell, *Preface to Estates in Land and Future Interests* 31–32 (2d ed. 1984).

common-return days. See *dies communes in banco* (1) under DIES.

common rule ex parte. (1842) *Hist.* A court-docket entry reflecting that the case would be decided by a majority vote and would proceed even if a notified party did not appear. *See Billington v. Sprague*, 22 Me. 34 (1842).

Commons. (15c) HOUSE OF COMMONS.

common scheme. See COMMON DESIGN.

common school. See *public school* under SCHOOL (1).

common scold. See SCOLD.

common serjeant. (16c) A judicial officer, appointed by the City of London, who helps the recorder in criminal trials.

common-situs picketing. See PICKETING.

common-source doctrine. (1938) The principle that a defendant in a trespass-to-try-title action who claims under a source common to both the defendant and the plaintiff may not demonstrate title in a third source that is paramount to the common source because doing so amounts to an attack on the source under which the defendant claims title.

common stock. See STOCK.

common-stock equivalent. A security that is exchangeable for common stock and thus is considered to be the same as common stock. • Common-stock equivalents include certain types of convertible securities, stock options, and warrants.

common-stock fund. See MUTUAL FUND.

common-stock ratio. (1928) The relationship of outstanding common stock to the corporation's total capitalization. • The common-stock ratio measures the relative claims of stockholders to earnings (earnings per share and payout ratio), cash flow (cash flow per share), and equity (book value per share). Cf. PAYOUT RATIO.

common substitution. See SUBSTITUTION (4).

common suit. See *common plea* (1) under PLEA (3).

common tenancy. See *tenancy in common* under TENANCY.

common thief. See THIEF.

common traverse. See TRAVERSE.

common trust fund. See TRUST FUND.

common venture. See *common adventure* under ADVENTURE.

common wall. See *party wall* under WALL.

commonweal (**kom**-ən-weel). (15c) The general welfare; the common good.

commonwealth. (15c) **1.** A country, state, or other political unit <the Commonwealth of Pennsylvania>. **2.** A political unit that has local autonomy but is voluntarily united with the United States <Puerto Rico and the Northern Mariana Islands are commonwealths>. Cf. DEPENDENCY; INSULAR AREA; TERRITORY (2). **3.** A loose association of countries that recognize one sovereign <the British Commonwealth>. • In this context, in Great Britain, the term *British* has been dropped from *British Commonwealth*; BrE speakers refer simply to *the Commonwealth.* — Abbr. Commw.; comm.

> "The Commonwealth is a voluntary association of independent States most of which are former British colonies. While the term 'commonwealth,' meaning 'common welfare' or 'public good,' has been used to describe various political communities . . . , it is generally associated with the grouping of States that evolved out of the British Empire. The majority of Commonwealth members are English-speaking and share in most instances similar legal systems based on common law. Though no longer united through common allegiance to the British Crown, all Member States of the association acknowledge the British monarch as the Head of the Commonwealth." Charlotte Steinorth, "Commonwealth," in 2 *The Max Planck Encyclopedia of Public International Law* 462, 463 (Rüdiger Wolfrum ed., 2012).

4. The central (federal) power in Australia. — Abbr. (in sense 4) Cwth.

commonwealth attorney. (1847) (*often cap.*) A prosecutor in some jurisdictions, such as Virginia. — Also termed *Commonwealth's Attorney.*

commonwealth court. See COURT.

common without stint. See COMMON (1).

commorancy (**kom**-ə-rən-see). (16c) **1.** Temporary residency. **2.** *English law.* Permanent residency in a certain place.

commorant (**kom**-ə-rənt). (17c) **1.** Someone who dwells in a place temporarily. **2.** *English law.* Someone who resides permanently in a certain place.

commorientes (kə-mor-ee-**en**-teez). [fr. Latin *commorior* "to die together"] (18c) **1.** (*pl.*) Persons who die at the same time, often of the same cause, such as spouses who die in an accident. **2.** *Civil law.* The rule establishing presumptions of survivorship for purposes of succession regarding such persons. See *simultaneous death* under DEATH; UNIFORM SIMULTANEOUS DEATH ACT.

commorientes provision. (1941) A testamentary provision that accounts for the possibility that persons, esp. family members, may die together in circumstances in which it cannot be determined who died first.

commotion. See CIVIL COMMOTION.

commune (**kom**-yoon), *n.* (17c) A community of people who share property and responsibilities.

commune forum (kə-**myoo**-nee **for**-əm). [Latin "common place of justice"] (18c) *Hist.* The seat of the principal English courts, esp. those that do not go on circuit.

commune placitum (kə-**myoo**-nee **plas**-ə-təm). [Latin "common plea"] (18c) *Hist.* A common plea between persons, as opposed to a plea of the Crown (i.e., a criminal action). Pl. ***communia placita.***

commune vinculum (kə-**myoo**-nee **ving**-kyə-ləm). [Latin "common bond"] (17c) *Hist.* A relationship or tie between persons; esp., the bond between lord and tenant, or the relationship between blood relatives.

communia (kə-**myoo**-nee-ə). [Latin] *Hist.* Things owned in common, such as running water, the air, and the sea.

communia placita non tenenda in scaccario (kə-**myoo**-nee-ə **plas**-ə-tə non tə-**nen**-də in skə-**kair**-ee-oh). [Law Latin "common pleas are not held in the Exchequer"] (17c) *Hist.* A writ directed to the Treasurer and Barons of the Exchequer, forbidding them from holding pleas between common persons, i.e., pleas in which the Crown was not a party.

communia precepta. (kə-**myoo**-nee-ə pree-**sep**-tə). (18c) [Latin] *Hist.* Common precepts or rules. — Also spelled *communia precepta.*

> "Laws are given as a common rule of life for the whole people of a kingdom, and hence they are called *communia praecepta.*" 1 John Erskine, *An Institute of the Law of Scotland* 9 (James Badenach Nicolson ed., rev. ed. 1871).

communibus annis (kə-**myoo**-ni-bəs **an**-is). [Latin] (17c) *Hist.* On the average of years; on the annual average.

> "[T]he money arising from corn rents is, *communibus annis,* almost double to the rents reserved in money." 2 William Blackstone, *Commentaries on the Laws of England* 322 (1766).

communication. (14c) **1.** The interchange of messages or ideas by speech, writing, gestures, or conduct; the process of bringing an idea to another's perception. **2.** The messages or ideas so expressed or exchanged.

▸ **absolutely privileged communication.** A defamatory statement not creating liability even if made with malice or in bad faith.

▸ **conditionally privileged communication.** (1889) A defamatory statement that creates liability only if made with malice or in bad faith • One category of conditionally privileged communications comprises statements made by a person with an interest in a subject to someone who also has an interest in that subject, such as an employer giving a defamatory job review of a former employee to a potential future employer. — Also termed *qualifiedly privileged communication.*

▸ **confidential communication.** (18c) A communication made within a certain protected relationship and legally protected from compelled disclosure in a legal proceeding unless the protected party waives that protection. • Among confidential communications are those between husband and wife, attorney and client, and priest and penitent. See PRIVILEGE (3).

▸ **ex parte communication.** (1804) A communication between counsel and the court when opposing counsel is not present. • Such communications are ordinarily prohibited.

▸ **privileged communication.** (1809) A communication that is protected by law from compelled disclosure in a legal proceeding or that cannot be used against the person who made it. • Examples include an informant's communication to a government agency and statements made in a legislative session by a legislator. See PRIVILEGE (3).

communication of acceptance. (1842) Words or acts indicating an offeree's intention to enter into a legally binding contract with the offeror on the terms stipulated in the offer.

communication right. (1939) *Copyright.* The power of a copyright owner to authorize or prohibit the transmission of a work to the public by means of interactive on-demand systems such as the Internet. • This right is included in the WIPO Copyright Treaty and the European Commission's Directive on the Information Society.

communicative evidence. See *testimonial evidence* under EVIDENCE.

communi consensu (kə-**myoo**-nɪ kən-**sen**-s[y]oo). [Latin] By common consent.

communi dividundo. See *actio de communi dividundo* under ACTIO.

communings (kə-**myoo**-nings), *n.* (18c) *Scots law.* Contract negotiations.

communio bonorum (kə-**myoo**-nee-oh bə-**nor**-əm). [Latin "community of goods"] (18c) *Civil law.* Commonly owned goods, esp. those held in common by a husband and wife. Pl. ***communiones bonorum.***

communio rei vel juris (kə-**myoo**-nee-oh **ree**-ɪ vel **joor**-is). [Latin] *Hist.* Joint ownership of a thing or right.

communis consensus (kə-**myoo**-nis kən-**sen**-səs). [Latin] *Hist.* Common consent.

communis error (kə-**myoo**-nis **e**-ror). [Latin] (17c) *Scots law.* A common error; esp., a long-standing error in practice that the court would uphold even though the practice has no legal basis. • The phrase appears in the maxim *communis error facet jus.*

communism. (19c) **1.** A political doctrine, based on Marxism, advocating the abolition of capitalism by ground-roots revolution; specif., a social and political doctrine advocating the abolition of private ownership in favor of common ownership of the means of production and the goods produced, each person contributing as able and receiving as needed. Cf. CAPITALISM. **2.** Totalitarian government.

communis opinio (kə-**myoo**-nis ə-**pin**-ee-oh). [Latin "common opinion"] (17c) *Hist.* A generally accepted belief about a point of law. • If held unanimously by those learned in the law, this common belief had the force of law in classical Rome.

> "*Communis opinio* is evidence of what the law is, — not where it is an opinion merely speculative and theoretical, floating in the minds of persons, but where it has been made the ground-work and *substratum* of practice." 1 Alexander M. Burrill, *A Law Dictionary and Glossary* 330 (2d ed. 1867) (quoting Lord Ellenborough).

communis opinio doctorum (kə-**myoo**-nis ə-**pin**-ee-oh dok-**tor**-əm). [Latin "learned common opinion"] *Hist.*

Scholarly agreement on points of Roman law, collected by the glossators of Justinian's texts in the later Middle Ages.

communis paries (kə-**myoo**-nis **par**-ee-eez). [Latin "common wall"] *Civil law.* See *party wall* under WALL. Pl. ***communes parietes.***

communis patria (kə-**myoo**-nis **pay**-tree-ə). [Law Latin] (17c) *Hist.* The common country; a place deemed home to all.

> "Under the old diligence of apprising, directed against heritable rights, the messenger executing the diligence held his court in the head borough of the shire where the lands lay, but afterwards it became the practice to hold these courts in Edinburgh as *communis patria* to all Scotland." John Trayner, *Trayner's Latin Maxims* 86 (4th ed. 1894).

communis scriptura (kə-**myoo**-nis skrip-**t[y]oor**-ə *or* kəm-**myoo**-nəs skrip-**tyuur**-ə). [Latin "common writing"] *Hist.* See CHIROGRAPH.

communis stipes (kə-**myoo**-nis **stɪ**-peez). [Latin "common trunk"] (18c) *Hist.* A common ancestor.

communitization (kə-myoo-nə-tə-**zay**-shən), *n.* (1940) *Oil & gas.* The aggregating of small tracts sufficient for the granting of a well permit under applicable well-spacing rules; POOLING. Cf. UNITIZATION. — **communitize** (kə-**myoo**-nə-tɪz), *vb.*

community. (14c) **1.** A neighborhood, vicinity, or locality. **2.** A society or group of people with similar rights or interests. **3.** Joint ownership, possession, or participation. **4.** The husband and wife considered as a single entity in a community-property state. • For example, if property is owned by husband and wife as their community property, the owner is sometimes said to be the community.

community account. See ACCOUNT.

community-based order. See COMMUNITY-SERVICE ORDER.

community control. A criminal sentence whose terms include intensive and strict supervision of an offender in the community, as by restricting the offender's movements and activities and conducting electronic surveillance, and providing severe sanctions for violations of any of the sentence's terms.

community correctional center. See JAIL.

community debt. See DEBT.

Community Development Financial Institution Fund. A fund in the U.S. Department of the Treasury created to expand available credit, investment capital, and financial services in distressed urban and rural communities. — Abbr. CDFI Fund.

community estate. (1876) In a community-property state, the total of the assets and debts making up a married couple's property owned in common. Cf. COMMUNITY PROPERTY.

community grant. See GRANT (4).

community land trust. See TRUST (3).

community lease. See LEASE.

Community mark. See *Community trademark* under TRADEMARK.

community-notification law. See MEGAN'S LAW.

community obligation. See OBLIGATION.

community of interest. (17c) **1.** Participation in a joint venture characterized by shared liability and shared opportunity for profit. See JOINT VENTURE. **2.** A common grievance that must be shared by all class members to maintain the class action. See CLASS ACTION. **3.** *Labor law.* A criterion used by the National Labor Relations Board in deciding whether a group of employees should be allowed to act as a bargaining unit. • The Board considers whether the employees have similar duties, wages, hours, benefits, skills, training, supervision, and working conditions. See BARGAINING UNIT.

community of profits. (1842) The right of partners to share in the partnership's profits.

Community patent. See PATENT (3).

Community Patent Convention. A 1975 treaty that, for patent purposes, treats the European Union as a single state and allows a patent applicant to obtain patent protection in all European Union countries through a single blanket filing and examination procedure. • If the application is approved, the European Patent Office issues a single Community patent. The treaty's full name is the Convention for the European Patent for the Common Market. — Abbr. CPC.

community policing. (1969) A law-enforcement technique in which police officers are assigned to a particular neighborhood or area to develop relationships with the residents for the purpose of enhancing the chances of detecting and thwarting criminal activity.

community property. (1820) Assets owned in common by husband and wife as a result of their having been acquired during the marriage by means other than an inheritance by, or a gift or devise to, one spouse, each spouse generally holding a one-half interest in the property. • Only nine states have community-property systems: Arizona, California, Idaho, Louisiana, Nevada, New Mexico, Texas, Washington, and Wisconsin. A community-property regime is elective in Alaska. See *marital property* under PROPERTY; TITLE DIVISION. Cf. COMMUNITY ESTATE; SEPARATE PROPERTY.

▸ **quasi-community property.** (1947) Personal property that, having been acquired in a non-community-property state, would have been community property if acquired in a community-property state. • If a community-property state is the forum for a divorce or administration of a decedent's estate, state law may allow the court to treat quasi-community property as if it were community property when it determines the spouses' interests.

community-property state. (1907) A state in which spouses hold property that is acquired during marriage (other than property acquired by one spouse by inheritance, devise, or gift) as community property. See COMMUNITY PROPERTY. Cf. COMMON-LAW STATE (2).

community service. (1901) Socially valuable work performed without pay. • Community service is often required as part of a criminal sentence, esp. one that does not include incarceration.

community-service order. (1971) A court order requiring a person convicted of a crime to perform a certain number of hours of community service, often in addition to or as an alternative to imprisonment. — Also termed *community-work order; community-based order; community-service condition.*

Community trademark. See TRADEMARK.

Community Trademark Treaty. A 1996 agreement allowing a trademark registrant to file a single application with the European Trademark Office for trademark protection in all European Union countries instead of filing a separate application in each country. • The trademark registrant need not be a citizen of a member country to file an application.

community trust. (1915) An agency organized to administer funds placed in trust for public-health, educational, and other charitable purposes in perpetuity.

community-work order. See COMMUNITY-SERVICE ORDER.

commutation (kom-yə-**tay**-shən), *n.* (15c) **1.** An exchange or replacement. **2.** *Criminal law.* The executive's substitution in a particular case of a less severe punishment for a more severe one that has already been judicially imposed on the defendant. Cf. PARDON; REPRIEVE. • Commutation may be based on the discovery of pertinent facts that were not known or available when the sentenced was decided, or that arose and were developed afterward. It may also be based on the executive's statutorily or constitutionally granted discretion, regardless of the facts. Under § 1-2.113 of the US DOJ Manual, commutation is rarely granted but may be considered for old age, illness, disparity, or undue severity of sentence. **3.** *Commercial & civil law.* The substitution of one form of payment for another. — **commute,** *vb.* — **commutative,** *adj.*

commutation of payments. (1915) *Workers' compensation.* A substitution of lump-sum compensation for periodic payments. • The lump sum is equal to the present value of the future periodic payments.

commutation of taxes. (1846) A tax exemption resulting from a taxpayer's paying either a lump sum or a specific sum in lieu of an ad valorem tax.

Commutation of Tithes Act. *Hist.* An act of Parliament that permitted tithes to be levied and collected in the form of cash rents rather than labor and goods in kind.

commutation tax. See TAX.

commutative contract. See CONTRACT.

commutative justice. See JUSTICE (4).

commuted value. See VALUE (2).

Commw. *abbr.* COMMONWEALTH.

compact (**kom**-pakt), *n.* (14c) An agreement or covenant between two or more parties, esp. between governments or states.

▸ **family compact.** (18c) An agreement to further common interests made between related people or within a group that behaves as a family. • Historically, some international treaties among countries ruled by monarchs have been called family compacts because of intermarriage among the royal houses.

▸ **interstate compact.** (1903) A voluntary agreement between states, esp. U.S. states that enact the agreement into state law upon federal congressional approval. Cf. INTERSTATE AGREEMENT.

Compact Clause. (1925) *Constitutional law.* U.S. Const. art. I, § 10, cl. 3, which forbids a state from entering into a contract with another state or a foreign country without congressional approval.

companion bill. See BILL (3).

companionship services. (1977) Assistance provided to someone who needs help with personal matters such as bathing and dressing. • This type of service (in contrast to housecleaning) is exempt from the federal Fair Labor Standards Act's minimum-wage and overtime requirements.

company. (13c) **1.** A corporation — or, less commonly, an association, partnership, or union — that carries on a commercial or industrial enterprise. **2.** A corporation, partnership, association, joint-stock company, trust, fund, or organized group of persons, whether incorporated or not, and (in an official capacity) any receiver, trustee in bankruptcy, or similar official, or liquidating agent, for any of the foregoing. Investment Company Act § 2(a)(8) (15 USCA § 80a-2(a)(8)). — Abbr. co.; com.

▸ **bonding company.** (1901) A company that insures a party against a loss caused by a third party.

▸ **controlled company.** (1901) A company that is under the control of an individual, group, or corporation that owns most of the company's voting stock. Cf. *subsidiary corporation* under CORPORATION.

▸ **dead-and-buried company.** (1993) A business that has dissolved, leaving no assets.

▸ **defunct company. 1.** A corporation whose registration with the state has been canceled. **2.** A business that has terminated all operations and been dissolved.

▸ **deposit company.** (1880) An institution whose business is the safekeeping of securities or other valuables deposited in boxes or safes leased to the depositors. See DEPOSITARY; DEPOSITORY.

▸ **development-stage company.** (1977) *Securities.* A company that devotes substantially all its efforts to establishing a new business in which the principal operations either have not yet begun or have begun but are not yet generating significant revenue.

▸ **diversified holding company.** (1937) A holding company that controls several unrelated companies or businesses.

▸ **diversified investment company.** (1941) An investment company that by law must invest 75% of its assets, but may not invest more than 5% of its assets in any one company or hold more than 10% of the voting shares in any one company.

▸ **face-amount certificate company.** (1941) An investment company that is engaged or proposes to engage in the business of issuing face-amount certificates of the installment type, or that has been engaged in this business and has such a certificate outstanding. See *investment company.*

▸ **growth company.** (1959) A company whose earnings have increased at a rapid pace and that usu. directs a high proportion of income back into the business.

▸ **guaranty company.** See *surety company.*

▸ **holding company.** (1906) A company formed to control other companies, usu. confining its role to owning stock and supervising management. • It does not participate in making day-to-day business decisions in those companies.

▸ **interlocking companies.** (1912) Companies that are financially interdependent and have directors in common on their boards.

▸ **investment company.** (1847) A company formed to acquire and manage a portfolio of diverse assets by investing money collected from different sources. • The Investment Company Act of 1940 defines the term as an issuer of securities that (1) is, holds itself out to be, or proposes to be engaged primarily in the business of investing, reinvesting, or trading in securities; (2) is engaged or proposes to engage in the business of issuing face-amount certificates of the installment type, or has been engaged in this business and has such a certificate outstanding; or (3) is engaged or proposes to engage in the business of investing, reinvesting, owning, holding, or trading in securities, and owns or proposes to acquire investment securities having a value exceeding 40% of the value of the issuer's total assets (exclusive of government securities and cash items) on an unconsolidated basis. 15 USCA § 80a-2(a)(16). — Also termed *investment trust.* See REAL-ESTATE INVESTMENT TRUST; MUTUAL FUND.

▸ **joint-stock company.** (18c) **1.** An unincorporated association of individuals possessing common capital, the capital being contributed by the members and divided into shares, of which each member possesses a number proportionate to the member's investment. **2.** A partnership in which the capital is divided into shares that are transferable without the express consent of the partners. — Also termed *joint-stock association*; *stock association.*

> "The joint stock association or company developed early in English company law, the term being used to distinguish companies which operated on a joint account and with a 'joint stock' (in trade) of their members from companies (now obsolete) each member of whom traded on one's separate account with one's own stock in trade. . . . In American jurisdictions, the joint stock association is generally an unincorporated business enterprise with ownership interests represented by shares of stock." Henry G. Henn & John R. Alexander, *Laws of Corporations* § 50, at 109 (3d ed. 1983).

▸ **limited company.** (1862) A company in which the liability of each shareholder is limited to the amount individually invested. • A corporation is the most common example of a limited company.

▸ **limited-liability company.** (1856) A statutorily authorized business entity that is characterized by limited liability for and management by its members and managers, and taxable as a partnership for federal income-tax purposes. • Formerly, limited-liability companies were also required to limit transferability of interests. — Abbr. LLC. — Also termed *limited-liability corporation.*

▸ **management company.** Any investment company that is neither a face-amount certificate company nor a unit-investment trust. See *investment company*; *face-amount certificate company*; *unit-investment trust* under TRUST (3).

▸ **mutual company.** (1912) A company that is owned by its customers rather than by a separate group of stockholders. • Many insurance companies are mutual companies, as are many federal savings-and-loan associations. See MUTUAL INSURANCE COMPANY.

▸ **parent company.** See *parent corporation* under CORPORATION.

▸ **personal holding company.** (1924) A holding company that is subject to special taxes and that usu. has a limited number of shareholders, with most of its revenue originating from passive income such as dividends, interest, rent, and royalties.

▸ **private limited company.** (1889) A company whose shares are not traded on the stock market and can pass to another person only with the agreement of all current shareholders.

▸ **railroad company.** See *railroad corporation* under CORPORATION.

▸ **reporting company.** A company that, because it issues publicly traded securities, must comply with the reporting requirements of the Securities Exchange Act of 1934.

▸ **safe-deposit company.** See DEPOSITARY (1).

▸ **shelf company.** (1982) A company that is formed without a particular purpose and may not actually operate until some purpose for its existence arises, usu. when sold to a buyer. • After being formed, shelf companies are usu. allowed to age before being offered for sale. The benefits of a shelf company to a buyer include time saved by not having to form a company, the appearance of longevity, and easier access to credit. If the company is incorporated, it is also termed *shelf corporation.*

▸ **shell company.** (1958) See *shell corporation* under CORPORATION.

▸ **small-business investment company.** See SMALL-BUSINESS INVESTMENT COMPANY.

▸ **surety company.** (1884) A company authorized to engage in the business of entering into guaranty and suretyship contracts and acting as a surety on bonds, esp. bail, fidelity, and judicial bonds. — Also termed *guaranty company.*

▸ **title company.** (1892) A company that examines real-estate titles for any encumbrances, claims, or other flaws, and issues title insurance. — Also termed *title-guaranty company.* See TITLE SEARCH.

▸ **trust company.** (1834) A company that acts as a trustee for people and entities and that sometimes also operates as a commercial bank. — Also termed (if incorporated) *trust corporation.* See TITLE (1), (2).

company breaker. See CORPORATE RAIDER.

company law. See CORPORATE LAW.

company-run dividend-reinvestment plan. See DIVIDEND-REINVESTMENT PLAN.

company secretary. See CORPORATE SECRETARY.

company's paper. See *commercial paper* under PAPER.

company union. See UNION.

comparable (**kom**-pər-ə-bəl), *n.* (*usu. pl.*) (19c) A piece of property used as a comparison to determine the value of a similar piece of property. — **comparable,** *adj.*

comparable accommodation. (1942) A standard used for determining the maximum allowable rent in rent-regulated housing. • In applying this standard, a court reviews the prevailing rent for substantially similar housing units in the same area.

comparable-sales approach. See MARKET APPROACH.

comparables analysis. See MARKET APPROACH.

comparable worth. (1983) **1.** The analogous value that each of two or more employees brings to a business through his or her work. **2.** The idea that employees who perform identical work should receive identical pay, regardless of their sex; the doctrine that men and women who perform work of equal value should receive comparable pay.

comparatio literarum (kom-pə-**ray**-shee-oh lit-ə-**rair**-əm). [Latin "comparison of writings"] (17c) *Hist.* The act of comparing writings to ascertain authorship. • Even under Roman law, handwriting experts (*comparatores*) sometimes testified about a document's authenticity.

comparatist. (1930) A comparative-law scholar.

comparative advertising. See ADVERTISING.

comparative criminology. See CRIMINOLOGY.

comparative disparity. (1977) *Constitutional law.* The degree of underrepresentation of a particular group among potential jurors on a venire, as judged against the group's percentage of the general population. • Comparative disparity is calculated by subtracting a group's percentage of representation on the venire from the group's percentage of the population — that is, calculating the absolute disparity in the group's representation — then dividing that percentage by the group's percentage-representation in the population. For example, if African-Americans make up 12% of a county's population and 8% of the potential jurors on the venire, the absolute disparity for African-Americans is 4%. And the comparative disparity is 33%, because 4 divided by 12 is .33, or 33%. Many courts criticize the comparative-disparity analysis, favoring instead an absolute-disparity analysis, because the comparative-disparity analysis is said to exaggerate the underrepresentation. The reason for calculating the disparity is to evaluate a claim that the jury was not impartial because it was not selected from a pool of jurors that fairly represented the makeup of the jurisdiction. See DUREN TEST; FAIR-CROSS-SECTION REQUIREMENT; STATISTICAL-DECISION THEORY. Cf. ABSOLUTE DISPARITY.

comparative fault. See *comparative negligence* under NEGLIGENCE.

comparative history of law. 1. See *descriptive comparative law* under COMPARATIVE LAW. **2.** COMPARATIVE LEGAL HISTORY.

comparative-impairment test. (1974) *Conflict of laws.* A test that asks which of two or more forums would have its policies most impaired by not having its law applied in the case.

comparative interpretation. See INTERPRETATION (1).

comparative jurisprudence. See COMPARATIVE LAW.

comparative law. (1839) The scholarly study of the similarities and differences between the legal systems of different jurisdictions, such as between civil-law and common-law countries. — Also termed *comparative jurisprudence*; *comparative legal studies.* See INTERNATIONAL LAW.

> "Comparative law has been described as the 'Cinderella of the Legal Sciences.' It has gained a foothold in the domain of the law, but its position is by no means secure, and comparative studies must often be carried on in an atmosphere of hostility or, at best, in a chilly environment of indifference. The English Universities have been stimulated into action which takes the form of the encouragement of comparative research, and the rendering of such other support to the subject as is possible, in view of the limited financial resources available for the purpose. But most practitioners in England, as elsewhere, view comparative law with doubt and suspicion, and their attitude towards comparative lawyers is summed up in Lord Bowen's famous pleasantry that 'a jurist is a man who knows a little about the law of every country except his own.'" H.C. Gutteridge, *Comparative Law: An Introduction to the Comparative Method of Legal Study and Research* 23 (1946).

> "What is known as comparative jurisprudence — namely, the study of the resemblances and differences between different legal systems — is not a separate branch of jurisprudence co-ordinate with the analytical, historical, and ethical, but is merely a particular method of that science in all its branches. We compare English law with Roman law either for the purpose of analytical jurisprudence, in order the better to comprehend the conceptions and principles of each of those systems; or for the purpose of historical jurisprudence, in order that we may better understand the course of development of each system; or for the purpose of ethical jurisprudence, in order that we may better judge the practical merits and demerits of each of them. Apart from such purposes the comparative study of law would be merely futile." John Salmond, *Jurisprudence* 7–8 n.(c) (Glanville L. Williams ed., 10th ed. 1947).

▸ **descriptive comparative law.** (1932) The inventory of legal systems (past and present) as a whole, as well as of individual rules that these systems establish for several categories of legal relations. • Descriptive comparative law is sometimes considered one of three subsets of comparative law, the other two being comparative legislation and comparative history of law. See COMPARATIVE LEGISLATION; COMPARATIVE LEGAL HISTORY.

> "*Descriptive Comparative Law.* This is a term which is somewhat loosely employed and embraces many types of comparative work of varying degrees of merit. There is a noticeable tendency to treat any investigation into foreign law as coming under this heading, but such an extension of the meaning of the term is unjustifiable. We may at once dismiss any such claim, so far as it relates to a mere compilation of facts concerning a single legal system, because in such a case there cannot be any comparison. Nor is such a claim enhanced merely because the compilation takes the form of a parallel or tabular statement of facts relating to several systems, which leaves it to a reader to discover for himself what differences may exist. But any statement of divergences between two or more systems would seem to be admissible under this heading, even though it may be pedestrian in character and unworthy of being dignified as legal research." H.C. Gutteridge, *Comparative Law: An Introduction to the Comparative Method of Legal Study and Research* 8 (1946).

comparative legal history. (1858) A species of comparative law seeking to establish a universal history of law, so that the succession of social phenomena influencing the evolution of the legal world might be better understood. • This field is closely allied to ethnological jurisprudence, folklore, legal sociology, and jurisprudence. — Also termed *comparative history of law.* Cf. *descriptive comparative law* under COMPARATIVE LAW; COMPARATIVE LEGISLATION.

comparative legal studies. See COMPARATIVE LAW.

comparative legislation. (1840) A species of comparative law seeking to define the common link for modern statutory doctrines, concerned with the development of legal study as a social science and with awakening an international legal consciousness. Cf. *descriptive comparative law* under COMPARATIVE LAW; COMPARATIVE LEGAL HISTORY.

comparative negligence. See NEGLIGENCE.

comparative-negligence doctrine. (1904) *Torts.* The principle that reduces a plaintiff's recovery proportionally to the plaintiff's degree of fault in causing the damage, rather than barring recovery completely. • Most states have statutorily adopted the comparative-negligence doctrine. See NEGLIGENCE. Cf. CONTRIBUTORY-NEGLIGENCE DOCTRINE.

comparative nomogenetics. (1926) The study of the development of the world's legal ideas and systems. • This term, like *comparative nomoscopy* and *comparative nomothetics*, was devised by John Henry Wigmore. *See* John Henry Wigmore, *A Panorama of the World's Legal Systems* 1120–21 (libr. ed. 1936).

comparative nomoscopy. (1926) The description of the world's legal systems.

comparative nomothetics. (1926) The analysis of the merits of the world's legal systems.

comparative rectitude. (1913) *Archaic. Family law.* The degree to which one spouse is less culpable than the other in damaging the marriage, so that even though both spouses are at fault, the less culpable spouse may successfully petition for a separation or divorce. • Comparative rectitude tempers the doctrine of recrimination by making a divorce possible even though both parties are at fault. The evaluation of comparative rectitude is now virtually obsolete because of the prevalence of no-fault divorce. See RECRIMINATION (2).

comparative responsibility. The apportionment of liability between a tortious wrongdoer and a plaintiff whose own negligence was also a cause of the injury in question. See NEGLIGENCE.

comparative-sales approach. See MARKET APPROACH.

comparator (kəm-**par**-ə-tər *or* kom-pə-**ray**-tər). (1883) Something with which something else is compared; esp., something or someone treated differently from something or someone else and used as evidence of unlawful treatment of the latter <the female plaintiffs alleged illegal wage discrimination and contrasted their pay with that of male comparators>.

comparuit ad diem (kəm-**pair**-oo-wit ad **dɪ**-əm), *n.* [Latin "he appeared to the day"] (18c) *Hist.* A plea averring that the defendant appeared in court as required and did not forfeit the bail bond.

compassing (**kəm**-pə-sing). (13c) *Hist.* The act of contriving or plotting, esp. of something underhanded. • The Treason Act of 1351 criminalized the act of compassing the sovereign's death. — Also termed *imagining.*

compassionate leave. See LEAVE.

compassionate release. See *medical parole* under PAROLE.

compel, *vb.* (14c) **1.** To cause or bring about by force, threats, or overwhelming pressure <a lawyer cannot be compelled to testify about a privileged communication>. **2.** (Of a legislative mandate or judicial precedent) to convince (a court) that there is only one possible resolution of a legal dispute <the wording of the statute compels us to affirm>.

compellable, *adj.* (16c) Capable of or subject to being compelled, esp. to testify <an accused person's spouse is not a compellable witness for the prosecution>.

compellativus (kəm-pel-ə-**tɪ**-vəs). [fr. Latin *compellare* "to accuse"] *Hist.* An adversary or accuser.

compelling need. (18c) A need so great that irreparable harm or injustice would result if it is not met. • Generally, courts decide whether a compelling need is present based on the unique facts of each case. In some jurisdictions, however, statutes define "compelling need" or provide guidelines for determining whether one exists. See, e.g., 5 USCA § 552(a)(6)(E)(v) (defining "compelling need" for an expedited response to a Freedom of Information Act request).

compelling-state-interest test. (1966) *Constitutional law.* A method for determining the constitutional validity of a law, whereby the government's interest in the law and its purpose are balanced against an individual's constitutional right that is affected by the law. • Only if the government's interest is strong enough will the law be upheld. The compelling-state-interest test is used, e.g., in equal-protection analysis when the disputed law requires strict scrutiny. See STRICT SCRUTINY.

Compendium: Copyright Office Practices. A set of books setting forth guidelines, policies, and procedures for the examination of copyright applications by the U.S. Copyright Office. • Although the *Compendium* does not have legal force, it provides examiners and attorneys with authority and guidance for addressing registration and related questions.

compensable (kəm-**pen**-sə-bəl), *adj.* (17c) Capable of being or entitled to be compensated for <a compensable injury>. — Also termed *recompensable.*

compensable death. See DEATH.

compensable injury. See INJURY.

compensate (**kom**-pən-sayt), *vb.* (17c) **1.** PAY (3). **2.** To make an amendatory payment to; to recompense (for an injury) <the court ordered the defendant to compensate the injured plaintiff>.

compensated surety. See SURETY (1).

compensated-surety defense. See DEFENSE (1).

compensating balance. (1931) The amount of money a borrower from a bank is required to keep on deposit as a condition for a loan or a line of credit.

compensatio (kom-pen-**say**-shee-oh), *n.* [Latin "weighing; balancing"] (16c) *Roman law.* A defendant's claim to have the plaintiff's demand reduced by the amount that the plaintiff owes the defendant. See SETOFF (2).

compensatio criminis (kom-pen-**say**-shee-oh **krim**-ə-nis). [Latin] (17c) *Eccles. law.* A defendant's plea in a divorce action, alleging that the complainant is guilty of the same conduct that the defendant is charged with, esp. adultery. See RECRIMINATION (1).

> "The *compensatio criminis* is the standard canon law of England in questions of divorce, and it is founded on the principle that a man cannot be permitted to complain of the breach of a contract which he had first violated; and the same principle, it is to be presumed, prevails in the United States." 2 James Kent, *Commentaries on American Law* *100 (George Comstock ed., 11th ed. 1866).

compensatio injuriarum (kom-pen-**say**-shee-oh in-joor-ee-**air**-əm). [Latin "the compensation of wrongs"] *Scots law.* The setoff in a defamation action.

compensatio lucri cum damno (kom-pen-**say**-shee-oh **loo**-krɪ kəm **dam**-noh). [Latin] *Hist.* Compensation of profits with damages; set-off of profit and loss.

compensation (kom-pən-**say**-shən), *n.* (14c) **1.** Remuneration and other benefits received in return for services rendered; esp., salary or wages.

"*Compensation* consists of wages and benefits in return for services. It is payment for work. If the work contracted for is not done, there is no obligation to pay. [Compensation] includes wages, stock option plans, profit-sharing, commissions, bonuses, golden parachutes, vacation, sick pay, medical benefits, disability, leaves of absence, and expense reimbursement." Kurt H. Decker & H. Thomas Felix II, *Drafting and Revising Employment Contracts* § 3.17, at 68 (1991).

2. Payment of damages, or any other act that a court orders to be done by a person who has caused injury to another. • In theory, compensation makes the injured person whole. **3.** SETOFF (2). — **compensatory,** (kəm-**pen**-sə-tor-ee), **compensational** (kom-pən-**say**-shə-nəl), *adj.*

▸ **accrued compensation.** (1919) Remuneration that has been earned but not yet paid.

▸ **adequate compensation.** See *just compensation.*

▸ **deferred compensation.** (1926) **1.** Payment for work performed, to be paid in the future or when some future event occurs. **2.** An employee's earnings that are taxed when received or distributed rather than when earned, such as contributions to a qualified pension or profit-sharing plan.

▸ **just compensation.** (16c) Under the Fifth Amendment, a payment by the government for property it has taken under eminent domain — usu. the property's fair market value, so that the owner is theoretically no worse off after the taking. — Also termed *adequate compensation*; *due compensation*; *land damages.*

▸ **unemployment compensation.** (1921) Compensation paid at regular intervals by a state agency to an unemployed person, esp. one who has been laid off. — Also termed *unemployment insurance*; *unemployment benefit.*

▸ **unreasonable compensation.** (1946) *Tax.* Compensation that is not deductible as a business expense because the compensation is out of proportion to the services actually rendered or because it exceeds statutorily defined limits. IRC (26 USCA) § 162(m).

Compensation Clause. *Constitutional law.* The clause of the U.S. Constitution providing for federal judges to be paid. U.S. Const. art. III, § 1, cl. 2.

compensation neurosis. (1924) A neurotic mental condition in a plaintiff who has dwelled on the prospect of receiving personal-injury damages or other compensation, the principal effects being that the plaintiff unconsciously exaggerates and prolongs the symptoms of the injury or harm. • Compensation neurosis is not a distinct diagnosis recognized bythe psychiatric community.

compensation period. The time fixed by unemployment or workers'-compensation law during which an unemployed or injured worker is entitled to receive compensation.

compensatories. See *compensatory damages* (1) under DAMAGES.

compensatory damages. See DAMAGES.

compensatory mitigation. See ENVIRONMENTAL MITIGATION.

compensatory payment. *Family law.* A postmarital spousal payment made by the richer ex-spouse to the poorer one and treated as an entitlement rather than as a discretionary award. • Compensatory payments are set by statute and are based on a formula using the length of the marriage, differences in postdivorce income, role as primary caregiver, and other factors. The purpose is to compensate somewhat for disparate income levels after a marriage ends. Cf. ALIMONY.

compensatory time. See COMP TIME.

comperendinatio (kom-pər-en-də-**nay**-shee-oh), *n.* [Latin "to remand to the next day but one"] (16c) *Roman law.* An adjournment of an action, particularly one of the *actiones legis*, to hear the parties or their advocates a second time; a second hearing of the parties to a case. • The judge (judex) would decide the case at the conclusion of the second hearing. See LEGIS ACTIO.

competence, *n.* (17c) **1.** A basic or minimal ability to do something; adequate qualification, esp. to testify <competence of a witness>. **2.** The capacity of an official body to do something <the court's competence to enter a valid judgment>. **3.** Authenticity; admissibility <the documents were supported by a business-records affidavit, leaving their competence as evidence beyond doubt>. Cf. COMPETENCY. — **competent,** *adj.*

competence-competence doctrine. (1975) The principle that arbitrators may decide challenges to their own jurisdiction. — Also termed *compétence-compétence* (Fr.); *Kompetenz-Kompetenz* (Ger.).

"The principle that arbitrators have jurisdiction to consider and decide the existence and extent of their own jurisdiction is variously referred to as the 'competence-competence' doctrine, the 'Kompetenz-Kompetenz' doctrine, or the 'who decides' question. It is critical to appreciate that these various formulae can have very different, and sometimes contradictory, applications, depending on the national legal system and the circumstances in which they are used. . . . In particular, some national legal systems provide for the arbitrators to initially decide jurisdictional issues (subject to subsequent judicial review) while other legal systems permit initial judicial decisions on jurisdictional objections; similarly, some legal regimes accord a tribunal's decision on its own jurisdiction no or virtually no deference, while other systems accord such decisions extremely broad deference and binding effect." 1 Gary B. Born, *International Commercial Arbitration* 853–54 (2009).

competence to stand trial. See COMPETENCY (2).

competency, *n.* (16c) **1.** The mental ability to understand problems and make decisions. **2.** *Criminal law.* A criminal defendant's ability to stand trial, measured by the capacity to understand the charges and the proceedings, to consult meaningfully with counsel, and to assist in the defense. — Also termed (in sense 2) *competency to stand trial*; *fitness to stand trial*; (less good) *competence to stand trial*; (English & Scots law) *fitness to plead.* Cf. COMPETENCE. — **competent,** *adj.*

competency hearing. See PATE HEARING.

competency proceeding. See PROCEEDING.

competency to stand trial. (1949) See COMPETENCY (2).

competent contractor. See CONTRACTOR.

competent court. See *court of competent jurisdiction* under COURT.

competent evidence. See EVIDENCE.

competent jurisdiction. See JURISDICTION (2).

competent witness. See WITNESS.

competing presumption. See *conflicting presumption* under PRESUMPTION.

competition. (16c) The struggle for commercial advantage; the effort or action of two or more commercial interests to obtain the same business from third parties.

▸ **fair competition.** (17c) Open, equitable, and just competition between business competitors.

▸ **horizontal competition.** (1930) Competition between a seller and its competitors. • The Sherman Antitrust Act prohibits unreasonable restraints on horizontal competition, such as price-fixing agreements between competitors. — Also termed *primary-line competition.*

▸ **perfect competition.** (1884) A completely efficient market situation characterized by numerous buyers and sellers, a homogeneous product, perfect information for all parties, and complete freedom to move in and out of the market. • A perfectly competitive market is one in which no single firm has influence on the price of what it sells. Perfect competition rarely if ever exists, but antitrust scholars often use the concept as a standard for measuring market performance.

▸ **primary-line competition.** See *horizontal competition.*

▸ **secondary-line competition.** See *vertical competition.*

▸ **unfair competition.** See UNFAIR COMPETITION.

▸ **vertical competition.** (1954) Competition between participants at different levels of distribution, such as manufacturer and distributor. — Also termed *secondary-line competition.*

competition law. See ANTITRUST LAW (1).

competitive advantage. See ADVANTAGE.

competitive advertising. See ADVERTISING.

competitive bid. See BID (2).

competitive civil-service examination. (1897) A test designed to evaluate a person's qualifications for a civil-service position. • This type of examination may be open to all those seeking civil-service employment, or it may be restricted to those civil servants seeking a promotion. See CIVIL SERVICE.

competitive injury. A wrongful economic loss caused by a commercial rival, such as the loss of sales due to unfair competition; a disadvantage in a plaintiff's ability to compete with a defendant, caused by the defendant's unfair competition. • Most courts require that the plaintiff suffer a competitive injury in order to prevail in a misappropriation action or to have standing to prosecute a false-advertising action under 15 USCA § 1125(a)(1)(B). — Also termed *competitive harm.*

competitive seniority. See SENIORITY.

competitor click fraud. See FRAUD.

compilation (kom-pə-**lay**-shən), *n.* (15c) **1.** *Copyright.* A collection of literary works arranged in an original way; esp., a work formed by collecting and assembling preexisting materials or data that are selected, coordinated, or arranged in such a way that the resulting product constitutes an original work of authorship. • An author who creates a compilation owns the copyright of the compilation but not of the component parts. *See* 17 USCA § 101. Cf. *collective work, derivative work* under WORK (2). **2.** A collection of statutes, updated and arranged to facilitate their use. — Also termed *compiled statutes.* **3.** A financial statement that does not have an accountant's assurance of conformity with generally accepted accounting principles. • In preparing a compilation, an accountant does not gather evidence or verify the accuracy of the information provided by the client; rather, the accountant reviews the compiled reports to ensure that they are in the appropriate form and are free of obvious errors. — **compile,** *vb.*

compiled statutes. 1. See COMPILATION (2). **2.** See STATUTE.

complainant (kəm-**playn**-ənt). (15c) **1.** The party who brings a legal complaint against another; esp., the plaintiff in a court of equity or, more modernly, a civil suit.

> "A suit in equity, under the procedure of the English Court of Chancery, which was generally adopted in the American States prior to the code, is instituted by the plaintiff filing a bill of complaint. The plaintiff is usually called the complainant, in the Federal courts the complainant or plaintiff indifferently. The bill is in substance a petition to the chancellor, or judge of the court of equity, setting forth at large the grounds of the suit, and praying the process of the court, its subpoena, to bring the defendant into court and compel him to answer the plaintiff's bill, and, also, for such relief by decree or interlocutory remedy, by way of injunction, etc., as the plaintiff supposes himself entitled to." Edwin E. Bryant, *The Law of Pleading Under the Codes of Civil Procedure* 55 (2d ed. 1899).

2. Someone who, under oath, signs a statement (called a "complaint") establishing reasonable grounds to believe that some named person has committed a crime. — Also termed *affiant.*

complainantless crime. See *victimless crime* under CRIME.

complaint. (14c) **1.** The initial pleading that starts a civil action and states the basis for the court's jurisdiction, the basis for the plaintiff's claim, and the demand for relief. • In some states, this pleading is called a *petition.* **2.** *Criminal law.* A formal charge accusing a person of an offense. Fed. R. Crim. P. 3. Cf. INDICTMENT; INFORMATION.

▸ **amended complaint.** (1822) A complaint that modifies and replaces the original complaint by adding relevant matters that occurred before or at the time the action began. Fed. R. Civ. P. 15(d). • In some circumstances, a party must obtain the court's permission to amend its complaint. Fed. R. Civ. Pro. 15(a). — Also termed *substituted complaint.* Cf. *supplemental complaint.*

▸ **complaint for modification.** See *motion to modify* under MOTION (1).

▸ **counter-complaint.** (18c) A complaint filed by a defendant against the plaintiff, alleging that the plaintiff has committed a breach and is liable to the defendant for damages.

▸ **criminal complaint.** (17c) A formal charging instrument by which a person is accused of a crime, usu. a misdemeanor or violation in a sworn statement.

▸ **first complaint.** See FRESH COMPLAINT.

▸ **fresh complaint.** See FRESH COMPLAINT.

▸ **preliminary complaint.** (1833) A complaint issued by a court to obtain jurisdiction over a criminal suspect for a hearing on probable cause or on whether to bind the suspect over for trial.

▸ **short-form complaint.** (1911) A simplified, convenient, indorsed complaint typically used by pro se litigants. • As contrasted with a formal complaint, a short-form complaint may be used in certain actions normally requiring the use of a formal complaint, but may be construed as conferring jurisdiction while containing a defect, curable by amendment.

▸ **substituted complaint.** See *amended complaint.*

▸ **supplemental complaint.** (1821) An additional complaint that either corrects a defect in the original complaint or adds relevant matters that occurred after the action began. • Generally, a party must obtain the court's permission to file a supplemental complaint. Fed. R. Civ. Pro. 15(d). Cf. *amended complaint.*

▸ **third-party complaint.** (1938) A complaint filed by the defendant against a third party, alleging that the third party may be liable for some or all of the damages that the plaintiff is trying to recover from the defendant. Fed. R. Civ. P. 14.

▸ **well-pleaded complaint.** (1954) An original or initial pleading that sufficiently sets forth a claim for relief — by including the grounds for the court's jurisdiction, the basis for the relief claimed, and a demand for judgment — so that a defendant may draft an answer that is responsive to the issues presented. • In federal court, a well-pleaded complaint must raise a controlling issue of federal law, or else the court will not have federal-question jurisdiction over the lawsuit.

complementarity, *n.* (1911) **1.** The quality, state, or condition of being complementary. **2.** *Int'l law.* See COMPLEMENTARITY PRINCIPLE.

complementarity principle. (1998) *Int'l law.* The doctrine that a country with control of a person accused of violating international criminal law has the jurisdiction to charge and try a person. • Because the jurisdiction of the International Criminal Court is complementary to the criminal jurisdiction of countries, that tribunal can assert jurisdiction over the accused person only if the country is unable or unwilling to undertake a genuine investigation and prosecution. — Sometimes shortened to *complementarity.*

complementary goods. (1965) *Trademarks.* Products that are typically used together, such as pancake syrup and pancake mix, or motion-picture projectors and film. • Trademark law may prevent the use of a similar mark on complementary goods because consumers may be confused into thinking the goods come from a common source. The patent-misuse doctrine may provide a defense in an infringement suit if the plaintiff has used its patent rights to gain market control over unpatented complementary goods. — Also termed *complementary products.* See AUNT JEMIMA DOCTRINE; PATENT-MISUSE DOCTRINE.

complementary products. See COMPLEMENTARY GOODS.

complete conception of invention. See CONCEPTION OF INVENTION.

completed-and-accepted doctrine. The principle that once construction work has been completed and accepted by the owner, the contractor is not liable to third parties for patent defects even if the contractor was negligent.

completed-contract accounting method. See ACCOUNTING METHOD.

completed-elective forfeiture. See FORFEITURE.

completed gift. See GIFT.

complete diversity. See DIVERSITY OF CITIZENSHIP.

completed-operations insurance. See INSURANCE.

complete in itself, *adj.* (18c) (Of a legislative act) fully covering an entire subject.

complete integration. See INTEGRATION (2).

complete interdiction. See *full interdiction* under INTERDICTION (3).

complete jurisdiction. See JURISDICTION.

completely integrated contract. See INTEGRATED CONTRACT.

completeness doctrine. See RULE OF OPTIONAL COMPLETENESS.

complete-operation rule. (1945) *Insurance.* The principle that goods are covered against damage at any time during the shipping process, including the loading and unloading of the goods. • Under some circumstances, the rule has been extended to cover personal injuries that occur during the shipping process. See WAREHOUSE-TO-WAREHOUSE COVER. Cf. COMING-TO-REST DOCTRINE.

complete ownership. See *perfect ownership* under OWNERSHIP.

complete-preemption doctrine. (1987) The rule that a federal statute's preemptive force may be so extraordinary and all-encompassing that it converts an ordinary state-common-law complaint into one stating a federal claim for purposes of the well-pleaded-complaint rule. See *well-pleaded complaint* under COMPLAINT.

complete property. See PROPERTY.

complete voluntary trust. See *executed trust* under TRUST (3).

completion bond. See PERFORMANCE BOND.

complexity. (18c) **1.** The quality, state, or condition of being complex; intricacy <the complexity of the rule against perpetuities>. **2.** One of many details or features of something that make it hard to understand or deal with; something that complicates things <the complexities of the derivatives market>.

complex litigation. See LITIGATION.

complex trust. See TRUST (3).

compliance audit. See AUDIT.

complicated larceny. See *mixed larceny* under LARCENY.

complice (**kom**-plis). (15c) *Archaic.* An accomplice or accessory to a crime or immoral behavior.

complicit. See COMPLICITOUS.

complicitous, *adj.* Being an accomplice; participating in guilt. — Also termed (erroneously, on the model of *implicit*) *complicit.*

> "When a single offender acts alone, he or she is the sole perpetrator or principal. Problems arise when other people get involved. The degree of participation of others varies from a minimal contribution (giving advice, supplying tools or transportation) to taking charge and executing the commission of the crime. Those who counsel, assist, advise, or solicit are called accessories. They are *complicitous* in the acts of the perpetrator." George P. Fletcher, *Basic Concepts of Criminal Law* 188 (1998).

complicity (kəm-**plis**-ə-tee), *n.* (17c) **1.** Involvement in a crime together with other people; association or participation in a criminal act as an accomplice. • Under the Model Penal Code, a person can be an accomplice as a result of either that person's own conduct or the conduct of another (such as an innocent agent) for which that person is legally accountable. Model Penal Code § 2.06.

See ACCOMPLICE; *innocent agent* under AGENT. **2.** Involvement in or knowledge of a situation that is morally wrong or entails dishonesty.

> "The law of criminal complicity is riddled with obscurities and difficulties. It is almost entirely governed by the common law, and contains a fairly high proportion of opportunistic judicial decisions that lend no coherence to the rules. There is no settled name for this branch of the law: actual perpetrators of the offence itself are termed 'principals,' but others who are liable to conviction as parties to the crime may be termed accomplices, accessories, or secondary parties. There is also a fundamental doctrinal obscurity: are there simply two forms of liability, that of principals and of accomplices, or is there a third and separate doctrine of 'joint enterprise?' Judicial and academic opinions are divided, but this branch of criminal law is so malleable that it is unlikely that the outcome of any case would be held to depend on whether or not 'joint enterprise' exists as a separate set of rules." *English Public Law* § 24.58, at 1235-36 (David Feldman ed., 2004).

component-parts doctrine. A rule that the seller of a component part is liable if the component is defective and causes harm, or if the seller participates substantially in integrating the component into the final product's design and the component causes the product to be defective.

composite, *n.* A computer image or artist's rendering of the face of a criminal suspect compiled usu. from descriptions given by people who saw the crime take place. — Also termed (BrE) *identikit picture.*

composite mark. See *composite trademark* under TRADEMARK.

composite state. See STATE (1).

composite trademark. See TRADEMARK.

composite work. See WORK (2).

composition, *n.* (14c) **1.** An agreement to settle a dispute or debt whereby one party abates part of what is due or claimed; COMPROMISE (1). Cf. AMIABLE COMPOSITION. **2.** An agreement between a debtor and two or more creditors for the adjustment or discharge of an obligation for some lesser amount; an agreement among the debtor and two or more creditors that the debtor will pay the creditors less than their full claims in full satisfaction of their claims. • Consideration arises from the agreement by each creditor with each other to take less than full payment. Through the performance of this agreement, the debtor is discharged in full for the debts of the participating creditors. Composition agreements have been largely superseded by proceedings under the Federal Bankruptcy Act or by state insolvency laws. — Also termed *composition with creditors; creditors' composition; attermoiement.*

> "A composition by a debtor with his creditors, under which they agree to accept a part of their debts in satisfaction of the whole, is based upon the principle that all the creditors shall stand on an equal footing, and observe good faith towards each other; and therefore any secret arrangement between the debtor and a particular creditor, whereby he is placed in a more favored position than the others, is a fraud on them, and renders the composition agreement voidable." James W. Eaton, *Handbook of Equity Jurisprudence* § 144, at 304 (Archibald H. Throckmorton ed., 2d ed. 1923)

3. The compensation paid as part of such an agreement. **4.** *Hist.* A payment of money or chattels as satisfaction for an injury. • In Anglo-Saxon and other early societies, a *composition* with the injured party was recognized as a way to deter acts of revenge by the injured party. — **compose,** *vb.*

> "[T]he first theory of liability was in terms of a duty to buy off the vengeance of him to whom an injury had been done whether by oneself or by something in one's power. The idea is put strikingly in the Anglo-Saxon proverb, 'Buy spear from side or bear it,' that is, buy off the feud or fight it out. . . . As the social interest in peace and order — the general security in its lowest terms — comes to be secured more effectively by regulation and ultimate putting down of feud as a remedy, payment of composition becomes a duty rather than a privilege . . . . The next step is to measure the composition not in terms of the vengeance to be bought off but in terms of the injury. A final step is to put it in terms of reparation." Roscoe Pound, *An Introduction to the Philosophy of Law* 74 (rev. ed. 1954).

composition deed. See DEED.

composition of matter. (1811) *Patents.* One of the types of patentable statutory subject matter, consisting of combinations of natural elements whether resulting from chemical union or from mechanical mixture, and whether the substances are gases, fluids, powders, or solids. • This classification includes chemical compounds such as drugs and fuels, physical products such as plastics and particleboard, and new life forms made by genetic engineering. Its subject matter is always the substance itself, rather than the form or shape. — Often shortened to *composition.*

composition with creditors. See COMPOSITION (2).

compos mentis (kom-pəs **men**-tis), *adj.* [Latin "master of one's mind"] (17c) Of sound mind; having use of and control over one's own mental faculties. Cf. NON COMPOS MENTIS.

compossessio (kom-pə-**zes[h]**-ee-oh). [Latin] *Civil law.* Possession by two or more persons of a thing in common.

compos sui **(kom**-pəs **s[y]oo**-I), *adj.* [Latin "master of one's self"] (Of a person) having control over one's own limbs, or having the power of bodily motion.

compound (kom- *or* kəm-**pownd**), *vb.* (14c) **1.** To put together, combine, or construct. **2.** To compute (interest) on the principal and the accrued interest. **3.** To settle (a matter, esp. a debt) by a money payment, in lieu of other liability; to adjust by agreement. **4.** To agree for consideration not to prosecute (a crime). • Compounding a felony in this way is itself a felony. **5.** Loosely, to aggravate; to make (a crime, etc.) more serious by further bad conduct.

compound duty. See DUTY (4).

compounder (kom- *or* kəm-**pown**-dər). (16c) **1.** Someone who settles a dispute; the maker of a composition. — Also termed *amicable compounder.* See COMPOSITION (2). **2.** Someone who knows of a crime by another and agrees, for a promised or received reward, not to prosecute.

compounding a crime. (17c) The offense of either agreeing not to prosecute a crime that one knows has been committed or agreeing to hamper the prosecution. — Also termed *compounding a felony*; (archaically) *theftbote.* See STIFLING OF A PROSECUTION.

> "If a prosecuting attorney should accept money from another to induce the officer to prevent the finding of an indictment against that person this would be *compounding a crime* if the officer knew the other was guilty of an offense, but would be bribery whether he had such knowledge or not." Rollin M. Perkins & Ronald N. Boyce, *Criminal Law* 539 (3d ed. 1982).

compounding a felony. See COMPOUNDING A CRIME.

compound interest. See INTEREST (3).

compound journal entry. See ENTRY (2).

compound larceny. 1. See *mixed larceny* under LARCENY. **2.** See *aggravated larceny* under LARCENY.

compound offense. See OFFENSE (2).

compound policy. See *blanket policy* under INSURANCE POLICY.

comprehensive general-liability insurance. See *commercial general-liability insurance* under INSURANCE.

comprehensive insurance. See INSURANCE.

comprehensive interpretation. See *extensive interpretation* under INTERPRETATION (1).

Comprehensive National Cybersecurity Initiative. The federal government's strategy for Internet security by using counterintelligence to defend the United States' network infrastructure against a range of potential threats and enhancing the cybersecurity environment through education, coordination, and research. • The CNCI was established by President George W. Bush in 2006. It involves several agencies, including the Department of Homeland Security, the Office of Management and Budget, and the National Security Agency. — Abbr. CNCI.

comprehensive nonliteral similarity. See SIMILARITY.

comprehensive zoning. See ZONING.

comprehensive zoning plan. (1925) A general plan to control and direct the use and development of a large piece of property. See ZONING.

comprint (**kom**-print). (17c) *Hist. Copyright.* The surreptitious and supposedly illegal printing of another bookseller's copy of a work. • Despite the word's appearance as a legal term in dictionaries since 1706, no such offense ever existed. The term, which is properly a verb meaning "to share in printing (a book)," was first given this erroneous definition by John Kersey when he produced a new edition of Edward Phillips's *New World of English Words.* It has occasionally been copied by legal lexicographers ever since.

comprising, *adj.* **1.** Consisting of exclusively; embracing to the exclusion of others. • This usage reflects the sense in normal idiomatic writing outside the intellectual-property context. **2.** *Patents.* (In the transition between the preamble and the body of a patent claim) including or having, but not exclusively. • This term does not limit the claim to the specified elements, so a later patent applicant's product or process cannot avoid infringement by merely adding another claim element. Hence a claim reciting "a widget comprising A and B," for example, is infringed by any widget that includes A and B, even if C, D, or E might be present. *See Amgen, Inc. v. Hoechst Marion Roussel, Inc.*, 314 F.3d 1313 (Fed. Cir. 2003). See *closed-ended claim* under PATENT CLAIM. Cf. CONSISTING OF.

compromis (kom-prə-**mee**). [French] *Int'l law.* **1.** An agreement between two or more countries to submit an existing dispute to the jurisdiction of an arbitrator, an arbitral tribunal, or an international court. See *compromissory arbitration* under ARBITRATION.

▸ **ad hoc compromis** (ad hok kom-prə-**mee**). (1934) An agreement in which countries submit a particular dispute that has arisen between them to an ad hoc or institutionalized arbitral tribunal or to an international court. — Also termed *compromis proper*; *special agreement.*

▸ **general compromis.** (1952) An agreement in which countries submit all or a definite class of disputes that may arise between them to an arbitral institution, a court, or an ad hoc arbitral tribunal by concluding a general arbitration treaty or by including an arbitration clause in a treaty. — Also termed *abstract compromis*; *anticipated compromis.*

2. In international-law moot-court competitions, the record on which the arguments are based.

compromise, *n.* (15c) **1.** An agreement between two or more persons to settle matters in dispute between them; an agreement for the settlement of a real or supposed claim in which each party surrenders something in concession to the other. — Also termed *compromise and settlement*; (erroneously) *compromise settlement.* See COMPOSITION (1). **2.** A debtor's partial payment coupled with the creditor's promise not to claim the rest of the amount due or claimed. Cf. ACCORD; ACCORD AND SATISFACTION. — **compromise,** *vb.*

compromise and settlement. See COMPROMISE (1).

compromise verdict. See VERDICT (1).

compromis proper. See *ad hoc compromis* under COMPROMIS (1).

compromissarius (kom-prə-mi-**sair**-ee-əs). [Latin] *Roman law.* See ARBITRATOR.

compromissory arbitration. See *compromissory arbitration* under ARBITRATION.

compromissum (kom-prə-**mis**-əm), *n.* [Latin "mutual agreement"] *Roman law.* An agreement to submit a controversy to arbitration.

compte arrêté (**kawnt** a-ray-**tay**). [French "settled account"] An account stated in writing, and acknowledged to be correct on its face by the party against whom it is stated.

compter (**kown**-tər), *n.* (15c) *Hist.* A debtor's prison; specif., a sheriff-controlled prison for civil prisoners such as debtors and dissenters. — Also termed *counter.*

comp time. (1979) Time that an employee is allowed to take off from work instead of or in addition to receiving overtime pay. — Also termed *compensatory time.*

comptroller (kən-**troh**-lər). (15c) An officer of a business or a private, state, or municipal corporation who is charged with duties usu. relating to fiscal affairs, including auditing and examining accounts and reporting the financial status periodically. • The standard, traditional pronunciation is as given. The pronunciation /**komp**-troh-ler/, though common today, has traditionally been considered a mispronunciation. — Also spelled *controller.*

Comptroller General of the United States. The officer in the legislative branch of the federal government who heads the General Accountability Office. • The Comptroller General is appointed by the President with the advice and consent of the Senate. See GENERAL ACCOUNTABILITY OFFICE.

Comptroller of the Currency. A presidential appointee who serves as a director of both the Federal Deposit Insurance Corporation and the Neighborhood Reinvestment

Corporation. See OFFICE OF THE COMPTROLLER OF THE CURRENCY.

compulsion, *n.* (15c) **1.** The act of compelling; the quality, state, or condition of being compelled.

> "Compulsion can take other forms than physical force; but in whatever form it appears the courts have been indisposed to admit that it can be a defence for any crime committed through yielding to it and the law of the matter is both meagre and vague. It can best be considered under the heads of obedience to orders, martial coercion, duress *per minas*, and necessity." J.W. Cecil Turner, *Kenny's Outlines of Criminal Law* 54 (16th ed. 1952).

2. An uncontrollable inclination to do something regardless of the rationality of one's motivation. **3.** Objective necessity; duress. — **compel,** *vb.*

compulsory (kəm-**pəl**-sə-ree), *adj.* (16c) Required or compelled; mandated by legal process or by statute <compulsory counterclaim>.

compulsory, *n.* (16c) *Eccles. law.* An order that compels the attendance of a witness.

compulsory acquisition. *Australian law.* EMINENT DOMAIN.

compulsory appearance. See APPEARANCE.

compulsory arbitration. See *mandatory arbitration* under ARBITRATION.

compulsory-attendance law. (1906) A statute requiring minors of a specified age to attend school. — Also termed *compulsory-school-attendance law.* See AMISH EXCEPTION.

compulsory condition. See CONDITION (2).

compulsory counterclaim. See COUNTERCLAIM.

compulsory-counterclaim rule. (1942) The rule requiring a defending party to present every counterclaim arising out of the same transaction or occurrence that is the basis of the plaintiff's claim. Fed. R. Civ. P. 13(a). • Most courts hold that if a party does not timely bring a compulsory counterclaim, the party is estopped from asserting the claim.

compulsory disclosure. See DISCLOSURE (2).

compulsory insurance. See INSURANCE.

compulsory joinder. See JOINDER.

compulsory labor. See FORCED LABOR.

compulsory license. See LICENSE.

compulsory nonsuit. See NONSUIT (2).

compulsory novation. See NOVATION.

compulsory pilot. See PILOT (1).

compulsory pilotage. See PILOTAGE.

compulsory pooling. See POOLING.

compulsory process. See PROCESS (2).

Compulsory Process Clause. (1957) *Constitutional law.* The clause of the Sixth Amendment to the U.S. Constitution giving criminal defendants the subpoena power for obtaining witnesses in their favor.

compulsory purchase. *Rare.* **1.** See EMINENT DOMAIN. **2.** See EXPROPRIATION (1).

compulsory retirement. See RETIREMENT.

compulsory sale. See SALE.

compulsory-school-attendance law. See COMPULSORY-ATTENDANCE LAW.

compulsory surrender. 1. See EMINENT DOMAIN. **2.** See EXPROPRIATION (1).

compulsory unitization. See UNITIZATION.

compurgation (kom-pər-**gay**-shən), *n.* [Latin *con-* "together" + *purgare* "to clear or purge"] (17c) *Hist.* A medieval trial by which a defendant could have supporters (called *compurgators*), frequently 11 in number, testify that they believed the defendant was telling the truth. — Also termed *wager of law; trial by oath.* — **compurgatory,** *adj.*

> "If a defendant on oath and in a set form of words will deny the charge against him, and if he can get a certain number of other persons (compurgators) to back his denial by their oaths, he will win his case. If he cannot get the required number, or they do not swear in proper form, 'the oath bursts,' and he will lose. Though oaths were used in the Roman law of procedure, this institution of compurgation was not known to it. It was, however, common to the laws of many of the barbarian tribes who overran the Roman empire. Because it was so common and so widespread the church adopted it. . . . The case of *King v. Williams* in 1824 was the last instance of its use. It was finally abolished in 1833." 1 William Holdsworth, *A History of English Law* 305–08 (7th ed. 1956).

compurgator (**kom**-pər-gay-tər). (16c) *Hist.* Someone who appeared in court and made an oath in support of a civil or criminal defendant. — Also termed *oath-helper.* See COMPURGATION.

computer crime. See CRIME.

computer-generated evidence. See EVIDENCE.

computer-information transaction. (1999) *Copyright.* An agreement whose primary purpose is to create, modify, transfer, or license computer information or rights in computer information.

computer matching. (1988) The comparing of computer records in two separate systems to determine whether the same record exists in both systems. • The government, for example, uses computer matching to find persons who are both employed and receiving welfare payments and to find instances in which both divorced parents are claiming the same child on their income-tax returns. See COMPUTER MATCHING AND PRIVACY PROTECTION ACT OF 1988.

Computer Matching and Privacy Protection Act of 1988. An act that allows governmental agencies, with certain limitations, to compare computerized records to establish or verify eligibility for benefits or to recoup payments on benefits. 5 USCA § 552a. — Abbr. CMPPA. See COMPUTER MATCHING.

Computer Programs Directive. See DIRECTIVE ON THE LEGAL PROTECTION OF COMPUTER PROGRAMS.

Computer Software Protection Act of 1980. *Copyright.* An amendment to the Copyright Act of 1976, defining "computer program" as a literary work for copyright purposes and qualifying the exclusive rights of copyrighted-software owners. 17 USCA § 117.

Computer Software Protection Act of 1984. *Copyright.* An amendment to the Copyright Act of 1976, enacted to protect copyrighted computer programs against illegal copying. 17 USCA § 109.

Computer Software Rental Amendments Act. *Copyright.* A 1990 statute prohibiting computer-program purchasers from leasing, renting, or lending the software for commercial gain. 17 USCA § 109. — Abbr. CSRAA.

computus (**kom**-pyə-təs). [Latin *computo* "to count up; to reckon"] *Hist.* A writ to compel a guardian, bailiff, receiver, or accountant to render an accounting. — Also spelled *compotus.*

Comstock Act. See COMSTOCK LAW.

comstockery (**kom**-stok-ər-ee). (*often cap.*) (1895) Censorship or attempted censorship of art or literature that is supposedly immoral or obscene.

Comstock law (**kom**-stok). (1878) An 1873 federal statute that prohibited mailing "obscene, lewd, or lascivious" books or pictures, as well as "any article or thing designed for the prevention of conception or procuring of abortions." • The bill was named for Anthony Comstock (1844–1915), a New Yorker (not a legislator) who was an anti-obscenity crusader. Twenty-four states passed similar prohibitions on materials distributed within their borders. Collectively, the state and federal restrictions are known as "the Comstock laws." Because of the intolerance that led to these statutes, there was born an English word roughly equivalent to *prudery* — namely, *comstockery.* — Also termed *Comstock Act.*

con. *abbr.* (1889) **1.** Confidence <con game>. **2.** Convict <ex-con>. **3.** Contra <pros and cons>. **4.** (*cap.*) Constitutional <Con. law>.

con, *n.* See CONFIDENCE GAME.

conatus (kə-**nay**-təs). [Latin] *Hist.* An attempt, esp. to commit a crime.

concealed debtor. See DEBTOR.

concealed weapon. See WEAPON.

concealment, *n.* (14c) **1.** The act of preventing disclosure or refraining from disclosing; esp., the injurious or intentional suppression or nondisclosure of facts that one is obliged to reveal; COVER-UP. **2.** The act of removing from sight or notice; hiding. **3.** *Insurance.* The insured's intentional withholding from the insurer material facts that increase the insurer's risk and that in good faith ought to be disclosed. Cf. NONDISCLOSURE. — **conceal,** *vb.*

> "Concealment is an affirmative act intended or known to be likely to keep another from learning of a fact of which he would otherwise have learned. Such affirmative action is always equivalent to a misrepresentation and has any effect that a misrepresentation would have . . . ." Restatement (Second) of Contracts § 160 cmt. a (1979).

▸ **active concealment.** (1865) The concealment by words or acts of something that one has a duty to reveal.

▸ **fraudulent concealment.** (1801) The affirmative suppression or hiding, with the intent to deceive or defraud, of a material fact or circumstance that one is legally (or, sometimes, morally) bound to reveal. — Also termed *hidden fraud.*

▸ **passive concealment.** (1882) The act of maintaining silence when one has a duty to speak.

concealment rule. (1950) The principle that a defendant's conduct that hinders or prevents a plaintiff from discovering the existence of a claim tolls the statute of limitations until the plaintiff discovers or should have discovered the claim. — Also termed *fraudulent-concealment rule.*

concedo (kən-**see**-doh). [Latin] *Hist.* I grant. • This was formerly a term of conveyance.

concentration account. See ACCOUNT.

concentration camp. A prison in which large numbers of nonmilitary prisoners are kept, esp. during wartime in extremely poor conditions.

conception (kən-**sep**-shən), *n.* (13c) **1.** The act or process of forming an idea or notion, esp. one involving abstract thought. **2.** The idea or notion so formed. **3.** The mental faculty or power of abstract thought (as distinguished from the perception of tangible things). **4.** A product of the imagination or of creativity; esp., CONCEPTION OF INVENTION. **5.** The impregnation of an ovum; the onset of pregnancy.

▸ **artificial conception.** (1978) Either artificial insemination or implantation of an embryo into a woman's body.

conception of invention. (1859) *Patents.* The formation in the inventor's mind of a definite and permanent idea of a complete invention that is thereafter applied in practice. • Courts usu. consider conception when determining priority of invention. — Often shortened to *conception.*

▸ **complete conception of invention.** (1874) *Patents.* The point at which an inventor knows every feature of the process or device to be patented, such that a person with ordinary skill in the art could reproduce it without extensive research or experimentation. — Often shortened to *complete conception.*

conceptual uncertainty. See UNCERTAINTY.

conceptum (kən-**sep**-təm). [Latin "seized"] *Civil law.* A theft in which the stolen item was searched for and found in someone's possession and in the presence of witnesses. See *furtum conceptum* under FURTUM.

concerted action. (18c) An action that has been planned, arranged, and agreed on by parties acting together to further some scheme or cause, so that all involved are liable for the actions of one another. — Also termed *concert of action.*

concerted activity. *Labor law.* Action by employees concerning wages or working conditions; esp., a conscious commitment to a common scheme designed to achieve an objective. • Concerted activity is protected by the National Labor Relations Act and cannot be used as a basis for disciplining or discharging an employee.

concerted refusal to deal. (1939) *Antitrust.* An agreement between two or more persons or firms to not do business with a third party. • The parties to the agreement may or may not be competitors. Concerted refusals to deal may violate § 1 of the Sherman Act and are analyzed under either the per se rule or the rule of reason, depending on the nature of the agreement. See BOYCOTT; PER SE RULE; RULE OF REASON.

concert of action. See CONCERTED ACTION.

concert-of-action rule. See WHARTON'S RULE.

concessi (kən-**ses**-ɪ). [Latin] (16c) *Hist.* I have granted. • *Concessi* creates a covenant in a lease for years; it does not warrant title. *Concessi* often appeared in the phrase *demisi, concessi, et ad firmam tradidi* ("demised, granted, and let to farm"). Cf. DEDI.

> "Concessi (a word much used in Conveyances). In Law it creates a *Covenant*, as *Dedi* does a *Warranty*." Thomas Blount, *Nomo-Lexicon: A Law-Dictionary* (1670).

concessimus (kən-**ses**-ə-məs). [Latin] *Hist.* We have granted. • *Concessimus* is a term of conveyance that creates a joint covenant on the part of the grantors.

concessio (kən-**sesh**-ee-oh). [Latin] *Hist.* A grant. • A term of conveyance used to convey incorporeal property. Pl. ***concessiones.***

> "Grants, *concessiones*; the regular method by the common law of transferring the property of *incorporeal* hereditaments, or, such things whereof no livery can be had. For which reason all corporeal hereditaments, as lands and houses, are said to lie *in livery*; and the others, as advowsons, commons, rents, reversions, etc., to lie *in grant*. . . . These therefore pass merely by the delivery of the deed." 2 William Blackstone, *Commentaries on the Laws of England* 317 (1766).

concession, *n.* (15c) **1.** A government grant for specific privileges. **2.** The voluntary yielding to a demand for the sake of a settlement. **3.** A rebate or abatement. **4.** *Int'l law.* A contract in which a country transfers some rights to a foreign enterprise which then engages in an activity (such as mining) contingent on state approval and subject to the terms of the contract. **5.** *Int'l law.* A territory that, although within a country, is administered by some other entity than the state that holds sovereignty over it. — **concede,** *vb.* — **concessive,** *adj.*

concessionary, *adj.* (18c) **1.** Given as something one allows someone to have in order to end an argument or disagreement <concessionary measures by prison officials>. **2.** Specially reduced in price, as for children or senior citizens <concessionary fares are available>.

concession bargaining. (1983) *Labor law.* A type of collective bargaining in which the parties negotiate the employees' giving back previously gained improvements in wages, benefits, or working conditions in exchange for some form of job security, such as protection against layoffs. — Also termed *employee givebacks*; *union givebacks.* See COLLECTIVE BARGAINING.

concessit solvere (kən-**ses**-it **sol**-və-ree). [Latin "he agreed to pay"] (17c) *Hist.* A form of debt action on a simple contract. • The plaintiff alleged that the defendant had granted and agreed to pay to the plaintiff the sum sued for, but had not done so. The defendant responded with a plea of *nunquam indebitatus* ("never indebted"). See *indebitatus assumpsit* under ASSUMPSIT; NUNQUAM INDEBITATUS; *common count* under COUNT.

concessor (kən-**ses**-ər). (17c) *Hist.* A grantor. Cf. CONCESSUS.

concessum (kən-**ses**-əm), *p.pl.* [fr. Latin *concedere* "to grant"] *Hist.* Granted. • Judges used this term to signify their assent to a point made in argument; for example, a court might state that a particular proposition was *concessum per totam curiam* ("granted by the whole court").

concessus (kən-**ses**-əs). (16c) *Hist.* A grantee. Cf. CONCESSOR.

conciliation, *n.* (1803) **1.** The settlement of a dispute in an agreeable manner. **2.** The process of trying to get disputants to stop arguing and agree. **3.** More specifically, a process in which a neutral person meets with the parties to a dispute and explores how the dispute might be resolved; esp., a relatively unstructured method of dispute resolution in which a third party facilitates communication between parties in an attempt to help them settle their differences. • Some jurisdictions, such as California, have Family Conciliation Courts to help resolve problems within the family. — Also termed (in senses 2 & 3) *facilitation*; *conciliation procedure.* Cf. MEDIATION; ARBITRATION. — **conciliate,** *vb.* — **conciliative, conciliatory,** *adj.* — **conciliator,** *n.*

conciliation court. See *small-claims court* under COURT.

conciliation procedure. See CONCILIATION (2).

concilium (kən-**sil**-ee-əm). [Latin "council"] (1834) **1.** *Hist.* The sitting of a court to hear argument in a case; a motion requesting a day to present an argument. **2.** CONCILIUM PLEBIS.

concilium plebis (kən-**sil**-ee-əm **plee**-bis). [Latin "assembly of the people"] (18c) *Roman law.* An assembly of the plebs gathered together to enact legislation. — Often shortened to *concilium.* See PLEBISCITUM. Cf. *comitia tributa* under COMITIA.

> "Legislation was carried on to some extent by the *Comitia Tributa* and in an increasing degree by the assembly of the *plebs* alone, *concilium plebis*, which, in historical times, was also based on the tributal organisation. This assembly, presided over by a tribune of the *plebs*, was active from early times and there was early legislation on constitutional questions, enacted by that body and approved by the Senate, which was regarded as binding on the whole community. Its enactments, *plebiscita*, were often called, as binding the whole community, leges . . . ." W.W. Buckland, *A Text-book of Roman Law from Augustus to Justinian* 4 (Peter Stein ed., 3d ed. 1963).

> "The pressure of plebeian agitation had led to the creation of tribunes of the *plebs* (494 B.C.) for the protection of individual citizens from oppression, with the right to hold meetings of an assembly called the *Concilium Plebis*, which eventually became identical with the *Comitia Tributa*, except that it comprised only the plebeian members of the Roman people, without the patricians. The resolutions of this assembly (*plebiscita*) at first bound the plebeians only, but by an obscure development culminating in the passing of the *Lex Hortensia* of 287 B.C., they came to be binding as laws on the whole people, patricians and plebeians alike." William A. Hunter, *Introduction to Roman Law* 16 (F.H. Lawson ed., 9th ed. 1934).

concilium regis (kən-**sil**-ee-əm **ree**-jis). [Latin "assembly of the king"] (17c) *Hist.* A tribunal that, during the reigns of Edward I and Edward II, heard cases of extraordinary difficulty.

concio. See *contio.*

conclude, *vb.* (16c) **1.** To ratify or formalize (a treaty, convention, or contract) <it can be difficult to amend a contract that the parties have already concluded>. **2.** To bind; estop <the admissions concluded the party as a matter of law>. **3.** *Scots law.* To sign (a contract, letter, etc.) for the sale of real property. • This term most commonly appears in the phrase *conclude missives.*

conclusion, *n.* (14c) **1.** The final part of a speech or writing (such as a jury argument or a pleading). **2.** A judgment arrived at by reasoning; an inferential statement. **3.** The closing, settling, or final arranging of a treaty, contract, deal, etc. See OPINION (2). **4.** *Archaic.* An act by which one estops oneself from doing anything inconsistent with the act. **5.** See OPINION (3).

> "Conclusion is, when a man by his own act upon record hath charged himself with a duty or other thing . . . . So if the sheriff, upon a *capias* to him directed, returns that he hath taken the body, and yet hath not the body in court at the day of the return, he shall be amerced . . . ." *Termes de la Ley* 102–03 (1st Am. ed. 1812).

conclusional, *adj.* See CONCLUSORY.

conclusionary, *adj.* See CONCLUSORY.

conclusion of fact. (18c) A factual deduction drawn from observed or proven facts without resort to rules of law; an evidentiary inference. Cf. FINDING OF FACT.

conclusion of law. (17c) **1.** An inference on a question of law, made as a result of a factual showing, no further evidence being required; a legal inference. **2.** A judge's final decision on a legal point raised in a trial or hearing, particularly one that is vital to reaching a judgment. Cf. FINDING OF FACT; LEGAL CONCLUSION.

conclusion to the country. (1835) *Archaic.* The closing part of a pleading that requests the trial of an issue by a jury. Cf. GOING TO THE COUNTRY.

conclusive, *adj.* (17c) Authoritative; decisive; convincing <her conclusive argument ended the debate>. Cf. CONCLUSORY.

conclusive evidence. See EVIDENCE.

conclusive presumption. See PRESUMPTION.

conclusive proof. See *conclusive evidence* (1) under EVIDENCE.

conclusory (kən-**kloo**-zə-ree *or* -sə-ree), *adj.* (1923) Expressing a factual inference without stating the underlying facts on which the inference is based <because the plaintiff's allegations lacked any supporting evidence, they were merely conclusory>. — Also termed *conclusional; conclusionary.* Cf. CONCLUSIVE.

concomitant (kən-**kom**-ə-tənt), *adj.* (17c) Accompanying; incidental <concomitant actions>. — **concomitant,** *n.*

concomitant evidence. See EVIDENCE.

concord (**kon**-kord *or* **kong**-), *n.* (14c) **1.** An amicable arrangement between parties, esp. between peoples or countries; a compact or treaty. **2.** *Archaic.* An agreement to compromise and settle an action in trespass.

> "Concord is an Agreement made between two or more, upon a Trespass committed; and is divided into *Concord executory,* and *Concord executed* . . . one binds not, as being imperfect, but the other is absolute, and ties the Party." Giles Jacob, *A New Law-Dictionary* (8th ed. 1762).

3. *Archaic.* An in-court agreement in which a person who acquired land by force acknowledges that the land in question belongs to the complainant. See DEFORCE.

> "Next comes the *concord,* or agreement itself, after leave obtained from the court; which is usually an acknowledgment from the deforciants (or those who keep the other out of possession) that the lands in question are the right of the complainant." 2 William Blackstone, *Commentaries on the Laws of England* 350 (1766).

4. *Hist.* The settlement of a dispute.

▸ **final concord.** A written agreement between the parties to an action by which they settle the action in court, with the court's permission. — Also termed *finalis concordia; final peace.* See FINE (1).

concordat (kon- *or* kən-**kor**-dat). (17c) **1.** An agreement between a government and a church, esp. the Roman Catholic Church.

> "The qualification of a treaty as a concordat depends only upon its object and purpose, not upon the name or outward form chosen by the parties. Although the term originally was also used for treaties between States, it has increasingly become restricted to only those treaties concluded with the Holy See." Heribert Franz Köck, "Concordats," in 1 *Encyclopedia of Public International Law* 164 (1992).

2. *Hist. Eccles. law.* An agreement between ecclesiastical persons concerning a benefice, such as a resignation or promotion. See BENEFICE. **3.** An agreement between secular persons or entities.

concordatory (kən-**kor**-də-tor-ee), *adj.* (1896) Of, relating to, or involving a concordat, esp. one between church and state in France.

Concordia discordantium canonum (kon-**kor**-dee-ə dis-kor-**dan**-shee-əm kə-**nohn**-əm). [Latin "the harmony of the discordant canons"] *Hist.* A collection of ecclesiastical authorities compiled by Gratian, an Italian monk, ca. 1140. • Gratian analyzed questions of law by drawing conclusions from side-by-side comparisons of a variety of texts. Later canonist scholarship usu. proceeded from Gratian's work. — Also termed *Decretum Gratiani; Decretum.*

> "Another body of jurisprudence was coming into being. From humble beginnings the canon law had grown into a mighty system. Already it asserted its right to stand beside or above the civil law. The civil law might be the law of earth, *ius soli;* here was the law of heaven, *ius poli.* . . . Many men had been endeavouring to state that law, but the fame of earlier labourers was eclipsed by that of Gratian. A monk of Bologna, that city which was the centre of the new secular jurisprudence, he published . . . a book which he called *Concordia discordantium canonum,* but which was soon to become for all mankind simply the *Decretum Gratiani,* or yet more simply the *Decretum.* It is a great law-book. The spirit which animated its author was not that of a theologian, not that of an ecclesiastical ruler, but that of a lawyer. . . . The Decretum soon became an authoritative text-book and the canonist seldom went behind it. . . . The canonist had for it rather that reverence which English lawyers have paid to Coke upon Littleton . . . ." 1 Frederick Pollock & Frederic W. Maitland, *The History of English Law Before the Time of Edward I* 112–13 (2d ed. 1898).

concourse (**kon**-kors *or* **kong**-). (17c) *Scots law.* **1.** The simultaneous existence of two actions based on the same facts, esp. a civil action and a criminal action; the concurrence of a public prosecutor in a private prosecution. **2.** The concurrence of the public prosecutor to a criminal prosecution by a private person.

> "A private party may prosecute for the punishment of an offence perpetrated against himself, and for which the public prosecutor may refuse to prosecute at the public expense; but the concourse of the public prosecutor is necessary, and it cannot be refused; or if refused, the case may proceed at the instance of the private party. *Concourse* is distinguished from *Instance.* In the former case the public prosecutor merely concurs or consents, whilst in the latter case he is also a principal party prosecuting for the public interest." Hugh Barclay, *A Digest of the Law of Scotland* 162 (3d ed. 1865).

3. A conflict among creditors or claimants. See CONCURSUS (1).

concubinage (kon-**kyoo**-bə-nij), *n.* (14c) **1.** The relationship of a man and woman who cohabit without the benefit of marriage. **2.** The quality, state, or condition of being a concubine. **3.** *Hist.* A plea in a dower action made by a defendant who asserts that the plaintiff is the defendant's concubine rather than wife.

> "*Concubinage,* in common Acceptation is the Keeping of a Whore or Concubine: But in a legal Sense, it is used as an Exception against her that sueth for Dower, alledging thereby that she was not a Wife lawfully married to the Party, in whose Lands she seeks to be endowed, but his *Concubine.*" Giles Jacob, *A New Law-Dictionary* (8th ed. 1762).

concubinatus (kon-kyoo-bi-**nay**-təs), *n.* [Latin "concubinage"] (16c) *Roman law.* A permanent, monogamous union of a man and a woman who are not legally married. • *Concubinatus* was not prohibited by law, but carried fewer benefits than a legal marriage. Cf. JUSTAE NUPTIAE.

> "[C]oncubinage (*concubinatus*) . . . was something to which we have no precise analogue in modern law, for, so far from being prohibited by the law, it was regulated thereby, being treated as a lawful connexion. It is almost a sort of unequal marriage (and is practically so described by some of the jurists) existing between persons of different station — the man of superior rank, the woman of a rank so much inferior that it is not to be presumed that his union with her was intended to be a marriage." James Bryce, "Marriage and Divorce under Roman and English Law," in 3 *Select Essays in Anglo-American Legal History* 806–07 (1909).

concubine (**kong**-kyə-bɪn). (13c) **1.** *Archaic.* A woman who cohabits with a man to whom she is not married. • A concubine is often considered a wife without title. A concubine's status arises from the permanent cohabitation of a man and a woman as husband and wife although without the benefit of marriage. Cf. *common-law wife* under WIFE; COURTESAN. **2.** *Hist. Eccles. law.* A secondary or inferior wife, usu. in a polygamous marriage, who lacks the full rights and privileges of the first wife. • Although a concubine was expected to serve all the functions of a legitimate wife, she had no authority in the family or household, and was denied certain legal protections. For instance, her husband could easily disown her, she had no dower rights, and her children could not inherit from their father if he had children by his first wife. A concubine was also barred from certain spiritual comforts, such as churching after the birth of a child.

concubitor (kən-**kyoo**-bi-tor), *n.* (16c) Someone who keeps a concubine.

concur (kən-**kər**), *vb.* (15c) **1.** To agree; to consent. **2.** In a judicial opinion, to agree with the judgment in the case (usu. as expressed in the opinion of another judge), or the opinion of another judge, but often for different reasons or through a different line of reasoning. **3.** (Of a house in a bicameral legislature) to accept an amendment passed by the other house.

> "When a bill has been amended in the second house and passed with the amendment, it is returned by that house to the house of its origin with a message stating the facts and requesting the house where the bill originated to concur in the amendment." National Conference of State Legislatures, *Mason's Manual of Legislative Procedure* § 766, at 553 (2000).

4. *Civil law.* To join with other claimants in presenting a demand against an insolvent estate.

concurator (kon- *or* kən-**kyuur**-ə-tər). (18c) *Civil law.* A joint guardian or co-curator. See CURATOR.

concurrence. (15c) **1.** Agreement; assent. **2.** A vote cast by a judge in favor of the judgment reached, often on grounds differing from those expressed in the opinion or opinions explaining the judgment.

▸ **special concurrence.** (1852) A vote cast by a judge in favor of the result reached, but on grounds different from those expressed in the opinion explaining the court's judgment or in order to state views not expressed by the court. *See, e.g., Ex parte Wynn*, 804 So.2d 1153, 1153 (Ala. 2001) (Houston, J., concurring specially); *Ex parte Stonewall Ins. Co.*, 562 So.2d 1314 (Ala. 1990) (Maddox, J., concurring specially); *Toombs Cnty. v. O'Neal*, 330 S.E.2d 95, 98 (Ga. 1985) (Weltner, J., concurring specially).

3. A separate written opinion explaining such a vote. — Also termed (in sense 3) *concurring opinion.*

> "Though the judges of appellate courts do not feel obligated to explain their judicial votes in full by disclosing in every case the extent to which they agree or disagree with each thought expressed in the court's opinion, it is nevertheless common practice to express differences of opinion on some occasions through concurring opinions. Such concurring opinions often serve as the robins that foretell a new spring. They give notice of the possibility of change by expressing minority views that may become majority views in the future for a variety of reasons — among them, changing views and changing personnel of the court. Coincidentally, they reduce the force of the majority opinion as precedent, increasing the likelihood that the rule there stated will be abandoned at some time in the future." Robert E. Keeton, *Venturing to Do Justice: Reforming Private Law* 29 (1969).

4. Acceptance by one house in a bicameral legislature of an amendment passed by the other house. **5.** A coincidence of equal powers.

concurrency, *n.* (17c) **1.** *Archaic.* The quality, state, or condition of being concurrent in jurisdiction; joint right or authority. **2.** *Criminal procedure.* An identical duration for two or more criminal sentences assessed against the same defendant.

concurrent, *adj.* (14c) **1.** Operating at the same time; covering the same matters <concurrent interests>. **2.** Having authority on the same matters <concurrent jurisdiction>.

concurrent cause. See CAUSE (1).

concurrent condition. See CONDITION (2).

concurrent consideration. See CONSIDERATION (1).

concurrent covenant. See COVENANT (1).

concurrent estate. See ESTATE (1).

concurrent finding. See FINDING OF FACT.

concurrent interest. See *concurrent estate* under ESTATE (1).

concurrent jurisdiction. See JURISDICTION.

concurrent lease. See LEASE.

concurrent lien. See LIEN.

concurrent negligence. See NEGLIGENCE.

concurrent policy. See INSURANCE POLICY.

concurrent power. See POWER (3).

concurrent registration. (1947) *Trademarks.* The approved recording of identical or similar marks by multiple owners if each mark was commercially used before the owners applied for registration and the risk of consumer confusion is slight. • The U.S. Patent and Trademark Office may impose restrictions on each mark's use to prevent consumer confusion.

concurrent remedy. See REMEDY.

concurrent representation. See REPRESENTATION (2).

concurrent resolution. See RESOLUTION (1).

concurrent-sentence doctrine. (1969) The principle that an appellate court affirming a conviction and sentence need not hear a challenge to a conviction on another count if the conviction on the other count carries a sentence that is equal to or less than the affirmed conviction.

concurrent sentences. See SENTENCE.

concurrent tortfeasors. See TORTFEASOR.

concurrent writ. See WRIT.

concurring opinion. See CONCURRENCE (3).

concurso (kon- *or* kən-**kər**-soh), *n.* [Latin lit. "to run hither and thither"] *Civil law.* An action in which a creditor seeks to enforce a claim against an insolvent debtor.

concursus (kon- *or* kən-**kər**-səs). [Latin "a running together"] (16c) **1.** *Civil & Scots law.* An equitable proceeding in which two or more creditors claim, usu. adversely to each other, an interest in a fund or estate so that they can sort out and adjudicate all the claims on the fund. See CONCOURSE (3). **2.** *Civil law.* INTERPLEADER. **3.** *Eccles. law.* An examination to determine a person's fitness for parochial office.

concursus debiti et crediti (kən-**kər**-səs **deb**-i-tɪ et **cred**-i-tɪ). [Law Latin] *Scots law.* A running together of debt and credit. • The phrase appears in reference to requirements for supporting a plea of compensation.

> "Concursus debiti et crediti . . . . This is necessary to found a plea of compensation, for the parties must be debtor and creditor, each in his own right and at the same time. Thus, if A sue B for payment of a debt due by him, B may plead in compensation a debt due to him by A, and here there is the necessary concurrence. But, if the firm of which A is a partner suing B for a debt due by him to them, be met by the plea of compensation by B, on the ground of a private debt due by A, the plea will not be sustained, for there is no *concursus*; a company being regarded by the law as a separate person." John Trayner, *Trayner's Latin Maxims* 88–89 (4th ed. 1894).

concursus in delicto (kon- *or* kən-**kər**-səs in də-**lik**-toh). [Latin] Cooperation in crime.

concussio (kən-**kəsh**-ee-oh), *n.* [Latin] (17c) *Roman law.* The offense of extorting money or gifts by threat of violence. • In modern civil-law contexts, the term is often anglicized to *concussion.* — **concuss,** *vb.*

concussionary, *n.* (17c) *Archaic.* Someone who extorts from others under guise of authority; one who practices concussion.

condedit (kən-**dee**-dit *or* -**ded**-it). [Latin "he made (a will)"] *Eccles. law.* A defensive plea filed by a party in response to an ecclesiastical-court libel (i.e., complaint) questioning the veracity of a will or the competency of the testator. — Also spelled *condidit.*

condemn, *vb.* (14c) **1.** To judicially pronounce (someone) guilty; to judicially sentence. **2.** To determine and declare (property) to be assigned to public use. See EMINENT DOMAIN. **3.** To adjudge (a building) as being unfit for habitation. **4.** To adjudge (food or drink) as being unfit for human consumption. **5.** *Maritime law.* To declare (a vessel) to be forfeited to the government, to be a prize, or to be unfit for service.

condemnation (kon-dem-**nay**-shən), *n.* (14c) **1.** The act of judicially pronouncing someone guilty; conviction. **2.** The determination and declaration that certain property (esp. land) is assigned to public use, subject to reasonable compensation; the exercise of eminent domain by a governmental entity. See EMINENT DOMAIN.

▸ **constructive condemnation.** See *inverse condemnation.*

▸ **excess condemnation.** (1921) A taking of land in excess of the boundaries of the public project as designed by the condemnor.

▸ **inverse condemnation.** (1932) An action brought by a property owner for compensation from a governmental entity that has taken the owner's property without bringing formal condemnation proceedings. — Also termed *constructive condemnation; reverse condemnation;* (in civil law) *injurious affection.*

▸ **quick condemnation.** (1918) The immediate taking of possession of private property for public use, whereby the estimated compensation is deposited in court or paid to the condemnee until the actual amount of compensation can be established. — Also termed *quick-take.*

▸ **reverse condemnation.** See *inverse condemnation.*

3. An official pronouncement that a building is unfit for habitation; the act of making such a pronouncement. **4.** The official pronouncement that a thing (such as food or drink) is unfit for use or consumption; the act of making such a pronouncement. **5.** *Maritime law.* The declaration that a vessel is forfeited to the government, is a prize, or is unfit for service.

condemnation blight. (1969) **1.** The reduction in value that the property targeted for condemnation suffers in anticipation of the taking. **2.** The physical deterioration of property targeted for condemnation in anticipation of the taking.

condemnation money. (18c) **1.** Damages that a losing party in a lawsuit is condemned to pay. **2.** Compensation paid by an expropriator of land to the landowner for taking the property.

condemnation proceeding. (1806) A statutorily authorized lawsuit for the taking of private property for public use without the owner's consent. See EMINENT DOMAIN.

condemnatory (kən-**dem**-nə-tor-ee), *adj.* (16c) **1.** Condemning; expressing condemnation or censure. **2.** Of, relating to, or involving the use of eminent domain or expropriation.

condemnee (kon-dem-**nee**). (1890) One whose property is expropriated for public use or taken by a public-works project.

condemnor (kon-dem-**nor** *or* kən-**dem**-nər). (1890) A person or entity that expropriates property for public use. — Also spelled *condemner* (kən-**dem**-nər).

condensate. See DISTILLATE (1).

condescendence (kon-di-**sen**-dənts), *n.* (17c) *Scots law.* A statement of facts in a civil pleading, set out in consecutively numbered paragraphs, that the claimant relies on to justify the claim.

condictio (kən-**dik**-shee-oh), *n.* [fr. Latin *condicere* "to demand back"] *Roman & civil law.* A personal action in the nature of demanding something back, esp. by means of an extraordinary remedy; an action of debt. • In the sense here used, *debt* must be understood broadly to cover not only contractual but also quasi-contractual or tort claims. *Condictio* is usu. founded on an obligation to give or do a certain thing or service. — Also termed *condiction; action of debt.* Pl. **condictiones** (kən-dik-shee-**oh**-neez). — **condictitious, condictious** *adj.*

> "Condiction was a form of legal procedure . . . first applied to the recovery of a loan of a definite sum of money, and

afterwards applied to a loan of other things ('fungibles') where the return of the loan was required in quantity and quality, but not the identical things; in fact, where the borrower undertook to repay not *this*, but *so much* of the article and quality received. When condiction was applied to such things, it was said to be called *triticaria* ('relating to wheat') from one of the most important subjects, but this action (*condictio triticaria*) was afterwards extended so as to include all cases where things certain, other than coined money, were redemanded. In practice the term *triticaria* was not used, or Justinian has cut it out." 2 Henry John Roby, *Roman Private Law in the Times of Cicero and of the Antonines* 76 (1902).

"The principal *actio stricti juris* was the *condictio*, a general term with many applications. It might be brought for a certain sum of money (*condictio certae pecuniae*), or for some other certain thing (*condictio triticaria*), or to assert an illiquid claim (*condictio incerti*). The various forms of *condictio* were also distinguished according to the cause which gave rise to them, as *condictio furtiva, condictio indebiti*, and others . . . ." R.W. Lee, *The Elements of Roman Law* 435 (4th ed. 1956).

▸ ***condictio causa data, causa non secuta*** (kən-**dik**-shee-oh **kaw**-zə **day**-tə, **kaw**-zə non si-**kyoo**-tə). [Latin "claim for recovery, consideration having been given but consideration not having followed"] (18c) *Roman & civil law.* An action for recovery of money paid when the consideration for the payment has not been furnished. • The classic case in Scotland concerned an advance payment for ship's engines: war broke out, the engines were requisitioned but never supplied, and the payment was held to be recoverable. Pl. ***condictiones causa data, causa non secuta.***

▸ ***condictio certi*** (kən-**dik**-shee-oh **sər**-tɪ). [Latin "claim for recovery of a certain sum or thing"] An action based on a promise to do a thing, where the promise is certain.

▸ ***condictio ex causa furtiva*** (kən-**dik**-shee-oh eks **kaw**-zə fər-**tɪ**-və). See *condictio rei furtivae.*

▸ ***condictio ex lege*** (kən-**dik**-shee-oh eks **lee**-jee). [Latin "claim for recovery under a statute"] (18c) An action arising where a statute creates an obligation but provides no remedy.

"The *condictiones ex lege* were established on equitable grounds to meet cases growing out of a new law for which no formula had been provided. Sometimes they were called 'actiones in factum praescriptis verbis'; sometimes 'condictiones.'" John George Phillimore, *Private Law Among the Romans* 287 (1863).

▸ ***condictio furtiva*** (kən-**dik**-shee-oh fər-**tɪ**-və). See *condictio rei furtivae.*

▸ ***condictio incerti*** (kən-**dik**-shee-oh in-**sər**-tɪ). [Latin "claim for recovery of an uncertain amount"] An action to recover an uncertain amount.

▸ ***condictio indebiti*** (kən-**dik**-shee-oh in-**deb**-ə-tɪ). [Latin "claim for recovery of something not due"] (17c) An action to prevent the unjust enrichment of a defendant who had received money or property from the plaintiff by mistake. — Also termed *actio condictio indebiti* (though strictly speaking this is a solecism).

"The 'condictio indebiti' is a personal action arising from an obligation of natural equity, in which money not due, paid by mistake, is claimed as if it had been a loan. This arises from natural equity, it is numbered among the 'quasi contractus' in the Institutes. Not only therefore may the person who has paid the money employ this remedy, but he who is injured by such payment may have recourse to it, and might recover all that the receiver had gained." John George Phillimore, *Private Law Among the Romans* 281 (1863).

▸ ***condictio ob rem dati, re non secuta*** (kən-**dik**-shee-oh ahb rem **day**-tɪ, ree non si-**kyoo**-tə). [Latin "personal claim based on a transfer made for a purpose that has failed"] *Roman law.* A condiction for something handed over for a purpose that has failed, as for the settlement of a lawsuit when in fact the lawsuit has nevertheless continued.

▸ ***condictio ob turpem vel injustam causam*** (kən-**dik**-shee-oh ahb **tər**-pəm vel in-**jəs**-təm **kaw**-zəm). [Latin "personal claim based on an immoral or illegal cause"] *Roman law.* A personal claim by an innocent party to recover money or property paid for an immoral or illegal purpose. — Sometimes shortened to *condictio ob turpem causam.*

"The *condictio ob turpem vel iniustam causam* lay where the payment or conveyance had been made for an immoral or illegal purpose (e.g. to induce the recipient not to commit a crime, or to return what he had borrowed and was wrongfully refusing to return). But the plaintiff must not be equally tainted by the 'turpitude,' as he would be, for example, if the payment had been made to induce the recipient to commit a crime." Barry Nicholas, *An Introduction to Roman Law* 230 (1962).

▸ ***condictio rei furtivae*** (kən-**dik**-shee-oh **ree**-ɪ fər-**tɪ**-vee). [Latin "claim for recovery of a stolen thing"] An action to recover a stolen thing or its value if the thing could not be returned. • A *condictio rei furtivae* could be brought by an owner or pledgee against the thief or the thief's heirs. — Also termed *condictio furtiva; condictio ex causa furtiva.*

▸ ***condictio sine causa*** (kən-**dik**-shee-oh **sɪ**-nee **kaw**-zə). [Latin "claim for recovery of money or a thing given without consideration"] An action for the recovery of property transferred without consideration and in contemplation of a specific event that did not occur, such as a dowry made in view of a marriage that does not take place.

▸ ***condictio triticaria*** (kən-**dik**-shee-oh trɪ-ti-**kair**-ee-ə). [Latin "claim for recovery of wheat"] An action for the recovery of a specified quantity of a named commodity.

condiction. *Civil law.* See CONDICTIO.

condidit. See CONDEDIT.

condign justice. See JUSTICE (4).

conditio (kən-**dish**-ee-oh). [Latin] A condition.

▸ ***conditio per quam*** (kən-**dish**-ee-oh pər **kwam**). [Latin] *Hist.* Condition by means of which.

▸ ***conditio sine qua non.*** See SINE QUA NON.

▸ ***conditio si sine liberis decesserit*** (kən-**dish**-ee-oh sɪ **sɪ**-nee **lib**-ər-is di-**ses**-ər-it). [Latin "the condition if he should have died childless"] (18c) *Roman law.* An express or implied clause in a will providing that if the heir or legatee dies childless, the property is to go to another person, such as the testator's own descendants; a residuary clause.

condition, *n.* (14c) **1.** A future and uncertain event on which the existence or extent of an obligation or liability depends; an uncertain act or event that triggers or negates a duty to render a promised performance. • For example, if Jones promises to pay Smith $500 for repairing a car, Smith's failure to repair the car (an implied or constructive condition) relieves Jones of the promise to pay.

"'Condition' is used in this Restatement to denote an event which qualifies a duty under a contract. It is recognized that 'condition' is used with a wide variety of other meanings in legal discourse. Sometimes it is used to denote an event that limits or qualifies a transfer of property. In the law of trusts, for example, it is used to denote an event such as the death of the settlor that qualifies his disposition of property in trust. Sometimes it is used to refer to a term in an agreement that makes an event a condition, or more broadly to refer to any term in an agreement (e.g., 'standard conditions of sale'). For the sake of precision, 'condition' is not used here in these other senses." Restatement (Second) of Contracts § 224 cmt. a (1981).

"Strictly, a condition is a fact or event on the occurrence of which some legal right or duty comes into existence; a party may promise that this fact is so, or that the event will take place, but it is equally possible that no party to the contract promises this. An insurance company promises to pay £10,000 to an insured person if his house is destroyed by fire; the destruction of the house by fire is a condition of the insurer's promise to pay, but neither party promises to burn the house." P.S. Atiyah, *An Introduction to the Law of Contract* 146 (3d ed. 1981).

"Promises and the duties they generate can be either unconditional ('I promise to pay you $100,000') or conditional ('I promise to pay you $100,000 if your house burns down'). Lawyers use *condition* in several senses. Sometimes they use it to refer to the term in the agreement that makes the promise conditional. . . . However, lawyers also use *condition* to refer to an operative fact rather than to a term. According to the Restatement Second a condition is 'an event, not certain to occur, which must occur, unless occurrence is excused, before performance under a contract becomes due.' This use of the word has the support of leading writers." E. Allan Farnsworth, *Contracts* § 8.2, at 519–20 (3d ed. 1999).

2. A stipulation or prerequisite in a contract, will, or other instrument, constituting the essence of the instrument. • If a court construes a contractual term to be a condition, then its untruth or breach will entitle the party to whom it is made to be discharged from all liabilities under the contract.

▸ **affirmative condition.** See *positive condition.*

▸ **casual condition.** (1873) *Civil law.* A condition that depends on chance; one that is not within the power of either party to an agreement.

▸ **collateral condition.** (17c) A condition that requires the performance of an act having no relation to an agreement's main purpose.

▸ **compulsory condition.** (1876) A condition expressly requiring that a thing be done, such as a tenant's paying rent on a certain day.

▸ **concurrent condition.** (1840) A condition that must occur or be performed at the same time as another condition, the performance by each party separately operating as a condition precedent; a condition that is mutually dependent on another, arising when the parties to a contract agree to exchange performances simultaneously. — Also termed *condition concurrent.*

"*Conditions concurrent* are acts that the parties to a contract are under duties of performing concurrently, the act of each party being separately operative as a condition precedent. The act is not concurrent with the legal relation affected, but only with the act of the other party." William R. Anson, *Principles of the Law of Contract* 412–13 (Arthur L. Corbin ed., 3d Am. ed. 1919).

▸ **condition implied by law.** See *constructive condition.*

▸ **condition implied in law.** See *constructive condition.*

▸ **condition precedent** (prə-**seed**-ənt *also* **pres**-ə-dənt). (1818) An act or event, other than a lapse of time, that must exist or occur before a duty to perform something promised arises. • If the condition does not occur and is not excused, the promised performance need not be rendered. The most common condition contemplated by this phrase is the immediate or unconditional duty of performance by a promisor.

▸ **condition subsequent.** (1818) A condition that, if it occurs, will bring something else to an end; an event the existence of which, by agreement of the parties, discharges a duty of performance that has arisen.

"A condition subsequent affects an interest which is already vested; and it either diminishes or defeats that interest. Thus a conveyance to A and his heirs, but if he marry B, then to him only for his life, and an estate to C for years or for life or in fee, provided, however, that he is to lose it if D come back from Rome, or if he fail to erect a building upon it, are estates on condition subsequent.

"When a condition is seen to affect an estate, the courts prefer to treat it, if reasonably possible, as subsequent rather than precedent. This is a very strong and frequently illustrated preference; and it is also a conspicuous application of the general principle, running through all the common law, that a right or an interest once conveyed or transferred, which may be looked upon as great and important or as of lesser significance, shall be treated and construed preferably in the former sense. The determination of whether a condition is precedent or subsequent depends ultimately on the intention of the parties as ascertained from their language and all the facts of the case; but, when such intent does not clearly appear, the rule now followed, and based on this principle of preference, is that 'if the act or condition required do not necessarily precede the vesting of the estate, but may accompany or follow it, or if the act may as well be done after as before the vesting of the estate,' then the condition is subsequent." Alfred G. Reeves, *A Treatise on Special Subjects of the Law of Real Property* § 419, at 589–90 (1904).

"If . . . the deed or will uses such words as 'but if,' 'on condition that,' 'provided, however,' or 'if, however,' it will generally be assumed that a condition subsequent was intended." Thomas F. Bergin & Paul G. Haskell, *Preface to Estates in Land and Future Interests* 50 (2d ed. 1984).

▸ **constructive condition.** (1837) A condition contained in an essential contractual term that, though omitted by the parties from their agreement, a court has supplied as being reasonable in the circumstances; a condition imposed by law to do justice. • The cooperation of the parties to a contract, for example, is a constructive condition. — Also termed *implied-in-law condition; condition implied by law; condition implied in law.* Cf. *implied-in-fact condition.*

"[C]onstructive conditions are imposed by law to do justice. . . . The dividing line between an express condition . . . and constructive conditions is often quite indistinct. Yet, the distinction is often of crucial importance. The general rule governing an express condition is that it must be strictly performed. The general rule as to constructive conditions is that substantial compliance is sufficient." John D. Calamari & Joseph M. Perillo, *The Law of Contracts* § 11.8, at 402 (4th ed. 1998).

▸ **contingent condition.** (17c) An event that is outside either party's control but whose occurrence or nonoccurrence could determine whether a contractual promise is enforceable. • Examples include a pianist's agreement to entertain at an outdoor reception unless it rains, and a potential partner's agreement to manage a store if the other partners can secure funding.

▸ **copulative condition** (**kop**-yə-lə-tiv *or* -lay-tiv). (18c) A condition requiring the performance of more than one act. Cf. *disjunctive condition; single condition.*

▸ **dependent condition.** A mutual covenant that goes to the consideration on both sides of a contract.

▸ **disjunctive condition.** (17c) A condition requiring the performance of one of several acts to be chosen by the performer. Cf. *copulative condition; single condition.*

▸ **dissolving condition.** See *resolutory condition.*

▸ **express condition.** (16c) **1.** A condition that is the manifested intention of the parties. **2.** A condition that is explicitly stated in an instrument; a contractual condition that the parties have reduced to writing.

"[E]xpress conditions . . . are conditions created through the agreement of the parties. This is so whether the intention to have the duty subject to a condition be manifested in words, or through any other conduct or type of utterance." John Edward Murray Jr., *Murray on Contracts* § 143, at 290 (2d ed. 1974).

▸ **implied condition.** (17c) A condition that is not expressly mentioned, but is imputed by law from the nature of the transaction or the conduct of the parties to have been tacitly understood between them as a part of the agreement. See *constructive condition; implied-in-fact condition.*

▸ **implied-in-fact condition.** (1946) A contractual condition that the parties have implicitly agreed to by their conduct or by the nature of the transaction. Cf. *constructive condition.*

▸ **implied-in-law condition.** See *constructive condition.*

▸ **inherent condition.** (18c) A condition that is an intrinsic part of an agreement; a condition that is not newly imposed but is already present in an agreement.

▸ **lawful condition.** (16c) A condition that can be fulfilled without violating the law.

▸ **mixed condition.** (18c) *Civil law.* A condition that depends either on the will of one party and the will of a third person, or on the will of one party and the happening of a causal event.

▸ **negative condition.** (17c) A condition forbidding a party from doing a certain thing, such as prohibiting a tenant from subletting leased property; a promise not to do something, usu. as part of a larger agreement. See *negative easement* under EASEMENT. — Also termed *restrictive condition.*

▸ **positive condition.** (17c) A condition that requires some act, such as paying rent. — Also termed *affirmative condition.*

▸ **potestative condition** (**poh**-tes-tə-tiv). (17c) *Civil law.* A condition that it is within the power (*potestas*) or will of the obligor to fulfill. • A condition is purely potestative when its fulfillment depends solely on the will of a party. Louisiana no longer uses this term, instead providing that a condition that depends solely on the whim of the obligor makes the obligation null. La. Civ. Code art. 1770. Cf. *suspensive condition; resolutory condition.*

▸ **precondition.** (1825) A stipulated act or event that must occur before either party to a contract will be bound by the contract; a prerequisite.

▸ **preexisting condition.** (1921) *Insurance.* A physical or mental condition evident during the period before the effective date of a medical-insurance policy. • Typically, coverage for later treatment for such a condition is excluded if symptoms of the condition were present during the period before the policy was effective.

▸ **promissory condition.** (1874) A condition that is also a promise.

"The distinction between a condition which is also a promise, and a condition which is not the subject of a promise, is often one of great difficulty and importance, especially where the term is implied and not expressed, and it is unfortunate that legal usage has sanctioned the word 'condition' for two such different concepts. It would at least be desirable if lawyers could be persuaded to refer to conditions which are the subject of a promise as 'promissory conditions,' a usage which it is proposed to adopt here." P.S. Atiyah, *An Introduction to the Law of Contract* 147 (3d ed. 1981).

▸ **resolutory condition** (rə-**zol**-yə-tor-ee). (1839) *Civil law.* **1.** A condition that upon fulfillment terminates an already enforceable obligation and entitles the parties to be restored to their original positions. **2.** *Louisiana law.* A conditional obligation that may be immediately enforced but will come to an end when an uncertain event that is specified occurs. La. Civ. Code art. 1767. — Also termed *resolutive condition; dissolving condition.* Cf. *potestative condition.*

▸ **restrictive condition.** See *negative condition.*

▸ **single condition.** (17c) A condition requiring the performance of a specified thing. Cf. *copulative condition; disjunctive condition.*

▸ **suspensive condition.** (17c) *Civil law.* A condition that makes an obligation mandatory only if a specified but uncertain event occurs. Cf. *potestative condition.*

▸ **testamentary condition.** (1905) A condition that must be satisfied before a gift made in a will becomes effective.

▸ **triggering condition.** (1972) A circumstance that must exist before a legal doctrine applies; esp., in criminal law, a circumstance that must exist before an actor will be entitled to a justification defense.

▸ **unlawful condition.** (17c) A condition that cannot be fulfilled without violating the law.

3. Loosely, a term, provision, or clause in a contract.

"This term *condition* is generally used to describe any fact, subsequent to the formation of a contract, which operates to make the duty of a promisor immediately active and compelling. Such a fact may be described as such in a term of the contract or it may not. In either event, the *term* of the contract should not itself be called the *condition*. . . . It is not uncommon, popularly, to speak of a condition of the contract as synonymous with *term* or *provision* of the contract. This should be avoided." William R. Anson, *Principles of the Law of Contract* 226 n.1 (Arthur L. Corbin ed., 3d Am. ed. 1919).

"The word 'condition' is used in the law of property as well as in the law of contract and it is sometimes used in a very loose sense as synonymous with 'term,' 'provision,' or 'clause.' In such a sense it performs no useful service." *Id.* at 409.

4. A qualification attached to the conveyance of property providing that if a particular event does or does not take place, the estate will be created, enlarged, defeated, or transferred. **5.** A state of being; an essential quality or status. — **condition,** *vb.*

▸ **artificial condition.** A physical characteristic of real property, brought about by a person's affirmative act instead of by natural forces.

▸ **dangerous condition.** (1850) **1.** A property defect creating a substantial risk of injury when the property is used in a reasonably foreseeable manner. • A dangerous condition may result in waiver of sovereign immunity. **2.** A property risk that children, because of their immaturity, cannot appreciate or avoid. Cf. *attractive nuisance* under NUISANCE.

conditional, *adj.* (14c) Subject to or dependent on a condition <a conditional sale>.

conditional acceptance. See ACCEPTANCE (3).

conditional adjournment. See ADJOURNMENT (1).

conditional admissibility. See ADMISSIBILITY.

conditional assault. See ASSAULT.

conditional assignment. See ASSIGNMENT (2).

conditional bequest. See BEQUEST.

conditional contraband. See CONTRABAND.

conditional contract. See CONTRACT.

conditional conveyance. See CONVEYANCE (1).

conditional covenant. See COVENANT (1).

conditional creditor. See CREDITOR.

conditional delivery. See DELIVERY.

conditional devise. See DEVISE.

conditional discharge. *Criminal procedure.* A revocable sentence imposed usu. for a minor offense, such as a misdemeanor, a violation, or an infraction; a judicial agreement to impose no penalty for such an offense if the violator does not commit another offense, esp. within a certain time frame. — Abbr. CD.

conditional divorce. See *conversion divorce* under DIVORCE.

conditional driver's license. See DRIVER'S LICENSE.

conditional duty. See DUTY (1).

conditional endorsement. See *conditional indorsement* under INDORSEMENT.

conditional estate. See *estate on condition* under ESTATE (1).

conditional examination. (1847) *Criminal procedure.* A pretrial deposition usu. taken on motion with a showing of exceptional circumstances, as where an elderly witness may die before trial or otherwise be unavailable.

conditional fee. 1. See *fee simple conditional* under FEE SIMPLE. **2.** See CONTINGENT FEE.

conditional fee agreement. (1990) *English law.* A contract between a lawyer and a client that provides for the lawyer to receive a fee only if the client wins the case. • Unlike American contingent-fee arrangements, the lawyer does not receive a percentage of the damages awarded but instead charges the client a base fee plus a success fee, which is usu. calculated as a percentage of up to 100% of the base fee. See *success fee* under FEE (1).

conditional gift. See GIFT.

conditional guaranty. See GUARANTY (1).

conditional indorsement. See INDORSEMENT.

conditional judgment. See JUDGMENT (2).

conditional legacy. See LEGACY (1).

conditional license. See *provisional license* (1) under LICENSE.

conditional limitation. See LIMITATION (4).

conditionally privileged communication. See COMMUNICATION.

conditional national treatment. See NATIONAL TREATMENT.

conditional obligation. See OBLIGATION.

conditional offer. See OFFER (2).

conditional pardon. See PARDON (1).

conditional payment. See PAYMENT (2).

conditional plea. See PLEA (1).

conditional presumption. See *rebuttable presumption* under PRESUMPTION.

conditional privilege. See *qualified privilege* under PRIVILEGE (1).

conditional promise. See PROMISE.

conditional proof. See PROOF.

conditional purpose. (16c) **1.** An intention to do something, conditions permitting. **2.** *Criminal law.* A possible defense against a crime if the conditions make committing the crime impossible (e.g., "I will steal the money if it's there," and the money is not there).

conditional release. See RELEASE (8).

conditional revocation. See DEPENDENT RELATIVE REVOCATION.

conditional right. See RIGHT.

conditional sale. See SALE.

conditional sales contract. See *retail installment contract* under CONTRACT.

conditional sentence. See SENTENCE.

conditional use. See USE (1).

conditional-use permit. See SPECIAL-USE PERMIT.

conditional-use zoning. See *conditional zoning* under ZONING.

conditional will. See WILL.

conditional zoning. See ZONING.

condition concurrent. See *concurrent condition* under CONDITION (2).

condition implied by law. See *constructive condition* under CONDITION (2).

condition implied in law. See *constructive condition* under CONDITION (2).

conditioning the market. (1959) *Securities law.* Arousing and stimulating investor interest in an issuer's offering of securities. See DIRECTED SELLING EFFORTS; GUN-JUMPING.

condition of employment. (1875) A qualification or circumstance required for obtaining or keeping a job.

condition precedent. See CONDITION (2).

conditions of sale. (16c) The terms under which an auction will be conducted. • The conditions of sale are usu. placed in the auction room for public viewing before the sale.

condition subsequent. See CONDITION (2).

conditio per quam. See CONDITIO.

condominia (kon-də-**min**-ee-ə). *Civil law.* Coownerships or limited ownerships. • *Condominia* are considered part of the *dominium* of the property, and thus are more than mere rights in the property (i.e., *jure in re aliena*); examples of *condominia* include *emphyteusis, superficies, pignus, hypotheca, usufructus, usus,* and *habitatio.*

condominium (kon-də-**min**-ee-əm). (1962) **1.** Ownership in common with others. **2.** A single real-estate unit in a multi-unit development in which a person has both separate ownership of a unit and a common interest, along with the development's other owners, in the common areas. Cf. COOPERATIVE (2). Pl. (in sense 2) **condominiums.**

"The condominium concept is not new, despite its relatively recent introduction in the United States. Ownership of individual units in buildings can be traced back to ancient Babylon; it was quite common in ancient Rome and in medieval Europe. The earliest condominium statute is Article 664 of the Code Napoleon of 1804, a very brief provision which was later substantially expanded. Condominium statutes were adopted in most nations in Europe, and in Central and South America, before any were adopted in the United States." Roger A. Cunningham et al., *The Law of Property* § 2.2, at 34 n.26 (2d ed. 1993).

3. Joint sovereignty by two or more countries. **4.** A politically dependent territory under such sovereignty. Pl. (in senses 3 & 4) **condominia.**

condonation (kon-də-**nay**-shən), *n.* (17c) **1.** A victim's express or (esp.) implied forgiveness of an offense, esp. by treating the offender as if there had been no offense. • Condonation is not usu. a valid defense to a crime. **2.** *Hist. Eccles. law.* One spouse's express or implied forgiveness of a marital offense by resuming marital life and sexual intimacy. • For example, one spouse might impliedly forgive the other spouse's infidelity by continuing to live with him or her. If adultery is charged as a ground for divorce and condonation is proved, the forgiving spouse is barred from proof of that offense. Cf. COLLUSION (2); CONNIVANCE (2); RECRIMINATION (2); RECONCILIATION (2).

condone (kən-**dohn**), *vb.* (1851) To voluntarily pardon or overlook (esp. an act of adultery). — **condonable** (kən-**dohn**-ə-bəl), *adj.*

conducere aliquid faciendum (kən-**d**[y]**oo**-sə-ree **al**-i-kwid fay-shee-**en**-dəm). [Latin] *Roman law.* To bind oneself to perform work for pay. Cf. LOCARE ALIQUID FACIENDUM.

conducere aliquid utendum (kən-**d**[y]**oo**-sə-ree **al**-i-kwid yoo-**ten**-dəm). [Latin] *Roman law.* To pay for the use of an object; to hire. Cf. LOCARE ALIQUID UTENDUM.

conduct, *n.* (15c) Personal behavior, whether by action or inaction, verbal or nonverbal; the manner in which a person behaves; collectively, a person's deeds. • Conduct does not include the actor's natural death or a death that results from behavior consciously engaged in but not reasonably expected to have this result. — **conduct,** *vb.*

"The word 'conduct' . . . covers both acts and omissions. . . . In cases in which a man is able to show that his conduct, whether in the form of action or of inaction, was involuntary, he must not be held liable for any harmful result produced by it . . . ." J.W. Cecil Turner, *Kenny's Outlines of Criminal Law* 13 n.2, 24 (16th ed. 1952).

▸ **active conduct.** (17c) Behavior that involves a person doing something by exerting will on the external world. Cf. *passive conduct.*

▸ **assertive conduct.** (1968) *Evidence.* Nonverbal behavior that is intended to be a statement, such as pointing one's finger to identify a suspect in a police lineup. • Assertive conduct is a statement under the hearsay rule, and thus it is not admissible unless a hearsay exception applies. Fed. R. Evid. 801(a)(2). — Also termed *implied assertion.*

▸ **contumacious conduct** (kon-t[y]oo-**may**-shəs). (18c) A willful disobedience of a court order. See CONTUMACY.

▸ **corrupt conduct.** (18c) Conduct that might or actually does adversely affect the honest and impartial exercise of official functions by a public official.

▸ **dangerous conduct.** See *unreasonably dangerous conduct.*

▸ **disorderly conduct.** (17c) Behavior that tends to disturb the public peace, offend public morals, or undermine public safety. See BREACH OF THE PEACE.

"At common law there was no offense known as disorderly conduct, although the offense of breaching the peace made many public disturbances criminal. In addition, this offense could be based on behavior that might cause another to respond in a violent manner even though the party guilty of the breach of the peace acted quietly or secretly, as when a person challenged someone to a duel. The enactment of statutes making disorderly conduct punishable went beyond the common-law notion of a breach of the peace by including behavior that merely tended to disturb the safety, health, or morals of others or that was intended only to annoy another. Further definitions were added later." Francis Barry McCarthy, "Vagrancy and Disorderly Conduct," in 4 *Encyclopedia of Crime and Justice* 1589, 1589 (Sanford H. Kadish ed., 1983).

▸ **disruptive conduct.** (1959) Disorderly conduct in the context of a governmental proceeding. See CONTEMPT.

▸ **involuntary conduct.** (1894) Actions that a person ordinarily may not want to take but cannot avoid when taken because of the influence of duress or some mental or physical condition.

▸ **nonassertive conduct.** (1965) *Evidence.* Behavior, esp. nonverbal, that is not intended to be a statement, such as fainting while being questioned as a suspect by a police officer. • Nonassertive conduct is not a statement under the hearsay rule, and thus it is admissible. Fed. R. Evid. 801.

▸ **outrageous conduct.** (18c) Conduct so extreme that it exceeds all reasonable bounds of human decency; behavior that is extremely shocking, offensive, or unfair. See *emotional distress* under DISTRESS (4).

▸ **passive conduct.** (1859) Behavior that does not involve exerting will on the external world. Cf. *active conduct.*

▸ **tortious conduct.** (1827) An act or omission that subjects the actor to liability under the principles of tort law.

▸ **unduly dangerous conduct.** See *unreasonably dangerous conduct.*

▸ **unprofessional conduct.** (1836) Behavior that is immoral, unethical, or dishonorable, esp. when judged by the standards of the actor's profession.

▸ **unreasonably dangerous conduct.** (1929) Conduct that involves undue risk under the circumstances. — Sometimes shortened to *dangerous conduct.* — Also termed *unduly dangerous conduct.*

▸ **wrongful conduct.** (1807) An act taken in violation of a legal duty; an act that unjustly infringes on another's rights. — Also termed *wrongful act.*

conductio (kən-**dək**-shee-oh), *n.* [Latin "a hiring"] (17c) *Roman law.* The hiring or leasing of services or property.

See *locatio conductio* under LOCATIO. Pl. ***conductiones*** (kən-dək-shee-**oh**-neez).

conduct money. See *witness fee* under FEE (1).

conductor (kən-**dək**-tər *or* -tor), *n.* [Latin "one who hires"] (17c) *Roman law.* **1.** A lessee or a person who hires the services of another; a hirer. **2.** A person hired to make a specific work; a contractor. • A contractor, esp. for the provision of public services, was also called *manceps* or *redemptor.* See MANCEPS; LOCATOR (1).

conductor operarum (kən-**dək**-tər [*or* -tor] op-ə-**rair**-əm). [Latin "a hirer of labor"] *Roman law.* Someone who hires another's labor, esp. manual labor, at a stated price; an employer.

conduct unbecoming a member of the bar. (1908) Behavior contrary to professional standards; esp., actions that show an unfitness to discharge continuing obligations to clients or the courts, and are therefore contrary to the administration of justice. *See In re Snyder,* 472 U.S. 634, 645, 105 S.Ct. 2874, 2881 (1985).

conductus (kən-**dək**-təs), *n.* [fr. Latin *conducere* "to hire"] *Roman law.* A person or thing hired by a *conductor.*

conduit taxation. See *pass-through taxation* under TAXATION (1).

confabulation (kən-fab-yə-**lay**-shən), *n.* (15c) **1.** The unconscious or, less often, conscious filling in of gaps in a person's own memory by imagining or fabricating events that do not necessarily have a basis in fact. • The person typically has no intention to deceive but instead believes the fabricated memories to be real. Confabulation in this psychological sense may result in a false allegation or confession of criminal conduct, often as a result of a mental disorder. **2.** A conference or discussion, esp. of an informal nature; a chat. — **confabulate,** *vb.*

confarreatio (kən-far-ee-**ay**-shee-oh), *n.* [Latin] (16c) *Roman law.* A religious ceremony used to wed members of the patrician class in ancient Rome. • By this ceremony, the wife was brought into the husband's family and placed under the husband's protection (*manus*). See MANUS (1). Cf. COEMPTIO; USUS (3). Pl. ***confarreationes*** (kən-far-ee-ay-shee-**oh**-neez).

> "Anciently, there were three modes in which marriage might be contracted according to Roman usage, one involving a religious solemnity, the other two the observance of certain secular formalities. By the religious marriage of *Confarreation*; by the higher form of civil marriage, which was called *Coemption*; and by the lower form, which was termed *Usus*, the Husband acquired a number of rights over the person and property of his wife, which were on the whole in excess of such as are conferred on him in any system of modern jurisprudence. But in what capacity did he acquire them? Not as *Husband*, but as *Father*. By the Confarreation, Coemption, and Usus, the woman passed *in manum viri*, that is, in law she became the *Daughter* of her husband. She was included in his Patria Potestas. . . . These three ancient forms of marriage fell, however, gradually into disuse, so that, at the most splendid period of Roman greatness, they had almost entirely given place to a fashion of wedlock — old apparently, but not hitherto considered reputable — which was founded on a modification of the lower form of civil marriage." Henry S. Maine, *Ancient Law* 149 (10th ed. 1884).

> "*Confarreatio* was a religious ceremony performed in the house of the bridegroom, to which the bride had been conveyed in the state, in the presence of at least ten witnesses and the *Pontifex Maximus*, or one of the higher priests. A set form of words (*carmen — verba concepta*) was repeated, and a sacred cake made of *Far* (*farreus panis*) — whence the term *Confarreatio* — was either tasted by or broken over the parties who sat during the performance of various rites, side by side, on a wooden seat made of an ox-yoke covered with the skin of the sheep which had previously been offered in sacrifice." William Ramsay, *A Manual of Roman Antiquities* 295 (Rodolfo Lanciani ed., 15th ed. 1894).

confectio (kən-**fek**-shee-oh), *n.* [Latin "a completing"] *Hist.* The act of making or executing a written instrument. Pl. ***confectiones*** (kən-fek-shee-**oh**-neez).

confederacy, *n.* (14c) **1.** A league of states or countries that have joined for mutual support or joint action; an alliance. **2.** An association of two or more persons, usu. for unlawful purposes; CONSPIRACY. **3.** The fact or condition of being allied or associated.

confederacy clause. (1892) *Archaic.* A clause in a complaint charging that the defendant or defendants have combined with others (who may yet be named as defendants) to defraud or deprive the plaintiff of personal rights.

confederate, *n.* (15c) Someone who helps someone else do something, esp. something secret or illegal; esp., a coconspirator or accomplice.

confederation. (15c) **1.** A group of people, political parties, or organizations that have unified for political purposes or trade. **2.** A league or union of states or countries, each of which retains its sovereignty but also delegates some rights and powers to a central authority. • The United States, for example, was first organized under the Articles of Confederation. Cf. FEDERATION.

> "A confederation is a union, more or less complete, of two or more states which before were independent. It aims to secure a common good, external, as mutual protection against powerful neighbors, or internal, as commerce and community of justice by means of common institutions." Theodore D. Woolsey, *Introduction to the Study of International Law* § 108, at 173 (5th ed. 1878).

▸ **confederation of states.** (18c) A confederation involving a central government that exists and exercises certain powers but does not control all the external relations of the member states. • For international purposes there exists not one but a number of states. Cf. *federal state* under STATE (1). — Often shortened to *confederation.*

> "A confederation is a governmental entity created by independent sovereign States that join together to perform some governmental functions under common authority . . . . A confederation is a stronger form of association than an alliance . . . , but is weaker than a federation. The individual member units retain their status as sovereign States, and are separately recognized as members of the international community. This distinguishes a confederation from a federation in which the constituent States surrender their sovereignty to a central authority retaining only internal constitutional autonomy. A confederation may also include additional territories that are dependent territories of one or more of the constituent States or, indeed, of the confederation itself. In order for an entity to be a confederation it must have institutions with authority to make specified decisions. These institutions may take the form of legislative or executive bodies or judicial institutions. The institutions need not be elaborate, but they must be more than mere diplomatic consultations or negotiations. A treaty merely creating standards or rules is not enough to establish a confederation. The confederation may, however, rely primarily on its constituent members to carry out its decisions." Fred L. Morrison, "Confederations of States," in 2 *The Max Planck Encyclopedia of Public International Law* 601, 602 (Rüdiger Wolfrum ed., 2012).

3. *Archaic.* An alliance; esp., in a negative sense, a conspiracy. 4. An organization consisting of private groups united by common interests or goals.

confer, *vb.* 1. To grant (something) as a gift, benefit, or honor; BESTOW <conferring an honorary degree>. 2. To bring together for the sake of scrutiny or comparison (usu. abbreviated *cf.*) <Cf. [this] *with* [that]>. 3. To hold a conference; to consult with one another <the parties are required to confer>.

conferee (kon-fər-**ee**). See MANAGER (2).

conference. (16c) 1. CONVENTION (3). 2. A meeting between the two houses of a bicameral legislature. See *conference committee* under COMMITTEE (1).

"It is proper for either house to request a conference with the other on any matter of difference or dispute between them. When a conference is requested, the subject of the conference should always be stated. One house may request a conference to inquire or protest concerning an offense or default on the part of a member or officer of the other house. When there is a question concerning procedure, or when an unparliamentary message has been sent, instead of replying directly, a conference should be requested. When there are questions as to procedure between the two houses, the proper procedure is to discuss the matter by a conference committee; also, where one house desires to formally present a question to the other, the question should be submitted through a conference committee." National Conference of State Legislatures, *Mason's Manual of Legislative Procedure* § 764, at 551 (2000).

3. A meeting held to deliberate on a subject and usu. decide how to proceed.

▸ **conference in chambers.** See *in-chambers conference.*

▸ **in-chambers conference.** (1945) A meeting in the judge's offices, esp. one during the pendency of a lawsuit, the attendees typically being the judge, counsel, and perhaps litigants, usu. for the purpose of advancing the proceedings or facilitating settlement of the dispute. — Also termed *conference in chambers.*

conference committee. See COMMITTEE (1).

conference in chambers. See *in-chambers conference* under CONFERENCE.

Conference of Chief Justices. An organization consisting of the highest judicial officers of all the states in the United States, the District of Columbia, the Commonwealth of Puerto Rico, the Commonwealth of the Northern Mariana Islands, and the territories of American Samoa, Guam, and the Virgin Islands. • Established in 1949, the organization seeks to improve the administration of justice in various ways, as by supporting adequate judicial funding, promoting the independence and effectiveness of state judicial systems, and advancing professionalism and lawyer competence. Since 1983, the organization has operated as a nonprofit corporation. — Abbr. CCJ.

confess, *vb.* (16c) To admit (an allegation) as true; to make a confession. — **confessor,** *n.*

confessed judgment. See CONFESSION OF JUDGMENT.

confessing error. A plea admitting to an assignment of error. See ASSIGNMENT OF ERROR.

confessio in judicio (kən-**fesh**-ee-oh in joo-**dish**-ee-oh). [Latin "confession in court"] *Hist.* An in-court confession.

confession, *n.* (14c) 1. A criminal suspect's oral or written acknowledgment of guilt, often including details about the crime. Cf. ADMISSION; STATEMENT (3).

"A confession is an acknowledgment in express words, by the accused in a criminal case, of the truth of the main fact charged or of some essential part of it." 3 John H. Wigmore, *Evidence in Trials at Common Law* § 821, at 308 (James H. Chadbourn ed., 4th rev. ed. 1970).

"The distinction between admissions in criminal cases and confessions by the accused is the distinction in effect between admissions of fact from which the guilt of the accused may be inferred by the jury and the express admission of guilt itself." William P. Richardson, *The Law of Evidence* § 394, at 268 (3d ed. 1928).

▸ **coerced-compliant confession.** (1995) A confession by a suspect who knows that he or she is innocent but is overcome by fatigue, the questioner's tactics, or a desire for some potential benefit. — Also termed *coerced-compliant false confession.*

▸ **coerced confession.** (1937) A confession that is obtained by threats or force.

▸ **direct confession.** (17c) A statement in which an accused person acknowledges having committed the crime.

▸ **extrajudicial confession.** (1813) A confession made out of court, and not as a part of a judicial examination or investigation. • Such a confession must be corroborated by some other proof of the corpus delicti, or else it is insufficient to warrant a conviction. Cf. *judicial confession.*

▸ **implied confession.** (16c) A confession in which the person does not plead guilty but invokes the mercy of the court and asks for a light sentence.

▸ **indirect confession.** (18c) A confession that is inferred from the defendant's conduct.

▸ **interlocking confession.** (1973) 1. A confession by one of two or more suspects whose statements are substantially the same and consistent concerning the elements of the crime. 2. A defendant's self-incriminating statement that implicates a codefendant and contains essentially the same information as the codefendant's self-incriminating statement.

▸ **involuntary confession.** (1830) A confession induced by the police or other law-enforcement authorities who make promises to, coerce, or deceive the suspect.

▸ **judicial confession.** (16c) A plea of guilty or some other direct manifestation of guilt in court or in a judicial proceeding. Cf. *extrajudicial confession.*

▸ **naked confession.** (18c) A confession unsupported by any evidence that a crime has been committed, and therefore usu. highly suspect.

▸ **oral confession.** (18c) A confession that is not made in writing. • Oral confessions are admissible, though as a practical matter police interrogators prefer to take written or recorded confessions since juries typically view these as being more reliable.

▸ **persuaded confession.** (1997) A false confession by a suspect who has no knowledge of a crime but adopts a belief in his or her guilt.

▸ **plenary confession** (**plee**-nə-ree *or* **plen**-ə). (1907) A complete confession; one that is believed to be conclusive against the person who made it.

▸ **relative confession.** (1898) *Hist.* A confession of guilt coupled with an accusation against another person as a participant in the crime. • If the accusation against the other person was proved, the accusing defendant was pardoned. If not, the defendant was convicted on the confession. *See State v. Willis*, 41 A. 820, 825 (Conn. 1898). See APPROVER (1).

▸ **threshold confession.** (1962) A spontaneous confession made promptly after arrest and without interrogation by the police. • The issue whether the defendant's statement is a threshold confession usu. arises when the defendant challenges the admissibility of the confession on grounds that he or she suffered an impermissibly long delay before being brought before a magistrate. Courts generally admit this type of confession into evidence if the confession was given before the delay occurred.

▸ **voluntary confession.** (16c) A confession given freely, without any benefit or punishment promised, threatened, or expected.

2. More broadly, any avowal or acknowledgment of an inculpatory or sinful act. **3.** An acknowledgment of belief in (another, esp. a deity). **4.** PENANCE (3).

confession and avoidance. (17c) A plea in which a defendant admits allegations but pleads additional facts that deprive the admitted facts of an adverse legal effect. • For example, a plea of contributory negligence (before the advent of comparative negligence) was a confession and avoidance. — Also termed *avoidance; plea in confession and avoidance; plea of confession and avoidance.* Cf. *affirmative defense* under DEFENSE (1).

confession of judgment. (18c) **1.** A person's agreeing to the entry of judgment upon the occurrence or nonoccurrence of an event, such as making a payment. **2.** A judgment taken against a debtor by the creditor, based on the debtor's written consent. **3.** The paper on which the person so agrees, before it is entered. — Also termed *confessed judgment; cognovit judgment; statement of confession; warrant of confession; judgment by confession.* See COGNOVIT. Cf. WARRANT OF ATTORNEY (2).

confessor (kən-**fes**-ər), *n.* (12c) **1.** Someone who admits guilt or culpability of a crime, fault, or error. **2.** Someone who avows faith, esp. in the face of persecution. **3.** A priest who administers the sacrament of penance. See PENANCE (3). **4.** Someone who leads a model Christian life and acquires a reputation for piety.

confidence. (14c) **1.** Assured expectation; firm trust; faith <the partner has confidence in the associate's work>. **2.** Reliance on another's discretion; a relation of trust <she took her coworker into her confidence>. **3.** A communication made in trust and not intended for public disclosure; specif., a communication protected by the attorney–client or similar privilege <the confidences between lawyer and client>. • Under the ABA Code of Professional Responsibility, a lawyer cannot reveal a client's confidence unless the client consents after full disclosure. DR 4-101. Cf. SECRET (2). — **confide,** *vb.*

confidence game. (1856) A dishonest trick played on someone in order to cheat the person out of money; specif., a means of obtaining money or property whereby a person intentionally misrepresents facts to gain the victim's trust so that the victim will transfer money or property to the person. — Also termed *con game; con; confidence trick.* Cf. BUNCO.

confidence man. (1849) Someone who defrauds a victim by first gaining the victim's confidence and then, through trickery, obtaining money or property; a swindler. • The equivalent term *confidence woman* is exceptionally rare, even though women are often involved in confidence games. — Often shortened to *con man.* See CONFIDENCE GAME. Cf. BUNCO STEERER.

confidence trick. See CONFIDENCE GAME.

confidential, *adj.* (18c) **1.** (Of information) meant to be kept secret; imparted in confidence <confidential settlement terms>. **2.** (Of a relationship) based on or characterized by trust and a willingness to impart secrets to the other <a confidential relationship between attorney and client>.

confidential adoption. See *closed adoption* under ADOPTION (1).

confidential communication. See COMMUNICATION.

confidential document. See DOCUMENT (2).

confidential informant. See CONFIDENTIAL SOURCE. — Abbr. CI.

confidential information. (18c) Knowledge or facts not in the public domain but known to some, esp. to those having a fiduciary duty not to misuse the knowledge or facts for their own advantage.

confidentiality, *n.* (1834) **1.** Secrecy; the state of having the dissemination of certain information restricted. **2.** The trusting relation between two people who have an especially close bond — as between lawyer and client, guardian and ward, or spouses — with regard to the faith that is placed in the one by the other.

> "The difference between 'secrecy' and 'confidentiality' is difficult to establish. A trade secret tends to have independent, legitimate, commercial value in and of itself, whereas confidential information may or may not have commercial value. For example, the secret formula for a popular soft drink would be considered a trade secret, whilst the menu choices for a film star's wedding breakfast would be confidential information. In a case where someone, without permission, photographed an 'installation' put together to be photographed for a record sleeve, and sold that photograph for commercial publication, a court decided that there was no possibility of an action for breach of copyright because the 'installation' was not an artistic work. Instead, an action for breach of confidence was successful. When the *Daily Mail* published extracts of the Prince of Wales' diaries, both his copyright and confidentiality were infringed." Ruth Soetendorp, "Confidential Information," in *The New Oxford Companion to Law* 197, 197 (Peter Cane & Joanne Conaghan eds., 2008).

confidentiality agreement. (1970) *Trade secrets.* A promise not to disclose trade secrets or other proprietary information learned in the course of the parties' relationship. • Confidentiality agreements are often required as a condition of employment. — Also termed *nondisclosure agreement.*

confidentiality clause. See CLAUSE.

confidentiality statute. (1975) A law that seals adoption records and prevents an adopted child from learning the identity of his or her biological parent and prevents the biological parent from learning the identity of the adoptive parents. — Also termed *sealed-record statute.*

confidential marriage. See MARRIAGE (1).

confidential relationship. See RELATIONSHIP.

confidential source. (1922) Someone who provides information to a law-enforcement agency or to a journalist on the express or implied guarantee of anonymity. • Confidentiality is protected both under the Federal Freedom of Information Act (for disclosures to law enforcement) and under the First Amendment (for disclosures to journalists). — Abbr. C/S. — Also termed *confidential informant.*

confinee. (1956) A person held in confinement.

confinement, *n.* (16c) The act of imprisoning or restraining someone; the quality, state, or condition of being imprisoned or restrained <solitary confinement>. See SOLITARY CONFINEMENT. — **confine,** *vb.*

confirm, *vb.* (13c) **1.** To give formal approval to <confirm the bankruptcy plan>. **2.** To verify or corroborate <confirm that the order was signed>. **3.** To make firm or certain <the judgment confirmed the plaintiff's right to possession>.

confirmatio (kon-fər-**may**-shee-oh). [Latin "confirmation"] *Hist.* A confirmation of a voidable estate. See CONFIRMATION (3).

▸ ***confirmatio crescens*** (kon-fər-**may**-shee-oh **kres**-enz). [Latin "growing confirmation"] A confirmation that enlarges an estate.

▸ ***confirmatio diminuens*** (kon-fər-**may**-shee-oh di-**min**-yoo-enz). [Latin "diminishing confirmation"] (18c) A confirmation that decreases the services that a tenant must perform.

▸ ***confirmatio perficiens*** (kon-fər-**may**-shee-oh pər-**fish**-ee-enz). [Latin "perfecting confirmation"] (18c) A confirmation that ratifies a wrongful and defeasible title, or makes a conditional estate absolute.

confirmatio ad omissa vel male appretiata (kon-fər-**may**-shee-oh ad oh-**mis**-ə vel **mal**-ee ə-pree-shee-**ay**-tə). [Law Latin] *Scots law.* Confirmation (by an executor) of subjects omitted or wrongly valued in a previously provided inventory.

Confirmatio Chartarum (kon-fər-**may**-shee-oh kahr-**tair**-əm). [Latin "confirmation of the charters"] *Hist.* A declaration first made by Henry III in 1225 confirming the guarantees of Magna Carta and the Charter of the Forest. • It was not enrolled until 1297, when, during the reign of Edward I, it was enacted, thus introducing these charters into the common law. — Also spelled *Confirmatio Cartarum.*

> "For lawyers, the really important date is neither 1215 nor 1225, when Henry's Charter took its final form, but 1297, when Edward I, in his *Inspeximus*, confirmed the Charter of 1225 and the Forest Charter, which was issued at the same time (*Confirmatio Chartarum*). The important element in the *Confirmatio* is the statement that the Charter might be pleaded in every royal court, either to support a claim or a defense. The Charter becomes in this way part of the law — the Common Law — which, in 1297, was already a definite concept although it was not yet quite the equivalent of the law of England. Until then, the political aspects of the Charter had been much the more important." Max Radin, *Handbook of Anglo-American Legal History* 156 (1936).

confirmation, *n.* (14c) **1.** The act of giving formal approval; the ratification or strengthening of an earlier act <Senate confirmation hearings>. **2.** The act of verifying or corroborating; evidence that verifies or corroborates <the journalist sought confirmation of the district attorney's remarks>. **3.** The ratification of a voidable estate; a type of conveyance in which a voidable estate is made certain or a particular estate is increased <deed of confirmation>. **4.** The act by which a court enters judgment on an arbitration award. • The result of confirmation is that the award has the same force as any other court judgment. *See* 9 USCA § 13. **5.** *Civil law.* A declaration that corrects a null provision of an obligation in order to make the provision enforceable. **6.** *Commercial law.* A bank's agreement to honor a letter of credit issued by another bank.

▸ **silent confirmation.** (1994) A bank's confirmation of a letter of credit based on the request of the letter's beneficiary rather than the issuing bank.

7. *Wills & estates.* The ratification or reaffirmation of an already-effective will by republishing all or part of it, either by re-signing the will or by executing a confirmatory codicil. Cf. RATIFICATION. — **confirmatory** (kən-**fər**-mə-tor-ee), *adj.*

confirmation buy. (1995) *Criminal law.* An undercover agent's purchase of contraband, typically for the purpose of confirming the suspect's identity or proving the suspect's knowledge.

confirmation of sale. A court's approval — usu. in the form of a docket entry or order — of the terms of a court-ordered sale.

confirmation slip. (1907) The form verifying a purchase or sale of a security, usu. mailed by the broker to the investor. — Also termed *transaction slip; sold note.*

confirmatio perficiens. See CONFIRMATIO.

confirmavi (kon-fər-**may**-vɪ). [Latin] *Hist.* I have confirmed. • The emphatic word in a deed of confirmation. See CONFIRMATION (3).

confirmed letter of credit. See LETTER OF CREDIT.

confirmee (kon-fər-**mee**). (17c) *Hist.* The grantee of a deed of confirmation. See CONFIRMATION (3).

confirming bank. See BANK.

confirmor (kən-**fər**-mər *or* -mor). (17c) *Hist.* The grantor of a deed of confirmation. See CONFIRMATION (3).

confiscable (kən-**fis**-kə-bəl *or* **kon**-fə-skə-bəl), *adj.* (18c) (Of property) liable to confiscation; subject to forfeiture <confiscable contraband>.

confiscare (kon-fi-**skair**-ee), *vb.* [Latin *con* "together" + *fiscus* "treasury"] *Hist.* To seize (property) for the government.

confiscate (**kon**-fə-skayt), *vb.* (16c) **1.** To appropriate (property) as forfeited to the government. **2.** To seize (property) by authority of law.

confiscation (kon-fi-**skay**-shən), *n.* (16c) **1.** Seizure of property for the public treasury. **2.** Seizure of property by actual or supposed authority. — **confiscatory** (kən-**fis**-kə-tor-ee), *adj.* — **confiscator** (**kon**-fə-skay-tər), *n.*

confiscatory rate. See RATE (2).

confitens reus (**kon**-fə-tenz **ree**-əs). [Latin "confessing accused"] *Hist.* An accused person who admits committing the offense.

conflict. 1. See CONFLICT OF LAWS. **2.** See CONFLICT OF INTEREST.

conflict check. A lawyer's ascertainment of whether any prior or existing representation would preclude the lawyer from undertaking a new representation, usu. of a new client.

conflict defender. (1992) A lawyer who has arranged to serve as assigned counsel in cases in which the public defender's office has a conflict of interest between two of its clients.

conflict diamond. (1999) A diamond that originated in an area controlled by forces or factions opposed to a legitimate, internationally recognized government, and is used to fund military action against that government. • Congress enacted the Clean Diamond Trade Act in 2003 to stop trade in conflict diamonds. 19 USCA §§ 3901 et seq. — Also termed *blood diamond.*

conflicting evidence. See EVIDENCE.

conflicting presumption. See PRESUMPTION.

conflict of authority. (1822) **1.** A disagreement between two or more courts, often courts of coordinate jurisdiction, on a point of law. **2.** A disagreement between two or more treatise authors or other scholars, esp. in an area in which scholarly authority is paramount, such as public or private international law.

conflict of interest. (1843) **1.** A real or seeming incompatibility between one's private interests and one's public or fiduciary duties. **2.** A real or seeming incompatibility between the interests of two of a lawyer's clients, such that the lawyer is disqualified from representing both clients if the dual representation adversely affects either client or if the clients do not consent. *See* Model Rules of Prof'l Conduct R. 1.7(a) (2013). — Often shortened to *conflict.*

▸ **thrust-upon conflict.** (1997) A conflict of interest that arises during an attorney's representation of two clients but did not exist and was not reasonably foreseeable when each client's representation began, and arises through no fault of the attorney's. • Some states may require that the conflict be of a type that clients may waive under the rules of professional responsibility. This situation may create an exception to the hot-potato rule. See HOT-POTATO RULE.

conflict of laws. (1827) **1.** A difference between the laws of different states or countries in a case in which a transaction or occurrence central to the case has a connection to two or more jurisdictions. — Often shortened to *conflict.* Cf. CHOICE OF LAW.

> "When a court is called upon to decide an ordinary case or controversy, the operative facts upon which judgment is based have, or are assumed to have, occurred within the territorial limits of the state or country where the court sits. Very often, however, the operative facts, or a part of them, have a connection with some other jurisdiction. Thus, a court may have to determine the validity or legal effect of an agreement as a contract in a case where the agreement was reached in another state or country, or the offer was accepted there. Again, a tort claim may be predicated upon injury which has been incurred outside the territorial limits of the state where the court sits. Or, the validity of a marriage celebrated abroad or that of a foreign divorce may be the factor upon which the conflicting claims of the parties depend. In the field of property the issue may turn upon the legal effect of an attempted transfer in one jurisdiction of property, real or personal, located in another or upon that of a foreign will. In cases such as these, which are illustrative only and not exhaustive, the foreign fact element raises questions of the effect to be given at the forum to foreign law. That branch of the law which deals with questions of the operative effect at the forum of foreign law because of a foreign fact element in the case is sometimes called Private International Law but in this country more usually Conflict of Laws." George Wilfred Stumberg, *Principles of Conflict of Laws* 1 (2d ed. 1951).

▸ **conflict of personal laws.** (1905) **1.** A difference of laws between a jurisdiction's general laws and the laws of a racial or religious group, such as a conflict between federal law and American Indian tribal law. **2.** A difference between personal laws. See PERSONAL LAW.

▸ **false conflict of laws.** (1966) **1.** A situation resembling but not embodying an actual conflict because the potentially applicable laws do not differ, because the laws' underlying policies have the same objective, or because one of the laws is not meant to apply to the case before the court. **2.** The situation in which, although a case has a territorial connection to two or more states whose laws conflict with one another, there is no real conflict because one state has a dominant interest in having its law chosen to govern the case — hence there is no real conflict. **3.** The situation in which the laws of all states that are relevant to the facts in dispute either are the same or would produce the same decision in the case. — Often shortened to *false conflict.*

2. The body of jurisprudence that undertakes to reconcile such differences or to decide what law is to govern in these situations; the principles of choice of law. — Often shortened (in sense 2) to *conflicts.* — Also termed (in international contexts) *private international law; international private law.* See *private international law* under INTERNATIONAL LAW.

> "The phrase [conflict of laws], although inadequate, because it does not cover questions as to jurisdiction, or as to the execution of foreign judgments, is better than any other." Thomas E. Holland, *The Elements of Jurisprudence* 421 (13th ed. 1924).

conflict-of-laws rules. (1917) The legal principles relied on to determine preliminary issues of applicable law where more than one jurisdiction is involved in a dispute. • Specifically, a court seeking to reconcile the varying principles of different legal systems must (1) determine that it has jurisdiction over the matter, (2) apply either its own jurisdiction's rules or those of another legal system involved in the litigation, and (3) decide whether any foreign judgment already issued is to be followed.

conflict of personal laws. See CONFLICT OF LAWS (1).

conflict out, *vb.* (1981) To disqualify (a lawyer or judge) on the basis of a conflict of interest <the judge was conflicted out of the case by his earlier representation of one of the litigants>.

conflict preemption. See *obstacle preemption* under PREEMPTION.

conflicts. See CONFLICT OF LAW (2).

conformed copy. See COPY (1).

conforming, *adj.* (1956) Being in accordance with contractual obligations <conforming goods> <conforming conduct>. UCC § 2-106(2).

conforming use. See USE (1).

Conformity Act. *Hist.* An 1872 federal statute providing that the practice and procedure in federal district courts (other than in equity and admiralty matters) must conform to the practice and procedure used by the state courts for like cases. • The Federal Rules of Civil Procedure (effective in 1938) superseded the Conformity Act.

> "[E]ven where there was conformity, it was to be 'as near as may be,' and this was understood by the Court to make the Conformity Act 'to some extent only directory and

advisory' and to permit the federal judge to disregard a state practice that would, in his view, 'unwisely encumber the administration of the law, or tend to defeat the ends of justice.' With all these exceptions to conformity, and with the judge left somewhat at large to decide when he would conform, it is hardly surprising that the result was, in the view of a distinguished commentator, 'a mixture of conflicting decisions, which have served to cloud the whole subject in hideous confusion and shifting certainty.'" Charles Alan Wright, *The Law of Federal Courts* § 61, at 425–26 (5th ed. 1994) (quoting *Indianapolis & St. Louis Ry. Co. v. Horst*, 93 U.S. 291, 300–01 (1876)).

conformity hearing. (1970) **1.** A court-ordered hearing to determine whether the judgment or decree prepared by the prevailing party conforms to the decision of the court. **2.** A hearing before a federal agency or department to determine whether a state-submitted plan complies with the requirements of federal law. • This type of hearing is common in cases involving social services.

confront, *vb.* **1.** To stand face-to-face with, esp. defiantly; to present a bold front to. **2.** To oppose or be opposed by; to encounter (difficulties, obstacles, etc.). **3.** To bring into the presence of; to put face-to-face with. **4.** To set in opposition for comparison; to compare.

confrontation. (17c) **1.** A face-to-face disagreement between two people or groups, esp. one involving vehemence and anger <Senate-floor confrontation between the two parties>. **2.** A fight or battle <military confrontations in the Dead Sea>.

"CONFRONTATION, in its massive form, is not a technique which can be used every day. It is suitable, really, only for cases where a great mass of material has been collected, where the witness to be attacked is believed to have feet of clay, and the intention is to strike a knock-out blow. On the other hand in its lesser form, as an auxiliary to the other techniques, it is in constant use. In probing, it is used to trap a witness who has been led on to elaborate the details of his story until they can be challenged; in gentle insinuation, it is used quietly to convince a witness that he has made an honest mistake; in firm insinuation it is used to surmount evasion and denials; finally, in undermining it is used for the same purpose, for example by confronting the witness with a certificate of a conviction which he has refused to admit, or with a previous contradictory statement." John H. Munkman, *The Technique of Advocacy* 115 (1951).

Confrontation Clause. (1913) The Sixth Amendment provision generally guaranteeing a criminal defendant's right to confront an accusing witness face-to-face and to cross-examine that witness. • This right may be overridden if the witness is esp. vulnerable, as with a child who is an alleged victim of sexual abuse. Even then, the defendant's attorney must have an opportunity to examine the witness while the defendant observes by means of closed-circuit television or the like. *See Maryland v. Craig*, 497 U.S. 836, 110 S.Ct. 3157 (1990).

confrontation right. See *right of confrontation* under RIGHT.

confusio (kən-**fyoo**-zhee-oh), *n.* [fr. Latin *confundere* "to pour together"] **1.** *Roman law.* An inseparable mixture of liquid property belonging to different owners. Cf. COMMIXTIO. **2.** *Roman law.* The extinction of a right or duty that occurs when the roles of creditor and debtor become united in one person. **3.** *Scots law.* A doctrine whereby a lesser right is absorbed into a greater right and is thus extinguished. • For example, if a debtor acquired the rights of a creditor, the debt would become meaningless.

"When the rights of both creditor and debtor come to be vested in the one person, in the same legal capacity, as by succession, gift or purchase, the obligation is extinguished, unless the creditor has an interest to maintain the obligation in being or the intention appears that *confusio* was not to operate. Obligations are not necessarily extinguished *confusione* where there is a legal relationship, independent of the pecuniary interests thereof, capable of revival by a subsequent separation of interests, as in the case of superior and vassal, and dominant and servient tenements in relation to servitude." 2 David M. Walker, *Principles of Scottish Private Law: Law of Obligations* 170 (1988).

confusio bonorum (kən-**fyoo**-zhee-oh bə-**nor**-əm). See CONFUSION OF GOODS.

confusion. **1.** CONFUSION OF GOODS. **2.** MERGER (9). **3.** *Trademarks.* A consumer's mistaken belief about the origin of goods or services. See LIKELIHOOD-OF-CONFUSION TEST.

▸ **direct confusion.** See *forward confusion.*

▸ **forward confusion.** (1986) Confusion occurring when consumers are likely to believe mistakenly that the infringing company's products are from the same source as the trademark owner's. • In forward-confusion cases, the infringing company is usu. smaller than the owner. Thus, consumers may believe the infringer to be an affiliate of the owner. — Also termed *direct confusion.*

▸ **reverse confusion.** (1968) Confusion occurring when consumers are likely to believe mistakenly — usu. through widespread advertising and promotion by the infringing company — that the trademark owner's products are actually those of the infringer. • Reverse confusion often injures the owner's reputation and goodwill. In an action for reverse confusion, the trademark owner is typically the smaller company.

confusion of boundaries. (18c) The branch of equity that deals with the settlement of disputed or uncertain real-property boundaries.

confusion of debts. See MERGER (9).

confusion of goods. (18c) The mixture of things of the same nature but belonging to different owners so that the identification of the things is no longer possible. • If this occurs by common consent of the owners, they are owners in common, but if the mixture is done willfully by one person alone, that person loses all right in the property unless (1) the goods can be distinguished and separated among owners, or (2) the mixing person's goods are equal in value to the goods with which they were intermingled. *Confusion of goods* combines the civil-law concepts of *confusio* (a mixture of liquids) and *commixtio* (a mixture of dry items). — Also termed *intermixture of goods; confusio bonorum.*

confusion of rights. See MERGER (9).

confusion of titles. (1825) *Civil law.* The merger of two titles to the same land in the same person. Cf. MERGER (9).

confutation (kon-fyoo-**tay**-shən), *n.* **1.** The act or process of disproving by convincing demonstration of falsity or illogic. **2.** The complete statement by which one engages in this act or process.

confute (kən-**fyoot**), *vb.* **1.** To prove (an argument, etc.) to be wrong, false, or invalid; to disprove completely. **2.** To prove (a person) to be in the wrong by irresistible argument.

con game. See CONFIDENCE GAME.

congeable (**kon**-jee-ə-bəl), *adj.* [fr. French *congé* "permission"] (16c) *Hist.* Lawful; permissible.

congé d'accorder (kawn-**zhay** da-kor-**day**). [Law French] *Hist.* Leave to accord. • Courts used this phrase in fictitious land-title lawsuits to grant the defendant permission to agree with the plaintiff's allegations. See FINE (1).

congé d'emparler (kawn-**zhay** dawm-pahr-**lay**). [French] *Hist.* Leave to imparl. • This phrase was formerly used by a defendant to request leave of court for additional time to file a responsive pleading. See IMPARLANCE.

congeries (kon-**jeer**-eez *or* **kon**-jə-reez). (17c) A collection or aggregation <a congeries of rights>.

congestion charging. (1994) A method of reducing traffic in major cities, esp. in city centers, by charging drivers a fee to go beyond a certain point on the roads into the cities.

conglomerate (kən-**glom**-ər-it), *n.* (1967) A corporation that owns unrelated enterprises in a wide variety of industries. — Also termed *conglomerate corporation.* — **conglomerate** (kən-**glom**-ə-rayt), *vb.* — **conglomerate** (kən-**glom**-ər-it), *adj.*

conglomerate merger. See MERGER (8).

congress, *n.* (16c) **1.** A formal meeting of delegates or representatives; CONVENTION (4). **2.** (*cap.*) The legislative body of the federal government, created under U.S. Const. art. I, § 1 and consisting of the Senate and the House of Representatives. — **congressional,** *adj.*

> "The word 'congress' had been used since the 17th century to denote a formal meeting of deputies or plenipotentiaries of several princes to treat about the conditions of peace or to adjust some other important political interests. The Congress which framed the Peace of Westphalia in 1648 laid the foundations of modern diplomacy and was the forerunner of many important gatherings of ambassadors. In colonial America the word had been used for such conferences of the colonies for a number of years and, in 1765, the Massachusetts General Court thought it 'highly expedient that there should be a meeting to consider of a general Congress.' At first, the word seems to have been limited in meaning to its original connotation and Samuel Adams in 1773 spoke of a Congress and then an Assembly of States, as if the latter term alone should be used of a true law making body; but when the Second Continental Congress found it necessary to become an organ of administration and law making, it continued to use the old name. At the present day, it is customary to speak of Congress, without prefixing an article, but the Constitution always speaks of *the* Congress." Paul S. Reinsch, *American Legislatures and Legislative Methods* 4 (1907).

3. SEXUAL INTERCOURSE.

Congressional Budget Office. An office in the legislative branch of the federal government responsible for forecasting economic trends, making cost estimates, conducting special studies in budget-related areas, and issuing annual reports that discuss federal spending and revenue levels and the allocation of funds. • It was established by the Congressional Budget and Impoundment Control Act of 1974. — Abbr. CBO

congressional committee. See COMMITTEE (1).

congressional district. See DISTRICT.

Congressional Globe. A privately issued record of the proceedings in Congress. • The *Globe* was the sole record of congressional speeches and statements from 1833 until the publicly printed *Congressional Record* appeared in 1873. It contains the congressional debates of the 23d through the 42d Congress.

congressional immunity. See IMMUNITY (1).

congressional intent. See LEGISLATIVE INTENT.

congressional power. See POWER (3).

Congressional Record. The official record of the daily proceedings in the U.S. Senate and House of Representatives. • Members of Congress are allowed to edit their speeches before printing, and they may insert material never actually spoken by obtaining permission from their respective houses to revise or extend their remarks.

congressional-reference case. See CASE (1).

Congressional Research Service. A nonpartisan agency in the Library of Congress that researches and analyzes legislative issues for congressional committees and individual members of Congress. • Congress created the agency in 1914 as the Legislative Reference Service. It was renamed in 1970. — Abbr. CRS.

congressional survey. See *government survey* under SURVEY (2).

Congress of Authors and Artists. *Copyright.* A 19th-century convention of writers, artists, librarians, and others promoting universal copyright protection. • The Congress, which met in 1858, 1861, and 1877, passed resolutions that helped lay the groundwork for the Berne Convention. See BERNE CONVENTION.

Congress of the Confederation. The second, loosely structured form of national government in the United States, created by the Articles of Confederation in 1781 and serving until the United States Constitution became operative in 1789. • Although the Articles formally named the governing body the Congress of the Confederation, it was still often called the Continental Congress.

conjectio (kən-**jek**-shee-oh), *vb.* [Latin "an inference"] *Hist.* A conclusion drawn from evidence; a fact inferred from the evidence presented. Pl. ***conjectiones*** (kən-jek-shee-**oh**-neez).

conjectio causae (kən-**jek**-shee-oh **kaw**-zee). [Latin "putting together of a cause"] *Roman law.* A summary presentation of a case before the court by the parties or their advocates.

conjectural choice, rule of. (1956) The principle that no basis for recovery is presented when all theories of causation rest only on conjecture. See CONJECTURE.

conjectura pietatis (kən-**jek**-chə-rə pı-ə-**tay**-tis). [Latin] *Hist.* A conclusion arising from a natural duty.

conjecture (kən-**jek**-chər), *n.* (14c) A guess; supposition; surmise. — **conjecture** (kən-**jek**-chər), *vb.* — **conjectural** (kən-**jek**-chər-əl), *adj.*

conjoint (kən-**joynt**), *n.* A person connected with another in a joint interest, obligation, or undertaking, such as a cotenant or spouse. — **conjoint,** *adj.*

conjoint robbery. See ROBBERY.

conjoint will. See *joint will* under WILL.

conjudex (kon-**joo**-deks). [fr. Latin *con* "together" + *judex* "judge"] *Hist.* An associate judge.

conjugal (**kon**-jə-gəl), *adj.* (16c) Of, relating to, or involving the married state, often with an implied emphasis on sexual relations between spouses <the prisoner was

allowed a private bed for conjugal visits>. See MARRIED (2).

conjugal rights. (18c) The rights and privileges arising from the marriage relationship, including the mutual rights of companionship, support, and sexual relations. • Loss of conjugal rights amounts to loss of consortium. See CONSORTIUM.

conjugal union. See MARRIAGE (1).

conjugal visit. (1958) An opportunity for physical contact granted to a prisoner and the prisoner's spouse, usu. in the form of an overnight stay at the prison. • Some jurisdictions allow conjugal visits between unmarried partners.

conjugium (kən-**joo**-jee-əm), *n.* [fr. Latin *con* "together" + *jugum* "yoke"] *Roman law.* The condition of being married.

conjunct (kən-**jəngkt** *or* **kon**-jəngkt), *adj.* (17c) *Civil law.* (Of persons) so closely related to a person (such as an insolvent) as to be disqualified from acting as a judge or witness in a case involving that person.

conjuncta (kən-**jəngk**-tə). [Latin] *Civil law.* Things (usu. words or phrases) that are joined together. Cf. DISJUNCTA.

conjunctim (kən-**jəngk**-tim), *adv.* [Latin] *Roman law.* Conjointly. • Heirs instituted *conjunctim*, for example, became coheirs with equal shares. Cf. DISJUNCTIM.

conjunctim et divisim (kən-**jəngk**-tim et də-**VI**-zim *or* -sim). [Latin] *Hist.* Jointly and severally.

conjunctio animorum (kən-**jəngk**-shee-oh an-ə-**mor**-əm). [Latin] *Scots law.* The mutual consent of parties to a marriage.

conjunctis viribis (kən-**jənk**-tis **veer**-i-bis), *adv.* (17c) With combined forces; with united powers.

conjunctive denial. See DENIAL (3).

conjunctive/disjunctive canon. The doctrine that in a legal instrument, *and* joins a conjunctive list to combine items, while *or* joins a disjunctive list to create alternatives. • Negatives, plurals, and various specific wordings create many nuances.

conjunctive obligation. See OBLIGATION.

conjuratio (kon-juu-**ray**-shee-oh). [Latin] CONJURATION.

conjuration (kon-jə-**ray**-shən). (14c) *Hist.* **1.** A plot or compact made by persons who swear to each other to do something that will result in public harm. **2.** The offense of attempting a conference with evil spirits to discover some secret or effect some purpose; witchcraft; sorcery.

> "*Coniuration* (*coniuratio*) is the very French word drawne from the latine, which as it is compounded of (*con* & *iuro*) so it signifieth a compact or plot, made by men combining themselves together by oath or promise, to do some publique harme. But in our common lawe, it is especially used for such as have personall conference with the devill or evill spirit, to know any secret, or to effect any purpose. And the difference that I have observed (how truly let those judge that be beter skilled in these maters) betweene coniuration and witchcraft, is because the one seemeth, by prayers and invocation of Gods powerfull names, to compell the devill, to say or doe what he commandeth him: the other dealeth rather by a friendly and voluntarie conference or agreement betweene him or her and the devill or familiar, to have her or his desires and turnes served in lieu of blood, or other gift offered unto him, especially of his or her soule." John Cowell, *The Interpreter* (1607).

conjurator (**kon**-jə-ray-tər). (16c) *Hist.* Someone who swears an oath with others; a coconspirator.

con man. See CONFIDENCE MAN.

connected plea. See PLEA (1).

connecting factor. (1950) *Conflict of laws.* A factual or legal circumstance that helps determine the choice of law by linking an action or individual with a state or jurisdiction. • An example of a connecting factor is a party's domicile within a state. See POINT OF ATTACHMENT.

connecting-up doctrine. (1986) The rule allowing evidence to be conditionally admitted if the offering party promises to show relevance by adducing other evidence.

connexity (kə-**nek**-sə-tee). (17c) Connectedness; the quality of being connected. • In some states, *connexity* expresses the relationship that must exist between a foreign party (such as a corporation) and the state for a plaintiff to maintain personal jurisdiction over the party; generally, the claim must arise from a transaction connected with the activities of the party in the state.

connivance (kə-**NI**-vənts), *n.* (16c) **1.** The act of indulging or ignoring another's wrongdoing, esp. when action should be taken to prevent it. **2.** *Family law.* As a defense to divorce, one spouse's corrupt consent, express or implied, to have the other commit adultery or some other act of sexual misconduct. • Consent is an essential element of connivance. The complaining spouse must have consented to the act complained of. Cf. COLLUSION (2); CONDONATION (2); RECRIMINATION (2). — **connive** (kə-**NIV**), *vb.*

connive (kə-**NIV**), *vb.* (17c) **1.** To knowingly overlook another's wrongdoing. **2.** Loosely, to conspire.

connubial (kon-[y]**oo**-bee-əl), *adj.* See MARRIED (2).

connubium. See CONUBIUM.

conqueror, *n.* [fr. Law French *conquerir* "to acquire"] (13c) *Hist.* **1.** Someone who acquires territory by force during war with the intention of exercising sovereignty. See CONQUEST (1). **2.** The first person who acquired land by purchase; one who first brought an estate into a family. See CONQUEST (2); PURCHASE (2).

conqueror, *vb.* [Latin] To complain. • *Conqueror* served as a declaratory statement in petitions, often by introducing the complaint: *Conqueror quod ....* ("I complain that ....").

conquest. (12c) **1.** *Int'l law.* An act of force by which, during a war, a belligerent occupies territory within an enemy country with the intention of extending its sovereignty over that territory. • That intention is usu. explained in a proclamation or some other legal act. **2.** *Hist.* The acquisition of land by any method other than descent, esp. by purchase. **3.** *Hist.* The land so acquired. Cf. PURCHASE (3).

> "What we call *purchase, perquisitio*, the feudists called *conquest, conquaestus*, or *conquisitio*: both denoting any means of acquiring an estate out of the common course of inheritance. And this is still the proper phrase in the law of Scotland: as it was, among the Norman jurists, who stiled the first purchasor (that is, he who first brought the estate into the family which at present owns it) the conqueror or *conquereur*. Which seems to be all that was meant by the appellation which was given to William the Norman, when his manner of ascending the throne of England was, in his own and his successors' charters, and by the historians of the times, entitled *conquaestus*, and himself *conquaestor* or *conquisitor*; signifying, that he was the first of his family who acquired the crown of England, and from whom therefore all future claims by descent must be derived: though now, from our disuse of the feodal sense of the

word, together with the reflection on his forcible method of acquisition, we are apt to annex the idea of *victory* to this name of *conquest* or *conquisition*; a title which, however just with regard to the *crown*, the conqueror never pretended with regard to the *realm* of England; nor, in fact, ever had." 2 William Blackstone, *Commentaries on the Laws of England* 242–43 (1766).

conquet. See ACQUET (1).

conquisitio (kən- *or* kəng-kwi-**zish**-ee-oh). [Latin "search"] See CONQUEST (2). — Also termed *conquisition.*

conquisitor (kən- *or* kəng-**kwiz**-ə-tər). [Latin "one who searches"] See CONQUEROR (1).

consanguine brother. See BROTHER.

consanguineo. See COSINAGE.

consanguine sister. See SISTER.

consanguineus (kon-sang-**gwin**-ee-əs), *n.* [Latin "related by blood"] (16c) *Hist.* A person related to another by blood; a consanguineous relative.

consanguineus frater (kon-sang-**gwin**-ee-əs **fray**-tər). [Latin "blood brother"] (18c) *Hist.* A half-brother by the same father.

consanguineus uterinus (kon-sang-**gwin**-ee-əs yoo-tə-**rI**-nəs). [Latin "blood relative by the uterus"] *Hist.* A half-sibling by the same mother.

consanguinitas (kon-sang-**gwin**-ə-tas), *n.* [Latin "relationship by blood"] (16c) *Roman law.* The relationship between siblings who have the same father.

consanguinity (kon-sang-**gwin**-ə-tee), *n.* (14c) The relationship of persons of the same blood or origin. See *prohibited degree* under DEGREE. Cf. AFFINITY (2), (3); *relative by affinity* under RELATIVE; AFFINITAS AFFINITATIS. — **consanguineous,** *adj.*

"In the mode of computing the degrees of consanguinity, the civil law . . . begins with the intestate, and descends from that ancestor to the next heir, reckoning for each person, as well in the ascending as descending lines. According to this rule of computation, the father of the intestate stands in the first degree, his brother in the second, and his brother's children in the third. Or, the grandfather stands in the second degree, the uncle in the third, the cousins in the fourth, and so on in a series of genealogical order. In the canon law, which is also the rule of the common law, in tracing title by descent, the common ancestor is the terminus a quo. The several degrees of kinship are deduced from him. By this method, the brother of A is related to him in the first degree instead of being in the second . . . for he is but one degree removed from the common ancestor. The uncle is related to A in the second degree, for though the uncle be but one degree from the common ancestor, yet A is removed two degrees from the grandfather, who is the common ancestor." 4 James Kent, *Commentaries on American Law* *412–13 (George Comstock ed., 11th ed. 1866).

▸ **collateral consanguinity.** (16c) The relationship between persons who have the same ancestor but do not descend or ascend from one another (for example, uncle and nephew, cousins, etc.).

▸ **lineal consanguinity.** (18c) The relationship between persons who are directly descended or ascended from one another (for example, mother and daughter, great-grandfather and grandson, etc.).

conscience. (13c) **1.** The moral sense of right or wrong; esp., a moral sense applied to one's own judgment and actions. **2.** In law, the moral rule that requires justice and honest dealings between people.

conscience clause. (1873) A legislative provision that allows a person to claim an exemption from compliance, usu. on religious-freedom grounds.

conscience of the court. (17c) **1.** The court's equitable power to decide issues based on notions of fairness and justice. See EQUITY (4). **2.** A standard applied by the court in deciding whether a party or a jury has acted within acceptable limits. • Thus, in some cases, a jury's award of damages is upset because it is said to "shock the conscience of the court." See SHOCK THE CONSCIENCE.

conscience-stricken, *adj.* (1816) Feeling extremely guilty about something one has done that was wrong; experiencing intense contrition.

conscientia illaesa (kon-s[h]ee-**en**-shee-ə i-**lee**-sə *or* -zə). [Latin] *Hist.* An unviolated conscience; good faith.

conscientia rei alienae (kon-s[h]ee-**en**-shee-ə **ree**-I ay-lee-**ee**-nee *or* al-ee-). [Law Latin] *Scots law.* The knowledge that property held by one person actually belongs to another.

conscientious belief. See BELIEF.

conscientious objection. (18c) A personal disapproval of participating in some specific conduct, usu. of a military or political nature, on moral grounds. • A conscientious objection generally requires something more than intellectual persuasion, amounting to a compulsive and complete aversion to particular behavior. It may or may not be based on religion, but it must be sincerely held.

conscientious objector. (1916) Someone who objects on moral grounds to participating in some type of required behavior, usu. of a military or political nature; esp., a person who for moral or religious reasons is opposed to participating in any war and who may be excused from military conscription but remains subject to serving in civil work for the country's health, safety, or interest. *See* 50 USCA § 456. Cf. PACIFIST. — **conscientious objection,** *n.* — **conscientiously object,** *vb.*

conscionable (**kon**-shə-nə-bəl), *adj.* (16c) Conforming with good conscience; just and reasonable <a conscionable bargain>. Cf. UNCONSCIONABLE. — **conscionableness, conscionability,** *n.*

conscious avoidance. See *deliberate indifference* under INDIFFERENCE.

conscious-avoidance direction. See *willful-blindness instruction* under JURY INSTRUCTION.

conscious-avoidance instruction. See *willful-blindness instruction* under JURY INSTRUCTION.

conscious indifference. See INDIFFERENCE.

consciously parallel. (1950) *Antitrust.* Of, relating to, or characterizing the conduct of a party who has knowledge of a competitor's action (such as raising prices) and who makes an independent decision to take the same action. • In some cases this is viewed as evidence of a conspiracy.

consciousness of guilt. (17c) The awareness of an accused that he or she has engaged in blameworthy conduct, usu. as demonstrated by evidence that the accused has tried to avoid the consequences of a crime, as by lying before or during the trial or by fleeing before or after arrest.

conscious parallelism. (1951) *Antitrust.* An act of two or more businesses in a concentrated market intentionally engaging in monopolistic conduct. — Also termed *tacit collusion; oligopolistic price coordination.*

conscious-presence test. (1941) A method for judging whether a testator is in the presence of a witness to a will, whereby if the testator can sense the presence of the witness — even if the witness cannot be seen — the witness is present. Restatement (Third) of Property: Wills and Other Donative Transfers § 3.1. — Also termed *conscious presence.* See PRESENCE-OF-THE-TESTATOR RULE. Cf. LINE-OF-SIGHT TEST.

conscius fraudis (**kon**-s[h]ee-əs **fraw**-dis). [Latin] See PARTICEPS FRAUDIS.

conscription. See DRAFT (2).

consecratio capitis (kon-sə-**kray**-shee-oh **kap**-i-tis). [Latin "consecrating the body"] *Roman law.* The act of declaring a wrongdoer an outlaw who could be killed on sight; the punishing of criminal behavior by relegating an offender to the gods, i.e., leaving the person outside divine and human protection. See SACER; OUTLAWRY.

consecutive sentences. See SENTENCE.

consecutive tortfeasors. See TORTFEASOR.

consensual (kən-**sen**-shoo-əl), *adj.* (18c) **1.** Having, expressing, or occurring with full consent <consensual relations>. **2.** Created or existing by mutual consent without formalities such as a written document or ceremony <consensual marriage>. — Also termed *consentaneous; consentient.*

consensual contract. See CONTRACT.

consensual crime. See *victimless crime* under CRIME.

consensual encounter. (1981) **1.** A sexual experience in which both or all participants willingly engage. **2.** *Criminal law.* An interaction between a person and a police officer who noncoercively asks for and is granted permission to search the person or his or her property.

consensual marriage. See MARRIAGE (1).

consensual offense. See *victimless crime* under CRIME.

consensual search. See *consent search* under SEARCH (1).

consensus. (1861) A general agreement; collective opinion. See *general consent* under CONSENT (2).

> "The regular method for the chair to use is to ask the members, 'Is it the consensus of this meeting that . . . is agreed to?' or, 'Is it the will of the assembly that . . . is agreed to?' or, 'Is there an objection?' Consensus has been used successfully throughout the years by Quakers, Indians, New England town meetings, and others as a decision-making procedure. It permits compromise. In small groups where less formality is required, it is a simple method for making decisions.
>
> "General consent is an equivalent to consensus, when done without objection. Otherwise, a formal vote must be taken." Floyd M. Riddick & Miriam H. Butcher, *Riddick's Rules of Procedure* 56 (1985).

consensus ad idem (kən-**sen**-səs ad ɪ-dem). [Latin] (1868) An agreement of parties to the same thing; a meeting of minds. — Also termed *consensus in idem; consensus in idem, placitum et conventio.*

> "Agreement between the parties or *consensus in idem* is the basis of contractual obligation . . . ." 2 David M. Walker, *Principles of Scottish Private Law* 11 (4th ed. 1988).

consent, *n.* (14c) **1.** A voluntary yielding to what another proposes or desires; agreement, approval, or permission regarding some act or purpose, esp. given voluntarily by a competent person; legally effective assent. • Consent is an affirmative defense to assault, battery, and related torts, as well as such torts as defamation, invasion of privacy, conversion, and trespass. Consent may be a defense to a crime if the victim has the capacity to consent and if the consent negates an element of the crime or thwarts the harm that the law seeks to prevent. *See* Model Penal Code § 2.11.

> "The consent [to a contract] is none the less 'genuine' and 'real,' even though it be induced by fraud, mistake, or duress. Consent may be induced by a mistaken hope of gain or a mistaken estimate of value or by the lie of a third person, and yet there is a contract and we do not doubt the 'reality of the consent.' Fraud, mistake, and duress are merely collateral operative facts that co-exist with the expressions of consent and have a very important effect upon the resulting legal relations." William R. Anson, *Principles of the Law of Contract* 199 n.1 (Arthur L. Corbin ed., 3d Am. ed. 1919).

▸ **blank consent.** See BLANK CONSENT.

▸ **express consent.** (16c) Consent that is clearly and unmistakably stated.

▸ **implied consent.** (17c) **1.** Consent inferred from one's conduct rather than from one's direct expression. — Also termed *implied permission.* **2.** Consent imputed as a result of circumstances that arise, as when a surgeon removing a gall bladder discovers and removes colon cancer.

▸ **informed consent.** (1938) **1.** A person's agreement to allow something to happen, made with full knowledge of the risks involved and the alternatives. • For the legal profession, informed consent is defined in Model Rule of Professional Conduct 1.0(e). **2.** A patient's knowing choice about a medical treatment or procedure, made after a physician or other healthcare provider discloses whatever information a reasonably prudent provider in the medical community would give to a patient regarding the risks involved in the proposed treatment or procedure. — Also termed *knowing consent.*

▸ **knowing consent.** See *informed consent.*

▸ **parental consent.** (17c) Consent given on a minor's behalf by at least one parent, or a legal guardian, or by another person properly authorized to act for the minor, for the minor to engage in or submit to a specified activity.

▸ **voluntary consent.** (16c) Consent that is given freely and that has not been coerced.

2. *Parliamentary law.* ADOPTION (5). — **consent,** *vb.* — **consensual,** *adj.*

▸ **general consent.** (16c) **1.** Adoption without objection, regardless of whether every voter affirmatively approves. **2.** See *unanimous consent* (1).

▸ **unanimous consent.** (17c) **1.** Adoption with every voter's approval. **2.** See *general consent* (1). • The terms "general consent" and "unanimous consent" have distinct but interchangeable meanings. Some parliamentary manuals treat them as synonymous; others distinguish them; and still others distinguish them, but in exactly the opposite way.

> "Motions that appear to have no opposition because they are relatively unimportant, uncontroversial, or because approval is obvious, permit the chair to say, 'The motion, without objection, is adopted' (or agreed to), without putting the motion to a formal vote. General consent

implies that no one cared enough to oppose the motion or proposition. Unanimous consent implies that everyone was in agreement. If there is even one objection, the request is denied and the question must be put to a vote for adoption." Floyd M. Riddick & Miriam H. Butcher, *Riddick's Rules of Procedure* 97 (1985).

"'Unanimous consent' does not necessarily imply that every member is in favor of the proposed action; it may only mean that the opposition, feeling that it is useless to oppose or discuss the matter, simply acquiesces." Henry M. Robert, *Robert's Rules of Order Newly Revised* § 4, at 52 (10th ed. 2001).

consent agenda. See *consent calendar* under CALENDAR (4).

consent agreement. *Trademarks.* An agreement in which one holder of a registered trademark consents to another's use and registration of a similar mark. • A party seeking to register a mark with a governmental agency may submit a consent agreement to overcome a potential refusal by the agency to register the mark on grounds the marks could be confused.

consentaneous, *adj.* See CONSENSUAL.

consent calendar. 1. *Family law.* A schedule of informal hearings involving a child, usu. arranged when it appears that the child's best interests will be served if the case is heard informally. • The child and all interested parties must first consent before the case goes on the consent calendar. **2.** For the parliamentary sense relating to a deliberative assembly's business, see *consent calendar* under CALENDAR (4).

consent clause. See AUTHORIZATION CLAUSE.

consent decree. See DECREE.

consent dividend. See DIVIDEND.

consentient, *adj.* See CONSENSUAL.

consenting adult. See ADULT.

consent judgment. See *agreed judgment* under JUDGMENT (2).

consent jurisdiction. See JURISDICTION.

consent-once-removed doctrine. (1993) *Criminal law.* The rule that police may enter a private place without a warrant if a confidential informant or undercover police officer has already entered by consent and has witnessed criminal activity.

consent order. See *consent decree* under DECREE.

consent search. See SEARCH (1).

consent theory. (1916) **1.** The notion that people make decisions as free agents who enter into relationships with other free agents, and that the aggregation of all such relationships within a territory becomes the basis for political governance. • Under this theory, contractual obligations can be understood only if viewed as being part of a broader system of legal entitlements. **2.** *Int'l law.* The view that the consent of states is the basis of all obligations between the states, as with treaties and other types of binding agreements.

consent to be sued. (1872) Agreement in advance to be sued in a particular forum. See COGNOVIT CLAUSE.

consent to marry. (16c) *Family law.* An agreement freely given by two marriageable persons, of at least the age of consent, to enter into a marriage. — Also termed *consent to marriage.*

consent to notice. (1996) A provision stating that notice required by a document may be given beforehand or to a designated person.

consequence. (14c) A result that follows as an effect of something that came before. See EFFECT.

▸ **avoidable consequence.** (17c) A result that could be or might have been prevented or mitigated by exercising due care to prevent or correct the underlying condition. See MITIGATION-OF-DAMAGES DOCTRINE.

"The doctrine of contributory negligence differs from that of avoidable consequences in an important respect. Contributory negligence takes away the cause of action itself; for the question of avoidable consequences to arise, it is necessary that a cause of action should first exist. But the principle from which they spring is the same, — that the defendant cannot be held responsible for anything of which the real cause is the plaintiff's negligence; or as the Supreme Court of the United States has said: 'One who by his negligence has brought an injury upon himself cannot recover damages for it.' The difference between contributory negligence and the doctrine of avoidable consequences is continually seen in personal injury cases. A railway collision occurs, which is due to the negligence of the company, and in which the plaintiff's arm is broken; he is entitled to damages. It appears that but for the fact that his arm was outside the car window at the time, he would not have been injured; his cause of action is gone. It appears that he has a cause of action, but that owing to his neglect to procure proper surgical advice, he has lost his arm altogether; for this head of damage he cannot recover." Arthur George Sedgwick, *Elements of the Law of Damages* 73–74 (2d ed. 1909) (citations omitted).

▸ **collateral consequence.** (17c) **1.** (*usu. pl.*) Any unforeseen or unplanned results of an action taken — esp. adverse ones. **2.** (*usu. pl.*) *Criminal law.* The indirect implications of a criminal conviction, esp. as it may affect the defendant's immigration status, property forfeitures, civil-litigation posture, etc. **3.** A penalty for committing a crime, in addition to the penalties included in the criminal sentence. • An example is the loss of a professional license. When a collateral consequence exists, a defendant's appeal of a conviction does not become moot when the criminal sentence is completed.

▸ **natural consequence.** (16c) Something that predictably occurs as the result of an act <plaintiff's injuries were the natural consequence of the car wreck>. — Also termed *natural and probable consequence.*

"The rule is usually phrased: 'The injury must be the *natural* and *probable* result of the negligence.' The term 'natural' has two meanings, *viz.*, such as takes place according to the processes of nature, and such as takes place according to human experience. In the first sense everything that takes place at all is natural. In the second sense it has the same meaning as 'probable,' 'ordinary,' 'usual,' 'not unlikely,' 'likely,' and several other synonyms." Leon Green, *Are Negligence and "Proximate" Cause Determinable by the Same Test?*, 1 Tex. L. Rev. 243, 245 (1923).

▸ **probable consequence.** (16c) An effect or result that is more likely than not to follow its supposed cause.

▸ **proximate consequence.** (1840) A result following an unbroken sequence from some event, esp. one resulting from negligence.

consequent, *adj.* (16c) **1.** Occurring as the natural result or necessary effect of a particular action, event, or situation; following as a natural result, a necessary effect, or a logical conclusion <poverty and its consequent crime rates>. **2.** Of, relating to, or involving correct reasoning;

characterized by correctness of thought; logical <Russell was thoroughly consequent in his analysis>.

consequential, *adj.* **1.** Having great importance; significant <a consequential election>. **2.** Flowing from a cause; resulting from a particular event or situation <consequential damages>.

consequential contempt. See CONTEMPT.

consequential damages. See DAMAGES.

consequential economic loss. See ECONOMIC LOSS.

consequential injury. See *consequential loss* under LOSS.

consequentialism. (1969) **1.** *Ethics.* An ethical theory that judges the rightness or wrongness of actions according to their consequences. • One of the best-known types of consequentialism is utilitarianism. **2.** *Constitutional law.* An interpretive theory that judges the rightness or wrongness of a judge-interpreter's reading according to its extratextual consequences. Cf. FORMALISM. **3.** In punishment theory, an account that justifies punishment by reference to the good consequences that the practice produces or is likely to produce, principally by means of deterrence, rehabilitation, incapacitation, or moral education. • As a theory of the justification for punishment, consequentialism is customarily contrasted with retributivism. See UTILITARIANISM. Cf. MIXED THEORY OF PUNISHMENT; RETRIBUTIVISM; UTILITARIAN-DETERRENCE THEORY; VIRTUE ETHICS. — **consequentialist,** *adj.*

▸ **side-constrained consequentialism.** See *negative retributivism* under RETRIBUTIVISM.

consequential loss. See LOSS.

consequential-loss insurance. See INSURANCE.

consequential mental harm. See MENTAL HARM.

conservation. (1875) *Environmental law.* The supervision, management, and maintenance of natural resources such as animals, plants, forests, etc., to prevent them from being spoiled or destroyed; the protection, improvement, and use of natural resources in a way that ensures the highest social as well as economic benefits.

▸ **heritage conservation.** See HISTORIC PRESERVATION.

conservation agreement. See *conservation easement* under EASEMENT.

conservation area. (1936) Land that has been officially designated as being important either to culture or to wildlife, both animals and plants, and has been set aside for maintaining as nearly as possible its pristine condition; specif., land that is subject to a conservation easement or conservation agreement.

conservation covenant. (1950) See *conservation easement* under EASEMENT.

conservation easement. See EASEMENT.

conservation land trust. See TRUST (3).

conservation park. (1978) Public land that is managed so as to preserve its natural condition, esp. its plants and animals, or to ensure that any commercial uses of its natural resources are ecologically sustainable.

conservation restriction. See *conservation easement* under EASEMENT.

conservation servitude. See *conservation easement* under EASEMENT.

conservation trust. See *land trust* (2) under TRUST (3).

conservatism. **1.** Collectively, the principles or theories of those who advocate preserving what is firmly established, and opposing changes in orthodoxy, esp. in politics and religion. **2.** The doctrine espoused by a conservative party. Cf. LIBERALISM.

conservative, *adj.* (14c) **1.** Predisposed to traditional attitudes, beliefs, and teachings; favoring established traditions, social stability, and gradual developments as opposed to abrupt changes. Cf. LIBERAL (2); PROGRESSIVE (1). **2.** (Of styles, tastes, etc.) not trendy or conspicuously fashionable. **3.** (Of estimates, guesses, etc.) marked by moderation or caution; deliberately lower than what the facts will probably bear out.

conservator (kən-**sər**-və-tər *or* **kon**-sər-vay-tər), *n.* (15c) A guardian, protector, or preserver. • *Conservator* is the modern equivalent of the common-law *guardian.* Judicial appointment and supervision are still required, but a conservator has far more flexible authority than a guardian, including the same investment powers that a trustee enjoys. The Uniform Probate Code uses the term *conservator,* and Article 5 is representative of modern conservatorship laws. — **conservatorship,** *n.*

▸ **managing conservator.** (1974) **1.** A person appointed by a court to manage the estate or affairs of someone who is legally incapable of doing so; GUARDIAN (1). **2.** In the child-custody laws of some states, the parent who has primary custody of a child, with the right to establish the child's primary domicile. See CUSTODY.

▸ **possessory conservator.** (1974) See *noncustodial parent* under PARENT.

conservator of the peace. See PEACE OFFICER.

conservator's deed. See *guardian's deed* under DEED.

conserve, *vb.* (14c) **1.** To take care of; to care for. **2.** To protect from change, destruction, or depletion. **3.** To reduce or minimize the use of.

consideratio. *Roman law.* See CONSIDERATION (4).

consideration, *n.* (16c) **1.** Something (such as an act, a forbearance, or a return promise) bargained for and received by a promisor from a promisee; that which motivates a person to do something, esp. to engage in a legal act. • Consideration, or a substitute such as promissory estoppel, is necessary for an agreement to be enforceable. *See* Restatement (Second) of Contracts § 81 (1979).

> "A 'consideration' has been explained to be 'any act of the plaintiff from which the defendant, or a stranger, derives a benefit or advantage, or any labour, detriment, or inconvenience sustained by the plaintiff, however small the detriment or inconvenience may be, if such act is performed, or inconvenience suffered by the plaintiff with the assent, express or implied, of the defendant, or, in the language of pleading, at the special instance and request of the defendant.'" Thomas E. Holland, *The Elements of Jurisprudence* 286 (13th ed. 1924).

> "A consideration in its widest sense is the reason, motive, or inducement, by which a man is moved to bind himself by an agreement. It is not for nothing that he consents to impose an obligation upon himself, or to abandon or transfer a right. It is in *consideration* of such and such a fact that he agrees to bear new burdens or to forgo the benefits which the law already allows him." John Salmond, *Jurisprudence* 359 (Glanville L. Williams ed., 10th ed. 1947).

> "The word 'consideration' has been around for a long time, so it is tempting to think we have had a theory of consideration for a long time. In fact until the nineteenth century

the word never acquired any particular meaning or stood for any theory." Grant Gilmore, *The Death of Contract* 18 (1974).

"In the late fifteenth and early sixteenth centuries the word 'consideration' was very familiar to lawyers, and although it had not yet acquired a special legal meaning (and indeed was not to do so during the period under discussion) it had already begun to develop legal associations. Most commonly it was used in statutes. . . . In the statutes of Henry VI it became quite common for the draftsman, after he had rehearsed the circumstances to introduce the enacting part with a clause in the following (or similar) form: 'The King, considering the premisses, of the Assent and Request aforesaid, hath ordained and established . . . .' In the course of time the matters which were considered, and to which consideration was given, came themselves to be called 'the considerations.' [By the late 15th century] the considerations were the matters considered; they were the factors which Parliament or the King was supposed to have had in mind in legislating, and which moved or motivated the enactment. Loosely the word could be treated as synonymous with 'cause,' and both in statutes and elsewhere causes and considerations were often mentioned in the same breath. But 'cause' does not mean exactly the same thing as 'consideration'; it lacks the suggestion of what was in the mind, what was considered, what motivated." A.W.B. Simpson, *Legal Theory and Legal History* 332 (1987).

▸ **adequate consideration.** (17c) Consideration that is fair and reasonable under the circumstances of the agreement. Cf. *sufficient consideration.*

"Although courts have not lost the habit of speaking of an 'adequate,' a 'sufficient,' or a 'valuable' consideration, the bargain test as epitomized in the Restatement imposes no such additional requirement." E. Allan Farnsworth, *Contracts* § 2.11, at 69–70 (3d ed. 1999).

▸ **and other good and valuable consideration.** See *other consideration.*

▸ **concurrent consideration.** (1847) Consideration arising at the same time as other consideration, or where the promises are simultaneous.

▸ **continuing consideration.** An act or performance extending over time.

▸ **due consideration. 1.** See DUE CONSIDERATION. **2.** See *sufficient consideration.*

▸ **executed consideration.** (18c) A consideration that has been wholly given; past consideration as opposed to present or future consideration.

▸ **executory consideration** (eg-**zek**-yə-tor-ee). (18c) A consideration that is to be given only after formation of the contract; present or future consideration as opposed to past consideration.

▸ **express consideration.** (17c) Consideration that is specifically stated in an instrument.

▸ **fair consideration.** (18c) **1.** Consideration that is roughly equal in value to the thing being exchanged; consideration given for property or for an obligation in either of the following circumstances: (1) when given in good faith as an exchange for the property or obligation, or (2) when the property or obligation is received in good faith to secure a present advance or prior debt in an amount not disproportionately small as compared with the value of the property or obligation obtained. — Also termed *fair and valuable consideration.* **2.** Consideration that is honest, reasonable, and free from suspicion, but not strictly adequate or full.

▸ **future consideration.** (1979) **1.** Consideration to be given in the future; esp., consideration that is due after the other party's performance. **2.** Consideration that is a series of performances, some of which will occur after the other party's performance. **3.** Consideration the specifics of which have not been agreed on between the parties. Cf. *past consideration.*

▸ **good and valuable consideration.** See *valuable consideration.*

▸ **good consideration.** (18c) **1.** Consideration based on natural love or affection or on moral duty <good consideration, being based purely on affection, does not amount to valuable consideration>. • Such consideration is usu. not valid for the enforcement of a contract. — Also termed *meritorious consideration*; *moral consideration.*

"A good consideration is that of *blood*, or the natural love and affection which a person has to his children, or any of his relatives. . . . A good consideration is not of itself sufficient to support a promise, any more than the moral obligation which arises from a man's passing his word; neither will the two together make a binding contract; thus a promise by a father to make a gift to his child will not be enforced against him. The consideration of natural love and affection is indeed good for so little in law, that it is not easy to see why it should be called a *good* consideration . . . ." Joshua Williams, *Principles of the Law of Personal Property* 95–96 (11th ed. 1881).

"Stated simply, good or meritorious consideration is nothing more than motive or moral obligation." 3 *Williston on Contracts* § 7:16, at 325–26 (Richard A. Lord ed., 4th ed. 1992).

2. Loosely, valuable consideration; consideration that is adequate to support the bargained-for exchange between the parties <his agreement to pay the offering price was good consideration for the sale>.

▸ **gratuitous consideration** (grə-**t**[y]**oo**-i-təs). (1880) Consideration that, not being founded on any detriment to the party who gives it, will not support a contract; a performance for which a party was already obligated.

▸ **grossly inadequate consideration.** (1827) Consideration whose value is so much less than the fair value of the object acquired that it may not support finding that the transaction is a valid exchange. • Depending on the surrounding circumstances, the transaction may actually be fraud, a gift, or something else other than a sale and purchase.

▸ **illegal consideration.** (18c) Consideration that is contrary to the law or public policy, or prejudicial to the public interest. • Such consideration does not support a contract.

▸ **illusory consideration.** (1827) Consideration consisting of a promise to perform a public duty or to perform under a preexisting contract. • The promise is unenforceable because the person making the promise was already obliged to perform. See *illusory promise* under PROMISE.

▸ **immoral consideration.** (18c) A consideration that so offends societal norms as to be invalid. • A contract supported by immoral consideration is usu. voidable or unenforceable. — Also termed *turpis causa.*

▸ **implied consideration.** (18c) Consideration that is inferred by law from the parties' actions.

▸ **impossible consideration.** (1855) Consideration stemming from a promise or performance that cannot be fulfilled.

▸ **inadequate consideration.** (18c) Consideration that is not fair or reasonable under the circumstances of the agreement. Cf. *adequate consideration.*

▸ **invented consideration.** (1977) Fictional consideration created by a court to prevent the invalidation of a contract that lacks consideration.

▸ **legal consideration.** See *valuable consideration.*

▸ **legally sufficient consideration.** See *sufficient consideration.*

▸ **meritorious consideration.** See *good consideration.*

▸ **moral consideration.** See *good consideration.*

▸ **nominal consideration.** (18c) Consideration that is so insignificant as to bear no relationship to the value of what is being exchanged (e.g., $10 for a piece of real estate). • Such consideration can be valid, since courts do not ordinarily examine the adequacy of consideration (although they do often inquire into such issues as fraud and duress). — Also termed *peppercorn.*

"Offers made in consideration of one dollar paid or promised are often irrevocable . . . . The irrevocability of an offer may be worth much or little to the offeree, and the courts do not ordinarily inquire into the adequacy of the consideration bargained for. Hence a comparatively small payment may furnish consideration for the irrevocability of an offer proposing a transaction involving much larger sums. But gross disproportion between the payment and the value of the option commonly indicates that the payment was not in fact bargained for but was a mere formality or pretense. In such a case there is no consideration . . . . Nevertheless, such a nominal consideration is regularly held sufficient to support a short-time option proposing an exchange on fair terms. The fact that the option is an appropriate preliminary step in the conclusion of a socially useful transaction provides a sufficient substantive basis for enforcement, and a signed writing taking a form appropriate to a bargain satisfies the desiderata of form. In the absence of statute, however, the bargaining form is essential: a payment of one dollar by each party to the other is so obviously not a bargaining transaction that it does not provide even the form of an exchange." Restatement (Second) of Contracts § 87 cmt. b (1979).

▸ **other consideration.** (18c) Additional things of value to be provided under the terms of a contract, usu. unspecified in the contract, deed, or bill of sale, because they are too numerous to conveniently list, or to avoid public knowledge of the total amount of consideration. — Also termed *other good and valuable consideration.*

▸ **past consideration.** (18c) An act done or a promise given by a promisee before making a promise sought to be enforced. • Past consideration is not consideration for the new promise because it has not been given in exchange for this promise (although exceptions exist for new promises to pay debts barred by limitations or debts discharged in bankruptcy). See PREEXISTING-DUTY RULE. Cf. *future consideration.*

"A past consideration is, in effect, no consideration at all; that is to say, it confers no benefit on the promisor, and involves no detriment to the promisee in respect of his promise. It is some act or forbearance in time past by which a man has benefited without thereby incurring any legal liability." William R. Anson, *Principles of the Law of Contract* 149 (Arthur L. Corbin ed., 3d Am. ed. 1919).

"'Past Consideration.' The quotation marks suggest that there is something wrong with this phrase. Past consideration, or something given, done, or suffered in the past which purportedly supports a subsequent promise, is no consideration. If a benefit has been conferred upon the promisor or if the promisee has suffered a detriment in the past and there is a subsequent promise to pay therefor, there is no bargain for such past value. Therefore, it cannot constitute consideration." John Edward Murray Jr., *Cases and Materials on Contracts* 427 (2d ed. 1976).

▸ **sham consideration.** Consideration that is of apparent value but not actual value because it does not actually exist or is never actually delivered. • Sham consideration is often used to make a gift appear to be a contracted-for bargain.

▸ **sufficient consideration.** (17c) Enough consideration as a matter of law to support a contract. — Also termed *due consideration; legally sufficient consideration.* Cf. *adequate consideration.*

▸ **valuable consideration.** (17c) Consideration that is valid under the law; consideration that either confers a pecuniarily measurable benefit on one party or imposes a pecuniarily measurable detriment on the other. — Also termed *good and valuable consideration; legal consideration.*

"By a valuable consideration is meant something of value given or promised by one party in exchange for the promise of the other. . . . The thing thus given by way of consideration must be of some *value.* That is to say, it must be material to the interests of one or the other or both of the parties. It must either involve some gain or benefit to the promisor by way of recompense for the burden of his promise, or it must involve some loss or disadvantage to the promisee for which the benefit of the promise is a recompense." John Salmond, *Jurisprudence* 360 (Glanville L. Williams ed., 10th ed. 1947).

2. *Parliamentary law.* The process by which a deliberative assembly disposes of a motion; DELIBERATION. • Consideration begins after the chair has stated the question on the motion; it ends with the chair putting the question on the motion (or on a subsidiary motion that disposes of the first motion and the assembly voting on it). It also includes debate and may also include (among other things) amendment and referral to a committee.

▸ **consideration by paragraph.** See *consideration seriatim.*

▸ **consideration seriatim.** (1875) Consideration serially, whereby a deliberative assembly considers a long or complex motion in a series of readily divisible parts before voting on the entire motion. — Also termed *consideration by paragraph* (in which case a "paragraph" means not a literary paragraph but any readily divisible part of a motion, which may include more than one literary paragraph); *serial consideration.*

"When a proposition, motion or resolution has many parts (paragraphs, sections, or clauses), or many articles (as a set of bylaws which is up for revision or amendment), it is best and most prudent that *no* vote be taken on each separate part. Instead, a single vote covering all its parts should be taken after each of them has been duly considered, amended, and perfected. *Seriatim* (Lat.) literally means 'serially,' and when applied to several or more parts of a parliamentary proposal or question it means consideration paragraph by paragraph or part by part.

"Hence, under the doctrine of consideration by paragraph, or *seriatim*, each part is discussed and may be amended and perfected to suit; then, without putting it to a vote for final adoption, the next part or paragraph is similarly open to discussion and amendment, but is not voted on for final adoption yet; and, in like manner, each additional part is perfected in turn until all the parts of a proposal have been considered." George Demeter, *Demeter's Manual of Parliamentary Law and Procedure* 146 (1969).

▸ **informal consideration.** Consideration without limit on how often a member may speak to the same question. • Informal consideration achieves the same freedom of debate as consideration in committee of the whole or quasi committee of the whole, without the fiction of the assembly resolving itself into a committee. See *committee of the whole* under COMMITTEE (1).

▸ **serial consideration.** See *consideration seriatim.*

3. Something that may be taken into account when forming an opinion.

▸ **irrelevant consideration.** (1824) A fact, statement, or other thing that is unrelated to the question to be decided or has no effect on the outcome.

4. *Hist.* A court's judgment. — Also termed (in Roman law) *consideratio.*

consideration, failure of. See FAILURE OF CONSIDERATION.

consideration, want of. See WANT OF CONSIDERATION.

consideratum est per curiam (kən-sid-ə-**ray**-təm est pər **kyoor**-ee-əm). [Latin] *Hist.* It is considered by the court. • This was the formal language preceding the judgment of a common-law court. — Sometimes shortened to *consideratum est.* Cf. IDEO CONSIDERATUM EST.

> "A judgment is the decision or sentence of the law, given by a court of justice, as the result of proceedings instituted therein for the redress of an injury. The language of the judgment is not, therefore, that 'it is decreed,' or 'resolved,' by the court, but that 'it is considered by the court,' *consideratum est per curiam*, that the plaintiff recover his debt, etc. In the early writers, *considerare*, *consideratio* always means the judgment of a court." 1 John Bouvier, *Bouvier's Law Dictionary* 619 (Francis Rawle ed., 8th ed. 1914).

consign (kən-**sɪn**), *vb.* (16c) **1.** To transfer to another's custody or charge. **2.** To give (goods) to a carrier for delivery to a designated recipient. **3.** To give (merchandise or the like) to another to sell, usu. with the understanding that the seller will pay the owner for the goods from the proceeds.

consignation (kon-sig-**nay**-shən), *n.* (16c) **1.** A debtor's delivery of money to an authorized third party after the creditor refuses to accept the payment. • Unlike a tender, a valid consignation discharges the debtor. Cf. TENDER (1). **2.** CONSIGNMENT (1).

consignator (kən-**sig**-nə-tor), *n.* (17c) A person authorized to accept delivery of money from a debtor if a creditor refuses to accept it. See CONSIGNATION.

consignee (kon-sɪ-**nee** *or* kən-). (18c) **1.** One to whom goods are consigned. • A consignee acts as the agent of the consignor. **2.** The person named in a bill to whom or to whose order the bill promises delivery. See AGENCY (1). Cf. CONSIGNOR.

consignment (kən-**sɪn**-mənt). (17c) **1.** The act of consigning goods for custody or sale. — Also termed (archaically) *consignation.* **2.** A quantity of goods that are sent somewhere, esp. in a single shipment, usu. to be sold. **3.** Under the UCC, a transaction in which a person delivers goods to a merchant for the purpose of sale, and (1) the merchant deals in goods of that kind under a name other than the name of the person making delivery, is not an auctioneer, and is not generally known by its creditors to be substantially engaged in selling others' goods, (2) with respect to each delivery, the aggregate value of the goods is $1,000 or more at the time of delivery, (3) the goods are not consumer goods immediately before delivery, and (4) the transaction does not create a security interest that secures an obligation. UCC § 9-102(a)(20). • A consignment creates an agency relationship. **4.** See *bailment for sale* under BAILMENT (1).

▸ **commercial consignment.** (1919) A consignment made by a merchant who delivers goods to another for the purpose of sale, lease, or other disposal when both parties deal in goods of that kind in the ordinary course of business.

consignment sale. See SALE.

consignor (kən-**sɪ**-nər *or* kon-sɪ-**nor**). (18c) **1.** Someone who dispatches goods to another on consignment. **2.** The person named in a bill as the person from whom goods have been received for shipment. Cf. CONSIGNEE.

consiliarius (kən-sil-ee-**air**-ee-əs), *n.* [fr. Latin *consilium* "advice"] (16c) **1.** *Roman law.* Someone who advises a magistrate; one who sits with the judge and assists in deciding cases. See CONCILIUM (1). **2.** *Hist.* A counselor learned in law. **3.** APOCRISARIUS.

consimili casu. See CASU CONSIMILI.

consistent-meaning canon. See PRESUMPTION OF CONSISTENT USAGE.

consisting of. *Patents.* Of, relating to, or involving the inclusion of the elements or steps recited in the body of a patent claim and the exclusion of any unlisted elements or steps that materially affect the properties of the claimed invention. — Also termed *consisting essentially of.* Cf. COMPRISING.

consistorial court. See CONSISTORY COURT.

consistorium (kon-sis-**tor**-ee-əm), *n.* [Latin] (16c) *Roman law.* In the later Empire, the emperor's privy council that functioned both as a general council of state and as a supreme court of law.

consistory court (kən-**sis**-tər-ee). (16c) *Eccles. law.* In England, a diocesan court exercising jurisdiction over the clergy and church property, such as a cemetery, and other ecclesiastical matters. • Consistory courts are presided over by the bishop's chancellor or the chancellor's commissary. — Also termed *consistorial court.* Cf. BISHOP'S COURT.

consobrini (kon-sə-**brɪ**-nɪ), *n. pl.* [Latin] (17c) *Roman law.* First cousins; children of brothers and sisters, or, more precisely, of two sisters.

consol (**kon**-sol *or* kən-**sol**). See *annuity bond* under BOND (3).

Consolato del Mare (kawn-soh-**lah**-toh del **mah**-ray). [Italian "consulate of the sea"] *Hist. Maritime law.* An influential collection of European maritime customs, referred to by commercial judges (*consuls*) in ports of the kingdom of Aragon and other Mediterranean maritime towns. • The *Consolato del Mare* was compiled in the 14th century and soon became one of the leading maritime codes of Europe. It is widely believed to be a Spanish work, but some historians suggest its origin is actually Italian. — Also written *Consolat de Mar.*

consolidate, *vb.* (16c) **1.** To combine or unify (separate items) into one mass or body, esp. in order to make them more effective or easier to deal with. **2.** *Civil procedure.* To combine, through court order, two or more actions involving the same parties or issues into a single action ending in a single judgment or, sometimes, in separate judgments. **3.** *Corporations.* To unite (two or more corporations or other organizations) to create one new corporation or other organization. See CONSOLIDATION.

consolidated appeal. See APPEAL (2).

consolidated bond. See BOND (3).

consolidated financial statement. See FINANCIAL STATEMENT (1).

consolidated laws. See CODE (1).

consolidated mortgage. See MORTGAGE.

Consolidated Omnibus Budget Reconciliation Act of 1985. A federal statute requiring employers that offer group health coverage to their employees to continue to do so for a prescribed period (usu. 18 to 36 months) after employment has terminated so that the former employee can continue to benefit from group-health rates until becoming a member of another health-insurance plan. • The statute temporarily continues group-health coverage for a person no longer entitled to receive it, such as a terminated employee or an overage dependent. "Qualifying events" justifying the continuation of group-health-insurance benefits include divorce, legal separation, or the death of a spouse. So COBRA often provides critical transitional coverage until a separated, divorced, or surviving spouse and children can arrange for new health insurance. The period of transitional coverage is up to 36 months, and an applicant spouse of the employee must make written application to the employer within 60 days of the separation or divorce. — Abbr. COBRA.

> "In the absence of any type of statutory vesting provision (which would render benefits nonforfeitable), terminated employees were generally left without health care coverage while they were looking for another job. While some state insurance laws provide for limited continuation coverage or individual conversion options, these alternatives were not available in all states . . . . Thus, COBRA was designed to fill this void, by providing a statutorily mandated mechanism for enabling terminated employees (and their eligible family members) to continue to have access to group health coverage at group rates until they can get another job or otherwise arrange for replacement coverage." I.M. Golub et al., *COBRA Handbook* § 1.1, at 1-2 (1994).

consolidated return. See TAX RETURN.

consolidated school district. See SCHOOL DISTRICT.

consolidated security. See SECURITY (4).

consolidated sentence. See *general sentence* under SENTENCE.

consolidating act. See *consolidating statute* under STATUTE.

consolidating statute. See STATUTE.

consolidation, *n.* (15c) **1.** The act or process of uniting; the quality, state, or condition of being united. **2.** *Legislation.* The combination into a single statutory measure of various legislative provisions that have previously been scattered in different statutes. **3.** *Civil procedure.* The court-ordered unification of two or more actions, involving the same parties and issues, into a single action resulting in a single judgment or, sometimes, in separate judgments. Fed. R. Civ. P. 42(a). — Also termed *consolidation of actions.* Cf. JOINDER; SEVERANCE (2). **4.** A judicial order that combines charges in two or more separate accusatory instruments into a single accusatory instrument.

▸ **procedural consolidation.** See JOINT ADMINISTRATION.

▸ **substantive consolidation.** (1975) *Bankruptcy.* The merger of two or more bankruptcy cases, usu. pending against the same debtor or related debtors, into one estate for purposes of distributing the assets, usu. resulting in the two estates sharing assets and liabilities, and in the extinguishment of duplicate claims and claims between the debtors.

5. *Corporations.* The unification of two or more corporations or other organizations by dissolving the existing ones and creating a single new corporation or organization. — Also termed (with respect to corporations) *consolidation of corporations.* Cf. MERGER (8). **6.** *Corporations. Archaic.* A union of the stock, property, or franchises of two or more companies whereby the conduct of their affairs is permanently — or for a long period — put under one management, whether the agreement between them is by lease, sale, or other form of contract, and whether the effect is the dissolution of one, both, or neither of the companies. — **consolidate,** *vb.* — **consolidatory** (kən-sol-ə-**day**-tər-ee), *adj.*

consolidation loan. See LOAN.

consolidation of actions. See CONSOLIDATION (3).

consolidation of corporations. See CONSOLIDATION (5).

consolidation of mortgages. *Hist.* The equitable right of a mortgagee who holds multiple mortgages on real property owned by the same person to refuse to release one mortgage unless all the mortgages are redeemed.

consonant statement. See STATEMENT.

consorting, *n.* (17c) **1.** A uniting in company with; an associating with. **2.** *Australian law.* The habitual keeping of company with one or more convicted or reputed criminals.

consortium (kən-**sor**-shee-əm). (1836) **1.** The benefits that one person, esp. a spouse, is entitled to receive from another, including companionship, cooperation, affection, aid, financial support, and (between spouses) sexual relations <a claim for loss of consortium>. See LOSS OF CONSORTIUM; CONJUGAL RIGHTS.

▸ **filial consortium** (**fil**-ee-əl). (1977) A child's society, affection, and companionship given to a parent.

▸ **parental consortium.** (1976) A parent's society, affection, and companionship given to a child.

▸ **spousal consortium.** (1976) A spouse's society, affection, and companionship given to the other spouse.

2. *Hist.* The services of a wife or daughter, the loss of which gives rise to a cause of action. • A husband could, for example, bring an action against a person who had injured his wife, "whereby he lost the help or companionship (of his wife)" (*per quod consortium amisit*). **3.** A group of companies that join or associate in an enterprise <several high-tech businesses formed a consortium to create a new supercomputer>. **4.** *Roman law.* A community of undivided goods existing among coheirs after the death of the head of their family (paterfamilias). Pl. **consortiums, consortia.**

consortium vitae (kən-**sor**-shee-əm **VI**-tee). [Law Latin] *Hist.* Cohabitation; the agreement between two parties to live together.

consortship (**kon**-sort-ship). (1836) *Maritime law.* An agreement by which salvors agree to work together to salvage wrecks, the recovery being apportioned among the salvors. • Consortships reduce interference among competing salvors and help prevent collisions at sea between operators attempting to salvage the same wreck.

conspicuous, *adj.* (1534) (Of a term or clause) clearly visible or obvious. • Whether a printed clause is conspicuous as a matter of law usu. depends on the size and style of the typeface. Under the UCC, a term or clause is conspicuous if it is written in a way that a reasonable person against whom it is to operate ought to notice it. *See* UCC § 1-201(b)(10). See FINE PRINT.

conspicuous place. (18c) For purposes of posting notices, a location that is reasonably likely to be seen.

conspiracy, *n.* (14c) An agreement by two or more persons to commit an unlawful act, coupled with an intent to achieve the agreement's objective, and (in most states) action or conduct that furthers the agreement; a combination for an unlawful purpose. 18 USCA § 371. • Conspiracy is a separate offense from the crime that is the object of the conspiracy. A conspiracy ends when the unlawful act has been committed or (in some states) when the agreement has been abandoned. A conspiracy does not automatically end if the conspiracy's object is defeated. *See* Model Penal Code § 5.03(7); *U.S. v. Jiminez Recio*, 537 U.S. 270, 123 S.Ct. 819 (2003). — Also termed *criminal conspiracy*. Cf. ATTEMPT (2); SOLICITATION (2).

> "*Conspiracie* (*conspiratio*) though both in Latine and French it be used for an agreement of men, to doe any thing either good or bad: yet in our lawyers bookes, it is alway taken in the evill part." John Cowell, *The Interpreter* (1607).

> "[Conspiracy is an] elastic, sprawling and pervasive offense, . . . so vague that it almost defies definition. Despite certain elementary and essential elements, it also, chameleon-like, takes on a special coloration from each of the many independent offenses on which it may be overlaid. It is always 'predominantly mental in composition' because it consists primarily of a meeting of minds and an intent." *Krulewitch v. U.S.*, 336 U.S. 440, 445–48, 69 S.Ct. 716, 719–20 (1949) (Jackson, J., concurring).

> "When two or more persons combine for the purpose of inflicting upon another person an injury which is unlawful in itself, or which is rendered unlawful by the mode in which it is inflicted, and in either case the other person suffers damage, they commit the tort of conspiracy." P.H. Winfield, *A Textbook of the Law of Tort* § 128, at 434 (5th ed. 1950).

▸ **bathtub conspiracy.** See *intra-enterprise conspiracy*.

▸ **chain conspiracy.** (1959) A single conspiracy in which each person is responsible for a distinct act within the overall plan, such as an agreement to produce, import, and distribute narcotics in which each person performs only one function. • All participants are interested in the overall scheme and liable for all other participants' acts in furtherance of that scheme.

▸ **circle conspiracy.** See *wheel conspiracy*.

▸ **civil conspiracy.** (1901) An agreement between two or more persons to commit an unlawful act that causes damage to a person or property.

▸ **conspiracy in restraint of trade.** See RESTRAINT OF TRADE.

▸ **conspiracy to defraud.** (18c) **1.** A secret plan by two or more people to cheat a person or organization. **2.** The common-law and (in some jurisdictions) statutory offense consisting in an agreement between two or more persons to use dishonest means that will harm or imperil the economic interests of another, or that will influence the exercise of a public duty. • Traditionally, the defrauding need not have been the primary purpose of the fraudfeasors' conduct; it is enough for the fraudfeasors to know that their actions will necessarily result in the defrauding of victims.

▸ **conspiracy to infringe.** (1908) *Intellectual property.* An agreement by two or more persons to commit an act that would interfere with the exclusive rights of a patent, copyright, or trademark owner. • This action is commonly recognized in trademark law. 18 USCA § 371; 17 USCA § 506(a)(1). The Copyright Act does not provide a basis for alleging a conspiracy to infringe, but an action is recognized by some states. The Patent Act provides no basis for an action asserting conspiracy to infringe because patent law covers only acts, not threats of acts.

▸ **conspiracy to injure.** (18c) **1.** A tort that occurs when two or more persons combine to harm someone else, whether physically, mentally, or economically. **2.** *English law.* A tort that occurs when two or more persons combine to damage another's business through means other than normal commercial competition.

▸ **conspiracy to monopolize.** (1890) *Antitrust.* A conspiracy to take exclusive control of a commercial market. • Under § 2 of the Sherman Act, a conspiracy to monopolize exists if there is a conspiracy or concerted action directed at a substantial part of interstate commerce with the intent to acquire monopoly power.

▸ **hub-and-spoke conspiracy.** See *wheel conspiracy*.

▸ **intracorporate conspiracy.** (1960) A conspiracy existing between a corporation and its own officers, agents, or employees. • To be prosecutable under federal law, the conspiracy must involve at least two persons (i.e., not just the corporation and one person). 18 USCA § 371. A corporation cannot conspire with its employees, and its employees, acting in the scope of their employment, conspire among themselves. *McAndrew v. Lockheed Martin Corp.*, 206 F.3d 1031, 1035 (11th Cir. 2000).

▸ **intra-enterprise conspiracy.** (1965) *Antitrust.* A conspiracy existing between two subsidiaries, divisions, or other parts of the same firm. — Also termed *bathtub conspiracy*.

▸ **rimless-wheel conspiracy.** (1973) See *wheel conspiracy*.

▸ **seditious conspiracy.** (1893) A criminal conspiracy to forcibly (1) overthrow or destroy the U.S. government, (2) oppose its authority, (3) prevent the execution of its laws, or (4) seize or possess its property. 18 USCA § 2384.

▸ **wheel conspiracy.** (1959) A conspiracy in which a single member or group (the "hub") separately agrees with two or more other members or groups (the "spokes"). • The person or group at the hub is the only party liable for all the conspiracies. — Also termed *rimless-wheel conspiracy*; *circle conspiracy*; *hub-and-spoke conspiracy*.

conspirator, *n.* (15c) Someone who takes part in a conspiracy.

▸ **unindicted conspirator.** See *unindicted coconspirator* under COCONSPIRATOR.

conspiratorial, *adj.* (1856) **1.** Of, relating to, or involving a conspiracy or one or more conspirators <conspiratorial plotting>. **2.** (Of an expression, tone of voice, or mannerism) suggesting the presence of a conspiracy <conspiratorial whispers>.

conspire, *vb.* (14c) To engage in conspiracy; to join in a conspiracy.

constable (**kon**-stə-bəl), *n.* (13c) **1.** A peace officer responsible for minor judicial duties, such as serving writs and warrants, but with less authority and smaller jurisdiction than a sheriff. **2.** In the United Kingdom, a police officer; also, the title of a police officer. — Also termed (redundantly) *police constable.* — **constabulary** (kən-**stab**-yə-ler-ee), *adj.* — **constabulary** (police station or force), *n.*

▸ **special constable.** Someone in the United Kingdom who holds down a regular job but also works as an unpaid police officer.

constablewick (**kon**-stə-bəl-wik). (17c) *Hist.* In the United Kingdom, the territorial jurisdiction of a constable. Cf. BAILIWICK (1).

constant dollars. (1925) The value of current money expressed as a percentage of its buying power in a previous year as determined by the consumer price index. • This value is used as a measure of inflation.

constat (**kon**-stat), *n.* [Latin "it is settled"] (16c) *Hist.* A certificate made by the Clerk of the Pipe and the auditors of the Exchequer at the request of a person intending to plead in the Court of Exchequer for the discharge of some item. • The *constat* certified what appeared on record.

constat de persona (**kon**-stat dee pər-**soh**-nə). [Law Latin] (17c) *Hist.* It is evident what person was meant. • A writing that misidentified a person was enforceable if the true identity of the person was evident from the remainder of the document. See DUMMODO CONSTET DE PERSONA.

constat de subjecto (**kon**-stat dee səb-**jek**-toh). [Law Latin] *Hist.* It is clear as to the subject matter (of a transaction).

constate (kən-**stayt**), *vb.* (18c) To establish, constitute, or ordain. • *Constate* usu. appears in relation to corporate documents; for example, a corporation is constated by its charter, organic law, or grant of powers to it.

constituency. (1831) **1.** The body of citizens dwelling in a defined area and entitled to elect a representative. **2.** The residents of an electoral district, esp. those who vote. **3.** An area of a country that elects a representative to the legislature. — Sense 3 is especially common in BrE.

constituency-based quorum. See *interest-based quorum* under QUORUM.

constituent, *adj.* (17c) **1.** (Of a component) that helps make up or complete a unit or a whole <a constituent element of the criminal offense>. **2.** (Of an assembly) able to frame or amend a constitution <a constituent council>.

constituent, *n.* (17c) **1.** Someone who gives another the authority to act as a representative; a principal who appoints an agent. **2.** Someone who is represented by a legislator or other elected official. **3.** One part of something that makes up a whole; an element. — **constituency,** *n.*

constituent element. An essential component of a crime or cause of action.

constituere (kon-sti-**tyoo**-ə-ree), *vb.* [Latin "to appoint"] *Hist.* To appoint (someone). • *Constituere* was used principally in powers of attorney: *attornavi et in loco meo constitui* ("I have attorned and put in my place").

constitute, *vb.* **1.** To give legal or appropriate procedural form to (something); to establish by law. **2.** To appoint to an office, function, or rank. **3.** To make up or form.

constituted annuity. See ANNUITY.

constituted authority. See AUTHORITY (3).

constitutio (kon-sti-**t[y]oo**-shee-oh), *n.* [Latin "a decree"] **1.** *Roman law.* An imperial decree; a law issued by the emperor; later, in the plural form *constitutiones,* a collection of laws. • The *constitutiones* took various forms, including *orationes* (laws submitted to the Senate), *edicta* (laws — usu. of a general character — put forth by the emperor), *mandata* (administrative directives to imperial officials), *decreta* (decisions by the emperor in legal cases), and *rescripta* (the emperor's responses to questions posed by litigants or imperial officials). Over time, the rapidly increasing number of *constitutiones* prompted their arrangement into collections such as the Theodosian Code and the Code of Justinian. They were the sole form of legislation after the third century A.D. — Also termed (collectively) *constitutiones principum.* See THEODOSIAN CODE; JUSTINIAN CODE. Pl. ***constitutiones*** (kon-sti-t[y]oo-shee-**oh**-neez).

> "The name *constitutiones*, applied to the law-making utterances of the Roman emperors, had a very different meaning from our word 'constitution,' used to denote the fundamental, organic law of the state. Every official public document issuing from the emperor, and creating, declaring, or modifying law, was a *constitutio*. . . . [A]nd it is hardly necessary to say that, although professing to come from the person of the emperor, they were actually composed by jurists, and usually by those who stood first in their profession." James Hadley, *Introduction to Roman Law* 6–7 (1881).

2. *Civil law.* A settlement achieved without a trial; the sum paid according to the settlement. **3.** *Hist. English law.* In England, a statute; a provision of a statute. Pl. ***constitutiones*** (kon-sti-t[y]oo-shee-**oh**-neez).

constitution. (18c) **1.** The entire plan or philosophy on which something is constructed. **2.** The fundamental and organic law of a country or state that establishes the institutions and apparatus of government, defines the scope of governmental sovereign powers, and guarantees individual civil rights and civil liberties; a set of basic laws and principles that a country, state, or organization is governed by. **3.** The written instrument embodying this fundamental law, together with any formal amendments.

> "The form of government of the individual states, as in the case of the federal government, is defined by state constitutions. In general, these constitutions resemble the federal constitution and establish three separate branches of government. The chief executive officers of the states are the governors, who have been popularly elected in most states throughout most of the history of the nation. While elected federal government officials have uniform terms of office and responsibilities under the Constitution, the governors and other officers of the various states are elected according to a pastiche of state constitutional requirements and for terms and at times that vary widely from one state to another. Governors exercise the executive powers of the state governments, although the extent of their power has varied immensely across time and in the different states. Both legislative and judicial systems, which to a large degree resemble the federal pattern, also exist at the state level. The legislative functions in most states are performed by bicameral legislatures, although

in the early years of the twentieth century several states adopted a single legislative body (unicameral) for their lawmaking functions. A hierarchical system of courts also exists within the various states ranging from municipal or local courts through Courts of Appeals to State Supreme Courts." Erik W. Austin, *Political Facts of the United States Since 1789* 66–67 (1986).

"Constitutions came earlier than democracy. During the late Middle Ages and early modern times, constitutions were mainly devices for establishing rights and limiting powers, functions that are still emphasized in certain academic literature on constitutions. But as the old powers to be limited were autocratic, constitutionalism advanced almost naturally, together with the expansion of suffrage rights and democratization. A constitution is usually defined as 'a set of rules' for making collective decisions. Enforceable decisions made by means of rules can solve human coordination and cooperation dilemmas. However, different rules may favor different decisions with differently distributed benefits. Two sets of rules can be distinguished: (a) those 'to regulate the allocation of functions, powers and duties among the various agencies and offices of government,' and (b) those to 'define the relationships between these and the public,' which in democracy are based on elections." Josep M. Colomer, "Comparative Constitutions," in *The Oxford Handbook of Political Science* 176, 176 (Robert E. Goodin ed., 2009) (citations omitted).

▸ **federal constitution. 1.** *Constitutional law.* See *United States Constitution.* **2.** A country's constitution.

▸ **flexible constitution.** (1885) *Constitutional law.* A constitution that has few or no special amending procedures. • The British Constitution is an example. Parliament can alter constitutional principles and define new baselines for government action through ordinary legislative processes. The Canadian Constitution also grants its legislature some limited ability to amend the Constitution by legislation.

▸ **rigid constitution.** (1885) *Constitutional law.* A constitution whose terms cannot be altered by ordinary forms of legislation, only by special amending procedures. • The U.S. Constitution is an example. It cannot be changed without the consent of three-fourths of the states. U.S. Const. art. V.

▸ **state constitution.** A constitution, often modeled after the federal constitution, ratified by the citizens of an individual state.

▸ **United States Constitution.** *Constitutional law.* The 1787 document ratified by the original thirteen colonies to reform and restructure the national government and establish the relationship between the federal government and the states collectively and the relationships between the individual states. • Before the Constitution was drafted, the governing bodies were the Continental Congress and its successor, the Congress of the Confederation. — Sometimes shortened to *Constitution.* — Also termed *federal constitution.*

▸ **unwritten constitution.** (1804) **1.** The customs and values, some of which are expressed in statutes, that provide the organic and fundamental law of a state or country that does not have a single written document functioning as a constitution. • In British constitutional law, the constitution is a collection of historical documents, statutes, decrees, conventions, traditions, and royal prerogatives. Documents and statutes include Magna Carta (1215), the Bill of Rights (1689), and the European Communities Act (1972). **2.** The implied parts of a written constitution, encompassing the rights, freedoms, and processes considered to be essential, but not explicitly defined in the written document. • Many aspects of an unwritten constitution are based on custom and precedent. The U.S. Constitution does not, for example, give the Supreme Court the power to declare laws unconstitutional but the Court does so without question. Nor does the Constitution expressly guarantee a right of privacy, but the Supreme Court has declared that the right exists and is protected. See PENUMBRA; RIGHT OF PRIVACY.

3. A country's history of government and institutional development. • This was the standard definition before the United States produced the first written constitution. It remains current in the United Kingdom and other countries that have unwritten constitutions. **4.** *Parliamentary law.* A governing document adopted by an organization for its internal governance and its external dealings. • The constitution may be an organization's most authoritative governing document, but if the organization has also received a charter or adopted articles of incorporation or association, then the constitution is subordinate to them. If the organization has also adopted bylaws, then the bylaws are subordinate to (and usu. more easily amended than) the constitution. The constitution and bylaws are sometimes contained in a single document. See *governing document* under DOCUMENT (2). Cf. BYLAW (1).

constitutional, *adj.* (18c) **1.** Of, relating to, or involving a constitution <constitutional rights>. **2.** Proper and valid under a constitution <constitutional actions>.

constitutional-avoidance rule. The doctrine that a case should not be resolved by deciding a constitutional question if it can be resolved in some other fashion.

constitutional challenge. See CHALLENGE (1).

constitutional convention. See CONVENTION (3).

constitutional corporation. See CORPORATION.

constitutional court. See COURT; ARTICLE III COURT.

constitutional-doubt canon. The doctrine that a statute should be interpreted in a way that avoids placing its constitutionality in doubt. — Also termed *presumption against unconstitutionality; no-constitutional-doubt canon.* See PRESUMPTION OF VALIDITY; PRESUMPTION AGAINST INEFFECTIVENESS; UT RES MAGIS VALEAT QUAM PEREAT (2).

"The constitutional-doubt canon is sometimes lumped together with the rule that 'if a case can be decided on either of two grounds, one involving a constitutional question, the other a question of statutory construction or general law, the Court will decide only the latter.' The two rules together are sometimes called the 'rules of constitutional avoidance.' But it promotes clarity to keep the two separate. The constitutional-doubt canon is a rule of interpretation; the rule that statutory grounds will be considered first is a rule of judicial procedure. Often, but not always, both rules will be invoked in the same case: In the process of considering the statute first, the court may find that one of its interpretations must be rejected as constitutionally doubtful." Antonin Scalia & Bryan A. Garner, *Reading Law: The Interpretation of Legal Texts* 251 (2012) (citations omitted).

constitutional-fact doctrine. (1937) **1.** The rule that federal courts are not bound by an administrative agency's findings of fact when the facts involve whether the agency has exceeded constitutional limitations on its power, esp. regarding personal rights. • The courts reviewed the facts de novo to afford protection of constitutional rights.

Although it has not been overruled or wholly discredited, this rule has fallen out of favor. **2.** The rule that a federal appellate court is not bound by a trial court's findings of fact when constitutional rights are implicated, specifically in citizenship-determination and First Amendment cases. *See, e.g., Bose Corp. v. Consumers Union*, 466 U.S. 485, 104 S.Ct. 1949 (1984). Cf. JURISDICTIONAL-FACT DOCTRINE.

constitutional freedom. (1822) A basic liberty guaranteed by the Constitution or Bill of Rights, such as the freedom of speech. — Also termed *constitutional protection*; *constitutional liberty.*

constitutional guarantee. A promise contained in the United States Constitution that supports or establishes an inalienable right, such as the right to due process.

constitutional homestead. See HOMESTEAD (1).

constitutional immunity. See IMMUNITY (1).

constitutionalism. (1832) **1.** The theory that a government should be based on a constitution. **2.** Adherence to this theory. Cf. POPULAR CONSTITUTIONALISM.

constitutionality, *n.* (18c) The quality, state, or condition of being acceptable according to a constitution <the constitutionality of the senator's bill is questionable>.

constitutionalize, *vb.* (1831) **1.** To provide with a constitution <constitutionalize the new government>. **2.** To make constitutional; to bring in line with a constitution <the court plans to constitutionalize the segregated school district>. **3.** To make a constitutional question out of (a question of law); to subject (an issue, etc.) to the burden of passing constitutional muster <the dissenter accused the majority of unnecessarily constitutionalizing the issue>. **4.** To lodge (an evidentiary objection) at least in part on the basis of a constitutional violation, as in "Objection, hearsay. Also, Confrontation Clause violation." — Also termed *federalize.*

constitutional law. (18c) *Constitutional law.* **1.** The body of law deriving from the U.S. Constitution and dealing primarily with governmental powers, civil rights, and civil liberties. **2.** The body of legal rules that determine the constitution of a state or country with an unwritten constitution. Cf. STATUTORY LAW; COMMON LAW. **3.** The field of law dealing with aspects of constitutional provisions, such as restrictions on government powers and guarantees of rights.

constitutional liberty. See CONSTITUTIONAL FREEDOM.

constitutional limitation. (18c) A constitutional provision that restricts the powers of a governmental branch, department, agency, or officer.

constitutional majority. See *majority of all the members* under MAJORITY.

constitutional malice. See *actual malice* (2) under MALICE.

constitutional monarchy. See *limited monarchy* under MONARCHY.

constitutional office. A public position that is created by a constitution, rather than by a statute.

constitutional officer. See OFFICER (1).

constitutional option. See NUCLEAR OPTION.

constitutional power. (18c) *Constitutional law.* A governmental authority or capacity that, in a government formed under a constitution, is enumerated or implied as being vested in a particular branch or official; a legislative, executive, or judicial power granted by or deriving from a constitution.

constitutional prohibition. See PROHIBITION (1).

constitutional protection. See CONSTITUTIONAL FREEDOM.

constitutional question. (18c) *Constitutional law.* A legal issue resolvable by the interpretation of a constitution, rather than a statute.

constitutional right. (18c) *Constitutional law.* A right guaranteed by a constitution; esp., one guaranteed by the U.S. Constitution or by a state constitution.

▸ **fundamental constitutional right.** *Constitutional law.* A right that is specifically identified in a constitution or has been found to be protected under the Due Process or Equal Protection Clause.

constitutional taking. See TAKING (2).

constitutional tort. See TORT.

Constitution Day. See CONSTITUTION DAY AND CITIZENSHIP DAY.

Constitution Day and Citizenship Day. An American federal holiday to commemorate the signing of the U.S. Constitution on September 17, 1787, and to honor people who have become U.S. citizens. • Originally, the holiday was called Constitution Day (1911) and later also called Citizenship Day (1952), and both were observed on September 17. In 2004, it was renamed in an amendment to the Omnibus Spending Bill of 2004.

constitutiones principum (kon-sti-t[y]oo-shee-**oh**-neez prin-**sip**-ə). [Latin] See CONSTITUTIO (1).

constitution-making. (18c) *Constitutional law.* The drafting and bringing into effect of a constitution. — **constitution-maker,** *n.*

> "Constitution-making is 'a pre-eminently political act.' 'It is a decision-making process carried out by political actors, responsible for selecting, enforcing, implementing, and evaluating societal choices; and it is shaped by the sociopolitical order in which it takes place and, in turn, it strongly influences that order.' The participants are aware that they are involved in 'higher law-making' and this creates special expectations, roles, and rules. Constitution-makers may rise above ordinary attitudes of 'business as usual' and are capable of adapting [sic: adopting?] non-parochial, long-term perspectives. . . . [Yet] [t]he great pages of the history of constitution-making are full of human pettiness and, increasingly, institutional self-interest." Claude Klein & András Sajó, "Constitution-Making: Process and Substance," in *The Oxford Handbook of Comparative Constitutional Law* 419, 420 (Michel Rosenfeld & András Sajó eds., 2012).

Constitutions of Clarendon. *Hist.* A 12th-century statement of customary law, produced during the reign of Henry II, intended to limit the jurisdiction of the ecclesiastical courts and narrow the clergy's exemption from secular justice.

> "During the first half of the twelfth century the claims of the church were growing, and the duty of asserting them passed into the hands of men who were not mere theologians but expert lawyers. Then, as all know, came the quarrel between Henry and Becket. In the Constitutions of Clarendon (1164) the king offered to the prelates a written treaty, a treaty which, so he said, embodied the 'customs' of his ancestors, more especially of his grandfather. Becket, after some hesitation, rejected the constitutions. The dispute waxed hot; certain of the customs were condemned by the pope. The murder followed . . . . [F]rom [Henry's] time onwards the lay courts, rather than the spiritual, are the aggressors and the victors in almost every contest." 1

Frederick Pollock & Frederic W. Maitland, *The History of English Law* 124–25 (2d ed. 1898).

constitutor (**kon**-stə-t[y]oo-tər), *n.* [Latin "an orderer, arranger"] *Roman law.* A person who, by agreement, becomes responsible for the payment of another's debt.

constitutum (kon-sti-**t[y]oo**-təm), *n.* [Latin "agreed arrangement"] *Roman law.* **1.** An agreement to pay an existing debt, either one's own or another's, on a fixed day. • A *constitutum* was not a novation; the creditor could still sue the original debtor. It differed from a stipulation because it had to be for an existing debt. If the promise was to pay one's own debt, it was called *constitutum debiti proprii.* If it was to pay another's debt, then it was *constitutum debiti alieni.* **2.** The fixing of a day for the repayment of money owed.

constitutum debiti (kon-sti-**t[y]oo**-təm **deb**-ə-tɪ). [Latin "debt agreement"] *Roman law.* See CONSTITUTUM (1).

constitutum debiti alieni (kon-sti-**t[y]oo**-təm **deb**-ə-tɪ **ay**-lee-ə-nɪ). [Latin "debt agreement"] *Roman law.* See CONSTITUTUM (1).

constitutum debiti proprii (kon-sti-**t[y]oo**-təm **deb**-ə-tɪ **proh**-pree-ɪ). [Latin "debt agreement"] *Roman law.* See CONSTITUTUM (1).

constitutum possessorium (kon-sti-**t[y]oo**-təm pah-ses-**sor**-ee-əm). [Latin "possessory agreement"] *Roman law.* **1.** A type of constructive delivery in which mediate possession is transferred while the immediate control or custody remains in the transferor. See *mediate possession* under POSSESSION. **2.** The agreement by which this transfer is brought about. • In the context of a security interest, the pledged property may remain in the possession of the debtor, but as bailee of the creditor. For the other two types of constructive delivery, see ATTORNMENT; BREVI MANU. — Also termed *traditio longa manu* (trə-**dish**-ee-oh **long**-gə **man**-yoo).

"[Another] form of constructive delivery is that which the commentators on the civil law have termed *constitutum possessiorum* . . . . Any thing may be effectually delivered by means of an agreement that the possessor of it shall for the future hold it no longer on his own account but on account of someone else. . . . [I]f I buy goods from a warehouseman, they are delivered to me so soon as he has agreed with me that he will hold them as warehouseman on my account. The position is then exactly the same as if I had first taken actual delivery of them, and then brought them back to the warehouse, and deposited them there for safe custody." John Salmond, *Jurisprudence* 306 (Glanville L. Williams ed., 10th ed. 1947).

construction, *n.* (14c) **1.** The act of building by combining or arranging parts or elements; the thing so built. **2.** The act or process of interpreting or explaining the meaning of a writing (usu. a constitution, statute, or other legal instrument); the ascertainment of a document's sense in accordance with established judicial standards; INTERPRETATION. — **construct** (in sense 1), *vb.* — **construe** (in sense 2), *vb.*

"Construction, as applied to written law, is the art or process of discovering and expounding the meaning and intention of the authors of the law with respect to its application to a given case, where that intention is rendered doubtful either by reason of apparently conflicting provisions or directions, or by reason of the fact that the given case is not explicitly provided for in the law." Henry Campbell Black, *Handbook on the Construction and Interpretation of the Laws* 1 (1896).

"Some authors have attempted to introduce a distinction between 'interpretation' and 'construction.' Etymologically there is, perhaps, such a distinction; but it has not been accepted by the profession. For practical purposes any such distinction may be ignored, in view of the real object of both interpretation and construction, which is merely to ascertain the meaning and will of the lawmaking body, in order that it may be enforced." William M. Lile et al., *Brief Making and the Use of Law Books* 337 (Roger W. Cooley & Charles Lesley Ames eds., 3d ed. 1914).

"There is no explanation of the distinction between interpretation and construction [in Blackstone], nor can it be inferred from the matters dealt with under each head. The distinction is drawn in some modern works, but it is not taken in this book because it lacks an agreed basis. Some writers treat interpretation as something which is only called for when there is a dispute about the meaning of statutory words, while speaking of construction as a process to which all statutes, like all other writings, are necessarily subject when read by anyone. Others treat interpretation as something which is mainly concerned with the meaning of statutory words, while regarding construction as a process which mainly relates to the ascertainment of the intention of the legislature." Rupert Cross, *Statutory Interpretation* 18 (1976).

"The terms *construction* and *interpretation* are conventionally used interchangeably by most lawyers. Sometimes a more precise use is advocated whereby construction is the broader process which encompasses both the interpretation of the express terms of the contract and the neighboring technique of the *implication* of terms into an agreement. The speech of Lord Steyn in *Equitable Life Assurance Society v Hyman* has echoes of this usage, insisting on a two-state process of interpreting the express terms, and then identifying any implied terms. Lord Steyn saw both techniques as part of the overall process of construction. This more rarefied usage is not widespread, and in this work interpretation and construction are used interchangeably." Gerard McMeel, *The Construction of Contracts* 11–12 (2d ed. 2007).

▸ **broad construction.** See *liberal interpretation* under INTERPRETATION (1).

▸ **construction *ut res magis valeat quam pereat*** (kən-**strək**-shən ət rays [*or* reez *or* rez] **may**-jis **vay**-lee-at kwam **peer**-ee-at). [Latin "a construction that gives effect to the matter rather than having it fail"] (18c) A construction arrived at when alternative readings are possible, one of which (usu. the broader reading) would achieve the manifest purpose of the document and one of which (usu. the narrower reading) would reduce it to futility or absurdity, whereby the interpreter chooses the one that gives effect to the document's purpose.

▸ **contemporaneous construction.** (1804) An interpretation given at or near the time when a writing was prepared, usu. by one or more persons involved in its preparation. — Also termed *practical construction; practical interpretation; contemporaneous and practical interpretation.* See CONTEMPORANEOUS-CONSTRUCTION DOCTRINE.

▸ **equitable construction.** See *liberal interpretation* under INTERPRETATION (1).

▸ **fair construction.** See FAIR READING.

▸ **liberal construction.** See *liberal interpretation* under INTERPRETATION (1).

▸ **literal construction.** See *strict interpretation* under INTERPRETATION (1).

▸ **loose construction.** See *liberal interpretation* under INTERPRETATION (1).

▸ **practical construction.** **1.** See *contemporaneous construction.* **2.** See PRAGMATISM (2).

▸ **pragmatic construction.** See PRAGMATISM (2).

▸ **purposive construction.** See *purposive interpretation* under INTERPRETATION (1).

▸ **statutory construction.** See STATUTORY CONSTRUCTION.

▸ **strict construction.** See *strict interpretation* under INTERPRETATION (1).

3. According to some theorists, the judicial imputation of meaning where the text is silent.

construction bond. See BOND (3).

construction contract. See CONTRACT.

construction financing. See *interim financing* under FINANCING.

constructionism. (1845) A judicial approach to interpreting the text of statutes, regulations, constitutions, and the like.

▸ **broad constructionism.** See *liberal constructionism.*

▸ **liberal constructionism.** (1963) **1.** Broad interpretation of a text's language, including the use of related writings to clarify the meanings of the words, and possibly also a consideration of meaning in both contemporary and current lights. **2.** The view that despite the Tenth Amendment, the federal government may do things that the Constitution does not expressly say it may do. — Also termed *broad constructionism*; *loose constructionism.*

▸ **loose constructionism.** See *liberal constructionism.*

▸ **strict constructionism,** *n.* (1892) **1.** The doctrinal view of judicial construction holding that judges should interpret a document or statute (esp. one involving penal sanctions) according to its literal terms, without looking to other sources to ascertain the meaning. **2.** The view that under the Tenth Amendment, the federal government cannot do anything that the Constitution does not expressly say it may do. — Also termed *literal canon*; *literal rule.* See TEXTUALISM. — **strict constructionist,** *n.*

constructionist. (1838) Someone who interprets a controlling text, such as a statute, constitution, or the like.

▸ **broad constructionist.** See *liberal constructionist.*

▸ **liberal constructionist.** (1901) **1.** A decision-maker who derives the meaning of a text's language not only from the words but from reasonable inferences drawn from the words and from other sources, such as a statute's legislative history. • A liberal constructionist may also consider the reasonableness of an interpretation under modern social mores. **2.** One who advocates the idea that the federal government may do things that the Constitution does not expressly say it may do. — Also termed *broad constructionist, loose constructionist.* See *liberal constructionism* under CONSTRUCTIONISM. Cf. *strict constructionist.*

▸ **loose constructionist.** See *liberal constructionist.*

▸ **strict constructionist.** (1838) **1.** A decision-maker who derives a text's meaning narrowly and applies the text according to that meaning. See ORIGINALISM; *strict constructionism* under CONSTRUCTIONISM. Cf. *liberal constructionist.*

> "Under the stimulus of political agitation in the early days of the republic over the powers conferred by the constitution two rival schools of interpretations sprang up. The ones terming themselves strict constructionists held that the language of the constitution should be construed literally and conservatively, while the other party held with equal fervor that the instrument should be construed liberally and according to the spirit rather than the letter, so that they were denominated loose constructionists." Jesse Franklin Brumbaugh, *Legal Reasoning and Briefing* 129 (1917).

2. One who advocates the idea that the federal government cannot do anything that the Constitution does not expressly say it may do.

construction lien. See *mechanic's lien* under LIEN.

construction loan. See *building loan* under LOAN.

construction mortgage. See MORTGAGE.

construction statute. See STATUTE.

construction warranty. See WARRANTY (2).

constructive, *adj.* (17c) Legally imputed; existing by virtue of legal fiction though not existing in fact. • Courts usu. give something a constructive effect for equitable reasons <the court held that the shift supervisor had constructive knowledge of the machine's failure even though he did not actually know until two days later>. See LEGAL FICTION. Cf. ACTUAL.

constructive abandonment. **1.** *Family law.* See *constructive desertion* under DESERTION. **2.** *Intellectual property.* See ABANDONMENT (11).

constructive acceptance. See ACCEPTANCE (1).

constructive adverse possession. See ADVERSE POSSESSION (1).

constructive amendment of indictment. See AMENDMENT OF INDICTMENT.

constructive assent. See ASSENT.

constructive authority. See AUTHORITY (1).

constructive bailment. See BAILMENT (1).

constructive breach. See *anticipatory breach* under BREACH OF CONTRACT.

constructive breaking into a house. See *constructive housebreaking* under HOUSEBREAKING.

constructive condemnation. See *inverse condemnation* under CONDEMNATION (2).

constructive condition. See CONDITION (2).

constructive conditional institute. See INSTITUTE (5).

constructive contempt. See *indirect contempt* under CONTEMPT.

constructive contract. See *implied-in-law contract* under CONTRACT.

constructive conversion. See CONVERSION (2).

constructive crime. See CRIME.

constructive custody. See CUSTODY (1).

constructive delivery. See DELIVERY.

constructive desertion. See DESERTION.

constructive discharge. See DISCHARGE (7).

constructive dismissal. See *constructive discharge* under DISCHARGE (7).

constructive dividend. See DIVIDEND.

constructive emancipation. See EMANCIPATION.

constructive escape. See ESCAPE (2).

constructive eviction. See EVICTION.

constructive force. See FORCE.

constructive fraud. See FRAUD.

constructive housebreaking. See HOUSEBREAKING.

constructive intent. See INTENT (1).

constructive juristic realism. See LEGAL REALISM.

constructive knowledge. See KNOWLEDGE (1).

constructive larceny. See LARCENY.

constructive loss. See *constructive total loss* (1) under LOSS.

constructive malice. See *implied malice* under MALICE.

constructive murder. See *felony murder* under MURDER.

constructive notice. See NOTICE (3).

constructive occupancy. See OCCUPANCY (1).

constructive offense. See *constructive crime* under CRIME.

constructive parent. See *equitable parent* under PARENT (1).

constructive payment. See PAYMENT (2).

constructive possession. See POSSESSION.

constructive presence. See PRESENCE.

constructive-receipt doctrine. (1936) The rule that gross income under a taxpayer's control before it is actually received (such as accumulated interest income that has not been withdrawn) must be included by the taxpayer in gross income, unless the actual receipt is subject to significant constraints. IRC (26 USCA) § 451.

constructive reduction to practice. See REDUCTION TO PRACTICE.

constructive search. See SEARCH (1).

constructive seisin. See *seisin in law* under SEISIN.

constructive seizure. See SEIZURE.

constructive service. 1. See SERVICE (7). **2.** See DOCTRINE OF CONSTRUCTIVE SERVICE (2).

constructive taking. See TAKING (1).

constructive total loss. See LOSS.

constructive transfer. See TRANSFER.

constructive treason. See TREASON.

constructive trespass. See *trespass to chattels* under TRESPASS.

constructive trust. See TRUST (3).

constructive trustee. See TRUSTEE (1).

constructive use. *Trademarks.* The imputed use of a trademark based on the filing of an application in the U.S. Patent and Trademark Office averring a bona fide intent to use it, followed by registration.

constructivism. (1936) **1.** A Kantian method for arriving at principles of justice, which are constructed or created by a hypothetical framework (or set of constructs) within which an individual may choose between competing principles. • In this sense the term was introduced by John Rawls in his influential essay *Kantian Constructivism in Moral Theory*, 77 J. Phil. 515 (1980). But it had already been used in scientific, philosophical, and literary contexts, in reference to art. **2.** *Int'l law.* The view that important aspects of international relations are historically and sociologically contingent, as opposed to being inevitable consequences of human nature or of other characteristics of world politics. • In this sense, the term appears to have been first used by Nicholas Onuf in 1989.

construe (kən-**stroo**), *vb.* (14c) To analyze and explain the meaning of (a sentence or passage) <the court construed the language of the statute>.

constuprate (**kon**-st[y]ə-prayt), *vb.* (16c) *Archaic.* To rape or violate (a person). — **constupration,** *n.*

consuetude (**kon**-swi-t[y]ood), *n.* (14c) Custom or habit; usage having the force of law. —**consuetudinary** (kon-swi-**t[y]ood**-i-ner-ee), *adj.*

consuetudinary (kon-swi-**t[y]oo**-di-nair-ee), *n.* [fr. Latin *consuetudo* "custom"] *Hist. Eccles. law.* A book containing the rites and forms of divine offices or customs of abbeys and monasteries. — Also termed ***consuetudinarius.***

consuetudinary law. See LAW.

Consuetudines Feudorum (kon-swə-**t[y]oo**-di-neez fyoo-**dor**-əm). [Law Latin "the customs of fiefs"] *Hist.* See FEUDORUM LIBRI.

consuetudinibus et serviciis (kon-swə-t[y]oo-**din**-ə-bəs et sər-**vish**-ee-is). [Law Latin "customs and services"] (17c) *Hist.* A writ of right that lay against a tenant who withheld rent or services from the lord.

consuetudo (kon-swə-**t[y]oo**-doh), *n.* [Latin "custom"] **1.** *Roman law.* Custom; long-established usage or practice. **2.** *Hist.* Customary law. • *Consuetudo* generally bears this sense, referring to law that has been long approved by the will of the people. It is a broad term that includes both the common law and the statutory law of England. **3.** *Hist.* A duty or tax.

consuetudo anglicana (kon-swə-**t[y]oo**-doh ang-gli-**kay**-nə). [Law Latin "the custom of England"] *Hist.* The English common law, as distinguished from Roman or civil law.

consuetudo curiae (kon-swə-**t[y]oo**-doh **kyoor**-ee-ee). [Latin] *Hist.* The custom or practice of a court.

consuetudo mercatorum (kon-swə-**t[y]oo**-doh mər-kə-**tor**-əm). [Latin "the custom of merchants"] *Hist.* See LAW MERCHANT. — Also termed *consuetudo mercatoria.*

consul (**kon**-səl), *n.* (14c) **1.** A governmental representative living in a foreign country to oversee commercial and other matters involving the representative's home country and its citizens in that foreign country. • Consuls are not diplomatic agents, so unless a treaty provides otherwise, they do not enjoy diplomatic privileges and immunities. But consuls are entitled to consular immunities, which protect them from local law and jurisdiction in the exercise of their consular functions. — **consular** (**kon**-sə-lər), *adj.* — **consulship** (**kon**-səl-ship), *n.*

> "The commercial agents of a government, residing in foreign parts, and charged with the duty of promoting the commercial interests of the state, and especially of its individual citizens or subjects, are called consuls. These, under the regulations of some countries, are of different grades, being either consuls-general, consuls, or vice-consuls, from whom consular agents differ little." Theodore D. Woolsey, *Introduction to the Study of International Law* § 99, at 159 (5th ed. 1878).

> "Consuls are commercial, not diplomatic agents. They reside abroad for the purpose of protecting the individual interests of traders, travellers, and mariners belonging to

the State which employs them. . . . They exercise jurisdiction over their countrymen, their persons are inviolable, their residences may be used as asylums in the case of war or tumult, and in fact they possess more than the ordinary diplomatic immunities." T.J. Lawrence, *A Handbook of Public International Law* 86–87 (10th ed. 1925).

"Consuls are not diplomatic agents; they perform various services for a state or its subjects in another state, without, however, representing the former in the full sense. They may be nationals of either state, and generally they are made subject to the authority of the diplomatic representative of the state for which they act. They watch over commercial interests of the state for which they act; collect information for it; help its nationals with advice, administer their property if they die abroad, and register their births, deaths, and marriages; they authenticate documents for legal purposes, take depositions from witnesses, visa passports, and the like." J.L. Brierly, *The Law of Nations* 216 (5th ed. 1955).

"The usual criterion used for the distinction between diplomats and consuls is the representative character of the former of which the latter are devoid. However, this distinction is not altogether correct. Undoubtedly diplomatic agents have a general representative character since in all matters and relations they represent their country in the state to which they are accredited. Consuls, on the other hand, as state organs, also represent their country in another state, but only in matters within their competence. Thus, the representative character of consuls is, like their competence, specific, and secondary to that of diplomatic agents." Constantin Economidès, "Consuls," in 1 *Encyclopedia of Public International Law* 770 (1992).

▸ **consul general.** (18c) A high-ranking consul appointed to a strategically important region and often having supervisory powers over other regions or other consuls.

2. *Roman law.* One of two chief magistrates elected annually during the Republic to exercise supreme authority. • Under the Empire, the consulship was reduced to a sinecure, held by appointees of the emperor or the emperor himself.

"The principal inheritors of the royal authority and dignity were the two consuls elected by the comitia centuriata. They enjoyed equal powers. In the calendar the year was distinguished by their names. They convoked and initiated legislation in either comitia. In special emergencies, particularly in times of grave crisis, either consul might appoint a dictator who exercised supreme authority, but not beyond six months, unless re-appointed. . . . It was abolished by Justinian in a.d. 541, though later emperors continued to assume the title." R.W. Lee, *The Elements of Roman Law* 14 (4th ed. 1956).

consular court. See COURT.

consular immunity. See IMMUNITY (1).

consular invoice. See INVOICE.

consular jurisdiction. (17c) The exercise of a judicial function by a consul in a foreign territory, as by performing a wedding ceremony between nationals of the country represented by the consul.

consular law. (1845) The law relating to consuls, developed through custom and multitudes of bilateral consular agreements.

consular marriage. See MARRIAGE (1).

consular privilege. See *consular immunity* under IMMUNITY (1).

consular relations. (18c) *Int'l law.* The aggregate of relations established between two countries through the exercise of consuls' functions on behalf of a sending state within the territory of a receiving state. See *sending state* and *receiving state* under STATE (1).

consulate (**kon**-sə-lit). (18c) **1.** The office or jurisdiction of a consul <the senator advised the businessman to notify the U.S. consulate in Kuwait before visiting the country>. **2.** The location of a consul's office or residence <the family was staying on the second floor, just above the Turkish consulate>.

▸ **foreign consulate.** (1882) The consulate of a foreign country in the receiving state.

3. Government by consuls <after the French Revolution, the Directory was overthrown and the Consulate was created>. • This sense of *consulate* is based on the original Roman meaning ("chief magistrate") — not on the modern sense of an overseas representative of a country.

consules electi (**kon**-s[y]uu-leez i-**lek**-tɪ). [Latin] *Hist.* Consuls elect.

consules missi (**kon**-s[y]uu-leez **mis**-ɪ). [Latin] *Hist.* Officials on mission.

consul general. See CONSUL (1).

consultation, *n.* (15c) **1.** The act of asking the advice or opinion of someone (such as a lawyer). **2.** A meeting in which parties consult or confer. **3.** *Int'l law.* The interactive methods by which states seek to prevent or resolve disputes. — **consult,** *vb.* — **consulting, consultative,** *adj.*

consultative exam. (1978) As a foundation for an expert opinion, a check-up performed by a qualified medical professional to determine whether a person has a mental or physical disability, and, if so, the extent of the disability and expectations for improvement.

consulting expert. See EXPERT.

consumable, *n.* (1802) A thing (such as food) that cannot be used without changing or extinguishing its substance. Cf. NONCONSUMABLE. — **consumable,** *adj.*

consume, *vb.* **1.** To destroy the substance of, esp. by fire; to use up or wear out gradually, as by burning or eating <the house was consumed by fire>. **2.** To expend wastefully; to waste; to squander <he consumed all his resources within four months>. **3.** To use up (time, resources, etc.), whether fruitfully or fruitlessly <45% of the paper we consume is recycled>. **4.** To eat or drink; to devour <no alcohol may be consumed on these premises>. **5.** To engage the attention or interest of fully; to obsess <she was consumed with guilt after her father's death>.

consumer. (15c) **1.** Someone who buys goods or services for personal, family, or household use, with no intention of resale; a natural person who uses products for personal rather than business purposes. **2.** Under some consumer-protection statutes, any individual. 15 USCA §§ 1679a(1), 1681a(c).

"The term 'consumer' has various legal meanings. It can be used broadly, to mean citizens who 'consume' or use goods or services, ranging from plumbing to health services and education. Usually it is used in a more restrictive way. Many statutory provisions, designed to protect purchasers of goods and services, contain specific measures applicable only to consumers. The statutory definitions of 'consumer' often contain slight variations, but there are certain common core features. 'Consumer' normally means a private individual acquiring goods or services. In some instances, in addition to natural persons, it can also include businesses such as sole-traders and partnerships, for example, under consumer credit measures. Occasionally, even companies come within the definition, if acting outside their normal business activities — for example a manufacturing company buying a car for a director." Deborah Parry, "Consumer," in *The New Oxford Companion to Law* 213, 213 (Peter Cane & Joanne Conaghan eds., 2008).

consumer boycott. See BOYCOTT.

consumer claim. (1929) A person's legal claim based on having purchased defective goods or services for a noncommercial purpose.

consumer confusion. (1944) *Trademarks.* The incorrect perception formed by a purchaser or user about a product's or service's manufacturer or origin. • The mistake usu. occurs when a product or service is marketed in a way that makes it appear to be affiliated with a well-known product, service, or provider. — Also termed *actual consumer confusion*; *user confusion*; *actual user confusion*.

consumer-contemplation test. (1979) A method of imposing product liability on a manufacturer if the evidence shows that a product's danger is greater than that which a reasonable consumer would expect. — Also termed *consumer-user-contemplation test*; *consumer-expectation test.* Cf. RISK–UTILITY TEST.

consumer contract. See CONTRACT.

consumer credit. See CREDIT (4).

Consumer Credit Code. See UNIFORM CONSUMER CREDIT CODE.

consumer-credit insurance. See INSURANCE.

Consumer Credit Protection Act. A federal statute that broadly regulates aspects of consumer credit, including lending practices, credit reporting, and debt collection. 15 USCA §§ 1601–1693r. • Enacted in 1968, the statute safeguards consumers in the use of credit by (1) requiring full disclosure of the terms of loan agreements, including finance charges, (2) restricting the garnishment of wages, and (3) regulating the use of credit cards. It originally consisted of five subchapters, of which the best known is the Truth in Lending Act. Later amendments have added other provisions, including five new subchapters: the Credit Repair Organizations Act, the Fair Credit Reporting Act, the Equal Credit Opportunity Act, the Fair Debt Collection Practices Act, and the Electronic Fund Transfer Act. Many states have adopted similar consumer-credit-protection acts. — Abbr. CCPA. — Also termed *Truth in Lending Act* (TILA). See UNIFORM CONSUMER CREDIT CODE.

consumer-credit sale. See SALE.

consumer-credit transaction. (1954) A transaction by which a person receives a loan to buy consumer goods or services. • Consumer-credit transactions are usu. subject to regulations enacted for the consumer's protection.

consumer debt. See DEBT.

consumer-expectation test. See CONSUMER-CONTEMPLATION TEST.

consumer finance company. See FINANCE COMPANY.

Consumer Financial Protection Bureau. An independent federal agency that regulates consumer financial products and services. • The Bureau protects consumers by restricting unfair or deceptive business practices, by promoting financial education, by taking consumer complaints, and by enforcing federal consumer-financial-protection laws. It was established by the Dodd–Frank Act in 2010 and began operating in 2011. — Abbr. CFPB.

consumer fraud. See FRAUD.

consumer goods. See GOODS.

consumer-goods transaction. (1950) *Secured transactions.* A transaction in which (1) an individual incurs an obligation primarily for a personal, family, or household purpose, and (2) a security interest in consumer goods secures the obligation. UCC § 9-102(a)(24).

consumerism. (1915) **1.** Advocacy to protect people from unfair prices, misleading advertisements, unconscionable consumer contracts, etc. **2.** The belief in the overarching importance of a robust consumer economy.

consumer law. (1966) The area of law dealing with consumer transactions — that is, a person's obtaining credit, goods, real property, or services for personal, family, or household purposes. — Also termed *consumer-transactions law.*

consumer lease. See LEASE.

consumer loan. See LOAN.

consumer price index. (1945) An index that tracks the price of goods and services purchased by the average consumer and that is published monthly by the U.S. Bureau of Labor Statistics. • The consumer price index is used to monitor periodic changes in the rate of inflation. It shows how much prices have increased or declined during a particular period. — Abbr. CPI. — Also termed *cost-of-living index.* Cf. PRODUCER PRICE INDEX.

consumer product. (1949) An item of personal property that is distributed in commerce and is normally used for personal, family, or household purposes. 15 USCA § 2301(1).

Consumer Product Safety Commission. An independent federal regulatory commission that develops safety standards for consumer products and promotes research into the causes and prevention of product-related deaths, illnesses, and injuries. • It was established in 1972. 15 USCA §§ 2051 et seq. — Abbr. CPSC.

consumer-product-safety standard. (1972) A standard established by government regulation, industry practice, or corporate policy to prevent or reduce the risk of injury caused to a user or bystander by an article that is manufactured and sold for personal, domestic, or household use or consumption.

consumer-protection law. (1954) A state or federal statute designed to protect consumers against unfair trade and credit practices involving consumer goods, as well as to protect consumers against faulty and dangerous goods.

consumer report. Under the federal Fair Credit Reporting Act, any communication by a consumer-reporting agency that is collected, used, or expected to be used as a factor in establishing the consumer's eligibility for credit, insurance, or employment, or for any other permissible purpose; specif., those communications bearing on a consumer's creditworthiness, credit standing, credit capacity, character, general reputation, personal characteristics, or mode of living. 15 USCA § 1681a(d). See CREDIT REPORT.

consumer-reporting agency. Under the federal Fair Credit Reporting Act, someone who, for fees, dues, or on a cooperative nonprofit basis, regularly engages in the practice of assembling or evaluating consumer-credit information or other information about consumers for the purpose of furnishing consumer reports to third parties, and who uses any means or facility of interstate commerce to prepare or furnish consumer reports. 15 USCA § 1681a(f). See CREDIT BUREAU; CREDIT-REPORTING BUREAU.

consumer sale. See SALE.

consumer transaction. (1951) A bargain or deal in which a party acquires property or services primarily for a personal, family, or household purpose.

consumer-transactions law. See CONSUMER LAW.

consumer-user-contemplation test. See CONSUMER-CONTEMPLATION TEST.

consumer warranty. See *manufacturer's warranty* under WARRANTY (1).

consummate (kən-**səm**-it *or* **kon**-sə-mit), *adj.* (15c) Completed; fully accomplished. • *Consummate* was often used at common law to describe the status of a contract or an estate, such as the transformation of a husband's interest in his wife's inheritance from that of a tenant by the curtesy *initiate* to a tenant by curtesy *consummate* upon the wife's death (assuming that a child had been born during the marriage). See *curtesy consummate* under CURTESY. — **consummation,** *n.*

consummate (**kon**-sə-mayt), *vb.* (16c) **1.** To bring to completion; esp., to make (a marriage) complete by sexual intercourse. **2.** To achieve; to fulfill. **3.** To perfect; to carry to the highest degree.

consummate dower. See DOWER.

consummate lien. See LIEN.

consummation of marriage. (16c) *Family law.* The first postmarital act of sexual intercourse between a husband and wife. • Under canon law, a refusal to consummate the marriage may be grounds for an annulment or for divorce. But this is not so at common law or under modern state law.

consumption. (14c) The act of destroying a thing by using it; the use of a thing in a way that exhausts it.

consumption tax. See TAX.

contagion. *Int'l law.* A discredited doctrine holding that revolution or abhorrent practices in a neighboring state justify its invasion and the overthrow of its government on the grounds of national security. • The doctrine was employed by the Holy Alliance (1815–1848) in Europe to invade countries where revolutions were brewing. — Also termed *doctrine of contagion.*

containing by estimate. (18c) *Archaic.* More or less. • This phrase usu. appears in deeds in which measurements are made by metes and bounds. It is redundant when the phrase "more or less" is used.

containment. (1947) *Int'l law.* The act of keeping something under control or stopping it from becoming more widespread or powerful; esp., a policy of restricting the ideological or territorial expansion of one's enemy. • This was the basic policy of the United States during the Cold War.

contango (kən-**tang**-goh), *n.* (1853) *Securities.* **1.** A pricing structure in which futures prices get progressively higher as maturities get progressively longer; also, a market in which long-term futures or options contracts sell at a premium over short-term contracts. — Also termed *normal market.* **2.** The premium so paid. • The premium paid for securities with longer maturities reflects the cost of holding the securities for future delivery. Cf. BACKWARDATION.

contemn (kən-**tem**), *vb.* (16c) To treat (as laws or court orders) with contemptuous disregard. See CONTEMPT.

contemnor (kən-**tem**-ər *or* -nər *or* -nor). (16c) Someone who is guilty of contempt before a governmental body, such as a court or legislature. — Also spelled *contemner.*

contemplation of bankruptcy. (18c) The thought of declaring bankruptcy because of the inability to continue current financial operations, often coupled with action designed to thwart the distribution of assets in a bankruptcy proceeding. — Also termed *contemplation of insolvency.*

contemplation of death. (18c) The thought of dying, not necessarily from imminent danger, but as the compelling reason to transfer property to another. See *gift causa mortis* under GIFT.

contemplation of insolvency. See CONTEMPLATION OF BANKRUPTCY.

contemporanea expositio (kən-tem-pə-**ray**-nee-ə eks-pə-**zish**-ee-oh). [Latin "contemporaneous exposition"] (17c) The doctrine that the best meaning of a statute or document is the one given by those who enacted it or signed it, and that the meaning publicly given by contemporary or long professional usage is presumed to be the correct one, even if the language may have a popular or an etymological meaning that is very different.

> "The rule as to *contemporanea expositio* was first laid down by Coke (2 Inst. ed. Thomas, p. 2, n. (1)), in speaking of Magna Charta, in the following terms: — 'This and the like were the forms of ancient Acts and graunts, and the ancient Acts and graunts must be construed and taken as the law was holden at that time when they were made.' The earlier statutes were in the form of charters, and no difference was at first made between the construction of a statute and that of any other instrument. Coke's rule has been adopted by the English Courts, and for modern use is best expressed by Lord Esher in *Sharpe v. Wakefield* (1888), 22 Q.B.D. 241: 'The words of a statute must be construed as they would have been the day after the statute was passed, unless some subsequent Act has declared that some other construction is to be adopted or has altered the previous statute.'" William Feilden Craies, *A Treatise on Statute Law* 88 (2d ed. 1911).

contemporaneous, *adj.* (17c) Living, occurring, or existing at the same time.

contemporaneous and practical interpretation. See *contemporaneous construction* under CONSTRUCTION (2).

contemporaneous construction. See CONSTRUCTION (2).

contemporaneous-construction doctrine. (1956) The rule that the initial interpretation of an ambiguous statute by an administrative agency or lower court is entitled to great deference if the interpretation has been used over a long period.

contemporaneous interpretation. See LIVING CONSTITUTIONALISM.

contemporaneous-objection rule. (1965) The doctrine that a timely and proper objection to the admission of evidence must be made at trial to afford the trial court an opportunity to conduct a meaningful inquiry into possible prejudice before or promptly after verdict and to preserve the issue for appeal. • An objection is timely if it is made as soon as practicable and is proper if made formally on the record.

contemporary community standards. (1957) The gauge by which a fact-finder decides whether material is obscene, judging by its patent offensiveness and its prurience in the locale at a given time. See OBSCENITY (1).

contempt, *n.* (14c) **1.** The act or state of despising. **2.** The quality, state, or condition of being despised. **3.** Conduct that defies the authority or dignity of a court or legislature. • Because such conduct interferes with the administration of justice, it is punishable, usu. by fine or imprisonment. Fed. R. Civ. P. 45(e); Fed. R. Crim. P. 42; 18 USCA § 401. See CONTUMACY. — Also termed *contempt of court; judicial contempt.*

> "Contempt is a disregard of, or disobedience to, the rules or orders of a legislative or judicial body, or an interruption of its proceedings by disorderly behavior or insolent language, in its presence or so near thereto as to disturb the proceedings or to impair the respect due to such a body." Edward M. Dangel, *Contempt* § 1, at 2 (1939).

▸ **civil contempt.** (1884) The failure to obey a court order that was issued for another party's benefit. • A civil-contempt proceeding is coercive or remedial in nature. The usual sanction is to confine the contemnor until he or she complies with the court order. The act (or failure to act) complained of must be within the defendant's power to perform, and the contempt order must state how the contempt may be purged. Imprisonment for civil contempt is indefinite and for a term that lasts until the defendant complies with the decree.

▸ **common-law contempt.** See *criminal contempt.*

▸ **consequential contempt.** (1840) **1.** Contempt that, although not amounting to gross insolence or direct opposition, tends to create a universal disregard of the power and authority of courts and judges. **2.** See *indirect contempt.*

▸ **constructive contempt.** See *indirect contempt.*

▸ **contempt of Congress.** (1924) Deliberate interference with the duties and powers of Congress, such as a witness's refusal to answer a question from a congressional committee. • Contempt of Congress is a criminal offense. 2 USCA § 192.

▸ **contempt of sovereignty.** (1921) *Int'l law.* The minor diplomatic offense of interference in domestic affairs by a foreign representative, esp. by making a public statement about an issue currently being debated in the legislature.

▸ **criminal contempt.** (1841) An act that obstructs justice or attacks the integrity of the court. • A criminal-contempt proceeding is punitive in nature. The purpose of criminal-contempt proceedings is to punish repeated or aggravated failure to comply with a court order. All the protections of criminal law and procedure apply, and the commitment must be for a definite period. — Also termed *common-law contempt.*

> "Criminal contempt is a crime in the ordinary sense; it is a violation of the law, a public wrong which is punishable by fine or imprisonment or both." *Bloom v. Illinois,* 391 U.S. 194, 201, 88 S.Ct. 1477, 1481 (1968).

▸ **direct contempt.** (1863) A contempt (such as an assault of a testifying witness) committed in the immediate vicinity of a court; esp., a contempt committed in a judge's presence. • A direct contempt is usu. immediately punishable when the transgression occurs.

▸ **indirect contempt.** (1896) Contempt that is committed outside court, as when a party disobeys a court order. • Indirect contempt is punishable only after proper notice to the contemnor and a hearing. — Also termed *constructive contempt; consequential contempt.*

contempt of court. See CONTEMPT (3).

contempt power. (1885) The power of a governmental body (such as Congress or a court) to punish someone who shows contempt for the process, orders, or proceedings of that body.

contempt proceeding. See PROCEEDING.

contemptuous, *adj.* (16c) Showing that one thinks someone or something deserves no respect; ostentatiously disdainful.

contemptuous damages. See *nominal damages* under DAMAGES.

contenement (kən-**ten**-ə-mənt). (12c) *Hist.* **1.** Freehold land held by a feudal tenant, esp. land used to support the tenant. • Magna Carta (1215) exempted this property from seizure.

> "*Contenement,* (*contenementum*) seemeth to be the free hould land, which lyeth to a mans tenement or dwelling house, that is in his owne occupation. For *magna carta. ca.* 14. you have these words: A free man shall not be amerced for a small fault, but after the quantity of the fault: and for a great fault, after the maner thereof, saving to him his contenement or free hould. And a merchant likewise shal be amerced saving to him his merchandies: and any other villaine then owers, shal be amerced saving his wainage . . . ." John Cowell, *The Interpreter* (1607).

2. A person's reputation or standing in the community. • Though *contenement* as used in this sense is also rooted in the ownership of land, it may stem from the Law French *contenance* ("countenance") rather than the Law Latin *contenementum* ("with tenement"), as used in sense 1.

> "Contenement signifies his Countenance, Credit, or Reputation, which he hath, together with, and by reason of his Freehold; and in this sense does the Statute of 1 Edw. 3 and *Old Nat. Br.* use it, where *Countenance* is used for *Contenement*: The Armor of a Soldier is his Countenance; the Books of a Schollar, his Countenance; and the like." Thomas Blount, *Nomo-Lexicon: A Law-Dictionary* (1670).

content, *n.* (1867) *Maritime law.* A written declaration of a departing vessel's destination, the kind and quantity of cargo it is carrying, and other particulars, submitted to a customs inspector for approval and permission for the vessel to leave port. Cf. MANIFEST, *n.*

content-based discrimination. See DISCRIMINATION (3).

content-based restriction. (1973) *Constitutional law.* A restraint on the substance of a particular type of speech. • This type of restriction is presumptively invalid but can survive a constitutional challenge if it is based on a compelling state interest and its measures are narrowly drawn to accomplish that end. *Boos v. Barry,* 485 U.S. 312, 108 S.Ct. 1157 (1998). See SPEECH (1).

contention. (14c) **1.** A strong opinion that someone expresses; esp., a legal or factual position stated openly by counsel <his main contention is that he owed the driver no duty>. **2.** Argument or disagreement between people; controversy, strife, or dispute <a source of contention>. **3.** Earnest effort in the face of opposition; a stubborn competition with rivals <Jones's contention against the establishment proved fruitless>.

contention interrogatory. See INTERROGATORY.

contentious jurisdiction. See JURISDICTION.

contentious possession. See *hostile possession* under POSSESSION.

contentious work. (17c) Legal work involving litigation — as opposed to purely transactional, consultative, advisory, or clerical work.

content-neutral. See NEUTRAL.

contents unknown. (18c) A statement placed on a bill of lading to show that the carrier does not know what is inside shipped containers. • Carriers use this phrase in an attempt to limit their liability for damage to the goods shipped. *Shipper's load and count* is also used.

content-valid test. (1973) A job-applicant examination that bears a close relationship to the skills required by the job. • Content-validation studies are often performed in employment-discrimination cases that contest the validity of an examination.

conterminous, *adj.* (17c) **1.** Sharing a common boundary; having the same area, context, or meaning <the surveyor set a new line between the conterminous counties>. — Also termed *coterminous.* **2.** Enclosed within a common boundary <all 48 conterminous states of this country>. **3.** See COTERMINOUS.

contest (kən-**test**), *vb.* (17c) **1.** To strive to win or hold; contend <he chose to contest for the prize>. **2.** To litigate or call into question; challenge <they want to contest the will>. **3.** To deny an adverse claim or assert a defense to it in a court proceeding <she contests that charge>. — **contest** (**kon**-test), *n.*

contestability clause (kən-tes-tə-**bil**-ə-tee). (1922) *Insurance.* A policy provision setting forth when and under what conditions the insurer may contest a claim or void the policy based on a representation or omission made when the policy was issued. • Contestability clauses usu. lapse after two years. — Also termed *contestable clause.* Cf. INCONTESTABILITY CLAUSE.

contestant. (17c) **1.** Someone who contests the validity of a will, trust, or other legal instrument. — Also termed *objectant*; *caveator.* **2.** *Trademarks.* Someone who challenges the placement of a trademark on the Principal Register. • The term refers to a challenger in (1) an interference proceeding, (2) an opposition proceeding before a mark is placed on the Principal Register, or (3) a cancellation proceeding after the mark is placed on the Principal Register. **3.** *Patents.* A party to an interference proceeding in the U.S. Patent and Trademark Office. — Also termed (in sense 3) *interferant.*

contestatio litis (kon-tes-**tay**-shee-oh **lI**-tis). [Latin "contestation of suit"] See LITIS CONTESTATIO.

contestation of suit (kon-tes-**tay**-shən). (17c) *Eccles. law.* The point in an action when the defendant answers the plaintiff's libel (i.e., complaint); the plea and joinder of an issue. — Also termed *litis contestatio.*

contested divorce. See DIVORCE.

contested hearing. See HEARING.

context, *n.* (16c) **1.** The surrounding text of a word or passage, used to determine the meaning of that word or passage <his remarks were taken out of context>. **2.** Setting or environment <in the context of foreign relations>. — **contextual,** *adj.*

context-based fiduciary relationship. See FIDUCIARY RELATIONSHIP.

context rule. *Contracts.* The principle that a court may look to extrinsic evidence to determine the intended meaning of a contract, even though the language itself is clear and unambiguous. • The court may consider (1) the subject matter and purpose of the contract, (2) the circumstances surrounding the making of the contract, (3) the subsequent conduct of the parties to the contract, (4) the reasonableness of the parties' respective interpretations, (5) statements made by the parties in preliminary negotiations, (6) usages of trade, and (7) the course of dealing between the parties. This rule does not make extrinsic evidence admissible for other purposes, such as adding to, modifying, or contradicting the contract's terms, unless a party can show that the actual language resulted from fraud, accident, or mistake. Restatement (Second) of Contracts §§ 212, 214(c) (1981).

contextual zoning. See ZONING.

contiguity (kon-ti-**gyoo**-ə-tee), *n.* (17c) The quality, state, or condition of being contiguous <contiguity existed between the two adjoining tracts of land>.

contiguous (kən-**tig**-yoo-əs), *adj.* (17c) **1.** Touching at a point or along a boundary; ADJOINING <Texas and Oklahoma are contiguous>. **2.** Near in time or sequence; successive <contiguous thunder and lightning>.

contiguous zone. (1926) *Int'l law.* An area abutting and extending beyond the territorial sea, in which countries have limited powers to enforce customs as well as fiscal, sanitary, and immigration laws.

Continental Congress. The first national governmental assembly in the United States, formed in 1774 to protest British treatment of the colonies. • The Second Continental Congress, commencing in 1775, adopted the Declaration of Independence and served as the national government until the Articles of Confederation were ratified in 1781. The successor government continued to call itself the Continental Congress even though the Articles of Confederation formally named it the Congress of the Confederation. See CONGRESS OF THE CONFEDERATION.

continental shelf. (1892) *Int'l law.* The submerged border of a continent where the seabed constitutes a relatively shallow landmass, usu. sloping gradually to a point of steeper descent, extending beyond a state's territorial sea through the natural prolongation of its land territory to the outer edge of the submerged continental margin, or 200 nautical miles from the baselines from which the breadth of the territorial sea is measured, whichever distance is greater. *United Nations Convention on the Law of the Sea* art. 76 (1982).

contingency (kən-**tin**-jən-see). (16c) **1.** An event that may or may not occur in the future; a possibility. **2.** The condition of being dependent on chance; uncertainty. **3.** CONTINGENT FEE.

contingency beneficiary. See *contingent beneficiary* (1) under BENEFICIARY.

contingency fee. See CONTINGENT FEE.

contingency reserve. See *contingent fund* under FUND (1).

contingency with a double aspect. (18c) A contingent remainder existing along with a second remainder, the latter remainder taking effect only if the first fails. • In the following example, this type of remainder would arise if A never has children: "to A for life, and if A has children, then to the children and their heirs forever; and if A dies without children, then to B and B's heirs forever." See *contingent remainder* under REMAINDER.

contingent (kən-**tin**-jənt), *adj.* (14c) **1.** Possible; uncertain; unpredictable <the trust was contingent, and the contingency never occurred>. **2.** Dependent on something that might or might not happen in the future; conditional <her acceptance of the position was contingent upon the firm's agreeing to guarantee her husband a position as well>.

contingent annuity. See ANNUITY.

contingent beneficiary. See BENEFICIARY.

contingent claim. See CLAIM (4).

contingent condition. See CONDITION (2).

contingent creditor. See CREDITOR.

contingent debt. See DEBT.

contingent demand. See DEMAND (1).

contingent estate. See ESTATE (1).

contingent fee. (17c) A fee charged for a lawyer's services only if the lawsuit is successful or is favorably settled out of court. • Contingent fees are usu. calculated as a percentage of the client's net recovery (such as 25% of the recovery if the case is settled, and 33% if the case is won at trial). — Also termed *contingency fee*; *contingency*; *conditional fee*.

▸ **reverse contingent fee.** (1979) A fee in which a defense lawyer's compensation depends in whole or in part on how much money the lawyer saves the client, given the client's potential liability — so that the lower the settlement or judgment, the higher the lawyer's fee. • For example, if a client might be liable for up to $2 million, and agrees to pay the lawyer 40% of the difference between $1 million and the amount of the settlement or judgment, then a settlement of $800,000 would result in a fee of $80,000 (40% of the $200,000 under the threshold amount of $1 million). — Also termed *negative contingent fee*; *defense contingent fee*; *reverse bonus*.

contingent fund. See FUND (1).

contingent guaranty. See GUARANTY (1).

contingent interest. See INTEREST (2).

contingent-interest mortgage. See MORTGAGE.

contingent legacy. See LEGACY.

contingent liability. See LIABILITY.

contingent ownership. See OWNERSHIP.

contingent remainder. See REMAINDER (1).

contingent right. See RIGHT.

contingent trust. See TRUST (3).

contingent use. See USE (4).

contingent-value right. See RIGHT.

contingent will. See WILL.

continual claim. (16c) *Hist.* A formal claim to a tract of land made by an out-of-possession owner who is deterred from taking possession by a menace of some type. • The claim — called *continual* because it had to be renewed annually — preserved the claimant's right to the land. The owner had to make the claim as near to the land as could be done safely. This procedure gave the disseised person the same benefits (such as the right to devise the land) as a legal entry. The continual claim was abolished early in the 19th century.

> "Continual claim is, where a man hath right to enter into certain lands whereof another is seised in fee, or fee tail, and dares not enter for fear of death or beating, but approaches as nigh as he dares, and makes claim thereto within the year and day before the death of him that hath the lands . . . ." *Termes de la Ley* 114 (1st Am. ed. 1812).

continual injury. See INJURY.

continuance, *n.* (14c) **1.** The act of keeping up, maintaining, or prolonging <continuance of the formal tradition>. **2.** Duration; time of continuing <the senator's continuance in office>. **3.** *Procedure.* The adjournment or postponement of a trial or other proceeding to a future date <motion for continuance>. Cf. RECESS (1). — **continue,** *vb.*

continuando (kən-tin-yoo-**an**-doh). [Law Latin "by continuing"] (17c) *Hist.* An allegation charging that the trespass or other wrongful act complained of constitutes a continuing tort against the plaintiff's property.

> "In trespasses of a permanent nature, where the injury is continually renewed, (as by spoiling or consuming the herbage with the defendant's cattle) the declaration may allege the injury to have been committed by *continuatione* from one given day to another, (which is called laying the action with a *continuando*) and the plaintiff shall not be compelled to bring separate actions for every day's separate offence." 3 William Blackstone, *Commentaries on the Laws of England* 212 (1768).

continuation. (1931) *Patents.* A patent application that is based on the same disclosure and claiming the same invention as a rejected parent application but containing some change in the scope of the claims. • A continuation application maintains the original filing date for prior-art and interference purposes, as long as it is filed while the parent application is still pending, has at least one inventor in common with the parent application, and refers to the parent application. — Also termed *continuation application*; *continuation-in-whole application*; *continuing application*; *file-wrapper continuation application*. Cf. CONTINUATION-IN-PART; *continued-prosecution application* under PATENT APPLICATION; REQUEST FOR CONTINUED EXAMINATION.

continuation agreement. (1942) *Partnership.* An agreement among the partners that, in the event of dissolution, the business of the partnership can be continued without the necessity of liquidation. Cf. BUY–SELL AGREEMENT (1).

> "Normally, a continuation agreement would have some type of provision for purchasing the interest of a deceased or expelled partner. However, such a provision is not necessary. Courts have enforced agreements that give the estate of the deceased partner nothing." Harold Gill Reuschlein & William A. Gregory, *The Law of Agency and Partnership* § 269, at 461 (2d ed. 1990).

continuation application. 1. See CONTINUATION. **2.** See CONTINUATION-IN-PART.

continuation-application laches doctrine. (2004) *Patents.* An equitable defense to patent infringement, based on an assertion that the patentee deliberately delayed the issuance of the patent-in-suit by filing multiple continuing applications that added new patent claims to cover products marketed or processes used after the original application was filed. — Also termed *prosecution laches doctrine.* See SUBMARINE PATENT.

continuation-in-part. (1926) *Patents.* A patent application filed by the same applicant during the pendency of an earlier application, repeating a substantial part of the earlier application but adding to or subtracting from the claims. 35 USCA § 120. • This type of application contains new technical descriptions from the inventor or reflects improvements made since the parent application was filed. A claim in a continuation-in-part application is entitled to the benefit of the parent application's filing date if the claimed subject matter is the same, but the new matter takes the filing date of the continuation-in-part application. Continuation-in-part applications are usu. filed to describe and claim later-discovered improvements to an invention, or to distinguish the invention from some prior-art reference. — Abbr. CIP. — Also termed *continuation-in-part application*; *continuation application*; *continuing application*; *file-wrapper continuation application.* Cf. CONTINUATION.

continuation-in-part application. See CONTINUATION-IN-PART.

continuation-in-whole application. See CONTINUATION.

continued bond. See *annuity bond* under BOND (3).

continued-custody hearing. See *shelter hearing* under HEARING.

continued meeting. See MEETING.

continued-prosecution application. See PATENT APPLICATION.

continuing, *adj.* (14c) **1.** Uninterrupted; persisting <a continuing offense>. **2.** Not requiring renewal; enduring <continuing stockholders> <continuing jurisdiction>.

continuing act. See ACT (2).

continuing annuity. See *survivorship annuity* under ANNUITY.

continuing application. See PATENT APPLICATION.

continuing breach. See BREACH OF CONTRACT.

continuing-claim doctrine. See CONTINUING-VIOLATION DOCTRINE.

continuing consideration. See CONSIDERATION (1).

continuing contract. See CONTRACT.

continuing covenant. See COVENANT (1).

continuing damages. See DAMAGES.

continuing guaranty. See GUARANTY (1).

continuing harm. See *continuing injury* under INJURY.

continuing injury. See INJURY.

continuing judicial education. (1964) Continuing legal education for judges, usu. organized and sponsored by a governmentally subsidized body and often involving topics such as judicial writing, efficient decision-making, caseload management, and the like. — Abbr. CJE.

continuing jurisdiction. See JURISDICTION.

continuing-jurisdiction doctrine. (1966) **1.** The rule that a court retains power to enter and enforce a judgment over a party even though that party is no longer subject to a new action. **2.** *Family law.* The rule that once a court has acquired jurisdiction over a child-custody or support case, that court continues to have jurisdiction to modify orders, even if the child or a parent moves to another state.

continuing legal education. (1948) **1.** The process or system through which lawyers extend their learning beyond their law-school studies, usu. by attending seminars designed to sharpen lawyering skills or to provide updates on legal developments within particular practice areas. • In many jurisdictions, lawyers have annual or biennial requirements to devote a given number of hours (usu. 12–15) to continuing legal education. **2.** The enhanced skills or knowledge derived from this process. **3.** The business field in which educational providers supply the demand for legal seminars, books, audiotapes, and videotapes designed to further the education of lawyers. — Abbr. CLE.

continuing nuisance. See NUISANCE.

continuing objection. See OBJECTION (1).

continuing offense. See OFFENSE (2).

continuing part-time judge. See JUDGE.

continuing threat of harm. (1972) A condition or situation that presents a high risk of injury at intervals or over an extended period, whether or not an injury has actually occurred. • The condition or situation can be a behavior that is subject to repetition, as with unfair-competition practices or stalking, or an enduring state, such as environmental contamination. — Also termed *threat of continuing harm*; *continuing threat of injury*; *threat of continuing injury.* Cf. *continuing injury* under INJURY.

continuing trespass. See TRESPASS.

continuing trust. See TRUST (3).

continuing violation. See VIOLATION (2).

continuing-violation doctrine. (1977) *Employment law.* The judge-made rule that if an employer's discriminatory acts are of an ongoing nature, the statute of limitations will be extended to allow the plaintiff to recover even when a claim based on those acts would otherwise be time-barred; the rule that the statute of limitations does not bar a claim or prosecution for an act that occurs as part of a series of related or recurring acts. • Each act is treated as a separate violation. — Also termed *continuing-claim doctrine*; *doctrine of continuing violation.*

continuing warranty. See *promissory warranty* under WARRANTY (3).

continuing wrong. See WRONG.

continuity (kon-ti-**n[y]oo**-ə-tee). **1.** *Int'l law.* The principle that upheavals and revolutions within a country — as well as changes in governmental forms, the extent of a country's territory, and measures taken during a military occupation — do not affect the existence of the country and therefore cannot lead to its extinction. **2.** *Patents.* The rule that a continuation or divisional patent application carries the effective filing date of its parent application if (1) the parent application fully discloses the same invention, (2) there is at least one common inventor, and (3) the parent application was still pending when the latter application was filed. • A continuation-in-part application carries the effective filing date for everything disclosed in the parent application, but not for new material. 35 USCA § 120. — Also termed *doctrine of continuity.* Cf. HIATUS.

continuity of business enterprise. (1980) *Tax.* A doctrine covering acquisitive reorganizations whereby the acquiring corporation must continue the target corporation's historical business or must use a significant portion of the target's business assets in a new business to qualify the acquisition as a tax-deferred transaction.

continuity-of-enterprise doctrine. See SUBSTANTIAL-CONTINUITY DOCTRINE.

continuity-of-entity doctrine. See MERE-CONTINUATION DOCTRINE.

continuity of existence. See CONTINUITY-OF-LIFE DOCTRINE.

continuity of interest. (1974) **1.** *Tax.* A doctrine covering acquisitive reorganizations whereby a target corporation's shareholders must retain a share in the acquiring corporation to qualify the acquisition as a tax-deferred transaction. **2.** A judicial requirement for divisive reorganizations whereby a target corporation's shareholders must retain an interest in both the distributing and the controlled corporations to qualify the exchange as a tax-deferred transaction. — Abbr. COI.

continuity-of-life doctrine. (1999) The principle that the withdrawal, incapacity, bankruptcy, or death of the owner of an entity (esp. a corporation) does not end the entity's existence. — Also termed *continuity of existence.*

continuous-adverse-use principle. (1999) The rule that the uninterrupted use of land — along with the other elements of adverse possession — will result in a successful claim for adverse possession. — Also termed *uninterrupted-adverse-use principle.* See ADVERSE POSSESSION.

continuous crime. See CRIME.

continuous easement. See EASEMENT.

continuous injury. See *continual injury* under INJURY.

continuous offense. See *continuous crime* under CRIME.

continuous-operations clause. (1955) *Oil & gas.* A provision in an oil-and-gas lease giving the lessee the right to continue any drilling well that was begun before the lease expired and to begin drilling more wells. See OPERATIONS CLAUSE.

continuous policy. See *perpetual policy* under INSURANCE POLICY.

continuous-representation doctrine. (1974) The principle that the limitations period for bringing a legal-malpractice action is tolled as long as the lawyer against whom the action is brought continues the representation that is related to the negligent act or omission.

continuous servitude. See *continuous easement* under EASEMENT.

continuous-treatment doctrine. (1962) The principle that the limitations period for bringing a medical-malpractice action is tolled while the patient continues treatment that is related to the negligent act or omission.

continuous trigger. See TRIPLE TRIGGER.

continuous vegetative state. See *persistent vegetative state* under VEGETATIVE STATE.

continuum juris (kən-**tin**-yoo-əm **joor**-is). [Latin] *Hist.* Continuity of law.

contio (**kon**-shee-oh), *n.* [Latin] *Roman law.* **1.** A public meeting to which participants have been summoned by a magistrate. **2.** A speech delivered at a public meeting. — Also spelled *concio.* Pl. ***contiones*** (kon-shee-**oh**-neez).

contor. See COUNTER.

contort (**kon**-tort), *n.* (1974) **1.** (*usu. pl.*) The overlapping domain of contract law and tort law.

> "I have occasionally suggested to my students that a desirable reform in legal education would be to merge the first-year courses in Contracts and Torts into a single course which we could call Contorts." Grant Gilmore, *The Death of Contract* 90 (1974).

2. A specific wrong that falls within that domain. **3.** *Informal.* A constitutional tort. See *constitutional tort* under TORT.

contra (**kon**-trə), *prep.* (15c) Against or contrary to. • As a citation signal, *contra* denotes that the cited authority supports a contrary view. In old law reports, *contra* often identifies the defendant's attorney (*pro querente* refers to the plaintiff's).

> "Observe in the note citing cases in support of a proposition mentioned in the text whether any of the cases follow the word *contra,* which means that a contrary rule has been laid down in them." Frank Hall Childs, *Where and How to Find the Law* 78–79 (1922).

contra account. See ACCOUNT.

contraband (**kon**-trə-band), *n.* (16c) **1.** Illegal or prohibited trade; smuggling. **2.** Goods that are unlawful to import, export, produce, or possess. — **contraband,** *adj.*

▸ **absolute contraband.** (1908) Goods used primarily for war, such as arms and ammunition, as well as clothing and equipment of a military character.

▸ **conditional contraband.** (1915) Goods susceptible of being used for warlike and peaceful purposes, such as coal and food. — Also termed *ancipitis usus* (an-**sip**-i-təs **yoo**-səs).

▸ **contraband per se.** (1901) Property whose possession is unlawful regardless of how it is used. Cf. *derivative contraband.*

▸ **derivative contraband.** (1965) Property whose possession becomes unlawful when it is used in committing an illegal act. Cf. *contraband per se.*

contra bonos mores (**kon**-trə **boh**-nohs **mor**-eez). [Latin "against good morals"] (17c) Offensive to the conscience and to a sense of justice. • Contracts *contra bonos mores* are voidable. — Also termed *contra bonos mores et decorum; adversus bonos mores.*

> "Whatever is *contra bonos mores et decorum,* the principles of our law prohibit, and the King's court, as the general censor and guardian of the public manners, is bound to restrain and punish." *Jones v. Randall,* 98 E.R. 706, 707 (1774).

contracausator (kon-trə-kaw-**zay**-tər). (18c) *Hist.* A criminal; a person prosecuted for a crime.

contraceptivism. (1946) *Hist.* The criminal offense of distributing or prescribing contraceptives.

contra constitutionem (**kon**-trə kon-sti-t[y]oo-shee-**oh**-nəm). [Latin] Against the constitution.

contract, *n.* (14c) **1.** An agreement between two or more parties creating obligations that are enforceable or otherwise recognizable at law <a binding contract>. **2.** The writing that sets forth such an agreement <a contract is

valid if valid under the law of the residence of the party wishing to enforce the contract>.

"The term contract has been used indifferently to refer to three different things: (1) the series of operative acts by the parties resulting in new legal relations; (2) the physical document executed by the parties as the lasting evidence of their having performed the necessary operative acts and also as an operative fact in itself; (3) the legal relations resulting from the operative acts, consisting of a right or rights *in personam* and their corresponding duties, accompanied by certain powers, privileges, and immunities. The sum of these legal relations is often called 'obligation.' The present editor prefers to define contract in sense (3) . . . ." William R. Anson, *Principles of the Law of Contract* 13 n.2 (Arthur L. Corbin ed., 3d Am. ed. 1919).

"A contract is a promise, or a set of promises, for breach of which the law gives a remedy, or the performance of which the law in some way recognizes as a duty. This definition may not be entirely satisfactory since it requires a subsequent definition of the circumstances under which the law does in fact attach legal obligation to promises. But if a definition were attempted which should cover these operative facts, it would require compressing the entire law relating to the formation of contracts into a single sentence." 1 Samuel Williston, *A Treatise on the Law of Contracts* § 1, at 1–2 (Walter H.E. Jaeger ed., 3d ed. 1957) (footnote omitted).

"The term 'contract' is also used by lay persons and lawyers alike to refer to a document in which the terms of a contract are written. Use of the word in this sense is by no means improper so long as it is clearly understood that rules of law utilizing the concept 'contract' rarely refer to the writing itself. Usually, the reference is to the agreement; the writing being merely a memorial of the agreement." John D. Calamari & Joseph M. Perillo, *The Law of Contracts* § 1.1, at 3 (4th ed. 1998).

3. A promise or set of promises by a party to a transaction, enforceable or otherwise recognizable at law; the writing expressing that promise or set of promises <when the lessor learned that the rooms were to be used for the delivery of blasphemous lectures, he declined to perform his contract>. *See* Restatement (Second) of Contracts § 2 (1979).

"The promissory element present in every contract is stressed in a widely quoted definition: 'A contract is a promise, or set of promises, for breach of which the law gives a remedy, or the performance of which the law in some way recognizes as a duty.' [1 Samuel Williston, *Contracts* § 1.1 (4th ed. 1990).] This, like similar definitions, is somewhat misleading. While it is true that a promise, express or implied, is a necessary element in every contract, frequently the promise is coupled with other elements such as physical acts, recitals of fact, and the immediate transfer of property interests. In ordinary usage the contract is not the promise alone, but the entire complex of these elements." John D. Calamari & Joseph M. Perillo, *The Law of Contracts* § 1.1, at 1–2 (4th ed. 1998).

4. Broadly, any legal duty or set of duties not imposed by the law of tort; esp., a duty created by a decree or declaration of a court <an obligation of record, as a judgment, recognizance, or the like, is included within the term "contract">. **5.** The body of law dealing with agreements and exchange <the general theory of contract>. **6.** The terms of an agreement, or any particular term <there was no express contract about when the money was payable>. **7.** Loosely, a sale or conveyance.

"Sometimes the word 'contract' is used to designate a transaction involving the exchange of goods or land for money. When money is exchanged for goods, this constitutes a sale. When money is exchanged for land, this constitutes a conveyance. Sales and conveyances may be the result of a previous contract but they are not the contracts in themselves. There is no undertaking or commitment to do or refrain from doing anything in the future. This indispensable element of contract is missing." John Edward Murray Jr., *Murray on Contracts* § 2, at 5 (2d ed. 1974).

8. Loosely, an enforceable agreement between two or more parties to do or not to do a thing or set of things; a compact <when they finally agreed, they had a contract>. — **contract,** *vb.* — **contractual,** *adj.*

"A contract is an agreement in which a party undertakes to do, or not to do, a particular thing." *Sturges v. Crowninshield*, 17 U.S. (4 Wheat) 122, 143 (1819).

▸ **absolute simulated contract.** *Civil law.* A simulated contract that the parties intend to be wholly ineffective. La. Civ. Code art. 2026. See *simulated contract.*

▸ **accessory contract.** (1836) A contract entered into primarily for the purpose of carrying out a principal contract; esp., a contract entered into for the purpose of obtaining by surety, mortgage, etc. the fulfillment of the provisions of an earlier contract. • The principal types are suretyship, indemnity, pledge, warranty, and ratification. Cf. *principal contract.*

▸ **adhesion contract.** (1949) A standard-form contract prepared by one party, to be signed by another party in a weaker position, usu. a consumer, who adheres to the contract with little choice about the terms. — Also termed *contract of adhesion*; *adhesive contract*; *adhesory contract*; *adhesionary contract*; *take-it-or-leave-it contract*; *leonine contract.*

"Some sets of trade and professional forms are extremely one-sided, grossly favoring one interest group against others, and are commonly referred to as contracts of adhesion. From weakness in bargaining position, ignorance, or indifference, unfavored parties are willing to enter transactions controlled by these lopsided legal documents." Quintin Johnstone & Dan Hopson Jr., *Lawyers and Their Work* 329–30 (1967).

"Dangers are inherent in standardization . . . for it affords a means by which one party may impose terms on another unwitting or even unwilling party. Several circumstances facilitate this imposition. First, the party that proffers the form has had the advantage of time and expert advice in preparing it, almost inevitably producing a form slanted in its favor. Second, the other party is usually completely or at least relatively unfamiliar with the form and has scant opportunity to read it — an opportunity often diminished by the use of fine print and convoluted clauses. Third, bargaining over terms of the form may not be between equals or, as is more often the case, there may be no possibility of bargaining at all. The form may be used by an enterprise with such disproportionately strong economic power that it simply dictates the terms. Or the form may be a take-it-or-leave-it proposition, often called a contract of adhesion, under which the only alternative to complete adherence is outright rejection." E. Allan Farnsworth, *Contracts* § 4.26, at 296–97 (3d ed. 1999).

▸ **aleatory contract** (**ay**-lee-ə-tor-ee). [fr. Latin *aleator* "gambler," fr. *alea* "the throwing of dice"] (1891) A contract in which at least one party's performance depends on some uncertain event that is beyond the control of the parties involved. • Most insurance contracts and life annuities are of this type. — Also termed *hazardous contract*; *wagering contract.* Cf. *certain contract.*

"A contract is aleatory when, because of the nature or according to the parties' intent, the performance of either party's obligation, or the extent of the performance, depends on an uncertain event." La. Civ. Code art. 1912.

▸ **alternative contract.** (1871) A contract in which the performing party may elect to perform one of two or more specified acts to satisfy the obligation; a contract that provides more than one way for a party to complete performance, usu. permitting that party to choose the manner of performance. — Also termed *alternative-methods-of-performance contract.*

▸ **assessment contract.** (1899) A contract in which the payment of a benefit is dependent on the collection of an assessment levied on persons holding similar contracts. See *assessment insurance* under INSURANCE.

▸ **best-efforts contract.** (1956) A contract in which a party undertakes to use best efforts to fulfill the promises made rather than to achieve a specific result; a contract in which the adequacy of a party's performance is measured by the party's ability to fulfill the specified obligations. • Although the obligor must use best efforts, the risk of failure lies with the obligee. To be enforceable, a best-efforts term must generally set some kind of goal or guideline against which the efforts may be measured. See BEST EFFORTS.

▸ **bilateral contract.** (1866) A contract in which each party promises a performance, so that each party is an obligor on that party's own promise and an obligee on the other's promise; a contract in which the parties obligate themselves reciprocally, so that the obligation of one party is correlative to the obligation of the other. — Also termed *mutual contract*; *reciprocal contract*; (in civil law) *synallagmatic contract.* See COUNTERPROMISE.

> "In a bilateral contract a promise, or set of promises on one side, is exchanged for a promise or a set of promises on the other side. In a unilateral contract, on the other hand, a promise on one side is exchanged for an act (or a forbearance) on the other side. Typical examples of bilateral contracts are contracts of sale, the buyer promising to pay the price and the seller promising to deliver the goods. A typical example of a unilateral contract is a promise of a reward for the finding of lost property followed by the actual finding of the property." P.S. Atiyah, *An Introduction to the Law of Contract* 32 (3d ed. 1981).

▸ **blanket contract.** (1894) A contract covering a group of products, goods, or services for a fixed period.

▸ **bona fide contract** (**boh**-nə fɪd *or* **fɪ**-dee). (18c) A contract in which equity may intervene to correct inequalities and to adjust matters according to the parties' intentions.

▸ **build-to-print contract.** (1986) A contract requiring the contractor to build a product according to exact technical specifications provided by the customer. • The design specifications are explicit and are often coupled with performance specifications, so the contractor has little discretion in how to perform. Much governmental contracting is build-to-print. — Also termed *design-specification contract.* Cf. *performance contract* (2).

▸ **certain contract.** (17c) A contract that will be performed in a stipulated manner. Cf. *aleatory contract.*

▸ **collateral contract.** (1809) A side agreement that relates to a contract that, if unintegrated, can be supplemented by evidence of the side agreement; an agreement made before or at the same time as, but separately from, another contract. See COLLATERAL-CONTRACT DOCTRINE.

> "The term 'collateral contract' has no very precise meaning in the law. It is generally used as a label for a contract which is collateral, or by the side of, another contract. A great many examples of implied or constructive contracts created by the Courts are collateral in a broad sense. . . . [A]lthough the normal presumption is that the parties intend a written contract to be exclusive evidence of their intentions, it is always open to a party to show that in fact the writing did not exclusively represent their intentions, because of a 'collateral' contract made during the negotiations but not incorporated in the written instrument." P.S. Atiyah, *An Introduction to the Law of Contract* 80–81, 161 (3d ed. 1981).

▸ **commutative contract** (kə-**myoo**-tə-tiv *or* **kom**-yə-tay-tiv). (1827) **1.** *Civil law.* A contract in which, at the time it is formed, the parties' obligations and advantages are certain and determinate. • This definition applied in Louisiana law before the civil code was revised in 1984. **2.** *Louisiana law.* A contract in which one party's performance is correlative to the performance of the other, so that nonperformance by either affords a defense to the other. La. Civ. Code art. 1911. Cf. *independent contract*; *synallagmatic contract.*

▸ **conditional contract.** (17c) An agreement that is enforceable only if another agreement is performed or if another particular prerequisite or condition is satisfied. — Also termed *hypothetical contract.*

▸ **conditional sales contract.** See *retail installment contract.*

▸ **consensual contract.** (18c) *Hist.* A contract arising from the mere consensus of the parties, without any formal or symbolic acts performed to fix the obligation. • Although the consensual contract was known to the common law, it originated in Roman law, where it embraced four types of contracts in which informal consent alone was sufficient: (1) an agency agreement (*mandatum*), (2) a partnership agreement (*societas*), (3) a sale (*emptio venditio*), or (4) a letting or hiring (*locatio conductio*). Cf. *real contract.*

> "[T]he peculiarity of these Consensual Contracts is that *no* formalities are required to create them out of the Pact. Much that is indefensible, and much more that is obscure, has been written about the Consensual Contracts, and it has even been asserted that in them the *consent* of the Parties is more emphatically given than in any other species of agreement. But the Consensual merely indicates that the Obligation is here annexed at once to the *Consensus.* The Consensus, or mutual assent of the parties, is the final and crowning ingredient in the Convention, and it is the special characteristic of agreements falling under one of the four heads of Sale, Partnership, Agency, and Hiring, that, as soon as the assent of the parties has supplied this ingredient, there is *at once* a Contract. The Consensus draws with it the Obligation, performing, in transactions of the sort specified, the exact functions which are discharged, in the other contracts, by the *Res* or Thing . . . ." Henry S. Maine, *Ancient Law* 322–23 (10th ed. 1884).

▸ **construction contract.** (1864) A contract setting forth the specifications for a building project's construction. • This type of contract is usu. secured by performance and payment bonds to protect both the owner and the subcontractors.

▸ **constructive contract.** See *implied-in-law contract.*

▸ **consumer contract.** (1909) A contract between a merchant seller and an individual who buys or contracts to buy goods that, at the time of contracting, are intended by the buyer to be used primarily for personal, family, or household purposes.

▸ **continuing contract.** (1828) A contract calling for periodic performances.

▸ **contract for deed.** (1825) See *installment land contract.*

▸ **contract for sale.** (1808) **1.** A contract for the present transfer of property for a price. — Also termed *contract of sale.* **2.** A contract to sell goods at a future time. — Also termed (in sense 2) *contract to sell.*

▸ **contract for services.** (1840) A contract for a job undertaken by an independent contractor, as opposed to an employee.

▸ **contract implied in fact.** See *implied-in-fact contract.*

▸ **contract implied in law.** See *implied-in-law contract.*

▸ **contract in restraint of trade.** (1811) A contract that limits the free exercise of business or trade; esp., a contract stipulating that one who sells a business cannot open a similar business within a specified distance of the business being sold within a specified period.

▸ **contract of adhesion.** See *adhesion contract.*

▸ **contract of affreightment.** See CONTRACT OF AFFREIGHTMENT.

▸ **contract of beneficence.** See *gratuitous contract.*

▸ **contract of benevolence.** See *gratuitous contract.*

▸ **contract of carriage.** See CONTRACT OF AFFREIGHTMENT.

▸ **contract of employment.** See *employment contract.*

▸ **contract of indemnity.** See *indemnity contract.*

▸ **contract of insurance.** See INSURANCE POLICY.

▸ **contract of marriage.** See *marriage contract.*

▸ **contract of pledge.** (18c) **1.** PAWN. **2.** *Civil law.* A real contract by which a debtor gives a creditor property to hold as security for a debt or the performance of a promise. • The contract is also called a *pawn,* when the property is movable, and an *antichresis,* when the property is immovable. See (in sense 2) PAWN; ANTICHRESIS. Cf. *pignorative contract.*

"[A] pledge is a personal security in the Common law, while it is a real security in the Civil law. Hence, the contract of pledge is a personal contract in the Common law, and a real contract in the Civil law." Henry Denis, *A Treatise on the Law of the Contract of Pledge as Governed by Both the Common Law and the Civil Law* 1 (1898).

"The contract of pledge is in general a contract wholly implied in law. No written contract is necessary, and generally none is made. If there be a written contract, it is generally made either to show that the transaction is a pledge and not a sale, or to provide a special mode for enforcing the lien. A mortgage under the registry laws must necessarily be made by a written transfer, while a pledge, though it may be constituted in writing, is ordinarily made by delivery of the property without any writing, the contract of the parties being wholly implied in law. A delivery of property as security for a debt without a written conveyance cannot be a mortgage, but must be a pledge." Leonard A. Jones, *A Treatise on the Law of Collateral Securities and Pledges* 8 (Edward M. White ed., 3d ed. 1912).

▸ **contract of record.** (1855) A contract that is declared by a court and entered into the court's record. • Contracts of record include judgments, recognizances, and (in England) statutes staple.

"Contracts of record are not really contracts at all, but are transactions which, being entered on the records of certain courts called 'courts of record,' are conclusive proof of the facts thereby appearing, and could formerly be enforced by action of law as if they had been put in the shape of a contract." 1 Stewart Rapalje & Robert L. Lawrence, *A Dictionary of American and English Law* 282 (1883).

"A contract of record is in point of fact no contract at all, and has nothing whatever to do with the law of contracts. These so-called contracts are the obligations incurred by a judgment or recognizance of a Court of Record. They came to be called contracts only because they were enforceable by the same type of action as was used for genuinely contractual cases in the old common-law system of procedure." P.S. Atiyah, *An Introduction to the Law of Contract* 31 (3d ed. 1981).

▸ **contract of sale.** See *contract for sale* (1).

▸ **contract of service.** **1.** See CONTRACT OF SERVICE. **2.** See *employment contract.*

▸ **contract of subscription.** See SUBSCRIPTION (3).

▸ **contract to pledge.** (1866) **1.** An agreement purporting to create a present pledge without a bailment. **2.** An agreement to make a future bailment for the purpose of security. See PLEDGE (3).

▸ **contract to satisfaction.** See *satisfaction contract.*

▸ **contract to sell.** See *contract for sale* (2).

▸ **contract *uberrimae fidei*** (yoo-ber-ə-mee fɪ-dee-ɪ). (1916) A contract in which the parties owe each other duties with the utmost good faith.

"In a certain restricted group of contracts good faith is peculiarly necessary owing to the relationship between the parties, and in these cases — known as contracts *uberrimae fidei* — there is a full duty to disclose all material facts. The typical instance of such contracts is the contract of insurance. Here the duty to disclose all material facts to the insurer arises from the fact that many of the relevant circumstances are within the exclusive knowledge of one party, and it would be impossible for the insurer to obtain the facts necessary for him to make a proper calculation of the risk he is asked to assume without this knowledge." P.S. Atiyah, *An Introduction to the Law of Contract* 221–22 (3d ed. 1981).

▸ **contract under hand.** (18c) *Archaic.* A contract entered into by individual signature by a duly authorized person, as opposed to a contract executed under seal or by deed.

▸ **contract under seal.** (1827) A formal contract that requires no consideration and has the seal of the signer attached. • A contract under seal must be in writing or printed on paper or parchment and is conclusive between the parties when signed, sealed, and delivered. Delivery is made either by actually handing it to the other party (or party's representative) or by stating an intention that the deed be operative even though it is retained in the possession of the party executing it. Modern statutes have mostly eliminated the special effects of a sealed contract. — Also termed *sealed contract; agreement under seal; special contract; deed; covenant; specialty; specialty contract; common-law specialty.* See SEAL. Cf. *sealed instrument* under INSTRUMENT.

"The only formal contract of English law is the *contract under seal,* sometimes also called a deed and sometimes a specialty. It is the only *formal contract,* because it derives its validity neither from the fact of agreement, nor from the consideration which may exist for the promise of either party, but from the *form* in which it is expressed." William R. Anson, *Principles of the Law of Contract* 82 (Arthur L. Corbin ed., 3d Am. ed. 1919).

"Contracts under seal also bear little resemblance to ordinary contracts, although here at least the liability is based on a promise. A contract under seal, that is to say a deed, . . . is a written promise or set of promises which derives its validity from the form, and the form alone, of the executing instrument. In point of fact the 'form' of the deed is nowadays surprisingly elastic. The only necessities are that the deed should be intended as such, and should be signed, sealed, and delivered. The sealing, however, has now become largely a fiction, an adhesive wafer simply being attached to the document in place of a genuine seal. Similarly, 'delivery' is not literally necessary, provided that there is a clear intention that the deed should be operative." P.S. Atiyah, *An Introduction to the Law of Contract* 31 (3d ed. 1981).

▸ **cost-plus contract.** (1920) A contract in which payment is based on a fixed fee or a percentage added to the actual cost incurred; esp., a construction contract in which the owner pays to the builder the actual costs of material and labor plus a fixed percentage over that amount.

▸ **de facto contract of sale.** (1918) A contract that passes property but is defective in some element.

▸ **dependent contract.** (1831) A contract conditioned or dependent on another contract.

▸ **deposit contract.** (1906) An agreement between a financial institution and its customer governing the treatment of deposited funds and the payment of checks and other demands against the customer's account.

▸ **design-specification contract.** See *build-to-print contract.*

▸ **destination contract.** (1958) A contract in which the seller bears the risk of loss until the goods arrive at the destination. UCC § 2-509. Cf. *shipment contract.*

▸ **discharged contract.** See *void contract* (2).

▸ **divisible contract.** See *severable contract.*

▸ **dual contract.** (1849) One of two contracts entered by the same parties for the same transaction, sometimes so that one contract may be used to defraud a person or entity (such as a lender) as to the terms of the parties' actual agreement.

▸ **employment contract.** (1927) A contract between an employer and employee in which the terms and conditions of employment are stated. — Also termed *contract of employment*; *contract of service*; *service contract.*

▸ **engineering, procurement, and construction contract.** (1991) A fixed-price, schedule-intensive construction contract — typical in the construction of single-purpose projects, such as energy plants — in which the contractor agrees to a wide variety of responsibilities, including the duties to provide for the design, engineering, procurement, and construction of the facility; to prepare start-up procedures; to conduct performance tests; to create operating manuals; and to train people to operate the facility. — Abbr. EPC contract. — Also termed *turnkey contract.* See SINGLE-PURPOSE PROJECT.

▸ **entire contract. 1.** A nonseverable contract that cannot be supplemented by anything external to the contract. **2.** A contract that has been completely performed. **3.** See *indivisible contract.*

▸ **entire-output contract.** See *output contract.*

▸ **escrow contract.** (1908) The contract among buyer, seller, and escrow holder, setting forth the rights and responsibilities of each. See ESCROW.

▸ **evergreen contract.** (1962) A contract that renews itself from one term to the next in the absence of contrary notice by one of the parties.

▸ **exclusive contract.** See EXCLUSIVE-DEALING ARRANGEMENT.

▸ **executed contract.** (18c) **1.** A contract that has been fully performed by both parties. **2.** A signed contract.

▸ **executory contract** (eg-**zek**-yə-tor-ee). (18c) **1.** A contract that remains wholly unperformed or for which there remains something still to be done on both sides, often as a component of a larger transaction and sometimes memorialized by an informal letter agreement, by a memorandum, or by oral agreement.

"If a contract is wholly executory, and the legal duties of the parties are as yet unfulfilled, it can be discharged by mutual consent, the acquittance of each from the other's claims being the consideration for the promise of each to waive his own." William R. Anson, *Principles of the Law of Contract* 138 (Arthur L. Corbin ed., 3d Am. ed. 1919).

2. *Bankruptcy.* A contract under which debtor and nondebtor each have unperformed material obligations and the debtor, if it ceased further performance, would have no right to the other party's continued performance.

▸ **express contract.** (17c) A contract whose terms the parties have explicitly set out. — Also termed *special contract.* Cf. *implied contract.*

▸ **financial contract.** *Securities.* An arrangement that (1) takes the form of an individually negotiated contract, agreement, or option to buy, sell, lend, swap, or repurchase, or other similar individually negotiated transaction commonly entered into by participants in the financial markets; (2) involves securities, commodities, currencies, interest or other rates, other measures of value, or any other financial or economic interest similar in purpose or function; and (3) is entered into in response to a request from a counterparty for a quotation, or is otherwise entered into and structured to accommodate the objectives of the counterparty to such an arrangement.

▸ **fixed-price contract.** (1922) A contract in which the buyer agrees to pay the seller a definite and predetermined price regardless of increases in the seller's cost or the buyer's ability to acquire the same goods in the market at a lower price.

▸ **formal contract.** (17c) A contract made through the observance of certain prescribed formalities. • Among the formal contracts are the contract under seal, the recognizance, the negotiable instrument, and the letter of credit. See *formal agreement* under AGREEMENT. Cf. *informal contract.*

▸ **form contract.** See *standard form contract.*

▸ **forward contract.** (1874) An agreement to buy or sell a particular nonstandardized asset (usu. currencies) at a fixed price on a future date. • Unlike a futures contract, a forward contract is not traded on a formal exchange. — Also termed *forward agreement.* Cf. FUTURES CONTRACT.

▸ **futures contract.** See FUTURES CONTRACT.

▸ **gambling contract.** (1809) An agreement to engage in a gamble; a contract in which two parties wager something, esp. money, for a chance to win a prize. • Where gambling is legal, contracts related to legal gambling activities are enforceable. — Also termed *gaming contract.* See *wagering contract* (1).

"Generally, under or apart from statutes so providing, or prohibiting such contracts or transactions, gambling contracts and transactions are illegal and void and cannot be enforced; and such contracts are void ab initio. . . . A gambling contract is invalid, no matter what outward form it may assume, and no ingenuity can make it legal." 38 C.J.S. *Gaming* § 26, at 138–39 (1996).

▸ **government contract.** (18c) A contract, esp. for the purchase of goods and services, to which a government or government agency is a party. See *procurement contract.*

▸ **gratuitous contract** (grə-t[y]**oo**-i-təs). (18c) **1.** A contract made for the benefit of a promisee who does not give consideration to the promisor. — Also termed *contract of beneficence; contract of benevolence.* Cf. *onerous contract.* **2.** *Civil law.* A contract in which one party promises to give a benefit to the other party without expecting or gaining any benefit in return. — Also termed *voluntary contract.*

▸ **grubstake contract.** (1888) A contract between two parties in which one party provides the grubstake — money and supplies — and the other party prospects for and locates minerals on public land. • Each party acquires an interest in the minerals as agreed to in the contract. Grubstake contracts are used chiefly in the western United States. In some states, such as Alaska, a request for grubstake money is considered the offer of a security and must be registered. — Also termed *grubstaking contract.*

▸ **guaranteed-sale contract.** (1980) A contract between a real-estate agency and a property owner in which the agency agrees to buy the property at a guaranteed price after a specified length of time if it has not been sold under the listing agreement. • The guaranteed price is usu. a substantial discount from the listed price. — Also termed *guaranteed-purchase contract.*

▸ **guaranty contract.** See GUARANTY (1).

▸ **hazardous contract.** See *aleatory contract.*

▸ **hedging contract.** (1848) A contract of purchase or sale that amounts to insurance against changing prices by which a dealer contracts to buy or sell for future delivery the same amount of a commodity as he or she is buying or selling in the present market.

▸ **hypothetical contract.** See *conditional contract.*

▸ **illegal contract.** (18c) A promise that is prohibited because the performance, formation, or object of the agreement is against the law. • Technically speaking, an illegal contract is not a contract at all because it cannot be enforced, so the phrase is a misnomer. Cf. *unenforceable contract; void contract.*

"An illegal contract is exceptionally difficult to define. It does not merely mean a contract contrary to the criminal law, although such a contract would indubitably be illegal. But a contract can well be illegal without contravening the criminal law, because there are certain activities which the law does not actually prohibit, but at the same time regards as contrary to the public interest and definitely to be discouraged, for instance, prostitution. While a void contract is not necessarily illegal, an illegal contract is often void. However, the consequences of an illegal contract differ somewhat from those usually produced by a simply void contract, so illegal contracts are usually accorded separate treatment." P.S. Atiyah, *An Introduction to the Law of Contract* 38 (3d ed. 1981).

▸ **illusory contract.** (18c) An agreement in which one party gives as consideration a promise that is so insubstantial as to impose no obligation. • The insubstantial promise renders the agreement unenforceable.

▸ **immoral contract.** (18c) An agreement that so flagrantly violates societal norms as to be unenforceable.

▸ **implied contract.** (17c) **1.** An implied-in-law contract. **2.** An implied-in-fact contract. Cf. *express contract.*

▸ **implied-in-fact contract.** (1913) A contract that the parties presumably intended as their tacit understanding, as inferred from their conduct and other circumstances. — Also termed *contract implied in fact; inferred contract.*

▸ **implied-in-law contract.** (1932) An obligation created by law for the sake of justice; specif., an obligation imposed by law because of some special relationship between the parties or because one of them would otherwise be unjustly enriched. • An implied-in-law contract is not actually a contract, but instead is a remedy that allows the plaintiff to recover a benefit conferred on the defendant. — Also termed *quasi-contract; contract implied in law; constructive contract.* See UNJUST ENRICHMENT. Cf. QUANTUM MERUIT.

"The term 'quasi contracts' may with propriety be applied to all noncontractual obligations which are treated, for the purpose of affording a remedy, as if they were contracts. So interpreted, the subject includes: (1) judgments and other so-called contracts of record; (2) a number of official and statutory obligations, such as the official obligation of a sheriff to levy execution and pay over the proceeds, and the statutory obligation of the owner of a vessel to pay pilotage; and (3) obligations arising from 'unjust enrichment,' i.e. the receipt by one person from another of a benefit the retention of which is unjust." Frederic Campbell Woodward, *The Law of Quasi Contracts* § 1, at 1–2 (1913).

"[A]dventurous courts have turned to the idea of a 'contract implied in law,' a 'quasi-contract' — not really a contract, a legal fiction necessary to promote the ends of justice and, in particular, to prevent 'unjust enrichment.'" Grant Gilmore, *The Death of Contract* 73–74 (1974).

"Since . . . claims for the redress of unjust enrichment did not fit comfortably into either the category of contract or that of tort, they came to be described as claims in *quasi-contract.* Some of them were originally characterized as being in *quantum meruit* (as much as he deserved), a form of action used for claims to payment for services. This procedural term has persisted and is sometimes used inexactly as a synonym for the more general term *quasi-contract*, which refers to any money claim for the redress of unjust enrichment." E. Allan Farnsworth, *Contracts* § 2.20, at 103 (2d ed. 1990).

▸ **impossible contract.** (17c) An agreement that the law will not enforce because there is no feasible way for one of the parties to perform. See IMPOSSIBILITY (3).

▸ **indemnity contract.** (1835) A contract by which the promisor agrees to reimburse a promisee for some loss irrespective of a third person's liability. — Also termed *contract of indemnity.*

▸ **independent contract.** (1801) A contract in which the mutual acts or promises of the parties have no relation to each other, either as equivalents or as consideration. Cf. *commutative contract.*

▸ **indivisible contract.** (1808) A contract under which the parties' obligations are interdependent, so no party can demand performance from another unless it also performs or is ready and willing to do so. — Also termed *entire contract.*

▸ **inferred contract.** See *implied-in-fact contract.*

▸ **informal contract.** (1850) **1.** A contract other than one under seal, a recognizance, or a negotiable instrument;

specif., that derives its force not from the observance of formalities but because of the presence in the transaction of certain elements that are usu. present when people make promises with binding intent — namely mutual assent and consideration (or a device other than consideration). • An informal contract may be made with or without a writing. Most modern contracts are informal. — Also termed *bargain*; *simple contract*. **2.** See *parol contract*. Cf. *formal contract*.

> "In general, there are five essential elements to the formation of an informal contract. These are: (1) mutual assent; (2) consideration or some other validation device; (3) two or more contracting parties (no person may contract with himself); (4) parties having legal capacity to contract; (5) the absence of any statute or common-law rule declaring the particular transaction to be void. The fourth and fifth elements are essential to the creation of any contract, formal or informal. The first, second and third elements are essential to the formation of informal contracts." John Edward Murray Jr., *Murray on Contracts* § 17, at 28 (2d ed. 1974).

▸ **innominate contract** (i-**nom**-ə-nit). (18c) *Roman & civil law.* A contract not classifiable under any particular name; a contract for which the law supplies nothing in addition to the express agreement of the parties. La. Civ. Code art. 1914. • This type of contract was developed late in classical Roman law. Although the agreements were reciprocal, they did not become operational without at least part performance. — Also termed *innominate real contract*. Cf. *nominate contract*.

▸ **installment contract.** (1896) A contract requiring or authorizing the delivery of goods in separate lots, or payments in separate increments, to be separately accepted. • Under the UCC, this type of agreement will be considered one contract even if it has a clause stating that each delivery is a separate contract. UCC § 2-612(1).

▸ **installment land contract.** (1909) A contract for the sale of land providing that the buyer will receive immediate possession of the land and pay the purchase price in installments over time, but that the seller will retain legal title until all payments are made. — Also termed *contract for deed*; *land contract*; *land sales contract*.

▸ **integrated contract.** See INTEGRATED CONTRACT.

▸ **interstate contract.** (1882) **1.** A contract whose parties are residents of different American states. **2.** A contract made between denizens of different nations. • Private international law may be used to resolve conflicts in such an agreement.

▸ **invalid contract.** (18c) An agreement that is either void or voidable. — Also termed *invalid agreement*.

▸ **investment contract.** See INVESTMENT CONTRACT.

▸ **joint contract.** (17c) A contract in which two or more promisors are together bound to fulfill its obligations, or one in which two or more promisees are together entitled to performance. Cf. *severable contract*.

▸ **land contract.** See *installment land contract*.

▸ **land sales contract.** See *installment land contract*.

▸ **leonine contract.** See *adhesion contract*.

▸ **letter contract.** (1949) In federal contract law, a written contract with sufficient provisions to permit the contractor to begin performance.

▸ **leverage contract.** See LEVERAGE CONTRACT.

▸ **literal contract.** (18c) **1.** *Roman law.* A type of written contract originally created by — and later evidenced by — an entry of the sum due on the debit side of a ledger, binding a signatory even though the signatory receives no consideration. • Literal contracts were often used for novations. See LITTERIS OBLIGATIO.

> "Though an obligation could be created by a literal contract in the time of Gaius, the so-called literal contract of Justinian was not, in itself, a means of *creating* an obligation, but was the *evidence* of an obligation created in some other way . . . . The true literal contract, as described by Gaius, may be defined as a means of creating an obligation to pay money by a fictitious entry . . . in the creditor's account book . . . with the consent of the intended debtor. A, with B's consent, enters the fact that B is indebted to him . . . and thereupon B is under an obligation to pay, though no money has passed between them." R.W. Leage, *Roman Private Law* 316–17 (C.H. Ziegler ed., 2d ed. 1930).

2. *Civil law.* A contract fully evidenced by a writing and binding on the signatory.

▸ **marine contract.** See *maritime contract*.

▸ **maritime contract.** (17c) A contract that is recognized in admiralty jurisdiction. • In general, a maritime contract relates to a vessel in its use as such, to navigation on navigable waters, to transportation by sea, or to maritime employment. — Also termed *marine contract*.

▸ **marketing contract.** (1920) **1.** A business's agreement with an agency or other association for the promotion of sales of the business's goods or services. **2.** An agreement between a cooperative and its members, by which the members agree to sell through the cooperative, and the cooperative agrees to obtain an agreed price.

▸ **marriage contract.** (16c) A form of mutual consent required for a matrimonial relationship to exist according to the law of the place where the consent takes place. — Also termed *contract of marriage*.

▸ **mixed contract.** (17c) **1.** *Civil law.* A contract in which the respective benefits conferred are unequal. **2.** A contract for the sale of both goods and services. • The UCC may apply to a mixed contract if the predominant purpose is for the sale of goods.

▸ **mutual contract.** See *bilateral contract*.

▸ **naked contract.** See NUDUM PACTUM.

▸ **nominate contract** (**nom**-ə-nit). (17c) *Civil law.* A contract distinguished by a particular name, such as sale, insurance, or lease, the very use of which determines some of the rules governing the contract and the contractual rights of the parties, without the need for special stipulations. • The contracts are generally divided into four types, real (arising from something done), oral (arising from something said), literal (arising from something written), and consensual (arising from something agreed to). La. Civ. Code art. 1914. Cf. *innominate contract*.

▸ **nude contract.** See NUDUM PACTUM.

▸ **nugatory contract.** A contract that is either wholly worthless to one party or of only trivial value to that party.

▸ **onerous contract.** (17c) *Civil law.* A contract in which each party is obligated to perform in exchange for the other's promise of performance. La. Civ. Code art. 1909. Cf. *gratuitous contract*.

▸ **option contract.** See OPTION (2).

▸ **oral contract.** A contract that has been agreed to but not fully reduced to writing; *parol contract* (1).

"A simple contract in writing differs from a specialty chiefly in not being under seal. A written contract is one which, in all its terms, is in writing.

"A contract partly in writing and partly oral is, in legal effect, an oral contract. It occurs where an incomplete writing, or one expressing only a part of what is meant, is by oral words rounded into the full contract; or where there is first a written contract, and afterward it is changed orally." Joel Prentiss Bishop, *Commentaries on the Law of Contracts* §§ 163–64, at 60 (1887).

▸ **output contract.** (1904) A contract in which a seller promises to supply and a buyer to buy all the goods or services that a seller produces during a specified period and at a set price. • The quantity term is measured by the seller's output. An output contract assures the seller of a market or outlet for the period of the contract. — Also termed *entire-output contract.* Cf. *requirements contract.*

▸ **parol contract** (pə-**rohl** *or* **par**-əl). (18c) **1.** A contract or modification of a contract that is not in writing or is only partially in writing. — Also termed *oral contract*; *parol agreement*; (loosely) *verbal contract.* **2.** At common law, a contract not under seal, although it could be in writing. — Also termed *informal contract*; *simple contract.* See PAROL-EVIDENCE RULE.

▸ **pay-or-play contract.** (1924) A contract in which one party agrees to perform and the other agrees to pay for the promised performance even if performance is never demanded. • Pay-or-play contracts are usu. made in the entertainment industry.

▸ **performance contract.** (1947) **1.** A contract that requires a party to act personally and does not allow substitution. • People who provide unique personal services often make performance contracts. **2.** A contract that allows the contractor to choose the means to achieve the end result. • The product's specifications may be loose and allow the contractor latitude in deciding how to perform. Cf. *build-to-print contract.*

▸ **personal contract.** (17c) **1.** A contract that binds a person but not that person's heirs or assignees because the contract requires a personal performance for which there is no adequate substitute. **2.** A contract that binds a representative as an individual rather than binding the person or entity represented. • For instance, contracts made by a decedent's personal representative traditionally bind the representative, not the estate, unless expressly agreed otherwise. **3.** A real-property-related contract that is treated as personal property, not as a substitute for the real property. • Examples include oil-and-gas royalty contracts and property-insurance policies.

▸ **pignorative contract** (**pig**-nə-ray-tiv). (18c) *Civil law.* A contract of sale in which the owner of real property, instead of relinquishing possession of the property that is theoretically sold, gives the counterparty a lien; a contract of pledge, hypothecation, or mortgage of realty. Cf. *contract of pledge* (2).

▸ **precontract.** (15c) A contract that precludes a party from entering into a comparable agreement with someone else. • Historically, a precontract was usu. a promise to marry. It formed an impediment to marriage with any person other than the promisee. The legal impediment was extinguished and revived several times until it was finally abolished in 1752 by 26 Geo. 2, ch. 33, § 13. Cf. LETTER OF INTENT; BETROTHAL (1).

▸ **principal contract.** (1876) A contract giving rise to an accessory contract, as an agreement from which a secured obligation originates. Cf. *accessory contract.*

▸ **private contract.** (16c) An agreement between private parties affecting only private rights.

▸ **procurement contract.** (1942) A contract in which a government receives goods or services. • A procurement contract, including the bidding process, is usu. subject to government regulation. — Also termed *government contract.* See FEDERAL ACQUISITION REGULATION.

▸ **public contract.** (17c) A contract that, although it involves public funds, may be performed by private persons and may benefit them.

▸ **quasi-contract.** See *implied-in-law contract.*

▸ **real contract.** (17c) *Hist.* A contract in which money or other property passes from one party to another; a contract requiring something more than mere consent, such as the lending of money or handing over of a thing. • This term, derived from Roman law, referred to contracts concerning both personal and real property. Real contracts included transactions in the form of *commodatum*, *depositum*, *mutuum*, and *pignus*. Cf. *consensual contract.*

"The essence of . . . *the real contracts*, was that, at the time the agreement was made, one party, by delivering something belonging to him to the other party to the contract, imposed on that other an obligation to return the thing itself or, in the case of things intended to be consumed, an equivalent in kind. As the Roman lawyers expressed it, the contractual obligation was created by something being handed over . . . ." R.W. Leage, *Roman Private Law* 292 (C.H. Ziegler ed., 2d ed. 1930).

"The term 'real contract' is in common use in the Civil law, and though not commonly used by judges or writers in the common law, nevertheless describes certain obligations enforced in England from very early times. A real contract is an obligation arising from the possession or transfer of a res." 1 Samuel Williston, *A Treatise on the Law of Contracts* § 8, at 19 (Walter H.E. Jaeger ed., 3d ed. 1957).

▸ **reciprocal contract.** See *bilateral contract.*

▸ **referral sales contract.** See REFERRAL SALES CONTRACT.

▸ **relative simulated contract.** *Civil law.* A simulated contract that the parties intend to have some effects, but not necessarily those recited in the contract. La. Civ. Code art. 2027. See *simulated contract.*

▸ **requirements contract.** (1932) A contract in which a buyer promises to buy, and a seller to supply, all the goods or services that a buyer needs during a specified period. • The quantity term is measured by the buyer's requirements. A requirements contract assures the buyer of a source for the term of the contract. Cf. *output contract.*

▸ **retail installment contract.** (1935) A contract for the sale of goods under which the buyer makes periodic payments and the seller retains title to or a security interest in the goods. — Also termed *retail installment contract and security agreement*; *conditional sales contract.* Cf. *chattel mortgage* under MORTGAGE.

▸ **satisfaction contract.** (1912) A contract by which one party agrees to perform to the satisfaction of the other. — Also termed *contract to satisfaction.*

▸ **sealed contract.** See *contract under seal.*

▸ **self-determination contract.** (1978) Under the Indian Self-Determination and Education Assistance Act, an agreement under which the federal government provides funds to an Indian tribe and allows the tribe to plan and administer a program that would otherwise be administered by the federal government. 25 USCA § 450b(j).

▸ **service contract.** (1902) **1.** A contract to perform a service; esp., a written agreement to provide maintenance or repairs on a consumer product for a specified term. **2.** See *employment contract.*

▸ **severable contract.** (1854) A contract that includes two or more promises each of which can be enforced separately, so that failure to perform one of the promises does not necessarily put the promisor in breach of the entire contract. — Also termed *divisible contract; several contract.* See SEVERABILITY CLAUSE. Cf. *joint contract.*

> "A *severable* contract . . . is one the consideration of which is, by its terms, susceptible of apportionment on either side, so as to correspond to the unascertained consideration on the other side, as a contract to pay a person the worth of his services so long as he will do certain work; or to give a certain price for every bushel of so much corn as corresponds to a sample." *Wharton's Law Lexicon* 215 (Ivan Horniman ed., 13th ed. 1925).

▸ **shipment contract.** (1893) A contract in which a seller bears the risk of damage to the items sold only until they are brought to the place of shipment. • If a contract for the sale of goods does not address the terms of delivery, it is presumed to be a shipment contract. UCC §§ 2-319, 2-504, 2-509. Cf. *destination contract.*

> "In the jargon of commercial lawyers, a contract that requires or authorizes the seller to send the goods to the buyer but does not require that he deliver them at any particular destination is called a 'shipment contract.' Generally, in shipment contracts, risk of loss passes to the buyer at the point of shipment, which is also the point of 'delivery,' while in 'destination contracts' (seller must deliver at a particular destination) risk passes upon seller's tender at destination." 1 James J. White & Robert S. Summers, *Uniform Commercial Code* § 3-5, at 128–29 (4th ed. 1995).

▸ **simple contract. 1.** See *informal contract* (1). **2.** See *parol contract* (2).

▸ **simulated contract.** (1817) *Civil law.* A contract that, by mutual agreement, does not express the true intent of the parties. La. Civ. Code art. 2025. • A simulated contract is absolute when the parties intend that the contract will impose no obligations; no obligations are enforceable on the parties by such a contract. A simulated contract is relative if the parties intend it to impose obligations different from those recited in the contract; the intended obligations are enforceable if all relevant conditions are met. A simulated contract may affect the rights of third parties. — Also termed *simulation.* See *action en declaration de simulation* under ACTION (4).

▸ **special contract.** (17c) **1.** See *contract under seal.* **2.** A contract with peculiar provisions that are not ordinarily found in contracts relating to the same subject matter. **3.** See *express contract.*

▸ **specialty contract.** See *contract under seal.*

▸ **standard-form contract.** (1923) A usu. preprinted contract containing set clauses, used repeatedly by a business or within a particular industry with only slight additions or modifications to meet the specific situation. • Because standard-form contracts usu. favor the drafting party, they can amount to adhesion contracts. As with contract interpretation generally, courts offset the drafting party's advantage by construing ambiguities in the light least favorable to the drafting party. See CONTRA PROFERENTEM. — Often shortened to *form contract.* — Also termed *standardized contract.* See *adhesion contract.*

> "[U]niformity of terms in contracts typically recurring in a business enterprise is an important factor in the exact calculation of risks. Risks that are difficult to calculate can be excluded altogether. Unforeseeable contingencies affecting performance, such as strikes, fire, and transportation difficulties can be taken care of. . . . Standardized contracts have thus become an important means of excluding or controlling the ['irrational factors' that could persuade a court or jury to decide against a powerful defendant]." Friedrich Kessler, *Contracts of Adhesion — Some Thoughts About Freedom of Contract*, 43 Colum. L. Rev. 629, 631–32 (1943).

▸ **statutory contract.** (1832) A contract for which a statute prescribes certain terms. • Statutes often govern the contracts made by public entities, but also some by private persons. For example, a statute may define and set minimum standards for terms in home-improvement contracts.

▸ **stock-option contract.** (1945) A negotiable instrument that gives the holder the right to buy or sell — for a specified price within a fixed time limit — a certain number of shares of the corporation's stock. See STOCK OPTION.

▸ **subcontract.** (18c) A secondary contract made by a party to the primary contract for carrying out the primary contract, or a part of it.

▸ **subscription contract.** See SUBSCRIPTION (3).

▸ **substituted contract.** (1833) A contract made between parties to an earlier contract so that the new one takes the place of and discharges the earlier one. • A substituted contract differs from a novation (as "novation" is traditionally defined) in that the latter requires the substitution for the original obligor of a third person not a party to the original agreement; when the obligee accepts the third party, the agreement is immediately discharged. In contrast to both substituted contract and novation, an executory accord does not immediately discharge an obligation; rather, the obligation is discharged on performance, often by a third person, rather than the original obligor. Cf. NOVATION; ACCORD (2).

> "[A] substituted contract immediately discharges the prior claim which is merged into the new agreement. Consequently, in the absence of an express agreement to the contrary, the original claim can no longer be enforced. In the event of a breach, any action would have to be brought on the substituted agreement. . . . The concept of 'substituted contract' was created largely to circumvent the unsatisfactory rules that until recently governed executory accords. Now that these rules have been modernized, the next step should be the reabsorption of the substituted contract into the executory accord. . . . [T]he untidy distinction between executory accords and substituted contracts should not be allowed to complicate litigation about routine claim settlements." John D. Calamari & Joseph M. Perillo, *The Law of Contracts* § 21.6, at 803 (4th ed. 1998).

▸ **supply contract.** A buy–sell agreement under which the seller agrees to furnish good or services either for a specified period of time or indefinitely. • A supply contract may specify quantities to be delivered at certain times, it may be a requirements or output contract, or it may specify indefinite quantities.

▸ **synallagmatic contract** (sin-ə-lag-**mat**-ik). [fr. Greek *synallagma* "mutual agreement"] (1826) *Civil law.* A contract in which the parties obligate themselves reciprocally, so that the obligation of each party is correlative to the obligation of the other. La. Civ. Code arts. 1908, 1911. • A synallagmatic contract is characterized by correlative obligations, whereas a commutative contract is characterized by correlative performances. The term *synallagmatic contract* is essentially the civil-law equivalent of the common law's *bilateral contract.* Cf. *commutative contract.*

▸ **tacit contract.** (17c) A contract in which conduct takes the place of written or spoken words in the offer or acceptance (or both).

▸ **take-it-or-leave-it contract.** See *adhesion contract.*

▸ **take-or-pay contract.** (1960) A contract requiring the buyer to either purchase and receive a minimum amount of a product ("take") or pay for this minimum without taking immediate delivery ("pay"). • These contracts are often used in the energy and oil-and-gas industries.

▸ **task-order contract.** (1995) A contract under which a vendor agrees to render services or deliver products as ordered from time to time. • Governments use this type of contract when the quantities that will be needed or the times for performance are uncertain. The contract may describe the services or products generally, but it must specify the period of performance, the number of option periods, and the total minimum and maximum quantity of products or services that the government will acquire under the contract. When exercising its contractual rights, the government issues task orders to specify the product or service requirements, which may vary with each order. — Sometimes shortened to *task order.*

▸ **third-party-beneficiary contract.** (1921) A contract that directly benefits a third party and that gives the third party a right to sue any of the contracting parties for breach.

▸ **tonnage contract.** See CONTRACT OF AFFREIGHTMENT.

▸ **turnkey contract.** See *engineering, procurement, and construction contract.*

▸ **unconscionable contract.** See *unconscionable agreement* under AGREEMENT.

▸ **unenforceable contract.** (1842) An otherwise valid contract that, because of some technical defect, cannot be fully enforced; a contract that has some legal consequences but that may not be enforced in an action for damages or specific performance in the face of certain defenses, such as the statute of frauds. — Also termed *agreement of imperfect obligation.* Cf. *illegal contract; void contract.*

"The difference between what is voidable and what is unenforceable is mainly a difference between substance and procedure. A contract may be good, but incapable of proof owing to lapse of time, want of written form, or failure to affix a revenue stamp. Writing in the first cases, a stamp in the last, may satisfy the requirements of law and render the contract enforceable, but it is never at any time in the power of either party to avoid the transaction. The contract is unimpeachable, only it cannot be proved in court." William R. Anson, *Principles of the Law of Contract* 19-20 (Arthur L. Corbin ed., 3d Am. ed. 1919).

"Courts are . . . fond of condemning the unenforceable agreement as 'illegal.' This is misleading insofar as it suggests that some penalty is necessarily imposed on one of the parties, apart from the court's refusal to enforce the agreement. In some cases, the conduct that renders the agreement unenforceable is also a crime, but this is not necessarily or even usually so. It is therefore preferable to attribute unenforceability to grounds of public policy rather than to 'illegality.'" E. Allan Farnsworth, *Contracts* § 5.1, at 323 (3d ed. 1999).

▸ **unilateral contract.** (1855) A contract in which only one party makes a promise or undertakes a performance.

"[M]any unilateral contracts are in reality gratuitous promises enforced for good reason with no element of bargain." P.S. Atiyah, *An Introduction to the Law of Contract* 126 (3d ed. 1981).

"If A says to B, 'If you walk across the Brooklyn Bridge I will pay you $100,' A has made a promise but has not asked B for a return promise. A has asked B to perform, not a commitment to perform. A has thus made an offer looking to a unilateral contract. B cannot accept this offer by promising to walk the bridge. B must accept, if at all, by performing the act. Because no return promise is requested, at no point is B bound to perform. If B does perform, a contract involving two parties is created, but the contract is classified as unilateral because only one party is ever under an obligation." John D. Calamari & Joseph M. Perillo, *The Law of Contracts* § 2-10(a), at 64-65 (4th ed. 1998).

▸ **valid contract.** (17c) A contract that is fully operative in accordance with the parties' intent. — Also termed *valid agreement.*

▸ **variable annuity contract.** (1959) *Securities.* An annuity whose payments vary according to how well the fund (usu. made up of common stocks) that backs it is performing. SEC Rule 0-1(e)(1) (17 CFR § 270.0-1(e)(1)). See *variable annuity* under ANNUITY.

▸ **verbal contract.** See *parol contract* (1).

▸ **voidable contract.** (18c) A contract that can be affirmed or rejected at the option of one of the parties; a contract that is void as to the wrongdoer but not void as to the party wronged, unless that party elects to treat it as void. — Also termed *voidable agreement.* Cf. *void contract.*

"A voidable contract is a contract which, in its inception, is valid and capable of producing the results of a valid contract, but which may be 'avoided,' i.e. rendered void at the option of one (or even, though rarely, of both) of the parties." P.S. Atiyah, *An Introduction to the Law of Contract* 37-38 (3d ed. 1981).

▸ **void contract.** (17c) **1.** A contract that is of no legal effect, so that there is really no contract in existence at all. • A contract may be void because it is technically defective, contrary to public policy, or illegal. — Also termed *void agreement.* Cf. *illegal contract; unenforceable contract; voidable contract.*

"Strictly speaking, a 'void contract' is a contradiction in terms; for the words describe a state of things in which, despite the intention of the parties, no contract has been made. Yet the expression, however faulty, is a compendious way of putting a case in which there has been the outward semblance without the reality of contract." William R. Anson, *Principles of the Law of Contract* 18 (Arthur L. Corbin ed., 3d Am. ed. 1919).

"A valid contract is, of course, simply a contract of full force and effect, not vitiated in any way. A so-called void contract, on the other hand, is really a contradiction in terms inasmuch as a contract has already been defined in terms applicable only to a valid contract. However, the term is convenient and is universally used. For purposes of exposition, it is convenient to treat void contracts as falling, broadly speaking, into main categories. On the one hand, are cases where one of the normal requirements for the creation of a contract is absent, while, on the other hand, are cases where all the normal requirements are satisfied, but the contract is void because the law disapproves of its purpose or the terms by which it seeks to achieve that purpose. Typical examples of contracts which are void because one of the normal requirements is absent are contracts in which the acceptance of an offer has not been communicated or in which a promise is given gratuitously. Typical examples of contracts which are void because of their terms or objects are wagering contracts, and contracts prejudicial to family relations." P.S. Atiyah, *An Introduction to the Law of Contract* 36–37 (3d ed. 1981).

2. A contract that has been fully performed. — Also termed *discharged contract.*

"Not only is the term 'void contract' in itself technically inaccurate, but a contract is sometimes said to be void, not because it was destitute of legal effect from its commencement, but because it has been fully performed, and so has ceased to have legal operation. It would be more proper to describe such a contract as 'discharged.'" William R. Anson, *Principles of the Law of Contract* 20 (Arthur L. Corbin ed., 3d Am. ed. 1919).

3. Loosely, a voidable contract.

"Again the word 'void' has been used, even by judges and the framers of statutes, where 'voidable' is meant. One illustration will suffice. By 17 *Geo. III*, c. 50, failure to pay certain duties at an auction is stated to make a bidding 'nul and void to all intents,' but this does not entitle a purchaser who has repented of his bargain to avoid the contract by his own wrong, that is by refusal to pay the statutory duty. The contract is voidable at the option of the party who has not broken the condition imposed by law." William R. Anson, *Principles of the Law of Contract* 20–21 (Arthur L. Corbin ed., 3d Am. ed. 1919).

▸ **voluntary contract.** See *gratuitous contract* (2).

▸ **wagering contract.** (18c) **1.** A contract made entirely for sport, the performance depending on the happening of an uncertain event. See *gambling contract.*

"Although wagering and gaming agreements were generally enforceable under the English common law, they were condemned in most American states, in part because they were thought to encourage shiftlessness, poverty, and immorality, and in party because they were regarded as too frivolous to be worthy of judicial attention. Irwin v. Williar, 110 U.S. 499 (1884) ('In England it is held that the contracts, although wagers, were not void at common law, . . . while generally, in this country, all wagering contracts are held to be illegal and void as against public policy.')" E. Allan Farnsworth, *Contracts* § 5.2 n.4, at 326–27 (3d ed. 1999).

2. A contract in which performance depends on a business transaction or outcome. • With this type of wagering contract, a business person is protected from a trade risk. **3.** See *aleatory contract.*

▸ **written contract.** (17c) A contract whose terms have been reduced to writing.

"Written contracts are also commonly signed, but a written contract may consist of an exchange of correspondence, of a letter written by the promisee and assented to by the promisor without signature, or even of a memorandum or printed document not signed by either party. Statutes relating to written contracts are often expressly limited to contracts signed by one or both parties. Whether such a limitation is to be implied when not explicit depends on the purpose and context." Restatement (Second) of Contracts § 95 cmt. c (1979) (citations omitted).

▸ **yellow-dog contract.** See YELLOW-DOG CONTRACT.

contract, freedom of. See FREEDOM OF CONTRACT.

contract bond. See PERFORMANCE BOND.

contract carrier. See *private carrier* under CARRIER (1).

Contract Clause. See CONTRACTS CLAUSE.

contract damages. Remedies available for a breach of contract. See *compensatory damages, consequential damages, liquidated damages, punitive damages* under DAMAGES; SPECIFIC PERFORMANCE.

contract debt. See DEBT.

contract demurrage. See DEMURRAGE (1).

contractee. (1875) *Rare.* A person with whom a contract is made.

contract for deed. See *installment land contract* under CONTRACT.

contract for sale. See CONTRACT.

contract for services. See CONTRACT.

contract implied in fact. See *implied-in-fact contract* under CONTRACT.

contract implied in law. See *implied-in-fact contract* under CONTRACT.

contract in, *vb.* (1927) **1.** To arrange for a person or company outside one's own organization to come in and do a particular job <we contract in our janitorial services>. **2.** To agree officially to take part in something <all members must contract in>.

contracting out, *n.* (1881) **1.** The excluding by agreement of statutory provisions that would otherwise govern the terms or performance of contractual obligations. **2.** OUTSOURCING.

contracting state. (18c) A country that has consented to be bound by a treaty.

contract in restraint of trade. See CONTRACT.

contract labor. See INDEPENDENT CONTRACTOR.

contract loan. See *add-on loan* under LOAN.

contract manufacturing. (1955) The production of goods in accordance with the designs and specifications of a customer who then sells the product under its own brand. • In ordinary contract manufacturing, the customer does not furnish the raw materials. Cf. TOLL MANUFACTURING.

contract–market differential. The difference between the contract price and the market price at the place and time of delivery.

contract not to compete. See *covenant not to compete* under COVENANT (1).

contract not to sue. See *covenant not to sue* under COVENANT (1).

contract of adhesion. See *adhesion contract* under CONTRACT.

contract of affreightment (ə-**frayt**-mənt). (18c) *Maritime law.* An agreement for the carriage of goods by water, esp. by more than one voyage between specified ports over a specified period on payment for each voyage performed. • A contract of affreightment may employ a bill of lading, a charterparty, or both to ship the goods. — Abbr. COA; CoA. — Also termed *contract of carriage*; *tonnage contract.* See CHARTERPARTY.

"When a shipowner, or person having for the time being as against the shipowner the right to make such an agreement, agrees to carry goods by water, or to furnish a ship for the purpose of so carrying goods, in return for a sum of money to be paid to him, such a contract is called a *contract of affreightment* and the sum to be paid is called *freight*. When the agreement is to carry a complete cargo of goods, or to furnish a ship for that purpose, the contract of affreightment is almost always contained in a document called a *charterparty*, the shipowner letting the ship for the purpose of carrying, or undertaking to carry, the charterer hiring the ship for such purpose, or undertaking to provide a full cargo." William Lennox McNair, Alan Abraham Mocatta & Michael J. Mustill, *Scrutton on Charterparties and Bills of Lading* 1 (17th ed. 1964).

contract of beneficence. See *gratuitous contract* under CONTRACT.

contract of benevolence. See *gratuitous contract* under CONTRACT.

contract of carriage. See CONTRACT OF AFFREIGHTMENT.

contract of employment. See *employment contract* under CONTRACT.

contract of guaranty. See GUARANTY (1).

contract of indemnity. See *indemnity contract* under CONTRACT.

contract of insurance. See INSURANCE POLICY.

contract of marriage. See *marriage contract* under CONTRACT.

contract of pledge. See CONTRACT.

contract of record. See CONTRACT.

contract of sale. See *contract for sale* (1) under CONTRACT.

contract of service. (18c) **1.** An agreement to enter into an apprenticeship.

▸ **beneficial contract of service.** (1906) *Archaic.* A minor's agreement to enter into an apprenticeship, historically binding the minor if it furnishes him or her with a means of livelihood, with the skills necessary to pursue an occupation, or with other beneficial experience.

2. See *employment contract* under CONTRACT.

contractor. (16c) **1.** A party to a contract. **2.** More specif., one who contracts to do work for or supply goods to another; esp., a person or company that agrees to do work or provide goods for another company <a roofing contractor>.

▸ **competent contractor.** (1854) A contractor who has the knowledge, skill, experience, and available equipment to do the work that he or she is employed to do without creating an unreasonable risk of injury to others and who has the personal characteristics necessary to carry out the work.

▸ **general contractor.** (18c) Someone who contracts for the completion of an entire project, including purchasing all materials, hiring and paying subcontractors, and coordinating all the work. — Also termed *original contractor; prime contractor.*

▸ **independent contractor.** See INDEPENDENT CONTRACTOR.

▸ **subcontractor.** See SUBCONTRACTOR.

contract out, *vb.* (1894) **1.** To arrange to have a job done by a person or company outside one's own organization <we contracted out the catering to the deli downstairs>. **2.** To agree officially not to take part in some system or scheme, such as a pension plan <we contracted out of Obamacare when it was still possible to do so>.

contract rate. See INTEREST RATE.

contract right. See RIGHT.

Contracts Clause. (1875) *Constitutional law.* The clause of the U.S. Constitution prohibiting states from passing any statute that would impair private contractual obligations. • The Supreme Court has generally interpreted this clause so that states can regulate private contractual obligations if the regulation is reasonable and necessary to serve an important public purpose. U.S. Const. art. I, § 10, cl. 1. — Also termed *Contract Clause; Obligation of Contracts Clause.*

contract-specification defense. (1966) An affirmative defense that immunizes a contractor from liability for a defect in a product when the contractor has manufactured or performed according to detailed contractual orders. • The defense applies to specialized, single-use components and protects a component supplier from claims of negligent design if the component conforms to the contractual specifications — unless the specifications are obviously dangerous. Under modern notions of strict liability, courts have increasingly rejected this defense. Cf. GOVERNMENT-CONTRACTOR DEFENSE; GOVERNMENT-AGENCY DEFENSE.

contract system. *Hist.* The practice of leasing prisoners out to private parties for the prisoners' labor.

contract theory. (1870) **1.** The study of the factors underlying the rationale for enforcing contractual obligations. **2.** The study of how and why people and organizations construct and enter into legal agreements. • In this sense, contract theory draws on principles of financial and economic behavior.

contract to pledge. See CONTRACT.

contract to satisfaction. See *satisfaction contract* under CONTRACT.

contract to sell. See *contract for sale* (2) under CONTRACT.

contractual bailment. See BAILMENT (1).

contractual duty. See DUTY (1).

contractual fault. See FAULT.

contractual indemnity. See INDEMNITY.

contractual limitation period. (1910) The contractually specified span of time within which any breach-of-contract lawsuit must be commenced, beginning when the breach occurs.

contractual obligation. See OBLIGATION.

contractual right. See RIGHT.

contract *uberrimae fidei*. See CONTRACT.

contract under hand. See CONTRACT.

contract under seal. See CONTRACT.

contractus (kən-**trak**-təs). [Latin] *Roman law.* A contract; an agreement between two or more parties, usu. to create an actionable bond between them. See CONTRAHERE.

"The texts of the Roman Law do not supply a definition of contract. The words contractus — contrahere — like 'contract' in English, are used in various senses, sometimes wider, sometimes narrower. Labeo gives contractus the meaning of a reciprocal obligation, such as purchase and sale, hire, partnership. But when the Romans speak of obligation arising from contract, they mean obligations arising from convention or agreement. In Roman law it was far from being the case that all agreements which might be expected to produce a legal obligation did so." R.W. Lee, *The Elements of Roman Law* 285 (4th ed. 1956).

contractus bonae fidei, vel stricti juris (kən-**trak**-təs **boh**-nee fɪ-dee-ɪ, vel **strik**-tɪ **joor**-ɪ). [Latin] (17c) *Roman law.* A contract of good faith or of strict law; a contract requiring that the parties perform their duties in good faith. • In an action brought on a *contractus bonae fidei*, the plaintiff had to assert that he had not acted in bad faith. All consensual contracts were considered *contractus bonae fidei*. The phrase was typically used when a remedy was being sought for a breach. Judges enforced contracts of good faith (e.g., contracts of sale) according to the requirements of good faith and contracts of strict law (e.g., stipulations) according to their strict terms. — Sometimes shortened to *contractus bonae fidei*.

contract zoning. See ZONING.

contradictio in adjecto. [Latin] (17c) A contradiction in terms; an oxymoron.

contradictory judgment. See JUDGMENT (2).

contradictory motion. See MOTION (1).

contradistinction. (17c) Distinction by contrary qualities or by contrast; a comparison by way of pointing out salient differences <contracts in contradistinction to torts>.

contra executionem (**kon**-trə ek-si-kyoo-shee-**oh**-nəm). [Law Latin] (17c) *Hist.* Against execution. • The phrase referred to the presumption in favor of a defendant's objections to the manner of execution against the defendant's property.

contrafactio (kon-trə-**fak**-shee-oh). [Law Latin] *Hist.* The act of counterfeiting. • The word appeared frequently in the phrase *contrafactio sigilli regis* ("counterfeiting the king's seal").

contra factum proprium (**kon**-trə **fak**-təm **proh**-pree-əm). [Latin] Against one's own deed.

contra fidem tabularum nuptialium (**kon**-trə fɪ-dəm tab-yə-**lair**-əm nəp-shee-**ay**-lee-əm). [Law Latin] (17c) *Scots law.* Against the provisions of the marriage contract. • The phrase usu. referred to antenuptial contracts.

contra formam collationis (**kon**-trə **for**-məm kə-lay-shee-**oh**-nis). [Latin "against the form of a collation"] (17c) *Hist.* A writ to regain lands given to a religious society in exchange for perpetual alms. • The writ was usu. sought by an heir of the person who had given the land away.

contra formam feoffmenti (**kon**-trə **for**-məm feef-**men**-tɪ). [Latin "contrary to the form of the feoffment"] *Hist.* A writ that commanded a landowner to stop demanding from a tenant more services than those included in the tenant's deed to the land. — Also spelled *contra formam feoffamenti*.

"Contra formam feoffamenti is a writ that lies where a man before the statute of *quia emptores terrarum*, made 18 Ed. 1, infeoffed another by deed to do certain service; if the feoffor or his heirs distrain him to do other service than is comprised in the deed, then the tenant shall have this writ, commanding him not to distrain him to do other service than is comprised in the deed." *Termes de la Ley* 116 (1st Am. ed. 1812).

contra formam statuti (**kon**-trə **for**-məm stə-**tyoo**-tɪ). [Law Latin] (17c) Contrary to the form of the statute. See AGAINST THE FORM OF THE STATUTE.

contrahere (kən-**tray**-hə-ree), *vb.* [Latin "draw together"] *Roman law.* **1.** To establish or enter into a formal relationship, as between husband and wife, creditor and debtor, by mutual agreement. **2.** To commit a crime. **3.** To accept an inheritance. **4.** Generally, to perform any act of legal significance. See CONTRACTUS.

contra hereditatem jacentem (**kon**-trə hə-red-i-**tay**-təm jə-**sen**-təm). [Law Latin] (18c) *Hist.* Against a succession that the heir has not taken up; against a fallen inheritance. • The phrase appeared in reference to a creditor's right to pursue a debtor's estate for recovery of a debt even though the heir did not take up the succession.

contra jus belli (**kon**-trə jəs **bel**-ɪ). [Latin] (18c) Against the law of war.

contra jus commune (**kon**-trə jəs kə-**myoo**-nee). [Latin] Against common right or law; contrary to the rule of the common law.

contra legem (**kon**-trə **lee**-jəm). [Latin] (16c) **1.** Contrary to law; against the law. **2.** EQUITY CONTRA LEGEM.

contra legem terrae (**kon**-trə **lee**-jəm **ter**-ee). [Latin] (18c) Against the law of the land.

contra libertatem matrimonii (**kon**-trə lib-ər-**tay**-təm ma-tri-**moh**-nee-ɪ). [Latin] (18c) *Hist.* Against freedom of marriage. • The phrase appeared in reference to marriage restraints, some of which were illegal.

***contra mundum* doctrine.** (2010) *English law.* The principle that an injunction issued against a news organization is binding on any other person or organization that receives notice of the injunction.

"Probably the most striking difference between England and the United States on national security law is the *contra mundum* doctrine in U.K. law that bans everyone (not just media), everywhere, at all times from communicating any information that is subject to judicial injunctions." Kyu Ho Youm, *Comparative Media Law and Ethics: The Wide View*, Comm. Law., Sept. 2010, at 7.

contra non producta (**kon**-trə non prə-**dək**-tə). [Law Latin "against things not produced"] (17c) *Scots law.* In a reduction action, a decree declaring that a challenged deed is void.

contra non valentem. See DOCTRINE OF CONTRA NON VALENTEM.

contra omnes gentes (**kon**-trə **om**-neez **jen**-teez). [Latin] (16c) *Hist.* Against all people. • These were the traditional words of warranty in a deed.

contra omnes mortales (**kon**-trə **ahm**-neez mor-**tay**-leez). [Law Latin] (17c) *Hist.* Against all mortals. • This language was contained in an absolute warranty.

contra pacem (**kon**-trə **pay**-səm). [Latin] (17c) *Hist.* Against the peace. • This term was used in indictments to signify that the alleged offense was against the public peace.

contra pietatem (**kon**-trə pɪ-ə-**tay**-təm). [Latin] *Hist.* Contrary to natural duty.

contraplacitum (kon-trə-**plas**-ə-təm). [Latin] *Hist.* A counterplea.

contra proferentem (**kon**-trə prof-ə-**ren**-təm). [Latin "against the offeror"] (17c) The doctrine that, in the interpretation of documents, ambiguities are to be construed unfavorably to the drafter. — Also spelled *contra proferentes*. — Also termed *ambiguity doctrine*.

contrarius consensus (kən-**trair**-ee-əs kən-**sen**-səs). [Latin] *Hist.* Agreement to the contrary.

contrariwise, *adv.* (15c) **1.** By contrast; on the contrary. **2.** In the opposite way or direction; in the reverse order.

contrarotulator (kon-trə-roch-yə-**lay**-tər *or* kon-trə-**roh**-tyə-lay-tər). [Latin "controller"] (17c) *Hist. English law.* A person responsible for collecting and managing funds on behalf of the Crown or other government office. • A variety of controllers existed in England, including the *contrarotulator custumarum* (controller of the customs), *contrarotulator hospitii domini regis* (controller of the king's household), and *contrarotulator pipae* (controller of the pipe — i.e., an officer who collected debts due to the Exchequer).

contrary to law. (16c) Illegal; unlawful; conflicting with established law.

contrary to the evidence. (16c) (Of an argument, finding, etc.) conflicting with the weight of the evidence presented at a contested hearing.

contra spolium (**kon**-trə **spoh**-lee-əm). [Law Latin "against the spoil"] (17c) *Scots law.* A real action for the recovery of stolen movable property.

contra tabulas. See BONORUM POSSESSIO CONTRA TABULAS.

contravene (kon-trə-**veen**), *vb.* (16c) **1.** To violate or infringe (the law, a rule, etc.); to defy <the soldier contravened the officer's order and then went AWOL>. **2.** To come into conflict with; to be contrary to <the court held that the regulation contravenes public policy>.

contravening equity. See EQUITY (5).

contravention (kon-trə-**ven**-shən). (16c) **1.** An act violating a legal condition or obligation; esp., historically, an entail heir's act that conflicts with the entail provision. **2.** *French law.* A criminal breach of a law, treaty, or agreement; a minor violation of the law. • A contravention is traditionally punishable by *peines de police*, usu. a fine not exceeding 15 francs and imprisonment not exceeding three days. See *public-welfare offense* under OFFENSE (2).

> "We might get [terminological] help from the practice of Continental Europe in which three classes of punishable offenses are maintained — crimes, delicts, and contraventions. The last word is used for those minor violations of regulations, all of them necessary enough for public safety and convenience, which are so numerous and so detailed in our lives. It is a convenient term and is widely used in the United States for just such acts, but it has not yet been made official. The Continental practice has the advantage of using the word crimes only for really serious offenses, which is in conformity with popular feeling on the subject." Max Radin, *The Law and You* 92 (1948).

3. *Scots law.* An action brought for breach of a peace bond. See LAWBURROWS. **4.** *Hist. Scots law.* An act committed in violation of a legal condition or obligation, esp. one done contrary to a deed by an heir to an entailment.

contravindicate, *vb. Roman law.* [Late Latin *contravindicare* "to claim against"] (Of a defendant) to counterclaim; esp., to allege an affirmative defense. — **contravindication,** *n.*

contrectatae (kon-trek-**tay**-tee). [Latin "things meddled with"] *Scots law.* Things that a person (such as a thief) either improperly used or tampered with.

contrectation (kon-trek-**tay**-shən), *n.* [fr. Latin *contrectare* "to touch or handle"] **1.** *Hist.* A touching or handling; manipulation. **2.** *Civil law.* The act of laying hands on another's property with the intent of taking, misappropriating, or misusing it; the handling and removal of goods in such a way as to amount to theft if they are not restored to their original place. • This term implied a greater culpability than simply taking property without the owner's permission and, under Roman law, was an element of theft (*furtum*).

contributing cause. See CAUSE (1).

contributing to the delinquency of a minor. (1913) The offense of an adult's engaging in conduct involving a minor — or in the presence of a minor — likely to result in delinquent conduct. • Examples include encouraging a minor to shoplift, enabling underage drinking, and soliciting sex for money. — Often shortened to *contributing to delinquency*. See JUVENILE DELINQUENCY. Cf. IMPAIRING THE MORALS OF A MINOR.

contributio lucri et damni (kon-tri-**byoo**-shee-oh **loo**-krɪ et **dam**-nɪ). [Latin] (18c) *Scots law.* Distribution of or sharing in profit and loss. • The phrase referred to one test for determining whether a partnership existed.

contribution. (14c) **1.** Something that one gives or does in order to help an endeavor be successful. **2.** An amount of money one gives in order to help pay for something. **3.** A regular payment one makes to one's employer or to the government to help pay for one's future benefits such as social security, a pension, etc. **4.** A piece of writing, a song, a poem, etc. that forms a part of a larger work such as a magazine, book, broadcast, recording, etc. **5.** The right that gives one of several persons who are liable on a common debt the ability to recover proportionately from each of the others when that one person discharges the debt for the benefit of all; the right to demand that another who is jointly responsible for a third party's injury supply part of what is required to compensate the third party. — Also termed *right of contribution*. **6.** One tortfeasor's right to collect from joint tortfeasors when, and to the extent that, the tortfeasor has paid more than his or her proportionate share to the injured party, the shares being determined as percentages of causal fault. **7.** The actual payment by a joint tortfeasor of a proportionate share of what is due. Cf. INDEMNITY. **8.** *Maritime law.* A share of the loss resulting from a ship's sacrifice of cargo, payable by each party whose property was spared to the party whose property was sacrificed. **9.** WAR CONTRIBUTION.

contribution agreement. See SUPPORT AGREEMENT.

contribution bar. (1976) Preclusion of a defendant having contribution rights against other defendants, who have settled their dispute with the plaintiff, from seeking contribution from them. • The bar is usu. allowed in exchange for a credit against any judgment the plaintiff obtains against the nonsettling defendant.

contribution claim. (1896) A defendant's claim to recover part of his or her liability to a plaintiff from another defendant or some third party who, it is asserted, should share in the liability. — Also termed *claim for contribution*.

contribution clause. See COINSURANCE CLAUSE.

contributione facienda (kon-tri-byoo-shee-**oh**-nee fay-shee-**en**-də). [Latin "writ for making contribution"] (16c)

Hist. A writ to compel a tenant in common to contribute to a fellow tenant who has paid more than the tenant's share of a sum for which all the tenants are liable.

> "*Contributione facienda* is a writ that lieth in case where more are bound to one thing, & one is put to the whole burden. . . . If tenents in comon or joynt, hold a mill (*pro indiviso*) & equally take the profits therof, the mill falling to decay, & one or more of them refusing to contribute toward the reparation therof, the rest shall have this writ . . . ." John Cowell, *The Interpreter* (1607).

contribution margin. (1948) The difference between a product's selling price and its variable production costs. • The contribution margin measures the amount of funds available for profit and payment of fixed costs.

contribution mortgage. See MORTGAGE.

contributory (kən-**trib**-yə-tor-ee), *adj.* (15c) **1.** Being one of the causes of a particular result. **2.** Tending to bring about a particular result. **3.** (Of a pension fund or insurance plan) paid for by both the employer and the employees. Cf. NONCONTRIBUTORY.

contributory, *n.* (15c) **1.** Someone who contributes or who has a duty to contribute. **2.** A contributing factor. **3.** *Hist.* Someone who, as a result of being or representing a past or present member of a corporation, is liable to contribute to the corporation's debts upon its winding up.

contributory infringement. See INFRINGEMENT.

contributory mortgage. See MORTGAGE.

contributory negligence. See NEGLIGENCE.

contributory-negligence doctrine. (1911) *Torts.* The principle that completely bars a plaintiff's recovery if the damage suffered is partly the plaintiff's own fault. • Most states have abolished this doctrine and have adopted instead a comparative-negligence analysis. See FAULT; NEGLIGENCE. Cf. COMPARATIVE-NEGLIGENCE DOCTRINE.

contributory pension plan. See PENSION PLAN.

control, *n.* (16c) The direct or indirect power to govern the management and policies of a person or entity, whether through ownership of voting securities, by contract, or otherwise; the power or authority to manage, direct, or oversee <the principal exercised control over the agent>.

▸ **ceded control.** Control that has been surrendered or given up.

▸ **corporate control.** *Corporations.* **1.** Ownership of more than 50% of the shares in a corporation. — Also termed *effective control*; *working control.* **2.** The power to vote enough of the shares in a corporation to determine the outcome of matters that the shareholders vote on.

▸ **effective control. 1.** The physical retention of possession of an item or its maintenance in a secure place. **2.** See *corporate control* (1).

▸ **superintending control.** (1850) The general supervisory control that a higher court in a jurisdiction has over the administrative affairs of a lower court within that jurisdiction.

▸ **working control.** (1897) **1.** The effective control of a corporation by a person or group who owns less than 50% of the stock. **2.** See *corporate control* (1).

control, *vb.* (15c) **1.** To exercise power or influence over <the judge controlled the proceedings>. **2.** To regulate or govern <by law, the budget office controls expenditures>. **3.** To have a controlling interest in <the five shareholders controlled the company>.

control group. (1937) The persons with authority to make decisions on a corporation's behalf.

control-group test. (1969) A method of determining whether the attorney–client privilege protects communications made by corporate employees, whereby those communications are protected only if made by an employee who is a member of the group with authority to direct the corporation's actions as a result of the communications. • The U.S. Supreme Court rejected the control-group test in *Upjohn Co. v. U.S.*, 449 U.S. 383, 101 S.Ct. 677 (1981). Cf. SUBJECT-MATTER TEST.

controlled buy. See CONTROLLED PURCHASE.

controlled company. See COMPANY.

controlled corporate groups. See CONTROLLED GROUP.

controlled corporation. See CORPORATION.

controlled debate. See DEBATE.

controlled foreign corporation. See CORPORATION.

controlled group. (1934) *Tax.* Two or more corporations whose stock is substantially held by five or fewer persons. • The Internal Revenue Code subjects these entities (such as parent-subsidiary or brother-sister groups) to special rules for computing tax liability. IRC (26 USCA) §§ 851(c)(3), 1563(a). — Also termed *controlled corporate groups.*

controlled purchase. (1957) The purchase of contraband by an undercover officer or an informant for the purpose of setting up an arrest of the seller. — Also termed *controlled buy.*

controlled-securities-offering distribution. See *securities-offering distribution* (1) under DISTRIBUTION.

controlled substance. (1970) A drug that is illegal to possess or use without a doctor's prescription; specif., any type of drug whose manufacture, possession, and use is regulated by law, including a narcotic, a stimulant, or a hallucinogen. See DRUG.

controlled-substance act. (1970) A federal or state statute that is designed to control the distribution, classification, sale, and use of certain drugs. • Most states have enacted these laws, which are usu. modeled on the Uniform Controlled Substances Act.

controlled-substance schedule. See DRUG SCHEDULE.

controlled time. See *controlled debate* under DEBATE.

controller. See COMPTROLLER.

controlling interest. See INTEREST (2).

controlling person. See CONTROL PERSON.

controlling shareholder. See SHAREHOLDER.

control person. (1958) *Securities.* Someone who has actual control of or significant influence over the issuer of securities, as by directing corporate policy. • The control person is subject to many of the same requirements applicable to the sale of securities by the issuer. — Also termed *controlling person.*

> "[T]he question of who is a control person is highly factual and is not dependent upon ownership of any specific percentage. For example, it has been held that someone owning eight percent of a company's stock was not a control person . . . ." 1 Thomas Lee Hazen, *Treatise on the Law of Securities Regulation* § 4.24, at 279 (3d ed. 1995).

control premium. See PREMIUM (3).

control stock. Stock belonging to a control person at the time of a given transaction. — Also termed *control shares.*

control test. See IRRESISTIBLE-IMPULSE TEST.

control theory. (1949) The theory that people will engage in criminal behavior unless certain personally held social controls (such as a strong investment in conventional, legitimate activities or a belief that criminal behavior is morally wrong) are in place to prevent them from doing so. Cf. ROUTINE-ACTIVITIES THEORY; RATIONAL-CHOICE THEORY; STRAIN THEORY.

control-your-kid law. See PARENTAL-RESPONSIBILITY STATUTE.

controver (kən-**troh**-vər). *Hist.* Someone who concocts false news.

controversy. (14c) **1.** A disagreement or a dispute, esp. in public. **2.** A justiciable dispute.

▸ **public controversy.** (17c) A controversy involving issues that are debated publicly and that have significant ramifications for persons other than those embroiled in it. • A participant in a public controversy may be deemed a public figure for purposes of a defamation suit arising from the controversy. See PUBLIC FIGURE.

> "The nature and extent of an individual's involvement in a public controversy is determined by three factors: (1) the extent to which participation in it is voluntary; (2) the extent to which there is access to channels of effective communication in order to counteract false statements; and (3) the prominence of the role played in the public controversy." 50 Am. Jur. 2d *Libel and Slander* § 75, at 390 (1995).

▸ **separable controversy.** (1881) A claim that is separate and independent from the other claims being asserted in a suit. • This term is most often associated with the statute that permits an entire case to be removed to federal court if one of the claims, being separate and independent from the others, presents a federal question that is within the jurisdiction of the federal courts. 28 USCA § 1441(c).

3. *Constitutional law.* A case that requires a definitive determination of the law on the facts alleged for the adjudication of an actual dispute, and not merely a hypothetical, theoretical, or speculative legal issue. — Also termed (in senses 2 & 3) *actual controversy.* See CASE-OR-CONTROVERSY REQUIREMENT.

> "What is a 'case or controversy' that is justiciable in the federal courts? The answer of Chief Justice Hughes is classic if cryptic. He said: 'A *controversy* in this sense must be one that is appropriate for judicial determination. A justiciable controversy is thus distinguished from a difference or dispute of a hypothetical character; from one that is academic or moot. The controversy must be definite and concrete, touching the legal relations of parties having adverse legal interests. It must be a real and substantial controversy admitting of specific relief through a decree of a conclusive character, as distinguished from an opinion advising what the law would be upon a hypothetical state of facts.' [*Aetna Life Ins. Co. v. Haworth*, 300 U.S. 227, 240–41, 57 S.Ct. 461, 464 (1937).] Unfortunately, this definition, though often quoted, turns upon labels that the Court had used in the past to describe cases before it, and the labels themselves are 'elastic, inconstant, and imprecise.'" Charles Alan Wright, *The Law of Federal Courts* § 12, at 60–61 (5th ed. 1994).

controvert (**kon**-trə-vərt *or* kon-trə-**vərt**), *vb.* (16c) To dispute or contest; esp., to deny (as an allegation in a pleading) or oppose in argument <the allegations in Peck's pleadings were never adequately controverted>.

contubernium (kon-t[y]uu-**bər**-nee-əm). [Latin] (16c) *Roman law.* A marriage-like union between slaves. • Contubernium was recognized in the United States. Before slavery was abolished, only one Southern court gave a marriage between slaves legal effect upon manumission. *See Girod v. Lewis*, 6 Mart. (O.S.) 559, 559–60 (La. 1819). In 1825, the Louisiana legislature passed a law expressly making such marriages invalid.

> "No such thing as marriage among slaves was, or could be, recognized by the law. As slaves were wholly subject to the disposal of their masters, no unions having the character of permanence or sacredness could exist among them: such a union, if it existed, would abridge the master's power of absolute control. Among slaves there could only be *contubernium*, cohabitation of the sexes for a longer or shorter time, but no legal *matrimonium*." James Hadley, *Introduction to Roman Law* 111 (1881).

> "There was . . . among slaves a permitted cohabitation called contubernium, but it brought with it no civil rights. . . . [C]ohabitation, . . . in a state of slavery, was not marriage, or evidence of marriage. It conferred no rights upon the offspring, and created no legal disabilities on the part of the father from forming a valid marriage, whenever he became in a condition which would authorize him to contract one." Adrienne D. Davis, *The Private Law of Race and Sex: An Antebellum Perspective*, 51 Stan. L. Rev. 221, 245 (1999).

contumace capiendo. See DE CONTUMACE CAPIENDO.

contumacious conduct. See CONDUCT.

contumacy (**kon**-t[y]uu-mə-see), *n.* (15c) Contempt of court; the refusal of a person to follow a court's order or direction. See CONTEMPT. — **contumacious,** *adj.*

contumax. (15c) *Hist.* **1.** A person found to be in contempt of court. **2.** Someone who is accused of a crime but refuses to appear and answer the charge.

contumelious (kon-t[y]oo-**mee**-lee-əs), *adj.* (15c) Insolent, abusive, spiteful, or humiliating.

contumely (**kon**-t[y]uu-mə-lee *or* kən-**t[y]oo**-mə-lee), *n.* (14c) Insulting language or treatment; scornful rudeness.

contutor (kən-**t[y]oo**-tər), *n.* [Latin] *Roman law.* A coguardian of a ward. • Appointment as a coguardian could be accomplished by testament or by court order.

conubium (kə-**n[y]oo**-bee-əm), *n.* [fr. Latin *con* "together" + *nubere* "to marry"] *Roman law.* **1.** The legal capacity to wed. **2.** The collection of rights that accompany a marriage between persons who have the capacity to marry. — Also spelled *connubium.* — Also termed *jus connubii.* See CONCUBINATUS; JUSTAE NUPTIAE. Cf. COMMERCIUM.

> "The word *connubium* denotes properly the right to intermarry with Roman citizens; and hence to contract a Roman marriage, according to the peculiar forms and with the peculiar incidents and effects of marriage between Roman citizens. Chief among these incidents or effects was the *patria potestas*, or life-long control of the father over his children, which, as we shall soon see, was among the most remarkable peculiarities of the Roman system. In general, *connubium* embraces the peculiar rights of Roman citizens, so far as they pertain to family relations." James Hadley, *Introduction to Roman Law* 116 (1881).

conurbation (kon-ər-**bay**-shən). (1915) A group of towns that have spread and joined together to form a highly populated area, often with a large city at its center.

conusance (**kon**-yə-zənts). (16c) *Hist.* **1.** Cognizance; jurisdiction. • The word *conusance* is actually an archaic form of *cognizance.* See COGNIZANCE (1); CLAIM OF COGNIZANCE. **2.** JUDICIAL NOTICE. **3.** An acknowledgment (of a debt, act, or opposing claim). • Examples of *conusance* include an acknowledgment in replevin that the defendant took the sued-for goods, or an acknowledgment in a land transfer (by *fine*) that the grantee is entitled to the land. See FINE (1).

conusant (**kon**-yə-zənt), *adj.* (17c) (Of a person) having cognizance or knowledge. See COGNIZANCE.

conusee (kon-yə-**zee**). See COGNIZEE.

conusor (**kon**-yə-zər *or* -zor). See COGNIZOR.

conuzee. See COGNIZEE.

convene, *vb.* (15c) **1.** To call together, esp. for a formal meeting; to cause to assemble. **2.** *Eccles. law.* To summon to respond to an action. See CONVENTIO (1).

> "When the defendant was brought to answer, he was said to be convened, — which the canonists called *conventio*, because the plaintiff and defendant met to contest." 1 John Bouvier, *Bouvier's Law Dictionary* 668 (Francis Rawle ed., 8th ed. 1914).

3. *Civil law.* To bring an action; to sue.

convenience account. See ACCOUNT.

convening authority. (1898) *Military law.* An officer (usu. a commanding officer) with the power to convene, or who has convened, a court-martial.

convening order. (1921) *Military law.* An instrument that creates a court-martial. • The convening order specifies (1) the type of court-martial and its time and place, (2) the names of the panel members and of the trial and defense counsel, (3) the name of the military judge, if one has been detailed, and (4) if necessary, the authority by which the court-martial has been convened.

conventicle (kən-**ven**-tə-kəl). [fr. Latin *conventiculum* "small assembly"] (14c) **1.** An assembly of a clandestine or unlawful character. **2.** An assembly for religious worship; esp., a secret meeting for worship not sanctioned by law. **3.** A place where such meetings are held.

conventio (kən-**ven**-shee-oh). [fr. Latin *convenire* "to come together"] **1.** *Eccles. law.* The act of convening the parties to an action by summoning the defendant. **2.** *Hist.* An agreement or convention; an agreement between two or more persons respecting a legal relation between them. See CONVENTION (1).

> "Conventio is a word much used both in Ancient and Modern Law-pleadings, for an Agreement or Covenant." Thomas Blount, *Nomo-Lexicon: A Law-Dictionary* (1670).

convention. (15c) **1.** An agreement or compact, esp. one among countries; a multilateral treaty <the Geneva Convention>. See TREATY.

▸ **antidiscrimination convention.** (1968) *Int'l law.* An international convention imposing on the signatory countries duties to take measures in their national laws to prohibit specified types of discrimination.

2. A special deliberative assembly elected for the purpose of framing, revising, or amending a constitution. — Also termed *constitutional convention.* See CONSTITUTION (1).

> "Constitutional conventions may be classified as follows: (1) authorized, (2) popular, and (3) revolutionary. An *authorized* convention is one which is provided for by the existing constitution and which is held pursuant to those existing constitutional provisions. . . . A *popular* convention is one which is held in a state where the constitution is *silent* on the matter of conventions, or which is held in *disregard* of provisions in the existing constitution relative to conventions, but which is duly called by the electors of the state voting at a regular and legally authorized election. . . . A *revolutionary* convention is one which is held under no color of legal authority." Homer Hendricks, *Some Legal Aspects of Constitutional Conventions*, 2 Tex. L. Rev. 195, 195–96 (1924).

3. An assembly or meeting of members belonging to an organization or having a common objective <an ABA convention>. — Also termed *conference.* **4.** *Parliamentary law.* A deliberative assembly that consists of delegates elected or appointed from subordinate or constituent organizations within a state or national organization, or elected directly from the organization's membership or from defined geographic or other constituencies into which the membership is grouped, and that usu. exercises the organization's highest policymaking authority <a national political convention>. — Also termed *assembly; congress; convocation; delegate assembly; general assembly.* See HOUSE OF DELEGATES. **5.** *Parliamentary law.* A session of a convention (in sense 4), consisting of a series of consecutive meetings separated by short recesses or adjournments, often during a convention (in sense 3) that includes educational and social programs for the benefit of delegates and other members. **6.** A generally accepted rule or practice; usage or custom <the court dispensed with the convention of having counsel approach the bench>.

Convention Against Torture. An international human-rights instrument, adopted by the General Assembly of the United Nations in December 1984 (taking effect in 1987), aiming to prevent torture around the world by obligating state parties to ensure that all acts of torture are offenses under their criminal law punishable by appropriate penalties.

conventional, *adj.* (16c) **1.** Customary; orthodox; traditional <conventional motion practice>. **2.** Depending on, or arising from, the agreement of the parties, as distinguished from something arising by law <conventional subrogation>. **3.** Arising by treaty or convention <conventional international law>.

conventional custom. See CUSTOM (1).

conventional interest. See INTEREST (3).

conventionalism. (1837) **1.** A jurisprudential conception of legal practice and tradition holding that law is a matter of respecting and enforcing legal and social rules.

> "Conventionalism makes two postinterpretive, directive claims. The first is positive: that judges must respect the established legal conventions of their community except in rare circumstances. It insists, in other words, that they must treat as law what convention stipulates as law. Since convention in Britain establishes that acts of Parliament are law, a British judge must enforce even acts of Parliament he considers unfair or unwise. This positive part of conventionalism most plainly corresponds to the popular slogan that judges should follow the law and not make new law in its place. The second claim, which is at least equally important, is negative. It declares that there is no law — no right flowing from past political decisions — apart from the law drawn from those decisions by techniques that are themselves matters of convention, and therefore that on some issues there is no law either way." Ronald Dworkin, *Law's Empire* 116 (1986).

2. The view that the grounds of a developed legal system are determined by a series of traditions that remain relatively limited, so as to leave some cases legally unregulated. *See* Scott J. Shapiro, *Legality* 297 (2011).

conventionality thesis. (2001) In legal philosophy, the positivist view that the criteria of legality are fixed by agreement among legal officials; specif., the view that any legal rule that officials follow and apply is a matter of coordinated agreement, analogous to the rule of the road (driving on the right or left side).

conventional law. (17c) A rule or system of rules agreed on by persons for the regulation of their conduct toward one another; law constituted by agreement as having the force of special law between the parties, by either supplementing or replacing the general law of the land. • The most important example is conventional international law, but there are many lesser examples such as rules and regulations of a country club or professional association, or the rules of golf, basketball, or any other game. — Also termed (in international law) *treaty-made law; treaty-created law; treaty law.* See CONVENTION (1).

conventional lien. See LIEN.

conventional lineup. See LINEUP.

conventional loan. See *conventional mortgage* under MORTGAGE.

conventional mortgage. See MORTGAGE.

conventional obligation. See OBLIGATION.

conventional remission. See REMISSION (1).

conventional sequestration. See SEQUESTRATION (5).

conventional servitude. See SERVITUDE (3).

conventional subrogation. See SUBROGATION.

Convention application. See PATENT APPLICATION.

convention article. A provision in an international treaty or convention.

conventione (kən-ven-shee-**oh**-nee). [Latin] *Hist.* A writ for the breach of a written covenant. • This writ was often used when parties wished to convey land by fine. — Also termed *writ of covenant.* See FINE (1).

Convention for the European Patent for the Common Market. See COMMUNITY PATENT CONVENTION.

Convention for the Protection of Performers, Producers of Phonograms, and Broadcasting Organizations. See ROME CONVENTION ON RELATED RIGHTS.

Convention for the Protection of Producers of Phonograms Against Unauthorized Duplication of Their Phonograms. See GENEVA PHONOGRAMS CONVENTION.

Convention on the Grant of European Patent. See EUROPEAN PATENT CONVENTION.

Convention Relating to the Distribution of Program-Carrying Signals Transmitted by Satellite. See BRUSSELS SATELLITE CONVENTION.

conventual writ. See WRIT.

conventus (kən-**ven**-təs), *n.* [Latin] **1.** An assembly. • *Conventus magnatum vel procerum* ("the assembly of the nobles") was an ancient name for Parliament. **2.** CONVENTUS JURIDICUS. Pl. ***conventus.***

conventus juridicus (kən-**ven**-təs juu-**rid**-i-kəs). [Latin "judicial assembly"] (17c) *Roman law.* A court session held by a provincial governor in the leading cities of the province. — Sometimes shortened to *conventus.*

converse-Erie doctrine. See REVERSE-ERIE DOCTRINE.

conversion, *n.* (14c) **1.** The act of changing from one form to another; the process of being exchanged.

▸ **equitable conversion.** (18c) A change in the nature of property so that real property is treated as personal property, or vice versa, in certain circumstances. • Equitable conversion is based on the maxim that equity regards as done that which ought to be done. The most common situation involves transferring real property as the parties to a contract intended before the seller experienced a change in circumstances, such as marriage or death, that could affect title to the property. When a contract is made, the buyer acquires equitable title to the property, and the seller retains legal title. But the seller's interest is treated as one in personal property rather than in real property because the seller's true interest is in the proceeds (usu. personal property such as cash); the legal title is security for the buyer's payment. Courts usu. apply the doctrine of equitable conversion to recognize the transfer of equitable title, including the right of possession, to the buyer when the contract was signed. The buyer then acquires legal title by performing under the contract.

▸ **forced conversion.** (1958) The conversion of a convertible security by the issuer, after a call for redemption. • An issuer will typically force a conversion when the price of the security to which the convertible is converted exceeds the redemption value.

2. *Tort & criminal law.* The wrongful possession or disposition of another's property as if it were one's own; an act or series of acts of willful interference, without lawful justification, with an item of property in a manner inconsistent with another's right, whereby that other person is deprived of the use and possession of the property. — **convert,** *vb.* — **conversionary,** *adj.*

> "There are three distinct methods by which one man may deprive another of his property, and so be guilty of a conversion and liable in an action for trover — (1) by wrongly taking it, (2) by wrongly detaining it, and (3) by wrongly disposing of it. The term conversion was originally limited to the third of these cases. To convert goods meant to dispose of them, or make away with them, to deal with them, in such a way that neither owner nor wrongdoer had any further possession of them: for example, by consuming them, or by destroying them, or by selling them, or otherwise delivering them to some third person. Merely to take another's goods, however wrongfully, was not to convert them. Merely to detain them in defiance of the owner's title was not to convert them. The fact that conversion in its modern sense includes instances of all three modes in which a man may be wrongfully deprived of his goods, and not of one mode only, is the outcome of a process of historical development whereby, by means of legal fictions and other devices, the action of trover was enabled to extend its limits and appropriate the territories that rightly belonged to other and earlier forms of action." R.F.V. Heuston, *Salmond on the Law of Torts* 94 (17th ed. 1977).

> "By conversion of goods is meant any act in relation to goods which amounts to an exercise of dominion over them, inconsistent with the owner's right of property. It does not include mere acts of damage, or even an asportation which does not amount to a denial of the owner's right of property; but it does include such acts as taking possession, refusing to give up on demand, disposing of the goods to a third person, or destroying them." William Geldart, *Introduction to English Law* 143 (D.C.M. Yardley ed., 9th ed. 1984).

▸ **constructive conversion.** (1832) Conversion consisting of an action that in law amounts to the appropriation of property. • Constructive conversion could be, for example, an appropriation that was initially lawful.

▸ **conversion by detention.** Conversion by detaining property in a way that is adverse to the owner or other lawful possessor. • The mere possession of property without title is not conversion. The defendant must have shown an intention to keep it in defiance of the owner or lawful possessor.

▸ **conversion by estoppel.** A judicial determination that a conversion has taken place — though in truth one has not — because a defendant is estopped from offering a defense. • This occurs, for example, under the traditional rule that a bailee is estopped from denying the bailor's title even if the bailor has no title to the chattel.

▸ **conversion by taking.** (1905) Conversion by taking a chattel out of the possession of another with the intention of exercising permanent or temporary dominion over it, despite the owner's entitlement to use it at all times.

▸ **conversion by wrongful delivery.** (1917) Conversion by depriving an owner of goods of possession by delivering them to someone else.

▸ **conversion by wrongful destruction.** Conversion by willfully consuming or otherwise destroying a chattel belonging to another person.

▸ **conversion by wrongful disposition.** Conversion by depriving an owner of goods by giving some other person a lawful title to them.

▸ **direct conversion.** The act of appropriating the property of another to one's own benefit, or to the benefit of a third person. • A direct conversion is per se unlawful, and the traditional requirements of demand and refusal of the property do not apply.

▸ **fraudulent conversion.** Conversion that is committed by the use of fraud, either in obtaining the property or in withholding it.

▸ **innocent conversion.** See *technical conversion.*

▸ **involuntary conversion.** (1876) The loss or destruction of property through theft, casualty, or condemnation.

▸ **negligent conversion.** See *technical conversion.*

▸ **technical conversion.** (1871) The taking of another's personal property by one who acts in good faith and mistakenly believes that he or she is lawfully entitled to the property. — Also termed *innocent conversion*; *negligent conversion.*

conversionary act. See ACT (2).

conversion divorce. See DIVORCE.

conversion premium. (1950) *Securities.* The surplus at which a security sells above its conversion price.

conversion price. (1910) *Securities.* The contractually specified price per share at which a convertible security can be converted into shares of another security, usu. common stock.

conversion ratio. (1932) **1.** The number of units of a security into which a convertible security may be converted. **2.** The ratio of the face amount of the convertible security to the conversion price.

conversion right. (1909) A right or option granted by a corporation to a shareholder or other security holder to convert a security into another type of security of the corporation. • A conversion right usu. enables holders of preferred stock and debt holders to convert the securities or debt into common stock.

conversion rule. See SPECIFIC-PURPOSE RULE.

conversion security. See SECURITY (4).

conversion statute. (1977) A law under which a state official or court oversees the sale or transfer of control of an organization in order to protect public assets.

conversion value. (1903) A convertible security's value as common stock. • For example, a bond that can be converted into ten shares of stock worth $40 each has a conversion value of $400. See BOND CONVERSION.

converter, *n.* (16c) Someone who wrongfully possesses or disposes of another's property; esp., one who engages in a series of acts of willful interference, without lawful justification, with an item of property in a manner inconsistent with another's right, whereby that other person is deprived of the use and possession of the property.

▸ **innocent converter.** (1898) Someone who takes another's chattel tortiously but in good faith and without knowledge that he or she has no entitlement to it.

convertible arbitrage. See *kind arbitrage* under ARBITRAGE.

convertible bond. See BOND (3).

convertible collision insurance. See INSURANCE.

convertible debenture. See DEBENTURE (3).

convertible debt. 1. See DEBT. **2.** See *convertible security* under SECURITY (4).

convertible divorce. See *conversion divorce* under DIVORCE.

convertible insurance. See INSURANCE.

convertible security. See SECURITY (4).

convertible stock. See *convertible security* under SECURITY (4).

convertible subordinated debenture. See DEBENTURE (3).

convey, *vb.* (14c) To transfer or deliver (something, such as a right or property) to another, esp. by deed or other writing; esp., to perform an act that is intended to create one or more property interests, regardless of whether the act is actually effective to create those interests.

conveyance (kən-**vay**-ənts), *n.* (15c) **1.** The voluntary transfer of a right or of property.

▸ **absolute conveyance.** (17c) A conveyance in which a right or property is transferred to another free of conditions or qualifications (i.e., not as a security). Cf. *conditional conveyance.*

▸ **conditional conveyance.** (18c) A conveyance that is based on the happening of an event, usu. payment for the property; a mortgage. Cf. *absolute conveyance.*

▸ **derivative conveyance.** See *secondary conveyance.*

▸ **innocent conveyance.** (18c) *Hist.* A leaseholder's conveyance of the leaseholder's property interest — that is, something less than a fee simple. • The conveyance is of an equitable interest.

▸ **involuntary conveyance.** See *involuntary alienation* under ALIENATION (1).

▸ **mesne conveyance** (meen). (18c) An intermediate conveyance; one occupying an intermediate position in the chain of title between the first grantee and the present holder.

▸ **original conveyance.** See *primary conveyance.*

▸ **present conveyance.** (17c) A conveyance made with the intent that it take effect at once rather than in the future.

▸ **primary conveyance.** (18c) A conveyance that creates an estate. • Examples of primary conveyances include feoffment, gift, grant, lease, exchange, and partition. — Also termed *original conveyance.* Cf. *secondary conveyance.*

"Of conveyances by the common law, some may be called *original*, or *primary* conveyances; which are those by means whereof the benefit or estate is created or first arises: others are *derivative* or *secondary*; whereby the benefit or estate, originally created, is enlarged, restrained, transferred, or extinguished." 2 William Blackstone, *Commentaries on the Laws of England* 309 (1766).

▸ **secondary conveyance.** (18c) A conveyance that follows an earlier conveyance and that serves only to enlarge, confirm, alter, restrain, restore, or transfer the interest created by the primary conveyance. — Also termed *derivative conveyance*; *derivative deed.* Cf. *primary conveyance.*

▸ **voluntary conveyance.** (17c) A conveyance made without valuable consideration, such as a deed in favor of a relative.

2. The transfer of a property right that does not pass by delivery of a thing or merely by agreement. **3.** The transfer of an interest in real property from one living person to another, by means of an instrument such as a deed. **4.** The document (usu. a deed) by which such a transfer occurs. **5.** A means of transport; a vehicle. **6.** *Bankruptcy.* A transfer of an interest in real or personal property, including an assignment, a release, a monetary payment, or the creation of a lien or encumbrance. — Also termed (in sense 6) *bond for deed.* See FRAUDULENT CONVEYANCE; PREFERENTIAL TRANSFER.

conveyance in fraud of creditors. See FRAUDULENT CONVEYANCE (1).

conveyancer (kən-**vay**-ən-sər). (17c) A lawyer who specializes in real-estate transactions. • In England, a *conveyancer* is a solicitor or licensed conveyancer who examines title to real estate, prepares deeds and mortgages, and performs other functions relating to the transfer of real property.

conveyancing (kən-**vay**-ən-sing). (17c) The act or work of drafting and preparing legal instruments, esp. those (such as deeds or leases) that transfer an interest in real property.

"*Conveyancing* is the art or science of preparing documents and investigating title in connection with the creation and assurance of interests in land. Despite its connection with the word 'conveyance,' the term in practice is not limited to use in connection with old system title but is used without discrimination in the context of all types of title." Peter Butt, *Land Law* 7 (2d ed. 1988).

"Conveyancing may be regarded as the application of the law of real property in practice." Robert E. Megarry & M.P. Thompson, *A Manual of the Law of Real Property* 125 (6th ed. 1993).

conveyancing counsel. (18c) *English law.* Three to six lawyers who are appointed by the Lord Chancellor to assist the High Court of Justice with opinions in matters of property titles and conveyancing. — Also termed *conveyancing counsel of the Supreme Court*; (formerly) *conveyancing counsel to the Court of Chancery.*

conveyee (kən-vay-**ee**). (18c) One to whom property is conveyed.

conveyor (kən-**vay**-ər *or* -or). (16c) Someone who transfers or delivers title to another.

conviciandi animo (kən-vish-ee-**an**-dı **an**-ə-moh). [Latin] *Hist.* With the intention of insulting; with the intention of bringing into contempt.

convicium (kən-**vish**-ee-əm), *n.* [Latin] *Roman law.* Reproach, abuse, revilement, or clamor directed at a person.

convict (**kon**-vikt), *n.* (15c) Someone who has been found guilty of a crime and is serving a sentence of confinement for that crime; a prison inmate.

convict (kən-**vikt**), *vb.* (15c) To prove or officially announce (a criminal defendant) to be guilty of a crime after proceedings in a law court; specif., to find (a person) guilty of a criminal offense upon a criminal trial, a plea of guilty, or a plea of nolo contendere (no contest).

convicted felon. See FELON.

conviction (kən-**vik**-shən), *n.* (15c) **1.** The act or process of judicially finding someone guilty of a crime; the state of having been proved guilty. **2.** The judgment (as by a jury verdict) that a person is guilty of a crime.

▸ **misconviction.** See MISCONVICTION.

▸ **summary conviction.** (18c) A conviction of a person for a violation or minor misdemeanor as the result of a trial before a magistrate sitting without a jury.

▸ **wrongful conviction. 1.** A conviction of a person for a crime that he or she did not commit. **2.** Broadly, a conviction that has been overturned or vacated by an appellate court.

3. At the end of an impeachment trial, a legislative body's declaration that the defendant is guilty of misconduct. **4.** A strong belief or opinion.

▸ **abiding conviction.** (17c) A settled conviction; a definite conviction based on a thorough examination of the case.

conviction rate. (1928) Within a given area or for a given time, the number of convictions (including plea bargains) as a percentage of the total number of prosecutions undertaken.

convict-labor system. (1902) A work program for prisoners to produce goods for either state use or sale in the public market. See STATE ACCOUNT SYSTEM; STATE-USE SYSTEM.

convincing, *adj.* (17c) Causing one to believe that something is true or right; persuasive.

convivium (kən-**viv**-ee-əm). [Latin "banquet"] *Hist.* Tenure that binds the tenant to provide meat and drink for the lord at least once a year.

convocation. (14c) **1.** CONVENTION (4). **2.** The process of arranging for a large meeting to be held. See *call to order* under CALL (1). **3.** A large formal meeting of a group of people, esp. church officials. See *provincial synod* under SYNOD. **4.** The ceremony held when students graduate from a college or university.

convoy, *n.* (16c) A group of vehicles or vessels traveling together for safety, esp. with armed escorts. • The term also applies figuratively to groups traveling together for convenience. — **convoy,** *vb.*

convoyed sale. See SALE.

conuzor. See COGNIZOR.

COO. *abbr.* CHIEF OPERATING OFFICER.

co-obligee. (1833) One of two or more persons to whom an obligation is owed. See OBLIGEE.

co-obligor. (18c) **1.** One of two or more persons who have undertaken an obligation. See OBLIGOR. **2.** Someone who is under a duty of contribution. See CONTRIBUTION (1).

cool blood. (17c) *Criminal law.* In the law of homicide, a condition in which the defendant's emotions are not in such an excited state that they interfere with his or her faculties and reason. — Also termed *cool state of blood.* See COLD BLOOD. Cf. HEAT OF PASSION.

***Cooley* doctrine.** (1936) *Constitutional law.* The principle that Congress has exclusive power under the Commerce Clause to regulate the national as well as the local aspects of national commercial matters, and that the states may regulate those aspects of interstate commerce so local in character as to require diverse treatment. • The Supreme Court has abandoned the *Cooley* doctrine in favor of a balancing test for Commerce Clause cases. *Cooley v. Port Bd. of Wardens*, 53 U.S. (12 How.) 299 (1851).

cooling-off period. (1913) **1.** An automatic delay between a person's taking some legal action and the consequence of that action. **2.** A period during which a buyer who has signed a sales agreement may cancel a purchase. **3.** An automatic delay between the filing of divorce papers and the divorce hearing. **4.** *Securities.* A period (usu. at least 20 days) between the filing of a registration and the effective registration. **5.** During a dispute, a period during which a rule precludes any action to be taken by either side. • In labor disputes, a statutory cooling-off period forbids employee strikes and employer lockouts. **6.** A period of time when two or more people or groups that are disputing something voluntarily agree to go away and think about how to improve the situation.

cooling time. (1874) *Criminal law.* Time to recover cool blood after great excitement, stress, or provocation, so that one is considered able to contemplate, comprehend, and act with reference to the consequences that are likely to follow. See COOL BLOOD.

> "[O]ne who controls his temper time after time, following repeated acts of provocation, may have his emotion so bottled-up that the final result is an emotional explosion . . . . [I]n such a case the 'cooling time' begins to run not from earlier acts, but from 'the last straw.' . . . As was the position in regard to the adequacy of the provocation, so the early holding was that the cooling time was a matter of law for the court." Rollin M. Perkins & Ronald N. Boyce, *Criminal Law* 100 (3d ed. 1982).

cool state of blood. See COOL BLOOD.

co-op. See COOPERATIVE.

cooperation. (18c) **1.** An association of individuals who join together for a common benefit. **2.** *Patents.* A unity of action to a common end or result, not merely joint or simultaneous action. **3.** *Int'l law.* The voluntary coordinated action of two or more countries occurring under a legal régime and serving a specific objective.

cooperation agreement. (1924) **1.** Any contract by which the parties bind themselves to work jointly and productively toward some mutually beneficial end. **2.** *Maritime law.* A contract between shipowners or others having rights in vessels to work together in marketing and chartering their vessels. **3.** A contract between the government and either a defendant or a witness stipulating to a lesser punishment in exchange for cooperating in the prosecution of another person.

▸ **horizontal cooperation agreement.** (1994) A cooperation agreement between competitors, esp. for such purposes as research and development, production, purchasing, or commercialization.

cooperation clause. (1925) *Insurance.* A policy provision requiring that the insured assist the insurer in investigating and defending a claim.

cooperative, *n.* (1883) **1.** An organization or enterprise (as a store) owned by those who use its services. **2.** A dwelling (as an apartment building) owned by its residents, to whom the apartments are leased. — Often shortened to *coop*; *co-op.* Cf. CONDOMINIUM (2).

cooperative adoption. See ADOPTION (1).

cooperative cause. See CAUSE (1).

cooperative corporation. See CORPORATION.

cooperative federalism. See FEDERALISM.

cooperative law. (1982) A dispute-resolution method by which the parties and their attorneys agree first to use nonadversarial strategies in an attempt to reach a binding agreement, with the possibility of litigation if a settlement fails, typically with the same attorneys involved in the litigation. Cf. COLLABORATIVE LAW; MEDIATION (1).

Cooperative State Research, Education, and Extension Service. An agency in the U.S. Department of Agriculture responsible for coordinating departmental research activities with those of academic and land-grant institutions. — Abbr. CSREES.

co-opt, *vb.* (1969) **1.** To add as a member. **2.** To assimilate; absorb.

co-optation (koh-ahp-**tay**-shən), *n.* (16c) The act of selecting a person to fill a vacancy (usu. in a close corporation). — **co-optative,** *adj.*

coordinate jurisdiction. See *concurrent jurisdiction* under JURISDICTION.

coordinate liability. See LIABILITY.

coordination-of-benefits clause. See COB CLAUSE.

coowner, *n.* (1858) Someone who is in concurrent ownership, possession, and enjoyment of property with one or more others; a tenant in common, a joint tenant, or a tenant by the entirety. — **coown,** *vb.* — **coownership,** *n.*

COPA. *abbr.* CHILD ONLINE PROTECTION ACT.

cop a plea, *vb.* (1914) *Slang.* (Of a criminal defendant) to plead guilty to a lesser charge as a means to avoid standing trial for a more serious offense. See PLEA BARGAIN.

coparcenary (koh-**pahr**-sə-ner-ee), *n.* (16c) An estate that arises when two or more persons jointly inherit from one ancestor, the title and right of possession being shared equally by all. • Coparcenary was a form of coownership created by common-law rules of descent upon intestacy when two or more persons together constituted the decedent's heirs. Typically, this situation arose when the decedent was survived by no sons but by two or more daughters, so that the daughters took as coparceners. — Also termed *parcenary*; *tenancy in coparcenary*. — **coparcenary,** *adj.*

> "Coparcenary is converted into separate ownership (i) by partition, or (ii) by the union in one parcener of all the shares, and it is converted into a tenancy in common if one parcener transfers her share to a stranger." G.C. Cheshire, *Modern Law of Real Property* 553 (3d ed. 1933).

coparcener (koh-**pahr**-sə-nər). (16c) A person to whom an estate descends jointly, and who holds it as an entire estate; a person who has become a concurrent owner as a result of descent. — Also termed *parcener*; (archaically) *coparticeps*.

> "Coparceners constitute a single heir, and they occupy a position intermediate between joint tenants and tenants in common. Like joint tenants they have unity of title, interest and possession; like tenants in common, their estate is not subject to the doctrine of survivorship, and if there are three coparceners and one dies, her share passes separately to her heirs or devisee, not to the survivors, though the unity of possession continues. It follows that unity of time is not necessary to constitute coparcenary, for if a man has two daughters to whom his estate descends and one dies leaving a son, such son and the surviving daughter will be coparceners." G.C. Cheshire, *Modern Law of Real Property* 553 (3d ed. 1933).

coparticeps (koh-**pahr**-tə-seps). [fr. Latin *particeps* "sharing"] See COPARCENER.

copartner. (16c) A member of a partnership; PARTNER.

> "*Copartner* need not exist alongside *partner*. The joint relationship (i.e., that the existence of one partner implies the existence of one or more other partners) is clear to all native speakers of English. . . . Because *copartner* adds nothing to the language of the law, it should be avoided." Bryan A. Garner, *Garner's Dictionary of Legal Usage* 223 (3d ed. 2011).

copartnership. (16c) See PARTNERSHIP. • The terms *copartnership* and *partnership* are equally old — each having first appeared in the 1570s.

coparty. (1906) A litigant or participant in a legal transaction who has a like status with another party; a party on the same side of a lawsuit. — Also termed *joint party*. See CODEFENDANT; COPLAINTIFF.

copayment. (1966) A fixed amount that a patient pays to a healthcare provider according to the terms of the patient's health plan. — Often shortened to *copay*.

copending, *adj.* (1904) *Patents.* (Of serial applications filed in the same patent prosecution) before the U.S. Patent and Trademark Office at or near the same time and concerning the same invention. • A continuation or divisional application that is copending with its parent application benefits from the parent's earlier filing date.

copending patent. See PATENT (3).

copia libelli deliberanda. See DE COPIA LIBELLI DELIBERANDA.

coplaintiff. (18c) One of two or more plaintiffs in the same litigation. — Also termed *joint plaintiff*. Cf. CODEFENDANT.

coprincipal. (17c) **1.** One of two or more participants in a criminal offense who either perpetrate the crime or aid a person who does so. **2.** One of two or more persons who have appointed an agent whom they both have the right to control.

copromisor. (1847) One of two or more persons who make a legally binding promise, which might be joint, joint and several, or several. — Also written *co-promisor*.

copulative condition. See CONDITION (2).

copy, *n.* (14c) **1.** An imitation or reproduction of an original. • In the law of evidence, a copy is generally admissible to prove the contents of a writing. Fed. R. Evid. 1003. See BEST-EVIDENCE RULE.

▸ **archival copy.** See ARCHIVAL COPY.

▸ **attested copy.** See *certified copy*.

▸ **certified copy.** (18c) A duplicate of an original (usu. official) document, certified as an exact reproduction usu. by the officer responsible for issuing or keeping the original. — Also termed *attested copy*; *exemplified copy*; *verified copy*.

▸ **conformed copy.** (1937) An exact copy of a document bearing written explanations of things that were not or could not be copied, such as a note on the document indicating that it was signed by a person whose signature appears on the original.

▸ **examined copy.** (18c) A copy (usu. of a record, public book, or register) that has been compared with the original or with an official record of an original.

▸ **exemplified copy.** See *certified copy*.

▸ **true copy.** (16c) A copy that, while not necessarily exact, is sufficiently close to the original that anyone can understand it.

▸ **verified copy.** See *certified copy*.

2. *Copyright.* The physical form in which a creative work is fixed and from which the work can be reproduced or perceived, with or without the aid of a special device. 17 USCA § 101. **3.** *Copyright.* An expressive work that is substantially similar to a copyrighted work and not produced coincidentally and independently from the same source as the copyrighted work. • Proof of copying in an infringement action requires evidence of the defendant's access to the original work and substantial similarity of the defendant's work to the original. See *substantial similarity* under SIMILARITY.

> "The noun 'copy' ordinarily connotes a tangible object that is a reproduction of the original work; the courts have generally found no reason to depart from this usage in the law of copyright." 1 Melville B. Nimmer & David Nimmer, *Nimmer on Copyright* § 4.08[B], at 4-47 (Supp. 1995).

copycat drug. See *generic drug* under DRUG.

copyhold. (15c) *Hist.* A base tenure requiring the tenant to provide the customary services of the manor, as reflected in the manor's court rolls. • Copyhold tenure descended from pure villeinage; over time, the customs of the manor, as reflected on the manor's rolls, dictated what services a lord could demand from a copyholder. This type of tenure was abolished by the Law of Property Act of 1922, which converted copyhold land into freehold or leasehold land. — Also termed *copyhold tenure*; *customary estate*; *customary freehold*; *tenancy by the verge*; *tenancy par la verge*; *tenancy by the rod*. See *base tenure* under TENURE (2); VILLEINAGE.

> "Out of the tenure by villeinage, copyhold tenure developed. . . . By the end of the fifteenth century, to hold by copy of the court roll, to be a 'copyholder,' was a definite advantage, and, in most cases the holders had for many generations been personally free. The fusing of several

different types of payment had also gone on, so that there was little difference between a holder in socage who had commuted the services for a sum of money and a copyholder who had done the same, except the specific dues of *heriot* and *merchet*. In Coke's time, a very large part of the land of England was still held by copyhold." Max Radin, *Handbook of Anglo-American Legal History* 371 (1936).

"[L]and held on an unfree tenure could be transferred only by a surrender and admittance made in the lord's court. The transaction was recorded on the court rolls and the transferee given a copy of the entry to prove his title; he thus held 'by copy of the court roll,' and the tenure became known as 'copyhold.'" Robert E. Megarry & M.P. Thompson, *A Manual of the Law of Real Property* 22 (6th ed. 1993).

▸ **privileged copyhold.** (1824) *Hist.* A copyhold subject only to the customs of the manor and not affected by the nonconforming dictates of the current lord.

copyholder. (16c) *Hist.* A tenant by copyhold tenure. — Also termed *tenant by the verge*; *tenant par la verge.*

"The lord still held a court, and that court kept records of all transactions affecting the lands. These records were called the rolls of the court. When, for instance, a tenant sold his interest to a third party, the circumstances of the sale would be recorded, and the buyer would receive a copy of the court rolls in so far as they affected his holding. Inasmuch as he held his estate by copy of court roll, he came to be called a copyholder." G.C. Cheshire, *Modern Law of Real Property* 24 (3d ed. 1933).

copyhold tenant. See *customary tenant* under TENANT (1).

copying, *n.* The duplication of an original thing.

▸ **domestic copying.** The act of making one or more copies of a thing, esp. a copyright-protected work, to use for private purposes.

copying claims. *Patents.* The amendment of a patent application to include claims from another's patent or patent application for the purpose of declaring an interference to determine ownership of the claimed invention.

copyleft. (1976) *Slang.* A software license that allows users to modify or incorporate open-source code into larger programs on the condition that the software containing the source code is publicly distributed without restrictions.

copylefted software. (1991) *Slang.* Free software whose distribution terms forbid the addition of restrictions if the software is redistributed in its original or a modified form. • Not actually a legal term, this phrase is popularly used as the antithesis of copyright by Internet free-software promoters. See FREEWARE.

copyright, *n.* (18c) **1.** The right to copy; specifically, a property right in an original work of authorship (including literary, musical, dramatic, choreographic, pictorial, graphic, sculptural, and architectural works; motion pictures and other audiovisual works; and sound recordings) fixed in any tangible medium of expression, giving the holder the exclusive right to reproduce, adapt, distribute, perform, and display the work. **2.** The body of law relating to such works. • Copyright law is governed by the Copyright Act of 1976. 17 USCA §§ 101 et seq. — Abbr. c. Cf. COPYRIGHT ACT OF 1976. — **copyright,** *vb.* — **copyrighted,** *adj.* — **copyrightable,** *adj.*

"[C]opyright is a monopoly of limited duration, created and wholly regulated by the legislature; and . . . an author has, therefore, no other title to his published works than that given by statute." Ethan S. Drone, *A Treatise on the Law of Property in Intellectual Productions* 2 (1879).

"What is copyright? From copyright law's beginnings close to three centuries ago, the term has meant just what it says: the right to make copies of a given work — at first it meant simply written work — and to stop others from making copies without one's permission." Paul Goldstein, *Copyright's Highway* 3 (1994).

"Before the 1976 Copyright Act swept virtually all copyrightable subject matter within the exclusive domain of federal protection, the term 'copyright' implied a statutory right created by Congress in order to 'Promote the Progress of Science.' Our first copyright act, in 1790, protected only maps, charts, and books. Protection gradually was extended to musical compositions and graphic works. In the middle of the nineteenth century, photography was developed and then protected, followed at the end of the century by motion pictures (although they were protected as photographs). As the twentieth century comes to a close, digital technology and multimedia forms of authorship seriously challenge the gradual, compartmentalized approach to granting new rights and new subject matter . . . ." 1 William F. Patry, *Copyright Law and Practice* 1 (1994).

▸ **ad interim copyright.** (1945) *Hist.* A limited five-year U.S. copyright granted to the author of a foreign edition of an English- language book or periodical if, within six months after its publication abroad, the author deposited one complete copy of that edition in the U.S. Copyright Office and requested ad interim copyright protection. • An ad interim copyright was granted as an exception to the 1909 Copyright Act's manufacturing clause, which limited copyright protection for English-language books and periodicals to those printed in the U.S. If the copyright owner published the work in the U.S. during the period of ad interim protection and complied with the Act's manufacturing requirements, full copyright protection related back to the date of first publication. Otherwise, the work went into the public domain at the end of five years.

▸ **common-law copyright.** (1829) A property right that arose when the work was created, rather than when it was published. • Under the Copyright Act of 1976, which took effect on January 1, 1978, common-law copyright was largely abolished for works created after the statute's effective date. But the statute retained the common law's recognition that the property right arose when the work was created rather than when it was published. The common-law copyright still applies in a few areas: notably, a common-law copyright received before January 1, 1978 remains entitled to protection. 17 USCA § 301. — Also termed *right of first publication.*

▸ **future copyright.** (1906) A copyright that will come into existence upon the occurrence of a particular event.

copyrightability test. (1992) A judicial test for determining whether a contributor to a joint work is an author for legal purposes, based on whether the contributor's effort is an original expression that could qualify for copyright protection on its own. • This test has been adopted by a majority of courts. Cf. DE MINIMIS TEST.

copyrightable, *adj.* (1895) Eligible for copyright protection.

copyrightable work. See WORK (2).

Copyright Act of 1790. The first U.S. copyright law, which, like England's Statute of Anne, gave authors copyright protection for 14 years, renewable for another 14 years, after which time the work then entered the public domain.

Copyright Act of 1909. A major revision of U.S. copyright law, extending the term of protection from 14 to 28 years (renewable for a second 28-year term); measuring the copyright term from the time of publication rather than the time of registration with the Copyright Office; and expanding coverage to all writings. • The Act retained the formalities for securing a copyright and required that a copyright mark appear on the work. It governed U.S. copyrights issued between July 1, 1909 and December 31, 1977. Although the 1976 Copyright Act supplanted the 1909 Act, the 1909 Act still applies to some pre-1978 claims and affects certain other rights of copyright owners. — Also termed *1909 Copyright Act.*

Copyright Act of 1976. A major revision of U.S. copyright law, extending the term of protection to the life of the author plus 50 years, measured from the date of creation; greatly expanding the types of works that qualify for protection; dropping the requirement that the work be published before it can be protected; making fair use a statutory defense to a claim in infringement; and preempting state common-law copyright. 17 USCA §§ 101 et seq. • This is the current federal statute that governs copyright registrations and rights. — Also termed *1976 Copyright Act.*

Copyright and the Challenge of Technology. See GREEN PAPER ON COPYRIGHT AND THE CHALLENGE OF TECHNOLOGY.

copyright application. (1932) A written request for copyright protection made by a work's creator, filed with the U.S. Copyright Office and accompanied by a filing fee and either a deposit copy of the work or approved identifying material. • A registrant who does not meet the deposit requirement of the Copyright Act of 1976 risks losing copyright protection. *See, e.g., Coles v. Wonder,* 283 F.3d 798 (6th Cir. 2002).

copyright bug. See COPYRIGHT NOTICE.

Copyright Clause. (1940) *Constitutional law.* U.S. Const. art. I, § 8, cl. 8, which gives Congress the power to secure to authors the exclusive rights to their writings for a limited time.

copyright clearinghouse. (1967) An organization that licenses members' works to applicants for specific purposes. • A clearinghouse usu. licenses only one type or class of works, such as songs, photographs, cartoons, or written materials.

copyright infringement. See INFRINGEMENT.

copyright legend. See COPYRIGHT NOTICE.

copyright-management information. (1995) The name and other identifying information about the creator, performer, or copyright owner of a creative work. See DIGITAL MILLENNIUM COPYRIGHT ACT.

copyright misuse. (1962) In an infringement action, an affirmative defense based on the copyright owner's use of a license to restrain trade or in any other manner that is against public policy. • The defense, roughly parallel to the declining patent-misuse defense, was invoked, for example, to prevent the American Medical Association from enforcing its copyright in its medical-procedure codes after licensing them to the U.S. government for use in the Medicaid program. *See Practice Mgmt. Info. Corp. v. Am. Med. Ass'n,* 121 F.3d 516 (9th Cir. 1997).

copyright notice. (1889) A notice that a work is copyright-protected, usu. placed in each published copy of the work. • A copyright notice takes the form © (year of publication) (name of basic copyright owner). Since March 1, 1989, such notice is not required for a copyright to be valid (although the notice continues to provide certain procedural advantages). The phrase "all rights reserved" is usu. no longer required. — Sometimes termed *copyright bug; copyright legend; notice of copyright.* See ALL RIGHTS RESERVED; BUENOS AIRES CONVENTION.

Copyright Office. See UNITED STATES COPYRIGHT OFFICE.

Copyright Office Circulars. *Copyright.* A series of publications available from the U.S. Copyright Office providing basic information about registration, fees, compulsory licenses, and other aspects of the copyright process.

copyright owner. (1886) **1.** Someone who holds an exclusive right or rights to copyrighted material. 17 USCA § 101. **2.** Someone who is named as the owner on any copyright notice attached to a work and who is registered with the U.S. Copyright Office as the owner.

Copyright Royalty Tribunal. A former board in the legislative branch of the federal government responsible for establishing and monitoring copyright royalty rates for published and recorded materials. • Its functions are now performed by copyright arbitration royalty panels. — Abbr. CRT.

Copyright Term Extension Act. See SONNY BONO COPYRIGHT TERM EXTENSION ACT.

copyright troll. (2006) A person, usu. an entity, that acquires from the owners of copyrighted works the right to sue infringers of those works. • The right to sue does not, by itself, convey standing under the Copyright Act because it is not included in § 106 of the Act, which lists the six exclusive rights that establish standing. — Sometimes shortened to *troll.*

coram (**kor**-əm), *prep.* [Latin] (Of a person) before; in the presence of.

coram domino rege (**kor**-əm **dom**-ə-noh **ree**-jee). [Latin] *Hist.* Before our lord the king.

coram ipso rege (**kor**-əm **ip**-soh **ree**-jee). [Latin] (17c) *Hist.* In the presence of the king himself. — Also termed *coram ipso domino rege.*

> "The court of king's bench (so called because the king used formerly to sit there in person, the style of the court still being *coram ipso rege*) is the supreme court of common law in the kingdom . . . ." 3 William Blackstone, *Commentaries on the Laws of England* 41 (1768).

coram judice (**kor**-əm **joo**-di-see). (16c) **1.** In the presence of a judge. **2.** JURISDICTION.

coram nobis (**kor**-əm **noh**-bis). [Latin "before us"] (16c) **1.** *Hist.* A writ of error taken from a judgment of the King's Bench. • "Before us" refers to the sovereign, in contrast to the writ *coram vobis* ("before you"), which refers to any court other than King's Bench, esp. the Court of Common Pleas. **2.** A writ of error directed to a court for review of its own judgment and predicated on alleged errors of fact. — Also termed *writ of error coram nobis; writ of coram nobis;* (misspelled) *quorum nobis.*

***coram nobis* motion.** See MOTION (1).

coram non judice (**kor**-əm non **joo**-di-see). [Latin "not before a judge"] (16c) **1.** Outside the presence of a judge. **2.** Before a judge or court that is not the proper one or that cannot take legal cognizance of the matter.

coram paribus (**kor**-əm **par**-ə-bəs). [Latin] (18c) *Hist.* Before one's peers. • This phrase appeared in deed attestations.

Coram Rege Court. See KING'S BENCH.

coram sectatoribus (**kor**-əm sek-tə-**tor**-ə-bəs). [Law Latin] (18c) *Hist.* Before the suitors.

coram vobis (**kor**-əm **voh**-bis), *n.* [Latin "before you"] (16c) *Hist.* **1.** A writ of error directed to a court other than the King's Bench, esp. the Court of Common Pleas, to review its judgment.

> "Certain errors in the process of the court, committed by the defaults of the clerks, or as to matters of fact, could be remedied by the court itself. The writ issued for this purpose was called a writ of error 'coram vobis' if the error was in the Common Pleas; 'coram nobis' if it was in the King's Bench." 1 William Holdsworth, *A History of English Law* 224 (7th ed. 1956).

2. A writ of error sent by an appellate court to a trial court to review the trial court's judgment based on an error of fact. — Also termed *writ of error coram vobis; writ of coram vobis.*

Cordon Rule. (1958) A rule of the U.S. Senate requiring any committee that is reporting a bill to show in some detail how it would change current law. • The rule is named for Senator Guy Cordon (1890–1969) of Oregon, who proposed it. The analogous rule in the U.S. House of Representatives is the Ramseyer rule. See RAMSEYER RULE.

core earnings. See *operating earnings* under EARNINGS.

core political speech. See SPEECH (1).

core proceeding. (1983) *Bankruptcy.* **1.** A proceeding involving claims that substantially affect the debtor-creditor relationship, such as an action to recover a preferential transfer. • In such a proceeding, the bankruptcy court, as opposed to the district court, conducts the trial or hearing and enters a final judgment. Cf. RELATED PROCEEDING. **2.** In federal courts, an action involving subject matter that is clearly within the confines of federal bankruptcy law and the management of the bankrupt's estate. • A federal bankruptcy court may also hear noncore matters that have an independent basis for subject-matter jurisdiction, such as a federal question. For a nonexclusive list of core proceedings, see 28 USCA § 157(b)(2).

core rights. (1973) **1.** Human rights that are generally recognized and accepted throughout the world. • These rights include freedom from extrajudicial execution, torture, and arbitrary arrest and detention. Core rights are embodied in many human rights conventions, including the Universal Declaration of Human Rights, the International Covenant on Civil and Political Rights, and the International Covenant on Economic, Social and Cultural Rights. See *natural right* under RIGHT. **2.** Fundamental rights claimed within a social, cultural, or other context. • These are not universally recognized rights. For example, the ability to vote may be a fundamental right of citizens in one country but only a privilege limited to selected people in another.

corespondent. (1857) **1.** A coparty who responds to a petition, such as a petition for a writ of certiorari. **2.** In some states, a coparty who responds to an appeal. **3.** *Family law.* In a divorce suit based on adultery, the person with whom the spouse is accused of having committed adultery; specif., a person whose name is given in a divorce as someone who has had sex with the spouse of the person who seeks the divorce. See RESPONDENT.

core work product. See *opinion work product* under WORK PRODUCT.

corium forisfacere (**kor**-ee-əm for-is-**fay**-sə-ree). [Law Latin "to forfeit skin"] *Hist.* To whip (a person, esp. a servant) as punishment. — Also termed *corium perdere.*

corium redimere (**kor**-ee-əm ri-**dim**-ər-ee). [Latin] *Hist.* To redeem one's skin. • This referred to a person who paid restitution for an offense.

cornage (**kor**-nij). [fr. Anglo-French *corne* "horn"] (1872) *Hist.* **1.** A form of tenure entitling a landowner to rent based on the number of horned cattle owned by the tenant; a tax or tribute on horned cattle levied in feudal times. • Cornage may have developed into a type of serjeanty or knight-service tenure that obligated the tenant to blow a horn to warn of invaders, esp. along the border with Scotland. See KNIGHT-SERVICE; SERJEANTY. **2.** A tribute of corn due only on special occasions, as distinguished from a regularly provided service. **3.** A tax or tribute on horned cattle levied in feudal times. **4.** A type of grand-sergeanty military tenure in which the tenant was bound to blow a horn to alert others whenever an enemy approached. • This term has often been spelled *coraage* or *coraagium*, stemming perhaps from a spelling error in the 1569 edition of Bracton's *De Legibus et Consuetudinibus Angliae.* Sense 4, according to the *Oxford English Dictionary,* is an "erroneous explanation given by Littleton" based on a misreading of Bracton. — Also termed (in senses 1, 3 & 4) *horn tenure.* See BRACTON.

Cornelian law. See LEX CORNELIA.

corner, *n.* (17c) **1.** The common end of two survey lines; an angle made by two boundary lines.

▸ **existent corner.** (1924) A corner whose location can be verified by an original landmark, a surveyor's field notes, or other reliable evidence.

▸ **lost corner.** (1801) A point in a land description, such as a landmark or natural object, whose position cannot be reasonably determined from traces of the original marks or other acceptable evidence. • The location can be determined by reference to one or more independent points remaining in the description.

▸ **obliterated corner.** (1837) A corner that can be located only with evidence other than that put in place by the original surveyor.

2. The acquisition of control over all or a dominant quantity of a commodity with the purpose of artificially enhancing the price, carried out by purchases and sales of the commodity — and of options and futures — in a way that depresses the market price so that the participants are enabled to purchase the commodity at satisfactory prices and withhold it from the market for a time, thereby inflating its price. • A corner accomplished by confederation, with the purpose of raising or depressing prices and operating on the market, is a criminal conspiracy if the means are unlawful.

corner influence. (1921) *Property.* In an appraisal, the additional value of a corner lot, esp. one zoned for commercial purposes, attributable to factors such as increased light and air, easier ingress and egress, greater accessibility by pedestrian and automotive traffic, and more space for displays and advertisements.

cornering the market. (1881) The act or process of acquiring ownership or control of a large portion of the available supply of a commodity or security, permitting manipulation of the commodity's or security's price.

***Corn Products* doctrine.** (1956) *Tax.* The principle that a capital asset should be narrowly defined to exclude inventory-related property that is integrally tied to the day-to-day operations of a business. *Corn Prods. Refining Co. v. C.I.R.*, 350 U.S. 46, 76 S.Ct. 20 (1955).

corody (**kor**- *or* **kahr**-ə-dee). (15c) *Hist.* An allowance of money, accommodation, food, or clothing given by a religious house to any person who signed over personal or real property or both in exchange or to a royal servant at the Crown's request. • The amount of property required from a person who purchased a corody depended on the person's age and remaining life expectancy. The Crown was entitled to a corody for a retired royal servant only from houses that the Crown had founded. Theoretically, the cost of a retired royal servant's care would come from the royal purse. But since the royal purse did not always open, royal servants were not always accepted as corodiaries. Cf. LIFE-CARE CONTRACT. — Also spelled *corrody.* — **corodiary** (kə-**roh**-dee-air-ee), **corrodiary,** *n.*

> "Corrody is a partition for one's sustenance. Be it bread, ale, herring, a yearly robe, or sum of money for the robe. So of a chamber, and stable for my horses, when the same is coupled with other things . . . ." Henry Finch, *Law, or a Discourse Thereof* 162 (1759).

corollary (**kor**- *or* **kahr**-ə-ler-ee), *n.* (14c) A proposition that follows from a proven proposition with little or no additional proof; something that naturally follows.

corona (kə-**roh**-nə). [Latin] *Hist.* The Crown. • This term formerly appeared in criminal pleadings, e.g., *placita coronae* ("pleas of the Crown").

coronation case. (1903) *Hist.* Any of the many lawsuits for breach of contract resulting from the postponement of the coronation of Edward VII because of his illness. • The English courts generally held that the contracts were void on grounds of frustrated purpose, esp. those reciting as their purpose the viewing of coronation events. In one case, however, the defendant had agreed to hire a ship for watching the naval review by King Edward VII and for a day's cruise around the fleet. The court held that the contract was not frustrated by the cancellation of the naval review — the day's cruise around the fleet was still possible, and indeed, the ship could have been used for many other purposes.

coronator (**kor**- *or* **kahr**-ə-nay-tər). [fr. Latin *corona* "crown"] A coroner. See CORONER (2).

> "The formal title of *custos* (or occasionally *conservator*) *placitorum corone* continued to be used throughout the Middle Ages, but the more convenient shorter forms *coronarius*, which was confined to a short period around 1200, and rapidly gained greater currency. The English form was 'coroner' or 'crowner.'" R.F. Hunnisett, *The Medieval Coroner* 1 n.1 (1961).

coronatore eligendo. See DE CORONATORE ELIGENDO.

coronatore exonerando. See DE CORONATORE EXONERANDO.

coroner (**kor**- *or* **kahr**-ə-nər). (14c) **1.** A public official whose duty is to investigate the causes and circumstances of any death that occurs suddenly, suspiciously, or violently. See MEDICAL EXAMINER. **2.** *Hist.* A royal official with county-wide jurisdiction to investigate deaths, to hold inquests, and to assume the duties of the sheriff if need be. • The coroner acted as a check on the sheriff, a local officer whose growing power threatened royal control over the counties. The coroner reported criminal activity to the king's justices in eyre. When the eyre court arrived in a county, it collected the coroner's roll to learn what had occurred in the county during the eyre's absence. The justices fined the coroner if he failed to produce the roll, or if they learned of criminal activity in the county from a source other than the roll.

> "The office of coroner was established in September 1194, when the justices in eyre were required to see that three knights and one clerk were elected in every county as 'keepers of the pleas of the crown.' These were the first county coroners. . . . Throughout the Middle Ages the coroner could be ordered to perform almost any duty of an administrative or inquisitorial nature within his bailiwick, either alone or with the sheriff, but there were other duties which belonged more specifically to his office and which he performed without being ordered. These consisted of holding inquests upon dead bodies, receiving adjurations of the realm made by felons in sanctuary, hearing appeals, confessions of felons and appeals of approvers, and attending and sometimes organising exactions and outlawries promulgated in the county court. These were the 'crown pleas' which the coroner had to 'keep' . . . ." R.F. Hunnisett, *The Medieval Coroner* 1 (1961).

coroner's court. See COURT.

coroner's inquest. See INQUEST (1).

coroner's jury. See JURY.

coroner's verdict. See VERDICT (3).

coronial, *adj.* (1898) Of, relating to, or involving a coroner or coroner's office.

corpnership. [portmanteau fr. *corporation* + *partnership*] (1958) *Slang.* A limited partnership (usu. having many public investors as limited partners) whose general partner is a corporation.

corpora delicti (**kor**-pə-rə də-**lik**-tɪ or –tee). [Latin] *Hist.* Objects of the offense. See CORPUS DELICTI.

corporale sacramentum (kor-pə-**ray**-lee sak-rə-**men**-təm). See *corporal oath* under OATH.

corporal oath. See OATH.

corporal punishment. See PUNISHMENT (1).

corporate, *adj.* (16c) Of, relating to, or involving a corporation, esp. a business corporation <corporate bonds>.

corporate acquisition. (1911) The takeover of one corporation by another if both parties retain their legal existence after the transaction. Cf. MERGER (8). — Also termed *business acquisition.*

corporate agent. See AGENT.

corporate alias. See ALIAS.

corporate authority. (1817) **1.** The power rightfully wielded by officers of a corporation. **2.** In some jurisdictions, a municipal officer, esp. one empowered to represent the municipality in certain statutory matters.

corporate body. See CORPORATION.

corporate bond. See BOND (3).

corporate books. (1846) Written records of a corporation's activities and business transactions.

corporate capacity. See CAPACITY (2).

corporate charter. See CHARTER (3).

corporate citizenship. (1889) Corporate status in the state of incorporation, though a corporation is not a constitutional citizen for the purposes of the Privileges and Immunities Clauses in Article IV § 2 and in the 14th Amendment to the U.S. Constitution.

corporate control. See CONTROL.

corporate counsel. See COUNSEL.

corporate crime. See CRIME.

corporate criminality. (1910) **1.** The quality, state, or condition of a corporation having incurred criminal responsibility. **2.** The principle that an incorporated body is a legal entity capable of incurring criminal responsibility.

corporate culture. (1966) A prevalent attitude or atmosphere created by a company's rules, policies, practices (esp. hiring practices), and communications from management, such as those touching on compliance or noncompliance with legal requirements.

corporate deposition. See *30(b)(6) deposition* under DEPOSITION (2).

corporate distribution. See DISTRIBUTION.

corporate domicile. See DOMICILE.

corporate entity. See ENTITY.

corporate franchise. See FRANCHISE (2).

corporate governance. (1948) The system or framework of rules and standards by which a company is — or companies generally are — managed, controlled, and held accountable, esp. as regards the integrity, transparency, and responsibility achieved by management and, more specifically, the board of directors.

corporate immunity. See IMMUNITY (2).

corporate indenture. See INDENTURE (2).

corporate law. (1821) Collectively, the statutes, rules, regulations, and legal doctrines relating to the ways in which corporations operate. — Also termed (BrE) *company law.*

corporate liability. See LIABILITY.

corporate merger. See MERGER (8).

corporate-mortgage trust. (1941) A financing device in which debentures are issued and secured by property held in trust. • An independent trustee protects the interests of those who purchase the debentures.

corporate name. See NAME.

corporate offense. See *corporate crime* under CRIME.

corporate officer. See OFFICER (1).

corporate-opportunity doctrine. (1942) The rule that a corporation's directors, officers, and employees are precluded from using information gained as such to take personal advantage of any business opportunities that the corporation has an expectancy right or property interest in, or that in fairness should otherwise belong to the corporation. • In a partnership, the analogous principle is termed the *firm-opportunity doctrine.*

> "The corporate opportunity doctrine prohibits a director or officer from improperly taking advantage of a business opportunity that belongs to the corporation. A corporate fiduciary breaches her duty to loyalty to the corporation if the fiduciary misappropriates a corporation's business opportunity for such fiduciary's own benefit. The remedy that may be invoked for such a breach is the ordering of a constructive trust whereby the defendant fiduciary is deemed to hold in trust the subject property (or profit) for the benefit of the corporation. Based on the rationale of unjust enrichment, a constructive trust may be ordered even where the corporation has not incurred any damages or injury." Marc I. Steinberg, *Lawyering and Ethics for the Business Attorney* 67–68 (3d ed. 2011).

corporate-owned life insurance. See LIFE INSURANCE.

corporate purpose. (18c) The general scope of the business objective for which a corporation was created. • A statement of corporate purpose is commonly required in the articles of incorporation.

corporate raider. (1955) A person or business that attempts to take control of a corporation, against its wishes, by buying its stock and replacing its management, often for the purpose of selling off its assets. — Often shortened to *raider.* — Also termed *hostile bidder; unfriendly suitor; company breaker.* Cf. WHITE KNIGHT.

corporate resolution. See RESOLUTION (2).

corporate seal. See SEAL.

corporate secretary. (1904) A corporate officer of high position who deals with administrative and legal matters; SECRETARY (2). — Also termed *company secretary.*

corporate speech. See SPEECH.

corporate stock. See STOCK.

corporate trustee. See TRUSTEE (1).

corporate veil. (1927) The legal assumption that the acts of a corporation are not the actions of its shareholders, so that the shareholders are exempt from liability for the corporation's actions. See PIERCING THE CORPORATE VEIL.

corporate welfare. See WELFARE (2).

corporation, *n.* (15c) An entity (usu. a business) having authority under law to act as a single person distinct from the shareholders who own it and having rights to issue stock and exist indefinitely; a group or succession of persons established in accordance with legal rules into a legal or juristic person that has a legal personality distinct from the natural persons who make it up, exists indefinitely apart from them, and has the legal powers that its constitution gives it. — Also termed *corporation aggregate; aggregate corporation; body corporate; corporate body.* See COMPANY. — **incorporate,** *vb.* — **corporate,** *adj.*

> "A corporation is an artificial being, invisible, intangible, and existing only in contemplation of law. . . . [I]t possesses only those properties which the charter of its creation confers upon it." *Trustees of Dartmouth College v. Woodward*, 17 U.S. (4 Wheat.) 518, 636 (1819).

▸ **acquired corporation.** (1931) The corporation that no longer exists after a merger or acquisition.

▸ **admitted corporation.** (1939) A corporation licensed or authorized to do business within a particular state. — Also termed *qualified corporation; corporation qualified to do business.*

▸ **aggregate corporation.** See *corporation aggregate.*

▸ **aggressor corporation.** (1967) A corporation that attempts to obtain control of a publicly held corporation by (1) a direct cash tender, (2) a public exchange offer to shareholders, or (3) a merger, which requires the agreement of the target's management.

▸ **alien corporation.** See *foreign corporation.*

▸ **brother-sister corporation.** See *sister corporation.*

▸ **business corporation.** (1868) A corporation formed to engage in commercial activity for profit. Cf. *nonprofit corporation.*

▸ **C corporation.** A corporation whose income is taxed through it rather than through its shareholders. • Any corporation not electing S-corporation tax status under the Internal Revenue Code is a C corporation by default. — Also termed *subchapter-C corporation.* Cf. *S corporation.*

▸ **charitable corporation.** (17c) A nonprofit corporation that is dedicated to benevolent purposes and thus entitled to special tax status under the Internal Revenue Code. — Also termed *eleemosynary corporation.* See CHARITABLE ORGANIZATION.

▸ **civil corporation.** (16c) Any corporation other than a charitable or religious corporation.

▸ **clearing corporation.** (1941) A corporation whose capital stock is held by or for a national security exchange or association registered under federal law such as the Securities Exchange Act of 1934. • Such a corporation normally works with an exchange to confirm, deliver, and settle transactions.

▸ **close corporation.** (1840) A corporation whose stock is not freely traded and is held by only a few shareholders (often within the same family). • The requirements and privileges of close corporations vary by jurisdiction. — Also termed *closely held corporation*; *closed corporation*; (when family owned) *family corporation.*

▸ **collapsible corporation.** (1955) A corporation formed to give a short-term venture the appearance of a long-term investment in order to portray income as capital gain, rather than profit. • The corporation is typically formed for the sole purpose of purchasing property. The corporation is usu. dissolved before the property has generated substantial income. Cf. *collapsible partnership* under PARTNERSHIP.

▸ **common-law corporation.** See *corporation by prescription.*

▸ **conglomerate corporation.** See CONGLOMERATE.

▸ **constitutional corporation.** (1845) A corporation formed in compliance with, or by reference to, a provision contained in a constitution.

▸ **controlled corporation.** (1901) **1.** A corporation in which the majority of the stock is held by one individual or firm. **2.** A corporation in which a substantial amount (but less than a majority) of the stock is held by one individual or firm. • Some states presume control with as little as 10%.

▸ **controlled foreign corporation.** (1931) *Tax.* A foreign corporation in which more than 50% of the stock is owned by U.S. citizens who each own 10% or more of the voting stock. • These shareholders (known as *U.S. shareholders*) are required to report their pro rata share of certain passive income of the corporation. IRC (26 USCA) §§ 951–964. — Abbr. CFC.

▸ **cooperative corporation.** (1927) An entity that has a corporate existence, but is primarily organized for the purpose of providing services and profits to its members and not for corporate profit. • The most common kind of cooperative corporation is formed to purchase real property, such as an apartment building, so that its shareholders may lease the apartments. See COOPERATIVE (1).

▸ **corporation aggregate.** (17c) **1.** See CORPORATION. **2.** *Hist.* A corporation made up of a number of individuals. — Also termed *aggregate corporation.* Cf. *corporation sole* (1).

> "The first division of corporations is into *aggregate* and *sole*. Corporations aggregate consist of many persons united together into one society, and are kept up by a perpetual succession of members, so as to continue forever: of which kind are the mayor and commonalty of a city, the head and fellows of a college, the dean and chapter of a cathedral church." 1 William Blackstone, *Commentaries on the Laws of England* 457 (1765).

> "The corporation aggregate is the typical corporation, which, at any given time, normally contains a number of individuals as members. This number may be great or small, varying from the hundreds of thousands of burgesses of a large borough to the two members of a private joint-stock company. It is even said that a corporation aggregate would not necessarily cease to exist if all its members died, leaving no successors; and this is, probably, sound doctrine." Edward Jenks, *The Book of English Law* 118 (P.B. Fairest ed., 6th ed. 1967).

▸ **corporation by estoppel.** (1903) A business that is deemed, by operation of law, to be a corporation because a third party dealt with the business as if it were a corporation, thus preventing the third party from holding a shareholder or officer of the corporation individually liable. See ESTOPPEL.

▸ **corporation by prescription.** (17c) A corporation that, though lacking a charter, has acquired its corporate status through a long period of operating as a corporation. • Such an entity may engage in any enterprises that are not manifestly inconsistent with the purposes for which it is assumed to have been created. For example, the University of Cambridge is a corporation by prescription. — Also termed *common-law corporation.*

▸ **corporation de facto.** See *de facto corporation.*

▸ **corporation de jure.** See *de jure corporation.*

▸ **corporation for profit.** See *for-profit corporation.*

▸ **corporation qualified to do business.** See *admitted corporation.*

▸ **corporation sole.** (18c) **1.** A series of successive persons holding an office; a continuous legal personality that is attributed to successive holders of certain monarchical or ecclesiastical positions, such as kings, bishops, rectors, vicars, and the like. • This continuous personality is viewed, by legal fiction, as having the qualities of a corporation. Cf. *corporation aggregate* (2).

> "It would have been quite possible to explain in the same way the devolution of the lands of the Crown, or of a bishopric, or of a rectory, from the sovereign, bishop, or rector, to his successor; but English law has preferred to introduce for this purpose the fiction, peculiar to itself, of a 'corporation sole.'" Thomas E. Holland, *The Elements of Jurisprudence* 350–51 (13th ed. 1924).

> "English Law knows another kind of corporation, the 'corporation sole,' in which the group consists, not of a number of contemporary members, but of a succession of single members, of whom only one exists at any given time. This kind of corporation has been described by eminent legal writers as a 'freak'; but it is a freak which undoubtedly has a legal existence. It has been said that the Crown is the only common law lay corporation sole; though the Master of Trinity College, Cambridge, has been claimed as another example, and statutory examples, such as the Public Trustee and the Treasury Solicitor, are conspicuous.

> But the examples of ecclesiastical corporations sole are numerous. Every diocesan bishop, every rector of a parish, is a corporation sole, and can acquire and hold land (and now also personal property) even during the vacancy of the see or living, for the benefit of his successors, and can bind his successors by his lawful conveyances and contracts. But, obviously, the distinction between the bishop or rector, in his personal and in his corporate character, is even harder to grasp than that between the members of a corporation aggregate and the corporation itself . . . ." Edward Jenks, *The Book of English Law* 118–19 (P.B. Fairest ed., 6th ed. 1967).

2. See *sole corporation.*

▸ **dead corporation.** See *dissolved corporation.*

▸ **de facto corporation** (di **fak**-toh). (1876) An incompletely formed corporation whose existence operates as a defense to personal liability of the directors, officers, and shareholders who in good faith thought they were operating the business as a duly formed corporation. — Also termed *corporation de facto.*

▸ **de jure corporation** (di **joor**-ee). (1877) A corporation formed in accordance with all applicable laws and recognized as a corporation for liability purposes. — Also termed *corporation de jure.*

▸ **dissolved corporation.** (18c) A corporation whose charter has expired or been revoked, relinquished, or voluntarily terminated. — Also termed *dead corporation.*

▸ **domestic corporation.** (1819) **1.** A corporation that is organized and chartered under the laws of a state. • The corporation is considered *domestic* by the chartering state. Cf. *foreign corporation.* **2.** *Tax.* A corporation created or organized in the United States or under federal or state law. IRC (26 USCA) § 7701(a)(4).

▸ **dormant corporation.** (1934) **1.** An inactive corporation; a legal corporation that is presently not operating. **2.** A corporation whose authority to do business has been revoked or suspended either by operation of law (as by failure to pay franchise taxes) or by an act of the government official responsible for the corporation's authority.

▸ **dummy corporation.** (1899) A corporation whose only function is to hide the principal's identity and to protect the principal from liability. — Also termed *dummy company.*

▸ **ecclesiastical corporation** (i-klee-zee-**as**-tə-kəl). (17c) *English law.* A corporation that is organized for spiritual purposes or for the administration of property held for religious uses. — Also termed *religious corporation.* Cf. *lay corporation.*

> "Ecclesiastical corporations. Corporations created for the furtherance of religion . . . . They are of two kinds: (1) corporations sole, i.e., bishops, certain deans, parsons and vicars; and (2) corporations aggregate, i.e., deans and chapters, and formerly prior and convent, abbot and monks, and the like. Such corporations are called 'religious corporations,' or 'religious societies,' in the United States." 1 Stewart Rapalje & Robert L. Lawrence, *A Dictionary of American and English Law* 432 (1883).

▸ **eleemosynary corporation.** See *charitable corporation.*

▸ **family corporation.** See *close corporation.*

▸ **foreign corporation.** (18c) A corporation that was organized and chartered under the laws of another state, government, or country <in Arizona, a California corporation is said to be a foreign corporation>. — Also termed *alien corporation.* Cf. *domestic corporation.*

> "'Foreign' is defined as 'not native or domestic.' This is the meaning given to the word in the various judicial definitions of foreign corporations. With respect to a particular state or country, a corporation created by or under the laws of that state or country is a 'domestic corporation,' and any corporation that owes its existence to the laws of another state, government or country is a 'foreign corporation.' The difference between a domestic and a foreign corporation of the same kind is one of status, determined by considerations that are external to the corporation and not internal or organic. Moreover, foreign corporations of all classes fall equally within the definition. In many jurisdictions foreign corporations are defined by statute, and the statutory definitions do not differ in substance from that stated above." 17 William Meade Fletcher, *Fletcher Cyclopedia of the Law of Private Corporations* § 8290, at 6–7 (1998).

▸ **for-profit corporation.** (1939) A corporation organized for the purpose of making a profit; a business corporation. — Also termed *corporation for profit; moneyed corporation.*

▸ **government corporation.** See *public corporation* (3).

▸ **joint-venture corporation.** (1958) A corporation that has joined with one or more individuals or corporations to accomplish some specified project.

▸ **lay corporation.** (17c) *English law.* A corporation made up of laypersons, and existing for a business or charitable purpose. Cf. *ecclesiastical corporation.*

▸ **limited-liability corporation.** See *limited-liability company* under COMPANY.

▸ **migratory corporation.** (1904) A corporation formed under the laws of another state than that of the incorporators' residence for the purpose of carrying on a significant portion of its business in the state of the incorporators' residence or in a state other than where it was incorporated.

▸ **moneyed corporation.** (1834) **1.** A corporation that uses money capital in its business, esp. one (such as a bank) that engages in the exchange or lending of money. **2.** See *for-profit corporation.*

▸ **multinational corporation.** (1960) A company with operations in two or more countries, generally allowing it to transfer funds and products according to price and demand conditions, subject to risks such as changes in exchange rates or political instability. — Also termed *transnational corporation.*

▸ **multistate corporation.** (1951) A corporation incorporated under the laws of two or more states.

▸ **municipal corporation.** See MUNICIPAL CORPORATION.

▸ **municipal corporation de facto.** See MUNICIPAL CORPORATION.

▸ **nonprofit corporation.** (1908) A corporation organized for some purpose other than making a profit, and usu. afforded special tax treatment. — Often shortened to *nonprofit.* — Also termed *not-for-profit corporation.* Cf. *business corporation.*

▸ **nonstock corporation.** (1907) A corporation that does not issue shares of stock as evidence of ownership but instead is owned by its members in accordance with a charter or agreement. • Examples are mutual insurance companies, charitable organizations, and private clubs.

▸ **not-for-profit corporation.** See *nonprofit corporation.*

▸ **parent corporation.** (1893) A corporation that has a controlling interest in another corporation (called a *subsidiary corporation*), usu. through ownership of more than one-half the voting stock. — Often shortened to *parent*. — Also termed *parent company*.

▸ **political corporation.** See *public corporation* (2).

▸ **private corporation.** (17c) A corporation founded by and composed of private individuals principally for a nonpublic purpose, such as manufacturing, banking, and railroad corporations (including charitable and religious corporations). — Also termed *quasi-individual*.

▸ **professional corporation.** (1958) A corporation providing services of a type requiring a professional license. • A professional corporation may be made up of architects, accountants, lawyers, physicians, veterinarians, or the like. — Abbr. P.C.

▸ **public corporation.** (17c) **1.** A corporation whose shares are traded to and among the general public. — Also termed *publicly held corporation*. **2.** A corporation that is created by the state as an agency in the administration of civil government. — Also termed *political corporation*. **3.** A government-owned corporation that engages in activities that benefit the general public, usu. while remaining financially independent. • Such a corporation is managed by a publicly appointed board. — Also termed (in sense 3) *government corporation*; *public-benefit corporation*.

> "A public corporation is a corporation created by the state for public purposes only, as an instrumentality to increase the efficiency of government, supply the public wants, and promote the public welfare. This class of corporations includes not only the municipal corporation, but also agencies of government, called 'quasi corporations,' whose objects are not the making of private profit nor supplying the wants of the members." Henry H. Ingersoll, *Handbook of the Law of Public Corporations* 11 (1904).

▸ **publicly held corporation.** See *public corporation* (1).

▸ **public-service corporation.** (1894) A corporation whose operations serve a need of the general public, such as public transportation, communications, gas, water, or electricity. • This type of corporation is usu. subject to extensive governmental regulation.

▸ **qualified corporation.** See *admitted corporation*.

▸ **quasi-corporation.** (1839) An entity that exercises some of the functions of a corporation but that has not been granted corporate status by statute; esp., a public corporation with limited authority and powers (such as a county or school district). — Also sometimes termed *quasi-municipal corporation*. Cf. MUNICIPAL CORPORATION.

> "In America a certain class of corporations are described as quasi corporations, by which is intended to express that the bodies so described are loosely organized, and possess only a part of the usual corporate powers and attributes. Quasi corporations represent the lower order of corporate life, and vary in their functions according to the purposes which they are intended to serve. Such are counties, townships, school districts, and the like." Henry H. Ingersoll, *Handbook of the Law of Public Corporations* § 3, at 7 (1904).

▸ **quasi-public corporation.** (1869) A for-profit corporation providing an essential public service. • An example is an electric company or other utility.

▸ **railroad corporation.** (1831) A corporation organized to construct, maintain, and operate railroads. — Also termed *railroad company*.

> "A railroad company or corporation is usually regarded as a private corporation, and justly so, as contrasted with a strictly public corporation, such as a city, county, township, or the like governmental subdivision, but it is not a private corporation in the strict sense that an ordinary business corporation is, for it is charged with duties of a public nature that distinguish it from a purely and strictly private corporation." 1 Byron K. Elliott & William F. Elliott, *A Treatise on the Law of Railroads* § 3, at 7 (3d ed. 1921).

▸ **registered corporation.** (1928) A publicly held corporation, a security of which is registered under § 12 of the Securities Exchange Act of 1934. • The corporation is subject to the Act's periodic disclosure requirements and proxy regulations. 15 USCA § 78*l*.

▸ **religious corporation.** (18c) A corporation created to carry out some ecclesiastical or religious purpose. See *ecclesiastical corporation*.

▸ **S corporation.** (1961) A corporation whose income is taxed through its shareholders rather than through the corporation itself. • Only corporations with a limited number of shareholders can elect S-corporation tax status under Subchapter S of the Internal Revenue Code. — Also termed *subchapter-S corporation*; *tax-option corporation*. Cf. *C corporation*.

▸ **shelf corporation.** See *shelf company* under COMPANY.

▸ **shell corporation.** (1969) A corporation that has no active business and usu. exists only in name as a vehicle for another company's business operations. — Also termed *shell company*.

▸ **sister corporation.** (1941) One of two or more corporations controlled by the same, or substantially the same, owners. — Also termed *brother-sister corporation*.

▸ **small-business corporation.** (1898) **1.** A corporation having no more than 100 shareholders and otherwise satisfying the requirements of the Internal Revenue Code provisions permitting a subchapter S election. IRC (26 USCA) § 1361(b). See *S corporation*. **2.** A corporation receiving money for stock (as a contribution to capital and paid-in surplus) totaling not more than $1,000,000, and otherwise satisfying the requirements of the Internal Revenue Code section 1244(c) thereby enabling the shareholders to claim an ordinary loss on worthless stock. IRC (26 USCA) § 1244(c).

▸ **sole corporation.** (17c) A corporation consisting of one incorporated office filled by one person and administered without a board of directors, ownership shares, or other diffusion of control; a corporation having or acting through only a single member. — Also termed *corporation sole*.

▸ **spiritual corporation.** (16c) A corporation whose members are spiritual persons, such as bishops, rectors, and abbots.

▸ **stock corporation.** (1873) A corporation in which the capital is contributed by the shareholders and divided into shares represented by certificates.

▸ **subchapter-C corporation.** See *C corporation*.

▸ **subchapter-S corporation.** See *S corporation*.

▸ **subsidiary corporation.** (1882) A corporation in which a parent corporation has a controlling share. — Often shortened to *subsidiary*; *sub.*

▸ **surviving corporation.** (1891) A corporation that acquires the assets and liabilities of another corporation by a merger or takeover.

▸ **target corporation.** (1967) A corporation over which control is being sought by another party. See TAKEOVER.

▸ **tax-option corporation.** See *S corporation.*

▸ **thin corporation.** (1947) A corporation with an excessive amount of debt in its capitalization. See *thin capitalization* under CAPITALIZATION.

▸ **trading corporation.** (18c) A corporation whose business involves the buying and selling of goods.

▸ **tramp corporation.** (1890) A corporation chartered in a state where it does not conduct business.

▸ **transnational corporation.** See *multinational corporation.*

▸ **trust corporation.** See *trust company* under COMPANY.

▸ **U.S.-owned foreign corporation.** (1969) A foreign corporation in which 50% or more of the total combined voting power or total value of the stock is held directly or indirectly by U.S. citizens. IRC (26 USCA) § 904(g)(6). • If the dividend or interest income paid by a U.S. corporation is classified as a foreign source, the U.S. corporation is treated as a U.S.-owned foreign corporation. IRC (26 USCA) § 861.

Corporation Act. *Hist.* A 1661 English statute (13 Car. 2, St. 2, ch. 1) prohibiting the holding of public office by anyone who would not take the Anglican sacrament and the oaths of supremacy and allegiance. • The Corporation Act belonged to the general category of Test Acts. It was repealed by the Promissory Oaths Act of 1871. See TEST ACT.

corporation borough. See BOROUGH.

corporation counsel. See COUNSEL.

corporation court. See COURT.

Corporation for National and Community Service. A federal corporation that fosters civic responsibility, provides educational opportunity for those who contribute services, and oversees AmeriCorps (the domestic Peace Corps), Learn and Serve America, and the National Senior Service Corps. • It was established in 1993. 42 USCA § 12651.

corporatism. (1890) The power and influence that large corporations either have or are thought to have.

corporator (**kor**-pə-ray-tər). (18c) **1.** A member of a corporation. **2.** INCORPORATOR.

> "Usually, a member of a corporation, in which sense it includes a stockholder; also, one of the persons who are the original organizers or promoters of a new corporation. The corporators are not the corporation, for either may sue the other." William C. Anderson, *A Dictionary of Law* 266 (1889).

corporeal (kor-**por**-ee-əl), *adj.* (15c) Having a physical, material existence; TANGIBLE <land and fixtures are corporeal property>. Cf. INCORPOREAL. — **corporeality,** *n.*

corporeal hereditament. See HEREDITAMENT.

corporeal ownership. See OWNERSHIP.

corporeal possession. See POSSESSION.

corporeal property. See PROPERTY.

corporeal thing. See THING (1).

corps diplomatique (**kor** dee-plə-ma-**teek**). DIPLOMATIC CORPS.

corpus (**kor**-pəs), *n.* [Latin "body"] (1844) **1.** The property for which a trustee is responsible; the trust principal. — Also termed *res*; *trust estate*; *trust fund*; *trust property*; *trust res*; *trust.* **2.** PRINCIPAL (4). Pl. **corpora** (**kor**-pə-rə), **corpuses** (**kor**-pə-səz).

corpus comitatus (**kor**-pəs kom-ə-**tay**-təs). [Latin "the body of a county"] (17c) *Hist.* **1.** The area within a territorial jurisdiction rather than on the "high seas" and hence where admiralty jurisdiction did not originally extend. See INFRA CORPUS COMITATUS. **2.** The denizens of an entire county, as opposed to just part of it.

corpus corporatum (**kor**-pəs kor-pə-**ray**-təm). [Latin] (18c) *Hist.* A corporate body; a corporation.

corpus cum causa (**kor**-pəs kəm **kaw**-zə). [Law Latin "the body with the cause"] (16c) *Hist.* A writ issuing out of Chancery to remove both a person and a record from an inferior court in order to review a judgment issued by the inferior court.

> "The first use of the writ to challenge imprisonment was in cases of privilege; an officer of a central court, or a litigant there, could be released from imprisonment in another court by writ of privilege in habeas corpus form. The Court of Chancery at the same time developed a similar procedure for reviewing the cause of imprisonment in an inferior tribunal; this species of writ was called *corpus cum causa*, and it became a common remedy against the misuse of borough jurisdiction in the fifteenth century." J.H. Baker, *An Introduction to English Legal History* 168 (3d ed. 1990).

corpus delicti (**kor**-pəs də-**lik**-tı *or* -tee). [Latin "body of the crime"] (1705) **1.** The fact of a transgression; ACTUS REUS. • The phrase reflects the simple principle that a crime must be proved to have occurred before anyone can be convicted for having committed it.

> "[T]he definition of 'corpus delicti' often becomes important. (a) Essentially it signifies merely the fact of the specific loss or injury sustained, e.g., death of a victim or burning of a house. (b) To this is added also, by most courts, the criminal agency of some person (i.e., not mere accident). (c) A few courts also include evidence of the accused's identity with the deed; but this is absurd, for it virtually signifies making 'corpus delicti' synonymous with the whole charge. — Many courts treat this rule with a pedantic and unpractical strictness." John H. Wigmore, *A Students' Textbook of the Law of Evidence* 310 (1935).

> "One of the important rules of evidence in criminal cases is that which requires proof of the *corpus delicti.* Literally defined this term means 'the body of the offense,' or 'the substance of the crime.' In popular language it is used to describe the visible evidence of the crime, such as the dead body of a murdered person. Properly used, however, it is applicable to any crime and relates particularly to the act element of criminality; that is, that a certain prohibited act has been committed or result accomplished and that it was committed or accomplished by a criminal human agency." Justin Miller, "The Criminal Act," in *Legal Essays in Tribute to Orrin Kip McMurray* at 469, 478 (Max Radin & Alexander M. Kidd eds., 1935).

> "The phrase 'corpus delicti' does not mean dead body, but body of the crime, and every offense has its corpus delicti. Its practical importance, however, has been very largely limited to the homicide cases. It concerns the usability in a criminal case of a confession made by the defendant outside of court." Rollin M. Perkins & Ronald N. Boyce, *Criminal Law* 140 (3d ed. 1982).

2. Loosely, the material substance on which a crime has been committed; the physical evidence of a crime, such as the corpse of a murdered person. • Despite the common misunderstanding, a victim's body could be evidence of a homicide but the prosecutor does not have to locate or present the body to meet the corpus delicti requirement. Pl. **corpora delicti.**

corpus delicti rule. (1926) *Criminal law.* The doctrine that in order to secure a conviction, the prosecution must establish the corpus delicti with corroborating evidence. • The doctrine prohibits the prosecution from proving the corpus delicti based solely on a defendant's extrajudicial statements.

corpus juris (**kor**-pəs **joor**-is). [Latin "body of law"] (1832) **1.** The law as the sum or collection of laws <*Corpus Juris Secundum*>. **2.** CORPUS JURIS CIVILIS — Abbr. C.J.

corpus juris Angliae (**kor**-pəs **joor**-is **ang**-glee-ee). (1954) The entire body of English law, comprising the common law, statutory law, equity, and special law in its various forms.

Corpus Juris Canonici (**kor**-pəs **joor**-is kə-**non**-ə-sI). [Latin] *Hist.* The body of the canon law, compiled from the decrees and canons of the Roman Catholic Church. • The *Corpus Juris Canonici* emerged during the 12th century, beginning with the publication of Gratian's *Decretum* (c. 1140). In addition to the *Decretum*, it includes Raymond of Peñaforte's *Liber Extra* (1234), the *Liber Sextus* of Pope Boniface VIII (1298), the *Clementines* of Pope Clement V (1313), the *Extravagantes Joannis* of Pope John XXII (1325), and *Extravagantes Communes* published by Pope John's successors (1499–1502). In 1582, the entire collection was edited by a commission of church dignitaries and officially named the *Corpus Juris Canonici*. It remained the Catholic Church's primary body of law until the promulgation of the Code of Canon Law in 1917, now replaced by that of 1983.

> "After Gratian, later papal enactments, called 'decretals,' were collected and issued by the authority of various popes. . . . A revised edition of such 'decretals' . . . was presented to Pope Gregory IX in 1234 — only a short while, therefore, after the final form of Magna Carta in 1225 — and issued by him with statutory force. The revision freely made changes in the text of the enactments and the resulting compilation in four 'books' was regarded as a 'Code,' corresponding to the 'Code' of Justinian, just as the *Decretum* of Gratian corresponded to the Digest. . . . All these compilations and collections were, from the sixteenth century on, known as the *Corpus Juris Canonici*, the 'Body of Canon Law,' and formed the basis of the law administered in the Church courts." Max Radin, *Handbook of Anglo-American Legal History* 33–34 (1936).

Corpus Juris Civilis (**kor**-pəs **joor**-is sə-**vil**-is *or* sə-**vI**-lis). The body of the civil law, compiled and codified under the direction of the Roman emperor Justinian in A.D. 528–556. • The collection includes four works in Latin — the Institutes, the Digest (or Pandects), the Code, and the Novels. The title *Corpus Juris Civilis* was not original, or even early, but was modeled on the *Corpus Juris Canonici* and given in the 16th century and later to editions of the texts of the four component parts of the Roman law. — Often shortened to *Corpus Juris*. See ROMAN LAW. Cf. JUSTINIAN CODE.

corpus possessionis (**kor**-pəs pə-zes[h]-ee-**oh**-nis). [Latin] *Roman law.* The physical aspect of possession. See *animus possidendi* under ANIMUS.

corpus pro corpore (**kor**-pəs proh **kor**-pə-ree). [Latin] (18c) *Hist.* Body for body. • This phrase commonly expressed the liability of a surety in a civil action (a mainpernor). See MAINPRISE.

correal (**kor**-ee-əl *or* kə-**ree**-əl), *adj.* [fr. Latin *correus* "codebtor"] (1875) *Roman law.* Of, relating to, or involving liability that is joint and several; pertaining to a joint obligation or engagement enforceable against any one of two or more joint debtors or by any one of two or more joint creditors. • A *correal* debtor who paid an entire obligation had no right of action against a codebtor. See CORREUS; SOLIDARY.

> "If Aulus, having first obtained from Titius the promise of a hundred aurei, turned to Seius and said, *Spondesne mihi, Sei, cosdem centum aureos dare?* (Do you engage, Seius, to give me the same one hundred aurei?), then if Seius answered, *Spondeo*, there was one single obligation for a hundred aurei, binding in full on each of the two debtors. Aulus could demand a hundred from Titius or a hundred from Seius, and in case of non-payment could sue either one, taking his choice between them, for the full amount. If either paid the hundred, whether willingly or by compulsion, the other was released: for there was but one debt, and that was now discharged. This kind of obligation is called correal obligation (correal, from *con*, and *reus* or *rei*, connected parties, parties associated in a common debt or credit)." James Hadley, *Introduction to Roman Law* 258 (1881).

correality (kor-ee-**al**-ə-tee), *n.* (1875) The quality, state, or condition of being correal; the relationship between parties to an obligation that terminates when an entire payment is made by one of two or more debtors to a creditor, or a payment is made by a debtor to one of two or more creditors. Cf. SOLIDARITY.

> "But there were circumstances, apart from indivisibility, in which each of the parties might be liable in full. . . . Several were liable or entitled, each *in solidum*, under an obligation, but the thing was due only once. Satisfaction by, or to, one of those liable, or entitled, ended the whole obligation, and action by one of the joint creditors, or against one of the debtors, not only 'novated' the obligation between the actual parties, but destroyed it altogether as against the others. This relation is commonly called correality (*correi debendi vel credendi*)." W.W. Buckland, *A Manual of Roman Private Law* 349–50 (2d ed. 1939).

correal obligation. See OBLIGATION.

corrected policy. See INSURANCE POLICY.

correction, *n.* (14c) **1.** Generally, the act or an instance of making right what is wrong <mark your corrections in red ink>. **2.** A change in business activity or market price following and counteracting an increase or decrease in the activity or price <the broker advised investors to sell before the inevitable stock-market correction>. See DOWN REVERSAL. **3.** (*usu. pl.*) The punishment and treatment of a criminal offender through a program of imprisonment, parole, and probation <Department of Corrections>. — **correct,** *vb.* — **corrective** (in senses 1 & 2), **correctional** (in sense 3), *adj.*

correction, house of. See *house of correction* under HOUSE.

correctional institution. See PRISON.

correctional services. (1936) Any and all services relating directly to prisons and prisoners.

correctional system. (1879) A network of governmental agencies that administer a jurisdiction's prisons and parole system.

correction of inventorship. *Patents.* The process or act by which the incorrect naming of an inventor in a patent application or patent is corrected to identify one or more true inventors. • With an application, inventorship is corrected by filing an appropriate amendment. With a patent, it is corrected by filing a petition with the Commissioner of Patents. Inventorship may be corrected to add or delete inventors, or to replace the original sole inventor with another inventor.

corrective advertising. (1971) Advertising that informs consumers that earlier advertisements contained a deceptive claim, and that provides consumers with corrected information. • This type of advertising may be ordered by the Federal Trade Commission.

corrective justice. See JUSTICE (4).

corrective rape. See RAPE (2).

corrector of the staple. (17c) *Hist.* A clerk who records merchants' transactions at a market or staple. See STAPLE (2).

correi credendi (**kor**-ee-I kri-**den**-dI). [Latin] (17c) *Roman law.* Joint creditors. — Also termed *correi stipulandi* (stip-yə-**lan**-dI). See STIPULATIO.

> "The mode for *stipulatio* is stated in the Institutes. Of several stipulators (*correi credendi*, active correality) each asks the debtor and he answers once for all. Of several promisors (*correi debendi*, passive correality) the creditor asks each and they answer together." W.W. Buckland, *A Manual of Roman Private Law* 350 (2d ed. 1939).

correi debendi (**kor**-ee-I di-**ben**-dI). [Latin] (17c) *Roman & Scots law.* Joint debtors. — Also termed *correi promittendi* (proh-mi-**ten**-dI). See STIPULATIO.

> "*Correi Debendi* — The name given by the Roman law to persons *jointly* bound. . . . In the Scotch law, if bound *severally*, and not *jointly and severally*, each is bound only for *his share*, whatever be the responsibility of the others." Hugh Barclay, *A Digest of the Law of Scotland* 196 (3d ed. 1865).

correi stipulandi. See CORREI CREDENDI.

correlation. (16c) A connection between two ideas, facts, phenomena, etc., esp. when one may be the cause of the other.

correlative (kə-**rel**-ə-tiv), *adj.* (16c) **1.** Related and mutually dependent; closely corresponding. **2.** Having or involving a reciprocal or mutually interdependent relationship <the term *right* is correlative with *duty*>. See LEGAL CORRELATIVE. — **correlative,** *n.*

correlative-rights doctrine. (1938) **1.** *Water law.* The principle that adjoining landowners must limit their use of a common water source to a reasonable amount. **2.** *Oil & gas.* The rule that a lessee's or landowner's right to capture oil and gas from the property is restricted by the duty to exercise that right without waste or negligence. • This is a corollary to the rule of capture. Cf. RULE OF CAPTURE (4).

correspondence audit. See AUDIT.

correspondent, *n.* (17c) **1.** The writer of a letter or letters. **2.** A person employed by the media to report on events. **3.** A securities firm or financial institution that performs services for another in a place or market that the other does not have direct access to. — **correspond,** *vb.*

correspondent bank. See BANK.

corresponding promise. See PROMISE.

corresponding secretary. See SECRETARY (3).

correus (**kor**-ee-əs), *n.* [Latin] *Roman law.* **1.** A codebtor in a contract; a joint debtor. **2.** A co-creditor in a contract; a joint creditor. See STIPULATIO. Pl. ***correi*** (**kor**-ee-I).

corrigendum (kor-ə-**jen**-dəm), *n.* [Latin "correction"] (1850) An error in a printed work discovered after the work has gone to press. — Also termed *erratum.* Pl. **corrigenda** (kor-ə-**jen**-də).

corroborate (kə-**rob**-ə-rayt), *vb.* (16c) To strengthen or confirm; to make more certain <the witness corroborated the plaintiff's testimony>.

corroborated, *adj.* (1822) (Of a statement or claim) supported by independent evidence that is both credible and admissible. Cf. UNCORROBORATED.

corroborating evidence. See EVIDENCE.

corroborating witness. See WITNESS.

corroboration (kə-rob-ə-**ray**-shən), *n.* (16c) **1.** Confirmation or support by additional evidence or authority <corroboration of the witness's testimony>. **2.** Formal confirmation or ratification <corroboration of the treaty>. **3.** *Patents & Trademarks.* Confirmation or support by additional evidence of the date of invention or of a trademark's first use. — **corroborate,** *vb.* — **corroborative** (kə-**rob**-ə-rə-tiv), *adj.* — **corroborator** (kə-**rob**-ə-ray-tər), *n.*

▸ **cross-corroboration.** (1953) **1.** Corroboration by multiple independent sources. **2.** *Criminal law.* (Of evidence that requires corroboration) corroboration by a source that itself usu. requires corroboration. • For example, even though one accomplice cannot corroborate another accomplice's testimony, an accomplice is allowed to corroborate a defendant's confession.

corroboration rule. (1922) *Criminal law.* The doctrine that a conviction cannot be based on a defendant's admission alone but must be supported by additional proof that a crime charged was actually committed.

corroboration warning. (1941) A judge's instruction to the jury that it should not convict a defendant on the basis of suspect evidence, such as a confession or an accomplice's testimony, that is uncorroborated unless the jury is satisfied beyond all reasonable doubt that the defendant is guilty. See *suspect evidence* under EVIDENCE.

corroborative evidence. See *corroborating evidence* under EVIDENCE.

corrody. See CORODY.

corrupt, *adj.* (14c) **1.** Having unlawful or depraved motives; given to dishonest practices, such as bribery. **2.** *Archaic.* (Of a person) subject to corruption of blood.

> "[T]here are divers offences made Treason by Act of Parliament, whereof, though a Man be Attaint, yet his Blood, by Provisoes therein, is not corrupt, nor shall he forfeit any thing . . . ." Thomas Blount, *Nomo-Lexicon: A Law-Dictionary* (1670).

corrupt, *vb.* (13c) **1.** To change (someone's behavior, morals, or principles) from good to bad; to pervert the integrity of. **2.** To change the traditional and established form of (culture, language, etc.) so that it becomes worse than it was before. **3.** To destroy or diminish the quality and usefulness of (an electronic or mechanical device or its components). **4.** *Archaic.* To impose corruption of blood on (a person).

corrupt conduct. See CONDUCT.

corrupting, *n.* See IMPAIRING THE MORALS OF A MINOR.

corruption. (14c) **1.** Depravity, perversion, or taint; an impairment of integrity, virtue, or moral principle; esp., the impairment of a public official's duties by bribery.

"The word 'corruption' indicates impurity or debasement and when found in the criminal law it means depravity or gross impropriety." Rollin M. Perkins & Ronald N. Boyce, *Criminal Law* 855 (3d ed. 1982).

2. A fiduciary's or official's use of a station or office to procure some benefit either personally or for someone else, contrary to the rights of others; an act carried out with the intent of giving some advantage inconsistent with official duty or the rights of others.

corruption in office. See *official misconduct* under MISCONDUCT.

corruption of a minor. See IMPAIRING THE MORALS OF A MINOR.

corruption of blood. (16c) A defunct doctrine, now considered unconstitutional, under which a person loses the ability to inherit or pass property as a result of an attainder or of being declared civilly dead. — Also termed *corruption of the blood.* See ATTAINDER; *civil death* (1) under DEATH.

"Corruption of blood is, when any one is attainted of felony or treason, then his blood is said to be corrupt; by means whereof neither his children, nor any of his blood, can be heirs to him, or to any other ancestor, for that they ought to claim by him. And if he were a noble or gentleman before, he and all his children are made thereby ignoble and ungentle . . . ." *Termes de la Ley* 125 (1st Am. ed. 1812).

corruptly, *adv.* (16c) In a corrupt or depraved manner; by means of corruption or bribery. • As used in criminal-law statutes, *corruptly* usu. indicates a wrongful desire for pecuniary gain or other advantage.

corrupt-motive doctrine. (1962) *Criminal law.* The rule that conspiracy is punishable only if the agreement was entered into with an evil purpose, not merely with an intent to do the illegal act. • This doctrine — which originated in *People v. Powell*, 63 N.Y. 88 (1875) — has been rejected by the Model Penal Code. — Also termed *Powell doctrine.*

corrupt-practices act. (1897) A federal or state statute that regulates campaign contributions and expenditures as well as their disclosure. — Abbr. CPA.

corsnaed, *n.* See *ordeal of the morsel* under ORDEAL.

corsned, *n.* See *ordeal of the morsel* under ORDEAL.

Corte de Justicia Centroamericana. See CENTRAL AMERICAN COURT OF JUSTICE.

corvée seigneuriale (kor-**vay** sen-yuu-ree-**ahl**). [French] *Hist.* Services due the lord of the manor. — Often shortened to *corvée.*

cosen, *vb.* See COZEN.

cosening, *n.* See COZENING.

cosign, *vb.* (1967) To sign a document along with another person, usu. to assume obligations and to supply credit to the principal obligor. — **cosignature,** *n.*

cosignatory, *n.* (1865) One of a group of people who sign a legal document for their department, organization, country, etc.; someone who signs a document jointly with others.

cosignature. See SIGNATURE.

cosigner. See COMAKER.

cosinage (**kəz**-ən-ij). (15c) *Hist.* A writ used by an heir to secure the right to land held by a great-great-grandfather or certain collateral relatives. — Also spelled *cosenage; cousinage.* — Also termed *consanguineo; de consanguineo; de consanguinitate.* Cf. AIEL; BESAYEL.

"[T]here is the closest possible affinity between the Mort d'Ancestor and the action of Cosinage. If I claim the seisin of my uncle, I use the one; if I claim the seisin of a first cousin, I use the other. But procedurally, the two stand far apart." 2 Frederick Pollock & Frederic W. Maitland, *History of English Law Before the Time of Edward I* 569 (2d ed. 1899).

cosmetic damages. See DAMAGES.

cost, *n.* (13c) **1.** The amount paid or charged for something; price or expenditure. Cf. EXPENSE.

▸ **aboriginal cost.** (1979) The cost of an asset incurred by the first company to use it for public utilities.

▸ **acquisition cost.** (1926) **1.** An asset's net price; the original cost of an asset. — Also termed *historical cost; original cost.* **2.** See LOAD.

▸ **advance cost.** (1877) **1.** A cost projected to be incurred by a client, as for litigation expenses, and therefore requested by counsel to be paid beforehand. **2.** A client's payment to cover such a projected cost.

▸ **after cost.** A delayed expense; an expense, such as one for repair under a warranty, incurred after the principal transaction.

▸ **applied cost.** A cost appropriated to a project before it has been incurred.

▸ **average cost.** (18c) The sum of the costs of beginning inventory and the costs of later additions divided by the total number of available units.

▸ **average variable cost.** (1959) The average cost per unit of output, arrived at by dividing the total variable expenses of production by the total units of output. Cf. LONG-RUN INCREMENTAL COST.

▸ **avoidable cost.** (1934) A cost that can be averted if production is held below a certain level so that additional expenses will not be incurred.

▸ **carrying cost.** (1922) **1.** *Accounting.* The variable cost of stocking one unit of inventory for one year. • Carrying cost includes the opportunity cost of the capital invested in the inventory. — Also termed *cost of carrying.* **2.** A current charge or noncapital expenditure made to prevent the causing or accelerating of the termination of a defeasible estate, as well as the sums spent on repairs required by the duty to avoid permissive waste.

▸ **common cost.** See *indirect cost.*

▸ **cost of completion.** (1852) *Contracts.* An element of damages based on the expense that would be incurred by the nonbreaching party to finish the promised performance.

▸ **direct cost.** (1818) The amount of money for material, labor, and overhead to produce a product.

▸ **distribution cost.** (1920) Any cost incurred in marketing a product or service, such as advertising, storage, and shipping.

▸ **fixed cost.** (1894) A cost whose value does not fluctuate with changes in output or business activity; esp., overhead expenses such as rent, salaries, and depreciation. — Also termed *fixed charge*; *fixed expense*.

▸ **flotation cost.** (*usu. pl.*) (1948) A cost incurred in issuing additional stock.

▸ **historical cost.** See *acquisition cost* (1).

▸ **implicit cost.** See *opportunity cost*.

▸ **indirect cost.** (1850) A cost that is not specific to the production of a particular good or service but that arises from production activity in general, such as overhead allocations for general and administrative activities. — Also termed *common cost*.

▸ **long-run incremental cost.** See LONG-RUN INCREMENTAL COST.

▸ **manufacturing cost.** (1828) The cost incurred in the production of goods, including direct and indirect costs.

▸ **marginal cost.** (1891) The additional cost incurred in producing one more unit of output.

▸ **mitigation cost.** (1969) A party's expenditures to reduce an existing harm so that further damage might be halted, slowed, or diminished.

▸ **mixed cost.** A cost that includes fixed and variable costs.

▸ **net book cost.** (1936) The cost of property when it was first acquired or devoted to public use, minus accumulated depreciation. — Also termed *rate-base value*.

▸ **net cost.** (18c) The cost of an item, arrived at by subtracting any financial gain from the total cost.

▸ **opportunity cost.** (1894) The cost of acquiring an asset measured by the value of an alternative investment that is forgone <her opportunity cost of $1,000 in equipment was her consequent inability to invest that money in bonds>. — Also termed *implicit cost*.

▸ **original cost.** See *acquisition cost* (1).

▸ **prime cost.** (1808) The true price paid for goods on a bona fide purchase.

▸ **prophylactic cost.** (1989) A party's expenditures to prepare property to withstand or prevent potential future harm. • These costs are not related to any existing property damage and are usu. not recoverable under insurance contracts.

▸ **replacement cost.** (1928) The cost of a substitute asset that is equivalent to an asset currently held. • The new asset has the same utility but may or may not be identical to the one replaced.

▸ **social cost.** (1862) The cost to society of any particular practice or rule <although automobiles are undeniably beneficial to society, they carry a certain social cost in the lives that are lost every year on the road>.

▸ **sunk cost.** (1916) A cost that has already been incurred and that cannot be recovered.

▸ **tangible cost.** (1938) *Oil & gas.* A particular expense associated with drilling, such as the costs incurred for materials and land. • Drilling and testing costs are considered intangible.

▸ **transaction cost.** (*usu. pl.*) (1945) A cost connected with a process transaction, such as a broker's commission, the time and effort expended to arrange a deal, or the cost involved in litigating a dispute.

▸ **unit cost.** (1911) The cost of a single unit of a product or service; the total manufacturing cost divided by the number of units.

▸ **variable cost.** (1953) The cost that varies in the short run in close relationship with changes in output.

2. (*pl.*) The charges or fees taxed by the court, such as filing fees, jury fees, courthouse fees, and reporter fees. — Also termed *court costs*. **3.** (*pl.*) The expenses of litigation, prosecution, or other legal transaction, esp. those allowed in favor of one party against the other. • Some but not all states allow parties to claim attorney's fees as a litigation cost. — Also termed (in sense 3) *litigation costs*; (in senses 2 & 3) *legal costs*.

▸ **accruing costs.** (1871) Costs and expenses incurred after judgment.

▸ **costs of increase.** See COSTS OF INCREASE.

▸ **costs of the day.** (1828) Costs incurred in preparing for trial.

▸ **costs to abide event.** (1858) Costs incurred by a successful party who is entitled to an award of those costs incurred at the conclusion of the matter; esp., appellate court's order for payment of costs to the party who finally prevails in a proceeding that has been returned to a lower court.

▸ **interlocutory costs.** (1831) Costs incurred during the pendency of an appeal.

▸ **legal costs.** (18c) Attorney's fees and other expenditures related to a lawsuit.

▸ **taxable cost.** (1872) A litigation-related expense that the prevailing party is entitled to as part of the court's award.

cost accounting. See *cost-accounting method* under ACCOUNTING METHOD.

cost-accounting method. See ACCOUNTING METHOD.

cost and freight. (1819) A mercantile-contract term allocating the rights and duties of the buyer and the seller of goods with respect to delivery, payment, and risk of loss, whereby the seller must (1) clear the goods for export, (2) arrange for transportation by water, and (3) pay the costs of shipping to the port of destination. • When the goods are safely stowed on the receiving ship while docked, the seller's delivery is complete; the risk of loss then passes to the buyer. This term is used only when goods are transported by sea or inland waterway. — Abbr. CF; CFR; C&F; CandF. Cf. COST, INSURANCE, AND FREIGHT; FREE ON BOARD.

cost approach. (1949) A method of appraising real property, based on the cost of building a new structure with the same utility, assuming that an informed buyer would pay no more for the property than it would cost to build a new structure having the same usefulness. Cf. MARKET APPROACH; INCOME APPROACH.

cost basis. See BASIS (2).

cost-benefit analysis. (1963) An analytical technique that weighs the costs of a proposed decision, holding, or project against the expected advantages, economic or otherwise; a way of calculating the methods or plans that will bring the most advantages for the smallest cost, esp. in business. — Abbr. CBA.

cost bill. See *bill of costs* under BILL (2).

cost bond. See BOND (2).

cost-book mining company. (1857) An association of persons organized for the purpose of working mines or lodes, whose capital stock is divided into shares that are transferable without the consent of other members. • The management of the mine is entrusted to an agent called a purser.

cost depletion. (1934) *Oil & gas.* The recovery of an oil-and-gas producer's basis (i.e., investment) in a producing well by deducting the basis proportionately over the producing life of the well. Treas. Reg. § 1.611-2. Cf. PERCENTAGE DEPLETION.

cost-effective, *adj.* (1967) Bringing the best possible profits or advantages for the lowest possible costs <cost-effective means of reducing carbon-monoxide emissions>.

cost-effectiveness analysis. (1955) A method of weighing the worth of an activity or project that might gain or has gained political or corporate approval, the assessment turning on the known or projected costs as against benefits that often cannot be measured directly in monetary terms. — Abbr. CEA.

cost, insurance, and freight. (1906) A mercantile-contract term allocating the rights and duties of the buyer and the seller of goods with respect to delivery, payment, and risk of loss, whereby the seller must (1) clear the goods for export, (2) arrange for transportation by water, (3) procure insurance against the buyer's risk of damage during carriage, and (4) pay the costs of shipping to the port of destination. • The seller's delivery is complete (and the risk of loss passes to the buyer) when the goods are loaded on the receiving ship while docked in the port of shipment. This term is used only when goods are transported by sea or inland waterway. — Abbr. CIF. Cf. COST AND FREIGHT; FREE ON BOARD.

> "'C.i.f.' is a mercantile symbol that is commonly used in international sales contracts. It is defined by section 2-320 of the UCC and by the Incoterms — 1953 and the Revised American Foreign Trade Definitions — 1941. Under all of these definitions the letters 'c.i.f.' mean that the price covers the cost of the goods, the cost of insuring them for the benefit of the order of the buyer, and the cost of carrying\ them to the named point, almost always the destination. Like the other mercantile symbols, the meaning of 'C.I.F.' may be varied by agreement." William D. Hawkland, *Uniform Commercial Code Series* § 2-320:01 (1984).

▸ **CIF destination.** (1960) A contractual term denoting that the price includes in a lump sum the cost of the goods and the insurance and freight to the named destination. — Also termed *CIF place of destination.*

cost justification. (1938) Under the Robinson-Patman Act, an affirmative defense against a charge of price discrimination dependent on the seller's showing that it incurs lower costs in serving those customers who are paying less. 15 USCA § 13(a).

cost-of-capital method. (1955) A means of measuring a utility's cost of acquiring debt and equity capital. • Regulatory commissions often use this method to determine a fair rate of return for the utility's investors.

cost of carrying. See *carrying cost* under COST (1).

cost of completion. See COST (1).

cost of living, *n.* (1896) The amount of money one needs to pay for food, clothes, and other necessaries <wages in line with the cost of living>.

cost-of-living adjustment. (1921) *Labor law.* A contractual or statutory provision that provides benefits usu. by granting an automatic monetary increase directly tied to the increase in the cost of living. • This automatic increase is used when determining federal pensions, military pensions, and some veterans benefits; it may also affect the private economy in the form of rent increases, salary decisions, and even court settlements. Cost-of-living adjustments are usu. measured by the consumer price index. — Abbr. COLA. See CONSUMER PRICE INDEX.

cost-of-living clause. (1953) A provision (as in a contract or lease) that gives an automatic wage, rent, or benefit increase tied in some way to cost-of-living rises in the economy. • A cost-of-living clause may also cover a decrease, though this is rare. See INFLATION.

cost-of-living index. See CONSUMER PRICE INDEX.

cost-plus contract. See CONTRACT.

cost price. See PRICE.

cost-push inflation. See INFLATION.

costs de incremento. See COSTS OF INCREASE.

costs of collection. (1833) Expenses incurred in receiving payment of a note; esp., attorney's fees incurred in the effort to collect a note.

costs of increase. (1836) Costs of court awarded in addition to what a jury awards. • Juries usu. awarded the successful party only a small sum for costs. A party wishing to recoup the additional costs had to file an affidavit of increase setting forth what further costs were incurred by taking the matter through trial. — Also termed *costs de incremento.* See *affidavit of increase* under AFFIDAVIT.

costs of the day. See COST (3).

costs to abide event. See COST (3).

cosurety. (1847) A surety who shares the cost of performing suretyship obligations with another. See SURETY.

cosuretyship. (1855) The relation between two or more sureties who are bound to answer for the same duty of the principal, and who are jointly responsible for any loss resulting from the principal's default.

cotarius (kə-**tair**-ee-əs). [Law Latin] (18c) *Hist.* A socage-tenure serf who holds land by paying rent and providing some personal services to the lord. • Both *cotarius* and *coterellus* serfs were also known as *cottagers.* Cf. COTERELLUS.

cotenancy. See TENANCY.

coterellus (kot-ə-**rel**-əs). [Law Latin] (18c) *Hist.* A serf who inhabits a cottage; a servile tenant whose person, issue, and goods are at the disposal of the lord. — Also spelled *coterell.* Cf. COTARIUS.

> "Coterellus. . . . A cottager. Considered by Spelman and others, the same with *cotarius.* But Cowell makes the distinction that the *cotarius* had free socage tenure, and paid a stated firm (rent) in provisions or money, with some occasional customary service; whereas the *coterellus* seemed to have held in mere villenage, and had his person and issue and goods disposed at the pleasure of the lord." 1 Alexander M. Burrill, *A Law Dictionary and Glossary* 387 (2d ed. 1867).

coterminous (koh-**tər**-mə-nəs), *adj.* (18c) **1.** (Of ideas or events) coextensive in time or meaning <Judge Smith's tenure was coterminous with Judge Jasper's>. **2.** CONTERMINOUS (1).

cotland (**kot**-lənd). (16c) *Hist.* Land held by a cottager, whether in socage or villeinage tenure.

cotortfeasor (koh-**tort**-fee-zər). (1834) Someone who, together with another, has committed a tort. See TORTFEASOR.

cotrustee. (18c) One of two or more persons in whom the administration of a trust is vested. • The cotrustees form a collective trustee and exercise their powers jointly. — Also termed *joint trustee*. See TRUSTEE (1).

cotset (**kot**-set). (1809) *Hist.* A villein who provides labor to a lord in exchange for a cottage and plot of land. — Also termed *cotsetus*.

cottier (**kot**-ee-ər). (14c) **1.** *Hist.* A serf who lives in a cottage; a cottager. • Over time, *cottier* has come to refer to a day laborer or a rural dweller. **2.** *Hist. Irish law.* A tenant who leases a house and a small (usu. two acre or less) plot of land.

couchant and levant (**kow**-chənt / **lev**-ənt), *adj.* See LEVANT AND COUCHANT.

council. (12c) **1.** A deliberative assembly; specif., a group of people elected or chosen to make rules, laws, or decisions, or to give advice <the U.N. Security Council>.

- ▸ **city council.** See CITY COUNCIL.
- ▸ **common council.** (18c) **1.** In some cities, the lower branch of a city council. **2.** In some cities, the city's governing board.
- ▸ **district council.** (1888) A body of people elected to organize local services such as education or healthcare in a given area.
- ▸ **general council.** (15c) A body of people elected to represent all the citizens of a territory or members of an organization.
- ▸ **select council.** (1830) In some cities, the upper branch of a city council.

2. An administrative or executive body.

councillor. See COUNCILOR.

Council of Economic Advisers. A three-member council in the Executive Office of the President responsible for analyzing the national economy and advising the President on economic matters. • Created by the Employment Act of 1946, it now functions under Reorganization Plan No. 9 of 1953. Its members are appointed by the President with the advice and consent of the Senate. — Abbr. CEA.

Council of Europe. An organization of European nations, founded in 1949, that promotes cooperation, social progress, and economic growth between its members. • The Council, unlike the European Union, has no lawmaking powers. Its membership is open to non-European Union nations.

Council of the North. *Hist.* A body used by the Tudors to administer the northern parts of England (esp. Yorkshire) during the 16th and 17th centuries. • The council probably predated the Tudors, but Henry VIII revived it. In addition to enforcing Crown policy in the northern territories, the appointees (many of whom were lawyers) exercised wide criminal and civil jurisdiction. The Council disbanded ca. 1640.

Council on Environmental Quality. A three-member council in the Executive Office of the President responsible for developing and recommending national policy on environmental quality. • The council was created by the National Environmental Policy Act of 1969. Its members are appointed by the President with the advice and consent of the Senate. 42 USCA §§ 4321 et seq., 4371 et seq. — Abbr. CEQ.

councilor, *n.* (15c) Someone who serves on a council, esp. at the local level. — Also spelled *councillor*. — **councilorship,** *n.*

counsel, *n.* (13c) **1.** Advice or assistance; opinion given as the result of consultation <the lawyer's counsel was to petition immediately for a change of immigration status>. **2.** One or more lawyers who, having the authority to do so, give advice about legal matters; esp., a courtroom advocate <the client acted on advice of counsel>. — In the singular, also termed *counselor*; *counselor-at-law*. Cf. ATTORNEY; LAWYER. **3.** *English law.* A member of the bar; BARRISTER.

- ▸ **advisory counsel.** (1866) **1.** An attorney retained merely to give advice on a particular matter, as distinguished from one (such as trial counsel) actively participating in a case. **2.** See *standby counsel*.
- ▸ **amicus counsel.** (1952) **1.** An attorney appointed by the court to advise it about a defendant's competency to stand trial. • The attorney may communicate with the defendant's lawyer but does not represent or assist the defendant in any way. **2.** An attorney who represents an amicus curiae. — Also termed (in sense 1) *counsel amicus curiae*.
- ▸ **appellate counsel.** (1921) A lawyer who represents a party on appeal. • The term is often used in contrast with *trial counsel*.
- ▸ **appointed counsel.** See *assigned counsel*.
- ▸ **assigned counsel.** (17c) An attorney appointed by the court to represent a person, usu. an indigent person. — Also termed *court-appointed attorney*; *court-appointed counsel*; *appointed counsel*.
- ▸ **corporate counsel.** (1898) An in-house attorney for a corporation. Cf. *in-house counsel*.
- ▸ **corporation counsel.** (1822) A city attorney in an incorporated municipality. See CITY ATTORNEY.
- ▸ **counsel amicus curiae.** See *amicus counsel* (1).
- ▸ **counsel of record.** See *attorney of record* (1) under ATTORNEY.
- ▸ **court-appointed counsel.** See *assigned counsel*.
- ▸ ***Cumis* counsel.** (1987) An independent attorney hired by a defendant in a lawsuit in which the damages may be covered by the defendant's insurer but a conflict of interest between the defendant and the insurer makes it unreasonable for an attorney selected by the insurer to represent the defendant. • The term derives from *San Diego Federal Credit Union v. Cumis Ins. Society, Inc.*, 162 Cal. App. 3d 358 (1984), in which the concept was first clearly articulated.
- ▸ **duty counsel.** See *duty solicitor* under SOLICITOR.
- ▸ **general counsel.** (1848) **1.** A lawyer or law firm that represents a client in all or most of the client's legal matters, but that sometimes refers extraordinary matters — such as litigation and intellectual-property cases — to other lawyers. **2.** The most senior lawyer in a corporation's legal department, usu. also a corporate officer.
- ▸ **house counsel.** See *in-house counsel*.

▸ **independent counsel.** (1920) An attorney hired to provide an unbiased opinion about a case or to conduct an impartial investigation; esp., an attorney appointed by a governmental branch or agency to investigate alleged misconduct within that branch or agency. See *special prosecutor* under PROSECUTOR. Cf. *special counsel.*

▸ **in-house counsel.** (1974) One or more lawyers employed by a company. — Also termed *house counsel; inside counsel;* (when employed by a corporation) *corporate counsel.* Cf. *corporate counsel.*

▸ **inside counsel.** See *in-house counsel.*

▸ **junior counsel.** (17c) **1.** The younger or lower-ranking of two or more attorneys employed on the same side of a case, esp. someone charged with the less important aspects of the case. **2.** *English law.* The barrister who assists Queen's Counsel.

▸ **King's Counsel.** See KING'S COUNSEL.

▸ **lead counsel.** (1956) **1.** The more highly ranked lawyer if two or more are retained; the lawyer who manages or controls the case or cases, esp. in class actions or multidistrict litigation. — Also termed *senior counsel; attorney in charge.* **2.** QUEEN'S COUNSEL; KING'S COUNSEL. — Also termed *leading counsel.*

▸ **local counsel.** (1859) One or more lawyers who practice in a particular jurisdiction and are retained by nonresident counsel to help prepare and try a case or to complete a transaction in accordance with that jurisdiction's law, rules, and customs.

▸ **of counsel. 1.** A lawyer employed by a party in a case; esp., one who — although not the principal attorney of record — is employed to assist in the preparation or management of the case or in its presentation on appeal. **2.** A lawyer who is affiliated with a law firm, though not as a member, partner, or associate.

▸ **opposing counsel.** One or more lawyers who represent an adverse party.

▸ **parallel-track settlement counsel.** See *settlement counsel.*

▸ **Queen's Counsel.** See QUEEN'S COUNSEL.

▸ **senior counsel. 1.** See *lead counsel.* **2.** See KING'S COUNSEL; QUEEN'S COUNSEL.

▸ **settlement counsel.** One or more lawyers retained specifically to negotiate a settlement of a claim or lawsuit as opposed to appearing in court in litigation on behalf of a client. • Typically retained to expedite a favorable resolution of a dispute, settlement counsel often work on resolving disputes even as trial counsel pursue their litigation strategies. Settlement counsel engagements are often designed to reduce costs and risks associated with litigation, attain an early settlement or reach other specific settlement objectives. —Also termed *parallel-track settlement counsel.* See ALTERNATIVE DISPUTE RESOLUTION.

▸ **shadow counsel.** (1986) See *standby counsel.*

▸ **special counsel.** (1854) An attorney employed by the state or a political subdivision to assist in a particular case when the public interest so requires. — Also termed *special attorney.* Cf. *independent counsel.*

▸ **standby counsel.** (1961) *Criminal law.* **1.** A lawyer appointed by the court to be prepared to represent a defendant who waives the right to counsel, so as to ensure both that the defendant receives a fair trial and that undue delays are avoided. • The court may appoint standby counsel over a defendant's objection. The counsel may also provide some advice and guidance to the defendant during the self-representation. **2.** A court-appointed or privately hired lawyer who is prepared to assume representation of a client if the client's primary lawyer withdraws or is fired by the client, or if a pro se defendant's self-representation ends. — Also termed *advisory counsel; shadow counsel.* Cf. *hybrid representation* under REPRESENTATION (2).

▸ **trial counsel.** (1928) **1.** A lawyer who represents a party at trial. • The term is often used in contrast with *appellate counsel.* **2.** *Military law.* The person who prosecutes a case on the government's behalf.

counsel, assistance of. See ASSISTANCE OF COUNSEL.

counsel, right to. See RIGHT TO COUNSEL.

counsel amicus curiae. See *amicus counsel* under COUNSEL.

counsel and procure. See AID AND ABET.

counseled, *adj.* **1.** Advised; having been given the advice of another, esp. an expert <a fully counseled patient decided to leave>. **2.** Of, relating to, or involving lawyers in their capacity as counselors <the settlement agreement was counseled and above-board>.

counseling, *n.* (14c) **1.** The furnishing of legal advice to a client. **2.** The furnishing of advice or guidance, esp. by a knowledgeable person such as a life coach, a psychologist, or a psychotherapist; specif., professional advice or guidance of an individual, a couple, or a family through established psychological methods such as personality profiling, case-history data, personal interviews, and testing for aptitudes and interests.

counselor. A lawyer; one who, having the authority to do so, gives advice about legal matters; esp., a courtroom advocate. See COUNSEL (2).

counselor-at-law. See COUNSEL (2).

count, *n.* (14c) **1.** *Criminal law.* The part of a charging instrument alleging that the suspect has committed a distinct offense. **2.** *Civil procedure.* In a complaint or similar pleading, the statement of a distinct claim. Cf. DECLARATION (7).

> "This word . . . is in our old law-books used synonymously with declaration . . . . But when the suit embraces two or more causes of action (each of which of course requires a different statement), or when the plaintiff makes two or more different statements of one and the same cause of action, each several statement is called a count, and all of them, collectively, constitute the declaration." 1 John Bouvier, *A Law Dictionary* 245 (1839).

▸ **alternative count.** (1870) An ancillary count in an indictment, information, or presentment stated to be distinct from, and usu. less serious than, the immediately preceding count, in such a way that the jury, if not satisfied that the defendant is guilty of the preceding count, may acquit on that count but find the defendant guilty of the second one.

▸ **common count.** (18c) *Hist.* In a plaintiff's pleading in an action for debt, boilerplate language that is not founded on the circumstances of the individual case but is intended to guard against a possible variance and to enable the plaintiff to take advantage of any ground of liability that the proof may disclose. • In the action for indebitatus assumpsit, the common count stated that the defendant had failed to pay a debt as promised. See *indebitatus assumpsit* under ASSUMPSIT.

▸ **general count.** (17c) A count that states the plaintiff's claim without undue particularity.

▸ **money count.** *Hist.* A count, usu. founded on a simple contract, giving rise to a claim for payment of money.

"Simple contracts, express or implied, resulting in mere debts, are of so frequent occurrence as causes of action, that certain concise forms of counts were devised for suing upon them. These are called the '*indebitatus*' or 'money counts.'" 2 Stewart Rapalje & Robert L. Lawrence, *A Dictionary of American and English Law* 833 (1883).

▸ **multiple counts.** (1941) Several separate causes of action or charged offenses contained in a single pleading or indictment.

▸ **omnibus count** (**ahm**-ni-bəs). (1872) A count that combines into one count all money claims, claims for goods sold and delivered, claims for work and labor, and claims for an account stated.

▸ **phone count.** (1990) A count in an indictment based on using a "communication facility" in the commission of a felony. • The phrase *communication facility* includes various types of electronic means of communicating with others. *See* 21 USCA § 843(b).

▸ **separate count.** (18c) One of two or more criminal charges contained in one indictment, each charge constituting a separate indictment for which the accused may be tried.

▸ **several count.** (18c) One of two or more counts in a pleading, each of which states a different cause of action.

▸ **special count.** (18c) A section of a pleading in which the plaintiff's claim is stated with great particularity — usu. employed only when the pleading rules require specificity.

3. A canvassing. See CANVASS (2). 4. *Hist.* The plaintiff's declaration, or initial pleading, in a real action. See DECLARATION (7). 5. *Patents.* The part of a patent application that defines the subject matter in a priority contest (i.e., an *interference*) between two or more applications or between one or more applications and one or more patents. See INTERFERENCE (3).

count, *vb.* (17c) **1.** In pleading, to declare or state; to narrate the facts that state a claim. **2.** *Hist.* To plead orally; to plead or argue a case in court.

count bargain. See *charge bargain* under PLEA BARGAIN.

counted vote. See VOTE (4).

counter. (14c) **1.** *Hist.* An advocate or professional pleader; one who counts (i.e., orally recites) for a client. • Counters had coalesced into an identifiable group practicing before the Common Bench by the beginning of the 13th century. They were the leaders of the medieval legal profession, and over time came to be known as *serjeants at law.* — Also spelled *countor; contor; counteur.* See SERJEANT-AT-LAW.

"No English reference to a countor has been found before the thirteenth century. But the advantage of having a third person to recite the count must have become evident soon after 1200 if not before. Not only might an independent and learned friend be less liable to blunder, but, given the principle that an advocate might be disavowed (*deadvocatus*), his blunders would be harmless." J.H. Baker, *The Order of Serjeants at Law* 9 (1984).

2. COMPTER.

counteraction. See COUNTERCLAIM.

counteraffidavit. See AFFIDAVIT.

counterbalance, *vb.* (17c) To have a more or less equal and opposite effect on (something); to counteract the power or effect of <remote housing is counterbalanced by significantly lower rents>.

counterbond. See BOND (2).

countercharge, *n.* (18c) **1.** An opposing charge or onslaught; esp., an opposing accusation. **2.** A responsive allegation of wrongdoing.

counterclaim, *n.* (18c) A claim for relief asserted against an opposing party after an original claim has been made; esp., a defendant's claim in opposition to or as a setoff against the plaintiff's claim. — Also termed *counteraction; countersuit; cross-demand.* Cf. CROSS-CLAIM. — **counterclaim,** *vb.* — **counterclaimant,** *n.*

"Under [Fed. R. Civ. P.] Rule 13 the court has broad discretion to allow claims to be joined in order to expedite the resolution of all controversies between the parties in one suit. Rule 13(c) specifically provides that the counterclaimant is not limited by recovery sought by the opposing party but may claim relief in excess of that amount. Further, the general legal rule is that it is immaterial whether a counterclaim is legal or equitable for purposes of determining whether it properly is brought under Rule 13. . . . The expectation is that this liberal joinder policy will further the elimination of circuity of action and multiple litigation." 6 Charles Alan Wright et al., *Federal Practice and Procedure* § 1403, at 15–16 (2d ed. 1990).

▸ **compulsory counterclaim.** (1938) A counterclaim that must be asserted to be cognizable, usu. because it relates to the opposing party's claim and arises out of the same subject matter. • If a defendant fails to assert a compulsory counterclaim in the original action, that claim may not be brought in a later, separate action (with some exceptions). *See* Fed. R. Civ. P. 13(a).

▸ **permissive counterclaim.** (1924) A counterclaim that need not be asserted to be cognizable, usu. because it does not arise out of the same subject matter as the opposing party's claim or involves third parties over which the court does not have jurisdiction. • Permissive counterclaims may be brought in a later, separate action. *See* Fed. R. Civ. P. 13(b).

counter-complaint. See COMPLAINT.

counterdeed. See DEED.

counterespionage. See ESPIONAGE.

counterfeisance (kown-tər-**fee**-zənts). (16c) *Archaic.* The act of counterfeiting.

counterfeit, *adj.* (14c) Made to look genuine in an effort to deceive; produced by fakery, esp. with an intent to defraud.

counterfeit, *vb.* (14c) To unlawfully forge, copy, or imitate an item, esp. money or a negotiable instrument (such as a security or promissory note) or other officially issued item of value (such as a postage stamp or a food stamp), or to possess such an item without authorization and with the intent to deceive or defraud by presenting the item as genuine. • Counterfeiting includes producing or selling an item that displays a reproduction of a genuine trademark, usu. to deceive buyers into thinking they are purchasing genuine merchandise. *See* 18 USCA §§ 470 et seq. — **counterfeiting,** *n.* — **counterfeit,** *n.*

"Literally a *counterfeit* is an imitation intended to pass for an original. Hence it is spurious or false, and *to counterfeit* is to make false. For this reason the verbs *counterfeit* and *forge* are often employed as synonyms and the same is true to some extent of the corresponding nouns. No error is involved in this usage but it is important to distinguish between the words as far as possible when used as the labels of criminal offenses. In the most restricted sense, [c]ounterfeiting is the unlawful making of false money in the similitude of the genuine. At one time under English statutes it was made treason. Under modern statutes it is a felony." Rollin M. Perkins & Ronald N. Boyce, *Criminal Law* 431–32 (3d ed. 1982).

Counterfeit Access Device and Computer Fraud and Abuse Act of 1984. A federal statute that criminalizes various computer-related activities such as accessing without permission a computer system belonging to a bank or the federal government, or using that access to improperly obtain anything of value. 18 USCA § 1030.

counterfeit document. See DOCUMENT (2).

counterfeiter. (15c) Someone who forges or otherwise makes a copy or an unauthorized imitation of something (esp. a document, currency, or another's signature) with the intent to deceive or defraud.

counterfeiting, *n.* (15c) The unlawful forgery, copying, or imitation of an item, esp. money or a negotiable instrument (such as a security or promissory note) or other officially issued item of value (such as a postage stamp), or the unauthorized possession of such an item, with the intent to deceive or defraud by claiming or passing the item as genuine. *See* 18 USCA §§ 470 et seq. — **counterfeit,** *vb.* — **counterfeit,** *n.* — **counterfeit,** *adj.*

counterfeit mark. See *counterfeit trademark* under TRADEMARK.

counterfeit recording. (1975) *Copyright.* An unauthorized copy of a copyright-protected recording's sounds, artwork, label, trademark, or packaging. — Also termed *bootleg recording.*

counterfeit trademark. See TRADEMARK.

counterfoil (kown-tər-foyl), *n.* (18c) A detachable part of a writing on which the particulars of the main part are summarized. • The most common example is a check stub, on which the date, the payee, and the amount are typically noted.

counterletter. (17c) *Civil law.* A document in which the parties to a simulated contract record their true intentions. La. Civ. Code art. 2025. • For example, the record owner of real property may acknowledge in a counterletter that another person actually owns the property; the counterletter may then be used when the property is to be reconveyed after a period. A counterletter can have no effect against a third party acting in good faith. See *simulated contract* under CONTRACT.

countermand (kown-tər-mand), *n.* (16c) **1.** A contradictory command that overrides or annuls a previous one. **2.** An action that has the effect of voiding something previously ordered; a revocation. — **countermand** (kown-tər-**mand** *or* **kown-**), *vb.*

counteroffer, *n.* (18c) *Contracts.* An offeree's new offer that varies the terms of the original offer and that ordinarily rejects and terminates the original offer. • A late or defective acceptance is considered a counteroffer. See MIRROR-IMAGE RULE. — **counteroffer,** *vb.* — **counterofferor,** *n.*

counterpart. (15c) **1.** In conveyancing, a corresponding part of an instrument <the other half of the indenture — the counterpart — could not be found>. **2.** One of two or more copies or duplicates of a legal instrument <this lease may be executed in any number of counterparts, each of which is considered an original>.

"Formerly 'part' was used as the opposite of 'counterpart,' in respect to covenants executed in duplicate, but now each copy is called a 'counterpart.'" 2 Stewart Rapalje & Robert L. Lawrence, *A Dictionary of American and English Law* 927 (1883).

"Counterparts are not nowadays written on the same parchment, but that which is executed by the grantor of an interest is called the '*original*,' while that which is executed by the party to whom the interest passes — for example, a lessee — is called the '*counterpart*.'" G.C. Cheshire, *Modern Law of Real Property* 674 (3d ed. 1933).

counterpart writ. See WRIT.

counterparty. One's opposite number, esp. in a transaction; the party with whom one is consummating a contract.

counterplea. (16c) *Hist.* An answer or replication to a plea whereby arguments are made why the plea should not be admitted.

"Questions arising upon the right to oyer are now generally settled upon application to the court or a judge. But this is not the only course; for if a party demands oyer, in a case where, upon the face of the pleading, his adversary conceives it to be not demandable, the latter may *demur*; or if he has any matter of fact to allege as a ground why the oyer cannot be demanded, he may *plead* such matter. If he pleads, the allegation is called a *counter-plea to the oyer*; all pleadings of this incidental kind, diverging from the main series of the allegations, being termed *counter-pleas*. Again, on the counter-plea, in all these cases, there may happen to be a replication, and other subsequent pleadings; and so the parties may come to *issue* in law or in fact on this collateral subject, in the same manner as upon any principal matter in controversy." Henry John Stephen, *A Treatise on the Principles of Pleading in Civil Actions* 78–79 (Samuel Williston ed., 5th ed. 1895).

counterpromise, *n.* (18c) A promise made in exchange for another party's promise <a promise supported by a counterpromise is binding in its inception>. See *bilateral contract* under CONTRACT. — **counterpromise,** *vb.*

counter-roll. (17c) *Hist.* A record kept by an officer as a check on another officer's record, esp. the rolls maintained by a sheriff and a coroner.

countersign, *vb.* (16c) To write one's own name next to someone else's to verify the other signer's identity. — **countersignature,** *n.*

countersuit. See COUNTERCLAIM.

counterterrorism. (1943) The individual and collective measures taken to combat terrorism in all its manifestations. See TERRORISM.

countertrade. (1978) A type of international trade in which purchases made by an importing country are linked to offsetting purchases made by the exporting country.

"Countertrade is barter in modern clothes. It developed rapidly as a form of doing business with the USSR and Eastern European nations in the 1970s and 1980s, before the major economic and political reforms tended to diminish its emphasis as a means of doing business." Ralph H. Folsom & Michael W. Gordon, *International Business Transactions* § 2.1, at 46 (1995).

countervailable subsidy. See SUBSIDY (2).

countervailing duty. See DUTY (4).

countervailing equity. See EQUITY (5).

counter will. See *mutual will* under WILL.

counteur. See COUNTER.

countez (**kawn**-teez). [Law French] *Hist.* A direction given by a clerk of a court to a crier, after a jury was sworn, to count the jury members.

> "Of this ignorance we may see daily instances, in the abuse of two legal terms of ancient French; one, the prologue to all proclamations, '*oyez*, or hear ye,' which is generally pronounced most unmeaningly, 'O yes:' the other, a more pardonable mistake, viz., when a jury are all sworn, the officer bids the crier number them, for which the word in law-french is, '*countez*;' but we now hear it pronounced in very good English, 'count these.'" 4 William Blackstone, *Commentaries on the Laws of England* 334 n.s (1769).

Counting House of the King's Household. See BOARD OF GREEN CLOTH.

countor. See COUNTER.

country. (14c) **1.** A country or political state; STATE (1). **2.** The territory of such a country or state.

county. (14c) The largest territorial division for local government within a state, generally considered to be a political subdivision and a quasi-corporation. • Every county exists as a result of a sovereign act of legislation, either constitutional or statutory, separating it from the rest of the state as an integral part of its territory and establishing it as one of the primary divisions of the state for purposes of civil administration. — Abbr. co.

> "A county is a part of the realm, intirely governed by one sheriff under the king, but all subject to the general government of the realm; and therefore every county is as it were an intire body of itself, so that upon a feoffment of lands in many towns in one county, livery of seisin made in one parcel in any one of the towns in the name of all, sufficeth for all the lands in all the other towns within the same county: but upon a feoffment of lands in divers counties, there must be livery of seisin in every county." Henry Finch, *Law, or a Discourse Thereof* 79 (1759).

▸ **foreign county.** (16c) Any county separate from that of a county where matters arising in the former county are called into question, though both may lie within the same state or country.

county agent. See *juvenile officer* under OFFICER (1).

county attorney. (18c) An attorney who represents a county in civil matters and, in some jurisdictions, prosecutes criminal offenders.

county auditor. See AUDITOR.

county bond. See BOND (3).

county commissioner. See COMMISSIONER.

county court. See COURT.

county judge. See JUDGE.

county officer. See OFFICER (1).

county palatine (**pal**-ə-tɪn *or* -tin). (15c) *Hist. English law.* A county in which the lord held certain royal privileges, such as the right to pardon a felon or to have indictments recite that offenses were committed against the lord's — rather than the king's — peace. • In England, there were three such counties: Chester, Durham, and Lancaster. The separate legal systems in these counties were slowly eliminated; the last vestiges of a separate system were abolished by the Courts Act (1971). Cf. *proprietary government* under GOVERNMENT (3).

> "The counties palatine were Chester, Durham, and Lancaster. Whatever may be the precise date at which these counties became 'Palatine,' it seems likely that there was in Saxon times a jurisdiction equivalent to that of the Palatine earl, and originating in usurpation and necessity. The Central Government was too far away both before and after the Conquest to control effectually the administration of the Marches, which were always turbulent and lawless districts." A.T. Carter, *A History of English Legal Institutions* 192 (4th ed. 1910).

county property. (18c) Property that a county is authorized to acquire, hold, or sell.

county purpose. (1855) An objective pursued by a county; esp., one that a county levies taxes for.

county seat. (1831) The municipality where a county's principal offices are located. — Also termed *county town.*

county supervisor. See *county commissioner* under COMMISSIONER.

county town. See COUNTY SEAT.

county warrant. See WARRANT (3).

coup d'état (koo day-**tah**). [French "stroke of state"] (17c) A sudden, usu. violent, change of government through seizure of power; a quick and often violent attempt by a group to take control of the government. — Often shortened to *coup.*

coupon (**koo**-pon). (1822) An interest or dividend certificate that is attached to another instrument, such as a bond, and that may be detached and separately presented for payment of a definite sum at a specified time. — Also termed *interest coupon.*

coupon bond. See BOND (3).

coupon interest rate. See *coupon rate* under INTEREST RATE.

coupon note. See NOTE (1).

coupon rate. See INTEREST RATE.

coupon security. See SECURITY (4).

coupon yield. See YIELD.

Cour de Cassation. See COURT OF CASSATION.

courier. (14c) A messenger, esp. a person or business employed to transport and deliver documents, correspondence, parcels, and other items. • In international law, the term denotes a messenger duly authorized by a sending state to deliver a diplomatic pouch.

▸ **diplomatic courier.** A courier employed by a national government to safeguard, transport, and deliver a diplomatic pouch. • The courier is granted diplomatic immunity until the job is completed. See DIPLOMATIC POUCH; DIPLOMATIC IMMUNITY (1).

course of business. (17c) The normal routine in managing a trade or business. — Also termed *ordinary course of business; regular course of business; ordinary course; regular course.*

course of dealing. (16c) An established pattern of conduct between parties in a series of transactions (e.g., multiple sales of goods over a period of years). • If a dispute arises, the parties' course of dealing can be used as evidence of how they intended to carry out the transaction. Cf. COURSE OF PERFORMANCE; *trade usage* under USAGE (1).

course of employment. (17c) Events that occur or circumstances that exist as a part of one's employment; esp., the time during which an employee furthers an employer's goals through employer-mandated directives. Cf. SCOPE OF EMPLOYMENT; ZONE OF EMPLOYMENT.

course of performance. (18c) A sequence of previous performance by either party after an agreement has been entered into, when a contract involves repeated occasions for performance and both parties know the nature of the performance and have an opportunity to object to it. • A course of performance accepted or acquiesced in without objection is relevant to determining the meaning of the agreement. Cf. COURSE OF DEALING; *trade usage* under USAGE (1).

course of trade. See *trade usage* under USAGE (1).

court, *n.* (12c) **1.** A tribunal constituted to administer justice; esp., a governmental body consisting of one or more judges who sit to adjudicate disputes <a question of law for the court to decide>. **2.** The judge or judges who sit on such a tribunal <the court asked the parties to approach the bench>. **3.** A legislative assembly <in Massachusetts, the General Court is the legislature>. **4.** A place where justice is judicially administered; the locale for legal proceedings <an out-of-court statement>. **5.** The building where the judge or judges convene to adjudicate disputes and administer justice <the lawyers agreed to meet at the court at 8:00 a.m.>. — Also termed (in senses 1 & 2) *law court*; (in sense 5) *courthouse*.

▸ **admiralty court.** See ADMIRALTY (1).

▸ **Appeal Court.** See COURT OF APPEAL.

▸ **appeals court.** See *appellate court.*

▸ **appellate court.** (18c) A court with jurisdiction to review decisions of lower courts or administrative agencies. — Also termed *appeals court*; *appeal court*; *court of appeals*; *court of appeal*; *court of review.*

> "Appellate courts are among the most important institutions of governance in the United States. Through their review of trial court and administrative agency decisions they ensure that those bodies function lawfully and that litigants receive justice under law. Moreover, they provide authoritative interpretations of statutory and constitutional provisions and control the shaping of the common law in response to ever-changing circumstances; they are thus major sources of law." Daniel John Meador & Jordana Simone Bernstein, *Appellate Courts in the United States* v (1994).

▸ **Archdeacon's court.** See COURT OF ARCHDEACON.

▸ **Article I Court.** See ARTICLE I COURT.

▸ **Article III Court.** See ARTICLE III COURT.

▸ **Bail Court.** See BAIL COURT.

▸ **Bankruptcy Court.** See BANKRUPTCY COURT.

▸ **baronial court.** (18c) *Hist.* A feudal court established by the owner of extensive lands held directly of the king under military tenure.

▸ **base court.** (16c) *Archaic.* An inferior court.

▸ **basement court.** See BASEMENT COURT.

▸ **bedside court.** (1924) *Rare.* A judicial proceeding convened at the bedside of a litigant or witness too sick or physically incapacitated to attend the normal place for such a proceeding.

▸ **bishop's court.** See BISHOP'S COURT.

▸ **borough court.** See BOROUGH COURT.

▸ **business court.** (1914) A court that handles exclusively commercial litigation. • In the late 20th century, business courts emerged as a way to unclog the general dockets and to dispose of commercial cases more efficiently and consistently. — Also termed *commercial court*; *commercial division.*

▸ **byrlaw court.** See BYRLAW COURT.

▸ **Central Criminal Court.** See CENTRAL CRIMINAL COURT.

▸ **children's court.** See *juvenile court* (1).

▸ **church court.** See *ecclesiastical court.*

▸ **circuit court.** (17c) **1.** A court usu. having jurisdiction over several counties, districts, or states, and holding sessions in all those areas. See CIRCUIT; CIRCUIT-RIDING. **2.** *English law.* A court that meets in small towns within a particular area whenever a judge visits from a larger town. **3.** UNITED STATES COURT OF APPEALS.

▸ **city court.** See *municipal court.*

▸ **civil court.** (16c) A court with jurisdiction over noncriminal cases. — Abbr. Civ. Ct.

▸ **claims court.** See *court of claims.*

▸ **closed court.** See CLOSED COURT.

▸ **Commerce Court.** *Hist.* A federal court that had the power to review and enforce determinations of the Interstate Commerce Commission. • The Commerce Court existed from 1910 to 1913.

▸ **commercial court.** (1831) **1.** See *business court.* **2.** *English law.* A court that hears business disputes under simplified procedures designed to expedite the trials. • This court was created in 1971 as part of the Queen's Bench Division of the High Court of Justice.

▸ **commissary court.** (17c) **1.** A court of general ecclesiastical jurisdiction presided over by four commissioners appointed by the Crown from the Faculty of Advocates. **2.** *Scots law.* A sheriff or county court that appoints and confirms the executors of decedents who have personal property in Scotland. **3.** *Hist. Scots law.* A supreme court in which matters of probate and divorce were decided. • This court was established in Edinburgh in 1563 to hear cases that had previously come under the jurisdiction of the ecclesiastical commissary court. It was absorbed by the Court of Session in 1836.

▸ **commissioner's court.** (1847) In certain states, a court having jurisdiction over county affairs and often functioning more as a managerial group than as a judicial tribunal.

▸ **common pleas court.** See COURT OF COMMON PLEAS.

▸ **commonwealth court.** (1885) **1.** In some states, a court of general jurisdiction. **2.** In Pennsylvania, a court that hears suits against the state and reviews decisions of state agencies and officials.

▸ **competent court.** See *court of competent jurisdiction.*

▸ **conciliation court.** See *small-claims court.*

▸ **consistory court.** See CONSISTORY COURT.

▸ **constitutional court.** (1823) **1.** A court named or described and expressly protected in a constitution; esp., ARTICLE III COURT. **2.** A court whose jurisdiction is solely or primarily over claims that legislation (and sometimes executive action) is inconsistent with a country's constitution. • Germany, for example, has state constitutional courts and a Federal Constitutional Court.

▸ **consular court** (**kon**-sə-lər). (18c) A court held by the consul of one country within the territory of another. • Consular courts are created by treaty, and their jurisdiction is usu. limited to civil cases. The last of the U.S. consular courts (Morocco) was abolished in 1956.

▸ **coroner's court.** (17c) *English law.* A common-law court that holds an inquisition if a person died a violent or unnatural death, died in prison, or died suddenly when the cause is not known. • The court also has jurisdiction over treasure trove.

▸ **corporation court.** (1830) In some jurisdictions, a court that serves an incorporated municipality. See *municipal court.*

▸ **county court.** (16c) **1.** A court with powers and jurisdiction dictated by a state constitution or statute. • The county court may govern administrative or judicial matters, depending on state law. — Also termed *parish court*; (in Latin) *curia comitatus.* **2.** See *probate court.*

▸ **court above.** (17c) A court to which a case is appealed. — Also termed *higher court*; *upper court.*

▸ **court a quo** (ay **kwoh**). (1845) A court from which a case has been removed or appealed.

▸ **court baron.** See COURT BARON.

▸ **court below.** (17c) A trial court or intermediate appellate court from which a case is appealed. — Also termed *lower court.*

▸ **court christian.** See *ecclesiastical court.*

▸ **court de facto.** See *de facto court* (1).

▸ **court merchant.** (17c) *Hist.* A court of limited jurisdiction that decided controversies arising between merchants, dealers, shipmasters, supercargoes, and other, usu. transient, people connected with trade. • Cases were usu. tried before a jury of merchants.

▸ **court not of record.** (1829) An inferior court that is not required to routinely make a record of each proceeding and usu. does not.

▸ **court of appeals.** (17c) **1.** An intermediate appellate court. — Also termed (as in California and England) *court of appeal.* See *appellate court.* **2.** In New York and Maryland, the highest appellate court within the jurisdiction. See also COURT OF APPEAL.

▸ **court of chivalry.** See HIGH COURT OF CHIVALRY.

▸ **court of claims.** (17c) A court with the authority to hear claims made against a state (or its political subdivision) for cases in which the state has waived sovereign immunity. — Also termed *claims court.* See UNITED STATES COURT OF FEDERAL CLAIMS.

▸ **court of competent jurisdiction.** (18c) A court that has the power and authority to do a particular act; one recognized by law as possessing the right to adjudicate a controversy. — Also termed *competent court.*

▸ **court of domestic relations.** See *family court.*

▸ **court of equity.** (16c) A court that (1) has jurisdiction in equity, (2) administers and decides controversies in accordance with the rules, principles, and precedents of equity, and (3) follows the forms and procedures of chancery. Cf. *court of law.*

▸ **court of final appeal.** (18c) **1.** See *court of last resort.* **2.** *Eccles. law.* (*cap.*) JUDICIAL COMMITTEE OF THE PRIVY COUNCIL.

▸ **court of first instance.** See *trial court.*

▸ **court of general jurisdiction.** (18c) A court having unlimited or nearly unlimited trial jurisdiction in both civil and criminal cases. — Also termed *general-jurisdiction court.*

▸ **court of impeachment.** See COURT FOR THE TRIAL OF IMPEACHMENTS.

▸ **court of inquiry.** (17c) **1.** *Hist.* In English law, a court appointed by the monarch to ascertain whether it was proper to use extreme measures against someone who had been court-martialed. **2.** *Hist.* In American law, an agency created under articles of war and vested with the power to investigate the nature of a transaction or accusation of an officer or soldier. **3.** In some jurisdictions, a court in which a magistrate examines witnesses in relation to any offense that the magistrate has a good-faith reason to believe was committed. **4.** *English law.* A group of people chosen to discover the facts about some event, such as a serious accident.

▸ **court of instance.** See *trial court.*

▸ **court of last resort.** (17c) The court having the authority to handle the final appeal of a case, such as the U.S. Supreme Court.

▸ **court of law.** (16c) **1.** Broadly, any judicial tribunal that administers the laws of a state or country. **2.** A court that proceeds according to the course of the common law, and that is governed by its rules and principles. Cf. *court of equity.*

▸ **court of limited jurisdiction.** (18c) A court with jurisdiction over only certain types of cases, or cases in which the amount in controversy is limited.

▸ **court of ordinary.** See *probate court.*

▸ **court of original jurisdiction.** (18c) A court where an action is initiated and first heard.

▸ **court of record.** (18c) **1.** A court that is required to keep a record of its proceedings. • The court's records are presumed accurate and cannot be collaterally impeached. See OF RECORD (2).

> "The distinction that we still draw between 'courts of record' and courts that are 'not of record' takes us back to early times when the king asserts that his own word as all that has taken place in his presence is incontestable. This privilege he communicates to his own special court; its testimony as to all that is done before it is conclusive. If any question arises as to what happened on a previous occasion, the justices decide this by recording or bearing record (*recordantur, portant recordum*). Other courts . . . may and, upon occasion, must bear record; but their records are not irrefragable . . . . We easily slip into saying that a court whose record is incontrovertible is a court which has record (*habet recordum*) or is a court of record, while a court whose record may be disputed has no record (*non habet recordum*) and is no court of record." 2 Frederick Pollock & Frederic W. Maitland, *History of English Law Before the Time of Edward I* 669 (2d ed. 1899).

2. A court that may fine and imprison people for contempt.

> "A court of record is, strictly speaking, a court which has power to fine and imprison." Lancelot Feilding Everest, *Everest and Strode's Law of Estoppel* 13 (1923).

▸ **court of review.** See *appellate court.*

▸ **court of special jurisdiction.** See *limited court.*

▸ **court of special session.** (1813) A court that has no stated term and is not continuous, but is organized only for hearing particular cases, esp. criminal cases. — Also termed *court of special sessions.*

> "By a recent statute, Courts of Special Sessions of the Peace, shall be held by a single Magistrate now authorized to sit as a member of a Court of Special Sessions; and all offences triable before such Courts, may be tried before such single Magistrate with or without a jury, at the election of the prisoner; and all provisions of law applicable to the powers, duties and proceedings of such Courts, shall apply to such Magistrate and the proceedings before him. A court of Special Sessions may be formed, either by a Judge of the County Courts, or by a Justice of the Peace of the same county." J. Benedict, *Benedict's Treatise: Containing a Summary of the Jurisdiction, Powers, and Duties of Justices of the Peace in the State of New York* 385 (2d ed. 1847).

▸ **court of summary jurisdiction.** See *magistrate's court.*

▸ **criminal court.** (17c) A court with jurisdiction over criminal matters.

▸ **Crown Court.** See CROWN COURT.

▸ **Dean of Guild Court.** See DEAN OF GUILD COURT.

▸ **de facto court** (di **fak**-toh). (1870) **1.** A court functioning under the authority of a statute that is later adjudged to be invalid. — Also termed *court de facto.* **2.** A court established and acting under the authority of a *de facto* government.

▸ **dependency court.** (1950) A court having jurisdiction over matters involving abused and neglected children, foster care, the termination of parental rights, and (sometimes) adoption.

▸ **diocesan court** (dɪ-**ahs**-i-sin). (18c) *Eccles. law.* A court exercising general or limited jurisdiction (as determined by patent, local custom, or legislation) of matters arising within a bishop's diocese. • Diocesan courts include the consistory court, the courts of the commissaries, and the courts of archdeacons.

▸ **district court.** (18c) **1.** A trial court having general jurisdiction within its judicial district. — Abbr. D.C. **2.** *Scots law.* A local court, usu. staffed by lay magistrates, with jurisdiction over petty crimes.

▸ **divided court.** See DIVIDED COURT.

▸ **divisional court.** (18c) An English court made up of two or more judges from the High Court of Justice sitting in special cases that cannot be disposed of by one judge. • Each division of the High Court has a divisional court, e.g., the Divisional Court of the Family Division. With the exception of the Divisional Court of the Chancery Division, which has jurisdiction to review land-registration appeals from the county court, almost all judicial appeals are from decisions of a magistrates' court. The Divisional Court of the Queen's Bench Division hears appeals from the Crown Court or the magistrates' court by way of case stated in criminal prosecutions, which is the most frequent use of a divisional court.

▸ **domestic court.** (1801) **1.** A court having jurisdiction at the place of a party's residence or domicile. **2.** See *family court.*

▸ **domestic-relations court.** See *family court.*

▸ **drug court.** (1971) A court that hears cases against nonviolent adults and juveniles, who are often first-time offenders and who are usu. charged with possession of a controlled substance or with committing a minor drug-related crime. • Drug courts focus on treatment rather than on incarceration. Cf. *problem-solving court.*

▸ **ecclesiastical court** (i-klee-zee-**as**-ti-kəl). (16c) **1.** A religious court that hears matters concerning a particular religion. **2.** In England, a court having jurisdiction over matters concerning the Church of England (the established church) as well as the duties and rights of the people serving it, but whose modern jurisdiction is limited to matters of ecclesiastical discipline and church property. — Also termed *church court*; *court christian*; *spiritual court*; (in Latin) *christianitatis curia*; *curia christianitatis.*

> "The ecclesiastical courts exercised a jurisdiction which played a part of the development of the English legal system, and their work was not confined to controlling the clergy and doctrines of the Church. The jurisdiction of these courts was of particular significance before the Reformation, but, in certain matters and especially in matrimonial causes and the law of succession to property on death (testate and intestate succession), it remained of importance till the middle of the nineteenth century." 1 A.K.R. Kiralfy, *Potter's Historical Introduction to English Law and Its Institutions* 211 (4th ed. 1958).

▸ **en banc court.** See *full court.*

▸ **examining court.** (18c) A lower court (usu. presided over by a magistrate) that determines probable cause and sets bail at a preliminary hearing in a criminal case.

▸ **family court.** (1923) A court having jurisdiction over matters involving divorce, child custody and support, paternity, domestic violence, and other family-law issues. — Also termed *family-law court*; *domestic-relations court*; *court of domestic relations*; *domestic court.*

▸ **federal circuit court.** UNITED STATES COURT OF APPEALS.

▸ **federal court.** (18c) A court having federal jurisdiction, including the U.S. Supreme Court, circuit courts of appeals, district courts, bankruptcy courts, and tax courts. — Also termed *United States court.*

▸ **foreign court.** (16c) **1.** The court of a foreign country. **2.** The court of another state.

▸ **forty-days court.** See COURT OF ATTACHMENTS.

▸ **franchise court.** See FRANCHISE COURT.

▸ **full court.** (16c) A court session that is attended by all the court's judges; an en banc court. — Also termed *full bench.*

▸ **General Court.** See GENERAL COURT.

▸ **general-jurisdiction court.** See *court of general jurisdiction.*

▸ **High Commission Court.** See COURT OF HIGH COMMISSION.

▸ **High Court.** **1.** See HIGH COURT OF JUSTICE. **2.** See HIGH COURT OF JUSTICIARY.

▸ **High Court of Admiralty.** See HIGH COURT OF ADMIRALTY.

▸ **High Court of Chivalry.** See HIGH COURT OF CHIVALRY.

▸ **High Court of Delegates.** See COURT OF DELEGATES.

▸ **High Court of Errors and Appeals.** See COURT OF ERRORS AND APPEALS.

▸ **High Court of Justice.** See HIGH COURT OF JUSTICE.

▸ **High Court of Justiciary.** See HIGH COURT OF JUSTICIARY.

▸ **higher court.** See *court above.*

▸ **highest court.** (16c) The court of last resort in a particular jurisdiction; a court whose decision is final and cannot be appealed because no higher court exists to consider the matter. • The U.S. Supreme Court, for example, is the highest federal court.

▸ **hot court.** (1972) A court, esp. an appellate court, that is familiar with the briefs filed in the case, and therefore with the issues, before oral argument. • Typically, a hot court controls the oral argument with its questioning, as opposed to listening passively to set presentations of counsel.

▸ **housing court.** (1953) A court dealing primarily with landlord-and-tenant matters, including disputes over maintenance, lease terms, and building and fire codes.

▸ **hundred court.** (16c) *Hist. English law.* In England, a larger court baron, held for all inhabitants of a particular hundred rather than a manor, in which the free suitors were the judges (jurors) and the steward the register. • A hundred court was not a court of record, and it resembled a court-baron in all respects except for its larger territorial jurisdiction. The last hundred court was abolished in 1971. — Also termed *hundred moot.* See COURT BARON.

▸ **immigration court.** (*usu. cap.*) An administrative court in the U.S. Department of Justice that hears removal and deportation proceedings. • The Board of Immigration Appeals hears appeals from this court. See BOARD OF IMMIGRATION APPEALS.

▸ **impeachment court.** See COURT FOR THE TRIAL OF IMPEACHMENTS.

▸ **inferior court.** (17c) **1.** Any court that is subordinate to the chief appellate tribunal within a judicial system. **2.** A court of special, limited, or statutory jurisdiction, whose record must show the existence of jurisdiction in any given case to give its ruling presumptive validity. — Also termed *lower court.*

▸ **inquisitorial court.** (18c) A court in which the inquisitorial system prevails.

> "We should remember that in the 'inquisitorial court' the roles of prosecutor, defender, and judge are combined in one person or group of persons. It is no accident that such a court commonly holds its sessions in secret. The usual explanation for this is that the methods by which it extracts confessions cannot stand public scrutiny. But the reason runs deeper. The methods employed by an inquisitorial court, even if open to the public, could scarcely be a secret of meaningful observation by an outsider. It is only when the roles of prosecutor, defender, and judge are separated that a process of decision can take on an order and coherence that will make it understandable to an outside audience and convince that audience that all sides of the controversy have been considered." Lon L. Fuller, *Anatomy of the Law* 35–36 (1968).

▸ **instance court.** (1837) **1.** See *trial court.* **2.** *Hist. English law.* The admiralty court in England that exercised original jurisdiction in all cases except those involving prizes.

▸ **insular court.** (1901) A federal court with jurisdiction over U.S. island territories, such as the Virgin Islands.

▸ **intermediate court.** (1834) An appellate court that is below a court of last resort.

▸ **international court.** A body with jurisprudential authority created by treaty or by an international organization to hear and decide cases of international law.

▸ **International Court of Justice.** See INTERNATIONAL COURT OF JUSTICE.

▸ **International Criminal Court.** See INTERNATIONAL CRIMINAL COURT.

▸ **International Trade Court.** See UNITED STATES COURT OF INTERNATIONAL TRADE.

▸ **J.P. court.** See *justice court.*

▸ **justice court.** (16c) A court, presided over by a justice of the peace, that has jurisdiction to hear minor criminal cases, matters involving small amounts of money, or certain specified claims (such as forcible-entry-and-detainer suits). — Also termed *justice-of-the-peace court*; *J.P. court.*

▸ **juvenile court.** (1903) **1.** A court having jurisdiction over cases involving children under a specified age, usu. 18. • Illinois enacted the first statewide juvenile-court act in 1899. Today every state has a specialized juvenile or family court with exclusive original delinquency jurisdiction. — Also termed *children's court.* **2.** A court having special jurisdiction over orphaned, delinquent, dependent, and neglected children. • This type of juvenile court is created by statute and derives its power from the specific wording of the statute, usu. having exclusive original jurisdiction over matters involving abuse and neglect, adoption, status offenses, and delinquency. Generally, juvenile courts are special courts of a paternal nature that have jurisdiction over the care, custody, and control of children (as defined by the statute). The jurisdiction of the juvenile court is exercised as between the state (for the child) and the parents of the child and is not concerned with a custody controversy that does not affect the morale, health, or welfare of the child. A juvenile court is not a criminal court. The primary concern of a juvenile court is the child's immediate welfare. See UNIFORM JUVENILE COURT ACT.

▸ **kangaroo court.** (1849) **1.** A self-appointed tribunal or mock court in which the principles of law and justice are disregarded, perverted, or parodied. • Kangaroo courts may be assembled by various groups, such as prisoners in a jail (to settle disputes between inmates) and players on a baseball team (to "punish" teammates who commit fielding errors). **2.** A court or tribunal characterized by unauthorized or irregular procedures, esp. so as to render a fair proceeding impossible. **3.** A sham legal proceeding. • The term's origin is uncertain, but it appears to be an Americanism. It has been traced to 1853 in the American West. "Kangaroo" might refer to the illogical leaps between "facts" and conclusions, or to the hapless defendant's quick bounce from court to gallows.

▸ **King's Court.** See CURIA REGIS (1).

▸ **land court.** A court having jurisdiction over land-related matters, including (1) exclusive original jurisdiction of applications for registration of land titles and related questions, writs of entry and petitions to clear title to real estate, petitions to determine the validity and extent of municipal zoning ordinances, bylaws, and regulations, and proceedings for foreclosure and redemption from tax titles; (2) original concurrent jurisdiction of declaratory judgment proceedings, shared with the supreme judicial, superior, and probate courts; and (3) original concurrent equity jurisdiction in land-related matters, except for cases of specific performance of land contracts. • Land courts today exist in the United States only in Massachusetts and Hawaii. — Also termed (Fr.) *justice foncière.*

▸ **landed-estates court.** (1858) *Hist. English law.* A statutorily established tribunal to dispose of encumbered real estate more promptly and easily than could be accomplished through the ordinary judicial machinery. • This type of court was first established in Ireland by acts of 11 & 12 Vict., ch. 48 and 12 & 13 Vict., ch. 77. The purpose of the court was to enable the owner, or any lessee of an unexpired term of 63 years or less, of encumbered land to apply to commissioners to direct a sale. The court served as a court of record and was called the Incumbered Estates Court. A later act abolished that court and created a new permanent tribunal called the Landed Estates Court. 21 & 22 Vict., ch. 72.

▸ **legatine court.** (17c) A court held by a papal legate and having ecclesiastical jurisdiction.

▸ **legislative court.** (1828) A court created by a statute, as opposed to one created by a constitution. — Also termed (in federal law) *Article I court.*

▸ **levy court.** (18c) *Hist.* A court in the District of Columbia that exercised many of the functions typical of county commissioners or county supervisors in the states, such as constructing and repairing roads and bridges.

▸ **limited court.** (18c) A court having special jurisdiction conferred by statute, such as a probate court. — Also termed *court of special jurisdiction.*

▸ **liquidation court.** (1947) Any court in which a liquidation proceeding takes place.

▸ **local court.** (18c) A court whose jurisdiction is limited to a particular territory, such as a state, municipal, or county court.

▸ **lord mayor's court.** (17c) *Hist.* A court of law and equity that had jurisdiction in civil cases arising within the city of London and acted as the appellate court from the Chamberlain Court. • It was abolished by the Court Act of 1971.

▸ **lower court. 1.** See *court below.* **2.** See *inferior court.*

▸ **magistrate's court** (**maj**-i-strayts *or* -strits). (1904) **1.** A court with jurisdiction over minor criminal offenses. • Such a court also has the power to bind over for trial persons accused of more serious offenses. — Also termed *police court.* **2.** A court with limited jurisdiction over minor criminal and civil matters. — Sometimes spelled (esp. in England) *magistrates' court.* — Also termed (in England) *court of petty sessions*; *court of summary jurisdiction.*

▸ **maritime court.** See ADMIRALTY (1).

▸ **mayor's court.** (18c) A municipal court in which the mayor presides as the judge, with jurisdiction over minor criminal (and sometimes civil) matters, traffic offenses, and the like.

▸ **military court.** (17c) A court that has jurisdiction over members of the armed forces and that enforces the Code of Military Justice. See CODE OF MILITARY JUSTICE.

▸ **military court of inquiry.** (1822) A military court that has special and limited jurisdiction and that is convened to investigate specific matters and, traditionally, to determine whether further procedures are warranted. 10 USCA § 935.

▸ **moot court.** See MOOT COURT.

▸ **municipal court.** (17c) A court having jurisdiction (usu. civil and criminal) over cases arising within the municipality in which it sits. • A municipal court's civil jurisdiction to issue a judgment is often limited to a small amount, and its criminal jurisdiction is limited to petty offenses. — Also termed *city court.*

▸ **naturalization court.** See NATURALIZATION COURT.

▸ **nisi prius court.** See NISI PRIUS.

▸ **open court.** See OPEN COURT.

▸ **ordinary's court.** See *probate court.*

▸ **orphan's court.** See *probate court.*

▸ **Palace Court.** See PALACE COURT.

▸ **parish court.** See *county court* (1).

▸ **peacemaker's court.** (1909) *American Indian law.* A tribal court that adjudicates, arbitrates, or mediates some disputes, usu. according to traditional and statutory tribal law.

▸ **people's court.** See PEOPLE'S COURT.

▸ **piepowder court.** See PIEPOWDER COURT.

▸ **police court.** See *magistrate's court* (1).

▸ **policy court.** An appellate court, usu. a court of last resort, that must consider a decision's effects not only on the litigants but also on public policy.

▸ **practice court. 1.** See MOOT COURT. **2.** (*cap.*) See BAIL COURT.

▸ **prerogative court.** (18c) In New Jersey, a probate court. See *probate court.*

▸ **pretorial court.** (1841) *Hist.* A 17th-century Maryland court that had jurisdiction over capital and other serious crimes. • It consisted of three judges: the colony's lord proprietor or his lieutenant-general, the Secretary or Register of the Council of State, and one other member of the Council.

▸ **prize court.** (18c) A court having jurisdiction to adjudicate the captures made at sea in time of war. See PRIZE (2). Cf. COURT OF APPEALS IN CASES OF CAPTURE.

▸ **probate court.** (18c) A court with the power to declare wills valid or invalid, to oversee the administration of estates and (in some states) to appoint guardians and approve the adoption of minors. — Also termed *surrogate's court*; *surrogate court*; *court of ordinary*; *ordinary's court*; *county court*; *orphan's court* (o.c.). See PROBATE.

▸ **problem-solving court.** (2000) A specialized court that matches community resources to defendants and litigants whose problems or cases may benefit from those resources. • In criminal cases, a problem-solving court tries to promote solutions to underlying behavioral problems that may lead to misconduct by providing treatment rather than imprisonment. For example, it may match offenders with resources for drug-abuse, domestic-violence, or mental-health treatment, often with close court supervision. In civil cases, a problem-solving court may help the parties try to resolve disputes through counseling or mediation rather than litigation. — Also termed *boutique court*. See BOUTIQUE COURT. Cf. *drug court*.

▸ **provisional court.** (1856) A federal court with jurisdiction and powers governed by the order granting its authority, such as a temporary court established in a conquered or occupied territory.

▸ **Quarter Sessions Court.** See COURT OF GENERAL QUARTER SESSIONS OF THE PEACE.

▸ **recorder's court.** (1827) A court having jurisdiction over felony cases. • This court exists in only a few jurisdictions, such as Michigan, where the recorder's court hears felony cases arising within the Detroit city limits.

▸ **register's court.** (1810) *Hist.* A probate court in Pennsylvania or Delaware. See *probate court*.

▸ **rogue court.** (1993) A court that fails to apply controlling law in making its decisions.

▸ **sheriff's court.** (17c) *Scots law.* The principal inferior court in Scotland, having both civil and criminal jurisdiction. — Also termed *sheriff court*.

▸ **small-claims court.** (1923) A court that informally and expeditiously adjudicates claims that seek damages below a specified monetary amount, usu. claims to collect small accounts or debts. — Also termed *small-debts court*; *conciliation court*.

▸ **spiritual court.** See *ecclesiastical court*.

▸ **state court.** (18c) A court of the state judicial system, as opposed to a federal court.

▸ **superior court.** (18c) **1.** In some states, a trial court of general jurisdiction. **2.** In Pennsylvania, an intermediate court between the trial court and the chief appellate court.

▸ **supreme court.** See SUPREME COURT.

▸ **Supreme Court of the United States.** See SUPREME COURT OF THE UNITED STATES.

▸ **Supreme Judicial Court.** (18c) The highest appellate court in Maine and Massachusetts.

▸ **surrogate's court.** See *probate court*.

▸ **tax court.** See TAX COURT.

▸ **teen court.** (1968) A group of teenagers who (1) hear cases involving juveniles, usu. first-time offenders, who have acknowledged their guilt or responsibility, and (2) impose sanctions within a fixed range, usu. involving counseling, community service, or restitution. • Some local jurisdictions in more than half the states have provided for this type of tribunal. The juvenile offender consents to the assessment of punishment by this jury of peers. The American Bar Association encourages the formation of these kinds of courts. — Also termed *youth court*.

▸ **Teind Court.** See TEIND COURT.

▸ **territorial court.** (1814) A U.S. court established in a U.S. territory (such as the Virgin Islands) and serving as both a federal and state court. • The Constitution authorizes Congress to create such court. U.S. Const. art. IV, § 3, cl. 2.

▸ **three-judge court.** (1894) A court made up of three judges; esp., a panel of three federal judges convened to hear a trial in which a statute is challenged on constitutional grounds. • Three-judge courts were virtually abolished in 1976 when Congress restricted their jurisdiction to constitutional challenges to congressional reapportionments. Occasionally, Congress creates three-judge courts in special legislation, as with the 2002 campaign-finance law. Appeals from a three-judge court go directly to the Supreme Court. *See* 28 USCA § 2284.

▸ **traffic court.** (1917) A court with jurisdiction over prosecutions for parking violations and infractions of road law.

▸ **trial court.** (18c) A court of original jurisdiction where the evidence is first received and considered. — Also termed *court of first instance*; *instance court*; *court of instance*.

▸ **tribal court.** See TRIBAL COURT.

▸ **unified family court.** (1931) In some jurisdictions, a court that hears all family matters, including matters of divorce, juvenile delinquency, adoption, abuse and neglect, and criminal abuse. • A unified family court also hears matters typically heard in family court (in jurisdictions that have statutory family courts) or in courts of general jurisdiction, such as divorce, paternity, and emancipation proceedings. Proponents of unified family courts cite the benefits of having all family-related matters heard by one court — for instance, the benefit of having a child testify only once rather than forcing the child to testify in one court in a divorce proceeding, in a different court in criminal proceedings against an abuser, and in yet another in a civil proceeding initiated by Child Protective Services.

▸ **United States Claims Court.** See UNITED STATES COURT OF FEDERAL CLAIMS.

▸ **United States court.** See *federal court*.

▸ **United States Court of International Trade.** See UNITED STATES COURT OF INTERNATIONAL TRADE.

▸ **United States Customs Court.** See UNITED STATES CUSTOMS COURT.

▸ **United States District Court.** See UNITED STATES DISTRICT COURT.

▸ **United States Supreme Court.** See SUPREME COURT OF THE UNITED STATES.

▸ **United States Tax Court.** See TAX COURT, U.S.

▸ **upper court.** See *court above*.

▸ **vice-admiralty court.** See VICE-ADMIRALTY COURT.

▸ **Wood-Plea Court.** See WOOD-PLEA COURT.

▸ **World Court.** See INTERNATIONAL COURT OF JUSTICE.

▸ **youth court.** See *teen court*.

court administrator. See ADMINISTRATOR (1).

court-annexed ADR. See ALTERNATIVE DISPUTE RESOLUTION.

court-annexed arbitration. See ARBITRATION.

court-appointed attorney. See *assigned counsel* under COUNSEL.

court-appointed counsel. See *assigned counsel* under COUNSEL.

court-appointed expert. See *independent expert* under EXPERT.

court-appointed special advocate. (1977) A trained volunteer appointed by a court to represent the interests of a child in an abuse or neglect case. — Abbr. CASA. Cf. *guardian ad litem* under GUARDIAN (1).

Court Appointed Special Advocates. A federally funded program in which trained laypersons act on behalf of children in abuse and neglect cases. • The CASA program began in 1977 in Seattle, Washington. In 1989, the American Bar Association endorsed using a combination of CASA volunteers and attorneys in abuse and neglect cases. CASA volunteers are sanctioned by the ABA as permissible guardians ad litem. — Abbr. CASA.

court a quo. See COURT.

court baron. (16c) *Hist.* A manorial court that had jurisdiction over amounts in controversy of 40 shillings or less. • According to some authorities, the court baron developed into two courts: the customary court baron for disputes involving copyholders, and the court baron proper (also known as the freeholders' court baron), in which freeholders were allowed to hold court concerning minor disputes. — Also termed *freeholder's court baron.*

> "In Coke's day it was said that the lord of a manor had one court, 'a court baron,' for his freeholders and another court, 'a customary court,' for his copyholders, and that in the latter the lord or his steward was the judge. Now over his unfree men the lord had, according to the law of the king's court, almost unlimited power; short of maiming them he might do what he liked with them; and every tenant of an unfree tenement was a tenant at will. Nevertheless in the court rolls and the manuals for stewards which come to us from the thirteenth and fourteenth centuries we cannot discover two courts or two methods of constituting the court. Freeholders and serfs are said to owe suit to the same halimoot, and so far as we can see, the *curia* which pronounces judgment is always the same body." 1 Frederick Pollock & Frederic W. Maitland, *The History of English Law Before the Time of Edward I* 593 (2d ed. 1898).

court below. See COURT.

court calendar. (1852) A list of matters scheduled for trial or hearing; DOCKET (2).

court christian. See *ecclesiastical court* under COURT.

court clinic. (1921) A medical clinic, established for the benefit of the courts, to which a judge may send a defendant for psychiatric evaluation or, esp. in the case of a juvenile, to explore why the defendant committed the offense and what treatment is appropriate.

> "Court Clinics have developed in two ways: one, in which the clinic has its own social workers to take case histories and to investigate the past of the offenders, and the second is when the Clinic utilizes the probation department as historians and as therapists. In both types of clinics, a history is taken, appropriate psychological tests are given to the offender, with particular reference to his intelligence, and a physical examination and a psychiatric examination are made. Usually these clinics have a meeting in which the whole staff discuss the cases when a diagnosis is made and, finally a report is sent to the referring judge, informing him as to the probable reason why the offender has committed the offense, the appropriate treatment if any is necessary, and the probably outcome of the case if the treatment procedures recommended are carried out." *Encyclopedia of Criminology* 79–80 (Vernon C. Branham & Samuel B. Kutash eds., 1949).

court commissioner. See COMMISSIONER.

court costs. See COST (2).

court crier. See CRIER (1).

court day. See DAY.

court de facto. See *de facto court* (1) under COURT.

courtesan. (16c) **1.** A court mistress. **2.** A loose woman. **3.** A prostitute. — Also spelled *courtezan.* Cf. CONCUBINE.

courtesy. 1. Respect; politeness exhibited as a matter of habit; civility. **2.** An act done out of respect or civility; a kind favor.

▸ **professional courtesy. 1.** Comity, respect, and decorum among professionals. **2.** An act of courtesy between professionals. **3.** A favor done for a fellow professional without charge.

3. CURTESY.

courtesy supervision. (1970) Oversight of a parolee by a correctional agency located in a jurisdiction other than where the parolee was sentenced. • Courtesy supervision is usu. arranged informally between correctional authorities in cases in which the offense is not serious and the parolee's rehabilitative needs are better served in another jurisdiction.

Court for Consideration of Crown Cases Reserved. *Hist.* A court established in 1848 to review questions of law arising in criminal cases. • Trial judges posed the post-verdict questions of law to the Court, which decided whether error had been committed. The Court was abolished in 1907, and its jurisdiction was transferred to the Court of Criminal Appeal. — Also termed *Court for Crown Cases Reserved.*

> "It was an old practice for the judge, in case of a conviction, if he felt a doubt as to the law, to respite judgment or sentence, and discuss the matter informally with the other judges. If they thought that the prisoner had been improperly convicted, he was pardoned. Statutory authority was given to this practice in 1848 by the establishment of the court for Crown Cases Reserved. All the judges were members of this court; and five, of whom the Lord Chief Justice must be one, formed a quorum." 1 William Holdsworth, *A History of English Law* 217 (7th ed. 1956).

Court for Crown Cases Reserved. See COURT FOR CONSIDERATION OF CROWN CASES RESERVED.

Court for Divorce and Matrimonial Causes. *Hist.* A court that exercised jurisdiction over family issues, such as legitimacy and divorce. • The Court, which was established in 1857, acquired the matrimonial jurisdiction previously exercised by the ecclesiastical courts. It consisted of the Lord Chancellor, the Chief Justices of the Queen's Bench and Common Pleas, the Chief Baron of Exchequer, the senior puisne judges of the last three courts, and the Judge Ordinary. In most instances, the Judge Ordinary heard the cases. The Judicature Act of 1873 abolished the Court and transferred its jurisdiction to the Probate Divorce and Admiralty Division (now Family Division) of the High Court of Justice.

Court for the Correction of Errors. *Hist.* A court having jurisdiction to review a lower court. • The name was formerly used in New York and South Carolina.

Court for the Relief of Insolvent Debtors. *Hist.* A court located in London that had jurisdiction over bankruptcy matters. • The Bankruptcy Act of 1861 abolished the Court.

court for the trial of impeachments. (18c) A tribunal empowered to try a government officer or other person brought before it by the process of impeachment. • The U.S. Senate and the British House of Lords have this authority, as do the upper houses of most state legislatures. — Also termed *impeachment court*; *court of impeachment*.

court hand. (17c) *Hist.* A script style used by English court clerks, the words being abbreviated and contracted according to a set of common principles for maintaining brevity and uniformity. • This type of writing, along with the use of Latin (except for technical or untranslatable phrases), was banned early in the 18th century in an effort to make court records more accessible to nonlawyers.

> "[T]echnical Latin continued in use from the time of its first introduction, till the subversion of our ancient constitution under Cromwell; when, among many other innovations in the law, some for the better and some for the worse, the language of our records was altered and turned into English. But, at the restoration of king Charles, this novelty was no longer countenanced; the practicers finding it very difficult to express themselves so concisely or significantly in any other language but the Latin. And thus it continued without any sensible inconvenience till about the year 1730, when it was again thought proper that the proceedings at law should be done into English, and it was accordingly so ordered by statute 4 Geo. II. c. 26. . . . What is said of the alteration of language by the statute 4 Geo. II. c. 26 will hold equally strong with respect to the prohibition of using the ancient immutable *court hand* in writing the records of other legal proceedings; whereby the reading of any record that is forty years old is now become the object of science, and calls for the help of an antiquarian." 3 William Blackstone, *Commentaries on the Laws of England* 322–23 (1768).

courthouse. See COURT (5).

courthouse steps. (1941) The figurative location of settlement negotiations that occur shortly before trial commences, regardless of the literal location of the negotiations <the parties settled the lawsuit on the courthouse steps>.

court lands. (1848) *Hist.* The part of a manor used for the lord's household. — Also termed (in Latin) *curtiles terrae*.

court leet (**kort** leet). (16c) *Hist.* A feudal court responsible for receiving frankpledges and notices of criminal accusations. • Courts leet exercised both governmental and judicial powers, but they declined in the 14th century after the justices in eyre began to take over serious criminal cases. The court met once or twice a year, and was presided over by the lord's steward, a lawyer who acted as judge. See SHERIFF'S TOWN.

court-martial, *n.* (18c) **1.** *Hist.* A committee formed for the purpose of carrying out martial law. See MARTIAL LAW.

> "The courts-martial, as they are called, by which martial law . . . is administered, are not, properly speaking, courts-martial or courts at all. They are merely committees formed for the purpose of carrying into execution the discretionary power assumed by the Government." James Fitzjames Stephen, *A General View of the Criminal Law of England* 118 (2d ed. 1890).

2. An ad hoc military court convened under military authority to try someone, particularly a member of the armed forces, accused of violating the Uniform Code of Military Justice. Pl. **courts-martial.** — **court-martial,** *vb.*

> "[C]ourts-martial are not a part of the federal judicial system, and the procedure in such courts is regulated by the Articles of War, Army Regulations, orders of the President, and military custom." *Altmayer v. Sanford*, 148 F.2d 161, 162 (5th Cir. 1945).

▸ **BCD special court-martial.** (1962) A special court-martial in which a possible punishment is a bad-conduct discharge (a "BCD").

▸ **general court-martial.** (17c) A proceeding that is presided over by a military judge, and no fewer than five members (who serve as jurors), and that has jurisdiction over all the members of the armed forces. • It is the highest military trial court.

▸ **special court-martial.** (18c) A proceeding that is presided over by a military judge and no fewer than three members (who serve as jurors) to hear noncapital offenses and prescribe a sanction of hard labor, dismissal, or extended confinement (up to one year). • It is the intermediate level of courts-martial.

▸ **summary court-martial.** (1819) A proceeding presided over by a single commissioned officer who is jurisdictionally limited in what sanctions can be imposed. • It is the lowest level of courts-martial.

court-martial order. (18c) A written order containing the result of a court-martial trial.

Court-Martial Reports. A publication containing the opinions of the U.S. Court of Military Appeals and select decisions of the Courts of Military Review. • This publication appeared during the years 1951–1975. — Abbr. CMR.

court merchant. See COURT.

court not of record. See COURT.

Court of Admiralty. See HIGH COURT OF ADMIRALTY.

court of ancient demesne. (17c) *Hist.* A court made up of freeholders of land held by the Crown (i.e., an *ancient demesne*). • The freeholders acted as judges much the same way that freeholders of an ordinary manor would in a court baron. See *ancient demesne* under DEMESNE; COURT BARON.

Court of Appeal. An English court of civil and criminal appellate jurisdiction established by the Judicature Acts of 1873 and 1875. • The court is made up of the Lord Chancellor, Lord Chief Justice, Master of the Rolls, President of the Family Division, Vice-Chancellor of the Chancery Division, former Lord Chancellors, Lords of Appeal in Ordinary, and Lords Justices of Appeal. In practice it is made up of the Master of Rolls and the Lords Justices. It sits in several divisions, each having three members. — Abbr. C.A. — Also termed (informally) *Appeal Court*.

Court of Appeal in Chancery. *Hist.* An English court of intermediate appeal in equity cases, established in 1851 and abolished in 1873–1875, when its jurisdiction was transferred to the Court of Appeal.

court of appeals. See COURT.

Court of Appeals, U.S. See UNITED STATES COURT OF APPEALS.

Court of Appeals for the Armed Forces. See UNITED STATES COURT OF APPEALS FOR THE ARMED FORCES.

Court of Appeals for the Federal Circuit. See UNITED STATES COURT OF APPEALS FOR THE FEDERAL CIRCUIT.

Court of Appeals for Veterans Claims. The federal court that reviews decisions of the Board of Veterans Appeals.

Court of Appeals in Cases of Capture. *Hist.* A court responsible for reviewing state-court decisions concerning British ships captured by American privateers during the Revolution. • Congress established the court under the Articles of Confederation. It was the first federal court in the United States and the chief United States court from 1780 to 1787. Cf. *prize court* under COURT.

Court of Archdeacon (ahrch-**dee**-kən). *Hist. Eccles. law.* An inferior ecclesiastical court that had jurisdiction over cases arising within the archdeaconry and probate matters. • Appeal was to the Bishop's Court. The Court of Archdeacon was abolished in 1967. — Also termed *Archdeacon's Court*; *Archdiaconal Court* (ahr-kə-dɪ-**ak**-ən-əl).

Court of Arches. *Eccles. law.* The ecclesiastical court of the province of Canterbury, responsible for appeals from provincial diocesan courts. • The Pope heard appeals from the Court of Arches until the break with Rome prompted a transfer of the appellate jurisdiction to the Court of Delegates. The Judicial Committee of the Privy Council now hears certain appeals from the Court of Arches. — Also termed *Arches Court of Canterbury*; *Court of Canterbury*; *Court of the Official Principal*. Cf. CHANCERY COURT OF YORK.

> "The Court of Arches is the provincial court of the Archbishop of Canterbury. It is held by a judge generally called the *Dean of the Arches*. Its jurisdiction was important while testamentary cases were dealt with in the Ecclesiastical Courts. The name is derived from the fact that the court was originally held in the Church of St. Mary-le-Bow (*Ecclesia Beatae Mariae de Arcubus*), the steeple of which is raised on stone pillars formed archwise like bent bows." W.J.V. Windeyer, *Lectures on Legal History* 184 n.11 (2d ed. 1949).

Court of Assistants. *Hist.* A colonial body organized in Massachusetts Bay Colony in 1630 to act as a legislature and court for the colony. Cf. GENERAL COURT.

> "The court of assistants, made up of governor, deputy governor, and magistrates, heard appeals from lower courts, and took original jurisdiction in certain cases — for example, cases of divorce. Below it were the county courts." Lawrence M. Friedman, *A History of American Law* 40 (2d ed. 1985).

Court of Attachments. *Hist.* An inferior forest court with jurisdiction over trespasses of the royal forests. • The judges of this court (the *verderers*) met every 40 days to hear charges made by the royal foresters. Major trespass cases were heard by the justices in eyre. — Also termed *wood-mote*; *forty-days court*. See VERDERER.

Court of Audience. *Hist. Eccles. law.* A court in which the Archbishop of York or Canterbury exercised personal jurisdiction. • This court was abolished in 1963.

> "Just as the bishop did not deprive himself of all jurisdiction by delegation to an official or commissary, so the archbishop did not originally deprive himself of all jurisdiction by delegation to the official principal. He possessed a jurisdiction concurrent with that of the court of the Arches, which was exercised in the court of Audience. In later times this jurisdiction was exercised by the judge of the court of Audience. At one time the archbishop may have exercised a considerable part of this jurisdiction in this court." 1 William Holdsworth, *A History of English Law* 601 (7th ed. 1956).

Court of Augmentations. *Hist.* A court established in 1536 by Henry VIII to determine controversies arising from the royal policy of taking over property owned by monasteries. • The court was merged into the Court of Exchequer in 1554.

Court of Canterbury. See COURT OF ARCHES.

Court of Cassation (ka-**say**-shən). The highest court of France. • The court's name derives from its power to quash (*casser*) the decrees of inferior courts. — Also termed (more formally) *Cour de Cassation*.

court of chancery. See CHANCERY (1).

court of chivalry. See HIGH COURT OF CHIVALRY.

Court of Civil Appeals. (1892) An intermediate appellate court in some states, such as Alabama and (formerly) Texas.

court of claims. 1. See COURT. **2.** (*cap.*) See UNITED STATES COURT OF FEDERAL CLAIMS.

Court of Common Bench. See COURT OF COMMON PLEAS.

Court of Common Pleas. (16c) **1.** *Hist.* A superior court having jurisdiction of all real actions and common pleas (i.e., actions between subjects). • The Court was presided over by a chief justice with four (later five) puisne judges. In 1873 it became the Common Pleas Division of the High Court of Justice. In 1881 it merged into the Queen's Bench Division. — Also termed *banc le common pleas*. **2.** An intermediate-level court in some states, such as Arkansas. **3.** A trial court of general jurisdiction in some states, such as Ohio, Pennsylvania, and South Carolina. — Also termed *Court of Common Bench*. — Abbr. C.P.

> "*Common pleas* is the kings Court now held in *Westminster* hall, but in auncient time moveable, as appeareth by the statute called *Magna charta* . . . . [U]ntill the time that *Henry* the third granted the great charter, there were but two courts in all, called the Kings courts: whereof one was the Exchequer, and the other, the kings bench, which was then called (*curia Domini regis*) and (*aula regis*) because it followed the court or king: and that upon the grant of that charter, the court of common pleas was erected and setled in one place certaine: viz. at *Westminster* . . . . All civill causes both reall and personall are, or were in former times, tryed in this court, according to the strict lawe of the realme: and by *Fortescue, cap. 50* it seemeth to have bene the onely court for reall causes." John Cowell, *The Interpreter* (1607).

court of competent jurisdiction. See COURT.

court of conscience. *Hist.* A local English court that had jurisdiction over small-debt cases. • The court was so called because its judgments were supposed to reflect equity and good conscience. County courts assumed the jurisdiction of the courts of conscience in 1846.

Court of Convocation. *Eccles. law.* An assembly of high-ranking provincial officials and representatives of the lower clergy having jurisdiction over cases of heresy, schism, and other ecclesiastical matters.

Court of Criminal Appeals. (1856) **1.** For each armed service, an intermediate appellate court that reviews court-martial decisions. • The court was established by the Military Justice Act of 1968. 10 USCA §§ 859–876. — Formerly termed *Court of Military Review* (CMR). **2.** In some jurisdictions, such as Texas and Oklahoma, the highest appellate court that hears criminal cases.

Court of Customs and Patent Appeals. *Hist.* An Article III court created in 1929 to hear appeals in customs and patent cases. • This court was abolished in 1982 and was superseded by the U.S. Court of Appeals for the Federal Circuit. — Abbr. CCPA. See UNITED STATES COURT OF APPEALS FOR THE FEDERAL CIRCUIT.

Court of Delegates. *Hist. Eccles. law.* A court serving as the final court of appeal for admiralty and ecclesiastical matters. • The Court was established in 1534 to serve in the stead of the Papal Curia when the English Church severed its ties with the Papacy. Six delegates, appointed to hear only one case, made up the Court, usu. three persons trained in common law and three in civil law. This mixture led to confused rulings and unreliable precedents that hindered the Court's credibility and ultimately led to its dissolution. The Court was abolished in 1833 and its jurisdiction transferred to the Judicial Committee of the Privy Council. — Also termed *High Court of Delegates.*

> "The crown had an absolute discretion as to the person to be appointed. But, as the lawyers of Doctors' Commons were the only lawyers acquainted with canon or civil law, certain of them were usually included in the commission. . . . It is not surprising to find that the [Court of Delegates] was unsatisfactory. It was a shifting body, so that no general rules of procedure could be established. It did not as a rule give reasons for its decisions. Its members were only paid a guinea a day; and consequently it was usually composed of the junior civilians. On them, the judges of the common law courts, appointed as delegates, were obliged to rely for their law. In consequence of the dissatisfaction felt at its working the Ecclesiastical Commission of 1832, in a special report, recommended the transfer of its jurisdiction to the Privy Council . . . ." 1 William Holdsworth, *A History of English Law* 605 (7th ed. 1956).

court of domestic relations. See *family court* under COURT.

Court of Earl Marshal. 1. See COURT OF THE LORD HIGH CONSTABLE AND EARL MARSHAL. **2.** See HIGH COURT OF CHIVALRY.

court of equity. See COURT.

court of error. (18c) **1.** *Hist.* Formerly, the Court of Exchequer Chamber and the House of Lords. • Appeals from common-law courts lay to the Court of Exchequer Chamber, and then to the House of Lords until 1873, when the Judicature Act gave jurisdiction of superior-court appeals to the Court of Appeal. Cf. COURT OF EXCHEQUER CHAMBER. **2.** Generally, a court having jurisdiction to review a lower court's rulings.

Court of Errors and Appeals. *Hist.* Formerly, the court of last resort in New Jersey and New York. — Also termed *High Court of Errors and Appeals.*

Court of Exchequer (eks-**chek**-ər *or* **eks**-chek-ər). *Hist.* A former English superior court responsible primarily for adjudicating disputes about the collection of public revenue. • In 1873 it became the Exchequer Division of the High Court of Justice. In 1881 that Division was merged into the Queen's Bench Division. See QUEEN'S BENCH DIVISION. Cf. CHAMBER OF ACCOUNTS.

Court of Exchequer Chamber. *Hist.* **1.** An informal assembly of common-law judges who (sometimes with the Lord Chancellor) gathered to discuss important cases that had adjourned pending an opinion from the Court. • This body never became a court of law in a technical sense, but judges gave great weight to its decisions. The last reported decision of this body is from 1738.

> "Earlier than these two statutory courts was the practice, which apparently originated about the time of Edward I, of informal meetings of the judges in the Exchequer Chamber to decide matters connected with litigation. . . . The purpose of the meeting was to bring before the judges a point of law which caused difficulty and which had arisen in a case being heard before one or other of the courts. Any resolution passed did not constitute a judgment; it was left to the court concerned to make the appropriate decree, and the official record made no reference to the informal decision. . . . Civil cases were debated in the Exchequer Chamber as late as the seventeenth century, and criminal cases continued to be 'reserved' for full discussion by all the common law judges until the nineteenth century." A.K.R. Kiralfy, *Potter's Outlines of English Legal History* 202–04 (5th ed. 1958).

2. A court created by statute in 1357 to hear appeals from the Court of Exchequer. **3.** A court created by statute in 1585 to hear appeals from the King's Bench. • This court consisted of all the justices of the Common Pleas and the Barons of Exchequer who were serjeants. At least six judges were necessary to render a judgment.

> "Parliament was only occasionally summoned in the sixteenth century; and as Parliament was the only court which could amend errors of the King's Bench, the want of a court which could hold regular sessions was much felt. To supply this want a new court of Exchequer Chamber was created in 1585 for the purpose of amending the errors of the King's Bench." 1 William Holdsworth, *A History of English Law* 244 (7th ed. 1956).

4. A court charged with hearing appeals from the common-law courts of record. • This court was created in 1830 by combining the courts created by the statutes of 1357 and 1585. Appeals from one common-law court were heard by judges from the other two courts.

> "This complicated system of appellate courts was abolished in 1830, when a new Court of Exchequer Chamber was set up as the court of error from each of the three common law courts. It was composed of the judges of the two common law courts other than those of the court appealed from. At the same time the right of the King's Bench to hear error from the Common Pleas was abolished. From the judgment of this new court a further appeal still lay to the House of Lords. This court was thus, until the Judicature Act, 1873, a court of intermediate appeals. Its jurisdiction after the Judicature Act passed to the Court of Appeal which was then created." W.J.V. Windeyer, *Lectures on Legal History* 144 (2d ed. 1949).

Court of Faculties. *Eccles. law.* An archbishop's tribunal that grants special dispensations (such as a marriage license) and decides questions relating to monuments and mortuary matters. See MASTER OF THE FACULTIES.

Court of Federal Claims, U.S. See UNITED STATES COURT OF FEDERAL CLAIMS.

court officer. See OFFICER OF THE COURT.

court-officer's deed. See DEED.

court of final appeal. See COURT.

court of first instance. See *trial court* under COURT.

court of general jurisdiction. See COURT.

Court of General Quarter Sessions of the Peace. *Hist.* **1.** *English law.* A court of criminal jurisdiction held in each county (or borough) once in every quarter of a year. • The court was made up of a county's justices of the peace. It committed certain cases to the Assizes. Quarter Sessions were abolished in 1971, with most jurisdiction transferred to the Crown Court. — Often shortened to *Quarter Sessions; Sessions.*

> "The court of general *quarter sessions* of the peace is a court that must be held in every county, once in every quarter of a year . . . . It is held before two or more justices of the peace, one of which must be of the *quorum.* The jurisdiction of this court, by statute 34 Edw. III. c. I. extends to the trying and determining all felonies and trespasses whatsoever, though they seldom, if ever, try any greater offence than small felonies within the benefit of clergy . . . ." 4 William Blackstone, *Commentaries on the Laws of England* 268 (1769).

2. A court held in some states four times a year with jurisdiction over misdemeanors and occasionally tasks of an administrative nature, such as the care of public roads and bridges. — Often shortened to *Quarter Sessions Court.* — Also termed *Court of Quarter Sessions of the Peace.*

Court of Great Sessions in Wales. *Hist.* A common-law court established in 1543 in Wales with jurisdiction equivalent to that of the English assizes. • The Court of Great Sessions was bound to follow English law, but not necessarily English case precedent. — Also termed *King's Great Sessions in Wales.*

> "There was no outcry when, in 1536, 'the sinister usages and customs' of the Welsh were abrogated and Welsh subjects were granted the same laws and liberties as the English. . . . A new system of courts, called the Great Sessions in Wales, was set up. The courts were to sit twice a year in four circuits, each comprising three counties, and to each circuit were appointed justices 'learned in the laws of this realm.' These courts operated alongside the English courts, and they had the same jurisdiction in Wales as the King's Bench and Common Pleas had in England. . . . In 1830 the Great Sessions were abolished, and by complete procedural assimilation England and Wales became at last one unified jurisdiction, two extra circuits being added to the English assize system." J.H. Baker, *An Introduction to English Legal History* 37–38 (3d ed. 1990).

Court of High Commission. *Hist. Eccles. law.* A tribunal responsible for inquiring into religious offenses such as the holding of heretical opinions, and absence from church. • Functioning as a court, the High Commission also prosecuted violations of the Acts of Supremacy and Uniformity (1559), the statutes that gave the Crown supreme power over the Church of England. The Commission's broad powers and use of civil-law procedures in ways counter to the common law (such as compelling suspects to testify against themselves) sparked opposition to its existence. Its close relationship with the Court of Star Chamber hastened its demise (along with the Star Chamber) in 1641. — Also termed *High Commission Court.*

> "[T]he court of the king's *high commission* in causes ecclesiastical . . . was intended to vindicate the dignity and peace of the church, by reforming, ordering, and correcting the ecclesiastical state and persons, and all manner of errors, heresies, schisms, abuses, offences, contempts, and enormities. Under the shelter of which very general words, means were found in that and the two succeeding reigns, to vest in the high commissioners extraordinary and almost despotic powers, of fining and imprisoning; which they exerted much beyond the degree of the offence itself, and frequently over offences by no means of spiritual cognizance. For these reasons this court was justly abolished by Statute 16 Car. I, c. 11. And the weak and illegal attempt that was made to revive it, during the reign of King James the second, served only to hasten that infatuated prince's ruin." 3 William Blackstone, *Commentaries on the Laws of England* 67–68 (1768).

Court of Honor. *Hist.* **1.** *English law.* A feudal court of the manor. **2.** *English law.* A court with jurisdiction to hear complaints concerning either affronts to honor or encroachments in precedence rights, heraldry, or coat-armor. **3.** A tribunal of army officers convened to review and punish any dereliction from a code of honor.

Court of Hustings (həs-tingz). *Hist.* **1.** *English law.* A local court with jurisdiction over real and mixed actions, held in the Guildhall of London before the Recorder, the Lord Mayor, and Sheriff (the latter two officials serving as honorary judges). • This court dates from before the Conquest. **2.** Formerly, a local court in Virginia. — Also termed *curia burgi.* See HUSTING.

court of impeachment. See COURT FOR THE TRIAL OF IMPEACHMENTS.

court of inquiry. See COURT.

court of instance. See *trial court* under COURT.

Court of International Trade, U.S. See UNITED STATES COURT OF INTERNATIONAL TRADE.

Court of Justice of the European Communities. See EUROPEAN COURT OF JUSTICE.

Court of Justice Seat. See COURT OF THE CHIEF JUSTICE IN EYRE.

Court of Justiciary, High. See HIGH COURT OF JUSTICIARY.

Court of King's Bench. See KING'S BENCH.

court of last resort. See COURT.

court of law. See COURT.

court of limited jurisdiction. See COURT.

Court of Magistrates and Freeholders. *Hist.* A South Carolina court with criminal jurisdiction over alleged offenses committed by slaves and free persons of color.

Court of Military Appeals. See UNITED STATES COURT OF APPEALS FOR THE ARMED FORCES.

Court of Military Review. See COURT OF CRIMINAL APPEALS (1).

court of nisi prius. See NISI PRIUS.

Court of the Official Principal. See COURT OF ARCHES.

court of ordinary. See *probate court* under COURT.

court of original jurisdiction. See COURT.

Court of Orphans. *Hist.* In Maryland and Pennsylvania, a court that exercised probate jurisdiction.

Court of Oyer and Terminer (oy-ər an[d] tər-mə-nər). (17c) **1.** *Hist.* An assize court commissioned by the Crown to pass through the counties two or more times a year and hear felonies and treason cases. • The judges sat by virtue of several commissions, each of which, strictly speaking, created a separate and distinct court. A judge with an *oyer and terminer* commission, for example, was allowed to hear only cases of felony and treason; he could not try persons charged with other criminal offenses. But if the judge also carried a commission of *gaol delivery* (as most did), he could try all prisoners held in gaol for any offense; in this way most Courts of Oyer and Terminer gathered full criminal jurisdiction. The jurisdiction of the assize courts was taken over by the Crown Court in 1971. See ASSIZE (1); COMMISSION OF OYER AND TERMINER; COMMISSION OF GAOL DELIVERY. **2.** In some states, a court of higher criminal jurisdiction.

Court of Oyer and Terminer and General Gaol Delivery. *Hist.* **1.** A court that carries the commissions of *oyer and terminer* and *gaol delivery.* See COMMISSION OF OYER AND TERMINER; COMMISSION OF GAOL DELIVERY. **2.** In Pennsylvania, a court of criminal jurisdiction.

Court of Peculiars. *Hist. Eccles. law.* A branch of the Court of Arches that had jurisdiction over the provincial parishes of Canterbury that were exempt from the jurisdiction of the diocesan bishop and responsible to the metropolitan only. • The Court of Peculiars was abolished in the 19th century. See COURT OF ARCHES; PECULIAR.

court of petty sessions. See *magistrate's court* (2) under COURT.

court of piepowder. See PIEPOWDER COURT.

Court of Pleas. *Hist.* A court of the county palatine of Durham, England having a local common-law jurisdiction. • It was abolished in 1873, and its jurisdiction was transferred to the High Court. — Also termed *Court of Pleas of Durham.*

Court of Policies of Insurance. *Hist.* A court that determines in a summary way insurance-policy issues arising between merchants. • The Court's jurisdiction extended only to London, and appeal was taken to the Court of Chancery. The Court was abolished in 1863. — Also termed *Court of Policies of Assurance.*

Court of Private Land Claims. *Hist.* A federal court — in existence from 1891 to 1895 — with jurisdiction to hear private parties' claims to public-domain land located in the southwestern part of the United States and deriving from Spanish or Mexican grants.

Court of Probate. **1.** *Hist.* A court established in 1857 to receive the testamentary jurisdiction formerly held by the ecclesiastical courts. • In 1873 the Court was merged into the High Court of Justice, where its jurisdiction was exercised by the Probate Divorce and Admiralty (now Family) Division. **2.** See *probate court* under COURT.

Court of Quarter Sessions of the Peace. See COURT OF GENERAL QUARTER SESSIONS OF THE PEACE.

Court of Queen's Bench. See QUEEN'S BENCH.

court of record. See COURT.

Court of Regard. *Hist.* A forest court responsible for looking into matters of waste and encroachment onto forest land (i.e., *purpresture*). • The Court also ensured that the feet of all mastiffs — a breed allowed in royal forests as guard dogs — within the forest were declawed and cut so as to prevent them from chasing deer.

Court of Requests. *Hist.* A royal court whose jurisdiction was mainly civil, though it exercised quasi-criminal jurisdiction in offenses such as riot and forgery. • Dating from 1483, the Court of Requests was a part of the Privy Council. It was disbanded in 1641 when Parliament limited the Privy Council's judicial functions.

> "The Court of Requests was a minor Court of Equity, which was originally a committee of the King's Council to hear poor men's causes and those of the King's servants, but was established as a separate Court by Wolsey at Whitehall. . . . The Lord Privy Seal was president of the Court of Requests and, therefore, the Court maintained a close connection with the Council, but, after the two Masters of Requests took practically complete control towards the end of the reign of Henry VIII, it became to all intents and purposes an independent Court. . . . [A]lthough the nature of the Court was more closely akin to the Council, the actual jurisdiction had much in common with the Chancery, but it occasionally entertained cases of a *quasi*-criminal character, such as riots, forgery and other offences remedied by the Star Chamber." Harold Potter, *An Historical Introduction to English Law and Its Institutions* 165 (3d ed. 1948).

> "The establishment of the court of Requests was due to the large increase in the judicial business of the Council and the Chancery under the Tudors. . . . It was related both to the judicial side of the Council, which . . . came, in the course of the Tudor period, to be known as the court of Star Chamber, and to the court of Chancery . . . . [F]rom the end of Henry VIII's reign onwards, the legal assessors of the court assumed entire control, with the result that it became a court which was quite separate from the court of Star Chamber. These legal assessors were styled Masters of Requests, and from their title the court got its name." 1 William Holdsworth, *A History of English Law* 412–13 (7th ed. 1956).

court of review. See *appellate court* under COURT.

Court of Session. *Scots law.* The supreme Scottish civil court. • Its jurisdiction corresponds generally to the English High Court of Justice. The Court of Session is divided into Outer House and Inner House. In Outer House, one judge hears cases of first instance. The Outer House's jurisdiction corresponds generally to the English High Court of Justice. The Outer House has two appellate chambers, the First and Second Division, in which three-judge panels sit. The Inner House's jurisdiction corresponds generally to the English Court of Appeal. The Court of Session also has several Lords Ordinary, who sit individually as trial judges. — Also termed *Supreme Civil Court in Scotland.*

court of sessions. *Hist.* In some colonies and American states, a court having jurisdiction over criminal cases and some administrative duties. • In California, for example, courts of sessions were established in 1851, upon statehood, to undertake county administrative, tax, and criminal-court functions, without appellate review. Their functions were gradually replaced by boards of supervisors and district courts during the late 19th century.

Court of Shepway. *Hist.* The Court of the Lord Warden of the Cinque Ports, exercising civil jurisdiction. • The civil jurisdiction of the Cinque Ports was abolished in 1855. See CINQUE PORTS.

court of special jurisdiction. See *limited court* under COURT.

court of special session. See COURT.

Court of Star Chamber. See STAR CHAMBER (1).

court of summary jurisdiction. See *magistrate's court* (2) under COURT.

Court of Swainmote. See COURT OF SWEINMOTE.

Court of Sweinmote (**swayn**-moht). *Hist.* A medieval forest court with jurisdiction over a variety of matters, esp. the right to graze animals during the summer when deer were fawning. • The forest freeholders (the *sweins*) made up the jury of the Court. By the 14th century, the Court's jurisdiction had expanded, and it acquired a form similar to the eyre courts. — Also spelled *Court of Swainmote.*

Court of Teinds. See TEIND COURT.

Court of the Chief Justice in Eyre (air). *Hist.* An eyre court responsible for trying offenses against the forest laws. • The jurisdiction of this Court was similar to that of the Court of Sweinmote. — Also termed *Court of Justice Seat.*

Court of the Earl Marshal. **1.** COURT OF THE LORD HIGH CONSTABLE AND EARL MARSHAL. **2.** HIGH COURT OF CHIVALRY.

Court of the Lord High Admiral. See HIGH COURT OF ADMIRALTY.

Court of the Lord High Constable and Earl Marshal. *Hist.* A court having jurisdiction over diverse military matters, such as treason, prisoners of war, and disputed coats of arms. • The Lord High Constable and the Earl Marshal were the top military officials of the Norman kings. After the office of Lord High Constable was forfeited in 1521, the court continued on as the *Court of the Earl Marshal,* but its jurisdiction was reduced to questions of chivalry only. Cf. HIGH COURT OF CHIVALRY.

Court of the Lord High Steward. *Hist.* A court commissioned to try a peer indicted for treason or a felony. • The Court met only if the House of Lords was not in session. The Lord High Steward sat as a judge and decided questions of law, and the peers decided facts only. The Court last sat in 1688.

Court of the Lord High Steward of the Universities. *Hist.* A court convened to try scholars, esp. Oxford or Cambridge students, who have been indicted for treason, felony, or mayhem.

Court of the Marshalsea (mahr-shəl-see). *Hist.* A court that moved about with the king, and had jurisdiction over certain cases arising within 12 miles of the king's residence (an area known as the *verge*). • The Court's steward and marshal acted as judges of the Court, and heard criminal cases and the common pleas of debt, covenant, and certain trespasses. The court's migratory nature made it inconvenient for litigants, and prompted its abolition in 1849. — Also termed *Court of the Steward and Marshal.* Cf. PALACE COURT.

> "Coke points out that all the Acts passed concerning this court restrained, or explained, but never added to its jurisdiction. He decided, in the *Case of the Marshalsea*, that it could not try the newer forms of action such as assumpsit and trover. Its once general jurisdiction had passed to the court of King's Bench, and the attitude of that court to the more limited court of the Marshalsea made the court of the Marshalsea almost useless. There were complaints in the seventeenth century of the conduct of its officials; and, as it was obliged to follow the king in his progresses, it was a court extremely inconvenient to use." 1 William Holdsworth, *A History of English Law* 208 (7th ed. 1956).

Court of the Official Principal. See COURT OF ARCHES.

Court of the Steward and Marshal. See COURT OF THE MARSHALSEA.

Court of the Steward of the King's Household. *Hist.* A court having jurisdiction over criminal cases involving a member of the royal household. • This court's jurisdiction was at first limited to acts of violence by the king's servants toward a member of the king's council, but it was later given broader criminal authority. The Court was abolished in 1828.

Court of Verge. 1. See VERGE (1). **2.** See VERGE (2).

Court of Veterans Appeals, U.S. See UNITED STATES COURT OF VETERANS APPEALS.

Court of Wards and Liveries. *Hist.* A court created in 1540 to assert the Crown's right to income from a variety of feudal tenures. • The Court's unpopularity led to its abolition in 1660.

> "[I]nquests of office were more frequently in practice than at present, during the continuance of the military tenures among us: when, upon the death of every one of the king's tenants, an inquest of office was held, called an *inquisitio post mortem*, to enquire of what lands he died seised, who was his heir, and of what age, in order to entitle the king to his marriage, wardship, relief, *primer-seisin*, or other advantages, as the circumstances of the case might turn out. To superintend and regulate these enquiries, the court of wards and liveries was instituted by statute 32 Hen. VIII c. 46 which was abolished at the restoration of king Charles the second, together with the oppressive tenures upon which it was founded." 3 William Blackstone, *Commentaries on the Laws of England* 258 (1768).

courtoisie internationale. See COMITY.

court order. See ORDER (2).

court-ordered arbitration. See *court-annexed arbitration* under ARBITRATION.

court-packing plan. (1937) A unsuccessful proposal — made in 1937 by President Franklin D. Roosevelt — to increase the number of U.S. Supreme Court justices from nine to fifteen. • The ostensible purpose of the proposal was to increase the court's efficiency, but President Roosevelt wanted to appoint justices who would not block his administration's New Deal programs.

court papers. (17c) All documents that a party files with the court, including pleadings, motions, notices, and the like. — Often shortened to *papers.* — Also termed *suit papers.*

court probation. See *bench probation* under PROBATION.

court recorder. See RECORDER (3).

court reporter. (1894) **1.** Someone who records judicial proceedings and testimony, stenographically or by electronic or other means, and when requested, prepares a transcript <the deposition could not start until the court reporter arrived>. — Also termed (BrE) *official shorthand writer.* Cf. *court recorder* under RECORDER. **2.** REPORTER OF DECISIONS.

court roll. (15c) *Hist.* A record of a manor's tenures; esp., a record of the terms by which the various tenants held their estates. • Copyhold tenure, for example, developed from the practice of maintaining court rolls. See COPYHOLD.

courtroom. (17c) The part of a courthouse where trials and hearings take place, often one of many such parts, each one usu. having a raised bench, a witness stand or box, an enclosed area for jurors; an identical set of tables for counsel, and a gallery for observers. Cf. *judge's chamber* under CHAMBER.

courtroom deputy. See DEPUTY.

courtroom privilege. See *judicial privilege* under PRIVILEGE (1).

court rule. 1. COURT RULES. **2.** RULE OF COURT.

court rules. (17c) Regulations having the force of law and governing practice and procedure in the various courts, such as the Federal Rules of Civil Procedure, the Federal Rules of Criminal Procedure, the U.S. Supreme Court Rules, and the Federal Rules of Evidence, as well as any local rules that a court promulgates. — Also termed *rules of court.*

courts of the franchise. See FRANCHISE COURT.

court system. (18c) The network of courts in a jurisdiction.

court trial. See *bench trial* under TRIAL.

court witness. See WITNESS.

cousin. (13c) **1.** A child of one's aunt or uncle. — Also termed *first cousin; full cousin; cousin-german.* **2.** A relative descended from one's ancestor (such as a grandparent) by two or more steps in a diverging line. **3.** Any distant relative by blood or marriage; a kinsman or kinswoman.

▸ **cousin-german.** (14c) A first cousin; a child of a full sibling of one's mother or father. See GERMAN.

▸ **cousin-in-law.** (1874) **1.** The husband or wife of one's cousin. **2.** A cousin of one's husband or one's wife.

▸ **cousin once removed.** (17c) **1.** A child of one's cousin. **2.** A cousin of one's parent.

▸ **cousin twice removed.** (18c) **1.** A grandchild of one's cousin. **2.** A cousin of one's grandparent.

▸ **first cousin.** See COUSIN (1).

▸ **second cousin.** (17c) A person related to another by descending from the same great-grandfather or great-grandmother.

▸ **third cousin.** (17c) A person related to another by descending from the same great-great-grandfather or great-great-grandmother.

coutumier (koo-too-**myay**). A collection of the customs, usages, and forms of practice in use over many centuries in France. • The *Grand Coutumier* was projected by Charles VII in 1453 but not completed until 1609.

covenant (**kəv**-ə-nənt), *n.* (14c) **1.** A formal agreement or promise, usu. in a contract or deed, to do or not do a particular act; a compact or stipulation.

▸ **absolute covenant.** (17c) A covenant that is not qualified or limited by any condition. Cf. *conditional covenant.*

▸ **active covenant.** (1933) A covenant that obligates the promisor to do something. See *affirmative covenant.* Cf. *passive covenant.*

▸ **affirmative covenant.** (18c) A covenant that obligates a party to do some act; esp., an agreement that real property will be used in a certain way. • An affirmative covenant is more than a restriction on the use of property. For the real-property sense, see *affirmative covenant* under COVENANT (4). Cf. *negative covenant.*

▸ **assertory covenant** (ə-**sər**-tə-ree). One that affirmatively states certain facts; an affirming promise under seal.

▸ **auxiliary covenant** (awg-**zil**-yə-ree). (18c) A covenant that does not relate directly to the primary subject of the agreement, but to something connected to it. Cf. *principal covenant.*

▸ **collateral covenant** (kə-**lat**-ə-rəl). (17c) A covenant entered into in connection with the grant of something but not immediately related to the thing granted; esp., a covenant in a deed or other sealed instrument extraneous to the property being conveyed. Cf. *inherent covenant.*

▸ **concurrent covenant.** (1819) A covenant that requires performance by one party at the same time as another's performance.

▸ **conditional covenant.** (17c) A covenant that is qualified by a condition. Cf. *absolute covenant.*

▸ **conservation covenant.** See *conservation easement* under EASEMENT.

▸ **continuing covenant.** (18c) A covenant that requires the successive performance of acts, such as an agreement to pay rent in installments.

▸ **covenant in deed.** See *express covenant.*

▸ **covenant in law.** See *implied covenant.*

▸ **covenant in restraint of trade.** (1827) See *covenant not to compete.*

▸ **covenant not to compete.** (1978) A promise, usu. in a sale-of-business, partnership, or employment contract, not to engage in the same type of business for a stated time in the same market as the buyer, partner, or employer. • Noncompetition covenants are valid to protect business goodwill in the sale of a company. In employment contexts, requiring the employee, after leaving the employment, not to do a particular type of work, they are disfavored as restraints of trade. Courts generally enforce them for the duration of the relationship, but provisions that extend beyond that relationship must be reasonable in scope, time, and territory. — Also termed *noncompetition agreement; noncompete covenant; noncompetition covenant; restrictive covenant; covenant in restraint of trade; promise not to compete; contract not to compete.*

▸ **covenant not to execute.** (18c) A covenant in which a party who has won a judgment agrees not to enforce it. • This covenant is most common in insurance law.

▸ **covenant not to sue.** (18c) A covenant in which a party having a right of action agrees not to assert that right in litigation. — Abbr. CNS. — Also termed *contract not to sue.*

> "A covenant not to sue is a promise by the creditor not to sue either permanently or for a limited period. If the promise is one never to sue it operates as a discharge just as does a release. The theory is that should the creditor sue despite his promise not to, the debtor has a counterclaim for damages for breach of the creditor's covenant not to sue which is equal to and cancels the original claim. . . . If the covenant is not to sue for a limited time, the modern view is that the covenant may be raised as an affirmative defense to any action brought in violation of the covenant." John D. Calamari & Joseph M. Perillo, *The Law of Contracts* § 21-11, 878–79 (3d ed. 1987).

▸ **dependent covenant.** (18c) A covenant that imposes a duty that depends on the other party's prior performance. • Until the performance, the other party does not have to perform. Cf. *concurrent covenant; independent covenant.*

▸ **executed covenant.** (1894) A covenant that has been fully performed.

▸ **executory covenant** (eg-**zek**-yə-tor-ee). (18c) A covenant that remains unperformed in whole or in part.

▸ **express covenant.** (17c) A covenant created by the words of the parties. — Also termed *covenant in deed.* Cf. *implied covenant.*

> "Express covenants are such as are created by the express words of the parties in a deed, declaratory of their intention. As the good of society requires that contracts entered into with the solemnity incident to deeds or covenants should be inviolably observed and strictly executed, the law has decreed, that where a man expressly covenants to do an act which he would not otherwise be bound by law to perform, he has, by his own deliberate act, imposed on himself a responsibility, from which in general he cannot be relieved, and is compellable, if he neglect such duty, to make compensation in damages to the party injured." Thomas Platt, *A Practical Treatise on the Law of Covenants* 25–26 (1829).

▸ **implied covenant.** (17c) A covenant that can be inferred from the whole agreement and the conduct of the parties. — Also termed *covenant in law.* See *implied term* under TERM (2). Cf. *express covenant.*

▸ **implied covenant of good faith and fair dealing.** (1924) An implied covenant to cooperate with the other party to an agreement so that both parties may obtain the full benefits of the agreement; an implied covenant to refrain from any act that would injure a contracting party's right to receive the benefit of the contract.

• Breach of this covenant is often termed *bad faith*. See BAD FAITH (2).

▸ **implied covenant of habitability.** See *implied warranty of habitability* under WARRANTY (2).

▸ **implied negative covenant.** (1890) A covenant binding a grantor not to permit use of any reserved right in a manner that might destroy the benefits that would otherwise inure to the grantee.

▸ **independent covenant.** (17c) A covenant that imposes a duty that does not depend on the other party's prior performance. Cf. *dependent covenant.*

"Where the performance of one covenant depends upon the performance of another, the precedent condition must be performed, before an action can be maintained on the other covenant. Covenants are to be regarded as dependent, according to the intention of the parties and the good sense of the case; and technical words will give way to such intention. Courts will not hold covenants to be independent, so that one party may refuse and yet enforce performance, unless there is no other way of construing it. But where one act is to be done by one party before another act, which is the consideration of it, is to be done by the other, the covenants to do those acts are independent." W.B. Martindale, *A Treatise on the Law of Conveyancing* § 174, at 158–59 (Lyne S. Metcalfe ed., 2d ed. 1889).

▸ **inherent covenant.** (18c) A covenant that relates directly to land, such as a covenant of quiet enjoyment. Cf. *collateral covenant.*

▸ **intransitive covenant.** (1878) A covenant whose performance does not pass from the original covenantor to the covenantor's representatives. Cf. *transitive covenant.*

▸ **joint covenant.** (17c) A covenant that binds two or more covenantors together. Cf. *several covenant.*

▸ **negative covenant.** (18c) A covenant that requires a party to refrain from doing something; esp., in a real-estate financing transaction, the borrower's promise to the lender not to encumber or transfer the real estate as long as the loan remains unpaid. Cf. *affirmative covenant.*

▸ **noncompete covenant.** See *covenant not to compete.*

▸ **noncompetition covenant.** (1956) See *covenant not to compete.*

▸ **passive covenant.** (1816) A covenant that obligates the promisor to refrain from doing something. Cf. *active covenant.*

▸ **positive covenant.** (1827) A covenant that requires a party to do something (such as to erect a fence within a specified time).

▸ **principal covenant.** (1860) A covenant that relates directly to the principal matter of an agreement. Cf. *auxiliary covenant.*

▸ **protection covenant.** See PROTECTION COVENANT.

▸ **restrictive covenant.** See *covenant not to compete.* (For the real-property sense, see *restrictive covenant* under COVENANT (4).)

▸ **several covenant.** (18c) A covenant that binds two or more covenantors separately. — Also termed *separate covenant.* Cf. *joint covenant.*

▸ **transitive covenant.** A covenant whose duty of performance passes from the original covenantor to the covenantor's representatives. Cf. *intransitive covenant.*

2. TREATY. **3.** A common-law action to recover damages or specific performance for breach of contract under seal. — Also termed *action of covenant.* **4.** A promise made in a deed or implied by law; esp., an obligation in a deed burdening or favoring a landowner. See *contract under seal* under CONTRACT.

"A *covenant* is properly defined as a promise made in deed, although in practice the term is used rather more loosely to mean simply an obligation affecting a landowner whether created by deed or not." Peter Butt, *Land Law* 334–35 (2d ed. 1988).

"In their nature, covenants are first cousins to easements appurtenant. The burdened land corresponds to a servient tenement, the benefitted land, to a dominant tenement. In concept, the main difference between easements and covenants is that, whereas an easement allows its holder to go upon and to do something upon the servient tenement, the beneficiary of a covenant may not enter the burdened land, but may require the owner of that land to do, or more likely not to do, something on that land." Roger A. Cunningham et al., *The Law of Property* § 8.13, at 467 (2d ed. 1993).

▸ **affirmative covenant.** (18c) An agreement that real property will be used in a certain way. • An affirmative covenant is more than a restriction on the use of property. It requires the owner to undertake certain acts on the property. For a more general definition of this term, see *affirmative covenant* under COVENANT (1).

▸ **appurtenant covenant.** See *covenant appurtenant.*

▸ **covenant against encumbrances.** (1807) A grantor's promise that the property has no visible or invisible encumbrances. • In a special warranty deed, the covenant is limited to encumbrances made by the grantor. — Also termed *warranty against encumbrances; general covenant against encumbrances.* Cf. *special covenant against encumbrances.*

▸ **covenant appurtenant** (ə-pər-tə-nənt). (1899) A covenant that is connected with the grantor's land; a covenant running with the land. — Also termed *appurtenant covenant.* Cf. *covenant in gross.*

▸ **covenant for further assurances.** (18c) A covenant to do whatever is reasonably necessary to perfect the title conveyed if it turns out to be imperfect. — Also termed *warranty of further assurances.* See *further assurance* under ASSURANCE.

▸ **covenant for possession.** (1869) A covenant giving a grantee or lessee possession of land.

▸ **covenant for quiet enjoyment.** (17c) **1.** A covenant insuring against the consequences of a defective title or any other disturbance of the title. **2.** A covenant ensuring that the tenant will not be evicted or disturbed by the grantor or a person having a lien or superior title. • This covenant is sometimes treated as being synonymous with *covenant of warranty.* — Also termed *covenant of quiet enjoyment.*

▸ **covenant for title.** (18c) A covenant that binds the grantor to ensure the completeness, security, and continuance of the title transferred. • This covenant usu. includes the covenants for seisin, against encumbrances, for the right to convey, for quiet enjoyment, and of warranty. — Also termed *title covenant; deed warranty.*

"These covenants [for title] were five in number: first, that the grantor was seised of the estate which he purported to convey, called the covenant for seisin; secondly, that he had a good right to convey it; thirdly, that the grantor should quietly possess and enjoy the premises without interruption, called the covenant for quiet enjoyment; fourthly, that such should be the case free and clear from all incumbrances, called the covenant against incumbrances; and fifthly, that such other assurances should be thereafter executed as might be necessary to perfect or conform the title, called the covenant for further assurance." William Henry Rawle, *A Practical Treatise on the Law of Covenants for Title* 17 (5th ed. 1887).

▸ **covenant in gross.** (17c) A covenant that does not run with the land. Cf. *covenant appurtenant.*

▸ **covenant of good right to convey.** See *covenant of seisin.*

▸ **covenant of habitability** (hab-ə-tə-**bil**-ə-tee). See *implied warranty of habitability* under WARRANTY (2).

▸ **covenant of nonclaim.** (1848) A covenant barring a grantor or the grantor's heirs from claiming title in the conveyed land.

▸ **covenant of quiet enjoyment.** See *covenant for quiet enjoyment.*

▸ **covenant of seisin** (**see**-zin). (18c) A covenant, usu. appearing in a warranty deed, stating that the grantor has an estate, or the right to convey an estate, of the quality and size that the grantor purports to convey. • For the covenant to be valid, the grantor must have both title and possession at the time of the grant. — Also termed *covenant of good right to convey; right-to-convey covenant.*

▸ **covenant of warranty.** (18c) A covenant by which the grantor agrees to defend the grantee against any lawful or reasonable claim of superior title by a third party and to indemnify the grantee for any loss sustained by the claim. • This covenant is sometimes treated as being synonymous with *covenant for quiet enjoyment.* The covenant is not breached if the grantor fails to defend the grantee against an invalid claim. See WARRANTY (1).

▸ **covenant running with the land.** (18c) A covenant intimately and inherently involved with the land and therefore binding subsequent owners and successor grantees indefinitely • The chief examples are these: (1) covenants for the maintenance of fences and walls; (2) covenants for the building and use of party-walls; (3) covenants for the leaving open of ways or parks; (4) covenants restricting building to a particular line; and (5) covenants restricting the kinds of buildings in a specified locale. — Also termed *covenant that* (or *which*) *runs with the land; real covenant.*

"A covenant which runs with the land is a promise by the grantor of land to be active or passive in the use of related land for the benefit of the granted land, or a promise by the grantee of land to be active or passive in its use for the benefit of related land of the grantor, which promise must be signed by the promisor in the deed or as a separate instrument under seal at about the same time; and of which promise the effect is to bind the promisor and his lawful successors to the burdened land for the benefit of the promisee and his lawful successors to the benefited land, and to give each the power to enforce his right in his own name." Henry Upson Sims, *Covenants Which Run with Land, Other Than Covenants for Title* 17–18 (1901).

▸ **covenant running with the title.** (1894) **1.** A covenant that relates to the land but has a specific or reasonably determinable expiration time. **2.** See *covenant running with the land.*

▸ **covenant to convey.** (18c) A covenant in which the covenantor agrees to transfer an estate's title to the covenantee.

▸ **covenant to renew.** (18c) An executory contract that gives a lessee the right to renew the lease.

▸ **covenant to stand seised** (seezd). (17c) *Archaic.* A covenant to convey land to a relative. • This covenant could not be used to convey land to a stranger; the only consideration that supports the covenant is the relationship by blood or marriage.

▸ **environmental covenant.** (1990) A real covenant to remediate contaminated land.

▸ **future covenant.** (18c) A covenant that can be breached only upon interference with the possession of the grantee or the grantee's successors. • The covenants in this class are the covenant for further assurances, the covenant for quiet enjoyment, and the covenant of warranty. The distinction between future and present covenants becomes important in determining when the statute of limitations begins to run. Cf. *present covenant.*

▸ **general covenant against encumbrances.** See *covenant against encumbrances.*

▸ **implied reciprocal covenant.** (1948) A presumption that a promisee has, in return for a promise made respecting land, impliedly made a promise to the promisor respecting other land. — Also termed *implied reciprocal servitude.*

▸ **personal covenant.** (17c) A covenant that creates a personal right or obligation enforceable only between the covenanting parties and that is not binding on the heirs or assigns of the parties. Cf. *covenant running with the land.*

▸ **present covenant.** (18c) A covenant that can be breached only at the time of conveyance. • The three covenants in this class are the covenant against encumbrances, the covenant of right to convey, and the covenant of seisin. Cf. *future covenant.*

▸ **protection covenant.** See PROTECTION COVENANT.

▸ **real covenant.** See *covenant running with the land.*

▸ **restrictive covenant.** (1811) **1.** A private agreement, usu. in a deed or lease, that restricts the use or occupancy of real property, esp. by specifying lot sizes, building lines, architectural styles, and the uses to which the property may be put. • Some restrictive covenants, such as race-based restrictions on transfers, are unenforceable but do not necessarily void the deed. — Also termed *restrictive covenant in equity; equitable easement; equitable servitude.* **2.** See *covenant not to compete* under COVENANT (1).

▸ **right-to-convey covenant.** See *covenant of seisin.*

▸ **special covenant against encumbrances.** (1860) A grantor's promise that the property is free of encumbrances created by the grantor only, not the grantor's predecessors. See *special warranty deed* under DEED. Cf. *covenant against encumbrances.*

▸ **title covenant.** See *covenant for title.*

covenant, *vb.* (14c) To promise or undertake in a covenant; to agree formally.

covenantal, *adj.* (1863) Of, relating to, or involving a covenant.

covenant appurtenant. See COVENANT (4).

covenantee (kəv-ə-nən-**tee**). (17c) The person to whom a promise by covenant is made; one entitled to the benefit of a covenant.

covenanter. See COVENANTOR.

covenant in gross. See COVENANT (4).

covenant in restraint of trade. See *covenant not to compete* under COVENANT (1).

covenant marriage. See MARRIAGE (1).

covenant not to compete. See COVENANT (1).

covenant of good right to convey. See *covenant of seisin* under COVENANT (4).

covenant of seisin. See COVENANT (4).

covenantor (**kəv**-ə-nən-tər *or* kəv-ə-nən-**tor**). (17c) The person who makes a promise by covenant; one subject to the burden of a covenant. — Also spelled *covenanter.*

covenant running with the land. See COVENANT (4).

covenant that runs with the land. See *covenant running with the land* under COVENANT (4).

covenant to protect against drainage. See PROTECTION COVENANT.

covenant which runs with the land. See *covenant running with the land* under COVENANT (4).

Coventry Act (**kəv**-ən-tree *or* **kov**-). *Hist.* An 1803 English statute establishing the death penalty for anyone who, with malice aforethought, did "cut out or disable the tongue, put out an eye, slit the nose, cut off a nose or lip, or cut off or disable any limb or member of any subject; with the intention in so doing to maim or disfigure him."

> "[At common law,] an injury such as cutting off [a man's] ear or nose did not constitute mayhem . . . , because it did not result in permanent disablement, but merely disfigured the victim. This was corrected by an early English statute. It seems that an assault was made upon Sir John Coventry on the street by persons who waylaid him and slit his nose in revenge for obnoxious words uttered by him in Parliament. This emphasized the weakness of the law of mayhem, and the so-called 'Coventry Act' was passed [in 1803]." Rollin M. Perkins & Ronald N. Boyce, *Criminal Law* 239–40 (3d ed. 1982).

coventurer (koh-**ven**-chər-ər). (1913) Someone who undertakes a joint venture with one or more persons. — Also termed *co-adventurer.* Cf. JOINT VENTURE.

cover, *n.* The purchase on the open market, by the buyer in a breach-of-contract dispute, of goods to substitute for those promised but never delivered by the seller. • Under UCC § 2-712, the buyer can recover from the seller the difference between the cost of the substituted goods and the original contract price.

coverage, *n.* (1912) **1.** Inclusion of a risk under an insurance policy; the risks within the scope of an insurance policy. — **cover,** *vb.*

▸ **dependent coverage.** (1949) An insurance provision for protection of an insured's dependents.

▸ **full coverage.** (1916) Insurance protection that pays for the full amount of a loss with no deduction.

2. The ratio between corporate pretax income and corporate liability for bond interest payments.

coverage opinion. See OPINION (2).

coverage ratio. (1975) A measurement of a firm's ability to cover its financing charges.

cover-all clause. See MOTHER HUBBARD CLAUSE (2).

cover-baron. See COVERT BARON.

covered-interest arbitrage. See ARBITRAGE.

covered security. See SECURITY (4).

covered wages. See WAGE.

cover letter. See TRANSMITTAL LETTER.

cover note. (1914) A written statement by an insurance agent confirming that coverage is in effect. • The cover note is distinguished from a binder, which is prepared by the insurance company.

covert action. See *covert mission* under MISSION.

covert baron (**kəv**-ərt **bar**-ən). [Law French] (16c) *Hist.* The condition or status of a married woman at common law. — Also written *cover-baron.* — Also termed *covert de baron; baron covert.*

> "By marriage, the husband and wife are one person in law: that is, the very being or legal existence of the woman is suspended during the marriage, or at least is incorporated and consolidated into that of the husband: under whose wing, protection, and *cover,* she performs every thing; and is therefore called in our law-french a *feme-covert;* is said to be *covert-baron,* or under the protection and influence of her husband, her *baron,* or lord; and her condition during her marriage is called her *coverture.*" 1 William Blackstone, *Commentaries on the Laws of England* 430 (1765).

covert-entry search warrant. See SEARCH WARRANT.

covert-listening device. See LISTENING DEVICE.

covert mission. See MISSION.

covert operation. See *covert mission* under MISSION.

coverture (**kəv**-ər-chər *also* -tyoor), *n.* (16c) *Archaic.* The condition of being a married woman <under former law, a woman under coverture was allowed to sue only through the personality of her husband>. See *feme covert* under FEME. — **covert** (**kəv**-ərt), *adj.*

> "*Coverture,* is a french word signifying any thing that covereth, as apparell, a coverlet . . . . It is particularly applied in our common lawe, to the estate and condition of a maried woman, who by the lawes of our realme, is in (*potestate viri*) and therefore disabled to contract with any, to the preiudice of her selfe or her husband, without his consent and privity; or at the least, without his allowance and confirmation." John Cowell, *The Interpreter* (1607).

> "*Coverture* is by law applied to the state and condition of a married woman, who is *sub potestati viri,* (under the power of her husband) and therefore unable to contract with any to the damage of herself or husband, without his consent and privity, or his allowance and confirmation thereof. When a woman is married she is called a *Femme couvert,* and whatever is done concerning her during marriage is said to be done during coverture." *The Pocket Lawyer and Family Conveyancer* 96 (3d ed. 1833).

cover-up, *n.* (1927) An attempt to prevent authorities or the public from discovering the truth about something; esp., the concealment of wrongdoing by a conspiracy of deception, nondisclosure, and destruction of evidence, usu. combined with a refusal to cooperate with investigators. • A cover-up often involves obstruction of justice. — **cover up,** *vb.*

covin (**kəv**-ən). (14c) *Hist.* A secret conspiracy or agreement between two or more persons to injure or defraud another. — Also spelled *covine.*

> "Covin is a secret assent determined in the hearts of two or more, to the prejudice of another: As if a tenant for term of life, or tenant in tail, will secretly conspire with another, that the other shall recover against the tenant for life the

> land which he holds, &c. in prejudice of him in the reversion." *Termes de la Ley* 129 (1st Am. ed. 1812).

covinous (**kəv**-ə-nəs), *adj.* (16c) *Hist.* Of a deceitful or fraudulent nature.

cowboy lawyer. See *Rambo lawyer* under LAWYER.

coworker. (17c) Someone with whom one works, usu. in the same department or in a similar position.

coyote (kI-**yoh**-tee), *n.* (1923) *Slang.* Someone who is paid to smuggle illegal immigrants, esp. from Latin America into the United States. See PEOPLE-SMUGGLING.

cozen (**kəz**-ən), *vb.* (16c) *Hist.* To cheat or defraud. — Also spelled *cosen.*

cozening (**kəz**-ən-ing). (16c) *Hist.* A deceitful practice; the offense of cheating, or fraudulent dealing. — Also spelled *cosening.* Cf. STELLIONATUS.

> "*Cosening* is an offence unnamed, whereby any thing is done guilefully in or out of contracts, which cannot be fitly termed by any speciall name. It is called *stellionatus* in the civile law . . . ." John Cowell, *The Interpreter* (1607).

C.P. *abbr.* COURT OF COMMON PLEAS.

CPA. *abbr.* **1.** See *certified public accountant* under ACCOUNTANT (1). **2.** See *continued-prosecution application* under PATENT APPLICATION. **3.** CORRUPT-PRACTICES ACT.

CPC. *abbr.* **1.** Certificate of probable cause. See *certificate of appealability* under CERTIFICATE. **2.** COMMUNITY PATENT CONVENTION.

CPD. *abbr.* OFFICE OF COMMUNITY PLANNING AND DEVELOPMENT.

CPI. *abbr.* CONSUMER PRICE INDEX.

CPS. *abbr.* CHILD PROTECTIVE SERVICES.

CPSA. *abbr.* CHILD STATUS PROTECTION ACT.

CPSC. *abbr.* CONSUMER PRODUCT SAFETY COMMISSION.

CPT. *abbr.* CARRIAGE PAID TO.

CR. *abbr.* **1.** Conditional release. **2.** Crime report.

C.R. *abbr.* CURIA REGIS.

CRAC. A mnemonic acronym used mostly by law students and their legal-writing professors, esp. as a method of preparing legal-research memos — the letters standing for conclusion, rule, analysis, conclusion. Cf. CREAC; IRAC.

crack, *n.* (1985) A highly addictive crystalline form of cocaine resembling hard, brittle bits of plastic. — Also termed *crack cocaine.*

crack, *vb.* (17c) *Slang.* **1.** To open (a lock). **2.** To decode (security information); esp., to decipher or discover (a code, a password, etc. needed to break into a computer, network, server, or database). **3.** To bypass (an encryption or a security device, esp. one designed to prevent unauthorized access, as in a cable television box, or copying, as in a DVD player). **4.** To hack (a computer, network, server, or database) with the intention of causing damage or disruption. Cf. HACK.

crack cocaine. See CRACK, *n.*

crack house. (1985) *Slang.* A drug house where chemically purified, rock-like cocaine is sold. See DRUG HOUSE.

cracking, *n.* A gerrymandering technique in which a geographically concentrated political or racial group that is large enough to constitute a district's dominant force is broken up by district lines and dispersed throughout two or more districts. Cf. PACKING; STACKING (2).

craft union. See UNION.

cramdown, *n.* (1954) Court confirmation of a Chapter 11 bankruptcy plan despite the opposition of certain creditors. • Under the Bankruptcy Code, a court may confirm a plan — even if it has not been accepted by all classes of creditors — if the plan (1) has been accepted by at least one impaired class, (2) does not discriminate unfairly, and (3) is fair and equitable. 11 USCA § 1129(b). — **cram down,** *vb.*

crash-and-dash. See RAM RAID.

crashworthiness doctrine. (1969) *Products liability.* The principle that the manufacturer of a product will be held strictly liable for injuries occurring in a collision, even if the collision results from an independent cause, to the extent that a defect in the product causes injuries above and beyond those that would have occurred in the collision itself. — Also termed *second-collision doctrine; second-impact doctrine; enhanced-injury doctrine.*

crassa ignorantia (**kras**-ə ig-nə-**ran**-shee-ə). *Hist.* Gross ignorance, esp. in circumstances where a person was able to acquire knowledge and should have done so.

crassa negligentia (**kras**-ə neg-li-**jen**-shee-ə). [Latin] (17c) *Hist.* Crass negligence; gross negligence.

> "In the Civil Law: *Crassa negligentia* is termed *magna culpa* or *lata culpa*, and it is in some cases deemed equivalent to fraud or deceit . . . . In the Common Law: it is defined to be the want of that care which every man of common sense, under the circumstances, takes of his own property." 1 Henry C. Adams, *A Juridical Glossary* 510 (1886).

crastino (**kras**-tə-noh). [Law Latin] *Hist.* Tomorrow; on the morrow. • The return day of writs, so-called because the court terms always began on a saint's day; writs were therefore returnable the day after.

CRAT. *abbr.* See *charitable-remainder annuity trust* under TRUST (3).

CRD. *abbr.* CERTIFICATE OF RELIEF FROM DISABILITIES.

CREAC. A mnemonic acronym used mostly by law students and their legal-writing professors, esp. as a method of preparing legal-research memos — the letters standing for conclusion, rule, explanation, analysis, conclusion. Cf. CRAC; IRAC.

creancer (**kree**-ən-sər). [Law French] (14c) *Hist.* A creditor. — Also spelled *creansour.*

create a blank. (1829) *Parliamentary law.* To amend a motion by striking out one or more terms and replacing them with blanks rather than different terms. • This form allows a vote on several competing proposals at one time, rather than the usual process of voting separately on each proposal. See *amendment by striking out and inserting* under AMENDMENT (3); BLANK (2).

creationism. (1860) The teaching of the biblical version of the creation of the universe. • The United States Supreme Court held unconstitutional a Louisiana statute that forbade the teaching of the theory of evolution unless biblical creation was also taught. The Court found the law violated the Establishment Clause of the First Amendment because it lacked a "clear secular purpose." *Edwards v. Aguillard*, 482 U.S. 578, 107 S.Ct. 2573 (1987). See ANTI-EVOLUTION STATUTE.

▸ **scientific creationism.** (1972) A doctrine holding that the biblical account of creation is supported by scientific evidence.

creation science. (1970) The interpretation of scientific evidence, arguments, and knowledge to support creationism. See CREATIONISM.

creative sentence. See *alternative sentence* under SENTENCE.

creative work. See *work of authorship* under WORK (2).

creativity. *Copyright.* The degree to which a work displays imaginativeness beyond what a person of very ordinary talents might create. • Labor and expense are not elements of creativity; for that reason, they are not protected by copyright. *Feist Pubs. Inc. v. Rural Tel. Serv. Co.*, 499 U.S. 340, 111 S.Ct. 1282 (1991). Cf. ORIGINALITY, SWEAT-OF-THE-BROW DOCTRINE.

> "Where creativity refers to the nature of the work itself, originality refers to the nature of the author's contribution to the work. Thus, a public domain painting may evince great creativity, but if a copyright claimant adds nothing of his own to it, by way of reproduction or otherwise, then copyright will be denied on the basis of lack of originality. Conversely, a work may be entirely the product of the claimant's independent efforts, and hence original, but may nevertheless be denied protection as a work of art if it is completely lacking in any modicum of creativity." 1 Melville B. Nimmer & David Nimmer, *Nimmer on Copyright* § 2.08[B][2], at 2-88 (Supp. 1995).

creator. See SETTLOR (1).

creature. See ANIMAL.

creature of statute. (1854) A doctrine, governmental agency, etc. that would not exist but for a legislative act that brought it into being.

credendi causa (krə-**den**-dɪ **kaw**-zə), *adv.* [Latin] For the sake of credit.

credential. (*usu. pl.*) (17c) **1.** A document or other evidence that proves one's authority or expertise. **2.** A testimonial that a person is entitled to credit or to the right to exercise official power. **3.** The letter of credence given to an ambassador or other representative of a foreign country. **4.** *Parliamentary law.* Evidence of a delegate's entitlement to be seated and vote in a convention or other deliberative assembly. • Before the meeting begins, the evidence usu. takes the form of a certificate or proof of election or appointment, which the delegate presents to a credentials committee so that the committee can list the delegate on its roster. During the meeting, the evidence usu. takes the form of a badge or card that the credentials committee issues to each delegate on its roster. See *credentials committee* under COMMITTEE (1). — **credential,** *vb.*

credentials committee. See COMMITTEE (1).

credibility, *n.* (16c) The quality that makes something (as a witness or some evidence) worthy of belief. — **credible,** *adj.*

credible evidence. See EVIDENCE.

credible witness. See WITNESS.

credit, *n.* (16c) **1.** Belief; trust <the jury gave credit to Benson's version>. **2.** One's ability to borrow money; the faith in one's ability to pay debts <a customer with good credit>. **3.** The time that a seller gives the buyer to make the payment that is due <30 days' credit>. **4.** The availability of funds either from a financial institution or under a letter of credit <the bank extended a line of credit to the customer>.

▸ **bank credit.** (18c) Credit that a bank makes available to a borrower.

▸ **consumer credit.** (1925) Credit extended to an individual to facilitate the purchase of consumer goods and services.

▸ **installment credit.** (1926) Consumer credit scheduled to be repaid in two or more payments, usu. at regular intervals. • The seller ordinarily exacts finance charges.

▸ **noninstallment credit.** (1959) Consumer credit arranged to be repaid in a single payment. • Examples include doctors' and plumbers' bills.

▸ **revolving credit.** (1885) A consumer-credit arrangement that allows the borrower to buy goods or secure loans on a continuing basis as long as the outstanding balance does not exceed a specified limit. — Also termed *open credit; revolving charge account.* Cf. *revolver loan* under LOAN.

5. LETTER OF CREDIT <the bank issued a credit in favor of the exporter>. **6.** A deduction from an amount due; an accounting entry reflecting an addition to revenue or net worth <confirm that the credit was properly applied to my account>. Cf. DEBIT. **7.** TAX CREDIT <the $500 credit reduced their income-tax liability by $500>.

▸ **accumulated-earnings credit.** (1954) *Tax.* A deduction allowed in arriving at a corporation's accumulated taxable income. • It offsets the base on which the tax is assessed by reducing the taxable base by the greater of $250,000 or the accumulated earnings retained for the reasonable needs of the corporation, reduced by the net capital gain. IRC (26 USCA) § 535. See *accumulated-earnings tax* under TAX.

credit, *vb.* (17c) **1.** To believe <the jury did not credit this testimony>. **2.** To enter (as an amount) on the credit side of an account <the account was credited with $500>.

creditable. (17c) **1.** Worthy of being believed; credible <creditable evidence>. **2.** Capable of being ascribed or credited <creditable service time>. **3.** Reputable; respectable <creditable witness>.

credit accident and health insurance. See *credit disability insurance* under INSURANCE.

credit account. See CHARGE ACCOUNT.

credit balance. (1942) *Accounting.* The status of an account when the sum of the credit entries exceeds the sum of the debit entries.

credit bureau. (1874) An organization that compiles information on people's creditworthiness and publishes it in the form of reports that are used chiefly by merchants and service-providers who deal directly with customers. • The practices of credit bureaus are regulated by federal (and often state) law. Most bureaus are members of the Associated Credit Bureaus of America. — Also termed *commercial agency; mercantile agency.* Cf. CREDIT-REPORTING BUREAU.

credit card. (1888) **1.** An identification card used to obtain items on credit, usu. on a revolving basis. See *revolving credit* under CREDIT (4). Cf. DEBIT CARD. **2.** Any card, plate, coupon book, or other credit device existing for the purpose of obtaining money, labor, or services on credit.

15 USCA § 1602(*l*). **3.** A card, plate, coupon book, or other credit device existing for the purpose of obtaining money, property, labor, or services on credit. 15 USCA § 1602(k).

credit-card cramming. (2001) **1.** A credit-card issuer's practice of charging consumers for optional goods or services that the consumers have not agreed to pay or do not understand. • For example, the credit-card crammer may offer the consumer a free service for a limited period without making it clear that if the service is not canceled when the period ends, it will be automatically renewed for a fee. **2.** A single act of charging a consumer's credit card without authorization, particularly for goods or services that the consumer did not agree to or receive.

credit-card crime. (1970) The offense of using a credit card to purchase something with knowledge that (1) the card is stolen or forged, (2) the card has been revoked or canceled, or (3) the card's use is unauthorized.

credit-card insurance. See INSURANCE.

credit-card offense. See CREDIT-CARD CRIME.

credit-default swap. An agreement to purchase a debt in exchange for the seller's promise to compensate the buyer if the debtor defaults. — Abbr. CDS.

credit disability insurance. See INSURANCE.

credit freeze. See FREEZE (1).

credit insurance. See INSURANCE.

credit involuntary-unemployment insurance. See INSURANCE.

credit life insurance. See LIFE INSURANCE.

credit line. See LINE OF CREDIT.

credit memorandum. (1913) A document issued by a seller to a buyer confirming that the seller has credited (i.e., reduced) the buyer's account because of an error, return, or allowance.

credit mobilier. (1856) A company or association that carries on a banking business by making loans on the security of personal property.

creditor. (15c) **1.** One to whom a debt is owed; one who gives credit for money or goods. — Also termed *debtee.* **2.** *Roman law.* One to whom any obligation is owed, whether contractual or otherwise. Cf. DEBITOR. **3.** A person or entity with a definite claim against another, esp. a claim that is capable of adjustment and liquidation. **4.** *Bankruptcy.* A person or entity having a claim against the debtor predating the order for relief concerning the debtor. Cf. DEBTOR.

▸ **attaching creditor.** (18c) A creditor who has caused an attachment to be issued and levied on the debtor's property.

▸ **bona fide creditor.** (1827) A creditor who receives payment for value that it has provided and who may therefore be allowed to keep the payment even if it was made by mistake or with money wrongfully taken from another party, so long as the recipient had no notice of the problem and is not to blame for it. • The recipient is known then as a bona fide creditor, by analogy to the position of a *bona fide purchaser.* So if an insurance company mistakenly pays a hospital to cover treatment of a patient, but then discovers that the patient was not entitled to coverage, many courts will reject the insurer's claim for recovery against the hospital. — Also termed *bona fide payee.*

> "As a general rule, equitable concepts of unjust enrichment dictate that when a payment is made based upon a mistake of fact, the payor is entitled to restitution unless the payee has, in reliance on the payment, materially changed its position. Restitution will be denied, however, if the mistaken payment is made to a bona fide creditor of a third person — a creditor without fault because it made no misrepresentations to the payor and because it had no notice of the payor's mistake at the time the payment was made." *City of Hope Nat'l Med. Ctr. v. Superior Court,* 8 Cal. App. 4th 633, 636–37 (1992) (internal citations omitted).

▸ **bond creditor.** (18c) A creditor whose debt is secured by a bond.

▸ **catholic creditor.** (18c) *Scots law.* Someone who has a security interest in more than one piece of the debtor's property.

▸ **certificate creditor.** A creditor of a municipal corporation who receives a certificate of indebtedness rather than payment because the municipality cannot pay the debt. Cf. *warrant creditor.*

▸ **conditional creditor.** (1932) *Civil law.* A creditor who has either a future right of action or a right of action in expectancy.

▸ **contingent creditor.** (18c) Someone who will be owed a debt at some future time if some event occurs.

▸ **creditor at large.** (1852) A creditor who has not established the debt by reducing it to judgment, or who has not otherwise secured a lien on any of the debtor's property. See *unsecured creditor.*

▸ **domestic creditor.** (18c) A creditor who resides in the same state or country as the debtor or the debtor's property.

▸ **double creditor.** (1889) A creditor who has a lien on two funds. Cf. *single creditor.*

▸ **execution creditor.** (18c) A judgment creditor who has caused an execution to issue on the judgment.

▸ **foreign creditor.** (18c) A creditor who resides in a different state or country from that of the debtor or the debtor's property.

▸ **gap creditor.** (1957) *Bankruptcy.* A creditor who extends credit to, lends money to, or has a claim arise against the debtor in the period between the filing of an involuntary bankruptcy petition and the entry of the order for relief. • Under the Bankruptcy Code, a gap creditor's claim receives second priority, immediately below administrative claims. 11 USCA §§ 502(f), 507(a)(2).

▸ **general creditor.** See *unsecured creditor.*

▸ **hypothetical creditor.** (1943) *Bankruptcy.* An actual or code-created judicial-lien creditor or bona fide purchaser who establishes a bankruptcy trustee's status under the Bankruptcy Code's priority scheme, claiming property through the debtor at the time of the bankruptcy filing. 11 USCA § 544. — Also termed *hypothetical lien creditor.*

▸ **joint creditor.** (18c) A creditor who is entitled, along with another creditor, to demand payment from a debtor.

▸ **judgment creditor.** See JUDGMENT CREDITOR.

▸ **junior creditor.** (18c) A creditor whose claim accrued after that of another creditor; a creditor who holds a debt that is subordinate to another's.

▸ **known creditor.** (18c) A creditor whose identity or claim is either known or reasonably ascertainable by the debtor. • Known creditors are entitled to notice of the debtor's bankruptcy or corporate dissolution, as well as notice of any deadline for filing proofs of claim.

▸ **lien creditor.** (1821) A creditor whose claim is secured by a lien on the debtor's property; specif., someone who is (1) a creditor that has acquired a lien by attachment, levy, or the like, (2) an assignee for the benefit of creditors from the time of assignment, (3) a trustee in bankruptcy from the date of the filing of the bankruptcy petition, or (4) a receiver in equity from the time of appointment. UCC § 9-102(a)(52).

▸ **preferred creditor.** (18c) A creditor with a superior right to payment, such as a holder of a perfected security interest as compared to a holder of an unsecured claim.

▸ **principal creditor.** (17c) A creditor whose claim or demand greatly exceeds the claims of other creditors.

▸ **prior creditor.** (17c) A creditor who is given priority in payment from the debtor's assets.

▸ **secondary creditor.** (18c) A creditor whose claim is subordinate to a preferred creditor's.

▸ **secured creditor.** (1858) A creditor who has the right, on the debtor's default, to proceed against collateral and apply it to the payment of the debt. UCC § 9-102(a)(73). — Also termed *secured party*.

"'Secured party' means: (A) a person in whose favor a security interest is created or provided for under a security agreement, whether or not any obligation to be secured is outstanding; (B) a person that holds an agricultural lien; (C) a consignor; (D) a person to which accounts, chattel paper, payment intangibles, or promissory notes have been sold; (E) a trustee, indenture trustee, agent, collateral agent, or other representative in whose favor a security interest or agricultural lien is created or provided for; or (F) a person that holds a security interest under Section 2-401, 2-505, 2-711(3), 2A-508(5), 4-210, or 5-118." UCC § 9-102(a)(73).

▸ **single creditor.** (18c) In the marshaling of assets, a creditor with a lien on one fund. See RULE OF MARSHALING ASSETS. Cf. *double creditor.*

▸ **specialty creditor.** (1826) A creditor to whom an heir is liable for a decedent's debts to the extent of the land inherited. • Historically, unless the creditor obtained a judgment against the debtor before the debtor's death, the creditor's right of action on the debt was limited to the decedent's lawful heir. If the debtor devised the land to a stranger, the creditor's claim was defeated. See HEIR (1).

"There were three exceptions to this rule that a fee simple estate was not liable to the creditors of the deceased. Debts due to the Crown and debts due to *judgment* creditors were enforceable against the land notwithstanding the death of the owner, and thirdly, if the fee simple tenant had in his lifetime executed a deed whereby he covenanted for himself and his heirs to pay a sum of money, the creditor (called a *specialty creditor*) could make the heir liable for the debt to the extent of the land which had descended to him. But this privilege of the specialty creditor was not at first enforceable against an equitable fee simple, and it was strictly limited to a right of action against the *heir* of the deceased, so that the creditor was defrauded of his money if the deceased devised his land to a stranger." G.C. Cheshire, *Modern Law of Real Property* 738 (3d ed. 1933).

▸ **subsequent creditor.** (18c) A creditor whose claim comes into existence after a given fact or transaction, such as the recording of a deed or the execution of a voluntary conveyance.

▸ **unsecured creditor.** (1838) A creditor who, upon giving credit, takes no rights against specific property of the debtor. — Also termed *general creditor.* See *creditor at large.*

▸ **warrant creditor.** A creditor of a municipal corporation who is given a municipal warrant for the amount of the claim because the municipality lacks the funds to pay the debt. Cf. *certificate creditor.*

creditor beneficiary. See BENEFICIARY.

creditor dominii (**kred**-i-tor də-**min**-ee-ɪ). [Law Latin] *Hist.* The creditor who is entitled to ownership of an object; a secured creditor.

creditor's bill. (1826) An equitable suit in which a judgment creditor seeks to reach property that cannot be reached by the process available to enforce a judgment. — Also termed *creditor's suit.*

creditor's claim. See CLAIM (5).

creditors' committee. (1874) *Bankruptcy.* A committee comprising representatives of the creditors in a Chapter 11 proceeding, formed to negotiate the debtor's plan of reorganization. • Generally, a committee has no fewer than 3 and no more than 11 members and serves as an advisory body. 11 USCA § 1102. — Also termed *committee of creditors.*

creditors' composition. See COMPOSITION (2).

creditors' meeting. See MEETING.

creditor's petitition. See *involuntary petition* under PETITION (1).

creditors' rights. (17c) **1.** The interests or claims of a person who or entity that is owed a debt. **2.** The procedures, usu. defined by statute, to collect these interests or claims, such as garnishment of wages or the seizure and sale of property. **3.** The branch of law relating to these procedures. — Also spelled *creditor's rights.*

creditors' scheme of arrangement. See SCHEME OF ARRANGEMENT.

creditor's suit. See CREDITOR'S BILL.

creditors' voluntary winding up. See *involuntary winding up* under WINDING UP.

credit plan. (1918) A financing arrangement under which a borrower and a lender agree to terms for a loan's repayment with interest, usu. in installments.

▸ **open-end credit plan.** (1967) A plan under which a creditor reasonably expects repeated transactions, prescribes terms for those transactions, and includes a finance charge that may be periodically computed on the outstanding balance. 15 USCA § 1602(j).

credit property insurance. See INSURANCE.

credit rating. (1958) An evaluation of a potential borrower's ability to repay debt, prepared by a credit bureau at the request of a lender.

Credit Repair Organizations Act. A 1996 federal statute amending the Consumer Credit Protection Act to regulate the advertising and business practices of credit-repair organizations that use any instrumentality of interstate commerce or the mails. 15 USCA §§ 1679–1679j. — Abbr. CROA.

credit report. (1898) **1.** A credit bureau's report on a person's financial status, usu. including the approximate amounts and locations of a person's bank accounts, charge accounts, loans, and other debts, bill-paying habits, defaults, bankruptcies, foreclosures, marital status, occupation, income, and lawsuits. See CREDIT BUREAU. **2.** The report of a credit-reporting bureau, usu. including highly personal information gathered through interviews with a person's friends, neighbors, and coworkers. See CREDIT-REPORTING BUREAU.

credit-reporting bureau. (1904) An organization that, on request, prepares investigative reports not just on people's creditworthiness but also on personal information gathered from various sources, including interviews with neighbors, friends, and coworkers. • These reports are used chiefly by employers (for prospective employees), insurance companies (for applicants), and landlords (for prospective tenants). — Also termed *investigating bureau.* Cf. CREDIT BUREAU.

creditrix (**kred**-ə-triks), *n.* [fr. Latin *credere* "to lend, entrust"] (17c) *Civil law. Archaic.* A female creditor.

credit sale. See SALE.

credit service charge. See SERVICE CHARGE (2).

credit-shelter trust. See *bypass trust* under TRUST (3).

credit slip. (1903) A document that allows a store customer to either purchase another item or receive cash or credit for merchandise the customer has returned to the store.

credit union. (1881) A cooperative association that offers low-interest loans and other consumer banking services to persons sharing a common bond — often fellow employees and their family members. • Most credit unions are regulated by the National Credit Union Administration. State-chartered credit unions are also subject to regulation by the chartering state, and they may be regulated by state banking boards.

creditworthy, *adj.* (1840) (Of a potential borrower) financially sound enough that a lender will extend credit in the belief that default is unlikely; fiscally healthy. — **creditworthiness,** *n.*

credo. 1. A guiding principle; a motto. **2.** A collection of guiding principles; a personal code.

creeping acquisition. See ACQUISITION.

creeping tender offer. See *creeping acquisition* under ACQUISITION.

C reorganization. See REORGANIZATION (2).

crescendo rental. See RENTAL (1).

cretion (**kree**-shən), *n.* [fr. Latin *cernere* "to decide"] (1880) *Roman law.* **1.** A method or form of accepting an inheritance by an heir who is appointed in a testament. • Cretion usu. had to be declared within 100 days from the date an heir received notice of the appointment.

> "In the old law it was the practice to fix a time limit, usually of one hundred days, within which the heir was to make a formal acceptance, with the addition that if he failed to do so, he was to be disinherited and a substitute was to take the inheritance in his place. This formal acceptance was known as cretio from the Latin verb *cernere* — to decide. The practice had fallen into disuse before Justinian, who formally abolished it." R.W. Lee, *The Elements of Roman Law* 199 (4th ed. 1956).

2. The period within which an heir might decide whether to accept an inheritance. — Also termed (in Latin) *cretio* (**kree**-shee-oh). — **cretionary** (**kree**-shən-er-ee), *adj.*

crew member. See SEAMAN.

CRF. *abbr.* CRIMINAL-REFERRAL FORM.

crib, *n.* [Origin unknown] (14c) *Hist.* An enclosure at the side of a court where the apprentices stood to learn the law. • For a full history of this term and its variants, see J.H. Baker, "The Pecunes," in *The Legal Profession and the Common Law* 171, 173 (1986). — Also spelled *cribbe; crubbe.* — Also termed *pecune.*

cri de pais. See CRY DE PAIS.

crier (**krɪ**-ər). (15c) **1.** An officer of the court who makes public pronouncements as required by the court. Cf. BAILIFF (1). — Also termed *court crier.* **2.** An auctioneer. **3.** TOWN CRIER. — Also spelled *cryer.*

criez la peez (**krɪ**-eez lə **peez**). [Law French] *Hist.* Rehearse the concord (or peace). • This phrase was used to confirm the conveyance of land by fine. The serjeant or countor in attendance read the phrase aloud in court. See FINE (1).

crim. con. (18c) *abbr.* CRIMINAL CONVERSATION.

crime. (14c) An act that the law makes punishable; the breach of a legal duty treated as the subject-matter of a criminal proceeding. — Also termed *criminal wrong.* See OFFENSE (2).

> "Understanding that the conception of *Crime,* as distinguished from that of *Wrong* or *Tort* and from that of *Sin,* involves the idea of injury to the State of collective community, we first find that the commonwealth, in literal conformity with the conception, itself interposed directly, and by isolated acts, to avenge itself on the author of the evil which it had suffered." Henry S. Maine, *Ancient Law* 320 (17th ed. 1901).

> "It is a curious fact that all the minor acts enumerated in the penal code of a state like, say, New York are in law called crimes, which term includes both murder and overparking. It is a strong term to use for the latter, and of course the law has for centuries recognized that there are more serious and less serious crimes. At the common law, however, only two classes were recognized, serious crimes or felonies, and minor crimes or misdemeanors." Max Radin, *The Law and You* 91 (1948).

▸ **administrative crime.** (1943) An offense consisting of a violation of an administrative rule or regulation that carries with it a criminal sanction.

▸ **antecedent crime.** See PRIOR CONVICTION.

▸ **assimilative crime.** A state-law crime committed in a place within federal jurisdiction or tried in a federal court.

▸ **bankruptcy crime.** See BANKRUPTCY CRIME.

▸ **capital crime.** See *capital offense* under OFFENSE (2).

▸ **commercial crime.** (1900) A crime that affects commerce; esp., a crime directed toward the property or revenues of a commercial establishment. • Examples include robbery of a business, embezzlement, counterfeiting, forgery, prostitution, illegal gambling, and extortion. *See* 26 CFR § 403.38.

▸ **common-law crime.** (1827) A crime that is punishable under the common law, rather than by force of statute. — Also termed *common-law offense.* Cf. *statutory crime.*

▸ **complainantless crime.** See *victimless crime.*

▸ **computer crime.** (1971) A crime involving the use of a computer, such as sabotaging or stealing electronically stored data. — Also termed *cybercrime.*

▸ **consensual crime.** See *victimless crime.*

▸ **constructive crime.** (1829) A crime that is built up or created when a court enlarges a statute by altering or straining the statute's language, esp. to drawing unreasonable implications and inferences from it. — Also termed *implied crime; presumed crime.*

▸ **continuous crime.** (1907) **1.** A crime that continues after an initial illegal act has been consummated; a crime that involves ongoing elements. • An example is illegal U.S. drug importation. The criminal act is completed not when the drugs enter the country, but when the drugs reach their final destination. **2.** A crime (such as driving a stolen vehicle) that continues over an extended period. Cf. *instantaneous crime.*

▸ **corporate crime.** (1934) A crime committed by a corporation's representatives acting on its behalf. • Examples include price-fixing and consumer fraud. Although a corporation as an entity cannot commit a crime other than through its representatives, it can be named as a criminal defendant — Also termed *organizational crime.* Cf. *occupational crime.*

▸ **credit-card crime.** See CREDIT-CARD CRIME.

▸ **crime against humanity.** See CRIME AGAINST HUMANITY.

▸ **crime against international law.** See CRIME AGAINST THE LAW OF NATIONS.

▸ **crime against nature.** See SODOMY.

▸ **crime against peace.** See CRIME AGAINST PEACE.

▸ **crime against the environment.** See ENVIRONMENTAL CRIME.

▸ **crime against the law of nations.** See CRIME AGAINST THE LAW OF NATIONS.

▸ **crime malum in se.** See MALUM IN SE.

▸ **crime malum prohibitum.** See MALUM PROHIBITUM.

▸ **crime of omission.** (18c) An offense that carries as its material component the failure to act.

▸ **crime of passion.** (18c) A crime committed in the heat of an emotionally charged moment, with no opportunity to reflect on what is happening. See HEAT OF PASSION.

▸ **crime of violence.** See *violent crime.*

▸ **crime without victims.** See *victimless crime.*

▸ **cybercrime.** See *computer crime.*

▸ **economic crime.** A nonphysical crime committed to obtain a financial gain or a professional advantage.

> "There are two major styles of economic crime. The first consists of crimes committed by businessmen as an adjunct to their regular business activities. Businessmen's responsibilities give them the opportunity, for example, to commit embezzlement, to violate regulations directed at their areas of business activity, or to evade the payment of taxes. This style of economic crime is often called white-collar crime. The second style of economic crime is the provision of illegal goods and services or the provision of goods and services in an illegal manner. Illegal provision of goods and services requires coordinated economic activity similar to that of normal business, but all of those engaged in it are involved in crime. The madam operating a brothel has many concerns identical to the manager of a resort hotel, and the distributor of marijuana must worry about the efficacy of his distribution system just as does a distributor of any other product. This type of economic crime is often called organized crime because the necessity of economic coordination outside the law leads to the formation of criminal groups with elaborate organizational customs and practices." Edmund W. Kitch, "Economic Crime," in 2 *Encyclopedia of Crime and Justice* 670, 671 (Sanford H. Kadish ed., 1983).

▸ **enhanced crime.** (1928) An offense that has a greater degree of severity than the normal offense of the same kind, usu. because of aggravating circumstances.

▸ **environmental crime.** See ENVIRONMENTAL CRIME.

▸ **expressive crime.** (1972) A crime committed for the sake of the crime itself, esp. out of frustration, rage, or other emotion rather than for financial gain. Cf. *instrumental crime.*

▸ **federal crime.** See FEDERAL CRIME.

▸ **general-intent crime.** (1955) A crime that involves performing a particular act without intending a further act or a further result.

▸ **hate crime.** (1984) A felony or misdemeanor motivated by the perpetrator's prejudice, usu. an intense bigotry, on the basis of the victim's race, color, national origin, ancestry, gender, religion, religious practice, age, disability, or sexual orientation. • Certain groups have lobbied to expand the definition by statute to include a crime motivated by the victim's disability, gender, or sexual orientation. Cf. *hate speech* under SPEECH (1).

▸ **high crime.** (17c) *Constitutional law.* A crime that is very serious, though not necessarily a felony. • Under the U.S. Constitution, a government officer's commission of a "high crime" is, along with treason and bribery, grounds for removal from office. U.S. Const. art. II, § 4. See IMPEACHABLE OFFENSE.

▸ **honor crime.** (1997) A crime motivated by a desire to punish a person who the perpetrator believes has injured a person's or group's sense of honor. • The term is most often applied to crimes committed against Muslim women by members of their own families for behavior that leads to perceived social harm, esp. loss of family honor. The term also extends to non-Muslims and covers many acts of violence, including assault, rape, infanticide, and murder. When the crime involves a death, it is also termed *honor killing.*

▸ **implied crime.** See *constructive crime.*

▸ **inchoate crime.** See *inchoate offense* under OFFENSE (2).

▸ **index crime.** See *index offense* under OFFENSE (2).

▸ **infamous crime** (in-fə-məs). (16c) **1.** At common law, a crime for which part of the punishment was infamy, so that one who committed it would be declared ineligible to serve on a jury, hold public office, or testify. • Examples are perjury, treason, and fraud. **2.** A crime punishable by imprisonment in a penitentiary. • The Fifth Amendment requires a grand-jury indictment for the prosecution of infamous (or capital) crimes, which include all federal felony offenses. See *indictable offense* under OFFENSE (2). Cf. *noninfamous crime.*

> "At common law an infamous crime was one . . . inconsistent with the common principles of honesty and humanity. Infamous crimes were treason, felony, all offenses found in fraud and which came within the general notion of the crimen falsi of the civil law, piracy, swindling, cheating,

barratry, and the bribing of a witness to absent himself from a trial, in order to get rid of his evidence." Justin Miller, *Handbook of Criminal Law* § 8, at 25 (1934).

▸ **instantaneous crime.** (1887) A crime that is fully completed by a single act, as arson or murder, rather than a series of acts. • The statute of limitations for an instantaneous crime begins to run with its completion. Cf. *continuous crime.*

▸ **instrumental crime.** (1971) A crime committed to further another end or result; esp., a crime committed to obtain money to purchase a good or service. Cf. *expressive crime.*

▸ **intellectual-property crime.** See INTELLECTUAL-PROPERTY CRIME.

▸ **international crime.** See INTERNATIONAL CRIME.

▸ **major crime.** See FELONY (1).

▸ **maritime crime.** (18c) **1.** A crime committed aboard or against a marine vessel, its passengers or crew, or an offshore installation. **2.** The use of a marine vessel or offshore installation to facilitate the commission of an unlawful act.

▸ **noninfamous crime.** (1989) A crime that does not qualify as an infamous crime. Cf. *infamous crime.*

▸ **occupational crime.** (1964) A crime that a person commits for personal gain while on the job. Cf. *corporate crime.*

▸ **organizational crime.** See *corporate crime.*

▸ **organized crime.** See ORGANIZED CRIME.

▸ **personal-condition crime.** See *status crime.*

▸ **personal crime.** (1841) A crime (such as rape, robbery, or pickpocketing) that is committed against an individual's person.

▸ **political crime.** See POLITICAL OFFENSE.

▸ **predatory crime.** (1921) A crime that involves preying on and victimizing individuals. • Examples include robbery, rape, and carjacking.

▸ **preliminary crime.** See *inchoate offense* under OFFENSE (2).

▸ **presumed crime.** See *constructive crime.*

▸ **prior crime.** See PRIOR CONVICTION.

▸ **quasi-crime.** (18c) *Hist.* **1.** An offense not subject to criminal prosecution (such as contempt or violation of a municipal ordinance) but for which penalties or forfeitures can be imposed. • The term includes offenses that give rise to *qui tam* actions and forfeitures for the violation of a public duty. **2.** An offense for which someone other than the actual perpetrator is held liable, the perpetrator being presumed to act on the command of the responsible party. See *quasi-delict* (1) under DELICT (1).

▸ **serious crime. 1.** See *serious offense* under OFFENSE (2). **2.** See FELONY (1).

▸ **signature crime.** (1974) A distinctive crime so similar in pattern, scheme, or modus operandi to previous crimes that it identifies a particular defendant as the perpetrator.

▸ **spontaneous crime.** (1974) A criminal act that occurs suddenly and without premeditation in response to an unforeseen stimulus. • For example, a husband who discovers his wife in bed with another man and shoots him could be said to have committed an effectively spontaneous crime.

▸ **status crime.** (1961) A crime of which a person is guilty by being in a certain condition or of a specific character. • An example of a status crime is vagrancy. — Also termed *status offense; personal-condition crime.*

▸ **statutory crime.** (1940) A crime punishable by statute.— Also termed *statutory offense.* Cf. *common-law crime.*

▸ **street crime.** (1966) A crime generally directed against a person in public, such as mugging, theft, or robbery. — Also termed *visible crime.*

▸ **strict-liability crime.** (1954) An offense for which the action alone is enough to warrant a conviction, with no need to prove a mental state; specif., a crime that does not require a mens rea element, such as traffic offenses and illegal sales of intoxicating liquor.

▸ **substantive crime.** See *substantive offense* under OFFENSE (2).

▸ **vice crime.** A crime of immoral conduct, such as gambling or prostitution.

▸ **victimless crime.** (1964) A crime that is considered to have no direct victim, usu. because only consenting adults are involved. • Examples are possession of illicit drugs and deviant sexual intercourse between consenting adults. — Also termed *consensual crime; crime without victims; complainantless crime.*

"When a man's house has been robbed or his brother murdered, he is likely to take this complaint vigorously to the police and demand action. His presence on the scene dramatizes the need for law enforcement and gives sense and purpose to the work of the police and district attorney. In contrast, the absence of a prosecuting witness surrounds 'crimes without victims' with an entirely different atmosphere. Here it is the police who must assume the initiative. If they attempt to work without the aid of informers, they must resort to spying, and this spying is rendered all the more distasteful because what is spied upon is sordid and pitiable." Lon L. Fuller, *Anatomy of the Law* 44 (1968).

▸ **violent crime.** (18c) A crime that has as an element the use, attempted use, threatened use, or substantial risk of use of physical force against the person or property of another. 18 USCA § 16; USSG § 2E1.3. — Also termed *crime of violence.* See *violent offense* under OFFENSE.

▸ **visible crime.** See *street crime.*

▸ **war crime.** See WAR CRIME.

▸ **white-collar crime.** See WHITE-COLLAR CRIME.

crime against humanity. (1860) *Int'l law.* A brutal crime that is not an isolated incident but that involves large and systematic actions, often cloaked with official authority, and that shocks the conscience of humankind; an inhumane act such as persecution on political, racial, or religious grounds, regardless of whether it is permitted by the domestic law of the country where perpetrated. • Among the specific crimes that fall within this category are mass murder, extermination, enslavement, deportation, and other inhumane acts perpetrated against a population, whether in wartime or not. *See* Statute of the International Criminal Court, art. 3 (37 ILM 999).

crime against international law. See CRIME AGAINST THE LAW OF NATIONS.

crime against peace. (1945) *Int'l law.* An international crime in which the offenders plan, prepare, initiate, or wage a war of aggression or a war in violation of international peace treaties, agreements, or assurances.

crime against the law of nations. (1839) *Int'l law.* **1.** A crime punishable under internationally prescribed criminal law or defined by an international convention and required to be made punishable under the criminal law of the member states. **2.** A crime punishable under international law; an act that is internationally agreed to be of a criminal nature, such as genocide, piracy, or engaging in the slave trade. — Also termed *crime against international law.*

crime against the person. See CRIMES AGAINST PERSONS.

crime-fraud exception. (1973) **1.** The doctrine that neither the attorney–client privilege nor the attorney-work-product privilege protects attorney–client communications that are in furtherance of a current or planned crime or fraud. *Clark v. U.S.*, 289 U.S. 1, 53 S.Ct. 465 (1933); *In re Grand Jury Subpoena Duces Tecum*, 731 F.2d 1032 (2d Cir. 1984). **2.** An exception to the marital-facts privilege denying protection when the disputed communication was in furtherance of criminal activity.

crime insurance. See INSURANCE.

crime laboratory. A forensic-science laboratory that examines and analyzes evidence from criminal cases. — Also termed *crime lab; forensic lab; police lab.*

crime malum in se. See MALUM IN SE.

crime malum prohibitum. See MALUM PROHIBITUM.

crimen (**krɪ**-mən), *n.* [Latin] **1.** An accusation or charge of a crime. **2.** A crime. Pl. ***crimina*** (**krim**-ə-nə).

▸ ***crimen expilatae hereditatis*** (**krɪ**-mən eks-pə-**lay**-tee hə-red-i-**tay**-tis). *Roman law.* A false claimant's willful spoliation of an inheritance.

▸ ***crimen falsi*** (**krɪ**-mən **fal**-sɪ *or* **fawl**-sɪ). [Latin "the crime of falsifying"] (17c) **1.** A crime in the nature of perjury. — Also termed *falsum.* **2.** Any other offense that involves some element of dishonesty or false statement. *See* Fed. R. Evid. 609(a)(2).

> "The starting point [for perjury] seems to have been the so-called *crimen falsi*, — crime of falsifying. In the beginning, perhaps, one convicted of perjury was deemed too untrustworthy to be permitted to testify in any other case, and the idea grew until the term '*crimen falsi*' included any crime involving an element of deceit, fraud or corruption." Rollin M. Perkins & Ronald N. Boyce, *Criminal Law* 26 (3d ed. 1982).

▸ ***crimen feloniae imposuit*** (**krɪ**-mən fə-**loh**-nee-ee im-**poz**-yə-wit). To accuse or charge with a felony.

▸ ***crimen furti*** (**krɪ**-mən **fər**-tɪ). [Latin "the crime of stealing"] See THEFT.

▸ ***crimen incendii*** (**krɪ**-mən in-**sen**-dee-ɪ). [Latin "the crime of burning"] See ARSON.

▸ ***crimen innominatum*** (**krɪ**-mən i-nom-ə-**nay**-təm). [Latin "the nameless crime"] See SODOMY.

▸ ***crimen majestatis*** (**krɪ**-mən maj-ə-**stay**-tis). [Latin "crime against majesty"] (17c) *Hist.* High treason; any crime against the king's person or dignity; LESE MAJESTY. • Under Roman law, *crimen majestatis* denoted any enterprise by a Roman citizen or other person against the republic or the emperor. — Also termed *crimen laesae majestatis.* See LESE MAJESTY. Cf. PERDUELLIO.

▸ ***crimen plagii*** (**krɪ**-mən **play**-jee-ɪ). [Latin] *Roman law.* See PLAGIUM.

▸ ***crimen raptus*** (**krɪ**-mən **rap**-təs). [Latin "the crime of rape"] See RAPE (2).

▸ ***crimen repetundarum*** (**krɪ**-mən rep-ə-tən-**dair**-əm). [Latin "accusation of (money) to be repaid"] (17c) *Roman law.* **1.** A charge of extortion brought against a Roman provincial governor. **2.** Any act of misgovernment or oppression on the part of a magistrate or official.

▸ ***crimen roberiae*** (**krɪ**-mən rə-**beer**-ee-ee). [Latin "the crime of robbery"] ROBBERY.

crime of omission. See CRIME.

crime of passion. See CRIME.

crime of violence. See *violent crime* under CRIME.

crimes against persons. (1827) A category of criminal offenses in which the perpetrator uses or threatens to use force. • Examples include murder, rape, aggravated assault, and robbery. — Also termed *crimes against the person.* Cf. *offense against the person* under OFFENSE (2).

crimes against property. (1827) A category of criminal offenses in which the perpetrator seeks to derive an unlawful benefit from — or do damage to — another's property without the use or threat of force. • Examples include burglary, theft, and arson (even though arson may result in injury or death). — Also termed *property crimes.* Cf. *offense against property* under OFFENSE (2).

crimes against the person. See CRIMES AGAINST PERSONS.

crime-scene re-creation. (2004) The simulation of the setting of a crime for purposes of conducting an experiment purporting to reconstruct actual events, often to show a jury what presumably occurred. • The proponent of such evidence must demonstrate a substantial similarity of conditions. For the evidence to be admissible, the conditions need not be identical but must be sufficiently similar to provide a fair comparison. *U.S. v. Birch*, 39 F.3d 1089, 1092 (10th Cir. 1994). Some crime-scene reenactments are produced using computer-generated evidence (CGE). — Also termed *crime-scene reenactment; crime-scene reconstruction.*

crime score. (1952) A number assigned from an established scale, indicating the relative seriousness of an offense based on the nature of the injury or the extent of property damage. • Prosecutors use crime scores and defendant scores to promote uniform treatment of similar cases and to assess which cases need extensive pretrial preparation. Cf. DEFENDANT SCORE.

crime statistics. (1905) Figures compiled by a governmental agency to show the incidence of various types of crime within a defined geographic area during a specified time.

crime wave. (1889) A sudden major increase in the amount of crime in an area.

crime without victims. See *victimless crime* under CRIME.

crimina extraordinaria (**krim**-ə-nə ek-stror-də-**nair**-ee-ə). [Latin] (16c) *Roman law.* Extraordinary crimes; crimes not brought before a *quaestio perpetua.* • These crimes carried no fixed penalty and were punished according to the judge's discretion.

criminal, *adj.* (15c) **1.** Of, relating to, or involving a crime; in the nature of a crime <criminal mischief>. **2.** Of, relating to, or involving the part of the legal system that is concerned with crime; connected with the administration of penal justice <the criminal courts>. **3.** Wrong, dishonest, and unacceptable.

criminal, *n.* (17c) **1.** Someone who is involved in illegal activities; one who has committed a criminal offense. **2.** Someone who has been convicted of a crime.

▸ **career criminal.** See RECIDIVIST.

▸ **dangerous criminal.** (18c) A criminal who has either committed a violent crime or used force in trying to escape from custody.

▸ **episodic criminal.** (1976) **1.** Someone who commits crimes sporadically. **2.** Someone who commits crimes only during periods of intense stress, as in the heat of passion.

▸ **habitual criminal.** See RECIDIVIST.

▸ **state criminal.** (17c) **1.** Someone who has committed a crime against the state (such as treason); a political criminal. **2.** FELON. **3.** Someone who has committed a crime under state law.

criminal abandonment. See ABANDONMENT (4).

criminal abortion. See ABORTION.

criminal act. See ACT (2).

criminal action. See ACTION (4).

criminal anarchy. See ANARCHY.

criminal anthropology. (1882) **1.** A branch of anthropology dealing with the mental and physical characteristics of criminals. **2.** CRIMINOLOGY.

criminal arrest. See ARREST (2).

criminal assault. See ASSAULT.

criminal attempt. See ATTEMPT.

criminal bankruptcy. See *bankruptcy fraud* under FRAUD.

criminal battery. See BATTERY (1).

criminal behavior. (17c) Conduct that causes social harm and is defined and punished by law. — Also termed *criminal conduct.*

criminal capacity. See CAPACITY (3).

criminal charge. See CHARGE (1).

criminal code. See PENAL CODE.

criminal coercion. See COERCION (2).

criminal complaint. See COMPLAINT (2).

criminal conduct. See CRIMINAL BEHAVIOR.

criminal conspiracy. See CONSPIRACY.

criminal contempt. See CONTEMPT.

criminal conversation. (18c) *Archaic.* A tort action for adultery, brought by a husband against a third party who engaged in sexual intercourse with his wife. • Criminal conversation has been abolished in most jurisdictions. — Abbr. crim. con. See HEARTBALM STATUTE.

> "An action (whether of trespass or case is uncertain, but probably trespass) formerly lay against one who had committed adultery with the wife of the plaintiff. It was known as an action for criminal conversation. The wife's consent was irrelevant. The action was distinct from that of enticement: one may commit adultery without enticing a wife away from her husband. The action was no doubt a necessity when divorce could only be obtained by Act of Parliament: as Parliament was not a tribunal suitable for trying allegations of adultery it was reasonable to require the petitioner to establish the truth of his allegations before a court of law. The action might also have been justified on the ground that the plaintiff is in substance complaining of the invasion of privacy of his marriage, and the insult thereby caused to his honour as a husband." R.F.V. Heuston, *Salmond on the Law of Torts* 358 (17th ed. 1977).

criminal court. See COURT.

criminal-court judge. See JUDGE.

criminal damage to property. (1946) **1.** Injury, destruction, or substantial impairment to the use of property (other than by fire or explosion) without the consent of a person having an interest in the property. **2.** Injury, destruction, or substantial impairment to the use of property (other than by fire or explosion) with the intent to injure or defraud an insurer or lienholder. Cf. ARSON.

criminal defamation. See DEFAMATION.

criminal defendant. (18c) Someone who is accused in a criminal proceeding.

criminal defense. 1. The field of criminal law concerning the rights of a defendant accused of a crime and the legal theories that negate elements of crimes. **2.** The particular legal theory used in defense of a particular criminal defendant. **3.** See DEFENSE (1). **4.** An attorney who represents a person accused of a crime.

criminal desertion. See DESERTION.

criminal-disposition report. (1990) In some jurisdictions, a form filled out by court personnel at the outset and again at the end of a criminal case and sent to a government department or division that tracks statistics about criminal caseloads and outcomes.

criminal facilitation. 1. See AID AND ABET. **2.** See FACILITATION (2).

criminal forfeiture. See FORFEITURE.

criminal fraud. See FRAUD.

criminal history record. See RAP SHEET.

criminal homicide. See HOMICIDE.

criminal infringement. See INFRINGEMENT.

criminal instrument. (1901) **1.** Something made or adapted for criminal use. Model Penal Code § 5.06(1)(a). **2.** Something commonly used for criminal purposes and possessed under circumstances showing an unlawful purpose. Model Penal Code § 5.06(1)(b). — Also termed *instrument of crime.*

criminal-instrumentality rule. (1942) The principle that when a criminal act is committed, that act — rather than the victim's negligence that made the crime possible — will be considered to be the crime's proximate cause.

criminal intent. (17c) **1.** See INTENT (1). **2.** MENS REA.

criminalism. (1866) **1.** A pathological tendency toward criminality. **2.** *Archaic.* The branch of psychiatry dealing with habitual criminals.

criminalist (krim-ə-nəl-ist). (17c) **1.** Someone who practices criminalistics as a profession. **2.** *Archaic.* One versed in criminal law. **3.** *Archaic.* A psychiatrist who treats criminals. **4.** *Archaic.* A habitual criminal.

criminalistics (krim-ə-nə-**lis**-tiks), *n.* (1943) The science of crime detection, usu. involving the subjection of physical evidence to laboratory analysis, including ballistic testing, blood-fluid and tissue analysis, and other tests. Cf. CRIMINOLOGY. — **criminalistic,** *adj.*

criminaliter (krim-ə-**nay**-lə-tər), *adv.* [Latin] Criminally <answerable both *civiliter* and *criminaliter*>. Cf. CIVILITER (1).

criminality (krim-ə-**nal**-ə-tee). (17c) **1.** The quality, state, or condition of being criminal. **2.** An act or practice that constitutes a crime. See DOUBLE CRIMINALITY.

▸ **dual criminality.** See DOUBLE CRIMINALITY.

criminalization (krim-ə-nəl-ə-**zay**-shən), *n.* (1945) **1.** The act or an instance of making a previously lawful act criminal, usu. by passing a statute. Cf. DECRIMINALIZATION; CIVILIZATION. **2.** The process by which a person develops into a criminal. — **criminalize,** *vb.*

criminalize (**krim**-ə-nəl-ɪz), *vb.* (17c) To make illegal; to outlaw.

criminal jurisdiction. See JURISDICTION.

criminal justice. (16c) **1.** The methods by which a society deals with those who are accused of having committed crimes. See LAW ENFORCEMENT (1). Cf. CIVIL JUSTICE. **2.** The field of study pursued by those seeking to enter law enforcement as a profession. • Many colleges offer degrees in criminal justice, typically after two to four years of study. — Also termed (in sense 2) *police science*; *law enforcement.*

criminal-justice system. (1929) The collective institutions through which an accused offender passes until the accusations have been disposed of or the assessed punishment concluded. • The system typically has three components: law enforcement (police, sheriffs, marshals), the judicial process (judges, prosecutors, defense lawyers), and corrections (prison officials, probation officers, and parole officers). — Also termed *law-enforcement system.*

criminal law. (18c) The body of law defining offenses against the community at large, regulating how suspects are investigated, charged, and tried, and establishing punishments for convicted offenders. — Also termed *penal law.*

> "The criminal law represents the pathology of civilization." Morris R. Cohen, *Reason and Law* 70 (1961).

> "Often the term 'criminal law' is used to include all that is involved in 'the administration of criminal justice' in the broadest sense. As so employed it embraces three different fields, known to the lawyer as (1) the substantive criminal law, (2) criminal procedure, and (3) special problems in the administration and enforcement of criminal justice. . . . The phrase 'criminal law' is more commonly used to include only that part of the general field known as the substantive criminal law . . . ." Rollin M. Perkins & Ronald N. Boyce, *Criminal Law* 1, 5 (3d ed. 1982).

> "The term 'criminal law' carries more meaning — and more controversy — than one might expect. The problem is finding the appropriate term for the field of law that both defines specific offenses such as theft and homicide and also lays down the general principles of criminal responsibility. The conventional term for this field in Continental European legal cultures is not criminal law but 'penal law' (*Strafrecht, derecho penal, driot pénal, diritto penale,* etc.). Of course one can say 'criminal law' in all of these languages, and in various times and various places the phrase *Kriminalrecht* or 'criminal law' did have currency, but the pattern of modern usage has changed, and this change is rich with paradox. These two terms — criminal law and penal law — highlight different features of the overall body of the criminal law. 'Criminal law' suggests that the field is about defining who criminals are and determining the appropriate way of dealing with them. That is, the idea of *criminal* law begins with the classification of those who violate the law as offenders and leaves open the appropriate response to protect society, be it civil commitment or punishment. The term 'penal law' highlights one form of social response to criminal behavior, namely the sanction of punishment by the state. The term 'criminal law,' therefore, is broader, for it includes within its ambit the responses of protective commitment for the criminally insane, licensing regulations, and other administrative techniques for protecting the public from dangerous people." 1 George P. Fletcher, *The Grammar of Criminal Law: American, Comparative, and International* 69–70 (2007).

criminal lawyer. See LAWYER.

criminal letter. *Scots law.* A summons.

criminal libel. See LIBEL (2).

criminally negligent homicide. See *negligent homicide* under HOMICIDE.

criminal miscarriage. *Hist.* See ABORTION (1).

criminal mischief. See MALICIOUS MISCHIEF.

criminal neglect of family. See NONSUPPORT.

criminal negligence. See NEGLIGENCE.

criminal nonsupport. See NONSUPPORT.

criminal offense. See OFFENSE (2).

criminal operation. (1893) *Hist.* See ABORTION (1).

criminal plea. See PLEA (1).

criminal policy. (1893) The branch of criminal science concerned with protecting against crime. • It draws on information provided by criminology, and its subjects for investigation are (1) the appropriate measures of social organization for preventing harmful activities, and (2) the treatment to be accorded to those who have caused harm, i.e., whether the offenders should receive warnings, supervised probation, or medical treatment, or whether they should suffer serious deprivations of life or liberty such as imprisonment or capital punishment.

criminal possession. See POSSESSION.

criminal principal. See PRINCIPAL (2).

criminal procedure. (18c) The rules governing the mechanisms under which crimes are investigated, prosecuted, adjudicated, and punished. • It includes the protection of accused persons' constitutional rights.

criminal proceeding. (*often pl.*) (16c) A judicial hearing, session, or prosecution in which a court adjudicates whether a person has committed a crime or, having already fixed guilt, decides on the offender's punishment; a criminal hearing or trial.

criminal process. See PROCESS (2).

criminal prosecution. See PROSECUTION (2).

criminal protector. (1978) An accessory after the fact to a felony; one who aids or harbors a wrongdoer after the commission of a crime.

criminal record. (18c) An official record kept by the police of any crimes a person has committed.

criminal-referral form. (1985) A form once required by federal regulatory authorities (from 1988 to 1996) for reporting every instance when a bank employee or affiliate committed or aided in committing a crime such as credit-card fraud, employee theft, or check-kiting. • This form, like the suspicious-transaction report, has since been superseded by the suspicious-activity report. — Abbr. CRF. See SUSPICIOUS-ACTIVITY REPORT.

criminal registration. See REGISTRATION (1).

criminal responsibility. **1.** See RESPONSIBILITY (2). **2.** See RESPONSIBILITY (3).

criminal restitution. See RESTITUTION (4).

criminal sanction. See SANCTION (3).

criminal science. (1891) The study of crime with a view to discovering the causes of criminality, devising the most effective methods of reducing crime, and perfecting the means for dealing with those who have committed crimes. • The three main branches of criminal science are criminology, criminal policy, and criminal law.

criminal sexual act. See SODOMY.

criminal sexual battery. See *sexual battery* under BATTERY (1).

criminal sexual conduct. **1.** RAPE (2). **2.** See *sexual assault* under ASSAULT. **3.** See FIRST-DEGREE SEXUAL CONDUCT.

criminal sexual conduct in the first degree. See FIRST-DEGREE SEXUAL CONDUCT.

criminal solicitation. See SOLICITATION (2).

criminal statute. See *penal statute* under STATUTE.

criminal syndicalism. See SYNDICALISM.

criminal syndicate. See SYNDICATE.

criminal term. See TERM (5).

criminal trespass. See TRESPASS.

criminal wheel. **1.** See WHEEL (1). **2.** See WHEEL (2).

criminal wrong. See CRIME.

criminate, *vb.* See INCRIMINATE.

crimination (krim-ə-**nay**-shən), *n.* (16c) **1.** INCRIMINATION. **2.** An accusation or strong censure.

criminative (**krim**-ə-nay-tiv), *adj.* (18c) Of, relating to, or involving incrimination or accusation. Cf. INFIRMATIVE.

crimin laesae majestatis. See LESE MAJESTY.

criminogenic (krim-ə-nə-**jen**-ik), *adj.* (1918) Tending to cause crime or criminality. — **criminogenesis,** *n.*

criminology (krim-ə-**nol**-ə-jee), *n.* (1872) The study of crime, criminals, and criminal punishment as social phenomena; the study of the causes of crime and the treatment of offenders, comprising (1) criminal biology, which examines causes that may be found in the mental and physical constitution of an offender (such as hereditary tendencies and physical defects), and (2) criminal sociology, which deals with inquiries into the effects of environment as a cause of criminality. — Also termed *criminal anthropology.* Cf. CRIMINALISTICS; PENOLOGY. — **criminological** (krim-ə-nə-**loj**-ə-kəl), *adj.* — **criminologist,** *n.*

▸ **comparative criminology.** (1931) The scholarly study of the similarities and differences between the criminal-justice systems of different countries.

▸ **environmental criminology.** (1981) The scholarly study of areas where crime occurs and of why offenders are active in those areas. — Also termed *geography of crime; ecology of crime.*

crimping. (18c) *Hist.* The offense of decoying and confining persons to force them into military service. Cf. IMPRESSMENT (3).

CRIMS. *abbr.* Criminal-records information-management system.

criss-cross agreement. See *cross-purchase agreement* under AGREEMENT.

crit. (1985) An adherent to the critical-legal-studies school of thought. — Also termed *CLSer; Critic; critter.*

▸ **fem-crit.** (1985) A feminist adherent of critical legal studies.

criteria contaminants. See *criteria pollutants* under POLLUTANT.

criteria pollutants. See POLLUTANT.

criterion. (17c) A standard, rule, or test on which a judgment or decision can be based or compared; a reference point against which other things can be evaluated; a characterizing mark or trait. Pl. **criteria.**

Critic. See CRIT.

critical date. *Patents.* The date, one year before the effective filing date of a patent application, before which an invention placed on sale in the United States cannot be patented in the United States. See *effective filing date* under DATE.

critical evidence. See EVIDENCE.

critical habitat. See HABITAT.

critical jurisprudence. See JURISPRUDENCE.

critical legal studies. (1978) (*sometimes cap.*) **1.** A school of thought advancing the idea that the legal system perpetuates the status quo in terms of economics, race, and gender by using manipulable concepts and by creating an imaginary world of social harmony regulated by law. • The Marxist wing of this school focuses on socioeconomic issues. Fem-crits emphasize gender hierarchy, whereas critical race theorists focus on racial subordination. See *fem-crit* under CRIT; CRITICAL RACE THEORY. **2.** The body of work produced by adherents to this school of thought. — Abbr. CLS.

critical limitation. (1940) *Patents.* A limitation essential either to the operativeness of an invention or to the patentability of a patent claim for the invention.

critical race theory. (1989) (*sometimes cap.*) **1.** A reform movement within the legal profession, particularly within academia, whose adherents believe that the legal system has disempowered racial minorities. • Critical race theorists observe that even if the law is couched in neutral language, it cannot be neutral because those who fashioned it had their own subjective perspectives that, once enshrined in law, have disadvantaged minorities and even perpetuated racism. **2.** The body of work produced by adherents to this theory. — Abbr. CRT.

critical stage. (1962) *Criminal procedure.* A point in a criminal prosecution when the accused's rights or defenses might be affected by the absence of legal representation. • Under the Sixth Amendment, a critical stage triggers the accused's right to appointed counsel. Examples of critical stages include preliminary hearings, jury selection, and (of course) trial. Cf. ACCUSATORY STAGE.

critter. See CRIT.

CRMO. *abbr.* Chief risk-management officer. See CHIEF RISK OFFICER.

CRO. *abbr.* CHIEF RISK OFFICER.

CROA. *abbr.* CREDIT REPAIR ORGANIZATIONS ACT.

cronyism (**kroh**-nee-iz-əm), *n.* (1950) *Derogatory.* The practice of unfairly giving the best jobs to one's friends when one is in a position of power; specif., partiality to friends and toadies as demonstrated esp. by the appointing of sycophants to political office with little or no regard for their qualifications. Cf. NEPOTISM.

crop insurance. See INSURANCE.

crop rent. See RENT (1).

crops. (13c) Products that are grown, raised, and harvested. • Crops usu. are from the soil, but fruit grown on trees are also considered crops.

▸ **annual crops.** (17c) **1.** Crops that must be planted each year, such as cotton, wheat, barley, corn, carrots, potatoes, and melons. **2.** Crops for which the produce in any single year is mainly the result of attention and care exerted in the same agricultural year, such as hops and sugar cane.

▸ **away-going crops.** (18c) A tenant's crops that were sown and will not be ready to harvest before the tenancy expires. • The tenant retains the ownership of the crop after the tenancy expires.

▸ **basic crops.** (1953) Crops (such as wheat and corn) that are usu. subject to government-price supports.

▸ **growing crops.** (17c) Crops that are in the process of growth. • Growing crops are goods under UCC § 2-105(1). Judicial decisions vary on the growth stage at which a crop becomes a growing crop and on whether pasturage grass is a growing crop. Cf. FARM PRODUCT.

▸ **standing crops.** (17c) Crops that have not been harvested or otherwise severed from the land.

cross, *n.* **1.** CROSS-EXAMINATION. **2.** A sale of a large amount of publicly traded stock between two private parties. • Although the transaction does not happen on the exchange floor, it typically requires exchange permission.

cross-accusation. See ACCUSATION.

cross-action. 1. See ACTION (4). **2.** See CROSS-CLAIM.

cross-appeal. See APPEAL (2).

cross-bill. See BILL (2).

cross-claim, *n.* (1825) A claim asserted between codefendants or coplaintiffs in a case and that relates to the subject of the original claim or counterclaim. *See* Fed. R. Civ. P. 13(g). — Also termed *cross-action; cross-suit.* Cf. COUNTERCLAIM. — **cross-claim,** *vb.* — **cross-claimant,** *n.*

> "The courts have not always distinguished clearly between a cross-claim and a counterclaim, and have used one name where the other is proper under the rules, perhaps because in some states, and in the old equity practice, the term cross-complaint or cross-bill is used for what the rules regard as a counterclaim. Under Rule 13 a counterclaim is a claim against an opposing party, while a cross-claim is against a co-party. Further there is not the same freedom in asserting cross-claims that the rules provide for counterclaims. An unrelated claim against an opposing party may be asserted as a permissive counterclaim, but only claims related to the subject matter of the original action, or property involved therein, are appropriate as cross-claims." Charles Alan Wright, *The Law of Federal Courts* § 80, at 574 (5th ed. 1994).

cross-collateral. See COLLATERAL.

cross-collateral clause. (1965) An installment-contract provision allowing the seller, if the buyer defaults, to repossess not only the particular item sold but also every other item bought from the seller on which a balance remained due when the last purchase was made. — Also termed *dragnet clause.*

cross-collateralization. See *cross-collateral* under COLLATERAL.

cross-complaint. (1854) **1.** A claim asserted by a defendant against another party to the action. — Also termed (in some jurisdictions) *cross-petition.* **2.** A claim asserted by a defendant against a person not a party to the action for a matter relating to the subject of the action. **3.** *Criminal procedure.* A criminal charge lodged by a criminal defendant against the complainant who filed the initial criminal charge.

cross-corroboration. See CORROBORATION.

cross-default clause. (1979) A contractual provision under which default on one debt obligation triggers default on another obligation.

cross-defendant. (18c) The party against whom a cross-claim is asserted. Cf. CROSS-PLAINTIFF.

cross-demand. See DEMAND (1).

crossed check. See CHECK.

cross-elasticity of demand. (1939) *Antitrust.* A relationship between two products, usu. substitutes for each other, in which a price change for one product affects the price of the other.

cross-error. See ERROR (2).

cross-examination, *n.* (18c) The questioning of a witness at a trial or hearing by the party opposed to the party in whose favor the witness has testified. • The purpose of cross-examination is to discredit a witness before the fact-finder in any of several ways, as by bringing out contradictions and improbabilities in earlier testimony, by suggesting doubts to the witness, and by trapping the witness into admissions that weaken the testimony. The cross-examiner is typically allowed to ask leading questions but is traditionally limited to matters covered on direct examination and to credibility issues. — Also termed *cross-interrogation.* Cf. DIRECT EXAMINATION; RECROSS-EXAMINATION. — **cross-examine,** *vb.*

cross-interrogatory. See INTERROGATORY.

cross-license. See LICENSE.

cross-marriage. See MARRIAGE (1).

cross-motion. See MOTION (1).

cross-offer, *n.* (1931) *Contracts.* An offer made to another in ignorance that the offeree has made essentially the same offer to the offeror. — **cross-offer,** *vb.* — **cross-offeror,** *n.*

cross-ownership. See OWNERSHIP.

cross-petition. See CROSS-COMPLAINT (1).

cross-plaintiff. (18c) The party asserting a cross-claim. Cf. CROSS-DEFENDANT.

cross-purchase agreement. See AGREEMENT.

cross-purchase buy-sell agreement. (1989) **1.** BUY-SELL AGREEMENT (1). **2.** A partnership insurance plan in which each partner individually buys and maintains enough insurance on the life or lives of other partners to purchase a deceased or expelled partner's equity.

cross-question. See QUESTION (1).

cross-rate. (1920) The exchange rate between two currencies expressed as the ratio of two foreign exchange rates in terms of a common third currency (usu. the U.S. dollar). • Foreign-exchange-rate dealers use cross-rate tables to look for arbitrage opportunities. See ARBITRAGE.

cross-reference, *n.* (1834) An explicit citation to a related provision within the same or a closely related document; esp., in a patent application the explicit citation in a continuing patent application to all interrelated applications, back to the original filing. • A cross-reference alone does not incorporate the disclosure of the parent application. Cf. INCORPORATION BY REFERENCE (1), (2). — **cross-reference,** *vb.*

cross-remainder. See REMAINDER (1).

cross-stream guaranty. See GUARANTY (1).

cross-suit. See CROSS-CLAIM.

crowd financing. See CROWDFUNDING.

crowdfunding. (2005) Collectively, fundraising efforts that involve the use of the Internet to appeal to potential donors who might support the fundraiser's purpose, as with charitable undertakings, artistic endeavors, political campaigning, research and development, etc. — Also termed *crowd financing; crowdsourced fundraising.*

crowdsourced fundraising. See CROWDFUNDING.

crowdsourcing. (2005) The activity or practice of involving a great many people to develop ideas, produce content, or accomplish huge or tedious tasks, as by soliciting help via the Internet. • The word originated as a convenient compound to denote "outsourcing to the crowd."

Crown. (16c) *English law.* The sovereign in his or her official capacity as a governing power. See KING; QUEEN (1).

> "In modern times it has become usual to speak of the Crown rather than of the King, when we refer to the King in his public capacity as a body politic. We speak of the property of the Crown, when we mean the property which the King holds in right of his Crown. So we speak of the debts due by the Crown, of legal proceedings by and against the Crown, and so on. The usage is one of great convenience, because it avoids a difficulty which is inherent in all speech and thought concerning corporations sole, the difficulty, namely, of distinguishing adequately between the body politic and the human being by whom it is represented and whose name it bears." John Salmond, *Jurisprudence* 341–42 (Glanville L. Williams ed., 10th ed. 1947).

Crown case. (18c) *English law.* A criminal action.

Crown Court. An English court having jurisdiction over major criminal cases. • Crown Courts date from 1971, when they assumed the criminal jurisdiction of the Assize Courts and all the jurisdiction of the Courts of Quarter Sessions.

crown jewel. (1983) A company's most valuable asset, esp. as valued when the company is the subject of a hostile takeover. • A common antitakeover device is for the target company to sell its crown jewel to a third party so that the company will be less attractive to an unfriendly suitor.

crown-jewel defense. (1983) An antitakeover device in which the target company agrees to sell its most valuable assets to a third party if a hostile bid is tendered, so that the company will be less attractive to an unfriendly suitor. Cf. SCORCHED-EARTH DEFENSE; PAC-MAN DEFENSE.

Crown land. See LAND.

Crown loan. See LOAN.

CRS. *abbr.* CONGRESSIONAL RESEARCH SERVICE.

CRT. *abbr.* (1996) **1.** CRITICAL RACE THEORY. **2.** See *charitable-remainder trust* under TRUST (3). **3.** COPYRIGHT ROYALTY TRIBUNAL.

crucial evidence. See *critical evidence* under EVIDENCE.

cruel and abusive treatment. See ABUSE (2).

cruel and inhumane treatment. See *extreme cruelty* under CRUELTY.

cruel and unusual punishment. See PUNISHMENT (1).

cruelty. (13c) The intentional and malicious infliction of mental or physical suffering on a living creature, esp. a human; abusive treatment; outrage. — Also termed *cruel treatment.* Cf. ABUSE; INHUMAN TREATMENT; INDIGNITY.

> "When William Blake opined that 'Cruelty has a human heart,' he posited the physical and emotional forms which cruelty may take. But when is one party so cruel to the other that it goes to the heart of the marriage and justifies dissolution? A New York court defined cruelty as bodily harm, or a reasonable apprehension of bodily harm, which endangers life, limb, or health and renders marital cohabitation unsafe or improper. Some states are reluctant to permit divorce when there has been only emotional suffering without physical harm. And in a marriage of long duration, some courts require that the cruelty be more extreme to justify divorce than if the relationship has been brief. Acts constituting the ground must continue over an extended period of time unless they are so severe as to shock the conscience, or raise the probability that it would be unsafe for the innocent party if the couple remain together." Walter Wadlington & Raymond C. O'Brien, *Family Law in Perspective* 73 (2001).

▸ **animal cruelty.** (18c) A malicious or criminally negligent act that causes an animal to suffer pain or death.

▸ **cruelty to a child.** See *child abuse* under ABUSE.

▸ **cruelty to animals.** See *animal cruelty.*

▸ **extreme cruelty.** (17c) As a ground for divorce, one spouse's physical violence toward the other spouse, or conduct that destroys or severely impairs the other spouse's mental health. — Also termed *cruel and inhumane treatment.* Cf. ABUSE (2).

▸ **legal cruelty.** (18c) Cruelty that will justify granting a divorce to the injured party; specif. conduct by one spouse that endangers the life, person, or health of the other spouse, or creates a reasonable apprehension of bodily or mental harm.

▸ **mental cruelty.** (1898) As a ground for divorce, one spouse's course of conduct (not involving actual violence) that creates such anguish that it endangers the life, physical health, or mental health of the other spouse. See *emotional distress* under DISTRESS (4).

▸ **physical cruelty.** (1874) As a ground for divorce, actual personal violence committed by one spouse against the other.

cruelty to a child. See *child abuse* under ABUSE.

cruelty to children. See *child abuse* under ABUSE.

***Crummey* power.** (1997) The right of a beneficiary of a *Crummey* trust to withdraw gifts made to the trust up to a maximum amount (often the lesser of the annual exclusion or the value of the gift made to the trust) for a certain period after the gift is made. • The precise characteristics of a Crummey power are established by the settlor of a Crummey trust. Typically, the power is exercisable for 30 days after the gift is made and permits withdrawals up to $5,000 or 5% of the value of the trust. A beneficiary may allow the power to lapse without making any demand for distribution. See *Crummey trust* under TRUST (3); *annual exclusion* (1) under EXCLUSION (1).

***Crummey* trust.** See TRUST (3).

Crusades. (16c) A series of military expeditions undertaken by British and European Christians in the 11th, 12th, and 13th centuries to take control of the biblical holy lands then occupied by Muslims.

***Cruz* waiver.** (1999) A plea bargain under which the defendant agrees that if the defendant does not appear at the sentencing hearing, the court may impose a greater sentence. *People v. Cruz*, 44 Cal. 3d 1247 (1988).

cry de pais (krɪ də **pay**). [Law French] *Hist.* The cry of the country. • The hue and cry after an offender, as raised by the country (i.e., the people). — Also spelled *cri de pais.* See HUE AND CRY (1).

cryer. See CRIER.

cryptanalysis (krip-tə-**nal**-i-sis), *n.* (1923) The scrutiny of coded messages, esp. linguistic codes involving plentiful slang, for the purpose of understanding communications among participants in organized crime.

crystal meth. (1969) *Slang.* A highly addictive synthetic d-methamphetamine that resembles shiny blue-white rocks or fragments of glass.

C/S. *abbr.* Confidential source. — Also termed *CI* (confidential informant).

CSAAS. *abbr.* CHILD-SEXUAL-ABUSE-ACCOMMODATION SYNDROME.

CSB. Criminal sexual battery. See *sexual battery* under BATTERY (1).

CSC. *abbr.* CIVIL SERVICE COMMISSION.

CSE agency. *abbr.* CHILD-SUPPORT-ENFORCEMENT AGENCY.

CSI. *abbr.* Crime-scene investigation.

***CSI* effect.** (2004) *Slang.* The supposed influence of the television show *CSI: Crime Scene Investigation* in leading jurors to expect quick and definitive analysis and resolution of all crime-scene issues.

CSO. *abbr.* Court security officer.

CSRAA. *abbr.* COMPUTER SOFTWARE RENTAL AMENDMENTS ACT.

CSREES. *abbr.* COOPERATIVE STATE RESEARCH, EDUCATION, AND EXTENSION SERVICE.

CSRT. *abbr.* COMBATANT STATUS REVIEW TRIBUNAL.

CSV. See *cash surrender value* under VALUE (2).

c.t.a. *abbr.* See *administration cum testamento annexo* under ADMINISTRATION.

Ct. Cl. *abbr.* Court of Claims. See UNITED STATES COURT OF FEDERAL CLAIMS.

CTEA. *abbr.* SONNY BONO COPYRIGHT TERM EXTENSION ACT.

CTF. *abbr.* See *common trust fund* under TRUST FUND.

CTL. *abbr.* See *constructive total loss* under LOSS.

CTR. *abbr.* **1.** CASH-TRANSACTION REPORT. **2.** CURRENCY-TRANSACTION REPORT.

CTW. *abbr.* Consent to withdraw.

cucking stool. See CASTIGATORY.

cuckold (**kək**-əld), *n.* (13c) *Archaic.* A man whose wife has had sex with another man; the husband of an adulteress. • The English language has no correlative term for the female counterpart to a cuckold. The name derives from the cuckoo, the female of which species lays its eggs in another bird's nest.

cuckold (**kək**-əld), *vb.* (16c) *Archaic.* (Of a wife or her lover) to make a cuckold of; specif., to subject (a husband) to the humiliation or other negative feelings attendant upon a wife's sexual infidelity.

cui ante divortium (kɪ [*or* kwɪ *or* kwee] **an**-tee də-**vor**-shee-əm). [Law Latin "to whom before divorce"] (16c) *Hist.* A writ of entry enabling a divorced woman to recover land that she had held in fee but that her husband had sold without her permission during the marriage. • The name of this writ derives from the words within it: *cui ipsa ante divortium inter eos celebratum, contradicere non potuit* ("whom she, before the divorce between them, could not gainsay"). The writ was abolished in 1833. — Also termed *sur cui ante divortium.*

Cui bono? [Latin] (17c) For whose advantage?; Who benefits?. • The exclamation may be used to ask who benefited from the results of a crime, usu. to cast suspicion without offering evidence of guilt. Despite the literal meaning, the term is more often used to mean "what's the good of it?" or "what benefits are there?"

cui in vita (kɪ [*or* kwɪ *or* kwee] in-**vɪ**-tə). [Law Latin "to whom in the life"] (16c) *Hist.* A writ of entry enabling a woman to recover land that she had held in fee but that her deceased husband had sold without her permission. • It is so called from the words of the writ: *cui ipsa in vita sua contradicere non potuit* ("whom she, in his lifetime, could not gainsay"). — Also termed *sur cui in vita.*

> "Cui in vita, is a writ of entry, which a Widow hath against him, to whom her Husband alienated her Lands or Tenements in his life time, which must specifie, that *During his life*, she could not withstand it." Thomas Blount, *Nomo-Lexicon: A Law-Dictionary* (1670).

cujus contrarium est verum (**k[y]oo**-jəs kən-**trair**-ee-əm est **veer**-əm). [Latin] *Hist.* The contrary of which is the truth.

cujus haeredibus maxime prospicitur (**k[y]oo**-jəs hə-**red**-i-bəs **mak**-sə-mee proh-**spis**-i-tər). [Latin] *Hist.* Whose heirs are chiefly regarded.

> "Cujus haeredibus maxime prospicitur . . . . This is a rule of construction to be attended to in ascertaining from the terms of a destination, in whom the fee of a property is vested, the ordinary rule being, that he is the fiar whose heirs are preferred. Thus, a conveyance to 'A and B jointly, and the heirs of B,' gives A merely a joint right of liferent, and gives B the fee. Under such a destination, B is so absolutely the fiar that his rights cannot be impaired by any acts, even onerous, of A, who is held, as we have said, to be a liferenter." John Trayner, *Trayner's Latin Maxims* 121 (4th ed. 1894).

culpa (**kəl**-pə). [Latin] **1.** *Roman & civil law.* Fault, neglect, or negligence; unintentional wrong. See NEGLIGENCE. Cf. DILIGENTIA; CASUS (1); DOLUS (1). **2.** *Roman law.* Conduct that made a party to a contract, or quasi-contract, liable to the other party.

▸ ***culpa in eligendo*** (**kəl**-pə in el-i-**jen**-doh). [Latin] *Hist.* Fault in selecting.

▸ ***culpa in vigilando*** (**kəl**-pə in vij-i-**lan**-doh). [Latin] *Hist.* Fault in supervising.

▸ ***lata culpa*** (**lay**-tə **kəl**-pə). [Latin "grave fault"] (16c) Gross negligence amounting to bad faith (*dolus*). • This phrase occurs most commonly in bailment law and in the law of the transport of persons. — Also termed *culpa lata.* See *gross negligence* under NEGLIGENCE.

▸ ***levis culpa*** (**lee**-vis **kəl**-pə). [Latin "slight fault"] (18c) **1.** Ordinary negligence. **2.** Failure to act as the ideal paterfamilias should. — Also termed *culpa levis; culpa levis in concreto.* See *ordinary negligence* under NEGLIGENCE.

> "If *culpa levis* is negligence arising from the lack of such diligence as the average businessman would show, the *culpa levissima*, as contrasted with it, is a failure of compliance with some severer standard not necessarily specified save by reference to the *culpa levis*. Or again, if *culpa levissima* marks shortcomings in very exact diligence, then *culpa levis* is failure to reach the accustomed standard." 1 Thomas Beven, *Negligence in Law* 26 (3d ed. 1908).

▸ ***levissima culpa*** (lə-**vis**-ə-mə **kəl**-pə). [Latin "the slightest fault"] Slight negligence. — Also termed *culpa levissima.* See *slight negligence* under NEGLIGENCE.

culpabilis (kəl-**pay**-bə-lis), *adj.* [Latin] *Hist.* Guilty.

culpability (kəl-pə-**bil**-ə-tee), *n.* (17c) **1.** Moral blameworthiness; the quality of being culpable. **2.** The mental state that must be proved for a defendant to be held liable for a crime. • Except in cases of absolute liability, criminal culpability under the Model Penal Code requires proof that the defendant "acted purposely, knowingly, recklessly, or negligently, as the law may require, with respect to each material element of the offense." Model Penal Code § 2.02. See MENS REA. Cf. ACTUS REUS.

> "At times the Court seems to differentiate between the two [meanings] by casting the punishment-phase determination as one about the defendant's moral culpability, as opposed to his purely legal culpability at the guilt phase. In this respect, a defendant's moral culpability for murder may be greater or lesser, depending on aggravating and mitigating circumstances, even though his legal culpability remains the same." Phyllis L. Crocker, *Concepts of Culpability and Deathworthiness*, 66 Fordham L. Rev. 21, 35–36 (1997).

culpable (**kəl**-pə-bəl), *adj.* (14c) **1.** Guilty; blameworthy. **2.** Involving the breach of a duty.

culpable accident. See ACCIDENT.

culpable homicide. 1. See HOMICIDE. **2.** See MANSLAUGHTER.

culpable intoxication. See *voluntary intoxication* under INTOXICATION.

culpable mental state. See MENTAL STATE.

culpable neglect. See NEGLECT.

culpable negligence. See NEGLIGENCE.

***culpa-in-contrahendo* doctrine.** [Law Latin "fault in contracting"] (1963) The principle that parties must act in good faith during preliminary contract negotiations; esp., the principle that a breach by the offeror after the offeree has begun performance of a unilateral contract and is stopped by the offeror before completion will give rise to liability in tort.

culpa lata. See *lata culpa* under CULPA.

culpa levis. See *levis culpa* under CULPA.

culpa levis in concreto. See *levis culpa* under CULPA.

culpa levissima. See *levissima culpa* under CULPA.

culprit. (17c) **1.** A person accused or charged with the commission of a crime. **2.** Someone who is guilty of a crime. • *Culprit* may be a running together of *cul*, shortened from the Latin *culpabilis* ("guilty"), and *prit*, from Old French *prest* ("ready"), two words formerly used to orally plead at the outset of a criminal case.

> "When the prisoner hath thus pleaded not guilty, *non culpabilis* . . . the clerk of the assise, or clerk of the arraigns, on behalf of the crown replies, that the prisoner is guilty, and that he is ready to prove him so. This is done by two monosyllables in the same spirit of abbreviation, '*cul. prit.*' which signifies first that the prisoner is guilty, (*cul. culpable*, or *culpabilis*) and then that the king is ready to prove him so; *prît, praesto sum*, or *paratus verificare*. . . . How our courts came to express a matter of this importance in so odd and obscure a manner . . . can hardly be pronounced with certainty. It may perhaps, however, be accounted for by supposing that these were at first short notes, to help the memory of the clerk, and remind him what he was to reply; or else it was the short method of taking down in court, upon the minutes, the replication and averment; '*cul. prît*': which afterwards the ignorance of succeeding clerks adopted for the very words to be by them spoken. But however it may have arisen, the joining of issue . . . seems to be clearly the meaning of this obscure expression; which has puzzled our most ingenious etymologists, and is commonly understood as if the clerk of the arraigns, immediately on plea pleaded, had fixed an opprobrious name on the prisoner, by asking him, '*culprit*, how wilt thou be tried?'" 4 William Blackstone, *Commentaries on the Laws of England* 333–34 (1769).

cultura (kəl-**t[y]oor**-ə). [Law Latin] *Hist.* A piece of tillable land; tillage.

cultural agreement. (1939) *Int'l law.* A bilateral or multilateral agreement between countries for the purpose of furthering cultural or intellectual relations.

cultural defense. See DEFENSE (1).

cultural property. (1944) *Int'l law.* Movable and immovable property that has cultural significance, whether in the nature of antiquities and monuments of a classical age or important modern items of fine arts, decorative arts, and architecture. • Some writers prefer the term *cultural heritage*, which more broadly includes intangible cultural things such as folklore, crafts, and skills.

culvertage (**kəl**-vər-tij), *n.* (17c) *Hist.* **1.** The status of villeinage. **2.** The condition of being reduced to villeinage or serfdom by forfeiture and degradation.

cum astrictis multuris (kəm ə-**strik**-tis məl-**t[y]oor**-is). [Law Latin] *Hist.* With defined payments for grinding; with astricted multures. • The phrase appeared in reference to portions of grain that the landholder was bound to pay a certain mill in exchange for grinding the remainder of the grain. See MOLITURAE.

cum aucupationibus, venationibus, et piscationibus (kəm awk-yə-pay-shee-**oh**-nə-bəs, vi-nay-shee-**oh**-nə-bəs et pi-skay-shee-**oh**-nə-bəs). [Latin] *Scots law.* With fowlings, huntings, and fishings. • The phrase was part of a clause granting the legal right to hunt and fish on the conveyed land if the right was accompanied by actual possession of the land for a specific period.

cum beneficio inventarii. See BENEFICIUM INVENTARII.

cum communi pastura (kəm kə-**myoo**-nɪ **pas**-chər-ə). [Law Latin] *Hist.* With common pasturage. • This phrase granted a servitude of pasture, not a right of common, on property.

cum curiis earumque exitibus (kəm **kyoor**-ee-is ee-ə-**rəm**-kwee ek-**sit**-i-bəs). [Law Latin] *Hist.* With courts, and the results or profits of the same. • The phrase appeared in reference to the right of the Baron courts to any of those courts' profits, as distinguished from the obligation of the King's courts to turn over all profits to the King.

cum curiis et bloodwitis (kəm **kyoor**-ee-is et **bləd**-wi-tis). [Law Latin] *Scots law.* With the power of holding courts and fining for blood. • Property disposed of *cum curiis et bloodwitis* entitled the purchaser of a barony to cumulative jurisdiction over barony matters.

cum decimis inclusis et nunquam antea separatis (kəm **des**-ə-mis in-**kloo**-sis et **nəm**-kwam **an**-tee-ə sep-ə-**ray**-tis). [Law Latin] *Scots law.* With the tithes included, and never before separated. • This phrase exempted conveyed land from the payment of tithes.

cum dividend. (1877) With dividend. • Stocks purchased cum dividend entitle the buyer to any pending declared dividends. Cf. EX DIVIDEND.

cum domibus, aedificiis (kəm **dom**-ə-bəs, ee-di-**fish**-ee-is). [Law Latin] *Scots law.* With houses, buildings. • These words in a conveyance included within the conveyance every structure erected on the conveyed land.

cum effectu (kəm i-**fek**-t[y]oo). [Latin] *Hist.* With effect; in effect.

> "Prescription does not run against any one . . . unless he is able to act in defence of his right *cum effectu* . . . . Under the old feudal system the casualty of ward was not incurred except where the vassal alienated his lands *cum effectu*. Thus, if the vassal was interdicted and disponed without the consent of his interdictors, his conveyance being reducible was not effectual, and the casualty was not incurred." John Trayner, *Trayner's Latin Maxims* 127–28 (4th ed. 1894).

cum excessu moderaminis (kəm ek-**ses**-[y]oo mod-ə-**ray**-mə-nis). [Law Latin] *Scots law.* In excess of the limits. • The phrase appeared in reference to the legal limits on the use of violence as a means of self-defense.

cum fabrilibus, brasinis, et brueriis (kəm fə-**bril**-ə-bəs, brə-**sɪ**-nəs, et broo-**er**-ee-is). [Law Latin] *Scots law.* With forges, maltkilns, and breweries. • A tenant was restricted from building these structures on land unless the tenant first obtained the superior's permission.

cum fossa et furca (kəm **fos**-ə et **fər**-kə). [Law Latin] *Hist.* With pit and gallows. • In ancient charters, this phrase granted Baron courts the right to try capital offenses and to inflict capital punishment.

cum grano salis (kəm **gray**-noh **say**-lis *or* kuum **grah**-noh **sah**-lis). [Latin] (17c) With a grain of salt; with allowance for exaggeration; with reservations.

cum herezeldis (kəm her-ə-**zel**-dis). [Latin] *Scots law.* With herezelds; with the best things that move. • The phrase appeared in reference to a tenant's best horse, cow, or other animal, when the animal was customarily transferred to the landlord on the death of the tenant.

cum imperio (kəm im-**peer**-ee-oh). [Latin] With sovereignty.

***Cumis* counsel.** See COUNSEL.

cum libera et plena administratione (kəm **lib**-ər-ə et **plee**-nə ad-min-ə-stray-shee-**oh**-nee). [Law Latin] *Scots law.* With full and free power of administration. • The phrase appeared in reference to the powers that one could grant to certain agents, such as attorneys.

cum libero exitu et introitu (kəm **lib**-ər-ə **ek**-si-t[y]oo et in-**troh**-ə-t[y]oo). [Law Latin] *Hist.* With free exit and entry.

cum maritagio (kəm mar-ə-**tay**-jee-oh). [Law Latin] *Scots law.* With the marriage portion. • The phrase appeared in reference to the required payment to a superior upon the marriage of the superior's ward.

cum molendinis et multuris (kəm mə-**len**-di-nis et **məl**-chər-is). [Law Latin] *Scots law.* With mills and multures. Cf. MOLITURAE.

cum nota (kəm **noh**-tə). [Latin] *Scots law.* With a distinguishing mark. • The phrase appeared in reference to otherwise inadmissible testimony that a judge could allow after considering the testimony's merit or believability.

cum omni causa (kəm **ahm**-nɪ **kaw**-zə). [Latin] *Roman law.* With every advantage derived from a given transaction, such as a sale.

cum onere (kəm **on**-ə-ree). [Latin] With the burden. • An item acquired *cum onere* is taken subject to existing burdens and charges.

cum onere debitorum defuncti (kəm **on**-ər-ee deb-i-**tor**-əm di-**fəngk**-tɪ). [Latin] *Hist.* With the burden of the decedent's debts. • The phrase appeared in reference to an heir's position after entering a succession.

cum pertinentiis (kəm pər-tə-**nen**-shee-is). [Latin] With the appurtenances. • In a conveyance of land, the conveyance included not only everything belonging to the land, but also rights incident to it.

cum piscariis (kəm pis-**kair**-ee-is). [Law Latin] *Scots law.* With fishings. • The phrase was used to convey an express grant of fishing rights without the necessity of also possessing the right for a prescribed period. Cf. CUM PISCATIONIBUS.

cum piscationibus (kəm pis-kay-shee-**oh**-nə-bəs). [Law Latin] *Hist.* With fishing or fisheries. • The phrase was used to convey the express grant of fishing rights only if the grant was accompanied by possession of the right for a prescribed period. Cf. CUM PISCARIIS.

cum rights. With rights. • A *cum rights* purchaser of stock is entitled to rights that have been declared but not distributed, such as the right to purchase additional shares at a stated price. — Also termed *rights on*.

cum satis furore ipso puniatur (kəm **sat**-is fyuu-**ror**-ree **ip**-soh pyoo-nee-**ay**-tər). [Latin] *Hist.* Since he is sufficiently punished by the insanity itself. • The phrase appeared in reference to the principle that an insane person is not criminally responsible for his or her acts. It was a forerunner to the modern insanity defense.

cum sua causa et labe (kəm **s[y]oo**-ə **kaw**-zə et **lay**-bee). [Latin] *Hist.* With its advantages and its defects.

cum suo onere (kəm **s[y]oo**-oh **on**-ər-ee). [Latin] *Hist.* With its burden. • The phrase appeared in reference to a vassal's land encumbrances that the superior was bound to accept upon the vassal's resignation.

cum testamento annexo (kəm tes-tə-**men**-toh ə-**nek**-soh). See *administration cum testamento annexo* under ADMINISTRATION.

cum titulo (kəm **tich**-[y]ə-loh). [Law Latin] *Hist.* With the title.

cumulatio criminum (kyoo-myə-**lay**-shee-oh **krim**-ə-nəm). [Law Latin] *Hist.* The accumulation of crimes; the charging of more than one crime in an indictment.

cumulative, *adj.* **1.** Including all the amounts previously added <cumulative dividends>. **2.** (Of evidence) tending to prove the same thing <cumulative testimony>. **3.** Gaining volume, strength, or severity by addition or repetition <cumulative penalties>. **4.** Formed by adding new material or parts of the same kind; consisting of portions gathered or collected one after another <cumulative error>.

cumulative approach. See UNITY OF ART.

cumulative dividend. See DIVIDEND.

cumulative-effects doctrine. (1987) The rule that a transaction affecting interstate commerce in a trivial way may be taken together with other similar transactions to establish that the combined effect on interstate commerce is not trivial and can therefore be regulated under the Commerce Clause.

cumulative error. See ERROR (2).

cumulative-error analysis. (1983) Appellate scrutiny of whether all of the individual harmless errors made in a trial had the cumulative effect of prejudicing the outcome. • If they did, the harmless errors taken together may amount to reversible error.

cumulative evidence. See EVIDENCE.

cumulative income bond. See *income bond* under BOND (3).

cumulative legacy. 1. See *accumulative legacy* under LEGACY (1). **2.** See *additional legacy* under LEGACY (1).

cumulatively harmful behavior. See HARMFUL BEHAVIOR.

cumulative offense. See OFFENSE (2).

cumulative preference share. See *cumulative preferred stock* under STOCK.

cumulative preferred stock. See STOCK.

cumulative punishment. See PUNISHMENT (1).

cumulative remedy. See REMEDY.

cumulative sentences. See *consecutive sentences* under SENTENCE.

cumulative stock. See *cumulative preferred stock* under STOCK.

cumulative supplement. See POCKET PART.

cumulative testimony. See TESTIMONY.

cumulative traverse. See TRAVERSE.

cumulative voting. See VOTING.

cumulative zoning. See ZONING.

cum virginitas vel castitas corrupta restitui non possit (kəm vər-**jin**-i-tas vel **kas**-ti-tas kə-**rəp**-tə ri-**stich**-[y]oo-ɪ). [Latin] *Hist. & Scots law.* Since virginity or chastity once violated cannot be restored. • The phrase was use to explain the basis for imposing severe punishment for rape.

cunnilingus. The sexual act involving oral stimulation of a person's vulva or clitoris.

CUPOS. *abbr.* A cohabiting unmarried person of the opposite sex. • Although this term is intended to be synonymous with "POSSLQ" (a person of the opposite sex sharing living quarters), it is more literally precise because it excludes married persons. See POSSLQ.

cur. *abbr.* CURIA (3).

cura (**kyoor**-ə), *n.* [Latin] *Roman law.* A guardianship that protects the interests of minors who are between puberty and the age of 25, or incapacitated persons. Cf. TUTELA. Pl. ***curae.***

> "*Cura* was a form of guardianship indicated by the necessities of the case, with respect to persons who, though *sui juris*, were in need of protection. It was not regarded as a substitute for *patria potestas* as *tutela* was. . . . It extended to the person as well as the property, and in the latter respect is much the same as in the case of the *tutela* of infants." R.W. Leage, *Roman Private Law* 122 (C.H. Ziegler ed., 2d ed. 1930).

▸ ***cura furiosi*** (**kyoor**-ə fyoor-ee-**oh**-sɪ). A guardianship for an insane person who was mentally incapacitated.

> "The cura furiosi empowered and bound the curator to manage the property of the lunatic on the lunatic's behalf." Rudolph Sohm, *The Institutes: A Textbook of the History and System of Roman Private Law* 492 (James Crawford Ledlie trans., 3d ed. 1907).

▸ ***cura minoris*** (**kyoor**-ə mi-**nor**-is). A form of guardianship for a minor under 25 whose capacity of action was complete, but whose judgment might be defective. Pl. ***cura minorum.***

▸ ***cura prodigi*** (**kyoor**-ə **prah**-də-jɪ). A form of guardianship for a spendthrift, usu. at the request of the person's agnatic family.

> "The cura prodigi differed from the cura furiosi in that the prodigus, unlike the furiosus, was himself capable of performing any act by which he acquired a right or benefit. The appointment of a curator, however, precluded the prodigus from performing any act which operated to alienate property or to subject him to a liability; any such act, in order to be effectual, had to be concluded either by the curator on behalf of the prodigus or by the prodigus with the approval of the curator." Rudolph Sohm, *The Institutes: A Textbook of the History and System of Roman Private Law* 492 (James Crawford Ledlie trans., 3d ed. 1907).

cura animarum (**kyoor**-ə an-ə-**mair**-əm). [Law Latin] (17c) *Hist. Eccles. law.* The cure of souls; the care of souls.

curable error. See ERROR (2).

cur. adv. vult. *abbr.* CURIA ADVISARI VULT.

curate (**kyuur**-it). (14c) *Eccles. law.* **1.** A person in charge of a parish; a pastor. **2.** A member of the clergy who receives a stipend or salary to assist a vicar, rector, or pastor; an assistant to a parish priest.

curatio (kyə-**ray**-shee-oh), *n.* [fr. Latin *cura* "care"] *Roman law.* **1.** The power or duty of managing the interests of a youth or incapacitated person. **2.** The office of a curator. See CURA. Pl. ***curationes*** (kyə-ray-shee-**oh**-neez).

curative admissibility. See ADMISSIBILITY.

curative-admissibility doctrine. (1975) The rule that otherwise inadmissible evidence will be admitted to rebut inadmissible evidence placed before the fact-finder by the adverse party. • The doctrine applies when a motion to strike cannot cure the prejudice created by the adverse party. — Also termed *doctrine of curative admissibility.*

curative direction. See *curative instruction* under JURY INSTRUCTION.

curative instruction. See JURY INSTRUCTION.

curative law. See *curative statute* under STATUTE.

curative statute. See STATUTE.

curator (**kyuur**-ə-tər *or* **kyuur**-ay-tər *or* kyuu-**ray**-tor), *n.* (15c) **1.** *Roman law.* (*ital.*) Someone who manages the affairs of another; a guardian. See CURA. Pl. ***curatores*** (kyər-ə-**tor**-eez).

> "Although the control of a *Tutor* ceased when the *Pupillus* had attained manhood and become invested with his political rights, it must have frequently happened that the youth would be involved in business which he would be incapable of regulating with advantage at that early age, and would, at all events, if wealthy, be open to fraud and imposition. Hence arose the practice of nominating a *Curator*, whose authority extended to the twenty-fifth year of the ward, but who did not necessarily, like a *Tutor*, exercise a general superintendence, being frequently nominated for one special purpose. . . . *Curatores* were appointed also to manage the affairs of persons beyond the age of twenty-five, who, in consequence of being insane, deaf and dumb, or affected with some incurable disease, were incapable of attending to their own concerns." William Ramsay, *A Manual of Roman Antiquities* 299-300 (Rodolfo Lanciani ed., 15th ed. 1894).

▸ **curator ad litem** (kyuu-**ray**-tor ad **lɪ**-təm). (18c) A curator appointed by a court to represent the interests of a youth, or an incapacitated or unborn person, during the proceedings before the court.

▸ ***curator bonis*** (kyuu-**ray**-tor **boh**-nis). [Latin "a guardian of property"] (18c) **1.** *Roman law.* A guardian appointed to care for property, esp. for the benefit of creditors. **2.** *Scots law.* A person appointed by a court to manage an estate, esp. of a minor or an insane person. — Also termed *curator ad bona.*

▸ ***curator bonorum*** (kyuu-**ray**-tor bə-**nor**-əm). (17c) A person appointed by a court to administer the estate of an insolvent person.

> "It is sometimes necessary for the public interest that the commonwealth should appoint a person or persons to watch over an estate. Where this was done, not on account of any personal defect in the proprietor, the person so appointed was called 'curator bonorum.' The necessity for such interference arose where property was to be administered for a body of creditors." John George Phillimore, *Private Law Among the Romans* 289-90 (1863).

2. A temporary guardian or conservator appointed by a court to care for the property or person of a minor or incapacitated person.

▸ **interim curator.** (1885) *Archaic.* A person appointed by a justice of the peace to hold a felon's property until a royal administrator could be assigned the task.

3. *Civil law.* A guardian who manages the estate of a minor, an absent person, or an incapacitated person. Pl. ***curatores.***

▸ **curator ad hoc** (kyuu-**ray**-tor ad **hok**). (1819) A court-appointed curator who manages a single matter or transaction. See *special guardian* under GUARDIAN (1).

▸ ***curator datur rei.*** See *curator rei.*

▸ ***curator rei*** (kyuu-**ray**-tor **ree**-ɪ). [Latin] *Scots law.* A guardian of an estate, as distinguished from a tutor, who is a guardian of a person. — Also termed *curator datur rei.*

4. *Parliamentary law.* An officer charged with custody of an organization's valuable property.

curator ad bona (kyuu-**ray**-tor ad **boh**-nə). See *curator bonis* under CURATOR (1).

curator datur rei. See *curator rei* under CURATOR (3).

curatorship. (16c) The office of a curator or guardian.

▸ **dative curatorship.** See *dative tutorship* under TUTORSHIP.

curatory, *n.* (16c) *Scots law.* The management by a curator of the affairs of someone incapable, esp. consent to the legal acts of a minor to cure the minor's legal incapacity.

curatrix (kyuu-**ray**-triks). (1846) *Archaic.* A female curator.

curb. See TRADING CURB.

curb-crawling. The offense or practice of driving slowly along the side of the road to find and solicit a prostitute, esp. a streetwalker. — Also spelled (BrE) *kerb-crawling.* — **curb-crawler,** *n.*

curbstone stockbroker. See *street stockbroker* under STOCKBROKER.

Curcio **hearing.** See HEARING.

cure, *n.* **1.** A seller's right under the UCC to correct a nonconforming delivery of goods, usu. within the contract period. UCC § 2-508. **2.** *Maritime law.* Restoration to health after disease or injury; medical attention and nursing care during a period of convalescence. See MAINTENANCE AND CURE; MAXIMUM CURE. — **curative,** *adj.*

cure, *vb.* (14c) To remove one or more legal defects to correct one or more legal errors. • For example, curing title involves removing defects from title to unmarketable land so that title becomes marketable.

cure by verdict. See AIDER BY VERDICT.

cure of default. A debtor's act to correct its failure to perform, or to refrain from performing, according to the terms of an agreement.

curfew (**kər**-fyoo). (14c) **1.** *Hist.* A law requiring that all fires be extinguished at a certain time in the evening, usu. announced by the ringing of a bell. **2.** A regulation that forbids people (or certain classes of them, such as minors) from being outdoors or in vehicles during specified hours.

curia (**kyoor**-ee-ə), *n.* [Latin] (16c) **1.** *Roman law.* One of 30 divisions (three tribes of ten *curiae*) into which the Roman people were said to be divided by Romulus. See *comitia curiata* under COMITIA. **2.** *Roman law.* A legislative gathering, esp. of the Roman Senate; the building used for the gathering. **3.** *Hist.* A judicial tribunal held in the sovereign's palace; a royal court. — Abbr. *cur.* **4.** *Hist.* A court. **5.** The papal court, including its functionaries and officials.

> "The word *curia* in classical Latin is used in a number of ways. Apparently, it meant at first a subdivision of the people. It was also used, by a transfer which is not too clear, for the building in which the Roman Senate met. By an almost inevitable development it became the word for the Senate itself and later the ordinary designation for the Council in municipalities of the later Empire. . . . How much of this was still recalled in Medieval times, we cannot tell, but . . . in the early Middle Ages, *curia* was a common word to describe both the groups of men who generally were found in attendance on pope, emperor, king or prince, and the groups which were summoned by him to give him counsel. The *curia* in the latter sense, however, was not really a casual group of persons, summoned spasmodically to advise the king or any other person. It had come to be in Feudal Europe the ordinary Latin word for the general meeting of the lord's vassals, which itself grew out of the Germanic *mot* or *thing*. . . . The *Curia* of the king was in theory a larger and more important example of the same

kind of assemblage." Max Radin, *Handbook of Anglo-American Legal History* 46–48 (1936).

curia admiralitatis (**kyoor**-ee-ə ad-mə-ral-ə-**tay**-tis). [Law Latin] See HIGH COURT OF ADMIRALTY.

curia advisari vult (**kyoor**-ee-ə ad-və-**sair**-I **vəlt**). [Latin] (17c) The court will be advised; the court will consider. • This phrase signaled a court's decision to delay judgment pending further consideration. In England, the phrase is still used in all Court of Appeal decisions when the judgment is reserved; that is, not delivered after the hearing. — Abbr. *cur. adv. vult*; *c.a.v.*

curia baronis (**kyoor**-ee-ə bə-**roh**-nis). [Law Latin] See COURT BARON.

curia burgi (**kyoor**-ee-ə **bər**-jI). See COURT OF HUSTINGS.

curia cancellaria. See CANCELLARIA.

curia Christianitatis (**kyoor**-ee-ə kris-tee-an-ə-**tay**-tis). [Law Latin "a court Christian"] (16c) *Hist.* An ecclesiastical court. See *ecclesiastical court* under COURT.

curia claudenda (**kyoor**-ee-ə klaw-**den**-də). See DE CURIA CLAUDENDA.

curia comitatus (**kyoor**-ee-ə kom-ə-**tay**-təs). [Law Latin] See *county court* (1) under COURT.

curia domini (**kyoor**-ee-ə **dom**-ə-nI). [Law Latin "lord's court"] *Hist.* A lord's house or hall, used as a meeting place for tenants during court sessions.

curia magna (**kyoor**-ee-ə **mag**-nə). [Law Latin "great court"] (17c) *Hist.* An ancient name for Parliament.

curia palatii (**kyoor**-ee-ə pə-**lay**-shee-I). [Law Latin "court of the palace"] (18c) PALACE COURT.

Curia Regis (**kyoor**-ee-ə **ree**-jis). [Latin "king's court"] *Hist.* (*sometimes not cap.*) **1.** The chief court in early Norman England, established by William the Conqueror, • The *curia regis* was a body of advisers who traveled with the king, advising him on political matters and acting as an appellate court in important or complicated cases. Over time the functions of the *curia regis* became exclusively judicial in nature. — Abbr. C.R. — Also termed *King's Court*; *aula regis.*

"[W]e are tempted to use terms which are more precise than those that were current in the twelfth century. In particular we are wont to speak of *the* Curia Regis without remembering that the definite article is not in our documents. Any court held in the king's name by the king's delegates is Curia Regis. Thus the institution of what in course of time will be a new tribunal, a Court of King's Bench or a Court of Common Pleas, may be found in some small rearrangement, some petty technical change, which at the moment passes unnoticed." 1 Frederick Pollock & Frederic W. Maitland, *The History of English Law Before the Time of Edward I* 153 (2d ed. 1898).

"[A small] body collects round the king, a body of administrators selected from the ranks of the baronage and of the clergy. At its head stands the chief-justiciar, the king's right-hand man, his viceroy when the king is, as often he is, in his foreign dominions. . . . This body when it sits for financial purposes constitutes the Exchequer (*Scaccarium*), so called from the chequered cloth which lies on the table, convenient for the counting of money. Also it forms a council and court of law for the king; it is a *curia Regis*, the king's court, and its members are *justitiarii*, justiciars or justices of this court. Under Henry I they are sent into the counties to collect taxes and to hold pleas; they are then *justitiarii errantes, justitiarii itinerantes*. During the whole period the term *curia Regis* seems loosely used to cover both the sessions of this permanent body and the assembly of the tenants in chief; the former may perhaps be regarded as a standing committee of the latter." F.W. Maitland, *The Constitutional History of England* 63–64 (1908; repr. 1955).

"The focal point of royal government was the *curia regis* (king's court), the body of advisers and courtiers who attended the king and supervised the administration of the realm. It was not a specific court of law, any more than the eyre was, but rather was the descendant of the Anglo-Saxon *witengemot* (meeting with the *witan*, or royal advisers) and the ancestor of the king's council which later subdivided into parliament and the privy council." J.H. Baker, *An Introduction to English Legal History* 20 (3d ed. 1990).

2. The sessions of this court.

curing title. (18c) The act of removing defects from a land title to make it marketable.

currency. (17c) An item (such as a coin, government note, or banknote) that circulates as a medium of exchange. See LEGAL TENDER.

▸ **blocked currency.** (1934) Currency or bank deposits that, by government restriction, may be used only within the country where they are located.

▸ **fiat currency.** See *soft currency.*

▸ **foreign currency.** Currency that is approved by another country's government, though it may circulate as a medium of exchange elsewhere.

▸ **fractional currency.** (1863) Paper money worth less than one dollar; esp., the currency issued by the federal government from 1863 to 1876. • For the historical equivalent, see SHIN PLASTER (2).

▸ **hard currency.** (1851) Currency backed by reserves, esp. gold and silver reserves. • The value of hard currency can be reliably expected to remain stable or increase, and as such is well-traded internationally. — Also termed *hard money.* See *real money* (1) under MONEY. Cf. *fiat money* under MONEY.

▸ **national currency.** (18c) Currency approved by a national government and placed in circulation as a medium of exchange. See LEGAL TENDER.

▸ **postal currency.** (1865) *Hist.* A fractional currency bearing a facsimile of postage stamps. • The United States Post Office issued these miniature notes in the 19th century until 1876. They were exchangeable for postage stamps, accepted for payments to the government in amounts up to $5, and could be exchanged for federal currency in multiples of $5. They were also used as small change when people hoarded coins during the Civil War. — Also termed *postage currency.*

▸ **soft currency.** (1927) Currency not backed by reserves and therefore subject to sharp fluctuations in value. — Also termed *fiat currency*; *fiat money*; *soft money.* See *fiat money* under MONEY.

▸ **United States currency.** (1803) Currency issued under the authority of the federal government.

currency arbitrage. See ARBITRAGE.

currency market. See *foreign-exchange market* under MARKET.

currency swap. See SWAP.

currency-transaction report. (1974) An Internal Revenue Service form that a bank is required to file whenever a customer engages in banking business that involves cash or a cash equivalent of at least $10,000, or any suspicious transaction. • The report is on blue paper, much like the skin color of the cartoon characters called Smurfs, so it is also termed (in slang) a *smurf.* — Abbr. CTR.

current account. See ACCOUNT.

current-account mortgage. See *offset mortgage* under MORTGAGE.

current asset. See ASSET.

current-cost accounting. (1938) A method of measuring assets in terms of replacement cost. • This approach accounts for inflation by recognizing price changes in a company's assets and restating the assets in terms of their current cost.

currente termino (kər-**ren**-tee **tər**-mi-noh). [Law Latin] *Scots law.* During the currency of the term. • The phrase might be used in leases.

current expense. See *operating expense* under EXPENSE.

current funds. See FUNDS (2).

current income. See INCOME.

current liability. 1. See *short-term debt* under DEBT. **2.** See LIABILITY.

current market value. (18c) The price at which an asset can be sold within the present accounting period. — Abbr. CMV.

current money. See MONEY.

current obligation. See OBLIGATION.

current revenue. See *current income* under INCOME.

current wages. See WAGE.

current yield. See YIELD.

currit quattuor pedibus (**kər**-it **kwah**-too-ər **ped**-ə-bəs). [Law Latin] It runs on four feet; it runs on all fours. See ON ALL FOURS.

cursitor (**kər**-sə-tər). (16c) *Hist.* A chancery clerk responsible for making out original writs. • *Cursitor* derives from the writs *de cursu* that the clerks wrote out.

cursitor baron. (17c) *Hist.* An officer of the Court of Exchequer with administrative, but not judicial, duties. • Over time, as the Barons of the Exchequer took on more judicial rather than fiscal duties, the need for someone with financial experience became apparent. So in 1610 a cursitor baron was appointed to sit alongside the judges. The office was abolished in 1856.

cursor (**kər**-sər). *Eccles. law.* An inferior officer of the papal court.

curtesy (**kər**-tə-see). (16c) At common law, a husband's right, upon his wife's death, to a life estate in the land that his wife owned during their marriage, assuming that a child was born alive to the couple. • This right has been largely abolished. Traditionally, the full phrase was *estate by the curtesy of England* (or *Scotland*). — Also spelled (esp. in Scots law) *courtesy.* — Also termed *tenancy by the curtesy.* Cf. DOWER.

> "An estate by the curtesy, or, as it is more commonly called, by curtesy, is that to which a husband is entitled, upon the death of the wife, in the lands or tenements of which she was seised in possession, in fee simple, or in tail, during their coverture, provided they have had lawful issue born alive, which might have been capable of inheriting the estate. It is a freehold estate for the term of his natural life." 2 Emory Washburn, *A Treatise on the American Law of Real Property* 162–63 (4th ed. 1876).

▸ ***curtesy consummate*** (**kər**-tə-see kən-**səm**-it *or* **kon**-sə-mit). (18c) The interest the husband has in his wife's estate after her death.

▸ ***curtesy initiate*** (**kər**-tə-see i-**nish**-ee-it). (18c) The interest the husband has in his wife's estate after the birth of issue capable of inheriting, and before the death of the wife.

curtilage (**kər**-tə-lij). (14c) The land or yard adjoining a house, usu. within an enclosure. • Under the Fourth Amendment, the curtilage is an area usu. protected from warrantless searches. — Also termed (in Latin) *curtillium.* See OPEN-FIELDS DOCTRINE. Cf. MESSUAGE.

curtiles terrae (kər-**tɪ**-leez **ter**-ee). [Law Latin] See COURT LANDS.

curtillium (kər-**til**-ee-əm). [Law Latin] See CURTILAGE.

cushion. See EQUITY (7).

cushion bond. See BOND (3).

custode admittendo (kə-**stoh**-dee ad-mi-**ten**-doh). See DE CUSTODE ADMITTENDO.

custode amovendo (kə-**stoh**-dee ay-moh-**ven**-doh). See DE CUSTODE AMOVENDO.

custodes libertatis angliae auctoritate parliamenti (kə-**stoh**-deez lib-ər-**tay**-tis **ang**-glee-ee awk-tor-ə-**tay**-tee parl-[y]ə-**men**-tɪ). [Latin] (17c) *Hist.* Guardians of the liberty of England by the authority of Parliament. • The style of all writs and judicial process that issued during the period between the execution of Charles I (January 1649) and the proclamation of Oliver Cromwell as Lord Protector (December 1653).

custodes pacis (kə-**stoh**-deez **pay**-sis). [Latin] (16c) *Hist.* Guardians (or *conservators*) of the peace. See PEACE OFFICER.

custodes treugarum (kəs-**toh**-deez troo-**gahr**-əm). [Latin] *Hist.* Keepers of the truce.

custodiae causa (kə-**stoh**-dee-ee **kaw**-zə). [Latin] *Scots law.* For keeping; for preserving. • The phrase described a bailment's purpose.

custodial account. See ACCOUNT.

custodia legis. See IN CUSTODIA LEGIS.

custodial interference. (1964) *Family law.* **1.** The abduction of a child or the inducement of a minor child to leave the parent legally entitled to custody or not to return to the parent entitled to legal custody. **2.** Any hindrance to a parent's rightful access to a child. • The Restatement (Second) of Torts § 700 (1977) provides for an action in tort by the parent entitled to custody against one who, with knowledge that the parent does not consent, either takes the child or compels or induces the child to leave or not to return to the parent legally entitled to custody.

custodial interrogation. See INTERROGATION.

custodial parent. See PARENT (1).

custodial release. See RELEASE (8).

custodial responsibility. (1942) *Family law.* Physical child custody and supervision, usu. including overnight responsibility for the child. • This term encompasses visitation and sole, joint, and shared custody. Both parents share responsibility for the child regardless of the amount of time they spend with the child. See CUSTODY.

custodial sentence. See PRISON SENTENCE.

custodial trust. See TRUST (3).

custodian, *n.* (18c) **1.** A person or institution that has charge or custody (of a child, property, papers, or other valuables); GUARDIAN. See CAREGIVER. **2.** *Bankruptcy.* A prepetition agent who has taken charge of any asset belonging to the debtor. 11 USCA § 101(11). — **custodianship,** *n.*

▸ **child custodian.** A person who has either legal or physical custody of a child. See CUSTODY (2).

▸ **custodian of evidence.** A custodian responsible for securing and controlling access to evidence and maintaining the evidence in exactly the condition it was in when received.

▸ **custodian of property.** A custodian responsible for managing real or personal property. • The custodian's duties generally include securing, safeguarding, and maintaining the property in the condition received and accounting for any changes in it.

custodian bank. See BANK.

custodian of evidence. See CUSTODIAN.

custodian of property. See CUSTODIAN.

custodian's deed. See DEED.

custodia terrae et haeredis. See DE CUSTODIA TERRAE ET HAEREDIS.

custody, *n.* (15c) **1.** The care and control of a thing or person for inspection, preservation, or security.

▸ **constructive custody.** (1822) Custody of a person (such as a parolee or probationer) whose freedom is controlled by legal authority but who is not under direct physical control.

▸ **involuntary protective custody.** (1975) *Criminal law.* A prison's removal of an inmate from the general prisoner population at the discretion of the administrators, usu. on the basis of concern for the inmate's safety. — Abbr. IPC.

▸ **penal custody.** (18c) Custody intended to punish a criminal offender.

▸ **physical custody.** See PHYSICAL CUSTODY (1).

▸ **preventive custody.** (1976) Custody intended to prevent further dangerous or criminal behavior.

▸ **protective custody.** (1929) **1.** The government's confinement of a person for that person's own security or well-being, such as a witness whose safety is in jeopardy or an incompetent person who may harm him- or herself or others. **2.** *Family law.* An arrangement intended to protect a child from abuse, neglect, or danger whereby the child is placed in the safety of a foster family after being removed from a home or from the custody of the person previously responsible for the child's care. **3.** An arrangement made by law-enforcement authorities to safeguard a person in a place other than the person's home because of criminal threats to harm the person.

2. *Family law.* The care, control, and maintenance of a child awarded by a court to a responsible adult. • Custody involves legal custody (decision-making authority) and physical custody (caregiving authority), and an award of custody usu. grants both rights. In a divorce or separation proceeding between the parents, the court usu. awards custody to one of them, unless both are found to be unfit, in which case the court may award custody to a third party, typically a relative. In a case involving parental dereliction, such as abuse or neglect, the court may award custody to the state for placing the child in foster care if no responsible relative or family friend is willing and able to care for the child. — Also termed *child custody*; *legal custody*; *managing conservatorship*; *parental functions*. See *managing conservator* (2) under CONSERVATOR; PARENTING PLAN.

▸ **divided custody.** (1905) An arrangement by which each parent has exclusive physical custody and full control of and responsibility for the child part of the time, with visitation rights in the other parent. • For example, a mother might have custody during the school year, and the father might have custody during the summer vacation.

▸ **joint custody.** (1870) An arrangement by which both parents share the responsibility for and authority over the child at all times, although one parent may exercise primary physical custody. • In most jurisdictions, there is a rebuttable presumption that joint custody is in the child's best interests. Joint-custody arrangements are favored unless there is so much animosity between the parents that the child or children will be adversely affected by a joint-custody arrangement. An award of joint custody does not necessarily mean an equal sharing of time; it does, however, mean that the parents will consult and share equally in the child's upbringing and in decision-making about upbringing. In a joint-custody arrangement, the rights, privileges, and responsibilities are shared, though not necessarily the physical custody. In a joint-custody arrangement, physical custody is usu. given to one parent. In fact, awards of joint physical custody, in the absence of extraordinary circumstances, are usu. found not to be in the best interests of the child. — Also termed *shared custody*; *joint managing conservatorship*.

> "The statutes, and the cases as well, differ over the definition of joint custody. It is most often defined as meaning only that both parents will share in the decisions concerning the child's care, education, religion, medical treatment and general welfare." Homer H. Clark Jr., *The Law of Domestic Relations in the United States* § 19.5, at 815 (2d ed. 1988).

▸ **legal custody.** (18c) **1.** CUSTODY (2). **2.** CUSTODY (3). **3.** The authority to make significant decisions on a child's behalf, including decisions about education, religious training, and healthcare.

▸ **physical custody.** (18c) **1.** PHYSICAL CUSTODY (2). **2.** PHYSICAL CUSTODY (3).

▸ **residential custody.** See PHYSICAL CUSTODY (2).

▸ **shared custody.** See *joint custody*.

▸ **sole custody.** (1870) An arrangement by which one parent has full control and sole decision-making responsibility — to the exclusion of the other parent — on matters such as health, education, religion, and living arrangements.

▸ **split custody.** (1942) An arrangement in which one parent has custody of one or more children, while the other parent has custody of the remaining children. • Split custody is fairly uncommon, since most jurisdictions favor keeping siblings together.

3. The detention of a person by virtue of lawful process or authority. — Also termed *legal custody*. — **custodial,** *adj.*

custody decree. See DECREE.

custody determination. (1948) *Family law.* A court order determining custody and visitation rights. • The order typically does not include any instructions on child support or other monetary obligations.

custody evaluation. See HOME-STUDY REPORT.

custody hearing. See HEARING.

custody interference. See CUSTODIAL INTERFERENCE.

custody of the law. (17c) The condition of property or a person being under the control of legal authority (as a court or law officer). See IN CUSTODIA LEGIS.

custody proceeding. (1937) *Family law.* An action to determine who is entitled to legal or physical custody of a child. • Legal custody gives one the right to make significant decisions regarding the child, and physical custody gives one the right to physical care and control of the child. See CUSTODY; *custody hearing* under HEARING.

custody release. See RELEASE (8).

custom, *n.* (13c) **1.** A practice that by its common adoption and long, unvarying habit has come to have the force of law. See USAGE (1). — **customary,** *adj.*

> "**Origin and nature of general customs.** — Customs are either general or particular. General customs form one of the legal sources of the common law. It is a matter of historical observation that long before any supreme political authority has come into being a series of practical rules determine the main relations of family life, the conditions of ownership, the punishment of the more violent forms of moral wrongdoing, and the adjustment of contracts. The mode in which such rules are formulated seems to be the following: A spontaneous practice is first followed, and if good and useful, is generally copied over and over again, the more so as habit and association always render the imitation of an old and familiar practice easier than inventing a new and untried one. It is the peculiarity of the class of customs which are the true germs of future law that they are being constantly brought to mind and tested by application to actions. Customs prescribing the formalities and conditions of marriage are brought into distinct consciousness on the formation of every fresh family. The incessantly active vicissitudes of birth and death in every community call for an unintermittent series of decisions upon the competing claims of survivors in matters of ownership, and upon the responsibilities of those who may already be called 'personal representatives' in matters of contract. The main machinery for the conversion of desultory and uncertain customs into fixed rules are the decisions which are constantly demanded for the purpose of ascertaining the nature and extent of an alleged custom. These decisions may be made by a casually selected arbitrator, a village council, or any man or body of men agreed upon, or any person who may have authority to hear the matter. The grounds of decision may be personal mercy, expediency or analogy. Such decisions tend to crystalize and solidify until they frequently become as certain and definite as the rules of established law." William P. Fishback, *A Manual of Elementary Law* § 30, at 29–30 (Arnold Bennett Hall ed., rev. ed. 1896).

▸ **conventional custom.** (18c) A custom that operates only indirectly through the medium of agreements, so that it is accepted and adopted in individual instances as conventional law between the parties to those agreements. — Also termed *usage.* See USAGE (1).

▸ **general custom.** (16c) **1.** A custom that prevails throughout a country and constitutes one of the sources of the law of the land. **2.** A custom that businesses recognize and follow. See *trade usage* under USAGE (1).

▸ **international custom.** A uniform and consistent practice in relationships between nations that serves as evidence of a generally accepted law.

▸ **legal custom.** (17c) A custom that operates as a binding rule of law, independently of any agreement on the part of those subject to it. — Often shortened to *custom.*

▸ **local custom.** (17c) A custom that prevails in some defined locality only, such as a city or county, and constitutes a source of law for that place only. — Also termed *particular custom; special custom.*

2. (*pl.*) Duties imposed on imports or exports. **3.** (*pl.*) The agency or procedure for collecting such duties.

customal, *n.* See CUSTOMARY.

custom and usage. (15c) General rules and practices that have become the norm through unvarying habit and common use. Cf. CUSTOM (1); USAGE.

customary, *n.* (16c) A record of all the established legal and quasi-legal practices within a community. — Also termed *custumal; customal.*

customary court baron. See COURT BARON.

customary dispatch. See DISPATCH (4).

customary easement. See EASEMENT.

customary estate. See COPYHOLD.

customary freehold. See COPYHOLD.

customary international law. See INTERNATIONAL LAW.

customary interpretation. See INTERPRETATION (1).

customary law. (16c) Law consisting of customs that are accepted as legal requirements or obligatory rules of conduct; practices and beliefs that are so vital and intrinsic a part of a social and economic system that they are treated as if they were laws. — Also termed *consuetudinary law.*

> "Customary law may be defined as those rules of human action, established by usage and regarded as legally binding by those to whom the rules are applicable, which are adopted by the courts and applied as sources of law, because they are generally followed by the political society as a whole, or by some part of it." G.W. Keeton, *The Elementary Principles of Jurisprudence* (2d ed. 1949).

> "In contrast with the statute, *customary law* may be said to exemplify *implicit law.* Let us, therefore, describe customary law in terms that will reveal to the maximum this quality of implicitness. A custom is not declared or enacted, but grows or develops through time. The date when it first came into full effect can usually be assigned only within broad limits. Though we may be able to describe in general the class of persons among whom the custom has come to prevail as a standard of conduct, it has no definite author; there is no person or defined human agency we can praise or blame for its being good or bad. There is no authoritative verbal declaration of the terms of the custom; it expresses itself not in a succession of words, but in a course of conduct." Lon L. Fuller, *Anatomy of the Law* 71 (1968).

customary seisin. See *quasi-seisin* under SEISIN.

customary tenant. See TENANT (1).

customer. (15c) **1.** A buyer or purchaser of goods or services; esp., the frequent or occasional patron of a business establishment. **2.** A person having an account with a bank or for whom a bank has agreed to collect items — including a bank that carries an account with another bank. **3.** A buyer or other person who causes an issuer to issue a credit — including a bank that procures issuance or confirmation on behalf of that bank's customer. **4.** *Hist.* Someone who collects customs; a toll-gatherer. **5.** *Hist.* A customary tenant.

customers' goods. See GOODS.

customer's man. See *registered representative* under REPRESENTATIVE.

customer's person. See *registered representative* under REPRESENTATIVE.

customhouse. (15c) A building or office, esp. at a port, where duties or customs are collected and where ships are cleared for entering or leaving the port. — Also spelled *customshouse.*

customhouse broker. See BROKER.

customhouse certificate. See CERTIFICATE.

custom of York. See YORK, CUSTOM OF.

customs, *n.* (*usu. cap.*) A government bureau that examines goods presented for entry into the country and collects taxes due on them. See UNITED STATES CUSTOMS SERVICE.

Customs and Border Protection. See UNITED STATES CUSTOMS AND BORDER PROTECTION.

Customs and Patent Appeals, Court of. See COURT OF CUSTOMS AND PATENT APPEALS.

customs broker. See *customhouse broker* under BROKER.

customs clearance. (1863) **1.** The passing of goods through customs so that they may lawfully enter or leave the country. **2.** A document given by a customs official to a shipper to show that the applicable customs duty has been paid and the goods may be lawfully shipped abroad.

Customs Cooperation Council. A specialized intergovernmental organization for the study of customs questions. • Established in 1952, the Council has its headquarters in Brussels. — Abbr. CCC.

Customs Court, U.S. See UNITED STATES CUSTOMS COURT.

customs duty. See DUTY (4).

customs-enforcement zone. See CUSTOMS ZONE.

customs frontier. (1851) *Int'l law.* The territorial boundary at which a country imposes customs duties.

customshouse. See CUSTOMHOUSE.

customs union. (1903) *Int'l law.* A combination of two or more countries within a single customs area with a common external tariff, though each participating country remains politically independent. • The effect is that tariffs originally levied on the traffic of goods between those countries are abolished or else successively dismantled according to an agreed-on scheme, and that common tariffs are imposed on imports from nonmembers.

customs zone. The area of land and sea that are subject to control by a nation's customs agency. — Also termed *customs-enforcement zone*; (more specif.) *sea-customs zone*; *land-customs zone.*

custos (**kəs**-tahs *also* **kəs**-təs). [Latin] *Hist.* A keeper, protector, or guardian.

Custos Brevium (**kəs**-tahs **bree**-vee-əm). [Law Latin "keeper of the writs"] *Hist.* A clerk who receives and files the writs returnable to the Courts of King's Bench and Common Pleas. • The office was abolished in 1837. — Also termed *Keeper of the Briefs.*

custos maris (**kəs**-tahs **mar**-is). [Law Latin "warden of the sea"] (17c) *Hist.* A high-ranking naval officer; an admiral. — Also termed *seaward*; *seward.*

custos morum (**kəs**-tahs **mor**-əm). [Law Latin] Custodian of morals <H.L.A. Hart believed that courts should not be seen as the *custos morum*>. • This name was sometimes used in reference to the Court of King's Bench.

> "[H]e [Viscount Simonds] approved the assertion of Lord Mansfield two centuries before that the Court of King's Bench was the *custos morum* of the people and had the superintendency of offences *contra bonos mores.*" Patrick Devlin, *The Enforcement of Morals* 88 (1968).

custos placitorum coronae (**kəs**-tahs plas-ə-**tor**-əm kə-**roh**-nee). [Law Latin] See CORONATOR.

Custos Rotulorum (**kəs**-tahs roch-yə-**lor**-əm *or* rot-yə-**lor**-əm). [Law Latin "keeper of the pleas of the Crown"] *Hist.* The principal justice of the peace in a county, responsible for the rolls of the county sessions of the peace. — Also termed *Keeper of the Rolls.*

Custos Sigilli. See KEEPER OF THE GREAT SEAL.

custos spiritualium (**kəs**-tahs spir-i-choo-**ay**-lee-əm *or* -tyoo-**ay**-lee-əm). [Law Latin "keeper of the spiritualities"] (17c) *Eccles. law.* A member of the clergy responsible for a diocese's spiritual jurisdiction during the vacancy of the see.

custos terrae (**kəs**-tahs **ter**-ee). [Law Latin "keeper of the land"] (17c) *Hist.* Guardian, warden, or keeper of the land.

custuma (**kəs**-chə-mə *or* **kəs**-tyə-mə). [French *coustum* "toll" or "tribute"] *Hist.* A duty or impost.

custumal, *n.* See CUSTOMARY.

cut, *n. Criminal procedure.* **1.** A peremptory challenge. **2.** *Slang.* A drug dilutant. **3.** A share of (a sum or amount).

cut, *vb. Criminal procedure.* **1.** To make a peremptory challenge. **2.** *Slang.* To dilute (a controlled substance) by adding material that adds volume to the mixture. **3.** To distribute (a sum or amount).

cutoff date. See DATE.

cutpurse. (14c) *Hist.* Someone who steals by cutting purses; a pickpocket.

cut slip, *n.* (1990) A judge's order to release a prisoner.

cut the baby in half. See SPLIT THE BABY.

cutting agent. See ADULTERANT (2).

CVA. *abbr.* United States Court of Veterans Appeals. See UNITED STATES COURT OF APPEALS FOR VETERANS CLAIMS.

CVR. *abbr.* CONTINGENT-VALUE RIGHT.

CVSA. *abbr.* Computer voice-stress analysis.

CVSG. *abbr.* (1993) A call for the view of the Solicitor General — an invitation from the U.S. Supreme Court for the Solicitor General's views on a pending petition for writ of certiorari in a case in which, though the government is not a party, governmental interests are involved.

C/W. *abbr.* Complaining witness.

Cwth. *abbr.* COMMONWEALTH (4).

CXT. *abbr.* See *common external tariff* under TARIFF (2).

cyberbullying. (1998) The abuse, coercion, harassment, or threatening of another person through electronic media, such as computer websites, e-mail, and text messages. See BULLY, *vb.*

cybercrime. See *computer crime* under CRIME.

cyberlaw (SI-bər-law). (1994) The field of law dealing with the Internet, encompassing cases, statutes, regulations, and disputes that affect people and businesses interacting through computers. • Cyberlaw addresses issues of online speech and business that arise because of the nature of the medium, including intellectual property rights, free speech, privacy, e-commerce, and safety, as well as questions of jurisdiction. — Also termed *cyberspace law.*

> "Much of the hoopla about 'cyberspace law' relates more to climbing the steep learning curve of [the Internet's] technological complexities than to changes in fundamental legal principles. To the extent there was 'new' law, it was almost entirely case-by-case development, in accordance with accepted and well-understood basic legal principles, albeit applied to new technology and new circumstances." Jay Dratler Jr., *Cyberlaw* § 1.01, at 1-3 (2001).

cyberoffense. See *computer crime* under CRIME.

cyberpatent. See *business-method patent* and *Internet patent* under PATENT (3).

cyberpayment. (1994) A transfer of money over the Internet, usu. through a payment service. — Also termed *Internet payment.*

cyberpiracy. (1995) *Trademarks.* The act of registering a well-known name or mark (or one that is confusingly similar) as a website's domain name, usu. for the purpose of deriving revenue. • One form of cyberpiracy is cybersquatting. Another is using a similar name or mark to mislead consumers. For example, a site called Nikee.com that sells Nikee branded athletic shoes and sporting goods would draw customers away the famous Nike brand. — **cyberpirate,** *n.*

cyberspace law. See CYBERLAW.

cybersquatting. (1997) The act of reserving a domain name on the Internet, esp. a name that would be associated with a company's trademark, and then seeking to profit by selling or licensing the name to the company that has an interest in being identified with it. • The practice was banned by federal law in 1999. See ANTICYBERSQUATTING CONSUMER PROTECTION ACT.

cyberstalking. (1995) The act of threatening, harassing, or annoying someone through multiple e-mail messages, as through the Internet, esp. with the intent of placing the recipient in fear that an illegal act or an injury will be inflicted on the recipient or a member of the recipient's family or household.

cyberterrorism. See TERRORISM.

cybertheft. (1994) The act of using an online computer service, such as one on the Internet, to steal someone else's property or to interfere with someone else's use and enjoyment of property. • Examples of cybertheft are hacking into a bank's computer records to wrongfully credit one account and debit another, and interfering with a copyright by wrongfully sending protected material over the Internet.

cyclical (SI-klə-kəl *or* **sik**-lə-kəl), *adj.* (Of a stock or an industry) characterized by large price swings that occur because of government policy, economic conditions, and seasonal changes.

cy pres (see **pray** *or* SI). [Law French "as near as"] (1885) **1.** The equitable doctrine under which a court reforms a written instrument with a gift to charity as closely to the donor's intention as possible, so that the gift does not fail. • Courts use *cy pres* esp. in construing charitable gifts when the donor's original charitable purpose cannot be fulfilled. It is also used to distribute unclaimed portions of a class-action judgment or settlement funds to a charity that will advance the interests of the class. More recently, courts have used cy pres to distribute class-action-settlement funds not amenable to individual claims or to a meaningful pro rata distribution to a nonprofit charitable organization whose work indirectly benefits the class members and advances the public interest. Cf. DOCTRINE OF APPROXIMATION.

> "The *cy pres* doctrine has been much discussed, if not a little severely criticised, and in many cases misunderstood. . . . The *cy pres* doctrine is one under which Courts of Chancery act, when a gift for charitable uses cannot be applied according to the exact intention of the donor. In such cases the courts will apply the gift, as nearly as possible (*cy pres*) in conformity with the presumed general intention of the donor; for it is an established maxim in the interpretation of wills, that a court is bound to carry the will into effect if it can see a general intention consistent with the rules of law, even if the particular mode or manner pointed out by the testator cannot be followed." George T. Bispham, *The Principles of Equity* § 104, at 113–14 (11th ed. 1931).

> "Although the reason for the adoption of the cy pres rule by the English chancery court in the middle ages is not known, various hypotheses as to the motives of the court have been suggested. The most plausible theory is that the chancellors, being ecclesiastics and trained in Roman law, resurrected this civil law doctrine in order to save gifts made for religious purposes and thereby subject the property to church control. Justification for the use of the doctrine was laid on the shoulders of the donor, the idea being that since the object of the testator in donating the money to charity was to obtain an advantageous position in the kingdom of heaven, he ought not to be frustrated in this desire because of an unexpected or unforeseen failure." Edith L. Fisch, *The Cy Pres Doctrine in the United States* 4 (1950).

2. A statutory provision that allows a court to reform a will, deed, or other instrument to avoid violating the rule against perpetuities. See RULE AGAINST PERPETUITIES.

cyrographarius (SI-roh-grə-**fair**-ee-əs). [Law Latin] *Hist.* See CHIROGRAPH (4).

cyrographum (SI-**rog**-rə-fəm). [Law Latin] See CHIROGRAPH (2).

czar. 1. A government official who advises on policy in a particular area <energy czar>. **2.** An emperor or absolute monarch, esp. in Russia before 1917. <Czar Alexander>. — Also spelled *tsar.*

▸ **drug czar.** (1971) *Slang.* The Director of National Drug Control Policy, who directs the international and domestic executive-branch agencies focused on antidrug activities. • The title first appeared in print in a 1982 United Press International news story.

D

D. *abbr.* **1.** DISTRICT. **2.** DEFENDANT. **3.** DIGEST.

D.A. *abbr.* (1934) **1.** DISTRICT ATTORNEY. **2.** See *deposit account* under ACCOUNT.

dactylography (dak-tə-**log**-rə-fee), *n.* (1884) The scientific study of fingerprints as a method of identification. — Also termed *dactyloscopy.* — **dactylographic** (dak-til-ə-**graf**-ik), *adj.*

dactyloscopy. See DACTYLOGRAPHY.

DAF. *abbr.* DELIVERED AT FRONTIER.

dailia. See DALUS.

dailus. See DALUS.

daily balance. (1859) The final daily accounting for a day on which interest is to be accrued or paid.

▸ ***average daily balance.*** (1902) The average amount of money in an account (such as a bank account or credit-card account) during a given period. • This amount serves as the basis for computing interest or a finance charge for the period.

daily newspaper. See NEWSPAPER.

***Dairy Queen* rule.** *Intellectual property.* In an infringement case, the principle that an injured party's claim for an accounting of the infringer's profits raises a question for the jury. • In *Dairy Queen, Inc. v. Wood,* 369 U.S. 469, 82 S.Ct. 894 (1962), the Supreme Court held that a claim for an accounting is not actually a request for equitable relief but for legal relief of money damages. The Court declared that "the constitutional right to trial by jury cannot be made to depend upon the choice of words used in the pleadings." *Id.* at 477–78.

daisy chain. A series of purchases and sales of the same stock by a small group of securities dealers attempting to drive up the stock's price to attract unsuspecting buyers' interest. • Once the buyers have invested (i.e., are caught up in the chain), the traders sell for a quick profit, leaving the buyers with overpriced stock. This practice is illegal.

dalus (day-ləs), *n.* [Law Latin "a dale"] *Hist.* **1.** A dale; a ditch. **2.** A measure of land being a thin strip of pasture between two plowed furrows. — Also termed *dailus; dailia.*

damage, *adj.* Of, relating to, or involving monetary compensation for loss or injury to a person or property <a damage claim> <a damage award>. — Also termed *damages* <a damages claim>. Cf. DAMAGES.

damage, *n.* (14c) **1.** Loss or injury to person or property; esp., physical harm that is done to something or to part of someone's body <actionable damage resulting from negligence>. **2.** By extension, any bad effect on something.

damage-cleer (**dam**-ij **kleer**), *n.* [fr. Latin *damna clericorum* "clerk's compensation"] (17c) *Hist.* A set fee payable by a plaintiff to the Court of the Common Pleas, King's Bench, or Exchequer before execution on an award of damages. • The fee — later abolished by statute — was originally a gratuity to the court clerks for preparing special pleadings. — Also spelled *damage cleere.* — Also termed *damna clericorum.*

> "Damage cleere, *damna clericorum,* was assessed by the tenth part in the common pleas, and by the twentieth part in the king's bench and exchequer, of all damages, exceeding five marks, recovered either by verdict, confession, or judgment of the court, in all actions upon the case, covenant, trespass, battery, false imprisonment, dower, and all others, wherein the damages were uncertain, which the plaintiff was obliged to pay to the prothonotary, or chief officer of that court, wherein they were recovered before he could have execution for them. But this is taken away by 17 Car. 2, c. 6." *Termes de la Ley* 141 (1st Am. ed. 1812).

damage feasant (**dam**-ij **fez**-ənt *or* **fee**-zənt), *n.* [fr. French *faisant dommage*] (16c) *Hist.* Doing damage. • This phrase usu. refers to injury to a person's land caused by another person's animals trespassing on the property and eating the crops or treading the grass. By law, the owner of the damaged property could distrain and impound the animals until compensated by the animals' owner. But the impounder had to feed the animals and could not sell or harm them. The term was introduced during the reign of Edward III. — Also spelled *damage faisant.* — Also termed *damnum facientes.*

damage money. See *danger pay* under PAY (1).

damage rule. See LEGAL-INJURY RULE.

damages, *n. pl.* (16c) Money claimed by, or ordered to be paid to, a person as compensation for loss or injury <the plaintiff seeks $8,000 in damages from the defendant>. — **damage,** *adj.*

> "*The term defined*: A sum of money adjudged to be paid by one person to another as compensation for a loss sustained by the latter in consequence of an injury committed by the former or the violation of some right." Martin L. Newell, *A Treatise on the Law of Malicious Prosecution, False Imprisonment, and the Abuse of Legal Process* 491 (1892).

> "Damages are the sum of money which a person wronged is entitled to receive from the wrongdoer as compensation for the wrong." Frank Gahan, *The Law of Damages* 1 (1936).

▸ **accelerated-market damages.** See *headstart damages.*

▸ **accumulative damages.** (1817) Statutory damages allowed in addition to amounts available under the common law. — Also termed *enhanced damages.*

▸ **actual damages.** (18c) An amount awarded to a complainant to compensate for a proven injury or loss; damages that repay actual losses. — Also termed *compensatory damages; tangible damages; real damages.*

▸ **added damages.** See *punitive damages.*

▸ **additional damages.** (1826) Damages usu. provided by statute in addition to direct damages. • Additional damages can include expenses resulting from the injury, consequential damages, or punitive damages.

▸ **benefit-of-the-bargain damages.** (1955) Damages that a breaching party to a contract must pay to the aggrieved party, equal to the amounts that the aggrieved party would have received, including profits, if the contract had been fully performed. — Also termed *loss-of-bargain damages; expectation loss.*

▸ **common-law damages.** (18c) A court-ordered monetary award intended to return an injured party, as nearly as possible, to the position that party occupied before suffering harm.

▸ **compensatory damages** (kəm-**pen**-sə-tor-ee). (1817) **1.** Damages sufficient in amount to indemnify the injured person for the loss suffered. — Often shortened to *compensatories.* **2.** See *actual damages.*

▸ **consequential damages.** (17c) Losses that do not flow directly and immediately from an injurious act but that result indirectly from the act. — Also termed *indirect damages.*

▸ **contemptuous damages.** See *nominal damages.*

▸ **continuing damages.** (1886) **1.** Ongoing damages arising from the same injury. **2.** Damages arising from the repetition of similar acts within a definite period.

▸ **contract damages.** See CONTRACT DAMAGES.

▸ **cosmetic damages.** The amount awarded to compensate for personal disfigurement.

▸ **damages for lost expectations.** See *expectation damages.*

▸ **damages ultra** (əl-trə). (1838) Additional damages claimed by a plaintiff who is not satisfied with the amounts the defendant paid into court.

▸ **diminution damages.** See *stigma damages.*

▸ **diminutive damages.** See *nominal damages.*

▸ **direct damages.** See *general damages.*

▸ **discretionary damages.** (1854) Damages (such as mental anguish or pain and suffering) that are not precisely measurable but are determined by the subjective judgment of a jury. — Also termed *indeterminate damages.*

▸ **double damages.** (18c) Damages that, by statute, are twice the amount that the fact-finder determines is owed or twice the amount of actual damages awarded. • In some cases, double damages are awarded in addition to actual damages, so the effect is the same as treble damages.

▸ **enhanced damages.** (1872) **1.** See *accumulative damages.* **2.** *Patents.* Damages for patent infringement in an amount up to three times that of compensatory damages, at the discretion of the court, based on the egregiousness of the defendant's conduct, including the willfulness of the infringement. 35 USCA § 284.

▸ **equitable damages.** See *equitable remedy* under REMEDY.

▸ **estimated damages.** See *liquidated damages.*

▸ **excess damages.** (1924) Damages awarded to an insured — beyond the coverage provided by an insurance policy — because the insurer did not settle the claim within policy limits. • If the insurer acted in bad faith in not settling, the insured may have a claim to recover the excess damages from the insurer. — Also termed *excess-liability damages.*

▸ **excessive damages.** (18c) A jury award that grossly exceeds the amount warranted by law based on the facts and circumstances of the case; unreasonable or outrageous damages, which are subject to reduction by remittitur. See REMITTITUR.

▸ **exemplary damages.** See *punitive damages.*

▸ **expectation damages.** (1939) Compensation awarded for the loss of what a person reasonably anticipated from a transaction that was not completed. — Also termed *expectancy damages; lost-expectation damages; damages for lost expectations.*

▸ **extraordinary damages.** See *special damages.*

▸ **fee damages.** (1892) Damages awarded to the owner of property abutting an elevated railroad for injury caused by the railroad's construction and operation. • The term is used because the damage is to the property owner's easements of light, air, and access, which are parts of the fee.

▸ **foreseeable damages.** (1932) Damages that a breaching party knew or should have known when the contract was made would be likely to result from a breach.

▸ **future damages.** (17c) Money awarded to an injured party for an injury's residual or projected effects, such as those that reduce the person's ability to function. • Examples are expected pain and suffering, loss or impairment of earning capacity, and projected medical expenses.

▸ **general damages.** (18c) Damages that the law presumes follow from the type of wrong complained of; specif., compensatory damages for harm that so frequently results from the tort for which a party has sued that the harm is reasonably expected and need not be alleged or proved. • General damages do not need to be specifically claimed. — Also termed *direct damages; necessary damages.*

▸ **gross damages.** (1845) The total damages found before adjustments and offsets.

▸ **headstart damages.** (1988) Damages for profits lost by a corporate plaintiff because of competition from a defendant who misappropriated or misused the plaintiff's property. — Also termed *accelerated-market damages.*

▸ **hedonic damages** (hi-**don**-ik). (1985) Damages that attempt to compensate for the loss of the pleasure of being alive. • Such damages are not allowed in most jurisdictions. — Also termed (erroneously) *hedonistic damages.*

▸ **imaginary damages.** See *punitive damages.*

▸ **inadequate damages.** (18c) Damages insufficient to fully and fairly compensate the parties; damages bearing no reasonable relation to the plaintiff's injuries, indicating prejudice, mistake, or other fact to support setting aside a jury's verdict.

▸ **incidental damages.** (18c) **1.** Losses reasonably associated with or related to actual damages. **2.** A seller's commercially reasonable expenses incurred in stopping delivery or in transporting and caring for goods after a buyer's breach. UCC § 2-710. **3.** A buyer's expenses reasonably incurred in caring for goods after a seller's breach. UCC § 2-715(1).

> "What are incidental damages? The Code does not define incidental damages; rather 2-715(1) lists many expenses that are included as incidental damages. However, Comment 1 to 2-715 stresses that those listed 'are not intended to be exhaustive' but are merely illustrative of the typical kinds of incidental expenses that can be recovered under 2-715:

(1) those associated with rightful rejection (for instance, inspection and storage); (2) those associated with a proper revocation of acceptance; and (3) those involved in effecting cover." 1 James J. White & Robert S. Summers, *Uniform Commercial Code* § 10-3, at 561–62 (4th ed. 1995).

▸ **indeterminate damages.** See *discretionary damages.*

▸ **indirect damages.** See *consequential damages.*

▸ **intervening damages.** (1886) Continuing damages that accrue during the pendency and prosecution of an unsuccessful appeal. • A lower court may include intervening damages in an award.

▸ **irreparable damages** (i-**rep**-ə-rə-bəl). (1874) Damages that cannot be easily ascertained because there is no fixed pecuniary standard of measurement, e.g., damages for a repeated public nuisance. — Also termed *nonpecuniary damages.*

▸ **land damages.** See *just compensation* under COMPENSATION.

▸ **lawful damages.** (1873) Those damages fixed by law and ascertained in a court of law.

▸ **liquidated damages.** (18c) An amount contractually stipulated as a reasonable estimation of actual damages to be recovered by one party if the other party breaches. • If the parties to a contract have properly agreed on liquidated damages, the sum fixed is the measure of damages for a breach, whether it exceeds or falls short of the actual damages. — Also termed *stipulated damages; estimated damages.* See LIQUIDATED-DAMAGES CLAUSE. Cf. *unliquidated damages;* PENALTY CLAUSE.

"Where the terms of a contract specify a sum payable for non-performance, it is a question of construction whether this sum is to be treated as a *penalty* or as *liquidated damages*. The difference in effect is this: The amount recoverable in case of a penalty is not the sum named, but the damage actually incurred. The amount recoverable as liquidated damages is the sum named as such. In construing these terms a judge will not accept the phraseology of the parties; they may call the sum specified 'liquidated damages,' but if the judge finds it to be a penalty, he will treat it as such." William R. Anson, *Principles of the Law of Contract* 470 (Arthur L. Corbin ed., 3d Am. ed. 1919).

"The distinction between a penalty and genuine liquidated damages, as they are called, is not always easy to apply, but the Courts have made the task simpler by laying down certain guiding principles. In the first place, if the sum payable is so large as to be far in excess of the probable damage on breach, it is almost certainly a penalty. Secondly, if the same sum is expressed to be payable on any one of a number of different breaches of varying importance, it is again probably a penalty, because it is extremely unlikely that the same damage would be caused by these varying breaches. Thirdly, where a sum is expressed to be payable on a certain date, and a further sum in the event of default being made, this latter sum is prima facie a penalty, because mere delay in payment is unlikely to cause damage. Finally, it is to be noted that the mere use of the words 'liquidated damages' is not decisive, for it is the task of the Court and not of the parties to decide the true nature of the sum payable." P.S. Atiyah, *An Introduction to the Law of Contract* 316–17 (3d ed. 1981).

▸ **loss-of-bargain damages.** See *benefit-of-the-bargain damages.*

▸ **lost-expectation damages.** See *expectation damages.*

▸ **lost-profits damages.** See LOST-PROFITS.

▸ **lost-volume damages.** The amount of profit lost because of lower sales.

▸ **measurable damages.** Damages whose amount can be determined with a high degree of certainty.

▸ **moratory damages** (**mor**-ə-tor-ee *or* **mahr**-). (1901) *Civil law.* Damages for a delay in performing an obligation. La. Civ. Code arts. 1989, 1994. • There must be a default before these damages can be recovered, while compensatory damages are recoverable for both a failure of performance and for a defective performance.

▸ **multiple damages.** (1927) Statutory damages (such as double or treble damages) that are a multiple of the amount that the fact-finder determines to be owed. — Also termed *multiplied damages.* See *double damages; treble damages.*

"[T]he statutory multiple damages differ from the common law punitive damages in that punitive damages involved no fixed sum or limit. The fixed limit of multiple damages not only reduces their threat to the defendant and the potential for abuse, it also reduces the possibility of a measured deterrence. Likewise, because the enhancement of the award is fixed by the statutory multiple, there is no occasion for introducing evidence of the defendant's wealth as there is in the case of common law punitive damages . . . . Perhaps a more important distinction is that multiple damages statutes may be enacted for entirely non-punitive purposes. Specifically, some double or treble damages statutes, and also specified 'civil penalties,' are intended to provide a kind of liquidated damages for actual losses that cannot be proved or that are otherwise unrecognized by the law." 1 Dan B. Dobbs, *Law of Remedies* § 3.12, at 543 (2d ed. 1993).

▸ **necessary damages.** See *general damages.*

▸ **nominal damages.** (18c) **1.** A trifling sum awarded when a legal injury is suffered but there is no substantial loss or injury to be compensated. **2.** A small amount fixed as damages for breach of contract without regard to the amount of harm. — Also termed *contemptuous damages; diminutive damages.* Cf. *substantial damages.*

"Nominal damages are damages awarded for the infraction of a legal right, where the extent of the loss is not shown, or where the right is one not dependent upon loss or damage, as in the case of rights of bodily immunity or rights to have one's material property undisturbed by direct invasion. The award of nominal damages is made as a judicial declaration that the plaintiff's right has been violated." Charles T. McCormick, *Handbook on the Law of Damages* § 20, at 85 (1935).

"Nominal damages are awarded if the plaintiff establishes a breach of contract or a tort of the kind that is said to be 'actionable *per se*' but fails to establish a loss caused by the wrong. In the case of tort not actionable *per se* as, for example, negligence, if the plaintiff fails to establish a loss, the action will be dismissed. The practical significance of a judgment for nominal damages is that the plaintiff thereby establishes a legal right. The judgment has the effect of a declaration of legal rights and may deter future infringements or may enable the plaintiff to obtain an injunction to restrain a repetition of the wrong. The obtaining of nominal damages will also, in many cases, entitle a plaintiff to costs . . . . [Also,] nominal damages might serve as a peg upon which to hang an award of exemplary damages." S.M. Waddams, *The Law of Damages* 477–78 (3d ed. 1997).

▸ **noneconomic damages.** See *nonpecuniary damages.*

▸ **nonpecuniary damages.** (1900) **1.** Damages that cannot be measured in money. — Also termed *noneconomic damages.* **2.** See *irreparable damages.*

▸ **particular damages.** See *special damages.*

▸ **pecuniary damages** (pə-**kyoo**-nee-er-ee). (17c) Damages that can be estimated and monetarily compensated. • Although this phrase appears in many old cases, it is now widely considered a redundancy — since damages are always pecuniary.

▸ **permanent damages.** (1853) Damages for past, present, and future harm that cannot be avoided or remedied.

▸ **presumptive damages.** See *punitive damages.*

▸ **prospective damages.** (1840) Future damages that, based on the facts pleaded and proved by the plaintiff, can reasonably be expected to occur.

▸ **proximate damages.** (1870) Compensation for reasonably foreseeable harm that directly, immediately, and naturally results from the act complained of. Cf. *speculative damages* (1).

▸ **punitive damages.** (1848) Damages awarded in addition to actual damages when the defendant acted with recklessness, malice, or deceit; specif., damages assessed by way of penalizing the wrongdoer or making an example to others. • Punitive damages, which are intended to punish and thereby deter blameworthy conduct, are generally not recoverable for breach of contract. The Supreme Court has held that three guidelines help determine whether a punitive-damages award violates constitutional due process: (1) the reprehensibility of the conduct being punished; (2) the reasonableness of the relationship between the harm and the award; and (3) the difference between the award and the civil penalties authorized in comparable cases. *BMW of North America, Inc. v. Gore*, 517 U.S. 559, 116 S.Ct. 1589 (1996). — Also termed *exemplary damages; vindictive damages; punitory damages; presumptive damages; added damages; aggravated damages; speculative damages; imaginary damages; smart money; punies.*

"Although compensatory damages and punitive damages are typically awarded at the same time by the same decisionmaker, they serve distinct purposes. The former are intended to redress the concrete loss that the plaintiff has suffered by reason of the defendant's wrongful conduct. The latter, which have been described as 'quasi-criminal,' operate as 'private fines' intended to punish the defendant and to deter future wrongdoing. A jury's assessment of the extent of a plaintiff's injuries is essentially a factual determination, whereas its imposition of punitive damages is an expression of its moral condemnation" *Cooper Indus. v. Leatherman Tool*, 532 U.S. 424, 432, 121 S.Ct. 1678, 1683 (2001).

▸ **putative damages.** (1897) Damages that are alleged; claimed but unproved damages.

▸ **real damages.** See *actual damages.*

▸ **reliance damages.** (1938) Damages awarded for losses incurred by the plaintiff in reliance on the contract. • Reliance damages restore the plaintiff to the economic condition the plaintiff enjoyed before the contract was formed.

"Reliance damages are . . . 'real' losses in a much more tangible way than losses of expectations. The distinction is nicely illustrated by *McRae v. Commonwealth Disposals Commission* . . . . In this case, . . . the defendants sold a shipwrecked tanker which they advertised as lying on a certain reef in the Pacific, and the plaintiffs spent a substantial sum of money equipping a salvage expedition to go in search of the ship. The ship was wholly non-existent, and the plaintiffs were held entitled to damages. Here it was clear that the plaintiffs had incurred substantial expenses — real losses — in reliance on the contract, and the Australian High Court awarded these reliance damages to the plaintiffs." P.S. Atiyah, *An Introduction to the Law of Contract* 311 (3d ed. 1981).

▸ **reliance-loss damages.** (2006) A reimbursement for losses or expenses that the plaintiff suffers in reliance on the defendant's contractual promise that has been breached.

▸ **remote damages.** See *speculative damages* (1).

▸ **rescissory damages** (ri-**sis**-ə-ree *or* ri-**siz**-). (1974) Damages awarded to restore a plaintiff to the position occupied before the defendant's wrongful acts.

▸ **restitution damages.** (1939) Damages awarded to a plaintiff when the defendant has been unjustly enriched at the plaintiff's expense.

"Suppose A pays money to B in pursuance of a contract which turns out to be void, or perhaps is subsequently frustrated: clearly A cannot sue B for breach of contract. B's promise to perform his side of the bargain is vitiated by the mistake or the frustrating event, so A's lost expectations are losses which he must just put up with. But his claim to repayment of the money is evidently much stronger: for this money is a tangible loss to A and a tangible enrichment to B. So in this sort of case the money will often be recoverable, though English lawyers think of this as a quasi-contractual claim to recover money as on a total failure of consideration, and not a contractual claim to restitution damages. There is, however, no strong reason for refusing to call this a contractual action, any more than there is a reason for calling an action for damages quasi-contractual." P.S. Atiyah, *An Introduction to the Law of Contract* 312 (3d ed. 1981).

▸ **severance damages.** (1853) In a condemnation case, damages awarded to a property owner for diminution in the fair market value of land as a result of severance from the land of the property actually condemned; compensation awarded to a landowner for the loss in value of the tract that remains after a partial taking of the land.

▸ **special damages.** (17c) Damages that are alleged to have been sustained in the circumstances of a particular wrong. • To be awardable, special damages must be specifically claimed and proved. *See* Fed. R. Civ. P. 9(g). — Often shortened to *specials.* — Also termed *particular damages; extraordinary damages.*

▸ **speculative damages.** (1804) **1.** Damages that are so uncertain to occur that they will not be awarded. — Also termed *remote damages.* **2.** See *punitive damages.*

▸ **statutory damages.** (1847) Damages provided by statute (such as a wrongful death and survival statute), as distinguished from damages provided under the common law.

▸ **stigma damages.** (1985) Damages resulting from a temporary harm that causes the fully restored property to be viewed as less valuable after the harm and produces a permanent loss of value. — Also termed *diminution damages.*

▸ **stipulated damages.** See *liquidated damages.*

▸ **substantial damages.** (1836) A considerable sum awarded to compensate for a significant loss or injury. Cf. *nominal damages.*

"Substantial damages . . . are the result of an effort at measured compensation, and are to be contrasted with nominal damages which are in no sense compensatory, but merely symbolic." Charles T. McCormick, *Handbook on the Law of Damages* § 20, at 85 (1935).

▸ **tangible damages.** See *actual damages.*

▸ **temperate damages.** (18c) *Rare.* Reasonable damages.

▸ **temporary damages.** (18c) Damages allowed for an intermittent or occasional wrong, such as a real-property injury whose cause can be removed or abated.

▸ **tort damages.** Monetary compensation for tangible and intangible harm to persons and property as the result of a tort. See TORT.

▸ **treble damages.** (18c) Damages that, by statute, are three times the amount of actual damages that the fact-finder determines is owed. — Also termed *triple damages.*

▸ **uncertain damages.** (17c) Damages that are not clearly the result of a wrong. • The rule against allowing recovery of uncertain damages refers to these damages, not damages that are uncertain only in amount.

▸ **unliquidated damages.** (18c) Damages that cannot be determined by a fixed formula and must be established by a judge or jury. Cf. *liquidated damages.*

▸ **vindictive damages.** See *punitive damages.*

damages, mitigation of. See MITIGATION-OF-DAMAGES DOCTRINE.

damages clause. See SURFACE-DAMAGE CLAUSE.

damages for detention. See *noncontract demurrage* under DEMURRAGE (1).

dame. (13c) **1.** The legal title of the wife of a knight or baronet. **2.** The female equivalent of a knight. **3.** A form of address to a woman of high rank. **4.** A matron. **5.** *Slang.* A woman. — Also termed (in senses 1 & 2) *domina.*

damna (**dam**-nə), *n.* [fr. Latin *damnum* "damage; loss"] *Hist.* **1.** Damages, exclusive of costs. **2.** Damages, inclusive of costs. **3.** The abbreviation of *damna clericorum,* the Latin equivalent to *damage-cleer,* being a portion of damages constituting the clerk's fee. See DAMAGE-CLEER.

damna clericorum (**dam**-nə kler-ə-**kor**-əm), *n.* See DAMAGE-CLEER.

damnatus (dam-**nay**-təs), *n.* [fr. Latin *damnare* "to condemn"] (16c) **1.** *Roman law.* A person condemned, esp. in a capital case. **2.** *Hist.* Something prohibited by law; something that is unlawful, as in *damnatus coitus* ("unlawful sexual connection").

damn-fool doctrine. (1990) *Insurance.* The principle that an insurer may deny (esp. liability) coverage when an insured engages in behavior that is so ill-conceived that the insurer should not be compelled to bear the loss resulting from the insured's actions. — Also termed *damned-fool doctrine.*

> "The 'damn foolish acts' concept is not a perfect predictor of judicial decisions, both because of its own imprecision and because other considerations, such as a desire to assure an innocent third party a source of indemnification, may influence a court. However, especially when . . . the insured who acted foolishly has sufficient resources to provide compensation to the injured persons, analysis of a coverage issue on the basis of a 'damn fool' doctrine is frequently a very effective approach both to predicting and to understanding outcomes." Robert E. Keeton & Alan I. Widiss, *Insurance Law: A Guide to Fundamental Principles, Legal Doctrines, and Commercial Practices* § 5.4, at 541 (1988).

damnification, *n.* (17c) Something that causes damage <damnification in the form of a penalty>.

damnify, *vb.* (16c) To cause loss or damage to; to injure <the surety was damnified by the judgment obtained against it>.

damni injuria actio (**dam**-nɪ in-**joor**-ee-ee **ak**-shee-oh). [Latin "an action for wrongful damage"] See *actio damni injuria* under ACTIO.

damnosa aut lucrosa (dam-**noh**-sə awt loo-**kroh**-sə). [Latin] *Hist.* Disadvantageous or advantageous. • The heir to a succession had to determine whether it was hurtful or advantageous to him to take up the estate before actually doing so. See ANNUS DELIBERANDI.

damnosa hereditas (dam-**noh**-sə hə-**red**-i-tas), *n.* [Latin "an injurious inheritance"] **1.** *Roman & civil law.* An inheritance more onerous than beneficial, esp. because it is burdened with debt. **2.** *English law.* A bankrupt debtor's property that creditors will disclaim under the bankruptcy laws because debt on the property will exceed revenues. **3.** Generally, anything that is acquired but turns out to be disadvantageous. — Also spelled *damnosa haereditas.*

damnous (**dam**-nəs), *adj.* (1870) Causing loss or damage.

damno vitando. **1.** See CERTANS DE DAMNO VITANDO. **2.** See IN DAMNO VITANDO.

damnum (**dam**-nəm), *n.* [Latin] (1828) A loss; damage suffered. See AD DAMNUM CLAUSE. Pl. **damna.**

> "Generally speaking, the word damnum meant any harm whatever. In a narrower sense it was held to mean any diminution of the loser's patrimony." John George Phillimore, *Private Law Among the Romans* 105 (1863).

damnum absque injuria (**dam**-nəm **ab**-skwee in-**joor**-ee-ə). [Latin "damage without wrongful act"] (17c) Loss or harm that is incurred from something other than a wrongful act and occasions no legal remedy. • An example is a loss from fair trade competition. — Also termed *damnum sine injuria; absque injuria damnum; absque injuria.* Cf. INJURIA ABSQUE DAMNO.

damnum cum injuria (**dam**-nəm kəm in-**joor**-ee-ə). (1896) Legal damage coupled with legal wrong, these two being necessary to give rise to an actionable right that results in liability.

damnum emergens (**dam**-nəm i-**mər**-jenz). [Latin "damage arising"] (17c) *Hist.* An actual realized loss (such as a decline in the value of property) as opposed to an expected future loss (such as loss of profit); consequential loss.

> "These kinds of damage are distinguished by the commentators as damnum emergens and lucrum cessans, which may be rendered 'positive damage' and 'loss of profit.' The first may be immediate (e.g., my slave is killed or has lost an eye), or consequential (I have lost his services — I have incurred medical expenses — he was one of a troupe of singers and the whole troupe is less valuable in consequence of his death or injury). Where there is no pecuniary loss there is no action. An action does not lie . . . for striking a slave if his value to me has not been depreciated by the blow nor for trespass to land unattended by damage." R.W. Lee, *The Elements of Roman Law* 394 (4th ed. 1956).

damnum et interesse (dam-**nəm** et in-tər-**es**-ee). [Latin] *Scots law.* The loss and damage sustained.

> "Damnum et interesse. — The loss and interest; or, as the words may also be translated, damage, and its issues or consequences. The words are used by Erskine in treating of the liability of cautioners who become bound to see a specific act performed. Failing performance, the cautioners are liable to the creditors for the *damnum et interesse* — that is, the actual and consequential damage suffered through non-performance on the part of the debtor." John Trayner, *Trayner's Latin Maxims* 134 (4th ed. 1894).

damnum facientes (**dam**-nəm fay-shee-**en**-teez), *n.* See DAMAGE FEASANT.

damnum fatale (**dam**-nəm fə-**tay**-lee). [Latin "unavoidable damage"] *Roman law.* Damage caused by an unavoidable circumstance, such as a storm or a shipwreck, for which bailees or others will not be held liable. • But an exception was made for damages resulting from theft.

> "The liability of innkeepers, carriers, and stable keepers, at Roman law, was provided for in the praetor's edict. They were under an obligation to restore all goods which the guests or passengers had with them, or left in their charge, and they could not defend themselves by showing the utmost degree of diligence. Unavoidable accident, which no human prudence would avert or provide against, *damnum fatale*, or overwhelming force, *vis maior*, were, however, an adequate defense . . . . It was particularly noted that theft by a third person would not be permitted as a defense and the reason assigned was the fact that travelers have scarcely any chance to protect themselves against collusion between the innkeeper and the thief." Max Radin, *Handbook of Roman Law* 254 (1927).

damnum infectum (**dam**-nəm in-**fek**-təm). [Latin "damage not done"] *Roman law.* Loss not yet suffered but threatened or apprehended, as when a neighbor's building is likely to collapse onto one's property.

damnum injuria datum (**dam**-nəm in-**joor**-ee-ə **day**-təm). [Latin "damage causing injury"] *Roman law.* Willful or negligent damage to corporeal property; damage for which compensation was given under the Aquilian law. • In this phrase, the word *damnum* refers to economic loss, not the physical damage (if any). See *actio legis Aquiliae* under ACTIO.

> "There are cases in which the law will suffer a man knowingly and wilfully to inflict harm upon another, and will not hold him accountable for it. Harm of this description — mischief that is not wrongful because it does not fulfil even the material conditions of responsibility — is called *damnum sine injuria*, the term *injuria* being here used in its true sense of an act contrary to law (*in jus*), not in its modern and corrupt sense of harm." John Salmond, *Jurisprudence* 372–73 (Glanville L. Williams ed., 10th ed. 1947).

> "There are many forms of harm of which the law takes no account. Damage so done and suffered is called *damnum sine injuria*, and the reasons for its permission by the law are various and not capable of exhaustive statement. For example, the harm done may be caused by some person who is merely exercising his own rights; as in the case of the loss inflicted on individual traders by competition in trade, or where the damage is done by a man acting under necessity to prevent a greater evil." R.F.V. Heuston, *Salmond on the Law of Torts* 13 (17th ed. 1977).

> "What did *damnum iniuria* actually mean? Loss and unlawful injury. The phrase *damnum iniuria* comprises two nouns in the nominative and in asyndeton. They are used to describe the loss and unlawful injury (or harm or detriment) for which the lex Aquilia gave remedies. Ultimately, therefore, the scope of *damnum iniuria* depended on the way the jurists interpreted the provisions of the statute. As Ulpian explains in D.47.10.1 pr and 9.2.5.1, by his time *iniuria* in *damnum iniuria* had come to mean *damnum*, more particularly loss caused by fault, even though unintentional. But that was the result of a development that had taken place over the best part of 500 years." Alan Rodger, "What Did *Damnum Iniuria* Actually Mean?" in *Mapping the Law: Essays in Memory of Peter Birks* 421, 437 (Andrew Burrows & Alan Rodger eds., 2006).

damnum sine injuria. See DAMNUM ABSQUE INJURIA.

Dan (dan), *n.* [fr. Latin *dominus*] (14c) *Archaic. English law.* In England, an honorable title for a man; the English equivalent to the Spanish *Don.* • The term was replaced by the terms *Master, Mister,* and *Sir.*

D&C. (1960) *abbr.* DILATION AND CURETTAGE.

D&E. *abbr.* See *dilation-and-evacuation abortion* under ABORTION.

D&O liability insurance. See *directors' and officers' liability insurance* under INSURANCE.

danelaw (**dayn**-law). (bef. 12c) *Hist.* **1.** A system of rules, introduced by the Danes during their invasions of England primarily in the ninth century and maintained principally in the midland and eastern counties where the invasions occurred. • Danelaw was the prevailing law in these regions from the reign of King Edgar to Edward the Confessor, who compiled a uniform law that included some Danelaw components. **2.** The counties in England where the Danish law was enforced primarily in the ninth and tenth centuries — Also termed *danelage; lex Danorum; denelage.*

> "The Danish invasions of the ninth century subjected the eastern parts of the island to new Scandinavian influences. Where the Danes conquered, their 'Danelaw' prevailed. The very word 'law' is believed to have been given to the English language by the Danes." J.H. Baker, *An Introduction to English Legal History* 3 (3d ed. 1990).

danger. (13c) **1.** Peril; exposure to harm, loss, pain, or other negative result. **2.** A cause of peril; a menace.

▸ **apparent danger.** (16c) **1.** Obvious danger; real danger. — Also termed *patent danger.* **2.** *Criminal law.* The perceived danger in one person's actions toward another, as a result of which it seems necessary for the threatened person to use force in self-defense. See SELF-DEFENSE.

▸ **deterrent danger.** (1959) An obvious danger that an occupier of land creates to discourage trespassers, such as a barbed-wire fence or spikes on the top of a wall.

▸ **hidden danger.** See *latent danger.*

▸ **imminent danger.** (16c) **1.** An immediate, real threat to one's safety that justifies the use of force in self-defense. **2.** *Criminal law.* The danger resulting from an immediate threatened injury sufficient to cause a reasonable and prudent person to defend himself or herself.

▸ **latent danger.** A danger that is not obvious or visible. — Also termed *hidden danger.*

▸ **patent danger.** See *apparent danger* (1).

▸ **retributive danger.** (1931) A concealed danger that an occupier of land creates to injure trespassers. • A retributive danger is lawful only to the extent that it could be justified if the occupier had inflicted the injury personally or directly to the trespasser. Thus, a spring gun or a land mine is an unlawful means of defending land against a trespasser.

▸ **seeming danger.** (17c) Danger that a reasonable person would perceive to be real, even if it is not.

▸ **unavoidable danger.** (16c) **1.** Inescapable danger. **2.** A danger that is unpreventable, esp. by a person operating a vessel.

danger-creation doctrine. (2000) The theory that if a state's affirmative conduct places a person in jeopardy, then the state may be liable for the harm inflicted on that person by a third party. • This is an exception to the general principle that the state is not liable for an injury that a third party inflicts on a member of the public. — Also termed *danger-creation exception.* Cf. SPECIAL-RELATIONSHIP DOCTRINE.

dangeria, *n. Hist.* Payment by forest tenants to the lord so that they can plow and sow in the same season as pannage. See PANNAGE.

danger-invites-rescue doctrine. See RESCUE DOCTRINE.

danger of navigation. See PERIL OF THE SEA.

danger of river. See PERIL OF THE SEA.

danger of the sea. See PERIL OF THE SEA.

dangerous, *adj.* (15c) **1.** (Of a condition, situation, etc.) perilous; hazardous; unsafe <a dangerous intersection>. **2.** (Of a person, an object, etc.) likely to cause serious bodily harm <a dangerous weapon> <a dangerous criminal>.

▸ **imminently dangerous.** (1834) (Of a person, behavior, activity, or thing) reasonably certain to place life and limb in peril. • This term is relevant in several legal contexts. For example, if a mental condition renders a person imminently dangerous to self or others, he or she may be committed to a mental hospital. And the imminently dangerous behavior of pointing a gun at someone's head could subject the actor to criminal and tort liability. Further, the manufacturer of an imminently dangerous product may be held to a strict-liability standard in tort.

▸ **inherently dangerous.** (1887) (Of an activity or thing) requiring special precautions at all times to avoid injury; dangerous per se. See DANGEROUS INSTRUMENTALITY; INHERENTLY DANGEROUS ACTIVITY.

dangerous animal. See ANIMAL.

dangerous condition. See CONDITION (5).

dangerous conduct. See *unreasonably dangerous conduct* under CONDUCT.

dangerous criminal. See CRIMINAL.

dangerous dog. See DOG (1).

dangerous-dog law. (1988) A state or local rule that defines, regulates, and restricts dogs considered dangerous or vicious to the public and that establishes punishments for a dog owner's violations, as by fining the owner, physically restraining the dog, or euthanizing the dog. — Also termed *dog-bite legislation.* Cf. BREED-SPECIFIC LEGISLATION.

dangerous-dog registry. (2007) A government-created website or list of dogs declared dangerous by law or by a court, along with the dog owners' addresses. • The registry lets the public see whether dangerous dogs live nearby.

dangerous drug. See DRUG.

dangerous exposure. See EXPOSURE.

dangerous instrumentality. (1857) An instrument, substance, or condition so inherently dangerous that it may cause serious bodily injury or death without human use or interference. • It may serve as the basis for strict liability. See ATTRACTIVE-NUISANCE DOCTRINE. Cf. *deadly weapon* under WEAPON.

dangerous lunatic. See LUNATIC.

dangerous occupation. See OCCUPATION (1).

dangerous product. See PRODUCT.

dangerous-propensity test. See DANGEROUS-TENDENCY TEST.

dangerous-proximity test. (1973) *Criminal law.* A common-law test for the crime of attempt, focusing on whether the defendant is dangerously close to completing the offense. • Factors include the gravity of the potential crime, the apprehension of the victim, and the uncertainty of the crime's occurrence. See ATTEMPT (2).

dangerous situation. (1898) Under the last-clear-chance doctrine, the circumstance in which a plaintiff operating a motor vehicle has reached a position (as on the path of an oncoming train) that cannot be escaped by the exercise of ordinary care. — Also termed *situation of danger.* See LAST-CLEAR-CHANCE DOCTRINE.

dangerous-tendency test. (1938) A propensity of a person or animal to inflict injury. • The test is used, esp. in dog-bite cases, to determine whether an owner will be held liable for injuries caused by the owner's animal. — Also termed *dangerous-propensity test.*

dangerous weapon. See WEAPON.

danger pay. See PAY, *n.* (1).

danger–utility test. See RISK–UTILITY TEST.

danism (**dan**-iz-əm), *n.* [fr. Greek *daneismos* "a loan"] (17c) *Hist.* The lending of money on usury.

***Darden* hearing.** (1979) *Criminal procedure.* An ex parte proceeding to determine whether disclosure of an informant's identity is pertinent to establishing probable cause when there is otherwise insufficient evidence to establish probable cause apart from the arresting officer's testimony about an informant's communications. • The defense attorney may be excluded from the hearing but can usu. submit questions to be used by the judge in the examination. *People v. Darden,* 313 N.E.2d 49 (N.Y. 1974).

dare (**dair**-ee), *vb.* [Latin "to give"] *Roman law.* **1.** To give; to transfer (something, esp. property). • The transfer can be made to discharge a debt, to create an obligation, or to make a gift. **2.** To appoint a representative.

dare ad remanentiam (**dair**-ee ad rem-ə-**nen**-shee-əm), *vb.* [Latin "to give in fee or forever"] To transfer (esp. a remainder) in fee or forever.

DARPA. *abbr.* DEFENSE ADVANCED RESEARCH PROJECTS AGENCY.

darraign (də-**rayn**), *vb.* [fr. Latin *derationare;* fr. French *disrener*] (13c) *Hist.* **1.** To displace; to disarrange. **2.** To respond to an accusation; to settle a dispute. — Also spelled *deraign; dereyne.*

darreign presentment. See *assize of darrein presentment* under ASSIZE (8).

darrein (**dar**-ayn), *adj.* [fr. French *dernier* "the last"] The last, as in *darrein presentment* ("the last presentment"). See DARREIN CONTINUANCE; *assize of darrein presentment* under ASSIZE (8).

darrein continuance (**dar**-ayn kən-**tin**-yoo-ənts), *n.* [fr. French *dernier continuance* "the last continuance"] (17c) *Hist.* Every plea of a new matter after the last entry of a plea on the record. • Every entry of a pleading after the first pleading on the record was called a *continuance.* — Also spelled *dareyne continuance.*

darrein presentment (**dar**-ayn pri-**zent**-mənt), *n.* See *assize of darrein presentment* under ASSIZE (8).

darrein seisin (**dar**-ayn **see**-zin), *n.* [French "last seisin"] (18c) *Hist.* A tenant's plea in a writ of right. See SEISIN.

DAT. *abbr.* DESK-APPEARANCE TICKET.

database. (1962) A compilation of information arranged in a systematic way and offering a means of finding specific elements it contains, often today by electronic means. • Unless the information itself is original, a database is not protected by U.S. copyright law. Elsewhere, it may be protected as a distinct class of "literary works," or it may be the subject of *sui generis* intellectual-property laws. See SWEAT-OF-THE-BROW DOCTRINE.

Database Directive. See DIRECTIVE ON THE LEGAL PROTECTION OF DATABASES.

data-mining. (1962) The use of a computer to examine large amounts of information to discover things that are not otherwise easily known.

data protection. (1975) Any method of securing information, esp. information stored on a computer, from being either physically lost or seen by an unauthorized person.

date. (14c) **1.** The day when an event happened or will happen <date of trial>. **2.** A period of time in general <at a later date>. **3.** An appointment at a specified time <no dates are available>.

▸ **answer date.** See *answer day* under DAY.

▸ **appearance date.** See *answer day* under DAY.

▸ **commencement date.** See *effective date.*

▸ **cutoff date.** (1937) A deadline; esp., in the sale of a note or other interest-paying asset, the last date on which the seller is entitled to any interest due on the note or asset.

▸ **date of bankruptcy.** (1809) *Bankruptcy.* The date when a court declares a person to be bankrupt; the date of bankruptcy adjudication. • This date may coincide with the voluntary-filing date.

▸ **date of cleavage.** (1909) *Bankruptcy.* The filing date of a voluntary-bankruptcy petition. • With a few exceptions, only the debts existing at this time are dischargeable.

▸ **date of injury.** (1831) *Torts.* The inception date of an injury; the date of an accident causing an injury.

▸ **date of invention.** (1896) *Patents.* For purposes of a patent application, the date when the creation was reduced to practice. • If the invention has not been built, the date of invention is the date when the patent application is filed, since that is a constructive reduction to practice.

▸ **date of issue.** (17c) **1.** *Commercial law.* An arbitrary date (for notes, bonds, and other documents in a series) fixed as the beginning of the term for which they run; the date that a stock or bond bears on its face, not the date on which it is actually signed, delivered, or put into circulation. • When a bond is delivered to a purchaser, it is considered "issued." But this concept is distinguishable from the "date of issue," which remains fixed, regardless of the date of sale or delivery. **2.** *Insurance.* The date specified in the policy as the "date of issue," not the date on which the policy is executed or delivered, and regardless of other dates that may be specified in the policy or elsewhere, such as the date that the policy is to "take effect."

▸ **date of maturity.** (1714) *Commercial law.* The date when a debt falls due, such as a debt on a promissory note or bond. — Also termed *maturity date.*

▸ **date of record.** See *record date* (1).

▸ **declaration date.** (1938) *Corporations.* The date when corporate directors declare a dividend. Cf. DIVIDEND DATE; EX-DIVIDEND DATE.

▸ **dividend date.** See DIVIDEND DATE.

▸ **due date.** (1843) The date on which something is supposed to happen, esp. as a matter of requirement.

▸ **effective date.** (1909) The date on which a statute, contract, insurance policy, or other such instrument becomes enforceable or otherwise takes effect. • This date sometimes differs from the date on which the instrument was enacted or signed. — Also termed *commencement date.*

▸ **effective filing date.** (1927) *Patents.* The date that a patent application is considered to have been filed. • The actual filing date may be later, as for a continuing application. But under the doctrine of continuity, the child application is usu. entitled to the filing date of the parent application to prove priority. — Also termed *parent filing date.* See DOCTRINE OF CONTINUITY.

▸ **filing date.** (18c) **1.** Generally, the date when any document is delivered to the appropriate authority. **2.** *Patents.* The date when a patent application is filed. • The filing date closes the door on prior art; starts the clock on the period of eligibility to file in other countries; sets the priority date for public use, disclosure, or sale; and (absent other evidence) establishes the date of constructive reduction to practice. **3.** *Trademarks.* The date when a trademark application is filed.

▸ **maturity date.** See *date of maturity.*

▸ **parent filing date.** See *effective filing date.*

▸ **payable date.** *Corporations.* The official date on which shareholder dividends or distributions become payable. — Also termed *record date.*

▸ **payment date.** *Corporations.* The date on which stock dividends or interest checks are paid to shareholders.

▸ **priority date.** (1933) **1.** *Patents.* The date that will determine which applicant will get a patent in an interference proceeding. • The priority date is also the cut-off date for prior art. In the United States the priority date is the date of invention; in the rest of the world it is the date the patent application was filed. Cf. FIRST-TO-FILE SYSTEM; FIRST-TO-INVENT SYSTEM. **2.** *Immigration.* The filing date of a petition for immigration based on the status of an immediate relative, on family sponsorship, or on employment.

▸ **record date.** (1886) *Corporations.* **1.** The date on which a stockholder must own shares to be entitled to vote or receive a dividend. — Also termed *date of record.* See EX-DIVIDEND DATE. **2.** See *payable date.*

▸ **settlement date.** (1921) **1.** The date on which an investor must pay the broker for securities purchased. **2.** The date on which a seller must deliver negotiable certificates for securities sold. **3.** ACCOUNT DAY. **4.** The date on which a real-estate purchaser pays for and takes title to the real estate. Cf. CLOSING. —Also termed *settlement day.*

▸ **submission date.** (1847) **1.** The date that a case is to be submitted to a court for determination. **2.** The date on which an investor must pay the broker for securities purchased. **3.** The date on which a seller must deliver negotiable certificates for securities sold.

date certain. (18c) A fixed or appointed day; a specified day, esp. a date fixed by an instrument such as a deed. Cf. TIME CERTAIN (1). — Also termed (in French law) *date certaine* (**dat** sair-**tayn**).

date of record. See *record date* (1) under DATE.

date rape. See RAPE (2).

date stamp. (1818) **1.** A device used for printing the date on documents. **2.** The mark that such a device makes. — **date-stamp,** *vb.*

datio (**day**-shee-oh), *n.* [fr. Latin *dare* "to give"] *Roman law.* **1.** An act of giving, as in *datio in solutum* ("giving in payment"). **2.** An appointment, as in *datio tutoris* ("appointment of a guardian"). Pl. ***dationes*** (day-shee-**oh**-neez).

datio in solutum (**day**-shee-oh in sə-**l[y]oo**-təm). *Roman law.* The discharging of an obligation by the giving and acceptance of something other than the thing due.

dation (**day**-shən), *n.* [fr. Latin *dare* "to give"] *Civil law.* A grant of something the recipient is actually entitled to, such as an office.

dation en paiement (**day**-shən in **pay**-mənt *or* da-**syon** ahn pay-**mon**), *n.* [French "a giving in payment"] *Civil law.* **1.** An exchange of something instead of money to satisfy a debt. See ACCORD AND SATISFACTION. **2.** *Louisiana law.* A contract in which the obligor gives a thing to the obligee, who accepts it in payment of a debt. La. Civ. Code art. 2655. • *Dation en paiement* requires court approval after petition and notice. **3.** A method of satisfying a mortgage debt by transferring the mortgaged property when the mortgage exceeds the property's value and the mortgage-holder is willing to accept the property in satisfaction of the debt.

dative (**day**-tiv), *n.* [fr. French *datif* "of giving"] (16c) **1.** *Roman & civil law.* An appointment made by judicial or magisterial authority; esp., something granted that is not provided by law or a will. • In Scotland, an executor-dative is a court-appointed executor. **2.** *Hist.* Something that can be given or retracted at will, such as an appointment to a nonperpetual office. — Also spelled *datif.*

dative curatorship. See *dative tutorship* under TUTORSHIP.

dative executor. See EXECUTOR (2).

dative-testamentary executor. See *dative executor* under EXECUTOR.

dative tutorship. See TUTORSHIP.

datum (**day**-təm), *n.* [fr. Latin *dare* "to give"] (17c) **1.** A piece of information. Pl. **data. 2.** *Hist.* Something given or executed. **3.** A date.

datus bonis (**day**-təs **boh**-nis). [Latin] *Scots law.* (Of a person) appointed to manage an estate.

***Daubert* hearing** (**dow**-bərt or doh-**behr**). (1993) A hearing conducted by federal district courts, usu. before trial, to determine whether proposed expert testimony meets the federal requirements for relevance and reliability, as clarified by the Supreme Court in *Daubert v. Merrell Dow Pharms., Inc.*, 509 U.S. 579, 113 S.Ct. 2786 (1993).

***Daubert* test.** (1993) *Evidence.* A method that federal district courts use to determine whether expert testimony is admissible under Federal Rule of Evidence 702, which generally requires that expert testimony consist of scientific, technical, or other specialized knowledge that will assist the fact-finder in understanding the evidence or determining a fact in issue. • In its role as "gatekeeper" of the evidence, the trial court must decide whether the proposed expert testimony meets the requirements of relevance and reliability. The court applies the test outside the jury's presence, usu. during a pretrial *Daubert* hearing. At the hearing, the proponent must show that the expert's underlying reasoning or methodology, and its application to the facts, are scientifically valid. In ruling on admissibility, the court considers a flexible list of factors, including (1) whether the theory can be or has been tested, (2) whether the theory has been subjected to peer review or publication, (3) the theory's known or potential rate of error and whether there are standards that control its operation, and (4) the degree to which the relevant scientific community has accepted the theory. *Daubert v. Merrell Dow Pharms., Inc.*, 509 U.S. 579, 113 S.Ct. 2786 (1993). Similar scrutiny must be applied to nonscientific expert testimony. *Kumho Tire Co. v. Carmichael*, 526 U.S. 137, 119 S.Ct. 1167 (1999). Variations of the *Daubert* test are applied in the trial courts of most states.

> "Francophones and gallicism-lovers be warned: *Daubert* is pronounced /**daw**-bərt/, not /doh-**bayr**/. The confusion over how to pronounce *Daubert* began (and apparently should have ended) in the Supreme Court when the Chief Justice said /**daw**-bərt/ in oral argument. The Dauberts' lawyer then chose to mispronounce his clients' name repeatedly rather than correct the Chief Justice. And so the /**daw**-bərt/ pronunciation was established ex cathedra by a Chief Justice who went uncorrected." Bryan A. Garner, *Garner's Dictionary of Legal Usage* 246 (3d ed. 2011) (citations omitted).

***Daubert* trilogy.** (1999) The three U.S. Supreme Court cases that govern the federal standards for admissibility of expert testimony: *Daubert v. Merrell Dow Pharms. Inc.*, 509 U.S. 579 (1993); *General Electric v. Joiner*, 522 U.S. 136 (1997); and *Kumho Tire Co. v. Carmichael*, 526 U.S. 137 (1999). • The *Daubert* trilogy, coupled with Federal Rule of Evidence 702, which was amended in response to the many cases applying *Daubert* (including *Kumho Tire*), requires the trial court in its capacity as "gatekeeper" of the evidence to exclude unreliable expert testimony. See DAUBERT TEST; EVIDENTIARY RELIABILITY; RELIABILITY.

daughter. (bef. 12c) A parent's female child; a female child in a parent–child relationship.

daughter-in-law. (14c) The wife of one's son.

Davis-Bacon Act. A 1931 federal statute regulating the minimum-wage rates payable to employees of federal public-works projects. 40 USCA § 276a.

day. (bef. 12c) **1.** Any 24-hour period; the time it takes the earth to revolve once on its axis <we have a day to prepare a mandamus petition>. **2.** The period between the rising and the setting of the sun <day or night>. — Also termed *natural day.* **3.** Sunlight <we can see it in the day>. **4.** The period when the sun is above the horizon, along with the period in the early morning and late evening when a person's face is discernible. **5.** Any specified time period, esp. as distinguished from other periods <the good old days> <a day's work>. — Also termed (in senses 2–4) *daytime.* Cf. NIGHT.

▸ **adjournment day.** (18c) **1.** The day on which an organization, such as a court or legislature, adjourns. **2.** *Hist.* A later day appointed by the judges at regular sittings at nisi prius to try an issue of fact not then ready for trial.

▸ **adjournment day in error.** (1868) *Hist.* A day scheduled for completion of matters not finished on the affirmance day of the term.

▸ **affirmance day general.** *Hist.* In the Court of Exchequer, a day appointed after the beginning of every term to affirm or reverse judgments.

▸ **answer day.** (1859) *Civil procedure.* The last day for a defendant to file and serve a responsive pleading in a lawsuit. • Under the Federal Rules of Civil Procedure, a defendant generally must serve an answer (1) within 20 days after being served with the summons and complaint, or (2) if a defendant timely waives service at the plaintiff's request, within 60 days after the request for waiver was sent. Fed. R. Civ. P. 4(d), 12(a). — Also termed *answer date*; *appearance date*; *appearance day.*

▸ **appointed day.** (16c) **1.** A day designated for some special event, such as a conference, meeting, symposium, etc. **2.** The day selected for a statute to come into effect.

▸ **artificial day.** (14c) The period from the rising to the setting of the sun. — Also termed *solar day*; *civil day*; *dies solaris.*

▸ **astronomical day.** See *solar day* (2).

▸ **banking day.** See BANKING DAY.

▸ **business day.** (1826) A day that most institutions are open for business, usu. a day on which banks and major stock exchanges are open, excluding Saturdays, Sundays, and certain major holidays.

▸ **calendar day.** (1847) A consecutive 24-hour day running from midnight to midnight. — Also termed *natural day.*

▸ **civil day.** See *artificial day.*

▸ **clear day.** (1868) One of many full, consecutive days between (1) the date when a period, measured in days, begins and (2) the date when an event that ends the period occurs. • For example, if a statute or contract requires a party to give another party five clear days of notice of a hearing, and the hearing is scheduled to be held on the 31st day of the month, the party giving notice must do so by the 25th day of the month so that five full (clear) days elapse between but not including the 25th and 31st.

▸ **common day.** (1829) *English law.* In England, an ordinary court day.

▸ **court day.** (1822) A day on which a particular court is open for court business. *See* Fed. R. Civ. P. 6(a); Fed. R. Crim. P. 45(a).

▸ **day of demurrage.** (1985) *Maritime law.* A day beyond the days allowed for loading or unloading cargo. • A fine is usu. assessed for each day of delay. See DEMURRAGE. Cf. LAYDAY.

▸ **dedication day.** (16c) *Hist.* A day on which people from several villages gathered in one place to celebrate the feast day of the saint and patron of a church.

▸ **entire day.** An undivided day, rather than parts of two or more days aggregated to form a 24-hour period. • An entire day must have a legal, fixed, precise time to begin and end. A statute referring to an *entire day* contemplates a 24-hour period beginning and ending at midnight.

▸ **ferial day** (**feer**-ee-əl). (14c) *Hist.* **1.** A day free from labor, pleading, and service of process; a holiday. **2.** A working day, under a 1449 statute (27 Hen. 6, ch. 5).

▸ **judicial day.** See *juridical day.*

▸ **juridical day** (juu-**rid**-i-kəl). (17c) A day on which legal proceedings can be held. — Also termed *judicial day.* Cf. *nonjudicial day*; NONJURIDICAL.

▸ **law day.** See LAW DAY.

▸ **lay day.** See LAYDAY.

▸ **legislative day.** (1836) A day that begins when a legislative body reconvenes after a recess or adjournment, and ends when the body next recesses or adjourns until a different calendar day. • A legislative day may extend over several calendar days.

▸ **love day.** (13c) *Hist.* **1.** A day when neighbors amicably settled a dispute. **2.** A day when one neighbor helped another without payment.

▸ **motion day.** See MOTION DAY.

▸ **natural day.** (14c) **1.** The 24-hour period from midnight to midnight. — Also termed *calendar day.* **2.** The period between sunrise and sunset. — Also termed *artificial day.*

▸ **nonjudicial day.** (18c) A day when courts do not sit or when legal proceedings cannot be conducted, such as a Sunday or legal holiday. See LEGAL HOLIDAY (1); NON JURIDICUS. Cf. *juridical day.*

▸ **peremptory day.** (16c) A day assigned for trial or hearing, without further opportunity for postponement.

▸ **quarter day.** (15c) *Hist.* One of four days during a year that money owed (such as rent) was legally or customarily payable. • In England and Wales the quarter days are Lady Day, March 25; Midsummer Day, June 24; Michaelmas Day, September 29; and Christmas Day, December 25. In Scotland the traditional quarter or term days are Candlemas, February 2; Whitsunday (or Whitsuntide), May 15; Lammas, August 1; and Martinmas, November 11. Scotland's statutory quarter or term days are the 28th of February, May, August, and November. If a document specifies a different date for a quarter day, then the specified date controls. — Also termed (in Scots law) *term day.*

▸ **return day.** (17c) **1.** A day on which a defendant must appear in court (as for an arraignment). **2.** A day on which a defendant must file an answer. **3.** A day on which a proof of service must be returned to court. — Also termed *rule day.* **4.** A day on which a writ of execution must be returned to court. **5.** A day specified by law for counting votes in an election. — Also termed *return date.*

▸ **rule day.** See *return day* (3).

▸ **solar day.** (18c) **1.** See *artificial day.* **2.** The 24-hour period from noon to noon. — Also termed *astronomical day.*

▸ **term day.** *Scots law.* See *quarter day.*

daybook. (16c) A merchant's original record of daily transactions.

day fine. See FINE (5).

day in court. (16c) **1.** The right and opportunity, in a judicial tribunal, to litigate a claim, seek relief, or defend one's rights. **2.** The right to be notified and given an opportunity to appear and to be heard when one's case is called.

day job. (1886) The normal job from which one earns most of one's money — esp. as contrasted with a less lucrative endeavor that one enjoys more.

daylight-saving time. (1909) The period during the summer when clocks are one hour ahead of standard time. — Also termed *daylight savings time.*

day loan. See LOAN.

day of demurrage. See DAY.

day order. See ORDER (8).

day rule. See DAY WRIT.

days in bank. (16c) Particular days set aside by the Court of Common Pleas for specific matters, including the appearance of parties and service of process. — Also termed *dies in banco.*

> "There are in each of these terms stated days called *days in bank, dies in banco;* that is, days of appearance in the court of common pleas. They are generally at the distance of about a week from each other, and regulated by some festival of the church. On some one of these days in bank all original writs must be made returnable . . . ." 3 William Blackstone, *Commentaries on the Laws of England* 277 (1768).

daysman (**dayz**-mən). (15c) *Hist.* **1.** An arbitrator; an elected judge; an umpire. **2.** A day laborer. — Also spelled *deiesman.*

days of grace. (16c) **1.** GRACE PERIOD (1). **2.** *Int'l law.* A timed exemption from prize law that is granted to enemy merchant ships when they are caught unawares by the outbreak of war.

daytime. 1. See DAY (2). **2.** See DAY (3). **3.** See DAY (4).

day trading. See TRADING.

daywork. (bef. 12c) **1.** Short-term employment that is intended to last only for a day, or for a few days. **2.** *Hist. English law.* In England, a measure of land being the amount of arable land that can be plowed in a day. — Also termed *daywere.*

daywork drilling contract. See DRILLING CONTRACT.

day writ. (1809) *English law.* A Queen's Bench writ allowing a prisoner to leave prison to conduct business (such as attending trial at the Court of Assizes), as long as the prisoner returns by 9:00 p.m. — Also termed *day rule.*

D.B. *abbr.* DOMESDAY BOOK.

d/b/a. *abbr.* Doing business as. • The abbreviation usu. precedes a person's or business's assumed name <Paul Smith d/b/a Paul's Dry Cleaners>. It signals that the business may be licensed or incorporated under a different name. Cf. TRADENAME.

d.b.e. *abbr.* DE BENE ESSE.

d.b.n. *abbr.* See *administration de bonis non* under ADMINISTRATION.

d.b.n.c.t.a. *abbr.* See *administration de bonis non cum testamento annexo* under ADMINISTRATION.

DBO. *abbr.* Death benefit only. See *survivor's income benefit plan* under EMPLOYEE BENEFIT PLAN.

D.C. *abbr.* **1.** DISTRICT OF COLUMBIA. **2.** See *district court* (1) under COURT.

DCAA. *abbr.* DEFENSE CONTRACT AUDIT AGENCY.

DCF. See *discounted cash flow* under CASH FLOW.

DCMA. *abbr.* DEFENSE CONTRACT MANAGEMENT AGENCY.

DCO. *abbr.* DELAYED-COMPLIANCE ORDER.

DD. *abbr.* See *downward departure* under DEPARTURE (1).

DDoS. *abbr.* DISTRIBUTED DENIAL-OF-SERVICE ATTACK.

DDP. *abbr.* **1.** DELIVERED DUTY PAID. **2.** DISCLOSURE DOCUMENT PROGRAM.

DDU. *abbr.* DELIVERED DUTY UNPAID.

de (də *or* duu). [French] Of; about. • This is a French preposition often used to show the genitive case, as in *brefe de droit* ("writ of right").

de (dee *or* day). [Latin] Of; about; concerning; respecting; by; from; out of; affecting. • This preposition is used in the titles of English statutes, of original and judicial writs, and of court proceedings.

DEA. *abbr.* DRUG ENFORCEMENT ADMINISTRATION.

deacon. (bef. 12c) *Eccles. law.* **1.** In some Christian churches, a religious official who is just below the rank of a priest. • In certain churches, a deacon is a cleric who assists the priest in various duties, including the presentation of the sacrament. It is the third order below bishops and priests. A deacon is not allowed to consecrate the Holy Communion or pronounce absolution but can perform most of the other priestly duties. **2.** An elected or appointed officer of a church who assists a minister or priest in various duties. See DIACONATE. Cf. ARCHDEACON. — **diaconal** (dɪ-**ak**-ə-nəl), *adj.*

dead-and-buried company. See COMPANY.

dead asset. See ASSET.

deadbeat. (1863) *Slang.* **1.** Someone who does not pay debts or financial obligations (such as child-support payments, fines, and legal judgments), usu. with the suggestion that the person is also adept or experienced at evading creditors. **2.** Someone who is lazy and has no specific goals or plan for his or her life.

deadbeat dad. (1983) *Slang.* A father who has not paid or who is behind in making child-support payments.

deadbeat mom. (1987) *Slang.* **1.** A mother who has not paid or who is behind in making child-support payments. • This term is used far less frequently than either *deadbeat dad* or *deadbeat parent,* probably because nearly ten times as many men as women fail to support (or are ordered to support) their children financially after divorce. **2.** An able-bodied mother whose income is derived from welfare payments, not from gainful employment.

Deadbeat Parents Punishment Act. A 1998 federal statute that makes it a felony, punishable by up to two years in prison, for failure to pay child support if the obligor has crossed state lines in an attempt to avoid paying the support. • The Act provides felony penalties if (1) a person travels across state lines intending to evade a child-support obligation that is over $5,000 or that has remained unpaid longer than one year, or (2) a person willfully fails to pay support for a child living in a different state if that obligation is greater than $10,000 or if it remains unpaid for more than two years. The Act supersedes the Child Support Recovery Act of 1994. The greatest change in the new statute is the provision regarding the obligor's crossing of state lines in an effort to evade the support obligation. 18 USCA § 228. — Abbr. DPPA. See CHILD SUPPORT RECOVERY ACT OF 1994.

deadborn. See *deadborn child* under CHILD.

dead corporation. See *dissolved corporation* under CORPORATION.

dead freight. See FREIGHT.

deadhand control. (1952) The convergence of various legal doctrines that allow a decedent's control of wealth to influence the conduct of a living beneficiary; esp., the use of executory interests that vest at some indefinite and remote time in the future to restrict alienability and to ensure that property remains in the hands of a particular family or organization. • Examples include the lawful use of conditional gifts, contingent future interests, and the *Claflin*-trust principle. The Rule Against Perpetuities restricts certain types of deadhand control, which is sometimes referred to either as the power of the *mortua manus* (dead hand) or as trying to retain property *in mortua manu*. Historically, deadhand-control problems concerned devises of land to religious corporations. See MORTMAIN; RULE AGAINST PERPETUITIES.

dead letter. (17c) **1.** A law or practice that, although not formally abolished, is no longer used, observed, or enforced. **2.** A piece of mail that can be neither delivered nor returned because it lacks correct addresses for both the intended recipient and the sender.

deadline. A cutoff date for taking some action.

deadlock, *n.* (18c) **1.** A state of inaction resulting from opposition, a lack of compromise or resolution, or a failure of election. See *tie vote* under VOTE (3). **2.** *Corporations.* The blocking of corporate action by one or more factions of shareholders or directors who disagree about a significant aspect of corporate policy. — **deadlock,** *vb.*

deadlocked jury. See *hung jury* under JURY.

deadlock instruction. See ALLEN CHARGE.

deadly force. See FORCE.

deadly weapon. See WEAPON.

deadly weapon per se. See WEAPON.

dead man's part. (18c) **1.** *Archaic.* By custom in certain places, the portion of a dead man's estate set aside for mass services; later, that portion set aside as payment for the administrator. • That portion ranged from one-third (if the deceased had a wife and children) to the entire estate (if the deceased had no wife or children).

> "If the deceased leaves a widow and children, his substance . . . is divided into three parts; one of which belongs to the widow, another to the children, and the third to the administrator: if only a widow, or only children, they shall respectively, in either case, take one moiety, and the administrator the other: if neither widow nor child, the administrator shall have the whole. And this portion, or *dead man's* part, the administrator was wont to apply to his own use, till the statute I Jac. II. c. 17 declared that the same should be subject to the statute of distributions." 2 William Blackstone, *Commentaries on the Laws of England* 518 (1766).

> "If a testator leaves neither wife nor child, he can give away the whole of his movable goods. If the testator leaves wife but no child, or child but no wife, his goods must, after his debts have been paid, be divided into two halves; one of these can be disposed of by his will, it is 'the dead's part,' the other belongs to the widow, or (as the case may be) to the child or children." 2 Frederick Pollock & Frederic W. Maitland, *History of English Law Before the Time of Edward I* 349 (2d ed. 1899).

2. *Scots law.* The part of the movable estate that may be disposed of by will in any way the testator wishes; specif., the part of a dead man's personal estate not legally reserved for his spouse or children and capable of being bequeathed by will or falling upon intestacy to his next-of-kin. — Also termed *dead's part.*

dead man's statute. (1879) A law prohibiting the admission of a decedent's statement as evidence in certain circumstances, as when an opposing party or witness seeks to use the statement to support a claim against the decedent's estate. — Also termed *dead person's statute.*

dead marriage. See MARRIAGE (1).

de admensuratione dotis (dee ad-men-s[y]uu-ray-shee-**oh**-nee **doh**-tis), *n.* [Law Latin "of the admeasurement of dower"] See *admeasurement of dower* under ADMEASUREMENT.

dead person's statute. See DEAD MAN'S STATUTE.

dead pledge. *Archaic.* See MORTGAGE (1).

dead rent. (1860) A mining-lease payment, either in addition to or as part of the royalty, that must be made whether or not the mine is working. • The purpose of the provision is to secure the working of the mine. See *delay rental* under RENTAL.

dead-ship doctrine. (1963) *Maritime law.* The rule that admiralty law no longer applies to a ship when its purpose has been so changed that it is no longer a vessel because it has no further navigation function.

dead's part. See DEAD MAN'S PART.

dead stock. (17c) Goods that remain in inventory because there is no market for them.

dead storage. (1905) The stowage of goods, esp. motor vehicles, for a long time in a public storage area, as opposed to the daily or regular stowage of goods in active use. Cf. LIVE STORAGE.

dead time. See TIME.

dead use. A future use.

de advisamento consilii nostri (dee ad-vɪ-zə-**men**-toh kən-**sil**-ee-ɪ **nos**-trɪ). [Law Latin] With or by the advice of our council. • This phrase was formerly used in writs of summons to Parliament.

de aequitate (dee ee-kwə-**tay**-tee). [Latin] In equity.

de aestimato (dee es-ti-**may**-toh). [Latin "for the estimation of something in money"] *Roman law.* An action available to an owner of goods against a person who received the goods but failed, after a certain period, to either pay the owner an agreed price after finding a purchaser or return the goods to the owner. • The transaction, or *aestimatum*, was an innominate contract often used by traveling merchants or second-hand dealers who, after purchasing items, could then resell them at higher prices or return them to the owner. — Also termed *actio aestimatoria.*

de aetate probanda (dee ee-**tay**-tee proh-**ban**-də), *n.* [Law Latin "of (about) proving age"] (17c) *Hist.* A writ ordering the sheriff to summon a jury to determine whether an heir of a tenant holding an estate directly of the Crown was old enough to receive the estate.

deafforest. See DISAFFOREST.

deal, *n.* (15c) **1.** An act of buying and selling; the purchase and exchange of something for profit <a business deal>. **2.** An arrangement for mutual advantage <the witness accepted the prosecutor's deal to testify in exchange for immunity>. **3.** An indefinite quantity <a great deal of money>.

deal, *vb.* (bef. 12c) **1.** To distribute (something) <to deal drugs>. **2.** To transact business with (a person or entity) <to deal with the competitor>. **3.** To conspire with (a person or entity) <to deal for the account>.

deal-breaker, *n.* (1979) Something that is so unacceptable that it makes one decide not to go forward with a purchase, relationship, job, etc.

dealer, *n.* (17c) **1.** Someone who purchases goods or property for sale to others; a retailer. **2.** A person or firm that buys and sells securities for its own account as a principal, and then sells to a customer. See DEAL, *n.* & *vb.*

▸ **broker-dealer.** See *broker-dealer* under BROKER.

▸ **registered dealer.** (1942) A dealer registered or required to be registered under the Securities Exchange Act of 1934.

dealership. (1916) A business that sells a particular company's products, such as cars, esp. as part of a franchise relationship.

dealer's talk. See PUFFING (1).

dealing. (*often pl.*) (15c) **1.** The business activities or relationships that someone is involved in <her financial dealings>. **2.** The activity of buying, selling, or doing business with people <fair dealing>. See FAIR DEALING.

de allocatione facienda (dee al-ə-kay-shee-**oh**-nee fay-shee-**en**-də), *n.* [Law Latin "for making allowance"] (18c) *Hist.* A writ directed to the treasurer and barons of the Exchequer allowing certain officers (such as accountants and customs collectors) to have in their accounts the funds necessary to make certain payments.

de alode parentum (dee **al**-ə-dee pə-**ren**-təm). [Law Latin] *Hist.* From freehold of one's parents.

> "De alode parentum. — Lands descending by inheritance from parents were said to be so acquired, in contradistinction to lands held in feu . . . and to those acquired by a singular title. Subsequently the phrase acquired a more comprehensive signification, as all lands were, in process of time, termed allodial, in which the holder had a right of absolute property, without rendering any service therefor, or recognising any superior therein, and of which he had an unlimited power of disposal." John Trayner, *Trayner's Latin Maxims* 137 (4th ed. 1894).

de alto et basso (dee **al**-toh et **bas**-oh), *n.* [Law Latin "of high and low"] *Hist.* The total submission of all differences — great or small — to arbitration.

deal with the devil. See DEVIL'S BARGAIN.

de ambitu (dee **am**-bi-tyoo). [Latin "of going around"] (17c) Of devious methods of securing a position, as through bribery. • Several Roman laws (such as the *Lex Julia de Ambitu*) dealt with these methods, such as prohibiting electoral bribery.

de ampliori gratia (dee am-plɪ-**or**-ɪ **gray**-shee-ə). [Latin] Of more abundant or more full grace.

dean. (14c) **1.** *Eccles. law.* An officer who leads a chapter, parish, or other subdivision of a diocese, usu. upon a bishop's request or appointment.

> "A dean and chapter are the council of the bishop, to assist him with their advice in affairs of religion, and also in the temporal concerns of his see . . . . All ancient deans are elected by the chapter, by *conge d'eslire* from the king, and letters missive of recommendation; in the same manner as bishops: but in those chapters, that were founded by Henry VIII out of the spoils of the dissolved monasteries, the deanery is donative . . . . The chapter, consisting of canons or prebendaries, are sometimes appointed by the king, sometimes by the bishop, and sometimes elected by each other." 1 William Blackstone, *Commentaries on the Laws of England* 370–71 (1765).

2. In a school, college, or university, the administrative or academic head. • In larger schools, there may be several kinds of deans, such as a dean of admissions and a dean of student affairs. Within a university, there may be deans of specific schools. **3.** The head or commander of a group of ten, such as ten soldiers or ten monks. — **decanal** (**dek**-ə-nəl), *adj.*

de anno bissextili (dee **an**-oh bis-sek-**stɪ**-lɪ), *n.* [Law Latin "of the bissextile year"] *Hist.* A law of Henry III advising the justices of the bench that in a case requiring something to be done within a year, the leap-year day and the day before should be counted as one day.

de annua pensione (dee **an**-yoo-ə pen-shee-**oh**-nee), *n.* [Law Latin "of annual pension"] (18c) *Hist.* A royal writ demanding payment from an abbey or prior, of a yearly pension for the king's chaplain named in the writ.

de annuo reditu (dee **an**-yoo-oh **red**-i-tyoo), *n.* [Law Latin "for a yearly rent"] *Hist.* A writ to recover an annuity payable in goods or money.

Dean of Guild. *Scots law.* In certain burghs, the head of the Guild or Merchant Company, with jurisdiction in maritime and mercantile disputes.

Dean of Guild Court. *Scots law.* The court presided over by the Dean of Guild. • In modern times the court dealt with municipal affairs, esp. building regulations. All such courts were abolished in 1975.

Dean of the Arches. *English law.* The presiding judge of the Court of Arches. See COURT OF ARCHES.

de apostata capiendo (dee ə-**pos**-tə-tə kap-ee-**en**-doh), *n.* [Law Latin "of the taking of an apostate"] (18c) *Hist.* A writ ordering a sheriff to apprehend and return to a monastery a person who had entered the monastery, professed the religious order, and then left and wandered around the country.

de arbitratione facto (dee ahr-bi-tray-shee-**oh**-nee **fak**-toh), *n.* [Law Latin "of arbitration had"] *Hist.* A writ staying an action already settled by arbitration.

de arrestandis bonis ne dissipentur (dee ar-ə-**stan**-dis **boh**-nis nee dis-ə-**pen**-tər), *n.* [Law Latin "of goods arrested lest they be dispersed"] *Hist.* A writ to seize goods from a party to ensure that the goods do not disappear while a lawsuit is pending.

de arrestando ipsum qui pecuniam recepit (dee ar-ə-**stan**-doh **ip**-sə kwɪ pə-**kyoo**-nee-əm ri-**see**-pit), *n.* [Law Latin "for the apprehension of one who took the king's money"] (18c) *Hist.* A writ ordering the arrest of a person who took the king's money for war service, and then hid to keep from serving.

de asportatis religiosorum (dee as-por-**tay**-tis ri-lij-ee-oh-**sor**-əm), *n.* [Law Latin "concerning the property of religious persons carried away"] *Hist.* A statute of Edward I passed to curb alienation of clerical possessions, including the removal of those possessions to foreign countries.

de assisa proroganda (dee ə-SI-zə proh-rə-**gan**-də), *n.* [Law Latin "of the proroguing of an assize"] *Hist.* A writ ordering justices to postpone an assize because a party is busy in the Crown's service.

death. (bef. 12c) The ending of life; the cessation of all vital functions and signs. — Also termed *decease*; *demise*.

▸ **accidental death.** (17c) A death that results from an unusual event, one that was not voluntary, intended, expected, or foreseeable. — Also termed *death by misadventure.*

▸ **brain death.** (1964) The bodily condition of showing no response to external stimuli, no spontaneous movements, no breathing, no reflexes, and a flat reading (usu. for a full day) on a machine that measures the brain's electrical activity. • In 1971, Kansas became the first state to enact a statutory definition of the term. Before that, heart transplants raised the question of when — and whether — death had occurred. Early cases dealing with this problem include a tort case (wrongful death), *Tucker v. Lower*, No. 2831 (Richmond, Va., L. & Eq. Ct., May 23, 1972) (jury accepted the defendants' definition of brain death); a criminal case (vehicular homicide), *People v. Flores*, No. 20190 (Sonoma Co. Mun. Ct. Dec. 19, 1973), No. N746-C (Sonoma Co. Super. Ct. July 23, 1974) (defendant acquitted because no statute defined brain death); and a criminal case (murder), *People v. Lyons*, 15 Crim. L. Rep. 2240, No. 56072 (Alameda Co. Super. Ct. May 21, 1974) (court accepted prosecutor's definition of brain death and convicted defendant). — Also termed *legal death.* Cf. *heart–lung death*; *higher-brain death.*

▸ **brain-stem death.** See *whole-brain death.*

▸ **civil death.** (16c) **1.** *Archaic.* At common law, the loss of rights — such as the rights to vote, make contracts, inherit, and sue — by a person who has been outlawed or convicted of a serious crime, or who is considered to have left the temporal world for the spiritual by entering a monastery. See NONPERSON (1). Cf. DE CATALLIS FELONUM.

> "In one large department of law the fiction [civil death] is elegantly maintained. A monk or nun can not acquire or have any proprietary rights. When a man becomes 'professed in religion,' his heir at once inherits from him any land that he has, and, if he has made a will, it takes effect at once as though he were naturally dead." 1 Frederick Pollock & Frederic W. Maitland, *History of English Law* 434 (2d ed. 1898).

> "Civil death arises from outlawry; it seems doubtful whether there are any other circumstances to which the phrase is now applicable." William R. Anson, *Principles of the Law of Contract* 193 n.(b) (Arthur L. Corbin ed., 3d Am. ed. 1919).

2. In some states, the loss of rights — such as the rights to vote and hold public office — by a person serving a life sentence or awaiting execution. Cf. *civil disability* under DISABILITY (3). **3.** The state of a corporation that has formally dissolved or become bankrupt, leaving an estate to be administered for the benefit of shareholders and creditors. — Also termed (in senses 2 & 3) *legal death.*

▸ **compensable death.** (1924) *Workers' compensation.* A death that, because it occurred in the course of employment, entitles the employee's heirs to compensation.

▸ **death by misadventure.** See DEATH BY MISADVENTURE.

▸ **death by one's own hand.** See SUICIDE (1).

▸ **death in custody.** A death that occurs while the person is held by police, in prison, or another authority.

▸ **heart–lung death.** (1975) The irreversible permanent stoppage of a person's circulatory system (heartbeat) and respiratory system (breathing). Cf. *brain death.*

▸ **higher-brain death.** (1982) The irreversible permanent loss of brain functions such as memory, personality, cognition, emotion, and consciousness — sometimes described as the functions that are responsible for "personhood." Cf. *brain death.*

▸ **immediate death.** (16c) **1.** See *instantaneous death.* **2.** A death occurring within a short time after an injury or seizure, but not instantaneously.

> "A distinction has been made between 'instantaneous' and 'immediate' death . . . . As an example of 'immediate' rather than 'instantaneous' death . . . the situation in which a blow on the head produces unconsciousness and renders the victim incapable of intelligent thought, speech, or action for several minutes until he dies." 22A Am. Jur. 2d *Death* § 43, at 159 (1988).

▸ **instantaneous death.** (18c) Death occurring in an instant or within an extremely short time after an injury or seizure. • It is a factor in determining an award of damages for the victim's pain and suffering. — Sometimes also termed *immediate death.*

> "Although the possibility of a death that is truly simultaneous with the injury that caused it has been denied, it has been pointed out that death may be so contemporaneous with the fatal injury as to be instantaneous in the sense that there could be no recovery for the victim's pain and suffering. Ordinarily, death is not regarded as instantaneous if an appreciable length of time elapsed between the injury and the death. Indeed, even where the injury causing the death is necessarily fatal and death results therefrom in a few moments, it has been held that although it would commonly be called an instantaneous death, still if the injured person survives the injury for a brief period, it may not be said that the death is instantaneous . . . . In such case it is immaterial that the period of time between the injury and death is short." 22A Am. Jur. 2d *Death* § 43, at 158 (1988).

▸ **intestate death.** (17c) The death of someone who does not have a valid will.

▸ **legal death.** **1.** See *brain death.* **2.** See *civil death* (2). **3.** See *civil death* (3).

▸ **natural death.** (15c) **1.** Bodily death, as opposed to civil death. **2.** Death from causes other than accident or violence; death from natural causes. — Also termed *mors naturalis.* See NATURAL-DEATH ACT. Cf. *violent death.*

▸ **presumptive death.** (1856) Death inferred from proof of the person's long, unexplained absence, usu. after seven years. See ENOCH ARDEN LAW.

▸ **simultaneous death.** (1878) The death of two or more persons in the same mishap, under circumstances that make it impossible to determine who died first.

See UNIFORM SIMULTANEOUS DEATH ACT; COMMON DISASTER; COMMORIENTES.

▸ **violent death.** (16c) Death accelerated by human intervention and resulting from a sharp blow, explosion, gunfire, or the like. Cf. *natural death*.

▸ **whole-brain death.** (1979) The irreversible loss of all major brain regions, including the brain stem. — Also termed *brain-stem death*.

▸ **wrongful death.** (16c) A death caused by a tortious injury; a death caused by someone's negligent or willful act or omission. See WRONGFUL-DEATH ACTION.

death, contemplation of. See CONTEMPLATION OF DEATH.

death action. See WRONGFUL-DEATH ACTION.

deathbed declaration. See *dying declaration* under DECLARATION (6).

deathbed deed. See DEED.

death benefit. See BENEFIT (2).

death-benefit-only plan. See *survivor's income benefit plan* under EMPLOYEE BENEFIT PLAN.

death by misadventure. (18c) **1.** ACCIDENTAL KILLING. **2.** See *accidental death* under DEATH. **3.** *Archaic.* A defense to a murder charge on the ground that the defendant lacked the requisite mental state for murder. • The defense was abolished as redundant because the prosecution had to prove state of mind anyway as an essential element of murder.

death by one's own hand. See SUICIDE (1).

death case. (1907) **1.** A criminal case in which the death penalty may be or has been imposed. **2.** WRONGFUL-DEATH ACTION.

death certificate. (1888) An official document issued by a public registry verifying that a person has died, with information such as the date and time of death, the cause of death, and the signature of the attending or examining physician.

death-damage statute. *Archaic.* See WRONGFUL-DEATH STATUTE.

death duty. 1. See DUTY (4). **2.** See *estate tax* under TAX.

death in custody. See DEATH.

death-knell doctrine. (1972) A rule allowing an interlocutory appeal if precluding an appeal until final judgment would moot the issue on appeal and irreparably injure the appellant's rights. • Once recognized as an exception to the final-judgment rule, the doctrine was limited by the U.S. Supreme Court in *Coopers & Lybrand v. Livesay*, 437 U.S. 463, 98 S.Ct. 2454 (1978). There, the Court held that the death-knell doctrine does not permit an immediate appeal of an order denying class certification. But the doctrine still applies in some contexts. For example, the doctrine allows an immediate appeal of the denial of a temporary restraining order when the lack of an appeal would leave nothing to be considered in the trial court. *Woratzeck v. Arizona Bd. of Executive Clemency*, 117 F.3d 400 (9th Cir. 1997). — Also termed *death-knell exception*. Cf. FINAL-JUDGMENT RULE.

Death on the High Seas Act. A 1920 federal statute permitting a wrongful-death action to be filed in U.S. district court for a death occurring on the high seas. 46 USCA app. §§ 761–767. — Abbr. DOHSA.

death penalty. (1848) **1.** CAPITAL PUNISHMENT. **2.** A penalty that makes a person or entity ineligible to participate in an activity that the person or entity previously participated in. • The penalty is usu. imposed because of some type of gross misconduct. **3.** See *death-penalty sanction* under SANCTION.

death-penalty sanction. See SANCTION (3).

death-qualified jury. See JURY.

death rate. (1859) The number of deaths for every 100 or every 1,000 people in a particular place during a particular year.

death row. (1950) The area of a prison where those who have been sentenced to death are confined.

death sentence. See SENTENCE.

deathsman. (16c) An executioner; a hangman.

death-spiral deal. (1999) A convertible security for which the conversion price depends on the market price less a percentage discount on the date of conversion. — Also termed *toxic convert*.

death statute. (1910) A law that protects the interests of a decedent's family and other dependents, who may recover in damages what they would reasonably have received from the decedent if the death had not occurred. Cf. SURVIVAL STATUTE.

death tax. 1. See *estate tax* under TAX. **2.** See *inheritance tax* under TAX.

death toll. The total number of people who die in an accident, terrorist incident, war, etc.

death trap. (1835) **1.** A structure or situation involving an imminent risk of death. **2.** A situation that, although seemingly safe, is actually quite dangerous.

death warrant. See WARRANT (1).

de attornato recipiendo (dee a-tor-**nay**-toh ri-sip-ee-**en**-doh), *n.* [Law Latin "of receipt of an attorney"] (17c) *Hist.* A writ requiring a court to receive and admit an attorney for a party.

de audiendo et terminando (dee aw-dee-**end**-doh et tər-mi-**nan**-doh), *n.* [Law Latin "for hearing and determining"] (16c) *Hist.* A writ or commission directing certain justices to hear and resolve particular cases resulting from a riot, including those involving heinous misdemeanors, breaches of the peace, and trespass. Cf. COMMISSION OF OYER AND TERMINER.

de averiis captis in withernamium (dee ə-**veer**-ee-is **kap**-tis in with-ər-**nay**-mee-əm), *n.* [Law Latin "for taking cattle in withernam"] *Hist.* A writ directing a sheriff to detain a defendant's cattle because the defendant had unlawfully taken the plaintiff's cattle out of the county. • The defendant's cattle would be detained until the sheriff could replevy the plaintiff's cattle.

de averiis replegiandis (dee ə-**veer**-ee-is ri-plee-jee-**an**-dis), *n.* [Law Latin "of replevying beasts"] *Hist.* A writ ordering a sheriff to replevy someone's beasts or chattels that had been unlawfully taken and detained. • This is the old writ of replevin.

de banco (dee *or* də **bang**-koh). [Law Latin] Of the bench. • In England, the term applied to justices of the Court of Common Pleas.

debar, *vb.* To officially prohibit or exclude (someone) from doing, attaining, or having (something), or from entering a place or condition; to shut out, prevent, or interdict by authority.

debarment, *n.* (17c) The act of precluding someone from having or doing something; exclusion or hindrance. — **debar,** *vb.*

debasement. (17c) **1.** The act of reducing the value, quality, or purity of something; esp., the act of lowering the value of coins by either reducing the weight of gold and silver in the coins or increasing the coins' alloy amounts. **2.** Degradation. **3.** The quality, state, or condition of being degraded. — **debase,** *vb.*

debatable, *adj.* **1.** Of, relating to, or involving points that admit of contention or dispute; open to question or controversy; not settled <debatable questions>. **2.** *Parliamentary law.* (Of a motion) permitted to be debated <an amendment is debatable whenever the motion being amended is debatable>.

debate, *n.* (15c) *Parliamentary law.* Formal consideration of a motion's merits in the form of speeches for, against, or otherwise addressing the motion. See CONSIDERATION (2). — **debatable,** *adj.* — **debatability,** *n.*

▸ **controlled debate.** (1992) Debate in which designated managers, usu. a partisan leader, lead each side and allot time for speeches. — Also termed *controlled time.*

▸ **extended debate.** (1836) Debate that continues beyond an otherwise applicable limit. See EXTEND DEBATE.

▸ **floor debate.** (1884) The legislative process of debating a proposed bill before an entire chamber rather than before a committee.

▸ **limited debate.** (1906) Debate with restrictions. See LIMIT DEBATE.

▸ **pro–con debate.** (1975) A debate that adheres to the parliamentary principle that speeches should alternate between opposing viewpoints. • Sometimes those seeking the floor on one side outnumber those on the other side, in which case the chair may allow two (or more) speeches in a row on the same side of the question.

debate, *vb.* **1.** To contend in words about; to dispute argumentatively on <to debate the tax issue on television>. **2.** To deliberate or consider carefully before making a decision; to meditate about (a question) by weighing alternatives <to debate what course to take>. **3.** To argue publicly; to engage in oral controversy <to debate about the relationship between poverty and crime>. **4.** To ponder in one's own mind (the pros and cons of a situation) <to debate about the advantages and disadvantages of making the telephone call>.

debate agenda. See *debate calendar* under CALENDAR (4).

debate calendar. See CALENDAR (4).

debauch (di-**bawch**), *vb.* (16c) **1.** *Archaic.* To draw (a person) away from duty; to lead (a person) astray. **2.** To corrupt (a person) with lewdness; to seduce (someone). **3.** To mar or spoil (a person or thing).

debauchery (di-**bawch**-ə-ree), *n.* (17c) Excessive indulgence in sensual pleasures; sexual immorality or excesses. — **debauch,** *vb.*

debellatio (deb-ə-**lay**-shee-oh). [Latin] (1933) *Int'l law.* A means of ending a war and acquiring territory when one of the belligerent countries has been so soundly defeated that its adversary is able to decide alone the fate of the defeated country's territory; conquest followed by annexation. — Also termed *subjugation.*

> "[There are] three possible alternative meanings of *debellatio* in international law. The first is that *debellatio* denotes the change wrought by the conquest and total subjugation of a State together with that State's annexation by the conqueror. The second view is that *debellatio* corresponds to the total defeat of an enemy State, its occupation, and the elimination of a vital component of Statehood; in this view, *debellatio* implies the extinction of the old State, but it leaves open the legal future of the occupied territory (annexation or the founding of one or more new States). The third view is that *debellatio* only describes a factual situation and that even the elimination of all the State organs combined with the occupation of the territory does not exclude the continuing existence of that State. It is mainly the second and the third meanings of *debellatio* which have been advocated for the situation of Germany since the end of World War II." Karl-Ulrich Meyn, "*Debellatio,*" in 1 *Encyclopedia of Public International Law* 166 (1992).

de bene esse (dee **bee**-nee **es**-ee *also* day **ben**-ay **es**-ay), *adv.* [Law Latin "of well-being"] (17c) **1.** As conditionally allowed for the present; in anticipation of a future need <Willis's deposition was taken *de bene esse*>. **2.** Loosely, for what it is worth. — Abbr. *d.b.e.* — ***de bene esse,*** *adj.*

> "To take or do anything 'de bene esse' is to allow or accept it for the time being until it comes to be more fully examined, when it may be accepted or rejected. The phrase was used at least as early as 1272, and seems to be one of the many legal borrowings from the Church, which in turn had borrowed from philosophers who found classical Latin inadequate for their musings on the nature of being." R.E. Megarry, *Miscellany-at-Law* 36 (1955).

debenture (di-**ben**-chər). [fr. Latin *debentur* "there are owed"] (15c) **1.** A debt secured only by the debtor's earning power, not by a lien on any specific asset. • Originally, this was the first word of a deed detailing sums acknowledged to be owed. **2.** An instrument acknowledging such a debt. — Also termed *certificate of indebtedness.* **3.** A bond that is backed only by the general credit and financial reputation of the corporate issuer, not by a lien on corporate assets. — Also termed *debenture bond; unsecured bond; naked debenture; plain bond.* Cf. BOND (3).

> "The word 'debenture' in its archaic sense was applied to a form given under seal as an acknowledgment for goods supplied to the Royal Household, and as such probably meant a charge on Public Funds. The term was further applied to drawback certificates issued for repayment, on the exportation of goods, of duty which had already been paid upon them, and this term is still so used by H.M. Customs. . . . The word is now, however, generally used to indicate an acknowledgment of indebtedness given under seal by an incorporated company, containing a charge on assets of the company, and carrying an agreed rate of interest until payment, but the variety of the forms which a debenture may take makes it difficult to find a good general definition in any reported case." Thomas Froude & Eric V.E. White, *The Practice Relating to Debentures* 1 (1935).

▸ **convertible debenture.** (1908) A debenture that the holder may change or convert into some other security, such as stock.

▸ **convertible subordinated debenture.** (1961) A debenture that is subordinate to another debt but can be converted into a different security.

▸ **fixed and floating debenture.** See *fixed and floating charge* under CHARGE (7).

▸ **sinking-fund debenture.** (1893) A debenture that is secured by periodic payments into a fund established to retire long-term debt.

▸ **subordinate debenture.** (1929) A debenture that is subject to the prior payment of ordinary debentures and other indebtedness.

4. *English law.* A company's security for a monetary loan. • The security usu. creates a charge on company stock or property. **5.** A customhouse certificate providing for a refund of the duties on imported goods when the importer reexports the goods rather than selling them in the country where they were imported.

debenture bond. See DEBENTURE (3).

debenture indenture. See INDENTURE (2).

debenture stock. (1863) **1.** Stock that is issued under a contract providing for periodic, fixed payments. **2.** *English law.* A type of bond representing money borrowed by a company using its property or other fixed assets as security.

debet et detinet (**dee**-bet *or* **deb**-et et **det**-i-net *or* **det**-ə-nət). [Law Latin] (17c) *Hist.* He owes and detains. • This phrase was used in declarations in actions for debt when the original creditor sued the original debtor. The declaration stated that the defendant "owes to" as well as "detains from" the plaintiff the debt or thing in question; thus, the action was said to be "in the *debet et detinet.*" But if the action was brought against someone other than the original debtor (such as an executor, for a debt due from the testator), then the action was said to be "in the *detinet* alone." Cf. DETINET.

debet sine breve (**dee**-bet *or* **deb**-et **sɪ**-nee **breev** *or* **bree**-vee), *n.* [Law Latin "debt without a writ"] **1.** An action for debt commenced under a bill rather than a writ. **2.** A debt confessed by judgment. — Abbr. *d.s.b.* — Also termed *debitum sine breve; debit sans breve.* See CONFESSION OF JUDGMENT.

de bien et de mal (də **byen** ay də **mal**). [Law French]. See DE BONO ET MALO (1).

de biens le mort (də **beenz** lə **mor**[**t**]). [Law French] *Hist.* Of the goods of the deceased.

de bigamis (dee **big**-ə-mis), *n.* [Law Latin "concerning men twice married"] *Hist.* The statute of 4 Edw. I. st. 3, so called from the opening words of the fifth chapter. See BIGAMUS.

debit. (15c) **1.** A sum charged as due or owing; esp., a decrease in the amount of money in a bank account, as because one has withdrawn money from it. **2.** A record that in financial accounting shows money to have been spent or to be owed; esp., in bookkeeping, an entry made on the left side of a ledger or account, noting an increase in assets or a decrease in liabilities. **3.** An account balance showing that something remains due to the holder of the account. Cf. CREDIT (6).

▸ **direct debit.** (1976) An instruction that one gives to a bank to pay money directly from one's account, usu. regularly, to a particular person, business, or other organization.

debita fundi (**deb**-i-təm **fən**-dɪ). [Law Latin] (17c) *Scots law.* Debts attaching to the soil; debts affecting the land.

debita laicorum (**deb**-i-tə lay-ə-**kor**-əm), *n.* [Law Latin "debts of laity"] *Hist.* The debts recoverable in civil courts.

debit card. (1975) A card used to pay for purchases by electronic transfer from the purchaser's bank account. Cf. CREDIT CARD.

debiti et crediti contributio (**deb**-i-tɪ et **kred**-i-tɪ kon-tri-**byoo**-shee-oh). [Law Latin] *Civil law.* A balancing of debit and credit. • The phrase appeared in reference to setoff.

debit note. See *debit receipt* under RECEIPT.

debitor (**deb**-i-tor), *n. Roman law.* Someone who has a legal obligation to someone else. Cf. CREDITOR (2). Pl. ***debitores.***

debitorem locupletem esse (deb-i-**tor**-əm lok-yoo-**plee**-təm **es**-ee). [Latin] *Hist.* That the debtor is solvent. • In assigning a debt, a creditor might sometimes warrant that the debtor had the money to pay it.

debitor non praesumitur donare (**deb**-i-tor non pri-**zyoo**-mi-tur doh-**nair**-ee), *n.* [Law Latin "a debtor is not presumed to make a gift"] (17c) *Hist.* The presumption that any payment from a debtor is intended to satisfy the debt, unless the disposition clearly shows the debtor's intent to make a donation.

debito tempore (**deb**-i-toh **tem**-pə-ree). [Latin] *Hist.* In due time.

debit receipt. See RECEIPT (2).

debitrix (**deb**-ə-triks), *n.* [Latin] *Archaic. Civil law.* A female debtor.

debit sans breve. See DEBET SINE BREVE.

debitum (**deb**-i-təm), *n.* [Latin "a debt"] *Roman law.* Money or other thing that is actually owed, where there is both a duty and liability to repay; an actionable debt. Cf. INDEBITUM.

debitum fructuum (**deb**-i-təm **frək**-choo-əm). [Law Latin "a debt on the fruits"] *Hist.* A debt from the fruit of the land, not from the land itself. • Tithes, for example, were usu. payable *debitum fructuum.*

debitum fundi (**deb**-i-təm **fən**-dɪ). Scots law. [Latin "a debt of the land"] A debt consisting of a lien on land.

debitum in diem (**deb**-i-təm in **dɪ**-əm). [Latin "a debt to a date"] (18c) *Hist.* A debt payable at a future date. • The phrase appeared in reference to a debt that is due but for which the time for payment had not yet arrived. See UBI DIES CESSIT, LICET NONDUM VENERIT.

debitum in praesenti solvendum in futuro (**deb**-i-təm in pri-**zen**-tɪ sol-**ven**-dəm in fyoo-**t**[**y**]**oor**-oh). [Latin] A present debt (or obligation) to be paid at a future time; a debt or obligation complete when contracted, but of which the performance cannot be required until some future period.

debitum reale (**deb**-i-təm ree-**ay**-lee). [Law Latin] (17c) *Hist.* A real debt; a debt on land, as distinguished from a personal obligation.

debitum sine breve. See DEBET SINE BREVE.

debitum subesse (**deb**-i-təm səb-**es**-ee). [Latin] *Hist.* That the debt is due.

de bonis asportatis (dee **boh**-nis as-pər-**tay**-tis). See *trespass de bonis asportatis* under TRESPASS.

de bonis non (dee **boh**-nis **non**). See *administration de bonis non* under ADMINISTRATION.

de bonis non administratis (dee **boh**-nis **non** ad-min-ə-**stray**-tis). [Law Latin] *Hist.* (17c) Of the goods not administered. • When the first administrator of an intestate estate dies or is removed, the second administrator is called an administrator *bonis non*, who administers the goods not administered by the previous executor.

de bonis non amovendis (dee **boh**-nis non ay-moh-**ven**-dis), *n.* [Latin "of goods not to be moved"] (18c) *Hist.* A writ directing the sheriffs of London to make sure that a defendant's goods are not removed while the defendant's writ of error on a judgment is pending.

de bonis propriis (dee **boh**-nis **proh**-pree-is), *n.* [Law Latin "of his own goods"] (17c) *Hist.* A judgment allowing execution on an administrator's individual property rather than the property of an estate, as when the administrator mismanages the estate. Cf. DE BONIS TESTATORIS.

de bonis testatoris (dee **boh**-nis tes-tə-**tor**-is), *n.* [Law Latin "of the goods of the testator"] (17c) *Hist.* A judgment awarding execution on a testator's property, rather than the individual property of an administrator. Cf. DE BONIS PROPRIIS.

de bonis testatoris ac si (dee **boh**-nis tes-tə-**tor**-is ak **SI**). [Law Latin "from the goods of the testator if he has any, and if not, from those of the executor"]. *Hist.* A judgment holding an executor responsible if the testator's estate is insufficient or if the executor falsifies a pleading as a release.

de bonne memoire (də **bawn mem**-wahr). [Law French] Of sound mind; of good memory. — Also spelled *de bone memorie.* See MIND AND MEMORY; COMPOS MENTIS.

de bono et malo (dee **boh**-noh et **mal**-oh), *n.* [Law Latin "for good and evil"] (18c) *Hist.* **1.** For good and evil. • A criminal defendant indicated full submission to the jury's verdict by placing himself or herself at the jury's mercy *de bono et malo.* — Also termed *de bien et de mal.* **2.** A special writ of jail delivery issued by the justices of assize to enable them to try all criminal defendants who were in jail where the court traveled. • Formerly, the judges were required to issue a separate writ for every prisoner. This was replaced by a general commission of jail delivery.

> "[T]hey have . . . a commission of general *gaol delivery*; which empowers them to try and deliver every prisoner, who shall be in the gaol when the judges arrive at the circuit town, whenever indicted, or for whatever crime committed. It was anciently the course to issue special writs of gaol delivery for each particular prisoner, which were called the writs *de bono et malo*: but, these being found inconvenient and oppressive, a *general* commission for all the prisoners has long been established in their stead. So that, one way or other, the gaols are cleared, and all offenders tried, punished, or delivered, twice in every year: a constitution of singular use and excellence." 4 William Blackstone, *Commentaries on the Laws of England* 267 (1769).

de bono gestu (dee **boh**-noh **jes**-t[y]oo). [Law Latin] (17c) For good behavior.

debt. (13c) **1.** Liability on a claim; a specific sum of money due by agreement or otherwise <the debt amounted to $2,500>. **2.** The aggregate of all existing claims against a person, entity, or state <the bank denied the loan application after analyzing the applicant's outstanding debt>. **3.** A nonmonetary thing that one person owes another, such as goods or services <her debt was to supply him with 20 international first-class tickets on the airline of his choice>. **4.** A common-law writ by which a court adjudicates claims involving fixed sums of money <he brought suit in debt>. — Also termed (in sense 4) *writ of debt.*

> "The action of debt lies where a party claims the recovery of a debt; that is, a liquidated or certain sum of money due him. The action is based upon contract, but the contract may be implied, either in fact or in law, as well as express; and it may be either a simple contract or a specialty. The most common instances of its use are for debts: (a) Upon unilateral contracts express or implied in fact. (b) Upon quasi-contractual obligations having the force and effect of simple contracts. (c) Upon bonds and covenants under seal. (d) Upon judgments or obligations of record. (e) Upon obligations imposed by statute." Benjamin J. Shipman, *Handbook of Common-Law Pleading* § 52, at 132 (Henry Winthrop Ballantine ed., 3d ed. 1923).

▸ **active debt.** (18c) *Civil law.* A debt due to another person.

▸ **ancestral debt.** (2002) An ancestor's debt that an heir can be compelled to pay.

▸ **antecedent debt.** (18c) **1.** *Contracts.* An old debt that may serve as consideration for a new promise if the statute of limitations has run on the old debt. See PREEXISTING-DUTY RULE. **2.** *Bankruptcy.* A debtor's prepetition obligation that existed before a debtor's transfer of an interest in property. • For a transfer to be preferential, it must be for or on account of an antecedent debt. See PREFERENTIAL TRANSFER.

▸ **bad debt.** (17c) A debt that is uncollectible and that may be deductible for tax purposes. Cf. *zombie debt.*

▸ **bonded debt.** (18c) A debt secured by a bond; a business or government debt represented by issued bonds.

▸ **book debt.** (17c) A debt that comes due in the ordinary course of business, as an integral part of doing business.

▸ **community debt.** (1877) A debt that is chargeable to the community of husband and wife. See COMMUNITY PROPERTY.

▸ **consumer debt.** (1935) A debt incurred by someone primarily for a personal, family, or household purpose. • Some jurisdictions also treat debt incurred for an agricultural purpose as a consumer debt.

> "What are 'consumer' debts? Section 101(8) defines a consumer debt as follows: 'consumer debt means debt incurred by an individual primarily for a personal, family, or household purpose.' The touchstone is the debtor's use of the money. The nature of the collateral, the business of the creditor and the form of the loan are all irrelevant. A loan of $25,000 from a Credit Union to pay for a child's education is a consumer debt, but the same loan used to finance the opening of an accounting business is not a consumer debt. This is so irrespective of the nature of the collateral put up for the debt." David G. Epstein et al., *Bankruptcy* § 7-45, at 579 (1993).

▸ **contingent debt.** (17c) A debt that is not presently fixed but that may become fixed in the future with the occurrence of some event.

▸ **contract debt.** (18c) An amount, usu. fixed, payable under a contract.

▸ **convertible debt.** (1858) A debt whose security may be changed by a creditor into another form of security.

▸ **debt by simple contract.** See *simple-contract debt.*

▸ **debt by special contract.** See *special-contract debt.*

▸ **debt by specialty contract.** See *special-contract debt.*

▸ **debt contracted.** **1.** A debt arising from a contract. **2.** More broadly, arising from either a contract or tort.

"Illustrations of what Mr. Bishop calls 'the elasticity of statutes' may be found in the meaning which different courts have attached to the words 'debt,' or the expression 'debt contracted,' in statutes imposing upon stockholders a personal liability to pay the corporate debts. . . . In such a statute the word 'debt,' and the words 'debts contracted,' have been held to embrace a judgment recovered in an action for slander; and the same expression has been held to embrace a judgment for costs in an action for a tort, and also a judgment in an action for deceit, since in the latter case the plaintiff might have waived the tort and sued upon the contract." Seymour D. Thompson, *A Treatise on the Liability of Stockholders in Corporations* § 57, at 62–63 (1879).

▸ **debt of record.** (17c) A debt evidenced by a court record, such as a judgment.

▸ **desperate debt.** (16c) **1.** Uncollectable debt. **2.** A debt taken on by one who is either insolvent or on the verge of insolvency.

▸ **distressed debt.** (1991) A debt instrument issued by a company that is financially troubled and in danger of defaulting on the debt, or in bankruptcy, or likely to default or declare bankruptcy in the near future.

▸ **exigible debt.** (1936) A liquidated and demandable debt; a matured claim.

▸ **fixed debt.** (1847) Generally, a permanent form of debt commonly evidenced by a bond or debenture; long-term debt. — Also termed *fixed liability*.

▸ **floating debt.** (18c) Short-term debt that is continuously renewed to finance the ongoing operations of a business or government.

▸ **forgiven debt.** (17c) Debt that the creditor has written off as uncollectible.

▸ **fraudulent debt.** (18c) A debt created by fraudulent practices.

▸ **funded debt.** (18c) **1.** A state or municipal debt to be paid out of an accumulation of money or by future taxation. **2.** Secured long-term corporate debt meant to replace short-term, floating, or unsecured debt.

▸ **future debt.** *Scots law.* A debt that is to become due at some definite future date, as distinguished from a pure or contingent debt.

▸ **general debt.** (16c) A governmental body's debt that is legally payable from general revenues and is backed by the full faith and credit of the governmental body.

▸ **hypothecary debt.** (1883) A lien on an estate.

▸ **individual debt.** (*usu. pl.*) (18c) Debt personally owed by a partner, rather than by the partnership.

▸ **installment debt.** (1927) A debt that is to be repaid in a series of payments at regular times over a specified period.

▸ **judgment debt.** (18c) A debt that is evidenced by a legal judgment or brought about by a successful lawsuit against the debtor.

▸ **junior debt.** See *subordinate debt*.

▸ **legal debt.** (17c) A debt recoverable in a court of law.

▸ **liquidated debt.** (18c) A debt whose amount has been determined by agreement of the parties or by operation of law.

▸ **liquid debt.** (17c) A debt that is due immediately and unconditionally.

▸ **long-term debt.** (1917) Generally, a debt that will not come due within the next year.

▸ **mutual debts.** (18c) Cross-debts of the same kind and quality between two persons. Cf. SETOFF (2).

▸ **national debt.** See NATIONAL DEBT.

▸ **nondischargeable debt.** (1908) A debt (such as one for delinquent taxes) that is not released through bankruptcy.

▸ **passive debt.** (1835) A debt that, by agreement between the debtor and creditor, is interest-free.

▸ **preferential debt.** (1880) A debt that is legally payable before others, such as an employee's wages.

▸ **privileged debt.** (18c) A debt that has priority over other debts if a debtor becomes insolvent; a secured debt.

▸ **public debt.** (16c) A debt owed by a municipal, state, or national government.

▸ **pure debt.** See *pure obligation* under OBLIGATION.

▸ **secured debt.** (18c) A debt backed by collateral.

▸ **senior debt.** (1927) A debt that takes priority over other debts. • Senior debts are often secured by collateral.

▸ **short-term debt.** (1918) Collectively, all debts and other liabilities that are payable within one year. — Also termed *current liability*.

▸ **simple-contract debt.** (1814) A debt that is either oral or written but is not of record and not under seal. — Also termed *debt by simple contract*.

▸ **special-contract debt.** (18c) A debt due, or acknowledged to be due, by an instrument under seal, such as a deed of covenant or sale, a lease reserving rent, or a bond. — Also termed *debt by special contract*; *debt by specialty contract*; *specialty debt*.

"Any contract in short whereby a determinate sum of money becomes due to any person, and is not paid but remains in action merely, is a contract of debt. And, taken in this light, it comprehends a great variety of acquisition; being usually divided into debts of *record*, debts by *special*, and debts by simple contract." 2 William Blackstone, *Commentaries on the Laws of England* 464 (1766).

▸ **subordinate debt.** (1945) A debt that is junior or inferior to other types or classes of debt. • Subordinate debt may be unsecured or have a low-priority claim against property secured by other debt instruments. — Also termed *junior debt*.

▸ **subprime debt.** (1998) The debt created by a loan made to a borrower with a high risk of default. See PRIME LENDING RATE.

▸ **unliquidated debt.** (18c) A debt that has not been reduced to a specific amount, and about which there may be a dispute.

▸ **unsecured debt.** (1843) A debt not supported by collateral or other security.

▸ **zombie debt.** (2006) *Slang.* Old debt that a creditor or collector has given up on collecting and sold to another party who undertakes fresh collection efforts. Cf. *bad debt*.

debt adjustment. See DEBT POOLING (1).

debt capital. See CAPITAL.

debt collector. (1852) **1.** Someone whose business or job is to seek payment of past-due bills and other outstanding debts. **2.** Under the Fair Debt Collection Practices Act, someone who uses an instrumentality of interstate commerce or the mails in any business whose principal purpose is collecting consumer debts, who regularly collects or attempts to collect consumer debts owed or due or asserted to be owed or due to another, or who collects consumer debts under a name that implies a third party's involvement. See FAIR DEBT COLLECTION PRACTICES ACT.

debt consolidation. (1926) **1.** See DEBT POOLING (1). **2.** The replacement of multiple loans from one or more lenders with a single loan from one lender, usu. with a lower monthly payment and a longer repayment period.

debtee. *Archaic.* See CREDITOR (1).

debt-equity ratio. See DEBT-TO-EQUITY RATIO.

debt-equity swap. A transaction in which a creditor accepts an ownership interest to settle a debt.

debt financing. See FINANCING.

debt instrument. (1953) A written promise to repay a debt, such as a promissory note, bill, bond, or commercial paper.

debt limitation. (1845) A ceiling placed on borrowing by an individual, business, or government. • The constitutions of many states prohibit the states from incurring debt in excess of a stated amount. Other state constitutions allow states to incur debt above a stated amount only through a vote of the people. — Also termed *limitation on indebtedness.*

debt of record. See DEBT.

debtor. (13c) **1.** Someone who owes an obligation to another, esp. an obligation to pay money; esp., the person who owes payment or other performance of a secured obligation, whether or not that person owns or has rights in the collateral — including the seller of accounts, contract rights, or chattel paper. **2.** *Bankruptcy.* Someone who files a voluntary petition or against whom an involuntary petition is filed. — Also termed *bankrupt.*

> "Section 101 [of the Bankruptcy Code] also introduces us to the language of modern bankruptcy practice. It tells us, for instance, that the person whom a bankruptcy case concerns is a *debtor.* A person or a firm in bankruptcy is no longer called a *bankrupt.* Although that word retains some currency among lay people, among bankruptcy lawyers it sounds old-fashioned and precious." Douglas G. Baird, *Elements of Bankruptcy* 6 (2001).

3. *Secured transactions.* Someone who (1) has a property interest — other than a security interest or other lien — in collateral, even if the person is not an obligor, (2) is a seller of accounts, chattel paper, payment intangibles, or promissory notes, or (3) is a consignee. UCC § 9-102(a)(28). — Abbr. Dr. Cf. CREDITOR.

▸ **absconding debtor.** (18c) A debtor who flees from creditors to avoid having to pay a debt. • Absconding from a debt was formerly considered an act of bankruptcy. See *act of bankruptcy* under ACT (2).

▸ **absent debtor.** (18c) A debtor who lacks the intent to defraud creditors but is beyond the geographic reach of ordinary service of process.

▸ **account debtor.** (1940) A person obligated on an account, chattel paper, or general intangible. • The UCC exempts from the definition of *account debtor* a person obligated to pay a negotiable instrument, even if the instrument constitutes chattel paper. UCC § 9-102(a)(3).

▸ **common debtor.** (17c) *Scots law.* A debtor whose property has been arrested by more than one creditor.

▸ **concealed debtor.** (18c) A debtor who hides from creditors, usu. with the intent to defraud the creditors or to avoid service of process, but does not leave the community or move out of state.

▸ **joint debtor.** (17c) One of two or more debtors jointly liable for the same debt.

▸ **judgment debtor.** See JUDGMENT DEBTOR.

▸ **new debtor.** (18c) *Secured transactions.* Someone who becomes bound as debtor under a security agreement previously entered into by another person. UCC §§ 9-102(a)(56), 9-203(d).

▸ **solvent debtor.** (17c) A debtor who owns enough property to cover all outstanding debts and against whom a creditor can enforce a judgment.

debtor-in-possession. (1806) *Bankruptcy.* A Chapter 11 or 12 debtor that continues to operate its business as a fiduciary to the bankruptcy estate. • With certain exceptions, the debtor-in-possession has all the rights, powers, and duties of a Chapter 11 trustee. — Abbr. DIP.

debtor rehabilitation. See REHABILITATION (3).

Debtor's Act of 1869. An English statute that, among other things, (1) abolished imprisonment for debt except in certain cases, as when a debtor owed a debt to the Crown or a debtor had money but refused to pay a debt, (2) abolished arrest by mesne process, that is, by compelling the defendant to appear and give bail unless it was believed that the defendant would leave the country, (3) made it a misdemeanor to obtain credit under false pretenses or to defraud creditors, and (4) defined how warrants and judgment orders would be executed.

debtor's examination. (1834) *Bankruptcy.* A meeting between a debtor and his or her creditors during which the creditors ask the debtor questions designed to uncover information about the location and extent of the debtor's assets and the dischargeability of debts. • The examination may be conducted under § 343 of the Bankruptcy Code or Rule 2004 of the Federal Rules of Bankruptcy Procedure. The bankruptcy trustee may be present and preside over the initial § 343 examination, which is held shortly after the bankruptcy filing. But the party (usu. a creditor) who requests a Rule 2004 examination presides over the meeting, which can be held at any time. *See* 11 USCA § 343; Fed. R. Bankr. P. 2004.

debtor's exemption. See EXEMPTION (2).

debtor's petition. See *voluntary petition* under PETITION (1).

debtor's property. See PROPERTY OF THE DEBTOR.

debt pooling. (1957) **1.** *Bankruptcy.* An arrangement by which a person's debts are consolidated and creditors agree to accept lower monthly payments or to take less money. — Also termed *debt consolidation*; *debt adjustment.* **2.** An arrangement under which a debtor agrees to pay (1) a sum of money periodically or otherwise to a third person who will then distribute the money among certain specified creditors in accordance with a plan, and (2) a fee to the third person for his or her services as distributor. • Debt-pooling in this manner is generally illegal if the arrangement is not made with a bank, attorney, judicial officer, retail-merchants' association, or nonprofit organization that provides debt-counseling services.

debt ratio. (1932) A corporation's total long-term and short-term liabilities divided by the firm's total assets. • A low debt ratio indicates conservative financing and thus usu. an enhanced ability to borrow in the future. — Also termed *debt-to-total-assets ratio*.

debt relief. (1932) An arrangement whereby poor countries are allowed not to pay back all the money lent to them by richer countries.

debt retirement. (1928) Repayment of debt; RETIREMENT (3).

debt security. See SECURITY (4).

debt service. (1930) **1.** The funds needed to meet a long-term debt's annual interest expenses, principal payments, and sinking-fund contributions. **2.** Payments due on a debt, including interest and principal.

debt subordination. See *debt-subordination agreement* under SUBORDINATION AGREEMENT.

debt-subordination agreement. See SUBORDINATION AGREEMENT.

debt-to-equity ratio. (1954) A corporation's long-term debt divided by its owners' equity, calculated to assess its capitalization. — Also termed *debt-equity ratio*; *debt-to-net-worth ratio*.

debt-to-total-assets ratio. See DEBT RATIO.

debt-validation notice. Written communication asserting that the recipient owes a certain amount of money and giving the recipient a stated time for demanding proof of the debt or for disputing the debt before legal action is taken. • Under the Fair Debt Collection Practices Act, collectors must send a debt-validation notice before taking action.

DeCA. *abbr.* DEFENSE COMMISSARY AGENCY.

de caetero (dee **see**-tə-roh) [Latin "about the other"] Henceforth; in the future. — Also spelled *de cetero*.

de calceto reparando (dee **kal**-sə-toh rep-ə-**ran**-doh), *n.* [Law Latin "for repairing a causeway"] *Hist.* A writ directing a sheriff to distrain residents of a place to repair a road.

decalvatio (dee-kal-**vay**-shee-oh). *Hist.* The act of cutting off a person's hair to symbolize a total loss of honor. • Although some early legal historians interpreted this Germanic practice as scalping, a leading historian of the early 20th century insisted that it referred only to the cutting of hair. See Munroe Smith, *The Development of European Law* 99 (1928).

decanatus (dek-ə-**nay**-təs), *n.* [Law Latin] *Hist.* A group of ten people; a decenary. See DECANUS.

decania (di-**kay**-nee-ə), *n.* [Law Latin] *Hist.* A dean's office; a dean's territory.

decanus (di-**kay**-nəs), *n.* [fr. Greek *dekanos* "a dean"] **1.** *Roman law.* An officer commanding ten soldiers. **2.** *Eccles. & civil law.* A leader of ten people, as in *decanus monasticus* ("dean of ten monks"). **3.** The dean of a cathedral.

de capitalibus dominus feodi (dee kap-ə-**tay**-lə-bəs **dom**-ə-nəs **fee**-ə-dɪ). [Law Latin] *Hist.* From the highest lord of the fee. • This term was primarily used in old charters to state that the tenure of an estate was to be held of the chief lord of the fee, rather than of the immediate grantor.

decapitation (dee-kap-ə-**tay**-shən). (17c) *Hist.* The act of cutting off a head; a beheading. • This was once a common method of capital punishment.

de capite minutis (dee **kap**-ə-tee mi-**n[y]oo**-tis). [Latin "of those who have lost their status"] *Roman law.* A title in the *Digest*, referring to people who lost their civil status. See CAPITIS DEMINUTIO.

decarceration. See DISIMPRISONMENT.

de cartis reddendis (dee **kahr**-tis ri-**den**-dis), *n.* [Law Latin "for restoring charters"] *Hist.* A writ ordering redelivery of a charter or deed; a writ of detinue. See DETINUE.

De Catallis Felonum. *Hist.* A 1326 statute providing that a felon forfeited his or her personal property and also lost all rights and means of acquiring property. • This statute is one of the earliest written laws imposing civil death. Cf. *civil death* (1) under DEATH.

de catallis reddendis (dee kə-**tal**-is ri-**den**-dis), *n.* [Law Latin "of chattels to be restored"] (18c) *Hist.* A writ ordering a bailee to deliver chattels kept from the owner. • This was replaced by the writ of detinue. See DETINUE.

de cautione admittenda (dee kaw-shee-**oh**-nee ad-mi-**ten**-də), *n.* [Law Latin "of security to be taken"] (16c) *Hist.* A writ commanding a bishop who had ordered an excommunicated person held for contempt, even though the prisoner had offered bail and promised to obey the church in the future, to take the offered security and order the prisoner's release.

decease, *n.* See DEATH.

decease, *vb.* (15c) To die; to cease living in the biological sense.

deceased, *n.* See DECEDENT.

decedent (di-**see**-dənt), *n.* (16c) A dead person, esp. one who has died recently. • This term is little used outside law. It typically appears in legal proceedings or administrative inquiries. — Also termed *deceased*.

▸ **nonresident decedent.** (1870) A decedent who was domiciled outside the jurisdiction in question (such as probate jurisdiction) at the time of death.

decedent's estate. See ESTATE (3).

deceit, *n.* (14c) **1.** The act of intentionally leading someone to believe something that is not true; an act designed to deceive or trick <the juror's deceit led the lawyer to believe that she was not biased>. **2.** A false statement of fact made by a person knowingly or recklessly (i.e., not caring whether it is true or false) with the intent that someone else will act on it. See *fraudulent misrepresentation* under MISREPRESENTATION. **3.** A tort arising from a false representation made knowingly or recklessly with the intent that another person should detrimentally rely on it <the new homeowner sued both the seller and the realtor for deceit after discovering termites>. See FRAUD; MISREPRESENTATION. — **deceive,** *vb.*

> "The tort of deceit consists in the act of making a wilfully false statement with the intent that the plaintiff shall act in reliance on it, and with the result that he does so act and suffers harm in consequence. . . . There are four main

elements in this tort: (1) there must be a false representation of fact; (2) the representation must be made with knowledge of its falsity; (3) it must be made with the intention that it should be acted on by the plaintiff, or by a class of persons which includes the plaintiff, in the manner which resulted in damage to him; (4) it must be proved that the plaintiff has acted upon the false statement and has sustained damage by so doing." R.F.V. Heuston, *Salmond on the Law of Torts* 387 (17th ed. 1977).

deceitful plea. See *sham pleading* under PLEADING (1).

decem tales (**des**-em **tay**-leez), *n.* [Law Latin "ten such people"] (17c) *Hist.* A writ directing a sheriff to summon ten people for a jury panel when a sufficient number have not already appeared.

decemviri litibus judicandis (di-**sem**-və-rɪ **lɪ**-ti-bəs joo-də-**kan**-dis). [Latin "ten persons to decide lawsuits"] (18c) *Roman law.* A group of five senators and five knights who assisted the elected magistrate in deciding legal disputes concerning liberty. — Also spelled *decemviri stlitibus judicandis.*

decenary. [fr. Latin *decena* "a tithing"] (17c) *Hist.* A town or district consisting of ten freeholding families. • A freeholder of the decenary (a *decennarius*) was bound by frankpledge to produce any wrongdoer living in the decenary. — Also spelled (incorrectly) *decennary.* — Also termed *decenna; tithing.* Cf. FRANKPLEDGE.

"The civil division of the territory of England is into counties, of those counties into hundreds, of those hundreds into tithings or towns. Which division, as it now stands, seems to owe its original to king Alfred; who, to prevent the rapines and disorders which formerly prevailed in the realm, instituted tithings; so called from the Saxon, because *ten* freeholders, with their families, composed one. These all dwelt together, and were sureties or free pledges to the king for the good behavior of each other; and, if any offence was committed in their district, they were bound to have the offender forthcoming. And therefore anciently no man was suffered to abide in England above forty days, unless he were enrolled in some tithing or decennary." 1 William Blackstone, *Commentaries on the Laws of England* 110 (1765).

decency. (16c) The quality, state, or condition of being proper, as in speech or dress; the quality of being seemly.

decenna (di-**sen**-ə), *n.* [fr. Latin *decem* "ten"] See DECENARY.

decennarius (des-ə-**nair**-ee-əs), *n.* [Law Latin "a deciner"] One of ten families of freeholders comprising a decenary. See DECENARY.

decennary. See DECENARY.

deception. 1. The act of deliberately causing someone to believe that something is true when the actor knows it to be false. **2.** A trick intended to make a person believe something untrue.

deceptive act. (1939) As defined by the Federal Trade Commission and most state statutes, conduct that is likely to deceive a consumer acting reasonably under similar circumstances. — Also termed *deceptive practice; deceptive sales practice.*

deceptive advertising. See FALSE ADVERTISING.

deceptive practice. See DECEPTIVE ACT.

deceptive sales practice. See DECEPTIVE ACT.

deceptive warranty. See WARRANTY (2).

decern (di-**sərn**), *vb.* (15c) *Scots law.* To decree; to give final judgment.

"Before the judgment or interlocutor of any court in Scotland can be extracted, to the effect of warranting execution, it must import a decree. Hence, all extractable judgments close with the word 'decern.'" William Bell, *Bell's Dictionary and Digest of the Law of Scotland* 287 (George Watson ed., 7th ed. 1890).

de certificando (dee sər-ti-fi-**kan**-doh), *n.* [Law Latin "about something to be certified"] (18c) A writ requiring something to be certified, similar to certiorari. See CERTIFICANDO DE RECOGNITIONE STAPULAE.

decertification. The withdrawal or revocation of certification. See CERTIFICATION.

decertify, *vb.* (1918) **1.** To revoke the certification of. **2.** To remove the official status of (a labor union) by withdrawing the right to act as a collective-bargaining agent. **3.** (Of a court) to overrule a previous order that created a class for purposes of a class action; to officially undo (a class). Cf. CERTIFY. — **decertification,** *n.*

de certiorando (dee sər-shee-ə-**ran**-doh), *n.* [Law Latin "about certification"] A writ ordering a sheriff to certify a fact.

decessit sine prole (di-**ses**-it sɪ-nee **proh**-lee). [Latin] Died without issue. See SINE PROLE.

decessus (di-**ses**-əs), *n.* [fr. Latin *decedere* "to depart"] **1.** *Roman law.* A death. **2.** A departure. • This term has been used in both the civil and common law, esp. in reference to the desertion of a ground in a previous pleading in favor of another. See DEPARTURE.

de cetero. See DE CAETERO.

de champertia (dee kam-**pər**-shee-ə), *n.* [Law Latin "about champerty"] *Hist.* A writ ordering justices of the bench to enforce the champerty laws. See CHAMPERTOR; CHAMPERTY.

de char et de sank (də **shahr** ay də **sangk**). [Law French] *Hist.* Of flesh and blood.

de chimino (dee **kim**-ə-noh), *n.* [Law Latin "writ of way"] *Hist.* A writ to enforce a right-of-way.

deciare. One-tenth of an are; ten square meters. Cf. ARE.

de cibariis utendis (dee si-**bair**-ee-əs yoo-**ten**-dis), *n.* [Law Latin "of victuals to be used"] *Hist.* The statute of 10 Edw. 3 ch. 3 restraining entertainment expenses. • This was one of several statutes limiting luxury spending.

deciding vote. See *casting vote* under VOTE (1).

decies tantum (**desh**-ee-eez *or* **dee**-shee-eez **tan**-təm), *n.* [Law Latin "ten times as much"] (16c) *Hist.* A writ ordering a juror who accepted a bribe for a verdict to pay ten times the bribery amount, half to the suing party and half to the Crown.

"Decies tantum is a writ that lies where a juror in any inquest takes money of the one part or other, to give his verdict; then he shall pay ten times as much as he hath received: and every one that will sue may have this action, and shall have the one half, and the king the other . . . . And the same law is of all other actions popular, where one part is to the king, the other to the party that sues. Also the embracers, who procure such inquests, shall be punished in the same manner, and they shall have imprisonment a year. But no justice shall inquire thereof *ex officio*, but only at the suit of the party." *Termes de la Ley* 146 (1st Am. ed. 1812).

decimae (**des**-ə-mee), *n.* [fr. Latin *decem* "ten"] *Eccles. law.* **1.** The tenth part of the annual profits of a benefice originally payable to the Pope, and later to the Crown by 26 Hen. 8, ch. 3.

"The tenths, or *decimae*, were the tenth part of the annual profit of each living . . . which was also claimed by the holy see . . . . But this claim of the pope met with a vigorous resistance from the English parliament; and a variety of acts were passed to prevent and restrain it . . . . But the popish clergy, blindly devoted to the will of a foreign master, still kept it on foot; sometimes more secretly, sometimes more openly and avowedly . . . . And, as the clergy expressed this willingness to contribute so much of their income to the head of the church, it was thought proper (when in the same reign the papal power was abolished, and the king was declared the head of the church of England) to annex this revenue to the crown . . . ." 1 William Blackstone, *Commentaries on the Laws of England* 274 (1765).

2. Tithes paid to the church, often in grain or wool.

decimae garbales (des-i-mee gahr-**bay**-leez). [Law Latin] (17c) *Hist. Eccles. law.* Tithe sheaves; grain tithes. • The parish rector was entitled to each tenth sheaf of the cut grain as a tithe.

decimae rectoriae (**des**-i-mee rek-**tor**-ee-ee). [Law Latin] *Hist. Eccles. law.* Parsonage tithes; that is, fixed tithes payable to the parson of a parish. • The right to levy such tithes could not be lost by prescription.

decimae vicariae (**des**-i-mee VI-**kair**-ee-ee). [Law Latin] *Hist. Eccles. law.* Vicarage tithes. • Vicars received tithes from various sources (such as from wool or eggs) according to need or custom. The right to levy them could not be lost by prescription.

decimation (des-ə-**may**-shən). (16c) **1.** A major destruction of people; a great loss of life. **2.** *Hist.* A tithing; a payment of the tenth part. **3.** *Hist.* A punishment, esp. by death, of every tenth person by lot. • Under Roman law, *decimatio* referred to the punishment by lot of every tenth soldier in a legion for mutiny or cowardice.

decision, *n.* (16c) **1.** A judicial or agency determination after consideration of the facts and the law; esp., a ruling, order, or judgment pronounced by a court when considering or disposing of a case. See JUDGMENT (2); OPINION (1). — **decisional,** *adj.*

▸ **appealable decision.** (1870) A decree or order that is sufficiently final to receive appellate review (such as an order granting summary judgment), or an interlocutory decree or order that is immediately appealable, usu. by statute (such as an order denying immunity to a police officer in a civil-rights suit). — Also termed *reviewable issue.* See COLLATERAL-ORDER DOCTRINE.

▸ **final decision.** See *final judgment* under JUDGMENT (2).

▸ **interlocutory decision.** See *interlocutory order* under ORDER (2).

▸ **unreasonable decision.** (1962) An administrative agency's decision that is so obviously wrong that there can be no difference of opinion among reasonable minds about its erroneous nature.

2. *Parliamentary law.* VOTE (4). **3.** *Parliamentary law.* The chair's ruling on a point of order. See *appeal from the decision of the chair* under APPEAL.

decisional law. See CASELAW.

decision coalition. (1978) A discernible voting bloc on a court, usu. based on judicial or political philosophy.

decisionism. [fr. German *Dezisionismus*] The legal philosophy that the decisions of political and legal bodies produce moral and legal precepts. • Under decisionism, a decision is valid if made by a proper authority or by using a proper method, regardless of the decision's content.

decision-making, *n.* (1953) The process or practice of making important choices or judgments, esp. after a period of discussion or thought.

decision-making responsibility. (1956) The authority to come to a binding resolution of an issue. • For example, in child-rearing, decision-making responsibility involves the authority to make significant decisions on a child's behalf, including decisions about education, religious training, and healthcare.

decision on the merits. See *judgment on the merits* under JUDGMENT (2).

decisive oath. See OATH.

decisory oath. See *decisive oath* under OATH.

***Decker* test.** See SUBJECT-MATTER TEST.

***Deck* rule.** (2005) The doctrine that a defendant cannot be tried while wearing handcuffs or other physical restraints unless the trial judge first holds a special hearing and makes specific findings about why the restraints are necessary. *Deck v. Missouri*, 544 U.S. 622 (2005).

declaim, *vb.* (14c) To make a speech in public in oratorical style; to speak loudly, esp. with pronounced gesticulations, so that people notice.

declamatory, *adj.* (16c) **1.** (Of speech or writing) expressing opinions or beliefs with great vehemence. **2.** *Pejorative.* (Of speech or writing) noisy and empty; stilted.

declarant (di-**klair**-ənt), *n.* (17c) **1.** Someone who has made a statement <in accordance with the rules of evidence, the statement was offered to prove the declarant's state of mind>. **2.** Someone who has signed a declaration, esp. one stating an intent to become a U.S. citizen <the declarant grew up in Italy>. **3.** AFFIANT (1). — **declarant,** *adj.*

declaration, *n.* (15c) **1.** A formal statement, proclamation, or announcement, esp. one embodied in an instrument. Cf. AFFIDAVIT.

▸ **declaration of alienage.** (18c) A declaration by a person with dual citizenship of a wish to renounce the citizenship of one state. • For the declaration to be effective, the person making it must be of full age and not under any disability.

▸ **declaration of default.** (18c) A creditor's notice to a debtor regarding the debtor's failure to perform an obligation, such as making a payment.

▸ **declaration of dividend.** (1837) A company's setting aside of a portion of its earnings or profits for distribution to its shareholders; the formal announcement that such a distribution has been proposed or authorized. See DIVIDEND.

▸ **declaration of homestead.** (1856) A statement required to be filed with a state or local authority to prove property ownership in order to claim homestead-exemption rights. See HOMESTEAD.

▸ **declaration of intention.** (1812) An alien's formal statement resolving to become a U.S. citizen and to renounce allegiance to any other government or country. — Also termed *first paper.*

▸ **declaration of legitimacy.** (1861) A formal or legal pronouncement that a child is legitimate.

▸ **declaration of trust.** (17c) **1.** The act by which the person who holds legal title to property manifests the intention to hold that title as trustee for the benefit of at least one other person or for certain specified purposes. See *self-declared trust* under TRUST (3). **2.** The instrument that creates a trust. — Also termed (in sense 2) *trust instrument*; *trust deed*; *trust agreement*.

▸ **judicial declaration.** (17c) *Hist. Scots law.* **1.** A party's statement, made in court and transcribed, about a case's material facts. **2.** An accused's statement, made after an arrest and taken down in writing.

2. *Int'l law.* The part of a treaty containing the stipulations under which the parties agree to conduct their actions; TREATY (1). **3.** *Int'l law.* A country's unilateral pronouncement that affects the rights and duties of other countries.

▸ **declaration of war.** (16c) A country's announcement that it is officially engaged in war against another country.

4. A document that governs legal rights to certain types of real property, such as a condominium or a residential subdivision. **5.** A listing of the merchandise that a person intends to bring into the United States. • This listing is given to U.S. Customs when one enters the country. **6.** *Evidence.* An unsworn statement made by someone having knowledge of facts relating to an event in dispute.

▸ **deathbed declaration.** See *dying declaration*.

▸ **declaration against interest.** (1940) A statement by a person who is not a party to a suit and is not available to testify at trial, discussing a matter that is within the declarant's personal knowledge and is adverse to the declarant's pecuniary, proprietary, or penal interest. • Such a statement is admissible into evidence as an exception to the hearsay rule. Fed. R. Evid. 804(b)(3). — Also termed *self-disserving declaration*; *statement against interest*. See *admission against interest* under ADMISSION (1).

▸ **declaration against penal interest.** (1926) *Criminal law.* A person's incriminating statement — an exception to the hearsay rule. — Abbr. DAPI.

▸ **declaration of pain.** (1891) A person's exclamation of present pain, which operates as an exception to the hearsay rule. Fed. R. Evid. 803(3).

▸ **declaration of peace.** See DECLARATION OF PEACE.

▸ **declaration of solvency.** See DECLARATION OF SOLVENCY.

▸ **declaration of state of mind.** (1843) A person's state-of-mind statement that operates as an exception to the hearsay rule. Fed. R. Evid. 803(3).

▸ **dying declaration.** (18c) A statement by a person who believes that death is imminent, relating to the cause or circumstances of the person's impending death. • The statement is admissible in evidence as an exception to the hearsay rule. — Also termed *deathbed declaration*; *antemortem statement*; *statement under belief of impending death*.

> "[A] rule peculiar to criminal cases is the exception to the rule respecting hearsay evidence which renders dying declarations as to the cause of death admissible in trials for murder or manslaughter. . . . The earliest emphatic statement of it . . . is to be found in Woodcock's case, decided in 1789 . . . . This case refers to a decision in 1720 . . . and to the case of *R. v Reason and Tranter*, decided in 1722. That case, however, says nothing as to any limitation on the rule. A series of cases from 1678 to 1765 show that during that period declarations of deceased persons as to the cause of their death were admitted even though the declarants had hopes of recovery when they were made." 1 James Fitzjames Stephen, *A History of the Criminal Law of England* 447–48 (1883).

▸ **self-disserving declaration.** See *declaration against interest*.

▸ **self-serving declaration.** (1881) An out-of-court statement made to benefit one's own interest.

7. *Common-law pleading.* The plaintiff's first pleading in a civil action. • It is an amplification of the original writ on which the action is founded, with the additional circumstances of the time and place of injury. In a real action, the declaration is called a *count*. Today the equivalent term in English law is *statement of claim*; in most American jurisdictions, it is called a *petition* or *complaint*. — Also termed *narratio*. See COUNT (1), (2); PLEADING (quot.). Cf. PLEA (2).

> "The declaration is a statement of all material facts constituting the plaintiff's cause of action in a methodical and legal form. It consists of the following parts: (a) Statement of title of court. (b) Statement of venue in the margin. (c) The commencement. (d) The body, or statement of the cause of action. (e) The conclusion." Benjamin J. Shipman, *Handbook of Common-Law Pleading* § 76, at 192 (Henry Winthrop Ballantine ed., 3d ed. 1923).

▸ **declaration in chief.** (18c) A declaration for the principal cause of action.

8. A formal, written statement — resembling an affidavit but not notarized or sworn to — that attests, under penalty of perjury, to facts known by the declarant. • Such a declaration, if properly prepared, is admissible in federal court with the same effect as an affidavit. 28 USCA § 1746. — Also termed *declaration under penalty of perjury*; *unsworn declaration under penalty of perjury*. Cf. AFFIDAVIT; *sworn statement* under STATEMENT. **9.** *Int'l law.* An oral or written statement, unilaterally made, by which a state expresses its will, intent, or opinion when acting in the field of international relations. **10.** See *declaratory judgment* under JUDGMENT (2). **11.** DECLARATION OF RIGHTS. — **declare,** *vb.*

declaration after final rejection. See *affidavit after final rejection* under AFFIDAVIT.

declaration against interest. See DECLARATION (6).

declaration against penal interest. See DECLARATION (6).

declaration date. See DATE.

declaration in chief. See DECLARATION (7).

declaration of a desire for a natural death. See LIVING WILL.

declaration of alienage. See DECLARATION (1).

declaration of continued use. See DECLARATION OF USE.

declaration of default. See DECLARATION (1).

declaration of delinquency. (1903) **1.** A court's official statement of how and when a probationer or parolee is alleged by police and prosecutors to have violated the terms of probation or parole. • The term may also apply to allegations about a defendant who has been conditionally discharged. **2.** In some states, a court's formal declaration that a juvenile has committed an act that would be a crime if the juvenile had been an adult when the act was committed.

declaration of dividend. See DECLARATION (1).

declaration of estimated tax. (1946) A required IRS filing by certain individuals and businesses of current estimated tax owed, accompanied by periodic payments of that amount. • The requirement ensures current collection of taxes from taxpayers (such as self-employed persons) whose incomes are not fully taxed by payroll withholding. IRC (26 USCA) §§ 6315, 6654.

declaration of homestead. See DECLARATION (1).

declaration of incontestability. (1990) *Trademarks.* A sworn statement submitted by the owner of a registered mark after five years of registration, averring that the mark has been in continuous use in commerce for at least five consecutive years since registration, that the mark has not become generic, that there has been no final adverse decision to ownership in the mark, and that there is no pending proceeding in the U.S. Patent and Trademark Office or courts involving the mark. • The statement entitles the mark to immunity from some legal challenges under § 15 of the Lanham Act. — Also termed *affidavit of incontestability; affidavit under § 15; declaration under § 15; Section 15 affidavit; Section 15 declaration.*

Declaration of Independence. The formal proclamation of July 4, 1776, in the name of the people of the American colonies, asserting their independence from the British Crown and announcing themselves to the world as an independent country.

declaration of indulgence. *Hist. English law.* A royal prerogative by which the king declared it his royal will and pleasure that all penal laws, esp. including those of an ecclesiastical nature, be suspended.

declaration of intention. See DECLARATION (1).

declaration of invalidity of marriage. See ANNULMENT (2).

declaration of legitimacy. See DECLARATION (1).

declaration of no defenses. See WAIVER OF DEFENSES.

declaration of pain. See DECLARATION (6).

Declaration of Paris. An international agreement, signed by Great Britain, France, Turkey, Sardinia, Austria, Prussia, and Russia in 1856 (at the end of the Crimean War), providing that (1) privateering is illegal, (2) with the exception of contraband, a neutral flag covers an enemy's goods, (3) with the exception of contraband, neutral goods cannot be confiscated under a hostile flag, and (4) a blockade must work to be binding. • The agreement was later adopted by most other maritime powers, except the United States and a few others.

> "The Declaration of Paris is one of the greatest triumphs won by commercial interests over the strict rules of maritime warfare. Its importance resides in its first three articles. Article 4 did no more than formulate a principle acknowledged for more than a century. Construed strictly it requires an impossibility; for no blockade, however strict, can always 'prevent access to the coast of the enemy.' But it is clear that the words were meant to be understood in a reasonable sense as merely prohibitory of ineffective or 'paper' blockades . . . . Article 1 struck at a most objectionable practice. The current of opinion had long been running strongly against the use of privateers. . . . Article 2 . . . has provoked an enormous amount of controversy. Together with Article 3 it amounted to a new departure in the law of maritime capture. Up to 1856 the great naval powers had been divided between the old principle that the liability of goods to capture should be determined by the character of their owner, and the more modern principle . . . that the character of the ship in which the goods were laden should settle their fate." 1 R.H. Inglis Palgrave, *Palgrave's Dictionary of Political Economy* 520–21 (Henry Higgs ed., 2d ed. 1925).

declaration of peace. A government's announcement that a state of war has ended. • This declaration legally and officially ends a civil or international war.

declaration of restrictions. (1950) *Property.* A statement of all the covenants, conditions, and restrictions affecting a parcel of land, usu. imposed and recorded by a developer of a subdivision. • The restrictions usu. promote a general plan of development by requiring all lot owners to comply with the specified standards, esp. for buildings. The restrictions run with the land. — Sometimes also written *declarations of restrictions.*

declaration of rights. 1. An action in which a litigant requests a court's assistance not because any rights have been violated but because those rights are uncertain. • Examples include suits for a declaration of legitimacy, for declaration of nullity of marriage, and for the authoritative interpretation of a will. **2.** See *declaratory judgment* under JUDGMENT (2). — Often shortened to *declaration.*

declaration of solvency. *English law.* **1.** A corporate board's statement that the company is capable of paying its debts made by its directors a statutorily specified time before a formal resolution for a voluntary winding up. **2.** A document prepared by a company seeking voluntary liquidation and listing the company's assets and liabilities to show that it can repay its debts within the coming year. • The declaration must be filed with the Registrar of Companies. **3.** A debtor's statement attesting that a transfer of real property for no money, occurring before bankruptcy, took place by reason of (1) natural love and affection, (2) was not intended to defraud creditors, and (3) was intended to benefit the recipient, and (4) preceded any inability of the donor to satisfy the creditors' claims without the property.

declaration of state of mind. See DECLARATION (6).

Declaration of Taking Act. The federal law regulating the government's taking of private property for public use under eminent domain. 40 USCA §§ 3114 et seq. • Fair compensation must be paid for the property.

declaration of trust. See DECLARATION (1).

declaration of use. (1954) *Trademarks.* A sworn statement submitted by a registered mark's owner averring that the registered mark is currently in use in commerce, and providing a specimen or facsimile of the mark's use. • The § 8 affidavit must be filed (1) between the fifth and sixth year following registration, and (2) within the year before the end of every ten-year period after the date of registration. If a registered mark's owner fails to file a § 8 affidavit within the required time, the U.S. Patent and Trademark Office may cancel the registration. The term comes from § 8 of the Lanham Act. — Also termed *affidavit of continued use; affidavit of use; affidavit under § 8; declaration of continued use; declaration under § 8; Section 8 declaration; statement of use.* Cf. INCONTESTABILITY STATUS; CANCELLATION (4).

declaration of war. See DECLARATION (3).

Declaration of War Clause. See WAR CLAUSE.

declaration under penalty of perjury. See DECLARATION (8).

declaration under § 8. See DECLARATION OF USE.

declaration under § 15. See DECLARATION OF INCONTESTABILITY.

declarator. See *action of declarator* under ACTION (4).

declarator of trust (di-**klar**-ə-tər *or* di-**klair**-ə-tər *or* -tor). (17c) A common-law action against a trustee who holds property under a title *ex facie* for the trustee's own benefit.

declaratory (di-**klar**-ə-tor-ee *or* di-**klair**-), *adj.* (16c) **1.** Clear; manifest <a declaratory statute>. **2.** Explanatory <a declaratory judgment>.

declaratory, *n.* See *action of declarator* under ACTION (4).

declaratory act. See *declaratory statute* under STATUTE.

declaratory decree. See *declaratory judgment* under JUDGMENT (2).

declaratory judgment. See JUDGMENT (2).

declaratory-judgment act. (1921) A federal or state law permitting parties to bring an action to determine their legal rights and positions regarding a controversy not yet ripe for adjudication, as when an insurance company seeks a determination of coverage before deciding whether to cover a claim. 28 USCA §§ 2201–2202. — Abbr. DJA. See *declaratory judgment* under JUDGMENT (2).

declaratory part of a law. A portion of a law clearly defining rights to be observed or wrongs to be avoided.

declaratory precedent. See PRECEDENT (2).

declaratory relief. See RELIEF (3).

declaratory statute. See STATUTE.

declaratory theory. (1895) The belief that judges' decisions never make law but instead merely constitute evidence of what the law is. • This antiquated view — held by such figures as Coke and Blackstone — is no longer accepted.

> "There are . . . at least three good reasons why the declaratory theory should have persisted for some time after the modern English doctrine [of precedent] had begun to take shape. In the first place, it appealed to believers in the separation of powers, to whom anything in the nature of judicial legislation would have been anathema. Secondly, it concealed a fact which Bentham was anxious to expose, namely, that judge-made law is retrospective in its effect. If in December a court adjudges that someone is liable, in consequence of his conduct during the previous January, it would certainly appear to be legislating retrospectively, unless the liability is based on an earlier Act of Parliament, or unless the court is simply following a previous decision. A way of disguising the retrospective character of such a judgment would be to maintain the doctrine that the court really was doing no more than state a rule which anyone could have deduced from well-known principles or common usage, for the conduct in question would then have been prohibited by the law as it stood in January. The third reason for the persistence of the declaratory theory may be thought to justify its retention in a revised form today. When confronted with a novel point, judges always tend to speak as though the answer is provided by the common law." Rupert Cross & J.W. Harris, *Precedent in English Law* 30 (4th ed. 1991).

declared trust. See *express trust* under TRUST (3).

Declare War Clause. See WAR CLAUSE.

de claro die (dee **klair**-oh **dɪ**-ee). [Law Latin "by clear day"] (16c) By daylight.

de clauso fracto (dee **klaw**-zoh **frak**-toh). [Law Latin] (17c) Of a breach of close. See CLAUSUM FREGIT.

de clerico admittendo (dee **kler**-ə-koh ad-mi-**ten**-doh), *n.* [Law Latin "for admitting a clerk"] (17c) *Hist.* A writ of execution commanding a bishop to accept a nominee for a vacant benefice. • A benefice's patron could enforce the right to fill a vacancy (the right of *presentation*) in the Court of Common Pleas by writ of *quare impedit.* — Also termed *admittendo clerico; ad admittendum clericum.* Cf. ADVOWSON; PRESENTATION (2); QUARE IMPEDIT.

de clerico capto per statutum mercatorium deliberando (dee **kler**-ə-koh **kap**-toh pər stə-**tyoo**-təm mər-kə-**tor**-ee-əm di-lib-ə-**ran**-doh), *n.* [Law Latin "for delivering a clerk arrested on a statute merchant"] *Hist.* A writ ordering the release of a clerk imprisoned for breaching a statute merchant. — Often shortened to *de clerico capto per statutum mercatorium.*

de clerico convicto commisso gaolae in defectu ordinarii deliberando. See CLERICO CONVICTO COMMISSO GAOLAE IN DEFECTU ORDINARII DELIBERANDO.

de clerico infra sacros ordines constituto, non eligendo in officium (dee **kler**-ə-koh **in**-frə **sak**-rohs **or**-di-neez kon-sti-**tyoo**-toh, non el-i-**jen**-doh in ə-**fish**-ee-əm). [Law Latin "for not electing a clerk in holy orders to office"] *Hist.* A writ ordering a cleric's release from secular office. • The writ was addressed to the bailiff or other person who had forced a cleric to take a bailiwick or other secular office.

de clero (dee **kleer**-oh), *n.* [Law Latin "concerning the clergy"] The statute of 25 Edw. 3 addressing clerical matters, including presentations and indictments.

declination (dek-lə-**nay**-shən). (14c) **1.** A deviation from proper course <declination of duty>. **2.** An act of refusal <declination of a gift>. **3.** A document filed by a fiduciary who chooses not to serve. **4.** At common law, a plea to the court's jurisdiction by reason of the judge's personal interest in the lawsuit. — Also termed (esp. in sense 2) *declinature.*

declinatory exception (di-**klɪn**-ə-tor-ee). See EXCEPTION (1).

declinatory plea. (17c) *Hist.* A pretrial plea claiming benefit of clergy. — Also termed *plea of sanctuary.* See BENEFIT OF CLERGY.

decline-to-prosecute letter. (2009) A letter by which a prosecutor's office, esp. a district attorney's office, states its intention not to prosecute a potential criminal defendant for a particular offense. — Abbr. DP letter.

declining-balance depreciation method. See DEPRECIATION METHOD.

decoctor (di-**kok**-tər *or* -tor), *n.* [fr. Latin *deciquere* "to waste"] *Roman law.* A bankrupt; a defaulting debtor.

decode, *vb.* (1896) **1.** To discover the meaning of; to decipher (a set of secret signs or letters). **2.** (Of a computer) to receive and change (data) into a usable and understandable form. **3.** (Of a television, radio, or similar device) to receive and change (digital signals) into sound or pictures, or both. **4.** To figure out the meaning of (a communication).

de coelo usque ad inferos (dee **kɪ**-loh **əs**-kwee ad in-**fər**-ohs). [Latin] From heaven to the center of the earth. • This phrase expressed a common-law maxim about the extent of a real-property owner's ownership interest in the property.

decollatio (dee-kah-**lay**-shee-oh), *n.* [fr. Latin *de* "off" + *collum* "neck"] (17c) *Hist.* In England and Scotland, an act of beheading. See DECAPITATION.

decolonization. (1938) *Int'l law.* The process by which a colonial power divests itself of sovereignty over a colony — whether a territory, a protectorate, or a trust territory — so that the colony is granted autonomy and eventually attains independence. — **decolonize,** *vb.*

de communi dividundo. See *actio de communi dividundo* under ACTIO.

de comon droit (də **kah**-mən **droyt**). [Law French] *Hist.* By the common law; of common right. See COMMON LAW.

de computo (dee **kom**-pyə-toh), *n.* [Law Latin "of account"] (17c) *Hist.* A writ ordering a defendant to either give a reasonable accounting to the plaintiff or explain why such an accounting should not be required. • This was the foundation for an action of account. See ACCOUNT (3).

de concilio curiae (dee kən-**sil**-ee-oh **kyoor**-ee-ee). [Law Latin] By the advice of the court; by the direction of the court. — Also spelled *de consillio curiae.*

De Conflictu Legum (dee kən-**flik**-too **lee**-gəm), *n.* [Latin] Concerning the conflict of laws. • This is a title to several works on the conflict of laws.

De Conjunctim Feoffatis (dee kən-**jəngk**-təm fee-**fay**-tis), *n.* [Law Latin "concerning persons jointly enfeoffed"] *Hist.* The title of the statute of Edward I preventing delays caused by tenants pleading, in novel disseisins or other actions, that someone else was jointly seised with them.

de consanguineo (dee kon-sang-**gwin**-ee-oh), *n.* See COSINAGE.

de consanguinitate (dee kon-sang-gwin-i-**tay**-tee), *n.* See COSINAGE.

de consilio (dee kən-**sil**-ee-oh). [Law Latin] Of counsel. • This term often referred to the advice or counsel to commit a crime.

deconstruction, *n.* (1969) A method used in philosophy and literary criticism to argue and purportedly demonstrate that no single explanation of the meaning of a piece of writing is correct. • In critical legal studies, deconstruction is a method of analyzing legal principles or rules by breaking down the supporting premises to show that these premises might also advance the opposite rule or result. — Also termed *trashing.* — **deconstructionist,** *adj.* & *n.*

de continuando assisam (dee kən-tin-yoo-**an**-doh ə-**sɪ**-zəm), *n.* [Law Latin "for continuing an assize"] A writ to continue an assize.

de contumace capiendo (dee kon-tyə-**may**-see kap-ee-**en**-doh), *n.* [Law Latin "for arresting a contumacious person"] (17c) *Hist.* A writ issuing out of the Court of Chancery at the request of an ecclesiastical court that has found a person to be in contempt. • This writ came into use after the Ecclesiastical Courts Act of 1813 removed ecclesiastical courts' power to excommunicate litigants who failed to comply with a court order. Cf. EXCOMMUNICATO CAPIENDO.

> "In 1812 the case of Mary Ann Dix — a woman not of age, who was imprisoned for two years on a writ de excommunicato capiendo for not paying costs in a suit for defamation — aroused the Legislature. In the following year it was enacted that excommunication should cease to exist as part of the process of the ecclesiastical courts to enforce appearance, and as a punishment for contempt. . . . [F]or the writ de excommunicato capiendo was substituted the writ de contumace capiendo; and the rules applying to the older writ were made applicable to the new." 1 William Holdsworth, *A History of English Law* 632 (7th ed. 1956).

de copia libelli deliberanda (dee **koh**-pee-ə li-**bel**-ɪ di-lib-ə-**ran**-də), *n.* [Law Latin "for delivering a copy of a libel"] (17c) *Hist. Eccles. law.* A writ ordering an ecclesiastical-court judge (such as the Dean of Arches) to provide the defendant with a copy of the plaintiff's complaint.

de coronatore eligendo (dee kor-ə-nə-**tor**-ee el-i-**jen**-doh), *n.* [Law Latin "for electing a coroner"] (16c) *Hist.* A writ ordering a sheriff to call an election of a coroner to fill a vacant office. See CORONER (2).

de coronatore exonerando (dee kor-ə-nə-**tor**-ee eg-zon-ə-**ran**-doh), *n.* [Law Latin "for removing a coroner"] (18c) A writ ordering the sheriff to remove a coroner from office for a reason stated in the writ. See CORONER (2).

> "The coroner is chosen for life: but may be removed, either by being made sheriff, or chosen verderor, which are offices incompatible with the other; or by the king's writ *de coronatore exonerando,* for a cause to be therein assigned, as that he is engaged in other business, is incapacitated by years or sickness, hath not a sufficient estate in the county, or lives in an inconvenient part of it." 1 William Blackstone, *Commentaries on the Laws of England* 336 (1765).

de corpore comitatus (dee **kor**-pə-ree kom-ə-**tay**-təs). [Law Latin] (17c) From the body of the county. • This term was esp. used to distinguish a body of the county at large from a smaller area or *de vicineto* ("from a neighborhood").

de corrodio habendo (dee kə-**roh**-dee-oh hə-**ben**-doh), *n.* [Law Latin "writ for having a corody"] (18c) *Hist.* A writ to obtain an allowance, esp. of meat or other sustenance, from a religious house for a royal servant living there.

decorum. (16c) **1.** Conduct that befits the dignity of a place or an occasion, esp. a formal one; propriety in speech, manner, conduct, and dress. **2.** *Parliamentary law.* The customs of formality and courtesy observed by the members and chair in conducting business. — **decorous,** *adj.*

decoy, *n.* (17c) An undercover law-enforcement officer or agent who acts as the willing subject of an attempted or completed crime in an attempt to lure a potential criminal defendant into a situation that establishes the grounds for a prosecution.

decoy, *vb.* (17c) *Slang.* To entice (a person) without force; to inveigle <the victim was decoyed out of her home> <the defendant was decoyed into the county and then served with process>. See ENTRAPMENT.

decoy duck. See BY-BIDDER.

decoy letter. (1836) A letter prepared and mailed to detect a criminal who has violated the postal or revenue laws.

decreased capacity. See CAPACITY (4).

decreasing term insurance. See INSURANCE.

decreasing-term life insurance. See *decreasing term insurance* under INSURANCE.

decree, *n.* (14c) **1.** Traditionally, a judicial decision in a court of equity, admiralty, divorce, or probate — similar to a judgment of a court of law <the judge's decree in favor of the will's beneficiary>. **2.** A court's final judgment. **3.** Any court order, but esp. one in a matrimonial case <divorce decree>. See JUDGMENT (2); ORDER (2); DECISION.

> "The chief differences between decrees in equity and judgments at common law are as follows: The former are pronounced by courts of equity; the latter, by courts of

law. The former result from an investigation and determination of the rights of the parties by the means provided and according to the principles recognized in equity jurisprudence; the latter result from an investigation and determination made by the more limited means and more inflexible rules of the common law. The former may be adjusted to all the varieties of interest and of circumstance, and may contain such directions as are needed to carry them into effect, both in letter and in spirit; the latter are in an invariable form, general in terms, and absolute for plaintiff or defendant. And the former often enforce rights not recognized by the common law . . . . The term 'judgment' is frequently used in a broad sense to include decrees in equity." 1 A.C. Freeman, *A Treatise of the Law of Judgments* § 12, at 23–24 (Edward W. Tuttle ed., 5th ed. 1925).

▸ **agreed decree.** (1911) A final judgment, the terms of which are agreed to by the parties.

▸ **consent decree.** (1831) A court decree that all parties agree to. — Also termed *consent order.*

▸ **custody decree.** (1913) A decree awarding or modifying child custody. • The decree may be included in the decree for a related proceeding — such as a divorce — or it may be a separate order.

▸ **decree absolute.** (1826) A ripened decree nisi; a court's decree that has become unconditional because the time specified in the decree nisi has passed. — Also termed *order absolute*; *rule absolute*; *absolute order*; *absolute rule.*

▸ **decree absolvitor** (ab-**zol**-vi-tər *or* -tor), *n.* (1809) *Scots law.* A judgment for a defendant, either by a dismissal of a claim or by an acquittal. — Also termed *decreet absolvitor.*

▸ **decree ad factum praestandum.** (1830) *Scots law.* A court order requiring that a party specifically perform an act, such as to deliver property. See IMPRISONMENT FOR DEBT.

▸ **decree arbitral** (**ahr**-bi-trəl), *n.* (18c) *Scots law.* **1.** An arbitration award. **2.** A form for an arbitration award. — Also termed *decreet arbitral.*

▸ **decree cognitionis causa** (kog-nish-ee-**oh**-nis **kaw**-zə), *n.* (1804) *Scots law.* A judgment in a suit involving a plaintiff creditor suing a debtor's heir to attach the heir's lands. — Also termed *decreet cognitionis causa.*

▸ **decree condemnator** (kon-dem-**nay**-tər *or* -tor), *n.* (18c) *Scots law.* A judgment for the plaintiff. — Also termed *decreet condemnator.*

▸ **decree dative.** (18c) *Scots law.* A decree appointing an executor.

▸ **decree nisi** (**NI**-SI). (18c) A court's decree that will become absolute unless the adversely affected party shows the court, within a specified time, why it should be set aside. — Also termed *nisi decree*; *order nisi*; *rule nisi.* See NISI.

▸ **decree of constitution.** (18c) *Scots law.* A judgment declaring the extent of a debt or obligation.

▸ **decree of distribution.** (1841) An instrument by which heirs receive the property of a deceased person.

▸ **decree of forthcoming.** (18c) *Scots law.* A court order that commands a third party in possession of a debtor's property to deliver the property to the creditor for liquidation or satisfaction of a debt. — Also termed *decree of furthcuming.*

▸ **decree of insolvency.** (18c) A probate-court decree declaring an estate's insolvency.

▸ **decree of locality.** (18c) *Scots law.* A Teind Court order allocating what share of a clergyman's stipend will be paid by each heir in the parish.

▸ **decree of modification.** (18c) *Scots law.* A Teind Court order modifying a stipend for the clergy.

▸ **decree of nullity.** (17c) A decree declaring a marriage to be void *ab initio.* See ANNULMENT; NULLITY OF MARRIAGE.

▸ **decree of registration.** (18c) **1.** A court order that quiets title to land and directs recording of the title. **2.** *Scots law.* CONFESSION OF JUDGMENT.

▸ **decree of valuation.** (18c) *Scots law.* A decree of the Teind Court determining the extent and value of a heritor's teinds.

▸ **decree *pro confesso*** (proh kən-**fes**-oh). (1821) *Equity practice.* A decree entered in favor of the plaintiff as a result of the defendant's failure to timely respond to the allegations in the plaintiff's bill; esp., a decree entered when the defendant has defaulted by not appearing in court at the prescribed time. — Also termed *decree taken pro confesso.*

"A decree pro confesso in equity is similar to a default judgment in an action at law. If a defendant in an equity suit fails to answer the plaintiff's petition within the prescribed time period, the bill will be taken pro confesso, and a decree entered in favor of the plaintiff . . . . However, whereas a default judgment in an action at law effects an admission of pleaded facts and conclusions of law . . . a decree pro confesso in an equity action admits only the material and well pleaded facts in the petition and does not admit the legal claims upon which the plaintiff seeks relief." 27A Am. Jur. 2d *Equity* § 249, at 733–34 (1996).

▸ **deficiency decree.** See *deficiency judgment* under JUDGMENT (2).

▸ **divorce decree.** (1870) A final judgment in a suit for divorce. • A divorce decree dissolves the marriage and usu. resolves all matters concerning property and children. Generally, matters concerning children can be modified in a post-divorce action if there has been a substantial change in circumstances. — Also termed *divorce order.*

▸ **final decree.** See *final judgment* under JUDGMENT (2).

▸ **foreign decree.** (18c) **1.** A decree issued by a court in another jurisdiction within the same country, such as a court in another state or province. **2.** A decree issued by a court in another country.

▸ **interlocutory decree.** See *interlocutory judgment* under JUDGMENT (2).

decree nunc pro tunc. See *judgment nunc pro tunc* under JUDGMENT (2).

decree of furthcuming. See *decree of forthcoming* under DECREE.

decreet (di-**kreet**), *n.* [fr. Latin *decretum*] (14c) *Archaic Scots law.* A court's final judgment; a decree. • *Decree* is now the usual term.

▸ ***decreet absolvitor*** (ab-**zol**-vi-tər *or* -tor), *n.* See *decree absolvitor* under DECREE.

▸ ***decreet arbitral*** (**ahr**-bi-trəl), *n.* See *decree arbitral* under DECREE.

▸ ***decreet cognitionis causa*** (kog-nish-ee-**oh**-nis **kaw**-zə), *n.* See *decreet cognitionis causa* under DECREE.

▸ ***decreet condemnator*** (kon-dem-**nay**-tər *or* -tor), *n.* See *decree condemnator* under DECREE.

decree taken pro confesso. See *decree pro confesso* under DECREE.

decrementum maris (dek-rə-**men**-təm **mar**-is). [Latin "decrease of the sea"] (16c) The receding of the sea from the land.

decrepit (di-**krep**-it), *adj.* (15c) (Of a person) disabled; physically or mentally incompetent to such an extent that the individual would be helpless in a personal conflict with a person of ordinary health and strength.

decreta (di-**kree**-tə), *n.* [Latin "decisions"] *Roman law.* Judgments of magistrates; esp., sentences pronounced by the emperor as the supreme judge. See DECRETUM.

> "*Decreta.* In Roman law decisions of magistrates given after investigation of a case by *cognitio* . . . and in particular, decisions of the emperor as judge of first instance after trial by *cognitio*, or as a judge of appeal. As the highest authority in the State the emperor could interpret the law freely and even introduce new principles. Consequently imperial decisions were authoritative interpretations of the law or even innovatory and regarded as statements binding for the future, and as such quoted by the jurists. They were not only communicated to the parties but recorded in the records of the imperial court and private persons might obtain copies of them." David M. Walker, *The Oxford Companion to Law* 343 (1980).

decretal (di-**kree**-təl), *adj.* (15c) Of, relating to, or involving a decree.

decretal child support. See CHILD SUPPORT.

decretal interdict. See INTERDICT (1).

decretal order. See ORDER (2).

decretals (di-**kree**-təlz), *n.* (14c) *Eccles. law.* Canonical epistles written either by the Pope or by the Pope and his cardinals to settle controversial matters; esp., the second part of the *Corpus Juris Canonici*, canonical epistles consisting mainly of (1) *Decretales Gregorii Noni*, a collection by Raymundus Barcinius, chaplain to Gregory IX, dating from about 1227; (2) *Decretales Bonifacii Octavi*, a collection by Boniface VIII in the year 1298; (3) *Clementinae*, a collection of Clement V, published in the year 1308; and (4) the *Extravagantes*, a collection by John XXII and other bishops. — Also termed (in Law Latin) *Decretales*. See CANON LAW.

decretist (di-**kree**-tist), *n.* (15c) In medieval universities, a law student; esp., a student or commentator on Gratian's *Decretum*.

decretum (di-**kree**-təm), *n.* [Latin "a decision having mandatory force"] (17c) **1.** *Roman law.* A decision of a magistrate, esp. a judgment by the emperor at first instance or on appeal. • A *decretum* of the emperor was a type of imperial constitution. **2.** *Eccles. law.* An ecclesiastical law, as distinguished from a secular law. See DECRETA. Pl. ***decreta.***

Decretum Gratiani (di-**kree**-təm gray-shee-**ay**-nɪ), *n.* [Latin "Gratian's decree"] See CONCORDIA DISCORDANTIUM CANONUM.

decriminalization, *n.* (1945) The legislative act or process of legalizing an illegal act <many doctors seek the decriminalization of euthanasia>. Cf. CRIMINALIZATION (1). — **decriminalize,** *vb.*

decrowning. (17c) The act of depriving someone of a crown.

decry (di-**krɪ**), *vb.* (17c) To speak disparagingly about (someone or something).

de cujus (dee **kyoo**-jəs *or* **kɪ**-əs). [Latin "from whom"] **1.** The person by or through whom another claimed something. **2.** The person whose legal position is in issue.

de curia claudenda (dee **kyoor**-ee-ə klaw-**den**-də), *n.* [Law Latin "of enclosing a court"] (17c) *Hist.* A writ ordering a person to build a wall or fence around his or her house to avoid disturbing a neighbor.

decurio (di-**kyoor**-ee-oh), *n.* [Latin "a decurion"] (16c) *Roman law.* A municipal senator belonging to a municipal council responsible for managing the internal affairs of the municipality. Pl. ***decuriones.***

de cursu (dee **kər**-s[y]oo). [Law Latin] Of course. • This term usu. refers to regular, formal proceedings as distinguished from incidental, summary proceedings.

de custode admittendo (dee kə-**stoh**-dee ad-mi-**ten**-doh), *n.* [Law Latin "of admitting a guardian"] *Hist.* A writ to admit a guardian.

de custode amovendo (dee kə-**stoh**-dee ay-moh-**ven**-doh), *n.* [Law Latin "of removing a guardian"] (18c) *Hist.* A writ to remove a guardian.

de custodia terrae et haeredis (dee kə-**stoh**-dee-ə **ter**-ee et **her**-ə-dis), *n.* [Law Latin "of right of ward"] *Hist.* A writ allowing a guardian in a knight's service to obtain custody of an infant ward.

dedbote. See *Godbote* under BOTE (3).

de debito (dee **deb**-i-toh), *n.* [Law Latin "of debt"] (17c) *Hist.* A writ of debt. — Sometimes shortened to *debito.*

de debitore in partes secando (dee deb-i-**tor**-ee in **pahr**-teez si-**kan**-doh). [Latin "of cutting a debtor in pieces"] (18c) *Roman law.* The title of a law in the Twelve Tables, meaning either literally to cut a debtor into pieces or merely to divide the debtor's estate. See TWELVE TABLES.

> "DE DEBITORE IN PARTES SECANDO . . . . [S]ome writers contending for the literal signification, while others have supposed it to be only a figurative expression . . . . The latter view has been adopted by Montesquieu, Bynkershoek, Heineccius and Taylor . . . . The literal meaning, on the other hand, is advocated by Aulus Gellius and other writers of antiquity, and receives support from an expression (*semoto omni cruciatu*) in the Roman Code itself . . . . This is also the opinion of Gibbon, Gravina, Pothier, Hugo and Niebuhr." 1 Alexander Burrill, *A Law Dictionary and Glossary* 432 (2d ed. 1867).

de deceptione (dee di-sep-shee-**oh**-nee), *n.* [Law Latin "of deceit"] (18c) *Hist.* A writ available to a party who was deceived and damaged by someone acting in the party's name.

de deoneranda pro rata portionis (dee dee-on-ə-**ran**-də proh **ray**-tə por-shee-**oh**-nis), *n.* [Law Latin "of the disburdening of a pro rata share"] (17c) *Hist.* A writ for someone who is forced to pay rent that others are supposed to contribute to proportionately.

dedi (**dee**-dɪ). [Latin] *Hist.* I have given. • *Dedi* is a conveyancing term that implies a warranty of title. Cf. CONCESSI.

> "Dedi is a warranty in law to the feoffee and his heirs: as if it be said in a feoffment A. B. hath given and granted, &c. it is a warranty." *Termes de la Ley* 148 (1st Am. ed. 1812).

dedication, *n.* (1809) *Property.* The donation of land or creation of an easement for public use. — **dedicate,** *vb.* — **dedicatory,** *adj.*

▸ **common-law dedication.** (1858) A dedication made without a statute, consisting in the owner's appropriation of land, or an easement in it, for the benefit or use of the public, and the acceptance, by or on behalf of the land or easement. — Often shortened to *dedication.*

▸ **dedication by adverse user.** (1895) A dedication arising from the adverse, exclusive use by the public with the actual or imputed knowledge and acquiescence of the owner.

▸ **express dedication.** (1836) A dedication explicitly manifested by the owner.

▸ **implied dedication.** (1837) A dedication presumed by reasonable inference from the owner's conduct.

▸ **statutory dedication.** (1852) A dedication for which the necessary steps are statutorily prescribed, all of which must be substantially followed for an effective dedication.

▸ **tacit dedication.** (1926) A dedication of property for public use arising from silence or inactivity and without an express agreement.

dedication and reservation. (1962) A dedication made with reasonable conditions, restrictions, and limitations.

dedication day. See DAY.

de die in diem (dee **dɪ**-ee in **dɪ**-əm). [Law Latin] From day to day; daily.

dedi et concessi (**dee**-dɪ et kən-**ses**-ɪ). [Law Latin] (16c) I have given and conveyed. • These were the words generally used to convey a gift.

dedimus et concessimus (**ded**-ə-məs et kən-**ses**-i-məs). [Law Latin] We have given and granted. • These words were used in a conveyance when there was more than one grantor or when the grant was from the Crown.

dedimus potestatem (**ded**-ə-məs poh-tes-**tay**-təm). [Law Latin "we have given power"] (16c) **1.** A commission issuing from the court before which a case is pending, authorizing a person named in the commission to compel the attendance of certain witnesses, to take their testimony on the written interrogatories and cross-interrogatories attached to the commission, to reduce the answers to writing, and to send it sealed to the court issuing the commission. **2.** *English law.* In England, a chancery writ commissioning the persons named in the writ to take certain actions, including administering oaths to defendants and justices of the peace. • The writ was formerly used to commission a person to take action such as acknowledging a fine and appointing an attorney for representation in court. Before the Statute of Westminster (1285), an attorney could not appear on behalf of a party without this writ. — Also termed *dedimus potestatem de attorno faciendo.*

> "Dedimus potestatem is a writ that lies where a man sues in the king's court, or is sued, and cannot well travel, then he shall have this writ directed to some justice, or other discreet person in the country, to give him power to admit some man for his attorney, or to levy a fine, or to take his confession, or his answer, or other examination, as the matter requires." *Termes de la Ley* 148 (1st Am. ed. 1812).

deditícii (ded-i-**tish**-ee-ɪ *or* dee-di-**tɪ**-shee-ɪ), *n. pl.* [Latin "those who have surrendered"] (17c) *Roman law.* The lowest class of freemen whose members were ineligible for Roman citizenship, including enemies granted freedom in exchange for surrender, or, under the *Lex Aelia Sentia,* manumitted slaves convicted of a crime in a court, or branded or put in chains by their former owners. • *Dediticii* who were formerly slaves were not allowed to live within 100 miles of Rome. Justinian abolished this status. — Also spelled *dedititii.* — Sing. ***dediticius, dedititius.***

> "Dediticii . . . were not reduced to slavery, but to a condition quite analogous. They were not allowed to make a will, or to take under one; they never obtained Roman citizenship, and they could not come within one hundred miles of the city of Rome." Andrew Stephenson, *A History of Roman Law* § 119, at 324 (1912).

> "Slaves who before manumission had been subjected to degrading punishment (e.g. had been branded or made to fight in the arena) were given, on manumission, a special status, viz. that of enemies surrendered at discretion (*dediticii*). A *dediticius,* though free and not a slave, had none of the rights of a citizen, could never under any circumstances better his position (e.g. become a citizen), and was not allowed to live within 100 miles of Rome." R.W. Leage, *Roman Private Law* 67 (C.H. Ziegler ed., 2d ed. 1942).

dedition (di-**dish**-ən), *n.* [fr. Latin *deditio* "give up"] (16c) A surrender of something, such as property.

de diversis regulis juris antiqui (dee di-**vər**-sis **reg**-yə-lis **joor**-is an-**tɪ**-kwɪ). [Latin "of various rules of ancient law"] *Roman law.* The last title in the Digest, containing 211 maxims. See DIGEST (2).

de dolo malo (dee **doh**-loh **mal**-oh). [Latin] (16c) Of or based on fraud. See ACTIO DE DOLO MALO.

de domo reparanda (dee **doh**-moh rep-ə-**ran**-də), *n.* [Law Latin "to repair a house"] (18c) *Hist.* A writ ordering a cotenant to contribute to the expenses of maintaining common property.

De Donis Conditionalibus (dee **doh**-nis kən-dish-ee-ə-**nal**-i-bəs). A 1285 English statute that gave rise to the ability to create a fee tail. — Often shortened to *De Donis.* — Sometimes written *de donis conditionalibus.*

> "[T]he statute *de donis* of 13 Edw. I. . . . was intended to check the judicial construction, that had, in a great degree, discharged the conditional fee from the limitation imposed by the grant. Under that statute, fees conditional were changed into estates tail . . . ." 4 James Kent, *Commentaries on American Law* *444 (George Comstock ed., 11th ed. 1866).

> "Entails, as authorised by the statute *De Donis,* were certainly intended by the Legislature to be perpetual and inviolable. But that intention never took full effect, and before two centuries were over it was wholly set at naught. This is the first of several surprises which the learner of English legal history meets with on his way. He must not expect to find Acts of Parliament in the thirteenth or even the sixteenth century carried into execution as they are in our own time. Statutes had to be administered through judges and lawyers, who were stubborn instruments. They constantly preferred their own mind to that of the Parliament, and would contrive and encourage every means of counterworking a statute they disliked, short of disobedience to its express terms." Frederick Pollock, *The Land Laws* 68–69 (3d ed. 1896).

> "[A]fter *De Donis,* the formula 'to A and the heirs of his body' gave to A an estate known as an *estate in fee tail.* Because A had no power to transfer an estate in fee simple absolute, it became theoretically possible for persons like O to tie up the ownership of land in a single family for hundreds of years. We say *theoretically possible* because by 1472 a way would be found for the tenant in tail (as A was

called) to transfer an estate in fee simple absolute despite *De Donis.*" Thomas F. Bergin & Paul G. Haskell, *Preface to Estates in Land and Future Interests* 29 (2d ed. 1984).

de dote assignanda (dee **doh**-tee as-ig-**nan**-də), *n.* [Law Latin "for assigning dower"] (17c) *Hist.* A writ ordering a royal escheater to provide dower to a widow of a tenant holding an estate directly from the Crown.

de dote unde nil habet (dee **doh**-tee **ən**-dee nil **hay**-bet), *n.* [Law Latin "of dower whereof she has none"] (18c) A writ ordering a tenant interfering with a widow's right to dower to provide a reasonable dower. — Also termed *writ of dower.* Cf. UNDE NIHIL HABET.

> "DE DOTE UNDE NIL HABET. This is a writ of right in its nature . . . . It must be brought by the widow as demandant, against the tenant of the freehold, that is, the heir or his alienee, and its effect is to enable the former to recover from the latter the seisin of a third part of the tenements in demand, to be set forth to her in severalty by metes and bounds, together with damages and costs." 1 Alexander M. Burrill, *A Law Dictionary and Glossary* 433 (2d ed. 1867).

deductible, *adj.* (1856) Capable of being subtracted, esp. from taxable income. See DEDUCTION (2).

deductible, *n.* (1929) **1.** Under an insurance policy, the portion of the loss to be borne by the insured before the insurer becomes liable for payment. Cf. SELF-INSURED RETENTION.

▸ **straight deductible.** (1991) A deductible that is a specified, fixed amount.

2. The insurance-policy clause specifying the amount of this portion.

deductible loss. See LOSS.

deduction, *n.* (15c) **1.** The act or process of subtracting or taking away. **2.** *Tax.* An amount subtracted from gross income when calculating adjusted gross income, or from adjusted gross income when calculating taxable income. — Also termed *tax deduction.* Cf. EXEMPTION (3); TAX CREDIT.

▸ **above-the-line tax deduction.** (1973) A nonitemized tax deduction that reduces gross income because it is subtracted from total income. • Examples of above-the-line deductions are certain moving expenses, education expenses, and alimony expenses.

▸ **additional standard deduction.** (1956) The sum of the additional amounts that a taxpayer who turns 65 or becomes blind before the close of the taxable year is entitled to deduct.

▸ **below-the-line tax deduction.** (1971) An expense that can be subtracted from adjusted gross income before the tax liability is determined. • Examples of below-the-line deductions are charitable donations and certain medical and interest expenses.

▸ **charitable deduction.** (1925) A deduction for a contribution to a charitable enterprise that has qualified for tax-exempt status in accordance with IRC (26 USCA) § 501(c)(3) and is entitled to be deducted in full by the donor from the taxable estate or from gross income. See CHARITABLE CONTRIBUTION (2); CHARITABLE ORGANIZATION.

▸ **deduction in respect of a decedent.** (1949) A deduction that accrues to the point of death but is not recognizable on the decedent's final income-tax return because of the accounting method used, such as an accrued-interest expense of a cash-basis debtor. — Abbr. DRD.

▸ **dividend-received deduction.** (1957) A deduction allowed to a corporate shareholder for dividends received from a domestic corporation. IRC (26 USCA) §§ 243–247. — Abbr. DRD.

▸ **itemized deduction.** (1943) An expense (such as a medical expense, home-mortgage interest, or a charitable contribution) that can be subtracted from adjusted gross income to determine taxable income.

▸ **marital deduction.** (1949) A federal tax deduction allowed for lifetime and testamentary transfers from one spouse to another. IRC (26 USCA) §§ 2056, 2523.

▸ **miscellaneous itemized deduction.** (1955) Generally, an itemized deduction of job or investment expenses; a deduction other than those allowable in computing adjusted gross income, those enumerated in IRC (26 USCA) § 67(b), and personal exemptions. • This type of deduction is allowed only to an itemizing taxpayer whose total miscellaneous itemized deductions exceed a statutory percentage of adjusted gross income. — Abbr. MID.

▸ **standard deduction.** (1944) A specified dollar amount that a taxpayer can deduct from adjusted gross income, instead of itemizing deductions, to determine taxable income.

3. The portion of a succession to which an heir is entitled before a partition. **4.** The act or process of reasoning from general propositions to a specific application or conclusion; the use of knowledge or information one already has in order to understand something or form an opinion. — Also termed *top-down reasoning.* **5.** The understanding or opinion one forms by reasoning from a general proposition to a specific application or conclusion. Cf. INDUCTION (2). — **deduct** (in senses 1–3), *vb.* — **deduce** (in sense 4), *vb.*

deduction for new. See NEW-FOR-OLD (1).

deduction in respect of a decedent. See DEDUCTION (2).

deductis debitis (di-**dək**-tis **deb**-i-tis). [Latin] (17c) *Hist.* The debts being deducted. • Before an estate could be ascertained, the debts had to be deducted.

deductive reasoning. See REASONING.

de ea re ita censuere (dee **ee**-ə ree ɪ-tə sen-**s[y]oo**-ə-ree). [Latin] Concerning that matter they have so decreed. • This phrase was used to record decrees of the Roman senate. — Abbr. *d.e.r.i.c.*

deed, *n.* (bef. 12c) **1.** Something that is done or carried out; an act or action. **2.** A written instrument by which land is conveyed. **3.** At common law, any written instrument that is signed, sealed, and delivered and that conveys some interest in property. See *special contract* & *contract under seal* under CONTRACT. — Also termed (in senses 2 & 3) *evidence of title.* Cf. CONVEYANCE; BILL OF SALE. — **deed,** *vb.*

> "A deed is a writing sealed and delivered. For if either a parchment without writing be delivered as one's deed, yet it is not his deed, though an obligation be afterwards written in it: or if it be a writing but not sealed at the time of the delivery of it as his deed, it is a scrole and not his deed. Or if I make and seal a deed, and the party take it without my delivery, I may plead it is not my deed." Henry Finch, *Law, or a Discourse Thereof* 108 (1759).

"What then is a deed? Unfortunately the word is not free from ambiguity. In the original and technical sense a deed is a written instrument under the seal of the party executing it. Because, however, of the wide use of such instruments in the conveyance of real estate, it has come to mean in popular acceptance any formal conveyance for the transfer of land or of an interest therein. The dual use of the term has crept into the language of courts and law writers, so that in the reading of cases it is difficult to determine whether the word is used in the first and original sense, or whether it connotes a formal instrument of the type ordinarily employed for the conveyance of land." Ray Andrews Brown, *The Law of Personal Property* § 46, at 118–19 (2d ed. 1955).

"All deeds are documents, but not all documents are deeds. For instance, a legend chalked on a brick wall, or a writing tattooed on a sailor's back may be documents but they are not deeds. A deed is, therefore, a particular kind of document. It must be a *writing* and a writing on *paper* or its like, e.g., vellum or parchment. Any instrument under seal is a deed if made between private persons. It must be *signed, sealed,* and *delivered.* A deed must either (a) effect the transference of an interest, right or property, or (b) create an obligation binding on some person or persons, or (c) confirm some act whereby an interest, right, or property has already passed." Gerald Dworkin, *Odgers' Construction of Deeds and Statutes* 1 (5th ed. 1967).

▸ **absolute deed.** (17c) A deed that conveys title without condition or encumbrance. — Also termed *deed absolute.*

▸ **administrator's deed.** (1845) A document that conveys property owned by a person who has died intestate. — Also termed *court-officer's deed.*

▸ **assignee's deed.** (1841) *Wills & estates.* A deed, usu. in a form prescribed by statute, by which an assignee acting for the benefit of an estate's creditors transfers real property to the creditors.

▸ **bargain-and-sale deed.** (1972) A deed that conveys property to a buyer for valuable consideration but that lacks any guarantee from the seller about the validity of the title. See BARGAIN AND SALE.

▸ **beneficiary deed.** (1990) A deed that automatically conveys the property to a designated person upon the property owner's death. — Also termed *transfer-on-death deed; TOD deed.*

▸ **chancery deed.** See *special master's deed.*

▸ **clerk and master's deed.** See *special master's deed.*

▸ **composition deed.** (18c) A deed reflecting the terms of an agreement between a debtor and a creditor to discharge or adjust a debt.

▸ **conservator's deed.** See *guardian's deed.*

▸ **counterdeed.** (18c) A secret deed, executed either before a notary or under a private seal, that voids, invalidates, or alters a public deed.

▸ **court-officer's deed.** (1955) **1.** See *administrator's deed.* **2.** See *executor's deed.* **3.** A document executed by the trustee of a court-supervised trust to convey trust property.

▸ **custodian's deed.** (1918) A deed conveying property to a custodian under the Uniform Gifts to Minors Act.

▸ **deathbed deed.** (18c) *Rare.* A deed executed by a grantor shortly before death. • The grantor need not be aware that he or she is near death when the deed is executed.

▸ **deed absolute.** See *absolute deed.*

▸ **deed in fee.** (18c) A deed conveying the title to land in fee simple, usu. with covenants.

▸ **deed in lieu of foreclosure.** (1934) A deed by which a borrower conveys fee-simple title to a lender in satisfaction of a mortgage debt and as a substitute for foreclosure. • This deed is often referred to simply as "deed in lieu."

▸ **deed inter partes.** A deed made among several persons.

▸ **deed of covenant.** (17c) A deed to do something, such as a document providing for periodic payments by one party to another (usu. a charity) for tax-saving purposes. • The transferor can deduct taxes from the payment and, in some cases, the recipient can reclaim the deducted tax.

▸ **deed of distribution.** (17c) A fiduciary's deed conveying a decedent's real estate.

▸ **deed of gift.** (16c) A deed executed and delivered without consideration. — Also termed *gratuitous deed.*

▸ **deed of inspectorship.** (1856) *Hist.* An instrument reflecting an agreement between a debtor and a creditor to appoint a receiver to oversee the winding up of the debtor's affairs on behalf of the creditor.

▸ **deed of partition.** (18c) A deed that divides land held by joint tenants, tenants in common, or coparceners.

▸ **deed of reconveyance.** (18c) A deed conveying title to real property from a trustee to a grantor when a loan is repaid. Cf. *deed of trust.*

▸ **deed of release.** (17c) A deed that surrenders full title to a piece of property upon payment or performance of specified conditions.

▸ **deed of separation.** (18c) An instrument governing a spouse's separation and maintenance.

▸ **deed of settlement.** (17c) **1.** A deed to settle something, such as the distribution of property in a marriage. **2.** *English law.* A deed formerly used to form a joint-stock company.

▸ **deed of trust.** (17c) A deed conveying title to real property to a trustee as security until the grantor repays a loan. • This type of deed resembles a mortgage. — Also termed *trust deed; trust indenture; indemnity mortgage; common-law mortgage.* Cf. *deed of reconveyance.*

▸ **deed poll.** (16c) A deed made by and binding on only one party, or on two or more parties having similar interests. • It is so called because traditionally the parchment was "polled" (that is, shaved) so that it would be even at the top (unlike an indenture). — Also spelled *deed-poll.* Cf. INDENTURE.

▸ **deed to lead uses.** (1855) A common-law deed prepared before an action for a fine or common recovery to show the object of those actions.

▸ **deed under seal.** A deed that is marked with the owner's seal indicating that the deed is authentic and needs no consideration.

▸ **deed without covenants.** See *quitclaim deed.*

▸ **defeasible deed.** (1802) A deed containing a condition subsequent causing title to the property to revert to the grantor or pass to a third party.

▸ **defective deed. 1.** A deed rendered ineffective by an irremediable flaw, such as forgery or lack of delivery.

2. A deed that is effective but voidable. • The grantor may rescind the deed.

▸ **derivative deed.** See *secondary conveyance* under CONVEYANCE.

▸ **disentailing deed.** (1841) *Hist.* A tenant-in-tail's assurance that the estate tail will be barred and converted into an estate in fee. • The Fines and Recoveries Act (3 & 4 Will. 4 ch. 74) introduced this way of barring an entail. It authorized nearly every tenant in tail, if certain conditions were met, to dispose of the land in fee simple absolute and thus to defeat the rights of all persons claiming under the tenant.

▸ **donation deed.** (1891) A deed granted by the government to a person who either satisfies the statutory conditions in a donation act or redeems a bounty-land warrant. See DONATION ACT; BOUNTY-LAND WARRANT.

▸ **enhanced-life-estate deed.** See *Lady Bird deed.*

▸ **executor's deed.** (1817) *Wills & estates.* A document that conveys property owned by a person who has died testate. — Also termed *court-officer's deed.*

▸ **full-covenant-and-warranty deed.** See *warranty deed.*

▸ **general warranty deed.** See *warranty deed.*

▸ **gift deed.** (1864) A deed given for a nominal sum or for love and affection.

▸ **good deed.** A deed that conveys good title as opposed to a deed that is merely good in form. — Also termed *lawful deed.*

▸ **grant deed.** (1891) A deed containing, or having implied by law, some but not all of the usual covenants of title; esp., a deed in which the grantor warrants that he or she (1) has not previously conveyed the estate being granted, (2) has not encumbered the property except as noted in the deed, and (3) will convey to the grantee any title to the property acquired after the date of the deed.

▸ **gratuitous deed.** See *deed of gift.*

▸ **guardian's deed.** (1824) A document that conveys property owned by a minor or a legally incompetent person. — Also termed *conservator's deed.*

▸ **inclusive deed.** See *inclusive grant* under GRANT (4).

▸ **indented deed.** See INDENTURE (1).

▸ **Lady Bird deed.** A deed that allows a property owner to transfer ownership of the property to another while retaining the right to hold and occupy the property and use it as if the transferor were still the sole owner. • This type of deed is used in a few states as an estate-planning tool to avoid probate. It enables a person to qualify for Medicaid while keeping a private home, or to make a gift without having to pay federal gift taxes. The name was accidentally coined in the 1980s by the Florida lawyer who invented this type of deed and used the names of the Lyndon Baines Johnson family in a sample deed. — Also termed *enhanced-life-estate deed.*

▸ **latent deed.** (17c) A deed kept in a strongbox or other secret place, usu. for 20 years or more.

▸ **lawful deed.** See *good deed.*

▸ **master's deed.** See *special master's deed.*

▸ **master's in chancery deed.** See *special master's deed.*

▸ **mineral deed.** (1920) A conveyance of an interest in the minerals in or under the land.

▸ **mortgage deed.** (17c) The instrument creating a mortgage. • A mortgage deed typically must contain (1) the name of the mortgagor, (2) words of grant or conveyance, (3) the name of the mortgagee, (4) a property description sufficient to identify the mortgaged premises, (5) the mortgagor's signature, and (6) an acknowledgment. To be effective and binding, a mortgage deed must also be delivered.

▸ **onerous deed.** (18c) *Scots law.* A deed given in exchange for a valuable consideration, often as part of a marriage settlement.

▸ **quitclaim deed.** (18c) A deed that conveys a grantor's complete interest or claim in certain real property but that neither warrants nor professes that the title is valid. — Often shortened to *quitclaim.* — Also termed *deed without covenants.* Cf. *warranty deed.*

> "A quitclaim deed purports to convey only the grantor's *present interest in the land,* if any, rather than the land itself. Since such a deed purports to convey whatever interest the grantor has at the time, its use excludes any implication that he has good title, or any title at all. Such a deed in no way obligates the grantor. If he has no interest, none will be conveyed. If he acquires an interest after executing the deed, he retains such interest. If, however, the grantor in such deed has complete ownership at the time of executing the deed, the deed is sufficient to pass such ownership. . . . A seller who knows that his title is bad or who does not know whether his title is good or bad usually uses a quitclaim deed in conveying." Robert Kratovil, *Real Estate Law* 49 (6th ed. 1974).

▸ **receiver's deed.** (1849) A document executed by a receiver to convey property owned by a debtor to a creditor.

▸ **referee's deed.** (1858) A document that conveys real property sold by court order, esp. for a partition or a foreclosure.

▸ **release deed.** (18c) A deed that is issued once a mortgage has been discharged, explicitly releasing and reconveying to the mortgagor the entire interest conveyed by an earlier deed of trust. — Also termed *reconveyance; satisfaction; release.*

▸ **sheriff's deed.** (18c) A deed that gives ownership rights in property bought at a sheriff's sale.

▸ **special master's deed.** (1892) (*usu. cap.*) A deed executed by a master in chancery to convey property as ordered by the court. — Also termed *special master's in chancery deed; clerk and master's deed; master's deed; master's in chancery deed; chancery deed.*

▸ **special master's in chancery deed.** See *special master's deed.*

▸ **special warranty deed.** (1808) **1.** A deed in which the grantor covenants to defend the title against only those claims and demands of the grantor and those claiming by and under the grantor. **2.** In a few jurisdictions, a quitclaim deed. Cf. *warranty deed.*

▸ **statutory deed.** (1832) A warranty-deed form prescribed by state law and containing certain warranties and covenants even though they are not included in the printed form.

▸ **support deed.** (1947) A deed by which a person (usu. a parent) conveys land to another (usu. a son or daughter) with the understanding that the grantee will support the grantor for life. • Support deeds often result in litigation.

▸ **tax deed.** (1853) A deed showing the transfer of title to real property sold for the nonpayment of taxes. See *office grant* under GRANT (4); *tax sale* under SALE. Cf. TAX CERTIFICATE.

▸ **title deed.** (18c) A deed that evidences a person's legal ownership of property. See TITLE.

▸ **transfer-on-death (TOD) deed.** See *beneficiary deed.*

▸ **trust deed.** See *deed of trust.*

▸ **warranty deed.** (1802) A deed containing one or more covenants of title; esp., a deed that expressly guarantees the grantor's good, clear title and that contains covenants concerning the quality of title, including warranties of seisin, quiet enjoyment, right to convey, freedom from encumbrances, and defense of title against all claims. — Also termed *general warranty deed; full-covenant-and-warranty deed.* See WARRANTY (1). Cf. *quitclaim deed; special warranty deed.*

▸ **wild deed.** (1914) A recorded deed that is not in the chain of title, usu. because a previous instrument connected to the chain of title has not been recorded.

deed abstract. See ABSTRACT OF DEED.

deedbote. See *Godbote* under BOTE (3).

deed box. (1834) *Archaic.* A box in which deeds of land title are traditionally kept. • Such a box is considered an heirloom in the strict sense. See HEIRLOOM (1).

deed-merger doctrine. (1975) *Property.* The principle that contractual promises about the title to real property are merged into the terms of the deed when the buyer accepts the deed. — Sometimes shortened to *merger doctrine.* — Also termed *deed-merger rule; merger of deed and contract.*

deed of agency. (1846) A revocable, voluntary trust for payment of a debt.

deed of crime. See ACTUS REUS (2).

deed of feoffment. See FEOFFMENT (3).

deed of inspectorship. See DEED.

deed of reconveyance. See DEED.

deed of trust. See DEED.

deed under seal. See DEED.

deed warranty. See *covenant for title* under COVENANT (4).

de ejectione custodiae (dee ee-jek-shee-**oh**-nee kəs-**toh**-dee-ee). [Latin "ejectment of a ward"] *Hist.* A writ available to a guardian after being ejected from the ward's land during the ward's minority. • The writ lay to recover the land or person of the ward, or both. The French equivalent was *ejectment de garde.*

de ejectione firmae (dee ee-jek-shee-**oh**-nee **fər**-mee). [Latin "ejectment of farm"] (17c) *Hist.* A writ or action of trespass to obtain the return of lands or tenements to a lessee for a term of years that had been ousted by the lessor or by a reversioner, remainderman, or stranger. • The lessee was then entitled to a writ of ejection to recover, at first, damages for the trespass only, but later the term itself, or the remainder of it, with damages. This action is the foundation of the modern action of ejectment. See EJECTMENT. — Often shortened to *ejectione firmae.*

> "A writ then of *ejectione firmae*, or action of trespass in *ejectment*, lieth, where lands or tenements are let for a term of years; and afterwards the lessor, reversioner, remainder-man, or any stranger, doth eject or oust the lessee of his term. In this case he shall have his writ of *ejection*, to call the defendant to answer for entering on the lands so demised to the plaintiff for a term that is not yet expired, and ejecting him. And by this writ the plaintiff shall recover back his term, or the remainder of it, with damages." 3 William Blackstone, *Commentaries on the Laws of England* 199 (1768).

> "The action of *ejectione firmae*, which had been getting into practice ever since the reign of Henry VII, did, during the long reign of Queen Elizabeth, establish itself as the regular and only remedy for obtaining possession of freeholds and inheritances, and for trying of titles. The reports of this time are full of ejectments." 3 W.F. Finlason, *Reeves' History of the English Law* 759 (rev. ed. 1869).

deem, *vb.* (bef. 12c) **1.** To treat (something) as if (1) it were really something else, or (2) it has qualities that it does not have <although the document was not in fact signed until April 21, it explicitly states that it must be deemed to have been signed on April 14>. **2.** To consider, think, or judge <she deemed it necessary>.

> "'Deem' has been traditionally considered to be a useful word when it is necessary to establish a legal fiction either positively by 'deeming' something to be what it is not or negatively by 'deeming' something not to be what it is. . . . All other uses of the word should be avoided . . . . Phrases like 'if he deems fit' or 'as he deems necessary' or 'nothing in this Act shall be deemed to . . .' are objectionable as unnecessary deviations from common language. 'Thinks' or 'considers' are preferable in the first two examples and 'construed' or 'interpreted' in the third. . . . 'Deeming' creates an artificiality and artificiality should not be resorted to if it can be avoided." G.C. Thornton, *Legislative Drafting* 99 (4th ed. 1996).

deemed income. See INCOME.

deemed transferor. (1988) *Tax.* Someone who holds an interest in a generation-skipping trust on behalf of a beneficiary, and whose death will trigger the imposition of a generation-skipping transfer tax. • A *deemed transferor* is often a child of the settlor. For example, a grandfather could establish a trust with income payable for life to his son (who, because he is only one generation away from his father, is also known as a *nonskip person*) with the remainder to his grandson, a beneficiary also known as the *skip person.* When the son dies, the trust will be included in his gross estate for determining the generation-skipping transfer tax. IRC (26 USCA) §§ 2601–2663. See GENERATION-SKIPPING TRANSFER; *generation-skipping transfer tax* under TAX; *generation-skipping trust* under TRUST (3); SKIP PERSON; NONSKIP PERSON.

deeming provision. A clause in a statute that makes a presumption about a significant fact or treats something as equivalent to another thing. • For example, a deeming provision may state that something put into the U.S. mail is presumed received within four days. Or it may state that an electronic signature is the same as a handwritten signature for purposes of the statute.

deep issue. See ISSUE (1).

deep link. *Intellectual property.* A webpage hyperlink that, when clicked, opens a page on another website other than that site's home page. • Some plaintiffs have argued, with mixed success, that bypassing their home page in this manner deprives them of advertising revenue. Deep linking does not violate copyright if the portal provided does not copy any of the linked page's content. And if there is no confusion about the source of the information, deep linking does not constitute unfair competition.

deep pocket. (1965) **1.** (*pl.*) Substantial wealth and resources <the plaintiff nonsuited the individuals and targeted the corporation with deep pockets>. **2.** A person or entity with substantial wealth and resources against which a claim may be made or a judgment may be taken <that national insurance company is a favorite deep pocket among plaintiff's lawyers>.

Deep Rock doctrine. (1942) *Bankruptcy.* The principle by which unfair or inequitable claims presented by controlling shareholders of bankrupt corporations may be subordinated to claims of general or trade creditors. • The doctrine is named for a corporation that made fraudulent transfers to its parent corporation in *Taylor v. Standard Gas & Elec. Co.*, 306 U.S. 307, 59 S.Ct. 543 (1939).

de escaeta (dee es-**kee**-tə), *n.* [Law Latin "of escheat"] *Hist.* A writ authorizing a lord to recover land when the lord's tenant died without an heir. See ESCHEAT.

de-escalating price. See PRICE.

de-escalation clause. (1989) A contractual provision to decrease the price of something if specified costs decrease. Cf. ESCALATOR CLAUSE (1).

de escambio monetae (dee es-**kam**-bee-oh mə-**nee**-tee), *n.* [Law Latin "of exchange of money"] *Hist.* A writ authorizing a merchant to prepare a bill of exchange.

de essendo quietum de theolonio (dee e-**sen**-doh kwi-**ee**-təm dee thee-ə-**loh**-nee-oh), *n.* [Law Latin "of being quit of toll"] (17c) *Hist.* A writ authorizing a person who is exempt from paying a toll to enforce the exemption without harassment. — Also spelled *de essendo quietum de tolonio.*

de essentia (dee e-**sen**-shee-ə). [Law Latin] *Hist.* Of the essence; essential.

de essonio de malo lecti (dee e-**soh**-nee-oh dee **mal**-oh **lek**-tɪ), *n.* [Law Latin "of essoin of *malum lecti* (sickness of bed)"] (18c) *Hist.* A writ ordering a determination whether a person is truly sick after the person has issued an essoin claiming sickness as an excuse for not appearing in court.

de estoveriis habendis (dee es-tə-**veer**-ee-is hə-**ben**-dis), *n.* [Law Latin "for having estovers"] (18c) *Hist.* A writ allowing a wife divorced *a mensa et thoro* ("from bed and board") to recover alimony or estovers. — Often shortened to *estoveriis habendis.*

> "In case of divorce *a mensa et thoro*, the law allows alimony to the wife which is that allowance, which is made to a woman for her support out of her husband's estate; being settled at the discretion of the ecclesiastical judge, on consideration of all the circumstances of the case. This is sometimes called her *estovers* for which, if he refuses payment, there is; (besides the ordinary process of excommunication) a writ at common law *de estoveriis habendis*, in order to recover it . . . . It is generally proportioned to the rank and quality of the parties. But in case of elopement, and living with an adulterer, the law allows her no alimony." 1 William Blackstone, *Commentaries on the Laws of England* 429 (1765).

de estrepamento (dee e-strep-ə-**men**-toh), *n.* [Law Latin "of enstrepment"] *Hist.* A writ to prevent waste by a tenant while a suit to recover the land is pending against the tenant. • Because this writ was only auxiliary to a real action to recover land, and because equity afforded the same relief by injunction, the writ fell into disuse and was abolished by 3 & 4 Will. 4, ch. 27. — Also termed *writ of estrepement.* See ESTREPEMENT.

de eu et trene (də **yoo** ay **trayn**). [French] *Hist.* Of water and whip of three cords. • This term referred to a neife who, as a servant, could be corporally punished. See NEIFE.

de eve et de treve (də **ev** ay də **trev**). [Law French] *Hist.* From grandfather and great-grandfather's great-grandfather. • This phrase described the ancestral rights of lords to their villeins.

de excommunicato capiendo (dee eks-kə-myoo-ni-**kay**-toh kap-ee-**en**-doh), *n.* [Law Latin "for taking an excommunicated person"] (16c) *Hist. Eccles. law.* A writ ordering a sheriff to imprison an excommunicated person until the person reconciled with the church. • It was replaced by the writ *de contumace capiendo.* See DE CONTUMACE CAPIENDO.

de excommunicato deliberando (dee eks-kə-myoo-ni-**kay**-toh di-lib-ə-**ran**-doh), *n.* [Law Latin "for delivering an excommunicated person"] (18c) *Hist. Eccles. law.* A writ releasing an excommunicated person from prison upon a certification by the person's superior that the person has reconciled with the church.

de excommunicato recapiendo (dee eks-kə-myoo-ni-**kay**-toh ri-kap-ee-**en**-doh), *n.* [Law Latin "for retaking an excommunicated person"] *Hist. Eccles. law.* A writ ordering the rearrest of an excommunicated person who had been released but had not reconciled with the church or given security for a reconciliation.

de excusationibus (dee ek-skyoo-zay-shee-**oh**-ni-bəs). [Latin "of excuses"] *Roman law.* The first title of the 27th book of the Digest, containing a person's legal excuses from serving as *tutor* or *curator.* • It is primarily drawn from the Greek work of Herennius Modestinus. See DIGEST (2).

de executione facienda in withernamium (dee ek-sə-kyoo-shee-**oh**-nee fay-shee-**en**-də in with-ər-**nay**-mee-əm), *n.* [Law Latin "for making execution in withernam"] (18c) *Hist.* A writ of execution in withernam. • This is a type of *capis in withernam* directing the sheriff to take from the defendant goods equal in value to the goods that the defendant took from the plaintiff.

de executione judicii (dee ek-sə-kyoo-shee-**oh**-nee joo-**dish**-ee-ɪ), *n.* [Law Latin "of execution of judgment"] (17c) *Hist.* A writ ordering a sheriff or bailiff to execute a judgment.

de exemplificatione (dee ig-zem-pli-fi-kay-shee-**oh**-nee), *n.* [Law Latin "of exemplification"] (18c) A writ ordering the transcription of an original record.

de exoneratione sectae (dee ig-zon-ə-ray-shee-**oh**-nee **sek**-tee), *n.* [Law Latin "of exoneration of suit"] *Hist.* A writ exempting the king's ward from being sued in any court lower than the Court of Common Pleas (such as a county court, hundred court, leet, or court baron) during the time of the wardship.

de expensis civium et burgensium (dee ek-**spen**-sis **siv**-ee-əm et bər-**jen**-see-əm), *n.* [Law Latin "for levying the expenses of burgesses"] (17c) *Hist.* A writ ordering the sheriff to levy the expenses of each citizen and burgess of Parliament.

de expensis militum levandis (dee ek-**spen**-sis **mil**-ə-təm lə-**van**-dis), *n.* [Law Latin "for levying the expenses of knights"] (18c) *Hist.* A writ ordering the sheriff to levy an allowance for knights of the shire in Parliament.

deface (di-**fays**), *vb.* (14c) **1.** To mar or destroy (a written instrument, signature, or inscription) by obliteration, erasure, or superinscription; to spoil the surface or appearance of. **2.** To detract from the value of (a coin) by punching, clipping, cutting, or shaving. **3.** To mar or injure (a building, monument, or other structure). — **defacement,** *n.*

defacere. See DIFFACERE.

de facto (di **fak**-toh *also* dee *or* day), *adj.* [Law Latin "in point of fact"] (17c) **1.** Actual; existing in fact; having effect even though not formally or legally recognized <a de facto contract>. **2.** Illegitimate but in effect <a de facto government>. Cf. DE JURE.

de facto adoption. See ADOPTION (1).

de facto arrest. See ARREST (2).

de facto blockade. See BLOCKADE.

de facto contract of sale. See CONTRACT.

de facto corporation. See CORPORATION.

de facto court. See COURT.

de facto dissolution. See DISSOLUTION (3).

de facto father. See *de facto parent* under PARENT (1).

de facto government. See GOVERNMENT (3).

de facto judge. See JUDGE.

de facto marriage. See MARRIAGE (1).

de facto merger. See MERGER (8).

de facto mother. See *de facto parent* under PARENT (1).

de facto officer. See *officer de facto* under OFFICER (1).

de facto parent. See PARENT (1).

de facto segregation. See SEGREGATION (2).

de facto stepparent adoption. See *second-parent adoption* under ADOPTION (1).

de facto taking. See TAKING (2).

defalcation (dee-fal-**kay**-shən), *n.* (15c) **1.** The fraudulent misappropriation of money held in trust; financial wrongdoing involving a breach of trust; EMBEZZLEMENT. **2.** Loosely, the failure to meet an obligation; a nonfraudulent default. **3.** *Archaic.* A deduction; a setoff. — **defalcate** (di-**fal**-kayt *or* dee-), *vb.* — **defalcator,** *n.*

defalk (di-**fawlk**), *vb.* (15c) *Archaic.* To deduct (a debt); to set off (a claim).

de falso judicio (dee **fal**-soh *or* **fawl**-soh joo-**dish**-ee-oh), *n.* [Law Latin "of false judgment"] (17c) *Hist.* A writ of false judgment; a writ to reverse an inferior court's ruling.

de falso moneta (dee **fal**-soh *or* **fawl**-soh mah-**nee**-tə), *n.* [Law Latin "of false money"] *Hist.* The statute of Edward I providing that persons importing certain coins (called "pollards" and "crokards") would forfeit both their goods and their lives.

defamacast (di-**fam**-ə-kast). (1962) Defamation by television or radio broadcast. • The word was first used in *American Broadcasting-Paramount Theatres, Inc. v. Simpson*, 126 S.E.2d 873, 879 (Ga. Ct. App. 1962). Although Prosser called it "a barbarous word" (William Prosser, *The Law of Torts* 753 [4th ed. 1971]), another authority has said that "[t]he word seems to be quite apt" (Laurence H. Eldredge, *The Law of Defamation* § 12, at 77 [1978]). See DEFAMATION.

defamation, *n.* (14c) **1.** Malicious or groundless harm to the reputation or good name of another by the making of a false statement to a third person. • If the alleged defamation involves a matter of public concern, the plaintiff is constitutionally required to prove both the statement's falsity and the defendant's fault. **2.** A false written or oral statement that damages another's reputation. See LIBEL; SLANDER. Cf. DISPARAGEMENT. — **defame,** *vb.*

> "Defamation is the publication of a statement which tends to lower a person in the estimation of right-thinking members of society generally; or which tends to make them shun or avoid that person." P.H. Winfield, *A Textbook of the Law of Tort* § 72, at 242 (5th ed. 1950).

> "The wrong of defamation consists in the publication of a false and defamatory statement concerning another person without lawful justification. That person must be in being. Hence not only does an action of defamation not survive for or against the estate of a deceased person, but a statement about a deceased or unborn person is not actionable at the suit of his relatives, however great their pain and distress, unless the statement is in some way defamatory of them." R.F.V. Heuston, *Salmond on the Law of Torts* 138 (17th ed. 1977).

> "For entirely too long a period of time, English and American law have recognized two distinct kinds of defamation based solely on the form in which it is published. Oral defamation is slander; written defamation is libel. Libel is a crime and a tort which subjects the defamer to tort liability without proof of special damages. Slander is not a common law crime and, with certain exceptions, does not subject the defamer to liability unless there is proof of special damages. Under this distinction in form alone the defamatory letter read only by its addressee and burned to ashes after being read is a more serious defamation than a defamatory statement spoken to an audience of 3,000 community leaders and molders of public opinion. This is utterly absurd and completely indefensible . . . ." Laurence H. Eldredge, *The Law of Defamation* § 12, at 77 (1978).

> "Defamation . . . is involved in two related harms, libel and slander. A familiar statement is that libel is written whereas slander is oral. This covers the idea in a general way but tends to mislead because defamation may be published without the use of words and hence be neither written nor oral. Thus libel may be perpetrated by hanging a person in effigy and slander, by sign or gesture." Rollin M. Perkins & Ronald N. Boyce, *Criminal Law* 489 (3d ed. 1982).

▸ **criminal defamation.** Defamation that is defined as a crime by statute.

▸ **defamation per quod.** (1915) Defamation that either (1) is not apparent but is proved by extrinsic evidence showing its injurious meaning or (2) is apparent but is not a statement that is actionable per se.

▸ **defamation per se.** (1928) A statement that is defamatory in and of itself and is not capable of an innocent meaning.

▸ **oral defamation.** See SLANDER.

▸ **trade defamation.** (1933) The damaging of a business by a false statement that tends to diminish the reputation of that business. • Trade defamation may be trade libel if it is recorded, or trade slander if it is not. — Also termed *commercial defamation.* Cf. TRADE DISPARAGEMENT.

▸ **written defamation.** See LIBEL (1), (2).

defamation privilege. See *litigation privilege* under PRIVILEGE (1).

defamatory, *adj.* (16c) (Of a statement or communication) tending to harm a person's reputation, usu. by subjecting the person to public contempt, disgrace, or ridicule, or by adversely affecting the person's business.

"A communication is defamatory if it tends so to harm the reputation of another as to lower him in the estimation of the community or to deter third persons from associating or dealing with him." Restatement (First) of Torts § 559 (1938).

"No exhaustive definition of 'defamatory' emerges from the cases for, as Lord Reid once said, it is not for the judges to 'frame definitions or to lay down hard and fast rules. It is their function to enunciate principles and much that they say is intended to be illustrative or explanatory and not to be definitive' [*Cassell & Co. Ltd. v. Broome* (1972) AC 1027, 1085]. One can nevertheless achieve a working description by combining two statements, namely: a defamatory statement is one which injures the reputation of another by exposing him to hatred, contempt, or ridicule, or which tends to lower him in the esteem of right-thinking members of society." R.W.M. Dias & B.S. Markesinis, *Tort Law* 423–24 (2d ed. 1989).

defamatory communication. See DEFAMATORY STATEMENT.

defamatory libel. See LIBEL (1).

defamatory matter. A statement that (1) imputes a crime or official misconduct in public office to a person, (2) is likely to impair a person's ability to perform in an occupation, calling, or office, or (3) exposes the person to general hatred, contempt, or ridicule.

defamatory propaganda. See PROPAGANDA.

defamatory statement. (1841) A statement that tends to injure the reputation of a person referred to in it. • The statement is likely to lower that person in the estimation of reasonable people and in particular to cause that person to be regarded with feelings of hatred, contempt, ridicule, fear, or dislike. — Also termed *defamatory communication.*

defames (di-**fay**-meez or di-**fahm**), *adj.* [Law French] Infamous.

default (di-**fawlt** *also* **dee**-fawlt), *n.* (13c) The omission or failure to perform a legal or contractual duty; esp., the failure to pay a debt when due.

default (di-**fawlt**), *vb.* (16c) **1.** To be neglectful; esp., to fail to perform a contractual obligation. **2.** To fail to appear or answer. **3.** To enter a default judgment against (a litigant).

defaultant (di-**fawl**-tənt), *adj.* (1884) In default; having defaulted. See DEFAULTER.

default clause. A contract provision defining what constitutes an act of default and the consequences of it. See DEFAULT.

defaulter. (17c) **1.** Someone who is in default. **2.** Someone who misappropriates or fails to account for money held in the person's official or fiduciary capacity. — Also termed *defaultant.*

default judgment. (16c) **1.** A judgment entered against a defendant who has failed to plead or otherwise defend against the plaintiff's claim. **2.** A judgment entered as a penalty against a party who does not comply with an order, esp. an order to comply with a discovery request. *See* Fed. R. Civ. P. 55(b). — Also termed *judgment by default.* See JUDGMENT (2).

▸ ***nil dicit* default judgment** (nil **dɪ**-sit). [Latin "he says nothing"] (2002) A judgment for the plaintiff entered after the defendant fails to file a timely answer, often after the defendant appeared in the case by filing a preliminary motion. — Often shortened to *nil dicit.* — Also termed *nihil dicit; nihil dicit default judgment; judgment by nil dicit.*

▸ **no-answer default judgment.** (1979) A judgment for the plaintiff entered after the defendant fails to timely answer or otherwise appear.

▸ **post-answer default judgment.** (1979) A judgment for the plaintiff entered after the defendant files an answer, but fails to appear at trial or otherwise provide a defense on the merits.

default jurisdiction. See JURISDICTION.

default of issue. See FAILURE OF ISSUE.

default rule. See RULE (1).

default summons. See SUMMONS.

defeasance (di-**feez**-ənts), *n.* (15c) **1.** An annulment or abrogation; VOIDANCE. **2.** The fact or an instance of bringing an estate or status to an end, esp. by conditional limitation. **3.** A condition upon the fulfillment of which a deed or other instrument is defeated or made void; a contractual provision containing such a condition. — Also termed *defeasance clause.* **4.** *Hist.* A collateral deed made simultaneously with a conveyance and containing a condition by which the main deed might be defeated or made void. — Also spelled *defeazance.* — **defease,** *vb.*

"A defeazance is a collateral deed, made at the same time with a feoffment or other conveyance, containing certain conditions, upon the performance of which the estate then created may be *defeated* or totally undone." 2 William Blackstone, *Commentaries on the Laws of England* 327 (1766).

defeasance clause. (1856) A mortgage provision stating that the conveyance to the mortgagee will be ineffective if the mortgagor pays the debt on time. See DEFEASANCE (3).

defeasible, *adj.* (16c) (Of an act, right, agreement, or position) capable of being annulled or avoided <defeasible deed>. See *fee simple defeasible* under FEE SIMPLE. — **defeasibility,** *n.*

defeasible deed. See DEED.

defeasible estate. See ESTATE (1).

defeasible fee simple. See *fee simple defeasible* under FEE SIMPLE.

defeasible interest. See INTEREST (2).

defeasible remainder. See REMAINDER (1).

defeasible title. See TITLE (2).

defeasive, *adj.* (1921) *Rare.* Capable of defeating <a counterclaim defeasive of the plaintiff's right to recovery>.

defeat, *vb.* (14c) **1.** To deprive (someone) of something expected, usu. by an antagonistic act <to defeat the opponent in an election>. **2.** To annul or render (something) void <to defeat title>. **3.** To vanquish; to conquer (someone or something) <to defeat the armies>. **4.** To frustrate (someone or something) <the expenditures defeat the bill's purpose>.

defeating the due course of justice. See PERVERTING THE COURSE OF JUSTICE.

defeating the ends of justice. See PERVERTING THE COURSE OF JUSTICE.

defect, *n.* (15c) An imperfection or shortcoming, esp. in a part that is essential to the operation or safety of a product. — **defective,** *adj.*

▸ **apparent defect.** See *patent defect.*

▸ **birth defect.** See BIRTH DEFECT.

▸ **design defect.** (1954) An imperfection occurring when the seller or distributor could have reduced or avoided a foreseeable risk of harm by adopting a reasonable alternative design, and when, as a result of not using the alternative, the product or property is not reasonably safe. — Also termed *defective design*. Cf. *manufacturing defect*.

▸ **fatal defect.** (18c) A serious defect capable of nullifying a contract.

▸ **hidden defect.** (1896) A product imperfection that is not discoverable by reasonable inspection and for which a seller or lessor is generally liable if the flaw causes harm. • Upon discovering a hidden defect, a purchaser may revoke a prior acceptance. UCC § 2-608(1)(b). — Also termed *latent defect*; *inherent defect*.

▸ **latent defect.** See *hidden defect*.

▸ **manufacturing defect.** (1925) An imperfection in a product that departs from its intended design even though all possible care was exercised in its assembly. Cf. *design defect*.

▸ **marketing defect.** (1980) **1.** The failure to adequately warn of a potential risk of harm that is known or should have been known about a product or its foreseeable use. **2.** The failure to adequately instruct the user about how to use a product safely.

▸ **patent defect.** (1827) A defect that is apparent to a normally observant person, esp. a buyer on a reasonable inspection. — Also termed *apparent defect*.

▸ **product defect.** (1967) An imperfection in a product that has a manufacturing defect or design defect, or is faulty because of inadequate instructions or warnings. See *manufacturing defect*; *design defect*; *marketing defect*.

defect, *vb.* To desert from duty or obedience; esp., to leave one's own country or group in order to go to or join an opposing one.

defect in title. (18c) **1.** Of a particular piece of property, an encumbrance or claim properly recorded in a public record. — Also termed *patent defect in title*. **2.** Of a particular piece of property, an unrecorded encumbrance or claim that is unknown to a seller and not easily discovered. — Also termed (in sense 2) *latent defect in title*.

defection. Abandonment of allegiance or duty; the forsaking of a person or cause; desertion.

defective, *adj.* (14c) **1.** (Of a position, right, act, or process) lacking in legal sufficiency <defective execution of documents> <defective service of process>. **2.** (Of a product) containing an imperfection or shortcoming in a part essential to the product's safe operation <defective wiring caused the accident>. **3.** *Archaic.* (Of a person) having a pronounced intellectual or physical disability. • Older authorities refer to "defective" persons as being "markedly subnormal in intelligence or ability," but this type of terminology is considered unacceptably stigmatizing in modern usage.

defective condition. (1823) An unreasonably dangerous state that might well cause physical harm beyond that contemplated by the ordinary user or consumer who purchases the product. See PRODUCTS LIABILITY.

defective deed. See DEED.

defective design. See *design defect* under DEFECT.

defective goods. See GOODS.

defective manufacture. See *defective product* under PRODUCT.

defective performance. See PERFORMANCE (1).

defective pleading. See PLEADING (1).

defective process. See PROCESS (2).

defective product. See PRODUCT.

defective record. See RECORD.

defective title. See TITLE (2).

defective trust. See TRUST (3).

defective verdict. See VERDICT (1).

defect of form. (17c) An imperfection in the style, manner, arrangement, or nonessential parts of a legal document, as distinguished from a substantive defect. Cf. DEFECT OF SUBSTANCE.

defect of parties. (18c) A failure to include all indispensable parties in a lawsuit.

defect of reason. (16c) *Archaic.* **1.** Mental illness. **2.** Mental retardation.

defect of substance. (18c) An imperfection in the substantive part of a legal document, as by omitting an essential term. Cf. DEFECT OF FORM.

defectus (di-**fek**-təs), *n.* [fr. Latin *deficere* "to be deficient"] *Hist.* A defect; a deficiency.

defectus sanguinis (di-**fek**-təs **sang**-gwi-nis). [Latin "defect of blood".] *Hist.* A failure of issue, often resulting in an escheat. See ESCHEAT.

defence. See DEFENSE.

defend, *vb.* (14c) **1.** To do something to protect someone or something from attack. **2.** To use arguments to protect someone or something from criticism or to prove that something is right. **3.** To do something to stop something from being taken away or to make it possible for something to continue. **4.** To deny, contest, or oppose (an allegation or claim) <the corporation vigorously defended against the shareholder's lawsuit>. **5.** To represent (someone) as an attorney; to act as legal counsel for someone who has been sued or prosecuted <the accused retained a well-known lawyer to defend him>.

defendant (di-**fen**-dənt). (14c) A person sued in a civil proceeding or accused in a criminal proceeding. — Abbr. D. Cf. PLAINTIFF.

▸ **John Doe defendant.** (1917) An anonymous defendant labeled "John Doe" because the plaintiff does not, at the time of filing suit, know the person's name. • John Doe defendants are common in several situations, as in police-brutality lawsuits in which the plaintiff does not know the names of the officers allegedly at fault, or in some copyright-infringement lawsuits where defendants are identified only by Internet addresses. See JOHN DOE.

▸ **target defendant.** (1959) In a case with multiple defendants, the one whom the plaintiff considers the primary source for any recovery of damages. • Among several defendants, one is usu. the most blameworthy or has the most insurance or greatest assets, or both.

defendant in error. (18c) *Archaic.* In a case on appeal, the prevailing party in the court below. See APPELLEE; RESPONDENT (1).

defendant score. (1982) A number taken from an established scale, indicating the relative seriousness of the defendant's criminal history. Cf. CRIME SCORE.

defendant's gain. (1882) The amount of money or the value of property that a criminal defendant has obtained by committing a crime. • Some states, such as New York, consider the defendant's gain when assessing a criminal fine or ordering restitution.

defendemus (di-**fen**-də-məs). [fr. Latin *defendere*] We will defend. • This term was used in conveyancing to require the donor and the donor's heirs to defend the donee against any attempted encumbrance not specifically agreed to. Although *defendemus* was not a warranty, it became part of the warranty clause "shall and will warrant and forever defend."

defender. (15c) **1.** Someone who defends, such as the defendant in a lawsuit, a person using self-defense, or defense counsel. **2.** PUBLIC DEFENDER.

defendere (di-**fen**-də-ree), *vb.* [Law Latin] To deny; to defend.

defendere se per corpus suum (di-**fen**-də-ree see pər **kor**-pəs s[y]**oo**-əm), *vb.* [Law Latin "to defend himself by his own body"] *Hist.* To agree to a trial by judicial combat; to agree to a duel.

defendere unica manu (di-**fen**-də-ree **yoo**-nə-kə **man**-yoo), *n.* [Law Latin "to defend with one hand"] *Hist.* A denial of an accusation under oath.

Defender of the Faith. See DEFENSOR FIDEI.

defendour (day-fon-**duur**), *n.* [Law French] *Hist.* A defendant; the party accused in an appeal.

defeneration (dee-fen-ə-**ray**-shən), *n.* [fr. Latin *de* "of" + *foenero* "to lend on usury"] (17c) *Hist.* The act of lending money at a usurious interest rate.

defenestration (dee-fen-ə-**stray**-shən). (17c) The act of throwing someone or something out a window. — **defenestrate,** *vb.*

defense (di-**fen[t]s**). (16c) **1.** A defendant's stated reason why the plaintiff or prosecutor has no valid case; esp., a defendant's answer, denial, or plea <her defense was that she was 25 miles from the building at the time of the robbery>.

> "Defence is defined to be that which is alleged by a party proceeded against in an action or suit, as a reason why the plaintiff should not recover or establish that which he seeks by his complaint or petition." Edwin E. Bryant, *The Law of Pleading Under the Codes of Civil Procedure* 240 (2d ed. 1899).

▸ **actus reus defense.** (1978) A criminal defendant's argument that the physical act constituting a crime never occurred. See ACTUS REUS. Cf. *state-of-mind defense.*

▸ **affirmative defense.** (1837) A defendant's assertion of facts and arguments that, if true, will defeat the plaintiff's or prosecution's claim, even if all the allegations in the complaint are true. • The defendant bears the burden of proving an affirmative defense. Examples of affirmative defenses are duress (in a civil case) and insanity and self-defense (in a criminal case). — Also termed *plea in avoidance; plea in justification.* Cf. *negative defense;* CONFESSION AND AVOIDANCE.

▸ ***Atkins* defense.** (2004) A criminal defendant's assertion that his or her low IQ qualifies the defendant as mentally retarded and thus ineligible for the death penalty. • The term is derived from *Atkins v. Virginia,* 536 U.S 304 (2002), in which the Supreme Court held that executing mentally retarded persons is a violation of the Eighth Amendment ban of cruel and unusual punishment. — Also termed *low-IQ defense.*

▸ **bulk-supplier defense.** (1987) A products-liability defense sometimes available to a component manufacturer or raw-material supplier when injury has been caused by a finished product, unless the component itself was defective.

▸ **capacity defense.** (1967) A defense based on the defendant's inability to be held accountable for an illegal act or the plaintiff's inability to prosecute a lawsuit (as when the plaintiff was a corporation, but has lost its corporate charter). See CAPACITY (2), (3).

▸ **change-of-position defense.** (1959) In an unjust-enrichment lawsuit, a defendant's claim to have incurred extraordinary expenses or liabilities in reliance on apparently being entitled to the enrichment, the changed circumstances making it inequitable for the defendant to be required to disgorge gains or otherwise make restitution.

▸ **choice-of-evils defense.** See *lesser-evils defense.*

▸ **claim-of-right defense.** (1955) *Criminal procedure.* In a prosecution for larceny, embezzlement, or other theft, a defendant's claim to superior ownership or possession of the property taken, esp. as security for a debt owed to the defendant. • The defense is not recognized in all jurisdictions, and is never a defense to a charge of robbery. — Also termed *self-help defense.*

▸ **collateral defense** (kə-**lat**-ə-rəl). (1970) *Criminal law.* A defense of justification or excuse not involving a rebuttal of the allegation and therefore collateral to the elements that the prosecutor must prove. See EXCUSE (2); JUSTIFICATION (2).

▸ **compensated-surety defense.** *Insurance.* A defense that may preclude a compensated surety or insurer from recovering against a third party who would be liable to the insured, unless the surety or insurer can show superior equities to the third party. See DOCTRINE OF SUPERIOR EQUITIES (2).

▸ **criminal defense.** See CRIMINAL DEFENSE.

▸ **cultural defense.** (1986) **1.** A criminal defendant's assertion that because an admitted act is not a crime in the perpetrator's culture or native land, it should not be judged by the laws of the place where it was committed. • This cultural defense is asserted as an affirmative defense to a criminal charge. **2.** The defense that the actor's mental state at the time the alleged crime was committed was heavily influenced by cultural factors. • This is not a complete defense but a mitigating one, pleaded to reduce the charges, the sentence, or both. See FEMALE GENITAL MUTILATION.

▸ **defense of habitation.** (1871) The defense that conduct constituting a criminal offense is justified if an aggressor unjustifiably threatens the defendant's place of abode or premises and the defendant engages in conduct that is (1) harmful to the aggressor, (2) sufficient to protect that place of abode or premises, and (3) reasonable in relation to the harm threatened. — Also termed *defense of premises.* See CASTLE DOCTRINE.

▸ **defense of honest mistake.** (1897) The affirmative defense that the accused person's misrepresentation was unintentional and made in good faith.

▸ **defense of honesty.** See *honesty defense.*

▸ **defense of illegality.** A defendant's affirmative defense that a contract is prohibited by law or that a contract is unenforceable because of some failure to comply with the law.

▸ **defense of inequitable conduct.** (1961) *Patents.* A defense to an action for patent infringement, made by charging the plaintiff with breaching the duty of candor and good faith. • To succeed, the defendant must show that, in the patent prosecution, the plaintiff intentionally withheld material information from or misled the examiner. Inequitable conduct is a combination of two former defenses: unclean hands and fraud on the Patent Office.

▸ **defense of innocent dissemination.** (1967) A defense to defamation on the basis that the accused person did not know the statement was defamatory and that this lack of knowledge was not due to negligence. — Often shortened to *innocent dissemination.*

▸ **defense of premises.** See *defense of habitation.*

▸ **derivative defense.** (1972) A defense that rebuts the criminal elements that a prosecutor must establish to justify the submission of a criminal case to a jury.

▸ **designer defense.** (1998) A novel defense based on diminished capacity attributed to stress or impairment. • The phrase derives from the fact that the defense is tailored to the defendant and the circumstances of the crime. Examples include extraordinary reactions to snack food (the Twinkie defense), unconsciousness or sleepwalking, and postpartum psychosis. See AUTOMATISM.

▸ **dilatory defense** (**dil**-ə-tor-ee). (1845) A defense that temporarily obstructs or delays a lawsuit but does not address the merits. • Examples of dilatory defenses include misjoinder, nonjoinder, res judicata, misnomer, lack of capacity to sue, another action pending, statute of limitations, prematurity, unripeness, release, and settlement.

▸ **dwelling defense.** See CASTLE DOCTRINE.

▸ **eleemosynary defense.** See *charitable immunity* under IMMUNITY (2).

▸ **emergency defense.** See NECESSITY (4).

▸ **empty-suit defense.** (2002) A defense in which a high-ranking officer or director in an organization claims ignorance of any wrongdoing by subordinates.

▸ **entrapment-by-estoppel defense.** See *public-authority defense.*

▸ **equitable defense.** (18c) A defense formerly available only in a court of equity but now maintainable in a court of law. • Examples include mistake, fraud, illegality, failure of consideration, forum non conveniens, laches, estoppel, and unclean hands.

▸ **exculpatory defense.** (1848) *Criminal law.* A defense that, if believed, would exonerate a defendant (in a trial) or potential defendant (before a grand jury) of all criminal liability.

▸ **frivolous defense.** (18c) A defense that has no basis in fact or law.

▸ **full defense.** A technical common-law defensive plea, stated at length and without abbreviation. • This plea is obsolete because of the pleading requirements in federal and state rules of civil procedure.

▸ **gay-panic defense.** (1989) A heterosexual defendant's claim that he or she panicked and killed a homosexual victim because the victim made an unwanted sexual advance on the defendant. — Also termed *homosexual-panic defense; homosexual-advance defense.*

▸ **general defense.** See GENERAL DEFENSE (1).

▸ **general-justification defense.** See *lesser-evils defense.*

▸ **homosexual-advance defense.** See *gay-panic defense.*

▸ **homosexual-panic defense.** See *gay-panic defense.*

▸ **honesty defense.** (1989) *Rare.* An assertion that the defendant acted honestly and in good faith. • This defense, almost unique to civil suits, is rarely raised. For example, a defendant may assert honesty as a defense to a charge of fraudulent misrepresentation. — Also termed *defense of honesty.* Cf. CLAIM OF RIGHT (1).

▸ **hypothetical-person defense.** See HYPOTHETICAL-PERSON DEFENSE.

▸ **imperfect defense.** (1835) A defense that fails to meet all legal requirements and usu. results only in a reduction in grade or sentence rather than an acquittal, as when a defendant is charged with manslaughter rather than murder because the defendant, while defending another, used unreasonable force to repel the attack. See *imperfect self-defense* under SELF-DEFENSE (1). Cf. *perfect defense.*

▸ **inconsistent defense.** (1852) A defense so contrary to another defense that the acceptance of one requires abandonment of the other. • A person accused of murder, for example, cannot claim both self-defense and the alibi of having been in a different city when the murder took place.

▸ **innocent-owner defense.** (1983) In forfeiture action, an affirmative defense in which the owner of property (such as real estate or money) asserts that another person committed the wrongful act or omission while using the property without the owner's knowledge or consent. *See* 18 USCA § 983(d). See *civil forfeiture* under FORFEITURE.

▸ **insanity defense.** See INSANITY DEFENSE.

▸ **intoxication defense.** (1966) *Criminal law.* A criminal defendant's claim that inebriation or drug use prevented the defendant from having the mental state (mens rea) necessary to prove culpability. See "BESOTTED" TEST.

▸ **issuable defense.** (1847) *Common-law pleading.* A plea on the merits setting forth a legal defense. Cf. *issuable plea* under PLEA (3).

▸ **justification defense.** See JUSTIFICATION DEFENSE.

▸ **legal defense.** (17c) A complete and adequate defense in a court of law.

▸ **lesser-evils defense.** (1982) The defense that, while the defendant may have caused the harm or evil that would ordinarily constitute a criminal offense, in the present case the defendant has not caused a net harm or evil because of justifying circumstances and therefore should be exculpated. — Also termed *choice-of-evils defense; necessity; general-justification defense.* See NECESSITY (4).

▸ **low-IQ defense.** See *Atkins defense.*

▸ **mens rea defense.** See *state-of-mind defense.*

▸ **meritorious defense** (mer-ə-**tor**-ee-əs). (18c) **1.** A defense that addresses the substance or essentials of a case rather than dilatory or technical objections. **2.** A defense that appears likely to succeed or has already succeeded.

▸ **mistake-of-fact defense.** See MISTAKE-OF-FACT DEFENSE.

▸ **mitigating defense.** (1864) *Criminal law.* A criminal defendant's claim that, if true, reduces the severity of the offense without eliminating criminal liability altogether.

▸ **necessity defense.** See JUSTIFICATION (2); *lesser-evils defense.*

▸ **negative defense.** (1877) A defendant's outright denial of the plaintiff's allegations without additional facts pleaded by way of avoidance. See GENERAL DEFENSE (1). Cf. *affirmative defense.*

▸ **neutral-reportage defense.** See NEUTRAL-REPORTAGE PRIVILEGE.

▸ **new-value defense.** (1986) *Bankruptcy.* A defense to a suit to recover preferential payments whereby the transferee of the payments can reduce liability by the amount of consideration or value that the transferee provided to the transferor after a suspect transfer.

▸ **ostrich defense.** (1985) A criminal defendant's claim not to have known of the criminal activities of an associate. Cf. WHITE-HEART-EMPTY-HEAD RULE.

▸ **outrageous-conduct defense.** (1977) *Criminal law.* A defense based on egregious government conduct that created the crimes at issue.

▸ **partial defense.** (1818) A defense going either to part of the action or toward mitigation of damages.

▸ **pass-on defense.** (1962) An antitrust defense that a member of the distributive chain who was overcharged or undercharged passed on the price adjustment to reflect the charge and thereby suffered no damage. — Also termed *passing on.*

▸ **peremptory defense** (pər-**emp**-tər-ee). (1860) A defense that questions the plaintiff's legal right to sue or contends that the right to sue has been extinguished.

▸ **perfect defense.** (1817) A defense that meets all legal requirements and results in the defendant's acquittal. See *perfect self-defense* under SELF-DEFENSE (1). Cf. *imperfect defense.*

▸ **pretermitted defense** (pree-tər-**mit**-id). (1947) A defense available to a party that must be pleaded at the right time or be waived.

▸ **public-authority defense.** (1976) *Criminal law.* A criminal defendant's position that a government official, such as a police officer, led him or her to believe, reasonably, that the conduct charged as illegal was authorized. — Also termed *entrapment-by-estoppel defense.*

▸ **self-help defense.** See *claim-of-right defense.*

▸ **sham defense.** (1853) A fictitious, untrue defense, made in bad faith.

▸ **sleepwalking defense.** See AUTOMATISM.

▸ **SODDI.** See SODDI DEFENSE.

▸ **state-of-mind defense.** (1959) A criminal defendant's argument that mens rea was lacking when an offense was allegedly committed. • The insanity defense is a type of state-of-mind defense. — Also termed *mens rea defense.* See MENS REA. Cf. *actus reus defense.*

▸ **true defense.** A defense admitting that a defendant committed the charged offense, but seeking to avoid punishment based on a legal excuse (such as insanity) or justification (such as self-defense).

▸ **unconsciousness defense.** See AUTOMATISM.

▸ **XYY-chromosome defense.** See XYY-CHROMOSOME DEFENSE.

2. A defendant's method and strategy in opposing the plaintiff or the prosecution; a doctrine giving rise to such a method or strategy <the lawyer advised her client to adopt a passive defense and to avoid taking the witness stand>.

▸ **empty-chair defense.** (1981) A trial tactic in a multiparty case whereby one defendant attempts to put all the fault on a defendant who plea-bargained or settled before trial or on a person who was neither charged nor named as a party.

▸ **malicious defense.** (1911) *Torts.* A defendant's use of unfair, harassing, or illegal tactics to advance a frivolous or unmeritorious defense. • The elements of the tort are (1) the defendant's initiation, continuation, or procurement of proceedings; (2) knowledge that the defense lacks merit; (3) the assertion of the defense for a purpose other than to properly adjudicate the claim, such as to harass, annoy, or injure, or to cause unnecessary delay or needless increase in the cost of litigation; (4) termination of the suit in the plaintiff's favor; and (5) harm to the plaintiff resulting from the proceeding. Damages are the same as in an action for malicious prosecution. A minority of states recognize the tort. Cf. MALICIOUS PROSECUTION.

▸ **Stalingrad defense.** (1986) The strategy of wearing down the plaintiff by tenaciously fighting by whatever means anything the plaintiff presents and appealing every ruling favorable to the plaintiff, rather than presenting a meritorious case. • The tactic is named for the Russian city besieged by the Germans in World War II. The defenders refused to surrender and used every available tactic and tool to hold the attackers at bay until winter cut the enemy's supply lines, leaving the attackers with inadequate resources with which to continue the siege.

3. One or more defendants in a trial, as well as their counsel <the defense rests>. **4.** *Commercial law.* A basis for avoiding liability on a negotiable instrument <the drawer asserted a real defense against the holder in due course>.

▸ **absolute defense.** See *real defense.*

▸ **limited defense.** See *personal defense.*

▸ **personal defense.** (1950) An ordinary defense in a contract action — such as failure of consideration or nonperformance of a condition — that the maker or drawer of a negotiable instrument is precluded from raising against a person who has the rights of a holder in due course. *See* UCC § 3-305(b). • A personal defense can be asserted only against a transferee who is not a holder in due course. — Also termed *limited defense.*

▸ **real defense.** A type of defense that is good against any possible claimant, so that the maker or drawer of a negotiable instrument can raise it even against a holder in due course. • The ten real defenses are (1) fraud in the factum, (2) forgery of a necessary signature, (3) adjudicated insanity that, under state law, renders the contract void from its inception, (4) material alteration of the instrument, (5) infancy, which renders the contract voidable under state law, (6) illegality that renders the underlying contract void, (7) duress, (8) discharge in bankruptcy, or any discharge known to the holder in due course, (9) a suretyship defense (for example, if the holder knew that one indorser was signing as a surety or accommodation party), and (10) a statute of limitations (generally three years after dishonor or acceptance on a draft and six years after demand or other due date on a note). — Also termed *absolute defense; universal defense.*

▸ **universal defense.** See *real defense.*

5. Measures taken by a country or individual to protect against an attack. See SELF-DEFENSE (2); NATIONAL DEFENSE (1).

▸ **self-defense.** See SELF-DEFENSE.

6. A country's military establishment. See NATIONAL DEFENSE (2). — Also spelled in all senses (esp. BrE) *defence.* **7.** TAKEOVER DEFENSE.

Defense Advanced Research Projects Agency. An agency in the U.S. Department of Defense responsible for military research and development. • The Agency was founded in 1958 as a response to the Soviet Union's launch of Sputnik and has since played a prominent role in the development of many advanced technologies, including networked computers. — Abbr. DARPA.

defense attorney. (1827) A lawyer who represents a defendant in a civil or criminal case. — Also termed *defense counsel; defense lawyer.*

defense au fond en droit (di-**fen[t]s** oh **foh*n*** *on* **drwah**). *Civil law.* A demurrer.

Defense Commissary Agency. An agency in the U.S. Department of Defense responsible for providing goods and services to members of the armed forces at reduced prices. • The Agency was founded in 1990 as the first post-Cold War consolidation of service agencies. — Abbr. DeCA.

defense contingent fee. See *reverse contingent fee* under CONTINGENT FEE.

Defense Contract Audit Agency. An agency in the U.S. Department of Defense responsible for conducting contract audits and for providing accounting and financial advice to all Department components responsible for procurement and contract administration. • The Agency was formed in 1965 as a culmination of 20 years of effort to coordinate and set uniform standards for military-contract auditing. — Abbr. DCAA.

Defense Contract Management Agency. A unit in the U.S. Department of Defense responsible for managing contracts to ensure that supplies and services are delivered on time and within cost and that they meet performance requirements. • The Agency was established as the Defense Contract Management Command within the Defense Logistics Agency in 1990. It was given independent existence as an agency and renamed in 2000. — Abbr. DCMA.

defense counsel. See DEFENSE ATTORNEY.

Defense Department. An executive department of the federal government, responsible for coordinating and overseeing military affairs and the agencies responsible for national security. • The Department was established as the National Military Establishment in 1947, by combining the War and the Navy Departments. Its name was changed to Department of Defense in 1949. The Department's components include the Army, the Air Force, the Navy, the Marine Corps, and the Joint Chiefs of Staff. It is headed by the Secretary of Defense, who is answerable to the President as Commander-in-Chief. — Also termed *Department of Defense* (DOD).

Defense Finance and Accounting Service. A unit in the U.S. Department of Defense responsible for providing professional finance and accounting services and for overseeing the Department's day-to-day finance and accounting activities. • The Service was formed in 1991 as a result of post-Cold War consolidation efforts. — Abbr. DFAS.

Defense Information Systems Agency. An agency in the U.S. Department of Defense responsible for developing and operating information systems to provide combat support for the armed forces. • The Agency is the 1991 successor to the Defense Communications Agency, which was formed in 1960 in a consolidation of separate service functions. — Abbr. DISA.

Defense Intelligence Agency. A combat-support unit in the U.S. Department of Defense responsible for developing and managing foreign military intelligence in support of military planning and operations and of weapons-systems acquisition. • The Agency was established in 1961 in a consolidation of separate service intelligence agencies. — Abbr. DIA.

Defense Investigative Services. See DEFENSE SECURITY SERVICE.

defense lawyer. See DEFENSE ATTORNEY.

Defense Legal Services Agency. An agency in the U.S. Department of Defense responsible for providing legal services to all agencies in the Department. • The General Counsel of the Department directs its operations. — Abbr. DLSA.

Defense Logistics Agency. A unit in the U.S. Department of Defense responsible for providing worldwide logistics support for military missions both in peace and in war. • Established in 1961 as the Defense Supply Agency, it was renamed in 1977 and reorganized in succeeding years. The Agency also supports nonmilitary agencies overseas. — Abbr. DLA.

defense-month. See FENCE-MONTH.

Defense Nuclear Facilities Safety Board. An independent federal board that sets standards for the design, construction, operation, and decommissioning of defense nuclear facilities of the U.S. Department of Energy. • It was established in 1988. 42 USCA §§ 2286–2286i.

defense of habitation. See DEFENSE (1).

defense of honest mistake. See DEFENSE (1).

defense of honesty. See *honesty defense* under DEFENSE (1).

defense of illegality. See DEFENSE (1).

defense of inequitable conduct. See DEFENSE (1).

defense of innocent dissemination. See DEFENSE (1).

Defense of Marriage Act. A federal statute that (1) provides that no state can be required to recognize or give effect to same-sex marriages, (2) defines the term "marriage" for purposes of federal law as the union of a man and a woman as husband and wife, and (3) defines "spouse" for purposes of federal law as being only a person of the opposite sex. 1 USCA § 7; 28 USCA 1738C. • The Defense of Marriage Act was enacted in response to the fear that if one state sanctioned same-sex marriages, other states might then have to give full faith and credit to those marriages. Key parts of the statute were invalidated in *U.S. v. Windsor*, 133 S.Ct. 2675 (2013). — Abbr. DOMA.

defense of others. (1942) A justification defense available if one harms or threatens another when defending a third person. See JUSTIFICATION (2).

defense of premises. See *defense of habitation* under DEFENSE (1).

defense of property. (1918) A justification defense available if one harms or threatens another when defending one's property. See JUSTIFICATION (2).

defense of self. See SELF-DEFENSE (1).

Defense of the Realm Act. *Hist. English law.* A 1914 statute, dating from the outset of the hostilities in World War I, that suspended Magna Carta and gave England's homeland-security officials the authority to detain without charges both aliens and citizens considered subversives or pro-Axis sympathizers. — Abbr. DORA.

Defense Security Cooperation Agency. A unit in the U.S. Department of Defense responsible for fostering and overseeing security-cooperation arrangements and for promoting security relationships with U.S. friends and allies. — Abbr. DSCA.

Defense Security Service. A unit in the U.S. Department of Defense responsible for conducting personnel investigations and providing industrial-security products and services to the Department and other agencies. • Established in 1972, the agency was formerly known as the Defense Investigative Service. — Abbr. DSS.

Defense Threat Reduction Agency. A unit in the U.S. Department of Defense responsible for reducing the risk of and defending against attacks that involve nuclear, chemical, biological, or other weapons of mass destruction. • The Agency was created in 1998. — Abbr. DTRA.

defensiva (dee-fen-**sɪ**-və), *n.* [Latin "a protector"] *Hist.* A warden of the Marches, being one of many lords appointed by the Crown to defend England's borders.

defensive allegation. See ALLEGATION.

defensive collateral estoppel. See COLLATERAL ESTOPPEL.

defensive democracy. See *militant democracy* under DEMOCRACY.

defensive disclosure. (1983) *Patents.* The deliberate publication of details about an invention in order to render it prior art and preclude others from getting a patent on the same invention. • This action can be taken formally, by filing for public disclosure through the Statutory Invention Registration and publishing the abstract in the Official Gazette of the U.S. Patent and Trademark Office, or privately, by publishing it in an independent journal that will probably be consulted by a patent examiner. — Also termed *defensive publication.* See STATUTORY INVENTION REGISTRATION.

defensive-force justification. See JUSTIFICATION (2).

defensive lockout. See LOCKOUT (1).

defensive-posture memorandum. See DEFENSIVE PROFILE.

defensive profile. (2002) The set of strategies devised by a company to discourage others from attempting a hostile takeover.

defensive-profile memorandum. *Corporations.* An outline of a company's strategy against a hostile takeover. — Also termed *defensive-posture memorandum.*

defensive publication. See DEFENSIVE DISCLOSURE.

defensive treaty. See TREATY (1).

defensor (di-**fen**-sər *or* -sor), *n.* [fr. Latin *defendere* "to forbid"] (14c) **1.** *Roman law.* A defender of another's interests in court; an advocate, esp. for a corporation. Cf. PROCURATOR LITIS. **2.** *Roman law.* DEFENSOR CIVITATIS. **3.** *Hist. Eccles. law.* An advocate or patron of a church; a church warden. **4.** *Hist.* A guardian; a protector; a defender.

defensor civitatis (di-**fen**-sər siv-i-**tay**-tis). [Latin "defender of the city"] (17c) *Roman law.* An officer conducting public business, including protecting people, esp. the poor, from legal injustices, adjudicating certain minor offenses and pecuniary matters, and acting as a notary in the execution of a will or other transfer. — Often shortened to *defensor.*

defensor fidei (di-**fen**-sər **fɪ**-dee-ɪ), *n.* [Latin "defender of the faith"] (16c) *Hist.* A unique title of the sovereign of England, first granted in 1521 by Pope Leo X to Henry VIII for writing against Martin Luther. • The Pope later withdrew the title because of Henry's harsh regulation of the church, but the title was again bestowed on the King by Parliament in 1544. The term is similar to the application of "Catholic" to the Spanish sovereign and "Most Christian" to the French sovereign. — Also termed *Defender of the Faith.*

defensum (di-**fen**-səm), *n.* [Law Latin "an inclosure"] *Hist.* **1.** A portion of an open field allotted for corn or hay but not for feeding. **2.** A wood partially enclosed to prevent the cattle from damaging the undergrowth. **3.** A prohibition.

defer, *vb.* (17c) **1.** To postpone; to delay until a later date <to defer taxes to another year>. **2.** To show deference to (another); to yield to the opinion of <because it was a political question, the courts deferred to the legislature>.

deference. (17c) **1.** Conduct showing respect for somebody or something; courteous or complaisant regard for another. **2.** A polite and respectful attitude or approach, esp. toward an important person or venerable institution whose action, proposal, opinion, or judgment should be presumptively accepted. — **deferential,** *adj.*

deferential review. See REVIEW.

deferment, *n.* (17c) **1.** The act of delaying; postponement <deferment of a judicial decision>. **2.** *Military law.* A delay in serving in the military. **3.** *Military law.* A delay in serving confinement that results from a court-martial until the sentence has been approved and its execution has been ordered. • The convening authority may grant a deferment. — **defer,** *vb.*

deferral of taxes. (1955) The postponement of paying a tax from one year to another, as by contributing money to a traditional IRA, for which earnings and contributions will be taxed only when the money is withdrawn.

deferral state. (1977) Under the Age Discrimination in Employment Act (ADEA), a state that has its own anti-discrimination legislation and enforcement mechanism, so that the time to file a federal lawsuit under the ADEA is postponed until state remedies have been exhausted.

deferred adjudication. 1. See *deferred judgment* under JUDGMENT (2). **2.** See DEFERRED PROSECUTION (1).

deferred-adjudication probation. See *deferred judgment* under JUDGMENT (2).

deferred annuity. See ANNUITY.

deferred charge. (1917) An expense not currently recognized on an income statement but carried forward on the balance sheet as an asset to be written off in the future <insurance premiums are a deferred charge>.

deferred claim. (1900) A claim postponed to a future accounting period.

deferred compensation. See COMPENSATION.

deferred credit. (1891) A credit (such as a premium on an issued bond) that is required to be spread over later accounting periods.

deferred-deposit loan. See *payday loan* under LOAN.

deferred dividend. See DIVIDEND.

deferred-dividend policy. See INSURANCE POLICY.

deferred expense. See EXPENSE.

deferred income. See INCOME.

deferred-interest bond. See BOND (3).

deferred judgment. See JUDGMENT (2).

deferred lien. See LIEN.

deferred pay. See PAY (1).

deferred payment. (1831) A principal-and-interest payment that is postponed; an installment payment.

deferred-payment annuity. See *deferred annuity* under ANNUITY.

deferred prosecution. (1946) **1.** An agreement between the prosecution and a defendant to either drop or delay prosecution in exchange for some type of cooperation. — Also termed *pretrial intervention; deferred adjudication.* **2.** See *deferred judgment* under JUDGMENT (2).

deferred revenue. See *prepaid income* under INCOME.

deferred sentence. See SENTENCE.

deferred stock. See STOCK.

defiance (di-fɪ-ənts). (13c) **1.** A challenge to meet in combat or contest; hence, a call on someone to prove an allegation. **2.** Behavior demonstrating that one refuses to do what someone else tells one to do, esp. because of a lack of respect; contemptuous opposition or disregard openly expressed in words or actions. — **defiant,** *adj.*

deficiency, *n.* (17c) **1.** A lack, shortage, or insufficiency of something that is necessary. **2.** A shortfall in paying taxes; the amount by which the tax properly due exceeds the sum of the amount of tax shown on a taxpayer's return. — Also termed *tax deficiency; income-tax deficiency; deficiency in tax.* **3.** The amount still owed when the property secured by a mortgage is sold at a foreclosure sale for less than the outstanding debt; esp., the shortfall between the proceeds from a foreclosure sale and an amount consisting of the principal debt plus interest plus the foreclosure costs. See *deficiency judgment* under JUDGMENT (2). **4.** The amount still owed after the collateral securing an obligation is disposed of after default for less than the outstanding debt. UCC § 9-615(d)(2).

deficiency assessment. See ASSESSMENT (2).

deficiency bill. See BILL (3).

deficiency decree. See *deficiency judgment* under JUDGMENT (2).

deficiency dividend. See DIVIDEND.

deficiency in tax. See DEFICIENCY (2).

deficiency judgment. See JUDGMENT (2).

deficiency letter. (1924) **1.** An IRS letter to a taxpayer detailing the ways in which a tax return seems to be deficient. See NINETY-DAY LETTER; THIRTY-DAY LETTER. **2.** An SEC letter to a registrant of a securities offering, detailing the ways in which the registration statement seems not to conform to federal disclosure requirements. — Also termed *letter of comment; letter of comments.*

deficiency notice. See NINETY-DAY LETTER.

deficiency suit. (1927) An action to recover the difference between a mortgage debt and the amount realized on foreclosure. See *deficiency judgment* under JUDGMENT (2).

deficient, *adj.* (16c) **1.** Not having or containing enough of something; lacking an adequate or proper supply or amount <a statement of facts deficient in important details>. **2.** Not good enough; unacceptable in quality <deficient social services>.

deficit. (18c) **1.** The difference between the amount of something that one needs and the lower amount that one actually has; a deficiency in the amount or quality of something.

▸ **trade deficit.** (1887) In economics, the excess of merchandise imports over merchandise exports during a specific period. — Also termed *trade gap.* Cf. *trade surplus* under SURPLUS.

2. An excess of expenditures or liabilities over revenues or assets.

deficit spending. (1938) The practice of making expenditures in excess of income, usu. from borrowed funds rather than actual revenues or surplus.

de fide instrumentorum (dee fɪ-dee in-strə-men-**tor**-əm). [Latin] (17c) *Roman & Scots law.* On the reliance to be placed on written documents. • The phrase appeared in reference to actions of rescission based on forgery.

de fideli administratione officii (dee fi-**dee**-lı ad-min-ə-stray-shee-**oh**-nee ə-**fish**-ee-ı). [Law Latin "of faithful administration of office"] *Scots law.* An oath to faithfully execute the duties of one's public office or duty. — Often shortened to *de fideli administratione.*

defile (di-**fıl**), *vb.* (14c) **1.** To make dirty; to physically soil. **2.** To make less pure and good, esp. by showing disrespect; to dishonor. **3.** To make ceremonially unclean; to desecrate. **4.** To morally corrupt (someone). **5.** *Archaic.* To debauch (a person); to deprive (a person) of chastity.

defilement (di-**fıl**-mənt), *n.* (16c) **1.** An act of defiling. **2.** A condition of being defiled.

define, *vb.* (14c) **1.** To state or explain explicitly. **2.** To fix or establish (boundaries or limits). **3.** To set forth the meaning of (a word or phrase).

defined-benefit pension plan. See PENSION PLAN.

defined-benefit plan. See EMPLOYEE BENEFIT PLAN.

defined-contribution pension plan. See *defined-contribution plan* under EMPLOYEE BENEFIT PLAN.

defined-contribution plan. See EMPLOYEE BENEFIT PLAN.

defined pension plan. See PENSION PLAN.

defined term. In legal drafting, a word or phrase given a specific meaning for purposes of the document in which it appears; a definiendum. See INTERPRETIVE-DIRECTION CANON.

de fine force (dee **fı**-nee fors). [Law French] Of pure necessity.

de fine non capiendo pro pulchre placitando (dee **fı**-nee non kap-ee-**en**-doh proh **pəl**-kree plas-ə-**tan**-doh), *n.* [Law Latin "of not taking a fine for amending a bad pleading"] (18c) *Hist.* A writ prohibiting the imposition of a fine for bad pleading. See BEAUPLEADER.

de fine pro redisseisina capiendo (dee **fı**-nee proh ree-dis-**see**-zin-ə kap-ee-**en**-doh), *n.* [Law Latin "of a fine paid for one imprisoned for redisseisin"] *Hist.* A writ releasing a person who paid a reasonable fine after being imprisoned for a redisseisin.

de finibus levatis (dee **fı**-nə-bəs lə-**vay**-tis), *n.* [Law Latin "concerning fines levied"] *Hist.* The statute requiring any levied fines to be read solemnly in open court. 27 Edw. 1.

definite failure of issue. See FAILURE OF ISSUE.

definite sentence. See SENTENCE.

definitio (def-ə-**nish**-ee-oh), *n.* [fr. Latin *definire* "definition"] *Civil law.* **1.** A definition; an explanation of something. **2.** The establishment of a general rule. **3.** A boundary. Pl. ***definitiones.***

definition. (14c) The meaning of a term as explicitly stated in a drafted document such as a contract, a corporate bylaw, an ordinance, or a statute; a definiens.

> "*Definitions of Words and of Things.* In principle, to define is to give the meaning of words, that is to establish a relationship between a thing and a sign. Thus the aim of every definition is to enable specified objects to be recognized by means of a word; consequently this definition becomes at the same time that of a word and that of a thing. The proposed distinction might to better advantage be termed subjective and objective definition. As there exists between a word and a thing or an idea no necessary relation, every one has logically the right to create for himself a terminology according to his own fancy, to call 'red' what others call 'green,' 'good' what is 'evil,' to apply the word 'marriage' to a definition of the testament, etc. It is very seldom, no doubt, that any one thus abuses himself without a motive in upsetting the meaning of words fixed by usage. But usage never gives to words a meaning which is strictly accurate. When there is need of precision in expression, everyone uses more or less this faculty of defining. The most ordinary words of everyday language never have so definite a meaning but they may be understood differently by different persons. Book, table, chair, door, etc., may not express exactly the same thing for everybody. In the domain of abstraction, the unlimited right of everyone to choose his language is absolutely indispensable to the development of thought. Each new conception demands a new definition. One may use old verses for new subjects, but old definitions answer no purpose as regards new ideas. And even without any spirit of innovation whatever, abstract ideas especially in the domain of the moral sciences are so fluctuating that whoever wishes to use them must put forth personal effort to restrict their meaning." 13 Pierre de Tourtoulon, *Philosophy in the Development of Law* § 1, at 329–30 (Martha McC. Read trans., 1922).

▸ **lexical definition.** (1875) A dictionary-style definition of a word, purporting to give the full meaning of a term.

▸ **stipulative definition.** (1989) A definition that, for purposes of the document in which it appears, arbitrarily clarifies a term with uncertain boundaries or that includes or excludes specified items from the ambit of the term.

definitive judgment. See *final judgment* under JUDGMENT (2).

definitive partition. See PARTITION (2).

definitive sentence. See *determinate sentence* under SENTENCE.

deflation, *n.* (1920) A general decline in the price of goods and services; esp., a reduction in the amount of money in a country's economy, so that prices fall or stop rising. Cf. INFLATION; DISINFLATION. — **deflate,** *vb.* — **deflationary,** *adj.*

deforce, *vb.* (15c) **1.** To keep (lands) from the true owner by means of force. **2.** To oust another from possession by means of force. **3.** To detain (a creditor's money) unjustly and forcibly. — **deforciant,** *n.*

> "The character of the action of debt is well illustrated by the form of the writ as given by Glanville. It directs the sheriff to order the debtor to render a stated sum which he owes to the plaintiff, 'and whereof the plaintiff complains that the defendant unjustly deforces him,' and, if he will not obey, he is to be summoned before the King's Court. The plaintiff is 'deforced' of money just as in a writ of right he is 'deforced' of land. It is true that the term 'deforces' disappeared from the writ shortly after Glanville's time, the word *debet* taking its place; but this seems to have been a matter of form, not of substance. The plaintiff sought to recover the money due as his property." William F. Walsh, *Outlines of the History of English and American Law* 411 (1924).

deforcement. (17c) **1.** An act of keeping lands from the true owner by force. **2.** An act of ousting another from possession by means of force. **3.** An act of detaining a creditor's money unjustly and forcibly.

deforciant (di-**for**-shənt), *n.* [fr. Law Latin *deforcians* "a deforcer"] (16c) **1.** Someone who prevents another from taking possession of property. **2.** The defendant in an action of fine. See FINE (1).

deforciare (di-for-shee-**air**-ee), *vb.* [fr. Law Latin *defortiare* "to deforce"] *Hist.* To withhold property (such as land and tenements) from the true owner. See DEFORCE (1), (2).

deforciatio (di-for-shee-**ay**-shee-oh), *n.* [Law Latin "a distress"] *Hist.* A seizure of goods to satisfy a debt.

de forisfactura maritagii (dee for-is-fak-**tyoor**-ə mar-ə-**tay**-jee-ɪ), *n.* [Law Latin "of forfeiture of marriage"] *Hist.* A writ forfeiting a marriage.

defossion (di-**fosh**-in), *n.* [fr. Latin *de* "down" + *fodere* "dig"] (18c) The punishment of being buried alive.

de frangentibus prisonam (dee fran-**jen**-ti-bəs **priz**-ə-nəm), *n.* [Latin "of those who break prison"] *Hist.* The statute providing that an escaped prisoner will not be put to death or forfeit a limb simply for escaping from prison unless the original crime required that penalty upon conviction. 1 Edw. 2.

defraud, *vb.* (14c) To cause injury or loss to (a person or organization) by deceit; to trick (a person or organization) in order to get money. See FRAUD.

defraudation (dee-fraw-**day**-shən). (16c) The perpetration of a fraud; the act of committing fraud.

defrauder. See FRAUDFEASOR.

defray, *vb.* (16c) To reduce (expenses that someone else has incurred) by contributing money; esp., to bear the expense of.

defrock, *vb.* (16c) To officially remove from the priesthood by reason of wrongdoing or misconduct.

defunct, *adj.* (16c) Not existing or useful anymore; extinct; dissolved; terminated <defunct corporation>.

defunct company. See company.

defunct marriage. See MARRIAGE (1).

defunctus (di-**fəngk**-təs), *adj.* [Latin] Dead, as in *defunctus sine prole* ("dead without (leaving) issue").

defund, *vb.* (1948) To withdraw all monetary support from; to take away all funding for.

de furto (dee **fər**-toh), *n.* [Latin "of theft"] *Hist. English law.* In England, a type of criminal appeal.

de futuro (dee fyuu-**t[y]uur**-oh). [Latin] *Hist.* Regarding the future; at a future time. • The phrase usu. appeared in reference to a marriage promise, which was not binding if it mentioned marriage at a future date. Cf. DE PRAESENTI.

degaster (day-gas-**tay**), *vb.* [fr. Old French *dégaster* "to spoil"] To waste.

de gestu et fama (dee **jes**-ty[y]oo et **fay**-mə), *n.* [Law Latin "of behavior and reputation"] (16c) *Hist.* A writ available to a person whose character and reputation had been impeached.

degradation (deg-rə-**day**-shən). (16c) **1.** A reduction in rank, degree, or dignity; specif., censure of a clergy member by divestiture of holy orders, either by word or by a solemn divestiture of robes and other insignia. Cf. DEPOSITION (4); DEPRIVATION (4). **2.** A moral or intellectual decadence or degeneration; a lessening of a person's or thing's character or quality <degradation of resources>. **3.** A wearing down of something, as by erosion.

de gratia (dee **gray**-shee-ə). [Latin] Of favor; by grace, as in *de speciali gratia* ("of special grace or favor").

degree. (13c) **1.** Generally, a classification or specification <degrees of proof>. **2.** An incremental measure of guilt or negligence; a level based on the seriousness of an offense <murder in the first degree>. Cf. DEGREE OF CRIME; GRADE; *graded offense* under OFFENSE (2). **3.** A stage in a process; a step in a series of steps toward an end <the statute went through several degrees of development>. **4.** A stage in intensity <a high degree of legal skill is required>. **5.** The qualification awarded to a student who has successfully completed a full course of study in a college or university <law degree>. — Also termed *academic degree.* Cf. DIPLOMA (3). **6.** In the line of descent, a measure of removal determining the proximity of a blood or marital relationship <the council member did not participate in the vote because he was related to one of the bidders within the first degree of consanguinity>. • In the civil law, and in the degree-of-relationship system used by many American jurisdictions, an intestate estate passes to the closest of kin, counting degrees of kinship. To calculate the degree of relationship of the decedent to the claimant, one counts the steps (one for each generation) up from the decedent to the nearest common ancestor of the decedent and the claimant, and on down to the claimant from the common ancestor. The total number of steps is the degree of relationship. For example, a decedent's cousin stands in the fourth degree of relationship. Degrees of relationship are used not only to determine who is the closest heir but also to establish the incest prohibition in marriage requirements. — Also termed *degree of kin; degree of relationship; degree of descent.* See AFFINITY (2); CONSANGUINITY.

- ▸ **equal degree.** (16c) A relationship between two or more relatives who are the same number of steps away from a common ancestor.
- ▸ **forbidden degree.** See *prohibited degree.*
- ▸ **Levitical degrees.** See *prohibited degree.*
- ▸ **prohibited degree.** (17c) A degree of relationship so close (as between brother and sister) that marriage between the persons is forbidden by law. • Generally, with slight variations from jurisdiction to jurisdiction, the law forbids marriages between all persons lineally related and within the third civil-law degree of relationship. That is, aunt–nephew and uncle–niece relations are prohibited. Prohibited degrees are also known as *Levitical degrees,* since the incest prohibition is pronounced in the Bible in Leviticus 18:6–18. — Also termed *forbidden degree.*

degree of care. (17c) A standard of care to be exercised in a given situation. See CARE.

degree of crime. (1826) **1.** A division or classification of a single crime into several grades of guilt, according to the circumstances surrounding the crime's commission, such as aggravating factors present or the type of injury suffered. Cf. DEGREE (2); GRADE; *graded offense* under OFFENSE (2). **2.** A division of crimes generally, such as felonies or misdemeanors.

degree of descent. See DEGREE (6).

degree of kin. See DEGREE (6).

degree of negligence. (18c) One of the varying levels of negligence typically designated as slight negligence, ordinary or simple negligence, and gross negligence. See NEGLIGENCE.

> "Although the common law concept of degrees of negligence has been criticized or repudiated in many jurisdictions, the usefulness of the view at common law that degrees of negligence exist is still recognized in a number of jurisdictions, particularly in regard to the distinction between ordinary and gross negligence. Furthermore,

legislators have not been dissuaded from using the degrees of negligence concept when it is helpful to achieve a legislative purpose." 57A Am. Jur. 2d *Negligence* § 233, at 274 (1989).

degree of proof. 1. See STANDARD OF PROOF. **2.** BURDEN OF PRODUCTION.

degree of relationship. See DEGREE (6).

de haerede deliberando illi qui habet custodiam terrae (dee hi-**ree**-dee di-lib-ə-**ran**-doh **il**-ɪ kwɪ **hay**-bət kə-**stoh**-dee-əm **ter**-ee), *n.* [Law Latin "for delivering an heir to him who has wardship of the land"] (18c) *Hist.* A writ ordering the sheriff to deliver an heir to a person who had wardship.

de haerede rapto et abducto (dee hi-**ree**-dee **rap**-toh et ab-**dək**-toh), *n.* [Law Latin "of an heir ravished and carried away"] *Hist.* A writ allowing a lord to recover a ward who had been taken by another person.

de haeretico comburendo (dee hi-**ret**-i-koh kom-byə-**ren**-doh), *n.* [Law Latin "of burning a heretic"] (17c) *Hist.* **1.** A writ ordering the execution by burning of a convicted heretic who refused to recant, or was convicted of heresy again after recanting. • The writ was abolished in 1677. 29 Car. II, c.9. — Also termed *writ de haeretico comburendo.*

"[W]e find among our ancient precedents a writ *de haeretico comburendo*, which is thought by some to be as ancient as the common law itself. However, it appears from thence, that the conviction of heresy by the common law was not in any petty ecclesiastical court, but before the archbishop himself in a provincial synod; and that the delinquent was delivered over to the king to do as he should please with him: so that the crown had a control over the spiritual power, and might pardon the convict by issuing no process against him; the writ *de haeretico comburendo* being not a writ of course, but issuing only by the special direction of the king in council." 4 William Blackstone, *Commentaries on the Laws of England* 46–47 (1769).

"But the case of Sawtre (1400) is a clear case in which the rule of the canon law was applied. He was convicted of heresy before the Bishop of Norwich and recanted his heresy. He fell again into heresy, and was condemned by the archbishop and his provincial Council, as a relapsed heretic. On this conviction the king issued a writ de haeretico comburendo. This case clearly shows that the common law recognized the rule of the canon law . . . ." 1 William Holdsworth, *A History of English Law* 617 (7th ed. 1956).

2. The first English penal law against heresy, enacted in 1401 (2 Hen. 4, ch. 15). • The law authorized the burning of defendants who relapsed or refused to abandon their heretical opinions.

"The first English statute that denounced the penalty of death against heretics was passed in the year 1401. Whether before that statute the law that was in force in our land demanded or suffered that such persons should be burnt is a question that has been eagerly debated; on it in the days of Elizabeth and James I depended the lives of Anabaptists and Arians; it has not yet lost its interest; but it is a question that buzzes in a vacuum, for until Lollardy became troublesome there was too little heresy in England to beget a settled course of procedure." 2 Frederick Pollock & Frederic Maitland, *The History of English Law Before the Time of Edward I* 544 (1899).

deherison (dee-**her**-i-zən). See DISINHERITANCE.

de homagio respectuando (dee hə-**may**-jee-oh ri-spek-tyoo-**an**-doh), *n.* [Law Latin "for respiting or postponing homage"] (18c) *Hist.* A writ to postpone an homage. See HOMAGE.

de homine capto in withernamium (dee **hom**-ə-nee **kap**-toh in wi<u>th</u>-ər-**nay**-mee-əm), *n.* [Law Latin "for taking a man in withernam"] (18c) *Hist.* A writ to seize and jail a person who took a bondman out of the county to keep the bondman from being replevied. • The defendant was jailed without bail until the bondman was returned. See WITHERNAM.

de homine replegiando (dee **hom**-ə-nee ri-plee-jee-**an**-doh), *n.* [Law Latin "for replevying a man"] (17c) A writ to replevy a person out of jail or out of the custody of another person after giving security that the replevied person will answer any charge.

"The writ *de homine replegiando* lies to replevy a man out of prison, or out of the custody of any private person, (in the same manner that chattels taken in distress may be replevied . . .) upon giving security to the sheriff that the man shall be forthcoming to answer any charge against him. And, if the person be conveyed out of the sheriff's jurisdiction, the sheriff may return that he is eloigned . . . upon which a process issues . . . to imprison the defendant himself, without bail . . . till he produces the party. But this writ is guarded with so many exceptions, that it is not an effectual remedy in numerous instances, especially where the crown is concerned." 3 William Blackstone, *Commentaries on the Laws of England* 129 (1768).

dehors (də-**hor** *or* də-**horz**). [Law French] (18c) Outside; beyond the scope of <the court cannot consider the document because it is dehors the record>.

de identitate nominis (dee ɪ-den-tə-**tay**-tee **nom**-ə-nis), *n.* [Law Latin "of identity of name"] (16c) *Hist.* A writ to free a person mistaken for someone else with the same name and then falsely arrested and imprisoned. — Also termed *de idemptitate nominis.*

de idiota inquirendo (dee id-ee-**oh**-tə in-kwɪ-**ren**-doh *or* in-kwə-**ren**-doh). [Latin "of inquiring concerning an idiot"] (17c) *Hist.* A writ directing the sheriff to open an inquiry before a jury of 12 into whether a person is an idiot, that is, mentally incapable of managing his or her personal affairs.

Dei gratia (**dee**-ɪ **gray**-shee-ə). [Latin] By the grace of God. • This phrase was often used in rulers' titles to show that their authority was by divine right. It was also formerly used in titles of magistrates and other officers.

de iis qui ponendi sunt in assisis (dee **ɪ**-əs kwɪ pə-**nen**-dɪ sənt in ə-**sɪ**-zəz), *n.* [Law Latin "of those who are to be put on assises"] *Hist.* The statute establishing juror qualifications. 21 Edw. 1.

dei judicium (**dee**-ɪ joo-**dish**-ee-əm). [Latin "God's judgment"] A trial by ordeal. See ORDEAL.

deimmobilization. (1930) The process by which component parts of immovable property become movable through damage, deterioration, detachment, or juridical act. La. Civ. Code. art 468.

de incremento (dee in-krə-**men**-toh). [Law Latin "of increase"] *Hist.* Additional. • Costs *de incremento* are costs awarded by a court in addition to costs awarded by the jury.

de industria (dee in-**dəs**-tree-ə). [Latin] *Hist.* Designedly; on purpose.

de ingressu (dee in-**gres**-[y]oo), *n.* [Law Latin "of entry"] (18c) *Hist.* A writ allowing entry into lands or tenements.

de injuria (dee in-**joor**-ee-ə). [Law Latin "of injury"] (18c) *Hist.* Of injury. • A traverse *de injuria*, contained in a replication in a trespass action, denies the defendant's excuse for the wrong done. See TRAVERSE.

de inofficioso testamento (dee in-ə-fish-ee-**oh**-soh tes-tə-**men**-toh). [Latin] *Roman law.* Concerning an inofficious or undutiful will. See INOFFICIOSUS; QUERELA INOFFICIOSI TESTAMENTI.

de integro (dee **in**-tə-groh), *n.* [Latin] Again; a second time.

de intrusione (dee in-troo-zhee-**oh**-nee), *n.* [Law Latin "of intrusion"] *Hist.* A writ available to a reversioner when the tenant dies and a stranger occupies the land.

dejeration (dej-ə-**ray**-shən). (17c) The act of taking a solemn oath.

de jure (di **joor**-ee *also* dee *or* day), *adj.* [Law Latin "as a matter of law"] (17c) Existing by right or according to law <de jure segregation during the pre-*Brown* era>. Cf. DE FACTO; DE GRATIA.

de jure corporation. See CORPORATION.

de jure condendo (di **joor**-ee kən-**den**-doh). [Latin] Of law to be established.

de jure gestionis (di **joor**-ee jes-chee-**oh**-nis). [Latin] Of the law of management or administration.

de jure government. See GOVERNMENT (3).

de jure imperii (di **joor**-ee im-**peer**-ee-ɪ). [Latin] Of the law of sovereignty.

de jure officer. See *officer de jure* under OFFICER (1).

de jure segregation. See SEGREGATION (2).

de lana caprina (rixari) (dee **lay**-nə kə-**prɪ**-nə rik-**sair**-ɪ). [Latin] *Hist.* To contend about a goat's hair; to dispute about nothing.

delantal (di-**lan**-təl). [Old English] *Hist.* See UTLAND.

de la plus belle (də lah ploo **bel**), *adj.* [Law French] *Hist.* Of the most fair. • This term described a form of dower assigned out of the husband's best tenements. The term was used in military tenures but was abolished by statute. 12 Car. 2, ch. 24. — Also termed *de la pluis beale.*

delate (di-**layt**), *vb.* (16c) To accuse, to inform against, to denounce in court, esp. a Scottish ecclesiastical court. — **delation,** *n.* — **delator,** *n.*

de latere (dee **lat**-ər-ee). [Latin] Of collaterals; from the side.

delatio (di-**lay**-shee-oh), *n.* [fr. Latin *deferre* "to denounce"] *Roman & civil law.* **1.** An accusation. **2.** Information.

delator (di-**lay**-tər), *n.* [Latin] (16c) *Roman law.* **1.** An informer. **2.** An accuser; esp., a person who made a practice of informing on and prosecuting others, esp. for fiscal offenses. • This was at first encouraged, but later the informer became subject to the death penalty. Pl. ***delatores.***

delatura (del-ə-**tyoor**-ə), *n.* [fr. Latin *deferre* "to denounce"] *Hist.* A reward given to an informer.

Delaware trust. See *asset-protection trust* (1) under TRUST (3).

delay, *n.* (13c) **1.** The act of postponing or slowing <the continuance was sought for no purpose other than delay>. Cf. VEXATIOUS DELAY. **2.** An instance at which something is postponed or slowed <the delay in starting the trial made it difficult for all of the witnesses to attend>. **3.** The period during which something is postponed or slowed <during the delay, the case settled>. **4.** *Civil law.* The period within which a party to a suit must take some action, such as perfecting an appeal or responding to a written-discovery request <the delay for responding to written interrogatories is 15 days after the date they are served on the responding party>.

delayed appeal. See APPEAL (2).

delayed-compliance order. (1977) *Environmental law.* An order issued by the Environmental Protection Agency or by a state agency to an existing source of pollutants, whereby the deadline for complying with an implementation plan is postponed. — Abbr. DCO. See IMPLEMENTATION PLAN.

delayed-death exception. (1993) An exemption from the double-jeopardy bar occurring when the victim of a physical injury dies after the perpetrator has been convicted of assault, battery, or some other offense involving physical injury, the perpetrator then becoming prosecutable for homicide.

delayed funds availability. (1991) A hold that a bank places on uncollected funds that are represented by a deposited check. — Abbr. DFA.

delayed rental. See RENTAL.

delayed sentence. See SENTENCE.

delay rental. See RENTAL (1).

delay tactic. (*often pl.*) (1905) A deliberate action taken in order to gain an advantage by putting something off until a later time; esp., one in a series of court filings, postponements, and other actions carried out solely to frustrate the speedy resolution of a dispute or to cause an opposing party vexation and expense. — Also termed *delaying tactic; dilatory tactic.*

del bien estre (del **been es**-tər). [Law French] *Hist.* Of well-being. See DE BENE ESSE.

del credere (del **kred**-ə-ray *or* **kray**-də-ray), *adj.* [Italian] (18c) Of belief or trust.

> "'*Del credere*' agents for the sale of goods, in consideration of a higher payment than usual, become responsible for the solvency of the person to whom they sell them." Thomas E. Holland, *The Elements of Jurisprudence* 304 (13th ed. 1924).

***del credere* agent.** See AGENT.

***del credere* bailiff.** See FACTOR (3).

***del credere* commission.** (18c) A factor's commission that is increased because the factor guarantees the payment to the principal of all debts that become due through the agency relationship.

***del credere* factor.** See *del credere agent* under AGENT.

delectus personarum (di-**lek**-təs pər-sə-**nahr**-əm). [Latin "choice of persons"] (1828) The rule that when personal relations are important, a person cannot be compelled to associate with another person; specif., the principle that one has the right to select the person or persons with whom one might form a partnership. — Also termed *delectus personae* (di-**lek**-təs pər-**soh**-nee). [Latin "choice of the person"]

> "The requirement of a contract for the creation of a partnership is founded upon the principle of delectus personarum, or right of selection, and this in turn grows out of the nature and consequences of the relation. 'When a man enters into a partnership, he certainly commits his dearest rights to the discretion of every one who forms a part of that partnership.' 'It is an imprudent thing for a man to enter into partnership with any person, unless he has the

most implicit confidence in his integrity.' Within the scope of the partnership one partner may bind his copartners by his contracts and acts, may pledge their credit and may convey a perfect title to the firm chattels. The property or money which one puts into a partnership venture ceases to be his exclusively and comes under the control and disposition of his copartners. Because of the powers of partners to subject one another to liability and to deal with common property, and because of the mutual confidence and trust required in the relation, this right of selection of one's associates is a fundamental principle, not only in the establishing, but also in the continuance, of the relation. It therefore follows that no person can be introduced as a partner without the consent of himself and of all those who for the time being are members of the firm." Eugene Allen Gilmore, *Handbook on the Law of Partnership* 71–72 (1911) (citations omitted).

"The law does not choose partners for people. So intimate and confidential is the relation, so important and dangerous, if abused, are the powers of one partner to subject the others to liability, that the law leaves the choice of partners to the parties themselves, and does not attempt to force a partner upon another without the latter's consent. This right to choose one's own partner — the *delectus personarum*, as it is often called — is properly regarded as one of the most important characteristics of partnership." Floyd R. Mechem, *Elements of the Law of Partnership* 7 (2d ed. 1920).

delegable duty. See DUTY (1).

delegate (**del**-ə-git), *n.* (15c) **1.** Someone who represents or acts for another person or a group; esp., someone who has been elected or chosen to speak, vote, or make decisions for a group. **2.** *Parliamentary law.* A voting member of a convention, whether entitled to vote as an elected or appointed delegate (in sense 1), as an upgraded alternate, or ex officio. See CONVENTION (4); ALTERNATE; EX OFFICIO.

▸ **instructed delegate.** (1899) A delegate bound to vote according to a constituency's expressed wishes. Cf. *uninstructed delegate*; UNIT RULE (2).

▸ **uninstructed delegate.** (1962) A delegate who is not instructed and may therefore vote according to his or her conscience. Cf. *instructed delegate.*

delegate, *vb.* (16c) **1.** To send as a representative with authority to act; to depute <to delegate Jones to represent the board before the commission>. **2.** To give part of one's power or work to someone in a lower position within one's organization <delegated legislative functions>. **3.** To choose someone to do a particular job, or to be a representative of a group or organization <she was delegated to organize the conference>. **4.** *Civil law.* To assign (one's debtor) to one's creditor in place of oneself <because Smith owed Johnson money, and Johnson owed Luna the same amount, Johnson delegated Smith to stand in his stead on the Luna debt>.

delegate assembly. See CONVENTION (4).

delegated legislation. **1.** See LEGISLATION (3). **2.** REGULATION (3).

delegated power. See POWER (3).

delegatee (del-ə-gə-**tee**). (1875) An agent or representative to whom a matter is delegated.

delegation, (del-ə-**gay**-shən), *n.* (1612) **1.** The act of entrusting another with authority or empowering another to act as an agent or representative <delegation of contractual duties>. — **delegate** (**del**-ə-gayt), *vb.* — **delegable** (**del**-ə-gə-bəl), *adj.* **2.** A group of representatives for a company, organization, etc. <a large delegation from Texas>.

delegation doctrine. (1883) *Constitutional law.* The principle (based on the separation-of-powers concept) limiting Congress's ability to transfer its legislative power to another governmental branch, esp. the executive branch. • Delegation is permitted only if Congress prescribes an intelligible principle to guide an executive agency in making policy. — Also termed *nondelegation doctrine.*

delegation of duties. (1893) *Contracts.* A transaction by which a party to a contract arranges to have a third party perform the party's contractual duties.

delegation of powers. (1854) A transfer of authority by one branch of government to another branch or to an administrative agency. See DELEGATION DOCTRINE.

de legatis et fidei commissis (dee li-**gay**-tis et **fɪ**-dee-ɪ kə-**mis**-is). [Latin] Of legacies and trusts. • This is a title in the Pandects.

delegator (**del**-i-gay-tər or -tor). (1875) Someone who delegates (a responsibility, etc.) to another.

de lege (dee **lee**-jee). [Latin] Of the written law.

de lege condenda (dee **lee**-jee kən-**den**-də). [Latin "from the law to be built"] The law that someone believes ought to be made.

de lege ferenda (dee **lee**-jee fə-**ren**-də). [Latin "from law to be passed"] (1905) *Int'l law.* A proposed principle that might be applied to a given situation instead or in the absence of a legal principle that is in force. See LEX FERENDA. Cf. DE LEGE LATA.

de lege lata (dee **lee**-jee **lay**-tə). [Latin "from law passed"] (1904) *Int'l law.* **1.** Existing law. **2.** The principle that a court should decide based on actual law and not on how it thinks the law ought to be. Cf. DE LEGE FERENDA.

delegitimation. The act of making unlawful something that was lawful; a withdrawal of authorization.

deleterious (del-ə-**teer**-ee-əs), *adj.* (1643) **1.** Poisonous <deleterious toxins>. **2.** Unwholesome; psychologically or physically harmful <deleterious influence>.

de libera falda (dee **lib**-ər-ə **fal**-də *or* **fawl**-də), *n.* [Law Latin "of free fold"] (18c) *Hist.* A writ allowing a free feeding, esp. of sheep on land. • This was a form of *quod permittat.*

de libera piscaria (dee **lib**-ər-ə pi-**skair**-ee-ə), *n.* [Law Latin "of free fishery"] (17c) *Hist.* A writ allowing an exclusive right to fish on public navigable water. • This writ was a form of *quod permittat.*

deliberate (di-**lib**-[ə]-rit), *adj.* (15c) **1.** Intentional; premeditated; fully considered. **2.** Unimpulsive; slow in deciding.

deliberate (di-**lib**-ə-rate), *vb.* (16c) (Of a court, jury, etc.) to weigh and analyze all the evidence after closing arguments <the jury deliberated for 12 hours before reaching a verdict>.

deliberate ambiguity. See *calculated ambiguity* under AMBIGUITY (1).

deliberate elicitation. (1966) *Criminal procedure.* The purposeful yet covert drawing forth of an incriminating response (usu. not during a formal interrogation) from a suspect whose Sixth Amendment right to counsel has attached but who has not waived that right. • Deliberate elicitation may occur, for example, when a police officer engages an arrested suspect in conversation on the way to the police station. Deliberate elicitation violates the Sixth Amendment. *Massiah v. U.S.*, 377 U.S. 201, 84 S.Ct. 1199 (1964). See MASSIAH RULE.

deliberate indifference. See INDIFFERENCE.

deliberate-indifference direction. See JEWELL INSTRUCTION.

deliberate-indifference instruction. See JEWELL INSTRUCTION.

deliberate nondisclosure. See NONDISCLOSURE.

deliberate speed, with all. (1817) As quickly as the maintenance of law and order and the welfare of the people will allow, esp. with respect to the desegregation of public schools. *Brown v. Board of Educ.*, 347 U.S. 483, 74 S.Ct. 686 (1954).

deliberation, *n.* (14c) The act of carefully considering issues and options before making a decision or taking some action; esp., the process by which a jury reaches a verdict, as by analyzing, discussing, and weighing the evidence. See CONSIDERATION (2). — **deliberate** (di-**lib**-ə-rayt), *vb.*

deliberative assembly. See ASSEMBLY (1).

deliberative oratory. See ORATORY.

deliberative-process privilege. See PRIVILEGE (1).

de libero homine exhibendo (dee **lib**-ər-oh **hom**-ə-nee ek-si-**ben**-doh). [Latin "for the production of a free man"] (17c) *Roman law.* An interdict requiring a free person to be produced before a magistrate.

de libero passagio (dee **lib**-ər-oh pə-**say**-jee-oh), *n.* [Law Latin "of free passage"] (17c) *Hist.* A writ allowing free passage over water. • This was a form of *quod permittat.*

de libertate probanda (dee lib-ər-**tay**-tee proh-**ban**-də), *n.* [Law Latin "for proving liberty"] (16c) *Hist.* A writ directing a sheriff to take security from a person accused of being a villein and to protect that person from harassment until the person's status was determined by the justices of assize.

de libertatibus allocandis (dee lib-ər-**tay**-tə-bəs al-ə-**kan**-dis), *n.* [Law Latin "for allowing liberties"] (17c) *Hist.* A writ allowing a person entitled to certain liberties to obtain them.

de licentia transfretandi (dee lɪ-**sen**-shee-ə trans-frə-**tan**-dɪ), *n.* [Law Latin "of permission to cross the sea"] (18c) *Hist.* A writ ordering wardens of seaports, on certain conditions, to permit any person named in the writ to cross the sea.

delict (di-**likt**), *n.* [Latin *delictum* "an offense"] (16c) *Roman & civil law.* **1.** A violation of the law; esp., a wrongful act or omission giving rise to a claim for compensation; TORT. — Also termed (in Roman law) *delictum*; (in French law) *délit.*

> "A delict is a civil wrong. It is an infringement of another's interests that is wrongful irrespective of any prior contractual undertaking to refrain from it — though there may also be one. It entitles the injured party to claim compensation in civil proceedings — though criminal proceedings aimed at punishing the wrongdoer may also ensue." P.Q.R. Boberg, *The Law of Delict* 1 (1984).

▸ **private delict.** (17c) A wrong regarded primarily as a matter of compensation between individuals.

▸ **public delict.** (17c) A wrong for which the community as a whole takes steps to punish the offender. Cf. *public tort* under TORT.

▸ **quasi-delict.** (17c) **1.** *Roman law.* A residuary category of private wrongs, characterized by either vicarious or strict liability.

> "QUASI-DELICT . . . . Justinian enumerates four cases of obligations said to arise quasi ex delicto. The implication seems to be that in all of them the law creates a liability though the defendant may not in fact be to blame. The cases are the following: — (1) The judge who 'makes the case his own' . . . incurs a penalty fixed by the magistrate at discretion . . . . (2) If anything was thrown, or poured, from an upper room . . . the occupier was liable for double the damage . . . . (3) If a thing was kept placed or suspended over a way used by the public . . . there was a penalty . . . which might be recovered from the occupier . . . . (4) Shipowners, innkeepers and stable-keepers were liable for damage or theft committed by slaves or free persons in their employ . . . ." R.W. Lee, *The Elements of Roman Law* 401–02 (4th ed. 1956).

2. See *quasi-offense* under OFFENSE (3). **3.** *Scots law.* Tortious conduct that is negligent, as opposed to intentional.

delictal. See DELICTUAL.

deliction (di-**lik**-shən). (1966) The loss of land by gradual, natural changes, such as erosion resulting from a change in the course of a river or stream. Cf. ACCRETION (2); ALLUVION; AVULSION (2); EROSION.

delictual (di-**lik**-chə-wəl), *adj.* (1875) Of, relating to, or involving a delict; TORTIOUS. — Also termed *delictal.*

delictual fault. See FAULT.

delictum. See DELICT.

delimination. (1896) The act of marking a boundary or fixing a limit.

delimit (di-**lim**-it), *vb.* (1852) To mark (a boundary); to fix (a limit).

delimitation. (1836) A fixing of precise limits or boundaries.

delineational gerrymandering. See GERRYMANDERING.

delinquency, *n.* (17c) **1.** A failure or omission; a violation of a law or duty. **2.** Illegal or immoral behavior or actions, esp. by young people. See JUVENILE DELINQUENCY. **3.** A debt that is overdue in payment.

delinquency charge. See CHARGE (7).

delinquency jurisdiction. See JURISDICTION.

delinquent, *adj.* (17c) **1.** (Of a person) failing to perform an obligation. **2.** (Of a person) guilty of serious antisocial or criminal conduct. **3.** (Of an obligation) past due or unperformed.

delinquent, *n.* (15c) **1.** Someone who fails to perform an obligation. **2.** A person guilty of serious antisocial or criminal conduct. **3.** JUVENILE DELINQUENT.

delinquent child. See CHILD.

delinquent minor. See JUVENILE DELINQUENT.

delinquent tax. See TAX.

de liquido in liquidum (dee **lik**-wi-doh in **lik**-wi-dəm). [Law Latin] (17c) *Scots law.* Of a liquid claim against a liquid claim. • The phrase appeared in reference to the extinguishment of a claim by setoff.

delirium. (16c) **1.** A disordered mental state, often occurring during illness. **2.** Exaggerated excitement. **3.** A delusion; a hallucination.

delirium tremens. (1813) An illness characterized by hallucinations and violent trembling, induced by excessive consumption of alcohol over a long period. — Abbr. d.t.'s. — Also termed *mania a potu; settled insanity.*

delisting, *n.* (1929) The suspension of the privilege of having a security listed on an exchange. • Delisting results from failing to meet the exchange's listing requirements, as by not complying with the minimum net-asset requirement. Cf. DEREGISTRATION. — **delist,** *vb.*

délit. See DELICT.

deliverance. (14c) **1.** A jury's verdict. **2.** A judicial opinion or judgment. **3.** A court's order directing that a person in custody be released; esp., such an order by an ecclesiastical court. — Also termed *writ of deliverance.* **4.** *Archaic.* In a replevin action, a writ ordering the redelivery of goods to the owner.

▸ **second deliverance.** (16c) *Hist.* A second replevin remedy after the plaintiff has been nonsuited and the distrained property has been returned to the defendant. — Also termed *writ of second deliverance.*

> "And at the common law, the plaintiff might have brought another replevin, and so *in infinitum,* to the intolerable vexation of the defendant. Wherefore the statute of Westm. 2, c. 2 restrains the plaintiff, when nonsuited, from suing any fresh replevin, but allows him a *judicial* writ issuing out of the original record, and called a writ of *second deliverance,* in order to have the same distress again delivered to him, on giving the like security as before. And, if the plaintiff be a second time nonsuit, or if the defendant has judgment upon verdict . . . he shall have a writ or *return irreplevisable*; after which no writ of second deliverance shall be allowed." 3 William Blackstone, *Commentaries on the Laws of England* 150 (1767).

5. Such a release (as in sense 3) or redelivery (as in sense 4). **6.** The quality, state, or condition of being saved from harm or danger.

delivered at frontier. (1937) A mercantile-contract term allocating the rights and duties of the buyer and the seller of goods with respect to delivery, payment, and risk of loss, whereby the seller must (1) clear the goods for export, (2) arrange and pay for transportation, and (3) deliver the goods to a specified place on the importing country's border. • The seller's delivery is complete (and the risk of loss passes to the buyer) when the goods arrive at the designated point and are placed at the disposal of the buyer. This term is generally used when the delivery place is on land, but it places no explicit restrictions on the mode of carriage. If the delivery place is a border port and delivery is complete either onboard or alongside the vessel, the term *delivered ex ship* or *delivered ex quay* is preferred. — Abbr. DAF. Cf. DELIVERED EX SHIP; DELIVERED EX QUAY.

delivered duty paid. (1854) A mercantile-contract term allocating the rights and duties of the buyer and the seller of goods with respect to delivery, payment, and risk of loss, whereby the seller must (1) clear the goods for export, (2) bear the costs of carriage, (3) pay the buyer's import duties, and (4) make the goods available to the buyer on board the carrier at the destination. • The seller's delivery is complete (and the risk of loss passes to the buyer) when the seller's carrier arrives at the agreed destination. This term is generally used when the delivery place is on land, but it places no explicit restrictions on the mode of carriage. If the delivery point is a port and delivery is complete either onboard or alongside the vessel, the term *delivered ex ship* or *delivered ex quay* is preferred. — Abbr. DDP. Cf. DELIVERED DUTY UNPAID; DELIVERED EX SHIP; DELIVERED EX QUAY.

delivered duty unpaid. (1991) A mercantile-contract term allocating the rights and duties of the buyer and the seller of goods with respect to delivery, payment, and risk of loss, whereby the seller must (1) clear the goods for export, (2) bear the costs of carriage (apart from unloading charges and import duties), and (3) make the goods available to the buyer on board the carrier at the destination. • The seller's delivery is complete (and the risk of loss passes to the buyer) when the seller's carrier arrives at the agreed destination. The buyer is responsible for all import duties. This term is generally used when the delivery place is on land, but it places no explicit restrictions on the mode of carriage. If the delivery point is a port and delivery is complete either onboard or alongside the vessel, the term *delivered ex ship* or *delivered ex quay* is preferred. — Abbr. DDU. Cf. DELIVERED DUTY PAID; DELIVERED EX SHIP; DELIVERED EX QUAY.

delivered ex quay. (1873) A mercantile-contract term allocating the rights and duties of the buyer and the seller of goods with respect to delivery, payment, and risk of loss, whereby the seller must (1) clear the goods for export, (2) bear the costs of transportation to the port named by the importing buyer, and (3) place the goods alongside the ship in the port of destination. • The seller's delivery is complete (and the risk of loss passes to the buyer) when the goods are unloaded in the destination port. This term is used only when goods are transported by sea or inland waterway. — Abbr. DEQ. Cf. DELIVERED EX SHIP; FREE ALONGSIDE SHIP.

delivered ex ship. (1864) A mercantile-contract term allocating the rights and duties of the buyer and the seller of goods with respect to delivery, payment, and risk of loss, whereby the seller must clear the goods for export and bear the costs of transportation (apart from unloading charges and import duties) to the importing country's port of destination. • The seller's delivery is complete (and the risk of loss passes to the buyer) when the seller's carrier arrives at the destination port. This term is used only when goods are transported by sea or inland waterway. — Abbr. DES. Cf. DELIVERED EX QUAY; FREE ON BOARD.

delivery, *n.* (15c) **1.** The formal act of voluntarily transferring something; esp., the act of bringing goods, letters, etc. to a particular person or place. **2.** The thing or things so brought and transferred. Cf. LIVERY (1). — **deliver,** *vb.*

▸ **absolute delivery.** (1808) A delivery that is complete upon the actual transfer of the instrument from the grantor's possession. • Such a delivery does not usu. depend on recordation.

▸ **actual delivery.** (17c) The act of giving real and immediate possession to the buyer or the buyer's agent.

▸ **conditional delivery.** (18c) A delivery that passes possession subject to the happening of a specified event. • Possession passes immediately; title remains conditional.

▸ **constructive delivery.** (18c) An act that amounts to a transfer of title by operation of law when actual transfer is impractical or impossible. • For example, the delivery of a deposit-box key by someone who is ill and immobile may amount to a constructive delivery of the box's contents even though the box may be miles away. For the three traditional types of constructive delivery, see ATTORNMENT; CONSTITUTUM POSSESSORIUM; TRADITIO BREVI MANU.

▸ **good delivery.** *Securities.* A security's delivery when the certificate (1) is in good condition, (2) belongs to the person transferring it, (3) is properly indorsed, and (4) is accompanied by any legal documents necessary for its negotiability.

▸ **jail delivery.** See JAIL DELIVERY.

▸ **second delivery.** (17c) A legal delivery by the depositary of a deed placed in escrow.

▸ **symbolic delivery.** (18c) The constructive delivery of the subject matter of a sale or gift by the actual delivery of an article that represents the item, that renders access to it possible, or that provides evidence of the title to it, such as the key to a warehouse or a bill of lading for goods on shipboard.

▸ **unconditional delivery.** (18c) A delivery that immediately passes both possession and title and that takes effect immediately.

delivery bond. See *forthcoming bond* under BOND (2).

delivery in escrow. (1842) The physical transfer of something to an escrow agent to be held until some condition is met, at which time the agent will release it. • An example of such a delivery is a stock buyer's transfer of cash to a bank that will give the seller the cash upon receiving the stock certificates. This type of delivery creates immediate conditional rights in the promisee. The device may be used to create an option contract in which the promisee has the option. See ESCROW.

delivery of deed. (18c) The collective words or actions by which a grantor manifests an intent that the deed be immediately effective to transfer an interest in land to a grantee. • The classic form of delivery occurs when the grantor physically hands the deed to the grantee. But a deed can also be delivered by words or other conduct of the grantor showing an intent to be immediately bound by the deed, without any physical transfer of the document: "As a deed may be delivered to the party without words, so may a deed be delivered by words without any act of delivery." 1 *Coke on Littleton* 36A (1628).

delivery of verdict. The declaration of a jury's findings of fact at the end of a trial.

delivery order. (18c) A written order to deliver goods, directed to a warehouseman, carrier, or other person who ordinarily issues warehouse receipts or bills of lading. UCC § 7-102(a)(5).

de lucranda dote (dee loo-**kran**-də **doh**-tee). [Latin "of being enriched by the dowry"] (17c) *Hist.* A spousal agreement giving a husband the right to retain his wife's dowry upon her death.

***De Luna* dilemma.** (1971) *Criminal law.* The problem posed when one of the two criminal codefendants claims that the other codefendant is the sole culprit, so that the trials must be severed. *De Luna v. U.S.*, 308 F.2d 140 (5th Cir. 1962).

de lunatico inquirendo (dee loo-**nat**-ə-koh in-kwə-**ren**-doh), *n.* [Law Latin "for inquiring about a lunatic"] (17c) *Hist.* A writ or commission to determine whether a person is a lunatic. — Also termed *commission of lunacy.*

delusional belief. See BELIEF.

dem. *abbr.* DEMISE.

de magna assisa eligenda (dee **mag**-nə ə-**SI**-zə el-i-**jen**-də), *n.* [Law Latin "of choosing the grand assize"] (18c) *Hist.* A writ ordering a sheriff to summon 4 knights to give oaths before the justices of assize and then choose 12 more knights to form a grand assize to determine who had the right in a writ of right.

demain. See DEMESNE.

de malo (dee **mal**-oh). [Law Latin] Of illness. • This term defined certain legal excuses, such as *de malo lecti* ("of illness in bed"), *de malo veniendi* ("of illness or misfortune in coming where the court is"), and *de malo villae* ("of illness in town where the court is").

demand, *n.* (13c) **1.** The assertion of a legal or procedural right.

▸ **contingent demand.** (18c) A demand that cannot be fixed because it depends on the occurrence of a contingency.

▸ **cross-demand.** (18c) A party's demand opposing an adverse party's demand. See COUNTERCLAIM; CROSS-CLAIM.

▸ **demand in reconvention.** See *reconventional demand.*

▸ **incidental demand.** (18c) *Civil law.* A plea by which a party other than the plaintiff asserts a claim that is related to the plaintiff's suit. • Examples include a cross-claim, a demand against a third party, an intervention, and a reconventional demand. La. Code Civ. Proc. art. 1031.

▸ **legal demand.** (17c) A lawful demand made by an authorized person.

▸ **main demand.** (18c) *Civil law.* A plaintiff's principal or primary claim against one or more defendants, contained in an original or validly amended pleading. — Also termed *principal demand; principal action.*

▸ **reconventional demand.** (1881) *Civil law.* A plea by which a defendant asserts any claim that it has against the plaintiff, or any offset against the plaintiff's claim. • This plea is similar to the common-law counterclaim. La. Code Civ. Proc. 1061 et seq. — Also termed *demand in reconvention.*

▸ **stale demand.** A demand that has become barred by prescription, a statute of limitations, laches, or similar doctrine.

2. *Parliamentary law.* A request, usu. invoking a right, that must be granted on a single member's motion. See REQUEST. **3.** A request for payment of a debt or an amount due. **4.** In economics, the intensity of buyer pressure on the availability and cost of a commodity or service. **3.** A request for payment of a debt or an amount due.

▸ **personal demand.** (17c) An in-person demand for payment on the drawer, maker, or acceptor of a bill or note.

4. In economics, the intensity of buyer pressure on the availability and cost of a commodity or service.

▸ **aggregate demand.** (18c) **1.** The total amount spent on goods and services in an economy during a specific period. **2.** The total demand for a firm's products and services during a specific period.

▸ **derived demand.** (1895) Product demand that is related to another product's demand.

demand, *vb.* (14c) **1.** To claim as one's due; to require; to seek relief. **2.** To summon; to call into court.

demandant. (15c) *Archaic.* The plaintiff in a real action (the defendant being called a *tenant*). See *real action* under ACTION (4).

demand clause. (1919) A provision in a note allowing the holder to compel full payment if the maker fails to meet an installment. Cf. ACCELERATION CLAUSE.

demand deposit. See DEPOSIT (2).

demand draft. See *sight draft* under DRAFT (1).

demand for assurances. A request for a guarantee or promise that a party will fulfill its contractual obligations. — Also termed *request for assurances.*

demand for document inspection. See REQUEST FOR PRODUCTION.

demand for relief. See PRAYER FOR RELIEF.

demand in reconvention. See *reconventional demand* under DEMAND (1).

demand instrument. (1924) An instrument payable on demand, at sight, or on presentation, as opposed to an instrument that is payable at a set future date. — Also termed *demand note.*

demand letter. (1911) A letter by which one party explains its legal position in a dispute and requests that the recipient take some action (such as paying money owed), or else risk being sued. • Under some statutes (esp. consumer-protection laws), a demand letter is a prerequisite for filing a lawsuit.

demand loan. See *call loan* under LOAN.

demand note. 1. See NOTE (1). **2.** See DEMAND INSTRUMENT.

demand of oyer. (18c) *Hist.* The assertion of a party's right to hear, read, or inspect a deed of which profert is made by the opposing party in a pleading. See OYER (3); PROFERT.

demand of view. (1838) *Hist.* In a real action, a request by a defendant (called a tenant) to see the thing at issue to ascertain its identity and the circumstances of the claim. • If a real action was brought against a tenant who did not know what land was at issue, the tenant might demand a view. See VIEW (4).

demand-pull inflation. See INFLATION.

demand registration rights. See REGISTRATION RIGHTS.

demandress. *Archaic.* A female demandant. See DEMANDANT.

demand to produce. *Criminal procedure.* A written request by either defense counsel or a prosecutor for opposing counsel to disclose information relating to a criminal charge. — Abbr. DTP.

de manucaptione (dee man-yə-kap-shee-**oh**-nee), *n.* [Law Latin "of manucaption"] (17c) *Hist.* A writ ordering a sheriff to release on sufficient bail an accused felon whose initial offer of bail had been rejected.

de manutenendo (dee man-yə-tə-**nen**-doh), *n.* [Law Latin "of maintenance"] *Hist.* A writ against a person who has wrongfully meddled in a lawsuit by providing assistance to a party to continue the litigation. See MAINTENANCE (8).

demarcation (dee-mahr-**kay**-shən). (18c) **1.** The point at which one area of work, responsibility, etc. ends and another begins. **2.** The process of deciding on or marking the border between two areas, esp. of land.

demarcation dispute. *Labor law.* **1.** A disagreement over which type of union worker has the right to perform a particular class or type of work. **2.** A disagreement over which union or two or more has the right to represent employees.

demarcation line. (18c) *Int'l law.* A provisional border having the function of separating territories under different jurisdictions, usu. established when the political situation does not admit a final boundary arrangement. — Also termed *line of demarcation.*

démarche (day-**mahrsh**). [French "gait; walk"] (17c) An oral or written diplomatic statement, esp. one containing a demand, offer, protest, threat, or the like. — Also spelled *demarche.* See AIDE-MÉMOIRE.

de maritagio amisso per defaltam (dee mar-ə-**tay**-jee-oh ə-**mis**-oh pər də-**fawl**-təm), *n.* [Law Latin] *Hist.* A writ available to a tenant of a frankmarriage to regain land lost by default.

dematerialized security. See *uncertificated security* under SECURITY (4).

de me (dee **mee**). [Latin] Of me. • This phrase appeared in feudal grants to confirm that a superior lord's permission was not needed for the conveyance. This was distinguished from a conveyance *a me de superiore meo* ("from me of my superior"), in which the estate is to be held of the superior, and is invalid unless confirmed by the superior. Cf. A ME.

demean, *vb.* (14c) **1.** To conduct (oneself); to behave. • This neutral sense, corresponding to *demeanor,* appears frequently in older legal texts — esp. in oaths in which newly sworn-in lawyers swear to "demean themselves with propriety," etc. **2.** To do something that causes people to lose respect for (someone or something).

demeaning, *adj.* (1880) Exhibiting less respect for a person or a group of people than they deserve, or causing them to feel embarrassed, ashamed, or scorned.

demeanor. (15c) Outward appearance or behavior, such as facial expressions, tone of voice, gestures, and the hesitation or readiness to answer questions. • In evaluating credibility, the jury may consider the witness's demeanor.

demeanor evidence. See EVIDENCE.

demease (di-**meez**), *n. Hist.* Death. See DEMISE.

de medietate linguae (dee mee-dee-ə-**tay**-tee **ling**-gwee). [Law Latin] (17c) Of half-tongue. • This term describes a jury made up of an equal number of natives and aliens. Edward III originally provided for such a jury in commercial cases when one party was an alien. It was later extended to criminal cases. If enough aliens could not be found, trial proceeded with the available number.

de medio (dee **mee**-dee-oh), *n.* [Law Latin "of mesne"] *Hist.* A writ against a mesne (i.e., middle) lord to protect an undertenant from harassment by a paramount lord for rent actually due from the mesne lord. — Also termed *writ of mesne.*

de melioribus damnis (dee mee-lee-**or**-ə-bəs **dam**-nis). [Law Latin] (18c) Of the better damages. • This term describes a plaintiff's election of the defendant against which to take judgment when the jury has mistakenly awarded separate damages against two or more defendants for a joint tort. Under these circumstances, the plaintiff could take a judgment against the defendant that had been assessed the greatest damages, and then enter a nolle prosequi against the others.

demembration (dee-mem-**bray**-shən), *n.* (16c) The cutting off of a limb; dismemberment; mutilation.

demented, *adj.* (17c) Not of sound mind; insane.

dementenant en avant (də-men-tə-**nahnt** on ə-**vahnt**). [Law French] From this time forward.

de mercatoribus (dee mər-kə-**tor**-ə-bəs), *n.* [Latin "of merchants"] *Hist.* The title of two statutes enacted in the 11th and 13th years of the reign of Edward I, providing that the land of a business debtor could be held by a creditor as security until the debt was paid.

> "But by the statute *de mercatoribus* . . . the whole of a man's lands was liable to be pledged in a statute merchant, for a debt contracted in trade; though one-*half* of them was liable to be taken in execution for any other debt of the owner." 1 William Blackstone, *Commentaries on the Laws of England* 161 (1765).

demerge, *vb.* (1980) To make (one part of a large company, esp. one that has grown through mergers and acquisitions) into a separate company; to spin off (a subsidiary).

demerit. (15c) **1.** A bad quality or feature of something. **2.** A mark showing that a student has behaved badly at school.

demesne (di-**mayn** *or* di-**meen**), *n.* [French] (14c) **1.** At common law, land held in one's own right, and not through a superior; esp., land attached to a manor and reserved for the court's own use. **2.** Domain; realm. — Also spelled *demain.*

▸ **ancient demesne.** (16c) *Hist.* A manor that was held by the Crown at the time of William the Conqueror and was recorded in the Domesday Book.

▸ **demesne as of fee.** (16c) *Hist.* Complete ownership of something.

> "But there is this distinction between the two species of hereditaments: that, of a corporeal inheritance a man shall be said to be seised *in his demesne, as of fee*; of an incorporeal one, he shall only be said to be seised *as of fee*, and not in his demesne. For, as incorporeal hereditaments are in their nature collateral to, and issue out of, lands and houses, their owner hath no property, *dominicum*, or demesne, in the *thing* itself, but hath only something derived out of it; resembling the *servitutes*, or services, of the civil law." 2 William Blackstone, *Commentaries on the Laws of England* 106 (1766).

demesne land. See LAND.

demesne land of the Crown. See *Crown land* under LAND.

demesnial (di-**may**-nee-əl *or* di-**meen**-ee-əl), *adj.* (1857) Of, relating to, or involving a demesne.

demi (**dem**-ee), *n.* [French] (16c) Half; the half. • The term is most often a combining form, as in *demi-sangue.*

***de micromis* party.** See PARTY (2).

demidietas (dem-ee-**dɪ**-ə-tas), *n.* [Law Latin] A half; a moiety.

demilitarization. (1918) *Int'l law.* The process by which a country obligates itself not to station military forces — or to maintain military installations — in specified areas or zones within its territory.

demilitarized zone. (1921) *Int'l law.* A territorial area in a country or between countries in which no military forces or military installations are stationed or maintained.

demimark. (1863) *Hist.* Half a mark; money equal to six shillings and eight pence, required to be tendered in a writ of right to force the demandant to prove seisin. — Also termed *half-mark.*

de minimis (də **min**-ə-mis), *adj.* [Latin "of the least"] (1952) **1.** Trifling; negligible. **2.** (Of a fact or thing) so insignificant that a court may overlook it in deciding an issue or case. • For example, under the Code of Judicial Conduct, *de minimis* describes an interest so insignificant that it does not raise a reasonable question of the judge's impartiality. **3.** DE MINIMIS NON CURAT LEX.

de minimis non curat lex (də **min**-ə-mis non **kyoor**-at **leks**). [Latin] (16c) The law does not concern itself with trifles. — Often shortened to *de minimis.*

***de minimis* party.** See PARTY (2).

***de minimis* test.** (1994) *Copyright.* A judicial test for determining whether a contributor to a joint work is an author for legal purposes, based on whether the joint effort itself is an original expression that qualifies for copyright protection. • This test has been rejected in favor of the copyrightability test by most courts that have addressed the issue. Cf. COPYRIGHTABILITY TEST.

de minis (dee **min**-is), *n.* [Latin "of threats"] (17c) *Hist.* A writ ordering a person to keep the peace when the person has threatened another person with bodily harm or property destruction.

deminutio (dee-mi-**n[y]oo**-shee-oh), *n.* [fr. Latin *deminuere* "taking away"] *Roman law.* A deprivation or loss. • The term appeared, for example, in the phrase *capitis deminutio* "the loss of civil status." — Also spelled *diminutio.* See CAPITIS DEMINUTIO. Pl. ***deminutiones*** (dee-mi-n[y]oo-shee-**oh**-neez).

demi-sangue (**dem**-ee-sang). [Law French] *Hist.* Half-blood; blood on either the father's or the mother's side. — Also termed *demy-sangue.* See *half-blood* under BLOOD.

demise (di-**mɪz**), *n.* (15c) **1.** The conveyance of an estate usu. for a term of years, a lease <the demise of the land for one year>. **2.** The instrument by which such a conveyance is accomplished <the demise set forth the terms of the transfer>. **3.** The passing of property by descent or bequest <a testator's demise of $100,000 to charity>. **4.** The death of a person or (figuratively) of a thing; the end of something that used to exist <the corporation's untimely demise>. — Abbr. dem. See DEATH. — **demise,** *vb.*

▸ **demise of the Crown.** (17c) The immediate, automatic transfer of a kingdom to a successor upon a sovereign's death or long absence from the throne.

> "The king never dies. Henry, Edward, or George may die; but the king survives them all. For immediately upon the decease of the reigning prince in his natural capacity, his kingship or imperial dignity, by act of law, without any . . . interval, is vested at once in his heir; who is, *eo instanti,*

king to all intents and purposes. And so tender is the law of supposing even a possibility of his death, that his natural dissolution is generally called his *demise* . . . an expression which signifies merely a transfer of property; for . . . when we say the demise of the crown, we mean only that, in consequence of the disunion of the king's body natural from his body politic, the kingdom is transferred or demised to his successor; and so the royal dignity remains perpetual." 1 William Blackstone, *Commentaries on the Laws of England* 242 (1765).

▸ **joint demise.** (18c) In an ejectment action, a demise made by two or more persons in one declaration.

▸ **separate demise.** (18c) In an ejectment action, a demise made solely by the lessor.

▸ **several demise.** (*often pl.*) (18c) *Hist.* In an ejectment action, a list of demises by all people potentially owning the property at issue, used to ensure that the plaintiff had proved a lease from the person actually having title. See EJECTMENT.

▸ **single demise.** (18c) In an ejectment action, a declaration containing one demise. See EJECTMENT.

demise charter. See *bareboat charter* under CHARTER (8).

demise charterer. See *bareboat charter* under CHARTER (8).

demise charterparty. See *bareboat charter* under CHARTER (8).

demised premises. See PREMISES.

demisi (di-**mɪ**-zɪ). [fr. Latin *demittere*] I have demised. • This was the operative phrase in a lease.

demissio (di-**mish**-ee-oh), *n.* [fr. Latin *demittere* "to demise"] *Hist.* A lease or other transfer. • In an ejectment action, this term was used in the phrase *ex demissione* ("on the demise") to show that a nominal plaintiff (a fictitious person) held an estate on a demise from the real plaintiff.

de mittendo tenorem recordi (dee mi-**ten**-doh tə-**nor**-əm ri-**kor**-dɪ), *n.* [Law Latin "of sending the tenor of a record"] *Hist.* A writ to certify a record under seal.

demobilization. (1866) A dismissal of troops from active service.

democracy, *n.* (16c) **1.** Government by the people, either directly or through representatives elected by the people; specif., a system of government in which every citizen of the country can vote to elect its government officials. **2.** A country that has a government that has been elected by the people of the country. **3.** A situation or system in which everyone is equal and has the right to vote, make decisions, etc. Cf. REPUBLIC.

"Democracy seems to have scored a historic victory over alternative forms of governance. Nearly everyone today, whether of the left, center, or right, claims adherence to democratic principles. Political regimes of all kinds throughout the world style themselves as democracies — although there may be vast differences between statement and execution in some of these cases. Democracy seems to bestow an aura of legitimacy on modern political life: rules, laws, policies, and decisions appear justified when they are 'democratic.' This was not always so. The great majority of political thinkers, from ancient Greece to the present day, have been highly critical of the theory and practice of democracy. A uniform commitment to democracy is a very recent phenomenon." David Held, "Democracy," in 1 *The Oxford Companion to American Politics* 255, 255–56 (David Coates ed., 2012).

▸ **direct democracy.** A democracy in which the people directly make policy and law decisions. — Also termed *true democracy; pure democracy.*

▸ **militant democracy.** (1852) A democratic regime that is ready and willing to adopt preemptive, ostensibly illiberal measures to prevent the destruction of that regime by those aiming to subvert democracy, esp. by voting it out of existence. — Also termed *defensive democracy; fighting democracy.*

▸ **pure democracy.** See *direct democracy.*

▸ **representative democracy.** A democracy in which the people elect representatives to make law and policy decisions for them. — Also termed *representative government.*

▸ **social democracy. 1.** A political and economic theory based on both socialistic ideas and democratic principles, whereby capitalism is supposed to give way to government-owned industries and legally enforced transfers of wealth, all of which is to be accomplished by democratic means. **2.** A welfare state with a government based on this theory.

"The term 'Social Democracy' has an odd history. Now the name for politics of the moderate left, it originally denoted a Marxist approach to socialism (by contrast, for example, with Fabianism). Social democratic parties in Continental Europe, such as the Austrian one led by figures like Karl Renner, were explicitly and avowedly Marxist in approach. Only since the Second World War have European Social Democrats made the final break with Marxism, a crucial turning-point (or mark of a change already achieved in substance) being the Bad Godesberg congress of the West German SPD in 1959. By now, at any rate, it is clear enough that 'social democracy' has come to be regarded by most English-speaking people as a philosophy of the moderate left, or even the centre, of the political spectrum. We may take it as an alternative to, rather than a form of 'socialism.'" Neil MacCormick, *Legal Right and Social Democracy* 1 (1982).

▸ **true democracy.** See *direct democracy.*

democratic, *adj.* (16c) **1.** Controlled by representatives who are elected by the people of a country <the democratic process>. **2.** Organized on the principle that everyone has a right to be involved in making decisions <a democratic style of management>. **3.** Organized according to the principle that all people in a society are equally important, whatever their material worth or social class <a democratic society>. **4.** (*cap.*) Of, relating to, or involving the Democratic Party of the United States <the Democratic nominee for Vice President>.

democratize, *vb.* (18c) To reform the way (a government, company, committee, etc.) is organized to make it more democratic.

de moderata misericordia capienda (dee mod-ə-**ray**-tə miz-ə-ri-**kor**-dee-ə kap-ee-**en**-də), *n.* [Law Latin "for taking a moderate amercement"] *Hist.* A writ ordering a bailiff to take a moderate penalty from a party who had been excessively penalized in a court not of record. • The writ was founded on Magna Carta.

de modo decimandi (dee **moh**-doh des-ə-**man**-dɪ), *n.* [Law Latin] (17c) *Eccles. law.* Of a mode of tithing. • This refers to any special kind of tithing by custom that is different from the general law that usu. required the tenth part of an annual increase. For example, it could mean a twelfth part of a quantity of hay rather than a tenth part or a couple of hens instead of a normal tithing of eggs. — Also termed *modus decimandi*; *modus*.

de momento in momentum (dee mə-**men**-toh in mə-**men**-təm). [Latin] (17c) *Scots law.* From moment to moment. • The phrase appeared in reference to terms for counting. For example, a minor's age was counted *de momento in momentum* until the last moment of 21 years. The years of prescription were also thus computed.

demonetization. (1852) A disuse of a metal in coinage; a withdrawal of the value of a metal as money <the demonetization of gold in the United States>.

demonstratio (dem-ən-**stray**-shee-oh), *n.* [fr. Latin *demonstrare* "to show"] *Roman law.* **1.** A description, as in *falsa demonstratio* (a false description of something or someone in a will). **2.** Under the formulary procedure, the statement of facts in a formula, forming the basis of a claim. See FORMULA (1). Pl. ***demonstrationes*** (dem-ən-stray-shee-**oh**-neez).

> "Demonstratio is the specification of a particular thing or person , inserted in a written instrument, in order to guard against mistake." John George Phillimore, *Private Law Among the Romans* 102 (1863).

demonstrative bequest. See BEQUEST.

demonstrative devise. See DEVISE.

demonstrative evidence. See EVIDENCE.

demonstrative legacy. See LEGACY (1).

de morte antecessoris (dee **mor**-tee an-ti-**ses**-ər-is). [Law Latin] (17c) *Scots law.* Concerning the death of the ancestor. • The phrase occurs in the *brieve of mortancestry*, equivalent to the English *mort d'ancestor.*

demote, *vb.* (1893) To lower (usu. a person) in rank, position, pay, or other status. See DEGRADATION (1).

de munere regio (dee **myoo**-nər-ə **ree**-jee-oh). [Law Latin] *Scots law.* By royal gift. • The phrase described land held under feudal tenure.

demur (di-**mər**), *vb.* (17c) **1.** To file a demurrer. See DEMURRER. **2.** To object to the legal sufficiency of a claim alleged in a pleading without admitting or denying the truth of the facts stated. **3.** To object to the legal sufficiency of a claim alleged in a pleading while admitting the truth of the facts stated.

demurrable (di-**mər**-ə-bəl), *adj.* (1827) (Of a claim, pleading, etc.) subject to a demurrer <a demurrable pleading>. See DEMURRER.

demurrage (di-**mər**-ij). (*usu. pl.*) (17c) *Maritime law.* **1.** Liquidated damages owed by a charterer to a shipowner for the charterer's failure to load or unload cargo by the agreed time.

▸ **contract demurrage.** (1975) Demurrage paid by a vessel's charterer if the time to load or unload the vessel at port takes longer than that agreed on in the charterer's contract with the shipowner. Cf. DISPATCH MONEY.

▸ **noncontract demurrage.** (1975) Demurrage not provided by contract, but ordered by a court. — Also termed *damages for detention.*

> "After the . . . days on contract demurrage have expired, the charterer of course still remains liable for further delay, but the liability now is one for noncontract demurrage, which will be fixed by the court just as would any other unliquidated claim for damages. Non-contract demurrage may also be referred to as 'damages for detention.'" Grant Gilmore & Charles L. Black Jr., *The Law of Admiralty* § 4-8, at 212 (2d ed. 1975).

2. A charge due for the late return of ocean containers or other equipment. **3.** The time during which a freighter may detain the ship on certain terms, after the expiration of the lay days. See LAYDAY.

demurrage lien. See LIEN.

demurrant (di-**mər**-ənt). (1809) Someone who demurs; esp., a litigant who files a demurrer.

demurrer (di-**mər**-ər). [Law French *demorer* "to wait or stay"] (16c) A pleading stating that although the facts alleged in a complaint may be true, they are insufficient for the plaintiff to state a claim for relief and for the defendant to frame an answer. • In most jurisdictions, such a pleading is now termed a *motion to dismiss*, but *demurrer* is still used in a few states, including California, Nebraska, and Pennsylvania. See PLEADING (quot.). Cf. DENIAL (3).

> "The word 'demurrer,' derived from the Latin *demorari*, or the French *demorrer*, meaning to 'wait or stay,' imports that the party demurring waits or stays in his proceedings in the action until the judgment of the court is given whether he is bound to answer to so insufficient a pleading. Each party may demur to what he deems an insufficient pleading of the other. The demurrer was *general* when it was to matter of substance; it was *special* when it was made to matter of form, and must specifically point out the defect." Edwin E. Bryant, *The Law of Pleading Under the Codes of Civil Procedure* 15 (2d ed. 1899).

▸ **demurrer *ore tenus.*** (1838) An oral demurrer. See ORE TENUS.

> "The codes either expressly or by implication require all pleadings to be in writing. To this proposition there is the apparent exception that objections to the jurisdiction of the court, or to the sufficiency of a pleading, that it does not state a cause of action or defence, may be raised on the trial by what is sometimes called a demurrer *ore tenus* (that is, orally, — by word of mouth)." Edwin E. Bryant, *The Law of Pleading Under the Codes of Civil Procedure* 179 (2d ed. 1899).

▸ **general demurrer.** See *general exception* (1) under EXCEPTION (1).

▸ **parol demurrer.** (18c) *Hist.* A suspension of proceedings during the minority of an infant.

▸ **speaking demurrer.** (18c) A demurrer that cannot be sustained because it introduces new facts not contained in the complaint.

▸ **special demurrer.** (17c) A demurrer that states grounds for an objection and specifically identifies the nature of the defect, such as that the pleading violates the rules of pleading or practice. • If a pleading is defective in form but not substance, the defect must be pointed out by a special demurrer.

demurrer book. (18c) *Hist.* A record of the demurrer issue used by the court and counsel in argument.

demurrer to evidence. (17c) A party's objection or exception that the evidence is legally insufficient to make a case. • Its effect, upon joinder in the demurrer by the opposite party, is that the jury is discharged and the demurrer is entered on record and decided by the court. A demurrer to evidence admits the truth of all the evidence and the legal deductions from that evidence.

demurrer to interrogatories. (18c) The objection or reason given by a witness for failing to answer an interrogatory.

demutualization, *n.* (1970) The process of converting a mutual insurance company (which is owned by its policyholders) to a stock insurance company (which is owned by outside shareholders), usu. as a means of increasing the insurer's capital by allowing the insurer to issue shares. • About half the states have demutualization statutes authorizing such a conversion. — **demutualize,** *vb.*

demy-sangue. See DEMI-SANGUE.

den and strond (den an[d] **strond).** (18c) *Hist.* Permission for a ship to run aground or strand itself.

denarius (di-**nair**-ee-əs), *n.* [Law Latin "penny"] **1.** *Roman law.* The principal silver coin used by the Romans. **2.** *Hist.* An English penny; a pence. **3.** *(pl.) Slang.* Money in general. — Also termed (in senses 1 & 3) *denier.* Pl. ***denarii.***

denarius Dei (di-**nair**-ee-əs **dee**-ɪ), *n.* [Law Latin "God's penny"] *Hist.* Earnest money exchanged by contracting parties, so called because the money was originally given either to the church or to the poor. • The *denarius Dei* was not part of the consideration. — Also termed *argentum dei.* See ARRA; GOD'S PENNY.

denationalization. (1921) **1.** *Int'l law.* The unilateral act of a country in depriving a person of nationality, whether by administrative decision or by operation of law. • Strictly, the term does not cover a person's renunciation of citizenship. **2.** The act of returning government ownership and control of an industry or function to private ownership and control. Cf. PRIVATIZATION. — **denationalize,** *vb.*

de nativo habendo (dee nə-**tɪ**-voh hə-**ben**-doh), *n.* [Law Latin "about a serf to be held"] (16c) *Hist.* A writ directing a sheriff to apprehend and return a runaway serf to the serf's lord. • A trial on the writ would determine the lord's ownership status. — Also termed *nativo habendo.*

de natura brevium (dee nə-**tyoor**-ə **bree**-vee-ə). [Latin] Concerning the nature of writs. • This was a common title of textbooks on English medieval law.

denaturalization. (1811) The process by which a government deprives a naturalized citizen of all rights, duties, and protections of citizenship. *See* 8 USCA § 1451. — **denaturalize,** *vb.*

denelage. See DANELAW.

denial, *n.* (16c) **1.** A statement that something is not true, esp. after someone else has suggested that it is or might be true; a disaffirmation. **2.** A refusal or rejection; esp., a court's refusal to grant a request presented in a motion or petition <denial of the motion for summary judgment>.

▸ **wrongful denial.** The improper or erroneous refusal to recognize something that is valid.

3. A defendant's response controverting the facts that a plaintiff has alleged in a complaint; a repudiation <the worker filed a denial alleging that physical contact never occurred>. See PLEADING (quot.). Cf. DEMURRER.

▸ **conjunctive denial.** (1860) A response that controverts all the material facts alleged in a complaint.

▸ **disjunctive denial.** (1920) A response that controverts the truthfulness of two or more factual allegations of a complaint in the alternative.

▸ **general denial.** (16c) A response that puts in issue all the material assertions of a complaint or petition. — Also termed *general plea.*

▸ **qualified general denial.** (1844) A general denial of all the allegations except the allegations that the pleader expressly admits.

> "The qualified general denial most frequently is used when a limited number of allegations in the complaint are to be admitted. This form of denial also is employed when defendant cannot expressly deny an averment in his opponent's pleading and therefore cannot submit a general denial, although defendant wants to put plaintiff to his proof on that averment by interposing a denial of knowledge or information sufficient to form a belief or a denial on information and belief." 5 Charles Alan Wright & Arthur Miller, *Federal Practice and Procedure* § 1266, at 405 (2d ed. 1990).

▸ **specific denial.** (1850) A separate response applicable to one or more particular allegations in a complaint.

4. A deprivation or withholding <denial of due process>. — **deny,** *vb.*

▸ **bad-faith denial.** A denial made dishonestly, unreasonably, or without grounds.

▸ **denial of claim.** The rejection of an application for benefits. — Also termed (in insurance) *denial of insurance claims.*

▸ **tortious denial of benefits.** See *wrongful denial of benefits.*

▸ **wrongful denial of benefits.** The improper, often baseless refusal to recognize a valid claim for financial assistance. — Also termed *tortious denial of benefits.*

denial of justice. *Int'l law.* A defect in a country's organization of courts or administration of justice, resulting in the country's violating its international legal duties to protect aliens. • A denial of justice is a wrongful act under international law. — Also termed *justitia denegata; déni de justice; refus de justice.*

denial of natural justice. An unjustified and unjustifiable act that violates rules, principles, or notions of fundamental law.

denial-of-service attack. (1993) A malicious strike against a computer, website, network, server, or database designed to render it inaccessible, usu. by overwhelming it with activity or by forcing it to malfunction. — Abbr. DoS attack. — Also termed *nuke.*

▸ **distributed denial-of-service attack.** (1999) A denial-of-service attack carried out by distributing a virus that causes infected computers to try to access the target computer at the same time. — Abbr. DDoS attack.

déni de justice. See DENIAL OF JUSTICE.

denier, *n.* **1.** (də-**nyay**) [French fr. Latin *denarius*] DENARIUS (1). **2.** DENARIUS (3). **3.** (di-**nɪ**-ər). [Law French] *Hist.* Denial; refusal, as in refusal to pay rent when demanded.

Denier à Dieu (də-**nyay** ah **dyuu** *or* **dyoo**). [French "God's money"] *French law.* Earnest money exchanged by contracting parties. See DENARIUS DEI.

denization (den-ə-**zay**-shən). (17c) The act of making a person a denizen. See DENIZEN. — Also termed *indenization.*

denize (den-ɪz *or* di-**nɪz**), *vb.* (16c) To make (a person) a denizen. See DENIZEN.

denizen (den-ə-zən). (15c) **1.** A person given certain rights in a foreign country or living habitually in a foreign country. **2.** *English law.* A person whose status is midway between being an alien and a natural-born or naturalized subject. See ENDENIZEN.

Denman's Act. *Hist.* **1.** The (English) Evidence Act of 1843, providing that no person offered as a witness can be excluded because of incapacity due to a past crime or an interest in the proceedings. — Also termed *Lord Denman's Act.* **2.** The (English) Criminal Procedure Act of 1865 that allowed defense counsel to sum up evidence as allowed in a civil trial, to prove contradictory statements made by an adverse witness, to prove a previous criminal conviction of an adverse witness, and to compare samples of disputed handwriting. — Also termed *Mr. Denman's Act.*

denominate, *vb.* (16c) **1.** To formally give a name or epithet to. **2.** To officially set the value of (something) according to an established system or a type of money. **3.** To show, point out, or indicate.

denomination. (15c) **1.** An act of naming. **2.** A collective designation, esp. of a religious sect; specif., a religious group that has different beliefs from other groups within the same religion. **3.** The value shown on a coin, stamp, or paper money.

de non alienando (dee non ay-lee-ə-**nan**-doh). [Law Latin] (17c) *Scots law.* For not alienating. • The phrase was used to restrict the transfer of property.

de non alienando sine consensu superiorum (dee **non** ay-lee-ə-**nan**-doh **sɪ**-nee kən-**sen**-s[y]oo s[y]oo-peer-ee-**or**-əm). [Law Latin] *Scots law.* Concerning the nonalienation of the lands without the consent of the superior. • The phrase was frequently present in a charter to a vassal.

de non contrahendo debito (dee non kon-trə-**hen**-doh **deb**-i-toh). [Law Latin] *Scots law.* Against the contraction of debt. • The phrase was inserted in an entail to prevent the heir from incurring debt.

de non decimando (dee **non** des-ə-**man**-doh), *n.* [Law Latin "of not paying tithes"] (17c) *Eccles. law.* A claim for release from paying a tithe. — Also termed *modus de non decimando.*

> "A prescription *de non decimando* is a claim to be entirely discharged of tithes, and to pay no compensation in lieu of them. Thus the king by his prerogative is discharged from all tithes. So a vicar shall pay no tithes to the rector, nor the rector to the vicar . . . . But these privileges are personal to both the king and the clergy; for their tenant or lessee shall pay tithes . . . . And from this original have sprung all the lands, which, being in lay hands, do at present claim to be tithe-free: for, if a man can show his lands to have been such abbey lands, and also immemorially discharged of tithes . . . this is now a good prescription, *de non decimando.* But he must show both these requisites for abbey lands, without a special ground of discharge, are not discharged of course; neither will any prescription *de non decimando* avail in total discharge of tithes, unless it relates to such abbey lands." 2 William Blackstone, *Commentaries on the Laws of England* 31–32 (1766).

de non procedendo ad assisam (dee **non** proh-sə-**den**-doh ad ə-**sɪ**-zəm), *n.* [Law Latin "of not proceeding to take an assize"] (18c) *Hist.* A writ ordering justices not to hold an assize in a particular case.

de non residentia clerici regis (dee **non** rez-ə-**den**-shee-ə **kler**-ə-sɪ **ree**-jis), *n.* [Law Latin "of the nonresidence of a parson employed in royal service"] (17c) *Hist.* A writ to excuse a parson from nonresidence because the parson is busy serving the Crown. See NONRESIDENCE (1).

de non sane memorie (dee **non** sayn **mem**-ə-ree). [Law French] (17c) Of unsound memory; of unsound mind. See MIND AND MEMORY; NON COMPOS MENTIS.

denotative fact. See FACT.

denounce, *vb.* (13c) **1.** To condemn openly; to express strong disapproval of someone or something, esp. in a very public way. **2.** To declare (an act or thing) to be a crime and prescribe a punishment for it. **3.** To accuse or inform against; esp., to give information to the police or other law-enforcement authorities about someone's illegal activities, esp. illegal political activities. **4.** To give formal notice to a foreign country of the termination of (a treaty).

denouncement. (16c) **1.** An act of accusation or condemnation <denouncement of a thief>. **2.** A declaration of a threatened action <denouncement of war> <denouncement of a treaty>. **3.** An application for a grant to work a mine that is either newly discovered or forfeited <the denouncement was granted>. • Historically, denouncements were also granted under Spanish-American law. **4.** *Archaic.* A formal announcement; a declaration <a denouncement of a doctrine>. — Also termed *denunciation.* — **denunciatory, denunciative,** *adj.*

de novi operis nuntiatione. See NOVI OPERIS NUNTIATIO.

de novo (di **noh**-voh *or* dee), *adj.* (1536) Anew.

- ▸ **hearing de novo.** See HEARING.
- ▸ **trial de novo.** See TRIAL.
- ▸ ***venire facias de novo*** (və-**nɪ**-ree **fay**-shee-əs dee **noh**-voh). See VENIRE FACIAS.

de novo damus (di **noh**-voh **day**-məs). [Law Latin "we give anew"] (17c) *Scots law.* The novodamus clause in a renewal of a gift or previous charter. See NOVODAMUS.

de novo judicial review. See JUDICIAL REVIEW.

de novo review. **1.** See *appeal de novo* under APPEAL. **2.** See *de novo judicial review* under JUDICIAL REVIEW.

density zoning. See *cluster zoning* under ZONING.

denumeration. (18c) An act of making a present payment.

denunciation. See DENOUNCEMENT.

denuntiatio (di-nən-shee-**ay**-shee-oh), *n.* [Latin] **1.** *Roman & civil law.* A declaration intended to protect or set in motion the enforcement of the declarer's right; esp., a report of a crime. **2.** *Hist.* A summons; a public notice. **3.** *Scots law.* The Crown's public denunciation of a debtor as a rebel and an outlaw when the debtor has disobeyed an order to pay. Pl. ***denuntiationes.***

denuntiatio belli (di-nən-shee-**ay**-shee-oh **bel**-ɪ). [Latin "declaration of war"). A declaration of war. See *declaration of war* under DECLARATION (3).

deny the appeal. See AFFIRM (1).

deodand (**dee**-ə-dand). (16c) *Hist.* Something (such as an animal) that has done wrong and must therefore be forfeited to the Crown. • Deodand was abolished in 1846.

> "In the oldest records, we see no attempt to distinguish the cases in which the dead man was negligent from those in which no fault could be imputed to him, and the large number of deodands collected in every eyre suggests that many horses and boats bore the guilt which should have been ascribed to beer. A drunken carter is crushed beneath the wheels of his cart; the cart, the cask of wine that was in it and the oxen that were drawing it are all deodand. Bracton apparently thought it an abuse to condemn as deodand a thing that had not moved; he would distinguish

between the horse which throws a man and the horse off which a man stupidly tumbles, between the tree that falls and the tree against which a man is thrown. We do not see these distinctions in the practice of the courts." 2 Frederick Pollock & Frederic W. Maitland, *History of English Law Before the Time of Edward I* 474 n.4 (2d ed. 1899).

"[W]hen in 1716 the coroner's jury of Yarmouth declared a stack of timber which had fallen on a child to be forfeited as a deodand, it was ransomed for 30s., which was paid over to the child's father." J.W. Cecil Turner, *Kenny's Outlines of Criminal Law* 7 (16th ed. 1952).

de odio et atia (dee **oh**-dee-oh et **ay**-shee-ə), *n.* [Law Latin "of hatred and malice"] (18c) *Hist.* A writ ordering a sheriff to summon a 12-member jury to inquire whether a prisoner jailed for murder was charged for a good reason or only because of ill-will and to determine whether bail should be set. • If the prisoner was accused out of spite or had committed the crime in self-defense, then another writ called *tradas in ballim* would have been issued ordering the sheriff to release the prisoner on bail if the sheriff could find 12 good citizens of the county to vouch for the prisoner. This writ, similar to *habeas corpus,* was first mentioned in Magna Carta. — Also termed *breve de bono et malo.*

"The right to personal liberty is guarded by the writ of *habeas corpus,* preceded by the writ *de odio et atia* referred to in Cap. 36 of Magna Carta: 'Nothing shall be given or demanded of another for the writ of inquisition of life or limb, but is shall be given gratis and never denied.' The right to be informed at once upon arrest of the nature and cause of the accusation is a different and independent constitutional right from that to a grand jury or the process of indictment; although many State Constitutions confound the two. The right to be informed of the nature and cause of the accusation is instantaneous upon arrest, or at least arises as soon as the accused is brought before a magistrate." Frederic Jesup Stimson, *The Law of the Federal and State Constitutions of the United States* 19 (1908).

de onerando pro rata portione (dee on-ə-**ran**-doh proh **ray**-tə por-shee-**oh**-nee), *n.* [Law Latin "of charging according to a ratable proportion"] (17c) *Hist.* A writ for a joint tenant or cotenant who is distrained for more rent than is proportionately required.

deontological duty. See *ethical duty* under DUTY (2).

deontological jurisprudence. See *critical jurisprudence* under JURISPRUDENCE.

deontology. (1826) The philosophy of ethics, rights, and duties as a matter of natural law; the scholarly study of moral and ethical duties. • The term most commonly appears in discussions of ethical theories (such as that of Immanuel Kant) that see right moral action as related to the fulfillment of duties rather than as the achievement of certain good consequences (as in utilitarianism). Moral rights in one's one intellectual property are often considered deontological issues. — **deontological,** *adj.*

de pace et legalitate tenenda (dee **pay**-see et lə-gal-ə-**tay**-tee tə-**nen**-də). [Latin] *Hist.* A writ for keeping the peace and adherence to the laws (or good behavior). — Also termed *de pace et legalitate tuenda.*

de pace et plagis (dee **pay**-see et **play**-jis), *n.* [Law Latin "of breach of peace and wounds"] (18c) *Hist.* A type of criminal appeal used in cases of assault, wounding, and breach of the peace.

de pace et roberia (dee **pay**-see et roh-**beer**-ee-ə), *n.* [Law Latin "of breach of peace and robbery"] *Hist.* A type of criminal appeal used in cases of robbery and breach of the peace.

de parco fracto (dee **pahr**-koh **frak**-toh), *n.* [Law Latin "of pound breach"] (17c) *Hist.* A writ against someone, esp. an owner, who breaks into a pound to rescue animals that have been legally distrained and impounded.

"And, being thus in the custody of the law, the taking them back by force is looked upon as an atrocious injury, and denominated a *rescous,* for which the distreinor has a remedy in damages, either by writ of *rescous,* in case they were going to the pound, or by writ *de parco fracto,* or *pound-breach,* in case they were actually impounded." 3 William Blackstone, *Commentaries on the Laws of England* 146 (1768).

de partitione facienda (dee pahr-tish-ee-**oh**-nee fay-shee-**en**-də), *n.* [Law Latin] (16c) *Hist.* A writ to partition lands or tenements.

department, *n.* (18c) **1.** A division of a greater whole; a subdivision <a legal department>. **2.** A country's division of territory, usu. for governmental and administrative purposes, as in the division of a state into counties <France has regional departments similar to states>. **3.** A principal branch or division of government <legislative department>; specif., a division of the executive branch of the U.S. government, headed by a secretary who is a member of the President's cabinet <Department of Labor>. — Also termed *government department*; *governmental department.* — **departmental,** *adj.*

departmentalism. *Constitutional law.* The doctrine, prominent in the decades shortly after ratification of the Constitution but defended only sporadically since the late 19th century, that the three branches of the national government have separate and coordinate authority to interpret the Constitution and that no branch is bound by the interpretations advanced by another. • Particularly opposed to the theory of judicial supremacy, departmentalism has in recent years also been embraced as a cognate or allied doctrine by some popular constitutionalists. Cf. JUDICIAL SUPREMACY; JUDICIAL REVIEW; POPULAR CONSTITUTIONALISM. — **departmentalist,** *adj.* & *n.*

Department of Agriculture. The cabinet-level department of the federal government responsible for improving farm income, developing foreign markets for U.S. farm products, conducting agricultural research, and inspecting and grading food products. • Created in 1862, it is headed by the Secretary of Agriculture. — Abbr. USDA.

Department of Commerce. The cabinet-level department of the federal government responsible for promoting the country's international trade, economic growth, and technical advancement. • Designated as a department in 1913, it is headed by the Secretary of Commerce. — Abbr. DOC.

Department of Defense. See DEFENSE DEPARTMENT.

Department of Defense Dependents Schools. A unit in the U.S. Department of Defense responsible for operating schools from kindergarten through grade 12 for the dependents of military and civilian personnel stationed overseas. — Abbr. DoDDS.

Department of Education. The cabinet-level department of the federal government responsible for advising the President on federal education policy, and administering and coordinating most federal programs of assistance to education. • Headed by the Secretary of Education, the Department includes the Office of Bilingual Education and Minority Languages Affairs (OBEMLA), the Office of Educational Research and Improvement (OERI), the Office of Elementary and Secondary Education (OESE), the Office of Postsecondary Education (OPE), the Office of Special Education and Rehabilitative Services (OSERS), the Office of Student Financial (OSF), the Office of Vocational and Adult Education (OVAE), and ten regional offices. — Abbr. DOE.

Department of Energy. The cabinet-level department of the federal government responsible for advising the President on energy policies, plans, and programs, and for providing leadership in achieving efficient energy use, diversity in energy sources, and improved environmental quality.• Headed by the Secretary of Energy, it oversees a comprehensive national energy plan, including the research, development, and demonstration of energy technology; energy conservation; the nuclear-weapons program; and pricing and allocation. — Abbr. DOE.

Department of Health and Human Services. The cabinet-level department of the federal government responsible for matters of health, welfare, and income security. • It was originally established by Reorganization Plan No. 1 of 1953 under the title Department of Health, Education, and Welfare. The Department is headed by the Secretary of Health and Human Services. — Abbr. HHS.

Department of Homeland Security. The cabinet-level department of the federal government responsible for ensuring security within the U.S. borders and in its territories and possessions. • The Department has five major divisions: Border and Transportation Security, Emergency Preparedness and Response, Science and Technology, Information Analysis and Infrastructure, and Management. It was established in 2002 and began operating in 2003. — Abbr. DHS.

Department of Housing and Urban Development. The cabinet-level department of the federal government responsible for overseeing programs that are concerned with housing needs and fair-housing opportunities, and with improving and developing the country's communities. • It was established in 1965 by the Department of Housing and Urban Development Act. 42 USCA §§ 3532–3537. It is headed by the Secretary of Housing and Urban Development. — Abbr. HUD.

department of human services. See DEPARTMENT OF PUBLIC WELFARE. — Abbr. DHS.

department of interior. See DEPARTMENT OF THE INTERIOR.

Department of Justice. The federal executive division that is responsible for federal law enforcement and related programs and services. • The U.S. Attorney General heads this department, which has separate divisions for prosecuting cases under federal antitrust laws, tax laws, environmental laws, and criminal laws. The department also has a civil division that represents the U.S. government in cases involving tort claims and commercial litigation. — Abbr. DOJ.

> "Established by the Judiciary Act of 1870, the U.S. Department of Justice handles most of the legal work of the federal government, including investigations and enforcement of federal law. It assists in prosecutions in lower federal courts through its role overseeing the U.S. attorneys and represents the government before the Supreme Court. In addition, the department provides legal advice and opinions to the president and heads of the executive departments. The U.S. attorney general administers the Department of Justice and serves as a member of the cabinet and a presidential adviser. Seventy-six men have served in that capacity; in 1993, Janet Reno became the first woman attorney general. The attorney general's office, created by the Judiciary Act of 1789, predates the Justice Department by eighty years. Initially, the duties of the attorney general were almost exclusively legal, centering on Supreme Court litigation and advice to the executive branch on questions of law. But with the growth of the department and expansion of its activities, the attorney general's post has become primarily administrative." Nancy V. Baker, "Justice, Department of," in *A Historical Guide to the U.S. Government* 345, 345 (George Thomas Kurian ed., 1998).

Department of Labor. The cabinet-level department of the federal government responsible for promoting the welfare of wage earners and for improving working conditions and opportunities for profitable employment. • Headed by the Secretary of Labor, it was created in 1913. 29 USCA § 551. — Abbr. DOL.

department of public welfare. (1909) A state-government agency that administers public-assistance programs of all types, such as food stamps and housing vouchers. • In many communities, this department is now called the Department of Human Services or Department of Social Services. — Abbr. DPW.

Department of Social Services. See CHILD PROTECTIVE SERVICES. — Abbr. DSS.

Department of State. The cabinet-level department of the federal government responsible for advising the President in formulating and executing foreign policy. • Headed by the Secretary of State, the Department negotiates treaties and other agreements with foreign countries; speaks for the United States before the United Nations and other international organizations; and represents the United States at international conferences. It was established in 1789 as the Department of Foreign Affairs and was renamed the Department of State later the same year. 22 USCA 2651–2728. Foreign affairs are handled through six bureaus: African Affairs, European Affairs, East Asian and Pacific Affairs, Near East Affairs, South Asian Affairs, and Western Hemisphere Affairs. — Also termed *State Department.*

Department of the Interior. The cabinet-level department of the federal government responsible for managing the country's public lands and minerals, national parks, national wildlife refuges, and western water resources, and for upholding federal trust responsibilities to Indian tribes. • The Department also has responsibility for migratory-wildlife conservation; historical preservation; endangered species; surface-mined-lands preservation and restoration; mapping; and geological, hydrological, and biological science. It was created in 1849 and reorganized in 1950. Headed by the Secretary of the Interior, it administers several agencies, including the Bureau of Land Management, the Bureau of Indian Affairs, the U.S. Fish and Wildlife Service, and the U.S. Geological Survey. — Also termed *Interior Department.*

Department of the Navy. See NAVY DEPARTMENT.

Department of the Treasury. The cabinet-level department of the federal government responsible for recommending tax and fiscal policies, collecting taxes, disbursing U.S. government funds, enforcing tax laws, and manufacturing coins and currency. • Created by Congress in 1789, it is headed by the Secretary of the Treasury. — Also termed *Treasury Department.*

Department of Transportation. The federal executive division responsible for programs and policies concerning transportation. • Through a series of specialized agencies, this department oversees aviation, highways, railroads, mass transit, the U.S. merchant marine, and other programs. — Abbr. DOT.

Department of Veterans Affairs. The cabinet-level department of the federal government responsible for operating programs that benefit veterans of military service and their families. • It is headed by the Secretary of Veterans Affairs. — Abbr. VA. — Formerly termed *Veterans Administration.*

departure, *n.* (15c) **1.** A deviation or divergence from a standard rule, regulation, measurement, or course of conduct <an impermissible departure from sentencing guidelines>.

▸ **downward departure.** (1981) In the federal sentencing guidelines, a court's discretionary imposition of a sentence more lenient than the standard guidelines propose, as when the facts militate in favor of a lesser punishment. — Abbr. DD. — Also termed *downward sentence departure.* See FEENEY AMENDMENT; DIVERSION PROGRAM. Cf. *upward departure.*

▸ **forbidden departure.** (1996) An impermissible deviation from the federal sentencing guidelines based on race, sex, national origin, creed, religion, or socioeconomic status.

▸ **lateral departure.** (1993) In the federal sentencing guidelines, a sentence allowing a defendant to avoid incarceration through community or home confinement. — Also termed *lateral sentencing.*

▸ **upward departure.** (1981) In the federal sentencing guidelines, a court's imposition of a sentence harsher than the standard guidelines propose, as when the court concludes that a criminal's history did not take into account additional offenses committed by the prisoner. — Also termed *upward sentence departure.* Cf. *downward departure.*

2. A variance between a pleading and a later pleading or proof <the departure between the plaintiff's pleadings and the actual evidence was significant>. **3.** A party's desertion of the ground (either legal or factual) taken in the immediately preceding pleading and resort to another ground <the defendant's departure from the asserted alibi necessitated a guilty plea>. — **depart,** *vb.*

departure in despite of court. *Hist.* A failure of a defendant (called a tenant) in a real action to appear on demand. • A tenant, having once appeared in a real action, was considered to be constructively present until again called. So if the tenant failed to appear when demanded, the tenant was said to have departed in despite (in contempt) of court.

departure order. See ORDER (2).

dépeçage (dep-ə-**sahzh**). [French "dismemberment"] A court's application of different state laws to different issues in a legal dispute; choice of law on an issue-by-issue basis.

depeculation (dee-pek-yə-**lay**-shən). (17c) *Hist.* Embezzlement from the public treasury. Cf. PECULATION. — **depeculate,** *vb.*

dependence. (16c) **1.** A relationship between two persons or things whereby one is sustained by the other or relies on the other for support or necessities <our dependence on oil>. **2.** The quality, state, or condition of being addicted to drugs, alcohol, etc. <alcohol dependence>. **3.** The quality, state, or condition of being strongly affected by another thing <the mutual dependence of economic freedom and democracy>.

dependency. (16c) A land or territory geographically distinct from the country governing it, but belonging to the country and governed by its laws. • The Philippines was formerly a dependency of the United States. Cf. COMMONWEALTH (2); TERRITORY (1).

dependency court. See COURT.

dependency exemption. See EXEMPTION (3).

dependency hearing. See *shelter hearing* under HEARING.

dependent, *n.* (16c) **1.** Someone who relies on another for support; one not able to exist or sustain oneself without the power or aid of someone else.

▸ **lawful dependent.** (1908) **1.** Someone who receives an allowance or benefits from the public, such as social security. **2.** Someone who qualifies to receive a benefit from private funds as determined by the laws governing the distribution.

▸ **legal dependent.** (1909) Someone who is dependent according to the law; a person who derives principal support from another and usu. may invoke laws to enforce that support.

▸ **partial dependent.** (1914) *Workers' compensation.* A person whose partial reliance on an employee covered under workers'-compensation law for support entitles him or her to receive death benefits if the employee is killed on the job.

2. *Tax.* A person, such as a child or parent, for whom a taxpayer may be able to claim a personal exemption if the taxpayer provides more than half of the person's support during the taxable year. • Besides support, other criteria must be met as well. IRC (26 USCA) § 152. — Also spelled (BrE, both senses 1 & 2) *dependant.* — **dependent,** *adj.*

dependent child. See CHILD.

dependent claim. See PATENT CLAIM.

dependent condition. See CONDITION (2).

dependent contract. See CONTRACT.

dependent covenant. See COVENANT (1).

dependent coverage. See COVERAGE (1).

dependent intervening cause. (1950) A cause of an accident or injury that occurs between the defendant's behavior and the injurious result, but that does not change the defendant's liability. See *intervening cause* under CAUSE (1).

dependent obligation. See *conditional obligation* under OBLIGATION.

dependent promise. See PROMISE.

dependent relative revocation. (1855) A common-law doctrine that undoes an otherwise effective revocation of a will when there is evidence that the testator's revocation was conditional rather than absolute. • One rationale for the doctrine is that the testator's intent to revoke the will was conditional rather than absolute. More often, the rationale is a theory of the second-best: the court seeks a solution that comes as close as possible to reaching the frustrated dispositive result that the testator intended. Typically, the doctrine applies when a testator has physically revoked the will and believes that a new will is valid, although this belief is mistaken. The doctrine undoes only the revocation; it does not always accomplish the testator's intent or validate an otherwise invalid will. — Also termed *dependent-relative-revocation doctrine; conditional revocation; mistakenly induced revocation; ineffective revocation; doctrine of ineffective revocation.*

dependent state. See *nonsovereign state* under STATE (1).

de perambulatione facienda (dee pə-ram-byə-lay-shee-**oh**-nee fay-shee-**en**-də), *n.* [Law Latin "for making perambulation"] (17c) *Hist.* A writ ordering the sheriff to go with 12 knights of the county to settle a boundary dispute by walking about to determine the proper boundary between adjacent towns or lordships.

de placito (dee **plas**-ə-toh), *n.* [Law Latin] Of a plea. • These words were used in a declaration describing the particular action being brought, as in *de placito debit* ("of a plea of debt").

de plagis et mahemio (dee **play**-jis et mə-**hee**-mee-oh), *n.* [Law Latin "of wounds and mayhem"] *Hist.* A type of criminal appeal used in cases of wounding and maiming.

de plano (dee **play**-noh). [Latin "from ground level"] (16c) **1.** *Roman law.* Informally; in a summary manner. • The praetor would administer justice *de plano* when he stood on the same level with the parties instead of sitting on an elevated bench. **2.** *Hist.* Clearly; manifestly, as in *de bigamis.* See DE BIGAMIS. **3.** *Hist.* By collusion. **4.** *Scots law.* Forthwith.

de plegiis acquietandis (dee **plee**-jee-is ə-kwi-ə-**tan**-dis), *n.* [Law Latin "for acquitting or releasing pledges"] (18c) *Hist.* A writ ordering repayment to a surety by a principal who had failed to make a required payment that the surety then had to cover.

depletable economic interest. (1940) A mineral-land interest subject to depletion by the removal (by drilling or mining) of the mineral that is the subject of the interest.

depletion, *n.* (17c) An emptying, exhausting, or wasting of an asset, esp. of a finite natural resource such as oil. — **deplete,** *vb.* — **depletive,** *adj.*

depletion allowance. See ALLOWANCE (3).

depletion reserve. (1915) *Accounting.* A charge to income reflecting the decrease in the value of a wasting asset, such as an oil reserve.

deplore, *vb.* (16c) **1.** To disapprove of (something) strongly and to condemn it both severely and publicly. **2.** To expose deep regret or concern for; to regard with grief or sorrow.

deploy, *vb.* (18c) **1.** To organize one or more (soldiers, pieces of military equipment, etc.) so as to be in the right place at the desired time. **2.** To use (something) for a particular purpose, esp. ideas, arguments, skills, etc. <a job requiring you to deploy a good deal of ingenuity>.

depolicing. The practice of law-enforcement officers who intentionally overlook suspicious behavior or ignore small crimes, such as traffic violations, esp. by members of ethnic minorities, in order to avoid being accused of racism or racial profiling. See RACIAL PROFILING.

depone (di-**pohn**), *vb.* (16c) *Scots law.* To testify. See DEPOSE.

de ponendo sigillum ad exceptionem (dee pə-**nen**-doh si-**jil**-əm ad ek-sep-shee-**oh**-nəm), *n.* [Law Latin "for putting a seal to an exception"] *Hist.* A writ directing justices of assize to preserve exceptions taken by a party in a case.

deponent (di-**poh**-nənt), *n.* (16c) **1.** Someone who testifies by deposition. **2.** A witness who gives written testimony for later use in court; AFFIANT (1). — **depone,** *vb.*

▸ **absent deponent.** (1954) **1.** A person who fails to appear at a deposition after being subpoenaed. **2.** A deponent who is not available to appear at trial.

depopulatio agrorum (dee-pop-yoo-**lay**-shee-oh ə-**gror**-əm), *n.* [Law Latin "depopulating the county"] (18c) *Hist.* The crime of destroying or ravaging a country. • A person could not claim the benefit of clergy for this crime.

depopulation. (15c) **1.** A substantial reduction in population. **2.** *Hist.* A species of waste by which the kingdom's population was diminished. See DEPOPULATIO AGRORUM.

deportable, *adj.* (1891) (Of an alien) subject to removal from a country after an illegal entry.

deportable alien. See ALIEN.

deportatio (dee-por-**tay**-shee-oh), *n.* [fr. Latin *deportare* "to carry away"] *Roman law.* Permanent exile of a condemned criminal involving loss of citizenship and, usu., forfeiture of all property. Cf. RELEGATIO.

> "Deportatio. Perpetual banishment of a person condemned for a crime. It was the severest form of banishment since it included additional penalties, such as seizure of the whole property, loss of Roman citizenship, confinement to a definite place. Under the Principate it replaced the former *interdictio aqua et igni.* The emperor could grant the deportee full amnesty, which restored him to his former rights (*postliminium*). Places of *deportatio* were islands (*in insulam*) near the Italian shore or an oasis in the Libyan desert." Adolf Berger, *Encyclopedic Dictionary of Roman Law* 432 (1953).

deportation (dee-por-**tay**-shən), *n.* (16c) The act or an instance of removing a person to another country; esp., the expulsion or transfer of an alien from a country. Cf. TRANSPORTATION (2). — **deport,** *vb.*

> "Deportation, or removal, is the process by which a noncitizen may be expelled from a country for violations of immigration law. In the United States deportation is a highly structured, bureaucratized process that applies to any 'alien,' a legal term meaning 'any person not a citizen or national of the United States.' Deportation may apply both to noncitizens who have entered the United States legally and also to others. U.S. deportation law has two basic forms, reflecting distinct goals: extended border control and post-entry social control. Extended border control seeks to remove those noncitizens who have evaded the rules that govern legal entry. Post-entry social control regulates those who have been legally admitted but who then engage in any of various prohibited behaviors. An array of fast-track mechanisms also exists, such as expedited removal, administrative removal, and reinstatement of removal. Indeed, much of the evolution of deportation law in the late twentieth and early twenty-first centuries has involved what is termed 'deformalization,' in which procedural rights are severely restricted. Harsh substantive changes to the U.S. deportation system, implemented in 1996, have resulted in the deportation of millions of noncitizens—many undocumented but also hundreds of thousands with legal immigration status. Many are barred from ever returning." Daniel Kanstroom, "Deportations and Repatriations," in 1 *The Oxford Encyclopedia of American Social History* 259, 259–60 (Lynn Dumenil ed., 2012).

deportation order. See ORDER (2).

deportee. (1895) Someone who has been deported or has been ordered to be deported.

deportment. (17c) **1.** The way one behaves in public; one's bearing, esp. as it affects one's professionalism or unprofessionalism. **2.** The way a person stands and talks, esp. when viewed with reference to propriety.

depose (di-**pohz**), *vb.* (14c) **1.** To examine (a witness) in a deposition <the defendant's attorney will depose the plaintiff on Tuesday>. **2.** To testify; to bear witness <the affiant deposes and states that he is at least 18 years old>. **3.** To remove from office or from a position of power; dethrone <rebels sought to depose the dictator>.

deposit, *n.* (17c) **1.** The act of giving money or other property to another who promises to preserve it or to use it and return it in kind; esp., the act of placing money in a bank for safety and convenience. — Also termed (when made at a bank) *bank deposit.* **2.** The money or property so given.

▸ **demand deposit.** (1907) A bank deposit that the depositor may withdraw at any time without prior notice to the bank.

▸ **direct deposit.** (1972) The payment of money by transferring the payment directly into the payee's bank account, usu. by electronic transfer.

▸ **frozen deposit.** (1942) A bank deposit that cannot be withdrawn, as when the financial institution is insolvent or an account is restricted.

▸ **general deposit.** (1810) **1.** A bank deposit of money that is commingled with other depositors' money. • A deposit made in the ordinary course of business is presumed to be general. **2.** A bank deposit that is to the depositor's credit, thus giving the depositor a right to the money and creating a debtor–creditor relationship between the bank and the depositor. • A bank is not required to return the actual money deposited as a general deposit, as it must with a special deposit; the bank need return only an equivalent sum.

▸ **special deposit.** (18c) A bank deposit that is made for a specific purpose, that is kept separately, and that is to be returned to the depositor. • The bank serves as a bailee or trustee for a special deposit by special agreement or under circumstances sufficient to create a trust. — Cf. *specific deposit.*

> "Where money or any other thing is received by a bank for safe-keeping and return of the identical money or thing, the transaction is termed a 'special deposit.' In such case the relation between the bank and the depositor is that of bailee and bailor. Where the bailment is gratuitous, the bank is liable only for such loss as results from its gross negligence." Francis B. Tiffany, *Handbook of the Law of Banks and Banking* 12 (1912).

▸ **specific deposit.** (1826) A bank deposit of money that may be commingled with the bank's own funds but is intended for a specific purpose. — Also termed *deposit for a specific purpose.* Cf. *special deposit.*

> "Where money is received by a bank, not for deposit on general account or for safe-keeping and return, but to apply to a specific purpose, the transaction is often termed a 'specific deposit.' In such case, although the money is to be mingled with the bank's own funds, it is generally, but not universally, held that the bank holds the deposit or fund as a trustee." Francis B. Tiffany, *Handbook of the Law of Banks and Banking* 12 (1912).

▸ **time deposit.** (1950) A bank deposit that is to remain for a specified period or for which notice must be given to the bank before withdrawal. — Also termed *term deposit.*

3. Money placed with a person as earnest money or security for the performance of a contract. • The money will be forfeited if the depositor fails to perform. — Also termed *security deposit.* **4.** *Copyright.* The placing of two copies of a published work with the Library of Congress within three months of publication. • This requirement is independent of copyright registration. **5.** *Civil law.* A contract by which a depositor delivers a thing to a depositary for safekeeping. La. Civ. Code arts. 2926, 2929. • A deposit may be either an onerous or a gratuitous contract. — Also termed *depositum; naked deposit; gratuitous deposit.* See *gratuitous bailment* under BAILMENT (1).

▸ **involuntary deposit.** (1904) A deposit made by accidentally leaving or placing personal property in another's possession. See *involuntary bailment* under BAILMENT (1).

▸ **necessary deposit.** (1832) A bailment, usu. made by reason of emergency or other necessity, that prevents the depositor from freely choosing the depositary. • A necessary deposit occurs, for example, when a person entrusts goods to a stranger during a fire.

> "Deposits, in the civil law, are divisible into two kinds: necessary and voluntary. A necessary deposit is such as is made by the party upon some sudden emergency, and from some pressing necessity, as, for instance, in case of a fire, a shipwreck, or other overwhelming calamity; and it is, therefore, confided to any person, with whom the depositor meets, without any proper opportunity for reflection or choice; and thence it is called *Miserabile depositum.* A voluntary deposit is such as arises without any such calamity, from the mere consent and agreement of the parties. This distinction was material in the civil law in respect to the remedy; for, in voluntary deposits, the action was only *in simplum,* in the other, it is *in duplum,* or twofold, whenever the depositary was guilty of any default. The common law has made no such distinction; and, therefore, in a necessary deposit, the remedy is limited to damages coextensive with the wrong." Joseph Story, *Commentaries on the Law of Bailments* § 44, at 45–6 (Edmund H. Bennett ed., 8th ed. 1870).

▸ **quasi-deposit.** (1832) An involuntary deposit made when one party lawfully possesses property merely by finding it.

▸ **voluntary deposit.** (1844) A deposit made by the mutual consent of the bailor and bailee.

6. *Patents.* The placing of a sample of microorganisms or cell lines with the U.S. Patent and Trademark Office to satisfy the enablement requirement. • The practice is not statutory but has been established by regulation and caselaw. 37 CFR §§ 1.801–809. — Also termed *enablement by deposit; patent deposit.*

deposit account. See ACCOUNT.

depositary. (17c) **1.** A person or institution that one leaves money or valuables with for safekeeping <a title-insurance officer is the depositary of the funds>. • When a depositary is a company, it is often termed a *safe-deposit company.* Cf. DEPOSITORY. **2.** A gratuitous bailee. See DEPOSIT (5).

depositary bank. See BANK.

deposit box. See SAFE-DEPOSIT BOX.

deposit certificate. See CERTIFICATE OF DEPOSIT (1).

deposit company. See COMPANY.

deposit contract. See CONTRACT.

deposit for a specific purpose. See *specific deposit* under DEPOSIT (2).

deposit in court. The placing of money or other property that represents a person's potential liability in the court's temporary custody, pending the outcome of a lawsuit. — Also termed *deposit into court*; *deposit into the registry of the court.*

deposit insurance. See INSURANCE.

deposit into the registry of the court. See DEPOSIT IN COURT.

deposition (dep-ə-**zish**-ən). (14c) **1.** A witness's out-of-court testimony that is reduced to writing (usu. by a court reporter) for later use in court or for discovery purposes. *See* Fed. R. Civ. P. 30; Fed. R. Crim. P. 15. — Also termed *examination before trial.* **2.** The session at which such testimony is recorded.

> "Definition of the term 'Deposition' (Depositio). In the civil law it meant simply the testimony of a witness. In very old English practice, simply the written testimony of a witness. In modern practice it means the testimony of a witness given or taken down in writing, under oath or affirmation, before a commissioner, examiner, or other judicial officer, in answer to interrogatories and cross-interrogatories, and usually subscribed by the witness. A deposition is therefore distinguished from an affidavit, which is always an *ex parte* statement drawn up in writing without any formal interrogation, and signed and sworn to by the party making it, although in affidavits the party making it is constantly called a deponent, and said to depose. Depositions were not formerly the ordinary incidents of common-law courts, but were subsequently introduced on the ground of necessity, where the oral testimony of a witness could not be obtained. But in courts of chancery it was quite frequently the case that this was the only kind of testimony which was taken, as was the case in the ecclesiastical courts." Edward P. Weeks, *A Treatise on the Law of Depositions* § 3, at 3–4 (1880).

▸ **apex deposition.** (1992) The deposition of a person whose position is at the highest level of a company's hierarchy. • Courts often preclude an apex deposition unless (1) the person to be deposed has particular knowledge regarding the claim, and (2) the requesting party cannot obtain the requested — and discoverable — information through less intrusive means.

▸ **corporate deposition.** See *30(b)(6) deposition.*

▸ **deposition *de bene esse*** (dee **bee**-nee **es**-ee *also* day **ben**-ay **es**-ay). (18c) A deposition taken from a witness who will likely be unable to attend a scheduled trial or hearing. • If the witness is not available to attend trial, the testimony is read at trial as if the witness were present in court. See *testimony de bene esse* under TESTIMONY.

▸ **deposition on written questions.** (1970) A deposition given in response to a prepared set of written questions, as opposed to a typical oral deposition. *See* Fed. R. Civ. P. 31. — Formerly also termed *deposition on written interrogatories.*

> "The advantage of a deposition on written questions is that counsel for the parties need not go to some distant place to be present at the taking of the deposition. Instead they serve on each other questions and cross questions — and even redirect and recross questions — that they wish to have put to the deponent. These are then sent to the officer who is to take the deposition. The officer puts the questions to the witness, records the answers, and transcribes and files the deposition as with an oral deposition. The officer is merely to record what the witness says in response to the various questions propounded to him or her." Charles Alan Wright, *The Law of Federal Courts* § 85, at 618–19 (5th ed. 1994).

▸ **naturalization deposition.** *Hist.* A formal statement made by a witness in support of someone's naturalization petition. See NATURALIZATION PETITION.

▸ **oral deposition.** (1910) A deposition given in response to oral questioning by a lawyer.

▸ **supporting deposition.** (1959) *Criminal procedure.* A sworn statement of a complaining witness or police office in factual substantiation of an accusatory instrument.

▸ **30(b)(6) deposition.** (1979) Under the Federal Rules of Civil Procedure, the deposition of an organization, through the organization's designated representative. • Under Rule 30(b)(6), a party may take the deposition of an organization, such as a corporation. The notice of deposition (or subpoena) may name the organization and may specify the matters to be covered in the deposition. The organization must then designate a person to testify about those matters on its behalf. Fed. R. Civ. P. 30(b)(6). Most states authorize a similar procedure under state-court procedural rules. — Also termed *corporate deposition.*

3. The written record of a witness's out-of-court testimony. **4.** *Eccles. law.* The involuntary release of a clergyman from the exercise of his office. Cf. DEGRADATION (1); DEPRIVATION (4). **5.** The natural process of depositing a substance on rocks or soil.

deposition hearing. See HEARING.

deposition on written interrogatories. See *deposition on written questions* under DEPOSITION (2).

deposition on written questions. See DEPOSITION (2).

deposition subpoena. See SUBPOENA.

deposition subpoena duces tecum. See *subpoena duces tecum* under SUBPOENA.

deposit of title deeds. (1827) A pledge of real property as security for a loan, by placing with the lender, as pledgee, the title-deed to the land.

depositor, *n.* (17c) Someone who makes a deposit. See DEPOSIT.

depository (di-**poz**-ə-tor-ee), *n.* (17c) A place where one can leave money or valuables for safekeeping <the grade school's depository for used books>. Cf. DEPOSITARY (1).

depository bond. See BOND (2).

depository institution. (1932) **1.** An organization formed under state or federal law, authorized by law to receive deposits, and supervised and examined by a government agency for the protection of depositors. **2.** A trust company or other institution authorized by law to exercise fiduciary powers similar to those of a national bank. • The term does not include an insurance company, a Morris Plan bank, an industrial loan company, or similar bank unless its deposits are insured by a federal agency.

depository-transfer check. See CHECK.

Depository Trust Corporation. The principal central clearing agency for securities transactions on the public markets. — Abbr. DTC.

deposit premium. (1920) The initial premium paid by an insured pending the final premium adjustment.

deposit ratio. (1934) The ratio of total deposits to total capital.

deposit slip. (1890) A bank's written acknowledgment of an amount received on a certain date from a depositor.

depositum (di-**poz**-i-təm), *n. Roman law.* The gratuitous deposit of goods for the benefit of the depositor. • The depositee was liable only for *dolus.* See DOLUS (1). Cf. *gratuitous bailment* under BAILMENT (1); DEPOSIT (5); LOCATIO.

> "The Depositum was a contract of the law of nations, specified by a particular designation, *bonae fidei*, complete by delivery, according to which a moveable thing was delivered to be safely and gratuitously kept to be restored to the person who had so deposited it whensoever he required it. Gratuitously, [it is said,] because if anything was paid, it was locatio." John George Phillimore, *Private Law Among the Romans* 241 (1863).

deposit warrant. See WARRANT (2).

de post disseisina (dee **pohst** dis-**see**-zin-ə), *n.* [Law Latin "of past disseisin"] *Hist.* A writ for recovery of land by a person who had previously recovered the land from a disseisor by a *praecipe quod reddat* or on a default or reddition, but who was again disseised by the same disseisor.

depot (**dee**-poh), *n.* (18c) **1.** A place where goods are stored until they are needed; a warehouse. **2.** A place where buses are kept and repaired. **3.** A railroad or bus station.

de praerogativa regis (dee pri-rog-ə-**tɪ**-və **ree**-jis). See PRAEROGATIVA REGIS.

de praesenti (dee pri-**zen**-tɪ). [Law Latin] *Hist.* At present; of the present. • A consent to marriage *de praesenti* constitutes marriage in itself. — Also spelled *de presenti.* Cf. DE FUTURO.

depraved, *adj.* (14c) **1.** (Of a person or crime) completely evil or morally unacceptable; perverted. **2.** (Of a crime) heinous; morally horrendous.

depraved-heart murder. See MURDER.

depraved-indifference murder. See *depraved-heart murder* under MURDER.

depravity (di-**prav**-i-tee), *n.* (17c) **1.** The quality, state, or condition of being morally bad, thoroughly evil, or ethically reprehensible; moral degeneracy; wickedness. **2.** A wicked act or habit.

deprecate (**dep**-ri-kayt), *vb.* (17c) To disapprove of strongly; to criticize. — **deprecatory,** *adj.*

depreciable life. See USEFUL LIFE.

depreciation (di-pree-shee-**ay**-shən), *n.* (1862) A reduction in the value or price of something; specif., a decline in an asset's value because of use, wear, obsolescence, or age. Cf. APPRECIATION; AMORTIZATION (2). — **depreciate,** *vb.* — **depreciable,** *adj.*

▸ **accelerated depreciation.** (1936) Depreciation recorded using a method that writes off the cost of an asset more rapidly than the straight-line method.

▸ **accumulated depreciation.** (1916) The total depreciation currently recorded on an asset. • On the balance sheet, an asset's total cost less accumulated depreciation reflects the asset's book value. — Also termed *accrued depreciation.*

▸ **annual depreciation.** (1862) The yearly decrease in a property's value due to regular wear and tear.

▸ **economic depreciation.** (1926) A reduction in the value of an asset due to a shortening of the asset's economic life.

▸ **functional depreciation.** (1910) Depreciation that results from the replacement of equipment that is not yet worn out but that is obsolete in light of new technology or improved methodology allowing more efficient and satisfactory production.

depreciation method. (1915) A set formula used in estimating an asset's use, wear, or obsolescence over the asset's useful life or some portion thereof. • This method is useful in calculating the allowable annual tax deduction for depreciation. See USEFUL LIFE.

▸ **accelerated depreciation method.** (1964) A depreciation method that yields larger deductions in the earlier years of an asset's life and smaller deductions in the later years.

▸ **annuity depreciation method.** (2001) A depreciation method that allows for a return of imputed interest on the undepreciated balance of an asset's value. • The imputed interest is subtracted from the current depreciation amount before it is credited to the accumulated depreciation accounts.

▸ **declining-balance depreciation method.** (1947) A method of computing the annual depreciation allowance by multiplying the asset's undepreciated cost each year by a uniform rate that may not exceed double the straight-line rate or 150 percent.

▸ **double-declining depreciation method.** (1996) A depreciation method that spreads over time the initial cost of a capital asset by deducting in each period twice the percentage recognized by the straight-line method and applying that double percentage to the undepreciated balance existing at the start of each period.

▸ **replacement-cost depreciation method.** A depreciation method that fixes an asset's value by the price of its substitute.

▸ **sinking-fund depreciation method.** (1956) A depreciation method that accounts for the time value of money by setting up a depreciation-reserve account that earns interest, resulting in a gradual yearly increase in the depreciation deduction.

▸ **straight-line depreciation method.** (1930) A depreciation method that writes off the cost or other basis of the asset by deducting the expected salvage value from the initial cost of the capital asset, and dividing the difference by the asset's estimated useful life.

▸ **sum-of-the-years'-digits depreciation method.** A method of calculating the annual depreciation allowance by multiplying the depreciable cost basis (cost minus salvage value) by a constantly decreasing fraction, which is represented by the remaining years of useful life at the beginning of each year divided by the total number of years of useful life at the time of acquisition. — Sometimes shortened to *SYD method.*

▸ **unit depreciation method.** (1980) A depreciation method — directly related to the productivity of the asset — that divides the asset's value by the estimated total number of units to be produced, and then multiplies the unit cost by the number of units sold during the year, representing the depreciation expense for the year.

▸ **units-of-output depreciation method.** (2004) A method by which the cost of a depreciable asset, minus salvage value, is allocated to the accounting periods benefited based on output (as miles, hours, number of times used, and the like).

depreciation reserve. (1913) An account built up to offset the depreciation of property because of time and use, so that at the end of the property's service there is enough money to replace the property.

depredation. (15c) An act of taking or destroying something; esp., a plundering and pillaging.

de presenti. See DE PRAESENTI.

depression. (18c) **1.** A period of economic stress that persists over an extended period, accompanied by poor business conditions and high unemployment. Cf. RECESSION. **2.** A medical condition that makes one deeply unhappy and anxious and can prevent one from living a normal life.

"The medical definition of depression is a sustained abnormality in a person's mood, or feelings of despair, hopelessness, and self-hatred. A depressive episode is defined as a period lasting at least two weeks in which a person feels depressed or becomes unable to experience any pleasure, accompanied by some of the following: changes in sleep patterns, changes in appetite, changes in sexual desire, loss of interest in things that were previously interesting, loss of pleasure in life (anhedonia), loss of energy, inability to concentrate, slowing of reflexes and bodily movements (psychomotor retardation), feelings of guilt, and thoughts of suicide. The quality, intensity, and disruptive nature of the symptoms appear to be most relevant clinically. Depression is an affect state that can vary in intensity from relatively mild to profound, from a subtle experience to a severely disabling clinical disorder. Depression can be a relatively appropriate, if somewhat excessive, response to an accurate appraisal of reality, or it can be based on severe reality distortions." PDM Task Force, *Psychodynamic Diagnostic Manual* 109-10 (2006).

3. Less clinically, a feeling of sadness that makes one feel little if any hope for the future. **4.** A portion of a surface that is lower than the other parts.

deprivation. (15c) **1.** An act of taking away <deprivation of property>. **2.** A withholding of something that one needs, esp. in order to be healthy <deprivation of food>. **3.** The quality, state, or condition of being without something that is necessary <sleep deprivation>. **4.** A removal or degradation from office, esp. an ecclesiastical office <deprivation of the bishop>. Cf. DEPOSITION (4); DEGRADATION (1).

deprived child. See CHILD.

***Deprizio* doctrine.** (1990) *Bankruptcy.* The rule that a debtor's payment to an outside creditor more than 90 days before a bankruptcy filing is voidable as a preferential transfer if the payment also benefits an inside creditor. *Levit v. Ingersoll Rand Fin. Corp. (In re V.N. Deprizio Constr. Co.)*, 874 F.2d 1186 (7th Cir. 1989).

de procedendo ad judicium (dee proh-sə-**den**-doh ad joo-**dish**-ee-əm), *n.* [Law Latin "for proceeding in an assise"] (17c) *Hist.* A chancery writ ordering a lower court to proceed to judgment in a case that had been wrongfully stayed. • If the lower-court justices refused, they could be punished for contempt. See PROCEDENDO.

de proprietate probanda (dee prə-prɪ-ə-**tay**-tee prə-**ban**-də), *n.* [Law Latin "for proving property"] (17c) *Hist.* A writ ordering a sheriff to investigate the ownership of distrained goods claimed by a defendant in a replevin action.

"If therefore the distreinor claims any such property, the party replevying must sue out a writ *de proprietate probanda*, in which the sheriff is to try, by an inquest, in whom the property previous to the distress subsisted. And if it be found to be in the distreinor, the sheriff can proceed no farther; but must return the claim of property to the court of king's bench or common pleas, to be there farther prosecuted, if thought advisable, and there finally determined." 3 William Blackstone, *Commentaries on the Laws of England* 148 (1768).

depublished opinion. See OPINION (1).

depute, *n.* (15c) *Scots law.* A person appointed to act in an official capacity or as another official's representative.

deputy, *n.* (15c) **1.** A person appointed or delegated to act as a substitute for another, esp. for an official. **2.** Someone whose job is to help a sheriff, marshal, etc. **3.** In some countries, such as France, a member of parliament. — **deputize, depute,** *vb.*

▸ **courtroom deputy.** (1973) The deputy clerk assigned to a particular courtroom or a particular judge.

▸ **general deputy.** (17c) **1.** A deputy appointed to act in another officer's place and execute all ordinary functions of the office. **2.** See *deputy sheriff* under SHERIFF (1).

▸ **special deputy.** (16c) A deputy specially appointed to serve a particular purpose, such as keeping the peace during a riot.

deputy sheriff. See SHERIFF (1).

DEQ. *abbr.* DELIVERED EX QUAY.

de quarantina habenda (dee kwahr-ən-**tɪ**-nə hə-**ben**-də), *n.* [Law Latin "of return of quarantine"] (17c) *Hist.* A writ ordering a sheriff to give a widow possession of part of her husband's estate, after she had been wrongfully ejected but before dower is assigned. See QUARANTINE (4).

de quo (dee **kwoh**). [Latin] Of which. • These were formal words used in a writ of entry, as in a writ of entry "in the quo" or "in the *quibus*." — Also termed *de quibus*.

deraign, *n.* (13c) *Archaic.* The process of proving, vindicating, or maintaining a legal right. • Historically, a deraign commonly took the form of a duel or trial by combat. — Also termed *deraignment*.

deraign, *vb.* (13c) *Archaic.* **1.** To prove, justify, vindicate, or settle (a right or claim). **2.** To dispute or contest. **3.** *Hist.* To settle (a dispute) by battle or duel.

deraignment. See DERAIGN, *n.*

deranged, *adj.* (18c) Behaving in a crazy or dangerous way, usu. as a result of mental illness.

de raptu virginum (dee **rap**-t[y]oo **vər**-jə-nəm), *n.* [Latin "of the ravishment of virgins"] (18c) *Hist.* A writ for taking an appeal in a rape case.

de rationabilibus divisis (dee rash-ən-ə-**bil**-i-bəs di-**vɪ**-sis), *n.* [Law Latin "of the fixing of reasonable boundaries"] (17c) *Hist.* A writ to settle the boundaries between property owners of different towns when one owner claimed a trespass by the other.

de rationabili parte bonorum (dee rash-[ee]-ə-**nay**-bə-lı **pahr**-tee bə-**nor**-əm), *n.* [Law Latin "of reasonable share of goods"] (16c) *Hist.* A writ allowing the wife and children of a dead man to recover a reasonable share of his goods from his executors after his debts were paid. • This writ was usu. founded on custom rather than the general law.

de recenti (dee ri-**sen**-tı). [Law Latin] *Scots law.* Recently. • The term adds weight to a statement that is made or an event (such as an arrest) that occurs soon after an incident. In a theft case, for example, the presumption of guilt was greater when the suspect was identified soon after the theft occurred.

derecho de autor. See AUTHOR'S RIGHT.

derecho indiano. *Hist. Spanish law.* The law of the Indies; specif., during the colonization of North and South America, the law of the New World.

de recordo et processu mittendis (dee ri-**kor**-doh et proh-**ses**-[y]oo mi-**ten**-dis), *n.* [Law Latin "of the sending of the record and process of a cause to a superior court"] A type of writ of error.

de recto (dee **rek**-toh), *n.* [Law Latin] A writ of right to recover both the seisin and the property. — Also termed *breve de recto.* See WRIT OF COURSE.

de recto de advocatione (dee **rek**-toh dee ad-və-kay-shee-**oh**-nee), *n.* [Law Latin "of the right of advowson"] (17c) *Hist.* A writ restoring a person's right to present a clerk to a benefice when that right had been interfered with. • It was abolished by St. 3 & 4 Will. 4, ch. 27.

de recto de rationabili parte (dee **rek**-toh dee rash-[ee]-ə-**nay**-bə-lı **pahr**-tee), *n.* [Law Latin "of right of reasonable part"] (17c) *Hist.* A writ allowing one coparcener or blood relative owning land in fee simple to obtain a rightful share from the other. • It was abolished by St. 3 & 4 Will. 4, ch. 27.

de recto patens (dee **rek**-toh **pay**-tenz), *n.* [Law Latin "of right patent"] *Hist.* The highest writ of right under the law given to an owner in fee simple to recover the possession and use of land from the freehold tenant. — Also termed *breve magnum de recto.*

de redisseisina (dee ree-dis-**see**-zin-ə), *n.* [Law Latin "of redisseisin"] *Hist.* A writ for recovery of land or rent by a person who had previously recovered the land or rent by an assize of novel disseisin, but who was again disseised by the same disseisor. • This writ is similar to *de post disseisina.* See DE POST DISSEISINA; DISSEISIN.

deregistration, *n.* The point at which an issuer's registration under section 12 of the Securities Exchange Act of 1934 is no longer required because of a decline in the number of holders of the issuer's securities. 15 USCA § 78*l*. • Deregistration is triggered when the number of holders falls below a certain number or when required by an administrative order. Cf. DELISTING. — **deregister,** *vb.*

deregulate, *vb.* (1964) To remove government rules and controls from (businesses, usu. of particular types) <deregulating the airline industry>.

deregulation, *n.* (1963) The reduction or elimination of governmental control of business, esp. to permit free markets and competition.

▸ **financial deregulation.** (1981) The lessening of governmental oversight and intervention in the business of financial institutions. • Among other effects, regulation of financial contracts is relaxed and competition for depositors and borrowers increases.

deregulation clause. (1981) *Oil & gas.* A gas-contract provision specifying how the price of gas will be calculated and what the buyer's and seller's obligations will be if regulated natural gas becomes deregulated.

de rei gestae veritate (dee **ree**-ı **jes**-tee ver-i-**tay**-tee). [Law Latin] *Scots law.* Of the truth of the thing done. • A witness to a deed that had been lost could testify to the deed's existence and to the truthfulness of the statements contained in it.

derelict (**der**-ə-likt), *adj.* (17c) **1.** Forsaken; abandoned; cast away <derelict property>. See *quasi-derelict* under DERELICT. **2.** Lacking a sense of duty; in breach of a legal or moral obligation <the managers were derelict in their duties>. **3.** (Of a building) in bad condition from long disuse; run-down and dilapidated.

derelict, *n.* (17c) **1.** Personal property abandoned or thrown away by the owner with no intent to claim it any longer, such as a ship deserted at sea.

▸ **quasi-derelict.** (1833) A ship that has been deserted or abandoned temporarily or involuntarily, as when the crew is dead or otherwise incapable of navigating the ship.

2. Land uncovered by water receding from its former bed. **3.** A street person or vagrant; a hobo.

dereliction (der-ə-**lik**-shən), *n.* (16c) **1.** The forsaking of a legal or moral obligation with no intent to reassume it; abandonment <dereliction of duty>.

▸ **dereliction in the performance of duties.** (1903) *Military law.* Willful or negligent failure to perform assigned duties; culpable inefficiency in performing assigned duties.

▸ **dereliction of duty.** A deliberate or accidental failure to do what should be done, esp. as part of one's job; remissness.

2. The state of a building that is run-down and dilapidated. **3.** An increase of land caused by the receding of a sea, river, or stream from its usual watermark. See RELICTION.

derelict-official act. (1912) A statute that mandates forfeiture of office if the holder willfully neglects or fraudulently fails to perform official duties.

de reparatione facienda (dee rep-ə-ray-shee-**oh**-nee fay-shee-**en**-də). (17c) *Hist.* **1.** An action brought by a joint tenant to compel a cotenant to contribute to the repair of jointly held property. **2.** A writ issued in such an action. • The writ had to issue before repairs were undertaken. There was no remedy after repairs began.

de replegiore de averiis. See DE AVERIIS REPLEGIANDIS.

de rescussu (dee ri-**skəs**-[y]oo), *n.* [Law Latin "of rescue"] (17c) *Hist.* A writ available when cattle were distrained or persons were arrested, and then rescued.

de retorno habendo (dee ri-**tor**-noh hə-**ben**-doh). [Law Latin] (17c) For having a return. • This term applied to (1) a judgment for a defendant in a replevin action, (2) a writ of execution for a defendant awarded judgment in a replevin action, and (3) a surety provided by a plaintiff at the beginning of a replevin action.

d.e.r.i.c. *abbr.* DE EA RE ITA CENSUERE.

de rien culpable (dee **reen kəl**-pə-bəl). [Law French] Guilty of nothing; not guilty.

de rigore juris (dee ri-**gor**-ee **joor**-is). [Latin] Of the law's strictness.

derivation. (16c) The origin of something, esp. a word, phrase, or idea. — **derive,** *vb.*

derivation clause. (1979) A deed-of-trust provision that provides information about the transfer of a property, esp. the source of the title, such as the name of the previous grantor and the recording date of the deed. See *deed of trust* under DEED.

derivative, *adj. Copyright.* Of, relating to, or constituting a work that is taken from, translated from, adapted from, or in some way further develops a previous work. • Copyright protection includes the exclusive right in derivative works, such as a screenplay adapted from a book, or a variant musical arrangement.

derivative, *n.* (1985) **1.** Something that has developed from or been produced from something else. See *derivative work* under WORK (2). **2.** A financial instrument whose value depends on or is derived from the performance of a secondary source such as an underlying bond, currency, or commodity. — Also termed *derivative instrument*; *derivative security.*

> "Derivatives transactions may be based on the value of foreign currency, U.S. Treasury bonds, stock indexes, or interest rates. The values of these underlying financial instruments are determined by market forces, such as movements in interest rates. Within the broad panoply of derivatives transactions are numerous innovative financial instruments whose objectives may include a hedge against market risks, management of assets and liabilities, or lowering of funding costs; derivatives may also be used as speculation for profit." *Procter & Gamble Co. v. Bankers Trust Co.*, [1996–1997 Transfer Binder] Fed. Sec. L. Rep. (CCH) ¶ 99,229, at 95,238 (S.D. Ohio 1996).

> "As the price of a derivative is separate from, although linked to, the price of the underlying, and the price of the underlying changes over time (or exhibits volatility), the pricing or valuation of a derivative requires, as an input to the calculation, a prediction of the extent to which changes in the price of the underlying will occur. Derivatives are useful because the future price of the underlying is uncertain, and participants in the derivative markets either wish to decrease their exposures to these uncertain prices, because they wish to hedge against the risk of unfavourable movements, or to increase their exposures to these uncertain prices, because they wish to speculate on favourable movements." John-Peter Castagnino, *Derivatives: The Key Principles* 5 (3d ed. 2009).

derivative acquisition. See ACQUISITION.

derivative action. (18c) **1.** *Corporations.* A suit by a beneficiary of a fiduciary to enforce a right belonging to the fiduciary; esp., a suit asserted by a shareholder on the corporation's behalf against a third party (usu. a corporate officer) because of the corporation's failure to take some action against the third party. • If the claim involves a serious wrongdoing by those in control of the organization, a conflict may arise between the lawyer's duty to the organization and the lawyer's relationship with the board, and the lawyer may not be able to defend the action. *See* Fed. R. Civ. P. 23.1. — Also termed *derivative suit*; *shareholder derivative suit*; *stockholder derivative suit*; *representative action.* Cf. DIRECT ACTION (3). **2.** A lawsuit arising from an injury to another person, such as a husband's action for loss of consortium arising from an injury to his wife caused by a third person.

derivative contraband. See CONTRABAND.

derivative conveyance. See *secondary conveyance* under CONVEYANCE (1).

derivative deed. See *secondary conveyance* under CONVEYANCE.

derivative defense. See DEFENSE (1).

derivative entrapment. See ENTRAPMENT.

derivative estate. See ESTATE (1).

derivative evidence. See EVIDENCE.

derivative instrument. See DERIVATIVE (2).

derivative-jurisdiction doctrine. (1964) The principle that a case is not properly removable unless it is within the subject-matter jurisdiction of the state court from which it is removed.

derivative lease. See SUBLEASE.

derivative liability. See LIABILITY.

derivative market. See MARKET.

derivative possession. See POSSESSION.

derivative power. See POWER (3).

derivative security. See DERIVATIVE (2).

derivative settlement. See SETTLEMENT (2).

derivative suit. See DERIVATIVE ACTION (1).

derivative title. See TITLE (2).

derivative-use immunity. See *use immunity* under IMMUNITY (3).

derivative work. See WORK (2).

derived demand. See DEMAND (4).

derogable, *adj.* Capable of being reduced or limited.

derogable authority. See AUTHORITY (1).

derogation (der-ə-**gay**-shən), *n.* (15c) **1.** The partial repeal or abrogation of a law by a later act that limits its scope or impairs its utility and force <statutes in derogation of the common law>. **2.** Disparagement; depreciation in value or estimation <some argue that the derogation of family values has caused an increase in crime>. **3.** Detraction, prejudice, or destruction (of a grant or right) <an attorney may be punished for derogation from professional integrity>. **4.** The ignoring of a responsibility or duty <in derogation of his official duties>. — **derogate** (**der**-ə-gayt), *vb.*

derogation canon. The traditional doctrine that statutes in derogation of the common law should be strictly construed.

derogation clause. (1935) *Int'l law.* A reservation in a treaty allowing a signator to refuse to comply with certain provisions. • For example, a signator may be allowed to suspend some or all of its treaty obligations during a war or other national emergency. If a treaty lacks an express derogation clause, then general principles governing suspension or termination of treaties govern.

derogation from grant. (1889) A provision in an instrument of transfer (such as a deed) that diminishes, avoids, or otherwise limits the grant itself.

derogatory clause. (16c) **1.** A statutory or contractual provision proclaiming that the document in which it appears, or a part of the document, cannot be repealed or amended. • Such provisions are considered ineffective. See REPEALABILITY CANON.

"The one thing a sovereign legislature cannot do is truncate its own sovereignty by restricting its successors. A parliament sovereign today must also be sovereign tomorrow. What is technically called a *clausula derogatoria* is therefore ineffective: *non impedit clausula derogatoria quo minus ab eadem potestate res dissolvantur a qua constituuntur* (a derogatory clause does not prevent things from being dissolved by the same power which created them)." F.A.R. Bennion, *Statutory Interpretation* § 140, at 313 (3d ed. 1997).

2. A clause that a testator inserts secretly in a will, containing a provision that any later will not having that precise clause is invalid. • A derogatory clause seeks to protect against a later will extorted by undue influence, duress, or violence. — Also termed *clausula derogativa*; *clausula derogatoria*.

DES. *abbr.* DELIVERED EX SHIP.

de salva gardia (dee **sal**-və **gahr**-dee-ə), *n.* [Law Latin "of safeguard"] (18c) *English law.* A writ issued to protect strangers from harm while pursuing their legal rights in England.

de salvo conductu (dee **sal**-voh kən-**dək**-t[y]oo). [Law Latin "of safe conduct"] A writ of safe conduct.

de sa vie (də sa **vee**). [Law French] Of one's own life, as distinguished from *pur autre vie* ("for another's life").

descend, *vb.* (15c) To pass (a decedent's property) by intestate succession.

descendant (di-**sen**-dənt), *n.* (17c) Someone who follows in the bloodline of an ancestor, either lineally or collaterally. • Examples are children and grandchildren. Cf. ASCENDANT. — **descendant,** *adj.*

▸ **collateral descendant.** (18c) Loosely, a blood relative who is not strictly a descendant, such as a niece or nephew.

▸ **direct descendant.** See *lineal descendant.*

▸ **lineal descendant.** (17c) A blood relative in the direct line of descent. • Children, grandchildren, and great-grandchildren are lineal descendants. — Also termed *direct descendant.*

▸ **matrilineal descendant.** (1949) A lineal descendant traced back exclusively through female relatives from a founding female ancestor. Cf. *patrilineal descendant.*

▸ **patrilineal descendant.** (1946) A lineal descendant traced back exclusively through male relatives from a founding male ancestor. Cf. *matrilineal descendant.*

descendibility of future interests. (1936) The legal possibility that a future interest (such as a remainder or an executory interest) can legally pass by inheritance.

descendible, *adj.* (15c) (Of property) capable of passing by descent or being inherited. See HERITABLE.

descent, *n.* (15c) **1.** The acquisition of real property by law, as by inheritance; the passing of intestate real property to heirs. See SUCCESSION (2). Cf. DISTRIBUTION (1); PURCHASE (3). **2.** The fact or process of originating from a common ancestor. Cf. ASCENT. — **descend,** *vb.*

▸ **collateral descent.** (16c) Descent in a collateral or oblique line, from brother to brother or cousin to cousin. • With collateral descent, the donor and donee are related through a common ancestor. Cf. *collateral descendant* under DESCENDANT.

▸ **direct-line descent.** See *lineal descent.*

▸ **immediate descent.** (17c) **1.** A descent directly to an heir, as from a grandmother to granddaughter, brought about by the earlier death of the mother. **2.** A direct descent without an intervening link in consanguinity, as from mother to daughter.

▸ **lineal descent.** (16c) Descent in a direct or straight line, as from father or grandfather to son or grandson. — Also termed *direct-line descent.*

▸ **maternal-line descent.** Descent between two persons, traced through the mother of the younger.

▸ **mediate descent.** (17c) **1.** A descent not occurring immediately, as when a granddaughter receives land from her grandmother, which first passed to the mother. **2.** A direct descent occurring through a link in consanguinity, as when a granddaughter receives land from her grandfather directly.

"The law categorizes descents as either lineal or collateral, and as mediate or immediate. The term mediate or immediate descent may denote either the passing of the estate, or the relationship between the intestate and the heir. The classification of descents as mediate or immediate describes the proximity of the descent, while the characterization as lineal or collateral refers to the direction of the descent." 23 Am. Jur. 2d, *Descent and Distribution* § 49, at 787–88 (1983).

▸ **paternal-line descent.** Descent between two persons, traced through the father of the younger.

descent and distribution. (18c) **1.** See *intestate succession* under SUCCESSION (2). **2.** Broadly, the rules by which a decedent's property is passed, whether by intestate succession or by will. See DISTRIBUTION.

"The descent and the distribution of property are governed in the States of the United States by statutes. In most States there exist two distinct statutes, one known as the 'Statute of Descents' and the other as the 'Statute of Distributions.' Those who take realty under the Statute of Descents, as heirs, are often different from those who take personal property by distribution. It is the theory of the law that the rules of descent and distribution make a disposition of the property which is what the average man would provide were he to make a will. It is his family which has the first claim upon him while living, and it is the family which is usually favored by the statutes relating to succession. Inasmuch, however, as the Statutes of Descent and of Distributions of the different States differ widely in their provisions, it would be impossible to present them in detail. In most Sates personalty does not go to the same set of successors as does real property. There are, however, a few States where the heir takes the chattels as well." Walter Denton Smith, *A Manual of Elementary Law* § 377, at 222 (1896).

descent cast. (17c) *Hist.* The devolution of realty that has been acquired by disseisin, abatement, or intrusion, onto an heir whose ancestor died intestate. • This tolled the real owner's right of entry until the owner brought a legal action. — Also termed *descent that tolls entry.*

description. (14c) **1.** A delineation or explanation of something by an account setting forth the subject's characteristics or qualities <description of a patentable process>. **2.** A representation by words or drawing of something seen or heard or otherwise experienced <description of the criminal> <description of the accident>. **3.** An enumeration or specific identification of something <description of items in the estate>. **4.** LEGAL DESCRIPTION. **5.** *Patents.* In a U.S. patent application, the section that (1) comprehensively characterizes the invention in language that is clear and complete enough to enable anyone of ordinary skill in the relevant art to make and use the invention;

(2) explains the best mode for using the invention; and (3) usu. includes an explanation of drawings that are part of the application. • The detailed description typically makes up the largest portion of the application's specification. — Also termed (in sense 5) *enabling disclosure*; *written description*.

descriptio personae (di-**skrip**-shee-oh pər-**soh**-nee). [Law Latin] (18c) Description of the person. • This phrase, typically used to identify or describe a person in a contract or deed, is not essential to a document's validity. Cf. DESIGNATIO PERSONAE.

descriptive canon. See CANON (1).

descriptive comparative law. See COMPARATIVE LAW.

descriptive mark. See *descriptive trademark* under TRADEMARK.

descriptive trademark. See TRADEMARK.

descriptive word. (1877) *Trademarks.* A term that portrays a general characteristic or function of a product or service. • A descriptive word may not be registered as a trademark unless it has acquired secondary meaning in the minds of consumers such that it is directly associated with one brand.

> "A trader cannot appropriate to his exclusive use words or symbols which (in the application he is to make of them) are public property. The right of all to use descriptive words in their ordinary and usual meaning must not be restricted. No sign or form of words may be appropriated as a trade-mark, for use in its primary meaning, which, from the nature of the fact conveyed by that primary meaning, others may employ with equal truth, and with equal right, for the same purpose." Harry D. Nims, *The Law of Unfair Competition and Trade-Marks* 524 (1929).

de scutagio habendo (dee skyoo-**tay**-jee-oh hə-**ben**-doh), *n.* [Law Latin "for having scutage"] (18c) *Hist.* **1.** A writ ordering a tenant-in-chief by knight's service to serve in a war, send a substitute, or pay a sum of money. **2.** A writ authorizing a lord who had served in the war or paid the required fine, to recover the scutage from his knights' fees. See SCUTAGE.

> "Such a baron, having proved that he fulfilled his contract or paid his fine, will have a royal writ *de scutagio habendo*, whereby the sheriff will be ordered to cause him to have the scutage due from his tenants. Still, before he can get his scutage, he has to obtain something that the king is apt to treat as a favour." 1 Frederick Pollock & Frederic W. Maitland, *The History of English Law Before the Time of Edward I* 270 (2d ed. 1898).

desecrate, *vb.* (17c) To divest (a thing) of its sacred character; to spoil, defile, or profane (a sacred thing).

desecration. 1. The act of damaging a sacred place or object or treating it disrespectfully. **2.** The act of making a sacred or venerable thing profane. **3.** *Eccles. law.* The act of dismissing or degrading a person from holy orders.

▸ **desecration of a venerated object.** The desecration of a tangible thing that is highly respected, such as a national flag or a military monument.

de secta ad molendinum (dee **sek**-tə ad mə-**len**-di-nəm), *n.* [Law Latin "of suit at mill"] (17c) *Hist.* A writ forcing a person to continue grinding corn at a particular mill, as was customary, or to give a good reason why the custom should not be continued.

> "There are also other services, due by ancient *custom* and *prescription* only. Such is that of doing suit to another's mill: where the persons, resident in a particular place, by usage time out of mind have been accustomed to grind their corn at a certain mill; and afterwards any of them go to another mill, and withdraw their suit . . . from the ancient mill. This is not only a damage, but an injury, to the owner . . . . And for this injury the owner shall have a writ *de secta ad molendinum* commanding the defendant to do his suit at that mill . . . or show good cause to the contrary: in which action the validity of the prescription may be tried, and if it be found for the owner, he shall recover damages against the defendant." 3 William Blackstone, *Commentaries on the Laws of England* 234–35 (1768).

de sectis non faciendis (dee **sek**-tis non fay-shee-**en**-dis), *n.* [Law Latin "of not doing services"] *Hist.* A writ exempting a ward or dowress from performing certain services.

desegregation, *n.* (1951) **1.** The abrogation of policies that separate people of different races into different institutions and facilities (such as public schools). **2.** The state of having had such policies abrogated. Cf. INTEGRATION (4); SEGREGATION. — **desegregate,** *vb.*

de seisina habenda (dee **see**-zin-ə hə-**ben**-də), *n.* [Law Latin "of holding seisin"] *Hist.* A writ ordering the sovereign to deliver seisin of lands and tenements to a lord, after holding them for the allowed year and a day because the lord's tenant committed a felony.

deselect, *vb.* (1979) **1.** *English law.* (Of voters) to refuse to choose a sitting Member of Parliament as the candidate in the next election. **2.** To remove from a list of choices on a computer.

Desert Act. See CAREY ACT.

deserter. (17c) *Int'l law.* A soldier who leaves the military without permission; specif., a member of the armed forces who leaves national military service with the intention of reneging on military obligations either permanently or for the duration of a military operation. • A deserter illegally abandons a military force, often by seeking refuge in a foreign territory or by joining enemy forces.

desertion, *n.* (16c) The willful and unjustified abandonment of a person's duties or obligations. • In family law, the five elements of spousal desertion are (1) a cessation of cohabitation, (2) the lapse of a statutory period, (3) an intention to abandon, (4) a lack of consent from the abandoned spouse, and (5) a lack of spousal misconduct that might justify the abandonment. — Also termed *gross neglect of duty*; (more specif.) *military desertion.* Cf. ABANDONMENT (2), (4). — **desert,** *vb.*

▸ **constructive desertion.** (1894) One spouse's misconduct that forces the other spouse to leave the marital abode. • The actions of the offending spouse must be serious enough that the spouse who is forced from the home finds the continuation of the marriage to be unendurable or dangerous to his or her safety and well-being, and finds it necessary to seek safety outside the marital domicile. — Also termed *constructive abandonment.*

▸ **criminal desertion.** (18c) One spouse's willful failure without just cause to provide for the care, protection, or support of the other spouse who is in ill health or needy circumstances.

▸ **military desertion.** The leaving of active military service with no intention of returning, esp. to avoid danger, or the participation in a foreign armed service without U.S. authorization. *See* UCMJ art. 85 (2012).

▸ **obstinate desertion.** (1846) Desertion by a spouse who persistently refuses to return to the marital home, so that the other spouse has grounds for divorce. • Before the advent of no-fault divorce, this term was commonly used in divorce statutes. The term was often part of the longer phrase *willful, continued, and obstinate desertion.*

▸ **willful, continued, and obstinate desertion.** See *obstinate desertion.*

Desert Land Act. See CAREY ACT.

deserts. See JUST DESERTS.

design, *n.* (16c) **1.** A plan or scheme. **2.** Purpose or intention combined with a plan.

▸ **formed design.** (1861) *Criminal law.* The deliberate and fixed intention to kill, though not necessarily a particular person. See PREMEDITATION.

3. The pattern or configuration of elements in something, such as a work of art. **4.** *Patents.* The drawing or the depiction of an original plan for a novel pattern, model, shape, or configuration that is chiefly decorative or ornamental. • If it meets other criteria, a design may also be protectable as a trademark. — **design,** *vb.*

design around, *vb.* (1923) *Patents.* To make something that performs the same function or has the same physical properties as (a patented product or process) but in a way different enough from the original that it does not infringe the patent. Cf. DOCTRINE OF EQUIVALENTS.

designate, *n.* (16c) See DESIGNEE.

designate, *vb.* **1.** To choose (someone or something) for a particular job or purpose <the forest was designated a conservation area>. **2.** To represent or refer to (something) using a particular symbol, sign, name, etc. <lakes are designated by blue spaces on the map>.

designated driver. (1982) Someone who agrees to drink little if any alcohol when two or more friends or coworkers go to a place where alcohol is being served so that he or she can drive the others home safely.

designated public forum. See PUBLIC FORUM.

designating petition. (1940) A document used to designate a candidate for a political-party nomination at a primary election or for election to a party position.

designation. (14c) **1.** The act of choosing someone or something for a particular purpose or of giving the person or thing a particular description <the designation of Cheng as lead counsel>. **2.** A name or title <the designation known as solicitor general>.

designatio personae (dez-əg-**nay**-shee-oh pər-**soh**-nee). [Law Latin] Designation of the person by class or category rather than by name, as "the children of A." • This phrase was used to specifically identify a person in a contract or deed, often as a word of limitation (e.g., "to my eldest son"). Cf. DESCRIPTIO PERSONAE.

design claim. See PATENT CLAIM.

design defect. See DEFECT.

design-defect exclusion. See EXCLUSION (3).

designedly, *adv.* (17c) Willfully; intentionally.

designee. (1925) Someone who has been designated to perform some duty or carry out some specific role. — Also termed *designate* (**dez**-ig-nət), *n.*

designer defense. See DEFENSE (1).

designer drug. See DRUG.

design patent. See PATENT (3).

design review. (1962) A process by which a building permit is withheld until the proposed building meets the architectural standards established by land-use regulations. — Also termed *architectural review.*

design specification. See STATEMENT OF WORK.

design-specification contract. See *build-to-print contract* under CONTRACT.

desist, *vb.* (16c) To stop or leave off. See CEASE-AND-DESIST ORDER.

desk-appearance ticket. (1972) *Criminal law.* A written police instruction directing a defendant charged with an offense to appear in court at a specified time. — Abbr. DAT.

desk audit. See AUDIT.

deskill, *vb.* (1941) To reduce or remove the need for a skill in (a job), usu. by a change in machinery or technology.

desk job. (1965) *Employment law.* An occupation that requires mostly working at a desk in an office.

de solemnitate (dee sə-lem-ni-**tay**-tee). [Law Latin] (17c) *Scots law.* As a solemnity. • The phrase appeared in reference to certain deed requirements essential to the deed's validity. Cf. EX SOLEMNITATE.

de son tort (də sawn [*or* son] **tor**[**t**]). [Law French "by his own wrongdoing"] Wrongful.

▸ **executor *de son tort.*** See EXECUTOR.

▸ **trustee *de son tort.*** See TRUSTEE (1).

de son tort demesne (də sawn **tor**[**t**] di-**mayn**). [Law French] Of a person's own wrong. • This is the law French equivalent of the Latin phrase *de injuria.* See DE INJURIA.

desperate debt. See DEBT.

despitus (di-**spɪ**-təs *or* **des**-pi-təs). [Law Latin] **1.** Contempt. **2.** A contemptible person.

despoil (di-**spoil**), *vb.* (14c) **1.** To deprive (a person or place) of possessions illegally by violence or by clandestine means, esp. in time of war. **2.** To mar the appearance of (a place) by taking or damaging things. — **despoliation** (di-spoh-lee-**ay**-shən), **despoilment,** *n.*

desponsation (dee-spon-**say**-shən). (14c) *Archaic.* The act of betrothal; the act of contracting for marriage.

despot (**des**-pət), *n.* (16c) **1.** A ruler with absolute power and authority. **2.** A tyrant who uses power in cruel and unfair ways. — **despotic** (di-**spot**-ik), *adj.*

despotism (**des**-pə-tiz-əm). (18c) **1.** A government by a ruler with absolute, unchecked power. **2.** Total power or controlling influence.

de statu defunctorum (dee **stay**-t[y]oo dee-fəngk-**tor**-əm). [Law Latin] *Scots law.* Concerning the status of the decedent. • The phrase was often used to refer to questions about the decedent's legitimacy.

de statuto mercatorio (dee stə-**tyoo**-toh mər-kə-**tor**-ee-oh), *n.* [Law Latin "of statute merchant"] (18c) *Hist.* A writ ordering the imprisonment of someone who forfeits a statute-merchant bond until the debt has been paid. See STATUTE MERCHANT.

de statuto stapulae (dee stə-**tyoo**-toh **stay**-pyə-lee), *n.* [Law Latin "of statute staple"] *Hist.* A writ to seize the property of and imprison a person who forfeits a staple-statute bond. See STATUTE STAPLE.

destination. (18c) **1.** The predetermined end of a course, as of a voyage or package. **2.** The act of appointment, esp. in a will; a designation. **3.** *Scots law.* The nomination of heirs — esp. in a certain order — by law or under a will.

> "The series of heirs called to the succession of heritable or moveable property, either by the provision of the law or by the will of the proprietor, is, generally speaking, termed a destination; but the term is usually applied, in a more limited sense, to a nomination of successors in a certain order, regulated by the will of the proprietor." William Bell, *Bell's Dictionary and Digest of the Law of Scotland* 320 (George Watson ed., 7th ed. 1890).

4. *Scots law.* The line of successors so appointed.

destination bill of lading. See BILL OF LADING.

destination contract. See CONTRACT.

destination du père de famille (des-tee-nah-**syawn** doo **pair** də fa-**mee**). [French "destination of the father of the family"] (1846) **1.** *Civil law.* The legal standing of the owner of two estates that would be subject to a servitude if they were not owned by the same person. • When the two estates cease to be owned by the same owner, a servitude comes into existence if (1) the servitude is apparent from external signs, such as a roadway or a pipeline, or (2) the common owner recorded a declaration establishing the destination. La. Civ. Code art. 741. **2.** *Hist.* A property use that the owner has intentionally established on one part of the property in favor of another part.

destinatione (des-ti-nay-shee-**oh**-nee). [Law Latin] *Hist.* By destination or appointment of an heir. • The phrase appeared in reference to the process, made possible through a destination clause, by which an heir was appointed to a succession in a certain order. See DESTINATION.

destitute (**des**-ti-t[y]oot), *adj.* (14c) **1.** Deprived; bereft. **2.** Not possessing the necessaries of life; lacking possessions and resources; indigent.

destitutive fact. See *divestitive fact* under FACT.

destroy, *vb.* **1.** To damage (something) so thoroughly as to make unusable, unrepairable, or nonexistent; to ruin <destroying evidence>. **2.** To annihilate; to take the life of <the civilization was completely destroyed>. **3.** To kill (an animal) by reason of mercy, illness, or dangerousness <the dog had to be destroyed>. **4.** To counteract; to nullify <the sun destroys the light of the stars in daytime>. **5.** To show to be false; to disprove <that theory destroys itself>. **6.** To render of no avail; to neutralize <she destroyed her opponent's arguments>.

destroyed will. See WILL.

destructibility, *n.* (18c) The capability of being destroyed by some action, turn of events, or operation of law. — **destructible,** *adj.*

destructibility of contingent remainders. (1918) *Property.* The common-law doctrine requiring a future interest to vest by the time it is to become possessory or else be totally destroyed, the interest then reverting to the grantor. • The doctrine could be avoided by the use of trustees to preserve contingent remainders. This doctrine has been abolished in all but a few American jurisdictions; the abolishing statutes are commonly termed *antidestructibility statutes.* — Also termed *destructibility rule; rule of the destructibility of contingent remainders.*

> "The destructibility rule still exists in its old common-law form in Florida. Various authors have suggested that it also exists unchanged in Arkansas, North Carolina, Oregon, Pennsylvania, South Carolina, and Tennessee; but there are no statutes or recent decisions to clarify the rule's status in these states." Thomas F. Bergin & Paul G. Haskell, *Preface to Estates in Land and Future Interests* 79 n.46 (2d ed. 1984).

destructible trust. See TRUST (3).

destruction. (14c) **1.** The act or process of demolishing, devastating, or overthrowing <the destruction of the rainforests>. **2.** The quality, state, or condition of being ruined or annihilated; loss <the death and destruction rampant in the area>. **3.** That which causes demolition, devastation, or ruin <a fool's tongue is his destruction>.

desuetude (**des**-wə-t[y]ood). (15c) **1.** The longtime discontinuance of a practice or custom; obsolescence through disuse. **2.** The civil-law doctrine holding that if a statute or treaty is left unenforced long enough, it ceases to have legal effect even though it has not been repealed. • This doctrine has no applicability in common-law systems. — Also termed (in sense 2) *desuetudinous repealer.* — **desuetudinous,** *adj.*

> "[T]he doctrine of desuetude has had in all legal systems a very limited and cautious application. For the anachronistic statute a better remedy may be found through reinterpretation in the light of new conditions; as Gray remarks with some irony. 'It is not as speedy or as simple a process to interpret a statute out of existence as to repeal it, but with time and patient skill it can often be done.'" Lon L. Fuller, *Anatomy of the Law* 38 (1968) (quoting John Chipman Gray, *The Nature and Sources of Law* 192 (1921)).

> "There is no doctrine of desuetude in English law, so a statute never ceases to be in force merely because it is obsolete. Normally there must be an express repeal, but the whole or part of an enactment may be impliedly repealed by a later statute." Rupert Cross, *Statutory Interpretation* 3 (1976).

desuetude canon. The doctrine that a statute is not repealed by nonuse or desuetude. — Also termed *antidesuetude canon.*

desuetudinous repealer. See DESUETUDE (2).

de superoneratione pasturae (dee soo-pə-roh-nə-ray-shee-**oh**-nee **pas**-tyə-ree), *n.* [Law Latin "of surcharge of pasture"] *Hist.* A judicial writ against a person who was initially brought into county court for putting too many cattle on pasture, and later was impleaded in the same court on the same charge, and the cause was removed to the superior court at Westminster.

de tabulis exhibendis (dee **tab**-yə-lis ek-si-**ben**-dis). [Latin] *Roman law.* Of producing the tablets of a will. • This was a subject covered under Roman exhibitory interdicts governing the production of documents. A will of a deceased person had to be produced and opened to determine whether the applicant had rights under it.

> "'*De tabulis exhibendis,*' was exhibitory. It lay against the person possessing or fraudulently ceasing to possess . . . any testamentary writing of a deceased person. . . . The object of it was to compel the witnesses of the will to attest their signatures before the Praetor — if they would not attend voluntarily, they might be coerced; anyone might apply for it who took an interest under the will." John George Phillimore, *Private Law Among the Romans* 168–69 (1863).

detachiare (di-tak-ee-**air**-ee *or* di-tash-ee-**air**-ee), *vb.* [Law Latin] *Hist.* To seize a person or property by a writ of attachment or other legal remedy.

detainee. (1928) **1.** A person held in custody, confined, or delayed by an authority, such as law enforcement or a government. **2.** A prisoner held indefinitely without trial, esp. for political reasons.

▸ **ghost detainee.** See *secret detainee.*

▸ **secret detainee.** (1991) Someone who is held, usu. without being formally charged with a crime or facing any other legal proceedings, in an undisclosed place, and whose detention is unknown to anyone other than the detaining authority. — Also termed *ghost detainee.* See *secret detention* under DETENTION (1).

detainer. (17c) **1.** The action of detaining, withholding, or keeping something in one's custody.

▸ **DHS detainer.** See *immigration detainer.*

▸ **forcible detainer.** See FORCIBLE DETAINER.

▸ **ICE detainer.** See *immigration detainer.*

▸ **immigration detainer.** (1986) A notice by the Department of Homeland Security to a federal, state, or local law-enforcement agency to (1) request information about a non-U.S. citizen who is about to be released from that agency's custody, and (2) request that the agency retain custody of that person for additional time to allow the DHS time and opportunity to assume custody and determine whether the person is subject to removal from the United States. — Also termed *DHS detainer; ICE detainer.*

▸ **unlawful detainer.** (18c) The unjustifiable retention of the possession of real property by one whose original entry was lawful, as when a tenant holds over after lease termination despite the landlord's demand for possession.

2. The confinement of a person in custody. **3.** A writ authorizing a prison official to continue holding a prisoner in custody. **4.** Someone who detains someone or something. **5.** *Criminal law.* A request sent by a criminal-justice agency to a prison, jail, or asylum requesting either that a certain inmate be held for the agency or that the agency be notified a reasonable time before the inmate is released.

de tallagio non concedendo (dee tə-**lay**-jee-oh non kon-sə-**den**-doh), *n.* [Law Latin "of not granting tallage"] *Hist.* The title of a statute declaring that no taxes will be imposed by the king or his heirs without the consent of the archbishops, bishops, earls, barons, knights, and other freemen of the realm. • The statute has been used to support the constitutional doctrine disallowing taxation except by Parliament. 34 Edw. 1 st. 4.

detection. (15c) The act of discovering or revealing something that is hidden or barely perceptible, esp. to solve a crime. — **detect,** *vb.*

> "There is a clear distinction between inducing a person to do an unlawful act and setting a trap to catch him in the execution of a criminal plan of his own conception. There is also a distinction between the terms 'detection' and 'entrapment,' as applied to the activities of law enforcement officers. Legitimate detection of crime occurs when officers test a suspected person by offering him an opportunity to transgress the law in such manner as is usual in the activity alleged to be unlawful. On the other hand, entrapment occurs when officers induce a person to violate the law when he would not otherwise do so." 21 Am. Jur. 2d *Criminal Law* § 202 (1981).

detection dog. See DOG (1).

de tempore cujus contrarium memoria hominum non existit (dee **tem**-pə-ree **k[y]oo**-jəs kən-**trair**-ee-əm mə-**mor**-ee-ə **hom**-ə-nəm non eg-**zis**-tit). [Latin] From time whereof the memory of man does not exist to the contrary. See LEGAL MEMORY.

de tempore in tempus et ad omnia tempora (dee **tem**-pə-ree in **tem**-pəs et ad **om**-nee-ə **tem**-pə-rə). [Latin] From time to time, and at all times.

de temps dont memorie ne court (də **tahn** dawn **mem**-ə-ree nə **koor**). [Law French] From time whereof memory does not run; time out of human memory. • This Law French phrasing was a forerunner of Blackstone's classic formulation: "time whereof the memory of man does not run to the contrary." 1 William Blackstone, *Commentaries on the Laws of England* 460–61 (1765). See LEGAL MEMORY.

détente (day-**tahnt**). [French] (1908) **1.** The relaxation of tensions between two or more parties, esp. countries. **2.** A policy promoting such a relaxation of tensions. **3.** A period during which such tensions are relaxed. Cf. ENTENTE; ALLIANCE.

detentio (di-**ten**-shee-oh), *n.* [Latin] **1.** *Roman law.* See *possessio naturalis* under POSSESSIO. **2.** *Hist.* Detention; detainment, as opposed to *captio* ("taking"). See *possessio naturalis* under POSSESSIO.

detention, *n.* (15c) **1.** The act or an instance of holding a person in custody; confinement or compulsory delay. — **detain,** *vb.*

▸ **arbitrary detention.** (18c) The detention of a person without due process of law; the indefinite or unreasonable delayed holding of a suspect or defendant without bringing the person before a competent court, esp. in a case involving terrorism or illegal immigration. — Also termed *detention without charge; detention without trial.*

▸ **detention without trial.** The indefinite detention of a suspect or an accused person without any plans for subjecting the person to prosecution. — Also termed *arbitrary detention.*

▸ **home detention.** See HOUSE ARREST.

▸ **immigration detention.** (1933) The detention of a noncitizen suspected of illegal entry, unauthorized arrival, or a visa violation, or of a noncitizen subject to removal or awaiting deportation.

▸ **investigative detention.** (1968) The holding of a suspect without formal arrest during the investigation of the suspect's participation in a crime. • Detention of this kind is constitutional only if probable cause exists.

▸ **pretrial detention.** (1962) **1.** The holding of a defendant before trial on criminal charges either because the established bail could not be posted or because release was denied. **2.** In a juvenile-delinquency case, the court's authority to hold in custody, from the initial hearing until the probable-cause hearing, any juvenile charged with an act that, if committed by an adult, would be a crime. • If the court finds that releasing the juvenile would create a serious risk that before the return date the juvenile might commit a criminal act, it may order the juvenile detained pending a probable-cause hearing. Juveniles do not have a constitutional right to bail. The Supreme Court upheld the constitutionality of such statutes in *Schall v. Martin,* 467 U.S. 253, 104 S.Ct. 2403 (1984). — Also termed *temporary detention.*

▸ **preventive detention.** (1952) Confinement imposed usu. on a criminal defendant who has threatened to escape, poses a risk of harm, or has otherwise violated the law while awaiting trial, or on a mentally ill person who may cause harm.

▸ **prolonged detention.** The indefinite, long-term detention of a person awaiting trial.

▸ **secret detention.** (1948) The holding of a suspect in an undisclosed place, without formal charges, a legal hearing, or access to legal counsel, and without the knowledge of anyone other than the detaining authority. See *secret detainee* under DETAINEE.

2. Custody of property; esp., an employee's custody of the employer's property without being considered as having legal possession of it.

▸ **detention of goods.** The withholding of another's personal property.

detention center. (1948) A place where people are temporarily kept and prevented from escaping, esp. people who have entered the country illegally or are thought to have committed crimes.

detention hearing. See HEARING.

detention in a reformatory. (1866) A juvenile offender's sentence of being sent to a reformatory school for some period.

detention of goods. See DETENTION (2).

detention without charge. See *arbitrary detention* under DETENTION (1).

detention without trial. See DETENTION (1).

determinable, *adj.* (15c) **1.** Liable to end upon the happening of a contingency; terminable <fee simple determinable>. **2.** Able to be determined or ascertained <the delivery date is determinable because she kept the written invoice>. — **determinability,** *n.*

determinable easement. See EASEMENT.

determinable estate. See ESTATE (1).

determinable fee. 1. See *fee simple determinable* under FEE SIMPLE. **2.** See *base fee* under FEE (2).

determinable freehold. See *determinable estate* under ESTATE (1).

determinable sentence. See SENTENCE.

determinant, *n.* (17c) Something that strongly influences an outcome, esp. what a person does or how a person behaves.

determinate (dee-**tər**-mi-nət), *adj.* **1.** Having defined limits; fixed; definite <of a determinate length>. **2.** Predetermined; settled; positive <a determinate rule>.

> "Laws properly so-called are a species of *commands*. But being a Command, every law properly so-called flows from a *determinate source*, or emanates from a *determinate author*. In other words, the author from whom it proceeds is a *determinate* rational being, or a *determinate* body or aggregate of rational beings. For whenever a Command is expressed or intimated, one party signifies a wish that another shall do or forbear: and the latter is obnoxious to an evil which the former intends to inflict in case the wish be disregarded. But every *signification* of a wish made by a single individual, or made by a body of individuals *as a body or collective whole*, supposes that the individuals or body is certain or *determinate*. And every intention or purpose held by a single individual, or held by a body of individuals as a body or collective whole, involves the same supposition." Thomas Alfred Walker, *The Science of International Law* 7 (1893).

determinate hospitalization. A fixed period of hospitalization, usu. by civil commitment.

determinate obligation. See OBLIGATION.

determinate sentence. See SENTENCE.

determinate sentencing. See *mandatory sentencing* under SENTENCING.

determination, *n.* (14c) **1.** The act of deciding something officially; esp., a final decision by a court or administrative agency <the court's determination of the issue>.

▸ **initial determination.** (1953) The first determination made by the Social Security Administration of a person's eligibility for benefits.

2. The act of finding the precise level, amount, or cause of something <accurate determination of why the flight veered off course>. **3.** The resolve to do something difficult <her determination to learn Mandarin>. **4.** The ending or expiration of an estate or interest in property, or of a right, power, or authority <the easement's determination after four years>. — **determine,** *vb.*

determination letter. (1929) A letter issued by the Internal Revenue Service in response to a taxpayer's request, giving an opinion about the tax significance of a transaction, such as whether a nonprofit corporation is entitled to tax-exempt status. — Also termed *ruling letter.*

determinative judgment. See *final judgment* under JUDGMENT (2).

determinism. (*sometimes cap.*) (1838) The belief that what one does and what happens to one are caused by things outside one's control; specif., a philosophy that human behavior is governed primarily by preexisting conditions, such as family or environmental factors, and is not influenced by will. — **deterministic,** *adj.*

de termino moto (dee **tər**-mə-noh **moh**-toh). [Law Latin] (18c) *Hist.* The common-law offense of moving or defacing landmarks. • This was considered a serious crime because of the importance that agrarian laws attached to landmarks.

deterrence, *n.* (1861) The act or process of discouraging certain behavior, particularly by fear; esp., as a goal of criminal law, the prevention of criminal behavior by fear of punishment. Cf. REHABILITATION (1); RETRIBUTION (1). — **deter,** *vb.* — **deterrent,** *adj.*

▸ **general deterrence.** (1949) A goal of criminal law generally, or of a specific conviction and sentence, to discourage people from committing crimes.

▸ **personal deterrence.** See *specific deterrence.*

▸ **special deterrence.** (1955) See *specific deterrence.*

▸ **specific deterrence.** A goal of a specific conviction and sentence to dissuade the offender from committing crimes in the future. — Also termed *personal deterrence; special deterrence.*

deterrence theory. 1. *Criminal law.* The principle that the threat of punishment deters people from committing crimes. **2.** UTILITARIAN-DETERRENCE THEORY.

deterrent, *n.* (1824) Something that impedes; something that prevents <a deterrent to crime>.

deterrent danger. See DANGER.

deterrent punishment. See PUNISHMENT (1).

de theolonio (dee thee-ə-**loh**-nee-oh), *n.* [Law Latin "of toll"] (18c) *Hist.* A writ of trespass available to a person prevented from taking toll. See TOLL.

de tigno juncto (dee **tig**-noh **jəngk**-toh). See *actio de tigno juncto* under ACTIO.

detinet (**det**-i-net). [Latin "he detains"] A holding back; detention. • An action in debt may be in detinet when the plaintiff alleges that the defendant wrongfully kept goods, as distinguished from wrongfully taking them. An action in debt may also be in *detinet* when it is brought by or against someone other than an original party to the debt, such as an executor. An action of replevin is in *detinet* when the defendant retains possession of the property until after the judgment. Cf. DEBET ET DETINET.

detinue (**det**-i-nyoo *or* -noo). (15c) A common-law action to recover personal property wrongfully taken or withheld by another. Cf. REPLEVIN; TROVER.

> "A claim in detinue lies at the suit of a person who has an immediate right to the possession of the goods against a person who is in actual possession of them, and who, upon proper demand, fails or refuses to deliver them up without lawful excuse. Detinue at the present day has two main uses. In the first place, the plaintiff may desire the specific restitution of his chattels and not damages for their conversion. He will then sue in detinue, not in trover. In the second place, the plaintiff will have to sue in detinue if the defendant sets up no claim of ownership and has not been guilty of trespass; for the original acquisition in *detinue sur bailment* was lawful." R.F.V. Heuston, *Salmond on the Law of Torts* 111 (17th ed. 1977).

▸ **detinue of goods in frankmarriage.** *Hist.* A writ allowing a divorced wife to obtain the goods given to her during the marriage.

▸ **detinue sur bailment** (**det**-i-nyoo sər **bayl**-mənt) [Law French] *Hist.* An action to recover property that the defendant acquired by bailment but refuses to return.

detinuit (di-**tin**-yoo-it). [Latin "he has detained"] (Of property) the former condition of being withheld. • An action is said to be *in the detinuit* when the plaintiff has already recovered possession of the property claimed under a writ of replevin. See *replevin in the detinuit* under REPLEVIN.

detour, *n.* (1936) *Torts.* An employee's minor deviation from the employer's business for personal reasons. • Because a detour falls within the scope of employment, the employer is still vicariously liable for the employee's actions. Cf. FROLIC.

detournement (di-**tuurn**-mənt), *n.* [French *détournement* "a rerouting, hijacking"] (1937) An employee's misappropriation of the employer's funds.

detraction, *n.* [fr. Latin *detrahere* "to take away"] (14c) **1.** The act or an instance of saying things about someone or something to make the person or thing seem less good or worthy than is actually the fact. **2.** The removal of personal property from one state to another after transfer of title by a will or inheritance. **3.** *Eccles, law.* The act of revealing someone's unknown crimes or serious faults.

de transgressione (dee trans-gresh-ee-**oh**-nee), *n.* [Law Latin "of trespass"] The general name of various writs of trespass. See TRESPASS.

de transgressione, ad audiendum et terminandum (dee trans-gresh-ee-**oh**-nee, ad aw-dee-**en**-dəm et tər-mi-**nan**-dəm), *n.* [Law Latin "of trespass, for determining and hearing a misdemeanor"] *Hist.* A commission for hearing and determining an outrage or misdemeanor.

detriment. (15c) **1.** Any loss or harm suffered by a person or property; harm or damage. **2.** *Contracts.* The relinquishment of some legal right that a promisee would have otherwise been entitled to exercise. — Also termed *legal detriment.* Cf. BENEFIT (2).

> "A promise or an act may be a detriment although *on balance* the promisor is making a good bargain. Thus a promise to pay £10,000 for a Rolls Royce worth £12,000, is none the less a detriment, and a good consideration for a promise to deliver the car." P.S. Atiyah, *An Introduction to the Law of Contract* 101 (3d ed. 1981).

▸ **detriment to a promisee.** (1947) *Contracts.* Consideration offered by a promisee to a promisor, esp. in a unilateral contract.

detrimental, *adj.* (17c) Causing harm, damage, or loss; injurious or hurtful <the detrimental effects of smog>.

detrimental reliance. See RELIANCE.

detunicari (di-tyoo-ni-**kair**-ɪ), *vb.* [Latin "to be revealed"] To discover; to lay open.

de una parte (dee **yoo**-nə **pahr**-tee), *n.* [Latin] Of one party. • A deed is *de una parte* when only one party grants something to another, as distinguished from a deed *inter partes.* See INTER PARTES.

deuterogamy (d[y]oo-tər-**og**-ə-mee), *n.* [fr. Greek *deuterogamia* "second marriage"] (17c) A second marriage after the death of or divorce from the first spouse, or after an annulment of a first marriage. — Also termed *digama; digamy.* Cf. BIGAMY (2).

de uxore rapta et abducta (dee ək-**sor**-ee **rap**-tə et ab-**dək**-tə), *n.* [Law Latin "of seizing and carrying away a man's wife"] (18c) *Hist.* A writ of trespass for a man whose wife had been raped and taken away. • At common law, the husband could recover damages but not possession of his wife.

devadiatus (di-vad-ee-**ay**-təs), *n.* [Law Latin] *Hist.* A defendant without a surety. — Also termed *divadiatus.*

devaluation, *n.* (1914) **1.** The attempt to make someone or something seem less important or worthy. **2.** The reduction in the value of one currency in relation to another currency. • In modern usage, the word implies a monetary authority's official lowering of a country's currency within a fixed exchange-rate system. Cf. REVALUATION. — **devalue,** *vb.*

devastation. (17c) **1.** An executor's squandering or mismanagement of the deceased's estate. **2.** An act of destruction. **3.** WASTE (1).

devastaverunt (di-vas-tə-**veer**-ənt). [Latin pl. of *devastavit* "he (or she) has wasted"] They have wasted. • This word usu. referred to both an executor's waste of a decedent's property and the action against the executor for that waste.

devastavit (dev-ə-**stay**-vit), *n.* [Latin "he (or she) has wasted"] (18c) The mismanagement of a decedent's estate by an administrator; esp., a fiduciary's failure to administer an estate or trust promptly and properly, as by spending extravagantly or misapplying assets. • A fiduciary who commits waste in this way becomes personally liable to those having claims on the assets, such as creditors and beneficiaries.

de vasto (dee **vas**-toh), *n.* [Law Latin "of waste"] A writ allowing a reversioner or remainderman to compel a tenant for life or for years to appear and answer for the waste and resulting damage to the plaintiff's inheritance. See WASTE (1).

developed water. See WATER.

developer, *n.* (1938) **1.** A person or company whose business is to buy land and then either to build on it or to improve the existing buildings there <Texas land developers>. — Also termed (for raw land) *land developer.* **2.** A person or company that designs or creates new products <software developer>.

developing country. (1964) *Int'l law.* A country that is not as economically or politically advanced as the main industrial powers. • Developing countries are located mostly in Africa, Asia, Eastern Europe, the Middle East, and Latin and South America. — Also termed *developing state; underdeveloped country; less-developed country; Third World country.*

> "Pertinent terminology has undergone extensive changes in the past 40 years. At the very start, before the category found its way into official texts, economic and political writings referred mainly to 'poor' or 'backward' countries. In the late 1940s, the term 'underdeveloped countries' came into common usage in economic literature and in the jargon of international organizations. It was replaced in the 1950s by the term 'less developed countries,' for which the current 'developing countries' was eventually substituted. These terms are essentially interchangeable as they refer to the same group and kind of countries. However, variations in the use of the term reflect significant changes in the perception of the central issue, namely, economic development, as well as responses to justified sensitivities on the part of the countries principally concerned." A.A. Fatouros, "Developing States," in 1 *Encyclopedia of Public International Law* 1017 (1992).

development. (1885) **1.** A substantial human-created change to improved or unimproved real estate, including the construction of buildings or other structures. **2.** An activity, action, or alteration that changes undeveloped property into developed property.

developmental disability. See DISABILITY (2).

developmental neglect. See NEGLECT.

development-stage company. See COMPANY.

de ventre inspiciendo (dee **ven**-tree in-spish-ee-**en**-doh), *n.* [Law Latin "of (or for) inspecting the belly"] (16c) *Hist.* **1.** A writ allowing a presumptive heir to summon a jury of matrons to verify the pregnancy of a widow suspected of feigning the pregnancy to produce a supposed heir. — Also termed *ad ventrem inspiciendum.* See *venire facias tot matronas* under VENIRE FACIAS.

> "And this gives occasion to a proceeding at common law, where a widow is suspected to feign herself with child, in order to produce a supposititious heir to the estate: an attempt which the rigor of the Gothic constitutions esteemed equivalent to the most atrocious theft, and therefore punished with death. In this case with us the heir presumptive may have a writ *de ventre inspiciendo* to examine whether she be with child, or not . . . and, if the widow be upon due examination found not pregnant, any issue she may afterwards produce, though within nine months, will be bastard." 1 William Blackstone, *Commentaries on the Laws of England* 444 (1765).

2. A writ providing a temporary stay of execution if a jury of matrons determines that a woman scheduled for execution and claiming pregnancy is "quick with child." • The execution would be postponed until after the birth, but if the woman became pregnant a second time before execution, she had no remedy. — Sometimes shortened to *ventre inspiciendo.* — Also spelled *de ventre in spiciendo.*

de verbo in verbum (dee **vər**-boh in **vər**-bəm). [Law Latin] (17c) Word for word.

devest (di-**vest**), *vb.* (16c) **1.** *Hist.* To deprive (a person) of possession, title, or property. **2.** To take; to draw away. — Also spelled *divest.*

deviance, *n.* (1941) The quality, state, or condition of departing from established norms, esp. in social customs; the condition of being different, esp. in a bad or abnormal way. — **deviate** (**dee**-vee-ayt), *vb.* — **deviant,** *adj.* & *n.* — **deviate** (**dee**-vee-ət), *n.*

deviation. (17c) **1.** Generally, a change from a customary or agreed-on course of action; a noticeable difference from what is expected or acceptable <deviation from the normal procedure>. **2.** The difference between a number or measurement in a set and the average of all numbers or measurements in that set <standard deviation>. **3.** *Employment law.* A departure from one's course of employment to tend to a personal matter. • A deviation from the course of employment may be an issue in disputes about workers' compensation or about the employer's tort liability to third parties based on the employee's actions. See COURSE OF EMPLOYMENT. Cf. FROLIC. **4.** *Insurance.* A departure by an insured party from a routine course of action, resulting in increased risk of some loss that the insured is indemnified against. **5.** *Maritime law.* A departure from the terms expressed in a bill of lading or other transportation contract.

> "For both geographic deviations and quasi-deviations, the contractual voyage is the benchmark against which the carrier's performance is to be measured. If the parties agreed to an indirect route, the carrier commits no deviation in following it; if the parties agreed to deck carriage, the carrier may stow the cargo on deck. All deviations 'have one common, indispensable element — a violation of the terms of the bill of lading.'" Michael F. Sturley, "Deviation Defined," in 2A *Benedict on Admiralty* 122 (7th rev. ed. 2002) (quoting *Rockwell Int'l Corp. v. M/V Incotrans Spirit,* 707 F. Supp. 272, 273 (S.D. Tex. 1989), *aff'd,* 998 F.2d 316 (5th Cir. 1993)).

▸ **quasi-deviation.** (1974) A deviation from an agreed-on shipping term other than a deviation in course or destination (e.g., an unreasonable delay or the unauthorized carriage of cargo on deck).

▸ **reasonable deviation.** (1924) A deviation that is justified by circumstances. • If a deviation is reasonable, the carrier does not lose its usual limitations and exemptions under the Carriage of Goods by Sea Act.

▸ **unreasonable deviation.** (1848) A deviation that is not justified by circumstances. • An unreasonable deviation causes the carrier to lose the benefit of its usual limitations and exemptions under the Carriage of Goods by Sea Act.

deviation doctrine. (1948) **1.** A principle allowing variation from a term of a will or trust to avoid defeating the document's purpose. **2.** A principle allowing an agent's activity to vary slightly from the scope of the principal's permission. See DEVIATION (3). **3.** *Maritime law.* The rule that a carrier loses the benefit of its limitations and exemptions under the Carriage of Goods by Sea Act if a deviation from the terms of the bill of lading is unreasonable, but does not if it is reasonable.

deviation-well survey. An examination to determine whether a well is bottomed under another person's land.

device. (14c) **1.** A scheme to trick or deceive; a stratagem or artifice, as in the law relating to fraud. **2.** *Patents.* A mechanical invention, as differentiated in patent law from a chemical discovery. • A device may be an apparatus or an article of manufacture. See MACHINE. **3.** *Trademarks.* A design, pattern, color, or other emblematic thing capable of identifying and distinguishing one's goods or services from those sold by others.

de vicineto (dee vi-**sin**-ə-toh *or* -**SI**-nə-toh). [Law Latin] (18c) From a vicinage; from a neighborhood. • This term was generally used in reference to a jury pool. See DE CORPORE COMITATUS.

de vi laica amovenda (dee **VI** **lay**-ə-kə ay-moh-**ven**-də), *n.* [Law Latin "of removing a lay force"] *Hist.* A writ allowing a person claiming rights to a church to order a sheriff to remove a group of laymen who, with another parson, had taken control of the church and prevented the new parson from entering.

devil, *n. English law.* A junior barrister who acts as an unpaid aid to a senior barrister. See DEVILING.

deviling (**dev**-ə-ling). (1875) **1.** The act of a barrister's handing a brief over to another to handle a case. **2.** The pupillage or training period in which a junior barrister (known as a "devil") drafts pleadings or other documents for a senior barrister who approves them, signs them, and is ultimately responsible for the work. — Also spelled *devilling.*

devil on the neck. (16c) *Hist.* A torture device made of irons that fastened to a person's neck and legs and then wrenched together to either gradually or quickly break the person's back. • It was often used to coerce confessions.

devil's advocate. (18c) A person who expresses a contrary opinion to encourage further analysis or discussion of a subject; esp., one who pretends to dispute so as to improve the discussion.

devil's bargain. (18c) *Slang.* A deal or agreement that accomplishes a desired result, but only with a severe consequence or sacrifice. — Also termed *deal with the devil; pact with the devil.*

devisable, *adj.* (16c) **1.** Capable of being bequeathed by a will. **2.** Capable of being invented. **3.** Feigned.

devisavit vel non (dev-ə-**say**-vit [*or* -**zay**-vit] vel **non**), *n.* [Law Latin "he (or she) devises or not"] *Hist.* An issue directed from a chancery court to a court of law to determine the validity of a will that has been contested, as by an allegation of fraud or testamentary incapacity. See VEL NON.

devise (di-**VIZ**), *n.* (15c) **1.** The act of giving property by will. • Although this term traditionally referred to gifts of real property — and in British usage the term is still confined to real property — in American usage the term has been considerably broadened. In both the Restatement of Property and the Uniform Probate Code, a disposition of any property by will is a devise. In the United States today, it is pedantry to insist that the noun *devise* be restricted to real property. **2.** The provision in a will containing such a gift. **3.** Property disposed of in a will. **4.** A will disposing of property. Cf. TESTAMENT (1); BEQUEST; LEGACY. — **devise,** *vb.*

▸ **alternative devise.** (18c) A devise that, under the terms of the will, is designed to displace another devise if one or more specified events occur. — Also termed *secondary devise.*

▸ **conditional devise.** (18c) A devise that depends on the occurrence of some uncertain event.

▸ **demonstrative devise.** (1956) A devise, usu. of a specific amount of money or quantity of property, that is primarily payable from a designated source, but that may be payable from the estate's general assets if the designated property is insufficient. *See* Restatement (Third) of Property: Wills and Other Donative Transfers § 5.1 (1999). Cf. *pecuniary devise.*

▸ **executory devise.** (17c) An interest in land, created by will, that takes effect in the future and depends on a future contingency; a limitation, by will, of a future estate or interest in land when the limitation cannot, consistently with legal rules, take effect as a remainder. • An executory devise, which is a type of conditional limitation, differs from a remainder in three ways: (1) it needs no particular estate to support it, (2) with it a fee simple or lesser estate can be limited after a fee simple, and (3) with it a remainder can be limited in a chattel interest after a particular estate for life is created in that interest. See *conditional limitation* under LIMITATION.

> "The reason of the institution of the executory devise was to support the will of the testator; for when it was evident that he intended a contingent remainder, and when it could not operate as such by the rules of law, the limitation was then, out of indulgence to wills, held to be good as an executory devise. They are not mere possibilities, but certain and substantial interests and estates, and are put under such restraints only as have been deemed requisite to prevent the mischiefs of perpetuities, or the existence of estates that were unalienable." 4 James Kent, *Commentaries on American Law* *264 (George Comstock ed., 11th ed. 1866).

▸ **failed devise.** See *lapsed devise.*

▸ **general devise.** (18c) **1.** A devise, usu. of a specific amount of money or quantity of property, that is payable from the estate's general assets. *See* Restatement (Third) of Property: Wills and Other Donative Transfers § 5.1 (1999). **2.** A devise that passes the testator's lands without specifically enumerating or describing them.

▸ **lapsed devise.** (18c) A devise that fails because the testator outlives the named recipient. — Also termed *failed devise; failed gift.*

▸ **pecuniary devise.** (18c) A demonstrative devise consisting of money. Cf. *demonstrative devise.*

▸ **primary devise.** (18c) A devise to the first person named as taker. • For example, a devise of "Blackacre to A, but if A does not survive me then to B" names A as the recipient of the primary devise and B as the recipient of the secondary or alternative devise.

▸ **residuary devise.** (18c) A devise of the remainder of the testator's property left after other specific devises are taken.

▸ **secondary devise.** See *alternative devise.*

▸ **specific devise.** (18c) A devise that passes a particular piece of property.

▸ **younger-generation devise.** (1992) An alternative devise to a descendant of the recipient of a primary devise. Unif. Probate Code § 2-603. • A devise of "Blackacre to A, but if A does not survive me then to A's child B" creates a younger-generation devise in A's descendant, B. See *alternative devise.*

devise, *vb.* (14c) To give (property, esp. real property) by will.

"The modern convention which sets apart 'devise' for 'realty' and 'bequeath' for 'personalty' is modern; in the middle ages, the English word . . . is the equivalent of the French word." 2 Frederick Pollock & Frederic W. Maitland, *History of English Law Before the Time of Edward I* 338 (2d ed. 1899).

devisee (dev-ə-**zee** *or* di-vɪ-**zee**). (16c) A recipient of property by will. Cf. LEGATEE.

▸ **first devisee.** (17c) The first devisee designated to receive an estate under a will.

▸ **next devisee.** (18c) The devisee who receives the remainder of an estate in tail, as distinguished from the first devisee. See FEE TAIL.

▸ **residuary devisee.** (18c) The person named in a will to receive the testator's remaining property after the other devises are distributed.

deviser. (16c) Someone who invents or contrives <the deviser of these patents>.

devisor. (16c) Someone who disposes of property (usu. real property) in a will.

devoir (də-**vwahr** *or* **dev**-wahr). (16c) *Hist.* A duty; a tax. — Also spelled *devoire.*

"Devoire is as much as to say a duty. It is used in the statute of 2 R. 2, cap. 3, where it is provided, that all the western merchants, being of the king's amity, shall pay all manner of customs and subsidies, and other *devoire of Calais.*" *Termes de la Ley* 168 (1st Am. ed. 1812).

devolution (dev-ə-**loo**-shən), *n.* (16c) **1.** The act or an instance of transferring one's rights, duties, or powers to another, as when a national government gives power to a group or organization at a lower or more local level. **2.** The passing of such rights, duties, or powers by transfer or succession <the federal government's devolution of police power to the states>. — **devolutionary,** *adj.* — **devolutionist,** *n.*

devolutive appeal. See APPEAL (2).

devolve (di-**vahlv**), *vb.* (16c) **1.** To transfer (rights, duties, powers, etc.) to another. **2.** (Of land, money, etc.) to pass by transmission or succession. See DEVOLUTION.

devy (də-**vɪ**), *vb.* [Law French] To die.

de warrantia chartae (dee wə-**ran**-shee-ə **kahr**-tee), *n.* [Law Latin "of a warranty of charter"] (18c) *Hist.* A writ allowing a tenant enfeoffed with a warranty, who was impleaded in an assize or other action in which the tenant could not call on the warranty, to compel the feoffor to assist the tenant with a plea or defense, or else to pay damages and the value of the land, if it is recovered against the tenant.

"This we still make use of in the form of common recoveries, which are grounded on a writ of entry; a species of action that we may remember relies chiefly on the weakness of the tenant's title, who therefore vouches another person to warrant it . . . . In assises indeed, where the principal question is whether the demandant or his ancestors were or were not in possession till the ouster happened, and the title of the tenant is little (if at all) discussed, there no voucher is allowed; but the tenant may bring a writ of *warrantia chartae* against the warrantor, to compel him to assist him with a good plea or defence, or else to render damages and the value of the land, if recovered against the tenant." 3 William Blackstone, *Commentaries on the Laws of England* 299 (1768).

de warrantia diei (dee wə-**ran**-shee-ə dɪ-**ee**-ɪ), *n.* [Law Latin "of warranty of day"] (18c) *Hist.* A writ ordering a judge not to default a party for nonappearance because the Crown warranted that the party was busy in its service.

dextrarius (dek-**strair**-ee-əs). *Hist.* One at the right hand of another.

dextras dare (**dek**-strəs **dair**-ee), *vb.* [Latin "to give right hands"] **1.** To shake hands to show friendship. **2.** To give oneself up to the power of another.

Dezisionismus. See DECISIONISM.

DFA. *abbr.* DELAYED FUNDS AVAILABILITY.

DFAS. *abbr.* DEFENSE FINANCE AND ACCOUNTING SERVICE.

DFP. *abbr. Criminal procedure.* Dismissal for failure to prosecute.

DFR. *abbr.* See *duty of fair representation* under DUTY (2).

DHS. *abbr.* **1.** DEPARTMENT OF HOMELAND SECURITY. **2.** Department of human services. See DEPARTMENT OF PUBLIC WELFARE.

DHS detainer. See *immigration detainer* under DETAINER (1).

DIA. *abbr.* DEFENSE INTELLIGENCE AGENCY.

diaconate (dɪ-**ak**-ə-nit), *n.* [Law Latin] (18c) **1.** A deacon's office. **2.** Deacons collectively. See DEACON.

diaconus (dɪ-**ak**-ə-nəs), *n.* [Law Latin] A deacon. See DEACON.

diagnosis (dɪ-əg-**noh**-sis). (17c) **1.** The determination of a medical condition (such as a disease) by physical examination or by study of its symptoms. **2.** The result of such an examination or study. Cf. PROGNOSIS.

▸ **clinical diagnosis.** (1840) A diagnosis from a study of symptoms only.

▸ **physical diagnosis.** (1885) A diagnosis from physical examination only.

diagnostic commitment. See COMMITMENT.

dialectic (dɪ-ə-**lek**-tik), *n.* (16c) **1.** A school of logic that teaches critical examination of the truth of an opinion, esp. by discussion or debate. • The method was applied by ancient philosophers, such as Plato and Socrates, primarily in the context of conversational discussions involving questions and answers, and also by more modern philosophers, such as Immanuel Kant, who viewed it as a theory of fallacies, and G.W.F. Hegel, who applied the term to his philosophy proceeding from thesis, to antithesis, to synthesis. **2.** An argument made by critically examining logical consequences. **3.** A logical debate. **4.** A disputant; a debater. Pl. **dialectics.**

diallage (dɪ-**al**-ə-jee), *n.* [fr. Greek *diallagē* "interchange"] (18c) A rhetorical figure of speech in which arguments are placed in several points of view, and then brought to bear on one point.

Dialogus de Scaccario (dɪ-**al**-ə-gəs dee skə-**kair**-ee-oh), *n.* [Law Latin "a dialogue of or about the Exchequer"] *Hist.* A treatise, written during the reign of Henry II, on the Court of Exchequer, set up in imaginary dialogue form between a master and a disciple. • Although some originally attributed the work to Gervase of Tilbury, it was probably written by Richard Fitz Nigel, the bishop of London under Richard I, and the former Treasurer of the Exchequer.

> "The Dialogus de Scaccario is an anonymous book, but there can be little doubt that we are right in ascribing it to Richard Fitz Neal: that is to say, to Richard the son of that Nigel, bishop of Ely . . . . The book stands out as an unique book in the history of medieval England, perhaps in the history of medieval Europe. A high officer of state, the trusted counsellor of a powerful king, undertakes to explain to all whom it may concern the machinery of government. He will not deal in generalities, he will condescend to minute details. Perhaps the book was not meant for the general public so much as for the numerous clerks who were learning their business in the exchequer, but still that such a book should be written, is one of the wonderful things of Henry's wonderful reign." 1 Frederick Pollock & Frederic W. Maitland, *The History of English Law Before the Time of Edward I* 161–62 (2d ed. 1898).

dianatic (dɪ-ə-**nat**-ik). See DIANOETIC.

dianoetic (dɪ-ə-noh-**et**-ik), *n.* [Greek *dianoetikos*, fr. *dia-* "through" + *noein* "to revolve in the mind"] (1856) *Archaic.* A form of logical reasoning that proceeds from one subject to another. — Also termed (erroneously) *dianatic.*

diarchy. See DYARCHY.

diarium (dɪ-**air**-ee-əm), *n.* [fr. Latin *dies* "day"] *Roman law.* An allowance (usu. of food) needed for a day; a daily allowance of food or pay. Pl. ***diaria*** (dɪ-**air**-ee-ə).

diatim (dɪ-**ay**-təm). [fr. Latin *dies* "day"] Every day; daily.

dica (**dɪ**-kə), *n.* [Law Latin] An account tally. See TALLY (1).

dicast (**dɪ**-kast *or* **dik**-ast), *n.* [Greek *dikastes*] (1822) *Hist.* An ancient Greek officer sitting as both judge and juror. • Each dicast was generally a free citizen over the age of 30. The dicasts sat together in groups of between 100 to 500, according to each case's importance, and decided cases by a majority.

dice-loading rule. A canon of construction, usu. of dubious validity, that skews a fair reading, such as the supposed canon that an ambiguity in a federal statute should be resolved in favor of American Indians.

dicis causa (**dɪ**-sis **kaw**-zə). [Latin] (17c) *Roman law.* For form's sake; on the surface. • The phrase appeared in reference to transactions completed in a certain form to conceal their true purpose.

dictate, *vb.* (16c) **1.** To pronounce orally for transcription. **2.** To order; to command authoritatively.

dictation. (17c) **1.** The act of speaking words to be transcribed. **2.** The words so transcribed.

dictator. (bef. 12c) **1.** *Roman law.* An absolute ruler appointed in an emergency for a term of six months and subject to reappointment.

> "In special emergencies, particularly in times of grave crisis, either consul might appoint a dictator who exercised supreme authority, but not beyond six months, unless reappointed. This was, in effect, a temporary reversion to monarchy." R.W. Lee, *The Elements of Roman Law* 14 (4th ed. 1956).

2. A person, esp. a ruler, with absolute authority.

dictatorship, *n.* (16c) **1.** Government by a ruler who has complete power; authoritarian rule or despotic control <military dictatorship>. — Also termed *monocracy.* **2.** A country that is ruled by one person who has complete power <communist dictatorship>. **3.** The office or term of office of a dictator <his dictatorship lasted three years>.

dictum (**dik**-təm), *n.* (16c) **1.** A statement of opinion or belief considered authoritative because of the dignity of the person making it. **2.** A familiar rule; a maxim. **3.** OBITER DICTUM. Pl. **dicta.**

> "As a dictum is by definition no part of the doctrine of the decision, and as the citing of it as a part of the doctrine is almost certain to bring upon a brief maker adverse comment, lawyers are accustomed to speak of a dictum rather slightingly, and sometimes they go so far as to intimate a belief that the pronouncing of a dictum is the doing of a wrong. Yet it must not be forgotten that dicta are frequently, and indeed usually, correct, and that to give an occasional illustration, or to say that the doctrine of the case would not apply to some case of an hypothetical nature, or to trace the history of a doctrine, even though it be conceded, as it must, that such passages are not essential to the deciding of the very case, is often extremely useful to the profession." William M. Lile et al., *Brief Making and the Use of Law Books* 307 (Roger W. Cooley & Charles Lesley Ames eds., 3d ed. 1914).

▸ ***dictum proprium*** (**dik**-təm **proh**-pree-əm). A personal or individual dictum that is given by the judge who delivers an opinion but that is not necessarily concurred in by the whole court and is not essential to the disposition of the case. — Also termed (loosely) *dictum propria.*

▸ ***gratis dictum*** (**gray**-tis **dik**-təm). (17c) **1.** A voluntary statement; an assertion that a person makes without being obligated to do so. **2.** A court's stating of a legal principle more broadly than is necessary to decide the case. **3.** A court's discussion of points or questions not raised by the record or its suggestion of rules not applicable in the case at bar.

▸ **judicial dictum.** (1829) An opinion by a court on a question that is directly involved, briefed, and argued by counsel, and even passed on by the court, but that is not essential to the decision and therefore not binding even if it may later be accorded some weight. Cf. OBITER DICTUM.

▸ **obiter dictum.** See OBITER DICTUM.

▸ ***simplex dictum*** (**sim**-pleks **dik**-təm). An unproved or dogmatic statement. See IPSE DIXIT.

dictum de Kenilworth (**dik**-təm dee **ken**-əl-wərth), *n.* [Law Latin "edict of Kenilworth"] *Hist.* A declaration of an agreement between Edward I and the barons who had opposed him under the leadership of Simon de Montfort. • The agreement, which concerned rent on the lands forfeited in the rebellion, was so called because it was made at Kenilworth castle in Warwickshire in A.D. 1266. It was published in the *Statutes of the Realm* and 52 Hen. 3.

dictum page. See *pinpoint citation* under CITATION (3).

dictum propria. See *dictum proprium* under DICTUM.

diebus feriatis (**dɪ**-ə-bəs feer-ee-**ay**-tis). [Latin] *Hist.* On holidays.

diei dictio (dɪ-**ee**-ɪ **dik**-shee-oh). [Latin "appointing a day"] *Roman law.* **1.** A magistrate's notice summoning the accused to appear on a fixed day for trial. **2.** The service of a summons. — Also written *diei dictitio, diem dicere.*

diem clausit extremum (**dɪ**-əm **klaw**-zit ek-**stree**-məm), *n.* [Law Latin "he closed his last day"] (16c) *Hist.* **1.** A chancery writ, founded on the statute of Marlbury, ordering the county escheator, after the death of a chief tenant of the Crown, to summon a jury to determine the amount and value of land owned by the chief tenant, to determine the next heir, and to reclaim the property for the Crown. • It was a type of inquisition post mortem.

> "Diem clausit extremum is a writ that lies where the king's tenant that holds in chief, dies; then this writ shall be directed to the excheator, to inquire of what estate he was seised, who is next heir, and his age, and of the certainty and value of the land, and of whom it is holden; and the inquisition shall be returned into the chancery, which is commonly called *the office after the death of that person.*" *Termes de la Ley* 169 (1st Am. ed. 1812).

2. An Exchequer writ ordering a sheriff to summon a jury to investigate a Crown debtor's place of death and amount of property owned, and to levy the property of the deceased's heirs and executors. • It was repealed by the Crown Proceedings Act of 1947.

> "And there is another writ of diem clausit extremum awarded out of the exchequer, after the death of an accomptant or debtor of his majesty, to levy the debt of his heir, executor, administrator's lands or goods." *Termes de la Ley* 169 (1st Am. ed. 1812).

dies (**dɪ**-eez), *n.* [Latin] A day; days. Pl. ***dies.***

▸ ***dies ad quem*** (**dɪ**-eez ad **kwem**), *n.* [Latin "the day to which"] *Civil law.* An ending date for a transaction; the ending date for computing time, such as the day on which interest no longer accrues.

▸ ***dies amoris*** (**dɪ**-eez ə-**mor**-is), *n.* [Law Latin] *Hist.* A day of favor; esp., a day set by the court for the defendant to make an appearance. • This was usu. the fourth day of the term, which was the first day the court normally sat for business. In addition, the defendant usu. had three days of grace from the summons to appear, but an appearance on the fourth day *quarto die post* ("on the fourth day thereafter") was usu. sufficient.

▸ ***dies a quo*** (**dɪ**-eez ay **kwoh**), *n.* [Latin "the day from which"] *Civil law.* A transaction's commencement date; the date from which to compute time, such as a day when interest begins to accrue. La. Civ. Code art. 1784.

▸ ***dies cedit*** (**dɪ**-eez **see**-dit). [Latin "the time begins to run"] *Roman & Scots law.* The day on which an interest, esp. a legacy, vests; the day on which a conditional obligation becomes due. • An interest usu., but not always, vested on the day of the testator's death. — Also termed *dies cedens.* Cf. *dies venit.*

> "A legacy was due, or became a valid right, either at the death of the testator or the occurrence of a condition precedent. This vesting of the property or the accruing of an obligation determined the content and nature of the interests involved. What the legatary got was discovered by examining what the legacy actually carried with it on the day when it became vested. To express the fact that the legacy had become vested, the technical expression *dies cedit* was used." Max Radin, *Handbook of Roman Law* 434–35 (1927).

▸ ***dies comitiales*** (**dɪ**-eez kə-mish-ee-**ay**-leez). [Latin] *Roman law.* The 190 days in the year when an election could be held or the people could assemble as a legislative body. • The praetors could not hold court while a legislative assembly was in session.

▸ ***dies communes in banco*** (**dɪ**-eez kə-**myoo**-neez in **bang**-koh), *n.* [Law Latin "common days before the bench"] **1.** Regular appearance dates in court. — Also termed *common-return days.* **2.** An enactment printed under the Statutes of Henry III, regulating continuances and writ return dates.

▸ ***dies datus*** (**dɪ**-eez **day**-təs), *n.* [Law Latin "a given day"] A continuance, esp. for a defendant before a declaration is filed; a time of respite in a case. • A continuance granted after the filing of the declaration is called an *imparlance.* See IMPARLANCE.

▸ ***dies datus in banco*** (**dɪ**-eez **day**-təs in **bang**-koh), *n.* [Law Latin] A day given before the bench, as distinguished from a day at nisi prius.

▸ ***dies datus partibus*** (**dɪ**-eez **day**-təs **pahr**-tə-bəs), *n.* [Law Latin "a day given to the parties"] A continuance; an adjournment.

▸ ***dies datus prece partium*** (**dɪ**-eez **day**-təs **pree**-see **pahr**-shee-əm), *n.* [Law Latin "a day given at the prayer of the parties"] A day given at the parties' request.

▸ ***dies Dominicus*** (**dɪ**-eez də-**min**-i-kəs), *n.* [Latin] The Lord's day; Sunday.

▸ ***dies excrescens*** (**dɪ**-eez ek-**skree**-sənz), *n.* [Law Latin "the increasing day"] The additional day in a leap year.

▸ ***dies fasti*** (**dɪ**-eez **fas**-tɪ). [Latin] *Roman law.* A day when justice could be administered; a day when the praetor could officially pronounce the three words "*do,*" "*dico,*" and "*addico.*" — Also termed *triverbial days.* Cf. NEFASTUS.

▸ ***dies feriati*** (**dɪ**-eez fer-ee-**ay**-tɪ), *n.* [Latin] *Roman & civil law.* A holiday; holidays.

▸ ***dies gratiae*** (**dɪ**-eez **gray**-shee-ee), *n.* [fr. Law French *jour de grace*] *Hist.* A day of grace, usu. granted to the plaintiff.

▸ ***dies in banco.*** See DAYS IN BANK.

▸ ***dies intercisi*** (**dɪ**-eez in-tər-**sɪ**-zɪ). [Latin "divided days"] *Roman law.* A day when the courts were open for only part of the day.

▸ ***dies juridicus*** (**dɪ**-eez juu-**rid**-i-kəs), *n.* [Latin] (17c) A day when justice can be administered. • This term was derived from the civil-law term *dies fasti.* See *dies fasti.*

▸ ***dies legitimus*** (**dɪ**-eez lə-**jit**-i-məs). [Latin] *Roman law.* A lawful day; a law day.

▸ ***dies marchiae*** (**dɪ**-eez **mahr**-kee-ee), *n.* [Law Latin "a day of the march"] *Hist.* In the reign of Richard II, the annual day set aside for the wardens of the English and Scottish borders to hold peace talks and resolve differences.

▸ ***dies nefasti*** (**dɪ**-eez nee-**fas**-tɪ), *n.* **1.** NEFASTUS (2). **2.** See *dies non juridicus.*

▸ ***dies non*** (**dɪ**-eez non). See *dies non juridicus.*

▸ ***dies non juridicus*** (**dɪ**-eez non juu-**rid**-i-kəs), *n.* [Law Latin "a day not juridical"] (17c) A day exempt from court proceedings, such as a holiday or a Sunday. — Often shortened to *dies non.*

▸ ***dies pacis*** (**dɪ**-eez **pay**-sis), *n.* [Law Latin "day of peace"] *Hist.* A day of peace. • The days were originally divided into two categories: *dies pacis ecclesiae* ("a day of the peace of the church") and *dies pacis regis* ("a day of the Crown's peace").

▸ ***dies religiosi*** (**dɪ**-eez ri-lij-ee-**oh**-sɪ). [Latin] *Roman law.* Religious days on which it was unlawful to transact legal or political business.

▸ ***dies solaris*** (dɪ-eez sə-**lair**-is), *n.* [Law Latin "a solar day"] See *solar day* under DAY.

▸ ***dies solis*** (dɪ-eez **soh**-lis). [Latin "day of the sun"] *Roman law.* Sunday.

▸ ***dies utiles*** (dɪ-eez **yoo**-tə-leez). [Latin "available days"] *Roman law.* A day when something can be legally done, such as an application to the praetor to claim an inheritance.

▸ ***dies venit*** (dɪ-eez **vee**-nit). [Latin "the day has come"] *Roman & Scots law.* The date when an interest is both vested and actionable. • It is usu. the day when the heir accepts the inheritance and a legatee can claim payment of a legacy. — Also termed *dies veniens.* Cf. *dies cedit.*

"But the legacy, though vested, is not yet so completely the property of the legatary that he may bring an action for it. To express the fact that such a right of action accrues, the term *dies venit* was used. In general, it may be said that *dies veniens* occurred when, and not until, the *heres* has actually entered upon the inheritance. But, of course, if the legacy was conditional, the *heres* may enter before the condition happens. In that case, *dies veniens* will occur simultaneously with *dies cedens*; i.e., the legacy will vest and the bequest become actionable at the same moment." Max Radin, *Handbook of Roman Law* 435 (1927).

▸ ***dies votorum*** (dɪ-eez voh-**tor**-əm), *n.* [Latin "a day of vows"] A wedding day.

diet. (13c) **1.** A regimen, esp. of food. **2.** (*cap.*) A country's parliamentary assembly, as in Israel, Japan, or some eastern European countries. **3.** A governing body's meeting day for legislative, political, or religious purposes; specif., a national assembly of various European countries, such as the diet of the German empire, which was summoned by the emperor regularly to perform various functions, including levying taxes, enacting laws, and declaring war. **4.** *Scots law.* A day to perform a duty, such as a court sitting day, an appearance day, and a criminal pleading or trial day. — Also spelled *dyet.*

"In procedure on indictment there are two diets, the pleading diet, when the accused is called to plead, and the trial diet when, if he has pled not guilty, he is tried." David M. Walker, *The Oxford Companion to Law* 357 (1980).

dieta (dɪ-**ee**-tə), *n.* [fr. Latin *dies* "day"] *Hist.* **1.** A day's journey. **2.** A day's work. **3.** A day's expenses.

dietary law. (1883) Any of the body of laws observed by members of various faiths regulating what foods may be eaten, how the foods must be prepared and served, and what combinations and contacts (e.g., between meat and milk) are prohibited.

di. et fi. (**dɪ** et **fɪ**). *abbr.* DILECTO ET FIDELI.

Dieu et mon droit (**dyuu** ay maw*n* **drwah**). [French "God and my right"] The motto of the royal arms of England. • It was first used by Richard I and, with the exception of Elizabeth I, was continually used from Edward III to William III, who used the motto *je maintiendrey.* Queen Anne used Elizabeth I's motto, *semper eadem,* but *Dieu et mon droit* has been used since her death.

Dieu son acte (**dyuu** saw*n* **akt**), *n.* [Law Latin "an act of God"] *Hist.* An act of God, beyond human control.

diffacere (di-**fay**-sə-ree), *vb.* [fr. Old French *deffacer*] *Hist.* To deface; to mutilate. — Also termed *disfacere; defacere.*

different-department rule. (1896) *Employment law.* A doctrine holding that people who work for the same employer are not fellow servants if they do not do the same work or do not work in the same department. • This rule, which creates an exception to the fellow-servant doctrine, has been rejected by many jurisdictions. See FELLOW-SERVANT RULE; FELLOW SERVANT.

differential, *n.* (18c) A difference between things, as between the wages of people doing different types of jobs within the same industry or profession.

differential pricing. (1946) *Antitrust.* The setting of the price of a product or service differently for different customers. See PRICE DISCRIMINATION.

differentia specifica (dif-ə-**ren**-shee-ə spə-**sif**-i-kə). [Latin] *Hist.* Specific difference.

differentiate, *vb.* (1816) **1.** To discover, recognize, and usu. express the differences between things or people. **2.** To be a quality, characteristic, or feature that makes one thing or person clearly different from another. **3.** To behave differently toward someone or something, esp. in an unfair way.

different-victim exception. (1987) *Criminal law.* An exemption from the double-jeopardy bar holding that a separate trial for an offense is permissible if the second trial involves another victim.

difforciare (di-for-shee-**air**-ee), *vb.* [Law Latin "to deny"] *Hist.* To keep (something) from someone; to deny (something) to someone.

diffused surface water. See WATER.

DIF system. See DISCRIMINANT FUNCTION.

digama (**dig**-ə-mə). See DEUTEROGAMY.

digamy (**dig**-ə-mee). See DEUTEROGAMY.

digest, *n.* (14c) **1.** An index of legal propositions showing which cases support each proposition; a collection of summaries of reported cases, arranged by subject and subdivided by jurisdiction and court. • The chief purpose of a digest is to make the contents of reports available and to group together those cases bearing on some specific point. The American Digest System covers the decisions of all American courts of last resort, state and federal, from 1658 to present. — Abbr. D.; Dig.

"An important and numerous class of books included in the general division designated as books of secondary authority is the group known by the generic name of 'Digests.' A Digest is essentially an index to Cases. But it is much more than an ordinary index, for it indicates the holdings and (in some, though not all, publications) the facts of each case. Any particular digest is a summary of the case law coming within its scope, and its units are summaries of particular points of particular cases. What the syllabi of a reported case are to that case, a digest is to many cases. Were a digest simply a collection of citations to cases, arranged logically according to the contents of such cases, it would be a search book; but, being a summary of the case law, it is a book of secondary authority." William M. Lile et al., *Brief Making and the Use of Law Books* 68 (Roger W. Cooley & Charles Lesley Ames eds., 3d ed. 1914).

2. *Civil law.* (*cap.*) A compilation and systematic statement of the various areas of law; chiefly, the Pandects of Justinian in 50 books, known as the *Digest.* — Also termed *digesta; digests.* See PANDECT (2); CORPUS JURIS CIVILIS.

digital agenda. (1995) *Copyright.* A series of 10 proposed changes to copyright law announced by WIPO in 1999 and designed to protect intellectual-property rights on the Internet while promoting e-commerce. — Also termed *WIPO digital agenda.*

digital body-cavity search. See *manual body-cavity search* under SEARCH (1).

digital cash. See *e-money* under MONEY.

digital certificate. (1992) A publicly available computer-based record that identifies the certifying authority and the subscriber who was issued a digital signature for electronically transmitted documents and that also provides the person's public key for decrypting the digital signature. • Subscribers register with certification authorities to obtain digital signatures. Certificates may include additional information, including issuance and expiration dates, and recommended reliance limits for transactions relying on the certificate. The certificate also serves as an electronic notarization when attached to an electronic document by the sender.

digital fingerprinting. See STEGANOGRAPHY.

Digital Millennium Copyright Act. *Copyright.* A 1998 federal law harmonizing United States copyright protection with international law, limiting copyright liability for Internet service providers, and expanding software owners' ability to copy programs. • Among many other provisions, the statute extends copyright protection to computer programs, movies, and other audiovisual works worldwide; attempts to regulate cyberspace; forbids devices whose purpose is to evade digital antipiracy tools; and bars the production or distribution of falsified copyright-management information. The statute also limits the liability of Internet service providers against claims of direct and indirect copyright infringement based on content provided by third parties. 17 USCA §§ 1301–1332. — Abbr. DMCA.

digital performance right. *Copyright.* The exclusive right of the owner of copyright in a sound recording to perform the work publicly by means of a digital audio transmission. • The Copyright Act was amended in 1995 to include this right.

digital sampling. See SAMPLING.

digital signature. See SIGNATURE.

digital watermarking. See STEGANOGRAPHY.

dignitary, *adj.* (18c) Of, relating to, or involving one's interest in personal dignity, as contrasted with one's interest in freedom from physical injury and property damage. • Tort actions that compensate a plaintiff for a dignitary insult rather than physical injury or property damage include false-light privacy and negligent infliction of emotional distress.

dignitary, *n.* (17c) **1.** Someone who holds a high rank or honor. **2.** *Eccles. law.* Someone who, by virtue of holding a superior office stands above ordinary priests and canons.

dignitary tort. See TORT.

dignitas (**dig**-nə-tahs). An axiom; a self-evident truth.

dignity, *n.* (13c) **1.** The quality, state, or condition of being noble; the quality, state, or condition of being dignified. **2.** An elevated title or position, whether civil or ecclesiastical. **3.** A person holding an elevated title; a dignitary. **4.** A right to hold a title of nobility, which may be hereditary or for life, usu. regarded as an incorporeal hereditament or as real property.

> "Dignities may be hereditary, such as peerages . . . or for life, such as life peerages and knighthoods. The dignities of peerages and baronetcies are created by writ or letters patent, that of knighthood by dubbing as knight. A dignity of inheritance may also exist by prescription. Dignities of inheritance are incorporeal hereditaments having been originally annexed to the possession of certain lands or created by a grant of those lands and are generally limited to the grantee and his heirs or his heirs of the body. If heirs are not mentioned, the grantee holds for life only. The heirs are determined by the rules which governed the descent of land prior to 1926." David M. Walker, *The Oxford Companion to Law* 358 (1980).

5. An axiom; DIGNITAS.

dijudication (dɪ-joo-də-**kay**-shən). (16c) *Archaic.* A judicial determination.

diktat (dik-**taht** or [BrE] **dik**-tat), *n.* (1922) An order that is forced on people by a ruler or government; an authoritarian decree.

dilapidation. (*often pl.*) (17c) Gradual ruin or decay through misuse or neglect; esp., damage to a building resulting from acts of either commission or omission. • A dilapidation may give rise to liability if it constitutes an act of waste, a breach of contract, or a statutory violation. — **dilapidate,** *vb.* — **dilapidator,** *n.*

dilapidations, action for (də-lap-ə-**day**-shənz). (18c) *Hist.* An action brought by a new incumbent of a benefice for damages rising from the disrepair of the houses or buildings on the benefice. • The incumbent — whether of a rectory, a vicarage, or a chapel — sued the executors or administrators of the incumbent's deceased predecessor (who was not liable for the disrepairs while living). The incumbent of a benefice was bound to maintain the parsonage, farm buildings, and chancel in good and substantial repair, restoring and rebuilding when necessary, according to the original plan. But the incumbent did not have to supply or maintain anything in the nature of ornament.

dilation and curettage. (1913) A surgical procedure in which a woman's cervix is dilated and the tissue in the uterus is removed using a metal instrument (called a *curette*). • This procedure may be performed in different situations, such as abnormal bleeding or after a miscarriage, but is now rarely used as a method of abortion. — Abbr. D&C. — Also termed *dilatation and curettage.* See *dilation-and-evacuation abortion* under ABORTION.

dilation-and-evacuation abortion. See ABORTION.

dilatory (**dil**-ə-tor-ee), *adj.* (15c) **1.** Designed or tending to cause delay <the judge's opinion criticized the lawyer's persistent dilatory tactics>. **2.** Given to or characterized by tardiness. — **dilatoriness,** *n.* — **dilatorily,** *adv.*

dilatory defense. See DEFENSE (1).

dilatory exception. See EXCEPTION (1).

dilatory fiduciary. See FIDUCIARY.

dilatory motion. See MOTION (1).

dilatory plea. See PLEA (3).

dilatory tactic. See DELAY TACTIC.

dilecto et fideli (di-**lek**-toh et fi-**dee**-lɪ). [Law Latin] To his beloved and faithful. • This phrase was used in various writs. — Abbr. *di. et fi.*

diligence. (14c) **1.** Constant application to one's business or duty; persevering effort to accomplish something undertaken. **2.** The attention and care required from a person in a given situation; care; heedfulness. • The Roman-law equivalent is *diligentia*. See DILIGENTIA.

> "Care, or the absence of *negligentia*, is *diligentia*. The use of the word diligence in this sense is obsolete in modern English, though it is still retained as an archaism of legal diction. In ordinary usage, diligence is opposed to idleness, not to carelessness." John Salmond, *Jurisprudence* 393 n.(i) (Glanville L. Williams ed., 10th ed. 1947).

▸ **common diligence. 1.** See *due diligence* (1). **2.** See *ordinary diligence*.

▸ **due diligence.** (18c) **1.** The diligence reasonably expected from, and ordinarily exercised by, a person who seeks to satisfy a legal requirement or to discharge an obligation. — Also termed *reasonable diligence; common diligence*. **2.** *Corporations & securities*. A prospective buyer's or broker's investigation and analysis of a target company, a piece of property, or a newly issued security. • A failure to exercise due diligence may sometimes result in liability, as when a broker recommends a security without first investigating it adequately. **3.** *Criminal law*. The prosecutorial burden of meeting all speedy-trial requirements in bringing a criminal defendant to justice.

▸ **extraordinary diligence.** Extreme care that a prudent person of unusual fastidiousness exercises to secure rights or property.

▸ **great diligence.** (15c) The diligence that a very prudent person exercises in handling his or her own property like that at issue. — Also termed *high diligence*.

▸ **low diligence.** See *slight diligence*.

▸ **necessary diligence.** (16c) The diligence that a person is required to exercise to be legally protected.

▸ **ordinary diligence.** (18c) The diligence that a person of average prudence would exercise in handling his or her own affairs. — Also termed *common diligence*.

▸ **reasonable diligence.** (18c) **1.** A fair degree of diligence expected from someone of ordinary prudence under circumstances like those at issue. **2.** See *due diligence* (1).

▸ **slight diligence.** (1836) The diligence that a person of less than common prudence takes with his or her own concerns. — Also termed *low diligence*.

▸ **special diligence.** (16c) The diligence expected from a person practicing in a particular field of specialty under circumstances like those at issue.

3. *Patents*. Speed and perseverance in perfecting an invention. • Diligence is one factor in deciding which of two or more independent inventors will be granted a patent: if the first inventor cannot prove reasonable diligence in reducing the invention to practice, a later inventor may take priority. **4.** *Scots law*. A court-issued warrant to compel something, such as the attendance of a witness or the enforcement of an unpaid judgment debt. **5.** *Scots law*. Any legal process available to a creditor to seize a debtor's property to compel the debtor to answer an action for debt, to preserve the property as security for a judgment that the creditor may obtain, or to liquidate the property in satisfaction of a judgment already obtained. • Forms of diligence include adjudication, arrestment, inhibition, poinding, and sequestration for rent. Until the mid-20th century, a debtor could also be imprisoned. The term *diligence* is also sometimes used to denote a warrant that may be granted to compel a witness's attendance or to compel production of documents. See EXECUTION (3).

diligence against the heritage. (18c) *Scots law*. A writ of execution allowing a creditor to proceed against a debtor's real property.

diligent, *adj*. (14c) **1.** Careful and attentive; persistent in doing something; industrious; assiduous <a diligent student>. **2.** Carried out with care and constant effort <a diligent search>.

diligentia (dil-ə-**jen**-shee-ə), *n*. [Latin] *Roman law*. Carefulness; diligence. • The failure to exercise *diligentia* might make a person liable if contractually obliged to look after another's interests, or it might result in tort liability. See DILIGENCE. Cf. NEGLIGENTIA.

> "The texts distinguish two standards of diligence, a higher and a lower. The higher is the diligence which the good father of a family habitually exhibits in his own affairs (diligentia exacta or exactissima — diligentia boni patrisfamilias). The lower is the diligence which the person in question exhibits in his own affairs (diligentia quam suis rebus). This may, in fact, reach a high degree of diligence or it may not. But, at least, where this standard is applied nothing extraordinary is expected. It is a concrete standard. It is enough that the person in question pursues his normal course. According to a traditional terminology, where the first standard is applied, there is said to be liability for culpa levis in abstracto — slight negligence in the abstract; in the second case there is liability for culpa levis in concreto — slight negligence in the concrete." R.W. Lee, *The Elements of Roman Law* 288 (4th ed. 1956).

▸ ***diligentia exactissima*** (dil-ə-**jen**-shee-ə eks-ak-**tis**-ə-mə). [Latin] Extraordinary diligence that a head of a family habitually exercises in business. — Also termed *diligentia exacta; diligentia boni patrisfamilias*. See *extraordinary diligence* under DILIGENCE (2).

▸ ***diligentia media*** (dil-i-**jen**-shee-ə **mee**-dee-ə). [Law Latin] *Scots law*. Middle level of diligence; the level of diligence that a person of ordinary prudence exercises in his or her own affairs. — Also termed *diligentia quam suis rebus* (dil-ə-**jen**-shee- ə kwam **s[y]oo**-is **ree**-bəs); *diligentia quam in suis rebus; ordinary diligence* under DILIGENCE (2).

▸ ***diligentia quam suis rebus.*** See *diligentia media*.

▸ ***exacta diligentia*** (eg-**zak**-tə dil-ə-**jen**-shee-ə). [Latin] *Roman law*. Great care.

diligent inquiry. (16c) A careful and good-faith probing to ascertain the truth of something.

diligiatus (də-lij-ee-**ay**-təs), *n*. [fr. Latin *dis*- "apart" + *ligius* "under legal protection"] A person cast out of the law's protection; an outlaw.

Dillon's rule. (1918) The doctrine that a unit of local government may exercise only those powers that the state expressly grants to it, the powers necessarily and fairly implied from that grant, and the powers that are indispensable to the existence of the unit of local government. • For the origins of this rule, see 1 John F. Dillon, *The Law of Municipal Corporations* § 89, at 115 (3d ed. 1881).

diluent, *n*. See ADULTERANT (2).

dilutant (dɪ-**loot**–ənt), *n*. (1884) An additive that makes a liquid, gas, or other substance weaker; esp., an adulterant that diminishes the concentration of the substance to which it is added. See ADULTERANT (2).

dilution. (17c) **1.** The act or an instance of diminishing a thing's strength or lessening its value; the weakening or thinning out of something. **2.** *Corporations.* The reduction in the monetary value or voting power of stock by increasing the total number of outstanding shares. **3.** *Constitutional law.* The limitation of the effectiveness of a particular group's vote by legislative reapportionment or political gerrymandering. • Such dilution violates the Equal Protection Clause. — Also termed *vote dilution.* **4.** *Trademarks.* The impairment of a famous trademark's strength, effectiveness, or distinctiveness through the use of the mark on an unrelated product, usu. blurring the trademark's distinctive character or tarnishing it with an unsavory association. • Trademark dilution may occur even when the use is not competitive and when it creates no likelihood of confusion. The elements of trademark dilution are (1) ownership of a famous mark and (2) actual dilution. But a plaintiff does not have to prove actual loss of sales or profits. *Moseley v. V Secret Catalogue, Inc.*, 537 U.S. 418, 123 S.Ct. 1115 (2003). See BLURRING; TARNISHMENT. — **dilute,** *vb.*

Dilution Act. See FEDERAL TRADEMARK DILUTION ACT.

dilution by blurring. See BLURRING.

dilution doctrine. (1948) *Trademarks.* The rule protecting a trademark from a deterioration in strength, as when a person seeks to use the mark for an unrelated product.

dimidietas (dim-ə-**dı**-ə-tas), *n.* [Law Latin] *Hist.* Half of something; a moiety.

dimidium (di-**mid**-ee-əm), *n.* [Latin "half"] *Hist.* **1.** Half; a half — as in *dimidium unius libratae* ("half a pound"). **2.** An undivided half of something.

dimidius (di-**mid**-ee-əs), *adj.* [Latin "half"] *Hist.* **1.** Half; doubled. **2.** Loosely, incomplete.

diminished capacity. See CAPACITY (3).

diminished responsibility. See *diminished capacity* under CAPACITY (3).

diminutio. See DEMINUTIO.

diminution (dim-ə-**n[y]oo**-shən), *n.* (14c) **1.** The act or process of decreasing, lessening, or taking away. **2.** An incompleteness or lack of certification in a court record sent from a lower court to a higher one for review. **3.** *Trademarks.* BLURRING. — **diminish** (in sense 1), *vb.*

diminution damages. See *stigma damages* under DAMAGES.

diminution-in-value method. (1980) A way of calculating damages for breach of contract based on a reduction in market value that is caused by the breach.

diminution-of-estate doctrine. *Bankruptcy.* The principle that funds under a debtor's control and made part of a debtor's bankruptcy estate cannot be transferred without creating a disadvantage to creditors.

diminutive damages. See *nominal damages* under DAMAGES.

dimissoriae litterae (dim-ə-**sor**-ee-ee **lit**-ər-ee), *n.* [Latin "dimissory letters"] *Eccles. law.* See DIMISSORY LETTERS.

dimissory letters (**dim**-ə-sor-ee). (16c) **1.** *Hist. Eccles. law.* Documents allowing a clergy member to leave one diocese for another. **2.** *Eccles. law.* Documents provided by one bishop to enable another bishop to ordain a candidate already ordained in the former bishop's diocese.

dimpled chad. See CHAD.

DIN. *abbr. Criminal law.* Department identification number — that is, a number assigned to an inmate upon entry into a correctional system, esp. a state one, the number often being an abbreviated code indicating the year of entry into the system, a code name of the prison, and the specific number assigned to the inmate.

diocesan (dı-**os**-ə-sən), *adj.* (16c) Of or belonging to a diocese; of, relating to, or involving the relationship between a bishop and the clergy within the diocese.

diocesan court. See COURT.

diocesan mission. (18c) A mission performing its work in a single diocese.

diocesan synod. See SYNOD.

diocese (**dı**-ə-sees *or* -sis). (14c) **1.** *Roman law.* A division of the later Roman Empire into groups of provinces. **2.** *Eccles. law.* A territorial unit of the church, governed by a bishop, and further divided into parishes. **3.** *Eccles. law.* A bishop's jurisdiction. • Several dioceses together are governed by an archbishop.

dioichia (dı-**oy**-kee-ə), *n.* [fr. Latin *diocesis* "a diocese"] A district over which a bishop exercises his spiritual functions.

DIP. *abbr.* DEBTOR-IN-POSSESSION.

diploma. (17c) **1.** *Roman law.* A letter giving permission to use the imperial post. **2.** *Hist.* A royal charter; letters patent. **3.** A document that evidences or memorializes graduation from a school or society. Cf. DEGREE (5). **4.** A document that evidences a license or privilege to practice a profession, such as medicine.

diplomacy, *n.* (18c) *Int'l law.* **1.** The art and practice of conducting negotiations between national governments.

> "Diplomacy may be defined as the conduct of international relations by negotiation. It is a process through which nations attempt to realize their national interests. It is, of course, not always an instrument of political order. Its object at times may be the intensification of a struggle between nations, or it may be a neutral tool that regards order as irrelevant to the pursuit of the national interest. But more often than not, diplomacy is an important instrument of political order, for the very process of negotiation implies that nations settle their differences through peaceful change within the framework of a given system rather than by resorting to the overthrow of the system through violence. When a nation has decided in favor of war, the instrument of diplomacy becomes superfluous. But so long as the national interest dictates the avoidance of war, diplomacy works on behalf of peace." John G. Stoessinger, *The Might of Nations: World Politics in Our Time* 217 (rev. ed. 1965).

> "According to Satow's classic definition, diplomacy is the application of intelligence and tact to the conduct of official relations between the governments of independent States, extending sometimes also to other relations with vassal States. But in stricto sensu, looking at the most precise and technical meaning of this concept, it is a science as well as an art, with one specific purpose: to accomplish foreign policy in the most accurate way, trying to persuade the counterpart. As a peaceful alternative to war, one of its main functions is the minimization of friction." Eduardo Jara Roncati, "Diplomacy," in 3 *The Max Planck Encyclopedia of Public International Law* 97, 97–98 (Rüdiger Wolfrum ed., 2012).

▸ **open diplomacy.** (1873) Diplomacy carried on with free access to interested observers and members of the press.

▸ **parliamentary diplomacy.** (1950) The negotiations and discussions carried out in international organizations according to their rules of procedure.

▸ **secret diplomacy.** (1878) Diplomacy carried on behind closed doors. — Also termed *quiet diplomacy.*

▸ **shuttle diplomacy.** (1974) Diplomatic negotiations assisted by emissaries, who travel back and forth between negotiating countries. • In legal contexts, the term usu. refers to a similar approach used by a mediator in negotiating the settlement of a lawsuit. The mediator travels back and forth between different rooms, one of which is assigned to each side's decision-makers and counsel. The mediator relays offers and demands between the rooms and, by conferring with the parties about their positions and about the uncertainty of litigation, seeks to reach an agreed resolution of the case. The mediator does not bring the parties together in the same room.

2. Loosely, foreign policy. **3.** The collective functions performed by a diplomat. — **diplomatic,** *adj.*

diploma privilege. A set of course and grade requirements that allow a person to be admitted to the practice of law without taking a bar exam.

diplomat. (1813) Someone who officially represents a government in a foreign country; specif., a representative of one sovereign state at the capital or court of another. — Also termed *diplomatist.*

diplomatic, *n.* See DIPLOMATICS.

diplomatic agent. See AGENT.

diplomatic bag. See DIPLOMATIC POUCH.

diplomatic corps. (1889) *Int'l law.* The ambassador and other diplomatic personnel assigned by their government to a foreign capital.

diplomatic courier. See COURIER.

diplomatic immunity. (1911) The general exemption of diplomatic ministers from the operation of local law, the exception being that a minister who is plotting against the security of the host country may be arrested and sent out of the country. • A minister's family shares in diplomatic immunity to a great, though ill-defined, degree. This immunity and the various exceptions to it are governed by the Foreign Service Immunities Act, 28 USCA §§ 1604 et seq. — Also termed *diplomatic privilege.* Cf. *consular immunity* under IMMUNITY (1).

diplomatic marriage. See *consular marriage* under MARRIAGE (1).

diplomatic mission. A select group of people that officially represents a country or an international intergovernmental organization while present in and officially received by another country.

diplomatic passport. See PASSPORT.

diplomatic pouch. (1914) **1.** A bag or container used for sending official government documents to diplomats working abroad; specif., a bag containing official correspondence, documents, or articles intended exclusively for official communications of a country with its missions, consular posts, or delegations. **2.** The contents of the bag. — Also termed *diplomatic bag; valise diplomatique.*

diplomatic precedence. See PRECEDENCE (1).

diplomatic privilege. See DIPLOMATIC IMMUNITY.

diplomatic protection. (1872) Protection given by one country's representatives to a person, usu. its citizen, against another country's alleged violation of international law.

> "The term diplomatic protection is not altogether precise. First, not only diplomatic agents and missions and other foreign offices may and do exercise diplomatic protection, but also, at a different level, consuls, and, although very rarely, military forces. Secondly, the term diplomatic protection does not clearly denote the boundary line to other diplomatic activities for the benefit of individuals, such as mere promotion of interests in one's own nationals in a foreign State, or friendly intercessions with foreign authorities. Thus, diplomatic or consular actions to obtain concessions or other government contracts for nationals from the receiving State, or the arrangement of legal defense for a justly imprisoned national are not diplomatic protection in our sense; they are usually neither directed against the other State nor based on a real or alleged violation of international law. All these last-mentioned activities may be called diplomatic protection only if the term is taken in a very broad sense." William Karl Geck, "Diplomatic Protection," in 1 *Encyclopedia of Public International Law* 1046 (1992).

diplomatic rank. See RANK.

diplomatic relations. (1814) *Int'l law.* The customary form of permanent contact and communication between sovereign countries; esp., the arrangement between two countries that each will keep representation at an embassy in the other's country.

diplomatic representation. See REPRESENTATION (5).

diplomatics. (1803) The science of deciphering and authenticating ancient writings. • The principles were largely developed by the Benedictine Dom Mabillon in his 1681 work entitled *De re diplomatica.* — Also termed *diplomatic (n.).*

> "Diplomatics, the science derived from the study of ancient diplomas, so called from being written on two leaves, or on double tablets. The Romans used the term more specially for the letters of license to use the public conveyances provided at the different stations, and generally for public grants. Subsequently it attained a more extended signification, and in more modern times has been used as a general term for ancient imperial and ecclesiastical acts and grants, public treaties, deeds of conveyance, letters, wills, and similar instruments, drawn up in forms and marked with peculiarities varying with their dates and countries. With the revival of literature, the importance of such documents in verifying facts and establishing public and private rights led to their being brought together from the historical works and the monastic registers in which they had been copied, or, in rarer instances, from public and ecclesiastical archives where the originals were still preserved. Then arose questions of authenticity, and doubts of the so-called originals; disputants defended or condemned them; and, in order to establish principles for distinguishing the genuine from the forged, treatises were written on the whole subject of these diplomas." 7 *Encyclopaedia Britannica* 220 (9th ed. 1907).

Diplomatic Security Service. See BUREAU OF DIPLOMATIC SECURITY.

diplomatist. See DIPLOMAT.

diptych (**dip**-tik), *n.* [fr. Latin *diptycha* fr. Greek *diptycha* "two-leaved"] (17c) **1.** *Roman law.* Two tablets usu. made of wood or metal and tied with string through holes at the edges so that they could fold over (like a book with two leaves). • Diptychs were often used to send letters, and the text was sometimes written using a stylus, once on the inside waxed leaves and again on the outside, so that it could be read without opening the tablets. **2.** *Hist. Eccles. law.* Tablets used by the church, esp. to register names of those making supplication, and to record births, marriages, and deaths. **3.** *Hist. Eccles. law.* The registry of those names.

"The recitation of the name of any prelate or civil ruler in the diptychs was a recognition of his orthodoxy; its omission, the reverse. The mention of a person after death recognized him as having died in the communion of the church, and the introduction of his name into the list of saints or martyrs constituted canonization. In liturgics the diptychs are distinguished as *the diptychs of the living* and the *diptychs of the dead*, the latter including also the commemoration of the saints . . . . In the Western Church the use of the diptychs died out between the ninth and the twelfth century; in the Eastern Church it still continues." 2 *The Century Dictionary and Cyclopedia* (1895).

"Diptychs were used in the time of the Roman empire for sending letters . . . . The consula and quaestors used, on assuming office, to send diptychs containing their names and portraits to their friends . . . . The early Christians used tablets thus made in the celebration of divine worship . . . . They were placed on . . . the pulpits, or reading desks, which may still be seen in ancient basilicas at the west end of the choir or presbytery; and from them were read to the congregation of the faithful the names of the celebrating priests, of those who occupied the superior positions in the Christian hierarchy, of the saints, martyrs, and confessors, and, in process of time, also of those who had died in the faith. . . . The inscription on the diptychs of deaths and baptisms, naturally led to the insertion of *dates*, and the diptychs seem thus to have grown into calendars, and to have been the germ from which necrologies, lists of saints, and almanacs have been developed." 7 *Encyclopaedia Britannica* 223-24 (9th ed. 1907).

dirationare (di-ray-shee-ə-**nair**-ee), *vb.* [fr. Latin *dis* "thoroughly" + *ratiocinari* "to reason"] *Hist.* **1.** To prove; to establish one's right. **2.** To disprove; to refute (an allegation).

direct (di-**rekt**), *adj.* (14c) **1.** (Of a thing) straight; undeviating <a direct line>. **2.** (Of a thing or a person) straightforward <a direct manner> <direct instructions>. **3.** Free from extraneous influence; immediate <direct injury>. **4.** Of, relating to, or involving passing in a straight line of descent, as distinguished from a collateral line <a direct descendant> <a direct ancestor>. **5.** (Of a political action) effected by the public immediately, not through representatives <direct resolution> <direct nomination>.

direct, *n.* See DIRECT EXAMINATION.

direct, *vb.* (14c) **1.** To aim (something or someone). **2.** To cause (something or someone) to move on a particular course. **3.** To guide (something or someone); to govern. **4.** To instruct (someone) with authority. **5.** To address (something or someone).

direct action. (1912) **1.** A lawsuit by an insured against his or her own insurance company rather than against the tortfeasor and the tortfeasor's insurer. **2.** A lawsuit by a person claiming against an insured but suing the insurer directly instead of pursuing compensation indirectly through the insured. **3.** A lawsuit to enforce a shareholder's rights against a corporation. Cf. DERIVATIVE ACTION (1).

direct-action statute. (1921) A statute that grants an injured party direct standing to sue an insurer instead of the insured tortfeasor. • Under Rhode Island's direct-action statute, for example, an injured party may bring a direct action against an insurer when good-faith efforts to serve process on the insured are unsuccessful. These statutes exist in several states, including Alabama, Arkansas, Louisiana, Minnesota, New York, Pennsylvania, and Wisconsin.

direct adoption. See *private adoption* under ADOPTION (1).

direct affinity. See AFFINITY.

direct aggression. See AGGRESSION.

direct and proximate cause. See *proximate cause* under CAUSE (1).

direct appeal. See APPEAL (2).

direct attack. 1. An attack on a judgment made in the same proceeding as the one in which the judgment was entered; specif., seeking to have the judgment vacated or reversed or modified by appropriate proceedings in either the trial court or an appellate court. • Examples of direct attacks are motions for new trial and appeals. Cf. COLLATERAL ATTACK. **2.** The taking of independent proceedings in equity to prevent the enforcement of a judgment.

direct beneficiary. See *intended beneficiary* under BENEFICIARY.

direct cause. See *proximate cause* under CAUSE (1).

direct charge-off accounting method. See ACCOUNTING METHOD.

direct confession. See CONFESSION (1).

direct confusion. See *forward confusion* under CONFUSION.

direct-consequences test. *Torts.* A court's standard for determining whether a negligent act caused an by assessing whether it occurred reasonably close time and place and without any unforeseeable intervening causes. • This test was originally articulated by then Judge Benjamin Cardozo in . *Railroad Co.*, 162 N.E. 99 (N.Y. 1928).

direct contempt. See CONTEMPT.

direct conversion. See CONVERSION (2).

direct cost. See COST (1).

direct damages. See *general damages* under DAMAGES.

direct debit. See DEBIT.

direct democracy. See DEMOCRACY.

direct deposit. See DEPOSIT (2).

direct descendant. See *lineal descendant* under DESCENDANT.

direct discrimination. See DISCRIMINATION (3).

direct dismissal. *Criminal procedure.* The dropping of a local criminal charge, without prejudice, upon a prosecutor's motion grounded on the impending presentment of charges to a grand jury for indictment.

direct economic loss. See ECONOMIC LOSS.

directed selling effort. (1988) *Securities law.* Any activity engaged in by a securities issuer that might condition the market for the securities being offered in reliance on Regulation S of the Securities Act of 1933. • Such activities include advertising the offering of the securities in general-circulation publications. Securities Act of 1933, Rule 902(c). See CONDITIONING THE MARKET.

directed verdict. See VERDICT (1).

direct estoppel. See COLLATERAL ESTOPPEL.

direct evidence. See EVIDENCE.

direct examination. (1859) The first questioning of a witness in a trial or other proceeding, conducted by the party who called the witness to testify. — Often shortened to *direct*. — Also termed *examination-in-chief*. Cf. CROSS-EXAMINATION; REDIRECT EXAMINATION.

> "A witness is first questioned by the party calling him. This is known as 'examination-in-chief.' Counsel conducting it may not, on any point in dispute, ask 'leading questions,' that is to say, questions where the witness is lured into a position in which he can in the end only answer yes or no. Thus it would not be correct to frame a question: 'You did go to Edinburgh on the 25th of last month, did you not?' The proper way of putting it is: 'Where did you go on the 25th of last month?' The object of the rule is, first, to prevent examining counsel from suggesting in any way the answer he wants, and also to compel an inattentive or lazy witness to give some thought to the question asked. In short, the important question is, not what the witness wants to say, but what he ought to say." Jean Duhamel & J. Dill Smith, *Some Pillars of English Law* 108–09 (Reginald Hall ed. and trans., 1st English ed. 1959).

direct impleading. See IMPLEADING.

direct inconsistency. See INCONSISTENCY.

direct infringement. See INFRINGEMENT.

direct injury. See INJURY.

direct interest. See INTEREST (2).

direction (di-**rek**-shən). (15c) **1.** The course taken in relation to the point toward or away from which something or someone is moving; a point to or from which a person or thing moves <the storm moved in a northerly direction>. **2.** The course on which something is aimed <the direction of the trial>. **3.** An act of guidance <under the chair's direction>. **4.** An order; an instruction on how to proceed <the judge's direction to the jury>. See JURY INSTRUCTION. **5.** The address to the court contained on a bill of equity <the direction on the bill>. **6.** A board of directors; a board of managers <the direction met on Wednesday>.

directions hearing. See HEARING.

directive. See ADVANCE DIRECTIVE.

Directive Harmonizing the Term of Copyright and Certain Related Rights. *Copyright.* A 1993 European Commission initiative setting the term of most copyright protection at the life of the author plus 70 years. • The directive extended coverage in most member countries to match that of Germany, whose term was the longest on the Continent. In 2006, it was repealed. Its provisions were incorporated into the Directive on the Term of Protection of Copyright and Certain Related Rights. — Also termed *Duration Directive*.

Directive on Certain Aspects of Electronic Commerce in the Internal Market. *Copyright.* A 2000 European Commission initiative that harmonizes members' laws governing commercial use of the Internet, including electronic contracts, the liability of service providers, unsolicited commercial e-mail, and related issues. — Also termed *Electronic Commerce Directive*; *E-Commerce Directive*.

Directive on Markets in Financial Instruments. (2004) *Securities.* A 2004 initiative from the European Council and Parliament to create a harmonized structure within which investment firms and banks conduct business and establish branches in member states. — Abbr. MiFID. — Also termed *markets-in-financial-instruments directive*.

Directive on Rental, Lending and Certain Neighboring Rights. *Copyright.* A 1992 European Commission initiative setting rules for reimbursing copyright owners for home rental and public lending of videotapes and other copies of works, and establishing the rights of performers, producers, broadcasters, and cable distributors. — Also termed *Rental and Related Rights Directive*; *Rental Directive*.

Directive on the Coordination of Certain Rules Concerning Copyright and Neighbouring Rights Applicable to Satellite Broadcasting and Cable Retransmission. *Copyright.* A 1993 European Commission initiative requiring members, among other things, to (1) recognize the right of a copyright owner to decide whether the work may be relayed by either cable or satellite, and (2) define the "place" of a satellite broadcast as the location where the signal originates. — Also termed *Cable and Satellite Directive*.

Directive on the Legal Protection of Computer Programs. *Copyright.* A 1991 European Commission initiative requiring members to protect computer software by copyright rather than by patent or some *sui generis* set of legal rights. • The purpose of the Directive was to harmonize copyright laws among the members of the European Commission. It standardized the degree of originality required for software to qualify for copyright protections. — Also termed *Computer Programs Directive*; *Software Directive*.

Directive on the Legal Protection of Databases. *Copyright.* A 1996 European Commission initiative that sets uniform copyright protection among members for databases of original content and requires a *sui generis* system of protection for databases that do not qualify for copyright protection because their content is not original. — Also termed *Database Directive*.

Directive on the Term of Protection of Copyright and Certain Related Rights. See DIRECTIVE HARMONIZING THE TERM OF COPYRIGHT AND CERTAIN RELATED RIGHTS.

directive to physicians. See LIVING WILL.

direct line. See LINE.

direct-line descent. See *lineal descent* under DESCENT.

direct loss. See LOSS.

directly, *adv.* (16c) **1.** In a straightforward manner. **2.** In a straight line or course. **3.** Immediately.

direct notice. See NOTICE (3).

director (di-**rek**-tər). (15c) **1.** Someone who manages, guides, or orders; a chief administrator. **2.** A person appointed or elected to sit on a board that manages the affairs of a corporation or other organization by electing and exercising control over its officers. — Also termed *trustee*. See BOARD OF DIRECTORS. Cf. OFFICER (1).

▸ **affiliated director.** See *outside director*.

▸ **associate director.** A director who has more limited powers and duties than a full or regular director.

▸ **class director.** (1977) **1.** A director whose term on a corporate board is staggered with those of the other directors to make a hostile takeover more difficult. **2.** A director elected or appointed to a corporate board to represent a special interest group, e.g., the preferred stockholders.

▸ **director general.** (1866) The head of a large organization, esp. in England <director general of the BBC>. — Also written *director-general*.

▸ **dummy director.** (1904) A board member who is a mere figurehead and exercises no real control over the corporation's business. — Also termed *accommodation director*; *nominal director.*

▸ **independent director.** See *outside director.*

▸ **inside director.** (1961) A director who is also an employee, officer, or major shareholder of the corporation.

▸ **interlocking director.** (1913) A director who simultaneously serves on the boards of two or more corporations that deal with each other or have allied interests.

▸ **managing director.** (1834) The director principally in charge of a large company's or organization's day-to-day operations.

▸ **outside director.** (1859) A nonemployee director with little or no direct interest in the corporation. — Also termed *affiliated director*; *independent director.*

▸ **provisional director.** (1962) A director appointed by a court to serve on a close corporation's deadlocked board of directors.

▸ **public director.** (1974) A director elected from outside a corporation's shareholders or an organization's membership to represent the public interest.

directorate (di-**rek**-tə-rət), *n.* (1837) **1.** The office of a director or governing board. **2.** A governmental division or corporate department in charge of a particular activity or subject matter <regional directorate of public works>. **3.** Collectively, the directors who run a company or other organization; BOARD OF DIRECTORS <the company's directorate>. **4.** *European law.* An agency responsible for administering the affairs of a particular branch of European Union governance.

direct order of alienation. (1852) *Real estate.* The principle that a grantee who assumes the debt on a mortgaged property is required to pay the mortgage debt if the original mortgagor defaults.

director general. See DIRECTOR.

Director of Public Prosecutions. *English law.* An officer (usu. a barrister or solicitor of ten years' standing) who advises the police and prosecutes criminal cases in England, Wales, and Northern Ireland under the supervision of the Attorney General. • This title, or a similar one, is used in various countries, including Australia, Canada, China, Northern Ireland, the Republic of Ireland, and South Africa. In Scotland, the equivalent officer is the *procurator fiscal.*

Director of the Mint. An officer appointed by the President, with the advice and consent of the Senate, to control and manage the U.S. Mint and its branches.

Director of the United States Patent and Trademark Office. The presidential appointee in charge of the U.S. Patent and Trademark Office. • Until a 2000 reorganization, the PTO chief was the Commissioner of Patents and Trademarks. The Director is also the Under Secretary of Commerce for Intellectual Property. — Formerly termed *Commissioner of Patents and Trademarks.*

directors' and officers' liability insurance. See INSURANCE.

directorship, *n.* (18c) **1.** The position of a board member. **2.** The period during which such a position is held.

▸ **interlocking directorships.** (1912) **1.** The situation in which a director or top executive of one corporation also serves as a director of another. **2.** The situation in which a person closely related to a director or top executive of one corporation serves as a director of another corporation.

directory, *n.* (17c) **1.** A book containing an alphabetical list of names, addresses, and telephone numbers, esp. those of a city's or area's residents and businesses. **2.** Any organization's publication containing information on its members or business, such as a legal directory. **3.** *Eccles. law.* A church's book of directions for conducting worship. • One of the primary directories is the Directory for the Public Worship of God, prepared by the Assembly of Divines in England in 1644 to replace the Book of Common Prayer, which had been abolished by Parliament (and was later reinstated). The Directory was ratified by Parliament in 1645 and adopted by the Scottish Parliament and General Assembly of the Church of Scotland that same year. A directory in the Roman Catholic Church contains instructions for saying the mass and offices each day of the year. **4.** A small governing body; specif., the five-member executive body that governed France from 1795–1799 during the French Revolution until it was overthrown by Napoleon and succeeded by the consulate.

directory call. (1812) *Property.* In a land description, a general description of the areas in which landmarks or other calls are found. See CALL (5); LOCATIVE CALLS.

directory provision. (1835) A statutory or contractual sentence or paragraph in which a directory requirement appears.

directory requirement. (1865) A statutory or contractual instruction to act in a way that is advisable, but not absolutely essential — in contrast to a mandatory requirement. • A directory requirement is frequently introduced by the word *should* or, less frequently, *shall* (which is more typically a mandatory word).

directory statute. See STATUTE.

directory trust. See TRUST (3).

direct-participation program. (1978) An investment vehicle that is financed through the sale of securities not traded on an exchange or quoted on NASDAQ and that provides flow-through tax consequences to the investors. — Abbr. DPP.

direct payment. See PAYMENT (2).

direct placement. (1939) **1.** The sale by a company, such as an industrial or utility company, of an entire issue of securities directly to a lender (such as an insurance company or group of investors), instead of through an underwriter. • This type of offering is exempt from SEC filing requirements. **2.** See *private adoption* under ADOPTION (1).

direct-placement adoption. See *private adoption* under ADOPTION (1).

direct possession. See *immediate possession* under POSSESSION.

direct provocation. See PROVOCATION.

direct question. See QUESTION (1).

direct-reduction mortgage. See MORTGAGE.

direct selling. (1916) **1.** Selling to a customer without going through a dealer. **2.** Selling to a retailer without going through a wholesaler.

direct skip. (1988) *Tax.* A generation-skipping transfer of assets, either directly or through a trust. • A direct skip may be subject to a generation-skipping transfer tax — either a gift tax or an estate tax. IRC (26 USCA) §§ 2601–2602. See GENERATION-SKIPPING TRANSFER; *generation-skipping transfer tax* under TAX; SKIP PERSON.

direct tax. See TAX.

Direct Tax Clauses. (1895) *Constitutional law.* The provisions in the U.S. Constitution requiring direct taxes to be apportioned among the states according to their respective numbers (U.S. Const. art. I, § 2, cl. 3) and prohibiting capitation or other direct taxes except in proportion to the census (U.S. Const. art. I, § 9, cl. 4). • An additional provision of Article I, § 2 concerning computation of taxes is affected by § 2 of the Fourteenth Amendment, and both clauses are affected by the Sixteenth Amendment concerning income taxes.

direct trust. See *express trust* under TRUST (3).

diribitores (di-rib-ə-**tor**-eez), *n. pl.* [Latin "sorters of votes"] *Roman law.* Officers who distributed voting ballots to the citizens in a *comitia.* See COMITIA.

diriment impediment. See IMPEDIMENT.

diritto connessi. [Italian] NEIGHBORING RIGHT.

diritto d' autore. [Italian] AUTHOR'S RIGHT.

dirt-for-debt transfer. (1994) A transaction in which a bankrupt debtor satisfies all or part of a secured debt by transferring the collateral to the creditor.

dirty, *adj.* (16c) **1.** Marked or covered with stains, spots, mud, grime, or other unwanted substances. **2.** Connected with sex in an offensive way. **3.** Unfair, immoral, or dishonest. **4.** Containing or possessing illegal drugs. **5.** (Of a bomb) containing a radioactive substance that worsens the danger or deadliness of the bomb. **6.** (Of a sports event) involving competitors who have illegally used performance-enhancing drugs.

dirty trick. (*usu. pl.*) (18c) Dishonest, surreptitious, and usu. illegal activity by a political group or other individual or organization carried out to harm the reputation or success of a rival.

DISA. *abbr.* DEFENSE INFORMATION SYSTEMS AGENCY.

disability. (16c) **1.** The inability to perform some function; esp., the inability of one person to alter a given relation with another person. **2.** An objectively measurable condition of impairment, physical or mental, esp. one that prevents a person from engaging in meaningful work <his disability entitled him to workers'-compensation benefits>. — Also termed *handicap; incapacity.*

> "An important distinction must be made between the word *impairment* and the word *disability.* [In the field of Social Security,] an impairment only refers to the type of medical problems a person has. Two people might have exactly the same *impairment*, yet only one of them qualify for *disability. Disability* is a legal term, meaning that someone cannot engage in meaningful work with the impairment that he has. If an impairment Meets or Equals a Listing . . . , then the difference between the meaning of the two words is not very important — two different people with the same impairment that Meets or Equals a Listing will always both qualify for disability benefits. The difference becomes important, when a case is being evaluated for possible allowance for vocational reasons; then the same impairment in two different people could result in allowance of benefits for one and denial of benefits for the other." David A. Morton III, *Medical Proof of Social Security Disability* 2 (1983).

> "The Supreme Court has cautioned that [the Americans with Disabilities Act] requires that disabilities be evaluated 'with respect to an individual' and must be determined based on whether an impairment substantially limits the 'major life activities of such individual.' The Court conceded that 'some impairments may invariably cause a substantial limitation of a major life activity,' but '[t]he determination of whether an individual has a disability is not necessarily based on the name or diagnosis of the impairment the person has, but rather on the effect of that impairment on the life of the individual.' As a result, courts are reluctant to characterize any particular impairment as a per se disability under ADA. And the fact that an impairment is considered to be a disability under a different set of criteria for some purpose other than the ADA has no bearing on the determination of whether an individual is disabled within the meaning of ADA." Harold S. Lewis Jr. & Elizabeth J. Norman, *Employment Discrimination Law and Practice* 485–86 (2001).

▸ **absolute disability.** *Hist.* A disability that attaches to a person and to that person's successors and descendants. • Examples of absolute disabilities include outlawry and treason. — Also termed *perpetual disability.*

▸ **developmental disability.** (1973) An impairment of a person's mental or physical functioning or adaptive behavior, normally manifested before the age of 22 and often as a severe, chronic condition. — Also termed *intellectual disability; intellectual impairment.*

▸ **intellectual disability.** See *developmental disability.*

▸ **legal disability.** (17c) A court-determined lack of capability to act for oneself in managing or administering financial affairs, usu. because the person is a minor or has a mental impairment.

▸ **partial disability.** (1848) A worker's inability to perform all the duties that he or she could do before an accident or illness, even though the worker can still engage in some gainful activity on the job.

▸ **permanent disability.** (1804) A disability that will indefinitely prevent a worker from performing some or all of the duties that he or she could do before an accident or illness.

▸ **personal disability.** A disability that applies only to an individual, such as infancy or incompetency.

▸ **physical disability.** (1826) An incapacity caused by a physical defect or infirmity, or by bodily imperfection or mental weakness.

▸ **short-term disability.** A disability that lasts only a short time (often three to six months).

▸ **temporary disability.** (18c) A disability that exists until an injured worker is as far restored as the nature of the injury will permit.

▸ **temporary total disability.** (1908) Total disability that is not permanent.

▸ **total disability.** (18c) A worker's inability to perform employment-related duties because of a physical or mental impairment.

3. Incapacity in the eyes of the law <most of a minor's disabilities are removed when he or she turns 18>. — Also termed *incapacity.*

▸ **canonical disability.** (18c) A canonical impediment (usu. impotence). See *canonical impediment* under IMPEDIMENT.

▸ **civil disability.** (18c) The condition of a person who has had a legal right or privilege revoked as a result of a criminal conviction, as when a person's driver's license is revoked after a DWI conviction. Cf. *civil death* (2) under DEATH.

disability accommodation. 1. See ACCOMMODATION. **2.** See *reasonable accommodation* under ACCOMMODATION.

disability benefits. See DISABILITY COMPENSATION.

disability clause. (1862) *Insurance.* A life-insurance-policy provision providing for a waiver of premiums during the policyholder's period of disability, and sometimes providing for monthly payments equal to a percentage of the policy's face value.

disability compensation. (1913) Payments from public or private funds to a disabled person who cannot work, such as social-security or workers'-compensation benefits. — Also termed *disability benefits.*

disability discrimination. See DISCRIMINATION (3).

disability insurance. See INSURANCE.

disability retirement plan. See EMPLOYEE BENEFIT PLAN.

disable, *vb.* (15c) **1.** To deprive (someone or something) of the ability to function; to weaken the capability of (someone or something). **2.** To impair; to diminish. **3.** To legally disqualify (someone); to render (someone) legally incapable.

disabled access. See *handicapped access* under ACCESS (1).

disabled adult. See ADULT.

disabled person. See PERSON (1).

disablement, *n.* (15c) **1.** The act of incapacitating or immobilizing. **2.** The imposition of a legal disability.

disabling restraints. (1963) Limits on the alienation of property. • These restraints are sometimes void as being against public policy.

disabling statute. See STATUTE.

disabuse, *vb.* (17c) To persuade (someone) no longer to believe what is untrue; to convince (someone) of the untruth of an incorrect idea; to rid of a false conception.

disadvantaged, *adj.* (17c) **1.** Having been prejudiced by something that hinders or prevents success. **2.** Having social problems such as low income or lack of education, both of which make it difficult for a person to succeed.

disadvantaged person. See PERSON (1).

disadvocare (dis-ad-və-**kair**-ee), *vb.* [Law Latin] To deny; to disavow.

disaffirm (dis-ə-**fərm**), *vb.* (16c) **1.** To repudiate; to revoke consent; to disclaim the intent to be bound by an earlier transaction. **2.** To declare (a voidable contract) to be void.

disaffirmance (dis-ə-**fərm**-ənts). (17c) **1.** An act of denial; a repudiation, as of an earlier transaction. **2.** A declaration that a voidable contract (such as one entered into by a minor) is void. — Also termed *disaffirmation.*

> "Disaffirmance is an operative act whereby the legal relations created by an infant's contract are terminated and discharged and other legal relations substituted. Inasmuch as the infant's executory promise does not operate to create any legal duty in him (the infant being at all times at liberty or *privileged* not to perform), his disaffirmance is not the discharge of such a duty. A return promise by an adult, however, creates a legal duty and the infant has a correlative right *in personam.* A disaffirmance terminates these." William R. Anson, *Principles of the Law of Contract* 181 (Arthur L. Corbin ed., 3d Am. ed. 1919).

disafforest (dis-ə-**for**-əst *or* -**fahr**-əst), *vb.* [fr. French *desaforester*] (16c) *Hist.* To free lands from the restrictions of the forest laws and return them to the status of ordinary lands. — Also termed *deafforest.*

disagreement. (15c) **1.** A difference of opinion; a lack of agreement. **2.** A quarrel. **3.** An annulment; a refusal to accept something, such as an interest in an estate.

disallow, *vb.* (14c) To officially reject (something) because a rule has been broken or an incorrect procedure has been followed. — **disallowance,** *n.*

disalt (dis-**awlt**), *vb.* (17c) *Hist.* To disable (a person).

disappeared person. (1944) **1.** Someone who has been absent from home for a specified number of continuous years (often five or seven) and who, during that period, has not communicated with the person most likely to know his or her whereabouts. See SEVEN-YEARS'-ABSENCE RULE; MISSING PERSON. **2.** *Human-rights law.* Someone who has been illegally detained or kidnapped, often by governmental authorities or soldiers, and whose current whereabouts and condition are unknown and undiscoverable.

disappearing quorum. See QUORUM.

disapprobation. (17c) **1.** The act of condemning; esp., formal disapproval of someone or something, esp. on moral grounds. **2.** An unfavorable opinion, whether held in the mind or publicly expressed. — **disapprobate,** *vb.*

disappropriation. (18c) **1.** *Eccles. law.* The alienation of church property from its original use; the severance of property from church ownership or possession. **2.** The release of property from individual ownership or possession.

disapproval. (17c) **1.** The act of censuring or condemning. **2.** A negative decision on or attitude toward someone or something; a sentiment that someone or something is bad or unsuitable.

disapprove, *vb.* (17c) **1.** To pass unfavorable judgment on (something); to reject. **2.** To think of unfavorably.

disarmament. (18c) *Int'l law.* The act of taking away or giving up weapons; esp., the negotiated or voluntary reduction of military arms, esp. nuclear weapons, to a greatly reduced level or to nil. Cf. ARMS CONTROL.

disaster. (16c) A calamity; a catastrophic emergency. See COMMON DISASTER. — **disastrous,** *adj.*

disaster area. (1953) A region officially declared to have suffered a catastrophic emergency, such as a flood or hurricane, and therefore eligible for government aid.

disaster loss. See LOSS.

disaster relief. See RELIEF (2).

Disaster Relief Act. A federal statute that provides a means by which the federal government can help state and local governments to relieve suffering and damage resulting from disasters such as hurricanes, tornadoes, floods, earthquakes, volcanic eruptions, landslides, mudslides, drought, fire, and explosions. • A 1974 amendment established a process for the President to declare affected communities disaster areas. A 1988 amendment (Stafford Disaster Relief and Emergency Assistance Act) constitutes the statutory authority for most federal disaster-response activities, esp. those relating to the Federal Emergency Management Agency (FEMA).

disavow (dis-ə-**vow**), *vb.* (14c) To disown; to disclaim knowledge of or responsibility for; to repudiate <the company disavowed the acts of its agent>. — **disavowal,** *n.*

disbar, *vb.* (17c) To expel (a lawyer) from the legal profession or bar; to officially revoke the privilege to practice law, usu. for disciplinary violations or criminal behavior. — Also termed *strike off.*

disbarment, *n.* (1862) The expulsion of a lawyer from the bar or from the practice of law, usu. because of some disciplinary violation; the official act by which an attorney is deprived of the privilege of practicing law. • One who has *passed the bar,* been *called to the bar,* or been *admitted to the bar* is privileged to stand inside the wooden barrier that separates the gallery from the actual courtroom, particularly the judge's bench, and conduct business with the court. So this term literally describes the loss of the privilege. Although disbarment is typically a permanent removal from the practice of law, in some jurisdictions a disbarred attorney may (after a certain period) petition for readmission. In England and Wales, only a barrister is disbarred; a solicitor is struck off the roll, so the expulsion of a solicitor is termed *striking off the roll.* See STRUCK OFF.

disbocatio (dis-bə-**kay**-shee-oh), *n.* [fr. Law Latin *dis-* + *boscus* "wood"] *Hist.* The conversion of forest to pasture.

disbursement (dis-**bərs**-mənt), *n.* (16c) **1.** The act of paying out money, commonly from a fund or in settlement of a debt or account payable <dividend disbursement>. **2.** The money so paid; an amount of money given for a particular purpose. — **disburse,** *vb.*

DISC. *abbr.* DOMESTIC INTERNATIONAL SALES CORPORATION.

discarcare (dis-kahr-**kair**-ee), *vb.* [fr. Latin *dis-* + *carcare* "to charge"] *Hist.* To unload (cargo), usu. from a ship. — Also termed *discargare.*

disceptatio causae (di-sep-**tay**-shee-oh **kaw**-zee). [Latin "debate about a case"] *Roman law.* The argument by the advocates of both sides of a dispute.

discharge (**dis**-chahrj), *n.* (15c) **1.** Any method by which a legal duty is extinguished; esp., the payment of a debt or satisfaction of some other obligation.

▸ **discharge by performance.** *Contracts.* The satisfaction of an obligation by carrying out its requirements.

▸ **discharge for breach.** *Contracts.* The release of an innocent party to a contract from any obligations under the contract because the other party has failed to perform a prerequisite or simultaneous obligation.

2. *Bankruptcy.* The release of a debtor from monetary obligations upon adjudication of bankruptcy; DISCHARGE IN BANKRUPTCY. Cf. RELEASE (1). **3.** The dismissal of a case. **4.** The canceling or vacating of a court order. **5.** The act or an instance of permitting a person to leave a place, such as a hospital or prison; esp., the release of a prisoner from confinement.

▸ **absolute discharge.** (16c) *English criminal law.* A court's unconditional release of a person convicted of a criminal offense on grounds that punishment would be inexpedient and useless, considering the nature of the offense and the character of the offender.

▸ **automatic discharge.** (1923) The extinguishment of responsibility without any requirement of a deliberate action, as with a self-executing termination of a contract.

▸ **unconditional discharge.** (18c) **1.** A release from an obligation without any conditions attached. **2.** A release from confinement without any parole requirements to fulfill.

6. The relieving of a witness, juror, or jury from further responsibilities in a case. — Also termed *discharge of witness; discharge of juror; discharge of jury.* **7.** The firing of an employee.

▸ **constructive discharge.** (1830) An employer's creation of working conditions that leave a particular employee or group of employees little or no choice but to resign, as by fundamentally changing the working conditions or terms of employment; an employer's course of action that, being detrimental to an employee, leaves the employee almost no option but to quit. — Also termed *constructive dismissal.*

▸ **retaliatory discharge.** (1967) A discharge that is made in retaliation for the employee's conduct (such as reporting unlawful activity by the employer to the government) and that clearly violates public policy. • Federal and state statutes may entitle an employee who is dismissed by retaliatory discharge to recover damages.

▸ **wrongful discharge.** (1825) A discharge for reasons that are illegal or that violate public policy. — Also termed *wrongful dismissal.*

8. The dismissal of a member of the armed services from military service <the sergeant was honorably discharged>.

▸ **administrative discharge.** (1949) A military-service discharge given by administrative means and not by court-martial.

▸ **bad-conduct discharge.** (1907) A punitive discharge that a court-martial can give a member of the military, usu. as punishment for repeated minor offenses. — Abbr. BCD.

▸ **dishonorable discharge.** (1857) The most severe punitive discharge that a court-martial can give to a member of the military; an order to a member of the armed forces to leave the military on grounds of morally unacceptable behavior. • A dishonorable discharge may result from conviction for an offense recognized in civilian law as a felony or of a military offense requiring severe punishment. Only a general court-martial can give a dishonorable discharge.

▸ **general discharge.** (1922) One of the administrative discharges given to a member of the military who does not qualify for an honorable discharge.

▸ **honorable discharge.** (17c) A formal final judgment passed by the government on a soldier's entire military record, and an authoritative declaration that he or she has left the service in a status of honor. • Full veterans' benefits are given only to a person honorably discharged.

▸ **undesirable discharge.** (1925) One of the administrative discharges given to a member of the military who does not qualify for an honorable discharge.

9. *Parliamentary law.* A motion by which a deliberative assembly, having referred a matter to a committee, takes the matter's further consideration out of the committee and back into its own hands. — Also termed *discharge a committee; withdrawal.* — **discharge** (dis-**chahrj**), *vb.*

dischargeability proceeding. (1979) *Bankruptcy.* A hearing to determine whether a debt is dischargeable or is subject to an exception to discharge. 11 USCA § 523.

dischargeable claim. (1912) *Bankruptcy.* A claim that can be discharged in bankruptcy.

discharge a committee. See DISCHARGE (9).

discharge by performance. See DISCHARGE (1).

discharged contract. See *void contract* (2) under CONTRACT.

discharge for breach. See DISCHARGE (1).

discharge hearing. (1927) *Bankruptcy.* A hearing at which the court informs the debtor either that a discharge has been granted or the reasons why a discharge has not been granted. See REAFFIRMATION HEARING.

discharge in bankruptcy. (1820) **1.** The release of a debtor from personal liability for prebankruptcy debts; specif., discharge under the United States Bankruptcy Code. **2.** A bankruptcy court's decree releasing a debtor from that liability.

discharge of juror. See DISCHARGE (6).

discharge of jury. See DISCHARGE (6).

discharge of witness. See DISCHARGE (6).

discharging bond. See BOND (2).

disciplinary, *adj.* (15c) **1.** Of, relating to, or involving the punishment of someone who has not obeyed the rules. **2.** Of, relating to, or involving trying to make people obey the rules.

disciplinary action. A measure taken by someone in authority to punish or cub behavior that does not meet or conform to communicated and expected standards of performance.

disciplinary authority. 1. A tribunal or regulatory body charged with enforcing rules and standards of professional responsibility. **2.** The duly exercised power to enforce rules and ethical guidelines.

disciplinary proceeding. (1900) An action brought to reprimand, suspend, or expel a licensed professional or other person from a profession or other group because of unprofessional, unethical, improper, or illegal conduct. • A disciplinary proceeding against a lawyer may result in the lawyer's being suspended or disbarred from practice.

disciplinary rule. (*often cap.*) (1890) A mandatory regulation stating the minimum level of professional conduct that a professional must sustain to avoid being subject to disciplinary action. • For lawyers, the disciplinary rules are found chiefly in the Model Code of Professional Responsibility. — Abbr. DR. Cf. ETHICAL CONSIDERATION.

discipline, *n.* (13c) **1.** Punishment intended to correct or instruct; esp., a sanction or penalty imposed after an official finding of misconduct, such as punishment or penalties (often termed "sanctions") imposed by a disciplining agency on an attorney who has breached a rule of professional ethics. • Three types of discipline are common: disbarment, suspension, and reprimand (public or private). **2.** A method of training people to control their behavior and obey rules. **3.** Control gained by enforcing compliance or order. **4.** The ability to control one's own behavior so that one does what is expected or necessary; esp., in the military, a state of mind inducing instant obedience to a lawful order, no matter how unpleasant or dangerous such compliance might be. **5.** An area of knowledge or teaching; a field of study, esp. one taught in higher education. — **discipline,** *vb.*

disclaim, *vb.* (15c) **1.** To state, usu. formally, that one has no responsibility for, knowledge of, or involvement with (something); to make a disclaimer about. **2.** To renounce or disavow a legal claim to. **3.** To utter a denial. **4.** To deny as authoritative.

disclaimer, *n.* (15c) **1.** A statement that one is not responsible for or involved with something, or that one has no knowledge of it. **2.** A renunciation of one's own legal right or claim, such as a renunciation of a patent claim, usu. to save the remainder of the application from being rejected. See RENUNCIATION (2). **3.** A repudiation of another's legal right or claim. **4.** A writing that contains such a renunciation or repudiation.

▸ **disclaimer of warranty.** (1881) An oral or written statement intended to limit a seller's liability for defects in the goods sold. • In some circumstances, printed words must be specific and conspicuous to be effective.

▸ **patent disclaimer.** See *statutory disclaimer.*

▸ **qualified disclaimer.** (1889) **1.** A disclaimer with a restriction or condition attached. • In this sense it is *qualified* because it carries the restriction or condition. **2.** A person's refusal to accept an interest in property so that he or she can avoid having to pay estate or gift taxes. • To be effective under federal tax law, the refusal must be in writing and must be executed no later than nine months from the time when the interest was created. In this sense, it is *qualified* in the sense of being within the lawful exemption. IRC (26 USCA) § 2518.

▸ **statutory disclaimer.** (1928) *Patents.* A patent applicant's amendment of a specification to relinquish one or more claims to the invention. 35 USCA § 253. • Before the statute was enacted, a single invalid claim was grounds for denying a patent. — Also termed *patent disclaimer.* See SPECIFICATION (3).

▸ **terminal disclaimer.** (1958) A patent applicant's statement shortening the term of the patent. • To revive an abandoned application for a design application or for a utility or plant application filed before June 8, 1995, the applicant must disclaim a period equal to the duration of abandonment. A terminal disclaimer may also be required in an application for an obvious variation on an existing patent with a common inventor or owner: to avoid a double-patenting rejection the inventor agrees that both patents will expire on the same day. 37 CFR 1.321.

disclose, *vb.* (14c) To make (something) known or public; to show (something) after a period of inaccessibility or of being unknown; to reveal.

disclosed principal. See PRINCIPAL (1).

disclosure, *n.* (16c) **1.** The act or process of making known something that was previously unknown; a revelation of facts <a lawyer's disclosure of a conflict of interest>. See DISCOVERY.

▸ **defensive disclosure.** See DEFENSIVE DISCLOSURE.

▸ **full disclosure.** (17c) A complete revelation of all material facts.

▸ **inadvertent disclosure.** The accidental revelation of confidential information, as by sending it to a wrong e-mail address or by negligently allowing another person to overhear a conversation.

▸ **public disclosure of private facts.** (1964) The public revelation of some aspect of a person's private life without a legitimate public purpose. • The disclosure is actionable in tort if the disclosure would be highly objectionable to a reasonable person. See INVASION OF PRIVACY.

▸ **supplemental disclosure.** The disclosure of additional facts and information, usu. because of previous unavailability. — Also termed *supplementary disclosure*.

▸ **voluntary disclosure of offense.** (1957) A person's uncoerced admission to an undiscovered crime. • Under the federal sentencing guidelines, a lighter sentence may be allowed. See USSG 5K2.16.

2. The mandatory divulging of information to a litigation opponent according to procedural rules. — Also termed *pretrial disclosure; compulsory disclosure; automatic disclosure; discovery disclosure.* See DISCOVERY (2). — **disclosural,** *adj.*

> "Rule 26(a) [of the Federal Rules of Civil Procedure] reflects a shift away from the traditional method of obtaining discovery through the service of written demands toward requiring automatic disclosure by the parties of information that would invariably be requested. The goal of automatic disclosure is the creation of a more efficient and expeditious discovery process. . . . Rule 26(a)(1) provides for the initial disclosure of specified information relating to witnesses, documents, and insurance agreements. Rule 26(a)(2) provides for the disclosure of information regarding experts who may be used at trial. Rule 26(a)(3) provides for specified pretrial disclosures regarding witnesses, evidence, and objections." Jay E. Grenig & Jeffrey S. Kinsler, *Handbook of Federal Civil Discovery and Disclosure* § 1.15, at 65–66 (2d ed. 2002).

▸ **accelerated disclosure.** See *accelerated discovery* under DISCOVERY.

▸ **initial disclosure.** *Civil procedure.* In federal practice, the requirement that parties make available to each other the following information without first receiving a discovery request: (1) the names, addresses, and telephone numbers of persons likely to have relevant, discoverable information, (2) a copy or description of all relevant documents, data compilations, and tangible items in the party's possession, custody, or control, (3) a damages computation, and (4) any relevant insurance agreements. Fed. R. Civ. P. 26(a)(1)(A)–(D).

3. *Patents.* A document explaining how an invention works in sufficient detail for one skilled in the art to be able to understand and duplicate the invention; everything revealed about an invention in the patent application, including drawings, descriptions, specifications, references to prior art, and claims. • An invention disclosure statement is sometimes attested by a knowledgeable witness, who signs and dates the disclosure document to establish the inventor's identity and the date of the invention before the patent application is prepared. An inventor can file a disclosure document with the U.S. Patent and Trademark Office before submitting a patent application, but the document's date has no relationship to the later application's effective filing date. — Also termed *disclosure document.* See ENABLEMENT REQUIREMENT; *information-disclosure statement* under DISCLOSURE STATEMENT. Cf. ENABLING SOURCE; DEFENSIVE DISCLOSURE. **4.** *Patents.* PUBLICATION (1).

disclosure document. 1. *Securities.* A statement provided to prospective investors to explain an investment fund's fee structure and style of trading, as well as the potential risks of investing. **2.** *Patents.* See DISCLOSURE (3).

Disclosure Document Program. *Patents.* A U.S. Patent and Trademark Office program allowing an inventor to file a preliminary description of an invention and establish its date of conception before applying for a patent. • The document can help establish a date of inventive effort for use in a later interference. — Abbr. DDP. Cf. *provisional application* under PATENT APPLICATION.

disclosure statement. A document containing relevant information that a reasonable person would find important in making a decision about a transaction or application.

▸ **information-disclosure statement.** (1999) *Patents.* A document submitted in the patent-application process in which the inventor reveals all known relevant prior art during the patentability search. • The statement must disclose all known patents, publications, and other references of prior art. The U.S. Patent and Trademark Office provides a form, "Information Disclosure Citation," for this purpose. — Abbr. IDS. — Also termed *statement of prior-art references.*

▸ **loan-disclosure statement.** A document setting forth the terms and conditions of a loan, including the amount borrowed, the interest rate, repayment methods, and the rights and responsibilities of the borrower and the lender.

▸ **property-disclosure statement.** A seller's statement either that a property has a problem and disclosing the nature of the problem, or that the seller is unaware of any problem.

discommon (dis-**kom**-ən), *vb.* (15c) **1.** To deprive of the right of common (e.g., the right to pasture). **2.** To deprive (something, esp. land) of commonable character. • A person could discommon land by separating or enclosing it. **3.** To deprive (someone) of the privileges of a place, such as the right to use common land or to enjoy a church fellowship.

dis. con. *abbr.* Disorderly conduct.

disconformity. See NEW MATTER.

discontinuance (dis-kən-**tin**-yoo-ənts), *n.* (14c) **1.** The termination of a lawsuit by the plaintiff; a voluntary dismissal or nonsuit. See DISMISSAL; NONSUIT (1); *judgment of discontinuance* under JUDGMENT (2). **2.** The termination of an estate-tail by a tenant in tail who conveys a larger estate in the land than is legally allowed. — **discontinue,** *vb.*

> "Such is . . . the injury of *discontinuance*; which happens when he who hath an estate-tail, maketh a larger estate of the land than by law he is entitled to do: in which case the estate is good, so far as his power extends who made it, but no farther. As if tenant in tail makes a feoffment in fee-simple, or for the life of the feoffee, or in tail; all which are beyond his power to make, for that by the common law extends no farther than to make a lease for his own life: the entry of the feoffee is lawful during the life of the feoffer; but if he retains the possession after the death of the feoffor, it is an injury, which is termed a discontinuance;

the ancient legal estate, which ought to have survived to the heir in tail, being gone, or at least suspended, and for a while discontinued." 3 William Blackstone, *Commentaries on the Laws of England* 171–72 (1768).

discontinuee, *n.* (16c) A person whose acquisition of an entailed estate causes a discontinuance of the fee tail heirs' right to the estate. Cf. DISCONTINUOR.

discontinuing easement. See *discontinuous easement* under EASEMENT.

discontinuor, *n.* (18c) A tenant in tail whose conveyance of the entailed estate causes a discontinuance. Cf. DISCONTINUEE.

discontinuous easement. See EASEMENT.

discontinuous servitude. See *discontinuous easement* under EASEMENT.

disconvenable (dis-kən-**vee**-nə-bəl), *adj.* [Law French] *Archaic.* Unfit; improper.

discount, *n.* (17c) **1.** A reduction from the full amount or value of something, esp. a price. **2.** An advance deduction of interest when a person lends money on a note, bill of exchange, or other commercial paper, resulting in its present value. See PRESENT VALUE. **3.** The amount by which a security's market value is below its face value. — Also termed *bond discount.* Cf. PREMIUM (3). — **discount,** *vb.*

▸ **bulk discount.** See *volume discount.*

▸ **cash discount.** (1889) **1.** A seller's price reduction in exchange for an immediate cash payment. **2.** A reduction from the stated price if the bill is paid on or before a specified date.

▸ **functional discount.** (1936) **1.** A supplier's price discount given to a purchaser based on the purchaser's role (such as warehousing or advertising) in the supplier's distributive system. • This type of discount typically reflects the value of services performed by the purchaser for the supplier. If a functional discount constitutes a reasonable reimbursement for the purchaser's actual marketing functions, it does not constitute unlawful price discrimination and does not violate antitrust laws. **2.** A supplier's price discount based on the purchaser's relative distance from the supplier in the chain of distribution. • For example, a wholesaler or distributor usu. receives a greater discount than a retailer.

▸ **quantity discount.** See *volume discount.*

▸ **trade discount.** (1889) **1.** A discount from list price offered to all customers of a given type — for example, a discount offered by a lumber dealer to building contractors. **2.** The difference between a seller's list price and the price at which the dealer actually sells goods to the trade.

▸ **volume discount.** (1939) A price decrease based on a large-quantity purchase. — Also termed *bulk discount; quantity discount.*

discount bond. See BOND (3).

discount broker. See BROKER.

discounted cash flow. See CASH FLOW.

discounted-cash-flow method. See *discounted cash flow* under CASH FLOW.

discount interest. See INTEREST (3).

discount loan. See LOAN.

discount market. See MARKET.

discount rate. See INTEREST RATE.

discount share. See *discount stock* under STOCK.

discount stock. See STOCK.

discount yield. See YIELD.

discoverable, *adj.* Subject to pretrial discovery <the defendant's attorney argued that the defendant's income-tax returns were not discoverable during the liability phase of the trial>.

discovered-peril doctrine. See LAST-CLEAR-CHANCE DOCTRINE.

discoveree. (1969) A party who is required to respond to a litigant's discovery request or order. Cf. DISCOVERER (1).

discoverer. 1. A litigant who seeks information or materials from another party by means of a discovery request. — Also termed *discovering party.* Cf. DISCOVEREE. **2.** *Patent law.* See INVENTOR. *See* 35 USCA § 101.

discovering party. See DISCOVERER (1).

discovert (dis-**kəv**-ərt), *adj.* (14c) **1.** *Archaic.* Uncovered; exposed. **2.** Not married, esp. a widow or a woman who has never married.

discovery, *n.* (16c) **1.** The act or process of finding or learning something that was previously unknown <after making the discovery, the inventor immediately applied for a patent>. Cf. INVENTION (2). **2.** Compulsory disclosure, at a party's request, of information that relates to the litigation <the plaintiff filed a motion to compel discovery>. *See* Fed. R. Civ. P. 26–37; Fed. R. Crim. P. 16. • The primary discovery devices are interrogatories, depositions, requests for admissions, and requests for production. Although discovery typically comes from parties, courts also allow limited discovery from nonparties. **3.** The facts or documents disclosed <the new associate spent all her time reviewing discovery>. **4.** The pretrial phase of a lawsuit during which depositions, interrogatories, and other forms of discovery are conducted. — **discover,** *vb.* — **discoverable,** *adj.*

"Discovery has broad scope. According to Federal Rule 26, which is the model in modern procedural codes, inquiry may be made into 'any matter, not privileged, that is relevant to the subject matter of the action.' Thus, discovery may be had of facts incidentally relevant to the issues in the pleadings even if the facts do not directly prove or disprove the facts in question." Geoffrey C. Hazard Jr. & Michele Taruffo, *American Civil Procedure: An Introduction* 115 (1993).

▸ **abusive discovery.** See DISCOVERY ABUSE (1).

▸ **accelerated discovery.** (1973) A party's production of relevant evidence to an opponent at a time earlier than would otherwise be required by rule or standing order of the court. • The accelerated discovery is usu. carried out in compliance with a specific court order or the parties' agreement. — Also termed *accelerated disclosure.*

▸ **administrative discovery.** Discovery conducted under the rules for an administrative hearing. See ADMINISTRATIVE HEARING.

▸ **document discovery.** The use of devices to request an opponent's production of documents containing information relevant to litigation.

▸ **jurisdictional discovery.** (1961) Discovery that is limited to finding facts relevant to whether the court has jurisdiction. • A court may allow limited jurisdictional discovery before it rules on a motion to dismiss for lack of jurisdiction.

▸ **merits discovery.** (1975) Discovery to uncover facts that support the claim or defense, or that might lead to other facts that will support the allegations of a legal proceeding.

▸ **postjudgment discovery.** (1967) Discovery conducted after judgment has been rendered, usu. to determine the nature of the judgment debtor's assets or to obtain testimony for use in future proceedings. — Also termed *posttrial discovery.*

▸ **pretrial discovery.** (1939) Discovery conducted before trial to reveal facts and develop evidence. • Modern procedural rules have broadened the scope of pretrial discovery to prevent the parties from surprising each other with evidence at trial.

▸ **reciprocal discovery.** (1913) **1.** The corresponding rights and duties of both sides of litigation to engage in discovery; esp., the prosecution's right to the disclosure of information and documents from a criminal defendant. **2.** See *reverse Jencks material* under JENCKS MATERIAL.

▸ **reverse discovery.** See *reverse Jencks material* under JENCKS MATERIAL.

discovery abuse. (1975) **1.** The misuse of the pretrial discovery process, esp. by making overbroad requests for information that is unnecessary or beyond the scope of permissible disclosure or by conducting discovery for an improper purpose. — Also termed *abusive discovery.*

> "The term 'discovery abuse' has been used as if it were a single concept, but it includes several different things. Thus, it is useful to subdivide 'abuse' into 'misuse' and 'overuse.' What is referred to as 'misuse' would include not only direct violation of the rules, as by failing to respond to a discovery request within the stated time limit, but also more subtle attempts to harass or obstruct an opponent, as by giving obviously inadequate answers or by requesting information that clearly is outside the scope of discovery. By 'overuse' is meant asking for more discovery than is necessary or appropriate to the particular case. 'Overuse,' in turn, can be subdivided into problems of 'depth' and of 'breadth,' with 'depth' referring to discovery that may be relevant but is simply excessive and 'breadth' referring to discovery requests that go into matters too far removed from the case." Charles Alan Wright, *The Law of Federal Courts* § 81, at 580 (5th ed. 1994).

2. The failure to respond adequately to proper discovery requests. — Also termed *abuse of discovery.*

discovery disclosure. See DISCLOSURE (2).

discovery immunity. (1975) An exemption provided by statute, caselaw, or court rules to exclude certain documents and information from being disclosed during discovery.

discovery policy. See *claims-made insurance* under INSURANCE.

discovery rule. (1916) *Civil procedure.* The rule that a limitations period does not begin to run until the plaintiff discovers (or reasonably should have discovered) the injury giving rise to the claim. • The discovery rule usu. applies to injuries that are inherently difficult to detect, such as those resulting from medical malpractice. See STATUTE OF LIMITATIONS; ACCRUAL RULE. Cf. OCCURRENCE RULE.

discovery sanction. See SANCTION (3).

discovery scope. See SCOPE OF DISCOVERY.

discovery vein. See VEIN.

discredit, *vb.* (16c) **1.** To disbelieve; to put no faith in. **2.** To destroy or impair the credibility of (a witness, a piece of evidence, or a theory); to lessen the degree of trust to be accorded to (a witness or document). — **discredit,** *n.*

discreet (di-**skreet**), *adj.* (14c) Wise in avoiding potential errors or in choosing the best, most creditable means for accomplishing an end, esp. when confidentiality is required; prudent; judicious; discerning.

discrete (di-**skreet**), *adj.* (14c) Individual; separate; distinct.

discrete and insular class. See CLASS (1).

discrete and insular minority. See MINORITY.

discretion (di-**skresh**-ən). (14c) **1.** Wise conduct and management exercised without constraint; the ability coupled with the tendency to act with prudence and propriety. **2.** Freedom in the exercise of judgment; the power of free decision-making.

▸ **sole discretion.** (17c) An individual's power to make decisions without anyone else's advice or consent.

3. *Criminal & tort law.* The capacity to distinguish between right and wrong, sufficient to make a person responsible for his or her own actions. **4.** A public official's power or right to act in certain circumstances according to personal judgment and conscience, often in an official or representative capacity. — Also termed *discretionary power.*

▸ **administrative discretion.** (17c) A public official's or agency's power to exercise judgment in the discharge of its duties.

▸ **judicial discretion.** (17c) The exercise of judgment by a judge or court based on what is fair under the circumstances and guided by the rules and principles of law; a court's power to act or not act when a litigant is not entitled to demand the act as a matter of right. — Also termed *legal discretion.*

▸ **prosecutorial discretion.** (1960) **1.** *Criminal law.* A prosecutor's power to choose from the options available in a criminal case, such as filing charges, prosecuting, not prosecuting, plea-bargaining, and recommending a sentence to the court. **2.** *Immigration law.* A federal authority's discretion not to immediately arrest or endeavor to remove an illegal immigrant because the immigrant does not meet the federal government's immigration-enforcement priorities.

discretion, abuse of. See ABUSE OF DISCRETION.

discretionary (di-**skresh**-ə-ner-ee), *adj.* (18c) (Of an act or duty) involving an exercise of judgment and choice, not an implementation of a hard-and-fast rule exercisable at one's own will or judgment. • A court's discretionary act may be overturned only after a showing of abuse of discretion.

discretionary abstention. See *permissive abstention* under ABSTENTION.

discretionary account. See ACCOUNT.

discretionary act. (18c) A deed involving an exercise of personal judgment and conscience. — Also termed *discretionary function.* See DISCRETION; ABUSE OF DISCRETION.

discretionary bail. See BAIL (4).

discretionary commitment. See COMMITMENT.

discretionary damages. See DAMAGES.

discretionary duty. See DUTY (2).

discretionary function. See DISCRETIONARY ACT.

discretionary immunity. See IMMUNITY (1).

discretionary income. See INCOME.

discretionary judgment. See JUDGMENT (2).

discretionary order. See ORDER (8).

discretionary power. 1. See POWER (3). **2.** See DISCRETION (4).

discretionary promise. See PROMISE.

discretionary review. See REVIEW.

discretionary sentencing. See *indeterminate sentencing* under SENTENCING.

discretionary-transfer statute. See TRANSFER STATUTE.

discretionary trust. See TRUST (3).

discretion statement. (1953) *Hist. English law.* In an action for divorce or judicial separation, a written request for the court to consider granting a judgment favorable to a spouse who has admittedly committed a matrimonial offense, esp. adultery.

> "In a suit for divorce or judicial separation, the defendant's own adultery is a discretionary bar. The petitioner asking the court to exercise its discretion to grant a decree notwithstanding his own adultery must lodge in the Divorce Registry a statement, known as a `discretion statement,' dated and signed by him or his solicitor, stating that the court will be asked to exercise its discretion on his behalf notwithstanding his own adultery, and setting forth particulars of his acts of adultery and of the facts which it is material for the court to know for the purpose of exercising its discretion." N. Simon Tessy, *Is a Discretion Statement Really Necessary?*, 21 Mod. L. Rev. 48, 48 (1958).

discriminant function (di-**skrim**-ə-nənt). (1966) An IRS method of selecting tax returns to be audited. • The method consists of (1) using a computer program to identify returns with a high probability of error (such as those showing a disproportionate amount of deductible expenses), and (2) having examiners manually review the selected returns to determine which ones should be audited. — Also termed *DIF system*.

discriminatee (di-skrim-ə-nə-**tee**). (1951) A person unlawfully discriminated against.

discrimination, *n.* (1866) **1.** The intellectual faculty of noting differences and similarities. **2.** The effect of a law or established practice that confers privileges on a certain class or that denies privileges to a certain class because of race, age, sex, nationality, religion, or disability. • Federal law, including Title VII of the Civil Rights Act, prohibits employment discrimination based on any one of those characteristics. Other federal statutes, supplemented by court decisions, prohibit discrimination in voting rights, housing, credit extension, public education, and access to public facilities. State laws provide further protections against discrimination. **3.** Differential treatment; esp., a failure to treat all persons equally when no reasonable distinction can be found between those favored and those not favored.

> "The dictionary sense of 'discrimination' is neutral while the current political use of the term is frequently non-neutral, pejorative. With both a neutral and a non-neutral use of the word having currency, the opportunity for confusion in arguments about racial discrimination is enormously multiplied. For some, it may be enough that a practice is called discriminatory for them to judge it wrong. Others may be mystified that the first group condemns the practice without further argument or inquiry. Many may be led to the false sense that they have actually made a moral argument by showing that the practice discriminates (distinguishes in favor of or against). The temptation is to move from '*X* distinguishes in favor of or against' to '*X* discriminates' to '*X* is wrong' without being aware of the equivocation involved." Robert K. Fullinwider, *The Reverse Discrimination Controversy* 11–12 (1980).

▸ **affirmative discrimination.** See *reverse discrimination.*

▸ **age discrimination.** (1930) Discrimination based on age. • Federal law prohibits discrimination in employment against people who are age 40 or older. Cf. AGEISM.

▸ **benign discrimination.** See *reverse discrimination.*

▸ **content-based discrimination.** (1976) A state-imposed restriction on the content of speech, esp. when the speech concerns something of slight social value and is vastly outweighed by the public interest in morality and order. • Types of speech subject to content-based discrimination include obscenity, fighting words, and defamation. *R.A.V. v. City of St. Paul*, 505 U.S. 377, 383–84, 112 S.Ct. 2538, 2543 (1992).

▸ **direct discrimination.** (1869) Differential treatment of a person or a particular group of people based on race, gender, or other characteristic.

▸ **disability discrimination.** Discrimination based on a person's actual, perceived, or past physical or mental impairment.

▸ **employment discrimination.** (1932) Discrimination against an employee, former employee, or job applicant by an employer based on a characteristic or status such as race, age, religion, disability, or sexual orientation. • Employment discrimination may be lawful if an employer can show that there is a valid job-related reason for it. *See* TITLE VII OF THE CIVIL RIGHTS ACT OF 1964.

▸ **gender discrimination.** See *sex discrimination.*

▸ **indirect discrimination.** Discrimination arising from the application of a provision, criterion, or policy in such a way that a particular definable group is disadvantaged.

▸ **institutionalized discrimination.** See *systemic discrimination.*

▸ **invidious discrimination** (in-**vid**-ee-əs). (1856) Discrimination that is offensive or objectionable, esp. because it involves prejudice or stereotyping.

▸ **lawful discrimination.** (1893) **1.** Discrimination based on a criterion that is not characteristic of a protected class; discrimination that is not statutorily forbidden. **2.** Discrimination against a member of a protected class that is legally permitted for a valid purpose. • For example, a church-affiliated private school may hire only adherents of a certain religion.

▸ **national-origin discrimination.** (1949) Discrimination based on the country or place where a person was born or a person's ancestors lived; discrimination based on a person's ethnicity (or presumed ethnicity), cultural heritage, or association with a certain ethnic group or organization.

▸ **positive discrimination.** See AFFIRMATIVE ACTION.

▸ **racial discrimination.** (1891) Discrimination based on race.

▸ **religious discrimination.** (1908) Discrimination based on a person's religious or spiritual beliefs or association. — Also termed *religion discrimination.*

▸ **reverse discrimination.** (1964) Preferential treatment of minorities, esp. through affirmative-action programs, in a way that adversely affects members of a majority group; specif., the practice of giving unfair treatment to a group of people who have traditionally been privileged in an attempt to be fair to the group of people unfairly treated in the past. — Also termed *benign discrimination; affirmative discrimination.* See AFFIRMATIVE ACTION.

▸ **sex discrimination.** (1885) Discrimination based on gender, esp. against women. • The Supreme Court has established an intermediate-scrutiny standard of review for gender-based classifications, which must serve an important governmental interest and be substantially related to the achievement of that objective. *Craig v. Boren*, 429 U.S. 190, 97 S.Ct. 451 (1976). The terminology is gradually shifting. Increasingly in medicine and sociology, *gender* is distinguished from *sex. Gender* refers to the psychological and societal aspects of being male or female; *sex* refers specifically to the physical aspects. — Also termed *gender discrimination.*

▸ **sexual-orientation discrimination.** (1979) Discrimination based on a person's predisposition or inclination to be romantically or sexually attracted to a certain type of person (i.e., heterosexuality, homosexuality, bisexuality, or asexuality), or based on a person's gender identity (i.e., a person's internal sense of gender).

▸ **systemic discrimination.** (1969) An ingrained culture that perpetuates discriminatory policies and attitudes toward certain classes of people within society or a particular industry, profession, company, or geographic location. • Examples of systemic discrimination include excluding women from traditionally male jobs, holding management trainee programs on evenings and weekends, and asking unlawful preemployment screening questions. — Also termed *institutionalized discrimination; systematic discrimination.*

▸ **viewpoint discrimination.** (1979) Content-based discrimination in which the government targets not a particular subject, but instead certain views that speakers might express on the subject; discrimination based on the content of a communication. • If restrictions on the content of speech are reasonable and not calculated to suppress a particular set of views or ideas, a governmental body may limit speech in a nonpublic forum to expressions that serve a specific purpose. For example, an agency holding a workshop to inform state employees of laws related to the agency's functions may reasonably prohibit the expression of opinions regarding the motives of the legislators. But if speech favorable to the legislators' intent is allowed and opponents are denied the opportunity to respond, the restriction would constitute viewpoint discrimination. — Also termed *viewpoint-based discrimination.*

4. The effect of state laws that favor local interests over out-of-state interests. • Such a discriminatory state law may still be upheld if it is narrowly tailored to achieve an important state interest. Cf. FAVORITISM. — **discriminate,** *vb.* — **discriminatory,** *adj.*

discriminatory harassment. See HARASSMENT.

discriminatory price. See PRICE.

discriminatory purpose. A design or desire to restrict the rights of a class of people, esp. a protected class.

discriminatory tariff. See TARIFF (2).

discussion. (16c) **1.** The act of exchanging views on something; a debate. **2.** *Civil law.* A creditor's act of exhausting all remedies against the principal debtor before proceeding with a lawsuit against the guarantor. See BENEFIT OF DISCUSSION.

disease. (14c) **1.** A deviation from the healthy and normal functioning of the body <the drug could not be linked to his disease>. **2.** (*pl.*) Special classes of pathological conditions with similar traits, such as having similar causes and affecting similar organs <respiratory diseases> <occupational diseases>. **3.** Any disorder; any depraved condition.

▸ **functional disease.** (1886) A disease that prevents, obstructs, or interferes with an organ's special function, without anatomical defect or abnormality in the organ itself.

▸ **industrial disease.** See OCCUPATIONAL DISEASE.

▸ **occupational disease.** See OCCUPATIONAL DISEASE.

▸ **organic disease.** (17c) A disease that is caused by an injury to, or lesion or malfunction in, an organ.

disembarrass, *vb.* (18c) To free from embarrassment; to extricate or disentangle one thing from another.

disembodied technology. (1972) *Intellectual property.* Know-how or knowledge that is in the form of information only. • Disembodied technology includes proprietary technology and information in the public domain. Cf. EMBODIED TECHNOLOGY.

disenfranchise (dis-ən-**fran**-chɪz), *vb.* (17c) To deprive (someone) of a right, esp. the right to vote; to prevent (a person or group of people) from having the right to vote. — Also termed *disfranchise.*

disenfranchised, *adj.* (17c) Not having rights, esp. not the right to vote, and therefore feeling alienated from society.

disenfranchisement (dis-ən-**fran**-chiz-mənt *or* -**fran**-chɪz-mənt). (18c) **1.** The act of depriving a member of a corporation or other organization of a right, as by expulsion. **2.** The act of taking away the right to vote in public elections from a citizen or class of citizens. — Also termed *disfranchisement.*

disengagement letter. A letter from an attorney to a client announcing the intention to end the attorney–client relationship.

disentailing assurance. See DISENTAILMENT.

disentailing deed. See DEED.

disentailing statute (dis-ən-**tayl**-ing). (1939) A statute regulating or prohibiting disentailing deeds. See *disentailing deed* under DEED.

disentailment (dis-ən-**tayl**-mənt), *n.* (1886) The act or process by which a tenant in tail bars the entail on an estate and converts it into a fee simple, thereby nullifying the rights of any later claimant to the fee tail. — Also termed *disentailing assurance.* See BARRING OF ENTAIL. — **disentail,** *vb.*

disentitle (dis-ən-**tɪt**-əl), *vb.* (17c) To deprive (someone) of a title or claim <the plaintiffs' actions disentitled them to recover damages>.

disentitlement provision. A clause in a statute or legal instrument setting forth limitations on claims and rights.

disestablish, *vb.* (1838) To formally oust (a church) as the official church of one's country; to remove (a church) from the privileged position of being governmentally installed and recognized. — **disestablishment,** *n.*

disfacere. See DIFFACERE.

disfigurement (dis-**fig**-yər-mənt). (17c) An impairment or injury to the appearance of a person or thing.

disfranchise. See DISENFRANCHISE.

disfranchisement. See DISENFRANCHISEMENT.

disgavel (dis-**gav**-əl), *vb.* (17c) *Hist.* To convert (gavelkind land) into ordinary freehold land. See GAVELKIND.

disgorgement, *n.* (15c) The act of giving up something (such as profits illegally obtained) on demand or by legal compulsion. — **disgorge,** *vb.*

disgrading. (16c) *Hist.* **1.** The act of degrading. **2.** The depriving of an order; the depriving of a dignity.

> "Disgrading, or degrading, is when a man having taken upon him a dignity temporal or spiritual, is afterwards thereof deprived, be he knight, clerk or other. Whereof if a clerk be delivered to his ordinary, and cannot clear himself of the offence whereof he is convicted by the jury, he shall be disgraded for it; which is nothing else but the deprivation of him from those orders he hath taken upon him, as priesthood, deaconship, or otherwise. . . . In like manner there is disgrading of a knight . . . . And it is worthy the observation, that by the canon law there are two kinds of disgradings; the one summary, by word only, and the other solemn, by devesting the party disgraded from those ornaments and rites which are the ensigns of his order or degree." *Termes de la Ley* 175–76 (1st Am. ed. 1812).

disguise, *n.* **1.** Apparel worn to conceal one's identity. **2.** The application of a façade to misrepresent the true nature of a thing. **3.**The act of concealment or misrepresentation.

disguised dividend. See *informal dividend* under DIVIDEND.

disguised donation. See DONATION (1).

disguised installment sale. See INSTALLMENT SALE.

disherison (dis-**her**-ə-zən). See DISINHERITANCE.

disheritor (dis-**her**-ə-tər *or* -tor). (17c) *Archaic.* Someone who deprives someone of an inheritance.

dishonest. 1. (Of a person) demonstrating a lack of integrity or probity; untrustworthy, and therefore tending to cheat people. **2.** (Of documents, profits, etc.) fraudulent; resulting from a lack of candor, fairness, and straightforwardness. **3.** (Of an action) not involving straightforward dealing; discreditable; underhanded; fraudulent. **4.** *Hist.* Unchaste; lewd.

> "All these adjectives [*dishonest, deceitful, lying, untruthful,* and *mendacious*] describe someone whose words or actions lack integrity and candor, and therefore credibility. *Dishonest* is broad, implying perhaps an instance or the habit of skewing the truth <a dishonest assertion>, but it may also imply an instance or the habit of stealing or cheating <a dishonest merchant>. *Deceitful* typically suggests a positive intent to mislead, especially by misrepresenting the true character either of oneself or of what is being sold or negotiated, by indulging in falsehoods, by defrauding, or by double-dealing <a deceitful negotiator>. *Lying,* the most brutal and frequent of these adjectives, connotes a habit of stating falsehoods as opposed to a single instance <a lying scoundrel>, although this connotation is absent when the word is used not as an adjective but as a participial verb (that is, 'You're lying!' could refer to only one instance, as opposed to a habit). *Untruthful* is a less inflammatory adjective, implying that someone's statements don't square with reality — and the term applies most often not to people but to their assertions <an untruthful report> <an untruthful financial statement>. *Mendacious,* a literary term, is essentially a heightened equivalent of *lying* <a mendacious villain>." Bryan A. Garner, *Garner's Dictionary of Legal Usage* 284 (3d ed. 2011).

dishonest act. See FRAUDULENT ACT.

dishonesty. Deceitfulness as a character trait; behavior that deceives or cheats people; untruthfulness; untrustworthiness.

dishonor, *vb.* (14c) **1.** To refuse to accept or pay (a negotiable instrument) when presented. See NOTICE OF DISHONOR; WRONGFUL DISHONOR. **2.** To deface or defile (something, such as a flag). — **dishonor,** *n.*

dishonorable discharge. See DISCHARGE (8).

disimprisonment. (17c) The release of a prisoner; the removal of a prisoner from confinement. — Also termed *disincarceration; decarceration.* Cf. INCARCERATION.

disincarcerate, *vb.* (17c) To release (a person) from jail; to set free.—Also termed *disimprison.*

disincarceration. See DISIMPRISONMENT.

disincentive, *n.* (1946) A deterrent (to a particular type of conduct), often created, intentionally or unintentionally, through legislation <federal tax law creates a disincentive to marriage> <sales taxes provide a disincentive to excessive consumer spending>.

disinflation. (1948) A period or process of slowing down the rate of inflation. Cf. DEFLATION.

disinherison (dis-in-**her**-ə-zən), *n.* See DISINHERITANCE.

disinherit, *vb.* (15c) To take away from (someone, esp. one's son or daughter) any claim to receive one's property after death.

disinheritance, *n.* (16c) **1.** The act by which an owner of an estate deprives a would-be heir of the expectancy to inherit the estate. • A testator may expressly exclude or limit the right of a person or a class to inherit property that the person or class would have inherited through intestate succession, but only if the testator devises all the property to another. **2.** The quality, state, or condition of being disinherited. — Also termed *disherison; disinherison; deherison.* See *forced heir* under HEIR.

▸ **negative disinheritance.** (1939) The act by which a testator attempts to exclude a person from inheritance without disposing of the property to another. • Negative disinheritance is ineffective at common law, although today it may be permitted by statute.

disinter (dis-in-**tər**), *vb.* (17c) **1.** To exhume (a corpse). **2.** To remove (something) from obscurity. — **disinterment** (dis-in-**tər**-mənt), *n.*

disinterested, *adj.* (17c) **1.** Free from bias, prejudice, or partiality and therefore able to judge the situation fairly; not having a pecuniary interest in the matter at hand <a disinterested witness>. **2.** Loosely, UNINTERESTED. Cf. UNINTERESTED. — **disinterest, disinterestedness,** *n.*

disinterested witness. See WITNESS.

disintermediation. (1966) **1.** The process of bank depositors' withdrawing their funds from accounts with low interest rates to put them into investments that pay higher returns. **2.** The selling of products directly to consumers through the Internet rather than selling first to a wholesaler and then to a shop — so that manufacturers are brought directly into contact with end users.

disinvestment, *n.* (1936) **1.** The consumption of capital. **2.** The taking of one's money out of a company by selling one's shares in it; esp., the withdrawal of investments, often on political grounds. — Also termed (in sense 2) *divestment.* — **disinvest,** *vb.*

disjoinder (dis-**joyn**-dər). (1936) The undoing of the joinder of parties or claims. See JOINDER. Cf. MISJOINDER (1); NONJOINDER (1).

disjuncta (dis-**jəngk**-tə), *n. pl.* [Latin] *Roman & civil law.* Things (usu. words or phrases) that are separated or opposed. — Also spelled *disiuncta.* Cf. CONJUNCTA.

disjunctim (dis-**jəngk**-təm), *adv.* [Latin] *Roman law.* Separately; severally. • A condition imposed *disjunctim,* for example, would bind the persons severally, rather than jointly. — Also spelled *disiunctim.* Cf. CONJUNCTIM.

disjunctive allegation. See ALLEGATION.

disjunctive condition. See CONDITION (2).

disjunctive denial. See DENIAL (3).

disjunctive obligation. See *alternative obligation* under OBLIGATION.

disme (dɪm), *n.* [Law French] (17c) A tithe; a tenth part, as in a tithe due the clergy equal to the tenth of all spiritual livings as required by the statute 25 Edw. 3, st. 7. • This is the Law French equivalent to the Latin *decimae.* It was once the spelling of the American 10-cent piece, the *dime.* See DECIMAE. Pl. ***dismes.***

dismember, *vb.* (13c) **1.** To cut a body into pieces and tear it apart, esp. by detaching all limbs. **2.** To divide a county, area, or organization into smaller parts.

dismemberment. (18c) **1.** The cutting off of a limb or body part. **2.** *Int'l law.* The disappearance of a country as a result of a treaty or an annexation, whereby it becomes part of one or more other countries. **3.** *Int'l law.* The reduction of a country's territory by annexation or cession, or the secession of one part. **4.** *Int'l law.* The extinguishment of a country and the creation of two or more new countries from the former country's territory.

dismemberments of ownership. (1882) *Civil law.* The three elements composing the right of ownership, namely the usus, the fructus, and the abusus. • The right of ownership may be dismembered and its components conveyed in the form of independent real rights, such as the right of use, the right of usufruct, and the right of security. See ABUSUS; FRUCTUS; USUS.

dismiss, *vb.* (15c) **1.** To send (something) away; specif., to terminate (an action or claim) without further hearing, esp. before the trial of the issues involved. **2.** To release or discharge (a person) from employment. See DISMISSAL.

dismissal, *n.* (1885) **1.** Termination of an action or claim without further hearing, esp. before the trial of the issues involved; esp., a judge's decision to stop a court case.

▸ **constructive dismissal.** (1908) See *constructive discharge* under DISCHARGE (7).

▸ **dismissal agreed.** A court's dismissal of a lawsuit with the acquiescence of all parties. • Among other possibilities, the parties may have settled out of court or chosen to have their dispute arbitrated or mediated. — Also termed *agreed dismissal.*

▸ **dismissal for failure to prosecute.** See *dismissal for want of prosecution.*

▸ **dismissal for lack of prosecution.** See *dismissal for want of prosecution.*

▸ **dismissal for want of equity.** (1859) A court's dismissal of a lawsuit on substantive, rather than procedural, grounds, usu. because the plaintiff's allegations are found to be untrue or because the plaintiff's pleading does not state an adequate claim.

▸ **dismissal for want of prosecution.** (1831) A court's dismissal of a lawsuit because the plaintiff has failed to pursue the case diligently toward completion. — Abbr. DWOP. — Also termed *dismissal for failure to prosecute; dismissal for lack of prosecution.*

▸ **dismissal without prejudice.** (1831) A dismissal that does not bar the plaintiff from refiling the lawsuit within the applicable limitations period. See WITHOUT PREJUDICE.

▸ **dismissal with prejudice.** (1898) A dismissal, usu. after an adjudication on the merits, barring the plaintiff from prosecuting any later lawsuit on the same claim. • If, after a dismissal with prejudice, the plaintiff files a later suit on the same claim, the defendant in the later suit can assert the defense of res judicata (claim preclusion). See RES JUDICATA; WITH PREJUDICE.

▸ **involuntary dismissal.** (1911) A court's dismissal of a lawsuit because the plaintiff failed to prosecute or failed to comply with a procedural rule or court order. Fed. R. Civ. P. 41(b).

▸ **voluntary dismissal.** (1834) A plaintiff's dismissal of a lawsuit at the plaintiff's own request or by stipulation of all the parties. Fed. R. Civ. P. 41(a).

2. A release or discharge from employment. See DISCHARGE (7).

▸ **dismissal for cause.** (1877) A dismissal of a contract employee for a reason that the law or public policy has recognized as sufficient to warrant the employee's removal.

3. *Military law.* A court-martial punishment for an officer, commissioned warrant officer, cadet, or midshipman, consisting of separation from the armed services with dishonor. • A dismissal can be given only by a general court-martial and is considered the equivalent of a dishonorable discharge. — **dismiss,** *vb.*

dismissal compensation. See SEVERANCE PAY.

dismissal order. See ORDER (2).

dismissed for want of equity. (18c) (Of a case) removed from the court's docket for substantive reasons, usu. because the plaintiff's allegations are found to be untrue or because the plaintiff's pleading does not state an adequate claim. See *dismissal for want of equity* under DISMISSAL (1).

dismissed for want of prosecution. (18c) (Of a case) removed from the court's docket because the plaintiff has failed to pursue the case diligently toward completion. See *dismissal for want of prosecution* under DISMISSAL (1).

dismissed without prejudice. (18c) (Of a case) removed from the court's docket in such a way that the plaintiff may refile the same suit on the same claim. See *dismissal without prejudice* under DISMISSAL (1); WITHOUT PREJUDICE.

dismissed with prejudice. (18c) (Of a case) removed from the court's docket in such a way that the plaintiff is foreclosed from filing a suit again on the same claim or claims. See *dismissal with prejudice* under DISMISSAL (1); WITH PREJUDICE.

dismission. (16c) *Archaic.* **1.** An act of dismissing <dismission of the jury>. **2.** A removal, esp. from office or position <dismission of the employee>. **3.** A decision that a suit cannot be maintained <dismission of the case>.

dismortgage. See REDEMPTION (4).

Disneyland parent. See PARENT (1).

disobedient, *adj.* (15c) Not observant of the commands or prohibitions of authority; deliberately not doing what one is told to do by people in positions of authority, such as parents and teachers.

disobedient child. See *incorrigible child* under CHILD.

disobey, *vb.* (14c) **1.** To refuse to do what one is commanded to do; to disregard or ignore the authority or commands of. **2.** To refuse to obey (a rule, law, etc.); to break.

disorder. (1877) **1.** A lack of proper arrangement <disorder of the files>. **2.** An irregularity <a disorder in the proceedings>. **3.** A public disturbance; a riot <civil disorder>. **4.** A disturbance in mental or physical health <an emotional disorder> <a liver disorder>.

disorderly conduct. See CONDUCT.

disorderly house. (16c) **1.** A dwelling where people carry on activities that are a nuisance to the neighborhood. **2.** A dwelling where people conduct criminal or immoral activities. • Examples are brothels and drug houses. — Also termed (more narrowly) *bawdy house*; *house of prostitution*; *house of ill fame*; *house of ill repute*; *lewd house*; *assignation house*; *house of assignation*.

> "The keeping of one type of disorderly house — the bawdy house — is punished because it violates the social interest in maintaining proper standards of morality and decency. . . . As included here a house may be disorderly for other reasons. Any house in which disorderly persons are permitted to congregate, and to disturb the tranquillity of the neighborhood by fighting, quarreling, swearing or any other type of disorder, is a disorderly house; and the keeping thereof is a misdemeanor at common law." Rollin M. Perkins & Ronald N. Boyce, *Criminal Law* 487 (3d ed. 1982).

disorderly person. (18c) **1.** A person guilty of disorderly conduct. **2.** Someone who breaches the peace, order, decency, or safety of the public, as defined by statute. • The offense of being a disorderly person is usu. a misdemeanor.

> "Ordinarily, a person who is guilty of disorderly conduct is a 'disorderly person,' but where statutes define 'a disorderly person' and distinguish acts which may constitute the offense of disorderly conduct, the distinction is to be preserved and the different provisions relative to the different offenses particularly followed." 27 C.J.S. *Disorderly Conduct* § 1(1), at 509 (1959).

disparagare (di-spar-ə-**gair**-ee), *vb.* [Law Latin fr. Law French *disparager* "to disparage"] *Hist.* **1.** To disparage. **2.** To bring together unequal persons, as in a marriage between persons of unequal lineage. Cf. PARAGE.

disparagatio (di-spar-ə-**gay**-shee-oh), *n.* [Law Latin] *Hist.* Disparagement in marriage.

disparagation (di-spar-ə-**gay**-shən), *n.* [Law French] *Hist.* **1.** Disparagement. **2.** A marriage below one's station.

disparage, *vb.* (16c) **1.** To speak slightingly of; to criticize (someone or something) in a way showing that one considers the subject of discussion neither good nor important. **2.** To degrade in estimation by disrespectful or sneering treatment.

disparagement (di-**spar**-ij-mənt), *n.* (16c) **1.** A derogatory comparison of one thing with another <the disparagement consisted in comparing the acknowledged liar to a murderer>. **2.** The act or an instance of unfairly castigating or detracting from the reputation of someone or something <when she told the press the details of her husband's philandering, her statements amounted to disparagement>. • Although many disparagements are untruthful or otherwise unfair, falsity is not a requirement. Any statement cast in a negative light may amount to a disparagement in the general sense. **3.** *Torts.* A false and injurious statement that discredits or detracts from the reputation of another's character, property, product, or business. • To recover in tort for disparagement, the plaintiff must prove that the statement caused a third party to take some action resulting in specific pecuniary loss to the plaintiff. — Also termed *injurious falsehood*. — More narrowly termed *slander of title*; *trade libel*; *slander of goods*. See TRADE DISPARAGEMENT. Cf. *trade defamation* under DEFAMATION. **4.** Reproach, disgrace, or indignity <self-importance is a disparagement of greatness>. **5.** *Hist.* The act or an instance of pairing an heir in marriage with someone of an inferior social rank <the guardian's arranging for the heir's marriage to a chimney sweep amounted to disparagement>.

> "DISPARAGEMENT . . . The matching an heir in marriage under his degree or against decency. Under the law down to 1660, if a tenant of land held by knight's service died leaving an infant heir, the lord of whom the land was held was entitled to the marriage of the heir, that is, to bestow him or her in marriage. It was necessary, however, that the proposed marriage should be without disparagement, that is, suitable to the heir, and not to a person of inferior rank, or of deformed body, or weak mind, or having any other characteristics which prevented the marriage being considered equal or fitting; otherwise the heir was said to be disparaged. Disparagements were of several kinds, of which the principal were: *propter vitium animi*, as where the proposed wife or husband was an idiot, etc.; *propter vitium sanguinis* (as in the case of villeins, "men of trade," etc.); and *propter vitium corporis*, by reason of some bodily defect." 1 *Jowitt's Dictionary of English Law* 725 (Daniel Greenberg ed., 2010) (citations omitted).

disparaging direction. See *disparaging instruction* under JURY INSTRUCTION.

disparaging instruction. See JURY INSTRUCTION.

disparaging mark. See *disparaging trademark* under TRADEMARK.

disparaging trademark. See TRADEMARK.

disparate impact (**dis**-pə-rit). (1973) The adverse effect of a facially neutral practice (esp. an employment practice) that nonetheless discriminates against persons because of their race, sex, national origin, age, or disability and that is not justified by business necessity. • Discriminatory intent is irrelevant in a disparate-impact claim. — Also termed *adverse impact*.

disparate treatment. (1933) The practice, esp. in employment, of intentionally dealing with persons differently because of their race, sex, national origin, age, or disability. • To succeed on a disparate-treatment claim, the plaintiff must prove that the defendant acted with discriminatory intent or motive.

> "Claims brought on behalf of a group of employees come in two varieties: claims of intentional discrimination (or disparate treatment) and claims of discriminatory impact (or disparate impact). The difference between these types of claims is significant, so much so that constitutional law only recognizes claims of disparate treatment, not disparate impact. Yet these two kinds of claims resemble one another, especially in the statistical evidence that the plaintiff must present in order to establish liability. . . . [C]lass claims of disparate treatment emphasize the historical perspective and its negative conception of equality as colorblindness, while class claims of disparate impact emphasize the remedial perspective and its goal of eliminating the effects of past discrimination." George Rutherglen, *Employment Discrimination Law* 56 (2001).

disparity (di-**spar**-ə-tee). (16c) Inequality; a difference in quantity or quality between two or more things.

dispatch (di-**spach** *also* **dis**-pach), *n.* (16c) **1.** A prompt sending off of something <a dispatch of the letter agreement>. **2.** A prompt completion of something <dispatch of a business transaction>. **3.** Something quickly sent <the dispatch was mailed>. **4.** *Maritime law.* The required diligence in discharging cargo <dispatch is required on all charters>.

▸ **customary dispatch.** (1880) Dispatch that follows the rules, customs, and usages of the port where cargo is discharged.

▸ **quick dispatch.** (1828) A speedy dispatch that does not strictly follow the customs of the port, esp. to avoid delays resulting from a crowded wharf.

5. *Maritime law.* DISPATCH MONEY.

dispatch money. (1891) *Maritime law.* An amount paid by a shipowner to a vessel's charterer if the vessel's cargo is unloaded at the port sooner than provided for in the agreement between the charterer and the shipowner. — Also termed *dispatch*. Cf. *contract demurrage* under DEMURRAGE.

> "Some charters contain a provision for 'dispatch money,' which is in the nature of a reward to the charterer for loading or unloading more rapidly than provided for — i.e., in less time than the stipulated 'lay days.' Dispatch, where payable, is usually stated, just as is demurrage, in terms of a rate per day and pro rata part thereof." Grant Gilmore & Charles L. Black Jr., *The Law of Admiralty* § 4-8, at 212 (2d ed. 1975).

dispatch rule. See MAILBOX RULE.

dispauper (dis-**paw**-pər), *vb.* (17c) To disqualify from being a pauper; to deprive (a person) of the ability to sue *in forma pauperis*. See IN FORMA PAUPERIS.

dispensable, *adj.* (17c) **1.** Being neither necessary nor important and therefore easy to get rid of. **2.** That may be the subject of dispensation; pardonable.

dispensary (di-**spen**-sər-ee), *n.* (17c) **1.** A place where drugs are prepared or distributed. **2.** An institution, usu. for the poor, where medical advice and medicines are distributed for free or at a discounted rate.

dispensation (dis-pen-**say**-shən). (17c) **1.** An exemption from a law, duty, or penalty; permission to do something that is ordinarily forbidden <special dispensation to annul the marriage>. **2.** The act of providing people with something as part of a governmental or other official process <the dispensation of justice>. **3.** A political or religious system that has control over people's lives at a particular time <the Mosaic dispensation then prevailing within the church>.

dispense with the reading of the minutes. (1909) *Parliamentary law.* To forgo reciting the secretary's proposed minutes at the regular time. • The reading is not forgone altogether, but simply postponed. If the proposed minutes have been printed and circulated, then their correction and approval is in order without reading them aloud, and a motion to dispense with reading them is superfluous.

dispersonare (dis-pər-sə-**nair**-ee), *vb.* [Latin] *Hist.* To scandalize, disparage, or slander.

displaced person. See PERSON (1).

displaced-persons camp. (1948) *Int'l. law.* In a country in the throes of war, natural disaster, ethnic cleansing, or some similar extraordinary event, a temporary settlement where citizens who have become homeless are temporarily provided with the basic necessities of life and given assistance in resettling or emigrating.

displacement. (17c) **1.** Removal from a proper place or position <displacement of a file> <displacement of an officer>. **2.** A replacement; a substitution <displacement of one lawyer with another>. **3.** A forced removal of a person from the person's home or country, esp. because of war <displacement of refugees>. **4.** A shifting of emotional emphasis from one thing to another, esp. to avoid unpleasant or unacceptable thoughts or tendencies <emotional displacement>.

display oratory. See *epideictic oratory* under ORATORY.

display right. (1944) *Copyright.* A copyright owner's exclusive right to show or exhibit a copy of the protected work publicly, whether directly or by technological means. • For example, this right makes it illegal to transmit a copyrighted work over the Internet without permission.

dispone (dis-**pohn**), *vb.* [fr. Middle English *disponen* fr. Old French *disponer* "dispose"] (14c) **1.** *Archaic.* To dispose; to arrange. **2.** *Scots law.* To convey, transfer, or otherwise alienate (property).

disponee. One to whom a grant or conveyance is made. See ALIENEE.

disponent (dis-**poh**-nənt). (17c) **1.** Of, relating to, or involving a sale, grant, or conveyance. **2.** Preparing or adapting for some specific purpose one has in mind.

disponent owner. See OWNER.

disponer (dis-**poh**-nər), *n.* (17c) *Scots law.* Someone who legally conveys his or her property to another.

disponible (dis-**poh**-ni-bəl), *adj.* (1899) (Of property) capable of being granted or conveyed; that may be sold.

dispono (dis-**poh**-noh), *vb.* [Latin] *Scots law.* I grant or convey (land, etc.). • This is traditionally the main verb in a grant.

disponor. See ALIENOR.

disposable, *adj.* (17c) **1.** Intended to be used but once, usu. for a short time, and then discarded <disposable container>. **2.** Available to be used <disposable income>.

disposable earnings. See *disposable income* under INCOME.

disposable income. See INCOME.

disposable portion. (1816) The portion of property that can be willed to anyone the testator chooses.

disposal. *Patents.* A patent application's termination by withdrawal, rejection, or grant. • In some countries, the meaning is limited to rejection.

disposing capacity. See *testamentary capacity* under CAPACITY (3).

Disposing Clause. *Constitutional law.* The clause of the U.S. Constitution giving Congress the power to dispose of property belonging to the federal government. U.S. Const. art. IV, § 3, cl. 2.

disposing mind. See *testamentary capacity* under CAPACITY (3).

disposition (dis-pə-**zish**-ən), *n.* (14c) **1.** The act of transferring something to another's care or possession, esp. by deed or will; the relinquishing of property <a testamentary disposition of all the assets>.

▸ **testamentary disposition.** (17c) A disposition to take effect upon the death of the person making it, who retains substantially entire control of the property until death.

2. A final settlement or determination <the court's disposition of the case>.

▸ **ambulatory disposition.** (1878) **1.** A judgment or sentence that is subject to amendment or revocation. **2.** A testamentary provision that is subject to change because the testator is still alive and capable of making a new will. • Sense 2 corresponds to the first sense of *disposition* above. See AMBULATORY.

▸ **informal disposition.** (1849) The termination of a case by means other than trial; any action that leads to disposition without conviction and without a judicial determination of guilt, such as guilty pleas and decisions not to prosecute.

3. Temperament or character; personal makeup <a surly disposition>. — **dispose,** *vb.* — **dispositive,** *adj.*

dispositional hearing. See *disposition hearing* under HEARING.

disposition hearing. See HEARING.

disposition without a trial. (1888) The final determination of a criminal case without a trial on the merits, as when a defendant pleads guilty or admits sufficient facts to support a guilty finding without a trial.

dispositive (dis-**poz**-ə-tiv), *adj.* (17c) **1.** Being a deciding factor; (of a fact or factor) bringing about a final determination. **2.** Of, relating to, or effecting the disposition of property by will or deed.

dispositive clause. (17c) *Scots law.* In a deed, the clause of conveyance by which the grantor describes the property conveyed, its conditions or burdens, the name of the grantee, and the destination to heirs. See DESTINATION (3).

dispositive fact. See FACT.

dispositive motion. See MOTION (1).

dispositive treaty. See TREATY (1).

dispossess (dis-pə-**zes**), *vb.* (16c) To take property or land away from; to oust or evict (someone) from property. See DISPOSSESSION.

dispossession (dis-pə-**zesh**-ən), *n.* (16c) Deprivation of, or eviction from, rightful possession of property; the wrongful taking or withholding of possession of land from the person lawfully entitled to it; OUSTER (1).

dispossessor. (16c) Someone who dispossesses.

dispossess proceeding. (1888) A summary procedure initiated by a landlord to oust a defaulting tenant and regain possession of the premises. See FORCIBLE ENTRY AND DETAINER.

disproportionate, *adj.* (16c) Having too much or too little in relation to something else; not suitable in comparison with something else in size, amount, importance, etc. — Also termed *disproportional.*

disprove, *vb.* (14c) To refute (an assertion); to prove (an allegation) false.

dispunishable, *adj.* (16c) *Archaic.* (Of an offense) not punishable; not answerable.

disputable presumption. See *rebuttable presumption* under PRESUMPTION.

disputatio fori (dis-pyoo-**tay**-shee-oh **for**-I). [Latin] *Roman law.* Argument before a court; the practice of legal advocacy.

disputation, *n.* **1.** The act of debating or disputing. **2.** A discussion on a subject about which the participants cannot agree; a controversial argument. **3.** An academic exercise in which participants orally defend a thesis by formal logic.

disputatious, *adj.* (1660) **1.** Tending to argue; inclined to contend or wrangle; disposed to controversy. **2.** Of, relating to, or involving disputation or controversy.

dispute, *n.* (16c) A conflict or controversy, esp. one that has given rise to a particular lawsuit. — **dispute,** *vb.*

▸ **arbitrable dispute.** (1924) A dispute that can properly be resolved by arbitration.

▸ **major dispute.** *Labor law.* Under the Railway Labor Act, a disagreement about basic working conditions, often resulting in a new collective-bargaining agreement or a change in the existing agreement. • Under the Act, two classes of disputes — major and minor — are subject to mandatory arbitration. 45 USCA § 155. — Also termed *new-contract dispute.*

▸ **minor dispute.** *Labor law.* Under the Railway Labor Act, a disagreement about the interpretation or application of a collective-bargaining agreement, as opposed to a disagreement over the formation of a new agreement. 45 USCA § 155.

dispute resolution. See ALTERNATIVE DISPUTE RESOLUTION.

dispute-resolution procedure. *Intellectual property.* A mechanism for resolving international grievances over intellectual-property protection, conducted by the World Trade Organization under the TRIPs agreement. • The procedure begins with a complaint by one country against another, followed by consultations between the countries, a WTO panel report on the issue, and (potentially) trade sanctions against one of the countries. — Abbr. DRP.

Dispute Settlement Body. The session of the World Trade Organization in which disputes among member governments about trade agreements are settled. — Abbr. DSB.

disqualification, *n.* (18c) **1.** Something that incapacitates, disables, or makes one ineligible; esp., a bias or conflict of interest that prevents a judge or juror from impartially hearing a case, or that prevents a lawyer from representing a party.

▸ **vicarious disqualification.** (1949) Disqualification of all the lawyers in a firm or in an office because one of the lawyers is ethically disqualified from representing the client at issue. — Also termed *imputed disqualification.*

"In general, disqualification of a lawyer from representation, at least in multiple client-conflict scenarios, means disqualification of that lawyer's entire firm from the same representation. When a lawyer has been exclusively or chiefly responsible for the representation of a client and that lawyer changes jobs, there is little question but that the imputed-disqualification rule will apply to disqualify the new firm from representing the opponent of the first client. But because lawyers often work for large organizations, . . . a question may arise about the application of the imputation rule when a lawyer has left employment . . . . If the lawyer had little or no responsibility in the first organization for the representation or if the lawyer can be effectively shielded from the representation in the new organization, or both, there may be no useful purpose served by imputing the lawyer's disqualification to the new organization . . . ." James E. Moliterno & John M. Levy, *Ethics of the Lawyer's Work* 151 (1993).

2. The act of making ineligible; the fact or condition of being ineligible. Cf. RECUSAL. **3.** A punishment that may be imposed after an official has been impeached and removed from office, precluding the official from holding another office or enjoying any benefits of having held office. — **disqualify,** *vb.*

"An attempt has been made to evade the conclusion that disqualification may be adjudged without removal, by a resort to grammatical construction. It is said that the words 'Judgment . . . shall not extend further than to removal and disqualification to hold and enjoy any office' necessarily mean that removal must precede disqualification and be a part of the judgment. This, if true, would lead to a sequence which no one can sanction. It is that disqualification must necessarily follow removal. For if, as is contended, the conjunction 'and' between the words 'removal' and 'disqualification' makes the two penalties [for impeachment] parts of an indivisible judgment, then *disqualification* must be adjudged whatever *removal* is. This would lead to this absurd, harsh, cruel, and unjust consequence: That a judge who was unfit for his place by reason of intoxication, when impeached, *must be disqualified forever* from holding any other Federal office. He could not be removed without also being disqualified." William Worth Belknap et al., *Proceeding of the Senate Sitting for the Trial of William W. Belknap* 1100–01 (1876) (opinion of Senator Thomas M. Norwood).

disrate, *vb.* (1811) To reduce to a lower rank, esp. to reduce a ship or petty officer's rank.

disrationare (dis-ray-shee-ə-**nair**-ee), *n.* [Law Latin fr. Law French *desreigner* "to deraign"] *Hist.* To prove; to establish a title.

disregard, *n.* (17c) **1.** The action of ignoring or treating without proper respect or consideration. **2.** The quality, state, or condition of being ignored or treated without proper respect or consideration.

▸ **reckless disregard.** (1820) **1.** Conscious indifference to the consequences of an act. **2.** *Defamation.* Serious indifference to truth or accuracy of a publication. • "Reckless disregard for the truth" is the standard in proving the defendant's actual malice toward the plaintiff in a libel action. **3.** The intentional commission of a harmful act or failure to do a required act when the actor knows or has reason to know of facts that would lead a reasonable person to realize that the actor's conduct both creates an unreasonable risk of harm to someone and involves a high degree of probability that substantial harm will result.

disregard, *vb.* To ignore or treat as unimportant; to pass by as undeserving of notice <the judge admonished the jury to disregard the prosecutor's statement about the defendant's not testifying>.

disregarding the corporate entity. See PIERCING THE CORPORATE VEIL.

disregard of the law. See MANIFEST DISREGARD OF THE LAW.

disrepair. (18c) A state of being in need of restoration after deterioration or damage.

disrepute. (17c) A lack or loss of reputation; a bad name; dishonor.

disruptive conduct. See CONDUCT.

disseise (dis-**seez**), *vb.* (14c) To wrongfully deprive (a person) of the freehold possession of property. — Also spelled *disseize.*

disseisee (dis-see-**zee**). (16c) Someone who is wrongfully deprived of the freehold possession of property. — Also spelled *disseizee.* — Also termed *disseisitus.*

disseisin (dis-**see**-zin), *n.* (14c) The act of wrongfully depriving someone of the freehold possession of property; DISPOSSESSION. — Also spelled *disseizin.*

"The disseised owner of land loses, of course, with the *res* the power of present enjoyment. But this is not all. He retains, it is true, the right *in rem*; or, to use the common phrase, he has still a right of entry and a right of action. But by an inveterate rule of our law, a right of entry and a chose in action were strictly personal rights. Neither was assignable. It follows, then, that the disseisee cannot transfer the land. In other words, as long as the disseisin continues, the disseised owner is deprived of the two characteristic features of property, — he has neither the present enjoyment nor the power of alienation." J.B. Ames, *The Disseisin of Chattels,* 3 Harv. L. Rev. 23, 25 (1889).

▸ **disseisin by election.** (18c) A legal fiction by which a property owner is allowed to claim that he or she has been disseised, regardless of whether this is actually true, in order to have a remedy against an adverse claimant.

▸ **equitable disseisin.** (1831) The wrongful deprivation of the equitable ownership, possession, or the fruits of ownership or possession.

▸ **fresh disseisin.** (17c) The right at common law of a person disseised of land to forcefully eject the disseisor from the land without resort to law, as long as the ejection occurred soon after the disseisin.

disseisitrix. See DISSEISORESS.

disseisitus. See DISSEISEE.

disseisor (dis-**see**-zər *or* -zor). (15c) Someone who wrongfully deprives another of the freehold possession of property. — Also spelled *disseizor.*

disseisoress (dis-**see**-zər-is). (16c) *Hist.* A female disseisor. — Also termed *disseisitrix.*

dissemble (di-**sem**-bəl), *vb.* (16c) **1.** To give an erroneous impression of, as by pretense or falsified semblance; to cover up (something) by deception <to dissemble the facts>. **2.** To put on false appearances; to disguise reality <although purporting to be a prince of his home country, he was merely dissembling>. **3.** *Archaic.* To physically disguise <to dissemble oneself by wearing a mask>.

dissemination (di-sem-i-**nay**-shən), *n.* (17c) **1.** The act of spreading, diffusing, or dispersing; esp., the circulation of defamatory matter. **2.** The extension of the influence or establishment of a thing, such as an idea, book, or document.

dissensus (di-**sen**-səs), *n.* [Latin "disagreement"] (1962) *Roman law.* **1.** A lack of agreement. **2.** A mutually agreed annulment of a contractual obligation; an undoing of the *consensus* that created the obligation.

dissent (di-**sent**), *n.* (16c) **1.** A disagreement with a majority opinion, esp. among judges. **2.** See *dissenting opinion* under OPINION (1). **3.** A withholding of assent or approval. **4.** The act of a surviving spouse who, as statutorily authorized in many states, refuses a devise and elects instead a statutory share. See ELECTIVE SHARE. — **dissent** (di-**sent**), *vb.*

dissent and appraisal, right of. See APPRAISAL REMEDY.

dissenters' right. See APPRAISAL REMEDY.

dissentiente (di-sen-shee-**en**-tee). [Latin] Dissenting. • When used with a judge's name, it indicates a dissenting opinion.

dissenting opinion. See OPINION (1).

dissenting shareholder. See SHAREHOLDER.

dissignare (di-sig-**nair**-ee), *vb.* [Law Latin] To break open a seal.

dissimulate, *vb.* (17c) **1.** To hide one's true feelings or thoughts, esp. by lying. **2.** To give a false appearance to; to make a false show or pretense of.

dissipation, *n.* (17c) The use of an asset for an illegal or inequitable purpose, such as a spouse's use of community property for personal benefit when a divorce is imminent. — **dissipate,** *vb.*

dissociate, *vb.* (17c) **1.** To regard (two things or people) as separate and not connected to each other. **2.** To do or say something to show (oneself) not to be in agreement with the views or actions of someone with whom one has been connected.

dissociative amnesia. See REPRESSED-MEMORY SYNDROME.

dissolute, *adj.* (15c) (Of a person or thing) lacking restraint; wanton; devoted to pleasure <dissolute person> <a dissolute lifestyle>.

dissolution (dis-ə-**loo**-shən), *n.* (14c) **1.** The act of bringing to an end; termination. **2.** The cancellation or abrogation of a contract, with the effect of annulling the contract's binding force and restoring the parties to their original positions. See RESCISSION. **3.** The termination of a corporation's legal existence by expiration of its charter, by legislative act, by bankruptcy, or by other means; the event immediately preceding the liquidation or winding-up process.

▸ **de facto dissolution.** (1847) The termination and liquidation of a corporation's business, esp. because of an inability to pay its debts.

▸ **involuntary dissolution.** (1867) The termination of a corporation administratively (for failure to file reports or pay taxes), judicially (for abuse of corporate authority, management deadlock, or failure to pay creditors), or through involuntary bankruptcy.

▸ **voluntary dissolution.** (1819) A corporation's termination initiated by the board of directors and approved by the shareholders.

4. The termination of a previously existing partnership upon the occurrence of an event specified in the partnership agreement, such as a partner's withdrawal from the partnership, or as specified by law. Cf. WINDING UP. **5.** *Patents.* The dismissal of an interference contest before a final judgment and an express award of priority. • The effect of dissolving an interference is that junior parties fail to meet their burden of proof, so the senior party retains priority. **6.** *Parliamentary law.* An adjournment sine die without any provision for reconvening the same deliberative assembly, even if another assembly of the same kind (such as a legislative body or a convention) will eventually convene. — **dissolve,** *vb.*

dissolution bond. See *discharging bond* under BOND (2).

dissolution of marriage. (16c) **1.** DIVORCE. **2.** *Archaic.* A divorce-like remedy available when both spouses have signed a separation agreement that deals with (1) the issue of alimony (providing either some or none), and (2) if there are children, the issues of support, custody, and visitation. • Under a dissolution of marriage in this sense, the court is bound by the separation agreement and cannot later modify alimony payments. Courts in jurisdictions where the term has been used in this specific sense traditionally distinguish it from *divorce*, which was formerly available only on certain grounds and which allowed the court to modify alimony payments.

dissolved corporation. See CORPORATION.

dissolving condition. See *resolutory condition* under CONDITION (2).

dissuade, *vb.* (16c) To persuade (someone) not to do something <to dissuade the expert from testifying>. — **dissuasive,** *adj.*

distaff right. (18c) *Hist.* A woman's legal right.

distance selling. The sale of goods or services by a business to a consumer when the parties do not meet in person, as with sales by telephone, through mail order, or on the Internet.

distillate. (1864) *Oil & gas.* **1.** The "wet" element of natural gas that may be removed as a liquid. — Also termed *condensate*; *natural gas.* **2.** Any product of the process of distillation.

distincte et aperte (dis-**tingk**-tee et ə-**pər**-tee). [Law Latin] Distinctly; openly. • This phrase was formerly used in writs of error to refer to the return required to be made.

distinct invention. See INVENTION.

distinctive mark. See *distinctive trademark* under TRADEMARK.

distinctive name. See NAME.

distinctiveness, *n. Trademarks.* The quality of a trademarked word, symbol, or device that identifies the goods or services of a particular merchant and distinguishes them from the goods or services of others. — Also termed *acquired distinctiveness.* — **distinctive,** *adj.*

distinctive trademark. See TRADEMARK.

distinguish, *vb.* (15c) **1.** To note a significant factual, procedural, or legal difference in (an earlier case), usu. to minimize the case's precedential effect or to show that it is inapplicable <the lawyer distinguished the cited case from the case at bar>.

> "In practice, courts do not concede to their predecessors the power of laying down very wide rules; they reserve to themselves the power to narrow such rules by introducing into them particular facts of the precedent case that were treated by the earlier court as irrelevant. This process is known as 'distinguishing.'" John Salmond, *Jurisprudence* 192 (Glanville L. Williams ed., 10th ed. 1947).

2. To make a distinction <the court distinguished between willful and reckless conduct>. — **distinction,** *n.*

distinguishable, *adj.* (16c) (Of a case or law) different from, and thereby not controlling or applicable in, a given case or situation.

distinguishable variation. (1939) *Copyright.* A detectable difference between two works. • Distinguishable variation is the standard for determining whether a work that is based on a work in the public domain can itself be copyrighted. Examples include translations of books and mezzotints of paintings. Some nontrivial originality is also required: exact copies are not protectable.

distinguishing mark. (17c) A physical indication or feature that identifies or delineates one person or thing from another <the voting ballots contained distinguishing marks so that they could not be counted>. See DISTINCTIVENESS.

distracted, *adj.* (17c) **1.** (Of a person) not concentrating. **2.** (Of a person) disordered.

distractio (di-**strak**-shee-oh), *n.* [Latin fr. *distrahere* "to draw apart"] *Roman law.* A separation or division into parts; an alienation or sale, such as a creditor's sale of a pledge.

distractio bonorum (di-**strak**-shee-oh bə-**nor**-əm). [Latin "the sale of goods"] (1918) *Roman law.* A curator bonorum's sale of the property in an insolvent estate to satisfy creditors' claims.

distraction doctrine. (1999) The rule that a plaintiff may not be guilty of contributory negligence if the plaintiff's attention was diverted from a known danger by a sufficient cause. See *contributory negligence* under NEGLIGENCE.

distractio pignoris (di-**strak**-shee-oh pig-**nor**-is). [Latin "the sale of something pledged"] *Roman law.* A creditor's sale of something pledged or hypothecated to obtain satisfaction on a debt.

distrahere (dis-**tray**-hə-ree), *vb.* [fr. Latin *dis* "apart" + *trahere* "to draw"] To draw apart; to sell; to dissolve, as in a contract.

distrain, *vb.* (13c) **1.** To force (a person, usu. a tenant), by the seizure and detention of personal property, to perform an obligation (such as paying overdue rent). **2.** To seize (goods) by distress, a legal remedy entitling the rightful owner to recover property wrongfully taken. — Also spelled *distrein.* — **distraint,** *n.*

distrainee. (1875) Someone who is, or whose property is, distrained; one deprived of property by distress.

distrainer. (17c) Someone who seizes property under a distress. — Also spelled *distrainor; distreinor.*

distraint. See DISTRESS (3).

distrein, *vb.* See DISTRAIN.

distress, *n.* (13c) **1.** The seizure of another's property to secure the performance of a duty, such as the payment of overdue rent. **2.** The legal remedy authorizing such a seizure; the procedure by which the seizure is carried out.

> "Distress . . . may be defined as the taking, either with legal process, or extra-judicially subject to the performance of some necessary condition precedent, by a private individual or by an officer of the court, of a personal chattel, out of the possession of a wrongdoer or defaulter and into the custody of the law to be impounded as a pledge in order to bring pressure to bear upon the owner of the chattel to redress an injury, to perform a duty, or to satisfy a lawful demand, subject, however, to the right of the owner to have the chattel returned to him [up]on the injury being redressed, or the duty performed, or the demand satisfied or [up]on security being given so to do." F.A. Enever, *History of the Law of Distress* 7–8 (1931).

> "The word *distress* is derived from *distringere,* meaning to put into a strait or pound. In early English custumals the word used is *nam,* which is of Scandinavian derivation and indicates a taking. In the Latin legal documents of early medieval times *pignorare* is used as well as *distringere* to denote the act of distraining, but whereas *distringere* is used in relation to distress for rent and services, *pignorare* is applied to distress for debts." F.A. Enever, *History of the Law of Distress* 3 (1931).

▸ **distress damage feasant.** (1829) The right to seize animals or inanimate chattels that are damaging or encumbering land and to keep them as security until the owner pays compensation.

▸ **distress infinite.** (15c) A distress that the sheriff can repeat from time to time to enforce the performance of something, as in summoning a juror or compelling a party to appear in court. • The goods must be returned after the delinquent person performs his or her duty.

> "[F]or the most part it is provided that distresses be reasonable and moderate; but, in the case of distress for fealty or suit of court, no distress can be unreasonable, immoderate, or too large: for this is the only remedy to which the party aggrieved is entitled, and therefore it ought to be such as is sufficiently compulsory; and, be it of what value it will, there is no harm done, especially as it cannot be sold or made away with, but must be restored immediately on satisfaction made. A distress of this nature, that has no bounds with regard to its quantity, and may be repeated from time to time until the stubbornness of the party is conquered, is called a *distress infinite.*" 3 William Blackstone, *Commentaries on the Laws of England* 231 (1768).

▸ **grand distress.** (16c) *Hist.* In a *quare impedit* action in which the defendant has failed to appear, a distress of the defendant's goods and lands to compel the defendant's appearance.

▸ **second distress.** (15c) A supplementary distress allowed when goods seized under the first distress are insufficient to satisfy the claim.

3. The property seized. — Also termed *distraint.* **4.** Pain or suffering that affects the body, a body part, or the mind.

▸ **emotional distress.** (1933) A highly unpleasant mental reaction (such as anguish, grief, fright, humiliation, or fury) that results from another person's conduct; emotional pain and suffering. • Emotional distress, when severe enough, can form a basis for the recovery of tort damages. — Also termed *emotional harm*; *mental anguish*; *mental distress*; *mental suffering*. See INTENTIONAL INFLICTION OF EMOTIONAL DISTRESS; NEGLIGENT INFLICTION OF EMOTIONAL DISTRESS. Cf. *mental cruelty* under CRUELTY.

> "Emotional distress passes under various names, such as mental suffering, mental anguish, mental or nervous shock, or the like. It includes all highly unpleasant mental reactions, such as fright, horror, grief, shame, humiliation, embarrassment, anger, chagrin, disappointment, worry, and nausea. It is only where it is extreme that the liability arises. Complete emotional tranquility is seldom attainable in this world, and some degree of transient and trivial emotional distress is a part of the price of living among people. The law intervenes only where the distress inflicted is so severe that no reasonable man could be expected to endure it. The intensity and the duration of the distress are factors to be considered in determining its severity. Severe distress must be proved; but in many cases the extreme and outrageous character of the defendant's conduct is in itself important evidence that the distress has existed." Restatement (Second) of Torts § 46 cmt. j (1965).

▸ **mental distress.** See *emotional distress*.

5. A situation in which a vessel, aircraft, etc. is in trouble or danger and needs help. **6.** Problems and hardships caused by a lack of resources.

distressed debt. See DEBT.

distressed goods. See GOODS.

distressed property. See PROPERTY.

distress sale. See SALE.

distress warrant. See WARRANT (1).

distributable net income. See INCOME.

distribute (di-**strib**-yoot), *vb.* (15c) **1.** To apportion; to divide among several. **2.** To arrange by class or order. **3.** To deliver. **4.** To spread out; to disperse.

distributed denial-of-service attack. See DENIAL-OF-SERVICE ATTACK.

distributee (di-strib-yoo-**tee**), *n.* (1870) **1.** A beneficiary entitled to payment. **2.** An heir, esp. one who obtains personal property from the estate of an intestate decedent.

▸ **expectant distributee.** (1934) A prospective heir whose interest depends on a contingency; an expectant heir. — Also termed *expectant beneficiary*. See *prospective heir* under HEIR.

▸ **legal distributee.** (1832) A person lawfully entitled to take property under a will.

distribution, *n.* (14c) **1.** The passing of personal property to an intestate decedent's heirs; specif., the process of dividing an estate after realizing its movable assets and paying out of them its debts and other claims against the estate. Cf. DESCENT (1). **2.** The act or process of apportioning or giving out. — **distribute,** *vb.*

▸ **controlled-securities-offering distribution.** See *securities-offering distribution* (1).

▸ **corporate distribution.** (1925) A corporation's direct or indirect transfer of money or other property, or incurring of indebtedness to or for the benefit of its shareholders, such as a dividend payment out of current or past earnings.

▸ **distribution in kind.** (1819) A transfer of property in its original state, such as a distribution of land instead of the proceeds of its sale. — Also termed *distribution in specie*.

▸ **distribution in specie.** See *distribution in kind*.

▸ **liquidating distribution.** (1924) A distribution of trade or business assets by a dissolving corporation or partnership. — Also termed *distribution in liquidation*.

▸ **nonliquidating distribution.** (1941) A distribution of assets by a corporation or partnership that is not going out of business, such as a distribution of excess capital not necessary for current operations.

▸ **partnership distribution.** (1942) A partnership's payment of cash or property to a partner out of earnings or as an advance against future earnings, or a payment of the partners' capital in partial or complete liquidation of the partner's interest.

▸ **probate distribution.** (1933) The judicially supervised apportionment and division — usu. after the payment of debts and charges — of assets of an estate among those legally entitled to share.

▸ **secondary distribution. 1.** The public sale of a large block of previously issued stock. — Also termed *secondary offering*. See OFFERING. **2.** The sale of a large block of stock after the close of the exchange.

▸ **securities-offering distribution. 1.** An issuer's public offering of securities through a formal underwriting agreement with a broker-dealer. — Also termed *controlled-securities-offering distribution*. **2.** An issuer's public offering of securities on an informal basis, with or without brokers. — Also termed (in both senses) *uncontrolled-securities-offering distribution*.

▸ **trust distribution.** (1949) The cash or other property paid or credited to a trust beneficiary.

▸ **uncontrolled-securities-offering distribution.** See *securities-offering distribution*.

distribution channel. (1923) One of several routes through which a manufacturer's or distributor's goods are marketed. • In trademark law, identical or similar marks that are used in the same channel may lead to consumer confusion. — Also termed *channel of trade*; *channel of distribution*.

distribution cost. See COST (1).

distribution in kind. See DISTRIBUTION.

distribution in liquidation. See *liquidating distribution* under DISTRIBUTION.

distribution in specie. See *distribution in kind* under DISTRIBUTION.

distribution license. See LICENSE.

distribution right. (1936) *Copyright.* A copyright holder's exclusive right to sell, lease, or otherwise transfer copies of the protected work to the public. Cf. FIRST-SALE DOCTRINE (1).

distributive (di-**strib**-yə-tiv), *adj.* (15c) Of, relating to, or involving the apportionment, division, or assignment of separate items or shares; pertaining to distribution.

distributive clause. (1821) A will or trust provision governing the distribution of income and gifts.

distributive deviation. (1967) A trustee's authorized or unauthorized departure from the express distributional terms of a trust. • A trustee must apply to the court for authority to deviate from the terms of a trust. In American law, courts rarely authorize deviation unless all the beneficiaries consent and there is no material purpose of the settlor yet to be served. Some state statutes provide that deviation is permitted if the court finds that deviation would effectuate the settlor's intention, though the modification is not expressly authorized by the trust's provisions. The Pulitzer trust illustrates the possibility that extraordinary circumstances not anticipated by the settlor may justify deviation, despite an express prohibition within the trust. Joseph Pulitzer set up a testamentary trust with shares of *World* newspaper stock; his will directed that the sale of these shares was not authorized under any circumstances. Nonetheless, the court later approved the stock sale when given evidence that because of hemorrhaging losses, the trust's continuation was jeopardized. *In re Pulitzer's Estate*, 249 N.Y.S. 87 (Sur. Ct. 1931).

distributive finding. (1838) A jury's decision partly in favor of one party and partly in favor of another.

distributive justice. See JUSTICE (4).

distributive-phrasing canon. The doctrine that distributive phrasing in a legal instrument applies each expression to its appropriate referent. See REDDENDO SINGULA SINGULIS.

distributive share. (18c) **1.** The share that an heir or beneficiary receives from the legal distribution of an estate. **2.** The portion (as determined in the partnership agreement) of a partnership's income, gain, loss, or deduction that is passed through to a partner and reported on the partner's tax return. **3.** The share of assets or liabilities that a partner or partner's estate acquires after the partnership has been dissolved.

distributor. (1884) A wholesaler, jobber, or other manufacturer or supplier that sells chiefly to retailers and commercial users.

distributorship. (1825) A company that has an arrangement to sell the products of another company; esp., a franchise held by a person or company who sells merchandise, usu. in a specific area to individual customers <a car distributorship>.

▸ **dual distributorship.** (1962) A business structure in which one party operates a branch or dealership on the same market level as one or more of its customers.

district. (17c) **1.** A territorial area into which a country, state, county, municipality, or other political subdivision is divided for judicial, political, electoral, or administrative purposes. **2.** A territorial area in which similar local businesses or entities are concentrated, such as a theater district or an arts district. — Abbr. D.

▸ **assessment district.** (1862) *Tax.* A usu. municipal subdivision in which separate assessments of taxable property are made.

▸ **congressional district.** (1804) A geographical unit of a state from which one member of the U.S. House of Representatives is elected.

▸ **consolidated school district.** See SCHOOL DISTRICT.

▸ **election district.** (18c) A subdivision of a state, county, or city that is established to facilitate an election or to elect governmental representatives for that subdivision.

▸ **floterial district** (floh-**teer**-ee-əl). (1952) A legislative district that includes several separate districts or political subdivisions that independently would not be entitled to additional representation, but whose conglomerate population entitles the district to another seat in the legislative body being apportioned.

▸ **influence district.** A voting district in which a racial or ethnic minority group does not constitute a majority of the voters, but does make up a sufficient proportion of the voters to constitute an influential minority, thus being able to elect its preferred candidate with a reasonable number of crossover votes from other groups. Cf. *majority-minority district.*

▸ **land district.** A federally created state or territorial division containing a U.S. land office that manages the disposition of the district's public lands.

▸ **legislative district.** (1840) A geographical subdivision of a state for the purpose of electing legislative representatives.

▸ **levee district.** (1872) A local or regional political subdivision organized to construct and maintain levees within its territory at public expense.

▸ **majority-minority district.** (1988) A voting district in which a racial or ethnic minority group makes up a majority of the voting citizens.

▸ **metropolitan district.** A special district, embracing parts of or entire cities and towns in a metropolitan area, created by a state to provide unified administration of one or more common services, such as water supply or public transportation.

▸ **mineral district.** (1812) A particular region of the country where valuable minerals are typically found and mined.

▸ **municipal utility district.** See MUNICIPAL UTILITY DISTRICT.

▸ **school district.** See SCHOOL DISTRICT.

▸ **special district.** A political subdivision that is created to bypass normal borrowing limitations, to insulate certain activities from traditional political influence, to allocate functions to entities reflecting particular expertise, and to provide a single service within a specified area <a transit authority is a special district>.

▸ **stock-law district.** (1885) A district in which cattle or other stock are prohibited from running free.

▸ **taxing district.** (1860) A district — constituting the whole state, a county, a city, or other smaller unit — throughout which a particular tax or assessment is ratably apportioned and levied on the district's inhabitants.

▸ **water district.** (1876) A geographical subdivision created by a state or local government entity to provide the public with a water supply.

district attorney. (18c) A public official appointed or elected to represent the state in criminal cases in a particular judicial district; PROSECUTOR (1). — Abbr. D.A. — Also termed *public prosecutor*; *state's attorney*; *prosecuting attorney.* Cf. UNITED STATES ATTORNEY.

▸ **on-call district attorney.** (2010) A district attorney who is assigned at a specific time to be in contact with police and the court to recommend bail amounts and to provide police with miscellaneous advice on matters that may arise.

▸ **riding district attorney.** A district attorney or assistant district attorney who works closely with the police, responding directly to crime scenes, taking statements from witnesses or suspects at a police station, drafting search-warrant applications, or attending lineups. — Also termed *ride-along DA*.

district clerk. See CLERK (2).

district council. See COUNCIL (1).

district court. See COURT.

district-court magistrate. See MAGISTRATE.

districting. (1879) The act of drawing lines or establishing boundaries between geographic areas to create voting districts. See APPORTIONMENT (3); GERRYMANDERING.

districtio (di-**strik**-shee-oh), *n.* [Law Latin "distraint"] *Hist.* **1.** A distress; a distraint. **2.** The right of distress. **3.** Something (such as a good or animal) that can be distrained. **4.** A territory within which distraint can be exercised. **5.** Any compulsory proceeding.

district judge. See JUDGE.

District of Columbia. The seat of the U.S. government, situated on the Potomac River between Maryland and Virginia. • Neither a state nor a territory, it is constitutionally subject to the exclusive jurisdiction of Congress. — Abbr. D.C.

district parish. See PARISH.

district school. See SCHOOL (1).

distringas (di-**string**-gas), *n.* [Law Latin "you are to distrain"] (15c) **1.** A writ ordering a sheriff to distrain a defendant's property to compel the defendant to perform an obligation, such as appearing in court or giving up a chattel to a plaintiff awarded judgment in a detinue action. **2.** A writ ordering the sheriff to seize jurors' goods to compel them to appear for jury service. **3.** An equitable process of execution against a corporation that has refused to obey a summons. **4.** *Hist.* An order, issued initially from the Court of Exchequer, then the Court of Chancery, and finally the High Court of Justice, for someone interested in purchasing Bank of England stock, temporarily restraining the bank officers from transferring the stock or paying a dividend on it. • This proceeding was used to prevent fraudulent dealing by a trustee or other stockholder. The relief was only temporary, and if the bank received a request from the stockholder to permit a stock deal, the bank had to warn the distringing party to promptly obtain a restraining order or a writ of injunction, or else the stock deal would go through.

distringas juratores (di-**string**-gas joor-ə-**tor**-eez), *n.* [Law Latin "you are to distrain the jurors"] (18c) *Hist.* A writ ordering the sheriff to distrain jurors or their property to compel their appearance before the judges of assize and nisi prius for jury duty on an appointed day.

distringas nuper vicecomitem (di-**string**-gas **n[y]oo**-pər **vi**-see-**kom**-i-təm), *n.* [Law Latin "you are to distrain the late sheriff"] (17c) *Hist.* **1.** A writ ordering a sheriff's successor to distrain the former sheriff's property until the former sheriff brings in a defendant to answer the plaintiff's charge, sells goods attached under a *fieri facias*, or performs some other obligation that the former sheriff should have completed while still in office. **2.** A writ calling on an ex-sheriff to account for the proceeds taken in execution.

distringas vice comitem (di-**string**-gas **vi**-see **kom**-i-təm), *n.* [Law Latin "you are to distrain the sheriff"] *Hist.* A *distringas* writ ordering the coroner to distrain the sheriff for not executing a writ of *venditioni exponas*. See VENDITIONI EXPONAS.

distringere (di-**strinj**-ə-ree), *vb.* [Latin] To distrain; to coerce; to compel. • The first-person form of the verb was *distringo* ("I distrain").

disturbance, *n.* (13c) **1.** An act causing annoyance or disquiet, or interfering with a person's pursuit of a lawful occupation or the peace and order of a neighborhood, community, or meeting. **2.** At common law, a wrong done to an incorporeal hereditament by hindering the owner's enjoyment of it.

disturbance of a public meeting. (1900) The unlawful interference with the proceedings of a public assembly.

> "Generally speaking, any conduct which, being contrary to the usages of the particular sort of meeting and class of persons assembled, interferes with its due progress and services, or is annoying to the congregation in whole or in part, is a disturbance; and a meeting may be said to be 'disturbed' when it is agitated, aroused from a state of repose, molested, interrupted, hindered, perplexed, disquieted, or diverted from the object of the assembly." 27 C.J.S. *Disturbance of Public Meetings* § 1, at 817 (1959).

disturbance of common. (18c) At common law, a wrongful interference with, or impediment to, another's right to commonable property, such as a wrongful fencing or surcharge on the common.

> "The disturbance of *common* comes next to be considered; where any act is done, by which the right of another to his common is incommoded or diminished. This may happen, in the first place, where one who hath no right of common, puts his cattle into the land; and thereby robs the cattle of the commoners of their respective shares of the pasture. Or if one, who hath a right of common, puts in cattle which are not commonable, as hogs and goats; which amounts to the same inconvenience" 3 William Blackstone, *Commentaries on the Laws of England* 237 (1768).

disturbance of franchise. (1837) At common law, a wrongful interference with a liberty or privilege.

> "Disturbance of *franchises* happens when a man has the franchise of holding a court-leet, of keeping a fair or market, of free-warren, of taking toll, of seizing waifs or estrays, or (in short) any other species of franchise whatsoever, and he is disturbed or incommoded in the lawful exercise thereof." 3 William Blackstone, *Commentaries on the Laws of England* 236 (1768).

disturbance of patronage. (18c) A wrongful obstruction of a patron from presenting a clerk to a benefice.

disturbance of public worship. (1841) Any conduct that interferes with the peaceful, lawful assembly of people for religious exercises.

disturbance of tenure. (18c) A stranger's ouster of a tenant from a tenancy. • The tenant's lord could recover damages for the ouster.

disturbance of the peace. See BREACH OF THE PEACE.

disturbance of ways. (1851) An impediment to a person's lawful right-of-way, as by an obstruction.

disturber. See IMPEDITOR.

disturbing the peace. See BREACH OF THE PEACE.

disunity. (17c) A situation in which a group of people cannot agree or work with each other; a lack of concord or harmony.

diswarren, *vb.* (18c) To change (land) from use as a warren to use for some other purpose, such as pasturage or a housing development. See WARREN.

dittay (**dit**-ay), *n.* (15c) *Scots law.* **1.** The grounds for an indictment. **2.** An indictment.

divadiatus. See DEVADIATUS.

diverse, *adj.* (13c) **1.** Of, relating to, or involving different types <the attorney handles diverse cases ranging from probate matters to criminal law>. **2.** (Of a person or entity) having a different citizenship from the party or parties on the other side of the lawsuit <the parties are diverse because the plaintiffs are citizens of Illinois and the defendant is a New York citizen>. See *diversity jurisdiction* under JURISDICTION. **3.** (Of a group of people) including people of different races, sexes, nationalities, and cultural backgrounds <the school has a diverse student body>.

diversification, *n.* (1939) **1.** A company's movement into a broader range of products, usu. by buying firms already serving the market or by expanding existing operations <the soft-drink company's diversification into the potato-chip market has increased its profits>. **2.** The act of investing in a wide range of companies to reduce the risk if one sector of the market suffers losses <the prudent investor's diversification of the portfolio among 12 companies>.

diversified holding company. See COMPANY.

diversified investment company. See COMPANY.

diversify, *vb.* (15c) **1.** (Of a business, company, country, etc.) to increase the range of goods or services produced or provided <lead smelters forced to diversify from their core business>. **2.** To make (something) change so that there is more variety <they diversified their business during the expansion>. **3.** To put money into several different types of investments instead of only one or two <she spread the risk by diversifying into real estate and precious metals>.

diversion, *n.* (17c) **1.** A deviation or alteration from the natural course of things; esp., the unauthorized alteration of a watercourse to the detriment of a lower riparian owner, or the unauthorized use of funds. **2.** A distraction or pastime. — **divert,** *vb.*

diversion program. (1972) *Criminal law.* **1.** A pretrial program that refers certain criminal defendants. esp. youth offenders and first-time offenders, to rehabilitative community programs, the charges being placed on hold until, and ultimately reduced or dismissed after, benchmarks such as counseling for mental health, drug abuse, or employment are met. — Also termed *pretrial diversion*; *pretrial intervention.* Cf. *deferred judgment* under JUDGMENT (2). **2.** A community-based program or set of services designed to prevent the need for court intervention in matters of child neglect, minor juvenile delinquency, truancy, or incorrigibility. • Sustained by government funding, the program provides services quickly and in a nonadversarial manner so that there is no need for a formal court trial. — Abbr. DP. — Also termed *diversionary program.*

Diversité des courts (di-vər-si-**tay** də **koort**). [Law French] A treatise on courts written in French, supposedly by Fitzherbert during the reign of Edward III. • It was printed initially in 1525 and again in 1534. — Also spelled *Diversité des courtes.*

> "[F]or in the ancient treatise, entitled *diversité de courtes* . . . we have a catalogue of the matters of conscience then cognizable by *subpoena* in chancery, which fall within a very narrow compass." 3 William Blackstone, *Commentaries on the Laws of England* 53 (1768).

diversity, *adj.* (1928) Of, relating to, or involving diversity jurisdiction <a diversity case>.

diversity, *n.* (1848) **1.** The fact of including many different types of people or things. **2.** Ethnic, socioeconomic, and gender heterogeneity within a group; the combination within a population of people with different backgrounds or ideas. • The Supreme Court has found diversity in education to be a compelling government interest that can support a narrowly tailored affirmative-action plan. *Grutter v. Bollinger*, 123 S.Ct. 2325 (2003). **3.** DIVERSITY OF CITIZENSHIP. **4.** *Hist.* A plea that a prisoner to be executed is not the one that was accused and found guilty, at which point a jury is immediately impaneled to try the issue of the prisoner's identity.

diversity jurisdiction. See JURISDICTION.

diversity of citizenship. (1876) A basis for federal-court jurisdiction that exists when (1) a case is between citizens of different states, or between a citizen of a state and an alien, and (2) the matter in controversy exceeds a specific value (now $75,000). 28 USCA § 1332. • For purposes of diversity jurisdiction, a corporation is considered a citizen of both the state of incorporation and the state of its principal place of business. An unincorporated association, such as a partnership, is considered a citizen of each state where at least one of its members is a citizen. — Often shortened to *diversity.* See *diversity jurisdiction* under JURISDICTION.

▸ **complete diversity.** (1925) In a multiparty case, diversity between both sides to the lawsuit so that all plaintiffs have different citizenship from all defendants. • Complete diversity must exist for a federal court to have diversity jurisdiction over the matter. The rule of complete diversity was first laid down by Chief Justice Marshall in *Strawbridge v. Curtiss*, 7 U.S. (3 Cranch) 267 (1806).

▸ **manufactured diversity.** (1968) Improper or collusively created diversity of citizenship for the sole or primary purpose of creating federal jurisdiction. • Manufactured diversity is prohibited by 28 USCA § 1359.

Diversity of Citizenship Clause. (1911) *Constitutional law.* U.S. Const. art. III, § 2, cl. 1, giving the federal judiciary power to hear cases between citizens of different states or between a state and a citizen of a different state. • Congress has passed two laws limiting the federal courts' power: the diversity statute (28 USCA § 1332) and the removal statute (28 USCA § 1441).

divertee. (1922) A defendant who participates in a diversion program. See DIVERSION PROGRAM.

dives costs (**dɪ**-veez), *n.* (1828) Ordinary court costs granted to a successful party, as distinguished from limited costs (such as out-of-pocket costs) allowed to a successful pauper who sued or defended *in forma pauperis.* • The term derives from the name of Dives, the supposed name of the rich man in the parable of the rich man and Lazarus (*Luke* 16:19–31). *Dives* is a Latin word meaning "rich."

divest, *vb.* (17c) **1.** To rid (oneself) of (something) by selling or donating <the judge had long since divested himself of investments in Fortune 100 companies>. **2.** To take away from <they divested the former dictator of all his wealth>. **3.** (Of a company, investor, etc.) to sell (assets, investments, etc.) <the pressure on companies in the 1970s to divest apartheid-related investments>.

divestitive fact. See FACT.

divestitive publication. See PUBLICATION (2).

divestiture (di-ves-tə-chər *or* dɪ-), *n.* (17c) **1.** The loss or surrender of an asset or interest. **2.** A court order to a party to dispose of assets or property. **3.** *Antitrust.* A court order to a defendant to rid itself of property, securities, or other assets to prevent a monopoly or restraint of trade. — **divest,** *vb.*

divestiture order. See ORDER (2).

divestment, *n.* (1844) **1.** *Property.* The cutting short of an interest in property before its normal termination. **2.** The complete or partial loss of an interest in an asset, such as land or stock. **3.** DISINVESTMENT (2).

divide-and-pay-over rule. (1916) *Wills & estates.* The principle that if the only provisions in a testamentary disposition are words ordering that payment be made at some time after the testator's death, time will be of the essence and the interest is future and contingent rather than vested and immediate.

divided court. (18c) An appellate court whose opinion or decision in a particular case is not unanimous, esp. when the majority is slim, as in a 5-to-4 decision of the U.S. Supreme Court.

divided custody. See CUSTODY (2).

divided-damages rule. (1929) *Maritime law.* The obsolete principle that when two parties are jointly liable to a third party for a tort, each party is liable for only half the damages. • The courts now apply a comparative-negligence standard.

dividend. (17c) A portion of a company's earnings or profits distributed pro rata to its shareholders, usu. in the form of cash or additional shares.

▸ **accumulated dividend.** (1862) A dividend that has been declared but not yet paid. — Also termed *accrued dividend.*

▸ **accumulative dividend.** See *cumulative dividend.*

▸ **asset dividend.** (1941) A dividend paid in the form of property, usu. the company's product, rather than in cash or stock. — Also termed *property dividend.*

▸ **bond dividend.** (1905) A dividend in which a shareholder receives a bond instead of scrip, property, or money.

▸ **bonus stock dividend.** (1988) A dividend paid to a shareholder whose entitlement to receive the dividend may be satisfied by the issue of company shares. — Also termed *bonus share dividend.*

▸ **capital-gain dividend.** (1951) A taxable payment to a mutual-fund shareholder. • The payment is the shareholder's proportional share of the net capital gains realized by securities sales from the mutual fund's portfolio. — Also termed *capital-gain distribution.*

▸ **cash dividend.** (1866) A dividend paid to shareholders in the form of money.

▸ **consent dividend.** (1938) A dividend that is not actually paid to the shareholders, but is taxed to the shareholders and increases the basis in their stock investment. • A corporation declares a consent dividend to avoid or reduce an accumulated-earnings or personal-holding-company penalty tax.

▸ **constructive dividend.** (1920) A taxable benefit derived by a shareholder from the corporation even though the benefit was not designated a dividend. • Examples include excessive compensation, bargain purchases of corporate property, or shareholder use of corporate property for personal reasons.

▸ **cumulative dividend.** (1882) A dividend that grows from year to year when not paid. • A cumulative dividend is usu. on preferred shares, and it must be paid in full before common shareholders may receive any dividend. If the corporation does not pay a dividend in a particular year or period, it is carried over to the next year or period and must be paid before the common shareholders receive any payment. — Also termed *accumulative dividend.* Cf. *noncumulative dividend.*

▸ **deferred dividend.** (1883) A dividend that is declared, but is payable at a future date.

▸ **deficiency dividend.** (1939) A dividend paid to reduce or avoid personal-holding-company tax in a prior year.

▸ **disguised dividend.** See *informal dividend.*

▸ **extraordinary dividend.** (1856) A dividend paid in addition to a regular dividend, usu. because of exceptional corporate profits during the dividend period. — Also termed *extra dividend; nonrecurring dividend; special dividend.*

▸ **final dividend.** The last dividend declared by the end of a fiscal year.

▸ **fixed-return dividend.** A dividend that is constant throughout the investment's life.

▸ **guaranteed dividend.** (1838) **1.** A preferred-stock dividend that must be paid. • If the corporation cannot immediately pay the dividend, it accrues. See *cumulative dividend.* **2.** A dividend whose payment is promised by a third party if the corporation can't pay the dividend.

▸ **informal dividend.** (1937) A payment of salary, rent, interest, or the like to or for a shareholder as a substitute for a dividend. — Also termed *disguised dividend.*

▸ **liability dividend.** See *scrip dividend.*

▸ **liquidation dividend.** (1924) A dividend paid to a dissolving corporation's shareholders, usu. from the capital of the corporation, upon the decision to suspend all or part of its business operations. — Also termed *liquidating dividend.*

▸ **nimble dividend.** (1948) A dividend paid out of current earnings when there is a deficit in the account from which dividends may be paid. • Some state statutes prohibit nimble dividends.

▸ **noncumulative dividend.** (1911) A dividend that does not accrue for the benefit of a preferred shareholder if there is a passed dividend in a particular year or period. Cf. *cumulative dividend.*

▸ **nonrecurring dividend.** See *extraordinary dividend.*

▸ **passed dividend.** (1902) A dividend that is not paid when due by a company that has a history of paying regular dividends.

▸ **preferred dividend.** (1882) A dividend paid to preferred shareholders, who are generally paid a fixed amount and take priority over common shareholders.

▸ **property dividend.** See *asset dividend.*

▸ **reinvested dividend.** (1968) A dividend that is used to purchase additional shares in the corporation, instead of being taken in cash by the shareholder. See DIVIDEND-REINVESTMENT PLAN.

▸ **scrip dividend.** (1869) A dividend paid in certificates entitling the holder to ownership of capital stock to be issued in the future. • This type of dividend may signal that the corporation's cash flow is poor. — Also termed *liability dividend.*

▸ **special dividend.** See *extraordinary dividend.*

▸ **stock dividend.** (1856) A dividend paid in stock expressed as a percentage of the number of shares already held by a shareholder.

▸ **unpaid dividend.** (1874) A declared but unpaid dividend.

▸ **year-end dividend.** (1952) An extra dividend paid at the end of the fiscal year depending on the amount of the profits.

dividenda (div-i-**den**-də), *n.* [fr. Latin *dividere* "to divide"] *Hist.* Something to be divided; an indenture.

dividend addition. (1887) An amount added to the face value of a life-insurance policy and purchased by using a dividend as a single premium payment.

dividend-credit rule. (1956) The principle that a corporate reserve fund amassed from unpaid dividends on preferred stock must be used to pay subsequent dividends on preferred stock before dividend payments on common stock. — Also termed *cast-iron-pipe doctrine.*

dividend date. (1907) The date on which a corporation distributes dividends to record owners of stock shares. See *record date* under DATE. Cf. EX-DIVIDEND DATE.

dividend imputation. (1966) *Tax.* A system of taxation under which some or all of the income tax paid by a corporation on its distributed earnings is attributed to the shareholders through a tax credit. • The tax credit reduces or eliminates the effect of double taxation of dividends. — Also termed *imputation system.*

dividend income. See INCOME.

dividend-payout ratio. (1954) A profitability ratio computed by dividing annual dividends per share by earnings per share.

dividend preference. (1929) The right of a holder of preferred shares to receive a dividend before the company pays dividends to holders of common shares. See *preferred stock* under STOCK.

dividend-received deduction. See DEDUCTION (2).

dividend-reinvestment plan. (1969) A stock-purchase program that allows investors to reinvest their dividends, and perhaps convert additional voluntary payments, into shares of the entity's common stock, usu. with no sales charge, and sometimes at a discount from the stock's market price. • Although the investor never receives the cash, it is still treated as income to the investor. An investor may be allowed to make optional cash purchases of additional stock. — Abbr. DRIP; DRP.

▸ **brokerage-run dividend-reinvestment plan.** A formal or informal program managed by a brokerage and allowing shareholders to reinvest dividends in a portfolio, often at no cost. • Brokerage-run plans are usu. limited to dividend reinvestment.

▸ **company-run dividend-reinvestment plan.** A program operated by a corporation for its own shareholders. • Company-run plans may offer additional features such as IRAs.

▸ **transfer-agent-run dividend-reinvestment plan.** A program administered by a financial institution for several companies. • An investor can participate in more than one DRIP program simultaneously and also make additional cash investments in multiple companies.

dividend-stripping, *n.* The purchase of stock shortly before a dividend is declared followed by the sale of the same stock after the record date for payment of the dividend has passed.

dividend yield. (1910) The current annual dividend divided by the market price per share.

divide the assembly. *Parliamentary law.* To order that a standing vote be taken. — Also termed *challenge the vote; divide the house; doubt the vote.* See *standing vote* under VOTE (4).

divide the house. See DIVIDE THE ASSEMBLY.

divide the question. (1827) *Parliamentary law.* To break a long or complex motion, usu. one covering more than one subject, into shorter motions that the assembly considers independently.

divinare (div-i-**nair**-ee), *vb.* [Latin] To foretell or divine (something).

divinatio (div-i-**nay**-shee-oh), *n.* [Latin] *Roman law.* A preliminary process for deciding which of two or more applicants had the best claim to conduct a criminal prosecution against an accused.

divine law. (15c) Law that emanates from a supernatural source, such as a deity. Cf. NATURAL LAW.

divine right of kings. (18c) The political theory that the sovereign is a direct representative of God and has the right to rule absolutely by virtue of royal birth.

> "Divine Right of Kings . . . originated in the mediaeval concept of God's award of temporal power to civil rulers and spiritual power to the Church. It was claimed by the earlier Stuart kings in England, and explains many of their attitudes in the struggle which developed between them and Parliament for political sovereignty . . . . The principle of divine right was submerged during the Commonwealth but re-emerged under James II, but disappeared with his flight and abdication." David M. Walker, *The Oxford Companion to Law* 366 (1980).

divine service. (15c) **1.** *Hist.* A feudal tenure by which monasteries and religious houses held land. • Under this tenure, lands were granted for the good of the grantor's soul, and the tenants were obligated to perform special divine functions, such as singing at a certain number of masses or distributing a specified amount in alms. **2.** A public worship service.

divisa (di-vɪ-zə), *n.* [fr. French *diviser* "to divide"] **1.** A division, as of goods by a will; a devise. **2.** A boundary of neighboring lands. **3.** A court held on such a boundary to settle the tenants' disputes.

divisibility of copyright. The principle that a right in the bundle of rights that make up a copyright may be transferred to another owner.

divisible, *adj.* Capable of being divided.

divisible asset. See *divisible property* under PROPERTY.

divisible contract. See *severable contract* under CONTRACT.

divisible divorce. See DIVORCE.

divisible harm. See HARM.

divisible obligation. See OBLIGATION.

divisible offense. See OFFENSE (2).

divisible promises. See PROMISE.

divisible property. See PROPERTY.

divisim (di-vɪ-zəm). [Law Latin] *Hist.* Severally; separately.

division. (14c) **1.** The separating of something into two or more different parts. **2.** The way those parts are separated or shared. **3.** A group that does a particular job within a large organization. **4.** A large military group. **5.** *Parliamentary law.* A standing vote. See *standing vote* under VOTE (4). — Also termed *division of the assembly; division of the house; division vote; standing division.* **6.** *Parliamentary law.* The separation of a long or complex motion, usu. one covering more than one subject, into shorter motions that the assembly considers independently. — Also termed *division of the question.* See DIVIDE THE QUESTION. **7.** *Patents.* RESTRICTION (4).

divisional application. See PATENT APPLICATION.

divisional bond. See BOND (3).

divisional court. See COURT.

divisional security. See SECURITY (4).

division of fees. See FEE-SPLITTING.

division of loss. (1859) The determination of which parties share legal responsibility for a financial detriment and in what shares the detriment is to be borne. See LOSS.

division of powers. (18c) The allocation of power between the national government and the states. • Under the Tenth Amendment, powers not delegated to the federal government are reserved to the states or to the people. See FEDERALISM. Cf. SEPARATION OF POWERS.

> "Just as the Colossus once strode the wine-dark waters of the harbor of Rhodes, so the separation of powers (along with its vertical counterpart, sometimes called the 'division of powers' that constitutes federalism) commands and pervades American constitutional law." 1 Laurence B. Tribe, *American Constitutional Law* § 2-3, at 124 (3d ed. 2000).

division of property. See PROPERTY SETTLEMENT (1).

division of the assembly. See DIVISION (5).

division of the house. See DIVISION (5).

division of the question. See DIVISION (6).

division order. (1898) *Oil & gas.* A contract for the sale of oil or gas, specifying how the payments are to be distributed. • Royalty owners enter into division orders to sell minerals and to instruct how payments are to be made under a mineral lease. Working-interest owners also commonly sign division orders to instruct purchasers how payments are to be divided.

division vote. See *standing vote* under VOTE (4); DIVISION (5).

divisum imperium (di-vɪ-zəm im-**peer**-ee-əm), *n.* [Latin "a divided empire"] Divided jurisdiction; alternate jurisdiction, as of courts.

> "This main sea begins at the low-water-mark. But between the high-water-mark and the low-water-mark, where the sea ebbs and flows, the common law and admiralty have *divisum imperium*, an alternate jurisdiction; one upon the water, when it is full sea; the other upon the land, when it is an ebb." 1 William Blackstone, *Commentaries on the Laws of England* 107 (1765).

divorce. (14c) The legal ending of a marriage; specif., the legal dissolution of a marriage by a court. — Also termed *marital dissolution; dissolution of marriage.* Cf. ANNULMENT. — **divorce,** *vb.*

> "When used without qualification, the term [*divorce*] imports a dissolution of the marriage relation between husband and wife, that is, a complete severance of the tie by which the parties were united. However, in its common and wider use, the term includes the dissolution of a valid marriage, a formal separation of married persons, and the annulment of a marriage void from the beginning.
>
> "So, while the term 'divorce' has sometimes been broadly defined or applied to include both decrees of nullity and decrees of dissolution of marriage, especially where the marriage was not void but only voidable at the option of the injured party, this has been declared to be not in accord with modern usage, and generally, the term denotes only dissolution or suspension of a marital relation, and does not include annulment of an invalid marriage." 27A C.J.S. *Divorce* § 2, at 31-32 (1986).

▸ **absolute divorce.** See *divorce a vinculo matrimonii.*

▸ **bifurcated divorce.** See *divisible divorce.*

▸ **collaborative divorce.** (1999) A divorce negotiated in a nonadversarial forum, usu. between spouses who, with or without a lawyer, are assisted as needed by a team of neutral experts in law, mental health, and financial matters (such as taxes and real estate).

▸ **conditional divorce.** See *conversion divorce.*

▸ **contested divorce.** (1857) **1.** A divorce that one spouse opposes in court. **2.** A divorce in which the spouses litigate. • In this sense, although both spouses may want the divorce, they disagree on the terms of the divorce decree. Cf. *uncontested divorce.*

▸ **conversion divorce.** (1970) A divorce granted after (1) a legal separation has been granted or the parties have signed a separation agreement, and (2) the parties have lived separately for a statutorily prescribed period. — Also termed *convertible divorce; conditional divorce.*

▸ **divisible divorce.** (1943) A divorce whereby the marriage itself is dissolved but the issues incident to the divorce, such as alimony, child custody, and visitation, are reserved until a later proceeding. • This type of divorce can be granted when the court has subject-matter jurisdiction but lacks personal jurisdiction over the defendant-spouse. The doctrine of divisible divorce was recognized by the Supreme Court in *Estin v. Estin*, 334 U.S. 541, 68 S.Ct. 1213 (1948), and *Vanderbilt v. Vanderbilt*, 354 U.S. 416, 77 S.Ct. 1360 (1957). — Also termed *bifurcated divorce.* See DOCTRINE OF DIVISIBLE DIVORCE.

▸ **divorce *a mensa et thoro*** (ay **men**-sə et **thor**-oh). [Latin "(divorce) from board and hearth"] (18c) *Hist.* A partial or qualified divorce by which the parties were separated and allowed or ordered to live apart, but remained technically married; legal separation. • This type of divorce, abolished in England in 1857, was the forerunner of modern judicial separation. — Also termed *separation a mensa et thoro; divorce from bed and board; separation from bed and board; limited divorce; legal separation; judicial separation*. See SEPARATION (1).

> "[The Ecclesiastical Courts] grant also what is called a divorce *a mensa et thoro*, or rather what we should call a judicial separation, i.e. they release the parties from the duty of living together on grounds of cruelty or misconduct. . . ." William Geldart, *Introduction to English Law* 38 (D.C.M. Yardley ed., 9th ed. 1984).

▸ **divorce *a vinculo matrimonii*** (ay **ving**-kyə-loh ma-trə-**moh**-nee-ɪ). [Latin "(divorce) from the chains of marriage"] (17c) A total divorce of husband and wife, dissolving the marriage tie and releasing the parties wholly from their matrimonial obligations. • At common law, but not always in canon law, this type of divorce bastardized any children from the marriage and was granted on grounds that existed before the marriage. In England, the Matrimonial Causes Act of 1857 introduced statutory divorce *a vinculo matrimonii*. — Usu. shortened to *divorce*. — Also termed *absolute divorce*. Cf. *limited divorce*.

▸ **Dominican divorce.** See *Mexican divorce*.

▸ **ex parte divorce** (eks **pahr**-tee). (1870) **1.** A divorce proceeding in which only one spouse participates or appears in court. **2.** A divorce obtained by one spouse in a foreign jurisdiction without any appearance by the other spouse. • An ex parte divorce can change only marital status; it does not affect in personam rights of the absent spouse.

▸ **fault divorce.** (1966) A divorce granted to one spouse on the basis of some proven wrongful act (grounds for divorce) by the other spouse. • Although all states now have some form of no-fault divorce, some jurisdictions still consider a spouse's fault in precipitating the divorce, esp. when dividing marital property or when awarding alimony. Traditionally, the common grounds for a fault divorce were adultery, abandonment, imprisonment, and physical or mental cruelty; the defenses to alleged fault in a petition for divorce were condonation, connivance, collusion, recrimination, and insanity. Section 303(e) of the Uniform Marriage and Divorce Act has abolished the defenses to divorce. Cf. *no-fault divorce*.

▸ **foreign divorce.** (1831) A divorce obtained outside the state or country in which one spouse resides. Cf. *ex parte divorce* (2).

▸ **Haitian divorce.** See *Mexican divorce*.

▸ **hotel divorce.** (1964) *Slang.* A form of collusive divorce — occurring before widespread passage of no-fault divorce laws — in which the spouses agree to fake an adultery scene to create "fault." Cf. *no-fault divorce*.

> "Clearly a lawyer may not originate or participate in a scheme to make it appear to the court that a ground for divorce has occurred when this is not the fact. Such is the case in the so-called 'hotel divorces,' prevalent in jurisdictions where adultery is the only ground for divorce, and based on the principle that intercourse will be presumed from apparently uninhibited opportunity." Henry S. Drinker, *Legal Ethics* 123–24 (1953).

▸ **irreconcilable-differences divorce.** Divorce granted on the grounds of persistent and unresolvable disagreements between the spouses. — Abbr. ID divorce.

▸ **legislative divorce.** (1849) *Hist.* The legal termination of a particular marriage, through a statute enacted by the legislature rather than by a court's decree. • In the 18th century, Colonial American legislatures granted these special statutes. In 1816, the House of Burgesses of Virginia granted a divorce to Rachel Robards Jackson, the wife of then President Andrew Jackson, from a former spouse. Mrs. Jackson's untimely death was attributed to her reaction to the scandal that she had married Jackson before the divorce was procured. Now only state courts have authority to grant decrees of divorce. — Also termed *parliamentary divorce*.

▸ **limited divorce.** (1831) **1.** A divorce that ends the legal relationship of marriage by court order but does not address financial support, property distribution, or care and custody of children. • In the days before no-fault divorce, a spouse might seek a quick divorce in a state with a short residency requirement (such as Nevada). Then courts in the home state would give full faith and credit only to the dissolution of the marital res, while maintaining sole jurisdiction over property-division, support, and custody issues. **2.** Loosely, a legal separation. **3.** See *divorce a mensa et thoro*. Cf. *divorce a vinculo matrimonii*.

▸ **mail-order divorce.** (1922) *Slang.* An invalid decree of divorce obtained by parties who are not physically present or domiciled in the jurisdiction purporting to grant the divorce. • Such a divorce is not recognized in the United States because of the absence of the usual bases for jurisdiction.

▸ **Mexican divorce.** (1928) A divorce obtained in Mexico by mail order or by the appearance of one spouse who does not have a Mexican domicile. • Neither type is recognized in the United States. — Also termed *Dominican divorce* (if granted in the Dominican Republic); *Haitian divorce* (if granted in Haiti).

▸ **migratory divorce.** (1911) A divorce obtained in a jurisdiction other than the marital domicile; esp., a divorce obtained by a spouse who moves to, or temporarily resides in, another state or country to get the divorce.

▸ **no-fault divorce.** (1969) A divorce in which the parties are not required to prove fault or grounds beyond a showing of the irretrievable breakdown of the marriage or irreconcilable differences. • The system of no-fault divorce has been adopted throughout the United States. By 1974, 45 states had adopted no-fault divorce; by 1985, every state but New York had adopted some form of it. In New York — one of the last bastions of fault grounds for divorce — the closest equivalent is a conversion divorce one year after legal separation or a legal-separation agreement. Cf. *fault divorce*; *hotel divorce*.

▸ **parliamentary divorce.** See *legislative divorce*.

▸ **pro–con divorce.** (1944) *Slang.* An uncontested divorce granted after only the plaintiff appears at the proceeding (since the defendant contests nothing).

▸ **quickie divorce.** (1948) *Slang.* A fast divorce granted with minimal paperwork. — Also termed *quick divorce*.

▸ **rabbinical divorce.** (1893) A divorce granted by a rabbinical court. • This type of divorce affects the relationship of the parties under the tenets of Judaism and is required in order for a Jewish woman to remarry in accordance with Judaic law. In the United States, it is not generally a divorce recognized in civil courts. — Also termed *get.*

▸ **uncontested divorce.** (1877) A divorce that is unopposed by the spouse who did not initiate it. Cf. *contested divorce.*

divorcé. (1877) A man who is divorced. See DIVORCÉE.

divorce agreement. (1912) A contractual agreement that sets out divorcing spouses' rights and responsibilities regarding property, alimony, custody, visitation, and child support. • The divorce agreement usu. becomes incorporated by court order as a part of the divorce decree and thus is enforceable by contempt, among other remedies. — Also termed *agreement incident to divorce; marital settlement agreement; separation agreement.* Cf. PROPERTY SETTLEMENT.

divorce decree. See DECREE.

divorcée. (1814) **1.** A woman who is divorced. **2.** In BrE, a man or woman who is divorced. • In BrE, *divorcee* (no accent) does the work that requires two words — *divorcé* and *divorcée* — in AmE. See DIVORCÉ.

divorce from bed and board. See *divorce a mensa et thoro* under DIVORCE.

divorce order. 1. See *divorce decree* under DECREE. **2.** *Family law.* An order issued by the court during divorce proceedings.

divorce proctor. (1912) **1.** A person (such as a guardian) who is appointed to protect the interest of the state or children in a divorce action. **2.** A public official provided for by a state statute to appear in fault-based divorce cases to advise the court about the merits of the case. *See, e.g., Greene v. Greene,* 309 S.W.2d 403 (Tenn. Ct. App. 1958). — Sometimes shortened to *proctor.*

divortium (di-**vor**-shee-əm), *n.* [Latin] **1.** *Roman law.* Divorce; a severance of the marriage tie. • In classical law, no grounds were required. Cf. REPUDIUM. **2.** *Eccles. law.* A decree allowing spouses to separate or declaring their marriage invalid.

> "Owing to the fact that the church had but slowly made up her mind know to know no such thing as a divorce in our acceptation of that term (i.e., the dissolution of a valid marriage) the term *divortium* is currently used to signify two very different things, namely (1) the *divortium quoad torum,* which is the equivalent of our 'judicial separation,' and (2) what is very often called the *divortium quoad vinculum* but is really a declaration of nullity. The persistence of the word *divortium* in the latter case is a trace of an older state of affairs, but in medieval practice the decree of nullity often served the purpose of a true divorce; spouses who had quarrelled began to investigate their pedigrees and were unlucky if they could discover no *impedimentum dirimens.*" 2 Frederick Pollock & Frederic W. Maitland, *History of English Law Before the Time of Edward I* 393 n.5 (2d ed. 1899; repr. 1959).

divortium aquarum (di-**vor**-shee-əm ə-**kwair**-əm). [Latin] *Hist.* Division of waters.

diyya (**dee**-yə), *n.* [Arabic "bloody money"] A fine or monetary compensation paid by an admitted killer to the family of the victim. — Also spelled *diyat; diya.* Cf. WERGILD.

D.J. See *district judge* under JUDGE.

DJA. *abbr.* DECLARATORY-JUDGMENT ACT.

DJIA. *abbr.* DOW JONES INDUSTRIAL AVERAGE.

DLA. *abbr.* DEFENSE LOGISTICS AGENCY.

DL/C. See *documentary letter of credit* under LETTER OF CREDIT.

DLOP. *abbr.* Dismissal for lack of prosecution. See *dismissal for want of prosecution* under DISMISSAL (1).

DLOP docket. See *DWOP docket* under DOCKET (2).

DLSA. *abbr.* DEFENSE LEGAL SERVICES AGENCY.

DMCA. *abbr.* DIGITAL MILLENNIUM COPYRIGHT ACT.

DNA. *abbr.* (1944) Deoxyribonucleic acid; the double-helix structure in cell nuclei that carries the genetic information of most living organisms.

DNA dragnet, *n.* (1993) *Criminal law.* During a crime investigation, the mass collection by police of biological samples from individuals, whether or not there is reason to suspect a given individual committed the crime. • The samples are used to produce DNA profiles for comparison to DNA believed to be from the perpetrator. — Also termed (in English law) *blooding.*

DNA exoneration. (1997) The use of DNA evidence, usu. after a conviction, to prove that an innocent person was wrongfully convicted; exculpation by means of DNA evidence.

DNA identification. (1987) A method of scientific identification based on a person's unique genetic makeup; specif., the comparison of a person's deoxyribonucleic acid (DNA) — a patterned chemical structure of genetic information — with the DNA in a biological specimen (such as blood, tissue, or hair) to determine whether the person is the source of the specimen. • DNA evidence is used in criminal cases to identify a victim's remains, to link a suspect to a crime, or to exonerate an innocent suspect. It is also used to establish paternity. — Also termed *DNA fingerprinting; genetic fingerprinting; DNA profiling; DNA typing.* Cf. HUMAN-LEUKOCYTE ANTIGEN TEST.

DNR order. *abbr.* DO-NOT-RESUSCITATE ORDER.

DNS. *abbr.* DOMAIN-NAME SYSTEM.

do (doh). [Latin] *Hist.* I give. • This term was considered the oldest and aptest for a feoffment and gift.

DOC. *abbr.* DEPARTMENT OF COMMERCE.

DOCCS. *abbr.* The Department of Corrections and Community Supervision.

dock, *n.* (15c) **1.** A structure that encloses water, often between two piers, in which ships are received for loading, unloading, safekeeping, or repair. **2.** The part of a warehouse or other building (usu. elevated with oversized doors) at which trucks are received for loading and unloading. **3.** *English law.* In a criminal court, the enclosure in which the prisoner is placed during trial <it was through his own deliberate choice that Mr. Bourne found himself in the dock at the Old Bailey, charged with a felony>. See BAIL DOCK.

dockage. (18c) A charge for the use of a dock, esp. while a vessel is undergoing repairs.

dock charter. See CHARTER (8).

docket, *n.* (15c) **1.** A formal record in which a judge or court clerk briefly notes all the proceedings and filings in a court case <review the docket to determine the filing date>. — Also termed *judicial record; bench docket; docket sheet.*

▸ **appearance docket.** (18c) A list of the parties and lawyers participating in an action, together with a brief abstract of the successive steps in the action.

▸ **judgment docket.** (1826) A book that a court clerk keeps for the entry or recordation of judgments, giving official notice of existing judgment liens to interested parties. — Also termed *judgment book; judgment file; judgment record; judgment roll.*

2. A schedule of pending cases <the case is third on Monday's trial docket>. — Also termed *court calendar; cause list; trial calendar.*

▸ **DWOP docket.** A list of cases that the court has set for possible dismissal for want of prosecution. — Also termed *doowop docket; DLOP docket.* See *dismissal for want of prosecution* under DISMISSAL (1).

▸ **preferred docket.** (1993) A list of cases set for trial, arranged in order of priority. • Criminal cases are, for example, generally given precedence over civil cases on the preferred docket because of the constitutional right to a speedy trial.

3. DOCKET CALL <the agreed judgment was signed at the court's uncontested docket call on May 24>. **4.** *Parliamentary law.* A list of each motion, report, election, and other business that awaits a deliberative assembly's consideration, from which a board or officer prepares and circulates an agenda for each meeting or for a series of upcoming meetings <in planning the meeting, the chair worked from an exhaustive docket>. See AGENDA. **5.** A written abstract that provides specific information (usu. about something attached); esp., a label <check the docket to determine the goods' destination and value>. **6.** *Hist.* A notary's attestation at the end of a deed or other instrument; esp., the attestation at the end of an instrument of seisin. — Also spelled *docquet.* See MANU ALIENA.

docket, *vb.* (17c) **1.** To make a brief entry in the docket of the proceedings and filings in a court case <to docket the filing date>. **2.** To abstract and enter in a book <to docket a judgment>. **3.** To schedule (a case) for trial or some other event <the case was docketed for a May trial>.

docket call. (1899) A court session in which attorneys (and sometimes parties) appear in court to report the status of their cases. • For example, they may announce readiness for trial or report the suit's settlement. — Often shortened to *docket.*

docket entry. (1822) A note made in the court's formal record of proceedings and filings. See DOCKET (1).

docket fee. See FEE (1).

docket number. (1866) A number that the court clerk assigns to a case on the court's docket.

docket order. See ORDER (2).

docket sheet. See DOCKET (1).

dock identification. *English law.* An in-court declaration by an eyewitness to a crime that the defendant in the dock was the person who committed the crime or was present at the scene of the crime. —Also termed *in-court identification.*

dockmaster. (18c) *English law.* An officer who directs the mooring and removal of ships to avoid the obstruction of commerce.

dock receipt. (1916) *Maritime law.* An interim document issued by a maritime carrier to evidence the delivery of goods at the dock. • Generally, a dock receipt entitles the designated person to receive a bill of lading, waybill, or other transport document. — Also termed *dock warrant; dock statement.* See DOCUMENT OF TITLE.

dock sale. See SALE.

dock statement. **1.** *English law.* A jury speech made by a defendant who, not being under oath, cannot be cross-examined and is not in the witness box. **2.** DOCK RECEIPT.

dock warrant. See DOCK RECEIPT.

DOCS. *abbr. Criminal law.* The Department of Correctional Services.

doctor, *n.* (14c) **1.** *Hist.* In Roman Catholic canon law, an honorary title for a scholar. **2.** A title of a person who has acquired an advanced degree in academics, or has achieved an honorable distinction. **3.** A physician. — Abbr. Dr.

doctor, *vb.* (18c) **1.** To treat medically. **2.** To repair or restore to a working condition. **3.** To alter or modify, usu. in a deceptive or false manner. **4.** To add something harmful to (food or drink).

Doctor of Juridical Science. A graduate law degree, beyond the J.D. and the LL.M. • It is the most advanced law degree obtainable, offered by only a few American as well as some foreign law schools. — Abbr. S.J.D.; J.S.D. — Also termed *Doctor of Judicial Science; Doctor of the Science of Jurisprudence; Doctor of the Science of Law.*

Doctor of Jurisprudence. See JURIS DOCTOR.

Doctor of Law. See JURIS DOCTOR.

Doctor of Laws. An honorary degree bestowed on one who has achieved great distinction. — Abbr. LL.D. Cf. JURIS DOCTOR; MASTER OF LAWS.

Doctor of the Science of Jurisprudence. See DOCTOR OF JURIDICAL SCIENCE.

Doctor of the Science of Law. See DOCTOR OF JURIDICAL SCIENCE.

doctor–patient privilege. See PRIVILEGE (3).

doctor–patient relationship. See RELATIONSHIP.

Doctors' Commons. *Hist. Informal.* The College of Doctors of Law, which trained specialists in admiralty and ecclesiastical law and housed admiralty and ecclesiastical courts from the 16th century to the 19th. • The College was dissolved in the 1860s after its functions were absorbed by the High Court. — Sometimes written *Doctors' Common.* — Also termed *College of Civilians.*

doctrine. (14c) **1.** A principle, esp. a legal principle, that is widely adhered to. **2.** *Archaic.* HOLDING (1).

doctrine against irrepealability. See REPEALABILITY CANON.

doctrine of abstention. See ABSTENTION DOCTRINE.

doctrine of acquired rights. See ACQUIRED-RIGHTS DOCTRINE.

doctrine of adverse domination. See ADVERSE-DOMINATION DOCTRINE.

doctrine of approximation. (1845) A doctrine that authorizes a court to vary the details of a trust's administration to preserve the trust and to carry out the donor's intentions. — Also termed *equitable doctrine of approximation.* Cf. CY PRES.

doctrine of capture. See RULE OF CAPTURE.

doctrine of claim differentiation. See CLAIM DIFFERENTIATION.

doctrine of coercion. See COERCION.

doctrine of completeness. See RULE OF OPTIONAL COMPLETENESS.

doctrine of constructive service. (1855) **1.** See *constructive service* under SERVICE (7). **2.** *Employment law.* The common-law principle that a wrongfully discharged person may sue on the breached contract for the wages that he or she would have earned during the remaining contract period. • In a jurisdiction that has adopted this principle, it is an exception to the mitigation-of-damages doctrine. — Often shortened to *constructive service.* Cf. MITIGATION-OF-DAMAGES DOCTRINE.

doctrine of contagion. See CONTAGION.

doctrine of continuing violation. See CONTINUING-VIOLATION DOCTRINE.

doctrine of continuity. See CONTINUITY (2).

doctrine of *contra non valentem* (**kon**-trə non və-**len**-təm). (1938) The common-law rule that a limitations or prescriptive period does not begin to run against a plaintiff who is unable to bring an action, usu. because of the defendant's culpable act, such as concealing material information that would give rise to the plaintiff's claim. — Often shortened to *contra non valentem.* — Sometimes misspelled *valentum.*

doctrine of contra proferentem. See CONTRA PROFERENTEM.

doctrine of cumulative error. See CUMULATIVE ERROR.

doctrine of curative admissibility. See CURATIVE-ADMISSIBILITY DOCTRINE.

doctrine of discovered peril. See LAST-CLEAR-CHANCE DOCTRINE.

doctrine of divisible divorce. The view that dissolution of a marriage is in rem, affecting marital status, and can be decided separately from issues related to child custody and property rights. See *divisible divorce* under DIVORCE.

doctrine of election (18c). A doctrine holding that when a person has contracted with an agent without knowing of the agency and later learns the principal's identity, the person may enforce the contract against either the agent or the principal, but not both. See ELECTION (1); ELECTION OF REMEDIES.

doctrine of entireties (en-tɪ-ər-teez). (1891) In customs law, the rule that when an entry consists of parts that assemble to form an article different from any of the parts, the proper classification will be of the whole article, rather than the individual components. • For example, an unassembled product consisting of an empty decorative glass, powdered wax in a cellophane bag, wicks, and fragrance, boxed together and sold as one product may be properly classified as a candle.

doctrine of equitable indemnity. See *equitable indemnity* under INDEMNITY.

doctrine of equivalents. (1856) *Patents.* A judicially created theory for finding patent infringement when the accused process or product falls outside the literal scope of the patent claims. • The doctrine evolved to prevent parties from evading liability for patent infringement by making trivial changes to avoid the literal language of the patent claims. *Graver Tank & Mfg. Co. v. Linde Air Prods. Co.*, 339 U.S. 605, 70 S.Ct. 854 (1950). In determining whether infringement exists under the doctrine, the court must first determine whether "the accused product or process contain[s] an element identical or equivalent to each claimed element of the patented invention." *Warner-Jenkinson Co. v. Hilton Davis Chem. Co.*, 520 U.S. 17, 39–40, 117 S.Ct. 1040, 1054 (1997). If it does, it infringes on the patent if the differing element performs substantially the same function in substantially the same way to get the same result as the patented product or process. Prosecution-history estoppel is not an absolute bar to a patentee who seeks to invoke the doctrine of equivalents to prove infringement on a claim that was voluntarily amended. *Festo v. Shoketsu Kinzoku Kogyo Kabushiki Co.*, 535 U.S. 722, 122 S.Ct. 1831 (2002). — Also termed *equivalents doctrine; doctrine of equivalence; doctrine of equivalency; doctrine of substantial equivalents; nonliteral infringement.* Cf. *literal infringement* under INFRINGEMENT.

▸ **reverse doctrine of equivalents.** (1976) The doctrine preventing infringement liability when the invention is substantially described by the claims of another's patent but performs the same or a similar function in a substantially different way.

doctrine of estates. (18c) *Hist.* The rule that a person cannot own land, but can merely own an estate in it, authorizing the person to hold it for some period of time. • This doctrine answers the question of the duration of an estate. Cf. DOCTRINE OF TENURES.

doctrine of finality. See FINALITY DOCTRINE.

doctrine of general average. (1833) *Maritime law.* A rule allowing a carrier to require cargo owners and the shipowner to contribute pro rata to the cost of protecting the ship and its cargo.

doctrine of identification. (1876) *Hist. English law.* The rule that if a person traveling in a conveyance is injured in an accident that occurs because of someone else's negligence, and the driver of the conveyance is contributorily negligent, the passenger cannot claim damages against the tortfeasor since the passenger is "identified" with the contributorily negligent driver. • The leading authority for this doctrine was *Thorogood v. Bryan*, 8 C.B. 115 (1849), but the Court of Appeal repudiated the doctrine as unsound in *The Bernina* [1887], 13 App. Cas. 1 (1888).

doctrine of illusory coverage. (1996) A rule requiring an insurance policy to be interpreted so that it is not merely a delusion to the insured; specif., a rule of contract interpretation or reformation that avoids an interpretation that would result in never triggering an insured's coverage or having the insurer incur no risk. • Courts avoid interpreting insurance policies in such a way that an insured's coverage is never triggered and the insurer bears no risk.

doctrine of imputed knowledge. (1869) *Agency law.* The rule that a principal is deemed to know facts known to his or her agent if they are within the scope of the agent's duties to the principal, unless the agent has acted adversely to the principal. • The doctrine serves as a bridge for the applicability of defenses that a third party may assert against a principal in which knowledge is a necessary element, including *in pari delicto.* See ADVERSE-AGENT DOCTRINE; IMPUTED KNOWLEDGE; IN PARI DELICTO DOCTRINE.

doctrine of incontrovertible physical facts. See PHYSICAL-FACTS RULE.

doctrine of ineffective revocation. See DEPENDENT RELATIVE REVOCATION.

doctrine of inherency. See INHERENCY DOCTRINE.

doctrine of intervening rights. See INTERVENING RIGHTS.

doctrine of legal unities. See LEGAL-UNITIES DOCTRINE.

doctrine of marital privacy. See MARITAL-PRIVACY DOCTRINE.

doctrine of necessaries. (1870) **1.** The rule holding a parent or spouse liable to anyone who sells goods or provides medical services to that person's child or spouse if the goods or services are required for sustenance, support, or healthcare. **2.** *Archaic.* The common-law rule holding a husband or father liable to anyone who sells goods to his wife or child if the goods are required for sustenance or support. See NECESSARIES.

doctrine of notice. See NOTICE DOCTRINE.

doctrine of obligation. (1879) *English law.* The rule that if a foreign court of competent jurisdiction has adjudicated a certain sum to be due from one person to another, the liability to pay that sum becomes a legal obligation enforceable domestically by a debt action. • Once the plaintiff proves the judgment, the burden shifts to the defendant to show why the obligation should not be performed. The doctrine was established by Baron Parke in *Russell v. Smyth*, 9 M. & W. 810, 819 (1842). — Often shortened to *obligation.*

doctrine of optional completeness. See RULE OF OPTIONAL COMPLETENESS.

doctrine of original public meaning. See ORIGINALISM (1).

doctrine of our federalism. See OUR FEDERALISM.

doctrine of *parens patriae.* See PARENS PATRIAE (2).

doctrine of practical location. See AGREED-BOUNDARY DOCTRINE.

doctrine of precedent. (18c) **1.** The rule that precedents not only have persuasive authority but also must be followed when similar circumstances arise. • This rule developed in the 19th century and prevails today. See STARE DECISIS. **2.** A rule that precedents are reported, may be cited, and will probably be followed by courts. • This is the rule that prevailed in England until the 19th century.

doctrine of preclusion of inconsistent positions. See *judicial estoppel* under ESTOPPEL.

doctrine of relation back. See RELATION BACK.

doctrine of res judicata. See RES JUDICATA.

doctrine of revestment. A rule by which a court regains jurisdiction after the entry of final judgment when the former opposing parties have actively participated in proceedings inconsistent with the court's judgment.

doctrine of scrivener's error. (1992) A rule permitting a typographical error in a document to be reformed by parol evidence, if the evidence is precise, clear, and convincing. See *clerical error* under ERROR (2).

doctrine of separate spheres. See SEPARATE-SPHERES DOCTRINE.

doctrine of specialty. (1935) *Int'l law.* The principle, included as a provision in most extradition treaties, under which a person who is extradited to a country to stand trial for certain criminal offenses may be tried only for those offenses and not for any other pre-extradition offenses. — Also termed *specialty doctrine.* See EXTRADITION.

doctrine of spousal unity. See SPOUSAL-UNITY DOCTRINE (1).

doctrine of subsequent negligence. See LAST-CLEAR-CHANCE DOCTRINE.

doctrine of substantial equivalents. See DOCTRINE OF EQUIVALENTS.

doctrine of substituted judgment. See SUBSTITUTED-JUDGMENT DOCTRINE.

doctrine of superior equities. (1932) **1.** An equitable doctrine applicable to all cases in equity whereby the court determines which party is most deserving of a favorable outcome. **2.** *Insurance.* A rule by which an insurer is unable to recover from anyone whose equities are equal or superior to the insurer's; esp., a rule that a right of subrogation may be invoked against another party only if that party's guilty conduct renders the party's equity inferior to that of the insured. — Also termed *risk-stops-here rule.*

doctrine of tenures. (18c) *Hist.* The rule that all land is held of the Crown, either directly or indirectly, on some type of tenure. • This doctrine answers the question of the manner in which an estate is held. — Also termed *doctrine of tenure.* Cf. DOCTRINE OF ESTATES.

doctrine of the captain of the ship. See CAPTAIN-OF-THE-SHIP DOCTRINE.

doctrine of the conclusiveness of the judgment. See *judicial estoppel* under ESTOPPEL.

doctrine of the last antecedent. See RULE OF THE LAST ANTECEDENT.

doctrine of the last preceding antecedent. RULE OF THE LAST ANTECEDENT.

doctrine of ultimate negligence. See LAST-CLEAR-CHANCE DOCTRINE.

doctrine of unanimous consent. *Corporations. Archaic.* The once-prevalent rule that contracts between a corporation and its shareholders or between individual shareholders cannot be changed, except in a few nonfundamental aspects, without the consent of all the shareholders. • In modern American law, statutes allow contracts to be modified by a majority of shareholders.

doctrine of unconstitutional conditions. See UNCONSTITUTIONAL-CONDITIONS DOCTRINE.

doctrine of uses. The principle that one person may have the right to the rents and profits from land while another has seisin and possession. Cf. STATUTE OF USES.

doctrine of vested rights. See VESTED-RIGHTS DOCTRINE.

doctrine of worthier title. See WORTHIER-TITLE DOCTRINE.

doctrine of zealous advocacy. See PRINCIPLE OF PARTISANSHIP.

document, *n.* (15c) **1.** Something tangible on which words, symbols, or marks are recorded. *See* Fed. R. Civ. P. 34(a). • Most traditionally, of course, the term embraced any piece of paper with information on it. Today the term also embraces any information stored on a computer, electronic storage device, or any other medium. **2.** (*pl.*) The deeds, agreements, title papers, letters, receipts, and other written instruments used to prove a fact.

▸ **ancient document.** (1846) *Evidence.* A document that is presumed to be authentic because its physical condition strongly suggests authenticity, it has existed for 20 or more years, and it has been maintained in proper custody (as by coming from a place where it is reasonably expected to be found). Fed. R. Evid. 901(b)(8). — Also termed *ancient writing.*

▸ **confidential document.** (1848) A document that has been prepared either by or for a person who has a legal duty not to disclose its contents.

▸ **counterfeit document.** (1901) A forged document, esp. one that reproduces a trademark or other identifying feature for purposes of deception.

▸ **document of authority.** See *governing document.*

▸ **electronic document.** Any electronic media content, other than a computer program or system file, intended to be used in an electronic or printed form. — Also termed *e-document.*

▸ **executed document.** A document that has been fully and properly signed by all the parties. • For an ambiguity stemming from an allied use of *executed,* see *executed contract* under CONTRACT.

▸ **false document.** (18c) A document that is not genuine. — Also termed *bogus document*; *fake document.*

▸ **foreign document.** (1816) A document that originated in, or was prepared or executed in, a foreign state or country.

▸ **forged document.** (1820) A document that is fraudulent; esp., either one that has been fabricated to seem genuine or a real document that has been altered to seem genuine as altered.

▸ **governing document.** (1876) *Parliamentary law.* A document that defines or organizes an organization, or grants or establishes its authority and governance. • An organization's governing documents may include a charter, articles of incorporation or association, a constitution, bylaws, and rules. A charter or articles of incorporation or association, if they have been granted or adopted, are an organization's most authoritative governing document, followed by the constitution, bylaws, and rules, in that order. — Also termed *document of authority.* See CHARTER (4), (5); ARTICLES OF INCORPORATION; ARTICLES OF ASSOCIATION (2); CONSTITUTION (4); BYLAW (1); SUBORDINATION (2).

▸ **hot document.** (1995) A document that directly supports a litigant's allegation. See SMOKING GUN.

▸ **public document.** (17c) A document issued or published by a political body or otherwise connected with public business. Cf. *public record* under RECORD.

3. *Evidence.* Under the best-evidence rule, a physical embodiment of information or ideas, such as a letter, contract, receipt, account book, blueprint, or X-ray plate; esp., the original of such an embodiment. *See* Fed. R. Evid. 1001 et seq.

> "[A] document . . . is an instrument on which is recorded, by means of letters, figures, or marks, matter which may be evidentially used. In this sense the term 'document' applies to writings; to words printed, lithographed, or photographed; to seals, plates, or stones on which inscriptions are cut or engraved; to photographs and pictures; to maps and plans. So far as concerns admissibility, it makes no difference what is the thing on which the words or signs offered may be recorded. . . . 'Document,' it will be therefore seen, is a term at once more comprehensive and more exact than 'instrument in writing,' a term at one time generally used in the same relation. An 'instrument in writing,' it might well be argued, does not include printed books; and it clearly does not include engravings on wood or stone. 'Document,' however, includes not merely books, but any other thing on which is impressed a meaning which, emanating from one party, is calculated to affect the rights of another party." 2 Francis Wharton, *A Treatise on the Law of Evidence in Criminal Issues* 1090 (O.N. Hilton ed., 10th ed. 1912) (citations omitted).

document, *vb.* (18c) **1.** To support with records, instruments, or other evidentiary authorities <document the chain of custody>. **2.** To record; to create a written record of <document a file>.

documentary credit. (1922) **1.** Credit extended on a document of title or any other legal document. **2.** A financing arrangement in which a financial institution authorizes or makes a payment to a third party (usu. an exporter) at a customer's request. • This financing method facilitates international transactions by providing the importer with necessary credit and the exporter with an expedited cash payment.

documentary demand for payment. See *documentary draft* (1) under DRAFT (1).

documentary draft. See DRAFT (1).

documentary evidence. See EVIDENCE.

documentary instruction. (2008) A written agreement between an importer and exporter covering the relegation of various documents relating to the shipment and disposition of goods.

documentary letter of credit. See LETTER OF CREDIT.

documentary-originals rule. See BEST-EVIDENCE RULE.

documentary sale. See SALE.

documentary stamp. (1899) A stamp required to be affixed to a deed or other instrument before it is recorded.

documentary-stamp transfer tax. See *stamp tax* under TAX.

documentation. (1888) **1.** Official documents, reports, and the like used to prove that something is true or correct <provide supporting documentation>. **2.** The act of recording information in a tangible medium <his documentation of the event was mostly on film>. **3.** The preparation of documents for use or filing. **4.** The act or process of furnishing a ship with papers.

document discovery. See DISCOVERY.

document draft. See DRAFT (3).

document of authority. See *governing document* under DOCUMENT (2).

document of title. (18c) A written description, identification, or declaration of goods authorizing the holder (usu. a bailee) to receive, hold, and dispose of the document and the goods it covers. • Documents of title, such as bills of lading, warehouse receipts, and delivery orders, are generally governed by Article 7 of the UCC. See BAILMENT (1)–(3).

▸ **negotiable document of title.** (1877) A document of title that actually stands for the goods it covers, so that any transfer of the goods requires a surrender of the document. UCC § 7-104(a).

▸ **nonnegotiable document of title.** (1919) A document of title that merely serves as evidence of the goods it covers. UCC § 7-104(b).

document request. See REQUEST FOR PRODUCTION.

documentum (dok-yə-**men**-təm), *n.* [Latin] *Roman law.* **1.** Proof. **2.** A document. • This term appeared in post-classical imperial constitutions.

DOD. *abbr.* Department of Defense. See DEFENSE DEPARTMENT.

Dodd–Frank Act. A 2010 federal statute whose stated purposes include promoting the financial stability of the United States by improving accountability and transparency in the financial system. • The statute affects nearly every federal agency with jurisdiction over finance or consumer protection, and nearly every segment of the financial-services industry. — Also termed *Dodd–Frank Wall Street Reform & Consumer Protection Act.*

Dodd–Frank Wall Street Reform & Consumer Protection Act. See DODD–FRANK ACT.

DoDDS. *abbr.* DEPARTMENT OF DEFENSE DEPENDENTS SCHOOLS.

do, dico, addico (**doh**, **dɪ**-koh, ə-**dɪ**-koh *or* **dik**-oh, ə-**dik**-oh). [Latin] I give, I say, I adjudge. • These formal words were spoken by the Roman praetor in the exercise of his jurisdiction on *dies fasti*, specific days on which court decisions could be announced. They could not be officially spoken on *dies nefasti*. *Do* refers to the granting of actions, exceptions, and the appointment of judges; *dico* refers to the pronouncement of judgments; and *addico* refers to the adjudication of controverted property.

DOE. *abbr.* **1.** DEPARTMENT OF EDUCATION. **2.** DEPARTMENT OF ENERGY.

Doe, Jane. See JANE DOE.

Doe, John. See JOHN DOE.

***D'Oench Duhme* doctrine** (dench **doom**). (1986) The rule that estops a borrower from asserting a claim or defense against a federal successor to a failed financial institution, if the claim or defense is based on a side or secret agreement or representation, unless the agreement or representation has been (1) put into writing, (2) executed by the financial institution and borrower when the loan was issued, (3) approved by the financial institution's board of directors or loan committee, and (4) made a permanent part of the financial institution's records. *D'Oench, Duhme & Co. v. FDIC*, 315 U.S. 447, 62 S.Ct. 676 (1942) (now partially codified at 12 USCA § 1823(e), and otherwise of questionable standing in light of *O'Melveny & Myers v. FDIC*, 512 U.S. 79, 114 S.Ct. 2048 (1994)).

do equity. (Of one who seeks an equitable remedy) to treat or offer to treat the other party as fairly as is necessary, short of abandoning one's own legal rights, to bring about a fair result. • The phrase derives from the maxim, "One who seeks equity must do equity." See UNCLEAN-HANDS DOCTRINE.

d'office (daw-**fees**). [Law French] Of office; officially. • This is similar to the Latin phrase *ex officio.*

dog. (bef. 12c) **1.** The common domesticated animal having four legs, fur, and a tail, and frequently kept as a pet or trained to guard people or places; *canis lupus familiaris*, commonly known as the domestic dog (even when feral).

▸ **arson dog.** (1993) A police dog trained to detect accelerants at the site of a fire.

▸ **assistance dog.** See *service dog.*

▸ **attack dog.** (1943) **1.** See *guard dog.* **2.** See WATCHDOG (2).

▸ **cadaver dog.** (1996) A dog trained to detect the scent of a human corpse, esp. one that is hidden. — Also termed *human-remains detection dog.* Cf. *search dog.*

▸ **dangerous dog.** (17c) A dog legally classified as one whose behavior poses a threat to the safety of humans and other animals based on its actions, its breed, or the actions of its owner. • The legal definition varies depending on city, county, or state law. See DANGEROUS-DOG LAW; DANGEROUS-DOG REGISTRY.

▸ **detection dog.** A dog trained to use its senses, esp. the sense of smell, to detect particular substances or items such as explosives, illegal drugs, or blood. — Also termed *sniffer dog; sniffing dog; drug-sniffing dog.*

▸ **guard dog.** A large, usu. aggressive dog trained to protect property or people by barking loudly when it detects an intruder and to attack or restrain the intruder. — Also termed *attack dog; watchdog.*

▸ **guide dog.** (1932) See *service dog.*

▸ **hearing-ear dog.** See *service dog.*

▸ **human-remains detection dog.** See *cadaver dog.*

▸ **K-9 dog.** See *police dog.*

▸ **police dog.** (1836) A dog trained specif. to work with law-enforcement officers. • In some jurisdictions, a police dog has legal status similar to a human law-enforcement officer. — Also termed *K-9 dog; K9 dog; K9 officer.*

▸ **search dog.** (1967) A dog trained to use its sense of smell to locate live, missing people, esp. those buried under rubble after a catastrophe such as an earthquake or bombing. — Also termed *search-and-rescue dog.*

▸ **seeing-eye dog.** See *service dog.*

▸ **service dog.** (1930) A dog trained to assist a disabled person with everyday tasks of living and alert the person to threats. • A service dog may be identified by the type of disability it's trained for. — Also termed *assistance dog; guide dog;* (for the blind) *seeing-eye dog;* (for the deaf) *hearing-ear dog.*

▸ **sniffer dog.** (1978) See *detection dog.*

▸ **tracking dog.** (1927) A dog trained to find and follow the scent of a particular object. Cf. *cadaver dog; search dog.*

▸ **watchdog.** (17c) **1.** See *guard dog.* **2.** See WATCHDOG (2).

2. *Slang.* Something undesirable, esp. a lawsuit <the cases assigned to the new lawyer were all dogs>. **3.** *Securities. Slang.* A stock or other investment that suffers public disdain and repeated price declines or poor performance. **4.** *Slang.* A thing of poor quality. **5.** *Slang.* A person, esp. a man, who has done something bad.

dog-bite legislation. See DANGEROUS-DOG LAW.

dog-draw. (16c) *Hist.* The apprehension of someone who was chasing a deer in a forest with a dog. • Dog-draw was one of the ways a man could be convicted of stealing deer from the King's forest. It could result in his being hanged on the nearest tree with his own bowstring.

> "Dog-draw is an apparent deprehension of an offender against venison in the forest. There are four kinds of them observed by Manwood, part. 2, cap. 18, num. 9, of his Forest Laws, that is, dog-draw, stable-stand, back-bear, and bloody-hand. Dog-draw is, when one is found drawing after a deer by the scent of a hound led in his hand." *Termes de la Ley* 181 (1st Am. ed. 1812).

dogma (**dawg**-mə *or* **dahg**-), *n.* (16c) **1.** A philosophy, opinion, or tenet that is strongly held, is believed to be authoritative, and is followed steadfastly, usu. to the exclusion of other approaches to the same subject matter. **2.** A formally stated and proclaimed doctrine of faith. Pl. **dogmas, dogmata** (-mə-tə).

DOHSA (**doh**-shə). *abbr.* DEATH ON THE HIGH SEAS ACT.

doing business. (17c) The act of engaging in business activities; specif., the carrying out of a series of similar acts for the purpose of realizing a pecuniary benefit, or otherwise accomplishing a goal, or doing a single act with the intention of starting a series of such acts; esp., a nonresident's participation in sufficient business activities in a foreign state to allow the state's courts to exercise personal jurisdiction over the nonresident. See BUSINESS (1); D/B/A/; DOING-BUSINESS STATUTE; LONG-ARM STATUTE; MINIMUM CONTACTS.

doing-business statute. (1923) A state law defining the acts that constitute undertaking business there, usu. for the purpose of establishing the circumstances under which the state's courts may exercise personal jurisdiction over a nonresident. See MINIMUM CONTACTS; LONG-ARM STATUTE.

DOJ. *abbr.* DEPARTMENT OF JUSTICE.

DOL. *abbr.* DEPARTMENT OF LABOR.

dol (dohl *or* dol), *n.* [French "deceit; fraud"] *Civil law.* Fraud committed in inducing another to enter into a contract. See *fraud in the inducement* under FRAUD. Cf. FRAUDE.

dole, *n.* (bef. 12c) **1.** A share of something that is jointly owned but divisible. **2.** A giving or distribution of food or money to the needy. **3.** *Slang.* Welfare benefits received from a governmental agency. **4.** *Scots law.* Criminal intent; the equivalent of mens rea.

do, lego (**doh**, **lee**-goh). [Latin] *Hist.* I give and bequeath. • In Roman law, this was the phrase used to make a bequest.

dole-land. (1805) *Hist.* Jointly owned land in which each owner or user has an assigned portion with distinct landmarks. • The share may be allotted annually on a rotating basis or permanently. — Also termed *dole-meadow*; *dole-moor.*

dole-meadow. See DOLE-LAND.

dole-moor. See DOLE-LAND.

***Dole* test.** (1990) **1.** A four-part test used to determine the constitutionality of a condition attached by Congress under its Spending Clause power to the receipt of federal money. • The spending must be in pursuit of the general welfare, and the condition must be unambiguous, related to some federal interest, and not barred by any other provision of the Constitution. *South Dakota v. Dole*, 483 U.S. 203, 107 S.Ct. 2793 (1987). **2.** (*not italicized*) A random drug test given to employees. • It is named for the man who developed a urine-screening test for drugs, Dr. Vincent Dole.

doli actio. See *actio de dolo malo* under ACTIO.

doli capax (**doh**-lɪ **kay**-paks), *adj.* [Latin "capable of wrong"] *Roman law.* Capable of committing a crime or tort; esp., old enough to determine right from wrong. — Also termed *capax doli.* Cf. DOLI INCAPAX.

> "In criminal cases, an infant of the age of *fourteen* years may be capitally punished for any capital offence: but under the age of *seven* he cannot. The period between *seven* and *fourteen* is subject to much incertainty: for the infant shall, generally speaking, be judged *prima facie* innocent; yet if he was *doli capax*, and could discern between good and evil at the time of the offence committed, he may be convicted and undergo judgment and execution of death, though he hath not attained to years of puberty or discretion. 1 William Blackstone, *Commentaries on the Laws of England* 452–53 (1765).

doli incapax (**doh**-lɪ in-**kay**-paks), *adj.* [Latin "incapable of wrong"] *Roman law.* Incapable of committing a crime or tort. — Also termed *incapax doli.* Cf. DOLI CAPAX.

dollar-cost averaging, *n.* (1952) The investment practice of purchasing a fixed dollar amount of a type of security at regular intervals.

dollarization, *n.* A foreign country's use of the U.S. dollar as its local currency.

dolo (**doh**-loh), *n.* [Spanish] *Spanish law.* Fraud or deceit; bad or mischievous design.

dolo circumventus (**doh**-loh sər-kəm-**ven**-təs). [Latin] (17c) *Hist.* Overreached by fraud.

dolose (də-**lohs** *or* **doh**-lohs). [Latin] (1859) *Hist.* Fraudulent; deceitful; malicious.

dolus (**doh**-ləs). [Latin "device; artifice"] (17c) *Roman & civil law.* **1.** Conduct intended to deceive someone; bad faith. • Although there may be *dolus* without fraud, fraud always includes *dolus.* Cf. CASUS (1); CULPA (1).

- ▸ ***dolus bonus*** (**doh**-ləs **boh**-nəs). [Latin "good deceit"] (17c) Shrewdness or justifiable deceit, as when a person lies to an attacker to prevent an assault. • *Dolus bonus* does not produce any legal consequences.
- ▸ ***dolus dans locum contractui*** (**doh**-ləs danz **loh**-kəm kən-**trak**-choo-ɪ). [Latin] Fraud or deceit giving rise to the contract; specif., a fraudulent misrepresentation that, having been made by one of the parties to the contract and relied on by the other, was actually instrumental in inducing the latter to enter into the contract.
- ▸ ***dolus incidens*** (**doh**-ləs **in**-si-denz). [Law Latin "incidental fraud"] *Hist.* Fraud that does not affect the essential terms of an agreement.
- ▸ ***dolus malus*** (**doh**-ləs **mal**-əs). [Latin "bad *or* evil deceit"] (16c) **1.** Evil or fraudulent design or intent; an unjustifiable deceit. **2.** DOLUS (2).

> "The dolus malus might either affect the substance or the incidents of a contract; e.g., it might either induce a person to sell, who but for the fraud would not have sold at all . . . or it might induce a person to buy at a higher price than he would otherwise have given, what he was however resolved to purchase." John George Phillimore, *Private Law Among the Romans* 97 (1863).

▸ ***dolus specialis*** (**doh**-ləs spesh-ee-**ay**-lis). [Latin] *Hist.* Special deceit.

2. Intentional aggression; willful injury, esp. to another's property. — Also termed *dolus malus; fraus.*

"In the twelfth century the resuscitated Roman law introduced some new ideas. Men began to contrast, as Glanvill does, civil with criminal causes, to speak of *dolus* and *culpa* and *casus,* and to lay stress on the psychical element in crime." 2 Frederick Pollock & Frederic W. Maitland, *History of English Law Before the Time of Edward I* 477 (2d ed. 1899).

"Although the word *malitia* is not unknown to the Roman lawyers, the usual and technical name for wrongful intent is *dolus,* or more specifically *dolus malus. Dolus* and *culpa* are two forms of *mens rea.* In a narrower sense, however, *dolus* includes merely that particular variety of wrongful intent which we term fraud — that is to say, the intent to deceive. From this limited sense it was extended to cover all forms of wilful wrongdoing. The English term fraud has never received an equally wide extension." John Salmond, *Jurisprudence* 385 (Glanville L. Williams ed., 10th ed. 1947).

▸ ***dolus directus.*** [Latin] Foresight of and desire to produce the primary or direct consequences of an action.

▸ ***dolus eventualis.*** [Latin] Awareness of the probable outcome of an action.

▸ ***dolus indirectus.*** [Latin] Awareness of the secondary or indirect, but not necessarily desired, effects of an action that are certain to result.

DOMA. *abbr.* DEFENSE OF MARRIAGE ACT.

domain (doh-**mayn**), *n.* (15c) **1.** The territory over which sovereignty is exercised <the 19th-century domains of the British Empire>. **2.** An estate in land <the family domain is more than 6,000 acres>. **3.** The complete and absolute ownership of land <his domain over this land has now been settled>. See EMINENT DOMAIN; PUBLIC DOMAIN.

domain name. (1987) The words and characters that website owners designate for their registered Internet addresses; specif., the first part of a website's address beginning usu. with "www." and ending with ".com," ".org," or some other letters that show something about the origin of the website. • All domain names have at least two levels. The first-level domain name identifies the registrant's category as, e.g., a commercial site (.com), governmental institution (.gov), educational institution (.edu), nonprofit group (.org), or discussion group (.net). The second-level domain name is the unique identifier for the user in a particular category <rhapsangel.com> <rhapsangel.org>. Second-level domain names may be protected under trademark law, but first-level domain names are not. Although the entire domain name may be validly registered as a trademark, trademark rights are not automatically created by registering a domain name. See INTERNET-PROTOCOL ADDRESS.

▸ **top-level domain name.** The highest level of domain names in the hierarchical Domain Name System of the Internet under the management and control of the Internet Corporation for Assigned Names and Numbers (ICANN). • Top-level domain names are the predefined suffixes attached to Internet domain names, such as .com, .gov, .edu, .org, and .net. ICANN began adding hundreds of new domain names to the original 22 in 2014.

domain-name infringement. See INFRINGEMENT.

domain-name system. The conventions for identifying the various servers and websites on the Internet. — Abbr. DNS.

domboc. See DOOMBOOK.

Dombrowski **doctrine.** (1965) A short-lived rule that entitled a person to seek a federal-court injunction to prevent prosecution under a broad or vague state statute that affects rights guaranteed by the First Amendment. *Dombrowski v. Pfister,* 380 U.S. 479, 85 S.Ct. 1116 (1965). • The doctrine was greatly cut back six years after it was announced, when the Supreme Court ruled that a speculative First Amendment chilling effect does not justify federal-court intervention in state affairs. *Younger v. Harris,* 401 U.S. 37, 91 S.Ct. 746 (1971).

domebook. See DOOMBOOK.

Domesday Book (**doomz**-day). The census or survey, commissioned by William the Conqueror in 1085 and substantially completed in 1086, of England's landholdings, buildings, people, and livestock. See REVELAND. — Abbr. D.B. — Also spelled *Doomsday Book.*

"*Domesday Book* had several variant names — *Liber de Wintonia, Rotulus Wintoniae, Scriptura Thesauri Regis, Liber Regis, Liber Judiciarius, Censualis Angliae, Angliae Notitia et Lustratio, Rotulus Regis, Liber de Thesauro, Exchequer Domesday.* . . . *Domesday Book* had as its main object a fiscal one, and a limited fiscal one at that. Beyond that it does not profess to go, and if we get any further information from it as to contemporary law and society, we get it as an indirect consequence." Percy H. Winfield, *The Chief Sources of English Legal History* 110–11 (1925).

domestic, *adj.* (15c) **1.** Of, relating to, or involving one's own country <domestic affairs>. **2.** Of, relating to, or involving one's own jurisdiction <in Alaska, a domestic corporation is an Alaskan one>. **3.** Of, relating to, or involving the family or the household <a domestic dispute>.

domestic abuse. See *domestic violence* under VIOLENCE.

domestic animal. See ANIMAL.

domestic asset-protection trust. See *asset-protection trust* (1) under TRUST (3).

domesticated animal. See ANIMAL.

domestication. The taming or bringing under control of a wild, living thing so that humans can use it.

domestic authority. (1833) **1.** The legal power to use nondeadly force when reasonably necessary to protect a person for whom one is responsible. **2.** The legal privilege a parent has to discipline a child as long as it involves nonexcessive force for a true parental purpose. **3.** Collectively, agents of one's own country, as opposed to the agents of another country.

domestic bill. See BILL (6).

domestic care. Healthcare and daily-living services provided to a senior citizen or disabled person in the person's own home as an alternative to a hospital or nursing home.

domestic copying. See COPYING.

domestic corporation. See CORPORATION.

domestic court. See COURT.

domestic creditor. See CREDITOR.

domestic dispute. (1890) A disturbance, usu. at a residence and usu. within a family, involving violence and often resulting in a call to a law-enforcement agency. — Also termed *domestic disturbance*; *family disturbance*. See *domestic violence* under VIOLENCE.

domestic disturbance. See DOMESTIC DISPUTE.

domestic export. See EXPORT (1).

domestic fixture. See FIXTURE.

domestic guardian. See GUARDIAN (1).

Domestic International Sales Corporation. (1970) A U.S. corporation, esp. a subsidiary whose income is primarily attributable to exports. • Income tax on part of a DISC's income is usu. deferred, resulting in a lower overall corporate tax for the parent than it would otherwise incur. IRC (26 USCA) §§ 991–997. — Abbr. DISC.

domestic judgment. See JUDGMENT (2).

domestic jurisdiction. *Int'l law.* A state's jurisdiction over matters that are internal to that state and governed only by that particular state's laws.

domestic partnership. (1845) **1.** A nonmarital relationship between two persons of the same or opposite sex who live together as a couple for a significant period of time. **2.** A relationship that an employer or governmental entity recognizes as equivalent to marriage for the purpose of extending employee-partner benefits otherwise reserved for the spouses of employees. Cf. CIVIL UNION; *same-sex marriage* under MARRIAGE (1). — **domestic partner,** *n.*

domestic-partnership law. (1983) A legislative enactment, formerly often a municipal ordinance, that grants unmarried adults living in economically or emotionally based relationships, regardless of their sexual preference, some of the rights of a civil marriage without attempting to change the traditional definition of marriage.

domestic-partnership period. (2004) The period beginning when domestic partners begin living together and ending when the partners stop sharing a primary residence. See DOMESTIC PARTNERSHIP.

domestic-partnership property. See PROPERTY.

Domestic Policy Council. See OFFICE OF POLICY DEVELOPMENT.

domestic relations. 1. Traditionally, family law together with employment law. **2.** FAMILY LAW (1).

> "The domestic relations are the relations existing between the members of a family or household. According to the usual classification, these relations are four in number, namely, the relations of (1) husband and wife; (2) parent and child; (3) guardian and ward; (4) master and servant. The relation of master and servant as a purely domestic relation is now of small importance, and the law relating thereto will be found discussed in connection with other branches of the law, especially the law of contracts, agency, and torts." Joseph R. Long, *A Treatise on the Law of Domestic Relations* § 1, at 1 (1905).

domestic-relations court. See *family court* under COURT.

domestic-relations exception. (1950) The exclusion of suits regarding the granting of divorce, alimony, and child custody from federal diversity jurisdiction. • The domestic-relations exemption to federal diversity jurisdiction originated as dictum in *Barber v. Barber*, 62 U.S. (21 How.) 582 (1858). Although federal courts do not have jurisdiction to grant divorces, award alimony, or determine child custody, they may hear other diversity matters involving family members such as tort claims or suits seeking to enforce alimony orders. *Ankenbrandt v. Richards*, 504 U.S. 689, 112 S.Ct. 2206 (1992).

domestic-relations law. See FAMILY LAW (1).

domestic-remedies rule. See EXHAUSTION-OF-LOCAL-REMEDIES RULE.

domestic servant. (17c) A household servant. — Often shortened to *domestic*.

domestic terrorism. See TERRORISM.

domestic tort. See *marital tort* under TORT.

domestic tribunal. See TRIBUNAL.

domesticus (də-**mes**-ti-kəs), *n.* [Latin] *Hist.* Steward; judge's assistant; assessor.

domestic violence. See VIOLENCE.

domicellus (dom-ə-**sel**-əs), *n.* [Law Latin] (18c) *Hist. French law.* **1.** A king's natural son.

> "*Domicellus*, Is an old obsolete . . . Word, anciently given as an Appellation or Addition to the King's natural Sons in *France*, and sometimes to the eldest Sons of Noblemen there; from whence we borrowed these Additions: As several natural Children of *John of Gaunt*, Duke of *Lancaster*, are stiled *Domicelli* by the Charter of Legitimation. . . . But according to *Thorn*, the *Domicelli* were only the better Sort of Servants in Monasteries." Giles Jacob, *A New Law-Dictionary* (8th ed. 1762).

2. A young lord. **3.** A knight's son.

domicile (**dom**-ə-sɪl), *n.* (15c) **1.** The place at which a person has been physically present and that the person regards as home; a person's true, fixed, principal, and permanent home, to which that person intends to return and remain even though currently residing elsewhere. Domicile may be divided into (1) domicile of origin, (2) domicile of choice, and (3) domicile by operation of law. — Also termed *permanent abode*; *habitancy*.

> "By domicile we mean home, the permanent home; and if you do not understand your permanent home, I am afraid that no illustration drawn from foreign writers or foreign languages will very much help you to it." *Whicker v. Hume* (1858) 7 H.L.C. 124, 160 (per Lord Cranworth).

> "It is difficult to give a definition of domicil that will cover at once domicil by operation of law and domicil by choice. The idea of domicil certainly includes the idea of place and the idea of settled connection with the place. Domicil of choice is so closely connected with the idea of home that it seems desirable to include that idea in any definition, and yet the idea is not applicable to many kinds of domicil by operation of law. It has therefore seemed best to state this element in the alternative. If a home is in the place, that is sufficient. If there is no home, or if the party is not *sui juris*, then the place is assigned by law without his will." 1 Joseph H. Beale, *A Treatise on the Conflict of Laws* § 9.1, at 89–90 (1935).

> "A person's domicile is the place with which that person is most closely associated — his or her 'home' with all the connotations of that word. A person can be domiciled in a nation, a state of the United States, a city, or a house within a city. He or she can have a domicile within a broader geographical designation without having a domicile in a narrower geographical designation. For example, a person may be domiciled in a state without being domiciled within any particular city within the state. For interstate choice-of-law purposes, it is the state in which a person is domiciled that is significant." Russell J. Weintraub, *Commentary on the Conflict of Laws* § 2.2, at 14 (4th ed. 2001).

2. The residence of a person or corporation for legal purposes. — Also termed (in sense 2) *legal residence*; *domicile by operation of law*. Cf. RESIDENCE; PLACE OF BUSINESS. — Also spelled (BrE) *domicil*.

> "Tax statutes frequently speak in terms of residence, intending it to be the equivalent of domicile. For example, the New York estate tax speaks in terms of residence and

non-residence. Similarly . . . , the United States imposes an estate tax on any resident or citizen of the U.S. Although both statutes use the term 'residence,' its usage has been construed to mean 'domicile.'" Robert C. Lawrence III, *International Tax and Estate Planning* § 1.03(a)(4), at 8–9 (1989).

▸ **after-acquired domicile.** (1858) A domicile established after the facts relevant to an issue arose. • An after-acquired domicile cannot be used to establish jurisdiction or choice of law.

▸ **commercial domicile.** (1839) **1.** A domicile acquired by a nonresident corporation conducting enough activities to permit taxation of the corporation's property or activities located outside the bounds of the taxing state. **2.** A domicile acquired by a person or company freely residing or carrying on business in enemy territory or enemy-occupied territory. — Also termed *quasi-domicile.*

▸ **corporate domicile.** (1890) The place considered by law as the center of corporate affairs, where the corporation's functions are discharged; the legal home of a corporation, usu. its state of incorporation or the state in which it maintains its principal place of business. • For purposes of determining whether diversity jurisdiction exists in federal court, a corporation is considered a citizen of both its state of incorporation and the state of its principal place of business. See DIVERSITY OF CITIZENSHIP.

▸ **domicile by operation of law.** Domicile established independently of a person's intention or residence, usu. created by the parent–child relationship.

▸ **domicile of birth.** See *domicile of origin.*

▸ **domicile of choice.** (1878) **1.** A domicile established by physical presence within a state or territory, coupled with the intention to make it home. **2.** The domicile that a person chooses after reaching majority or being emancipated.

▸ **domicile of origin.** (1831) The domicile of a person at birth, derived from the custodial parent or imposed by law. — Also termed *natural domicile*; *domicile of birth*; *original domicile.* See *necessary domicile.*

"Domicil is sometimes divided into domicil of birth, that by operation of law, and that of choice. Domicil of origin in modern times is domicil in the place where his parents at his birth were domiciled." Theodore D. Woolsey, *Introduction to the Study of International Law* § 71, at 105 n.2 (5th ed. 1878).

"Domicile of origin is the domicile the law assigns to each person at birth, usually the domicile of the father in the case of a legitimate child and of the mother in the case of an illegitimate child. Domicile of origin has particular significance in English law. If one abandons one's domicile of choice without attaining a new one, the domicile of origin 'revives' until a new domicile of choice is attained. In contrast, U.S. jurisdictions generally will not find a domicile abandoned until a new one has been adopted." Robert C. Lawrence III, *International Tax and Estate Planning* § 1.03(a)(1), at 4 (1989).

▸ **domicile of succession.** (1874) The domicile that determines the succession of a person's estate.

▸ **domicile of trustee.** (1939) The domicile where a trustee is appointed.

▸ **elected domicile.** (1850) A contractually agreed domicile between parties for purposes of the contract.

▸ **foreign domicile.** (18c) A domicile established by a citizen or subject of one sovereignty within the territory of another.

▸ **matrimonial domicile.** (1838) A domicile that a husband and wife, as a married couple, have established as their home. — Also termed *marital domicile*; *matrimonial home.*

▸ **municipal domicile.** (1875) A person's residence in a county or municipality, as distinguished from the person's state or national domicile.

▸ **national domicile.** (1868) A domicile considered in terms of a particular country rather than a locality or subdivision of a country.

▸ **natural domicile.** See *domicile of origin.*

▸ **necessary domicile.** (1856) A domicile legally fixed and independent of choice, as in the domicile of origin. See *domicile of origin*; *domicile by operation of law.*

▸ **original domicile.** See *domicile of origin.*

▸ **quasi-domicile.** See *commercial domicile.*

▸ **quasi-national domicile.** (1879) A person's state of residence, as distinguished from the person's national or local domicile.

domiciliary (dom-ə-**sil**-ee-er-ee), *adj.* (18c) Of, relating to, or involving domicile <domiciliary jurisdiction>.

domiciliary (dom-ə-**sil**-ee-er-ee), *n.* (1845) Someone who resides in a particular place with the intention of making it a principal place of abode; one who is domiciled in a particular jurisdiction. Cf. RESIDENT, *n.*; CITIZEN (1).

domiciliary administration. See ADMINISTRATION.

domiciliary administrator. See ADMINISTRATOR (2).

domiciliary letters testamentary. See LETTERS TESTAMENTARY.

domiciliary parent. See PARENT (1).

domiciliate (dom-ə-**sil**-ee-ayt), *vb.* (18c) To establish a domicile; to fix a place of residence.

domiciliation (dom-i-sil-ee-**ay**-shən), *n.* (1816) The act of establishing a domicile.

domicilium (dom-ə-**sil**-ee-əm), *n.* [Law Latin] *Roman law.* DOMICILE.

domicilium ex proprio motu (dom-i-**sil**-ee-əm eks **proh**-pree-oh **moh**-t[y]oo). [Latin] *Hist.* Domicile on one's own initiative.

domicilium necessarium (dom-i-**sil**-ee-əm nes-ə-**sair**-ee-əm). [Latin] *Hist.* Necessary or compulsory domicile.

domicilium originis (dom-i-**sil**-ee-əm ə-**rij**-i-nis). [Latin] *Hist.* Domicile of origin (or nativity).

domigerium (dom-ə-**jeer**-ee-əm), *n.* [Law Latin] *Hist.* **1.** Power over someone. **2.** Danger. **3.** Power to impose a fine or to inflict a penalty.

domina (**dom**-ə-nə), *n.* [Law Latin] (18c) **1.** A lady. **2.** A peeress. Cf. DAME (1), (2).

dominant estate. See ESTATE (4).

dominant-jurisdiction principle. (1995) The rule that the court in which a case is first filed maintains the suit, to the exclusion of all other courts that would also have jurisdiction. Cf. FIRST-TO-FILE RULE.

dominant position. *Business law.* The market situation of a business that can behave in disregard of suppliers and customers and as if it has little or no competition, allowing it to set prices, supplies, production levels, product quality, means of distribution, etc. according to its own discretion.

dominant praedium. See *praedium dominans* under PRAEDIUM.

dominant property. See *dominant estate* under ESTATE (4).

dominant tenant. See TENANT (1).

dominant tenement. See *dominant estate* under ESTATE (4).

dominate, *vb.* (17c) **1.** To master (someone or something); to control (someone or something). **2.** Predominate.

dominating patent. See *fencing patent* under PATENT (3).

dominatio (dom-ə-**nay**-shee-oh), *n.* [Latin] *Hist.* Lordship; rule.

domination. 1. The act or activity of exercising thorough control over someone or something. **2.** Control by the exercise of power or constituted authority; dominion; government. **3.** Mental control; esp., the emotional dominion by someone with superior ability or resources over an inferior, often with arbitrary and capricious sway. **4.** *Patents.* The effect that an earlier patent (usu. a basic one) has on a later patent (esp. one for improvements on the patented device) because the earlier patent's claims are so broad or generic that the later patent's invention will always infringe on the earlier patent's claims. • Because the patent system is based on exclusion of others from an invention's subject matter, the earlier, basic patent's claims "dominate" the later-invented improvement. If the improvement is patented and worked, it infringes the basic patent. But the basic patent's owner cannot practice the improvement without infringing on the improvement's patent. This stand-off effect encourages improvement and basic-patentees to seek licenses or cross-licenses with each other. See BLOCKING PATENT.

dominical (də-**min**-ə-kəl), *adj.* (16c) Of, relating to, or involving a Sunday; pertaining to the Lord's day.

Dominican divorce. See *Mexican divorce* under DIVORCE.

dominicide (də-**min**-ə-sɪd), *n.* [fr. Latin *dominus* "master" + *caedo* "to kill"] (17c) *Hist.* **1.** The crime of killing one's lord or master. **2.** Someone who kills his or her lord or master.

dominicum (də-**min**-ə-kəm), *n.* [Latin "domain"] **1.** *Hist.* Domain; lordship. **2.** *Hist.* Land ownership, esp. that retained by a lord for his own possession, as distinguished from the rights given to a tenant. **3.** *Eccles. law.* A church or other religious building.

dominicum antiquum (də-**min**-ə-kəm an-**tɪ**-kwəm), *n.* [Law Latin] *Hist.* Ancient domain.

dominion. (14c) **1.** Control; possession <dominion over the car>. **2.** Sovereignty <dominion over the nation>. **3.** FOREIGN DOMINION.

dominium (də-**min**-ee-əm), *n.* [fr. Latin *dominus* "lord"] (1823) **1.** *Roman & civil law.* Absolute ownership including the right to possession and use; a right of control over property that the holder might retain or transfer at pleasure. • *Dominium* was subject to any servitudes, planning restrictions, etc. This term gradually came to also mean merely ownership of property, as distinguished from the right to possession or use.

> "*Dominium* is the Roman term for the rights of an owner against all the world: and the contrast of *dominium* and *obligatio* is the nearest approach that can be made, in classical Roman language, to the distinction marked by the modern terms *in rem* and *in personam.*" Frederick Pollock, *A First Book of Jurisprudence* 83 (1896).

> "The one word *dominium* has to assume so many shades of meaning. The tenant *qui tenet terram in dominio*, is *dominus rei* and has *dominium rei*; but then he has above him one who is his *dominus*, and for the rights of this lord over him and over his land there is no other name than *dominium.*" 2 Frederick Pollock & Frederic W. Maitland, *The History of English Law Before the Time of Edward I* 4 (2d ed. 1899).

▸ ***dominium directum*** (də-**min**-ee-əm di-**rek**-təm), *n.* [Law Latin] (18c) **1.** *Civil law.* Legal, not equitable, ownership; specif., the nominal right of ownership retained by one who has granted to another an exclusive right of enjoyment over a thing. **2.** *Feudal law.* The right of the superior of land over a tenant.

▸ ***dominium directum et utile*** (də-**min**-ee-əm di-**rek**-təm et **yoo**-tə-lee), *n.* [Law Latin] *Civil law.* Complete ownership of property, including both title and exclusive use.

▸ ***dominium eminens*** (də-**min**-ee-əm **em**-ə-nenz), *n.* [Law Latin] (17c) *Civil law.* Eminent domain. See EMINENT DOMAIN.

▸ ***dominium ex jure quiritium*** (də-**min**-ee-əm eks **joor**-ee kwɪ-**rish**-ee-əm). *Roman law.* Ownership exercised by Roman citizens in the most complete manner (*pleno jure*), the property being domestic (not foreign) and having been acquired according to all the forms of law. — Also termed *dominium quiritarium*; *dominium legitimum.*

▸ ***dominium legitimum*** (lə-**jit**-i-məm). See *dominium ex jure quiritium.*

▸ ***dominium plenum*** (də-**min**-ee-əm **plee**-nəm), *n.* [Law Latin] (17c) *Civil law.* Full ownership combining *dominium directum* and *dominium utile.* — Also termed *plenum dominium.*

▸ ***dominium quiritarium*** (kwɪ-rə-**tair**-ee-əm). See *dominium ex jure quiritium.*

▸ ***dominium utile*** (də-**min**-ee-əm **yoo**-tə-lee), *n.* [Law Latin] (17c) *Civil law.* Equitable ownership; a beneficial right to use property; the right of a tenant to use the soil and its profits.

> "The special characteristic of Feudal land was that ownership in it was split into two kinds, the *dominium directum* of the superior (lord) and the *dominium utile* of the vassal. The feudists correctly insisted that this was not a form of joint ownership, not yet of ownership burdened with an easement or a 'usufruct,' but that two kinds of ownership were present, and that each of these persons, the lord and the vassal, was properly called 'owner' or *dominus.* The lord's *dominium directum* gave him a reversion in the case of forfeiture of failure of issue and the enjoyment of whatever the *naturalia* and *accidentalia* were. The vassal's *dominium utile* gave him the immediate enjoyment of the land itself." Max Radin, *Handbook of Anglo-American Legal History* 148 (1936).

▸ ***nudum dominium*** (də-**min**-ee-əm **n[y]oo**-dəm). [Latin "bare ownership"] *Roman Law.* Ownership divorced from present possession or use.

▸ ***plenum dominium.*** See *dominium plenum.*

2. *Hist.* Lordship; sovereignty.

"The Latin word for ownership, *dominium*, is particularly confusing, since in medieval times it is also the word for lordship." J.H. Baker, *An Introduction to English Legal History* 255 (3d ed. 1990).

domino volente (**dom**-ə-noh və-**len**-tee). [Law Latin "the owner being willing"] With the owner's consent.

dominus (**dom**-ə-nəs), *n.* [Latin "lord"] **1.** *Roman law.* An owner of a thing or inheritance. **2.** *Roman law.* The master of a slave. **3.** *Roman law.* The title of the emperor in the later empire. **4.** *Hist.* A lord; a feudal superior, as in *dominus rex* ("the lord of the king"), *dominus capitalis* ("a chief lord"), *dominus medius* ("an intermediate lord"), and *dominus ligius* ("a liege lord"). **5.** *Hist. Eccles. law.* Lord; sir. • This is a title of distinction usu. given to a knight, a clergyman, a lord of a manor, or another gentleman of quality. **6.** *Civil law.* Someone who possesses something by right. Pl. ***domini.***

dominus directus (**dom**-ə-nəs di-**rek**-təs). [Law Latin] (17c) *Hist.* The immediate feudal superior.

dominus litis (**dom**-ə-nəs **lɪ**-tis), *n.* [Latin] (17c) **1.** *Civil law.* The party who makes the decisions in a lawsuit, usu. as distinguished from the attorney. **2.** *Maritime law.* A third person who represents an absent party in a case. — Also termed *litis dominium.*

dominus navis (**dom**-ə-nəs **nay**-vis), *n.* [Latin] *Civil law.* The absolute owner of a shipping vessel.

dominus omnium bonorum (**dom**-ə-nəs **ahm**-nee-əm bə-**nor**-əm). [Law Latin] (17c) *Hist.* Proprietor of all movable goods. • The phrase formerly described a husband who owned goods in common with his wife.

domitae naturae (**dom**-ə-tee nə-**tyoor**-ee). [Latin] (17c) *Hist.* Of a tame nature; not wild. • This term usu. refers to long-domesticated animals, such as sheep or cattle, in which a person has absolute property rights. But it can also refer to naturally wild animals that have been tamed. Cf. FERAE NATURAE.

dommage moral. See *nonpecuniary loss* under LOSS.

dommage survenu (daw-**mazh** suur-və-**noo**). [French] Damage sustained. • This is from article 17 of the Warsaw Convention providing for compensatory damages, rather than awards for loss of society or punitive damages, for bodily injury that a passenger suffers while on board an aircraft, or while boarding or disembarking.

domo reparanda (**doh**-moh rep-ə-**ran**-də), *n.* [Latin "to repair a house"] (17c) *Hist.* **1.** A writ available to a person to force a neighbor who owns a decrepit house to repair it because the person is worried that the neighbor's house will fall and cause injury. **2.** A writ by which a tenant in common could compel a cotenant to share in the expenses of repairing property held in common.

Dom. Proc. *abbr.* DOMUS PROCERUM.

domus (**doh**-məs), *n.* [Latin] A house; an abode.

domus conversorum (**doh**-məs kon-vər-**sor**-əm), *n.* [Law Latin "house of the converts"] (17c) *Hist.* An institution, established by Henry III for converted Jews, that continued until Edward III expelled Jews from the kingdom and converted the institution to a chancery record office.

Domus Dei (**doh**-məs **dee**-ɪ), *n.* [Law Latin] (16c) House of God. • This term was applied to all churches in medieval England, as well as to various hospitals and religious houses, such as the Hospital of St. Julian in Southampton.

Domus Procerum (**doh**-məs **pros**-ə-rəm), *n.* [Latin "house of nobles"] The House of Lords. — Abbr. *Dom. Proc.*; *D.P.*

donatarius (doh-nə-**tair**-ee-əs), *n.* [Latin] A donee; a gift recipient.

donate, *vb.* (18c) To give (property or money) without receiving consideration for the transfer. — **donation,** *n.* — **donative** (**doh**-nə-tiv), *adj.*

donated stock. See STOCK.

donated surplus. See SURPLUS.

donatio (doh-**nay**-shee-oh). [Latin] A gift.

donatio ante nuptias (doh-**nay**-shee-oh an-tee **nəp**-shee-əs), *n. Hist.* A gift given by a prospective spouse to his or her betrothed in contemplation of the marriage; esp., BRIDEPRICE.

donatio causa mortis (doh-**nay**-shee-oh **kaw**-zə **mor**-tis), *n.* See *gift causa mortis* under GIFT. Pl. ***donationes causa mortis.***

"[A] *donatio mortis causa* must have all the essentials of a gift *inter vivos*; but the law attaches to the former the condition that it must be executed during the donor's last sickness, in contemplation of death, and upon the condition that he die from the then sickness; for if he survives, the gift, *ipso facto*, is revoked." W.W. Thornton, *A Treatise of the Law Relating to Gifts and Advancements* 1 (1893).

donatio inofficiosa (doh-**nay**-shee-oh in-ə-fish-ee-**oh**-sə). [Latin "inofficious gift"] *Roman law.* A gift so large that it diminishes an heir's birthright portion of the donor's property.

donatio inter virum et uxorem (doh-**nay**-shee-oh **in**-tər **vɪ**-rəm et ək-**sor**-əm). [Latin] (18c) *Roman law.* Donation between husband and wife. • With a few exceptions (such as suitable anniversary gifts), a donation between spouses was invalid, but might be confirmed if the donor died without revoking it.

donatio inter vivos (doh-**nay**-shee-oh **in**-tər **vɪ**-vohs). See *inter vivos gift* under GIFT.

donatio mortis causa, *n.* See *gift causa mortis* under GIFT. Pl. ***donationes mortis causa.***

donation. (16c) **1.** A gift, esp. to a charity; something, esp. money, that someone gives to a person or an organization by way of help.

▸ **disguised donation.** (1829) A transaction intended as a donation but labeled, characterized, or concealed as another type of transaction. • For example, a transaction styled as a sale in which the price is only nominal may be a donation in disguise. La. Civ. Code art. 2464.

"The Louisiana jurisprudence distinguishes 'sham transactions,' which have no effect at all, from 'disguised donations,' which are intended by the parties to be valid, but are not represented as donations on their face." *Wooley v. Lucksinger*, 14 So.3d 311, 470 (La. Ct. App. 2008).

▸ **donation purely gratuitous.** (1832) *Louisiana law.* An unconditional inter vivos gift. Cf. *onerous donation.*

▸ **onerous donation.** (1832) *Civil law.* An inter vivos gift burdened with a condition imposed by the donor. • There is no gift unless the gift's value is more than twice as much as the condition's value to the donor. La. Civ. Code arts. 1524, 1526. Cf. *donation purely gratuitous.*

▸ **remunerative donation.** (1834) *Civil law.* An inter vivos gift made to compensate a person for services rendered.

• It is not a gift unless the value of the property given is more than twice as much as the value of the services. La. Civ. Code arts. 1525, 1526.

2. The act of giving something, esp. money, to help a person or an organization. **3.** *Eccles. law.* A method of acquiring a benefice by deed of gift alone, without presentation, institution, or induction.

donation act. (18c) *Hist. Property.* A statute granting public lands to settlers who satisfy certain conditions or to veterans as a reward for military service. See *donation land, bounty land* under LAND.

donation claim. See CLAIM (3).

donation deed. See DEED.

donation land. See LAND.

donatio propter nuptias (doh-**nay**-shee-oh **prahp**-tər **nəp**-shee-əs). [Latin "a gift on account of marriage"] (16c) *Roman law.* A gift from a husband to his wife equivalent to her dowry and subject to similar conditions. • It was formerly called *donatio ante nuptias* ("gift before marriage") because it was not allowed after the marriage celebration. Justinian later changed the law and the name. See DOS.

donatio velata (doh-**nay**-shee-oh vi-**lay**-tə). [Latin] *Hist.* A veiled gift; a concealed gift.

donative (**don**-ə-tiv *or* **doh**-nə-tiv), *adj.* (16c) **1.** Of, relating to, or characterized by a donation <a donative transfer>. **2.** Subject to a donation <an advowson donative>.

donative advowson. See *advowson donative* under ADVOWSON.

donative intent. See INTENT (1).

donative trust. See TRUST (3).

donator (**doh**-nay-tər *or* doh-**nay**-tər *also* -tor), *n.* [Latin] (15c) A donor; a person who makes a gift.

donatory (**don**-ə-tor-ee *or* **doh**-nə-tor-ee), *n.* (17c) *Scots law.* A recipient of a gift; specif., a donee of the Crown.

> "A donatory is the donee or receiver of a gift or donation. In practice, the term is applied exclusively to the person to whom the Crown makes a gift, as of escheat, *ultimus haeres*, or the like." William Bell, *Bell's Dictionary and Digest of the Law of Scotland* 299 (George Watson ed., 1882).

donec (**doh**-nek). [Latin] *Hist.* As long as; while; until; within a certain time. • This term was used in old conveyances.

donec probetur in contrarium (**doh**-nek proh-**bee**-tər in kən-**trair**-ee-əm). [Latin] Until proof is given to the contrary.

donee (doh-**nee**). (16c) **1.** One to whom a gift is made; the recipient of a gift. **2.** The person in whose favor a power of appointment is created or reserved. See DONEE OF POWER.

donee beneficiary. See BENEFICIARY.

donee of power. (18c) Someone who has been given a power of appointment, i.e., the power to dispose of someone else's property. — Often shortened to *donee.* See DONEE (2). Cf. DONOR (3).

donor. (15c) **1.** Someone who gives something without receiving consideration for the transfer. **2.** SETTLOR (1). **3.** The person who creates or reserves a power of appointment. Cf. DONEE OF POWER.

donor-advised fund. See *donor-advised trust* under TRUST (3).

donor-advised trust. See TRUST (3).

donor card. See ORGAN-DONOR CARD.

do-not-resuscitate order. (1978) A document, executed by a competent person, directing that if the person's heartbeat and breathing both cease while in a hospital, nursing home, or similar facility, no attempts to restore heartbeat or breathing should be made. — Abbr. DNR order. — Also termed *advance directive.*

▸ **out-of-hospital do-not-resuscitate order.** (1996) A do-not-resuscitate order, executed by a person who has been diagnosed by a physician as having a terminal condition, directing healthcare professionals to withhold certain life-sustaining treatments when acting outside a hospital or similar facility. — Abbr. OOH-DNR order.

donum (**doh**-nəm), *n.* [Latin "a gift"] *Roman law.* A gift.

donum gratuitum. See *gratuitous gift* under GIFT.

doom, *n.* (bef. 12c) *Hist.* **1.** A statute or law. **2.** A judgment; esp., a sentence in a criminal matter. **3.** Justice; fairness. **4.** A trial; the process of adjudicating. — Also spelled *dome.*

> "The word 'doom' is, perhaps, best translated as 'judgment.' It survived in occasional use until the fourteenth century. Wyclif's translation of the Bible, rendering the verse, 'For with what judgment ye judge, ye shall be judged,' as 'For in what dome ye demen, ye schuln be demed.' The distinction which we make to-day between the legislator, who makes the law, and the judge, who interprets, declares and applies it, was not known to our Anglo-Saxon ancestors. The dooms were judgments in the sense that they were declarations of the law of the people." W.J.V. Windeyer, *Lectures on Legal History* 1 (2d ed. 1949).

doombook, *n.* [fr. Saxon *dombec*] (bef. 12c) *Hist.* A code, compiled under Alfred, containing maxims of common law, judicial forms, and criminal penalties. • The code existed until the reign of Edward IV, when it was lost. — Also termed *domebook* (**doom** buuk); *domboc; liber judicialis of Alfred.*

Doomsday book. See DOMESDAY BOOK.

door-closing statute. (1960) A state law closing or denying access to local courts unless a plaintiff meets specified conditions; esp., a statute requiring a foreign corporation to "qualify" before doing business in the state, including registering with the secretary of state, paying a fee or tax, and appointing an agent to receive service of process.

doorkeeper. *Parliamentary law.* An officer charged with regulating access to the chamber or hall where a deliberative assembly meets. — Also termed *guard.*

doorstep loan. See LOAN.

doowop docket. *Slang.* See *DWOP docket* under DOCKET (2).

dope. (1889) **1.** A thick liquid used esp. for medicinal purposes. **2.** *Slang.* A drug, esp. a narcotic.

DORA. *abbr.* DEFENSE OF THE REALM ACT.

dormant (**dor**-mənt), *adj.* (15c) Inactive; suspended; latent <a dormant judgment>. — **dormancy,** *n.*

dormant claim. (18c) A claim that is in abeyance.

Dormant Commerce Clause. See COMMERCE CLAUSE.

dormant corporation. See CORPORATION.

dormant execution. See EXECUTION (4).

dormant judgment. See JUDGMENT (2).

dormant legislative intent. See LEGISLATIVE INTENT.

dormant partner. See *silent partner* under PARTNER.

dormant title. See TITLE (2).

dorsum (**dor**-səm). [Latin] *Hist.* The back. • This term usu. appeared as part of the phrase *in dorso* to indicate that an instrument had been signed on the back. *In dorso recordi,* for example, meant "on the back of the record."

> "In the first place then the payee, or person to whom or whose *order* such bill of exchange or promissory note is payable, may by endorsement, or writing his name in *dorso* or on the back of it, assign over his whole property to the bearer, or else to another person by name . . . ." 2 William Blackstone, *Commentaries on the Laws of England* 468 (1766).

dos (dos), *n.* [Latin] **1.** *Roman law.* Dowry.

> "Dos was a gift made to the husband on the part of the wife as her contribution towards the expenses of the joint establishment. It was made by the wife or by another person on her behalf, usually before marriage and conditionally on the marriage taking place; but it might also be made or increased after marriage." R.W. Lee, *The Elements of Roman Law* 150 (4th ed. 1956).

▸ ***dos adventitia*** (dos ad-ven-**tish**-ee-ə). [Latin] (18c) *Roman law.* A dowry brought by a bride to her husband when furnished by someone other than the bride or her father.

▸ ***dos profectitia*** (dos proh-fek-**tish**-ee-ə). [Latin] (17c) *Roman law.* A dowry brought by a bride to her husband when furnished by the bride's father or the bride herself.

▸ ***dos receptitia*** (dos ree-sep-**tish**-ee-ə). [Latin] *Roman law.* A dowry (whether *adventitia* or *profectitia*) that is specially stipulated to be returnable to the giver when the marriage ends.

2. *Hist.* Dower.

DoS attack. DENIAL-OF-SERVICE ATTACK.

dos rationabilis. See *dower by the common law* under DOWER.

dossier (**dos**-ee-ay), *n.* [French] (1880) A file or brief; a bundle of papers relating to a particular matter.

DOT. *abbr.* DEPARTMENT OF TRANSPORTATION.

dot (dot *or* dawt), *n.* [French fr. Latin *dos*] (1855) *Civil law.* Dowry; the property that a woman brings to the marriage to help with marriage expenses. • The income is usu. controlled by the husband, while the principal remains the wife's separate property.

dotage (**doh**-tij). (14c) **1.** Senility; feebleness of a person's mind in old age. **2.** Foolish affection; excessive fondness.

dotal (**doht**-əl), *adj.* (16c) Of, relating to, or involving a dowry. See DOWRY.

dotalitium (doh-tə-**lish**-ee-əm), *n.* [Law Latin] (18c) *Hist.* Dower.

> "[S]ome have ascribed the introduction of dower to the Normans, as a branch of *their* local tenures; though we cannot expect any feodal reason for its invention, since it was not a part of the pure, primitive, simple law of feuds, but was first of all introduced into that system (wherein it was called . . . *dotalitium*) by the emperor Frederick the second; who was contemporary with our king Henry III. It is possible therefore that it might be with us the relic of a Danish custom: since, according to the historians of that country, dower was introduced into Denmark by Swein, the father of our Canute the great, out of gratitude to the Danish ladies, who sold all their jewels to ransom him when taken prisoner by the Vandals." 2 William Blackstone, *Commentaries on the Laws of England* 129–30 (1766).

dotal property. See PROPERTY.

dotation (doh-**tay**-shən), *n.* (14c) **1.** The act of giving a dowry. **2.** An endowment, esp. of funds for a charitable institution such as a hospital.

dot-com, *adj.* (2000) Of, relating to, or involving a person or company whose business is done on the Internet.

dote (doht), *vb.* (13c) **1.** To be silly due to old age. **2.** To bestow excessive fondness.

dote assignanda (**doh**-tee as-ig-**nan**-də). See DE DOTE ASSIGNANDA.

dote unde nil habet (**doh**-tee **ən**-dee nil **hay**-bet). See DE DOTE UNDE NIL HABET.

dotis administratio (**doh**-tis ad-min-ə-**stray**-shee-oh). See DE ADMENSURATIONE DOTIS.

dotissa (doh-**tis**-ə), *n.* [Law Latin] A dowager.

double agent. See AGENT.

double adultery. See ADULTERY.

double assessment. See ASSESSMENT (2).

double audit. See AUDIT.

double-bill, *vb.* (1913) To charge two different clients or customers for the same time or expense; to charge two different customers for services rendered to each customer at the same time.

double-blind sequential lineup. See LINEUP.

double-breasted operation. (1976) An arrangement in which a business owner operates both a union business and a similar nonunion business, to compete for both types of business contracts. — Also termed *open-shop–closed-shop operation.*

double-breasting. (1983) *Labor law.* The practice by a common owner of dividing its employees between two companies, one that is unionized and is party to a collective-bargaining agreement, and one that is nonunion. — Also termed *dual-shop operation.*

double commission. See COMMISSION (5).

double complaint. See DUPLEX QUERELA.

double creditor. See CREDITOR.

double criminality. (1934) *Int'l law.* The punishability of a crime in both the country where a suspect is being held and a country asking for the suspect to be handed over to stand trial. • Double criminality is a requirement for extradition. — Also termed *dual criminality.*

double damages. See DAMAGES.

double-declining depreciation method. See DEPRECIATION METHOD.

double-dipping, *n.* (1975) An act of seeking or accepting essentially the same benefit twice, either from the same source or from two different sources, as in simultaneously accepting retirement and unemployment benefits. — **double-dipper,** *n.*

double entendre. (17c) A word or phrase that can be interpreted in two different ways — one of them usu. both subtle and either sexual or scatological.

double-entry bookkeeping. See BOOKKEEPING.

double forgery. See FORGERY.

double-fraction problem. (1957) *Oil & gas.* A common ambiguity that arises when the owner of a fractional interest conveys or reserves a fractional interest. • For example, if the owner of an undivided half interest in minerals conveys "an undivided half interest in the minerals," it is unclear whether the intention is to convey the owner's entire half interest or half of the owner's half interest.

double gibbet. See GIBBET.

double hearsay. See HEARSAY.

double indemnity. See INDEMNITY.

double insurance. See INSURANCE.

double Irish. A tax-avoidance strategy used by multinational corporations to shift income from a high-tax country to a lower-tax country by making payments between two or more related Irish-incorporated entities. • The name comes from Irish tax law, which does not tax the income of foreign subsidiaries of Irish corporations, even though the subsidiaries are incorporated in Ireland. This is also termed *double-Irish arrangement.* It may be combined with the use of a shell company in a nation such as the Netherlands, Luxembourg, or Switzerland to further reduce tax liabilities. This scheme is also termed *Dutch sandwich, Luxembourgish sandwich,* or *Swiss sandwich.*

double jeopardy. (1847) The fact of being prosecuted or sentenced twice for substantially the same offense. • Double jeopardy is prohibited by the Fifth Amendment. In 2005, the United Kingdom abolished the rule for certain serious offenses, such as murder and hijacking. A court may quash an acquittal and order a retrial if new and compelling evidence of the defendant's guilt is discovered, and the evidence was not available before the acquittal. Only one retrial is allowed. Cf. FORMER JEOPARDY.

Double Jeopardy Clause. (1928) The Fifth Amendment provision stating, "nor shall any person be subject for the same offence to be twice put in jeopardy of life or limb." • The clause, which was ratified in 1791, does not prevent postacquittal appeals by the government if those appeals could not result in the defendant's being subjected to a second trial for substantially the same offense before a second fact-trier. *See U.S. v. Wilson,* 420 U.S. 332, 95 S.Ct. 1013 (1975).

double-nexus test. A court's determination whether a taxpayer has standing to challenge an action of the federal government because there is (1) a logical link between taxpayer's status and the type of legislative enactment challenged, and (2) a nexus between that status and the precise nature of the alleged constitutional infringement. • This is an exception to the general rule that a taxpayer has no standing to challenge an action of the federal government. It was first announced in *Flast v. Cohen,* 392 U.S. 83, 104–05, 88 S.Ct. 1942, 1955 (1968). — Also termed *double-nexus analysis.*

double patenting. (1898) **1.** The obtaining of two patents covering the same invention. • An inventor is not allowed to receive more than one patent on one invention. 37 CFR 1.56. **2.** The issuance or obtaining of a patent for an invention that differs from an already patented invention only in some unpatentable detail. — Also termed *obviousness double patenting.*

▸ **judicially created double patenting.** (1985) The attempt to patent an invention that is an obvious variation of another invention by the same inventor when the first invention has already been patented or has a pending application. • Double patenting is grounds for rejecting a patent application, limiting the term of a patent through a terminal disclaimer, or invalidating a patent. *In re Longi,* 225 U.S.P.Q. 645 (Fed. Cir. 1985). A double-patenting challenge can be overcome by filing a terminal disclaimer. 37 CFR 1.321. — Also termed *obviousness-type double patenting.*

▸ **obviousness-type double patenting.** (1966) **1.** DOUBLE PATENTING (2). **2.** See *judicially created double patenting.*

▸ **same-invention double patenting.** See *statutory double patenting.*

▸ **statutory double patenting.** (1997) The attempt to patent an invention that is the same subject matter as another invention by the same inventor, when the first invention has already been patented or has a pending patent application. • Any double patenting is grounds for invalidating a patent claim or rejecting a claim in a patent application. 35 USCA § 101. — Also termed *same-invention double patenting.*

double plea. See PLEA (3).

double pleading. See DUPLICITY (3).

double possession. See POSSESSION.

double probate. See PROBATE (1).

double proof. See PROOF.

double-proxy marriage. See MARRIAGE (3).

double punishment. See PUNISHMENT (1).

double quarrel. See DUPLEX QUERELA.

double recovery. See RECOVERY.

double rent. See RENT (1).

double standard. (1900) A pair of principles that permit, esp. in a hypocritical way, greater opportunity or greater leniency for one class of people than for another, usu. based on a difference such as gender or race. See DISCRIMINATION (3).

double-talk, *n.* Complicated, subtle, often equivocal speech cunningly used to engender confusion or perpetrate deceit.

double taxation. See TAXATION (1).

double-taxation treaty. (1935) *Int'l law.* An international agreement designed to ameliorate the legal and financial consequences to taxpayers who have income that is taxable by two countries.

double use. See USE (1).

double value. Twice the value of something; specif., a penalty payable by a tenant to a landlord of twice the yearly value of lands held by the tenant, who refused to leave when the landlord provided written notice of intent to possess the property. • The penalty was provided under the Landlord and Tenant Act (1730). St. 4 Geo. 2. ch. 28, s. 1.

double voucher. (17c) In a common-recovery suit, a voucher first by the fictitious tenant to the real tenant, and then by the real tenant to the common vouchee. • The use of a fictitious tenant was necessary because if the recovery had been obtained directly against the real tenant, it would be effective only to the limited extent that the real tenant actually possessed an interest in the estate. But if recovery was obtained against another party, it would be effective against any latent interest that the real tenant might assert in the estate. See COMMON RECOVERY.

> "The recovery, here described, is with a *single* voucher only; but sometimes it is with *double* . . . or farther voucher, as the exigency of the case may require. And indeed it is now usual always to have a recovery with double voucher at the least; by first conveying an estate of freehold to any indifferent person, against whom the *praecipe* is brought; and then he vouches the tenant in tail, who vouches over the common vouchee. For, if a recovery be had immediately against tenant in tail, it bars only such estate in the premises of which he is then actually seised; whereas if the recovery be had against another person, and the tenant in tail be vouched, it bars every latent right and interest which he may have in the lands recovered." 2 William Blackstone, *Commentaries on the Laws of England* 359 (1766).

double waste. See WASTE (1).

double will. See *mutual will* under WILL.

doubt, reasonable. See REASONABLE DOUBT.

doubtful title. See TITLE (2).

doubt the vote. See DIVIDE THE ASSEMBLY.

doulocracy. See DULOCRACY.

doun (doon *or* dohn), *n.* [Law French] A gift.

do ut des (**doh** ət **deez**). [Latin "I give that you may give"] (16c) *Roman law.* An innominate contract in which a party gives something in exchange for something that the other party is to give. See *innominate contract* under CONTRACT.

do ut facias (**doh** ət **fay**-shee-əs). [Latin "I give that you may do"] (16c) *Roman law.* An innominate contract in which a person gives something to another person who is to do or perform certain work. See *innominate contract* and *bilateral contract* under CONTRACT.

dovetail seniority. (1964) The combination of seniority lists from merging companies into one list that allows employees to keep their premerger seniority.

Dow (dow). See DOW JONES INDUSTRIAL AVERAGE.

dowable (**dow**-ə-bəl), *adj.* (16c) **1.** Capable of being endowed <the widow received the dowable estate>. **2.** Capable of receiving dower <the woman was dowable of the estate>.

dowager (**dow**-ə-jər). (16c) A widow holding property or title — esp. a life estate in real property — received from her deceased husband.

dowager-queen. (16c) The widow of the king of England.• If she is also the mother of the reigning monarch, she may also by known as the *queen mother.* — Also written *dowager queen.* — Also termed *queen dowager*; *queen mother.*

> "A queen *dowager* is the widow of the king, and as such enjoys most of the privileges belonging to her as queen consort. But it is not high treason to conspire her death; or to violate her chastity . . . because the succession to the crown is not thereby endangered. Yet still, . . . no man can marry a queen dowager without special licence from the king, on pain of forfeiting his lands and goods. . . . A queen dowager, when married again to a subject, doth not lose her regal dignity, as peeresses dowager do their peerage when they marry commoners." 1 William Blackstone, *Commentaries on the Laws of England* 217 (1765).

dower (**dow**-ər). (14c) At common law, a wife's right, upon her husband's death, to a life estate in one-third of the land that he owned in fee. • With few exceptions, the wife could not be deprived of dower by any transfer made by her husband during his lifetime. Although most states have abolished dower, many states retaining the concept have expanded the wife's share to a life estate in all the land that her husband owned in fee. — Also termed *dowment*; *maritagium.* Cf. CURTESY.

▸ **consummate dower** (kən-**səm**-it *or* **kon**-sə-mit). (1894) A widow's interest in her deceased husband's estate until that interest is legally assigned to her. — Also termed *dower consummate.*

▸ **dower *ad ostium ecclesiae*** (ad **ahs**-tee-əm e-**klee**-z[h]ee-ee), *n.* [Law Latin "dower at the church door"] (16c) *Hist.* An endowment of dower made by a man to his wife at the church door or porch, usu. as part of the marriage ceremony.

> "DOWER AD OSTIUM ECCLESIAE . . . . This appears to have been the original English dower . . . . It was formerly the most usual species of dower, and, though latterly fallen into disuse, was not abolished until the statute of 3 & 4 Will. IV. c. 105, s. 13 . . . . The wife might be endowed of personalty or goods as well as of lands, and a trace of this ancient kind of dower is still distinctly preserved in the marriage ritual of the church of England, in the expression 'with all my worldly goods I thee endow.'" 1 Alexander M. Burrill, *A Law Dictionary and Glossary* 520 (2d ed. 1867).

▸ **dower by custom.** (17c) *Hist.* Dower that is determined by custom rather than the general law. — Also termed *dower by particular custom.*

> "Dower by . . . *custom*; as that the wife shall have half the husband's lands, or in some places the whole, and in some only a quarter." 2 William Blackstone, *Commentaries on the Laws of England* 132 (1766).

▸ **dower by particular custom.** See *dower by custom.*

▸ **dower by the common law.** (17c) The regular dower, consisting of a life interest in one-third of the lands that the husband held in fee. — Also termed *dos rationabilis* (dos rash-[ee]-ə-**nab**-ə-ləs).

▸ **dower consummate.** See *consummate dower.*

▸ **dower *ex assensu patris*** (eks ə-**sen**-s[y]oo **pa**-tris), *n.* [Law Latin "dower by the father's assent"] (17c) *Hist.* A type of dower *ad ostium ecclesiae* made while the husband's father is alive and consents to the endowment to his son's wife.

▸ **dower inchoate.** See *inchoate dower.*

▸ **election dower.** (1883) A widow's right to take a statutory share of her deceased husband's estate if she chooses to reject her share under a will. See RIGHT OF ELECTION.

▸ **equitable dower.** See *equitable jointure* under JOINTURE (1).

▸ **inchoate dower** (in-**koh**-it). (1862) A wife's interest in her husband's estate while both are living. — Also termed *dower inchoate.*

doweress. See DOWRESS.

Dow Jones Industrial Average. A stock-market-performance indicator that consists of the price movements in the stocks of 30 leading industrial companies in the

United States. — Abbr. DJIA. — Often shortened to *Dow.* — Also termed *Dow Jones Average.*

dowle stones (dohl). Rocks used as land boundaries. See CALL (5); LOCATIVE CALLS.

dowment. See DOWER.

down market. See *bear market* under MARKET.

down payment. See PAYMENT (2).

down reversal. *Securities.* A sudden market-price decline after a rising trend. • The term applies to the early stage of the decline; if the decline continues for several months, it is termed a *bear market.* — Also termed *correction; market correction.*

downright evidence. (1877) *Rare.* A preponderance of evidence.

downside. (1930) *Securities.* **1.** A downward movement of stock prices. **2.** The potential of a downward movement in stock prices. Cf. UPSIDE.

downside risk. (1972) *Securities.* A likely risk that stock prices will drop.

downside trend. (1982) *Securities.* The portion of the market cycle that shows declining stock prices. — Also termed *down trend.*

downsizing. (1975) Reducing the number of employees, usu. to decrease labor costs and to increase efficiency.

downstream, *adj. Oil & gas.* Of, relating to, or involving the process by which hydrocarbons are brought to market, including refining, processing, petrochemical transportation, and marketing of refined hydrocarbon products. Cf. UPSTREAM.

downstream guaranty. See GUARANTY (1).

downstream merger. See MERGER (8).

down trend. See DOWNSIDE TREND.

downward departure. See DEPARTURE (1).

downward sentence departure. See *downward departure* under DEPARTURE (1).

dowress (**dow**-ris). (16c) *Archaic.* **1.** A woman legally entitled to dower. **2.** A tenant in dower. — Also spelled *doweress.*

dowry (**dow**-ree). (14c) *Archaic.* The money, goods, or property that a woman brings to her husband in marriage. — Also termed *marriage portion; maritagium* (mair-ə-**tay**-jee-əm); *maritage* (**mair**-i-tij).

dozen peers. *Hist.* During the reign of Henry III, 12 peers assembled by the barons to be the King's advisers.

DP. *abbr.* DIVERSION PROGRAM.

D.P. *abbr.* DOMUS PROCERUM.

DPA. *abbr.* Deferred-prosecution agreement.

DP letter. *abbr.* DECLINE-TO-PROSECUTE LETTER.

DPP. *abbr.* DIRECT-PARTICIPATION PROGRAM.

DPPA. *abbr.* DEADBEAT PARENTS PUNISHMENT ACT.

DPW. *abbr.* DEPARTMENT OF PUBLIC SERVICES.

Dr. *abbr.* **1.** DEBTOR. **2.** DOCTOR.

DR. *abbr.* DISCIPLINARY RULE.

DRA. *abbr.* DRIVER-RESPONSIBILITY ASSESSMENT.

draconian (dray- *or* drə-**koh**-nee-in), *adj.* (18c) (Of a law) harsh, severe, strict, and even cruel. • This term derives from *Draco,* the name of the ancient Athenian lawgiver. — Also termed *draconic.*

draff (draf). (13c) Refuse; dregs; sweepings of dust and dirt. • In weighing commodities, it is excluded from the waste allowance for goods sold by weight.

draft, *n.* (17c) **1.** An unconditional written order signed by one person (the *drawer*) directing another person (the *drawee* or *payor*) to pay a certain sum of money on demand or at a definite time to a third person (the *payee*) or to bearer. • A check is the most common example of a draft. — Also spelled *draught.* — Also termed *bill of exchange; letter of exchange.* Cf. NOTE (1).

▸ **bank draft.** (1835) A draft drawn by one financial institution on another.

▸ **bearer draft.** See *bearer check* under CHECK.

▸ **clean draft.** (1939) A draft with no shipping documents attached.

▸ **demand draft.** See *sight draft.*

▸ **documentary draft.** (1922) **1.** A payment demand conditioned on the presentation of a document, such as a document of title, invoice, certificate, or notice of default. — Also termed *documentary demand for payment.* **2.** A negotiable or nonnegotiable draft with accompanying documents, securities, or other papers to be delivered against honor of the draft.

▸ **export draft.** (1921) A draft drawn by a domestic seller on a foreign buyer, directing the buyer to pay the trade amount to the seller or the seller's bank.

▸ **foreign draft.** (1870) A draft drawn in one country or state but payable in another. — Also termed *foreign bill of exchange; international bill of exchange.*

▸ **inland draft.** (1855) A draft drawn and payable in the same state or country.

▸ **order draft.** See *order check* under CHECK.

▸ **overdraft.** See OVERDRAFT.

▸ **sales draft.** (1910) A draft drawn on a purchaser of goods proportioned to their price and insuring payment for them. — Also termed *sales bill; sales bill of exchange.*

▸ **share draft.** (1978) A demand that a member draws against a credit-union share account, payable to a third party. • A share draft is similar to a check that is written to draw funds out of a checking account at a bank.

▸ **sight draft.** (1842) A draft that is payable on the bearer's demand or on proper presentment to the drawee. — Also termed *demand draft.*

▸ **time draft.** (1847) A draft that contains a specified payment date. UCC § 3-108. — Also termed *time bill.*

▸ **trade draft.** A draft that instructs a commercial enterprise or its agent to pay the amount specified.

2. The compulsory enlistment of persons into military service <his illness disqualified him from the draft>. — Also termed *conscription; military draft.* **3.** An initial or preliminary version; a piece of writing not yet in its finished form <the second draft of the contract>.

▸ **document draft.** A first or intermediate version of a writing.

draft, *vb.* (18c) **1.** To write or compose (a plan, letter, report, etc.) in its initial form, which will need to be revised and polished before it is finished <to draft a contract>. **2.** To recruit or select (someone) <to draft someone to run for political office> <to draft someone into the armed services>.

draft board. (1918) A civilian board that registers and selects persons for mandatory military service. See SELECTIVE SERVICE SYSTEM.

draft card. A notification sent to someone informing the recipient that he or she has been drafted into the armed forces.

draft dodger. Someone who illegally avoids joining the armed forces despite having been ordered to join.

drafter. (1884) Someone who draws or frames a legal document, such as a will, contract, or legislative bill. — Also termed *draftsman.*

drafting. (1878) The skill, technique, and practice of preparing operative legal documents such as statutes, rules, regulations, contracts, and wills setting forth the rights, duties, privileges, and liabilities of people and legal entities. — Also termed *legal drafting.*

> "[T]he approach to drafting and the approach to interpretation must always go hand in hand." Francis G. Jacobs, "Approaches to Interpretation in a Plurilingual Legal System," in *A True European: Essays for Judge David Edward* 297, 299–300 (Mark Hoskins & William Robinson eds., 2003).

draftsman. See DRAFTER.

dragnet. 1. A net that is pulled along the bottom of a river, creek, or lake to dredge up things that may be there. **2.** By extension, a system in which the police look for criminals using systematic and thorough methods.

dragnet arrest. See ARREST (2).

dragnet clause. 1. See MOTHER HUBBARD CLAUSE (1). **2.** See CROSS-COLLATERAL CLAUSE.

dragnet lien. See LIEN.

Drago doctrine. (1906) The principle asserted by Luis Drago, Minister of Foreign Affairs of the Argentine Republic, in a December 29, 1902 letter to the Argentine Minister in Washington, in which Drago, responding to the forcible coercion of Venezuela's unpaid loans by Great Britain and others, argued that no public debt should be collected from a sovereign state by force or through the occupation of American territory by a foreign power. • The subject was presented at the Hague Conference of 1907, when a modified version of the Drago doctrine was adopted.

drain, *n.* (16c) **1.** The act of drawing a liquid off gradually; the act of emptying. **2.** The act of gradually exhausting. **3.** A conduit for draining liquid, as a ditch or a pipe.

drain, *vb.* (bef. 12c) **1.** To draw (a liquid) off gradually <the farmer drained water from the property>. **2.** To exhaust gradually <the facility has drained the area's natural resources>. **3.** To empty gradually <the water drained>.

drainage district. (1857) A political subdivision authorized to levy assessments for making drainage improvements within its area.

drainage rights. (1871) The interest that a property owner has in the natural drainage and flow of water on the land.

dram (dram). (15c) **1.** An apothecary measurement of fluid equal to an eighth of an ounce. **2.** A small amount of anything, esp. liquor.

drama, *n.* (16c) **1.** A presentation of a story portrayed by words and actions or actions alone; a play. Cf. DRAMATIC COMPOSITION.

> "The term [*drama*] is applied to compositions which imitate action by representing the personages introduced in them as real and as employed in the action itself. The varieties of the drama differ more or less widely, both as to the objects imitated and as to the means used in the imitation. But they all agree as to the *method* or *manner* which is essential to the dramatic art, viz., *imitation in the way of action.*" 7 *Encyclopaedia Britannica* 338 (9th ed. 1907).

2. An event or series of events having conflicting and exciting elements that capture people's attention.

drama-pricing. (2006) A seller's tactic of dramatically dropping the price of something, esp. real estate, to attract a buyer. — Also termed *trauma-pricing.*

dramatic composition. (17c) *Copyright.* A literary work setting forth a story, incident, or scene intended to be performed by actors, often with a musical accompaniment. Cf. DRAMA (1).

dramatic work. See WORK (2).

dram shop. (18c) *Archaic.* A place where alcoholic beverages are sold; a bar or saloon. — Also spelled *dram-shop; dramshop.* — Also termed *grog-shop; drinking shop.*

dram-shop act. (1859) A statute allowing a plaintiff to recover damages from a commercial seller of alcoholic beverages for the plaintiff's injuries caused by a customer's intoxication. — Also termed *civil-liability act; civil-damage law.*

dram-shop liability. (1995) Civil liability of a commercial seller of alcoholic beverages for personal injury caused by an intoxicated customer. • Claims based on a similar type of liability have been brought against private citizens for personal injury caused by an intoxicated social guest.

draught. See DRAFT (1).

draw, *vb.* (13c) **1.** To create and sign (a draft) <draw a check to purchase goods>. **2.** To prepare or frame (a legal document) <draw up a will>. **3.** To take out (money) from a bank, treasury, or depository <she drew $6,000 from her account>. **4.** To select (a jury) <the lawyers began voir dire and had soon drawn a jury>.

draw and quarter, *vb.* (16c) **1.** *Hist.* To attach each of a person's limbs to a different horse, and then cause each horse to pull until the victim is torn apart. • This was an ancient form of execution reserved for acts of treason. Cf. HANGED, DRAWN, AND QUARTERED. **2.** (*fig.*) To punish or criticize severely.

drawback. (17c) **1.** A disadvantage of a situation, plan, product, etc. **2.** A government allowance or refund on import duties when the importer reexports imported products rather than selling them domestically. 19 USCA § 1313.

drawee (draw-ee). (18c) The person or entity that a draft is directed to and that is requested to pay the amount stated on it. UCC § 3-103(a)(4). • The drawee is usu. a bank that is directed to pay a sum of money on an instrument. UCC § 4-105(3). — Also termed *payor; payor bank.*

drawee bank. See *payor bank* under BANK.

drawee institution. See *payor bank* under BANK.

drawer. (17c) **1.** Someone who directs a person or entity, usu. a bank, to pay a sum of money stated in an instrument — for example, a person who writes a check. UCC § 3-103(a)(5). See MAKER. **2.** Under the UCC, a person who signs or is identified in a draft as a person ordering payment. UCC § 3-103(a)(5).

drawing. (1832) **1.** *Patents.* A specially prepared figure included with a patent application to explain and describe the invention. • A drawing is required when necessary to understand the invention. 35 USCA § 113. **2.** *Trademarks.* A graphic or textual depiction of a trademark, filed as part of an application for the mark to be placed on the primary register. • The drawing serves as the element that is published in the *Official Gazette.* It must include the applicant's name and address, the type of goods or services it will identify, and the date of first use or a statement of intent to use it in commerce.

▸ **formal drawing.** (1940) A drawing that complies with the formatting requirements of the U.S. Patent and Trademark Office, as set forth in 37 CFR 1.84, and is stamped "Approved" by the PTO Drafter. Cf. *informal drawing.*

▸ **front-page drawing.** A drawing submitted with the patent application and selected by the examiner as the application's representative drawing. • The drawing is reproduced on the front page of the published application or patent.

▸ **informal drawing.** (1969) A drawing that does not comply with the formatting requirements of the U.S. Patent and Trademark Office. • A drawing may be submitted as informal by the patent applicant, or declared informal by the PTO Drafter. Cf. *formal drawing.*

▸ **original drawing.** (1845) A drawing submitted with the original application.

▸ **special-form drawing.** (2003) A drawing of a trademark that contains some graphical element, such as a logo, a picture, or a special type style. • A stylized or special-form drawing must be submitted in black-and-white, with a description of the colors to be used on the final mark. — Also termed *stylized drawing.*

▸ **substitute drawing.** (1925) A drawing submitted after the original application has been filed. • A substitute drawing is often a formal drawing filed to replace an informal drawing.

▸ **typed drawing.** (1983) A drawing of a trademark that is purely textual, with no graphical component. • A typed drawing consists solely of the words, letters, and numbers that make up the mark, typed in all-capitals. — Also termed *typed-form drawing.*

drawing account. See ACCOUNT.

drawing lots. (13c) An act of selection or decision-making based on pure chance, with the result depending on the particular lot drawn. • Jurors are usu. instructed by the court not to base their verdict on drawing lots or similar methods of chance.

drawlatch. (14c) *Hist.* A thief; a robber who waits until homes are empty, then draws the homes' door latches to steal what is inside.

drayage. (18c) A charge for transporting property.

drayman. (16c) **1.** *Hist.* The driver of a horse- or mule-drawn low, sideless, flatbed wagon used to transport goods. • The wagon was called a *dray.* **2.** *Archaic.* The driver of a vehicle used to deliver a brewery's beverages. **3.** The driver of a truck that carries shipping containers between a port or railyard and the shippers or recipients. Cf. CARTMAN (2).

DRD. *abbr.* **1.** See *deduction in respect of a decedent* under DEDUCTION (2). **2.** DIVIDEND-RECEIVED DEDUCTION.

DRE. *abbr.* DRUG-RECOGNITION EXPERT.

dread-disease insurance. See INSURANCE.

dreit dreit. See DROIT-DROIT.

D reorganization. See REORGANIZATION (2).

drift of the forest. (17c) *Hist.* A periodic examination of forest cattle by officers who drive them to an enclosed place to determine their ownership or common status.

> "Drift of the forest is nothing else but an exact view or examination taken once, twice, or oftener in a year as occasion shall require, what beasts there are in the forest, to the end that the common in the forest be not over-charged, that the beasts of foreigners that have no common there be not permitted, and that beasts not commonable may be put out." *Termes de la Ley* 185–87 (1st Am. ed. 1812).

drift-stuff. (1853) Any material floating at random in water without a discoverable source. • Drift-stuff is usu. the property of the riparian owner.

drilling contract. (1907) *Oil & gas.* A well-drilling agreement between a drilling contractor, who owns drilling rigs and associated equipment, and the owner or lessor of the mineral rights. • The contract spells out the rights and duties of the parties. In general, the more control the interest-owner retains over the contractor, the more liability the owner is exposed to for damages the drilling causes.

▸ **daywork drilling contract.** (1980) *Oil & gas.* A contract under which the lease operator hires a drilling rig and oilfield workers, pays an amount based on the time spent in drilling operations, and retains the right to direct drilling operations. • This type of contract gives the lease operator broad control over the drilling contractor, so courts in turn impose broad liability on the lease operator for any damages that result from the drilling. Cf. *footage drilling contract; turnkey drilling contract.*

▸ **footage drilling contract.** (1937) *Oil & gas.* A drilling contract under which the drilling contractor is paid to drill to a specified formation or depth, is paid a set amount per foot drilled, and is given broad control over how to do the work. • The risk of unexpected delays, as well as most liabilities, is on the contractor rather than the lease operator under this type of contract. Cf. *daywork drilling contract; turnkey drilling contract.*

▸ **turnkey drilling contract.** (1921) *Oil & gas.* A drilling contract under which the drilling contractor promises to perform specified functions for an agreed price. • The lease operator has little or no discretion to control the drilling contractor, and so assumes little or no liability for damages the drilling may cause. Cf. *daywork drilling contract; footage drilling contract.*

drilling-delay rental clause. (1986) *Oil & gas.* A provision in an oil-and-gas lease giving the lessee the right to maintain the lease from period to period during the primary term by paying delay rentals instead of starting drilling operations. • Lessees use drilling-delay rental clauses because courts have said that they obviate any implied covenant to drill a test well on the premises. They are accepted by lessors because they provide for periodic income from the lease. See *"or" lease*, *"unless" lease* under LEASE.

drinking age. See AGE.

drinking-driver program. (1979) In some states, an educational course for people convicted of a drunk-driving offense. • When the course has been completed, the participant's driver's license is usu. restored, subject to case-specific conditions. See DRIVING WHILE INTOXICATED.

drinking shop. See DRAM SHOP.

drink-spiking. See SPIKING.

DRIP. *abbr.* DIVIDEND-REINVESTMENT PLAN.

drip rights. A servitude allowing water dripping off a person's roof to fall on a neighbor's land. Cf. AQUAE IMMITTENDAE; *servitus stillicidii* under SERVITUS.

driver. (15c) **1.** Someone who steers and propels a vehicle. **2.** Someone who herds animals; a drover. **3.** A piece of software that allows a computer to work with another piece of hardware such as a mouse or a printer.

driver-responsibility assessment. (2001) In some states, an additional financial penalty imposed on a drunk-driving convict, such as a yearly payment of a specified amount to the department of motor vehicles. — Abbr. DRA.

driver's education. (1950) A training course, taken usu. by teenagers, that teaches one how to drive a car. • Completion of the course, whose requirements vary by state, is typically a condition for acquiring a driver's license. In the United States, this prerequisite generally applies only to minors; legal adults need only pass a driver's test.

driver's license. (1882) The state-issued certificate authorizing a person to operate a motor vehicle; an official document or card stating the owner is legally allowed to drive. • It is also often used as a form of identification. — Also termed (in some states) *driver license*; (BrE) *driving licence.*

▸ **commercial driver's license.** (1951) A driver's license issued specifically for the operation of commercial vehicles. • Such a license is required by federal law but is issued under state law.

▸ **conditional driver's license.** (1942) A limited driver's license that allows some driving privileges to a participant in a diversion program. — Also termed *occupational driver's license*; *restricted driver's license*; *post-revocation conditional license.*

▸ **hardship license.** (1968) **1.** See HARDSHIP PRIVILEGE. **2.** A restricted driver's license issued to a 14- to 16-year-old driver (below the minimum driving age) who demonstrates a necessity to drive. • In states that issue such licenses, the driver is usually required to demonstrate a serious hardship—e.g., family financial or medical problems—that leaves the driver with no other practical way of getting to and from school or work. These licenses typically restrict driving privileges such as the number of passengers allowed, the hours permitted for driving, and the routes the driver may take.

▸ **occupational driver's license.** See *conditional driver's license.*

▸ **post-revocation conditional license.** (1998) A restricted-use driver's license discretionarily accorded to a convicted motorist who is eligible for relicensure but who must comply with specific terms, such as an ignition-interlock device. See *conditional driver's license.*

▸ **provisional driver's license.** (1950) A driver's license showing that one is still becoming proficient and must complete a period of training before obtaining an unrestricted license. — Also termed *learner's permit.*

▸ **restricted driver's license.** See *conditional driver's license.*

▸ **restricted-use license.** (1976) A driver's license permitting its holder to have limited driving privileges. — Abbr. RUL.

driver's test. (1874) The official test that one must pass in order to be legally allowed to drive on public roads. — Also termed *driving test.*

driving, *n.* (15c) The act of directing the course of something, such as an automobile or a herd of animals.

driving under the influence. (1924) The offense of operating a motor vehicle in a physically or mentally impaired condition, esp. after consuming alcohol or drugs. • Generally, this is a lesser offense than driving while intoxicated. But in a few jurisdictions the two are synonymous. — Abbr. DUI. — Also termed *driving while ability-impaired* (DWAI); *driving under the influence of liquor* (DUIL); *driving while intoxicated* (DWI); *operating under the influence* (OUI); *operating while intoxicated* (OWI); *operating a motor vehicle while intoxicated* (OMVI); *operating a motor vehicle under the influence* (OMVUI). Cf. DRIVING WHILE INTOXICATED.

driving while ability-impaired. See DRIVING UNDER THE INFLUENCE.

driving while black. (1990) *Slang.* A law-enforcement officer's stopping of an African-American motorist for a minor traffic offense because the officer is suspicious that the motorist is or has been engaged in criminal activity; specif., the racial profiling of a black driver. — Abbr. DWB. — Also termed (of Hispanics) *driving while brown.* See RACIAL PROFILING.

driving while intoxicated. (1913) **1.** The offense of operating a motor vehicle in a physically or mentally impaired condition after consuming enough alcohol to raise one's blood alcohol content above the statutory limit (.08% in many states), or after consuming drugs. • Penalties vary widely; for example, the maximum penalty in Missouri and Louisiana is a $500 fine and six months in jail, while the penalties in New York range from $500 to $5,000 in fines and up to four years in jail. **2.** DRIVING UNDER THE INFLUENCE. — Abbr. DWI. — Also termed *drunk driving*; *operating a vehicle while intoxicated* (OMVI). Cf. DRIVING UNDER THE INFLUENCE; BWI.

▸ **baby DWI.** (2007) Under a zero-tolerance statute that severely restricts drinking while driving for those under the age of 21, a driving-while-intoxicated charge for operating a motor vehicle after consuming even a very low amount of alcohol (as low as .02% blood alcohol content). See ZERO-TOLERANCE LAW.

▸ **common-law DWI.** (1985) A driving-while-intoxicated charge to be proved not by a chemical test but by testimony about the defendant's physical condition and erratic, unsafe driving.

▸ **felony DWI.** (1975) A driving-while-intoxicated charge prosecutable as a felony because of an aggravating circumstance, esp. if a minor under a specified age (often 15 or below) was a passenger, the driver had a previous DWI within a specified period (often ten years), or the driver caused an injury accident.

▸ **per se DWI.** (1975) A strict-liability statute that eliminates the need for the state to prove intoxication if the defendant's blood alcohol content is above a specified level.

DRL. *abbr.* BUREAU OF DEMOCRACY, HUMAN RIGHTS, AND LABOR.

DRM. See *direct-reduction mortgage* under MORTGAGE.

drofland (**drohf**-lənd). (17c) *Hist.* A socage tenure that required the holder to drive the landlord's cattle to fairs and markets.

droit (drwah *or* droyt). [French "right"] (15c) **1.** A legal right or claim. **2.** The whole body of law.

droit administratif. (**drawh** ad-mee-nee-strə-**teef**). **1.** *French law.* Administrative law. **2.** In English, more specifically, the rules of European administrative laws that exempt governmental agents from liability except through legal actions conducted in administrative tribunals.

> "[I]t is necessary to contrast the administrative law of the common-law countries with the *droit administratif* of the Continental countries. The difference between them lies in a divergency of constitutional conceptions, particularly in the relation of the ordinary courts to the administrative machinery. Unlike the administrative law of Anglo-American countries, *droit admnistratif* seems to possess a very definite and logical character. It is the law administered by special administrative courts having jurisdiction of all controversies in which executive acts are brought into question. For the prosecution of crime and suits between private parties the ordinary courts of civil and criminal jurisdiction are available; but in any suit in which a public official becomes a party, only the administrative courts are deemed competent." William Seagle, *The Quest for Law* 330–31 (1941).

droit-close (droyt **klohz**), *n.* [Law French] (17c) *Hist.* A writ against a lord on behalf of a tenant in ancient demesne holding land by charter in fee simple, in fee-tail, for life, or in dower.

droit common (droyt **kom**-ən), *n.* [Law French] The common law. — Also termed *droit coutumier.* See COMMON LAW (2).

droit coutumier. See DROIT COMMON.

droit d'accession (**drwah** dak-ses-**syawn**), *n.* [French "right of accession"] *Civil law.* The right of the owner of a thing to whatever is produced by it or is united with it, either naturally or artificially. La. Civ. Code arts. 483, 490, 507. • The equivalent of the Roman *specificatio*, the right includes, for example, the right of a landowner to new land deposited on a riverbank and the right of an orchard owner to the fruit of the trees in the orchard. See ACCESSION (5).

> "DROIT D'ACCESSION . . . . The civil law rule is that if the thing can be reduced to the former matter it belongs to the owner of the matter, e.g. a statue made of gold; but if it cannot so be reduced it belongs to the person who made it, e.g. a statue made of marble." 1 John Bouvier, *Bouvier's Law Dictionary* 941 (Francis Rawle ed., 8th ed. 1914).

droit d'accroissement (**drwah** da-krwas-**mawn**), *n.* [French] *French law.* A right of survivorship by which an heir's interest is combined with the interest of a coheir who either has refused or is unable to accept the interest.

droit d'aubaine (**drwah** doh-**ben**), *n.* [Law French "right of alienage"] *Hist.* With certain exceptions, a sovereign's right to a deceased alien's property, regardless of whether the alien had a will. • This right was primarily exercised in France where it was revived in some form by Napoleon after its initial abolishment in 1790. It was ultimately abolished in 1819. — Also spelled *droit d'aubaigne; droit d'aubenage.* — Also termed *jus albanagii; jus albinatus.*

> "Under the French rule of law, known as the *droit d'aubaine* . . . the whole property of an alien dying in France without leaving children born in that country escheated to the crown. The royal right was not universally exacted, and at a very early period special exceptions were introduced in favour of certain classes. Thus Louis XI exempted merchants of Brabant, Flanders, Holland, and Zealand from the operation of the law, and a similar privilege was extended by Henri II to merchants of the Hanse towns, and from Scotland." 1 R.H. Inglis Palgrave, *Palgrave's Dictionary of Political Economy* 68 (Henry Higgs ed., 2d ed. 1925).

> "In France by the fourteenth century it was accepted that a stranger might acquire and possess but not inherit or transmit by will or on intestacy. In 1386 the French king assumed the seigneurial *droit d'aubaine* or right to inherit. In treaties in the seventeenth and eighteenth centuries the right was frequently renounced. Louis XVI in 1787 abolished the right as against subjects of Great Britain without reciprocity. The constituent Assembly abolished the right in 1790 and it was commonly abolished elsewhere in the early nineteenth century." David M. Walker, *The Oxford Companion to Law* 378 (1980).

droit d'auteur (**drwah** doh-**tər**), *n.* [French "author's right"] The copyright system used in France and other civil-law countries and differing from common-law copyright by giving more protection to an author's moral right. See AUTHOR'S RIGHT.

droit de bris (**drwah** də **bree**), *n.* [Law French "right of a wreck"] *Hist.* A right claimed by lords of the coasts of France to fragments of shipwrecks, including persons or property that had washed ashore. • The right was exercised primarily in Bretagne but was abrogated by Henry III as duke of Normandy, Aquitaine, and Guienne, in a charter granted in A.D. 1226. — Also termed *droit de bris sur le naufrages.* Cf. DROIT DE NAUFRAGE.

droit de cuissage. See DROIT DU SEIGNEUR.

droit de détraction (**drwah** də day-trak-**syawn**), *n.* [French "the right of withdrawal"] *Int'l law.* A tax on property acquired by succession or by will and then removed to another state or country.

droit de garde (**drwah** də **gahrd**), *n.* [French "right of ward"] *Hist. French law.* A king's right to wardship of a noble vassal who has not reached majority.

droit de gite (**drwah** də **zheet**), *n.* [French "right of lodging"] *Hist. French law.* A duty of a commoner holding land in the royal domain to provide lodging and food to a royal party traveling on royal business.

droit de greffe (**drwah** də **gref**), *n.* [French "a right concerning the clerk's office"] *Hist. French law.* The Crown's privilege to sell offices connected with the custody of judicial records or official acts.

droit de maitrise (**drwah** də may-**treez**), *n.* [French "a right of mastership"] *Hist. French law.* A required payment to the Crown by an apprentice who has become a master worker.

droit de naufrage (**drwah** də noh-**frazh**), *n.* [French] *Hist. French law.* The right of a sovereign or a lord owning a seashore to seize the wreckage of a shipwreck and kill the crew or sell them as slaves. Cf. DROIT DE BRIS.

droit de prise (**drwah** də **preez**), *n.* [French "a right of prize"] *Hist. French law.* A commoner's duty to supply articles on credit to the royal household for domestic consumption.

droit de quint (**drwah** də **kant**), *n.* [French "the right of a fifth"] *Hist. French law.* A required payment made by a noble vassal to the king each time ownership of the vassal's fief changed.

droit de suite (**drwah** də **sweet**), *n.* [French "right to follow"] (18c) **1.** A creditor's right to recover a debtor's property after it passes to a third party. **2.** *Copyright.* An artist's resale royalty; the right of a work's creator to benefit from appreciation in the value of the work by receiving a portion of the profit from its later resales. • A *droit de suite* is recognized in all member states of the European Union and in California.

> "The *droit de suite* (literally translated as the right to follow the work) enables artists to claim a portion of the price for which a work is resold. The idea is that an artist may sell a painting for a low price at a time when they are unknown and have little bargaining power. In due course, as the artist's reputation develops, the painting may be resold for continually increasing sums. . . . The right is seen to be justified not only because it encourages creation, but also because the artist is conceived (through the authorial link) as being responsible for the increase in value (economic success of their works)." Lionel Bently & Brad Sherman, *Intellectual Property Law* 281 (2001).

droit d'exécution (**drwah** dek-say-kyoo-**syawn**), *n.* [French "right of execution"] *French law.* **1.** A stockbroker's right to sell the stock bought for a client who later refuses it. **2.** A stockbroker's right to sell deposited securities to secure the broker against a loss in buying for a client.

droit-droit (drwah-drwah), *n.* [Law French "double right"] (18c) *Hist.* The unification of the right of possession with the right of property. — Also termed *jus duplicatum; dreit dreit.*

> "A complete title to lands, tenements, and hereditaments. For it is an ancient maxim of the law, that no title is completely good, unless the right of possession be joined with the right of property; which right is then denominated a double right, *jus duplicatum,* or *droit droit.* And when to this double right the actual possession is also united . . . then, and then only, is the title completely legal." 2 William Blackstone, *Commentaries on the Laws of England* 199 (1766).

droit du seigneur (**drwah** də sen-**yuur**). [French "right of the lord"] (1825) *Hist.* **1.** A supposed customary right of a feudal lord to have sexual intercourse with a tenant's bride on her wedding night. **2.** A supposed custom requiring sexual abstinence by a couple on their wedding night. — Also spelled *droit de seigneur.* — Also termed *jus primae noctis; ius primae noctis; jus primae nocte; droit de cuissage; right-of-right night.*

droit écrit (**drwaht** ay-**kree**), *n.* [French "the written law"] *French law.* The civil law; the *corpus juris civilis.*

droit foncier (drwah fahn-see-**ay**), *n.* [French] The law of property.

droit international (**drwaht** an-tair-nah-syoh-**nahl**), *n.* [French] International law.

droit maritime (**drwah** ma-ree-**teem**). [French] Maritime law.

droit moral (**drwah** maw-**ral**). [French] The doctrine of moral right, which entitles artists to prevent others from altering their works. • The basic rights protected by this doctrine are (1) the right to create, (2) the right to disclose or publish, (3) the right to withdraw from publication, (4) the right to be identified with the work, and (5) the right to ensure the integrity of the work, including the right to object to any mutilation or distortion of the work. These rights are sometimes called *moral rights.* See MORAL RIGHT.

droit naturel (**drwah** na-tuu-**rel**), *n.* [French] Natural law.

droits civils (**drwah** see-**veel**), *n.* [French] *French law.* Private rights not connected to a person's civil status. • Foreigners had certain rights that could be enforced when there was reciprocity with the foreigner's home country.

droits of admiralty (droyts), *n.* (18c) The Lord High Admiral's rights in connection with the sea, such as the right to recover proceeds from shipwrecks, enemy goods confiscated at the beginning of hostilities, jetsam, flotsam, treasure, deodand, fines, forfeitures, sturgeons, whales, and other large fishes. • The droit proceeds are paid to the Exchequer's office for the public's use. See PRIZE (2).

> "The crown had originally certain rights to property found upon the sea, or stranded upon the shore. The chief kinds of property to which the crown was thus entitled were, great fish (such as whales or porpoises), deodands, wreck of the sea, flotsam, jetsam, and lagan, ships or goods of the enemy found in English ports or captured by uncommissioned vessels, and goods taken or retaken from pirates . . . . After the rise of the court of Admiralty the Lord High Admiral became entitled to these droits by royal grant . . . . The right to droits carried with it a certain jurisdiction. Inquisitions were held into these droits at the ports, or the Vice-Admirals or droit gatherers reported them to the Admiral. The large terms of the Admiral's Patents incited them, or their grantees, to frequent litigation with private persons or other grantees of the crown . . . . The Admiralty droits . . . are now transferred to the consolidated fund." 1 William Holdsworth, *A History of English Law* 559–61 (7th ed. 1956).

droitural (**droy**-chə-rəl), *adj.* [fr. Old French *droiture* "right"] (18c) Of, relating to, or involving an interest in property, as distinguished from actual possession.

droit voisins (**drwah** vwah-**san**), *n.* [French] NEIGHBORING RIGHT.

dromones (drə-**moh**-neez), *n. pl.* (14c) *Hist.* **1.** Large ships. **2.** War vessels of recognized navies, usu. prepared for hostilities. — Also termed *dromos; dromunda.*

Droop quota. (1894) In some proportional-representation elections, the minimum number of votes needed to win a legislative seat. • The quota is determined by a formula based on the reciprocal of the number of representatives plus one — or 1/(n + 1), where "n" is the number of representatives being elected. The term is named for the developer of the election format, Henry Richmond Droop (1831–1884).

drop. *English law.* A rule *nisi* that is not adopted because the members of a court are equally divided on the issue. • The rule is dropped rather than discharged or made absolute.

drop-dead date. (1982) The date by which one must have completed something because any later efforts are useless and ineffective; esp., the date by which performance is required as a condition. Cf. TIME-IS-OF-THE-ESSENCE CLAUSE.

drop-dead provision. (1985) *Contracts.* A clause in an agreement or order allowing a party to take action without notice if the other party fails to perform certain acts.

drop-down clause. (1987) *Insurance.* An insurance-policy provision requiring an excess insurer to provide coverage to the insured even though the underlying coverage has not been exhausted, usu. because the underlying insurers are insolvent.

drop letter. (1847) A letter addressed to someone in the delivery area of the post office where the letter was posted.

drop-shipment delivery. (1917) A manufacturer's shipment of goods directly to the consumer rather than initially to a wholesaler. • If the wholesaler takes the order, it may receive part of the profit from the sale. — Often shortened to *drop-ship.*

drop shipper. (1964) A wholesaler who arranges to have goods shipped directly from a manufacturer to a consumer. See DROP-SHIPMENT DELIVERY.

dropsy testimony. See TESTIMONY.

drove, *n.* (bef. 12c) **1.** A group of animals driven in a herd. **2.** A large group of people in motion.

drover's pass. (1863) A free pass issued by a railroad company to the cattle's drover, who accompanies the cattle on the train.

DRP. *abbr.* **1.** DIVIDEND-REINVESTMENT PLAN. **2.** DISPUTE-RESOLUTION PROCEDURE.

drug, *n.* (14c) **1.** A substance intended for use in the diagnosis, cure, treatment, or prevention of disease. **2.** A natural or synthetic substance that alters one's perception or consciousness. See CONTROLLED SUBSTANCE.

▸ **addictive drug.** (1965) A drug (such as heroin or nicotine) that, usu. after repeated consumption, causes physical dependence and results in well-defined physiological symptoms upon withdrawal.

▸ **adulterated drug.** (1855) A drug that does not have the strength, quality, or purity represented or expected.

▸ **copycat drug.** See *generic drug.*

▸ **dangerous drug.** (1884) A drug that has potential for abuse or injury, usu. requiring a label warning that it cannot be dispensed without a prescription.

▸ **designer drug.** (1983) A chemical substance that is created to duplicate the pharmacological effects of controlled substances, often by using the same chemicals contained in controlled substances, but manipulating their formulas.

▸ **ethical drug.** (1940) A drug that can be dispensed only with a doctor's prescription. Cf. *proprietary drug.*

▸ **gateway drug.** (1982) A drug (such as marijuana) that is not in itself particularly dangerous but that some believe will lead people to experiment with more dangerous drugs such as cocaine or heroin.

▸ **generic drug.** (1961) A drug containing the active ingredients but not necessarily the same excipient substances (such as binders or capsules) as the pioneer drug marketed under a brand name. — Also termed *copycat drug.* See *pioneer drug.*

▸ **new drug.** A drug that experts have not recognized as safe and effective for use under the conditions prescribed. 21 USCA § 321(p)(1). • The Food and Drug Administration must approve all new drugs before they can be marketed.

▸ **orphan drug.** (1975) A prescription drug developed to treat diseases affecting fewer than 200,000 people in the United States (such as a rare cancer) or whose developmental costs are not reasonably expected to be recovered from the drug's sales. 21 USCA § 360bb.

▸ **pioneer drug.** The first drug that contains a particular active ingredient that is approved by the FDA for a specified use.

▸ **precompounded prescription drug.** (1962) A drug that is distributed from the manufacturer, to the pharmacist, and then to the consumer without a change in form.

▸ **proprietary drug.** (1877) A drug that is prepared and packaged for the public's immediate use. • Proprietary drugs may be sold over the counter. Cf. *ethical drug.*

drug abuse. (1903) The detrimental state produced by the repeated consumption of a narcotic or other potentially dangerous drug, other than as prescribed by a doctor to treat an illness or other medical condition.

drug addict. See ADDICT.

drug-assistance program. (1985) **1.** A governmental program to ensure access to necessary prescription medicines for needy people who are uninsured or underinsured or who otherwise lack health coverage. **2.** Rehabilitative counseling, and monitoring, usu. in a nonresidential setting, for detecting and treating users of illegal drugs.

drug baron. (1917) Someone who leads an organization that buys and sells large quantities of illegal drugs.

drug court. See COURT.

drug czar. See CZAR.

drug dealer. (1917) Someone who sells illegal drugs or who sells legal drugs through illegal outlets.

drug dependence. (1905) The psychological or physiological need for a drug.

Drug Enforcement Administration. An agency in the U.S. Department of Justice responsible for enforcing federal controlled-substances laws through investigations and prosecutions, and for coordinating operations with federal, state, and local law-enforcement agencies and with foreign governments. — Abbr. DEA.

drug-factory presumption. (1986) The doctrine that a suspect found in a private room where drugs are being made or mixed, or preparations are underway to make or mix them, is legally assumed to have knowing possession of the drugs and their preparatory ingredients. — Also termed *room doctrine.*

drug-free zone. (1986) An area in which the possession or distribution of a controlled substance results in an increased penalty. • Drug-free zones are often established, for example, around public schools.

druggie. (1966) *Slang.* See JUNKIE.

druggist. (17c) Someone who mixes, compounds, dispenses, or otherwise deals in drugs and medicines, usu. either as a proprietor of a drugstore or as a pharmacist.

drug house. (1983) *Slang.* A structure, usu. a dwelling, in a residential neighborhood that is known or reputed to be used as a venue for the illegal sale of controlled substances. • Many drug houses are also called by the specific substances sold there, such as *crack house* or *meth house.*

drug kingpin. (1978) An organizer, leader, manager, financier, or supervisor of a drug conspiracy; a person who has great authority in running an illegal drug operation. — Also termed *drug lord.*

drug paraphernalia. (1920) *Criminal law.* Any type of equipment, product, or material that is primarily designed or intended for the unlawful manufacture, processing, or hiding of a controlled substance, or for the introduction of a controlled substance into the human body, when possession of the substance is unlawful. 21 USCA § 863(d).

Drug Price Competition and Patent Term Restoration Act of 1984. See HATCH–WAXMAN ACT.

drug-recognition exam. (1996) A test or series of tests performed by a police officer to determine whether a suspect is under the influence of drugs. • One example is the horizontal-gaze-nystagmus test. See HORIZONTAL-GAZE-NYSTAGMUS TEST.

drug-recognition expert. (1986) A person trained to identify various types of drugs and alcohol, to understand the effects that drugs and alcohol have on people, and to recognize the signs and symptoms of drug and alcohol intoxication. — Abbr. DRE.

drug rehabilitation. (1929) **1.** The process of helping people live without alcohol or illegal drugs after they have become addicted. **2.** A program or system designed to help people undergo this process. — Often shortened to *rehab.*

drug runner. (1916) Someone who takes illegal drugs across international borders. Cf. MULE.

drug schedule. (1965) A classification system for controlled substances, which are placed into five categories (schedules) based on the drug's acceptable medical use, its potential for abuse, and its potential for physical or psychological dependency. • Schedule I drugs, such as heroin and LSD, are the most dangerous because of the high potential for abuse and dependence; Schedule V drugs, such as over-the-counter cough medicine, are considered the least dangerous. — Also termed *controlled-substance schedule.*

drug-sniffing dog. See *detection dog* under DOG (1).

drug test. (1863) A laboratory analysis of a biological specimen for the presence of a specific drug or a metabolite of it. • Specimens include hair, saliva, blood, urine, or breath.

drug trafficking. See TRAFFICKING.

drug-treatment program. (1968) A series of classes that teach and condition those with a history of substance abuse, together with follow-up sessions that monitor enrolees' progress.

drummer. (1827) **1.** A commercial agent who travels around taking orders for goods to be shipped from wholesale merchants to retail dealers; a traveling sales representative. **2.** A traveling salesperson.

drummer floater insurance. See INSURANCE.

drungarius (drəng-**gair**-ee-əs), *n.* [Law Latin] *Hist.* **1.** A commander of a band of soldiers. **2.** A naval commander.

drungus (**drəng**-gəs), *n.* [Law Latin] *Hist.* A band of soldiers.

drunk, *adj.* (14c) Intoxicated; (of a person) under the influence of intoxicating liquor to such a degree that the normal capacity for rational thought and conduct is impaired. — **drunk,** *n.*

drunkard. (16c) **1.** Someone who habitually consumes intoxicating substances excessively; esp., one who is often intoxicated. **2.** ALCOHOLIC. • This term may also be used to refer to a drug addict. — Also termed *habitual drunkard.*

drunk driving. The driving of a motor vehicle after drinking too much alcohol. See DRIVING WHILE INTOXICATED.

drunkenness. (bef. 12c) **1.** A state of intoxication; inebriation; the condition resulting from a person's ingestion of excessive amounts of intoxicating liquors sufficient to affect the person's normal capacity for rational thought and conduct. **2.** A habitual state of intoxication. — Also termed *alcohol impairment; alcoholic impairment.*

▸ **excessive drunkenness.** (1832) A state of drunkenness in which a person is so far deprived of reason and understanding that he or she is incapable of understanding the character and consequences of an act.

drunkometer (drəng-**kom**-ə-tər). See BREATHALYZER.

Dru Sjodin National Sex Offender Public Website. A national sex-offender registry maintained by the U.S. Department of Justice under 42 USCA § 16920.

dry, *adj.* (bef. 12c) **1.** Free from moisture; desiccated <dry land>. **2.** Unfruitful; destitute of profitable interest; nominal <a dry trust>. **3.** (Of a jurisdiction) prohibiting the sale or use of alcoholic beverages <a dry county>.

dry-benching. See DRY-LABBING.

dry cargo. See CARGO.

dry check. See *bad check* under CHECK.

dry conspiracy. (1987) *Criminal law. Slang.* A drug case in which the police, despite investigating several suspects, recover no contraband at all. Cf. WET CONSPIRACY.

dry exchange. (16c) Something that pretends to pass on both sides of a transaction, but passes on only one side.

> "Dry exchange . . . seems to be a subtil term invented to disguise usury, in which something is pretended to pass on both sides, whereas in truth nothing passes on the one side." *Termes de la Ley* 185 (1st Am. ed. 1812).

> "DRY EXCHANGE . . . . A euphemism applied to the 'coverture' or 'colouring' of the stringent statutes passed during the Tudor period against usury . . . . Usury, which was condemned by religion and law alike during the middle ages, was from the middle of the 16th century no longer to be confounded with the legitimate employment of capital; but the sentiment which inspired the above enactments was that of governing classes associated with the landed interest." 1 R.H. Inglis Palgrave, *Palgrave's Dictionary of Political Economy* 643 (Henry Higgs ed., 2d ed. 1925).

dry hole. (1883) *Oil & gas.* An oil or gas well that is incapable of producing enough minerals to justify the cost of completing it and putting it into production.

dry-hole agreement. (1950) *Oil & gas.* A support agreement in which the contributing party agrees to make a cash contribution to the drilling party in exchange for geological or drilling information if the well drilled is unproductive. See SUPPORT AGREEMENT.

dry-hole clause. (1937) *Oil & gas.* A provision in an oil-and-gas lease specifying what a lessee must do to maintain the lease for the remainder of the primary term after drilling an unproductive well. • A dry-hole clause is intended to make clear that the lessee may maintain the lease by paying delay rentals for the remainder of the primary term.

dry-labbing, *n.* (1991) *Criminal law. Slang.* The act or practice of a police laboratory's reporting results without concluding all the required or requested tests. — Also termed *dry-benching.*

dry mortgage. See MORTGAGE.

dry presumption. See PRESUMPTION.

dry receivership. See RECEIVERSHIP.

dry rent. See RENT (1).

dry trust. See TRUST (3).

dry use. See USE (4).

DS. *abbr.* BUREAU OF DIPLOMATIC SECURITY.

d.s.b. *abbr.* DEBET SINE BREVE.

DSB. *abbr.* DISPUTE SETTLEMENT BODY.

DSCA. *abbr.* DEFENSE SECURITY COOPERATION AGENCY.

DSS. *abbr.* **1.** DEPARTMENT OF SOCIAL SERVICES. **2.** DEFENSE SECURITY SERVICE.

DTC. *abbr.* DEPOSITORY TRUST CORPORATION.

DTP. *abbr.* DEMAND TO PRODUCE.

DTRA. *abbr.* DEFENSE THREAT REDUCTION AGENCY.

d.t.'s. (1861) *abbr.* DELIRIUM TREMENS.

dual agent. See AGENT.

dual-and-successive-prosecution policy. See PETITE POLICY.

dual-capacity doctrine. (1914) The principle that makes an employer — who is normally shielded from tort liability by workers'-compensation laws — liable in tort to an employee if the employer and employee stand in a secondary relationship that confers independent obligations on the employer. — Also termed *dual-persona doctrine.* Cf. DUAL-PURPOSE DOCTRINE.

dual carriageway. See CARRIAGEWAY.

dual citizenship. (1890) **1.** A person's status as a citizen of two countries, as when the person is born in the United States to parents who are citizens of another country, or one country still recognizes a person as a citizen even though that person has acquired citizenship in another country. **2.** The status of a person who is a citizen of both the United States and the person's country of residence.

dual contract. See CONTRACT.

dual criminality. (1974) See DOUBLE CRIMINALITY.

dual distributor. (1945) A firm that sells goods simultaneously to buyers on two different levels of the distribution chain; esp., a manufacturer that sells directly to both wholesalers and retailers.

dual distributorship. See DISTRIBUTORSHIP.

dual employment. See MOONLIGHTING.

dual fund. See MUTUAL FUND.

dual inheritance. See INHERITANCE.

dualism. *Int'l law.* The doctrine that because domestic and international law are distinct and separate, international law is ineffective unless domestic law is adapted to incorporate or conform to international law. Cf. MONISM.

duality of art. (1964) *Copyright.* The twofold nature of applied art as both functional and aesthetic. • The United States takes a duality-of-art approach to copyright, protecting applied art only when the item could stand alone as an identifiable work of art even if it did not perform the function it was designed to do. — Also termed *noncumulative approach.* Cf. UNITY OF ART.

dual juries. See JURY.

dual listing. See LISTING (2).

dual motive. See MOTIVE.

dual-persona doctrine (**d**[y]**oo**-əl pər-**soh**-nə). (1982) See DUAL-CAPACITY DOCTRINE.

dual practice. 1. A lawyer's solicitation of and provision of nonlegal services to clients. • An example occurs when a lawyer offers accounting services to clients; the lawyer remains fully subject to governing codes in both legal and accounting matters. **2.** Professional practice by a lawyer and a nonlawyer in the same office. • The nonlawyer may not own or operate the law office, nor may the lawyer help the nonlawyer engage in the unauthorized practice of law.

dual-priorities rule. (1978) The principle that partnership creditors have priority for partnership assets and that individual creditors have priority for a partner's personal assets. • This rule has been abandoned by the bankruptcy laws and the Revised Uniform Partnership Act. The bankruptcy code now allows partnership creditors access to all assets of bankrupt partners, not just those remaining after payment to individual creditors. — Also termed *jingle rule.*

dual-prosecution rule. (1981) The principle that the federal government and a state government may both prosecute a defendant for the same offense because both governments are separate and distinct entities. See DUAL-SOVEREIGNTY DOCTRINE.

dual-purpose doctrine. (1953) The principle that an employer is liable for an employee's injury that occurs during a business trip even though the trip also serves a personal purpose. Cf. DUAL-CAPACITY DOCTRINE.

dual-purpose fund. See *dual fund* under MUTUAL FUND.

dual representation. See *concurrent representation* under REPRESENTATION (2).

dual-residential parent. See PARENT (1).

dual-shop operation. See DOUBLE-BREASTING.

dual-sovereignty doctrine. (1957) **1.** The rule that the federal and state governments may both prosecute a person for a crime without violating the constitutional protection against double jeopardy, if the person's act violated both jurisdictions' laws. See DUAL-PROSECUTION RULE.

duarchy (**d[y]oo**-ahr-kee), *n.* [fr. Greek *duo* "two" + *archia* "rule"] See DIARCHY.

dubii juris (**d[y]oo**-bee-ɪ **joor**-is). [Latin] *Hist.* Of doubtful law. • The phrase appeared in reference to an unsettled legal point.

dubitante (d[y]oo-bi-**tan**-tee). [Latin] Doubting. • This term was usu. placed in a law report next to a judge's name, indicating that the judge doubted a legal point but was unwilling to state that it was wrong. — Also termed *dubitans.*

> "[E]xpressing the epitome of the common law spirit, there is the opinion entered *dubitante* — the judge is unhappy about some aspect of the decision rendered, but cannot quite bring himself to record an open dissent." Lon L. Fuller, *Anatomy of the Law* 147 (1968).

dubitatur (d[y]oo-bi-**tay**-tər). [Latin] It is doubted. • This phrase indicates that a point of law is doubtful. — Also termed *dubitavit.*

ducat (**dək**-it). (14c) A gold coin used as currency, primarily in Europe and first appearing in Venice in the early 1100s, with the motto *sit tibi, Christe, dato, quem tu regis, iste Ducatus* ("let this duchy which thou rulest be dedicated to thee, O Christ"). • It survived into the 20th century in several countries, including Austria and the Netherlands.

ducatus (d[y]ə-**kay**-təs), *n.* [Law Latin] A duchy; a dukedom.

duces tecum (**d[y]oo**-səs **tee**-kəm *also* **tay**-kəm). [Latin] (17c) Bring with you. See *subpoena duces tecum* under SUBPOENA.

duces tecum licet languidus (**d[y]oo**-səs **tee**-kəm **lɪ**-set **lang**-gwə-dəs), *n.* [Law Latin "bring with you, although sick"] (18c) *Hist.* A habeas corpus writ ordering a sheriff to bring someone into court despite a return by the sheriff noting that the person was too ill to come.

Duchy Court of Lancaster (**dəch**-ee **kort** əv **lang**-kə-stər). *Hist. English law.* A court with special equity jurisdiction, similar to the equity courts of chancery, in which the Duchy of Lancaster's chancellor or deputy presides over issues primarily relating to land held by the Crown in right of the Duchy.

Duchy of Lancaster (**dəch**-ee əv **lang**-kə-stər). Land, in the county of Lancaster, the Savoy in London, and around Westminster, that originally belonged to the Duke of Lancaster and later belonged to the Crown in right of the Duchy.

ducking stool. See CASTIGATORY.

due, *adj.* (14c) **1.** Just, proper, regular, and reasonable <due care> <due notice>. **2.** Immediately enforceable <payment is due on delivery>. **3.** Owing or payable; constituting a debt <the tax refund is due from the IRS>.

due administration of justice. See ADMINISTRATION OF JUSTICE.

due and payable. (Of a debt) owed and subject to immediate collection because a specified date has arrived or time has elapsed, or some other condition for collectibility has been met. See DUE (3). Cf. PAYABLE.

due-bill. See IOU.

due care. See *reasonable care* under CARE (2).

due compensation. See *just compensation* under COMPENSATION.

due consideration. (16c) **1.** The degree of attention properly paid to something, as the circumstances merit. **2.** See *sufficient consideration* under CONSIDERATION (1).

due course, payment in. See PAYMENT IN DUE COURSE.

due-course holder. See HOLDER IN DUE COURSE.

due course of law. See DUE PROCESS.

due date. See DATE.

due day. See BOON DAY.

due deference. (17c) The appropriate degree of respect with which a reviewing authority must consider the decision of a primary decision-maker.

due diligence. See DILIGENCE (2).

due-diligence information. (1986) *Securities.* Information that a broker-dealer is required to have on file and make available to potential customers before submitting quotations for over-the-counter securities. • The informational requirements are set out in SEC Rule 15c2-11 (17 CFR § 240.15c2-11).

due influence. (17c) The sway that one person has over another, esp. as a result of temperate persuasion, argument, or appeal to the person's affections. Cf. UNDUE INFLUENCE.

duel. (15c) **1.** TRIAL BY COMBAT. **2.** A single combat; specif., a prearranged combat with deadly weapons fought between two or more persons under prescribed rules, usu. in the presence of at least two witnesses, to resolve a previous quarrel or avenge a deed. • In England and the United States, death resulting from a duel is treated as murder, and seconds may be liable as accessories. — Also termed *monomachy; single combat.* Cf. MUTUAL COMBAT.

> "[A] duel which did not end in death was only a misdemeanour, till the passing of Lord Ellenborough's Act, 43 Geo. 3, c. 58, passed in 1803 . . . . A duel which did end fatally might be either murder or manslaughter, according to the following distinctions: — If the duel was on a sudden falling out, if the parties fought in hot blood and on the spot and one was killed, the offence was only manslaughter, however aggravated the case might be. . . . If a fatal duel took place when the parties were in cool blood, it was held to be murder, and of this there has never been any doubt whatever in this country, though juries not unfrequently acquitted in such cases if they sympathized with the prisoner." 3 James Fitzjames Stephen, *A History of the Criminal Law of England* 100 (1883).

> "Dueling is distinguished from other offenses in that it has none of the elements of sudden heat and passion, and is usually carried out with some formality. A duel has been distinguished from an 'affray' in that an affray occurs on a sudden quarrel while a duel is always the result of design." 28A C.J.S. *Dueling* § 2, at 154 (1996).

dueling, *n.* (17c) The common-law offense of fighting at an appointed time and place after an earlier disagreement. • If one of the participants is killed, the other is guilty of murder, and all who are present, abetting the crime, are guilty as principals in the second degree.

> "Dueling is prearranged fighting with deadly weapons, usually under certain agreed or prescribed rules. . . . It is a misdemeanor at common law to fight a duel, even though no death result, to challenge another to a duel, intentionally to provoke such a challenge, or knowingly to be the bearer of such a challenge." Rollin M. Perkins & Ronald N. Boyce, *Criminal Law* 243 (3d ed. 1982).

duellum (d[y]oo-**el**-əm), *n.* [fr. Latin *duo* "two"] *Hist.* See TRIAL BY COMBAT.

due negotiation. See NEGOTIATION.

due notice. See NOTICE (3).

due-on-encumbrance clause. (1971) A mortgage provision giving the lender the option to accelerate the debt if the borrower further mortgages the real estate without the lender's consent. • All state laws on the enforcement of due-on-sale clauses have been preempted, and the subject is now governed exclusively by the Garn Act. 12 USCA § 1701j-3.

due-on-sale clause. (1967) A mortgage provision that gives the lender the option to accelerate the debt if the borrower transfers or conveys any part of the mortgaged real estate without the lender's consent.

due posting. (1893) **1.** The stamping and placing of letters or packages in the U.S. mail. **2.** The proper entry of an item into a ledger. **3.** Proper publication; proper placement of an item (such as an announcement) in a particular place, as on a particular wall.

due process. (16c) The conduct of legal proceedings according to established rules and principles for the protection and enforcement of private rights, including notice and the right to a fair hearing before a tribunal with the power to decide the case. — Also termed *due process of law*; *due course of law*. See FUNDAMENTAL-FAIRNESS DOCTRINE.

> "The words '*due process*' have a precise technical import, and are only applicable to the process and proceedings of the courts of justice; they can never be referred to an act of legislature." Alexander Hamilton, Remarks on an Act for Regulating Elections, New York Assembly, 6 Feb. 1787, in 4 *Papers of Alexander Hamilton* 34, 35 (Harold C. Syrett ed., 1962).

> "The words, 'due process of law,' were undoubtedly intended to convey the same meaning as the words, 'by the law of the land,' in *Magna Charta*." *Murray's Lessee v. Hoboken Land & Improvement Co.*, 59 U.S. (18 How.) 272, 276 (1856).

> "Due process of law in each particular case means, such an exertion of the powers of government as the settled maxims of law sanction, and under such safeguards for the protection of individual rights as those maxims prescribe for the class of cases to which the one in question belongs." Thomas M. Cooley, *A Treatise on the Constitutional Limitations* 356 (1868).

> "An elementary and fundamental requirement of due process in any proceeding which is to be accorded finality is notice reasonably calculated, under all the circumstances, to apprise interested parties of the pendency of the action and afford them an opportunity to present their objections. . . . The notice must be of such nature as reasonably to convey the required information." *Mullane v. Central Hanover Bank & Trust Co.*, 339 U.S. 306, 314, 70 S.Ct. 652, 657 (1950).

▸ **economic substantive due process.** (1957) The doctrine that certain social policies, such as the freedom of contract or the right to enjoy property without interference by government regulation, exist in the Due Process Clause of the 14th Amendment, particularly in the words "liberty" and "property."

▸ **procedural due process.** (1934) The minimal requirements of notice and a hearing guaranteed by the Due Process Clauses of the 5th and 14th Amendments, esp. if the deprivation of a significant life, liberty, or property interest may occur. • The Supreme Court has ruled that the fundamental guarantees of due process apply to children as well as to adults and that they apply in situations in which a juvenile may be deprived of liberty even though the juvenile proceedings may be labeled civil rather than criminal. *In re Gault*, 387 U.S. 1, 87 S.Ct. 1428 (1967). In that case, the Court held that an accused child was entitled to notice of the charges, the privilege against self-incrimination, the right to confront witnesses, and the right to summon witnesses on his or her own behalf. Justice Abe Fortas wrote the majority opinion in *Gault*, and Chief Justice Earl Warren predicted that it would come to be called the "Magna Carta for juveniles."

▸ **substantive due process.** (1933) The doctrine that the Due Process Clauses of the 5th and 14th Amendments require legislation to be fair and reasonable in content and to further a legitimate governmental objective.

> "The doctrine of substantive due process is so called because the inquiry focuses not on the legal procedure by which one is convicted and punished (deprived of life, liberty, or property) for violating the law, but rather on the law itself and whether a person may legitimately be required to obey such a law. One typical formulation of this doctrine is that it forbids government to deprive a person of life, liberty, or property 'arbitrarily,' that is, without sufficient grounds to do so. The origins of substantive due process are embedded in two phenomena of the traditional era. First, there was a strand of judicial review — based not on the Constitution, but on principles of natural justice; this . . . was a minority position and a deviation from the main principles of the era. Second, there were a number of cases, primarily in state courts, that were rooted in an analysis of the intrinsic requirements of 'law.' These two phenomena were united especially in their orientation toward property rights." Christopher Wolfe, *The Rise of Modern Judicial Review: From Constitutional Interpretation to Judge-Made Law* 145 (1986).

Due Process Clause. (1890) *Constitutional law.* The constitutional provision that prohibits the government from unfairly or arbitrarily depriving a person of life, liberty, or property. • There are two Due Process Clauses in the U.S. Constitution, one in the 5th Amendment applying to the federal government, and one in the 14th Amendment applying to the states (although the 5th Amendment's Due Process Clause also applies to the states under the incorporation doctrine). Cf. EQUAL PROTECTION CLAUSE.

due process of law. See DUE PROCESS.

due-process rights. (1930) The rights (as to life, liberty, and property) so fundamentally important as to require compliance with due-process standards of fairness and justice. See DUE PROCESS; DUE PROCESS CLAUSE; FUNDAMENTAL-FAIRNESS DOCTRINE.

due proof. (16c) Sufficient and properly submitted evidence to produce a result or support a conclusion, such as an entitlement to benefits supported by an insurance policy. • The evidence need not be the best proof possible. *Metropolitan Life Ins. Co. v. Frisch*, 65 N.E. 2d 852, 855 (Ind. App. 1946).

***Duhig* rule.** (1956) *Oil & gas.* A rule of title interpretation developed to deal with the common problem of overconveyance of fractional interests by giving priority to the granted interest over the reserved interest. *Duhig v. Peavy Moore Lumber Co., Inc.*, 144 S.W.2d 878 (Tex. 1940). • The rule is not accepted in all states and is generally limited to conveyances by warranty deed.

DUI. (1969) *abbr.* DRIVING UNDER THE INFLUENCE.

DUIL. *abbr.* Driving under the influence of liquor. See DRIVING UNDER THE INFLUENCE.

duke. (12c) **1.** A sovereign prince; a ruler of a duchy. **2.** The first order of nobility in the United Kingdom below the royal family.

"But after the Norman conquest, which changed the military policy of the nation, the kings themselves continuing for many generations *dukes* of Normandy, they would not honour any subjects with that title, till the time of Edward III; who, claiming to be the king of France, and thereby losing the ducal in the royal dignity, in the eleventh year of his reign created his son, Edward the black prince, duke of Cornwall: and many, of the royal family especially, were afterwards raised to the honour. However, in the reign of queen Elizabeth, A.D. 1572, the whole order became utterly extinct: but it was revived about fifty years afterwards by her successor, who was remarkably prodigal of honours, in the person of George Villiers duke of Buckingham." 1 William Blackstone, *Commentaries on the Laws of England* 385 (1765).

Duke of Exeter's Daughter. (17c) A torture rack in the Tower of London, named after the Duke of Exeter, Henry VI's minister who assisted in introducing it to England. — Also termed *brake*.

"The rack . . . to extort a confession from criminals, is a practice of a different nature . . . . And the trial by rack is utterly unknown to the law of England; though once when the dukes of Exeter and Suffolk . . . had laid a design to introduce the civil law into this kingdom as the rule of government, for a beginning thereof they erected a rack for torture; which was called in derision the duke of Exeter's daughter, and still remains in the tower of London: where it was occasionally used as an engine of state, not of law, more than once in the reign of queen Elizabeth." 4 William Blackstone, *Commentaries on the Laws of England* 320–21 (1769).

Duke of York's Laws. A body of laws compiled in 1665 by Governor Nicholls for the more orderly government of the New York colony. • The laws were gradually extended to the entire province.

dulocracy (d[y]oo-**lok**-rə-see), *n.* [fr. Greek *doulos* "servant" + *kratein* "to rule"] (1824) A government in which servants or slaves have so many privileges that they essentially rule. — Also spelled *doulocracy*.

duly, *adv.* (14c) In a proper manner; in accordance with legal requirements.

duly constituted authority. See *constituted authority* under AUTHORITY (3).

dum (dəm). [Latin] While; provided that.

dumb bidding. (1840) An auction bidding process in which the minimum acceptance price is placed under the object for sale — unbeknownst to the bidders — and no bids are accepted until they meet that price. • Dumb bidding was initially intended to avoid the taxes imposed on auction sales by the statute of 1779, 19 Geo. 3, ch. 56, §§ 5–6, but the courts determined that the practice was fraudulent.

dum fervet opus (dəm **fər**-vet **oh**-pəs). [Latin] While the action is fresh; in the heat of action. • This term usu. referred to matters of testimony.

dum fuit infra aetatem (dəm **fyoo**-it **in**-frə ee-**tay**-təm), *n.* [Law Latin "while he was within age"] (16c) *Hist.* A writ allowing a person of full age to recover lands feoffed while the person was an infant. • The remedy was also available to the person's heirs. It was later replaced by the action of ejectment. See EJECTMENT.

dum fuit in prisona (dəm **fyoo**-it in **priz**-ə-nə), *n.* [Law Latin "while he was in prison"] *Hist.* A writ restoring a man to his estate after he transferred the estate under duress of imprisonment. See DURESS OF IMPRISONMENT.

dummodo (**dəm**-ə-doh). [Latin] So that; provided that. • This term was used as a limitation in conveyances, as in *dummodo solverit talem redditum* (**dəm**-ə-doh **sol**-və-rit **tay**-lem **red**-i-təm), meaning "provided he shall pay such a rent."

dummodo constet de persona (**dəm**-ə-doh **kon**-stet dee pər-**soh**-nə). [Latin] *Hist.* Provided it be evident who is the person meant. See CONSTAT DE PERSONA.

dummodo vassalli conditio non sit deterior (**dəm**-ə-doh **vas**-ə-lɪ kən-**dish**-ee-oh non sit di-**teer**-ee-or). [Law Latin] *Hist.* Provided the vassal's condition be not made worse. • The phrase was used as a limitation in a conveyance. See DUMMODO.

dummy, *adj.* (1846) Sham; make-believe; pretend <dummy corporation>. **dummy,** *n.* (1866) **1.** A party who has no interest in a transaction, but participates to help achieve a legal goal. **2.** A party who purchases property and holds legal title for another. Cf. STRAW MAN (3).

dummy bid. See BID (1).

dummy company. See *dummy corporation* under CORPORATION.

dummy corporation. See CORPORATION.

dummy director. See DIRECTOR.

dummy shareholder. See SHAREHOLDER.

dum non fuit compos mentis (dəm non **fyoo**-it **kom**-pəs **men**-tis), *n.* [Law Latin "while he was of unsound mind"] (16c) *Hist.* A writ allowing heirs to recover an estate transferred by someone of unsound mind.

dump, *vb.* (18c) **1.** To drop (something) down, esp. in a heap; to unload. **2.** To sell (products) at an extremely low price; specif., to sell (products) in a foreign market at a lower price than at home.

dumping. (1857) **1.** The act of selling a large quantity of goods at less than fair value. **2.** Selling goods abroad at less than the market price at home. See ANTIDUMPING LAW.

"Dumping involves selling abroad at a price that is less than the price used to sell the same goods at home (the 'normal' or '*fair*' value). To be unlawful, dumping must threaten or cause material injury to an industry in the export market, the market where prices are lower. Dumping is recognized by most of the trading world as an unfair practice (akin to price discrimination as an antitrust offense)." Ralph H. Folsom & Michael W. Gordon, *International Business Transactions* § 6.1 (1995).

"Dumping has traditionally been defined as the type of price discrimination between national markets, in which a producer sells at a lower price abroad than in his home market (price dumping . . .). It is often considered unfair that a producer, who benefits from protection in his home market and therefore can charge high prices there, subsequently uses the artificially high profits generated on the protected home market to subsidize low-priced export sales. As originally envisaged by economists such as [Jacob] Viner, anti-dumping action would be justified against predatory dumping only. It is assumed that in this type of dumping, exporters maintain the dumped prices as long as the competition in the importing country is not eliminated . . . . Then, when the competition is eliminated, the exporters increase their prices and in the long run, therefore, the consumers lose as well. However, predatory dumping has never been proven to exist. Anti-dumping laws have also seldom contained a predatory intent requirement, presumably because of the difficulty of proving such intent. Over time, a second form of dumping, so-called cost dumping, has been treated as actionable. Under this concept, anti-dumping duties may effectively be imposed on producers that sell below full cost of production in an export market. The ADA provides detailed — although arbitrary — rules for determining under which circumstances sales below cost in the domestic market may be ignored for purposes of determining normal value." Edwin Vermulst, "Anti-Dumping," in 1 *The Max Planck Encyclopedia of Public International Law* 436, 437 (Rüdiger Wolfrum ed., 2012).

3. The disposal of waste matter into the environment.

Dumping Act. A federal antidumping law requiring the Secretary of the Treasury to notify the U.S. International Trade Commission (USITC) whenever the Secretary determines that goods are likely to be sold abroad at less than their fair value, so that the USITC can take appropriate action. 19 USCA § 1673.

dumping duty. See *antidumping tariff* under TARIFF (2).

dump-truck lawyer. (1986) *Slang.* A public defender who spends little time or effort and exhibits little skill mounting a defense on behalf of an indigent defendant. • This derogatory term arises from criminal defendants' common perception (typically a misperception) that public defenders prefer to dump cases by making plea bargains rather than spend time preparing for trial. *People v. Clark*, 833 P.2d 561, 590 (Cal. 1992); *People v. Huffman*, 139 Cal. Rptr. 264, 267 n.2 (Cal. App. 1977). — Often shortened to *dump truck.*

dum se bene gesserit (dəm see **bee**-nee **jes**-ər-it). [Latin "while he behaves himself properly"] *Hist.* During good conduct. Cf. QUAMDIU BENE SE GESSERINT.

dum sola (dəm **soh**-lə). [Latin] While single. • This phrase was used to limit conveyances, esp. to women, as in *dum sola fuerit* ("while she remains single"), *dum sola et casta vixerit* ("while she remains single and chaste"), and *dum sola et casta* ("while she is unmarried and lives chastely").

dun (dən), *vb.* (17c) To demand payment from (a delinquent debtor) <his creditors are dunning him daily>. — **dun,** *n.*

***Dunaway* hearing.** (1983) *Criminal law.* A pretrial hearing to determine whether evidence was obtained in violation of Fourth Amendment protections against unreasonable search and seizure, specif., whether a defendant's statement, esp. one to police, should be suppressed because it was obtained after an arrest without probable cause, the prosecution having the burden to show either probable cause or attenuation. • The name derives from *Dunaway v. New York*, 442 U.S. 200, 99 S.Ct. 2249 (1979). See PROBABLE CAUSE (1); ATTENUATION DOCTRINE.

dungeon. (14c) **1.** The bottom part of a fortress or tower, often used as a prison. — Also termed *dungeon-keep.* **2.** A dark underground prison.

dunnage (**dən**-ij). (15c) Anything, esp. pieces of wood, that are put underneath or between cargo on a vessel to prevent the cargo from bruising or getting wet from water leaking into the hold.

duodecemvirale judicium (d[y]oo-oh-des-əm-və-**ray**-lee joo-**dish**-ee-əm). [Latin] A trial by 12 persons; a trial by jury.

duodecima manus (d[y]oo-oh-**des**-ə-mə **man**-əs). [Latin] (18c) Twelve men.

"The manner of waging and making law is this. He that has waged, or given security, to make his law, brings with him into court eleven of his neighbours: . . . for by the old Saxon constitution every man's credit in courts of law depended upon the opinion which his neighbours had of his veracity. The defendant then, standing at the end of the bar, is admonished by the judges of the nature and danger of a false oath. . . . And thereupon his eleven neighbours or compurgators shall avow upon their oaths that they believe in their consciences that he saith the truth . . . . It is held indeed by later authorities . . . that fewer than eleven compurgators will do: but Sir Edward Coke is positive that there must be this number . . . for as wager of law is equivalent to a verdict in the defendant's favor, it ought to be established by the same or equal testimony, namely, by the oath of *twelve* men. And so indeed Glanvil expresses it, ...'*jurabit duodecima manu*' . . . ." 3 William Blackstone, *Commentaries on the Laws of England* 343 (1768).

duodena (d[y]oo-ə-**dee**-nə). [Latin] **1.** A jury of twelve. **2.** A dozen of anything.

duopoly (d[y]oo-**op**-ə-lee). (1895) A market in which there are only two sellers of a product.

duopsony (d[y]oo-**op**-sə-nee). (1935) A market in which there are only two buyers of a product.

duoviri (d[y]oo-**oh**-və-rɪ *or* d[y]oo-oh **vɪ**-rɪ). See DUUMVIRI.

duplex querela (**d[y]oo**-pleks kwə-**ree**-lə). (17c) **1.** *Hist. Eccles. law.* An appeal by a clerk to the archbishop in response to the bishop's delaying or wrongfully refusing to do justice. **2.** *Eccles. law.* An appeal to a person's immediate superior, as when a bishop appeals to an archbishop. — Also termed *double quarrel; double complaint.*

"During the sixteenth century, at least in the Province of Canterbury, cases dealing with presentation to benefices were 'regularized' by assigning them to a separate legal category, called the Duplex querela. This legal remedy was similar to an appeal, brought before the Court of Arches or the archbishop's Court of Audience by a cleric who had been presented to a bishop, who had refused to admit him and had admitted someone else in his place. The 'double' nature of the action came from naming as defendants both the bishop and the party who had been admitted, allegedly contrary to right. In theory, the Duplex querela could be brought in any area of ecclesiastical competence — for instance, where a bishop's court refused to appoint one person as administrator of a decedent's estate and appointed someone else instead. However, this remedy was used almost exclusively in beneficial matters. A successful action elicited an order from the Court of Arches that the plaintiff be admitted to the benefice. It was said in justification that the defendant bishop's negligence had caused the right to admit to pass to his superior, the archbishop." R.H. Helmholz, 1 *The Oxford History of the Laws of England* 490 (2004).

duplex valor maritagii (**d[y]oo**-pleks **val**-ər mar-ə-**tay**-jee-ɪ), *n.* [Law Latin "double the value of a marriage"] (18c) *Hist.* A ward's forfeiture of double the value of a marriage made without the guardian's consent. • In the quotation that follows, Blackstone uses the accusative form (*duplicem valorem maritagii*) because the phrase follows the verb *forfeited.*

"For, while the infant was in ward, the guardian had the power of tendering him or her a suitable match, without *disparagement*, or inequality: which if the infants refused, they forfeited the value of the marriage . . . to their guardian; that is, so much as a jury would assess, or any one would *bona fide* give to the guardian for such an alliance: . . . and, if the infants married themselves without the guardian's consent, they forfeited double the value, *duplicem valorem maritagii*. This seems to have been one of the greatest hardships of our ancient tenures." 2 William Blackstone, *Commentaries on the Laws of England* 70 (1766).

duplicate (**d[y]oo**-pli-kit), *n.* (16c) **1.** A reproduction of an original document having the same particulars and effect as the original. *See* Fed. R. Evid. 101(4). **2.** A new original, made to replace an instrument that has been lost or destroyed. — Also termed (in sense 2) *duplicate original.* — **duplicate** (**d[y]oo**-pli-kit), *adj.*

"A 'duplicate' is defined for purposes of the best evidence rule as a counterpart produced by the same impression as the original, or from the same matrix, or by means of photography including enlargements and miniatures, by mechanical or electronic recording, by chemical reproduction, or by other equivalent techniques which accurately reproduce the original; copies subsequently produced manually, either handwritten or typed, are not within this definition." 29A Am. Jur. 2d *Evidence* § 1085 (1994).

duplicate (**d[y]oo**-pli-kayt), *vb.* (17c) **1.** To copy exactly <he duplicated the original document>. **2.** To double; to repeat <she duplicated the performance>.

duplicate-claiming rejection. See REJECTION.

duplicate original. 1. One of several identical agreements or documents executed in duplicate; an admissible duplicate under Fed. R. Evid.1003. **2.** DUPLICATE, *n.* (2).

duplicate taxation. See *double taxation* under TAXATION (1).

duplicate will. See WILL.

duplicatio (d[y]oo-pli-**kay**-shee-oh), *n.* [fr. Latin *duplicare* "to double"] **1.** *Roman & civil law.* A defendant's answer to the plaintiff's replication, similar to a rejoinder in common law. — Also termed (in Scots law) *duply.* See REPLICATION. **2.** The fourth in a series. **3.** A duplication of a transaction.

duplicative (doo-**plik**-ə-tiv *also* **doo**-pli-kay-tiv), *adj.* (1870) **1.** Having or characterized by having overlapping content, intentions, or effect <duplicative sources> <duplicative evidence> <duplicative regulations>. **2.** Duplicate; having or characterized by having identical content <duplicative database> <duplicative backup>.

duplicatum jus (d[y]oo-pli-**kay**-təm **jəs**), *n.* [Law Latin "double right"] A double right, such as *droit droit* (both the "right of possession and right of property").

duplicitous (d[y]oo-**plis**-i-təs), *adj.* (1890) **1.** Given to a tricky doubleness in character, speech, or conduct; esp., deceitful in behaving or speaking differently with different persons in relation to the same matter, with the intent of fooling one or more of them. **2.** (Of a pleading, esp. an indictment) alleging two or more matters in one plea; characterized by double pleading.

duplicitous appeal. See APPEAL (2).

duplicitous indictment. See INDICTMENT.

duplicitous information. See INFORMATION.

duplicity (d[y]oo-**plis**-i-tee), *n.* (15c) **1.** Dishonest behavior that is designed to deceive someone; deceitfulness; double-dealing. **2.** The charging of the same offense in more than one count of an indictment. **3.** The pleading of two or more distinct grounds of complaint or defense for the same issue. — Also termed *double pleading.* Cf. *alternative pleading* under PLEADING (2); *double plea* under PLEA (3).

"One offence only may be stated in a single indictment or count; if more than one offence is charged, the indictment is bad for duplicity. Two averments which seem to charge two offences may in reality be two ways of stating the same offence; in such a case, since one offence only is charged, the indictment is not double. Thus in burglary, a single breaking with intent to commit two felonies is but one crime, and charging a breaking with two intents is not double. The same is true of a conspiracy to commit two offences . . . . So an indictment for murder is good which charges a killing by several means; a killing might be accomplished by the use of several means, and it would be a single offence. Where two averments are made with the same meaning and for the same purpose, either of which would be sufficient alone, the indictment is not thereby rendered double . . . . If one of the charges is insufficiently stated, so that no conviction could legally be had for that crime on the indictment, it is to be disregarded as mere surplusage, and the indictment is not double." Joseph Henry Beale, *A Treatise on Criminal Pleading and Practice* 103–04 (1899) (citations omitted.)

duplum (**d[y]oo**-pləm). [Latin] *Roman & civil law.* Double the price of something; esp., a measure of damages equal to double a thing's value. • This measure was used for certain delicts. Cf. SIMPLUM.

duply. See DUPLICATIO (1).

durable goods. See GOODS.

durable lease. See LEASE.

durable power of attorney. See POWER OF ATTORNEY.

durables. See *durable goods* under GOODS.

durante (d[y]ə-**ran**-tee). [Law Latin] While; during, as in *durante minore aetate* ("during minority"), *durante viduitate* ("during widowhood"), *durante virginitate* ("during virginity"), and *durante vita* ("during life"). • The term was often used in conveyancing.

durante absentia (d[y]ə-**ran**-tee ab-**sen**-shee-ə). [Law Latin] During absence. • This term referred to the administration of an estate while the executor was out of the county or otherwise absent. During the executor's absence, the administration sometimes continued because a delay until the executor's return would impair the estate settlement.

durante bello (d[y]ə-**ran**-tee **bel**-oh), *adv.* [Latin] While the war lasts.

durante bene placito (d[y]ə-**ran**-tee **bee**-nee **plas**-ə-toh). [Law Latin] During good pleasure. • This phrase was used in the royal writ granting tenure *durante bene placito* to the king' judges.

durante furore (d[y]ə-**ran**-tee fyuu-**ror**-ee). [Law Latin] *Hist.* While the insanity endures. • The phrase appeared in reference to the rule prohibiting the state from prosecuting an insane person. The state could, however, prosecute the person once the insanity ended.

durante minore aetate (dyoo-**rant**-ee mi-**nor**-ee I-**taht**-ee), *adv.* [Latin] During the state of minority.

durante viduitate (dyoo-**rant**-ee vid-yə-wi-**taht**-ee), *adv.* [Latin] During the state of widowhood; for as long as a woman remains in viduity. See VIDUITY.

duration. (14c) **1.** The length of time something lasts <the duration of the lawsuit>.

▸ **duration of interest.** (1847) The length of time a property interest lasts.

▸ **duration of trust.** (1887) The length of time a trust exists.

2. A length of time; a continuance in time <an hour's duration>.

durational-residency requirement. (1970) The requirement that one be a state resident for a certain time, such as one year, as a precondition to the exercise of a specified right or privilege. • When applied to voting, this requirement has been held to be an unconstitutional denial of equal protection because it burdens voting rights and impairs the fundamental personal right of travel.

Duration Directive. See DIRECTIVE HARMONIZING THE TERM OF COPYRIGHT AND CERTAIN RELATED RIGHTS.

***Duren* test.** (1980) *Constitutional law.* A test to determine whether a jury's composition violates the fair-cross-section requirement and a criminal defendant's Sixth Amendment right to an impartial jury. • Under the test, a constitutional violation occurs if (1) a distinctive group is not fairly and reasonably represented in the jury pool in relation to its population in the community, (2) the underrepresentation is the result of a systematic exclusion of the group from the jury-selection process, and (3) the government cannot reasonably justify the discrepancy. *Duren v. Missouri,* 439 U.S. 357, 99 S.Ct. 664 (1979). See FAIR-CROSS-SECTION REQUIREMENT; STATISTICAL-DECISION THEORY; ABSOLUTE DISPARITY; COMPARATIVE DISPARITY.

duress (d[y]uu-**res**). (13c) **1.** Strictly, the physical confinement of a person or the detention of a contracting party's property. • In the field of torts, duress is considered a species of fraud in which compulsion takes the place of deceit in causing injury.

"Duress consists in actual or threatened violence or imprisonment; the subject of it must be the contracting party himself, or his wife, parent, or child; and it must be inflicted or threatened by the other party to the contract, or else by one acting with his knowledge and for his advantage." William R. Anson, *Principles of the Law of Contract* 261–62 (Arthur L. Corbin ed., 3d Am. ed. 1919).

"Few areas of the law of contracts have undergone such radical changes in the nineteenth and twentieth centuries as has the law governing duress. In Blackstone's time relief from an agreement on grounds of duress was a possibility only if it was coerced by actual (not threatened) imprisonment or fear of loss of life or limb. 'A fear of battery . . . is no duress; neither is the fear of having one's house burned, or one's goods taken away or destroyed'; he wrote, 'because in these cases, should the threat be performed, a man may have satisfaction by recovering equivalent damages: but no suitable atonement can be made for the loss of life, or limb.' Today the general rule is that any wrongful act or threat which overcomes the free will of a party constitutes duress. This simple statement of the law conceals a number of questions, particularly as to the meaning of 'free will' and 'wrongful.'" John D. Calamari & Joseph M. Perillo, *The Law of Contracts* § 9-2, at 337 (3d ed. 1987).

2. Broadly, a threat of harm made to compel a person to do something against his or her will or judgment; esp., a wrongful threat made by one person to compel a manifestation of seeming assent by another person to a transaction without real volition. • Duress practically destroys a person's free agency, causing nonvolitional conduct because of the wrongful external pressure. A marriage that is induced by duress is generally voidable. **3.** The use or threatened use of unlawful force — usu. that a reasonable person cannot resist — to compel someone to commit an unlawful act. • Duress is a recognized defense to a crime, contractual breach, or tort. See Model Penal Code § 2.09. See COERCION.

"[In most states,] the age-old rule of duress — that the doing of a prohibited act is not a crime if reasonably believed to be necessary to save from death or great bodily injury — together with the equally ancient exception in the form of the 'inexcusable choice,' are as firm today as ever except for the realization that they cover only part of the field." Rollin M. Perkins & Ronald N. Boyce, *Criminal Law* 1064 (3d ed. 1982).

"Among defenses, necessity needs to be distinguished from duress. Necessity is generally regarded as a justification, while duress is held to be an excuse. This means that the person who acts under necessity chooses to act in a way that the law ultimately approves. The person who acts under duress acts in a way that the law disapproves and seeks to discourage, but he acts under circumstances which make conviction and punishment inappropriate and unfair. This is so because to act under duress is to act under pressures that a person of reasonable firmness would not be able to resist. Thus, both the theory of necessity and the theory of duress refer to the pressure of exigent and extraordinary situations, but they do so in different ways." Thomas Morawetz, "Necessity," in 3 *Encyclopedia of Crime and Justice* 957, 959 (Sanford H. Kadish ed., 1983).

▸ **duress of circumstances.** See NECESSITY (1).

▸ **duress of goods.** (18c) **1.** The act of seizing personal property by force, or withholding it from an entitled party, and then extorting something as the condition for its release. **2.** Demanding and taking personal property under color of legal authority that either is void or for some other reason does not justify the demand. — Also termed *duress of property.*

▸ **duress of imprisonment.** (16c) The wrongful confining of a person to force the person to do something.

▸ **duress of property.** See *duress of goods.*

▸ **duress of the person.** (1881) Compulsion of a person by imprisonment, by threat, or by a show of force that cannot be resisted.

▸ **duress per minas** (pər mɪ-nəs). [Law Latin] (18c) Duress by threat of loss of life, loss of limb, mayhem, or other harm to a person.

"Duress *per minas* is either for fear of loss of life, or else for fear of mayhem, or loss of limb. And this fear must be upon sufficient reason . . . . A fear of battery, or being beaten, though never so well grounded, is no duress; neither is the fear of having one's house burned, or one's goods taken away and destroyed; because in these cases, should the threat be performed, a man may have satisfaction by recovering equivalent damages: but no suitable atonement can be made for the loss of life, or limb." 1 William Blackstone, *Commentaries on the Laws of England* 127 (1765).

"Duress *per minas* is a very rare defence; so rare that Sir James Stephen, in his long forensic experience, never saw a case in which it was raised. It has, however, been thought that threats of the immediate infliction of death, or even of grievous bodily harm, will excuse *some* crimes that have been committed under the influence of such threats." J.W. Cecil Turner, *Kenny's Outlines of Criminal Law* 58 (16th ed. 1952).

▸ **economic duress.** (1929) An unlawful coercion to perform by threatening financial injury at a time when one cannot exercise free will. — Also termed *business compulsion.*

"Courts have shown a willingness to recognize the concept of 'economic duress.' For instance it has been held that a defence on these grounds may be available to the purchaser of a ship from a shipbuilder, if the latter extracts a promise of extra payment as a condition of delivery of the ship." P.S. Atiyah, *An Introduction to the Law of Contract* 230 (3d ed. 1981).

▸ **moral duress.** (1828) An unlawful coercion to perform by unduly influencing or taking advantage of the weak financial position of another. • Moral duress focuses on the inequities of a situation while economic duress focuses on the lack of will or capacity of the person being influenced.

Durham (dər-əm). One of the three remaining county palatines in England, the others being Chester and Lancaster. • Its jurisdiction was vested in the Bishop of Durham until the statute 6 & 7 Will. 4, ch. 19 vested it as a separate franchise and royalty in the Crown. The jurisdiction of the Durham Court of Pleas was transferred to the Supreme Court of Judicature by the Judicature Act of 1873, but Durham continued to maintain a Chancery Court according to the Palatine Court of Durham Act of 1889. See COUNTY PALATINE.

***Durham* rule.** (1954) *Criminal law.* A test for the insanity defense, holding that a defendant is not criminally responsible for an act that was the product of mental disease or defect (*Durham v. U.S.*, 214 F.2d 862 (D.C. Cir. 1954)). • Formerly used in New Hampshire and the District of Columbia, the *Durham* rule has been criticized as being too broad and is no longer accepted in any American jurisdiction. — Also termed *product test.* See INSANITY DEFENSE.

***Durrett* rule.** (1981) *Bankruptcy.* The principle that a transfer of property in exchange for less than 70% of the property's value should be invalidated as a preferential transfer. *Durrett v. Washington Nat'l Ins. Co.*, 621 F.2d 201 (5th Cir. 1980); 11 USCA § 548. • This rule has been applied most frequently to foreclosure sales. But it has essentially been overruled by the U.S. Supreme Court, which has held that, at least for mortgage foreclosure sales, the price received at a regularly conducted, noncollusive sale represents a reasonably equivalent value of the property, and the transfer is presumed valid. *BFP v. Resolution Trust Corp.*, 511 U.S. 531, 114 S.Ct. 1757 (1994).

***Dusky* standard.** (1967) *Criminal law.* The measure for whether a criminal defendant is mentally competent to stand trial, the test being whether the defendant has a rational and factual understanding of the charges and potential penalties, plus the ability to cooperate and assist counsel with the defense. *Dusky v. U.S.*, 362 U.S. 402 (1960).

Dutch auction. See AUCTION.

Dutch-auction tender method. See *Dutch auction* (3) under AUCTION.

Dutch lottery. See LOTTERY.

Dutch sandwich. See DOUBLE IRISH.

Dutch standard. **1.** (*usu. pl.*) *Environmental law.* A reference value for the presence of an environmental pollutant, used in environmental investigation, remediation, and cleanup. **2.** *Hist.* A glass jar filled with sugar of a known degree of refinement, with which a sugar sample is compared to determine its quality of refinement. • Major Dutch sugar traders produced sets of jars containing sugars of different colors, from raw to refined, for use in judging the quality of sugar. Tariffs on imported sugar were based on quality, so customs offices used the Dutch sugar standards to examine samples and determine the proper duties.

dutiable (d[y]oo-tee-ə-bəl), *adj.* (18c) Subject to a duty; of, relating to, or involving goods that must have a duty paid on them <dutiable goods>.

duty. (13c) **1.** A legal obligation that is owed or due to another and that needs to be satisfied; that which one is bound to do, and for which somebody else has a corresponding right.

> "There is a duty if the court says there is a duty; the law, like the Constitution, is what we make it. Duty is only a word with which we state our conclusion that there is or is not to be liability; it necessarily begs the essential question. . . . [M]any factors interplay: the hand of history, our ideas of morals and justice, the convenience of administration of the rule, and our social ideas as to where loss should fall." William L. Prosser, *Palsgraf Revisited*, 52 Mich. L. Rev. 1, 15 (1953).

> "A classic English definition [of *duty*] from the late nineteenth century holds that, when circumstances place one individual in such a position with regard to another that thinking persons of ordinary sense would recognize the danger of injury to the other if ordinary skill and care were not used, a duty arises to use ordinary skill and care to avoid the injury. A much quoted American judicial definition of duty emphasizes its relational aspects, with a focus on the foreseeability of risk to those 'within the range of apprehension.' At about the same time, one of the most creative of American law teachers defined duty as a complex of factors, including administrative, economic, and moral ones, to be applied by judges in their analyses of the legal strength of personal injury cases." Marshall S. Shapo, *The Duty to Act* xi–xii (1977).

> "While courts frequently say that establishing 'duty' is the first prerequisite in an individual tort case, courts commonly go on to say that there is a 'general duty' to 'exercise reasonable care,' to avoid subjecting others to 'an unreasonable risk of harm,' or to comply with the 'legal standard of reasonable conduct.' Though cast in the language of duty, these formulations merely give the expression to the point that negligence is the standard of liability." Restatement (Third) of Torts § 6 cmt. a (Discussion Draft 1999).

▸ **absolute duty.** (16c) **1.** A duty to which no corresponding right attaches. • According to John Austin's legal philosophy, there are four kinds of absolute duties: (1) duties not regarding persons (such as those owed to God and to lower animals), (2) duties owed to persons indefinitely (i.e., to the community as a whole), (3) self-regarding duties (such as the duty not to commit suicide), and (4) duties owed to the sovereign. 1 John Austin, *The Providence of Jurisprudence Determined* 400 (Sarah Austin ed., 2d ed. 1861). **2.** A duty as to which nothing but lapse of time remains necessary to make immediate performance by the promisor obligatory.

▸ **active duty.** See *positive duty.*

▸ **affirmative duty.** (17c) A duty to take a positive step to do something.

▸ **conditional duty.** (17c) A duty that is conditioned on the occurrence of an event other than the lapse of time.

▸ **contractual duty.** (1882) **1.** A duty arising under a particular contract. **2.** A duty imposed by the law of contracts.

▸ **delegable duty.** (1908) A duty that may be transferred to another to perform. See ASSIGNMENT (6).

▸ **duty of care and skill.** The duty to act with the diligence and the prevailing standards for the locality for the kind of work performed and to use any special skills the actor has to perform the work. — Also termed *duty of care, skill, and diligence.*

▸ **duty of care, skill, and diligence.** See *duty of care and skill.*

▸ **duty of confidence.** The duty to guard another person's secrets against disclosure.

▸ **duty to act.** (17c) A duty to take some action to prevent harm to another, and for the failure of which one may be liable depending on the relationship of the parties and the circumstances.

▸ **duty to defend.** *Insurance.* The obligation of an insurer to provide an insured with a legal defense against claims of liability, within the terms of the policy. • The duty to defend applies if the terms of the policy and the facts of the claim allow an ambiguity about whether the insurer will have a duty to indemnify the insured. It does not apply if no such ambiguity exists.

▸ **duty to indemnify.** (1852) An obligation to compensate another for the other's loss. • The duty arises under the terms of an agreement, which governs the extent of the duty. An insurance policy is fundamentally an indemnification agreement, but the duty is often made a part of other contracts as well.

▸ **duty to obey the law.** A person's duty to abide by and act within the statutes and common laws that regulate behavior.

▸ **duty to protect.** See *duty to warn.*

▸ **duty to rescue.** *Torts.* An obligation to save a person in peril. • The duty arises when a person created the hazardous situation that placed another in peril, and where there is a special relationship, such as parent and child. See *special relationship* under RELATIONSHIP; RESCUE DOCTRINE.

▸ **duty to retreat.** See RETREAT RULE.

▸ **duty to settle.** (1860) *Insurance.* The obligation of an insurer to negotiate and settle third-party claims against an insured in good faith.

▸ **duty to speak.** (16c) A requirement (not strictly a duty) to say something to correct another's false impression. • For example, a duty to speak may arise when a person has, during the course of negotiations, said something that was true at the time but that has ceased to be true before the contract is signed.

▸ **duty to warn.** *Torts.* The obligation to notify a person about a known hazard or a known threat presented by another person. — Also termed *duty to protect.* See TARASOFF LETTER.

▸ **equitable duty.** (17c) A duty enforceable in a court of chancery or in a court having the powers of a court in chancery.

▸ **imperfect duty.** (1861) **1.** A duty that, though recognized by law, is not enforceable against the person who owes it. **2.** A duty that is not fit for enforcement but should be left to the discretion and conscience of the person whose duty it is.

▸ **implied duty of cooperation.** (1963) A duty existing in every contract, obligating each party to cooperate with, or at least not to wrongfully hinder, the other party's performance. • Breach of this implied duty excuses performance.

▸ **legal duty.** (17c) A duty arising by contract or by operation of law; an obligation the breach of which would give a legal remedy <the legal duty of parents to support their children>.

▸ **moral duty.** (16c) A duty the breach of which would be a moral wrong. — Also termed *natural duty.*

▸ **negative duty.** (17c) A duty that forbids someone to do something; a duty that requires someone to abstain from something. — Also termed *passive duty.*

▸ **noncontractual duty.** (1911) A duty that arises independently of any contract.

▸ **nondelegable duty** (non-**del**-ə-gə-bəl). (1902) **1.** *Contracts.* A duty that cannot be delegated by a contracting party to a third party. • If a contracting party purports to delegate the duty, the other party can rightfully refuse to accept performance by the third party. **2.** *Torts.* A duty for which the principal retains primary (as opposed to vicarious) responsibility for due performance even if the principal has delegated performance to an independent contractor. • For example, a landlord's duty to maintain common areas, though delegated to a service contractor, remains the landlord's responsibility if someone is injured by improper maintenance.

▸ **passive duty.** See *negative duty.*

▸ **perfect duty.** A duty that is not merely recognized by the law but is actually enforceable.

▸ **positive duty.** A duty that requires a person either to do some definite action or to engage in a continued course of action. — Also termed *active duty.*

▸ **preexisting duty.** (1823) A duty that one is already legally bound to perform. See PREEXISTING-DUTY RULE.

▸ **quasi-judicial duty.** (1856) A discretionary judicial duty that a nonjudicial officer may perform under some circumstances.

2. Any action, performance, task, or observance owed by a person in an official or fiduciary capacity.

▸ **deontological duty.** See *ethical duty.*

▸ **discretionary duty.** (18c) A duty that allows a person to exercise judgment and choose to perform or not perform. Cf. *ministerial duty.*

▸ **duty of attendance.** The duty to be present at official meetings or in court.

▸ **duty of candor** (**kan**-dər). (1949) **1.** A duty to disclose material facts; esp., a lawyer's duty not to allow a tribunal to be misled by false statements, either of law or of fact, that the lawyer knows to be false. **2.** A duty of a director seeking shareholder approval of a transaction to disclose to the shareholders all known material facts about the transaction. — Also termed *ethical duty of candor.* See CANDOR.

▸ **duty of candor and good faith.** (1973) *Patents.* A patent applicant's responsibility to disclose to the U.S. Patent and Trademark Office all known information relevant to the invention's patentability, esp. prior art, novelty, and embodiment. • If an applicant fails to be candid in disclosing all relevant information, the PTO may reject the application. If the patent is issued and undisclosed but relevant information is discovered later, the patent may be invalidated, and the applicant charged with fraud on the PTO, even if the undisclosed information might not have barred the patent's issuance. 37 CFR 1.56.

▸ **duty of fair representation.** (1948) A labor union's duty to represent its member employees fairly, honestly, and in good faith. — Abbr. DFR.

▸ **duty of faithful service.** See *fiduciary duty.*

▸ **duty of fidelity.** See *fiduciary duty.*

▸ **duty of good faith and fair dealing.** (1934) A duty that is implied in some contractual relationships, requiring the parties to deal with each other fairly, so that neither prohibits the other from realizing the agreement's benefits. See GOOD FAITH; BAD FAITH.

▸ **duty of loyalty.** (16c) See *fiduciary duty.*

▸ **duty of obedience.** The duty to carry out instructions and abide by restrictions on behavior. • This duty may be limited to lawful activities.

▸ **duty of prudent investment.** A fiduciary's duty to use another's assets to generate income while applying the same care that a reasonable, prudent person would use for oneself.

▸ **duty of utmost good faith.** See *utmost good faith* under GOOD FAITH.

▸ **duty to act for proper purposes.** *English law.* The duty of a corporate director to exercise authorized powers only for reasons that are expressly or impliedly covered by the company's charter.

▸ **duty to avoid conflicts of interest.** See *fiduciary duty.*

▸ **duty to disclose.** A person's duty to reveal or provide relevant information in connection with litigation, a transaction, an application, etc.

▸ **duty to disclose adverse authority.** A lawyer's duty to point out to a court contrary precedents in the controlling jurisdiction. — Also termed *duty to disclose adverse precedent.* See *duty of candor.*

▸ **duty to inform.** Professional obligation to ensure that a client or patient understands, as fully as possible, the potential benefits and harm of a decision that the client faces.

▸ **duty to investigate.** A duty to learn facts about an event or situation.

▸ **duty to provide security.** The responsibility of a person or entity who owns or controls premises to take measures to protect people who enter the premises against harm by others.

▸ **duty to treat.** A healthcare professional's obligation to treat a person's injury or illness when there is an agreement or an expectation to do so as a condition of employment.

▸ **ethical duty.** A duty imposed by a standard of ethics. — Also termed *deontological duty.*

▸ **fiduciary duty** (fi-**d**[y]**oo**-shee-er-ee). (1842) A duty of utmost good faith, trust, confidence, and candor owed by a fiduciary (such as an agent or a trustee) to the beneficiary (such as the agent's principal or the beneficiaries of the trust); a duty of utmost good faith, trust, confidence, and candor owed by a fiduciary (such as a lawyer or corporate officer) to the beneficiary (such as a lawyer's client or a shareholder); a duty to act with the highest degree of honesty and loyalty toward another person and in the best interests of the other person (such as the duty that one partner owes to another). • For example, directors have a duty not to engage in self-dealing to further their own personal interests rather than the interests of the corporation. — Also termed *duty of loyalty; duty of fidelity; duty of faithful service; duty to avoid conflicts of interest.* See FIDUCIARY; FIDUCIARY RELATIONSHIP.

▸ **ministerial duty.** (1837) A duty that requires neither the exercise of official discretion nor judgment. Cf. *discretionary duty.*

▸ **proprietary duty.** (1923) A duty owed by a governmental entity while engaged in a proprietary, rather than governmental, activity.

3. DUTY OF CARE. **4.** A tax imposed on a commodity or transaction, esp. on imports; IMPOST. • A duty in this sense is imposed on things, not persons.

▸ **account duty.** (1905) An inheritance tax payable by a decedent's beneficiary.

▸ **ad valorem duty.** (18c) A tax calculated as a percentage of an imported product's value. Cf. *compound duty; specific duty.*

▸ **antidumping duty.** See *antidumping tariff* under TARIFF (2).

▸ **compound duty.** (18c) A tax based on a combination of imported goods' weight, volume, or item count, plus a percentage of their value. Cf. *ad valorem duty; specific duty.*

▸ **countervailing duty.** (18c) A tax imposed on manufacturers of imported goods to protect domestic industry by offsetting subsidies given by foreign governments to those manufacturers.

▸ **customs duty.** (18c) A tax levied on an imported or exported commodity; esp., the federal tax levied on goods shipped into the United States.

▸ **death duty.** (18c) An estate tax or inheritance tax. — Also termed *estate duty.*

▸ **dumping duty.** See *antidumping tariff* under TARIFF (2).

▸ **duty of detraction.** (1953) A tax on property acquired by succession or will and then removed from one state to another.

▸ **estate duty.** (1891) *Hist. English law.* A tax imposed on the principal value of all property that passed on death. • Estate duties were first imposed in 1889. A capital transfer tax replaced it in 1975. Since 1986, an inheritance tax has applied instead, with exceptions for certain transactions entered into before then. See *death duty.*

▸ **import duty.** (17c) A tax on the importation of a product. — Also termed *duty on import.*

▸ **legacy duty.** See *legacy tax* under TAX.

▸ **probate duty.** (1826) A tax assessed by the government either on every will admitted to probate or on the gross value of the decedent's personal property.

▸ **specific duty.** (18c) A tax calculated on an import's weight, volume, or item count. Cf. *ad valorem duty; compound duty.*

▸ **succession duty.** (1836) A tax payable by the successor to real property, esp. when the successor has not purchased the property for value but has succeeded to the property in some other way.

▸ **tonnage duty.** (18c) A charge imposed on a commercial vessel for entering, remaining in, or leaving a port., usu. assessed on the basis of the ship's weight. • U.S. Const. art. I, § 10, cl. 3 prohibits the states from levying tonnage duties. — Also termed *tonnage tax; tonnage.*

▸ **unascertained duty.** (1804) A preliminary, estimated payment to a customs collector of the duty that will be due on final accounting. • An importer pays this duty to receive permission to land and sell the goods.

5. Service in a branch of the armed forces; military service.

duty-bound, *adj.* (1908) Required by legal or moral obligation to do something <Jones is duty-bound to deliver the goods by Friday>.

duty counsel. See *duty solicitor* under SOLICITOR.

duty-free, *adj.* (17c) Of, relating to, or involving products of foreign origin that are not subject to import or export taxes.

duty of attendance. See DUTY (2).

duty judge. See JUDGE.

duty of candor. See DUTY (2).

duty of care. *Torts.* A legal relationship arising from a standard of care, the violation of which subjects the actor to liability.

> "The terms 'duty of care,' 'breach,' 'causation,' and 'remoteness' are used in a variety of senses by different persons, and differently even by the same person, thus leading to confusion and traps for the unwary. 'Duty of care' is sometimes used in the sense of the recognition by law that there can be liability in the given type of situation, as can be seen in *Weller & Co. and Another v. Foot and Mouth Disease Research Institute*, where the plaintiffs lost on a preliminary point because the judge ruled that the kind of damage for which they sued was not cognizable as an abstract matter of law. At other times a 'duty of care' is said to be 'owed to' a plaintiff only when there is foreseeability of harm to him in the particular circumstances, as in *Roe v. Minister of Health*, where Denning LJ said: 'There is no duty of care owed to a person when you could not reasonably foresee that he might be injured by your conduct.'" R.W.M. Dias & B.S. Markesinis, *Tort Law* 57 (2d ed. 1989).

▸ ***employer's duty of care.*** *English law.* An employer's responsibility to take all reasonable steps to protect employees' health, safety, and well-being.

duty of care and skill. See DUTY (1).

duty of care, skill, and diligence. See *duty of care and skill* under DUTY (1).

duty of confidence. See DUTY (1).

duty of faithful service. See *duty of loyalty* under DUTY (2).

duty of fidelity. See *duty of loyalty* under DUTY (2).

duty of loyalty. See *fiducuary duty* under DUTY (2).

duty of minimization. See MINIMIZATION REQUIREMENT.

duty of obedience. See DUTY (2).

duty of prudent investment. See DUTY (2).

duty of the flag. (17c) *Hist.* A maritime ceremony by which a foreign vessel struck her flag and lowered her topsail upon meeting the British flag. • The ceremony was an acknowledgment of British sovereignty over the British seas.

duty of tonnage (**tən**-ij). See *tonnage duty* under DUTY (4).

duty of utmost good faith. See *utmost good faith* under GOOD FAITH.

duty of water. (17c) The amount of water necessary to irrigate a given tract.

duty on import. See *import duty* under DUTY (4).

duty solicitor. See SOLICITOR.

duty to act for proper purposes. See DUTY (2).

duty to avoid conflicts of interest. See *fiduciary duty* under DUTY (2).

duty-to-defend clause. (1964) *Insurance.* A liability-insurance provision obligating the insurer to take over the defense of any lawsuit brought by a third party against the insured on a claim that falls within the policy's coverage. See *duty to defend* under DUTY (1).

duty to disclose. See DUTY (2).

duty to disclose adverse authority. See DUTY (2).

duty to disclose adverse precedent. See *duty to disclose adverse authority* under DUTY (2).

duty to investigate. See DUTY (2).

duty to mitigate (**mit**-i-gayt). (1891) A nonbreaching party's or tort victim's duty to make reasonable efforts to limit losses resulting from the other party's breach or tort. • Not doing so precludes the party from collecting damages that might have been avoided. See MITIGATION-OF-DAMAGES DOCTRINE.

> "There is probably no more fundamental proposition in the law of damages than that an aggrieved party may not recover damages for any loss that he could have reasonably avoided. This 'doctrine of avoidable consequences' is often called the 'duty' to mitigate damages. This is something of a misnomer because the doctrine does not contemplate a duty in the sense that its breach is actionable. The rule is just that one may not recover damages for losses that could have been reasonably mitigated. Although the [Uniform Commercial] Code rarely speaks directly to this concept, the courts have made clear that the unavoidable loss principle is implicit in every damage remedy. The courts usually justify this implication from the mandate in Section 1-305 that remedies 'be liberally administered' so that compensation to the injured party is achieved without penalty to the breacher." 1 Roy Ryden Anderson, *Damages Under the Uniform Commercial Code* § 1:6, at 11 (2013–2014).

duty to obey the law. See DUTY (1).

duty to protect. See *duty to warn* under DUTY (1).

duty to provide security. See DUTY (2).

duty to recognize. *Int'l law.* A postulated obligation within the international community to acknowledge the statehood of an entity that bears all the marks of a national government. *See* James Crawford, *Brownlie's Principles of Public International Law* 148 (8th ed. 2012).

duty to rescue. See DUTY (1).

duty to retreat. See RETREAT RULE.

duty to treat. See DUTY (2).

duty to warn. See DUTY (1).

duumviri (d[y]oo-**əm**-və-rɪ), *n. pl.* [fr. Latin *due* "two" + *viri* "men"] **1.** *Roman law.* Magistrates elected or appointed in pairs to hold an office or perform a function.

▸ ***duumviri municipales*** (d[y]oo-**əm**-və-rɪ myoo-nis-ə-**pay**-leez). [Latin] (18c) Two judicial magistrates annually elected in towns and colonies.

▸ ***duumviri navales*** (d[y]oo-**əm**-və-rɪ nə-**vay**-leez). [Latin] (16c) Two officers appointed to man, equip, and refit the navy.

2. Two peers in authority. — Also termed *duoviri.*

dux (dəks), *n.* [fr. Latin *ducere* "to lead"] **1.** *Roman law.* An army commander. **2.** *Roman law.* A military governor of a province. • This term was eventually used also as a title of distinction. **3.** *Hist.* Duke; a title of nobility. See DUKE.

DV. *abbr.* See *domestic violence* under VIOLENCE.

DWAI. *abbr.* Driving while ability-impaired — the New York equivalent of driving under the influence. See DRIVING UNDER THE INFLUENCE.

DWAID. *abbr.* Driving while ability-impaired by drugs.

DWAIDA. *abbr.* Driving while ability-impaired by drugs combined with alcohol.

DWB. (1990) *abbr.* DRIVING WHILE BLACK.

dwell, *vb.* (13c) **1.** To remain; to linger <the case dwelled in her memory>. **2.** To reside in a place permanently or for some period <he dwelled in California for nine years>.

dwelling defense. See CASTLE DOCTRINE.

dwelling-house. (15c) **1.** The house or other structure in which one or more people live; a residence or abode. **2.** *Real estate.* The house and all buildings attached to or connected with the house. **3.** *Criminal law.* A building, a part of a building, a tent, a mobile home, or another enclosed space that is used or intended for use as a human habitation. • The term has referred to connected buildings in the same curtilage but now typically includes only the structures connected either directly with the house or by an enclosed passageway. — Often shortened to *dwelling.* — Also termed (archaically) *mansion house*; (more broadly) *dwelling place.*

▸ **quasi-dwelling-house.** (1823) *Hist.* Any outbuilding, such as a barn, that is in proximity to the building used as a residence. See BURGLARY (1).

> "A 'dwelling house' or 'dwelling' has been defined in connection with the crime of arson as any house intended to be occupied as a residence, or an enclosed space, permanent or temporary, in which human beings usually stay, lodge, or reside. If a building is not used exclusively as a dwelling, it is characterized as a dwelling if there is internal communication between the two parts of the building. Dwellings include mobile homes and a boat, if the person resides on it." 5 Am. Jur. 2d *Arson and Related Offenses* § 13, at 789 (1995).

DWI. *abbr.* (1950) DRIVING WHILE INTOXICATED.

DWOP (**dee**-wop *or* **doo**-wop). *abbr.* Dismissal without prejudice. See *dismissal for want of prosecution* under DISMISSAL (1).

DWOP docket. See DOCKET (2).

dyarchy (dɪ-ahr-kee), *n.* [fr. Greek *dy* "two" + *archein* "rule"] (1835) A government jointly ruled by two people, such as William and Mary of England. — Also termed *diarchy.*

> "Dyarchy. A term applied by Mommsen to the Roman principate . . . a period in which he held that sovereignty was shared between the princes and the senate. The term has also been given to a system of government, promoted as a constitutional reform in India by Montagu and Chelmsford and introduced by the Government of India Act, 1919. It marked the introduction of democracy into the executive of the British administration of India by dividing the provincial executives into authoritarian and popularly responsible sections composed respectively of councillors appointed by the Crown and ministers appointed by the governor and responsible to the provincial legislative councils . . . . The system ended when full provincial autonomy was granted in 1935." David M. Walker, *The Oxford Companion to Law* 386 (1980).

dyathanasia, (dɪ-ath-ə-**nay**-zhə), *n.* (1975) The act of permitting death to occur naturally by withholding, terminating, or not offering life-prolonging treatments or intervention. — Also termed *passive mercy killing.* See EUTHANASIA.

Dyer Act. A 1919 federal law making it unlawful either (1) to transport a stolen motor vehicle across state lines, knowing it to be stolen, or (2) to receive, conceal, or sell such a vehicle, knowing it to be stolen. 18 USCA §§ 2311–2313. — Also termed *National Motor Vehicle Theft Act.*

dyet. See DIET.

dying declaration. See DECLARATION (6).

dying without issue. See FAILURE OF ISSUE.

dynamite charge. See ALLEN CHARGE.

dynamite instruction. See ALLEN CHARGE.

dynasty. (15c) **1.** A powerful family line that continues in power for a long time; esp., a family of kings or other rulers whose parents, grandparents, etc. have ruled the country for many years <the Hapsburg dynasty in Austria>. **2.** A period of time when a particular family ruled a country for many years <a vase from the Ming Dynasty> **3.** A powerful group of individuals who control a particular industry or field and who control their successors <a literary dynasty> <a banking dynasty>.

dynasty trust. See TRUST (3).

dysnomy (**dis**-nə-mee), *n.* [fr. Greek *dys* "bad" + *nomos* "law"] (1965) The enactment of bad legislation. Cf. EUNOMY.

dyvour (dɪ-vər). (16c) *Scots law.* Someone who is heavily in debt or bankrupt.

E

EA. *abbr.* ENVIRONMENTAL ASSESSMENT.

EAA. *abbr.* EQUAL ACCESS ACT OF 1984.

eadem persona cum defuncto (ee-**ay**-dəm pər-**soh**-nə kəm di-**fəngk**-toh). [Law Latin] (17c) *Hist.* The same person as the decedent. • An heir having full title to the decedent's property was legally viewed to be the same person as the decedent.

ea intentione (**ee**-ə in-ten-shee-**oh**-nee). [Latin] With that intent.

EAJA. *abbr.* EQUAL ACCESS TO JUSTICE ACT.

E&O insurance. See *errors-and-omissions insurance* under INSURANCE.

earl. (12c) A title of nobility, formerly the highest in England but now the third highest, ranking between a marquis and a viscount. • This title corresponds with the French *comte* and the German *graf.* Originating with the Saxons, this title is the most ancient of the English peerage. William the Conqueror first made the title hereditary, giving it in fee to his nobles. No territorial, private, or judicial rights now accompany the title; it merely confers nobility and a hereditary seat in the House of Lords.

earldom. (12c) **1.** The rank, dignity, or jurisdiction of an earl. • Only the dignity remains now, the jurisdiction having been given over to the sheriff. See DIGNITY. **2.** The property belonging to an earl.

earles-penny. (18c) *Hist.* Money given in part payment; EARNEST. — Also termed *earl's penny.*

Earl Marshal of England. (13c) A great officer of state, who historically had jurisdiction over several courts, including the court of chivalry and the court of honor. • Under this office is the herald's office, or college of arms. The Earl Marshal was also a judge of the Marshalsea court, now abolished. This office is quite ancient. Since 1672, it has been hereditary in the family of Howards, Dukes of Norfolk. — Often shortened to *Earl Marshal.*

earl's penny. See EARLES-PENNY.

early neutral evaluation. In dispute resolution, a preliminary objective assessment by a disinterested expert about the strength of each party's case and the likely outcome if the parties go to trial. — Abbr. ENE.

early voting. See VOTING.

earmark, *n.* (16c) **1.** Originally, a mark on the ear — a mode of marking sheep and other animals.

> "When now-a-days we say that 'money has no ear-mark,' we are alluding to a practice which in all probability played a large part in ancient law. Cattle were ear-marked or branded, and this enabled their owner to swear that they were his in whosesoever hands he might find them. The legal supposition is, not that one ox is indistinguishable from another ox, but that all oxen, or all oxen of a certain large class, are equivalent. The possibility of using them as money has rested on this supposition." 2 Frederick Pollock & Frederic W. Maitland, *History of English Law Before the Time of Edward I* 151–52 (2d ed. 1899).

2. A mark put on something (such as a coin) to distinguish it from another. **3.** An indication of an underlying quality, state, or condition, esp. fraud <concealment is an earmark of fraud>. See BADGE OF FRAUD.

earmark, *vb.* (16c) **1.** To mark with an earmark. **2.** To set aside for a specific purpose or recipient.

earmarking doctrine. (1987) *Bankruptcy.* The principle that borrowed funds set aside for the lender are not part of a debtor's bankruptcy estate and may be transferred without disadvantage to other creditors; specif., an equitable principle that when a new lender makes a loan to enable a debtor to pay off a specified creditor, the funds are specifically set aside for that creditor so that, if the debtor lacks control over the disposition of the funds, they do not become part of the debtor's estate and thus subject to a preference.

earn, *vb.* (bef. 12c) **1.** To acquire by labor, service, or performance. **2.** To do something that entitles one to a reward or result, whether it is received or not.

earned income. See INCOME.

earned-income credit. See *earned-income tax credit* under TAX CREDIT.

earned-income tax credit. See TAX CREDIT.

earned land. See LAND.

earned premium. See PREMIUM (1).

earned surplus. See *retained earnings* under EARNINGS.

earned time. See TIME.

earner. (17c) **1.** Someone who produces income through personal efforts or property or both. **2.** Property or an asset that produces income for its owner.

earnest, *n.* (13c) **1.** A nominal payment or token act that serves as a pledge or a sign of good faith, esp. as the partial purchase price of property. • Though not legally necessary, an earnest may help the parties come to an agreement. **2.** EARNEST MONEY.

earnest money. (16c) A deposit paid (often in escrow) by a prospective buyer (esp. of real estate) to show a good-faith intention to complete the transaction, and ordinarily forfeited if the buyer defaults. • Although earnest money has traditionally been a nominal sum (such as a nickel or a dollar) used in the sale of goods, it is not a mere token in the real-estate context: it is generally a percentage of the purchase price and may be a substantial sum. — Also termed *earnest; bargain money; caution money; hand money.* Cf. BINDER (2); *down payment* under PAYMENT.

> "The amount of earnest money deposited rarely exceeds 10 percent of the purchase price, and its primary purpose is to serve as a source of payment of damages should the buyer default. Earnest money is *not* essential to make a purchase agreement binding if the buyer's and seller's exchange of mutual promises of performance (that is, the buyer's promise to purchase and the seller's promise to sell at a specified price and terms) constitutes the consideration for the contract." John W. Reilly, *The Language of Real Estate* 131 (4th ed. 1993).

earnest-penny. See GOD'S PENNY.

earning asset. See ASSET.

earning capacity. (1872) A person's ability or power to earn money, given the person's talent, skills, training, and experience. • Earning capacity is one element considered when measuring the damages recoverable in a personal-injury lawsuit. And in family law, earning capacity is considered when awarding child support and spousal maintenance (or alimony) and in dividing property between spouses upon divorce. — Also termed *earning power.* See LOST EARNING CAPACITY.

earnings. (16c) Revenue gained from labor or services, from the investment of capital, or from assets. See INCOME.

▸ **appropriated retained earnings.** (1974) Retained earnings that a company's board designates for a distinct use, and that are therefore unavailable to pay dividends or for other uses. — Also termed *appropriated surplus; surplus revenue; suspense reserve.*

▸ **earnings before interest and taxes.** (1973) *Corporations.* A company's income calculated without deductions for interest expenses and taxes, used as a measure of the company's ability to generate cash flow from ongoing operations.— Abbr. EBIT.

▸ **earnings before interest, taxes, and depreciation.** *Corporations.* A company's income without deductions for interest expenses, taxes, depreciation expenses, or amortization expenses, used as an indicator of a company's profitability and ability to service its debt. — Abbr. EBITDA.

▸ **earnings per share.** See EARNINGS PER SHARE.

▸ **future earnings.** See *lost earnings.*

▸ **gross earnings.** See *gross income* under INCOME.

▸ **lost earnings.** (1877) Wages, salary, or other income that a person could have earned if he or she had not lost a job, suffered a disabling injury, or died. • Lost earnings are typically awarded as damages in personal-injury and wrongful-termination cases. There can be past lost earnings and future lost earnings. Both are subsets of this category, though legal writers sometimes loosely use *future earnings* as a synonym for *lost earnings.* Cf. LOST EARNING CAPACITY.

▸ **net earnings.** See *net income* under INCOME.

▸ **normalized earnings.** (1969) *Corporations.* Earnings adjusted for inflation and to remove elements that are extraordinary, nonrecurring, nonoperating, or otherwise unusual.

▸ **ongoing earnings.** See *operating earnings.*

▸ **operating earnings.** (1908) Business income calculated in violation of generally accepted accounting principles by including income items and excluding various business expenses. • Many companies use operating earnings to favorably skew their price-earnings (P/E) ratios. Because the rationales for the underlying calculations vary from company to company, and from period to period within a company, operating earnings are almost always artificially inflated and unreliable. The term *operating earnings* is meaningless under generally accepted accounting principles. — Also termed *pro forma earnings; economic earnings; core earnings; ongoing earnings; earnings excluding special items.* See PRICE-EARNINGS RATIO.

▸ **pretax earnings.** (1951) Net earnings before income taxes.

▸ **pro forma earnings.** See *operating earnings.*

▸ **real earnings.** Earnings that are adjusted for inflation so that they reflect actual purchasing power.

▸ **retained earnings.** (1932) A corporation's accumulated income after dividends have been distributed. — Also termed *earned surplus; undistributed profit.*

▸ **surplus earnings.** (18c) The excess of corporate assets over liabilities within a given period, usu. a year.

earnings and profits. *Corporations.* In corporate taxation, the measure of a corporation's economic capacity to make a shareholder distribution that is not a return of capital. • The distribution will be dividend income to the shareholders to the extent of the corporation's current and accumulated earnings and profits. Cf. *accumulated-earnings tax* under TAX; *accumulated taxable income* under INCOME.

earnings before interest and taxes. See EARNINGS.

earnings before interest, taxes, and depreciation. See EARNINGS.

earnings excluding special items. See *operating earnings* under EARNINGS.

earnings per share. (1908) *Corporations.* A measure of corporate value by which the corporation's net income is divided by the number of outstanding shares of common stock. • Investors benefit from calculating a corporation's earnings per share, because it helps the investors determine the fair market value of the corporation's stock. — Abbr. EPS.

▸ **fully diluted earnings per share.** (1969) A corporation's net income — assuming that all convertible securities had been transferred to common equity and all stock options had been exercised — divided by the number of shares of the corporation's outstanding common stock.

earnings-price ratio. See *earnings yield* under YIELD.

earnings report. See INCOME STATEMENT.

earnings yield. See YIELD.

earnout. (1971) *Business law.* A payment contingent on the occurrence of a future event; esp., a payment by a buyer to a seller contingent on the business being sold meeting or exceeding sales or earnings goals. • An earnout provision in a merger or acquisition reduces the buyer's risk because part of the purchase price is paid in the future based on the earnings or performance of the business. — Also written *earn-out.*

earnout agreement. (1977) *Business law.* An agreement for the sale of a business whereby the buyer first pays an agreed amount up front, leaving the final purchase price to be determined by the business's future profits. • The seller usu. helps manage the business for a period after the sale. — Sometimes shortened to *earnout.*

earthquake insurance. See INSURANCE.

earwig, *vb. Slang.* To engage a judge in ex parte communications. — **earwigging,** n.

earwitness. (16c) A witness who testifies about something that he or she heard but did not see. Cf. EYEWITNESS.

eased land. *Real estate.* Land encumbered by a conservation easement or, less often, other easement.

easement (**eez**-mənt). (14c) An interest in land owned by another person, consisting in the right to use or control the land, or an area above or below it, for a specific limited purpose (such as to cross it for access to a public road). • The land benefiting from an easement is called the *dominant estate*; the land burdened by an easement is called the *servient estate.* Unlike a lease or license, an easement may last forever, but it does not give the holder the right to possess, take from, improve, or sell the land. The primary recognized easements are (1) a right-of-way, (2) a right of entry for any purpose relating to the dominant estate, (3) a right to the support of land and buildings, (4) a right of light and air, (5) a right to water, (6) a right to do some act that would otherwise amount to a nuisance, and (7) a right to place or keep something on the servient estate. — Also termed *private right-of-way*; *easement agreement.* See SERVITUDE (1). Cf. PROFIT À PRENDRE.

▸ **access easement.** (1933) An easement allowing one or more persons to travel across another's land to get to a nearby location, such as a road. • The access easement is a common type of easement by necessity. — Also termed *easement of access*; *easement of way*; *easement of passage.*

▸ **adverse easement.** See *prescriptive easement.*

▸ **affirmative easement.** (1881) An easement that forces the servient-estate owner to permit certain actions by the easement holder, such as discharging water onto the servient estate. — Also termed *positive easement.* Cf. *negative easement.*

> "Positive easements give rights of entry upon the land of another, not amounting to profits, to enable something to be done on that land. Some are commonplace, examples being rights of way across the land of another and rights to discharge water on to the land of another. Others are more rare, such as the right to occupy a pew in a church, the right to use a kitchen situated on the land of another for the purpose of washing and drying clothes, and the right to use a toilet situated on the land of another." Peter Butt, *Land Law* 305 (2d ed. 1988).

▸ **agricultural-preservation easement.** See *land-conservation easement.*

▸ **apparent easement.** (1851) A visually evident easement, such as a paved trail or a sidewalk.

▸ **appendant easement.** See *easement appurtenant.*

▸ **appurtenant easement.** See *easement appurtenant.*

▸ **avigational easement.** (1962) An easement permitting unimpeded aircraft flights over the servient estate. — Also termed *avigation easement*; *aviation easement*; *flight easement*; *navigation easement.*

▸ **common easement.** (18c) An easement allowing the servient landowner to share in the benefit of the easement. — Also termed *nonexclusive easement.*

▸ **conservation easement.** (1965) *Property.* A real-estate covenant binding a parcel of land in a way that preserves a native plant or animal, a natural or physical feature of the land, or some aspect of the land that has some historical, cultural, or scientific significance. • The easement is a recorded, perpetual, individually tailored agreement creating a nonpossessory interest in real property, the interest being held by a government entity or by a qualified nonprofit. It permanently restricts or imposes affirmative obligations on the property's owner or lessee to retain or protect natural, scenic, or open-space values of real property, ensure its availability for agricultural, forest, recreational, or open-space use, protect natural resources and habitat, maintain or enhance air or water quality, or preserve the historical, architectural, archeological, or cultural aspects of the real property while allowing the landowner to continue to own and use the land, sell it, or transfer it to heirs. — Also termed *conservation agreement*; *conservation covenant*; *conservation servitude*; *conservation restriction.*

▸ **continuous easement.** (1863) An easement that may be enjoyed without a deliberate act by the party claiming it, such as an easement for drains, sewer pipes, lateral support of a wall, or light and air. — Also termed (in Louisiana) *continuous servitude.* Cf. *discontinuous easement.*

▸ **customary easement.** An easement that belongs to the public in general as established by traditional use. — Also termed *easement by custom.*

▸ **determinable easement.** (1889) An easement that terminates on the happening of a specific event.

▸ **discontinuous easement.** (1867) An easement that can be enjoyed only if the party claiming it deliberately acts in some way with regard to the servient estate. • Examples are a right-of-way and the right to draw water. — Also termed *discontinuing easement*; *noncontinuous easement*; *nonapparent easement*; (in Louisiana) *discontinuous servitude.* Cf. *continuous easement.*

▸ **easement appurtenant.** (1810) An easement created to benefit another tract of land, the use of easement being incident to the ownership of that other tract. — Also termed *appurtenant easement*; *appendant easement*; *pure easement*; *easement proper.* Cf. *easement in gross.*

▸ **easement by custom.** See *customary easement.*

▸ **easement by estoppel.** (1907) A court-ordered easement created from a voluntary servitude after a person, mistakenly believing the servitude to be permanent, acted in reasonable reliance on the mistaken belief.

▸ **easement by express grant.** See *express easement.*

▸ **easement by express reservation.** See *express easement.*

▸ **easement by implication.** See *implied easement.*

▸ **easement by implication from description of land.** See *implied easement.*

▸ **easement by implied grant.** See *implied easement.*

▸ **easement by implied reservation.** See *implied easement.*

▸ **easement by necessity.** (1865) An easement created by operation of law because the easement is indispensable to the reasonable use of nearby property, such as an easement connecting a parcel of land to a road. — Also termed *easement of necessity*; *necessary way.*

▸ **easement by prescription.** See *prescriptive easement.*

▸ **easement for air.** See *light-and-air easement.*

▸ **easement for light.** See *light-and-air easement.*

▸ **easement for light and air.** See *light-and-air easement.*

▸ **easement for support.** An easement prohibiting a landowner from depriving the adjoining land and the structures on it of the land's vertical or horizontal support.

▸ **easement in gross.** (1866) An easement benefiting a particular person and not a particular piece of land. • The beneficiary need not, and usu. does not, own any land adjoining the servient estate. Cf. *easement appurtenant.*

▸ **easement of access.** See *access easement.*

▸ **easement of convenience.** (1880) An easement that increases the facility, comfort, or convenience of enjoying the dominant estate or some right connected with it.

▸ **easement of natural support.** See *lateral support* under SUPPORT (4).

▸ **easement of necessity.** See *easement by necessity.*

▸ **easement of passage.** See *access easement.*

▸ **easement of prior use.** See *prior-use easement.*

▸ **easement of way.** See *access easement.*

▸ **easement proper.** See *easement appurtenant.*

▸ **equitable easement.** (1869) **1.** An implied easement created by equity when adjacent lands have been created out of a larger tract. • Such an easement is usu. created to allow implied privileges to continue. **2.** See *restrictive covenant* (1) under COVENANT (4).

▸ **exclusive easement.** (1848) An easement that the holder has the sole right to use. Cf. *common easement.*

▸ **façade easement.** A recorded agreement between the owner of a building and a land trust or government agency permanently prohibiting alteration of the building façade to protect its historic value while allowing the owner to continue to own and use the building, sell it, or transfer it to heirs.

▸ **flight easement.** See *avigational easement.*

▸ **floating easement.** (1878) An easement that, when created, is not limited to any specific part of the servient estate.

▸ **flowage easement.** (1894) A common-law easement that gives the dominant-estate owner the right to flood a servient estate, as when land near a dam is flooded to maintain the dam or to control the water level in a reservoir.

▸ **implied easement.** (1867) An easement created by law after an owner of two parcels of land uses one parcel to benefit the other to such a degree that, upon the sale of the benefited parcel, the purchaser could reasonably expect the use to be included in the sale. — Also termed *easement by implication, way of necessity; easement by implied grant; easement by implied reservation.*

▸ **inchoate easement.** The use of another person's land never having ripened into a right because the landowner interrupted the use or no evidence supports the view that the landowner knew of and acquiesced to the use. — Also termed *inchoate prescriptive easement.*

▸ **ingress-and-egress easement.** The right to use land to enter and leave another's property.

▸ **intermittent easement.** (1965) An easement that is usable or used only from time to time, not regularly or continuously.

▸ **land-conservation easement.** (1984) *Property.* An easement arising from an agreement between a landowner and a land trust to provide for the protection of the land in its natural state while perhaps also allowing the property to be used for agricultural or low-impact recreational activities. • The easement runs with the land. — Also termed *land-conservation agreement; land-preservation easement; agricultural-preservation easement.*

▸ **light-and-air easement.** (1940) A negative easement that prevents an adjoining landowner from constructing a building that would prevent light or air from reaching the dominant estate. — Also termed *air-and-light easement; easement for light and air; air easement; light easement.* See *negative easement.* Cf. *solar easement.*

▸ **mineral easement.** (1888) An easement that permits the holder to enter the property to remove minerals from it.

▸ **navigation easement.** (1950) **1.** An easement giving the federal government the right to regulate navigable waters, even when the regulation interferes with private water rights. **2.** See *avigational easement.*

▸ **negative easement.** (1861) An easement that prohibits the servient-estate owner from doing something, such as building an obstruction. Cf. *affirmative easement.*

> "Negative easements . . . confer no right of entry, but consist essentially of the right to prevent something being done; examples are the right to the flow of air through defined aperture, the right to receive light for a building, the right to the support of a building, and (possibly) the right to require a neighbouring landowner to repair fences." Peter Butt, *Land Law* 305 (2d ed. 1988).

▸ **noise easement.** (1961) An easement that allows the dominant estate's owner to generate noise that travels onto the servient-estate owner's property.

▸ **nonapparent easement.** See *discontinuous easement.*

▸ **noncontinuous easement.** See *discontinuous easement.*

▸ **nonexclusive easement.** See *common easement.*

▸ **positive easement.** See *affirmative easement.*

▸ **prescriptive easement.** (1838) An easement created from an open, adverse, and continuous use over a statutory period. — Also termed *easement by prescription; adverse easement.* See ADVERSE POSSESSION.

▸ **prior-use easement.** An implied easement arising from reasonable necessity for enjoyment and use of the property, and previous usage for those purposes. — Also termed *easement by prior use; easement from prior use; easement of prior use.*

▸ **private easement.** (1805) An easement whose enjoyment is restricted to one specific person or a few specific people.

▸ **public easement.** (1803) An easement for the benefit of an entire community, such as the right to travel down a street or a sidewalk.

▸ **pure easement.** See *easement appurtenant.*

▸ **quasi-easement.** (1860) **1.** An easement-like right occurring when both tracts of land are owned by the same person. • A quasi-easement may become a true easement if the landowner sells one of the tracts. **2.** An obligation or license that relates to land but that is not a true easement — for example, a landowner's obligation to maintain the fence between the landowner's tract and someone else's tract.

▸ **reciprocal negative easement.** (1897) An easement created when a landowner sells part of the land and restricts the buyer's use of that part, and, in turn, that same restriction is placed on the part kept by the landowner. • Such an easement usu. arises when the original landowner creates a common scheme of development for smaller tracts that are carved out of the original tract.

▸ **reserved easement.** (1925) An easement created by the grantor of real property to benefit the grantor's retained property and to burden the granted property.

▸ **secondary easement.** (1843) An easement that is appurtenant to the primary or actual easement; the right to do things that are necessary to fully enjoy the easement itself.

▸ **shadow easement.** (1896) An easement that allows the dominant estate's owner to erect a structure that casts a shadow on the servient estate.

▸ **solar easement.** (1982) An easement created to protect the dominant estate's exposure to direct sunlight. • A solar easement is often created to prevent the servient-estate owner from constructing any building that would cause shadows on the dominant estate, thus interfering with the use of a solar-energy system. Cf. *light-and-air easement.*

> "Solar easements . . . remain difficult to describe because of the relationship of the sun to the earth. Shadow variables include land slope, terrain, solar orientation, latitude, time of day, and height of potential obstructions. Lawyers, engineers, land planners, title companies and others have expressed concern over the complexity required to write a solar easement containing highly detailed, technical information often included in these easements." Sandy F. Kraemer, *Solar Law* 42 (1978).

▸ **timber easement.** (1982) An easement that permits the holder to cut and remove timber from another's property. — Also termed *timber rights.*

easement agreement. See EASEMENT.

easement by custom. See *customary easement* under EASEMENT.

easement by express grant. See *express easement* under EASEMENT.

easement by express reservation. See *express easement* under EASEMENT.

easement by implied grant. See *implied easement* under EASEMENT.

easement by implied reservation. See *implied easement* under EASEMENT.

easement for air. See *light-and-air easement* under EASEMENT.

easement for light. See *light-and-air easement* under EASEMENT.

easement for light and air. See *light-and-air easement* under EASEMENT.

easement for support. See EASEMENT.

Easter-offerings. (17c) *Eccles. law.* Small sums of money paid as personal tithes to the parochial clergy by the parishioners at Easter. • Under the Recovery of Small Tithes Act (1695), Easter-offerings were recoverable before justices of the peace. St. 7 & 8 Will. 3, ch. 6. — Also termed *Easter-dues.*

Easter sittings. (1834) *English law.* A term of court beginning on April 15 of each year and usu. ending on May 8, but sometimes extended to May 13. • This was known until 1875 as *Easter term.* Cf. HILARY SITTINGS; MICHAELMAS SITTINGS; TRINITY SITTINGS.

Easter Term. See EASTER SITTINGS.

East Greenwich (eest **gren**-ich). *Hist.* The name of a royal manor in the county of Kent, England. • Historically, this manor was mentioned in royal grants or patents as descriptive of the tenure of free socage.

East India Company. *Hist.* The company that was originally established to pursue exclusive trade between England and India, and that later became more active in political affairs than in commerce. • In 1858, the Government of India Act transferred governance over the company's territories to the Crown. The company was dissolved in 1874. St. 21 & 22 Vict., ch. 106.

EAT. *abbr.* Earnings after taxes.

eat inde sine die (**ee**-ət **in**-dee **sɪ**-nee **dɪ**-ee) [Latin] Let him go thence without day. • These words were used on a defendant's acquittal, or when a prisoner was to be discharged, to signify that the matter be dismissed without any further judicial proceedings. See GO HENCE WITHOUT DAY.

eaves-drip. (bef. 12c) **1.** The dripping of water from the eaves of a house onto adjacent land. **2.** An easement permitting the holder to allow water to drip onto the servient estate. See DRIP RIGHTS; STILLICIDIUM.

eavesdropping. (17c) The act of secretly listening to the private conversation of others without their consent; a clandestine attempt to overhear or intercept others' private communication. Cf. LISTENING DEVICE; WIRETAPPING.

EB. *abbr.* BUREAU OF ECONOMIC AND BUSINESS AFFAIRS.

EBA. *abbr.* Enterprise bargaining agreement. See *certified agreement* under AGREEMENT.

ebba et fluctus (**eb**-ə et **flək**-təs), *n.* [Latin "ebb and flow"] *Hist.* The ebb and flow of tide; ebb and flood. • The time of one ebb and flood, plus an additional 40 days, was anciently granted to a person who was excused from court for being beyond seas. See EBB AND FLOW; ESSOIN; BEYOND SEAS.

ebb and flow. (bef. 12c) The coming and going of the tides. • This expression was formerly used to denote the limits of admiralty jurisdiction. The tidewater limitation was abandoned in *The Genesee Chief v. Fitzhugh*, 53 U.S. (12 How.) 443 (1851).

ebdomadarius (eb-dom-ə-**dair**-ee-əs), *n.* [Latin "weekly"] (18c) *Eccles. law.* An officer in a cathedral church who supervises the regular performance of divine service and prescribes the duties of choir members.

EBE. *abbr.* ENTRAPMENT BY ESTOPPEL.

EBIT. *abbr.* See *earnings before interest and taxes* under EARNINGS.

EBITDA. *abbr.* See EARNINGS.

ebriety, *n.* (16c) *Rare.* A state or habit of intoxication; inebriation.

EC. *abbr.* (1973) **1.** ETHICAL CONSIDERATION. **2.** European Community. See EUROPEAN UNION. **4.** See EMERGENCY CONTRACEPTIVE PILL.

ecclesia (i-**klee**-z[h]ee-ə), *n.* [Latin fr. Greek *ekklesia* "assembly"] (16c) **1.** A place of religious worship. **2.** A Christian assembly; a church.

ecclesiarch (i-**klee**-zee-ahrk), *n.* (18c) The ruler of a church.

ecclesiastic (i-klee-zee-**as**-tik), *n.* (17c) A clergyman; a priest; one consecrated to the service of the church.

ecclesiastical (i-klee-zee-**as**-ti-kəl), *adj.* (15c) Of, relating to, or involving the church, esp. as an institution. — Also termed *ecclesiastic.*

ecclesiastical authorities. (1821) The church's hierarchy, answerable to the Crown, but set apart from the rest of the citizens, responsible for superintending public worship and other religious ceremonies and for administering spiritual counsel and instruction. • In England, the several levels of the clergy are (1) archbishops and bishops, (2) deans and chapters, (3) archdeacons, (4) rural deans, (5) parsons (under whom are included appropriators) and vicars, and (6) curates. Church-wardens, sidesmen, parish clerks, and sextons are also considered types of ecclesiastical authorities because their duties are connected with the church. Cf. *ecclesiastical court* under COURT.

ecclesiastical commissioners. (1836) *Hist. English law.* A group of people empowered to suggest measures to improve the established church's efficiency, to be ratified by orders in council. • This body of commissioners, established in 1836 by the Ecclesiastical Commissioners Act (St. 6 & 7 Will. 4, ch. 77), has been dissolved. Its functions, rights, and property are now vested in the church commissioners.

ecclesiastical controversy. (1829) A civil claim based on the decision of a religious association's tribunal against one or more members of the association. • If the decision relates solely to matters within the church, such as church governance or questions of faith, secular courts have no jurisdiction to hear what is effectively an appeal. *See Watson v. Jones*, 80 U.S. 679, 728–29 (1871).

ecclesiastical corporation. See CORPORATION.

ecclesiastical court. See COURT.

ecclesiastical jurisdiction. (16c) Jurisdiction over ecclesiastical cases and controversies, such as that exercised by ecclesiastical courts.

ecclesiastical law. (16c) **1.** The body of law derived largely from canon and civil law and administered by the ecclesiastical courts. **2.** The law governing the doctrine and discipline of a particular church; esp., Anglican canon law. — Also termed *jus ecclesiasticum*; *law spiritual.* Cf. CANON LAW.

ecclesiastical marriage. See MARRIAGE (1).

ecclesiastical matter. (16c) A matter that concerns church doctrine, creed, or form of worship, or the adoption and enforcement, within a religious association, of laws and regulations to govern the membership, including the power to exclude from such an association those deemed unworthy of membership.

ecclesiastical sentence. (16c) The judgment in an ecclesiastical case.

ecclesiastical tenure. See *tenure by divine service* under TENURE (2).

ecclesiastical things. (16c) Property (such as buildings and cemeteries) given to a church to support the poor or for any other pious use.

ecclesiastical-tithe rentcharge. See RENTCHARGE.

ecdicus (**ek**-də-kəs), *n.* [Greek *ekdikos* "legal representative"] (17c) *Hist.* The attorney, proctor, or advocate of an organization. • A church's attorney, for example, was known as an *episcoporum ecdicus.*

e-check. See CHECK.

echevin (esh-ə-**van**), *n.* (17c) *French law.* A municipal officer corresponding with the position of alderman or burgess, and sometimes having civil jurisdiction to hear and determine certain minor cases.

echouement (ay-shoo-**mawn**), *n.* In French marine law, stranding. See STRANDING.

ECHR. *abbr.* **1.** EUROPEAN COMMISSION OF HUMAN RIGHTS. **2.** EUROPEAN COURT OF HUMAN RIGHTS.

ECJ. *abbr.* EUROPEAN COURT OF JUSTICE.

ECOA. *abbr.* EQUAL CREDIT OPPORTUNITY ACT.

ecological terrorism. See *ecoterrorism* under TERRORISM.

ecology of crime. See *environmental criminology* under CRIMINOLOGY.

e-commerce. (1993) The practice of buying and selling goods and services through online consumer services and of conducting other business activities using an electronic device and the Internet. • The *e*, a shortened form of *electronic*, has become a popular prefix for other terms associated with electronic transactions. — Also termed *electronic commerce.* See ELECTRONIC TRANSACTION.

E-Commerce Directive. See DIRECTIVE ON CERTAIN ASPECTS OF ELECTRONIC COMMERCE IN THE INTERNAL MARKET.

e-commerce insurance. See INSURANCE.

econometrics (ee-kon-ə-**me**-triks). (1931) The branch of economics that expresses economic theory in mathematical terms and that seeks to verify theory through statistical methods.

economic coercion. See COERCION (2).

economic crime. See CRIME.

economic-cure trade embargo. See EMBARGO (3).

economic depreciation. See DEPRECIATION.

Economic Development Administration. A unit in the U.S. Department of Commerce responsible for helping to develop local economies and distressed areas by making grants for public works and development facilities that are designed to reduce persistent unemployment in economically distressed areas. • The agency was created in 1965 by the Public Works and Economic Development Act. — Abbr. EDA.

economic discrimination. (1919) Any form of discrimination within the field of commerce, such as boycotting a particular product or price-fixing. See BOYCOTT; PRICE DISCRIMINATION; PRICE-FIXING.

economic duress. See DURESS (3).

economic earnings. See *operating earnings* under EARNINGS.

Economic Espionage Act. *Trade secrets.* A 1996 federal statute criminalizing the misappropriation of trade secrets and providing criminal penalties for industrial espionage by or for a foreign entity. • The Act also applies to one who knowingly receives, purchases, or possesses stolen trade-secret information. 18 USCA §§ 1831–1839. — Sometimes termed *Industrial Espionage Act.*

economic frustration. See *commercial frustration* under FRUSTRATION (1).

economic goodwill. See GOODWILL.

economic-harm rule. See ECONOMIC-LOSS RULE.

economic indicator. (1903) A statistical measure used to describe the state of the economy or to predict its direction • Typical economic indicators include housing starts, gross domestic product, unemployment rates, and the Consumer Price Index. See INDICATOR.

▸ **lagging economic indicator.** (1980) An economic indicator (such as new-home sales) that tends to respond to the direction of the economy. — Often shortened to *lagging indicator.*

▸ **leading economic indicator.** (1964) An economic indicator (such as interest rates) that tends to predict the future direction of the economy. — Often shortened to *leading indicator.*

economic injury. See INJURY.

economic jurisprudence. See JURISPRUDENCE.

economic life. The duration of an asset's profitability, usu. shorter than its physical life.

economic loss. (1905) A monetary loss such as lost wages or lost profits. • The term usu. refers to a type of damages recoverable in a lawsuit. For example, in a products-liability suit, economic loss includes the cost of repair or replacement of defective property, as well as commercial loss for the property's inadequate value and consequent loss of profits or use.

▸ **consequential economic loss.** (1945) Economic loss that proximately results from a defective product and that is beyond direct economic loss. • Examples include lost profits and loss of goodwill or business reputation.

▸ **direct economic loss.** Economic loss flowing directly from insufficient product quality. • The most common type is loss-of-bargain damages — the difference between the actual value of goods accepted and the value they would have had if they had been delivered as promised or warranted.

economic-loss rule. (1976) *Torts.* **1.** The principle that a plaintiff generally cannot recover for financial harm that results from injury to the person or property of another. • Many states recognize an exception to this rule when the defendant commits fraud or negligent misrepresentation, or when a special relationship exists between the parties (such as an attorney–client relationship). **2.** The principle that a buyer cannot recover in tort from the seller of a product when the product causes damage only to itself. **3.** The principle that a party generally may not recover in tort for financial harm that results from the defendant's failure to perform under a contract. **4.** Any principle that broadly inhibits recovery for the negligent infliction of pure financial harm. — Also termed *economic-harm rule*; *economic-loss doctrine.*

"One way the courts have attempted to draw a line between tort and warranty is to bar recovery for 'economic loss' in tort. In some states this common law doctrine has achieved the status of the 'economic loss doctrine,' meaning that once loss is defined as 'economic' it cannot be recovered at least in negligence or strict tort and perhaps not in fraud or misrepresentation." 1 James J. White & Robert S. Summers, *Uniform Commercial Code* § 10-5, at 581 (4th ed. 1995).

"It seems impossible to formulate a single economic loss rule. Instead, the problem of recovery for pure economic loss that is unaccompanied by physical harm to person or property occurs in a number of contexts that may invoke differing concerns of policy." Dan B. Dobbs, *An Introduction to Non-Statutory Economic Loss Claims*, 48 Ariz. L. Rev. 713, 733 (2006).

economic migrant. See *economic refugee* under REFUGEE.

economic obsolescence. See OBSOLESCENCE.

economic offense. See *economic crime* under CRIME.

economic-out clause. See MARKET-OUT CLAUSE.

economic-realities test. (1956) A method by which a court determines the true nature of a business transaction or situation by examining the totality of the commercial circumstances. • Courts often use this test to determine whether a person is an employee or an independent contractor. Factors include whether the alleged employer controls the details of the work and whether taxes are withheld from payments made to the worker.

economic refugee. See REFUGEE.

economic rent. (1880) **1.** The return gained from an economic resource (such as a worker or land) above the minimum cost of keeping the resource in service. **2.** Rent that yields a fair return on capital and expenses.

Economic Research Service. An agency in the U.S. Department of Agriculture responsible for compiling and analyzing information about domestic and international agricultural developments. — Abbr. ERS.

economic right. (*usu. pl.*) (1911) *Copyright.* A legal interest and power that concerns a financial benefit from a work, as distinguished from a moral interest that a creator has in a creation. • The term is mostly used in civil-law countries that recognize creators' moral rights.

economics. (18c) The social science dealing with the production, distribution, and consumption of goods and services.

Economics and Statistics Administration. A unit in the U.S. Department of Commerce responsible for maintaining high-quality standards of statistical reporting in the federal government and for responding to the needs of the Department of Commerce and the rest of the executive branch for statistical information and analysis. • The unit comprises the Bureau of the Census, the Bureau of Economic Analysis, and STAT-USA. — Abbr. ESA.

economic strike. See STRIKE (1).

economic-substance doctrine. (1981) *Tax.* The principle that a transaction must be treated as a sham for tax purposes if (1) the transaction has no genuine business purpose, and (2) there is no reasonable possibility that it will generate a profit in the absence of tax benefits.

economic substantive due process. See DUE PROCESS.

economic tort. See *business tort* under TORT.

economic unit. (1962) *Eminent domain.* In a partial-condemnation case, the property that is used to determine the fair-market value of the portion that is taken by eminent domain. • The land taken may be a large or small portion of the entire property. To determine how much property to include in an economic unit, three factors are weighed: (1) unity of use, (2) unity of ownership, and (3) contiguity. Of these, the most important is unity of use. See LARGER PARCEL.

economic value. See *exchange value* under VALUE (2).

economic warfare. See WARFARE.

economic waste. *Oil & gas.* Overproduction or excessive drilling of oil or gas.

economist. (16c) A professional who studies economics and the economy; a specialist in economics.

economy. (15c) **1.** The management or administration of the wealth and resources of a community (such as a city, state, or country). **2.** The sociopolitical organization of a community's wealth and resources. **3.** Restrained, thrifty, or sparing use of resources; efficiency.

▸ **balanced economy.** An economy in which the monetary values of imports and exports are equal.

▸ **black economy.** See SHADOW ECONOMY.

▸ **closed economy.** (1927) The economy of a country that does not trade with any other countries.

▸ **judicial economy.** See JUDICIAL ECONOMY.

▸ **market economy.** (1929) An economic system in which companies are not controlled by the government but decide what they want to produce or sell based on what they believe they can profit from. • Prices are determined by market forces rather than regulation.

▸ **overheated economy.** (1910) An economy that, although it has a high level of economic activity, has the capacity to cause interest rates and inflation to rise.

▸ **political economy.** (17c) A social science dealing with the economic problems of government and the relationship between political policies and economic processes.

▸ **shadow economy.** See SHADOW ECONOMY.

▸ **underground economy.** See SHADOW ECONOMY.

economy of scale. (*usu. pl.*) (1944) A decline in a product's per-unit production cost resulting from increased output, usu. due to increased production facilities; savings resulting from the greater efficiency of large-scale processes.

e contra (ee **kon**-trə). [Latin] On the contrary.

e-contract, *n.* (1999) **1.** POINT-AND-CLICK AGREEMENT. **2.** Any type of contract formed in the course of e-commerce by (1) the interaction of two or more individuals using electronic means, such as e-mail, (2) the interaction of an individual with an electronic agent, such as a computer program, or (3) the interaction of at least two electronic agents that are programmed to recognize the existence of a contract. • Sections 202–17 of the Uniform Computer Information Transactions Act provide rules for the formation, governance, and basic terms of an e-contract. Traditional contract principles and remedies usu. apply to e-contracts. — Also termed *electronic contract.* See ELECTRONIC AGENT.

e-contract, *vb.* (1997) To form a binding agreement by means of a computer or other electronic or automated technology.

e converso (ee kən-**vər**-soh). [Latin] Conversely; on the other hand; on the contrary.

ecosabotage. See *ecoterrorism* under TERRORISM.

ecoterrorism. See TERRORISM.

ecovandalism. See *ecoterrorism* under TERRORISM.

ECP. See EMERGENCY CONTRACEPTIVE PILL.

ECPA. *abbr.* ELECTRONIC COMMUNICATIONS PRIVACY ACT.

ECU. *abbr.* (1970) EUROPEAN CURRENCY UNIT.

ecumenical (ek-yə-**men**-ə-kəl), *adj.* (16c) **1.** General; universal. **2.** Interreligious; interdenominational.

E.D. *abbr.* Eastern District, in reference to U.S. judicial districts.

EDA. *abbr.* ECONOMIC DEVELOPMENT ADMINISTRATION.

EDGAR. *Securities.* The automated system used by the U.S. Securities and Exchange Commission to collect, validate, index, accept, and forward submissions from companies and others who are required by law to file forms with the SEC. • EDGAR is an acronym for electronic data-gathering, analysis, and retrieval.

edge lease. See LEASE.

EDI agreement. *abbr.* (1987) Electronic Data Interchange agreement; an agreement that governs the transfer or exchange of data, such as purchase orders, between parties by computer. • Electronic data transmitted under an EDI agreement is usu. formatted according to an agreed standard, such as the American National Standards Institute ANSI X12 standard or the U.N. EDIFACT standard.

edict (**ee**-dikt), *n.* [fr. Latin *edictum*] (14c) A formal decree, demand, or proclamation issued by the sovereign of a country. • In some countries, an edict has legal force equivalent to that of a statute. For Roman law edicts, see EDICTUM.

▸ **perpetual edict.** See *edictum perpetuum* under EDICTUM.

▸ **praetorian edict** (pri-**tor**-ee-ən). See *edictum praetoris* under EDICTUM.

edictal (ee-**dik**-təl), *adj.* (17c) Of, relating to, consisting of, or pronounced in one or more edicts. — **edictally,** *adv.*

edictal citation. (18c) *Scots & Roman–Dutch law.* A form of summons to appear in court, treated as having been served by public proclamation when personal service is impossible (as when a defendant is out of Scotland or cannot be found). — Also termed *edictal intimation.* See *substituted service* under SERVICE (7).

edictal interdict. See INTERDICT (1).

edictal intimation. See EDICTAL CITATION.

edicta magistratuum. See JUS HONORARIUM.

Edicts of Justinian. *Roman law.* Thirteen constitutions or laws of Justinian, appended to the Greek collection of the Novels in the Venetian manuscript. • The Edicts were confined to administrative matters in the provinces of the Roman Empire. They were not known to the glossators.

edictum (ə-**dik**-təm), *n.* [Latin] *Roman law.* **1.** In imperial Rome, an edict or mandate; an ordinance or law proclaimed by the emperor. • An edict was a constitution of the emperor acting on his own initiative, differing from a rescript in not being returned in the way of answer; from a decree in not being given in judgment; and from both in not being founded on solicitation. As an imperial constitution, it had the force of law. **2.** A declaration by a magistrate relevant to his jurisdiction or area of competence;

esp., the pronouncement of a magistrate of the principles by which he proposed to act in office. See *edictum annuum*; FORMULA (1). Pl. ***edicta.***

▸ ***edictum aedilicium*** (ee-**dik**-təm ee-də-**lish**-ee-əm). A curule aedile's edict regarding sales in the public market; esp., an edict giving remedies for sales of defective goods, animals, or slaves. • An aedile could, for instance, declare that sellers would be strictly liable for latent defects in goods, and dictate how dogs and wild animals for sale should be confined to protect the public. — Also written *aedilitium edictum*. Pl. ***edicta aedilicia.***

▸ ***edictum annuum*** (**an**-yoo-əm). An edict issued by a praetor at the beginning of the one-year term of office. Pl. ***edicta annua.***

▸ ***edictum perpetuum*** (pər-**pech**-oo-əm). (17c) The urban praetor's edict in its permanent form, edited by Julian in A.D. 131 and given legislative force. • This term originally had the narrower sense of the praetors' general edicts as opposed to edicts issued in specific cases. — Also termed *perpetual edict*; *lex annua*. Pl. ***edicta perpetua.***

▸ ***edictum praetoris*** (pri-**tor**-əs). (17c) The proclamation issued by a praetor at the start of the year's term, explaining the grounds on which a formula would be granted. — Also termed *praetorian edict*. See *edictum annuum*; FORMULA (1).

▸ ***edictum provinciale*** (prə-vin-shee-**ay**-lee). An edict or system of rules for the administration of justice, modeled on edictum praetoris, issued by the provincial governors in the Roman Empire. Pl. ***edicta provincialia.***

▸ ***edictum repentinum*** (rep-ən-**tɪ**-nəm). [Latin] *Roman law.* A supplementary edict issued to deal with some emergency. • This term was contrasted with *edictum perpetuum*. Pl. ***edicta repentina.***

▸ ***Edictum Theodorici*** (thee-ə-də-**rɪ**-sɪ). A collection of laws applicable to both Romans and Goths, issued by Theodoric, king of the Ostrogoths, at Rome about A.D. 500, or perhaps by Theodoric III, king of the Visigoths in Gaul about A.D. 460.

▸ ***edictum tralatitium*** (tral-ə-**tish**-ee-əm). A praetor's edict that retained all or a principal part of the predecessor's edict, with only such additions as appeared necessary to adapt it to changing social conditions or juristic ideas. • This had become standard practice by the end of the Republic. — Also spelled *edictum tralacticium* (tral-ək-**tish**-ee-əm). Pl. ***edicta tralatitia.***

edile (ee-dɪl). See AEDILE.

editorial privilege. See *journalist's privilege* (2) under PRIVILEGE (3).

editus (**ed**-ə-təs), *adj. Hist.* **1.** (Of a statute or rule) enacted; promulgated. **2.** (Of a child) born; brought forth.

e-document. See *electronic document* under DOCUMENT (2).

educational expense. See EXPENSE.

educational institution. (1842) **1.** A school, seminary, college, university, or other educational facility, though not necessarily a chartered institution. **2.** As used in a zoning ordinance, all buildings and grounds necessary to accomplish the full scope of educational instruction, including those things essential to mental, moral, and physical development.

educational neglect. See NEGLECT.

educational trust. See TRUST (3).

education individual retirement account. See INDIVIDUAL RETIREMENT ACCOUNT.

education voucher. See *tuition voucher* under VOUCHER.

EEC. *abbr.* (1958) European Economic Community. See EUROPEAN UNION.

EEOC. *abbr.* EQUAL EMPLOYMENT OPPORTUNITY COMMISSION.

EEZ. *abbr.* EXCLUSIVE ECONOMIC ZONE.

effect, *n.* (14c) **1.** Something produced by an agent or cause; a result, outcome, or consequence. **2.** The result that an instrument between parties will produce on their relative rights, or that a statute will produce on existing law, as discovered from the language used, the forms employed, or other materials for construing it.

effect, *vb.* (16c) To bring about; to make happen <the improper notice did not effect a timely appeal>.

effective, *adj.* (14c) **1.** (Of a statute, order, contract, etc.) in operation at a given time <effective June 1>. • A statute, order, or contract is often said to be effective beginning (and perhaps ending) at a designated time. **2.** Performing within the range of normal and expected standards <effective counsel>. **3.** Productive; achieving a result <effective cause>.

effective assignment. See ASSIGNMENT (2).

effective assistance of counsel. See ASSISTANCE OF COUNSEL.

effective cause. See *immediate cause* under CAUSE (1).

effective control. See CONTROL.

effective date. See DATE.

effective filing date. See DATE.

effective marginal tax rate. See TAX RATE.

effective possession. See *constructive possession* under POSSESSION.

effective rate. See INTEREST RATE.

effective tax rate. See *average tax rate* under TAX RATE.

effective vote. See VOTE (1).

effects, *n. pl.* (17c) Movable property; goods <personal effects>.

▸ **household effects.** See *household goods* under GOODS.

▸ **personal effects.** (1818) Items of a personal character; esp., personal property owned by a decedent at the time of death.

effects doctrine. See AFFECTS DOCTRINE.

effeirs (e-**feerz**), *adv. Scots law.* As appropriate; correctly. • The term ordinarily appears in the phrase *as affeirs*.

effets (e-fe *or* e-fets), *n. pl.* [French] **1.** Bills of exchange. **2.** Goods; movables; chattels.

▸ ***effets mobiliers*** (moh-beel-**yay** *or* moh-bə-**leerz**). Funds; stocks.

efficacy. The power to make an intended result occur; the capacity to produce effects. — **efficacious,** adj. — **efficaciousness,** n.

▸ **legal efficacy.** The quality of having significance or force under law to produce certain effects.

efficient adequate cause. See *proximate cause* under CAUSE (1).

efficient breach. See BREACH OF CONTRACT.

efficient-breach theory. (1980) *Contracts.* The view that a party should be allowed to breach a contract and pay damages, if doing so would be more economically efficient than performing under the contract. • This relatively modern theory stems from the law-and-economics movement. See BREACH OF CONTRACT.

efficient cause. See *proximate cause* under CAUSE (1).

efficient intervening cause. See *intervening cause* under CAUSE (1).

efficient proximate cause. See *proximate cause* under CAUSE (1).

effigy (**ef**-ə-jee), *n.* (16c) A figure, image, or other representation; esp., a crude representation of someone who is disliked. • Effigies are sometimes hanged, burned, or otherwise abused to express public disapproval or ridicule.

effluent (**ef**-loo-ənt), *n.* (1859) Liquid waste that is discharged into a river, lake, or other body of water.

effluxion of time (i-**flək**-shən). (17c) The expiration of a lease term resulting from the passage of time rather than from a specific action or event. — Also termed *efflux of time.*

efforcialiter (e-for-shee-**ay**-lə-tər), *adv.* [Latin] *Hist.* Forcibly. • This adverb referred primarily to military force.

effraction (ə-**frak**-shən). (19c) *Archaic.* A breach made by the use of force; BURGLARY (1).

effractor (i-**frak**-tər). [Latin] (17c) *Hist.* Someone who breaks through; a burglar. See HOUSEBREAKING. Pl. **effractors, *effractores*** (ef-rak-**tor**-eez).

effusio sanguinis (e-**fyoo**-zhee-oh **sang**-gwi-nis). [Latin] (18c) *Hist.* **1.** The shedding of blood. **2.** The fine or penalty imposed for the shedding of blood. • The Crown granted to many lords of manors the power to collect this fine. — Also termed *bloodwite; bloodwit.* Cf. WERGILD.

EFT. *abbr.* Electronic funds transfer. See FUNDS TRANSFER.

EFTA. *abbr.* ELECTRONIC FUND TRANSFER ACT.

e.g. *abbr.* [Latin *exempli gratia*] (17c) For example <an intentional tort, e.g., battery or false imprisonment>. Cf. I.E.

egalitarian, *adj.* (1885) Of, relating to, or involving the belief that all people are equal and should have the same rights and opportunities in life, and often the same outcomes. — **egalitarian,** *n.*

egalitarianism. (1932) The belief in human equality, esp. when that entails the removing of all inequalities among people; specif., a philosophy that promotes human equality in social, religious, political, and economic rights and privileges.

egg donation. (1980) *Family law.* A type of assisted-reproductive therapy in which eggs are removed from one woman and transplanted into the uterus of another woman who carries and delivers the child. • In egg donation, the egg is usu. fertilized in vitro. See IN VITRO FERTILIZATION; ASSISTED-REPRODUCTIVE TECHNOLOGY.

eggshell-skull plaintiff. See PLAINTIFF.

eggshell-skull rule. (1961) *Torts.* The principle that a defendant is liable for a plaintiff's unforeseeable and uncommon reactions to the defendant's negligent or intentional act. • Under this rule, for example, if one person negligently scrapes another who turns out to be a hemophiliac, the negligent defendant is liable for the full extent of the plaintiff's injuries even though the harm to another plaintiff would have been minor. — Also termed *eggshell-plaintiff rule; thin-skull rule; special-sensitivity rule; old-soldier's rule.*

EGM. *abbr.* See *extraordinary general meeting* under MEETING.

ego, talis (**ee**-goh, **tay**-lis). [Latin] I, such a one. • This phrase was used in describing the forms of old deeds.

egrediens et exeuns (e-**gree**-dee-enz et **ek**-see-ənz). [Latin "stepping out and exiting"] *Common-law pleading.* Going forth and issuing out of (land).

egregious (i-**gree**-jəs), *adj.* (16c) Extremely or remarkably bad; flagrant <the defendant's egregious behavior>.

egress (**ee**-gres). (16c) **1.** The act of going out or leaving. **2.** The right or ability to leave; a way of exit. Cf. INGRESS.

EHM. *abbr. Criminal law.* Electronic home monitoring.

ei abest (**ee**-I **ab**-est). [Latin] *Roman law.* It is wanting to him. • The phrase appeared in reference to any diminution in a person's assets.

EIB. *abbr.* EXPORT–IMPORT BANK OF THE UNITED STATES.

EIC. *abbr.* Earned-income credit. See EARNED-INCOME TAX CREDIT.

eight ball. (1989) *Criminal law. Slang.* An eighth of an ounce (3.5 grams) of a controlled substance, esp. cocaine, heroin, or methamphetamines.

eight-corners rule. (1989) *Insurance.* The principle that a liability insurer's duty to defend its insured — generally triggered if the plaintiff's claims against the insured are within the policy's coverage — is assessed by reviewing the claims asserted in the plaintiff's complaint, without reference to matters outside the four corners of the complaint plus the four corners of the policy. — Also termed *allegations-of-the-complaint rule.* Cf. FOUR-CORNERS RULE.

1891 Copyright Amendment Act. See CHACE ACT.

Eighteenth Amendment. The constitutional amendment — ratified in 1919 and repealed by the 21st Amendment in 1933 — that prohibited the manufacture, sale, transportation, and possession of alcoholic beverages in the United States. See PROHIBITION (3).

Eighth Amendment. The constitutional amendment, ratified as part of the Bill of Rights in 1791, prohibiting excessive bail, excessive fines, and cruel and unusual punishment.

eight-hour law. (1867) A statute that sets eight hours as the standard workday for some jobs and that usu. requires a higher pay rate for work beyond eight hours. • One example is the federal Fair Labor Standards Act. See WAGE-AND-HOUR LAW.

8-K. An SEC form that a registered corporation must file if a material event affecting its financial condition occurs between the due dates for regular SEC filings. — Also termed *Form 8-K.* Cf. 10-K.

83(b) election. (1970) *Tax.* An employee's choice to treat an employer's grant of unvested property, usu. stock, as being vested immediately and as currently taxable on the amount the employer paid for it. • The alternative is for the employee to wait until the property vests and pay taxes on its value at that time. An 83(b) election is typically used when the property is expected to have a dramatic increase in value before the employee's interest in it vests. IRC (26 USCA) § 83(b).

eigne (ayn), *adj.* [Law French] (15c) *Hist.* **1.** (Of a child) eldest; first-born. **2.** (Of title) superior; prior. **3.** (Of an estate) entailed. See ENTAILED. • This adjective traditionally follows the noun it modifies in sense 1 <bastard eigne> but precedes the noun in senses 2 and 3 <eigne title>. — Also spelled *eign*; *eygne*; *eisne*; *aisne*. — Also termed (in Law Latin) *einetius.*

▸ **bastard eigne.** (17c) *Hist.* An illegitimate son whose parents afterward marry and have a second son (*mulier puisne*) for lawful issue.

eignesse (ay-**nes**), *n.* [French] See ESNECY.

eik (eek). *Scots law.* An appendix or postscript to a formal document.

EIN. *abbr.* See TAX-IDENTIFICATION NUMBER.

einecia (I-**nee**-shee-ə), *n.* [Law Latin fr. French *ainé* "being born before"] (17c) Eldership. See ESNECY.

einetia. See EISNETIA.

einetius (I-**nee**-shee-əs), *n.* See EIGNE.

EIR. *abbr.* Environmental-impact report. See ENVIRONMENTAL-IMPACT STATEMENT.

eire (air), *n. Hist.* A journey; route; circuit. See EYRE.

eirenarcha (I-rə-**nahr**-kə), *n.* [from Greek *eirene* "peace" + *archein* "to rule"] (17c) *Roman law.* A provincial justice of the peace; a person charged with maintaining order. — Also spelled (in Latin) *irenarcha.*

EIS. *abbr.* ENVIRONMENTAL-IMPACT STATEMENT.

eisegesis (I-sə-**jee**-səs). The act of reading into a text one's own desired meaning. Cf. EXEGESIS. — **eisegete,** *n.*

eisne (ayn), *adj.* See EIGNE.

eisnetia (IZ-**nee**-shee-ə), *n.* [Law Latin] The share of the oldest son; the portion of an estate acquired by primogeniture. — Also spelled *einetia.* Cf. ESNECY.

EITC. *abbr.* EARNED-INCOME TAX CREDIT.

either-or order. See *alternative order* under ORDER (8).

eiusdem generis. See EJUSDEM GENERIS.

eject, *vb.* (15c) **1.** To cast or throw out. **2.** To oust or dispossess; to put or turn out of possession. **3.** To expel or thrust out forcibly (e.g., disorderly patrons). — **ejector,** *vb.*

ejection, *n.* (16c) **1.** An expulsion by action of law or by actual or threatened physical force. See OUSTER. **2.** EJECTMENT (2).

ejectione custodiae. See DE EJECTIONE CUSTODIAE.

ejectione firmae. See DE EJECTIONE FIRMAE.

ejectment. (16c) **1.** The ejection of an owner or occupier from property. **2.** A legal action by which a person wrongfully ejected from property seeks to recover possession, damages, and costs. **3.** The writ by which such an action is begun. • The essential allegations in an action for ejectment are that (1) the plaintiff has title to the land, (2) the plaintiff has been wrongfully dispossessed or ousted, and (3) the plaintiff has suffered damages. — Also termed *action of ejectment*; *action for the recovery of land*; *ejection.* See FORCIBLE ENTRY AND DETAINER. Cf. EVICTION; OUSTER.

> "The evolution of the action of ejectment from its primitive form as a mere action of trespass, enabling a lessee of lands to recover damages when ousted of his possession, through a series of most ingenious fictions, which were afterwards added to enable him to recover possession as well, until its final establishment as the proper method of trying all disputed titles to real property, presents to the student of legal science one of the most interesting studies that the history of the law affords. Few remedies have passed through so many changes of form, both in pleading and practice, and yet retained the same distinctive character that marked their origin." George W. Warvelle, *A Treatise on the Principles and Practice of the Action of Ejectment* § 4, at 4–5 (1905).

> "Any person wrongfully dispossessed of land may sue for the specific restitution of it in an action of ejectment. Originally this action was a special variety of trespass and available only to leaseholders. But in time and by the aid of the most elaborate fictions it came to be used by freeholders also. All these fictions have now been swept away; in theory even the term ejectment has been replaced by the term action for the recovery of land. The older term is, however, replaced in practice." R.F.V. Heuston, *Salmond on the Law of Torts* 41 (17th ed. 1977).

▸ **equitable ejectment.** (1820) A proceeding brought to enforce specific performance of a contract for the sale of land and for other purposes. • Though in the form of an ejectment action, this proceeding is in reality a substitute for a bill in equity.

▸ **justice ejectment.** (1900) A statutory proceeding to evict a tenant who has held over after termination of the lease or breach of its conditions.

ejectment bill. (18c) *Equity practice.* A bill in equity brought to recover real property and an accounting of rents and profits, without setting out a distinct ground of equity jurisdiction (and thus demurrable).

ejectment de garde. See DE EJECTIONE CUSTODIAE.

ejector, *n.* (17c) Someone who ejects, puts out, or dispossesses another.

▸ **casual ejector.** (17c) The nominal defendant in an ejectment action who, under a legal fiction, is supposed to come casually or by accident onto the premises and to eject the lawful possessor.

ejectum (i-**jek**-təm), *n.* Something that is cast out, esp. by the sea. See FLOTSAM. Cf. JETSAM; LAGAN (1); WAVESON.

ejectus (ee-**jek**-təs), *n.* [Latin] *Hist.* A whoremonger; a pimp.

ejercitoria (ay-hair-see-tor-**ee**-ə), *n.* [Spanish] *Spanish law.* An action lying against a shipowner on the contracts or obligations made by the master for repairs or supplies. • This action corresponds to the *actio exercitoria* of Roman law. See *action exercitoria* under ACTIO.

ejido (ay-**hee**-doh), *n.* [fr. Latin *exitus* "a going out"] (19c) *Spanish law.* Common land or pasture; esp., land used in common by inhabitants of a city, pueblo, or town for such things as pasture, wood, and threshing-ground; commons. — Also termed *exidos*; *exedos.* See COMMON (2).

EJJ. *abbr.* See *extended juvenile jurisdiction* under JURISDICTION.

ejuration (ej-ə-**ray**-shən). (17c) The renouncing or resigning of one's place.

ejusdem generis (ee-**jəs**-dəm **jen**-ə-ris *also* ee-**joos**- *or* ee-**yoos**-). [Latin "of the same kind or class"] (17c) **1.** A canon of construction holding that when a general word or phrase follows a list of specifics, the general word or phrase will be interpreted to include only items of the same class as those listed. • For example, in the phrase *horses, cattle, sheep, pigs, goats, or any other farm animals,* the general language *or any other farm animals* — despite its seeming breadth — would probably be held to include only four-legged, hoofed mammals typically found on farms, and thus would exclude chickens. — Also termed *Lord Tenterden's rule.* Cf. EXPRESSIO UNIUS EST EXCLUSIO ALTERIUS; NOSCITUR A SOCIIS; RULE OF RANK. **2.** Loosely, NOSCITUR A SOCIIS.

> "Of these canons, *ejusdem generis,* still occasionally applied today, provides that when a list of specific words is followed by a broader or more general term, the broader term is interpreted to include only potential members of a class similar to those denoted by the specific words. An example from the sixteenth century is the *Archbishop of Canterbury's Case,* in which the King's Bench used the principle in interpreting a statute that contained a list of 'inferior' means of conveyance, followed by the phrase 'or any other means.' Even though 'any other means' would seem to include all other types of conveyance, the court limited this catchall phrase to other inferior means of conveyance, and held that it did not include a superior conveyance by an act of Parliament. Obviously, these canons or maxims presuppose both a careful drafting of the text and a close reading by the judges interpreting it." Peter M. Tiersma, *Parchment Paper Pixels: Law and the Technologies of Communication* 152 (2010).

ejusdem negotii (ee-**jəs**-dəm ni-**goh**-shee-ɪ). [Latin] *Hist.* Part of the same transaction.

elaborare (i-lab-ə-**rair**-ee), *vb.* [Latin] *Hist.* To gain, acquire, or purchase, as by labor and industry.

elaboratus (i-lab-ə-**ray**-təs), *n.* [Latin] *Hist.* Property acquired by labor.

Elastic Clause. See NECESSARY AND PROPER CLAUSE.

elbow clerk. See CLERK (5).

elder abuse. See *abuse of the elderly* under ABUSE.

Elder Brethren. A distinguished body of men elected as masters of Trinity House, an institution incorporated in the reign of Henry VIII and charged with many duties in marine affairs, such as superintending lighthouses. • The full title of the corporation is Elder Brethren of the Holy and Undivided Trinity.

elder law. (1986) The field of law dealing with the elderly, including such issues as estate planning, retirement benefits, social security, age discrimination, and healthcare.

elder statesman. See STATESMAN.

elder title. (15c) A title of earlier date but one that becomes operative simultaneously with, and prevails over, a title of newer origin.

elected domicile. See DOMICILE.

electee. (16c) **1.** A person chosen or elected. **2.** A person to whom the law gives a choice about status.

electing small-business trust. See TRUST (3).

electio est creditoris (i-**lek**-shee-oh est kred-i-**tor**-is). [Law Latin] (16c) *Scots law.* The creditor has the election or choice. • The phrase appeared in reference to the creditor's right to apply payments to one debt or another. Cf. ELECTIO EST DEBITORIS.

> "Electio est creditoris . . . . This has reference to a creditor's right to apply indefinite payments, made by his debtor, to that debt or obligation which is least secured; but where the debtor at the time of payment appropriates the sum paid, towards extinction of a particular debt, it must be so applied." John Trayner, *Trayner's Latin Maxims* 184 (4th ed. 1894).

electio est debitoris (i-**lek**-shee-oh est deb-i-**tor**-is). [Law Latin] (16c) *Scots law.* The debtor has the election or choice. • If the law provided alternative methods of fulfilling an obligation, the debtor could choose the method of payment. Cf. ELECTIO EST CREDITORIS.

election, *n.* (13c) **1.** The exercise of a choice; esp., the act of choosing from several possible rights or remedies in a way that precludes the use of other rights or remedies <the taxpayers' election to file jointly instead of separately>. See ELECTION OF REMEDIES. **2.** The doctrine by which a person is compelled to choose between accepting a benefit under a legal instrument and retaining some property right to which the person is already entitled; an obligation imposed on a party to choose between alternative rights or claims, so that the party is entitled to enjoy only one <the prevailing plaintiff was put to an election between out-of-pocket damages and lost profits>. — Also termed *equitable election.* See RIGHT OF ELECTION. **3.** The process of selecting a person to occupy an office (usu. a public office), membership, award, or other title or status <the 2004 congressional election>. Cf. *two-round voting* under VOTING. — **elect,** *vb.* — **elective,** *adj.*

> "'Election' is 'a choice by the major part of those who have a right to choose,' and who exercise that right. If the electors are unanimous, or but a few dissent from the the choice of the larger number, it is easy to determine the election by the view. So if there be no competitor to dispute the choice, nor any proposed, there can be no doubt who is the person elected, though some, or even the larger part of the electors do not give their voices." Arthur Male, *A Treatise on the Law and Practice of Elections* 100–01 (1818).

▸ **by-election.** (1880) An election specially held to fill a vacant post. — Also spelled *bye-election.* Cf. *general election.*

▸ **election at large.** (1753) An election in which a public official is selected from a major election district rather than from a subdivision of the larger unit. — Also termed *at-large election.*

▸ **free election.** (15c) An election in which the political system and processes guarantee that each voter will be allowed to vote according to conscience.

▸ **general election.** (16c) **1.** An election that occurs at a regular interval of time. — Also termed *regular election.* **2.** An election for all seats, as contrasted with a by-election. Cf. *by-election.*

▸ **midterm election.** See *off-year election.*

▸ **municipal election.** (1832) The election of municipal officers.

▸ **off-year election.** (1919) An election conducted at a time other than the presidential election year. — Also termed *midterm election.*

▸ **popular election.** (16c) An election by people as a whole, rather than by a select group.

▸ **primary election.** (1835) A preliminary election in which a political party's registered voters nominate the candidate who will run in the general election. — Often shortened to *primary.*

▸ **recall election.** (1904) An election in which voters decide whether to remove an elected official from office before the term ends. — Also termed *recall referendum*; *representative recall.*

▸ **regular election.** See *general election* (1).

▸ **representation election.** (1925) An election held by the National Labor Relations Board to decide whether a certain union will represent employees in a bargaining unit. See BARGAINING UNIT.

▸ **retention election.** A nonpartisan election in which the electorate decides whether a state judge will remain in office. — Also termed *retention judicial election*; *retention referendum.* See MISSOURI PLAN.

▸ **runoff election.** (1954) An election held after a general election, in which the two candidates who received the most votes — neither of whom received a majority — run against each other so that the winner can be determined. Cf. *two-round voting* under VOTING.

▸ **special election.** (1836) An election that occurs in an interim between general elections, usu. to fill a sudden vacancy in office. Cf. *by-election.*

4. *Patents.* A patent applicant's choice of a single invention to continue prosecuting under the original application, after an examiner has required a restriction. See RESTRICTION (4).

▸ **election of species.** (1919) A patent applicant's choice of one alternative over others after an examiner determines that a generic claim is not allowable.

election, doctrine of. A doctrine holding that when a person has contracted with an agent without knowing of the agency and later learns of the principal's identity, the person may enforce the contract against either the agent or the principal, but not both. See ELECTION (1).

election, estoppel by. See *estoppel by election* under ESTOPPEL.

election board. (1837) **1.** A panel of inspectors or commissioners appointed for each election precinct to determine voter qualification, to supervise the polling, and often to ascertain and report the results. **2.** A local agency charged with the conduct of elections.

election by spouse. See RIGHT OF ELECTION.

election contest. A challenge by an election's loser against the winner, calling for an analysis of the election returns, which may include reviewing voter qualifications or recounting the ballots.

election district. See DISTRICT.

election dower. See DOWER.

election fraud. (18c) Illegal conduct committed in an election, usu. in the form of fraudulent voting. • Examples include voting twice, voting under another person's name (usu. a deceased person), or voting while ineligible.

election judge. (1872) **1.** A person appointed to supervise an election at the precinct level; a local representative of an election board. **2.** *English law.* One of two puisne judges of the Queen's Bench Division of the High Court selected to try election petitions.

election of a devise. A person's choice between retaining real property in his or her possession that a testator has given to another person, and accepting a gift of real property under the will. See DEVISE.

election of a legacy. A person's choice between retaining real property in his or her possession that a testator has given to another person, and accepting a gift of personal property under the will. See LEGACY.

election of performance. *Contracts.* **1.** A person's choice of time, place, or manner to carry out a required task. **2.** After a contract has been materially breached, the nonbreaching party's choice between continuing or ceasing to perform.

election of remedies. (18c) **1.** A claimant's act of choosing between two or more concurrent but inconsistent remedies based on a single set of facts. **2.** The affirmative defense barring a litigant from pursuing a remedy inconsistent with another remedy already pursued, when that other remedy has given the litigant an advantage over, or has damaged, the opposing party. • This doctrine has largely fallen into disrepute and is now rarely applied. **3.** The affirmative defense that a claimant cannot simultaneously recover damages based on two different liability findings if the injury is the same for both claims, thus creating a double recovery. Cf. *alternative relief* under RELIEF (3).

election of species. See ELECTION (4).

election petition. (1832) *English law.* A petition for inquiry into the validity of a Parliament member's election, when the member's return is allegedly invalid for bribery or other reason.

election returns. (1837) The report made to the board of canvassers or the election board, by those charged with tallying votes, of the number of votes cast for a particular candidate or proposition.

Elections Clause. (1929) *Constitutional law.* U.S. Const. art. I, § 4, cl. 1, giving states the duty to determine the time, place, and manner for electing senators and representatives, and also giving Congress the power to alter or preempt the election rules prescribed by the states. — Also termed *Times, Places, and Manner Clause.*

elective franchise. See FRANCHISE (1).

elective office. (1822) An office that is filled by popular election rather than by appointment.

elective share. (1931) *Wills & estates.* The percentage of a deceased spouse's estate, set by statute, that a surviving spouse (or sometimes a child) may choose to receive instead of taking under a will or in the event of being unjustifiably disinherited. — Also termed *forced share*; *statutory share*; *statutory forced share.* See RIGHT OF ELECTION.

> "In many states today, common-law dower and curtesy have been wholly replaced by statutes that make the surviving spouse an 'heir' of the deceased spouse and fix a *minimum* percentage of the decedent's estate (real and personal) to which the survivor will be entitled regardless of efforts of the deceased spouse to prevent it *by will*. This statutory minimum — called the *statutory forced share* — is typically an estate in fee simple, not merely a life estate. A serious disadvantage to the surviving spouse under many of these statutes, however, is that the minimum percentage applies only to property owned by the decedent *at death*. Both husbands and wives can, under such statutes, defeat their spouses' forced shares by *inter vivos* transfer." Thomas F.

Bergin & Paul G. Haskell, *Preface to Estates in Land and Future Interests* 37–38 (2d ed. 1984).

elector. (15c) **1.** A member of the electoral college chosen to elect the U.S. President and Vice President. — Also termed *presidential elector.* **2.** A voter.

▸ **qualified elector.** (1809) A legal voter; a person who meets the voting requirements for age, residency, and registration and who has the present right to vote in an election. See VOTER.

3. Someone who chooses between alternative rights or claims. **4.** *Hist.* The title of certain German princes who had a voice in electing the Holy Roman Emperors. • This office sometimes became hereditary and was connected with territorial possessions.

electoral college. (*often cap.*) (17c) **1.** The body of electors chosen from each state to formally elect the U.S. President and Vice President by casting votes based on the popular vote. **2.** Any similar body in another polity.

electoral process. (1851) **1.** The method by which a person is elected to public office in a democratic society. **2.** The taking and counting of votes.

electoral register. See ELECTORAL ROLL; REGISTER (2).

electoral roll. The official list of all registered voters in a given area. — Also termed *electoral register.*

electorate. The body of citizens who have the right to vote.

electric chair. (1889) **1.** A chair that is wired so that electrodes can be fastened to a condemned person's body and a lethal charge passed through the body for the purpose of carrying out a death penalty. • The electric chair was first used in 1890 at the Auburn State Prison in New York. **2.** By extension, the penalty of death by electrocution.

electronic agent. Any electronic or automated means, such as a computer program, that can independently initiate or respond to an action or message without a human's review. • Because an electronic agent is not a person, it is not an agent as defined by the common law. See AGENT.

electronic ballot. See BALLOT (2).

electronic cash. See *e-money* under MONEY.

electronic chattel paper. See CHATTEL PAPER.

electronic check. See *e-check* under CHECK.

electronic-check conversion. (1985) In a discrete electronic-funds transfer, the process by which a paper check is used as the source of information for the check number, account number, and bank-routing number. • The check itself is not considered the method of payment. — Often shortened to *check conversion.* See *e-check* under CHECK.

electronic commerce. See E-COMMERCE.

Electronic Commerce Directive. See DIRECTIVE ON CERTAIN ASPECTS OF ELECTRONIC COMMERCE IN THE INTERNAL MARKET.

Electronic Communications Privacy Act. A federal statute that limits the circumstances under which the federal and state government may gain access to oral, wire, and electronic communications. 18 USCA § 2510. — Abbr. ECPA.

electronic contract. See E-CONTRACT.

electronic currency. See *e-money* under MONEY.

Electronic Data Interchange agreement. See EDI AGREEMENT.

electronic document. See DOCUMENT (2).

electronic funds transfer. See FUNDS TRANSFER.

Electronic Fund Transfer Act. A 1978 federal statute amending the Consumer Credit Protection Act to regulate the use of electronic systems to transfer funds and to provide a basic framework establishing the rights, liabilities, and responsibilities of participants in such systems. • The statute covers fund transfers at automated-teller machines, cash-dispensing machines, and other electronic terminals, and transfers made by means of telephones and computers. 15 USCA §§ 1693–1693r. — Abbr. EFTA.

electronic mail. See E-MAIL.

electronic-monitoring device. (1976) *Criminal law.* A usu. computerized instrument that allows police or others to keep track of the whereabouts of a person or vehicle or of the movements and activities of people around a building or a room, esp. by GPS positioning, video surveillance, or audio surveillance. • An ankle bracelet is one such device often used in criminal law. See ANKLE BRACELET.

electronic signature. See SIGNATURE.

Electronic Signatures in Global and National Commerce Act. See E-SIGN ACT.

electronic surveillance. 1. See EAVESDROPPING. **2.** See WIRETAPPING.

electronic transaction. (1975) A transaction formed by electronic messages in which the messages of one or both parties will not be reviewed by an individual as an expected step in forming a contract.

eleemosynae (el-ə-**mos**-ə-nee), *n. pl.* (16c) *Eccles. law.* Possessions belonging to the church.

eleemosynaria (el-ə-mos-ə-**nair**-ee-ə), *n.* (17c) *Hist.* **1.** The place in a religious house or church where the common alms were deposited, to be distributed to the poor by the almoner. **2.** The office of almoner.

eleemosynarius (el-ə-mos-ə-**nair**-ee-əs), *n.* [Law Latin] (16c) *Hist.* **1.** An almoner, or chief officer, who received the eleemosynary rents and gifts and distributed them to pious and charitable uses. **2.** The name of an officer (Lord Almoner) of the English kings, in former times, who distributed the royal alms or bounty.

eleemosynary (el-ə-**mos**-ə-ner-ee), *adj.* (17c) Of, relating to, or assisted by charity; not-for-profit <an eleemosynary institution>.

eleemosynary corporation. See *charitable corporation* under CORPORATION.

eleemosynary defense. See *charitable immunity* under IMMUNITY (2).

eleganter (el-ə-**gan**-tər), *adv. Civil law.* Accurately; with discrimination; neatly.

elegit (ə-**lee**-jit). [Latin "he has chosen"] (16c) *Hist.* A writ of execution (first given by 13 Edw., ch. 18) either on a judgment for a debt or damages or on the forfeiture of a recognizance taken in the king's court. • Under it, the defendant's goods and chattels were appraised and, except for plow beasts, delivered to the plaintiff to satisfy the debt. If the goods were not sufficient to pay the debt, then the portion of the defendant's freehold lands held at the time of judgment was also delivered to the plaintiff, to hold until the debt was satisfied out of rents and profits or until the defendant's interest expired. During this period the plaintiff was called *tenant by elegit*, and the estate an *estate by elegit*. The writ was abolished in England in 1956, and it is no longer used anywhere in the United States.

element. (13c) **1.** A constituent part of a claim that must be proved for the claim to succeed <Burke failed to prove the element of proximate cause in prosecuting his negligence claim>. **2.** *Patents.* A discretely claimed component of a patent claim. • For a prior-art reference to anticipate a claim, it must teach each and every claim element. To recover for patent infringement, the plaintiff must prove that the accused product infringes every element of at least one claim, either literally or under the doctrine of equivalents. — Also termed (in sense 2) *limitation*. See DOCTRINE OF EQUIVALENTS.

elemental fact. See *ultimate fact* under FACT.

elementary law. Collectively, the fundamental principles that are embodied in and operate through governmental institutions, whose foundations rest on the whole fabric of a country's legal system and jurisprudence; the very most basic principles on which a system of laws is based. Cf. FUNDAMENTAL LAW.

elements of crime. (1909) The constituent parts of a crime — usu. consisting of the actus reus, mens rea, and causation — that the prosecution must prove to sustain a conviction. • The term is more broadly defined by the Model Penal Code in § 1.13(9) to refer to each component of the actus reus, causation, the mens rea, any grading factors, and the negative of any defense.

Eleventh Amendment. The constitutional amendment, ratified in 1795, prohibiting a federal court from hearing an action against a state by a person who is not a citizen of that state. See *sovereign immunity* under IMMUNITY (1).

ELI. *abbr.* See *employers'-liability insurance* under INSURANCE.

eligible, *adj.* (15c) Fit and proper to be selected or to receive a benefit; legally qualified for an office, privilege, or status. — **eligibility,** *n.*

elimination. (17c) *Hist.* The act of banishing or turning out of doors; rejection.

elinguation (ee-ling-**gway**-shən). (18c) *Hist.* The punishment of cutting out a person's tongue. — **elinguate,** *vb.*

elisor (i-**lɪ**-zər). (17c) A person appointed by a court to assemble a jury, serve a writ, or perform other duties of the sheriff or coroner if either is disqualified. — Also spelled *eslisor.*

Elkins Act. A 1903 federal statute that strengthened the Interstate Commerce Act by prohibiting rebates and other forms of preferential treatment to large carriers. 49 USCA §§ 41–43 (superseded).

ell (el). (bef. 12c) *Hist.* A measure of length corresponding to the modern yard.

Ellenborough's Act (**el**-ən-brəz). *English law.* An 1803 statute dealing with offenses against the person and criminalizing abortion in England and Ireland. • The statute was introduced in Parliament by Edward Law (1750–1818), the first Baron Ellenborough. St. 43 Geo. 3, ch. 58. — Also termed *Lord Ellenborough's Act*; *Malicious Shooting or Stabbing Act.*

***Ellerth–Faragher* defense.** See FARAGHER–ELLERTH DEFENSE.

elogium (i-**loh**-jee-əm), *n. Civil law.* **1.** A will or testament. **2.** A clause or provision in a will or testament.

eloign (i-**loyn**), *vb.* (15c) **1.** To remove (a person or property) from a court's or sheriff's jurisdiction. **2.** To remove to a distance; conceal. — Also spelled *eloin.* — **eloigner,** *n.*

eloignment (i-**loyn**-mənt), *n.* (17c) The getting of a thing or person out of the way, or removing it to a distance, so as to be out of reach.

elongata (ee-lawng-**gay**-tə). [Latin] **1.** *adj.* Eloigned; carried away to a distance. **2.** ELONGATUS.

elongatus (ee-lawng-**gay**-təs). [Latin "eloigned"] A return made by a sheriff to a writ *de homine replegiando*, stating that the party to be replevied has been eloigned, or conveyed out of the sheriff's jurisdiction. — Also termed *elongata.*

elongavit (ee-lawng-**gay**-vit). [Latin "he has eloigned"] In a proceeding by foreign attachment, the serjeant-at-mace's return that the garnishee has eloigned the goods, so that they cannot be appraised. • Upon such a return, judgment was given for the plaintiff that an inquiry be made into the eloigned goods. The inquiry was then set for trial and an assessment made by a jury.

elope, *vb.* (17c) **1.** *Archaic.* To run away; escape. **2.** *Archaic.* To abandon one's husband and run away with a lover. **3.** To run away secretly for the purpose of getting married, often without parental consent. — **elopement,** *n.*

eloquence (**el**-ə-kwents). **1.** The condition, state, or quality of expressing strong, sincere emotions in vivid and appropriate speed; the faculty, art, or an instance of expressing thoughts in well-chosen words that listeners or readers find pleasing and persuasive. **2.** Discourse characterized by uncommonly apt and fluent language.

> "Eloquence consists, it is true, more in the harmonious structure of thought, and in the depth and sublimity of feeling, than in the adoption of measured language, the manufacture of phrases, or the graceful fall of well-turned periods. Those who bestow more attention upon words than upon reason and sentiment, never yet were, and never can be eloquent; they are mere tuners of accents; and either speak holliday, or make fritters of the King's English. 'Like the screech-owl — they are all noise and feather, without flesh or blood.'" 1 David Paul Brown, *The Forum: Or Forty Years Full Practice at the Philadelphia Bar* 158 (1856).

elsewhere, *adv.* (bef. 12c) In another place. • In shipping articles, this term, following the designation of the port of destination, must be construed either as void for uncertainty or as subordinate to the principal voyage stated in the preceding words.

eluviation (i-loo-vee-**ay**-shən). (1899) Movement of soil caused by excessive water in the soil.

EM. *abbr. Criminal law.* Electronic monitoring.

e-mail, *n.* (1982) A communication exchanged between people by computer, through either a local area network or the Internet. — Also spelled *email.* — Also termed *electronic mail.* — **e-mail,** *vb.*

e-mail spoofing. See SPOOFING.

emanation. (16c) **1.** The act of coming or flowing forth from something. **2.** That which flows or comes forth from something; an effluence.

emancipate, *vb.* (17c) **1.** To set free from legal, social, or political restraint; esp., to free from slavery or bondage. **2.** To release (a child) from the control, support, and responsibility of a parent or guardian. — **emancipative, emancipatory,** *adj.* — **emancipator,** *n.*

emancipated minor. See MINOR (1).

emancipatio. See EMANCIPATION (3).

emancipation. (17c) **1.** The act by which one who was under another's power and control is freed. **2.** A surrender and renunciation of the correlative rights and duties concerning the care, custody, and earnings of a child; the act by which a parent (historically a father) frees a child and gives the child the right to his or her own earnings. • This act also frees the parent from all legal obligations of support. Emancipation may take place by agreement between the parent and child, by operation of law (as when the parent abandons or fails to support the child), or when the child gets legally married or enters the armed forces. **3.** *Roman law.* The enfranchisement of a son by his father, accomplished through the formality of an imaginary sale. • Justinian substituted the simpler proceeding of a manumission before a magistrate. — Also termed (in sense 3) *emancipatio.* Cf. MANCIPATION.

▸ **constructive emancipation.** (1841) Emancipation by law, as opposed to a voluntary act of the parent. • Constructive emancipation may occur in several ways, as by (1) conduct of the parent that is inconsistent with the performance of parental duties, (2) marriage of the child, or (3) the child's service in the armed forces.

▸ **partial emancipation.** (1844) Emancipation that frees a child for only a part of the period of minority, or from only a part of the parent's rights, or for only some purposes.

emancipation act. See MARRIED WOMEN'S PROPERTY ACTS.

Emancipation Proclamation. An executive proclamation, issued by President Abraham Lincoln on January 1, 1863, declaring that all persons held in slavery in designated states and districts were freed.

emancipist, *n. Australian law.* Someone who has served a sentence for a crime and has been released from prison.

embargo, *n.* (16c) **1.** A government's wartime or peacetime detention of an offending country's private ships found in the ports of the aggrieved country <the President called off the embargo of Iraq's ships after the war ended>. — Also spelled *imbargo.* — Also termed *hostile embargo.*

> "A *hostile* embargo is a kind of reprisal by one nation upon vessels within its ports belonging to another nation with which a difference exists, for the purpose of forcing it to do justice. If this measure should be followed by war, the vessels are regarded as captured, if by peace, they are restored." Theodore D. Woolsey, *Introduction to the Study of International Law* § 118, at 187 (5th ed. 1878).

2. A country's detention of all ships in its own ports, including its own, to promote safety and to preclude transportation to an offending country <the embargo of all U.S. ships traveling to Iraq remained in effect until hostilities subsided>. — Also termed *civil embargo.*

> "A *civil embargo* may be laid for the purpose of national welfare or safety, as for the protection of commercial vessels against the rules of belligerent powers which would expose them to capture. Such was the measure adopted by the United States in December 1807, which detained in port all vessels except those which had a public commission, and those that were already laden or should sail in ballast. The right to adopt such a measure of temporary non-intercourse is undoubted." Theodore D. Woolsey, *Introduction to the Study of International Law* § 118, at 187 (5th ed. 1878).

3. The unilateral or collective restrictions on the import or export of goods, materials, capital, or services into or from a specific country or group of countries for political or security reasons <for a time, the industrialized countries placed an embargo on all goods from Libya>. — Also termed *trade embargo; economic-cure trade embargo.* **4.** The conscription of private property for governmental use, such as to transport troops <the Army's embargo of the company jet to fly General White to Washington>. **5.** A temporary prohibition on disclosure <the embargo on the press release expired at 11:59 p.m.>. — **embargo,** *vb.*

embassador. See AMBASSADOR.

embassy. (1534) **1.** The building in which a diplomatic body is located; esp., the residence of the ambassador. **2.** A body of diplomatic representatives headed by an ambassador; a diplomatic mission on the ambassadorial level. **3.** The mission, business, and function of an ambassador. Cf. LEGATION.

Ember Days. (bef. 12c) *Eccles. law.* The days — which the ancient church fathers called *quatuor tempora jejunii* — that are observed on the Wednesday, Friday, and Saturday following (1) Quadragesima Sunday (the first Sunday in Lent), (2) Whitsuntide, or Holyrood Day, in September, and (3) St. Lucy's day, about the middle of December. • Almanacs refer to the weeks in which these days fall as *Ember Weeks*; they are now chiefly noticed because, by tradition, the Sundays following Ember Days are used to ordain priests and deacons, although the canon law allows bishops to ordain on any Sunday or holiday.

embezzlement, *n.* (15c) The fraudulent taking of personal property with which one has been entrusted, esp. as a fiduciary. • The criminal intent for embezzlement — unlike larceny and false pretenses — arises after taking possession (not before or during the taking). — Also termed *defalcation; peculation.* See LARCENY; FALSE PRETENSES. — **embezzle,** *vb.* — **embezzler,** *n.*

> "Embezzlement is not a common-law crime. It is the result of legislative efforts to make provision for an unreasonable gap which appeared in the law of larceny as it developed. Under the early English statute embezzlement was made a misdemeanor, but under most modern American statutes it is either a felony or a misdemeanor depending upon the value of the property converted." Rollin M. Perkins & Ronald N. Boyce, *Criminal Law* 351 (3d ed. 1982).

emblem. (15c) **1.** A flag, armorial bearing, or other symbol of a country, organization, or movement. **2.** Loosely, something that is used to symbolize something else.

emblemata Triboniani (em-**blee**-mə-tə trə-boh-nee-**ay**-nɪ). [Latin] *Roman law.* Alterations, modifications, and additions to the writings of the older jurists that were combined to form the Digest or Pandects, and generally termed interpolations. • Justinian appointed a commission over which Tribonian presided to harmonize contradictions, delete obsolete matter, and bring the law up to date. This term is considered old-fashioned by modern Romanists. See INTERPOLATION.

emblements (**em**-blə-mənts). (15c) **1.** The growing crop annually produced by labor, as opposed to a crop occurring naturally. • Emblements are considered personal property that the executor or administrator of a deceased tenant may harvest and take regardless of who may have since occupied the land. — Also termed *fructus industriales.* **2.** The tenant's right to harvest and take away such crops after the tenancy has ended.

"At common law those products of the earth which are annual, and are raised by yearly manurance and labor, and essentially owe their annual existence to the cultivation by man, [are] termed 'emblements' and sometimes '*fructus industriales.*'" *Sparrow v. Pond*, 52 N.W. 36 (Minn. 1892).

"The law of emblements has its origin and matrix, in the privilege, recognized at least as early as the fifteenth century, of the tenant for an uncertain term, to harvest and remove, even after the tenancy had terminated, the annual crop, which he had planted and nurtured." Ray Andrews Brown, *The Law of Personal Property* § 159, at 806 (2d ed. 1955).

emblers de gentz (**em**-blərz də **jents**). [Law French] A theft from the people. • The phrase occurs in the old English rolls of Parliament — for example, "Whereas divers murders, *emblers de gentz*, and robberies are committed. . . ."

embodied technology. (1972) *Intellectual property.* Know-how or knowledge that is manifest in products and equipment, including software. Cf. DISEMBODIED TECHNOLOGY.

embodiment. *Patents.* **1.** The tangible manifestation of an invention.

"An 'invention' is *intellectual* property. It is a mental construct formed and contained within the inventor's mind and has no physical structure or reality. An 'embodiment' of an invention, however, is a specific physical form of the invention. Each embodiment exists in the real world. It can be 'reduced to practice'; i.e., it is either actually built or could be built." Morgan D. Rosenberg, *The Essentials of Patent Claim Drafting* xvii (2012).

2. The method for using this tangible form. **3.** The part of a patent application or patent that describes a concrete manifestation of the invention. • Embodiments are less common in software or process patents than in manufacturing-related patents.

embossed seal. See NOTARY SEAL.

embrace, *vb.* (15c) To attempt to influence (a judge or juror) by corruption, or to behave in a way that might have a corrupting influence; to engage in embracery.

embracee (em-bray-**see**). The bribe-taker in the offense of embracery.

embracer (im-**brays**-ər). [fr. Old French *embraseor* "one who kindles or instigates," fr. *embraser* "to set fire to"] (15c) The bribe-giver in the offense of embracery; one who attempts to influence a judge or a juror by means of corruption. — Also spelled *embraceor.*

embracery (im-**brays**-ə-ree), *n.* (15c) **1.** The attempt to corrupt or wrongfully influence a judge or juror, esp. by threats or bribery. — Also spelled *imbracery.* — Also termed *jury-tampering; laboring a jury.* Cf. JURY-FIXING; JURY-PACKING. — **embrace,** *vb.* — **embracer,** *n.*

"The word 'embracery' . . . has tended to disappear. It is included in some of the codes but the tendency has been to divide this common-law offense into two parts, placing that which is appropriate thereto in sections on bribery and the remainder in provisions dealing with obstruction of justice." Rollin M. Perkins & Ronald N. Boyce, *Criminal Law* 552 (3d ed. 1982).

2. The procuring for oneself or another a place on a jury, with the purpose of affecting the outcome.

embryo (**em**-bree-oh). (16c) A developing but unborn or unhatched animal; esp., an unborn human from conception until the development of organs (i.e., until about the eighth week of pregnancy). Cf. FETUS; ZYGOTE.

▸ **embryo *formatus*** (for-**may**-təs). *Eccles. law.* A human embryo organized into human shape and endowed with a soul. • Though rejected in the early doctrine of the Christian church, the distinction between the embryo *formatus* and *informatus* was accepted by Gratian (regarded as the founder of canon law) in his *Decretum* (ca. 1140), in which he said that abortion is not murder if the fetus has not yet been infused with a soul. Though he did not specify the time of formation or animation, by the 16th century canonists accepted that the time of formation and animation was the 40th day after conception for the male fetus and the 80th day for the female. — Also termed *embryo animatus.*

▸ **embryo *informatus*** (in-for-**may**-təs). *Eccles. law.* A human embryo before it has been endowed with a soul. — Also termed *embryo inanimatus.*

▸ **preembryo.** See ZYGOTE.

▸ **proembryo.** See ZYGOTE.

embryo adoption. See ADOPTION (1).

emend (i-**mend**), *vb.* (15c) To remove the mistakes from (a piece of writing); to edit (a text) for corrections.

emenda (ee-**men**-də), *n. pl.* [Latin "amends"] Things given in reparation for a trespass.

emendatio (ee-men-**day**-shee-oh), *n.* [Latin] *Hist.* The power of amending and correcting abuses, according to certain rules and measures.

▸ ***emendatio panis et cerevisiae*** (ee-men-**day**-shee-oh **pan**-is et ser-ə-**vizh**-ee-ee). [Latin "the correction of bread and ale"] The power of supervising and correcting (assizing) the weights and measures of bread and ale.

emendation (ee-men-**day**-shən). (16c) **1.** Correction or revision, esp. of a text. **2.** *Hist.* The correction of an error or wrongdoing; atonement for a criminal offense, esp. by the payment of money. • As criminal law developed over time, emendation by payment of *wer* or *wite* gradually faded away and was replaced by harsher punishments.

e mera gratia (ee **meer**-ə **gray**-shee-ə). [Latin] Out of mere grace or favor.

emergency. 1. A sudden and serious event or an unforeseen change in circumstances that calls for immediate action to avert, control, or remedy harm. **2.** An urgent need for relief or help.

Emergency Alert System. A national warning system in the United States used to alert the public to weather emergencies, such as floods, hurricanes, and tornadoes, and enabling the President of the United States to speak to the people on ten minutes' notice. • Established in 1997, it replaced the Emergency Broadcast System (1963–97), which itself replaced CONELRAD (1951–63), which stood for "Control of Electromagnetic Radiation."

emergency circumstances. See *exigent circumstances* under CIRCUMSTANCE.

emergency contraceptive pill. A drug taken orally after unprotected sexual intercourse or contraceptive failure in order to prevent pregnancy by disrupting or delaying ovulation or fertilization. — Abbr. ECP; EC. — Also termed *morning-after pill.* See *medication abortion* under ABORTION. Cf. ABORTION PILL.

Emergency Court of Appeals. *Hist.* A temporary court, established during World War II, whose purpose was to review wage- and price-control matters. • The court was created in 1942 and abolished in 1962. Cf. TEMPORARY EMERGENCY COURT OF APPEALS.

emergency defense. See NECESSITY (4).

emergency doctrine. (1929) **1.** A legal principle exempting a person from the ordinary standard of reasonable care if that person acted instinctively to meet a sudden and urgent need for aid. — Also termed *imminent-peril doctrine*; *sudden-emergency doctrine*; *sudden-peril doctrine*; *sudden-peril rule.* **2.** A legal principle by which consent to medical treatment in a dire situation is inferred when neither the patient nor a responsible party can consent but a reasonable person would do so. — Also termed (in sense 2) *emergency-treatment doctrine.* Cf. GOOD SAMARITAN DOCTRINE; RESCUE DOCTRINE. **3.** The principle that a police officer may conduct a search without a warrant if the officer has probable cause and reasonably believes that immediate action is needed to protect life or property. • For example, the officer might see the need to protect someone in distress, to assist a crime victim, or to investigate what appears to be impending danger — Also termed *emergency exception; rescue doctrine.* See *exigent circumstances* under CIRCUMSTANCE.

emergency-employment doctrine. (1937) The principle that an employee may enlist another's help in dealing with an emergency that falls within the scope of the employee's duties and that could not be overcome without the assistance of the other person.

emergency exception. See EMERGENCY DOCTRINE (3).

emergency jurisdiction. See JURISDICTION.

emergency power. See POWER.

Emergency Preparedness and Response Directorate. The former division of the U.S. Department of Homeland Security responsible for coordinating relief and recovery efforts and for developing and coordinating plans to prevent terrorism and to minimize risks of danger from natural disasters. • The Directorate included the Federal Emergency Management Agency and also coordinated efforts with the Strategic National Stockpile and the National Disaster Medical System from the Department of Health and Human Services, the Nuclear Incident Response Team from the Department of Energy, the Domestic Emergency Support Teams from the Department of Justice, the National Domestic Preparedness Office of the Federal Bureau of Investigation, and state and local emergency responders. It was abolished in July 2005.— Abbr. EPR.

emergency protective order. See PROTECTIVE ORDER.

emergency search. See SEARCH (1).

emergency-treatment doctrine. See EMERGENCY DOCTRINE (2).

emergency warrant. See WARRANT (1).

emerita. See EMERITUS.

emeritus. (18c) An honorary title conferred on a former officer or professor who has honorably retired, usu. after serving for an extended period well beyond the norm. • The term is loosely used as an adjective meaning "honored," but it is not a synonym for "former," "retired," or "immediate past" (as in "immediate past president"). See HONORARY. Pl. **emeriti.** Fem. **emerita.** Fem. pl. **emeritae.**

emigrant (**em**-ə-grənt), *n.* (18c) Someone who leaves his or her country for any reason with the intent to establish a permanent residence elsewhere. Cf. IMMIGRANT.

emigrant agent. See AGENT.

emigration (em-ə-**gray**-shən), *n.* (17c) The act of leaving a country with the intent not to return and to reside elsewhere. Cf. IMMIGRATION. — **emigrate,** *vb.*

> "Emigration is usually defined as the voluntary removal of an individual from his home State with the intention of residing abroad. However, not all emigration is voluntary; there sometimes exists forced emigration, even mass emigration. Emigration may also be due to flight for political reasons or expulsion. One then speaks of refugees or exiles." Paul Weis, "Emigration," in 2 *Encyclopedia of Public International Law* 76 (1995).

emigré (**em**-ə-gray *or* em-ə-**gray**), *n.* [French] (18c) Someone who is forced to leave his or her country for political reasons. — Also spelled *émigré.*

eminence (**em**-ə-nənts). (*usu. cap.*) (17c) *Eccles. law.* An honorary title given to cardinals of the Roman Catholic Church. • Until the pontificate of Urban VIII, cardinals were called *illustrissimi* and *reverendissimi.*

éminence grise (ay-mee-nahn[t]s **greez**). [French "gray eminence"] (1838) **1.** Someone who possesses unofficial power, often secretly, through someone else; an undisclosed or confidential power-broker. **2.** Loosely, a respected figure in a particular field; an elder statesman. See *elder statesman* under STATESMAN (1). Pl. **éminence grises.**

eminent domain. (18c) The inherent power of a governmental entity to take privately owned property, esp. land, and convert it to public use, subject to reasonable compensation for the taking. — Also (rarely) termed *compulsory purchase*; (in Scots law) *compulsory surrender*; (in Australia) *compulsory acquisition.* See CONDEMNATION (2); EXPROPRIATION; TAKING (2).

> "The term 'eminent domain' is said to have originated with Grotius, the seventeenth century legal scholar. Grotius believed that the state possessed the power to take or destroy property for the benefit of the social unit, but he believed that when the state so acted, it was obligated to compensate the injured property owner for his losses. Blackstone, too, believed that society had no general power to take the private property of landowners, except on the payment of a reasonable price. The just compensation clause of the fifth amendment to the Constitution was built upon this concept of a moral obligation to pay for governmental interference with private property. . . . No provision for the power of eminent domain appears in the federal Constitution. The Supreme Court, however, has said that the power of eminent domain is an incident of federal sovereignty and an 'offspring of political necessity.' The Court has also noted that the fifth amendment's limitation on taking private property is a tacit recognition that the power to take private property exists." John E. Nowak & Ronald D. Rotunda, *Constitutional Law* § 11.11, at 424–25 (4th ed. 1991) (quoting *Bauman v. Ross*, 167 U.S. 548, 574, 17 S.Ct. 966, 976 (1897)).

Eminent Domain Clause. (1903) The Fifth Amendment provision providing that private property cannot be taken for public use without just compensation. See TAKINGS CLAUSE.

emissary. (17c) One sent on a special mission as another's agent or representative, esp. to promote a cause or to gain information.

emission. **1.** The production or sending out of heat, light, gas, radiation, carbon, smoke, etc. **2.** (*often pl.*) A pollutant that is released into the air, esp. from engines or smokestacks. — **emit,** *vb.*

emission-reduction credit. A certification that a business has reduced its discharge of a pollutant by a stated volume. • The certificates can be bought and sold. — Abbr. ERC. — Also termed *certified emission-reduction credit* (CERC). See EMISSIONS TRADING.

emissions cap. A maximum limit set by an authority on the amount of a pollutant that may be released into the air. See EMISSIONS PERMIT.

emissions credit. (1981) *Environmental law.* Official approval to produce a particular amount of a substance that can be harmful to the environment, usu. given to a company by the governmental department responsible for environmental policies, such as the Environmental Protection Agency.

emissions permit. A license issued by an authority granting the holder permission to discharge a specific volume of a pollutant. • The total number of permits one holder receives cannot exceed the emissions cap. If the holder needs more, they must be purchased in the open market. — Also termed *allowance*; *carbon credit.* See EMISSIONS CAP; EMISSIONS TRADING.

emissions trading. (1982) The open-market buying and selling of emissions permits and emission-reduction credits. • A business that has reached its emissions cap can purchase more permits or credits to meet its actual emissions volume. — Also termed *cap and trade.* See EMISSIONS PERMIT; EMISSION-REDUCTION CREDIT.

emit, *vb.* (16c) **1.** To give off or discharge into the air <emit light>. **2.** To issue with authority <emit a new series of currency>. — **emission,** *n.*

EMIT test. (1984) *abbr.* Enzyme-multiplied-immunoassay-technique test, a drug test (a urine test) administered by corrections officers as well as probation and parole officers.

emolument (i-**mol**-yə-mənt), *n.* (*usu. pl.*) (15c) Any advantage, profit, or gain received as a result of one's employment or one's holding of office.

Emoluments Clause. (1991) *Constitutional law.* **1.** The clause of the United States Constitution preventing members of Congress from continuing to serve in Congress after accepting an appointment to another federal office, and also prohibiting such an appointment if the office was created or its emoluments increased while the Senator or Representative served in Congress. U.S. Const. art. I, § 6, cl. 2. — Also written *Emolument Clause.* **2.** FOREIGN EMOLUMENTS CLAUSE.

e-money. See MONEY.

emotional abuse. See ABUSE.

emotional distress. See DISTRESS (4).

emotional-distress damages. See *nonpecuinary loss* under LOSS.

emotional disturbance. See EXTREME MENTAL OR EMOTIONAL DISTURBANCE.

emotional harm. See *emotional distress* under DISTRESS (4).

emotional incapacity. (1904) **1.** The inability to control one's emotions or express appropriate emotions because of a mental disorder. **2.** *Hist. Evidence.* (Of a witness) hostility or partiality rooted in bias, corruption, or interest. • At common law, an interested witness was not competent to testify on grounds of emotional incapacity. *See State v. Craft*, 41 So. 550, 551 (La. 1906).

emotional insanity. See INSANITY.

empanel, *vb.* (15c) To swear in (a jury) to try an issue or case. — Also spelled *impanel.* — **empanelment, empaneling,** *n.*

empaneled jury. See JURY

emparnours (em-**pahr**-nərz), *n. pl.* [French] *Hist.* Persons who undertook lawsuits on behalf of others.

emperor. (13c) **1.** The title of the sovereign ruler of an empire. **2.** The chief of a confederation of states of which kings are members. • The rulers of the Roman world adopted the designation *emperor* after the fall of the republic. The title was later assumed by those — including Napoleon — who claimed to be their successors in the Holy Roman Empire. The sovereigns of Japan and Morocco are often called *emperors*, as were, in Western speech, the former sovereigns of Turkey and China. The title denotes a power and dignity superior to that of a king. It appears to be the appropriate style of the executive head of a federal government constructed on the monarchial principle and comprising several distinct kingdoms or other quasi-sovereign states, as with the German empire from 1871 to 1918.

emphasis added. (1945) A citation signal indicating that the writer quoting another's words has italicized or otherwise emphasized some of them. — Also termed *emphasis supplied.*

emphyteusis (em-fi-**t[y]oo**-sis), *n.* [Greek "implanting"] (16c) *Greek, Roman & civil law.* A contract by which one person delivered to another (the *emphyteuta*) a tract of land, either in perpetuity or for a long period of time, in exchange for the obligation to cultivate the land and to pay annual rental. • In Roman law, the land was state-owned (*ager vectigalis*). In the 5th century, *emphyteusis* was officially recognized as distinct from ownership or a lease. The land's lessee or tenant, called an *emphyteuta*, had to bear any burdens imposed on the land. Although the *emphyteusis* was alienable, the owner had to consent to the sale. (Cf. SUPERFICIARIUS.) Unlike a usufruct, *emphyteusis* did not terminate with the death of the *emphyteuta.* Perpetual *emphyteusis* was abolished in the 18th century.

emphyteuta (em-fi-**t[y]oo**-tə), *n.* [Latin] (18c) *Greek, Roman & civil law.* The person to whom an *emphyteusis* is granted; the lessee or tenant under a contract of *emphyteusis.* See FEE FARM.

> "The 'emphyteuta' had the right to the produce. He might change, so long as by doing so he did not worsen, the character of the farm. He might hypothecate or altogether alienate his right, subject to the condition of offering to the owner of the soil the opportunity of preemption." John

George Phillimore, *Private Law Among the Romans* 147 (1863).

emphyteutic (em-fi-**t**[y]**oo**-tik), *adj.* [Latin] (17c) *Civil law.* Founded on, growing out of, or having the character of an *emphyteusis*; held under an *emphyteusis.*

empire. (14c) The jurisdiction of an emperor; the region over which an emperor's dominion extends.

empirical (em-**pir**-i-kəl), *adj.* (16c) Of, relating to, or based on experience, experiment, or observation <the expert's theory was not supported by empirical data>. — Also termed *empiric.*

emplazamiento (em-plah-zah-**myen**-toh), *n.* [Spanish] *Spanish law.* A summons; esp., a court-issued citation requiring the addressee to appear at a designated time and place.

emplead. See IMPLEAD.

emploi (om-**plwah**), *n.* [French] *French law.* Equitable conversion. • When property covered by the *régime dotal* is sold, the purchaser must ensure that the sale proceeds are reinvested for the wife's benefit. See *régime dotal* under REGIME.

employ, *vb.* (15c) **1.** To make use of. **2.** To hire. **3.** To use as an agent or substitute in transacting business. **4.** To commission and entrust with the performance of certain acts or functions or with the management of one's affairs.

employable, *adj.* Having the qualifications or skills necessary to get a job; capable of obtaining steady work.

employee. (1822) Someone who works in the service of another person (the employer) under an express or implied contract of hire, under which the employer has the right to control the details of work performance. — Also spelled *employe.* Cf. AGENT; INDEPENDENT CONTRACTOR.

▸ **borrowed employee.** (1932) An employee whose services are, with the employee's consent, lent to another employer who temporarily assumes control over the employee's work. • Under the doctrine of respondeat superior, the borrowing employer is vicariously liable for the borrowed employee's acts. But the borrowing employer may also be entitled to assert immunity under workers'-compensation laws. — Also termed *borrowed servant; loaned employee; loaned servant; employee pro hac vice; special employee.* See RESPONDEAT SUPERIOR.

▸ **full-time employee.** (1919) One who is hired to work at least the normal number of hours in a workweek as defined by an employer or a statute, usu. 35 to 40 hours.

▸ **part-time employee.** (1915) One who is hired to work fewer hours (usu. substantially fewer) than the normal number in a workweek as defined by an employer or a statute.

▸ **probationary employee.** (1900) A recently hired employee whose ability and performance are being evaluated during a trial period of employment; PROBATIONER (2).

▸ **public employee.** See CIVIL SERVANT.

▸ **seasonal employee.** (1932) An employee who is engaged to work for only a certain time of the year when a business anticipates a cyclical increase in demand.

▸ **statutory employee.** (1929) *Workers' compensation.* An employee who is covered, or required to be covered, by the employer's workers'-compensation insurance and who therefore has no independent tort claim against the employer for unintentional injuries suffered on the job. See *statutory employer* under EMPLOYER.

employee benefit plan. (1942) A written stock-purchase, savings, option, bonus, stock-appreciation, profit-sharing, thrift, incentive, pension, or similar plan solely for employees, officers, and advisers of a company. • The term includes an employee-welfare benefit plan, an employee-pension benefit plan, or a combination of those two. *See* 29 USCA § 1002(3). But the term excludes any plan, fund, or program (other than an apprenticeship or training program) in which no employees are plan participants. — Often shortened to *plan.* Cf. PENSION PLAN.

▸ **defined-benefit plan.** (1974) A plan established and maintained by an employer primarily to provide systematically for the payment of definitely determinable benefits to employees over a period of years, usu. for life, after retirement; any pension plan that is not a defined-contribution plan. • Retirement benefits under a defined-benefit plan generally are based on a formula that includes such factors as years of service and compensation. If the trust funding the plan lacks sufficient assets to pay the promised benefits, ERISA requires the employer to cover the shortfall. 29 USCA § 1002(35). Cf. *defined-contribution plan.*

▸ **defined-contribution plan.** (1974) Under ERISA, an employee retirement plan in which each participant has a separate account — funded by the employee's contributions and the employer's contributions (usu. in a preset amount) — and each participant's benefits are based solely on what has accumulated in the participant's account. 29 USCA § 1002(34). — Also termed *defined-contribution pension plan; individual account plan.* Cf. *defined-benefit plan.*

▸ **disability retirement plan.** (1968) **1.** A plan that is invoked when a covered person is disabled from working to normal retirement age. **2.** A plan that provides increased benefits if a person retires because of a disability.

▸ **employee-stock-ownership plan.** (1957) A type of profit-sharing plan that invests primarily in the employer's stock. • Employee-stock-ownership plans receive special tax benefits and can borrow money to fund employee stock purchases, which makes them a useful corporate finance tool. IRC (26 USCA) § 4975(e)(7). — Abbr. ESOP.

▸ **excess-benefit plan.** (1977) An employee benefit plan maintained by an employer solely for the purpose of providing benefits for certain employees in excess of limitations on contributions and benefits imposed by the Internal Revenue Code. 29 USCA § 1002(36).

▸ **401(k) plan.** (1986) A retirement and savings plan that allows an employee to elect to have a portion of his or her pretax salary contributed to a defined-contribution plan. • Employers often match all or part of the employee's contributions. Employees usu. can choose investments from a list of options. IRC (26 USCA) § 401(k).

▸ **403(b) plan.** (1984) A retirement plan for employees of public educational systems and certain tax-exempt organizations that is funded by pretax employee contributions much like a 401(k) plan, but may also provide for employer contributions. IRC (26 USCA) § 403(b). — Also termed *tax-sheltered annuity*; *tax-deferred annuity*.

▸ **457 plan.** (1989) A type of deferred-compensation plan for employees of state and local governments and tax-exempt organizations that operates much like a 401(k) plan, but (except for governmental plans) is unfunded. IRC (26 USCA) § 457.

▸ **governmental plan.** (1974) Under ERISA, an employee benefit plan established or maintained for its employees by the federal government, state or local governments, or their agencies or instrumentalities. 29 USCA § 1002(32). • If a collective-bargaining agreement between a labor union and a governmental entity includes a benefit plan, that plan may be a governmental plan if it is funded by and covers only employees of the governmental entity. — Also termed *governmental employee benefit plan*; *government plan*.

▸ **individual account plan.** See *defined-contribution plan*.

▸ **Keogh plan.** See KEOGH PLAN.

▸ **medical-expense reimbursement plan.** (1970) An arrangement provided by an employer to reimburse employees for medical expenses, including vision and dental expenses, that are not covered under a medical plan available to all employees. • Some plans may also be used to substitute for health insurance, or to pay for medical expenses in excess of insurance-policy limits. IRC (26 USCA) 105. — Abbr. MERP.

▸ **money-purchase plan.** (1960) A defined-contribution plan that provides for mandatory employer contributions without regard to employer profits. • Contributions are frequently stated as a percentage of employee compensation.

▸ **nonqualified deferred-compensation plan.** (1967) An unfunded compensation arrangement, frequently offered to executives, that defers compensation and the recognition of its accompanying taxable income to a later date. • It is termed "nonqualified" because it does not qualify for favorable tax treatment under IRC (26 USCA) § 401(a). The plan avoids the restrictions on qualified plans, esp. the limits on contributions and benefits and rules against discrimination in favor of highly compensated employees. — Abbr. NQDC. — Also termed *nonqualified executive-compensation plan*; *unfunded deferred-compensation plan*.

> "Generally, a nonqualified deferred compensation plan is an agreement or promise by an employer to certain individuals to pay compensation to those individuals at some future date. A nonqualified plan may also be a series of deferred compensation agreements between an employer and certain individuals that are considered to be a plan of benefits. These types of plans do not qualify for the special tax treatment afforded to plans that meet the qualification requirements of Section 401(a) of the Internal Revenue Code . . . ." Bruce J. McNeil, *Nonqualified Deferred Compensation Plans* 1 (1994).

▸ **pension plan.** See PENSION PLAN.

▸ **profit-sharing plan.** See PROFIT-SHARING PLAN.

▸ **qualified plan. 1.** See *qualified pension plan* under PENSION PLAN. **2.** See *qualified profit-sharing plan* under PROFIT-SHARING PLAN.

▸ **retirement plan.** (1860) An employee benefit plan — such as a pension plan or Keogh plan — provided by an employer (or a self-employed person) for an employee's retirement.

▸ **SIMPLE plan.** (2003) An arrangement under which an individual retirement account or annuity is established for each eligible employee and funded by elective pretax employee contributions, much as with a 401(k) plan, and certain matching or minimum employer contributions. • The plan can be attractive to employers because it is easier to administer than a 401(k) plan. The name is a loose acronym for "Savings Incentive Match Plan for Employees." IRC (26 USCA) § 408(p).

▸ **simplified employee pension plan.** (1985) An arrangement under which an individual retirement account or annuity is established for each eligible employee and funded by discretionary employer contributions. IRC (26 USCA) § 408(k). • A simplified employee pension plan operates much like a 401(k) plan, in that the employee contributions can be made by deferred compensation and the employer can contribute. But the plan is attractive to small employers because it is much easier to administer than a 401(k) plan and gives the employer complete discretion on whether to make an annual contribution. IRC (26 USCA) § 408(k). — Abbr. SEP; SEP-IRA.

▸ **split-funded plan.** (1982) A retirement plan combining elements of both life-insurance and investment plans.

▸ **survivor-income benefit plan.** (1978) An agreement between an employer and an employee whereby the employer agrees that if the employee dies before retirement, the employer will pay a specified or determinable amount to the employee's spouse or other designated beneficiary. • Typically, a formula is used, so the benefit amount may be a multiple of the employee's salary (e.g., two times the average base pay in the three years preceding death) or based on the length of employment. — Abbr. SIB. — Also written *survivor's-income benefit plan*. — Also termed *death-benefit-only plan* (DBO).

▸ **target benefit plan.** (1979) A money-purchase plan that sets a "target" benefit for each participant and mandates employer contributions determined by an actuarial cost method designed to fund the target benefit.

▸ **unfunded deferred-compensation plan.** See *nonqualified deferred-compensation plan*.

▸ **welfare plan.** Under ERISA, any plan, fund, or program established or maintained by an employer or an employee organization for the purpose of providing to participants or their beneficiaries any number of potential benefits: medical, surgical, or hospital care or benefits; benefits in the event of sickness, accident, disability, death or unemployment; vacation benefits; apprenticeship or other training programs; daycare centers; scholarship funds; prepaid legal services; or holiday and severance benefits. 29 USCA § 1002(1).

employee givebacks. See CONCESSION BARGAINING.

employee-liability exclusion. See EXCLUSION (3).

employee misconduct. See MISCONDUCT (1).

employee pro hac vice. See *borrowed employee* under EMPLOYEE.

Employee Retirement Income Security Act. A federal statute that regulates private pension plans and employee benefit plans and that established the Pension Benefit

Guaranty Corporation. 29 USCA §§ 1001 et seq. — Abbr. ERISA.

"ERISA was adopted in 1974 in response to highly publicized instances of fraud and mismanagement in employee pension funds, which had resulted in thousands of workers losing retirement benefits accumulated over a lifetime of work. ERISA was intended primarily as an instrument for regulating pensions, as its title suggests, and most of its substantive provisions address protection of retirement benefits. ERISA also, however, applies to employee welfare benefit plans, and thus covers employer provided health insurance, the dominant vehicle for private finance of health care in the United States." Barry R. Furrow et al., *Health Law* § 2-9, at 48 (2d ed. 2000).

employee stock option. See STOCK OPTION (2).

employee-stock-ownership plan. See EMPLOYEE BENEFIT PLAN.

Employee's Withholding Allowance Certificate. See W-4 FORM.

employer. (16c) A person, company, or organization for whom someone works; esp., one who controls and directs a worker under an express or implied contract of hire and who pays the worker's salary or wages. Cf. PRINCIPAL (1).

▸ **equal-opportunity employer.** (1962) An employer who agrees not to discriminate against any job applicant or employee on the basis of race, color, religion, sex, natural origin, age, or disability. — Abbr. EOE.

▸ **general employer.** An employer who transfers an employee to another employer for a limited period. See *borrowed employee* under EMPLOYEE.

▸ **special employer.** An employer who has borrowed an employee for a limited period and has temporary responsibility for and control over the employee's work.

▸ **statutory employer.** (1927) *Workers' compensation.* Someone who employs a statutory employee. See *statutory employee* under EMPLOYEE.

employer–employee relationship. See RELATIONSHIP.

employer-identification number. See TAX-IDENTIFICATION NUMBER.

employer's duty of care. See DUTY OF CARE.

employers' liability. See WORKERS' COMPENSATION.

employers'-liability insurance. See INSURANCE.

employment. (15c) **1.** The relationship between master and servant. See MASTER AND SERVANT. **2.** The act of employing. **3.** The quality, state, or condition of being employed; the condition of having a paying job. **4.** Work for which one has been hired and is being paid by an employer.

▸ **casual employment.** (1831) Work that is occasional, irregular, or for a short time — often associated with day labor.

▸ **employment at will.** (1887) Employment that is usu. undertaken without a contract and that may be terminated at any time, by either the employer or the employee, without cause. • Employment at will is the default rule in 49 states. Montana, by statute, is the exception. — Also termed *at-will employment*; *hiring at will.*

"Surprisingly, the employment at will doctrine is not an ancient one. On the contrary, it dates only from the period in the mid-nineteenth century that saw the transformation of the employment relation from one of status to one of contract. The relentless logic of the contract approach dictated the rule that the employee had only such rights as were expressly agreed to in his contract of employment — no more and no less. This meant that there was no implication that an indefinite hiring would last for a year or any other presumed period, since if the parties had wanted a particular term they would have expressly agreed to it." 1 Lex K. Larson, *Unjust Dismissal* § 1.01, at 1-3 (1992).

"The doctrine of employment at will prescribed that an employee without a contract for a fixed term could be hired or fired for any reason or no reason at all. . . . [The] rule provided that employees categorized as 'at will' had no legal interest in continuing job security. Whereas early American masters had some responsibility to the public as well as to their servants when they turned dependent servants out on the world, under [this] formulation, masters could simply fire employees who had no contracts." Mark A. Rothstein et al., *Employment Law* § 1.4, at 9-10 (1994).

▸ **gainful employment.** (17c) Work that a person can pursue and perform for money.

▸ **hazardous employment.** (17c) High-risk work; work involving extra peril. • In the context of workers' compensation, hazardous employment often requires an employer to carry workers'-compensation coverage or its equivalent, regardless of the number of employees.

▸ **joint employment.** A job in which the essential terms and conditions of the employee's work are controlled by two or more entities, as when a company hires a contractor to perform a task and retains control over the contractor's employees in matters such as hiring, firing, discipline, conditions of employment, promulgation of work rules, assignment of day-to-day job duties, and issuance of operating instructions.

▸ **permanent employment.** (18c) Work that, under a contract, is to continue indefinitely until either party wishes to terminate it for some legitimate reason.

▸ **seasonal employment.** (1919) An occupation possible only during limited parts of the year, such as a summer-camp counselor, a baseball-park vendor, or a shopping-mall Santa.

▸ **temporary employment.** (17c) Work for a specific need or fixed duration, usu. agreed on beforehand.

▸ **underemployment.** (1907) Work that does not make the best or most use of a person's skills, experience, or availability to perform.

employment agency. (19c) A business that procures, for a fee, employment for people and employees for employers. • Whether the employer or the employee pays the fee depends on the terms of the agreement. See FINDER (1).

employment-and-indemnity clause. *Maritime law.* A charterparty provision for the hire of the ship and the charterer's indemnification of the shipowner against any loss of cargo caused by the master's compliance with the charterer's orders. • The term *employment* in this phrase refers to the employment of the ship as a carrier.

Employment and Training Administration. A unit in the U.S. Department of Labor responsible for developing plans for training dislocated and unemployed workers, including young people and those who are disabled; and for interpreting federal workforce-security laws as they apply to the states.

employment capacity. 1. A person's ability to work or to acquire the skills and knowledge necessary to work. **2.** The number of jobs that an employer can sustain.

employment contract. See CONTRACT.

employment discrimination. See DISCRIMINATION (3).

employment law. See LABOR LAW.

employment-practices-liability insurance. See INSURANCE.

employment protection. *Employment law.* The system of laws, agreements, and processes that guard the rights of employees. • Examples include the right to maternity leave and complaint procedures in corporate human-resource departments.

employment-related-practices exclusion. See EXCLUSION (3).

Employment Standards Administration. A unit in the U.S. Department of Labor responsible for enforcing various laws and administering programs relating to minimum-wage and overtime standards, registration of farm-labor contractors, wage rates to be paid and the nondiscrimination and affirmative-action programs to be followed by government contractors and subcontractors, workers'-compensation programs for federal and certain private employers, financial integrity and the internal organizational practices of labor unions, and certification of employee protection for federally sponsored transportation programs. • The Administration operates through four divisions that have regional offices or administrators in various cities: the Office of Federal Contract Compliance Programs, the Wage and Hour Division, the Office of Labor-Management Standards, and the Office of Workers' Compensation Programs. — Abbr. ESA.

emporium (em-**por**-ee-əm), *n.* (16c) **1.** A place for wholesale trade in commodities carried by sea. • The term is sometimes applied to a seaport town, but properly signifies only a particular place in such a town. **2.** An important marketplace. **3.** A large retail store that sells a wide variety of goods.

empresario (em-pre-**sahr**-ee-oh), *n.* [Spanish] (1840) **1.** *Spanish law.* A businessperson; one who invests in or manages a business; esp., a land developer. **2.** *Hist.* A person receiving extensive land grants as consideration for bringing people into Mexico (esp. into what would become Texas) and settling them on the land for the purpose of increasing the population, developing the country's resources, and controlling the aboriginal peoples.

emptio (**emp**-shee-oh), *n.* [Latin "purchase"] *Roman & civil law.* The act of buying; a purchase. — Also spelled *emtio.* Pl. ***emptiones.***

▸ ***emptio bonorum*** (bə-**nor**-əm). [Latin "purchase of goods"] A type of forced assignment for the benefit of creditors, involving a public sale of an insolvent debtor's estate whereby the purchaser succeeded to all the debtor's property, rights, and claims, and became responsible for the debtor's debts and liabilities to an extent fixed before the transfer.

▸ ***emptio et venditio*** (et ven-**dish**-ee-oh). [Latin "purchase and sale"] A contract of sale. • The double name reflects that both the buyer and seller had duties and rights in the transaction. In Roman law, agreement on the thing to be sold and its price were essential. The buyer could enforce the contract by *actio empti,* and the seller could enforce by *actio venditi.* — Also termed *emptio venditio.* See VENDITIO.

> "The emergence of the consensual contract of sale (*emptio venditio*) at latest in the second century BC was a critical moment in the history of Roman commerce. Previously sale must have depended on an exchange of stipulations, in which the seller promised to deliver the object of sale, and the buyer promised to pay the price. That had various drawbacks: formality; the fact that routine terms (e.g. warranties about the quality of the goods sold) had each individually to be spelled out and formally promised in every contract; and the fact that the buyer and seller (or their slaves on their behalf) must meet face to face in order to make the contract by oral exchange of question and answer. The development of the consensual contract of sale overcame all of these disadvantages. The contract of sale automatically implied warranties on the part of the seller about his or her title to the goods and about their quality. The law already set out the essentials which applied to a contract: the whole point of the contract was that without need for express stipulation certain legal effects were automatically produced." David Johnston, "Logic and Experience in Roman Law," in *Mapping the Law: Essays in Memory of Peter Birks* 513, 515 (Andrew Burrows & Alan Rodger eds., 2006).

▸ ***emptio perfecta*** (**emp**-tee-oh per-**fek**-tə), *n.* [Latin "perfected sale"] A fully completed sale. — Also termed *perfect sale.*

> "In order to transfer the risk to the buyer, it was necessary that there should be *emptio perfecta.* The obligation of the parties to go forward might be complete, yet the sale might not be perfect. To make a perfect sale it was necessary for the bargain to be unconditional, to relate to specific goods, and for the price to be certain." Samuel Williston, *The Risk of Loss After an Executory Contract of Sale in the Civil Law,* 9 Harv. L. Rev. 72, 73 (1895).

▸ ***emptio rei facta a pluribus ementibus*** (**emp**-shee-oh **ree**-ɪ **fak**-tə ay **pluur**-ə-bəs i-**men**-tə-bəs). [Latin] *Hist.* A purchase made by many buyers. La. Civ. Code art. 2450. • An *emptio rei facta a pluribus ementibus* did not automatically create a partnership among the purchasers.

▸ ***emptio rei speratae*** (**ree**-ɪ spə-**ray**-tee). [Latin "purchase of a hoped-for thing"] (1947) The purchase of a thing not yet in existence or not yet in the seller's possession; e.g., a future crop. La. Civ. Code art. 2451. • The price of such a purchase typically depended on the actual yield and thus could fluctuate.

▸ ***emptio spei*** (**spee**-ɪ). [Latin "purchase of a hope"] (1850) An *emptio rei speratae* in which the price is fixed, regardless of actual gain. • Even if the future event, such as the casting of a net, produced nothing, the buyer had to pay.

▸ ***emptio venditio.*** See *emptio et venditio.*

emptor (**emp**-tor *or* -tər), *n.* [Latin] (1875) *Civil law.* A buyer; purchaser. — Also spelled *emtor.* See *caveat emptor* under CAVEAT (1). Pl. ***emptores.***

emptor familiae. See FAMILIAE EMPTOR.

emptrix (**em**[**p**]-trəks), *n.* [Latin] *Civil law.* A female buyer. — Also spelled *emtrix.* Pl. ***emptrices.***

empty-chair defense. See DEFENSE (2).

empty-chair doctrine. See ADVERSE-INTEREST RULE.

empty-suit defense. See DEFENSE (1).

emtio. See EMPTIO.

emtor. See EMPTOR.

emtrix. See EMPTRIX.

enable, *vb.* (15c) To give power to do something; to make able.

enablement. (1971) *Patents.* The disclosure in a patent application; specif. the description of the subject matter clear and complete enough to teach a person of ordinary skill in the art how to make and use the invention. • If the artisan would still be unable to work the invention without undue experimentation after reading the description — in light of the information known in the art as of the filing date of the patent application — the patent application will be rejected for lack of enablement. 35 USCA § 112. Cf. NONENABLEMENT.

enablement by deposit. See DEPOSIT (6).

enablement requirement. (1971) *Patents.* The rule that the specification of a patent application must describe the invention so that a person with ordinary skill in the art could make and use the invention without undue experimentation. • A specification that meets this requirement is referred to as *enabling.* Cf. ENABLING SOURCE; BEST-MODE REQUIREMENT.

enabling act. See *enabling statute* under STATUTE.

enabling clause. See CLAUSE.

enabling disclosure. See DESCRIPTION (5).

enabling power. See POWER OF APPOINTMENT.

enabling source. *Patents.* A document that defeats the patentability of an invention because the information provided made it possible — before the patent application was filed — for a person skilled in the art to make the invention. Cf. ENABLEMENT REQUIREMENT.

enabling statute. 1. See STATUTE. **2.** *Hist.* (*cap.*) The Lease Act (1540), by which tenants in tail, husbands seised in right of their wives, and others were empowered to make leases for their lives or for 21 years. St. 32 Hen. 8, ch. 28.

enact, *vb.* (15c) **1.** To make into law by authoritative act; to pass <the statute was enacted shortly before the announced deadline>. **2.** (Of a statute) to provide <the statute of frauds enacts that no action may be brought on certain types of contracts unless the plaintiff has a signed writing to prove the agreement>. — **enactor,** *n.*

enacted law. See LAW.

enacting clause. See CLAUSE.

enacting words. (17c) The statutory phrasing denoting that an act is taking effect as law. • The most common enacting words are *Be it enacted that....* — Also termed *words of enactment.*

enactive (en-**ak**-tiv), *adj.* (17c) **1.** Having the power to establish a new law; capable of enacting. **2.** ENACTORY (1).

enactment, *n.* (18c) **1.** The action or process of making into law <enactment of a legislative bill>. **2.** A statute <a recent enactment>.

> "As the term is generally used, an 'enactment' is a legal *proposition* laid down in an Act or other legislative text with the effect that, when facts fall within an indicated area called the factual outline, specified legal consequences called the legal thrust are called forth. The proposition constituting an enactment may, as is most usual, be embodied in a single sentence of the Act or other instrument. Or it may fall to be collected from two or more sentences, whether consecutive or not." F.A.R. Bennion, *Statutory Interpretation* 305 (1997).

enactor (en-**ak**-tər), *n.* (17c) A person or body that enacts or decrees; esp., one that establishes a new law.

enactory (i-**nak**-tə-ree), *adj.* (19c) **1.** Of, relating to, constituting, or by an enactment; esp., instituting a new right or duty by means of enactment. **2.** ENACTIVE (1).

enajenación (e-nah-hen-ah-**syohn**), *n.* [Spanish] *Spanish law.* Alienation; the transfer of land.

en arere (en ə-**reer**). [Law French] In time past.

en autre droit (en **oh**-trə **droyt** *or* on **noh**-trə **drwah**). [French] In the right of another, as when an executor sues on behalf of the estate. — Also spelled *in autre droit.* See AUTRE DROIT.

en banc (en **bangk** *or* on **bongk**). [Law French "on the bench"] *adv.* & *adj.* (1863) With all judges present and participating; in full court <the court heard the case en banc> <an en banc rehearing>. — Also spelled *in banc; in bank.* — Also termed *in banco.*

en banc court. See *full court* under COURT.

en banc sitting. See SITTING.

enbancworthy, *adj.* (1968) *Slang.* (Of an appellate case) worthy of being considered en banc <the Fifth Circuit concluded that two of the four issues are truly enbancworthy>. — **enbancworthiness,** *n.*

en bloc (on **blok** *or* en **blok**), *adj.* & *adv.* [French] (1861) As a whole; as a unit. • In parliamentary law, this term can refer to a series of resolutions or other motions that are disposed of with a single vote. — Also termed *en grosse; en gros.*

enbrever (en-**bree**-vər), *vb.* [Law French] **1.** To abbreviate. **2.** To put into a schedule.

encheson (en-**chee**-zən), *n.* [Law French] The occasion, cause, or reason for which something is done. — Also spelled *encheason.*

enclave (**en**-klayv *or* **on**-). (19c) *Int'l law.* An isolated part of a country's territory entirely surrounded by the territory of one foreign country, so that any communication with the main part of the country must pass through the territory of the foreign country. • Although international enclaves were once common, they are now relatively rare; examples include Baarle-Hertog, a Belgian enclave in the Netherlands, and Kaliningrad, a Russian enclave between Lithuania and Poland. — Also termed *international enclave.*

▸ **federal enclave.** (1943) Territory or land that a state has ceded to the United States. • Examples of federal enclaves are military bases, national parks, federally administered highways, and federal Indian reservations. The U.S. government has exclusive authority and jurisdiction over federal enclaves.

▸ **quasi-enclave.** (1955) An isolated part of a country's territory that, though not entirely surrounded by the territory of a foreign country, is inaccessible by way of the country's own territory because of topographical features such as impassable mountains.

Enclave Clause. *Constitutional law.* The provision giving Congress power to govern the District of Columbia, and to purchase land from states for forts, arsenals, and other necessary purposes. U.S. Const. art. I, § 8, cl. 17.

enclose, *vb.* (14c) **1.** To surround or encompass; to fence or hem in on all sides. **2.** To place (something) in a parcel or envelope. — Also spelled *inclose.* **enclosed land.** See LAND.

enclosed please find. See TRANSMITTAL LETTER.

enclosure. (15c) **1.** Something enclosed in a parcel or envelope. **2.** Land surrounded by some visible obstruction; CLOSE (1). **3.** An artificial fence around one's estate. — Also spelled *inclosure*.

encoding warranty. See WARRANTY (1).

encomienda (en-koh-mee-**en**-dah), *n.* [Spanish] (1810) *Spanish law.* **1.** A royal grant to a private person of a certain portion of territory in the Spanish colonies, together with the concession of a certain number of the native inhabitants, on the feudal principle of commendation. **2.** A royal grant of privileges to the military orders of Spain. **3.** A mandate for a person to do a specific commission. **4.** Something given by mandate; esp., a parcel.

encourage, *vb.* (15c) *Criminal law.* To instigate; to incite to action; to embolden; to help. See AID AND ABET.

encroach, *vb.* (16c) **1.** To enter by gradual steps or stealth into the possessions or rights of another; to trespass or intrude. **2.** To gain or intrude unlawfully onto another's lands, property, or authority. — Formerly also spelled *incroach*.

encroachment, *n.* (16c) **1.** An infringement of another's rights. **2.** An interference with or intrusion onto another's property <the court remedied the encroachment by ordering the defendant to cut down the tree limb hanging over the plaintiff's yard>. — Formerly also spelled *incroachment*. See TRESPASS.

encumbrance, *n.* (16c) A claim or liability that is attached to property or some other right and that may lessen its value, such as a lien or mortgage; any property right that is not an ownership interest. • An encumbrance cannot defeat the transfer of possession, but it remains after the property or right is transferred. — Also spelled *incumbrance*. — **encumber,** *vb.*

> "Encumbrances are not confined to the law of property, but pertain to the law of obligations also. Choses in action may be mortgaged, settled in trust, or otherwise made the subject-matter of *jura in re aliena*, no less than land and chattels." John Salmond, *Jurisprudence* 435–36 n.(k) (Glanville L. Williams ed., 10th ed. 1947).

> "'Encumbrance' means a right, other than an ownership interest, in real property. The term includes mortgages and other liens on real property." UCC § 9-102(a)(32).

▸ **mesne encumbrance** (meen). An intermediate encumbrance; an encumbrance that first occurred both earlier and later than other encumbrances.

encumbrancer. (1858) One having a legal claim, such as a lien or mortgage, against property.

end, *n.* (12c) **1.** An object, goal, or purpose. **2.** A result; a termination point.

endangered species. See SPECIES (1).

endangering the welfare of a child. See CHILD ENDANGERMENT. — Abbr. EWOC; EWC.

endangerment, *n.* (17c) The act or an instance of putting someone or something in danger; exposure to peril or harm. See CHILD ENDANGERMENT; RECKLESS ENDANGERMENT. — **endanger,** *vb.*

endeavor, *n.* (15c) A systematic or continuous effort to attain some goal; any effort or assay to accomplish some goal or purpose.

endeavor, *vb.* (15c) To exert physical or intellectual strength toward the attainment of an object or goal.

en déclaration de simulation (on dek-lah-rah-**syawn** də sim-[y]ə-lah-**syawn**). [French "in order to declare (something) a pretence"] *Civil law.* An action to void a contract; esp., one brought to remove a cloud from title and bring back, for any legal purpose, to the true owner's estate the thing sold.

en demeure (on də-**myuur**). [French "in default"] *Civil law.* Of a debtor who fails to pay on demand according to the terms of the obligation.

endenizen (en-**den**-ə-zən), *vb.* (16c) To recognize as a legal resident; to naturalize. — Also spelled *endenize*; *indenizen*; *indenize*. See DENIZEN. — **endenization,** *n.*

endless-chain scheme. See PYRAMID SCHEME.

end lines. (1874) *Mining law.* A claim's lines, as platted or laid down on the ground, that mark its boundaries on the shorter dimension, where the claim crosses the vein, in contrast to side lines, which mark the longer dimension and follow the course of the vein. • With reference to the apex rule, if the claim as a whole crosses the vein instead of following its course, the end lines will become the side lines and vice versa. See APEX RULE. Cf. SIDE LINES.

endnote. (1926) A note that, instead of appearing at the bottom of the page (as a footnote does), appears at the end of the book, chapter, or paper. Cf. FOOTNOTE (1).

endogenous insemination. See *artificial insemination by husband* under ARTIFICIAL INSEMINATION.

endorse, *vb.* See INDORSE.

endorsed bond. See *guaranteed bond* (1) under BOND (3).

endorsee. See INDORSEE.

endorsement, *n.* (16c) **1.** INDORSEMENT. **2.** An amendment to an insurance policy; a rider. — **endorse,** *vb.* — **endorseable,** *adj.*

endorsement test. *Constitutional law.* A court's examination of a government or government-sanctioned practice to determine whether it endorses a particular religion by appearing to favor, prefer, or promote that religion over other beliefs and thus violates the Establishment Clause of the First Amendment. • The test is drawn from *Allegheny County v. ACLU*, 492 U.S. 573, 109 S.Ct. 3086 (1989).

endorser. See INDORSER.

endow, *vb.* (14c) **1.** To give money or property to, esp. as a source of continuing or permanent income. **2.** *Hist.* To provide (a woman) with a dower.

endowment. (15c) **1.** A gift of money or property to an institution (such as a university) for a specific purpose, esp. one whose principal is kept intact indefinitely and only the interest income from that principal is used. **2.** The act of giving this money or property. **3.** *Hist.* The assigning or giving of a dower to a woman.

endowment insurance. 1. See INSURANCE. **2.** See *endowment life insurance* under LIFE INSURANCE.

endowment life insurance. See LIFE INSURANCE.

endowment policy. See INSURANCE POLICY.

end position. (1964) One's legal and financial position on the signing of a contract, including the choices now available, such as renewal and renegotiation.

end user. See USER (2).

ENE. *abbr.* Early neutral evaluation.

***Enelow–Ettelson* rule** (en-ə-loh–**et**-əl-sən). (1972) The defunct doctrine that an order staying federal-court proceedings pending the determination of an equitable defense (such as arbitration) is an injunction appealable under 28 USCA § 1292(a)(1) if the proceeding stayed was an action that could have been maintained as an action at law before the merger of law and equity. *Enelow v. New York Life Ins. Co.*, 293 U.S. 379, 55 S.Ct. 310 (1935); *Ettelson v. Metropolitan Life Ins. Co.*, 317 U.S. 188, 63 S.Ct. 163 (1942).

enemy. (13c) **1.** Someone who opposes or inflicts injury on another; an antagonist. **2.** An opposing military force. **3.** A state with which another state is at war. — Also termed *public enemy.* **4.** A person possessing the nationality of the state with which one is at war. — Also termed *enemy subject.* **5.** A foreign state that is openly hostile to another whose position is being considered.

▸ **alien enemy.** See ALIEN.

▸ **public enemy.** (16c) **1.** A notorious criminal who is a menace to society; esp., one who seems more or less immune from successful prosecution. **2.** ENEMY (3). **3.** A social, health, or economic condition or problem that affects the public at large and is difficult to control <teenage smoking has been declared a public enemy in this country>.

enemy alien. See *alien enemy* under ALIEN.

enemy combatant. See COMBATANT.

enemy's property. *Int'l law.* Property used in illegal commerce or trading with a public enemy, whether that property belongs to an ally or a citizen. • This term is esp. common in prize courts. The illegal traffic makes the property hostile, and allows penal consequences to attach to the property itself.

enemy subject. See ENEMY (4).

Energy, Department of. See DEPARTMENT OF ENERGY.

en fait (on **fay**), *adv.* [French] In fact; actually.

enfeoff (en-**fef** *or* en-**feef**), *vb.* (15c) To put (a person) in legal possession of a freehold interest; to transfer a fief to. — Formerly spelled *infeoff.* — Also termed *feoff*; *infeudate*; (in Law Latin) *feoffare.*

enfeoffment (en-**fef**-mənt *or* en-**feef**-), *n.* (15c) **1.** At common law, the act or process of transferring possession and ownership of an estate in land. — Also termed *infeudation*; *infeudatio.* **2.** The property or estate so transferred. **3.** The instrument or deed by which one obtains such property or estate. — Also spelled *infeoffment.* — Also termed *feoffment*; (in Scots law) *infeftment.*

enforce, *vb.* (14c) **1.** To give force or effect to (a law, etc.); to compel obedience to. **2.** Loosely, to compel a person to pay damages for not complying with (a contract).

enforced disappearance. (1985) *Int'l law.* The deprivation of a person's liberty by the State or persons acting with the State's knowledge, followed by the State's refusal to acknowledge that the person was deprived of liberty or concealment of the person's whereabouts or fate, so that the person is unprotected by the law. See DISAPPEARED PERSON (2).

enforcement, *n.* (15c) The act or process of compelling compliance with a law, mandate, command, decree, or agreement.

▸ **enforcement of foreign judgment.** A court's enforcement of a judgment by a court outside the court's territory after determining that the judgment should be recognized. • A foreign judgment may be recognized and enforced if it meets five conditions: (1) the court that made the judgment had jurisdiction; (2) the judgment is final between the parties; (3) the losing party had a chance to be heard during the proceedings; (4) no fraud was worked on the foreign court; and (5) enforcement is not against the public policy of the enforcing state.

▸ **enforcement of judgment.** A court's action to compel a person to comply with the terms of a judgment, usu. one made by that court. • A prevailing party may ask a court to enforce its order so that the party can collect the damages awarded.

▸ **extrajudicial enforcement.** See SELF-HELP.

▸ **law enforcement.** See LAW ENFORCEMENT.

▸ **remedial enforcement.** See *secondary right* under RIGHT.

▸ **sanctional enforcement.** See *secondary right* under RIGHT.

▸ **secondary enforcement.** See *secondary right* under RIGHT.

▸ **selective enforcement.** See SELECTIVE ENFORCEMENT.

▸ **specific enforcement.** See *primary right* under RIGHT.

enforcement notice. *Real estate.* Legal notification that a person who is developing or altering real property without a permit must comply with local planning regulations.

enforcement of foreign judgment. See ENFORCEMENT.

Enforcement of Foreign Judgments Act. A uniform law, adopted by most states, that gives the holder of a foreign judgment essentially the same rights to levy and execute on the judgment as the holder of a domestic judgment. • The Act defines a *foreign judgment* as any judgment, decree, or order (of a court in the United States or of any other court) that is entitled to full faith and credit in the state. See FULL FAITH AND CREDIT.

enforcement of judgment. See ENFORCEMENT.

enforcement order. See ORDER (2).

enforcement power. (1939) The authority by which Congress may enforce a particular constitutional amendment's provisions by appropriate legislation. • Enforcement power is granted to Congress under the 13th, 14th, 15th, 19th, 23rd, 24th, and 26th Amendments.

enfranchise, *vb.* (15c) **1.** To grant voting rights or other rights of citizenship to (a person or class). **2.** To set free, as from slavery.

enfranchisement (en-**fran**-chiz-mənt *or* -chɪz-mənt), *n.* (16c) **1.** The granting of voting rights or other rights of citizenship to a class of persons. **2.** The act of making free, as from slavery.

enfranchisement of copyhold. (18c) *Hist.* The conversion of copyhold into freehold tenure, by (1) a conveyance of the fee simple from the lord of the manor to the copyholder, (2) a release by the lord of all seigniorial rights, or (3) a release by the copyholder to the lord of the copyholder's interest in the estate. See COPYHOLD.

engage, *vb.* (15c) To employ or involve oneself; to take part in; to embark on.

engagement, *n.* (17c) **1.** A contract or agreement involving mutual promises; esp., an agreement to establish a lawyer–client relationship relating to a specific transaction or dispute. **2.** An agreement to marry; the period after which a couple has agreed to marry but before they do so. — Also termed (in sense 2) *betrothal*; *betrothment.*

engagement fee. See RETAINER (3).

engagement letter. (1972) A document identifying the scope of a professional's services to a client and outlining the respective duties and responsibilities of both; esp., a letter from a lawyer agreeing to represent a person or entity in some legal matter and formally establishing an attorney–client relationship.

engagement slip. (1933) A note sent by a lawyer to a court informing the court that the lawyer is professionally engaged in a second court on a given day and thus cannot appear before the first court on that day as scheduled. • The term is used in Pennsylvania.

engender, *vb.* (14c) To cause; to bring about; to occasion.

engineering, procurement, and construction contract. See CONTRACT.

***England* procedure.** (1974) A procedure by which — after a federal court has referred a case back to state court under the *Pullman* abstention doctrine, and the state court has adjudicated the state-court issues — a litigant may return to federal court to have the federal claims adjudicated. *England v. Louisiana State Bd. of Med. Examiners*, 375 U.S. 411, 84 S.Ct. 461 (1964). See *Pullman abstention* under ABSTENTION.

English Bill of Rights. A 1689 act of Parliament that limits the powers of the monarchy to act without the consent of Parliament, prohibits challenges to the freedom of speech in Parliament, and grants basic freedoms and privileges to the general public. 1 W.&M., sess. 2, ch. 2. • The Act's formal name is An Act Declaring the Rights and Liberties of the Subject and Settling the Succession of the Crown. Among other provisions, the monarch cannot unilaterally suspend laws, raise taxes, or raise an army, and a person accused of a crime cannot be subjected to cruel and unusual punishment or burdened by excessive bail. Some of its provisions were adopted into the United States Bill of Rights.

English Constitution. The basic principles and documents of English law, esp. those that define the powers of and limits on the monarchy and Parliament and that establish the rights and privileges of the people. • The essential constitutional documents include Magna Carta (1215), the Petition of Right (1628), the Habeas Corpus Act (1679), the Bill of Rights (1689), the Parliament Acts (1911 and 1949), the Human Rights Act (1998), and the Equality Act (2010). See MAGNA CARTA; PETITION OF RIGHT; HABEAS CORPUS ACT; ENGLISH BILL OF RIGHTS.

English rule. The requirement that a losing litigant must pay the winner's costs and attorney's fees. — Also termed *loser-pays rule*. Cf. AMERICAN RULE (1).

Englishry, presentment of. PRESENTMENT OF ENGLISHRY.

en gros (on **groh**). [French] (18c) Total; by wholesale; IN GROSS. — Also spelled *en grosse*. See EN BLOC.

engross, *vb.* (15c) **1.** *Hist.* To handwrite (a document, esp. a deed) in a style characterized by large letters. • This method of writing, which was derived from ancient court hand, was also used in transcribing wills well into the 19th century. See COURT HAND. **2.** To prepare a copy of (a legal document, such as a deed) for execution. **3.** To prepare a copy of (a bill or mandate) before a final legislative vote. **4.** *Hist.* To buy large quantities of (a stock or commodity) in an effort to corner the market and control the price. **5.** To absorb or fully occupy. — Formerly also spelled *ingross*. Cf. ENROLL (2). — **engrossment,** *n.*

engrossed bill. See BILL (3).

engrosser, *n.* (15c) **1.** Someone who engrosses legal documents. **2.** *Hist.* Someone who buys large quantities of a commodity in an effort to control the price.

Engrosser of the Great Roll. See CLERK OF THE PIPE.

engrossing, *n.* (16c) *Hist.* The practice of buying large quantities of commodities or merchandise with the intent of gaining a monopoly and selling them at a very high price. • Engrossing was a misdemeanor in England until 1834. — Also termed *engrossment*. See CORNERING THE MARKET.

> "Engrossing . . . is the getting into one's possession, or buying up, of corn or other dead victuals, with intent to sell them again. This must of course be injurious to the public, by putting it in the power of one or two rich men to raise the price of provisions at their own discretion." 4 William Blackstone, *Commentaries on the Laws of England* 158 (1769).

engrossment, *n.* (16c) **1.** The preparation of a legal document (such as a deed) for execution. **2.** The drafting of a resolution or bill just before a final vote on the matter in the legislature. **3.** ENGROSSING.

enhanced, *adj.* (16c) Made greater; increased <because of his recidivism, Monte was subject to an enhanced sentence after his latest conviction>.

enhanced crime. See CRIME.

enhanced damages. See DAMAGES.

enhanced-injury claim. *Torts.* A cause of action in which a defendant's liability stems from the defendant's negligence or defective product that resulted in harm caused by another to be more serious than it would have been.

enhanced-injury doctrine. See CRASHWORTHINESS DOCTRINE.

enhanced-life-estate deed. See *Lady Bird deed* under DEED.

enhanced offense. See *enhanced crime* under CRIME.

enhanced sentence. See SENTENCE.

enhancement. (16c) **1.** The act of augmenting, as with a sentence in a criminal prosecution or damages in a civil action; the quality, state, or condition of being enhanced. **2.** *Criminal law.* An upward adjustment to a defendant's offense level under applicable sentencing guidelines <the use of a deadly weapon led to an enhancement of the sentence>. See UPWARD ADJUSTMENT.

enhancement fact. (1978) A fact that is constitutionally required to be proved before a sentence may be increased beyond the applicable sentencing guidelines.

enheritance (on-nair-ee-**tahns**), *n.* [Law French] See INHERITANCE.

enitia pars (ə-**nish**-ee-ə **pahrz**). [Latin] (17c) The share of the eldest. • In English law, this describes the lot or share chosen by the eldest of coparceners when they make a voluntary partition. The first choice (*primer election*) belongs to the eldest.

enjoin, *vb.* (13c) **1.** To legally prohibit or restrain by injunction <the company was enjoined from selling its stock>. **2.** To prescribe, mandate, or strongly encourage <the graduating class was enjoined to uphold the highest professional standards>. — Also spelled *injoin.* — **enjoinment** (in sense 1), *n.* — **enjoinder** (in sense 2), *n.*

enjoinable, *adj.* (18c) Capable of being prohibited by injunction <an enjoinable nuisance>.

enjoy, *vb.* (15c) To have, possess, and use (something) with satisfaction; to occupy or have the benefit of (property).

enjoyment, *n.* (16c) **1.** Possession and use, esp. of rights or property. **2.** The exercise of a right.

- ▸ **adverse enjoyment.** (18c) The possession or use of land under a claim of right against the property owner.
- ▸ **beneficial enjoyment.** (18c) The possession and benefit of land or other property, but without legal title.
- ▸ **present enjoyment.** (18c) The immediate possession and use of land or other property.
- ▸ **quiet enjoyment.** (18c) The possession of land with the assurance that the possession will not be disturbed by a superior title. See *covenant for quiet enjoyment* under COVENANT (4).

en juicio (en **hwee**-syoh), *adv.* [Spanish] Judicially; in a court of law.

enlarge, *vb.* (14c) **1.** To increase in size or extend in scope or duration <the court enlarged the time allotted for closing arguments>. **2.** To free from custody or imprisonment <at common law, an action for escape lay when a prisoner was wrongly enlarged>. Cf. AT LARGE. — **enlargement,** *n.*

enlargement of time. (18c) A usu. court-ordered extension of the time allowed to perform an action, esp. a procedural one.

enlarger l'estate (en-**lahr**-jər lə-**stayt**). [Law French] *Hist.* A release that enlarges an estate and consists of a conveyance of the ulterior interest to the tenant. • If an estate was held by a tenant for life or years, with the remainder to another in fee, and if the one in remainder released all rights to the tenant and his or her heirs (through an *enlarger l'estate*), the tenant then held the estate in fee.

enlisted member. (1841) *Military law.* A person in an enlisted grade; a person in military service below the grade of officer or warrant officer. — Also termed *enlisted man.*

enlistment, *n.* (18c) Voluntary entry into a branch of the armed services. — **enlist,** *vb.*

en masse (en **mas**). [French] (18c) In a mass; in a large group all at once; all together.

enmity. (14c) **1.** An intense feeling of hatred toward someone, esp. when the feeling is mutual; antagonism. **2.** The quality, state, or condition of being an enemy; mutual hostility.

en mort mayne (en **mort** mayn). [French "in dead hand"] In mortmain. See MORTMAIN.

Enoch Arden law (**ee**-nək **ahrd**-ən). (1923) A statute that grants a divorce or an exemption from liability so that a person can remarry when his or her spouse has been absent without explanation for a specified number of years (usu. five or seven). • This type of law is named after a Tennyson poem, in which the eponymous hero, having been shipwrecked for years on a desert island, returns home to find that his wife has remarried. He selflessly conceals his identity from her so that she can remain with her new husband. — Also spelled *Enoc Arden law.* See *presumptive death* under DEATH; ABANDONMENT (4). Cf. SEVEN-YEARS'-ABSENCE RULE.

enorm (i-**norm**), *adj.* (15c) *Hist.* (Of a crime or other wrong) monstrously evil; wicked.

enormia (i-**nor**-mee-ə), *n.* [Latin] *Common-law pleading.* Unlawful or wrongful acts; wrongs. • This word, esp. as part of the phrase *et alia enormia* ("and other outrages"), appeared regularly in writs and declarations of trespass.

enorm lesion (i-**norm lee**-zhən). See LAESIO ENORMIS.

enormous, *adj.* (16c) Aggravated; excessively large <enormous crimes>.

en owel main (en **ow**-əl **mayn**). [Law French] In equal hand.

enpleet (en-**pleet**), *vb. Hist.* See IMPLEAD.

enquête (on-**ket**), *n.* [French] *Eccles. law.* An examination of witnesses (taken down in writing) by or before an authorized judge for the purpose of gathering testimony to be used in a trial. — Also termed *enquest* (on[g]-**kwes**[**t**]).

enquest. See ENQUÊTE.

en recouvrement (on ray-koo-vrə-**mon**). [French "for purpose of recovery"] *French law.* An indorsement on a bill of exchange that does not transfer the property in the bill of exchange but merely gives the indorsee the authority to recover the amount of the bill.

enregister, *vb.* REGISTER.

enrégistrement (on-ray-zhees-trə-**mon**), *n.* [French] *French law.* Registration. • This formality is performed by a clerk who inscribes a government register with a summary analysis of a deed or other document. The clerk then puts a stamped or sealed note on the deed or document, indicating the date on which it was registered.

enrichment. (17c) The receipt of a benefit. Cf. UNJUST ENRICHMENT.

enroll, *vb.* (14c) **1.** To register or transcribe (a legal document, as a deed) into an official record on execution. — Formerly also spelled *inroll.* **2.** To prepare (a bill passed by the legislature) for the executive's signature. Cf. ENGROSS.

enrolled, *adj.* (1840) Registered; recorded.

enrolled agent. (1922) Someone who, though neither a certified public accountant nor an attorney, has been admitted to practice before the IRS, either by passing an examination or by working for the IRS in a technical area for at least five years. • The enrolled agent is one of four types of persons who are allowed to practice before the IRS, the other three being attorneys, certified public accountants, and persons who are admitted to represent either themselves or others in a particular case.

enrolled bill. See BILL (3).

enrolled-bill rule. (1914) The conclusive presumption that a statute, once formalized, appears precisely as the legislature intended, thereby preventing any challenge to the drafting of the bill.

> "Under the 'enrolled bill rule,' an enrolled bill, properly authenticated and approved by the governor, is conclusive as to regularity of its enactment. Ordinarily, the courts will not go behind the enrolled bill to determine its validity. The supreme court can look behind the enrolled bill only to determine whether the constitutional mandate relative to vote and journal entry upon the final passage have been complied with." National Conference of State Legislatures, *Mason's Manual of Legislative Procedure* § 702, at 497 (2000).

enrollment, *n.* (16c) **1.** The act of recording or registering in a list, catalogue, or roll.

▸ **enrollment of vessels.** (1824) *Maritime law.* The recording and certification of vessels used in coastal or inland navigation, as distinguished from the "registration" of vessels used in foreign commerce. • *Enrollment* and *registry* are used to distinguish certificates granted to two classes of vessels. Enrollment evidences the national character of a vessel engaged in coasting trade or home traffic; registry is used to declare the nationality of a vessel engaged in foreign trade. Cf. REGISTRY (5).

2. The preparation of a final, perfect copy of a bill as passed by a legislature. Cf. ENGROSSMENT (2). **3.** The process of arranging to become a student at a school, college, university, etc. **4.** The number of students at a school, college, university, etc. — Also spelled (archaically) *inrollment*; (BrE) *enrolment.*

Enrollment Office. *Hist.* A department of the Court of Chancery responsible for storing enrolled deeds and judgments. • The Enrollment Office was abolished in 1879; its duties were transferred to the Central Office.

en route (en *or* on **root**). [French] (18c) On the way; in the course of transportation or travel.

enschedule, *vb.* (17c) *Archaic.* To insert in a list, account, or writing.

enseal, *vb.* (14c) *Archaic.* To seal (a document).

enserver (en-**sər**-vər), *vb.* [Law French] To make subject to a service or servitude.

ensign, *n.* **1.** A ship's flag indicating what nation the ship belongs to, esp. on a military vessel. **2.** An officer of the lowest commission rank in the United States Navy.

ens legis (enz **lee**-jis). [Law Latin] A creature of the law; an artificial being as opposed to a natural person. • The term describes an entity, such as a corporation, that derives its existence entirely from the law.

entail, *n.* (14c) A fee abridged or limited to the owner's issue or class of issue rather than descending to all the heirs. See BARRING OF ENTAIL; FEE TAIL. — Also termed (in Scots law) *tailzie.* — **entailable,** *adj.*

> "*Entail* is fee entailed, viz; abridged, limited, and tied to certain conditions at the will of the donor; where lands are given to, or settled on others." *The Pocket Lawyer and Family Conveyancer* 97 (3d ed. 1833).

▸ **quasi-entail.** (1810) An estate *pur autre vie* that is granted to a person and the heirs of the person's body. • The interest so granted is not properly an estate-tail (because it is not granted by inheritance), but it is similar enough that the interest will go to the heir of the body as special occupant during the life of the *cestui que vie,* in the same manner as an estate of inheritance would descend if limited to the grantee and the heirs of his body.

entail, *vb.* (14c) **1.** To make necessary; to involve <responding to this onerous discovery will entail countless hours of work>. **2.** To limit the inheritance of (an estate) to only the owner's issue or class of issue, so that none of the heirs can transfer the estate <the grantor entailed the property through a so-called "tail female">. See FEE TAIL. — **entailable,** *adj.*

entailed, *adj.* (16c) Settled or limited to specified heirs or in tail <entailed gifts>.

entailed estate. See FEE TAIL.

entailed interest. See INTEREST (2).

entailment, *n.* (17c) **1.** The act of entailing an estate. **2.** An estate so entailed.

entencion (en-**ten**-shən), *n.* [Law French] *Hist.* A plaintiff's count or declaration.

entendment. *Archaic.* See INTENDMENT.

entente (ahn-**tahnt**). [French "intent, understanding"] (19c) *Int'l law.* **1.** An understanding that two or more countries have for carrying out a common policy or course of action. • An *entente* is looser than an alliance but stronger than the countries' merely having good relations. **2.** The countries having such an understanding. Cf. ALLIANCE; DÉTENTE.

enter, *vb.* (13c) **1.** To come or go into; esp., to go onto (real property) by right of entry so as to take possession <the landlord entered the defaulting tenant's premises>. **2.** To put formally before a court or on the record <the defendant entered a plea of no contest>. **3.** To become a party to <they entered into an agreement>. See ENTRY.

enterceur (en-tər-**sər**), *n.* [Law French] A party claiming goods; one who has placed goods in the hands of a third party.

entering wedge. See SLIPPERY SLOPE.

enter judgment. (Of a court) to note a final disposition in the official record of a case. See JUDGMENT (2).

enterpleder. *Archaic.* See INTERPLEADER (1).

enterprise, *n.* (15c) **1.** An organization or venture, esp. for business purposes.

▸ **governmental enterprise.** (1850) An enterprise undertaken by a governmental body, such as a parks department that creates a public park. — Also termed *government enterprise.*

2. Under federal anti-racketeering law, an individual, partnership, corporation, association, union, other legal entity, or group of individuals associated in fact, although not a legal entity. • The enterprise must be ongoing and must exist as an entity separate from the allegedly illegal activity that it engages in. 18 USCA § 1961(4). See RACKETEER INFLUENCED AND CORRUPT ORGANIZATIONS ACT. **3.** One or more persons or organizations that have related activities, unified operation or common control, and a common business purpose. • Under the Fair Labor Standards Act, an employee who is employed by an enterprise is entitled to minimum-wage and overtime benefits. 29 USCA §§ 201 et seq.

enterprise bargaining agreement. See *certified agreement* under AGREEMENT. — Abbr. EBA.

enterprise corruption. (1986) *Criminal law.* The wrongful participation in the control over or investment of proceeds from criminal activities.

enterprise goodwill. See GOODWILL.

enterprise liability. See LIABILITY.

enterprise organizations. See BUSINESS ENTERPRISES.

enterprise value. See VALUE (2).

enterprise zone. (1978) An economically depressed area in which the government encourages business activity, as by lowering taxes, providing subsidies, or making other financial concessions for businesses that move there.

entertain, *vb.* (15c) **1.** To bear in mind or consider; esp., to give judicial consideration to <the court then entertained motions for continuance>. **2.** To amuse or please. **3.** To receive (a person) as a guest or provide hospitality to (a person). **4.** *Parliamentary law.* To recognize and state (a motion); to receive and take into consideration <the chair will entertain the motion>.

entertainment expense. See EXPENSE.

entertainment law. (1953) The field of law dealing with the legal and business issues in the entertainment industry (such as film, music, and theater), and involving the representation of artists and producers, the negotiation of contracts, and the protection of intellectual-property rights.

enthrone, *vb.* (17c) **1.** To ceremonially establish (a monarch) in the position to rule. **2.** By extension, to seat (a person) in a place or position of authority and influence. — **enthronement,** *n.*

enthymeme (**en**-thə-meem). (1552) **1.** A syllogism in which one of the premises is suppressed; specif., an argument in which a legal or factual premise is unexpressed but implied. See SYLLOGISM.

▸ **enthymeme of the first order.** A syllogism in which the major premise is suppressed, as in "Because Socrates is a man, he will die."

▸ **enthymeme of the second order.** A syllogism in which the minor premise is suppressed, as in "Because all men are mortal, Socrates will die."

2. *Archaic.* In Aristotelian logic, a syllogism that is at most persuasive or probable, whether or not a premise has been suppressed. — **enthymematic,** *adj.*

entice, *vb.* (14c) To lure or induce; esp., to wrongfully solicit (a person) to do something.

enticement, *n.* (14c) **1.** The act or an instance of wrongfully soliciting or luring a person to do something. **2.** *Hist.* The tort of inducing a man's wife to leave him or to remain away from him against his will.

enticement of a child. (1931) *Criminal law.* The act or offense of inviting, persuading, or attempting to persuade a child to enter a vehicle, building, room, or secluded place with the intent of committing an unlawful sexual act against the child. — Often shortened to *enticement.*

enticement of a parent. (1950) *Rare. Torts.* The tortious interference with a child's rights and interests in maintaining the parent–child relationship, usu. caused by a third person who induces a parent to abandon the child. • Actions based on enticement, where they are recognized, are rarely successful because many states do not recognize a child's legal right to a parent's consortium or affection.

entire, *adj.* (14c) **1.** Whole; complete in all its parts. **2.** Not divisible into parts.

entire-agreement clause. (1960) **1.** INTEGRATION CLAUSE. **2.** A provision in an insurance contract stating that the entire agreement between the insured and insurer is contained in the contract, often including the application (if attached), declarations, insuring agreement, exclusions, conditions, and endorsements. — Also termed *entire-contract clause.*

entire benefit. See *entire use* under USE (4).

entire blood. See *full blood* under BLOOD.

entire contract. See CONTRACT.

entire-contract clause. See ENTIRE-AGREEMENT CLAUSE.

entire-controversy doctrine. (1970) The principle that a plaintiff or defendant who does not assert all claims or defenses related to the controversy in a legal proceeding is not entitled to assert those claims or defenses in a later proceeding. — Also termed *single-controversy doctrine.* Cf. *compulsory counterclaim* under COUNTERCLAIM; RES JUDICATA (2).

entire day. See DAY.

entire interest. See INTEREST (2).

entire-market-value rule. (1942) *Patents.* The principle that when a single patented feature of a multicomponent product drives demand for that product, a royalty may be based on revenues attributable to the product as a whole. • This rule is an exception to the general rule that a royalty should be based on the smallest salable feature that practices the patent. *See LaserDynamics, Inc. v. Quanta Computer, Inc.*, 694 F.3d 51 (Fed. Cir. 2012). — Sometimes shortened to *market-value rule.*

entire-output contract. See *output contract* under CONTRACT.

entire tenancy. See TENANCY.

entirety (en-**tɪ**-ər-tee). (16c) **1.** The whole, as opposed to a moiety or part. **2.** Something (such as certain judgments and contracts) that the law considers incapable of being divided into parts.

entirety, tenancy by the. See *estate by entirety* under ESTATE (1).

entirety clause. (1940) *Oil & gas.* A mineral-lease or deed provision specifying that royalties must be apportioned if the property is subdivided after the lease is granted. • For the lessee, the clause makes it clear that the lessee's duties will increase if the lessor transfers a part of the leased premises. For the lessor, the clause avoids the non-apportionment rule.

entire use. See USE (4).

entitle, *vb.* (14c) **1.** To grant a legal right to or qualify for. **2.** *Eccles. law.* To ordain as a minister. — Formerly also spelled *intitle.*

entitlement. (19c) An absolute right to a (usu. monetary) benefit, such as social security, granted immediately upon meeting a legal requirement.

entitlement issue. See *open offer* under OFFER (2).

entitlement program. (1971) A government program guaranteeing certain benefits, such as financial aid or government-provided services, to people or entities that meet the criteria set by law. • Some examples of entitlement programs are unemployment benefits, Social Security, food stamps, and agricultural price-support plans. Qualified beneficiaries have an enforceable right to participate in the programs.

entity. An organization (such as a business or a governmental unit) that has a legal identity apart from its members or owners.

▸ **corporate entity.** (1862) A corporation's status as an organization existing independently of its shareholders. • As a separate entity, a corporation can, in its own name, sue and be sued, lend and borrow money, and buy, sell, lease, and mortgage property.

▸ **public entity.** (1926) A governmental entity, such as a state government or one of its political subdivisions.

entity assumption. (1972) The presumption that a business is a unit separate from its owners and from other firms.

entity theory of partnership. (1916) The theory that a partnership is an entity with a legal existence apart from the partners who make it up. • Under the Uniform Partnership Act, "[a] partnership is an entity distinct from its partners." UPA § 201 (1994). Cf. AGGREGATE THEORY OF PARTNERSHIP.

entrance permit. See ENTRY PERMIT.

entrant. 1. Someone who comes or goes into (a place), esp. a person who legally enters real property to take possession of it. **2.** Someone who goes into a field, marketplace, or event as a competitor. **3.** Someone who enters or becomes a member of a profession or of an institution, such as a university.

entrapment, *n.* (1899) **1.** A law-enforcement officer's or government agent's inducement of a person to commit a crime, by means of fraud or undue persuasion, in an attempt to cause a criminal prosecution against that person. **2.** The affirmative defense of having been so induced. • To establish entrapment (in most states), the defendant must show that he or she would not have committed the crime but for the fraud or undue persuasion. — **entrap,** *vb.*

> "Entrapment, so-called, is a relatively simple and very desirable concept which was unfortunately misnamed, with some resulting confusion. It is socially desirable for criminals to be apprehended and brought to justice. And there is nothing whatever wrong or out of place in setting traps for those bent on crime, provided the traps are not so arranged as likely to result in offenses by persons other than those who are ready to commit them. What the State cannot tolerate is having crime instigated by its officers who are charged with the duty of enforcing the law. . . . Obviously 'entrapment' is not the appropriate word to express the idea of official investigation of crime, but it is so firmly entrenched that it seems wiser to accept it with due explanation than attempt to supplant it . . . ." Rollin M. Perkins & Ronald N. Boyce, *Criminal Law* 1161 (3d ed. 1982).

▸ **derivative entrapment.** (1984) Entrapment in which the government uses a private person, acting either as an agent of the government or as an unwitting participant, to induce the subject of the entrapment to commit a crime.

▸ **entrapment by estoppel.** (1985) *Criminal law.* An affirmative defense that the defendant acted in reliance on a government official who had actual or apparent authority and assured or actively misled a defendant into reasonably believing that the defendant's conduct was legal. — Abbr. EBE.

▸ **objective entrapment.** (1970) Entrapment as judged by focusing on egregious law-enforcement conduct, not on the defendant's predisposition.

▸ **sentencing entrapment.** (1991) Entrapment of a defendant who is predisposed to commit a lesser offense but who is unlawfully induced to commit a more serious offense that carries a more severe sentence. — Also termed *sentence entrapment*; *sentence-factor manipulation.*

entrapment-by-estoppel defense. See *public-authority defense* under DEFENSE (1).

entrebat (on-trə-**ba**), *n.* [Law French] An intruder or interloper.

entrenched legislation. See LEGISLATION (3).

entrepôt (on-trə-**poh**), *n.* [French] (18c) *French law.* A building or place where goods from abroad may be deposited and from which those goods may then be exported to another country without paying a duty.

entrepreneur (on-trə-prə-**nər** *or* **-noor**), *n.* (19c) Someone who initiates and assumes the financial risks and accepts the rewards of a new enterprise and who usu. undertakes its management. Cf. INTRAPRENEUR.

entrepreneurial rights. See NEIGHBORING RIGHTS.

entrust, *vb.* (16c) To give (a person) the responsibility for something, usu. after establishing a confidential relationship. — Also spelled (archaically) *intrust.* See NEGLIGENT ENTRUSTMENT. — **entrustment,** *n.*

entrusting, *n. Commercial law.* The transfer of possession of goods to a merchant who deals in goods of that type and who may in turn transfer the goods and all rights to them to a purchaser in the ordinary course of business. UCC § 2-403(2).

entry, *n.* (13c) **1.** The act, right, or privilege of entering real property <they were given entry into the stadium>. — Also termed *entry onto land.*

▸ **forcible entry.** See FORCIBLE ENTRY.

▸ **lawful entry.** (17c) **1.** The entry onto real property by a person not in possession, under a claim or color of right, and without force or fraud. **2.** The entry of premises under a search warrant. See SEARCH WARRANT.

▸ **open entry.** (18c) A conspicuous entry onto real property to take possession; an entry that is neither clandestine nor carried out by secret artifice or stratagem and that (by law in some states) is accomplished in the presence of two witnesses.

▸ **reentry.** See REENTRY.

▸ **unlawful entry.** (17c) **1.** The crime of intentionally entering another's real property, by fraud or other illegal means, without the owner's consent. Cf. TRESPASS (1). **2.** An alien's crossing of a border into a country without proper documents.

2. An item written in a record; a notation <Forney made a false entry in the books on March 3>.

▸ **blind entry.** (1872) An accounting entry that indicates only the debited and credited amounts without any explanation.

▸ **compound journal entry.** (1941) A journal entry requiring more than one debit and credit (as when revenue is received partly in cash and partly in securities).

▸ **journal entry.** (1874) An entry in an accounting journal of equal debits and credits, with occasional explanations of the recorded transactions.

3. The placement of something before the court or on the record. **4.** *Copyright.* The deposit of a title of work with the Register of Copyrights to secure its protection. **5.** *Immigration.* Any entrance of an alien into the United States, whether voluntary or involuntary. **6.** *Criminal law.* The unlawful coming into a building to commit a crime.

entry, right of. See POWER OF TERMINATION.

entry, writ of. See WRIT OF ENTRY.

entry *ad communem legem* (ad kə-**myoo**-nəm **lee**-jəm). [Latin] (17c) *Hist.* **1.** Entry at common law. **2.** AD COMMUNEM LEGEM.

entry *ad terminum qui praeteriit* (ad **tər**-mə-nəm kwI pri-**ter**-ee-it). See AD TERMINUM QUI PRAETERIIT.

entry fiction. (1982) The assumption, for purposes of immigration and deportation proceedings, that an excludable alien is to be treated as if detained at the border despite his or her physical presence in the United States.

entry for marriage in speech. See *causa matrimonii praelocuti* under CAUSA (1).

entry *in casu consimili* (**en**-tree in **kay**-s[y]oo kən-**sim**-ə-lI). [Latin] See CASU CONSIMILI.

entryman (**en**-tree-mən), *n.* (1886) *Archaic.* Someone who enters public land and stakes a claim with the intention of settling.

entry of judgment. (17c) The ministerial recording of a court's final decision, usu. by noting it in a judgment book or civil docket. Cf. RENDITION OF JUDGMENT.

entry on the roll. (17c) *Hist.* **1.** A clerk's notation on a parchment roll of the proceedings and issues in a particular case. • Before parties began submitting written pleadings, they would appear (in person or through counsel) in open court and state their respective contentions orally until they settled on the issue or precise point in dispute. During the progress of these oral statements, an appointed officer of the court would prepare minutes of the various proceedings on a parchment roll that then became the official record of the suit. Even after the practice of oral pleadings had fallen into disuse, proceedings continued to be entered "on the roll." This practice was abolished early in the 19th century. **2.** A future interest created in a transferor who conveys an estate on condition subsequent.

entry onto land. See ENTRY (1).

entry permit. A printed or written document that grants a person access to a place. — Also termed *entrance permit.*

enumerate (i-**n**[y]**oo**-mə-rayt), *vb.* (17c) To count off or designate one by one; to list. — **enumeration,** *n.*

enumerated motion. See MOTION (1).

enumerated power. See POWER (3).

enumerated-powers doctrine. *Constitutional law.* The principle that Congress may act only for the purposes and activities expressly mentioned in the text of the Constitution.

enumerated right. See RIGHT.

enumerator. (1856) A person appointed to collect census papers or schedules.

enunciate (i-**nən**-see-ayt), *vb.* (17c) **1.** To state publicly; to announce or proclaim <the court enunciated a new doctrine yesterday>. **2.** To articulate or pronounce <enunciate your syllables more clearly when you speak>. — **enunciation,** *n.* — **enunciable,** *adj.* — **enunciator,** *n.*

enure. See INURE.

en ventre sa mere (on **von**-trə sa **mair**). [Law French "in utero"] (18c) (Of a fetus) in the mother's womb <child *en ventre sa mere*>. • This phrase refers to an unborn child, usu. in the context of a discussion of that child's rights. If the child is *en ventre sa mere* at the time of a decedent's death and is subsequently born alive, the child is treated as having been in existence at the time of the decedent's death for purposes of inheritance. — Also spelled *in ventre sa mere.* See VENTER.

> "An infant *in ventre sa mere,* or in the mother's womb, is supposed in law to be born for many purposes." 1 William Blackstone, *Commentaries on the Laws of England* 126 (1765).

en vie (on **vee**). [Law French "in life"] Alive.

environment. 1. The natural world in which living things dwell and grow. **2.** The conditions affecting the development, growth, or performance of a person or thing. **3.** The physical conditions of a particular place where a living person or thing exists. — **environmental,** *adj.*

environmental assessment. See ENVIRONMENTAL-IMPACT STATEMENT.

environmental audit. See AUDIT.

environmental covenant. See COVENANT (4).

environmental crime. (1972) *Environmental law.* A statutory offense involving harm to the environment, such as a violation of the criminal provisions in the Clean Air Act Amendments of 1970, the Federal Water Pollution Control Act of 1972 (commonly called the Clean Water Act), or the Endangered Species Act of 1973. • Although the most significant environmental-crime statutes were enacted in the 1970s, they date back to the late 19th century, with statutes such as the Pure Food and Drug Act of 1896 and the assorted statutes that ultimately became the Rivers and Harbors Act of 1899. — Also termed *crime against the environment.*

environmental criminology. See CRIMINOLOGY.

environmental effect. (1967) *Environmental law.* A natural or artificial disturbance of the physical, chemical, or biological components that make up the environment.

environmental-impact statement. (1971) *Environmental law.* **1.** A document that the National Environmental Policy Act (42 USCA § 4332(2)(c)) requires a federal agency to produce before undertaking a major project or legislative proposal so that better decisions can be made about the positive and negative environmental effects of an undertaking. **2.** In some states, a public document used by a government agency to analyze the significant environmental effects of a proposed project, to identify alternatives, and to disclose possible ways to reduce or avoid possible environmental damage. **3.** Generally, the estimation and evaluation of the possible environmental, economic, and social effects of a project or program on its location before making major decisions about the project or program. — Abbr. EIS. — Also termed *environmental-impact report* (EIR); *environmental assessment.*

environmental law. (1971) The field of law dealing with the maintenance and protection of the environment, including preventive measures such as the requirements of preparing environmental-impact statements, as well as measures to assign liability and provide cleanup for incidents that harm the environment. • Because most environmental litigation involves disputes with governmental agencies, environmental law is heavily intertwined with administrative law.

environmental mitigation. (1978) A project or program designed to offset the effects of human activities on an existing historic or natural resource, such as a wetland, an endangered species, or an archaeological site. — Also termed *compensatory mitigation*; *mitigation banking.*

environmental offense. See ENVIRONMENTAL CRIME.

Environmental Protection Agency. An independent federal agency in the executive branch responsible for setting pollution-control standards in the areas of air, water, solid waste, pesticides, radiation, and toxic materials; enforcing laws enacted to protect the environment; and coordinating the antipollution efforts of state and local governments. • The commission was created by Reorganization Plan No. 3 of 1970. — Abbr. EPA.

environmental risk assessment. See RISK ASSESSMENT.

environmental terrorism. See *ecoterrorism* under TERRORISM.

environmental tort. See TORT.

enviroterrorism. See *ecoterrorism* under TERRORISM.

envoy (**en**-voy). (17c) **1.** A high-ranking diplomat sent to a foreign country to execute a special mission or to serve as a permanent diplomatic representative. — Formerly also termed *envoy extraordinary.* **2.** A messenger or representative.

▸ **envoy extraordinary.** (17c) *Int'l law.* **1.** Someone who heads a legation rather than an embassy. • In current usage, the term is honorific and has no special significance. **2.** *Hist.* ENVOY (1).

envoy plenipotentiary. See *ambassador plenipotentiary* under AMBASSADOR.

enzyme-multiplied immunoassay technique. See EMIT TEST.

eo die (ee-oh **dɪ**-ee). [Latin] On that day; on the same day.

EOE. *abbr.* **1.** See *equal-opportunity employer* under EMPLOYER. **2.** Errors and omissions excepted. • This phrase is sometimes appended to an account stated to allow for slight errors. See *errors-and-omissions insurance* under INSURANCE.

eo instante (ee-oh in-**stan**-tee). [Latin] At that very instant. — Also spelled *eo instanti.*

eo intuitu (ee-oh in-**t[y]oo**-ə-too). [Latin] With or in that view; with that intent or object.

eo ipso (ee-oh **ip**-soh). [Latin] By that very act.

eo loci (ee-oh **loh**-sɪ). [Latin] In that state; in that condition.

eo loco (ee-oh **loh**-koh). [Latin] **1.** In that place. **2.** In that state; in that condition.

EOM. *abbr.* End of month. • This appears as a payment term in some sales contracts.

eo nomine (ee-oh **nahm**-ə-nee). [Latin] (17c) By or in that name <interest *eo nomine*>.

EPA. *abbr.* (1970) ENVIRONMENTAL PROTECTION AGENCY.

EPC. *abbr.* **1.** EUROPEAN PATENT CONVENTION. **2.** Engineering, procurement, and construction. See *engineering, procurement, and construction contract* under CONTRACT.

EPC contract. See *engineering, procurement, and construction contract* under CONTRACT.

ephemeral recording. (1954) *Copyright.* A temporary copy of a work that may be created and used by a broadcaster under a license or under a statutory exemption that waives the need to obtain the copyright owner's permission. • A broadcaster must still pay royalties, and usu. must destroy the ephemeral recording within a statutorily defined time after creation or use.

epideictic oratory. See ORATORY.

epidemiological evidence. See EVIDENCE.

e pili ana (ay **pee**-lee **ah**-nah). [Hawaiian] Adjoining. • This term usu. refers to land that adjoins a stream.

epimenia (ep-ə-**mee**-nee-ə), *n. pl.* [Latin] Expenses; gifts.

epiqueya (ep-ee-**kay**-ah), *n.* [Spanish] *Spanish law.* An equitable principle calling for the benign and prudent interpretation of the law according to the circumstances of the time, place, and person.

episcopacy (i-**pis**-kə-pə-see), *n.* (17c) *Eccles. law.* **1.** The office of a bishop. **2.** A form of church government by bishops. **3.** An office requiring oversight.

episcopalia (i-pis-kə-**pay**-lee-ə), *n. pl.* (19c) *Eccles. law.* Synodals, pentecostals, and other customary payments from the clergy to their diocesan bishop, collected by rural deans and forwarded to the bishop.

episcopate (i-**pis**-kə-pit), *n.* (17c) *Eccles. law.* **1.** A bishopric. **2.** The dignity or office of a bishop.

episcoporum ecdicus (i-pis-kə-**por**-əm **ek**-di-kəs). [Latin] *Eccles. law.* A bishop's proctor; a church lawyer.

episcopus (i-**pis**-kə-pəs), *n.* [Latin fr. Greek] **1.** *Roman law.* An overseer; an inspector, such as the municipal officer responsible for oversight of the bread and other provisions that served as the citizens' daily food. **2.** A bishop.

episcopus puerorum (i-**pis**-kə-pəs pyoo-ər-**or**-əm). [Latin "bishop of the boys"] (17c) *Hist. Eccles. law.* A layperson who would, on certain feasts, braid his hair, dress like a bishop, and act ludicrous. • This English custom outlasted several laws passed to abolish it.

episodic criminal. See CRIMINAL.

epistle (ee-**pis**-əl), *n.* (13c) *Roman & civil law.* A rescript replying to a magistrate or official body. See RESCRIPT (3).

epistola (i-**pis**-tə-lə), *n.* [Latin "letter"] *Hist.* A charter; a written instrument to convey lands or to assure contracts. See ASSURANCE. — Also spelled *epistula.*

epistulae (i-**pis**-tyoo-lee), *n. pl.* [Latin "letters"] *Roman law.* **1.** Rescripts; esp., opinions given by the emperors in cases submitted to them for decision. **2.** Opinions of *juris consulti*, such as Neratius, on questions of law in the form of letters to those consulting them. — Also spelled *epistolae.*

EPL insurance. See *employment-practices liability insurance* under INSURANCE.

e pluribus unum (ee **ploor**-ə-bəs [y]**oo**-nəm). [Latin] (18c) One out of many. • This is the motto on the official seal of the United States and on several U.S. coins.

EPO. *abbr.* **1.** See *emergency protective order* under PROTECTIVE ORDER. **2.** EUROPEAN PATENT OFFICE. **3.** EXCLUSIVE-PROVIDER ORGANIZATION.

epoch (**ep**-ək), *n.* (17c) **1.** A period of time marked by distinctive features or noteworthy events. **2.** A time when a new computation is begun; a time from which memorable dates are counted. — **epochal** (**ep**-ə-kəl), *adj.*

EPR. *abbr.* EMERGENCY PREPAREDNESS AND RESPONSE DIRECTORATE.

EPS. *abbr.* EARNINGS PER SHARE.

e-quaintance. [fr. *e-* "electronic" + *acquaintance*, the result being an odd morphological blend] (2000) *Slang.* A person known to someone else only through social media, cyberchatting, or the like.

Equal Access Act of 1984. A federal statute that prohibits school districts receiving federal funds and allowing extracurricular activities to be held in their facilities from denying secondary-school students the right to meet for religious and other purposes in public-school facilities. 20 USCA § 4071. • The constitutionality of the Act was upheld in *Board of Education of Westside Community Schools v. Mergens*, 496 U.S. 226, 110 S.Ct. 2356 (1990). — Abbr. EAA.

equal-access rule. (1989) *Criminal law.* The doctrine that contraband found on a defendant's premises will not support a conviction if other persons have had the same access to the premises as the defendant. • To invoke this defense successfully, the defendant must show that other persons did in fact have equal access to the premises; speculative evidence that trespassers might have come onto the premises will not bar a conviction.

Equal Access to Justice Act. A 1980 federal statute that allows a prevailing party in certain actions against the government to recover attorney's fees and expert-witness fees. Pub. L. No. 96-481, title II, 94 Stat. 2325 (codified as amended in scattered sections of 5, 15, and 28 USCA). — Abbr. EAJA.

equal and uniform taxation. See TAXATION (1).

Equal Credit Opportunity Act. A federal statute that prohibits creditors from discriminating against credit applicants on the basis of race, color, religion, national origin, age, sex, or marital status with respect to any aspect of a credit transaction. 15 USCA §§ 1691(a)–(f). — Abbr. ECOA.

equal degree. See DEGREE.

equal-dignities rule. (1949) *Agency.* The doctrine that an agent can perform all acts requiring a writing signed by the principal only if the agent's authority is set forth in a writing. • This rule is an adjunct to the statute of frauds and applies when one or more of the signatories to a contract acted through an agent. — Also termed *equal-dignity rule.*

Equal Employment Opportunity Commission. An independent federal commission that investigates claims of employment discrimination based on race, color, religion, sex, national origin, or age and enforces antidiscrimination statutes through lawsuits. • It was created by Title VII of the Civil Rights Act of 1964. The EEOC encourages mediation and other nonlitigious means of resolving employment disputes. A claimant must file a charge of discrimination with the EEOC before pursuing a claim under Title VII of the Civil Rights Act and certain other employment-related statutes. — Abbr. EEOC.

equal-footing doctrine. (1949) The principle that a state admitted to the Union after 1789 enters with the same rights, sovereignty, and jurisdiction within its borders as did the original 13 states.

equality. (15c) The quality, state, or condition of being equal; esp., likeness in power or political status. See EQUAL PROTECTION.

> "We need not repeat the burning irony of Anatole France: 'The law in its majesty draws no distinction but forbids rich and poor alike from begging in the streets or from sleeping in the public parks.' Equality is meaningless under unequal conditions." Morris R. Cohen, *Reason and Law* 101 (1961).

▸ **political equality.** (17c) The sharing of governmental decisions in such a way that, in the setting of governmental policies, the preference of each citizen is assigned an equal value.

equality before the law. (18c) The status or condition of being treated fairly according to regularly established norms of justice; esp., in British constitutional law, the notion that all persons are subject to the ordinary law of the land administered by the ordinary law courts, that officials and others are not exempt from the general duty of obedience to the law, that discretionary governmental powers must not be abused, and that the task of superintending the operation of law rests with an impartial, independent judiciary.

> "A number of distinct meanings are normally given to the provision that there should be equality before the law. One meaning is that equality before the law only connotes the equal subjection of all to a common system of law, whatever its content. . . . A second theory asserts that equality before the law is basically a procedural concept, pertaining to the application and enforcement of laws and the operation of the legal system. . . . A third meaning normally borne by declarations that all are equal before the law, perhaps no more than a variant of the second, is that State and individual before the law should be equal." Polyvios G. Polyviou, *The Equal Protection of the Laws* 1-2 (1980).

equality of states. (18c) *Int'l law.* The doctrine that all fully independent countries are equal under international law. • This doctrine does not, of course, mean that all countries are equal in power or influence, but merely that, as countries, they all have the same legal rights.

equalization, *n.* (18c) **1.** The raising or lowering of assessed values to achieve conformity with values in surrounding areas. **2.** *Tax.* The adjustment of an assessment or tax to create a rate uniform with another. — Also termed *equalization of taxes; fair and proper legal assessment.*

equalization board. (1875) A local governmental agency responsible for adjusting the tax rates in different districts to ensure an equitable distribution of the tax burden. — Also termed *board of equalization.*

equalization of taxes. See EQUALIZATION (2).

equalize, *vb.* (16c) To make equal; to cause to correspond or be the same in size, value, amount, or degree.

equal justice under the law. The principle that all persons should be treated the same by the judicial system. — Also termed *equal justice before the law.*

equal-knowledge rule. (1954) *Georgia law.* The principle that a complainant who was at least as aware as the defendant of the danger has no grounds for recovery because the consequences could have been readily avoided. Cf. SUPERIOR-KNOWLEDGE RULE.

equally divided. (16c) **1.** (Of property) apportioned per capita — not per stirpes — among heirs on the testator's death. • A provision in a will calling for property to be divided "share and share alike" has the same effect. **2.** (Of a court, legislature, or other group) having the same number of votes on each side of an issue or dispute.

equal-management rule. (1983) The doctrine that each spouse alone may manage community property unless the law provides otherwise. Cf. HEAD-AND-MASTER RULE.

equal-opportunity employer. See EMPLOYER.

equal-or-superior-knowledge rule. See SUPERIOR-KNOWLEDGE RULE.

equal pay. See PAY.

Equal Pay Act. A federal law mandating that all who perform substantially the same work must be paid equally without regard to gender. 29 USCA § 206.

equal protection. (1866) The 14th Amendment guarantee that the government must treat a person or class of persons the same as it treats other persons or classes in like circumstances. • In today's constitutional jurisprudence, equal protection means that legislation that discriminates must have a rational basis for doing so. And if the legislation affects a fundamental right (such as the right to vote) or involves a suspect classification (such as race), it is unconstitutional unless it can withstand strict scrutiny. — Also termed *equal protection of the laws; equal protection under the law.* See RATIONAL-BASIS TEST; STRICT SCRUTINY.

> "Equal protection does not require that all persons be dealt with identically, but it does require that a distinction made have some relevance to the purpose for which the classification is made." *Baxstrom v. Herold*, 383 U.S. 107, 111, 86 S.Ct. 760, 763 (1966).

> "As in all equal protection cases, . . . the crucial question is whether there is an appropriate governmental interest suitably furthered by the differential treatment." *Police Dep't v. Mosley*, 408 U.S. 92, 95, 92 S.Ct. 2286, 2290 (1972).

> "[T]he equal protection principle is exclusively associated with written Constitutions and embodies guarantees of equal treatment normally applied not only to the procedural enforcement of laws but also to the substantive content of their provisions. In other words, the equal protection of the laws is invariably treated as a substantive constitutional principle which demands that laws will only be legitimate if they can be described as just and equal." Polyvios G. Polyviou, *The Equal Protection of the Laws* 4 (1980).

Equal Protection Clause. (1899) *Constitutional law.* The 14th Amendment provision requiring the states to give similarly situated persons or classes similar treatment under the law. Cf. DUE PROCESS CLAUSE.

equal protection of the laws. See EQUAL PROTECTION.

equal protection under the law. See EQUAL PROTECTION.

Equal Rights Amendment. A failed constitutional amendment that, had it been ratified, would have constitutionally prohibited sex-based discrimination. • Congress passed the Amendment in 1972, but it failed in 1982, having been ratified by only 35 of the required 38 states. — Abbr. ERA.

equal-shares clause. (1993) *Insurance.* A clause requiring an insurer to pay its proportionate share of a claimed loss.

Equal Time Act. A federal law requiring that a broadcasting-facility licensee that permits a legally qualified candidate for public office to use the facility for broadcasting must afford an equal opportunity to all other candidates for the office. 47 USCA § 315.

equal-time doctrine. See FAIRNESS DOCTRINE. — Also termed *equal-time rule.*

eques (**ee**-kweez), *n.* [Latin] (16c) *Hist.* A knight.

equilocus (ee-kwə-**loh**-kəs), *n.* [Latin] An equal.

equip, *vb.* (16c) To furnish for service or against a need or exigency; to fit out; to supply with whatever is necessary for efficient action.

equipment, *n.* (17c) The articles or implements used for a specific purpose or activity (esp. a business operation). • Under the UCC, *equipment* includes goods if (1) the goods are used in or bought for a business enterprise (including farming or a profession) or by a debtor that is a nonprofit organization or a governmental subdivision or agency, and (2) the goods are not inventory, farm products, or consumer goods. UCC § 9-102(a)(33).

equipment trust. (1885) A financing device commonly used by railroads whereby a trustee and the railroad jointly buy equipment from a manufacturer, the trustee providing most of the purchase price and then leasing the equipment to the railroad, which pays either a note or a rental fee comprising interest, amortization for serial retirement, and the trustee's fee. See EQUIPMENT TRUST CERTIFICATE; *equipment trust bond* under BOND (3).

equipment trust bond. See EQUIPMENT TRUST CERTIFICATE.

equipment trust certificate. (1893) An official document evidencing a bond secured by tangible property, such as a railroad car or an airplane; specif., a security issued to pay for new equipment. • Title to the equipment is held jointly by a trustee until the note or rental fee has been paid off. — Also termed *trust certificate; equipment trust bond.* See EQUIPMENT TRUST.

equipment violation. (1960) A traffic violation for the malfunctioning or noncompliance of one's motor vehicle with applicable law, as when one's headlight or brake light does not work; one's exhaust pollutes excessively; one's license plate is obscured by grime or mud; or one's inspection sticker is missing or expired.

equitable (**ek**-wi-tə-bəl), *adj.* (16c) **1.** Just; consistent with principles of justice and right. **2.** Existing in equity; available or sustainable by an action in equity, or under the rules and principles of equity.

equitable abstention. See ABSTENTION.

equitable accounting. (1849) **1.** ACCOUNTING FOR PROFITS. **2.** ACCOUNTING (2).

equitable action. See *action in equity* under ACTION (4).

equitable-adjustment theory. (1979) The doctrine that in settling a federal contract dispute, the contracting officer should make a fair adjustment within a reasonable time before the contractor has to settle with its subcontractors, suppliers, and other creditors.

equitable adoption. See *adoption by estoppel* under ADOPTION (1).

equitable asset. See ASSET.

equitable assignment. See ASSIGNMENT (2).

equitable-benefit doctrine. (1974) *Bankruptcy.* The principle that allows a bankruptcy court to grant preferred status to claims for service rendered by persons other than bankruptcy officers, to the extent that the service benefited the estate, when the person filing the claim acted primarily for the benefit of the estate as a whole.

equitable charge. A security interest granted by a debtor to give the creditor the right to sue for recovery of the property if the debtor defaults. • The creditor does not have an ownership interest in or possession of the property.

▸ **fixed equitable charge.** An equitable charge that grants the creditor the right to recover against a specific asset.

equitable common injunction. See *common injunction* under INJUNCTION.

equitable construction. See *liberal interpretation* under INTERPRETATION (1).

equitable conversion. See CONVERSION (1).

equitable damages. See *equitable remedy* under REMEDY.

equitable defense. See DEFENSE (1).

equitable disseisin. See DISSEISIN.

equitable distribution. (1893) *Family law.* The division of marital property by a court in a divorce proceeding, under statutory guidelines that provide for a fair, but not necessarily equal, allocation of the property between the spouses. • With equitable distribution, when a marriage ends in divorce, property acquired during the marriage is divided equitably between the spouses regardless of who holds title to the property. The courts consider many factors in awarding property, including a spouse's monetary contributions, nonmonetary assistance to a spouse's career or earning potential, the efforts of each spouse during the marriage, and the length of the marriage. The court may take into account the relative earning capacity of the spouses and the fault of either spouse. Equitable distribution is applied in 47 states (i.e., all the states except California, Louisiana, and New Mexico, which are "equal division" community-property states). — Also termed *equitable division*; *assignment of property.* Cf. TITLE DIVISION; COMMUNITY PROPERTY.

equitable division. See EQUITABLE DISTRIBUTION.

equitable doctrine of approximation. See DOCTRINE OF APPROXIMATION.

equitable dower. See *equitable jointure* under JOINTURE.

equitable duty. See DUTY (1).

equitable easement. See EASEMENT.

equitable ejectment. See EJECTMENT.

equitable election. See ELECTION (2).

equitable estate. See ESTATE (1).

equitable estoppel. See ESTOPPEL.

equitable foreclosure. See FORECLOSURE.

equitable fraud. See *constructive fraud* (1) under FRAUD.

equitable-fund doctrine. See COMMON-FUND DOCTRINE.

equitable indemnity. See INDEMNITY.

equitable injunction. See INJUNCTION.

equitable interest. See INTEREST (2).

equitable jettison. See JETTISON.

equitable jointure. See JOINTURE.

equitable jurisdiction. See *equity jurisdiction* under JURISDICTION.

equitable levy. See *equitable lien* under LIEN.

equitable lien. See LIEN.

equitable life estate. See ESTATE (1).

equitable life tenant. See LIFE TENANT.

equitable maxim. See MAXIM.

equitable mortgage. See MORTGAGE.

equitable owner. See *beneficial owner* (1) under OWNER.

equitable ownership. See *beneficial ownership* (1) under OWNERSHIP.

equitable parent. See PARENT (1).

equitable partition. See PARTITION (2).

equitable-parent doctrine. (1987) *Family law.* The principle that a spouse who is not the biological parent of a child born or conceived during the marriage may, in a divorce action, be considered the child's natural father or mother if (1) the other spouse and the child both acknowledge a parent–child relationship, esp. when that other spouse has cooperated in the development of this relationship before the divorce action, (2) the nonbiologically related spouse wants parental rights, and (3) he or she is willing to take on the financial or custodial responsibility of raising a child. • The doctrine sometimes applies to nonspousal partners as well. Very few jurisdictions apply the doctrine. *See* Carolee Kvoriak Lezuch, *Michigan's Doctrine of Equitable Parenthood*, 45 Wayne L. Rev. 1529 (1999). — Also termed *equitable-parenthood doctrine.*

equitable recoupment. (1878) **1.** *Tax.* A doctrine allowing a taxpayer to offset previously overpaid taxes against current taxes due, even though the taxpayer is time-barred from claiming a refund on the previous taxes. **2.** *Tax.* A doctrine allowing the government to offset taxes previously uncollected from a taxpayer against the taxpayer's current claim for a refund, even though the government is time-barred from collecting the previous taxes. • In both senses, this type of recoupment can be asserted only if the statute of limitations has created an inequitable result. See RECOUPMENT (2). **3.** A principle that diminishes a party's right to recover a debt to the extent that the party holds money or property of the debtor to which the party has no right. • This doctrine is ordinarily a defensive remedy going only to mitigation of damages. The doctrine is sometimes applied so that a claim for a tax refund that is barred by limitations may nonetheless be recouped against a tax claim of the government. — Also termed *equitable-recoupment doctrine.* See SETOFF; RECOUPMENT (3).

equitable relief. See *equitable remedy* under REMEDY.

equitable remedy. See REMEDY.

equitable remuneration. See *compulsory license* (1) under LICENSE.

equitable rescission. See RESCISSION.

equitable-restraint doctrine. See *Younger abstention* (1) under ABSTENTION.

equitable reversion. See REVERSION (1).

equitable right. See RIGHT.

equitable right of redemption. See RIGHT OF REDEMPTION.

equitable right to setoff. (1895) The right to cancel cross-demands, usu. used by a bank to take from a customer's deposit accounts the amount equal to the customer's debts that have matured and that are owed to that bank. See SETOFF.

equitable seisin. See SEISIN.

equitable servitude. See *restrictive covenant* (1) under COVENANT (4).

equitable setoff. See SETOFF.

equitable subordination. See SUBORDINATION.

equitable subrogation. See SUBROGATION.

equitable title. See TITLE (2).

equitable tolling. (1963) **1.** The doctrine that the statute of limitations will not bar a claim if the plaintiff, despite diligent efforts, did not discover the injury until after the limitations period had expired, in which case the statute is suspended or tolled until the plaintiff discovers the injury. • Equitable tolling does not require misconduct such as concealment by the defendant. **2.** The doctrine that if a plaintiff files a suit first in one court and then refiles in another, the statute of limitations does not run while the litigation is pending in the first court if various requirements are met. • Among those requirements are (1) timely notice to the defendant; (2) no prejudice to the defendant; and (3) reasonable and good-faith conduct on the part of the plaintiff. **3.** A court's discretionary extension of a legal deadline as a result of extraordinary circumstances that prevented one from complying despite reasonable diligence throughout the period before the deadline passed.

equitable waste. See WASTE (1).

equity, *n.* (14c) **1.** Fairness; impartiality; evenhanded dealing <the company's policies require managers to use equity in dealing with subordinate employees>. **2.** The body of principles constituting what is fair and right; natural law <the concept of "inalienable rights" reflects the influence of equity on the Declaration of Independence>.

> "In its popular sense it [equity] is practically equivalent to natural justice. But it would be a mistake to suppose that equity, as administered by the Courts, embraces a jurisdiction as wide and extensive as that which would result from carrying into operation all the principles of natural justice. There are many matters of natural justice wholly unprovided for, from the difficulty of framing any general rules to meet them, and from the doubtful wisdom of a policy of attempting to give a legal sanction to duties of imperfect obligation, such as charity, gratitude and kindness. A large proportion of natural justice in its widest sense is thus not judicially enforced, but is left to the conscience of each individual." R.E. Megarry, *Snell's Principles of Equity* 1 (23d ed. 1947).

3. The recourse to principles of justice to correct or supplement the law as applied to particular circumstances; specif., the judicial prevention of hardship that would otherwise ensue from the literal interpretation of a legal instrument as applied to an extreme case or from the literal exclusion of a case that seems to fall within what the drafters of the instrument probably intended <the judge decided the case by equity because the statute did not fully address the issue>. — Also termed *natural equity.*

> "Lord Evershed, after referring to the old doctrine of the 'equity' of a statute, whereby the courts had a certain latitude in stretching it to cover cases not expressly dealt with, makes the interesting suggestion that it might be as well to revive this doctrine and confer on the judiciary the function of rendering an Act just and workable and of giving effect to sensible solutions, unless the terms of the Act itself precluded this. Such a change would doubtless entail a fundamental reversal of the present form of legislative drafting. Draftsmen and courts are at present engaged in a battle of wits, the draftsman seeking to anticipate the restrictive interpretations of the courts by inserting the most elaborately detailed provisions to ensure that particular situations are covered, which often has the unfortunate result of excluding from the effect of the statute equally relevant situations which were not actually thought of at the time." Dennis Lloyd, *Introduction to Jurisprudence* 388–89 (rev. ed. 1965).

4. The system of law or body of principles originating in the English Court of Chancery and superseding the common and statute law (together called "law" in the narrower sense) when the two conflict <in appealing to the equity of the court, she was appealing to the "king's conscience">; CHANCERY (2).

> "Equity is that system of justice which was developed in and administered by the High Court of Chancery in England in the exercise of its extraordinary jurisdiction. This definition is rather suggestive than precise; and invites inquiry rather than answers it. This must necessarily be so. Equity, in its technical and scientific legal sense, means neither natural justice nor even all that portion of natural justice which is susceptible of being judicially enforced. It has, when employed in the language of English law, a precise, definite and limited signification, and is used to denote a system of justice which was administered in a particular court — the nature and extent of which system cannot be defined in a single sentence, but can be understood and explained only by studying the history of that court, and the principles upon which it acts. In order to begin to understand what equity is, it is necessary to understand what the English High Court of Chancery was, and how it came to exercise what is known as its extraordinary jurisdiction. Every true definition of equity must, therefore, be, to a greater or lesser extent, a history." George T. Bispham, *The Principles of Equity* 1–2 (Joseph D. McCoy ed., 11th ed. 1931).

> "In its technical sense, equity may . . . be defined as a portion of natural justice which, although of a nature more suitable for judicial enforcement, was for historical reasons not enforced by the Common Law Courts, an omission which was supplied by the Court of Chancery. In short, the whole distinction between equity and law is not so much a matter of substance or principle as of form and history." R.E. Megarry, *Snell's Principles of Equity* 2 (23d ed. 1947).

> "The term 'equity' is an illustration of Mr. Towkington's proposition that some words have a legal meaning very unlike their ordinary one. In ordinary language 'equity' means natural justice; but the beginner must get that idea out of his head when dealing with the system that the lawyers call equity. Originally, indeed, this system was inspired by ideas of natural justice, and that is why it acquired its name; but nowadays equity is no more (and no less) natural justice than the common law, and it is in fact nothing else than a particular branch of the law of England. Equity, therefore, is law. The student should not allow himself to be confused by the lawyer's habit of contrasting 'law' and 'equity,' for in this context 'law' is simply an abbreviation for the common law. Equity *is* law in the sense that it is part of the law of England; it is not law only in the sense that it is not part of the common law." Glanville Williams, *Learning the Law* 25–26 (11th ed. 1982).

5. A right, interest, or remedy recognizable by a court of equity <there was no formal contract formation, so they sued for breach in equity>.

▸ **contravening equity** (kon-trə-**veen**-ing). (1888) A right or interest that is inconsistent with or contrary to a right sought to be enforced.

▸ **countervailing equity** (kown-tər-**vayl**-ing). (1824) A contrary and balancing equity, equally deserving of consideration.

▸ **latent equity** (**lay**-tənt). (18c) An equitable claim or right known only by the parties for and against whom it exists, or that has been concealed from one who is interested in the subject matter. — Also termed *secret equity.*

▸ **perfect equity.** (1821) An equitable title or right that, to be a legal title, lacks only the formal conveyance or other investiture that would make it cognizable at law; esp., the equity of a real-estate purchaser who has paid the full amount due but has not yet received a deed.

▸ **secret equity.** See *latent equity.*

6. The right to decide matters in equity; equity jurisdiction <the court decided that the wrong was egregious enough to ignore the statute of limitations and decide the case in equity>. **7.** The amount by which the value of or an interest in property exceeds secured claims or liens; the difference between the value of the property and all encumbrances on it <thanks to the real-estate boom, the mortgaged house still had high equity>. — Also termed *cushion.*

▸ **negative equity.** (1940) The difference between the value of an asset and the outstanding amount of the loan secured by the asset when the asset's current value is less than the loan's balance.

8. An ownership interest in property, esp. in a business <the founders gave her equity in the business in return for all her help>. See OWNERS' EQUITY; BOOK EQUITY; MARKET EQUITY.

▸ **private equity.** Corporate stock that is not traded on a public exchange. • Investors put capital directly into a private company or buy out a public company and delist the stock in exchange for the equity interest.

9. A share in a publicly traded company <he did not want to cash in his equity>.

equity, bill in. See BILL (2).

equity, court of. See COURT.

equity accounting method. See ACCOUNTING METHOD.

equity capital. See CAPITAL.

equity *contra legem* (**kon**-trə **lee**-jəm). (1969) *Int'l law.* The use of equity in derogation of the law, where, under the circumstances of the case, an exception to the law is needed to achieve an equitable and just result. — Sometimes shortened to *contra legem.* See EX AEQUO ET BONO. Cf. EQUITY INTRA LEGEM.

equity financing. See FINANCING.

equity insolvency. See INSOLVENCY.

equity *intra legem* (**in**-trə **lee**-jəm). (1983) A court's power to interpret and apply the law to achieve the most equitable result. — Sometimes shortened to *intra legem.* — Also written *equity infra legem.* Cf. EQUITY CONTRA LEGEM.

equity jurisdiction. See JURISDICTION.

equity jurisprudence. See JURISPRUDENCE.

equity kicker. See EQUITY PARTICIPATION.

equity loan. See *home equity loan* under LOAN.

equity of exoneration (eg-zon-ə-**ray**-shən). (1827) The right of a person who is secondarily liable on a debt to make the primarily liable party discharge the debt or reimburse any payment that the secondarily liable person has made. • One example is the right of a surety to call on the principal for reimbursement after the surety has paid the debt. Unlike contribution, which exists when the parties are equally liable, the equity of exoneration exists when parties are successively liable. — Also termed *right of exoneration.* See EXONERATION.

equity of partners. (1952) The right of each partner to have the firm's property applied to the firm's debts.

equity of redemption. (18c) *Real estate.* The right of a mortgagor in default to recover property before a foreclosure sale by paying the principal, interest, and other costs that are due. • A defaulting mortgagor with an equity of redemption has the right, until the foreclosure sale, to reimburse the mortgagee and cure the default. In many jurisdictions, the mortgagor also has a statutory right to redeem within six months after the foreclosure sale, and the mortgagor becomes entitled to any surplus from the sale proceeds above the amount of the outstanding mortgage. — Also termed *right of redemption; equitable right of redemption.* See CLOG ON THE EQUITY OF REDEMPTION; REDEMPTION (4); STATUTORY RIGHT OF REDEMPTION.

> "A mortgage is technically a conveyance of title to property as security for a debt. The law courts, with typical technicality, early adopted the rule that if the debt was not paid on the very day it was due, the debtor lost his land. The equity courts, however, with more liberality, and with more of a recognition of the real purpose of the transaction, recognized the fact that the securing of the debt, rather than the act of conveyance of title was the principal thing giving character to the transaction. Accordingly they alleviated the severity of the legal rule by, in effect, giving the land back to the debtor if he would pay the debt, even though it had not been paid on time. This equitable right to redeem, even after default in paying the debt when it was due, was called the 'equity of redemption.'" Charles Herman Kinnane, *A First Book on Anglo-American Law* 309 (2d ed. 1952).

equity of subrogation. (1850) The right of a person who is secondarily liable on a debt, and who pays the debt, to personally enforce any right that the original creditor could have pursued against the debtor, including the right to foreclose on any security held by the creditor and any right that the creditor may have to contribution from others who are liable for the debt. — Also termed *right of subrogation*; (in Scots law) *right of relief.* See SUBROGATION.

equity-of-the-statute rule. (1959) In statutory construction, the principle that a statute should be interpreted according to the legislators' purpose and intent, even if this interpretation goes well beyond the literal meaning of the text; the doctrine that the supposed fair application intended for an enactment is the interpreter's paramount concern, allowing departures from the statute's literal words. • This statute-specific ally of purposivism arose in the Middle Ages, mostly fell into disuse by the Renaissance, was thoroughly rejected for most of the 19th century, and has made spasmodic comebacks in

American law since then. See PURPOSIVISM. Cf. GOLDEN RULE; MISCHIEF RULE; PLAIN-MEANING RULE.

equity participation. (1947) The inclusion of a lender in the equity ownership of a project as a condition of the lender's granting a loan. — Also termed *equity kicker.*

equity pleading. See PLEADING (2).

equity *praeter legem* (**pree**-tər **lee**-jəm) (1969) *Hist.* The use of equity to fill a gap in the law. — Sometimes shortened to *praeter legem.*

equity ratio. (1935) **1.** The percentage relationship between a purchaser's equity value (esp. the amount of a down payment) and the property value. **2.** The measure of a shareholder's equity divided by total equity.

equity security. See SECURITY (4).

equity skimming. (1974) *Criminal law.* The practice of purportedly buying a dwelling that is subject to a federally insured loan and then converting the rents received from tenants to one's own use instead of applying them toward payment of the mortgage. • When the property is foreclosed on, the "buyer" is gone and the original owner is responsible for the delinquent mortgage.

equity stock. See STOCK.

equity term. See TERM (5).

equity to a settlement. (1838) A wife's equitable right, arising when her husband sues in equity for the reduction of her equitable estate to his own possession, to have all or part of that estate settled on herself and her children. — Also termed *wife's equity; wife's settlement.*

equivalence of advantages. See RECIPROCITY (2).

equivalent, *adj.* (15c) **1.** Equal in value, force, amount, effect, or significance. **2.** Corresponding in effect or function; nearly equal; virtually identical.

equivalent, *n. Patents.* An element that (1) existed before another element; (2) can perform the same function as the other element; and (3) is recognizable as a substitute for the other element. • For instance, mechanical devices are equivalents when one skilled in the art can recognize that each device would produce the same result. If the equivalent is known at the time an invention is conceived, the invention's patentability may be questioned. See ANALOG.

> "If a given substitute is an equivalent under certain circumstances or in certain settings, and is not an equivalent under certain other circumstances or in certain other settings, then the substitution is patentable, provided the claim contains express limitations to the circumstances or settings in which the substitution is nonequivalent." Roger Sherman Hoar, *Patent Tactics and Law* 43 (3d ed. 1950).

equivalents doctrine. See DOCTRINE OF EQUIVALENTS.

equivocal (i-**kwiv**-ə-kəl), *adj.* (17c) **1.** Of doubtful character; questionable. **2.** Having more than one meaning or sense; ambiguous.

equivocal plea. See PLEA (3).

equivocality test (i-kwiv-ə-**kal**-ə-tee). See RES IPSA LOQUITUR TEST.

equivocation (i-kwiv-ə-**kay**-shən). The purposeful use of words having a double meaning; esp., the intentional use of language that is subject to different interpretations, with the intent to mislead or deceive. — **equivocate,** *vb.* — **equivocal,** *adj.*

equuleus (i-**kwoo**-lee-əs), *n.* [Latin] *Roman law.* A rack in the shape of a horse, used for torture.

ERA. *abbr.* (1973) EQUAL RIGHTS AMENDMENT.

erase, *vb.* (14c) **1.** To rub or scrape out (something written); to obliterate. **2.** To obliterate (recorded material). **3.** To seal (criminal records) from disclosure. — **erasure,** *n.*

Erastian (i-**ras**-chən *or* i-**ras**-tee-ən). (17c) *Hist.* A follower of Thomas Erastus (1524–1583), who thought that offenses against religion and morality should be punished by the civil power and not by the censures of the church. • As a sect, Erastians had great influence in England, particularly among 17th-century common-law lawyers.

erasure of record. See EXPUNGEMENT OF RECORD.

ERC. *abbr.* EMISSION-REDUCTION CREDIT.

erciscundus (er-sis-**kən**-dəs), *adj.* [Latin] *Civil law.* To be divided. • A suit *judicium familiae erciscundae* was one to partition an inheritance.

erect, *vb.* (15c) **1.** To construct. **2.** To establish. • In England, *erect* is one of the formal words of incorporation in a royal charter, being part of the phrase, "We do incorporate, erect, ordain, name, constitute, and establish." See ERIGIMUS.

erectile dysfunction. See IMPOTENCE.

E reorganization. See REORGANIZATION (2).

erga omnes (ər-gə **om**-neez). [Latin] Toward all.

***erga omnes* obligations.** See OBLIGATIONS ERGA OMNES.

***erga omnes partes* obligations.** See OBLIGATIONS ERGA OMNES.

ergo (**ər**-goh *or* **air**-goh), *adv.* [Latin] (14c) Therefore; thus.

ergolabus (ər-goh-**lay**-bəs), *n.* [Latin] *Civil law.* Someone who contracts to perform work by personally furnishing the materials and labor.

***Erie*-bound,** *adj.* (1961) (Of a federal court) required to apply the *Erie* doctrine.

***Erie* doctrine** (**eer**-ee). (1943) The principle that a federal court exercising diversity jurisdiction over a case that does not involve a federal question must apply the substantive law of the state where the court sits. *Erie R.R. v. Tompkins,* 304 U.S. 64, 58 S.Ct. 817 (1938). Cf. REVERSE ERIE DOCTRINE.

***Erie/Klaxon* doctrine.** See KLAXON DOCTRINE.

erigimus (i-**rij**-ə-məs). [Latin] *Hist.* We erect. • This was one of the words used in a corporation's royal charter. See ERECT (2).

ERISA (ee- *or* ə-**ris**-ə). *abbr.* EMPLOYEE RETIREMENT INCOME SECURITY ACT.

eristic (e-**ris**-tik), *adj.* (17c) Of, relating to, or involving controversy or disputation. — Also termed *eristical.*

ermine (**ər**-min), *n.* (18c) The station of a judge; judgeship. • The term refers to the fur trimmings (made from the coats of white weasels called "ermine") adorning official robes of English judges. — **ermined,** *adj.*

erosion. (1841) The wearing away of something by action of the elements; esp., the gradual eating away of soil by the operation of wind, currents, or tides. Cf. ACCRETION (2); DELICTION; AVULSION (2); ALLUVION.

▸ **littoral erosion.** Erosion of coastlines caused by tides and waves.

▸ **riparian erosion.** Erosion of a stream's or river's banks caused by rushing water.

erotica. Materials such as literature and artworks intended to arouse sexual desire.

err (ər), *vb.* (14c) To make an error; to be incorrect or mistaken <the court erred in denying the motion for summary judgment>.

errant (**er**-ənt), *adj.* (14c) **1.** Fallible; incorrect; straying from what is proper <an errant judicial holding>. **2.** Traveling <a knight errant>.

errata sheet. (1932) An attachment to a deposition transcript containing the deponent's corrections upon reading the transcript and the reasons for those corrections. — Also termed *errata page.*

erratum (i-**ray**-təm *or* i-**rah**-təm), *n.* [Latin "error"] (16c) An error that needs correction. See CORRIGENDUM. Pl. **errata** (i-**ray**-tə *or* i-**rah**-tə).

erroneous (i-**roh**-nee-əs), *adj.* (15c) Incorrect; inconsistent with the law or the facts.

erroneous assessment. See ASSESSMENT (2).

erroneous extradition. See *extraordinary rendition* under RENDITION.

erroneous judgment. See JUDGMENT (2).

erroneous rendition. See RENDITION.

erroneous tax. See TAX.

erronice (i-**roh**-nə-see), *adv.* [Law Latin] Erroneously; through error or mistake.

error, *n.* (13c) **1.** An assertion or belief that does not conform to objective reality; a belief that what is false is true or that what is true is false; MISTAKE.

▸ **billing error.** Under the Fair Credit Billing Act, a mistake appearing on a creditor's statement of an obligor's account (1) reflecting an extension of credit not made (or not in the amount reflected), for which the obligor requests additional clarification, (2) reflecting goods or services not accepted or not delivered in accordance with the applicable agreement, (3) failing to reflect a payment made or a credit issued, (4) involving a computation error or similar accounting error by the creditor, or (5) falling within certain other statutory categories. 15 USCA § 1666(b).

▸ **bona fide error.** A violation that is unintentional and occurs despite procedures reasonably adapted to avoid any such error. • A bona fide error is sometimes a defense to a technical violation of a statute that otherwise imposes strict liability. *See, e.g.,* 15 USCA § 1640(c); 15 USCA § 1692k(c); 47 USCA § 227(c)(5). — Also termed *good-faith error.*

▸ **error *in corpore.*** See ERROR IN CORPORE.

▸ **error *in negotio.*** See ERROR IN NEGOTIO.

▸ **error *in qualitate.*** See ERROR IN QUALITATE.

▸ **error *in quantitate.*** See ERROR IN QUANTITATE.

▸ **error *in substantia.*** See ERROR IN SUBSTANTIA.

▸ ***error juris.*** See ERROR JURIS.

▸ **good-faith error.** See *bona fide error.*

▸ **reissuable error.** See REISSUABLE ERROR.

2. A mistake of law or of fact in a tribunal's judgment, opinion, or order.

▸ **assigned error.** An alleged error that occurred in a lower court and is pointed out in an appellate brief as grounds for reversal <appellants' two assigned errors appeared to the court to be harmless errors>. See ASSIGNMENT OF ERROR.

▸ ***Booker* error.** See BOOKER ERROR.

▸ ***Caldwell* error.** See CALDWELL ERROR.

▸ **clear error.** (18c) A trial judge's decision or action that appears to a reviewing court to have been unquestionably erroneous. • Even though a clear error occurred, it may not warrant reversal. — Also termed *clear and unmistakable error.*

▸ **clerical error.** (18c) An error resulting from a minor mistake or inadvertence and not from judicial reasoning or determination; esp., a drafter's or typist's technical error that can be rectified without serious doubt about the correct reading. • Among the numberless possible examples of clerical errors are omitting an appendix from a document; typing an incorrect number; mistranscribing or omitting an obviously needed word; and failing to log a call. A court can correct a clerical error in the record at any time, even after judgment has been entered. *See* Fed. R. Civ. P. 60(a); Fed. R. Crim. P. 36. — Also termed *scrivener's error; vitium clerici.* See VITIUM SCRIPTORIS.

▸ **cross-error.** (1838) An error brought by the party responding to a writ of error against the party petitioning for the writ.

▸ **cumulative error.** (1890) The prejudicial effect of two or more trial errors that may have been harmless individually. • The cumulative effect of multiple harmless errors may amount to reversible error. — Also termed *doctrine of cumulative error.* See CUMULATIVE-ERROR ANALYSIS.

▸ **curable error.** An error at trial that can be immediately corrected by the court upon objection. • A curable error is not grounds for reversal on appeal, unless an objection preserved the error and the trial court failed to fix the mistake. See *reversible error.*

▸ **error apparent of record.** See *plain error.*

▸ **error *in vacuo.*** See *harmless error.*

▸ **evidentiary error.** A court's error in admitting evidence.

▸ **fatal error.** See *reversible error.*

▸ **fundamental error.** See *plain error.*

▸ **harmful error.** See *reversible error.*

▸ **harmless error.** (1851) A trial-court error that does not affect a party's substantive rights or the case's outcome. • If the error is constitutional, reversal is required unless there is no reasonable possibility that the error might have contributed to the conviction — unless it was harmless beyond a reasonable doubt. If the error is statutory, the error is reversible only if there is a significant possibility that the jury would have acquitted had it not been for the error. *See* Fed. R. Civ. P. 61; Fed. R. Crim. P. 52. — Also termed *technical error; error in vacuo.* Cf. *substantial error.*

▸ **incurable error.** An error at trial that has a prejudicial effect on the outcome and is not remediable by the trial court. • No objection to an incurable error is required for reversal. See *substantial error*. Cf. *reversible error*.

▸ **invited error.** (1893) An error that a party cannot complain of on appeal because the party, through its conduct, encouraged or prompted the trial court to make the erroneous ruling.

▸ **jurisdictional error.** (1858) An error caused by a decision-maker's exceeding the power or authority statutorily conferred upon the tribunal.

▸ **manifest constitutional error.** (1985) An error by the trial court that has an identifiably negative impact on the trial to such a degree that the constitutional rights of a party are compromised. • A manifest constitutional error can be reviewed by a court of appeals even if the appellant did not object at trial.

▸ **manifest error.** (18c) An error that is plain and indisputable, and that amounts to a complete disregard of the controlling law or the credible evidence in the record.

▸ **obvious error.** See OBVIOUS ERROR.

▸ **plain error.** (1801) An error that is so obvious and prejudicial that an appellate court should address it despite the parties' failure to raise a proper objection at trial. • A plain error is often said to be so obvious and substantial that failure to correct it would infringe a party's due-process rights and damage the integrity of the judicial process. *See* Fed. R. Evid. 103(d). — Also termed *fundamental error*; *error apparent of record*.

▸ **prejudicial error.** See *reversible error*.

▸ **procedural error.** A mistake in complying with the rules or steps in the legal process.

▸ **reissuable error.** See REISSUABLE ERROR.

▸ **reversible error.** (1855) An error that affects a party's substantive rights or the case's outcome, and thus is grounds for reversal if the party properly objected at trial. — Also termed *harmful error*; *prejudicial error*; *fatal error*.

▸ **scrivener's error.** See *clerical error*.

▸ **structural error.** (1980) A defect in a trial mechanism or framework that, by deprivation of basic constitutional protections, taints the trial process, making it unreliable and rendering any punishment fundamentally unfair. • This error is per se prejudicial and requires automatic reversal. An example of structural error is the denial of right to counsel. Cf. *trial error*.

▸ **substantial error.** (1829) An error that affects a party's substantive rights or the outcome of the case. • A substantial error may require reversal on appeal. — Also termed ; *substantive error*. Cf. *harmless error*.

▸ **substantive error.** See *substantial error*.

▸ **technical error.** See *harmless error*.

▸ **trial error.** A mistake in or deviation from proper trial procedure during the presentation of a case to a jury, usu. without substantial or injurious effect or influence on the jury's decision-making process. • Such an error does not require automatic reversal but is instead subject to harmless-error analysis, in which the error is considered in the context of all the evidence presented to determine whether its admission was harmless. Examples of trial error include the incorrect receipt, admission, or rejection of evidence; the improper use of a defendant's post-*Miranda* silence; giving jury instructions with an erroneous conclusive presumption; and a prosecutor's improperly commenting on a defendant's silence at trial. *See Lockhart v. Nelson*, 488 U.S. 33, 40, 109 S.Ct. 285, 290 (1988). Cf. *structural error*.

3. An appeal <a proceeding in error>.

error, assignment of. See ASSIGNMENT OF ERROR.

error, writ of. See WRIT OF ERROR.

error apparent of record. See *plain error* under ERROR (2).

error calculi (**er**-or **kal**-kyuu-lɪ). [Latin] (1832) *Roman & civil law.* An error in calculation.

> "If it occurs in a judgment and is fully evident, no appeal is necessary. The judge himself may correct it. In public administration, *error calculi* is without any legal effect. A reexamination and correction (*retractatio*) is admissible even after ten or twenty years." Adolf Berger, *Encyclopedic Dictionary of Roman Law* 456 (1953).

error *de persona* (dee pər-**soh**-nə). [Latin "error of the person"] (17c) A mistake about a person's identity. Cf. ERROR NOMINIS.

errore acerrimo non affectato insimulatove (e-**ror**-ee ə-**ser**-i-moh non af-ek-**tay**-toh in-sim-yuu-lə-**toh**-vee). [Latin] *Hist.* Through error of the most pointed or positive character, not merely pretended or feigned.

errore lapsus (e-**ror**-ee **lap**-səs). [Latin] (17c) *Hist.* Mistaken through inadvertence. • This type of mistake was usu. not sufficient to invalidate a contract.

error *in corpore* (**kor**-pə-ree). (18c) A mistake involving the identity of a particular object, as when a party buys a horse believing it to be the one that the party had already examined and ridden, when in fact it is a different horse

error in fact. See *mistake of fact* (1) under MISTAKE.

error in law. See *mistake of law* (1) under MISTAKE.

error *in negotio* (ni-**goh**-shee-oh). (1944) A mistake about the type of contract that the parties actually wanted to enter.

error *in qualitate* (kwah-lə-**tay**-tee). (1974) A mistake affecting the quality of the contractual object.

error *in quantitate* (kwahn-tə-**tay**-tee). (2004) A mistake affecting the amount of the contractual object.

error in substantia, *n.* (səb-**stan**-shee-ə). A substantial error, as in understanding the nature of an article purchased.

error *in vacuo* (in **vak**-yoo-oh). [Latin "error in a void"] See *harmless error* under ERROR (2).

error *juris* (**er**-or **joor**-is). [Latin] *Hist.* Error in law.

error *nominis* (**nahm**-ə-nis). [Latin "error of name"] (1844) A mistake of detail in a person's name, such as spelling, or a mistaken name as a whole. Cf. ERROR DE PERSONA; IDEM SONANS.

error of fact. See *mistake of fact* (1) under MISTAKE.

error-of-judgment rule. (1921) The doctrine that a professional is not liable to a client for advice or an opinion given in good faith and with an honest belief that the advice was in the client's best interests, but that was based on a mistake either in judgment or in analyzing an unsettled area of the professional's business. • For example, an attorney who makes an error in trial tactics involving an unsettled area of the law may, under certain circumstances, defeat a malpractice claim arising from the tactical error. — Also termed *judgmental immunity.*

error of law. See *mistake of law* (1) under MISTAKE.

errors, assignment of. See ASSIGNMENT OF ERRORS.

errors-and-omissions insurance. See INSURANCE.

ERS. *abbr.* ECONOMIC RESEARCH SERVICE.

ESA. *abbr.* **1.** ECONOMICS AND STATISTICS ADMINISTRATION. **2.** EMPLOYMENT STANDARDS ADMINISTRATION.

ESBT. *abbr.* See *electing small-business trust* under TRUST (3).

escalation clause. See ESCALATOR CLAUSE.

escalator clause. (1930) **1.** A contractual provision that allows pricing to be adjusted by increasing or decreasing the contract price according to changing market conditions, such as higher or lower taxes or operating costs. Cf. DE-ESCALATION CLAUSE. **2.** A provision in a divorce decree or divorce agreement providing for the automatic increase of alimony payments upon the occurrence of any of various triggering events, such as cost-of-living increases or an increase in the obligor's salary. • Escalation clauses for child support are often unenforceable. **3.** *Oil & gas.* A provision in a long-term gas contract allowing the base price of the gas to be adjusted either up or down as the market changes. — Also termed *escalation clause; fluctuating clause.*

escambium. See CAMBIUM (2).

escape, *n.* (14c) **1.** The act or an instance of breaking free from confinement, restraint, or an obligation. **2.** An unlawful departure from legal custody without the use of force. — Also termed *actual escape; prisoner escape.* Cf. PRISON BREACH.

> "In the technical sense an 'escape' is an unauthorized departure from legal custody; in a loose sense the word is used to indicate either such an unlawful departure or an avoidance of capture. And while the word is regularly used by the layman in the broader sense, it usually is limited to the narrower meaning when used in the law, — although this is not always so." Rollin M. Perkins & Ronald N. Boyce, *Criminal Law* 559 (3d ed. 1982).

▸ **constructive escape.** (1822) A prisoner's obtaining more liberty than the law allows, while not fully regaining freedom.

▸ **escape from custody.** A detained person's violent or nonviolent escape from law-enforcement officers or a place of temporary detention. Cf. PRISON BREACH.

3. At common law, a criminal offense committed by a peace officer who allows a prisoner to depart unlawfully from legal custody. — Also termed *voluntary escape; prisoner escape.* — **escape,** *vb.*

▸ **negligent escape.** (16c) The offense committed by a peace officer who negligently allows a prisoner to depart from legal custody.

> "Escapes are either voluntary, or negligent. Voluntary are such as are by the express consent of the keeper, after which he never can retake his prisoner again, (though the plaintiff may retake him at any time) but the sheriff must answer for the debt. Negligent escapes are where the prisoner escapes without his keeper's knowledge or consent; and then upon fresh pursuit the defendant may be retaken, and the sheriff shall be excused, if he has him again before any action brought against himself for the escape." 3 William Blackstone, *Commentaries on the Laws of England* 415–16 (1768).

escape clause. (1945) A contractual provision that allows a party to avoid performance under specified conditions; specif., an insurance-policy provision — usu. contained in the "other insurance" section of the policy — requiring the insurer to provide coverage only if no other coverage is available. Cf. EXCESS CLAUSE; PRO RATA CLAUSE.

escapee. (19c) Someone who has escaped confinement; esp., a prisoner or other inmate who has escaped from lawful custody.

> "The word 'escapee' is employed at times by those who are not careful in the use of language. They probably think this word is comparable to 'arrestee' or 'employee.' But the arrestee did not do the arresting and the employee did not do the employing. The employee does the work but that makes him a worker, not a workee." Rollin M. Perkins & Ronald N. Boyce, *Criminal Law* 560 (3d ed. 1982).

▸ **escapee at large.** An escapee who has not been recaptured.

escape period. (1946) *Labor law.* A time sometimes stipulated in a union contract during which workers may withdraw from the union near the end of one term covered by the contract and before the start of the next.

escape warrant. See WARRANT (1).

escapium (e-**skay**-pee-əm), *n.* [Law Latin] That which comes by chance or accident. • In medieval Latin, the term often referred to the escape of a prisoner or the straying of cattle.

escheat (es-**cheet**), *n.* (14c) **1.** *Hist.* The reversion of land ownership back to the lord when the immediate tenant dies without heirs. See WRIT OF ESCHEAT. **2.** Reversion of property (esp. real property) to the state upon the death of an owner who has neither a will nor any legal heirs. **3.** Property that has so reverted. See *heirless estate* under ESTATE (3). — **escheat,** *vb.* — **escheatable,** *adj.*

> "Escheat, from the French *eschoir,* to fall incidentally, was the casual descent of lands and tenements to the lord *propter defectum sanguinis* [for lack of inheritable blood], that is, when the tenant died without heirs; which was a part of the feudal system in every country." George Crabb, *A History of English Law* 79 (1st Am. ed. 1831).

> "All escheats, under the English law, are declared to be strictly feudal, and to import the extinction of tenure. . . . The rule [was] that if lands were held in trust and the *cestui que trust* without heirs, the lands did not escheat to the crown, but the trustee, being *in esse* and in the legal seisin of the land, took the land discharged of the trust, and bound as owner for the feudal services. But as the feudal tenures do not exist in this country, there are no private persons who succeed to the inheritance by escheat; and the state steps in the place of the feudal lord, by virtue of its sovereignty, as the original and ultimate proprietor of all the lands within its jurisdiction." 4 James Kent, *Commentaries on American Law* *423–24 (George Comstock ed., 11th ed. 1866).

escheat grant. See GRANT (4).

escheator (es-**cheet**-ər). (14c) *Hist.* A royal officer appointed to assess the value of property escheating to the Crown. • Corrupt officers led many to associate the escheator with fraudulent conduct, giving rise to the word *cheat* as used in the modern sense. — Also termed *cheater.*

escheat patent. See *escheat grant* under GRANT (4).

escheccum (es-**chek**-əm), *n.* [Latin] *Hist.* A jury or inquisition.

***Escobedo* rule** (es-kə-**bee**-doh). (1964) *Criminal procedure.* The principle that a statement by an unindicted, targeted suspect in police custody is inadmissible at trial unless the police warn the suspect of the right to remain silent and provide an opportunity for the suspect to consult with retained or appointed counsel. • This rule was a precursor to the *Miranda* rule. *Escobedo v. Illinois*, 378 U.S. 478, 84 S.Ct. 1758 (1964). See MIRANDA RULE.

escot (e-**skot**), *n.* (17c) *Hist. English law.* A tax paid in boroughs and corporations to support the community.

escribano (es-kree-**bah**-noh), *n.* [Spanish] *Spanish law.* A notary; specif., an officer who has authority to set down in writing, and attest to, transactions and contracts between private persons, as well as judicial acts and proceedings.

escritura (es-kree-**toor**-ah), *n.* [Spanish] *Spanish law.* A written instrument, such as a contract; esp., a deed that either is prepared by an *escribano* or notary of a corporation or council (*concejo*) or is sealed with a monarchical or governmental seal.

escritura publica (es-kree-**toor**-ah **pəb**-li-kə). See PUBLIC WRITING (2).

escroquerie (es-**kroh**-kə-ree), *n.* [French] Fraud; swindling; cheating.

escrow (**es**-kroh), *n.* (16c) **1.** A legal document or property delivered by a promisor to a third party to be held by the third party for a given amount of time or until the occurrence of a condition, at which time the third party is to hand over the document or property to the promisee <the agent received the escrow two weeks before the closing date>. **2.** An account held in trust or as security <the earnest money is in escrow>. — Also termed *escrow account*; *impound account*; *reserve account.* See *escrow account* under ACCOUNT. **3.** The holder of such a document, property, or deposit <the attorney performed the function of escrow>. • Although an escrow holder is often termed an "escrow agent," the holder is not an agent as defined by the common law. — Also termed *escrow agent.* See ESCROW AGENT. **4.** The general arrangement under which a legal document or property is delivered to a third person until the occurrence of a condition <creating an escrow>. — **escrow,** *vb.*

> "Like 'scroll' and 'scrawl,' the word 'escrow' is derived from the Norman-French word for a writing or a written instrument. It has come in practice to refer to a security device: one or both parties to a transaction deposit property or an instrument with a third party until some condition has occurred. The property or instrument may be referred to as 'the escrow'; the delivery is said to be 'in escrow.'" Restatement (Second) of Contracts § 103 cmt. a (1979).

escrow account. See *impound account* under ACCOUNT.

escrow agent. (1911) The third-party depositary of an escrow; ESCROW (3). • An escrow holder is not a common-law agent because the holder does not act subject to the control of the parties to the escrow agreement. — Also termed *escrow holder*; *escrowee*; *escrow officer.*

escrow agreement. (1882) The instructions given to the third-party depositary of an escrow.

escrow contract. See CONTRACT.

escrow deposit. See *escrow account* under ACCOUNT.

escrowee. See ESCROW AGENT.

escrow holder. See ESCROW AGENT.

escrowl (es-**krohl**), *n. Hist.* (17c) **1.** An escrow. **2.** A scroll.

escrow officer. See ESCROW AGENT.

escuage (**es**-kyoo-ij). [French, fr. Latin *escuagium*] See SCUTAGE.

ESI. *abbr.* Electronically stored information.

E-Sign Act. The short name for the Electronic Signatures in Global and National Commerce Act, a 2000 federal statute that establishes the legal equivalency of electronic contracts, electronic signatures, and other electronic records with their paper counterparts. • The E-Sign Act applies to all types of transactions, whether in interstate or foreign commerce, unless a specific exception applies. Among the few exceptions are documents related to family law and probate law, most documents required by the Uniform Commercial Code, court documents, and a list of notices that directly impact the lives of consumers (e.g., a notice of termination of utility services or a notice of eviction).

esketores (es-kə-**tor**-eez), *n. pl. Hist.* Robbers; destroyers of others' lands or fortunes.

eskipper (ə-**skip**-ər), *vb.* To ship. — Also termed *eskippare* (es-kə-**pair**-ee).

eskippeson (ə-**skip**-[ə]-sən), *n.* Shippage; passage by sea. — Also termed *skippeson.*

eslisor (es-lɪ-zər). See ELISOR.

esne (**ez**-nee), *n.* (bef. 12c) *Hist.* A hireling of servile condition; a hired laborer or a slave.

esnecy (**es**-ni-see), *n.* (17c) *Hist.* Seniority; the condition, right, or privilege of the eldest-born. • The term esp. applied to the privilege of the eldest among coparceners to make a first choice of shares upon a voluntary partition. — Also termed *aesnecia.*

ESOP (**ee**-sop). *abbr.* See *employee-stock-ownership plan* under EMPLOYEE BENEFIT PLAN.

espera (**es**-pə-rə), *n.* A period fixed by law or by a court within which certain acts are to be performed (such as payment of a debt).

espionage (**es**-pee-ə-nahzh). (18c) The activity of using spies to collect information about what another government or company is doing or plans to do.

▸ **counterespionage.** (1899) The process or practice of trying to stop spying activities against one's own country, organization, etc., esp. by means of espionage.

▸ **industrial espionage.** (1962) *Intellectual property.* The surreptitious taking of secret information from one company in order to help another company; specif., one company's spying on another to steal trade secrets or other proprietary information.

Espionage Act. A federal statute that criminalizes and punishes espionage, spying, and related crimes. 18 USCA §§ 793 et seq. • Two Espionage Acts were passed. The 1917 act criminalized false statements intended to interfere with the war effort; to willfully cause or attempt to cause dissension in the armed forces; or to willfully obstruct national recruiting and enlistment activities. This act remains enforceable "when the United States is at war." The 1918 act criminalized speech intended to obstruct war-bond sales; to generate scorn or contempt for democratic government, the flag, or the uniform of the Army or Navy; to urge reduced production of war materials with the intent to hinder the war effort; or to express support for a national enemy or opposition to the United States' cause. The act's constitutionality was upheld by the U.S. Supreme Court before it was repealed in 1921.

esplees (es-**pleez**), *n. pl.* (17c) *Archaic.* **1.** Products yielded from land. **2.** Rents or other payments derived from land. **3.** Land itself. — Also termed *explees.*

espousals (ə-**spow**-zəlz), *n.* (14c) Mutual promises between a man and a woman to marry one another. Cf. BETROTHAL (1).

> "Espousals were of two kinds: sponsalia per verba de futuro, which take place if man and woman promise each other that they will hereafter become husband and wife; sponsalia per verba de praesenti, which take place if they declare that they take each other as husband and wife now, at this very moment." 2 Frederick Pollock & Frederic W. Maitland, *History of English Law Before the Time of Edward I* 368 (2d ed. 1899).

espouse, *vb.* (15c) **1.** To marry. **2.** To dedicate oneself to and advocate for (a cause).

esquire (**es**-kwɪr *or* e-**skwɪr**). (15c) **1.** *Hist.* A candidate for knighthood who assisted knights in martial endeavors. **2.** *Hist.* A member of the gentry whose rank was inferior to that of a knight. **3.** *Archaic.* A landed gentleman; a member of the landed gentry. **4.** (*usu. cap. as an honorific*) A title of courtesy commonly appended after the name of a lawyer. • It is traditionally considered a solecism to put it after one's own name — as opposed to someone else's name. — Abbr. Esq.

> "Heralds and experts on honour for a long time regarded serjeants either as inferior to esquires or at most as being equals by reason of office. James Whitelocke, a barrister with historical interests and a future serjeant, said in 1601 that becoming a serjeant carried with it the status of esquire, so that the proper description was 'A.B. esquire, serjeant at law.' Chief Justice Dyer, however, argued in 1580 that the name of esquire was 'drowned' on creation as a serjeant, the latter being a higher degree; and the same point of view was urged in 1611 by the serjeants in a precedence dispute. It was probably not until the eighteenth century that the heralds accepted the priority of serjeants before esquires. By that time the rank of esquire had begun its decline, and according to the courts it belonged to all barristers at law by virtue of their profession." J.H. Baker, *The Order of Serjeants at Law* 52 (1984).

essence, of the. See OF THE ESSENCE.

essence test. (1969) *Labor law.* A test under which an arbitrator's interpretation of a collective-bargaining agreement must be upheld if it derives in any rational way from the agreement, viewed in light of the agreement's language, its context, and any other evidence of the parties' intention.

essendi quietum de tolonio (e-**sen**-dɪ kwɪ-**ee**-təm dee tə-**loh**-nee-oh). [Latin "a writ to be free of a toll"] (16c) *Hist.* A writ available to a citizen or a burgess of any city or town who, by charter or prescription, is exempt from a particular toll.

essential, *adj.* (14c) **1.** Of, relating to, or involving the essence or intrinsic nature of something. **2.** Of the utmost importance; basic and necessary. **3.** Having real existence; actual.

essential contract theory. (2000) The view that contracts are primarily relations rather than discrete transactions, so that even a simple transaction can be understood as involving a wider social and economic context. • This view was originally developed by Ian R. Macneil in response to Grant Gilmore's *The Death of Contract* (1974). *See* Ian R. Macneil, *The Many Futures of Contract,* 47 Cal. L. Rev. 691 (1974). — Also (and earlier) termed *relational contract theory.*

essential-elements test. *Criminal law.* A means of ascertaining whether an out-of-state conviction counts as comparable to an in-state conviction by assessing whether the basic components of the crime are fairly identical. • The essential-elements test is used for various purposes, including the determination whether an out-of-state felony conviction can serve as a predicate for sentencing an offender as a persistent felon.

essential-facilities doctrine. *Antitrust.* The principle that a firm with substantial power in a market cannot use an essential facility so as to create a bottleneck and prevent competitors from entering the market.

essential facility. *Antitrust.* A tangible or intangible operation, process, manufacturing plant, or other thing that is under the control of a monopolist, but is fundamentally necessary for effective competition.

essential finding. See FINDING OF FACT.

essentialia (e-sen-shee-**ay**-lee-ə). [Law Latin "essentials"] (1890) *Scots law.* Terms or qualities essential to the existence of a particular right or contract. Cf. ACCIDENTALIA.

> "Essentialia. This term, applied to a contract, or right, or other subject of law, signifies those things which are essential to the very being of the contract or right, as such, and any alteration in which would make the contract or right resolve into one of another kind." William Bell, *Bell's Dictionary and Digest of the Law of Scotland* 406 (George Watson ed., 7th ed. 1890).

essentialia feudi (e-sen-shee-**ay**-lee-ə **fyoo**-dɪ). [Law Latin] (1838) *Scots law.* The essential terms of a feudal right. Cf. ACCIDENTALIA FEUDI.

essential mistake. See MISTAKE.

essential reliance. See RELIANCE.

essential term. See *fundamental term* under TERM (2).

essoin (e-**soyn**), *n.* [fr. Old French *essoi(g)ne* "excuse"] (14c) *Hist.* **1.** An excuse for not appearing in court on an appointed day in obedience to a summons. **2.** The offering or presentation of such an excuse. — Also spelled *essoign.*

> "The first return-day of every term, properly speaking, is the first day of that term; and on that day the court used formerly to sit . . . to hear the *essoigns,* or excuses, of such as did not appear according to the summons of the writ. This day therefore came to be called the *essoign*-day of the term." 1 George Crompton, *Practice Common-Placed: Rules and Cases of Practice in the Courts of King's Bench and Common Pleas* liv (3d ed. 1787).

essoin, *vb.* [fr. Old French *essoi(g)nier* "to excuse"] (14c) *Hist.* To present an excuse for not appearing in court as ordered. — Also spelled *essoign.*

> "Upon the summons, the defendant either appeared, or *essoigned,* or made default. If he did the former, the plaintiff declared against him, and the cause was proceeded in by the court; and if he did the latter, the plaintiff had liberty to take out further process against him. But if he *essoigned,* that is, sent an excuse to the court why he could not attend, he was to send it by the *return day of the writ* which if he did, a further process did not issue against him." 1 George Crompton, *Practice Common-Placed: Rules and Cases of Practice in the Courts of King's Bench and Common Pleas* liv (3d ed. 1787).

essoin day. (17c) *Hist. English law.* The first general return day of the term, when the courts sat to receive essoins. • By the Law Terms Act (1830), essoin days were eliminated as a part of the term. St. 11 Geo. 4; 1 Will. 4, ch. 70, § 6.

essoin *de malo villae* (dee **mal**-oh **vil**-ee). (16c) *Hist.* A procedure by which a defendant, who was in court the first day but was then taken ill without pleading, would send two essoiners to state in court that the defendant was detained by sickness in a particular village and thus unable to attend. • This essoin would be accepted unless the plaintiff could show its falsity.

essoiner (e-**soyn**-ər), *n.* (17c) *Hist.* A person making an essoin. — Also termed *essoiniator* (e-**soyn**-ee-ay-tər).

essoin roll. (17c) *Hist.* A roll on which essoins were entered, together with the day to which they were adjourned.

establish, *vb.* (14c) **1.** To settle, make, or fix firmly; to enact permanently <one object of the Constitution was to establish justice>. **2.** To make or form; to bring about or into existence <Congress has the power to establish Article III courts>. **3.** To prove; to convince <the House managers tried to establish the President's guilt>.

established, *adj.* (17c) **1.** Having existed for a long period of time; already in long-term use <an established legal rule>. **2.** Known to do a particular job well because of a long-term track record <an established legal author>.

established church. 1. See CHURCH (2). **2.** See *state religion* under RELIGION.

established religion. See *state religion* under RELIGION.

established royalty. See ROYALTY (1).

establishment, *n.* (15c) **1.** The act of establishing; the quality, state, or condition of being established. **2.** An institution or place of business. **3.** A group of people who are in power or who control or exercise great influence over something.

Establishment Clause. (1959) *Constitutional law.* The First Amendment provision that prohibits the federal and state governments from establishing an official religion, or from favoring or disfavoring one view of religion over another. U.S. Const. amend. I. Cf. FREE EXERCISE CLAUSE.

establishment of religion. A government's acts officially recognizing a church as a national institution supported by the government. Cf. DISESTABLISH.

estadal (es-tah-**dahl**), *n.* [Spanish] *Hist.* In Spanish America, a measure of land of 16 square varas, or yards.

estadia (es-tah-**dee**-ah), *n.* [Spanish] *Spanish law.* **1.** A delay in a voyage, or in the delivery of cargo, caused by the charterer or consignee, who becomes liable for demurrage. **2.** The time for which the party who has chartered a vessel, or is bound to receive the cargo, must pay demurrage because of a delay in performing the contract. — Also termed *sobrestadia* (soh-bray-stah-**dee**-ah).

estandard (ə-**stan**-dərd), *n.* [Law French] A standard of weights and measures.

est a scavoir (ay ah skah-**vwahr**). [Law French, prob. fr. Latin *est sciendum* "it is to be known"] It is to be understood or known; to wit. • This expression is common in Sir Thomas de Littleton's 15th-century *Treatise on Tenures,* written in Law French. See SCIENDUM EST.

estate. (15c) **1.** The amount, degree, nature, and quality of a person's interest in land or other property; esp., a real-estate interest that may become possessory, the ownership being measured in terms of duration. See *periodic tenancy* under TENANCY.

▸ **absolute estate.** (16c) A full and complete estate that cannot be defeated.

> "The epithet *absolute* is used to distinguish an estate extended to any given time, without any condition to defeat or collateral limitation to determine [i.e., terminate] the estate in the mean time, from an estate subject to a condition or collateral limitation. The term absolute is of the same signification with the word pure or simple, a word which expresses that the estate is not determinable by any event besides the event marked by the clause of limitation." G.C. Cheshire, *Modern Law of Real Property* 54 (3d ed. 1933).

▸ **base estate.** *Hist.* An estate held at the will of the lord, as distinguished from a freehold.

▸ **concurrent estate.** (18c) Ownership or possession of property by two or more persons at the same time. • In modern practice, there are three types of concurrent estates: tenancy in common, joint tenancy, and tenancy by the entirety. — Also termed *concurrent interest.*

> "A concurrent estate is simply an estate — whether present or future, defeasible or non-defeasible, in fee simple, in tail, for life, or for years — that is owned by *two or more persons at the same time.* O transfers 'to A and B and their heirs.' A and B own a present concurrent estate in fee simple absolute." Thomas F. Bergin & Paul G. Haskell, *Preface to Estates in Land and Future Interests* 53 (2d ed. 1984).

▸ **conditional estate.** See *estate on condition.*

▸ **contingent estate.** (17c) An estate that vests only if a specified event does or does not happen. — Also termed *estate on contingency; estate on condition; estate upon condition.* Cf. *estate on condition.*

▸ **defeasible estate.** (17c) An estate that may come to an end before its maximum duration has run because of the operation of a special limitation, a condition subsequent, or an executory limitation. • If an estate is defeasible by operation of a special limitation, it is called a *determinable estate.*

▸ **derivative estate.** (18c) A particular interest that has been carved out of another, larger estate. Cf. *original estate.*

▸ **determinable estate.** (17c) An estate that is defeasible by operation of a special limitation. — Also termed *determinable freehold.*

▸ **equitable estate.** (17c) An estate recognized in equity, such as a trust beneficiary's interest. See EQUITY.

> "[A] legal estate was a right *in rem,* an equitable estate a right *in personam,* that is to say, the former conferred a right enforceable against the whole world, the latter one which could be enforced only against a limited number of persons." G.C. Cheshire, *Modern Law of Real Property* 54 (3d ed. 1933).

▸ **equitable life estate.** (1831) An interest in real or personal property that lasts for the life of the holder of the estate and that is equitable as opposed to legal in its creation. • An example is a life estate held by a trust beneficiary.

▸ **estate *ad remanentiam*** (ad rem-ə-**nen**-shee-əm). An estate in fee simple.

▸ **estate at sufferance.** See *tenancy at sufferance* under TENANCY.

▸ **estate at will.** See *tenancy at will* under TENANCY.

▸ **estate by curtesy.** (18c) An estate owned by a wife, to which the husband is entitled upon her death. See CURTESY.

▸ **estate by elegit.** (18c) An estate held by a judgment creditor, entitling the creditor to the rents and profits from land owned by the debtor until the debt is paid. See ELEGIT.

▸ **estate by entirety.** (1876) A common-law estate in which each spouse is seised of the whole of the property. • An estate by entirety is based on the legal fiction that a husband and wife are a single unit. The estate consists of five unities: time, title, interest, possession, and marriage. The last of these unities distinguishes the estate by entirety from the joint tenancy. A joint tenancy can exist with any number of persons, while an estate by entirety can be held only by a husband and wife and is not available to any other persons. And it can be acquired only during the marriage. This estate has a right of survivorship, but upon the death of one spouse, the surviving spouse retains the entire interest rather than acquiring the decedent's interest. Most jurisdictions have abolished this estate. — Also termed *estate by the entirety*; *estate by entireties*; *estate by the entireties*; *tenancy by the entirety*; *tenancy by the entireties*. Cf. *joint tenancy* and *tenancy in common* under TENANCY.

▸ **estate by purchase.** (17c) An estate acquired in any manner other than by descent. See PURCHASE.

▸ **estate by statute staple.** (1856) An estate in a defendant's land held by a creditor under the statute staple until the debt was paid. See STATUTE STAPLE.

▸ **estate by the curtesy of England.** See CURTESY.

▸ **estate for a term.** See *tenancy for a term* under TENANCY.

▸ **estate for life.** See *life estate*.

▸ **estate for years.** See *tenancy for a term* under TENANCY.

▸ **estate in common.** See *tenancy in common* under TENANCY.

▸ **estate in fee.** See FEE SIMPLE.

▸ **estate in fee simple.** See FEE SIMPLE.

▸ **estate in fee tail.** See FEE TAIL.

▸ **estate *in gage*.** An estate that has been pledged as security for a debt. See MORTGAGE.

▸ **estate in partnership.** (1913) A joint estate that is vested in the members of a partnership when real estate is purchased with partnership funds and for partnership purposes.

▸ **estate in possession.** (17c) An estate in which a present interest passes to the tenant; an estate in which the tenant is entitled to receive the rents and other profits arising from the estate.

▸ **estate in remainder.** See REMAINDER (1).

▸ **estate in reversion.** See REVERSION (1).

▸ **estate in severalty** (**sev**-ə-rəl-tee). (18c) An estate held by a tenant separately, without any other person being joined or connected in interest.

▸ **estate in tail.** See FEE TAIL.

▸ **estate *in vadio*** (in **vad**-ee-oh). An estate in gage or pledge. See MORTGAGE.

▸ **estate less than freehold.** (18c) An estate for years, an estate at will, or an estate at sufferance.

▸ **estate on condition.** (18c) An estate that vests, is modified, or is defeated upon the occurrence or nonoccurrence of some specified event. • While an estate on limitation can revert without any action by the grantor or the grantor's heirs, an estate on condition requires the entry of the grantor or the grantor's heirs to end the estate whenever the condition occurs. — Also termed *estate on conditional limitation*; *conditional estate*; *estate upon condition*. Cf. *estate on limitation*.

▸ **estate on conditional limitation.** See *estate on condition*.

▸ **estate on condition expressed.** (18c) A contingent estate in which the condition upon which the estate will fail is stated explicitly in the granting instrument.

▸ **estate on condition implied.** (18c) A contingent estate having some condition that is so inseparable from the estate's essence that it need not be expressed in words.

▸ **estate on limitation.** (18c) An estate that automatically reverts back to the grantor according to a provision, usu. regarding the passage of a determined time period, designated by words such as "during," "while," and "as long as." See *fee simple determinable* under FEE SIMPLE. Cf. *estate on condition*.

▸ **estate *pur autre vie*.** See *life estate pur autre vie*.

▸ **estate tail.** See FEE TAIL.

▸ **estate tail quasi.** An estate granted by a life tenant, who, despite using language of conveyance that is otherwise sufficient to create an estate tail, is unable to grant in perpetuity.

▸ **executed estate.** See REMAINDER (1).

▸ **expectant estate.** See *future interest* under INTEREST (2).

▸ **fast estate.** See *real property* under PROPERTY.

▸ **freehold estate.** See FREEHOLD.

▸ **future estate.** See *future interest* under INTEREST (2).

▸ **joint estate.** (15c) Any of the following five types of estates: (1) a joint tenancy, (2) a tenancy in common, (3) an estate in coparcenary (a common-law estate in which coheirs hold as tenants in common), (4) a tenancy by the entirety, or (5) an estate in partnership.

▸ **landed estate.** (18c) An interest in real property, esp. suburban or rural land, as distinguished from real estate situated in a city. — Also termed *landed property*.

▸ **leasehold estate.** See LEASEHOLD.

▸ **legal estate.** (17c) An interest enforced in law rather than in equity.

▸ **legal life estate.** See *life estate*.

▸ **life estate.** (18c) An estate held only for the duration of a specified person's life, usu. the possessor's. • Most life estates — created, for example, by a grant "to Jane for life" — are beneficial interests under trusts, the corpus often being personal property, not real property. — Also termed *estate for life*; *legal life estate*; *life tenancy*. See LIFE TENANT.

▸ **life estate *pur autre vie*** (pər **oh**-trə **vee**). (1888) A life estate for which the measuring life — the life whose duration determines the duration of the estate — is someone's other than the possessor's. — Also spelled *life estate per autre vie.*

▸ **marital estate.** See *marital property* under PROPERTY.

▸ **mesne estate.** (17c) *Hist.* An estate held by a feudal lord who received it from a superior lord. See MESNE LORD.

▸ **next eventual estate.** (1836) An estate taking effect upon an event that terminates the accumulation of undisposed rents and profits; an estate taking effect when the existing estate terminates.

▸ **nonancestral estate.** (1868) An estate from any source other than the owner's ancestors. — Also termed *nonancestral property.*

▸ **nonfreehold estate.** (1937) Any estate in real property without seisin, such as an estate for years, from period to period, at will, or at sufferance; any estate except a fee simple, fee tail, or life estate.

▸ **original estate.** An estate that is the first of one or more derivative estates, bearing to each other the relation of a particular estate and a reversion.

▸ **particular estate.** An estate or interest less than a fee simple, such as a fee tail, a life estate, or a term for years. • It is so called because the estate is a mere part (*particula*) of the fee simple.

▸ **periodic estate.** See *periodic tenancy* under TENANCY.

▸ **possessory estate.** (18c) An estate giving the holder the right to possess the property, with or without an ownership interest in the property.

▸ **present estate.** An estate in immediate possession; one vested at the present time, as distinguished from a future estate. See *present interest* under INTEREST (2).

▸ **qualified estate.** (18c) Any estate that is not absolute and unconditional; a limited or conditional estate.

▸ **reversionary estate.** See REVERSION.

▸ **separate estate.** The individual property of one of two persons who stand in a marital or business relationship. See SEPARATE PROPERTY.

▸ **settled estate.** (18c) An estate created or limited under a settlement; an estate in which the powers of alienation, devising, and transmission according to the ordinary rules of descent are restrained by the settlement's terms.

▸ **stipendiary estate** (stɪ-**pen**-dee-er-ee). (1880) *Hist.* An estate granted in return for services, usu. of a military kind.

▸ **vested estate.** (18c) An estate with a present right of enjoyment or a present fixed right of future enjoyment.

2. All that a person or entity owns, including both real and personal property.

▸ **bankruptcy estate.** See BANKRUPTCY ESTATE.

3. The property that one leaves after death; the collective assets and liabilities of a dead person.

> "The word 'estate' was probably adopted because in early days it was possible to ascertain a man's status or position in life by discovering the particular kind of tenure by which he held his lands. The *quality* of his tenure gave a clue to his status. The baron for example ought in theory to be the holder of a barony; he has the status of a baron because he has the estate of a baron. . . . [O]ne of the distinguishing marks of [the] freehold estates was the uncertainty of their duration. They were invariably held either for life, or for some other space of time dependent upon an event which might not happen within a lifetime, and thus a freehold estate came to be regarded as one which involved the performance of free services only, but as one which endured for an uncertain time. In this way, the word 'estate' came to denote the *quantity* of a man's interest in land." G.C. Cheshire, *Modern Law of Real Property* 26 (3d ed. 1933).

▸ **adjusted gross estate.** (1932) **1.** The total value of a decedent's property after subtracting administration expenses, funeral expenses, creditors' claims, and casualty losses. • The value of the adjusted gross estate is used in computing the federal estate tax. Cf. *net probate estate* under PROBATE ESTATE. **2.** See *gross estate* (1).

▸ **ancestral estate.** (1850) An estate that is acquired by descent or by operation of law with no other consideration than that of blood.

▸ **augmented estate.** (1967) A refinement of the elective share to which a surviving spouse is entitled, whereby the "fair share" is identified as something other than the traditional one-third of the probate estate. • The current version of the Uniform Probate Code uses a sliding scale that increases with each year of marriage. Under the UPC, a surviving spouse has accrued full marital-property rights after 15 years of marriage. This percentage of spousal entitlement is applied to a reconceptualization of the decedent's estate to take into account more than just the assets remaining in the probate estate at death. Also added into the calculation are the value of certain inter vivos transfers that the decedent made to others in a way that depleted the probate estate; the value of similar transfers made to others by the spouse as well as the value of the marital property owned by the spouse at the decedent's death; and the value of inter vivos transfers of property made by the decedent to the spouse. The Uniform Probate Code adopted this version of the augmented-estate concept in an attempt to equalize the treatment of surviving spouses in non-community-property states vis-à-vis community- property states. Unif. Probate Code § 2-202. See ELECTIVE SHARE.

▸ **decedent's estate.** (18c) The real and personal property that a person possesses at the time of death and that passes to the heirs or testamentary beneficiaries.

▸ **estate of inheritance.** (16c) An estate that may descend to heirs.

▸ **gross estate.** (1833) **1.** The total value of a decedent's property without any deductions. **2.** Loosely, adjusted gross estate.

▸ **heirless estate.** (1956) The property of a person who dies intestate and without heirs. See ESCHEAT.

▸ **insolvent estate.** (17c) An estate whose assets are insufficient to cover its debts, taxes, and administrative expenses.

▸ **net estate.** See *net probate estate* under PROBATE ESTATE.

▸ **net probate estate.** See PROBATE ESTATE.

▸ **probate estate.** See PROBATE ESTATE.

▸ **residuary estate.** (18c) The part of a decedent's estate remaining after payment of all debts, expenses, statutory claims, taxes, and testamentary gifts (special, general, and demonstrative) have been made. — Also termed *residual estate; residue; residuary; residuum.*

▸ **taxable estate.** (18c) A decedent's gross estate reduced by allowable deductions (such as administration costs and ESOP deductions). IRC (26 USCA) § 2051. • The taxable estate is the amount that is subject to the federal unified transfer tax at death.

4. A tract of land, esp. one affected by an easement.

"The old definitions of this word [*estate*] generally confine it to lands or realty. Thus, according to Lord Coke, '*state* or *estate* signifieth such inheritance, freehold, term for years, &c., as any man hath in *lands* or tenements.' *Co. Litt.* 345a. So Cowell defines it to be 'that title or interest which a man hath in *lands* or tenements,' and the same definition is given in the *Termes de la Ley*. And this limited sense of the word has been relied on, in argument, in some cases . . . . But, according to the settled modern doctrine, the term *estate* is of much more extensive import and application, being indeed *genus generalissimum*, and clearly comprehending things personal as well as real; person as well as real estate." 1 Alexander M. Burrill, *A Law Dictionary and Glossary* 561 (2d ed. 1867).

▸ **dominant estate.** (18c) An estate that benefits from an easement. — Also termed *dominant tenement*; *dominant property*; *upper estate*. Cf. *servient estate*.

▸ **lower estate.** See *servient estate*.

▸ **real estate.** See *real property* under PROPERTY.

▸ **servient estate** (sər-vee-ənt). (18c) An estate burdened by an easement. — Also termed *servient tenement*; *servient property*; *lower estate*. Cf. *dominant estate*.

▸ **upper estate.** See *dominant estate*.

estate agent. See *real-estate agent* under AGENT.

estate duty. See DUTY (4).

estate freeze. (1986) An estate-planning maneuver whereby an owner of a closely held business exchanges common stock for dividend-paying preferred stock and gives the common stock to his or her children, thus seeking to guarantee an income in retirement and to avoid estate tax on future appreciation in the business's value.

estate from period to period. See *periodic tenancy* under TENANCY.

estate in expectancy. See *future interest* under INTEREST (2).

estate in fee. See FEE SIMPLE.

estate in freehold. See FREEHOLD.

estate in lands. (16c) **1.** Property that one has in lands, tenements, or hereditaments. **2.** The conditions or circumstances under which a tenant stands in relation to the leased property.

estate in remainder. See REMAINDER (1).

estate planning. (1938) **1.** The preparation for the distribution and management of a person's estate at death through the use of wills, trusts, insurance policies, and other arrangements, esp. to reduce administration costs and transfer-tax liability. **2.** A branch of law that involves the arrangement of a person's estate, taking into account the laws of wills, taxes, insurance, property, and trusts.

estates of the realm. (16c) *English law.* **1.** The lords spiritual, the lords temporal, and the commons of the United Kingdom. — Also termed *the three estates*. **2.** In feudal Europe, the clergy, nobles, and commons. • Because the lords spiritual had no separate assembly or negative in their political capacity, some authorities reduce the estates in the United Kingdom to two, the lords and commons. In England (until about the 14th century), the three estates of the realm were the clergy, barons, and knights. In legal practice, the lords spiritual and lords temporal are usu. collectively designated simply as *lords*.

estate's property. See PROPERTY OF THE ESTATE.

estate tax. See TAX.

estate trust. See TRUST (3).

***ester* in judgment** (es-tər). [Law French] To appear before a tribunal, as either plaintiff or defendant.

estimated damages. See *liquidated damages* under DAMAGES.

estimated tax. See TAX.

estimated useful life. See USEFUL LIFE.

estop (e-stop), *vb.* (15c) To bar or prevent by estoppel.

estoppage (e-stop-ij), *n.* (18c) The quality, state, or condition of being estopped.

estoppel (e-stop-əl), *n.* (16c) **1.** A bar that prevents one from asserting a claim or right that contradicts what one has said or done before or what has been legally established as true. **2.** A bar that prevents the relitigation of issues. **3.** An affirmative defense alleging good-faith reliance on a misleading representation and an injury or detrimental change in position resulting from that reliance. Cf. WAIVER (2). — **estop,** *vb.*

"'Estoppe,' says Lord Coke, 'cometh of the French word *estoupe*, from whence the English word stopped; and it is called an estoppel or conclusion, because a man's own act or acceptance stoppeth or closeth up his mouth to allege or plead the truth.' [Co. Litt. 352a.] Estoppel may also be defined to be a legal result or 'conclusion' arising from an admission which has either been actually made, or which the law presumes to have been made, and which is binding on all persons whom it affects." Lancelot Feilding Everest, *Everest and Strode's Law of Estoppel* 1 (3d ed. 1923).

"In using the term 'estoppel,' one is of course aware of its kaleidoscopic varieties. One reads of estoppel by conduct, by deed, by laches, by misrepresentation, by negligence, by silence, and so on. There is also an estoppel by judgment and by verdict; these, however, obviously involve procedure. The first-named varieties have certain aspects in common. But these aspects are not always interpreted by the same rules in all courts. The institution seems to be flexible." John H. Wigmore, "The Scientific Role of Consideration in Contract," in *Legal Essays in Tribute to Orrin Kip McMurray* 641, 643 (Max Radin & Alexander M. Kidd eds., 1935).

▸ **administrative collateral estoppel.** See COLLATERAL ESTOPPEL.

▸ **assignee estoppel.** (1970) *Patents.* The equitable doctrine that bars the assignee of a patent from contesting the patent's validity under some circumstances, as when the assignee seeks to avoid royalty payments, to void an assignment contract, or to mitigate damages related to the assignee's fraudulent acquisition of the patent. • The doctrine prevents an assignee from simultaneously attacking and defending the validity of the same patent.

▸ **assignor estoppel.** (1959) *Patents.* Estoppel barring someone who has assigned the rights to a patent from later attacking the patent's validity. *Westinghouse Elec. & Mfg. Co. v. Formica Insulation Co.*, 266 U.S. 342, 45 S.Ct. 117 (1924). • The doctrine was narrowed by *Diamond Scientific Co. v. Ambico, Inc.*, 848 F.2d 1220 (Fed. Cir. 1988), in which the court held that in some circumstances equity may outweigh the public-policy reasons behind the estoppel doctrine.

► **collateral estoppel.** See COLLATERAL ESTOPPEL.

► **equitable estoppel.** (18c) **1.** A defensive doctrine preventing one party from taking unfair advantage of another when, through false language or conduct, the person to be estopped has induced another person to act in a certain way, with the result that the other person has been injured in some way. • This doctrine is founded on principles of fraud. The five essential elements of this type of estoppel are that (1) there was a false representation or concealment of material facts, (2) the representation was known to be false by the party making it, or the party was negligent in not knowing its falsity, (3) it was believed to be true by the person to whom it was made, (4) the party making the representation intended that it be acted on, or the person acting on it was justified in assuming this intent, and (5) the party asserting estoppel acted on the representation in a way that will result in substantial prejudice unless the claim of estoppel succeeds. — Also termed *estoppel by conduct*; *estoppel in pais*. **2.** See *promissory estoppel*.

► **estoppel by acquiescence.** Estoppel arising from a party's failure to respond to a claim within a reasonable time after receiving notice of the claim, thereby giving rise to a presumption of acceptance.

► **estoppel by agreement.** Estoppel based on the terms of a contract between the parties expressly or impliedly showing a mutual acceptance of certain facts or assumptions. — Also termed *estoppel by convention*.

► **estoppel by conduct.** See *equitable estoppel*.

► **estoppel by contract.** (1874) A bar that prevents a person from denying a term, fact, or performance arising from a contract that the person has entered into.

► **estoppel by convention.** See *estoppel by agreement*.

► **estoppel by deed.** (1841) Estoppel that prevents a party to a deed from denying anything recited in that deed if the party has induced another to accept or act under the deed; esp., estoppel that prevents a grantor of a warranty deed, who does not have title at the time of the conveyance but who later acquires title, from denying that he or she had title at the time of the transfer. See AFTER-ACQUIRED-TITLE DOCTRINE. — Also termed *estoppel by warranty*.

> "The apparent odiousness of some classes of estoppel, chiefly estoppels by deed, seems to result not so much from the nature of an estoppel, as from the highly technical rules of real property law upon which it operated, and with which it was associated. Estoppels by record, indeed, stand upon a considerably higher footing than estoppels by deed . . . ." Lancelot Feilding Everest, *Everest and Strode's Law of Estoppel* 10 (1923).

► **estoppel by election.** (1906) The intentional exercise of a choice between inconsistent alternatives that bars the person making the choice from the benefits of the one not selected.

► **estoppel by inaction.** See *estoppel by silence*.

► **estoppel by judgment.** See COLLATERAL ESTOPPEL.

► **estoppel by laches.** (1894) An equitable doctrine by which some courts deny relief to a claimant who has unreasonably delayed or been negligent in asserting a claim.

► **estoppel by misrepresentation.** (1882) An estoppel that arises when one makes a false statement that induces another person to believe something and that results in that person's reasonable and detrimental reliance on the belief.

► **estoppel by negligence.** (1875) An estoppel arising when a negligent person induces someone to believe certain facts, and then the other person reasonably and detrimentally relies on that belief. Cf. *assisted misrepresentation* under MISREPRESENTATION.

► **estoppel by record.** See COLLATERAL ESTOPPEL.

► **estoppel by representation.** (1863) An estoppel that arises when one makes a statement or admission that induces another person to believe something and that results in that person's reasonable and detrimental reliance on the belief; esp., equitable estoppel.

► **estoppel by silence.** (1872) Estoppel that arises when a party is under a duty to speak but fails to do so. — Also termed *estoppel by standing by*; *estoppel by inaction*.

► **estoppel by standing by.** See *estoppel by silence*.

► **estoppel by verdict.** See COLLATERAL ESTOPPEL.

► **estoppel by warranty.** See *estoppel by deed*.

► **estoppel in pais.** See *equitable estoppel*.

► **estoppel on the record.** See *prosecution-history estoppel*.

► **file-wrapper estoppel.** See *prosecution-history estoppel*.

► **judicial estoppel.** (1886) Estoppel that prevents a party from contradicting previous declarations made during the same or an earlier proceeding if the change in position would adversely affect the proceeding or constitute a fraud on the court. — Also termed *doctrine of preclusion of inconsistent positions*; *doctrine of the conclusiveness of the judgment*.

► **legal estoppel.** (1818) Estoppel recognized in law (as distinguished from equitable estoppel or estoppel in pais), such as an estoppel resulting from a recital or other statement in a deed or official record, and precluding any denial or assertion concerning a fact.

► **marking estoppel.** (1973) *Patents.* Estoppel that prevents a party from asserting that a product is not covered by a patent if that party has marked the product with a patent number. • This type of estoppel has been questioned in recent years, and has been sharply limited by some courts.

► **promissory estoppel.** (1924) The principle that a promise made without consideration may nonetheless be enforced to prevent injustice if the promisor should have reasonably expected the promisee to rely on the promise and if the promisee did actually rely on the promise to his or her detriment. — Also termed (inaccurately) *equitable estoppel*.

> "One of the earlier attempts at a doctrine of enforceability because of action in reliance was to state a rule that a promise might become enforceable by reason of 'promissory estoppel.' The use of this phrase made some headway, because it satisfied the need of the courts for a justification of their enforcement of certain promises in the absence of any bargain or agreed exchange. Nevertheless, the phrase is objectionable. The word estoppel is so widely and loosely used as almost to defy definition yet, in the main, it has been applied to cases of misrepresentation of facts and not to promises. The American Law Institute was well advised in not adopting this phrase and in stating its rule in terms of action or forbearance in reliance on the promise." Arthur Linton Corbin, *Corbin on Contracts* 204 (one-vol. ed., 1952).

"The doctrine of promissory estoppel is equitable in origin and nature and arose to provide a remedy through the enforcement of a gratuitous promise. Promissory is distinct from equitable estoppel in that the representation at issue is promissory rather than a representation of fact. 'Promissory estoppel and estoppel by conduct are two entirely distinct theories. The latter does not require a promise.'" Ann Taylor Schwing, *California Affirmative Defenses* § 34:16, at 35 (2d ed. 1996) (quoting *Division of Labor Law Enforcement v. Transpacific Transp. Co.*, 88 Cal. App. 3d 823, 829 (Cal. Ct. App. 1979)).

▸ **prosecution-history estoppel.** (1983) *Patents.* The doctrine limiting a patent-holder's invocation of the doctrine of equivalents by eliminating from the claims those elements that the holder surrendered or abandoned during the prosecution of the patent. — Also termed *estoppel on the record; file-wrapper estoppel.* See DOCTRINE OF EQUIVALENTS.

▸ **quasi-estoppel.** (1823) An equitable doctrine preventing one from repudiating an act or assertion if it would harm another who reasonably relied on the act or assertion.

▸ **technical estoppel.** (1802) **1.** An estoppel arising from a matter of record or from a deed made by the party who is claimed to be estopped. • Estoppels by deed or by record are called "technical" because the rules of estoppel apply with certainty in appropriate cases. **2.** COLLATERAL ESTOPPEL. See *estoppel by deed.*

estoppel-asserter. (1900) Someone who relied on an alleged misrepresentation and seeks to have the person who made the representation held liable for the resulting harm or loss. • The asserter must be the person to whom the misrepresentation was directly made. — Also termed *estoppel-raiser.*

estoppel by acquiescence. See ESTOPPEL.

estoppel by agreement. See ESTOPPEL.

estoppel by convention. See *estoppel by agreement* under ESTOPPEL.

estoppel certificate. (1897) **1.** A signed statement by a party (such as a tenant or a mortgagee) certifying for another's benefit that certain facts are correct, such as that a lease exists, that there are no defaults, and that rent is paid to a certain date. • A party's delivery of this statement estops that party from later claiming a different state of facts. **2.** See WAIVER OF CLAIMS AND DEFENSES.

estoppel-denier. (1900) Someone who allegedly made a misrepresentation to another and seeks to avoid liability for the misrepresentation and show that a contradictory statement is true.

estoppel per rem judicatam (pər rem joo-di-**kay**-təm). See COLLATERAL ESTOPPEL.

estoppel-raiser. See ESTOPPEL-ASSERTER.

estover (e-**stoh**-vər). (*usu. pl.*) (16c) **1.** Wood that a tenant is allowed to take for fuel, the manufacture or repair of agricultural instruments, and the erection and maintenance of fences and hedges; necessary supplies. — Also termed *bote.* See BOTE (1); *common of estovers* under COMMON (1). **2.** The tenant's right to obtain that wood. **3.** ALIMONY.

estoveriis habendis (es-tə-**veer**-ee-is hə-**ben**-dis). [Latin] *Hist.* See DE ESTOVERIIS HABENDIS.

estrange, *vb.* (15c) **1.** To separate, to keep away (a person or thing), or to keep away from (a person or thing). **2.** To destroy or divert affection, trust, and loyalty. — **estrangement,** *n.*

estray (e-**stray**), *n.* (16c) **1.** A valuable tame animal found wandering and ownerless; an animal that has escaped from its owner and wanders about. • At common law, an estray belonged to the Crown or to the lord of the manor, but today the general rule is that it passes to the state in trust for the true owner, who may regain it by proving ownership. An animal cannot be an estray when on the range where it was raised and where its owner permits it to run, and esp. when the owner is known to the party who takes the animal. **2.** FLOTSAM. **3.** Anything that has gone out of its usual, normal, or intended place.

▸ **free estray.** Freight that, having reached the incorrect destination, is redirected to its correct destination at no charge.

estreat (e-**street**), *n.* (15c) A copy or duplicate of some original writing or record, esp. of a fine or amercement imposed by a court, extracted from the record, and certified to one who is authorized and required to collect it. — Also termed (in Scots law) *extract*; (archaic) *extractum.*

"Estreat (*extractum*) is used for the true copy or note of some original writing of record, and especially of fines and amerciaments, imposed in the rolls of a court, to be levied by the bailiff or other officer." Edward Bullingbrooke, *The Duty and Authority of Justices of the Peace and Parish Officers for Ireland* 249 (rev. ed. 1788).

estreat, *vb.* (16c) To take out a forfeited recognizance from the recordings of a court and return it to the court to be prosecuted.

estrepe (e-**streep**), *vb.* (17c) **1.** To strip; to despoil; to commit waste on an estate, as by cutting down trees or removing buildings. **2.** To injure the value of a reversionary interest by stripping or spoiling the estate. See WASTE (1).

estrepement (e-**streep**-mənt), *n.* (16c) A species of aggravated waste, by stripping or devastating land to the injury of the reversioner, esp. pending a suit for possession. See DE ESTREPAMENTO.

et, *conj.* [Latin] And • This conjunction was the introductory word of several Latin and Law French phrases that were once common.

et adjournatur (et aj-ər-**nay**-tər). [Latin] *Hist.* And it is adjourned. • This phrase was used in the old reports, when argument of a case was adjourned to another day, or where a second argument was had.

et al. (et **al** *or* **ahl**). *abbr.* (1883) **1.** [Latin *et alii* or *et alia*] And other persons <the office of Thomas Webb et al.>. **2.** [Latin *et alibi*] And elsewhere.

et alii e contra (et **ay**-lee-ɪ ee **kon**-trə). [Latin "and others on the other side"] *Hist.* A phrase often used in the Year Books, describing a joinder in issue.

et alius (et **ay**-lee-əs). [Latin] And another.

et allocatur (et al-ə-**kay**-tər). [Latin] And it is allowed.

etc. *abbr.* (15c) ET CETERA.

et cetera (et **set**-ər-ə). [Latin "and others"] (12c) And other things. • The term usu. indicates additional, unspecified items in a series. — Abbr. etc.

et de ceo se mettent en le pays (ay də **say**-oh sə me-**tawn** on lə **pay**). [Law French] *Hist.* And of this they put themselves upon the country. See CONCLUSION TO THE COUNTRY; GOING TO THE COUNTRY.

et de hoc ponit se super patriam (et dee hok **poh**-nit see **s[y]oo**-pər **pay**-tree-əm). [Latin] *Hist.* And of this he puts himself upon the country. • This was the formal conclusion of a common-law plea in bar by way of traverse.

et ei legitur in haec verba (et **ee**-ɪ **lee**-jə-tər in **heek vər**-bə). [Latin] *Hist.* And it is read to him in these words. • This phrase was formerly used in entering the prayer of oyer on the record.

eternal law. See NATURAL LAW.

ETF. *abbr.* EXCHANGE-TRADED FUND.

et habeas ibi tunc hoc breve (et **hay**-bee-əs **ib**-ɪ təngk hok **bree**-vee). [Latin] *Hist.* And that you have then and there this writ. • These were the formal words directing the return of a writ. The literal translation was retained in the later form of a considerable number of writs.

et habuit (et **hab**-yoo-it). [Latin "and he had [it]"] *Hist.* A common phrase in the Year Books, indicating that a party's application or demand was granted.

ethical, *adj.* (16c) **1.** Of, relating to, or involving moral obligations that one person owes another; esp., in law, pertaining to legal ethics <the ethical rules regarding confidences>. See LEGAL ETHICS. **2.** Conforming to moral norms or standards of professional conduct <refusing to identify the informant was a perfectly ethical act>.

ethical absolutism. See MORAL ABSOLUTISM.

ethical code. See CODE OF ETHICS.

ethical consideration. (*often cap.*) A structural component of the ethical canons set forth in the legal profession's Model Code of Professional Responsibility, containing a goal or ethical principle intended to guide a lawyer's professional conduct. • Ethical considerations are often used in the interpretation and application of the Model Rules of Professional Conduct. — Abbr. EC. Cf. DISCIPLINARY RULE.

ethical drug. See DRUG.

ethical duty. See DUTY (2).

ethical duty of candor. See *duty of candor* under DUTY (2).

ethical jurisprudence. See JURISPRUDENCE.

ethical relativism. See MORAL RELATIVISM.

ethical wall. (1988) A screening mechanism maintained by an organization, esp. a law firm, to protect client confidences from improper disclosure to lawyers or staff who are not involved in a particular representation. • The screening mechanism is designed to prevent lawyer or law-firm disqualification from certain representations because of conflicts of interest, as when a newly hired lawyer previously worked for an opposing party. — Also termed *screening mechanism*; *Chinese wall*; *firewall.*

ethics. 1. A system of moral tenets or principles; the collective doctrines relating to the ideals of human conduct and character. **2.** The study of behavior as judged by moral right and wrong, including the sources, principles, and enforcement of behavioral standards. See LEGAL ETHICS.

> "As used here, *ethics* refers to imperatives regarding the welfare of others that are recognized as binding upon a person's conduct in some more immediate and binding sense than *law* and in some more general and impersonal sense than *morals*. This definition is narrower than those of the philosophers. At least in some such definitions, law, morals, and ethics are a part of a general subject that includes all aspects of the concept of obligation. Moreover, among the various systems of ethics there are ones that deny the existence or even the intelligibility of an imperative regarding the welfare of others. In these systems, the sense of self is the only thing that can or should be given regard or, indeed, the only thing that can be said to exist. But in these systems it also seems impossible coherently to condemn another person's conduct as unethical, which is the problem that both lawyers and their ethical critics are concerned with. So while acknowledging the place in the philosophical universe of what are termed ethical egoism and radical ethical passivity, our concern here is with the relationships between rules that are believed to exist and the conduct they are thought to refer to." Geoffrey C. Hazard Jr., *Ethics in the Practice of Law* 1-2 (1978).

▸ **situational ethics.** See SITUATIONAL ETHICS.

▸ **virtue ethics.** See VIRTUE ETHICS.

ethics opinion. A reasoned decision written by a body with disciplinary authority on a matter involving professional responsibility.

ethnic cleansing. (1991) The elimination of a particular people from an area or country because of their racial or national identity; specif., the officially sanctioned forcible and systematic diminution or elimination of targeted ethnic minorities from a geographic area, usu. by confiscating real and personal property, ordering or condoning mass murders and mass rapes, and expelling the survivors. • In theory, the purpose of ethnic cleansing is to drive all members of the victimized group out of a territory. In practice, ethnic cleansing is nearly synonymous with genocide as mass murder is a characteristic of both. Ethnic cleansing additionally includes mass rapes for two cultural reasons: (1) the victims are often put to death by their relatives or commit suicide, and (2) any children born are regarded as belonging to the father's ethnic group, not the mother's. Both acts — murder and rape — are intended to diminish or extinguish the victimized minority. Cf. GENOCIDE.

ethnic minority. See MINORITY (3).

ethnic profiling. See RACIAL PROFILING.

ethnocentric, *adj.* (1891) Characterized by or based on the idea that one's own race or nation is better than any other. — **ethnocentrism,** *n.*

ethnological jurisprudence. See JURISPRUDENCE.

et hoc genus omne (et hok **jee**-nəs **om**-nee). [Latin] *Hist.* And all that kind of thing.

et hoc paratus est verificare (et hok pə-**ray**-təs est ver-ə-fi-**kair**-ee). [Latin] And this he is prepared to verify. • This phrase traditionally concluded a plea in confession and avoidance, or any pleading that contained new affirmative matter. A pleading containing this phrase was technically said to "conclude with a verification," as opposed to a simple denial.

et hoc petit quod inquiratur per patriam (et hok **pet**-it kwod in-kwə-**ray**-tər pər **pay**-tree-əm). [Latin "and this he prays may be inquired of by the country"] *Archaic.* The conclusion of a plaintiff's pleading that tendered an issue to the country. See CONCLUSION TO THE COUNTRY.

ethos (**ee**-thahs *or* **ee**-thohs), *n.* (1851) The set of ideas and moral attitudes that characterize a person, group, institution, country, etc.

etiam causa non cognita (**ee**-shee-əm **kaw**-zə non **kog**-ni-tə). [Latin] *Hist.* Even where the cause is not known;

absent an investigation. • Some decrees could be issued without a full factual inquiry or trial.

etiam in articulo mortis (**ee**-shee-əm in ahr-**tik**-yə-loh **mor**-tis). [Latin] *Scots law.* Even at the point of death. • The phrase appeared in reference to a circumstance under which one could revoke a will.

etiam in lecto (**ee**-shee-əm in **lek**-toh). [Law Latin] *Hist.* Even upon deathbed.

E-ticket. (1997) A traffic citation that is electronically generated, mailed, and filed, as for running a red light or speeding.

et inde petit judicium (et **in**-dee **pet**-it joo-**dish**-ee-əm). [Latin "and thereupon he prays judgment"] *Archaic.* A clause found at the end of a pleading, requesting judgment in that party's favor.

etiquette of the profession. See LEGAL ETIQUETTE.

et modo ad hunc diem (et **moh**-doh ad **həngk dɪ**-əm). [Latin "and now at this day"] *Archaic.* The formal beginning of an entry of appearance or of a continuance.

et non (et **non**). [Latin "and not"] *Archaic.* A phrase formerly used in pleading to introduce the negative averments of a special traverse. See ABSQUE HOC.

et seq. (et **sek**). *abbr.* [Latin *et sequens* "and the following one," *et sequentes* (masc.) "and the following ones," or *et sequentia* (neuter) "and the following ones"] (18c) And those (pages or sections) that follow <11 USCA §§ 101 et seq.>.

et sic (et **sik**). [Latin "and so"] *Archaic.* The introductory words of a special conclusion to a plea in bar, intending to render the plea positive and not argumentative.

et sic ad judicium (et **sik** ad joo-**dish**-ee-əm). [Latin] *Archaic.* And so to judgment.

et sic ad patriam (et **sik** ad **pay**-tree-əm). [Latin] *Hist.* And so to the country. • This phrase was used in the Year Books to record an issue to the country.

et sic de anno in annum quamdiu ambobus partibus placuerit (et **sik** dee **an**-oh in **an**-əm **kwam**-dee-yoo **am**-bə-bəs **pahr**-tə-bəs plak-yoo-**air**-it). *Hist.* And so, from year to year, so long as both parties please, or are agreed. • The phrase appeared in reference to tacit relocation. See TACIT RELOCATION.

et sic fecit (et **sik fee**-sit). [Latin] *Archaic.* And he did so.

et sic pendet (et **sik pen**-dit). [Latin] *Hist.* And so it hangs. • This phrase was used in the old reports to signify that a point was left undetermined.

et sic ulterius (et **sik** əl-**teer**-ee-əs). [Latin] *Archaic.* And so on; and so further; and so forth.

et uxor (et **ək**-sor). [Latin] *Archaic.* And wife. • This phrase was formerly common in case names and legal documents (esp. abstracts of title) involving a husband and wife jointly. It usu. appears in its abbreviated form, *et ux.* <conveyed the land to Donald Baird et ux.>. See UXOR.

et vir (et **veer**). [Latin] *Archaic.* And husband. See VIR.

EU. *abbr.* (1990) EUROPEAN UNION.

Euclidean zoning. See ZONING.

eundo et redeundo (ee-**ən**-doh et red-ee-**ən**-doh). [Latin] *Hist.* Going and returning. • This phrase was once used to describe vessels in transit.

eundo, morando, et redeundo (ee-**ən**-doh, mə-**ran**-doh, et red-ee-**ən**-doh). [Latin] *Hist.* Going, remaining, and returning. • This phrase was once used to describe a person (for example, a witness or legislator) who is privileged from arrest while traveling to the place where assigned duties are to be performed, while remaining there, and while returning.

eunomy (**yoo**-nə-mee), *n.* (19c) A system of good laws that lead to civil order and justice. — Also termed *eunomia.* Cf. DYSNOMY. — **eunomic,** *adj.*

euphemism. An alternative term or phrase intended to be less offensive or in some other way more acceptable than the term or phrase it replaces (e.g., as by calling a serious lie a "fib").

Euratom. A European Union organization that coordinates the development and use of nuclear energy in Europe. • It was created in 1958 and merged with the European Economic Community in 1967. It is governed by the Council of the European Union.

eureka model. (1993) *Patents.* The view that the inventive process is the product of a stroke of luck rather than labor. • The notion is used to counter labor-based theories justifying intellectual-property rights, since no labor is involved in a "eureka" discovery. Cf. LABOR–DESERT MODEL; VALUE-ADDED MODEL.

eureka moment. (1997) *Slang.* The instant when an inventor realizes the answer to a question or the significance of a discovery. — Also termed *flash of genius.*

Euribor. *abbr.* (1997) EURO INTERBANK OFFERED RATE.

euro (**yuur**-oh). (1981) The official currency of most countries in the European Union. • On January 1, 1999, the euro became the single currency of the participating countries. Euro notes and coins began circulating on January 1, 2002.

Eurodollar. (1960) United States currency held in a bank outside the U.S., usu. in Europe, and used to settle international transactions.

Euro Interbank Offered Rate. (1998) A measure of what major international banks charge each other for large-volume, short-term loans of euros, based on interest-rate data provided daily by a panel of representative banks across Europe. — Abbr. Euribor. Cf. LONDON INTERBANK OFFERED RATE.

European Commission of Human Rights. A body of the Council of Europe charged with overseeing the operation of the European Convention on Human Rights. • The commission was abolished in 1998. The European Court of Human Rights absorbed its functions. See EUROPEAN COURT OF HUMAN RIGHTS. — Abbr. ECHR.

European Community. See EUROPEAN UNION.

European Convention on Human Rights and Fundamental Freedoms. A 1950 international agreement to protect human rights. • The European Commission for Human Rights and the European Court for Human Rights were created under the convention's terms.

European Copyright Directive. An official instruction of the European Union designed to promote uniformity in certain aspects of copyright law and related rights, esp. on the Internet. • Officially titled Directive 2001/29 on the Harmonisation of Certain Aspects of Copyright and Related Rights in the Information Society, this is the

European Union equivalent of the Digital Millennium Copyright Act. Among other provisions, the directive provides broad exclusive rights of reproduction and distribution to copyright holders, and requires E.U. member countries to prohibit the circumvention of technical measures and devices intended to prevent the alteration or reproduction of copyrighted works.

European Court of Human Rights. The judicial body of the Council of Europe. • The court was set up in 1959 and was substantially changed in 1994–1998. As of 2008, the court had 47 judges, each elected by the Council of Europe's Parliamentary Assembly. The court adjudicates alleged violations of the civil and political rights enumerated in the Convention for the Protection of Human Rights and Fundamental Freedoms. — Abbr. ECHR.

European Court of Justice. A European Union court composed of one judge from each member country and several advocate judges, established to ensure that EU treaties and legislation are interpreted and applied consistently throughout the EU. — Abbr. ECJ. — Also termed *Court of Justice of the European Communities.*

European Currency Unit. A monetary unit that was the precursor of the euro. • Created in 1979, it was an artificial currency used by the members of the European Union as their internal accounting unit. It ceased to exist in January 1999, when it was replaced by the euro. — Abbr. ECU; ecu. See EURO.

European Economic Community. See EUROPEAN UNION.

European law. (1844) **1.** The law of the European Union. **2.** More broadly, the law of the European Union, together with the conventions of the Council of Europe, including the European Convention on Human Rights. **3.** More broadly still, all the law current in Europe, including the law of European organizations, the North Atlantic Treaty Organization, and all the bilateral and multilateral conventions in effect, as well as European customary law.

European option. See OPTION (5).

European Patent Convention. A 1973 treaty allowing a patent applicant to obtain patent protection in all signatory countries, mostly European Union members, through a single blanket filing and examination procedure. • The Community patent is valid in any member country in which it is registered. The procedure is administered through the European Patent Office in Munich, Germany and The Hague, Netherlands. — Abbr. EPC. — Also termed *Convention on the Grant of European Patent.*

European Patent Office. The office that receives filings, conducts examinations, and issues Community patents applied for under the European Patent Convention. • The office is located in Munich, Germany, and The Hague, Netherlands. — Abbr. EPO.

European Patent Organization. A centralized patent-grant system, established in 1978, comprising a legislative body (the Administrative Council) and an executive body (the European Patent Office).

European-style option. See *European option* under OPTION (5).

European Union. An association of European countries whose purpose is to achieve full economic unity (and eventual political union) by agreeing to eliminate barriers to the free movement of capital, goods, and labor among the member-countries. • The European Union was formed as the European Economic Community (EEC) by the Treaty of Rome in 1957, and later renamed the European Community (EC). The European Community became the European Union when the Maastricht Treaty on European Union took effect in November 1993. — Abbr. EU.

Eurozone. The parts of the European Union in which the euro is the standard currency.

> "Eurozone designates the EC Member States that have introduced the euro as their common currency; they form a separate zone. Seventeen states are currently members of this zone and comprise Austria, Belgium, Cyprus, Estonia, Finland, France, Germany, Greece, Ireland, Italy, Luxembourg, Malta, the Netherlands, Portugal, Slovakia, Slovenia and Spain. Denmark and the United Kingdom are exempt from introducing the euro as a result of the opt-out clauses that are to be found in protocols to the Treaty of Maastricht. The other EC Member States will introduce the euro as soon as the Council has established that they satisfy the conditions for sharing a single currency." Ninon Colneric, "European Community," in 1 *The Max Planck Encyclopedia of European Private Law* 565, 567 (Jürgen Basedow et al. eds., 2012).

euthanasia (yoo-thə-**nay**-zhə), *n.* (1869) The act or practice of causing or hastening the death of a person who suffers from an incurable or terminal disease or condition, esp. a painful one, for reasons of mercy. • Euthanasia is sometimes regarded by the law as second-degree murder, manslaughter, or criminally negligent homicide. In 2001, the Netherlands became the first country to legalize euthanasia. — Also termed *mercy killing.* See LIVING WILL; ADVANCE DIRECTIVE. Cf. *assisted suicide* under SUICIDE (1); DYATHANASIA. — **euthanasic** (yoo-thə-**nay**-zik), *adj.*

> "The translation of the Greek word *euthanasia* — 'easy death' — contains an ambiguity. It connotes that the means responsible for death are painless, so that the death is an easy one. But it also suggests that the death sought would be a relief from a distressing or intolerable condition of living (or dying), so that death, and not merely the means through which it is achieved, is good or right in itself. Usually, both aspects are intended when the term *euthanasia* is used; but when that is not the case, there can be consequences in legal analysis." Alexander Morgan Capron, "Euthanasia," in 2 *Encyclopedia of Crime and Justice* 709, 709 (Sanford H. Kadish ed., 1983).

▸ **active euthanasia.** (1954) Euthanasia performed by a facilitator (such as a healthcare practitioner) who not only provides the means of death but also carries out the final death-causing act; euthanasia committed through the use of techniques or instrumentalities for hastening death.

▸ **involuntary euthanasia.** (1950) Euthanasia of a competent, nonconsenting person; euthanasia that occurs when the person is capable of requesting to be killed but has not done so.

▸ **nonvoluntary euthanasia.** (1975) Euthanasia of an incompetent, and therefore nonconsenting, person; euthanasia that occurs when the person killed is incapable of either making or refusing to make a request to be killed.

> "The opinion of Judge Reinhardt for eight judges of the Ninth Circuit in *Compassion in Dying v Washington* uses the term 'euthanasia' in an almost uniquely eccentric way, as the *unrequested* putting to death of persons suffering from incurable and distressing disease. Almost all other English-speakers call that *non-voluntary euthanasia*, and so shall I. I shall assume Ronald Dworkin's agreement, since he defines euthanasia simply as 'deliberately killing a person

out of kindness' — not very serviceable as a legal definition, but compatible with common usage and not with the Ninth Circuit's. The official Dutch definition of 'euthanasia' is precisely opposite to the Ninth Circuit's, but equally eccentric: termination of life 'by someone other than the person concerned *upon the request of the latter*.' Almost everyone in the English-speaking world calls that '*voluntary euthanasia*,' and so shall I." John Finnis, *Human Rights and Common Good* 253 (2011) (citations omitted).

▸ **passive euthanasia.** (1968) The act of allowing a terminally ill person to die by either withholding or withdrawing life-sustaining support such as a respirator or feeding tube; euthanasia committed through omitting to supply sustenance or treatment that, but for the decision and intent to terminate life, would have been supplied.

▸ **voluntary euthanasia.** (1932) Euthanasia performed with the terminally ill person's consent; euthanasia that occurs after the person killed has requested to be killed.

euthanize (**yoo**-thə-nɪz), *vb.* (1873) To put to death by euthanasia. • This term is used chiefly in reference to animals. — Also termed *euthanatize.*

evacuee (ee-vak-yə-**wee**) (1886) Someone who has been evacuated, esp. because of a natural disaster or an imminent man-made danger, such as war. • This loanword from French dates from World War I. Cf. *displaced person* under PERSON (1); REFUGEE.

evaluative fact. See FACT.

evaluative mediation. See MEDIATION.

Evarts Act (**ev**-ərts). An 1891 federal statute that established the circuit courts of appeals (now U.S. courts of appeals) and fixed the contemporary method of federal appellate review.

evasion. 1. See TAX EVASION. **2.** See PLEADING (quot.).

evasive, *adj.* (17c) Tending or seeking to evade; elusive; shifting. • If a pleading requiring a response is evasive, the responding party may move for a more definite statement. Fed. R. Civ. P. 12(e).

evasive answer. See ANSWER (2).

even date. The same date. • This jargonistic phrase is sometimes used in one instrument to refer to another instrument with the same date, esp. when both relate to the same transaction (as a deed and a mortgage).

even-handed, *adj.* (17c) Fair and impartial; according fair and equal treatment to everyone alike.

evenings. (17c) *Hist.* The delivery at evening or night to a customary tenant of a gratuity in the form of a portion of the grass, corn, or other crop that the tenant cuts, mows, or reaps for the lord.

even lot. See *round lot* under LOT (3).

event-driven audit. See AUDIT.

eventuality. (18c) Something that might happen; a possibility, esp. a negative one.

evergreen contract. See CONTRACT.

evergreening, *n. Patents.* A strategy employed by a patent owner to retain royalties on a patent by extending the term on a patent that is about to expire.

evict, *vb.* (15c) **1.** To expel (a person, esp. a tenant), from real property, usu. by legal process. — Also termed *put out.* **2.** *Archaic.* To recover (property or title) from a person by legal process. — **evictor,** *n.*

eviction. (16c) The act or process of legally dispossessing a person of land or rental property. See FORCIBLE ENTRY AND DETAINER. Cf. EJECTMENT.

▸ **actual eviction.** (18c) A physical expulsion of a person from land or rental property.

▸ **constructive eviction.** (1826) **1.** A landlord's act of making premises unfit for occupancy, often with the result that the tenant is compelled to leave. **2.** The inability of a land purchaser to obtain possession because of paramount outstanding title. • Such an eviction usually constitutes a breach of the covenants of warranty and quiet enjoyment.

▸ **eviction by paramount title.** (1830) An eviction by judicially establishing title superior to that under which the possessor claims. — Also termed *eviction by title paramount.*

▸ **eviction by title paramount.** See *eviction by paramount title.*

▸ **partial eviction.** (18c) An eviction, either constructive or actual, from a portion of a tenant's premises.

▸ **retaliatory eviction.** (1966) An eviction — nearly always illegal — commenced in response to a tenant's complaints or involvement in activities with which the landlord does not agree.

▸ **summary eviction.** (1907) An eviction accomplished through a simplified legal procedure, without the formalities of a full trial.

▸ **total eviction.** (1832) An eviction that wholly deprives the tenant of any right in the premises.

evidence, *n.* (14c) **1.** Something (including testimony, documents, and tangible objects) that tends to prove or disprove the existence of an alleged fact; anything presented to the senses and offered to prove the existence or nonexistence of a fact <the bloody glove is the key piece of evidence for the prosecution>. **2.** See *fact in evidence* under FACT. **3.** The collective mass of things, esp. testimony and exhibits, presented before a tribunal in a given dispute <the evidence will show that the defendant breached the contract>. **4.** The body of law regulating the admissibility of what is offered as proof into the record of a legal proceeding <under the rules of evidence, the witness's statement is inadmissible hearsay that is not subject to any exception>. — Also termed (in sense 4) *rules of evidence; law of evidence.* — **evidence,** *vb.*

"Evidence is any matter of fact which is furnished to a legal tribunal, otherwise than by reasoning or a reference to what is noticed without proof, as the basis of inference in ascertaining some other matter of fact." James B. Thayer, *Presumptions and the Law of Evidence*, 3 Harv. L. Rev. 141, 142 (1889).

"The 'rules of evidence' are such precepts in the general subject of judicial administration as determine the manner in which a designated fact submitted to judicial decision may be proved; whether such a fact may be proved at all; if so, who are competent to prove it and under what conditions. In the aggregate, these rules constitute the 'law of evidence.'" 1 Charles Frederic Chamberlayne, *A Treatise on the Modern Law of Evidence* § 2, at 4 (1911).

"Evidence, broadly defined, is the means from which an inference may logically be drawn as to the existence of a fact; that which makes evident or plain. Evidence is the demonstration of a fact; it signifies that which demonstrates, makes clear, or ascertains the truth of the very fact or point in issue, either on the one side or on the other. In legal acceptation, the term 'evidence' includes all the means by which any alleged matter of fact, the truth of which is submitted to investigation, is established or disproved. 'Evidence' has also been defined to mean any species of proof legally presented at the trial of an issue, by the act of the parties and through the medium of witnesses, records, documents, concrete objects, and the like." 31A C.J.S. *Evidence* § 3, at 67–68 (1996).

▸ **adminicular evidence.** (1911) *Rare.* Corroborating or auxiliary evidence presented for the purpose of explaining or completing other evidence.

▸ **admissible evidence.** (18c) Evidence that is relevant and is of such a character (e.g., not unfairly prejudicial, based on hearsay, or privileged) that the court should receive it. — Also termed *competent evidence; proper evidence; legal evidence.*

▸ **autoptic evidence.** See *demonstrative evidence.*

▸ **background evidence.** (1939) Evidence that, being both relevant and explanatory of noncontroversial events — while not being unfairly prejudicial — is admitted to explain a sequence of events so as to minimize speculation by a fact-finder. • Background evidence is often said to "complete the narrative."

▸ **best evidence.** (17c) Evidence of the highest quality available, as measured by the nature of the case rather than the thing being offered as evidence. • The term is usu. applied to writings and recordings. If the original is available, it must be offered rather than a copy or oral rendition. Fed. R. Evid. 1002. — Also termed *primary evidence; original evidence.* See BEST-EVIDENCE RULE. Cf. *secondary evidence.*

"In some circumstances, 'best evidence' may mean that evidence which is more specific and definite as opposed to that which is merely general and indefinite or descriptive. However, 'best evidence' or 'primary evidence' is variously defined as that particular means of proof which is indicated by the nature of the fact under investigation as the most natural and satisfactory, or as that kind of proof which under any possible circumstances affords the greatest certainty of the fact in question; or as evidence which carries on its face no indication that better remains behind." 32A C.J.S. *Evidence* § 1054, at 417 (1996).

▸ **character evidence.** (1949) Evidence regarding someone's general personality traits or propensities, of a praiseworthy or blameworthy nature; evidence of a person's moral standing in a community. Fed. R. Evid. 404, 405, 608. • Character evidence is usu., but not always, prohibited if offered to show that the person acted in conformity with that character. Cf. *reputation evidence.*

▸ **circumstantial evidence.** (18c) **1.** Evidence based on inference and not on personal knowledge or observation. — Also termed *indirect evidence; oblique evidence.* Cf. *direct evidence* (1). **2.** All evidence that is not given by eyewitness testimony.

"*Indirect* evidence (called by the civilians, *oblique*, and more commonly known as *circumstantial* evidence) is that which is applied to the principal fact, indirectly, or through the medium of other facts, by establishing certain circumstances or minor facts, already described as evidentiary, from which the principal fact is extracted and gathered by a process of special inference . . . ." Alexander M. Burrill, *A Treatise on the Nature, Principles and Rules of Circumstantial Evidence* 4 (1868).

"Some circumstantial evidence is very strong, as when you find a trout in the milk." Henry David Thoreau, Journal, 11 Nov. 1850, in 2 *Journal of Henry D. Thoreau* 94 (Bradford Torrey & Francis H. Allen eds., 1962).

"Evidence of some collateral fact, from which the existence or non-existence of some fact in question may be inferred as a probable consequence, is termed circumstantial evidence." William P. Richardson, *The Law of Evidence* § 111, at 68 (3d ed. 1928).

"Testimonial evidence readily defines itself by its name; it is any assertion by a human being, offered to evidence the truth of the matter asserted. Circumstantial evidence is any and all other evidence. Scientifically the term 'circumstantial' is indefensible, for it does not correlate with 'testimonial'; a more correct equivalent would be 'nontestimonial.' But no one has yet invented an acceptable substitute for 'circumstantial.'" John H. Wigmore, *A Students' Textbook of the Law of Evidence* 38 (1935).

▸ **classified evidence.** Secret or confidential information that a party seeks to discover or present as evidence. See CLASSIFIED INFORMATION.

▸ **clear and convincing evidence.** (17c) Evidence indicating that the thing to be proved is highly probable or reasonably certain. • This is a greater burden than preponderance of the evidence, the standard applied in most civil trials, but less than evidence beyond a reasonable doubt, the norm for criminal trials. — Also termed *clear and convincing proof.* See REASONABLE DOUBT. Cf. PREPONDERANCE OF THE EVIDENCE.

▸ **communicative evidence.** See *testimonial evidence.*

▸ **competent evidence. 1.** See *admissible evidence.* **2.** See *relevant evidence.*

▸ **computer-generated evidence.** (1972) Evidence created by using a computer to provide a re-creation, simulation, or reconstruction of an event (usu. a crime scene or accident), esp. as it may be used as substantive evidence or as demonstrative evidence. • To be introduced as substantive evidence, it must be relevant, sufficiently reliable, and probative to a degree that outweighs the danger of unfair prejudice. As demonstrative evidence, it need only be helpful to understanding a witness's testimony and not be based on erroneous or misleading information. See ACCIDENT RECONSTRUCTION; CRIME-SCENE RE-CREATION. — Abbr. CGE.

▸ **conclusive evidence.** (17c) **1.** Evidence so strong as to overbear any other evidence to the contrary. — Also termed *conclusive proof.* **2.** Evidence that so preponderates as to oblige a fact-finder to come to a certain conclusion.

▸ **concomitant evidence.** (17c) Circumstantial evidence that, at the time of the act, the alleged doer of the act was present and actually did it.

▸ **conflicting evidence.** (1803) Evidence that comes from different sources and is often irreconcilable.

▸ **corroborating evidence.** (17c) Evidence that differs from but strengthens or confirms what other evidence shows (esp. that which needs support). — Also termed *corroborative evidence.* Cf. *cumulative evidence.*

▸ **credible evidence.** (17c) Evidence that is worthy of belief; trustworthy evidence.

▸ **critical evidence.** (18c) Evidence strong enough that its presence could tilt a juror's mind. • Under the Due Process Clause, an indigent criminal defendant is usu.

entitled to an expert opinion of the merits of critical evidence. — Also termed *crucial evidence.*

▸ **crucial evidence.** See *critical evidence.*

▸ **cumulative evidence.** (18c) Additional evidence that supports a fact established by the existing evidence (esp. that which does not need further support). Cf. *corroborating evidence.*

▸ **demeanor evidence.** (1909) The behavior and appearance of a witness on the witness stand, to be considered by the fact-finder on the issue of credibility.

▸ **demonstrative evidence** (di-**mon**-strə-tiv). (17c) Physical evidence that one can see and inspect (i.e. an explanatory aid, such as a chart, map, and some computer simulations) and that, while of probative value and usu. offered to clarify testimony, does not play a direct part in the incident in question. • This term sometimes overlaps with and is used as a synonym of real evidence. — Also termed *illustrative evidence; autoptic evidence; autoptic proference; real evidence; tangible evidence.* See *nonverbal testimony* under TESTIMONY. Cf. *real evidence; testimonial evidence.*

"There remains a source of proof, distinct from either circumstantial or testimonial evidence, viz., what the tribunal *sees or hears* by its own senses. Whether this should be termed 'evidence' or not is a question of words, open to difference of view. But it is universally conceded to be an available source of proof. Bentham's term for it, 'real evidence,' came into wide vogue, but is ambiguous. The term 'autoptic proference' (etymologically meaning 'showing to the tribunal's own vision') is preferable." John H. Wigmore, *A Students' Textbook of the Law of Evidence* 39 (1935).

▸ **derivative evidence.** (1961) Evidence that is later discovered by using evidence that was illegally obtained. • The evidence is inadmissible because of the primary taint unless it would inevitably have been discovered anyway. See EXCLUSIONARY RULE; FRUIT-OF-THE-POISONOUS-TREE DOCTRINE. Cf. *primary evidence* (2).

▸ **direct evidence.** (16c) **1.** Evidence that is based on personal knowledge or observation and that, if true, proves a fact without inference or presumption. — Also termed *positive evidence.* Cf. *circumstantial evidence; negative evidence.* **2.** See *original evidence* (1).

"As commonly used, direct evidence is the immediate perception of the tribunal or the statement of a witness as to the existence of a constituent fact." 1 Charles Frederic Chamberlayne, *A Treatise on the Modern Law of Evidence* § 15, at 16 (1911).

"A little reflection shows that no disputed case will ordinarily be proved solely by circumstantial or solely by testimonial evidence. Ordinarily there is evidence of *both kinds*. The matter has been obscured by the use of the term 'direct evidence,' — a term sometimes used to mean testimonial evidence in general, but sometimes also limited to apply only to testimony directly asserting the fact-in-issue. . . . The term 'direct' evidence has no utility." John H. Wigmore, *A Students' Textbook of the Law of Evidence* 40 (1935).

▸ **documentary evidence.** (18c) Evidence supplied by a writing or other document, which must be authenticated before the evidence is admissible.

▸ **downright evidence.** See DOWNRIGHT EVIDENCE.

▸ **epidemiological evidence.** Evidence based on studies of how a disease is caused, spread, and controlled in a population.

▸ **evidence aliunde.** See *extrinsic evidence* (1).

▸ **evidence-in-chief.** (18c) The collective evidence presented during a litigant's presentation of its case or defense. See CASE-IN-CHIEF.

▸ **exclusive evidence.** (18c) The only facts that have, or are allowed by law to have, any probative force at all on a particular matter in issue.

"[T]here is an important class of rules declaring certain facts to be exclusive evidence, none other being admissible. The execution of a document which requires attestation can be proved in no other way than by the testimony of an attesting witness, unless owing to the death or some other circumstance his testimony is unavailable. A written contract can generally be proved in no other way than by the production of the writing itself, whenever its production is possible." John Salmond, *Jurisprudence* 485 (Glanville L. Williams ed., 10th ed. 1947).

▸ **exculpatory evidence** (ek-**skəl**-pə-tor-ee). (18c) Evidence tending to establish a criminal defendant's innocence. Fed. R. Crim. P. 16. • The prosecution has a duty to disclose exculpatory evidence in its possession or control when the evidence may be material to the outcome of the case. See BRADY MATERIAL.

▸ **expert evidence.** (16c) Evidence about a scientific, technical, professional, or other specialized issue given by a person qualified to testify because of familiarity with the subject or special training in the field. — Also termed *expert testimony.* Fed. R. Evid. 702–705. See DAUBERT TEST.

▸ **extrajudicial evidence.** (18c) Evidence that does not come directly under judicial cognizance but nevertheless constitutes an intermediate link between judicial evidence and the fact requiring proof. • It includes all facts that are known to the tribunal only by way of inference from some form of judicial evidence. See JUDICIAL NOTICE. Cf. *judicial evidence.*

▸ **extrinsic evidence.** (17c) **1.** Evidence relating to a contract but not appearing on the face of the contract because it comes from other sources, such as statements between the parties or the circumstances surrounding the agreement. • Extrinsic evidence is usu. not admissible to contradict or add to the terms of an unambiguous document. — Also termed *extraneous evidence; parol evidence; evidence aliunde.* **2.** Evidence that is not legitimately before the court. Cf. *intrinsic evidence.* **3.** Evidence that is calculated to impeach a witness's credibility, adduced by means other than cross-examination of the witness. • The means may include evidence in documents and recordings and the testimony of other witnesses. *See* Fed. R. Evid. 608(b) & note.

"Under [Federal Rule of Evidence] 608(b), if the witness denies engaging in untruthful misconduct, the cross-examiner must 'take the witness' answer,' meaning the questioner may not introduce extrinsic evidence to contradict the witness' denial through other witness testimony or the introduction of impeaching documents, or indeed any other evidence than the cross-examination, even if the questioner waits until it is his turn to put on evidence." Paul F. Rothstein, *The Federal Rules of Evidence* 312 (3d ed. 2003).

▸ **eyewitness-identification evidence.** See *identification evidence.*

▸ **fabricated evidence.** (18c) False or deceitful evidence that is unlawfully created, usu. after the relevant event, in an attempt to achieve or avoid liability or conviction. — Also termed *fabricated fact.*

▸ **false evidence.** See *false testimony* under TESTIMONY.

▸ **forensic evidence.** (18c) Evidence used in court; esp., evidence arrived at by scientific means (as with nuclear or mitochondrial DNA, toxicological and chemical analysis), by interpretation of patterns (as with fingerprints, handwriting, etc.), or by a combination of experiential and scientific analysis (as with explosive and fire-debris analysis, blood-spatter analysis). — Also termed *forensic-science evidence.*

▸ **foundational evidence.** (1946) Evidence that determines the admissibility of other evidence.

▸ **404(b) evidence.** Evidence of a defendant's prior bad acts admitted as evidence to prove the defendant's motive, opportunity, intent, preparation, plan, knowledge, identity, absence of mistake, or lack of accident rather than to establish a proclivity toward bad character. • Generally, a prosecutor wishing to use this type of evidence must notify the defendant of that intention before the trial, but a judge may waive that requirement on a showing of good cause. — Also termed *uncharged-crimes evidence.*

▸ **fresh evidence.** (17c) **1.** Evidence that was not available at the time of a trial but merits requiring a new trial. **2.** New evidence discovered at any time before or after a trial. **3.** Evidence present at the time of an incident or investigation.

▸ **habit evidence.** (1921) Evidence of personal and organizational habits, which may (with or without corroboration) be admissible as a means of proving that conduct conformed to the habit or routine practice. Fed. R. Evid. 406.

▸ **hearsay evidence.** See HEARSAY.

▸ **hypnotically refreshed evidence.** See *hypnotically refreshed testimony* under TESTIMONY.

▸ **identification evidence.** (1925) An eyewitness's testimony about the identity of a crime's perpetrator. — Also termed *eyewitness-identification evidence.*

▸ **illegally obtained evidence.** (1924) Evidence obtained by violating a statute or a person's constitutional or other rights, esp. the Fourth Amendment guarantee against unreasonable search and seizure, the Fifth Amendment right to remain silent, or the Sixth Amendment right to counsel.

▸ **illustrative evidence.** See *demonstrative evidence.*

▸ **immaterial evidence.** (18c) **1.** Evidence lacking in probative value. **2.** Evidence offered to prove a matter that is not in issue.

▸ **impeachment evidence.** (1861) Evidence used to undermine a witness's credibility. Fed. R. Evid. 607–610.

▸ **impertinent evidence.** See *irrelevant evidence.*

▸ **incompetent evidence.** (18c) Evidence that is for any reason inadmissible.

▸ **incriminating evidence.** (1878) Evidence tending to establish guilt or from which a fact-trier can infer guilt.

▸ **inculpatory evidence** (in-**kəl**-pə-tor-ee). (1849) Evidence showing or tending to show one's involvement in a crime or wrong.

▸ **indirect evidence.** See *circumstantial evidence* (1).

▸ **indispensable evidence.** (18c) Evidence without which a particular fact cannot be proved.

▸ **individualized evidence.** (1985) Forensic evidence consisting in the matching of a specimen to a particular individual or other source (as with DNA, fingerprints, writing samples, tool marks, bite marks, and specimens such as hair).

▸ **insufficient evidence.** (17c) Evidence that is inadequate to prove or support a finding of something. • This term usu. describes a case that is not strong enough to even get to the fact-finder.

▸ **intrinsic evidence.** (17c) **1.** Evidence brought out by the examination of the witness testifying. **2.** Evidence existing within a writing. Cf. *extrinsic evidence* (2).

▸ **irrelevant evidence.** (18c) Evidence not tending to prove or disprove a matter in issue. Fed. R. Evid. 401–403. — Also termed *impertinent evidence.* See IRRELEVANT.

▸ **judicial evidence.** (17c) Evidence produced in court, consisting of all facts brought to the attention of or admitted into evidence before the tribunal. Cf. *extrajudicial evidence.*

▸ **legal evidence.** (17c) **1.** See *admissible evidence.* **2.** All admissible evidence, both oral and documentary, of such a character that it reasonably and substantially proves the point rather than merely raising suspicion or conjecture.

▸ **lifestyle evidence.** See LIFESTYLE EVIDENCE.

▸ **material evidence.** (17c) Evidence having some logical connection with the facts of the case or the legal issues presented. Cf. *relevant evidence*; *immaterial evidence.*

▸ **mathematical evidence.** (18c) **1.** Loosely, evidence that establishes its conclusions with absolute certainty. **2.** Evidence relating to mathematical or statistical matters, or probabilities.

▸ **mediate evidence.** See *secondary evidence.*

▸ **medical evidence.** (18c) Evidence furnished by a doctor, nurse, or other qualified medical person testifying in a professional capacity as an expert, or by a standard treatise on medicine or surgery.

▸ **moral evidence.** (17c) Loosely, evidence that depends on a belief, rather than complete and absolute proof. • Generally, moral evidence is testimonial.

▸ **multiple evidence.** (1926) Evidence with probative or other value on more than one issue but usu. admitted into evidence for one specific purpose. • Impeachment evidence, for example, may not be probative on a particular issue but may nonetheless affect the jury's perceptions of several issues.

▸ **negative evidence.** (17c) Evidence suggesting that an alleged fact does not exist, such as a witness's testifying that he or she did not see an event occur. • Negative evidence is generally regarded as weaker than positive evidence because a positive assertion that a witness saw an event is a stronger statement than an assertion that a witness did not see it. But a negative assertion will sometimes be considered positive evidence, depending on the witness's opportunity to see the event. For instance, testimony that the witness watched the entire game and saw no riot in the stands is stronger than testimony stating only that the witness did not see a riot. — Also termed *negative testimony.* Cf. *direct evidence* (1).

▸ **newly discovered evidence.** (18c) Evidence existing at the time of a motion or trial but then unknown to a party, who, upon later discovering it, may assert it as grounds for reconsideration or a new trial. *See* Fed. R. Civ. P. 60(b).

▸ **no evidence.** See NO EVIDENCE.

▸ **oblique evidence.** See *circumstantial evidence* (1).

▸ **opinion evidence.** (1955) A witness's belief, thought, inference, or conclusion concerning a fact or facts. Fed. R. Evid. 701–705. See OPINION (3); OPINION RULE.

"In a sense all testimony to matter of fact is opinion evidence; i.e. it is a conclusion formed from phenomena and mental impressions." James B. Thayer, *A Preliminary Treatise on Evidence at the Common Law* 524 (1898).

▸ **oral evidence.** See *testimonial evidence.*

▸ **original evidence.** (18c) **1.** A witness's statement that he or she perceived a fact in issue by one of the five senses, or that the witness was in a particular physical or mental state. — Also termed *direct evidence.* Cf. HEARSAY. **2.** See *best evidence.*

▸ **parol evidence** (pə-**rohl** *or* **par**-əl). (18c) **1.** Evidence of oral statements. **2.** See *extrinsic evidence* (1). See PAROL-EVIDENCE RULE.

"The Admission of parol Evidence to explain Doubts or Difficulties arising upon Instruments, has been for a long Time watched over by Courts of Justice with a jealous Eye; it is considered as an unfound Mode of Interpretation, and some of the modern Judges have expressed themselves of Opinion, that Justice would have been better and more fairly administered, if parol Evidence had never been admitted. But as the Province of Judges is merely to dispense the Law as they find it settled, and they have considered themselves bound to admit this Kind of Evidence in certain Cases in which it has been allowed and established by prior Adjudications. One of the Instances in which such Evidence has been admitted is, in Cases of *wrong* or *imperfect* Descriptions of Legatees, and to *ascertain* Legatees when their Names have been *misspelled*, or *mistaken*." R.S. Donnison Roper, *A Treatise upon the Law of Legacies* 21 (1800).

▸ **partial evidence.** (17c) Evidence that establishes one of a series of facts.

▸ **personal evidence.** See TESTIMONY.

▸ **positive evidence.** See *direct evidence* (1).

▸ **preappointed evidence.** (1850) Evidence prescribed in advance (as by statute) for the proof of certain facts.

▸ **preliminary evidence.** (18c) Evidence that is necessary to begin a hearing or trial and that may be received conditionally in anticipation of other evidence linking it to issues in the case. Fed. R. Evid. 104.

▸ **presumptive evidence.** (17c) **1.** Evidence deemed sufficient to establish another fact unless discredited by other evidence. **2.** *Archaic.* Circumstantial evidence as distinct from testimonial evidence. — Also termed *probable evidence.*

▸ **prima facie evidence** (**prɪ**-mə **fay**-shə). (18c) Evidence that will establish a fact or sustain a judgment unless contradictory evidence is produced.

"The legislative branch may create an evidential presumption, or a rule of 'prima facie' evidence, i.e., a rule which does not shut out evidence, but merely declares that certain conduct shall suffice as evidence until the opponent produces contrary evidence." John H. Wigmore, *A Students' Textbook of the Law of Evidence* 237 (1935).

▸ **primary evidence.** **1.** See *best evidence.* **2.** *Criminal procedure.* Evidence directly discovered in a search, as distinguished from derivative evidence later developed from that primary evidence. • If the search was illegal, whether the evidence is primary or derivative is part of the analysis for whether it must be excluded as fruit of the poisonous tree or allowed because it would inevitably have been discovered anyway. See PRIMARY-EVIDENCE RULE; INEVITABLE-DISCOVERY RULE. Cf. *derivative evidence.*

▸ **privileged evidence.** (1897) Evidence that is exempt from production to an opposing party or tribunal (with certain, limited exceptions) because it is covered by one or more statutory or common-law protections, such as the attorney–client privilege. See *privileged communication* under COMMUNICATION.

▸ **probable evidence.** See *presumptive evidence.*

▸ **probative evidence** (**proh**-bə-tiv). (1877) Evidence that tends to prove or disprove a point in issue. Cf. *relevant evidence.*

▸ **proffered evidence** (**prof**-ərd). (1904) **1.** Evidence that is offered to the court to obtain a ruling on its admissibility. **2.** Evidence whose admissibility depends on the existence or nonexistence of a preliminary fact.

▸ **proper evidence.** See *admissible evidence.*

▸ **prospectant evidence** (prə-**spek**-tənt). (1924) Circumstantial evidence existing before someone does an act and suggesting that the person might or might not do the act. • This evidence typically falls into any of five categories: (1) moral character or disposition, (2) physical and mental capacity, (3) habit or custom, (4) emotion or motive, and (5) plan, design, or intention.

"The first section of this chapter illustrates one of the classifications of circumstantial evidence adopted by Wigmore. His division of the subject into 'prospectant,' 'concomitant,' and 'retrospectant' evidence involves the use of strange words, but it has the merit of stressing the main types of argument by which the relevance of one fact to another may be established." Rupert Cross, *Evidence* 28 (3d ed. 1967).

▸ **Queen's evidence.** (17c) *English law.* Testimony provided by one criminal defendant, usu. under a promise of pardon, against another criminal defendant. — Also termed (when a king reigns) *King's evidence.* See *state's evidence.*

▸ **real evidence.** (17c) **1.** Physical evidence (such as clothing or a knife wound) that itself plays a direct part in the incident in question. — Also termed *physical evidence.* **2.** See *demonstrative evidence.*

"Anything which is believed for any other reason than that someone has said so, is believed on real evidence." John Salmond, *Jurisprudence* 480 (Glanville L. Williams ed., 10th ed. 1947).

▸ **rebuttal evidence.** (1859) Evidence offered to disprove or contradict the evidence presented by an opposing party. • Rebuttal evidence is introduced in the rebutting party's answering case; it is not adduced, e.g., through cross-examination during the case-in-chief of the party to be rebutted. — Also termed *rebutting evidence.*

▸ **relevant evidence.** (18c) Evidence tending to prove or disprove a matter in issue. • Relevant evidence is both probative and material and is admissible unless excluded by a specific statute or rule. Fed. R. Evid.

401–403. — Also termed *competent evidence.* Cf. *material evidence; probative evidence.*

▸ **reputation evidence.** (1888) Evidence of what one is thought by others to be. • Reputation evidence may be introduced as proof of character when character is in issue or is used circumstantially. Fed. R. Evid. 405(a). — Also termed *reputational evidence.* Cf. *character evidence.*

▸ **retrospectant evidence** (re-trə-**spek**-tənt). (1929) Circumstantial evidence that, although it occurs after an act has been done, suggests that the alleged doer of the act actually did it <when goods have been stolen, and the thief is sought, a person's later possession of those goods amounts to retrospectant evidence that this person took them>. — Also termed *traces.* Cf. *prospectant evidence.*

▸ **satisfactory evidence.** (17c) Evidence that is sufficient to satisfy an unprejudiced mind seeking the truth. — Also termed *sufficient evidence; satisfactory proof.*

▸ **scientific evidence.** (17c) Fact or opinion evidence that purports to draw on specialized knowledge of a science or to rely on scientific principles for its evidentiary value. See DAUBERT TEST.

▸ **secondary evidence.** (17c) Evidence that is inferior to the primary or best evidence and that becomes admissible when the primary or best evidence is lost or inaccessible. • Examples include a copy of a lost instrument or testimony regarding a lost instrument's contents. — Also termed *mediate evidence; mediate testimony; substitutionary evidence. See* Fed. R. Evid. 1004. Cf. *best evidence.*

▸ **secondhand evidence.** See HEARSAY.

▸ **secret evidence.** (1983) Classified information that may be used against a defendant in an immigration proceeding but withheld from the defendant, the defendant's lawyer, and the public on national-security grounds. • The use of secret evidence was made easier under the Anti-Terrorism and Effective Death Penalty Act of 1996.

▸ **signature evidence.** (1987) Highly distinctive evidence of a person's prior bad acts. • While ordinarily inadmissible, signature evidence will be admitted if it shows, for example, that two crimes were committed through the same planning, design, scheme, or modus operandi, and in such a way that the prior act and the current act are uniquely identifiable as those of the defendant. *See* Fed. R. Evid. 404(b).

▸ **slight evidence.** (18c) A small quantity of evidence; esp., the small amount of evidence sufficient to remove a presumption from a case or for a rational fact-finder to conclude that something essential has not been established beyond a reasonable doubt. See SLIGHT-EVIDENCE RULE.

▸ **social-framework evidence.** (1988) Evidence derived from social-science research to help determine factual issues in a specific case. • Examples are testimony about eyewitness inaccuracy based on studies of human memory, the likelihood of a defendant's being a threat to society in the future based on studies of other individuals convicted of similar crimes and their subsequent behavior, and testimony about battering and its effects. *See* W. Laurens Walker and John Monahan, *Social Frameworks: A New Use of Social Science in Law,* 73 Va. L. Rev. 559, 559–70 (1987). Social-framework evidence has been widely admitted in courts around the country.

▸ **state's evidence.** (1886) Testimony provided by one criminal defendant — under a promise of immunity or reduced sentence — against another criminal defendant. See TURN STATE'S EVIDENCE.

▸ **subsequent-act evidence.** (1979) *Criminal law.* Evidence of a criminal defendant's bad behavior after the alleged commission of an offense, admissible under Federal Rule of Evidence 404(b) if the behavior is relevant to intent, motive, opportunity, identity, or the absence of mistake or accident.

▸ **substantial evidence.** (17c) **1.** Evidence that a reasonable mind could accept as adequate to support a conclusion; evidence beyond a scintilla. See SUBSTANTIAL-EVIDENCE RULE. **2.** The product of adequately controlled investigations, including clinical studies, carried out by qualified experts that establish the effectiveness of a drug under FSA regulations. 21 USCA § 355(e).

▸ **substantive evidence** (**səb**-stən-tiv). (18c) Evidence offered to help establish a fact in issue, as opposed to evidence directed to impeach or to support a witness's credibility.

▸ **substitutionary evidence.** See *secondary evidence.*

▸ **sufficient evidence.** See *satisfactory evidence.*

▸ **suspect evidence.** (1952) Evidence that is admissible but of a type that may turn out to be incorrect or untrue. • For example, evidence given by an accomplice is suspect because the accomplice may want to shift blame to the defendant.

▸ **tainted evidence.** (1876) Evidence that is inadmissible because it was directly or indirectly obtained by illegal means. See FRUIT-OF-THE-POISONOUS-TREE DOCTRINE.

▸ **tangible evidence.** (18c) Physical evidence that is either real or demonstrative. See *demonstrative evidence; real evidence.*

▸ **testimonial evidence.** (1831) A person's testimony offered to prove the truth of the matter asserted; esp., evidence elicited from a witness. — Also termed *communicative evidence; oral evidence.* Cf. *demonstrative evidence.*

> "An assertion is testimonial evidence whether made out of court or in court, if it is offered with a view to persuading the tribunal of the matter asserted." John H. Wigmore, *A Students' Textbook of the Law of Evidence* 120 (1935).

▸ **traditionary evidence.** (18c) Evidence derived from a deceased person's former statements or reputation. • Traditionary evidence is admissible to prove ancestry, ancient boundaries, or similar facts, usu. when no living witnesses are available to testify.

> "Traditionary evidence as to rights, or declarations as to pedigree, must be derived from those persons who were in a situation to know what the rights were, or, in the latter case, from such as were connected with the family." 1 Thomas Starkie, *A Practical Treatise on the Law of Evidence* 62 (2d Am. ed. 1828).

▸ **uncharged-crimes evidence.** See *404(b) evidence.*

▸ **unwritten evidence.** (18c) Evidence given orally, in court or by deposition.

evidence by inspection. See *demonstrative evidence* under EVIDENCE.

evidence code. (1877) A relatively comprehensive set of statutory provisions or rules governing the admissibility of evidence at hearings and trials.

evidence in chief. See EVIDENCE.

evidence of debt. See SECURITY (4).

evidence of indebtedness. See SECURITY (4).

evidence of insurability. (1905) Information — such as medical records or a medical examination — that an insurer may require to establish a potential insured's qualification for a particular insurance policy.

evidence of title. (17c) The means by which the ownership of land is satisfactorily demonstrated within a given jurisdiction. See DEED (2), (3).

> "There are four kinds of evidence of title: *abstract and opinion, certificate of title, title insurance* and *Torrens certificate*. The certificate of title is used extensively in the Eastern states, and some Southern states. In urban centers in a great many sections of the country, title insurance occupies a dominant position in real estate transactions. In farm areas the abstract and opinion method is common. To a great extent, the acceptability of a particular kind of evidence of title depends on the local custom." Robert Kratovil, *Real Estate Law* 170 (6th ed. 1974).

evidence locker. See PROPERTY ROOM.

evidence room. See PROPERTY ROOM.

evidence rules. See EVIDENCE (4).

evidencing feature. (1973) *Evidence.* A group of circumstances that, when taken as a whole, form a composite feature that can be reliably associated with a single object. • This term appears more frequently in criminal cases than in civil. In criminal cases, it usu. refers to evidence that establishes a perpetrator's identity, but in civil cases it often refers to evidence that an event did or did not occur. — Also termed *evidencing mark*; *evidential mark.*

evidencing mark. See EVIDENCING FEATURE.

evidentia (ev-i-**den**-shee-ə), *n.* [Law Latin] Evidence.

evidential, *adj.* (17c) Of, relating to, relying on, or constituting evidence; EVIDENTIARY (1).

evidential burden. See BURDEN OF PROOF (1).

evidential fact. See *evidentiary fact* (2) under FACT.

evidential mark. See EVIDENCING FEATURE.

evidential uncertainty. See UNCERTAINTY.

evidentiary (ev-i-**den**-shə-ree), *adj.* (1810) **1.** Having the quality of evidence; constituting evidence; evidencing. **2.** Of, relating to, or involving the rules of evidence or the evidence in a particular case.

evidentiary burden. See BURDEN OF PROOF (1).

evidentiary error. See ERROR (2).

evidentiary fact. See FACT.

evidentiary hearing. See HEARING; ADMINISTRATIVE PROCEEDING.

evidentiary privilege. See PRIVILEGE (3).

evildoer. (14c) Someone who commits crimes or engages in heinous acts, esp. terrorism; one who engages in gross wrongdoing. — **evildoing,** *n.*

evil-minded, *adj.* (16c) Having a wicked disposition or malicious thoughts; esp., immoral and cruel in such a way as to be likely to cause harm or injury.

evince, *vb.* (17c) To show, indicate, or reveal <in abstaining from the vote, Hariden evinced misgivings about the nomination>.

evocation (ev-ə-**kay**-shən). (17c) *French law.* The act of withdrawing a case from an inferior court and bringing it before a superior court.

evocative mark. See *suggestive trademark* under TRADEMARK.

evocative trademark. See *suggestive trademark* under TRADEMARK.

evolution statute. See ANTI-EVOLUTION STATUTE.

ewage (**yoo**-ij), *n.* [Law French] (18c) *Hist.* A toll paid for water passage.

EWC. *abbr.* ENDANGERING THE WELFARE OF A CHILD.

EWOC. *abbr.* ENDANGERING THE WELFARE OF A CHILD.

ex. (18c) **1.** Former <ex-wife>. **2.** Without <ex rights>. **3.** From <*ex cathedra*>. **4.** (*usu. cap.*) *abbr.* Exhibit <Ex. 4>. **5.** *abbr.* Example <this is but one ex. of several that might be cited>. **6.** (*cap.*) *abbr.* EXCHEQUER.

ex abundanti (eks ab-ən-**dan**-tɪ). [Latin "out of abundance"] *Archaic.* Abundantly; superfluously.

ex abundanti cautela (eks ab-ən-**dan**-tɪ kaw-**tee**-lə). [Latin] *Archaic.* Out of abundant caution; to be on the safe side.

exacerbate (ig-**zas**-ər-bayt), *vb.* (17c) To make worse; specif., to render more violent, severe, or seriously upsetting.

exacta diligentia. See DILIGENTIA.

exaction, *n.* (15c) **1.** The act of demanding more money than is due; extortion. **2.** A fee, reward, or other compensation, whether properly, arbitrarily, or wrongfully demanded. — **exact,** *vb.*

▸ **land-use exaction.** (1988) A requirement imposed by a local government that a developer dedicate real property for a public facility or pay a fee to mitigate the impacts of the project, as a condition of receiving a discretionary land-use approval. • A land-use exaction confers a public benefit, such as an easement or the payment of an impact fee, and is demanded by government from real-estate developers in exchange for the grant of a development permit. The U.S. Supreme Court has held that an exaction is a compensable taking under the Fifth Amendment unless the benefit exacted serves the same governmental purpose as the development restriction and imposes on the developer a burden roughly proportionate to the public harm the development will cause. *Nollan v. California Coastal Comm'n*, 43 U.S. 825 (1987); *Dolan v. City of Tigard*, 512 U.S. 374 (1994).

exactor. (16c) **1.** *Civil law.* A tax collector; a gatherer or receiver of money. **2.** *Hist.* A collector of public funds; a tax collector.

exact performance. See PERFORMANCE (1).

ex adverso (eks ad-**vər**-soh). [Latin] On the other side. • This term is sometimes applied to opposing counsel.

ex aequitate (eks ee-kwə-**tay**-tee). [Latin] According to equity; in equity.

ex aequo et bono (eks **ee**-kwoh et **boh**-noh). [Latin] According to what is equitable and good. • A decision-maker (esp. in international law) who is authorized to decide *ex aequo et bono* is not bound by legal rules and may instead follow equitable principles. For example, article 38(2) of the Statute of the International Court of Justice provides that the Court may "decide a case *ex aequo et bono* if the parties agree thereto." 37 ILM 999.

> "A long-standing debate surrounds whether *amiable composition* amounts to the same thing as decision-making *ex aequo et bono*, according to the 'right and good.' While the two notions are often used interchangeably, they may not be coextensive in all minds. Arbitrators who decide *ex aequo et bono* normally begin and end with a private sense of justice, going directly to a personal view of the right result. With *amiable composition* another option would present itself, directing arbitrators to start at rules of law, but depart only if needed to achieve a just result. The difference is significant, given that there is nothing inherently unjust [a]bout most norms of commercial law." William W. Park, *Arbitrators and Accuracy*, 1 J. Int'l Disp. Settlement 25, 50–51 (2010).

ex-all. Without all rights and privileges. • Securities sold ex-all reserve all rights and privileges, such as pending dividends, to the seller.

ex altera parte (eks **al**-tər-ə [*or* **awl**-] **pahr**-tee). [Latin] Of the other part.

examen (eg-**zay**-mən), *n.* [Law Latin] A trial; investigation.

examen computi (eg-**zay**-mən kəm-**pyoo**-tɪ). [Latin] The balance of an account.

examination. (14c) **1.** The questioning of a witness under oath. See DIRECT EXAMINATION; CROSS-EXAMINATION. **2.** *Bankruptcy.* The questioning of a debtor, esp. at the first meeting of creditors, concerning such matters as the bankrupt's debts and assets. **3.** An inquiry made at the U.S. Patent and Trademark Office, upon application for a patent, into the alleged invention's novelty and utility, and whether it interferes with any other pending application or in-force patent.

▸ **preliminary examination.** (1894) *Patents.* A patent office's initial review of an application, usu. to see whether the specification is properly set out and to prepare a search report.

4. *Banking.* The government's fact-finding mechanism for determining the soundness of a bank's finances and management. **5.** *Insurance.* A periodic investigation by a state insurance commission into the affairs and soundness of an insurance company licensed in that state. **6.** PRELIMINARY HEARING. **7.** A test, such as a bar examination. **8.** A close look at a person or thing to determine its condition.

▸ **mental examination.** *Criminal law.* An analysis performed by a mental-health professional to determine a defendant's mental state; esp., an examination of someone by a psychiatrist or psychologist to ascertain whether the person is or was mentally sound at a particular time and, if not, whether the condition is treatable. • A defendant in a criminal prosecution may undergo such an examination to determine competency to stand trial or to establish a defense based on some mental condition, such as insanity. — Also termed *mental evaluation*; (more narrowly) *psychiatric examination* or *psychiatric evaluation*. See INSANITY DEFENSE; COMPETENCY (2). Cf. *competency proceeding* under PROCEEDING; SUBSTANTIAL-CAPACITY TEST; INDEPENDENT MENTAL EVALUATION.

▸ **physical examination.** An examination of a person's body by a medical professional to determine whether the person is healthy, ill, or disabled.

▸ **postmortem examination.** See AUTOPSY (1).

▸ **psychiatric examination.** (1912) See *mental examination.*

examination before trial. See DEPOSITION (1).

examination-in-chief. See DIRECT EXAMINATION.

examination of title. See ABSTRACT OF TITLE.

examination on the voir dire. See VOIR DIRE.

examination *pro interesse suo* (**proh** in-tər-**es**-ee s[y]**oo**-oh). [Latin "according to his interest"] (1852) A judicial inquiry into the merits of a person's claim to sequestered property.

> "In practice, an examination pro interesse suo is an inquiry described as follows: When any person claims to be entitled to an estate or other property sequestered, whether by mortgage or judgment, lease or otherwise, or has a title paramount to the sequestration, he should apply to the court to direct an inquiry whether the applicant has any and what interest in the property sequestered." 79A C.J.S. *Sequestration* § 31, at 589 (1995).

examination system. (1899) *Patents.* A patent system in which an invention is subjected to official scrutiny to determine whether it qualifies for patent protection. Cf. REGISTRATION SYSTEM.

examined copy. See COPY (1).

examiner. (16c) **1.** One authorized to conduct an examination; esp., a person appointed by the court, esp. a court of equity, to administer an oath and take testimony. — Also formerly termed *examiner in chancery.* See MASTER (2). **2.** A patent officer responsible for determining the patentability of an invention submitted to the patent office. **3.** MEDICAL EXAMINER. **4.** BANK EXAMINER.

examiner in chancery. See EXAMINER (1).

examiner-in-chief. (1861) *Hist. Patents.* **1.** A member of the quasi-judicial body in the U.S. Patent and Trademark Office that formerly heard appeals of interference decisions and patent-application rejections. **2.** (*pl. cap.*) The body comprising those members; the predecessor of the Board of Appeals, the Board of Patent Interferences, and the present-day Board of Patent Appeals and Interferences.

examiner's amendment. (1923) *Patents & Trademarks.* Minor changes in the form of a patent or trademark application, made by the examiner rather than the applicant. • For example, the examiner may correct spelling and grammar rather than wait for the applicant to respond. A patent examiner may also amend or cancel claims if authorized by the applicant.

examiner's answer. (1911) *Patents.* The brief filed by a patent examiner with the Board of Patent Appeals and Interferences to rebut the arguments in an appeal brief and to defend the examiner's decision to reject the application. Cf. *appeal brief* under BRIEF (1).

examining authority. See AUTHORITY (3).

examining board. (1851) An appointed group of public officials responsible for conducting the tests required by those applying for occupational and professional licenses. — Also termed *board of examiners.*

examining court. See COURT.

examining group. (1938) *Patents.* A subunit of the Patent Office consisting of patent examiners who specialize in a particular area of technology.

examining trial. See PRELIMINARY HEARING.

example. *Patents.* A detailed description of an invention's embodiment. • Alternatives without detail may be referred to as *by example.* — Also termed *specific example; working example.*

exannual roll (eks-**an**-yoo-əl). (17c) *Hist. English law.* In England, a roll into which illeviable fines and desperate debts were transcribed and that was annually read to the sheriff upon his accounting to see what might be gotten.

ex ante (eks **an**-tee), *adj.* & *adv.* [Latin "from before"] (1937) Based on assumption and prediction, on how things appeared beforehand, rather than in hindsight; subjective; prospective <from an *ex ante* perspective>. Cf. EX POST.

ex arbitrio judicis (eks ahr-**bi**-tree-oh **joo**-di-sis). [Latin] *Civil law.* At, from, or upon the discretion of the judge.

exarch (**ek**-sahrk), *n.* **1.** *Hist.* A viceroy; esp., a provincial governor of the Byzantine Empire. **2.** *Eccles. law.* A patriarch's deputy, usu. a bishop, who visits the clergy, investigates ecclesiastical cases, and handles other church matters.

exarchate (ek-**sahr**-kət), *n.* An exarch's office, official dignity, or jurisdiction.

ex assensu curiae (eks ə-**sen**-s[y]oo **kyoor**-ee-ee *or* -ɪ). [Latin] By or with the consent of the court.

ex assensu patris (eks ə-**sen**-s[y]oo **pay**-tris). [Latin "by or with the consent of the father"] *Hist.* A species of dower *ad ostium ecclesiae,* under which a husband, by his father's express consent, would endow his wife with a parcel of the father's lands. • This type of dower was abolished in England by the Dower Act (1833). St. 3 & 4 Will. 4, ch. 105, § 13.

ex assensu suo (eks ə-**sen**-s[y]oo **s[y]oo**-oh). [Latin "with his assent"] Formal words in a default judgment for damages.

ex auditu (eks **aw**-di-t[y]oo). [Latin] *Hist.* By hearsay; by report.

ex bonis (eks **boh**-nis). [Latin] *Civil law.* Of, relating to, or involving goods or property.

ex bonis maternis (eks **boh**-nis mə-**tər**-nis). [Latin] *Hist.* Out of the goods succeeded to through the mother.

ex bonis paternis (eks **boh**-nis pə-**tər**-nis). [Latin] *Hist.* Out of the goods succeeded to through the father.

excambiator (eks-kam-bee-**ay**-tər), *n.* [Latin] (17c) *Hist.* An exchanger of lands; a broker.

excambion (eks-**kam**-bee-ahn), *n.* (16c) *Scots law.* **1.** The exchange of one piece of property for another, esp. an exchange of heritable estates. **2.** EXCAMBIUM (1).

excambium (eks-**kam**-bee-əm), *n.* [Latin] (16c) **1.** An exchange; a place where merchants meet to transact their business. — Also termed (in Scots law) *excambion.* **2.** An equivalent in recompense; a recompense in lieu of dower *ad ostium ecclesiae.*

ex capite (eks **kap**-i-tee). [Latin] On the ground of; by reason of. See LIEGE POUSTIE.

ex capite doli (eks **kap**-i-tee **doh**-lɪ). [Law Latin] *Hist.* On the ground of dole; for the reason of fraud. — Also termed *ex capite fraudis.*

ex capite inhibitionis (eks **kap**-i-tee in-hi-bish-ee-**oh**-nis). [Law Latin] *Scots law.* On the ground of inhibition. See INHIBITION (4).

ex capite interdictionis (eks **kap**-i-tee in-tər-dik-shee-**oh**-nis). [Law Latin] *Hist.* On the ground of interdiction. See INTERDICTION.

ex capite lecti (eks **kap**-i-tee **lek**-tɪ). [Law Latin] *Scots law.* On the ground of deathbed. • Under some circumstances, a legal heir could overturn a deed that a grantor made to the heir's detriment if the deed were made within 60 days before the grantor's death.

ex capite metus (eks **kap**-i-tee **mee**-təs). [Law Latin] *Scots law.* On the ground of fear. • A transaction could be rescinded if it were induced by serious threats.

ex capite minorennitatis et laesionis (eks **kap**-i-tee min-or-en-i-**tay**-tis et lee-z[h]ee-**oh**-nis). [Law Latin] *Scots law.* On the ground of minority and lesion. • The phrase appeared in reference to a ground upon which a minor could be restored against deeds granted by him during his minority. The phrase also referred to a basis on which a minor could set aside a deed (on the ground of lesion) if the deed were substantially onerous.

ex cathedra (eks kə-**thee**-drə *or* **kath**-ə-drə), *adv.* & *adj.* [Latin "from the chair"] (17c) By virtue of one's high office or position; with authority <ex cathedra pronouncements>.

ex causa (eks **kaw**-zə). [Latin] By title.

ex causa lucrativa (eks **kaw**-zə loo-krə-**tɪ**-və). [Latin] *Hist.* From a lucrative source; gratuitously.

ex causa mandati (eks **kaw**-zə man-**day**-tɪ). [Latin] *Scots law.* On account of the mandate; because of the mandate.

> "A mandatory is entitled to claim from the mandant reimbursement of all moneys disbursed, as well as relief from all obligations incurred, *ex causa mandati* — i.e., on account of the matter which the mandate authorised to be done or performed." John Trayner, *Trayner's Latin Maxims* 195 (4th ed. 1894).

ex causa potestatis (eks **kaw**-zə poh-tes-**tay**-tis). *Roman law.* Because of his position of authority. • Certain men could not marry women who were subject to their guardianship or control, and the reason was said to be *ex causa potestatis.*

> "Certain impediments to marriage in the civil law were described as being *ex causa potestatis.* Thus a tutor or curator could not marry his female ward until his office had terminated, or unless his accounts had been passed. A person administering a government or public office in a province, and the members of his family, were not permitted to intermarry with a person domiciled in his province, unless they had been betrothed to each other before he had accepted the office." Alexander Wood Renton & George Grenville Phillimore, *The Comparative Law of Marriage and Divorce* 6 (1910).

excellency. (*usu. cap.*) (16c) A title of honor given to certain high officials or dignitaries, such as governors, ambassadors, and Roman Catholic bishops or archbishops.

***Excelsior* list.** (1967) *Labor law.* A roster of the names and addresses of employees who are eligible to vote in a union election. • The NLRB requires an employer to file the list within seven days after the employer and a union reach a consent-election agreement. *Excelsior Underwear, Inc.,* 156 NLRB 1236 (1966).

exceptio (ek-**sep**-shee-oh), *n.* [Latin] *Hist.* **1.** An exception, plea, or objection. **2.** *Roman & civil law.* A defendant's plea admitting the claim in principle but alleging facts or legal provisions that negate it in this instance. **3.** A defense to a claim that is justly brought but that unjustly accuses the particular defendant named. Pl. ***exceptiones*** (ek-sep-shee-**oh**-neez).

▸ ***exceptio dilatoria*** (dil-ə-**tor**-ee-ə). (17c) A dilatory exception; an exception that defeated the action for a time and created a delay, such as an agreement not to sue within a certain time.

▸ ***exceptio doli mali*** (**doh**-lɪ **mal**-ɪ). An exception, defense, or plea of fraud. — Sometimes shortened to *exceptio doli.*

▸ ***exceptio dominii*** (də-**min**-ee-ɪ). A claim of ownership by the defendant in an action to recover property.

▸ ***exceptio dotis cautae non numeratae*** (**doh**-tis **kaw**-tee non n[y]oo-mə-**ray**-tee). A defense to an action for the restitution of dowry, asserting that, although promised, dowry was never paid.

▸ ***exceptio in factum*** (in **fak**-təm). An exception on the facts; an exception or plea founded on the peculiar circumstances of a case.

▸ ***exceptio in personam*** (in pər-**soh**-nəm). A plea or defense of a personal nature that only the person to whom it is granted by law may assert.

▸ ***exceptio in rem*** (in **rem**). A plea or defense that is not of a personal nature but is connected with the legal circumstances on which the suit is founded, and that may therefore be alleged by any party in interest, such as an heir or surety of the proper or original debtor.

▸ ***exceptio jurisjurandi*** (**joor**-is-juu-**ran**-dɪ). An exception of oath; an exception or plea that the matter had been sworn to. • This kind of exception was allowed if a debtor, at a creditor's instance, had sworn that nothing was due the creditor, but the creditor sued anyway.

▸ ***exceptio metus*** (**met**-əs). An exception, defense, or plea of fear or compulsion.

▸ ***exceptio non adimpleti contractus*** (non ad-im-**plee**-tɪ kən-**trak**-təs). An exception in a contract action involving mutual duties or obligations, to the effect that the plaintiff may not sue if the plaintiff's own obligations have not been performed.

▸ ***exceptio non numeratae pecuniae*** (ek-**sep**-shee-oh non n[y]oo-mə-**ray**-tee pi-**kyoo**-nee-ee). [Latin] *Roman law.* An exception or defense that money was not paid.

> "This was one of the Roman law exceptions, founded on the *obligatio literarum* of the Romans. The *obligatio literarum* was constituted by a writing, the granter of which acknowledged receipt from the creditor of a certain sum of money. But as the obligation was sometimes granted before the money was advanced, *spe numerandae pecuniae*, by the Roman law, the obligation, until the lapse of two years after its date and delivery, did not prove the receipt of the money; and the debtor against whom, within that time, a demand for repayment was made, might plead the *exceptio non numeratae pecuniae*; that is, that the money of which repayment was demanded, was truly never advanced. The exception was sufficient to elide the demand, unless the creditor proved that he had advanced the money." William Bell, *Bell's Dictionary and Digest of the Law of Scotland* 426 (George Watson ed., 7th ed. 1890).

▸ ***exceptio non solutae pecuniae*** (non sə-**loo**-tee pi-**kyoo**-nee-ee). A plea that the debt at issue in the suit had not been discharged by payment (as the adverse party alleged), notwithstanding the existence of a receipt or acquittance reflecting payment. Cf. *exception pecuniae non numeratae.*

▸ ***exceptio pacti conventi*** (**pak**-tɪ-kən-**ven**-tɪ). An exception of compact; a defense or plea that the plaintiff had agreed not to sue.

▸ ***exceptio pecuniae non numeratae*** (pi-**kyoo**-nee-ee non n[y]oo-mə-**ray**-tee). An exception or plea of money not paid; a defense by a party who was sued on a promise to repay money that was never received from the plaintiff. Cf. *exceptio non solutae pecuniae; pecunia non numerata* under PECUNIA.

▸ ***exceptio peremptoria*** (pər-emp-**tor**-ee-ə). (18c) A peremptory exception that forever destroyed the subject matter or ground of the action, such as the *exceptio doli mali* and the *exceptio metus.* — Also termed *exceptio perpetua.*

▸ ***exceptio plurium concubentium*** (**ploor**-ee-əm kon-kyoo-**ben**-shee-əm). *Rare.* The plea or defense in a paternity action that the plaintiff had several lovers around the time of conception.

▸ ***exceptio rei judicatae*** (**ree**-ɪ joo-də-**kay**-tee). (17c) An exception or plea of matter adjudged; a plea that the subject matter of the action had been determined in a previous action.

▸ ***exceptio rei venditae et traditae*** (**ree**-ɪ **ven**-də-tee et **trad**-ə-tee). An exception or plea of the sale and delivery [of a thing]. • This exception presumes a valid sale but, because no one can transfer a right greater than what is possessed, no valid transfer of property occurred, yet the real owner is nonetheless estopped from contesting the sale.

▸ ***exceptio senatusconsulti Macedoniani*** (sə-**nay**-təs-kən-**səl**-tɪ mas-ə-doh-nee-**ay**-nɪ). A defense to an action for the recovery of money loaned, on the ground that the loan was made to a person who was under another person's paternal power. • This defense is so named from the decree of the senate that forbade the recovery of such loans.

▸ ***exceptio senatusconsulti Velleiani*** (sə-**nay**-təs-kən-**səl**-tɪ vel-ee-**ay**-nɪ). A defense to an action on a contract of suretyship, on the ground that the surety was a woman and thus incapable of becoming bound for another. • This defense is so named from the decree of the senate forbidding such sureties.

▸ ***exceptio temporis*** (**tem**-pə-ris). (18c) An exception or plea that the time prescribed by law for bringing a particular action has expired.

exception, *n.* (14c) **1.** A formal objection to a court's ruling by a party who wants to preserve an overruled objection or rejected proffer for appeal <the prosecutor stated her exception to the court's ruling disallowing the witness's testimony>. • To make an exception or objection, attorneys sometimes say, "I except" or "I object." *Exception* properly refers only to an objection made after an initial objection or proffer is made and overruled. In most courts, an exception is no longer required to preserve the initial objection.

> The following quotation reflects former practice: "The exception must be distinguished from the objection. Many counsel are heard carelessly saying 'I except' when the thing they are doing is 'I object.' The exception serves an entirely distinct purpose from the objection, — a double purpose, in fact. It warns the judge and the other party that the excepter is not satisfied with the ruling and takes issue with a view to appeal; and it sums up and preserves the precise terms of the ruling. The proponent of the evidence

is the excepter if the ruling excludes the evidence; but if it admits the evidence, the opponent of the evidence is the excepter. Thus the excepter and the objector are not necessarily the same parties." John H. Wigmore, *A Students' Textbook of the Law of Evidence* 421 (1935).

▸ **catchall exception.** A broad exception to the hearsay rule, provided for in another rule of evidence. — Also termed *residual exception.*

▸ **declinatory exception** (di-**klɪn**-ə-tor-ee). (1829) *Louisiana law.* An exception to a court's jurisdiction. • Grounds for refusing to submit to a court's jurisdiction include lack of personal jurisdiction and insufficient service of process.

▸ **dilatory exception** (**dil**-ə-tor-ee). (1822) *Louisiana law.* An exception intended to delay but not dismiss an action.

▸ **general exception.** (16c) **1.** An objection pointing out a substantive defect in an opponent's pleading, such as the insufficiency of the claim or the court's lack of subject-matter jurisdiction; an objection to a pleading for want of substance. — Also termed *general demurrer.* Cf. SPECIAL EXCEPTION (1). **2.** An objection in which the excepting party does not specify the grounds of the objection.

▸ **peremptory exception.** (16c) *Louisiana law.* A defensive pleading asserting that no legal remedy exists for the plaintiff's alleged injury, that res judicata or prescription bars the claim, or that an indispensable party has not been included in the litigation.

▸ **residual exception.** See *catchall exception.*

▸ **special exception.** See SPECIAL EXCEPTION.

2. Something that is excluded from a rule's operation <employers with fewer than five employees are an exception to the rule>.

▸ **statutory exception.** (18c) A provision in a statute exempting certain persons or conduct from the statute's operation.

3. The retention of an existing right or interest, by and for the grantor, in real property being granted to another. **4.** The exclusion from a legal description of part of real property to prevent its conveyance to another. Cf. RESERVATION (1). — **except,** *vb.*

exceptionable (ek-**sep**-shən-ə-bəl), *adj.* (17c) Liable to objection; OBJECTIONABLE.

exceptional charge. See *special charge* under CHARGE (7).

exception clause. (1843) A clause that attempts to modify or exclude the prima facie obligations that arise when a legal instrument takes effect. Cf. EXEMPTION CLAUSE.

Exceptiones Petri (ek-sep-tee-**oh**-neez **pee**-tree). [Latin "excerpts by Peter"] An 11th-century short-form manual of rules for practical use, drawn from the *Corpus Juris Civilis.* • It was produced in Southern France and dedicated to Odilo, a magistrate of high standing.

exceptio plurium concubentium **defense. 1.** See *multiple access* under ACCESS (3). **2.** See *exceptio plurium concubentium* under EXCEPTIO.

exceptis excipiendis (ek-**sep**-tis ek-sip-ee-**en**-dis). [Latin] With all necessary exceptions.

exceptor, *n.* (17c) Someone who takes exception; an objector. — Also spelled *excepter.*

excerpta (ek-**sərp**-tə), *n. pl.* [Latin] Extracts.

ex certa scientia (eks **sər**-tə sɪ-**en**-shee-ə). [Latin] Of certain or sure knowledge. • This phrase was anciently used in patents, and imported full knowledge of the subject matter on the part of the sovereign.

excès de pouvoir (ek-**say** də poo-**vwahr**). [French "excess of power"] **1.** *Int'l law.* Beyond the powers (of a tribunal). **2.** *Administrative law.* Beyond the powers of an official.

excess, *n.* **1.** The amount or degree by which something is greater than another. **2.** The action of exceeding one's authority or overstepping a prescribed limit or going beyond one's rights. **3.** Immoderate or undue indulgence, esp. in food or drink. — **excessive,** *adj.*

excess-benefit plan. See EMPLOYEE BENEFIT PLAN.

excess clause. (1945) An insurance-policy provision — usu. contained in the "other insurance" section of the policy — that limits the insurer's liability to the amount exceeding other available coverage. • This clause essentially requires other insurers to pay first. Cf. ESCAPE CLAUSE; PRO RATA CLAUSE.

excess condemnation. See CONDEMNATION (2).

excess damages. See DAMAGES.

excess insurance. See INSURANCE.

excess insurer. See INSURER.

excessive assessment. See ASSESSMENT (2).

excessive bail. See BAIL (1).

excessive damages. See DAMAGES.

excessive drunkenness. See DRUNKENNESS.

excessive entanglement. (1970) *Constitutional law.* Impermissible merging, involvement, or intermixing of the spheres of government and religion whereby state and church functions are blurred or caused to overlap; intrusion by the government into an organization's religious administration, authority, concerns, or rights. • The excessive-entanglement test derives from the Establishment Clause, U.S. Const. amend. I, and includes both administrative entanglement and political disagreement regarding religious matters. *See Lemon v. Kurtzman,* 403 U.S. 602, 613, 91 S.Ct. 2105, 2111 (1971). — Also termed *excessive government entanglement.*

excessive execution. An exercise of a power of appointment exceeding the limits (express or statutory) set on the use of the power.

excessive fine. See FINE (5).

Excessive Fines Clause. (1986) *Constitutional law.* The clause of the Eighth Amendment to the U.S. Constitution prohibiting the imposition of excessive fines.

excessive force. See FORCE.

excessive government entanglement. See EXCESSIVE ENTANGLEMENT.

excessive price. See PRICE.

excessive punishment. See PUNISHMENT (1).

excessive sentence. See SENTENCE.

excessive verdict. See VERDICT (1).

excess judgment. See JUDGMENT (2).

excess jurisdiction. See EXCESS OF JURISDICTION (1).

excess-liability damages. See *excess damages* under DAMAGES.

excess limits. Insurance coverage against losses in excess of a specified limit.

excess-lines insurance. See *surplus-lines insurance* under INSURANCE.

excess margin. (1972) Equity in a brokerage firm's customer account that exceeds either the legal-minimum dollar amount for a margin account or the maintenance requirement.

excess of authority. (1805) An overreach of jurisdiction or mandate; esp., an arbitrator's act that exceeds the limits of power vested in that position. • The arbitrator's authority comes from the parties' arbitration agreement, subject to any mandatory limitations imposed by applicable law. Excess of authority is a ground for vacating an arbitration award under the Federal Arbitration Act and under state arbitration acts. Although the terminology is somewhat different, excess of authority is also a ground for denying recognition and enforcement of an award under the New York Convention.

excess of jurisdiction. (17c) **1.** A court's acting beyond the limits of its power, usu. in one of three ways: (1) when the court has no power to deal with the kind of matter at issue, (2) when the court has no power to deal with the particular person concerned, or (3) when the judgment or order issued is of a kind that the court has no power to issue. **2.** A court's departure from recognized and established requirements of law, despite apparent adherence to procedural form, the effect of which is a deprivation of one's constitutional right. — Also termed *excess jurisdiction.*

excess of privilege. (1889) **1.** An excessive publication of a privileged statement — that is, beyond the limits of the privilege. **2.** The improper and malicious use of the privilege to publish a statement.

excess policy. See *excess insurance* under INSURANCE.

excess-profits tax. See TAX.

excess reinsurance. See REINSURANCE.

excess reserve. See RESERVE (1).

excess theory. *Insurance.* The principle that a tortfeasor will be considered underinsured if the injured party's damages exceed the tortfeasor's liability-insurance coverage. • This principle allows an injured party to invoke underinsured-motorist coverage. Cf. GAP THEORY.

excess vote. See VOTE (1).

excess water. See WATER.

exchange, *n.* (14c) *Commercial law.* **1.** The act of transferring interests, each in consideration for the other.

▸ **1031 exchange.** See 1031 EXCHANGE.

▸ **bargained-for exchange.** See BARGAINED-FOR EXCHANGE.

▸ **like-kind exchange.** See LIKE-KIND EXCHANGE.

▸ **tax-free exchange.** See TAX-FREE EXCHANGE.

2. Money or negotiable instruments presented as payment; CURRENCY. See MEDIUM OF EXCHANGE. **3.** The interchange or conversion of money. See FOREIGN EXCHANGE. **4.** The payment of a debt using a bill of exchange or credit rather than money. **5.** An organization that brings together buyers and sellers of securities, commodities, and the like to promote uniformity in the customs and usages of merchants, to facilitate the speedy adjustment of business disputes, to gather and disseminate valuable commercial and economic information, and to secure to its members the benefits of cooperation in the furtherance of their legitimate pursuits. • The best-known exchanges are stock, produce, livestock, cotton, and grain exchanges. See LISTED SECURITY EXCHANGE; RECIPROCAL EXCHANGE. **6.** The building or hall where members of an exchange meet every business day to buy and sell for themselves, or as brokers for their customers, for present and future delivery. See SECURITIES EXCHANGE (1). — **exchange,** *vb.*

Exchange Act. See SECURITIES EXCHANGE ACT OF 1934.

exchange agreement. See AGREEMENT.

exchange broker. (17c) Someone who negotiates money or merchandise transactions for others.

exchange rate. (1896) The ratio for converting one country's money into another country's money. See FOREIGN EXCHANGE.

▸ **fixed exchange rate.** An exchange rate that remains constant despite fluctuations in supply and demand for a currency.

▸ **floating exchange rate.** A variable exchange rate that depends on the supply and demand for a particular currency.

exchange-rate mechanism. (1978) A system or method for controlling the exchange rate between the currencies of two countries.

exchange ratio. The number or fraction of shares that an acquiring company must give for each share of an acquired company.

exchange-traded fund. See FUND (1).

exchange value. See VALUE (2).

Exchequer (eks-**chek**-ər *or* **eks**-chek-ər). (14c) **1.** *English law.* The government department charged with collecting taxes and administering the national revenue; the treasury department. • The name is said to have derived from the checkered cloth, resembling a chessboard, that anciently covered the table on which certain of the king's accounts were tallied, the sums being marked and scored with counters. **2.** COURT OF EXCHEQUER. — Abbr. Ex.

Exchequer bill. (17c) *English law.* A bill of credit issued in England by the authority of Parliament; an instrument issued at the Exchequer, usu. under the authority of an act of Parliament passed for that specific purpose, containing an engagement on the part of the government to repay, with interest, the principal sums advanced.

Exchequer Chamber. *English law.* An English court of intermediate appeal from the common-law courts, namely, the Court of King's Bench, the Court of Common Pleas, and the Court of Exchequer. • It was established in 1822. — Also termed *Camera Scaccarii.*

Exchequer Division. *Hist. English law.* A division of the High Court of Justice, to which the business of the Court of Exchequer was specially assigned by section 34 of the Judicature Act of 1873, and later merged into the Queen's Bench Division in 1881.

excise, *n.* (15c) A tax imposed on the manufacture, sale, or use of goods (such as a cigarette tax), or on an occupation or activity (such as a license tax or an attorney occupation fee). — Also termed *excise tax*. Cf. *income tax* and *property tax* under TAX.

excise lieu property tax. See TAX.

excise tax. See EXCISE.

excision. See FEMALE GENITAL MUTILATION.

excited utterance. (1800) A statement about a startling event made under the stress and excitement of the event. • An excited utterance may be admissible as a hearsay exception. Fed. R. Evid. 803(2). Cf. PRESENT SENSE IMPRESSION.

excludable, *adj.* (1916) **1.** (Of evidence) subject to exclusion <excludable hearsay>. **2.** (Of an alien) ineligible for admission or entry into a country.

excludable alien. See ALIEN.

excludable time. See TIME.

exclude. See RIGHT TO EXCLUDE.

excludendo fiscum et relictam (eks-kloo-**den**-doh **fis**-kəm et ri-**lik**-təm). [Law Latin] *Hist.* To the exclusion of the rights of the Crown and of the widow.

exclusion, *n.* **1.** *Tax.* An item of income excluded from gross income. — Also termed *income exclusion*.

▸ **annual exclusion.** (1940) The amount allowed as nontaxable gift income during the calendar year. • The purpose of the annual exclusion is both to serve as an estate-planning mechanism (so that gifts made during the donor's lifetime remain nontestamentary and nontaxable) and to eliminate the administrative inconvenience of taxing relatively small gifts. In 2014, for an individual, the first $14,000 in gifts can be excluded; for married persons, the exclusion is $28,000 per couple for joint gifts, regardless of which spouse supplied the donated property. IRC (26 USCA) § 2503. — Also termed *annual gift-tax exclusion*.

2. *Evidence.* A trial judge's determination that an item offered as evidence may not be presented to the trier of fact (esp. the jury).— Also termed *judicial exclusion*. **3.** *Insurance.* An insurance-policy provision that excepts certain events or conditions from coverage. — **exclude,** *vb.* — **exclusionary,** *adj.*

▸ **automobile exclusion.** (1949) A provision in some commercial general liability policies, excluding coverage for damages arising from the use (including loading and unloading) of an automobile, aircraft, or other motor vehicle owned, operated, rented, or borrowed by the insured.

▸ **business-risk exclusion.** (1972) An exclusion in some commercial general liability policies, excluding coverage for common risks of doing business, including harm to the insured's product or work, damages arising from a product recall, damages arising from the insured's failure to perform under a contract, or damages arising from a failure of the insured's product to perform as intended.

▸ **design-defect exclusion.** (1974) A provision in some umbrella policies and some older commercial general liability policies, excluding coverage for bodily injury arising from the failure of the insured's product to perform its intended function because of a defect or deficiency in its design, formula, specifications, instructions, or advertising materials.

▸ **employee-liability exclusion.** (1989) A provision in some commercial general liability policies, excluding coverage for injury to an employee (or a member of the employee's family), arising from and in the course of employment with the insured. • This exclusion is generally intended to exclude from coverage all injuries covered by the workers'-compensation laws.

▸ **employment-related-practices exclusion.** (1995) A provision in some commercial general liability policies, excluding coverage for damages arising from an insured's employment practices, including any policy, action, or omission — such as coercion, demotion, evaluation, reassignment, discipline, defamation, harassment, humiliation, or discrimination — that is directed at the person injured.

▸ **expected/intended exclusion.** (1983) A provision in some commercial general liability policies, excluding coverage for property damage or bodily injury that is expected or intended by the insured, except any harm arising from the use of reasonable force to protect a person or property. • This exclusion is sometimes referred to as "exclusion a" because it is the first exclusion listed on most policies. — Also termed *exclusion a*; *intentional-injury exclusion*.

▸ **failure-to-perform exclusion.** (1993) A provision in some commercial general liability policies, excluding coverage for (1) the loss of use of undamaged property resulting from the insured's delay or failure in performing an obligation, or (2) a design defect or failure in the insured's product. — Also termed *loss-of-use exclusion*.

▸ **knowledge-of-falsity exclusion.** (1995) A provision in some commercial general liability policies, excluding coverage for damages arising from an oral or written communication made by the insured with knowledge that it is false.

▸ **named-insured exclusion.** (1949) An exclusion limiting liability-insurance coverage to a named insured whose injuries were caused by another named insured under the same insurance policy.

▸ **owned-property exclusion.** (1986) *Insurance.* A provision in a comprehensive general-liability insurance policy allowing only third parties who are injured on or by the insured's property to make liability claims against the insurer. • The provision ordinarily excludes coverage for (1) property owned, rented, occupied, sold, given away, or abandoned by the insured, (2) personal property in the care, custody, or control of the insured, and (3) property located where the insured and its employees work.

▸ **own-product exclusion.** (1998) A provision in some commercial general liability policies, excluding coverage for property damage to a product that is manufactured, sold, handled, distributed, or disposed of by the insured.

▸ **own-work exclusion.** (1997) A provision in some commercial general liability policies, excluding coverage for damage to the work or services performed by the insured.

▸ **pollution exclusion.** (1972) A provision in some commercial general liability policies, excluding coverage for bodily injury or property damages arising from the discharge, dispersal, release, or escape of chemicals, waste, acid, and other pollutants. • Pollution-exclusion clauses may take one of two forms: (1) sudden and accidental, and (2) absolute. The sudden-and-accidental clause, usu. limited to policies issued before 1985, contains an exception under which the damages are covered (i.e., exempted from the exclusion) if the discharge or other release was sudden and accidental. The absolute pollution exclusion, in most policies issued since 1985, does not contain this exception.

▸ **sistership exclusion.** (1966) A provision in some commercial general liability policies, excluding coverage for damages arising from the withdrawal, inspection, repair, replacement, or loss of use of the insured's product or work, to the extent that the product or work is withdrawn or recalled from the market because of a known or suspected defect or deficiency. — Also termed *recall exclusion.*

4. The fact of not including a person or thing.

▸ **categorical exclusion. 1.** An unconditional, general exclusion. **2.** *Environmental law.* A category of actions that are exempted from compliance with regulations or statutes, usu. because they will not have a significant individual or cumulative effect on the human environment.

exclusion a. See *expected/intended exclusion* under EXCLUSION (3).

exclusionary clause. 1. A sales-contract provision that limits the remedies available to a party if another party breaches the contract. **2.** *Insurance.* A provision in an insurance policy listing the exceptions to coverage and circumstances that prohibit recovery under the policy. — Also termed (in both senses) *exclusionary provision.*

exclusionary hearing. See HEARING.

exclusionary practice. (1945) *Antitrust.* A method by which a firm can gain or maintain monopoly power without the express or tacit cooperation of competing or potentially competing firms.

exclusionary rule. (1855) **1.** *Evidence.* Any rule that excludes or suppresses evidence <despite many exceptions, hearsay has long been inadmissible under an exclusionary rule>. — Also termed *exclusionary evidence rule.* **2.** *Criminal procedure.* A rule that excludes or suppresses evidence obtained in violation of an accused person's constitutional rights <in accordance with the exclusionary rule, the court did not admit the drugs into evidence because they had been obtained during a warrantless search of the defendant's home>. See FRUIT-OF-THE-POISONOUS-TREE DOCTRINE; GOOD-FAITH EXCEPTION.

> "The deterrence of unreasonable searches and seizures is a major purpose of the exclusionary rule. . . . But the rule serves other purposes as well. There is, for example, . . . 'the imperative of judicial integrity,' namely, that the courts do not become 'accomplices in willful disobedience of a Constitution they are sworn to uphold.' . . . A third purpose of the exclusionary rule . . . is that of 'assuring the people — all potential victims of unlawful government conduct — that the government would not profit from its lawless behavior, thus minimizing the risk of seriously undermining popular trust in the government.'" Wayne R. LaFave & Jerold H. Israel, *Criminal Procedure* § 3.1, at 107 (2d ed. 1992) (quoting *Elkins v. U.S.*, 364 U.S. 206, 80 S.Ct. 1437 (1960); *U.S. v. Calandra*, 414 U.S. 338, 94 S.Ct. 613 (1974) (dissent)).

3. NO-RECOURSE RULE.

exclusionary zoning. See ZONING.

exclusion clause. A contract term that excuses or exempts a party from liability under some circumstances.

exclusionist. (1822) Someone who seeks to exclude a person or group of people from some right or privilege.

exclusion-of-liability clause. See EXCULPATORY CLAUSE.

exclusion order. 1. A court order forbidding a person from going to or entering a place. **2.** An authority's order barring the admission of a person or goods to the country. **3.** *Intellectual property.* An order issued by the U.S. International Trade Commission in a § 337 investigation directing U.S. Customs to stop the importation of infringing products into the United States. See CEASE-AND-DESIST ORDER (2); SECTION 337 INVESTIGATION.

▸ **general exclusion order.** *Intellectual property.* An order to stop an entire class of goods from being imported by a party named in a § 337 investigation. Cf. *limited exclusion order.*

▸ **limited exclusion order.** *Intellectual property.* An order to stop importation of specified goods by a party named in a § 337 investigation. Cf. *general exclusion order.*

▸ **permanent exclusion order.** *Intellectual property.* An order to permanently stop importation of specified goods into the United States based on findings of a § 337 investigation.

▸ **temporary exclusion order.** *Intellectual property.* An order to temporarily stop importation of specified goods by a party to a § 337 investigation unless the party posts a bond.

exclusion period. *Insurance.* The length of time that must elapse before an insurer will provide healthcare-coverage for a preexisting medical condition.

exclusion zone. (1976) An area that people are not allowed to enter without special permission either because it is dangerous or because secret things occur there.

exclusive, *adj.* **1.** Limited to a particular person, group, entity, or thing <exclusive right>. **2.** Unable to be true if something else is true <mutually exclusive>. **3.** Whole; undivided <exclusive attention>.

exclusive agency. See AGENCY (1).

exclusive-agency listing. See LISTING (1).

exclusive agency to sell. See *exclusive agency* under AGENCY (1).

exclusive authorization-to-sell listing. See *exclusive-agency listing* under LISTING (1).

exclusive contract. See EXCLUSIVE-DEALING ARRANGEMENT.

exclusive control. (1890) Under the doctrine of res ipsa loquitur, a defendant's sole management of and responsibility for the instrumentality causing harm. • Exclusive control is a prerequisite to the doctrine's applicability. See RES IPSA LOQUITUR.

exclusive-dealing arrangement. (1943) An agreement requiring a buyer to purchase all needed goods or services from one seller. — Often shortened to *exclusive dealing.* — Also termed *exclusive contract.* See *requirements contract* under CONTRACT.

exclusive easement. See EASEMENT.

exclusive economic zone. (1972) *Int'l law.* An area just beyond the territorial sea, extending up to 200 nautical miles from the baseline of the territorial sea, in which the coastal country enjoys special authority for economic purposes. — Abbr. EEZ.

exclusive evidence. See EVIDENCE.

exclusive franchise. See *exclusive agency* under AGENCY (1).

exclusive jurisdiction. See JURISDICTION.

exclusive-jurisdiction clause. A contract provision specifying the only courts in which the parties can bring claims arising out of the contract.

exclusive license. See LICENSE.

exclusive listing. See *exclusive-agency listing* under LISTING (1).

exclusive ownership. See FEE SIMPLE.

exclusive possession. See POSSESSION.

exclusive power. See POWER (3).

exclusive-provider organization. A managed-care organization in which subscribers receive a discounted rate for medical services within a given network of approved providers, but have no coverage for care received outside the network. — Abbr. EPO. Cf. PREFERRED-PROVIDER ORGANIZATION.

exclusive right. See RIGHT.

exclusive right of sale. (1867) The right to sell a principal's products or to act as the seller's real-estate agent to the exclusion of all others, including the owner. — Also termed *exclusive right to sell.* Cf. *exclusive agency* under AGENCY (1).

exclusive sale. See SALE.

exclusive use. See USE (1).

exclusive-use clause. (1915) A lease provision enumerating conditions for a lessee's use of the leased property.

ex colore (eks kə-**lor**-ee). [Latin] By color; under color of; under pretense, show, or protection of.

ex comitate (eks kom-ə-**tay**-tee). [Latin] Out of comity or courtesy.

excommengement (eks-kə-**menj**-mənt), *n.* See EXCOMMUNICATION.

ex commodato (eks kom-ə-**day**-toh). [Latin "out of loan"] *Hist.* (Of a right of action) arising out of a loan.

excommunicant (eks-kə-**myoo**-ni-kənt), *n.* (16c) *Eccles. law.* **1.** An excommunicated person. **2.** *Rare.* An excommunicator.

excommunicate, *vb.* (16c) To punish (a person) by expulsion from the membership in a church, esp. the Roman Catholic Church.

excommunication, *n.* (15c) *Eccles. law.* Expulsion from a church or religious society, esp. as a formal sentence of censure pronounced by a spiritual court for an offense falling under ecclesiastical cognizance. • In England, an excommunicated person was formerly subject to various civil disabilities, such as an inability to be a juror, to be a witness in any court, or to sue to recover lands or money due. These penalties were abolished by the Ecclesiastical Courts Act (1813). St. 53 Geo. 3, ch. 127. — Also termed *excommengement.*

> "Closely allied to outlawry is excommunication; it is in fact an ecclesiastical outlawry, and, like temporal outlawry, though once it was the law's last and most terrible weapon against the obstinate offender, it is now regarded as a normal process for compelling the appearance in court of those who are accused. Indeed as regards the laity, since the spiritual courts can not direct a seizure of the body, lands, or goods, those courts must, if mere citations fail to produce an appearance, at once have recourse to their last weapon. Then, as ordained by William the Conqueror, the lay power comes to their aid. If the excommunicate does not seek absolution within forty days (this period seems to be fixed already in the twelfth century), the ordinary will signify this to the kind; a writ for the arrest of the offender will be issued, and he will be kept in prison until he makes his submission." 2 Frederick Pollock & Frederic W. Maitland, *History of English Law Before the Time of Edward I* 500 (2d ed. 1899).

> "Excommunication, as construed in law, is the official announcement by the superior authority of the termination of membership in a religious body and the forfeiture of spiritual privileges of the church. It is one of the methods of discipline in the nature of expulsion from membership in a fraternity, and the fact of expulsion from a church is conclusive proof that the person expelled is not a member of such church. Whether the excommunication was wrong or not can not be examined in the court of the State, and such expelled member can not maintain a suit in relation to church property nor vote for trustees." Charles M. Scanlan, *The Law of Church and Grave* 83 (1909).

excommunicato capiendo (eks-kə-myoo-ni-**kay**-toh kap-ee-**en**-doh). [Latin] (16c) *Hist. Eccles. law.* A writ that, being founded on a bishop's certificate of excommunication, required the sheriff to arrest and imprison the defendant. • The writ issued out of chancery and was returnable to the King's Bench. Cf. DE CONTUMACE CAPIENDO.

excommunicator. (17c) Someone who excommunicates.

excommunicato recapiendo (eks-kə-myoo-ni-**kay**-toh ri-kap-ee-**en**-doh). [Latin] *Hist. Eccles. law.* A writ commanding that an excommunicant — who had been committed to prison for obstinacy but who was unlawfully freed before agreeing to obey the church's authority — should be found, retaken, and imprisoned again.

ex comparatione scriptorum (eks kom-pə-ray-shee-**oh**-nee skrip-**tor**-əm). [Latin] By a comparison of writings or handwritings. • This term was formerly used in the law of evidence.

ex concessis (eks kən-**ses**-is). [Latin] From the premises granted; according to what has already been allowed.

ex consulto (eks kən-**səl**-toh). [Latin] With consultation or deliberation.

ex continenti (eks kon-tə-**nen**-tɪ). [Latin] *Civil law.* Immediately; without any interval or delay.

ex contractu (eks kən-**trak**-t[y]oo). [Latin "from a contract"] (17c) Arising from a contract <action *ex contractu*>. Cf. EX DELICTO (1).

ex-convict. A person who has been released from prison after serving a sentence.

ex coupon bond. See BOND (3).

exculpate (**ek**-skəl-payt *or* ek-**skəl**-payt), *vb.* (17c) To free from blame or accusation; esp., to prove not guilty. Cf. EXONERATE (1). — **exculpation** (ek- skəl-**pay**-shən), *n.* — **exculpatory** (ek-**skəl**-pə-tor-ee), *adj.*

exculpatory clause. (1891) A contractual provision relieving a party from liability resulting from a negligent or wrongful act. • A will or a trust may contain an exculpatory clause purporting to immunize a fiduciary from a breach of duty; the clause may reduce the degree of care and prudence required of the fiduciary. But courts generally find that if an exculpatory clause in a will or trust seeks to confer absolute immunity, it is void as being against public policy. See EXEMPTION CLAUSE. Cf. LIMITATION-OF-LIABILITY CLAUSE. — Also termed *exclusion-of-liability clause.*

exculpatory defense. See DEFENSE (1).

exculpatory evidence. See EVIDENCE.

exculpatory-no doctrine. (1977) *Criminal law.* The principle that a person cannot be charged with making a false statement for falsely denying guilt in response to an investigator's question. • This doctrine is based on the Fifth Amendment right against self-incrimination. But the U.S. Supreme Court has overruled this doctrine in federal law. *Brogan v. U.S.*, 522 U.S. 398, 118 S.Ct. 805 (1998).

ex curia (eks **kyoor**-ee-ə). [Latin] Out of court; away from the court.

excursus (ek-**skərs**-əs), *n.* **1.** A detailed discussion of a point, esp. by way of digression. **2.** A passage inserted in a treatise, dissertation, or other work to elucidate an obscure or important point in the text; specif., a scholarly footnote, usu. by a later commentator, that sheds light on some intricacy, complication, or cloudy matter in the main text. Pl. ***excursuses.***

excusable, *adj.* (14c) (Of an illegal act or omission) not punishable under the specific circumstances <excusable neglect>.

excusable assault. See ASSAULT.

excusable homicide. See HOMICIDE.

excusable neglect. See NEGLECT.

excusatio (ek-skyoo-**zay**-shee-oh), *n.* [Latin] *Roman & civil law.* An excuse or reason that exempts someone from some duty or obligation.

excusator (ek-skyoo-**zay**-tər), *n.* (17c) **1.** *Hist.* An excuser. **2.** In old German law, a defendant; one who wholly denies the plaintiff's claim.

excuse (ek-**skyoos**), *n.* (14c) **1.** A reason that justifies an act or omission or that relieves a person of a duty. **2.** *Criminal law.* A defense that arises because the defendant is not blameworthy for having acted in a way that would otherwise be criminal. • The following defenses are the traditional excuses: duress, entrapment, infancy, insanity, and involuntary intoxication. — Also termed *legal excuse*; *lawful excuse.* Cf. JUSTIFICATION (2). — **excuse** (ek-**skyooz**), *vb.* — **excusatory** (ek-**skyooz**-ə-tor-ee), *adj.*

▸ **partial excuse.** *Criminal law.* A defense that arises because the defendant, while partially blameworthy, is not fully culpable. • If successful, a partial excuse results in conviction on a lesser charge. The primary partial excuses reduce murder to manslaughter. See *imperfect defense* under DEFENSE (1). Cf. HEAT OF PASSION; *adequate provocation* under PROVOCATION; EXTREME MENTAL OR EMOTIONAL DISTURBANCE; *diminished capacity* under CAPACITY (3).

> "The criminal law has . . . adopted some partial excuses, but these have quite limited scopes. The most important are a set of mitigating doctrines that reduce a homicide that would otherwise be deemed murder to the lesser crime of manslaughter. The common law's 'provocation/passion' doctrine is the most hoary. An intentional killing which would otherwise be murder is reduced to voluntary manslaughter if the defendant killed while subjectively in the 'heat of passion' as a result of a provocation that would have caused a reasonable person to be in such a state. So, for example, a person engaged in mutual combat who was inflamed and intentionally killed his opponent would be guilty only of voluntary manslaughter. Although the rationale for the mitigation is contested, the most convincing explanation is that the defendant's rationality is compromised (but not entirely disabled) by the passion, and the passion is not fully the defendant's fault because it was aroused by a provocation that would have inflamed an objectively reasonable person." Stephen J. Morse, *Excusing and the New Excuse Defenses: A Legal and Conceptual Review*, 23 Crime & Just. 329, 335 (1998).

excuse by failure of presupposed conditions. See *commercial impracticability* under IMPRACTICABILITY.

excuss (ek-**skəs**), *vb.* (18c) To seize and detain by law.

excussion (ek-**skəsh**-ən), *n.* [Latin] *Roman & civil law.* A diligent prosecution of a remedy against a debtor; esp., the exhausting of a remedy against a principal debtor before resorting to a surety. — Also termed *excussio.*

ex-date. See EX-DIVIDEND DATE.

ex debito justitiae (eks **deb**-i-toh jəs-**tish**-ee-ee). [Latin] From or as a debt of justice; in accordance with the requirement of justice; of right; as a matter of right.

> "A *mandamus* will issue to enforce obedience to acts of parliament and to the king's charters, when it is said to be demandable *ex debito justitiae.*" S.S. Merrill, *Law of Mandamus* § 13, at 7 (1892).

ex debito naturali (eks **deb**-i-toh nach-ə-**ray**-lı). [Law Latin] *Scots law.* Arising from natural obligation. • The phrase appeared in reference to an obligation that was moral rather than legal.

ex defectu juris (eks di-**fek**-t[y]oo **joor**-is). [Law Latin] *Scots law.* From a defect in the right. • A seller had to warrant a purchaser against an eviction based on a defect in the seller's own right.

ex defectu natalium (eks di-**fek**-t[y]oo nə-**tay**-lee-əm). [Law Latin] *Hist.* From defect of parentage. • Formerly, this phrase appeared in reference to a basis on which the court rejected the will of a bastard who died without issue.

ex defectu sanguinis (eks di-**fek**-t[y]oo **sang**-gwə-nis). [Latin] *Hist.* From failure of blood; for want of issue.

ex delectu familiae (eks di-**lek**-t[y]oo fə-**mil**-ee-ee). [Law Latin] *Hist.* From choice of a certain family. • The phrase appeared in reference to the sovereign's right to bestow honors on those whom he chose.

ex deliberatione Dominorum Concilii (eks di-lib-ə-ray-shee-**oh**-nee dom-ə-**nor**-əm kən-**sil**-ee-ı). [Law Latin] *Hist.* After consideration by the Lords of Council.

> "Formerly all writs which passed the signet were procured by presentation of a bill (or petition) for such writ. The bill was perused and considered by the Lord Ordinary on the Bills, and if he was satisfied, the bill was passed and the writ issued: the latter bearing the words *ex deliberatione Dominorum Concilii* to signify that the bill had been considered. These words are still appended to almost all writs which pass the signet, but they are now only words of style, since the writs are now passed *periculo petentis* without being submitted to the Lords." John Trayner, *Trayner's Latin Maxims* 196–97 (4th ed. 1894).

ex delicto (eks də-**lik**-toh), *adj. & adv.* [Latin "from a wrong"] **1.** Arising from a crime or tort <action ex

delicto>. • Although *ex delicto* refers most commonly to a tort in modern usage, it referred historically to both torts and crimes. Cf. IN DELICTO; EX CONTRACTU. **2.** *Int'l law. Rare.* As a consequence of a crime or tort <because they were counterfeit, the goods were seized and condemned ex delicto>.

ex delicto trust. See TRUST (3).

ex demissione (eks də-mish-ee-**oh**-nee). [Latin "upon the demise"] *Hist.* A phrase forming part of the title of the old action of ejectment. — Abbr. *ex dem.*

ex directo (eks di-**rek**-toh). [Latin] Directly; immediately.

ex distribution. (1945) Without distribution. • Shares are traded ex distribution when they no longer carry the right to receive a distribution to be made to holders. — Abbr. X; XDIS.

ex diverso (eks di-**vər**-soh). [Latin] *Hist.* On the other hand; conversely.

ex dividend. (1830) Without dividend. • Shares are traded ex dividend when the seller, not the purchaser, is entitled to the next dividend payment because it will be made before the stock transfer is completed. The first day on which shares are traded ex dividend, the stock price will drop by an amount usu. approximating the amount of the dividend. — Abbr. XD.; X. Cf. CUM DIVIDEND.

ex-dividend date. (1930) The date on or after which the buyer of a security does not acquire the right to receive a recently declared dividend. — Also termed *ex-date.* Cf. DIVIDEND DATE.

ex dolo malo (eks **doh**-loh **mal**-oh). [Latin] Out of fraud; out of deceitful or tortious conduct.

exeat (**ek**-see-ət), *n.* (18c) **1.** Generally, permission to go outside (a place). **2.** Permission that a bishop grants to a priest to go out of his diocese. Cf. NE EXEAT (1).

execute, *vb.* (14c) **1.** To perform or complete (a contract or duty) <once the contract was fully executed, the parties owed no further contractual duties to each other>. **2.** To change (as a legal interest) from one form to another <the shifting use was executed into a valid legal estate>. **3.** To make (a legal document) valid by signing; to bring (a legal document) into its final, legally enforceable form <each party executed the contract without a signature witness>. **4.** To put to death, esp. by legal sentence <Johnson was executed shortly after midnight>. **5.** To enforce and collect on (a money judgment) <Williams asked the sheriff to execute on the judgment>.

executed, *adj.* (16c) **1.** (Of a document) that has been signed <an executed will>. **2.** That has been done, given, or performed <executed consideration>.

> "[T]he term 'executed' is a slippery word. Its use is to be avoided except when accompanied by explanation. . . . A contract is frequently said to be *executed* when the document has been signed, or has been signed, sealed, and delivered. Further, by executed contract is frequently meant one that has been fully performed by both parties." William R. Anson, *Principles of the Law of Contract* 26 n.* (Arthur L. Corbin ed., 3d Am. ed. 1919).

executed consideration. See CONSIDERATION (1).

executed contract. See CONTRACT.

executed covenant. See COVENANT (1).

executed document. See DOCUMENT (2).

executed estate. See REMAINDER (1).

executed fine. See FINE (1).

executed note. See NOTE (1).

executed remainder. See *vested remainder* under REMAINDER (1).

executed trust. See TRUST (3).

executed use. See USE (4).

executio (ek-sə-**kyoo**-shee-oh), *n.* [Latin] **1.** The performance or completion of a thing; the act of following through on a commitment. **2.** The doing of something thoroughly. **3.** Management or administration. **4.** *Hist.* Execution; the final process in an action.

executio bonorum (bə-**nor**-əm). [Latin] *Hist.* The management or administration of goods.

execution, *n.* (14c) **1.** The act of carrying out or putting into effect (as a court order or a securities transaction) <execution of the court's decree> <execution of the stop-loss order>. **2.** Validation of a written instrument, such as a contract or will, by fulfilling the necessary legal requirements <delivery of the goods completed the contract's execution>. **3.** Judicial enforcement of a money judgment, usu. by seizing and selling the judgment debtor's property <even if the plaintiff receives a judgment against the foreign debtor, execution is unlikely>. — Also termed (in Scots law) *diligence.* **4.** A court order directing a sheriff or other officer to enforce a judgment, usu. by seizing and selling the judgment debtor's property <the court issued the execution authorizing seizure of the car>. — Also termed *execution writ; writ of execution; execution of judgment; judgment execution; general execution; fieri facias.*

> "After judgment has been entered execution will issue, at the request of the party who is entitled thereto, but the time allowed for appeal from the judgment must have expired. Execution is a writ for the enforcement of a judgment, and is directed to such officers as have authority to make service within the jurisdiction. Execution ordinarily includes the amount of the debt or damage that has been ascertained to be due, together with costs. Executions are issued upon written order being presented to the clerk of courts by the party desiring it. There is no set form of such request, although some courts have printed blanks for the use of the public." Gleason L. Archer, *Law Office and Court Procedure* 290 (1910).

> "A writ of execution is an authorization to an executive officer, issued from a court in which a final judgment has been rendered, for the purpose of carrying such judgment into force and effect. It is founded upon the judgment, must generally be conformed to it in every respect, and the plaintiff is always entitled to it to obtain a satisfaction of his claim, unless his right has been suspended by proceedings in the nature of an appeal or by his own agreement." Benjamin J. Shipman, *Handbook of Common-Law Pleading* § 26, at 50 (Henry Winthrop Ballantine ed., 3d ed. 1923).

▸ **alias execution.** (17c) A second execution issued to enforce a judgment not fully satisfied by the original writ. Cf. *alias writ* under WRIT.

▸ **body execution.** (1875) A court order requiring an officer to take a named person into custody, usu. to bring the person before the court to pay a debt; CAPIAS.

▸ **close-jail execution.** (1934) A body execution stating that the person to be arrested should be confined in jail without the privilege of movement about the jailyard.

▸ **dormant execution.** (1826) An execution authorizing an officer to seize and hold property rather than sell it, until further notice.

▸ **junior execution.** (1850) An execution that is subordinate to another execution issued from an earlier judgment against the same debtor.

▸ **malicious execution.** (1855) An abuse of process by which a person, maliciously and without reasonable cause, issues an execution against the property of a judgment debtor.

▸ **special execution.** (17c) An execution authorizing a judgment to be satisfied from specified property.

▸ **speedy execution.** (16c) An execution issuing quickly (esp. by judges at nisi prius) after a trial.

5. *Criminal law.* The carrying out of a death sentence <the Supreme Court stayed the execution>. — **execute,** *vb.*

execution clause. The part of a deed containing the date, seal (if required), and signatures of the grantor, grantor's spouse, and witnesses.

execution creditor. See CREDITOR.

executione facienda in withernamium (ek-sə-kyoo-shee-**oh**-nee fay-shee-**en**-də in wi<u>th</u>-ər-**nay**-mee-əm). [Latin] (17c) *Hist.* A writ that lay for taking cattle of a person who had taken someone else's cattle out of the county so that the sheriff could not replevy them.

executione judicii (ek-sə-kyoo-shee-**oh**-nee joo-**dish**-ee-ɪ). [Latin] (16c) *Hist.* A writ directed to a judge of an inferior court to issue execution on a judgment in that court, or to return some reasonable cause why the judge has delayed execution.

executioner. (16c) Someone who puts another person to death to carry out a death sentence; esp., a person whose job is to carry out capital punishment on the state's behalf.

execution lien. See LIEN.

execution of judgment. See EXECUTION (4).

exécution parée (eg-zay-koo-**syawn** pa-**ray**). [French] *French law.* A right founded on an act approved and verified before a notary, by which a creditor may immediately — without citation or summons — seize and cause to be sold the debtor's property and keep the proceeds of the sale (to the extent of the indebtedness).

execution-proof. See JUDGMENT-PROOF.

execution sale. See SALE.

execution writ. See EXECUTION (4).

executive, *n.* (18c) **1.** The branch of government responsible for effecting and enforcing laws; the person or persons who constitute this branch. • The executive branch is sometimes said to be the residue of all government after subtracting the judicial and legislative branches. — Sometimes also termed *executive department.* Cf. LEGISLATURE; JUDICIARY (1).

▸ **chief executive.** (1876) The head of the executive branch of a government, such as the President of the United States.

2. A corporate officer at the upper levels of management. — Also termed *executive officer*; *executive employee.* — **executive,** *adj.*

executive administration. (17c) Collectively, high public officials who administer the chief departments of the government.

executive agency. (1850) An executive-branch department whose activities are subject to statute and whose contracts are subject to judicial review. • One example is the National Aeronautics and Space Agency.

executive agreement. (1942) An international agreement entered into by the President, without approval by the Senate, and usu. involving routine diplomatic or military matters. Cf. TREATY (1).

executive board. See BOARD OF DIRECTORS.

executive branch. (18c) The division of government charged with administering and carrying out the law; EXECUTIVE (1). — Also termed *executive branch of government.* Cf. JUDICIAL BRANCH; LEGISLATIVE BRANCH.

> "Dozens and dozens of separate agencies constitute the executive branch, many of them almost a law unto themselves. There are too many of them to count. Congress rarely puts any of them to sleep. (The late, unmourned Interstate Commerce Commission is a rare exception.) There is also the presidency itself. This has been, in many ways, *the* growth element of twentieth-century government. The president is not only the celebrity of celebrities, he is a man of enormous and growing power. (So far, of course, all presidents have been men.) One of the most significant developments of the twentieth century — one easily overlooked or forgotten — was the establishment of the Executive Office of the President in the 1930s; and the vast power it attracted to itself. The president's staff — not the cabinet, not the agencies, but the people who work in and for the White House — now number in the thousands. The president runs, in effect, a parallel government. Who gives the president advice on foreign policy? Not just the secretary of state; and sometimes not even primarily the secretary of state. There are foreign policy advisers 'in the White house'; and they often have more real say than the cabinet department which, in theory, runs foreign policy and advises the president. The president's economic advisers, his social advisers, his staff in general — these are, in many senses, the heart of the government." Lawrence M. Friedman, *American Law in the 20th Century* 599 (2002).

executive clemency. See CLEMENCY.

executive committee. See COMMITTEE (1).

executive department. See EXECUTIVE (1).

executive director. (18c) A salaried employee who serves as an organization's chief administrative and operating officer and heads its professional staff. — Also termed *executive secretary*; *staff director.*

executive employee. (1938) An employee whose duties include some form of managerial authority and active participation in the control, supervision, and management of the business. — Often shortened to *executive.*

executive immunity. See IMMUNITY (1).

executive officer. See EXECUTIVE (2).

executive order. (1862) An order issued by or on behalf of the President, usu. intended to direct or instruct the actions of executive agencies or government officials, or to set policies for the executive branch to follow. — Abbr. ex. ord.

executive pardon. See PARDON.

executive power. (17c) *Constitutional law.* The power to see that the laws are duly executed and enforced. • Under federal law, this power is vested in the President; in the states, it is vested in the governors. The President's enumerated powers are found in the U.S. Constitution, art. II, § 2; governors' executive powers are provided for in state constitutions. The other two great powers of government are the legislative power and the judicial power.

executive-practice canon. The doctrine that favors an interpretation conforming to executive practice at the time of a statute's enactment.

executive privilege. See PRIVILEGE (3).

executive right. (1893) *Oil & gas.* The exclusive right to lease specified land or mineral rights. • The executive right is one of the incidents of the mineral interest.

executive secretary. See EXECUTIVE DIRECTOR.

executive session. See SESSION (1).

executor, *n.* (13c) **1.** (**ek**-sə-kyoo-tər) Someone who performs or carries out some act. **2.** (eg-**zek**-yə-tər) A person named by a testator to carry out the provisions in the testator's will. Cf. ADMINISTRATOR (2). — Abbr. *exor.*

> "[T]he very name of executor purporteth in general one to execute somewhat, or to whom the execution of somewhat is committed or recommended. In one particular thereof an executor of a will must needs be such a one to whom the execution and performance of another man's will after his death is commended or committed; or who is constituted or authorized by the will maker to do him that friendly office. Hence it followeth necessarily, that a will is the only bed where an executor can be begotten or conceived; for where no will is, there can be no executor; and this is so conspicuous, and evidence to every low capacity, that it needs no proof or illustration." Thomas Wentworth, *The Office and Duty of Executors* 2–3 (Henry Jeremy & E.D. Ingraham eds., 1st Am. ed. fr. 14th London ed. 1832).

> "An executor is the person to whom the execution of the last will or testament of personal estate is by the testator's appointment confided." Simon Greenleaf Croswell, *Handbook on the Law of Executors and Administrators* § 1, at 3 (1897).

▸ **acting executor.** (18c) Someone who assumes the role of executor — usu. temporarily — but is not the legally appointed executor or the executor-in-fact. — Also termed *temporary executor.*

▸ **coexecutor.** See *joint executor.*

▸ **dative executor.** An executor appointed by a probate-court judge to administer an estate under intestacy laws. — Also termed *dative-testamentary executor.* See DATIVE (1). Cf. *executor ab episcopo constitutus.*

▸ **executor *ab episcopo constitutus*** (ab ə-**pis**-kə-poh kon-sti-**t[y]oo**-təs). [Law Latin] (17c) *Eccles. law.* An executor appointed by a bishop; an administrator to an intestate. — Also termed *executor dativus.* Cf. *dative executor.*

▸ **executor *a lege constitutus*** (ay [*or* ah] **lee**-jee kon-sti-**t[y]oo**-təs). [Law Latin] (17c) *Eccles. law.* One authorized by law to be an executor; the ordinary of the diocese.

▸ **executor *a testatore constitutus*** (ay [*or* ah] tes-tə-**tor**-ee kon-sti-**t[y]oo**-təs). [Law Latin] (17c) *Eccles. law.* An executor appointed by a testator. — Also termed *executor testamentarius.* Cf. *testamentary executor.*

▸ **executor dative.** See DATIVE (1).

▸ **executor *dativus.*** See *executor ab episcopo constitutus.*

▸ **executor *de son tort*** (də sawn [*or* son] **tor[t]**). [Law French "executor of his own wrong"] (17c) Someone who, without legal authority, takes on the responsibility to act as an executor or administrator of a decedent's property, usu. to the detriment of the estate's beneficiaries or creditors. See DE SON TORT.

> "*Executor de son tort* — or, executor of his own wrong. Is he that takes upon him the office of an executor by intrusion, not being so constituted by the testator." *The Pocket Lawyer and Family Conveyancer* 98 (3d ed. 1833).

▸ **executor *lucratus*** (loo-**kray**-təs). An executor who has assets of the testator, the latter having become liable by wrongfully interfering with another's property.

▸ **executor *testamentarius.*** See *executor a testatore constitutus.*

▸ **executor to the tenor.** *Eccles. law.* Someone who is not named executor in the will but who performs duties similar to those of an executor.

▸ **general executor.** (18c) An executor who has the power to administer a decedent's entire estate until its final settlement.

▸ **independent executor.** (1877) An executor who, unlike an ordinary executor, can administer the estate with very little supervision by the probate court. • Only a few states — mostly in the West and Southwest — allow testators to designate independent executors. But lawyers routinely write wills that relieve a trusted executor from obtaining appraisals, from providing inventories and surety bonds, and from obtaining court approval "to the maximum extent permitted by law." The Uniform Probate Code endorses independent administration, and it is the usual process unless a party demands court-supervised administration. — Also termed *nonintervention executor.*

▸ **joint executor.** (17c) One of two or more persons named in a will as executor of an estate. — Also termed *coexecutor.*

▸ **limited executor.** (18c) An executor whose appointment is restricted in some way, such as time, place, or subject matter.

▸ **literary executor.** (1868) *Copyright.* A limited-purpose executor appointed to manage copyrighted materials in an estate.

▸ **nonintervention executor.** See *independent executor.*

▸ **special executor.** (18c) An executor whose power is limited to a portion of the decedent's estate.

▸ **substituted executor.** (18c) An executor appointed to act in the place of an executor who cannot or will not perform the required duties.

▸ **temporary executor.** See *acting executor.*

▸ **testamentary executor.** An executor appointed by a testator and confirmed by the probate court. Cf. *executor a testatore constitutus.*

3. (eg-**zek**-yə-tər) *Patents.* Someone who represents a legally incapacitated inventor. — **executorial,** *adj.* — **executorship,** *n.*

executor fund. See FUND (1).

executor's bond. See BOND (2).

executor's deed. See DEED.

executor's year. See YEAR.

executory (eg-**zek**-yə-tor-ee), *adj.* (16c) **1.** Taking full effect at a future time <executory judgment>. **2.** To be performed at a future time; yet to be completed <executory contract>.

executory accord. See ACCORD (2).

executory bequest. See BEQUEST.

executory consideration. See CONSIDERATION (1).

executory contract. See CONTRACT.

executory covenant. See COVENANT (1).

executory devise. See DEVISE.

executory interest. (1833) A future interest, held by a third person, that either cuts off another's interest or begins after the natural termination of a preceding estate. Cf. REMAINDER.

> "What is an executory interest? Here is a pretty good definition: *An executory interest is any future interest created in a person other than the transferor that is not a remainder.* Here are five classic examples of executory interest: (1) O transfers 'to A for life; then, one day after A's death, to the heirs of A.' The transfer creates a springing executory interest in those who will be A's heirs. (2) O transfers 'to A for 200 years if he shall so long live, then to the heirs of A.' This transfer also creates a springing executory interest in A's prospective heirs. (3) O transfers 'to A and his heirs five years from the date of this deed.' A owns a springing executory interest. (4) O, when B is fifteen, transfers 'to A for life; then no sooner than one day after A's death, to B and his heirs if B ever reaches 21.' B owns a springing executory interest. (5) O transfers 'to A and his heirs; but if A marries X, to B and his heirs.' B owns a shifting executory interest." Thomas F. Bergin & Paul G. Haskell, *Preface to Estates in Land and Future Interests* 80 (2d ed. 1984).

▸ **shifting executory interest.** (1948) An executory interest that operates in defeasance of an interest created simultaneously in a third person.

▸ **springing executory interest.** (1948) An executory interest that operates in defeasance of an interest left in the transferor.

executory judgment. See JUDGMENT (2).

executory limitation. See LIMITATION (4).

executory process. (1829) *Civil law.* **1.** A process that can be resorted to either (1) when the right of a creditor arises from an act importing a confession of judgment, and that contains a privilege or mortgage in the creditor's favor, or (2) when the creditor demands the execution of a judgment that has been rendered by a different tribunal. **2.** An accelerated procedure, summary in nature, by which the holder of a mortgage or privilege evidenced by a confession of judgment seeks to effect an ex parte seizure and sale of the subject property.

executory remainder. See *contingent remainder* under REMAINDER (1).

executory sale. See SALE.

executory trust. See TRUST (3).

executory unilateral accord. (1940) An offer to enter a contract; OFFER (2).

executory use. See *springing use* under USE (4).

executory warranty. See WARRANTY (3).

executress. See EXECUTRIX.

executrix (eg-**zek**-yə-triks), *n.* (16c) *Archaic.* A female executor. — Abbr. exrx. — Also termed *executress.* See EXECUTOR. Pl. **executrixes** (eg-**zek**-yə-trik-səz), **executrices** (eg-zek-yə-**trɪ**-seez).

executry. (17c) *Scots law.* **1.** Executorship. See EXECUTOR (1), (2). **2.** The movable property of a decedent.

exedos (e-**he**-thohs), *n.* See EJIDOS.

exegesis (eks-ə-**jee**-səs). The explanation of the meaning of a text through close reading. Cf. EISEGESIS. — **exegetical,** *adj.* — **exegete,** *n.*

exemplar (eg-**zem**-plər *or* -plahr), *n.* (15c) **1.** An ideal example; the epitome of some characteristic <Justice Jackson was an exemplar of clear legal writing>. **2.** An ideal or typical example; a standard specimen <handwriting exemplars>. **3.** Nontestimonial identification evidence, such as fingerprints, voiceprints, and DNA samples <the suspect's fingerprints matched exemplars taken at the crime scene>. See VOICE EXEMPLAR. **4.** (*often pl.*) A known sample of a person's voice, handwriting, recorded footsteps, etc., for use in forensic comparison to determine whether a match in identity exists with a sample of questionable origin or identity <an exemplar of the defendant's voice seemed to match the 911 call>. See INDIVIDUALIZATION; VOICE EXEMPLAR.

exemplary, *adj.* (16c) **1.** Serving as an ideal example; commendable <exemplary behavior>. **2.** Serving as a warning or deterrent; admonitory <exemplary damages>.

exemplary damages. See *punitive damages* under DAMAGES.

exemplary punishment. See *deterrent punishment* under PUNISHMENT.

exemplary substitution. See SUBSTITUTION (5).

exemplification, *n.* (16c) An official transcript of a public record, authenticated as a true copy for use as evidence. — **exemplify,** *vb.*

exemplificatione (eg-zem-plə-fə-**kay**-shee-oh-nee). [Latin] A writ granted for the exemplification or transcript of an original record.

exemplified copy. See *certified copy* under COPY (1).

exempli gratia (eg-**zem**-plɪ **gray**-shee-ə *or* ek-**sem**-plee **grah**-tee-ə). [Latin] (17c) For example; for instance. — Abbr. e.g. or (rarely) ex. gr.

exemplum (eg-**zem**-pləm), *n.* [Latin] (19c) *Civil law.* A copy; a written authorized copy.

exempt, *adj.* (14c) Free or released from a duty or liability to which others are held <persons exempt from military service> <property exempt from sequestration>. — **exempt,** *vb.* — **exemptive,** *adj.*

exempt income. See INCOME.

exemption. (14c) **1.** Freedom from a duty, liability, or other requirement; an exception. See IMMUNITY (3); EXCEPTION (2). **2.** A privilege given to a judgment debtor by law, allowing the debtor to retain certain property without liability. — Also termed *debtor's exemption.*

▸ **exemption from garnishments.** A statutory protection of earnings or funds in bank accounts against seizure under certain circumstances.

3. *Tax.* An amount allowed as a deduction from adjusted gross income, used to determine taxable income. Cf. DEDUCTION (2).

▸ **dependency exemption.** (1920) A tax exemption granted to an individual taxpayer for each dependent whose gross income is less than the exemption amount and for each child who is younger than 19 or, if a student, younger than 24.

▸ **personal exemption.** (1920) An amount allowed as a deduction from an individual taxpayer's adjusted gross income.

exemption clause. (1840) A contractual provision providing that a party will not be liable for damages for which that party would otherwise have ordinarily been liable. Cf. EXCEPTION CLAUSE; EXCULPATORY CLAUSE; INDEMNITY CLAUSE.

> "An exemption clause may take many forms, but all such clauses have one thing in common in that they exempt a party from a liability which he would have borne had it not been for the clause. In some cases an exemption clause merely relieves a party from certain purely contractual obligations, for example, the duties of a seller in a contract of sale regarding the quality and fitness of the goods. In other cases exemption clauses go further and protect the party not merely from contractual liability but even from liability which would otherwise have arisen in tort. For example, a shipping company's ticket may exempt the company from liability to the passenger for any injuries, however caused. Now if the passenger is injured as a result of the negligence of the company's employees, that would, in the normal way, give rise to an action in tort for negligence, quite apart from the contract." P.S. Atiyah, *An Introduction to the Law of Contract* 167 (3d ed. 1981).

exemption equivalent. The maximum value of assets that one can transfer to another before incurring a federal gift and estate tax.

exemption from garnishments. See EXEMPTION (2).

exemption law. (1839) A law describing what property of a debtor cannot be attached by a judgment creditor or trustee in bankruptcy to satisfy a debt. See EXEMPT PROPERTY (1).

ex empto (eks **emp**-toh). [Latin] *Roman & civil law.* Out of purchase; founded on purchase.

exempt offering. See OFFERING.

exempt organization. (1932) An organization that is either partially or completely exempt from federal income taxation. See CHARITABLE ORGANIZATION.

exempt property. (1839) **1.** A debtor's holdings and possessions that, by law, a creditor cannot attach to satisfy a debt. • All the property that creditors may lawfully reach is known as *nonexempt property.* Many states provide a homestead exemption that excludes a person's house and household items, up to a certain amount, from the liens of most creditors. The purpose of the exemption is to prevent debtors from becoming destitute. See HOMESTEAD. Cf. NONEXEMPT ASSETS. **2.** Personal property that a surviving spouse is automatically entitled to receive from the decedent's estate.

exempt security. See SECURITY (4).

exempt transaction. (1929) A sale that falls outside the scope of a certain statute, such as the Securities Act of 1933 or the Securities Exchange Act of 1934.

exennium (eg-**zen**-ee-əm), *n.* [Latin] *Hist.* A gift, esp. one given at the new year.

ex eo ob quod mittitur (eks **ee**-oh ob kwod **mit**-i-tər). [Latin] For that purpose for which he is sent.

ex eo quod plerumque fit (eks **ee**-oh kwod pli-**rəm**-kwee fit). [Latin] *Hist.* From that which generally happens.

exequatur (ek-sə-**kway**-tər). [Latin "let it be executed"] (17c) A written official recognition and authorization of a consular officer, issued by the government to which the officer is accredited.

> "Consuls on exhibiting proof of their appointment, if not objectionable persons, receive an *exequatur*, or permission to discharge their functions within the limits prescribed, which permission can be withdrawn for any misconduct." Theodore D. Woolsey, *Introduction to the Study of International Law* § 100, at 162–63 (5th ed. 1878).

ex equitate (eks ek-wə-**tay**-tee). [Latin] *Hist.* According to equitable rules.

exercise, *vb.* (14c) **1.** To make use of; to put into action <exercise the right to vote>. **2.** To implement the terms of; to execute <exercise the option to buy the commodities>. — **exercise,** *n.*

Exercise Clause. See FREE EXERCISE CLAUSE.

exercise of judgment. (17c) The use of sound discretion — that is, discretion exercised with regard to what is right and equitable rather than arbitrarily or willfully.

exercise price. See *strike price* under PRICE.

exercise value. (1931) The value to an optionholder of using the option.

exercitalis (eg-zər-si-**tay**-lis), *n.* [Latin] A soldier; a vassal.

exercitor (eg-**zər**-si-tor), *n.* [Latin "an exercisor"] (17c) *Civil law.* The person to whom the profits of a ship temporarily belong, whether that person is the owner, charterer, or mortgagee. — Also termed *exercitor maris*; *exercitor navis.* Cf. SHIP'S HUSBAND.

exercitoria actio. See *actio exercitoria* under ACTIO.

exercitorial power (eg-zər-si-**tor**-ee-əl). (1876) The trust given to a shipmaster.

exercitor maris (eg-**zər**-si-tər **mar**-is). See EXERCITOR.

exercitor navis (eg-**zər**-si-tər **nay**-vis). See EXERCITOR.

exercituale (eg-zər-sich-oo-**ay**-lee), *n.* [Law Latin, fr. Latin *exercitus* "an army"] *Hist.* A heriot paid only in arms, horses, or military accouterments. See HERIOT.

exercitus (eg-**zər**-si-təs), *n.* [Latin "an army"] *Hist.* An army; an armed force. • Of indefinite number, the term was applied on various occasions to a gathering of 42 armed men, of 35, or even of 4.

ex eventu (eks i-**ven**-t[y]oo). [Latin] *Hist.* After the event; following the occurrence.

ex facie (eks **fay**-shee-ee *or* -shee *or* -shə). [Latin] (1861) *Archaic.* On the face of it; evidently; apparently. • The phrase typically referred to a defect appearing from the document itself, without further inquiry.

ex facto (eks **fak**-toh). [Latin "from a fact"] From or in consequence of a fact or action; actually; DE FACTO.

exfestucare (eks-fes-tə-**kair**-ee), *vb.* [Latin] *Hist.* To abdicate or resign; to surrender (an estate, office, or dignity) by the symbolic delivery of a staff or rod (*festuca*) to the transferee.

ex fictione juris (eks fik-shee-**oh**-nee **joor**-is). [Latin] (16c) By a fiction of law.

ex figura verborum (eks fi-**gyuur**-ə vər-**bor**-əm). [Law Latin] (18c) *Hist.* By the form of the words used. • A defective deed could not be fixed merely by calling it something else.

ex fraude creditorum (eks **fraw**-dee kred-kred-i-**tor**-əm). [Law Latin] *Hist.* On the ground of fraud toward creditors. • A preference could be set aside if it were made within 60 days of the bankruptcy filing.

exfrediare (eks-free-dee-**air**-ee), *vb.* [Latin] To break the peace; to commit open violence.

ex. gr. *abbr.* EXEMPLI GRATIA.

ex gratia (eks **gray**-shee-ə *or* **grah**-tee-ə). [Latin "by favor"] (18c) Made as a favor or gift, and not because of any legal duty; not legally necessary. — Also termed *a gratia.*

ex gratia payment. (1916) A payment not legally required; esp., an insurance payment not required to be made under an insurance policy.

ex gravi querela (eks **gray**-vI kwə-**ree**-lə). [Latin "from or on the grievous complaint"] (16c) *Hist.* A writ that lay for a person to whom any lands or tenements in fee were devised by will (within any city, town, or borough in which lands were devisable by custom), against an heir of the devisor who entered and detained them from the devisee. • The writ was abolished by the Real Property Limitation Act (1833). St. 3 & 4 Will. 4, ch. 27, § 36.

exhausted ballot. See *exhausted vote* under VOTE (1).

exhausted combination. See *old combination* under COMBINATION.

exhausted-combination rejection. See *old-combination rejection* under REJECTION.

exhausted vote. See VOTE (1).

exhaustion, *n.* **1.** The act of consuming something until nothing is left. **2.** The deprivation of a valuable quality or component by overuse or consumption. **3.** The pursuit of options until none remain. — **exhaust,** *vb.*

exhaustion doctrine. (1935) **1.** EXHAUSTION OF REMEDIES. **2.** *Criminal law.* The rule in habeas proceedings that a petitioner must raise an issue in the state courts before presenting it to a federal court. **3.** EXHAUSTION-OF-RIGHTS DOCTRINE.

exhaustion-of-domestic-remedies rule. See EXHAUSTION-OF-LOCAL-REMEDIES RULE.

exhaustion-of-local-remedies rule. (1958) *Int'l law.* The principle that a country should be allowed the opportunity to redress an alleged wrong through its own domestic legal system before the country's legal responsibility can be called into question by regional or international bodies. — Sometimes shortened to *local-remedies rule.* — Also termed *exhaustion-of-domestic-remedies rule; domestic-remedies rule; rule of prior exhaustion of local remedies; rule of prior exhaustion of domestic remedies.*

exhaustion of remedies. (1876) The doctrine that, if an administrative remedy is provided by statute, a claimant must seek relief first from the administrative body before judicial relief is available. • The doctrine's purpose is to maintain comity between the courts and administrative agencies and to ensure that courts will not be burdened by cases in which judicial relief is unnecessary. — Also termed *exhaustion-of-remedies doctrine; exhaustion of administrative remedies; exhaustion doctrine.*

> "The traditional rule can . . . be fairly simply stated. A litigant must normally exhaust state 'legislative' or 'administrative' remedies before challenging the state action in federal court. He or she need not normally exhaust state 'judicial' remedies. The rationale for this distinction is that until the administrative process is complete, it cannot be certain that the party will need judicial relief, but when the case becomes appropriate for judicial determination, he or she may choose whether to resort to a state or federal court for that relief. The word 'normally' is required in both branches of the rule." Charles Alan Wright, *The Law of Federal Courts* § 49, at 313 (5th ed. 1994).

▸ **vicarious exhaustion of remedies.** (1987) The rule that if one member of a class satisfies a requirement to exhaust administrative remedies, that is enough for all others similarly situated to be considered as having exhausted the remedies. — Often shortened to *vicarious exhaustion.*

exhaustion-of-rights doctrine. (1977) *Intellectual property.* The principle that once the owner of an intellectual-property right has placed a product covered by that right into the marketplace, the right to control how the product is resold within that internal market is lost. • Within a common market, such as the European Union, the doctrine also applies to the import and export of the goods between member countries. Cf. PATENT-EXHAUSTION DOCTRINE. — Often shortened to *exhaustion doctrine.*

exhaustion of state remedies. (1944) The doctrine that an available state remedy must be exhausted in certain types of cases before a party can gain access to a federal court. • For example, a state prisoner must exhaust all state remedies before a federal court will hear a petition for habeas corpus.

exhibere (ek-sə-**beer**-ee), *vb.* [Latin] **1.** To present (a tangible thing) so that it may be handled. **2.** To appear personally to defend against an action at law.

exhibit, *n.* (17c) **1.** A document, record, or other tangible object formally introduced as evidence in court. **2.** A document attached to and made part of a pleading, motion, contract, or other instrument.

exhibit, *vb.* (16c) *Archaic.* To bring a lawsuit by filing (a bill).

exhibitio billae (ek-sə-**bish**-ee-oh **bil**-ee). [Latin] *Hist.* The commencement of a suit by presenting or exhibiting a bill to the court.

exhibition. (1861) *Scots law.* An action to compel the production or delivery of documents.

exhibitionism, *n.* (1893) The indecent display of one's body. — **exhibitionist,** *adj.* & *n.*

exhibition value. (1922) In the motion-picture industry, the minimum receipts that distributors expect to realize from showing a particular film. — Also termed *minimum sale; price expectancy.*

exhibit list. (1929) **1.** A pretrial filing that identifies by number and description the exhibits a party intends to offer into evidence at trial. • Courts often require the exchange of exhibit lists before trial so that evidentiary disputes can be resolved with minimal disruption in the course of a jury trial. **2.** A document prepared during a trial by the clerk or a courtroom deputy to identify by number and description the exhibits that the parties have entered into evidence.

exhibitory interdict. See INTERDICT (1).

exhumation (eks-hyoo-**may**-shən *or* eg-zyoo-), *n.* (18c) The removal from the earth of something buried, esp. a human corpse for purposes of checking the cause of death; disinterment.— **exhume,** *vb.*

ex hypothesi (eks hI-**poth**-ə-sI). [Latin] (17c) Hypothetically; by hypothesis; on the assumption <conviction for a felony is *ex hypothesi* impossible in the case of suicide>.

exidos (e-**hee**-thohs), *n.* See EJIDOS.

exigency (**ek**-sə-jən-see), *n.* (16c) A state of urgency; a situation requiring immediate action. — Also termed *exigence.*

exigendary (ek-sə-**jen**-də-ree), *n.* See EXIGENTER.

exigent, *adj.* (17c) Requiring immediate action or aid; urgent <exigent circumstances>.

exigent (**ek**-sə-jənt), *n.* (15c) *Hist.* A judicial writ employed in the process of outlawry, commanding the sheriff to demand the defendant's appearance, from county court to county court, until he was outlawed — or, if the defendant appeared, to take him before the court to answer the plaintiff's action. See EXIGI FACIAS.

exigent circumstances. See CIRCUMSTANCE.

exigent-circumstances doctrine. (1967) *Criminal law.* The rule that emergency conditions may justify a warrantless search and seizure, esp. when there is probable cause to believe that evidence will be removed or destroyed before a warrant can be obtained.

exigenter (**ek**-sə-jen-tər), *n.* (16c) *Hist.* An officer of the court of common pleas responsible for preparing exigents and proclamations in the process of outlawry. • This office was abolished in 1837 by the Superior Courts (Officers) Act, St. 7 Will. 4, and 1 Vict., ch. 30. — Also termed *exigendary.*

exigent list. A list of cases set down for hearing on various incidental and ancillary motions and rules.

exigent search. See SEARCH (1).

exigible (**ek**-sə-jə-bəl), *adj.* (17c) Requirable; demandable (as a debt). Cf. PRESTABLE.

exigible debt. See DEBT.

exigi facias (**ek**-sə-jɪ **fay**-shee-əs). [Latin] That you cause to be demanded. • These were the emphatic words of the Latin form of the writ of exigent; the phrase was sometimes used as the name of the writ. See EXIGENT.

exile, *n.* (14c) **1.** Expulsion from a country, esp. from the country of one's origin or longtime residence; banishment.

▸ **forced exile.** (17c) Compelled removal or banishment from one's native country.

2. Someone who has been banished. **3.** A prolonged voluntary absence from one's home country. — **exile,** *vb.*

exilium (eg-**zil**-ee-əm), *n.* [Latin "exile"] *Hist.* **1.** Exile; the act of driving away or despoiling. **2.** A type of waste consisting in the driving away of an estate's bondservants and tenants by demolishing their homes or by enfranchising the bondservants and then turning them out of their homes.

Ex-Im Bank. See EXPORT-IMPORT BANK OF THE UNITED STATES.

ex incommodo (eks in-**kom**-ə-doh). [Latin] *Hist.* On account of inconvenience. • An argument based solely on inconvenience was usu. rejected.

ex incontinenti (eks in-kon-tə-**nen**-tɪ). [Latin] *Hist.* Without delay; in a summary manner.

ex industria (eks in-**dəs**-tree-ə). [Latin] With contrivance or deliberation; designedly; on purpose.

ex ingenio (eks in-**jen**-ee-oh). [Latin] *Hist.* According to the judgment of any one.

ex instrumentis de novo repertis (eks in-strə-**men**-tis dee **noh**-voh **rep**-ər-tis). [Law Latin] *Hist.* On account of documents newly or recently found. • The phrase appeared in reference to a basis for altering a decree. See INSTRUMENTA NOVITER REPERTA.

ex integro (eks **in**-tə-groh). [Latin] Anew; afresh.

ex intervallo (eks in-tər-**val**-oh). [Latin] *Hist.* At some interval.

existent corner. See CORNER (1).

existimatio (eg-zis-tə-**may**-shee-oh), *n.* [Latin] *Roman law.* **1.** The civil reputation belonging to a Roman citizen of unimpeached dignity or character; the highest standing of a Roman citizen. **2.** The decision or award of an arbiter. Pl. ***existimationes*** (eg-zis-tə-may-shee-**oh**-neez).

exit, *n.* (16c) **1.** A way out. See EGRESS. **2.** In a docket entry, an issuance of something (as a writ or process). • For example, *exit attachment* denotes that a writ of attachment has been issued in the case. — **exit,** *vb.*

exitus (**ek**-si-təs), *n.* [Latin] *Hist.* **1.** Children; offspring. **2.** The rents, issues, and profits of lands and tenements. **3.** An export duty. **4.** The conclusion of a pleading.

ex jure (eks **joor**-ee). [Latin] Of or by legal right.

ex jure naturae (eks **joor**-ee nə-**t[y]oor**-ee). [Latin] *Hist.* According to the law of nature.

ex jure representationis (eks **joor**-ee rep-ri-zen-tay-shee-**oh**-nis). [Law Latin] *Hist.* According to the law of representation.

ex justa causa (eks **jəs**-tə **kaw**-zə). [Latin] From a just or lawful cause; by a just or legal title.

ex justitia (eks jəs-**tish**-ee-ə). [Latin] From justice; as a matter of justice.

exlegalitas (eks-lə-**gay**-lə-tas), *n.* [Law Latin] *Hist.* **1.** Outlawry; outside the law's protection. **2.** Someone who is prosecuted as an outlaw.

ex legal municipal bond. See BOND (3).

exlegare (eks-lə-**gair**-ee), *vb.* [Law Latin] *Hist.* To outlaw; to deprive of the benefit and protection of the law.

ex lege (eks **lee**-jee *or* **lay**-gay). [Latin] By virtue of law; as a matter of law <property forfeited *ex lege*>.

> "Antecedent rights 'in personam' . . . either arise or do not arise out of a contract. . . . In the latter case, since they arise from facts of various kinds to which it pleases the Law to affix similar results, we shall describe them as rights 'ex lege'; and it will be convenient to consider the rights which arise thus variously before treating of those which arise solely from contract. . . . The rights which we describe as arising 'ex lege' were described by the Roman lawyers as arising 'quasi ex contractu,' and more simply, 'ex variis causarum figuris.'" Thomas E. Holland, *The Elements of Jurisprudence* 246–47 (13th ed. 1924).

ex legibus (eks **lee**-jə-bəs). [Latin "according to the laws"] *Hist.* To be interpreted according to both the letter and the spirit of the law.

exlex (**eks**-leks), *n.* [Law Latin] (1909) *Hist.* An outlaw; one who is outside the law's protection.

ex licentia regis (eks lɪ-**sen**-shee-ə **ree**-jis). [Latin] By the king's license.

ex locato (eks loh-**kay**-toh). [Latin] *Roman law.* From lease; out of letting. • This term referred to an action or right of action arising out of a contract of hiring, bailment for reward, or employment. See *actio locati* under ACTIO.

ex maiore cautela (eks may-**or**-ee kaw-**tee**-lə). [Latin] From greater caution.

ex maleficio, *adj.* [Latin] Tortious.

ex maleficio (eks mal-ə-**fish**-ee-oh), *adv.* [Latin] By malfeasance.

ex malitia (eks mə-**lish**-ee-ə). [Latin] *Hist.* From malice; maliciously. • In the law of defamation, the term refers to a publication that is false and without legal excuse.

ex malo regimine (eks **mal**-loh ri-**jim**-ə-nee). [Latin] *Hist.* From bad treatment.

ex mandato (eks man-**day**-toh). [Latin] *Hist.* According to the mandate; arising from a mandate.

ex mero motu (eks **meer**-oh **moh**-tyoo). [Latin "on his mere motion"] *Hist.* Voluntarily; without suggestion or influence from another person. • The phrase was formerly sometimes used in reference to a court, as an equivalent of *sua sponte* or *on its own motion.* See SUA SPONTE.

ex metu carceris (eks **mee**-t[y]oo **kahr**-sər-is). [Latin] *Hist.* From fear of imprisonment.

ex mora (eks **mor**-ə). [Latin] *Civil law.* From or in consequence of delay. • Interest is allowed *ex mora* — that is, if there has been delay in repaying borrowed money.

ex mora debitoris (eks **mor**-ə deb-i-**tor**-is). [Latin] *Hist.* On account of the debtor's delay. • The phrase appeared in reference to a basis for charging interest on a debt.

ex more (eks **mor**-ee). [Latin] According to custom.

ex mutuo (eks **myoo**-choo-oh). [Latin] From or out of loan. • In old English law, a debt was said to arise *ex mutuo* when one lent another anything that consisted in number, weight, or measure.

ex natura (eks nə-**t[y]oor**-ə). [Latin] *Hist.* Naturally; according to nature.

ex natura feudi (eks nə-**t[y]oor**-ə **fyoo**-dɪ). [Law Latin] *Hist.* According to the nature of the feudal right.

ex naturali jure (eks nach-ə-**ray**-lɪ **joor**-ee), *adv.* [Latin] By or according to natural law <*ex naturali jure* some time may be needed after a declaration of war before the war begins>. See NATURAL LAW.

ex natura rei (eks nə-**t[y]oor**-ə **ree**-ɪ). [Latin] *Hist.* According to the nature of the thing (or transaction).

ex necessitate (eks nə-ses-i-**tay**-tee). [Latin] Of or from necessity.

▸ ***ex necessitate legis*** (eks nə-ses-i-**tay**-tee **lee**-jis). From or by necessity of law.

▸ ***ex necessitate rei*** (eks nə-ses-i-**tay**-tee **ree**-ɪ). From the necessity or urgency of the thing or case.

ex nihilo (eks **nɪ**-hi-loh). [Latin] (16c) From nothing.

ex nobili officio (eks **nob**-i-lɪ ə-**fish**-ee-oh). [Latin "by virtue of its noble office"] *Scots law.* (Of a judicial act) done as a matter of equity. See NOBILE OFFICIUM.

ex officio (eks ə-**fish**-ee-oh), *adv.* & *adj.* [Latin] (16c) By virtue or because of an office; by virtue of the authority implied by office. • The term is often misused as a synonym for "nonvoting." Some meetings mistakenly label their regularly invited guests as "ex officio members" when in fact they are not members at all; others mistakenly refer to the nonvoting members as "ex officio members" even though some nonvoting members are present only in an individual capacity and not by virtue of office, or even though some voting members also serve ex officio. But an ex officio member is a voting member unless the applicable governing document provides otherwise.

> "Frequently boards include ex-officio members — that is, persons who are members of the board by virtue of an office or committee chairmanship held in the society, or in the parent state or national society or federation or some allied group; or — sometimes in boards outside of organized societies — by virtue of a public office. In the executive board of a society, if the ex-officio member of the board is under the authority of the society (that is, if he is a member, officer, or employee of the society), there is no distinction between him and the other board members. If the ex-officio member is not under the authority of the society, he has all the privileges of board membership, including the right to make motions and to vote, but none of the obligations — just as in a case, for example, where the governor of a state is ex officio a trustee of a private academy." Henry M. Robert, *Robert's Rules of Order Newly Revised* § 49, at 466 (10th ed. 2000).

ex officio information. (18c) *English law.* A criminal information filed by the attorney general ex officio on behalf of the Crown, in the Court of King's Bench, for offenses more immediately affecting the government, as distinguished from informations in which the Crown is the nominal prosecutor.

ex officio justice. (1855) A judge who serves on a commission or board only because the law requires the presence of a judge rather than because the judge was selected for the position.

ex officio member. See *member ex officio* under MEMBER (1).

ex officio service (eks ə-**fish**-ee-oh). (1845) A service that the law imposes on an official by virtue of the office held, such as that of a local justice of the peace to perform marriage ceremonies.

exogamous insemination. See *artificial insemination by donor* under ARTIFICIAL INSEMINATION.

exoine (e-**soyn**), *n.* [French "excuse"] *French law.* An act or instrument in writing containing the reasons why a party in a civil suit, or a person accused, has not appeared after being summoned. See ESSOIN.

exonerate (eg-**zon**-ə-rayt), *vb.* (16c) **1.** To free from responsibility <exonerate from the payment of the debt>. **2.** To clear of all blame; to officially declare (a person) to be free of guilt; EXCULPATE. **3.** To free from encumbrances <exonerate the property from the mortgage lien>. — **exonerative** (eg-**zon**-ər-ay-tiv *or* -ə-tiv), *adj.*

exoneration (eg-zon-ə-**ray**-shən). (16c) **1.** The removal of a burden, charge, responsibility, or duty. **2.** The right to be reimbursed by reason of having paid money that another person should have paid. **3.** The equitable right of a surety — confirmed by statute in many states — to proceed to compel the principal debtor to satisfy the obligation, as when, even though the surety would have a right of reimbursement, it would be inequitable for the surety to be compelled to perform if the principal debtor can satisfy the obligation. • When a testator leaves a gift of property encumbered by a mortgage or lien, the doctrine of exoneration operates to satisfy the encumbrance from the general assets of the estate. Many states have abandoned the common-law rule in favor of exoneration. See EQUITY OF EXONERATION; QUIA TIMET.

exoneration, suit for. See SUIT FOR EXONERATION.

exoneratione sectae (eg-zon-ə-ray-shee-**oh**-nee **sek**-tee). [Latin] (17c) *Hist.* A writ that lay for the Crown's ward, to be free from all suit during wardship.

exoneratione sectae ad curiam baron (eg-zon-ə-ray-shee-**oh**-nee **sek**-tee ad **kyoor**-ee-əm **bar**-ən). [Latin "by exoneration of the suit to the lord's court"] *Hist.* A writ issued by the guardian of the Crown's ward, forbidding the sheriff or steward of a particular court from distraining or taking other action against the ward.

exonerative fact. See FACT.

exoneree (eg-**zon**-ə-ree), *n. Slang.* Someone who is relieved of blame, responsibility, or accusation; esp., someone who is officially cleared from a wrongful criminal conviction. See EXONERATE (2).

exoneretur (eg-zon-ə-**ree**-tər). *Hist.* [Latin "let him be relieved or discharged"] (1824) A note, recorded on a bailpiece, of a court order to release a bail obligation after the court has sentenced the defendant to prison. Cf. BAILPIECE (1).

exor. *abbr.* EXECUTOR.

ex. ord. (*often cap.*) *abbr.* EXECUTIVE ORDER.

exordium (eg-**zor**-dee-əm). [Latin] (16c) An introduction in a discourse or writing, esp. in a will. • In a will, the exordium usu. contains statements of the testator's name and capacity to make the will. — Also termed *exordium clause*; *introductory clause.* See INTRODUCTORY CLAUSE.

exotics. See *invasive species* under SPECIES (1).

exotic species. See *alien species* under SPECIES (1).

ex paritate rationis (eks par-ə-**tay**-tee ray-shee-**oh**-nis *or* rash-ee-). [Law Latin] *Hist.* By a parity of reasoning.

ex parte, *adj.* (17c) Done or made at the instance and for the benefit of one party only, and without notice to, or argument by, anyone having an adverse interest; of, relating to, or involving court action taken or received by one party without notice to the other, usu. for temporary or emergency relief <an ex parte hearing> <an ex parte injunction>. • Despite the traditional one-sidedness of ex parte matters, some courts now require notice to the opposition before what they call an "ex parte hearing." — Sometimes spelled *exparte.* — **ex parte,** *adv.*

ex parte (eks **pahr**-tee), *adv.* [Latin "from the part"] (18c) On or from one party only, usu. without notice to or argument from the adverse party <the judge conducted the hearing ex parte>.

ex parte application. See *ex parte motion* under MOTION (1).

ex parte communication. See COMMUNICATION.

ex parte divorce. See DIVORCE.

ex parte hearing. See *ex parte proceeding* under PROCEEDING.

ex parte injunction. See INJUNCTION.

ex parte materna (eks **pahr**-tee mə-**tər**-nə). [Latin] On the mother's side; of the maternal line.

ex parte motion. See MOTION (1).

ex parte order. See ORDER (2).

ex parte paterna (eks **pahr**-tee pə-**tər**-nə). [Latin] On the father's side; of the paternal line.

ex parte proceeding. See PROCEEDING.

Ex Parte Quayle **action.** See QUAYLE ACTION.

ex parte reexamination. See REEXAMINATION.

ex parte trial. See TRIAL.

expatriate (ek-**spay**-tree-it), *n.* (18c) An expatriated person; esp., a person who lives permanently in a foreign country.

expatriate (ek-**spay**-tree-ayt), *vb.* (1812) **1.** To withdraw (oneself) from residence in or allegiance to one's native country; to leave one's home country to live elsewhere. **2.** To banish or exile (a person). — **expatriation,** *n.*

expectancy, *n.* (1811) **1.** *Property.* An estate with a reversion, a remainder, or an executory interest. **2.** *Wills & estates.* The mere hope or probability of inheriting; specif., possibility that an heir apparent, an heir presumptive, or a presumptive next of kin will acquire property by devolution on intestacy, or the possibility that a presumptive beneficiary will acquire property by will. — Also termed *bare expectancy.* Cf. *vested interest* under INTEREST (2). **3.** *Insurance.* The probable number of years in one's life. See LIFE EXPECTANCY.

expectancy damages. See *expectation damages* under DAMAGES.

expectancy table. See ACTUARIAL TABLE.

expectant, *adj.* (14c) Having a relation to, or being dependent on, a contingency; CONTINGENT.

expectant beneficiary. See *expectant distributee* under DISTRIBUTEE.

expectant distributee. See DISTRIBUTEE.

expectant estate. See *future interest* under INTEREST (2).

expectant heir. See HEIR.

expectant interest. See *future interest* under INTEREST (2).

expectant right. See RIGHT.

expectation, *n.* (16c) **1.** The act of looking forward; anticipation. **2.** A basis on which something is expected to happen; esp., the prospect of receiving wealth, honors, or the like.

> "[E]xpectation does not in itself amount to intention. An operating surgeon may know very well that his patient will probably die of the operation; yet he does not intend the fatal consequence which he expects. He intends the recovery which he hopes for but does not expect." John Salmond, *Jurisprudence* 379–80 (Glanville L. Williams ed., 10th ed. 1947).

▸ **legitimate expectation.** (18c) Expectation arising from the reasonable belief that a private person or public body will adhere to a well-established practice or will keep a promise.

expectation damages. See DAMAGES.

expectation interest. See INTEREST (2).

expectation loss. See *benefit-of-the-bargain damages* under DAMAGES.

expectation of life. See LIFE EXPECTANCY.

expectation of privacy. (1965) A belief in the existence of the right to be free of governmental intrusion in regard to a particular place or thing. • To suppress a search on privacy grounds, a defendant must show the existence of the expectation and that the expectation was reasonable.

expected/intended exclusion. See EXCLUSION (3).

expediente (ek-sped-ee-**en**-tee), *n.* [Spanish] *Spanish law.* **1.** The papers or documents constituting a grant or title to land from the government; esp., a historical record of proceedings relating to a grant of land by the sovereign. **2.** A legal or administrative case file; esp., the official record of all filings and orders in a lawsuit. **3.** A maneuver intended to achieve a particular result.

expediment (ek-**sped**-ə-mənt), *n.* (1848) The whole of one's goods and chattels.

expedited proceeding. See SHOW-CAUSE PROCEEDING.

expeditio brevis (ek-spə-**dish**-ee-oh **bree**-vəs). [Latin] *Archaic.* The service of a writ.

expeditionary force. (1816) A group of soldiers sent to another country to fight in a war.

expel, *vb.* (15c) To drive out or away; to eject, esp. with force. See EJECT; EVICT.

expenditor (ek-**spen**-də-tər). (15c) Someone who expends or disburses certain taxes; a paymaster.

expenditure. (18c) **1.** The act or process of spending or using money, time, energy, etc.; esp., the disbursement of funds <the expenditure of time and money on one's professional endeavors>. **2.** A sum paid out <expenditures on research and development>.

▸ **independent expenditure.** See INDEPENDENT EXPENDITURE.

expensae litis (ek-**spen**-see **lɪ**-tis). [Latin] (17c) Costs or expenses of a lawsuit, for which a successful party is sometimes reimbursed.

expense, *n.* (14c) An expenditure of money, time, labor, or resources to accomplish a result; esp., a business expenditure chargeable against revenue for a specific period. Cf. COST (1). — **expense,** *vb.*

▸ **accrued expense.** (1880) An expense incurred but not yet paid.

▸ **administrative expense.** See *general administrative expense.*

▸ **business expense.** (1858) An expense incurred to operate and promote a business; esp., an expenditure made to further the business in the taxable year in which the expense is incurred. • Most business expenses — unlike personal expenses — are tax-deductible.

▸ **capital expense.** (1913) An expense made by a business to provide a long-term benefit; a capital expenditure. • A capital expense is not deductible in the current year, but it can be depreciated or amortized.

▸ **capitalized expense.** (1933) An amortized expense.

▸ **current expense.** See *operating expense.*

▸ **deferred expense.** (1925) A cost incurred by a business when the business expects to benefit from that cost over a period beyond the current year. • An example is a prepaid subscription to a business periodical the cost of which will be recognized as an expense over a multiyear subscription period.

▸ **educational expense.** (1882) A deductible expense incurred either to maintain or to improve an existing job skill or to meet a job requirement such as one imposed by an employer.

▸ **entertainment expense.** (1936) An expense incurred while providing entertainment relating directly to or associated with a business purpose. • Entertainment expenses are tax-deductible in part.

▸ **extraordinary expense.** (16c) An unusual or infrequent expense, such as a write-off of goodwill or a large judgment. • As used in a constitutional provision authorizing a state to incur extraordinary expenses, the term denotes an expense for the general welfare compelled by an unforeseen condition such as a natural disaster or war. — Also termed *extraordinary item.*

▸ **fixed expense.** See *fixed cost* under COST (1).

▸ **funeral expense.** (*usu. pl.*) (18c) An expense necessarily and reasonably incurred in procuring the burial, cremation, or other disposition of a corpse, including the funeral or other ceremonial rite, a casket and vault, a monument or tombstone, a burial plot and its care, and a visitation (or wake).

▸ **general administrative expense.** (*usu. pl.*) (1907) An expense incurred in running a business, as distinguished from an expense incurred in manufacturing or selling; overhead. • Examples include executive and clerical salaries, rent, utilities, and legal and accounting services. — Also termed *administrative expense; general expense.* — Abbr. G&A.

▸ **home-office expense.** (1964) A tax deduction allowed for the expenses of operating a business from one's residence.

▸ **hospital expense.** (1828) An expense incurred in the course of medical treatment in a hospital as an inpatient or outpatient. See *medical expense.*

▸ **medical expense.** (1853) **1.** An expense for medical treatment or healthcare, such as drug costs and health-insurance premiums. • Medical expenses are tax-deductible to the extent that the amounts (less insurance reimbursements) exceed a certain percentage of adjusted gross income. **2.** (*usu. pl.*) In civil litigation, any one of many possible medical costs that the plaintiff has sustained or reasonably expects to incur because of the defendant's allegedly wrongful act, including charges for visits to physicians' offices, medical procedures, hospital bills, medicine, and recuperative therapy needed in the past and in the future. — Often shortened (in pl.) to *medicals.*

▸ **moving expense.** (1903) An expense incurred in changing one's residence. • If incurred for business reasons (as when one's job requires relocation), most moving expenses are tax-deductible.

▸ **operating expense.** (1861) An expense incurred in running a business and producing output. — Also termed *current expense.*

▸ **ordinary and necessary expense.** (1826) An expense that is normal or usual and helpful or appropriate for the operation of a particular trade or business and that is paid or incurred during the taxable year. • Ordinary and necessary expenses are tax-deductible. — Also termed *ordinary and necessary business expense.*

▸ **organizational expense.** (1941) An expense incurred while setting up a corporation or other entity.

▸ **out-of-pocket expense.** (1905) An expense paid from one's own funds.

▸ **personal expense.** An expense incurred by an individual for purposes other than business or an investment.

▸ **prepaid expense.** (1919) An expense (such as rent, interest, or insurance) that is paid before the due date or before a service is rendered.

▸ **travel expense.** (1905) An expense (such as for meals, lodging, and transportation) incurred while away from home in the pursuit of a trade or business. See TAX HOME.

expense account. (1872) Money that is available to someone who works for an organization, esp. to pay for meals and hotel expenses during work-related travel.

expense loading. See LOADING.

expense ratio. (1909) *Accounting.* The proportion or ratio of expenses to income.

expenses of administration. (18c) Expenses incurred by a decedent's representatives in administering the estate.

expenses of receivership. (18c) Expenses incurred by a receiver in conducting the business, including rent and fees incurred by the receiver's counsel and by any master, appraiser, and auditor.

expense stop. (1990) A lease provision establishing the maximum expenses to be paid by the landlord, beyond which the tenant must bear all remaining expenses.

expensilatio (ek-**spen**-sI-**lay**-shee-oh), *n.* [Latin] *Roman law.* An entry to the debit of one party in the account book of another party, esp. as part of a literal contract. See *literal contract* (1) under CONTRACT. Pl. ***expensilationes*** (ek-spen-sI-lay-shee-**oh**-neez).

expensis militum non levandis (ek-**spen**-sis mi-**lit**-əm non lə-**van**-dis). [Latin] *Hist.* A writ to prohibit the sheriff from levying any allowance for knights of the shire on persons who held lands in ancient demesne. See *ancient demesne* under DEMESNE.

experience-rated premium. See PREMIUM (1).

experience rating. (1921) *Insurance.* A method of determining the amount of the premium by analyzing the insured's loss record over time to assess (1) the risk that covered events will occur, and (2) the amount of probable damages if they do.

experimental use. See USE (1).

experimental-use defense. (1977) *Patents.* A defense to a claim of patent infringement raised when the construction and use of the patented invention was for scientific purposes only. • While still recognized, this defense is narrowly construed and today may apply only to research that tests the inventor's claims. 35 USCA § 271(e)(1).

experimental-use exception. (1964) *Patents.* An exception to the public-use statutory bar, whereby an inventor is allowed to make public use of an invention for more than one year when that use is necessary to test and improve the invention.

ex persona domini (eks pər-**soh**-nə **dah**-mi-nI). [Latin] From the person of the master.

> "Generally speaking, by the Roman law contractual rights could not be acquired through free persons who were strangers to the family. But a slave derived a standing to accept a promise to his master *ex persona domini*. Bracton says that contracts can be accepted for a principal by his agent; but he starts from the domestic relations in language very like that of the Roman jurisconsults. An obligation may be acquired through slaves or free agents in our power, if they take the contract in the name of their master." Oliver Wendell Holmes, "Agency" (part 2), in *Collected Legal Papers* 81, 82 (Harold J. Laski ed., 1920).

expert, *n.* (16c) Someone who, through education or experience, has developed skill or knowledge in a particular subject, so that he or she may form an opinion that will assist the fact-finder. Fed. R. Evid. 702. See DAUBERT TEST.

▸ **consulting expert.** (1897) An expert who, though retained by a party, is not expected to be called as a witness at trial. • A consulting expert's opinions are generally exempt from the scope of discovery. Fed. R. Civ. P. 26(b)(4)(B). — Also termed *nontestifying expert.*

▸ **court-appointed expert.** See *independent expert.*

▸ **impartial expert.** (1870) See *independent expert.*

▸ **independent expert.** (1882) An expert who is appointed by the court to present an unbiased opinion. — Also termed *court-appointed expert*; *impartial expert. See* Fed. R. Evid. 706.

▸ **testifying expert.** (1952) An expert who is identified by a party as a potential witness at trial. • As a part of initial disclosures in federal court, a party must provide to all other parties a wide range of information about a testifying expert's qualifications and opinion, including all information that the witness considered in forming the opinion. Fed. R. Civ. P. 26(a)(2)(b).

expert designation. The official naming of a witness who is thought to have enough special skills and knowledge to qualify him or her as someone whose expertise may aid the fact-finder in reaching a decision. See *expert witness* under WITNESS.

expert determination. An alternative-dispute-resolution method in which the parties mutually seek an expert's evaluation of emerging problems and possible solutions without using the forms of judicial process and without either side's defining an entrenched position. • The process is binding on the parties. Cf. ARBITRATION.

expert evidence. See EVIDENCE.

expertise (ek-spər-**teez**), *n.* Skill or knowledge in a particular subject; specialized experience that gives rise to a facility that comparatively few people possess.

expert opinion. See OPINION (3).

expert-reliance materials. (2006) Facts, documents, and other sources that provide data or information to an expert witness. • Often shortened to *reliance materials.*

expert testimony. See *expert evidence* under EVIDENCE.

expert witness. See WITNESS.

expert-witness fee. See FEE (1).

expiate, *vb.* (16c) To make amends or atonement for (an offense, wrong, sin, etc.); to show contrition for (a wrong committed) by accepting the punishment or trying to make matters right. — **expiation,** *n.*

ex pietate (eks pI-ə-**tay**-tee). [Latin] *Hist.* From natural affection and duty.

expilare (eks-pə-**lair**-ee), *vb.* [Latin] *Roman law.* In the law of inheritance, to spoil; to rob; to plunder. See CRIMEN EXPILATAE HEREDITATIS.

expilatio (eks-pə-**lay**-shee-oh), *n.* [Latin] *Roman law.* The offense of unlawfully appropriating goods belonging to a succession. • This offense was not technically theft (*furtum*) because the property belonged to neither the decedent nor an heir, since the latter had not yet taken possession. — Also termed *expilation*. Pl. ***expilationes*** (eks-pə-lay-shee-**oh**-neez).

expilator (eks-pə-**lay**-tər), *n.* [Latin] (17c) *Roman law.* A robber; a spoiler or plunderer. See EXPILATIO.

expiration, *n.* (16c) The ending of a fixed period of time; esp., a formal termination on a closing date <expiration of the insurance policy>. — Also termed *expiry.*

expiration date. (1803) The date after which something cannot or should not be used; esp., the date on which an offer, option, or the like ceases to exist. — Also termed *expiry date.*

expire, *vb.* (14c) **1.** (Of an official document) to be no longer legally effective; to become null at a time fixed beforehand <the contract expired on September 10>. **2.** (Of a period of time during which someone holds a position of authority) to come to an end <the president's term of office has expired>. **3.** (Of a person) to die; to cease living <the testator expired in July 2013>.

expiry. See EXPIRATION.

expiry date. See EXPIRATION DATE.

expiry of the legal. (17c) *Scots law.* The end of the period during which a debtor can redeem land awarded to a creditor by paying off the debt.

explanation. 1. The activity or process of expounding, interpreting, or making something intelligible; esp., the process of demonstrating by reasoning or investigation the causal or logical antecedents or conditions of some event or thing to be accounted for.

> "It would appear, indeed, that there is an *essential* complexity about what is ordinarily considered explanatory; that once the demand for explanation arises, an answer which does no more than represent what is to be explained as what we always find happening in such circumstances fails to explain it at all. . . . [S]ome sort of analysis besides mere certification as a recurring phenomenon, would seem to be essential. I assume, of course, that the demand for explanation arises out of a genuine puzzlement, and that the explanation is offered in good faith — not as a joke, or in order to silence the questioner. Thus, if the objection were raised that it is common practice for harassed parents to respond to their children's 'why' questions with 'That's what always happens,' I should insist that such a response, far from being an explanation, is just a way of registering either their inability or their unwillingness to give one." William Dray, *Laws and Explanations in History* 72–73 (1957).

2. The statement or statements made in this activity or process. **3.** The interpretation or meaning given to something by someone who expounds it. **4.** Reconciliation or reestablishment of mutual understanding between those who have been at variance.

explanatory-phrase rule. (1925) *Trademarks.* The principle that a senior user of a family-name trademark is entitled to a judicial remedy for unfair competition if the same family name appears on competing goods or services, the remedy being that the junior user must include on signs, labels, and advertisements an explanation that the company is not affiliated with the senior user's company. • The rule resolves two conflicting principles: (1) everyone has the right to use a family name in business, and (2) no one may use a family name in a way that unfairly hurts someone else's business.

explecia (ek-**splee**-shee-ə). [Law Latin] See EXPLETA.

explees (ek-**spleez**). See ESPLEES.

expleta (ek-**splee**-tə), *n. pl.* [Law Latin] *Hist.* The rents and profits of an estate. — Also termed *expletia; explecia.*

explicatio (eks-plə-**kay**-shee-oh), *n.* [Law Latin] *Civil law.* The fourth pleading in an action, consisting of the plaintiff's response to the defendant's rejoinder. • This is the civil-law equivalent of the common-law *surrejoinder.*

explicit, *adj.* **1.** Clear, open, direct, or exact. **2.** Expressed without ambiguity or vagueness; leaving no doubt.

exploding adjustable-rate mortgage. See MORTGAGE.

exploitation, *n.* (19c) The act of taking advantage of something; esp., the act of taking unjust advantage of another for one's own benefit or selfish ends. See SEXUAL EXPLOITATION. — **exploit,** *vb.* — **exploitative,** *adj.*

exploration manager. See LANDMAN (1).

export, *n.* (17c) **1.** A product or service created in one country and transported to another.

▸ **domestic export.** (1819) A product originally grown or manufactured in the United States, as distinguished from a product originally imported into the United States and then exported.

2. The process of transporting products or services to another country. Cf. IMPORT (1), (2).

export, *vb.* (15c) **1.** To send or carry abroad. **2.** To send, take, or carry (a good or commodity) out of the country; to transport (merchandise) from one country to another in the course of trade. **3.** To carry out or convey (goods) by sea.

exportation. (17c) The act of sending or carrying goods and merchandise from one country to another.

Export Clause. See IMPORT-EXPORT CLAUSE.

export declaration. (1920) A document — required by federal law — containing details of an export shipment.

export draft. See DRAFT (1).

Export-Import Bank of the United States. A federally chartered bank that finances the export of goods and services by direct lending or by issuing guarantees and insurance so that private banks can extend credit. • The bank was organized by Executive Order 6581 of 2 Feb. 1934. It became independent in 1945. 12 USCA §§ 635 et seq. — Often shortened to *Ex-Im Bank.* — Abbr. EIB.

export letter of credit. See LETTER OF CREDIT.

export quota. See QUOTA (2).

export tax. See TAX.

exposé (ek-spoh-**zay**), *n.* [French] (1803) **1.** A statement or account; an explanation. • In diplomatic language, the term describes a written explanation of the reasons for a certain act or course of conduct. **2.** Exposure of discreditable matter.

expositio (eks-pə-**zish**-ee-oh), *n.* [Latin] An explanation or interpretation; an exposition.

exposition de part (eks-poh-zee-**syawn** də **pahr**). [French] *French law.* The abandonment, in either a public or a private place, of a child that is unable to take care of itself.

expository jurisprudence. See JURISPRUDENCE.

expository statute. See *declaratory statute* under STATUTE.

ex post, *adj.* [Latin "from after"] (1937) Based on knowledge and fact; viewed after the fact, in hindsight; objective; retrospective. Cf. EX ANTE.

ex post facto (eks pohst **fak**-toh), *adj.* (18c) Done or made after the fact; having retroactive force or effect.

ex post facto, *adv.* [Latin "from a thing done afterward"] (17c) After the fact; retroactively.

Ex Post Facto Clause. (1848) *Constitutional law.* One of two clauses in the U.S. Constitution forbidding the enactment of ex post facto laws. U.S. Const. art. I, § 9, cl. 3; art. I, § 10, cl. 1.

ex post facto law. (18c) *Constitutional law.* A statute that criminalizes an action and simultaneously provides for punishment of those who took the action before it had legally become a crime; specif., a law that impermissibly applies retroactively, esp. in a way that negatively affects a person's rights, as by making into a crime an action that was legal when it was committed or increasing the punishment for past conduct. • Ex post facto criminal laws are prohibited by the U.S. Constitution. But retrospective civil laws may be allowed. See RETROACTIVE LAW.

exposure. (17c) The amount of liability or other risk to which a person is subject <the client wanted to know its exposure before it made a settlement offer>.

▸ **dangerous exposure.** *Maritime law.* Exposure that is reasonably foreseeable in the ordinary chances, mistakes, or hazards of navigation.

exposure of person. See INDECENT EXPOSURE.

exposure theory. (1978) *Insurance.* A theory of coverage providing that an insurer must cover a loss if the insurance was in effect when the claimant was exposed to the product that caused the injury. Cf. MANIFESTATION THEORY; ACTUAL-INJURY TRIGGER; TRIPLE TRIGGER.

express, *adj.* (14c) Clearly and unmistakably communicated; stated with directness and clarity. Cf. IMPLIED. — **expressly,** *adv.*

express abandonment. See ABANDONMENT (11).

express abrogation. See ABROGATION.

express acceptance. See ACCEPTANCE (3).

express active trust. See *active trust* under TRUST (3).

express actual knowledge. See *actual knowledge* (1) under KNOWLEDGE (1).

express-advocacy test. (1986) A rule distinguishing electioneering from ordinary political speech or the discussion of issues and candidates, the federal government being able to regulate only those public communications with explicit words for or against a federal candidate's election. *See Federal Election Comm'n v. Massachusetts Citizens for Life, Inc.*, 479 U.S. 238, 249, 107 S.Ct. 616, 623 (1986).

express agency. See AGENCY (1).

express aider. See AIDER BY SUBSEQUENT PLEADING.

express amnesty. See AMNESTY (1).

express assent. See ASSENT.

express assumpsit. See *special assumpsit* under ASSUMPSIT. **express assumption of risk.** See ASSUMPTION OF THE RISK.

express authority. See AUTHORITY (1).

express color. See COLOR.

express condition. See CONDITION (2).

express consent. See CONSENT (1).

express consideration. See CONSIDERATION (1).

express contract. See CONTRACT.

express covenant. See COVENANT (1).

express dedication. See DEDICATION.

express dissatisfaction. *Wills & estates.* A beneficiary's contesting of a will or objecting to any provision of the will in a probate proceeding.

express easement. See EASEMENT.

expressed, *adj.* (16c) Declared in direct terms; stated in words; not left to inference or implication.

express intention. See INTENTION.

expressio falsi (ek-**spres[h]**-ee-oh **fal**-sɪ *or* **fawl**-sɪ). [Latin] (17c) *Hist.* A false statement. • Such a statement might result in rescission of a contract. Cf. ALLEGATIO FALSI.

expression. 1. Writings, speech, or actions that show a person's ideas, thoughts, emotions, or opinions. **2.** The look on a person's face that usu. indicates a person's thoughts or emotions.

expression, freedom of. See FREEDOM OF EXPRESSION.

expressio unius est exclusio alterius (ek-**spres[h]**-ee-oh yoo-**nɪ**-əs est ek-**skloo**-zhee-oh al-tə-**rɪ**-əs). [Law Latin] A canon of construction holding that to express or include one thing implies the exclusion of the other, or of the alternative. • For example, the rule that "each citizen is entitled to vote" implies that noncitizens are not entitled to vote. — Also termed *inclusio unius est exclusio alterius*; *expressum facit cessare tacitum*; *negative-implication canon*. Cf. EJUSDEM GENERIS; NOSCITUR A SOCIIS; RULE OF RANK.

expressis verbis (ek-**spres**-is **vər**-bis), *adv.* [Latin "in express words"] *Hist.* In explicit terms; expressly.

expressive association, freedom of. See FREEDOM OF ASSOCIATION.

expressive crime. See CRIME.

expressive offense. See *expressive crime* under CRIME.

express malice. See MALICE.

express notice. See NOTICE (3).

express obligation. See *conventional obligation* under OBLIGATION.

express permission. See PERMISSION (2).

express power. See POWER (3).

express private passive trust. See TRUST (3).

express repeal. See REPEAL.

express republication. (18c) A testator's repeating of the acts essential to a will's valid execution, with the avowed intent of republishing the will. See REPUBLICATION (2).

express repudiation. See REPUDIATION.

express surrender. See SURRENDER (5).

express trust. See TRUST (3).

expressum facit cessare tacitum. See EXPRESSIO UNIUS EST EXCLUSIO ALTERIUS.

express waiver. See WAIVER (1).

express warranty. See WARRANTY (2).

expromissio (eks-prə-**mis[h]**-ee-oh), *n. Roman law.* A type of novation by which a creditor accepts a new debtor in place of a former one, who is then released.

expromissor (eks-prə-**mis**-ər), *n.* (17c) *Roman law.* Someone who exonerates another from an obligation and adopts it himself; specif., one who assumes another's debt and becomes solely liable for it by a stipulation with the creditor.

expromittere (eks-prə-**mit**-ə-ree), *vb. Roman law.* To undertake for another with the view of becoming liable in the other's place.

ex proposito (eks proh-**poz**-ə-toh). [Latin] *Hist.* Intentionally; by design.

expropriation, *n.* (15c) **1.** A governmental taking or modification of an individual's property rights, esp. by eminent domain; CONDEMNATION (2). — Also termed (in England) *compulsory purchase*; (in Scotland) *compulsory surrender.* Cf. APPROPRIATION (1). **2.** A voluntary surrender of rights or claims; the act of renouncing or divesting oneself of something previously claimed as one's own. — **expropriate,** *vb.* — **expropriator,** *n.*

ex proprio motu (eks **proh**-pree-oh **moh**-tyoo). [Latin] (17c) Of one's own accord.

ex proprio vigore (eks **proh**-pree-oh vi-**gor**-ee). [Latin] By their or its own force.

ex provisione hominis (eks prə-vizh-ee-**oh**-nee **hom**-ə-nis). [Latin] By the provision of man; by the limitation of the party, as distinguished from the disposition of the law.

ex provisione mariti (eks prə-vizh-ee-**oh**-nee mə-**rɪ**-tɪ *or* **mar**-ə-tɪ). [Latin] From the provision of the husband.

expulsion, *n.* (15c) An ejectment or banishment, either through depriving a person of a benefit or by forcibly evicting a person. — **expulsive,** *adj.*

expunction of record. See EXPUNGEMENT OF RECORD.

expunge (ek-**spənj**), *vb.* (17c) **1.** To remove from a record, list, or book; to erase or destroy <the trustee wrongfully expunged the creditor's claim against the debtor>. **2.** *Parliamentary law.* To declare (a vote or other action) null and outside the record. • Something expunged is noted in the original record as expunged and is redacted from all future copies. — Also termed *rescind and expunge*; *rescind and expunge from the minutes*; *rescind and expunge from the record.* — **expungement** (ek-**spənj**-mənt), **expunction** (ek-**spəngk**-shən), *n.*

> "Where it is desired not only to rescind an action but to express very strong disapproval, legislative bodies have voted to rescind the objectionable action and expunge it from the record. When a record has been expunged, the chief legislative officer should cross out the words or draw a line around them in the original minutes and write across them the words, 'Expunged by order of the senate (or house),' giving the date of the order. This statement should be signed by the chief legislative officer. The word 'expunged' must not be so blotted as not to be readable, as otherwise it would be impossible to determine whether more was expunged than ordered. When the minutes are printed or published, the expunged portion is omitted." National Conference of State Legislatures, *Mason's Manual of Legislative Procedure* § 444, at 296–97 (2000).

expungement of record. (1966) The removal of a conviction (esp. for a first offense) from a person's criminal record. — Also termed *expunction of record; erasure of record.*

expurgation (ek-spər-**gay**-shən), *n.* (15c) The act or practice of purging or cleansing, as by publishing a book without its obscene passages. — **expurgate** (**eks**-pər-gayt), *vb.* — **expurgator** (**eks**-pər-gay-tər), *n.*

expurgatory oath. See OATH.

ex quasi contractu (eks **kway**-zɪ kən-**trak**-t[y]oo). [Latin] From quasi-contract.

ex rel. *abbr.* [Latin *ex relatione* "by or on the relation of"] (1838) On the relation or information of. • A suit *ex rel.* is typically brought by the government upon the application of a private party (called a *relator*) who is interested in the matter. See RELATOR (1).

ex relatione (**eks** ri-lay-shee-**oh**-nee), *adv.* [Latin] By relation.

ex re nata (eks ree **nay**-tə). [Latin] According to a case that has arisen.

ex rights, *adv.* (1913) Without rights. • Shares are traded ex rights when the value of the subscription privilege has been deducted, giving the purchaser no right to buy shares of a new stock issue. — Abbr. X; XR. — Also termed *rights off.*

ex-rights date. (1934) The date on which a share of common stock no longer offers privilege subscription rights.

ex rigore juris (eks ri-**gor**-ee **joor**-is). [Latin] According to the rigor or strictness of the law; in strictness of law.

exrogare (eks-rə-**gair**-ee), *vb.* [Latin] See ABROGARE.

exrx. *abbr.* EXECUTRIX.

ex scriptis olim visis (eks **skrip**-tis **oh**-ləm **vɪ**-zis *or* -sis). [Latin "from writings formerly seen"] A method of handwriting proof available when a witness has seen other documents purporting to be in the party's handwriting and either has had further correspondence with the party about the documents' subject matter or has had some other type of communication with the party that would lead to a reasonable presumption that the documents were in the party's handwriting.

ex ship. (1838) Of or referring to a shipment of goods for which the liability or risk of loss passes to the buyer once the goods leave the ship.

ex situ (eks **si**-t[y]oo), *adv.* [Latin] Away from its place.

ex solemnitate (eks sə-lem-ni-**tay**-tee). [Latin] *Hist.* On account of its being required as a solemnity. Cf. DE SOLEMNITATE.

ex statuto (eks stə-**tyoo**-toh). [Latin] According to the statute.

ex stipulatu actio (eks stip-yə-**lay**-t[y]oo **ak**-shee-oh). [Latin] *Roman & civil law.* An action on a stipulation; an action given to recover marriage portions.

ex-stock dividend. (1920) Without stock dividend. • The phrase often denotes the interval between the announcement and payment of a stock dividend. A purchaser of shares during this interval is not entitled to the dividend, which goes to the seller.

ex sua natura (eks **s[y]oo**-ə nə-**t[y]oor**-ə). [Latin] *Hist.* In its own nature (or character).

ex tempore (eks **tem**-pə-ree), *adv.* [Latin "out of time"] (16c) **1.** *Archaic.* By lapse of time. **2.** Without any preparation; extemporaneously.

extend debate. (1853) *Parliamentary law.* To cancel or relax an otherwise applicable limit on debate. — Also termed *extend the limits of debate.* See DEBATE. Cf. CLOSE DEBATE; LIMIT DEBATE.

extended-coverage clause. (1932) *Insurance.* A policy provision that insures against hazards beyond those covered (or excluded) in the basic policy.

extended debate. See DEBATE.

extended family. See FAMILY.

extended first mortgage. See *wraparound mortgage* under MORTGAGE.

extended insurance. See INSURANCE.

extended jurisdiction. See JURISDICTION.

extended juvenile jurisdiction. See JURISDICTION.

extended policy. See INSURANCE POLICY.

extended-reporting-period endorsement. See TAIL COVERAGE.

extended service contract. See *extended warranty* under WARRANTY (2).

extended service warranty. See *extended warranty* under WARRANTY (2).

extended-term insurance. See INSURANCE.

extended ultra vires. See *broad ultra vires* under ULTRA VIRES.

extended warranty. See WARRANTY (2).

extendi facias (ek-**sten**-dɪ **fay**-shee-əs). [Latin "you are to cause to be executed"] See EXTENT (3).

extend the limits of debate. See EXTEND DEBATE.

extension, *n.* (17c) **1.** The continuation of the same contract for a specified period. Cf. RENEWAL (3). **2.** *Patents.* A continuation of the life of a patent for an additional statutorily allowed period. **3.** *Tax.* A period of additional time to file an income-tax return beyond its due date. **4.** A period of additional time to take an action, make a decision, accept an offer, or complete a task. — **extend,** *vb.*

extension agreement. (1869) An agreement providing additional time for the basic agreement to be performed.

extensive interpretation. See INTERPRETATION (1).

extensores (ek-sten-**sor**-eez), *n. pl. Hist.* Officers appointed to appraise and divide or apportion land; extenders or appraisers.

extent. (16c) *Hist.* **1.** A seizure of property in execution of a writ. **2.** A writ issued by the Exchequer to recover a debt owed to the Crown, under which the debtor's lands, goods, or body could all be seized to secure payment. — Also termed *writ of extent.*

▸ **extent in chief.** (18c) A writ of extent issued at the suit of the Crown.

▸ **extent in chief in the second degree.** (1835) A writ of extent issued against a debtor of a Crown debtor, so that it resembles a garnishment. See GARNISHMENT.

▸ **immediate extent.** (18c) A writ of extent issued without a commission of inquest or a scire facias.

3. A writ giving a creditor temporary possession of the debtor's property (esp. land). — Also termed *extendi facias.*

extenta manerii (ek-**sten**-tə mə-**neer**-ee-ɪ). [Latin "the extent of a manor"] An English statute (4 Edw., St. 1) directing the making of a survey of a manor and all its appendages.

extent in aid. (18c) *Hist.* A writ that a Crown debtor could obtain against a person indebted to the Crown debtor so that the Crown debtor could satisfy the debt to the Crown. • This writ, having been much abused because of some peculiar privileges that Crown debtors enjoyed, was abolished in 1947 by the Crown Proceedings Act.

extent in chief. See EXTENT (2).

extenuate (ek-**sten**-yoo-ayt), *vb.* (16c) To make less severe; to mitigate.

extenuating circumstance. See *mitigating circumstance* under CIRCUMSTANCE.

extenuation (ek-sten-yoo-**ay**-shən), *n.* (16c) The act or an instance of making the commission of a crime or tort less severe.

extern. See CLERK (4).

external act. See ACT (2).

externality. (*usu. pl.*) (1957) A consequence or side effect of one's economic activity, causing another to benefit without paying or to suffer without compensation. — Also termed *spillover*; *neighborhood effect.*

▸ **negative externality.** (1970) An externality that is detrimental to another, such as water pollution created by a nearby factory.

▸ **positive externality.** (1970) An externality that benefits another, such as the advantage received by a neighborhood when a homeowner attractively landscapes the property.

external obsolescence. See *economic obsolescence* under OBSOLESCENCE.

external sovereignty. See SOVEREIGNTY (3).

exterritorial. See EXTRATERRITORIAL.

exterritoriality. See EXTRATERRITORIALITY.

exterus (**ek**-stər-əs), *n.* [Latin] A foreigner or alien; one born abroad.

ex testamento (eks tes-tə-**men**-toh), *adv.* [Latin] By, from, or under a will or testament <succession *ex testamento* is the mode of devolution that the property of deceased persons ought primarily to follow>. Cf. AB INTESTATO.

extinct, *adj.* (15c) **1.** No longer in existence or use. **2.** (Of a debt) lacking a claimant.

extinctive fact. See *divestitive fact* under FACT.

extinctive prescription. See PRESCRIPTION (4).

extinguish, *vb.* (16c) **1.** To bring to an end; to put an end to. **2.** To terminate or cancel. **3.** To put out or stifle.

extinguishment, *n.* (16c) The cessation or cancellation of some right or interest. • For example, the extinguishment of a legacy occurs when the item bequeathed no longer exists or no longer belongs to the testator's estate.

extinguishment of copyhold. The destruction of copyhold by a uniting of freehold and copyhold interests in the same person and in the same right. • In England, under the 1922 Law of Property Act, copyholds were enfranchised and became either leasehold or, more often, freehold. See COPYHOLD.

extinguishment of debt. A debtor's satisfaction of an obligation to a creditor.

extinguishment of legacy. See ADEMPTION.

extinguishment of lien. (1800) A lien's discharge by operation of law.

extirpation (ek-stər-**pay**-shən), *n.* (16c) **1.** The act of completely removing or destroying something. **2.** Damage to land intentionally done by a person who has lost the right to the land.

extirpatione (ek-stər-pay-shee-**oh**-nee), *n.* [Latin] *Hist.* A writ issued either before or after judgment to restrain a person from maliciously damaging any house or extirpating any trees on land that the person had lost the right to possess.

extort, *vb.* (15c) **1.** To compel or coerce (a confession, etc.) by means that overcome one's power to resist. **2.** To gain by wrongful methods; to obtain in an unlawful manner; to exact wrongfully by threat or intimidation. — **extortive,** *adj.*

extortion, *n.* (14c) **1.** The offense committed by a public official who illegally obtains property under the color of office; esp., an official's collection of an unlawful fee. — Also termed *common-law extortion.*

> "The dividing line between bribery and *extortion* is shadowy. If one other than the officer corruptly takes the initiative and offers what he knows is not an authorized fee, it is bribery and not extortion. On the other hand, if the officer corruptly makes an unlawful demand which is paid by one who does not realize it is not the fee authorized for the service rendered, it is extortion and not bribery. In theory it would seem possible for an officer to extort a bribe under such circumstances that he would be guilty of either offense whereas the outraged citizen would be excused." Rollin M. Perkins & Ronald N. Boyce, *Criminal Law* 538 (3d ed. 1982).

2. The act or practice of obtaining something or compelling some action by illegal means, as by force or coercion. — Also termed *statutory extortion.* — **extortionate,** *adj.*

> "The distinction traditionally drawn between robbery by intimidation and blackmail or extortion is that a person commits robbery when he threatens to do *immediate* bodily harm, whereas he commits blackmail or extortion when he threatens to do bodily harm *in the future.*" James Lindgren, "Blackmail and Extortion," in 1 *Encyclopedia of Crime and Justice* 115, 115 (Sanford H. Kadish ed., 1983).

extortionate credit transaction. See LOANSHARKING.

extra (**ek**-strə), *prep.* [Latin] (1852) Beyond; except; without; out of; additional.

extra allowance. In New York practice, a sum in addition to costs that may, in the court's discretion, be awarded to the successful party in an unusually difficult case. See ALLOWANCE (4).

extracameral, *adj.* (1958) Of, relating to, or involving a legislator's actions outside the legislative chamber or a judge's actions outside the courtroom or chambers. Cf. INTRACAMERAL.

extra commercium (**eks**-trə kə-**mər**-shee-əm). [Latin] Outside commerce. • This phrase was used in Roman and civil law to describe property dedicated to public use and not subject to private ownership.

extract (**ek**-strakt), *n.* (17c) **1.** A portion or segment, as of a writing. **2.** *Scots law.* See ESTREAT.

extract (ek-**strakt**), *vb.* (16c) **1.** To draw out or forth; to pull out from a fixed position. **2.** To dig or otherwise take (something) from its place, as minerals from the earth.

extracta curiae (ek-**strak**-tə **kyoor**-ee-ee). *Hist.* The issues or profits of holding a court, arising from customary dues, fees, and amercements.

extraction. *Intellectual property.* The transfer of data from a database from the server where the database resides to a different computer or medium.

> "'Extraction' is something of a misnomer, given that the extracted contents will remain on the original database, and are accordingly copied from, not removed from, it. It is also somewhat illogical that the contents must be removed to another medium. Removal to the same medium should also constitute extraction." Ingrid Winternitz, *Electronic Publishing Agreements* 28 (2000).

extractum. See ESTREAT.

extra curtem domini (**eks**-trə **kər**-tem **dom**-ə-nɪ). [Law Latin] *Hist.* Beyond the domain of the superior. • A vassal was not usu. required to perform a service (such as transporting grain) beyond the superior's jurisdiction.

extraditable, *adj.* (1881) **1.** (Of a criminal) subject or liable to extradition <an extraditable felon>. **2.** (Of a crime) making an offender liable to extradition <murder is an extraditable offense>.

extradite (**ek**-strə-dɪt), *vb.* (1864) **1.** To surrender or deliver (a fugitive) to another jurisdiction; specif., to send (an accused person) back to the state or country where a crime may have happened for purposes of prosecution or punishment. **2.** To obtain the surrender of (a fugitive) from another jurisdiction.

extradition (ek-strə-**dish**-ən). (18c) The official surrender of an alleged criminal by one state or country to another having jurisdiction over the crime charged; the return of a fugitive from justice, regardless of consent, by the authorities where the fugitive is found. Cf. RENDITION (2); REQUISITION (6).

- ▸ **international extradition.** (1856) Extradition in response to a demand made by the executive of one country on the executive of another country. • This procedure is generally regulated by treaties.
- ▸ **interstate extradition.** (1876) Extradition in response to a demand made by the governor of one state on the governor of another state. • This procedure is provided for by the U.S. Constitution, by federal statute, and by state statutes.

Extradition Clause. (1878) *Constitutional law.* The clause of the U.S. Constitution providing that any accused person who flees to another state must, on request of the executive authority of the state where the crime was committed, be returned to that state. U.S. Const. art. IV, § 2, cl. 2.

extradition treaty. (1847) A treaty governing the preconditions for, and exceptions to, the surrender of a fugitive from justice by the country where the fugitive is found to another country claiming criminal jurisdiction over the fugitive.

extradition warrant. See WARRANT (1).

extra dividend. See *extraordinary dividend* under DIVIDEND.

extradotal property. See PROPERTY.

extra-elements test. (1985) *Intellectual property.* A judicial test for determining whether a state-law claim is preempted by federal intellectual-property statutes under the *Sears–Compco* doctrine, the criterion being that if the claim requires proof of an extra element that makes the action qualitatively different from an infringement action based on federal law, the state action is not preempted.

extra familiam (**eks**-trə fə-**mil**-ee-əm). [Latin] *Hist.* Outside the family. • The phrase appeared in reference to the status of a child after forisfamiliation. Cf. INTRA FAMILIAM.

extra feodum (**eks**-trə **fee**-ə-dəm). [Latin] Out of his fee; out of the seigniory.

extrahazardous, *adj.* (1831) Especially or unusually dangerous. • This term is often applied to exceptionally dangerous railroad crossings. — Also termed *ultrahazardous.*

extrahazardous activity. See ABNORMALLY DANGEROUS ACTIVITY.

extrahura (ek-strə-**hyoor**-ə), *n.* [Law Latin] *Hist.* An animal that wanders about or strays without its owner; ESTRAY.

extrajudicial, *adj.* (17c) Outside court; outside the functioning of the court system <extrajudicial confessions>. — Also termed *out-of-court.*

extrajudicial admission. See ADMISSION (1).

extrajudicial confession. See CONFESSION (1).

extrajudicial enforcement. See SELF-HELP.

extrajudicial evidence. See EVIDENCE.

extrajudicial oath. See OATH.

extrajudicial opinion. See OPINION (1).

extrajudicial remedy. See REMEDY.

extrajudicial statement. (1838) Any utterance made outside court. • It is usu. treated as hearsay under the rules of evidence.

extrajudicial tender. See TENDER (3).

extra judicium (**ek**-strə joo-**dish**-ee-əm). [Latin] Extrajudicial; out of court; beyond the jurisdiction.

extra jus (**ek**-strə **jəs**). [Latin] Beyond the law; more than the law requires.

extralateral right. See APEX RULE.

extralegal, *adj.* (17c) Beyond the province of law.

extra legem (**ek**-strə **lee**-jəm). [Latin] Out of the law; out of the protection of the law.

extramarital, *adj.* (1929) Of, relating to, or involving a sexual relationship that a married person has with someone other than the person's spouse.

extramural powers (ek-strə-**myuur**-əl). (1916) Powers exercised by a municipality outside its corporate limits.

extranational, *adj.* (1864) Beyond the territorial and governing limits of a country.

extraneous (ek-**stray**-nee-əs), *adj.* See EXTRINSIC.

extraneous evidence. See *extrinsic evidence* (1) under EVIDENCE.

extraneous offense. See OFFENSE (2).

extraneous question. (1808) A question that is beyond or beside the point to be decided.

extraneus (ek-**stray**-nee-əs), *n.* & *adj.* [Latin "outside"] **1.** *Hist.* Someone who is foreign-born; a foreigner. **2.** *Roman law.* An heir not born in the family of the testator; a citizen of a foreign state.

extraordinary, *adj.* (15c) **1.** Beyond what is usual, customary, regular, or common <extraordinary measures>. **2.** Of, relating to, or involving a degree of care, diligence, caution, or prudence that would be exercised by highly fastidious and thoughtful people, though falling short of any superhuman effort <extraordinary care>. **3.** Of, relating to, or involving a legal proceeding or procedure not normally required or resorted to <an extraordinary sitting of the court>. **4.** Of, relating to, or involving an occurrence, esp. an incident or accident, that would not have been foreseeable to someone of normal prudence <an extraordinary deluge>. **5.** Surpassing the common degree, measure, or allotment <extraordinary acuity>. **6.** Employed for an exceptional purpose or for a special occasion <envoy extraordinary>. • In sense 6, *extraordinary* frequently functions as a postpositive adjective (as in the bracketed illustration). **7.** Of, relating to, or involving a course of study or one or more lectures not considered part of the core curriculum but instead of secondary importance <an extraordinary elective>.

extraordinary average. See AVERAGE (3).

extraordinary care. See *great care* under CARE (2).

extraordinary circumstances. See CIRCUMSTANCE.

extraordinary damages. See *special damages* under DAMAGES.

extraordinary danger. See *extraordinary hazard* under HAZARD (1).

extraordinary diligence. See DILIGENCE (2).

extraordinary dividend. See DIVIDEND.

extraordinary expense. See EXPENSE.

extraordinary flood. A flood whose occurrence is not predictable and whose magnitude and destructiveness could not have been anticipated or provided against by the exercise of ordinary foresight; a flood so unusual that a person of ordinary prudence and experience could not have foreseen it. See ACT OF GOD.

extraordinary gain. See GAIN (3).

extraordinary general meeting. See MEETING.

extraordinary grand jury. See *special grand jury* under GRAND JURY.

extraordinary hazard. See HAZARD (1).

extraordinary interrogation technique. **1.** An unusual and extreme means of questioning a suspect or detainee to break down the person's resistance to answering, usu. by subjecting the person to pain or extreme discomfort or denying necessities such as sleep. **2.** TORTURE.

extraordinary item. See *extraordinary expense* under EXPENSE.

extraordinary loss. See LOSS.

extraordinary majority. See *supermajority* under MAJORITY.

extraordinary relief. See RELIEF (3).

extraordinary remedy. See REMEDY.

extraordinary rendition. See RENDITION (3).

extraordinary repair. (1828) As used in a lease, a repair that is made necessary by some unusual or unforeseen occurrence that does not destroy the building but merely renders it less suited to its intended use; a repair that is beyond the usual, customary, or regular kind.

extraordinary risk. See *extraordinary hazard* under HAZARD (1).

extraordinary session. See *special session* under SESSION (1).

extraordinary writ. See WRIT.

extraparochial (ek-strə-pə-**roh**-kee-əl), *adj.* (17c) Out of a parish; not within the bounds or limits of any parish.

extra paternam familiam (**eks**-trə pə-**tər**-nəm fə-**mil**-ee-əm). [Law Latin] *Hist.* Outside the father's family. Cf. INTRA PATERNAM FAMILIAM.

extrapolate (ek-**strap**-ə-layt), *vb.* (19c) **1.** To use known facts to make one or more educated guesses about unknown or future facts; specif., to estimate an unknown value or quantity on the basis of the known range, esp. by statistical methods. **2.** To deduce an unknown legal principle from a known case. **3.** To speculate about possible results based on known facts. — **extrapolative** (-lay-tiv *or* -lə-tiv), **extrapolatory** (-lə-tor-ee), *adj.* — **extrapolator** (-lay-tər), *n.*

extrapolation (ek-strap-ə-**lay**-shən), *n.* (19c) **1.** The process of estimating an unknown value or quantity on the basis of the known range of variables. **2.** The process by which a court deduces a legal principle from another case. **3.** The process of speculating about possible results, based on known facts.

extra praesentiam mariti (**eks**-trə pri-**zen**-shee-əm mə-**rɪ**-tɪ *or* **mar**-ə-tɪ). [Latin] Out of her husband's presence.

extra quattuor maria (**eks**-trə **kwah**-too-ər **mar**-ee-ə). [Latin] Beyond the four seas; out of the kingdom of England. • The reference is to the seas surrounding Great Britain. The phrase was traditionally applied to the impossibility of a husband's access to his wife at the time of conception.

extra regnum (**eks**-trə **reg**-nəm). [Latin] Out of the realm.

extras. (1894) *Construction law.* Contractual amendments in the nature of additions that were not originally part of the contract, requested by an owner of a building under construction. Cf. CHANGE ORDER (1).

extra session. See *special session* under SESSION (1).

extraterritorial, *adj.* (19c) Occurring outside a particular state or country; beyond the geographic limits of a particular jurisdiction. — Also termed *exterritorial.*

extraterritorial infringement. See INFRINGEMENT.

extraterritoriality. (19c) The freedom of diplomats, foreign ministers, and royalty from the jurisdiction of the country in which they temporarily reside. — Also termed *exterritoriality.* See DIPLOMATIC IMMUNITY.

extraterritoriality canon. The doctrine that a statute presumptively has no extraterritorial application (*statuta suo clauduntur territorio, nec ultra territorium disponunt*). — Also termed *presumption against extraterritoriality.*

extraterritorial jurisdiction. See JURISDICTION.

extraterritorial recognition of rights. See *private international law* under INTERNATIONAL LAW.

extra territorium (**eks**-trə ter-ə-**tor**-ee-əm). [Latin] Beyond or outside the territory.

extratextual, *adj.* Existing outside the literal or clearly implied meaning of a writing, esp. a legal instrument <extratextual sources>.

Extravagantes (ek-strav-ə-**gan**-teez), *n. pl.* [Law Latin "wanderings"] *Eccles. law.* Papal constitutions and decretal epistles of Pope John XXII and certain of his successors. • These epistles were so called because they were not digested or arranged with the other papal decretals, but appeared detached from canon law. The term remained even after the epistles were later included in the body of canon law.

extravagant interpretation. See INTERPRETATION (1).

extra viam (**eks**-trə **vɪ**-əm). [Latin "out of the way"] A plaintiff's responsive pleading in a trespass action, asserting that the defendant's claim of a right-of-way across the plaintiff's land is not a defense to the action because the defendant strayed from the supposed right-of-way.

extra vires (**eks**-trə **vɪ**-reez *or* **veer**-eez). See ULTRA VIRES.

extra work. See WORK (1).

extrema ratio (ek-**stree**-mə **ray**-shee-oh). [Latin] *Hist.* Extreme policy.

extreme cruelty. See CRUELTY.

extreme force. See *deadly force* under FORCE.

extreme indifference. See INDIFFERENCE.

extreme-indifference murder. See *depraved-heart murder* under MURDER.

extreme mental or emotional disturbance. (1959) *Criminal law.* A highly disturbed mental state that, under the Model Penal Code, can serve as an affirmative defense to murder. • This concept, which expands and replaces the common-law defense of heat of passion or adequate provocation, can reduce the offense to manslaughter. The test contains both objective and subjective elements: there must be a reasonable explanation of the extreme mental or emotional disturbance, but the reasonableness is considered from the "viewpoint of a person in the actor's situation under the circumstances as he believes them to be." Model Penal Code § 210.3.1(b). — Abbr. EMED. — Also termed *emotional disturbance; mental disturbance.* Cf. *partial excuse* under EXCUSE (2); HEAT OF PASSION; *adequate provocation* under PROVOCATION; *diminished capacity* under CAPACITY (3).

extrinsic, *adj.* (17c) From outside sources; of, relating to, or involving outside matters. — Also termed *extraneous.*

extrinsic ambiguity. See *latent ambiguity* under AMBIGUITY (1).

extrinsic evidence. See EVIDENCE.

extrinsic fraud. See FRAUD.

extrinsic material. See MATERIAL.

extrinsic test. (1977) *Copyright.* A test for determining whether two ideas or works are substantially similar by listing and analyzing like and unlike elements. • The test may be applied and decided by the trier of law rather than the trier of fact. Cf. INTRINSIC TEST.

ex turpi causa (eks **tər**-pɪ **kaw**-zə). [Latin] From an immoral consideration. • This phrase, a shortened form of the maxim *ex turpi causa non oritur actio* ("from an immoral consideration an action does not arise"), expresses the principle that a party does not have a right to enforce performance of an agreement founded on a consideration that is contrary to the public interest.

> "The doctrine *ex turpi causa* has made its way into the law as an extension of a moral principle. If it is misused, the principle suffers. Moreover, its misuse is a symptom of a disease of thought that debilitates the law and morals. This is the failure to recognize that there is a fundamental difference between the law that expresses a moral principle and the law that is only a social regulation. If only in the growth of English law that distinction had been maintained, much of the arbitrariness and the absurdities in the cases I have cited would have been avoided. There is a dictum of Lord Wright's which may some day be used as a foundation for a change of heart. Speaking of the maxim *ex turpi causa*, he said: 'In these days there are many statutory offences which are the subject of the criminal law and in that sense are crimes, but which would, it seems, afford no moral justification for a court to apply the maxim.' *Beresford* v. *Royal Insurance* (1937), 2 KB. at 220." Patrick Devlin, *The Enforcement of Morals* 60 (1968).

exuere patriam (eg-z[y]**oo**-ə-ree **pay**-tree-əm), *vb.* [Latin] To renounce one's country or native allegiance; to expatriate oneself.

exulare (eks-[y]ə-**lair**-ee), *vb.* [Latin] *Hist.* To exile or banish.

ex una parte (eks [y]**oo**-nə **pahr**-tee). [Latin] Of one part or side; on one side.

exuperare (eg-z[y]oo-pə-**rair**-ee), *vb.* [Latin] To overcome; to apprehend or take.

ex utraque parte (eks yoo-**tray**-kwee **pahr**-tee). [Latin] On both sides.

ex utriusque parentibus conjuncti (eks yoo-tree-**əs**-kwee pə-**ren**-ti-bəs kən-**jəngk**-tɪ). [Latin] Related on the side of both parents; of the whole blood.

ex vi aut metu (eks **vɪ** awt **mee**-t[y]oo). [Latin] *Hist.* On the ground of force or fear. • The phrase appeared in reference to a basis for rescinding a transaction.

ex visceribus (eks vi-**ser**-ə-bəs). [Latin "from the bowels"] From the vital part; from the very essence of (a thing).

ex visceribus verborum (eks vi-**ser**-ə-bəs vər-**bor**-əm). [Latin] From the mere words (and nothing else); from the words themselves.

ex visitatione Dei (eks viz-ə-tay-shee-**oh**-nee **dee**-ɪ). [Latin] **1.** By the dispensation of God; by reason of physical incapacity. • Anciently, when a prisoner who was being arraigned stood silently instead of pleading, a jury was impaneled to inquire whether the prisoner obstinately stood mute or was dumb *ex visitatione Dei*. **2.** By natural causes as opposed to violent ones. • This phrase sometimes appears in a coroner's report when death results from a disease or another natural cause.

ex visu scriptionis (eks **vɪ**-s[y]oo [*or* -z[y]oo] skrip-shee-**oh**-nis). [Latin] From the sight of the writing; from having seen a person write. • This phrase describes a method of proving handwriting.

ex vi termini (eks vɪ **tər**-mə-nɪ). [Law Latin] From or by the force of the term; from the very meaning of the expression used.

ex voluntate (eks vol-ən-**tay**-tee). [Latin] Voluntarily; from free will or choice.

EXW. *abbr.* EX WORKS.

ex warrants, *adv.* (1935) Without warrants. • Shares are traded ex warrants when they no longer carry the right to receive declared warrants that have been distributed to holders. — Abbr. X; XW.

ex works. (1938) From the factory. • This trade term defines the obligations of a buyer and a seller of goods with respect to delivery, payment, and risk of loss. The seller's delivery is complete (and the risk of loss passes to the buyer) when the goods are made available to the buyer at a location of the seller's choice without requiring a collecting vehicle to be loaded, as at the seller's showroom, factory, or warehouse. — Abbr. EXW.

ex-works price. See PRICE.

eyde (ayd), *n.* [Law French] Aid; assistance; relief; subsidy.

eye for an eye. See LEX TALIONIS.

eye of the law. (16c) The law as a personified perceiver; legal contemplation <dead people are no longer persons in the eye of the law>.

eyewitness. (16c) Someone who personally sees an event; esp., someone who has seen something happen, usu. a crime, and can describe it later . Cf. EARWITNESS.

eyewitness identification. (1939) A naming or description by which one who has seen an event testifies from memory about the person or persons involved. • For many years, courts and commentators have recognized that eyewitness identification is among the least reliable forms of evidence. In particular, DNA exonerations have proved that eyewitness identification is frequently inaccurate. *See U.S. v. Brownlee*, 454 F.3d 131, 141–42 (3d Cir. 2006). See MEMORY CORRUPTION.

eyewitness-identification direction. See *identification instruction* under JURY INSTRUCTION.

eyewitness-identification evidence. See *identification evidence* under EVIDENCE.

eyewitness-identification instruction. See *identification instruction* under JURY INSTRUCTION.

eygne (ayn), *n.* See EIGNE.

eyre (air). [Old French *eire* "journey, march"] (12c) *Hist.* A system of royal courts sent out into the counties by the Crown to investigate allegations of wrongdoing, to try cases, and to raise revenue for the Crown through the levy of fines. • The eyre system was abolished in the 13th century. See ARTICLES OF THE EYRE; JUSTICE IN EYRE.

> "In 1176 the itinerant justices were organised into six circuits . . . . The justices assigned to these circuits, who numbered as many as twenty or thirty at a time in the 1180s, were known as *justiciae errantes* (later *justiciarii in itinere*, justices in eyre); and the French word 'eyre' became the name of one of the most prominent forms of royal justice until the time of Edward III. Every so often a 'general eyre' would visit a county, bringing the king's government with it. . . . The general eyres were not merely law courts; they were a way of supervising local government through itinerant central government." J.H. Baker, *An Introduction to English Legal History* 19 (3d ed. 1990).

eyrer (**air**-ər), *vb.* [Law French] (12c) *Hist.* To travel or journey; to go about.

F

F. 1. *abbr.* The first series of the *Federal Reporter*, which includes federal decisions (trial and appellate) from 1880 to 1924. **2.** *Hist.* A letter branded on a felon who claimed benefit of clergy (which involved reciting the "neck verse," Psalm 51, to avoid execution) so that the felon could claim the benefit only once. • Without the benefit of clergy, the felon faced capital punishment. Those convicted for an affray (fray) or falsity were also so branded. The letter *T* was also sometimes branded on the hands of convicted thieves. The practice stopped in the 1800s. See T (1); NECK VERSE; BENEFIT OF CLERGY (1).

> "He that shall maliciously strike any person with a Weapon in Church or Churchyard, or draw any Weapon there with intent to strike, shall have one of his Ears cut off; and, if he have no Ears, then shall be marked on the Cheek with a hot Iron, having the Letter F, whereby he may be known for a *Fray-maker* or *Fighter*." Thomas Blount, *Nomo-Lexicon: A Law-Dictionary* (1670).

> "F, Is a Letter wherewith *Felons*, &c. are branded and marked with an hot Iron, on their being admitted to the Benefit of Clergy." Giles Jacob, *A New Law-Dictionary* (8th ed. 1762).

F.2d. *abbr.* The second series of the *Federal Reporter*, which includes federal appellate decisions from 1924 to 1993.

F.3d. *abbr.* The third series of the *Federal Reporter*, which includes federal appellate decisions from 1993.

FAA. *abbr.* **1.** FEDERAL AVIATION ADMINISTRATION. **2.** FEDERAL ARBITRATION ACT. **3.** FREE OF ALL AVERAGE.

fabricare (fab-rə-**kair**-ee), *vb.* [Law Latin "to make"] *Hist.* **1.** To make a coin, either lawfully or unlawfully. **2.** To forge, esp. a bill of lading. • The term sometimes appeared in a past-tense form in indictments: *fabricavit et contrafecit* ("[he] forged and counterfeited").

fabricate, *vb.* (15c) **1.** To frame, construct, or build. **2.** To prepare (something) according to standard or prepared specifications. **3.** To form by labor and art; to produce or manufacture. **4.** To invent, forge, or devise falsely. • To fabricate a story is to create a plausible version of events that is advantageous to the person relating those events. The term is softer than *lie*. See LIE, *vb.* (1).

fabricated evidence. See EVIDENCE.

fabricated fact. See *fabricated evidence* under EVIDENCE.

fabrication, *n.* **1.** False information invented to deceive others. **2.** MANUFACTURE.

fabric land. See LAND.

fabula (**fab**-yə-lə). [Law Latin] *Hist.* A contract or covenant, esp. a nuptial contract.

FAC. *abbr.* **1.** Failure to answer a (traffic) citation. • In some jurisdictions, if someone fails to respond after receiving a ticket, the court notifies the relevant administrative agency, which records this information and suspends the defendant's driver's license until the FAC is vacated and any fines or fees are paid. **2.** Foreign Affairs Committee. **3.** FEDERAL AUDIT CLEARINGHOUSE. **4.** FIRST AMENDMENT CENTER.

façade easement. See EASEMENT.

FACE. *abbr.* FREEDOM OF ACCESS TO CLINIC ENTRANCES ACT.

face, *n.* (13c) **1.** The surface of anything, esp. the front, upper, or outer part <the face of a clock>. **2.** By extension, the apparent or explicit part of a writing or record <the fraud must appear on the face of the record>. **3.** The inscribed side of a document, instrument, or judgment <although the contract appeared valid on its face, the buyer did not have the legal capacity to enter into it>. Cf. FOUR CORNERS.

face amount. (1869) **1.** PAR VALUE. **2.** *Insurance.* The principal payable under an insurance policy, as expressly stated by its terms. — Also termed *face value*; *face amount insured by the policy*; *face of policy*.

face-amount certificate. See STOCK CERTIFICATE.

face-amount certificate company. See COMPANY.

face-amount certificate of the installment type. See *face-amount certificate* (1) under STOCK CERTIFICATE.

face amount insured by the policy. See FACE AMOUNT.

face of policy. See FACE AMOUNT.

face rate. See *nominal rate* under INTEREST RATE.

face-sheet filing. *Bankruptcy.* A bankruptcy case filed without schedules or with incomplete schedules listing few creditors and debts, often to delay an eviction or foreclosure.

face-sheet PSI. See PRESENTENCE-INVESTIGATION REPORT.

face value. (1851) **1.** FACE AMOUNT. **2.** PAR VALUE.

facial, *adj.* (19c) Apparent; of, relating to, or involving the face of something; prima facie <the claim stated a facial case of undue influence>.

facial attack. (1966) A challenge to the sufficiency of a complaint, such as a motion to dismiss in federal practice.

facial challenge. See CHALLENGE (1).

facially sufficient, *adj.* (1972) **1.** (Of a document) appearing on the surface to be. • A search-warrant affidavit's facial sufficiency will not protect it from attack if the affidavit is based on false testimony by the officer making the affidavit. See FRANKS HEARING. **2.** (Of a complaint) able to withstand a motion to dismiss for failure to state a claim.

facially void. See VOID (1).

facias (**fay**-shee-əs). [Law Latin] That you cause. • *Facias* is used in writs as an emphatic word. See FIERI FACIAS; LEVARI FACIAS; SCIRE FACIAS. It also appears in the phrase *ut facias* ("so that you do"). See DO UT FACIAS; FACIO UT DES; FACIO UT FACIAS.

facies (**fay**-shee-eez). (17c) [Latin] The outward appearance or surface of a thing.

facile (*fas*-əl), *adj.* (16c) *Scots law.* (Of a mentally deficient person) so susceptible to outside influence as to need legal protection, as by a guardian or conservator.

facilitate, *vb.* (17c) **1.** To make the occurrence of (something) easier; to render less difficult. **2.** *Criminal law.*

To make the commission of (a crime) easier. • Property (such as a vehicle or home) that facilitates the commission of certain offenses and that may therefore be forfeited. **3.** *Mediation.* To use techniques designed to improve the flow of information between parties to a dispute.

facilitated negotiation. See MEDIATION.

facilitating practice. *Antitrust.* An activity that makes it possible or easier for business to coordinate pricing, distribution, or other behavior in ways that reduce or eliminate competition.

facilitation, *n.* (17c) **1.** CONCILIATION. Cf. MEDIATION. **2.** The act or an instance of aiding or helping; esp., in criminal law, the act of making it easier for another person to commit a crime. — Also termed *criminal facilitation.*

facilitative mediation. See MEDIATION.

facilitator. 1. Something that helps a process take place. **2.** Someone who helps a group of people engage in discussions or work together; esp., one who interacts with parties in negotiations, exchanging information and trying to further the process.

> "The term 'facilitator' is often used interchangeably with the term 'mediator,' but a facilitator does not typically become as involved in the substantive issues as does a mediator. The facilitator focuses more on the process involved in resolving a matter." U.S. Office of Personnel Management, *Alternative Dispute Resolution: A Resource Guide* 8–9 (2001).

facility and circumvention. (18c) *Scots law.* Conduct intended to persuade a person vulnerable to outside influence to act against his or her own interest. • Any contract brought under conditions of facility and circumvention (a type of fraud) would be voidable. — Sometimes shortened to *facility.* See FACILE.

facility-of-payment clause. (1909) **1.** *Insurance.* An insurance-policy provision allowing the appointment of a person to receive payment from the insurer on the beneficiary's behalf. • Its purpose is to protect an insurer that pays benefits to the designated beneficiary against a subsequent claimant who might have superior right to the proceeds. **2.** *Trusts.* A trust provision that allows anyone who owes money to an incapacitated beneficiary to discharge the debt by paying the money owed to the custodial trustee.

facio ut des (**fay**-shee-oh ət **deez**). [Latin "I do so that you give"] (17c) *Civil law.* **1.** An innominate contract in which a person agrees to do something for recompense. See *innominate contract* under CONTRACT. **2.** The consideration in such a contract.

facio ut facias (**fay**-shee-oh ət **fay**-shee-əs). [Latin "I do that you may do"] (17c) *Civil law.* **1.** An innominate contract in which a person agrees to do something for another person who agrees to do something in return, such as an agreement to marry. Cf. *bilateral contract* under CONTRACT. **2.** The consideration in such a contract. See *innominate contract* under CONTRACT.

> "These valuable considerations are divided by the civilians into four species. . . . The second species is, *facio, ut facias:* as when I agree with a man to do his work for him, if he will do mine for me; or if two persons agree to marry together; or to do any positive acts on both sides. Or, it may be to forbear on one side in consideration of something done on the other; as, that in consideration A, the tenant, will repair his house, B, the landlord, will not sue him for waste." 2 William Blackstone, *Commentaries on the Laws of England* 444 (1766).

facsimile (fak-**sim**-ə-lee). (17c) **1.** An exact copy. **2.** FAX.

facsimile signature. See SIGNATURE.

facsimile transmission. 1. See FAX (1). **2.** See FAX (3).

fact. (15c) **1.** Something that actually exists; an aspect of reality <it is a fact that all people are mortal>. • Facts include not just tangible things, actual occurrences, and relationships, but also states of mind such as intentions and the holding of opinions. **2.** An actual or alleged event or circumstance, as distinguished from its legal effect, consequence, or interpretation <the jury made a finding of fact>. — Also termed *historical fact.* **3.** An evil deed; a crime <an accessory after the fact>.

> "By *facts and circumstances* are meant all things and relations, whether natural or artificial, which really exist, whether their existence be perceptible by the senses, or otherwise." 1 Thomas Starkie, *A Practical Treatise on the Law of Evidence* 15 (2d Am. ed. 1828).

> "A *fact* is any act or condition of things, assumed (for the moment) as happening or existing." John H. Wigmore, *A Students' Textbook of the Law of Evidence* 7 (1935).

▸ **ablative fact.** See *divestitive fact.*

▸ **adjudicative fact** (ə-**joo**-di-kay-tiv *or* -kə-tiv). (1959) A controlling or operative fact, rather than a background fact; a fact that is particularly related to the parties to a proceeding and that helps the tribunal determine how the law applies to those parties. • For example, adjudicative facts include those that the jury weighs. *See* Fed. R. Evid. 201. Cf. *legislative fact.*

▸ **alienative fact** (**ay**-lee-ə-nay-tiv *or* **ay**-lee-ə-nə-tiv). (1902) A fact that divests a person of a right by transferring it to another.

▸ **ancient fact.** (17c) A fact about a person, thing, or event that existed or occurred a very long time ago, and about which no living person has firsthand knowledge. — Also termed *fact in pais.*

▸ **basic fact.** See *intermediate fact.*

▸ **collateral fact.** (18c) A fact not directly connected to the issue in dispute, esp. because it involves a different transaction from the one at issue. • Evidence of collateral facts is generally inadmissible.

▸ **collative fact.** See *investitive fact.*

▸ **denotative fact** (**dee**-noh-tay-tiv *or* di-**noh**-tə-tiv). (1982) A fact relevant to the use of a nonlegal term in a legal rule.

▸ **destitutive fact.** See *divestitive fact.*

▸ **dispositive fact** (dis-**poz**-ə-tiv). (1946) **1.** A fact that confers rights or causes the loss of rights. • A dispositive fact may be either an investitive or a divestitive fact. — Also termed *vestitive fact* (**ves**-tə-tiv). **2.** A fact that is decisive of a legal matter; evidence that definitively resolves a legal issue or controversy. See DISPOSITION.

▸ **divestitive fact** (di-**ves**-tə-tiv *or* dɪ-). (1973) A fact that causes the loss of rights; an act or event modifying or extinguishing a legal relation. — Also termed *extinctive fact; destitutive fact; ablative fact.*

▸ **elemental fact.** See *ultimate fact.*

▸ **evaluative fact.** (1986) A fact used to assess an action as being reasonable or negligent.

▸ **evidentiary fact** (ev-i-**den**-shə-ree) (1855) **1.** A fact that is necessary to the operation of an evidentiary rule or that is necessary for or leads to the determination of an ultimate fact. — Also termed *predicate fact.* **2.** A fact that furnishes evidence of the existence of some other fact. — Also termed *evidential fact.* **3.** See *fact in evidence.*

▸ **exonerative fact** (eg-**zon**-ər-ə-tiv *or* -ay-tiv). (1980) A divestitive fact that extinguishes a duty.

▸ **extinctive fact.** See *divestitive fact.*

▸ **fabricated fact.** See *fabricated evidence* under EVIDENCE.

▸ **fact in evidence.** (18c) A fact that a tribunal considers in reaching a conclusion; a fact that has been admitted into evidence in a trial or hearing. — Also written *fact-in-evidence.* — Also termed *evidentiary fact.*

"A *fact-in-evidence*, or, briefly, *evidence*, signifies any facts considered by the tribunal as data to persuade them to reach a reasoned belief upon a probandum. This process of thought by which the tribunal reasons from fact to probandum is termed *inference*." John H. Wigmore, *A Students' Textbook of the Law of Evidence* 7 (1935).

▸ **fact in issue.** (*usu. pl.*) (17c) **1.** *Hist.* A fact that one party alleges and that the other controverts. **2.** A fact to be determined by a fact-finder; PROBANDUM. See *factum probandum* under FACTUM. — Also written *fact-in-issue.* — Also termed *principal fact.*

"A *fact-in-issue* is a fact as to the correctness of which the tribunal, under the law of the case, must be persuaded; the term 'probandum' (thing to be proved) will here be used as the convenient single word." John H. Wigmore, *A Students' Textbook of the Law of Evidence* 7 (1935).

▸ **fact *in pais*.** See *ancient fact.*

▸ **fact material to risk.** (1882) *Insurance.* A fact that may increase the risk and that, if disclosed, might induce the insurer either to decline to insure or to require a higher premium.

▸ **foundational fact.** See *predicate fact.*

▸ **immaterial fact.** (1810) A fact that is not relevant to a matter in issue. Cf. *material fact.*

▸ **impositive fact.** An investitive fact that imposes duties.

▸ **inferential fact.** (1858) A fact established by conclusions drawn from other evidence rather than from direct testimony or evidence; a fact derived logically from other facts.

▸ **intermediate fact.** (1852) A fact that helps lead to an ultimate fact or is a necessary element to a chain of reasoning leading to a conclusion. — Also termed *basic fact.* See MIXED QUESTION OF LAW AND FACT.

▸ **investitive fact** (in-**ves**-tə-tiv). (1939) A fact that confers rights. — Also termed *collative fact* (kə-**lay**-tiv).

▸ **judicial fact.** (1862) See *judicially noticed fact.*

▸ **judicially noticed fact.** (1930) A fact that is not established by admissible evidence but may be accepted by the court because the fact is generally known within the trial court's territorial jurisdiction, or because its validity can be determined from sources whose accuracy cannot be reasonably questioned. *See* Fed. R. Evid. 201(b). — Also termed *judicial fact.* See JUDICIAL NOTICE.

▸ **juridical fact.** See *legal fact* (1).

▸ **jurisdictional fact.** (*usu. pl.*) (1837) A fact that must exist for a court to properly exercise its jurisdiction over a case, party, or thing. See JURISDICTIONAL-FACT DOCTRINE.

▸ **legal fact.** (18c) **1.** A fact that triggers a particular legal consequence, whether or not the actor intended that effect. — Also termed *juridical fact.* **2.** A fact concerning the state of the law.

▸ **legislative fact.** (1828) A fact that explains a particular law's rationality and that helps a court or agency determine the law's meaning and application. • Legislative facts are not ordinarily specific to the parties in a proceeding. Cf. *adjudicative fact.*

"[L]egislative fact includes matters needed to construe statutes or regulations, and factual assumptions a court makes when called upon to 'legislate.' Examples of the latter might include the fact that spouses will communicate less if they are not granted a privilege covering their confidences, or that marital harmony will be strained if spouses can be compelled to testify against each other — facts which might be useful in helping a court decide whether to create or continue a common-law marital privilege . . . . Obviously, legislative facts of this nature do not and cannot meet the indisputability criterion of the Rule [Fed. R. Evid. 201], nor are they required to." Paul F. Rothstein, *The Federal Rules of Evidence* 35–36 (3d ed. 2003).

▸ **material fact.** (1848) A fact that is significant or essential to the issue or matter at hand; esp., a fact that makes a difference in the result to be reached in a given case. • What constitutes a material fact is a matter of substantive law. Cf. *immaterial fact.*

▸ **minor fact.** (1813) A subordinate fact or circumstance. — Also termed *subsidiary fact.*

▸ **negative fact.** The absence or nonexistence of a quality, state, or condition. Cf. *positive fact.*

"The important consideration in connection with negative facts is the greatly increased difficulty of establishing by evidence the truth of a negative proposition, i.e., of proving the *nonexistence* of a fact. A positive fact — an existence — is capable of being verified. If physical, it may be verified, its existence ascertained, by perception, the employment of the sense faculties of the observer. If the fact be a psychological one, it may be recognized by a direct act of consciousness. As Bentham puts it, 'In most cases, we cannot perceive nonexistence or absence. We can only infer it from something existing and present which we do perceive.' This is, of course, not universally true. Certain negative facts, mere absences or nonexistences of their positive correlative terms seem capable of direct perception. Thus, cold is merely the nonexistence of heat, yet we may be fairly said to perceive it. In a certain sense, we may be said to perceive *darkness*, though simply the nonexistence or withdrawal of light. It is not an improper use of language to say that we are conscious of the absence or nonexistence of sound, i.e., of silence. In all such cases — as of the cessation of a customary or pleasurable state — we may be said to be conscious of a *lack*, to an extent which, coming to the consciousness through the sense, differs but slightly, if at all, from perception." 1 Charles Frederic Chamberlayne, *The Modern Law of Evidence* 86 (1911).

▸ **operative fact.** (1857) **1.** A fact that affects an existing legal relation, esp. a legal claim. • In the context of the hearsay rule, this term distinguishes out-of-court statements that are operative facts, and thus not hearsay (e.g., a party's saying "I agree to reimburse you" in a case for breach of oral contract), from out-of-court statements that relate only to operative facts (e.g., "Joel told me Mike said he would reimburse me"), and thus are hearsay. **2.** A fact that constitutes the transaction or event on which a claim or defense is based. • Some jurisdictions hold that claim preclusion bars litigation of a claim based on the same "core of operative facts" as a previously litigated action. *See Frier v. City of Vandalia*, 770 F.2d 699 (7th Cir. 1985) (applying Illinois law).

▸ **physical fact.** (1857) A fact having a physical existence, such as a fingerprint left at a crime scene.

▸ **positive fact.** The presence or existence of a quality, state, or condition. Cf. *negative fact*.

▸ **predicate fact** (**pred**-ə-kit). (1899) **1.** A fact from which a presumption or inference arises. **2.** A fact necessary to the operation of an evidentiary rule. • For example, there must be a conspiracy for the coconspirator exception to the hearsay rule to apply. — Also termed *foundational fact*; *evidentiary fact*.

▸ **presumed fact.** (1822) A fact whose existence can be justifiably inferred from facts established by evidence.

▸ **primary fact.** (18c) A fact that can be established by direct testimony and from which inferences are made leading to ultimate facts, esp. those based on the tort theory of public disclosure of private facts. See *ultimate fact*.

▸ **principal fact.** **1.** See *fact in issue*. **2.** See *ultimate fact*.

▸ **private fact.** (16c) A fact that has not been made public; esp., a fact that relates to the intimate or private aspects of a person's life. • Whether a fact is private often arises in invasion-of-privacy claims. Cf. *public fact*.

▸ **probative fact** (**proh**-bə-tiv). (1858) A fact in evidence used to prove an ultimate fact, such as skid marks used to show speed as a predicate to a finding of negligence. — Also termed *factum probans*.

▸ **psychological fact.** (1863) A fact that is related to mental state, such as motive or knowledge.

▸ **public fact.** (1955) For the purpose of an invasion-of-privacy claim, a fact that is in a public record or in the public domain. Cf. *private fact*.

▸ **relative fact.** (1862) A fact incidental to another fact; a minor fact. See *minor fact*.

▸ **simulated fact.** (1943) A fabricated fact intended to mislead; a lie.

▸ **subsidiary fact.** See *minor fact*.

▸ **translative fact** (trans- *or* tranz-**lay**-tiv). (1880) A fact by means of which a right is transferred from one person to another; a fact that fulfills the double function of terminating one person's right to an object and of originating another's right to it.

▸ **transvestitive fact.** (1883) A fact that is simultaneously investitive and divestitive.

> "When a person transfers the rights he has to another, the transfer divests him of the *potestas*, and invests that other with it. This is quite distinct from the creation or extinction of the *potestas*. A new descriptive term is wanted, and after the analogy of the other words, 'transvestitive' has been coined for the purpose." W.A. Hunter, *A Systematic and Historical Exposition of Roman Law* 141 (4th ed. 1903).

▸ **ultimate fact.** (18c) **1.** A fact essential to the claim or the defense. — Also termed *elemental fact*; *principal fact*. **2.** A fact that is found by making an inference or deduction from findings of other facts; specif., a factual conclusion derived from intermediate facts.

▸ **undisputed fact.** (18c) An uncontested or admitted fact.

▸ **vestitive fact.** See *dispositive fact* (1).

FACTA. *abbr.* **1.** FAIR & ACCURATE CREDIT TRANSACTIONS ACT. **2.** FOREIGN ACCOUNT TAX COMPLIANCE ACT.

facta (**fak**-tə). [Latin] *pl.* FACTUM.

facta concludentia (**fak**-tə kon-kloo-**den**-shee-ə). [Latin] *Hist.* Conclusive events.

FACT Act. *abbr.* FAIR & ACCURATE CREDIT TRANSACTIONS ACT.

facta praeterita (**fak**-tə pree-**tər**-i-tə). [Latin] *Hist.* Past events.

fact bargain. An agreement between a prosecutor and a defendant whereby the defendant stipulates that some facts are true in exchange for the prosecutor's not introducing certain other facts into evidence. Cf. *charge bargain*, *sentence bargain* under PLEA BARGAIN.

fact-finder. (1926) One or more persons who hear testimony and review evidence to rule on a factual issue. • The fact-finder may be the judge (in a bench trial) or a jury. — Often spelled *factfinder*. — Also termed *finder of fact*; *fact-trier* or *trier of fact* (in a judicial proceeding); *fact-finding board* (for a group or committee). See FINDING OF FACT.

fact-finding. (1909) **1.** The process of considering the evidence presented to determine the truth about a disputed point of fact. **2.** *Int'l law.* The gathering of information for purposes of international relations, including the peaceful settlement of disputes and the supervision of international agreements. • Examples of fact-finding include legislative tours to acquire information needed for making decisions at an international level. — Also termed *inquiry*.

> "[F]act-finding must be as impartial and as fair to the parties as procedural and evidentiary rules can render it without making the inquiry's task impossible, not merely for ethical reasons, but in order to maximize the credibility and impact of the facts found. To this end, fact-finders must develop procedures that sharply distinguish them from those bodies that assemble prosecutorial evidence." Thomas M. Franck & H. Scott Fairley, *Procedural Due Process in Human Rights Fact-Finding by International Agencies*, 74 Am. J. Int'l L. 308, 310 (1980).

3. A method of alternative dispute resolution in which an impartial third party determines and studies the facts and positions of disputing parties with a view toward clarifying the issues and helping the parties work through their dispute.

fact-finding board. See FACT-FINDER.

fact interrogatory. See *identification interrogatory* under INTERROGATORY.

faction. (16c) **1.** A subset within a larger group of people, the subset having different ideas from the others and engaging in a struggle to get those ideas accepted. **2.** A number of citizens, whether a majority or a minority, who are united and motivated by a common impulse or interest that is adverse to the rights of others or to the permanent or aggregate interests of the community. • This definition is adapted from *The Federalist*, No. 10. **3.** Partisanship marked by contentious quarreling. — **factional,** *adj.*

factionalism. (1904) Dissension between groups within an organization.

factio testamenti (**fak**-shee-oh tes-tə-**men**-tɪ). See TESTAMENTI FACTIO.

fact issue. See *issue of fact* under ISSUE (1).

facto (**fak**-toh), *adj.* In or by the fact. See DE FACTO; IPSO FACTO.

facto et animo (**fak**-toh et **an**-ə-moh). [Latin] In fact and intent <taking possession *facto et animo*>.

factor, *n.* [Latin "he who does"] (15c) **1.** An agent or cause that contributes to a particular result <punishment was a factor in the court's decision>. **2.** Someone who acts for another, esp. as a mercantile or colonial agent. **3.** An agent who is employed to sell property for the principal and who possesses or controls the property; a person who receives and sells goods for a commission <a factor was employed to sell goods for the company>. • A factor differs from a broker because the factor possesses or controls the property. — Also termed *mercantile agent; commission merchant; selling agent; purchasing agent; del credere bailiff.* Cf. BROKER (2).

> "A factor by the rules of common law and of mercantile usage is an agent to whom goods are consigned for the purpose of sale, and he has possession of the goods, power to sell them in his own name, and a general discretion as to their sale. He may sell them on the usual terms of credit, may receive the price, and give a good discharge to the buyer." William R. Anson, *Principles of the Law of Contract* 523 (Arthur L. Corbin ed., 3d Am. ed. 1919).

> "'Factor' and 'mercantile agent' are often used as though synonymous. In the Factor's Act, so called, passed toward the close of the reign of Queen Victoria it was provided: 'The expression 'mercantile agent' shall mean a mercantile agent having in the customary course of the business as such agent authority either to sell goods, or to consign goods for the purpose of sale, or to buy goods, or to raise money on the security of goods.' We are under the impression that at the present time in this country the word 'factor' is not much used by business men. They speak rather of commission merchants, or selling agents, or purchasing agents. But we believe that the legal definition of the word 'factor' today in this country accords with the statutory definition given above." Edward H. Warren, *The Rights of Margin Customers Against Wrongdoing Stockbrokers* 14 (1941).

4. Someone who buys accounts receivable at a discount <the company sold its receivables to a factor at only 5% of their stated value>. **5.** A person in charge of managing property, esp. real property. **6.** A garnishee <the factor held $400 of the debtor's property when the writ of garnishment was served>.

▸ **judicial factor.** (18c) *Scots law.* An administrator or factor specially appointed by the Court of Session to manage an estate.

factorage. (17c) **1.** The compensation paid to a factor for his or her services. **2.** The business of a factor.

factoring, *n.* (17c) The buying of accounts receivable at a discount. • The price is discounted because the factor (who buys them) assumes the risk of delay in collection and loss on the accounts receivable. See FACTOR (3).

factorize (**fak**-tə-rɪz), *vb.* (19c) **1.** GARNISH (2). **2.** GARNISH (3). — **factorization,** *n.*

factorizing process. (1837) A procedure or legal process by which a third party, rather than the creditor, attaches a debtor's property; GARNISHMENT. — Also termed *trustee process; process by foreign attachment.*

> "In Vermont and Connecticut, the [garnishee] is also sometimes called the factor, and the process [of garnishing], factorizing process." Charles D. Drake, *A Treatise on the Law of Suits by Attachment in the United States* § 451, at 386 (7th ed. 1891).

factor's act. (1833) A statute protecting one who buys goods from a factor or agent by creating the presumption that the agent was acting on the owner's behalf and with the owner's approval.

factor's lien. See LIEN.

factory act. (1838) A statute that regulates workers' hours, health, and safety. See FAIR LABOR STANDARDS ACT.

fact pleading. See *code pleading* under PLEADING (2).

fact question. See QUESTION OF FACT.

fact-trier. See FACT-FINDER.

factual cause. See *but-for cause* under CAUSE (1).

factual impossibility. See IMPOSSIBILITY.

factual issue. See *issue of fact* under ISSUE (1).

factual presumption. See *presumption of fact* under PRESUMPTION.

factum (**fak**-təm), *n.* [Latin] (18c) **1.** A fact, such as a person's physical presence in a new domicile.

▸ ***factum imprestabile*** (**fak**-təm im-pres-**tay**-bə-lee). [Law Latin] *Hist.* An act that cannot be performed; an impossibility.

▸ ***factum juridicum*** (**fak**-təm juu-**rid**-i-kəm). [Latin] A juridical fact. See *legal fact* (1) under FACT.

▸ ***factum probandum*** (**fak**-təm prə-**ban**-dəm). [Latin] (1838) A fact to be proved. See *fact in issue* (2) under FACT.

> "Evidence is *always a relative term.* It signifies a relation between two facts, the factum probandum, or proposition to be established, and the factum probans, or material evidencing the proposition. The former is necessarily to be conceived of as hypothetical; it is that which the one party affirms and the other denies, the tribunal being as yet not committed in either direction. The latter is conceived of for practical purposes as existent and is offered as such for the consideration of the tribunal. The latter is brought forward as a reality for the purpose of convincing the tribunal that the former is also a reality." John Henry Wigmore, *Evidence in Trials at Common Law* § 2, at 14–15 (Peter Tillers ed., 1983).

▸ ***factum probans*** (**fak**-təm **proh**-banz). [Latin] (1843) A probative or evidentiary fact; a subsidiary fact tending to prove a principal fact in issue. See *probative fact* under FACT.

▸ ***factum proprium et recens*** (**fak**-təm **proh**-pree-əm et **ree**-senz). [Law Latin] (1855) *Hist.* One's own act recently performed.

2. An act or deed, such as the execution of a will. • Over time, *factum* in this sense came to mean "charter" — that is, the act or deed of conveying land, reduced to written form. See FACTUM OF A WILL; *fraud in the factum* under FRAUD.

> "[I]t is only a short step to holding as a matter of law that a 'deed' — and by a deed (*fet, factum*) men are beginning to mean a sealed piece of parchment — has an operative force of its own which intentions expressed, never so plainly, in other ways have not. The sealing and delivering of the parchment is the contractual act. Further, what is done by 'deed' can only be undone by 'deed.'" 2 Frederick Pollock & Frederic W. Maitland, *The History of English Law Before the Time of Edward I* 220 (2d ed. 1899).

3. A statement of facts. **4.** BRIEF (1). Pl. **facta.**

factum of a will. (1847) The formal ceremony of making a will; a will's execution by the testator and attestation by the witnesses.

fact witness. See WITNESS.

fact work product. See WORK PRODUCT.

facultative certificate (fak-əl-tay-tiv). *Insurance.* (1983) A contract of reinsurance separately negotiated to cover risks under a single insurance policy. • Facultative reinsurance allows the reinsurer the "faculty" of assessing and possibly rejecting a particular risk (esp. if underwriting information is inadequate).

facultative obligation. See OBLIGATION.

facultative reinsurance. See REINSURANCE.

faculties. (16c) *Hist. Eccles. law.* **1.** An authorization granted to a person to do what otherwise would not be allowed. **2.** The extent of a husband's estate; esp., the ability to pay alimony. See ALLEGATION OF FACULTIES.

Faculties, Court of. See COURT OF FACULTIES.

Faculties, Master of the. See MASTER OF THE FACULTIES.

Faculty of Advocates. *Scots law.* The society comprising the members of the Scottish bar; specif., a body of independent lawyers who have been admitted to practice before the courts of Scotland. • Unlike the English bar, the advocates do not have chambers, but all share the facilities of Advocates' Library in Parliament House. The Faculty was founded in 1532.

faderfium (fah-th̲ər-fee-əm). *Hist.* A marriage gift to the bride from her father or brother.

faeder-feoh (fah-th̲ər-fee). *Hist.* Property brought by a wife to her husband at marriage. • If the husband died, the property reverted to the widow if the heir of the deceased husband refused consent to her second marriage. The property reverted to the widow's family if she returned to them.

fagot (fag-ət). (16c) *Hist.* **1.** A bundle of sticks, twigs, or branches, esp. as used to burn heretics at the stake. **2.** An embroidered figure of such firewood, required to be worn by heretics who had recanted as an emblem or reminder of the fate they might otherwise have suffered. **3.** The punishment or torture of being burned at the stake. — Also spelled *faggot.*

fail, *n.* A transaction between securities brokers in which delivery and payment do not occur at the prescribed time, usu. on the settlement date. — Also termed *fail contract.*

▸ **fail to deliver.** The nondelivery of securities from a selling broker to a buying broker by the settlement date.

▸ **fail to receive.** The failure of a buying broker to receive delivery of securities from the selling broker by the settlement date.

fail, *vb.* (13c) **1.** To be deficient or unsuccessful; to fall short of achieving something expected or hoped for <they failed to settle the dispute>. **2.** To become insolvent or bankrupt <two banks failed last week>. **3.** To lapse <the bequest failed as a result of ademption>. **4.** To stop functioning <the car's brakes failed>.

fail contract. See FAIL.

failed devise. See *lapsed devise* under DEVISE.

failed gift. 1. See *lapsed devise* under DEVISE. **2.** See *lapsed legacy* under LEGACY (1).

failed legacy. See *lapsed legacy* under LEGACY (2).

failed state. See STATE (1).

failing circumstances. 1. BANKRUPTCY (1). **2.** INSOLVENCY.

failing-company defense. *Antitrust.* A defendant corporation's argument that a merger should proceed because if the failing corporation were to merge, the overall effects of the merger on competition and the losses to stockholders and any affected communities would be less serious than they would be if the failing corporation were to cease operations entirely.

failing-company doctrine. (1956) *Antitrust.* The rule that allows an otherwise proscribed merger or acquisition between competitors when one is bankrupt or near failure. 15 USCA §§ 12–27. — Also termed *failing-firm defense.*

fail position. (1976) A situation existing when, after all transactions in a security have been netted out, a broker owes another broker more securities than it has coming in from other firms.

failure. (17c) **1.** Deficiency; lack; want. **2.** An omission of an expected action, occurrence, or performance. See LAPSE (2).

▸ **failure of a condition.** (1851) The nonoccurrence of an event that has been made a condition of the contract. • The usual result is that one or both of the parties need not perform. — Also termed *failure of a condition precedent.*

▸ **failure of consideration.** See FAILURE OF CONSIDERATION.

▸ **failure of good behavior.** (1937) A civil servant's act that is ground for removal.

▸ **failure of issue.** See FAILURE OF ISSUE.

▸ **failure of justice.** See MISCARRIAGE OF JUSTICE.

▸ **failure of proof.** (17c) A party's not having produced evidence establishing a fact essential to a claim or defense.

▸ **failure of record.** (1844) *Hist.* In a trial by record, a party's inability to produce the record and thereby prove a pleading; an absence of proof to support a party's pleading. • The other party was entitled to summary judgment. See *trial by record* under TRIAL.

▸ **failure of service.** The failure to serve required notice or process.

▸ **failure of title.** (18c) A seller's inability to establish a good claim to the property contracted for sale. Cf. *clear title* under TITLE (2).

▸ **failure of trust.** (1856) The invalidity of a trust because the instrument creating it has a defect or because of its illegality or other legal impediment.

▸ **failure of will.** (1920) The invalidity of a will that was not executed with necessary statutory formalities.

▸ **failure otherwise than on the merits.** (1963) The defeat of a plaintiff's claim by a procedural device without a decision on the existence of the claim's elements.

▸ **failure to appear.** See NONAPPEARANCE. — Abbr. FTA.

▸ **failure to appear in court.** See NONAPPEARANCE.

▸ **failure to bargain collectively.** (1935) An employer's refusal to discuss labor issues with a union.

▸ **failure to claim.** *Patents.* A finding by the U.S. Patent and Trademark Office or by a court that a patent applicant or patentee has forfeited the right to obtain a patent on a broader disclosed but unclaimed subject matter. • Any art outside the explicit claims, including foreseeable alteration of the claimed structure, is considered to be in the public domain.

▸ **failure to comply.** A person's failure to obey a lawful command or order, esp. a court's order.

▸ **failure to depart.** Noncompliance on the part of an alien with a final order of removal, having remained on U.S. soil. See 8 USCA § 1253(a).

▸ **failure to file return.** *Tax.* The failure of a person or entity that has taxable income to file a tax return with a state or federal revenue agency.

▸ **failure to make delivery.** (1838) Nondelivery or misdelivery. See NONDELIVERY; MISDELIVERY.

▸ **failure to meet obligations. 1.** See BANKRUPTCY (1). **2.** See INSOLVENCY.

▸ **failure to perform.** (17c) A party's not meeting its obligations under a contract; NONPERFORMANCE.

▸ **failure to protect.** *Family law.* The refusal or inability of a parent or guardian to prevent abuse of a child under his or her care.

▸ **failure to state a claim upon which relief can be granted.** (1867) A plaintiff's not having alleged facts in the complaint sufficient to maintain a claim. • This failure warrants dismissal of the complaint. *See* Fed. R. Civ. P. 12(b)(6). — Often shortened to *failure to state a claim.* — Also termed *failure to state a cause of action.*

▸ **failure to testify.** (1860) A party's, esp. a criminal defendant's, decision not to testify. • Under the Fifth Amendment, the prosecutor and the judge cannot comment to the jury on a criminal defendant's failure to testify. But comments on the failure are usu. permissible in a civil case.

▸ **failure to thrive.** See FAILURE TO THRIVE.

▸ **failure to warn.** A failure to comply with a duty to warn others of a risk or danger. • For example, a property owner must give notice that a dangerous, usu. hidden, condition exists on the premises. And a manufacturer must warn the public about a product's known and potential hazards.

failure of a condition precedent. See *failure of a condition* under FAILURE.

failure of consideration. (1803) *Archaic.* A seriously deficient contractual performance that causes a contract's basis or inducement to cease to exist or to become worthless. • Scholars disapprove of this term as misleading, since *failure of performance* is more accurate. Unlike *consideration,* the phrase *failure of consideration* relates not to the formation of a contract but to its performance. See CONSIDERATION (1). Cf. WANT OF CONSIDERATION.

> "An illustration will help indicate how the term is used. If C promises to build a structure for O and O promises to make payment when the work is completed, it is clear that there is consideration on both sides of this contract and that therefore a contract was formed upon the exchange of promises. If C fails to perform, the result is sometimes described as a 'failure of consideration.' 'Failure of consideration' simply means a failure to perform and as used covers both a material breach of constructive conditions and a failure to perform an express condition. The use of the term 'failure of consideration' in this sense appears to be an unnecessary invitation to confusion because the word consideration is being used in two different senses. Fortunately, the use of this phrase has gradually fallen into disuse. It is, however, still sufficiently widespread to be mentioned here. This volume nowhere utilizes 'failure of consideration' as an operative concept." John D. Calamari & Joseph M. Perillo, *The Law of Contracts* § 11-21, at 474-75 (3d ed. 1987).

▸ **partial failure of consideration.** (1808) A party's incomplete performance of a contract with multiple, severable performances, so that if some of the performances are not accomplished, the appropriate part of the agreement can be apportioned to whatever has been completed.

▸ **total failure of consideration.** (1809) A party's deficient contractual performance in a situation in which the contract is indivisible so that the deficiency voids the contract.

failure of good behavior. See FAILURE.

failure of issue. (17c) *Archaic.* The fact of a person's dying when the person has no surviving children or other descendants who are eligible to inherit the person's estate. — Also termed *dying without issue; definite failure of issue; default of issue.* See ISSUE (3).

> "There has been considerable litigation during the past several centuries over the meaning of a gift to 'A and his heirs, but if A shall die without issue, to B and his heirs.' First of all, what does 'die without issue' mean? The answer appears simple — you look to the time of A's death to determine whether or not he has any children or grandchildren. But that is not the way the English courts originally construed this language. The English adopted the so-called 'indefinite failure of issue' construction — if at any time in the future A's line of descent should come to an end, then there was a gift over to B and his heirs. The effect of this was a fee tail in A and a remainder in B. This seems a distortion of the language, and particularly unsuited to American circumstances since the fee tail never found a real home here. Most of our jurisdictions, by judicial decision or statute, adopted the so-called 'definite failure of issue' construction — you look to the date of A's death to determine whether he has issue, and to that time alone. If A has issue at that time, then the gift over to B fails. This seems to be the literal meaning of the words, and it is the only sensible conclusion in a system where the fee tail is virtually a dead letter. The English also struck down the constructional preference for indefinite failure by statute in the nineteenth century." Thomas F. Bergin & Paul G. Haskell, *Preface to Estates in Land and Future Interests* 236-37 (2d ed. 1984).

▸ **indefinite failure of issue.** (18c) A failure of issue whenever it happens, without any certain period within which it must happen.

failure of justice. See MISCARRIAGE OF JUSTICE.

failure of proof. See FAILURE.

failure-of-proof defense. (1982) The defense that a party's proof does not establish a fact essential to a claim or defense.

failure of record. See FAILURE.

failure of service. See FAILURE.

failure of title. See FAILURE.

failure of trust. See FAILURE.

failure of will. See FAILURE.

failure otherwise than on the merits. See FAILURE.

failure to appear. See NONAPPEARANCE.

failure to appear in court. See NONAPPEARANCE.

failure to bargain collectively. See FAILURE.

failure to claim. See FAILURE.

failure to comply. See FAILURE.

failure to depart. See FAILURE.

failure-to-disclose-best-mode rejection. See REJECTION.

failure to file return. See FAILURE.

failure to make delivery. See FAILURE.

failure to meet obligations. **1.** See BANKRUPTCY (1). **2.** See INSOLVENCY.

failure to perform. See FAILURE.

failure-to-perform exclusion. See EXCLUSION (3).

failure to protect. See FAILURE.

failure to state a cause of action. See *failure to state a claim upon which relief can be granted* under FAILURE.

failure to state a claim upon which relief can be granted. See FAILURE.

failure-to-supervise statute. See PARENTAL-LIABILITY STATUTE.

failure to testify. See FAILURE.

failure to thrive. (1967) *Family law.* **1.** A medical and psychological condition in which a child's height, weight, and motor development fall significantly below average growth rates. • Failure to thrive is sometimes asserted as a ground for alleging abuse or neglect by a parent or caregiver. **2.** A condition, occurring during the first three years of a child's life, in which the child suffers marked retardation or ceases to grow. — Abbr. FTT.

failure to warn. See FAILURE.

faint action. See FEIGNED ACTION.

faint pleader. (17c) A false, fraudulent, or collusive manner of pleading.

fair, *adj.* (bef. 12c) **1.** Characterized by honesty, impartiality, and candor; just; equitable; disinterested <everyone thought Judge Reavley to be fair>. **2.** Free of bias or prejudice <in jury selection, the lawyers tried to select a fair and impartial jury>. **3.** (Of an interpretation or reading) compellingly plausible based on the words of the legal instrument at issue. See FAIR READING. **4.** (Of a document) unblemished and unaltered <fair copy>. **5.** (Of an object considered for its value) reasonably good in kind, quality, or degree; free from any pronounced defect.

fair, *n.* (13c) *Hist.* A privileged market for the buying and selling of goods. • A fair was an incorporeal hereditament granted to a town by royal patent or franchise or established by prescription. The franchise to hold a fair conferred important privileges, and a fair, as a legally recognized institution, possessed distinctive legal characteristics, most of which are now obsolete. Cf. *market overt* under MARKET.

Fair and Accurate Credit Transactions Act. A 2003 amendment to the federal Fair Credit Reporting Act providing for free annual credit reports to consumers and establishing measures intended to help prevent identity theft. • One of the Act's better-known and more heavily litigated provisions prohibits merchants from printing the expiration date or more than the last five digits of the card number on a point-of-sale credit-card or debit-card receipt. 15 USCA § 1681c(g). — Abbr. FACTA; FACT Act.

fair-and-equitable requirement. (1970) *Bankruptcy.* A Bankruptcy Code standard requiring a forced, nonconsensual Chapter 11 plan (a "cramdown" plan) to provide adequately for each class of interests that has not accepted the plan. • In determining whether a cramdown plan is fair and equitable, a bankruptcy court must apply the Code's detailed statutory criteria, consider the plan as a whole, and weigh all the circumstances surrounding the treatment of each impaired class of interests. 11 USCA § 1129(b). See CRAMDOWN.

fair and impartial jury. See *impartial jury* under JURY.

fair and impartial trial. See FAIR TRIAL.

fair and proper legal assessment. See EQUALIZATION (2).

fair and reasonable value. See *fair market value* under VALUE (2).

fair and valuable consideration. See *fair consideration* (1) under CONSIDERATION (1).

fair averaging. **1.** A method of consolidating items based on technically and statistically valid data, esp. for determining flat grant amounts paid to recipients of general assistance programs where the grant amounts are based on the actual subsistence needs of the recipients. **2.** The process or activity of assessing taxes by using the average of the amount and price of goods acquired over a 12-month period rather than the amount and price at a particular time of year.

fair cash market value. See *fair market value* under VALUE (2).

fair cash value. See *fair value* under VALUE (2).

fair comment. (18c) A statement based on the writer's or speaker's honest opinion about a matter of public concern. • Fair comment is a common-law defense to libel or slander. For a statement to be considered a fair comment, it must be based on facts truly stated, it must be free from the imputation of corrupt or dishonorable motives on the part of the person whose conduct is criticized (except to the extent that the imputation is warranted by the facts truly stated), and it must be the honest statement of the writer's or speaker's real opinion.

fair competition. See COMPETITION.

fair consideration. See CONSIDERATION (1).

fair construction. See FAIR READING.

Fair Credit Billing Act. A federal statute that protects consumers from unfair billing practices, facilitates the correction of billing errors by credit-card companies, and makes those companies more responsible for the quality of goods purchased by cardholders. 15 USCA §§ 1666–1666j. — Abbr. FCBA.

Fair Credit Reporting Act. (1970) A 1970 federal statute that regulates disclosure and use of consumer-credit information and ensures the right of consumers to have access to and to correct their credit reports. 15 USCA §§ 1681–1681u. • Many states have enacted similar statutes. — Abbr. FCRA.

fair-cross-section requirement. (1975) *Constitutional law.* The principle that a person's right to an impartial jury, guaranteed by the Sixth Amendment, includes a requirement that the pool of potential jurors fairly represent the composition of the jurisdiction's population. • Although the pool of potential jurors need not precisely match the composition of the jurisdiction, the representation of each group must be fair — no group being systematically excluded or underrepresented. A minimal disparity in a particular group's representation, such as an absolute disparity of 10% or less, will not ordinarily violate this principle unless some aggravating factor exists. See DUREN TEST; ABSOLUTE DISPARITY; COMPARATIVE DISPARITY; STATISTICAL-DECISION THEORY.

fair dealing, *n.* (17c) **1.** The conduct of business with full disclosure, usu. by a corporate officer with the corporation. **2.** A fiduciary's transacting of business so that, although the fiduciary might derive a personal benefit, all interested persons are fully apprised of that potential and of all other material information about the transaction. Cf. SELF-DEALING. **3.** *Canadian law.* FAIR USE.

Fair Debt Collection Practices Act. A 1977 amendment to the Consumer Credit Protection Act regulating collection practices by debt collectors in connection with the collection of debt from consumers. 15 USCA §§ 1692–1692p. • Many states have enacted their own fair-debt-collection-practices statutes. The federal statute regulates primarily third-party debt collectors collecting debt owed (or at least originally owed) to another, but some state statutes also apply to first-party creditors collecting their own accounts. — Abbr. FDCPA.

fair hearing. See HEARING.

Fair Housing Act. A 1968 federal statute that prohibits discrimination on the basis of race, sex, religion, family status, or national origin in the sale or rental of a dwelling, esp. in the refusal to sell or rent. 42 USCA §§ 3601–3631. — Abbr. FHA. — Also termed *Title VIII of the Civil Rights Act of 1968.*

fair interpretation. See FAIR READING.

Fair Labor Standards Act. A 1938 federal statute that regulates minimum wages, overtime pay, and the employment of minors. • It applies to employees engaged in interstate commerce or employed by an entity engaged either in interstate commerce or in the production of goods for commerce. 29 USCA §§ 201–219. — Abbr. FLSA. — Also termed *Wage and Hours Act.*

fairly-debatable rule. (1956) **1.** *Insurance.* In some states, a test that requires an insurer to have a plausible basis for denying a claim in order to avoid bad-faith liability. **2.** *Zoning.* A doctrine that bars a court from interfering with a zoning decision that is supported by substantial evidence, even if it is one on which reasonable minds can differ.

fair market price. See *fair market value* under VALUE (2).

fair market value. See VALUE (2).

fair-market-value rule. See MARKET-VALUE RULE (2).

fair-minded, *adj.* (17c) Able and habitually inclined to understand situations and to judge people and their actions prudently and impartially; honest and judicious.

fairness. 1. The quality of treating people equally or in a reasonable way. **2.** The qualities of impartiality and honesty.

fairness doctrine. (1965) *Hist.* A federal law, based on an FCC rule, requiring the broadcast media to furnish a reasonable opportunity for the discussion of conflicting views on issues of public importance. • The FCC abandoned the fairness doctrine in 1987. — Also termed *equal-time doctrine.* Cf. EQUAL TIME ACT.

fairness opinion. See OPINION (2).

fair notice. See NOTICE (3).

fair-notice doctrine. The principle that a law, regulation, or order providing for criminal or civil penalties may not be enforced when the language is vague or when it may be reasonably interpreted in a way that makes the defendant's conduct lawful. Cf. VAGUENESS DOCTRINE.

fair on its face. (18c) (Of a document) having the appearance of being regular or legal and susceptible to being shown to be defective without extrinsic evidence.

fair pay. See PAY.

fair persuasion. See PERSUASION.

fair play. (17c) Equity, candor, honesty, and fidelity in dealings with another or others generally.

fair play and substantial justice. (1945) The fairness requirement that a court must meet in its assertion of jurisdiction over a nonresident defendant to comport with due process. *International Shoe Co. v. Washington,* 326 U.S. 310, 66 S.Ct. 154 (1945). See MINIMUM CONTACTS.

fair preponderance of the evidence. See PREPONDERANCE OF THE EVIDENCE.

fair presentation. 1. *Commercial law.* A materially accurate disclosure of a company's financial condition, achieved by selecting and using appropriate accounting policies, reasonably reflecting transactions that underlie the financial data, and making any additional necessary disclosures. **2.** *Criminal law.* The requirement that an applicant for a writ of habeas corpus, when in a state's custody, must show that (1) he or she has exhausted all available remedies in the state courts, (2) the state has offered no corrective process, or (3) circumstances exist that render a state's corrective process insufficient to protect the applicant's rights.

fair rate of return. See RATE OF RETURN.

fair reading. The interpretation that would be given to a text by a reasonable reader, fully competent in the language, who seeks to understand what the text meant at its adoption and who considers the purpose of the text but derives purpose only from the words actually used. — Also termed *fair construction; fair interpretation.* Cf. PURPOSIVISM.

fair-report privilege. (1965) The common-law protection extended to media reports about matters of public interest, such as official judicial and governmental proceedings, regardless of the reports' accuracy or whether they are defamatory. • In the United States and United Kingdom, this protection is augmented by statutes.

fair representation. *Labor law.* Union representation that adequately covers all union members in collective bargaining and handles employees' grievances both adequately and in good faith.

fair return on investment. See RETURN.

fair sale. See SALE.

fair-share clause. *Labor law.* A provision in a collective-bargaining contract requiring nonunion employees who benefit under the contract to pay the union for the union's representational expenses. • The amount payable is equal to the portion of a member's union dues that is earmarked for representational expenses. — Also termed *fair share of union dues.*

fair-share membership. See FINANCIAL-CORE MEMBERSHIP.

fair share of union dues. See FAIR-SHARE CLAUSE.

fair trade, *n.* (1881) **1.** The activity of manufacturing, buying, and selling goods in a way that is ethical and morally sound, as by ensuring that labor laws are complied with, the environment not damaged, and people fairly compensated. **2.** Commerce conducted under a fair-trade agreement. — **fair-trade,** *adj.* & *vb.*

fair-trade agreement. (1937) A commercial agreement that a seller will sell all of a producer's goods at or above a specified minimum price. • Fair-trade agreements were valid until 1975, when the Consumer Goods Pricing Act made them illegal. 15 USCA §§ 1, 45.

fair-trade law. (1936) A state statute that protects and enforces a fair-trade agreement. • At one time, many states had fair-trade laws. But when applied to interstate commerce, the laws may violate the Sherman Antitrust Act, so most states have repealed them.

fair trial. (17c) A trial by an impartial and disinterested tribunal in accordance with regular procedures; esp., a criminal trial in which the defendant's constitutional and legal rights are respected. — Also termed *fair and impartial trial.*

fair use. (1869) *Copyright.* A reasonable and limited use of a copyrighted work without the author's permission, such as quoting from a book in a book review or using parts of it in a parody. • Fair use is a defense to an infringement claim, depending on the following statutory factors: (1) the purpose and character of the use, (2) the nature of the copyrighted work, (3) the amount of the work used, and (4) the economic impact of the use. 17 USCA § 107. — Also termed (in Canadian law) *fair dealing.*

> "[Fair use is] the most troublesome [problem] in the whole law of copyright." *Dellar v. Samuel Goldwyn, Inc.*, 104 F.2d 661, 662 (2d Cir. 1939) (per curiam).

> "Fair use is a judicial safety valve, empowering courts to excuse certain quotations or copies of copyrighted material even though the literal terms of the Copyright Act prohibit them." Paul Goldstein, *Copyright's Highway* 84 (1994).

fair value. See VALUE (2).

fair-value accounting method. See ACCOUNTING METHOD.

fair-value law. (1952) A statute allowing a credit against a deficiency for the amount that the fair market value of land exceeds the price at foreclosure. — Also termed *fair-value legislation.*

fair warning. (1931) *Criminal law.* The requirement that a criminal statute define an offense with enough precision so that a reasonable person can know what conduct is prohibited. *See U.S. v. Harriss*, 347 U.S. 612, 617 (1954). — Also termed *fair notice.*

fair-warning challenge. (1975) *Criminal law.* A defense that no one should be held criminally liable for conduct that he or she could not reasonably understand to be prohibited. — Also termed *lack-of-fair-warning challenge.* Cf. RULE OF LENITY.

fair wear and tear. See WEAR AND TEAR.

fait (fay *or* fe). [Law French fr. Latin *factum*] (16c) Anything done; an act or deed. • The term *fait accompli* (fay *or* fe tə-kom-**plee**), meaning "a deed accomplished," which is not merely legal, is related to this word.

fait enrolle (fay *or* fe ton-**rohl**). [Law French] *Hist.* An enrolled deed of a sale of a freehold estate.

faith. 1. Trust that a promise will be carried out. **2.** Allegiance or loyalty to a person or to a duty. **3.** A firm belief in something that has little or no factual basis. **4.** A religion or religious belief.

Faith and Credit Clause. See FULL FAITH AND CREDIT CLAUSE.

faith and trust. See FLIM FLAM.

faithful, *adj.* **1.** Trustworthy in honoring vows, promises, or allegiances; loyal. **2.** (Of a person in a committed relationship) abstaining from sexual relations other than with one's partner. **3.** True in detail; accurate. **4.** Truthful; worthy of belief or confidence. Cf. UNFAITHFUL.

faithful-agent theory. The principal–agent model of interpretation in which courts are thought to be agents of the legislature with limited discretion in applying the legislature's directions as set forth in a statute. — Also termed *honest-agent theory.*

Faithfully Executed Clause. (1967) *Constitutional law.* The clause of the U.S. Constitution providing that the President must take care that the laws are carried out faithfully. U.S. Const. art. II, § 3.

faith-healing exemption. (1981) *Family law.* In a child-abuse or child-neglect statute, a provision that a parent who provides a child with faith healing (in place of standard medical treatment) will not, for that reason alone, be charged with abuse or neglect. • Nearly all states have enacted some form of faith-healing exemption. But the statutes differ greatly. For example, they differ on whether the exemption is available as a defense to manslaughter or only to murder charges brought against a parent whose child dies as a result of the parent's refusal to consent to medical treatment. — Also termed *religious-exemption statute; spiritual-treatment exemption.* Cf. *medical neglect* under NEGLECT.

faithless-agent rule. (2008) The doctrine that an agent who engages in misconduct forfeits the compensation related to the service that is improperly performed. — Also termed *faithless-agent doctrine.* Cf. FAITHLESS-SERVANT DOCTRINE.

faithless-servant doctrine. (1974) The common-law principle that an employer may refuse to pay compensation to an employee who is disloyal. • The doctrine originated in *Murray v. Beard*, 102 N.Y. 505, 508 (1886), and has been adopted by other states. It is based on the employee's duty of loyalty to an employer. Sometimes the faithless-servant doctrine is extended to agents. But an agent is a fiduciary, not a servant, and owes the principal more duties than loyalty. — Also termed *faithless-servant rule.* Cf. FAITHLESS-AGENT RULE.

fake, *n.* (19c) Something that is not what it purports to be. See FORGERY (2); IMPOSTOR.

fake, *vb.* (19c) To make or construct falsely. See COUNTERFEIT.

fake document. See *false document* under DOCUMENT (2).

fakement. (1819) *Slang.* **1.** An act of fraud or false pretense. **2.** The means or device by which a fraud is effected.

Falcidian law (fal-**sid**-ee-ən). (17c) *Roman law.* A law prescribing that one could give no more than three-fourths of one's property in legacies and that the heirs should receive at least one-fourth (the Falcidian portion). • If the testator violated this law, the heir had the right to deduct proportionally from each legatee as necessary. The law, proposed by the Roman tribune Falcidius, was enacted in 40 B.C. — Also termed *lex Falcidia*. See LEGITIME.

> "A large number of small legacies might [either] leave nothing for the heir . . . [or] make his part so small as to seem valueless in his eyes. But a Falcidian law, passed in the year 40 B.C., put an end to the whole difficulty. This law secured to the heir a quarter of the net value of the estate; the legatees could obtain only three-quarters: if the legatees named in the will amounted to more than this, they were diminished by proportional reductions. . . . Few measures have accomplished their purpose more satisfactorily than the Falcidian law, which remained in force through the history of the empire, and holds an important place in the system of Justinian." James Hadley, *Introduction to Roman Law* 321–22 (1881).

Falcidian portion. (1993) *Roman law.* The one-fourth part of an estate that one or more testamentary heirs are entitled to retain. La. Civ. Code art. 1494. — Also termed *quarta Falcidiana*. See *forced heir* under HEIR; LEGITIME. Cf. QUARTA TREBELLIANICA.

***Falconer* error.** (1992) A trial court's failure to instruct the jury that a guilty finding on a manslaughter charge requires acquittal on a murder charge. *Falconer v. Lane*, 905 F.2d 1129 (7th Cir. 1990).

faldage (**fahl**-dij), *n.* (17c) *Hist.* **1.** A landowner's right to require tenants to graze their sheep in designated temporary folds within a manor so that the manure will fertilize the field. — Also termed *foldage; fold soc.* **2.** A sum of money paid to the landowner by a sheep-owning tenant in lieu of keeping the animals in the landowner's temporary fold. — Also termed *faldfee*.

faldfee (**fahld**-fee), *n. Hist.* See FALDAGE (2).

faldworth (**fahld**-wərth), *n.* (18c) *Hist.* Someone who resides in a rural community where everyone above a certain age is responsible for the good conduct of all other members of the community and has reached that age of responsibility. • This was part of the frankpledge system. See DECENARY; FRANKPLEDGE.

fallacy. (15c) Any unsound, and usu. deceptive, argument or inference. • Both "formal" and "material" fallacies occur in a variety of recognized categories, knowledge of which is fundamental in the analysis of the validity of legal reasoning employed in any legal argument, esp. in judicial opinions. The presence of a fallacy in a legal argument is a defect — usu. deceptive and often fatal — in the legal reasoning.

- ▸ **fallacy of composition.** The error of inferring that a characteristic of one person or object is also a characteristic of a group as a whole. Cf. *fallacy of division*.
- ▸ **fallacy of division.** The error of assuming that a characteristic of something whole is also a characteristic of each component. Cf. *fallacy of composition*.
- ▸ **formal fallacy.** (1880) A fallacy involving flaws in the form of the argument, such as a violation of the formal rules of syllogistic reasoning.
- ▸ **material fallacy.** (18c) A fallacy involving flaws in the factual content of a logical argument.
- ▸ **moralistic fallacy.** The fallacy that whatever is good or right is inherently natural. Cf. *naturalistic fallacy*.
- ▸ **naturalistic fallacy.** The fallacy that natural things are inherently good or right and unnatural things are inherently bad or wrong. Cf. *moralistic fallacy*.
- ▸ **Parmenides' fallacy.** The fallacy of assuming that the present will not change when speculating how an action will affect the future. • Professor Philip Bobbit of the University of Texas named the term for the Greek philosopher Parmenides, who argued that the present is static and all change is illusion.

fallen angel. *Slang.* A company, institution, or borrower whose creditworthiness has significantly declined. Cf. RISING STAR.

fallacy of composition. See FALLACY.

fallacy of division. See FALLACY.

fallo (**fah**-yoh *or* **fɪ**-yoh), *n. Spanish law.* The mandate in a court's judgment; the dispositive sentence in a judicial pronouncement.

fall of the hammer. (1854) An auctioneer's closing of bidding <the bureau will be sold at the fall of the hammer>. • Traditionally, an auctioneer bangs a hammer, gavel, or other object when bidding is closed. In some circumstances, such as online auctions, an oral or written announcement that bidding is closed substitutes.

falsa causa. See CAUSA (2).

falsa demonstratio (**fal**-sə *or* **fawl**-sə dem-ən-**stray**-shee-oh). (1839) *Roman law.* A false designation; specif., an erroneous description of a person or thing in a legal instrument. • Generally, a simple error in description, grammar, or spelling will not void an instrument or even a single provision in it (such as a bequest by will). — Also termed *false demonstration*.

falsa moneta (**fal**-sə *or* **fawl**-sə mə-**nee**-tə). *Roman law.* Counterfeit money.

falsare (fal-**sair**-ee *or* fawl-), *vb.* [Law Latin] *Hist.* To counterfeit; to falsify, forge, or deceive.

falsarius (fal-**sair**-ee-əs *or* fawl-). [Law Latin] *Hist.* A counterfeiter. — Also spelled *falcarious*. — Also termed *falsonarius*.

falsâvert. (1900) Someone who changes his or her position prejudicially in reliance on a misrepresentation. • This is the neologism of the scholar John S. Ewart (1849–1933), who in coining the term complained that "[w]e are sadly in need of some short phrases wherewith to distinguish the actors in cases of estoppel." See DETRIMENTAL RELIANCE.

> "*Falsâvert* has the advantage of having for its first syllable a word familiar enough to all lawyers, and for its second that which is readily recognized (with the same meaning) in *convert* and *pervert*. *Falsâ* is preferable to *falso*, the last letter of which would frequently be taken as belonging to the *vert*, instead of to the first factor in the combination; and it is used as an adjective in the ablative having the word *re* understood — the whole word thus indicating one who has changed his position by reason of a falsity." John S. Ewart, *An Exposition of the Principles of Estoppel by Misrepresentation* iii–iv n.2 (1900).

false, *adj.* (12c) **1.** Untrue <a false statement>. **2.** Deceitful; lying <a false witness>. **3.** Not genuine; inauthentic <false coinage>. • What is false can be so by intent, by accident, or by mistake. **4.** Wrong; erroneous <false step>.

false, *vb.* (14c) **1.** *Scots law.* To make or prove false. **2.** *Archaic.* FALSIFY (1).

false action. See FEIGNED ACTION.

false advertising, *n.* (1911) **1.** The tortious and sometimes criminal act of distributing an advertisement that is untrue, deceptive, or misleading; esp., under the Lanham Act, an advertising statement that tends to mislead consumers about the characteristics, quality, or geographic origin of one's own or someone else's goods, services, or commercial activity. • Under § 43(a) of the Lanham Act, false advertising is actionable by anyone who reasonably believes that he or she has been or is likely to be damaged by the statement. An exaggerated opinion ("puffing") is an immaterial statement and therefore not actionable. **2.** At common law, a statement in a defendant's advertising about its own goods or services intended to deceive or confuse customers into buying those goods or services instead of the plaintiff's, thus causing actual damage to the plaintiff, esp. the loss of sales. — Also termed (in both senses) *deceptive advertising.*

false alarm. See ALARM.

false answer. See ANSWER (1).

false arrest. See ARREST (2).

false-association claim. (1992) *Intellectual property.* A claim based on the wrongful use of a distinctive name, mark, trade dress, or other device to misrepresent sponsorship, origin of goods or services, or affiliation. • The power to assert a false-association claim is not limited to trademark registrants. Any person who claims an injury caused by deceptive use of a trademark or its equivalent may have standing to bring suit. *See* 15 USCA § 1125(a)(1)(A).

false belief. See BELIEF.

false character. *Hist.* The crime of impersonating a servant's master or mistress. See IMPOSTOR. Cf. *false impersonation* under IMPERSONATION.

false check. See *bad check* under CHECK.

false claim. (16c) An assertion or statement that is untrue; esp., overbilling.

False Claims Act. A federal statute establishing civil and criminal penalties against persons who bill the government falsely, deliver less to the government than represented, or use a fake record to decrease an obligation to the government. 18 USCA §§ 286–287; 31 USCA §§ 3729–3733. • The Act may be enforced either by the attorney general or by a private person in a qui tam action. — Abbr. FCA. — Also termed *Lincoln Law.* See QUI TAM ACTION.

false conflict of laws. See CONFLICT OF LAWS (1).

false demonstration. See FALSA DEMONSTRATIO.

false designation of origin. (1920) *Trademarks.* A mark, design, or similar element that creates a misleading or erroneous impression of a good or product's source.

false document. See DOCUMENT (2).

false evidence. See *false testimony* under TESTIMONY.

falsehood. 1. A statement that is untrue, esp. one deliberately so; LIE <telling falsehoods>. **2.** The practice of telling lies; MENDACITY (3) <several acquaintances accused him of falsehood>. **3.** The state of not being true; falsity <the statement's truth or falsehood>. **4.** PERJURY.

false impersonation. See IMPERSONATION.

false-implication libel. See LIBEL (2).

false imprisonment. (14c) The restraint of a person in a bounded area without legal authority, justification, or consent. • False imprisonment is a common-law misdemeanor and a tort. It applies to private as well as governmental detention. *See* Restatement (Second) of Torts § 35 (1977). Cf. *false arrest* under ARREST (2).

> "[In the phrase *false imprisonment*,] false is . . . used not in the ordinary sense of mendacious or fallacious, but in the less common though well-established sense of erroneous or wrong; as in the phrases false quantity, false step, false taste, etc." R.F.V. Heuston, *Salmond on the Law of Torts* 123 n.38 (17th ed. 1977).

> "Some courts have described false arrest and false imprisonment as causes of action which are distinguishable only in terminology. The two have been called virtually indistinguishable, and identical. However, the difference between them lies in the manner in which they arise. In order to commit false imprisonment, it is not necessary either to intend to make an arrest or actually to make an arrest. By contrast, a person who is falsely arrested is at the same time falsely imprisoned." 32 Am. Jur. 2d *False Imprisonment* § 3 (1995).

false instrument. See INSTRUMENT.

false judgment. (16c) *Hist.* A writ filed to obtain review of a judgment of a court not of record. —Also termed *writ of false judgment.*

> "After judgment given, a writ also of *false judgment* lies to the courts at Westminster to rehear and review the cause, and not a writ of *error*; for this is not a court of record . . . ." 3 William Blackstone, *Commentaries on the Laws of England* 34 (1768).

> "In order to correct errors in a court not of record, the proper remedy was a writ of false judgment. It was an original writ issuing out of chancery and law where an erroneous judgment was claimed to have been rendered in a court not of record in which the suitors, i.e. persons bound to attend the court, were judges, such as a county court, a hundred court, or the court of a lord. Any one who had sustained damage by the judgment could bring the writ. It was not necessary for all the parties against whom the judgment was rendered to join as in a writ of error. The writ was made out by the cursitor and was to be served in court. If the lord refused to hold his court, there was a writ of *distringas* to compel him. The writ operated as a *supersedas* from the time of a service. After the Revolution there were statutes requiring a recognizance with two sureties in certain cases, but there was no such requirement till the last decade of the eighteenth century." Roscoe Pound, *Appellate Procedure in Civil Cases* 60 (1941).

false light. (1962) **1.** *Torts.* In an invasion-of-privacy action, a plaintiff's allegation that the defendant attributed to the plaintiff views that he or she does not hold and placed the plaintiff before the public in a highly offensive and untrue manner. *See* Restatement (Second) or Torts § 652E. • If the matter involves the public interest, the plaintiff must prove the defendant's malice. See *invasion of privacy by false light* under INVASION OF PRIVACY. Cf. DEFAMATION. **2.** (*usu. pl.*) *Maritime law.* A signal displayed intentionally to lure a vessel into danger. 18 USCA § 1658(b). — Also termed *false light or signal.*

false making. See FORGERY (1).

false marking. See MARKING.

false-memory syndrome. (1992) The supposed recovery of memories of traumatic or stressful episodes that did not actually occur, often in session with a mental-health therapist. • This term is most frequently applied to claims by adult children that repressed memories of prolonged and repeated child sexual abuse, usu. by parents, have surfaced, even though there is no independent evidence to substantiate the claims. — Abbr. FMS. Cf. REPRESSED-MEMORY SYNDROME.

False Memory Syndrome Foundation. An organization of parents who claim that their adult children have falsely accused them of childhood sexual abuse. • The organization was formed in 1992 to support people who claim to have been wrongly accused of child sexual abuse as a result of the purported recovery of repressed memories. — Abbr. FMSF. Cf. VICTIMS OF CHILD ABUSE LAWS.

false misrepresentation. (18c) See MISREPRESENTATION. • This phrase is redundant because the word *misrepresentation* includes the idea of falsity.

false news. (16c) *Hist.* The misdemeanor of spreading false information that causes discord between the monarch and the people or between important people in the realm. 3 Edw. ch. 34 (1550).

false oath. See PERJURY.

false patent marking. See *false marking* under MARKING.

false personation. See *false impersonation* under IMPERSONATION.

false plea. See *sham pleading* under PLEADING (1).

false positive. (1912) Something that is incorrectly shown or thought to be a particular thing, esp. after medical or scientific testing, or clinical research.

false pretenses. (18c) The crime of knowingly obtaining title to another's personal property by misrepresenting a fact with the intent to defraud. • Although unknown to English common law, false pretenses became a misdemeanor under a statute old enough to make it common law in the United States. Modern American statutes make it either a felony or a misdemeanor, depending on the property's value. — Also termed *obtaining property by false pretenses*; *fraudulent pretenses*; *larceny by false pretenses*. Cf. *larceny by trick* under LARCENY; EMBEZZLEMENT.

false promise. See PROMISE.

false report. (1827) *Criminal law.* The criminal offense of informing law enforcement about a crime that did not occur.

false representation. See MISREPRESENTATION.

false return. (16c) **1.** A process server's or other court official's written misrepresentation, usu. under oath, that process was served, that some other action was taken, or that something is true. See RETURN (2). **2.** A tax return on which taxable income is incorrectly reported or the tax is incorrectly computed. See TAX RETURN.

false statement. See STATEMENT.

false swearing. See PERJURY.

false testimony. See TESTIMONY.

false token. See TOKEN.

false verdict. See VERDICT (1).

false weight. (*usu. pl.*) (16c) A weight or measure that does not comply with governmentally prescribed standards or with the prevailing custom in the place and business in which the weight or measure is used.

falsi crimen. See *crimen falsi* under CRIMEN.

falsifiability (fal-si-fɪ-ə-**bil**-i-tee), *n.* (1937) The susceptibility of a hypothesis, theory, view, etc. to being proved false. • Using the scientific method, one seeks to establish a hypothesis that fits all or most of the known facts and then proceeds to attack that hypothesis at its weakest points by extracting from it predictions that can be shown to be false. The Supreme Court has endorsed falsifiability as important for courts in determining whether evidence is scientifically reliable. *See Daubert v. Merrell Dow Pharms., Inc.*, 509 U.S. 579, 593 (1993). The concept of falsifiability was most famously elaborated in Karl R. Popper's seminal book *Conjectures and Refutations* (1965). See SCIENTIFIC METHOD.

falsify, *vb.* (15c) **1.** To make deceptive; to counterfeit, forge, or misrepresent; esp., to tamper with (a document, record, etc.) by interlineation, obliteration, or some other means <the chiropractor falsified his records to help the plaintiff>. — Also termed (archaically) *false*. See COUNTERFEIT; FORGERY. **2.** *Rare.* To prove something to be false or erroneous <their goal in the appeal was to falsify the jury's verdict>. — **falsification,** *n.*

falsifying a record. (18c) The crime of making false entries or otherwise tampering with a public record with the intent to deceive or injure, or to conceal wrongdoing. 18 USCA §§ 1506, 2071, 2073; Model Penal Code § 224.4.

falsing of dooms, *n.* See APPEAL (2).

falsity, *n.* (13c) **1.** The quality, state, or condition of being untruthful or deceitful. **2.** An untrue statement; LIE. See FALSE.

falsonarius. See FALSARIUS.

falso retorno brevium (fal-soh [*or* **fawl**-soh] ri-**tor**-noh **bree**-vee-əm). [Law Latin] *Hist.* A writ against a sheriff for falsely returning a writ. See FALSE RETURN (1).

falsum (**fal**-səm *or* **fawl**-səm), *n.* [Latin] **1.** *Roman law.* A false statement. See *crimen falsi* under CRIMEN. **2.** *Roman law.* A crime involving forgery or falsification. • Until the later Roman Empire, the term applied to both documents and counterfeited coins. **3.** *Hist.* In early English common law, the forgery of currency or of the king's seal. • At common law, *falsum* was one of the 11 felonies or capital crimes.

***falsus in uno* doctrine** (**fal**-səs [*or* **fawl**-səs] in **yoo**-noh). [fr. Latin *falsus in uno, falsus in omnibus* "false in one thing, false in all"] (1956) The principle that if the fact-trier believes that a witness's testimony on a material issue is intentionally deceitful, the fact-trier is permitted to disregard all of that witness's testimony. • Once a mandatory jury instruction, this doctrine has been nearly universally rejected.

> "[T]here is an old maxim 'falsus in uno, falsus in omnibus' (false in one thing, false in all), which is often much overemphasized by counsel, though it is recognized by many courts in their charges to the jury. But this is only primitive psychology, and should be completely discarded." John H. Wigmore, *A Students' Textbook of the Law of Evidence* 181 (1935).

faltering-company exception. (1990) A provision in the Worker Adjustment and Retraining Notification Act exempting an employer from giving the required 60-day notice for a plant shutdown if (1) at the time notice was due, the employer was seeking capital or resources that would have allowed the employer to avoid or postpone a shutdown, and (2) the employer reasonably and in good faith believed that providing the notice would have precluded the employer from obtaining the necessary capital or other resources. 29 USCA § 2102(b)(1). See WORKER ADJUSTMENT AND RETRAINING NOTIFICATION ACT.

fama publica (**fay**-mə **pəb**-li-kə). [Latin "public repute"] (18c) *Hist.* A person's reputation in the community. • A person's *fama publica* could be used against him or her in a criminal proceeding. Cf. ILL FAME.

> "Now in the thirteenth century we find in the sheriff's turn a procedure by way of double presentment, and we may see it often, though not always, when a coroner is holding an inquest over the body of a dead man. The *fama publica* is twice distilled. The representatives of the vills make presentments to a jury of twelve freeholders which represents the hundred, and then such of these presentments as the twelve jurors are willing to 'avow,' or make their own, are presented by them to the sheriff. . . . From the very first the legal forefathers of our grand jurors are not in the majority of cases supposed to be reporting crimes that they have witnessed, or even to be the originators of the *fama publica*. We should be guilty of an anachronism if we spoke of them as 'endorsing a bill' that is 'preferred' to them; but still they are handing on and 'avowing' as their own a rumour that has been reported to them by others." 2 Frederick Pollock & Frederic W. Maitland, *The History of English Law Before the Time of Edward I* 643 (2d ed. 1899).

familia (fə-**mil**-ee-ə), *n.* (18c) [Latin] *Roman law.* **1.** All persons, free and slave, in the power of a paterfamilias; specif., a family, including household servants. See PATERFAMILIAS. **2.** One's legal relations through and with one's family, including all property, ancestral privileges, and duties.

> "*Familia* is used to signify (1) the master of a house and all who are subject to his authority, his wife, children, and slaves; (2) the *agnati* or relations through males; (3) the *cognati*, or all blood relations; (4) anciently, a person's patrimonium and *sacra privata* (e.g., *actio familiae erciscunde*); and (5) the slaves of a household." T. Whitcombe Greene, *Outlines of Roman Law* 42 (3d ed. 1875).

> "Familia. . . . A family or household, including servants, that is, hired persons (*mercenarii* or *conductitii*,) as well as bondsmen, and all who were under the authority of one master, (*dominus*). Bracton uses the word in the original sense, as denoting servants or domestics." 1 Alexander M. Burrill, *A Law Dictionary and Glossary* 603–04 (2d ed. 1867).

familiae emptor (fə-**mil**-ee-ee **emp**-tor). [Latin "estate purchaser"] (18c) *Roman law.* A trustee who received an inheritance by a fictitious purchase and distributed it as the testator instructed. — Also termed *emptor familiae.* See *mancipatory will* under WILL.

> "At some date, probably long before the XII Tables, men on the point of death, unable to make a true will because there was no imminent sitting of the *Comitia*, adopted the practice of conveying all their property . . . to a person who is described as the *familiae emptor*, and who is said by Gaius to be *in loco heredis*. Instructions were no doubt given to him as to the disposal of the property or part of it, but it is not clear that these were enforceable . . . ." W.W. Buckland, *A Manual of Roman Private Law* 175 (2d ed. 1939).

familiae erciscundae (fə-**mil**-ee-ee ər-sis-**kən**-dee). See *actio familiae erciscundae* under ACTIO.

familiares regis (fə-mil-ee-**air**-eez **ree**-jis). [Law Latin] *Hist.* **1.** Persons of the king's household. **2.** *English law.* The ancient title of the six clerks of chancery in England.

family, *n.* (14c) **1.** A group of persons connected by blood, by affinity, or by law, esp. within two or three generations. **2.** A group consisting of parents and their children. **3.** By extension, a group of people who live together and usu. have a shared commitment to a domestic relationship. See RELATIVE. — **familial,** *adj.*

▸ **blended family.** (1985) The combined families of persons with children from earlier marriages or relationships.

▸ **extended family.** (1942) **1.** The immediate family together with the collateral relatives who make up a clan; GENS. **2.** The immediate family together with collateral relatives and close family friends.

▸ **immediate family.** (18c) **1.** A person's parents, spouse, children, and siblings. **2.** A person's parents, spouse, children, and siblings, as well as those of the person's spouse. • Stepchildren and adopted children are usu. immediate family members. For some purposes, such as taxes, a person's immediate family may also include the spouses of children and siblings.

▸ **intact family.** (1936) A family in which both parents live together with their children.

family allowance. See ALLOWANCE (1).

Family and Medical Leave Act. A 1993 federal statute providing that employees may take unpaid, job-protected leave for certain family-based medical reasons, as when a family member is sick or when a child is born. 29 USCA §§ 2601 et seq. • The statute applies to businesses with 50 or more employees. An employee may take up to 12 weeks of unpaid leave per year under the Act. — Abbr. FMLA. Cf. FAMILY LEAVE.

family arrangement. (1817) An informal agreement among family members, usu. to distribute property in a manner other than what the law provides for. — Also termed *family settlement.*

family-automobile doctrine. See FAMILY-PURPOSE RULE.

family-autonomy doctrine. See PARENTAL-AUTONOMY DOCTRINE.

family-car doctrine. See FAMILY-PURPOSE RULE.

family compact. See COMPACT.

family corporation. See *close corporation* under CORPORATION.

family council. See FAMILY MEETING.

family court. See COURT.

family-court judge. See JUDGE.

family disturbance. See DOMESTIC DISPUTE.

Family Division. *English law.* A section of the High Court that has jurisdiction over family matters such as divorce and custody, as well as uncontested probate matters.

Family Educational Rights and Privacy Act. A federal statute that prescribes minimum standards for the maintenance and dissemination of student records by educational institutions that receive federal funding. 20 USCA § 1232g. • It applies only to schools that receive federal funding. — Abbr. FERPA. — Also termed *Buckley Amendment* (after its proponent, Senator James L. Buckley of New York).

family-expense statute. (1901) **1.** A state law that permits a charge against the property of a spouse for family debts such as rent, food, clothing, and tuition. **2.** A section of the federal tax code providing that a person may not deduct expenses incurred for family, living, or personal purposes. IRC (26 USCA) § 262. See NECESSARIES.

family farmer. See FARMER.

family-farmer bankruptcy. See CHAPTER 12 (2).

family history. Information about the health of a patient's close biological relatives indicating whether the patient may have hereditary tendencies toward certain diseases or disabling conditions.

family home. See HOME.

family-income insurance. See INSURANCE.

family independence agency. See CHILD PROTECTIVE SERVICES.

family law. (1919) **1.** The body of law dealing with marriage, divorce, adoption, child custody and support, child abuse and neglect, paternity, assisted reproductive technology, and other domestic-relations issues. • Juvenile delinquency is sometimes considered part of family law, though some categorize it only as criminal law. — Also termed *domestic relations*; *domestic-relations law.* **2.** (More broadly) all the law dealing with wills and estates, property, constitutional rights, contracts, employment, and finance as they relate to families.

> "Considered historically, family law began as a branch of public law, and only in recent times, whilst individualist theories have been dominant, has it become a branch of private law. Family law, administered by the *paterfamilias*, preceded the birth of the state, and is therefore older than other branches of public law. Later, the state was able to break down the corporate unity of the family, and to impose its commands directly upon the individual. Even today, however, it may be contended that the individual, in providing for the support and development in society of his family, is fulfilling a semipublic function." G.W. Keeton, *The Elementary Principles of Jurisprudence* 328 (2d ed. 1949).

family-law court. See *family court* under COURT.

family leave. See LEAVE.

family maintenance. See MAINTENANCE (6).

family medical leave. See LEAVE.

family meeting. *Hist. Civil law.* **1.** An advisory council called to aid the court in a family-law matter, such as arrangement of a guardianship for a minor or an incompetent adult. • If a person had no relatives, the court could summon friends of the person instead. **2.** A council of relatives of a minor assembled to advise the minor and to help administer the minor's property. — Also termed *family council.*

family of marks. (1954) *Trademarks.* A group of trademarks that share a recognizable characteristic so that they are recognized by consumers as identifying a single source. • An example of a family of marks is the variety of marks beginning with *Mc-* and identifying items served at McDonald's restaurants.

family of nations. (1818) *Int'l law.* The community of countries to which international law applies. • This term is now obsolescent. It is increasingly rejected as Eurocentric.

> "'The family of nations' is an aggregate of States which, as the result of their historical antecedents, have inherited a common civilisation, and are at a similar level of moral and political opinion." Thomas E. Holland, *The Elements of Jurisprudence* 396 (13th ed. 1924).

family partnership. See PARTNERSHIP.

family-partnership rules. (1946) **1.** The body of laws governing the conduct of partnerships between family members. **2.** Laws or regulations designed to prevent the shifting of income among partners, esp. family members, who may not be dealing at arm's length.

family-planning clinic. (1949) **1.** A facility that provides medical services or counseling related to reproductive health, such as birth-control options, pregnancy, sexually transmitted diseases, and infertility. — Also termed *reproductive-health clinic.* **2.** See ABORTION CLINIC.

family-pot trust. See TRUST (3).

family-purpose rule. (1927) *Torts.* The principle that a vehicle's owner is liable for injuries or damage caused by a family member's negligent driving. • Many states have abolished this rule. — Also termed *family-purpose doctrine*; *family-automobile doctrine*; *family-car doctrine.* Cf. GUEST STATUTE.

> "A number of jurisdictions have adopted the so-called 'family purpose' doctrine, under which the owner of a motor vehicle purchased or maintained for the pleasure of his family is liable for injuries inflicted by the negligent operation of the vehicle while it is being used by members of the family for their own pleasure, on the theory that the vehicle is being used for the purpose or business for which it was kept, and that the person operating it is therefore acting as the owner's agent or servant in using it." 8 Am. Jur. 2d *Automobiles and Highway Traffic* § 715, at 296 (1997).

family-responsibility leave. See LEAVE.

family reunification. See REUNIFICATION.

family settlement. 1. FAMILY ARRANGEMENT. **2.** See SETTLEMENT (1).

family shelter. See *women's shelter* under SHELTER (1).

family support. A combined award of child support and alimony that does not apportion the amount of each.

Family Support Act of 1988. A federal statute requiring states to develop and implement child-support guidelines. 42 USCA § 667. See CHILD-SUPPORT GUIDELINES.

family trust. See TRUST (3).

family violence. See *domestic violence* under VIOLENCE.

famosus (fə-**moh**-səs), *adj.* [Latin] *Hist.* **1.** (Of a statement) having a defamatory character. **2.** (Of an action) involving infamy if the defendant lost the case.

famosus libellus (fə-**moh**-səs li-**bel**-əs). [Latin] (17c) *Roman law.* **1.** A libelous writing. **2.** The species of injury that is caused by libel. **3.** The criminal offense of written libel.

famous mark. See *famous mark* under TRADEMARK.

famous trademark. See TRADEMARK.

fanciful mark. See *fanciful trademark* under TRADEMARK.

fanciful term. See *fanciful trademark* under TRADEMARK.

fanciful trademark. See TRADEMARK.

Fannie Mae (**fan**-ee **may**). See FEDERAL NATIONAL MORTGAGE ASSOCIATION.

FAO. *abbr.* (1946) FOOD AND AGRICULTURE ORGANIZATION.

FAPE. *abbr.* Free appropriate public education. • This is a right of children with disabilities to have access to free education, guaranteed by the Rehabilitation Act of 1973 and the Individuals with Disabilities Education Act. *See* 34 CFR § 100.33; 34 CFR § 300.13.

F. App. *abbr.* The *Federal Appendix*, a set of reports containing unpublished decisions (those not designated for publication) dated on or after January 1, 2001, from all federal courts of appeals except the Third, Fifth, and Eleventh Circuits. — Also abbreviated F. Appx; F. App'x.

FAR. (*often pl.*) *abbr.* **1.** FEDERAL AVIATION REGULATION <the pilot violated several FARs before the crash>. **2.** FEDERAL ACQUISITION REGULATION.

***Faragher–Ellerth* defense.** An employer's defense against a hostile-work-environment claim based on a showing that the employer acted with reasonable care to prevent and to correct hostile workplace conditions and took no adverse action against the employee, and that the employee unreasonably failed to act to avoid the harm, as by not following procedures to report antiharassment-policy violations. • The defense is named for two U.S. Supreme Court cases that created it: *Faragher v. City of Boca Raton*, 524 U.S. 775, 118 S.Ct. 2275 (1998), and *Burlington Industries, Inc. v. Ellerth*, 524 U.S. 742, 118 S.Ct. 2257 (1998). — Also written *Faragher/Ellerth defense.* — Also termed *Faragher–Ellerth affirmative defense*; *Ellerth–Faragher defense*; *Ellerth/Faragher defense*.

farley (**fahr**-lee). (17c) *Hist.* Money paid by a tenant in lieu of a chattel (or *heriot*). • The term originated in West Stanton, Devonshire, but even as its geographic range expanded, it invariably occurred in the west of England. See HERIOT.

farm, *n.* (14c) **1.** Land and connected buildings used for agricultural purposes. **2.** *Hist.* Rent. **3.** *Hist.* By extension, land for which the rent was paid. — Also termed and spelled *ferm*; *fearm*; *firme*.

farm, *vb.* (15c) **1.** To cultivate land; to conduct the business of farming. **2.** To lease. See FARM OUT.

Farm Credit Administration. An independent federal agency that regulates and examines the borrower-owned banks, cooperative associations, and other entities that make up the Federal Farm Credit System. • The agency was created in 1929 under the title "Federal Farm Board," became a federal agency in the Department of Agriculture in 1933, and again became independent in 1971. It supervises all federal farm-credit activities. — Abbr. FCA. See FEDERAL FARM CREDIT SYSTEM.

farmee. See FARMOUTEE.

farmer. (14c) A person whose business is farming.

▸ **family farmer.** (1946) A person, married couple, or entity whose income and debts primarily arise from a family-owned and -operated farm. • To qualify as a family farmer, specific debt, income, and asset thresholds and limits must be met as set forth in the Bankruptcy Code. Only a family farmer can file for Chapter 12 bankruptcy. 11 USCA § 101(18). See CHAPTER 12.

farmer bankruptcy. See CHAPTER 12 (2).

Farmers Home Administration. An agency in the U.S. Department of Agriculture responsible for making mortgages and insuring loans to farmers and for funding rural public-works projects. • The agency was abolished in 1994, when its functions were assumed by other agencies in the Department. — Abbr. FmHA; FHA. — Also written *Farmers' Home Administration*.

farminee. See FARMOUTEE.

farming operation. (1859) *Bankruptcy.* A business engaged in farming, tillage of soil, dairy farming, ranching, raising of crops, poultry, or livestock, or production of poultry or livestock products in an unmanufactured state. 11 USCA § 101(21). See CHAPTER 12.

farminor. See FARMOUTOR.

farm let, *vb.* (17c) *Hist.* To lease; to let land for rent. • *Farm-let* is a phrasal verb that commonly appeared in real-property leases; it corresponds with its Latin root, *ad firmam tradidi.*

> "A lease is properly a conveyance of any lands or tenements, (usually in consideration of rent or other annual recompense) made for life, for years, or at will, but always for a *less* time than the lessor hath in the premises: for if it be for the *whole* interest, it is more properly an assignment than a lease. The usual words of operation in it are, 'demise, grant, and to farm let; *dimisi, concessi, et ad firmam tradidi.*'" 2 William Blackstone, *Commentaries on the Laws of England* 317–18 (1766).

farmor. See FARMOUTOR.

farm out, *vb.* (17c) **1.** To turn over something (such as an oil-and-gas lease) for performance by another. • The term evolved from the Roman practice of transferring the right to collect taxes to a third party for a fee. That practice continued in England, Scotland, and France, but it has been long abolished. Cf. OUTSOURCING. **2.** *Hist.* To lease for a term. **3.** To exhaust farmland, esp. by continuously raising a single crop.

farmout agreement. (1943) *Oil & gas.* An agreement by which someone who owns an oil-and-gas lease (the *farmoutor* or *farmor*) agrees to assign to another (the *farmoutee* or *farmee*) an interest in the lease in return for drilling and testing operations on the lease. • For the farmouter, the agreement either (1) maintains the lease by securing production or complying with the implied covenant to develop or offset, or (2) obtains an interest in production without costs. For the farmoutee, the agreement obtains acreage that is not otherwise available or at lower cost than would otherwise be possible. A farmout agreement may also serve as a device to keep people and equipment gainfully employed. — Often shortened to *farmout.* — Also written *farm-out agreement.* See ASSIGNMENT (1), (2).

farmoutee (fahrm-ow-**tee**). (1964) An oil-and-gas sublessee to whom the lease is assigned by a farmoutor for purposes of drilling a well. — Also termed *farmee*; *farminee*.

farmoutor (**fahrm**-ow-tor *or* -tər). (1979) An oil-and-gas lessee who assigns the lease to another, a farmoutee, who agrees to drill a well. — Also spelled *farmouter.* — Also termed *farmor*; *farminor*.

farm products. (1886) Crops, livestock, and supplies used or produced in farming or products of crops or livestock in their unmanufactured states, if they are in the possession of a debtor engaged in farming. UCC § 9-102(a)(34). Cf. *growing crops* under CROPS.

Farm Service Agency. An agency in the U.S. Department of Agriculture responsible for administering farm-commodity, crop-insurance, and resource-conservation programs for farmers and ranchers and for making or guaranteeing farm-emergency and -operating loans through a network of state and county offices. — Abbr. FSA.

farthing (fahr-th̲ing). **1.** *Hist.* An area of land measured as one-quarter of a larger area (much as a farthing was one-quarter of a penny). • A farthing of land ranged from a quarter of a hide to a quarter of an acre. **2.** Something of little value or worth. • The British farthing coin was withdrawn from use in 1961.

farvand (fahr-vənd). (1857) *Hist. Maritime law.* Voyage or passage by water under a charterparty.

Faryndon's Inn. *Hist.* The ancient name of Serjeants' Inn. See SERJEANTS' INN.

FAS. *abbr.* (1888) **1.** FREE ALONGSIDE SHIP. **2.** FETAL ALCOHOL SYNDROME. **3.** FOREIGN AGRICULTURAL SERVICE.

fas (fas), *n.* [Latin] *Roman law.* **1.** Moral law thought to be of divine origin; divine law. • *Jus*, by contrast, is created by man. See JUS. **2.** What is right, proper, lawful, and permitted. Cf. NEFAS.

> "The first element to be noted in the Roman composite existing in primitive times, when religion and law were not distinguished, is *fas* — the will of the gods, embodied in rules that regulated not only ceremonials but the conduct of all men as such." Hannis Taylor, *The Science of Jurisprudence* 65 (1908).

> "It is true that the two spheres of *ius* and *fas* overlapped. . . . All this, however, concerned merely the question of where to draw the line between *ius* and *fas*; it did not blur the distinction between the two. From the standpoint of the history of Roman law, this distinction, consciously made from very early times, was of great importance, since it enabled the Romans to delimit the scope and the contents of strictly legal rules. This attitude may occasionally have caused a certain cold aloofness from purely human problems, but it undoubtedly contributed to the clarity of the legal system." Hans Julius Wolff, *Roman Law: An Historical Introduction* 51–52 (1951).

FASB (faz-bee). *abbr.* FINANCIAL ACCOUNTING STANDARDS BOARD.

FASB statement. (1981) An official pronouncement from the Financial Accounting Standards Board establishing a given financial-accounting practice as acceptable.

fascism. (1921) **1.** A totalitarian political ideology under which all economic and social aspects of life come under rigid government control or direction, and the state's interests supersede individual interests. **2.** A political system based on this ideology. — **fascist,** *adj.* & *n.*

fast estate. See *real property* under PROPERTY.

fasti (fas-tɪ). [Latin] (17c) *Roman law.* **1.** The days on which court can be held. • In this sense, *fasti* is a shortened form of *dies fasti.* **2.** A calendar of days on which court can be held. See *dies fasti* under DIES.

fast land. See LAND.

fast-track arbitration. See ARBITRATION.

fast-tracking, *n.* (1996) **1.** The expediting of judicial dispositions; esp., a court's method of accelerating the disposition of cases. • For example, a judge might order that all discovery must be finished within 90 days and that trial is set for 30 days later. **2.** More generally, the expedited promotion of something, such as a legislative bill or the career of a promising athlete. See ROCKET DOCKET. — **fast-track,** *vb.*

fatal, *adj.* (14c) **1.** Of, relating to, or involving death; producing death <the decision had fatal consequences> <fatal blow>. **2.** Providing grounds for legal or logical invalidity <a fatal defect in the contract> <a fatal flaw in the appellant's argument>.

fatal accident. See ACCIDENT.

fatal defect. See DEFECT.

fatal error. See *reversible error* under ERROR (2).

fatalism. (17c) **1.** The belief that there is nothing one can do to affect events or to prevent things from happening; the idea that all events are absolutely predetermined, or fixed by fate. **2.** The disposition to accept every event or occurrence as preordained or controlled by destiny. — **fatalist,** *n.* — **fatalistic,** *adj.*

fatality. (15c) **1.** A death in an accident, disaster, or violent attack <25 traffic fatalities>. **2.** The quality, state, or condition of causing death or destruction; esp., the fact that an activity or disease is certain to cause death <a 15% fatality rate>.

fatality hearing. (2005) A public-safety proceeding, often held before an administrative-law judge of the department of motor vehicles, to determine the cause of a traffic death and to consider the suspension or revocation of a driver's license. Cf. SAFETY HEARING.

fatal variance. See VARIANCE (1).

fate and transport. (1978) *Environmental law.* The physical condition and migration of contaminants and hazardous materials along environmental pathways such as air, water, and soil.

father. (bef. 12c) A male parent. See PARENT.

- ▸ **acknowledged father.** (18c) The admitted biological father of a child born to unmarried parents. See ACKNOWLEDGMENT (1).
- ▸ **adoptive father.** See *adoptive parent* under PARENT.
- ▸ **biological father.** (1951) The man whose sperm impregnated the child's biological mother. — Also termed *natural father; birth father; genetic father.*
- ▸ **birth father.** See *biological father.*
- ▸ **de facto father.** See *de facto parent* under PARENT (1).
- ▸ **filiated father.** The proven biological father of a child born to unmarried parents. See FILIATION.
- ▸ **foster father.** See *foster parent* under PARENT (1).
- ▸ **genetic father.** See *biological father.*
- ▸ **godfather.** See GODPARENT.
- ▸ **intentional father.** See *intentional parent* under PARENT (1).
- ▸ **legal father.** (16c) The man recognized by law as the male parent of a child. • A man is the legal father of a child if he was married to the child's natural mother when the child was born, if he has recognized or acknowledged the child, or if he has been declared the child's natural father in a paternity action. If a man consents to the artificial insemination of his wife, he is the legal father of the child that is born as a result of the artificial insemination even though he may not be the genetic father of the child.
- ▸ **natural father.** See *biological father.*
- ▸ **presumed father.** (1937) The man presumed to be the father of a child for any of several reasons: (1) because he was married to the child's natural mother when the child was conceived or born (even though the marriage

may have been invalid), (2) because the man married the mother after the child's birth and agreed either to have his name on the birth certificate or to support the child, or (3) because the man welcomed the child into his home and held out the child as his own. • This term represents a complicated category, and state laws vary in their requirements. See PRESUMPTION OF PATERNITY.

▸ **psychological father.** See *psychological parent* under PARENT (1).

▸ **putative father** (**pyoo**-tə-tiv). (16c) The alleged biological father of a child born out of wedlock.

▸ **stepfather.** (bef. 12c) The husband of one's mother by a later marriage. — Formerly also termed *vitricus*; *father-in-law.*

father-in-law. (14c) **1.** The father of a person's spouse. **2.** See *stepfather* under FATHER.

fatherly power. See *patria potestas* under POTESTAS.

***Fatico* hearing** (**fat**-ə-koh). (1979) *Criminal procedure.* A sentencing hearing at which the prosecution and the defense may present evidence about what the defendant's sentence should be. *U.S. v. Fatico*, 603 F.2d 1053 (2d Cir. 1979).

fatuum judicium (**fach**-oo-əm joo-**dish**-ee-əm). [Latin] *Archaic.* A foolish judgment or verdict.

fatwa. *Islamic law.* A legal ruling or opinion given by a recognized authority on Islamic law. Pl. **fatawa.**

fauces terrae (**faw**-seez **ter**-ee). [Latin "narrow passage of the land," lit. "jaws of the land"] (1815) A body of water that experiences tides and is partially enclosed by land. • This includes inlets, rivers, harbors, creeks, bays, basins, and similar aquatic bodies.

fault. (13c) **1.** An error or defect of judgment or of conduct; any deviation from prudence or duty resulting from inattention, incapacity, perversity, bad faith, or mismanagement. **2.** A breach of duty as an element of the tort of negligence. • Fault is a traditional element in determining the legal responsibility for an injury suffered by another. **3.** *Civil law.* The intentional or negligent failure to maintain some standard of conduct when that failure results in harm to another person. See NEGLIGENCE. Cf. LIABILITY (1).

▸ **contractual fault.** (1876) *Civil law.* Fault resulting from the intentional or negligent failure to perform an enforceable obligation in a contract.

▸ **delictual fault.** (1963) *Civil law.* Fault resulting from intentional or negligent misconduct that violates a legal duty.

▸ **inscrutable fault.** (1841) *Maritime law.* Fault ascribed to human error but for which no responsible party or parties can be identified.

> "'Inscrutable fault' exists when a collision clearly resulted from human fault but the court is unable to locate it or allocate the fault among the parties." *Atkins v. Lorentzen*, 328 F.2d 66, 69 (5th Cir. 1964).

fault-based liability. See *fault liability* under LIABILITY.

fault divorce. See DIVORCE.

fault-first method. (1996) A means by which to apply a settlement credit to a jury verdict, whereby the amount of the verdict is first reduced by the percentage of the plaintiff's comparative fault, and then the remainder the amount of any settlements the plaintiff has received on the claim is subtracted. See SETTLEMENT CREDIT. Cf. SETTLEMENT-FIRST METHOD.

faultless pardon. See PARDON (1).

fault liability. See LIABILITY.

fault of omission. (17c) Negligence resulting from a negative act; NONFEASANCE. See *negative act* under ACT (2).

***Fauntleroy* doctrine.** (1983) The principle that a state must give full faith and credit to another state's judgment, as long as the other state had proper jurisdiction, even if the judgment is based on a claim that is illegal in the state in which enforcement is sought. *Fauntleroy v. Lum*, 210 U.S. 230, 28 S.Ct. 641 (1908).

fautor (**faw**-tər). (14c) *Hist.* **1.** An abettor or supporter; an active partisan. **2.** Someone who encourages resistance to execution of process.

faux (foh), *adj.* [Law French] (17c) False or counterfeit.

faux (foh), *n.* [French "false"] *Civil law.* The fraudulent alteration of the truth. See CRIMEN FALSI.

faux action. A false action. See PLEADING.

faux money. Counterfeit money.

faux peys (foh **pay**). [French] False weights. See FALSE WEIGHT.

faux serement (foh ser-**mahn**). [French] A false oath.

favor, *n.* See BIAS.

favorable termination. *Criminal procedure.* In a criminal prosecution, a final determination on the merits in the defendant's favor. • Favorable termination is an element of the common-law tort of malicious prosecution. It was incorporated into § 1983 analysis in *Heck v. Humphrey*, 512 U.S. 477 (1994).

favored beneficiary. See BENEFICIARY.

favored nation. See MOST FAVORED NATION.

favored-nation clause. See MOST-FAVORED-NATION CLAUSE.

favorite of the law. (18c) A person or status entitled to generous or preferential treatment in legal doctrine.

> "It has long been said that the surety is a favorite of the law and his contract strictissimi-juris." Laurence P. Simpson, *Handbook on the Law of Suretyship* 94 (1950).

favoritism. (18c) Preference or selection, usu. invidious, based on factors other than merit. See NEPOTISM; PATRONAGE; CRONYISM. Cf. DISCRIMINATION (3).

favor legitimationis (**fay**-vər lə-jit-ə-may-shee-**oh**-nis). [Latin "(in) favor of legitimacy"] (1971) The principle that a court should attempt to uphold a child's legitimacy.

favor matrimonii (**fay**-vər ma-trə-**moh**-nee-I). [Latin "(in) favor of marriage"] (1956) The principle that a court should attempt to uphold the validity of a marriage.

favor negotii (**fay**-vər ni-**goh**-shee-I). [Latin "(in) favor of business"] (1959) The principle that favors upholding a contract against an interpretation that would render the contract illegal or unenforceable.

favor paternitatis (**fay**-vər pə-tər-nə-**tay**-tis). [Latin "(in) favor of paternity"] (1962) The principle that a court should interpret facts so as to uphold the paternity of a child.

favor solutionis (**fay**-vər sə-loo-shee-**oh**-nis). [Latin "(in) favor of payment"] *Conflict of laws.* The principle that a contract should be interpreted according to the applicable law governing performance.

favor testamenti (**fay**-vər tes-tə-**men**-tɪ). [Latin "(in) favor of the testament"] (1908) The principle that a court should attempt to uphold a will's validity.

fax, *n.* (1948) **1.** A method of transmitting over telephone lines an exact copy of a printing. **2.** A machine used for such a transmission. — Also termed *telecopier.* **3.** The communication sent or received by such a machine. — Also termed (and shortened from) *facsimile*; (in senses 1 & 3) *facsimile transmission.* — **fax,** *vb.*

FBA. *abbr.* FEDERAL BAR ASSOCIATION.

FBI. *abbr.* (1936) FEDERAL BUREAU OF INVESTIGATION.

FBOP. *abbr.* FEDERAL BUREAU OF PRISONS.

FBP. *abbr.* FEDERAL BUREAU OF PRISONS.

FCA. *abbr.* **1.** FARM CREDIT ADMINISTRATION. **2.** FREE CARRIER. **3.** FALSE CLAIMS ACT.

F. Cas. *abbr. Federal Cases,* a series of reported decisions (1789–1880) predating the *Federal Reporter.*

FCBA. *abbr.* FAIR CREDIT BILLING ACT.

FCC. *abbr.* (1937) FEDERAL COMMUNICATIONS COMMISSION.

FCFAA. *abbr.* FEDERAL COMPUTER FRAUD AND ABUSE ACT.

FCI. *abbr.* Federal corrections institution.

FCIC. *abbr.* FEDERAL CROP INSURANCE CORPORATION.

FCJ. *abbr.* Failure to comply with a judgment, esp. one imposed for a traffic violation. • The defendant's driver's license is suspended until the FCJ is remedied and the fines and fees are paid.

FCM. *abbr.* FUTURES-COMMISSION MERCHANT.

FCO. *abbr.* FOREIGN AND COMMONWEALTH OFFICE.

FCPA. *abbr.* FOREIGN CORRUPT PRACTICES ACT.

FCPV. *abbr.* Failure to comply with parking-violation tickets. • If a person has a certain number of unpaid parking tickets (often six) within a jurisdiction, the person will be barred from obtaining or renewing a driver's license.

FCRA. *abbr.* FAIR CREDIT REPORTING ACT.

FDA. *abbr.* FOOD AND DRUG ADMINISTRATION.

f/d/b/a. *abbr.* Formerly doing business as.

FDCA. *abbr.* FOOD, DRUG, AND COSMETIC ACT.

FDCPA. *abbr.* FAIR DEBT COLLECTION PRACTICES ACT.

FDIC. *abbr.* FEDERAL DEPOSIT INSURANCE CORPORATION.

feal (**fee**-əl), *adj.* (16c) *Archaic.* Faithful; loyal; constant. — Also spelled *fele.*

fealty (**feel**-tee *or* **fee**-əl-tee). (14c) **1.** *Hist.* In feudal law, the allegiance that a tenant or vassal owed to a lord. — Also termed *feodality.*

> "There was the possibility that if the entire top layer of the structure revolted, the king might be deprived of all support. To meet this possibility, the king also bound directly to himself all the important men in the lower strata of the [feudal] structure by an oath of loyalty. This was particularly effective for in medieval times the oath of fealty had all the sanction of the church, and in addition due to the necessity for feudal organization in times of disorder, had also a popular sanction in public opinion so that the man who broke his oath to his lord was one of the most execrable men to be found in the whole social organization." Charles Herman Kinnane, *A First Book on Anglo-American Law* 248 (2d ed. 1952).

2. By extension, fidelity, allegiance, or faithfulness more generally.

fear, *n.* The strong, negative feeling that a person experiences when anticipating danger or harm.

fearm. See FARM.

fear-of-cancer claim. (1985) *Torts.* A tort claim based on a plaintiff's mental anguish or emotional distress arising from the well-founded fear of developing cancer, where either (1) the plaintiff was exposed to asbestos or other carcinogenic agents, or (2) a physician's negligence gave rise to a potentially cancerous condition or permitted a cancer to develop unchecked. • The plaintiff must demonstrate (1) actual exposure to a disease-causing agent, and (2) the reasonableness of the emotional distress. *See Winik v. Jewish Hosp. of Brooklyn,* 293 N.E.2d 95 (N.Y. 1972); *Ferrara v. Galluchio,* 152 N.E.2d 249 (N.Y. 1958). — Also termed *cancerphobia claim.*

feasance (**fee**-zənts), *n.* (16c) The doing or accomplishment of an act, condition, or obligation. Cf. MALFEASANCE; MISFEASANCE; NONFEASANCE. — **feasor,** *n.*

feasant (**fez**-ənt *or* **fee**-zənt). *Archaic.* Doing or causing. See DAMAGE FEASANT.

feasibility. (17c) The possibility that something can be made, done, or achieved, or that it is reasonable; practicability. — **feasible,** *adj.*

feasibility standard. (1978) *Bankruptcy.* The requirement that, to obtain approval of the bankruptcy court, a Chapter 11 reorganization plan must be workable and have a reasonable likelihood of success.

feasor (**fee**-zər), *n.* (1808) An actor; a person who commits an act. See FRAUDFEASOR; TORTFEASOR.

feast, *n.* (13c) **1.** *Roman law.* An established holiday or festival in the ecclesiastical calendar, used as a date in a legal instrument. **2.** *Hist.* One of four principal days (feasts) of the year: March 25, the annunciation of the Virgin Mary; June 24, the birth of John the Baptist; September 28, the feast of St. Michael the Archangel; and December 21, the feast of St. Thomas the Apostle. • The four feast days were used as fixed dates (called "quarter-days") for paying rent; before 1875, they were used as a reference point to set terms of courts. — Also termed *feast day*; *feast-day.*

featherbedding. (1921) A union practice designed to increase employment and guarantee job security by requiring employers to hire or retain more employees than are needed. • The practice stems from employees' desire for job security in the face of technological improvement. The Taft–Hartley Act outlaws featherbedding, which it defines as any agreement or union demand for payment of wages for services that are not performed. 29 USCA § 401-531.

FEC. *abbr.* FEDERAL ELECTION COMMISSION.

FECA. *abbr.* **1.** FEDERAL EMPLOYEES' COMPENSATION ACT. **2.** FEDERAL ELECTION CAMPAIGN ACT.

feciales, *n.* See FETIALES.

fecial law. See FETIAL LAW.

Fed. *abbr.* **1.** FEDERAL. **2.** FEDERAL RESERVE SYSTEM.

FED. *abbr.* FORCIBLE ENTRY AND DETAINER.

Fed. Appx. *abbr.* FEDERAL APPENDIX.

Fed. Cir. *abbr.* UNITED STATES COURT OF APPEALS FOR THE FEDERAL CIRCUIT.

federal, *adj.* (18c) Of, relating to, or involving a system of associated governments with a vertical division of governments into national and regional components having different responsibilities; esp., pertaining to the national government of the United States. — Abbr. Fed.

Federal Acquisition Regulation. (*usu. pl.*) A federal regulation that governs contracting methods, requirements, and procedures with the federal government. 48 CFR ch. 1. — Also termed *Federal Procurement Regulation.* — Abbr. FAR.

federal act. (1874) A statute enacted by the U.S. Congress. See FEDERAL LAW.

federal agency. See AGENCY (3).

federal appeal. See APPEAL (2).

Federal Appendix. See F. APP.

Federal Arbitration Act. A federal statute providing for the enforcement of private agreements to arbitrate disputes related to interstate commerce or maritime contracts. • Under the Act, arbitration agreements are enforced in accordance with their terms, just as other contracts are, in both federal and state courts. The Act also sets out the grounds on which arbitration awards may be vacated and prescribes court procedures in support of arbitration. The Act supersedes substantive state laws that once frustrated enforcement of arbitration agreements. 9 USCA §§ 1–16. Chapter 2 of the Act implements the New York Convention, and Chapter 3 implements the Inter-American Convention on International Commercial Arbitration. — Abbr. FAA. — Also termed (archaically) *United States Arbitration Act.* Cf. UNIFORM ARBITRATION ACT.

Federal Audit Clearinghouse. A federal-government office within the Office of Management and Budget responsible for receiving, processing, and distributing to federal agencies the single-audit reporting packages of thousands of federal-assistance recipients. — Abbr. FAC.

Federal Aviation Act. (1958) A federal law establishing the Federal Aviation Administration. 49 USCA §§ 44720 et seq.

Federal Aviation Administration. The federal agency established in 1958 to be responsible for regulating air commerce, promoting civil aviation and a national system of airports, achieving efficient use of navigable airspace, developing and operating a common system of air-traffic control and air navigation, and developing and implementing programs and regulations relating to environmental effects of civil aviation. • Originally titled the Federal Aviation Agency, its name was changed in 1967 when it became a part of the Department of Transportation. The FAA was formerly charged with promoting safety in air transportation, but that task was transferred to the Transportation Security Administration after the terrorist attacks of 11 Sept. 2001. Abbr. FAA. — Formerly also termed *Federal Aviation Agency.*

Federal Aviation Regulation. (*usu. pl.*) A federal regulation governing the safety, maintenance, and piloting of civil aircraft. 14 CFR ch. 1. — Abbr. FAR.

Federal Bar Association. (1920) A voluntary association of federal judges and lawyers who have been admitted to practice in the federal courts. — Abbr. FBA.

Federal Bureau of Investigation. A division of the U.S. Department of Justice charged with investigating all violations of federal laws except those specifically assigned to another federal agency. • The division dates back to 1909, though it did not acquire its current name until 1935. — Abbr. FBI.

Federal Bureau of Prisons. The U.S. government unit responsible for the custody and care of federal offenders, whether incarcerated in federal, state-run, or privately operated facilities. • The Bureau was established in 1930 to centralize federal-prison administration and ensure consistency in prison operations. — Abbr. FBP; FBOP.

Federal Cases. See F. CAS.

federal census. See CENSUS.

Federal Circuit. See COURT OF APPEALS FOR THE FEDERAL CIRCUIT.

federal circuit court. See UNITED STATES COURT OF APPEALS.

federal citizen. See CITIZEN (1).

Federal Claims, U.S. Court of. See UNITED STATES COURT OF FEDERAL CLAIMS.

federal-comity doctrine. (1976) The principle encouraging federal district courts to refrain from interfering in each other's affairs. • Under this doctrine, a federal court has the discretion to transfer, stay, or dismiss a case that is duplicative of a case filed in another federal court. See COMITY (1).

federal common law. See COMMON LAW (1).

Federal Communications Commission. An independent federal commission that regulates interstate and foreign communications by radio, television, wire, satellite, and cable. • It was created by the Communications Act of 1934. 47 USCA §§ 151 et seq. — Abbr. FCC.

Federal Computer Fraud and Abuse Act. A law establishing criminal and civil liability for gaining unauthorized access to a computer and causing damage to it. • Damage is statutorily defined to include harm to the computer's data, programs, systems, and information either by compromising integrity or by impairing availability. — Abbr. FCFAA.

federal constitution. See CONSTITUTION (3).

Federal Corrupt Practices Act. A 1910 law regulating the federal-election campaign financing and spending activities of political parties. • The Federal Corrupt Practices Act was the first federal statute to require political parties to publicly disclose contributions and expenditures. It was replaced in 1971 by the Federal Election Campaign Act. — Abbr. FCPA. — Also termed *Publicity Act.*

federal court. See COURT.

federal covered security. See *covered security* under SECURITY (4).

federal crime. (1860) A criminal offense under a federal statute. • Most federal crimes are codified in Title 18 of the U.S. Code. — Also termed *federal offense.*

Federal Crop Insurance Corporation. A federally chartered corporation that protects farmers against financial losses from crop failure due to adverse weather conditions, insect infestation, plant disease, floods, fires, and earthquakes by encouraging the sale of insurance through licensed agents and brokers and by reinsuring private companies that issue insurance under brand names. • Created by the Agricultural Adjustment Act of 1938, the Corporation operates under the general supervision of the Secretary of Agriculture. — Abbr. FCIC.

Federal Deposit Insurance Corporation. An independent agency of the federal government responsible for protecting bank and thrift deposits by insuring accounts up to $250,000, examining banks that are not members of the Federal Reserve System, and liquidating failed institutions. • It was established in 1933 and began insuring banks in 1934. — Abbr. FDIC.

Federal Election Campaign Act. A 1971 federal statute requiring candidates for federal office to disclose the names of their contributors and how they spend those contributions. • A 1974 amendment placed legal limits on campaign contributions and created the Federal Election Commission. 2 USCA §§ 431 et seq. — Abbr. FECA. Cf. BIPARTISAN CAMPAIGN REFORM ACT.

Federal Election Commission. A ten-member independent federal commission that certifies payments to qualifying presidential campaigns in primary and general elections and to national-nominating conventions, audits campaign expenditures, and enforces laws requiring public disclosure of financial activities of presidential campaigns and political parties. • It was established by the Federal Election Campaign Act of 1971. 2 USCA § 437c. — Abbr. FEC.

Federal Emergency Management Agency. A unit in the Department of Homeland Security responsible for coordinating all emergency-preparedness activities of the federal government through its various regional offices. • FEMA also operates the National Flood Insurance Program and is responsible for fire protection and arson control. It was established as an independent agency in 1979 and became a unit in the Department of Homeland Security in 2003. — Abbr. FEMA.

Federal Employees' Compensation Act. A workers'-compensation law for federal employees. 5 USCA §§ 8101–8152 — Abbr. FECA. See WORKERS' COMPENSATION.

federal-employer-identification number. See TAX-IDENTIFICATION NUMBER.

Federal Employers' Liability Act. A workers'-compensation statute that provides death and disability benefits for employees of railroads engaged in interstate and foreign commerce. 45 USCA §§ 51–60 — Abbr. FELA.

federal enclave. See ENCLAVE.

Federal Energy Regulatory Commission. An independent five-member commission in the U.S. Department of Energy responsible for licensing natural-gas and hydroelectric power projects and for setting interstate rates on (1) transporting and selling natural gas for resale, (2) transporting and selling electricity at wholesale, and (3) transporting oil by pipeline. • It was created by the Department of Energy Organization Act of 1977. As enforcer of the Natural Gas Act, it succeeded the Federal Power Commission. — Abbr. FERC.

Federal Farm Credit Bank. One of a system of federally chartered institutions created to provide credit to farm-related enterprises. • The banks resulted from a merger of federal land banks and federal intermediate credit banks. They are supervised by the Farm Credit Administration.

Federal Farm Credit Banks Funding Corporation. A federal corporation that manages the sale of Federal Farm Credit System securities in the money and capital markets and also provides advisory services to banks in the Federal Farm Credit System. — Abbr. FFCBFC.

Federal Farm Credit System. The national cooperative system of banks and associations providing credit to farmers, agricultural concerns, and related businesses. • The system consists of the banks for cooperatives, the farm credit banks, and the Federal Farm Credit Banks Funding Corporation. It is supervised by the Farm Credit Administration and was originally capitalized by the federal government. The system is now self-funding and owned by its member-borrowers.

federal financial assistance. See FINANCIAL ASSISTANCE.

Federal Food Stamp Act. A federally funded program that provides needy families with financial assistance in obtaining a nutritionally adequate diet. • The Secretary of Agriculture administers the Act.

federal-funds rate. (1940) The interest rate at which banks lend to each other overnight. • The loans are usu. made by banks with excess reserves to those with temporarily insufficient reserves. — Often shortened to *fed funds.* — Also termed *fed-funds rate.*

federal government. See GOVERNMENT (3).

federal healthcare law. See AFFORDABLE CARE ACT; OBAMACARE.

Federal Highway Administration. An agency in the U.S. Department of Transportation responsible for granting aid to states for highway construction and improvement, providing matching grants to states for highway-safety programs, funding highways on federally owned land, seeking uniformity among the states in commercial motor-carrier registration and taxation, regulating the safety of motor carriers operating in interstate commerce, and training employees of state and local agencies engaged in highway work backed by federal aid. — Abbr. FHWA.

Federal Home Loan Bank. One of 12 federally chartered banks created in 1932 to extend secured loans to savings institutions that are members of the system and to community financial institutions that finance small businesses, small farms, and small agribusinesses. • The banks are supervised by the Federal Housing Finance Board. — Abbr. FHLB. — Sometimes shortened to *home loan bank.*

Federal Home Loan Bank Board. See FEDERAL HOUSING FINANCE BOARD.

Federal Home Loan Mortgage Corporation. A corporation that purchases both conventional and federally insured first mortgages from members of the Federal Reserve System and other approved banks. — Abbr. FHLMC. — Also termed *Freddie Mac.*

Federal Housing Administration. An agency in the U.S. Department of Housing and Urban Development responsible for facilitating mortgage lending by insuring mortgage loans on houses meeting the agency's standards. • It was created in 1934. — Abbr. FHA. See DEPARTMENT OF HOUSING AND URBAN DEVELOPMENT.

Federal Housing Finance Board. A five-member independent federal board that supervises the 12 Federal Home Loan Banks. • Formerly known as the Federal Home Loan Bank Board, it was established by the Federal Home Loan Bank Act of 1932. That Act was amended by the Financial Institutions Reform, Recovery, and Enforcement Act of 1989. 12 USCA §§ 1421 et seq. — Abbr. FHFB.

federal instrumentality, *n.* (1871) **1.** A means or agency used by the national government. **2.** A national agency or other entity immune from state control.

Federal Insurance Contributions Act. A federal statute imposing the social-security tax on employers and employees. IRC (26 USCA) §§ 3101–3127. — Abbr. FICA.

federal intermediate credit bank. See BANK.

federalism. (1787) The legal relationship and distribution of power between the national and regional governments within a federal system of government, and in the United States particularly, between the federal government and the state governments.

▸ **cooperative federalism.** (1947) Distribution of power between the federal government and the states whereby each recognizes the powers of the other while jointly engaging in certain governmental functions.

▸ **our federalism.** See OUR FEDERALISM.

Federalist Papers. *Constitutional law.* A series of 85 essays written by Alexander Hamilton, John Jay, and James Madison (under the pseudonym Publius) expounding and advocating the adoption of the U.S. Constitution. • Most of the essays were published in 1787 and 1788. — Also termed *The Federalist.*

Federalist Society. A national association of lawyers, law students, and others committed to conservative and libertarian viewpoints on political and social matters. • The group is based in Washington, D.C. Cf. NATIONAL LAWYERS GUILD.

federalize. See CONSTITUTIONALIZE.

Federal Judicial Center. An agency in the judicial branch of the federal government responsible for researching judicial administration and for training judges and employees of the federal judiciary. • Its director is appointed by a seven-member board presided over by the Chief Justice of the United States. 28 USCA § 620. — Abbr. FJC.

Federal Judicial Code. The portion (Title 28) of the U.S. Code dealing with the organization, jurisdiction, venue, and procedures of the federal court system, as well as court officers, personnel, and the Department of Justice.

federal jurisdiction. See JURISDICTION.

federal-juvenile-delinquency jurisdiction. See JURISDICTION.

Federal Kidnapping Act. A 1932 federal law punishing kidnapping for ransom or reward when the victim is transported interstate or internationally. • The law rebuttably presumes that a victim has been transported in violation of the law if the victim is not released within 24 hours. The Federal Kidnapping Act, by express provision, does not apply to the kidnapping of a minor by either parent. The law was enacted after the son of aviator Charles Lindbergh was kidnapped and murdered. For this reason, it is also termed *Lindbergh Act.* 18 USCA § 1201. Cf. PARENTAL KIDNAPPING PREVENTION ACT.

> "The Federal Kidnapping Act was passed in 1932 to close a dangerous loophole between state and federal law. At that time, marauding bands of kidnappers were preying upon the wealthy with ruthless abandon, seizing their victims for ransom while operating outside the reach of existing state laws. Knowing that authorities in the victim's home state were powerless once a hostage was transported across state lines, the criminals would kidnap their target in one state, then move quickly to the next. In response, Congress made kidnapping a federal crime when the victim was moved from one state to another, and comprehensive language was used to cover every possible variety of kidnapping followed by interstate transportation." 1 Am. Jur. 2d *Abduction and Kidnapping* § 14, at 185 (1994).

Federal Labor Relations Authority. An agency that protects the right of federal employees to organize, engage in collective bargaining, and select their own union representatives. • It was established under Reorganization Plan No. 2 of 1978 and began operating in 1979. 5 USCA §§ 7101–7135. — Abbr. FLRA.

federal labor union. See UNION.

federal land. See LAND.

Federal Land Bank. (1914) One of a system of 12 regional banks created in 1916 to provide mortgage loans to farmers. • Under the Agricultural Credit Act of 1987, the system was merged with federal intermediate credit banks to create the Federal Farm Credit System. — Abbr. FLB.

federal law. (18c) The body of law consisting of the U.S. Constitution, federal statutes and regulations, U.S. treaties, and federal common law. Cf. STATE LAW.

Federal Law Enforcement Training Center. An interagency law-enforcement training facility serving over 70 law-enforcement organizations in the federal government. • The Center was transferred from the Department of the Treasury to the Department of Homeland Security in 2003. — Abbr. FLETC.

federally recognized tribe. See INDIAN TRIBE.

federal magistrate. (1852) UNITED STATES MAGISTRATE JUDGE.

Federal Maritime Commission. An independent federal agency that regulates the waterborne foreign and domestic commerce of the United States by (1) ensuring that U.S. international trade is open to all countries on fair and equitable terms, (2) guarding against unauthorized monopolies in U.S. waterborne commerce, and (3) ensuring that financial responsibility is maintained to clean up oil spills and indemnify injured passengers. • The Agency was established in 1961. Its five commissioners are appointed by the President with the advice and consent of the Senate. — Abbr. FMC.

Federal Maritime Lien Act. A statute that confers an automatic lien on anyone who provides a vessel with any of a wide range of goods and services. 46 USCA §§ 31341–31343. — Abbr. FMLA.

Federal Mediation and Conciliation Service. An independent federal agency that tries to prevent the interruption of interstate commerce that could result from a labor–management dispute by helping the parties reach a settlement without resorting to a job action or strike. • The Service can intervene on its own authority or at the request of a party to the dispute. It also helps employers and unions select qualified arbitrators. The Service was established by the Labor Management Relations Act of 1947. 29 USCA § 172. — Abbr. FMCS. Cf. NATIONAL MEDIATION BOARD.

Federal Mine Safety and Health Review Commission. An independent five-member commission that (1) monitors compliance with occupational safety and health standards in the country's surface and underground coal, metal, and nonmetal mines, and (2) adjudicates disputes that arise under the Federal Mine Safety and Health Amendments Act of 1977. • It was established in 1977. 30 USCA §§ 801 et seq. —Abbr. FMSHRC.

federal minimum wage. See WAGE.

Federal Motor Carrier Safety Administration. A unit in the U.S. Department of Transportation responsible for regulating the operation of large trucks and buses. — Abbr. FMCSA.

Federal National Mortgage Association. A privately owned and managed corporation chartered by the U.S. government that provides a secondary mortgage market for the purchase and sale of mortgages guaranteed by the Veterans Administration and those insured under the Federal Housing Administration. — Abbr. FNMA. — Also termed *Fannie Mae*.

federal offense. See FEDERAL CRIME.

federal officer. See OFFICER (1).

Federal Parent Locator Service. A federal program operated in the U.S. Department of Health and Human Services and created to help enforce child-support obligations. • In an effort to increase the collection of child support and the enforcement of child-support orders. Congress authorized the use of all information contained in the various federal databases to help locate absent, delinquent child-support obligors. Although initially information could be released only if the family was receiving public assistance, any judgment obligee can now apply to receive the last known address of a delinquent child-support obligor. 42 USCA § 653. Abbr. FPLS.

Federal Power Commission. See FEDERAL ENERGY REGULATORY COMMISSION.

federal preemption. See PREEMPTION (5).

federal prison. See PRISON.

federal prison camp. (1931) A federal minimum-security detention facility. • Federal prison camps, which often do not have walls or fences, usu. house nonviolent inmates who are serving sentences shorter than a year plus one day and who are not considered escape risks. Cf. PRISON CAMP.

federal prisoner. See PRISONER (3).

Federal Procurement Regulation. See FEDERAL ACQUISITION REGULATION.

Federal Protective Service. A law-enforcement agency in the U.S. Department of Homeland Security responsible for protecting ambassadors, diplomatic staffs, and embassy property. • It was transferred from the General Services Administration in 2003. — Abbr. FPS.

federal question. In litigation, a legal issue involving the interpretation and application of the U.S. Constitution, an act of Congress, or a treaty. • Jurisdiction over federal questions rests with the federal courts, though not necessarily exclusively. 28 USCA § 1331.

federal-question jurisdiction. See JURISDICTION.

Federal Railroad Administration. A unit in the U.S. Department of Transportation responsible for promulgating and enforcing rail-safety regulations, administering rail-related financial-aid programs, conducting research on rail safety, and rehabilitating rail passenger service for the Northeast corridor. — Abbr. FRA.

Federal Register. A daily publication containing presidential proclamations and executive orders, federal-agency regulations of general applicability and legal effect, proposed agency rules, and documents required by law to be published. • The *Federal Register* is published by the National Archives and Records Administration. — Abbr. Fed. Reg.

> "*Federal Register.* For some time prior to 1936 considerable popular clamor was heard for some form of official governmental gazette, similar to those issued by continental or South American governments, in which would appear the daily orders, proclamations, administrative rulings, and decisions of the various agencies of the government. Strange as it may seem, the United States was about the only important nation without some form of an official publication of this character. With the expansion of the administrative agencies of the United States since 1933 and the promulgation of the thousands of Executive Orders, concerning which the public was comparatively ignorant, the demand, supported by a strong public opinion, became increasingly insistent. On one occasion a member of the United States Supreme Court was heard to comment on the confused state of our administrative law and the need for some systematic organization of these federal rules and orders.
>
> "As a result of this demand, Congress passed the Federal Register Act of July 16, 1935 (Title 44, sec. 301–314), providing for the publication of the Federal Register, and providing that the contents thereof shall be judicially noticed and without prejudice to any other mode of citation may be cited by volume and page number." Arthur Sydney Beardsley, *Legal Bibliography and the Use of Law Books* 147 (1937).

federal regulations. See CODE OF FEDERAL REGULATIONS.

Federal Reporter. See F. (1).

Federal Reporter Second Series. See F.2D.

Federal Reporter Third Series. See F.3D.

Federal Reserve Bank. One of the 12 central banks in the Federal Reserve System.

Federal Reserve Board of Governors. The board that supervises the Federal Reserve System and sets national monetary and credit policy. • The board consists of seven members nominated by the President and confirmed by the Senate for 14-year terms. — Often shortened to *Federal Reserve Board.* — Abbr. FRB.

federal reserve note. (1913) The paper currency in circulation in the United States. • Non-interest-bearing promissory notes are payable to their bearer on demand. The Federal Reserve Banks issue the notes in denominations of $1, $2, $5, $10, $20, $50, and $100. Until 1945, the United States Mint also printed $500, $1,000, $5,000, and $10,000 bills. Although the Federal Reserve System discontinued using bills larger than $100 in 1969, the outstanding bills remain legal tender. 31 USCA § 5103. Cf. GOLD CERTIFICATE; SILVER CERTIFICATE.

Federal Reserve System. The central bank that sets credit and monetary policy by fixing the reserves to be maintained by depository institutions, determining the discount rate charged by Federal Reserve Banks, and regulating the amount of credit that may be extended on any security. • The Federal Reserve System was established by the Federal Reserve Act of 1913. 12 USCA § 221. It comprises 12 central banks supervised by a Board of Governors whose members are appointed by the President and confirmed by the Senate. — Abbr. FRS; Fed.

Federal Retirement Thrift Investment Board. A board that administers the Thrift Savings Plan that allows federal employees to save funds for retirement. • It was established in 1986. 5 USCA § 8472. — Abbr. FRTIB.

Federal Rules Decisions. See F.R.D.

Federal Rules Enabling Act. A 1934 statute granting the U.S. Supreme Court the authority to adopt rules of civil procedure for federal courts. • For the rulemaking power of federal courts today, see 28 USCA §§ 2071–2072. See also Fed. R. Civ. P. 83; Fed. R. Crim. P. 57. The statute is usu. called the "Rules Enabling Act."

Federal Rules of Appellate Procedure. The rules governing appeals to the U.S. courts of appeals from lower courts, some federal-agency proceedings, and applications for writs. — Abbr. Fed. R. App. P.; FRAP.

Federal Rules of Bankruptcy Procedure. The rules governing proceedings under the Bankruptcy Code. — Abbr. Fed. R. Bankr. P.

Federal Rules of Civil Procedure. The rules governing civil actions in the U.S. district courts. — Abbr. Fed. R. Civ. P.; FRCP.

> "Chief Justice Hughes in 1935 appointed fourteen lawyers and law teachers as the Advisory Committee for the Federal Rules of Civil Procedure, with William D. Mitchell, former Attorney General, as chairman, and Charles E. Clark, then dean of the Yale Law School, as reporter, to recommend a draft of rules uniting law and equity. The committee proposed a system of rules that was approved by the Court with certain changes. In accordance with the Enabling Act, the rules were submitted to Congress for its acquiescence and, Congress having taken no exception to them, they became effective September 16, 1938. The rules thus produced bear the unmistakable imprint of the reporter, Charles E. Clark, and represent the largest single accomplishment in American civil procedure since the Field Code of 1848. Although they were not perfect and have been amended many times, experience with them has on the whole been satisfactory, and more than half of the states have adopted them in their entirety or in large part." Fleming James, Geoffrey C. Hazard Jr. & John Leubsdorf, *Civil Procedure* § 1.8, at 24–25 (5th ed. 2001).

Federal Rules of Criminal Procedure. The rules governing criminal proceedings in the U.S. district courts. — Abbr. Fed. R. Crim. P.

Federal Rules of Evidence. The rules governing the admissibility of evidence at trials in federal courts. — Abbr. Fed. R. Evid.; FRE.

Federal Savings and Loan Insurance Corporation. A federal agency created in 1934 to insure deposits in savings-and-loan associations and savings banks. • When this agency became insolvent in 1989, its assets and liabilities were transferred to an insurance fund managed by the FDIC. — Abbr. FSLIC. See RESOLUTION TRUST CORPORATION.

federal sentencing guidelines. See UNITED STATES SENTENCING GUIDELINES.

federal state. See STATE (1).

federal statute. See FEDERAL ACT.

Federal Supplement. See F.SUPP.

Federal Supplement Second Series. See F.SUPP.2D.

Federal Supply Service. A unit in the General Services Administration responsible for providing supplies to federal agencies worldwide. — Abbr. FSS.

Federal Technology Service. A unit in the General Services Administration that provides communications services worldwide to federal departments and agencies. — Abbr. FTS.

Federal Tort Claims Act. A statute that limits federal sovereign immunity and allows recovery in federal court for tort damages caused by federal employees, but only if the law of the state where the injury occurred would hold a private person liable for the injury. 28 USCA §§ 2671–2680 — Abbr. FTCA. See *sovereign immunity* under IMMUNITY (1).

> "Although it has been suggested that the maxim, 'the King can do no wrong' never had an existence in the United States, it has also been declared that in enacting the Federal Tort Claims Act, Congress recognized the manifold injustice that springs from the delimiting effect of the rule represented by that maxim. And it is said that in passing the Act, Congress intended to compensate the victims of negligence in the conduct of governmental activities in circumstances in which a private person would be liable, rather than leave just treatment to the caprice and legislative burden of individual private laws, and to eliminate the burden on Congress of investigating and passing on private bills seeking individual relief." 35 Am. Jur. 2d *Federal Tort Claims Act* § 1, at 296 (1967).

Federal Trade Commission. An independent five-member federal commission that administers various laws against business monopolies, restraint of trade, and deceptive trade practices. • It was established by the Federal Trade Commission Act of 1914. 15 USCA §§ 41–58. The commissioners are appointed by the President and confirmed by the Senate for a seven-year term. The President selects one of the commissioners to serve as chair. The Commission's body of rulings reaches into many state-law actions because many so-called "Little FTC Acts" of the states specify that FTC interpretations should provide a model for state-court decisions. — Abbr. FTC.

Federal Trademark Act. See LANHAM ACT.

Federal Trademark Dilution Act. A 1995 amendment to the Lanham Act (Trademark Act of 1946) that provides additional remedies against the dilution of famous trademarks. 15 USCA § 1125(c). — Sometimes shortened to *Dilution Act.* — Abbr. FTDA.

federal transfer. 1. The federal district court's right to move a civil action filed there to any other district or division where the plaintiff could have brought the action originally. 28 USCA § 1404(a). See CHANGE OF VENUE. **2.** An order directing the transfer of an inmate from a state correctional facility to the custody of the Federal Bureau of Prisons, usu. for increased security.

Federal Transit Administration. A unit in the U.S. Department of Transportation responsible for increasing public-transit ridership through demonstration projects and financial assistance. • Formerly called the Urban

Mass Transit Administration (UMTA), it was renamed in 1991. — Abbr. FTA.

Federal Unemployment Tax Act. The federal statute requiring employers to remit taxes based on employees' wages and salaries. 18 USCA §§ 1201 et seq. — Abbr. FUTA.

federal waters. See WATER.

federation. (18c) A league or union of states, groups, or peoples united under a strong central authority but retaining limited regional sovereignty, esp. over local affairs. Cf. CONFEDERATION.

fed funds. See FEDERAL FUNDS RATE.

fed-funds rate. See FEDERAL FUNDS RATE.

Fed. R. App. P. *abbr.* FEDERAL RULES OF APPELLATE PROCEDURE.

Fed. R. Bankr. P. *abbr.* FEDERAL RULES OF BANKRUPTCY PROCEDURE.

Fed. R. Civ. P. *abbr.* FEDERAL RULES OF CIVIL PROCEDURE.

Fed. R. Crim. P. *abbr.* FEDERAL RULES OF CRIMINAL PROCEDURE.

Fed. Reg. *abbr.* FEDERAL REGISTER.

Fed. R. Evid. *abbr.* FEDERAL RULES OF EVIDENCE.

Fed Wire. The Federal Reserve's computer network that allows nearly instantaneous domestic money and securities transfers among the Federal Reserve's offices, depository institutions, the U.S. Treasury, and other government agencies.

fee. (14c) **1.** A charge or payment for labor or services, esp. professional services.

▸ **attorney's fees.** See ATTORNEY'S FEE.

▸ **contingent fee.** See CONTINGENT FEE.

▸ **docket fee.** (1836) A fee charged by a court for filing a claim.

▸ **expert-witness fee.** (1892) A fee paid for the professional services of an expert witness.

▸ **financing fee.** The fee that a lender charges for a loan, calculated as a percentage of the loan amount. • A financing fee is often expressed in *points*, with one point equaling one percent. See POINT (3).

▸ **fixed fee.** (18c) **1.** A flat charge for a service; a charge that does not vary with the amount of time or effort required to complete the service. **2.** In a construction contract, a predetermined amount that is added to costs for calculating payments due under the contract.

▸ **franchise fee.** (1894) **1.** A fee paid by a franchisee to a franchisor for franchise rights. • Franchise fees are regulated by state laws. **2.** A fee paid to the government for a government grant of a franchise, such as the one required for operating a radio or television station.

▸ **interchange fee.** (1972) In the bank-payment-card industry (as with major credit-card networks), a fee paid by the acquiring (or "merchant") bank to the issuing bank for each card transaction. • An acquiring bank acquires the card-paid transactions and provides services to the relevant merchant, while the issuing bank issues cards to cardholders. The interchange fee is imposed by the system so that acquiring banks will share their merchant fees with issuing banks, which bear the greater risk of nonpayment. For a description of how the transaction and fees work, see *U.S. v. Visa U.S.A., Inc.*, 344 F.3d 229, 235 (2d Cir. 2003).

▸ **jury fee.** (1806) A fee, usu. a minimal one, that a party to a civil suit must pay the court clerk to be entitled to a jury trial.

▸ **loan-origination fee.** (1965) A fee charged by a lender to cover the administrative costs of making a loan.

▸ **maintenance fee.** See MAINTENANCE FEE.

▸ **management fee.** A fee charged by someone who manages something, esp. by an investment manager for supervisory services.

▸ **origination fee.** (1921) A fee charged by a lender for preparing and processing a loan.

▸ **probate fee.** (1894) Compensation paid with a probate court's approval to an attorney who performs probate-related services to the estate.

▸ **referral fee.** Compensation paid by one professional-service provider to another for directing a client to the payer's services.

▸ **success fee.** (1983) A bonus paid to a representative who performs exceptionally well in gaining favorable results; esp., a bonus that a client pays to an attorney if the attorney obtains something of value to the client. • For instance, a client might agree to pay a success fee for success in litigation, for favorable negotiations in a transaction, or for the successful conclusion of a corporate merger, acquisition, or loan. See CONDITIONAL FEE AGREEMENT.

▸ **witness fee.** (1878) **1.** A statutory fee that must be tendered with a subpoena for the subpoena to be binding. **2.** A fee paid by a party to a witness as reimbursement for reasonable expenses (such as travel, meals, lodging, and loss of time) incurred as a result of the witness's having to attend and testify at a deposition or trial. • Any other payment to a nonexpert witness is considered unethical. — Also termed (in English law) *conduct money*. Cf. *expert-witness fee*.

2. A heritable interest in land; esp., a fee simple absolute. — Also termed *fee estate*; *feod*; *feodum*; *feud*; *feudum*; *fief*. See FEE SIMPLE. Cf. FEU.

> "To *enfeoff* someone was to transfer to him an interest in land called a *fief* — or, if you prefer, a *feoff*, *feod*, or *feud*. Our modern word *fee*, a direct lineal descendant of *fief*, implies the characteristic of potentially infinite duration when used to describe an interest in land today; but in the earliest part of the feudal period, a *fief* might have been as small as a life interest. We shall see later that feoffment was *not* used to transfer interests 'smaller' than life interests — e.g., so-called *terms for years* — but for our purposes now we may simply note that transfers of interests for life or 'larger' were accomplished by livery of seisin." Thomas F. Bergin & Paul G. Haskell, *Preface to Estates in Land and Future Interests* 11 (2d ed. 1984).

▸ ***arriere fee*** (**ar**-ee-air *or* **ar**-ee-ər). (17c) *Hist.* A fee dependent on a superior one; a subfief. — Also termed *arriere fief*.

▸ **base fee.** (16c) A fee that has some qualification connected to it and that terminates whenever the qualification terminates. • An example of the words creating a base fee are "to A and his heirs, tenants of the manor of Tinsleydale," which would terminate when A or his heirs are no longer tenants of the manor of Tinsleydale.

Among the base fees at common law are the fee simple subject to a condition subsequent and the conditional fee. — Also termed *determinable fee*; *qualified fee*; *limited fee*. See *fee simple determinable* under FEE SIMPLE.

"A base fee is a particular kind of determinable fee. The two essentials of a base fee are (a) it continues only so long as the original grantor or any heirs of his body are alive; and (b) there is a remainder or reversion after it. . . . In effect a base fee was a fee simple which endured for as long as the entail would have continued if it had not been barred, and determined when the entail would have ended." Robert E. Megarry & M.P. Thompson, *A Manual of the Law of Real Property* 38–40 (6th ed. 1993).

▸ **determinable fee.** See *base fee*.

▸ **fee expectant.** (17c) *Rare.* A fee tail created when land is given to a man and wife and the heirs of their bodies. See FRANKMARRIAGE.

▸ **fee simple.** See FEE SIMPLE.

▸ **fee tail.** See FEE TAIL.

▸ **great fee.** *Hist.* In feudal law, a fee received directly from the Crown.

▸ **knight's fee.** See KNIGHT'S FEE.

▸ **lay fee.** (15c) *Hist.* A fee interest in land held by ordinary feudal tenure, such as socage, rather than by ecclesiastical tenure through frankalmoin. See FRANKALMOIN; SOCAGE.

▸ **limited fee.** See *base fee*.

▸ **plowman's fee.** *Hist.* A species of tenure for peasants or small farmers by which the land descended in equal shares to all the tenant's sons.

▸ **qualified fee.** See QUALIFIED FEE.

▸ **quasi-fee.** (1828) *Hist.* An estate in fee acquired wrongfully.

fee damages. See DAMAGES.

fee expectant. See FEE (2).

feeder judge. (1998) A judge, esp. a federal circuit judge, whose clerks frequently move on to become clerks for U.S. Supreme Court Justices.

feeder organization. (1951) *Tax.* An entity that conducts a business or trade for the benefit of a tax-exempt organization. • The feeder organization is not tax-exempt. IRC (26 USCA) § 502.

fee estate. See FEE (2).

fee farm. (14c) *Hist.* A species of tenure in which land is held in perpetuity at a yearly rent (fee-farm rent), without fealty, homage, or other services than those in the feoffment. — Also termed *feodi firma*; *firma feodi*. See EMPHYTEUSIS; RENTCHARGE.

"Now to all appearance the term *socage*, a term not found in Normandy, has been extending itself upwards; a name appropriate to a class of cultivating peasants has begun to include the baron or prelate who holds land at a rent but is not burdened with military service. . . . He is sometimes said to have *feodum censuale*; far more commonly he is said to hold 'in fee farm.' This term has difficulties of its own, for it appears in many different guises; a feoffee is to hold *in feofirma, in feufirmam, in fedfirmam, in feudo firmam, in feudo firma, ad firmam feodalem*, but most commonly, *in feodi firma*. The Old English language had both of the words of which this term is compounded, both *feoh* (property) and *feorm* (rent); but so had the language of France, and in Norman documents the term may be found in various shapes, *firmam fedium, feudifirmam*. But, whatever may be the precise history of the phrase, to hold in fee farm means to hold heritably, perpetually, at a rent; the fee, the inheritance, is let to farm." 2 Frederick Pollock & Frederic W. Maitland, *The History of English Law Before the Time of Edward I* 293 (2d ed. 1899).

fee-farm rent. See RENTCHARGE.

fee forfeiture. A court-ordered waiver or forced repayment of attorney's fees.

fee for service. A pricing-and-payment system in which a person can select and pay separately for particular services rather than a single payment for a bundle of services

fee interest. (1947) **1.** See FEE. **2.** See FEE SIMPLE. **3.** See FEE TAIL. **4.** *Oil & gas.* Ownership of both the surface interest and the mineral interest.

feemail (**fee**-mayl). (1994) *Slang.* **1.** An attorney's fee extorted by intimidation, threats, or pressure. **2.** The act or process of extorting such a fee. Cf. BLACKMAIL (1); GRAYMAIL; GREENMAIL (1), (2).

Feeney Amendment. An amendment to the 2003 Amber Alert Bill that (1) tightened judges' discretion to depart downward from federal sentencing guidelines, (2) required circuit courts to review all downward departures, and (3) required reports to Congress on individual judges' downward departures. • The Supreme Court overturned the statute two years later. *U.S. v. Booker*, 543 U.S. 220 (2005).

fee-sharing. See FEE SPLITTING.

fee-shifting, *n.* (1970) The transfer of responsibility for paying fees, esp. attorney's fees, from the prevailing party to the losing party. See AMERICAN RULE (1); ENGLISH RULE.

fee simple. (15c) An interest in land that, being the broadest property interest allowed by law, endures until the current holder dies without heirs; esp., a fee simple absolute. — Often shortened to *fee*. — Also termed *estate in fee simple*; *tenancy in fee*; *fee-simple title*; *exclusive ownership*; *feudum simplex*; *estate in fee*. See AND HIS HEIRS.

"[*Fee simple*] is a term not likely to be found in modern conversation between laymen, who would in all probability find it quite unintelligible. Yet to a layman of the 14th century the term would have been perfectly intelligible, for it refers to the elementary social relationship of feudalism with which he was fully familiar: the words 'fee' and 'feudal' are closely related. . . . The estate in fee simple is the largest estate known to the law, ownership of such an estate being the nearest approach to ownership of the land itself which is consonant with the feudal principle of tenure. It is 'the most comprehensive estate in land which the law recognises'; it is the 'most extensive in quantum, and the most absolute in respect to the rights which it confers, of all estates known to the law.' Traditionally, the fee simple has two distinguishing features: first, the owner ('tenant' in fee simple) has the power to dispose of the fee simple, either inter vivos or by will; second, on intestacy the fee simple descends, in the absence of lineal heirs, to collateral heirs — to a brother, for example, if there is no issue." Peter Butt, *Land Law* 35 (2d ed. 1988).

"**Fee simple.** Originally this was an estate which endured for as long as the original tenant or any of his heirs survived. 'Heirs' comprised any blood relations, although originally ancestors were excluded; not until the Inheritance Act 1833 could a person be the heir of one of his descendants. Thus at first a fee simple would terminate if the original tenant died without leaving any descendants or collateral blood relations (e.g., brothers or cousins), even if before his death the land had been conveyed to another tenant who was still alive. But by 1306 it was settled that where a tenant in fee simple alienated the land, the fee simple would continue as long as there were heirs of the new tenant and so on, irrespective of any failure of the original tenant's heirs. Thenceforward a fee simple was virtually eternal." Robert E. Megarry & M.P. Thompson, *A Manual of the Law of Real Property* 24–25 (6th ed. 1993).

▸ **fee simple absolute.** (18c) An estate of indefinite or potentially infinite duration (e.g., "to Albert and his heirs"). — Often shortened to *fee simple* or *fee*. — Also termed *fee simple absolute in possession.*

"Although it is probably good practice to use the word 'absolute' whenever one is referring to an estate in fee simple that is free of special limitation, condition subsequent, or executory limitation, lawyers frequently refer to such an estate as a 'fee simple' or even as a 'fee.'" Thomas F. Bergin & Paul G. Haskell, *Preface to Estates in Land and Future Interests* 24 (2d ed. 1984).

▸ **fee simple conditional.** (17c) **1.** An estate conveyed to a man conditionally upon his having an heir of his body. • If an heir was born alive (whether the child survived or not), the condition was fulfilled and the donee received a fee simple, which he could alienate. **2.** An estate restricted to some specified heirs, exclusive of others (e.g., "to Albert and his female heirs"). • The fee simple conditional is obsolete except in Iowa, Oregon, and South Carolina. — Also termed *general fee conditional; conditional fee.*

"The reader should be careful not to confuse this estate with estates having similar labels, such as the 'estate in fee simple subject to a condition subsequent' . . . ." Thomas F. Bergin & Paul G. Haskell, *Preface to Estates in Land and Future Interests* 29 n.19 (2d ed. 1984).

▸ **fee simple defeasible** (di-fee-zə-bəl). (18c) An estate that ends either because there are no more heirs of the person to whom it is granted or because a special limitation, condition subsequent, or executory limitation takes effect before the line of heirs runs out. — Also termed *defeasible fee simple; qualified fee.*

▸ **fee simple determinable.** (18c) An estate that will automatically end and revert to the grantor if some specified event occurs (e.g., "to Albert and his heirs while the property is used for charitable purposes"); an estate in fee simple subject to a special limitation. • The future interest retained by the grantor is called a *possibility of reverter.* — Abbr. FSD. — Also termed *determinable fee; qualified fee; fee simple subject to common-law limitation; fee simple subject to special limitation; fee simple subject to special interest; base fee; estate on limitation.*

"In theory, it should be easy to determine whether an instrument creates a fee simple determinable or a fee simple subject to a condition subsequent. If the instrument includes a special limitation (introduced by words such as 'so long as' or 'until') it creates a fee simple determinable, whether or not it also includes an express reverter clause. If the instrument includes an express condition or proviso ('on condition that' or 'provided that') and an express right to re-enter for breach of the stated condition, it creates a fee simple subject to a condition subsequent. But deeds and wills often fail to employ the appropriate words to create one of the two types of defeasible estate or the others. Instead deeds and wills often contain a confusing mixture of words appropriate for creation of both types of defeasible estate." William B. Stoebuck & Dale A. Whitman, *The Law of Property* 43 (3d ed. 2000).

▸ **fee simple subject to a condition subsequent.** (1874) An estate subject to the grantor's power to end the estate if some specified event happens (e.g., "to Albert and his heirs, on condition that no alcohol is sold on the premises"). • The future interest retained by the grantor is called a *power of termination* (or a *right of entry*). — Abbr. FSSCP. — Also termed *fee simple on a condition subsequent; fee simple subject to a power of termination; fee simple upon condition.*

▸ **fee simple subject to an executory limitation.** (1856) A fee simple defeasible that is subject to divestment in favor of someone other than the grantor if a specified event happens (e.g., "to Albert and his heirs, but if the property is ever used as a parking lot, then to Bob"). — Also termed *fee simple subject to an executory interest.*

▸ **fee simple subject to a power of termination.** See *fee simple subject to a condition subsequent.*

▸ **fee simple subject to common-law limitation.** See *fee simple determinable.*

▸ **fee simple subject to special interest.** See *fee simple determinable.*

▸ **fee simple subject to special limitation.** See *fee simple determinable.*

▸ **fee simple upon condition.** See *fee simple subject to a condition subsequent.*

fee-simple title. See FEE SIMPLE.

fee-splitting. (1913) **1.** The division of attorney's fees between two or more lawyers, esp. between the lawyer who handled a matter and the lawyer who referred the matter. • Some states consider this practice unethical. **2.** The division of attorney's fees between two or more lawyers who represent a client jointly but are not in the same firm. • Under most states' ethics rules, an attorney is prohibited from splitting a fee with a nonlawyer. — Also termed *fee-sharing; division of fees.*

fee statement. (1941) A lawyer's bill for services either already rendered or to be rendered, usu. including itemized expenses.

fee tail. (15c) An estate that is heritable only by specified descendants of the original grantee, and that endures until its current holder dies without issue (e.g., "to Albert and the heirs of his body"). • Most jurisdictions — except Delaware, Maine, Massachusetts, and Rhode Island — have abolished the fee tail. — Also termed *entailed estate; estate tail; estate in tail; estate in fee tail; tenancy in tail; entail; feodum talliatum.* See ENTAIL; TAIL.

"The old legal estate tail was throughout its history invariably associated with family settlements, and in particular with marriage settlements. . . . Medieval landowners sought to achieve [familial continuity and status] by perfecting a single estate which in itself would conform to three requirements: (1) While it should be an estate of inheritance it should devolve on lineal heirs only, and not on collaterals — in other words that it should descend only to the *heirs of the body* of the first grantee. (2) As a corollary, the estate should be such that if at any time the first grantee's issue should fail the estate itself should come to an end and the land revert to the original settlor or his heirs. (3) No owner of the estate for the time being should have power to dispose of the land in such a way as to prevent it descending on his death to the next heir of the body of the original grantee. All this was attempted by limiting land, not to 'A and his heirs,' which would give A a fee simple, but to '*A and the heirs of his body.*'" 1 *Stephen's Commentaries on the Laws of England* 150 (L. Crispin Warmington ed., 21st ed. 1950).

"If we cannot resist the temptation to say that *De Donis* permitted the creation of tailor-made estates, we can at least argue that it is not a pun. Our word 'tailor' and the word 'tail,' as used in 'fee tail,' come from the same source — the French *tailler*, to cut. The word 'tail' in 'fee tail' has nothing to do with that which wags the dog. The estate in fee tail was a *cut* estate — either cut in the sense that the collateral heirs were cut out, or cut in the sense that the estate was carved into a series of discrete life-possession periods to be enjoyed successively by A and his lineal heirs. . . . We know of no state in the United States that recognizes the estate in fee tail in its strict 1285–1472 form. Wherever it is recognized, the tenant in tail in possession may disentail it by simple deed." Thomas F. Bergin & Paul G. Haskell, *Preface to Estates in Land and Future Interests* 30, 32 (2d ed. 1984).

▸ **fee tail general.** (16c) A fee tail that is heritable by all of the property owner's issue by any spouse. • Formerly, a grant "to A and the heirs of his body" created a fee tail general.

▸ **fee tail special.** (17c) A fee tail that restricts the eligibility of claimants by requiring a claimant to prove direct descent from the grantee and meet the special condition in the grant. • For example, the words "to A and the heirs of his body begotten on his wife Mary" meant that only descendants of A and Mary could inherit; A's children by any other wife were excluded. An estate tail special could also be restricted to only male or only female descendants, as in "to A and the heirs male of his body."

feign (fayn), *vb.* (13c) To make up or fabricate; to make a false show of <he feigned an illness>.

feigned, *adj.* (14c) Pretended; simulated; fictitious.

feigned accomplice. See INFORMANT.

feigned action. (16c) *Hist.* An action brought for an illegal purpose on a pretended right. — Also termed *faint action*; *false action*.

feigned issue. (17c) *Hist.* A proceeding in which the parties, by consent, have an issue tried by a jury without actually bringing a formal action. • The proceeding was done when a court either lacked jurisdiction or was unwilling to decide the issue. — Also termed *fictitious issue*.

"The chancellor's decree is either *interlocutory* or *final*. It very seldom happens that the first decree can be final, or conclude the cause; for, if any matter of fact is strongly controverted, this court is so sensible of the deficiency of trial by written depositions, that it will not bind the parties thereby, but usually directs the matter to be tried by jury . . . . But, as no jury can be summoned to attend this court, the fact is usually directed to be tried at the bar of the court of king's bench or at the assises, upon a *feigned issue*. For, (in order to bring it there, and have the point in dispute, and that only, put in issue) an action is feigned to be brought, wherein the pretended plaintiff declares that he laid a wager of 5*l*. with the defendant that A was heir at law to B; and then avers that he is so; and therefore demands the 5*l*. The defendant allows the wager, but avers that A is not the heir to B; and thereupon the issue is joined . . . . These feigned issues seem borrowed from the *sponsio judicialis* of the Romans: and are also frequently used in the courts of law, by consent of the parties, to determine some disputed rights without the formality of pleading . . . ." 3 William Blackstone, *Commentaries on the Laws of England* 452 (1768).

feigned recovery. See COMMON RECOVERY.

FEIN. *abbr.* See TAX-IDENTIFICATION NUMBER.

***Feist* doctrine.** (1991) *Copyright.* The rule that "sweat of the brow" will not support U.S. copyright protection in an unoriginal collection of facts. *Feist Pubs. v. Rural Tel. Serv. Co.*, 499 U.S. 340, 111 S.Ct. 1282 (1991). Cf. SWEAT-OF-THE-BROW DOCTRINE.

FELA (fee-lə). *abbr.* FEDERAL EMPLOYERS' LIABILITY ACT.

fele (feel). [Law French] See FEAL.

fellatio (fə-lay-shee-oh), *n.* The sexual act involving oral stimulation of a person's penis. — **fellate,** *vb.*

fellow, *n.* (bef. 12c) **1.** One joined with another in some legal status or relation. **2.** A member of a college, board, corporate body, or other organization.

fellow-officer rule. (1971) *Criminal procedure.* The principle that an investigative stop or an arrest is valid even if the law-enforcement officer lacks personal knowledge to establish reasonable suspicion or probable cause as long as the officer is acting on the knowledge of another officer and the collective knowledge of the law-enforcement office. — Also termed *Whiteley rule*; *collective-knowledge rule*.

fellow servant. (16c) A coworker having the same employer; esp., an employee who is so closely related to another employee's work that there is a special risk of harm if either one is negligent. See FELLOW-SERVANT RULE; DIFFERENT-DEPARTMENT RULE.

▸ **superior fellow servant.** (1882) A worker that has the power of control or direction over a coworker. — Also termed *superior servant*.

fellow-servant rule. (1905) A common-law doctrine holding that an employer is not liable for an employee's injuries caused by a negligent coworker. • This doctrine has generally been abrogated by workers'-compensation statutes. In some jurisdictions, employees were considered fellow servants when they were working with one aim or result in view. In others, the relation of fellow servant was tested by the "doctrine of vice principal" or the "superior-servant rule," meaning that an employer is liable for injuries to an employee if they result from the negligence of another employee who is given power of control or direction over the injured employee. — Also termed *common-employment doctrine*. Cf. DIFFERENT-DEPARTMENT RULE.

felo-de-se (**fee**-loh *or* **fel**-oh dee **see**), *n.* (17c) See SUICIDE (2). Pl. **felones de se.**

"'*Felo de se*,' or felon of himself is freely spoken of by the early writers as self-murder. Hence one who killed himself before he arrived at the age of discretion or while he was *non compos mentis*, was not a *felo de se*, or suicide . . . . [B]y the early common law suicide was a felony and was punished by ignominious burial and forfeiture of goods and chattels to the king." Rollin M. Perkins & Ronald N. Boyce, *Criminal Law* 120 (3d ed. 1982).

felon, *n.* (13c) Someone who has been convicted of a felony. — Also termed *state criminal*; (redundantly) *convicted felon*.

felon-de-se. See SUICIDE (2).

felonia (fə-**loh**-nee-ə). [Latin "felony"] *Hist.* An offense that results in a vassal's forfeiting his fee.

"The attempt to derive *felonia* from *fel* 'poison' is merely a folk etymology which came into vogue when 'felony' meant a serious crime, and differed from treason. The word was well established in Feudal Law as the characteristic offense against the Feudal relationship. It will hardly do, therefore, to try to determine its meaning merely by reference to English usage . . . ." Max Radin, *Handbook of Anglo-American Legal History* 148 n.7 (1936).

felon-in-possession statute. (1972) A legislative act that makes it a felony for a person previously convicted of a specified crime, esp. a felony but also often a domestic-violence misdemeanor, to possess a firearm.

felonious (fə-**loh**-nee-əs), *adj.* (16c) **1.** Of, relating to, or involving a felony. **2.** Constituting or having the character of a felony. **3.** Proceeding from an evil heart or purpose; malicious; villainous. **4.** Wrongful; (of an act) done without excuse or color of right.

felonious assault. See ASSAULT.

felonious homicide. See HOMICIDE.

felonious intent. See *criminal intent* under INTENT (1).

felonious restraint. (1971) **1.** The offense of knowingly and unlawfully restraining a person under circumstances that expose the person to serious bodily harm. Model Penal Code § 212.2(a). **2.** The offense of holding a person in involuntary servitude. Model Penal Code § 212.2(b).

felon of oneself. See SUICIDE (2).

felony, *n.* (14c) **1.** A serious crime usu. punishable by imprisonment for more than one year or by death. • Examples include burglary, arson, rape, and murder. — Also termed *major crime; serious crime.* Cf. MISDEMEANOR.

> "Felony, in the general acceptation of our English law, comprizes every species of crime, which occasioned at common law the forfeiture of lands or goods." 4 William Blackstone, *Commentaries on the Laws of England* 94 (1769).

> "Amongst indictable crimes, the common law singled out some as being so conspicuously heinous that a man adjudged guilty of any of them incurred — not as any express part of his sentence but as a consequence that necessarily ensued upon it — a forfeiture of property, whether of his lands or of his goods or of both (in the case of treason). Such crimes came to be called 'felonies.' The other, and lesser, crimes were known as 'transgressions' or 'trespasses,' and did not obtain their present name of misdemeanours until a much later date. A felony is, therefore, a crime which either involved by common law such a forfeiture, or else has been placed by statute on the footing of those crimes which did involve it." J.W. Cecil Turner, *Kenny's Outlines of Criminal Law* 93 (16th ed. 1952).

▸ **atrocious felony.** (1814) *Archaic.* A serious, usu. cruel felony involving personal violence. • The common practice today is to refer to the specific type of crime alleged (e.g., first-degree murder or aggravated sexual assault).

▸ **serious felony.** (1874) A major felony, such as burglary of a residence or an assault that causes great bodily injury. • In many jurisdictions, a defendant's prior serious-felony convictions can be used to enhance another criminal charge.

▸ **substantive felony.** See *substantive offense* under OFFENSE (2).

▸ **treason felony.** See TREASON FELONY.

▸ **violent felony.** See *violent offense* under OFFENSE (2).

2. *Hist.* At common law, an offense for which conviction results in forfeiture of the defendant's lands or goods (or both) to the Crown, regardless of whether any capital or other punishment is mandated. • At early common law, the term *felony* included any offense for which a defendant who fled before trial could be summarily convicted, attainted, and outlawed, or that carried a right of appeal after conviction. Although treason carried the same penalties as a common-law felony, it was usu. defined as a separate class of crime. **3.** *Hist. Feudal law.* A grave act that resulted in the forfeiture of land granted by a superior.

felony-de-se. See SUICIDE (2).

felony DWI. See DRIVING WHILE INTOXICATED.

felony hearing. See PRELIMINARY HEARING.

felony injury to a child. (1990) The act of causing or allowing a child to suffer in circumstances likely to produce great bodily harm or death, or inflicting unjustifiable pain or mental suffering in those circumstances.

felony-merger doctrine. (1965) *Hist.* The common-law rule that when an act constitutes both a private tort and a criminal felony, the tort is subsumed into the felony and no private legal action is permitted.

felony murder. See MURDER.

felony-murder rule. (1943) *Criminal law.* The doctrine that if a person dies during the course of and in furtherance of a specified type of felony — even in immediate flight from the scene and even if the decedent was a perpetrator of the felony — the death is considered a murder regardless of intent. • Most states restrict this rule to inherently dangerous felonies such as rape, arson, robbery, and burglary. Cf. MISDEMEANOR-MANSLAUGHTER RULE.

felony offense. (1917) FELONY. • The phrase *felony offense* is a redundancy, since *felony* alone denotes the offense.

FEMA. *abbr.* (1978) FEDERAL EMERGENCY MANAGEMENT AGENCY.

female genital mutilation. (1979) **1.** Female circumcision. **2.** The act of cutting, or cutting off, one or more female sexual organs. • Female genital mutilation is practiced primarily among certain tribes in Africa, but it also occurs among some immigrant populations in the United States and in other Western countries. There are three commonly identified types: *sunna,* in which the hood of the clitoris is cut off; *excision,* in which the entire clitoris is cut off; and *infibulation,* in which the clitoris, the labia minora, and much of the labia majora are cut off. In the United States, Congress has outlawed female genital mutilation, specifically prohibiting the use of a cultural defense for persons accused of performing the act. 18 USCA § 16. — Abbr. FGM. — Often shortened to *female mutilation.* — Also termed *female circumcision; clitoridectomy.* See *cultural defense* under DEFENSE (1).

> "The two most common female genital mutilations are clitoridectomy and infibulation. Clitoridectomy, or female circumcision, refers to a variety of procedures ranging from excision of the prepuce of the clitoris (the Sunna circumcision practiced by many Muslim groups) to the removal of the entire clitoris and the labia minora. Among the Nandi the clitoris is burnt off with a hot coal. It is estimated that in 1995 there were some 20 to 80 million women in the world who had undergone some form of clitoridectomy. The practice is less common than male circumcision but occurs only in societies where male circumcision also occurs. Apart from Islamic groups, the major areas where the practice takes place are East and West Africa. Infibulation is almost entirely restricted to Muslim groups in the Horn of Africa, notably the Somali and Galla and a few other neighboring East African groups. It is sometimes called pharaonic circumcision, suggesting that the ancient Egyptians practiced it (there is no evidence that this was the case). Infibulation requires blocking access to the vagina, generally by sewing the labia majora together leaving only a small opening to accommodate urination and menstruation." Edgar A. Gregersen, "Genital Mutilation," in 2 *Encyclopedia of Cultural Anthropology* 531, 532 (David Levinson & Melvin Ember eds., 1996).

fem-crit. See CRIT.

feme (fem), *n.* (16c) [Law French] *Archaic.* **1.** A woman. **2.** A wife. — Also spelled *femme.*

▸***feme covert*** (fem **kəv**-ərt). [Law French "covered woman"] (17c) *Archaic.* A married woman. • The notion, as Blackstone put it, was that the husband was the one "under whose wing, protection, and cover, she performs every thing." 1 William Blackstone, *Commentaries on the Laws of England* 430 (1765). See COVERTURE.

▸***feme sole*** (fem **sohl**). [Law French] (17c) *Archaic.* **1.** An unmarried woman. **2.** A married woman handling the affairs of her separate estate. — Also termed (in sense 2) *feme sole trader; feme sole merchant.*

femicide (**fem**-ə-sɪd). (19c) **1.** The killing of a woman. **2.** Someone who kills a woman.

feminist jurisprudence. See JURISPRUDENCE.

femme. See FEME.

fence, *n.* (14c) **1.** Someone who receives stolen goods, usu. with the intent to sell them in a legitimate market.

> "The receivers of stolen goods almost never 'know' that they have been stolen, in the sense that they could testify to it in a courtroom. The business could not be so conducted, for those who sell the goods — the 'fences' — must keep up a more respectable front than is generally possible for the thieves." *U.S. v. Werner,* 160 F.2d 438, 441–42 (2d Cir. 1947).

> "The typical 'fence' takes over the stolen property and pays the thief a price. He purports to 'buy' the goods from the thief." Rollin M. Perkins & Ronald N. Boyce, *Criminal Law* 395 (3d ed. 1982).

2. A place where stolen goods are sold. See RECEIVING STOLEN PROPERTY. **3.** LAWFUL FENCE. **4.** *Scots law.* The formal warning to not interrupt or obstruct judicial or legislative proceedings. **5.** *Scots law.* A penalty of forfeiture prescribed in a statute or a contract.

fence, *vb.* (16c) **1.** To sell (stolen property) to a fence. **2.** *Scots law.* To open (a legislative or judicial sitting) by warning persons against obstructing or interrupting the legislature or court. **3.** *Scots law.* To threaten with forfeiture as a consequence of violating a law or breaching a contractual promise.

fence-month. (16c) *Hist.* The summer fawning season when it was unlawful to hunt deer. — Also termed *defense-month.*

fencing patent. See PATENT (3).

feneration (fen-ə-**ray**-shən). (16c) *Hist.* **1.** The act or practice of lending money with interest. **2.** USURY.

fenus (**fen**-əs), *n.* [Latin] *Roman law.* Simple interest.

fenus nauticum. See NAUTICUM FENUS.

feod (fyood). **1.** See FEE (2). **2.** See FEUD.

feodal (**fyoo**-dəl), *adj.* See FEUDAL.

feodal action. See FEUDAL ACTION.

feodality (fyoo-**dal**-ə-tee). See FEALTY.

feodal system. See FEUDALISM.

feodarum consuetudines (fee-ə-**dair**-əm [*or* fyoo-**dair**-əm] kon-swə-**t[y]oo**-də-neez). See FEUDARUM CONSUETUDINES.

feodary (**fyoo**-də-ree). (15c) *Hist.* An officer of the Court of Wards who traveled with the escheator from county to county in order to receive royal rents and estimate the value of land tenures for the Crown. See COURT OF WARDS AND LIVERIES.

feodatory (**fyoo**-də-tor-ee). See FEUDATORY.

feodi firma (**fee**-ə-dɪ *or* **fyoo**-dɪ **fər**-mə). See FEE FARM.

feodi firmarius (**fee**-ə-dɪ *or* **fyoo**-dɪ fər-**mair**-ee-əs). *Hist.* The tenant of a fee farm.

feodum (**fee**-ə-dəm *or* **fyoo**-dəm). [Law Latin] (17c) *Hist.* **1.** A fee; a heritable estate.

> "Feodum . . . A fee; the same as *feudum.* This is the word uniformly employed by Glanville and Bracton to denote an estate of inheritance, and an estate held of another by service, instead of *feudum,* which is invariably used by the continental feudists." 1 Alexander M. Burrill, *A Law Dictionary and Glossary* 615 (2d ed. 1867).

2. Part of a lord's estate held by a tenant (i.e., a seigniory). See SEIGNIORY (2). **3.** A payment for services rendered.

feodum antiquum. See *feudum antiquum* under FEUDUM.

feodum apertum. See *feudum apertum* under FEUDUM.

feodum laicum. See *feudum laicum* under FEUDUM.

feodum militis (**fee**-ə-dəm *or* **fyoo**-dəm **mil**-ə-tis). *Hist.* A knight's fee. — Also termed *feodum militare.*

feodum nobile (**fee**-ə-dəm *or* **fyoo**-dəm **noh**-bə-lee). See *feudum nobile* under FEUDUM.

feodum novum (**fee**-ə-dəm *or* **fyoo**-dəm **noh**-vəm). See *feudum novum* under FEUDUM.

feodum simplex (**fee**-ə-dəm *or* **fyoo**-dəm **sim**-pleks). (16c) A fee simple.

feodum talliatum (**fee**-ə-dəm *or* **fyoo**-dəm tal-ee-**ay**-təm). (17c) A fee tail. — Also spelled *feudum talliatum.*

feoff (**fef** *or* **feef**), *vb.* See ENFEOFF.

feoffamentum (fee-[ə]-fə-**men**-təm). [Law Latin] *Hist.* See FEOFFMENT.

feoffare (fee-[ə]-**fair**-ee), *vb.* [Law Latin] *Hist.* See ENFEOFF.

feoffator (fee-[ə]-**fay**-tər). [Law Latin] *Hist.* See FEOFFOR.

feoffatus (fee-[ə]-**fay**-təs). [Law Latin] *Hist.* See FEOFFEE.

feoffee (fef-**ee** *or* feef-**ee**). (15c) The transferee of an estate in fee simple; the recipient of a fief.

▸**feoffee to uses.** (18c) *Hist.* A person to whom land is conveyed for the use of a third party (called a *cestui que use*); one who holds legal title to land for the benefit of another. See CESTUI QUE USE; GRANT TO USES. Cf. TRUSTEE (1).

feoffer. See FEOFFOR.

feoffment (**fef**-mənt *or* **feef**-mənt). (14c) *Hist.* **1.** The act of conveying a freehold estate; a grant of land in fee simple. — Also termed *feoffment with livery of seisin.* **2.** The land so granted. **3.** The charter that transfers the land. — Also termed *deed of feoffment.*

▸**feoffment to uses.** (17c) An enfeoffment of land to one person for the use of a third party. • The feoffee was bound in conscience to hold the land according to the prescribed use and could derive no benefit from the holding.

> "Conveyances of freehold land could originally be made only by a feoffment with livery of seisin. This was a solemn ceremony carried out by the parties entering on the land, and the feoffor, in the presence of witnesses, delivering the seisin to the feoffee either by some symbolic act,

such as handing him a twig or sod of earth, or by uttering some words such as 'Enter into this land and God give you joy' and leaving him in possession of the land." Robert E. Megarry & H.W.R. Wade, *The Law of Real Property* 47 (5th ed. 1984).

feoffment with livery of seisin. See FEOFFMENT (1).

feoffor (**fef**- *or* **feef**-ər *or* -or). (15c) The transferor of an estate in fee simple. — Also spelled *feoffer.*

feorme (fərm). *Hist.* A portion of the land's produce owed by the grantee to the lord according to the terms of a charter.

ferae bestiae (**feer**-ee **bes**-tee-ee). [Latin] *Roman law.* Wild beasts. • Since a wild animal belonged to no one (*res nullius*), its captor acquired ownership by *occupatio.* See OCCUPATIO.

ferae naturae (**feer**-ee nə-**tyoor**-ee). [Latin "of a wild nature"] (17c) **1.** *adj.* (Of animals) wild; untamed; undomesticated. **2.** *n.* Wild animals. See RULE OF CAPTURE (2). Cf. DOMITAE NATURAE; MANSUETAE FERAE.

feral animal. See ANIMAL.

FERC (fərk). *abbr.* FEDERAL ENERGY REGULATORY COMMISSION.

FERC-out clause. (1984) *Oil & gas.* A provision in a contract to sell natural gas specifying that if a regulatory agency does not allow the price paid to the producer to be passed on to consumers, either the contract price will be reduced accordingly or the contract will be terminated. — Also termed *regulatory-out clause.*

ferdella terrae (fər-**del**-ə **ter**-ee). [Latin] (17c) *Hist.* **1.** Ten acres of land. **2.** A yard-land (twenty acres). — Also termed *ferdel.*

ferdfare (**fərd**-fair), *n.* [fr. Saxon *fird* "military service" + *fare* "a going"] (bef. 12c) *Hist.* **1.** A summons to military service. **2.** An exemption from military service. — Also spelled *firdfare; fyrdfare.*

ferdingus (**fər**-ding-gəs). *Hist.* A freeman of the lowest class.

***Feres* doctrine** (**feer**-is *or* **feer**-eez or **fer**-ez). (1955) *Torts.* The rule that a member of the military is barred from recovering damages from the United States on a claim brought under the Federal Tort Claims Act for injuries sustained in military service. *Feres v. U.S.*, 340 U.S. 135, 71 S.Ct. 153 (1950). — Also termed *Feres rule.* See ACTIVITY INCIDENT TO SERVICE.

feria (**feer**-ee-ə), *n.* [Law Latin] (1844) *Hist.* **1.** A weekday. **2.** A holiday. **3.** See *ferial day* under DAY. **4.** A fair. **5.** A ferry.

feriae (**feer**-ee-ɪ), *n. pl.* [Latin] *Roman law.* Religious and public holidays on which Romans suspended politics and lawsuits, and on which slaves enjoyed a partial break from labor.

ferial day. See DAY.

ferlingum. See FURLONG.

ferlingus. See FURLONG.

ferm. See FARM.

fermer. [Law French] *Hist.* **1.** A lessee, esp. one who holds lands for agricultural purposes. **2.** Someone who holds something (such as land or an incorporeal right) for a term.

FERPA. *abbr.* FAMILY EDUCATIONAL RIGHTS AND PRIVACY ACT.

ferriage (**fer**-ee-ij). (14c) *Hist.* The toll or fare paid for the transportation of persons or property on a ferry.

ferry, *n.* (bef. 12c) **1.** A boat or vessel used to carry persons or property across water, usu. with fixed terminals and short distances. **2.** The commercial transportation of persons or property across water. **3.** The place where a ferry passes across water, including the continuation of the highway on both sides of the water. **4.** The right, usu. exclusive, given by government franchise, to carry persons or property across water for a fee. — Also termed *ferry franchise.*

ferry, *vb.* (bef. 12c) To carry persons or property, usu. across water, for a fee.

ferry franchise. See FERRY (4).

fertile-octogenarian rule. (1856) The legal fiction, assumed under the rule against perpetuities, that a woman can become pregnant as long as she is alive. • The case that gave rise to this fiction was *Jee v. Audley*, 1 Cox 324, 29 Eng. Rep. 1186 (Ch. 1787). *See* W. Barton Leach, *Perpetuities: New Hampshire Defertilizes Octogenarians*, 77 Harv. L. Rev. 729 (1963). — Also termed *presumption-of-fertility rule.*

"Suppose testator bequeaths in trust to pay the income to A for her life, then to pay the income to the children of A for their lives, and upon the death of the survivor of such children, to pay the principal to the grandchildren of A. At the time of the testator's death A is 79 years old, and she has two children. Believe it or not, it has been held that the remainder to the grandchildren of A is violative of the rule against perpetuities and invalid. The law adopted the conclusive presumption that every person is capable of having children until the day he or she dies, as far as the rule against perpetuities is concerned. Consequently, A could have an additional child who would not be a life in being at the testator's death, and that child could have a child who would be born beyond the permissible period. The result of this hypothesis is to invalidate the remainder to the grandchildren. This situation is sometimes referred to as the case of the 'fertile octogenarian.' Remember that the class gift is invalid if it is possible that the interest of any one member of the class can violate the rule." Thomas F. Bergin & Paul G. Haskell, *Preface to Estates in Land and Future Interests* 188 (2d ed. 1984).

ferus, *adj.* [Latin] Fierce; wild; untamed; savage.

festing-man. *Hist.* A bondsman; a surety. See FRANKPLEDGE.

festing-penny. *Hist.* Earnest, or payment, given to a servant when hired.

festinum remedium (fes-**tɪ**-nəm ri-**mee**-dee-əm). [Latin] (17c) *Hist.* A speedy remedy. • It was used in cases, such as actions for dower or assize, where the redress of injury was given without unnecessary delay.

***Festo* doctrine.** (2003) *Patents.* The rule that the voluntary narrowing of a patent claim may give rise to prosecution-history estoppel. *Festo Corp. v. Shoketsu Kinzoku Kogyo Kabushiki Co.*, 304 F.3d 1289 (Fed. Cir. 2003).

festuca (fes-**tyoo**-kə). *Hist.* A rod, staff, or stick used as a pledge (or *gage*) of good faith by a party to a contract or as a token of conveyance of land. • In Roman law, a festuca was a symbol of ownership. — Also termed *fistuca; vindicta.* See LIVERY OF SEISIN.

"The *wed* or gage, however, was capable of becoming a symbol; an object which intrinsically was of trifling value might be given and might serve to bind a contract. Among the Franks, whom we must regard as being for many purposes our ancestors in law, it took the shape of the *festuca*. Whether this transition from the 'real' to the 'formal' can be accomplished without the intervention of sacral ceremonies seems doubtful. There are some who regard the *festuca* as a stout staff which has taken the place of a spear and is a symbol of physical power. Others see in it a little bit of stick on which imprecatory runes have been cut. It is hard to decide such questions, for, especially under the influence of a new religion, symbols lose their old meanings and are mixed up. Popular etymology confounds confusion." 2 Frederick Pollock & Frederic W. Maitland, *The History of English Law Before the Time of Edward I* 186 (2d ed. 1899).

festum (**fes**-təm). [Latin] A feast-day, holiday, or festival.

fetal alcohol syndrome. (1976) A variety of birth defects caused by the mother's alcohol consumption during pregnancy. • The birth defects include facial abnormalities, mental retardation, and growth deficiencies. — Abbr. FAS.

fetiales (fee-shee-**ay**-leez), *n. pl.* (16c) *Roman law.* The order of priests whose duties concerned international relations and treaties, including the declaration of war and peace. — Also spelled *feciales.*

"Feciales [were] . . . priests among the Romans, Etruscans, and other ancient nations of Italy, who acted as heralds of peace and war. Their persons were sacred from injury when engaged on any mission to a hostile state, as the persons of ambassadors, and messengers, under a flag of truce, are inviolate in the present time. Their duties in some few particulars resembled those of the heralds of the Middle Ages. The Roman feciales . . . formed a kind of college of heralds, instituted by Numa Pompilius, the second king of Rome, about 710 B.C." Samuel Orchart Beeton, *Beeton's Illustrated Dictionary of Religion, Philosophy, Politics, and Law* 240 (1886).

fetial law (**fee**-shəl). (16c) *Roman law.* A branch of law concerned with matters (such as treaties, embassies, and war declarations) affecting relations between peoples or countries. — Also spelled *fecial law.* — Also termed *jus fetiale.*

feticide (**fee**-tə-sɪd). (1842) **1.** The act or an instance of killing a fetus, usu. by assaulting and battering the mother; esp., the act of unlawfully causing the death of a fetus. **2.** An intentionally induced miscarriage. — Also spelled *foeticide.* — Also termed *child destruction.* Cf. INFANTICIDE (1). — **feticidal,** *adj.*

fetter, *n.* (*usu. pl.*) (bef. 12c) A chain or shackle for the feet. — **fetter,** *vb.*

fettering of property. (1888) The act of making the disposition or ownership of property more complex so that those with separate interests must cooperate if they are to handle their interests reasonably. • Fettering of property occurs whenever ownership is split into two or more interests, as when present and future interests are divided or when a tenancy in common is created.

fetus. (14c) A developing but unborn mammal, esp. in the latter stages of development. — Also spelled *foetus.* Cf. EMBRYO; ZYGOTE.

feu (fyoo), *n.* [fr. Law Latin *feudum* "a fee"] (15c) **1.** A right to land given to a person in exchange for service to be performed. **2.** *Scots law.* Land held by a vassal in return for an annual payment in money, crops, or services (called *feu duty*). • This type of tenure was abolished in Scotland in 2000. **3.** *Scots law.* A perpetual grant of land to be held in exchange for grain or money. **4.** A perpetual lease for a fixed rent. **5.** A piece of land held under a perpetual lease for a fixed rent. — Also spelled *few.* See FEE (2). — **feu,** *vb.* — **feu,** *adj.*

"Feu; in Latin *feudum*, was used to denote the feudal-holding, where the service was purely military; but the term has been used in Scotland in contradistinction to ward-holding, the military tenure of this country . . . for, even in the purest ages of the military system, innumerable instances are to be found of grants of land in the feudal form, where the vassal annually delivered victual, or performed agricultural services to his superior." William Bell, *Bell's Dictionary and Digest of the Law of Scotland* 456 (George Watson ed., 7th ed. 1890).

feu, *vb.* (18c) *Scots law.* To grant (land) by feu.

feu annual. (16c) *Scots law.* The yearly return generated by a feu.

feuar (**fyoo**-ər), *n.* (16c) *Scots law.* Someone who holds a feu. Cf. FEU; VASSAL.

feu charter. (18c) *Scots law.* The charter creating a feu tenure.

feud, *n.* (15c) *Hist.* **1.** A heritable estate in land conveyed from a feudal superior to a grantee or tenant, held on the condition of rendering services to the superior.

"It is believed that the forms *feud* and *fief* appear in England but late in the day under the influence of foreign books; they never became terms of our law. It is noticeable also that *feodum* was constantly used in the sense that our *fee* has when we speak of a lawyer's or doctor's fee; payments due for services rendered, at least if they are permanent periodic payments, are *feoda*; the judges, for example, receive *feoda*, not salaries. The etymological problem presented by the English *fee* seems no easy one, because at the Conquest the would-be Latin *feodum* or *feudum* (the *d* in which has puzzled philologists and does not always appear in Domesday Book) is introduced among a people which already has *feoh* as a word for property in general and cattle in particular." 2 Frederick Pollock & Frederic W. Maitland, *The History of English Law Before the Time of Edward I* 236 n.2 (2d ed. 1899).

▸ **impartible feud.** An indivisible feud; a feud not subject to partition. See *feudum individuum* under FEUD.

▸ **improper feud.** (18c) A nonmilitary feud; a feud that is base or servile in nature.

"These were the principal, and very simple, qualities of the genuine or original feuds; being then all of a military nature, and in the hands of military persons: though the feudatories, being under frequent incapacities of cultivating and manuring their own lands, soon found it necessary to commit part of them to inferior tenants . . . . But this at the same time demolished the ancient simplicity of feuds; and an inroad being once made upon their constitution, it subjected them, in a course of time, to great varieties and innovations. Feuds came to be bought and sold, and deviations were made from the old fundamental rules of tenure and succession; which were held no longer sacred, when the feuds themselves no longer continued to be purely military. Hence these tenures began now to be divided into *feoda propria et impropria*, proper and improper feuds . . . ." 2 William Blackstone, *Commentaries on the Laws of England* 57–58 (1766).

▸ **proper feud.** (18c) A feud based on military service.

2. The interest of the tenant in the land conveyed. **3.** The land itself conveyed. — Also termed (in senses 1–3) *fee; fief; feod; feude; feudum.* **4.** An enmity or private war existing between families or clans, esp. as a result of a murder.

"[In Anglo-Saxon times,] where wrong done to an individual is not regarded as an injury to the entire tribe, the wrongdoer is out of the peace only as regards the wronged party and his kin. The situation created by such wrongful deed is feud (Anglo Saxon *foehth*, Latin *faida*). The root meaning of the word is 'hatred.' Feud is legally sanctioned hostility. The recognition of feud by the law is found in the fact that revenge taken in lawful feud is not a breach of the peace. It is not a wrongful deed. It furnishes no basis for any claim for fine or punishment. The man slain in lawful feud is not to be avenged nor has compensation to be paid for his slaying." Munroe Smith, *The Development of European Law* 29 (1928).

▸ **blood feud.** (1858) A state of hostility between families in which one family seeks to avenge the killing of one of its members by killing a member of the other family. See VENDETTA.

"Anglo-Saxon polity preserved, even down to the Norman Conquest, many traces of a time when kinship was the strongest of all bonds. Such a stage of society, we hardly need add, is not confined to any one region of the world or any one race of men. . . . When it puts on the face of strife between hostile kindreds, it is shown in the war of tribal factions, and more specifically in the blood-feud. A man's kindred are his avengers; and, as it is their right and honour to avenge him, so it is their duty to make amends for his misdeeds, or else maintain his cause in fight. Step by step, as the power of the State waxes, the self-centred and self-helping autonomy of the kindred wanes. Private feud is controlled, regulated, put, one may say, into legal harness; the avenging and the protecting clan on the slain and the slayer are made pledges and auxiliaries of public justice." 1 Frederick Pollock & Frederic W. Maitland, *The History of English Law Before the Time of Edward I* 31 (2d ed. 1898).

feudal, *adj.* (17c) **1.** Of, relating to, or growing out of feudalism <feudal law>. **2.** Of, relating to, or involving a feud <feudal tenure>. — Also spelled (archaically) *feodal*. Cf. ALLODIAL.

feudal action. (1875) *Hist.* A real action; an action that concerned only real property.

feudalism (**fyood**-əl-iz-əm). (19c) **1.** A landholding system, particularly applying to medieval Europe, in which all are bound by their status in a hierarchy of reciprocal obligations of service and defense. • The lord was obligated to give the vassal (1) some land, (2) protection, and (3) justice. The lord guaranteed the quiet occupation of the land by the vassal and guaranteed to do right if the vassal became involved in a dispute. In return, the vassal owed the lord some type of service, called "tenure" (literally "means of holding"), because the different types of service were the methods by which the vassals held the property. **2.** The social, political, and economic system of medieval Europe. — Also termed *feudal system*; *feodal system*. — **feudalistic,** *adj.*

"What do we mean by feudalism? Some such answer as the following is the best that I can give — A state of society in which the main social bond is the relation between lord and man, a relation implying on the lord's part protection and defence; on the man's part protection, service and reverence, the service including service in arms. This personal relation is inseparably involved in a proprietary relation, the tenure of land — the man holds land of the lord, the man's service is a burden on the land, the lord has important rights in the land, and (we may say) the full ownership of the land is split up between man and lord." F.W. Maitland, *The Constitutional History of England* 143 (1908; repr. 1955).

"Modern historical research has taught us that, while it is a mistake to speak of a feudal *system*, the word 'feudalism' is a convenient way of referring to certain fundamental similarities which, in spite of large local variations, can be discerned in the social development of all the peoples of western Europe from about the ninth to the thirteenth centuries." J.L. Brierly, *The Law of Nations* 2 (5th ed. 1955).

feudal law. (16c) *Hist. English law.* The real-property law of land tenures that prevailed in England, esp. after the Norman Conquest. See FEUDARUM CONSUETUDINES.

feudal service. See SERVICE (6).

feudal system. See FEUDALISM.

feudal tenure. See TENURE (1).

feuda pecuniae (fyoo-də pi-**kyoo**-nee-ee). [Law Latin] *Hist.* A heritable right to money.

feudarum consuetudines (fyoo-**dair**-əm kon-swə-**t**[**y**]**oo**-də-neez). [Latin] The customs of feuds. • This was the name of a compilation of feudal laws and customs made in 12th-century Milan. It is regarded as an authoritative work in continental Europe. — Also spelled *feodarum consuetudines*.

feudary. See FEUDATORY.

feudatory, *adj.* (16c) *Hist.* (Of a vassal) owing feudal allegiance to a lord.

feudatory, *n.* (17c) *Hist.* The grantee of a feud; the vassal or tenant who held an estate by feudal service. — Also termed *feudary*; *feodatory*.

"Every receiver of lands, or feudatory, was therefore bound, when called upon by his benefactor, or immediate lord of his feud or fee, to do all in his power to defend him." 2 William Blackstone, *Commentaries on the Laws of England* 46 (1766).

feude. See FEUD.

feudee (fyoo-**dee**), *n.* (1875) *Hist.* The grantee of a feud; a feudal tenant.

feudist. (17c) A writer on feuds (for example, Cujacius, Spelman, or Craig).

Feudorum Libri (fyoo-**dor**-əm **lɪ**-brɪ). [Latin "the books of the feuds"] *Hist. English law.* The Books of Feuds, a five-book compilation of Lombardic feudal law published in Milan around 1152, during the reign of Henry III. • This unofficial compilation was the main source of tenure law among the countries in Europe. It was widely used in medieval law schools and courts in Italy, France, and Germany. The *Feudorum Libri* were probably known in England but had little effect other than influencing English lawyers to study their own tenure system more critically. — Also termed *Consuetudines Feudorum*; *Usus Feudorum*.

feudum (**fyoo**-dəm). [Law Latin] A fief or feud; a feodum. — Also termed *feodum*; *feum*. Pl. ***feuda*** (**fyoo**-də). See FEUD (1)–(3); FIEF; FEE (2).

"The Latin equivalent of *feodum* or *feudum* is the root of the words 'feudal' and 'subinfeudation.' The French form *fief* is favoured by some English historians, but it was not used in law-French." J.H. Baker, *An Introduction to English Legal History* 256 n.4 (3d ed. 1990).

▸ ***feudum antiquum*** (**fyoo**-dəm an-**tɪ**-kwəm), *n.* [Law Latin "ancient feud"] (18c) *Hist.* **1.** A feud that passed to a vassal from an intestate ancestor. **2.** A feud that ancestors had possessed for more than four generations. **3.** An ancient feud. — Also termed *feodum antiquum* (**fee**-ə-dəm *or* **fyoo**-dəm). See FEUD (1). Pl. ***feuda antiqua*** (**fyoo**-də an-**tɪ**-kwə).

▸ ***feudum apertum*** (**fyoo**-dəm ə-**pər**-təm). *Hist.* A feud that reverted to the lord because of a tenant's failure of issue, a crime by the tenant, or some other legal cause. — Also termed *feodum apertum*.

▸***feudum burgale*** (**fyoo**-dəm bər-**gay**-lee). [Law Latin] *Hist.* Land held feudally by burgage tenure — that is, tenure given in exchange for a tenant's watching and warding in a burgh. See WATCH AND WARD.

▸***feudum ex camera aut caverna*** (**fyoo**-dəm eks **kam**-ər-ə awt kə-**vər**-nə). [Law Latin "feu from a room or hole"] *Hist.* An annual gift of money, grain, or other items to a deserving person, esp. a soldier.

▸***feudum francum*** (**fyoo**-dəm **frangk**-əm). (1929) *Hist.* A free feud; a feud or fee that was noble and free from talliage and subsidies that vulgar feuds (*plebeia feuda*) were subject to.

▸***feudum hauberticum*** (**fyoo**-dəm haw-**bər**-tə-kəm). (17c) *Hist.* A feud that was held on the military service of appearing fully armed when summoned by the lord. See ARRIÈRE-BAN.

▸***feudum improprium*** (**fyoo**-dəm im-**proh**-pree-əm). (1847) *Hist.* A feud that was improper.

▸***feudum individuum*** (**fyoo**-dəm in-də-**vij**-oo-əm). *Hist.* A feud that was indivisible and descendible only to the eldest son.

▸***feudum laicum*** (**fyoo**-dəm **lay**-ə-kəm). *Hist.* A lay feud. — Also termed *feodum laicum*.

▸***feudum ligium*** (**fyoo**-dəm **lij**-ee-əm). (18c) *Hist.* **1.** A liege feud; a feud held immediately of the sovereign. **2.** A feud for which the vassal owed fealty to his lord against all other persons.

▸***feudum maternum*** (**fyoo**-dəm mə-**tər**-nəm). (18c) *Hist.* A feud that descended to the feudatory from the maternal side.

▸***feudum militare*** (**fyoo**-dəm mil-ə-**tair**-ee). (17c) *Hist.* A knight's feud. • It was held by knight-service and esteemed the most honorable species of tenure. — Also termed *feodum militis*; (in Norman law) *fief d'haubert* or *fief d'hauberk*.

▸***feudum nobile*** (**fyoo**-dəm **noh**-bə-lee). (17c) *Hist.* A feud for which the tenant did guard and owed fealty and homage. — Also termed *feodum nobile*.

▸***feudum novum*** (**fyoo**-dəm **noh**-vəm). [Law Latin] (17c) *Hist.* A new fee; a fee that began with the person of the feudatory, and that was not acquired by succession. — Also spelled *feodum novum*.

> "For if the feud, of which the son died seised, was really *feudum antiquum*, or one descended to him from his ancestors, the father could not possibly succeed to it, because it must have passed him in the course of descent, before it could come to the son . . . . And if it were *feudum novum*, or one newly acquired by the son, then only the descendants from the body of the feudatory himself could succeed, by the known maxim of the early feodal constitutions . . . which was founded as well upon the personal merit of the vassal, which might be transmitted to his children but could not ascend to his progenitors . . . ." 2 William Blackstone, *Commentaries on the Laws of England* 211–12 (1766).

▸***feudum novum ut antiquum*** (**fyoo**-dəm **noh**-vəm ət an-**tɪ**-kwəm). (17c) *Hist.* A new feud held with the qualities of an ancient feud.

▸***feudum paternum*** (**fyoo**-dəm pə-**tər**-nəm). (18c) *Hist.* **1.** A feud that the tenant's paternal ancestors had held for four generations. **2.** A feud descendible only to the heirs on the paternal side. **3.** A feud that could be held only by males.

▸***feudum proprium*** (**fyoo**-dəm **proh**-pree-əm). *Hist.* An original feud that is military in nature and held by military service.

▸***feudum rectum*** (**fyoo**-dəm **rek**-təm). [Law Latin] *Hist.* Lands held by military tenure.

▸***feudum simplex*** (**fyoo**-dəm **sim**-pleks). [Law Latin] *Hist.* FEE SIMPLE.

▸***feudum talliatum*** (**fyoo**-dəm tal-ee-**ay**-təm). See FEE TAIL.

feu duty. (16c) *Scots law.* The annual rent paid by the tenant of a feu. — Also termed *ground annual*.

feu farm. (15c) *Scots law.* A tenure of land held in exchange for a specified annual payment (called *feu duty*). • This type of tenure was converted to a freehold in 2000. — Also termed *feu tenure*. See FEU DUTY.

feuholding (**fyoo**-hohl-ding). (18c) *Hist.* A tenancy held by rendering produce or money instead of military service. — Also written *feu holding*.

feum. See FEUDUM.

feu tenure. See FEU FARM.

few. See FEU.

ff. *abbr.* **1.** And the pages following. **2.** (*often cap.*) FRAGMENTA.

FFCA. *abbr.* FULL FAITH AND CREDIT ACT.

FFCBFC. *abbr.* FEDERAL FARM CREDIT BANKS FUNDING CORPORATION.

FFL. *abbr.* Federal firearms license.

FGA. *abbr.* **1.** Free from general average. **2.** Foreign general average.

> "*F.G.A.* means Foreign General Average, and implies that, if goods become liable to general average, the rules to be applied will be those of the port of destination or refuge, i.e., the law of the place where the adjustment is made." 2 E.W. Chance, *Principles of Mercantile Law* 128 (P.W. French ed., 10th ed. 1951).

FGM. *abbr.* FEMALE GENITAL MUTILATION.

FHA. *abbr.* **1.** FARMERS HOME ADMINISTRATION. **2.** FEDERAL HOUSING ADMINISTRATION. **3.** FAIR HOUSING ACT.

FHA mortgage. See MORTGAGE.

FHEO. *abbr.* OFFICE OF FAIR HOUSING AND EQUAL OPPORTUNITY.

FHFB. *abbr.* FEDERAL HOUSING FINANCE BOARD.

FHLB. *abbr.* FEDERAL HOME LOAN BANK.

FHLBB. *abbr.* FEDERAL HOME LOAN BANK BOARD.

FHLMC. *abbr.* FEDERAL HOME LOAN MORTGAGE CORPORATION.

FHWA. *abbr.* FEDERAL HIGHWAY ADMINISTRATION.

fiancer (fyah*n*-say), *vb.* [Law French] To pledge one's faith.

fiant, *n.* (16c) *Hist.* **1.** A decree; commission. **2.** A warrant to the Chancery of Ireland for a grant under the great seal.

fiar, *n.* (16c) *Scots law.* Someone who holds an estate in fee, in contrast to a liferenter.

fiat (**fee**-aht *or* **fee**-at *or* **fɪ**-at *or* **fɪ**-ət), *n.* [Latin "let it be done"] (17c) **1.** An order or decree, esp. an arbitrary one <judicial fiat>. **2.** A court decree, esp. one relating to a routine matter such as scheduling <the court requires all

motions to contain a fiat — to be filled in by the court — setting the hearing date>. — Also termed *fiaunt.*

fiat currency. See *soft currency* under CURRENCY.

fiat justitia (fɪ-at jəs-**tish**-ee-ə). [Latin] *Hist.* Let justice be done. • This phrase signaled the Crown's commission to the House of Lords to hear an appeal.

> "*Fiat Justitia, ruat coelum,* says another maxim, as full of extravagance as it is of harmony: Go heaven to wreck — so justice be but done: — and what is the ruin of kingdoms, in comparison of the wreck of heaven?" Jeremy Bentham, *An Introduction to the Principles of Morals and Legislation* 13–14 n.1 (1823).

fiat money. See MONEY.

fiat ut petitur (fɪ-at ət **pet**-ə-tər). [Latin] (16c) Let it be done as it is asked. • An order granting a petition.

fiaunt. See FIAT.

fib, *n.* A falsehood, esp. a nonserious one told without evil intent; often, a white lie. See LIE, *n.* — **fib,** *vb.*

FICA (fɪ-kə). *abbr.* FEDERAL INSURANCE CONTRIBUTIONS ACT.

fickle-fiduciary rule. (2000) The principle that a partner or employee who breaches a fiduciary duty should forfeit all compensation, bonuses, and other benefits received after and during the breach. • The rule usu. applies to a person who engages in or assists a competing business, or resigns from employment to set up or work for a competing business. Traditionally, mitigating factors, including the absence of harm to the employer or partnership, are not considered in applying the rule. But some courts have found that if a strict application would produce unjustly harsh results, mitigating factors must be weighed.

ficta traditio (**fik**-tə trə-**dish**-ee-oh). [Latin] *Scots law.* A fictitious delivery. • The phrase invoked the rule that if the parties so intended, an item could be treated as having been delivered to a buyer in possession of it without the need for physical transfer. — Also termed *fictio brevis manus.*

fictio (**fik**-shee-oh), *n.* [Latin fr. *fingere* "to feign"] *Roman law.* A legal fiction; a legal assumption or supposition (such as that the plaintiff was a citizen) necessary to achieve certain legal results that otherwise would not be obtained. • Legal fictions allowed Roman magistrates (*praetors*) to expand the law beyond what was strictly allowed by the *jus civile.* This practice also occurred in English law — for example, the action of *common recovery,* which allowed a landowner to convey land that by law could not be alienated (such as land held in fee tail). Pl. ***fictiones*** (fik-shee-**oh**-neez).

fictio brevis manus (**fik**-shee-oh **bree**-vis **may**-nəs). [Law Latin] FICTA TRADITIO.

fictio juris. See LEGAL FICTION.

fiction. See LEGAL FICTION.

fictional action. See *collusive action* under ACTION (4).

fiction of law. See LEGAL FICTION.

fictitious, *adj.* (17c) Of, relating to, or involving a fiction, esp. a legal fiction.

fictitious action. See ACTION (4).

fictitious bid. See BID (1).

fictitious issue. See FEIGNED ISSUE.

fictitious name. 1. See *assumed name* under NAME. **2.** See ALIAS (1). **3.** See JOHN DOE.

fictitious party. See PARTY (2).

fictitious-payee rule. (1943) *Commercial law.* The principle that if a drawer or maker issues commercial paper to a payee whom the drawer or maker does not actually intend to have any interest in the instrument, an ensuing forgery of the payee's name will be effective to pass good title to later transferees. — Also termed *padded-payroll rule.*

fictitious person. See *artificial person* under PERSON (3).

fictitious promise. See *implied promise* under PROMISE.

fictitious seisin. See *seisin in law* under SEISIN.

fide-commissary. See CESTUI QUE TRUST.

fidecommittee. (18c) A beneficiary; CESTUI QUE TRUST. — Also termed *fideicommissary; fideicommissarius.*

> "In a particular case, a *cestuy que trust* is called by the Roman law, *fideicommissarius.* In imitation of this, I have seen him somewhere or other called in English a *fide-committee.* This term, however, seems not very expressive. A fide-committee, or, as it should have been, a *fidei*-committee, seems, literally speaking, to mean one who is committed to the good faith of another." Jeremy Bentham, *An Introduction to the Principles of Morals and Legislation* 226 n.1 (1823).

fideicomiso (fee-day-koh-**mee**-soh). *Mexican law.* A trust; esp., a trust that is established for the purpose of acquiring property in Mexico with a Mexican bank as trustee and a non-Mexican (who may be the settlor) as beneficiary. • The property is held in the name of the trust, but the beneficiary has all the rights and obligations of direct ownership, including the power to lease, sell, or devise the property. A Mexican fideicomiso usu. lasts 50 years and can be renewed for 50 more. Cf. FIDEICOMMISSUM.

fideicommissarius. See CESTUI QUE TRUST.

fideicommissary (fɪ-dee-ɪ **kom**-ə-ser-ee). See CESTUI QUE TRUST.

fideicommissary heir. See HEIR.

fideicommissary substitution. (1906) **1.** SUBSTITUTION (6). **2.** SUBSTITUTION (7).

fideicommissum (fɪ-dee-ɪ-kə-**mis**-əm). [Latin] (18c) **1.** *Roman law.* A devise or bequest coupled with a request to the heir as a matter of good faith to give some part of the inheritance, such as a particular object, or all the inheritance, to a third party. • A *fideicommissum* was a device to overcome some of the technicalities of the Roman will. Originally it created a mere moral obligation, but Augustus made it enforceable by legal process. **2.** *Roman & civil law.* An arrangement similar to a trust by which a testator gave property to a person for the benefit of another who could not, by law, inherit property. • Over time, this device was used to tie up property for generations, and most civil jurisdictions now prohibit or limit it. For example, in Louisiana, an arrangement in which one person bequeaths property to a second with a charge to preserve it and, at death, to restore it to a third person is a prohibited *fideicommissum.* Pl. ***fideicommissa.***

> "The many formalities with regard to the institution of heirs and the bequest of legacies, coupled with the fact that many persons, *e.g. peregrini,* were incapable of being instituted heirs, or of being given a legacy, led, in the late Republic, to testators leaving directions to their heirs in favour of given individuals, which, though not binding at law, they hoped their heirs would, in honour, feel bound

to carry out. The beginning of *fideicommissa*, therefore, was very like the early practice with regard to trusts in English law, and, as in the case of trusts, a time came when trusts were made binding legally as well as morally. . . . For brevity, the *fideicommissum* will here be called 'the trust,' the person upon whom it was imposed (*fiduciarius*) 'the trustee,' and the person in whose favour it was imposed (*fideicommissarius*) 'the beneficiary.'" R.W. Leage, *Roman Private Law* 252 (C.H. Ziegler ed., 2d ed. 1930).

fidejubere (fɪ-dee-yə-**beer**-ee), *vb.* [Latin] *Roman law.* To become a surety. • Forms of this word were spoken by the parties to a *stipulatio* that bound one party to become a surety for the other; the first party asked, "Do you pledge yourself?" ("*fidejubesne?*"), and the second responded, "I do pledge myself" ("*fidejubeo*"). See STIPULATIO.

fidejussion (fɪ-di-**jəsh**-ən). [fr. Latin *fidejussio*] (16c) *Roman law.* An act by which a person becomes an additional security for another; esp., an oral contract of suretyship entered into to fortify the obligation contracted by another. • The act does not remove the principal's liability but only adds to the surety's security. Fidejussion was one of the three types of adpromission, and the only type remaining in Justinian's law. — Also spelled *fidejussio*; *fideiussio*. See ADPROMISSION (1). — **fidejussionary,** *adj.*

fidejussor (fɪ-dee-**jəs**-or *or* -**jəs**-ər). (16c) **1.** *Roman law.* (*ital.*) A guarantor; a person who binds himself to pay another's debt. **2.** *Hist. Maritime law.* Someone who acts as bail for a defendant in the Court of Admiralty. — Also spelled *fideiussor.* Cf. ADPROMISSOR. — **fidejussory,** *adj.*

"The proceedings of the court of admiralty bear much resemblance to those of the civil law, but are not entirely founded thereon; and they likewise adopt and make use of other laws, as occasion requires; such as the Rhodian law, and the laws of Oleron. For the law of England, as has frequently been observed, doth not acknowledge or pay any deference to the civil law considered as such; but merely permits its use in such cases where it judged its determinations equitable, and therefore blends it, in the present instance, with other marine laws . . . . The first process in these courts is frequently by arrest of the defendant's person; and they also take recognizances or stipulation of certain fidejussors in the nature of bail, and in case of default may imprison both them and their principal." 3 William Blackstone, *Commentaries on the Laws of England* 108–09 (1768).

fidelissimi magistri omnium juris arcanorum conscii (fɪ-di-**lis**-i-mɪ **maj**-i-strɪ **om**-nee-əm **joor**-is ahr-kə-**nor**-əm **kon**-shee-ɪ). [Latin] *Hist.* Most faithful teachers, privy to all the mysteries of the law.

fidelitas (fi-**del**-ə-tas). [Latin "fidelity"] See FEALTY.

fidelitatis sacramentum (fi-del-i-**tay**-tis sak-rə-**men**-təm). [Law Latin] (17c) *Hist.* The oath of fealty that a vassal owed to a lord.

fidelity and guaranty insurance. See *fidelity insurance* under INSURANCE.

fidelity bond. See BOND (2).

fidelity guarantee. See *fidelity bond* under BOND (2).

fidelity-guarantee insurance. See *fidelity bond* under BOND (2).

fidelity guaranty insurance. See *fidelity insurance* under INSURANCE.

fidelity insurance. See INSURANCE.

fidem facere judici (fɪ-dəm **fay**-sə-ree **joo**-di-sɪ). [Latin] *Hist.* To convince the judge. • The phrase appeared in reference to the introduction of evidence to prove a case.

fidem mentiri (fɪ-dəm men-**tɪ**-rɪ). [Latin] *Hist.* To betray faith or fealty. • The term refers to a feudal tenant who did not keep the fealty sworn to the lord.

fidepromission (fɪ-dee-proh-**mish**-ən), *n.* [Latin "faith-promise"] (19c) *Roman law.* A contract of guaranty by stipulation. • Fidepromission was one of the three types of adpromission. See ADPROMISSION (1); STIPULATION (3). — **fidepromissor,** *n.*

fides (fɪ-deez). [Latin] Faith.

fides facta (fɪ-deez **fak**-tə). [Latin] (17c) *Hist.* Faith-making; faith-pledging. • Among the Franks and Lombards, certain transactions were guaranteed by symbolic, formal acts — making one's faith — such as the giving of a rod when property was transferred. See FESTUCA.

fiducia (fi-**d**[y]**oo**-shee-ə), *n.* [Latin "an entrusting"] *Roman law.* An early form of transfer of title by way of mortgage, deposit, etc., with a provision for reconveyance upon payment of the debt, termination of the deposit, etc. See WADSET (1).

"The Roman mortgage (*fiducia*) fell wholly out of use before the time of Justinian, having been displaced by the superior simplicity and convenience of the *hypotheca*; and in this respect modern Continental law has followed the Roman." John Salmond, *Jurisprudence* 443 (Glanville L. Williams ed., 10th ed. 1947).

fiducial, *adj.* (16c) Of, relating to, or characterized by confidence in and reliance on another person or thing <there must be a fiducial bond between a patient and a doctor>.

fiducial relationship. See *trust relationship* under RELATIONSHIP.

fiduciarius heres. See HERES.

fiduciarius tutor (fi-d[y]oo-shee-**air**-ee-əs **t**[y]**oo**-tər). *Roman law.* A fiduciary guardian; a person who by fulfilling a trust to free someone in power became his or her guardian.

fiduciary (fi-**d**[y]**oo**-shee-er-ee), *n.* (17c) **1.** Someone who is required to act for the benefit of another person on all matters within the scope of their relationship; one who owes to another the duties of good faith, loyalty, due care, and disclosure <the corporate officer is a fiduciary to the corporation>. **2.** Someone who must exercise a high standard of care in managing another's money or property <the beneficiary sued the fiduciary for investing in speculative securities>. — **fiduciary,** *adj.*

"'Fiduciary' is a vague term, and it has been pressed into service for a number of ends. . . . My view is that the term 'fiduciary' is so vague that plaintiffs have been able to claim that fiduciary obligations have been breached when in fact the particular defendant was not a fiduciary *stricto sensu* but simply had withheld property from the plaintiff in an unconscionable manner." D.W.M. Waters, *The Constructive Trust* 4 (1964).

▸ **dilatory fiduciary** (**dil**-ə-tor-ee). (1986) A trustee or other fiduciary who is unreasonably slow in administering an estate.

▸ **successor fiduciary.** (1929) A fiduciary who is appointed to succeed or replace a prior one.

▸ **temporary fiduciary.** (1967) An interim fiduciary appointed by the court until a regular fiduciary can be appointed.

fiduciary bond. See BOND (2).

fiduciary contract. (1837) *Hist.* An agreement by which one party delivers something to another on condition that the second party will return the thing to the first.

fiduciary debt. (1842) A debt founded on or arising from a fiduciary relationship, rather than from a solely contractual relationship.

fiduciary duty. See DUTY (2).

fiduciary heir. See HEIR.

fiduciary-out clause. (1987) *Mergers & acquisitions.* A merger-agreement provision that allows the target corporation to terminate the agreement without committing a breach if a specified condition occurs. • The most common condition is the receipt of a more favorable offer, but other conditions may also be specified.

fiduciary relationship. (1846) A relationship in which one person is under a duty to act for the benefit of another on matters within the scope of the relationship. • Fiduciary relationships — such as trustee–beneficiary, guardian–ward, principal–agent, and attorney–client — require an unusually high degree of care. Fiduciary relationships usu. arise in one of four situations: (1) when one person places trust in the faithful integrity of another, who as a result gains superiority or influence over the first, (2) when one person assumes control and responsibility over another, (3) when one person has a duty to act for or give advice to another on matters falling within the scope of the relationship, or (4) when there is a specific relationship that has traditionally been recognized as involving fiduciary duties, as with a lawyer and a client or a stockbroker and a customer. — Also termed *fiduciary relation*; *confidential relationship.* Cf. *special relationship* under RELATIONSHIP.

▸ **context-based fiduciary relationship.** A fiduciary relationship that arises from a factual context that indicates the placement of trust or confidence in another, vulnerability or dependence on another, substantial disparity in knowledge, and the ability to exert influence.

▸ **status-based fiduciary relationship.** (1992) A fiduciary relationship that is of a form generally accepted and prescribed, such as principal and agent, attorney and client, and trustee and beneficiary.

fiduciary-shield doctrine. (1978) *Corporations.* The principle that a corporate officer's act cannot be the basis for jurisdiction over the officer in an individual capacity.

fief (feef), *n.* **1.** See FEE. **2.** See FEUD. • Metaphorically, the term refers to an area of dominion, esp. in a corporate or governmental bureaucracy.

fief d'hauberk (**feef** doh-**bairk**). See *feudum militare* under FEUDUM.

fief d'haubert. See *feudum militare* under FEUDUM.

fiefdom. (1814) **1.** *Hist.* A small area ruled by a king or a lord. **2.** By extension, an area, organization, or part of an organization over which someone has complete control or significant power.

fief-tenant. *Hist.* The holder of a fief or fee; a feeholder or freeholder.

field audit. See AUDIT.

field book. (18c) A log or book containing a surveyor's notes that are made on-site and that describe by course and distance the running of the property lines and the establishment of the corners of a parcel of land.

Field Code. The New York Code of Procedure of 1848, which was the first comprehensive Anglo-American code of civil procedure and served as a model for the Federal Rules of Civil Procedure. • It was drafted by David Dudley Field (1805–1894), a major law-reformer. See *code pleading* under PLEADING (2).

field-interview form. (1975) A document that police fill out to document contact with an individual short of an arrest. — Also termed *field-interview card*; *field-interview notebook.*

field notes. (18c) The notes in a surveyor's field book.

field of invention. See CLASSIFICATION OF PATENTS (2).

field of search. See CLASSIFICATION OF PATENTS (2).

field-of-use restriction. (1971) *Intellectual property.* A license provision restricting the licensee's use of the licensed property to a defined product or service market or to a designated geographical area.

field sobriety test. See SOBRIETY TEST.

field stop. See STOP-AND-FRISK.

field-warehouse financing agreement. The loan agreement in a field-warehousing arrangement.

field warehousing. (1906) An inventory-financing method by which a merchant pledges its inventory, which is in the possession of a third person (a warehouser). • This is a method of financing an inventory that cannot economically be delivered to the creditor or third party. The borrower segregates part of the inventory and places it under the nominal control of a lender or third party, so that the lender has a possessory interest. Cf. *floor-plan financing* under FINANCING; PLEDGE.

> "Field warehousing is a way of bringing about the security relationship of a pledge. It is an arrangement for allowing the pledgor a more convenient access to the pledged goods, while the goods are actually in the custody and control of a third person on the pledgor's premises." *Business Factors, Inc. v. Taylor-Edwards Warehouse & Transfer Co.*, 585 P.2d 825, 828 (Wash. Ct. App. 1978).

> "Field warehousing is . . . an arrangement whereby a wholesaler, manufacturer, or merchant finances his business through the pledge of goods remaining on his premises. The arrangement is valid and effective where there is an actual delivery to the warehouseman by the bailor who has hired the warehouseman and given him exclusive possession of the warehouse goods." *In re Covington Grain Co.*, 638 F.2d 1362, 1365 (5th Cir. 1981).

fierding court (**fyər**-ding *or* **feer**-ding). (18c) *Hist.* An ancient court of inferior jurisdiction. • Four courts were in each district or hundred.

fieri (fɪ-ə-rɪ). [Latin] (17c) To be made; to be done. • *Fieri* usu. appears as part of the phrase *in fieri.* See IN FIERI.

fieri facias (fɪ-ə-rɪ **fay**-shee-əs). [Latin "that you cause to be done"] (15c) A writ of execution that directs a marshal or sheriff to seize and sell a judgment debtor's property to satisfy a money judgment; EXECUTION (4). — Abbr. *fi. fa.* (**fi** fay); *Fi. Fa.* — Also termed *execution writ*; *writ of execution.* Cf. LEVARI FACIAS.

> "It receives its name from the Latin words in the writ (*quod fieri facias de bonis et catallis*, that you cause to be made of the goods and chattels). It is the form of execution in common use in levying upon the judgment-debtor's personal property." John Bouvier, *Bouvier's Law Dictionary* (Francis Rawle ed., 8th ed. 1914).

"The writ of 'fieri facias' (commonly called a writ of 'fi fa'), which commanded literally 'that you cause to be made,' was an early common-law means of enforcing payment on a judgment; it was, in effect, an order to the sheriff of the court to enforce a judgment against the debtor by levy, seizure, and sale of his personalty to the extent needed to satisfy a judgment." 30 Am. Jur. 2d *Executions and Enforcement of Judgments* § 14, at 50–51 (1994).

▸ ***fieri facias de bonis ecclesiasticis*** (**fi**-ə-rɪ **fay**-shee-əs dee **boh**-nis e-klee-z[h]ee-**as**-tə-sis). [Latin "that you cause to be made of the ecclesiastical goods"] (1827) *Hist.* A writ of execution — used when the defendant was a beneficed clerk who had no lay fee — that commanded the bishop to satisfy the judgment from the ecclesiastical goods and chattels of the defendant within the diocese. • This was accomplished by issuing a sequestration to levy the debt out of the defendant's benefice. This writ was issued after a *fieri facias* had been returned *nulla bona*.

▸ ***fieri facias de bonis propriis*** (**fi**-ə-rɪ **fay**-shee-əs dee **boh**-nis **proh**-pree-is). [Latin "that you cause to be made of his own goods"] (17c) *Hist.* A writ that executes on an executor's property when a writ *fieri facias de bonis testatoris* is returned by the sheriff *nulla bona* or *devastavit* (a wasting of the testator's goods by the executor).

▸ ***fieri facias de bonis testatoris*** (**fi**-ə-rɪ **fay**-shee-əs dee **boh**-nis tes-tə-**tor**-is). [Latin "that you cause to be made of the testator's goods"] (17c) *Hist.* A writ of execution served on an executor for a debt incurred by the testator.

fieri feci (**fi**-ə-rɪ **fee**-sɪ). [Latin "I have caused to be made"] (17c) *Hist.* A sheriff's return on a *fieri facias* for which the sheriff has collected, in whole or in part, the sum to be levied on. • The return is usu. expressed by the word "satisfied."

FIF. *abbr.* Foreign-investment fund.

fi. fa. (*sometimes cap.*) *abbr.* FIERI FACIAS.

FIFO (**fi**-foh). *abbr.* (1945) FIRST-IN, FIRST-OUT.

FIFRA. *abbr.* Federal Insecticide, Fungicide, and Rodenticide Act. 7 USCA §§ 136–136y.

fifteenth. (14c) *Hist.* A tax of one-fifteenth of all the personal property of every subject. • The tax was levied at intervals by act of Parliament. Under Edward III, the value of the fifteenth was assessed and fixed at a specific sum and did not increase as the wealth of the kingdom increased — thus the tax ceased to actually be one-fifteenth. See QUOD PERSONA NEC PREBENDARII.

Fifteenth Amendment. The constitutional amendment, ratified in 1870, guaranteeing all citizens the right to vote regardless of race, color, or prior condition of servitude.

Fifth Amendment. The constitutional amendment, ratified with the Bill of Rights in 1791, providing that a person cannot be (1) required to answer for a capital or otherwise infamous offense unless a grand jury issues an indictment or presentment, (2) subjected to double jeopardy, (3) compelled to engage in self-incrimination on a criminal matter, (4) deprived of life, liberty, or property without due process of law, or (5) deprived of private property for public use without just compensation.

Fifth Amendment, pleading the. See TAKE THE FIFTH.

Fifty Decisions. Justinian's rulings that settled controversies and eliminated obsolete rules in the law. • The decisions were made in preparation for *Justinian's Digest.* — Also termed (in Latin) *Quinquaginta Decisiones.*

50 percent plus one. See HALF PLUS ONE.

50-percent rule. (1975) The principle that liability for negligence is apportioned in accordance with the percentage of fault that the fact-finder assigns to each party, that the plaintiff's recovery will be reduced by the percentage of negligence assigned to the plaintiff, and that the plaintiff's recovery is barred if the plaintiff's percentage of fault is 50% or more. — Also termed *modified-comparative-negligence doctrine; hybrid-comparative-negligence doctrine.* See *comparative negligence* under NEGLIGENCE; APPORTIONMENT OF LIABILITY. Cf. PURE-COMPARATIVE-NEGLIGENCE DOCTRINE.

fighting age. See AGE.

fighting democracy. See *militant democracy* under DEMOCRACY.

fighting words. (1917) **1.** Inflammatory speech that might not be protected by the First Amendment's free-speech guarantee because it might incite a violent response. **2.** Inflammatory speech that is pleadable in mitigation — but not in defense — of a suit for assault. — Also termed *fighting talk.*

fightwite (**fɪt**-wɪt). (bef. 12c) *Hist.* A fine imposed against one who participated in a breach of the peace.

filacer (**fil**-ə-sər). (15c) *Hist.* An officer of the Westminster superior courts who filed the writs on which process was made. • The office was abolished in 1837. — Also spelled *filazer.*

filacium. See FILUM.

filare (fi-**lair**-ee), *vb.* [Law Latin] *Hist.* To file.

filazer. See FILACER.

file, *n.* (17c) **1.** A court's complete and official record of a case <the associate went to the courthouse to verify that the motion is in the file>. **2.** A lawyer's complete record of a case <the paralegal stored the file in three drawers in her office>. **3.** A portion or section of a lawyer's case record <the janitor found the correspondence file behind the copy machine>. **4.** A case <Jonah was assigned the Watson file after Amy left the firm>.

file, *vb.* (16c) **1.** To deliver a legal document to the court clerk or record custodian for placement into the official record <Tuesday is the deadline for filing a reply brief>. • A document not suitable for filing will normally be stamped "lodged" and placed in the court file but not included in the record on appeal. — Also termed (BrE) *lodge.* **2.** To commence a lawsuit <the seller threatened to file against the buyer>. **3.** To record or deposit something in an organized retention system or container for preservation and future reference <please file my notes under the heading "research">. **4.** *Parliamentary law.* To acknowledge and deposit (a report, communication, or other document) for information and reference only without necessarily taking any substantive action.

filed-rate doctrine. (1928) A common-law rule forbidding a regulated entity, usu. a common carrier, to charge a rate other than the one on file with the appropriate federal regulatory authority, such as (formerly) the Interstate Commerce Commission. — Also termed *filed-tariff doctrine.* See TARIFF (2).

file history. See FILE WRAPPER.

file-transport protocol. (1989) A set of programmed rules enabling computers to exchange files over the Internet. — Abbr. FTP.

file wrapper. (1867) *Patents & Trademarks.* The complete record of proceedings in the Patent and Trademark Office from the initial application to the issued patent or trademark; specif., a patent or trademark-registration application together with all documentation, correspondence, and any other record of proceedings before the PTO concerning that application. — Also termed *file history; prosecution history.* Cf. CERTIFIED FILE HISTORY.

file-wrapper continuation. 1. See CONTINUATION. **2.** See CONTINUATION-IN-PART. — Abbr. FWC.

file-wrapper continuation application. 1. See CONTINUATION. **2.** See CONTINUATION-IN-PART.

file-wrapper estoppel. See *prosecution-history estoppel* under ESTOPPEL.

filia (**fil**-ee-ə), *n.* [Latin] A daughter. Pl. ***filiae.***

filial consortium. See CONSORTIUM (1).

filiality. See FILIATION (1).

filiated father. See FATHER.

filiation (fil-ee-**ay**-shən). (15c) **1.** The fact or condition of being a son or daughter; relationship of a child to a parent. • Despite Bentham's protest (see below), *filiation* is usual in this sense. — Also termed *filiality.*

> "In English we have no word that will serve to express with propriety the person who bears the relation opposed to that of parent. The word *child* is ambiguous, being employed in another sense, perhaps more frequently than in this: more frequently in opposition to *a person of full age*, an *adult*, than in correlation to a *parent*. For the condition itself we have no other word than filiation: an ill-contrived term, not analogous to *paternity* and *maternity*: the proper term would have been *filiality*: the word filiation is as frequently, perhaps, and more consistently, put for the act of establishing a person in the possession of the condition of filiality." Jeremy Bentham, *An Introduction to the Principles of Morals and Legislation* 276 n.2 (1823).

2. Judicial determination of paternity. See PATERNITY; *filiated father* under FATHER.

filiation order. See ORDER (2).

filibuster (**fil**-ə-bəs-tər), *n.* (18c) **1.** A dilatory tactic, esp. prolonged and often irrelevant speechmaking, employed in an attempt to obstruct legislative action. • The filibuster is common in the U.S. Senate, where the right to debate is usu. unlimited and where a filibuster can be terminated only by a cloture vote of two-thirds of all members. **2.** In a deliberative body, a member in the minority who resorts to obstructive tactics to prevent the adoption of a measure or procedure that is favored by the majority. — Also termed *filibusterer.* **3.** *Hist.* Someone who, together with others, works to invade and revolutionize a foreign state in disregard of international law. See CLOTURE.

filibuster, *vb.* (1853) **1.** To try to prevent or delay action in a legislature by protracted speechmaking. **2.** By extension, to use long-windedness as a delay tactic.

filicide (**fil**-i-sɪd). (17c) **1.** Someone who kills his or her own child. **2.** The act of killing one's own child. Cf. INFANTICIDE.

filing, *n.* (18c) A particular document (such as a pleading) in the file of a court clerk or record custodian <the lawyer argued that the plaintiff's most recent filing was not germane to the issue before the court>.

filing date. See DATE.

filing fee. (1864) A sum of money required to be paid to the court clerk before a proceeding can start.

filing status. (1968) *Tax.* One of the four categories under which a person files an income tax return. • Under federal law, the four categories are (1) single; (2) head of household; (3) married filing a joint return; and (4) married filing separate returns.

filiolus (fil-ee-**oh**-ləs). [Latin] *Hist.* A godson. — Also spelled (in old records) *filious.*

filius (**fil**-ee-əs), *n.* [Latin] **1.** A son. **2.** (*pl.*) Descendants. Pl. ***filii.*** Cf. HERES.

filiusfamilias (**fil**-ee-əs-fə-**mil**-ee-as), *n.* [Latin "the son of a family"] (18c) *Roman law.* An unemancipated son or daughter, grandson or granddaughter. — Also termed *homo alieni juris.*

> "Every Roman citizen is either a paterfamilias or a filiusfamilias, according as he is free from paternal power (homo sui juris) or not (homo alieni juris). Paterfamilias is the generic name for a homo sui juris, whether child or adult, married or unmarried. Filiusfamilias is the generic name for a homo alieni juris, whether son or daughter, grandson or granddaughter, and so on." Rudolph Sohm, *The Institutes: A Textbook of the History and System of Roman Private Law* 177 (James Crawford Ledlie trans., 3d ed. 1907).

filius mulieratus (**fil**-ee-əs myoo-lee-ə-**ray**-təs). [Law Latin] (17c) *Hist.* The eldest legitimate son of a woman who previously had an illegitimate son by the same father; a legitimate son whose older brother is illegitimate; MULIER PUISNE. Cf. *bastard eigne* under EIGNE.

filius nullius (**fil**-ee-əs nə-**lɪ**-əs). [Latin "son of nobody"] (17c) *Hist.* An illegitimate child. — Also termed *filius populi.*

> "I proceed next to the rights and incapacities which appertain to a bastard. The rights are very few, being only such as he can *acquire*; for he can *inherit* nothing, being looked upon as the son of nobody; and sometimes called *filius nullius*, sometimes *filius populi*." 1 William Blackstone, *Commentaries on the Laws of England* 447 (1765).

filius populi. See FILIUS NULLIUS.

fill, *n.* (1850) Dirt, sand, rock, or similar material dumped into wetlands, a ravine, or some other depression in the earth.

filla (**fil**-ə). *Hist.* The ribbon from which a seal hangs at the bottom of deeds and other legal documents.

fill a blank. (1897) *Parliamentary law.* To replace a blank in a motion by choosing among proposals from the floor. See BLANK (2); AMENDMENT (3).

fill-or-kill order. See ORDER (8).

filum (**fɪ**-ləm). [Latin "thread"] *Hist.* **1.** A thread or wire that holds (esp. legal) papers together to form a file. • This was the ancient method of filing legal papers. **2.** An imaginary thread or line passing through the middle of a stream or road. — Also termed (in sense 1) *filacium.*

▸ ***filum aquae*** (**fɪ**-ləm **ay**-kwee). [Latin "thread of water"] (18c) A line of water; the middle line of a stream of water, supposedly dividing it into two equal parts and usu. constituting the boundary between the riparian owners on each side. — Also termed *medium filum.*

▸ *filum forestae* (fɪ-ləm **for**-ə-stee). [Latin] The border of a forest.

▸ *filum viae* (fɪ-ləm **vɪ**-ee). [Latin] (1934) **1.** The middle line of a road. **2.** The boundary between landowners on each side of a road.

finable (fɪ-nə-bəl), *adj.* (15c) Liable to a fine; subject to having to pay a fine. — Also spelled *fineable.*

final, *adj.* (14c) **1.** (Of a judgment at law) not requiring any further judicial action by the court that rendered judgment to determine the matter litigated; concluded. **2.** (Of an equitable decree) not requiring any further judicial action beyond supervising how the decree is carried out. • Once an order, judgment, or decree is final, it may be appealed on the merits. Cf. INTERLOCUTORY.

▸ **final and conclusive.** Terminal and unappealable, except on grounds of procedural error, fraud, or mistake.

final agenda. See AGENDA.

final alimony. See *permanent alimony* under ALIMONY (1).

final and conclusive. See FINAL.

final appealable judgment. See *final judgment* under JUDGMENT (2).

final appealable order. See *final judgment* under JUDGMENT (2).

final argument. See CLOSING ARGUMENT.

final concord. See CONCORD.

final decision. See *final judgment* under JUDGMENT (2).

final-decision rule. See FINAL-JUDGMENT RULE.

final decree. See *final judgment* under JUDGMENT (2).

final dividend. See DIVIDEND.

final injunction. See *permanent injunction* under INJUNCTION.

finalis concordia (fi-**nay**-lis kən-**kor**-dee-ə). [Latin] (17c) A final or conclusive agreement. See *final concord* under CONCORD; FINE (1).

finality. The quality of being complete and unchangeable.

finality doctrine. (1942) The rule that a court will not judicially review an administrative agency's action until it is final. — Also termed *final-order doctrine*; *doctrine of finality*; *principle of finality*; *final-order rule.* Cf. FINAL-JUDGMENT RULE; INTERLOCUTORY APPEALS ACT.

finality rule. See FINAL-JUDGMENT RULE.

final judgment. See JUDGMENT (2).

final-judgment rule. (1931) The principle that a party may appeal only from a district court's final decision that ends the litigation on the merits. • Under this rule, a party must raise all claims of error in a single appeal. — Also termed *final-decision rule*; *finality rule.* 28 USCA § 1291. Cf. FINALITY DOCTRINE; INTERLOCUTORY APPEALS ACT; DEATH-KNELL DOCTRINE.

final-offer arbitration. See ARBITRATION.

final office action. See OFFICE ACTION.

final order. See ORDER (2).

final-order doctrine. See FINALITY DOCTRINE.

final-order rule. See FINALITY DOCTRINE.

final peace. See *final concord* under CONCORD.

final process. See PROCESS (2).

final receiver's receipt. (1875) The government's acknowledgment that it has received full payment from a person for public land, that it holds the legal title in trust for the person, and that it will in due course issue the person a land patent.

final rejection. See REJECTION.

final settlement. See SETTLEMENT (2).

final speech. See CLOSING ARGUMENT.

final submission. See CLOSING ARGUMENT.

finance, *n.* (18c) **1.** That aspect of business concerned with the management of money, credit, banking, and investments <after a brief career in finance, Andrea decided to go to law school>. **2.** The science or study of the management of money, etc. <Bill sought a degree in finance because he wanted to be an investment banker>.

finance, *vb.* (19c) To raise or provide funds.

finance bill. See BILL (6).

finance charge. (1922) An additional payment, usu. in the form of interest, paid by a retail buyer for the privilege of purchasing goods or services in installments. • This phrase is increasingly used as a euphemism for *interest.* See INTEREST (3).

finance company. (20c) A nonbank company that deals in loans either by making them or by purchasing notes from another company that makes the loans directly to borrowers.

▸ **commercial finance company.** (1948) A finance company that makes loans to manufacturers and wholesalers. — Also termed *commercial credit company.*

▸ **consumer finance company.** (1951) A finance company that deals directly with consumers in extending credit. — Also termed *small-loan company.*

▸ **sales finance company.** (1935) A finance company that does not deal directly with consumers but instead purchases consumer installment paper arising from the sale of consumer durables "on time." — Also termed *acceptance company.*

finance lease. See LEASE.

finance officer. See TREASURER.

financial ability. See ABILITY.

financial accounting. See ACCOUNTING (1).

Financial Accounting Standards Board. The independent body of accountants responsible for establishing, interpreting, and improving standards for financial accounting and reporting. — Abbr. FASB. Cf. GOVERNMENTAL ACCOUNTING STANDARDS BOARD.

financial advantage. See ADVANTAGE.

financial asset. See *current asset* under ASSET.

financial assistance. Any economic benefit, such as a scholarship or stipend, given by one person or entity to another.

▸ **federal financial assistance.** (1928) An economic benefit provided by the federal government to a recipient in the form of a trust, grant, or other federal program or activity. *See U.S. Dep't of Transp. v. Paralyzed Veterans of Am.*, 477 U.S. 597, 607, 106 S.Ct. 2705, 2712 (1986).

financial contract. See CONTRACT.

financial-core membership. (1970) Union membership in which a private-company employee pays the union's initiation fees and periodic dues but is not a full union member. • Financial-core membership is allowed only in states without a right-to-work law, where a union-security contract clause can require employees to pay financial-core membership dues but cannot require full union membership. The dues are limited to the amount required to support the union's representational activities, such as collective bargaining. *See Communications Workers of Am. v. Beck*, 487 U.S. 735, 744, 108 S.Ct. 2641, 2648 (1988). — Also termed (in public-employment sector) *fair-share membership*; *agency-shop membership*. See UNION-SECURITY CLAUSE.

Financial Crimes Enforcement Network. A unit in the U.S. Department of the Treasury responsible for supporting law-enforcement efforts against domestic and international financial crimes. — Abbr. FinCEN.

financial deregulation. See DEREGULATION.

financial futures. See FUTURES (1).

Financial Industry Regulatory Authority. An independent organization authorized by Congress to enforce the organization's rules governing securities broker-dealers. • For example, the Authority requires broker-dealers to be familiar with an investor's financial situation, needs, and investment objectives, and to use that knowledge fairly and honestly to recommend suitable investments. — Abbr. FINRA.

financial institution. (1821) A business, organization, or other entity that manages money, credit, or capital, such as a bank, credit union, savings-and-loan association, securities broker or dealer, pawnbroker, or investment company.

financial interest. See INTEREST (2).

financial intermediary. (1873) A financial entity — usu. a commercial bank — that advances the transfer of funds between borrowers and lenders, buyers and sellers, and investors and savers.

Financial Management Service. A unit in the U.S. Department of the Treasury responsible for developing and managing systems for moving the U.S. government's cash by assisting other agencies in collecting and disbursing funds; collecting and publishing financial information; and collecting delinquent debts. • The FMS has the power to engage agents to carry out payment and collection functions. — Abbr. FMS.

financial market. See MARKET.

financial planner. (1945) A person whose business is advising clients about personal finances and investments. • Upon completing a certification program, such a person is called a *certified financial planner*. — Abbr. CFP.

Financial Privacy Rule. A provision within the Gramm–Leach–Bliley Act requiring financial institutions to provide each consumer with a privacy notice as soon as the consumer relationship is established and annually afterward. • The privacy notice must explain what information is collected about the consumer, where the information is shared, how it is used and protected, and how the consumer can opt out of the information being shared with unaffiliated parties. 15 USCA §§ 6801–6809.

financial report. 1. See FINANCIAL STATEMENT. **2.** See ANNUAL REPORT.

financial-responsibility act. (1930) A state statute conditioning license and registration of motor vehicles on proof of insurance or other financial accountability.

financial-responsibility clause. (1946) *Insurance.* A provision in an automobile insurance policy stating that the insured has at least the minimum amount of liability insurance coverage required by a state's financial-responsibility law.

financial restatement. (2002) A report correcting material errors in a financial statement, esp. to adjust profits and losses after an accounting procedure has been disallowed.

financials. *Slang.* Financial statements.

financial secretary. 1. See SECRETARY (3). **2.** See TREASURER.

Financial Services Agency. The regulatory body that oversees the United Kingdom's financial-services industry, including exchanges and related entities. — Formerly termed *Securities and Investment Board.*

Financial Services Modernization Act of 1999. See GRAMM–LEACH–BLILEY ACT.

financial statement. (18c) **1.** A balance sheet, income statement, or annual report that summarizes an individual's or organization's financial condition on a specified date or for a specified period by reporting assets and liabilities. — Also termed *financial report.* Cf. FINANCING STATEMENT.

▸ **certified financial statement.** (1930) A financial statement examined and reported by an independent public or certified public accountant. SEC Rule 12b-2 (17 CFR § 240.12b-2).

▸ **consolidated financial statement.** (1903) The financial report of a company and all its subsidiaries combined as if they were a single entity.

▸ **normalized financial statement.** (2000) A statement in which some components have been adjusted to exclude anomalies, such as unusual and nonrecurring elements, and nonoperating assets or liabilities, so the statement may be compared with others.

2. INCOME-AND-EXPENSE DECLARATION.

financial year. See *fiscal year* under YEAR.

financier. A person who lends a large amount of money to a business or other entity for a project or activity.

financing, *n.* (19c) **1.** The act or process of raising or providing funds. **2.** Funds that are raised or provided. — **finance,** *vb.*

▸ **asset-based financing.** (1985) A method of lending in which lenders and investors look primarily to the cash flow from a particular asset for repayment.

▸ **construction financing.** See *interim financing.*

▸ **debt financing.** (1927) The raising of funds by issuing bonds or notes or by borrowing from a financial institution.

▸ **equity financing.** (1925) **1.** The raising of funds by issuing capital securities (shares in the business) rather than making loans or selling bonds. **2.** The capital so raised.

▸ **floor-plan financing.** (1926) A loan that is secured by merchandise and paid off as the goods are sold. • Usu.

such a loan is given by a manufacturer to a retailer or other dealer (as a car dealer). — Also termed *floor planning.* Cf. FIELD WAREHOUSING.

▸ **gap financing.** (1989) Interim financing used to fund the difference between a current loan and a loan to be received in the future, esp. between two long-term loans. See *bridge loan* under LOAN.

▸ **interim financing.** (1918) A short-term loan secured to cover certain major expenditures, such as construction costs, until permanent financing is obtained. — Also termed *construction financing.*

▸ **internal financing.** (1922) A funding method using funds generated through the company's operations rather than from stock issues or bank loans.

▸ **link financing.** (1991) The obtaining of credit by depositing funds in another's bank account to aid the other in obtaining a loan.

▸ **outside financing.** (1915) The raising of funds by selling stocks (equity financing) or bonds (debt financing).

▸ **permanent financing.** (1907) A long-term loan obtained to repay an interim loan, such as a mortgage loan that is used to repay a construction loan.

▸ **project financing.** (1948) A method of funding in which the lender looks primarily to the money generated by a single project as security for the loan. • This type of financing is usu. used for large, complex, and expensive single-purpose projects such as power plants, chemical-processing plants, mines, and toll roads. The lender is usu. paid solely or primarily from the money generated by the contracts for the facility's output (sometimes paid by customers directly into an account maintained by the lender), such as the electricity sold by a power plant. The lender usu. requires the facility to be developed and owned by a special-purpose entity (sometimes called a bankruptcy-remote entity), which can be a corporation, limited partnership, or other legal entity, that is permitted to perform no function other than developing, owning, and operating the facility. See SINGLE-PURPOSE PROJECT; SPECIAL-PURPOSE ENTITY; BANKRUPTCY-REMOTE ENTITY.

financing agency. See AGENCY (1).

financing fee. See FEE (1).

financing instrument. See *investment instrument* under INSTRUMENT.

financing statement. (1954) A document filed in the public records to notify third parties, usu. prospective buyers and lenders, of a secured party's security interest in goods or real property. *See* UCC § 9-102(a)(39). Cf. FINANCIAL STATEMENT.

FinCEN. *abbr.* FINANCIAL CRIMES ENFORCEMENT NETWORK.

find, *vb.* (bef. 12c) To determine a fact in dispute by verdict or decision <find guilty> <found that no duty existed>. Cf. HOLD, *vb.* (2).

finder. (13c) **1.** An intermediary who brings together parties for a business opportunity, such as two companies for a merger, a borrower and a financial institution, an issuer and an underwriter of securities, or a seller and a buyer of real estate. • A finder differs from a broker-dealer because the finder merely brings two parties together to make their own contract, while a broker-dealer usu. participates in the negotiations. See INTERMEDIARY. **2.** Someone who discovers an object, often a lost or mislaid chattel.

finder of fact. See FACT-FINDER.

finder's fee. (1937) **1.** The amount charged by one who brings together parties for a business opportunity. **2.** The amount charged by a person who locates a lost or missing item and returns it to its owner. — Also termed *finder's commission, finder's agreement.*

finder's-fee contract. (1959) An agreement between a finder and one of the parties to a business opportunity.

finding. See FINDING OF FACT.

finding of fact. (18c) A determination by a judge, jury, or administrative agency of a fact supported by the evidence in the record, usu. presented at the trial or hearing <he agreed with the jury's finding of fact that the driver did not stop before proceeding into the intersection>. — Often shortened to *finding.* See FACT-FINDER. Cf. CONCLUSION OF FACT; CONCLUSION OF LAW.

▸ **concurrent finding.** (*usu. pl.*) (1894) Identical factual findings by two different tribunals on a specific issue of fact.

▸ **essential finding.** (1902) *Military law.* A military tribunal's determination of a collateral pretrial motion.

▸ **general finding.** (1829) An undifferentiated finding in favor of one party.

▸ **special finding.** (17c) **1.** (*usu. pl.*) A finding of the necessary and ultimate facts to support a judgment in favor of one party. **2.** *Military law.* A military tribunal's finding that directly relates to the determination of guilt or innocence.

finding of no significant impact. *Environmental law.* A document stating the reasons why an action will not significantly affect the quality of the human environment. • The reasons must be supported by an environmental assessment. — Abbr. FONSI. See ENVIRONMENTAL ASSESSMENT.

fine, *n.* (13c) **1.** An amicable final agreement or compromise of a fictitious or actual suit to determine the true possessor of land. • The fine was formerly used as a form of conveyance to disentail an estate. — Also termed *final concord; finalis concordia.* See FOOT OF THE FINE.

> "A peculiar and persistent use of the writ [of covenant] was in levying a fine. A fine — *finalis concordia* — was the compromise of a suit, settled upon terms approved by the court. The dispute, while it might be a reality, was more often fictitious, and was chiefly used as a means of conveying land. . . . Soon after [Glanvill's] book was written, an innovation was made in the procedure which endured until 1833. The terms of the compromise, agreed by the parties and approved by the judges, were entered upon a threefold indenture, one of the parts being given to each of the litigants and the third — the 'foot' or bottom of the document — being kept among the records of the court. The parties thus obtained incontestable evidence and abundant security, and either could sue the other if the agreement were not implemented." C.H.S. Fifoot, *History and Sources of the Common Law: Tort and Contract* 256 (1949).

> "Unlike the recovery, which was a *real* action, the fine was a compromised fictitious *personal* action, originally designed as a method of ensuring security in conveyancing and only later being employed for the purpose of barring estates tail. In outline, it operated in the following manner. The intending purchaser brought an action, begun by writ

of covenant, against the intending vendor. The parties then applied to the court to compromise the action; by the terms of the compromise (*finis*) the intending vendor admitted that the land belonged to the intending purchaser because he had given it to him, and the terms of the compromise were recorded in the court records. The fine owed its popularity as a means of conveyancing to two factors, neither of which was present in the standard method of conveyance by means of feoffment. First, the enrolling in the court records provided evidence of the transaction which was both permanent and free from the danger of forgery. Secondly, the effect of the fine was to set running a short period of limitation at the expiration of which all claims to the land were barred. It was this second aspect which made the device attractive as a means of 'barring' fees tail." Peter Butt, *Land Law* 102–03 (2d ed. 1988).

▸ **executed fine.** *Hist.* A fine made on acknowledgment of the right of the grantee to land given to him as a gift from the grantor. • This was abolished in England in 1833. 3 & 4 Will. 4, ch. 74.

2. FINE FOR ALIENATION. **3.** A fee paid by a tenant to the landlord at the commencement of the tenancy to reduce the rent payments. **4.** *Hist.* A money payment from a tenant to the tenant's lord.

▸ **common fine.** (16c) A sum of money due from a tenant to a lord to defray the cost of a court leet or to allow the litigants to try the action closer to home. — Also termed *head-silver.*

5. A pecuniary criminal punishment or civil penalty payable to the public treasury. — **fine,** *vb.*

"This word is ambiguously taken in our law; for sometimes it is taken for a sum of money or mulct imposed or laid upon an offender for some offence done, and then it is also called a ransom. And sometimes it is taken for an income, or a sum of money paid at the entrance of a tenant into his land: [sometimes as a sum paid for the renewal of a lease, and denominated a fine for renewal:] and sometimes it is taken for a final agreement or conveyance upon record, for settling and securing of lands and tenements." 1 Edward Hilliard, *Sheppard's Touchstone of Common Assurances* 2B (Richard Preston ed., 7th ed. 1820) (brackets in original).

▸ **day fine.** A fine payable over time, usu. as a percentage of the defendant's earnings on a weekly or monthly basis.

▸ **excessive fine.** (16c) **1.** *Criminal law.* A fine that is unreasonably high and disproportionate to the offense committed. • The Eighth Amendment proscribes excessive fines. An example of an excessive fine is a civil forfeiture in which the property was not an instrumentality of the crime and the worth of the property was not proportional to the owner's culpability. **2.** A fine or penalty that seriously impairs one's earning capacity, esp. from a business.

▸ **fresh fine.** (1832) *Hist.* A fine levied within the past year.

fineable. See FINABLE.

Fine and Recovery Act. *Hist.* An 1833 English statute that abolished the use of fines as a method of conveying title to land. 3 & 4 Will. 4, ch. 74. See FINE (1).

fine annullando levato de tenemento quod fuit de antiquo dominico (fɪ-nee a-nə-**lan**-doh lə-**vay**-to dee ten-ə-**men**-toh kwod **fyoo**-it dee an-**tɪ**-kwoh də-**min**-ə-koh). [Latin "a fine to be annulled levied from a tenement which was of ancient demesne"] *Hist.* A writ for disannulling a conveyance of land in ancient demesne to the lord's prejudice.

fine capiendo pro terris (fɪ-nee kap-ee-**en**-doh proh **ter**-is). [Latin "a fine to be taken for lands"] (17c) *Hist.* A writ that an imprisoned felon could use in some circumstances to obtain release from jail and to recover lands and goods taken during imprisonment.

fine for alienation. (17c) *Hist.* A fee paid by a tenant to the lord upon the alienation of a feudal estate and substitution of a new tenant. • It was payable by all tenants holding by knight's service or tenants *in capite* by socage tenure. — Often shortened to *fine.*

fine for endowment. *Hist.* A fee paid by a widow of a tenant to the tenant's lord. • If not paid, the widow could not be endowed of her husband's land.

finem facere (fɪ-nəm **fay**-sə-ree). [Latin] *Hist.* **1.** To make a composition or compromise; to relinquish a claim in exchange for consideration.

"In the thirteenth century the king's justices wield a wide and a 'common law' power of ordering that an offender be kept in custody. They have an equally wide power of discharging him upon his 'making fine with the king.' We must observe the language of the time. In strictness they have no power to 'impose a fine.' No tribunal of this period, unless we are mistaken, is ever said to impose a fine. To order the offender to pay so much money to the king — this the judge may not do. If he did it, he would be breaking or evading the Great Charter, for an amercement should be affeered, not by royal justices, but by neighbours of the wrong-doer. What the judges can do is this: — they can pronounce a sentence of imprisonment and then allow the culprit to 'make fine,' that is to make an end (*finem facere*) of the matter by paying or finding security for a certain sum of money. In theory the fine is a bilateral transaction, a bargain; it is not 'imposed,' it is 'made.'" 2 Frederick Pollock & Frederic W. Maitland, *The History of English Law Before the Time of Edward I* 517 (2d ed. 1899).

2. To make a settlement of a penalty. • Magna Carta (ch. 55) specifically limited "[a]ll fines which were made with us unjustly and contrary to the law of the land . . ." (*Omnes fines qui injuste et contra legem terrae facti sunt nobiscum*).

fine non capiendo pro pulchre placitando (fɪ-nee non kap-ee-**en**-doh proh **pəl**-kree plas-ə-**tan**-doh). [Latin "a fine not to be taken for pleading fairly"] (17c) *Hist.* A writ prohibiting court officers from taking fines for fair pleading (i.e., *beaupleader*).

fine print. (1951) The part of an agreement or document — usu. in small, light print that is not easily noticeable — referring to disclaimers, restrictions, or limitations.

fine pro redisseisina capiendo (fɪ-nee proh re-dis-**see**-zin-ə kap-ee-**en**-doh). [Law Latin "a fine to be taken for again disseising"] (17c) *Hist.* A writ that entitled a person imprisoned for twice dispossessing someone (*redisseisin*) to release upon payment of a reasonable fine.

fines le roy (**fɪnz** lə **roy**). [Law French] *Hist.* The king's fines. • A fine or fee that was paid to the monarch for an offense or contempt.

fine sur cognizance de droit, comme ceo que il ad de son done (fɪn sər **kon**-ə-zənts də **droyt**, kom **say**-oh kweel **ad** də **sawn dawn**). [Law French "a fine upon acknowledgment of the right, as that which he has of his gift"] *Hist.* The most common fine of conveyance, by which the defendant (also called the *deforciant*) acknowledged in court that he had already conveyed the property to the cognizee. • This form of conveyance took the place of an actual livery of seisin. See FINE (1).

"But, in general, the first species of fine, '*sur cognizance de droit come ceo, etc.*,' is the most used, as it conveys a clean and absolute freehold, and gives the cognizee a seisin in law, without an actual livery; and is therefore called a fine executed, whereas the others are but executory." 2 William Blackstone, *Commentaries on the Laws of England* 353 (1766).

fine sur cognizance de droit tantum (**fIn** sər **kon**-ə-zənts də **droyt tan**-təm). [Law French "fine upon acknowledgment of the right merely"] *Hist.* A fine of conveyance that does not acknowledge a prior conveyance of land. • This type of fine was used to convey reversionary interests — that is, interests that did not require acknowledgment of an earlier livery of seisin. See FINE (1).

fine sur concessit (**fIn** sər kən-**ses**-it). [Law French] *Hist.* A species of conveyance in which the cognizor does not acknowledge the cognizee's preceding right in land but grants the cognizee an estate de novo, usu. for life or a term of years, by way of supposed composition. See FINE (1).

fine sur done, grant et render (**fIn** sər **dawn**, **grant** ay **ren**-dər). [Law French "fine upon gift, grant and render"] *Hist.* A double conveyance, consisting of a *fine sur cognizance de droit come ceo que il ad de son done* and a *fine sur concessit,* used to convey particular limitations of estates. • For example, after acknowledgment of the cognizee's right in the land, the cognizee would grant back to the cognizor or a third party some other estate in the land. See FINE (1).

finger, *vb.* (1930) *Slang.* To identify (a person) as a perpetrator, usu. of a crime <in his grand-jury testimony, Vinson fingered Bauer as the gunman>.

finger pillory. See PILLORY.

fingerprint, *n.* (1859) **1.** The distinctive pattern of lines on a human fingertip <no two fingerprints are identical>. **2.** The impression of a fingertip made on any surface <the detective found several fingerprints on the knife>. **3.** An ink impression of the pattern of lines on a fingertip, usu. taken during the booking procedure after an arrest <after Dick had his fingerprints taken, he was put in the drunk tank>. — Also termed *print; thumbprint.* Cf. DNA IDENTIFICATION. — **fingerprint,** *vb.* — **fingerprinting,** *n.*

fingerprint claim. See PATENT CLAIM.

finire (fi-**nI**-ree), *vb.* [Law Latin] *Hist.* **1.** To fine; to pay a fine. **2.** To end or finish a matter.

finis (**fI**-nis *or* **fin**-is). [Latin] (15c) *Hist.* **1.** Boundary or limit. **2.** The compromise of a fine of conveyance. See FINE (1).

> "The parties then applied to the court to compromise the action; by the terms of the compromise (*finis*) the intending vendor admitted that the land belonged to the intending purchaser because he had given it to him, and the terms of the compromise were recorded in the court records." Peter Butt, *Land Law* 102 (2d ed. 1988).

3. A fine, or payment of money made to satisfy a claim of criminal penalty.

finished goods. See GOODS.

finitio (fi-**nish**-ee-oh). [Law Latin] *Hist.* An ending; death.

finium regundorum actio (**fI**-nee-əm ri-gən-**dor**-əm **ak**-shee-oh). [Latin "action for regulating boundaries"] (17c) *Roman law.* An action for settling a boundary dispute.

FINRA. *abbr.* FINANCIAL INDUSTRY REGULATORY AUTHORITY.

FIO. *abbr.* Free in and out. • This bill-of-lading term means that the shipper supervises and pays for loading and unloading of cargo.

FIOS. *abbr.* Free in and out stowed. • This bill-of-lading term means that the shipper supervises and pays for loading, unloading, and stowing.

firdfare. See FERDFARE.

fire, *vb.* (1885) To discharge or dismiss a person from employment; to terminate as an employee.

firearm. (17c) A weapon that expels a projectile (such as a bullet or pellets) by the combustion of gunpowder or other explosive. — Also termed *gun.*

firebomb. See BOMB.

firebote. See *housebote* under BOTE (2).

firebug. See INCENDIARY (1).

fire department. (1855) The organization, usu. a branch of local government, that works to prevent fires and stop them from burning. — Also termed (BrE) *fire service.*

firefighter's rule. (1986) A doctrine holding that a firefighter, police officer, or other emergency professional may not hold a person, usu. a property owner, liable for unintentional injuries suffered by the professional in responding to the situation created or caused by the person. — Also termed *fireman's rule.*

fire insurance. See INSURANCE.

fireman's rule. See FIREFIGHTER'S RULE.

fire ordeal. See *ordeal by fire* under ORDEAL.

fire sale. See SALE.

fire service. See FIRE DEPARTMENT.

firewall. (18c) **1.** An interior wall between attached living areas or businesses designed to slow the spread of fire between units. **2.** Software designed to prevent unauthorized incoming access to a computer while allowing outgoing access to system servers and the Internet. **3.** ETHICAL WALL.

firing squad. (19c) **1.** A group of persons, esp. soldiers, assembled to carry out a capital-punishment sentence by shooting the prisoner with high-powered rifles at the same time from a short distance. **2.** A military detachment that fires a salute, usu. during the burial ceremony for the person being honored.

firm, *n.* (18c) **1.** The title under which one or more persons conduct business jointly. **2.** The association by which persons are united for business purposes. • Traditionally, this term has referred to a partnership, as opposed to a company. But today it frequently refers to a company. See LAW FIRM.

firma. [Latin] **1.** A lease. **2.** A corporation or partnership.

firma burgi (**fər**-mə **bər**-jI). [Law Latin "the farm of the borough"] (18c) *Hist.* A person's right to take the profits of a borough. • The monarch or the borough's lord granted this right to a person upon payment of a fixed sum.

firma feodi. See FEE FARM.

firma noctis. See NOCTEM DE FIRMA.

firmaratio (fər-mə-**ray**-shee-oh). [Law Latin] *Hist.* A tenant's right to the lands and tenements leased to him.

firmarius (fər-**mair**-ee-əs). [Law Latin] A person entitled to take rent or profits. Cf. FERMER (2).

firma social (feer-mah soh-**syahl**). [Spanish] *Spanish law.* An officially registered name of a corporation or partnership.

firm bid. See BID (2).

firm-commitment underwriting. See UNDERWRITING.

firme. See FARM.

firmitas (fər-mə-tas). [Law Latin] *Hist.* An assurance of some privilege by deed or charter.

firm offer. See *irrevocable offer* under OFFER.

firm opportunity. A law-firm lawyer's opportunity to profit individually from a venture from which the firm might benefit, as opposed to the individual lawyer, and as to which the lawyer must therefore defer to the firm and turn over any income to the firm.

firm-opportunity doctrine. See CORPORATE-OPPORTUNITY DOCTRINE.

First Amendment. The constitutional amendment, ratified with the Bill of Rights in 1791, guaranteeing the freedoms of speech, religion, press, assembly, and petition.

First Amendment Center. An advocacy group that works to preserve and protect First Amendment freedoms through education and the dissemination of information. — Abbr. FAC.

first-bite rule. See ONE-BITE RULE (1).

first-blush rule. (1971) The common-law principle that allows a court to set aside a verdict as excessive because the verdict causes the mind to immediately conclude that it resulted from passion or prejudice on the part of the jury.

first board. *Criminal law.* A prisoner's first appearance before a parole board, often just before completing the minimum length of an indeterminate sentence.

first cause. See *proximate cause* under CAUSE (1).

first chair, *n.* (1952) *Slang.* The lead attorney in court for a given case <despite having worked at the firm for six years, the associate had yet to be first chair in a jury trial>. Cf. SECOND CHAIR. — **first-chair,** *vb.*

first complaint. See FRESH COMPLAINT.

first cousin. See COUSIN (1).

first day. (*often cap.*) See SABBATH.

first-degree, *adj.* See DEGREE (2).

first-degree amendment. See *primary amendment* under AMENDMENT (3).

first-degree manslaughter. See *voluntary manslaughter* under MANSLAUGHTER.

first-degree murder. See MURDER.

first-degree principal. See *principal in the first degree* under PRINCIPAL (2).

first-degree sexual conduct. (1979) Sexual battery that involves an aggravating factor, as when the perpetrator commits the offense against a minor or when the perpetrator commits the offense in the course of committing another crime, such as a burglary. — Also termed *criminal sexual conduct in the first degree.*

first devisee. See DEVISEE.

first-filed rule. See FIRST-TO-FILE RULE.

first-filing rule. See FIRST-TO-FILE RULE.

first fruits. (14c) **1.** *Hist.* One year's profits from the land of a tenant *in capite*, payable to the Crown after the tenant's death. — Also termed *primer seisin.* **2.** *Hist. Eccles. law.* The first year's whole profits of a clergyman's benefice, paid by the incumbent to the Pope, or (after the break with Rome) to the Crown. • This revenue was later termed "Queen Anne's Bounty" when it was converted to a fund to benefit the poor. — Sometimes written *firstfruits.* — Also termed *primitiae*; *primitive*; *annates*; *annats*; *Queen Anne's Bounty.*

first-generation rights. See RIGHT.

firsthand knowledge. See *personal knowledge* under KNOWLEDGE (1).

first impression, case of. See CASE (1).

first-in, first-out. (1934) An accounting method that assumes that goods are sold in the order in which they were purchased — that is, the oldest items are sold first. — Abbr. FIFO. Cf. LAST-IN, FIRST-OUT; NEXT-IN, FIRST-OUT.

first instance, court of. See *trial court* under COURT.

first-inventor defense. (1999) *Patents.* In a suit alleging infringement of a business-method patent, a statutory affirmative defense made out by showing that the defendant was using the business method commercially for at least a year before the plaintiff filed the patent application. • The First Inventor Defense Act of 1999 is codified at 35 USCA § 273.

first lien. See LIEN.

First Lord of the Admiralty. *Hist.* In Great Britain, a minister and one of the lord commissioners who presided over the navy. • The First Lord was assisted by other lords, called Sea Lords, and various secretaries.

First Lord of the Treasury. *English law.* The chief officer in charge of the treasury. • Today, this position is held by the Prime Minister.

first magistrate. See MAGISTRATE (1).

first meeting. *Archaic. Criminal law.* The first contact between a killer and a victim after the killer has been informed of the victim's insulting words or conduct that provoked the killing. • If the killing occurred during the first meeting, a murder charge could be reduced to manslaughter. See HEAT OF PASSION.

first meeting of creditors. See *creditors' meeting* under MEETING.

first mortgage. See MORTGAGE.

first-mortgage bond. See BOND (3).

first name. See *personal name* under NAME.

first-named insured. See *primary insured* under INSURED.

first of exchange. (1839) *Archaic.* The first in a series of drafts (bills of exchange) drawn in duplicate or triplicate for safety in their delivery, the intention being that the acceptance and payment of any one of them, usu. the first to arrive, cancels the others in the set.

first offender. See OFFENDER.

first office action. See OFFICE ACTION.

first option to buy. See RIGHT OF PREEMPTION.

first paper. See *declaration of intention* under DECLARATION (1).

first-party insurance. See INSURANCE.

first-past-the-post voting. See *plurality voting* under VOTING.

first policy year. (1904) *Insurance.* The first year of a life-insurance policy that is to be automatically renewed annually. • This statutory phrase prohibits an insurer from using the policy's suicide exclusion as a defense — and refusing payment on the policy — when an insured commits suicide after the first year of the policy. The insurer can invoke the suicide exclusion as a defense to payment only if the insured commits suicide in the first policy year.

first purchaser. See PURCHASER (2).

first reading, *n. Legislation.* The introduction of a piece of legislation to the assembled legislators, usu. followed by substantive debate. • Sometimes, only the title is read aloud at the first reading. The legislation may be voted on immediately or referred to a committee.

first refusal, right of. See RIGHT OF FIRST REFUSAL.

first responder. (1976) A member of a police force, fire department, or medical-services unit with special training to be the initial person to help in an emergency.

first-sale doctrine. (1963) **1.** *Copyright.* The rule that the purchaser of a physical copy of a copyrighted work, such as a book or CD, may give or sell that copy to someone else without infringing the copyright owner's exclusive distribution rights. • With regard to that physical copy, the copyright owner's distribution right is said to be exhausted. 17 USCA § 109(a). **2.** *Patents.* The principle that the buyer of a patented article has the right to use, repair, and resell the article without interference from the patentee. • The patentee may still retain control of the article through terms in the license or sale contract. See PATENT-EXHAUSTION DOCTRINE.

first security. See *first lien* under LIEN.

first security interest. See *first lien* under LIEN.

first taker. See TAKER.

first-to-file rule. (1969) *Civil procedure.* **1.** The principle that, when two suits are brought by the same parties, regarding the same issues, in two courts of proper jurisdiction, the court that first acquires jurisdiction usu. retains the suit, to the exclusion of the other court. • The court with the second-filed suit ordinarily stays proceedings or abstains. But an exception exists if the first-filed suit is brought merely in anticipation of the true plaintiff's suit and amounts to an improper attempt at forum-shopping. See ANTICIPATORY FILING. **2.** The doctrine allowing a party to a previously filed lawsuit to enjoin another from pursuing a later-filed action. — Also termed *first-filing rule*; *first-filed rule*; *priority-jurisdiction rule.* Cf. DOMINANT-JURISDICTION PRINCIPLE.

first-to-file system. (1993) *Patents.* The practice of granting priority to the first person to file a patent application. • Most of the world uses a first-to-file patent system; the only major exception is the United States, which grants priority to the first inventor. Cf. FIRST-TO-INVENT SYSTEM.

first-to-invent system. (1974) *Patents.* The practice of awarding a patent to the first person to create an invention, rather than the first to file a patent application. • Because the first inventor is not necessarily the first person to file for a patent, an interference hearing is held to decide who is entitled to the patent. This system is used only in the United States. See CONCEPTION OF INVENTION; *priority of invention* under PRIORITY. Cf. FIRST-TO-FILE SYSTEM.

first user. See SENIOR USER.

first-year law students' examination. (1935) A test that an applicant for admission to the California Bar must pass to receive credit for legal study if the applicant does not attend a law school that has been approved by the American Bar Association or accredited by the California Committee of Bar Examiners. • Other requirements to become a licensed attorney in California include completing prelegal education, passing the professional-responsibility exam (MPRE), and passing the California bar exam, among other things. — Abbr. FYLSE; FYLSX. — Also termed (slang) *baby bar examination*; *baby bar.*

FISA. *abbr.* FOREIGN INTELLIGENCE SURVEILLANCE ACT.

FISC. *abbr.* UNITED STATES FOREIGN INTELLIGENCE SURVEILLANCE COURT.

fisc (fisk), *n.* [Latin *fiscus*] (16c) The public treasury. — Also spelled *fisk.*

fiscal (**fis**-kəl), *adj.* (16c) **1.** Of, relating to, or involving financial matters <fiscal year>. **2.** Of, relating to, or involving public finances or taxation <the city's sound fiscal policy>.

fiscal agent. See AGENT.

fiscal officer. See OFFICER (1).

fiscal period. See *fiscal year* under YEAR.

fiscal power. See POWER (3).

fiscal year. See YEAR.

fiscus (**fis**-kəs), *n.* [Latin "the basket" *or* "moneybag"] (17c) **1.** *Roman law.* The emperor's treasury. • In later Roman times, the term also included the treasury of the state. See AERARIUM. **2.** *Hist.* The treasury of a monarch (as the repository of forfeited property), a noble, or any private person. **3.** The treasury or property of the state as distinguished from the private property of the monarch. Cf. HANAPER.

fishery. (16c) **1.** A right or liberty of taking fish. • Fishery was an incorporeal hereditament under old English law. — Also termed *piscary.*

▸ **free fishery.** (17c) An exclusive right of fishery, existing by grant or prescription from the monarch, to take fish in public water such as a river or an arm of the sea. — Also termed *libera piscaria.*

▸ **right of fishery.** (18c) The right of persons to fish in public waters, subject to federal and state restrictions and regulations, such as fishing seasons, licensing, and catch limits.

▸ **several fishery.** (18c) A right to fish in waters that are neither on one's own land nor on the land of a person who granted the right to fish.

2. A fishing ground.

▸ **common fishery.** (18c) A fishing ground where all persons have a right to take fish. Cf. *common of piscary* under COMMON (1).

3. A stock of one or more species of fish or other aquatic wildlife considered for conservation or management purposes.

fishery zone. A marked portion of a country's coastal waters that a country claims as part of its territory along with all the commercially valuable sealife found within it, which may be caught only by the country's own citizens.

fishing expedition. (1874) An attempt, through broad discovery requests or random questions, to elicit information from another party in the hope that something relevant might be found; esp., such an attempt that exceeds the scope of discovery allowed by procedural rules. — Also termed *fishing trip.*

> "No longer can the time-honored cry of 'fishing expedition' serve to preclude a party from inquiring into the facts underlying his opponent's case." *Hickman v. Taylor,* 329 U.S. 495, 507, 67 S.Ct. 385, 392 (1947).

fish royal. (18c) *Hist.* Whales, sturgeon, and porpoises that, when thrown ashore or caught near the English coast, become Crown property.

fisk. See FISC.

fisticuffs, *n.* A pugilistic encounter; an instance of fistfighting.

fistuca. See FESTUCA.

fit and proper, *adj.* Having the necessary and desired qualities for a particular purpose.

fit and proper person. See PERSON (1).

fithwite. See FUTHWITE.

fitness for a particular purpose. See *implied warranty of fitness for a particular purpose* under WARRANTY (2).

fitness hearing. See *transfer hearing* under HEARING.

fitness to plead. See COMPETENCY (2).

fitness to stand trial. See COMPETENCY (2)

fit occupantis (fit ahk-yə-**pan**-tis). [Latin] *Hist.* It becomes the property of the captor.

Five Mile Act. *Hist.* A 1665 English statute prohibiting Puritan ministers from teaching or coming within five miles of any town where they had held office if they refused to pledge that they would not seek to overturn the Church of England. • The Act was repealed in 1689.

501(c)(3) organization. See CHARITABLE ORGANIZATION.

529 plan. (2000) A state-sponsored plan administered by certain investment companies to allow parents and others to accumulate pretax income to pay for a beneficiary's (usu. a child's) college education. • Anyone can contribute to an account set up under 529 plan guidelines. Withdrawals made for educational purposes are taxed at the beneficiary's tax rate; other withdrawals trigger an additional 10% penalty. IRC (26 USCA) § 529.

fix, *n.* (1816) **1.** A dose of an illegal drug <the defendant testified that he robbed the store because he needed to buy a fix>. **2.** A navigational reading.

fix, *vb.* (14c) **1.** To announce (an exchange price, interest rate, etc.) <interest was fixed at 6%>. **2.** To establish (a person's liability or responsibility) <you cannot fix liability on the defendant without evidence>. **3.** To agree with another to establish (a price for goods or services), often illegally <representatives of Acme and Widget secretly met to fix prices for their companies' products>. See PRICE-FIXING. **4.** To influence (an action or outcome, esp. a sports event) by improper or illegal means <after losing the election, the challenger claimed that the incumbent had fixed the election>.

fix a day to which to adjourn. *Parliamentary law.* A motion that provides for another meeting (called an *adjourned meeting* or a *continued meeting*) to continue the same session, but does not immediately end the current meeting. • This motion may be made and voted on while another motion is pending, and its adoption is often immediately followed by a motion to postpone the pending motion or to adjourn (i.e., to immediately end) the current meeting. — Also termed *fix the time to which to adjourn.* See *adjourn to a day certain* under ADJOURN.

fixation. *Copyright.* The process or result of recording a work of authorship in tangible form so that it can be copyrighted under federal law. • Fixation occurs, for instance, when a live television broadcast is transmitted and simultaneously recorded on videotape.

fix bail, *vb.* (18c) To set the amount and terms of bail <after hearing the officer's testimony, the judge fixed bail for the defendant at $100,000>. See BAIL.

fixed abode. See ABODE.

fixed and floating charge. See CHARGE (7).

fixed and floating debenture. See *fixed and floating charge* under CHARGE (7).

fixed and floating lien. See *fixed and floating charge* under CHARGE (7).

fixed annuity. See ANNUITY.

fixed asset. See *capital asset* (1) under ASSET.

fixed-benefit plan. See *defined pension plan* under PENSION PLAN.

fixed capital. See CAPITAL.

fixed charge. See *fixed cost* under COST (1).

fixed cost. See COST (1).

fixed debt. See DEBT.

fixed-dollar investment. See INVESTMENT (1).

fixed equitable charge. See EQUITABLE CHARGE.

fixed exchange rate. See EXCHANGE RATE.

fixed expense. See *fixed cost* under COST (1).

fixed fee. See FEE (1).

fixed in a tangible medium of expression. (1966) *Copyright.* (Of a work) embodied in a physical form that is made by the author or under the author's authority and that is either permanent or stable enough to be perceived, reproduced, or otherwise communicated. • A work consisting of sounds, images, or both that is being transmitted is "fixed" if it is recorded at the same time that it is transmitted.

fixed income. See INCOME.

fixed-income investment. See INVESTMENT (1).

fixed-income security. See SECURITY (4).

fixed interest rate. See INTEREST RATE.

fixed liability. See *fixed debt* under DEBT.

fixed-meaning canon. The doctrine that words must be given the meaning they had when the text was adopted; ORIGINALISM. • In the context of statutory construction, the Supreme Court of the United States has declared that the "'will of Congress' we look to is not a will evolving from Session to Session, but a will expressed and fixed in a particular enactment." *West Virginia Univ. Hosp., Inc. v. Casey*, 499 U.S. 83, 101 n.7 (1991). See ORIGINAL MEANING.

fixed opinion. See OPINION (3).

fixed price. See PRICE.

fixed-price contract. See CONTRACT.

fixed-rate mortgage. See MORTGAGE.

fixed-return dividend. See DIVIDEND.

fixed security. See SECURITY (4).

fixed sentence. See SENTENCE.

fixed sentencing. See *mandatory sentencing* under SENTENCING.

fixed sum. See SUM.

fixed-term, *adj.* (1981) Lasting for a stipulated period of time.

fixed-term lease. (1928) A lease for a fixed period of time, lacking an indefinite "so long thereafter" provision sometimes found in leases. Cf. HABENDUM CLAUSE.

fixed-term marriage. See *temporary marriage* under MARRIAGE (1).

fixed-term partnership. See PARTNERSHIP.

fixed-term work. See WORK (1).

fixed trust. See TRUST (3).

fixing a jury. See JURY-FIXING.

fixing prices. See PRICE-FIXING.

fixture. (18c) Personal property that is attached to land or a building and that is regarded as an irremovable part of the real property, such as a fireplace built into a home. *See* UCC § 9-102(a)(41). • Historically, personal property becomes a fixture when it is physically fastened to or connected with the land or building and the fastening or connection was done to enhance the utility of the land or building. If personal property has been attached to the land or building and enhances only the chattel's utility, it is not a fixture. For example, if bricks are purposely stacked to form a wall, a fixture results. But if the bricks are merely stacked for convenience until used for some purpose, they do not form a fixture. — Also termed *permanent fixture*; *immovable fixture*. Cf. IMPROVEMENT.

> "A fixture can best be defined as a thing which, although originally a movable chattel, is by reason of its annexation to, or association in use with land, regarded as a part of the land. . . . The law of fixtures concerns those situations where the chattel annexed still retains a separate identity in spite of annexation, for example a furnace or a light fixture. Where the chattel annexed loses such identity, as in the case of nails, boards, etc., the problem becomes one of accession." Ray Andrews Brown, *The Law of Personal Property* § 137, at 698 & n.1 (2d ed. 1955).

▸ **agricultural fixture.** (1874) A fixture erected on leased land for use in agricultural pursuits, such as tilling the land or keeping farm animals. • These fixtures may or may not be removable at the end of the lease.

▸ **domestic fixture.** (1855) Removable personal property provided by a tenant for the tenant's personal comfort and convenience while occupying leased premises. • This term frequently applies to items such as large kitchen appliances. See *tenant's fixture*. Cf. *ornamental fixture*.

▸ **ornamental fixture.** (1859) Removable personal property that a tenant attaches to leased premises to make them more attractive and comfortable. • This term sometimes overlaps with *domestic fixture* when an object is decorative as well as functional. See *tenant's fixture*. Cf. *domestic fixture*.

▸ **tenant's fixture.** (1832) Removable personal property that a tenant affixes to the leased property but that the tenant can detach and take away. — Also termed *movable fixture*. See *domestic fixture*; *ornamental fixture*.

▸ **trade fixture.** (1839) Removable personal property that a tenant attaches to leased land for business purposes, such as a display counter. • Despite its name, a trade fixture is not usu. treated as a fixture — that is, as irremovable.

fixture filing. (1972) The act or an instance of recording, in public real-estate records, a security interest in personal property that is intended to become a fixture. *See* UCC § 9-102(a)(40). • The creditor files a financing statement in the real-property records of the county where a mortgage on the real estate would be filed. A fixture-filing financing statement must contain a description of the real estate.

FJC. *abbr.* FEDERAL JUDICIAL CENTER.

FKA. *abbr.* Formerly known as. — Also rendered *F/K/A*; *fka*; *f/k/a*.

flag, *n.* (14c) **1.** A usu. rectangular piece of cloth, bunting, or other material decorated with a distinctive design and used as a symbol or signal. **2.** Something symbolized by the display of a flag, such as a ship or nationality. See DUTY OF THE FLAG; LAW OF THE FLAG.

▸ **flag of convenience.** (1958) *Int'l law.* A national flag flown by a ship not because the ship or its crew has an affiliation with the country, but because the lax controls and modest fees and taxes imposed by that country have attracted the owner to register it there. • After World War II, shipowners began registering their ships in countries such as Panama, Liberia, and Honduras to avoid expensive and restrictive national regulation of labor, safety, and other matters. Since the late 1950s, there has been increasing international pressure to require a "genuine link" between a ship and its flag state, but this reform has been slow in coming. — Abbr. FOC.

▸ **flag of truce.** (16c) *Int'l law.* A white flag used as a signal when one belligerent wishes to communicate with the other in the field. • The bearers of such a flag may not be fired on, injured, or taken prisoner, as long as they carry out their mission in good faith.

▸ **maritime flag.** (1872) A flag designated for use on a vessel to show in what country the vessel is registered.

flag desecration. (1919) The act of mutilating, defacing, burning, or flagrantly misusing a flag. • Flag desecration is constitutionally protected as a form of free speech. *U.S. v. Eichman*, 496 U.S. 310, 110 S.Ct. 2404 (1990).

flag mast. See MAST (1).

flagrans bellum (**flay**-granz **bel**-əm). [Latin "raging war"] (17c) A war currently being waged.

flagrans crimen (**flay**-granz **CRI**-mən). [Latin] A crime in the very act of its commission or of recent occurrence; a fresh crime.

flagrante bello (flə-**gran**-tee **bel**-oh). [Latin] (17c) During an actual state of war.

flagrante delicto. See IN FLAGRANTE DELICTO.

flag state. (1840) *Maritime law.* The state under whose flag a ship is registered. • A ship may fly the flag of one state only.

flag-state control. (1975) *Maritime law.* The exercise of authority by a state over vessels that fly under its flag to ensure compliance with domestic and international safety and environmental laws and regulations. Cf. COASTAL-STATE CONTROL; PORT-STATE CONTROL.

flash-bang diversionary device. (1985) A device that creates a bright flash of light and a loud sound (sometimes with smoke), deployed usu. during the execution of a no-knock search warrant to surprise and distract a suspect who may be dangerous or who may try to destroy evidence. — Also written *flashbang diversionary device.* — Often shortened to *flash-bang*; *flashbang.*— Also termed *stun grenade.* See *no-knock search warrant* under SEARCH WARRANT.

flash of genius. See EUREKA MOMENT.

flash-of-genius rule. (1943) *Patents.* The now-defunct principle that a device is not patentable if it was invented as the result of trial and error rather than as a "flash of creative genius." • The rule, which takes its name from language in *Cuno Engineering Corp. v. Automatic Devices Corp.*, 314 U.S. 84, 91, 62 S.Ct. 37, 41 (1941), was legislatively overturned in 1952. 35 USCA § 103.

flat, *adv.* (16c) Without an allowance or charge for accrued interest <the stock was sold flat>.

flat, *n.* (1824) A room or suite of rooms in a larger block; an apartment.

flat bond. See BOND (3).

flat call. See CALL (6).

flat cancellation. See CANCELLATION (2).

flat money. See *fiat money* under MONEY.

flat reinsurance. See REINSURANCE.

flat sentence. See *determinate sentence* under SENTENCE.

flat tax. See TAX.

flat time. See TIME.

Flavian municipal law. *Hist. Roman law.* See LEX IRNITANA.

flawed asset. See ASSET.

flawed-asset arrangement. An agreement between a bank and a customer whereby money deposited by the customer cannot be withdrawn until a specified event occurs, such as the customer's repayment of a loan from the bank.

FLB. *abbr.* FEDERAL LAND BANK.

fledwite (fled-wɪt). (16c) *Hist.* **1.** A discharge from an amercement (a fine) for a fugitive who turns himself or herself in to the monarch. **2.** The fine set on a fugitive as the price for obtaining freedom. **3.** The right to hold court and take an amercement for the offenses of beating and striking. — Also spelled *fleduite.* — Also termed *flighwite.*

flee, *vb.* **1.** To run away; to hasten off <her attackers turned and fled>. **2.** To run away or escape from danger, pursuit, or unpleasantness; to try to evade a problem <he fled at the sight of the police>. **3.** To vanish; to cease to be visible <the smirk soon fled from his face>. **4.** To abandon or forsake <she fled her native tribe>.

flee from justice. See FLIGHT.

fleet insurance. See INSURANCE.

Fleet marriage. See MARRIAGE (1).

Fleet Prison. *Hist.* A large London jail best known for holding debtors and bankrupts in the 18th and 19th centuries. • Formerly standing beside the Fleet River, it was opened in 1197 and operated almost continuously until it was closed and demolished in 1846.

fleme (fleem). (bef. 12c) *Hist.* An outlaw; a fugitive bondman or villein. — Also spelled *flem.* — Also termed *flyma.*

flemene frit (flee-mən frit). (18c) *Hist.* The harboring or aiding of a fleme (a fugitive). — Also termed and spelled *flemenes frinthe*; *flemensfirth*; *flyman frynth*; *flymena frynthe.*

flemeswite (fleemz-wɪt). (16c) *Hist.* The privilege to possess, or the actual possession of, the goods and fines of a fleme (a fugitive).

Fleta seu Commentarius Juris Anglicani (**flee**-tə syoo kom-ən-**tair**-ee-əs **joor**-is ang-glə-**kay**-nɪ). *Hist.* The title of an ancient treatise on English law, composed in the 13th century and first printed in 1647. • The work is largely derivative, being based on Bracton's *De Legibus et Consuetudinibus.* The unknown author may have been a judge or lawyer who wrote the treatise while in London's Fleet prison. — Often shortened to *Fleta.*

FLETC. *abbr.* FEDERAL LAW ENFORCEMENT TRAINING CENTER.

flexdollars. (1991) Money that an employer pays an employee, who can apply it to a choice of employee benefits.

flexible constitution. See CONSTITUTION (3).

flexible-rate mortgage. 1. See *adjustable-rate mortgage* under MORTGAGE. **2.** See *renegotiable-rate mortgage* under MORTGAGE.

flexible work. See WORK (1).

flextime. (1972) A work schedule that employees have discretion to alter as long as they work their required number of hours over a specified period (usu. a week). — Also termed *flexitime.*

flexweek. (1992) A four-day workweek, usu. consisting of four 10-hour days. — Also termed *flexiweek.*

flier policy. See INSURANCE POLICY.

flight. (bef. 12c) The act or an instance of fleeing, esp. to evade arrest or prosecution <the judge denied bail because the defendant is a flight risk>. — Also termed *flight from prosecution*; *flee from justice.*

flight easement. See *avigational easement* under EASEMENT.

flight from prosecution. See FLIGHT.

flighwite. See FLEDWITE.

flim flam. (16c) A scheme by which a person is tricked out of money; CONFIDENCE GAME. • The term originated as the name of a machine at the heart of a mid-19th-century patent case, *Sloat v. Spring*, 22 F. Cas. 330 (C.C.E.D. Pa. 1850). — Also termed *faith and trust.*

flip, *vb. Slang.* **1.** To buy and then immediately resell securities or real estate in an attempt to turn a profit. **2.** To refinance consumer loans. **3.** To turn state's evidence. See TURN STATE'S EVIDENCE.

▸ **quick flip.** *Slang.* **1.** *Real estate.* The hasty, usu. repeated transfer of property at a higher price, often through mortgage-fraud tactics such as an overstated appraisal of the property, overstated net worth of the buyer, or misrepresentations by the owner. **2.** *Criminal procedure.* A reversal of roles from suspect or accused to informant so quickly as to let police use the information to obtain a search warrant or to make an arrest before the informant has even been arraigned.

flip mortgage. See MORTGAGE.

flipping. *Slang.* **1.** The legitimate practice of buying something, such as goods, real estate, or securities, at a low price and quickly reselling at a higher price. **2.** The fraudulent practice of buying property at a low price, preparing a false appraisal or other documentation showing that property has a much greater value, and quickly reselling the property for an inflated price based on the false document.

Flip Wilson defense. (1989) *Criminal law. Slang.* A defense based on vague blame-shifting, as in "Society made me do it" or "Drugs made me do it." • Flip Wilson (1933–1998) was a comedian in the 1960s and 1970s whose catchphrase was "The devil made me do it."

float, *n.* (1915) **1.** The sum of money represented by outstanding or uncollected checks.

> "'Float' refers to the artificial balance created due to delays in processing credits and debits to an account." *In re Cannon*, 277 F.3d 838, 843 (6th Cir. 2002).

2. The delay between a transaction and the withdrawal of funds to cover the transaction. **3.** The amount of a corporation's shares that are available for trading on the securities market.

float, *vb.* (1833) **1.** (Of a currency) to attain a value in the international exchange market solely on the basis of supply and demand <the IMF allowed the peso to float>. **2.** To issue (a security) for sale on the market <PDQ Corp. floated a new series of preferred shares>. **3.** To arrange or negotiate (a loan) <the bank floated a car loan to Alice despite her poor credit history>.

floatage. See FLOTSAM.

floater. See *floating-rate note* under NOTE (1).

floater insurance. See INSURANCE.

floating, *adj.* (16c) Not fixed or settled; fluctuating; variable.

floating capital. See CAPITAL.

floating charge. **1.** See *floating lien* under LIEN. **2.** See CHARGE (7).

floating debt. See DEBT.

floating easement. See EASEMENT.

floating exchange rate. See EXCHANGE RATE.

floating-interest bond. See BOND (3).

floating lien. See LIEN.

floating policy. See INSURANCE POLICY.

floating rate. See INTEREST RATE.

floating-rate note. See NOTE (1).

floating security. See *floating charge* (1) under CHARGE (7).

floating stock. See STOCK.

floating zone. See ZONE.

floating zoning. See ZONING.

flood, *n.* (bef. 12c) An overflowing of water into an area normally dry; esp., the uncontrollable inundation by surface waters of an area that would not ordinarily be expected to be so affected. See *floodwater* under WATER.

floodgate. (*usu. pl.*) (13c) A restraint that prevents a release of a usu. undesirable result <the new law opened the floodgates of litigation>.

flood insurance. See INSURANCE.

floodplain. (19c) Land that is subject to floodwaters because of its level topography and proximity to a river or arroyo; esp., level land that, extending from a riverbank, is inundated when the flow of water exceeds the channel's capacity. — Also written *flood plain.*

floodwater. See WATER.

floor. (18c) **1.** *Parliamentary law.* The part of the hall where the members of a deliberative body meet to debate issues and conduct business; esp., a legislature's central meeting place where the members sit and conduct business, as distinguished from the galleries, corridors, or lobbies <the Senate floor> <nominations from the floor>. See *assignment of the floor* under ASSIGNMENT (6); CLAIM THE FLOOR; HAVE THE FLOOR; OBTAIN THE FLOOR; ON THE FLOOR; *privilege of the floor* under PRIVILEGE (5). **2.** The part of a courtroom between the judge's bench and the counsel table. **3.** The trading area where stocks and commodities are bought and sold on an exchange <the broker placed his buy order with the trader on the floor of the NYSE>. **4.** The lowest limit, such as the lowest interest rate allowed by law or the smallest permissible payment under a contract <the floor for that position is $25,000 per year>.

floor amendment. See AMENDMENT (3).

floor debate. See DEBATE.

floor-plan financing. See FINANCING.

floor planning. See *floor-plan financing* under FINANCING.

floor-plan rule. (1930) The principle by which a vehicle owner who has placed a vehicle for sale in a retail dealer's showroom is estopped to deny the title of an innocent purchaser from the dealer in the ordinary course of retail dealing.

floor price. See PRICE.

floor tax. See TAX.

flotage. See FLOTSAM.

flotation. See OFFERING.

flotation cost. See COST (1).

floterial district. See DISTRICT.

flotsam (**flot**-səm). (17c) Goods and debris, esp. those from a shipwreck, that float on the surface of a body of water. — Also termed *floatage*; *flotage*. Cf. JETSAM; LAGAN (1); WAVESON.

> "None of those goods which are called *jetsam* (from being *cast* into the sea while the ship is in danger, and after perisheth) or those called *flotsam* (from *floating* upon the sea after shipwreck) or those called *lagan*, or *ligan* (goods thrown overboard before the shipwreck, which sink to the bottom of the sea) are to be esteemed wreck, so long as they remain upon the sea, and are not cast upon the land by the sea; but if any of them are cast upon the land by the sea, they are wreck." Edward Bullingbrooke, *The Duty and*

Authority of Justices of the Peace and Parish Officers for Ireland 897 (rev. ed. 1788).

flowage. (19c) The natural movement of water from a dominant estate to a servient estate. • It is a privilege or easement of the owner of the upper estate and a servitude of the lower estate.

flowage easement. See EASEMENT.

flower bond. See BOND (3).

FLRA. *abbr.* FEDERAL LABOR RELATIONS AUTHORITY.

FLSA. *abbr.* FAIR LABOR STANDARDS ACT.

fluctuating clause. See ESCALATOR CLAUSE.

flyer policy. See *flier policy* under INSURANCE POLICY.

fly for it. *Hist.* To flee after allegedly committing a crime. • The ancient custom in criminal trials was to ask the jury after its verdict — even a not-guilty verdict — "Did he fly for it?" The purpose was to enable the jury to find whether the defendant had fled from justice. A defendant who had fled would forfeit personal property, even though found not guilty on the underlying charge.

flying freehold. See FREEHOLD.

flyma. See FLEME.

flyman frynth. See FLEMENE FRIT.

flymena frynthe. See FLEMENE FRIT.

fly-power assignment. See ASSIGNMENT (2).

flyspeck, *n. Insurance.* A potential trivial defect in title to real property, as a result of which a title-insurance company is likely to exclude any risk from that defect before issuing a policy. — **flyspeck,** *vb.*

FMC. *abbr.* FEDERAL MARITIME COMMISSION.

FMCS. *abbr.* FEDERAL MEDIATION AND CONCILIATION SERVICE.

FMCSA. *abbr.* FEDERAL MOTOR CARRIER SAFETY ADMINISTRATION.

FmHA. *abbr.* FARMERS' HOME ADMINISTRATION.

FMLA. *abbr.* **1.** FAMILY AND MEDICAL LEAVE ACT. **2.** FEDERAL MARITIME LIEN ACT.

fMRI. *abbr.* FUNCTIONAL MAGNETIC RESONANCE IMAGING.

FMS. *abbr.* **1.** FINANCIAL MANAGEMENT SERVICE. **2.** FALSE-MEMORY SYNDROME.

FMSF. *abbr.* FALSE MEMORY SYNDROME FOUNDATION.

FMSHRC. *abbr.* FEDERAL MINE SAFETY AND HEALTH REVIEW COMMISSION.

FMV. See *fair market value* under VALUE (2).

fn. *abbr.* FOOTNOTE, *n.*

FNCS. *abbr.* FOOD, NUTRITION, AND CONSUMER SERVICES.

FNMA. *abbr.* FEDERAL NATIONAL MORTGAGE ASSOCIATION.

FNS. *abbr.* FOOD AND NUTRITION SERVICE.

FNU LNU. *abbr.* (1999) *Criminal law. Slang.* First name unknown, last name unknown —sometimes used in an accusatory instrument in which a suspect is unknown or unidentified, as where there is a coconspirator about whom nothing is known.

FOB. *abbr.* (1890) FREE ON BOARD.

FOB destination. See FREE ON BOARD.

FOB shipping. See FREE ON BOARD.

FOC. See *flag of convenience* under FLAG.

focal species. See SPECIES (1).

foedus (**fee**-dəs). [Latin "league"] *Hist. Int'l law.* A treaty; league; compact.

foenus nauticum (**fee**-nəs **naw**-tə-kəm). [Latin] (16c) *Civil law.* Nautical or maritime interest; esp., an extraordinary rate of interest charged to underwrite a hazardous voyage. — Also termed *usura maritima.*

foesting-men. See HABENTES HOMINES.

foeticide. See FETICIDE.

foetus. See FETUS.

FOIA (**foy**-ə). *abbr.* FREEDOM OF INFORMATION ACT.

foiable (**foy**-ə-bəl), *adj.* (1981) *Slang.* (Of documents) subject to disclosure under the Freedom of Information Act (FOIA).

folcland. See FOLKLAND.

foldage. See FALDAGE (1).

folio (**foh**-lee-oh). [fr. Latin *folium* "leaf"] (15c) **1.** *Hist.* A leaf of a paper or parchment, numbered only on the front. • A folio includes both sides of the leaf, or two pages, with the letters "a" and "b" (or "r" and "v," signifying *recto* and *verso*) added to show which of the two pages was intended. **2.** *Hist.* A certain number of words in a legal document, used as a method of measurement. • In England, 72 or 90 words formed a folio; in the United States, 100 words. — **folio,** *vb.*

> "Folio . . . [a] certain number of words; in conveyances, etc., and proceedings in the High Court amounting to seventy-two, and in parliamentary proceedings to ninety." *Wharton's Law Lexicon* 368 (Ivan Horniman ed., 13th ed. 1925).

3. A page number on a printed book. **4.** A large book the pages of which are formed by folding a sheet of paper only once in the binding to form two leaves, making available four pages (both sides of each leaf).

folkland. (bef. 12c) *Hist.* Land held by customary law, without written title. — Also spelled *folcland.* Cf. BOOKLAND; LOANLAND.

> "In all discussions on Anglo-Saxon law bookland is contrasted with 'folkland.' The most recent and probably the most correct view is that folkland simply means land subject to customary law, as opposed to land which was held under the terms of a charter. It would seem that the view that folkland means public land or land of the people, though till recently generally accepted, must be abandoned as resting on insufficient evidence. It appears that folkland might either be land occupied by individuals or families or communities, or it might be waste or unoccupied land. The only characteristic which can be universally ascribed to it is, that it is not bookland." Kenelm E. Digby, *An Introduction to the History of the Law of Real Property* 15 (5th ed. 1897).

folk laws. See LEGES BARBARORUM.

folkmote. See HALLMOTE (3).

folkway. (1906) (*usu. pl.*) A social habit or cultural norm; a traditional pattern of life common to a people. • The term is thought to have been introduced by the American sociologist W.G. Sumner in his *Folkways* (1907). Cf. LAW-WAY.

> "[T]he most primitive mode is that of the folkways. Unconscious, habitual, uniform modes of acting, they call for little or no effort of choice, judgment, or will, and arise from the instinctive feelings of hunger, love, vanity, and fear; acquired by imitation they are rudimentary in the higher animals, and reach their highest potency in the smaller and more primitive groups, such as families and clans." Edward

D. Page, "Sympathy in Group and Institutional Survival," in *Formative Influences of Legal Development* 393, 393 (Albert Kocourek and John H. Wigmore eds., 1918).

follow, *vb.* (bef. 12c) To conform to or comply with; to accept as authority <the lawyer assumed that the Supreme Court would follow its own precedent>.

following-form policy. See INSURANCE POLICY.

following-orders defense. See NUREMBERG DEFENSE (1).

follow-the-fortunes doctrine. (1987) *Insurance.* The principle that a reinsurer must reimburse the reinsured for its payment of settled claims as long as the reinsured's payments were reasonable and in good faith. • This rule prevents a reinsurer from second-guessing a reinsured's good-faith decision to pay a claim arguably not covered under the original insurance policy. — Often shortened to *follow the fortunes.*

follow-the-settlements doctrine. (1995) *Insurance.* The principle that an indemnitor must accede to the actions of the indemnitee in adjusting and settling claims; esp., the principle that a reinsurer must follow the actions of the reinsured.

fons et origo (fonz et ə-rɪ-goh). [Latin] *Hist.* Source and origin.

fons et origo mali (fonz et ə-rɪ-goh **may**-lɪ). [Latin] *Hist.* Source and origin of evil.

FONSI. *abbr.* FINDING OF NO SIGNIFICANT IMPACT.

fons juris. See SOURCE OF LAW.

food adulteration. Making food impure by adding a foreign or inferior substance to it.

Food and Agriculture Organization. An agency of the United Nations dedicated to eliminate hunger and improve nutrition internationally by working to give people access to healthful food, increase agricultural productivity, reduce rural poverty, and increase global economic growth. • Created in 1945, the FAO is headquartered in Rome and includes seven departments. — Abbr. FAO.

Food and Drug Administration. A division of the U.S. Public Health Service in the Department of Health and Human Services responsible for ensuring that food is safe, pure, and wholesome; that human and animal drugs, biological products, and medical devices are safe and effective; and that certain other products, such as electronic products that emit radiation, are safe. • Created by the Pure Food and Drug Act of 1906, the agency today enforces the Food, Drug, and Cosmetic Act of 1938 and related statutes and regulations. 21 USCA §§ 301 et seq. — Abbr. FDA.

Food and Nutrition Service. An agency in the U.S. Department of Agriculture established to work toward ending hunger and obesity through various assistance programs, including the Special Supplemental Nutrition Program for Women, Infants, and Children (WIC), the Supplemental Nutrition Assistance Program (SNAP), and school meals, while supporting and promoting the U.S. agriculture industry. — Abbr. FNS. See FOOD, NUTRITION, AND CONSUMER SERVICES; SPECIAL SUPPLEMENTAL NUTRITION PROGRAM FOR WOMEN, INFANTS, AND CHILDREN; SUPPLEMENTAL NUTRITION ASSISTANCE PROGRAM.

food-disparagement law. See AGRICULTURAL-DISPARAGEMENT LAW.

Food, Drug, and Cosmetic Act. A 1938 federal law prohibiting the transportation in interstate commerce of adulterated or misbranded food, drugs, or cosmetics. • The Act superseded the Pure Food and Drug Act of 1906. — Abbr. FDCA.

Food, Nutrition, and Consumer Services. An agency group in the U.S. Department of Agriculture responsible for reducing hunger by educating children and needy people about healthy diets and by providing them access to food through the food-stamp and other programs. • This is an umbrella term for the two agencies responsible to the Under Secretary for Food, Nutrition, and Consumer Services: the Food and Nutrition Service (FNS) and the Center for Nutrition Policy and Promotion (CNPP). — Abbr. FNCS. See FOOD AND NUTRITION SERVICE; CENTER FOR NUTRITION POLICY AND PROMOTION.

food recall. See RECALL (2).

Food Safety and Inspection Service. An agency in the U.S. Department of Agriculture responsible for inspecting all types of meat, poultry, eggs, and related products to ensure safety and accurate labeling. — Abbr. FSIS.

food-spiking. See SPIKING.

Food Stamp Program. See SUPPLEMENTAL NUTRITION ASSISTANCE PROGRAM.

foolscap. (17c) *Archaic.* Writing or printing paper varying in size but in modern terms most closely approximating legal-size paper (11 x 17). • At 13 x 16, the pages could be folded to make pages 13 x 8. Foolscap got its name from jester's cap and bell traditionally used as a watermark. The spelling *fool's cap* refers not to the paper but instead to a jester's or dunce's cap.

> "Foolscap, the cap, usually of conical shape, with a cockscomb running up the centre of the back and with bells attached, worn by jesters and fools; also a conical cap worn by dunces. The name is given to a size of writing or printing paper, varying in size from 12 x 15 in. to 17 x 13½ in. The name is derived from the use of a 'fool's cap' as a watermark. A German example of the watermark dating from 1479 was exhibited in the Caxton Exhibition (1877). The *New English Dictionary* [now known as the *Oxford English Dictionary*—ed.] finds no trustworthy evidence for the introduction of the watermark by a German, Sir John Spielmann, at his papermill at Dartford in 1580, and states that there is no truth in the familiar story that the Rump Parliament substituted a fool's cap for the royal arms as a watermark on the paper used for the journals of parliament." 10 *Encyclopaedia Britannica* 616 (11th ed. 1910).

fool's test. The test formerly used by federal courts and by the Federal Trade Commission to determine whether an advertisement is deceptive, by asking whether even a fool might believe it. • The name comes from Isaiah: "wayfaring men, though fools, shall not err therein." The test was announced in *Charles of the Ritz Distrib. Corp. v. Fed. Trade Comm'n,* 143 F.2d 676 (2d Cir. 1944). It was replaced by a "reasonable consumer" test by the FTC in 1984. Cf. REASONABLE-CONSUMER TEST.

foot acre. See ACRE-FOOT.

footage drilling contract. See DRILLING CONTRACT.

foot-frontage rule. (1880) *Tax.* A method of property-tax assessment — used esp. to pay for improvements such as sidewalks and sewers — that considers only the lot's actual frontage on the line of improvement and ignores the depth of the lot and the number and character of other improvements or their value.

footgeld (**fuut**-geld). (16c) *Hist.* In forest law, a fine imposed for not making a dog incapable of hunting by either cutting out the ball of its paw or cutting off its claws. • The cutting was known as "expeditating" the dog. To be "free" or "quit" of footgeld was to be relieved of the duty to expedite one's dog.

footnote, *n.* (18c) **1.** A discrete unit of additional information that appears at the bottom of a page, usu. explaining, commenting on, or citing a source for a specific part of the text <the third edition had 400 footnotes>. • Footnotes are usu. signaled by superscript numbers, symbols, or sometimes characters in the text. Cf. ENDNOTE. **2.** An aside, caveat, or afterthought <he mentioned his earlier legal experience as a footnote to his speech>. **3.** Something of lesser importance or significance <the event was a footnote to legal history>. — Abbr. fn. *or* n.

footnote, *vb.* (1893) To provide additional information in the form of a footnote.

footnote 4. (1938) *Constitutional law.* Justice Harlan Fiske Stone's footnote in *U.S. v. Carolene Products Co.*, 304 U.S. 144, 58 S.Ct. 778 (1938), raising the question whether courts may use a higher degree of scrutiny to review legislation when prejudice against "discrete and insular minorities" may hamper the democratic safeguards that would ordinarily protect those minorities. • It is the most famous footnote in constitutional law, and legal scholars continue to debate its meaning and significance.

foot of the fine. (16c) *Hist.* At common law, the fifth and last part of a fine of conveyance. • This part included the entire matter, reciting the names of the parties and the date, place, and before whom it was acknowledged or levied. — Also termed *chirograph.* See FINE (1).

footprint. (16c) **1.** *Evidence.* The impression made on a surface of soil, snow, etc., by a human foot or a shoe, boot, or any other foot covering. **2.** *Real estate.* The shape of a building's base.

foot, *n.* The bottom or end of a writing <foot of the deed>.

FOP. *abbr.* Full order of protection — Also abbreviated FOOP.

for account of. (1826) A form of indorsement on a note or draft introducing the name of the person entitled to receive the proceeds.

Foraker Act (**for**-ə-kər). The original (1900) federal statute providing Puerto Rico with a civil government, but keeping it outside the U.S. customs area. *See* 48 USCA §§ 731–752.

foraneous (fə-**ray**-nee-əs), *adj.* [fr. Latin *forum* "marketplace"] (17c) Of, relating to, or involving a court or marketplace.

foraneus (fə-**ray**-nee-əs), *n.* [fr. Latin *foris* "without"] *Hist.* A foreigner; an alien; a stranger.

forathe (**for**-ayth). *Hist.* In forest law, one who can make an oath or bear witness for another.

forbannitus (for-**ban**-ə-təs). [Law Latin] *Hist.* **1.** A pirate; an outlaw. **2.** Someone who was banished. — Also termed *forisbanitus.*

forbarre (for-**bahr**), *vb.* [Law French] (16c) *Hist.* To preclude; to bar out; to estop.

forbatudus (for-bə-**t[y]oo**-dəs). [Law Latin] *Hist.* Someone who provokes a fight and dies in it.

forbearance, *n.* (16c) **1.** The act of tolerating or abstaining. **2.** The act of refraining from enforcing a right, obligation, or debt. • Strictly speaking, *forbearance* denotes an intentional negative act, while *omission* or *neglect* is an unintentional negative act. — **forbear,** *vb.*

> "The terms 'loan' and 'forbearance' are correlative. Permitting one to retain a loan of money after it has become due and payable is *forbearing* it. That is, *forbearance*, within the meaning of usury laws, is the giving of further time for the return of payment of money after the date upon which it became due." James Avery Webb, *A Treatise on the Law of Usury* 18 (1899).

> "Forbearance or a promise to forbear the exercise of a right, a privilege, or a power, is sufficient consideration for a promise. A request for forbearance where no time is stated is presumed to be for a reasonable time. Surrender or forbearance to sue a claim which is voidable by the exercise of a privilege given by law, involves the possibility of detriment and constitutes sufficient consideration for a counterpromise. The test of forbearance as detriment is whether the claimant had a legal right to bring suit. If the claim is invalid, as known to the claimant, he had no such right; his suit is no more than the wrongful exercise of a power. But even if invalid, in law or in fact, if the claimant reasonably and in good faith believes his claim to be valid, forbearance of the legal right to have his claim adjudicated constitutes detriment and consideration. It is to be emphasized, that even where forbearance is detrimental it must have been bargained for, expressly or impliedly, in order to constitute consideration." Laurence P. Simpson, *Handbook of the Law of Contracts* 119 (1954).

▸ **forbearance to sue.** The act of refraining from seeking a judicial remedy for a legal or equitable injury.

forbidden degree. See *prohibited degree* under DEGREE.

forbidden departure. See DEPARTURE (1).

for cause. (15c) For a legal reason or ground. • The phrase expresses a common standard governing the removal of a civil servant or an employee under contract. — **for-cause,** *adj.*

for-cause challenge, *n.* See *challenge for cause* under CHALLENGE (2).

force, *n.* (14c) Power, violence, or pressure directed against a person or thing.

▸ **actual force.** (16c) Force consisting in a physical act, esp. a violent act directed against a robbery victim. — Also termed *physical force.*

▸ **constructive force.** (1802) Threats and intimidation to gain control or prevent resistance; esp., threatening words or gestures directed against a robbery victim.

▸ **deadly force.** (16c) Violent action known to create a substantial risk of causing death or serious bodily harm. •Generally, a person may use deadly force in self-defense or in defense of another only if retaliating against another's deadly force. — Also termed *extreme force.* Cf. *nondeadly force.*

> "Under the common law the use of deadly force is never permitted for the sole purpose of stopping one fleeing from arrest on a misdemeanor charge . . . ." Rollin M. Perkins & Ronald N. Boyce, *Criminal Law* 1098 (3d ed. 1982).

▸ **excessive force.** (16c) Unreasonable or unnecessary force under the circumstances.

▸ **extreme force.** See *deadly force.*

▸ **independent force.** Force not stimulated by a situation created by the actor's conduct.

▸ **intervening force.** (1881) Force that actively produces harm to another after the actor's negligent act or omission has been committed.

▸ **irresistible force.** (16c) Force that cannot be foreseen or controlled, esp. that which prevents the performance of a contractual obligation; FORCE MAJEURE. See VIS MAJOR.

▸ **legal force.** See *reasonable force.*

▸ **nondeadly force.** (1961) **1.** Force that is neither intended nor likely to cause death or serious bodily harm; force intended to cause only minor bodily harm. **2.** A threat of deadly force, such as displaying a knife. — Also termed *moderate force.* Cf. *deadly force.*

▸ **physical force.** See *actual force.*

▸ **reasonable force.** (17c) Force that is not excessive and that is appropriate for protecting oneself or one's property. • The use of reasonable force will not render a person criminally or tortiously liable. — Also termed *legal force.*

> "One does not use jeweller's scales to measure reasonable force." *Reed v. Wastie*, [1972] Crim. L.R. 221 (per Lane, J.) (as quoted in Glanville Williams, *Textbook of Criminal Law* 451 (1978)).

▸ **unlawful force.** (16c) Force that is directed against a person without that person's consent, and that is a criminal offense or an actionable tort. Model Penal Code § 3.11.

force, *vb.* (14c) To compel by physical means or by legal requirement <Barnes used a gun to force Jillian to use her ATM card> <under the malpractice policy, the insurance company was forced to defend the doctor>.

force and arms. *Hist.* Violence. • The phrase was used in common-law pleading in declarations of trespass and in indictments to denote that the offending act was committed violently. See VI ET ARMIS.

force and effect, *n.* (16c) Legal efficacy <mailing the brief had the force and effect of filing it with the clerk>. • The term is now generally regarded as a redundant legalism.

forced abortion. See ABORTION.

forced arbitration. See *mandatory arbitration* under ARBITRATION.

forced conversion. See CONVERSION (1).

forced entry. (1918) The act or an instance of someone's getting into a building illegally by breaking a door, window, etc. Cf. FORCIBLE ENTRY.

forced exile. See EXILE (1).

forced heir. See HEIR.

forced labor. (1872) *Int'l law.* Work exacted from a person under threat of penalty; work for which a person has not offered himself or herself voluntarily. • Under the U.N. Convention on Civil and Political Rights (article 8), exemptions from this definition include (1) penalties imposed by a court, (2) compulsory military service, (3) action taken in an emergency, (4) normal civil obligations, and (5) minor communal services. — Also termed *compulsory labor.*

forced pooling. See *compulsory pooling* under POOLING.

forced portion. See LEGITIME.

forced resettlement. (1947) *Int'l law.* The involuntary transfer of individuals or groups within the jurisdiction of a country whether inside its own territory or into or out of occupied territory.

forced respite. See RESPITE.

forced sale. See SALE.

forced share. See ELECTIVE SHARE.

forced unitization. See *compulsory unitization* under UNITIZATION.

force majeure (fors ma-zhər). [Law French "a superior force"] (1883) An event or effect that can be neither anticipated nor controlled; esp., an unexpected event that prevents someone from doing or completing something that he or she had agreed or officially planned to do. • The term includes both acts of nature (e.g., floods and hurricanes) and acts of people (e.g., riots, strikes, and wars). — Also termed *force majesture; vis major; superior force.* Cf. ACT OF GOD; VIS MAJOR (1).

force-majeure clause. (1916) A contractual provision allocating the risk of loss if performance becomes impossible or impracticable, esp. as a result of an event or effect that the parties could not have anticipated or controlled.

force-the-vote provision. (2002) *Mergers & acquisitions.* A contractual clause requiring a company's board of directors to approve a merger transaction and submit it to the shareholders, who then vote on the merger regardless of whether the board recommends that the shareholders approve it when the vote is held.

forcible, *adj.* (15c) Effected by force or threat of force against opposition or resistance.

> "[In the law of trespass, the] term 'forcible' is used in a wide and somewhat unnatural sense to include any act of physical interference with the person or property of another. To lay one's finger on another person without lawful justification is as much a forcible injury in the eye of the law, and therefore a trespass, as to beat him with a stick. To walk peacefully across another man's land is a forcible injury and a trespass, no less than to break into his house *vi et armis.* So also it is probably a trespass deliberately to put matter where natural forces will take it on to the plaintiff's land." R.F.V. Heuston, *Salmond on the Law of Torts* 5 (17th ed. 1977).

forcible detainer. (17c) **1.** The wrongful retention of possession of property by one originally in lawful possession, often with threats or actual use of violence. **2.** FORCIBLE ENTRY AND DETAINER (2).

forcible entry. (17c) **1.** The act or an instance of violently and unlawfully taking possession of lands and tenements against the will of those in lawful possession. **2.** The act of entering land in another's possession by the use of force against another or by breaking into the premises. Cf. FORCED ENTRY.

forcible entry and detainer. (17c) **1.** The act of violently taking and keeping possession of lands and tenements without legal authority.

> "To walk across another's land, or to enter his building, without privilege, is a trespass, but this in itself, while a civil wrong, is not a crime. However, if an entry upon real estate is accomplished by violence or intimidation, or if such methods are employed for detention after a peaceable entry, there is a crime according to English law, known as forcible entry and detainer. This was a common-law offense in England, although supplemented by English statutes that

are old enough to be common law in this country. . . . It has sometimes been said that there are two separate offenses — (1) forcible entry and (2) forcible detainer. This may be true under the peculiar wording of some particular statute, but in general it seems to be one offense which may be committed in two different ways." Rollin M. Perkins & Ronald N. Boyce, *Criminal Law* 487–88 (3d ed. 1982).

2. A quick and simple legal proceeding for regaining possession of real property from someone who has wrongfully taken, or refused to surrender, possession. — Abbr. FED. — Also termed *forcible detainer.* See EVICTION; EJECTMENT.

"Forcible entry and detainer is a remedy given by statute for the recovery of possession of land and of damages for its detention. It is entirely regulated by statute, and the statutes vary materially in the different states." Benjamin J. Shipman, *Handbook of Common-Law Pleading* § 74, at 188 (Henry Winthrop Ballantine ed., 3d ed. 1923).

forcible touching. (1963) In some jurisdictions, a misdemeanor battery involving patting, squeezing, grabbing, or pinching the sexual or intimate parts of another person for the purpose of sexual gratification.

foreclose, *vb.* (15c) To terminate a mortgagor's interest in property; to subject (property) to foreclosure proceedings.

"Should the mortgagor default in his obligations under the mortgage, the mortgagee will seek to 'foreclose,' — i.e., 'end' or 'close' the mortgagor's rights in the security. After taking the appropriate statutory steps, the mortgagee will sell the mortgaged property. If the sale is to someone other than the mortgagor or the mortgagee (a 'third party' sale) the proceeds will go: first, to pay the costs of the foreclosure proceedings; second, to pay off the principal indebtedness and accrued interest; third, if there is anything left over (i.e., any 'equity' existed) this is paid to the mortgagor." Edward H. Rabin, *Fundamentals of Modern Real Property Law* 1087 (1974).

foreclosure (for-**kloh**-zhər). (18c) A legal proceeding to terminate a mortgagor's interest in property, instituted by the lender (the mortgagee) either to gain title or to force a sale in order to satisfy the unpaid debt secured by the property. Cf. REPOSSESSION.

"Every foreclosure has a point of time at which the title to the mortgaged premises is transferred absolutely from the mortgagor and his subsequent lienors to a purchaser or to a party who sustains the relations of a purchaser to the premises, whether the foreclosure be conducted by action and judicial sale, entry and possession, advertisement or otherwise. The principal object of a foreclosure is accomplished only when such a transfer has been effected. Other ends may also be sought, as a personal judgment of deficiency, but the extinguishment of the mortgage and the production of a perfect title is the first purpose of every method of foreclosure." Charles Hastings Wiltsie, *A Treatise on the Law and Practice of Foreclosing Mortgages on Real Property* § 1, at 2 (1893).

▸ **equitable foreclosure.** (1876) A foreclosure method in which the court orders the property sold, and the proceeds are applied first to pay the costs of the lawsuit and sale and then to the mortgage debt. • Any surplus is paid to the mortgagor.

▸ **judicial foreclosure.** (1839) A costly and time-consuming foreclosure method by which the mortgaged property is sold through a court proceeding requiring many standard legal steps such as the filing of a complaint, service of process, notice, and a hearing. • Judicial foreclosure is available in all jurisdictions and is the exclusive or most common method of foreclosure in at least 20 states.

▸ **mortgage foreclosure.** (1842) A foreclosure of the mortgaged property upon the mortgagor's default.

▸ **nonjudicial foreclosure.** (1916) **1.** See *power-of-sale foreclosure.* **2.** A foreclosure method that does not require court involvement.

▸ **power-of-sale foreclosure.** (1946) A foreclosure process by which, according to the mortgage instrument and a state statute, the mortgaged property is sold at a nonjudicial public sale by a public official, the mortgagee, or a trustee, without the stringent notice requirements, procedural burdens, or delays of a judicial foreclosure. • Power-of-sale foreclosure is authorized and used in more than half the states. — Also termed *nonjudicial foreclosure; statutory foreclosure.*

▸ **strict foreclosure.** (1823) A rare procedure that gives the mortgagee title to the mortgaged property — without first conducting a sale — after a defaulting mortgagor fails to pay the mortgage debt within a court-specified period. • The use of strict foreclosure is limited to special situations except in those few states that permit this remedy generally.

▸ **tax foreclosure.** (1869) A public authority's seizure and sale of property for nonpayment of taxes.

foreclosure decree. (1847) **1.** Generally, a decree ordering a judicial foreclosure sale. **2.** A decree ordering the strict foreclosure of a mortgage.

foreclosure sale. See SALE.

foregift. (18c) *Hist.* A premium paid for a lease in addition to rent; forehand rent. See FOREHAND RENT (1).

foregoer (for-**goh**-ər). (15c) *Hist.* A royal purveyor; a person who buys provisions for the Crown at an appraised (that is, reduced) price while the royal household travels about the country.

foregone conclusion. (17c) An inevitable result; a foreordained eventuality.

forehand rent. (18c) *Hist.* **1.** A premium paid by the tenant on the making of a lease, esp. on the renewal of a lease by an ecclesiastical corporation. **2.** Generally, rent payable before a lease begins.

foreign, *adj.* (13c) **1.** Of, relating to, or involving another country <foreign affairs>. **2.** Of, relating to, or involving another jurisdiction <the Arizona court gave full faith and credit to the foreign judgment from Mississippi>. — **foreigner,** *n.*

Foreign Account Tax Compliance Act. A 2010 federal statute enacted as part of the Hiring Incentives to Restore Employment (HIRE) Act to amend the Internal Revenue Code by targeting (1) tax noncompliance by U.S. taxpayers with foreign accounts, (2) U.S. taxpayers' reporting about certain foreign financial accounts and offshore assets, and (3) the reporting of foreign financial institutions about financial accounts held by U.S. taxpayers or foreign entities in which U.S. taxpayers hold a substantial ownership interest. 26 USCA §§ 1298f, 1471–1474, 6038D. — Abbr. FACTA.

foreign administration. See *ancillary administration* under ADMINISTRATION.

foreign administrator. See ADMINISTRATOR (2).

foreign affairs. (16c) Matters concerning politics, diplomatic relations, and business activities between a given country and all others; international relations considered from one particular country's point of view.

foreign agent. See AGENT.

Foreign Agricultural Service. An agency in the U.S. Department of Agriculture responsible for maintaining a worldwide agricultural intelligence and reporting system. — Abbr. FAS.

Foreign and Commonwealth Office. The formal name of the British government department responsible for dealing with matters concerning foreign countries. — Often shortened to *Foreign Office.* — Abbr. FCO.

foreign apposer. See APPOSER.

foreign arbitration award. See ARBITRATION AWARD.

foreign assignment. See ASSIGNMENT (2).

foreign bill. See BILL (6).

foreign bill of exchange. See *foreign draft* under DRAFT (1).

foreign bond. See BOND (3).

foreign consulate. See CONSULATE (2).

foreign corporation. See CORPORATION.

Foreign Corrupt Practices Act. A 1977 federal statute that prohibits United States citizens from offering or paying bribes to foreign officials in order to obtain or maintain a commercial interest, and requires companies whose securities are listed in the United States to comply with certain accounting practices. 15 USCA §§ 78dd-1 et seq. — Abbr. FCPA.

foreign county. See COUNTY.

foreign court. See COURT.

foreign creditor. See CREDITOR.

foreign currency. See CURRENCY.

foreign decree. See DECREE.

foreign divorce. See DIVORCE.

foreign document. See DOCUMENT (2).

foreign domicile. See DOMICILE.

foreign dominion. (16c) *Hist.* A country that at one time was a foreign state but that by conquest or cession has come under the British Crown.

foreign draft. See DRAFT (1).

foreign-earned-income exclusion. (1964) The Internal Revenue Code provision that excludes from taxation a limited amount of income earned by nonresident taxpayers outside the United States. • The taxpayer must elect between this exclusion and the foreign tax credit. IRC (26 USCA) § 911(a), (b). See *foreign tax credit* under TAX CREDIT.

Foreign Emoluments Clause. (2004) *Constitutional law.* The clause of the U.S. Constitution prohibiting titles of nobility and the acceptance of a gift, title, or other benefit from a foreign power. U.S. Const. art. I, § 9, cl. 8. — Sometimes shortened to *Emoluments Clause.*

foreigner. (15c) **1.** *Hist.* A person not an inhabitant of a particular city under discussion. **2.** A citizen of another country.

foreign exchange. (17c) **1.** The activity of making international monetary transactions; esp., the conversion of one currency to that of a different country. **2.** Foreign currency or negotiable instruments payable in foreign currency, such as traveler's checks.

foreign-exchange market. See MARKET.

foreign-exchange rate. (1916) The rate at which the currency of one country is exchanged for the currency of another country.

foreign-flag vessel. See VESSEL.

foreign guardian. See GUARDIAN (1).

foreign immunity. See IMMUNITY (1).

Foreign Intelligence Surveillance Act. A 1978 federal statute that established new procedures and courts to authorize electronic surveillance of foreign intelligence operations in the United States. • The Act established the Foreign Intelligence Surveillance Court and the Foreign Intelligence Court of Review. It allows the Attorney General to obtain warrants that authorize electronic surveillance of suspected foreign-intelligence operatives without public disclosure and without a showing of probable cause that criminal activity is involved. — Abbr. FISA.

Foreign Intelligence Surveillance Court. See UNITED STATES FOREIGN INTELLIGENCE SURVEILLANCE COURT.

Foreign Intelligence Surveillance Court of Review. See UNITED STATES FOREIGN INTELLIGENCE SURVEILLANCE COURT OF REVIEW.

foreign judgment. See JUDGMENT (2).

foreign jurisdiction. See JURISDICTION.

foreign jury. See JURY.

foreign law. (16c) **1.** Generally, the law of another country. **2.** *Conflict of laws.* The law of another state or of a foreign country.

foreign minister. See MINISTER (3).

foreign note. See NOTE (1).

foreign object. (17c) An item that appears where it does not belong; esp., an item introduced into a living body, such as a sponge that is left in a patient's body during surgery. • The discovery rule usu. tolls the statute of limitations for a medical-malpractice claim based on a foreign object. — Also termed *foreign substance.* See FOREIGN SUBSTANCE.

Foreign Office. See FOREIGN AND COMMONWEALTH OFFICE.

foreign port. See PORT.

foreign-relations law. See INTERNATIONAL LAW.

foreign secretary. (*usu. cap.*) (18c) The government minister in charge of a particular country's foreign office, esp. that of the United Kingdom.

foreign service. (19c) **1.** UNITED STATES FOREIGN SERVICE. **2.** FORINSEC SERVICE. **3.** *Hist.* A feudal service performed by a tenant outside the fee.

Foreign Service Institute. A unit in the U.S. Department of State responsible for training officers and employees of the Foreign Service as well as personnel in other agencies. — Abbr. FSI.

foreign-situs trust. See TRUST (3).

Foreign Sovereign Immunities Act. A federal statute providing individuals with a right of action against foreign governments, under certain circumstances, to the extent the claim arises from the private, as opposed to the public, acts of the foreign state. 28 USCA §§ 1602–1611. — Abbr.

FSIA. See RESTRICTIVE PRINCIPLE OF SOVEREIGN IMMUNITY.

"The Foreign Sovereign Immunities Act (FSIA) of 1976 was designed to provide a set of comprehensive regulations governing access to federal and state courts in this country for plaintiffs asserting claims against foreign states and instrumentalities thereof. The enactment of this legislation responded to the reality that increased contacts between American citizens and companies on the one hand, and foreign states and entities owned by foreign states on the other, as well as a constantly expanding range of government activities, had created the need for judicial fora in this country to resolve disputes arising out of these activities." 14A Charles Alan Wright et al., *Federal Practice and Procedure* § 3662, at 160-61 (2d ed. 1998).

foreign state. (16c) **1.** A foreign country. **2.** An American state different from the one under discussion.

foreign-state immunity. See *foreign immunity* under IMMUNITY (1).

foreign substance. (17c) A substance found in a body, organism, or thing where it is not supposed to be found <the plaintiff sued because she thought she saw — and later confirmed that she had found — a foreign substance (namely, a piece of glass) in her hamburger>. See FOREIGN OBJECT.

foreign support order. See SUPPORT ORDER.

foreign tax credit. See TAX CREDIT.

foreign trade zone. See FREE-TRADE ZONE.

foreign trust. See *foreign-situs trust* under TRUST (3).

foreign vessel. See VESSEL.

foreign voyage. See VOYAGE.

foreign water. See WATER.

forejudge, *vb.* (16c) **1.** To prejudge; to judge beforehand. **2.** Loosely, FORJUDGE.

foreman. (15c) **1.** See *presiding juror* under JUROR. **2.** Someone who directs the work of employees; an overseer, crew chief, or superintendent. — **foremanship,** *n.*

forematron. (1903) *Hist.* The presiding juror in an all-woman jury. See PRESIDING JUROR.

forensic (fə-**ren**-sik *also* -zik), *adj.* [fr. Latin *forensis* "public," fr. Latin *forum* "court"] (17c) **1.** Used in or suitable to courts of law or public debate <forensic psychiatry>. See FORENSIS. **2.** Rhetorical; argumentative <Tietjen's considerable forensic skills>. **3.** *Hist.* Exterior; foreign. **4.** Of, relating to, or involving the scientific methods used for investigating crimes.

forensic accounting. (1946) The application of accountancy principles to monetary issues that arise in courts, as in the apportionment of funds and of financial responsibilities upon a divorce or dissolution of a partnership.

forensic chemistry. (1832) The science of chemistry applied to legal questions. — Also termed *legal chemistry.*

forensic engineering. (1976) The use of engineering principles or analysis in a lawsuit, usu. through an expert witness's testimony.

forensic evidence. See EVIDENCE.

forensic lab. See CRIME LABORATORY.

forensic linguistics. (1973) The science or technique that evaluates the linguistic characteristics of written or oral communications, usu. to determine identity or authorship.

forensic medicine. (1845) The branch of medicine that establishes or interprets evidence using scientific or technical facts, such as ballistics. — Also termed *medical jurisprudence.*

"Forensic medicine provides one of the most fascinating of all chapters in medicine. The study of the body, usually dead, the quiet scientific assembly of the evidence it bears, and the construction of reasonable inferences based on these observations cannot fail to give interest and satisfaction. All branches of medicine from anatomy to obstetrics provide the basic knowledge application of which, shaped to conform with the needs of the law, forms the body of the subject. Truth — or the nearest reasonable approach to it permitted by what is observed — is the sole aim. Vagueness and theory have no place in forensic medicine, and the doctor is respected who properly says he does not know or is insufficiently informed to give opinion." Keith Simpson, *Forensic Medicine* 1 (2d ed. 1952).

forensic odontology. (1952) The application of dentistry to law, esp. in areas such as identifying human remains, comparing human bite marks, interpreting oral injury, and identifying dental malpractice.

forensic oratory. See ORATORY.

forensic pathology. (1959) The specific branch of medicine that establishes or interprets evidence dealing with diseases and disorders of the body, esp. those that cause death.

forensic psychiatry. (1918) The application of psychiatry in courts, esp. for the determination of competency to stand trial, criminal responsibility, parental fitness, liability to civil commitment, etc.

forensics (fə-**ren**-siks *also* -ziks). (1963) **1.** The art of argumentative discourse or debate. **2.** The branch of law enforcement dealing with legal evidence relating to firearms and ballistics.

forensic science. (1883) A broad range of evidence-related disciplines, some laboratory-based (as with nuclear and mitochondrial-DNA analysis, toxicology, and drug analysis), others based on interpretation of observed patterns (as with fingerprints, writing samples, tool marks, bite marks, and specimens), and still others based on a combination of experiential and scientific analysis (as with explosive and fire-debris analysis, blood-spatter analysis).

forensis (fə-**ren**-sis), *adj.* [fr. Latin *forum* "court"] *Roman law.* Of, relating to, or involving a court of law. • An advocate, for example, was sometimes known as a *homo forensis.* See FORENSIC.

fore-oath. *Hist.* An oath required of a plaintiff, complainant, or pursuer before suing unless the cause of the complaint was obvious.

foreperson. See *presiding juror* under JUROR.

foreseeability, *n.* (1928) The quality of being reasonably anticipatable. • Foreseeability, along with actual causation, is an element of proximate cause in tort law. — **foreseeable,** *adj.*

foreseeable damages. See DAMAGES.

foreshore. 1. The part of a seashore between the high-water and low-water marks. **2.** The strip of uncultivated land between the edges of a body of water and cultivated or developed land.

forest, *n.* (13c) **1.** *Hist.* A tract of land, not necessarily wooded, reserved to the king or a grantee, for hunting deer and other game. **2.** A franchise consisting of the right to keep wild game on grounds set apart for the chase. **3.** A dense growth of trees and underbrush on a large tract of land.

forestall (for-**stawl**), *vb.* (bef. 12c) **1.** To prevent (an event, result, etc.). **2.** *Hist.* To intercept or obstruct (as a person on a royal highway). **3.** *Hist.* To prevent (a tenant) from coming on the premises. **4.** *Hist.* To intercept (as a deer reentering a forest). **5.** *Hist.* To buy (goods) for the purpose of reselling at a higher price. • At common law, this was an indictable offense. See FORESTALLING THE MARKET. — Also spelled *forstall.*

"[A] growing town in England might have placed a higher value on grain than a neighboring town with a static population, yet traditional patterns of business might continue to send the same amount of grain to both towns. A forestaller would bid against the traditional buyer in the smaller town, obtain the grain, and resell it where it could command a higher price in the larger town. Forestalling did not harm allocative efficiency. Indeed, it was a highly effective means of reallocating scarce goods to their most highly valued uses — the very definition of efficiency. Rather, forestalling was objectionable, and thus prohibited as a restraint of trade, because the bidding process necessarily resulted in higher grain prices in many parts of the country." Stephen F. Ross, *Principles of Antitrust Law* 12 (1993).

forestaller, *n.* (15c) **1.** Someone who forestalls. **2.** *Hist.* One guilty of the offense of forestalling. See FORESTALL (5).

forestalling the market. (17c) *Hist.* **1.** The taking possession of commodities on their way to the market. **2.** The purchase of goods on their way to the market, with the intention of reselling them at a higher price. **3.** The deterrence of having sellers offer their goods at market at a reasonable price; specif., the crime of inhibiting normal trading by persuading sellers to raise their prices on goods or dissuading them from offering the goods in a particular market, or by purchasing as much as possible of certain goods before they reach the market to drive up prices.

forest law. (16c) *Hist.* The body of law protecting game and preserving timber.

forestry right. (1992) A land interest under which a person has the right to enter the land, establish and maintain a crop of trees, harvest them, and construct works for that purpose.

Forest Service. An agency in the U.S. Department of Agriculture responsible for managing the country's national forests. • The Forest Service also operates the Youth Conservation Corps and the Volunteers in the National Forest programs.

forethought. (14c) The thinking and planning that takes place before one does something; PREMEDITATION.

forfeiture (**for**-fi-chər), *n.* (14c) **1.** The divestiture of property without compensation. **2.** The loss of a right, privilege, or property because of a crime, breach of obligation, or neglect of duty. • Title is instantaneously transferred to another, such as the government, a corporation, or a private person. **3.** A destruction or deprivation of some estate or right because of the failure to perform some contractual obligation or condition.

"[When a condition] is not likely to occur until the obligee has relied on the expected exchange by, for example, performing or preparing to perform, . . . nonoccurrence of the condition results in the obligee's loss of its reliance interest when the obligee loses the right to that exchange. This loss of reliance interest is often described as 'forfeiture.'" E. Allan Farnsworth, *Contracts* § 8.4, at 533 (3d ed. 1999).

4. Something (esp. money or property) lost or confiscated by this process; a penalty, fine, or mulct. **5.** A judicial proceeding, the object of which is to effect a confiscation or divestiture. — **forfeit,** *vb.* — **forfeitable,** *adj.*

▸ **civil forfeiture.** (1867) An in rem proceeding brought by the government against property that either facilitated a crime or was acquired as a result of criminal activity.

▸ **completed-elective forfeiture.** (1917) A forfeiture accomplished by the exercise of the will of one of the parties interested, as when a lease becomes voidable upon the breach of a covenant and the lessor then elects to terminate the lease.

▸ **criminal forfeiture.** (1866) A governmental proceeding brought against a person to seize property as punishment for the person's criminal behavior.

▸ **forfeiture by wrongdoing.** (1976) *Criminal law.* **1.** The loss of a property right (as to a car or cash) by virtue of one's involvement in crime. **2.** A defendant's intentional or wrongful act of making a declarant unavailable to testify, thereby waiving the hearsay rule regarding the declarant's statement and waiving the right to confront the witness.

▸ **forfeiture of marriage.** (17c) *Hist.* A monetary penalty exacted by a lord from a ward who married without the lord's consent. • The penalty was a money payment double the value that the marriage would otherwise have been worth to the lord.

▸ **forfeiture of pay.** (17c) *Military law.* A punishment depriving the guilty party of all or part of his or her military pay.

▸ **potential-elective forfeiture.** (1917) A situation from which a forfeiture may or may not be accomplished, as when a lease becomes voidable upon the breach of a covenant and the lessor has not yet elected whether to terminate the lease.

▸ **real forfeiture.** (1917) A forfeiture that operates automatically, as when an estate is granted upon conditional limitation and terminates in accordance with the stipulation.

forfeiture by wrongdoing. See FORFEITURE.

forfeiture clause. (1804) **1.** A contractual provision stating that, under certain circumstances, one party must forfeit something to the other. • Forfeiture clauses are often held to be void, although they are similar to conditions and other qualifications of estates in land. **2.** NO-CONTEST CLAUSE.

forfeiture restraint. (1935) An attempt by an otherwise effective conveyance or contract to cause a later conveyance to terminate or to make some or all of the later conveyance subject to termination. — Sometimes shortened to *restraint.*

forgavel (for-**gav**-əl). (18c) *Hist.* A small reserved rent in money; quit-rent.

***Forgay* rule.** See PRACTICAL FINALITY. The name derives from *Forgay v. Conrad,* 47 U.S. (6 How.) 201 (1848). — Also termed *Forgay–Conrad doctrine.*

forged document. See DOCUMENT (2).

forgery, *n.* (16c) **1.** The act of fraudulently making a false document or altering a real one to be used as if genuine <the contract was void because of the seller's forgery>. • Though forgery was a misdemeanor at common law, modern statutes typically make it a felony. — Also termed *false making.* **2.** A false or altered document made to look genuine by someone with the intent to deceive <he was not the true property owner because the deed was a forgery>. — Also termed *fake.* **3.** Under the Model Penal Code, the act of fraudulently altering, authenticating, issuing, or transferring a writing without appropriate authorization. • Under the explicit terms of the Code, *writing* can include items such as coins and credit cards. Model Penal Code § 224.1(1). — **forge,** *vb.* — **forger,** *n.*

> "Forgery at the common law, is an offence in falsly and fraudulently making or altering any manner of record, or any other authentick matter of a publick nature; as a parish register, or any deed, will, privy seal, certificate of holy orders, protection of a parliament man, and the like. As for writings of an inferior nature, as private letters, and such like, the counterfeiting of them is not properly forgery; therefore in some cases it may be more safe to prosecute such offenders for a misdemeanor, or cheats. For by reason of the uncertainty of opinions, concerning proper forgeries at common law, indictments are generally brought upon some of the following statutes, and very few at common law. But if the indictment is at common law, and the offender is convicted, he may be pillored, fined, and imprisoned." Edward Bullingbrooke, *The Duty and Authority of Justices of the Peace and Parish Officers for Ireland* 323 (rev. ed. 1788) (citations omitted).

> "As the law then stood, forgery was variously defined as the making of a false instrument with intent to deceive (Buller, J.); a false signature made with intent to deceive; or the false making of an instrument which purports on the face of it to be good and valid for the purposes for which it was created, with a design to defraud (Eyre, B.); the false making of a note or other instrument with intent to defraud (Grose, J., on behalf of the twelve judges); fraudulently writing or publishing a false deed or writing, to the prejudice of the right of another (Comyns, C.B.); the fraudulent making or alteration of a writing to the prejudice of another man's right (Hawkins); a false making, a making *malo animo,* of any written instrument, for the purpose of fraud and deceit (East); and a fraudulent making or alteration of a writing to the prejudice of another man's right (Blackstone)." Leon Radzinowicz, *A History of English Criminal Law and Its Administration from 1750: The Movement for Reform, 1750–1833* 642 (1948) (citations omitted).

> "While it is true that there is a distinction between fraud and forgery, and forgery contains some elements that are not included in fraud, forgeries are a species of fraud. In essence, the crime of forgery involves the making, altering, or completing of an instrument by someone other than the ostensible maker or drawer or an agent of the ostensible maker or drawer." 37 C.J.S. *Forgery* § 2, at 66 (1997).

▸ **double forgery.** A draft having a forged payor signature and a forged indorsement.

forgiven debt. See DEBT.

fori disputationes (**for**-I dis-pyoo-tay-shee-**oh**-neez). [Latin "arguments of the court"] *Roman law.* Arguments or discussions before a court.

forinsec service (fə-**rin**-sik). (18c) *Hist.* The feudal services owed by a mesne (i.e., intermediate) lord, esp. those of a military nature. — Also termed *foreign service; forinsecum servitium.* Cf. INTRINSEC SERVICE.

> "The terminology of Bracton's day and of yet earlier times neatly expresses the distinction between the service which the tenant owes to his immediate lord by reason of the bargain which exists between them, and the service which was incumbent on the tenement whilst it was in the lord's hand. The former is intrinsec service, the latter forinsec service; the former is the service which is created by, which (as it were) arises within, the bargain between the two persons, *A* and *B*, whose rights and duties we are discussing; the latter arises outside that bargain, is 'foreign' to that bargain . . . . [T]he term is a relative one; what is 'intrinsec' between *A* and *B* is 'forinsec' as regards *C*." 1 Frederick Pollock & Frederic W. Maitland, *The History of English Law Before the Time of Edward I* 238, 239 n.2 (2d ed. 1898).

forinsecum servitium. See FORINSEC SERVICE.

forinsecus (fə-**rin**-sə-kəs), *adv.* [fr. Latin *foris* "without"] *Hist.* On the outside.

forinsecus (fə-**rin**-sə-kəs), *n.* [Latin] *Hist.* A foreigner; someone from another jurisdiction.

foris (**for**-is), *adj.* [Latin] Abroad; outdoors; without.

forisbanitus (for-is-**ban**-ə-təs). See FORBANNITUS.

forisbannire (for-is-bə-**nI**-ree), *vb.* [Law Latin "to banish"] *Hist.* To expel from a certain territory; to banish.

forisfacere (for-is-**fay**-sə-ree), *vb.* [fr. Latin *foris* "without" + *facere* "to make"] *Hist.* **1.** To forfeit (an estate or other property). • Literally, this means to make the property foreign to oneself. **2.** To violate the law; to do a thing against or without the law.

forisfactum (for-is-**fak**-təm), *adj.* [Law Latin] *Hist.* (Of property) forfeited.

forisfactus (for-is-**fak**-təs). [Law Latin] *Hist.* A criminal; esp., one who has forfeited his or her life by committing a capital offense.

▸ **forisfactus servus** (for-is-**fak**-təs **sər**-vəs). [Law Latin] *Hist.* A freed slave who has forfeited his or her freedom by committing a crime.

forisfamiliate (for-is-fə-**mil**-ee-ayt), *vb.* [fr. Latin *foris* "outside" + *familia* "family"] (16c) *Hist.* To emancipate (a son) from paternal authority by a gift of land. • This act usu. rendered the son ineligible to inherit more property. — Also termed (archaically) *forisfamiliare.*

forisfamiliated (for-is-fə-**mil**-ee-ay-tid), *adj.* (18c) *Hist.* (Of a son) emancipated from paternal authority and in possession of a portion of family land in lieu of inheritance.

> "If our English law at any time knew an enduring *patria potestas* which could be likened to the Roman, that time had passed away long before the days of Bracton. . . . Bracton, it is true, has copied about this matter some sentences from the Institutes which he ought not to have copied; but he soon forgets them, and we easily see that they belong to an alien system. Our law knows no such thing as 'emancipation,' it merely knows an attainment of full age. . . . In old times a forisfamiliated son, that is, one whom his father had enfeoffed, was excluded from the inheritance. This is already antiquated, yet Bracton can find nothing else to serve instead of an *emancipatio.*" 2 Frederick Pollock & Frederic W. Maitland, *The History of English Law Before the Time of Edward I* 438, 438 n.3 (2d ed. 1899).

forisfamiliation. (17c) *Scots law.* The liberation of a child from the father's tutelage, as when a child under the age of majority left home, was given seisin in a part of the father's land, or accepted something as a settled inheritance. Cf. EMANCIPATION (2).

forisjudicatio. See FORJUDGER.

forisjudicatus. See FORJUDGER.

forisjurare (for-is-jə-**rair**-ee), *vb.* [Law Latin] *Hist.* To forswear; to renounce under oath. — Also termed *forjurer.*

forisjurare parentilam (for-is-jə-**rair**-ee pə-**ren**-tə-ləm), *vb.* [Law Latin] *Hist.* To renounce parental authority. • One who did so lost all rights of heirship.

forisjurare provinciam (for-is-jə-**rair**-ee prə-**vin**-shee-əm), *vb.* [Law Latin] *Hist.* To renounce under oath allegiance to one's country.

forjudge, *vb.* (15c) **1.** *Hist.* To expel a person, esp. an officer or attorney, from court for some offense or misconduct. **2.** To deprive (a person) of a thing by a judgment; to condemn (a person) to lose a thing. — Also spelled (loosely) *forejudge.*

forjudger (for-**jəj**-ər), *n.* (15c) *Hist.* **1.** A judgment that deprives a person of a thing. **2.** A judgment of expulsion or banishment. — Also termed *forisjudicatio; forisjudicatus.*

forjurer. See FORISJURARE.

forjurer royalme (for-zhə-**ray** roy-**ohm**), *vb.* [Law French] *Hist.* To renounce the kingdom under oath; to abjure the realm.

form, *n.* (13c) **1.** The outer shape, structure, or configuration of something, as distinguished from its substance or matter <courts are generally less concerned about defects in form than defects in substance>. **2.** Established behavior or procedure, usu. according to custom or rule <the prosecutor followed the established form in her closing argument>. **3.** A model; a sample; an example <attorneys often draft pleadings by using a form instead of starting from scratch>. **4.** The customary method of drafting legal documents, usu. with fixed words, phrases, and sentences <Jones prepared the contract merely by following the state bar's form>. **5.** A legal document with blank spaces to be filled in by the drafter <the divorce lawyer used printed forms that a secretary could fill in>.

Form 8-K. See 8-K.

Form 10-K. See 10-K.

Form 10-Q. See 10-Q.

Form 990. *Tax.* The IRS form for extensive annual reporting by organizations, other than private foundations, that are exempt from income tax under §§ 501(c), 527, or 4947(a)(1) of the Internal Revenue Code. • Form 990-EZ is a short-form return used by organizations with gross receipts less than $200,000 and total assets less than $500,000.

Form 8283. *Tax.* The IRS form for annual reporting of noncash charitable contributions. • Donated property over $5,000 in value requires appraisal and signature of donee.

forma (**for**-mə). [Latin "form"] *Hist.* The prescribed form of judicial proceedings.

forma et figura judicii (**for**-mə et **fig**-yər-ə joo-**dish**-ee-ı). [Latin] *Hist.* The form and shape of judgment. • A form prescribed by statute.

formal, *adj.* (14c) **1.** Of, relating to, or involving established procedural rules, customs, and practices. **2.** Ceremonial.

formal abandonment. See *express abandonment* under ABANDONMENT (11).

formal acknowledgment. See ACKNOWLEDGMENT.

formal admission. See ADMISSION (1).

formal agreement. See AGREEMENT.

formal contract. See CONTRACT.

formal drawing. See DRAWING.

formal fallacy. See FALLACY.

formal impeachment. See IMPEACHMENT (3).

formalism (**for**-mə-liz-əm), *n.* **1.** LEGAL FORMALISM. **2.** An approach to law, and esp. to constitutional and statutory interpretation, holding that (1) where an authoritative text governs, meaning is to be derived from its words, (2) the meaning so derived can be applied to particular facts, (3) some situations are governed by that meaning, and some are not, and (4) the standards for deciding what constitutes following the rules is objectively ascertainable. **3.** Decision-making on the basis of form rather than substance; specif., an interpretive method whereby the judge adheres to the words rather than pursuing the text's unexpressed purposes (purposivism) or evaluating its consequences (consequentialism). Cf. ANTIFORMALISM; PURPOSIVISM; CONSEQUENTIALISM (2). — **formalist,** *n.*

> "Of all the criticisms leveled against textualism, the most mindless is that it is 'formalistic.' The answer to that is, *of course it's formalistic!* The rule of law is *about* form. If, for example, a citizen performs an act — let us say the sale of certain technology to a foreign country — which is prohibited by a widely publicized bill proposed by the administration and passed by both houses of Congress, *but not yet signed by the President,* that sale is lawful. It is of no consequence that everyone knows both houses of Congress and the President wish to prevent that sale. Before the wish becomes a binding law, it must be embodied in a bill that passes both houses and is signed by the President. Is that not formalism? A murderer has been caught with blood on his hands, bending over the body of his victim; a neighbor with a video camera has filmed the crime; and the murderer has confessed in writing and on videotape. We nonetheless insist that before the state can punish this miscreant, it must conduct a full-dress criminal trial that results in a verdict of guilty. Is that not formalism? Long live formalism. It is what makes a government a government of laws and not of men." Antonin Scalia, *A Matter of Interpretation* 25 (1997).

formalistic, *adj.* (1839) Of, relating to, or involving excessive adherence to matters of form, esp. at the expense of concerns about substance.

formality. (16c) **1.** (*usu. pl.*) An act, esp. an established form or conventional procedure, that must be done to make something legal. **2.** Something that is done as part of an official process but will not affect the outcome. **3.** *Hist.* (*pl.*) Robes worn by magistrates on solemn occasions. **4.** *Copyright.* (*usu. pl.*) A procedural requirement formerly required before receiving U.S. copyright protection. • Formalities included (1) a copyright notice appearing on the work, (2) actual publication, (3) registration with the Copyright Office, and (4) deposit of the work with the Library of Congress. The formality requirements eroded during the 20th century. Today, none are required, although registration remains a prerequisite for an infringement suit by U.S. authors in the United States.

formal law. (17c) Procedural law.

> "Procedure is by many German writers inappropriately called 'formal law.'" Thomas E. Holland, *The Elements of Jurisprudence* 358 n.2 (13th ed. 1924).

formal party. See *nominal party* under PARTY (2).

formal rejection. See REJECTION.

formal rulemaking. See RULEMAKING.

formal witness statement. See WITNESS STATEMENT (2).

forma pauperis. See IN FORMA PAUPERIS.

formata (for-**may**-tə). [Law Latin] *Eccles. law.* Canonical letters.

formata brevia. See BREVIA FORMATA.

formation. (15c) **1.** The process or action of forming something or of being formed. **2.** The thing being formed. 3. A particular arrangement, as of troops, vessels, or aircraft.

forma verborum (**for**-mə vər-**bor**-əm). [Latin] (17c) *Hist.* The form of the words.

formbook. (1830) A book that contains sample legal documents, esp. transaction-related documents such as contracts, deeds, leases, wills, trusts, and securities disclosure documents.

form contract. See *standard form contract* under CONTRACT.

formed design. See DESIGN (2).

formedon (for-mə-don). [fr. Latin *forma doni* "form of the gift"] (15c) *Hist.* A writ of right for claiming entailed property held by another. • A writ of formedon was the highest remedy available to a tenant in tail. — Also termed *writ of formedon.*

> "Called *formedon,* because the writ comprehended the *form of the gift.* It was of three kinds, in the *descender,* in the *remainder,* and in the *reverter.*" 1 Alexander M. Burrill, *A Law Dictionary and Glossary* 650 (2d ed. 1867).

▸ **formedon in the descender.** (17c) A writ of formedon brought by the issue in tail to recover possession of the land.

▸ **formedon in the remainder.** (16c) A writ of formedon brought by a remainderman under a grant or gift in tail to recover possession of the land.

▸ **formedon in the reverter.** (17c) A writ of formedon brought by a reversioner or donor of the grant or gift in tail to recover possession of the land.

former acquittal. See *autrefois acquit* under AUTREFOIS.

former adjudication. (18c) A judgment in a prior action that resulted in a final determination of the rights of the parties or essential fact questions and serves to bar relitigation of the issues relevant to that determination. • Collateral estoppel and res judicata are the two types of former adjudication. See COLLATERAL ESTOPPEL; RES JUDICATA.

former jeopardy. (1870) The fact of having previously been prosecuted for the same offense. • A defendant enters a plea of former jeopardy to inform the court that a second prosecution is improper. Cf. DOUBLE JEOPARDY.

former punishment. *Military law.* The rule that nonjudicial punishment for a minor offense may bar trial by court-martial for the same offense.

former testimony. See TESTIMONY.

form letter. (1909) **1.** A standard letter that is sent to many people over time, esp. because it relates to a matter of frequent recurrence. **2.** A mass-circulation letter, usu. one with a generic salutation (e.g., *Dear Patron of the Arts*) and no personalized message.

form of action. (17c) The common-law legal and procedural device associated with a particular writ, each of which had specific forms of process, pleading, trial, and judgment. • The 11 common-law forms of action were trespass, trespass on the case, trover, ejectment, detinue, replevin, debt, covenant, account, special assumpsit, and general assumpsit.

> "Forms of action are usually regarded as different methods of procedure adapted to cases of different kinds, but in fact the choice between forms of action is primarily a choice between different theories of substantive liability, and the scope of the actions measures the existence and extent of liability at common law. . . . The development and extension of the different forms of action is the history of the recognition of rights and liability in the law of torts, contracts, and property, and the essentials of rights of action." Benjamin J. Shipman, *Handbook of Common-Law Pleading* §§ 27, 30 at 54, 60 (Henry Winthrop Ballantine ed., 3d ed. 1923).

Form S-1. See S-1.

formula. [Latin "set form of words"] (17c) **1.** *Roman law.* A written document, prepared by a praetor and forwarded to a judex, identifying the issue to be tried and the judgment to be given by the judex. • It was based on model pleas formulated by the praetor in his edict and adapted by him or other magistrates in civil suits for the benefit of the judex who had to try the issue. These pleas were adapted to the circumstances of the case. The usual parts of a formula were (1) the *demonstratio,* in which the plaintiff stated the facts of the claim; (2) the *intentio,* in which the plaintiff specified the relief sought against the defendant; and (3) the *condemnatio,* in which the judex condemned (usu. to pay the plaintiff a sum) or acquitted the defendant. — Also termed *verba concepta* (**vər**-bə kən-**sep**-tə). Pl. **formulae** (**for**-myə-lee).

> "By the second century [*legis actiones*] . . . had become stereotyped; they were few, and the development of new forms seemed impossible. But with the introduction of the formulary procedure by the *lex Aebutia* (second century) a task of unprecedented importance was laid upon the jurisconsults. It was now the business of the plaintiff to present to the magistrate (the most important was the praetor) a draft statement of claim (*formula*); the defendant might propose modifications of the draft, for example the insertion of a special defence (*exceptio*); the magistrate too might make his authorization of the proposed formula conditional on the plaintiff accepting certain changes in it. The settling of the formula was thus an extremely technical process, for which professional help was indispensable, since neither the parties nor the magistrate, unless by exception he happened to be a jurist himself, would possess the requisite legal knowledge. The work of the pontiffs in composing the solemn words of the *legis actiones* was insignificant in comparison with the achievements of the jurists of the Hellenistic period in devising the formulae of the new procedure." Fritz Schultz, *History of Roman Legal Science* 50 (rev. ed. 1967).

2. *Common-law pleading.* A set form of words (such as those appearing in writs) used in judicial proceedings. Pl. **formulas.**

formula deal. (1946) An agreement between a movie distributor and an independent or affiliated circuit to exhibit a feature movie in all theaters at a specified percentage of the national gross receipts realized by the theaters.

formula direction. See *formula instruction* under JURY INSTRUCTION.

formulae (**for**-myə-lee). [Latin "set forms of words"] *Roman law.* Model pleas formulated by the praetor in his edict and adapted by him or other magistrates in civil suits for the benefit of the judex who had to try the issue. • These pleas were adapted to the circumstances of the case. — Also termed *verba concepta* (**vər**-bə kən-**sep**-tə).

formula instruction. See JURY INSTRUCTION.

formulary. (16c) **1.** *Hist.* A collection of the forms of proceedings (*formulae*) used in litigation, such as the writ forms kept by the Chancery. See WRIT SYSTEM. **2.** A list of drugs that Medicare or a health-maintenance organization will pay for.

formulary procedure. (1885) *Hist.* The common-law method of pleading and practice, which required formulaic compliance with the accepted forms of action even if through elaborate fictions. • In the 19th century, this type of procedure was replaced both in the United States and in England. See *code pleading* under PLEADING (2).

fornication, *n.* (14c) **1.** Voluntary sexual intercourse between two unmarried persons. • Fornication is still a crime (usu. a misdemeanor) in some states, such as Virginia. **2.** *Hist.* Voluntary sexual intercourse with an unmarried woman. • At common law, the status of the woman determined whether the offense was adultery or fornication — *adultery* was sexual intercourse between a man, single or married, and a married woman not his wife; *fornication* was sexual intercourse between a man, single or married, and a single woman. Cf. ADULTERY. — **fornicate,** *vb.* — **fornicator,** *n.*

> "Fornication was not a common-law crime but was made punishable by statute in a few states as a misdemeanor." Rollin M. Perkins & Ronald N. Boyce, *Criminal Law* 455 (3d ed. 1982).

fornix (**for**-niks). [Latin] *Hist.* **1.** A brothel. **2.** Fornication.

forprise (for-**prɪz**). (16c) *Hist.* **1.** An exception or reservation. • The term was frequently used in leases and conveyances.

> "Forprise . . . [a]n exception or reservation. . . . We still use it in Conveyances and Leases, wherein *Excepted* and *Forprised* is an usual expression." Thomas Blount, *Nomo-Lexicon: A Law-Dictionary* (1670).

2. An exaction. — **forprise,** *vb.*

for-profit corporation. See CORPORATION.

forschel (**for**-shəl). *Hist.* A strip of land next to a highway. — Also termed *forschet.*

forspeca (for-**spee**-kə). **1.** PROLOCUTOR (2). **2.** PARANYMPHUS.

forstall. See FORESTALL.

forswearing (for-**swair**-ing), *n.* (14c) **1.** The act of repudiating or renouncing under oath. **2.** PERJURY. — **forswear,** *vb.*

fortax (for-**taks**), *vb. Hist.* To tax wrongly or extortionately.

forthcoming, *n.* (17c) *Scots law.* **1.** An action through which arrestment is made available to an arrester. **2.** An order that perfects an arrestment by directing a debtor either to pay the money owed or to deliver the arrested goods to the creditor.

forthcoming bond. See BOND (2).

forthright, *adj.* (1855) **1.** Direct, honest, and candid; straightforward. **2.** Expressed without evasion or equivocation.

forthwith, *adv.* (14c) **1.** Immediately; without delay. **2.** Directly; promptly; within a reasonable time under the circumstances; with all convenient dispatch.

fortia (**for**-shə). [Law Latin] *Hist.* **1.** Force. • *Fortia* refers to force used by an accessory to allow the principal to commit the crime. **2.** Power, dominion, or jurisdiction.

fortia frisca (**for**-shə **fris**-kə). [Law Latin] *Hist.* See FRESH FORCE.

fortior (**for**-shee-ər *or* -or), *adj.* [Latin "stronger"] *Hist.* (Of evidence) involving a presumption that, because of the strength of a party's evidence, shifts the burden of proof to the opposing party.

fortuitous (for-**t[y]oo**-ə-təs), *adj.* (17c) Occurring by chance; accidental. • A fortuitous event may be highly unfortunate. Literally, the term is neutral, despite its common misuse as a synonym for *fortunate.*

fortuitous collision. See COLLISION.

fortuitous event. (1856) **1.** A happening that, because it occurs only by chance or accident, the parties could not reasonably have foreseen. **2.** An event that, so far as contracting parties are aware, depends on chance. **3.** *Louisiana law.* An event that could not have been reasonably foreseen at the time a contract was made. La. Civ. Code art. 1875. — Also termed *cas fortuit.* See FORCE MAJEURE; UNAVOIDABLE-ACCIDENT DOCTRINE.

Fortune 500. An annual compilation of the 500 largest U.S. corporations as ranked by gross revenues. • It is published in, and gets its name from, *Fortune* magazine.

forty, *n.* (1845) *Archaic.* Forty acres of land in the form of a square <the south forty>. • To determine a forty, a section of land (640 acres) was quartered, and one of those quarters was again quartered.

forty-days court. See COURT OF ATTACHMENTS.

forum, *n.* (15c) **1.** A public place, esp. one devoted to assembly or debate. See PUBLIC FORUM; NONPUBLIC FORUM. **2.** A court or other judicial body; a place of jurisdiction. Pl. **forums, fora.**

▸ **neutral forum.** A forum where all parties are equal and the decision-makers are impartial and disinterested.

▸ **public forum.** See PUBLIC FORUM.

forum actus (**for**-əm **ak**-təs). [Latin "the forum of the act"] (1888) *Hist.* The place where an act was done.

forum arresti (**for**-əm ə-**res**-tɪ). [Latin] *Hist.* Forum of the arrest.

forum competens (**for**-əm **kom**-pə-tenz). [Latin] (18c) *Hist.* A competent court; a court that has jurisdiction over a case.

forum connexitatis (**for**-əm kə-nek-si-**tay**-tis). [Latin] *Hist.* Forum of the connection.

forum conscientiae (**for**-əm kon-shee-**en**-shee-ee). [Latin "the forum of conscience"] (16c) *Hist.* The tribunal or court of conscience. • This court was usu. a court of equity. See COURT OF CONSCIENCE.

forum contentiosum (**for**-əm kən-ten-shee-**oh**-səm). [Latin "the forum of contention"] (17c) *Hist.* A court of justice; a place for litigation.

forum contractus (**for**-əm kən-**trak**-təs). [Latin "the forum of the contract"] (1836) *Hist.* **1.** The place where a contract was made, and thus the place of jurisdiction. **2.** The court of the place where a contract was made.

forum conveniens (**for**-əm kən-**vee**-nee-enz). [Latin "a suitable forum"] (1868) The court in which an action is most appropriately brought, considering the best interests and convenience of the parties and witnesses. Cf. FORUM NON CONVENIENS.

forum delicti (**for**-əm də-**lik**-tɪ). [Latin] *Hist.* Forum of the wrongdoing.

forum domesticum (**for**-əm də-**mes**-ti-kəm). [Latin] (1838) *Hist.* A domestic court. • This type of court decides matters (such as professional discipline) arising within the organization that created it.

forum domicilii (**for**-əm dom-ə-**sil**-ee-ɪ). [Latin] (17c) *Hist.* The forum or court of someone's domicile, usu. that of the defendant.

forum ecclesiasticum (**for**-əm e-klee-z[h]ee-**as**-ti-kəm). [Latin] (17c) *Hist.* An ecclesiastical court. — Also termed *judicium ecclesiasticum.*

forum externum (**for**-əm ek-**stər**-nəm), *n.* [Latin "external tribunal"] (17c) *Eccles. law.* A court dealing with legal cases relating to or involving the corporate life of the church.

forum inconveniens. See FORUM NON CONVENIENS.

forum internum (**for**-əm in-**tər**-nəm), *n.* [Latin "internal tribunal"] (17c) *Eccles. law.* A court of conscience; a court for matters of conscience or the confessional.

forum ligeantiae rei (**for**-əm lij-ee-**an**-shee-ee **ree**-ɪ). [Latin] (1886) *Hist.* The forum of the defendant's allegiance; the court or jurisdiction of the country to which the defendant owes allegiance.

forum loci patrimonii (**for**-əm **loh**-sɪ pat-ri-**moh**-nee-ɪ). [Latin] *Hist.* Forum of the site of the patrimony.

forum non competens (**for**-əm non **kom**-pə-tenz). [Latin] (1865) *Hist.* An inappropriate court; a court that lacks jurisdiction over a case.

forum non conveniens (**for**-əm non kən-**vee**-nee-enz). [Latin "an unsuitable court"] (1879) *Civil procedure.* The doctrine that an appropriate forum — even though competent under the law — may divest itself of jurisdiction if, for the convenience of the litigants and the witnesses, it appears that the action should proceed in another forum in which the action might also have been properly brought in the first place. — Also termed *forum inconveniens.*

> "Forum non conveniens allows a court to exercise its discretion to avoid the oppression or vexation that might result from automatically honoring plaintiff's forum choice. However, dismissal on the basis of forum non conveniens also requires that there be an alternative forum in which the suit can be prosecuted. It must appear that jurisdiction over all parties can be secured and that complete relief can be obtained in the supposedly more convenient court. Further, in at least some states, it has been held that the doctrine cannot be successfully invoked when the plaintiff is resident of the forum state since, effectively, one of the functions of the state courts is to provide a tribunal in which their residents can obtain an adjudication of their grievances. But in most instances a balancing of the convenience to all the parties will be considered and no one factor will preclude a forum non coveniens dismissal, as long as another forum is available." Jack H. Friedenthal et al., *Civil Procedure* § 2.17, at 87–88 (2d ed. 1993).

forum originis (**for**-əm ə-**rij**-ə-nis). [Latin] (17c) *Hist.* The forum or place either of a person's birth or of the father's citizenship, considered as a place of jurisdiction.

forum prorogatum (**for**-əm proh-roh-**gay**-təm). [Latin] *Hist.* The deferred forum.

forum regium (**for**-əm **ree**-jee-əm). [Latin] *Hist.* The king's court.

forum rei (**for**-əm **ree**-ɪ). [Latin] (18c) *Hist.* **1.** The forum of the defendant, i.e., the place where the defendant is domiciled or resides. **2.** FORUM REI SITAE.

forum rei gestae (**for**-əm **ree**-ɪ **jes**-tee). [Latin] (1861) *Hist.* The forum or court of a *res gesta* (thing done); the place where an act was done, considered as a place of jurisdiction.

forum rei sitae (**for**-əm **ree**-ɪ **sɪ**-tee). [Latin] (1885) *Hist.* The court where the thing or subject-matter in controversy is situated, considered as a place of jurisdiction. — Often shortened to *forum rei.*

forum seculare (**for**-əm sek-yə-**lair**-ee). [Latin] (1806) *Hist.* A secular court. — Also spelled *forum saeculare.*

forum-selection clause. (1970) A contractual provision in which the parties establish the place (such as the country, state, or type of court) for specified litigation between them. — Also termed *choice-of-exclusive-forum clause; prorogation clause; jurisdiction-prorogation clause.* Cf. CHOICE-OF-LAW CLAUSE.

forum-shopping. (1954) The practice of choosing the most favorable jurisdiction or court in which a claim might be heard. • A plaintiff might engage in forum-shopping, for example, by filing suit in a jurisdiction with a reputation for high jury awards or by filing several similar suits and keeping the one with the preferred judge. Cf. JUDGE-SHOPPING.

forum state. (1911) *Conflict of laws.* The state in which a lawsuit is filed.

for use. For the benefit or advantage of another. See USE.

forward agreement. See *forward contract* under CONTRACT.

forward and backward at sea. *Marine insurance.* From port to port in the course of a voyage, and not merely from one terminus to the other and back.

forward confusion. See CONFUSION.

forward contract. See CONTRACT.

forward cover. The purchase of a cash commodity to meet the obligation of a forward contract. See *forward contract* under CONTRACT.

forwarding agent. See AGENT.

forward-looking, *adj.* (18c) Of, relating to, or involving the future; contemplating events to come.

forward-looking statement. A business's announcement about something yet to happen, such as its possibilities or expectations for future operations or economic performance. • A forward-looking statement may be misleading if it is not clearly making predictions rather than stating facts.

forward market. See *futures market* under MARKET.

forward-rate agreement. (1996) A contract that specifies what the interest rate on an obligation will be on some future date. — Abbr. FRA.

forward triangular merger. See *triangular merger* under MERGER (8).

fossage (**fos**-ij), *n.* (18c) *Hist.* A duty paid to maintain a moat around a fortification.

foster, *adj.* (bef. 12c) **1.** (Of a relationship) involving parental care given by someone not related by blood or legal adoption <foster home>. **2.** (Of a person) giving or receiving parental care to or from someone not related by blood or legal adoption <foster parent> <foster child>.

foster, *vb.* (12c) **1.** To give care to or promote the growth and development of (something or someone); esp., to give parental care to (a child who is not one's natural or legally adopted child). **2.** To give aid or encouragement to; to sustain or promote.

fosterage, *n.* (17c) **1.** The act of caring for and esp. of rearing another's child. **2.** The entrusting of a child to another. **3.** The condition of being in the care of another. **4.** The act of encouraging or promoting.

foster care. (1876) **1.** A federally funded child-welfare program providing substitute care for abused and neglected children who have been removed by court order from their parents' or guardians' care or for children voluntarily placed by their parents in the temporary care of the state because of a family crisis. 42 USCA §§ 670–679a. • The state welfare agency selects, trains, supervises, and pays those who serve as foster parents. Cf. ADOPTION (1).

▸ **long-term foster care.** (1972) The placing of a child in foster care for extended periods, perhaps even for the child's entire minority, in lieu of family reunification, termination and adoption, or guardianship. • Although most courts do not generally find this arrangement to be in a child's best interests, sometimes it is the only possibility, as when the child, because of age or disability, is unlikely to be adopted or when, although the parent cannot be permanently reunited with the child, limited contact with the parent would serve the child's best interests. Under the Adoption and Safe Families Act, long-term foster care is the permanent placement of last resort.

2. The area of social services concerned with meeting the needs of children who participate in these types of programs.

foster-care drift. (1983) The phenomenon that occurs when children placed in foster care remain in that system, in legal limbo, for too many years of their developmental life before they are reunited with their parents or freed for adoption and placed in permanent homes. • The Adoption and Safe Families Act was enacted in 1997 to help rectify this problem. See ADOPTION AND SAFE FAMILIES ACT.

foster-care placement. (1968) The (usu. temporary) act of placing a child in a home with a person or persons who provide parental care for the child. Cf. OUT-OF-HOME PLACEMENT.

foster-care review board. (1991) A panel of screened and trained volunteers who routinely review cases of children placed in foster care, examine efforts at permanency planning, and report to the court.

foster child. See CHILD.

foster father. See *foster parent* under PARENT.

foster home. (19c) A household in which foster care is provided to a child who has been removed from his or her birth or adoptive parents, usu. for abuse or neglect. • A foster home is usu. an individual home, but it can also be a group home.

fosterlean (**fos**-tər-leen). (1902) *Hist.* Remuneration for rearing a foster child.

fosterling. (bef. 12c) See *foster child* under CHILD.

foster mother. See *foster parent* under PARENT.

foster parent. See PARENT (1).

foul bill of lading. See *unclean bill of lading* under BILL OF LADING.

foul play. (15c) **1.** Wrongdoing, esp. when it involves a person's murder. **2.** A dishonest, unfair, or rule-violating act, esp. one that happens during a sporting event.

foundation. (14c) **1.** The basis on which something is supported; esp., evidence or testimony that establishes the admissibility of other evidence <laying the foundation>. **2.** A fund established for charitable, educational, religious, research, or other benevolent purposes; an endowment <the Foundation for the Arts>.

▸ **private foundation.** (17c) A charitable organization that is funded by a single source, derives its income from investments rather than contributions, and makes grants to other charitable organizations. • A private foundation is generally exempt from taxation. IRC (26 USCA) § 509. — Also termed *private nonoperating foundation.*

▸ **private nonoperating foundation.** See *private foundation.*

▸ **private operating foundation.** (1978) A private foundation that conducts its own charitable program rather than making grants to other charitable organizations. • Most of the foundation's earnings and assets must be used to further its particular charitable purpose.

foundational evidence. See EVIDENCE.

foundational fact. See *predicate fact* under FACT.

founded on, *adj.* (16c) Having as a basis <the suit was founded on the defendant's breach of contract>.

founder, *n.* (14c) **1.** Someone who founds or establishes; esp., a person who supplies funds for an institution's future needs. **2.** SETTLOR (1).

founder's share. (*usu. pl.*) (1937) *English law.* In England, a share issued to the founder of a company as a part of the consideration for the business. • Now rare, a founder's share participates in profits only if the dividend on ordinary shares has been paid to a specified amount.

founding father. (1914) A prominent figure in the founding of an institution or esp. a country; specif., one who played a leading role in founding the United States of America, esp. in the Revolutionary War and the making of the U.S. Constitution.

foundling. (14c) A deserted or abandoned infant that is found and cared for by people other than its parents.

foundling hospital. (18c) A charitable institution, found esp. in Europe, the purpose of which is to care for abandoned children.

found property. See PROPERTY.

four, rule of. See RULE OF FOUR.

four corners. (1874) The face of a written instrument. • The phrase derives from the ancient custom of putting all instruments (such as contracts) on a single sheet of parchment, as opposed to multiple pages, no matter how long the sheet might be. At common law, this custom prevented people from fraudulently inserting materials into a fully signed agreement. The requirement was that every contract could have only four corners.

four-corners rule. (1948) **1.** The principle that a document's meaning is to be gathered from the entire document and not from its isolated parts. **2.** The principle that no extraneous evidence should be used to interpret an unambiguous document. Cf. PAROL-EVIDENCE RULE.

IV-D agency. See CHILD-SUPPORT-ENFORCEMENT AGENCY.

four-folding. (1822) *Hist.* The quadrupling of a property's taxable value for purposes of penalizing a person who falsely underreported the property's true taxable value.

> "In the State of Connecticut a number of men are chosen annually by each town, to receive from each inhabitant a list of the taxable property in his possession. This list is required by law; and is made up by the proprietor. The men, who receive it, are from their employment called *Listers*. If the proprietor gives in a false list, he is punished by having the falsified article increased on the list four-fold. . . . We therefore style this punishment *four-folding*." 4 Timothy Dwight, *Travels in New-England and New-York* 284 (1822).

401(k) plan. See EMPLOYEE BENEFIT PLAN.

402A action. (1969) A products-liability tort action, modeled after Section 402A of the Restatement (Second) of Torts. See PRODUCTS LIABILITY.

403(b) plan. See EMPLOYEE BENEFIT PLAN.

404(b) evidence. See EVIDENCE.

419 fraud. See *advance-fee fraud* under FRAUD.

457 plan. See EMPLOYEE BENEFIT PLAN.

Fourteenth Amendment. The constitutional amendment, ratified in 1868, whose primary provisions effectively apply the Bill of Rights to the states by prohibiting states from denying due process and equal protection and from abridging the privileges and immunities of U.S. citizenship. • The amendment also gave Congress the power to enforce these provisions, leading to legislation such as the civil-rights acts.

Fourth Amendment. The constitutional amendment, ratified with the Bill of Rights in 1791, prohibiting unreasonable searches and seizures and the issuance of warrants without probable cause. See PROBABLE CAUSE. Cf. ABANDONMENT DOCTRINE.

fourth estate. (1821) The journalistic profession; the news media. • The term comes from the British Parliament's reporters' gallery, whose influence was said to equal Parliament's three traditional estates: the Lords Spiritual, the Lords Temporal, and the Commons. (In France, the three estates were the clergy, the nobility, and the commons.)

Fourth of July. See INDEPENDENCE DAY (1).

fourth-sentence remand. See REMAND.

four unities. (1852) The four qualities needed to create a joint tenancy at common law — interest, possession, time, and title. See UNITY (2).

fovere consimilem causam (foh-**veer**-ee kən-**sim**-ə-ləm **kaw**-zəm). [Law Latin] *Hist.* To favor a similar case. • A judge who is disqualified for having a personal interest in a case may also be disqualified in a later case if the ruling in the former case could affect the ruling in the latter.

Fox's Libel Act. *Hist.* A 1792 statute that gave the jury in a libel prosecution the right of rendering a guilty or not-guilty verdict on the whole matter in issue. • The jury was no longer bound to find the defendant guilty if it found that the defendant had in fact published the allegedly libelous statement. The Act empowered juries to decide whether the defendant's statement conformed to the legal standard for libel.

foy (foy *or* fwah). [Law French] Faith; allegiance.

FPA. *abbr.* Free from particular average.

> "*F.P.A.* means Free from Particular Average; that is to say, the insured can recover only where the loss is total or is due to a general average sacrifice. The claims under the Sue and Labour clause are not affected by this stipulation." 2 E.W. Chance, *Principles of Mercantile Law* 128 (P.W. French ed., 10th ed. 1951).

FPAD. *abbr.* FREIGHT PAYABLE AT DESTINATION.

FPC clause. See AREA-RATE CLAUSE.

FPLS. *abbr.* FEDERAL PARENT LOCATOR SERVICE.

FPS. *abbr.* FEDERAL PROTECTIVE SERVICE.

Fr. *abbr.* **1.** French. **2.** FRAGMENTA.

FRA. *abbr.* **1.** FEDERAL RAILROAD ADMINISTRATION. **2.** FORWARD-RATE AGREEMENT.

fractional, *adj.* (1815) (Of a tract of land) covering an area less than the acreage reflected on a survey; of, relating to, or involving any irregular division of land containing either more or less than the conventional amount of acreage.

fractional currency. See CURRENCY.

fractional interest. See *undivided interest* under INTEREST (2).

fractional share. See SHARE (2).

fragmenta (frag-**men**-tə), *n. pl.* [Latin "fragments"] *Roman law.* Passages drawn from the writings of Roman jurists and compiled in Justinian's *Digest.* — Abbr. Fr.; Ff.

fragmented literal similarity. See SIMILARITY.

frame, *vb.* (14c) **1.** To plan, shape, or construct; esp., to draft or otherwise draw up (a document). **2.** To incriminate (an innocent person) with false evidence, esp. fabricated. — **framable, frameable,** *adj.*

frame-up, *n.* (1900) A plot to make an innocent person appear guilty.

framing. On the Internet, a website's display of another entity's webpage inside a bordered area, often without displaying the page's URL or domain name. • Framing may constitute a derivative work and may infringe on a copyright or trademark if done without giving credit to or obtaining permission from the other website's owner.

francbordus. See FREE-BORD.

franchise (**fran**-chIz), *n.* (14c) **1.** The right to vote. — Also termed *elective franchise.*

▸ **female franchise.** See *women's suffrage* under SUFFRAGE.

2. The government-conferred right or privilege to engage in a specific business or to exercise corporate powers. — Also termed *corporate franchise; general franchise.*

> "When referring to government grants (other than patents, trademarks, and copyrights), the term 'franchise' is often used to connote more substantial rights, whereas the term 'license' connotes lesser rights. Thus, the rights necessary for public utility companies to carry on their operations are generally designated as franchise rights. On the other hand, the rights to construct or to repair, the rights to practice certain professions, and the rights to use or to operate automobiles are generally referred to as licenses." 1 *Eckstrom's Licensing in Foreign and Domestic Operations* § 1.02[3], at 1-10 to 1-11 (David M. Epstein ed., 1998).

"In a violent conceptual collision, some franchisors maintain that a franchise is merely an embellished license and therefore revocable at will. Franchisees contend that a franchise is a license coupled with an interest, not subject to unlimited control by franchisors. As a result of this disagreement, legislative draftsmen have had difficulty defining 'franchise.'" 1 Harold Brown, *Franchising: Realities and Remedies* § 1.03[1], at 1-17 (rev. ed. 1993).

▸ **franchise appurtenant to land.** (1919) *Rare.* A franchise that is used in connection with real property and thus is sometimes characterized as real property.

▸ **general franchise.** (1871) A corporation's charter.

▸ **special franchise.** (1827) A right conferred by the government, esp. one given to a public utility, to use property for a public use but for private profit.

3. The sole right granted by the owner of a trademark or tradename to engage in business or to sell a good or service in a certain area. **4.** The business or territory controlled by the person or entity that has been granted such a right.

▸ **business franchise.** See *commercial franchise.*

▸ **commercial franchise.** (1968) A franchise using local capital and management by contracting with third parties to operate a facility identified as offering a particular brand of goods or services. — Also termed *business franchise.*

▸ **sports franchise.** (1961) **1.** A franchise granted by a professional sports league to field a team in that league. **2.** The team itself.

▸ **trial franchise.** (1980) A franchise having an initial term of limited duration, such as one year.

franchise, *vb.* (14c) To grant (to another) the sole right of engaging in a certain business or in a business using a particular trademark in a certain area.

franchise agreement. (1905) The contract between a franchisor and franchisee establishing the terms and conditions of the franchise relationship. • State and federal laws regulate franchise agreements.

franchise appurtenant to land. See FRANCHISE (2).

franchise clause. (1967) *Insurance.* A provision in a casualty insurance policy stating that the insurer will pay a claim only if it is more than a stated amount, and that the insured is responsible for all damages if the claim is under that amount. • Unlike a deductible, which the insured always has to pay, with a franchise clause, once the claim exceeds the stated amount, the insurer pays the entire claim.

franchise court. (1864) *Hist.* A privately held court that (usu.) exists by virtue of a royal grant, with jurisdiction over a variety of matters, depending on the grant and whatever powers the court acquires over time. • In 1274, Edward I abolished many of these feudal courts by forcing the nobility to demonstrate by what authority (*quo warranto*) they held court. If a lord could not produce a charter reflecting the franchise, the court was abolished. — Also termed *courts of the franchise.*

"Dispensing justice was profitable. Much revenue could come from the fees and dues, fines and amercements. This explains the growth of the second class of feudal courts, the *Franchise Courts.* They too were private courts held by feudal lords. Sometimes their claim to jurisdiction was based on old pre-Conquest grants . . . . But many of them were, in reality, only wrongful usurpations of private jurisdiction by powerful lords. These were put down after the famous *Quo Warranto* enquiry in the reign of Edward I." W.J.V. Windeyer, *Lectures on Legal History* 56–57 (2d ed. 1949).

franchisee. (1956) Someone who is granted a franchise.

franchise fee. See FEE (1).

franchiser. See FRANCHISOR.

franchise tax. See TAX.

franchisor. (19c) Someone who grants a franchise. — Also spelled *franchiser.*

francigena (fran-sə-**jee**-nə). [Law Latin *francus* "french" + Latin *genitus* "born"] *Hist.* **1.** A person born in France. **2.** Any alien in England; a foreigner. See FRENCHMAN.

francus (**frangk**-əs). [fr. French *franc* "free"] *Hist.* A freeman.

francus bancus. See FREE BENCH.

francus homo (**frangk**-əs **hoh**-moh). (17c) *Hist.* A free man.

francus tenens. See FRANK-TENANT.

frank, *adj.* [Law French] (13c) *Hist.* Free. — Also spelled *fraunc; fraunche; fraunke.*

frank, *n.* (bef. 12c) **1.** (*cap.*) A member of the Germanic people who conquered Gaul in the 6th century. • France received its name from the Franks. **2.** A signature, stamp, or mark affixed to mail as a substitute for postage. **3.** The privilege of sending certain mail free of charge, accorded to certain government officials, such as members of Congress and federal courts. — Also termed (in sense 3) *franking privilege.* — **frank,** *vb.*

frankalmoin (**frangk**-al-moyn). [Law French "free alms"] (16c) *Hist.* A spiritual tenure by which a religious institution held land, usu. with a general duty to pray for the donor. • This tenure differed from the tenure by *divine service,* which required certain church services, masses, or alms distributions. — Also spelled *frankalmoign; frankalmoigne.* — Also termed *almoign; almoin; free alms; libera eleemosyna.* See *spiritual tenure* under TENURE (2).

"Frankalmoin, or free alms, was a survival of Anglo-Saxon law, and implied simply an indefinite promise to pray for the soul of the donor; but since it was deemed a tenure by which the land was held, the general doctrine of 'services' was applied. On the other hand, in the case of Divine Service, which was much less frequently met with, the tenant promised a definite number of prayers, a duty which might be enforced in the King's courts." A.K.R. Kiralfy, *Potter's Outlines of English Legal History* 210 (5th ed. 1958).

frank bank. See FREE BENCH.

frank-chase. (16c) *Hist.* Free chase; a person's liberty or right to hunt or log within a certain area. • Others holding land within the frank-chase area were forbidden from hunting or logging in it. See CHASE.

frank-fee. (15c) *Hist.* Freehold land — land that one held to oneself and one's heirs — exempted from all services except homage; land held other than by ancient demesne or copyhold.

frank ferm. (18c) *Hist.* An estate in land held in socage, the nature of the fee having been changed from knight's service by enfeoffment for certain yearly services. — Also spelled *frank-ferme.*

franking machine. (1927) A device used by businesses and other organizations to put a mark on letters and parcels to show that postage has been paid.

franking privilege. See FRANK (3).

frank-law. (17c) *Hist.* The rights and privileges of a citizen or freeman; specif., the condition of being legally capable of giving an oath (esp. as a juror or witness). See LEGALIS HOMO.

> "Frank law . . . may be understood from Bracton's description of the consequences of losing it, among which the principal one was, that the parties incurred perpetual infamy, so that they were never afterwards to be admitted to oath, because they were not deemed to be *othesworth*, (that is, not worthy of making oath,) nor allowed to give testimony." 1 Alexander M. Burrill, *A Law Dictionary and Glossary* 657–58 (2d ed. 1867).

franklin (**frangk**-lin). (14c) *Hist.* A freeman; a freeholder; a gentleman. — Also spelled *francling*; *frankleyn*; *frankleyne.*

frankmarriage. (14c) *Hist.* An entailed estate in which the donor retains control of the land by refusing to accept feudal services from the donee (usu. the donor's daughter) for three generations. • If the donee's issue fail in that time, the land returns to the donor. A donor who accepted homage (and the corresponding services arising from it) from the donee risked losing control of the land to a collateral heir. After three generations — a time considered sufficient to demonstrate that the line was well established — the donee's heir could insist on paying homage; doing so transformed the estate into a fee simple. — Also termed *liberum maritagium.* See MARITAGIUM.

> "Only when homage has been done are we to apply the rule which excludes the lord from the inheritance. This is at the bottom of one of the peculiarities of the 'estate in frankmarriage.' When a father makes a provision for a daughter, he intends that if the daughter has no issue or if her issue fails — at all events if this failure occurs in the course of a few generations — the land shall come back to him or to his heir. Therefore no homage is done for the estate in frankmarriage until the daughter's third heir has entered, for were homage once done, there would be a danger that the land would never come back to the father or to his heir." 2 Frederick Pollock & Frederic W. Maitland, *The History of English Law Before the Time of Edward I* 291 (2d ed. 1899).

frankpledge. (bef. 12c) *Hist.* A promise given to the sovereign by a group of ten freeholders (a *tithing*) ensuring the group's good conduct. • The frankpledge was of Saxon origin, but continued after the Norman Conquest. The members of the group were not liable for an injury caused by an offending member, but they did act as bail to ensure that the culprit would appear in court. They were bound to produce a wrongdoer for trial. — Also termed *borrow*; *laughe.* See VIEW OF FRANKPLEDGE. Cf. DECENARY.

> "Since there was no elaborate group of royal officials, the policing of the country had to be arranged for in a special way. The commonest way was to hold each household responsible for the offenses of any member of it. A further step was taken when, in the time of Cnut, a group of ten men was formed who were responsible for each other, in the sense that every one was security, *borh*, for the good behavior of the others. This group was called *fri-borh*, frankpledge, and remained for a long time one of the chief police methods of England." Max Radin, *Handbook of Anglo-American Legal History* 33–34 (1936).

***Franks* hearing.** (1978) *Criminal procedure.* A proceeding in which a defendant seeks to suppress evidence based on the falsity of an affiant's declaration. • The defendant must establish that (1) the affiant deliberately misstated or omitted facts, and (2) the falsehood was necessary to the finding of probable cause. *See Franks v. Delaware*, 438 U.S. 154, 98 S.Ct. 2674 (1978).

frank-tenant. (17c) *Hist.* A freeholder. — Also termed *francus tenens.* See FREEHOLD.

frank-tenement. (16c) *Hist.* A free tenement; a FREEHOLD. • This term described both the tenure and the estate.

FRAP (frap). *abbr.* FEDERAL RULES OF APPELLATE PROCEDURE.

frater (**fray**-tər), *n.* [Latin] (18c) *Roman law.* A brother.

▸ ***frater consanguineus*** (**fray**-tər kon-sang-**gwin**-ee-əs). A brother or half-brother having the same father.

▸ ***frater germanus*** (**fray**-tər jər-**may**-nəs). (17c) A brother having both parents in common.

▸ ***frater nutricius*** (**fray**-tər n[y]oo-**trish**-ee-əs). (18c) A foster brother who was suckled by the same wet nurse.

▸ ***frater uterinus*** (**fray**-tər yoo-tə-**rI**-nəs). (18c) A brother or half-brother having the same mother.

fraternal, *adj.* (15c) **1.** Of, relating to, or involving the relationship of brothers. **2.** Of, relating to, or involving a fraternity or a fraternal benefit association.

fraternal benefit association. (1892) A voluntary organization or society created for its members' mutual aid and benefit rather than for profit, the members having dedicated themselves to a common and worthy cause, objective, or interest. • These associations often have a lodge system, a governing body, rituals, and a benefits system for their members. — Also termed *fraternal benefit society*; *fraternity*; *fraternal lodge*; *fraternal order.* Cf. FRIENDLY SOCIETY.

fraternal insurance. See INSURANCE.

fraternal lodge. See FRATERNAL BENEFIT ASSOCIATION.

fraternal order. See FRATERNAL BENEFIT ASSOCIATION.

fraternal society. See *benevolent association* under ASSOCIATION.

fraternity (frə-**tər**-ni-tee). [Latin *fraternitas* "brotherhood"] **1.** The quality, state, or condition of being brothers, or of being a brother; brotherliness. **2.** A body of men associated for some common interest <a fraternity of philosophers>. **3.** Men of the same class, profession, occupation, or taste <the legal fraternity>. **4.** FRATERNAL BENEFIT ASSOCIATION. **5.** In the legal philosophy of James Fitzjames Stephen, the love of the human species; a genuine desire to promote the happiness of fellow human beings. *See* Stephen, *Liberty, Equality, Fraternity* 273–338 (2d ed. 1874). Cf. SORORITY.

frater nutricius. See FRATER.

frater uterinus. See FRATER.

fratres conjurati (**fray**-treez kon-jə-**ray**-tI). [Latin "sworn brothers"] *Hist.* Sworn brothers or companions for the defense of their sovereign or for other purposes.

fratriage (**fra**-tree-ij *or* **fray**-). (18c) *Hist.* **1.** A younger brother's portion of his father's estate, received as an inheritance. • Under feudal law, even though the land was from the father's estate, the younger brother was bound to pay homage to the older brother. **2.** A portion of an inheritance given to coheirs. — Also termed *fratriagium.*

fratricidal, *adj.* (1804) **1.** Of, relating to, or involving the killing or killer of a sibling. **2.** By extension, pertaining to the killing of the members of one's own society or group.

fratricide (fra-trə-sɪd *or* **fray-**), *n.* (15c) **1.** The killing of one's brother or sister. **2.** Someone who has killed one's brother or sister. Cf. SORORICIDE.

fraud, *n.* (14c) **1.** A knowing misrepresentation or knowing concealment of a material fact made to induce another to act to his or her detriment. • Fraud is usu. a tort, but in some cases (esp. when the conduct is willful) it may be a crime. — Also termed *intentional fraud.*

> "Fraud has been defined to be, any *kind of artifice by which another is deceived.* Hence, all surprise, trick, cunning, dissembling, and other unfair way that is used to cheat any one, is to be considered as fraud." John Willard, *A Treatise on Equity Jurisprudence* 147 (Platt Potter ed., 1879).

2. A reckless misrepresentation made without justified belief in its truth to induce another person to act. **3.** A tort arising from a knowing or reckless misrepresentation or concealment of material fact made to induce another to act to his or her detriment. • Additional elements in a claim for fraud may include reasonable reliance on the misrepresentation and damages resulting from this reliance. **4.** Unconscionable dealing; esp., in contract law, the unfair use of the power arising out of the parties' relative positions and resulting in an unconscionable bargain. See DEFRAUD. — **fraudulent,** *adj.*

> "[T]he use of the term *fraud* has been wider and less precise in the chancery than in the common-law courts. This followed necessarily from the remedies which they respectively administered. Common law gave damages for a wrong, and was compelled to define with care the wrong which furnished a cause of action. Equity refused specific performance of a contract, or set aside a transaction, or gave compensation where one party had acted unfairly by the other. Thus 'fraud' at common law is a false statement . . . : fraud in equity has often been used as meaning unconscientious dealing — 'although, I think, unfortunately,' a great equity lawyer has said." William R. Anson, *Principles of the Law of Contract* 263 (Arthur L. Corbin ed., 3d Am. ed. 1919).

▸ **actual fraud.** (17c) A concealment or false representation through an intentional or reckless statement or conduct that injures another who relies on it in acting. — Also termed *fraud in fact; positive fraud; moral fraud.*

▸ **advance-fee fraud.** (1981) A criminal fraud in which the victim is persuaded by the perpetrator to pay "fees" in anticipation of receiving a much larger benefit that is ultimately never delivered. • The perpetrator usu. claims to have, or to represent someone with, a large sum of money that must be immediately transferred out of a foreign country for some compelling reason, such as to avoid seizure by a government. The criminal promises the victim a portion of the money in return for the victim's agreement to open a bank account in the victim's name. The victim then must pay "upfront fees" to the designated "bank" and others. Although the Internet has become a favorite tool for this fraud, it has been around for years, beginning with handwritten or typed letters and later faxes. Because advance-fee fraud is believed to have originated in Nigeria, it is also termed *419 fraud* after the section of the Nigerian penal code designed to punish those who defraud by this method.

▸ **affiliate click fraud.** (2006) Click fraud committed by a third party who agrees to host the ad in exchange for payment based on the number of clicks. See *click fraud.*

▸ **affinity fraud.** (2007) A fraud in which the perpetrator tailors the fraud to target members of a particular group united by common traits or interests that produce inherent trust. • The perpetrator often is or pretends to be a member of the group. Investment scams such as Ponzi or pyramid schemes are common forms of affinity fraud. When a religious group is targeted, it is usu. called *religious-affinity fraud.*

▸ **bank fraud.** (1843) The criminal offense of knowingly executing, or attempting to execute, a scheme or artifice to defraud a financial institution, or to obtain property owned by or under the custody or control of a financial institution, by means of false or fraudulent pretenses, representations, or promises. 18 USCA § 1344.

▸ **bankruptcy fraud.** (1815) A fraudulent act connected to a bankruptcy case; esp., any of several proscribed acts performed knowingly and fraudulently in a bankruptcy case, such as concealing assets or destroying, withholding, or falsifying documents in an effort to defeat bankruptcy-code provisions. *See* 18 USCA § 152. — Also termed *criminal bankruptcy; bankruptcy crime.*

▸ **civil fraud.** (18c) **1.** FRAUD (3). **2.** *Tax.* An intentional — but not willful — evasion of taxes. • The distinction between an intentional (i.e., *civil*) and willful (i.e., *criminal*) fraud is not always clear, but *civil fraud* carries only a monetary, noncriminal penalty. Cf. *criminal fraud;* TAX EVASION.

▸ **click fraud.** (2005) A scheme in which a person or robot repeatedly clicks on a merchant's pay-per-click advertisement on a website for purposes other than viewing the website or making a purchase.

▸ **collateral fraud.** See *extrinsic fraud* (1).

▸ **common-law fraud.** See *promissory fraud.*

▸ **competitor click fraud.** (2006) Click fraud committed by a business's competitor in order to increase the amount of money the advertising merchant must pay to the site hosting the ad. See *click fraud.*

▸ **constructive fraud.** (18c) **1.** Unintentional deception or misrepresentation that causes injury to another. **2.** See *fraud in law.* — Also termed *legal fraud; fraud in contemplation of law; equitable fraud; fraud in equity.*

> "In equity law the term fraud has a wider sense, and includes all acts, omissions, or concealments by which one person obtains an advantage against conscience over another, or which equity or public policy forbids as being to another's prejudice; as acts in violation of trust and confidence. This is often called constructive, legal, or equitable fraud, or fraud in equity." *Encyclopedia of Criminology* 175 (Vernon C. Branham & Samuel B. Kutash eds., 1949), s.v. "Fraud."

▸ **consumer fraud.** Any intentional deception, deceptive act or practice, false pretense, false promise, or misrepresentation made by a seller or advertiser of goods or services to induce a person or people in general to buy.

▸ **criminal fraud.** (18c) Fraud that is illegal by statute and may subject an offender to criminal penalties such as fines and imprisonment. • An example is the willful evasion of taxes accomplished by filing a fraudulent tax return. Cf. *civil fraud; larceny by trick* under LARCENY.

▸ **election fraud.** See ELECTION FRAUD.

▸ **equitable fraud.** See *constructive fraud* (1).

▸ **extrinsic fraud.** (1851) **1.** Fraud that is collateral to the issues being considered in the case; specif., intentional misrepresentation or deceptive behavior outside the transaction itself (whether a contract or a lawsuit), depriving one party of informed consent or full participation. • For example, a person might engage in extrinsic fraud by convincing a litigant not to hire counsel or answer by dishonestly saying the matter will not be pursued. — Also termed *collateral fraud*. **2.** Fraud that prevents a person from knowing about or asserting certain rights. Cf. *intrinsic fraud*.

▸ **419 fraud.** See *advance-fee fraud*.

▸ **fraud in contemplation of law.** See *fraud in law*.

▸ **fraud in equity.** See *constructive fraud* (1).

▸ **fraud in fact.** See *actual fraud*.

▸ **fraud in law.** (17c) Fraud that is presumed under the circumstances, without regard to intent, usu. through statutorily created inference. • Fraud may be presumed, for example, when a debtor transfers assets and thereby impairs creditors' efforts to collect sums due. This type of fraud arises by operation of law, from conduct that, if sanctioned, would (either in the particular circumstance or in common experience) secure an unconscionable advantage, irrespective of evidence of an actual intent to defraud. — Also termed *constructive fraud*.

▸ **fraud in the execution.** See *fraud in the factum* (1).

▸ **fraud in the factum.** (1848) **1.** Fraud occurring when a legal instrument as actually executed differs from the one intended for execution by the person who executes it, or when the instrument may have had no legal existence. • Compared to fraud in the inducement, fraud in the factum occurs only rarely, as when a blind person signs a mortgage when misleadingly told that the paper is just a letter. — Also termed *fraud in the execution*; *fraud in the making*. **2.** *Criminal law*. In the law of rape, misrepresentation about the nature of the act of penetration, whereby the other party's consent is nullified and the actor becomes criminally responsible. • For example, a doctor who secures his patient's consent to his inserting an object into her vagina commits fraud in factum, and is thus guilty of rape, if he has represented that the object will be a medical instrument but is instead his sexual organ. Cf. *fraud in the inducement*.

▸ **fraud in the inducement.** (1831) **1.** Fraud occurring when a misrepresentation leads another to enter into a transaction with a false impression of the risks, duties, or obligations involved; an intentional misrepresentation of a material risk or duty reasonably relied on, thereby injuring the other party without vitiating the contract itself, esp. about a fact relating to value or the ability to perform. — Also termed *fraud in the procurement*. **2.** *Criminal law*. Misrepresentation designed to elicit a person's consent to sexual activity but not concerning the nature of the activity itself, and therefore deemed not to vitiate any consent thereby secured. • For example, a man who secures a woman's consent to sexual intercourse after claiming, falsely, that he is a theatrical agent or that he wishes to marry her, commits fraud in the inducement, not fraud in the factum, and therefore has not committed the offense of rape. The factum–inducement distinction has proved difficult to apply in borderline cases and has been abandoned in most modern criminal codes. Cf. *fraud in the factum*.

▸ **fraud in the making.** See *fraud in the factum* (1).

▸ **fraud in the procurement.** See *fraud in the inducement* (1).

▸ **fraud on the community.** (1946) *Family law*. In a community-property state, the deliberate hiding or fraudulent transfer of community assets before a divorce or death for the purpose of preventing the other spouse from claiming a half-interest ownership in the property.

▸ **fraud on the court.** (1810) In a judicial proceeding, a lawyer's or party's misconduct so serious that it undermines or is intended to undermine the integrity of the proceeding. • Examples are bribery of a juror and introduction of fabricated evidence.

▸ **fraud on the market.** (1893) **1.** Fraud that occurs when an issuer of securities gives out misinformation that affects the market price of stock, effectively misleading people who buy or sell even though they did not rely on the statement itself or on anything derived from it other than the market price. **2.** The securities-law claim based on such fraud. See FRAUD-ON-THE-MARKET PRINCIPLE.

▸ **fraud on the Patent Office.** (1865) *Patents*. A defense in a patent-infringement action, attacking the validity of the patent on the grounds that the patentee gave the examiner false or misleading information or withheld relevant information that the examiner would have considered important in considering patentability. • The scope of prohibited acts is wider than that covered by common-law fraud, and today the defense is generally called "inequitable conduct before the PTO." If the defense is established, the entire patent is rendered unenforceable. See *defense of inequitable conduct* under DEFENSE (1).

▸ **healthcare fraud.** A healthcare provider's false statement or misrepresentation made in order to claim a higher payment for healthcare services than the provider is actually entitled to. — Also termed (specif.) *Medicaid fraud*; *Medicare fraud*.

▸ **hidden fraud.** See *fraudulent concealment* under CONCEALMENT.

▸ **identity fraud.** See IDENTITY THEFT.

▸ **insurance fraud.** (1877) Fraud committed against an insurer, as when an insured lies on a policy application or fabricates a claim.

▸ **intrinsic fraud.** (1832) Fraud that pertains to an issue involved in a judicial proceeding. • Examples include the use of fabricated evidence, perjured testimony, and false receipts or other commercial documents. Cf. *extrinsic fraud*.

▸ **legal fraud.** See *fraud in law*.

▸ **long-firm fraud.** (1930) The act of obtaining goods or money on credit by falsely posing as an established business and having no intent to pay for the goods or repay the loan.

▸ **mail fraud.** (1918) An act of fraud using the U.S. Postal Service, as in making false representations through the mail to obtain an economic advantage. 18 USCA §§ 1341–1347.

▸ **Medicaid fraud.** See *healthcare fraud*.

▸ **Medicare fraud.** See *healthcare fraud*.

▸ **moral fraud.** See *actual fraud*.

▸ **passport fraud.** See PASSPORT FRAUD.

▸ **positive fraud.** See *actual fraud.*

▸ **promissory fraud.** (1934) A promise to perform made when the promisor had no intention of performing the promise. — Also termed *common-law fraud.*

▸ **religious-affinity fraud.** See *affinity fraud.*

▸ **tax fraud.** See TAX EVASION.

▸ **wire fraud.** (1955) An act of fraud using electronic communications, as by making false representations on the telephone to obtain money. • The federal Wire Fraud Act provides that any artifice to defraud by means of wire or other electronic communications (such as radio or television) in foreign or interstate commerce is a crime. 18 USCA § 1343.

fraud, badge of. See BADGE OF FRAUD.

fraudare (fraw-**dair**-ee), *vb.* [Latin] *Roman law.* To defraud.

fraud by hindsight. (1941) *Securities.* A claim of fraud based on the assumption that a corporation deliberately misled investors by issuing optimistic financial statements or forecasts and later reporting worse-than-expected results. • Suits for fraud by hindsight were common in the early 1990s. Congress eliminated this claim in the Private Securities Litigation Reform Act of 1995. 15 USCA §§ 78u-4(b).

fraude (frawd). [French] *Civil law.* Fraud committed in performing a contract. Cf. DOL.

fraudfeasor (**frawd**-fee-zər). (1890) Someone who has committed fraud. — Also termed *defrauder.* See FEASOR.

fraud in the execution. See *fraud in the factum* under FRAUD.

fraud on creditors. See FRAUDULENT CONVEYANCE (1).

fraud on the community. See FRAUD.

fraud-on-the-market principle. (1994) *Securities.* The doctrine that, in a claim under the antifraud provisions of the federal securities laws, a plaintiff may presumptively establish reliance on a misstatement about a security's value — without proving actual knowledge of the fraudulent statement — if the stock is purchased in an open and developed securities market. • This doctrine recognizes that the market price of an issuer's stock reflects all available public information. The presumption is rebuttable. — Also termed *fraud-on-the-market theory.* See *fraud on the market* under FRAUD.

fraud on the power. (1828) *Wills & estates.* An appointment of a power made in favor of a permissible appointee but ineffective because the donee's purpose is to benefit an impermissible appointee.

frauds, statute of. See STATUTE OF FRAUDS.

fraudulent act. (17c) **1.** Conduct involving bad faith, dishonesty, a lack of integrity, or moral turpitude. **2.** Conduct satisfying the elements of a claim for actual or constructive fraud. — Also termed *dishonest act; fraudulent or dishonest act.*

fraudulent alienation. (17c) **1.** The transfer of an interest in property with an intent to defraud others, esp. creditors and lienholders. See FRAUDULENT CONVEYANCE (1). **2.** The transfer of an estate asset by the estate's administrator for little or no consideration.

fraudulent alienee. See ALIENEE.

fraudulent banking. (1890) The receipt of a deposit by a banker who knows at the time of the deposit that the bank is insolvent.

fraudulent claim. **1.** A claim for any benefit or payment based on a fraudulent misrepresentation. **2.** A false insurance claim. See FRAUD.

fraudulent concealment. See CONCEALMENT.

fraudulent-concealment rule. See CONCEALMENT RULE.

fraudulent conversion. See CONVERSION (2).

fraudulent conveyance. (17c) **1.** A transfer of an interest in property for little or no consideration, made for the purpose of hindering or delaying a creditor by putting the property beyond the creditor's reach; a transaction by which the owner of real or personal property seeks to place the property beyond the reach of creditors. — Also termed *conveyance in fraud of creditors; fraud on creditors.*

> "With respect to the general power which is exercisable by deed, it seems that the principle that the donee's creditors can reach the property subject to the exercised general power will have application only to the so-called fraudulent conveyance. That is to say, if the owned assets of the donee after the donative inter vivos exercise are sufficient to satisfy the creditors, then the exercise of the power will not subject the appointive property to the claims of the creditors; if, on the other hand, the owned assets of the donee are inadequate to satisfy creditors' claims after the exercise of the power, then the transfer resulting from the exercise is likely to fall into the category of the fraudulent conveyance and the creditors will be able to reach the appointive property in the hands of the appointee." Thomas F. Bergin & Paul G. Haskell, *Preface to Estates in Land and Future Interests* 173 (2d ed. 1984).

2. *Bankruptcy.* A prebankruptcy transfer or obligation made or incurred by a debtor for little or no consideration or with the actual intent to hinder, delay, or defraud a creditor. • A bankruptcy trustee may recover such a conveyance from the transferee if the requirements of 11 USCA § 548 are met. — Also termed *fraudulent transfer.* Cf. PREFERENTIAL TRANSFER.

fraudulent debt. See DEBT.

fraudulent joinder. See JOINDER.

fraudulent marriage. See MARRIAGE (1).

fraudulent misrepresentation. See MISREPRESENTATION.

fraudulent or dishonest act. See FRAUDULENT ACT.

fraudulent pretenses. See FALSE PRETENSES.

fraudulent representation. See *fraudulent misrepresentation* under MISREPRESENTATION.

fraudulent sale. See SALE.

fraudulent transfer. See FRAUDULENT CONVEYANCE (2).

fraudulent-use insurance. See *credit-card insurance* under INSURANCE.

fraus (fraws). [Latin] **1.** Deceit; cheating. • For example, a debtor who conveyed property with the specific intent (*fraus*) of defrauding a creditor risked having the conveyance rescinded. **2.** DOLUS (2).

fraus legis (fraws **lee**-jis). [Latin "fraud on the law"] (1879) *Roman law.* Evasion of the law; specif., doing something that is not expressly forbidden by statute, but that the law does not want done.

fray. See AFFRAY.

FRB. *abbr.* FEDERAL RESERVE BOARD OF GOVERNORS.

FRCA. *abbr.* FAIR-CREDIT-REPORTING ACT.

FRCP. *abbr.* FEDERAL RULES OF CIVIL PROCEDURE.

FRD. *abbr.* Federal Rules Decisions; that is, a series of reported federal court decisions (beginning in 1938) that construe or apply the Federal Rules of Civil and Criminal Procedure. • Also included are rule changes, ceremonial proceedings of federal courts, and articles on federal-court practice and procedure. — Often written *F.R.D.*

FRE. *abbr.* FEDERAL RULES OF EVIDENCE.

Freddie Mac. See FEDERAL HOME LOAN MORTGAGE CORPORATION.

free, *adj.* (bef. 12c) **1.** Having legal and political rights; enjoying political and civil liberty <a free citizen> <a free populace>. **2.** Not subject to the constraint or domination of another; enjoying personal freedom; emancipated <a free person>. **3.** Characterized by choice, rather than by compulsion or constraint <free will>. **4.** Unburdened <the land was free of any encumbrances>. **5.** Not confined by force or restraint <free from prison>. **6.** Unrestricted and unregulated <free trade>. **7.** Costing nothing; gratuitous <free tickets to the game>. — **freely,** *adv.*

free, *vb.* (bef. 12c) **1.** To liberate; esp., to allow (someone) to leave prison or some other place of confinement <to free the political prisoners>. **2.** To remove (a person, animal, or thing) from a constraint or burden <to free the country from its enormous debt>. **3.** To stop (someone) from suffering from something by removing it <to free the patient from pain>. **4.** To make available <to free some money for investment>.

free acceptance. See ACCEPTANCE (1).

free agency, *n.* (ca. 1955) A person's freedom from responsibility to anyone else in some aspect of his or her activities; esp., a professional athlete's ability to negotiate an employment contract with any team in a league, rather than being confined to the league's collective-bargaining system. • Free agency is usu. granted to veteran players who have been in the league for a certain number of years. Cf. RESERVE CLAUSE. — **free agent,** *n.*

free alms. See FRANKALMOIN.

free alongside ship. (1878) (Of goods or fright) delivered at the side of the ship free of charges, the buyer's liability then beginning. • This mercantile-contract term allocates the rights and duties of the buyer and the seller of goods with respect to delivery, payment, and risk of loss, whereby the seller must clear the goods for export, and deliver the goods to the wharf beside the buyer's chosen vessel. The seller's delivery is complete (and the risk of loss passes to the buyer) when the goods are placed on the wharf beside the vessel. The buyer is responsible for all costs of carriage. This term is used only when goods are transported by sea or inland waterway. UCC § 2-319. — Abbr. FAS. — Also termed *free overboard; free overside.* Cf. FREE ON BOARD; DELIVERED EX QUAY.

free and clear, *adj.* (18c) Unencumbered by any liens; marketable <free and clear title>.

free and common socage. See *free socage* under SOCAGE.

free and equal, *adj.* (1869) (Of an election) conducted so that the electorate has a reasonable opportunity to vote, with each vote given the same effect.

free bench. (15c) *Hist.* A widow's (and occasionally a widower's) interest in the deceased spouse's estate. • *Free bench* gave the surviving spouse a half interest in the estate until death or remarriage. — Also termed *francus bancus; frank bank; liber bancus.*

> "The bench in question was, we may guess . . . a bench at the fireside. The surviving spouse has in time past been allowed to remain in the house along with the children. In the days when families kept together, the right of the widower or widow to remain at the fireside may have borne a somewhat indefinite character. . . . By way of 'free bench' the surviving spouse now has the enjoyment of one-half of the land until death or second marriage, whether there has ever been a child of the marriage or no." 2 Frederick Pollock & Frederic W. Maitland, *The History of English Law Before the Time of Edward I* 419 (2d ed. 1899).

free-bord. (17c) *Hist.* **1.** A small strip of land (usu. 2½ feet wide and lying just outside a fence) that is adjacent to an owner's property and that the owner of the property is allowed to claim and use. **2.** The right of claiming that quantity of land. — Also spelled *freebord; free bord; freeboard.* — Also termed *francbordus.*

free carrier. (1981) A mercantile-contract term allocating the rights and duties of the buyer and the seller of goods with respect to delivery, payment, and risk of loss, whereby the seller must clear the goods for export and deliver them to the buyer's chosen carrier at a named place. • The seller's delivery is complete (and the risk of loss passes to the buyer) when the goods are loaded on the collecting vehicle or otherwise placed at the carrier's disposal. The buyer is responsible for all costs of carriage. There are no restrictions on the buyer's choice of carrier. — Abbr. FCA.

free chapel. (15c) *Hist. Eccles. law.* A church founded by the Crown (or by a person under royal grant) and not subject to the bishop's jurisdiction.

> "[T]hose onely are *Free-chappels,* which are of the King's Foundation, and by him exempted from the Jurisdiction of the Ordinary; but the King may licence a Subject to found such a Chappel, and by his Charter exempt it from the Ordinaries Visitation also. . . . [I]t is called *free,* in respect of its exemption from the Jurisdiction of the Diocesan . . . ." Thomas Blount, *Nomo-Lexicon: A Law-Dictionary* (1670).

free chase. See CHASE.

free city. (16c) *Int'l law.* A country-like political and territorial entity that, although independent in principle, does not have the full capacity to act according to general international law but is nevertheless a subject of international law.

> "Free cities are territorial entities that do not have full national sovereignty. Based on international treaties, some sovereign rights are exercised by foreign authorities such as international organizations or States. Free cities are sometimes, although not always, regarded as States . . . , but their status as subjects of international law is beyond debate. They are distinguished from free zones or free ports by having their own political status. The political reasons for the creation of free cities can be found in international conflicts over territorial sovereignty of the area in which they are situated." Christian Hattenhauer, "Free Cities," in 4 *The Max Planck Encyclopedia of Public International Law* 231, 231 (Rüdiger Wolfrum ed., 2012).

free collective bargaining. See COLLECTIVE BARGAINING.

free customs zone. See FREE-TRADE ZONE.

freedman (**freed**-mən). (16c) *Hist.* An emancipated slave; the ability to act without physical or legal restraint.

freedom. (bef. 12c) **1.** The quality, state, or condition of being free or liberated; esp., the right to do what one wants without being controlled or restricted by anyone. **2.** A political right.

freedom fighter. (1910) Someone who fights in a war against an oppressive, dishonest, and violent government.

freedom-of-access law. See OPEN-MEETING LAW.

Freedom of Access to Clinic Entrances Act. A 1994 federal statute that provides for criminal sanctions, private civil causes of action, and civil action by the U.S. Attorney General against a person who uses force, threat of force, or physical obstruction to injure, intimidate, or interfere with a provider or patient of reproductive services or who damages a reproductive-services facility. — Abbr. FACE.

freedom of assembly. See RIGHT OF ASSEMBLY.

freedom of association. (1889) *Constitutional law.* The right to join with others in a common undertaking that would be lawful if pursued individually. • This right is protected by the First Amendment to the U.S. Constitution. Cf. RIGHT OF ASSEMBLY.

> "Freedom of association can be regarded as a civil liberty insofar as it contemplates the ability of persons to form associations without intervention by the state. The notion emerged from early assertions of religious liberty, and can be traced back to the protestant movement, which emerged in Europe from the sixteenth century onwards. It was also a freedom utilized by an emergent capitalist class who sought to associate in incorporated bodies for commercial purposes. Freedom of association can further be understood in political terms as the right to organize political parties aimed at challenging the power of the ruling elite. Its significance therefore grew with the spread of democratic government, initially through revolution, in the seventeenth and eighteenth centuries." Tonia Novitz, "Freedom of Association," in *The New Oxford Companion to Law* 477 (Peter Cane & Joanne Conaghan eds., 2008).

▸ **freedom of expressive association.** (1984) The right of an individual to associate with others, without undue government interference, for the purpose of engaging in activities protected by the First Amendment, such as speech, assembly, and the exercise of religion.

▸ **freedom of intimate association.** (1980) The right to form and preserve certain intimate human relationships without intrusion by the state because the relationships safeguard individual freedom. • The group relationships protected by the right to freedom of intimate association are familial in nature and are characterized by deep attachments, a high degree of commitment, and the sharing of distinctly personal aspects of life. The exclusion of others is an essential characteristic of these relationships.

freedom of belief. (17c) **1.** The right to hold and display a belief in a practice, teaching, or observance without governmental interference. **2.** FREEDOM OF RELIGION.

freedom of choice. (1817) **1.** The liberty embodied in the exercise of one's rights. **2.** The liberty to exercise one's right of privacy, esp. the right to have an abortion. **3.** The parents' opportunity to select a school for their child in a unitary, integrated school system that is devoid of de jure segregation. — Also termed *right to choose; choice.*

freedom of conscience. (16c) **1.** The right to follow one's beliefs in matters of morality without governmental interference. **2.** Loosely, FREEDOM OF RELIGION.

freedom of contract. (1879) The doctrine that people have the right to enter into binding private agreements with others; a judicial concept that contracts are based on mutual agreement and free choice, and thus should not be hampered by undue external control such as governmental interference. • This is the principle that people are able to fashion their relations by private agreements, esp. as opposed to the assigned roles of the feudal system. As Maine famously said, "[T]he movement of progressive societies has been a movement from *Status* to *Contract*." Henry Sumner Maine, *Ancient Law* 165 (1864). — Also termed *liberty of contract; autonomy of the parties.*

> "Like most shibboleths, that of 'freedom of contract' rarely, if ever, received the close examination which its importance deserved, and even today it is by no means easy to say what exactly the nineteenth-century judges meant when they used this phrase. At least it may be said that the idea of freedom of contract embraced two closely connected, but none the less distinct, concepts. In the first place it indicated that contracts were based on mutual agreement, while in the second place it emphasized that the creation of a contract was the result of a free choice unhampered by external control such as government or legislative interference." P.S. Atiyah, *An Introduction to the Law of Contract* 5 (3d ed. 1981).

freedom of discussion. See FREEDOM OF EXPRESSION.

freedom of expression. (1877) *Constitutional law.* The freedom of speech, press, assembly, or religion as guaranteed by the First Amendment of the U.S. Constitution; the prohibition of governmental interference with those freedoms. — Also termed *freedom of discussion.* Cf. FREEDOM OF SPEECH.

freedom of ideas. See FREEDOM OF THOUGHT.

Freedom of Information Act. The federal statute that establishes guidelines for public disclosure of documents and materials created and held by federal agencies. 5 USCA § 552. • The basic purpose of the statute, or of a state statute modeled after it, is to give the public access to official information so that the public will be better informed and the government will be more accountable for its actions. — Abbr. FOIA. See REVERSE FOIA SUIT.

freedom of intimate association. See FREEDOM OF ASSOCIATION.

freedom of movement. (18c) The right to travel within the boundaries of a political entity.

freedom of petition. See RIGHT TO PETITION.

freedom of religion. (16c) *Constitutional law.* The right to adhere to any form of religion or none, to practice or abstain from practicing religious beliefs, and to be free from governmental interference with or promotion of religion, as guaranteed by the First Amendment and Article VI, § 3 of the U.S. Constitution. — Also termed *freedom of belief; freedom of conscience.* See FREEDOM OF BELIEF; FREEDOM OF CONSCIENCE.

freedom of speech. (17c) *Constitutional law.* The right to express one's thoughts and opinions without governmental restriction, as guaranteed by the First Amendment of the U.S. Constitution. — Also termed *free speech; liberty of speech.* Cf. FREEDOM OF EXPRESSION.

> "Freedom of speech is yet another jurisprudential field in which American and foreign constitutional tribunals have differed in their conceptions of democracy. Yet it is no exaggeration to say that the American emphasis on *freedom of speech* as the *sine qua non* of democracy has been influential all over the democratic world. The jurisprudence

of the foreign courts under discussion is studded with references to American free speech doctrine. Seminal free speech decisions in Germany, Canada, and South Africa have all taken their main cue from Benjamin Cardozo's oft-quoted remark that freedom of speech is 'the matrix, the indispensable condition of nearly every other form of freedom.' Yet, while foreign constitutional tribunals have relied heavily on American speech cases for the interpretation of their constitutions, they have not always accepted the latter's conclusions." Donald P. Kommers, "American Courts and Democracy: A Comparative Perspective," in *The Judicial Branch* 218 (Kermit L. Hall & Kevin T. McGuire eds., 2005).

Freedom of Speech Clause. See SPEECH CLAUSE.

freedom of testation. A person's power to choose how his or her estate will be distributed at death.

freedom of the city. (16c) *Hist.* An immunity or privilege from some burden, esp. from county jurisdiction and its privilege of municipal taxation and self-government, held under a royal charter.

freedom of the press. (17c) *Constitutional law.* The right to print and publish materials without governmental intervention, as guaranteed by the First Amendment of the U.S. Constitution. — Also termed *liberty of the press.*

"'Freedom of the press' has less significance than meets the eye. It is true, of course, that the First Amendment specifically guarantees freedom of the press as well as free speech, and the media often ascribe the freedom they enjoy to the Press Clause. Even the Supreme Court occasionally emits rhetoric that implies as much. But as a matter of positive law, the Press Clause actually plays a rather minor role in protecting the freedom of the press. Most of the freedoms the press receives from the First Amendment are no different from the freedoms everyone enjoys under the Speech Clause. The press is protected from most government censorship, libel judgments, and prior restraints not because it is the press but because the Speech Clause protects all of us from those threats." David A. Anderson, *Freedom of the Press*, 80 Texas L. Rev. 429, 430 (2002).

Freedom of the Press Clause. PRESS CLAUSE.

freedom of the seas. (17c) *Int'l law.* The principle that the seas beyond territorial waters are not subject to any country's control. • Ships on the high seas are subject only to the jurisdiction of the country whose flag they fly, except in cases of piracy, hijacking, hot pursuit from territorial waters, slave trading, and certain rights of approach by warships. — Also termed *mare liberum.*

freedom of thought. (16c) The right to develop, hold, or consider facts, viewpoints, or ideas independently of others' viewpoints. — Also termed *freedom of ideas.*

freedom-to-create statute. (1983) *Patents.* A law restricting an employer's ability to require employees to assign to the employer all rights to their inventions, even those independently developed.

freedom-to-operate search. See INFRINGEMENT SEARCH.

free election. See ELECTION (3).

free enterprise. (1890) **1.** The principle of allowing businesses to operate as much as possible without government control or regulation. **2.** A private and consensual system of production and distribution, usu. conducted for profit in a competitive environment that is relatively free of governmental interference. See CAPITALISM.

free entry, egress, and regress (ee-gres / ree-gres). (1831) *Hist.* A person's right to go on land as often as reasonably necessary. • A tenant could go on land to gather crops still growing after the tenancy expired.

free estray. See ESTRAY.

Free Exercise Clause. (1950) *Constitutional law.* The constitutional provision (U.S. Const. amend. I) prohibiting the government from interfering in people's religious practices or forms of worship. — Also termed *Exercise Clause.* Cf. ESTABLISHMENT CLAUSE.

free fishery. See FISHERY (1).

free-gas clause. (1913) *Oil & gas.* A provision in an oil-and-gas lease entitling the lessor or the surface owner to use gas produced from the leased property without charge. • Used commonly in colder states, free-gas clauses usu. limit how the gas may be used (e.g., domestic heating and light), how much gas may be used (e.g., not more than 300 MCF per year), or both.

freehold, *n.* (15c) **1.** An estate in land held in fee simple, in fee tail, or for term of life; any real-property interest that is or may become possessory. • At common law, these estates were all created by enfeoffment with livery of seisin. **2.** The tenure by which such an estate is held. — Also termed *freehold estate; estate in freehold; freehold interest; frank-tenement; liberum tenementum.* Cf. LEASEHOLD.

▸ **determinable freehold.** See *determinable estate* under ESTATE (1).

▸ **flying freehold.** *English law.* The part of a freehold property that encroaches on another owner's property, not on the ground but above it, as with a balcony that extends over the property line.

▸ **movable freehold.** (18c) Real property capable of being increased or diminished by natural causes, such as the land a seashore owner acquires or loses as water recedes or approaches.

▸ **perpetual freehold.** (17c) An estate given to a grantee for life, and then successively to the grantee's heirs for life. • The effect of this type of freehold was to keep land within a family in perpetuity, much like a fee tail.

"It took the form of a grant 'to A for life, remainder to A's son for life, remainder to that son's son for life,' and so on ad infinitum. Such a limitation, if valid, would have been an effective substitute for the fee tail. The courts, however, set their face against this 'perpetual freehold' (as it was sometimes termed), and in *Lovelace v. Lovelace* (1585) it was held that remainders which did not vest before the determination of the first life estate would fail ex post facto. Subsequently a number of other, not entirely convincing, reasons were found for invalidating perpetual freeholds, ultimately culminating in what is sometimes termed the 'old' rule against perpetuities, but, more commonly, the rule in *Whitby v. Mitchell*, taking its name from the case which marked its emphatic reiteration." Peter Butt, *Land Law* 136 (2d ed. 1988).

freeholder. (15c) *Hist.* Someone who possesses a freehold. — Also termed *charterer.*

freeholder's court baron. See COURT BARON.

freehold estate. See FREEHOLD.

freehold interest. See FREEHOLD.

freehold land society. (*usu. pl.*) (1851) *Hist. English law.* A society in England created to enable mechanics, artisans, and other workers to buy at the lowest possible price freehold land with a sufficient yearly value to entitle the owner to the right to vote in the county in which the land was located.

freehold reversion. See REVERSION.

free ice. *Hist.* Ice in navigable streams that does not belong to the adjacent riparian owner or to another with the right to appropriate it, but that belongs to the person who first appropriates it.

free law. (17c) *Hist.* The civil rights enjoyed by a freeman (as opposed to a serf). • Free law could be forfeited if the freeman was convicted of treason or an infamous crime.

free-lights doctrine. See ANCIENT-LIGHTS DOCTRINE.

freeman. (bef. 12c) **1.** Someone who enjoys all the civil and political rights belonging to the people under a free government. See FREE LAW. **2.** Someone who is not a slave. **3.** *Hist.* A member of a municipal corporation (a city or borough) who possesses full civic rights, esp. the right to vote. **4.** *Hist.* A freeholder. Cf. VILLEIN. **5.** *Hist.* An allodial landowner. Cf. VASSAL. — Also written *free man.*

***Freeman–Walter–Abele* test.** (1992) *Patents.* An obsolete two-step judicial test for determining whether a claimed invention is an unpatentable mathematical algorithm. • The test looks first to whether an algorithm is explicit or inherent in the claim, and second to whether a patent would wholly preempt others from using the algorithm. *In re Freeman*, 573 F.2d 1237 (CCPA 1978); *In re Walter*, 618 F.2d 758 (CCPA 1980); *In re Abele*, 684 F.2d 902 (CCPA 1982). The test has "little, if any, applicability" after *State St. Bank & Trust Co. v. Signature Fin. Group*, 149 F.3d 1368 (Fed. Cir. 1998).

free market. See *open market* under MARKET.

free of all average. (1858) *Maritime law.* Insurance that covers a total loss only. — Abbr. FAA.

free on board. (1886) (Of goods or freight) delivered free of charge on the means of conveyance, such as air, rail, or sea. • This is a mercantile-contract term allocating the rights and duties of the buyer and the seller of goods with respect to delivery, payment, and risk of loss, whereby the seller must clear the goods for export, and the buyer must arrange for transportation. The seller's delivery is complete (and the risk of loss passes to the buyer) when the goods pass into the transporter's possession. The buyer is responsible for all costs of carriage. UCC § 2-319. — Abbr. FOB. — Also termed *freight on board.* Cf. FREE ALONGSIDE SHIP; DELIVERED EX SHIP.

> "In an *F.O.B.* ('free on board') contract, the goods must be delivered on board by the seller, free of expense to the purchaser, and they are not at the latter's risk until actually delivered on board, when the property in them passes to him. The seller must also give the buyer sufficient notice to enable him to insure against loss during the sea transit. The buyer, on the other hand, must name a ship or authorize the seller to select one. The seller cannot sue for the price until the goods are loaded, and if his inability to load was caused by the buyer's failure to name an effective ship, his only remedy lies in damages. Similarly, *F.O.R.* means 'free on rail.'" 2 E.W. Chance, *Principles of Mercantile Law* 86–87 (P.W. French ed., 10th ed. 1951).

▸ **FOB destination.** (1915) A mercantile term denoting that the seller is required to pay the freight charges and bear the risk of loss as far as the buyer's named destination.

▸ **FOB shipping.** (1914) A mercantile term denoting that the seller is required to bear the risk of placing the goods on a carrier.

free overboard. See FREE ALONGSIDE SHIP.

free overside, *adj.* (1886) **1.** Exempt from charges until unloaded from a vessel. **2.** FREE ALONGSIDE SHIP.

free pardon. See PARDON.

free passage. 1. The ability or right of a vehicle or vessel to travel without hindrance. **2.** Travel without paying for the means of transportation. See STOWAWAY.

free port. 1. See PORT. **2.** FREE-TRADE ZONE.

free ride. (19c) A benefit obtained without paying a fair price or obtained at another's expense without contribution. • For example, a competitor who used aerial photographs of a plant-construction site to discover secret manufacturing techniques was judicially criticized for getting a free ride, in contrast to others who might spend time and effort legally reverse-engineering the same techniques.

free rider. (1937) Someone who obtains a free ride. — Also written *freerider.*

free-riding. See LEGISLATIVE FREE-RIDING.

free seas. See *high seas* under SEA.

free service. See SERVICE (6).

free ship. See SHIP.

free socage. See SOCAGE.

free software. See FREEWARE.

free speech. See FREEDOM OF SPEECH.

free state. See STATE (1).

Freestone rider. See PUGH CLAUSE.

free teind. See TEIND.

free tenure. See TENURE (2).

free trade, *n.* (17c) The open and unrestricted import and export of goods without barriers, such as quotas or tariffs, other than those charged only as a revenue source, as opposed to those designed to protect domestic businesses. Cf. *protective tariff* under TARIFF (2).

free-trade zone. (1899) A duty-free area within a country to promote commerce, esp. transshipment and processing, without entering into the country's market. — Abbr. FTZ. — Also termed *free-trade area; foreign trade zone; free customs zone; free port.*

freeware. (ca. 1983) Software, esp. based on open-source code, that is made generally available with express or implicit permission for anyone to use, copy, modify, and distribute for any purpose, including financial gain. • The term "free" refers to usage rights rather than price — a distinction important in two respects. First, a user may purchase the initial copy of freeware. Second, software available at no cost may not include permission for the software's user to copy, modify, or give away the software. — Also termed *free software.* Cf. PROPRIETARY SOFTWARE; SEMI-FREE SOFTWARE; SHAREWARE.

free warehouse. A lockable building or facility where goods in international commerce may be stored and guarded by Customs.

free warren. See WARREN.

freeze, *n.* (1942) **1.** A period when the government severely restricts or immobilizes certain commercial activity.

▸ **credit freeze.** (1922) A period when the government restricts bank-lending.

▸ **wage-and-price freeze.** (1943) A period when the government forbids the increase of wages and prices.

2. A recapitalization of a closed corporation so that the value of its existing capital is concentrated primarily in preferred stock rather than in common stock. • By freezing capital, the owner can transfer the common stock to heirs without taxation while continuing to enjoy preferred-stock income during the owner's lifetime, while the common stock grows.

freeze, *vb.* (1922) **1.** To cause to become fixed and unable to increase <to freeze interest rates> <to freeze prices>. **2.** To make immobile by government mandate or banking action <to freeze assets>. **3.** To cease physical movement, esp. when ordered by a law enforcement officer <the police officer shouted at the suspect to freeze>.

freezee, *n.* (1958) A person or entity subjected to a freeze-out.

freezeout, *n.* (1883) *Corporations.* A transaction in which a shareholder or group of shareholders obtains the entire common-equity interest in a company while the other shareholders receive cash, debt, or preferred stock in exchange for their common-equity shares. — Also termed *going-private transaction.* Cf. SQUEEZE-OUT.

> "A 'freeze-out' is usually accomplished by the merger of a corporation into its parent corporation, where the parent corporation owns a large percentage of the shares of the subsidiary, and the minority shareholders are entitled to minimal distributions of cash or securities. A 'freeze-out' may also be used to connote the situation where so large a number of equity shares are issued to the acquiring corporation that the public shareholders own less than 10 percent of the outstanding equity securities and, therefore, have no control over the corporation or any of its decisions. In such event, a short-form merger could later be used to eliminate the minority shareholders." 69A Am. Jur. 2d *Securities Regulation — State* § 245, at 971 n.60 (1993).

▸ **parent–subsidiary freezeout.** (1978) A transaction in which a parent company uses its majority ownership in a subsidiary to acquire the minority shareholders' interest.

▸ **pure freezeout.** A transaction in which company insiders or employees acquire all the public shares of the company, often with the help of lenders. — Also termed *management buyout.* See *management buyout* under BUYOUT.

▸ **second-step freezeout.** (1978) A freezeout that takes place as the final phase of a two-step takeover, after the initial phase in which a majority interest is acquired by the purchase of shares in a tender offer, on the open market, from the issuer, from a control group, or from an issuer–control-group combination.

freeze out, *vb.* (1861) **1.** To subject one to a freezeout. **2.** To exclude a person or entity, esp. a business competitor, from a market or a specific transaction <freezing out the competition>.

freeze-out merger. See *cash merger* under MERGER (8).

freight. (15c) **1.** Goods transported by water, land, or air; CARGO. **2.** The compensation paid to a carrier for transporting goods.

> "Freight, in the common acceptation of the term, means the price for the actual transportation of goods by sea from one place to another; but, in its more extensive sense, it is applied to all rewards or compensation paid for the use of ships, including the transportation of passengers." 3 James Kent, *Commentaries on American Law* *219 (George Comstock ed., 11th ed. 1866).

▸ **back freight.** (18c) An extra charge that a consignor of cargo incurs when delivery at an intended port is not feasible, covering the carrier's expenses for additional transport or storage of the cargo.

▸ **dead freight.** (17c) The amount paid by a shipper to a shipowner for the ship's unused cargo space.

freight absorption. See ABSORPTION (5).

freight at destination. See FREIGHT PAYABLE AT DESTINATION.

freight forwarder. (1865) *Maritime law.* A person or company whose business is to receive and ship goods for others. • A freight forwarder may be an agent of the cargo's owner or of the carrier, or may be an independent contractor acting as a principal and assuming the carrier's responsibility for delivering the cargo. — Also termed *third-party logistical service provider; forwarding agent.*

freighting voyage. See VOYAGE.

freight on board. See FREE ON BOARD.

freight paid at destination. See FREIGHT PAYABLE AT DESTINATION.

freight payable at destination. (1910) (In a shipping contract) a term indicating that shipping costs will be determined by weighing the cargo when it is offloaded from the ship, at which time payment will be due. • This method usu. applies to bulk cargo. — Abbr. FPAD. — Also termed *freight at destination; freight paid at destination.*

freight rate. See RATE (2).

frenchman. (bef. 12c) *Hist.* A stranger; a foreigner. • In early English law, this term was applied to all foreigners, even those not from France.

F reorganization. See REORGANIZATION (2).

fresh, *adj.* (13c) Recent; not stale; characterized by newness without any material interval.

fresh complaint. (1853) *Criminal law.* A reasonably prompt lodging of a grievance; esp., a victim's prompt report of a sexual assault to someone trustworthy. — Also termed *first complaint; prompt complaint; prompt outcry.*

fresh-complaint rule. (1952) *Evidence.* The principle that the testimony of a witness whom a victim of a sex crime promptly told about the crime is admissible to corroborate the victim's claim that a crime occurred. • The testimony is admissible to show that the complaint was made promptly, not for the truth of matter stated in the complaint. The theory is that a sexual-assault victim's credibility is bolstered if the victim reports the assault soon after it occurs. Most courts no longer recognize this theory.

fresh disseisin. See DISSEISIN.

fresh evidence. See EVIDENCE.

fresh fine. See FINE (5).

fresh force. (15c) *Hist.* Force, such as disseisin or deforcement, newly done. • This term refers to force used in a town, and for which a remedy (the Assize of Fresh Force) existed. See *assize of fresh force* under ASSIZE (8).

fresh pursuit. (17c) **1.** The right of a police officer to make a warrantless search of a fleeing suspect or of the place to which the suspect has fled, or to cross jurisdictional lines to arrest a fleeing suspect. **2.** The right of a person to use reasonable force to retake property that has just been taken. — Also termed *fresh suit; hot pursuit.*

fresh start. (1857) *Bankruptcy.* The favorable financial status obtained by a debtor who receives a release from personal liability on prepetition debts or who reorganizes debt obligations through the confirmation and completion of a bankruptcy plan.

fresh suit. See FRESH PURSUIT.

friable, *adj.* Easily crumbled or broken into small pieces.

Friday market. See MARKET.

friendly amendment. See AMENDMENT (3).

friendly fire. (1918) **1.** The use of weapons by one's own side in an armed conflict, esp. when it results in one or more casualties to that side. Cf. BLUE-ON-BLUE. **2.** A fire burning where it is intended to burn, even if still capable of causing unintended damage.

friendly-parent law. A statute that requires or allows a judge to consider as a factor in awarding custody the extent to which one parent encourages or thwarts the child's relationship with the other parent.

friendly-parent principle. (1991) *Family law.* The theory that if one parent is more likely to support the child's relationship with the other parent after a divorce is granted, then that more supportive parent should be awarded custody. • This theory has been criticized as fundamentally flawed because (1) a court may not consider the legitimate fears and concerns that motivate a parent's "unfriendly" behavior, and (2) the theory's simplicity discourages a parent from revealing anything negative about the other parent to the child, even if relevant to the child's safety, for fear of being viewed as too hostile. — Also termed *friendly-parent doctrine; friendly-parent paradigm.*

friendly society. (18c) In the United Kingdom, a voluntary association, supported by subscriptions or contributions, for the purpose of providing financial relief to ill members and to their widows and children upon death. • Friendly societies are regulated by statute. See *benevolent association* under ASSOCIATION. Cf. FRATERNAL BENEFIT ASSOCIATION.

friendly subpoena. See SUBPOENA.

friendly suit. (18c) A lawsuit in which all the parties have agreed beforehand to allow a court to resolve the issues. • Friendly suits are often filed by settling parties who wish to have a judgment entered.

friendly suitor. See WHITE KNIGHT.

friendly takeover. See TAKEOVER.

friend of the court. (1816) **1.** AMICUS CURIAE. **2.** In some jurisdictions, an official who investigates and advises the court in domestic-relations cases involving minors. • The friend of the court may also help enforce court orders in those cases.

friend-of-the-court brief. See *amicus brief* under BRIEF (1).

fright. (bef. 12c) Fear caused by a suddenly perceived danger; sudden terror or alarm. • In tort law, although fright alone without physical injury does not ordinarily constitute an element of damages, if the fright is a natural and direct result of the defendant's act, and if the fright naturally and directly causes an impairment of health or a loss of bodily power, then it may constitute an element of the injury to be considered by the fact-finder. — **frighten,** *vb.*

fringe benefit. See BENEFIT (2).

fringe meaning. The outer periphery of a word's or provision's meaning, well beyond the core sense but still often included within the literal sense if the interpreter is unconcerned about absurd results.

frisk, *n.* (18c) A pat-down search to discover a concealed weapon. — Also termed *pat-down.* See STOP-AND-FRISK. Cf. SEARCH (1). — **frisk,** *vb.*

frivolous, *adj.* (15c) Lacking a legal basis or legal merit; not serious; not reasonably purposeful <a frivolous claim>. — **frivolousness,** *n.* (or, less good) **frivolity,** *n.*

frivolous appeal. See APPEAL (2).

frivolous claim. See CLAIM (4).

frivolous defense. See DEFENSE (1).

frivolous objection. See OBJECTION (1).

frivolous suit. See SUIT.

FRM. See *fixed-rate mortgage* under MORTGAGE.

FRN. *abbr.* See *floating-rate note* under NOTE.

frolic (frol-ik), *n.* (1834) *Torts.* An employee's significant deviation from the employer's business for personal reasons. • A frolic is outside the scope of employment, and thus the employer is not vicariously liable for the employee's actions. Cf. DETOUR.

front, *n.* (14c) **1.** The side or part of a building or lot that is open to view, that is the principal entrance, or that faces out to the open (as to a lake or ocean); the foremost part of something <the property's front was its most valuable attribute>. **2.** A person or group that serves to conceal the true identity or activity of the person or group in control <the political party was a front for the terrorist group>. **3.** A political association similar to a party <popular front>.

frontage (frən-tij). (17c) **1.** The part of land abutting or lying between a building's front and a street, highway, or body of water <the property's value was so low because of its narrow frontage>. **2.** The linear distance of a frontage <the lot's frontage was 90 feet>.

frontage assessment. See ASSESSMENT (2).

frontager (frən-tij-ər), *n.* (17c) A person owning or occupying land that abuts a highway, river, seashore, or the like.

front-end load. See *loan fund* under MUTUAL FUND.

front-end money. See SEED MONEY.

front foot. (1863) A measurement used to calculate a frontage assessment. — Also termed *abutting foot.*

front-foot rule. (1872) The principle that an improvement cost is to be apportioned among several properties in proportion to their frontage, without regard to the benefits conferred on each property. — Also termed *front-foot plan.*

frontier. (15c) For trade purposes, an international boundary.

front money. See SEED MONEY.

front-page citation. See CITATION (4).

front-page drawing. See DRAWING.

frontpay. (1976) *Labor law.* Court-awarded compensation for the post-judgment effects of continuing employment discrimination. Cf. BACKPAY.

front-running, *n. Securities.* A broker's or analyst's use of nonpublic information to acquire securities or enter into options or futures contracts for his or her own benefit, knowing that when the information becomes public, the price of the securities will change in a predictable manner. • This practice is illegal. Front-running can occur in many ways. For example, a broker or analyst who works for a brokerage firm may buy shares in a company that the firm is about to recommend as a strong buy or in which the firm is planning to buy a large block of shares. See INSIDER TRADING.

front wages. See WAGE.

frottage. (ca. 1935) Sexual stimulation by rubbing the genitals against another person. • Frottage may be accomplished without removing clothing. When a child is involved, it is a form of sexual abuse.

frozen account. See *blocked account* under ACCOUNT.

frozen asset. See ASSET.

frozen deposit. See DEPOSIT (2).

FRS. *abbr.* FEDERAL RESERVE SYSTEM.

FRTIB. *abbr.* FEDERAL RETIREMENT THRIFT INVESTMENT BOARD.

fructuarius (frək-choo-**air**-ee-əs). [Latin "(one) entitled to fruits"] **1.** *Roman & civil law.* One having the usufruct of a thing (as of land and animals); a usufructuary. See USUFRUCTUARY. **2.** *Hist.* A lessee. Pl. ***fructuarii.***

> "The *fructuarius* had the use, and enjoyment of the profits, of the subject of the usufruct. This included the stock and instruments of a farm, the stakes necessary for his vines, and the working of mines and quarries and pits, already opened." David T. Oliver & W. Nalder Williams, *Willis and Oliver's Roman Law Examination Guide* 86 (3d ed. 1910).

fructus (**frək**-təs). [Latin "fruits"] **1.** *Roman & civil law.* The natural produce of land and animals; the profit from or increase in land and animals. • The owner of the land or animals acquired ownership by *separatio*, the separation of the fruit from the parent body. A *bona fide possessor* or an *emphyteuta* also acquired ownership by *separatio*, which allowed a nonowner to claim title from a thief. But in Justinian's law, a bona fide possessor had to account to a successful claimant for ownership for the principal thing and any unconsumed fruits. A tenant or usufructuary acquired title only by *perceptio*, and cannot claim title from a thief. See PERCEPTION. Cf. FRUCTUS CIVILES. **2.** USUFRUCT. Pl. ***fructus.***

fructus civiles (**frək**-təs sə-**vɪ**-leez). [Latin "civil fruits"] *Roman & civil law.* Income (such as rent or interest) that one receives from another for the use or enjoyment of a thing, esp. real property or loaned money. • In Roman law, *fructus civiles* included both minerals and the earnings of slaves.

fructus fundi (**frək**-təs **fən**-dɪ). [Latin "land fruits"] The fruits or produce of land.

fructus industriales (**frək**-təs in-dəs-tree-**ay**-leez). [Latin "industrial fruits"] The fruit or produce arising from labor or industry, such as cultivated crops. See EMBLEMENTS (1). Cf. FRUCTUS NATURALES.

fructus legis (**frək**-təs **lee**-jis). [Latin "fruits of the law"] The proceeds of judgment or execution.

fructus naturales (**frək**-təs nach-ə-**ray**-leez). [Latin "natural fruits"] The natural produce of land or plants and the offspring of animals. • *Fructus naturales* are considered part of the real property. Cf. FRUCTUS INDUSTRIALES.

fructus pecudum (**frək**-təs **pek**-yə-dəm). [Latin "fruits of the herd"] The produce or increase of flocks or herds.

fructus pendentes (**frək**-təs pen-**den**-teez). [Latin "hanging fruits"] (17c) Fruits not yet severed or gathered; fruits united with that which produces them.

fructus percepti (**frək**-təs pər-**sep**-tɪ). [Latin "gathered fruits"] (17c) *Roman & civil law.* Fruits that have been gathered.

fructus rei alienae (**frək**-təs **ree**-ɪ ay-lee-**ee**-nee *or* al-ee-). [Latin "fruits of another's property"] The fruits of another's property; fruits taken from another's estate.

fructus separati (**frək**-təs sep-ə-**ray**-tɪ). [Latin "separated fruits"] *Roman & civil law.* The produce of a thing after being separated from it, and so becoming in law "fruits."

fructus stantes (**frək**-təs **stan**-teez). [Latin "standing fruits"] Fruits that have not yet been severed from the stalk or stem.

fructuum perceptio (**frək**-choo-əm pər-**sep**-shee-oh). [Latin] *Roman & civil law.* The rightful taking of the produce of property by a person who does not own the property.

fruges (**froo**-jeez). [Latin "fruits" or "crops"] *Roman & civil law.* Edible produce or crops; esculents.

frugi aut bonae famae (**froo**-jɪ awt **boh**-nee **fay**-mee). [Latin] *Hist.* Frugal or of good reputation.

fruit. (14c) **1.** The produce or product of something (as of land or property). **2.** *Civil law.* Income or goods derived or produced from property without a diminution of the property's inherent value.

▸ **civil fruit.** (1823) *Civil law.* Revenue derived from a thing by operation of law or by reason of a juridical act, such as lease or interest payments, or certain corporate distributions. La. Civ. Code art. 551. See FRUCTUS CIVILES.

▸ **natural fruit.** (1823) *Civil law.* A product of the land or of animals. • Examples are crops and eggs. La. Civ. Code art. 2317. See FRUCTUS NATURALES.

3. Something (such as evidence) obtained during or resulting from an activity or operation <the fruit of the officer's search>. See FRUIT-OF-THE-POISONOUS-TREE DOCTRINE.

fruit-and-the-tree doctrine. (1979) *Tax.* The rule that an individual who earns income cannot assign that income to another person to avoid taxation.

fruit-of-the-poisonous-tree doctrine. (1948) *Criminal procedure.* The rule that evidence derived from an illegal search, arrest, or interrogation is inadmissible because the evidence (the "fruit") was tainted by the illegality (the "poisonous tree"). • Under this doctrine, for example, a murder weapon is inadmissible if the map showing its location and used to find it was seized during an illegal search. — Also termed *fruits doctrine.* See EXCLUSIONARY RULE; ATTENUATION DOCTRINE; INDEPENDENT-SOURCE RULE; INEVITABLE-DISCOVERY RULE.

fruits doctrine. See FRUIT-OF-THE-POISONOUS-TREE DOCTRINE.

fruits of a crime. (1854) The proceeds acquired through criminal acts.

frustra (**frəs**-trə). [Latin] *Hist.* In vain; to no purpose.

frustration, *n.* (16c) **1.** The prevention or hindering of the attainment of a goal, such as contractual performance.

▸ **commercial frustration.** (1918) An excuse for a party's nonperformance because of some unforeseeable and uncontrollable circumstance. — Also termed *economic frustration.*

▸ **self-induced frustration.** (1926) A breach of contract caused by one party's action that prevents the performance. • The phrase is something of a misnomer, since *self-induced frustration* is not really a type of frustration at all but is instead a breach of contract.

▸ **temporary frustration.** (1950) An occurrence that prevents performance and legally suspends the duty to perform for the duration of the event. • If the burden or circumstance is substantially different after the event, then the duty may be discharged.

2. *Contracts.* The doctrine that if a party's principal purpose is substantially frustrated by unanticipated changed circumstances, that party's duties are discharged and the contract is considered terminated. — Also termed *frustration of purpose.* Cf. IMPOSSIBILITY (4); IMPRACTICABILITY; MISTAKE. — **frustrate,** *vb.*

frustration of purpose. See FRUSTRATION (2).

frustrum terrae (**frəs**-trəm **ter**-ee). [Latin] (17c) *Hist.* A piece of land. • This usu. referred to a fragment of land remaining after a survey.

***Frye* test.** (1955) The defunct federal common-law rule of evidence on the admissibility of scientific evidence. • It required that the tests or procedures must have gained general acceptance in their particular field. *Frye v. U.S.*, 293 F. 1013 (D.C. Cir. 1923). In *Daubert v. Merrell Dow Pharms., Inc.*, 509 U.S. 579, 113 S.Ct. 2786 (1993), the Supreme Court held that scientific evidence must meet the requirements of the Federal Rules of Evidence, not the *Frye* test, to be admissible. — Also termed *general-acceptance test.* See DAUBERT TEST.

FSA. *abbr.* FARM SERVICE AGENCY.

FSI. *abbr.* FOREIGN SERVICE INSTITUTE.

FSIA. *abbr.* FOREIGN SOVEREIGN IMMUNITIES ACT.

FSIS. *abbr.* FOOD SAFETY AND INSPECTION SERVICE.

FSLIC. *abbr.* FEDERAL SAVINGS AND LOAN INSURANCE CORPORATION.

FSS. *abbr.* FEDERAL SUPPLY SERVICE.

FSSCP. *abbr.* Fee simple subject to a condition precedent. See FEE SIMPLE.

FST. See *field sobriety test* under SOBRIETY TEST.

F.Supp. *abbr.* Federal Supplement, a series of reported decisions of the federal district courts (from 1932 to 1998), the U.S. Court of Claims (1932 to 1960), and the U.S. Customs Court (from 1949 to 1998, but renamed the Court of International Trade in 1980). • It is the first of the Federal Supplement series. — Also abbreviated F. Supp.

F.Supp.2d. *abbr.* The second series of the Federal Supplement, which includes decisions of federal district courts and the Court of International Trade from 1997 to the present. • Some of the F.Supp. volumes contain cases from 1998 and some of the F.Supp.2d volumes contain cases decided in 1997. — Also abbreviated F. Supp. 2d

FTA. *abbr.* **1.** FEDERAL TRANSIT ADMINISTRATION. **2.** Failure to appear. See NONAPPEARANCE. **3.** Failed to appear.

FTC. *abbr.* FEDERAL TRADE COMMISSION.

FTCA. *abbr.* FEDERAL TORT CLAIMS ACT.

FTDA. *abbr.* FEDERAL TRADEMARK DILUTION ACT.

FTM. *abbr.* Forward triangular merger. See *triangular merger* under MERGER.

FTO search. 1. See INFRINGEMENT SEARCH. **2.** *abbr.* Foreign terrorist organization.

FTP. See FILE-TRANSPORT PROTOCOL.

FTS. *abbr.* FEDERAL TECHNOLOGY SERVICE.

FTT. *abbr.* FAILURE TO THRIVE.

FTZ. *abbr.* FREE-TRADE ZONE.

fudge, *vb.* **1.** To manipulate (esp. numbers or data) to arrive at a desired conclusion. **2.** To balk at or evade questioning. **3.** To use hyperbole, euphemism, or some other rhetorical device in an effort to spin or distort a message.

fuer (**fyoo**-ər). [Law French "to flee"] Flight from the law. — Also termed *fugere.*

▸ ***fuer in fait*** (**fyoo**-ər in **fay**). [Law French "flight in fact"] Actual flight from the law. — Also termed *fugere in facta.*

▸ ***fuer in ley*** (**fyoo**-ər in **lay**). [Law French "flight in law"] Legal flight from the law. • If an accused fails to appear, the law treats that failure as flight. — Also termed *fugere in lege.*

fuero (foo-**wer**-oh). *Spanish law.* **1.** A forum; court. **2.** The territory in which a court has the power to act; JURISDICTION (3). **3.** A privilege enjoyed by some but not others. **4.** A custom having the force of law. **5.** *Hist.* A collection of local, usu. customary, laws.

▸ ***Fuero Juzgo*** (**hooz**-goh). *Hist.* A 7th-century Visigothic code that was revised and incorporated into the laws of 13th-century Spain. • The code contains the earliest known laws of community property. In the 18th century, much of the Fuero Juzgo was incorporated into the Code Napoleon. In the 19th century, vestiges of the Fuero Juzgo were incorporated into the Spanish Civil Code.

▸ ***Fuero Real*** (ray-**ahl**). *Hist.* A collection of the ancient customs of Castile, collected by order of Alfonse X in 1255 to produce a uniform legal code, much of which was incorporated into local *fueros.* • Louisiana's system of acquets and gains was adapted from the Fuero Real.

fugam fecit (**fyoo**-gəm **fee**-sit). [Law Latin] *Hist.* He fled; he has made flight. • When a jury made this finding in a felony or treason trial, the defendant's property was subject to forfeiture.

fugere. See FUER.

fugere in facta. See *fuer in fait* under FUER.

fugere in lege. See *fuer in ley* under FUER.

fugitation (fyoo-jə-**tay**-shən). (18c) *Hist.* A sentence or declaration of fugitive status that was pronounced against an accused person for failing to answer a citation and appear. • The effect was that the person forfeited his or her goods and chattels. — **fugitate,** *vb.*

fugitive. (14c) **1.** Someone who flees or escapes; a refugee. **2.** A criminal suspect or a witness in a criminal case who flees, evades, or escapes arrest, prosecution, imprisonment, service of process, or the giving of testimony, esp. by fleeing the jurisdiction or by hiding. *See* 18 USCA § 1073. — Also termed (in sense 2) *fugitive from justice.*

fugitive-disentitlement doctrine. (1990) See FUGITIVE-FROM-JUSTICE DOCTRINE.

fugitive-dismissal rule. (1993) The principle that an appellate court may dismiss a criminal defendant's appeal if the defendant is a fugitive.

Fugitive Felon Act. A federal statute that makes it a felony to flee across state lines to avoid state-felony prosecution or confinement, or to avoid giving testimony in a state-felony case. 18 USCA § 1073.

fugitive from justice. See FUGITIVE.

fugitive-from-justice doctrine. (1935) *Criminal procedure.* The equitable rule that if a criminal defendant appeals from a conviction and then absconds or flees while the appeal is pending, the appellate court should dismiss the appeal. — Also termed *fugitive-disentitlement doctrine.*

fugitive resource. 1. See *mineral ferae naturae* under MINERAL. **2.** A natural resource that lacks a fixed location or boundary. • A fugitive resource is treated as common property rather than private property. Examples include schools of wild fish and flocks of game birds.

fugitive's goods. *Hist.* The goods that a person forfeited as a result of fleeing.

fugitive-slave laws. (1843) *Hist.* Federal statutes enacted in 1793 and 1850 providing for the surrender and return of slaves who had escaped and fled to a free territory or a free state. — Also termed *Fugitive Slave Acts.*

fugitive warrant. See WARRANT (1).

fugitivus (fyoo-jə-**tɪ**-vəs), *n.* [Latin] *Roman law.* A runaway slave; a fugitive.

fugue (fyoog). (16c) An abnormal state of consciousness in which one appears to function normally but on recovery has no memory of what one did while in that condition.

full adversary hearing. See *adjudication hearing* under HEARING.

full age. See *age of majority* under AGE.

full and final release. See *general release* under RELEASE (8).

full bench. See *full court* under COURT.

full blood. See BLOOD.

full-box method. (1954) *Criminal procedure. Slang.* A jury-selection process in which the prosecution and defense examine each veniremember in turn and immediately send a veniremember not struck for cause to the jury box until the number of veniremembers in the box is 12 plus the number of peremptory challenges granted to each side, the prosecution and defense then exercising their peremptory challenges until 12 jurors are sworn. • Only a portion of the full venire will usu. be examined before a jury is selected. Cf. STRUCK-BOX METHOD.

full cash value. See VALUE (2).

full copy. *Equity practice.* A complete transcript of a bill or other pleading, with all indorsements and a copy of all exhibits.

full court. See COURT.

full cousin. See COUSIN (1).

full-covenant-and-warranty deed. See *warranty deed* under DEED.

full coverage. See COVERAGE (1).

full-credit bid. See BID (1).

full-crew law. (1916) A statute that regulates the number of railroad employees required to operate a train, or airline employees required to operate an airplane.

full defense. See DEFENSE (1).

full disclosure. See DISCLOSURE (1).

full endorsement. See *irregular indorsement* and *special indorsement* under INDORSEMENT.

full faith and credit. (17c) The recognition, acceptance, and enforcement of the laws, orders, and judgments of another jurisdiction; specif., the recognition by one state of another state's legal decisions.

Full Faith and Credit Act. A federal statute requiring federal courts to give a state court's judgment the same preclusive effect as the judgment would have under state law. 28 USCA § 1738. *See Migra v. Warren City School Dist. Bd. of Educ.*, 465 U.S. 75, 81, 104 S.Ct. 892, 896 (1984). — Abbr. FFCA.

full-faith-and-credit bond. See *general-obligation bond* under BOND (3).

Full Faith and Credit Clause. (1896) *Constitutional law.* U.S. Const. art. IV, § 1, which requires states to give effect to the acts, public records, and judicial decisions of other states. — Also termed *Faith and Credit Clause.*

Full Faith and Credit for Child-Support Orders Act. A 1994 federal statute designed to facilitate interstate child-support collection. • Under the Act, the state first issuing a child-support order maintains continuing, exclusive jurisdiction to modify the order as long as the child or one or both of the litigants continue to reside there, unless all the contestants agree in writing to change jurisdiction. An order from one state may be registered for enforcement in another state. 28 USCA § 1738B.

full hearing. See HEARING; ADMINISTRATIVE PROCEEDING.

fullied. *Hist. slang.* See FULLY COMMITTED FOR TRIAL.

full indorsement. 1. See *irregular indorsement* under INDORSEMENT. **2.** See *special indorsement* under INDORSEMENT.

full interdiction. See INTERDICTION (3).

full member. See *voting member* under MEMBER (1).

full name. See NAME.

full ownership. See *perfect ownership* under OWNERSHIP.

full-paid stock. See STOCK.

full pardon. See *absolute pardon* under PARDON.

full partner. See *general partner* under PARTNER.

full payout lease. See *finance lease* under LEASE.

full performance. See PERFORMANCE.

full-performance doctrine. The rule that a party who has fully performed an oral agreement may seek to enforce the agreement against another. • The full-performance doctrine is an exception to the Statute of Frauds and also serves as an estoppel.

full powers. *Int'l law.* An official document designating a person to represent a country for (1) negotiating, adopting, or authenticating the text of a treaty, (2) expressing the consent of the country to be bound by a treaty, or (3) accomplishing any act with respect to the treaty.

full proof. See PROOF.

full-reporting clause. (1942) **1.** *Insurance.* An insurance-policy clause that requires the insured to reveal values and that penalizes the insured if the insured revealed less than required in the policy application. — Also termed *honesty clause.* **2.** An insurance-policy clause providing that the indemnity will not exceed the proportion of the loss that the last reported value bears to the actual value.

full right. (18c) The union of good title with actual possession.

full-service lease. See LEASE.

full settlement. See SETTLEMENT (2).

full-time employee. See EMPLOYEE.

full value. See *fair market value* under VALUE (2).

full warranty. See WARRANTY (2).

fully administered. (17c) A plea by an executor or administrator that he or she has completely and legally disposed of all the assets of the estate and that the estate has no remaining assets from which a new claim could be satisfied.

fully committed for trial, *adj.* (18c) *English law.* (Of a person) qualified to be indicted, arraigned, and tried. • Historically, a defendant went through two hearings that were essentially minitrials to determine whether the evidence against the defendant was sufficient to support the charges. If the hearing magistrate decided there was, then the defendant was fully committed for trial. In modern usage, it means only that the defendant has had at least two bail hearings and has not yet been indicted. — Often shortened to *fully committed.* — Formerly also termed (in slang) *fullied.*

fully diluted earnings per share. See EARNINGS PER SHARE.

fully funded, *adj.* (1930) **1.** Having sufficient financial resources to meet current payments, even upon bankruptcy <the company's pension plan was fully funded>. **2.** Having completely satisfied a funding requirement; paid <the construction loan was fully funded>. — Also termed *funded.*

fully managed fund. See MUTUAL FUND.

fully met. See ANTICIPATED.

fully paid face-amount certificate. See *face-amount certificate* (2) under STOCK CERTIFICATE.

fully paid share. See SHARE (2).

fumus boni juris (**fyoo**-məs **boh**-nɪ **joor**-is). [Latin] *Hist.* The smoke of good law.

function, *n.* (16c) **1.** Activity that is appropriate to a particular business or profession <a court's function is to administer justice>. **2.** Office; duty; the occupation of an office <presidential function>.

functional analog. See ANALOG.

functional depreciation. See DEPRECIATION.

functional discount. See DISCOUNT.

functional disease. See DISEASE.

functional feature. (1913) *Trademarks.* A design element that is either physically necessary to construct an article or commercially necessary to manufacture and sell it; a product's attribute that is essential to its use, necessary for its proper and successful operation, and utilitarian rather than ornamental in every detail. • A functional feature is not eligible for trademark protection.

functional immunity. See *immunity ratione materiae* under IMMUNITY (1).

functionalism. A methodological approach to law focusing on the effects of rules in practice, often as exhibited in judicial decisions, rather than on the precise statements of the rules themselves. *See* Ralf Michaels, "The Functional Method of Comparative Law," in *The Oxford Handbook of Comparative Law* 339 (M. Reimann & Reinhard Zimmermann eds., 2006). See LAW IN ACTION. Cf. LEGAL REALISM.

functionality. (19c) *Trademarks.* The quality of having a shape, configuration, design, or color that is so superior to available alternatives that giving the first user exclusive trademark rights would hinder competition.

▸ **aesthetic functionality.** (1981) A doctrine that denies protection to the design of a product or its container when the design is necessary to enable the product to function as intended.

functional limitation. (1901) *Patents.* In a patent application, the definition of an invention by what it does rather than what it is. • A functional limitation is not inherently invalid, but it is examined closely because it tends to be too broad, claiming every possible way of doing the same thing. MPEP 2173.05(g).

functional magnetic resonance imaging. (1993) A neuroimaging technique that enables researchers to observe metabolic correlates of neural activity. • Unlike MRI, which provides a visual structure of the brain, fMRI provides a visual representation of neural function. Scientific and legal scholars have debated its reliability as a means for detecting deception, propensity to commit crime, and neurological consistencies between categories of criminals. — Abbr. fMRI.

functional obsolescence. See OBSOLESCENCE.

functional rejection. See REJECTION.

functional utility. See UTILITY (2).

functionary. (18c) A public officer or employee; esp., one whose job involves unimportant or mundane duties.

functus officio (**fəngk**-təs ə-**fish**-ee-oh). [Latin "having performed his or her office"] (19c) (Of an officer or official body) without further authority or legal competence because the duties and functions of the original commission have been fully accomplished. • The term is sometimes abbreviated to *functus* <the court was *functus*>.

fund, *n.* (17c) **1.** A sum of money or other liquid assets established for a specific purpose <a fund reserved for unanticipated expenses>.

▸ **blended fund.** (1843) A fund created by income from more than one source, usu. from the sale of a testator's real and personal property.

▸ **changing fund.** (1969) A fund, esp. a trust fund, that changes its form periodically as it is invested and reinvested.

▸ **client-security fund.** (1958) A fund established usu. by a state or a state bar association to compensate persons for losses that they suffered because of their attorneys' misappropriation of funds or other misconduct.

▸ **contingent fund.** (18c) **1.** A fund created by a municipality for expenses that will necessarily arise during the year but that cannot be appropriately classified under any of the specific purposes for which taxes are collected. **2.** A fund segregated by a business to pay unknown costs that may arise in the future. — Also termed *contingency reserve.*

▸ **exchange-traded fund.** A mutual fund whose shares are bought and sold on a stock exchange. — Abbr. ETF.

▸ **executor fund.** (1985) A fund established for an executor to pay an estate's final expenses.

▸ **fund in court.** (18c) **1.** Contested money deposited with the court. See INTERPLEADER. **2.** Money deposited to pay a contingent liability.

▸ **general fund.** (17c) **1.** A government's primary operating fund; a state's assets furnishing the means for the support of government and for defraying the legislature's discretionary appropriations. • A general fund is distinguished from assets of a special character, such as trust, escrow, and special-purpose funds. **2.** A nonprofit entity's assets that are not earmarked for a specific purpose.

▸ **general revenue fund.** (1855) The fund out of which a municipality pays its ordinary and incidental expenses. — Abbr. GRF.

▸ **guaranty fund.** (1843) A private deposit-insurance fund, raised primarily by assessments on banks, and used to pay the depositors of an insolvent bank. • Guaranty funds preceded the FDIC's federal-deposit insurance, which began in 1933, though many funds continued until the savings-and-loan crisis in the 1980s. Massachusetts has a guaranty fund for uninsured deposits (deposits above $100,000) that are not covered by federal-deposit insurance.

▸ **imprest fund (im-prest).** (1937) A fund used by a business for small, routine expenses.

▸ **joint-welfare fund.** (1951) A fund that is established in collective bargaining to provide health and welfare benefits to union employees. • The fund is jointly managed by labor and management representatives. — Also termed *Taft–Hartley fund.*

▸ **paid-in fund.** (1942) A reserve cash fund established by a mutual insurance company to pay unforeseen losses. • The fund is in lieu of a capital stock account.

▸ **pooled-income fund.** See POOLED-INCOME FUND.

▸ **private fund.** (1940) An investment company that is exempt from the registration and other requirements of the Investment Company Act of 1940, usu. because investors in the fund are either few or else large and sophisticated. • Hedge funds are the best-known example of private funds. Until 2010, advisers to private funds were exempt from the registration requirement of the Investment Advisers Act. See HEDGE FUND; INVESTMENT ADVISER.

▸ **public fund.** (*usu. pl.*) (17c) **1.** The revenue or money of a governmental body. • The term includes not only coins and paper but also bank deposits and instruments representing investments of public money. **2.** The securities of a state or national government.

▸ **revolving fund.** (1928) A fund whose moneys are continually expended and then replenished, such as a petty-cash fund.

▸ **sinking fund.** (18c) A fund consisting of regular deposits that are accumulated with interest to pay off a long-term corporate or public debt. — Abbr. SF.

▸ **sovereign-wealth fund.** (2006) A fund through which government moneys are invested in securities issued by foreign companies or sovereigns.

▸ **strike fund.** See STRIKE FUND.

▸ **Taft–Hartley fund.** See *joint-welfare fund.*

▸ **trust fund.** See TRUST FUND.

▸ **unsatisfied-judgment fund.** (1953) A fund established by a state to compensate persons for losses stemming from an automobile accident caused by an uninsured or underinsured motorist.

2. (*usu. pl.*) Money or other assets, such as stocks, bonds, or working capital, available to pay debts, expenses, and the like <Sue invested her funds in her sister's business>.

▸ **commingled funds.** Funds belonging to two or more owners that have been pooled together.

▸ **current funds.** Assets that can be readily converted into cash.

3. A pool of investments owned in common and managed for a fee; MUTUAL FUND <a diverse portfolio of funds>. **4.** An investment company <hedge fund>. See HEDGE FUND.

fund, *vb.* (18c) **1.** To furnish money to (an individual, entity, or venture), esp. to finance a particular project. **2.** To use resources in a manner that produces interest. **3.** To convert (a debt, esp. an open account) into a long-term debt that bears interest at a fixed rate.

fundamental breach. See *repudiatory breach* under BREACH OF CONTRACT.

fundamental constitutional right. See CONSTITUTIONAL RIGHT.

fundamental error. See *plain error* under ERROR (2).

fundamental-fairness doctrine. (1969) The rule that applies the principles of due process to a judicial proceeding. • The term is commonly considered synonymous with *due process.*

fundamental interest. See FUNDAMENTAL RIGHT.

fundamental law. (17c) The organic law that establishes the governing principles of a country or state; esp., CONSTITUTIONAL LAW. — Also termed *organic law; ground-law.* Cf. NATURAL LAW; ELEMENTARY LAW.

fundamental-miscarriage-of-justice exception. (1986) The doctrine allowing a federal court in a habeas corpus proceeding to address a claim of constitutional error that, although ordinarily unreviewable, is subject to review because of a state-court procedural default that rendered the proceedings basically unfair. • For the exception to apply, among other things, the petitioner must show by a preponderance of the evidence that constitutional error resulted in the conviction of one who is actually innocent. If the defaulted claim applies only to sentencing, the exception permits review of the claim if the petitioner shows by clear and convincing evidence that, but for the constitutional error, no reasonable judge or jury would have imposed the sentence that the petitioner received.

fundamental mistake. See MISTAKE.

fundamental right. (17c) **1.** A right derived from natural or fundamental law. **2.** *Constitutional law.* A significant component of liberty, encroachments of which are rigorously tested by courts to ascertain the soundness of purported governmental justifications. • A fundamental right triggers strict scrutiny to determine whether the law violates the Due Process Clause or the Equal Protection Clause of the 14th Amendment. As enunciated by the Supreme Court, fundamental rights include voting, interstate travel, and various aspects of privacy (such as marriage and contraception rights). — Also termed *fundamental interest.* See STRICT SCRUTINY. Cf. SUSPECT CLASSIFICATION.

fundamental term. See TERM (2).

fundamental trend. See *major trend* under TREND.

fundatio (fən-**day**-shee-oh). [Latin "founding" or "foundation"] *Hist.* The founding of a corporation, particularly an eleemosynary corporation.

▸***fundatio incipiens*** (fən-**day**-shee-oh in-**sip**-ee-enz). [Latin "incipient foundation"] (18c) The incorporation or grant of corporate powers.

▸***fundatio perficiens*** (fən-**day**-shee-oh pər-**fish**-ee-enz). [Latin "perfecting foundation"] (1954) The endowment or gift of funds to a corporation.

funded. See FULLY FUNDED.

funded debt. See DEBT.

fund in court. See FUND (1).

funding, *n.* (18c) **1.** The process of financing capital expenditures by issuing long-term debt obligations or by converting short-term obligations into long-term obligations to finance current expenses; the process of creating a funded debt. **2.** The refinancing of a debt before its maturity. — Also termed *refunding.* **3.** The provision or allocation of money for a specific purpose, such as for a pension plan, by putting the money into a reserve fund or investments. **4.** The provision of financial resources to finance a particular activity or project, such as a research study. **5.** The transfer of property to a trust.

fundi publici (**fən**-dı **pəb**-lə-sı). [Latin] *Hist.* Public lands.

fundo annexa (**fən**-doh ə-**nek**-sə). [Latin] (18c) *Hist.* Things annexed to the soil.

fundraising. (1940) The activity of collecting pledges or donations for a specific cause, esp. one that involves not-for-profit endeavors. — Also written *fund-raising.*

funds transfer. A payment of money from one person or entity to another; esp., the process by which payment is made through a series of transactions between computerized banking systems, beginning with an originator's payment order and ending when a final payment order is received by the beneficiary's bank. • Commercial or wholesale funds transfers are governed by Article 4A of the UCC. Consumer funds transfers are regulated by the federal Electronic Fund Transfer Act (15 USCA §§ 1693 et seq.). — Also termed (specif.) *electronic funds transfer* (EFT).

fundus (**fən**-dəs). [Latin "land"] *Hist.* **1.** Land or ground in general, without consideration of its specific use. **2.** A farm.

▸***fundus emphyteuticarius*** (**fən**-dəs em-fə-tyoo-ti-**kair**-ee-əs). *Civil law.* Land held under a hereditary leasehold. See EMPHYTEUSIS.

▸***fundus instructus*** (**fən**-dəs in-**strək**-təs). [Latin] *Hist.* Land already provided with certain necessaries.

▸***fundus patrimonialis*** (**fən**-dəs pa-trə-moh-nee-**ay**-lis). [Latin] *Roman law.* Land belonging to the *patrimonium principis* (that is, property belonging to the emperor as such).

funeral expense. See EXPENSE.

fungibiles res (fən-**jib**-ə-leez **reez**). [Latin] *Civil law.* Fungible things.

fungibility. The quality of being interchangeable with another thing or quantity of a thing.

fungible (**fən**-jə-bəl), *adj.* (18c) Commercially interchangeable with other property of the same kind <corn and wheat are fungible goods, whereas land is not>. — **fungible,** *n.*

fungible goods. See GOODS.

fur (fər), *n.* [Latin] *Roman law.* A thief.

furandi animus (fyuu-**ran**-dı **an**-ə-məs). See *animus furandi* under ANIMUS.

furca (**fər**-kə), *n.* [Latin "fork"] (17c) *Roman law.* An instrument of punishment with two prongs to which the arms are tied. • In England, *furca* became another name for *gallows.*

furca et flagellum (**fər**-kə et flə-**jel**-əm). [Law Latin] *Hist.* Gallows and whip. • This referred to the basest of servile tenures — the tenant was completely at the mercy of the lord.

furca et fossa (**fər**-kə et **fahs**-ə). [Law Latin] (18c) *Hist.* Gallows and pit. • This phrase was used in ancient grants of criminal jurisdiction for punishing felons: hanging for men and drowning for women.

fur famosus (fər fə-**moh**-səs). [Latin] *Scots law.* A reputed thief.

Furian Caninian law. See LEX FURIA CANINIA.

furigeldum (fyər-ə-**jel**-dəm). [Law Latin *fur* "theft" + *geldum* "payment"] *Hist.* A fine paid for theft.

furlong (**fər**-lawng). (14c) One-eighth of a mile, or forty rods. — Also termed *ferlingus; ferlingum.*

furlough (**fər**-loh). (17c) **1.** A leave of absence from military or other employment duty. **2.** A brief release from prison. See *study release* under RELEASE. — **furlough,** *vb.*

fur manifestus (fər man-ə-**fes**-təs). [Latin "manifest thief"] *Roman law.* A thief caught in the act of stealing. • A *fur manifestus* could be put to death on the spot in either of two circumstances: (1) if the theft occurred at night, or (2) if the thief used a lethal weapon against the person who discovered the crime. Apart from this, the manifest thief was liable to pay the owner four times the value of the stolen property. — Also termed *manifest thief.*

furnisher. Under the federal Fair Credit Reporting Act, someone who provides information to a consumer reporting agency. *See* 15 USCA § 1681s-2.

furor brevis. See HEAT OF PASSION.

furta (fər-tə). *Hist.* A right or privilege from the monarch to try, condemn, and execute criminals within a jurisdiction.

further advance. 1. A second or later loan to a mortgagor by a mortgagee, either on the same security as the original loan or on an additional security. **2.** *Equity practice.* The agreed conversion of arrears of interest on a mortgage security into principal.

furtherance. (15c) The act or process of facilitating the progress of something or of making it more likely to occur; promotion or advancement.

further assurance. See ASSURANCE.

further direction. See *additional instruction* under JURY INSTRUCTION.

further-exploration covenant. (1956) *Oil & gas.* In an oil-and-gas lease, an implied promise that once production has been obtained from the leased property, the lessee will continue to explore other parts of the property and other formations under it. • Some jurisdictions hold that the covenant for further exploration does not exist independently of the covenant for reasonable development. See also REASONABLE-DEVELOPMENT COVENANT; REASONABLY-PRUDENT-OPERATOR STANDARD.

further instruction. See *additional instruction* under JURY INSTRUCTION.

furtive gesture. A surreptitious movement, esp. one seeming to be hiding something, seen by a police officer and providing reasonable suspicion to detain or search.

furtum (fər-təm), *n.* [Latin "theft"] *Roman law.* **1.** The offense of stealing movable property. • Under Roman law, *furtum* included not only the taking of another's property, but any handling of the property done with the intent of profiting by it. *Furtum* was not only a private wrong (*delictum*) prosecuted by the person suffering the loss. Cf. PECULATUS. **2.** The thing stolen.

> "'Furtum' is the fraudulent removal of a thing from the place in which it was for the sake of profit, either from the thing itself, or its use or possession, in violation of the law of nature." John George Phillimore, *Private Law Among the Romans* 185 (1863).

▸***furtum conceptum*** (fər-təm kən-**sep**-təm). [Latin] (1922) *Roman law.* A theft in which someone is discovered in possession of stolen property after a search with witnesses. • The possessor was liable to pay the owner three times the value of the stolen property. The possessor could bring an action against the thief and recover triple damages.

▸***furtum grave*** (fər-təm **gray**-vee *or* **grah**-vay). *Hist. Scots law.* An aggravated degree of theft that, in ancient times, was punishable by death.

▸***furtum manifestum*** (fər-təm man-ə-**fes**-təm). [Latin "open theft"] (17c) *Roman law.* A theft in which the thief is caught in the act. • A theft was "manifest" if the thief was caught on the day of the theft with the stolen property before reaching the place where he intended to take it. Fourfold damages were available by means of *actio furti.* (See *actio furti* under ACTIO.) A theft other than this type was known as *furtum nec manifestum.*

▸***furtum oblatum*** (fər-təm ə-**blay**-təm). [Latin "offered theft"] (1937) *Roman law.* **1.** A theft in which the thief offers stolen property to a person who is then found with the goods. • The person found in possession of the stolen goods could bring an action against the true thief. **2.** The planting of stolen goods.

▸***furtum possessionis*** (fər-təm pə-zes[h]-ee-**oh**-nis). [Latin "theft of possession"] (1922) *Roman law.* The owner's dishonest removal of a thing from the control of a pledgee, a bona fide possessor, a commodatary with a lien, or a usufructuary.

▸***furtum rei*** (fər-təm **ree**-ɪ). [Latin "theft of a thing"] (1947) *Roman law.* Ordinary theft, involving the dishonest taking of something to which the taker had no right.

▸***furtum usus*** (fər-təm **yoo**-səs *or* **yoo**-zəs). [Latin "theft of the use of a thing"] (1888) *Roman law.* **1.** A bailee's dishonest use of the thing bailed or lent. **2.** A creditor's dishonest use of a pledge (*pignus*) without contractual authority.

Fusian Caninian law. See LEX FURIA CANINIA.

fustigation (fəs-ti-**gay**-shən), *n.* (16c) **1.** *Hist.* The beating of someone with a stick or club. **2.** Harsh criticism. — **fustigate,** *vb.*

fustis (fəs-tis). *Hist.* **1.** A staff used in making livery of seisin. **2.** A baton or club.

FUTA. *abbr.* FEDERAL UNEMPLOYMENT TAX ACT.

futhwite (**footh**-wɪt). *Hist.* A fine for fighting or breaking the peace. — Also termed *fithwite.*

future-acquired property. See AFTER-ACQUIRED PROPERTY (1).

future advance. (1805) Money secured by an original security agreement even though it is lent after the security interest has attached.

future-advance clause. (1911) A contractual term in a security agreement covering additional loaned amounts on present collateral or collateral to be acquired in the future, regardless of whether the secured party is obliged to make the advances; esp., a provision in an open-end mortgage or deed of trust allowing the borrower to borrow additional sums in the future, secured under the same instrument and by the same security. • This type of clause makes a new security agreement unnecessary when the secured creditor makes a future loan to the debtor.

future-advances mortgage. See MORTGAGE.

future chose in action. See CHOSE.

future consideration. See CONSIDERATION (1).

future copyright. See COPYRIGHT.

future covenant. See COVENANT (4).

future damages. See DAMAGES.

future dangerousness. A person's, esp. a criminal defendant's, relative threat to others in the years ahead. • Future dangerousness is a major factor in criminal sentencing, in the civil commitment of people with serious mental disorders, and in the commitment of sexually violent predators. Psychiatrists often testify as experts to predict whether a defendant will be a continuing threat to society. The U.S. Supreme Court has sustained civil-commitment statutes that have "coupled proof of dangerousness with the proof of some additional actor, such as a 'mental illness' or 'mental abnormality'" (*Kansas v. Hendricks*, 521 U.S. 346, 358 (1997)), and civil commitment can be upheld as long as the person is both mentally ill and dangerous (*Foucha v. Louisiana*, 504 U.S. 71, 77 (1992)). Although there is much concern about the accuracy of these predictions, they are still generally admissible.

future debt. See DEBT.

future earnings. See *lost earnings* under EARNINGS.

future estate. See *future interest* under INTEREST (2).

future goods. See GOODS.

future interest. See INTEREST (2).

future performance. See PERFORMANCE (1).

futures, *n.* (1880) **1.** Standardized assets (such as commodities, stocks, or foreign currencies) bought or sold for future acceptance or delivery. — Also termed *financial futures.* **2.** FUTURES CONTRACT. **3.** Future claimants, esp. those who would become members of a class of persons injured by a defendant and thus included in a class action.

futures-commission merchant. (1937) An individual or firm that executes orders to buy and sell futures or futures options. — Abbr. FCM.

futures contract. (1915) An agreement to buy or sell a standardized asset (such as a commodity, stock, or foreign currency) at a fixed price at a future time, usu. during a particular time of a month. • Futures contracts are traded on exchanges such as the Chicago Board of Trade or the Chicago Mercantile Exchange. — Often shortened to *futures.* — Also termed *futures agreement; time-bargain.* Cf. *forward contract* under CONTRACT; LEVERAGE CONTRACT; OPTION.

futures market. See MARKET.

futures option. See OPTION (5).

futures trading. (1921) The buying and selling of futures contracts, usu. on formal exchanges.

future use. See *contingent use* under USE (4).

future value. See VALUE (2).

FWC. *abbr.* File wrapper continuation. See CONTINUATION; CONTINUATION-IN-PART.

FWS. *abbr.* UNITED STATES FISH AND WILDLIFE SERVICE.

FY. *abbr.* See *fiscal year* under YEAR.

FYLSE. *abbr.* FIRST-YEAR LAW STUDENTS' EXAMINATION.

FYLSX. *abbr.* FIRST-YEAR LAW STUDENTS' EXAMINATION.

fyrd. See *fyrdbote* under BOTE (1).

fyrdbote. See BOTE (1).

fyrdfare. See FERDFARE

G

GA. *abbr.* See *general average* under AVERAGE (3).

GAAP (gap). *abbr.* GENERALLY ACCEPTED ACCOUNTING PRINCIPLES.

GAAS (gas). *abbr.* GENERALLY ACCEPTED AUDITING STANDARDS.

gabel (gə-**bel**). *Hist.* **1.** A tax or duty on movables. **2.** GAVEL (2). — Also spelled *gabelle.* See LAND-GAVEL.

gabelle (gə-**bel**). (15c) *Hist.* **1.** A tax or duty on merchandise. **2.** A peasant villager, esp. one who pays rent or tribute. See GAVEL (1). — Also spelled *gabella; gavella.*

GAC. *abbr.* Guilty as charged.

gage (gayj), *n.* (14c) A pledge, pawn, or other thing deposited as security for performance. • An archaic use of this word corresponded to the way *wage* was formerly used in legal contexts: a *gager del ley*, for example, was an earlier form of *wager of law*, while *gager de deliverance* had the same meaning as *wager of deliverance.* Cf. WAGE, *vb.* (2).

> "A single root has sent out many branches which overshadow large fields of law. Gage, engagement, wage, wages, wager, wed, wedding, the Scottish wadset, all spring from one root. In particular we must notice that the word 'gage,' in Latin *vadium*, is applied indiscriminately to movables and immovables, to transactions in which a gage is given and to those in which a gage is taken. When a lord has seized his tenant's goods in distress they are in his hands a gage for the payment of the rent that is in arrear, and the sheriff is always taking gages from those who have no mind to give them. The notion expressed by the word seems to be that expressed by our 'security' . . . ." 2 Frederick Pollock & Frederic W. Maitland, *The History of English Law Before the Time of Edward I* 117–18 (2d ed. 1899).

gage, *vb.* (14c) To pawn or pledge; to give as security for. • *Gage* is an older form of *wage*, and often appeared as a phrase, *gager deliverance.*

> "Though the word *Gage* be retained, as it is a Substantive, yet as it is a verb, use hath turned the *Gage* into *Wage* so as it is oftener written *Wage*; as to *Wage Deliverance*, to give security, that a thing shall be delivered: For, if he that distrained, being sued, have not delivered the Cattle that were distrained, then he shall not onely avow the Distress, but *Gager Deliverance*, put in surety, that he will deliver them." Thomas Blount, *Nomo Lexicon: A Law-Dictionary* (1670).

gager (**gay**-jər), *n.* The giving of security; the transaction in which one gives a gage. See GAGE.

gager del ley. See WAGER OF LAW.

gag order. (1952) **1.** A judge's order directing parties, attorneys, witnesses, or journalists to refrain from publicly discussing the facts of a case. • When directed to the press, such an order is generally unconstitutional under the First Amendment. **2.** A judge's order that an unruly defendant be bound and gagged during trial to prevent further interruptions. — Also termed *gag rule.*

gain, *n.* (14c) **1.** An increase in amount, degree, or value.

▸ **abnormal gain.** (1880) **1.** An unforeseen surplus of output. **2.** An unforeseen instance of profitability. **3.** An uncharacteristic acquisition of additional weight.

▸ **pecuniary gain.** (18c) **1.** A gain of money or of something having monetary value. **2.** *Criminal law.* Any monetary or economic gain that serves as an impetus for the commission of an offense. • In most states, an offense and its punishment are aggravated if the offense was committed for pecuniary gain. Murder, for example, is often aggravated to capital murder if the murderer is paid to commit the crime. See SOLICITATION (2).

2. Excess of receipts over expenditures or of sale price over cost. See PROFIT (1). **3.** *Tax.* The excess of the amount realized from a sale or other disposition of property over the property's adjusted value. IRC (26 USCA) § 1001. — Also termed *realized gain*; *net gain*; (in senses 2 & 3) *business gain.* See AMOUNT REALIZED. Cf. LOSS (2).

> "[I]t may probably be said that when a tax law employs the phrase 'gains, profits, and income,' to describe what is taxable, the term 'gain' is inserted out of abundant caution, and intended to include an acquisition of the taxpayer which is not to be described as a 'profit,' and which might not be included in the term 'income' if that word were taken in a narrow sense. Properly speaking, 'gain' means that which is acquired or comes as a benefit, and in a statute laying an income tax it may mean money received within the year which is not the fruit of a business transaction nor of the labor or exertion of the individual, but something arising from fortuitous circumstances or conditions which he does not control. In this signification, the term would include money received as a legacy or money won on a wager." Henry Campbell Black, *A Treatise on the Law of Income Taxation under Federal and State Laws* § 33, at 80–81 (1913).

▸ **capital gain.** See CAPITAL GAIN.

▸ **extraordinary gain.** (16c) A gain that is both unusual and infrequent, such as the gain realized from selling a large segment of a business.

▸ **ordinary gain.** (1945) A gain from the sale or exchange of a noncapital asset. Cf. CAPITAL GAIN.

▸ **recognized gain.** (1951) The portion of a gain that is subject to income taxation. IRC (26 USCA) § 1001(c). See BOOT (1).

4. (*pl.*) *Civil law.* A type of community property that reflects the increase in property value brought about by the spouses' common skill or labor. See COMMUNITY PROPERTY; ACQUET.

gainage. See WAINAGE (2).

gainful employment. See EMPLOYMENT.

gainor. See SOCMAN.

gains, *n.* See GAIN.

GAL. *abbr.* See *guardian ad litem* under GUARDIAN (1).

gale (gayl). (17c) *Hist.* **1.** A periodic payment of rent. See GAVEL (2). **2.** Rent paid by a free miner (the *galee*) for the right to mine a plot of land. **3.** A license to mine a plot of land. • A gale could be conveyed or devised. **4.** The land so licensed.

***Gallagher* agreement.** (1977) A contract that gives one codefendant the right to settle with the plaintiff for a fixed sum at any time during trial and that guarantees payment of the sum regardless of the trial's outcome. *City of Tucson v. Gallagher*, 493 P.2d 1197 (Ariz. 1972). Cf. MARY CARTER AGREEMENT.

gallows. (bef. 12c) A wooden frame consisting of two upright posts and a crossbeam, from which condemned criminals are hanged by a rope.

gamalis (gə-**may**-lis). [Law Latin] *Hist.* **1.** A child born in lawful wedlock. **2.** A child born to betrothed but unmarried parents.

gambler. See COMMON GAMBLER.

gambling, *n.* (18c) The act of risking something of value, esp. money, for a chance to win a prize. • Gambling is regulated by state and federal law. 18 USCA §§ 1081 et seq. — Also termed *gaming*. See COMMON GAMBLER.

▸ **Indian gambling.** Gambling conducted by a federally recognized Indian tribe and regulated by federal law. — Also termed *Indian gaming*.

gambling contract. See CONTRACT.

gambling device. (1809) Any thing, such as cards, dice, or an electronic or mechanical contrivance, that allows a person to play a game of chance in which money may be won or lost. • Gambling devices are regulated by law, and the use or possession of a gambling device can be illegal. — Also termed *gaming device*.

gambling place. (1841) Any location where gambling occurs. 18 USCA § 1081. — Also termed *gaming house*; *gaming room*.

gambling policy. See *wager insurance* under INSURANCE.

gambling verdict. See *chance verdict* under VERDICT (1).

game, *n.* (13c) **1.** Wild animals and birds considered as objects of pursuit, for food or sport; esp., animals for which one must have a license to hunt. — Also termed *game animal*. **2.** A contest, for amusement or for a prize, whose outcome depends on the skill, strength, or luck of the players.

▸ **game of chance.** (17c) A game whose outcome is determined by luck rather than skill. See GAMBLING DEVICE.

> "Games of chance do not cease to be such merely because they call for the exercise of skill by the players, nor do games of skill cease to be so because at times . . . their result is determined by some unforeseen accident, usually called 'luck.' According to some cases, the test of the character of the game is not whether it contains an element of chance or an element of skill, but which of these is the dominating element that determines the result of the game. . . . And it has been said that 'it is the character of the game, and not the skill or want of skill of the player,' which determines whether a game is one of chance or skill." 38 Am. Jur. 2d *Gambling* § 4, at 109–10 (1968).

▸ **game of skill.** (18c) A game in which the outcome is determined by a player's superior knowledge or ability, not chance.

▸ **percentage game.** (1889) A game of chance from which the house collects an amount calculated as a percentage of the wagers made or the sums won. • Percentage games are illegal in many states.

game, *vb.* (16c) To gamble; to play for a stake.

game animal. See GAME (1).

game law. (18c) A federal or state statute that regulates the hunting of game, esp. one that forbids the capturing or killing of specified game either entirely or seasonally, describes the means for killing or capturing game in season, or restricts the number and type of game animals that may be killed or captured in season. 16 USCA §§ 661–667; 18 USCA §§ 41–47.

gamete intrafallopian transfer. (ca. 1984) A procedure in which mature eggs are implanted in a woman's fallopian tubes and fertilized with semen. — Abbr. GIFT. — Also termed *gamete intrafallopian-tube transfer*. Cf. ARTIFICIAL INSEMINATION; IN VITRO FERTILIZATION.; IN VIVO FERTILIZATION; ZYGOTE INTRAFALLOPIAN TRANSFER.

gaming. See GAMBLING.

gaming contract. See *gambling contract* under CONTRACT.

gaming device. See GAMBLING DEVICE.

gaming house. See GAMBLING PLACE.

gaming room. See GAMBLING PLACE.

ganancial (gə-**nan**-shəl), *adj.* (1843) Of, relating to, or consisting of community property <a spouse's ganancial rights>. See COMMUNITY PROPERTY.

G&A. *abbr.* See *general administrative expense* under EXPENSE.

gang. (15c) A group of persons who go about together or act in concert, esp. for antisocial or criminal purposes. • Many gangs have common identifying signs and symbols, such as hand signals and distinctive colors. — Also termed *street gang*. See GANG COLORS.

gang colors. The color of clothing or insignia used by gang members to identify themselves and their territory. • Certain types of clothing, such as hooded sweatshirts of a certain color, distinctive tattoos, and graffiti may also be gang colors.

gangland. (ca. 1912) The world of criminal gangs and organized crime.

gang loitering. See LOITERING.

gang rape. See RAPE (2).

gang-related loitering. See *gang loitering* under LOITERING.

gangster. (1886) A member of a criminal gang or an organized-crime syndicate.

Ganser's syndrome (**gahn**-zər *or* **gan**-sər). (1968) An abnormality characterized by the giving of irrelevant and nonsensical answers to questions. • Prisoners have been known to feign this syndrome in an attempt to obtain leniency.

gantlet (**gawnt**-lit). [fr. Swedish *gata* "lane" + *lopp* "course"] (15c) **1.** *Hist.* A former military punishment in which the offender was stripped to the waist and forced to run between two rows of soldiers who gave him lashes as he passed. **2.** A series of severe troubles or difficulties; an ordeal. — Also spelled *gauntlet*; (archaically) *gantlope*.

GAO. *abbr.* **1.** GOVERNMENT ACCOUNTABILITY OFFICE. **2.** *Hist.* General Accounting Office.

gaol. See JAIL.

gaol delivery. See JAIL DELIVERY.

gaoler. See JAILER.

gaol liberties. See JAIL LIBERTIES.

gap. 1. CASUS OMISSUS. **2.** GAP PERIOD. **3.** A blank space on a bill of exchange allowing an unauthorized change to be readily made to its face, as by enabling a fraudster to increase the amount payable on a check.

gap creditor. See CREDITOR.

gap-filler. (15c) A rule that supplies a contractual term that the parties failed to include in the contract. • For example, if the contract does not contain a sales price, UCC § 2-305(1) establishes the price as being a reasonable one at the time of delivery. Cf. *default rule* under RULE (1).

> "Contracts often have gaps in them, intentional or inadvertent. Gaps arise, too, out of the 'battle of the forms' under sections 2-204 and 2-207. Some gaps are more or less complete, others only partial. Article 2 of the Code includes numerous gap filler provisions which taken together constitute a kind of standardized statutory contract." 1 James J. White & Robert S. Summers, *Uniform Commercial Code* § 3-4 (4th ed. 1995).

gap financing. See FINANCING.

gap period. (1978) *Bankruptcy.* The duration of time between the filing of an involuntary bankruptcy petition and the entry of the order for relief. — Often shortened to *gap.*

gap report. (1984) In the making of federal court rules, a report that explains any changes made by an advisory committee in the language of a proposed amendment to a procedural rule after its publication for comment. • Before advisory committees began issuing gap reports in the early 1980s, there were complaints that the public record did not show why changes were made after the public-comment period. The five advisory committees — for appellate, bankruptcy, civil, criminal, and evidence rules — therefore began filing the reports to fill in the "gaps" in the record. Although the phrase is sometimes written in capital letters (*GAP report*), it is not an acronym.

gap theory. (1971) *Insurance.* The principle that a tortfeasor will be considered underinsured if his or her liability-insurance coverage — although legally adequate — is less than the injured party's underinsured-motorist coverage. • This principle allows an injured party to invoke underinsured-motorist coverage. Cf. EXCESS THEORY.

garageman's lien. See *mechanic's lien* under LIEN.

garandia (gə-**ran**-dee-ə). [Law Latin] *Hist.* A warranty. — Also spelled *garantia* (gə-**ran**-shee-ə).

garauntor (**gar**-ən-tər). [Law French] *Hist.* A warrantor of land. • A *garauntor* was obligated to defend the title and seisin of the alienee. If the alienee was evicted, the *garauntor* had to provide the alienee with other land of equal value.

***Garcia* hearing** (gahr-**see**-ə). (1981) *Criminal procedure.* A hearing held to ensure that a defendant who is one of two or more defendants represented by the same attorney understands (1) the risk of a conflict of interest inherent in this type of representation, and (2) that he or she is entitled to the services of an attorney who does not represent anyone else in the defendant's case. *U.S. v. Garcia,* 517 F.2d 272 (5th Cir. 1975). See CONFLICT OF INTEREST (2).

gard (gahrd). [Law French] *Hist.* **1.** Wardship or custody (of a person). **2.** A precinct (or *ward*) of a city. — Also spelled *garde; gardia.*

garde (gahrd). [French] **1.** *Civil law.* A relationship that gives rise to a person's liability when an injury is caused by a thing, whether animate or inanimate, that is considered by law to be that person's responsibility or to be in that person's custody. **2.** See GARD.

gardein (gahr-**deen**). [Law French] *Hist.* A guardian or keeper. — Also spelled *gardian; gardien; gardeyn.*

garden leave. See LEAVE.

gardia (**gahr**-dee-ə). GARD.

gardianus (gahr-dee-**ay**-nəs). [Law Latin] *Hist.* A guardian, defender, or protector; a warden. — Also spelled *guardianus.*

▸ ***gardianus ecclesiae*** (gahr-dee-**ay**-nəs e-**klee**-z[h]ee-ee). (17c) *Eccles. law.* A churchwarden.

garene (gə-**reen**). [Law French] See WARREN.

***Garmon* doctrine.** See *Garmon preemption* under PREEMPTION.

***Garmon* preemption.** See PREEMPTION.

***Garner* doctrine.** (1970) The rule that allows shareholder plaintiffs in a corporate derivative action to discover confidential communications between a corporate officer and the corporation's attorney. • The *Garner* doctrine does not apply to attorney work product, and the movant must show good cause. *Garner v. Wolfinbarger,* 430 F.2d 1093 (5th Cir. 1970). See DERIVATIVE ACTION (1).

garnish, *n.* (16c) *Hist.* Money exacted from a new prisoner by other prisoners or as a jailer's fee. • This practice was banned in England in 1815.

garnish, *vb.* [Old French *garnir* "to warn" "to prepare"] (16c) **1.** *Hist.* To notify or warn (a person) of certain debts that must be paid before the person is entitled to receive property as an heir. **2.** To subject (property) to garnishment; to attach (property held by a third party) in order to satisfy a debt. **3.** To notify (a person, bank, etc.) that a garnishment proceeding has been undertaken and that the one receiving notice may be liable as stakeholder or custodian of the defendant's property. — Also termed *garnishee;* (in senses 2 & 3) *factorize.* — **garnishable,** *adj.*

garnishee (gahr-ni-**shee**), *n.* (17c) A person or institution (such as a bank) that is indebted to or is bailee for another whose property has been subjected to garnishment. — Also termed *garnishee-defendant* (as opposed to the "principal defendant," i.e., the primary debtor).

garnishee (gahr-ni-**shee**), *vb.* See GARNISH.

garnisher. (16c) A creditor who initiates a garnishment action to reach the debtor's property that is thought to be held or owed by a third party (the *garnishee*). — Also spelled *garnishor.*

garnishment, *n.* (16c) **1.** A judicial proceeding in which a creditor (or potential creditor) asks the court to order a third party who is indebted to or is bailee for the debtor to turn over to the creditor any of the debtor's property (such as wages or bank accounts) held by that third party. • A plaintiff initiates a garnishment action as a means of either prejudgment seizure or postjudgment collection. Cf. SEQUESTRATION (4), (5).

> "Garnishment is a[n] . . . inquisitorial proceeding, affording a harsh and extraordinary remedy. It is an anomaly, a statutory invention sui generis, with no affinity to any action known to the common law. . . . It is a method of seizure; but it is not a 'levy' in the usual acceptation of that term. It is a proceeding by which a diligent creditor may legally obtain preference over other creditors; and it is in the nature of a creditor's bill, or a sequestration of the

effects of a debtor in the hands of his debtor." 38 C.J.S. *Garnishment* § 3, at 248–50 (2003).

▸ **wrongful garnishment.** (1896) **1.** An improper or tortious garnishment. **2.** A cause of action against a garnisher for improperly or tortiously filing a garnishment proceeding.

2. The judicial order by which such a turnover is effected. Cf. ATTACHMENT (1); SEQUESTRATION (5).

garnishment lien. See LIEN.

garnishor. See GARNISHER.

***Garrity* statement** (gar-ə-tee). (1967) A public employee's oral or written report (as of an incident) obtained under a threat of termination of employment. • A public employee usu. makes a *Garrity* statement in the course of an internal investigation (as by a police department). Because a *Garrity* statement is coerced, the statement and any evidence obtained as a result of it cannot be used in a later criminal prosecution against the public employee. The statement and evidence may be used only to evaluate the employee's performance. *Garrity v. New Jersey*, 385 U.S. 493, 87 S.Ct. 616 (1967).

***Garrity* warnings.** (1998) A set of admonitions given to a public employee, such as a police officer, whose conduct is undergoing an internal investigation and whose failure to cooperate may subject the employee to discipline or even discharge. *See Garrity v. State of New Jersey*, 385 U.S. 493 (1967).

garsumne. [Old English] A fine; an amercement.

GASB. *abbr.* GOVERNMENTAL ACCOUNTING STANDARDS BOARD.

gas-balancing agreement. (1967) *Oil & gas.* A contract among owners of the production of a gas well to balance production if one owner sells more of the gas stream than the other owners do.

gas chamber. (ca. 1945) A small, sealed room in which a capital punishment is carried out by strapping the prisoner into a chair and releasing poisonous fumes.

gas contract. (1882) *Oil & gas.* An agreement for the sale of natural gas.

gas sold. *Oil & gas.* Natural gas that is actually sold but not necessarily all that a well produces. • The term is used in natural-gas leases.

gastonette. (1988) A dilatory "dance" in which each of the two responsible parties waits until the other party acts — so that the delay seems interminable; esp., a standoff occurring when two courts simultaneously hear related claims arising from the same bases and delay acting while each court waits for the other to act first. • The term was coined by Judge Jon O. Newman in *In re McLean Industries, Inc.*, 857 F.2d 88, 90 (2d Cir. 1988), on the model of "After you, my dear Alphonse." "No, after you, Gaston." *See* Jon O. Newman, *Birth of a Word*, 13 Green Bag 2d 169, 169 (2010); Bryan A. Garner, *A Legal Lexicographer Looks at Law Reviews*, 16 Green Bag 2d 281, 283–84 (2013).

gas used. *Oil & gas.* Natural gas that is consumed while a well is in operation but that is not necessarily sold.

gate arrest. See *prison-gate arrest* under ARREST (2).

gateway drug. See DRUG.

GATS. *abbr.* GENERAL AGREEMENT ON TRADE IN SERVICES.

GATT (gat). *abbr.* (1948) GENERAL AGREEMENT ON TARIFFS AND TRADE. See TRIPS.

gauger (gay-jər). (15c) A surveying officer who examines containers of liquids to give them a mark of allowance, as containing the lawful measure.

gauntlet. See GANTLET.

gaval. See GAVEL (2).

gavel (gav-əl). (bef. 12c) **1.** *Hist.* A tribute, toll, or custom paid to a superior. **2.** *Hist.* An annual payment of rent or revenue, esp. payment in kind, such as gavel-corn, gavel-malt, or oat-gavel. — Sometimes spelled *gabel.* — Also termed *gale*; *gaval.* **3.** A mallet used by a presiding officer, often a judge, to bring a meeting or court to order.

gavelbred (gav-əl-bred). *Hist.* Rent payable in bread, corn, or some other provision; rent payable in kind.

gavelet (gav-əl-it). (14c) *Hist.* A writ used in Kent and London to recover rent from land held in gavelkind. See CESSAVIT.

gavelgeld (gav-əl-geld). *Hist.* **1.** Property that yields a profit or a toll. **2.** The tribute or toll itself.

gavelherte (gav-əl-hərt). *Hist.* A service of plowing performed by a customary tenant.

gaveling man (gav-əl-ing man *or* mən). *Hist.* See GAVELMAN.

gavelkind (gav-əl-kɪnd). (14c) *Hist.* **1.** A species of socage tenure arising in land that has descended equally to the decedent's sons. • It was widespread before 1066, when it was mainly superseded by primogeniture. This property-division technique was then largely limited to Kent. The person holding land in this manner enjoyed several advantages not available under the common law: the land could be disposed of by will, did not escheat for felony other than treason or for want of heirs, and was alienable by an heir at age 15. Gavelkind was abolished in 1925. Although the etymology of this term was much debated in the 19th century, the explanation given in the first quotation below appears to be the true one. **2.** Land that yields gavel service.

> "[G]*afol*, or *gavel*, was a word of frequent use before the Norman Conquest, and signified not only a tribute, tax, or custom, but also rent in general; and . . . under this term were comprehended all socage services whatsoever which lay in render or feasance, the word being often compounded with and applied to the particulars wherein the payment or performance of the service consisted; as corn-gavel, or gavel-corn, was a corn-rent, and gavel-earth was a service of 'earing' or ploughing. . . . The tenant from whom such services were due was called a gavel-man; and 'gavelkind' being taken as a compound of this word 'gavel' and 'gekynde,' which is nature, kind, quality (usually appearing under the form 'gafolcund' in the most ancient records), the proper signification of the term will be land of the kind or nature which yielded rent, or 'censual land,' which may be compared to rent-service land as distinguished from knight-service land, which being held by free military service yielded no 'cens' or rent in money, provision, or works: so that the lands held by the old English tenure are known in Kent as gavelkind which in other parts of the country are distinguished by the name of socage." Thomas Robinson, *Robinson on Gavelkind* 5–6 (Charles I. Elton & Herbert J.H. Mackay eds., 5th ed. 1897).

> "The term 'gavelkind' has by the modern usage acquired [a] signification more confined as to the properties contained under it, yet more extensive in point of place: since at this day it is generally used to denote the partibility of the land, exclusive of all other customary qualities; nor is the word 'gavelkind' in common parlance confined to Kentish lands,

but is equally and indifferently applied to all partible lands wherever they lie." *Id.* at 9.

"Archbishop Hubert Walter, who presided in the king's court . . . obtained from King John a charter empowering him and his successors to convert into military fees the tenements that were holden of their church in gavelkind. The archbishop's main object may have been to get money in the form of rents and scutages, instead of provender and boonworks, 'gavel-corn' and 'gavel-swine,' 'gavel-erth' and 'gavel-rip.' . . ." 2 Frederick Pollock & Frederic W. Maitland, *The History of English Law Before the Time of Edward I* 273 (2d ed. 1899).

gavelman (gav-əl-mən). (13c) *Hist.* A tenant who is liable for money rent in addition to a customary service to the lord. • A gavelman was formerly a villein who had been released from villenage in consideration of money rent. — Also termed *gaveling man.*

gavelmed (gav-əl-meed). (bef. 12c) *Hist.* A tenant's customary service of mowing the lord's meadowland or grass for hay. — Also spelled *gavelmead.*

gavelrep (gav-əl-reep). (17c) *Hist.* A tenant's duty to reap the lord's fields at the lord's command; BEDRIP. — Also spelled *gavelrip.*

gavel through. (1970) *Parliamentary law.* To put (a question) to a vote before any member can obtain the floor. • The practice of "gaveling through" a motion is improper under parliamentary law.

"It should be noted that, under legitimate parliamentary procedure, there is no such thing as 'gaveling through' a measure. The right of members to debate or introduce secondary motions cannot be cut off by the chair's attempting to put a question to vote so quickly that no member can get the floor — either when the chair first states the question or when he believes debate is ended. Debate is not closed by the presiding officer's rising to put the question." Henry M. Robert, *Robert's Rules of Order Newly Revised* § 43, at 374 (10th ed. 2000).

gavelwerk (gav-əl-wərk). (13c) *Hist.* Customary service, either by the tenant's own hands or with the aid of the tenant's carts or carriages.

gay marriage. See *same-sex marriage* under MARRIAGE (1).

gay-panic defense. See DEFENSE (1).

gay rights. The legal protections and entitlements accorded to homosexual men, lesbians, and bisexuals. • Normally the term does not refer to transsexuals and transgenders.

"Written human rights law is scanty when it comes to sexuality, or even homosexuality. There is nothing explicit on sexuality or sexual rights in the Universal Declaration of Human Rights (1948) ('UDHR'). The same is true of the global and regional human rights treaties elaborated on the basis of the UDHR, the International Covenant on Civil and Political Rights (1966) ('ICCPR'), the International Covenant on Economic, Social and Cultural Rights (1966) ('ICESCR'), the European Convention for the Protection of Human Rights and Fundamental Freedoms (1950) ('ECHR'), the American Convention on Human Rights (1969) ('ACHR'), and the African Charter on Human and Peoples' Rights (1981) ('AChHPR'). Only the Charter of Fundamental Rights of the European Union (2000) ('EU Charter'; which is now EU law according to Art. 6 Treaty on European Union [2008] OJ C115/1) contains a limited reference to gay rights as it prohibits any discrimination on the ground of sexual orientation in Art. 21. This reference is limited because it is confined to the context of equality rights. That means that these provisions do guarantee equal treatment of homo- and heterosexual persons and behaviour; but they do not say anything about liberty rights, about the regulation of sexuality and sexual behavior that can legitimately be made in general. In other words: those rights do not protect against undue inference with sexual life as such, they just guarantee that such inferences burden heterosexuals and homosexuals alike and to the same degree." Helmut Graupner, "Gay Rights," in 4 *The Max Planck Encyclopedia of Public International Law* 292, 292 (Rüdiger Wolfrum ed., 2012).

gaze nystagmus test. See HORIZONTAL-GAZE NYSTAGMUS TEST.

Gazette (gə-zet). (17c) An official newspaper of the British government in which acts of State, Crown appointments, notices of bankruptcy, and other legal matters are reported. • Although the *London Gazette* is the most famous, there are also publications called the *Edinburgh Gazette* and the *Belfast Gazette* with similar purposes.

gazump, *vb.* (1928) *BrE Slang.* (Of a house seller) to prevent (a buyer who has the house under contract) from going through with the sale at the stipulated price, usu. by selling instead to another buyer who, after the earlier bid is accepted, offers still more money to the seller <the Joneses couldn't keep up: they were gazumped at the last minute and lost the house they wanted>.

gazumping (gə-zəmp-ing). (20c) *BrE Slang.* The improper sale of a house, usu. by raising the price and selling to a different buyer after accepting an earlier offer. • Gazumping can take different forms, the usual one being when a seller raises the price after accepting the buyer's offer. But it may also occur when a competing buyer makes a higher bid than the one already accepted, thus encouraging the seller to back out of the earlier contract.

gazunder, *vb.* (1988) *BrE Slang.* (Of a house buyer) to prevent (a seller who has the house under contract) from going through at the stipulated price, usu. by saying that the sale can go forward only if the seller will lower the price from that originally agreed to.

G-Bay. See GUANTANAMO BAY.

g.b.h. *abbr.* Grievous bodily harm. See *serious bodily injury* under INJURY.

GBMI. *abbr.* GUILTY BUT MENTALLY ILL.

GCM. *abbr.* GENERAL COUNSEL'S MEMORANDUM.

GCV. *abbr.* GOING-CONCERN VALUE.

gdn. *abbr.* GUARDIAN.

GDP. *abbr.* (1962) GROSS DOMESTIC PRODUCT.

Geary Act. *Hist.* An 1892 statute requiring all Chinese residents of the United States to subject themselves to extensive government monitoring (under penalty of being deported), declaring that the burden of proof after any arrest would be on the Chinese arrestee and disallowing bail to Chinese immigrants in habeas corpus proceedings. • Named after California Congressman Thomas J. Geary (1854–1929), the Geary Act was held constitutional by the Supreme Court in 1893. *Fong Yue Ting v. U.S.*, 149 U.S. 698 (1893). Yet the law never had much effect besides creating racial controversy, since Congress never appropriated the money to enforce its provisions.

Gebrauchsmuster. [German] *Patents.* UTILITY MODEL. — Abbr. GM.

***Geders* rule.** (1976) *Criminal law.* The doctrine that a trial judge who bars contact between attorney and client unconstitutionally infringes on attorney–client privilege. *See Geders v. U.S.*, 425 U.S. 80 (1976).

geld, *n.* (15c) *Hist.* A tax paid to the Crown under Anglo-Saxon and Norman kings.

geldable (geld-ə-bəl), *adj.* (17c) *Hist.* (Of property) subject to tax or tribute. — Also spelled *gildable*.

GEM. See *growing-equity mortgage* under MORTGAGE.

gemot (gə-**moht**). (bef. 12c) *Hist.* A local judicial assembly; a public meeting. — Also spelled *gemote*. Cf. WITENAGEMOT.

> "The name of the popular assembly varied nearly as much as the names of the territorial divisions. Three of these names, however, are alone of importance here. The Franks used the word *mahl*, translated *mallum* in Latin; while elsewhere the word *thing* was commonly employed. The English gradually adopted the word *gemot*.
>
> "The general court, or assembly of the state, and the local assembly of the district, were, therefore, the law courts of higher and lower jurisdiction throughout the north of Europe. No doubt, the pressure of the circumstances did, in many cases, produce variations from this arrangement; but, amid all changes and convulsions, the state assembly still remained the one supreme court; the district assembly still remained the one district court, of what may be called the common or customary law. This is typical for of judicial constitution among the Germans. Its variations make the judicial history of modern Europe." Henry Adams, "The Anglo-Saxon Courts of Law," in *Essays in Anglo-Saxon Law* 1, 5-6 (1905).

gender-based harassment. See HARASSMENT.

gender discrimination. See *sex discrimination* under DISCRIMINATION (3).

gender/number canon. The doctrine that in a legal instrument, in the absence of a contrary indication, the masculine includes the feminine (and vice versa), and the singular includes the plural (and mostly vice versa). See BROUGHAM'S ACT.

gener (jee-nər), *n.* [Latin] *Roman law.* A son-in-law.

general acceptance. See ACCEPTANCE (1).

general-acceptance test. See FRYE TEST.

General Accounting Office. See GENERAL ACCOUNTABILITY OFFICE.

general act. See PUBLIC LAW (2).

general administration. See ADMINISTRATION.

general administrative expense. See EXPENSE.

general administrator. See ADMINISTRATOR (2).

general agency. See AGENCY (1).

general agent. **1.** See AGENT. **2.** See INSURANCE AGENT.

General Agreement on Tariffs and Trade. A multiparty international agreement — signed originally in 1948 — that promotes international trade by lowering import duties and providing equal access to markets. • More than 150 countries are parties to the agreement. — Abbr. GATT. See WORLD TRADE ORGANIZATION; GENERAL AGREEMENT ON TRADE IN SERVICES.

General Agreement on Trade in Services. A multiparty international agreement that promotes international trade in the service industry. • It resulted from the Uruguay Round negotiations in 1995. Its counterpart for goods is the GATT. — Abbr. GATS. See WORLD TRADE ORGANIZATION; GENERAL AGREEMENT ON TARIFFS AND TRADE.

general appearance. See APPEARANCE.

general assembly. (17c) **1.** The name of the legislative body in many states. **2.** (*cap.*) The deliberative body of the United Nations. **3.** CONVENTION (4).

general assignment. See ASSIGNMENT (2).

general assumpsit. See ASSUMPSIT.

general authority. See AUTHORITY (1).

general average. See AVERAGE (3).

general-average bond. See BOND (2).

general-average contribution. See *general average* under AVERAGE (3).

general average loss. See LOSS.

general-average statement. (1838) *Maritime law.* A statement containing an exact calculation of the general average and each party's contributory share. See AVERAGE (3).

general bad character. See *bad character* under CHARACTER.

general benefit. See BENEFIT (2).

general bequest. See BEQUEST.

general cargo. See CARGO.

general challenge. See *challenge for cause* under CHALLENGE (2).

general compromis. See COMPROMIS (1).

general consent. **1.** See BLANK CONSENT. **2.** See CONSENT (2).

general contractor. See CONTRACTOR.

general council. See COUNCIL (1).

general counsel. See COUNSEL.

General Counsel's Memorandum. *Tax.* **1.** A written discussion, issued by the office of the Chief Counsel of the IRS, on the merits of a legal issue involving tax law. **2.** A written explanation issued by the office of the Chief Counsel of the IRS to explain the IRS's positions in a revenue ruling or a technical-advice memorandum. — Abbr. GCM.

general count. See COUNT (2).

General Court. (17c) The name of the legislature in Massachusetts or New Hampshire. • "General Court" was a common colonial-era term for a body that exercised judicial and legislative functions. Cf. COURT OF ASSISTANTS.

general court-martial. See COURT-MARTIAL (2).

general covenant against encumbrances. See *covenant against encumbrances* under COVENANT (4).

general creditor. See *unsecured creditor* under CREDITOR.

general criminal intent. See *general intent* under INTENT (1).

general custom. See CUSTOM (1).

general damages. See DAMAGES.

general debt. See DEBT.

general defense. **1.** A denial in broad terms of at least one element in a complaint or charge. **2.** *Int'l law.* All legitimate means, military and nonmilitary, that may be used to protect a nation against external threats of any nature.

general deficiency bill. See *deficiency bill* under BILL (3).

general delivery. (1846) A post-office department that handles the delivery of mail when the recipient appears in person to collect it, usu. after traveling. — Also termed (BrE) *poste restante*.

general demurrer. See *general exception* (1) under EXCEPTION (1).

general denial. See DENIAL (3).

general deposit. See DEPOSIT (2).

general deputy. 1. See DEPUTY. **2.** See *deputy sheriff* under SHERIFF (1).

general deterrence. See DETERRENCE.

general devise. See DEVISE.

general direction. See *general instruction* under JURY INSTRUCTION

general-disability insurance. See INSURANCE.

general discharge. See DISCHARGE (8).

general-duty judge. See JUDGE.

general election. See ELECTION (3).

general employer. See EMPLOYER.

general endorsement. See *blank indorsement* under INDORSEMENT.

general exception. See EXCEPTION (1).

general exclusion order. See EXCLUSION ORDER (3).

general execution. See EXECUTION (4).

general executor. See EXECUTOR (2).

general expense. See *general administrative expense* under EXPENSE.

general federal common law. See COMMON LAW (1).

general fee conditional. See *fee simple conditional* under FEE SIMPLE.

general finding. See FINDING OF FACT.

general franchise. See FRANCHISE (2).

general fund. See FUND (1).

general good and welfare. See GOOD OF THE ORDER.

general guaranty. See GUARANTY (1).

general guardian. See GUARDIAN (1).

general hypothecation. See HYPOTHECATION.

***generalia* canon.** See GENERAL/SPECIFIC CANON.

generalia specialibus non derogant (jen-ə-**ray**-lee-ə spesh-ee-**ay**-lə-bəs non **der**-ə-gənt). [Latin "general things do not derogate from specific things"] The doctrine holding that general words in a later statute do not repeal an earlier statutory provision dealing with a special subject. • This principle illustrates the cautious approach that some courts have adopted in interpreting broad provisions, but there are many exceptions. See GENERAL/SPECIFIC CANON.

generalia verba sunt generaliter intelligenda (jen-ə-**ray**-lee-ə vər-bə suunt jen-ə-**ral**-i-tər in-tel-i-**jen**-də). See GENERAL-TERMS CANON.

general imparlance. See IMPARLANCE.

general improvement. See IMPROVEMENT.

general indorsement. See *blank indorsement* under INDORSEMENT.

general instruction. See JURY INSTRUCTION.

general intangible. See INTANGIBLE.

general intent. See INTENT (1).

general-intent crime. See CRIME.

general-intent offense. See *general-intent crime* under CRIME.

general issue. See ISSUE (1).

general jail delivery. See JAIL DELIVERY (2).

general jurisdiction. See JURISDICTION.

general-jurisdiction court. See *court of general jurisdiction* under COURT.

general jurisprudence. See JURISPRUDENCE.

general-justification defense. See *lesser-evils defense* under DEFENSE (1).

general knowledge. See KNOWLEDGE (1).

General Land Office. A former U.S. Interior Department division that exercised executive power relating to the public lands, including their survey, patenting, and sale or other disposition. • The General Land Office and the U.S. Grazing Service were consolidated into the Bureau of Land Management in 1946. — Abbr. GLO. See BUREAU OF LAND MANAGEMENT.

general law. See LAW.

general ledger. See LEDGER (1).

general legacy. See LEGACY (1).

general legal principle. See GENERAL PRINCIPLE OF LAW.

general legatee. See LEGATEE.

general legislation. See LEGISLATION (3).

general letter of credit. See LETTER OF CREDIT.

general-liability policy. See *comprehensive general-liability policy* under INSURANCE POLICY.

general lien. See LIEN.

general listing. See *open listing* under LISTING (1).

generally accepted accounting principles. (1930) The conventions, rules, and procedures that define approved accounting practices at a particular time. • These principles are issued by the Financial Accounting Standards Board for use by accountants in preparing financial statements. The principles include not only broad guidelines of general application but also detailed practices and procedures. — Abbr. GAAP. — Also termed *generally accepted accountancy principles.*

generally accepted auditing standards. The guidelines issued by the American Institute of Certified Public Accountants establishing an auditor's professional qualities and the criteria for the auditor's examination and required reports. — Abbr. GAAS.

general malice. See MALICE.

general manager. See MANAGER (1).

general maritime law. (18c) The body of U.S. legal precedents and doctrines developed through caselaw in maritime and admiralty litigation. • General maritime law is a branch of federal common law. It is distinguished from statutory law. — Abbr. GML. Cf. MARITIME LAW; LAW OF THE SEA.

> "The general maritime law is characterized by the expansive and dominant role played by federal courts in fashioning and applying its precepts to new situations. Large areas of maritime tort law have not been touched by legislation; these are left to the federal courts to define and fill. In areas preempted by legislation, federal courts may

not establish principles in derogation of the congressional mandate. However, in the framework of admiralty jurisdiction, federal courts may still play an active role in interpreting statutes, filling gaps, and coordinating legislation with the general maritime law." Thomas J. Schoenbaum, *Admiralty and Maritime Law* 122 (1987).

general meeting. See *regular meeting* under MEETING.

general mens rea. See *general intent* under INTENT (1).

general mortgage. See MORTGAGE.

general-mortgage bond. See BOND (3).

general *non est factum*. See NON EST FACTUM.

general objection. See OBJECTION (1).

general-obligation bond. See BOND (3).

general occupant. See OCCUPANT.

general officer. See OFFICER (2).

general order. See ORDER (4).

general owner. See OWNER.

general parliamentary law. See PARLIAMENTARY LAW.

general pardon. See AMNESTY.

general part. A restatement of the law, esp. one intended to be enacted, that arranges the rules into a logical order by placing the broadly applicable rules before the more specific ones so as to avoid constant repetition.

"Even in those legal systems that have codified it, the general part has never been exempt from criticism. In Germany [where it originated], hostility towards it reached its peak under the regime of National Socialism: the general part was removed from curricula, and the planned 'People's Code' (Volksgesetzbuch) intended to ban it from legislation as well. Nowadays the controversy over the general part has considerably subsided, but it is still not completely settled." Jan Peter Schmidt, "General Part," in 1 *The Max Planck Encyclopedia of European Private Law* 774, 775 (Jürgen Basedow et al. eds., 2012).

general partner. See PARTNER.

general partnership. See PARTNERSHIP.

general personal jurisdiction. See JURISDICTION.

general plea. See *general denial* under DENIAL (3).

general plea in bar. See PLEA IN BAR.

general power. See POWER OF APPOINTMENT.

general power of appointment. See POWER OF APPOINTMENT.

general power of attorney. See POWER OF ATTORNEY.

general prayer. See PRAYER FOR RELIEF.

general principle of law. (18c) **1.** A principle widely recognized by peoples whose legal order has attained a certain level of sophistication. **2.** *Int'l law.* A principle that gives rise to international legal obligations.

"[T]he adjective 'general' does not refer to several or many orders [i.e., legal systems] as do the general principles of national law, but indicates principles which are applied generally in all cases of the same kind which arise in international law (e.g. the principle of nonintervention)." Hermann Mosler, "General Principles of Law," in 2 *Encyclopedia of Public International Law* 512, 512 (1995).

3. A principle recognized in all kinds of legal relations, regardless of the legal system to which it belongs (state law, federal law, international law, etc.). — Also termed *general legal principle.*

general privilege. See PRIVILEGE (5).

general property. See PROPERTY.

general publication. See PUBLICATION (2).

general-public license. See *open-source license* under LICENSE.

general-purpose public figure. See *all-purpose public figure* under PUBLIC FIGURE.

general receiver. See *principal receiver* under RECEIVER (1).

general reference. See REFERENCE (1).

general release. See RELEASE (8).

general replication. See REPLICATION.

general reprisal. See REPRISAL (1).

general resolution. See RESOLUTION (2).

general retainer. See RETAINER.

general retention. See RETENTION.

general revenue. See REVENUE.

general revenue fund. See FUND (1).

general rule. See RULE.

general search warrant. See SEARCH WARRANT.

general sentence. See SENTENCE.

General Services Administration. The independent federal agency that constructs and operates buildings; manages government property and records; procures and distributes supplies; and provides management services in communications, traffic, and automatic data processing. • Its Office of Enterprise Development assists small businesses in dealing with the agency through GSA's 12 regional offices. The agency was created by the Federal Property and Administrative Services Act of 1949. 40 USCA § 751. — Abbr. GSA.

general session. See SESSION (1).

general ship. See SHIP.

general special imparlance. See IMPARLANCE.

general/specific canon. The doctrine that if there is a conflict in a legal instrument between a general provision and a specific provision, the specific provision prevails (*generalia specialibus non derogant*). — Also termed *generalia canon.*

"[T]he general/specific canon does not mean that the existence of a contradictory specific provision voids the general provision. Only its application to cases covered by the specific provision is suspended; it continues to govern all other cases. So if a lease provides in one clause that water is provided, and in another it provides that the tenant is responsible for all utilities, the tenant will still be liable to pay for all utilities other than water." Antonin Scalia & Bryan A. Garner, *Reading Law: The Interpretation of Legal Texts* 184 (2012).

general statute. **1.** See STATUTE. **2.** PUBLIC LAW (2). **3.** See *general law* under LAW.

general strike. See STRIKE (1).

general-subordination agreement. See SUBORDINATION AGREEMENT.

general synod. See SYNOD.

general tail. See *tail general* (1) under TAIL.

general tax. See TAX.

general tenancy. See TENANCY.

general term. See TERM (5).

general-terms canon. The doctrine that general terms in a legal instrument are to be given their general meaning. • The traditional maxim is *Generalia verba sunt generaliter intelligenda.*

general title. See TITLE (3).

general traverse. See TRAVERSE.

general truce. See TRUCE.

general trust. See *passive trust* under TRUST (3).

general usage. See USAGE (1).

general verdict. See VERDICT (1).

general-verdict rule. (1930) The principle that when a jury returns a general verdict on multiple causes of action (or theories of recovery), it is presumed on appeal that the jury found in the prevailing party's favor on each cause of action.

general verdict subject to a special case. See VERDICT (1).

general verdict with interrogatories. See VERDICT (1).

general warrant. See WARRANT (1).

general warranty. See WARRANTY (1).

general warranty deed. See *warranty deed* under DEED.

general welfare. See WELFARE (1).

General Welfare Clause. (1898) *Constitutional law.* U.S. Const. art. I, § 8, cl. 1, which empowers Congress to levy taxes and pay debts in order to provide for the country's general welfare. • The Supreme Court has broadly interpreted this clause to allow Congress to create, for example, the social-security system. — Also termed *Welfare Clause.*

general words. (18c) Semantically broad expression; esp., language used in deeds to convey not only the specific property described in the conveyance but also all easements, privileges, and appurtenances that may belong to the property.

generation. (14c) **1.** A single degree or stage in the succession of persons in natural descent. **2.** The average time span between the birth of parents and the birth of their children.

generation-skipping tax. See TAX.

generation-skipping transfer. (1979) *Wills & trusts.* A conveyance of assets to a "skip person," that is, a person more than one generation removed from the transferor. • For example, a conveyance either directly or in trust from a grandparent to a grandchild is a generation-skipping transfer subject to a generation-skipping transfer tax. IRC (26 USCA) §§ 2601–2663. See *generation-skipping transfer tax* under TAX; *generation-skipping trust* under TRUST (3); SKIP PERSON.

generation-skipping transfer tax. See TAX.

generation-skipping trust. See TRUST (3).

generic, *adj.* (1846) *Trademarks.* **1.** Common or descriptive, and thus not eligible for trademark protection; nonproprietary <a generic name>. **2.** Not having a trademark or brand name <generic drugs>.

genericalness. See GENERICNESS.

generic burglary. See BURGLARY.

generic claim. See PATENT CLAIM.

generic drug. See DRUG.

generic-drug law. (1977) A statute that allows pharmacists to substitute a generic drug for a brand-name drug under specified conditions. • Most states have enacted generic-drug laws to ensure that less-expensive generic drugs are available to consumers.

genericide (jə-**ner**-ə-sɪd). (1977) *Trademarks.* The loss or cancellation of a trademark that no longer distinguishes the owner's product from others' products. • Genericide occurs when a trademark becomes such a household name that the consuming public begins to think of the mark not as a brand name but as a synonym for the product itself. Examples of trademarks that have been "killed" by genericide include *aspirin* and *escalator.*

genericism (jə-**ner**-ə-siz-əm). See GENERICNESS.

generic name. (1872) *Trademarks.* A term that describes something generally without designating the thing's source or creator, such as the word *car* or *sink.* • A generic name cannot be protected as a trademark for the thing it denotes; e.g., *Apple* can be a trademark for computers but not for apples. — Also termed *generic term; generic mark; common descriptive name.*

genericness, *n.* (20c) The quality, state, or condition of being generic <an affirmative defense of genericness in a trademark suit>. — Also termed *genericalness; genericism.*

generic swap. See *plain-vanilla swap* under INTEREST-RATE SWAP.

generic term. See GENERIC NAME.

genetic child. See *natural child* (1) under CHILD.

genetic engineering. (ca. 1951) A method of creating new life forms and organic matter by gene-splicing and other techniques. • The Supreme Court has ruled that those creations are patentable. *Diamond v. Chakrabarty,* 447 U.S. 303, 100 S.Ct. 2204 (1980).

genetic father. See *biological father* under FATHER.

genetic fingerprinting. See DNA IDENTIFICATION.

Genetic Information Nondiscrimination Act. A 2008 federal statute prohibiting harassment and employment discrimination based on analyses of the genes of a person or a person's family. — Abbr. GINA.

genetic-marker test. (1976) A medical method of testing tissue samples used in paternity and illegitimacy cases to determine whether a particular man could be the father of a child. • This test represents a medical advance over blood-grouping tests. It analyzes DNA and is much more precise in assessing the probability of paternity. — Abbr. GMT. See PATERNITY TEST. Cf. BLOOD-GROUPING TEST; HUMAN-LEUKOCYTE ANTIGEN TEST.

genetic mother. See *biological mother* under MOTHER.

genetic parent. See *biological parent* under PARENT (1).

Geneva Conventions of 1949 (jə-**nee**-və). Four international agreements dealing with the protection of wounded members of the armed forces, the treatment of prisoners of war, and the protection of civilians during international armed conflicts. • Common Article 3 of the Conventions proclaims certain minimum standards of treatment that are applicable to noninternational armed conflicts. The humanitarian-law protection established in these four agreements was amplified in 1977 by the two Protocols Additional to the Geneva Conventions. In common parlance, people refer to the *Geneva Convention* as if there were just one agreement. See LIEBER CODE. Cf. LAWS OF WAR.

> "The term 'Geneva Conventions' refers to four conventions, the earliest of which dates from 1864, and which were revised, expanded, and completed in 1949. They have been signed and ratified by every state in the world and were the brainchild of Henry Dunant, a Swiss social activist. After witnessing the battle of Solferino in 1859, Dunant was moved to ameliorate the suffering of soldiers, and he subsequently founded the International Committee of the Red Cross in 1863. Meanwhile, attempts to codify the conduct of war and the treatment of soldiers were also emerging in the United States in response to the Civil War. In 1863 the Lieber Code, written by an American law professor named Francis Lieber, was issued and adopted by the Union government. The Confederacy initially denounced the code but subsequently adopted it, and it went on to form the basis of similar codes in the United Kingdom, Prussia, France, Spain, Russia, Serbia, Argentina, and the Netherlands. Though the Lieber Code and the Geneva Conventions both attempted to codify and thereby lessen the horrors of war, each had a different focus: the Lieber Code focused on permitted conduct by soldiers, and the Geneva Conventions focused on protecting the sick and wounded." Adriana Sinclair, "Geneva Conventions," in 1 *The Oxford Encyclopedia of American Military and Diplomatic History* 414, 414 (Timothy J. Lynch ed., 2013).

Geneva Phonograms Convention. A 1971 treaty requiring signatories to protect phonorecord producers against piracy and the importation of pirated copies, by copyright protection, unfair-competition law, or criminal sanctions. • The treaty was drafted by representatives from WIPO and UNESCO to correct weaknesses in the Rome Convention. — Also termed *Convention for the Protection of Producers of Phonograms Against Unauthorized Duplication of Their Phonograms; Phonograms Convention.*

genocidal rape. See *war rape* under RAPE (2).

genocide (**jen**-ə-sɪd). (ca. 1944) *Int'l law.* An international crime involving acts causing serious physical and mental harm with the intent to destroy, partially or entirely, a national, ethnic, racial, or religious group. • The widely ratified Genocide Convention of 1948 defines the crime. The International Criminal Court has jurisdiction to try those accused of genocide. Many countries also have criminal laws providing punishment for individuals convicted of genocide. Cf. ETHNIC CLEANSING; POGROM.

> "The . . . draft Convention on the Prevention and Punishment of the Crime of Genocide was adopted by the General Assembly on December 9, 1948 and unanimously recommended for adherence to the members of the United Nations. It came into force in October, 1950 . . . . The term 'genocide' was first proposed by Dr. Lemkin in the course of the war and incorporated on his suggestion into the Indictment of the Major German War Criminals. The [U.N. General] Assembly Resolution on Genocide of December 11, 1946, and the Convention of 1948, are also the result of a remarkable one-man campaign." Georg Schwarzenberger, *Power Politics: A Study of International Society* 634 (2d ed. 1951).

Genoese lottery (jen-oh-**eez** *or* **-ees**). See LOTTERY.

genotype. (19c) *Patents.* The genetic makeup of a living organism. • A patent on living matter must disclose its genotype rather than just describe its physical characteristics (phenotype) or behavior. Cf. PHENOTYPE. — **genotypic,** *adj.*

gens (jenz), *n.* [Latin] (19c) *Roman law.* A clan or group of families who share the same name and (supposedly) a common ancestor; extended family. • Members of a *gens* are freeborn and possess full civic rights. Pl. ***gentes.***

> "A wider group still is the *gens*, of great importance in early law though its importance was gone in classical times. This consisted of all who bore the same *nomen*, the gentile name." W.W. Buckland, *A Manual of Roman Private Law* 61 (2d ed. 1939).

gentes (**jen**-teez), *n.* [Latin] (19c) *Roman law.* The peoples or countries of the world, particularly the civilized peoples.

gentile (**jen**-tɪl). [fr. Latin *gentilis*] (1875) *Roman law.* A member of a *gens.* See GENS.

gentium privatum. See *private international law* under INTERNATIONAL LAW.

gentleman. (12c) *Hist.* **1.** A man of noble or gentle birth or rank; a man above the rank of yeoman. **2.** A man belonging to the landed gentry. • Today the term has no precise legal meaning.

gentleman's agreement. See GENTLEMEN'S AGREEMENT.

Gentleman Usher of the Black Rod. *English law.* An officer of the House of Lords who has various ceremonial duties, including the summoning of the members of the House of Commons to the House of Lords when a bill is to receive royal approval. • The office dates from the 14th century.

gentlemen's agreement. (1886) An unwritten agreement that, while not legally enforceable, is secured by the good faith and honor of the parties. — Also spelled *gentleman's agreement.*

gentrification, *n.* (1973) The restoration and upgrading of a deteriorated or aging urban neighborhood by middle-class or affluent persons, resulting in increased property values and often in displacement of lower-income residents. — **gentrify,** *vb.*

genuine, *adj.* (17c) **1.** (Of a thing) authentic or real; having the quality of what a given thing purports to be or to have <the plaintiff failed to question whether the exhibits were genuine>. **2.** (Of an instrument) free of forgery or counterfeiting <the bank teller could not determine whether the signature on the check was genuine>. UCC § 1-201(b)(19). — **genuineness,** *n.*

genuine issue of material fact. (1938) *Civil procedure.* In the law of summary judgments, a triable, substantial, or real question of fact supported by substantial evidence. • An issue of this kind precludes entry of summary judgment.

genus (**jee**-nəs *or* **jen**-əs). (16c) A general class comprising several species or divisions. • In legal usage, the terms *genus* and (sometimes) *species* invoke the taxonomic classification of life forms in biological science. For example, patent law is a species within the genus of intellectual property; burglary is a species within the genus of crime. In the law of sales, *genus* referred to fungibles, while *species* referred to specific, individual items. Cf. SPECIES (2).

genus claim. See *generic claim* under PATENT CLAIM.

genus nunquam perit (**jee**-nəs **nən**[g]-kwam **per**-it). [Latin] *Hist.* The class never perishes. • The phrase appeared in reference to a quantity of contracted-for goods of a certain class (rather than a single item), the destruction of which did not discharge the seller's obligation.

geodetic-survey system (jee-ə-**det**-ik). (1990) A federally created land-description method consisting of nationwide marks (or *benches*) made at longitude and latitude points. • The geodetic-survey system integrates most of the real property in the United States into one unified form of measurement.

geographical indication. *Intellectual property.* A territorial name that conveys an attribute of a product or the goodwill of producers of that place (e.g., "Champagne"). • The right to use a geographical indication with a product or service is typically shared by a community of producers. — Abbr. GI. —Also termed *geographic indicator; geographic indicator.* Cf. *geographically descriptive trademark* under TRADEMARK.

> "Geographical indications are protected in different ways. Many countries protect them under unfair competition law, especially prohibiting their use by persons not appropriately connected with the subject region. Other countries provide for the registration and protection of geographical indications, as such, and may include administrative systems for their regulation. Still other countries treat geographical indications as trademarks, including collective and certification marks." Frederick M. Abbott, Thomas Cottier & Francis Gurry, *International Intellectual Property in an Integrated World Economy* 281 (2007).

geographically descriptive trademark. See TRADEMARK.

geographic indicator. See GEOGRAPHICAL INDICATOR.

geographic market. See MARKET.

geographic name. See NAME.

geographic positioning system. See GPS.

geography of crime. See *environmental criminology* under CRIMINOLOGY.

geopolitics. *Int'l law.* (1901) **1.** The ideas and activities relating to the way in which a country's geography, natural resources, alliances, and population influence its political development and its relationships with other countries. **2.** The field of study relating to these ideas and activities.

***Georgia-Pacific* analysis.** (1985) *Patents.* A 15-factor test for setting a reasonable royalty in infringement suits. • Among other factors, the test considers what a prudent licensee would have paid while still being able to earn a profit. *Georgia-Pacific Corp. v. U.S. Plywood Corp.*, 318 F. Supp. 1116 (S.D.N.Y. 1970).

german (**jər**-mən), *adj.* (14c) Having the same parents or grandparents; closely related.

▸ **brother-german.** See BROTHER.

▸ **cousin-german.** See COUSIN (1).

▸ **sister-german.** See SISTER.

germane (jər-**mayn**), *adj.* (14c) Relevant; pertinent <the caselaw cited in the brief was not germane to the legal issue pending before the court>. • Under parliamentary law, debate and amendments are in order only if they are germane to the motion under consideration. — **germaneness,** *n.*

germanus (jər-**may**-nəs). [Latin] *Roman law.* **1.** *adj.* Having the same father and mother. See *frater germanus* under FRATER. **2.** *n.* A whole brother; a child of both of one's own parents.

gerrymandering (**jer**-ee-man-dər-ing *or* **ger**-ee-), *n.* (1812) **1.** The practice of dividing a geographical area into electoral districts, often of highly irregular shape, to give one political party an unfair advantage by diluting the opposition's voting strength. • When Massachusetts Governor Elbridge Gerry ran for reelection in 1812, members of his political party, the Anti-Federalists, altered the state's voting districts to benefit the party. One newly created district resembled a salamander, inspiring a critic to coin the word *gerrymander* by combining the governor's name, *Gerry,* with the ending of *salamander.* Gerry was not reelected governor, but was elected as James Madison's vice president. — Also termed *political gerrymandering.* **2.** The practice of dividing any geographical or jurisdictional area into political units (such as school districts) to give some group a special advantage. — Also termed *partisan gerrymandering; jurisdictional gerrymandering.* Cf. REAPPORTIONMENT. — **gerrymander,** *vb.*

▸ **delineational gerrymandering.** (1976) Gerrymandering by varying the districts' shape. • There are three kinds of delineational gerrymandering: cracking (or fracturing), packing, and stacking. See CRACKING; PACKING; STACKING (2).

▸ **institutional gerrymandering.** (1973) Gerrymandering by means of varying the number of representatives per district.

▸ **racial gerrymandering.** (1961) Gerrymandering along racial lines, or with excessive regard for the racial composition of the electorate.

gersum (**gər**-səm). (14c) *Hist.* **1.** Money paid for a thing; specif., compensation paid by a tenant to a superior on entering a holding. **2.** A penalty or amercement paid for an offense. — Also spelled *garsumme; gersuma; gersume; grassum.* **3.** GRESSUME.

gersumarius (jər-s[y]ə-**mair**-ee-əs). *Hist.* Finable; liable to be fined at the discretion of a feudal superior. • A villein who gave his daughter in marriage was *gersumarius* — he was liable to pay a fine to the lord.

Geschmacksmuster. *Patents.* [German] See *design patent* under PATENT.

Gestalt factors. (1990) The criteria that a court uses in a minimum-contacts analysis to determine the reasonableness of subjecting a nonresident to personal jurisdiction. • These fairness criteria include (1) the defendant's burden of making a personal appearance, (2) the forum state's interest in adjudicating the dispute, (3) the plaintiff's interest in obtaining convenient and effective relief, (4) the judicial system's interest in arriving at the most effective resolution of the controversy, and (5) the common interests of all sovereigns in promoting substantive social policies. These factors were articulated by the United States Supreme Court in *Burger King Corp. v. Rudzewicz,* 471 U.S. 462, 478, 105 S.Ct. 2174, 2185 (1985), but the Court has never used the term *Gestalt factors;* it was coined in *Donatelli v. National Hockey League,* 893 F.2d 459, 465 (1st Cir. 1990). See MINIMUM CONTACTS.

gestational carrier. See *surrogate mother* (1) under MOTHER.

gestational mother. See *birth mother* under MOTHER.

gestational surrogacy. See SURROGACY.

gestational surrogate. See *surrogate mother* (1) under MOTHER.

gestio (**jes**-chee-oh), *n.* [Latin] (16c) *Roman law.* **1.** Behavior or conduct. See GESTIO PRO HEREDE. **2.** The management of a thing, esp. a transaction. See NEGOTIORUM GESTIO. — Also termed *gestion.*

▸ ***negotiorum gestio*** (ni-goh-shee-**or**-əm **jes**-chee-oh). See NEGOTIORUM GESTIO.

gestio pro haerede (**jes**-chee-oh proh **her**-ə-dee). [Latin "behavior as heir"] (17c) *Roman & Hist. Scots law.* An appointed heir's conduct (such as selling or leasing the decedent's property) that indicates the heir's intent to receive the inheritance and thereby take on the estate's debts; more broadly, any behavior as an heir. — Also spelled *gestio pro haerede.*

gestor (**jes**-tor), *n.* [Latin] *Roman law.* **1.** Someone who carries on a business. **2.** NEGOTIORUM GESTOR. Pl. ***gestores.***

gestu et fama (**jes**-t[y]oo et **fay**-mə). [Latin "demeanor and reputation"] (16c) *Hist.* A writ used by a person who had been imprisoned because of a poor reputation in the community to gain release from jail pending the arrival of justices with commissions of gaol delivery. See COMMISSION OF GAOL DELIVERY.

gestum (**jes**-təm), *n.* [Latin] *Roman law.* A deed or an act; a thing done. • *Gestum* is synonymous with *factum.* See FACTUM (2).

gesture. (15c) A motion of the body calculated to express a thought or emphasize a certain point <the prosecutor was known for her dramatic gestures during closing argument>.

get, *n.* (19c) **1.** A rabbinical divorce; a Jewish divorce. **2.** Under Jewish law, a document signed by a rabbi to grant a divorce. • Under Jewish law, a Jewish divorce can be obtained only after the husband has given the get to the wife, who must voluntarily accept it. — Also spelled *gett.* See *rabbinical divorce* under DIVORCE. Pl. **gittin.**

get-up. See TRADE DRESS.

gewrit. (17c) *Hist.* A deed, charter, or similar writing.

ghost detainee. See *secret detainee* under DETAINEE.

ghosting. The assumption of the identity of a deceased person to conceal one's true identity. Cf. IDENTITY THEFT.

ghost officer. See POLICE OFFICER.

GI. *abbr.* GEOGRAPHIC INDICATION.

gibbet (**jib**-it), *n.* (13c) *Hist.* A post with one arm extending from the top, from which criminals are either executed by hanging or suspended after death as a warning to other potential offenders; a type of gallows.

▸ **double gibbet.** (17c) A gibbet with two arms extending from its top so that it resembles a capital "T."

gibbet law. See HALIFAX LAW.

GIC. See *guaranteed investment contract* under INVESTMENT CONTRACT.

GIFT. *abbr.* GAMETE INTRAFALLOPIAN TRANSFER.

gift, *n.* (12c) **1.** The voluntary transfer of property to another without compensation. **2.** A thing so transferred. — **gift,** *vb.*

> "[I]t is . . . well to here state the things essential to make a valid gift. The donor must have the capacity to make a gift; he must have an intention to make it; his intention must be to make it now, and not in the future; he must deliver, either actually or constructively, the thing given to the donee, releasing all dominion over the thing given and investing the donee with whatever dominion he possessed; there must be an acceptance by the donee; it must be irrevocable, unless the consent of both the donor and donee is first obtained; it must be without a valuable consideration, for if there be a valuable consideration, however small, for the transaction, it is a contract and not a gift; the thing given must not be indefinite, and the entire transaction must show a valid gift as a whole and not of a part." W.W. Thornton, *A Treatise of the Law Relating to Gifts and Advancements* 2-3 (1893).

▸ **absolute gift.** See *inter vivos gift.*

▸ **anatomical gift.** (1971) A testamentary donation of a bodily organ or organs, esp. for transplant or for medical research. • The procedures for making an anatomical gift are set forth in the Uniform Anatomical Gift Act, which has been adopted in every state.

▸ **antenuptial gift.** See *prenuptial gift.*

▸ **charitable gift.** (17c) An inter vivos or testamentary donation to a nonprofit organization for the relief of poverty, the advancement of education, the advancement of religion, the promotion of health, governmental, or municipal purposes, and other purposes the accomplishment of which is beneficial to the community. Restatement (Second) of Trusts § 368 (1959). • When the beneficiary is a religious organization or the gift is intended for a religious purpose, it is sometimes also termed *pious gift.*

▸ **class gift.** (1949) A gift to a group of persons, uncertain in number at the time of the gift but to be ascertained at a future time, who are all to take in definite proportions, the share of each being dependent on the ultimate number in the group.

> "The typical class gift is to 'children,' 'issue,' 'heirs,' 'brothers and sisters,' 'nieces and nephews,' 'grandchildren.' A class gift is one in which the donor intends to benefit a group or a class of persons, as distinguished from specific individuals; the class gift donor is said to be 'group-minded.' The class gift is one in which the donor intends that the number of donees, from the time of the delivery of the instrument of gift in the case of the inter vivos gift, or from the time of the execution of the will in the case of the testamentary gift, is subject to fluctuation by way of increase or decrease, or by way of increase only, or by way of decrease only, depending on the circumstances of the gift." Thomas F. Bergin & Paul G. Haskell, *Preface to Estates in Land and Future Interests* 136 (2d ed. 1984).

▸ **completed gift.** (1952) A gift that is no longer in the donor's possession and control. • Only a completed gift is taxable under the gift tax.

▸ **conditional gift.** A gift that is dependent on a condition. • The donor may revoke the gift before the condition is fulfilled because the gift is not final.

▸ ***gift causa mortis*** (**kaw**-zə **mor**-tis). (1802) A gift made in contemplation of the donor's imminent death. • The four essentials are that (1) the gift must be made because of the donor's present life-threatening illness or peril, (2) the donor must intend to make an immediate gift, (3) the donor must deliver the gift, and (4) the donee must accept the gift. Even though *causa mortis* is the more usual word order in modern law, the correct Latin phrasing is *mortis causa* — hence *gift mortis causa.* — Also termed *donatio causa mortis; donatio mortis causa; gift in contemplation of death; transfer in contemplation of death.* See CONTEMPLATION OF DEATH.

> "[Gifts causa mortis] are conditional, like legacies; and it is essential to them that the donor make them in his last illness, or in contemplation and expectation of death; and with reference to their effect after his death, they are good, notwithstanding a previous will; and if he recovers, the gift becomes void." 2 James Kent, *Commentaries on American Law* *444 (George Comstock ed., 11th ed. 1866).

> "A 'gift causa mortis' . . . is testamentary, and it is similar to testamentary disposition in the respect that there

remains with the donor the power to revoke the gift until his death. In some respects, a gift causa mortis may be said to resemble a contract, for mutual consent and the concurrent will of both parties are necessary to the validity of the transfer." 38A C.J.S. *Gifts* § 85, at 276–77 (1996).

▸ **gift in contemplation of death.** See *gift causa mortis.*

▸ **gift inter vivos.** See *inter vivos gift.*

▸ **gift in trust.** (18c) A gift of legal title to property to someone who will act as trustee for the benefit of a beneficiary.

▸ **gift over.** (18c) A property gift (esp. by will) that takes effect after the expiration of a preceding estate in the property (such as a life estate or fee simple determinable) <to Sarah for life, with gift over to Don in fee>.

▸ **gift splitting.** See *split gift.*

▸ **gratuitous gift.** (17c) A gift made without consideration, as most gifts are. • Strictly speaking, the term looks redundant, but it answers to the *donum gratuitum* of Roman law.

▸ **immediate gift.** (16c) A gift that upon receipt vests present rights in the donee.

▸ **imperfect gift.** (17c) A gift that lacks the legal formalities required to make it effective.

▸ **inter vivos gift** (**in**-tər **vɪ**-vohs *or* **vee**-vohs). (1848) A gift of personal property made during the donor's lifetime and delivered to the donee with the intention of irrevocably surrendering control over the property. — Also termed *gift inter vivos; lifetime gift; absolute gift.*

▸ **lifetime gift.** See *inter vivos gift.*

▸ **manual gift.** (1840) *Civil law.* A gift of movable, tangible property, made by delivery without any formalities. La. Civ. Code art. 1539.

▸ **onerous gift** (**ohn**-ə-rəs *or* **on**-ə-rəs). (1871) A gift made subject to certain conditions imposed on the recipient.

▸ **pious gift.** See *charitable gift.*

▸ **prenuptial gift** (pree-**nəp**-shəl). (1921) A gift of property from one spouse to another before marriage. • In community-property states, prenuptial gifts are often made to preserve the property's classification as separate property. — Also termed *antenuptial gift.*

▸ **split gift.** (1957) *Tax.* A gift that is made by one spouse to a third person and that, for gift-tax purposes, both spouses treat as being made one-half by each spouse; a gift in which the spouses combine their annual gift-tax exclusions. • A split gift, for example, is eligible for two annual exclusions of $10,000 each, or a total of $20,000 for one gift. — Also termed *gift-splitting; gift-splitting election.* See *annual exclusion* under EXCLUSION (1).

▸ **substitute gift.** (1934) A testamentary gift to one person in place of another who is unable to take under the will for some reason. — Also termed *substitutional gift.*

▸ **taxable gift.** (1922) A gift that, after adjusting for the annual exclusion and applicable deductions, is subject to the federal unified transfer tax. IRC (26 USCA) § 2503.

▸ **testamentary gift** (tes-tə-**men**-tə-ree *or* -tree). (18c) A gift made in a will.

▸ **vested gift.** (1820) An absolute gift, being neither conditional nor contingent, though its use or enjoyment might not occur until sometime in the future.

gift *causa mortis.* See GIFT.

gift deed. See DEED.

gift enterprise. (1858) **1.** A scheme for the distribution of items by chance among those who have purchased shares in the scheme. **2.** A merchant's scheme to increase sales without lowering prices by giving buyers tickets that carry a chance to win a prize. • Gift enterprises are regulated by state law. See LOTTERY.

gifting circle. See GIFTING CLUB.

gifting club. (2001) A type of pyramid scheme or Ponzi scheme in which recruits make "gifts" of money to other club members with the expectation that future recruits will make "gifts" to the present recruits. • Many gifting clubs limit membership to women. Club leaders usu. try to evade income-tax laws by claiming that the money paid in by a recruit is a tax-free "gift" to a club member and warning new recruits not to expect "gifts" in the future. Some states forbid gifting clubs as illegal pyramid schemes. Other states hold that the clubs are illegal lotteries. — Also termed *gifting circle; sisterhood; birthday club.* See PONZI SCHEME; PYRAMID SCHEME.

gift inter vivos. See *inter vivos gift* under GIFT.

gift in trust. See GIFT.

gift over. See GIFT.

gift splitting. See *split gift* under GIFT.

gift-splitting election. See *split gift* under GIFT.

Gifts to Minors Act. See UNIFORM TRANSFERS TO MINORS ACT.

gift tax. See TAX.

gift-tax exclusion. See *annual exclusion* under EXCLUSION (1).

***Giglio* material.** (1977) *Criminal law.* Information relating to or suggesting any agreement between the prosecution and any of its own witnesses — evidence that must be disclosed to the defense. • Failure to disclose *Giglio* material, even negligent failure, violates the defendant's due-process right to any exculpatory information in the prosecution's possession. *Giglio v. U.S.*, 405 U.S. 150 (1972). — Also termed *Giglio evidence.*

gilda mercatoria (**gil**-də mər-kə-**tor**-ee-ə). [Law Latin] (17c) *Hist.* A merchant guild; an incorporated society of merchants having exclusive trading rights within a town.

gild hall. See GUILD HALL (1).

GI loan. See *veteran's loan* under LOAN.

gilour (**gɪ**-lər). [Law French] *Hist.* A guiler; a person who cheats or deceives. • *Gilour* referred to a person who sold false goods, such as a person who sold pewter as silver.

gilt-edged, *adj.* (1873) (Of a security) having the highest rating for safety of investment; exceptionally safe as an investment.

GINA. *abbr.* GENETIC INFORMATION NONDISCRIMINATION ACT.

Ginnie Mae (**jin**-ee **may**). See GOVERNMENT NATIONAL MORTGAGE ASSOCIATION.

GIPSA. *abbr.* GRAIN INSPECTION, PACKERS, AND STOCKYARD ADMINISTRATION.

girth (gərth). [Old English] (13c) **1.** A measure of length, equal to a yard. • This term, which was used in Saxon and early English law, was taken from the circumference of a man's body. **2.** The area surrounding a church. **3.** A place of sanctuary. **4.** A band or strap that encircles the body of an animal to fasten something (usu. a saddle) to its back.

gisement (**jɪs**- *or* **jɪz**-mənt). [Law French] (16c) *Archaic.* See AGISTMENT.

giser (**jɪ**-sər), *vb.* [Law French] *Hist.* (Of an action) to lie; to be capable of being brought as a suit in court. • This verb, in its inflected form *gist*, appeared in such phrases as *ou assise ne gist point* ("when an assise does not lie"), *le action bien gist* ("the action well lies"), and *gist en le bouche* ("it lies in the mouth"), and *cest action gist* ("this action lies").

gisetaker (**jɪs**- *or* **jɪz**-tay-kər). *Archaic.* See AGISTER.

gist (jist). (18c) **1.** The ground or essence (of a legal action) <the gist of the crime>. **2.** The main point <she skimmed the brief to get the gist of it>. • This noun derives from the Law French verb *giser* "to lie." See GISER.

gist-of-the-action doctrine. (2000) The principle that a plaintiff who brings a tort claim arising from a contractual relationship must show that the contract and any contractual claim are collateral to the tort claim. • The doctrine prevents plaintiffs from recasting contract claims as tort claims. This term is most common in Pennsylvania but also appears in New Jersey, Delaware, the Virgin Islands, and elsewhere.

Gitmo. See GUANTANAMO BAY.

give, *vb.* (13c) **1.** To voluntarily transfer (property) to another without compensation <Jack gave his daughter a car on her birthday>. **2.** To confer by a formal act <the First Amendment gives all citizens the right to free speech>. **3.** To present for another to consider <the witness gave compelling testimony before the jury>. **4.** (Of a jury) to impose or award by verdict <the jury gave the defendant the death penalty> <the jury gave the plaintiff $1,000 in damages>.

give-and-take, *n.* (18c) A willingness between two people to try sympathetically to understand each other and, in the spirit of good faith, to engage in mutual concessions and compromises.

give bail, *vb.* (17c) To post security for one's appearance in court <the court ordered the accused to give bail in the amount of $10,000>. — Also termed *post bail.*

give color, *vb.* (16c) *Hist.* To admit, either expressly or impliedly by silence, that an opponent's allegations appear to be meritorious. • In common-law pleading, a defendant's plea of confession and avoidance had to give color to the plaintiff's allegations in the complaint or the plea would be fatally defective. See COLOR (2).

give, devise, and bequeath, *vb.* (17c) To transfer property by will <I give, devise, and bequeath all the rest, residue, and remainder of my estate to my beloved daughter Sarah>. • This wording has long been criticized as redundant. In modern usage, *give* ordinarily suffices. See BEQUEST.

given name. See *personal name* under NAME.

give way, *vb.* (1802) *Maritime law.* (Of a vessel) to deviate from a course, or to slow down, in accordance with navigation rules, so that a second vessel may pass without altering its course.

giving in payment. (1814) *Civil law.* The act of discharging a debt by giving something to the creditor (with the creditor's consent) other than what was originally called for. La. Civ. Code art. 2655. • The phrase is a translation of the French *dation en paiement* and derives from the Roman *datio in solutum.* See DATION EN PAIEMENT. Cf. ACCORD AND SATISFACTION.

gladius (**glay**-dee-əs), *n.* [Latin "sword"] *Roman law.* The emblem of the emperor's power, esp. the power to punish criminals. See JUS GLADII.

glaive (glayv). (14c) *Hist.* A sword, lance, or horseman's staff. • The glaive was one of the weapons allowed in a trial by combat.

glamour stock. See *growth stock* under STOCK.

Glanvill. The earliest great English legal treatise, dating from ca. 1187 and named after the Justiciar of Henry II, which attempted to expound English common law for the first time as a single national system. • Scholars believe that Glanvill himself had little or nothing to do with the book known as *Glanvill.* Cf. BRACTON. — Also spelled *Glanville.*

glass ceiling. (1984) An actual or supposed upper limit of professional advancement, esp. for women, as a result of discriminatory practices.

Glass–Steagall Act. A federal statute that protects bank depositors by restricting the securities-related business of commercial banks, specif. by prohibiting banks from owning brokerage firms or engaging in the brokerage business. 12 USCA § 378. • The Act was partly repealed in 1999 by the Gramm–Leach–Bliley Act. — Also termed *Banking Act of 1933.*

GLBA. *abbr.* GRAMM–LEACH–BLILEY ACT.

glebae ascriptitius. See ADSCRIPTUS GLEBAE.

glebae ascriptus. See ADSCRIPTUS GLEBAE.

glebe (gleeb). [fr. Latin *gleba* "clod of earth"] (15c) **1.** *Roman law.* The soil of an inheritance; an agrarian estate. • *Servi addicti glebae* ("slaves bound to the land") were serfs attached to and passing with the estate. **2.** *Eccles. law.* Land possessed as part of the endowment or revenue of a church or ecclesiastical benefice.

> "Diocesan glebe land forms the largest section of ecclesiastical conveyancing work by virtue of the large number of glebe properties which are held in each diocese. Such land is governed primarily by the Endowments and Glebe Measure 1976 . . . , which in technical terms defines 'glebe land' as 'land vested in the incumbent of a benefice (when the benefice is full) as part of the endowments of the benefice other than parsonage land'; and 'diocesan glebe land' as 'glebe land acquired by a diocesan board of finance under any provision of this Measure and any other land acquired by such a board, being land which by virtue of, or of any enactment amended by, a provision of this Measure is to be held as part of the diocesan glebe land of the diocese.'" David Rees, *Ecclesiastical Conveyancing* 8 (1989).

GLO. *abbr.* GENERAL LAND OFFICE.

global commons. (1971) *Int'l law.* One or more areas outside the jurisdiction of any country, such as the high seas, outer space, or Antarctica. • Some authorities suggest that cyberspace is also part of the global commons.

global fund. See MUTUAL FUND.

globalization. (1930) The mostly 21st-century activity of creating and developing one massive worldwide economy, made possible by modern communications, enhanced methods of shipping goods, relatively free trade, free flow of capital, and the free competition among labor markets, so that single businesses may operate in many different countries. — **globalize,** *vb.*

global positioning service. See GPS.

global positioning system. See GPS.

global village. (1959) The world as envisioned by someone who sees worldwide interconnections and interdependence, partly as a result of how electronic media and modern communications have limited people's isolation and effectively closed the physical distances that once separated one region of the world from another.

***Globe* election.** (1953) *Labor law.* The procedure by which a group of employees is given the opportunity to decide whether to be represented as a distinct group or to be represented as a part of a larger, existing unit. *Globe Machine & Stamping Co.*, 3 NLRB 294 (1937). — Also termed *self-determination election.*

Glomar response. A reply that neither confirms nor denies the existence of requested documents. • The name *Glomar* comes from the *Hughes Glomar Explorer*, a large vessel that was publicly listed as a research ship owned and operated by the Summa Corporation but was believed to be actually owned and operated by the U.S. government. *See Phillippi v. CIA*, 546 F.2d 1009 (D.C. Cir. 1976); Att'y General's Memorandum on the 1986 Amendments to the Freedom of Info. Act 26 (Dec. 1987). — Also termed *Glomar reply; glomarization.*

glomarization. See GLOMAR RESPONSE.

glos (glos), *n.* [Latin] *Roman law.* One's husband's sister.

gloss, *n.* (16c) **1.** A note inserted between the lines or in the margin of a text to explain a difficult or obscure word in the text <this edition of Shakespeare's works is bolstered by its many glosses on Elizabethan English>. **2.** A collection of explanations; a glossary <the hornbook's copious gloss>. **3.** (*usu. pl.*) A pronouncement about meaning; an interpretation <the statutory language needs no gloss>.

glossators (glah-**say**-tərz). (15c) (*usu. cap.*) A group of Italian jurisconsults who, from the 11th to the 13th centuries, were primarily responsible for the revival of the study of Roman law. • They originally worked by glossing (that is, explaining in the margin) difficult or unclear passages, and gradually their writings blossomed into full-blown commentaries and discussions. See POSTGLOSSATORS. — **glossatorial,** *adj.*

Gloucester, Statute of (**glos**-tər). *Hist.* A statute that allowed a successful plaintiff to recover costs in addition to damages. • The statute was enacted in Gloucester. 6 Edw. I, ch. 1 (1278).

glove silver. (18c) *Hist.* Money given as an incentive or reward to a court officer, esp. money given by a sheriff to an assize official when no prisoners were left by the assize for execution. • The name derives from the practice of giving money to servants, ostensibly to buy gloves with.

GMI. *abbr.* GUILTY BUT MENTALLY ILL.

GML. *abbr.* GENERAL MARITIME LAW.

GMT. *abbr.* GENETIC-MARKER TEST.

GNMA. *abbr.* GOVERNMENT NATIONAL MORTGAGE ASSOCIATION.

GNP. *abbr.* (1961) GROSS NATIONAL PRODUCT.

go bail, *vb.* (1822) *Archaic.* To act as a surety on a bail bond.

gobbledygook. (1944) Complicated language, esp. of the willfully obscure type, usu. found in official or technical documents prepared by writers whose purpose is something other than clear and easy communication. — Also spelled *gobbledegook.* Cf. LEGALDYGOOK.

Godbote. See BOTE (3).

godfather. See GODPARENT.

God-gild. *Hist.* Money paid or something offered for the service of God; esp., a payment of money or a gift (for example, land) to a church. See FRANKALMOIN.

godmother. See GODPARENT.

godparent. (1865) *Eccles. law.* A person, usu. a close family friend or relative, who accepts a parent's invitation to assume part of the responsibility for the religious education of a newly baptized child. • Often, too, there is an understanding that the godparent would help support and rear the child if the parents were to die or become incapacitated. The spiritual parent–child relationship creates a canonical impediment to marriage. — Also termed (more specifically) *godmother; godfather;* (in *eccles. law*) *sponsor.*

God's penny. (17c) *Hist.* Earnest money; a small sum paid on the striking of a bargain. — Also termed *denarius Dei; earnest-penny; godpenny.* See DENARIUS DEI. Cf. ARRA.

> "It is among the merchants that the giving of earnest first . . . becomes a form which binds both buyer and seller in a contract of sale. To all appearances this change was not accomplished without the intermediation of a religious idea. All over western Europe the earnest becomes known as the God's penny or Holy Ghost's penny (*denarius Dei*) . . . ." 2 Frederick Pollock & Frederic W. Maitland, *The History of English Law Before the Time of Edward I* 208 (2d ed. 1899).

go forward, *vb.* (1964) To commence or carry on with the presentation of a case in court <after the lunch recess, the judge instructed the plaintiff to go forward with its case>.

go hence without day. (18c) (Of a defendant to a lawsuit) to be finished with legal proceedings without any further settings on the court's calendar. • Thus, a defendant who "goes hence without day" succeeds in getting a case finally resolved, usu. by dismissal. The phrase derives from the Law French phrase *aller sans jour*, and over time defendants came to use it to request that the case against them be dismissed without the necessity of a day in court. — Sometimes shortened to *go without day; without day.* See SINE DIE.

going-and-coming rule. (1927) **1.** The principle that torts committed by an employee while commuting to or from work are generally outside the scope of employment. **2.** The principle that denies workers'-compensation benefits to an employee injured while commuting to or from work. Cf. COMMERCIAL-TRAVELER RULE.

going concern. (1881) A commercial enterprise actively engaging in business with the expectation of indefinite continuance. — Also termed *going business.*

going-concern value. See VALUE (2).

going price, *n.* (18c) The prevailing or current market value of something. See *fair market value* under VALUE (2).

going private. (1966) The process of changing a public corporation into a close corporation by terminating the corporation's status with the SEC as a publicly held corporation and by having its outstanding publicly held shares acquired by a single shareholder or a small group.

going-private transaction. See FREEZEOUT.

going public. (1961) The process of a company's selling stock to the investing public for the first time (after filing a registration statement under applicable securities laws), thereby becoming a public corporation.

going through the bar. (1831) *Hist.* A daily process in which the court would ask all barristers present whether they had motions to present. • This practice, which ended in 1873, was conducted according to seniority, except for the last day of a term, when the junior barristers were asked first.

going to the country. *Hist.* The act of requesting a jury trial. • A defendant was said to be "going to the country" by concluding a pleading with the phrase "and of this he puts himself upon the country." Similarly, a plaintiff would conclude a pleading with the phrase "and this the plaintiff prays may be enquired of by the country." — Also termed *go to the country.* Cf. CONCLUSION TO THE COUNTRY.

going value. See *going-concern value* under VALUE (2).

going witness. See WITNESS.

gold bond. See BOND (3).

gold certificate. (1864) *Hist.* A banknote issued by the United States Treasury from 1863 to 1934 and redeemable in gold. • When the United States abandoned the gold standard in 1933, Congress declared ownership of gold certificates illegal even though the Treasury continued to issue them until mid-1934. The certificates were legalized again in 1964, but they can no longer be redeemed for gold. They now have the same status as Federal Reserve notes, which are not redeemable for precious metal. Cf. FEDERAL RESERVE NOTE; SILVER CERTIFICATE.

gold clause. (1935) A provision calling for payment in gold. • Gold clauses, which are now void, were once used in contracts, bonds, and mortgages.

golden, *adj.* (13c) **1.** Made of gold. **2.** Having the color of gold. **3.** Special, successful, or peculiarly advantageous.

golden boot. See GOLDEN HANDSHAKE.

golden handcuffs. (1976) Employment advantages, such as high pay, that make it hard if not impossible for employees to consider leaving a particular employer because there would be no comparable advantages elsewhere. • As a result, the employee often stays in the position even if it is otherwise unrewarding or unpleasant.

golden handshake. (1960) *Corporations.* A generous compensation package offered to an employee, usu. as an inducement to retire or upon dismissal. — Also termed *golden boot.*

golden parachute. (1981) *Corporations.* An employment-contract provision that grants an upper-level executive lucrative severance benefits — including long-term salary guarantees or bonuses — if control of the company changes hands (as by a merger). Cf. TIN PARACHUTE.

> "Key executives may be provided with significant employment contract clauses that are triggered only by a change in the firm's control through a sale, merger, acquisition, or takeover. These contract clauses are commonly termed *golden parachutes*, and they generally provide that if control over the employer's business occurs and the new management terminates the executive, additional compensation will be received. . . . Golden parachutes are useful in providing long-term incentives for executives to enter industries in which takeover chances are above average. Generally, golden parachutes do not violate public policy." Kurt H. Decker & H. Thomas Felix II, *Drafting and Revising Employment Contracts* § 3.33, at 84 (1991).

golden rule. 1. The interpretive doctrine that words in a legal instrument should be given their ordinary sense, as understood in context, unless that would lead to some absurdity or inconsistency with the rest of the text; ORDINARY-MEANING CANON (1). • The term *golden rule* is a mostly British name for the doctrine. — Also termed *Baron Parke's Rule.* **2.** The doctrine that a judge may look beyond the ordinary meaning and consult extratextual sources if the result dictated by the words is absurd. **3.** The doctrine that a word or phrase is presumed to bear a consistent meaning throughout a text; PRESUMPTION OF CONSISTENT USAGE. • The phrase *golden rule* has been used in so many divergent senses by so many commentators that it is often seen as being best avoided altogether. Cf. ABSURDITY; MISCHIEF RULE; PLAIN-MEANING RULE; EQUITY-OF-THE-STATUTE RULE.

> "[T]he 'golden' rule . . . allows for a departure from the literal rule when the application of the statutory words in the ordinary sense would be repugnant to or inconsistent with some other provision in the statute or even when it would lead to what the court considers to be an absurdity. The usual consequence of applying the golden rule is that words which are in the statute are ignored or words which are not there are read in. The scope of the golden rule is debatable, particularly so far as the meaning of an 'absurdity' is concerned." Rupert Cross, *Statutory Interpretation* 14 (1976).

golden-rule argument. (1934) A jury argument in which a lawyer asks the jurors to reach a verdict by imagining themselves or someone they care about in the place of the injured plaintiff or crime victim. • Because golden-rule arguments ask the jurors to become advocates for the plaintiff or victim and to ignore their obligation to exercise calm and reasonable judgment, these arguments are widely condemned and are considered improper in most states.

golden share. See SHARE (2).

goldsmiths' notes. (17c) *Hist.* Bankers' cash notes; promissory notes given by bankers to customers as acknowledgments of the receipt of money. • This term derives from the London banking business, which originally was transacted by goldsmiths.

gold standard. (19c) **1.** The use of the value of gold as a fixed standard on which to base the value of money. **2.** A monetary system in which currency is convertible into its legal equivalent in gold or gold coin. • The United States adopted the gold standard in 1900 and abandoned it in 1934. Cf. PAPER STANDARD.

good, *adj.* (bef. 12c) **1.** Sound or reliable <a good investment>. **2.** Valid, effectual, and enforceable; sufficient under the law <good title>.

good, *n.* See GOODS.

good and lawful fence. See LAWFUL FENCE.

good and merchantable abstract of title. See ABSTRACT OF TITLE.

good and valuable consideration. See *valuable consideration* under CONSIDERATION (1).

good and workmanlike. (18c) (Of a product or service) characterized by quality craftsmanship; constructed or performed in a skillful way or method <the house was built in a good and workmanlike manner>.

good behavior. (16c) **1.** A standard by which judges are considered fit to continue their tenure, consisting in the avoidance of criminal behavior. **2.** Orderly conduct, which in the context of penal law allows a prisoner to reduce the time spent in prison. Cf. *good time* under TIME.

good cause. See CAUSE (2).

good cause shown. See *good cause* under CAUSE (2).

good character. See CHARACTER.

good consideration. See CONSIDERATION (1).

good deed. See DEED.

good delivery. See DELIVERY.

good faith, *n.* (18c) A state of mind consisting in (1) honesty in belief or purpose, (2) faithfulness to one's duty or obligation, (3) observance of reasonable commercial standards of fair dealing in a given trade or business, or (4) absence of intent to defraud or to seek unconscionable advantage. — Also termed *bona fides.* Cf. BAD FAITH. — **good-faith,** *adj.*

> "The phrase 'good faith' is used in a variety of contexts, and its meaning varies somewhat with the context. Good faith performance or enforcement of a contract emphasizes faithfulness to an agreed common purpose and consistency with the justified expectations of the other party; it excludes a variety of types of conduct characterized as involving 'bad faith' because they violate community standards of decency, fairness or reasonableness. The appropriate remedy for a breach of the duty of good faith also varies with the circumstances." Restatement (Second) of Contracts § 205 cmt. a (1979).

> "[G]ood faith is an elusive idea, taking on different meanings and emphases as we move from one context to another — whether the particular context is supplied by the type of legal system (e.g., common law, civilian, or hybrid), the type of contract (e.g., commercial or consumer), or the nature of the subject matter of the contract (e.g., insurance, employment, sale of goods, financial services, and so on)." Roger Brownsword et al., "Good Faith in Contract," in *Good Faith in Contract: Concept and Context* 1, 3 (Roger Brownsword ed., 1999).

▸ **utmost good faith.** The state of mind of a party to a contract who will freely and candidly disclose any information that might influence the other party's decision to enter into the contract. — Also termed *uberrima fides; uberrimae fidei.*

good-faith bargaining. (1938) *Labor law.* Negotiations between an employer and a representative of employees, usu. a union, in which both parties meet and confer at reasonable times with open minds and with a view to reaching an agreement. • The National Labor Relations Act requires good-faith bargaining, and failure to bargain in good faith is considered an unfair labor practice. 29 USCA §§ 151–169. See UNFAIR LABOR PRACTICE.

good-faith error. See *bona fide error* under ERROR (1).

good-faith exception. (1980) *Criminal procedure.* An exception to the exclusionary rule whereby evidence obtained under a warrant later found to be invalid (esp. because it is not supported by probable cause) is nonetheless admissible if the police reasonably relied on the notion that the warrant was valid. • The Supreme Court adopted the good-faith exception in *U.S. v. Leon,* 468 U.S. 897, 104 S.Ct. 3405 (1984).

good-faith improver. (1934) Someone who makes improvements to real property while actually and reasonably believing himself or herself to be the owner or lawful occupant. • The improver may be entitled to recover the value of the improvements from the true owner or to remove them. See IMPROVEMENT.

good-faith margin. See MARGIN.

good-faith mistake. (1905) An honest error that involves neither cynical sabotage nor subconscious bias against accomplishing something. — Also termed *honest error.*

good-faith purchaser. See *bona fide purchaser* under PURCHASER (1).

good-guy clause. See *good-guy guaranty* under GUARANTY (1).

good-guy guaranty. See GUARANTY (1).

good health. (15c) *Insurance.* A state of reasonable healthiness; a state of health free from serious disease. • Good health, a phrase often appearing in life-insurance policies, does not mean perfect health. — Also termed *sound health.*

> "As used in policies of insurance, there is no material difference between the terms 'sound health' and 'good health,' and generally it appears that the two terms are considered to be synonymous. Such expressions are comparative terms, and the rule followed generally is that the term 'good health' or 'sound health,' when used in an insurance contract, means that the applicant has no grave, important, or serious disease, and is free from any ailment that seriously affects the general soundness or healthfulness of his system." 43 Am. Jur. 2d *Insurance* § 1061, at 1069 (1982).

good judgment. See JUDGMENT (1).

good jury. See *special jury* under JURY.

good-military-character defense. See GOOD-SOLDIER DEFENSE (1).

good moral character, *n.* (18c) **1.** A pattern of behavior that is consistent with the community's current ethical standards and that shows an absence of deceit or morally reprehensible conduct. • An alien seeking to be naturalized must show good moral character in the five years preceding the petition for naturalization. **2.** A pattern of behavior conforming to a profession's ethical standards and showing an absence of moral turpitude. • Good moral character is usu. a requirement of persons applying to practice a profession such as law or medicine. See CHARACTER.

good offices. *Int'l law.* The involvement of one or more countries or an international organization in a dispute between other countries with the aim of contributing to its settlement or at least easing relations between the disputing countries.

good of the order. *Parliamentary law.* A time scheduled, usu. late in a meeting, for informal announcements, comments, and suggestions that do not seek the meeting's immediate action. — Also termed *general good and welfare; open forum; open microphone.*

Goodright. (18c) *Hist.* A name sometimes used as a fictitious plaintiff in an ejectment action. • "John Doe" was used more frequently. — Also termed *Goodtitle.* Cf. JOHN DOE.

good root of title. See ROOT OF TITLE.

goods. (bef. 12c) **1.** Tangible or movable personal property other than money; esp., articles of trade or items of merchandise <goods and services>. • The sale of goods is governed by Article 2 of the UCC. **2.** Things that have value, whether tangible or not <the importance of social goods varies from society to society>.

> "'Goods' means all things (including specially manufactured goods) which are movable at the time of identification to the contract for sale other than the money in which the price is to be paid, investment securities, (Article 8), and things in action. 'Goods' also includes the unborn young of animals and growing crops and other identified things attached to realty as described in the section on goods to be severed from realty (Section 2-107)." UCC § 2-105(1).

▸ **basic goods.** Goods that are used to make other goods. • For example, fabrics are basic goods used to make clothing. — Also termed *primary goods*; *fundamental goods*.

▸ **bulk goods.** Unpackaged goods that are stored, transported, and sold in variable, usu. very large, quantities.

▸ **bulky goods.** (17c) Goods that are obviously difficult to move because of their nature, their number, or their location.

▸ **capital goods.** (1890) Goods (such as equipment and machinery) used for the production of other goods or services. — Also termed *industrial goods*.

▸ **commingled goods.** (1906) Goods that are physically mixed or united with other goods in such a way that their individual identity is lost in a product or undifferentiated mass.

▸ **consumer goods.** (1888) Goods bought or used primarily for personal, family, or household purposes, and not for resale or for producing other goods. UCC § 9-102(a)(23).

▸ **customers' goods.** (1857) *Insurance.* Goods belonging to the customers of a casualty-insurance policyholder; goods held by a policyholder as a bailee.

▸ **defective goods.** Goods that are imperfect in some material respect.

▸ **distressed goods.** (1935) Goods sold at unusually low prices or at a loss.

▸ **durable goods.** (1891) Consumer goods that are designed to be used repeatedly over a long period; esp., large things (such as cars, televisions, and furniture) that most people do not buy often. — Also termed *durables*; *hard goods*.

▸ **finished goods.** Manufactured goods that are complete and ready for sale or distribution to consumers.

▸ **fungible goods** (**fən**-jə-bəl). (1892) Goods that are interchangeable with one another; goods that, by nature or trade usage, are the equivalent of any other like unit, such as coffee or grain. UCC § 1-201(b)(18).

▸ **future goods.** (1857) Goods that will come into being, such as those yet to be manufactured; goods that are not both existing and identified. • A purported present sale of future goods or any interest in them operates as a contract to sell. UCC § 2-105(2).

▸ **goods in transit.** (1836) Goods that have been shipped by the seller but have not yet been received by the purchaser.

▸ **goods used in manufacture.** (1929) **1.** Goods or materials used as an integral part of manufacturing other goods. **2.** Goods or materials consumed incidentally during the manufacturing process. **3.** Goods, including fixed assets such as machinery and buildings, that are necessary to the existence of the manufacturing process.

▸ **gray-market goods.** See PARALLEL IMPORTS.

▸ **hard goods.** See *durable goods*.

▸ **household goods.** (16c) Goods that are used in connection with a home. • This term usu. arises when a warehouser claims a lien on what he or she asserts are "household" goods. According to the UCC, a warehouser may claim a lien on a depositor's furniture, furnishings, and personal effects that are used in a dwelling. UCC § 7-209(d). — Also termed *household effects*.

▸ **industrial goods.** See *capital goods*.

▸ **mobile goods.** (1932) Goods that are normally used in more than one jurisdiction (such as shipping containers and road-construction machinery) and that are held by the debtor as equipment or leased by the debtor to others. • Under previous drafts of the Uniform Commercial Code, the procedure for perfecting a security interest in mobile goods was generally defined by the law of the state where the debtor is located. The current UCC does not distinguish mobile goods. See *ordinary goods*. UCC § 9-303.

▸ **nonconforming goods.** (1931) Goods that fail to meet contractual specifications, allowing the buyer to reject the tender of the goods or to revoke their acceptance. UCC §§ 2-601, 2-608. See PERFECT-TENDER RULE.

▸ **ordinary goods.** Goods that are anything other than mobile goods, minerals, or goods covered by a certificate of title. • The current UCC does not distinguish between ordinary and mobile goods.

▸ **prize goods.** (17c) Goods captured at sea during wartime.

▸ **soft goods.** (1854) Consumer goods (such as clothing) that are not durable goods.

▸ **stolen goods.** Goods that have been wrongfully taken from their owner; goods acquired by robbery, theft, or larceny.

Good Samaritan action. (1967) **1.** A deed performed gratuitously by a person to help another who is in peril. — Also termed *Good Samaritan act*. See GOOD SAMARITAN DOCTRINE; GOOD SAMARITAN LAW. **2.** A lawsuit brought by a person or group for the benefit of all or part of a community.

Good Samaritan doctrine (sə-**mar**-i-tən). (1952) *Torts.* The principle that a person who is injured while attempting to aid another in imminent danger, and who then sues the one whose negligence created the danger, will not be charged with contributory negligence unless the rescue attempt is an unreasonable one or the rescuer acts unreasonably in performing the attempted rescue. Cf. EMERGENCY DOCTRINE; RESCUE DOCTRINE; LOST-CHANCE DOCTRINE.

good-samaritan law. (1965) A statute that exempts from liability a person (such as an off-duty physician) who voluntarily renders aid to another in imminent danger but negligently causes injury while rendering the aid. • Some form of good-samaritan legislation has been enacted in all 50 states and in the District of Columbia. Under some circumstances, the term applies to a statutory provision that immunizes one from liability for accidental damage caused by a good-faith attempt to protect another. For example, § 230 of the Communications Decency Act protects cellphone-service providers that remove third-party applications under a good-faith belief that the applications may be harmful to subscribers. — Also written *Good Samaritan law.* — Also termed *good-samaritan statute; good-samaritan clause.* Cf. GOOD SAMARITAN DOCTRINE.

> "The so-called 'Good Samaritan Statutes' . . . do not require aid to be given. They merely encourage doctors to stop and give aid to strangers in emergency situations by providing that no physician who *in good faith* renders such aid shall be liable in civil damages as a result of acts or omissions in rendering such aid. Some states have enacted statutes that require a person who is able to do so with no danger or peril to himself to come to the aid of another who is exposed to grave physical harm." Rollin M. Perkins & Ronald N. Boyce, *Criminal Law* 661 (3d ed. 1982).

goods and chattels (**chat**-əlz), *n.* (16c) Loosely, personal property of any kind; occasionally, tangible personal property only. — Also termed *goods and effects; goods and merchandise.*

goods in transit. See GOODS.

good-soldier defense. (1988) **1.** A military defense used in courts-martial, allowing introduction of evidence of good military character, such as reputation and honorable-service awards, to persuade the judge or panel that the service-member could not have committed the crime that he or she is charged with. — Also termed *good-military-character defense.* **2.** NUREMBERG DEFENSE.

goods used in manufacture. See GOODS.

good time. See TIME.

good-time law. (1910) A statute allowing a prisoner's sentence to be reduced by a stated number of days for each month or year of good behavior while incarcerated. — Also termed *good-time statute.*

Goodtitle. See GOODRIGHT.

good title. See TITLE (2).

goodwill. (bef. 12c) A business's reputation, patronage, and other intangible assets that are considered when appraising the business, esp. for purchase; the ability to earn income in excess of the income that would be expected from the business viewed as a mere collection of assets. • Because an established business's trademark or servicemark is a symbol of goodwill, trademark infringement is a form of theft of goodwill. By the same token, when a trademark is assigned, the goodwill that it carries is also assigned. — Also written *good will.* — Also termed *enterprise goodwill; commercial goodwill; practice goodwill; economic goodwill.* Cf. *going-concern value* under VALUE (2).

> "[Goodwill] is only another name for reputation, credit, honesty, fair name, reliability." Harry D. Nims, *The Law of Unfair Competition and Trade-Marks* 36 (1929).

> "Good will is to be distinguished from that element of value referred to variously as going-concern value, going value, or going business. Although some courts have stated that the difference is merely technical and that it is unimportant to attempt to separate these intangibles, it is generally held that going-concern value is that which inheres in a plant of an established business." 38 Am. Jur. 2d *Good Will* § 2, at 913 (1968).

▸ **individual goodwill.** See *personal goodwill.*

▸ **personal goodwill.** (1884) Goodwill attributable to an individual's skills, knowledge, efforts, training, or reputation in making a business successful. — Also termed *professional goodwill; separate goodwill; individual goodwill.*

▸ **professional goodwill.** See *personal goodwill.*

▸ **separate goodwill.** See *personal goodwill.*

goose case. See WHITEHORSE CASE.

goosehorn, *n. Slang.* A bawdy house; a house of prostitution. See DISORDERLY HOUSE.

go over, *vb.* (1818) **1.** (Of a trial) to adjourn. **2.** (Of an inheritance) to bypass a named heir in favor of others if a specified condition occurs or has occurred. • For example, a testator may specify that if the named heir predeceases the testator or if the testator's widow remarries, that heir's share will pass to another designated or qualified heir.

gore (gor), *n.* (bef. 12c) **1.** *Hist.* A small, narrow slip of land. **2.** A small (often triangular) piece of land, such as may be left between surveys that do not close. **3.** In some New England states (such as Maine and Vermont), a county's subdivision that has little population and thus is not organized as a town.

Gothland sea laws. See LAWS OF VISBY.

go to protest. (1861) (Of commercial paper) to be dishonored by nonpayment or nonacceptance <the draft will go to protest>. See DISHONOR (1); PROTEST (2).

go to the country. See GOING TO THE COUNTRY.

gouging, *n.* The unlawful or unfair raising of prices. — Also termed *price-gouging.*

govern, *vb.* (14c) (Of a precedent) to control a point in issue <the *Smith* case will govern the outcome of the appeal>.

governing body. (17c) **1.** GOVERNMENT (2). **2.** A group of (esp. corporate) officers or persons having ultimate control <the board of directors is the governing body of XYZ, Inc.>.

governing document. See DOCUMENT (2).

government. (14c) **1.** The structure of principles and rules determining how a state or organization is regulated. **2.** The sovereign power in a country or state. **3.** An organization through which a body of people exercises political authority; the machinery by which sovereign power is expressed <the Canadian government>. • In this sense, the term refers collectively to the political organs of a country regardless of their function or level, and regardless of the subject matter they deal with. Cf. NATION; STATE.

▸ **central government.** See *federal government* (1).

▸ **de facto government** (di **fak**-toh). (1830) **1.** A government that has taken over the regular government and exercises sovereignty over a country. **2.** An independent government established and exercised by a group of a country's inhabitants who have separated themselves from the parent state. — Also termed *government de facto.*

▸ **de jure government.** (1875) A functioning government that is legally established. — Also termed *government de jure.*

▸ **federal government.** (18c) **1.** A national government that exercises some degree of control over smaller political units that have surrendered some degree of power in exchange for the right to participate in national political matters. — Also termed (in federal states) *central government*. **2.** The U.S. government. — Also termed *national government*.

▸ **government de facto.** See *de facto government*.

▸ **government de jure.** See *de jure government*.

▸ **immediate government.** A government in which the state exercises its sovereign powers directly. Cf. *representative government*.

"Immediate government is that form in which the state exercises directly the functions of government. This form of government must always be unlimited, no matter whether the state be monarchic, aristocratic, or democratic; for the state alone can limit the government, and, therefore, where the state is the government, its limitations can only be self-limitations, i.e. no limitations in public law. Nothing prevents immediate government from being always despotic government in fact, except a benevolent disposition. It is always despotic government in theory." 2 John W. Burgess, *Political Science and Comparative Constitutional Law* 1-2 (1891).

▸ **limited government.** A system, usu. constitutionally established, in which the reach of a government, esp. a national government, is purposely restricted so that (1) citizens may more fully control how local policy is shaped, (2) the free-market system allows people greater economic liberty, and (3) the government has minimal ability to abridge the people's civil liberties.

"In contradistinction to all despotisms and dictatorships, the Constitution of the United States establishes limited government by imposing positive restraints on the Federal Government and the states. In some matters the individual is protected against the Federal Government, in others against the state, and in still others against both. These limitations are not mere political theories or vague declarations of rights; they are rules of law expounded and applied by the courts, enforced by proper executive authorities, and respected as a creed." Charles A. Beard & William Beard, *The American Leviathan: The Republic in the Machine Age* 52-53 (1931).

▸ **local government.** (17c) The government of a particular locality, such as a city, county, or parish; a governing body at a lower level than the state government. • The term includes a school district, fire district, transportation authority, and any other special-purpose district or authority. — Also termed *municipal government*.

▸ **minority government.** (1859) In a parliamentary system, a government that does not have enough votes to control the parliament or to make decisions without the support of one or more other parties.

▸ **mixed government.** (16c) A government containing a blend of forms, as in democracy and monarchy.

▸ **municipal government.** See *local government*.

▸ **national government. 1.** See NATIONAL GOVERNMENT. **2.** See *federal government* (2).

▸ **proprietary government.** (18c) *Hist.* A government granted by the Crown to an individual, in the nature of a feudatory principality, with powers of legislation formerly belonging to the owner of a county palatine. Cf. COUNTY PALATINE.

▸ **provisional government.** (17c) A government temporarily established to govern until a permanent one is organized to replace it.

▸ **representative government.** A form of democracy established on the principle that the people elect individuals who will represent them in the state's exercise of its sovereign powers.—Also termed *representative democracy*. Cf. *immediate government*.

"Representative government may be limited or unlimited. If the state vests its whole power in the government, and reserves no sphere of autonomy for the individual, the government is unlimited; it is a despotism in theory, however liberal and benevolent it may be in practice. If, on the other hand, the state confers upon the government less than its whole power, less than sovereignty, either by enumerating the powers of government, or by defining and safeguarding individual liberty against them, the government is limited, or, as we now usually say, it is constitutional as to form." 2 John W. Burgess, *Political Science and Comparative Constitutional Law* 2-3 (1891).

▸ **republican government.** (17c) A government in the republican form; specif., a government by representatives chosen by the people.

▸ **state government.** (18c) The government of a state of the United States.

4. The executive branch of the U.S. government. **5.** The prosecutors in a given criminal case <the government has objected to the introduction of that evidence>. **6.** An academic course devoted to the study of government; political science <Bridges is enrolled in Government 101>.

Government Accountability Office. An office in the legislative branch of the federal government responsible for auditing the receipt and disbursement of U.S. government funds and conducting investigations for members of Congress and congressional committees. • Headed by the Comptroller General of the United States, it was formerly called the General Accounting Office, established by the Budget and Accounting Act of 1921. It was renamed in 2004. 31 USCA § 702. — Abbr. GAO.

government agency. See AGENCY (3).

government-agency defense. (1985) *Torts.* An affirmative defense that immunizes a contractor from liability upon proof that the contractor acted on the government's behalf as an agent or as a government officer. • This defense is extremely limited because of the difficulty of establishing the government–agent relationship. *See Yearsley v. W.A. Ross Constr. Co.*, 309 U.S. 18, 20–22, 60 S.Ct. 413, 414–15 (1940). Cf. GOVERNMENT-CONTRACTOR DEFENSE; CONTRACT-SPECIFICATION DEFENSE.

government-agency security. See *government security* under SECURITY (4).

government agent. See AGENT.

government-agent exception. The rule that criminal statutes do not apply to government agents in the lawful execution of their duties.

governmental, *adj.* (18c) Of, relating to, or involving a government <governmental powers>.

Governmental Accounting Standards Board. A body that establishes, interprets, and improves standards for accounting and financial reporting in state and local governments and is the official source of their generally accepted accounting procedures (GAAP). • Created in 1984, the Board is a division of the Financial Accounting Foundation, a private nonprofit organization. — Abbr. GASB. Cf. FINANCIAL ACCOUNTING STANDARDS BOARD.

governmental act. See GOVERNMENTAL FUNCTION.

governmental activity. See GOVERNMENTAL FUNCTION.

governmental employee benefit plan. See *governmental plan* under EMPLOYEE BENEFIT PLAN.

governmental enterprise. See ENTERPRISE (1).

governmental function. (1817) *Torts.* A government agency's conduct that is expressly or impliedly mandated or authorized by constitution, statute, or other law and that is carried out for the benefit of the general public. • Generally, a governmental entity is immune from tort liability for governmental acts. — Also termed *governmental act; governmental activity.* See PUBLIC-FUNCTION TEST. Cf. PROPRIETARY FUNCTION.

> "[A]ctivities of police or firefighters, though tortious, are usually considered governmental in the sense that they involve the kind of power expected of the government, even if its exercise in the specific case is wrongful. The city is immune as to such activities for this reason. On the other hand, if the city operates a local electric or water company for which fees are charged, this looks very much like private enterprise and is usually considered proprietary. . . . The difficult distinction between governmental and proprietary functions is even more troubling where the city's conduct combines both kinds of function at once. For example, operation of a sanitary sewer may be deemed governmental, but operation of a storm sewer may be deemed proprietary." W. Page Keeton et al., *Prosser and Keeton on the Law of Torts* § 131, at 1053–54 (5th ed. 1984).

governmental-function theory. (1936) *Constitutional law.* A principle by which private conduct is characterized as state action, esp. for due-process and equal-protection purposes, when a private party is exercising a public function. • Under this theory, for example, a political party (which is a private entity) cannot exclude voters from primary elections on the basis of race. — Also termed *public-function rationale.*

governmental immunity. See *sovereign immunity* under IMMUNITY (1).

governmental instrumentality. (1854) A constitutionally or legislatively created agency that is immune from certain kinds of liability, as for taxes or punitive damages.

governmental interest. (1872) A matter of public concern that is addressed by a government in law or policy. — Also termed *state interest.*

governmental-interest-analysis technique. See INTEREST-ANALYSIS TECHNIQUE.

governmental plan. See EMPLOYEE BENEFIT PLAN.

governmental secret. See STATE SECRET.

governmental trust. See TRUST (3).

governmental unit. (1904) A subdivision, agency, department, county, parish, municipality, or other unit of the government of a country or a state. • The term includes an organization with a separate corporate existence only if the organization can legally issue debt obligations on which interest is exempt from income taxation under national law. UCC § 9-102(a)(45).

government-annuity society. *Hist. English law.* One of several organizations formed in England to enable the working class to provide for themselves by purchasing, on advantageous terms, a government annuity for life or for a term of years.

government bond. **1.** See *savings bond* under BOND (3). **2.** See *government security* under SECURITY (4).

government-business enterprise. See BUSINESS ENTERPRISE.

government contract. See CONTRACT.

government-contractor defense. (1981) An affirmative defense that immunizes a government contractor from civil liability under state law when the contractor complies with government specifications. • Immunization is extended when two conditions are satisfied: (1) the supplier warned the government about any dangers presented by the goods about which the supplier had knowledge but the government did not, and (2) the government itself is immune from liability under the *Feres* doctrine. Essentially, this federal common-law defense, which has been applied in cases of negligence, strict liability, and breach of warranty, extends sovereign immunity over the contractor. The leading case on this defense is *Boyle v. United Techs. Corp.*, 487 U.S. 500, 108 S.Ct. 2510 (1988). — Also termed *Boyle defense; government-contract defense; government-contract-specification defense;* (in military context) *military-contractor defense.* See FERES DOCTRINE. Cf. GOVERNMENT-AGENCY DEFENSE.

government-contract-specification defense. See GOVERNMENT-CONTRACTOR DEFENSE.

government-controlled corporation. See *quasi-governmental agency* under AGENCY (3).

government corporation. See *public corporation* (3) under CORPORATION.

government de facto. See *de facto government* under GOVERNMENT (3).

government de jure. See *de jure government* under GOVERNMENT (3).

government department. See DEPARTMENT (3).

government enterprise. See *governmental enterprise* under ENTERPRISE.

government health warning. (1971) A notice required to be put on particular products, such as cigarettes, to warn people of health risks.

government immunity. See *sovereign immunity* under IMMUNITY (1).

government-in-exile. (1940) An individual or group of individuals residing in a foreign country while (1) claiming supreme authority over a country, (2) being recognized by the hosting country as the supreme authority over that other country, and (3) being organized to perform and actually performing some acts of state on behalf of the home country.

government insurance. See INSURANCE.

government land. See *public land* under LAND.

Government National Mortgage Association. A federally owned corporation in the U.S. Department of Housing and Urban Development responsible for guaranteeing mortgage-backed securities composed of FHA-insured or VA-guaranteed mortgage loans. • The Association purchases, on the secondary market, residential mortgages originated by local lenders; it then issues federally insured securities backed by these mortgages. — Abbr. GNMA. — Also termed *Ginnie Mae.*

government of laws. (16c) The doctrine that government must operate according to established, consistent legal principles and not according to the interests of those who happen to be in power at a given time; esp., the doctrine that judicial decisions must be based on the law, regardless of the character of the litigants or the personal predilections of the judge.

government plan. See *governmental plan* under EMPLOYEE BENEFIT PLAN.

Government Printing Office. An office in the legislative branch of the federal government responsible for printing and distributing congressional publications and publications of other agencies of the United States government. • The Office is supervised by the Congressional Joint Committee on Printing. It began operating in 1860. — Abbr. GPO.

government secret. See STATE SECRET.

government-securities interdealer broker. See BROKER.

government security. See SECURITY (4).

government survey. See SURVEY (2).

government-survey system. (1931) A land-description method that divides the United States into checks or tracts of ground, which are further broken down into smaller descriptions, such as metes and bounds.

government tort. See TORT.

government vessel. See VESSEL.

governor. (14c) The chief executive official of a U.S. state. • Governors are elected and usu. serve a two- or four-year term.

Governor-General. (16c) Someone who represents the British Crown in the Commonwealth countries that are not republics <Governor-General of Australia>.

governorship. (17c) **1.** The position of being governor. **2.** The period during which someone is governor.

governor's warrant. See WARRANT (1).

go without day. See GO HENCE WITHOUT DAY.

GPARM. See *graduated-payment adjustable-rate mortgage* under MORTGAGE.

GPO. *abbr.* GOVERNMENT PRINTING OFFICE.

GPS. *abbr.* (1974) Global positioning system; that is, a network of computers and earth-orbiting satellites that allows an earth-bound receiver to determine its precise location. • Developed and maintained by the U.S. Government, GPS is freely accessible globally. Russia operates a similar system (GLONASS), while others are in development by China (BDS), the European Union (Galileo), and India (IRNSS). — Also termed *geographic positioning system; global positioning service.*

grab-bag judge. See JUDGE.

grab law. (1884) The various means of debt collection involving remedies outside the scope of federal bankruptcy law, such as attachment and garnishment; aggressive collection practices.

grace period. (1945) **1.** A period of extra time allowed for taking some required action (such as making payment) without incurring the usual penalty for being late. • Insurance policies typically provide for a grace period of 30 days beyond the premium's due date, during which the premium may be paid without the policy's being canceled. Article 9 of the UCC provides for a 20-day grace period, after the collateral is received, during which a purchase-money security interest must be perfected to have priority over any conflicting security interests. — Also termed *days of grace; grace days.* **2.** *Patents.* The one-year interval allowed by the U.S. Patent Act between the time an invention is used in public, sold, offered for sale, or disclosed in a publication and the time the inventor applies for a patent. • Most countries follow the doctrine of absolute priority and do not allow a grace period. — Sometimes shortened to *grace.* Cf. STATUTORY BAR; *absolute novelty* under NOVELTY.

gradatim (grə-**day**-təm), *adv.* (16c) [Latin] Gradually; by successive degrees of relationship. • *Gradatim* refers to the step-by-step admission of successors when there is no heir next in line. See GRADUS.

grade, *n. Criminal law.* An incremental step in the scale of punishments for offenses, based on a particular offense's seriousness <several grades of murder>. See DEGREE (2); DEGREE OF CRIME; *graded offense* under OFFENSE (2).

graded offense. See OFFENSE (2).

grading. The fixing of a criminal offense at a level of seriousness, such as first degree, second degree, or third degree (in reference to a felony), or Class A, Class B, or Class C (in reference to a misdemeanor). See DEGREE OF CRIME.

gradual method. An intestate-inheritance scheme that gives priority to relatives who are nearest in degree of consanguinity. • This method dates back to the English Statute of Distributions (1670). Cf. PARENTELIC METHOD; UNIVERSAL-INHERITANCE RULE.

graduated lease. See LEASE.

graduated mortgage. See *graduated-payment mortgage* under MORTGAGE.

graduated-payment adjustable-rate mortgage. See MORTGAGE.

graduated-payment mortgage. See MORTGAGE.

graduated tax. See TAX.

gradus (**gray**-dəs), *n.* [Latin "step"] (18c) **1.** *Roman law.* A step or degree in the familial relationship. • The term identified a position in the order of succession under a will. **2.** *Hist.* A degree, rank, or grade; specif., the rank of a master-in-chancery or a serjeant-at-law.

graffarius. See GRAFFER.

graffer (**graf**-ər). (15c) *Hist.* A notary or scrivener. — Also termed *graffarius.*

graffium (**graf**-ee-əm). *Hist.* A register or cartulary of deeds and other documents establishing title to property, esp. real property. — Also spelled *grafium.*

grafio (**gray**-fee-oh). [Law Latin] *Hist.* **1.** A baron; a viscount. • A grafio was inferior to a count. **2.** A fiscal judge, responsible for collecting taxes and fines. • The term was chiefly used among early European countries.

graft, *n.* (14c) **1.** The act of using a position of trust to gain money or property dishonestly; esp., a public official's fraudulent acquisition of public funds. **2.** Money or property gained illegally or unfairly.

***Graham* factors.** (1966) *Patents.* A three-part test for determining obviousness under § 103 of the Patent Act of 1952, looking at (1) the scope and content of the prior art, (2) the differences between the prior art and the patent claims, and (3) the level of ordinary skill in the pertinent art.

Graham v. John Deere Co. of Kansas City, 383 U.S. 1, 86 S.Ct. 684 (1966). See NONOBVIOUSNESS.

Gramm–Leach–Bliley Act. A federal statute that repealed both the part of the Glass–Steagall Act prohibiting combinations among banking, securities, and insurance companies, and related conflict-of-interest provisions for such companies' officers, directors, and employees. • The Act also regulates the collection, disclosure, use, and protection of consumers' nonpublic personal information. — Abbr. GLBA. — Also termed *Financial Services Modernization Act of 1999*. See FINANCIAL PRIVACY RULE.

Grain Inspection, Packers, and Stockyards Administration. An agency in the U.S. Department of Agriculture responsible for helping to market meat, cereals, and related agricultural products, and for promoting fair trade practices. — Abbr. GIPSA.

grain rent. See *crop rent* under RENT (1).

grammar canon. The doctrine that words in a legal instrument are to be given the meaning that proper grammar and usage would assign them.

grammatical interpretation. See INTERPRETATION (1).

granage. (16c) *Hist.* A duty consisting of one-twentieth of the salt imported by an alien into London.

granatarius (gran-ə-**tair**-ee-əs). [Law Latin] *Hist.* An officer in charge of a granary, esp. one in charge of a religious house's granary.

grand, *adj.* (17c) Of, relating to, or involving a crime involving the theft of money or property valued more than a statutorily established amount, and therefore considered more serious than those involving a lesser amount <grand theft>. See *grand larceny* under LARCENY. Cf. PETTY.

grand assize. See ASSIZE (5).

grand bill of sale. See BILL OF SALE.

grand cape. See *cape magnum* under CAPE.

grandchild. See CHILD.

grand coutumier de pays et duché de Normandie (gron koo-t[y]oo-**myay** də **pay** ay də-**shay** də nor-man-**dee**). [French] *Hist.* A collection of the common or customary laws of the Duchy of Normandy. • The code was probably compiled in the 13th century, and it still remains the law of Jersey, except to the extent that it has been modified by later legislation and judicial decisions. See CLAMEUR DE HARO.

Grand Day. (17c) *English law.* **1.** *Hist.* One of four holy days on which the courts were not in session. • Each of the four court terms had a Grand Day. The four Grand Days were Candlemas Day (February 2), Ascension Day (March 25), St. John the Baptist Day (June 24), and All Saints' Day (November 1). The Inns of Court and of Chancery ceremoniously observed each Grand Day. **2.** A day in each term on which the Benchers of the Inns of Court host ceremonial dinners in their halls. See BENCHER. Cf. TERM (6).

grand distress. See DISTRESS (2).

grandfather, *vb.* (1953) To cover (a person) with the benefits of a grandfather clause <the statute sets the drinking age at 21 but grandfathers those who are 18 or older on the statute's effective date>.

grandfather clause. (1900) **1.** *Hist.* A clause in the constitutions of some Southern states exempting from suffrage restrictions the descendants of men who could vote before the Civil War. • The U.S. Supreme Court held that a clause of this kind in the Oklahoma Constitution violated the 15th Amendment. *Guinn v. U.S.*, 238 U.S. 347, 35 S.Ct. 926 (1915). **2.** A provision that creates an exemption from the law's effect for something that existed before the law's effective date; specif., a statutory or regulatory clause that exempts a class of persons or transactions because of circumstances existing before the new rule or regulation takes effect. **3.** In a government contract, a provision that immunizes the contractor against any changes in federal law that would otherwise adversely affect the contract. • For example, the government may promise to cover any increased costs that arise from a change in the law, even though the contractor would bear them for any other reason. **4.** In a construction contract, a general and inclusive provision that makes a party responsible for dealing with risks, whether expected or unexpected.

grandiloquence. Lofty, pompous, bombastic language, esp. in speech; a turgid, pretentious, antiquely elevated style. — **grandiloquent,** *adj.*

grand inquest. See INQUEST (4).

grand juror. See JUROR.

grand jury. (15c) A body of (usu. 16 to 23) people who are chosen to sit permanently for at least a month — and sometimes a year — and who, in ex parte proceedings, decide whether to issue indictments. *See* Fed. R. Crim. P. 6. • If the grand jury decides that evidence is strong enough to hold a suspect for trial, it returns a bill of indictment (a *true bill*) charging the suspect with a specific crime. — Also termed *accusing jury*; *presenting jury*; *jury of indictment*. Cf. *petit jury* under JURY.

> "Strictly speaking there is no obscurity surrounding the origin of the 'grand jury,' for it was not until the 42nd year of the reign of Edward III (A.D. 1368) that the modern practice of returning a panel of twenty-four men to inquire for the county was established and this body then received the name '*le graunde inquest*.' Prior to this time the accusing body was known only as an inquest or jury, and was summoned in each hundred by the bailiffs to present offences occurring in that hundred. When, therefore, this method of proceeding was enlarged by the sheriff returning a panel of twenty-four knights to inquire of and present offences for the county at large, we see the inception of the grand jury of the present day. But while it is true that our grand jury was first known to England in the time of Edward the Third, it is nevertheless not true that it was an institution of Norman origin or transplanted into England by the Normans." George J. Edwards Jr., *The Grand Jury, an Essay* 2 (1906).

> "The grand jury serves — or may serve — two distinct functions. One is a screening function; the grand jury evaluates evidence supporting possible charges and returns an indictment only in those cases in which the evidence amounts to at least probable cause. The other is an investigatorial function; the grand jury sometimes develops information that is of value in determining whether grounds for a charge exist and — perhaps incidentally — in proving that charge at the defendant's later criminal trial." Frank W. Miller et al., *Cases and Materials on Criminal Justice Administration* 546 (3d ed. 1986).

▸ **additional grand jury.** See *special grand jury*.

▸ **investigative grand jury.** (1960) A grand jury whose primary function is to examine possible crimes and develop evidence not currently available to the prosecution. — Also termed *investigatory grand jury*.

▸ **runaway grand jury.** (1959) A grand jury that acts essentially in opposition to the prosecution, as by calling its own witnesses, perversely failing to return an indictment that the prosecution has requested, or returning an indictment that the prosecution did not request.

▸ **screening grand jury.** (1990) A grand jury whose primary function is to decide whether to issue an indictment.

▸ **special grand jury.** (1854) A grand jury specially summoned, usu. when the regular grand jury either has already been discharged or has not been drawn; a grand jury with limited authority. — Also termed *additional grand jury*; *extraordinary grand jury.*

Grand Jury Clause. (1949) *Constitutional law.* The clause of the Fifth Amendment to the U.S. Constitution requiring an indictment by a grand jury before a person can be tried for serious offenses.

grand-jury witness. See WITNESS.

grand larceny. See LARCENY.

grand list. See ASSESSMENT ROLL.

grandparent application. See PATENT APPLICATION.

grandparent rights. (1983) A grandfather's or grandmother's rights in seeking visitation with a grandchild. • By statute in most states, in certain circumstances a grandparent may seek court-ordered visitation with a grandchild. Typically these circumstances include the death of the grandparents' child (the child's parent) and the divorce of the child's parents. But the United States Supreme Court has held that the primary, constitutionally protected right of decision-making regarding association with a child lies with the child's parents. As a general rule, if the parent is a fit and proper guardian and objects to visitation, the parent's will prevails. *Troxel v. Granville*, 530 U.S. 57, 120 S.Ct. 2054 (2000).

grandparent visitation. See VISITATION.

Grand Remonstrance (ri-**mon**-strənts). *Hist.* A protest document issued by the House of Commons in 1641, setting forth numerous political grievances against Charles I. • The document demanded three primary remedial measures: (1) improvements in the administration of justice, (2) appointment of trustworthy ministers, and (3) enforcement of the laws against Roman Catholics. It was the first major split between the Royalist and Parliamentary parties, and it led Charles to seek the arrest of the five members who pushed the document through the Commons.

grand serjeanty. See SERJEANTY.

Grand Survey. See *grand inquest* (2) under INQUEST (4).

grange (graynj). (14c) **1.** *Hist.* A farm furnished with all the necessities for husbandry, such as a barn, granary, and stables; esp., an outlying farm that belonged to a religious establishment or a feudal lord. **2.** (*cap.*) A social, educational, and political organization, formally called the National Grange of the Patrons of Husbandry, that informs its members about agriculture-related legislation and proposals, and represents farm interests in lobbying government. • Formed in 1867, the Grange soon became the foundation of the Granger Movement, a 19th-century political force that protested economic abuses that increased farmers' costs while forcing down prices for agricultural products. Movement followers (called Grangers) controlled several Midwest state legislatures and passed Granger laws that set maximum rates for railroads, warehouses, and grain elevators. Railroads and other interested parties challenged the constitutionality of these laws in what have become known as the Granger Cases.

Granger Cases (**grayn**-jər). Six U.S. Supreme Court decisions holding that the police power of the states enabled them, through legislation, to regulate fees charged by common carriers, warehouses, and grain elevators. • The cases, decided in 1876, arose out of grangers' (i.e., farmers') frustration with the inflated prices they were paying to store and transport their agricultural products. When several state legislatures passed laws regulating those prices, the affected businesses sued to have the laws overturned on grounds that they violated the Commerce Clause and the Due Process Clause of the 14th Amendment. The Court rejected these claims, holding that the activities involved affected the public interest and were therefore subject to the government's regulatory authority. See GRANGE (2).

Granger Movement. See GRANGE (2).

granny's law. (*often cap.*) (2007) Any statute that imposes harsher penalties for physical attacks on senior citizens.

grant, *n.* (13c) **1.** An agreement that creates a right or interest in favor of a person or that effects a transfer of a right or interest from one person to another. • Examples include leases, easements, charges, patents, franchises, powers, and licenses. **2.** The formal transfer of real property. **3.** The document by which a transfer is effected; esp., DEED. **4.** The property or property right so transferred.

▸ **cessate grant.** (1863) *English law.* A grant of probate made because of the executor's incapacity or after a limited grant has expired because its purpose has been served. — Also termed *cessate probate*; *supplemental grant of probate.*

▸ **community grant.** (1887) A grant of real property made by a government (or sometimes by an individual) for communal use, to be held in common with no right to sell. • A community grant may set out specific, communal uses for the property, such as for grazing animals or maintaining a playground. Cf. *private grant.*

▸ **escheat grant.** (18c) A government's grant of escheated land to a new owner. — Also termed *escheat patent.*

▸ **imperfect grant.** (1818) **1.** A grant that requires the grantor to do something before the title passes to another. Cf. *perfect grant.* **2.** A grant that does not convey all rights and complete title against both private persons and government, so that the granting person or political authority may later disavow the grant. *See Paschal v. Perex*, 7 Tex. 368 (1851).

▸ **inclusive grant.** (18c) A deed or grant that describes the boundaries of the land conveyed and excepts certain parcels within those boundaries from the conveyance, usu. because those parcels of land are owned or claimed by others. — Also termed *inclusive deed.*

▸ **office grant.** A grant made by a legal officer because the owner is either unwilling or unable to execute a deed to pass title, as in the case of a tax deed. See *tax deed* under DEED.

▸ **perfect grant.** (16c) A grant for which the grantor has done everything required to pass a complete title, and the grantee has done everything required to receive and enjoy the property in fee. Cf. *imperfect grant* (1).

▸ **private grant.** (17c) A grant of real property made to an individual for his or her private use, including the right to sell it. • Private grants made by a government are often found in the chains of title for land outside the original 13 states, esp. in former Spanish and Mexican possessions. Cf. *community grant*.

5. SUBSIDY (1).

grant, *vb.* (13c) **1.** To give or confer (something), with or without compensation <the parents granted the car to their daughter on her 16th birthday>. **2.** To formally transfer (real property) by deed or other writing <the Lewisons granted the townhouse to the Bufords>. **3.** To permit or agree to <the press secretary granted the reporter access to the Oval Office>. **4.** To approve, warrant, or order (a request, motion, etc.) <the court granted the continuance>. **5.** *Int'l law.* See SUBSIDY (3).

grantback, *n.* (1956) A license-agreement provision requiring the licensee to assign or license back to the licensor any improvements that the licensee might make to a patent or other proprietary right.

grant deed. See DEED.

grantee. (15c) One to whom property is conveyed.

grantee–grantor index. See INDEX (1).

grant-in-aid. (19c) **1.** A sum of money given by a governmental agency to a person or institution for a specific purpose; esp., federal funding for a state public program.

granting clause. (18c) The words that transfer an interest in a deed or other instrument, esp. an oil-and-gas lease. • In an oil-and-gas lease, the granting clause typically specifies the rights transferred, the uses permitted, and the substances covered by the lease.

grant of rights. *Copyright.* A copyright owner's prepublication assignment to the publisher of all rights in exchange for a payment or an advance on royalties.

grantor. (17c) **1.** Someone who conveys property to another. **2.** SETTLOR (1).

grantor–grantee index. See INDEX (1).

grantor-retained annuity trust. See TRUST (3).

grantor-retained income trust. See TRUST (3).

grantor-retained unitrust. See TRUST (3).

grantor's lien. See *vendor's lien* (1) under LIEN.

grant to uses. (1865) *Hist.* A conveyance of legal title to real property to one person for the benefit of another. • If, for example, A conveyed land to B and his heirs to the use of C and his heirs, B — the feoffee to uses — acquired seisin in and had possession of the land and was considered the legal owner. C — the cestui que use — was considered the equitable owner of the land and was entitled to the land's rents, profits, and benefits. Because the cestui que use did not have seisin in the land, he was not subject to feudal payments. From the 13th century forward, the grant to uses was an increasingly popular mode of conveyance. See CESTUI QUE USE; STATUTE OF USES; USE (4).

grass hearth. *Hist.* A tenant's customary service, consisting of the tenant's bringing his plow to the lord's land and plowing it for one day.

grassum (**gras**-əm). [Law Latin] (14c) **1.** *Scots law.* A single lease payment made in addition to the periodic payments due under an agreement; a payment in addition to the rent paid by a tenant to the landlord. Pl. **grassums.**

> "Grassum; an anticipation of rent in a gross or lump sum . . . . In questions with singular successors there is no limitation of the power to take grassums, only the rent must not be thereby diminished so as to be altogether elusory. In regard, however, to lands under entail, the heir in possession must administer the estate *secundum bonum et aequum*, taking no more of the annually accruing rents and profits than he leaves to descend to his successors. Hence, grassums, as being, in effect, anticipations of the future rents, to the prejudice of succeeding heirs, are held to be struck at by the prohibition against alienation." William Bell, *Bell's Dictionary and Digest of the Laws of Scotland* 492 (George Watson ed., 7th ed. 1890).

2. GRESSUME. **3.** GERSUM (1). **4.** GERSUM (2).

GRAT. *abbr.* See *grantor-retained annuity trust* under TRUST (3).

gratia curiae (**gray**-shee-ə **kyoor**-ee-ee *or* -ɪ). [Latin] (18c) Favor of the court. Cf. RIGOR JURIS.

gratia mandatarii (**gray**-shee-ə man-də-**tair**-ee-ɪ). [Latin] *Hist.* For the sake of the mandatary. • The phrase appeared in reference to the irrevocability of a mandate given solely for the mandatary's benefit.

> "Gratia mandatarii . . . . In the general case, a mandate, being for the benefit of the mandant, may be recalled by him at pleasure. Mandates, however, which are granted solely for the sake (or advantage) of the mandatary, such as the mandate contained in the registration clause of a deed, whereby the granter gives authority for its registration, are not revocable." John Trayner, *Trayner's Latin Maxims* 237 (4th ed. 1894).

gratification. (16c) *Archaic.* A voluntarily given reward or recompense for a service or benefit; a gratuity.

gratis (**grat**-is *or* **gray**-tis), *adj.* (15c) Free; without compensation.

gratis dictum. See DICTUM.

gratuitous (grə-**t[y]oo**-ə-təs), *adj.* (17c) **1.** Done or performed without obligation to do so; given without consideration in circumstances that do not otherwise impose a duty <gratuitous promise>. Cf. ONEROUS (3). **2.** Done unnecessarily <gratuitous obscenities>. — **gratuity,** *n.* — **gratuitousness,** *n.*

gratuitous agent. See AGENT.

gratuitous allowance. See ALLOWANCE (1).

gratuitous assignee. See ASSIGNEE.

gratuitous assignment. See ASSIGNMENT (2).

gratuitous bailment. See BAILMENT (1).

gratuitous benefit. See BENEFIT (4).

gratuitous consideration. See CONSIDERATION (1).

gratuitous contract. See CONTRACT.

gratuitous deed. See *deed of gift* under DEED.

gratuitous deposit. 1. See *gratuitous bailment* under BAILMENT (1). **2.** See DEPOSIT (5).

gratuitous gift. See GIFT.

gratuitous promise. See PROMISE.

gratuitous service. See SERVICE (3).

gratuitous surety. See SURETY (1).

gratuitous trust. See *donative trust* under TRUST (3).

gratuity. See BOUNTY.

gravamen (grə-**vay**-mən). (17c) The substantial point or essence of a claim, grievance, or complaint.

gravatio (grə-**vay**-shee-oh). [Law Latin] *Hist.* An accusation or impeachment.

grave-robbing. The criminal act of opening a tomb or grave to steal valuables or corpses, or any part of a corpse. — Also termed *grave robbery.*

graveyard insurance. See *wager insurance* under INSURANCE.

gravitas (**grav**-i-tahs *or* -tas). [Latin] Seriousness.

gravity. (16c) Seriousness of harm, an offense, etc., as judged from an objective legal standpoint.

graymail. (1978) A criminal defendant's threat to reveal classified information during the trial in the hope of forcing the government to drop the criminal charge. Cf. BLACKMAIL (1); GREENMAIL (1), (2); FEEMAIL.

gray market. See MARKET.

gray-market adoption. See *private adoption* under ADOPTION (1).

gray-market goods. See PARALLEL IMPORTS.

gray mule case. See WHITEHORSE CASE.

Greaser Law. *Hist. Slang.* A California anti-vagrancy statute that gave law-enforcement authorities broad discretion to arrest, fine, and jail people of Hispanic appearance who had no visible means of support. • This statute was enacted in 1855 and repealed in the mid-20th century. The term *greaser* is racially derogatory. — Also termed *Greaser Act.*

great bodily injury. See *serious bodily injury* under INJURY.

great care. See CARE (2).

Great Charter. See MAGNA CARTA.

great diligence. See DILIGENCE (2).

greater weight of the evidence. See PREPONDERANCE OF THE EVIDENCE.

great fee. See FEE (2).

Great Inquest. See *grand inquest* (2) under INQUEST (4).

Great Lakes rule. (1933) *Maritime law.* The statutory provision that an admiralty litigant is entitled to a jury trial in a contract or tort action if the lawsuit arises from the operation of a commercial vessel on the Great Lakes or the navigable waters connecting them. *See* 28 USCA § 1873.

Great Law, The. *Hist.* The first code of laws enacted in Pennsylvania, in 1682. • The code was enacted by an assembly called by William Penn.

great pond. A body of water larger than ten acres, and thus subject to public ownership. • This term applies in Maine, New Hampshire, and Massachusetts. — Also termed *public pond.*

Great Rolls of the Exchequer. See PIPE ROLLS.

great seal. See SEAL.

Great Survey. See *grand inquest* (2) under INQUEST (4).

great tithe. See TITHE.

Great Waters Program. A scheme created by Congress in 1990 to make the Environmental Protection Agency more directly responsible for protecting large bodies of fresh water and coastal waters from environmental harm caused by air pollution. Clean Air Act Amendments of 1990, 42 USCA § 7412(m).

Great Writ. See HABEAS CORPUS.

gree (gree), *n.* [Law French] (13c) *Hist.* A satisfaction received by a party for an offense or injury against the party. See SATISFACTION (1).

> "Gree comes of the French word *gree*, good liking: and it signifies in our law, contentment or satisfaction; as in the statute of 1 R. 2, c. 15, to make gree to the parties is to give them contentment or satisfaction for an offence done unto them." *Termes de la Ley* 247 (1st Am. ed. 1812).

greenback, *n.* (ca. 1862) *Slang.* A legal-tender note of the United States; any note issued by a federal reserve bank. • The term was coined in 1862 when the backs of American paper currency were first printed in green ink.

greenbelt. An undeveloped area of land around a city, esp. one set aside for parks or farmland or preserved as natural wilderness.

green card. (1962) A registration card evidencing a resident alien's status as a permanent U.S. resident. • The card was provided on green paper from 1946 to 1964, and in Spanish it was known as *la tarjeta verde* as early as 1952. By 1962, the translation had made its way into American English.

green-card marriage. See MARRIAGE (1).

green-circle wage. See WAGE.

Green Cloth. See BOARD OF GREEN CLOTH.

greenfields agreement. (1988) *Labor law.* A contract between a union and a new business that hasn't yet hired employees.

greenfield site. (ca. 1962) **1.** Land that has never been developed. • Such land is presumably uncontaminated. Cf. BROWNFIELD SITE. **2.** Property acquired as an investment, esp. for establishing a new business.

green goods. (1887) *Slang.* Counterfeit money.

greenhouse effect. The warming of a planet's surface and lower atmosphere caused by the presence of heat-trapping gases in the atmosphere. See GREENHOUSE GAS.

greenhouse gas. A gas or gaseous compound that allows sunlight to pass through to a planet's surface but absorbs and traps in the lower atmosphere heat radiated back from the surface. See GREENHOUSE EFFECT.

green-light, *vb.* (1941) To give permission or authority to proceed.

greenmail. (1983) **1.** The act or practice of buying enough stock in a company to threaten a hostile takeover and then selling the stock back to the corporation at an inflated price. **2.** The money paid for stock in the corporation's buyback. Cf. BLACKMAIL (1); FEEMAIL; GRAYMAIL. **3.** A shareholder's act of filing or threatening to file a derivative action and then seeking a disproportionate settlement.

green paper. (1967) A first-draft document of a policy proposal made for consultation, discussion, and debate to produce a consensus for the next draft; specif., a document produced by the British Government to set forth for discussion particular proposals for possible legislation. Cf. WHITE PAPER; GREEN PAPER ON COPYRIGHT AND THE CHALLENGE OF TECHNOLOGY.

Green Paper on Copyright and the Challenge of Technology. *Copyright.* A 1988 European Commission publication that laid out a plan to harmonize the copyright laws of member countries, esp. laws relating to information technology. • The Green Paper was followed by a series of directives that mandated uniform policies regarding copyright and new technologies. — Usu. shortened to *Green Paper.*

Green River ordinance. (1934) A local licensing law that protects residents from unwanted peddlers and salespersons, typically by prohibiting door-to-door solicitations without prior consent. • The ordinance takes its name from Green River, Wyoming, which enacted the first such law in the early 20th century before others came into vogue during the 1930s and 1940s throughout the United States.

greenspace. **1.** In urban planning, an open area with grass and trees and sometimes other vegetation, set aside for aesthetic or recreational purposes. — Also termed *urban open space.* Cf. GREENBELT. **2.** OPEN-SPACE PRESERVE.

green wax. (*pl.*) *Hist.* An Exchequer order (an *estreat*) directing a sheriff to collect the fines and amercements listed in the order. • The name derives from the color of the wax the Exchequer used on the estreat to certify its authenticity. See ESTREAT.

greeting, *n.* (*often pl.*) (bef. 12c) The salutation on a message, often a legal instrument such as a subpoena. • The word has persisted in many locales on writs, subpoenas, and even military-draft notices — perhaps through irony.

greffe. *Feudal law.* **1.** The register of the court of a fief. **2.** A prothonotary's office.

greffier (**gref**-ee-ər *or* gref-**yay**), *n.* [Law French] (16c) *Hist.* A registrar, esp. of a court; the court recordkeeper.

Gregorian calendar. See NEW STYLE.

Gregorian Code. See CODEX GREGORIANUS.

gremio juris, in. See IN GREMIO JURIS.

gremio legis, in. See IN GREMIO LEGIS.

Grenville Act. *Hist.* A 1770 English statute that transferred jurisdiction over parliamentary election petitions from the whole House of Commons to select committees. • The Act, sponsored by George Grenville, was designed to depoliticize the resolution of disputed elections. It was repealed in 1828 when it was superseded by statutes that gave to the courts jurisdiction over election disputes.

G reorganization. See REORGANIZATION (2).

Gresham's law. (19c) The principle that a debased currency will drive out valuable currency. • This economic principle is popularly attributed to Sir Thomas Gresham (1519–1579), even though earlier writers such as Oresme and Copernicus discussed it.

gressume (**gres**-əm). *Hist.* A fine paid by a copyhold tenant upon the transfer of a copyhold estate, esp. upon the death of the lord. — Also spelled *grasson*; *grassum*; *grossome*; *gersum.*

Gretna-Green marriage. See MARRIAGE (1).

greve. See REEVE.

grey market. See *gray market* under MARKET.

greywater. See WATER.

GRF. *abbr.* See *general revenue fund* under FUND (1).

grievance, *n.* (14c) **1.** An injury, injustice, or wrong that potentially gives ground for a complaint <a petition for a redress of grievances>. **2.** The complaint itself <the client filed a grievance with the state-bar committee>. **3.** *Labor law.* A complaint that is filed by an employee or the employee's union representative and that usu. concerns working conditions, esp. an alleged violation of a collective-bargaining agreement. See *grievance arbitration* under ARBITRATION; GRIEVANCE PROCEDURE. **4.** The belief that one has been treated unfairly or illegally.

grievance arbitration. See ARBITRATION.

grievance procedure. (1937) *Labor law.* A process, consisting of several steps, for the resolution of an employee's complaint. • The first step usu. occurs at the shop level and is handled by a supervisor. If the grievance is not resolved at the first step, the grievance is appealed in successive steps that vary among collective-bargaining agreements. The final step of the procedure is grievance arbitration. See *grievance arbitration* under ARBITRATION; GRIEVANCE (3).

grievant, *n.* (1958) *Labor law.* An employee who files a grievance and submits it to the grievance procedure outlined in a collective-bargaining agreement.

grieve, *vb.* To contest under a grievance procedure <the union urged the employee to grieve the suspension>. — **grievable,** *adj.*

grievous, *adj.* (13c) **1.** Very serious in causing great pain and suffering; inducing intense suffering or affliction <a grievous accident>. **2.** Causing mischief or destruction; fierce <grievous sharks>. **3.** Expressing or involving grief or distress <grievous misgivings>.

grievous bodily harm. See *serious bodily injury* under INJURY.

grift, *vb.* (1915) *Slang.* To obtain money or other property illicitly by adroit use of a scam, confidence game, or other fraudulent means. — **grifter,** *n.*

GRIT. *abbr.* See *grantor-retained income trust* under TRUST (3).

grith, *n. Hist.* **1.** Security; peace. **2.** KING'S PEACE. **3.** A place of security; sanctuary. See CHURCHGRITH.

grithbreach, *n. Hist.* **1.** BREACH OF THE PEACE. **2.** The penalty for breach of the peace.

grithman, *n. Hist.* Someone who has taken sanctuary.

GRM. *abbr.* GROSS-RENT MULTIPLIER.

grog-shop. See DRAM SHOP.

groin-grabbing. (1991) The act of fondling or touching a person's genitals through the person's clothing, usu. quickly, and esp. in a crowded space or while walking along a sidewalk in the opposite direction from the person. — Also termed *groin-groping.*

gross, *adj.* **1.** Conspicuous by reason of size or other attention-getting qualities; esp., obvious by reason of magnitude <a gross Corinthian column>. **2.** Undiminished by deduction; entire <gross profits>. **3.** Not specific or detailed; general <a gross estimate>. **4.** Coarse in meaning or sense <gross slang>. **5.** Repulsive in behavior or appearance; sickening <a gross fellow with gross habits>. **6.** Beyond all reasonable measure; flagrant <a gross injustice>.

gross, *n.* **1.** See *gross income* under INCOME. **2.** A group of 144 items; a dozen dozen.

gross, easement in. See *easement in gross* under EASEMENT.

gross adventure. See ADVENTURE.

gross average. See *general average* under AVERAGE (3).

gross charter. See CHARTER (8).

gross charterparty. See *gross charter* under CHARTER (8).

gross damages. See DAMAGES.

gross domestic product. (1951) The total value of all goods and services produced in a country during one year, apart from income received from abroad. — Abbr. GDP.

gross earnings. See *gross income* under INCOME.

gross estate. See ESTATE (3).

gross income. See INCOME.

gross-income multiplier. See GROSS-RENT MULTIPLIER.

gross-income tax. See TAX.

gross interest. See INTEREST (3).

gross lease. See LEASE.

grossly inadequate consideration. See CONSIDERATION (1).

gross margin. See *gross profit margin* under PROFIT MARGIN.

gross misconduct in the workplace. See MISCONDUCT (1).

gross misdemeanor. See MISDEMEANOR (1).

gross national product. (1947) The market value of all goods and services produced in a country within a year, used to measure a country's economic development and wealth. — Abbr. GNP.

gross neglect of duty. See DESERTION.

gross negligence. See NEGLIGENCE.

grossome. *Hist.* See GRESSUME.

gross premium. See PREMIUM (1).

gross profit. See PROFIT (1).

gross profit margin. See PROFIT MARGIN.

gross receipts. *Tax.* The total amount of money or other consideration received by a business taxpayer for goods sold or services performed in a taxable year, before deductions. IRC (26 USCA) § 448; 26 CFR § 1.448-1T (f)(2)(iv).

gross-receipts tax. See TAX.

gross-rent multiplier. (1960) The ratio between the market value of rent-producing property and its annual gross rental income. • The gross-rent multiplier is used as a method to estimate a property's market value. — Abbr. GRM. — Also termed *gross-income multiplier.*

gross sales. See SALE.

gross spread. See SPREAD (4).

gross up, *vb.* (1987) *Tax. Slang.* To add back to a decedent's gross estate the gift taxes paid by the decedent or the decedent's estate on gifts made by the decedent or the decedent's spouse during the three-year period preceding the decedent's death. IRC (26 USCA) § 2035.

gross weight. See WEIGHT (1).

gross yield. See YIELD.

Grotian (**groh**-shən), *n. International law.* An adherent to the basic tenants of Hugo Grotius (also known as Hugo van Groot — 1583–1645), who has become known as the "Father of International Law," who conceived of natural law as being independent of any divine power, and who formulated rules governing the relations between states by relying heavily on principles derived from Roman law.

> "The Grotians occupy an intermediate position between the pure Naturalists and the Positivists. They maintain the distinction elaborated by Grotius between the Natural Law of Nations, and the positive or voluntary law, based on custom, emphasizing the importance of both." G.W. Keeton, *The Elementary Principles of Jurisprudence* 244 (2d ed. 1949).

ground, *n.* (*usu. pl.*) (13c) The reason or point that something (as a legal claim or argument) relies on for validity <grounds for divorce> <several grounds for appeal>.

ground, *vb.* (14c) **1.** To provide a basis for (something, such as a legal claim or argument) <the decision was grounded on public policy>. **2.** To base (something, such as a legal principle or judicial decision) on <the court grounded the decision on common law> <strict liability is grounded on public policy>.

groundage (**grown**-dij), *n.* (15c) *Hist. Maritime law.* A tax or toll levied on a vessel lying in port; the tax or toll so paid.

ground annual. **1.** See *ground rent* under RENT (1). **2.** See FEU DUTY.

ground landlord. (17c) *Hist.* The grantor of an estate on which ground rent is reserved. See *ground rent* under RENT (1).

ground-law. A fundamental law. See FUNDAMENTAL LAW; *basic norm* under NORM.

> "If the power of a sovereign or of a government is limited by a ground-law, written or unwritten, a treaty cannot override that constitution." Theodore D. Woolsey, *Introduction to the Study of International Law* § 103, at 167 (5th ed. 1878).

ground lease. See LEASE.

groundless, *adj.* (17c) (Of a legal claim or argument) lacking a basis or a rationale <groundless cause of action>. See FRIVOLOUS.

ground of action. (17c) **1.** CAUSE OF ACTION (1). **2.** CAUSE OF ACTION (2).

ground rent. See RENT (1).

ground-rent lease. See *ground lease* under LEASE.

grounds for appeal. (18c) A trial court's errors of procedure or law that form a basis for asking an appellate court to review a case. — Also termed *grounds for review.*

groundswell. (1817) **1.** A broad, deep heaving of the sea, as in a tsunami. **2.** A sudden and usu. spontaneous increase in a particular sentiment among people, esp. involving political opinion.

groundwater. See WATER (1).

groundwork. (16c) Preliminary thought and activity that must occur before a plan can be successfully executed; a preparatory foundation.

ground writ. See WRIT.

group annuity. See ANNUITY.

group art unit. (1970) *Patents.* A U.S. Patent and Trademark Office division consisting of patent examiners who specialize in a particular invention's subject matter.

group boycott. See BOYCOTT.

group director. (1973) *Patents.* The person responsible for directing the operations of an examining group within the U.S. Patent and Trademark Office.

grouping-of-contacts theory. See CENTER-OF-GRAVITY DOCTRINE.

group insurance. See INSURANCE.

group libel. See LIBEL (2).

group litigation. (1936) A set of lawsuits on behalf of or against numerous persons recognized as one litigating entity, such as a civil-rights group.

group policy. See *master policy* under INSURANCE POLICY.

group right. See RIGHT.

growing crops. See CROPS.

growing-equity mortgage. See MORTGAGE.

growth. (1952) The gain, increase, or expansion in value of securities or of a business.

growth company. See COMPANY.

growth fund. See MUTUAL FUND.

growth industry. (1954) An industry or business sector whose revenues and earnings are rising at a faster rate than average.

growth management. (1974) *Land-use planning.* The regulation of a community's rate of growth through zoning ordinances, impact fees, and other measures. See ZONING.

growth stock. See STOCK.

GRT. *abbr.* See *gross-receipts tax* under TAX.

gruarii (groo-**air**-ee-I), *n. pl. Hist.* The principal officers of a forest. • These officers were charged with guarding and enforcing restrictions on the use of timber. See FOREST.

grubstake contract. See CONTRACT.

grubstaking contract. See *grubstake contract* under CONTRACT.

grundnorm. (*often cap.*) A fundamental norm, order, or rule that forms an underlying basis for a legal system. See *basic norm* under NORM; FUNDAMENTAL LAW.

> "In most civilized communities, the irresistible power of the State restrains itself by what German jurisprudence calls 'auto-limitation,' growing from that hidden tap-root of the social tree — a root lying deeper than any explicit constitution — which in Kelsen's system is the *Grundnorm.* We have very clear examples of it in our own society. The Sovereign possesses prerogative powers which it is almost inconceivable that she should ever exercise. Our textbooks tell us that the legislative power of Parliament is unlimited, but everybody knows that it is in fact limited by a multitude of restraints which lie ultimately in the 'consent of the governed.' No ruling authority in the civilized world dares be merely authoritarian." Carleton Kemp Allen, *Aspects of Justice* 72 (1958).

Grundy Tariff. See SMOOT–HAWLEY TARIFF ACT.

GRUT. *abbr.* See *grantor-retained unitrust* under TRUST (3).

GSA. *abbr.* GENERAL SERVICES ADMINISTRATION.

GSR. *abbr.* Gunshot residue.

GST. *abbr.* See *generation-skipping tax* under TAX.

GST supertrust. See *dynasty trust* under TRUST (3).

GSTT. *abbr.* See *generation-skipping transfer tax* under TAX.

GSW. *abbr.* Gunshot wound.

Guantanamo Bay. A U.S. military prison within the Guantanamo Bay Naval Base, Cuba. • The naval base was established in 1903. After the terrorist attacks of September 11, 2001, a prison camp was created on the base and opened in January 2002. Its declared purpose was to detain suspects and prisoners connected with terrorist acts or groups who were considered extraordinarily dangerous and to provide an optimal setting for interrogating them before releasing or prosecuting them or returning them to other nations. — Also termed *Gitmo*; *Guantanamo Bay detention camp*; *G-Bay.*

guarantee (gar-ən-**tee**), *n.* (17c) **1.** The assurance that a contract or legal act will be duly carried out. **2.** GUARANTY (1).

> "In practice, *guarantee*, n., is the usual term, seen often, for example, in the context of consumer warranties or other assurances of quality or performance. *Guaranty*, by contrast, is now used primarily in financial and banking contexts in the sense 'a promise to answer for the debt of another.' *Guaranty* is now rarely seen in nonlegal writing, whether in BrE or AmE." Bryan A. Garner, *Garner's Dictionary of Legal Usage* 399 (3d ed. 2011).

3. Something given or existing as security, such as to fulfill a future engagement or a condition subsequent. **4.** One to whom a guaranty is made. — Also termed (in sense 4) *creditor.* — Also spelled (in senses 1–3) *guaranty.*

> "A guarantee is a collateral engagement to answer for the debt, default or miscarriage of another person. The person who gives the guarantee, is termed the *surety* or *guarantor*; the person to whom it is given, the *creditor* or *guarantee*; and the person whose debt, default or miscarriage is the foundation of the guarantee, the *principal debtor*, or simply, *the principal.*" Henry Anselm de Colyar, *A Treatise on the Law of Guarantees and of Principal & Surety* 1 (3d ed. 1897).

guarantee, *vb.* (18c) **1.** To assume a suretyship obligation; to agree to answer for a debt or default. **2.** To promise that a contract or legal act will be duly carried out. **3.** To give security to.

guarantee bond. See *guaranty bond* under BOND (2).

guarantee clause. (1887) **1.** A provision in a contract, deed, or mortgage by which one person promises to pay the obligation of another. **2.** (*cap.*) U.S. Const. art. IV, § 4, under which the federal government ensures for the states both a republican form of government and protection from invasion or internal insurrection. • The U.S. Supreme Court has consistently treated claims under the Guarantee Clause as nonjusticiable political questions. *See Pacific States Tel. & Tel. Co. v. Oregon,* 223 U.S. 118, 82 S.Ct. 224 (1912). — Also termed (in sense 2) *Republican Form of Government Clause.*

guaranteed annual wage plan. (1981) *Labor law.* A wage-payment method in which the employer agrees either to pay employees a predetermined minimum sum each year or to provide a minimum number of hours of employment each year. • A wide variety of guaranteed annual wage plans are used. For example, an employer may agree to pay employees wages for each week in the year, even though work may not be available at certain times of the year. The purpose of such a plan is to provide a stable labor force year-round.

guaranteed bond. See BOND (3).

guaranteed dividend. See DIVIDEND.

guaranteed investment contract. See INVESTMENT CONTRACT.

guaranteed-purchase contract. See *guaranteed-sale contract* under CONTRACT.

guaranteed-sale contract. See CONTRACT.

guaranteed stock. See STOCK.

guarantee of title. (1836) *Property.* A warranty that the title to a piece of real property is vested in a particular person, given by a title company or abstract company, and based on a title searcher's opinion of the status of the property's title. The guarantee is usu. backed by insurance to cover damages resulting from the title searcher's oversight or negligence in finding recorded legal instruments. Cf. *title insurance* under INSURANCE.

guarantee stock. See STOCK.

guarantee treaty. See TREATY (1).

guarantor. (19c) Someone who makes a guaranty or gives security for a debt. • While a surety's liability begins with that of the principal, a guarantor's liability does not begin until the principal debtor is in default. — Also termed *guarantor surety.* Cf. SURETY (1).

"A guarantor either guarantees payment or collection, depending on the words used. 'Payment guaranteed' or equivalent words added to a signature mean the signer will pay the instrument if it is not paid when due without a need for the holder to resort to another party. 'Collection guaranteed' means resort must first be had to others." Fred H. Miller & Alvin C. Harrell, *The Law of Modern Payment Systems* § 5.02, at 195 (2003).

▸ **coguarantor.** (1875) One of two or more guarantors for the same debt.

"Little is gained by the use of the term coguarantor, inasmuch as most of the problems that arise, where either this term or the term cosurety would be proper, involve the relations between the guarantors and sureties themselves. The rights of cosureties and coguarantors inter se and their rights against the principal being the same, there is no advantage in attempting to suggest the form of their promise to the obligee by the use of the terms cosureties or coguarantors." Herschel W. Arant, *Handbook of the Law of Suretyship and Guaranty* 12 (1931).

▸ **guarantor of collectibility.** (1881) Someone who guarantees a debtor's solvency and is under a duty to pay only if the creditor is unable to collect from the principal debtor after exhausting all legal remedies, including demand, suit, judgment, and any supplementary proceedings.

▸ **guarantor of payment.** (1814) Someone who guarantees payment of a negotiable instrument when it is due without the holder first seeking payment from another party. • A guarantor of payment is liable only if "payment guaranteed" or equivalent words are added to the guarantor's indorsement.

▸ **officious guarantor.** Someone who guarantees a debt without being requested or having a legal duty to do so and who therefore may claim no reimbursement of money paid on the guaranty. See OFFICIOUS INTERMEDDLER.

guarantor surety. See GUARANTOR.

guaranty (**gar**-ən-tee), *n.* (16c) **1.** A promise to answer for the payment of some debt, or the performance of some duty, in case of the failure of another who is liable in the first instance; a collateral undertaking by one person to be answerable for the payment of some debt or performance of some duty or contract for another person who stands first bound to pay or perform. — Also termed *contract of guaranty.* • The term is most common in finance and banking contexts and is often contrasted with *warranty.* While a warranty relates to things (not persons), is not collateral, and need not be in writing, a guaranty is an undertaking that a person will pay or do some act, is collateral to the duty of the primary obligor, and must be in writing. The term is also contrasted with *surety.* A guaranty can exist only where there is some principal or substantive liability to which it is collateral. If there is no debt, default, or miscarriage of a third person either present or prospective, there can be no guaranty. On the spelling of *guaranty* vs. *guarantee,* see the quotation at GUARANTEE (2). — Also termed *guaranty contract.* See SURETYSHIP.

"Both guaranty and warranty are undertakings by one party to another to indemnify the party assured against some possible default or defect. But a guaranty relates to the future, as a collateral promise designed to protect the promisee from loss in case another fails to perform his duty. A warranty relates to the present or past, and is an independent promise designed to protect the promisee from loss in the event that the facts warranted are not as the promisor states them to be when the contract is made. A warranty is broken as soon as it is made if the facts are not as represented, and is enforceable though oral; whereas a guaranty is not breached until a future default occurs, and is unenforceable unless in writing." Laurence P. Simpson, *Handbook on the Law of Suretyship* 23 (1950).

"A transaction of guaranty involves at least three parties: a promisor, a creditor (the person to whom the promise is made), and a debtor — although at the time the promise is made, the person denominated the 'creditor' need not have extended the credit to the person denominated as the 'debtor.' The usual guaranty situation arises when the promisor makes a promise to the creditor either as to the solvency of the debtor or as to the payment of the debt." 38 Am. Jur. 2d *Guaranty* § 1, at 996 (1968).

▸ **absolute guaranty.** (18c) **1.** An unqualified promise that the principal will pay or perform. **2.** A guarantor's contractual promise to perform some act for the creditor — such as paying money or delivering property — if the principal debtor defaults.

▸ **conditional guaranty.** (1813) A guaranty that requires the performance of some condition by the creditor before the guarantor will become liable.

▸ **contingent guaranty.** (1843) A guaranty in which the guarantor will not be liable unless a specified event occurs.

▸ **continuing guaranty.** (1817) A guaranty that governs a course of dealing for an indefinite time or by a succession of credits. — Also termed *open guaranty.*

▸ **cross-stream guaranty.** (1986) A guaranty made by a company for the obligation of another company when both are owned by the same parent company or individual.

▸ **downstream guaranty.** (1986) **1.** A parent corporation's guaranty of a subsidiary's obligations. **2.** A guaranty made for a company by a guarantor who is also a partner, member, or stockholder of the company.

▸ **general guaranty.** (17c) **1.** A guaranty addressed to no specific person, so that anyone who acts on it can enforce it. **2.** A guaranty for the principal's default on obligations that the principal undertakes with anyone.

▸ **good-guy guaranty.** (2004) A limited guaranty by a third-person that leased property or collateral will be kept in good condition and returned to the lessor or lender if a default occurs. • Good-guy guaranties are most commonly associated with real-property leases. — Also written *good-guy guarantee.* — Also termed *good-guy clause.*

▸ **guaranty of collection.** (1843) A guaranty that is conditioned on the creditor's having first exhausted legal remedies against the principal debtor before suing the guarantor. See *guarantor of collectibility* under GUARANTOR.

▸ **guaranty of payment.** (1811) A guaranty that is not conditioned on the creditor's exhausting legal remedies against the principal debtor before suing the guarantor. See *guarantor of payment* under GUARANTOR.

▸ **irrevocable guaranty** (i-rev-ə-kə-bəl). (1898) A guaranty that cannot be terminated unless the other parties consent.

▸ **limited guaranty.** (1831) An agreement to answer for a debt arising from a single transaction. — Also termed *noncontinuing guaranty.*

▸ **open guaranty.** See *continuing guaranty.*

▸ **revocable guaranty.** (1936) A guaranty that the guarantor may terminate without any other party's consent.

▸ **special guaranty.** (18c) **1.** A guaranty addressed to a particular person or group of persons, who are the only ones who can enforce it. **2.** A guaranty that names a definite person as obligee and that can be accepted only by the person named.

▸ **specific guaranty.** (18c) A guaranty of a single debt or obligation.

▸ **upstream guaranty.** (1986) A guaranty made by a corporate subsidiary for the parent corporation's obligations.

2. GUARANTEE (1).

guaranty bond. See BOND (2).

guaranty company. See *surety company* under COMPANY.

guaranty contract. See GUARANTY (1).

guaranty fund. See FUND (1).

guaranty insurance. See INSURANCE.

guaranty letter of credit. See *standby letter of credit* under LETTER OF CREDIT.

guaranty stock. See STOCK.

guaranty treaty. See *guarantee treaty* under TREATY (1).

guard. See DOORKEEPER.

guardage. (17c) *Hist.* **1.** WARDSHIP. **2.** GUARDIANSHIP.

guard dog. See DOG (1).

guardhouse lawyer. See JAILHOUSE LAWYER.

guardian, *n.* (15c) **1.** Someone who has the legal authority and duty to care for another's person or property, esp. because of the other's infancy, incapacity, or disability. • A guardian may be appointed either for all purposes or for a specific purpose. — Abbr. gdn. — Also termed *custodian.* See CONSERVATOR. Cf. WARD (1).

▸ **chancery guardian** (**chan**-sər-ee). (1856) A guardian appointed by a court of chancery to manage both the person and the estate of the ward.

▸ **domestic guardian.** (17c) A guardian appointed in the state in which the ward is domiciled.

▸ **foreign guardian.** (1844) A guardian appointed by a court in a state other than the one in which the ward is domiciled. • A foreign guardian cares for the ward's property that is located in the state of appointment.

▸ **general guardian.** (16c) A guardian who has general care and control of the ward's person and estate.

▸ **guardian ad litem** (ad **lɪ**-tem *or* -təm). (18c) A guardian, usu. a lawyer, appointed by the court to appear in a lawsuit on behalf of an incompetent or minor party. — Abbr. GAL. — Also termed *special advocate*; *special guardian*; *law guardian*; *case guardian*; *litigation guardian.* Cf. NEXT FRIEND; *attorney ad litem* under ATTORNEY.

> "[I]t is necessary to determine whether the lawyer has been appointed as a guardian *ad litem* (GAL) charged with representing the child's best interests, or as an advocate, serving as counsel to the child . . . . From the distinction between guardian and advocate flow a series of important consequences, including such matters as whether the attorney may file motions and examine witnesses, whether the attorney may file a report with the court, and whether the attorney may testify. Moreover, in most jurisdictions a GAL has an absolute quasi-judicial immunity for lawsuits for negligence . . . . Although a non-lawyer cannot serve as counsel to the child, such an individual might be a GAL or 'special advocate' in some states. Courts have struggled to clarify these roles, and define how children's representatives may participate in different types of proceedings." Homer H. Clark Jr. & Ann Laquer Estin, *Domestic Relations: Cases and Problems* 1078 (6th ed. 2000).

▸ **guardian by custom.** (17c) *Hist.* Someone who, under local custom, had the right to act as a minor's guardian.

▸ **guardian by election.** (1846) A guardian chosen by a ward who would otherwise be without one.

▸ **guardian by estoppel.** See *quasi-guardian.*

▸ **guardian by nature.** (17c) *Hist.* The parental guardian of an heir apparent who has not yet reached the age of 21. • Although the common law recognized the father as a guardian by nature and the mother as one only after the father's death, most states have given both parents equal rights of guardianship over their children (see, e.g., N.Y. Dom. Rel. Law § 81). — Also termed *natural guardian.*

▸ **guardian by nurture.** (17c) *Hist.* The parental guardian of a child who is not the heir apparent, lasting until the child reaches the age of 14. — Also termed *guardian for nurture.*

> "There are also guardians *for nurture,* which are, of course, the father or mother, till the infant attains the age of fourteen years and, in default of father or mother, the ordinary usually assigns some discreet persons to take care of the infant's personal estate, and to provide for his maintenance and education." 1 William Blackstone, *Commentaries on the Laws of England* 449 (1765).

▸ **guardian by statute.** See *statutory guardian.*

▸ **guardian *de son tort*** (də sawn [*or* son] **tor**[t]). See *quasi-guardian.*

▸ **guardian for nurture.** See *guardian by nurture.*

▸ **guardian in chivalry.** (16c) *Hist.* A guardian who, by virtue of knight's service, had custody of the body and lands of a male heir under 21 or a female heir under 14. • This type of guardian had no accountability for profits.

▸ **guardian in socage.** (16c) *New York law.* A guardian for a child who has acquired lands by descent. • A guardian is usu. a relative who could not possibly inherit from the child. This type of guardianship applies to both the person and the property of the child and, historically, lasted only until the child was 14, when the child was allowed to select a guardian; now it lasts until the child reaches age 18 or is emancipated.

▸ **guardian of property.** See *guardian of the estate.*

▸ **guardian of the estate.** (1839) A guardian responsible for taking care of the property of someone who is incapable of caring for his or her own property because of infancy, incapacity, or disability. — Also termed *guardian of property.*

▸ **guardian of the person.** (16c) A guardian responsible for taking care of someone who is incapable of caring for himself or herself because of infancy, incapacity, or disability.

▸ **law guardian.** See *guardian ad litem.*

▸ **litigation guardian.** See *guardian ad litem.*

▸ **natural guardian.** (18c) **1.** *Hist.* The eldest son's father, until the son turned 21. **2.** In the absence of statute, the father of a legitimate child until the child reaches the age of 21. • A father of illegitimate children may be appointed as their guardian upon the mother's death. **3.** Most commonly and by statute, either the father or the mother of a minor child — each bearing the title simultaneously. • If one parent dies, the other is the natural guardian. See *guardian by nature.*

▸ **partial guardian.** (1976) A guardian whose rights, duties, and powers are strictly limited to those specified in a court order.

▸ **quasi-guardian.** (1832) A guardian who assumes that role without any authority. • Such a person may be made to account as guardian. — Also termed *guardian by estoppel; guardian de son tort.*

▸ **special guardian.** (17c) **1.** A guardian who has special or limited powers over the ward's person or estate. • Examples are guardians who have custody of the estate but not of the person, those who have custody of the person but not of the estate, and guardians ad litem. — Also termed (in civil law) *curator ad hoc.* See CURATOR (2). **2.** See *guardian ad litem.*

▸ **standby guardian.** (1969) A parent-designated guardian who is appointed to assume responsibility for a child at a future date if the child's parent becomes incapable of caring for the child but who does not divest the parent of custodial rights. • Several states have enacted statutes providing for a standby guardian in the case of a terminally ill single parent. A standby guardian assumes responsibility for a child during periods of the parent's incapacity and upon the parent's death.

▸ **statutory guardian.** (18c) A guardian appointed by a court having special statutory jurisdiction. — Also termed *guardian by statute.*

▸ **successor guardian.** (1927) An alternate guardian named in a parent's will against the possibility that the first nominee cannot or will not serve as guardian.

▸ **testamentary guardian.** (18c) A guardian nominated by a parent's will for the person and property of a child until the child reaches the age of majority.

2. *Hist.* A mesne lord who was entitled to treat an infant heir's lands for all practical purposes as the lord's own, enjoying fully their use and whatever profits they yielded. • At the end of the guardianship, when the heir reached majority, no accounting was owed by the mesne lord.

guardian of the poor. (17c) *Hist.* A person in charge of the relief and maintenance of the poor in a parish. • Guardians of the poor administered poor-relief funds raised under the Poor Relief Act of 1601. • The function is now performed by local authorities. — Also termed *overseer of the poor.*

guardian of the spiritualities. (17c) *Eccles. law.* Someone who exercises the spiritual and ecclesiastical jurisdiction of a diocese during a vacancy in the see or the absence of the bishop.

guardian of the temporalities. (17c) *Eccles. law.* The person to whom custody of the secular possessions of a vacant see or abbey is committed by the Crown. • Temporalities (secular possessions) are the land, revenue, and tenements that archbishops and bishops have had annexed to their sees.

guardian's deed. See DEED.

guardianship. (15c) **1.** The fiduciary relationship between a guardian and a ward or other incapacitated person, whereby the guardian assumes the power to make decisions about the ward's person or property. • A guardianship is almost always an involuntary procedure imposed by the state on the ward. Cf. CONSERVATOR; INTERDICTION. **2.** The duties and responsibilities of a guardian. — Also termed *guardage.*

▸ **ancillary guardianship.** (1899) A subservient and subsidiary guardianship in a state other than that in which guardianship is originally granted.

▸ **guardianship of the estate.** (1816) A guardianship in which the guardian can make decisions only about matters regarding the ward's assets and property.

▸ **guardianship of the person.** (1839) A guardianship in which the guardian is authorized to make all significant decisions affecting the ward's well-being, including the ward's physical custody, education, health, activities, personal relationships, and general welfare.

▸ **plenary guardianship.** (1984) A guardianship in which the guardian can make decisions about both the ward's estate and the ward's person.

▸ **standby guardianship.** (1983) A guardianship in which a parent designates a guardian to assume responsibility for a child at a future date, if the child's parent becomes incapable of caring for the child, but without divesting the parent of custodial rights.

guardianship action. See ACTION (4).

guardianship hearing. See HEARING.

guardianship order. (1920) A court's appointment of a fiduciary to make decisions about the care and management of a ward's person or property.

gubernator navis (g[y]oo-bər-**nay**-tər **nay**-vis). [Latin "ship helmsman"] *Roman law.* The pilot or steersman of a ship. • The *gubernator navis* could be sued for damages if he negligently caused a collision.

guerrilla warfare. See WARFARE.

guest. (13c) **1.** Someone who is entertained or to whom hospitality is extended. **2.** Someone who pays for services at an establishment, esp. a hotel or restaurant. **3.** In an automobile statute, one who accepts a ride in a motor vehicle without paying for it or conferring any other substantial benefit on the owner or operator, but accepts the ride for his or her own pleasure or business.

▸ **business guest.** (1942) *Torts.* See BUSINESS VISITOR (1).

▸ **social guest.** (1901) *Torts.* A guest who is invited to enter or remain on another person's property primarily for private entertainment as opposed to entertainment open to the general public. See LICENSEE (2).

guest statute. (1914) A law that bars a nonpaying passenger in a noncommercial vehicle from suing the host-driver for damages resulting from the driver's ordinary negligence. • Though once common, guest statutes remain in force in only a few states. — Also termed *automobile-guest statute.* Cf. FAMILY-PURPOSE RULE.

guidage. (15c) *Hist.* **1.** A toll or fee for guiding a traveler through strange or dangerous territory. **2.** The act of guiding a traveler through strange or dangerous territory.

guide dog. See *service dog* under DOG (1).

guild. (14c) **1.** A group of persons sharing a common vocation who unite to regulate the affairs of their trade in order to protect and promote their common vocation; specif., a voluntary society or fraternity of persons employed in the same trade or craft, formed for the mutual benefit and protection of its members, who pay a fee (a *geld* or *gild*) for its general expenses. — Also termed *trade guild.* **2.** *Hist.* A company or corporation.

guildhall. (14c) *Hist.* **1.** The meeting place of a guild. — Also spelled *gildhall.* **2.** The chief hall of a city, used for holding court and the meetings of the municipal corporation.

guild rent. See RENT (1).

guilt, *n.* (bef. 12c) The fact, state, or condition of having committed a wrong, esp. a crime; esp., a judicial finding to this effect <the state's burden was to prove guilt beyond a reasonable doubt>. Cf. INNOCENCE.

▸ **third-party guilt.** The fact, state, or condition of someone's having committed a wrong other than the defendant; esp., a judicial finding to this effect.

guiltless, *adj.* (14c) **1.** Free from guilt; not having committed a wrong <guiltless of the crime>. **2.** Having the quality or appearance of innocence <even though she confessed, the defendant looked guiltless>.

guilt phase. (1960) The part of a criminal trial during which the fact-finder determines whether the defendant committed a crime. Cf. PENALTY PHASE.

guilty, *adj.* (bef. 12c) **1.** Having committed a crime; responsible for a crime <guilty of armed robbery>. **2.** Responsible for a civil wrong, such as a tort or breach of contract <guilty of fraudulent misrepresentation>. — **guiltily,** *adv.*

guilty, *n.* **1.** A plea of a criminal defendant who does not contest the charges. **2.** A jury verdict convicting the defendant of the crime charged.

guilty but mentally ill. (1975) A jury verdict convicting the defendant of the crime charged but recognizing that the defendant's actions may have been related to mental illness that falls short of insanity. • Guilty-but-mentally-ill verdicts are treated like other guilty verdicts in that the defendant is still subject to imprisonment. *See* Jane Campbell Moriarty, ed., *The Role of Mental Illness in Criminal Trials* 3:17, 3-41 (2001) (3 vols.). — Abbr. GBMI; GMI. — Also termed *guilty but insane; guilty of the act, but so insane as not to be responsible.* See INSANITY DEFENSE.

> "Under the Michigan act, a defendant will be found not guilty by reason of insanity if he is determined to have been legally insane at the time of the offense. In contrast, a defendant will be found guilty but mentally ill when he is guilty of an offense and it is determined that he was mentally ill rather than legally insane at the time the offense was committed. A defendant found not guilty by reason of insanity is subjected to a psychiatric examination and is then either committed or discharged. A defendant found guilty but mentally ill, however, is treated for the present mental illness and also receives the sentence that would be imposed on one simply found 'guilty' of the crime. The effect of the scheme is to require hospitalization or confinement of all mentally ill offenders, including those who do not meet the standards establishing legal insanity." Jonas Robitscher & Andrew Ky Haynes, *In Defense of the Insanity Defense*, 31 Emory L.J. 9, 16 (1982).

guilty mind. See MENS REA.

guilty plea. See PLEA (1).

guilty verdict. See VERDICT (1).

gumshoe. (1900) *Slang.* A private detective.

gun. See FIREARM.

gun-control law. (1968) A statute or ordinance that regulates the sale, possession, or use of firearms. • Gun-control laws vary widely among the states, and many cities have gun-control ordinances. Federal law restricts and regulates the illegal sale, possession, and use of firearms. 18 USCA §§ 921–930. — Often shortened to *gun control.* See BRADY ACT.

Gun-Free Schools Act. A federal law designed to eliminate weapons in schools. 20 USCA § 7151. • The Gun-Free Schools Act provides that each state receiving federal funds for elementary and secondary schools must require school districts to expel for one year any student found to have brought a weapon to school. The Act does, however, provide for a case-by-case modification of the expulsion requirement.

gun-jumping. (1969) *Slang.* The act of unlawfully soliciting the public's purchase of securities before the SEC approves a registration statement; the making of offers after the filing of a registration statement, but before its effective date, when such offers violate the Securities Act. — Also termed *conditioning the market.* See REGISTRATION STATEMENT.

gunner. *Slang.* A law-school student who aggressively and overconfidently asks and attempts to answer questions during class, usu. arousing the disgust and derision of classmates.

GVR. *abbr.* Granted, vacated, and remanded. • The U.S. Supreme Court sometimes issues this mandate — granting certiorari, vacating the conviction, and remanding the case based on the certiorari petition alone.

gwalstow (**gwawl**-stoh). [fr. Old English *gwal* "gallows" + *stow* "place"] *Hist.* A place where criminals were executed.

gynecocracy (gɪ-nə-**kok**-rə-see *also* jin-ə *or* jɪ-nə-). (17c) Government by a woman or by women. — Also spelled *gynaecocracy.* Cf. MATRIARCHY.

gyve (jɪv). (14c) (*usu. pl.*) *Hist.* A shackle for the leg.

H

H. *abbr.* **1.** HOUSE OF REPRESENTATIVES. **2.** House report. **3.** See *house bill* under BILL (3). **4.** In the citation of English statutes, a named Henry. **5.** In the Year Books, the Hilary term. See YEAR BOOKS (3); HILARY SITTINGS. **6.** In tax assessments and other such official reports, a house.

habe (**hay**-bee). [Law Latin] A form of the salutatory expression *ave* ("hail"). — Also termed *have* (**hay**-vee).

habeas corpora juratorum (**hay**-bee-əs **kor**-pər-ə joor-ə-**tor**-əm). [Law Latin "that you have the bodies of the jurors"] (17c) *Hist.* A writ commanding the sheriff to bring in jurors and, if necessary, to take their lands and goods as security to ensure their attendance in court for a trial setting. • This writ issued from the Court of Common Pleas and served the same purpose as a *distringas juratores* in the King's Bench. The writ was abolished in 1852.

habeas corpus (**hay**-bee-əs **kor**-pəs). [Law Latin "that you have the body"] (18c) A writ employed to bring a person before a court, most frequently to ensure that the person's imprisonment or detention is not illegal (*habeas corpus ad subjiciendum*). • In addition to being used to test the legality of an arrest or commitment, the writ may be used to obtain judicial review of (1) the regularity of the extradition process, (2) the right to or amount of bail, or (3) the jurisdiction of a court that has imposed a criminal sentence. — Abbr. H.C. — Sometimes shortened to *habeas.* — Also termed *writ of habeas corpus*; *Great Writ.*

> "The writ of habeas corpus, by which the legal authority under which a person may be detained can be challenged, is of immemorial antiquity. After a checkered career in which it was involved in the struggles between the common-law courts and the Courts of Chancery and the Star Chamber, as well as in the conflicts between Parliament and the crown, the protection of the writ was firmly written into English law by the Habeas Corpus Act of 1679. Today it is said to be 'perhaps the most important writ known to the constitutional law of England . . . .'" Charles Alan Wright, *The Law of Federal Courts* § 53, at 350 (5th ed. 1994) (quoting *Secretary of State for Home Affairs v. O'Brien,* [1923] A.C. 603, 609).

▸ ***habeas corpus ad deliberandum et recipiendum*** (**hay**-bee-əs **kor**-pəs ad di-lib-ə-**ran**-dəm et ri-sip-ee-**en**-dəm). [Law Latin "that you have the body to consider and receive"] (17c) *Hist.* A writ used to remove a person for trial from one county to the county where the person allegedly committed the offense. Cf. EXTRADITION.

▸ ***habeas corpus ad faciendum et recipiendum*** (**hay**-bee-əs **kor**-pəs ad fay-shee-**en**-dəm et ri-sip-ee-**en**-dəm). [Law Latin "that you have the body to do and receive"] (17c) *Hist.* A writ used in civil cases to remove the case, and also the body of the defendant, from an inferior court to a superior court. — Also termed *habeas corpus cum causa.* See CERTIORARI.

▸ ***habeas corpus ad prosequendum*** (**hay**-bee-əs **kor**-pəs ad prahs-ə-**kwen**-dəm). [Law Latin "that you have the body to prosecute"] (1865) A writ used in criminal cases to bring before a court a prisoner to be tried on charges other than those for which the prisoner is currently being confined.

▸ ***habeas corpus ad respondendum*** (**hay**-bee-əs **kor**-pəs ad ree-spon-**den**-dəm). [Law Latin "that you have the body to respond"] (17c) *Hist.* A writ used in civil cases to remove a person from one court's custody into that of another court, in which the person may then be sued.

▸ ***habeas corpus ad satisfaciendum*** (**hay**-bee-əs **kor**-pəs ad sat-is-fay-shee-**en**-dəm). [Law Latin "that you have the body to make amends"] (17c) *English law.* In England, a writ used to bring a prisoner against whom a judgment has been entered to some superior court so that the plaintiff can proceed to execute that judgment.

▸ ***habeas corpus ad subjiciendum*** (**hay**-bee-əs **kor**-pəs ad səb-jis-ee-**en**-dəm). [Law Latin "that you have the body to submit to"] (17c) A writ directed to someone detaining another person and commanding that the detainee be brought to court. — Usu. shortened to *habeas corpus.*

▸ ***habeas corpus ad testificandum*** (**hay**-bee-əs **kor**-pəs ad tes-ti-fi-**kan**-dəm). [Law Latin "that you have the body to testify"] (17c) *Hist.* A writ used in civil and criminal cases to bring a prisoner to court to testify.

▸ ***habeas corpus cum causa.*** See *habeas corpus ad faciendum et recipiendum.*

Habeas Corpus Act. 1. One of the four great charters of English liberty (31 Car. 2, 1679), securing to English subjects speedy relief from all unlawful imprisonments. • The other three great charters are Magna Carta, the Petition of Right (3 Car. 1, 1628), and the Bill of Rights (1 Wm. & M. 1689). The Habeas Corpus Act does not apply in Scotland; the corresponding statute is the Criminal Procedure Act of 1701, ch. 6. **2.** A statute deriving ultimately from the English statute and enacted in the United States as a constitutional guarantee of personal liberty.

Habeas Corpus Clause. *Constitutional law.* The constitutional provision allowing suspension of the writ of habeas corpus only when necessary to protect the public in times of rebellion or invasion. U.S. Const. art. I, § 9, cl. 2.

habendum clause (hə-**ben**-dəm). (1829) **1.** The part of an instrument, such as a deed or will, that defines the extent of the interest being granted and any conditions affecting the grant. • The introductory words to the clause are ordinarily *to have and to hold.* — Also termed *to-have-and-to-hold clause.* **2.** *Oil & gas.* The provision in an oil-and-gas lease defining how long the interest granted to the lessee will extend. • Modern oil-and-gas leases typically provide for a primary term — a fixed number of years during which the lessee has no obligation to develop the premises — and a secondary term (for "so long thereafter as oil and gas produced") once development takes place. Most jurisdictions require production of paying quantities to keep the lease in effect. — Often shortened to *habendum.* — Also termed *term clause.*

> "*Habendum.* — This part of the deed was originally used to determine the interest granted, or to lessen, enlarge, explain or qualify the premises. But it cannot perform the

office of divesting the estate already vested by the deed; for it is void if it be repugnant to the estate granted. It has degenerated into a mere useless form; and the premises now contain the specification of the estate granted, and the deed becomes effectual without any habendum. If, however, the premises should be merely descriptive, and no estate mentioned, then the habendum becomes efficient to declare the intention; and it will rebut any implication arising from the silence of the premises." 4 James Kent, *Commentaries on American Law* *468 (George Comstock ed., 11th ed. 1866).

habendum et tenendum (hə-**ben**-dəm et tə-**nen**-dəm). [Law Latin] *Hist.* To have and to hold. • This formal phrase appeared in land deeds and defined the estate or interest being transferred. See HABENDUM CLAUSE; TENENDUM.

habentes homines (hə-**ben**-teez **hom**-ə-neez), *n.* [Law Latin "men who have"] *Hist.* Rich men. — Also termed *foestingmen.*

habere (hə-**beer**-ee), *vb.* [Latin "to have"] *Roman law.* To have (the right to) something. • This term was sometimes distinguished from *tenere* (to hold) and *possidere* (to possess), with *habere* referring to the right, *tenere* to the fact, and *possidere* to both.

"'Habere' has two meanings; for we say that the owner of a thing 'has' it and also that a nonowner who holds the thing 'has' it. Lastly, we use the word in relation to property deposited with us." *Digest of Justinian* 45.1.38.9 (Ulpian, Ad Sabinum 49).

habere facias possessionem (hə-**beer**-ee **fay**-shee-əs pə-zes[h]-ee-**oh**-nəm), *n.* [Law Latin "that you cause to have possession"] (17c) *Hist.* A writ giving a successful ejectment-action plaintiff the possession of the recovered land. • If the sheriff delivered more than the person was entitled to, a writ of *rehabere facias seisinam* could compel the sheriff to return the excess. — Often shortened to *habere facias* or *hab. fa.*

habere facias seisinam (hə-**beer**-ee **fay**-shee-əs **see**-zi-nəm), *n.* [Law Latin "that you cause to have seisin"] (16c) *Hist.* A writ of execution commanding the sheriff to give the applicant seisin of the recovered land. • This writ was the proper process for giving seisin of a freehold, as distinguished from giving only a chattel interest in land. See SEISIN.

habere facias visum (hə-**beer**-ee **fay**-shee-əs **vɪ**-səm *or* -zəm), *n.* [Law Latin "that you cause to have a view"] (17c) *Hist.* A writ allowing a litigant to inspect the lands in controversy.

habere licere (hə-**beer**-ee li-**seer**-ee), *vb.* [Latin "to allow to have"] *Roman law.* To stipulate to a purchaser's right to possess and enjoy property undisturbed. • The term denoted a seller's duty to indemnify the purchaser if the purchaser was evicted. An evicted purchaser could raise an action on the stipulation or, under Justinian, an *actio ex empto* against the seller.

hab. fa. *abbr.* HABERE FACIAS POSSESSIONEM.

habili et competente forma (**hab**-ə-lɪ et kom-pə-**ten**-tee **for**-mə). [Latin] *Hist.* In a fit and competent manner.

habili modo (**hab**-ə-lɪ **moh**-doh). [Latin] *Hist.* In a fit manner; sufficiently.

habilis causa transferendi dominii (**hab**-ə-lis **kaw**-zə trans-fə-**ren**-dɪ də-**min**-ee-ɪ). [Law Latin] *Hist.* An adequate title for transferring the property. • The phrase appeared in reference to the grantor's power and intention to convey the property; the title had to be sufficient to support the conveyance of property. — Also spelled *habilis causa transferrendi dominii.*

habit. 1. Something that a person does often, generally with little or no thought. **2.** A person's usual behavior. **3.** A strong physical or mental need for an addictive substance, such as a narcotic, alcohol, or nicotine.

"Habit is of a dark and subtle nature; it silently spreads its influence over the mind, which it weakens by degrees, until at length it is, in some cases, and these too of no rare deception, totally corrupted and debased; it usually comes in a pleasing form, that at once engages the imagination and lays the understanding asleep; by the gentleness of its operations it arouses no fear; by the smoothness of its voice it lulls every suspicion. When by these means it has secured its conquest, it so artfully entwines itself with the system of our nature, that we fondly imagine it to be a part of ourselves, nor do we cease to cherish it, until we fall [to] the miserable sacrifice of its power." [John Raithby,] *The Study and Practice of the Law* 388 (1798).

habitability. (1890) The condition of a building in which inhabitants can live free of serious defects that might harm health and safety <lack of running water adversely affects the apartment's habitability>.

habitability, implied warranty of. See *implied warranty of habitability* under WARRANTY (2).

habitable (**hab**-ə-tə-bəl), *adj.* (15c) (Of a place) good enough for people to live in; providing a minimal level of safety and comfort so as to make for passable living conditions.

habitancy (**hab**-ə-tən-see). (18c) **1.** DOMICILE (1). **2.** RESIDENCE.

habit and repute. [fr. Latin *habitus et reputatus* "held and reputed"] (17c) *Scots law.* A person's reputation. • Marriage could formerly be constituted if one was generally held and reputed to be married. And it was an aggravation of theft to be held and reputed a thief.

habitant (a-bee-**ton**), *n.* [French] (18c) **1.** *Hist. French law.* A person holding land in feudal tenure from a seignior. **2.** A native of Canada of French descent, esp. one from the farming class.

habitat. 1. A human dwelling. **2.** *Environmental law.* The place where a particular species of animal or plant is normally found.

▸ **critical habitat.** A specified geographic area containing features vital for conserving a threatened or endangered species. • The habitat may require special protection and management, and may include areas necessary for a species' recovery, even though it is not currently inhabited.

▸ **riparian habitat.** A habitat along the banks or shore of a body of water.

habitatio (hab-ə-**tay**-shee-oh), *n.* [Latin "dwelling"] *Roman law.* The right to dwell (in a place); the right of free residence in another's house; an urban servitude. • This right was usu. given by will and treated as a personal servitude. See *urban servitude* under SERVITUDE (2). Cf. USUFRUCT; USUS (1).

habitation. (14c) **1.** The activity of inhabiting; occupancy. **2.** A dwelling place; a domicile. **3.** *Civil law.* A nontransferable and nonheritable right to dwell in the house of another. La. Civ. Code art. 630. See RESIDENCE; DOMICILE. Cf. USUFRUCT.

habit evidence. See EVIDENCE.

habitual, *adj.* (17c) **1.** Customary; usual <habitual late sleeper>. **2.** Recidivist <habitual offender>.

habitual criminal. See RECIDIVIST.

habitual drunkard. See DRUNKARD.

Habitual Drunkards' Act. *English law.* An 1879 statute that legalized the confinement of male alcoholics. Cf. INEBRIATE ACT.

habitual offender. 1. See RECIDIVIST. **2.** See OFFENDER.

habitual residence. See RESIDENCE.

hable (**ab**-əl), *n.* [Law French] *Hist.* A port or harbor; a station for ships.

hacienda particular (ah-**syen**-dah [*or* hah-see-**en**-də] pahr-tee-koo-**lahr**), *n. Spanish law.* Private property.

hacienda pública (ah-**syen**-dah [*or* hah-see-**en**-də] **poo**-blee-kah), *n. Spanish law.* **1.** Public revenue or assets. **2.** The public treasury; economic ministry.

hacienda social (ah-**syen**-dah [*or* hah-see-**en**-də] soh-**syahl**), *n. Spanish law.* Property belonging to a corporation or partnership.

hack, *vb.* (1984) To surreptitiously break into the computer, network, servers, or database of another person or organization. Cf. CRACK.

hacker, *n.* (1976) Someone who surreptitiously uses or changes the information in another's computer system.

had. Commenced or begun, as used in a statute providing that no legal proceeding may be *had* (usu. followed by the words *or maintained*) <no action for foreclosure may be had or maintained until the debtor has been given at least 30 days' notice>.

hadbote. See BOTE (3).

hadgonel (**had**-gə-nel), *n. Hist.* A tax or mulct. See MULCT.

***Hadley v. Baxendale* rule.** (1930) *Contracts.* The principle that consequential damages will be awarded for breach of contract only if it was foreseeable at the time of contracting that this type of damage would result from the breach. *Hadley v. Baxendale,* 9 Exch. 341 (1854). • *Hadley v. Baxendale* is best known for its impact on a nonbreaching party's ability to recover consequential damages, but the case also confirmed the principle that the nonbreaching party may recover damages that arise naturally from the breach. See *foreseeable damages* under DAMAGES.

> "The rationale of the decision appears in Baron Alderson's noted statement of what came to be known as the two rules of *Hadley v. Baxendale.* The first rule was that the injured party may recover damages for loss that 'may fairly and reasonably be considered [as] arising naturally, i.e., according to the usual course of things, from such breach of contract itself.' . . . The second and more significant rule went to recovery of damages for loss other than that 'arising naturally' — to recovery of what have come to be known as 'consequential' damages. . . . By introducing this requirement of 'contemplation' for the recovery of consequential damages, the court imposed an important new limitation on the scope of recovery that juries could allow for breach of contract. The result was to impose a more severe limitation on the recovery of damages for breach of contract than that applicable to actions in tort or for breach of warranty, in which substantial or proximate cause is the test." E. Allan Farnsworth, *Contracts* § 12.14, at 822–23 (3d ed. 1999).

had-not test. See BUT-FOR TEST.

haec est conventio (**heek** est kən-**ven**-shee-oh). [Law Latin] *Hist.* This is the agreement. • These formal words commonly prefaced written agreements.

haec est finalis concordia (**heek** est fi-**nay**-lis kən-**kor**-dee-ə). [Law Latin] *Hist.* This is the final agreement. • These were the words that began a fine, a fictitious judicial proceeding formerly in use as a mode of conveying land. See FOOT OF THE FINE; FINE.

haec verba. See IN HAEC VERBA.

haeredibus et assignatis quibuscunque (hə-**red**-i-bəs et as-ig-**nay**-tis kwib-əs-**kəng**-kwee). [Law Latin] *Scots law.* To heirs and assignees whomsoever. • This was a simple destination phrase.

haereditas. See HEREDITAS.

haeres. See HERES.

haeretico comburendo. See DE HAERETICO COMBURENDO.

hafne (**hay**-vən), *n.* [Old English] (bef. 12c) A haven or port.

hafne court. *Hist. English law.* Haven courts; one of several courts anciently held in certain ports in England.

Hague Academy of International Law (hayg). A center for advanced studies in international law, both public and private, whose purpose is to facilitate the comprehensive and impartial examination of problems of international legal relations. • It was founded in the Netherlands in 1923 on the initiative of the Carnegie Endowment for International Peace and the Institut de Droit International. — Also termed *Académie de Droit International de La Haye.*

Hague Convention. The short name for any one of the many numerous international conventions that address different legal issues and attempt to standardize procedures between countries.

Hague Convention on Protection of Children and Cooperation in Respect of Intercountry Adoption. A 1993 international agreement to establish uniform procedures governing intercountry adoptions. • The Convention has not been widely adopted. The U.S. has signed but not ratified it.

Hague Convention on the Civil Aspects of International Child Abduction. An international convention, concluded in 1980, seeking to counteract cross-border child-snatching by noncustodial parents. • This convention created a legal mechanism available to parents seeking the return of, or access to, their children. Its purposes are to secure the prompt return of children who have been wrongfully taken from one country to another and to enforce custody and visitation rights in the contracting countries. The procedure is summary in nature and does not contemplate continuing hearings on the merits of a dispute. More than 80 countries are parties to the Convention, including the United States. 42 USCA §§ 11601–11610.

Hague Convention on the Service Abroad of Judicial and Extrajudicial Documents. An international convention, concluded on November 15, 1965, governing procedures for effecting service of process in a foreign country. • More than 35 countries are parties to the Convention, including the United States.

Hague Convention on the Taking of Evidence Abroad in Civil or Commercial Matters. An international convention, concluded on October 26, 1968, establishing procedures for obtaining evidence in a foreign country, such as taking a deposition abroad. • More than 27 countries are parties, including the United States.

Hague Rules. *Maritime law.* An international agreement adopted in 1924 at the International Convention for the Unification of Certain Rules of Law Relating to Bills of Lading, the primary purpose being to limit carriers' liability for certain losses.

Hague Tribunal. *Int'l law.* A permanent court of arbitration established by the Hague Peace Conference of 1899 to facilitate immediate recourse to arbitration to settle international differences. • The court was given jurisdiction over all international arbitrations, unless the parties agreed to institute a special tribunal. An international bureau was likewise established to serve as a registry for the court and to issue communications about the court's meetings. The court is "permanent" only in the sense that there is a permanent list of members from whom arbitrators in a given case are selected. Apart from making minor changes in the court, the Second Hague Conference of 1907 provided that, of the two arbitrators appointed by each party, only one should be a national of the appointing state.

haircut. (1986) **1.** *Securities.* The discount required by a regulatory authority on the value of stock that a brokerage firm holds in its own account at the time of filing a monthly report about the firm's net capital condition. **2.** The difference between the amount of a loan and the market value of the collateral securing the loan. **3.** In a Chapter 11 reorganization, the percentage of a principal debt that is "forgiven" by a creditor as the debtor reorganizes the debt by extending the time in which to pay it and reducing the total amount to be paid. See *haircut reorganization* under REORGANIZATION (1). **4.** The margin in a repurchase transaction — that is, the difference between the actual yield on the bid quote and the price used in the repurchase agreement. **5.** The margin requirement of a member of a futures or options exchange when undertaking a transaction. **6.** A commission or fee paid to a broker, salesperson, etc. — Sometimes shortened to *cut.*

haircut reorganization. See REORGANIZATION (1).

hairsplitting, *n.* (1826) The act or an instance of citing unimportant differences or oversubtle details while making an argument; the making of or insisting on trivial distinctions. — **hairsplitting,** *adj.*

Haitian divorce. See *Mexican divorce* under DIVORCE.

hale, *v.* (17c) To compel (a person) to go, esp. to court <hale a party into court>.

half, *n.* (bef. 12c) One of two equal parts into which a thing can be divided; MOIETY.

half blood. See BLOOD.

half brother. See BROTHER.

halfendeal (**hahv**-ən-deel), *n.* [fr. Law Latin *halfendele*] (bef. 12c) *Hist.* Half a thing; a moiety. — Also spelled *half endeal; half-endeal.*

half-life, *n. Finance.* The time until 50% of the principal of a bond issue has been redeemed.

half-mark. See DEMIMARK.

half nephew. See NEPHEW (1).

half niece. See NIECE.

half orphan. See ORPHAN (2).

half pay. See PAY (1).

half-pilotage. See PILOTAGE.

half plus one. (1887) *Parliamentary law.* A common but inexact (and often inaccurate) approximation for a majority. • For a body with 100 members, a majority is indeed half plus one, or 51. But for a body with an odd number of members, "half plus one" would not be a whole number. So "a simple majority" is a better choice for designating majority rule. — Also termed *50 percent plus one.* See MAJORITY (2).

half-proof. (16c) *Civil law.* **1.** Proof established by one witness, or by a private instrument. See UNUS NULLUS RULE. **2.** Prima facie proof that is nonetheless insufficient to support a sentence or decree.

half-seal. (16c) *Hist.* A seal used in the Court of Chancery to mark commissions to the Court of Delegates on the appeal of an ecclesiastical or maritime case. • The use of the seal ended when the Court of Delegates was abolished in 1832. See COURT OF DELEGATES.

half-secret trust. See TRUST (3).

half section. See SECTION.

half sister. See SISTER.

half-stock. See STOCK.

half-timer. (1865) *Hist. English law.* In England, a child excused from full-time attendance at school under the Factory and Workshop Act of 1908 so that the child could work part-time in a factory or workshop. • The Factory and Workshop Acts from 1901 to 1911 were repealed by the Factory and Workshop (Cotton Cloth Factories) Act of 1929 and the Factories Act of 1937.

half-time submission. (2005) *English law. Slang.* The assertion by the defense after the prosecution or plaintiff has rested its case and before the defense opens its case that the evidence is insufficient to prove the case. See NO CASE TO ANSWER.

half-tongue. (15c) *Hist. English law.* A jury empaneled to try an alien, and composed half of one nationality and half of another. • The use of this type of jury ended in 1914 with the passage of the Status of Aliens Act.

halfway house. (1970) A transitional housing facility designed to rehabilitate people who have recently left a prison or medical-care facility, or who otherwise need help in adjusting to unsupervised living. — Also termed *residential treatment center; residential treatment facility; residential community treatment center.*

half-year. See YEAR.

Halifax law. (16c) **1.** *Hist. English law.* The summary and unauthorized trial and execution (usu. by decapitation) of a person accused of a crime. • This term comes from the parish of Halifax, in England, where — according to custom in the forest of Hardwick — this form of private justice was anciently practiced by the free burghers against people accused of stealing. Thieves could be condemned to death by beheading on market day. The last such case is said to have occurred in 1650. — Also termed *gibbet law; Halifax inquest.* **2.** LYNCH LAW; more broadly, an irrevocable punishment carried out after a summary trial.

haligemot. See HALLMOTE.

hall. (bef. 12c) **1.** *Hist.* A manor house or chief mansion house. • It was called a *hall* because the magistrate's court was typically held there. **2.** A building or room of considerable size, used for meetings of bodies such as public assemblies, conventions, and courts. **3.** *Parliamentary law.* The room or other space in which a deliberative assembly meets.

hallage (**hawl**-ij), *n.* (17c) *Hist.* **1.** A fee or toll due for goods or merchandise sold in a hall used as a market. **2.** A toll payable to the lord of a fair or market for commodities sold in the common hall.

hallazgo (ah-**yahz**-goh), *n.* [Spanish] *Spanish law.* **1.** The finding and taking possession of ownerless property. **2.** The first occupant recognized by law.

halle-gemot (**hawl**-gə-moht), *n.* See HALLMOTE.

halligan tool. See HOOLIGAN TOOL.

hallmark. (18c) **1.** An official stamp affixed by goldsmiths and silversmiths on articles made of gold or silver to show genuineness. **2.** A mark of genuineness.

hallmoot. See HALLMOTE.

hallmote (**hahl**-moht), *n.* (bef. 12c) **1.** *Hist.* A court baron; specif., an annual court, presided over by the lord of the manor, to decide civil disputes between feudal tenants. • The court was usu. held in the manor's great hall. See COURT BARON. **2.** A trade guild's commercial court, in which guild members were tried for trade-related offenses against the guild. See GUILD (1). **3.** A convention of citizens in their public hall. — Also termed *folkmote.* — Also spelled (in senses 1–3) *hallmoot*; *halmote*; *halymote*; *halle-gemot*; *haligemote.* **4.** (Erroneously) an ecclesiastical court. • Although this definition appears in many secular legal dictionaries, it is unheard of in canon law. In sense 4, it is often (erroneously) spelled *holymote.*

halmote. See HALLMOTE.

halymote (**hal**-ə-moht). See HALLMOTE.

ham (ham *or* am). (bef. 12c) **1.** A place of dwelling; a village. • This word now usu. appears in compound form at the end of place names, such as *Buckingham* and *Cheltenham.* **2.** A small (esp. enclosed) pasture; a piece of land. — Also spelled *hamm.* Cf. HAMLET.

hamburger helper. [fr. a commercial cooking mix] *Criminal law. Slang.* Any dilutant commonly added to narcotics by drug dealers to add volume to controlled substances.

hamel. See HAMLET.

hameleta. See HAMLET.

hamesucken (**haym**-sək-ən), *n.* (bef. 12c) *Scots law.* **1.** Assault by a burglar on a householder within the house after breaking in to commit the assault or to commit theft. **2.** The crime of housebreaking or burglary accompanied by violence. • Deriving from Anglo-Saxon law (*hāmsōcn*), this term literally meant "breaching the peace of another's home." — Also spelled *hamesecken*; *hamesoken.* — Also termed *hamfare.*

> "Burglary, or nocturnal housebreaking, *burgi latrocinium*, which by our ancient law was called *hamesecken*, as it is in Scotland to this day, has always been looked upon as a very heinous offence . . . ." 4 William Blackstone, *Commentaries on the Laws of England* 223 (1769).

hamfare. See HAMESUCKEN.

hamlet. (bef. 12c) A small village; a part or member of a vill. • A hamlet in a rural community might consist of no more than a store, a church, and a few residences. — Also termed *hamel*; *hameleta*; *hamleta.* See VILL. Cf. HAM.

hamleta. See HAMLET.

hammer, *n.* **1.** The gavel used at an auction. **2.** *Slang.* A forced sale; a sale at public auction <her jewelry was brought to the hammer>. See *forced sale* under SALE.

hammer price. See PRICE.

Hammurabi, Code of. See CODE OF HAMMURABI.

hanaper (**han**-ə-pər), *n.* [Law Latin *hanaperium* "hamper"] (14c) *Hist.* **1.** A basket or hamper used by the Chancery to store writs and returns. **2.** The treasury of the Chancery, funded from the fees charged for writs. Cf. FISCUS.

Hanaper Office. *Hist.* An office formerly belonging to the common-law jurisdiction of the Chancery Court. • The term derives from the storage of writs in a hamper (*in hanaperio*). Crown writs, on the other hand, were stored in the Petty Bag Office. The Hanaper Office was abolished in 1842. See BAGA.

hand, *n.* (bef. 12c) **1.** A person's handwriting; HANDWRITING (1) <a holographic will must be in the testator's hand>. **2.** An instrumental part <he had a hand in the crime>. **3.** Someone who performs some work or labor <Hickory was one of the Gales' hired hands>. **4.** (*usu. pl.*) Possession <the cocaine was now in the hands of the police>. **5.** Assistance <the carpenter lent a hand to the project>. **6.** A measure of length equal to four inches, used in measuring the height of equines, esp. horses <the pony stood ten hands tall>. **7.** *Hist.* An oath <he gave his hand on the matter>. **8.** One of two sides or aspects of an issue or argument <on the one hand we can argue for imprisonment, on the other for leniency>.

hand, *vb.* (17c) To give; to deliver <he handed over the documents>.

handbill. (18c) A written or printed notice displayed, handed out, or posted, usu. to inform interested people of an event or of something to be done. • Posting and distribution of handbills is regulated by ordinance or statute in most localities.

handcuff, *n.* (*usu. pl.*) A pair of metal rings, usu. connected by a chair or bar, that can be fastened around the wrists as a physical restraint; MANACLE.

hand down, *vb.* (17c) To announce or file (a judgment) in a case. • The term was originally used in connection with an appellate-court opinion sent to the court below; it was later expanded to include any decision by a court on a case or point under consideration.

handfasting. 1. See *handfast marriage* (3) under MARRIAGE (1). **2.** See *handfast marriage* (4) under MARRIAGE (1).

handfast marriage. See MARRIAGE (1).

Hand formula. (1972) A balancing test for determining whether conduct has created an unreasonable risk of harm, first formulated by Judge Learned Hand in *U.S. v. Carroll Towing Co.*, 159 F.2d 169 (2d Cir. 1947). • Under this test, an actor is negligent if the burden of taking adequate precautions against the harm is outweighed by the probable gravity of the harm multiplied by the probability that the harm will occur. — Also termed *Learned Hand formula*; *Learned Hand test*; *Hand test*; *Hand rule.*

"The legal standard applicable to most unintentional tort cases is that of negligence, defined by Judge Learned Hand as follows: the defendant is guilty of negligence if the loss caused by the accident, multiplied by the probability of the accident's occurring, exceeds the burden of the precautions that the defendant might have taken to avert it. This is an economic test. . . . Although the Hand formula is of relatively recent origin, the method that it capsulizes has been the basic one used to determine negligence ever since negligence was first adopted as the standard to govern accident cases." Richard A. Posner, *Economic Analysis of Law* § 6.2, at 122–23 (2d ed. 1977).

handhabend (**hand**-hab-ənd), *adj.* (14c) *Hist.* (Of a thief) caught in possession of a stolen item.

handhabend, *n.* [fr. Old English *aet haebbendre handa* "at or with a having hand"] (bef. 12c) *Hist.* **1.** The bearing of stolen goods in hand or about the person. **2.** A thief or another person caught carrying stolen goods. **3.** Jurisdiction to try a person caught carrying stolen goods. — Also spelled *hand-habende.* Cf. BACKBEREND.

handicap. See DISABILITY (2).

handicapped access. See ACCESS (1).

handicapped child. See CHILD.

handle, *n. Securities.* The whole number of the price of a bid or offer of securities (e.g., 35), used esp. when the price has an additional fraction added to the whole number (e.g., 35⅝).

hand money. (1842) Money paid in hand to bind a bargain; earnest money paid in cash. See EARNEST MONEY.

hand note. See NOTE (1).

Hand rule. See HAND FORMULA.

handsale. (17c) *Hist.* **1.** A sale memorialized by shaking hands. **2.** The earnest money given immediately after the handshake to memorialize a sale. • In some northern European countries, shaking hands was necessary to bind a bargain. This custom sometimes persists for oral contracts. The Latin phrase for *handsale* was *venditio per mutuam manuum complexionem* ("a sale by the mutual joining of hands"). — Also spelled *handsel.*

hands-off agreement. (1986) A noncompete contractual provision between an employer and a former employee prohibiting the employee from using information learned during his or her employment to divert or to steal customers from the former employer.

hand up, *vb.* (1930) (Of a grand jury) to deliver (an indictment) to a criminal court.

hand uplifted. See UPLIFTED HAND.

handwriting. (15c) *Evidence.* **1.** A person's chirography; the cast or form of writing peculiar to a person, including the size, shape, and style of letters, and whatever gives individuality to one's writing. — Often shortened to *hand.* **2.** Something written by hand; a writing specimen. • Nonexpert opinion about the genuineness of handwriting, based on familiarity not acquired for litigation purposes, can authenticate a document. Fed. R. Evid. 901(b)(2).

hang, *vb.* (1848) **1.** (Of a jury) to be unable to reach a verdict <the jury was hung after 12 hours of continuous deliberation>. See *hung jury* under JURY. **2.** To suspend a person above the ground by a rope tied around the person's neck in order to cause the person's death. • The standard past tense of the verb in sense 2 is *hanged,* not *hung* — the latter being the standard past tense in all other uses of the verb. See HANGING.

hanged, drawn, and quartered. (16c) *Hist.* An ancient sentence for high treason, consisting of the prisoner's being drawn on a hurdle to the place of execution, hanged by the neck (but not until dead), disemboweled, and beheaded, and the body then divided into four pieces for the king's disposal. • The sentence was abolished in England in 1870. See TREASON.

hanging, *n.* (13c) The killing of someone by suspending the person above the ground by a rope around the person's neck. • Death is caused by asphyxiation (by being hoisted from the ground) or by a sudden breaking of the cervical vertebrae (by being dropped from a height). Hanging was a common form of capital punishment in the United States until the 1930s. See HANG.

hanging chad. See CHAD.

hanging in chains. (16c) *Hist. English law.* As the punishment in an atrocious case, the suspending of an executed murderer's body by chains near where the crime was committed. • Hanging in chains was abolished in 1834.

hanging judge. See JUDGE.

hangman. (14c) *Archaic.* An executioner; esp., someone whose job is to execute condemned criminals by hanging.

Hansard (**han**-sərd). *English law.* The official reports of debates in the British Parliament. • The name derives from Luke Hansard (1752–1828), printer of the *Journal of the House of Commons* from 1774 to 1828. The name has varied at different times. In 1892 it became the *Authorised Edition*; in 1909 the title was changed to the *Official Report*; and since 1943 the name *Hansard* has been added to *Official Report.* — Also termed *Hansard Official Report*; *Hansard's Debates.*

hanse (hans), *n.* [German] (14c) *Hist.* **1.** A merchant guild, esp. one engaging in trade abroad. **2.** A fee for entrance to the guild; an impost levied on merchants not belonging to the guild.

Hanseatic (han-see-**at**-ik), *adj.* (17c) *Hist.* **1.** Of, relating to, or involving the union of the Hanse Towns in Germany, usu. referred to as the *Hanseatic League.* **2.** Of, relating to, or involving a hanse or commercial alliance.

Hanse Towns (hans). *Hist.* The collective name of certain German cities — including Lübeck, Hamburg, and Bremen — that allied in the 12th century to protect and further their mutual commercial interests. • This alliance was usu. called the *Hanseatic League.* The League framed and promulgated a code of maritime law known as the *Laws of the Hanse Towns,* or *Jus Hanseaticum Maritimum.* The League's power peaked in the 14th century, then gradually declined until 1669, when the last general assembly was held. See HANSEATIC (1).

Hanse Towns, laws of the. *Hist.* A uniform maritime code drawn from the laws of the Hanse towns, esp. that of Lübeck, published in German at Lübeck in 1597 and revised and enlarged in 1614. — Also termed *Hanseatic code*; *Hanseatic laws.*

happiness, right to pursue. (1829) *Constitutional law.* The constitutional right to pursue any lawful business or activity that might yield the highest enjoyment, increase one's prosperity, or allow the development of one's faculties as long as it is not inconsistent with others' rights.

• This is considered a penumbral rather than explicit right under the U.S. Constitution. *See* the Declaration of Independence ¶ 2 (1776).

happy-slapping. (2005) *Slang.* An assault on a randomly chosen victim by a person or group while another person films the assault with the intention of later broadcasting copies of the recording. • Happy-slapping began in the early 2000s as a fad in London, in which a teenage victim was merely slapped or struck with an object such as a rolled-up newspaper while the assault was recorded on a cellphone camera. As the fad spread across England and into Europe, the perpetrators attacked victims of all ages, and the assaults occasionally escalated from mere slaps to serious bodily injury, rape, and even murder. — **happy-slap,** *vb.*

hara-kiri swap. See INTEREST-RATE SWAP.

harassment (hə-**ras**-mənt *or* **har**-əs-mənt). (18c) Words, conduct, or action (usu. repeated or persistent) that, being directed at a specific person, annoys, alarms, or causes substantial emotional distress to that person and serves no legitimate purpose; purposeful vexation. • Harassment is actionable in some circumstances, as when a creditor uses threatening or abusive tactics to collect a debt. — **harass** (hə-**ras** *or* **har**-əs), *vb.*

▸ **discriminatory harassment.** Harassment that denigrates, shows hostility to, or exhibits aversion toward a person or group (esp. of a protected class), thereby creating a hostile environment that unreasonably interferes with learning, living, or working. • Sexual harassment and gender-based harassment are forms of discriminatory harassment. See *gender-based harassment*; SEXUAL HARASSMENT.

▸ **gender-based harassment.** Harassment motivated by hostility and intended to enforce traditional heterosexual norms and roles and discourage what is seen as nontraditional behavior. See *discriminatory harassment.*

▸ **hostile-work-environment harassment.** See *hostile-environment sexual harassment* under SEXUAL HARASSMENT.

▸ **quid pro quo harassment.** See *quid pro quo sexual harassment* under SEXUAL HARASSMENT.

▸ **same-sex harassment.** See *same-sex sexual harassment* under SEXUAL HARASSMENT.

▸ **sexual harassment.** See SEXUAL HARASSMENT.

harbinger (**hahr**-bin-jər), *n.* (14c) **1.** *Hist. English law.* A royal officer who went ahead and was responsible for securing lodging for troops or for a traveling royal entourage. **2.** A person or thing that predicts what is to come <a harbinger of bad news>.

harbor, safe. See SAFE HARBOR.

harboring, *n.* (14c) The act of affording lodging, shelter, or refuge to a person, esp. a criminal or illegal alien.

harboring a criminal. See HARBORING A FUGITIVE.

harboring a fugitive. (1934) *Criminal law.* The crime of affording lodging, shelter, refuge, or other aid to a person seeking to avoid capture or punishment. • If the fugitive is suspected of committing a felony or has been convicted of a felony and has violated his or her parole or probation conditions, the term *harboring a felon* is commonly used. — Also termed *harboring a criminal; harboring an offender.*

harboring an illegal alien. (1974) The act of providing concealment from detection by law-enforcement authorities or shelter, employment, or transportation to help a noncitizen remain in the United States unlawfully, while knowing about or recklessly disregarding the noncitizen's illegal immigration status. • The crime of harboring an illegal alien does not require that the offender be involved in the smuggling of illegal aliens into the country. 8 USCA § 1324.

harboring an offender. See HARBORING A FUGITIVE.

harbor line. (1849) A line marking the boundary of a certain part of public water that is reserved for a harbor; esp., the line beyond which wharves and other structures may not extend.

hard, *adj.* **1.** (Of a market) having prices that are rising. **2.** (Of a currency) having excess demand and therefore tending to rise in value in relation to other currencies.

hard asset. See *real asset* under ASSET.

hardball, *adj.* Ruthless; uncompassionate. • Taken from the baseball term, *hardball* is distinguished from *softball,* which is played with a softer and bigger ball, making for an easier game and a more remote possibility of injury.

hard bargain. See BARGAIN.

hard case. (1836) **1.** A lawsuit involving equities that tempt a judge to stretch or even disregard a principle of law at issue. • Hence the expression, "Hard cases make bad law." **2.** A lawsuit in which no clear rule obviously governs the outcome.

> "It is an old saying that 'hard cases make bad law.' Its original meaning concerned cases in which the law had a hard impact on some person whose situation aroused sympathy. In such cases there was an inevitable, and often strong, temptation to offer a strained interpretation of the law to avoid the hard effect in the individual case. The slogan 'hard cases make bad law' amounted to an exhortation to refrain from bending the law on account of exceptional individual hardship. . . . 'Hard case' has over the past few decades changed its meaning, under the influence of Ronald Dworkin, who suggests (in effect) that such cases provide occasions to make good law. A hard case is now understood as a case where some difficulty of interpreting the law has arisen, where there are strong arguments for each of the rival understandings or interpretations of the law put forward by or on behalf of the parties." Neil MacCormick, *Rhetoric and the Rule of Law: A Theory of Legal Reasoning* 49–50 (2005).

hard commodity. See COMMODITY.

hard currency. See CURRENCY.

hard dollars. 1. Cash proceeds given to a seller. **2.** The part of an equity investment that is not deductible in the first year. Cf. SOFT DOLLARS.

hard goods. See *durable goods* under GOODS.

hard intellectual property. See INTELLECTUAL PROPERTY.

hard labor. (18c) Work imposed on prisoners as additional punishment, usu. for misconduct while in prison. • Several states (such as Louisiana, Maine, and New Jersey) impose hard labor as a sentence for a variety of crimes. Hard labor is also imposed in military sentencing. See PENAL SERVITUDE.

hard-look doctrine. (1979) *Administrative law.* The principle that a court should carefully review an administrative-agency decision to ensure that it did not result from expediency, pressure, or whim.

hard money. See MONEY.

hard sell. (1952) A sales practice characterized by slogans, aggressiveness, intimidation, and urgent decision-making. Cf. SOFT SELL.

hardship. (13c) **1.** Privation; suffering or adversity. **2.** The asperity with which a proposed construction of law would bear on a particular case, forming, for a nontextualist, a basis against the construction. See AB INCONVENIENTI; HARD CASE. **3.** *Family law.* A condition that makes it onerous or impossible for a child-support obligor to make the required child-support payment. **4.** *Zoning.* A ground for a variance under a zoning statute if the zoning ordinance as applied to a particular property is unduly oppressive, arbitrary, or confiscatory; esp., a ground for granting a variance based on the impossibility or prohibitive expense of conforming the property or its use to the zoning regulation. — Also termed *undue hardship; unnecessary hardship.* See VARIANCE (2).

hardship license. See DRIVER'S LICENSE.

hardship privilege. (1977) A limited driving privilege that lessens the effect of a driver's suspension pending a DWI prosecution. • The defendant must typically produce evidence from some third party to demonstrate that wholesale suspension would work a hardship either personally or to an employer, children, or others. — Also termed *hardship license; preconviction conditional license.*

hardware. Collectively, the equipment that makes up the physical parts of a computer, including its electronic circuitry together with keyboards, readers, scanners, and printers. Cf. SOFTWARE.

Hare–Ware voting. See *instant-runoff voting* under VOTING.

harm, *n.* (bef. 12c) Injury, loss, damage; material or tangible detriment.

- ▸ **accidental harm.** (17c) **1.** Harm not caused by a purposeful act. **2.** Harm not caused by a tortious act.
- ▸ **bodily harm.** (16c) Physical pain, illness, or impairment of the body.
- ▸ **divisible harm.** Harm that can be apportioned between two or more parties.
- ▸ **grievous bodily harm.** See *serious bodily injury* under INJURY.
- ▸ **indivisible harm.** Harm that cannot be apportioned between two or more defendants. See *joint and several liability* under LIABILITY.
- ▸ **mental harm.** See MENTAL HARM.
- ▸ **physical harm.** (18c) Any physical injury or impairment of land, chattels, or the human body.
- ▸ **serious bodily harm.** See *serious bodily injury* under INJURY.
- ▸ **social harm.** (1933) An adverse effect on any social interest that is protected by the criminal law.

> "If the phrase 'social harm' is used to include every invasion of any social interest which has been placed under the protection of a criminal sanction (whether by common law or by statute), every crime may be said to involve, in addition to other requirements, (1) the happening of social harm and (2) the fact that the act of some person was the cause of this harm." Rollin M. Perkins & Ronald N. Boyce, *Criminal Law* 830 (3d ed. 1982).

harmful behavior. (1900) Conduct that could injure another person, esp. a child.

- ▸ **cumulatively harmful behavior.** (1985) *Family law.* Seriously harmful parental (or caregiver) behavior that, if continued for a significant period, will over time cause serious harm to a child.
- ▸ **immediately harmful behavior.** (1985) *Family law.* Seriously harmful parental (or caregiver) behavior that could have caused serious injury to a child but that, because of the intervention of an outside force or a fortuitous event, did not result in any injury.
- ▸ **seriously harmful behavior.** (1985) *Family law.* Parental (or caregiver) behavior that could cause serious injury to a child in the person's care. • Some examples of seriously harmful behavior are physical battering, physical neglect, sexual abuse, and abandonment.

harmful child labor. See *oppressive child labor* under CHILD LABOR.

harmful error. See *reversible error* under ERROR (2).

harmless error. See ERROR (2).

harmless-error rule. 1. The doctrine that an unimportant mistake by a trial judge, or some minor irregularity at trial, will not result in a reversal on appeal. **2.** *Wills & estates.* The doctrine that a trivial, unintentional, or unimportant mistake in executing a will may be excused if there is clear and convincing evidence that the testator adopted the document as his or her will. • The rule allows a slightly defective will to be admitted to probate. *See* Restatement (Third) of Property (Wills and Other Donative Transfers) § 3.3 (1999); Unif. Probate Code § 2-503. Cf. STRICT-COMPLIANCE RULE.

harmonious-reading canon. The doctrine that the provisions of a legal instrument should be interpreted in a way that renders them compatible, not contradictory. — Also termed *anti-repugnance canon.*

harmony. (14c) Agreement or accord; conformity <the decision in *Jones* is in harmony with earlier Supreme Court precedent>. — **harmonize,** *vb.*

harm principle. (1959) The view that the legitimate purpose of criminal law is to deter anyone from harming or endangering others.

***Harris* motion.** *Criminal procedure.* A formal request by the defense to preclude use of a suppressed statement for impeachment on grounds that the statement was involuntary. *See Harris v. New York*, 401 U.S. 222 (1971).

***Harrison* motion.** A formal request to preclude the introduction of testimony from an earlier trial. *Harrison v. U.S.*, 392 U.S. 219 (1968).

harrow (**har**-oh *or* hə-**roh**), *n.* [fr. Old French *haro*] (14c) *Hist.* In Norman and early English law, an outcry (or hue and cry) after felons and malefactors. — Also spelled *haro.* See HUE AND CRY. Cf. CLAMEUR DE HARO.

Harter Act. *Maritime law.* An 1893 federal statute regulating a carrier's liability for the loss or damage of ocean cargo shipped under bills of lading. 46 USCA app. §§ 190–196. • The Act was the primary model for the Carriage of Goods by Sea Act, which has largely superseded it in practice. See CARRIAGE OF GOODS BY SEA ACT.

> "[T]he Harter Act [was] the world's first legislative attempt to allocate the risk of loss in ocean transportation between carrier and cargo interests." Michael F. Sturley, *Changing*

Liability Rules and Marine Insurance, 24 J. Mar. L. & Com. 119, 119 (1993).

Hart-Scott-Rodino Antitrust Improvement Act. A 1976 federal statute that generally strengthens the Justice Department's antitrust enforcement powers, esp. by requiring firms to give notice to the Federal Trade Commission and the Justice Department of an intent to merge if one of the firms has annual revenues or assets exceeding $100 million, and the acquisition price or value of the acquired firm exceeds $50 million. 15 USCA § 18(a). — Often shortened to *Hart-Scott-Rodino Act* (HSR Act).

hash, *vb.* (1984) To run (a document) through an encryption algorithm, usu. to secure the contents or to derive a number unique to the document. • The product of hashing is either run through the encryption algorithm in reverse to verify that the transmitted message has not been altered or combined with the sender's private-encryption key to produce a digital signature for the document.

hash number. (1999) A unique numerical code generated by encryption software for use in creating a digital signature. — Also termed *hashed number.* See DIGITAL SIGNATURE; HASH; KEY ENCRYPTION.

haspa (**has**-pə), *n.* [Law Latin] *Hist.* The hasp of a door, where livery of seisin was traditionally made within a structure located on the property being transferred.

hasta (**has**-tə), *n.* [Latin "spear"] **1.** *Roman law.* A sale by auction, indicated by a spear placed into the ground. • The phrase *hastae subicere* ("to put under the spear") meant to put up for sale at auction. **2.** *Hist.* A symbol used to invest a fief.

Hatch Act. A 1939 federal statute that restricts political-campaign activities by federal employees and limits contributions by individuals to political campaigns. 5 USCA §§ 1501–1508. • Senator Carl Hatch sponsored the Act following disclosures that Works Progress Administration officials were using their positions to campaign for the Democratic Party.

Hatch–Waxman Act. The popular name of the 1984 federal statute that provides incentives for the development of generic drugs and allows drug-patent owners to regain the time lost on a patent's term while awaiting the drug's approval by the Food and Drug Administration. — Also termed *Drug Price Competition and Patent Term Restoration Act of 1984.*

hate crime. See CRIME.

hate offense. See *hate crime* under CRIME.

hate speech. See SPEECH.

hat money. (17c) *Maritime law.* A small gratuity traditionally paid to the master (and sometimes the crew) of a ship for the care of the cargo. — Also termed *pocket money; primage.*

> "Primage and average, which are mentioned in bills of lading, mean a small compensation or duty paid to the master, over and above the freight, for his care and trouble as to the goods. It belongs to him of right, and it is not understood to be covered by the policy of insurance. For these charges, as well as for freight, the master has a lien on the cargo." 3 James Kent, *Commentaries on American Law* *232 n. (b) (George Comstock ed., 11th ed. 1866).

Hatsell's Precedents. *Parliamentary law.* A compilation of points of order decided in the House of Commons, published by the House's clerk, John Hatsell, in two volumes, the first in 1776 and the second in 1781. • Hatsell's compilation was a primary source for the manual that Thomas Jefferson compiled while presiding over the United States Senate.

hauber ([**h**]**aw**-bər), *n.* [Old French] *Hist.* A high lord; a great baron.

haulage royalty. See ROYALTY (2).

haustus (**haws**-təs), *n.* [Latin "a drawing"] *Roman law.* A species of rustic praedial servitude consisting in the right to draw water from a well or spring on another's property — the term being esp. common in the form *aquaehaustus.* • A right-of-way (*iter*) to the well was implied in the easement. See *servitude appurtenant* under SERVITUDE.

have. See HABE.

have and hold. See HABENDUM CLAUSE (1).

have the floor. (1888) *Parliamentary law.* To be entitled to speak after being recognized by the chair.

hawala (hə-**wah**-lə), *n.* [Hindi] (1916) A system for transferring money, usu. across national borders, based on trust and operating through networks based on family relationships or on regional or ethnic affiliations rather than through banks and financial institutions. • The system originated in India before the introduction of western banking practices. It is commonly used in immigrant communities. In Indian and Pakistani usage, "white hawala" refers to legitimate transactions and "black hawala" refers to money-laundering. — Also termed *hundi.*

hawaladar (hə-**wah**-lə-dər), *n.* [Hindi] (2000) A hawala operator.

hawker. (16c) An itinerant or traveling salesperson who sells goods in a public street, esp. one who, in a loud voice, cries out the benefits of the items offered for sale; a peddler. • A hawker is usu. required to have a license.

hawking. (16c) The act of offering, by outcry, goods for sale from door to door or on a public street.

haybote See BOTE (2).

hayward. (13c) *Hist.* **1.** An officer of a town or manor responsible for maintaining fences and hedges, esp. to prevent cattle from breaking through to an enclosed pasture. **2.** A cattle herder.

Hazantown agreement (**hay**-zən-town). (1980) A type of collective-bargaining agreement used in the garment industry, governing the relationship between a jobber and the contractors that produce the jobber's garments. • The agreement does not govern the relationship between the jobber and its own employees. It governs the relationship between the jobber and the contractors that manufacture the garments that the jobber sells, including covenants that the jobber will use only unionized contractors, will ensure that salaries and bonuses are appropriately paid, and will contribute to employee-benefit funds maintained on behalf of the contractor's employees. The term takes its name from Hazantown, Inc., the jobber involved in *Danielson v. Joint Bd. of Coat, Suit & Allied Garment Workers' Union*, 494 F.2d 1230 (2d Cir. 1974). — Also termed *jobber's agreement.*

hazard, *n.* (14c) **1.** Danger or peril; esp., a factor contributing to a peril. See PERIL.

▸ **extraordinary hazard.** (1919) *Workers' compensation.* An unusual occupational danger that is increased by the acts of employees other than the injured worker. — Also termed *extraordinary danger; extraordinary risk.*

▸ **imminent hazard.** (17c) An immediate danger; esp., in environmental law, a situation in which the continued use of a pesticide will probably result in unreasonable adverse effects on the environment or will involve an unreasonable danger to the survival of an endangered species. 7 USCA § 136(1).

▸ **occupational hazard.** (1917) A danger or risk that is peculiar to a particular calling or occupation. • Occupational hazards include both accidental injuries and occupational diseases.

2. *Insurance.* The risk or probability of loss or injury, esp. a loss or injury covered by an insurance policy.

▸ **moral hazard.** (1881) A hazard that has its inception in mental attitudes, such as dishonesty, carelessness, and insanity. • The risk that an insured will destroy property or allow it to be destroyed (usu. by burning) in order to collect the insurance proceeds is a moral hazard. Also, an insured's potential interest, if any, in the burning of the property is sometimes called a moral hazard.

▸ **physical hazard.** (1887) A hazard that has its inception in the material world, such as location, structure, occupancy, exposure, and the like.

3. *Hist.* An unlawful dice game in which the chances of winning are complicated by arbitrary rules.

hazarder (haz-ər-dər), *n.* (13c) *Hist.* A player in an unlawful game of dice. — Also spelled *hazardor.*

hazardous, *adj.* (16c) Risky; dangerous.

hazardous cargo. See CARGO.

hazardous contract. See *aleatory contract* under CONTRACT.

hazardous employment. See EMPLOYMENT.

hazardous negligence. See NEGLIGENCE.

hazardous substance. (1882) **1.** A toxic pollutant; an imminently dangerous chemical or mixture. **2.** See *hazardous waste* under WASTE (2).

hazardous waste. See WASTE (2).

hazardous-waste manifest. A shipping document that travels with hazardous waste from the point of generation to the final treatment, storage, and disposal facility. • The manifest is ordinarily signed by, and a copy retained by, each person in the chain of generation, transportation, and disposal to create a complete tracking of the hazardous waste.

hazard pay. See PAY, *n.* (1).

hazing, *n.* (1850) The practice of physically or emotionally abusing newcomers to an organization as a means of initiation. • In the early 19th century, *hazing* referred to beating. Hazing was a well-established custom in fraternities at Ivy League universities by the mid-19th century. (One college magazine referred to "the absurd and barbarous custom of hazing, which has long prevailed in the college." 1 Harvard Mag. 413 (1860)). The first death from hazing was reported at Yale in 1892 (*N.Y. Daily News*, June 28, 1892). In the late 20th century, many colleges and universities banned hazing, and many states passed antihazing statutes establishing criminal penalties. See ANTIHAZING STATUTE.

hazing statute. See ANTIHAZING STATUTE.

H.B. See *house bill* under BILL (3).

H.C. *abbr.* **1.** HOUSE OF COMMONS. **2.** HABEAS CORPUS.

HDC. *abbr.* HOLDER IN DUE COURSE.

he. (bef. 12c) A pronoun of the masculine gender, traditionally used and construed in statutes to include both sexes, as well as corporations. • It may also be read as *they.* Because of the trend toward nonsexist language, fastidious drafters avoid using the generic pronouns *he, him,* and *his* unless the reference is only to a male person. But they are often unavoidable, esp. in criminal statutes.

head-and-master rule. (1984) *Hist.* The doctrine that the husband alone is authorized to manage community property. • Some courts have held that the rule is unconstitutional gender-based discrimination. — Also termed *lord-and-master rule.* Cf. EQUAL-MANAGEMENT RULE.

headborough. See BORSHOLDER.

heading. (17c) A brief title or caption of a section of a statute, contract, or other writing. See TITLE-AND-HEADINGS CANON.

> "The headings prefixed to sections or sets of sections in some modern statutes are regarded as preambles to those sections. They cannot control the plain words of the statute, but they may explain ambiguous words . . . ." P. St. J. Langan, *Maxwell on the Interpretation of Statutes* 11 (12th ed. 1969).

headings canon. See TITLE-AND-HEADINGS CANON.

headlease. (1909) A primary lease under which a sublease has been granted. — Also spelled *head lease.* — Also termed *primary lease; chief lease.*

headlessor. (1933) A lessor on a lease of property that has been subleased.

head money. (16c) **1.** A tax on people who fit within a designated class; a poll tax. See *capitation tax* and *poll tax* under TAX. **2.** *Hist.* A bounty offered by a government for a prisoner taken at sea during a naval engagement. • This bounty is divided among the officers and crew in the same manner as prize money. See PRIZE MONEY. **3.** *Hist.* A tax or duty on shipowners for every immigrant brought into the United States. • It was imposed in 1882 by federal statute. — Also termed *head tax.* **4.** *Hist.* A bounty or reward paid to a person who killed a bandit or outlaw and produced the head as evidence. See BOUNTY (1); REWARD.

headnote. (1855) A case summary that appears before a printed judicial opinion in a law report, addresses a point of law, and usu. includes the relevant facts bearing on that point of law. — Also termed *syllabus; synopsis; reporter's syllabus.* Cf. SYLLABUS.

> "It is customary to prefix to each case a head-note, sometimes called a syllabus, showing the points decided. This head-note is usually the work of the reporter, but sometimes it is the work of the judges. By whomsoever made, a head-note is not final authority. Like the words of the opinion, the head-note is merely a guide, more or less trustworthy, to the doctrine of the case. Of course, the value of head-notes depends upon the accuracy of the writer of them and also upon the method pursued by him." Eugene Wambaugh, *The Study of Cases* § 27, at 35 (2d ed. 1894).

> "The syllabus or headnote is a brief statement of the propositions of law decided in the case, being in the nature of

a table of contents of the case. The modern method is to number each proposition in the syllabus, and to indicate, by corresponding figures, the exact place in the decision where the point mentioned in the syllabus can be found. Sometimes, especially in the older reports, the syllabus is inaccurate or misleading, and it is not safe to rely on it without first verifying it from the decision." Frank Hall Childs, *Where and How to Find the Law* 22 (1922).

headnote lawyer. See LAWYER.

head of family. (1845) Someone who supports one or more people related by birth, adoption, or marriage and with whom those persons maintain their permanent domicile. • The phrase *head of family* appears most commonly in homestead law. For a person to have the status of head of family, there must, of necessity, be at least two people in the family. — Also termed *head of a family.* Cf. HEAD OF HOUSEHOLD.

head of government. *Int'l law.* **1.** The person who holds the top office in a country's executive branch. **2.** HEAD OF STATE.

head of household. (1847) **1.** HEAD OF FAMILY. **2.** The primary income-provider within a family. **3.** For income-tax purposes, an unmarried or separated person (other than a surviving spouse) who provides a home for dependents for more than one-half of the taxable year. • A head of household is taxed at a lower rate than a single person who is not head of a household. Cf. HEAD OF FAMILY; HOUSEHOLDER.

head of state. *Int'l law.* The principal representative of a country. • In some political systems, one person is both the head of government and the head of state. In others, esp. parliamentary systems, an elected or hereditary figurehead is the head of state but not the head of government. Cf. HEAD OF GOVERNMENT (1).

head-of-state immunity. See IMMUNITY (1).

headquarters. (17c) **1.** A central place where people in authority are stationed; esp., the main campus, building, or offices used by a large company or organization having at least several satellite locations. **2.** The place from which military operations are controlled; specif., the temporary or permanent location of a commanding officer in a camp, garrison, etc., esp. that of the commander-in-chief.

headright. (1930) In American Indian law, a tribe member's right to a pro rata portion of income from a tribal trust fund set up under the Allotment Act of 1906. • This type of trust fund is funded largely by mineral royalties arising from land held or once held by the tribe member's tribe.

headright certificate. (1842) *Hist.* A certificate issued under authority of a Republic of Texas law of 1839 providing that a person was entitled to a grant of 640 acres if the person (1) had immigrated to the Republic between 1 October 1837 and 1 January 1840, (2) was a head of household, and (3) actually resided within the Republic with his or her family. • The grant was to be held under the certificate for three years and then conveyed by absolute deed to the settler.

headship. (16c) The position of being in charge of an organization.

head shop. (1967) A retail establishment that sells items intended for use with illegal drugs.

head-silver. See *common fine* under FINE (4).

heads of damage. (1855) The categories of damages claimed in a lawsuit.

headstart damages. See DAMAGES.

head-start injunction. See INJUNCTION.

headstream. (1817) The source of a river.

head tax. **1.** See *poll tax* under TAX. **2.** HEAD MONEY (3).

headwater. (18c) **1.** (*usu. pl.*) The part of a river or stream that is closest to its source. **2.** HEADSTREAM.

health. (bef. 12c) **1.** The quality, state, or condition of being sound or whole in body, mind, or soul; esp., freedom from pain or sickness. **2.** The relative quality, state, or condition of one's physical or mental well-being, whether good or bad.

▸ **good health.** See GOOD HEALTH.

▸ **public health.** (17c) **1.** The health of the community at large. **2.** The healthful or sanitary condition of the general body of people or the community en masse; esp., the methods of maintaining the health of the community, as by preventive medicine and organized care for the sick. • Many cities have a "public health department" or other agency responsible for maintaining the public health; federal laws dealing with health are administered by the Department of Health and Human Services.

▸ **sound health.** See SOUND HEALTH.

healthcare. Collectively, the services provided, usu. by medical professionals, to maintain and restore health. See MEDICINE (2).

healthcare fraud. See FRAUD.

healthcare-insurance receivable. (2007) An interest in or claim under an insurance policy, being a right to payment of a monetary obligation for healthcare goods or services provided. UCC § 9-102(a)(46).

healthcare lien. See LIEN.

healthcare proxy. See ADVANCE DIRECTIVE (1).

health insurance. See INSURANCE.

health-insurance order. (1991) *Family law.* An order requiring a parent either to obtain health insurance for a child or to add a child to an existing health-insurance policy. • Health-insurance orders often include dental insurance.

Health Insurance Portability and Accountability Act. A 1996 federal statute that provides additional health-insurance protections to employees by limiting the effect of preexisting conditions on an employee's ability to obtain insurance; permitting an employee to enroll a new dependent acquired by birth, adoption, or marriage; making it easier for people to maintain insurance coverage while changing jobs; and helping businesses employing fewer than 50 workers to obtain group insurance plans. • The Act is codified in various sections of 18 USCA, 26 USCA, 29 USCA, and 42 USCA. — Abbr. HIPAA.

health law. (18c) A statute, ordinance, or code that prescribes sanitary standards and regulations for the purpose of promoting and preserving the community's health.

health-maintenance organization. (1973) A group of participating healthcare providers that furnish medical services to enrolled members of a group health-insurance plan. — Abbr. HMO. Cf. MANAGED-CARE ORGANIZATION; PREFERRED-PROVIDER ORGANIZATION.

health officer. (1815) A government official charged with executing and enforcing health laws. • The powers of a health officer (such as the Surgeon General) are regulated by law.

heard and determined. (16c) (Of a case) having been presented to a court that rendered judgment.

hearing. (13c) **1.** A judicial session, usu. open to the public, held for the purpose of deciding issues of fact or of law, sometimes with witnesses testifying <the court held a hearing on the admissibility of DNA evidence in the murder case>. — Also termed *judicial hearing.* **2.** *Administrative law.* Any setting in which an affected person presents arguments to a decision-maker <a hearing on zoning variations>. **3.** In legislative practice, any proceeding in which legislators or their designees receive testimony about legislation that might be enacted <the shooting victim spoke at the Senate's hearing on gun control>. See PRELIMINARY HEARING. **4.** *Equity practice.* A trial. **5.** *English law.* ORAL ARGUMENT.

▸ **adjudication hearing.** (1947) **1.** *Administrative law.* An agency proceeding in which a person's rights and duties are decided after notice and an opportunity to be heard. See *procedural due process* under DUE PROCESS. Cf. *disposition hearing.* **2.** In child-abuse and neglect proceedings, the trial stage at which the court hears the state's allegations and evidence and decides whether the state has the right to intervene on behalf of the child. **3.** In a juvenile-delinquency case, a hearing at which the court hears evidence of the charges and makes a finding of whether the charges are true or not true. — Also termed *adjudicatory hearing; adjudicatory proceeding; adjudicative hearing.*

▸ **adjudicatory hearing** (ə-**joo**-di-kə-tor-ee). See *adjudication hearing.*

▸ **audibility hearing.** (1973) A pretrial or in-chambers assessment of whether an audio recording will be understandable by to jurors without their undue speculation about its content.

▸ **bifurcated hearing.** (1951) A multipart (esp. a two-part) hearing, the first part of which is to establish one requirement and the second part of which is to establish another, etc. • In a *Wade* hearing (see WADE HEARING), for example, it may be necessary to establish either a lack of suggestiveness in a lineup or an independent source for the identification. Only if the first (lack of suggestiveness) is not established will the second (independent source of identification) become necessary. Some judges refer to such a two-stage hearing as "bifurcated."

▸ **certification hearing.** See *transfer hearing.*

▸ **competency hearing.** (1958) *Criminal law.* A hearing to determine the physical and mental fitness of a defendant to be tried for a crime.

▸ **conformity hearing.** See CONFORMITY HEARING.

▸ **contested hearing.** (1872) A hearing in which at least one of the parties has objections regarding one or more matters before the court.

▸ **continued-custody hearing.** See *shelter hearing.*

▸ ***Curcio* hearing.** A hearing conducted when an attorney has an apparent conflict of interest so that the defendant may choose whether to make an informed, knowing, and intelligent waiver of the right to conflict-free counsel. *U.S. v. Curcio*, 680 F.2d 881, 888 (2d Cir. 1982).

▸ **custody hearing.** (1935) *Family law.* A judicial examination of the facts relating to child custody, typically in a divorce or separation proceeding. • Child-neglect and dependency matters are also often dealt with in custody hearings. — Also termed *custody proceeding.*

▸ ***Daubert* hearing.** See DAUBERT HEARING.

▸ **dependency hearing.** See *shelter hearing.*

▸ **deposition hearing.** A witness's out-of-court testimony under oath before a judge or officer of the court, usu. given because the witness will be unable to attend proceedings in court.

▸ **detention hearing.** (1959) **1.** *Criminal law.* A hearing to determine whether an accused should be released pending trial. • Such a hearing is usu. held soon after the defendant's arrest. See *pretrial detention* under DETENTION (1). **2.** *Family law.* A hearing held by a juvenile court to determine whether a juvenile accused of delinquent conduct should be detained, continued in confinement, or released pending an adjudicatory hearing. Cf. *adjudication hearing; disposition hearing.* **3.** See *shelter hearing.*

▸ **directions hearing.** A hearing at which the court reviews the management of a case and sets the timetable for the next steps in the preparation for trial.

▸ **discharge hearing.** See DISCHARGE HEARING.

▸ **dispositional hearing.** See *disposition hearing.*

▸ **disposition hearing.** (1960) *Family law.* **1.** In child-abuse and neglect proceedings, after an adjudication hearing at which the state proves its allegations, a hearing at which the court hears evidence and enters orders for the child's care, custody, and control. • Typically, the judge determines a plan for services aimed at reunifying or rehabilitating the family. **2.** In a juvenile-delinquency case, after an adjudication hearing at which the state proves its case against the juvenile or after a juvenile's pleading true to the charges against him, a hearing at which the court determines what sanctions, if any, will be imposed on the juvenile. • At a disposition hearing, the court balances the best interests of the child against the need to sanction the child for his or her actions. If the juvenile is adjudicated a delinquent, the probation staff prepares a social history of the youth and his family and recommends a disposition. After reviewing the social history and various recommendations, the court enters a disposition. Among the possible juvenile sanctions are a warning, probation, restitution, counseling, or placement in a juvenile-detention facility. Probation is the most common sanction. — Also termed *dispositional hearing.* Cf. *adjudication hearing.* **3.** See *permanency hearing.*

▸ **evidentiary hearing.** (1952) **1.** A hearing at which evidence is presented, as opposed to a hearing at which only legal argument is presented. **2.** See ADMINISTRATIVE PROCEEDING.

▸ **exclusionary hearing.** (1963) A pretrial hearing conducted to review and determine the admissibility of alleged illegally obtained evidence.

▸ **fair hearing.** (1831) A judicial or administrative hearing conducted in accordance with due process.

▸ **fatality hearing.** See FATALITY HEARING.

▸ ***Fatico* hearing.** See FATICO HEARING.

▸ **fitness hearing.** See *transfer hearing.*

▸ ***Franks* hearing.** See FRANKS HEARING.

▸ **full adversary hearing.** See *adjudication hearing.*

▸ **full hearing.** (17c) **1.** A hearing at which the parties are allowed notice of each other's claims and are given ample opportunity to present their positions with evidence and argument. **2.** See ADMINISTRATIVE PROCEEDING.

▸ ***Garcia* hearing.** See GARCIA HEARING.

▸ **guardianship hearing.** A hearing at which a court determines whether a person or the person's estate needs to be protected by a third party because the person is a minor or is unable to manage his or her affairs because of incapacity.

▸ **hearing de novo** (dee *or* di **noh**-voh). (18c) **1.** A reviewing court's decision of a matter anew, giving no deference to a lower court's findings. **2.** A new hearing of a matter, conducted as if the original hearing had not taken place.

▸ **hearing on the merits.** (18c) A formal proceeding before a judge who hears testimony under the rules of evidence and makes a final decision in the case.

▸ **independent-source hearing.** (1990) *Criminal procedure.* A hearing to determine whether evidence was obtained illegally, and if so, whether the evidence is admissible. See INDEPENDENT-SOURCE RULE.

▸ ***Jackson–Denno* hearing.** See JACKSON–DENNO HEARING.

▸ ***Kastigar* hearing.** (1975) *Criminal law.* A hearing at which the prosecution must establish by a preponderance of the evidence that the government's evidence derives from proper, nonimmunized sources. *Kastigar v. U.S.*, 406 U.S. 441, 92 S.Ct. 1653 (1972).

▸ ***Mapp* hearing.** See MAPP HEARING.

▸ **neglect hearing.** (1952) *Family law.* A judicial hearing involving alleged child abuse or some other situation in which a child has not been properly cared for by a parent or person legally responsible for the child's care. • At issue is the civil culpability of the parent or responsible party and the possible loss of children into foster care or — in extreme cases — the termination of parental rights.

▸ **omnibus hearing.** (1969) *Criminal procedure.* A hearing designed to bring judicial oversight to a criminal case at an early stage to make certain that the case is being handled expeditiously and properly. • At an omnibus hearing, the court is primarily interested in ensuring that discovery is being conducted properly, that any necessary evidentiary hearings have been scheduled, and that all issues ripe for decision have been decided.

▸ **permanency hearing.** (1832) *Family law.* Under the Adoption and Safe Families Act, a judicial proceeding to determine the future, permanent status of a child in foster care. • Under the Act, the term *permanency hearing* replaces the term *disposition hearing.* The permanency hearing must occur within 12 months of a child's being placed in foster care. The purpose of the hearing is to determine the final direction of the case, whether that means going forward with termination proceedings or continuing plans for family reunification. — Also termed *permanency-planning hearing.*

▸ **preliminary hearing.** See PRELIMINARY HEARING.

▸ **preliminary protective hearing.** See *shelter hearing.*

▸ **presentence hearing.** See PRESENTENCE HEARING.

▸ **pretrial hearing.** See PRETRIAL CONFERENCE.

▸ **probable-cause hearing.** See *shelter hearing.*

▸ **public hearing.** (18c) A hearing that, within reasonable limits, is open to anyone who wishes to observe. • Such a hearing is often characterized by the right to appear and present evidence in a case before an impartial tribunal.

▸ **reaffirmation hearing.** See REAFFIRMATION HEARING.

▸ **refusal hearing.** (1972) *Criminal procedure.* An administrative or judicial proceeding to determine whether a DWI or DUI defendant has declined to take a chemical test, such as a breath test, and, if so, the legal consequences of having done so. See BREATH TEST.

▸ **retention hearing.** (1971) *Criminal procedure.* **1.** A proceeding to decide whether a criminal defendant who has been found not guilty by reason of mental disease or insanity should be released. **2.** A proceeding to decide whether police-seized property, having been an instrumentality of a crime, should be released from police custody.

▸ **review hearing.** *Family law.* After a finding of child abuse or neglect, a hearing to assess the progress in the case plan. See CASE PLAN.

▸ **revocation hearing.** (1928) *Criminal procedure.* A hearing held to determine whether a parolee should be returned to prison for violating the terms of parole.

▸ ***Sell* hearing.** (2005) *Criminal law.* A hearing to consider whether a criminal defendant who has been found incompetent to stand trial can be forced to take medicine that will restore competency. *Sell v. U.S.*, 539 U.S. 166, 123 S.Ct. 2174 (2003).

▸ **sentencing hearing.** See PRESENTENCE HEARING.

▸ **shelter hearing.** (1975) *Family law.* A hearing shortly after the state's removal of a child for suspected abuse or neglect. • The hearing, generally held within 24 to 72 hours after the removal, is for the purpose of determining whether the state has adequate cause to maintain the children in protective care. — Also termed *shelter-care hearing; continued-custody hearing; preliminary protective hearing; probable-cause hearing; detention hearing; dependency hearing.*

▸ **suppression hearing.** (1955) *Criminal procedure.* A pretrial hearing in which a criminal defendant seeks to prevent the introduction of evidence alleged to have been seized illegally.

▸ **termination-of-parental-rights hearing.** (1973) *Family law.* A trial or court proceeding, usu. initiated by a state agency, that seeks to sever the legal ties between a parent and child, usu. so that the child can be adopted. • The standard of proof in a termination-of-parental-rights hearing is clear and convincing evidence. *Santosky v.*

Kramer, 455 U.S. 745, 102 S.Ct. 1388 (1982). — Abbr. TPR hearing. — Often shortened to *termination hearing*.

▸ **transfer hearing.** (1968) *Criminal procedure*. In a juvenile-court case, a hearing to determine whether the case should be transferred to adult criminal court so that the juvenile may be tried as an adult. • Every state, as well as the District of Columbia, has a transfer statute. The United States Supreme Court defined the due-process requirements for transfer hearings in *Kent v. U.S.*, 383 U.S. 541, 86 S.Ct. 1045 (1966). — Also termed *certification hearing*; *waiver hearing*; *fitness hearing*. See TRANSFER STATUTE; MANDATORY WAIVER; STATUTORY EXCLUSION.

▸ **trial-type hearing.** See ADMINISTRATIVE PROCEEDING.

▸ **uncontested hearing.** (1926) A hearing in which either (1) the parties are in agreement as to all matters before the court, or (2) one of the parties has failed to appear despite notice.

▸ **unfair hearing.** (1915) A hearing that is not conducted in accordance with due process, as when the defendant is denied the opportunity to prepare or consult with counsel.

▸ ***Wade* hearing.** See WADE HEARING.

▸ **waiver hearing.** See *transfer hearing*.

▸ ***Youngblood* hearing.** (1981) A hearing to determine the circumstances in which evidence was destroyed. *Arizona v, Youngblood*, 488 U.S. 51 (1998). See SPOLIATION.

hearing-ear dog. See *service dog* under DOG (1).

hearing examiner. See ADMINISTRATIVE-LAW JUDGE.

hearing officer. (1925) **1.** ADMINISTRATIVE-LAW JUDGE. **2.** See *judicial officer* (3) under OFFICER (1).

hearsay. (16c) **1.** Traditionally, testimony that is given by a witness who relates not what he or she knows personally, but what others have said, and that is therefore dependent on the credibility of someone other than the witness. • Such testimony is generally inadmissible under the rules of evidence. **2.** In federal law, a statement (either a verbal assertion or nonverbal assertive conduct), other than one made by the declarant while testifying at the trial or hearing, offered in evidence to prove the truth of the matter asserted. Fed. R. Evid. 801(c). — Also termed *hearsay evidence*; *secondhand evidence*. Cf. *original evidence* under EVIDENCE.

▸ **double hearsay.** (1921) A hearsay statement that contains further hearsay statements within it, none of which is admissible unless exceptions to the rule against hearsay can be applied to each level <the double hearsay was the report's statement that Amy had heard Joe admit running the red light>. Fed. R. Evid. 805. — Also termed *multiple hearsay*; *hearsay within hearsay*.

▸ **inferential hearsay.** (1967) Hearsay that is implied in testimony that suggests the contents of a conversation that is not explicitly disclosed by the testimony. • For example, a prosecutor might elicit inferential hearsay by asking a police-officer witness, "As the result of your discussions with Ms. Smith, did you conclude that she had engaged in embezzlement?" — Also termed *implicit hearsay*.

hearsay exception. (1895) Any of several deviations from the hearsay rule, allowing the admission of otherwise inadmissible statements because the circumstances surrounding the statements provide a basis for considering the statements reliable.

▸ **tender-years hearsay exception.** (1976) A hearsay exception for an out-of-court statement by a child ten years of age or younger, usu. describing an act of physical or sexual abuse, when the child is unavailable to testify and the court determines that the time, content, and circumstances of the statement make it reliable.

hearsay rule. (1896) The rule that no assertion offered as testimony can be received unless it is or has been open to test by cross-examination or an opportunity for cross-examination, except as provided otherwise by the rules of evidence, by court rules, or by statute. • The chief reasons for the rule are that out-of-court statements amounting to hearsay are not made under oath and are not subject to cross-examination. Fed. R. Evid. 802. Rule 803 provides 23 explicit exceptions to the hearsay rule, regardless of whether the out-of-court declarant is available to testify, and Rule 804 provides five more exceptions for situations in which the declarant is unavailable to testify.

> "[T]he great hearsay rule . . . is a fundamental rule of safety, but one overenforced and abused, — the spoiled child of the family, — proudest scion of our jury-trial rules of evidence, but so petted and indulged that it has become a nuisance and an obstruction to speedy and efficient trials." John H. Wigmore, *A Students' Textbook of the Law of Evidence* 238 (1935).

hearsay within hearsay. See *double hearsay* under HEARSAY.

heartbalm statute. (1940) A state law that abolishes the rights of action for monetary damages as solace for the emotional trauma occasioned by a loss of love and relationship. • The abolished rights of action include alienation of affections, breach of promise to marry, criminal conversation, and seduction of a person over the legal age of consent. Many states today have enacted heartbalm statutes primarily because of the highly speculative nature of the injury and the potential for abusive prosecution, as well as the difficulties of determining the cause of a loss. The terminology in this field is somewhat confusing, since a *heartbalm statute* abolishes lawsuits that were known as *heartbalm suits*; some scholars therefore call the abolitionary statutes *anti-heartbalm statutes*. But the prevailing term is *heartbalm statute*. — Also written *heart-balm statute*. — Also termed *heartbalm act*; *anti-heartbalm statute*; *anti-heartbalm act*.

> "Under the English common law, a broken engagement might be followed by a lawsuit for breach of promise to marry . . . . [T]he action came to look more like a tort action, in which damages might be given for the injury to the plaintiff's feelings, health and reputation and for expenses such as costs incurred in preparing for a wedding. Widespread criticism of the suit for breach of promise to marry (as well as related tort actions including seduction and alienation of affections) led to the passage of 'heart balm' statutes abolishing these claims in many jurisdictions in the United States beginning in the 1930's." Homer H. Clark Jr. & Ann Laquer Estin, *Domestic Relations: Cases and Problems* 47 (6th ed. 2000).

hearth money. (17c) *Hist. English law.* **1.** A tax of two shillings levied on every fireplace in England (14 Car. 2, ch. 10). • This extremely unpopular tax was enacted in 1662 during the reign of Charles II and abolished in 1688.

2. PETER-PENCE. — Also termed (in sense 1) *chimney money.*

heart-lung death. See DEATH.

heat of passion. (bef. 12c) Rage, terror, or furious hatred suddenly aroused by some immediate provocation, usu. another person's words or actions. • At common law, heat of passion could serve as a mitigating circumstance to reduce a murder charge to manslaughter if the provocation was objectively adequate, if there was inadequate time to cool off, and if the provocation and passion were causally linked to the homicide. — Also termed *sudden heat of passion; sudden heat; sudden passion; hot blood; sudden heat and passion; furor brevis.* See *adequate provocation* under PROVOCATION. Cf. *partial excuse* under EXCUSE (2); COLD BLOOD; COOL BLOOD.

> "To constitute the *heat of passion* included in this requirement it is not necessary for the passion to be so extreme that the slayer does not know what he is doing at the time; but it must be so extreme that for the moment his action is being directed by passion rather than by reason." Rollin M. Perkins & Ronald N. Boyce, *Criminal Law* 99 (3d ed. 1982).

heavy work. See WORK (1).

hebote. See HEREBOTE.

heckler's veto. (1965) **1.** The government's restriction or curtailment of a speaker's right to freedom of speech when necessary to prevent possibly violent reactions from listeners. • A common example is preventing or cutting short a speech that is provoking demonstrators and might lead to violence. The term was coined by Harry Kalven, *The Negro and the First Amendment* 141 (1965). **2.** An interruptive or disruptive act by a private person intending to prevent a speaker from being heard, such as shouting down the speaker, hurling personal insults, and carrying on loud side-conversations. — Also termed (in sense 2) *verbal terrorism.*

heckler's-veto doctrine. (1979) The principle that a public entity may not suppress a speaker's right of free speech solely because a crowd reacts negatively. • Under the doctrine, a court must determine whether a public disturbance was caused by the speaker or by the speaker's opponents. It originated in *Terminiello v. City of Chicago,* 337 U.S. 1, 4–5, 69 S.Ct. 894 (1949).

hedagium (hə-**day**-jee-əm), *n.* [Law Latin] *Hist.* A toll or custom due at a wharf for landing goods. • The Crown exempted particular persons and societies from this toll.

hedge, *vb.* (17c) To use two compensating or offsetting transactions to ensure a position of breaking even; esp., to make advance arrangements to safeguard oneself from loss on an investment, speculation, or bet, as when a buyer of commodities insures against unfavorable price changes by buying in advance at a fixed rate for later delivery. — **hedging,** *n.*

hedgebote. See *haybote* under BOTE (2).

hedge fund. (1967) A specialized investment group — usu. organized as a limited partnership or offshore investment company — that offers the possibility of high returns through risky techniques such as selling short or buying derivatives. • A hedge fund is exempt from the registration requirements of the Investment Company Act of 1940 and may therefore engage in transactions that would be illegal for a registered fund, such as selling short or leveraging through borrowing. Since 2010, investment advisers to hedge funds with substantial investments in the United States must register with the SEC.

hedging contract. See CONTRACT.

***Hedgpeth* harmlessness principle.** (2012) The doctrine that a jury instruction on multiple theories of guilt, one of which turns out to be invalid, is reviewable as a harmless error. *See Hedgpeth v. Pulido,* 555 U.S. 57, 129 S.Ct. 530 (2008).

hedonic damages. See DAMAGES.

hedonistic damages. See *hedonic damages* under DAMAGES.

hedonistic utilitarianism. See UTILITARIANISM.

heeding presumption. See PRESUMPTION.

heedlessness, *n.* (16c) The quality of being thoughtless and inconsiderate; esp., conduct involving the disregard of others' rights or safety. • Heedlessness is often construed to involve the same degree of fault as recklessness. See RECKLESSNESS. — **heedless,** *adj.*

hegemonism (hi-**jem**-ə-niz-əm). (19c) **1.** A philosophical position advocating hegemony. **2.** All forms of political extension by means of hegemony.

hegemony (hi-**jem**-ə-nee), *n.* (16c) **1.** Influence, authority, or supremacy over others <the hegemony of capitalism>. **2.** The striving for leadership or predominant authority of one state of a confederacy or union over the others; political domination <the former Soviet Union's hegemony over Eastern Europe>. — **hegemonic** (hej-ə-**mon**-ik), *adj.*

heightened scrutiny. See INTERMEDIATE SCRUTINY.

heinous (hay-nəs), *adj.* (14c) (Of a crime or its perpetrator) shockingly atrocious or odious. — **heinousness,** *n.*

heir (air). (13c) **1.** Someone who, under the laws of intestacy, is entitled to receive an intestate decedent's property. — Also termed *legal heir; heir at law; lawful heir; heir general; legitimate heir.* Cf. ANCESTOR.

> "Laymen — and sometimes first-year law students taking exams — wrongly assume that one who receives real property by will is an heir. Technically, the word 'heir' is reserved for one who receives real property by action of the laws of intestacy, which operate today only in the absence of a valid will." Thomas F. Bergin & Paul G. Haskell, *Preface to Estates in Land and Future Interests* 14 n.32 (2d ed. 1984).

2. In common-law jurisdictions, a person who inherits real or personal property, whether by will or by intestate succession; esp., by abstract designation, someone who serves merely to determine the quantity of an estate given by will.

> "Of the operation of the terms 'heirs' and 'heirs of the body,' In a will, or other instrument of conveyance. The general rule is, that those terms do not denote any particular person, to take by way of description, as devisee, grantee, or donee. Neither does any estate, by the use of those terms, vest in any person in character of heir; but only in the person of him who is named in the instrument of conveyance, who takes by purchase. But the heirs there named do not take as purchasers. They are words merely descriptive of the quantity of the estate given: As, if an estate is devised to A, and his heirs, forever; in this case, A alone takes the estate as a purchaser; and the terms, *his heirs forever,* denote what estate is limited by the devisee to A, viz., a fee simple, wholly in his power to alien or dispose of, as he pleases; and is, upon his death, descendible to dispose of, as he pleases; and is, upon his death, descendible to his heirs in general. If it be devised to A, and the heirs of his body, this denotes the estate to be an estate tail, descendible to no other heirs but to those of his body.

They serve, then, not as a designation of any person who is to take the estate, but only as descriptive of the quantity of the estate taken by the devisee." Tapping Reeve, *The Law of Baron and Femme* 60 (1862).

3. Popularly, a person who has inherited or is in line to inherit great wealth. **4.** *Civil law.* Someone who succeeds to the rights and occupies the place of, or is entitled to succeed to the estate of, a decedent, whether by an act of the decedent or by operation of law. • The term *heir* under the civil law has a more expansive meaning than under the common law.

▸ **afterborn heir.** (18c) One born after the death of an intestate from whom the heir is entitled to inherit. See *afterborn child* under CHILD.

▸ **apparent heir.** See *heir apparent.*

▸ **beneficiary heir** (ben-ə-**fish**-ee-er-ee). (1822) *Civil law.* An heir who accepts an inheritance but whose liability for estate debts is limited to the value of the inheritance. — Also termed *heir beneficiary.* See BENEFIT OF INVENTORY. Cf. *unconditional heir.*

▸ **bodily heir.** See *heir of the body.*

▸ **coheir** (koh-**air**). (16c) One of two or more persons to whom an inheritance descends.

▸ **collateral heir.** (17c) Someone who is neither a direct descendant nor an ancestor of the decedent, but whose kinship is through a collateral line, such as a brother, sister, uncle, aunt, nephew, niece, or cousin. Cf. *lineal heir.*

▸ **expectant heir.** (17c) An heir who has a reversionary or future interest in property, or a chance of succeeding to it. — Also termed *heir expectant.* See REVERSION (1); REMAINDER (1). Cf. *prospective heir.*

"The reader should be aware that one never has an 'heir' until one is dead; one merely has an 'heir expectant' . . . . Thus, to say that an heir 'owns' anything is conceptually difficult. But . . . some unborn heirs may be entitled to the protection of the courts, and thus be said to have estates." Thomas F. Bergin & Paul G. Haskell, *Preface to Estates in Land and Future Interests* 26 n.13 (2d ed. 1984).

▸ ***fideicommissary*** **heir** (fɪ-dee-ɪ-**kom**-i-sair-ee). (1913) *Roman & civil law.* A beneficiary of property who succeeds the direct (original) heir. See FIDEICOMMISSUM.

▸ **fiduciary heir.** (1860) *Roman & civil law.* An heir who takes property as a trustee on behalf of a person who is not eligible to receive the property immediately. See FIDEICOMMISSUM.

▸ **forced heir.** *Civil law.* (1813) A person whom the testator or donor cannot disinherit because the law reserves part of the estate for that person. • In Louisiana, only descendants are forced heirs. La. Civ. Code art. 1493. See LEGITIME.

▸ **heir apparent.** (14c) An heir who is certain to inherit unless he or she dies first or is excluded by a valid will. — Also termed *apparent heir.* Cf. *heir presumptive.*

"Heirs *apparent* are such, whose right of inheritance is indefeasible, provided they outlive the ancestor; as the eldest son or his issue, who must by the course of the common law be heirs to the father whenever he happens to die." 2 William Blackstone, *Commentaries on the Laws of England* 208 (1766).

▸ **heir beneficiary.** See *beneficiary heir.*

▸ **heir by adoption.** (15c) Someone who has been adopted by (and thus has become an heir to) the deceased. • By statute in most jurisdictions, an adopted child has the same right of succession to intestate property as a biological child unless the deceased clearly expresses a contrary intention. Jurisdictions differ on whether an adopted child may also inherit from his or her biological parents or family. The clear majority view, however, is that upon adoption, a complete severance of rights and obligations occurs and the child forfeits inheritance from all biological relatives.

▸ **heir by custom.** (17c) *Hist. English law.* In England, a person whose right of inheritance depends on a particular and local custom, such as gavelkind and borough English. See GAVELKIND; BOROUGH ENGLISH.

▸ **heir by devise.** (1842) One to whom lands are given by will.

▸ **heir conventional.** *Civil law.* Someone who is entitled to take a succession because of a contract or settlement.

▸ **heir expectant.** See *expectant heir.*

▸ **heir in tail.** See *heir special.*

▸ **heir male.** (15c) *Hist.* The nearest male blood-relation of a decedent.

▸ **heir of the blood.** (16c) An heir who succeeds to an estate because of consanguinity with the decedent, in either the ascending or descending line.

▸ **heir of the body.** (14c) (*usu. pl.*) *Archaic.* A lineal descendant of the decedent, excluding a surviving spouse, adopted children, and collateral relations. • The term of art *heirs of the body* was formerly used to create a fee tail <A conveys Blackacre to B and the heirs of his body>. — Also termed *bodily heir.*

▸ **heir presumptive.** (17c) An heir who will inherit if the potential intestate dies immediately, but who may be excluded if another, more closely related heir is born. — Also termed *presumptive heir.* Cf. *heir apparent.*

▸ **heirs and assigns.** (16c) A term of art formerly required to create a fee simple <A conveys Blackacre to B and his heirs and assigns>.

▸ **heir special.** (17c) *Hist.* An heir who receives property according to the nature of the estate held in fee tail. • Heirs special were said to receive property *per formam doni* ("by the form of the gift"). — Also termed *heir in tail.*

▸ **instituted heir.** See *testamentary heir.*

▸ **irregular heir.** (1837) *Hist. Louisiana law.* A person or entity who has a statutory right to take property from an estate in default of the testamentary or legal heirs.

▸ **joint heir.** (16c) **1.** A coheir. **2.** Someone who is or will be an heir to both of two designated persons at the death of the survivor of them, the word *joint* being here applied to the ancestors rather than the heirs.

▸ **known heir.** (16c) An heir who is present to claim an inheritance, the extent of which depends on there being no closer relative.

▸ **last heir.** *Hist.* The person — either the lord of the manor or the sovereign — to whom lands come by escheat when there is no lawful heir.

▸ **laughing heir.** (1943) *Slang.* An heir distant enough to feel no grief when a relative dies and leaves an inheritance (generally viewed as a windfall) to the heir.

▸ **lineal heir.** (16c) Someone who is either an ancestor or a descendant of the decedent, such as a parent or a child. Cf. *collateral heir.*

▸ **natural heir.** (16c) An heir by consanguinity as distinguished from an heir by adoption or a statutory heir (such as a person's spouse).

▸ **presumptive heir.** See *heir presumptive.*

▸ **pretermitted heir** (pree-tər-**mit**-id). (1841) A child or spouse who has been omitted from a will, as when a testator makes a will naming his or her two children and then, sometime later, has two more children who are not mentioned in the will. — Also termed (more specif.) *pretermitted child; pretermitted spouse.* See PRETERMITTED-HEIR STATUTE.

▸ **prospective heir.** (1855) An heir who may inherit but may be excluded; an heir apparent or an heir presumptive. Cf. *expectant heir.*

▸ **right heir.** (14c) **1.** *Hist.* The preferred heir to an estate tail, as distinguished from a general heir. • An estate tail would pass to a general heir only on the failure of the preferred heir and his line. **2.** HEIR (1).

▸ **substitute heir.** (1830) *Louisiana law.* A person named in a will as an alternate heir to another named person and who inherits if the first named heir dies before the testator.

▸ **testamentary heir** (tes-tə-**men**-tə-ree *or* -tree). (17c) *Civil law.* Someone who is appointed as an heir in the decedent's will. — Also termed *instituted heir.*

▸ **unconditional heir.** (1888) *Civil law.* Someone who expressly or tacitly chooses to inherit without any reservation or without making an inventory. Cf. *beneficiary heir.*

heirdom. (13c) The quality, state, or condition of being an heir; succession by inheritance.

heiress. (17c) **1.** *Archaic.* A female heir. See HEIR (1). **2.** A woman or girl who has inherited or is in line to inherit great wealth.

heir general. See HEIR (1).

heir-hunter. (1928) A person whose business is to track down missing heirs.

heirless estate. See ESTATE (3).

heirloom. (15c) **1.** An item of personal property that by local custom, contrary to the usual legal rule, descends to the heir along with the inheritance, instead of passing to the executor or administrator of the last owner. • Traditional examples are an ancestor's coat of arms, family portraits, title deeds, and keys. Blackstone gave a false etymology that many have copied: "The termination, *loom,* is of Saxon origin; in which language it signifies a limb or member; so that an heirloom is nothing else, but a limb or member of the inheritance." 2 William Blackstone, *Commentaries on the Laws of England* 427 (1766). In fact, *loom* derives from Old English *geloma* "utensil," and *loom* meant "implement, tool." **2.** Popularly, a treasured possession of great sentimental value passed down through generations within a family.

> "Heir-looms, strictly so called, are now very seldom to be met with. They may be defined to be such personal chattels as go, by force of a *special custom,* to the heir, along with the inheritance, and not to the executor or administrator of the last owner. The owner of an heir-loom cannot by his will bequeath the heir-loom, if he leave the land to descend to his heir; for in such a case the force of custom will prevail over the bequest, which, not coming into operation until after the decease of the owner, is too late to supersede the custom. . . . In popular language the term 'heir-loom' is generally applied to plate, pictures or articles of property which have been assigned by deed of settlement or bequeathed by will to trustees, in trust to permit the same to be used and enjoyed by the persons for the time being in possession, under the settlement or will, of the mansion-house in which the articles may be placed." Joshua Williams, *Principles of the Law of Personal Property* 13-14 (11th ed. 1881).

heir portioner. See PORTIONER (1).

heirship. (13c) **1.** The quality, state, or condition of being an heir. **2.** The relation between an ancestor and an heir.

hell-or-high-water clause. (1980) A clause in a personal-property lease requiring the lessee to continue to make full rent payments to the lessor even if the thing leased is unsuitable, defective, or destroyed.

hell-or-high-water rule. (1960) **1.** The principle that a personal-property lessee must pay the full rent due, regardless of any claim against the lessor, unless the lessee proves unequal bargaining power or unconscionability. **2.** *Insurance.* The principle that an insured's automobile-liability policy will cover the insured while using a vehicle owned by another if the insured uses the vehicle in a manner within the scope of the permission granted.

henceforth, *adv.* (14c) From now on <the newly enacted rule will apply henceforth>.

henfare. *Hist.* A fine for flight from an accusation of murder.

Henricus Vetus (hen-**rɪ**-kəs **vee**-təs). [Law Latin] Henry the Old (or *Elder*). • This term was used in early English charters to distinguish King Henry I from later kings of the same name.

Henry VIII clause. (1931) *English law.* A statutory provision that enables amendment or repeal by administrative regulation, thereby minimizing the degree of parliamentary scrutiny of any such changes. • The term derives from the Statute of Proclamations (1539), which gave King Henry VIII the power to legislate by proclamation.

heordpenny (**hərd**-pen-ee), *n.* See PETER-PENCE.

Hepburn Act. A 1906 federal statute that amended the Interstate Commerce Act to (1) increase the (now defunct) Interstate Commerce Commission's jurisdiction to include pipelines, (2) prohibit free passes except to employees, (3) prohibit common carriers from transporting any products (except timber) in which they had an interest, and (4) require joint tariffs and a uniform system of accounts.

heptarchy (**hep**-tahr-kee). (16c) **1.** A government by seven rulers. **2.** A country divided into seven governments, specif. the seven Anglo-Saxon kingdoms of Kent, Sussex, Essex, Wessex, East Anglia, Mercia, and Northumbria existing until the 9th century.

herald, *n.* (13c) **1.** *English & Scots law.* In England and Scotland, one of several officers responsible for keeping genealogical lists and tables, adjusting armorial bearings, and regulating the ceremonies at royal coronations and funerals. • There are six in England and three in Scotland. **2.** *Hist.* A messenger who announces royal or state proclamations, and who carries diplomatic messages (esp.

proclamations of war, peace, or truce) between kings or countries.

Heralds' College. *English law.* A royal corporation responsible in England for granting and recording armorial insignia and genealogies, and for dealing with matters of precedence. • The College was founded by Richard III in 1484, is governed by the Earl Marshal, and consists of three kings of arms, six heralds, and four pursuivants. The heralds' books, based on family-lineage inquiries made throughout England, are considered good evidence of pedigrees. The heralds' office is still allowed to make grants of arms and to grant name changes. — Also termed *College of Arms.*

herbage (**hər**-bij). (15c) *English law.* In England, an easement or liberty of pasturage on another's land.

herdwerch (**hərd**-wərk), *n. Hist.* Herdsmen's work, or customary labor, done by shepherds and inferior tenants at the lord's will. — Also spelled *heordwerch.*

hereafter, *adv.* (bef. 12c) **1.** From now on; henceforth <because of the highway construction, she will hereafter take the bus to work>. **2.** At some future time <the court will hereafter issue a ruling on the gun's admissibility>. **3.** HEREINAFTER <the exhibits hereafter referred to as Exhibit A and Exhibit B>.

here and there. See VALUE DATE.

herebannum (her-ə-**ban**-əm), *n.* [Law Latin fr. Old English *here* "army" + *bann* "proclamation"] *Hist.* **1.** A proclamation summoning the army into the field. **2.** A mulct or fine for not joining that army when summoned. **3.** A tax or tribute for the support of that army.

herebote (**her**-ə-boht), *n.* [fr. Old English *here* "army" + *bod* "command"] (17c) *Hist. English law.* In England, a royal edict summoning the people to the battlefield; an edict commanding subjects into battle. — Also spelled *herebode; hebote.*

hereby, *adv.* (13c) By this document; by these very words <I hereby declare my intention to run for public office>.

heredad (e-re-**dahd**), *n. Spanish law.* **1.** An inheritance or heirship. **2.** A piece of land under cultivation; a cultivated farm.

▸ ***heredad yacente*** (e-re-**dad** yah-**sen**-te). An inheritance not yet accepted. See *hereditas jacens* under HEREDITAS.

heredero (e-re-**der**-oh), *n. Spanish law.* **1.** An heir or legatee. **2.** An owner of a cultivated farm.

heredes. See HERES.

heredes alioqui successuri (hə-**ree**-deez ay-lee-**oh**-kwɪ sək-**ses**-ə-rɪ). [Latin] *Hist.* Heirs entitled otherwise to succeed. — Also termed *heredes alioquin successuri.*

heredes nati et facti (hə-**ree**-deez **nay**-tɪ et **fak**-tɪ). [Latin] *Hist.* Heirs born and made.

heredes proximi (hə-**ree**-deez **prok**-sə-mɪ), *n.* [Latin] Nearest or next heirs.

heredes proximi et remotiores (hə-**ree**-deez **prok**-sə-mɪ **et** ri-moh-shee-**or**-eez). [Latin] *Hist.* Heirs nearer and more remote.

heredes remotiores (hə-**ree**-deez ri-moh-shee-**or**-eez), *n.* [Latin] (18c) Heirs more remote; relatives other than children or descendants.

heredipeta (he-rə-**dip**-ə-tə), *n.* [Law Latin] *Hist.* A legacy-hunter; the seeker of an inheritance.

heredis institutio (hə-**ree**-dis in-sti-**t**[**y**]**oo**-shee-oh). See INSTITUTIO HEREDIS.

hereditament (her-ə-**dit**-ə-mənt *or* hə-**red**-i-tə-mənt). (15c) **1.** Any property that can be inherited; anything that passes by intestacy. **2.** Real property; land.

> "A tenement is anything which can be holden, that is, anything subject to tenure. Hereditaments are things which can be inherited; that is, which, on the death of the owner intestate, descend to the heir. Personal as well as real property may be a hereditament; for instance, heirlooms, which, though personal property, descend with the inheritance. Thus 'tenement' is a broader term than 'land,' and 'hereditament' broader than 'tenement.'" Earl P. Hopkins, *Handbook on the Law of Real Property* § 1, at 3 (1896).

▸ **corporeal hereditament** (kor-**por**-ee-əl). (18c) A tangible item of property, such as land, a building, or a fixture.

▸ **incorporeal hereditament** (in-kor-**por**-ee-əl). (18c) An intangible right in land, such as an easement. • The various types at common law were advowsons, annuities, commons, dignities, franchises, offices, pensions, rents, tithes, and ways.

> "There are two quite distinct classes of incorporeal hereditaments: 1. Those which may ripen into corporeal hereditaments. Thus a grant to A for life with remainder to B in fee simple gave B an incorporeal hereditament which becomes corporeal after A's death. 2. Those which can never become corporeal hereditaments but are merely rights over the land of another, e.g., rentcharges." Robert E. Megarry & M.P. Thompson, *A Manual of the Law of Real Property* 361 (6th ed. 1993).

hereditary, *adj.* (16c) Of, relating to, or involving inheritance; that descends from an ancestor to an heir.

hereditary, *n.* **1.** A person whose rank, title, status, office, or the like is acquired by inheritance rather than earned by skill and merit. **2.** See *hereditary lease* under LEASE. **3.** A country whose rule or leadership is passed by inheritance.

hereditary lease. See LEASE.

hereditary succession. See *intestate succession* under SUCCESSION (2).

hereditas (hə-**red**-i-tas), *n.* [Latin] **1.** *Roman law.* An inheritance by universal succession to a decedent. • This succession applied whether the decedent died testate or intestate, and whether in trust (*ex fideicommisso*) for another or not. The comparable right under Praetorian law was *bonorum possessio,* possession of an inheritance that could be the basis of a right to succeed. **2.** *Hist.* An estate transmissible by descent; an inheritance. — Also spelled *haereditas.*

▸ ***hereditas damnosa*** (hə-**red**-i-tas dam-**noh**-sə). (1930) A burdensome inheritance; an inheritance whose debts exceed its assets.

▸ ***hereditas jacens*** (hə-**red**-i-tas **jay**-senz). [Latin *iaceo* "to lie"] (18c) **1.** Property belonging to an estate before an heir accepts it. • This term had a similar meaning at common law. See ABEYANCE (2).

> "Hereditas jacens is the term applied to an inheritance which has not yet vested, an inheritance, that is to say, which has been 'delata' to a heres extraneus (i.e. voluntarius), but has not yet been acquired by him." Rudolph Sohm, *The Institutes: A Textbook of the History and System of Roman Private Law* 512 (James Crawford Ledlie trans., 3d ed. 1907).

2. *Hist.* A decedent's estate that has no heir or legatee to take it; an escheated estate. — Also termed *caduca*. See ESCHEAT. 3. *Hist.* An inheritance without legal owner and thus open to the first occupant.

▸ ***hereditas legitima*** (hə-**red**-i-tas lə-**jit**-i-mə). A succession or inheritance devolving by operation of law rather than by will. See INTESTACY.

▸ ***hereditas luctuosa*** (hə-**red**-i-tas lək-choo-**oh**-sə). A sad or mournful inheritance; one that disturbs the natural order of mortality (*turbato ordine mortalitatis*), as that of a parent inheriting a child's estate. • This term is more literary than legal. — Also termed *tristis successio*.

▸ ***hereditas paterna*** (hə-**red**-i-tas pə-**tər**-nə). [Latin] (18c) *Hist.* A succession that descends through the father.

▸ ***hereditas testamentaria*** (hə-**red**-i-tas tes-tə-men-**tair**-ee-ə). Testamentary inheritance; succession to an estate under a decedent's will.

heredity. (16c) **1.** *Archaic.* Intestate succession; the taking of an inheritance by common-law succession. **2.** The genetic transmission of characteristics from a parent to a child; the biological law by which characteristics of a living being tend to repeat themselves in the being's descendants. Cf. SOCIAL HEREDITY.

herein, *adv.* (bef. 12c) In this thing (such as a document, section, or paragraph) <the due-process arguments stated herein should convince the court to reverse the judgment>. • This term is inherently ambiguous.

hereinafter, *adv.* (16c) Later in this document <the buyer agrees to purchase the property described hereinafter>. — Also loosely termed *hereafter*.

hereinbefore, *adv.* (17c) In a preceding part of this document or writing.

herenach (**her**-ə-nak), *n.* [fr. Old Irish *airchinnich* "chief man"] (17c) An archdeacon. — Also spelled *erenach*.

hereof, *adv.* (bef. 12c) Of this thing (such as a provision or document); relating or belonging to this document <the conditions hereof are stated in section 3>.

hereon, *adv.* (bef. 12c) **1.** (Of position) on this (place, document, etc.). **2.** On this basis, matter, or subject. — Also termed (in senses 1 & 2) *hereupon*. **3.** On the occurrence of (a condition).

heres (**heer**-eez), *n.* [Latin] *Roman law.* A successor to the rights and liabilities of a deceased person; an heir. • Because the *heres* succeeded to both the rights and the debts of the decedent, the office combined that of a modern executor with that of an heir at law. The institution of the *heres* was the essential characteristic of a testament; if this was not done, the instrument was called a *codicillus*. — Also spelled (in Law Latin) *haeres*. Pl. ***heredes*** (hə-**ree**-deez) or (for *haeres*) ***haeredes.***

> "[E]very natural person who had rights, or was subject to obligations or duties, at the time of his death, necessarily had a successor or heir [*haeres*], who possessed all his rights and was subject to all his obligations and duties. Moreover, every person's successor or heir was either such a person as he himself appointed by his will (*haeres factus*), or, if he made no appointment, such person as was designated by law (*haeres natus*). An heir designated by law became such for his own benefit alone. An heir appointed by will was required to pay such legacies as were given by the will, subject to which he also took the inheritance for his own benefit. In respect to the obligations and duties to which the deceased was subject at the time of his death, there was no difference between the *haeres factus* and the *haeres natus*; for such obligations and duties fell, necessarily and by operation of law, upon the one and the other, without distinction. So completely, indeed, was the heir of the deceased person identified with the deceased, that the law made no distinction between the estate of the one and that of the other, nor between the debts of the one and those of the other." C.C. Langdell, *A Brief Survey of Equity Jurisdiction*, 4 Harv. L. Rev. 99, 101 (1890).

▸ ***fiduciarius heres*** (fi-d[y]oo-shee-**air**-ee-əs **heer**-eez). [Latin "fiduciary heir"] *Roman law.* A person formally named an heir in a testament, but in a fiduciary capacity, and charged to deliver the succession to the person designated by the testament.

▸ ***heres actu*** (**heer**-eez **ak**-t[y]oo). [Law Latin] *Hist.* Heir by appointment.

▸ ***heres astrarius*** (as-**trair**-ee-əs). [Law Latin "heir of the hearth"] An heir who has received, by conveyance, an ancestor's estate during the ancestor's lifetime.

▸ ***heres de facto*** (di **fak**-toh). [Law Latin "heir from fact"] *Hist.* **1.** An heir whose status arises from the disseisin or other wrongful act of the heir's ancestor. See DISSEISIN. **2.** An heir in fact, as distinguished from an heir by law (*de jure*).

▸ ***heres ex asse*** (**as**-ee). [Latin "sole heir"] (16c) *Roman law.* An heir to the whole estate.

▸ ***heres ex testamento*** (eks tes-tə-**men**-to). See *heres factus*.

▸ ***heres extraneus*** (ek-**stray**-nee-əs). [Latin "extraneous heir"] (1884) *Roman law.* An external heir; one who had not been subject to the testator's power (*potestas*) and hence not bound to accept the inheritance. Pl. ***heredes extranei*** (hə-**ree**-deez ek-**stray**-nee-ɪ).

▸ ***heres factus*** (**fak**-təs). [Latin "made heir"] (18c) An heir appointed by will; a testamentary heir. — Also termed *heres ex testamento*; *heres institutus*. Cf. *heres natus*.

▸ ***heres fideicommissarius*** (fɪ-dee-ɪ-kom-ə-**sair**-ee-əs). [Latin] *Roman law.* The person for whose benefit an estate was given by will to a fiduciary heir. • This office corresponds loosely to the *cestui que trust* of the common law. Cf. *heres fiduciarius*.

▸ ***heres fiduciarius*** (fi-d[y]oo-shee-**air**-ee-əs). [Latin "fiduciary heir"] (18c) *Roman law.* A person made heir by will, in trust for the benefit of another; an heir subject to a trust. Cf. *heres fideicommissarius*.

▸ ***heres in mobilibus*** (**heer**-eez in moh-**bil**-i-bəs). [Law Latin] (18c) *Hist.* Heir in movables.

▸ ***heres institutus*** (in-sti-**t[y]oo**-təs). See *heres factus*.

▸ ***heres legitimus*** (lə-**jit**-i-məs). [Latin "lawful heir"] (18c) *Roman law.* An heir entitled to succeed (on intestacy) by the laws of the Twelve Tables.

▸ ***heres natus*** (**nay**-təs). [Latin "heir by birth"] (18c) An heir by reason of birth; an heir at law or by intestacy. Cf. *heres factus*.

▸ ***heres necessarius*** (nes-ə-**sair**-ee-əs). [Latin "necessary heir"] (1852) *Roman law.* A slave freed on the testator's death and thus compelled to accept the inheritance.

▸ ***heres rectus*** (**rek**-təs). [Law Latin] *Hist.* A right or proper heir.

▸ ***heres suus*** (**s[y]oo**-əs). [Latin "one's own heir"] **1.** A decedent's proper or natural heir; a lineal descendant of the deceased. **2.** *Roman law.* A free person who was subject to the testator's power (*potestas*) but who could exercise full legal rights upon the testator's death.

▸ ***heres suus et necessarius*** (s[y]**oo**-əs et nes-ə-**sair**-ee-əs). [Latin "one's own and necessary heir"] A free person subject to the decedent's *potestas.* • These heirs were called *necessary* because they became heirs by law, not by the decedent's choice. But since this was also true of slaves, when named heirs in a will, the former class was designated *suus et necessarius* by way of distinction, the word *suus* denoting that the necessity arose from the relationship to the decedent.

▸ ***suus heres*** (s[y]**oo**-əs **heer**-eez). [Latin] (18c) *Roman law.* An heir in the power of the deceased, by whom acceptance of the inheritance was not necessary. See SUI HEREDES.

▸ ***ultimus heres*** (**əl**-ti-məs). (18c) The last or remote heir; the lord.

▸ ***unciarius heres*** (ən-shee-**air**-ee-əs **heer**-eez). [Latin] *Roman law.* An heir to one-twelfth of an estate or inheritance.

heresy (**her**-ə-see), *n.* (13c) **1.** Opinion or doctrine contrary to (usu. Roman Catholic) church dogma. **2.** *Hist. English law.* In England, an offense against religion, consisting not in totally denying Christianity, but in publicly denying some of its essential doctrines; an opinion on divine subjects devised solely by human reason, openly taught, and obstinately maintained. • This offense is now subject only to ecclesiastical correction and is no longer punishable by the secular law. — **heretical,** *adj.*

hereto, *adv.* (12c) To this document <the exhibits are attached hereto>.

heretofore, *adv.* (13c) Up to now; before this time <a question that has not heretofore been decided>.

hereunder, *adv.* (15c) **1.** Later in this document <review the provisions hereunder before signing the consent form>. **2.** In accordance with this document <notice hereunder must be provided within 30 days after the loss>.

hereunto, *adv.* (16c) To this.

hereupon, *adv.* (12c) **1.** HEREON (1). **2.** HEREON (2). **3.** (Of time or consequence) immediately after this.

herewith, *adv.* (bef. 12c) With or in this letter or document <enclosed herewith are three copies>.

herezeld. (15c) *Hist.* In a feudal system, a vassal's best animal (esp. the best horse, ox, or cow), given in tribute to the superior upon the vassal's death. — Also spelled *hereyeld; herield.*

herield. See HEREZELD.

heriot (**her**-ee-ət), *n.* [fr. Old English *here* "army" + *geatwa* "trappings"] (bef. 12c) *Hist.* A customary tribute of goods and chattels payable to the lord of the fee upon the tenant's death. • *Heriot* derives from an earlier feudal service consisting of military equipment returned to the lord on the tenant's death; over time it came to refer only to the chattel payment due at the tenant's death.

> "The heriot, which was an obligation that existed among the Saxons, has sometimes been confounded with the relief, but it has not been shown by Bracton, a writer in a subsequent reign, to be a distinct thing, the heriot being a voluntary present, made by the tenant at his death to his lord, of his best beast, or his second best, according to the custom of the place. It had not, like the relief, any respect to the inheritance." George Crabb, *A History of English Law* 78 (1st Am. ed. 1831).

> "We are told that the ancient heriot (*heregeatu*, military apparel) had at one time consisted of the horses and arms lent by the lord to his man which on the man's death were returned to the lord. . . . Turning to manorial surveys, we find it among the commonest of customs that when a tenant in villeinage dies, the lord shall have the best beast; sometimes a similar due is taken from the goods of the dead freeholder, and it is to these customary dues that the name 'heriot' permanently attaches itself." 1 Frederick Pollock & Frederic W. Maitland, *The History of English Law Before the Time of Edward I* 312, 317 (2d ed. 1898).

▸ **heriot custom.** (17c) A heriot due by custom. • This term is used primarily to distinguish a *heriot service* from an ordinary heriot.

▸ **heriot service.** (16c) A tribute arising from special reservation in a grant or lease of lands, and thus amounting to little more than rent.

herislit (**her**-ə-sleet *or* **hair**-), *n.* [Old English] *Hist.* **1.** The act of surrendering; laying down of arms. **2.** The crime of deserting from an army.

heritable (**her**-i-tə-bəl), *adj.* (14c) **1.** (Of property) capable of being inherited. **2.** (Of a person) capable of inheriting. — Also termed *inheritable.*

heritable blood. See BLOOD.

heritable bond. See BOND (2).

heritable jurisdiction. (17c) *Hist. Scots law.* The power of a laird to try his own people and hand down punishments, including death. • The laird or clan chief traditionally acted as a supreme court. There was no appeal from decisions and sentences were usu. carried out immediately. The Heritable Jurisdiction Act of 1748 abolished this power.

heritable obligation. See OBLIGATION.

heritable property. *Scots law.* See HERITAGE.

heritable security. See SECURITY (4).

heritage (**her**-i-tij), *n.* (13c) *Scots law.* Property that passed on death to the owner's heir; esp., land and all the property connected to it (such as a house). — Also termed *heritable property.*

heritage conservation. See HISTORIC PRESERVATION.

heritage preservation. See HISTORIC PRESERVATION.

Her Majesty's Stationery Office. See STATIONERY OFFICE.

hermaphrodite. See INTERSEX. — **hermaphroditic,** adj.

hermeneutics (hər-mə-**n[y]oo**-tiks), *n.* (18c) The art of interpreting texts, esp. as a technique used in critical legal studies. — **hermeneutical, hermeneutic,** *adj.*

Hermogenian Code. See CODEX HERMOGENIANUS.

hesia (**hee**-zhee-ə *or* **hee**-shee-ə), *n.* [Law Latin] An easement.

hetaerarcha (het-ər-**ahr**-kə), *n.* [Greek *hetaera* "association" + *archein* "to rule"] *Roman law.* The head of a society, corporation, or college.

hetaeria (hə-**teer**-ee-ə), *n.* [Greek "association"] (1849) *Roman law.* A society, guild, or college; a fraternity. — Also termed (in English) *hetaery.*

heterologous, *adj.* (1893) *Patents.* Of, relating to, or constituting the DNA of a foreign organism.

heterologous artificial insemination. See *artificial insemination by donor* under ARTIFICIAL INSEMINATION.

heterosexual, *adj.* (1892) **1.** Of, relating to, or characterized by sexual desire for a person of the opposite sex. **2.** Of or related to sexual intercourse involving people of different sexes.

heuristic (hyuu-**ris**-tik), *adj.* (1821) Of, relating to, or involving a method of learning or problem-solving by using trial-and-error and other experiential techniques <heuristic discovery methods>.

heuristics, *n.* (1860) The study of how people use their experience to answer questions and to improve their performance; specif., the study of learning and problem-solving through trial-and-error and other experiential techniques.

HEW. *abbr.* The Department of Health, Education, and Welfare, a former agency of the U.S. government created in 1953. • When the Department of Education was created in 1979, the name of HEW was changed to the Department of Health and Human Services (HHS).

Heydon's case, rule in. See MISCHIEF RULE.

HGN. *abbr.* Horizontal-gaze nystagmus. See HORIZONTAL-GAZE NYSTAGMUS TEST.

HGN test. *abbr.* HORIZONTAL-GAZE NYSTAGMUS TEST.

HHS. *abbr.* DEPARTMENT OF HEALTH AND HUMAN SERVICES.

hiatus. *Patents.* A gap between the time when a parent application ceases to be pending (by abandonment or issuance) and the time a continuing application is filed. • A hiatus breaks the chain of continuity, so that later applications are not entitled to the effective filing date of the parent application. Cf. CONTINUITY (2).

hidage (**hɪd**-ij), *n.* (12c) *Hist.* A tax, payable to the Crown, based on every hide of land. — Also spelled *hydage.* See HIDE.

> "Of the same nature with scutages upon knights'-fees were the assessments of hydage upon all other lands, and of talliage upon cities and burghs. But they all gradually fell into disuse, upon the introduction of subsidies, about the time of king Richard II and king Henry IV." 1 William Blackstone, *Commentaries on the Laws of England* 300 (1765).

hidalgo (hi-**dal**-goh *or* ee-**dahl**-goh), *n.* [fr. Spanish *hijo* "son" + *algo* "property"] (16c) In Spain, a man belonging to the lower nobility; a gentleman of property.

hidalguia (ee-dahl-**gee**-yə), *n.* [Spanish] In Spain, nobility by descent or lineage.

HIDC. *abbr.* HOLDER IN DUE COURSE.

hidden asset. See ASSET.

hidden danger. See *latent danger* under DANGER.

hidden defect. See DEFECT.

hidden fraud. See *fraudulent concealment* under CONCEALMENT.

hidden tax. See TAX.

hide, *n. Hist.* (bef. 12c) **1.** *English law.* In England, a measure of land consisting in as much as could be worked with one plow, variously estimated as from 30 to 120 acres but probably determined by local usage. • A hide was anciently employed as a unit of taxation. Cf. CARUCATE. **2.** As much land as would support one family or the dwellers in a mansion-house. — Also termed (in senses 1 & 2) *hide land.* **3.** A house; a dwelling-house.

hidegild (**hɪd**-gild), *n.* [Old English] (bef. 12c) *Hist.* A sum of money paid by a villein or servant to avoid a whipping. — Also spelled *hidgild; hydegeld; hudegeld.*

hidel (**hɪd**-əl *or* **hid**-əl), *n.* [Old English] (13c) *Hist.* A hiding-place; a place of protection or sanctuary.

hide land. 1. See HIDE (1). **2.** See HIDE (2).

hierarchical church. See CHURCH (2).

high bailiff. See BAILIFF (2).

High Commission Court. See COURT OF HIGH COMMISSION.

high commissioner. See COMMISSIONER.

High Court. 1. See HIGH COURT OF JUSTICE. **2.** See HIGH COURT OF JUSTICIARY.

High Court of Admiralty. *English law.* In England, a court exercising jurisdiction in matters relating to shipping, collision, and salvage cases. • The court dates from the 14th century, and much of its early history concerns prize and piracy cases. Its jurisdiction varied through the centuries, sometimes extending into criminal matters and other areas of law not related directly to maritime issues. The Judicature Acts of 1873–1875 merged the Court into the High Court as part of the Probate, Divorce, and Admiralty Division. The Administration of Justice Act of 1970 established a new Admiralty Court as part of the Queen's Bench Division of the High Court. It is regulated by the Supreme Court Act of 1981. — Also termed *Court of the Lord High Admiral; Court of Admiralty.* Cf. ADMIRALTY (1).

> "To the office of the Lord High Admiral (originally a naval official concerned with the command of the fleet and the suppression of piracy and wrecking) there was annexed a court which acquired a jurisdiction over civil cases of a maritime nature. Just how and when this happened is too cloudy and controversial for simple or even accurate summary, but by the time of Richard II (1377–1400) the admiral and vice-admiral were transacting enough judicial business to move Parliament to limit their jurisdiction by statute to 'a thing done upon the sea,' and in Tudor times the court was well established as a court of record, doing a large civil business. It slowly but surely took away most of their business from the local maritime courts in the port towns, and attracted the easily aroused jealousy of the common law courts, as well as the dislike of those who feared it as a prerogative court . . . . These factors resulted in the rather anticlimactic eclipse of the court for almost two centuries." Grant Gilmore & Charles L. Black Jr., *The Law of Admiralty* § 1-4, at 9–10 (2d ed. 1975).

High Court of Australia. The highest federal court in the Australian judicial system. • Established in 1901, the High Court is based in Canberra.

High Court of Chivalry. *Hist.* A court of honor having jurisdiction over matters relating to deeds of arms and war, armorial insignia, and precedence. — Also termed *Court of Chivalry; Court of Earl Marshal.* See COURT OF HONOR.

> "This *Curia Marescalli*, or High Court of Chivalry, was revived by James I as a court of honour, which not only tried the right to distinctions of honour and coat armour but also redressed affronts to honour such as slander. The slander jurisdiction was later denied, leaving it with a jurisdiction probably confined to disputes over armorial bearings, which are determined according to the law of arms. The court, which has only sat once since 1737, is the last English court to use the procedure of the civil law." J.H. Baker, *An Introduction to English Legal History* 142 (3d ed. 1990).

High Court of Delegates. See COURT OF DELEGATES.

High Court of Errors and Appeals. See COURT OF ERRORS AND APPEALS.

High Court of Justice. The superior civil court of England and Wales. — Often shortened to *High Court.*

High Court of Justiciary (jə-stish-ee-er-ee). *Scots law.* The superior criminal court of Scotland, acting both as a trial court and as a court of final criminal appeal. • Its judges are Lords Commissioners of Justiciary. — Often shortened to *High Court.*

high crime. See CRIME.

high-crime area. (1949) A geographic locale that purportedly has a significant incidence of crime — which can affect the evaluation of police conduct on a motion to suppress that alleges unlawful search and seizure.

high degree of care. See *great care* under CARE (2).

high diligence. See *great diligence* under DILIGENCE (2).

higher-brain death. See DEATH.

higher court. See *court above* under COURT.

higher scale. See SCALE (4).

highest and best use. See USE (1).

highest court. See COURT.

highest degree of care. See CARE (2).

highest proved value. See VALUE (2).

high flier. (1961) *Slang.* A security that has strongly attracted public interest so that investors pay an unusually high price.

highgrade, *vb.* (1907) **1.** To steal rich ore, as from a mine by a miner. **2.** To mine only esp. valuable ore (such as gold).

high-grade security. See SECURITY (4).

high justice. See JUSTICE (6).

high–low agreement. (1980) A settlement in which a defendant agrees to pay the plaintiff a minimum recovery in return for the plaintiff's agreement to accept a maximum amount regardless of the outcome of the trial. — Also termed *hilo settlement.*

highly prudent person. See REASONABLE PERSON.

high-managerial agent. See AGENT.

high misdemeanor. See MISDEMEANOR (1).

high offense. See *high crime* under CRIME.

high-probability rule. (1916) *Marine insurance.* The principle that an insured may abandon a vessel if it appears extremely likely that a total loss is imminent.

high seas. See SEA.

high sheriff. See SHERIFF (3).

high-test marriage. See *covenant marriage* under MARRIAGE (1).

high treason. See TREASON.

high-water line. See *high-water mark* under WATERMARK (1).

high-water mark. See WATERMARK (1).

highway. (bef. 12c) **1.** Broadly, any main route on land, on water, or in the air. **2.** A free and public roadway or street that every person may use. Cf. CARRIAGEWAY.

> "Every thoroughfare which is used by the public, and is, in the language of the English books, 'common to all the king's subjects,' is a highway, whether it be a carriage-way, a horse-way, a foot-way, or a navigable river. It is, says Lord Holt, the *genus* of all public ways." 3 James Kent, *Commentaries on American Law* *432 (George Comstock ed., 11th ed. 1866).

3. The main public road, esp. a wide one, connecting towns or cities. **4.** The entire width between boundaries of every publicly maintained way when part is open to public use for purposes of vehicular traffic.

▸ **common highway.** (16c) A highway for use by the public for any purpose of transit or traffic.

▸ **public highway.** (17c) A highway controlled and maintained by governmental authorities for general use.

highway act. (*usu. pl.*) (1807) One of a body of statutes governing the laying out, construction, repair, and use of highways. — Also termed *highway law.*

highwayman. (17c) A highway robber; a person who robs on a public road. • The term is most common in historical contexts. In the 17th and 18th centuries, it was common for highwaymen to stop carriages on the roads and rob people.

highway patrol. (1914) The police who enforce the law, esp. speed limits, on major roadways.

highway rate. (18c) *Hist. English law.* In England, a tax for the maintenance and repair of highways.

highway robbery. See ROBBERY.

highway tax. See TAX.

high-yield bond. See BOND (3).

high-yield debt obligation. See *high-yield bond* under BOND (3).

high-yield security. See *high-yield bond* under BOND (3).

higuela (ee-gay-lah), *n. Spanish law.* A receipt given by a decedent's heir, setting forth what property the heir has received from the estate, and kept as a record.

HIIP. *abbr.* High-impact incarceration program — an intensive substance-abuse-treatment program used in some states for pretrial supervision and for some probations.

hijack, *vb.* (1923) **1.** To commandeer (a vehicle, airplane, or ship), esp. at gunpoint. See CARJACK; SKYJACK. **2.** To steal or rob from (a vehicle or airplane in transit). **3.** *Hist.* To rob by trickery or violence; esp., to rob (a smuggler or bootlegger) and take illegal goods.

Hilary Rules. (19c) *Hist. English law.* A collection of English pleading rules designed to ease the strict pleading requirements of the special-pleading system, esp. by limiting the scope of the general issue in the formed actions and by forcing the defendant to set up affirmatively all matters other than a denial of the breach of duty or of the wrongful act. • Promulgated in England in the 1834 Hilary Term, these rules followed an 1828 initiative to examine procedural laws and other subjects and to report to Parliament changes that might be enacted. The rules had the unintended effect of extending the reach of strict-pleading requirements into new areas of law. Widespread dissatisfaction with the Hilary Rules led to the liberalization of the pleading system under the 1873–1875 Judicature Acts. — Formerly also termed *New Rules.*

> "The failure of the Hilary Rules . . . lay in their insistence on special pleading as it was understood late in the eighteenth century. That parties should plead precisely, and clarify as far as possible the issue between them, is one thing;

that their endeavours to do so should be judged by the extremely artificial standards of the old system, was quite another." Theodore F.T. Plucknett, *A Concise History of the Common Law* 416 (5th ed. 1956).

Hilary sittings. (1876) *English law.* In England, a term of court beginning on January 11 of each year and ending on the Wednesday before Easter. • The Hilary sittings were known as *Hilary term* until 1875. Cf. EASTER SITTINGS; MICHAELMAS SITTINGS; TRINITY SITTINGS.

hilo settlement. See HIGH-LOW AGREEMENT.

***Hilton* doctrine.** (1974) *Civil procedure.* The rule that in a dispute between parties to an oil-and-gas lease, royalty owners who would lose their rights if the defendant's lease were terminated are regarded as indispensable parties to a proceeding challenging the lease. *Hilton v. Atlantic Refining Co.*, 327 F.2d 217 (5th Cir. 1964).

Himalaya clause. (1974) *Maritime law.* A provision in a bill of lading extending the carrier's defenses and limitations under the Carriage of Goods by Sea Act to third parties, typically employees, agents, and independent contractors. • The Supreme Court has held that this type of clause must be strictly construed. *Robert C. Herd & Co. v. Krawill Machinery Corp.*, 359 U.S. 297, 79 S.Ct. 766 (1959). See CARRIAGE OF GOODS BY SEA ACT.

"The plaintiff was injured while a passenger on the cruise ship *The Himalaya*. She sued the master and the boatswain for their negligence because the carrier was contractually exempt from all liability. Because the contract did not have a 'Himalaya clause,' she succeeded. The carrier, having indemnified its employees, ultimately paid the damages. It thus lost its contractual exemption indirectly." Michael J. Sturley, *International Uniform Law in National Courts*, 27 Va. J. Int'l L. 729, 740 n.101 (1987).

hinc inde (**hink in**-dee). [Law Latin] *Scots law.* On either side. • The phrase usu. refers to the respective claims of parties to a lawsuit.

hinder, *vb.* (14c) **1.** (Of progress) to slow or make difficult. **2.** To hold back. **3.** (Of action) to impede, delay, or prevent.

hindering, *n.* (14c) The unlawful act of impeding or obstructing the processes of law enforcement, justice, or government.

hine (hɪn), *n. Hist. English law.* In England, a husbandry servant. — Also spelled *hind.*

hinefare (**hɪn**-fair), *n. Hist. English law.* In England, the loss or departure of a servant from the master.

hinegeld (**hɪn**-geld), *n. Hist. English law.* A ransom for an offense committed by a servant.

HIPAA (**hip**-ə). *abbr.* HEALTH INSURANCE PORTABILITY AND ACCOUNTABILITY ACT.

hipoteca (ee-poh-**tek**-ah), *n. Spanish law.* A mortgage of real property. See HYPOTHECATION.

Hippocratic oath. (18c) The solemn medical-ethics vow taken by newly certified physicians to treat the ill to the best of their ability, to respect and preserve the patient's privacy, and to teach the techniques of medicine to the next generation.

hire, *vb.* (bef. 12c) **1.** To engage the labor or services of another for wages or other payment. **2.** To procure the temporary use of property, usu. at a set price. **3.** To grant the temporary use of services <hire themselves out>.

hired gun. (1971) *Slang.* **1.** An expert witness who testifies favorably for the party paying his or her fee, often because of that financial relationship rather than because of the facts. **2.** A lawyer who stops at nothing to accomplish the client's goals, regardless of moral consequences.

hireling, *n.* (bef. 12c) Someone who is hired or serves for wages, esp. one who works only for the sake of payments.

hire purchase. See INSTALLMENT PLAN.

hire-purchase agreement. See LEASE-PURCHASE AGREEMENT.

hiring. See LOCATIO.

hiring at will. See *employment at will* under EMPLOYMENT.

his. (bef. 12c) A possessive pronoun of the masculine gender but traditionally used and construed to include both sexes. • Because of the trend toward nonsexist language, careful drafters now tend to avoid the generic use of *his* (and the personal pronouns *he* and *him*) unless the reference is only to a male person.

His Honor; Her Honor. (1827) **1.** A third-person title customarily given to a judge. **2.** A third-person title customarily given to the mayor of a city. **3.** A third-person title given by the Massachusetts Constitution to the lieutenant governor of the commonwealth. Cf. YOUR HONOR.

his testibus (his **tes**-tə-bəs). [Law Latin] *Hist.* These being witnesses. • The concluding clause of deeds and charters typically opened with these words, which stated the names of the witnesses to the instrument. This clause appeared in deeds and charters until the 16th century. — Also spelled *hijs testibus*; *hiis testibus.*

historian. *Parliamentary law.* An officer charged with compiling or contributing to an organization's official history.

historical cost. See *acquisition cost* (1) under COST (1).

historical fact. See FACT (2).

historical interpretation. See ORIGINALISM.

historical jurisprudence. See JURISPRUDENCE.

historic bay. See BAY.

historic building. A structure at least 50 years old and officially regarded by local, state, or federal government as having special value or significance. — Also termed *historic structure.*

historicism. See ORIGINALISM.

historic preservation. (1897) The effort to conserve, preserve, and protect artifacts and developed places, including structures and landscapes, of historical significance. — Also termed *heritage conservation*; *heritage preservation.*

historic-preservation law. (1965) An ordinance prohibiting the demolition or exterior alteration of certain historic buildings or of all buildings in a historic district.

historic site. (1870) A building, structure, area, or property that is significant in the history, architecture, archaeology, or culture of a country, state, or city, and has been so designated by statute. • A historic site usu. cannot be altered without the permission of the appropriate authorities.

historic structure. See HISTORIC BUILDING.

hit, *n.* (bef. 12c) **1.** A physical strike. **2.** *Criminal law.* A murder committed for money or on orders from a gang leader. **3.** *Criminal law.* An instance of the taking of a drug. **4.** *Intellectual property.* A single instance of a computer's connection to a webpage. • Counters keep track of how many visitors a webpage attracts, and a large number of hits is a major selling point for advertising. **5.** *Intellectual property.* A webpage identified by an Internet search engine as containing words matching a user's query. **6.** A creative work that is a popular or a commercial success.

hit-and-run, *n.* (1924) An accident, esp. a motor-vehicle accident, in which one or more of the drivers involved, usu. those at fault, leave the scene before law-enforcement officials arrive.

hit-and-run statute. (1931) A law requiring a motorist involved in an accident to remain at the scene and to give certain information to the police and others involved.

hither, *adv.* (bef. 12c) *Archaic.* Here <Come hither!>.

hitherto, *adv.* (13c) Until now; heretofore.

H.L. *abbr.* HOUSE OF LORDS.

HLA test. See HUMAN-LEUKOCYTE ANTIGEN TEST.

H.M. Customs and Excise. See H.M. REVENUE AND CUSTOMS.

HMO. *abbr.* (1971) HEALTH-MAINTENANCE ORGANIZATION.

H.M. Revenue and Customs. *English law.* The government department responsible for direct and indirect taxation in the United Kingdom. — Formerly termed *H.M. Customs and Excise.*

HOA. *abbr.* Homeowners' association. See ASSOCIATION.

hoard, *vb.* (bef. 12c) To acquire and hold (goods) beyond one's reasonable needs, usu. because of an actual or anticipated shortage or price increase <hoarding food and medical supplies during wartime>.

hobbler. (14c) *Hist. English law.* In England, a light horseman or bowman; a tenant bound by his tenure to maintain a small light horse for military service.

Hobbs Act. 1. A federal anti-racketeering act making it a crime to interfere with interstate commerce by extortion, robbery, or physical violence. 18 USCA § 1951. See RACKETEER INFLUENCED AND CORRUPT ORGANIZATIONS ACT. **2.** A federal statute vesting exclusive jurisdiction in the circuit courts over orders, rules, and regulations of certain federal agencies. 18 USCA § 2342.

hobby loss. See LOSS.

hoc. [Latin] This; with; by; in.

hoc intuitu (**hok** in-**t[y]oo**-ə-t[y]oo). [Law Latin] *Scots law.* In this prospect. • The phrase appeared in reference to deeds executed in expectation of an event, such as a marriage.

hoc loco (**hok loh**-koh). [Law Latin] *Hist.* In this place.

hoc nomine (**hok nahm**-ə-nee). [Law Latin] *Hist.* In this name.

hoc ordine (**hok or**-di-nee). [Law Latin] *Hist.* In this order.

hoc titulo (**hok tit**-yə-loh *or* **tich**-ə-loh). [Law Latin] *Hist.* Under this title.

hodgepodge. (15c) **1.** HOTCHPOT (1). **2.** An unorganized mixture.

hodgepodge act. (1883) A statute that deals with incongruous subjects.

> "*Hodge-Podge Act.* . . . Such acts, besides being evident proofs of the ignorance of the makers of them, or of their want of good faith, are calculated to create a confusion which is highly prejudicial to the interests of justice. . . . In many states bills, except general appropriation bills, can contain but one subject, which must be expressed in the title." 1 John Bouvier, *Bouvier's Law Dictionary* 1444 (Francis Rawle ed., 8th ed. 1914).

hold, *n.* **1.** An order to preserve something or to delay or postpone an action.

▸ **litigation hold.** A notice issued in anticipation of a lawsuit or investigation, ordering employees to preserve documents and other materials relevant to that lawsuit or investigation.

2. *Archaic. English law.* In England, tenure. • This word occurs most often in conjunction with others — for example, *freehold, leasehold* — and rarely in its separate form. See HOLDING (4).

hold, *vb.* (bef. 12c) **1.** To possess by a lawful title <Sarah holds the account as her separate property>. **2.** (Of a court) to adjudge or decide as a matter of law (as opposed to fact) <this court thus holds the statute to be unconstitutional>. Cf. FIND. **3.** To direct and bring about officially; to conduct according to law <we must hold an election every two years>. **4.** To keep in custody or under an obligation <I will ask the judge to hold you accountable>. **5.** To take or have an estate from another; to have an estate on condition of paying rent or performing service <James holds Hungerstream Manor under lease>. **6.** To conduct or preside at; to convoke, open, and direct the operations of <Judge Brown holds court four days a week>. **7.** To possess or occupy; to be in possession and administration of <Jones holds the office of treasurer>.

holdback, *n.* An amount withheld from the full payment of a contract pending the other party's completion of some obligation, esp. to ensure that a contractor finishes the work agreed on beforehand. • The terms of a holdback are typically expressed in the contract. The device gives the contractor an incentive to finish the work, and the other party security that the work will be finished. — **hold back,** *vb.*

holder. (14c) **1.** Someone who has legal possession of a negotiable instrument and is entitled to receive payment on it. **2.** A person with legal possession of a document of title or an investment security. **3.** Someone who possesses or uses property.

holder for value. (18c) Someone who has given value in exchange for a negotiable instrument. • Under the UCC, examples of "giving value" include acquiring a security interest in the instrument and accepting the instrument in payment of an antecedent claim. UCC § 3-303(a). — Also termed *bona fide holder for value.*

holder in due course. (1882) Someone who in good faith has given value for a negotiable instrument that is complete and regular on its face, is not overdue, and, to the possessor's knowledge, has not been dishonored. • Under UCC § 3-305, a holder in due course takes the instrument free of all claims and personal defenses, but subject to real defenses. — Abbr. HDC; HIDC. — Also termed *due-course holder.*

holder in good faith. (18c) Someone who takes property or an instrument without knowledge of any defect in its title.

holder of record. See STOCKHOLDER OF RECORD.

hold harmless, *vb.* (18c) To absolve (another party) from any responsibility for damage or other liability arising from the transaction; INDEMNIFY. — Also termed *save harmless.*

hold-harmless agreement. (1939) A contract in which one party agrees to indemnify the other. — Also termed *save-harmless agreement*. See INDEMNITY.

hold-harmless clause. See INDEMNITY CLAUSE.

holding, *n.* (15c) **1.** A court's determination of a matter of law pivotal to its decision; a principle drawn from such a decision. Cf. OBITER DICTUM; RATIO DECIDENDI. **2.** A ruling on evidence or other questions presented at trial. **3.** (*usu. pl.*) Legally owned property, esp. land or securities. **4.** *Hist.* In feudal law, tenure.

holding cell. See JAIL.

holding charge. (1949) A criminal charge of some minor offense filed to keep the accused in custody while prosecutors take time to build a bigger case and prepare more serious charges.

holding company. See COMPANY.

holding-company tax. See TAX.

holding over. 1. A tenant's action in continuing to occupy the leased premises after the lease term has expired. • Holding over creates a tenancy at sufferance, with the tenant being referred to as a *holdover.* See *tenancy at sufferance* under TENANCY. **2.** *Parliamentary law.* An officer's continued tenure beyond the term for which he or she was elected, usu. because a successor has not been elected or cannot yet assume the office.

holding period. (1935) *Tax.* The time during which a capital asset must be held to determine whether gain or loss from its sale or exchange is long-term or short-term.

holding zone. See ZONE.

hold order. (1945) A notation in a prisoner's file stating that another jurisdiction has charges pending against the prisoner and instructing prison officials to alert authorities in that other jurisdiction instead of releasing the prisoner.

hold out, *vb.* (16c) **1.** To represent (something) as true <hold themselves out as spouses>; esp., to represent (oneself or another) as having a certain legal status, as by claiming to be an agent or partner with authority to enter into transactions <even though he was only a promoter, Schwartz held himself out as the principal>. **2.** To refuse to yield or submit; to stand firm <Womack held out for a higher salary and better benefits>. **3.** To maintain, continue, or resist until the end <hold out against the siege>.

holdover clause. See TRAILER CLAUSE.

holdover tenancy. See *tenancy at sufferance* under TENANCY.

holdover tenant. See TENANT (1).

hold pleas. *Archaic.* To hear or try cases.

holdup. See STICKUP.

holiday. See LEGAL HOLIDAY.

holograph (**hol**-ə-graf), *n.* (17c) A document (such as a will or deed) that is handwritten by its author. • The majority rule is that a holographic will need not be entirely handwritten — only the "material provisions" — to take into account the popular use of fill-in-the-blank will forms. This is also the position of the Uniform Probate Code. — Also termed *olograph*; *autograph.* Cf. ONOMASTIC (2); SYMBOLIC. — **holographic,** *adj.*

holographic will. See WILL.

holymote. See HALLMOTE (4).

homage (**hom**-ij). (14c) In feudal times, a ceremony that a new tenant performed for the lord to acknowledge the tenure. • This was the most honorable service that a free tenant might do for a lord. In the ceremony, kneeling before the lord, the tenant placed his hands between the lord's hands while saying, "I become your man from this day forward, of life and limb and earthly honor, and to you will be faithful and loyal, and bear you faith, for the tenements that I claim to hold of you, saving the faith that I owe unto our sovereign lord the king, so help me God."

> "Homage is an oath of fidelity, acknowledging himself to be the lord's man: wherein the tenant must be ungirt, uncovered, kneel upon both knees, and hold both his hands together between the lord's hands sitting before him. This is to be done only to the lord himself." Henry Finch, *Law, or a Discourse Thereof* 143 (1759).

▸ ***homage ancestral*** (**hom**-ij an-**ses**-trəl). [Law French] A type of homage in which a tenant and the tenant's ancestors have held immemorially of another by the service of homage. • This long-standing relationship bound the lord to warrant the title and to hold the tenant clear of all services to superior lords. — Also spelled *homage auncestral* (aw-**mahzh** on-se-**stral**).

▸ ***homage liege*** (**hom**-ij **leej**). Homage due the sovereign alone as supreme lord, done without any saving or exception of the rights of other lords. — Also termed *homagium ligium* (hə-**may**-jee-əm **lɪ**-jee-əm).

homage jury. See JURY.

homagio respectuando (hə-**may**-jee-oh ri-spek-choo-**an**-doh), *n.* [Law Latin "homage to the respected"] (17c) *Hist.* A writ to the escheator commanding the delivery of seisin of lands to the heir of the king's tenant, even though the heir had not performed homage.

homagium (hə-**may**-jee-əm), *n.* [Law Latin] A formal ceremony in which a feudal tenant acknowledged the tenure granted by a lord; HOMAGE; MANHOOD (2).

▸ ***homagium ligium.*** See *homage liege* under HOMAGE.

▸ ***homagium planum*** (**play**-nəm), *n.* [Law Latin "plain homage"] (18c) *Hist.* A type of homage binding the homager to nothing more than fidelity, without obligation either of military service or of attendance in the superior's courts.

▸ ***homagium reddere*** (**red**-ə-ree), *n.* [Law Latin "to renounce homage"] (18c) *Hist.* The process, prescribed in feudal law by a set form and method, by which a vassal disowns and defies the lord.

▸ ***homagium simplex*** (**sim**-pleks), *n.* [Law Latin "simple homage"] *Hist.* A type of homage that acknowledges tenure, while reserving the rights of other lords.

hombre bueno (**awm**-bray **bway**-noh), *n. Spanish law.* **1.** An arbitrator chosen by the parties to a suit. **2.** A judge. **3.** A citizen in good standing; esp., one who is competent to testify in a suit.

home. (bef. 12c) A dwelling place.

▸ **family home.** A house that was purchased during marriage and that the family has resided in, esp. before a divorce. • In some jurisdictions, the court may award the family home to the custodial parent until (1) the youngest child reaches the age of 18 or is otherwise emancipated, (2) the custodial parent moves, or (3) the custodial parent remarries. In making such an award, the court typically reasons that it is in the best interests of the child to remain in the family home. — Also termed *marital home*; *marital residence*.

▸ **manufactured home.** (1973) *Secured transactions.* A structure, transportable in one or more sections, that when traveling is 8 body feet or more in width or 40 body feet or more in length, or, when erected on site, is 320 or more square feet, and that is built on a permanent chassis and designed to be used as a dwelling with or without a permanent foundation when connected to the required utilities, and that has within it plumbing, heating, air-conditioning, and electrical systems. UCC § 9-102(a)(53).

▸ **matrimonial home.** See *matrimonial domicile* under DOMICILE.

▸ **tax home.** See TAX HOME.

home confinement. (1986) A condition of probation or of post-incarceration release requiring a defendant to remain at home for a specific period, often while being monitored with a GPS tracking device. • A few departures to known destinations may be allowed.

home detention. See HOUSE ARREST.

home-equity line of credit. See *home-equity loan* under LOAN.

home equity loan. See LOAN.

home invasion. (1912) The illegal and forceful entry into a private dwelling for the purpose of committing a usu. violent crime while an occupant is present, often after tricking an occupant into opening the door.

homeland security. (2001) Collectively, the measures taken by the U.S. government after the terrorist attacks of 11 September 2001 to prevent further terrorism within the country.

homeless person. See PERSON (1).

homeless shelter. See SHELTER (1).

home loan bank. See FEDERAL HOME LOAN BANK.

home office. (1864) **1.** A corporation's principal office or headquarters. **2.** (*cap.*) *English law.* In England, the Department of the Secretary of State for Home Affairs, responsible for overseeing the internal affairs of the country. • Established in 1782, the Home Office has become one of the United Kingdom's major departments of state, with primary responsibility (since 2007) for counterterrorism and intelligence, security, and policing, and immigration.

home-office expense. See EXPENSE.

homeowners' association. 1. See ASSOCIATION. **2.** See OWNERS' ASSOCIATION (1).

homeowner's equity loan. See LOAN.

homeowner's insurance. See INSURANCE.

homeowner's policy. See INSURANCE POLICY.

Home Owners Warranty. A warranty and insurance program that, among other coverage, insures a new home for ten years against major structural defects. • The program was developed by the Home Owners Warranty Corporation, a subsidiary of the National Association of Home Builders. Builders often provide this type of coverage, and many states provide similar warranty protection by statute. — Also spelled *Home Owners' Warranty.* — Abbr. HOW.

home port. See PORT.

home-port doctrine. (1920) *Maritime law.* The rule mandating that a vessel engaged in interstate and foreign commerce is taxable only at its home port, usu. where the vessel is registered.

home rule. (1860) A state legislative provision or action allocating a measure of autonomy to a local government, conditional on its acceptance of certain terms. Cf. LOCAL OPTION.

> "Home rule in the United States was sometimes envisioned in its early days as giving the cities to whom such rule was granted full-fledged sovereignty over local affairs, thus bringing about dual state and local sovereignty along the national plan of federal and state governments. But such local sovereignty has never developed, nor have any clear-cut distinctions between state and local power." Osborne M. Reynolds Jr., *Handbook of Local Government Law* § 35, at 96 (1982).

home-rule charter. See CHARTER (2).

home secretary. (*usu. cap.*) (18c) The British government minister in charge of the Home Office.

homestall. (bef. 12c) *Hist.* Homestead.

home state. (1871) *Family law.* **1.** The state where a person is domiciled. **2.** In an interstate child-custody dispute governed by the Uniform Child Custody Jurisdiction and Enforcement Act, the state where a child has lived with a parent or a person acting as a parent for at least six consecutive months immediately before the proceeding.

home-state jurisdiction. See JURISDICTION.

homestead, *n.* (bef. 12c) **1.** The house, outbuildings, and adjoining land owned and occupied by a person or family as a residence. • As long as the homestead does not exceed in area or value the limits fixed by law, in most states it is exempt from forced sale for collection of a debt. — Also termed *homestead estate.* See HOMESTEAD LAW. — **homestead,** *vb.* — **homesteading,** *n.*

▸ **business homestead.** (1882) The premises on which a family's business is located. • In some states, business homesteads are exempt from execution or judicial sale for most kinds of debt.

▸ **constitutional homestead.** (1851) A homestead, along with its exemption from forced sale, conferred on the head of a household by a state constitution. — Also termed *statutory homestead*; *pony homestead.*

▸ **pony homestead.** See *constitutional homestead.*

▸ **probate homestead.** (1881) A homestead created by a probate court from a decedent's estate for the benefit of the decedent's surviving spouse and minor children. • Under most statutes providing for the creation of a probate homestead, it is exempt from forced sale for the collection of decedent's debts. The family can remain in the home at least until the youngest child reaches the age of majority. Many states allow the surviving spouse to live in the home for life. In a few states, such as Texas, the right to a probate homestead is constitutional. See *family allowance, spousal allowance* under ALLOWANCE (1); HOMESTEAD LAW. Cf. *life estate* under ESTATE (1).

▸ **statutory homestead.** See *constitutional homestead.*

2. A surviving spouse's right of occupying the family home for life. • In some states, the right is extended to other dependents of a decedent.

homesteader. (1872) Someone who acquires or occupies a homestead.

homestead estate. See HOMESTEAD.

homestead exemption. See HOMESTEAD LAW.

homestead-exemption statute. See HOMESTEAD LAW.

homestead law. (1847) A statute exempting a homestead from execution or judicial sale for debt, unless all owners, usu. a husband and wife, have jointly mortgaged the property or otherwise subjected it to creditors' claims. — Also termed *homestead exemption*; *homestead-exemption statute*; *homestead right.*

homestead right. See HOMESTEAD LAW.

home-study report. (1965) *Family law.* A summary of an investigation into a child's home, family environment, and background, usu. prepared by a social worker when a child has been removed from his or her home because of abuse or neglect, but also prepared after a similar investigation of the home of potential adoptive parents. — Often shortened to *home study.* — Also termed *custody evaluation*; *social study.*

home-style exemption. (1996) *Copyright.* A provision in the U.S. Copyright Act allowing for the public airing of radio and television broadcasts in public-accommodation establishments, such as bars and restaurants, with immunity from liability for infringement. • The exemption is so named because the equipment used for the airing must be a single receiver of the type typically found in homes. 17 USCA § 110(5).

homicidal, *adj.* (18c) **1.** Of, relating to, or involving homicide <homicidal incidents>. **2.** Likely to commit murder <homicidal maniac>.

homicide (hom-ə-sɪd), *n.* (14c) **1.** The killing of one person by another. **2.** Someone who kills another.

> "The legal term for killing a man, whether lawfully or unlawfully, is 'homicide.' There is no *crime* of 'homicide.' Unlawful homicide at common law comprises the two crimes of murder and manslaughter. Other forms of unlawful homicide have been created by statute: certain new forms of manslaughter (homicide with diminished responsibility, and suicide pacts), infanticide, and causing death by dangerous driving." Glanville Williams, *Textbook of Criminal Law* 204 (1978).

▸ **criminal homicide.** (1850) **1.** Homicide prohibited and punishable by law, such as murder or manslaughter. **2.** The act of purposely, knowingly, recklessly, or negligently causing the death of another human being. Model Penal Code § 210.1.

> "Criminal homicide is everywhere divided into categories that reflect the historical distinction in English law between murder and manslaughter. American statutory formations have varied the terminology and the precise classifications; many statutes create more than two forms of criminal homicide, for purposes of definition and/or punishment. These variations notwithstanding, it is usually possible to discern a category that corresponds to the common-law crime of murder, the paradigm of which is a deliberate killing without legal justification or excuse, and a category that corresponds to the common-law crime of manslaughter and comprises killings that either are committed in circumstances which substantially mitigate their intentional aspect or are not intentional. In common speech as well as in the law, *murder* refers to the most serious criminal homicides, and *manslaughter* to those that may be serious crimes for which a substantial penalty is imposed but lack the special gravity of murder." Lloyd L. Weinreb, "Homicide: Legal Aspects," in 2 *Encyclopedia of Crime and Justice* 855, 857 (Sanford H. Kadish ed., 1983).

▸ **criminally negligent homicide.** See *negligent homicide.*

▸ **culpable homicide.** (16c) *Scots law.* A wrongful act that results in a person's death but does not amount to murder. Cf. MANSLAUGHTER.

▸ **excusable homicide.** (18c) **1.** Homicide resulting from a person's lawful act, committed without intention to harm another. **2.** See *justifiable homicide* (1).

▸ **felonious homicide.** (18c) Homicide committed unlawfully, without legal justification or excuse. • This is the category into which murder and manslaughter fall.

▸ **homicide by abuse.** (1989) Homicide in which the perpetrator, under circumstances showing an extreme indifference to human life, causes the death of the perpetrator's dependent — usu. a child or mentally retarded person.

▸ **homicide by misadventure.** See ACCIDENTAL KILLING.

▸ **homicide per infortunium** (pər in-for-t[y]oo-nee-əm). [Latin "homicide by misfortune"] (1856) The unintentional killing of another while engaged in a lawful act; ACCIDENTAL KILLING. See PER INFORTUNIUM.

▸ **innocent homicide.** (1884) Homicide that does not involve criminal guilt.

▸ **justifiable homicide.** (18c) **1.** The killing of another in self-defense when faced with the danger of death or serious bodily injury. — Also termed *excusable homicide.* See SELF-DEFENSE (1). **2.** A killing mandated or permitted by the law, such as execution for a capital crime or killing to prevent a crime or a criminal's escape.

> "It should be noted that a justifiable homicide is not criminal, since it is a killing which the law has either commanded or permitted: the *actus* in such a case is not legally punishable, and therefore we may perhaps say that it is an *actus* of killing which is not *reus.* As we shall see in most cases of justifiable homicide the killing is intentional, and therefore the mental element of criminal responsibility is clearly present: but there is no crime committed since there is no *actus reus.*" J.W. Cecil Turner, *Kenny's Outlines of Criminal Law* 109 (16th ed. 1952).

> "English lawyers once distinguished between 'excusable' homicide (e.g. accidental non-negligent killing) and 'justifiable' homicide (e.g. killing in self-defence or in the arrest of a felon) and different legal consequences once attached to these two forms of homicide. To the modern lawyer this distinction has no longer any legal importance: he would simply consider both kinds of homicide to be cases where some element, negative or positive, required in the full definition of criminal homicide (murder or manslaughter) was lacking. But the distinction between these two different ways in which actions may fail to constitute a criminal offence is still of great moral importance. Killing in self-defence is an exception to a general rule making killing punishable; it is admitted because the policy or aims which in general justify the punishment of killing (e.g. protection of human life) do not include cases such as this. In the case of 'justification' what is done is regarded as something which the law does not condemn, or even welcomes." H.L.A. Hart, "Prolegomenon to the Principles of Punishment," in *Punishment and Responsibility* 1, 13 (1968).

▸ **negligent homicide.** (1859) Homicide resulting from the careless performance of a legal or illegal act in which the danger of death is apparent; the killing of a human being by criminal negligence. — Also termed *criminally negligent homicide.* See *criminal negligence* under NEGLIGENCE.

> "There is no common-law offense known as 'negligent homicide.' As a matter of the common law of crimes

any killing below the grade of manslaughter is innocent homicide. Some of the new penal codes have a classification scheme which (omitting degrees or other variations) divides criminal homicide into murder, manslaughter and criminally negligent homicide — or simply negligent homicide. For the most part, however, this has been achieved by removing from manslaughter the offense of homicide by criminal negligence and using this to constitute the newly named offense. Thus, though there are a few exceptions, most states will have no homicide offense which would be below common-law manslaughter." Rollin M. Perkins & Ronald N. Boyce, *Criminal Law* 116–17 (3d ed. 1982).

▸ **nonfelonious homicide.** (1896) A killing that is legally either excusable or justifiable. See *excusable homicide*; *justifiable homicide*.

▸ **public-service homicide.** (1995) *Slang.* The killing of a criminal by another criminal.

▸ **reckless homicide.** (1866) The unlawful killing of another person with conscious indifference toward that person's life. Cf. MANSLAUGHTER.

▸ **vehicular homicide.** (1952) The killing of a person as a result of the unlawful or negligent operation of a motor vehicle. — Also termed *automobile homicide*.

▸ **victim-precipitated homicide.** (1957) **1.** See *suicide-by-cop* under SUICIDE (1). **2.** A killing provoked by the victim who consciously intended to die at the hands of another person. • This term applies loosely to any assisted suicide. Unlike most types of homicide, the victim bears some of the responsibility for causing his or her own death.

▸ **willful homicide.** (1860) The act of intentionally causing a person's death, with or without legal justification.

homicide by misadventure. See ACCIDENTAL KILLING.

homicide per infortunium. See ACCIDENTAL KILLING.

homicidium (hom-ə-SI-dee-əm), *n.* [Latin "felling of a person"] Homicide.

▸ **homicidium ex casu** (eks **kay**-s[y]oo). Homicide by accident. See ACCIDENTAL KILLING.

▸ **homicidium ex justitia** (eks jəs-**tish**-ee-ə). Homicide in the administration of justice, or in the carrying out of a legal sentence. See *justifiable homicide* (2) under HOMICIDE.

▸ **homicidium ex necessitate** (eks nə-ses-i-**tay**-tee). Homicide from inevitable necessity, such as protecting one's person or property. See *justifiable homicide* (1) under HOMICIDE.

▸ **homicidium ex voluntate** (eks vol-ən-**tay**-tee). Voluntary or willful homicide. See *criminal homicide* under HOMICIDE.

▸ **homicidium in rixa** (hom-ə-SI-dee-əm in **rik**-sə). [Law Latin] (17c) *Scots law.* Homicide committed in the course of a brawl.

"Homicidium in rixa . . . . Such crime amounts only to culpable homicide, and the punishment being in the discretion of the judge, varies according to the particular circumstances of each case. It is not punished capitally, because this crime lacks the previous malice essential to the crime of murder." John Trayner, *Trayner's Latin Maxims* 244 (4th ed. 1894).

homily. See SERMON (1).

hominatio (hom-ə-**nay**-shee-oh), *n.* [Law Latin] *Hist.* HOMAGE.

homine capto in withernamium (**hom**-ə-nee **kap**-toh in wi<u>th</u>-ər-**nay**-mee-əm). [Law Latin "for taking a man in withernam"] (17c) *Hist.* A writ for the arrest of a person who had taken a bondman out of the country to prevent a replevy. See WITHERNAM.

homine replegiando (**hom**-ə-nee ri-plee-jee-**an**-doh). [Law Latin "for replevying a man"] (16c) *Hist.* A writ to replevy a man out of prison, or out of the custody of a private person.

homines (**hom**-ə-neez), *n.* [Latin "men"] *Hist.* Feudal tenants entitled to have their causes and other matters tried only in their lord's court. See HOMO.

▸ ***homines ligii*** (**lI**-jee-I). [Latin] (17c) *Hist.* Liege men; feudal tenants or vassals, esp. those who held immediately of the sovereign.

homing device. (1933) **1.** A technological means of locating a particular thing or target. **2.** A special part of a weapon that pinpoints its target.

homiplagium (hom-ə-**play**-jee-əm), *n.* [Law Latin] *Hist.* The maiming of a person.

hommes de fief (awm də **feef**), *n.* [French "men of the fief"] *Hist.* Feudal tenants; peers in the lords' courts. — Also termed *hommes feodaux*.

homo (**hoh**-moh), *n.* [Latin] *Hist.* **1.** A male human. **2.** A homo sapiens; a human being of either sex. **3.** A slave. **4.** A vassal; a feudal tenant. **5.** A retainer, dependent, or servant. See HOMINES. Pl. ***homines.***

▸ ***homo alieni juris*** (ay-lee- *or* al-ee-**ee**-nI **joor**-is). See FILIUSFAMILIAS.

▸ ***homo chartularius*** (kahr-chə-**lair**-ee-əs). (17c) A slave manumitted by charter.

▸ ***homo civitatis*** (**hoh**-moh siv-i-**tay**-tis). [Latin] *Hist.* Man of the city.

▸ ***homo commendatus*** (kom-ən-**day**-təs). A man who commends himself into another's power for protection or support.

▸ ***homo ecclesiasticus*** (e-klee-z[h]ee-**as**-ti-kəs). A church vassal; one bound to serve a church, esp. in an agricultural capacity.

▸ ***homo economicus*** (**hoh**-moh ee-kə-**nom**-i-kəs). [Latin] *Hist.* Economic man.

▸ ***homo exercitalis*** (eg-zər-shə-**tay**-lis). A man of the army; a soldier.

▸ ***homo feodalis*** (fyoo-**day**-lis). A fee man; a vassal or tenant who holds a fee.

▸ ***homo fiscalis*** (fis-**kay**-lis). A servant or vassal belonging to the treasury (*fiscus*). — Also termed *homo fiscalinus*.

▸ ***homo francus*** (**frangk**-əs). **1.** *English law.* In England, a freeman. **2.** A Frenchman.

▸ ***homo ingenuus*** (in-**jen**-yoo-əs). A free and lawful man; a yeoman.

▸ ***homo liber*** (**lI**-bər). **1.** A free man. **2.** A freeman lawfully competent to be a juror. **3.** An allodial proprietor, as distinguished from a feudal tenant. See ALLODIAL.

▸ ***homo ligius*** (**lI**-jee-əs). (1935) A liege man, esp. the vassal of a king.

▸ ***homo novus*** (**noh**-vəs). (17c) **1.** A new tenant or vassal; one invested with a new fee. **2.** A tenant pardoned after being convicted of a crime.

▸ ***homo pertinens*** (**pər**-tə-nenz). A feudal bondman or vassal; one belonging to the soil.

▸ ***homo politicus*** (**hoh**-moh pə-**lit**-i-kəs). [Latin] *Hist.* Political man.

▸ ***homo regius*** (**ree**-jee-əs). A king's vassal.

▸ ***homo Romanus*** (rə-**may**-nəs). A Roman. • A term used in Germanic law codes to describe the Roman inhabitants of Gaul and other former Roman provinces.

▸ ***homo sociologicus*** (**hoh**-moh soh-see-oh-**loj**-i-kəs). [Latin] *Hist.* Sociological man.

▸ ***homo sui juris*** (s[y]**oo**-I **joor**-is). See PATERFAMILIAS.

▸ ***homo trium litterarum*** (**trI**-əm lit-ə-**rair**-əm). [Latin "a man of three letters"] (17c) A thief. • The "three letters" refers to *f, u,* and *r,* for the Latin word *fur* ("thief").

homologación. See HOMOLOGATION.

homologare (hom-ə-lə-**gair**-ee), *vb.* [Law Latin] *Civil law.* **1.** To confirm or approve; to consent or assent. **2.** To confess.

homologate (hə-**mol**-ə-gayt), *vb.* (17c) *Civil law.* To approve or confirm officially <the court homologated the sale>.

homologation (hə-mol-ə-**gay**-shən). (17c) *Civil law.* **1.** Confirmation, esp. of a court granting its approval to some action. **2.** The consent inferred by law from a party's failure, for a ten-day period, to complain of an arbitrator's sentence, of an appointment of a syndic (or assignee) of an insolvent, or of a settlement of successions. **3.** A judge's approval of certain acts and agreements to render them more readily enforceable. — Also termed (in Spanish law) *homologación* (oh-moh-loh-gah-**syohn**). See *judgment homologating the tableau* under JUDGMENT (2).

homologous artificial insemination. See *artificial insemination by husband* under ARTIFICIAL INSEMINATION.

homologous insemination. See *artificial insemination by husband* under ARTIFICIAL INSEMINATION.

homophobia. (1969) A fear or hatred of homosexuals.

homosexual, *adj.* (1891) **1.** Of, relating to, or characterized by sexual desire for a person of the same sex. **2.** Of or related to sexual intercourse involving people of the same sex.

homosexual-advance defense. See *gay-panic defense* under DEFENSE (1).

homosexual marriage. See *same-sex marriage* under MARRIAGE (1).

homosexual-panic defense. See *gay-panic defense* under DEFENSE (1).

Hon. *abbr.* (18c) HONORABLE.

honest-agent theory. See FAITHFUL-AGENT THEORY.

honest claim. See CLAIM (3).

honest error. See GOOD-FAITH MISTAKE.

honeste vivere ([h]ə-**nes**-tee **vI**-və-ree). [Latin] *Roman law.* To live honorably. • This was one of the three general precepts in which Justinian expressed the requirements of the law. Cf. ALTERUM NON LAEDERE; SUUM CUIQUE TRIBUERE.

honest mistake. See MISTAKE.

honest-services doctrine. See INTANGIBLE-RIGHTS DOCTRINE.

honest-services law. (1997) A statute making it a crime to deprive someone else of the intangible right of honest services.

honesty. The character or quality of being truthful and trustworthy; esp., a disposition to behave in accordance with justice and honorable dealing, esp. as regards candor and truth-telling.

honesty clause. See FULL-REPORTING CLAUSE (1).

honesty defense. See DEFENSE (1).

honor, *n.* (13c) **1.** In the United States, a courtesy title given to judges and certain other public officials. **2.** (*often pl.*) *English law.* A dignity or privilege, degree of nobility, knighthood, or other title that flows from the Crown.

> "[W]e may collect three Distinctions of Honour, the first in Expression only, and founded upon virtuous and noble Actions, where no Reward has attended, but the general Reputation of a brave and spotless Character; which Honour may subsist in a private Life, without any popular or personal Distinction. The Second Kind of Honour, is that which is apply'd to signify the Privilege of Blood, which some bring into the world with them, or are by Succession rais'd to the highest Honours: and this Honour in Blood, is justly kept up and held in sacred Esteem in all civiliz'd and polite Nations. The third Notion of Honour, is, when Blood and Merit meet in the same Person; and this is, of all others, the most glorious; the Honour so acquir'd, lives in his Family, and perpetuates his Vertues to Posterity; whilst the Glory those by descents of Blood shine in, without some personal Distinction, is but the Reflection of their ancestors." *The Laws of Honour; or, A Compendious Account of the Ancient Derivation of All Titles, Dignities, Offices, Etc.* ii (1714).

3. *Hist.* A seigniory of several manors held under one baron or lord paramount.

honor, *vb.* (13c) **1.** To accept or pay (a negotiable instrument) when presented. **2.** To recognize, salute, or praise.

Honorable. (15c) A title of respect given to judges, members of the U.S. Congress, ambassadors, and the like <The Honorable Ruth Bader Ginsburg>. • Used primarily in writing, less often in speech, the title should always be coupled with the full name <The Honorable John Roberts> <Hon. John Roberts>. It is considered a solecism to omit the first name, as often happens in congressional hearings on the placards placed before those who testify <*Hon. Breyer>. — Abbr. Hon.

▸ **Most Honorable.** (16c) *English law.* A title of respect given to marquises and (collectively) to the Order of the Bath and to members of the Privy Council.

▸ **Right Honorable.** (15c) *English law.* A title of respect given to earls, viscounts, privy councilors, and various high civil functions, esp. judges on important appellate courts, as well as (sometimes) peers' children who have courtesy titles.

honorable discharge. See DISCHARGE (8).

honorable-engagement clause. (2003) *Reinsurance.* An arbitration provision in a reinsurance contract allowing the arbitrators to view the reinsurance arrangement reasonably — in line with the agreement's general purposes — rather than strictly according to the rules of law or an unduly technical interpretation of contractual language.

honorarium (on-ə-**rair**-ee-əm), *n.* (17c) **1.** A payment of money or anything else of value made to a person for services rendered for which fees cannot legally be or are not traditionally paid. **2.** A voluntary reward for that for which no remuneration could be collected by law; a voluntary donation in consideration of services that admit of no compensation in money. **3.** *Roman law.* A gratuitous payment, esp. for professional services, as distinguished from compensation for physical labor. Cf. MERCES. Pl. **honoraria; honorariums.**

honorary, *adj.* (16c) (Of a title or status) conferred in recognition of merit or service, but without the attendant rights, powers, or duties; nominal <honorary member>. • An honorary title or status may be granted without regard to whether the honoree ever held the title or status in fact. The honorary title conferred on a former officer who has honorably retired from office is often "emeritus" or "emerita." See EMERITUS.

honorary canon. See CANON (5).

honorary feud. *Hist. English law.* In England, a title of nobility descending to the eldest son only. See FEUD (1)–(3).

honorary services. *Hist. English law.* Special services rendered to the king by a person holding tenure of grand serjeanty. • The services usu. consisted of carrying the royal banner or sword, or serving at the king's coronation as a butler, as a champion, or in some other capacity.

honorary trust. See TRUST (3).

honor crime. See CRIME.

honor killing. See *honor crime* under CRIME.

honor offense. See *honor crime* under CRIME.

honor system. (1904) A protocol whereby members of a group agree to obey certain rules even though no one checks whether they are being followed.

hoodwink, *vb.* (17c) To deceive as if by blinding; to trick (someone) in a clever way so as to gain an advantage for oneself.

hooligan. (1898) **1.** An unruly or mischievous person who causes trouble; a street-gang member. • This term is often associated with boisterous fans of British sporting events. **2.** See HOOLIGAN TOOL.

hooligan tool. (2002) A steel bar used by police officers and firefighters to break open doors or windows. — Sometimes shortened to *hooligan.* — Also termed *halligan tool.*

horae juridicae (**hor**-ee juu-**rid**-i-see), *n. pl.* [Latin] (17c) *Hist.* Juridical hours. • The time during which judges sat in court to attend to judicial business. — Also termed *horae judicii* (hor-ee joo-**dish**-ee-ee).

horca (**or**-kah), *n. Spanish law.* **1.** A gallows. **2.** A stick for administering corporal punishment. **3.** A designated place for administering corporal punishment.

hordera (hor-**deer**-ə), *n.* [Law Latin] *Hist. English law.* In England, a treasurer. — Also termed *hordarius* (hor-**dair**-ee-əs).

horderium (hor-**deer**-ee-əm), *n.* [Law Latin] *Hist. English law.* In England, a hoard, treasury, or repository.

horizontal agreement. See *horizontal restraint* under RESTRAINT OF TRADE.

horizontal arrangement. See *horizontal restraint* under RESTRAINT OF TRADE.

horizontal competition. See COMPETITION.

horizontal cooperation agreement. See COOPERATION AGREEMENT.

horizontal equality. In per capita distribution of an estate, parity of distribution among members of the same generation. See PER CAPITA. Cf. VERTICAL EQUALITY.

horizontal-gaze nystagmus test (nis-**tag**-məs). (1985) *Criminal law.* A field-sobriety test for intoxication, in which the suspect is told to focus on an object (such as a pencil) and to track its movement, usu. from side to side, by moving only the eyes. • Intoxication is indicated if the eyes jerk or twitch while tracking the object. The test has been recognized as valid by the National Highway Transportation Safety Administration. — Abbr. HGN test. — Often shortened to *gaze-nystagmus test.* See DRUG-RECOGNITION EXAM; *field sobriety test* under SOBRIETY TEST.

horizontal integration. See *horizontal merger* under MERGER.

horizontal merger. See MERGER (8).

horizontal nonprivity. See NONPRIVITY.

horizontal price-fixing. See PRICE-FIXING.

horizontal privity. See PRIVITY (1).

horizontal-property act. (1971) A statute dealing with cooperatives and condominiums.

horizontal restraint. See RESTRAINT OF TRADE.

horizontal stare decisis. See STARE DECISIS.

horizontal union. See *craft union* under UNION.

hornbook. (16c) **1.** A book explaining the basics of a given subject. **2.** A textbook containing the rudimentary principles of an area of law. Cf. CASEBOOK.

> "*Hornbook* . . . The first book of children, covered with horn to keep it unsoiled." Samuel Johnson, *A Dictionary of the English Language* (1755).

hornbook law. See BLACKLETTER LAW.

hornbook method. (1895) A method of legal instruction characterized by a straightforward presentation of legal doctrine, occasionally interspersed with questions. • The hornbook method predominates in civil-law countries, and in certain fields of law, such as procedure and evidence. — Also termed *lecture method.* Cf. CASEBOOK METHOD; SOCRATIC METHOD.

horning, *n.* (16c) *Hist. Scots law.* The denunciation of a person as an outlaw. • The term comes from the old ceremony of proclaiming a person outlawed in which the king's messenger gave three blasts on a horn. — Also termed *putting to the horn.*

horn tenure. 1. See CORNAGE (1). **2.** See CORNAGE (3).

hors (or). [French] **1.** Out or out of. **2.** Outside.

hors de son fee (**or** də son **fee**), *n.* [French "out of his fee"] *Hist.* A defensive plea in an action for rent or services by which the defendant alleged that the land in question was outside the plaintiff's fee.

horse case. See WHITEHORSE CASE.

horsehead. See PUMPING UNIT.

horseshedding, *n.* (1850) The instructing of a witness favorable to one's case (esp. a client) about the proper method of responding to questions while giving testimony. • The term often connotes unethical witness-coaching techniques. Cf. SANDPAPERING. — Also spelled *horse-shedding.* — Also termed *woodshedding.* — **horseshedder,** *n.* — **horseshed,** *vb.*

hospitalaria. See HOSTILARIA.

hospital expense. See EXPENSE.

Hospitallers (**hos**-pi-təl-ərz). A military and religious order founded in the 11th century and so called because it built a hospital at Jerusalem to care for pilgrims. • The Crown seized all its lands and goods in England under the Grantees of Reversions Act (1540). The Hospitallers still functions in several countries as a humanitarian society.

hospital lien. See LIEN.

hospitator (**hos**-pə-tay-tər), *n.* [Law Latin] A host or entertainer.

▸ ***hospitator communis*** (kə-**myoo**-nis). A common innkeeper.

▸ ***hospitator magnus*** (**mag**-nəs). The marshal of a camp.

hospitia (hah-**spish**-ee-ə), *n.* [Latin] Inns.

▸ ***hospitia cancellariae*** (kan-sə-**lair**-ee-ɪ). Inns of chancery.

▸ ***hospitia communia*** (kə-**myoo**-nee-ə). Common inns.

▸ ***hospitia curiae*** (**kyoor**-ee-ɪ). (17c) Inns of court.

hospiticide (hah-**spit**-ə-sɪd), *n.* (17c) **1.** The murder of a host by a guest. **2.** A host who murders a guest.

hospitium (hah-**spish**-ee-əm), *n.* [Latin] (17c) An inn; a household.

hostage. (13c) **1.** An innocent person held captive by another who threatens to kill or harm that person if one or more demands are not met. • Hostage-taking is a federal crime. 18 USCA § 1203. Cf. KIDNAPPING. **2.** *Int'l law.* Someone who is given or taken into an enemy's custody in time of war, his or her freedom or life standing as security for the performance of some agreement made to the enemy by the belligerent power with whom the hostage is associated.

hostage-taking. (1906) **1.** The unlawful holding of an unwilling person as security that the holder's terms will be met by an adversary. **2.** The manipulation of a person or entity by seizing or threatening to seize something important so as to secure the demands against another party.

hostelagium (hos-tə-**lay**-jee-əm), *n.* [Law Latin] *Hist.* A right to receive lodging and entertainment, anciently reserved by lords in their tenants' houses.

hosteler (**hos**-tə-lər). (14c) **1.** Someone who stays in a youth hostel. **2.** A stableman. **3.** *Archaic.* Someone who receives and entertains guests, esp. at a monastery. **4.** *Archaic.* An innkeeper. See HOSTLER.

hostes (**hos**-teez), *n. pl.* [Latin] Enemies. Sing. ***hostis*** (**hos**-tis).

▸ ***hostes humani generis*** (hyoo-**may**-nɪ **jen**-ə-ris). (17c) Enemies of the human race; specif., pirates.

> "Despite Cicero's celebrated definition of pirates as *hostes humani generis*, there is no trace of the expression in (positive) international law. The 'criminals against humanity' — which included enslavers and sexual slavers, but not (yet) pirates or terrorists — come the closest today to those 'enemies of all humanity.' There being no mention on international treaties, what is it that scholars have meant when they referred to *hostes humani generis* in treatises on international law? The meaning was generally twofold: pirates were worthy of punishment; and, to put it plainly as did Grotius, any pirate 'is justiciable by any State anywhere.'" Joaquín Alcaide Fernández, "Hostes Humani Generis: Pirates, Slavers, and Other Criminals," in *The Oxford Handbook of the History of International Law* 120, 120–21 (Bardo Fassbender & Anne Peters eds., 2012) (citation omitted).

hosticide (**hos**-tə-sɪd), *n.* (1848) **1.** The killing of an enemy. **2.** Someone who kills an enemy.

hostilaria (hos-tə-**lair**-ee-ə), *n.* [Latin] A place or room in a religious house used to receive guests and strangers. — Also termed *hospitalaria* (hos-pə-tə-**ler**-[ee-]ə).

hostile, *adj.* (16c) **1.** ADVERSE. **2.** Showing ill will or a desire to harm. **3.** Antagonistic; unfriendly.

hostile act. See ACT OF HOSTILITY.

hostile amendment. See AMENDMENT (3).

hostile bidder. See CORPORATE RAIDER.

hostile embargo. See EMBARGO (1).

hostile-environment sexual harassment. See SEXUAL HARASSMENT.

hostile intent. (17c) *Int'l law.* The threat of imminent use of force against a nation's sovereign territory, extraterritorial interests, armed forces, or citizens and their property.

hostile possession. See POSSESSION.

hostile propaganda. See PROPAGANDA.

hostile takeover. See TAKEOVER.

hostile witness. See WITNESS.

hostile-work-environment harassment. See *hostile-environment sexual harassment* under SEXUAL HARASSMENT.

hostility. (15c) **1.** A state of enmity between individuals or countries. **2.** An act or series of acts displaying antagonism. **3.** (*usu. pl.*) Acts of war.

hostler ([**h**]**os**-lər). [fr. *hosteler*] (14c) *Archaic.* **1.** A stableman; an ostler. **2.** An innkeeper. • By the 16th century, this term had lost its "innkeeper" sense, and referred exclusively to a stableman.

hot bench. See BENCH.

hot blood. See HEAT OF PASSION.

hot cargo. (1938) *Labor law.* Goods produced or handled by an employer with whom a union has a dispute.

hot-cargo agreement. (1957) *Labor law.* A voluntary agreement between a union and a neutral employer by which the latter agrees to exert pressure on another employer with whom the union has a dispute, as by ceasing or refraining from handling, using, selling, transporting, or otherwise dealing in any of the products of an employer that the union has labeled as unfair. • Most agreements of this type were prohibited by the Landrum–Griffin Act of 1959. See LANDRUM–GRIFFIN ACT.

hot-cargo clause. See CARGO CLAUSE.

hot check. See *bad check* under CHECK.

hotchpot (**hoch**-pot), *n.* (16c) **1.** The blending of items of property to secure equality of division, esp. as practiced either in cases of divorce or in cases in which advancements of an intestate's property must be made up to the estate by a contribution or by an accounting. — Also termed *hotchpotch; hotchpot rule*. Cf. RAPPORT À SUCCESSION.

> "In some states . . . a child who has received his advancement in real or personal estate, may elect to throw the amount of the advancement into the common stock, and take his share of the estate descended, or his distributive share of the personal estate, as the case may be: and this is said to be bringing the advancement into *hotchpot*, and it is a proceeding which resembles the *collatio bonorum* in the civil law." 4 James Kent, *Commentaries on American Law* *419 (George Comstock ed., 11th ed. 1866).

> "[T]he distribution of the property among the children is subject to what is called the *hotchpot rule*, the purpose of which is to ensure that the shares of all the children shall be equal. The rule is that any money or property which the intestate has paid to, or settled on, or covenanted to settle on a child, either by way of advancement or in view of marriage, shall be brought into account and deducted from the share which is payable to that child under the intestacy." G.C. Cheshire, *Modern Law of Real Property* 783–84 (3d ed. 1933).

2. In a community-property state, the property that falls within the community estate. See COLLATIO BONORUM. **3.** MAIN POT.

hot court. See COURT.

hot document. See DOCUMENT (2).

hotel divorce. See DIVORCE.

hotelkeeper. See INNKEEPER.

hotelkeeper's lien. See LIEN.

hot-goods clause. (1938) *Labor law.* A clause in the Fair Labor Standards Act of 1938 prohibiting the sale of goods produced in violation of minimum-wage and overtime laws. • Exemptions to the hot-goods prohibition are provided for transporters and "innocent purchasers" who acquire the goods in good-faith reliance on the producer's written assurances that the goods were produced in compliance with the Fair Labor Standards Act of 1938. *See Citicorp Indus. Credit, Inc. v. Brock*, 483 U.S. 27, 28–29, 107 S.Ct. 2694, 2696 (1987).

hot issue. See ISSUE (2).

hot news. *Intellectual property.* Extremely time-sensitive or transient information that is usu. reliable for very brief periods, such as stock quotations.

hot-news test. (1997) *Intellectual property.* A judicial test for determining whether a misappropriation claim is preempted by the *Sears–Compco* doctrine, consisting in analyzing whether, in addition to the elements of copyright infringement, the claim also requires proof of (1) time-sensitive information collected at a cost to the plaintiff, (2) unfair use of that information by a directly competing defendant who has made no similar investment, and (3) a consequent threat to the plaintiff's commercial existence.

hot-potato rule. (1994) The principle that a lawyer may not unreasonably withdraw from representing a client. • The term comes from the rule's classic formulation: "a firm may not drop a client like a 'hot potato,' especially if it is in order to keep happy a far more lucrative client." *Picker Int'l, Inc. v. Varian Assocs., Inc.*, 670 F. Supp. 1363, 1365 (N.D. Ohio 1987). An exception may be allowed for a conflict of interest arising from circumstances beyond the control of the lawyer or the law firm. See *thrust-upon conflict* under CONFLICT OF INTEREST.

hot pursuit. (18c) **1.** See FRESH PURSUIT. **2.** *Int'l law.* The legitimate chase of a foreign vessel on the high seas just after that vessel has violated the law of the pursuing country while within that country's jurisdiction.

hot stock. See *hot issue* under ISSUE (2).

hot-water ordeal. See *ordeal by water* (2) under ORDEAL.

hour of cause. (16c) *Scots law.* The time at which a trial is to begin.

housage (**howz**-ij). (17c) **1.** A fee for storing goods. **2.** The quality, state, or condition of being housed or the action of housing.

house. (bef. 12c) **1.** A home, dwelling, or residence.

▸ **ancient house.** *Hist. English law.* In England, a house that has stood long enough to acquire an easement of support against the adjoining land or building.

▸ **bawdy house.** See DISORDERLY HOUSE (2).

▸ **disorderly house.** See DISORDERLY HOUSE.

▸ **dwelling-house.** See DWELLING-HOUSE.

▸ **house of correction.** (16c) **1.** A reformatory. **2.** A place for the confinement of juvenile offenders or those who have committed crimes of lesser magnitude. — Also termed *house of refuge*.

▸ **house of detention.** See JAIL.

▸ **house of ill fame.** **1.** See BROTHEL. **2.** See DISORDERLY HOUSE (2).

▸ **house of prostitution.** See DISORDERLY HOUSE (2).

▸ **house of refuge.** See *house of correction*.

▸ **house of worship.** (17c) A building or place set apart for and devoted to the holding of religious services or exercises or public worship; a church or chapel, or a place similarly used.

▸ **public house.** See PUBLIC HOUSE.

2. A branch of a legislature or a quorum of such a branch; esp., the lower chamber of a bicameral legislature. See LOWER HOUSE; UPPER HOUSE. **3.** HOUSE OF REPRESENTATIVES. **4.** HOUSE OF DELEGATES (1).

houseage (**howz**-ij). A fee paid for housing goods, as by a carrier or at a wharf.

house arrest. (1936) The confinement of a person who has been accused or convicted of a crime to his or her home, usu. ensuring the person's whereabouts by attaching an electronically monitored bracelet to the person. • Most house-arrest programs require the offender to work and permit leaving the home only for reasons such as work, medical needs, or community-service obligations. — Also termed *home detention*.

house bill. See BILL (3).

housebote. See BOTE (2).

housebreaking. (17c) The crime of breaking into a dwelling or other secured building, with the intent to commit a felony inside; esp., BURGLARY (1). • *Burglary* is now used more frequently than *housebreaking*. In England, for example, *housebreaking* was replaced in 1968 with statutory burglary, though the term is still used in Scots law. In some jurisdictions, *housebreaking* includes "breaking out" of a house that was entered without a breaking. — **housebreaker,** *n.*

> "The oldest term for this purpose [i.e., of distinguishing between common-law burglary and its statutory enlargements], still encountered at times, is 'housebreaking'; a

more recent suggestion is 'breaking and entering,' and peace officers sometimes speak of a 'breakin.'" Rollin M. Perkins & Ronald N. Boyce, *Criminal Law* 270 (3d ed. 1982).

▸ **constructive housebreaking.** (1863) A breaking made out by construction of law, as when a burglar gains entry by threat or fraud. — Also termed *constructive breaking into a house.*

housebreaking implement. See BURGLARY TOOL.

houseburning. (14c) *Hist.* The common-law misdemeanor of intentionally burning one's own house that is within city limits or that is close enough to other houses that they might be in danger of catching fire (even though no actual damage to them may result). — Also termed *combustio domorum.* Cf. ARSON.

house counsel. See *in-house counsel* under COUNSEL.

house-duty. (1851) *Hist. English law.* A tax first imposed in 1851 on inhabited houses. 14 & 15 Vict., ch. 36 (repealed 1924). • This tax replaced the window tax, which levied a duty on houses with more than six windows. See *window tax* under TAX.

household, *adj.* (14c) Belonging to the house and family; domestic.

household, *n.* (14c) **1.** A family living together. **2.** A group of people who dwell under the same roof. Cf. FAMILY. **3.** The contents of a house.

household effects. See *household goods* under GOODS.

household-employment tax. See *nanny tax* under TAX.

householder. (14c) **1.** Someone who keeps house with his or her family; the head or master of a family. **2.** Someone who owns or is in charge of a house. **3.** An occupier of a house. Cf. HEAD OF HOUSEHOLD. — **householdership,** *n.*

household goods. See GOODS.

house law. *Hist.* A regulatory code promulgated by the head of a royal or noble family, or of a prominent private family, governing intrafamily relationships and acts concerning events such as marriage, disposition of property, and inheritance. • Such a code had no legal authority but was enforced within the family by personal and economic sanctions.

house mark. See *house trademark* under TRADEMARK.

house of assignation. See DISORDERLY HOUSE (2).

House of Commons. The lower chamber of the British and Canadian parliaments being the more powerful of the two houses. — Abbr. H.C. — Often shortened to *Commons.*

house of correction. See HOUSE.

house of delegates. (18c) **1.** (*cap.*) The lower chamber of the state legislature in Maryland, Virginia, and West Virginia. **2.** (*often cap.*) The convention of many learned or professional associations, including the American Bar Association <the ABA House of Delegates>. — Often shortened to *House.* — Also termed *house of representatives.* See CONVENTION (4).

house of detention. See JAIL.

house of ill fame. 1. See BROTHEL. **2.** See DISORDERLY HOUSE (2).

house of ill repute. See DISORDERLY HOUSE (2).

House of Lords. (17c) The upper chamber of the British Parliament, of which the 11-member judicial committee provided judges who served as the final court of appeal in most civil cases from 1876 to 2009. • In practice, the Lords sat as committees, in later years usu. of five but occasionally of seven. Two committees might sit simultaneously. — Abbr. H.L. — Also termed *Lords; judicial House of Lords.*

"'House of Lords' is an ambiguous expression. It refers (1) to all the peers who choose to sit as the Upper House of the legislature (Parliament), and also (2) to a court consisting of the highest level of the judiciary." Glanville Williams, *Learning the Law* 8 (11th ed. 1982).

"The judicial House of Lords survived and consolidated its position as the final appellate court during the period 1914–45. There were still echoes, however, of the complex manoeuvrings of the 1870s over the need for a second tier of appeal. Lord Parmoor wrote in 1936 against 'constituting the House of Lords as the ultimate Court of Appeal,' partly because of the expense of 'a multiplicity of appeals.' A little earlier, in the wake of the Second Interim Report of the Business of Courts Committee, a restriction on civil appeals to the House of Lords — requiring leave from either the Court of Appeal or the House itself — had been provided for in the Administration of Justice (Appeals) Act 1934. Even so, there were suggestions that 'we could have contemplated with equanimity the entire abolition of the final appeal'; and in 1940 a legal writer claimed that it 'is difficult to justify two appeal courts.' One of the factors that helped to reinforce the House of Lords as the final appeal court was that it heard appeals from Scotland (in civil cases) and Northern Ireland as well as from England and Wales. In other words, it was the final appeal court for the United Kingdom, and the presence of Scottish Law Lords in particular was important. Scottish Law Lords in the period under review were Lord Shaw of Dunfermline (1909–29), Lord Dunedin (1913–32), Lord Thankerton (1929–48), and Lord Macmillan (1930–9 and 1941–7)." David G.T. Williams, "A Developing Jurisdiction, 1914–45," in *The Judicial House of Lords, 1876–2009* 198, 198 (Louis Blom-Cooper et al. eds., 2009) (citations omitted).

house of prostitution. See DISORDERLY HOUSE (2).

house of refuge. See *house of correction* under HOUSE.

House of Representatives. (18c) **1.** The lower chamber of the U.S. Congress, composed of 435 members — apportioned among the states on the basis of population — who are elected to two-year terms. **2.** The lower house of a state legislature. — Abbr. H.R.; (in senses 1 & 2) H. — Often shortened to *House.* **3.** HOUSE OF DELEGATES (1). — Often shortened (in all senses) to *House.* — Abbr. H.R.

house of worship. See HOUSE.

house trademark. See TRADEMARK.

housing. (14c) Structures built as dwellings for people, such as houses, apartments, and condominiums.

▸ **public housing.** (1913) Housing, usu. in the form of houses and apartments, built, owned, or operated by a governmental agency and usu. provided at a nominal cost for people with low incomes. — Also termed *publicly assisted housing.*

housing code. See BUILDING CODE.

housing court. See COURT.

housing development. (1939) A defined area containing many houses that have been built to a certain set of specific standards. — Also termed *housing estate.*

housing estate. See HOUSING DEVELOPMENT.

housing project. (1900) A group of apartments, town houses, or houses, usu. built with government money for poor families. — Also termed *projects.*

hovering act. (1808) *Int'l law.* A statute applying to a coastal country's criminal jurisdiction over ships, and persons aboard those ships, when the ships are outside the country's territory.

> "The notion of hovering acts evolved long before that of a belt of uniform width in the form of territorial waters. Great Britain's first anti-smuggling legislation to operate at a stated distance seaward was in 1719, applying to the master of any ship 'found at anchor or hovering within two leagues from the shore.' Later enactments extended this limit to three, then four, then eight leagues. A statute of 1794 gave power to seize and confiscate customable goods in vessels 'found at anchor, or hovering' inside specific straight lines drawn between lines on the British coasts, thus resembling the 'King's Chambers' of the Stuart era. In 1805 the British Parliament extended the seizure limit to 100 leagues (300 miles) from the coasts of Great Britain and Ireland in respect of vessels 'belonging wholly or in part to His Majesty's subjects, or whereof one-half of the persons on board shall be subjects of His Majesty.' Foreign-flag vessels could have fallen within this category. In the case of *Le Louis* (1817) 165 E.R. 1464, the British Admiralty judge Lord Stowell described these statutes as being permitted by 'the common courtesy of nations for their convenience.'" Geoffrey Marston, "Hovering Acts," in 2 *Encyclopedia of Public International Law* 884–85 (1995).

HOW. *abbr.* HOME OWNERS WARRANTY.

How say you? (18c) *Archaic.* (Asked of a jury) how do you find?

howsoever, *adv.* (14c) In whatever way; however.

H.R. *abbr.* HOUSE OF REPRESENTATIVES.

H.R. 10 plan. See KEOGH PLAN.

HSR Act. See HART–SCOTT–RODINO ANTITRUST IMPROVEMENT ACT.

HTML. *abbr.* (1993) HYPERTEXT MARKUP LANGUAGE.

http. *abbr.* (1992) HYPERTEXT TRANSFER PROTOCOL.

hub. (1991) *Criminal law. Slang.* A core prison around which other satellite prisons are located.

hub-and-spoke conspiracy. See *wheel conspiracy* under CONSPIRACY.

hub court. (2001) A central court that accepts certain types of recurrent cases, such as drug cases, from other courts within the same city or county.

huc usque (hək əs-kwee), *adv.* [Latin] *Hist.* Hitherto. • This term commonly appeared in pleadings. — Also spelled *hucusque.*

HUD. *abbr.* DEPARTMENT OF HOUSING AND URBAN DEVELOPMENT.

hudegeld. See HYDEGELD.

hue and cry. (15c) *Hist.* **1.** The public uproar that, at common law, a citizen was expected to initiate after discovering a crime. — Also termed *vociferatio*; *clamor.*

> "Hue and Cry is the old Common Law mode of pursuing, 'with horn and voice,' persons suspected of felony, or having inflicted a wound from which death is likely to ensue." 1 Joseph Chitty, *A Practical Treatise on the Criminal Law* 26 (2d ed. 1826).

> "All were obliged to pursue the criminal when the hue and cry was raised. Neglect of these duties entailed an amercement of the individual, the township or the hundred. The sheriffs and the constables were under special obligations, as conservatores pacis, to fulfil these duties." 1 William Holdsworth, *A History of English Law* 294 (7th ed. 1956).

2. The pursuit of a felon accompanying such an uproar. **3.** A written proclamation for the capture of a felon.

huggery. (18c) *English law. Rare.* A barrister's improperly ingratiating actions to curry favor with a solicitor for the purpose of gaining professional employment. • Although many consider huggery a breach of Bar etiquette, it is not expressly forbidden.

hui (**hoo**-ee), *n.* In Hawaiian law, an association of persons who own land together, usu. as tenants in common.

huissier (wee-**syay**), *n.* [French fr. *huis* "door"] (14c) **1.** *French law.* An usher of a court; an officer (such as a marshal) who serves process. **2.** *Hist. English law.* In England, a ministerial officer attached to a court, responsible for service of process, issuing executions, and maintaining order during court sessions.

hulk, *n.* (17c) *Hist. English law.* In England, a dismantled ship used as a prison. • Living conditions in hulks were notoriously poor, and their use as prisons ended as part of the broad prison-reform movements of the mid-19th century.

humanitarian, *adj.* (18c) **1.** Motivated by concerns for human welfare. **2.** Of or relating to a situation or event that involves widespread human suffering, esp. when aid or support is required on a large scale.

humanitarian doctrine. See LAST-CLEAR-CHANCE DOCTRINE.

humanitarian intervention. See INTERVENTION.

humanitarian law. (1955) *Int'l law.* Law dealing with such matters as the permissible use of weapons and other means of warfare, the treatment of prisoners of war and civilian populations in armed conflicts, and generally the direct impact of war on human life and liberty. • Most existing rules composing humanitarian law are codified in the Geneva Conventions and their protocols.

human-leukocyte antigen test. (1979) A medical process of analyzing the blood sample of a man in a paternity or legitimacy case by comparing certain indicators with the child's blood. — Abbr. HLA test. See BLOOD-GROUPING TEST. Cf. GENETIC-MARKER TEST.

human-remains detection dog. See *cadaver dog* under DOG (1).

human resources. (1965) An organization's department dealing with employment policies, training, and generally helping employees.

human rights. (18c) The freedoms, immunities, and benefits that, according to modern values (esp. at an international level), all human beings should be able to claim as a matter of right in the society in which they live. See UNIVERSAL DECLARATION OF HUMAN RIGHTS.

> "Human rights do not emerge exclusively from Western philosophical and political principles. The cultures of every world region contain important references to principles and standards of behavior in human relations. Amartya Sen tells of the Indian emperor Ashoka in the third century B.C.E. whose political inscriptions favored tolerance and individual freedom, both as part of state policy and in relations of different people to each other. The domain of toleration, Ashoka argued, must include everybody without exception." Andrew Clapham, "Human Rights," in *The Oxford Companion to Politics of the World* 368, 368 (Joel Krieger ed., 2d ed. 2001).

human shield. (1885) **1.** Someone who is taken and kept as a prisoner by a criminal who tries to use the person while trying to negotiate a way not to be caught, injured, or killed. **2.** Someone, usu. one among many, who is moved by a despot or dictator to a military target in order to make the destruction of that target by a superpower more difficult on the world stage because of the inevitable casualties involved.

human trafficking. See TRAFFICKING.

human will. See WILL (1).

hundi. See HAWALA.

hundred. (bef. 12c) **1.** Formerly, a county subdivision that had its own local court.

> "*The hundred* was a group of adjoining townships. It may have consisted of an area taxed at one hundred hides. Other explanations of the term 'hundred' are that the unit may have consisted of one hundred households, or the area had to supply one hundred fighting men for the national defence." L.B. Curzon, *English Legal History* 7 (2d ed. 1979).

2. The populace of such a subdivision. **3.** See *hundred court* under COURT. **4.** In the United States, a political division derived from the English county division. • Hundreds existed in colonial Delaware, Maryland, Pennsylvania, and Virginia. Today, they exist only in Delaware. — **hundredal (hun-dri-dəl),** *adj.*

hundredarius (hən-dri-**dair**-ee-əs), *n.* [Law Latin] *Hist.* **1.** HUNDREDARY. **2.** HUNDREDOR (1).

hundredary (hən-dri-der-ee), *n.* [Law Latin] (17c) *Hist.* The chief or presiding officer of a hundred. — Also termed *hundredarius.*

hundred court. See COURT.

hundredes earldor **(hən-dridz ərl-dər),** *n.* [Latinized Old English] *Hist.* The presiding officer in a hundred court. — Also termed *hundredes man.*

hundred moot. See *hundred court* under COURT.

hundredor (hən-dri-dər), *n.* (15c) *Hist.* **1.** A freeholder of a hundred who can sue in, or act as judge of, a hundred court. See *hundred court* under COURT. **2.** Someone who has been empaneled (or is fit to be empaneled) on a hundred-court jury, and who dwells within the hundred where the legal claim arose. **3.** An officer who has jurisdiction of a hundred and who holds the hundred court. **4.** The bailiff of a hundred. See HUNDRED (1), (2).

hundredpenny (hən-drəd-pen-ee), *n.* (12c) *Hist.* A tax or due that in medieval times was levied in a hundred. See HUNDRED (1), (2).

hundred rolls. (18c) *Hist.* Records that list the various feudal tenancies and feudal obligations existing among English lords and tenants. • The *hundred rolls* were compiled in 1274–1275 by royal commissioners from inquiries put to hundred-court juries in order to alert the Crown to the existence of feudal relationships that infringed on royal prerogatives (and thereby royal revenue).

hunger strike. (1889) A person's refusal to eat for a long time in order to protest something.

hung jury. See JURY.

hung parliament. See PARLIAMENT (1).

***Huntley* hearing.** (1965) In New York practice, a pretrial hearing in a criminal case to determine the admissibility of a defendant's statement. The hearing usu. follows a defendant's motion to suppress an involuntary statement. The name derives from *People v. Huntley*, 204 N.E.2d 179 (N.Y. 1965), in which the court held that a judge in a criminal trial must conduct a preliminary hearing to determine whether, beyond a reasonable doubt, a defendant's confession was made voluntarily.

hurto **(oor-toh),** *n. Spanish law.* Theft; larceny; stealing.

husband. (13c) A married man; a man who has a lawful, living spouse. • Etymologically, the word signified the *house bond*, the man who, according to Saxon ideas and institutions, held around him the family, for which he was legally responsible.

▸ **common-law husband.** (1896) The husband in a common-law marriage; a man who contracts an informal marriage with a woman and then holds himself out to the community as being married to her. See *common-law marriage* under MARRIAGE (1).

husbandlike and proper. (1893) (Of land cultivation or management) according to the locale's usual practices.

husbandman. (14c) *Archaic.* A farmer.

husbandria (həz-bən-**dree**-ə), *n.* [Law Latin] *Hist.* HUSBANDRY.

husbandry. (14c) **1.** Agriculture or farming; cultivation of the soil for food. • In some states, tools and equipment used in farming are exempt from forced sale for collection of a debt. **2.** Generally, care of a household; careful management of resources.

husband–wife immunity. See IMMUNITY (2).

husband–wife privilege. See *marital privilege* under PRIVILEGE (3).

huscarle (hoos-kahrl), *n.* [Old English] *Hist.* **1.** A house servant or domestic; a man of the household. **2.** A king's vassal, thane, or baron; an earl's man or vassal.

husfastne (hoos-fas[t]-ən), *n.* [Old English] *Hist.* Someone who holds house and land; a man bound to a frankpledge.

husgablum (hoos-gab-ləm), *n.* [Old English] *Hist.* A tax or tribute levied on a house; house rent.

hush money. (18c) *Criminal law. Slang.* Money paid to someone not to be candid or truthful about something illegal or embarrassing, esp. a bribe to suppress the dissemination of certain information.

husting. (*usu. pl.*) [Old English] (bef. 12c) **1.** *Hist.* A deliberative assembly, esp. one called by the king or other leader. **2.** *Hist.* COURT OF HUSTINGS. **3.** *Hist.* The raised platform used by officials of the Court of Hustings. **4.** *Hist.* The raised platform used to nominate candidates for Parliament. • This practice ended after passage of the Ballot Act in 1872. **5.** Any place where political campaign speeches are made. **6.** By extension, the activity of trying to persuade people to vote for oneself by making speeches.

HUT. *abbr.* Highway-use tax.

hutesium et clamor (h[y]oo-**tee**-z[h]ee-əm et **klam**-ər). [Law Latin] HUE AND CRY.

hybrid action. *Labor law.* A lawsuit in which a union member asserts claims against the employer for breach of a collective bargaining agreement, and against the union for breach of the duty of fair representation. — Also termed *hybrid suit.*

hybrid class action. See CLASS ACTION.

hybrid comparative negligence. See NEGLIGENCE.

hybrid-comparative-negligence doctrine. (1984) See 50-percent rule.

hybrid mark. See *composite trademark* under TRADEMARK.

hybrid power of appointment. See POWER OF APPOINTMENT.

hybrid representation. See REPRESENTATION (2).

hybrid security. See SECURITY (4).

hybrid suit. See HYBRID ACTION.

hybrid trademark. See *composite trademark* under TRADEMARK.

Hyde Amendment. 1. A federal statute that prohibits the use of Medicaid funds for abortions except when necessary to save the mother's life, and that prohibits federally funded family-planning programs from providing abortion counseling. • The bill was sponsored by Representative Henry Hyde of Illinois. **2.** A federal statute authorizing a criminal defendant to recover reasonable attorney's fees and litigation expenses if a court decides that the government's position was "vexatious, frivolous, or in bad faith." 18 USCA § 3006A.

hydegeld (**hɪd**-geld), *n. Hist. English law.* **1.** In England, a discharge for an assault on a trespassing servant. **2.** HIDEGILD. — Also spelled *hudegeld.*

***Hydraflow* test.** (1996) A principle for deciding when an inadvertent disclosure of a privileged document is a waiver of the attorney–client privilege, whereby the court considers the reasonableness of the precautions taken to prevent the inadvertent disclosure, the number of disclosures involved, the extent of the disclosure, the promptness of any efforts to remedy the disclosure, and whether justice would be best served by permitting the disclosing party to retrieve the document. *Hydraflow, Inc. v. Enidine, Inc.*, 145 F.R.D. 626 (W.D.N.Y. 1993). — Also termed *middle-of-the-road test.* Cf. LENIENT TEST; STRICT TEST.

hyperbole. Exaggeration, esp. to an excessive degree; specif., a manner of speaking that depicts something as being much bigger, smaller, worse, etc. than it really is.

hyperinjunction. See INJUNCTION.

hyperlink. (1988) *Intellectual property.* The part of a computer document, such as a picture or passage, on which a user can click to move to another document, usu. a related one; specif., an element on a webpage — usu. a word, phrase, or graphic, but sometimes a single pixel — that, when clicked on, takes the user to another part of the same website or to a different website. • A copyright violation occurs if someone knows or has reason to know that a link will be used for unauthorized copying and creates a link to encourage or contribute to wrongful copying. — Often shortened to *link.* — **hyperlink,** *vb.*

hyperliteralism. An interpretive approach that overstresses literal meaning, as by insisting that a book *manuscript* must be handwritten; that *decimation* must refer to the destruction of one-tenth of an army; or that the pronoun *he* (despite the legal and grammatical convention to the contrary) cannot refer to a female. • The adjective corresponding to *hyperliteralism* is either *hyperliteral* or *literalistic*, both pejorative.

hypertext. (1965) A way of preparing computer documents to make it possible to move from one document to another by clicking on words or pictures, esp. on the Internet.

hypertext markup language. (1992) The programming code used on websites to format text and provide links between resources. — Abbr. HTML.

hypertext transfer protocol. (1992) The set of programmed rules that enable computers to exchange information over the Internet. • Browsers use http to contact other computers. — Abbr. http.

hypnotically induced recollection. See *hypnotically refreshed testimony* under TESTIMONY.

hypnotically induced testimony. See *hypnotically refreshed testimony* under TESTIMONY.

hypnotically refreshed evidence. See *hypnotically refreshed testimony* under TESTIMONY.

hypnotically refreshed recollection. See *hypnotically refreshed testimony* under TESTIMONY.

hypnotically refreshed testimony. See TESTIMONY.

hypobolum (hi-**pob**-ə-ləm), *n.* [Latin fr. Greek] *Civil law.* A legacy given to a wife, in addition to her dowry, on the death of her husband. Pl. ***hypobola.***

hypothec (hɪ-**poth**-ek *or* hi-). (16c) *Civil law.* A mortgage given to a creditor on property to secure a debt; HYPOTHECA. Cf. HYPOTHÈQUE.

▸ **landlord's hypothec.** (18c) *Scots law.* The lessor's right of security for rent in articles, furniture, and equipment (other than tools of the tenant's trade) that the tenant brought onto the leased premises. • Unlike the English remedy of distress, the right of security is effected only by the lessor's application to the court for a decree of sequestration. Until 1880, a landlord could assert the lien against a tenant's crops and stock as well as personal property. See SEQUESTRATION FOR RENT.

▸ **mariner's hypothec. 1.** A lien that a seaman, freighter, or repairer can assert against a ship for payment of wages or other sums due. **2.** A shipowner's lien against the ship's cargo for the freight costs.

▸ **solicitor's hypothec.** A legal agent's lien for costs in excess of the costs recovered from an opposing party. • The lien may also apply to the retention of some documents, such as title deeds, as security for a client's outstanding account.

hypotheca (hɪ-pə-**thee**-kə *or* hip-ə-), *n.* [Latin fr. Greek] (16c) *Roman law.* A mortgage of property in which the debtor was allowed to keep, but not alienate, the property.

> "Yet another mode of creating a security is possible, by which not merely the ownership of a thing but its possession also remains with the debtor. This is called by the Roman lawyers and their modern followers 'hypotheca.' Hypothecs may arise by the direct application of a rule of law, by judicial decision, or by agreement." Thomas E. Holland, *The Elements of Jurisprudence* 235 (13th ed. 1924).

hypothecaria actio (hɪ-poth-ə-**kair**-ee-ə **ak**-shee-oh). [Latin] *Roman law.* A hypothecary action; an action to enforce a mortgage or to obtain the surrender of the thing mortgaged. — Also termed *actio hypothecaria.* See *hypothecary action* under ACTION (4).

hypothecarii creditores (hɪ-poth-ə-**kair**-ee-ɪ kred-ə-**tor**-eez). [Latin] *Roman law.* Hypothecary creditors; those who lent money on the security of a hypotheca.

hypothecary (hɪ-**poth**-ə-ker-ee), *adj.* (17c) Of, relating to, or involving a hypothec or hypothecation.

hypothecary action. See ACTION (4).

hypothecary debt. See DEBT.

hypothecate (hɪ-**poth**-ə-kayt), *vb.* (17c) To pledge (property) as security or collateral for a debt, without delivery of title or possession.

hypothecation (hɪ-poth-ə-**kay**-shən), *n.* (17c) The pledging of something as security without delivery of title or possession. — **hypothecator** (hɪ-**poth**-ə-kay-tər), *n.*

▸ **general hypothecation.** (1841) **1.** A debtor's pledge to allow all the property named in the security instrument to serve as collateral and to be used to satisfy the outstanding debt. **2.** See *tacit hypothecation* (1), (2).

▸ **tacit hypothecation.** (17c) **1.** *Civil law.* A type of lien or mortgage that is created by operation of law without the parties' express agreement. — Also termed *tacit mortgage.* **2.** See *maritime lien* under LIEN.

hypothecation bond. See BOND (2).

hypothèque (ee-poh-**tek**), *n. French law.* Hypothecation; the right vested in a creditor by the assignment to the creditor of real estate as security for a debt, whether or not accompanied by possession. • *Hypothèque* may be *légale,* as with the charge that the state has over the lands of its accountants, or that a married woman has over the lands of her husband; *judiciaire,* when it is the result of a judgment of a court of justice; or *conventionelle,* when it is the result of the parties' agreement. Cf. HYPOTHEC.

hypothesis (hɪ-**poth**-ə-səs). (16c) **1.** A supposition based on evidence but not proved; a proposed explanation, supported by evidence, that serves as a starting point for investigation. **2.** A theory or supposition proposed for the sake of debate.

hypothetical, *adj.* (16c) **1.** Involving tentative theory or supposition adopted provisionally; assumed or postulated merely for the sake of argument.

hypothetical, *n.* (17c) **1.** A proposition or statement that is presumed true for the sake of logical analysis or debate. • Hypotheticals are often used as teaching tools to illustrate the application of legal principles or to explore the potential consequences of words and actions. **2.** HYPOTHETICAL QUESTION.

hypothetical contract. See *conditional contract* under CONTRACT.

hypothetical creditor. See CREDITOR.

hypothetical lien creditor. See *hypothetical creditor* under CREDITOR.

hypothetical negotiation. (1960) A judicial construct used to calculate damages in a patent-infringement suit by arriving at a figure that would have been reasonable royalty acceptable to both parties.

hypothetical-person defense. (1979) An entrapment defense in which the defendant asserts that an undercover law-enforcement officer (or person acting at the law-enforcement officer's direction) encouraged the defendant to engage in the criminal conduct either by making false representations designed to convince the defendant that the conduct was not prohibited, or by using persuasive methods that created a substantial risk that the charged offense would be committed by a person who was not otherwise inclined to commit it. • This defense has been adopted by a minority of states and by the Model Penal Code. — Also termed *objective method.* See Model Penal Code § 2.13. Cf. SHERMAN–SORRELLS DOCTRINE.

hypothetical pleading. See PLEADING (1).

hypothetical question. (1826) A question posed on assumed facts, usu. changed facts, to discover or test how a given principle or rule would apply in one of several possible situations; esp., a judge's query posed to counsel to see what result a posited legal rule would yield under circumstances different from those in the case to be decided. — Also termed *abstract question.*

hypothetical tenant. (1981) *Hist.* A fictional person used for assessing property taxes based on what the person would pay to lease the property.

I

IAA. *abbr.* INVESTMENT ADVISERS ACT.

IABA. *abbr.* INTER-AMERICAN BAR ASSOCIATION.

IAC. *abbr.* Ineffective assistance of counsel. See ASSISTANCE OF COUNSEL.

IAD. *abbr.* INTERSTATE AGREEMENT ON DETAINERS ACT.

IADA. *abbr.* INTERSTATE AGREEMENT ON DETAINERS ACT.

IADC. *abbr.* INTERNATIONAL ASSOCIATION OF DEFENSE COUNSEL.

IAF. *abbr.* INTER-AMERICAN FOUNDATION.

IAIP. *abbr.* INFORMATION ANALYSIS AND INFRASTRUCTURE PROTECTION DIRECTORATE.

ib. See IBID.

IBC. *abbr.* Issuing a bad check; issuance of a bad check.

ibi. [Latin] There and then.

ibid. (**ib**-id). *abbr.* [Latin *ibidem*] (17c) In the same place. • This abbreviation, used in citations (mostly outside law), denotes that the reference is to a work cited immediately before, and that the cited matter appears on the same page of the same book (unless a different page is specified). — Also termed *ib.* Cf. ID.

IBM. *abbr.* IRRETRIEVABLE BREAKDOWN OF THE MARRIAGE.

ICA. *abbr.* **1.** INTERNATIONAL COMMODITY AGREEMENT. **2.** INVESTMENT COMPANY ACT.

ICANN. *abbr.* INTERNET CORPORATION FOR ASSIGNED NAMES AND NUMBERS.

ICC. *abbr.* **1.** INTERSTATE COMMERCE COMMISSION. **2.** INTERNATIONAL CRIMINAL COURT. **3.** An intensive confinement center, where federal shock imprisonment can occur under 18 USCA §§ 3621(e), 4046.

ICE. *abbr.* IMMIGRATION AND CUSTOMS ENFORCEMENT.

ICE detainer. See *immigration detainer* under DETAINER (1).

ICE number. (2003) [acronym for *in case of emergency*] A relative's or friend's telephone number stored usu. in a mobile phone so that people will know whom to call if the phone owner is seriously injured or ill.

ICJ. *abbr.* INTERNATIONAL COURT OF JUSTICE.

ICPC. *abbr.* INTERSTATE COMPACT ON THE PLACEMENT OF CHILDREN.

ICSID (**ik**-sid). *abbr.* INTERNATIONAL CENTRE FOR SETTLEMENT OF INVESTMENT DISPUTES.

ICWA. *abbr.* INDIAN CHILD WELFARE ACT.

id. (id). *abbr.* [Latin *idem*] (17c) The same. • *Id.* is used in a legal citation to refer to the authority cited immediately before <*id.* at 55>. Cf. IBID.

ID. *abbr.* (1955) **1.** Identification; IDENTITY CARD. **2.** IRRECONCILABLE DIFFERENCES. **3.** (In Canada) impaired driving.

IDA. *abbr.* INVESTMENT-DIRECTION AGREEMENT.

IDC. *abbr.* INTANGIBLE DRILLING COST.

ID card. See IDENTITY CARD.

ID divorce. See *irreconcilable-differences divorce* under DIVORCE.

IDEA. *abbr.* INDIVIDUALS WITH DISABILITIES EDUCATION ACT.

idea–expression dichotomy. (1967) *Copyright.* The fundamental rule that copyright law protects only specific expressions of an idea, not the idea itself.

idem per idem (I-dem pər I-dem). [Latin] The same for the same. • This phrase refers to an illustration that adds nothing to a matter under consideration.

idem sonans (I-dem **soh**-nanz), *adj.* [Latin] (1856) (Of words or names) sounding the same, regardless of spelling <the names Gene and Jean are *idem sonans*>. • In trademark law, the term designates a name that sounds close enough to a registered trademark to create confusion among consumers and infringe that mark. Hence the Steinway company was able to prevent a competitor from registering *Steinweg* for the name of its pianos. See *Grotrian, Helfferich, Schultz, Th. Steinweg Bachf. v. Steinway & Sons*, 523 F.2d 1331 (2d Cir. 1975). In most areas of the law, however, *idem sonans* is used only if there is an identical sounding of the syllables.

> "The names of parties should be correctly spelled, but misspelling which does not change the sound works no harm; it matters not how incorrectly names are spelled, if they are *idem sonans* (the same sound)." Edwin E. Bryant, *The Law of Pleading Under the Codes of Civil Procedure* 186 (2d ed. 1899).

idem sonans (I-dem **soh**-nanz), *n.* [Latin] (1848) A legal doctrine preventing a variant spelling of a name in a document from voiding the document if the misspelling is pronounced the same way as the true spelling.

identical-words presumption. See PRESUMPTION OF CONSISTENT USAGE.

identification direction. See *identification instruction* under JURY INSTRUCTION.

identification evidence. See EVIDENCE.

identification interrogatory. See INTERROGATORY.

identification of goods. (1887) A process that enables a buyer to obtain an identifiable (and therefore insurable) interest in goods before taking possession from the seller. • The goods are identified in any manner agreed to by the parties. UCC § 2-501.

identification parade. See LINEUP.

identified adoption. See *private adoption* under ADOPTION (1).

identify, *vb.* (18c) **1.** To prove the identity of (a person or thing) <the witness identified the weapon>. **2.** To look on as being associated (with) <the plaintiff was identified with the environmental movement>. **3.** To specify (certain goods) as the object of a contract <to identify the appliances to the contract>. See IDENTIFICATION OF GOODS.

identifying material. *Copyright.* A portion or representation of an entire work deposited with the U.S. Copyright Office. • A copyright registrant is required to deposit at least one complete copy of the work, and often two. If a trade secret would be disclosed by a deposit or the work's nature makes deposit difficult (as with a holograph), a substitution is acceptable. Common forms of identifying material are drawings, photocopies, and selected pages of software code and databases.

identikit. (1959) A compilation of pictures of facial features, used by police to create a composite image of a suspect from witness descriptions. • In BrE, the resulting image is called a *photofit.*

identikit picture. See COMPOSITE.

identitate nominis (I-den-ti-**tay**-tee **nom**-ə-nis). See DE IDENTITATE NOMINIS.

identity. (16c) **1.** Sameness in essential attributes; the condition of being the very same thing as has been described or asserted. **2.** The selfsame nature of two or more things; esp., in patent law, the sameness in two devices of the function performed, the way it is performed, and the result achieved. • Under the doctrine of equivalents, infringement may be found even if the accused device is not identical to the claimed invention. See DOCTRINE OF EQUIVALENTS. **3.** The distinguishing personality or attributes of an individual. **4.** More generally, the qualities and attitudes that a person or group of people have, differentiating them from others. **5.** *Evidence.* The authenticity of a person or thing. Cf. MISTAKEN IDENTITY.

identity card. (1900) A small piece of plastic or paper with a person's name, date of birth, and photograph on it for purposes of proving just who its owner is. — Abbr. ID card; ID.

identity fraud. See IDENTITY THEFT.

identity of interests. (18c) *Civil procedure.* A relationship between two parties who are so close that suing one serves as notice to the other, so that the other may be joined in the suit. Fed. R. Civ. P. 15(c)(1)(c).

identity of parties. (1803) *Civil procedure.* A relationship between two parties who are so close that a judgment against one prevents later action against the other because of res judicata.

identity parade. See LINEUP.

identity theft. (1964) *Criminal law.* The unlawful taking and use of another person's identifying information for fraudulent purposes; specif., a crime in which someone steals personal information about and belonging to another, such as a bank-account number or driver's-license number, and uses the information to deceive others usu. for financial gain. — Also termed *identity fraud.* Cf. GHOSTING.

ideo (I-dee-oh), *adv.* [Latin] Therefore; for that reason.

ideo consideratum est (I-dee-oh kən-sid-ə-**ray**-təm est). [Latin] *Hist.* Therefore it is considered. • These words often prefaced a judgment at common law, and they later came to refer to the judgment itself. Cf. CONSIDERATUM EST PER CURIAM.

ideological aggression. 1. See *hostile propaganda* under PROPAGANDA. **2.** See *subversive propaganda* under PROPAGANDA.

Ides (Idz), *n.* [fr. Latin *idus* (pl.)] (bef. 12c) *Roman law.* In the Roman calendar, the ninth day after the Nones, being the 15th of March, May, July, and October, and the 13th of the other months. • In the calculation of the day, Nones is the first day counted. Cf. CALENDS; NONES.

idiochira (id-ee-oh-**kI**-rə). [Greek "one's own hand"] *Hist.* An instrument executed privately, rather than before a public officer; esp., a deed written in one's own hand.

idiocy. (16c) *Archaic.* The condition of a person who, from birth, has never had any glimmering of reasoning or intellectual faculties. — Also termed *idiopathic insanity.*

idiopathic insanity. See IDIOCY.

idiot. (14c) *Archaic.* A person afflicted with profound mental retardation. • Because of its frequent derogatory uses, this term has largely fallen out of use in modern legal and medical contexts. Cf. IMBECILE.

idiota (id-ee-**oh**-tə). [Latin] (16c) *Civil law.* **1.** An unlearned, simple person. **2.** A private person; one not in public office.

idiota inquirendo (id-ee-**oh**-tə in-kwI-**ren**-doh *or* in-kwə-**ren**-doh). See DE IDIOTA INQUIRENDO.

id non agebatur (**id** non aj-ə-**bay**-tər). [Law Latin] *Hist.* That was not done.

idoneis argumentis (I-**doh**-nee-is ahr-gyoo-**men**-tis). [Law Latin] *Hist.* By suitable arguments.

idoneitas (I-doh-**nee**-ə-tas). [fr. Latin *idoneus* "suitable"] *Hist.* A person's ability or fitness. — Also termed *idoneity.*

idoneity. See IDONEITAS.

idoneum se facere; idoneare se (I-**doh**-nee-əm see **fay**-sə-ree; I-doh-nee-**air**-ee see). [Law Latin "to make oneself sufficient; to clear oneself"] *Hist.* To purge oneself, by oath, of a crime that one is accused of committing.

idoneus (I-**doh**-nee-əs), *adj.* [Latin] *Roman law.* (Of a person or thing) appropriate or suitable. • A responsible or solvent man, for example, was known as an *idoneus homo*, while a pledge of sufficient security was termed *idonea cautio.* — Also spelled (in English) *idoneous.*

IDP. *abbr.* Internally displaced person. See *displaced person* under PERSON (1).

IDS. *abbr.* See *information-disclosure statement* under DISCLOSURE STATEMENT.

i.e. *abbr.* [Latin *id est*] (17c) That is <the federal government's highest judicial body, i.e., the Supreme Court>. Cf. E.G.

IEP. *abbr.* INDIVIDUALIZED EDUCATION PROGRAM.

IET. *abbr.* See *interest-equalization tax* under TAX.

IFP. *abbr.* IN FORMA PAUPERIS.

IFP affidavit. See *poverty affidavit* under AFFIDAVIT.

IFRP. *abbr.* INMATE FINANCIAL RESPONSIBILITY PROGRAM.

ignis judicium (**ig**-nis joo-**dish**-ee-əm). [Latin] *Hist.* Trial by fire. See *ordeal by fire* under ORDEAL.

ignition-interlock device. (1986) A device installed in a motor vehicle to determine the driver's blood alcohol content before the vehicle can be started and to prevent its being started if the blood alcohol level registers as being above the acceptable limit. • In some jurisdictions, those convicted of DWI must bear the expense of installing such a device as a condition of being able to have a driver's license.

ignominy (ig-nə-min-ee). (16c) Public disgrace or dishonor. — **ignominious,** *adj.*

ignoramus (ig-nə-**ray**-məs). [Law Latin] (16c) *Hist.* We do not know. • This notation, when written on a bill of indictment, indicated the grand jury's rejection of the bill. See NOT FOUND; NO BILL. Cf. TRUE BILL.

> "When the grand jury have heard the evidence, if they think it a groundless accusation, they used formerly to endorse on the back of the bill, '*ignoramus*;' or, we know nothing of it; intimating, that, though the facts might possibly be true, that truth did not appear to them: but now they assert in English, more absolutely, 'not a true bill;' and then the party is discharged without farther answer." 4 William Blackstone, *Commentaries on the Laws of England* 301 (1769).

ignorantia (ig-nə-**ran**-shee-ə). [Latin] Ignorance; esp., ignorance of the law.

> "*Ignorantia* . . . . Divided in the civil law, into *ignorantia facti* (ignorance of fact) and *ignorantia juris* (ignorance of law). Lord Coke accepts this division . . . ." 2 Alexander M. Burrill, *A Law Dictionary and Glossary* 40 (2d ed. 1867).

ignorantia facti (ig-nə-**ran**-shee-ə **fak**-tɪ). [Latin] (17c) **1.** Ignorance of fact. **2.** IGNORANTIA FACTI EXCUSAT.

ignorantia facti excusat (ig-nə-**ran**-shee-ə **fak**-tɪ ek-**skyoo**-sat *or* -zat). [Latin] (17c) Ignorance of fact is an excuse; whatever is done under a mistaken impression of a material fact is excused or provides grounds for relief. • This maxim refers to the principle that acts done and contracts made under mistake or ignorance of a material fact are voidable. — Often shortened to *ignorantia facti.*

> "'*Ignorantia facti excusat,*' however, is obviously too sweeping even for a general statement of law, because it is clear (to mention only one point for the moment) that if a certain deed would constitute exactly the same crime under either of two factual situations, it will be no excuse that one was mistaken for the other." Rollin M. Perkins & Ronald N. Boyce, *Criminal Law* 1044 (3d ed. 1982).

ignorantia juris (ig-nə-**ran**-shee-ə **joor**-is). [Latin] (16c) **1.** Ignorance of law. • Under Roman law, this type of ignorance was less likely than *ignorantia facti* to excuse mistaken conduct, except in the case of minors and people, such as women, under some legal disability. **2.** IGNORANTIA JURIS NON EXCUSAT.

ignorantia juris haud excusat. See IGNORANTIA JURIS NON EXCUSAT.

ignorantia juris non excusat (ig-nə-**ran**-shee-ə **joor**-is non ek-**skyoo**-sat *or* -zat). [Latin] (17c) Lack of knowledge about a legal requirement or prohibition is never an excuse to a criminal charge. • In English, the idea is commonly rendered *ignorance of the law is no excuse.* — Often shortened to *ignorantia juris.* — Also termed *ignorantia juris neminem excusat* (ignorance of the law excuses no one); *ignorantia legis non excusat; ignorantia juris haud excusat.*

> "Almost the only knowledge of law possessed by many people is that ignorance of it is no excuse (*ignorantia juris non excusat*). This maxim was originally formulated at a time when the list of crimes, broadly speaking, represented current morality (*mala in se*), but we now have many other crimes that are the result of administrative or social regulation (*mala prohibita*), which are equally governed by the maxim. The rule is, then, that whereas ignorance of fact can excuse, to the extent that it negatives *mens rea* or fault, ignorance of the law generally does not." Glanville Williams, *Textbook of Criminal Law* 405 (1978).

ignorantia juris neminem excusat. See IGNORANTIA JURIS NON EXCUSAT.

ignorantia legis non excusat. See IGNORANTIA JURIS NON EXCUSAT.

ignoratio elenchi (ig-nə-**ray**-shee-oh e-**leng**-kɪ *or* ig-nə-**rah**-tee-oh i-**leng**-kee). [Law Latin "ignorance of the conclusion to be proved"] (16c) **1.** An advocate's misunderstanding of an opponent's position, manifested by an argument that fails to address the opponent's point; the overlooking of an opponent's counterargument. **2.** An advocate's attempt to prove something by marshaling evidence that is immaterial.

ignore, *vb.* (1801) **1.** To refuse to notice, recognize, or consider. **2.** (Of a grand jury) to reject (an indictment) as groundless; to no-bill (a charge). See NO BILL.

ignoring, *n. Family law.* A parent's or caregiver's pattern of depriving a child of essential intellectual or emotional stimulation or of otherwise stifling the child's emotional growth and intellectual development by being physically or emotionally unavailable. Cf. ISOLATING; REJECTING.

IIED. *abbr.* INTENTIONAL INFLICTION OF EMOTIONAL DISTRESS.

ILC. *abbr.* **1.** INTERNATIONAL LAW COMMISSION. **2.** See *irrevocable letter of credit* under LETTER OF CREDIT.

ill, *adj.* **1.** *Archaic.* Inherently bad or evil; of, relating to, or involving viciousness, perniciousness, or wickedness <ill cruelty>. **2.** *Archaic.* Mischievous, baneful, or deleterious <an ill wind blows>. **3.** Attended by evil and suffering; wretched and miserable <an ill fate>. **4.** Of, relating to, or involving threats, harshness, or bad import <ill news travels fast>. **5.** (Of a pleading) defective, bad, or null. **6.** In a bad moral state or condition; (of a person) quarrelsome, cross, and hostile <an ill temper>. **7.** Suffering from disease or debility and feeling unwell <feeling ill these days>. **8.** Not proper, polite, or polished <ill breeding>. **9.** *Archaic.* Unskillful; inexpert <I am ill at mathematics>.

illation (i-**lay**-shən). (16c) **1.** The act or process of inferring. **2.** An inference; that which is inferred.

illegal, *adj.* (17c) Forbidden by law; unlawful <illegal dumping> <an illegal drug>.

illegal abortion. See *criminal abortion* under ABORTION.

illegal alien. See ALIEN.

illegal bargain. See BARGAIN.

illegal consideration. See CONSIDERATION (1).

illegal contract. See CONTRACT.

illegal entry. (18c) **1.** *Criminal law.* The unlawful act of going into a building with the intent to commit a crime. • In some jurisdictions, illegal entry is a lesser included offense of burglary. **2.** *Immigration.* The unauthorized entrance of an alien into the United States by arriving at the wrong time or place, by evading inspection, or by fraud.

illegal immigrant. See *illegal alien* under ALIEN.

illegal interest. See USURY.

illegality, *n.* (17c) **1.** An act that is forbidden by law. **2.** The state of not being legally authorized.

> "A contract made *ultra vires* is void; but not [strictly speaking] on the ground of illegality. Lord Cairns . . . takes exception to the use of the term 'illegality,' pointing out that it is not the *object* of the contracting parties, but the *incapacity* of one of them, that avoids the contract." William R. Anson, *Principles of the Law of Contract* 190 (Arthur L. Corbin ed., 3d Am. ed. 1919).

"It must not be thought that illegality in the law of contract is co-terminous with illegality in the criminal law, for a contract may be illegal without involving any breach of the criminal law at all." P.S. Atiyah, *An Introduction to the Law of Contract* 257 (3d ed. 1981).

3. The quality, state, or condition of being unlawful; esp., DEFENSE OF ILLEGALITY. • The affirmative defense of illegality must be expressly set forth in the response to the opponent's pleading. Fed. R. Civ. P. 8(c).

illegally obtained evidence. See EVIDENCE.

illegal per se. (1855) Unlawful in and of itself.

illegal promise. See PROMISE.

illegal rate. See INTEREST RATE.

illegal search. See *unreasonable search* under SEARCH (1).

illegal strike. See STRIKE (1).

illegal subdivision. See SUBDIVISION.

illegal tax. See TAX.

illegal tax protester. See TAX PROTESTER.

illegal trade. See TRADE (1).

illegal trust. See TRUST (3).

illegal vote. See VOTE (1).

illegitimacy. (17c) **1.** Unlawfulness. **2.** The status of a person who is born outside a lawful marriage and who is not later legitimated by the parents. — Also termed *bastardy.* Cf. LEGITIMACY.

illegitimate, *adj.* (16c) **1.** (Of a child) born out of lawful wedlock and never having been legitimated <illegitimate son>. • Under modern ecclesiastical law, a child born out of wedlock may be automatically legitimated if the parents later marry. A child conceived while the mother is married but born after she is divorced or widowed is considered legitimate. **2.** Against the law; unlawful <illegitimate contract for the sale of contraband>. **3.** Improper <illegitimate conduct>. **4.** Incorrectly inferred <illegitimate conclusion>.

illegitimate child. See CHILD.

ill fame. (15c) Evil repute; notorious bad character. Cf. FAMA PUBLICA.

illicenciatus (il-ɪ-sen-shee-**ay**-təs). [Law Latin] Without license.

illicit (i[l]-**lis**-ət), *adj.* (16c) Illegal or improper <illicit relations>.

illicit cohabitation. See COHABITATION.

illicitum collegium (i-**lis**-ə-təm kə-**lee**-jee-əm). [Latin] (18c) *Roman law.* An illegal association; a *collegium* engaging in illegal activity. • Members of an *illicitum collegium* were subject to prosecution.

Illinois land trust. See *land trust* (1) under TRUST (3).

illiquid asset. See ASSET.

illness. 1. The quality, state, or condition of being sick; bodily or mental indisposition <his illness lasted three months>. • An illness may run the full gamut from slight to severe. **2.** A disease of the body or mind; disorder of health <a serious illness>. Cf. AILMENT.

illusory (i-**loo**-sə-ree), *adj.* (17c) Deceptive; based on a false impression.

illusory appointment. See APPOINTMENT (4).

illusory consideration. See CONSIDERATION (1).

illusory contract. See CONTRACT.

illusory promise. See PROMISE.

illusory tenant. See TENANT (1).

illusory-transfer doctrine. (1976) The rule that the law disregards an inter vivos gift over which the donor retains so much control that there is no good-faith intent to relinquish the transferred property. • The illusory-transfer doctrine is usu. applied to inter vivos trusts in which the settlor retains an excessive control or an interest — for instance, one in which the settlor retains the income for life, the power to revoke, and substantial managerial powers. The leading case on this doctrine is *Newman v. Dore*, 9 N.E.2d 966 (N.Y. 1937). See *colorable transfer* under TRANSFER.

illusory trust. See TRUST (3).

illustrative evidence. See *demonstrative evidence* under EVIDENCE.

ILP. *abbr.* INDEPENDENT-LIVING PROGRAM.

imaginary damages. See *punitive damages* under DAMAGES.

imaginative reconstruction. An interpretive approach whereby a judge seeks to resolve a *casus omissus* (an omitted case) or a *casus incogitatus* (an unthought-of situation) by putting himself or herself in the place of the enacting legislature and trying to divine what the collective body would have wanted done. Cf. PREFERENCE ELICITATION.

imagining. See COMPASSING.

imbargo. *Archaic.* See EMBARGO (1).

imbecile (**im**-bə-səl *or* -sil). (1802) *Archaic.* A person afflicted with severe mental retardation. • Formerly a clinical term, *imbecile* has fallen into disuse because of its frequent derogatory uses. Cf. IDIOT.

imbezzle. *Archaic.* Embezzle. See EMBEZZLEMENT.

imbracery. See EMBRACERY.

IMCO. *abbr.* INTERGOVERNMENTAL MARITIME CONSULTATIVE ORGANIZATION.

IME. *abbr.* **1.** INDEPENDENT MEDICAL EXAMINATION. **2.** INDEPENDENT MENTAL EVALUATION.

IMF. *abbr.* (1948) INTERNATIONAL MONETARY FUND.

imitation. *Trademarks.* An item that so resembles a trademarked item as to be likely to induce the belief that it is genuine. See SIMILARITY.

"The law of trade marks is of recent origin, and may be comprehended in the proposition that a dealer 'has a property in his trade mark.' The ownership is allowed to him, that he may have the exclusive benefit of the reputation which his skill has given to articles made by him, and that no other person may be able to sell to the public, as his, that which is not his. An imitation of his mark, with partial differences such as the public would not observe, does him the same harm as an entire counterfeit. If the wholesale buyer, who is most conversant with the marks, is not misled, but the small retailer or the consumer is, the injury is the same in law, and differs only in degree." *Clark v. Clark*, 25 Barb. 76 (N.Y. App. Div. 1857).

"It is no excuse that one using the trade-marks of another informs his dealers of the imitation, for succeeding sellers may not make similar disclosures." James Kent, 2 *Commentaries on American Law* *372 n. 8 (George Comstock ed., 11th ed. 1866).

IMLS. *abbr.* INSTITUTE OF MUSEUM AND LIBRARY SERVICES.

immaterial, *adj.* (1893) (Of evidence) tending to prove some fact that is not properly at issue; lacking any logical connection with the consequential facts. Cf. IRRELEVANT (1). — **immateriality,** *n.*

> "The rules of substantive law and of pleading are what determine immateriality; and if the probandum is immaterial, of course no evidence to prove it is wanted." John H. Wigmore, *A Students' Textbook of the Law of Evidence* 37 (1935).

immaterial alteration. See ALTERATION (2).

immaterial averment. See AVERMENT.

immaterial evidence. See EVIDENCE.

immaterial fact. See FACT.

immaterial issue. See ISSUE (1).

immaterial variance. See VARIANCE (1).

immatriculation. *Int'l law.* The grant of nationality to and enrollment on the national registry of a merchant ship, thereby giving the ship the right to fly the registering country's flag.

immaturity. See MINORITY (1).

immediate, *adj.* (15c) **1.** Occurring without delay; instant <an immediate acceptance>. **2.** Not separated by other persons or things <her immediate neighbor>. **3.** Having a direct impact; without an intervening agency <the immediate cause of the accident>. Cf. PROXIMATE. — **immediacy, immediateness,** *n.*

immediate annuity. See ANNUITY.

immediate breach. See BREACH OF CONTRACT.

immediate cause. See CAUSE (1).

immediate control. (1962) *Criminal procedure.* **1.** The area within an arrestee's reach. • A police officer may conduct a warrantless search of this area to ensure the officer's safety and to prevent the arrestee from destroying evidence. **2.** Vehicular management by which a driver continuously governs the vehicle's movement. • A driver's failure to maintain immediate control over the vehicle could be evidence of negligence.

immediate death. See DEATH.

immediate descent. See DESCENT.

immediate extent. See EXTENT (2).

immediate family. See FAMILY.

immediate gift. See GIFT.

immediate intent. See INTENT (1).

immediately-apparent requirement. (1978) *Criminal procedure.* The principle that a police officer must, through instant observation, have probable cause to believe that an item is contraband before seizing it. • This plain-view exception to the warrant requirement was first announced in *Coolidge v. New Hampshire*, 403 U.S. 443, 91 S.Ct. 2022 (1971).

> "An object may not be seized from a car merely because the police plain view of it was lawfully acquired; there must be probable cause that the object is a fruit, instrumentality or evidence of crime. And under the 'immediately apparent' requirement of *Coolidge v. New Hampshire*, this probable cause must be determined without examination of the object other than is justified by the purpose underlying police entry of the vehicle." Wayne R. LaFave & Jerold H. Israel, *Criminal Procedure* § 3.7, at 201 (2d ed. 1992).

immediately harmful behavior. See HARMFUL BEHAVIOR.

immediately pending motion. See MOTION (2).

immediate notice. See NOTICE (3).

immediate-notice clause. (1923) *Insurance.* An insurance-policy provision requiring the insured to notify the insurer as soon as possible after a claim arises. • A requirement in a policy for "prompt" or "immediate" notice — or that notice must be given "immediately," "at once," "forthwith," "as soon as practicable," or "as soon as possible" — generally means that the notice must be given within a reasonable time under the circumstances.

immediate past president. 1. See PRESIDENT. **2.** See EMERITUS.

immediate possession. See POSSESSION.

immediate right. See RIGHT.

immemorial (im-ə-**mor**-ee-əl), *adj.* (17c) Beyond memory or record; very old. See TIME IMMEMORIAL.

immemorial possession. See POSSESSION.

immemorial usage. See USAGE (1).

immigrant. (18c) Someone who enters a country to settle there permanently; a person who immigrates. Cf. EMIGRANT.

▸ **alien immigrant.** (1891) An immigrant who has not yet been naturalized.

▸ **undocumented immigrant.** See *illegal alien* under ALIEN.

immigrate, *vb.* To come to dwell or settle; to move into a country where one is not a native for the purpose of permanent residence.

immigration, *n.* (17c) The act of entering a country with the intention of settling there permanently. Cf. EMIGRATION. — **immigrate,** *vb.* — **immigrant,** *n.*

Immigration and Customs Enforcement. The investigative branch of the Department of Homeland Security responsible for enforcing criminal and civil federal laws pertaining to border control, customs, trade, and immigration. • The ICE was formed in 2003 by merging the investigative and interior enforcement divisions of the U.S. Customs Service and the Immigration and Naturalization Service. — Abbr. ICE.

Immigration and Nationality Act. A comprehensive federal law regulating immigration, naturalization, and the exclusion of aliens. 8 USCA §§ 1101–1537. — Abbr. INA. — Also termed *Nationality Act.*

Immigration and Naturalization Service. A former U.S. Department of Justice agency that administered the Immigration and Nationality Act and operated the U.S. Border Patrol. • The INS ceased to exist on 1 March 2003, when most of its functions were transferred to three new agencies within the Department of Homeland Security: (1) U.S. Citizenship and Immigration Services; (2) U.S. Immigration and Customs Enforcement (ICE), and (3) U.S. Customs and Border Protection. — Abbr. INS. See UNITED STATES CITIZENSHIP AND IMMIGRATION SERVICES.

Immigration Appeals Board. See BOARD OF IMMIGRATION APPEALS.

immigration court. See COURT.

immigration detainer. See DETAINER (1).

immigration detention. See DETENTION (1).

imminent danger. See DANGER.

imminent hazard. See HAZARD (1).

imminently dangerous. See DANGEROUS.

imminent-peril doctrine. See EMERGENCY DOCTRINE (1).

immiscere (i-**mis**-ə-ree), *vb.* [Latin] *Roman law.* To mix or mingle with; to meddle with. • This term took on the figurative sense of meddling in another's affairs (e.g., acting as if one were an heir), for which a person could be held accountable.

immobilia (im-ə-**bil**-ee-ə). Immovables. — Also termed *res immobiles* (**reez** i-**moh**-bə-leez).

immobilia situm sequuntur (im-ə-**bil**-ee-ə **SI**-təm sə-**kwən**-tər). [Latin] Immovable things follow their site. • This principle means that immovables are governed by the law of the place where they are fixed. — Sometimes shortened to *immobilia situm.* Cf. MOBILIA SEQUUNTUR PERSONAM.

immobilis, *adj.* (i-**moh**-bə-lis). [Latin] Immovable.

immobilize, *vb.* (1871) To make immobile; esp., to turn (movable property) into immovable property or to turn (circulating capital) into fixed capital.

immoral, *adj.* **1.** Inconsistent with what is right, honest, and commendable; contrary to standards of ethical rightness <to cause suffering deliberately is immoral>. **2.** Inimical to the general welfare <the immoral use of human shields>. **3.** Not following accepted standards of sexual behavior; habitually engaged in lewd or licentious practices <immoral sex>.

immoral consideration. See CONSIDERATION (1).

immoral contract. See CONTRACT.

immoral subject matter. (1959) **1.** *Patents.* Collectively, inventions that have no socially beneficial use. • In the past, patents were denied for some categories of inventions thought to constitute immoral subject matter, such as gambling devices. The doctrine is rarely used today. **2.** *Trademarks.* SCANDALOUS SUBJECT MATTER.

immovable, *n.* (*usu. pl.*) (16c) Property that cannot be moved; an object so firmly attached to land that it is regarded as part of the land. — Also termed *immovable thing.* See FIXTURE. Cf. MOVABLE. — **immovable,** *adj.*

> "Considered in its legal aspect, an immovable, that is to say, a piece of land, includes the following elements: — 1. A determinate portion of the earth's surface. 2. The ground beneath the surface down to the centre of the world. All the pieces of land in England meet together in one terminable point at the earth's centre. 3. Possibly the column of space above the surface *ad infinitum.*" John Salmond, *Jurisprudence* 428 (Glanville L. Williams ed., 10th ed. 1947).

immovable fixture. See FIXTURE.

immune, *adj.* (15c) Having immunity; exempt from a duty or liability.

immunity. (14c) **1.** Any exemption from a duty, liability, or service of process; esp., such an exemption granted to a public official or governmental unit. Cf. IMPUNITY.

▸ **absolute immunity.** (17c) A complete exemption from civil liability, usu. afforded to officials while performing particularly important functions, such as a representative enacting legislation and a judge presiding over a lawsuit. Cf. *qualified immunity.*

▸ **congressional immunity.** (1969) *Constitutional law.* Either of two special immunities given to members of Congress: (1) the exemption from arrest while attending a session of the body to which the member belongs, excluding an arrest for treason, breach of the peace, or a felony, or (2) the exemption from arrest or questioning for any speech or debate entered into during a legislative session. U.S. Const. art. I, § 6, cl. 1. See SPEECH OR DEBATE CLAUSE.

▸ **constitutional immunity.** (1852) Immunity created by a constitution.

▸ **consular immunity.** (1906) A legal immunity that protects foreign-government officials at a level below that of diplomat from being prosecuted or punished for any act performed as part of official duties. • Because consular immunity extends only to activities directly relating to consular functions, it is not as broad as diplomatic immunity. — Also termed *consular privilege.* Cf. DIPLOMATIC IMMUNITY.

▸ **diplomatic immunity.** See DIPLOMATIC IMMUNITY.

▸ **discretionary immunity.** (1965) A qualified immunity for a public official's acts, granted when the act in question requires the exercise of judgment in carrying out official duties (such as planning and policy-making). *See* 28 USCA § 2680(a).

> "Probably no one test will control the decision on discretionary immunity. Although the fact that the government has omitted to act is not in itself a defense, the discretionary immunity is frequently emphasized in nonfeasance cases. On the other hand, where the government's activity is affirmative, specific, and in violation of a statute, regulation, or constitutional provision imposing a duty upon government, courts are often willing to say there is no room for discretion." W. Page Keeton et al., *Prosser and Keeton on the Law of Torts* § 131, at 1041–42 (5th ed. 1984).

▸ **executive immunity.** (1941) **1.** The absolute immunity of the U.S. President or a state governor from civil damages for actions that are within the scope of official responsibilities. **2.** The qualified immunity from civil claims against lesser executive officials, who are liable only if their conduct violates clearly established constitutional or statutory rights. • Executive immunity generally protects an official while carrying out clearly established responsibilities about which a reasonable person would know. Cf. *executive privilege* under PRIVILEGE (3).

▸ **foreign immunity.** (1940) The immunity of a foreign sovereign, its agents, and its instrumentalities from litigation in U.S. courts. — Also termed *foreign-state immunity. See* Foreign Sovereign Immunities Act, 28 USCA § 1330.

▸ **functional immunity.** See *immunity ratione materiae.*

▸ **government immunity.** See *sovereign immunity.*

▸ **head-of-state immunity.** (1978) *Int'l law.* Customary immunity from the jurisdiction of a foreign court that is extended to the leader of a state for authorized official acts while in power.

▸ **immunity *ratione materiae.*** (1943) *Int'l law.* Immunity granted based on the applicant's employment in certain government functions. — Also termed *functional immunity.*

▸ **immunity *ratione personae.*** See *personal immunity.*

▸ **intergovernmental immunity.** (1935) The immunity between the federal and state governments based on their independent sovereignty. See INTERGOVERNMENTAL-IMMUNITY DOCTRINE.

▸ **judicial immunity.** (1850) The immunity of a judge from civil liability arising from the performance of judicial duties.

▸ **legislative immunity.** (1890) The immunity of a legislator from civil liability arising from the performance of legislative duties. See *congressional immunity*.

▸ **personal immunity.** *Int'l law.* Immunity granted to a person because of the office he or she holds. — Also termed *immunity ratione personae*.

▸ **prosecutorial immunity.** (1967) The absolute immunity of a prosecutor from civil liability for decisions made and actions taken in a criminal prosecution.

▸ **qualified immunity.** (1877) Immunity from civil liability for a public official who is performing a discretionary function, as long as the conduct does not violate clearly established constitutional or statutory rights. — Also termed *prima facie privilege*. Cf. *absolute immunity*.

▸ **sovereign immunity.** (1857) **1.** A government's immunity from being sued in its own courts without its consent. • Congress has waived most of the federal government's sovereign immunity. See FEDERAL TORT CLAIMS ACT; RESTRICTIVE PRINCIPLE OF SOVEREIGN IMMUNITY. **2.** A state's immunity from being sued in federal court by the state's own citizens. — Also termed *government immunity*; *governmental immunity*.

▸ **work-product immunity.** See WORK-PRODUCT RULE.

2. *Torts.* A doctrine providing a complete defense to a tort action. • Unlike a privilege, immunity does not negate the tort, and it must be raised affirmatively or it will be waived. Cf. PRIVILEGE (2).

▸ **charitable immunity.** (1935) The immunity of a charitable organization from tort liability. • This immunity has been eliminated or restricted in most states. — Also termed *eleemosynary defense*.

▸ **corporate immunity.** (1820) A corporate officer's immunity from personal liability for a tortious act committed while acting in good faith and within the course of performing corporate duties.

▸ **husband–wife immunity.** (1951) The immunity of one spouse from a tort action by the other spouse for personal injury. • The immunity arose from the age-old notion that a husband and wife were one in the eyes of the law, so that one could not injure the other — there being no "other." Most states and the District of Columbia have abolished interspousal tort immunity either by judicial opinion or by statute. Some states have abolished the rule only in specific instances such as intentional or vehicular torts. — Also termed *interspousal immunity*; *interspousal tort immunity*; *marital immunity*.

▸ **interspousal immunity.** See *husband–wife immunity*

▸ **judgmental immunity.** See ERROR-OF-JUDGMENT RULE.

▸ **marital immunity.** See *husband–wife immunity*.

▸ **parental immunity.** (1930) **1.** The principle that parents are not liable to their children, nor children to their parents, for tort claims. • This tort immunity did not exist at English common law; it was created by American courts, first appearing in *Hewellette v. George*, 9 So. 885 (Miss. 1891), overruled by *Glaskox ex rel. Denton v. Glaskox*, 614 So.2d 906 (1992). Many courts have abolished the doctrine for some purposes, such as actions by unemancipated minors against parents to recover for injuries sustained in motor-vehicle accidents. *See, e.g., Merrick v. Sutterlin*, 610 P.2d 891 (Wash. 1980) (en banc). Nor does the immunity apply when an injury is inflicted by the parent or child through willful, wanton, or criminal conduct. *See, e.g., Nudd v. Matsoukas*, 131 N.E.2d 525 (Ill. 1956). — Also termed *parent–child immunity*; *parental-immunity doctrine*. **2.** The principle that parents are not liable for damages caused by the ordinary negligence of their minor child. Cf. PARENTAL-LIABILITY STATUTE.

3. *Criminal law.* Freedom from prosecution granted by the government in exchange for the person's testimony. • By granting immunity, the government can compel testimony — despite the Fifth Amendment right against self-incrimination — because that testimony can no longer incriminate the witness.

▸ **letter immunity.** (1978) Immunity granted by a prosecutor in a letter to a grand-jury witness.

▸ **pocket immunity.** (1983) Immunity that results from the prosecutor's decision not to prosecute, instead of from a formal grant of immunity. — Also termed *informal immunity*.

▸ **testimonial immunity.** (1938) Immunity from the use of the compelled testimony against the witness. • Any information derived from that testimony, however, is generally admissible against the witness.

> "Testimonial immunity is a logical corollary to a person's fifth amendment right not to 'be compelled in any criminal case to be a witness against himself.' It provides that when a witness is compelled to testify for any reason, his testimony cannot be used against him in a subsequent criminal proceeding. It also follows that the immunity is not available where the witness testifies *voluntarily*, and that the protection applies only in a subsequent *criminal* prosecution in which the *witness* is subject to prosecution for an offense related to his earlier testimony." 2 Paul H. Robinson, *Criminal Law Defenses* § 205, at 482–83 (1984).

▸ **transactional immunity.** (1966) Immunity from prosecution for any event or transaction described in the compelled testimony. • This is the broadest form of immunity.

▸ **use immunity.** (1970) Immunity from the use of the compelled testimony (or any information derived from that testimony) in a future prosecution against the witness. • After granting use immunity, the government can still prosecute if it shows that its evidence comes from a legitimate independent source. — Also termed *use/derivative-use immunity*; *derivative-use immunity*.

4. Freedom of a person against having a given legal relation altered by someone else's act or omission.

immunity bath. (1906) *Slang.* **1.** *Criminal law.* Broad immunity granted to a witness as assurance that he or she will not be subject to prosecution. **2.** Legal protection against an adverse action in a civil suit. • For example, the business-judgment rule may be called an "immunity bath" if it protects a corporation from the effects of poor decisions. — Also termed (occas.) *bath*.

immunity *ratione materiae*. See IMMUNITY (1).

immunity *ratione personae*. See *personal immunity* under IMMUNITY (1).

immunize, *vb.* (1892) To grant immunity to <the new legislation immunized the police officers from liability>.

impacted area. (1915) A region that is affected by some event or phenomenon; esp., a region whose school population increases because of an influx of federal employees to work on a federal project or activity but whose tax revenue declines because of the U.S. government's immunity from local taxes.

impact rule. (1865) *Torts.* The common-law requirement that physical contact must have occurred for the recovery of damages for negligent infliction of emotional distress. • This rule has been abandoned in most jurisdictions. — Also termed *physical-impact rule.*

impair, *vb.* (17c) To diminish the value of (property or a property right). • This term is commonly used in reference to diminishing the value of a contractual obligation to the point that the contract becomes invalid or a party loses the benefit of the contract. See CONTRACTS CLAUSE.

impaired capital. See CAPITAL.

impairing the morals of a minor. (1931) *Criminal law.* The offense committed by an adult who engages in sex acts short of intercourse with a minor. • Examples of this conduct are fondling, taking obscene photographs, and showing pornographic materials. See SEXUAL RELATIONS (2). — Also termed *unlawful sexual conduct with a minor*; *corrupting*; *corruption of a minor.* Cf. CONTRIBUTING TO THE DELINQUENCY OF A MINOR.

impairment, *n.* (14c) The quality, state, or condition of being damaged, weakened, or diminished <impairment of collateral>; specif., a condition in which a part of a person's mind or body is damaged or does not work well, esp. when the condition amounts to a disability. — **impair,** *vb.*

▸ **intellectual impairment.** See *developmental disability* under DISABILITY (2).

▸ **severe impairment.** (1906) In social-security or disability law, a physical or mental impairment that greatly restricts a person's ability to perform ordinary, necessary tasks of daily life. See DISABILITY (2); MAJOR LIFE ACTIVITY.

impalement, *n.* (17c) *Hist.* An ancient mode of inflicting punishment by thrusting a sharp pole through a person's body. — Formerly also spelled *empalement.* — **impale,** *vb.*

impanel, *vb.* See EMPANEL.

impaneled jury. See JURY.

imparcare (im-pahr-**kair**-ee), *vb.* [Law Latin "to enclose"] *Hist.* To impound; to confine in prison. See CARCER.

imparl (im-**pahrl**), *vb.* (15c) **1.** *Hist.* To request or obtain an imparlance. **2.** To confer with the opposing party in an effort to settle a dispute amicably; to discuss settlement.

imparlance (im-**pahr**-lənts). (17c) *Hist.* **1.** A continuance granted in order to give the requesting party (usu. the defendant) further time to answer the adversary's previous pleading (esp. the plaintiff's writ, bill, or count), often so that the parties will have time to settle the dispute. • Imparlances were abolished in England in 1853. **2.** A petition for such a continuance. **3.** The permission granting such a continuance. — Formerly also spelled *emparlance.* — Also termed *licentia loquendi.*

> "After defence made, the defendant must put in his *plea.* But, before he pleads, he is entitled to demand one *imparlance*, or *licentia loquendi*, and may have more granted by consent of the plaintiff; to see if he can end the matter amicably without farther suit, by talking with the plaintiff . . . ." 3 William Blackstone, *Commentaries on the Laws of England* 298 (1768).

> "An imparlance is the time allowed by the court to either party, upon request, to answer the pleading of his opponent. Imparlance, from the French 'parler' — to speak — in its most common signification, means time to plead. Formerly the parties, in the course of oral pleadings, were allowed time to speak or confer with one another, so that they might endeavor to settle the matters in dispute, and later, when the pleadings came to be in writing, the court permitted a certain time for each to plead to or answer the pleading of his opponent. In modern practice the term is rarely used . . . ." Benjamin J. Shipman, *Handbook of Common-Law Pleading* § 234, at 405 (Henry Winthrop Ballantine ed., 3d ed. 1923).

▸ **general imparlance.** (17c) The allowance of time until the court's next term, without reserving to the defendant the benefit of any exception. • With this type of imparlance, the requesting defendant cannot later object to the jurisdiction of the court or plead any matter in abatement.

▸ **general special imparlance.** (18c) The allowance of time with a saving of all exceptions, so that a defendant might later plead not only in abatement but also to the jurisdiction.

▸ **special imparlance.** (17c) The allowance of time with a saving only of exceptions to the writ, bill, or count, but not to the court's jurisdiction.

impartial, *adj.* (16c) Not favoring one side more than another; unbiased and disinterested; unswayed by personal interest. — **impartiality,** *n.*

impartial chair. (1993) **1.** ARBITRATOR. **2.** MEDIATOR. — Also termed *impartial chairman.*

impartial chairman. See IMPARTIAL CHAIR.

impartial expert. See *independent expert* under EXPERT.

impartial jury. See JURY.

impartible (im-**pahr**-tə-bəl), *adj.* (14c) Indivisible <an impartible estate>.

impartible feud. See FEUD (1).

impasse (**im**-pas). A point in negotiations at which agreement cannot be reached. • A neutral third party (such as a mediator) is often called in to help resolve an impasse.

> "Not only is the employer free after impasse to implement changes already offered to the union, but either party is free after impasse to decline to negotiate further. Since impasse signifies that the parties have exhausted (at least temporarily) the avenues of bargaining, termination of bargaining at that point cannot be thought to demonstrate a cast of mind against reaching agreement." Robert A. Gorman, *Basic Text on Labor Law: Unionization and Collective Bargaining* 447 (1976).

impeach, *vb.* (14c) **1.** To charge with a crime or misconduct; esp., to formally charge (a public official) with a violation of the public trust <President Nixon resigned from office to avoid being impeached>. • Impeaching a federal official, such as the President, the Vice President, or a federal judge, requires that a majority of the U.S. House of Representatives vote to return at least one article of impeachment to the U.S. Senate, itemizing the charges and explaining their factual grounds. Even if an official is impeached, removal from office does not occur unless two-thirds of the senators who are present vote for conviction. **2.** To discredit the veracity of (a witness) <to impeach a witness on cross-examination>. **3.** To challenge the accuracy or authenticity of (a document) <the handwriting expert impeached the holographic will>.

impeachable offense. (1810) *Constitutional law.* An offense for which a public official may legally be impeached, during the first step in a two-step process that may, depending on the vote in the upper house of the legislature, lead to the official's removal from office. • The U.S. Constitution states that "[t]he President, Vice President and all civil Officers of the United States, shall be removed from Office on Impeachment for, and Conviction of, Treason, Bribery, or other high Crimes and Misdemeanors." U.S. Const. art. II, § 4. The meaning of this language was much debated during the impeachment and trial of President Bill Clinton, against whom two articles of impeachment were returned by the House of Representatives. The question arose concerning what type of misdemeanor will suffice, and whether the *high* in *high crimes* modifies *misdemeanors* as well. No definitive answer resulted from the proceedings.

impeachment. (16c) **1.** The act (by a legislature) of calling for the removal from office of a public official, accomplished by presenting a written charge of the official's alleged misconduct; esp., the initiation of a proceeding in the U.S. House of Representatives against a federal official, such as the President or a judge. — Also termed *formal impeachment.* • Congress's authority to remove a federal official stems from Article II, Section 4 of the Constitution, which authorizes the removal of an official for "Treason, Bribery, or other high Crimes and Misdemeanors." But the grounds on which an official can be removed do not have to be criminal in nature. They usu. involve some type of abuse of power or breach of the public trust. Articles of impeachment — which can be approved by a simple majority in the House — serve as the charging instrument for the later trial in the Senate. If the President is impeached, the Chief Justice of the Supreme Court presides over the Senate trial. The defendant can be removed from office by the vote of a two-thirds majority of the senators who are present. In the United Kingdom, impeachment is by the House of Commons and trial by the House of Lords. But no case has arisen there since 1801, and many British scholars consider impeachment obsolete. **2.** The act of discrediting a witness, as by catching the witness in a lie or by demonstrating that the witness has been convicted of a criminal offense. **3.** The act of challenging the accuracy or authenticity of evidence.

▸ **formal impeachment.** (1878) **1.** The discrediting of a witness's testimony by confronting the witness with his or her specific untruthful acts, prior convictions, prior inconsistent statements, or the like. **2.** IMPEACHMENT (1).

▸ **impeachment by omission.** (1973) The use of a significantly incomplete statement on an earlier occasion as a prior inconsistent statement.

4. *Archaic.* Hindrance, impediment, or obstruction; a restraint, esp. by means of a lawsuit. See IMPEACHMENT OF WASTE. **5.** *Archaic.* An accusation.

impeachment court. See COURT FOR THE TRIAL OF IMPEACHMENTS.

impeachment evidence. See EVIDENCE.

impeachment of verdict. (1821) A party's attack on a verdict, alleging impropriety by a member of the jury.

impeachment of waste. (16c) *Hist.* An action for waste against the tenant of the harmed property. — Also termed *impetitio vasti.*

> "[F]or above five hundred years past, all tenants for life or for any less estate, have been punishable or liable to be impeached for waste, both voluntary and permissive; unless their leases be made, as sometimes they are, without impeachment of waste . . . ." 2 William Blackstone, *Commentaries on the Laws of England* 283 (1766).

impechiare (im-pee-chee-**air**-ee), *vb.* [fr. Law French *empescher* "to impeach"] *Hist.* To impeach; to accuse.

impediens (im-**pee**-dee-enz). [Law Latin] *Hist.* Someone who hinders. • The defendant (or *deforciant*) in a fine of conveyance was sometimes so called. See FINE (1).

impediment (im-**ped**-ə-mənt). (14c) A hindrance or obstruction; esp., some fact (such as legal minority) that bars a marriage if known beforehand and, if discovered after the ceremony, renders the marriage either void or voidable.

▸ **canonical impediment.** (16c) A ground for annulment recognized by canon law and developed by the ecclesiastical courts of the Roman Catholic Church. • Canonical impediments include affinity, impotence, disparity of worship, and previous religious profession.

▸ **civil impediment.** (1832) A ground for annulment recognized by civil law of contracts, such as minority, unsoundness of mind, fraud, and duress. • The defects of fraud and duress may be waived so that the parties may confirm the marriage.

▸ **diriment impediment** (**dir**-ə-mənt im-**ped**-ə-mənt), *n.* [fr. Latin *dirimens impedimentum* "nullifying impediment"] (17c) A fact that raises an absolute bar to marriage and renders a contracted marriage void. • Diriment impediments include consanguinity within a prohibited degree and a prior undissolved marriage. — Also termed *impedimenta dirimentia.*

impedimenta dirimentia. See *diriment impediment* under IMPEDIMENT.

impedimentum rebus agendis (im-ped-ə-**men**-təm **ree**-bəs ə-**jen**-dis). [Law Latin] (17c) *Hist.* A hindrance to the transaction of business.

impeditor (im-**ped**-ə-tər). [Law Latin] *Hist.* Someone who interferes with a patron's right of advowson (that is, the right to appoint a clerk to a benefice). — Also termed *disturber.* See DE CLERICO ADMITTENDO.

impensae (im-**pen**-see), *n. pl.* [Latin] *Roman law.* Expenditures made on a thing.

▸ ***impensae necessariae*** (im-**pen**-see nes-ə-**sair**-ee-ee). Expenditures necessary to prevent deterioration, destruction, or loss of a thing — such as money expended for building repair or maintenance.

▸ ***impensae utiles*** (im-**pen**-see **yoo**-tə-leez). Useful expenditures that improve something and increase its selling value.

▸ ***impensae voluptariae*** (im-**pen**-see vol-əp-**tair**-ee-ee). Expenditures made on a thing for ornamental purposes only.

imperative authority. See AUTHORITY (4).

imperative law. See LAW.

imperative theory of law. (1909) The theory that law consists of the general commands issued by a country or other political community to its citizens and residents and enforced by courts with the sanction of physical force. • Imperative theorists believe that if there are rules predating or independent of the polity, those rules may closely resemble law or even substitute for it, but they are not law. See POSITIVE LAW. Cf. NATURAL LAW.

imperative words. (17c) Language having a binding effect by requiring certain actions or effects. • Words such as *must* are imperative. Cf. PRECATORY WORDS.

imperfect defense. See DEFENSE (1).

imperfect duty. See DUTY (1).

imperfect gift. See GIFT.

imperfect grant. See GRANT (4).

imperfect justification. See JUSTIFICATION (2).

imperfect obligation. See *moral obligation* under OBLIGATION.

imperfect ownership. See OWNERSHIP.

imperfect right. See RIGHT.

imperfect self-defense. See SELF-DEFENSE (1).

imperfect statute. See STATUTE.

imperfect title. See TITLE (2).

imperfect trust. See *executory trust* under TRUST (3).

imperfect usufruct. See *quasi-usufruct* (1) under USUFRUCT.

imperfect war. See WAR (1).

imperial state. See STATE (1).

imperitia (im-pə-**rish**-ee-ə), *n.* [Latin] *Roman law.* Lack of skill or competence; inexperience. • The Romans considered *imperitia* to be a type of *culpa* that gave rise to liability in tort or liability under a contract calling for the rendering of services (such as a *locatio conductio operis*). *Imperitus* could denote a person, such as a crafter who was incompetent.

imperium (im-**peer**-ee-əm), *n.* [Latin] (17c) *Roman law.* Power or dominion; esp., the legal authority wielded by superior magistrates under the Republic, and later by the emperor under the Empire. • *Imperium* implied the right of military command, the power of corporal punishment, and the power of life and death over citizens. It was symbolized by the lictors who carried the *fasces* and an ax, which symbolized those powers. *Imperium* was also used less technically in reference to lesser types of authority.

▸ ***imperium domesticum*** (im-**peer**-ee-əm də-**mes**-ti-kəm). [Latin "domestic power"] The power of the head of a household.

▸ ***imperium merum*** (im-**peer**-ee-əm **meer**-əm). [Latin "bare power" or "absolute executive power"] (17c) *Roman law.* A higher magistrate's power to use force to repress crime.

▸ ***imperium mixtum*** (im-**peer**-ee-əm **miks**-təm). [Latin "mixed power"] (17c) *Roman law.* A magistrate's authority to make and enforce decisions in civil and criminal matters.

impermissible comment on the evidence. See COMMENT ON THE EVIDENCE.

impersonal. See IN REM.

impersonation. (18c) The act of impersonating or imitating someone. — Also termed *personation.*

▸ **false impersonation.** (1878) The crime of falsely representing oneself as another person, often a law-enforcement officer, for the purpose of deceiving someone. *See* 18 USCA §§ 912–917. — Also termed *false personation.*

impertinent, *adj.* See IRRELEVANT.

impertinent evidence. See EVIDENCE.

impertinent matter. (18c) *Procedure.* In pleading, matter that is not relevant to the action or defense. • A federal court may strike any impertinent matter from a pleading. Fed. R. Civ. P. 12(f). Cf. SCANDALOUS MATTER.

impertinent question. See QUESTION (1).

impescare (im-pə-**skair**-ee), *vb.* [fr. Law French *empescher* "to impeach"] *Hist.* To impeach; to accuse.

impetitio vasti (im-pə-**tish**-ee-oh **vas**-tɪ). See IMPEACHMENT OF WASTE.

impetrare (im-pə-**trair**-ee), *vb.* [Latin] *Roman law.* To obtain by request. • This word often appeared in petitions requesting a *formula* for an action from a praetor. (See FORMULA (1).) It performed a similar function under English law for those seeking a writ from Chancery. The English verb *impetrate* derives from this Latinism.

impetration (im-pə-**tray**-shən). (15c) **1.** *Hist.* The act of petitioning for a writ. **2.** *Hist. Eccles. law.* The act of obtaining a papal benefice for bestowal by the king or other lay patron. — **impetrate,** *vb.*

impignorata (im-pig-nə-**ray**-tə). [Law Latin] *Hist.* Given in pledge; pledged or mortgaged.

impignoration (im-pig-nə-**ray**-shən), *n.* (16c) *Hist.* The act or an instance of pawning or pledging. — **impignorate,** *vb.*

impinge, *vb.* (17c) To encroach or infringe (*on* or *upon*) <impinge on the defendant's rights>.

implacitare (im-plas-ə-**tair**-ee), *vb.* [fr. Latin *placitum* "plea"] *Hist.* To implead; to sue.

implead, *vb.* (14c) **1.** To bring (someone) into a lawsuit; esp., to bring (a new party) into the action. Cf. INTERPLEAD. **2.** *Hist.* To bring an action against; to accuse. — Formerly also spelled *emplead*; *empleet.*

impleader, *n.* (1918) A procedure by which a third party is brought into a lawsuit, esp. by a defendant who seeks to shift liability to someone not sued by the plaintiff. Fed. R. Civ. P. 14. — Also termed *third-party practice*; *vouching-in.* Cf. INTERPLEADER; INTERVENTION (1).

impleading. (1875) The addition of another party, esp. a third party, into a lawsuit. Cf. INTERPLEADER; INTERVENTION (1).

- ▸ **direct impleading.** (1881) The addition of a specific defendant or third party.
- ▸ **indirect impleading.** (1936) The addition of a party who intervenes through interpleader.

implementation plan. An outline of steps needed to accomplish a particular goal; esp., in environmental law, a detailed outline of the timing and sequence of measures to be taken to meet environmental-quality standards by a specified time.

implicate, *vb.* (15c) **1.** To show (a person) to be involved in (a crime, misfeasance, etc.) <when he turned state's evidence, he implicated three other suspects>. **2.** To bring into play; to involve or affect <three judges were implicated in the bribery>. **3.** To be shown to be a cause <viruses have been implicated in the spread of some cancers>.

implication. (15c) **1.** The act of showing involvement in something, esp. a crime or misfeasance <the implication of the judges in the bribery scheme>. **2.** Something that is not directly stated but is inferable; an inference drawn from something said or observed <the implication was that the scheme involved several persons>.

- ▸ **necessary implication.** (18c) An implication so strong in its probability that anything to the contrary would be unreasonable.

implicit cost. See *opportunity cost* under COST (1).

implicit hearsay. See *inferential hearsay* under HEARSAY.

implied, *adj.* (16c) **1.** Not directly or clearly expressed; communicated only vaguely or indirectly <counsel's implied statement>. **2.** Recognized by law as existing inferentially <implied agreement>. Cf. EXPRESS.

implied abandonment. See ABANDONMENT (11).

implied abrogation. See ABROGATION.

implied acceptance. See ACCEPTANCE (3).

implied acquittal. See ACQUITTAL (1).

implied actual authority. See *implied authority* under AUTHORITY (1).

implied actual knowledge. See *actual knowledge* (2) under KNOWLEDGE (1).

implied admission. See ADMISSION (1).

implied agency. See AGENCY (1).

implied agent. See *apparent agent* under AGENT.

implied amnesty. See AMNESTY (1).

implied assent. See ASSENT.

implied assertion. See *assertive conduct* under CONDUCT.

implied assumption. See ASSUMPTION.

implied assumption of the risk. See ASSUMPTION OF THE RISK.

implied authority. See AUTHORITY (1).

implied bias. See BIAS.

implied coercion. See UNDUE INFLUENCE (1).

implied color. See COLOR.

implied condition. See CONDITION (2).

implied confession. See CONFESSION (1).

implied consent. See CONSENT (1).

implied-consent law. (1958) *Criminal law.* A statute establishing a presumption that the operator of a motor vehicle implicitly consents to having a chemical test administered to determine blood alcohol content, as long as the police have reason to believe that the person is intoxicated or otherwise under the influence. • When the operator is unconscious, the police may rely on such a statute to justify taking a blood sample without a court order.

implied consideration. See CONSIDERATION (1).

implied contract. See CONTRACT.

implied contractual indemnity. See INDEMNITY.

implied covenant. See COVENANT (1).

implied covenant of good faith and fair dealing. See COVENANT (1).

implied covenant of habitability. See *implied warranty of habitability* under WARRANTY (2).

implied crime. See *constructive crime* under CRIME.

implied dedication. See DEDICATION.

implied duty of cooperation. See DUTY (1).

implied easement. See EASEMENT.

implied indemnity. See INDEMNITY.

implied in fact, *adj.* (1865) Inferable from the facts of the case.

implied-in-fact condition. See CONDITION (2).

implied-in-fact contract. See CONTRACT.

implied in law, *n.* (1806) Imposed by operation of law and not because of any inferences that can be drawn from the facts of the case.

implied-in-law condition. See *constructive condition* under CONDITION (2).

implied-in-law contract. See CONTRACT.

implied intent. See INTENT (1).

implied intention. See INTENTION.

implied license. See LICENSE.

implied license by acquiescence. See LICENSE.

implied license by conduct. See LICENSE.

implied license by equitable estoppel. See LICENSE.

implied license by legal estoppel. See LICENSE.

implied-license doctrine. (1968) **1.** The principle that a person's specific conduct may be tantamount to a grant of permission to do something. **2.** The principle that in some specified circumstances a statute can be construed as supplying a necessary authority by operation of law.

implied malice. See MALICE.

implied negative covenant. See COVENANT (1).

implied notice. See NOTICE (3).

implied obligation. See *obediential obligation* under OBLIGATION.

implied obligation of cooperation. See OBLIGATION.

implied offense. See *constructive crime* under CRIME.

implied partnership. See *partnership by estoppel* under PARTNERSHIP.

implied permission. See PERMISSION (2).

implied power. See POWER (3).

implied promise. See PROMISE.

implied reciprocal covenant. See COVENANT (4).

implied reciprocal servitude. See *implied reciprocal covenant* under COVENANT (4).

implied repeal. See REPEAL.

implied repudiation. See REPUDIATION.

implied reservation. See RESERVATION (3).

implied-reservation-of-water doctrine. (1974) A legal doctrine permitting the federal government to use and control, for public purposes, water appurtenant to federal lands. See EMINENT DOMAIN.

implied right. See RIGHT.

implied surrender. See SURRENDER (5).

implied term. See TERM (2).

implied trust. 1. See *constructive trust* under TRUST (3). **2.** See *resulting trust* under TRUST (3).

implied waiver. See WAIVER (1).

implied warranty. See WARRANTY (2).

implied warranty of authority. See WARRANTY (2).

implied warranty of fitness for a particular purpose. See WARRANTY (2).

implied warranty of habitability. See WARRANTY (2).

implied warranty of merchantability. See WARRANTY (2).

imply, *vb.* (14c) **1.** To express or involve indirectly; to suggest <the opinion implies that the court has adopted a stricter standard for upholding punitive-damages awards>. Cf. INFER. **2.** (Of a court) to impute or impose on equitable or legal grounds <the court implied a contract between the parties>. **3.** To read into (a document) <citing grounds of fairness, the court implied a condition that the parties had not expressed>. See *implied term* under TERM (2). — **implication,** *n.*

> "Anglo-American judges, who continually evaluate facts, often use the phrase *by implication* (= by what is implied, though not formally expressed, by natural inference), along with its various cognates. Judges (by implication) draw 'natural inferences' and thereby decide that something or other was, in the circumstances, 'implied.' Through the process of hypallage — a semantic shift by which the attributes of the true subject are transferred to another subject — the word *imply* has come to be used in reference to what the judges do, as opposed to the circumstances. This specialized use of *imply* runs counter to popular lay use and is not adequately treated in English-language dictionaries.
>
> . . .
>
> "The lawyer's *imply* has directly encroached on the word *infer.* Whereas nonlawyers frequently use *infer* for *imply,* lawyers and judges conflate the two in the opposite direction, by using *imply* for *infer.* In analyzing the facts of a case, judges will *imply* one fact from certain others. (*From* is a telling preposition.) Nonlawyers believe they must be *inferring* an additional fact from those already known; if contractual terms are *implied,* they must surely be implied by the words or circumstances of the contract and not by the judges." Bryan A. Garner, *Garner's Dictionary of Legal Usage* 430, 430–31 (3d ed. 2011).

import, *n.* (16c) **1.** A product brought into a country from a foreign country where it originated <imports declined in the third quarter>. See PARALLEL IMPORTS. **2.** The process or activity of bringing foreign goods into a country <the import of products affects the domestic economy in significant ways>. Cf. EXPORT, *n.* **3.** Meaning; esp., implied meaning <the court must decide the import of that obscure provision>. **4.** Importance; significance <time will tell the relative import of Judge Kozinski's decisions in American law>.

importation. (17c) The bringing of goods into a country from a foreign country.

import duty. See DUTY (4).

imported litigation. See LITIGATION.

importer. (15c) A person or entity that brings goods into a country from a foreign country and pays customs duties.

Import–Export Clause. (1945) *Constitutional law.* U.S. Const. art. I, § 10, cl. 2, which prohibits states from taxing imports or exports. • The Supreme Court has liberally interpreted this clause, allowing states to tax imports as long as the tax does not discriminate in favor of domestic goods. — Also termed *Export Clause.*

import letter of credit. See LETTER OF CREDIT.

import quota. See QUOTA (2).

import recording. See BOOTLEG RECORDING (1).

importune (im-por-t[y]oon), *vb.* (16c) To solicit forcefully; to request persistently, and sometimes irksomely.

impose, *vb.* (17c) To levy or exact (a tax or duty).

imposition. (14c) An impost or tax.

impositive fact. See FACT.

impossibility. (14c) **1.** The fact or condition of not being able to occur, exist, or be done. **2.** A fact or circumstance that cannot occur, exist, or be done. **3.** *Contracts.* A fact or circumstance that excuses performance because (1) the obligation cannot be performed because of its nature, (2) the subject or means of performance has deteriorated, has been destroyed, or is no longer available, (3) the method of delivery or payment has failed, (4) a law now prevents performance, or (5) death or illness prevents performance. • Increased or unexpected difficulty and expense do not usu. qualify as an impossibility and thus do not excuse performance. — Also termed *impossibility of performance.* **4.** The doctrine by which such a fact or circumstance excuses contractual performance. Cf. FRUSTRATION (2); IMPRACTICABILITY. **5.** *Criminal law.* A fact or circumstance preventing the commission of a crime.

▸ **factual impossibility.** (1932) Impossibility due to the fact that the act cannot physically be accomplished, such as trying to pick an empty pocket. • Such an impossibility may be either absolute (impossible in any case, as by trying to stop the sun from rising) or relative (arising from the particular facts, as when A agrees to pay B, who is dead). Factual impossibility is not a defense to the crime of attempt. — Also termed *physical impossibility; impossibility of fact.*

▸ **legal impossibility.** (1831) **1.** Impossibility due to the fact that what the defendant intended to do is not illegal even though the defendant might have believed that he or she was committing a crime. • A legal impossibility might occur, for example, if a person goes hunting while erroneously believing that it is not hunting season. This type of legal impossibility is a defense to the crimes of attempt, conspiracy, and solicitation. — Also termed *impossibility of law; true legal impossibility.* **2.** Impossibility due to the fact that an element required for an attempt has not been satisfied. • This type of legal impossibility might occur, for example, if a person pulls the trigger of an unloaded gun pointed at another when the crime of attempt requires that the gun be loaded. This is a defense to the crime of attempt.

▸ **objective impossibility.** (1882) Impossibility due to the nature of the performance and not to the inability of the individual promisor.

▸ **subjective impossibility.** (1882) Impossibility due wholly to the inability of the individual promisor and not to the nature of the performance.

▸ **supervening impossibility.** (1867) Impossibility arising after the formation of a contract but before the time when the promisor's performance is due, and arising because of facts that the promisor had no reason to anticipate and did not contribute to the occurrence of.

"Contracting parties constantly take a voluntary risk, and it would make the whole basis of contract insecure if they were allowed to plead every and any kind of supervening impossibility. Moreover, a man need not undertake this kind of risk unless he chooses. He can deliberately exclude it by stipulations in his contract, if the other party is willing to contract with him on those terms." 2 *Stephen's Commentaries on the Laws of England* 82–83 (L. Crispin Warmington ed., 21st ed. 1950).

impossibility of fact. See FACTUAL IMPOSSIBILITY.

impossibility of law. See LEGAL IMPOSSIBILITY.

impossibility of performance. See IMPOSSIBILITY (3).

impossibility-of-performance doctrine. (1960) The principle that a party may be released from a contract on the ground that uncontrollable circumstances have rendered performance impossible. See *objective impossibility* under IMPOSSIBILITY. Cf. FRUSTRATION (2); IMPRACTICABILITY; FORCE MAJEURE.

impossible consideration. See CONSIDERATION (1).

impossible contract. See CONTRACT.

impost (**im**-pohst). (16c) A tax or duty, esp. a customs duty <the impost was assessed when the ship reached the mainland>. See DUTY (4).

impostor (im-**pos**-tər). (16c) Someone who pretends to be someone else to deceive others, esp. to receive the benefits of a negotiable instrument. — Also spelled *imposter.*

impostor rule. (1939) *Commercial law.* The principle that (1) an impostor's indorsement of a negotiable instrument is not a forgery, and (2) the drawer or maker who issues the instrument to the impostor is negligent and therefore liable to the holder for payment. • If a drawer or maker issues an instrument to an impostor, any resulting forgery of the payee's name will be effective in favor of a person paying on the instrument in good faith or taking it for value or collection. UCC § 3-404(a), (b).

impotence (**im**-pə-təns). (15c) **1.** Powerlessness; the quality, state, or condition of lacking strength or vigor. **2.** A man's inability to achieve an erection and therefore to have sexual intercourse. • Because an impotent husband cannot consummate a marriage, impotence has often been cited as a ground for annulment. — Also termed *impotency; physical incapacity; erectile dysfunction.* Cf. POTENCY (4).

"An impotent person, physically incapable of consummating the marriage, cannot contract a valid marriage. By impotency is meant, not mere barrenness or sterility, but incapacity preventing complete and natural sexual intercourse. The incapacity must exist at the time of the marriage, and must continue and be incurable, to authorize a decree of nullity. But a decree will be granted, although the impotency might be cured by an operation not dangerous to life, where the afflicted party refuses to submit to the operation. The mere fact that the parties were of advanced age at the time of their marriage will not defeat a suit to avoid the marriage on the ground of impotency, but this fact may strongly incline the court against granting the relief sought. Impotency is one of the canonical impediments, and renders the marriage voidable merely, and not void. The validity of a marriage, therefore, cannot be impeached on this ground after the death of one of the parties." Joseph R. Long, *A Treatise on the Law of Domestic Relations* 21–22 (1905).

3. *Hist.* Sterility. **4.** *Rare.* A woman's physical inability to engage in sexual intercourse.

impotency. See IMPOTENCE.

impound, *n.* The portion of a monthly mortgage payment that is earmarked to pay property taxes and property-insurance premiums. See *impound account* under ACCOUNT.

impound, *vb.* (15c) **1.** To place (something, such as a car or other personal property) in the custody of the police or the court, often with the understanding that it will be returned intact at the end of the proceeding. **2.** To take and retain possession of (something, such as a forged document to be produced as evidence) in preparation for a criminal prosecution.

impound account. 1. See ACCOUNT. **2.** See ESCROW (2).

impoundment. (17c) **1.** The act or an instance of impounding; the quality, state, or condition of being impounded. See IMPOUND. **2.** *Constitutional law.* The President's refusal to spend funds appropriated by Congress. • Although not authorized by the Constitution and seldom used, impoundment effectively gives the executive branch a line-item veto over legislative spending.

impracticability (im-prak-ti-kə-**bil**-ə-tee). (17c) *Contracts.* **1.** A fact or circumstance that excuses a party from performing an act, esp. a contractual duty, because (though possible) it would cause extreme and unreasonable difficulty. • For performance to be truly impracticable, the duty must become much more difficult or much more expensive to perform, and this difficulty or expense must have been unanticipated. **2.** The doctrine by which such a fact or circumstance excuses performance. Cf. FRUSTRATION (2); IMPOSSIBILITY (4).

▸ **commercial impracticability.** (1913) The occurrence of a contingency whose nonoccurrence was an assumption in the contract, as a result of which one party cannot perform. — Also termed *excuse by failure of presupposed conditions* (UCC § 2-615).

"The doctrines of Impossibility, Commercial Impracticability or as the Uniform Commercial Code knows it, Excuse by Failure of Presupposed Conditions, comprise unclimbed peaks of contract doctrine. Clearly, all of the famous early and mid-twentieth century mountaineers, Corbin, Williston, Farnsworth and many lesser men have made attempts on this topic but none has succeeded in conquering the very summit. . . . In spite of attempts by all of the contract buffs and even in the face of eloquent and persuasive general statements, it remains impossible to predict with accuracy how the law will apply to a variety of relatively common cases. Both the cases and the Code commentary are full of weasel words such as 'severe' shortage, 'marked' increase, 'basic' assumptions, and 'force majeure.'" James J. White & Robert S. Summers, *Uniform Commercial Code* § 3-9, at 155 (3d ed. 1988).

imprescriptible (im-prə-**skrip**-tə-bəl), *adj.* (16c) Not subject to prescription; not capable of being divested or acquired by prescription. See PRESCRIPTION (3).

imprescriptible right. See RIGHT.

impressment (im-**pres**-mənt), *n.* (18c) **1.** The act of forcibly taking something for public service. **2.** A court's imposition of a constructive trust on equitable grounds. See *constructive trust* under TRUST (3). **3.** *Hist.* The method by which armed forces were formerly expanded, when so-called press-gangs seized men off ships, usu. merchant ships, and forced them to serve in the military. Cf. CRIMPING. — **impress,** *vb.*

imprest fund. See FUND (1).

imprest money (**im**-prest). (16c) A payment made to a soldier or sailor upon enlistment or impressment.

imprimatur (im-pri-**may**-tər *or* -**mah**-tər). [Latin "let it be printed"] (17c) **1.** A license giving permission to publish a book. • Once required in England, the imprimatur is now encountered only rarely — in countries that censor the press. **2.** A general grant of approval; commendatory license or sanction, esp. by an important person.

imprimis (im-**prı**-mis), *adv.* [fr. Latin *in primis* "in the first"] (15c) In the first place; first in order. • The word *imprimis* formerly introduced a series of specified particulars, as at the beginning of the gifts made in a will. — Also termed *in primis.*

imprison, *vb.* (13c) **1.** To put into prison; to jail; incarcerate. **2.** To keep (a person) somewhere so that the person is not at liberty, while preventing any departure.

imprisonment, *n.* (14c) **1.** The act of confining a person, esp. in a prison <the imprisonment of Jackson by the authorities was entirely justified>. — Also termed *incarceration.* **2.** The quality, state, or condition of being confined <Jackson's imprisonment>. Cf. FALSE IMPRISONMENT. **3.** The period during which a person is not at liberty <14 years' imprisonment>.

> "Imprisonment, by whatever name it is called, is a harsh thing, and the discipline that must be exercised over human beings in close confinement can never be wholly agreeable to those subject to it. When an attempt is made to hide the harsh realities of criminal justice behind euphemistic descriptions, a corrupting irony may be introduced into ordinary speech that is fully as frightening as Orwell's 'Newspeak.'" Lon L. Fuller, *Anatomy of the Law* 57 (1968).

▸ **life imprisonment.** (18c) Confinement of a person in prison for the remaining years of his or her natural life. — Often shortened to *life.* — Also termed *life in prison.*

imprisonment for debt. (17c) *Hist.* Detention of a debtor by court order to force the debtor to pay certain civil obligations. • The remedy was usu. available only when the debt arose from nonpayment of taxes or fines owed to the Crown, or from the debtor's failure to pay court-ordered support or alimony, or from failure to obey a decree *ad factum praestandum.* — Also termed *civil imprisonment.* See *decree ad factum praestandum* under DECREE.

improbation. (16c) *Scots law.* An action to prove that a document is forged or otherwise false. — Also termed *proper improbation.*

▸ **reduction improbation.** (18c) *Scots law.* An action in which a person who may be harmed or affected by a document can demand the document's production in court. • The person bringing the action may ask the court either to determine the document's effects or to nullify the document. If the document is not produced, the court can automatically declare it false or forged.

improper, *adj.* (15c) **1.** Incorrect; unsuitable or irregular. **2.** Fraudulent or otherwise wrongful.

improper cumulation of actions. (1860) *Hist.* Under the common-law pleading system, the joining of inconsistent legal claims in one proceeding. • This is permitted under most modern pleading systems.

improper feud. See FEUD (1).

improper influence. See UNDUE INFLUENCE (2).

improper means of discovery. (1939) *Trade secrets.* A wrongful way of figuring out a competitor's trade secrets, as by misrepresentation, eavesdropping, or stealing.

improper motion. See MOTION (2).

improper party. See PARTY.

improper venue. See VENUE.

impropriate rector. See RECTOR (1).

impropriation (im-proh-pree-**ay**-shən). (16c) *Eccles. law.* The grant of an ecclesiastical benefice to the use of a lay person, whether individual or corporate. See LAY IMPROPRIATOR. Cf. APPROPRIATION (5). — **impropriate,** *vb.*

> "A church might also be appropriated to a layman, and the proper word to denote this was *impropriation* as distinct from *appropriation,* which was confined to the case of an allocation to a spiritual body." G.C. Cheshire, *Modern Law of Real Property* 333 (3d ed. 1933).

impropriety. 1. Behavior that is inappropriate or unacceptable under the circumstances; an inappropriate or unacceptable act or remark. **2.** Anything that is unsuitable, unseemly, or unbecoming.

▸ **appearance of impropriety.** Conduct or status that would lead a reasonable person to think that the actor is behaving or will be inclined to behave inappropriately or wrongfully. • Under the Code of Judicial Conduct, the test for an appearance of impropriety is whether the conduct would create in reasonable minds a perception that the judge has violated the Code or engaged in other conduct that reflects adversely on the judge's honesty, impartiality, temperament, or fitness to serve as a judge.

improve, *vb.* (16c) **1.** To increase the value or enhance the appearance of (something). **2.** To develop (land), whether or not the development results in an increase or a decrease in value. — **improver,** *n.*

improved land. See LAND.

improved value. (1834) *Real estate.* In the appraisal of real property, the value of the land plus that of any improvements.

improvement. (16c) An addition to property, usu. real estate, whether permanent or not; esp., one that increases its value or utility or that enhances its appearance. — Also termed *land improvement.* Cf. FIXTURE; MAINTENANCE (4).

▸ **beneficial improvement.** See *valuable improvement.*

▸ **general improvement.** (17c) An improvement whose primary purpose or effect is to benefit the public generally, though it may incidentally benefit property owners in its vicinity.

▸ **local improvement.** (1831) A real-property improvement, such as a sewer or sidewalk, financed by special assessment and specially benefiting adjacent property.

▸ **necessary improvement.** (17c) An improvement made to prevent the deterioration of property.

▸ **public improvement.** (17c) An improvement made to property owned by the state or any other political entity, such as a municipality.

▸ **valuable improvement.** (18c) An improvement that adds permanent value to the freehold. • Because of its nature, a valuable improvement would not typically be made by anyone other than the owner. A valuable improvement may be slight and of small value, as long as it is both permanent and beneficial to the property. — Also termed *beneficial improvement.*

▸ **voluntary improvement.** An improvement whose only purpose is ornamental.

improvement bond. See *revenue bond* under BOND (3).

improvement claim. See *Jepson claim* under PATENT CLAIM.

improvement invention. See INVENTION.

improvement patent. See PATENT (3).

improvidence (im-**prahv**-ə-dənts). (15c) A lack of foresight and care in the management of property, esp. as grounds for removing an estate administrator.

improvident (im-**prahv**-ə-dənt), *adj.* (16c) **1.** Lacking foresight and care in the management of property. **2.** Of, relating to, or involving a judgment arrived at by using misleading information or a mistaken assumption.

impruiare (im-proo-ee-**air**-ee), *vb.* [Law Latin] *Hist.* To improve (land).

impubes (im-**pyoo**-beez), *n.* [Latin] *Roman law.* A child under the age of puberty. • Under Roman law, this term referred to a male under 14 and a female under 12. Cf. INFANS; PUBES. Pl. ***impuberes*** (im-**pyoo**-bə-reez).

impugn (im-**pyoon**), *vb.* (14c) To challenge or call into question (a person's character, the truth of a statement, etc.); to challenge with arguments, accusations, or imputations of incorrectness, esp. on a question of morality. — **impugnment,** *n.*

impulse, *n.* (17c) A sudden urge or inclination that prompts an unplanned action.

▸ **uncontrollable impulse.** (1844) An impulse so overwhelming that it cannot be resisted. • In some jurisdictions, an uncontrollable impulse serves as a defense to criminal conduct committed as a result of the impulse. See IRRESISTIBLE-IMPULSE TEST.

impunity (im-**pyoo**-nə-tee). (16c) Exemption from punishment; immunity from the detrimental effects of one's actions <because she was a foreign diplomat, she was able to park illegally with impunity>. Cf. IMMUNITY (1).

imputation, *n.* (16c) The act or an instance of imputing something, esp. fault or crime, to a person; an accusation or charge <an imputation of negligence>.

imputation of payment. (1827) *Civil law.* The act of applying or directing a payment to principal or interest on a debt, or to a particular debt when there are two or more. La. Civ. Code arts. 1864, 1866.

imputation system. See DIVIDEND IMPUTATION.

impute (im-**pyoot**), *vb.* (14c) To ascribe or attribute; to regard (usu. something undesirable) as being done, caused, or possessed by <the court imputed malice to the defamatory statement>. — **imputation,** *n.* — **imputable,** *adj.* — **imputability,** *n.*

"The word 'impute' . . . means to bring into the reckoning, to attribute or to ascribe. It is sometimes used to attribute vicariously, — to ascribe as derived from another. This is included properly within the general import of the term but it is not its primary meaning. It may be used in many senses. Thus we may impute (ascribe) intent, knowledge, guilt, and so forth. Here it is used in the basic sense of imputing (ascribing) the fact itself. Harm has been done. Did the defendant do it? Usually such an inquiry is purely factual. What really happened? At times, however, when all the facts are known we have to ask: Will the law impute (attribute or ascribe) what happened to the defendant? That is what is meant here by 'imputability.'" Rollin M. Perkins & Ronald N. Boyce, *Criminal Law* 605 (3d ed. 1982).

imputed contributory negligence. See NEGLIGENCE.

imputed disqualification. See *vicarious disqualification* under DISQUALIFICATION (1).

imputed income. See INCOME.

imputed interest. See INTEREST (3).

imputed knowledge. See KNOWLEDGE; DOCTRINE OF IMPUTED KNOWLEDGE.

imputed liability. (1984) See *vicarious liability* under LIABILITY (2).

imputed negligence. See NEGLIGENCE.

imputed notice. See NOTICE (3).

in, *prep.* Under or based on the law of <to bring an action in contract>.

INA. *abbr.* IMMIGRATION AND NATIONALITY ACT.

in absentia (in ab-**sen**-shee-ə *or* ab-**sen**-shə). [Latin] (1886) In the absence of (someone); in (someone's) absence <tried in absentia>.

in abstracto. [Latin] (17c) In the abstract; theoretically.

inaccuracy rejection. See REJECTION.

in acquirenda possessione (in ak-wə-**ren**-də pə-zes[h]-ee-**oh**-nee). [Latin] In the course of acquiring possession.

in action. (18c) (Of property) attainable or recoverable through litigation. See *chose in action* under CHOSE.

inactive case. See CASE (1).

inactive stock. See STOCK.

inadequate assistance of counsel. See *ineffective assistance of counsel* under ASSISTANCE OF COUNSEL.

inadequate consideration. See CONSIDERATION (1).

inadequate damages. See DAMAGES.

inadequate remedy at law. (1817) A legal remedy (such as the award of damages) that does not sufficiently correct the wrong, as a result of which an injunction may be available to the disadvantaged party. See IRREPARABLE-INJURY RULE.

inadequate verdict. See VERDICT (1).

inadmissible, *adj.* (18c) **1.** (Of a thing) not allowable or worthy of being admitted. **2.** (Of evidence) excludable by some rule of evidence. **3.** (Of an alien) ineligible for admission into a country or (if the alien has already entered illegally) subject to removal.

inadmissible alien. See ALIEN.

in adversum (in ad-**vər**-səm). [Law Latin] (16c) Against an adverse party.

> "Where a decree is obtained against one who resists, it is termed 'a decree not by consent but *in adversum*.'" 1 John Bouvier, *Bouvier's Law Dictionary* 1518 (Francis Rawle ed., 8th ed. 1914).

inadvertence, *n.* (15c) An accidental oversight; a result of carelessness.

inadvertent disclosure. See DISCLOSURE (1).

inadvertent discovery. (1971) *Criminal procedure.* A law-enforcement officer's unexpected finding of incriminating evidence in plain view. • Even though this type of evidence is obtained without a warrant, it can be used against the accused under the plain-view exception to the warrant requirement.

inadvertent negligence. See NEGLIGENCE.

inaedificatio (in-ee-di-fi-**kay**-shee-oh), *n.* [Latin] *Roman law.* The building of a structure, such as a house, on another's land with one's own materials, or on one's own land with another's materials. • *Inaedificatio* was a form of *accessio*. Regardless of the source of the materials, the building became the landowner's property. See ACCESSIO.

in aemulationem (in ee-myə-lay-shee-**oh**-nəm). [Latin] With a desire to injure; with an intent to annoy.

in aemulationem vicini (in ee-myə-lay-shee-**oh**-nəm vɪ-**sɪ**-nɪ). [Latin] *Hist.* To the annoyance of a neighbor.

in aequali jure (in ee-**kway**-lɪ **joor**-ee). [Law Latin] In equal right.

in aequali manu (in ee-**kway**-lɪ **man**-yoo). [Law Latin] In equal hand. • This phrase refers to property held indifferently between two parties, as when the parties to an instrument deposit it in the hands of a neutral third person. — Also termed *in aequa manu.*

in aequo (in **ee**-kwoh). [Law Latin] In equity. Cf. EX AEQUO ET BONO.

inalienable, *adj.* (17c) Not transferable or assignable <inalienable property interests>. — Also termed *unalienable.*

inalienable interest. See INTEREST (2).

inalienable right. See RIGHT.

in alieno solo (in ay-lee- *or* al-ee-**ee**-noh **soh**-loh). [fr. Law French *en auter soile*] In another's land.

in alio loco (in **al**-ee-oh **loh**-koh). [Latin] In another's place. See CEPIT IN ALIO LOCO.

in ambiguo (in am-**big**-yoo-oh). [Law Latin] In doubt.

in apicibus juris (in ə-**pis**-ə-bəs **joor**-is). [Latin] Among the extremes (or most subtle doctrines) of the law.

in aquali manu. [Latin "in equal hand"] Held equally between two parties. — Also termed *in aquea manu.*

in aquea manu. See IN AQUALI MANU.

inarbitrable, *adj.* (18c) **1.** (Of a dispute) not capable of being arbitrated; not subject to arbitration. **2.** Not subject to being decided.

in arbitrio alieno (in ahr-**bi**-tree-oh ay-lee-**ee**-noh *or* al-ee-). [Law Latin] According to the judgment of someone else. • This term refers to property bequeathed to a trustee for the benefit of others, to be used in the trustee's discretion.

in arbitrium judicis (in ahr-**bi**-tree-əm **joo**-di-sis). [Latin] At the decision or discretion of the judge.

in arcta et salva custodia (in **ahrk**-tə et **sal**-və kə-**stoh**-dee-ə). [Latin] In close and safe custody.

in arrears (in ə-**reerz**), *adj. & adv.* (17c) **1.** Behind in the discharging of a debt or other obligation <the tenants were in arrears with the rent>. **2.** At the end of a term or period instead of the beginning <the interests, fees, and costs are payable in arrears>. See ARREAR.

in articulo mortis (in ahr-**tik**-yə-loh **mor**-tis). [Law Latin] At the point of death. Cf. IN EXTREMIS.

inasmuch as, *conj.* (14c) Because; since (in its causative meaning) <the jury was inconclusive on the question of Peter's guilt inasmuch as there was no specific finding about his conduct>. • This phrasal conjunction explains the way in which a writer or speaker believes that some conclusion is true.

inaudita altera parte (in-**aw**-di-tə *or* in-aw-**dɪ**-tə **al**-tə-rə **pahr**-tee). [Latin "without hearing the other party"] Ex parte. • The term is sometimes used in decisions of the European Court of Justice. See EX PARTE.

inauguration (i-naw-gyə-**ray**-shən), *n.* (16c) **1.** A formal ceremony inducting someone into office. **2.** A formal ceremony introducing something into public use. **3.** The formal commencement of a period of time or course of action. — **inaugurate** (i-**naw**-gyə-rayt), *vb.* — **inauguratory** (i-**naw**-gyə-rə-tor-ee), *adj.* — **inaugurator** (i-**naw**-gyə-ray-tər), *n.*

in autre droit (in **oh**-trə droyt). [Law French] See EN AUTRE DROIT.

in banc. See EN BANC.

in banco. See EN BANC.

in bank. See EN BANC.

in being. (17c) Existing in life <life in being plus 21 years>. • In property law, this term includes children conceived but not yet born. — Also termed *in esse.* See LIFE IN BEING.

> "The intentional killing of one not 'in being,' i.e. an unborn child, was until 1929 punishable neither as murder nor as infanticide. There can be no murder nor manslaughter of a child which dies before being born or even whilst being born, only of one that has been born and, moreover, been born alive." J.W. Cecil Turner, *Kenny's Outlines of Criminal Law* 104 (16th ed. 1952).

in blank. (1836) (Of an indorsement) not restricted to a particular indorsee. See *blank indorsement* under INDORSEMENT.

inboard, *adj.* (1830) *Maritime law.* (Of cargo) stowed between the boards (i.e., sides) of the vessel; esp., stowed inside or near the vessel's centerline.

in bonis. [Latin] (1831) Among the goods or property; in actual possession.

- ▸ ***in bonis defuncti*** (in **boh**-nis di-**fəngk**-tɪ). [Latin] Among the decedent's property.
- ▸ ***in bonis esse*** (in **boh**-nis **es**-ee *or* **es**-ay). [Latin "to be among the goods"] *Roman law.* **1.** To be someone's property. **2.** (Of property) held in possession without benefit of a solemn act (such as *mancipatio*) required to transfer ownership, until ownership might be acquired by the passage of time. See *bonitary ownership* under OWNERSHIP.

▸ ***in bonis habere*** (in **boh**-nis hə-**beer**-ee). See *bonitary ownership* under OWNERSHIP.

Inc. *abbr.* (1906) Incorporated.

in cahoots. See CAHOOTS.

in camera (in **kam**-ə-rə), *adv.* & *adj.* [Law Latin "in a chamber"] (1872) **1.** In the judge's private chambers. **2.** In the courtroom with all spectators excluded. **3.** (Of a judicial action) taken when court is not in session. — Also termed (in reference to the opinion of one judge) *in chambers.*

in camera inspection. (1953) A trial judge's private consideration of evidence.

in camera proceeding. See PROCEEDING.

in camera sitting. See SITTING.

in campo (in **kam**-poh). [Latin] *Hist.* In the field; before the court.

incapacitate (in-kə-**pas**-i-tayt), *vb.* (17c) **1.** To make (someone) too weak or too ill to work or function normally <he was incapacitated after the fall>. **2.** To stop (a system, piece of equipment, etc.) from working properly <the motor was incapacitated>.

incapacitated person. (1834) Someone who is impaired by an intoxicant, by mental illness or deficiency, or by physical illness or disability to the extent that personal decision-making is impossible.

incapacitation, *n.* (18c) **1.** The action of disabling or depriving of legal capacity. **2.** The quality, state, or condition of being disabled or lacking legal capacity.

incapacity. (17c) **1.** Lack of physical or mental capabilities. **2.** Lack of ability to have certain legal consequences attach to one's actions. • For example, a five-year-old has an incapacity to make a binding contract. — Also termed *legal incapacity.* **3.** DISABILITY (2). **4.** DISABILITY (3). Cf. INCOMPETENCY.

▸ **emotional incapacity.** See EMOTIONAL INCAPACITY.

▸ **testimonial incapacity.** (1867) The lack of capacity to testify.

incapax doli (in-**kay**-paks **doh**-lI). See CAPAX DOLI.

in capita. Individually. See PER CAPITA.

in capite (in **kap**-ə-tee). [Law Latin "in chief"] *Hist.* A type of tenure in which a person held land directly of the Crown. — Also termed *tenure in capite.*

incarceration, *n.* (16c) The act or process of confining someone; IMPRISONMENT. Cf. DISIMPRISONMENT. — **incarcerate,** *vb.* — **incarcerator,** *n.*

▸ **shock incarceration.** (1985) Incarceration in a military-type setting, usu. for three to six months, during which the offender is subjected to strict discipline, physical exercise, and hard labor. *See* 18 USCA § 4046. • After successfully completing the program, the offender is usu. placed on probation. See BOOT CAMP. Cf. *shock probation* under PROBATION.

incarcerative, *adj.* (1957) Of, relating to, or involving incarceration <incarcerative rehabilitation>.

in casu consimili. See CASU CONSIMILI.

in casu proviso (in **kay**-s[y]oo prə-**vI**-zoh). See CASU PROVISO.

in causa (in **kaw**-zə). [Latin] In the cause <the record in causa *Abercromby v. Graham* is closed>.

incendiarius (in-sen-dee-**air**-ee-əs), *n. Roman law.* A fire-starter; arsonist.

incendiary (in-**sen**-dee-er-ee), *n.* (15c) **1.** Someone who deliberately and unlawfully sets fire to property. — Also termed *arsonist; firebug.* **2.** An instrument (such as a bomb) or chemical agent designed to start a fire. — **incendiary,** *adj.*

incendiary speech. See SPEECH.

incendium (in-**sen**-dee-əm), *n.* [Latin] (17c) **1.** *Roman law.* Fire. **2.** *Hist.* ARSON (2).

incentive-pay plan. (1948) A compensation plan in which increased productivity is rewarded with higher pay.

incentive stock option. See STOCK OPTION (2).

incentive theory. (1954) *Intellectual property.* The proposition that society grants creators exclusive rights to their intellectual property in order to stimulate further creativity. • The Patent and Copyright Clause of the U.S. Constitution declares that the purpose of exclusive-right protection is "to Promote the Progress of Science and useful Arts." U.S. Const. art. I, § 8, cl. 8.

incentive-to-commercialize theory. (2000) *Patents.* The economic theory justifying the grant of patent rights based on how efficient the patent system is at bringing together diverse resources such as commercial backing, manufacturing capacity, marketing know-how, and other skills that the inventor alone would be unable to handle. — Also termed *incentive-to-invest theory; incentive-to-innovate theory; prospect theory.* Cf. INCENTIVE-TO-DESIGN-AROUND THEORY; INCENTIVE-TO-DISCLOSE THEORY; INCENTIVE-TO-INVENT THEORY.

incentive-to-design-around theory. (1999) *Patents.* The economic theory justifying the grant of patent rights based on their tendency to encourage others to design substitutes and improvements that are better or cheaper. Cf. INCENTIVE-TO-COMMERCIALIZE THEORY; INCENTIVE-TO-DISCLOSE THEORY; INCENTIVE-TO-INVENT THEORY.

incentive-to-disclose theory. (1992) *Patents.* The economic theory justifying the grant of patent rights based on the social benefit of having the information enter the public domain. • Without the incentive, the argument goes, the technical advancements would remain trade secrets and the duplication of research efforts would be a waste to society. Cf. INCENTIVE-TO- COMMERCIALIZE THEORY; INCENTIVE-TO-DESIGN-AROUND THEORY; INCENTIVE-TO-INVENT THEORY.

incentive-to-innovate theory. See INCENTIVE-TO-COMMERCIALIZE THEORY.

incentive-to-invent theory. (1989) *Patents.* The economic theory justifying the grant of patent rights based on their tendency to encourage new inventions that benefit society and that may not otherwise be developed. Cf. INCENTIVE-TO-COMMERCIALIZE THEORY; INCENTIVE-TO-DESIGN-AROUND THEORY; INCENTIVE-TO-DISCLOSE THEORY.

incentive-to-invest theory. See INCENTIVE-TO-COMMERCIALIZE THEORY.

incentive trust. See TRUST (3).

incentive zoning. See ZONING.

incerta persona (in-**sər**-tə pər-**soh**-nə). [Latin "uncertain person"] (1917) *Roman law.* A person (or corporate body) that could not inherit property, such as a person whose existence was uncertain or whom the testator could not identify by name (such as the first person to appear at the testator's funeral). Pl. ***incertae personae.***

> "Another change under Justinian was of much greater importance. Gifts of all kinds could now be made to *incertae personae* . . . ." W.W. Buckland, *A Text-book of Roman Law from Augustus to Justinian* 363 (Peter Stein ed., 3d ed. 1963).

incerto patre (in-sər-toh **pay**-tree). [Latin] *Hist.* From an uncertain father. • The phrase appeared in reference to illegitimate children.

incest, *n.* (13c) **1.** Sexual relations between family members or close relatives, including children related by adoption. • Incest was not a crime under English common law but was punished as an ecclesiastical offense. Modern statutes make it a felony.

> "Although incest under both English and American law is a distinct crime, its commission may involve any of eight different offenses: illegal marriage, consensual cohabitation by unmarried persons, fornication (consensual intercourse), forcible rape, statutory rape, child abuse, and juvenile delinquency (sexual relations between minor siblings or cousins). . . . The choice of crime charged is generally one of prosecutorial discretion. Unless one of the participants is a minor and the other an adult, both parties may be prosecuted for incest." Lois G. Forer, "Incest," in 3 *Encyclopedia of Crime and Justice* 880, 880 (Sanford H. Kadish ed., 1983).

2. Intermarriage between persons related in any degree of consanguinity or affinity within which marriage is prohibited — for example, through the uncle–niece or aunt–nephew relationship.

incestuosi (in-ses-choo-**oh**-sɪ). [Law Latin] (16c) *Hist.* Children begotten incestuously. Cf. ADULTERINI.

incestuous (in-**ses**-chə-wəs), *adj.* **1.** Involving sexual activity between people who are closely related in a family <incestuous relations between mother and son>. **2.** By metaphorical extension, involving a small group of people who spend time only with each other, not others outside the group <an incestuous political community>.

incestuous adultery. See ADULTERY.

in chambers. See IN CAMERA.

in-chambers conference. See CONFERENCE.

inchartare (in-kahr-**tair**-ee), *vb.* [Law Latin "to put in charter"] To grant by written instrument.

in chief. (17c) **1.** Principal, as opposed to collateral or incidental. **2.** Denoting the part of a trial in which the main body of evidence is presented. See CASE-IN-CHIEF.

***Inchmaree* clause** (**inch**-mə-ree). (1902) *Maritime law.* An insurance-policy provision that protects against risks not caused by nature, such as a sailor's negligence or a latent defect in machinery. • This term is taken from a British ship, the *Inchmaree*, whose sinking in 1884 gave rise to litigation that led to the clause bearing its name. *See Thames & Mersey Marine Ins. Co. v. Hamilton, Fraser & Co.*, [1887] L.R. 12 App. Cas. 484. — Also termed *additional-perils clause.*

> "The most celebrated decision of recent times under the 'general' clause was doubtless Thames & Mersey Marine Ins. Co. v. Hamilton, Fraser & Co., 12 App.Cas. 484 (1887). A pump, insured as part of the machinery of a vessel, clogged through valve failure and was damaged. The House of Lords held this accident arose neither through a 'peril of the sea' nor through a cause ejusdem generis with the enumerated perils. . . . This was a disquieting decision, for it more than suggested that many costly accidents that might be suffered by the expensive machinery on steam vessels were not covered by the standard marine policy. The result was the inclusion of the celebrated 'Inchmaree' clause in hull policies, extending special coverage not only to machinery breakage but to many other classes of loss not covered by the standard perils clause as restrictively construed." Grant Gilmore & Charles L. Black Jr., *The Law of Admiralty* § 4-8, at 74 n.90 (2d ed. 1975).

inchoate (in-**koh**-it), *adj.* (16c) Partially completed or imperfectly formed; just begun. Cf. CHOATE. — **inchoateness,** *n.*

> "The word 'inchoate,' not much used in ordinary discourse, means 'just begun,' 'undeveloped.' The common law has given birth to three general offences which are usually termed 'inchoate' or 'preliminary' crimes — attempt, conspiracy, and incitement. A principal feature of these crimes is that they are committed even though the substantive offence is not successfully consummated. An attempt fails, a conspiracy comes to nothing, words of incitement are ignored — in all these instances, there may be liability for the inchoate crime." Andrew Ashworth, *Principles of Criminal Law* 395 (1991).

inchoate crime. See *inchoate offense* under OFFENSE (2).

inchoate dower. See DOWER.

inchoate easement. See EASEMENT.

inchoate instrument. See INSTRUMENT (2).

inchoate interest. See INTEREST (2).

inchoate lien. See LIEN.

inchoate offense. See OFFENSE (2).

inchoate prescriptive easement. See *inchoate easement* under EASEMENT.

inchoate right. (17c) **1.** A right that has not fully developed, matured, or vested. **2.** *Patents.* An inventor's right that has not yet vested into a property right because the patent application is pending.

incidence (**in**-si-dən[t]s), *n.* The frequency with which something occurs, such as crime or disease; the number of times that something happens <the incidence of heroin use has fallen>.

incident, *adj.* (15c) Dependent on, subordinate to, arising out of, or otherwise connected with (something else, usu. of greater importance) <the utility easement is incident to the ownership of the tract>.

incident, *n.* (15c) **1.** A discrete occurrence or happening; an event, esp. one that is unusual, important, or violent <a major incident on the tollway>. **2.** A dependent, subordinate, or consequential part (of something else) <child support is a typical incident of divorce>. **3.** *Int'l law.* A serious disagreement between two countries <a serious diplomatic incident>.

incidental, *adj.* (17c) Subordinate to something of greater importance; having a minor role <the FAA determined that the wind played only an incidental part in the plane crash>.

incidental admission. See ADMISSION (1).

incidental authority. See AUTHORITY (1).

incidental beneficiary. See BENEFICIARY.

incidental damages. See DAMAGES.

incidental demand. See DEMAND (1).

incidental main motion. See MOTION (2).

incidental motion. See MOTION (2).

incidental power. See *incident power* under POWER (3).

incidental question. See QUESTION (2).

incidental reliance. See RELIANCE.

incidental use. See USE (1).

incidenter (in-si-**den**-tər). [Latin] *Hist.* Incidentally.

incident of ownership. (*usu. pl.*) (1821) Any right of control that may be exercised over a transferred life-insurance policy so that the policy's proceeds will be included in a decedent's gross estate for estate-tax purposes <because Douglas still retained the incidents of ownership after giving his life-insurance policy to his daughter, the policy proceeds were taxed against his estate>. • The incidents of ownership include the rights to change the policy's beneficiaries and to borrow against, assign, and cancel the policy.

incident power. See POWER (3).

incident room. (1971) A room in a police station or other place where police work on a particular crime or series of crimes. — Also termed *situation room.*

incident to employment. (1876) *Workers' compensation.* A risk that is related to or connected with a worker's job duties.

incidere (in-**sid**-ə-ree), *vb.* [Latin "fall into or on"] *Roman law.* To come within the scope of a law or to fall into a legal category; esp., to become involved in a situation that entangles a person in a legal action. • This term had a similar meaning under English law. For example, a person might become liable to (or "fall into") amercement (*incidere in misericordiam*). See AMERCEMENT.

incipitur (in-**sip**-i-tər). [Law Latin] *Hist.* It is begun. • This refers to the practice of entering the commencement of a pleading on the court roll.

incite, *vb.* (15c) To provoke or stir up (someone to commit a criminal act, or the criminal act itself). Cf. ABET.

incitee. (1951) Someone who has been incited, esp. to commit a crime.

inciteful, *adj.* (1971) Tending to incite <inciteful speech>.

incitement, *n.* (15c) **1.** The act or an instance of provoking, urging on, or stirring up. **2.** *Criminal law.* The act of persuading another person to commit a crime; SOLICITATION (2). — **inciteful,** *adj.*

> "An inciter is one who counsels, commands or advises the commission of a crime. It will be observed that this definition is much the same as that of an accessory before the fact. What, then, is the difference between the two? It is that in incitement the crime has not (or has not necessarily) been committed, whereas a party cannot be an accessory in crime unless the crime has been committed. An accessory before the fact is party to consummated mischief; an inciter is guilty only of an inchoate crime." Glanville Williams, *Criminal Law: The General Part* 612 (2d ed. 1961).

> "Emphasis upon the theory of one offense with guilt attaching to several is quite appropriate because it is still part of the groundwork of our legal philosophy, so far as perpetrators, abettors and inciters are concerned, despite the fact that some of the statutes require lipservice to the notion of a separate substantive offense, in the effort to avoid certain procedural difficulties. It explains how one may be guilty of a crime he could not perpetrate, by having caused or procured it as a result of his abetment or incitement." Rollin M. Perkins & Ronald N. Boyce, *Criminal Law* 732–33 (3d ed. 1982).

inciter. (15c) Someone who incites another to commit a crime; an aider or abettor.

inciting revolt. See MUTINY.

incivile (in-**siv**-ə-lee), *adj.* [Law Latin] Irregular; out of the due course of law.

incivism (**in**-si-viz-əm). (18c) Unfriendliness toward one's own country or its government; lack of good citizenship.

inclausa (in-**klaw**-zə). [Law Latin] *Hist.* An enclosure near a house; a home close. See CLOSE (1).

in clientela (in klɪ-ən-**tee**-lə). [Latin] In the relation between client and patron.

in-clinic abortion. See ABORTION.

inclose, *vb.* See ENCLOSE.

inclosure. See ENCLOSURE.

include, *vb.* (15c) To contain as a part of something. • The participle *including* typically indicates a partial list <the plaintiff asserted five tort claims, including slander and libel>. But some drafters use phrases such as *including without limitation* and *including but not limited to* — which mean the same thing. See NAMELY.

included offense. See *lesser included offense* under OFFENSE (2).

inclusionary-approach rule. (1981) The principle that evidence of a prior crime, wrong, or act is admissible for any purpose other than to show a defendant's criminal propensity as long as it is relevant to some disputed issue and its probative value outweighs its prejudicial effect.

inclusio unius est exclusio alterius. See EXPRESSIO UNIUS EST EXCLUSIO ALTERIUS.

inclusive deed. See *inclusive grant* under GRANT (4).

inclusive grant. See GRANT (4).

inclusive legal positivism. 1. See LEGAL POSITIVISM. **2.** INCORPORATIONISM.

inclusive survey. See SURVEY (2).

incognito (in-kog-**nee**-toh *or* in-**kog**-ni-toh), *adj.* or *adv.* [Latin "unknown"] (17c) Without making one's name or identity known <Binkley flew incognito to France>.

incola (**in**-kə-lə), *n.* [Latin "an inhabitant"] *Roman law.* A foreign resident without full civil rights; the inhabitant of a foreign colony. • The term is used particularly for provincial residents who were not Roman citizens. — Also termed (in English) *incolant.* Cf. PEREGRINUS.

incolant. See INCOLA.

income. (16c) The money or other form of payment that one receives, usu. periodically, from employment, business, investments, royalties, gifts, and the like. See EARNINGS. Cf. PROFIT.

- ▸ **accrued income.** (1869) Money earned but not yet received.
- ▸ **accumulated income.** (1835) Income that is retained in an account; esp., income that a trust has generated, but that has not yet been reinvested or distributed by the trustee.
- ▸ **accumulated taxable income.** (1941) *Tax.* The income of a corporation as adjusted for certain items (such as excess charitable contributions), less the dividends-paid deduction and the accumulated-earnings credit. • It serves as the base on which the

accumulated-earnings tax is imposed. See *accumulated-earnings tax* under TAX.

▸ **active income.** (1972) **1.** Wages; salary. **2.** Income from a trade or business.

▸ **adjusted gross income.** (1940) *Tax.* Gross income minus allowable deductions specified in the tax code. — Abbr. AGI.

▸ **adjusted ordinary gross income.** (1967) *Tax.* A corporation's gross income less capital gains and certain expenses. • The IRS uses this calculation to determine whether a corporation is a personal holding company. If 60% or more of a corporation's AOGI consists of certain passive investment income, the company has met the test for personal-holding-company classification. IRC (26 USCA) § 543(b). — Abbr. AOGI. See *personal holding company* under COMPANY.

▸ **aggregate income.** (1926) *Tax.* The combined income of a husband and wife who file a joint tax return.

▸ **assessable income.** See *taxable income.*

▸ **blocked income.** (1945) *Tax.* Money earned by a foreign taxpayer but not subject to U.S. taxation because the foreign country prohibits changing the income into dollars.

▸ **business income.** (1861) Any income realized as a result of commercial activity.

▸ **current income.** (1842) Income that is due within the present accounting period. — Also termed *current revenue.*

▸ **deemed income.** *Tax.* Income that is treated as available for an individual's use regardless of actual receipt.

▸ **deferred income.** (1918) Money received at a time later than when it was earned, such as a check received in January for commissions earned in November.

▸ **discretionary income.** (1947) The money remaining from one's income after one's bills have been paid and therefore available for such activities as entertainment, holidays, etc.; income remaining after all essentials have been paid for.

▸ **disposable income.** (1960) Income that may be spent or invested after payment of taxes and other primary obligations. — Also termed *disposable earnings.*

▸ **distributable net income.** (1918) *Tax.* The amount of distributions from estates and trusts that the beneficiaries will have to include in income.

▸ **dividend income.** (1930) *Tax.* The income resulting from a dividend distribution and subject to tax.

▸ **earned income.** (1894) Money derived from one's own labor or active participation; earnings from services. Cf. *unearned income* (2).

▸ **exempt income.** (1947) *Tax.* Income that is not subject to income tax.

▸ **fixed income.** (1810) Money received at a constant rate, such as a payment from a pension or annuity.

▸ **gross income.** (1843) *Tax.* Total income from all sources before deductions, exemptions, or other tax reductions. See IRC (26 USCA) § 61. — Sometimes shortened to *gross.* — Also termed *gross earnings.*

▸ **imputed income.** (1948) *Tax.* The benefit one receives from the use of one's own property, the performance of one's services, or the consumption of self-produced goods and services.

▸ **income in respect of a decedent.** (1945) *Tax.* Income earned by a person, but not collected before death. • This income is included in the decedent's gross estate for estate-tax purposes. For income-tax purposes, it is taxed to the estate or, if the estate does not collect the income, it is taxed to the eventual recipient. — Abbr. IRD.

▸ **investment income.** See *unearned income* (1).

▸ **net income.** (18c) *Tax.* Total income from all sources minus deductions, exemptions, and other tax reductions. • Income tax is computed on net income. — Also termed *net earnings.*

▸ **net operating income.** (1913) Income derived from operating a business, after subtracting operating costs.

▸ **nonoperating income.** (1915) Business income derived from investments rather than operations.

▸ **operating income.** See *ordinary income* (1).

▸ **ordinary income.** (1860) *Tax.* **1.** For business-tax purposes, earnings from the normal operations or activities of a business. — Also termed *operating income.* **2.** For individual income-tax purposes, income that is derived from sources such as wages, commissions, and interest (as opposed to income from capital gains).

▸ **other income.** Income not derived from an entity's principal business, such as earnings from dividends and interest.

▸ **passive income.** (1958) *Tax.* Income derived from a business, rental, or other income-producing activity that the earner does not directly participate in or has no immediate control over. See PASSIVE ACTIVITY. Cf. *portfolio income.*

▸ **passive investment income.** (1966) *Tax.* Investment income that does not involve or require active participation, such as gross receipts from royalties, rental income, dividends, interest, annuities, and gains from the sale or exchange of securities. IRC (26 USCA) § 1362(d)(3)(C). — Abbr. PII.

▸ **personal income.** (1851) The total income received by an individual from all sources.

▸ **portfolio income.** (1978) *Tax.* Income not derived in the ordinary course of a trade or business, such as interest earned on savings, dividends, royalties, capital gains, or other investment sources. • For tax purposes, losses on passive activities cannot be used to offset net portfolio income. Cf. *passive income.*

▸ **prepaid income.** (1935) Income received but not yet earned. — Also termed *deferred revenue.*

▸ **previously taxed income.** (1967) *Tax.* An S corporation's undistributed taxable income taxed to the shareholders as of the last day of the corporation's tax year. • This income could usu. be withdrawn later by the shareholders without tax consequences. PTI has been replaced by the accumulated adjustments account. — Abbr. PTI.

▸ **private income.** (18c) Money that someone receives regularly from working as an employee, as a business owner, or as an investor.

▸ **real income.** Income adjusted to allow for inflation or deflation so that it reflects true purchasing power.

▸ **regular income.** Income that is received at fixed or specified intervals.

▸ **split income.** (1949) *Tax.* An equal division between spouses of earnings reported on a joint tax return, allowing for equal tax treatment in community-property and common-law states.

▸ **taxable income.** (1856) *Tax.* Gross income minus all allowable deductions and exemptions; the amount of income used for calculation of income taxes owed by an individual or a company. • Taxable income is multiplied by the applicable tax rate to compute one's tax liability. See *income tax* under TAX. — Also termed *assessable income.*

▸ **unearned income.** (1921) **1.** Earnings from investments rather than labor. — Also termed *investment income.* **2.** Income received but not yet earned; money paid in advance. Cf. *earned income.*

▸ **unrelated-business income.** (1952) *Tax.* Gross income earned by a nonprofit corporation from activities unrelated to its nonprofit functions. • A nonprofit corporation's income is tax-exempt only to the extent that it is produced by activities directly related to its nonprofit purpose. — Abbr. UBI. — Also termed *unrelated-business taxable income.* IRC (26 USCA) § 512(a)(3)(A).

"The [Internal Revenue] Service has justified the unrelated business income tax as a means of preventing unfair competition between tax-exempt and for-profit providers. Thus, part of the analysis of whether income from a business venture is unrelated business taxable income focuses on the impact of the activity on competitors by inquiring whether the activity at issue is one generally offered by commercial enterprise. The categorization of a business activity of an exempt organization as related or unrelated to the exempt purpose of the organization follows very few bright-line rules. Approaches to the question of exempt purposes within the context of unrelated business income differ substantially from those used in the context of the qualification of an entity for exempt status itself." Barry R. Furrow et al., *Health Law* § 8-1, at 419 (2d ed. 2000).

income-and-expense declaration. (1982) *Family law.* In child-support litigation, a document that contains information on a parent's income, assets, expenses, and liabilities. — Also termed *financial statement.*

income approach. (1951) A method of appraising real property based on capitalization of the income that the property is expected to generate. — Also termed *income-capitalization approach.* Cf. MARKET APPROACH; COST APPROACH.

income averaging. (1946) *Tax.* A method of computing tax by averaging a person's current income with that of preceding years.

income-based plan. See CHAPTER 13.

income-basis method. A method of computing the rate of return on a security using the interest and price paid rather than the face value.

income beneficiary. See BENEFICIARY.

income bond. See BOND (3).

income-capitalization approach. See INCOME APPROACH.

income exclusion. See EXCLUSION (1).

income fund. See MUTUAL FUND.

income in respect of a decedent. See INCOME.

income property. See PROPERTY.

income-shifting. (1957) *Tax.* The practice of transferring income to a taxpayer in a lower tax bracket, such as a child, to reduce tax liability. • Often this is accomplished by forming a Clifford trust. See *Clifford trust* under TRUST (3); *kiddie tax* under TAX.

income statement. (1863) A statement of all the revenues, expenses, gains, and losses that a business incurred during a given period. — Also termed *statement of income; profit-and-loss statement; earnings report.* Cf. BALANCE SHEET.

income stock. See STOCK.

income support. See WELFARE (2).

income tax. See TAX.

income-tax deficiency. See DEFICIENCY (2).

income-tax return. See TAX RETURN.

income-tax withholding. See WITHHOLDING.

income-withholding order. (1986) A court order providing for the withholding of a person's income by an employer, usu. to enforce a child-support order. — Abbr. IWO. — Also termed *wage-withholding order; wage-assignment order; wage assignment.* Cf. *attachment of wages* under ATTACHMENT (1).

income yield. See CAPITALIZATION RATE.

in commendam (in kə-**men**-dəm). [Law Latin] *Civil law.* In trust. • The phrase typically refers to property held in a limited partnership. See *limited partnership* under PARTNERSHIP.

in common. (16c) Shared equally with others, undivided into separately owned parts. — Also termed *in communi.* See *tenancy in common* under TENANCY.

in communi (in kə-**myoo**-nɪ). [Law Latin] In common.

incommunicado (in-kə-myoo-ni-**kah**-doh), *adj.* [Spanish] (1844) **1.** Without any means of communication. **2.** (Of a prisoner) having the right to communicate with only a few designated people.

in communi forma (in kə-**myoo**-nɪ **for**-mə). [Law Latin] *Hist.* In common form; in general form rather than special form. — Also written *in forma communi.*

incommutable (in-kə-**myoot**-ə-bəl), *adj.* (18c) (Of an offense) not capable of being commuted. See COMMUTATION.

incompatibility, *n.* (1875) Conflict in personality and disposition, usu. leading to the breakup of a marriage. • Every state now recognizes some form of incompatibility as a no-fault ground for divorce. See *no-fault divorce* under DIVORCE. Cf. IRRECONCILABLE DIFFERENCES; IRRETRIEVABLE BREAKDOWN OF THE MARRIAGE.

Incompatibility Clause. (1972) *Constitutional law.* The clause of the U.S. Constitution prohibiting a person from simultaneously holding offices in both the executive and legislative branches of the federal government. U.S. Const. art. I, § 6, par. 2, cl. 2.

incompetence, *n.* (17c) **1.** The quality, state, or condition of being unable or unqualified to do something <the dispute was over her alleged incompetence as a legal assistant>. **2.** INCOMPETENCY <the court held that the affidavit was inadmissible because of the affiant's incompetence>.

incompetency, *n.* (17c) Lack of legal ability in some respect, esp. to stand trial or to testify <once the defense lawyer established her client's incompetency, the client did not have to stand trial>. — Also termed *legal incompetency; incompetence; mental incompetence; legal incompetence.* Cf. INCAPACITY. — **incompetent,** *adj.*

incompetency hearing. See PATE HEARING.

incompetent, *adj.* (16c) **1.** (Of a witness) unqualified to testify. **2.** (Of evidence) inadmissible. • This sense is often criticized, as in the quotation below. —Also termed *legally incompetent.*

> "[*Incompetent*] is constantly used loosely as equivalent to 'inadmissible' on any ground. This use should be avoided." John H. Wigmore, *A Students' Textbook of the Law of Evidence* 36 (1935).

incompetent, *n.* See LEGALLY INCAPACITATED PERSON.

incompetent evidence. See EVIDENCE.

incompetent witness. See WITNESS.

incomplete instrument. See INSTRUMENT (2).

incompleteness rejection. See REJECTION.

incomplete transfer. See TRANSFER.

in computo (in kəm-**pyoo**-toh). [Law Latin] In computation.

in concert. See ACTING IN CONCERT.

inconclusive, *adj.* (18c) (Of evidence) not leading to a conclusion or definite result.

in confinio majoris aetatis (in kən-**fin**-ee-oh mə-**jor**-is ee-**tay**-tis). [Latin] Having nearly attained majority. • A person that undertook an obligation *in confinio majoris aetatis* could be held liable despite the fact that the person pleaded minority status. See MAJORENNITATI PROXIMUS. Cf. IN CONFINIO MINORIS AETATIS.

in confinio minoris aetatis (in kən-**fin**-ee-oh mi-**nor**-is ee-**tay**-tis). [Latin] Having nearly attained minority. Cf. IN CONFINIO MAJORIS AETATIS.

in consequentiam (in kon-sə-**kwen**-shee-əm). [Latin] As a consequence.

in consideratione inde (in kən-sid-ə-ray-shee-**oh**-nee **in**-dee). [Law Latin] In consideration thereof.

in consideratione legis (in kən-sid-ə-ray-shee-**oh**-nee **lee**-jis). [Law Latin] **1.** In consideration or contemplation of law. **2.** In abeyance.

in consideratione praemissorum (in kən-sid-ə-ray-shee-**oh**-nee pree-mi-**sor**-əm). [Law Latin] In consideration of the premises.

in consimili casu (in kən-**sim**-ə-lɪ **kay**-s[y]oo). See CASU CONSIMILI.

inconsistency. (17c) **1.** A part of something that is incompatible with another part of the whole thing. **2.** A conflict between two things or different parts of one thing.

▸ **direct inconsistency.** (17c) An obvious conflict between two things, as when a state law regulates a matter differently from a federal law.

▸ **indirect inconsistency.** (1966) **1.** A conflict arising from the inclusion of a material fact or circumstance in a witness's testimony that, if true, should have been included in an earlier statement but wasn't. See *prior inconsistent statement* under STATEMENT. **2.** The equal application of two different laws, which may result in different outcomes.

▸ **legal inconsistency.** See *legally inconsistent verdict* under VERDICT (1).

inconsistent, *adj.* (17c) Lacking agreement among parts; not compatible with another fact or claim <inconsistent statements>.

inconsistent defense. See DEFENSE (1).

inconsistent presumption. See *conflicting presumption* under PRESUMPTION.

inconsistent statement. See *prior inconsistent statement* under STATEMENT.

in conspectu ejus (in kən-**spek**-t[y]oo **ee**-jəs). [Law Latin] In his sight or view.

in contemplation of death. See CONTEMPLATION OF DEATH.

incontestability clause. (1907) *Insurance.* An insurance-policy provision (esp. found in a life-insurance policy) that prevents the insurer, after a specified period (usu. one or two years), from disputing the policy's validity on the basis of fraud or mistake; a clause that bars all defenses except those reserved (usu. conditions and the payment of premiums). • Most states require that a life-insurance policy contain a clause making the policy incontestable after it has been in effect for a specified period, unless the insured does not pay premiums or violates policy conditions relating to military service. Some states also require similar provisions in accident and sickness policies. — Also termed *noncontestability clause; incontestable clause; uncontestable clause.* Cf. CONTESTABILITY CLAUSE.

incontestability status. (1973) *Trademarks.* A classification of a trademark that meets certain criteria — including commercial use for five years after being placed on the Principal Register — as immune from legal challenge. • Although incontestability does not confer absolute immunity, it makes a challenge much more difficult. 15 USCA § 1065.

incontestable clause. INCONTESTABILITY CLAUSE.

incontestable policy. See INSURANCE POLICY.

incontinenti (in-kon-ti-**nen**-tɪ), *adv.* [Law Latin] Immediately; without any interval or intermission. — Also spelled *in continenti.*

incontrovertible-physical-facts doctrine. See PHYSICAL-FACTS RULE.

inconvenience. See RULE OF INCONVENIENCE.

inconvenient forum. See FORUM NON CONVENIENS.

incorporamus (in-kor-pə-**ray**-məs). [Law Latin] *Hist.* We incorporate. • This word indicated an intent to incorporate.

> "All the other methods therefore whereby corporations exist, by common law, by prescription, and by act of parliament, are for the most part reducible to this of the king's letters patent, or charter of incorporation. The king's creation may be performed by the words '*creamus, erigimus, fundamus, incorporamus,*' or the like." 1 William Blackstone, *Commentaries on the Laws of England* 461 (1765).

incorporate, *vb.* (14c) **1.** To form a legal corporation <she incorporated the family business>. **2.** To combine with something else <incorporate the exhibits into the agreement>. **3.** To make the terms of another (esp. earlier) document part of a document by specific reference <the

codicil incorporated the terms of the will>; esp., to apply the provisions of the Bill of Rights to the states by interpreting the 14th Amendment's Due Process Clause as encompassing those provisions.

incorporated right. See RIGHT.

incorporation, *n.* (15c) **1.** The formation of a legal corporation. See ARTICLES OF INCORPORATION. **2.** *Constitutional law.* The process of applying the provisions of the Bill of Rights to the states by interpreting the 14th Amendment's Due Process Clause as encompassing those provisions. • In a variety of opinions since 1897, the Supreme Court has incorporated the First, Fourth, Sixth, and Ninth Amendments into the Fourteenth Amendment's Due Process Clause.

▸ **selective incorporation.** (1947) Incorporation of certain provisions of the Bill of Rights. • Justice Benjamin Cardozo, who served from 1932 to 1938, first advocated this approach.

▸ **total incorporation.** (1952) Incorporation of all of the Bill of Rights. • Justice Hugo Black, who served on the U.S. Supreme Court from 1937 to 1971, first advocated this approach.

3. INCORPORATION BY REFERENCE. — **incorporate,** *vb.*

incorporation by reference. (1886) **1.** A method of making a secondary document part of a primary document by including in the primary document a statement that the secondary document should be treated as if it were contained within the primary one. • With a contract, the document to be incorporated must be referred to and described in the contract in such a way that the document's identity is clear beyond doubt. With a will, the rule applies only to clearly identified writings that existed when the testator signed the will. Unif. Probate Code § 2-510. Not all jurisdictions follow this rule for either contracts or wills. — Often shortened to *incorporation.* — Also termed *adoption by reference.* **2.** *Patents.* The explicit inclusion in one patent application of information already contained in another document, such as another patent or patent application. • Generally, the reference must be to a U.S. patent or application if the information is essential (i.e., the description, enabling disclosure, or best mode), but otherwise it may be to a foreign patent or a nonpatent publication. Incorporation by reference is often used in a continuing application to cite the disclosure contained in a parent application. Cf. CROSS-REFERENCE. **3.** *Patents.* The inclusion in a patent claim of information from an external drawing or table. • Incorporation by reference is a necessity doctrine, available when there is no other practical way to convey the information in words, and when it is more concise and clear to refer the examiner to the graphic element.

incorporationism. The philosophical view that (1) law is made possible by an interdependent convergence of behavior and attitude, esp. in agreements that take the form of social conventions or rules, (2) authoritative legal pronouncements must distinguish some situations from others, and (3) the legality of norms can depend on their substantive moral merit, not just on their pedigree or social source. See Jules Coleman, *The Practice of Principle* (2001); W.J. Waluchow, *Inclusive Legal Positivism* (1994). — Also termed *soft positivism; inclusive legal positivism.* Cf. LEGAL POSITIVISM.

incorporator. (1883) Someone who takes part in the formation of a corporation, usu. by executing the articles of incorporation. — Also termed *corporator.*

in corpore (in **kor**-pə-ree). [Latin] (1906) In body or substance; in a material thing or object.

incorporeal (in-kor-**por**-ee-əl), *adj.* (15c) Having a conceptual existence but no physical existence; INTANGIBLE <copyrights and patents are incorporeal property>. Cf. CORPOREAL. — **incorporeality,** *n.*

incorporeal chattel. See *incorporeal property* under PROPERTY.

incorporeal hereditament. See HEREDITAMENT.

incorporeal ownership. See OWNERSHIP.

incorporeal possession. See POSSESSION.

incorporeal property. See PROPERTY.

incorporeal right. See RIGHT.

incorporeal thing. 1. See *incorporeal property* under PROPERTY. **2.** See THING (1).

in corporibus sed non in quantitatibus (in kor-**por**-ə-bəs sed non in kwon-ti-**tay**-tə-bəs). [Law Latin] In separate and distinct subjects, but not in things estimated in quantities. • The phrase appeared in reference to the best of a decedent's movable property to which an heir had a right. This property typically included animals and equipment but not wine or grain because wine and grain were estimated in quantities.

incorrigibility (in-kor-ə-jə-**bil**-ə-tee *or* in-kahr-), *n.* (14c) Serious or persistent misbehavior by a child, making reformation by parental control impossible or unlikely. Cf. JUVENILE DELINQUENCY. — **incorrigible,** *adj.*

incorrigible (in-**kor**-ə-jə-bəl *or* in-**kahr**-), *adj.* (14c) Incapable of being reformed; delinquent.

incorrigible child. See CHILD.

Incoterm (**in**[g]-koh-tərm). *Maritime law.* A standardized shipping term, defined by the International Chamber of Commerce, that apportions the costs and liabilities of international shipping between buyers and sellers. See EX WORKS; COST, INSURANCE, AND FREIGHT; COST AND FREIGHT; FREE ALONGSIDE SHIP; FREE ON BOARD.

in-court identification. See DOCK IDENTIFICATION.

increase (**in**-krees), *n.* (14c) **1.** The extent of growth or enlargement. **2.** *Archaic.* The produce of land or the offspring of human beings or animals. — **increase** (in-**krees**), *vb.*

increase, costs of. See COSTS OF INCREASE.

increased-risk-of-harm doctrine. See LOSS-OF-CHANCE DOCTRINE.

increment (**in**[g]-krə-mənt), *n.* (15c) A unit of increase in quantity or value. — **incremental,** *adj.*

▸ **unearned increment.** (1871) An increase in the value of real property due to population growth.

incremental cash flow. See CASH FLOW.

incrementum (in-krə-**men**-təm). [Latin] *Hist.* An increase. • This term appeared in various phrases, such as *costs de incremento* ("costs of increase"). See COSTS OF INCREASE.

increscitur (in-**kres**-i-tər). See ADDITUR.

incriminate (in-**krim**-ə-nayt), *vb.* (18c) **1.** To charge (someone) with a crime <the witness incriminated the murder suspect>. **2.** To identify (oneself or another) as being involved in the commission of a crime or other wrongdoing <the defendant incriminated an accomplice>. — Also termed *criminate.* — **incriminatory,** *adj.*

incriminating, *adj.* (18c) Demonstrating or indicating involvement in criminal activity <incriminating evidence>.

incriminating admission. See ADMISSION (1).

incriminating circumstance. See CIRCUMSTANCE.

incriminating evidence. See EVIDENCE.

incriminating statement. See STATEMENT.

incrimination. (18c) **1.** The act of charging someone with a crime. **2.** The act of involving someone in a crime. — Also termed *crimination.* See SELF-INCRIMINATION.

incroach, *vb. Archaic.* See ENCROACH.

incroachment. *Archaic.* See ENCROACHMENT.

in cujus rei testimonium (in **kyoo**-jəs **ree**-ɪ tes-tə-**moh**-nee-əm). [Law Latin] In witness whereof. • These words were used to conclude deeds. The modern phrasing of the testimonium clause in deeds and other instruments — beginning with *in witness whereof* — is a loan translation of the Latin.

inculpatae tutelae moderatio. See MODERAMEN INCULPATAE TUTELAE.

inculpate (in-**kəl**-payt *or* **in**-kəl-payt), *vb.* (18c) **1.** To accuse. **2.** To implicate (oneself or another) in a crime or other wrongdoing; INCRIMINATE. — **inculpation,** *n.* — **inculpatory** (in-**kəl**-pə-tor-ee), *adj.*

inculpatory evidence. See EVIDENCE.

incumbent (in-**kəm**-bənt), *n.* (15c) Someone who holds an official post, esp. a political one. — **incumbency,** *n.* — **incumbent,** *adj.*

incumbrance. See ENCUMBRANCE.

incur, *vb.* (15c) To suffer or bring on oneself (a liability or expense). — **incurrence,** *n.* — **incurrable,** *adj.*

incurable error. See ERROR (2).

in curia. [Latin] In court; into court.

incurramentum (in-kə-rə-**men**-təm). [fr. Latin *in* "upon" + *currere* "to run"] *Hist.* The incurring of a fine or penalty.

incurred risk. See ASSUMPTION OF THE RISK (2).

in cursu diligentiae (in **kər**-s[y]oo dil-ə-**jen**-shee-ee). [Law Latin] In the course of doing diligence — i.e., executing a judgment.

in cursu rebellionis (in **kər**-s[y]oo ri-bel-ee-**oh**-nis). [Law Latin] In the course of rebellion.

> "In cursu rebellionis . . . . All persons were formerly regarded as in rebellion against the Crown who had been put to the horn for non-fulfilment of a civil obligation; their whole moveable estate fell to the Crown as escheat; they might be put to death with impunity; and lost all their legal privileges. If the denunciation remained unrelaxed for year and day (which was the time known as the *cursus rebellionis*), the rebel was esteemed *civiliter mortuus*, and his heritage reverted to the superior . . . . Denunciation for civil obligation and its consequences were in effect abolished by the Act 20 Geo. II. c. 50." John Trayner, *Trayner's Latin Maxims* 257 (4th ed. 1894).

in custodia legis (in kə-**stoh**-dee-ə **lee**-jis). [Latin] In the custody of the law <the debtor's automobile was *in custodia legis* after being seized by the sheriff>. • The phrase is traditionally used in reference to property taken into the court's charge during pending litigation over it. — Also termed *in legal custody.*

in damno vitando (in **dam**-noh vɪ-**tan**-doh). [Latin] In endeavoring to avoid damage (or injury).

inde (**in**-dee), *adv.* [Latin] Thence; thereof. • This word appeared in several Latin phrases, such as *quod eat inde sine die* ("that he go thence without day").

indebitatus (in-deb-i-**tay**-təs), *p.pl.* [Law Latin] Indebted. See NUNQUAM INDEBITATUS.

indebitatus assumpsit (in-deb-i-**tay**-təs ə-**səm**[**p**]-sit). See ASSUMPSIT.

indebiti solutio (in-**deb**-i-tɪ sə-**l**[**y**]**oo**-shee-oh). [Latin] (18c) *Roman & Scots law.* Payment of what is not owed. • Money paid under the mistaken belief that it was owed could be recovered by *condictio indebiti.* See *condictio indebiti* under CONDICTIO.

> "*Indebiti Solutio* — When a person has paid in error what he was not bound to pay the law lays upon the person who has received payment a duty of restitution. . . . Payment (solutio) includes any performance whereby one person has been enriched at the expense of another. Usually it will be the handing over of money or of some other thing, but it may also consist in undertaking a new liability or in discharging an existing liability." R.W. Lee, *The Elements of Roman Law* 373–74 (4th ed. 1956).

indebitum (in-**deb**-i-təm), *n. & adj. Roman law.* A debt that in fact is not owed. • Money paid for a nonexistent debt could be recovered by the action *condictio indebiti.* Cf. DEBITUM.

> "A conditional debt if paid could be recovered as an *indebitum,* so long as the condition was outstanding." W.W. Buckland, *A Manual of Roman Private Law* 255 (2d ed. 1939).

indebtedness (in-**det**-id-nis). (17c) **1.** The quality, state, or condition of owing money. **2.** Something owed; a debt.

indecency, *n.* (16c) The quality, state, or condition of being outrageously offensive, esp. in a vulgar or sexual way. • Unlike obscene material, indecent speech is protected under the First Amendment. Cf. OBSCENITY. — **indecent,** *adj.*

> "*Obscenity* is that which is offensive to chastity. *Indecency* is often used with the same meaning, but may also include anything which is outrageously disgusting. These were not the names of common-law crimes, but were words used in describing or identifying certain deeds which were." Rollin M. Perkins & Ronald N. Boyce, *Criminal Law* 471 (3d ed. 1982).

indecent advertising. (1998) **1.** Signs, broadcasts, or other forms of communication that use grossly objectionable words, symbols, pictures, or the like to sell or promote goods, services, events, etc. **2.** *Archaic.* In some jurisdictions, the statutory offense of advertising the sale of abortifacients and (formerly) contraceptives.

indecent assault. (1861) *Criminal law.* The crime of making a sexual attack on someone by touching or threatening to touch the person, without engaging in rape. See *sexual assault* (2) under ASSAULT.

indecent assault by contact. See *sexual assault* (2) under ASSAULT.

indecent assault by exposure. See INDECENT EXPOSURE.

indecent exhibition. (1826) *Criminal law. Archaic.* The act of publicly displaying or offering for sale something (such as a photograph or book) that is outrageously offensive, esp. in a vulgar or sexual way.

indecent exposure. (1828) *Criminal law.* An offensive display of one's body in public, esp. of the genitals; specif., the crime of deliberately showing one's sex organs in a place where this action is likely to offend people. — Also termed *indecent assault by exposure; exposure of person.* Cf. LEWDNESS; OBSCENITY.

> "*Indecent exposure* of the person to public view is also a common-law misdemeanor. Blackstone did not deal with it separately. 'The last offense which I shall mention,' he said, 'more immediately against religion and morality, and cognizable by the temporal courts, is that of open and notorious *lewdness*; either by frequenting houses of ill fame, which is an indictable offense; or by some grossly scandalous and public indecency, for which the punishment is by fine and imprisonment.' In other words private indecency was exclusively under the jurisdiction of the ecclesiastical court but public indecency of an extreme nature was indictable." Rollin M. Perkins & Ronald N. Boyce, *Criminal Law* 473 (3d ed. 1982) (quoting 4 William Blackstone, *Commentaries on the Laws of England* 64 (1769)).

indecent liberties. (18c) Improper behavior, usu. toward another person, esp. of a sexual nature.

indecimable (in-**des**-ə-mə-bəl), *adj.* (17c) *Hist.* Not titheable; not liable for tithes.

indefeasible (in-də-**feez**-ə-bəl), *adj.* (16c) (Of a claim or right) not vulnerable to being defeated, revoked, or lost <an indefeasible estate>.

indefeasible remainder. See REMAINDER (1).

indefeasibly vested remainder. See *indefeasible remainder* under REMAINDER.

indefensus (in-də-**fen**-səs), *n.* [Latin "undefended"] *Roman law.* Someone who fails to make a defense or plea to an action. • The term later acquired a similar meaning in English law.

indefinite detainee. See NONREMOVABLE INMATE.

indefinite failure of issue. See FAILURE OF ISSUE.

indefinitely, *adv.* (15c) **1.** For a length of time with no definite end <postponed indefinitely>. **2.** Without giving clear or exact details <an indefinitely drafted contract>. See *postpone indefinitely* under POSTPONE.

indefinite payment. See PAYMENT (2).

indefinite postponement. See *postpone indefinitely* under POSTPONE.

indefinite sentence. See *indeterminate sentence* under SENTENCE.

indefinite sentencing. See INDETERMINATE SENTENCING.

in Dei nomine (in **dee**-I **nahm**-ə-nee). [Latin] *Hist.* In the name of God. • The opening phrase of certain writs.

in delicto (in də-**lik**-toh). [Latin] In fault. See IN PARI DELICTO. Cf. EX DELICTO (1).

indemnification (in-dem-nə-fi-**kay**-shən), *n.* (18c) **1.** The action of compensating for loss or damage sustained. **2.** The compensation so made. — **indemnificatory,** *adj.*

indemnifier. See INDEMNITOR.

indemnify (in-**dem**-nə-fI), *vb.* (17c) **1.** To reimburse (another) for a loss suffered because of a third party's or one's own act or default; HOLD HARMLESS. **2.** To promise to reimburse (another) for such a loss. **3.** To give (another) security against such a loss. — **indemnifiable,** *adj.*

indemnis (in-**dem**-nis), *adj.* [Latin] Free from loss or damage; harmless.

indemnitee (in-dem-nə-**tee**). (1884) Someone who receives indemnity from another.

indemnitor (in-**dem**-nə-tər *or* -tor). (1827) Someone who indemnifies another. — Also termed *indemnifier.*

indemnity (in-**dem**-nə-tee), *n.* (15c) **1.** A duty to make good any loss, damage, or liability incurred by another. **2.** The right of an injured party to claim reimbursement for its loss, damage, or liability from a person who has such a duty. **3.** Reimbursement or compensation for loss, damage, or liability in tort; esp., the right of a party who is secondarily liable to recover from the party who is primarily liable for reimbursement of expenditures paid to a third party for injuries resulting from a violation of a common-law duty. Cf. CONTRIBUTION (6), (7). — **indemnitory,** *adj.*

▸ **contractual indemnity.** (1924) Indemnity that is expressly provided for in an agreement.

▸ **double indemnity.** (1859) The payment of twice the basic benefit in the event of a specified loss, esp. as in an insurance contract requiring the insurer to pay twice the policy's face amount in the case of accidental death.

▸ **equitable indemnity.** (1809) **1.** A doctrine allowing a defendant in a tort action to allocate blame to a codefendant or cross-defendant, and thereby to proportionally reduce legal responsibility, even in the absence of contractual indemnity. • In this sense, equitable indemnity applies only among defendants who are jointly and severally liable to the plaintiffs. — Also termed *implied indemnity; doctrine of equitable indemnity.* **2.** See *implied contractual indemnity.* **3.** See *implied indemnity.*

▸ **implied contractual indemnity.** (1958) Indemnity that is not expressly provided for by an indemnity clause in an agreement but is nevertheless determined to be reasonably intended by the parties, based on equitable considerations. — Also termed *equitable indemnity.*

▸ **implied indemnity.** (1850) Indemnity arising from equitable considerations and based on the parties' relationship, as when a guarantor pays a debt to a creditor that the principal debtor should have paid. — Also termed *equitable indemnity.*

▸ **indemnity against liability.** (1838) A right to indemnity that arises on the indemnitor's default, regardless of whether the indemnitee has suffered a loss.

> "*Indemnity against Liability* — Where the indemnity is against liability, the cause of action is complete and the indemnitee may recover on the contract as soon as his liability has become fixed and established, even though he has sustained no actual loss or damage at the time he seeks to recover. Thus, under such a contract, a cause of action accrues to the indemnitee on the recovery of a judgment against him, and he may recover from the indemnitor without proof of payment of the judgment." 42 C.J.S. *Indemnity* § 22 (1991).

▸ **statutory indemnity.** (1866) Indemnity conferred by legislation. • Corporation statutes require that a corporation indemnify its personnel — in particular officers and directors — against costs incurred in the successful defense of a judicial, administrative, or investigative proceeding. Corporation statutes also typically authorize undertakings to advance defense costs to company personnel.

indemnity bond. See BOND (2).

indemnity clause. (1860) A contractual provision in which one party agrees to answer for any specified or unspecified liability or harm that the other party might incur. — Also termed *hold-harmless clause; save-harmless clause.* Cf. EXEMPTION CLAUSE.

indemnity contract. See CONTRACT.

indemnity costs. (1892) *English law.* In civil litigation, the prevailing party's reasonable expenses, including legal fees, that the court may order the opposing party to pay as compensation in addition to any other award.

indemnity insurance. See *first-party insurance* under INSURANCE.

indemnity land. (1901) **1.** Public land granted to a railroad company to help defray the cost of constructing a right-of-way. • This land indemnifies a railroad company for land given in a previous grant but later rendered unavailable for railroad use by a disposition or reservation made after the original grant. **2.** Federally owned land granted to a state to replace previously granted land that has since been rendered unavailable for the state's use. — Also termed *place land.*

indemnity mortgage. See *deed of trust* under DEED.

indemnity principle. (1917) *Insurance.* The doctrine that an insurance policy should not confer a benefit greater in value than the loss suffered by the insured.

indenization (in-den-i-**zay**-shən), *n.* See DENIZATION.

indenizen. See ENDENIZEN.

indent, *n.* (16c) **1.** *Hist.* An indented certificate of indebtedness issued by the U.S. government or a state government in the late 18th or early 19th century. **2.** A contract or deed in writing.

indent (in-**dent**), *vb.* (14c) *Hist.* **1.** To cut in a serrated or wavy line; esp., to sever (an instrument) along a serrated line to create multiple copies, each fitting into the angles of the other. See CHIROGRAPH; INDENTURE (1).

> "If a deed be made by more parties than one, there ought to be regularly as many copies of it as there are parties, and each should be cut or indented (formerly in acute angles *instar dentium,* but at present in a waving line) on the top or side, to tally or correspond with the other; which deed, so made, is called an indenture. . . . Deeds thus made were denominated *syngrapha* by the canonists; and with us *chirographa,* or hand-writings; the word *cirographum* or *cyrographum* being usually that which is divided in making the indenture . . . ." 2 William Blackstone, *Commentaries on the Laws of England* 295–96 (1766).

2. To agree by contract; to bind oneself. **3.** To bind (a person) by contract.

indented deed. See INDENTURE (1).

indenture (in-**den**-chər), *n.* (14c) **1.** A formal written instrument made by two or more parties with different interests, traditionally having the edges serrated, or indented, in a zigzag fashion to reduce the possibility of forgery and to distinguish it from a deed poll. — Also termed *indented deed.* Cf. *deed poll* under DEED. **2.** A deed or elaborate contract signed by two or more parties.

> "The distinction between a *deed poll* and an *indenture* is no longer important since 8 & 9 Vict. c. 106, § 5. Formerly a deed made by one party had a polled or smooth-cut edge, a deed made between two or more parties was copied for each on the same parchment, and the copies cut apart with indented edges, so as to enable them to be identified by fitting the parts together. Such deeds were called indentures. An indented edge is not now necessary to give the effect of an indenture to a deed purporting to be such." William R. Anson, *Principles of the Law of Contract* 84 (Arthur L. Corbin ed., 3d Am. ed. 1919).

> "An indenture was a deed with the top of the parchment indented, i.e., having an irregular edge. The deed was written out twice on a single sheet of parchment, which was then severed by cutting it with an irregular edge; the two halves of the parchment thus formed two separate deeds which could be fitted together to show their genuineness. This contrasted with a 'deed poll,' a deed to which there was only one party, which at the top had been polled, or shaved even." Robert E. Megarry & M.P. Thompson, *A Manual of the Law of Real Property* 129 (6th ed. 1993).

▸ **corporate indenture.** (1919) A document containing the terms and conditions governing the issuance of debt securities, such as bonds or debentures.

▸ **debenture indenture.** (1938) An indenture containing obligations not secured by a mortgage or other collateral. • It is a long-term financing vehicle that places the debenture holder in substantially the same position as a bondholder secured by a first mortgage.

▸ **trust indenture.** (1843) **1.** A document containing the terms and conditions governing a trustee's conduct and the trust beneficiaries' rights. — Also termed *indenture of trust.* **2.** See *deed of trust* under DEED.

3. *Hist.* A contract by which an apprentice or other person, such as a servant, is bound to a master, usu. for a term of years or other limited period. — **indentured,** *adj.*

indentured servant. See SERVANT.

indenture of a fine. *Hist.* A document engrossed by the chirographer of fines to reflect penalties assessed by the court. • The chirographer prepared indentures in duplicate on the same piece of parchment, then split the parchment along an indented line through a word, sentence, or drawing placed on the parchment to help ensure its authenticity. See CHIROGRAPHER OF FINES.

indenture of trust. See *trust indenture* under INDENTURE (2).

indenture trustee. See TRUSTEE (1).

independence, *n.* (17c) The quality, state, or condition of being independent; esp., a country's freedom to manage all its affairs, whether external or internal, without control by other countries.

Independence Day. (18c) **1.** July 4, when each year the United States celebrates its independence from England — from the date in 1776 when the Declaration of Independence was signed. — Also termed *Fourth of July.* **2.** The day every year when a given country celebrates its independence from another country that formerly controlled it.

independent, *adj.* (17c) **1.** Not subject to the control or influence of another <an independent investigation>. **2.** Not associated with another (often larger) entity <an independent subsidiary>. **3.** Not dependent or contingent on something else <an independent person>.

independent adjuster. See ADJUSTER.

independent adoption. See *private adoption* under ADOPTION (1).

independent advice. (1871) Counsel that is impartial and not given to further the interests of the person giving it. • Whether a testator or donor received independent advice before making a disposition is often an important issue in an undue-influence challenge to the property disposition. — Also termed *proper independent advice.*

independent agency. See AGENCY (3).

independent agent. See AGENT.

independent audit. See AUDIT.

independent-basis doctrine. (1970) *Criminal law.* The rule that even if a witness's identification of a criminal defendant was tainted by suggestiveness in a lineup, photo array, etc., the identification is nevertheless admissible in evidence if the prosecution presents corroborative evidence that is untainted. Cf. INDEPENDENT-SOURCE RULE.

independent claim. See PATENT CLAIM.

independent conception. See INDEPENDENT DEVELOPMENT.

independent contract. See CONTRACT.

independent contractor. (1841) *Labor law.* Someone who is entrusted to undertake a specific project but who is left free to do the assigned work and to choose the method for accomplishing it. • It does not matter whether the work is done for pay or gratuitously. Unlike an employee, an independent contractor who commits a wrong while carrying out the work usu. does not create liability for the one who did the hiring. — Also termed *contract labor.* Cf. EMPLOYEE.

independent counsel. See COUNSEL.

independent covenant. See COVENANT (1).

independent creation. (1916) *Copyright.* A defense asserting that a later work is not a derivative of an allegedly infringed work, but is a product of coincidentally parallel labor.

independent development. (1991) *Intellectual property.* A defense against an industrial-espionage charge wherein the user shows that the property was independently discovered or conceived. • Trademarks, symbols, inventions, and other types of intellectual property are all subject to independent development. — Also termed *independent conception.*

independent director. See *outside director* under DIRECTOR.

independent executor. See EXECUTOR (2).

independent expenditure. (1975) *Campaign-finance law.* An expenditure for a political activity, usu. advertising, that expressly advocates a particular candidate's election or defeat, made independently of the candidate's campaign. • To be considered independent, the activity must not be made with the cooperation, approval, or direct knowledge of any candidate, candidate's committee, or political party — or of any of their agents. While there are no limits on the amount that an individual or group may spend on an independent expenditure or the number of such expenditures they may make, the law requires that independent expenditures be reported and that their funding sources be disclosed.

independent expert. See EXPERT.

independent force. See FORCE.

independent intervening cause. See *intervening cause* under CAUSE (1).

independent invention. See INVENTION.

independent investigation committee. See SPECIAL LITIGATION COMMITTEE.

independent liability. See LIABILITY.

independent-living program. (1981) *Family law.* A training course designed to enable foster children who are near the age of majority to leave the foster-care system and manage their own affairs as adults. • Independent-living programs provide education, training, and financial and employment counseling. They also help many foster youth in locating suitable post-foster-care housing. Permanency planning orders or case plans can — but are not required to — provide for independent living as a goal for a child in long-term foster care and describe how it is to be accomplished. — Abbr. ILP. See AGING-OUT; PERMANENCY PLAN.

independent medical examination. See MEDICAL EXAMINATION.

independent mental evaluation. (1979) An assessment of a person's mental and emotional condition that is made by an impartial mental-health professional, such as a psychologist or psychiatrist. Cf. *mental examination* under EXAMINATION (8). — Abbr. IME.

independent obligation. See OBLIGATION.

independent personal representative. See *personal representative* under REPRESENTATIVE (1).

independent-practice association. (1983) A network of independent healthcare providers who contract with a health-maintenance organization (HMO) to provide services to the HMO's subscribers at negotiated rates. • Independent-practice associations generally remain free to accept patients who subscribe to other HMOs or who are not members of an HMO. — Abbr. IPA.

independent probate. See *informal probate* under PROBATE (1).

independent promise. See *unconditional promise* under PROMISE.

independent regulatory agency. See *independent agency* under AGENCY (3).

independent regulatory commission. See *independent agency* under AGENCY (3).

independent retirement account. See INDIVIDUAL RETIREMENT ACCOUNT.

independent-significance doctrine. (1968) *Wills & estates.* The principle that effect will be given to a testator's disposition that is not done solely to avoid the requirements of a will. • An example is a will provision that gives the contents of the testator's safe-deposit box to his niece. Because the safe-deposit box has utility ("significance") independent of the will, the gift of its contents at the testator's death is valid.

independent-source doctrine. See INDEPENDENT-SOURCE RULE.

independent-source hearing. See HEARING.

independent-source rule. (1968) *Criminal procedure.* The rule providing — as an exception to the fruit-of-the-poisonous-tree doctrine — that evidence obtained by illegal means may nonetheless be admissible if that evidence is also obtained by legal means unrelated to the original illegal conduct. — Also termed *independent-source doctrine.* See INDEPENDENT-BASIS DOCTRINE; FRUIT-OF-THE-POISONOUS-TREE DOCTRINE. Cf. INEVITABLE-DISCOVERY RULE.

independent state. See SOVEREIGN STATE.

independent union. See UNION.

indestructible trust. See TRUST (3).

indeterminacy, *n.* (17c) The quality of being indistinct, vague, imprecise, or poorly defined.

indeterminate, *adj.* (14c) Not definite, distinct, or precise; impossible to know about definitely or exactly.

> "[A] proposition of law (or legal proposition) is indeterminate if the materials of legal analysis — the accepted sources of law and the accepted methods of working with those sources such as deduction and analogy — are insufficient to resolve the question, Is this proposition or its denial a correct statement of the law? If a litigated case turns on an indeterminate legal proposition, a result favoring either the plaintiff or the defendant is equally well-supported by the legal materials." Mark V. Tushnet, "Defending the Indeterminacy Thesis," in *Analyzing Law: New Essays in Legal Theory* 223, 224–25 (Brian Bix ed., 1998).

indeterminate bond. See BOND (3).

indeterminate conditional release. A release from prison granted once the prisoner fulfills certain conditions. • The release can be revoked if the prisoner breaches other conditions.

indeterminate damages. See *discretionary damages* under DAMAGES.

indeterminate obligation. See OBLIGATION.

indeterminate sentence. See SENTENCE.

indeterminate sentencing. (1941) *Criminal law.* **1.** The practice of not imposing a definite term of confinement, but instead prescribing a range for the minimum and maximum term, leaving the precise term to be fixed in some other way, usu. based on the prisoner's conduct and apparent rehabilitation while incarcerated. — Also termed *indefinite sentencing.* **2.** See *indeterminate sentencing* under SENTENCING.

in detrimentum animi (in de-trə-**men**-təm **an**-ə-mɪ). [Latin] To the injury of the soul. • The phrase appeared in reference to the ground on which a person was prohibited from questioning a legal document that the person had sworn to never question.

index, *n.* (14c) **1.** An alphabetized listing of the topics or other items included in a single book or document, or in a series of volumes, usu. found at the end of the book, document, or series <index of authorities>.

- ▸ **grantee–grantor index.** (1961) An index, usu. kept in the county clerk's or recorder's office, alphabetically listing by grantee the volume and page number of the grantee's recorded property transactions. • In some jurisdictions, the grantee–grantor index is combined with the grantor–grantee index.
- ▸ **grantor–grantee index.** (1944) An index, usu. kept in the county clerk's or recorder's office, alphabetically listing by grantor the volume and page number of the grantor's recorded property transactions.
- ▸ **tract index.** (1858) An index, usu. kept in the county clerk's or recorder's office, listing, by location of each parcel of land, the volume and page number of the recorded property transactions affecting the parcel.

2. A number, usu. expressed in the form of a percentage or ratio, that indicates or measures a series of observations, esp. those involving a market or the economy <cost-of-living index> <stock index>.

- ▸ **advance-decline index.** (1957) A stock-market indicator showing the cumulative net difference between stock-price advances and declines.

index animi sermo (**in**-deks **an**-ə-mɪ **sər**-moh). [Latin] Speech is the index of the mind. • This maxim supports the concept that the language of a statute or instrument is the best guide to the drafter's intent.

indexation. See INDEXING.

index crime. See *index offense* under OFFENSE (2).

indexed bond. See BOND (3).

index fund. See MUTUAL FUND.

indexing. 1. The practice or method of adjusting wages, pension benefits, insurance, or other types of payments to compensate for inflation or cost-of-living increases. **2.** The practice of investing funds to track or mirror an index of securities. — Also termed *indexation.*

index lease. See LEASE.

index of authorities. (1881) An alphabetical list of authorities cited in a book or brief, usu. with subcategories for cases, statutes, and treatises. — Also termed *table of authorities; table of cases.*

index offense. See OFFENSE (2).

Index of Patents. An annual two-part publication of the U.S. Patent and Trademark Office, containing the year's List of Patentees (Part I) and Index to Subjects of Inventions (Part II), arranged by class and subclass.

Index of Trademarks. An annual publication of the U.S. Patent and Trademark Office, listing all trademarks registered in a given year.

Index to the U.S. Patent Classification System. An entry-level aid to using the Patent Office's classification system, comprising an estimated 65,000 common terms and phrases and referring each entry to a class and subclass within the system.

Indian child. (1978) Under the Indian Child Welfare Act, any unmarried person under the age of 18 who either is a member of an Indian tribe or is both eligible for membership in an Indian tribe and the biological child of a member of an Indian tribe. See INDIAN CHILD WELFARE ACT.

Indian Child Welfare Act. A federal statute that governs child-custody proceedings — including foster-care placement, preadoptive placement, adoptive placement, and termination of parental rights — in cases involving a child of American Indian descent. 25 USCA §§ 1911 et seq. • Congress enacted the Act to help protect the best interests of Indian children, to promote the stability and security of Indian tribes and families, and to counteract the disproportionate foster-care placement and adoption of Indian children by non-Indians. The Act provides minimum federal standards for removing Indian children from their families and for placing them in foster or adoptive homes that will provide an environment reflecting the values of the Indian culture. The

Act has an important jurisdictional feature: in a custody dispute involving an Indian child who resides in or is domiciled within an Indian reservation, the tribe and its tribal courts have exclusive jurisdiction. And in a custody dispute involving an Indian child who lives off a reservation, upon petition, any state court should usu. defer and transfer the case to the tribal court unless a party demonstrates good cause to the contrary. — Abbr. ICWA.

Indian Claims Commission. A federal agency — dissolved in 1978 — that adjudicated claims brought by American Indians, a tribe, or another identifiable group of Indians against the United States. • The U.S. Court of Federal Claims currently hears these claims.

Indian country. (17c) **1.** The land within the borders of all Indian reservations, together with the land occupied by an Indian community (whether or not located within a recognized reservation) and any land held in trust by the United States but beneficially owned by an Indian or tribe. See INDIAN LAND. **2.** *Hist.* Any region (esp. during the U.S. westward migration) where a person was likely to encounter Indians.

Indian gambling. See GAMBLING.

Indian gaming. See *Indian gambling* under GAMBLING.

Indian land. (17c) Land owned by the United States but held in trust for and used by American Indians. — Also termed *Indian tribal property.* See INDIAN COUNTRY. Cf. TRIBAL LAND.

Indian law. 1. The body of law dealing with American Indian tribes and their relationships to federal and state governments, private citizens, and each other. — Also termed *Native American Law; American Indian law.* **2.** The law of India.

Indian reservation. (1804) An area that the federal government has designated for use by an American Indian tribe, where the tribe generally settles and establishes a tribal government.

Indian Territory. A former U.S. territory — now a part of the state of Oklahoma — to which the Cherokee, Choctaw, Chickasaw, Creek, and Seminole tribes were forcibly removed between 1830 and 1843. • In the late 19th century, most of this territory was ceded to the United States, and in 1907 the greater part of it became the State of Oklahoma.

Indian title. (18c) A right of occupancy that the federal government grants to an American Indian tribe based on the tribe's immemorial possession of the area. • Congress does not recognize tribal ownership of the land, only possession. A tribe or nation must actually, exclusively, and continuously use the property to establish that it is the ancestral home. An individual may claim Indian title by showing that the individual or his or her lineal ancestors continuously occupied a parcel of land, as individuals, before the land was closed to settlers. — Also termed *aboriginal title; right of occupancy.* Cf. *aboriginal title* (1) under TITLE (2).

Indian tribal property. See INDIAN LAND.

Indian tribe. (18c) A group, band, nation, or other organized group of indigenous American people, including any Alaskan native village, that is recognized as eligible for the special programs and services provided by the U.S. government because of Indian status (42 USCA § 9601(36)); esp., any such group having a federally recognized governing body that carries out substantial governmental duties and powers over an area (42 USCA § 300f(14); 40 CFR § 146.3). • A tribe may be identified in various ways, esp. by past dealings with other tribes or with the federal, state, or local government, or by recognition in historical records. — Also termed *federally recognized tribe.*

indicare (in-di-**kair**-ee), *vb.* [Latin] **1.** *Roman law.* To accuse (someone) of a crime; to provide evidence against someone. **2.** *Civil law.* To show or discover. **3.** *Civil law.* To fix or tell the price of a thing. See INDICIUM.

indicator. (17c) *Securities.* An average or index that shows enough of a correlation to market trends or economic conditions that it can help analyze market performance.

▸ **coincident indicator.** (1961) An economic or market-activity index or indicator that shows changing trends near the same time that overall conditions begin to change.

▸ **economic indicator.** See ECONOMIC INDICATOR.

▸ **lagging indicator.** (1961) **1.** An index that indicates a major stock-market change sometime after the change occurs. **2.** See *lagging economic indicator* under ECONOMIC INDICATOR.

▸ **leading indicator.** (1957) **1.** A quantifiable index that predicts a major stock-market change. **2.** See *leading economic indicator* under ECONOMIC INDICATOR.

indicavit (in-di-**kay**-vit). [Law Latin "he has indicated"] (13c) *Hist.* A writ of prohibition by which a church patron removes to a common-law court an ecclesiastical-court action between two clerics who dispute each other's right to a benefice. • The writ was long available — nominally up to the 20th century — under the 1306 statute *De Conjunctim Feoffatis* (34 Edw. I). Actions concerning clerics' rights to a benefice were usu. tried in ecclesiastical courts, but they could be removed to a common-law court if the action involved a church patron in some way, as when one cleric was appointed by a certain patron and the other cleric was appointed by another patron. Cf. ADVOWSON.

indicia (in-**dish**-ee-ə), *n. pl.* (17c) **1.** *Roman law.* Evidence. **2.** (*pl.*) Signs; indications <the purchase receipts are indicia of ownership>.

indicia of title. (1830) A document that evidences ownership of personal or real property.

indicium (in-**dish**-ee-əm), *n.* [Latin] (17c) *Roman law.* **1.** The act of providing evidence against an accused. **2.** The act of promising recompense for a certain service. **3.** A sign or mark; esp., something used as a type of proof. See INDICARE.

indict (in-**dɪt**), *vb.* (17c) *Criminal law.* To charge (a person) with a crime by formal legal process, esp. by grand-jury presentation. — Also formerly spelled *endite; indite.*

indictable misdemeanor. See *serious misdemeanor* under MISDEMEANOR.

indictable offense. See OFFENSE (2).

indictee (in-dɪ-**tee**). (16c) *Criminal law.* Someone who has been indicted; one officially charged with a crime.

indictio (in-**dik**-shee-oh), *n.* [Latin] **1.** *Roman law.* An imperial proclamation establishing a 15-year period for the reassessment of property values for tax purposes.

• *Indictio* also referred to the 15-year cycle itself. **2.** A declaration or proclamation, such as a declaration of war (*indictio belli*). **3.** An indictment. Pl. ***indictiones*** (in-dik-shee-**oh**-neez).

indictment (in-**dɪt**-mənt), *n.* (14c) *Criminal law.* **1.** The formal written accusation of a crime, made by a grand jury and presented to a court for prosecution against the accused person. *See* Fed. R. Crim. P. 7. **2.** The act or process of preparing or bringing forward such a formal written accusation. See CHARGING INSTRUMENT. Cf. INFORMATION; PRESENTMENT (2).

> "Indictment cometh of the *French* word *enditer,* and signifieth in law, an accusation found by an inquest of twelve or more upon their oath. And as the *appeal* is ever the suit of the party, so the indictment is always the suit of the king, and, as it were, his declaration; and the party who prosecutes it, is a good witness to prove it. And when such accusation is found by a grand jury, without any bill brought before them, and afterwards reduced to a formal indictment, it is called a *presentment;* and when it is found by jurors returned to inquire of that particular offence only which is indicted, it is properly called an *inquisition.*" Edward Bullingbrooke, *The Duty and Authority of Justices of the Peace and Parish Officers for Ireland* 436 (rev. ed. 1788).

> "According to Lord Hale, an indictment is a plain, brief, and certain narrative of an offence committed by any person, and of those necessary circumstances that concur to ascertain the fact and its nature. . . . . The chief rule was that the indictment should be plain and certain. This was required in order that the accused should know what he was to answer, that he might not be tried again, that there might be a proper judgment, and that posterity might know what law was to be derived from the record." Franklin G. Fessenden, *Improvement in Criminal Pleading,* 10 Harv. L. Rev. 98, 100 (1896).

▸ **barebones indictment.** (1963) An indictment that cites only the language of the statute allegedly violated; an indictment that does not provide a factual statement.

> "What has been called 'a bare bones indictment using only statutory language' is quite common, and entirely permissible so long as the statute sets forth fully, directly, and expressly all essential elements of the crime intended to be punished." 1 Charles Alan Wright, *Federal Practice and Procedure* § 125, at 558-59 (3d ed. 1999).

▸ **duplicitous indictment** (d[y]oo-**plis**-ə-təs). (1914) **1.** An indictment containing two or more offenses in the same count. **2.** An indictment charging the same offense in more than one count.

▸ **John Doe indictment.** (1929) An indictment that, instead of naming a specific person, describes the defendant by use of a physical description, a DNA profile, fingerprints, or one or more photographs.

▸ **joint indictment.** (17c) An indictment that charges two or more people with an offense.

▸ **sealed indictment.** (1914) A criminal charge submitted to the grand jury without notice to the defendant and made public only when the defendant is arraigned. — Also termed *silent indictment.*

▸ **superseding indictment.** (1904) A second or later indictment that includes additional charges or corrects errors in an earlier one.

▸ **twin-count indictment.** (2002) An indictment charging two crimes of the same class, as opposed to a more serious crime and a lesser-included offense.

indictor (in-**dɪt**-ər *or* in-**dɪ**-tor). (17c) Someone who causes another to be indicted.

in diem (in **dɪ**-əm *or* **dee**-əm). [Latin] For each day; per day. Cf. PER DIEM.

in diem addictio. See ADDICTIO IN DIEM.

indifference. (15c) A lack of interest in or concern about something; apathy.

▸ **conscious indifference. 1.** *Criminal law.* See *deliberate indifference* (2). **2.** *Torts.* See *deliberate indifference* (3).

▸ **deliberate indifference. 1.** *Criminal law.* (1951) The careful preservation of one's ignorance despite awareness of circumstances that would put a reasonable person on notice of a fact essential to a crime. See JEWELL INSTRUCTION. **2.** *Criminal law.* Awareness of and disregard for the risk of harm to another person's life, body, or property. **3.** *Torts.* Conscious disregard of the harm that one's actions could do to the interests or rights of another. — Also termed *reckless indifference; conscious avoidance; conscious indifference;* (in senses 2 & 3) *gross indifference.*

▸ **extreme indifference.** (18c) *Criminal law.* Excessive disregard for the known risk of harm to another person's life, body, or property.

▸ **reckless indifference.** See *deliberate indifference.*

indigena (in-**dij**-ə-nə). [Latin "native"] *Hist.* A subject born within the English realm or naturalized by act of Parliament. Cf. ALIENIGENA.

indigence. See INDIGENCY.

indigency, *n.* (17c) The quality, state, or condition of a person who lacks the means of subsistence; extreme hardship or neediness; poverty. • For purposes of the Sixth Amendment right to appointed counsel, *indigency* refers to a defendant's inability to afford an attorney. — Also termed *indigence.* — **indigent,** *adj.* & *n.*

> "Supreme Court opinions speak generally of the rights of an 'indigent defendant' without offering any specific definition of 'indigency.' . . . The appellate courts agree that indigency is not a synonym for 'destitute.' . . . Among the factors to be considered in evaluating the individual's financial capacity are: (1) income from employment and such governmental programs as social security and unemployment compensation; (2) real and personal property; (3) number of dependents; (4) outstanding debts; (5) seriousness of the charge (which suggests the likely fee of a retained attorney); and (6) other legal expenses (such as bail bond)." Wayne R. LaFave & Jerold H. Israel, *Criminal Procedure* § 11.3(g), at 544 (2d ed. 1992).

indigenous rights. See RIGHT.

indigent (**in**-di-jənt), *n.* (15c) **1.** A poor person. **2.** Someone who is found to be financially unable to pay filing fees and court costs and so is allowed to proceed *in forma pauperis.* • The Supreme Court has recognized an indigent petitioner's right to have certain fees and costs waived in divorce and termination-of-parental-rights cases. *Boddie v. Connecticut,* 401 U.S. 371, 91 S.Ct. 780 (1971); *M.L.B. v. S.L.J.,* 519 U.S. 102, 117 S.Ct. 555 (1996). See PAUPER; IN FORMA PAUPERIS. — **indigent,** *adj.*

indigent defendant. (1882) Someone who is too poor to hire a lawyer and who, upon indictment, becomes eligible to receive aid from a court-appointed attorney and a waiver of court costs. See IN FORMA PAUPERIS. Cf. PAUPER.

indignity (in-**dig**-ni-tee), *n.* (16c) *Family law.* A ground for divorce consisting in one spouse's pattern of behavior calculated to humiliate the other. — Also termed *personal indignity.* Cf. CRUELTY.

indirect aggression. See AGGRESSION.

indirect attack. See COLLATERAL ATTACK.

indirect confession. See CONFESSION (1).

indirect contempt. See CONTEMPT.

indirect cost. See COST (1).

indirect damages. See *consequential damages* under DAMAGES.

indirect discrimination. See DISCRIMINATION (3).

indirect evidence. See *circumstantial evidence* (1) under EVIDENCE.

indirect impleading. See IMPLEADING.

indirect inconsistency. See INCONSISTENCY.

indirect infringement. See INFRINGEMENT.

indirect loss. See *consequential loss* under LOSS.

indirect notice. See *implied notice* under NOTICE (3).

indirect possession. See *mediate possession* under POSSESSION.

indirect provocation. See *adequate provocation* under PROVOCATION.

indirect-purchaser doctrine. (1976) *Antitrust.* The principle that in litigation for price discrimination, the court will ignore sham middle parties in determining whether different prices were paid by different customers for the same goods. • This doctrine gives standing to bring an antitrust action to a party who is not an immediate purchaser of a product. Thus, if a manufacturer sells a product to a retailer, but dictates the terms by which the retailer must sell the product to a consumer, a court will ignore the retailer and treat the consumer as the direct purchaser of the product.

indirect tax. See TAX.

indiscriminate attack. (1834) *Int'l law.* An aggressive act that (1) is not carried out for a specific military objective, (2) employs a means of combat not directed at a specific military objective, or (3) employs a means of combat the effects of which cannot be limited in accordance with an international protocol such as the Geneva Conventions of 1949 and their protocols or the Hague Conventions of 1899 and 1907.

indispensable-element test. (1976) *Criminal law.* A common-law test for the crime of attempt, based on whether the defendant acquires control over any thing that is essential to the crime. • Under this test, for example, a person commits a crime by buying the explosives with which to detonate a bomb. See ATTEMPT (2).

indispensable evidence. See EVIDENCE.

indispensable instrument. See INSTRUMENT (2).

indispensable party. See PARTY (2).

indistanter (in-di-**stan**-tər), *adv.* [Law Latin "immediately"] Forthwith; without delay.

indite. See INDICT.

individual, *adj.* (15c) **1.** Existing as an indivisible entity. **2.** Of, relating to, or involving a single person or thing, as opposed to a group.

individual account plan. See *defined-contribution plan* under EMPLOYEE BENEFIT PLAN.

individual asset. See ASSET.

individual debt. See DEBT.

individual goodwill. See *personal goodwill* under GOODWILL.

individualization. (1982) The use of forensic evidence to support a conclusion that involves matching a specimen to a particular source. — **individualize,** *vb.* — **individualized,** *adj.*

individualized educational placement. See INDIVIDUALIZED EDUCATION PROGRAM.

individualized education plan. See INDIVIDUALIZED EDUCATION PROGRAM.

individualized education program. (1976) *Family law.* A specially designed plan of educational instruction for a child with disabilities. • The individualized education program is a written plan that details the particular child's abilities, the child's educational goals, and the services to be provided. — Abbr. IEP. — Also termed *individualized education plan; individualized educational placement.* See *child with disabilities* under CHILD; INDIVIDUALS WITH DISABILITIES EDUCATION ACT.

individualized evidence. See EVIDENCE.

individual liberty. See *personal liberty* under LIBERTY.

individual property. See SEPARATE PROPERTY (1).

individual proprietorship. See SOLE PROPRIETORSHIP.

individual retirement account. (1974) A savings or brokerage account to which a person may contribute up to a specified amount of earned income each year. • The contributions, along with any interest earned in the account, are not taxed until the money is withdrawn after a participant reaches 59½ (or before then, if a 10% penalty is paid). — Abbr. IRA. — Also termed *independent retirement account.* Cf. KEOGH PLAN.

▸ **education individual retirement account.** (1997) An individual retirement account from which withdrawals may be made tax-free if the withdrawn funds are used for education costs. • Before 2002, annual contributions were limited to $500. In 2002, the contribution limit increased to $2,000 per year for families with incomes under $190,000.

▸ **Roth IRA.** (1991) An IRA in which contributions are nondeductible when they are made. • No further taxes are assessed on the contributions (or accrued interest) when the money is withdrawn (if all applicable rules are followed). This term takes its name from Senator William Roth, who sponsored the legislation creating this type of IRA.

individual right. 1. See *absolute right* under RIGHT. **2.** See *personal right* (1) under RIGHT.

Individuals with Disabilities Education Act. A federal statute that governs the public education of children with physical or mental handicaps and attempts to ensure that these children receive a free public education that meets their unique needs. • The Education of All Handicapped Children Act (enacted in 1975) was renamed the Individuals with Disabilities Education Act in 1990, and this Act was substantially amended in 1997. All states currently participate in this joint federal–state initiative. 20 USCA §§ 1400–1485. — Abbr. IDEA.

individual voluntary arrangement. (1992) *English law.* A formal out-of-court arrangement between a debtor and two or more lenders to freeze the interest rate of a debt and pay off a percentage of the debt over an agreed period, at the end of which time the remaining debt is canceled. • The arrangement is an alternative to filing for bankruptcy. It must be set up by an authorized insolvency practitioner but does not require court approval. — Abbr. IVA.

indivisible, *adj.* (14c) Not separable into parts; held by two or more people in undivided shares <an indivisible debt>.

indivisible contract. See CONTRACT.

indivisible harm. See HARM.

indivisible injury. See INJURY.

indivision. (1875) *Civil law.* Undivided ownership of property; the condition of being owned by coowners each having an undivided interest in the property.

indivisum (in-di-**VI**-səm *or* -zəm), *adj.* [Latin] *Roman law.* (Of property) held in common; not divided.

indorse, *vb.* (16c) To sign (a negotiable instrument), usu. on the back, either to accept responsibility for paying an obligation memorialized by the instrument or to make the instrument payable to someone other than the payee. — Also spelled *endorse.*

indorsee (in-dor-**see**). (18c) A person to whom a negotiable instrument is transferred by indorsement. — Also spelled *endorsee.*

▸ **indorsee in due course.** (1880) An indorsee who, in the ordinary course of business, acquires a negotiable instrument in good faith for value, before its maturity, and without knowledge of its dishonor.

indorsement, *n.* (16c) **1.** The placing of a signature, sometimes with an additional notation, on the back of a negotiable instrument to transfer or guarantee the instrument or to acknowledge payment. **2.** The signature or notation itself. — Also spelled *endorsement.* — **indorse,** *vb.*

> "The clever indorser can subscribe his or her name under a variety of magic phrases. The Code specifies the legal effect of some of these phrases. Qualified indorsements ('without recourse') limit the liability of the indorser if the instrument is dishonored. Restrictive indorsements such as 'for deposit only,' 'pay any bank,' and the like set the terms for further negotiation of the instrument. Their main purpose is to prevent thieves and embezzlers from cashing checks." 2 James J. White & Robert S. Summers, *Uniform Commercial Code* § 16-7, at 92–93 (4th ed. 1995).

▸ **accommodation indorsement.** (1888) An indorsement to an instrument by a third party who acts as surety for another party who remains primarily liable. See ACCOMMODATION PAPER.

▸ **anomalous indorsement.** See *irregular indorsement.*

▸ **blank indorsement.** (18c) An indorsement that names no specific payee, thus making the instrument payable to the bearer and negotiable by delivery only. UCC § 3-205(b). — Also termed *indorsement in blank; general indorsement.*

▸ **collection indorsement.** See *restrictive indorsement.*

▸ **conditional indorsement.** (1815) An indorsement that restricts the instrument in some way, as by limiting how the instrument can be paid or transferred; an indorsement giving possession of the instrument to the indorsee, but retaining title until the occurrence of some condition named in the indorsement. • Wordings that indicate this type of indorsement are "Pay to Brad Jones when he becomes 18 years of age" and "Pay to Brigitte Turner, or order, unless before payment I give you notice to the contrary." — Also termed *restricted indorsement; restrictive indorsement.* Cf. *special indorsement.*

> "Conditional indorsement. — This somewhat rare form of indorsement is one expressing a lawful condition, other than those conditions implied by the Law Merchant such as presentment and notice of dishonor. For example, 'pay A on his graduation', 'pay A on arrival at twenty-one', 'pay A on completion of house contract.' Unlike conditions expressed on the *face* of the instrument, a conditional *indorsement* does not destroy the negotiability of the instrument. Nor in making payment need the maker, drawee or acceptor inquire whether the condition has been fulfilled or not." Melville M. Bigelow, *The Law of Bills, Notes, and Checks* 193–94 (William Minor Lile ed., 3d ed. 1928).

▸ **full indorsement. 1.** See *irregular indorsement.* **2.** See *special indorsement.*

▸ **general indorsement.** See *blank indorsement.*

▸ **indorsement in blank.** See *blank indorsement.*

▸ **indorsement in full.** See *special indorsement.*

▸ **indorsement without recourse.** See *qualified indorsement.*

▸ **irregular indorsement.** (1741) An indorsement by a person who signs outside the chain of title and who therefore is neither a holder nor a transferor of the instrument. • An irregular indorser is generally treated as an accommodation party. — Also termed *anomalous indorsement; full indorsement.* See ACCOMMODATION PARTY.

▸ **qualified indorsement.** (1806) An indorsement that passes title to the instrument but limits the indorser's liability to later holders if the instrument is later dishonored. • Typically, a qualified indorsement is made by writing "without recourse" or "sans recourse" over the signature. UCC § 3-415(b). — Also termed *indorsement without recourse.* See WITHOUT RECOURSE.

> "A qualified indorsement is one that 'constitutes the indorser a mere *assignor* of the title to the instrument. It may be made by adding to the indorser's signature the words "without recourse", or any words of similar import. Such an indorsement does not impair the negotiable character of the instrument.' The purpose of such an indorsement is to pass title to the instrument without assuming a general indorser's liability. Though by no means confined to that class, it is more commonly used by persons holding paper in a representative capacity, in the transfer of the paper to the beneficial owner or owners — as in the case of agents, attorneys, executors, administrators, guardians, trustees and other fiduciaries." Melville M. Bigelow, *The Law of Bills, Notes, and Checks* 192–93 (William Minor Lile ed., 3d ed. 1928) (citations omitted).

▸ **restricted indorsement.** See *conditional indorsement.*

▸ **restrictive indorsement.** (18c) An indorsement that includes a condition (e.g., "pay Josefina Cardoza only if she has worked 8 full hours on April 13") or any other language restricting further negotiation (e.g., "for deposit only"). — Also termed *collection indorsement.* See *conditional indorsement.*

▸ **special indorsement.** (18c) An indorsement that specifies the person to receive payment or to whom the goods named by the document must be delivered. UCC § 3-205(a). — Also termed *indorsement in full; full indorsement.* Cf. *conditional indorsement.*

▸ **trust indorsement.** (1926) An indorsement stating that the payee becomes a trustee for a third person (e.g., "pay Erin Ray in trust for Kaitlin Ray"); a restrictive indorsement that limits the instrument to the use of the indorser or another person.

▸ **unauthorized indorsement.** (1840) An indorsement made without authority, such as a forged indorsement.

▸ **unqualified indorsement.** (1808) An indorsement that does not limit the indorser's liability on the paper. • It does not, for example, include the phrase "without recourse."

▸ **unrestrictive indorsement.** (1844) An indorsement that includes no condition or language restricting negotiation. — Also termed *unrestricted indorsement.*

indorsement in blank. See *blank indorsement* under INDORSEMENT.

indorsement in full. See *special indorsement* under INDORSEMENT.

indorsement without recourse. See *qualified indorsement* under INDORSEMENT.

indorser. (18c) Someone who transfers a negotiable instrument by indorsement; specif., one who signs a negotiable instrument other than as maker, drawer, or acceptor. — Also spelled *endorser.*

▸ **accommodation indorser.** (1820) An indorser who acts as surety for another person.

in dote aestimata (in **doh**-tee es-ti-**may**-tə). [Latin] *Roman & civil law.* When the dowry was valued. • When the dowry had been valued, the husband owed a sum of money representing the value and could dispose of the specific items of which the dowry was composed.

in dubio (in **d[y]oo**-bee-oh), *adv. & adj.* [Latin] In doubt.

induced abortion. See ABORTION.

induced infringement. See INFRINGEMENT.

inducement, *n.* (15c) **1.** The act or process of enticing or persuading another person to take a certain course of action. See *fraud in the inducement* under FRAUD.

▸ **active inducement.** (1942) *Patents.* The act of intentionally causing a third party to infringe a valid patent. • Active inducement requires proof of (1) an actual intent to cause the patent infringement and (2) knowledge of the patent.

2. *Contracts.* The benefit or advantage that causes a promisor to enter into a contract. **3.** *Criminal law.* An enticement or urging of another person to commit a crime. **4.** The preliminary statement in a pleading; esp., in an action for defamation, the plaintiff's allegation that extrinsic facts gave a defamatory meaning to a statement that is not defamatory on its face, or, in a criminal indictment, a statement of preliminary facts necessary to show the criminal character of the alleged offense. Cf. INNUENDO (2); COLLOQUIUM. — **induce,** *vb.*

inducement of breach of contract. See TORTIOUS INTERFERENCE WITH CONTRACTUAL RELATIONS.

induciae legales (in-**d[y]oo**-shee-ee lə-**gay**-leez). [Latin] (18c) *Civil & Scots law.* The days allowed after summons for a defendant to appear in court.

inducing infringement. See *infringement in the inducement* under INFRINGEMENT.

induct, *vb.* (14c) **1.** To put into possession of (something, such as an office or benefice). **2.** To admit as a member. **3.** To enroll (a person) for military service.

inductio (in-**dək**-shee-oh), *n.* [Latin] *Roman law.* The act of erasing a writing or part of it, as when a testator struck a legacy from a will. Pl. ***inductiones*** (in-dək-shee-**oh**-neez).

induction. (14c) **1.** The act or process of initiating <the induction of three new members into the legal fraternity>. **2.** The act or process of reasoning from specific instances to general propositions <after looking at several examples, the group reasoned by induction that it is a very poor practice to begin a new paragraph by abruptly bringing up a new case>. See BOTTOM-UP REASONING. Cf. DEDUCTION (4).

> "Induction is a procedure for arriving at natural laws, and at other generalizations, which state how events are related. From these general statements we can predict and anticipate events." O.C. Jensen, *The Nature of Legal Argument* 28 (1957).

inductive reasoning. See REASONING.

indulgence. (14c) **1.** A yielding to inclination, passion, or the propensity for gratifying one's desires, esp. to excess; self-gratification <unbridled indulgence>. **2.** The treatment of someone else by restraint, forbearance, or humoring <I beg your indulgence>. **3.** The habit of allowing oneself to do whatever one wants, or of allowing someone else to do whatever he or she wants <constant self-indulgence>. **4.** Something one wants to have or do for pleasure, not from necessity <his only indulgence was the occasional martini>. **5.** A favor granted; an act of leniency; the act of ignoring someone's faults or weaknesses <critical indulgence toward the flawed film>. **6.** An extension of time for contractual performance such as payment, usu. granted as a favor; esp., permission to defer the payment of a note <a one-week indulgence>. **7.** *Eccles. law.* The relaxation of a rule for someone's benefit; a theological dispensation; esp., PARDON (2) <a plenary indulgence granted by the pope>.

indult (in-**dəlt**). (16c) *Eccles. law.* A dispensation granted by the Pope to do or obtain something contrary to canon law. • Historically, indults were often used for political ends. An indult granted to a sovereign empowered the recipient to present an ecclesiastical benefice, usu. without papal interference. Less exalted bodies, such as the parliament of Paris and the college of cardinals, were sometimes granted similar privileges. — Also termed *indulto.*

indulto (in-**dəl**-toh). [Spanish] (17c) **1.** A pardon or amnesty. **2.** *Hist.* A duty paid on imported goods to the Spanish or Portuguese Crown.

in duplo (in **d[y]oo**-ploh), *adv. & adj.* [Law Latin] In double. • This term appeared in phrases such as *damna in duplo* ("double damages"). — Also termed (in Roman law) *in duplum.*

in duplum. See IN DUPLO.

in duriorem sortem (in d[y]uur-ee-**or**-əm **sor**-təm). [Latin] *Civil law.* To the debt that it was the debtor's interest to have first discharged. • The phrase appeared in reference to a debt that bound the debtor most quickly or to which a penalty was imposed.

industrial action. (1971) See JOB ACTION.

industrial board. (1900) A subentity of a government's labor department, usu. responsible for promulgating and enforcing rules and regulations under the labor laws.

industrial design. *Patents.* The shape, configuration, pattern, or ornament applied to a finished article of manufacture, often to distinguish the product's appearance. • A design patent may be issued to protect the product's characteristic appearance.

industrial-development bond. See BOND (3).

industrial disease. See OCCUPATIONAL DISEASE.

industrial dispute. See LABOR DISPUTE.

industrial espionage. See ESPIONAGE.

Industrial Espionage Act. See ECONOMIC ESPIONAGE ACT.

industrial estate. See INDUSTRIAL PARK.

industrial goods. See *capital goods* under GOODS.

industrial insurance. See *industrial life insurance* under LIFE INSURANCE.

industrial law. See LABOR LAW.

industrial life insurance. See LIFE INSURANCE.

industrial organization. See UNION.

industrial park. (1955) A piece of land, often in a suburb or at the edge of a city, where factories or businesses are located. — Also termed *industrial estate.*

industrial property. (1884) *Intellectual property.* Patented goods, industrial designs, trademarks, and copyrights that a business owns and may exclude others from using. • Employed in the Paris Convention, the term was not defined, but the treaty states that it is to be construed broadly.

industrial relations. (1904) *Labor law.* All dealings and relationships between an employer and its employees, including collective bargaining about issues such as safety and benefits. See LABOR RELATIONS.

industrial-revenue bond. See *industrial-development bond* under BOND (3).

industrial tribunal. (1891) *Labor law.* A court that adjudicates disagreements between workers and their employers.

industrial union. See UNION.

industry. (15c) **1.** Diligence in the performance of a task. **2.** Systematic labor for some useful purpose; esp., work in manufacturing or production. **3.** A particular form or branch of productive labor; an aggregate of enterprises employing similar production and marketing facilities to produce items having markedly similar characteristics.

industry-wide liability. See *enterprise liability* (1–3) under LIABILITY.

indutiae (in-**d**[y]**oo**-shee-ee), *n.* [Latin] **1.** *Roman & int'l law.* A truce or cessation of hostilities; an armistice. **2.** *Roman & civil law.* A delay allowed for performing an obligation or other legal business. **3.** *Maritime law.* A period of 20 days in which a bottomry-bond debtor may unload the ship's cargo and pay the bond. — Also spelled *induciae.*

in eadem causa (in ee-**ay**-dəm **kaw**-zə), *adv.* [Latin] In the same cause; in the same state or condition.

inebriate (in-**ee**-bree-ət), *n.* (18c) *Archaic.* An intoxicated person; esp., a habitual drunkard.

inebriate act. (1911) *Hist. English law.* A statute, esp. one of a series enacted in England from 1879 to 1900, dealing with the confinement of habitual drunkards, embracing both criminal inebriates and voluntary alcoholics, on the principle that drunkards are not classified as lunatics but can nevertheless be dangerous to themselves and others. Cf. HABITUAL DRUNKARDS' ACT.

inebriated (in-**ee**-bree-ay-tid), *adj.* (15c) Drunk; intoxicated.

ineffective assistance of counsel. See ASSISTANCE OF COUNSEL.

ineffective revocation. See DEPENDENT RELATIVE REVOCATION.

Ineligibility Clause. *Constitutional law.* The clause of the U.S. Constitution that prohibits a member of Congress from accepting an appointment to an executive office that was created, or the compensation for which was increased, during the member's service in Congress. U.S. Const. art. I, § 6.

ineligible, *adj.* (18c) (Of a person) legally disqualified to serve in office. — **ineligibility,** *n.*

in emulationem vicini (in em-yə-lay-shee-**oh**-nəm vi-**SI**-NI), *adj.* [Latin "in envy or hatred of a neighbor"] (Of a legal claim) brought for an act done solely to hurt or distress another, such as raising a high fence.

in eodem negotio (in ee-**oh**-dəm ni-**goh**-shee-oh). [Latin] Arising out of the same transaction.

inequitable (in-**ek**-wi-tə-bəl), *adj.* (17c) Not fair; opposed to principles of equity <an inequitable ruling>.

inequitable conduct. See *defense of inequitable conduct* under DEFENSE (1).

in equity. (15c) In a chancery court rather than a court of law; before a court exercising equitable jurisdiction.

inequity (in-**ek**-wi-tee), *n.* (16c) **1.** Unfairness; a lack of equity. **2.** An instance of injustice.

inertia selling. (1969) *English law.* The unlawful practice of sending unsolicited goods to individuals and then billing them for any unreturned goods.

inescapable peril. See PERIL (1).

in esse (in **es**-ee *also* **es**-ay). [Latin "in being"] (16c) In actual existence; IN BEING <the court was concerned only with the rights of the children *in esse*>. Cf. IN POSSE.

in essentialibus (in e-sen-shee-**al**-ə-bəs). [Law Latin] *Scots law.* In the essential parts. • An error in an essential term of an instrument (such as a deed) was usu. fatal.

inessential mistake. See *unessential mistake* under MISTAKE.

in est de jure (in **est** dee **joor**-ee). [Latin] It is implied as of right or by law.

in evidence. Having been admitted into evidence <the photograph was already in evidence when the defense first raised an objection to it>.

inevitability doctrine. See INEVITABLE-DISCLOSURE DOCTRINE (2).

inevitable accident. See *unavoidable accident* under ACCIDENT.

inevitable-accident doctrine. See UNAVOIDABLE-ACCIDENT DOCTRINE.

inevitable-disclosure doctrine. 1. INEVITABLE-DISCOVERY RULE. **2.** *Trade secrets.* The legal theory that a key employee, once hired by a competitor, cannot avoid misappropriating the former employer's trade secrets. • To justify an injunction, the plaintiff must prove that the former employee has confidential information and will not be able to avoid using that knowledge to unfairly compete against the plaintiff. Most courts have rejected this controversial doctrine on grounds that it effectively turns a nondisclosure agreement into a disfavored noncompetition agreement. The leading case upholding the doctrine is *PepsiCo, Inc. v. Redmond*, 54 F.3d 1262 (7th Cir. 1995), where the court quipped: "PepsiCo finds itself in the position of a coach, one of whose players has left, playbook in hand, to join the opposing team before the big game." — Also termed *inevitable-disclosure rule; inevitability doctrine; inevitable-misappropriation doctrine.*

inevitable-disclosure rule. See INEVITABLE DISCLOSURE DOCTRINE (2).

inevitable-discovery rule. (1963) *Criminal procedure.* The rule that evidence obtained indirectly from an illegal search is admissible, and the illegality of the search is harmless, if the evidence would have been obtained nevertheless in the ordinary course of police work. • The rule is an exception to the fruit-of-the-poisonous-tree doctrine. The prosecution bears the burden of establishing the inevitability of the discovery. — Also termed *inevitable-discovery doctrine; inevitable-disclosure doctrine.* See FRUIT-OF-THE-POISONOUS-TREE DOCTRINE. Cf. INDEPENDENT-SOURCE RULE.

inevitable-misappropriation doctrine. See INEVITABLE-DISCLOSURE DOCTRINE (2).

in excambio (in eks-**kam**-bee-oh), *adv.* [Law Latin] *Hist.* In exchange. • This phrase appeared in deeds of exchange.

inexcusable neglect. See NEGLECT.

in executione rei judicatae (in ek-si-kyoo-shee-**oh**-nee **ree**-I joo-di-**kay**-tee). [Latin] In execution of a judgment right already judicially determined.

in exitu (in **eks**-ə-t[y]oo *or* **eg**-zə-t[y]oo), *adv. & adj.* [Law Latin] *Hist.* In issue. • These words sometimes appeared in phrases such as *de materia in exitu* ("of the matter in issue").

in extenso (in ek-**sten**-soh). [Latin] (1826) In full; unabridged <set forth *in extenso*>.

in extremis (in ek-**stree**-mis). [Latin "in extremity"] (16c) **1.** In extreme circumstances. **2.** Near the point of death; on one's deathbed. • Unlike *in articulo mortis*, the phrase *in extremis* does not always mean at the point of death. Cf. IN ARTICULO MORTIS.

in facie curiae (in **fay**-shee-ee **kyoor**-ee-ee), *adv. & adj.* [Law Latin "in the face of the court"] In the presence of the court.

in facie ecclesiae (in **fay**-shee-ee e-**klee**-z[h]ee-ee), *adv. & adj.* [Law Latin "in the face of the church"] In the presence of the church. • A marriage solemnized in a parish church or public chapel was said to be *in facie ecclesiae.*

in faciendo (in fay-shee-**en**-doh), *adv. & adj.* [Law Latin "in doing"] In the performance of an act; in feasance. • The phrase appeared in reference to an obligation to perform an act. Cf. IN FACTO PRAESTANDO.

in fact. (18c) Actual or real; resulting from the acts of parties rather than by operation of law. Cf. IN LAW.

in facto (in **fak**-toh), *adv.* [Latin] In fact; in deed.

in facto praestando (in **fak**-toh pree-**stan**-doh). [Latin] In the performance of some act. Cf. IN FACIENDO.

in facto proprio (in **fak**-toh **proh**-pree-oh). [Latin] Concerning one's own act.

infamia (in-**fay**-mee-ə), *n.* [Latin] *Roman law.* **1.** Bad reputation; ill-fame. **2.** Loss of honor as a citizen.

infamia facti (in-**fay**-mee-ə **fak**-tI). (17c) Infamy in fact, though not yet judicially proved.

infamia juris (in-**fay**-mee-ə **joor**-is). (16c) Infamy established by judicial verdict.

infamis (in-**fay**-mis), *adj.* [Latin] *Roman law.* (Of a person or action) of ill-repute. • A person was automatically *infamis* if held liable for certain torts or breaches of fiduciary duty. This type of condemnation carried with it certain disabilities, such as disqualification from office or ineligibility to witness a formal transaction.

infamous (**in**-fə-məs), *adj.* (14c) **1.** (Of a person) having a bad reputation. **2.** (Of a person) deprived of some or all rights of citizenship after conviction for a serious crime. • Historically, a person convicted of almost any crime became infamous. **3.** (Of conduct) that is punishable by imprisonment.

infamous crime. See CRIME.

infamous offense. See *infamous crime* under CRIME.

infamous punishment. See PUNISHMENT (1).

infamy (**in**-fə-mee), *n.* (18c) **1.** Disgraceful repute. **2.** The loss of reputation or position resulting from a person's being convicted of an infamous crime. See *infamous crime* under CRIME.

infancy. (14c) **1.** MINORITY (1).

> "Every person is, at the common law, considered an infant, or minor, until he has reached the age of twenty-one years, which age is computed to be completed on the first instant of the day preceding the twenty-first anniversary of his birth. The period of infancy is wholly a matter of positive law, and the rights and liabilities of infants and their legal relations to others are wholly under the control of government." Lewis Hochheimer, *A Treatise on the Law Relating to the Custody of Infants* 1 (2d ed. 1891).

2. Early childhood.

▸ **natural infancy.** (17c) At common law, the period ending at age seven, during which a child was presumed to be without criminal capacity.

3. The beginning stages of anything.

infangthief (**in**-fang-theef). [fr. Old English *in* "in" + *fangen* "taken" + *theof* "thief"] (bef. 12c) *Hist.* A privilege held by a lord of a manor to try, and deal summarily with, a thief captured on the lord's land, esp. a thief captured with plunder. — Also spelled *infangthef.* Cf. OUTFANGTHIEF.

infans (**in**-fanz), *n.* [Latin] *Roman law.* A child under seven years old. • On turning seven years old, an *infans* became known as an *impubes.* An *infans* had no capacity in the law. Cf. IMPUBES.

infant, *n.* (14c) **1.** A newborn baby. **2.** MINOR (1).

> "An infant in the eyes of the law is a person under the age of twenty-one years, and at that period (which is the same in the French and generally in the American law) he or she is said to attain majority; and for his torts and crimes an infant may be liable; but for his contracts, as a general rule, he is not liable, unless the contract is for necessaries." John Indermaur, *Principles of the Common Law* 195 (Edmund H. Bennett ed., 1st Am. ed. 1878).

"[I]nfant — the one technical word that we have as a contrast for the person of full age — stands equally well for the new-born babe and the youth who is in his twenty-first year." 2 Frederick Pollock & Frederic W. Maitland, *History of English Law Before the Time of Edward I* 439 (2d ed. 1899).

"The common-law rule provided that a person was an infant until he reached the age of twenty-one. The rule continues at the present time, though by statute in some jurisdictions the age may be lower." John Edward Murray Jr., *Murray on Contracts* § 12, at 18 (2d ed. 1974).

infantia (in-**fan**-shee-ə), *n.* [Latin] *Roman law.* The period of a person's life from birth to seven years; early childhood.

infantiae proximus (in-**fan**-shee-ee **prok**-si-məs). [Latin] *Roman law.* Next to infancy. • A child was *infantiae proximus* when slightly over seven years of age.

infanticide (in-**fant**-ə-sɪd). (17c) **1.** The act of killing a newborn child, esp. by the parents or with their consent. • In archaic usage, the word referred also to the killing of an unborn child. — Also termed *child destruction*; *neonaticide.* Cf. FETICIDE; FILICIDE (2). **2.** The practice of killing newborn children. **3.** Someone who kills a newborn child. — Also termed *child-slaying.* Cf. ASSIDERATION; PROLICIDE. — **infanticidal,** *adj.*

in favorem libertatis (in fə-**vor**-əm lib-ər-**tay**-tis). [Law Latin] In favor of liberty.

in favorem vitae (in fə-**vor**-əm **vɪ**-tee), *adv.* [Law Latin] In favor of life.

infect, *vb.* (14c) **1.** To contaminate <the virus infected the entire network>. **2.** To taint with crime <one part of the city has long been infected with illegal drug-dealing>. **3.** To make (a ship or cargo) liable in the seizure of contraband, which is only a part of its cargo <claiming that the single package of marijuana had infected the ship, the Coast Guard seized the entire vessel>. — **infection,** *n.* — **infectious,** *adj.*

infection, doctrine of. (1901) *Int'l law.* The principle that any goods belonging to an owner of contraband and carried on the same ship as the contraband may be seized or otherwise treated in the same manner as the contraband itself.

infeft, *p.pl.* (15c) *Scots law.* Enfeoffed. See ENFEOFF.

infeftment. (15c) *Scots law.* ENFEOFFMENT (1).

in feodo simpliciter (in **fee**-ə-doh [*or* **fyoo**-doh] sim-**plis**-i-tər). [Law Latin] In fee simple. See FEE SIMPLE.

infeoff, *vb.* See ENFEOFF.

infeoffment. See ENFEOFFMENT.

infer, *vb.* (16c) To conclude from facts or from factual reasoning; to draw as a conclusion or inference. Cf. IMPLY (1).

inferable bias. See BIAS.

inference (**in**-fər-ənts), *n.* (16c) **1.** A conclusion reached by considering other facts and deducing a logical consequence from them.

▸ **adverse inference.** (1844) A detrimental conclusion drawn by the fact-finder from a party's failure to produce evidence that is within the party's control. • Some courts allow the inference only if the party's failure is attributable to bad faith. — Also termed *adverse presumption.* Cf. SPOLIATION (1).

2. The process by which such a conclusion is reached; the process of thought by which one moves from evidence to proof. — **infer,** *vb.* — **inferential,** *adj.* — **inferrer,** *n.*

inference-on-inference rule. (1939) The principle that a presumption based on another presumption cannot serve as a basis for determining an ultimate fact.

inference-stacking. (1979) The practice or an instance of piling one or more inferences on each other to arrive at a legal conclusion. — Also termed *pyramiding inferences.* See INFERENCE-ON-INFERENCE RULE.

inferential fact. See FACT.

inferential hearsay. See HEARSAY.

inferential pleading. See *argumentative pleading* under PLEADING (1).

inferior court. See COURT.

inferior judge. See JUDGE.

inferior officer. See OFFICER (1).

inferred authority. See *incidental authority* under AUTHORITY (1).

inferred contract. See *implied-in-fact contract* under CONTRACT.

infertile, *adj.* (16c) Unable to conceive or bear offspring; sterile. — **infertility,** *n.*

infeudate. See ENFEOFF.

infeudatio (in-fyoo-**day**-shee-oh). [Law Latin] *Scots law.* ENFEOFFMENT.

infeudation (in-fyoo-**day**-shən), *n.* (15c) Under the feudal system of landholding, the process of giving a person legal possession of land; ENFEOFFMENT (1). Cf. SUBINFEUDATION; SUPERINFEUDATION. — **infeudate,** *vb.*

"So thorough was the process by which the land of England became subject to fixed obligations to the king — the process generally referred to today as the *infeudation* of England — that by the time of the famous Domesday survey, a scant twenty years after Hastings, it was possible to assign to almost every rock and stone of English soil its precise duty to the Crown." Thomas F. Bergin & Paul G. Haskell, *Preface to Estates in Land and Future Interests* 3 (2d ed. 1984).

infibulation. See FEMALE GENITAL MUTILATION.

inficiari. See INFITIARI.

inficiatio. See INFITIATIO.

infidel (**in**-fə-dəl). (15c) **1.** Someone who does not believe in something specified, esp. a particular religion. **2.** *Hist.* Someone who violates a feudal oath of fealty.

infidelis (in-fi-**dee**-lis *or* -**del**-is). [Latin] *Hist.* **1.** INFIDEL (1). **2.** INFIDEL (2).

infidelitas (in-fi-**dee**-lə-tas *or* -**del**-ə-tas), *n.* [Latin] *Hist.* Infidelity; faithlessness to one's feudal oath.

"Many of the smaller misdeeds were regarded as exhibitions of an *infidelitas*, which, however, did not amount to a *felonia*." 2 Frederick Pollock & Frederic W. Maitland, *The History of English Law Before the Time of Edward I* 513–14 (2d ed. 1899).

infidelity. (15c) **1.** Unfaithfulness to an obligation. **2.** The sexual betrayal of one's spouse or committed partner; specif., participation in sexual relations with a person other than one's spouse or partner. Cf. ADULTERY.

infiduciare (in-fi-**d**[y]**oo**-shee-air-ee), *vb.* [Law Latin] To pledge property.

in fieri (in fɪ-ə-rɪ), *adj.* [fr. Latin *in* "in" + *fieri* "to be done"] (17c) (Of a legal proceeding) that is pending or in the course of being completed.

in fine (in fɪ-nee *or* fɪn), *adv.* [Latin] (15c) **1.** In short; in summary. **2.** At the end (of a book, chapter, section, etc.).

infirmative, *adj.* (17c) *Rare.* (Of evidence) tending to weaken or invalidate a criminal accusation <an infirmative fact>. Cf. CRIMINATIVE.

infirmative hypothesis. *Criminal law.* An approach to a criminal case in which the defendant's innocence is impermissibly assumed, and incriminating evidence is explained in a manner consistent with that assumption.

infirmity (in-**fər**-mə-tee), *n.* (14c) Physical weakness caused by age or disease; esp., in insurance law, an applicant's ill health that is poor enough to deter an insurance company from insuring the applicant. — **infirm,** *adj.*

infitiari (in-fish-ee-**air**-ɪ), *vb.* [Latin "to deny"] *Roman law.* To deny a plaintiff's allegation; esp., to deny liability on a debt. — Also spelled *inficiari.*

infitiatio (in-fish-ee-**ay**-shee-oh), *n.* [Latin] *Roman law.* The denial of a debt or liability; the denial of a plaintiff's allegation. — Also spelled *inficiatio.* Pl. ***infitationes*** (in-fish-ee-ay-shee-**oh**-neez).

in flagrante delicto (in flə-**gran**-tee də-**lik**-toh). [Latin "while the crime is ablaze"] (18c) In the very act of committing a crime or other wrong; red-handed <the sheriff caught them *in flagrante delicto*>. — Sometimes shortened to *flagrante delicto.*

inflammatory (in-**flam**-ə-tor-ee), *adj.* (18c) Tending to cause strong feelings of anger, indignation, or other type of upset; tending to stir the passions. • Evidence can be excluded if its inflammatory nature outweighs its probative value.

inflation, *n.* (14c) A general increase in prices coinciding with a fall in the real value of money. Cf. DEFLATION. — **inflationary,** *adj.*

> "Inflation is often initiated and must be sustained by expansive monetary and fiscal policies. Once begun, inflation frequently generates expectations of further inflation that retard its ultimate disappearance. Another contributing cause of continuing inflation is the attempt by all sellers, whether of land, labor, or capital, to capture a larger share of national income for themselves. Since only 100 percent of national income is available for division, each successful attempt by one seller to gain a larger share for himself by raising the price of his product necessarily results in a smaller share for the rest. They raise their own prices in retaliation. And rather than suffer the unemployment that would result if aggregate monetary demands were left at the former level, governments facilitate the process by expansionary monetary and fiscal measures. As this process continues over time, society experiences 'sellers' inflation,' often called 'cost-push' inflation. Atomistic competition cannot initiate this process. It continues because of monopolistic and oligopolistic sellers, including organized labor." 1 Phillip Aneeda & Donald F. Turner, *Antitrust Law* ¶ 108, at 20 (1978).

▸ **cost-push inflation.** (1952) Inflation caused by a rise in production costs.

▸ **demand-pull inflation.** (1957) Inflation caused by an excess of demand over supply.

inflation-indexed bond. See BOND (3).

inflation rate. (1947) The pace of change in the prices of goods and services in a particular period. • The primary indexes for measuring the rate are the Consumer Price Index and the Producer Price Index.

infliction of emotional distress. 1. INTENTIONAL INFLICTION OF EMOTIONAL DISTRESS. **2.** NEGLIGENT INFLICTION OF EMOTIONAL DISTRESS.

influence, *n.* (16c) **1.** Use of pressure, authority, or power, usu. indirectly, to induce action or change the decisions or acts of another; one or more inducements intended to alter, sway, or affect the will of another, but falling short of coercion. See DUE INFLUENCE; UNDUE INFLUENCE. **2.** The quality, state, or condition of being intoxicated from alcohol, narcotics, or other foreign substances introduced into the body. See UNDER THE INFLUENCE.

▸ **outside influence.** (1857) **1.** Information that reaches a juror without being introduced into evidence, affects the juror's deliberations or mental processes, and relates specifically to the defendant or case being tried. **2.** The fact or an instance of a juror's being exposed to communications about the present case with a source outside the jury.

influence district. See DISTRICT.

in force, *adj.* (17c) In effect; operative; binding.

in-force patent. See PATENT (3).

in forma communi (in **for**-mə kə-**myoo**-nɪ) See IN COMMUNI FORMA.

in forma delicti (in **for**-mə di-**lik**-tɪ). [Latin] In the form of a delict (or tort). See DELICT.

informal, *adj.* (16c) Not done or performed in accordance with normal forms or procedures <an informal proceeding>.

informal acknowledgment. See ACKNOWLEDGMENT.

informal action. See ACTION (4).

informal admission. See *extrajudicial admission* under ADMISSION (1).

informal agency action. (1971) Administrative-agency activity other than adjudication or rulemaking, such as investigation, publicity, or supervision. Cf. RULEMAKING.

informal application. See PATENT APPLICATION.

informal consideration. See CONSIDERATION (2).

informal contract. See CONTRACT.

informal disposition. See DISPOSITION (2).

informal dividend. See DIVIDEND.

informal drawing. See DRAWING.

informal immunity. See *pocket immunity* under IMMUNITY (3).

informal issue. See ISSUE (1).

informal marriage. See *common-law marriage* under MARRIAGE (1).

informal probate. See PROBATE (1).

informal proceeding. See PROCEEDING.

informal proof of claim. See PROOF OF CLAIM.

informal rulemaking. See RULEMAKING.

informal will. See WILL.

informal witness statement. See WITNESS STATEMENT (3).

informant. (17c) Someone who informs against another; esp., one who confidentially supplies information to the police about a crime, sometimes in exchange for a reward or special treatment. — Also termed *informer; feigned accomplice.*

▸ **citizen-informant.** (1951) A witness who, without expecting payment and with the public good in mind, comes forward and volunteers information to the police or other authorities.

▸ **common informant.** (1894) Someone who, in an administrative capacity, commences a prosecution on behalf, and with the authority, of a government agency or public instrumentality.

informant's privilege. See PRIVILEGE (3).

in forma pauperis (in **for**-mə **paw**-pə-ris), *adv.* [Latin "in the manner of a pauper"] (16c) In the manner of an indigent who is permitted to disregard filing fees and court costs <when suing, a poor person is generally entitled to proceed *in forma pauperis*>. *See* 28 USCA § 1915; Fed. R. App. P. 24. • For instance, in many jurisdictions, an indigent divorce petitioner's filing fees and court costs are waived. — Abbr. IFP.

***in forma pauperis* affidavit.** See *poverty affidavit* under AFFIDAVIT.

***in forma pauperis* motion.** (1963) A request to receive poor-person (or pauper) status in a civil case (where certain costs are waived) or criminal appeal (where an indigent appellant may be assigned appellate counsel and receive a free transcript, etc.). — Also termed *poor-person motion.*

in forma specifica (in **for**-mə spi-**sif**-i-kə). [Latin] In the specified form.

information. (15c) *Criminal procedure.* A formal criminal charge made by a prosecutor without a grand-jury indictment. *See* Fed. R. Crim. P. 7. • The information is used to prosecute misdemeanors in most states, and about half the states allow its use in felony prosecutions as well. — Also termed *bill of information.* See CHARGING INSTRUMENT. Cf. INDICTMENT; PRESENTMENT (2).

▸ **confidential information.** See CONFIDENTIAL INFORMATION.

▸ **duplicitous information.** (1912) An information that charges two or more offenses as one count.

▸ **substitute information in lieu of indictment.** (1936) An information that the prosecutor files to take the place of a previously returned indictment, usu. because the indictment is defective or because the prosecutor has added, altered, or deleted facts and allegations.

▸ **superseding information.** (1910) A second or later information that includes additional charges or corrects errors in an earlier one.

informational checkpoint. See CHECKPOINT.

informational member. See *nonvoting member* under MEMBER (1).

informational picketing. See PICKETING.

informational privacy. See PRIVACY.

informational report. See REPORT (1).

Information Analysis and Infrastructure Protection Directorate. The division of the U.S. Department of Homeland Security responsible for analyzing intelligence information gathered from the Central Intelligence Agency, the Defense Intelligence Agency, the Federal Bureau of Investigation, the National Security Administration, and other sources, and for issuing warnings about threats of terrorist attack. • The unit is also charged with evaluating weaknesses in the country's infrastructure and recommending ways to reduce vulnerability to attacks. — Abbr. IAIP.

information and belief, on. (1817) (Of an allegation or assertion) based on secondhand information that the declarant believes to be true. • For the historical precursor to this phrase, see INSINUATIO.

information-disclosure statement. See DISCLOSURE STATEMENT.

information in equity. (1845) An equitable action brought by a sovereign or a governmental unit to preserve or protect the public interest through a public remedy. • When the action is to abate a nuisance that affects public property, it is an equitable action for purpresture. See PURPRESTURE. Cf. INFORMATION OF INTRUSION.

information letter. (1974) A written statement issued by the Department of Labor — in particular, by the Pension and Welfare Benefits Administration — that calls attention to a well-established interpretation or principle of ERISA, without applying it to a specific factual situation.

information of intrusion. (17c) *Hist.* A proceeding for trespass onto real property owned or held by a sovereign, such as a state or federal government. • This was a common-law remedy for purpresture. See PURPRESTURE. Cf. INFORMATION IN EQUITY.

> "In England it [an information of intrusion] is filed by the king's attorney general for any trespass committed upon the lands of the crown. It is founded on no writ under seal, but merely on intimation of the king's officer who 'gives the court to understand and be informed' of the matter in question. 3 Bl. Com. 261; Cro. Jac. 212. In America — in Massachusetts and Virginia — the remedy is resorted to in case of an intrusion on escheated lands. Com. v. Andre, 20 Mass. (3 Pick.) 224; Com. v. Hite, 6 Leigh (Va.) 588. Massachusetts Gen. St. 141 authorizes information of intrusion to be filed by the district attorney in case of any intrusion upon lands held by the State in this county for the benefit or use of any tribe of Indians or any individual thereof, or any descendants of them." 10 *The American and English Encyclopedia of Law* 711 n.1 (John Houston Merrill et al. eds., 1889) (s.v. *information of intrusion*).

> "An information of intrusion, it may be added, was in the nature of an action for trespass *quare clausum fregit.*" R.E. Megarry, *A New Miscellany-at-Law* 141 (2005).

information return. See TAX RETURN.

Information Society Directive. *Copyright.* An initiative of the European Commission implementing the standards set by the WIPO Copyright Treaty, setting reproduction rights and establishing a "making-available" right. — Abbr. ISD.

informative advertising. See ADVERTISING.

informed consent. See CONSENT (1).

informed intermediary. See INTERMEDIARY.

informer. (14c) **1.** INFORMANT. **2.** A private citizen who brings a penal action to recover a penalty. • Under some statutes, a private citizen is required to sue the offender for a penalty before any criminal liability can attach. — Also termed *common informer.* See COMMON INFORMER.

informer's privilege. See *informant's privilege* under PRIVILEGE (3).

in foro (in **for**-oh), *adv.* [Latin] In a forum, court, or tribunal; in the forum.

in foro conscientiae (in **for**-oh kon-shee-**en**-shee-ee), *adv.* [Latin "in the forum of conscience"] Privately or morally rather than legally <this moral problem cannot be dealt with by this court, but only *in foro conscientiae*>.

in foro contentioso (in **for**-oh kən-ten-shee-**oh**-soh), *adv.* [Latin] *Hist.* In the forum of contention or litigation; in a contested action. — Also termed *in foro contradictorio.*

"A decree is said to be granted *in foro contentioso* where the action in which it is pronounced has been litigated, and parties fully heard on the merits of the case. But it is not necessary that parties should be fully heard to make the decree pronounced in the case a decree *in foro.*" John Trayner, *Trayner's Latin Maxims* 261 (4th ed. 1894).

in foro contradictorio. See IN FORO CONTENTIOSO.

in foro ecclesiastico (in **for**-oh e-klee-z[h]ee-**as**-ti-koh), *adv.* [Law Latin] In an ecclesiastical court.

in foro externo (in **for**-oh ek-**stər**-noh), *adv.* [Latin "in an external forum"] *Eccles. law.* In a court that is handling a case relating to or involving the corporate life of the church. See FORUM EXTERNUM.

in foro humano (in **for**-oh hyoo-**may**-noh), *adv.* In a human as opposed to a spiritual forum.

"[T]his may be murder or manslaughter in the sight of God, yet *in foro humano* it cannot come under the judgment of felony . . . ." 1 Hale P.C. 429.

in foro interno (in **for**-oh in-**tər**-noh), *adv.* [Latin "in an internal forum"] *Eccles. law.* In a court of conscience; in a court for matters of conscience or the confessional. See FORUM INTERNUM.

in foro saeculari (in **for**-oh sek-yə-**lair**-ɪ), *adv.* [Law Latin] In a secular court.

infra (**in**-frə), *adv.* & *adj.* [Latin "below"] (18c) Later in this text. • *Infra* is used as a citational signal to refer to a later-cited authority. In medieval Latin, *infra* also acquired the sense "within." Cf. INTRA; SUPRA.

infra aetatem (**in**-frə ee-**tay**-təm), *adj.* [Latin] Underage. — Also spelled *infra etatem.*

infra annos nubiles (**in**-frə **an**-ohs **n[y]oo**-bə-leez), *adj.* [Law Latin] Under marriageable years; i.e., not old enough to wed.

infra annum (**in**-frə **an**-əm), *adv.* [Law Latin] Under a year; within a year.

infra annum luctus (**in**-frə **an**-əm **lək**-təs), *adv.* [Latin] Within the year of mourning. • This phrase referred to the one-year period of mourning during which a widow was prohibited from remarrying.

infra civitatem (**in**-frə siv-i-**tay**-təm), *adv.* [Law Latin] Within the state.

infra corpus comitatus (**in**-frə **kor**-pəs kom-ə-**tay**-təs), *adv.* & *adj.* [Law Latin] Within the body of a county. • In English law, this phrase referred to a body of water that was completely enclosed by land, and therefore exempt from admiralty jurisdiction. See CORPUS COMITATUS.

infraction, *n.* (17c) A violation, usu. of a rule or local ordinance and usu. not punishable by incarceration. See VIOLATION (1). — **infract,** *vb.*

▸ **civil infraction.** (1971) An act or omission that, though not a crime, is prohibited by law and is punishable. • In some states, many traffic violations are classified as civil infractions.

infra dignitatem curiae (**in**-frə dig-ni-**tay**-təm **kyoor**-ee-ee), *adj.* [Law Latin "beneath the dignity of the court"] (Of a case) too trifling in amount or character to be entertained by a court.

infra furorem (**in**-frə fyə-**ror**-əm), *adv.* [Law Latin] During madness; while in a state of insanity.

infra hospitium (**in**-frə hah-**spish**-ee-əm). [Law Latin "within the inn"] The doctrine that an innkeeper is liable for goods deposited by a guest.

infra jurisdictionem (**in**-frə joor-is-dik-shee-**oh**-nəm), *adv.* & *adj.* [Law Latin] Within the jurisdiction.

infra praesidia (**in**-frə prə-**sid**-ee-ə). [Latin "within the defenses"] (17c) *Hist.* The international-law doctrine that someone who captures goods will be considered the owner of the goods if they are brought completely within the captor's power. • This term is a corruption of the Roman-law term *intra praesidia*, which referred to goods or persons taken by an enemy during war. Under the principle of *postliminium*, the captured person's rights or goods were restored to prewar status when the captured person returned. See POSTLIMINIUM.

"In war, when those who are our enemies have captured someone on our side and have taken him into their own lines [*intra praesidia*]; for if during the same war he returns he has *postliminium*, that is, all his rights are restored to him just as if he had not been captured by the enemy." *Digest of Justinian* 49.15.5.1 (Pomponius, Quintus Mucius 37).

infrastructure. (1927) The underlying framework of a system; esp., public services and facilities (such as highways, schools, bridges, sewers, and water systems) needed to support commerce as well as economic and residential development.

in fraudem creditorum (in **fraw**-dəm kre-di-**tor**-əm), *adv.* [Latin] In fraud of creditors.

in fraudem legis (in **fraw**-dəm **lee**-jis), *adv.* [Latin] In fraud of the law. • With an intent to evade the law.

infringement, *n.* (1572) *Intellectual property.* An act that interferes with one of the exclusive rights of a patent, copyright, or trademark owner. See INTELLECTUAL PROPERTY. Cf. PLAGIARISM. — **infringe,** *vb.*

▸ **contributory infringement.** (1888) **1.** The act of participating in, or contributing to, the infringing acts of another person. • The law imposes vicarious liability for contributory infringement. **2.** *Patents.* The act of aiding or abetting another person's patent infringement by knowingly selling a nonstaple item that has no substantial noninfringing use and is esp. adapted for use in a patented combination or process. • In the patent context, contributory infringement is statutorily defined in the Patent Act. 35 USCA § 271(c). **3.** *Copyright.* The act of either (1) actively inducing, causing, or materially contributing to the infringing conduct of another person, or (2) providing the goods or means necessary to help another person infringe (as by making facilities available for an infringing performance). • In the copyright context, contributory infringement is a common-law doctrine. **4.** *Trademarks.* A manufacturer's or distributor's conduct in knowingly supplying, for resale, goods bearing an infringing mark. — Also termed *indirect infringement.*

▸ **copyright infringement.** (1875) *Copyright.* The act of violating any of a copyright owner's exclusive rights granted by the federal Copyright Act, 17 USCA §§ 106, 602. • A copyright owner has several exclusive rights in copyrighted works, including the rights (1) to reproduce the work, (2) to prepare derivative works based on the work, (3) to distribute copies of the work, (4) for certain kinds of works, to perform the work publicly, (5) for certain kinds of works, to display the work publicly, (6) for sound recordings, to perform the work publicly, and (7) to import into the United States copies acquired elsewhere. — Also termed *infringement of copyright.*

▸ **criminal infringement.** *Copyright.* (1902) The statutory criminal offense of either (1) willfully infringing a copyright to obtain a commercial advantage or financial gain (17 USCA § 506; 18 USCA § 2319), or (2) trafficking in goods or services that bear a counterfeit mark (18 USCA § 2320). • Under the second category, the law imposes criminal penalties if the counterfeit mark is (1) identical with, or substantially indistinguishable from, a mark registered on the Principal Register of the U.S. Patent and Trademark Office, and (2) likely to confuse or deceive the public.

▸ **direct infringement.** (1853) **1.** *Patents.* The act of making, using, selling, offering for sale, or importing into the United States, without the patentee's permission, a product that is covered by the claims of a valid patent. 35 USCA § 271(a). **2.** *Trademarks.* The use of a mark in trade when that use causes a likelihood of confusion about the source of goods or services already identified by a similar mark. **3.** *Copyright.* The unauthorized copying, distributing, or displaying of — or the adapting of a derivative work from — a copyrighted work. Cf. *contributory infringement*; *infringement in the inducement.*

▸ **domain-name infringement.** (1996) *Trademarks.* Infringement of another's trademark or servicemark by the use of a confusingly similar Internet domain name.

▸ **extraterritorial infringement.** *Patents & copyright.* Foreign activities that alone or in combination with other acts in the United States constitute infringement.

▸ **indirect infringement. 1.** See *contributory infringement.* **2.** See *induced infringement.*

▸ **induced infringement.** (1964) The act of persuading another person to make, use, or sell a patented invention without authorization. — Also termed *indirect infringement.*

▸ **infringement by sale.** (1911) *Patents.* The unauthorized sale, resale, or offer of a possessory interest in a patented invention. — Also termed *infringement through sale.*

▸ **infringement in the inducement.** (1996) *Patents.* The act of actively and knowingly aiding and abetting direct infringement by another person. • Although sometimes used in copyright and trademark law to mean contributory infringement, the term is usu. reserved for the patent context. — Also termed *inducing infringement.* See AID OR ABET INFRINGEMENT. Cf. *direct infringement.*

▸ **innocent infringement.** (1850) *Intellectual property.* The act of violating an intellectual-property right without knowledge or awareness that the act constitutes infringement. • An innocent infringer may, in limited circumstances, escape liability for some or all of the damages. In the copyright context, damages may be limited if (1) the infringer was misled by the lack of a copyright notice on an authorized copy of the copyrighted work, distributed under the owner's authority before March 1989 (the effective date of the Berne Convention Implementation Act of 1988), and (2) the infringing act occurred before the infringer received actual notice of the copyright. 17 USCA § 405(b). In the trademark context, publishers and distributors of paid advertisements who innocently infringe a mark have no liability for damages. 15 USCA § 1114. In both contexts, the innocent infringer is immunized only from an award of monetary damages, not from injunctive relief. Cf. *willful infringement.*

▸ **literal infringement.** (1906) *Patents.* Infringement in which every element and every limitation of a patent claim is present, exactly, in the accused product or process. Cf. DOCTRINE OF EQUIVALENTS.

▸ **nonliteral infringement.** See DOCTRINE OF EQUIVALENTS.

▸ **patent infringement.** (1876) The unauthorized making, using, offering to sell, selling, or importing into the United States of any patented invention. 35 USCA § 271(a). — Also termed *infringement of patent.*

> "In determining whether an accused device or composition infringes a valid patent, resort must be had in the first instance to the words of the claim. If accused matter falls clearly within the claim, infringement is made out and that is the end of it." *Graver Tank & Mfg. Co. v. Linde Air Prods. Co.*, 339 U.S. 605, 607, 70 S.Ct. 854, 855 (1950).

▸ **trademark infringement.** (1893) The unauthorized use of a trademark — or of a confusingly similar name, word, symbol, or any combination of these — in connection with the same or related goods or services and in a manner that is likely to cause confusion, deception, or mistake about the source of the goods or services. — Also termed *infringement of trademark.* See LIKELIHOOD-OF-CONFUSION TEST.

▸ **vicarious infringement.** (1979) A person's liability for an infringing act of someone else, even though the person has not directly committed an act of infringement. • For example, a concert theater can be vicariously liable for an infringing performance of a hired band.

▸ **willful infringement.** (1837) An intentional and deliberate infringement of another person's intellectual property. Cf. *innocent infringement.*

infringement by sale. See INFRINGEMENT.

infringement of copyright. See COPYRIGHT INFRINGEMENT.

infringement of patent. See PATENT INFRINGEMENT.

infringement of trademark. See TRADEMARK INFRINGEMENT.

infringement opinion. See OPINION (2).

infringement search. (1932) *Patents.* A patent search aimed at discovering whether a product or method infringes any in-force patent. • An infringement search is usu. limited to the political territory where the patent is to be relied on. — Also termed *clear-to-use search*; *freedom-to-operate search*; *FTO search.* Cf. PATENTABILITY SEARCH; VALIDITY SEARCH.

infringement test. (1948) *Patents.* A means of determining whether a patent claim is dependent by asking if the claim would always be infringed if the independent claim on which it rests were infringed. • Since a dependent claim must incorporate all the elements of the independent claim, an infringement of the independent claim must also be an infringement of the dependent claim.

infringement through sale. See *infringement by sale* under INFRINGEMENT.

infringer. (16c) Someone who interferes with one of the exclusive rights of a patent, copyright, or trademark owner. See INFRINGEMENT.

in fructu (in **frək**-t[y]oo). [Latin] Among the fruit. • A bona fide possessor traditionally owned the fruits of the subject possessed but not the subject itself because the subject was not *in fructu*. For example, a person who possessed but did not own a goat was entitled to the goat's milk, wool, and offspring, but not the goat's meat.

in full. (17c) Constituting the whole or complete amount <payment in full>.

in full life. (Of a person) alive in fact and in law; neither naturally nor civilly dead.

in futuro (in fyə-**tyoor**-oh), *adv.* [Latin] In the future. Cf. IN PRAESENTI.

in generali passagio (in jen-ə-**ray**-lɪ pə-**say**-jee-oh), *adv.* [Law Latin] *Hist.* In the general passage (to the holy land with a company of Crusaders). • This type of pilgrimage excused an absence from court during the Crusades. Cf. SIMPLEX PASSAGIUM.

in genere (in **jen**-ər-ee). [Latin "in kind"] Belonging to the same class, but not identical.

ingenui (in-**jen**-yə-wɪ). *Roman law.* People born into freedom. • This term, denoting one type of *liberi* (free people), was commonly opposed to *libertini* (people born into slavery and later emancipated).

ingenuitas (in-jə-**n[y]oo**-ə-tas), *n.* [Latin] *Roman law.* The condition or status of a free-born person.

ingenuitas regni (in-jə-**n[y]oo**-ə-tas **reg**-nɪ). [Law Latin] *Hist.* The freemen, yeomanry, or commonalty of the kingdom. • This term was occasionally applied to the nobility.

ingenuus (in-**jen**-yoo-əs), *n.* [Latin] *Roman law.* A free-born person. • This term, denoting freeborn persons, was commonly opposed to *libertini* (people born into slavery and later emancipated). Cf. LATINI JUNIANI; SERVUS (1).

in globo (in **gloh**-boh), *adv.* [Latin "in a mass"] As an undivided whole rather than separately <settlement paid *in globo* to the three defendants>.

ingratitude, *n.* (14c) *Civil law.* Lack of appreciation for a generous or kind act, esp. for a gift received. • Under Louisiana law, a gift may be reclaimed on grounds of ingratitude if the recipient mistreats the giver by, for example, attempting to murder the giver or refusing to provide the giver with needed food. La. Civ. Code art. 1560.

ingratus (in-**gray**-təs), *adj.* [Latin] *Roman law.* (Of a person) ungrateful; (of conduct) marked by ingratitude. • Ungrateful acts or words (such as spiteful comments from a freedman toward a former master) could form the basis for a return to a prior inferior status.

in gremio juris (in **gree**-mee-oh **joor**-is), *adv.* & *adj.* [Law Latin] *Civil & Scots law.* In the bosom of the right. • This phrase describes a clause formerly inserted in an instrument to bind holders to its terms.

in gremio legis (in **gree**-mee-oh **lee**-jis), *adv.* & *adj.* [Law Latin] In the bosom of the law. • This figurative expression describes something that is under the protection of the law, such as a land title that is in abeyance.

ingress (**in**-gres). (15c) **1.** The act of entering. **2.** The right or ability to enter; access. Cf. EGRESS.

ingress-and-egress easement. See EASEMENT.

ingress, egress, and regress. (17c) The right of a lessee to enter, leave, and reenter the land in question.

ingressus (in-**gres**-əs). [Latin "ingress, entry"] (18c) *Hist.* The fee paid by an heir to a feudal lord to enter the estate of a decedent.

in gross. (16c) **1.** Undivided; still in one large mass. — Also termed *en gros*; *en grosse*. **2.** (Of a servitude) personal as distinguished from appurtenant to land. See *easement in gross* under EASEMENT.

ingross, *vb.* See ENGROSS.

ingrossator (in-groh-**say**-tər). [Law Latin] *Hist.* An engrosser; a clerk who writes records or instruments on parchment. • The Engrosser of the Great Roll, for example, was known as the *Ingrossator Magni Rotuli*. See CLERK OF THE PIPE.

inhabit, *vb.* (14c) To dwell in; to occupy permanently or habitually as a residence.

in hac parte (in hak **pahr**-tee). [Latin] On this part or side.

in haec verba (in heek **vər**-bə). [Latin] In these same words; verbatim.

in haereditate jacente (in hə-red-i-**tay**-tee jə-**sen**-tee). [Latin] In the estate of a person deceased.

inhaerere jurisdictioni (in-hi-**reer**-ee joor-is-dik-shee-**oh**-nɪ). [Latin] *Civil law.* To be necessarily connected with jurisdiction. • The phrase typically referred to a judge's inherent powers, such as the power to inflict punishment or to enforce a judgment.

inhere (in-**heer**), *vb.* (15c) To exist as a permanent, inseparable, or essential attribute or quality of a thing; to be intrinsic to something.

inherency doctrine. (1951) *Patents.* The rule that anticipation can be inferred despite a missing element in a prior-art reference if the missing element is either necessarily present in or a natural result of the product or process and a person of ordinary skill in the art would know it. • On one hand, the doctrine precludes patenting an existing invention by merely claiming an inherent element. On the other hand, it allows the later patentability of a substance, usu. a chemical compound, that was inadvertently created but not recognized or appreciated. See INHERENT ANTICIPATION. Cf. ALL-ELEMENTS-RULE.

inherent anticipation. (1969) *Patents.* An invention's lack of novelty arising from the existence of prior-art products or processes that necessarily possess the same characteristics. • Inherency differs from obviousness in that a lack of novelty must be based on fact, not mere possibility or probability. See INHERENCY DOCTRINE.

inherent authority. See AUTHORITY (1).

inherent condition. See CONDITION (2).

inherent covenant. See COVENANT (1).

inherent defect. See *hidden defect* under DEFECT.

inherent jurisdiction. See JURISDICTION.

inherently dangerous. See DANGEROUS.

inherently dangerous activity. (1957) An activity that can be carried out only by the exercise of special skill and care and that involves a grave risk of serious harm if done unskillfully or carelessly.

inherently dangerous work. See WORK (1).

inherent power. See POWER (3).

inherent-powers doctrine. (1937) *Constitutional law.* The principle that allows courts to deal with diverse matters over which they are thought to have intrinsic authority, such as (1) procedural rulemaking, (2) internal budgeting of the courts, (3) regulating the practice of law; and (4) general judicial housekeeping. • The power is based on interpretations of art. I, § 8, cl. 18 of the Constitution.

inherent right. See *inalienable right* under RIGHT.

inherent risk. See RISK.

inherent vice. See VICE.

inherit, *vb.* (14c) **1.** To receive (property) from an ancestor under the laws of intestate succession upon the ancestor's death. **2.** To receive (property) as a bequest or devise.

inheritable, *adj.* See HERITABLE.

inheritable blood. See *heritable blood* under BLOOD.

inheritable obligation. See *heritable obligation* under OBLIGATION.

inheritable security. See *heritable security* under SECURITY (4).

inheritance. (14c) **1.** Property received from an ancestor under the laws of intestacy. **2.** Property that a person receives by bequest or devise.

▸ **dual inheritance.** (1919) An adopted child's intestate inheritance through both his adopted family and his natural parent. • The problem of dual inheritance occurs only if a relative of the birth parent adopts the child. For instance, if a child's mother dies and the maternal grandparents adopt the grandchild, and if a grandparent then dies intestate, the child qualifies for two separate shares — one as a child and the other as a grandchild. In some jurisdictions, by statute, such a child is allowed to inherit only the adopted child's share. Under the Uniform Probate Code, the child takes the larger of the two shares.

▸ **several inheritance.** (16c) An inheritance that descends to two persons severally, as by moieties.

▸ **shifting inheritance.** (1835) Under intestacy laws, an inheritance that is transferred from an heir who was living when the intestate died to an afterborn heir who is more closely related to the intestate.

▸ **universal inheritance.** (1943) A system by which an intestate's estate escheats to the state only if the decedent leaves no surviving relatives, no matter how distant. • Universal inheritance has been almost universally abandoned in Anglo-American jurisdictions. See UNIVERSAL-INHERITANCE RULE.

inheritance tax. See TAX.

inheritor (in-**hair**-i-tər), *n.* (15c) Someone who inherits; HEIR.

inheritrix (in-**hair**-i-triks), *n. Archaic.* (16c) A female heir; HEIRESS.

inhibition (in-hi-**bish**-ən), *n.* (16c) **1.** *Eccles. law.* A writ issued by a superior ecclesiastical court, forbidding a judge from proceeding in a pending case. **2.** *Eccles. law.* An order issuing from an ecclesiastical court, prohibiting a member of the clergy from taking office or performing an unlawful action. **3.** *Hist.* A writ of prohibition. **4.** *Scots law.* An order issued by the Court of Session to prohibit a debtor from encumbering or alienating the debtor's heritable property to the prejudice of a creditor. See EX CAPITE INHIBITIONIS; (in senses 3 & 4) PROHIBITION (2).

in hoc (in **hok**), *adv.* [Latin] In this; in respect to this.

in hoc statu (in hok **stay**-t[y]oo). [Latin] In this position.

inhonestus (in-hə-**nes**-təs), *adj.* [Latin] *Roman law.* **1.** (Of a person) of ill repute. **2.** (Of conduct) morally shameful.

in-house counsel. See COUNSEL.

inhumane, *adj.* (16c) Extremely cruel; causing unacceptable suffering.

inhuman treatment. *Family law.* Physical or mental cruelty so severe that it endangers life or health. • Inhuman treatment is usu. grounds for divorce. — Also termed *inhumane treatment.* See CRUELTY.

in hypothesi (in hɪ-**pahth**-ə-sɪ). [Latin] In a supposed case; in a hypothetical case. Cf. IN THESI.

in iisdem terminis (in ee-**ɪs**-dem **tər**-mə-nis), *adv.* [Law Latin] In the same terms.

inimical (i-**nim**-ə-kəl), *adj.* (17c) **1.** Behaving like an enemy; hostile. **2.** Opposite or adverse in effect or tendency.

inimicitia capitalis (i-nim-ə-**sish**-ee-ə kap-i-**tay**-lis). [Latin] *Hist.* Deadly enmity.

in individuo (in in-di-**vid**-yoo-oh), *adv.* [Law Latin] In the distinct, identical, or individual form. See IN SPECIE.

in infinitum (in in-fə-**nɪ**-təm). [Latin "in infinity"] (16c) To infinity. • This phrase was in reference to a line of succession that is indefinite.

in initialibus (in i-nish-ee-**al**-ə-bəs). [Law Latin] In the preliminary stage. • The phrase appeared in reference to the point in the examination when the *initialia testimonii* took place to determine the witness's competence to testify. See INITIALIA TESTIMONII.

in initio (in i-**nish**-ee-oh). [Latin "in the beginning"] At the beginning or outset. Cf. AB INITIO.

in initio litis (in i-**nish**-ee-oh **lɪ**-tis). [Latin] In the beginning of the suit. • Many defenses had to be raised at this stage of a case.

in integrum (in in-**teg**-rəm), *adj.* [Latin] Entire; wholly undamaged.

in invitum (in in-**vɪ**-təm), *adv.* [Latin] Against an unwilling person <the nonparty appealed after being compelled to participate in the proceedings *in invitum*>. Cf. AB INVITO.

in ipso termino (in **ip**-soh **tər**-mi-noh). [Latin] At the very end; on the last day, as of a prescriptive period.

initial appearance. See APPEARANCE.

initial cause. See *proximate cause* under CAUSE (1).

initial determination. See DETERMINATION (1).

initial disclosure. See DISCLOSURE (2).

initialia testimonii (i-nish-ee-**ay**-lee-ə tes-tə-**moh**-nee-ɪ). [Law Latin "initial parts of testimony"] *Scots law.* The preliminary examination of a witness in order to determine the witness's competence to testify. Cf. IN INITIALIBUS.

initial margin requirement. See MARGIN REQUIREMENT.

initial-permission rule. (1940) *Insurance.* The principle that a nonowner driver of a vehicle will be treated as an omnibus insured under the owner-insured's policy when the owner-insured grants the driver permission to use the vehicle. • It makes no difference whether the nonowner driver uses the vehicle in a manner other than that contemplated by the owner-insured. Cf. SPECIFIC-PURPOSE RULE.

initial protest. See PROTEST (2).

initial public offering. See OFFERING.

initial surplus. See SURPLUS.

initiation of charges. (1950) *Military law.* The first report to the proper military authority of an alleged commission of an offense by a person subject to the Uniform Code of Military Justice. Cf. PREFERRING OF CHARGES.

initiative (i-**nish**-ə-tiv *or* i-**nish**-ee-ə-tiv). (1889) *Voting law.* An electoral process by which a percentage of voters can propose legislation and compel a vote on it by the legislature or by the full electorate. • Recognized in some state constitutions, the initiative is one of the few methods of direct democracy in an otherwise representative system. Cf. PLEBISCITE (1); REFERENDUM.

in itinere (in ɪ-**tin**-ər-ee), *adv.* [Latin] On a journey; on the way. • This term referred to the justices in eyre (justices *in itinere*) and to goods en route to a buyer. See EYRE; IN TRANSITU.

initium possessionis (i-**nish**-ee-əm pə-zes[h]-ee-**oh**-nis). [Latin "the beginning of the possession"] *Hist.* The right by which possession was first held.

injoin, *vb. Archaic.* See ENJOIN.

in judicio (in joo-**dish**-ee-oh), *adv. & adj.* [Latin] Before the judge. • The phrase is still sometimes used. Originally, in Roman law, *in judicio* referred to the second stage of a Roman formulary trial, held before a private judge known as a *judex*. — Also termed *apud judicem.* See FORMULA (1). Cf. IN JURE (2).

in judicio possessorio (in joo-**dish**-ee-oh pah-ses-**sor**-ee-oh). [Law Latin] In a possessory action.

injunction (in-**jəngk**-shən), *n.* (16c) A court order commanding or preventing an action. • To get an injunction, the complainant must show that there is no plain, adequate, and complete remedy at law and that an irreparable injury will result unless the relief is granted. — Also termed *writ of injunction*; *equitable injunction.* See IRREPARABLE-INJURY RULE.

> "In a general sense, every order of a court which commands or forbids is an injunction; but in its accepted legal sense, an injunction is a judicial process or mandate operating *in personam* by which, upon certain established principles of equity, a party is required to do or refrain from doing a particular thing. An injunction has also been defined as a writ framed according to the circumstances of the case, commanding an act which the court regards as essential to justice, or restraining an act which it esteems contrary to equity and good conscience; as a remedial writ which courts issue for the purpose of enforcing their equity jurisdiction; and as a writ issuing by the order and under the seal of a court of equity." 1 Howard C. Joyce, *A Treatise on the Law Relating to Injunctions* § 1, at 2–3 (1909).

▸ **affirmative injunction.** See *mandatory injunction.*

▸ **anti-antisuit injunction.** (1988) An injunction prohibiting a litigant subject to the jurisdiction of a local court from seeking in a foreign court to restrain the continuation of a proceeding in the local court. Cf. *antisuit injunction.*

▸ **antisuit injunction.** (1961) An injunction prohibiting a litigant from instituting other, related litigation, usu. between the same parties on the same issues. Cf. *anti-antisuit injunction.*

▸ **common injunction.** (18c) *Hist.* **1.** An injunction grantable as an order of course, without reference to the merits, when the defendant failed to appear or failed to timely plead, answer, or demur. **2.** *English law.* An injunction issued by a court of equity forbidding enforcement of a common-law judgment. • In some cases, common law and equity rules differed, which could lead to inconsistent remedies. A court of equity that ensured the equitable rule would prevail by issuing a common injunction. Common injunctions were abolished by the Judicature Act of 1873, § 24(5). — Also termed *equitable common injunction.*

▸ **equitable common injunction.** See *common injunction.*

▸ **ex parte injunction.** (1854) A preliminary injunction issued after the court has heard from only the moving party. — Also termed *temporary restraining order.*

▸ **final injunction.** See *permanent injunction.*

▸ **headstart injunction.** (1984) *Trade secrets.* An injunction prohibiting the defendant from using a trade secret for a period of time equal to the time between the date of the secret's theft and the date when the secret became public. • So named since that period is the "head start" the defendant unfairly gained over the rest of the industry.

▸ **hyperinjunction.** (2009) *English law. Slang.* A superinjunction that expressly applies its bar on discussing the subject matter or even the injunction's existence to journalists, Members of Parliament, and lawyers except for the recipient's council. • The first known hyperinjunction was issued in 2006. See GAG ORDER (1). Cf. *superinjunction.*

▸ **injunction pendente lite.** See *preliminary injunction.*

▸ **interlocutory injunction.** See *preliminary injunction.*

▸ **mandatory injunction.** (1843) An injunction that orders an affirmative act or mandates a specified course of conduct. — Also termed *affirmative injunction.* Cf. *prohibitory injunction.*

▸ **permanent injunction.** (1846) An injunction granted after a final hearing on the merits. • Despite its name, a permanent injunction does not necessarily last forever. — Also termed *perpetual injunction*; *final injunction.*

▸ **perpetual injunction.** See *permanent injunction.*

▸ **preliminary injunction.** (1828) A temporary injunction issued before or during trial to prevent an irreparable injury from occurring before the court has a chance to decide the case. • A preliminary injunction will be issued only after the defendant receives notice and an opportunity to be heard. — Also termed *interlocutory injunction; temporary injunction; provisional injunction; injunction pendente lite*. Cf. *ex parte injunction*; TEMPORARY RESTRAINING ORDER.

▸ **preventive injunction.** (1882) An injunction designed to prevent a loss or injury in the future. Cf. *reparative injunction*.

▸ **production injunction.** (1994) *Trade secrets*. A permanent injunction prohibiting specified conduct in a field or activity that the court has found to embrace misappropriated trade secrets.

▸ **prohibitory injunction.** (1843) An injunction that forbids or restrains an act. • This is the most common type of injunction. Cf. *mandatory injunction*.

▸ **provisional injunction.** See *preliminary injunction*.

▸ **quia-timet injunction** (**kwɪ**-ə **tɪ**-mət *or* **kwee**-ə **tim**-et). [Latin "because he fears"] (1913) An injunction granted to prevent an action that has been threatened but has not yet violated the plaintiff's rights. See QUIA TIMET.

▸ **reparative injunction** (ri-**par**-ə-tiv). (1955) An injunction requiring the defendant to restore the plaintiff to the position that the plaintiff occupied before the defendant committed a wrong. Cf. *preventive injunction*.

▸ **special injunction.** (18c) *Hist*. An injunction in which the prohibition of an act is the only relief ultimately sought, as in prevention of waste or nuisance.

▸ **superinjunction.** (2009) *Slang. English law*. (2009) A type of gag order that forbids the recipient not just to discuss the subject matter but also to reveal the existence of the injunction itself. • Since Members of Parliament are not restrained by the injunction because of parliamentary privilege, and because parliamentary proceedings may be reported without restriction, the existence and contents of a superinjunction may be made known indirectly. — Also written *super-injunction*. See GAG ORDER (1). Cf. *hyperinjunction*.

▸ **temporary injunction.** See *preliminary injunction*.

▸ **use injunction.** (1995) *Trade secrets*. A permanent injunction prohibiting the use of specified information that the court has found to constitute a trade secret.

injunctional. See INJUNCTIVE.

injunction bond. See BOND (2).

injunctive, *adj*. (15c) That has the quality of directing or ordering; of, relating to, or involving an injunction. — Also termed *injunctional*.

in jure (in **joor**-ee). [Latin "in law"] **1.** According to the law. **2.** *Roman law*. Before the praetor or other magistrate. • *In jure* referred to the first stage of a Roman formulary trial, held before the praetor or other judicial magistrate for the purpose of establishing the legal issues and their competence. Evidence was taken in the second stage, which was held before a judex. See FORMULA (1). Cf. IN JUDICIO.

in jure alterius (in **joor**-ee al-**teer**-ee-əs), *adv*. [Latin] In another's right.

in jure cessio (in **joor**-ee **sesh**-ee-oh). [Latin "a surrender in law"] *Roman law*. A fictitious trial held to transfer ownership of property; a collusive claim to formally convey property, esp. incorporeal property, by a court's assignment of ownership. • At trial, the transferee appeared before a praetor and asserted ownership of the property. The actual owner also appeared, but did not contest the assertion, and so allowed the transfer of the property to the plaintiff. *In jure cessio* was most often used to convey incorporeal property. — Also spelled *in iure cessio*.

in jure proprio (in **joor**-ee **proh**-pree-oh), *adv*. [Latin] In one's own right.

injuria (in-**joor**-ee-ə), *n*. [Latin] (1876) *Roman law*. **1.** WRONG. Cf. DAMNUM INJURIA DATUM; *actio injuriarum* under ACTIO. **2.** An assault on a person's reputation or body. Pl. ***injuriae*** (in-**joor**-ee-ee).

> "By *injuria* (or outrage), as the fourth ground of delict obligation, is meant some affronting wrong, calculated to wound the self-respect and touch the honor of the person injured, to humiliate or degrade him in the view of others." James Hadley, *Introduction to Roman Law* 243 (N.Y., D. Appleton & Co. 1881).

> "The term *injuria* [is best] used in its original and proper sense of *wrong* (*in jus*, contrary to law). The modern use of 'injury' as a synonym for damage is unfortunate but inveterate." R.F.V. Heuston, *Salmond on the Law of Torts* 13 nn.51–52 (17th ed. 1977).

injuria absque damno (in-**joor**-ee-ə **abs**-kwee **dam**-noh). [Latin "injury without damage"] (1843) A legal wrong that will not sustain a lawsuit because no harm resulted from it. — Also termed *injuria sine damno*. Cf. DAMNUM SINE INJURIA.

> "Just as there are cases in which damage is not actionable as a tort (*damnum sine injuria*), so conversely there are cases in which behaviour is actionable as a tort, although it has been the cause of no damage at all (*injuria sine damno*). Torts are of two kinds — namely, those which are actionable *per se*, and those which are actionable only on proof of actual damage resulting from them. Thus the act of trespassing upon another's land is actionable even though it has done the plaintiff not the slightest harm. Similarly, a libel is actionable *per se*, while slander (that is to say, oral as opposed to written defamation) is in most cases not actionable without proof of actual damage." R.F.V. Heuston, *Salmond on the Law of Torts* 14 (17th ed. 1977).

injuria sine damno. See INJURIA ABSQUE DAMNO.

injurious, *adj*. (15c) Harmful; tending to injure.

injurious affection. See *inverse condemnation* under CONDEMNATION (2).

injurious exposure. (1936) *Workers' compensation*. Contact with a substance that would cause injury if the person were repeatedly exposed to it over time. • An employer may be found liable for harm resulting from injurious exposure.

injurious falsehood. 1. See DISPARAGEMENT (3). **2.** See TRADE DISPARAGEMENT.

injurious words. (1832) *Louisiana law*. Slanderous or libelous language. See SLANDER; LIBEL (1), (2).

injury, *n*. (14c) **1.** The violation of another's legal right, for which the law provides a remedy; a wrong or injustice. See WRONG. **2.** *Scots law*. Anything said or done in breach of a duty not to do it, if harm results to another in person, character, or property. • Injuries are divided into real injuries (such as wounding) and verbal injuries (such as slander). They may be criminal wrongs (as with assault) or civil wrongs (as with defamation). **3.** Any harm or damage. • Some authorities distinguish *harm* from *injury*, holding that while *harm* denotes any personal loss or detriment, *injury* involves an actionable invasion of a legally protected interest. *See* Restatement (Second) of Torts § 7, cmt. a (1965). — **injure,** *vb.* — **injurious,** *adj.*

▸ **accidental injury.** (1800) An injury resulting from external, violent, and unanticipated causes; esp., a bodily injury caused by some external force or agency operating contrary to a person's intentions, unexpectedly, and not according to the usual order of events.

> "An accidental injury is a bodily injury caused by some external force or agency, operating contrary to the intention of the insured, unexpectedly, and not according to the usual order of events. The accident policy usually defines an accidental injury as one due to external, violent, and accidental causes." William Reynolds Vance, *Handbook of the Law of Insurance* § 232, at 566 (1904).

▸ **advertising injury.** (1977) Harm resulting from (1) oral or written speech that slanders or libels a person, or disparages a person's goods, products, or services; (2) oral or written speech that violates a person's right of privacy; (3) misappropriation of advertising ideas or style of doing business; or (4) infringement of copyright, esp. in a name or slogan.

▸ **antitrust injury.** (1958) Damage, loss, or harm caused by anticompetitive conduct that violates antitrust laws. • An example is a vertical maximum-price-fixing conspiracy that results in predatory pricing. *See Atl. Richfield Co. v. USA Petroleum Co.*, 495 U.S. 328, 334–35, 110 S.Ct. 1884, 1889 (1990).

▸ **bodily injury.** (16c) Physical damage to a person's body. — Also termed *personal injury*; *personal bodily injury*; *physical injury.* See *serious bodily injury*; *personal injury* (1).

▸ **civil injury.** (17c) Physical harm or property damage caused by breach of a contract or by a criminal offense redressable through a civil action.

▸ **compensable injury** (kəm-**pen**-sə-bəl). (1917) *Workers' compensation.* An injury caused by an accident arising from the employment and in the course of the employee's work, and for which the employee is statutorily entitled to receive compensation.

▸ **consequential injury.** See *consequential loss* under LOSS.

▸ **continual injury.** (16c) An injury that recurs at repeated intervals. — Also termed (but improperly) *continuous injury.*

▸ **continuing injury.** (1824) An injury that is still in the process of being committed. • An example is the constant smoke or noise of a factory. — Also termed *continuing harm.*

▸ **direct injury.** (17c) **1.** An injury resulting directly from violation of a legal right. **2.** An injury resulting directly from a particular cause, without any intervening causes.

▸ **economic injury.** *Torts.* An injury to a person's ability to enter into or profit from a business arrangement.

▸ **great bodily injury.** See *serious bodily injury.*

▸ **indivisible injury.** (1838) A single injury that has been caused by concurrent tortfeasors and that is not reasonably capable of being separated. • Traditionally, before tort-reform legislation, multiple tortfeasors were held jointly and severally liable for an indivisible injury. See *joint and several liability* under LIABILITY.

▸ **injury in fact.** (1809) An actual or imminent invasion of a legally protected interest, in contrast to an invasion that is conjectural or hypothetical. • An injury in fact gives the victim standing to bring an action for damages.

▸ **injury to reputation.** A diminution in any manner or degree of the esteem, goodwill, or confidence that people place in a person, firm, company, etc.

▸ **irreparable injury** (i-**rep**-ər-ə-bəl). (17c) An injury that cannot be adequately measured or compensated by money and is therefore often considered remediable by injunction. — Also termed *irreparable harm*; *nonpecuniary injury.* See IRREPARABLE-INJURY RULE.

> "The term 'irreparable injury,' however, is not to be taken in its strict literal sense. The rule does not require that the threatened injury should be one not physically capable of being repaired. If the threatened injury would be substantial and serious — one not easily to be estimated, or repaired by money — and if the loss or inconvenience to the plaintiff if the injunction should be refused (his title proving good) would be much greater than any which can be suffered by the defendant through the granting of the injunction, although his title ultimately prevails, the case is one of such probable great or 'irreparable' damage as will justify a preliminary injunction." Elias Merwin, *Principles of Equity and Equity Pleading* 426–27 (H.C. Merwin ed., 1895).

▸ **legal injury.** (18c) Violation of a legal right.

▸ **malicious injury.** (16c) **1.** An injury resulting from a willful act committed with knowledge that it is likely to injure another or with reckless disregard of the consequences. **2.** MALICIOUS MISCHIEF.

▸ **nonpecuniary injury.** See *irreparable injury.*

▸ **pecuniary injury.** (18c) An injury that can be adequately measured or compensated by money.

▸ **permanent injury.** (17c) **1.** A completed wrong whose consequences cannot be remedied for an indefinite period. **2.** *Property.* A lasting injury to land that causes it to revert to the grantor or vests immediate right of possession in a remainderman. Cf. *temporary injury.*

▸ **personal injury.** (16c) *Torts.* **1.** In a negligence action, any harm caused to a person, such as a broken bone, a cut, or a bruise; bodily injury. — Also termed *bodily injury.* **2.** Any invasion of a personal right, including mental suffering and false imprisonment. — Also termed *private injury.* **3.** For purposes of workers' compensation, any harm (including a worsened preexisting condition) that arises in the scope of employment. — Abbr. PI.

▸ **physical injury.** See *bodily injury.*

▸ **private injury.** See *personal injury* (2).

▸ **public injury.** (16c) A loss or an injury stemming from a breach of a duty or violation of a right that affects the community as a whole.

▸ **reparable injury** (**rep**-ər-ə-bəl). (1832) An injury that can be adequately compensated by money.

▸ **scheduled injury.** (1917) *Workers' compensation.* A partially disabling injury for which a predetermined amount of compensation is allowed under a workers'-compensation statute.

▸ **serious bodily injury.** (1843) Serious physical impairment of the human body; esp., bodily injury that creates a substantial risk of death or that causes serious, permanent disfigurement or protracted loss or impairment of the function of any body part or organ. Model Penal Code § 210.0(3). • Typically, the fact-finder must decide in any given case whether the injury meets this general standard. Generally, an injury meets this standard if it creates a substantial risk of fatal consequences or, when inflicted, constitutes mayhem. — Abbr. SBI. — Also termed *serious bodily harm; grievous bodily harm; great bodily injury.* Cf. MAYHEM (1).

▸ **temporary injury.** (1812) An injury that may be abated or discontinued at any time by either the injured party or the wrongdoer. Cf. *permanent injury.*

▸ **willful and malicious injury.** (1808) *Bankruptcy.* Under the statutory exception to discharge, damage to another entity (such as a creditor) caused by a debtor intentionally performing a wrongful act — without just cause or excuse — that the debtor knew was certain or substantially certain to cause injury. 11 USCA § 523(a)(6).

injury-in-fact trigger. See ACTUAL-INJURY TRIGGER.

injustice. (15c) **1.** An unjust state of affairs; unfairness. **2.** An unjust act.

in jus vocare (in **jəs** voh-**kair**-ee), *vb.* [Latin] *Roman law.* To summon a defendant to court.

in kind, *adv.* (17c) **1.** In goods or services rather than money <payment in cash or in kind>. **2.** In a similar way; with an equivalent of what has been offered or received <returned the favor in kind>. — **in-kind,** *adj.* <in-kind repayment>.

INL. *abbr.* BUREAU OF INTERNATIONAL NARCOTICS AND LAW ENFORCEMENT.

inlagare (in-lə-**gair**-ee), *vb.* [Law Latin] *Hist.* To restore (an outlaw) to the protection of the law. Cf. UTLAGARE.

inlagation (in-lə-**gay**-shən), *n.* [Law Latin] (17c) *Hist.* The act of restoring an outlaw to the protection of the law; inlawry. Cf. UTLAGATION.

inlagh (**in**-law). *Hist.* A person within the protection of the law, in contrast to an outlaw. Cf. UTLAGH.

inland. (15c) **1.** The interior part of a country or region, away from the coast or border. **2.** *Hist.* The portion of a feudal estate lying closest to the lord's manor and dedicated to the support of the lord's family. — Also termed (in sense 2) *inlantal.* Cf. UTLAND.

inland bill of exchange. See *domestic bill* (2) under BILL (6).

inland draft. See DRAFT (1).

inland marine insurance. See INSURANCE.

inland revenue. See INTERNAL REVENUE.

inland trade. See TRADE (1).

inland waters. See INTERNAL WATERS.

inlantal (**in**-lan-təl). *Hist.* See INLAND (2). — Also spelled *inlantale.*

in law. (15c) Existing in law or by force of law; in the contemplation of the law. Cf. IN FACT.

in-law, *n.* (1894) A relative by marriage.

inlaw, *vb.* (bef. 12c) *Archaic.* To place (an offender) under the protection of the law. Cf. OUTLAW (1).

> "The outlaw's life is insecure. . . . If the king inlaws him, he comes back into the world like a new-born babe, *quasi modo genius*, capable indeed of acquiring new rights, but unable to assert any of those that he had before his outlawry. An annihilation of the outlawry would have a different operation, but the inlawed outlaw is not the old person restored to legal life; he is a new person." 1 Frederick Pollock & Frederic W. Maitland, *History of English Law Before the Time of Edward I* 477 (2d ed. 1898).

inlawry. (1848) The restoration of an outlawed person's rights and protections under the law. See INLAGATION.

in lecto aegritudinis (in **lek**-toh ee-gri-**t[y]oo**-di-nis). [Law Latin] *Scots law.* On a bed of sickness. • The phrase appeared in reference either to the deathbed or to periods of illness that excused a person from fulfilling an obligation. See LIEGE POUSTIE.

in lecto mortali (in **lek**-toh mor-**tay**-lɪ), *adv.* & *adj.* [Latin] On the deathbed.

in legal custody. See IN CUSTODIA LEGIS.

in libera elemosina. See IN LIBERAM ELEMOSINAM.

in liberam baroniam (in **lib**-ər-əm bə-**roh**-nee-əm). [Law Latin] Into a free barony.

> "In former times, many persons holding certain feudal rights from the Crown were called barons, but in the strict legal sense, the title was only due to him whose lands had been erected or confirmed by the king *in liberam baroniam*. The advantages conferred by the right of barony were considerable. Such a right conferred on the baron both civil and criminal jurisdiction within his barony; and under the clause of union contained in his charter, he was enabled to take infeftment in the whole lands and rights of the barony in, what was at that time, an easy and inexpensive mode." John Trayner, *Trayner's Latin Maxims* 264 (4th ed. 1894).

in liberam elemosinam (in **lib**-ər-əm el-ə-mə-**sɪ**-nəm). [Latin "in free alms"] Of, relating to, or involving land given away for a charitable purpose; land given away to be held in frankalmoin. — Also spelled *in liberam eleemosinam.* — Also termed *in libera elemosina.* See FRANKALMOIN.

in liberam regalitatem (in **lib**-ər-əm ri-gal-ə-**tay**-təm). [Law Latin] Into a free regality. • The phrase appeared in reference to feudal land grants that were made by the Crown and that gave the grantees jurisdiction over criminal and civil matters in their territory equivalent to that of the Crown.

in libero sochagio (in **lib**-ər-oh sə-**kay**-jee-oh), *adv.* [Law Latin] In free socage. See SOCAGE.

in lieu of. (13c) Instead of or in place of; in exchange or return for <the creditor took a note in lieu of cash> <the defendant was released in lieu of $5,000 bond>.

in lieu tax. See TAX.

in limine (in **lim**-ə-nee), *adv.* [Latin "at the outset"] (18c) Preliminarily; presented to only the judge, before or during trial <a question to be decided in limine>. See MOTION IN LIMINE.

in-limine, *adj.* (1963) (Of a motion or order) raised preliminarily, esp. because of an issue about the admissibility of evidence believed by the movant to be prejudicial <in-limine motion>.

in linea recta (in **lin**-ee-ə **rek**-tə). [Latin] In the direct line (of succession).

in litem (in **lɪ**-tem *or* -təm), *adv.* [Latin] For a suit; to the suit. See AD LITEM.

in loco (in **loh**-koh). [Latin] (18c) In the place of.

in loco parentis (in **loh**-koh pə-**ren**-tis), *adv.* & *adj.* [Latin "in the place of a parent"] (18c) Of, relating to, or acting as a temporary guardian or caretaker of a child, taking on all or some of the responsibilities of a parent. • The Supreme Court has recognized that during the school day, a teacher or administrator may act *in loco parentis. See Vernonia*

Sch. Dist. v. Acton, 515 U.S. 646, 654, 115 S.Ct. 2386, 2391 (1995). See *person in loco parentis* under PERSON (1).

in loco parentis, *n.* Supervision of a young adult by an administrative body such as a university.

in lucro captando (in **loo**-kroh kap-**tan**-doh). [Latin] In endeavoring to gain an advantage.

in majorem cautelam (in mə-**jor**-əm kaw-**tee**-ləm), *adv.* [Latin] For a greater security.

in majorem evidentiam (in mə-**jor**-əm ev-ə-**den**-shee-əm). [Law Latin] For more certain proof; for more sure evidence.

in mala fide (in **mal**-ə **fɪ**-dee). [Latin] In bad faith. See BAD FAITH.

> "A possessor *in mala fide* is one who holds possession of a subject, in the knowledge that it is not his own, on a title which he knows, or has reasonable ground for believing to be a bad one." John Trayner, *Trayner's Latin Maxims* 266 (4th ed. 1894).

in mancipio (in man-**sip**-ee-oh), *adj.* [Latin] *Roman law.* In a state of civil bondage. • This status applied to a son whose father was sued in a noxal action and settled the claim by handing over his son. See NOXAL ACTION (1).

in manu mortua. See IN MORTUA MANU.

in-marriage. See MARRIAGE (1).

inmate. (16c) **1.** A person confined in a prison, hospital, or similar institution. **2.** *Archaic.* A person living inside a place; one who lives with others in a dwelling.

Inmate Financial Responsibility Program. A federal program for the payment by convicted prisoners of financial penalties while they are incarcerated or on supervised release. — Abbr. IFRP.

inmate record coordinator. (1983) In some jurisdictions, a state correctional officer who plans the schedules of prisoners, including attorney–client consultations. — Abbr. IRC.

in medias res (in **mee**-dee-əs **reez** *or* in **me**-dee-ahs **rays**), *adv.* [Latin] (18c) Into the middle of things; without preface or introduction.

in medio (in **mee**-dee-oh). [Law Latin] *Scots law.* In the middle; intermediate. • The phrase appeared in reference to a fund in controversy.

in meditatione fugae (in med-i-tay-shee-**oh**-nee **f[y]oo**-jee). [Law Latin] *Scots law.* Meditating flight; contemplating leaving the country. • Formerly, a debtor could be detained under a *fugae* warrant if the debtor had sufficient debt to warrant imprisonment, and if the debtor was attempting to leave the country. This type of warrant became obsolete when imprisonment for debt was abolished.

in mercy, *adv.* (17c) At a judge's discretion concerning punishment. • A judgment formerly noted (using the Law Latin phrase *in misericordia*) which litigant lost by stating that the unsuccessful party was in the court's mercy. A plaintiff held in mercy for a false claim, for example, was said to be *in misericordia pro falso clamore suo.*

in misericordia (in miz-ə-ri-**kor**-dee-ə). [Law Latin] See IN MERCY.

in mitigation. (18c) For the purpose of reducing or offsetting the seriousness of an act or making it easier to forgive.

in mitiori sensu (in mish-ee-**or**-ɪ **sens**-[y]oo), *adv.* [Law Latin] In a milder or more favorable sense. • This phrase appeared as part of the former rule applied in slander actions. A word capable of two meanings would be given the one more favorable to the defendant. Cf. INNOCENT-CONSTRUCTION RULE.

> "Within half a century of its first appearance, the action for words had become part of the everyday business of the common-law courts, in particular the King's Bench. In the early days there were often more slander cases in the rolls than *assumpsit* . . . . The judges apparently came to regret this aspect of their increased jurisdiction, especially since juries frequently awarded sums of money quite disproportionate to the harm and to the ability of the wrongdoer to pay . . . . [T]he principal effect of the judicial reaction was that a spirit of repression began to manifest itself . . . . The . . . most effective attack was launched in the 1570s, when the courts began the policy of construing ambiguous or doubtful words in the milder sense (*in mitiori sensu*) so that they would not be actionable." J.H. Baker, *An Introduction to English Legal History* 500–01 (3d ed. 1990).

in modum adminiculi (in **moh**-dəm ad-mi-**nik**-yə-lɪ). [Law Latin] As corroborating evidence.

in modum assisae (in **moh**-dəm ə-**sɪ**-zee), *adv.* [Law Latin] In the manner or form of an assize. See ASSIZE.

in modum juratae (in **moh**-dəm juu-**ray**-tee), *adv.* [Law Latin] In the manner or form of a jury.

in modum poenae (in **moh**-dəm **pee**-nee). [Latin] By way of penalty. • The phrase appeared in reference to the basis for charging interest.

in modum probationis (in **moh**-dəm proh-bay-shee-**oh**-nis). [Latin] In the form of proof. • The phrase appeared in reference to documents that a party provided to support a claim.

in modum simplicis querelae (in **moh**-dəm **sim**-plə-sis kwə-**ree**-lee). [Law Latin] By way of summary complaint.

in mora (in **mor**-ə), *adv.* & *adj.* [Latin] *Roman law.* In delay; in default. • This was said of a debtor who delayed performance or failed to perform.

in mortua manu (in **mor**-choo-ə **man**-yoo), *adj.* & *adv.* [Law Latin "in a dead hand"] (Of property) perpetually controlled according to a decedent's directions. • Land held by a religious society was described this way because the church could hold property perpetually without rendering feudal service. — Also termed *in manu mortua.* See DEADHAND CONTROL; MORTMAIN.

in mundo (in **mən**-doh *or* muun-doh). [Law Latin "in the world"] In a clean, fair copy.

> "Papers written '*in mundo*,' are what are usually termed extended, or clean copies." John Trayner, *Trayner's Latin Maxims* 268 (4th ed. 1894).

innavigable (in-**nav**-i-gə-bəl), *adj.* (16c) **1.** (Of a body of water) not capable of, or unsuitable for, navigation. **2.** *Marine insurance.* (Of a vessel) unfit for service. — Also termed *unnavigable.*

inner bar. (17c) *English law.* The group of senior barristers, called the Queen's Counsel or King's Counsel, who are admitted to plead within the bar of the court. Cf. OUTER BAR.

inner barrister. See BARRISTER.

inner cabinet. See CABINET.

inner-city post-traumatic-stress defense. See URBAN-SURVIVAL SYNDROME.

Inner House. *Scots law.* The appellate jurisdiction of the Court of Session. See COURT OF SESSION (1).

inning. (*pl.*) (16c) Land reclaimed from the sea.

innkeeper. (15c) Someone who, for compensation, keeps open a public house for the lodging and entertainment of travelers. • A keeper of a boarding house is usu. not considered an innkeeper. — Also termed *hotelkeeper.*

> "The definition of the black letter text, 'The innkeeper is one who holds himself out to the public to furnish either lodging alone, or lodging with some other form of entertainment, to transients for hire,' is substantially that of Prof. Goddard. It will be seen that this definition involves four elements: (1) A public holding out by the innkeeper (2) as one ready to furnish lodging at least (3) to transients (4) for hire." Armistead M. Dobie, *Handbook on the Law of Bailments and Carriers* 243 (1914).

> "The innkeeper is the person who on his own account carries on the business of an inn. In other words, he is the proprietor of the establishment. The person actually employed as manager, though he has the whole direction of the enterprise, is not an innkeeper if he is acting on behalf of someone else. Thus the salaried manager of a hotel owned or operated by a corporation is not held responsible as an innkeeper; the corporation is the innkeeper." John H. Sherry, *The Laws of Innkeepers* § 2.6, at 15 (rev. ed. 1981).

innkeeper's liability. See LIABILITY.

innkeeper's lien. See *hotelkeeper's lien* under LIEN.

innocence, *n.* (14c) The absence of guilt; esp., freedom from guilt for a particular offense. Cf. GUILT.

▸ **actual innocence.** (1839) *Criminal law.* The absence of facts that are prerequisites for the sentence given to a defendant. • In death-penalty cases, actual innocence is an exception to the cause-and-prejudice rule, and can result in a successful challenge to the death sentence on the basis of a defense that was not presented to the trial court. The prisoner must show by clear and convincing evidence that, but for constitutional error in the trial court, no reasonable judge or juror would find the defendant eligible for the death penalty. *See Sawyer v. Whitley*, 505 U.S. 333, 336, 112 S.Ct. 2514, 2517 (1992). Cf. CAUSE-AND-PREJUDICE RULE.

▸ **legal innocence.** (1813) *Criminal law.* The absence of one or more procedural or legal bases to support the sentence given to a defendant. • In the context of a petition for writ of habeas corpus or other attack on the sentence, legal innocence is often contrasted with actual innocence. Actual innocence, which focuses on the facts underlying the sentence, can sometimes be used to obtain relief from the death penalty based on trial-court errors that were not objected to at trial, even if the petitioner cannot meet the elements of the cause-and-prejudice rule. But legal innocence, which focuses on the applicable law and procedure, is not as readily available. Inadvertence or a poor trial strategy resulting in the defendant's failure to assert an established legal principle will not ordinarily be sufficient to satisfy the cause-and-prejudice rule or to establish the right to an exception to that rule. See CAUSE-AND-PREJUDICE RULE.

innocence proffer. (2003) *Criminal law.* A meeting at which a criminal defendant and his or her lawyer try to persuade one or more prosecutors to drop the charges because they are baseless or unsustainable.

innocent, *adj.* (14c) Free from guilt; free from legal fault. See NOT GUILTY (2).

innocent agent. See AGENT.

innocent-construction rule. (1958) The doctrine that an allegedly libelous statement will be given an innocuous interpretation if the statement is either ambiguous or harmless. Cf. IN MITIORI SENSU.

innocent conversion. See *technical conversion* under CONVERSION (2).

innocent converter. See CONVERTER.

innocent conveyance. See CONVEYANCE (1).

innocent dissemination. See *defense of innocent dissemination* under DEFENSE (1).

innocent homicide. See HOMICIDE.

innocent infringement. See INFRINGEMENT.

innocent junior user. See JUNIOR USER.

innocent misrepresentation. See MISREPRESENTATION.

innocent nondisclosure. See NONDISCLOSURE.

innocent owner. See OWNER.

innocent-owner defense. See DEFENSE (1).

innocent party. See PARTY (2).

innocent passage. (1828) *Int'l law.* The right of a foreign ship to pass through a country's territorial waters; the right of a foreign vessel to travel through a country's maritime belt without paying a toll. • The right of innocent passage is guaranteed in Article 17 of the United Nations Convention on the Law of the Sea. Passage is considered innocent as long as it is not prejudicial to the peace, good order, and security of the coastal country. — Also termed *right of innocent passage.* Cf. TRANSIT PASSAGE.

> "The term 'innocent passage' accurately denotes the nature of the right as well as its limitations. In the first place it is a right of 'passage,' that is to say, a right to use the waters as a thoroughfare between two points outside them; a ship proceeding through the maritime belt to a port of the coastal state would not be exercising a right of passage. In the second place the passage must be 'innocent'; a ship exercising the right must respect the local regulations as to navigation, pilotage, and the like, and, of course, it must not do any act which might disturb the tranquillity of the coastal state." J.L. Brierly, *The Law of Nations* 188-89 (5th ed. 1955).

innocent purchaser. See *bona fide purchaser* under PURCHASER (1).

innocent purchaser for value. See *bona fide purchaser* under PURCHASER (1).

innocent spouse. See SPOUSE.

innocent trespass. See TRESPASS.

innocent trespasser. See TRESPASSER.

innocuae utilitatis (i-**nok**-yoo-[w]ee yoo-til-ə-**tay**-tis). [Latin "useful without harming"] *Hist.* An act that is beneficial to one person and harmful to no one.

Inn of Chancery. *Hist.* Any of nine collegiate houses where students studied either to gain entry into an Inn of Court or to learn how to frame writs in order to serve in the chancery courts. • Over time, the Inns — Clement's, Clifford's, Lyon's, Furnival's, Thavies,' Symond's, Barnard's, Staples,' and the New Inn — became little more than dining clubs, and never exercised control over their members as the Inns of Court did. The Inns of Chancery were all dissolved in the 19th century. Cf. INN OF COURT.

Inn of Court. 1. Any of four autonomous institutions, at least one of which English barristers must join to receive their training and of which they remain members for life. • The four are Lincoln's Inn, the Middle Temple, the Inner Temple, and Gray's Inn. These powerful bodies examine candidates for the Bar, "call" them to the Bar, and award the degree of barrister.

> "It is impossible to fix with certainty the period when the professors and students of the common law first began to associate themselves together as a society, and form themselves into collegiate order; or to assign an exact date to the foundation of the Inns of Court, the original institution of which nowhere precisely appears. . . . After the fixing of the Court of Common Pleas by Magna Charta, the practitioners of the municipal law took up their residence in houses between the king's courts at Westminster and the city of London — forming then one community; and before the end of the reign of Edward II, they appear to have divided themselves into separate inns or colleges, at Temple Bar, Lincoln's Inn, and Gray's Inn." Robert H. Pearce, *A Guide to the Inns of Court and Chancery* 1–2 (1855).

2. (*pl.*) In the United States, an organization whose purpose is to emphasize practice skills, professionalism, and ethics, and to provide mentors to train students and young lawyers in the finer points of good legal practice. • Formally named the *American Inns of Court Foundation*, the organization has more than 100 local chapters whose members include judges, practicing attorneys, law professors, and law students.

innominate (i-**nom**-ə-nət), *adj.* (17c) *Civil law.* Unclassified; having no special name or designation. See *innominate contract* under CONTRACT.

innominate action. See ACTION (4).

innominate contract. See CONTRACT.

innominate obligations. (1949) Obligations having no specific classification or name because they are not strictly contractual, delictual, or quasi-contractual. • An example is the obligation of a trustee to a beneficiary. — Also termed *obligationes innominati.*

innominate real contract. See *innominate contract* under CONTRACT.

in nomine Dei, Amen (in **nahm**-ə-nee **dee**-ɪ, ay-**men**). [Latin] In the name of God, Amen. • This phrase formerly appeared at the beginning of a will or other instrument.

innotescimus (in-oh-**tes**-ə-məs). [Law Latin "we make known"] (17c) *Hist.* A certification, in the form of letters patent, of a charter of feoffment or other instrument not filed of record. • This term derives from the word of emphasis appearing at the end of the document. See LETTERS PATENT (1). Cf. EXEMPLIFICATION.

innovata lite dependente (in-oh-**vay**-tə **lɪ**-tee dee-pen-**den**-tee). [Law Latin] *Hist.* Innovations during the pendency of a suit. • The phrase appeared in reference to the interference with something that is the subject of a lawsuit. See PENDENTE LITE.

innovation. *Scots law.* See NOVATION.

innoxiare (i-nok-shee-**air**-ee), *vb.* [Law Latin] To purge (someone) of fault.

in nubibus (in **n[y]oo**-bi-bəs), *adv.* & *adj.* [Law Latin] (16c) In the clouds. • An expression for something that is under the protection of the law.

in nudis finibus contractus (in **n[y]oo**-dis **fin**-ə-bəs kən-**trak**-təs). [Law Latin] In the bare terms of a contract.

in nudis terminis (in **n[y]oo**-dis **tər**-mə-nis). [Law Latin "with bare limits"] In its bare terms. • The phrase appeared in reference to the simple terms of an instrument. See NUDUM PACTUM.

innuendo (in-yoo-**en**-doh). [Latin "by hinting"] (17c) **1.** An oblique remark or indirect suggestion, usu. of a derogatory nature. **2.** An explanatory word or passage inserted parenthetically into a legal document. • In criminal law, an innuendo is a statement in an indictment showing the application or meaning of matter previously expressed, the meaning of which would not otherwise be clear. In the law of defamation, an innuendo is the plaintiff's explanation of a statement's defamatory meaning when that meaning is not apparent from the statement's face. For example, the innuendo of the statement "David burned down his house" can be shown by pleading that the statement was understood to mean that David was defrauding his insurance company (the fact that he had insured his house is pleaded and proved by *inducement*). Cf. INDUCEMENT (4); COLLOQUIUM.

> "Innuendo (from *innuo*, to nod or beckon with the head) is a word used in declarations and law pleadings, to ascertain a person or thing which was named before . . . . If a man say, that such a one had the pox, innuendo the French pox, this will not be admitted, because the French pox was not mentioned before, and the words shall be construed in a more favourable sense. But, if in discourse of the French pox, one say, that such a one had the pox, innuendo the French pox, this will be admitted to render that certain which was uncertain before." 2 Richard Burn, *A New Law Dictionary* 24 (1792).

> "It is not a true innuendo to repeat the obvious meaning of defamatory words in other language, or in an embroidered or exaggerated way. Otherwise an ingenious pleader could perplex the judge and jury and harry the defendant by ringing the changes on the same words, creating numerous different causes of action, each requiring a separate verdict. A true innuendo relies on a conjunction of the words used and some extrinsic fact. Thus it is defamatory in itself to say that a man's affairs are being investigated by the Fraud Squad: but the statement does not support the innuendo that those affairs are being carried on fraudulently. Conversely, the statement 'X is a good advertiser' is innocent in itself, but carries a libellous innuendo if published to persons who know the extrinsic fact that X is an eminent member of the Bar." R.F.V. Heuston, *Salmond on the Law of Torts* 149 (17th ed. 1977). [The example about lawyers' advertising no longer has relevance to American law. — Eds.]

in nullius bonis (in nə-**lɪ**-əs **boh**-nis). See NULLIUS IN BONIS.

in nullo est erratum (in **nəl**-oh est i-**ray**-təm), *adj.* [Law Latin "in nothing is there error"] Of, relating to, or involving a demurrer that denies any error and at once refers a question of law to the court.

in obligatione (in ob-li-gay-shee-**oh**-nee). [Latin] Under an obligation.

in odium (in **oh**-dee-əm). [Latin] In detestation. • For example, a gift made to a woman who was later divorced for committing adultery was revoked *in odium* of her guilt.

in odium corrumpentis (in **oh**-dee-əm kor-əm-**pen**-tis). [Latin] In detestation of the person corrupting.

inofficiosus (in-ə-fish-ee-**oh**-səs), *adj.* [Latin "inofficious"] *Roman law.* Contrary to a natural duty of affection, used esp. of a will that unjustly disinherits a child or close relative. See QUERELA INOFFICIOSI TESTAMENTI.

inofficious testament. See TESTAMENT.

inofficious will. See *inofficious testament* under TESTAMENT.

in omnibus (in **ahm**-ni-bəs). [Latin] In all things; on all points <a case parallel *in omnibus*>.

inoperable mode. (1990) *Patents.* In a patent application, a disclosed way of working an invention that is not the best mode. • The term usu. designates a mode that is intended to misrepresent or deliberately conceal the best mode. That misrepresentation or concealment is inequitable conduct that will bar patentability or render an issued patent unenforceable.

inoperative, *adj.* (17c) **1.** Having no force or effect; not operative <an inoperative statute>. **2.** *Patents.* (Of an invention), the condition of not being capable of functioning as described in the patent application.

> "An invention is inoperative if an exemplification, built exactly as described in the patent, won't operate, or if further experiment and invention are required to make it operate." Roger Sherman Hoar, *Patent Tactics and Law* 37 (3d ed. 1950).

inops consilii (**in**-ahps kən-**sil**-ee-ı), *adj.* [Latin] (17c) Destitute of counsel; without legal counsel. • This term described actions taken without benefit of legal advice, as when a testator drafts a will without the help of an attorney.

> "[T]hat in devises by last will and testament, (which, being often drawn up when the party is *inops consilii*, and are always more favoured in construction than formal deeds, which are presumed to be made with great caution, forethought, and advice) in these devises, I say, remainders may be created in some measure contrary to the rules before laid down . . . ." 2 William Blackstone, *Commentaries on the Laws of England* 172 (1766).

in order. (1850) **1.** Ready for business <the meeting is in order>. **2.** Available and appropriate for consideration under the applicable rules <the motion is in order>. Cf. OUT OF ORDER (1).

inordinatus (in-or-də-**nay**-təs), *n.* [Latin "disorderly; unordained"] See INTESTATE.

in pacato solo (in pə-**kay**-toh **soh**-loh), *adv.* [Latin] In a country that is at peace.

in pace Dei et regis (in **pay**-see **dee**-ı et **ree**-jis), *adv.* [Law Latin] In the peace of God and the king. • This phrase was used in an appeal from a murder conviction.

in pais (in **pay** *or* **pays**). [Law French "in the country"] Outside court or legal proceedings. See *equitable estoppel* (1) under ESTOPPEL.

in paper. (18c) *Hist.* Of a proceeding that is within the jurisdiction of the trial court; that is, before the record is prepared for an appeal.

> "Formerly, the suitors were much perplexed by writs of error brought upon very slight and trivial grounds, as misspellings and other mistakes of the clerks, all which might be amended at the common law, while all the proceedings were in *paper*, for they were then considered in *fieri*, and therefore subject to the control of the courts." 3 William Blackstone, *Commentaries on the Laws of England* 407 (1768).

in pari causa (in **par**-ı **kaw**-zə), *adv.* [Latin "in an equal case"] In a case affecting two parties equally or in which they have equal rights <*in pari causa*, the possessor ordinarily defeats the nonpossessory claimant>.

in pari delicto (in **par**-ı də-**lik**-toh), *adv.* [Latin "in equal fault"] Equally at fault <the court denied relief because both parties stood *in pari delicto*>.

***in pari delicto* doctrine,** *n.* [Latin] (1917) The principle that a plaintiff who has participated in wrongdoing may not recover damages resulting from the wrongdoing. See DOCTRINE OF IMPUTED KNOWLEDGE. Cf. CLEAN-HANDS DOCTRINE.

in pari materia (in **par**-ı mə-**teer**-ee-ə). [Latin "in the same matter"] **1.** *adj.* On the same subject; relating to the same matter. • It is a canon of construction that statutes that are *in pari materia* may be construed together, so that inconsistencies in one statute may be resolved by looking at another statute on the same subject. See RELATED-STATUTES CANON; *cognate act* under ACT (3).

> "[I]t seems that the present position is that, when an earlier statute is *in pari materia* with a later one, it is simply part of its context to be considered by the judge in deciding whether the meaning of a provision in the later statute is plain." Rupert Cross, *Statutory Interpretation* 128 (1976).

2. *adv.* Loosely, in conjunction with <the Maryland constitutional provision is construed *in pari materia* with the Fourth Amendment>.

in patiendo (in pash-ee-**en**-doh), *adv.* & *adj.* [fr. Latin *patior* "suffer"] In suffering or permitting.

in patria potestate (in **pay**-tree-ə [*or* **pa**-tree-ə] poh-tes-**tay**-tee). [Latin] *Roman law.* (Of a person) in the power of the father or a senior male ascendant; subject to *patria potestas.* • Uncles and brothers never had power over nephews or younger brothers. See *patria potestas* under POTESTAS; SUB POTESTATE. Cf. SUI JURIS.

in patrimonio principis (in pa-trə-**moh**-nee-oh **prin**-si-pis). [Latin] See INTER REGALIA.

in pectore judicis (in **pek**-tə-ree **joo**-di-sis), *adv.* & *adj.* [Latin] In the breast of the court. See BREAST OF THE COURT.

in pejorem partem (in pə-**jor**-əm **pahr**-təm), *adv.* [Law Latin] In the worst part; on the worst side.

in pendente (in pen-**den**-tee). [Latin] In suspension; in abeyance.

inpenny and outpenny. (14c) *Hist.* A customary payment of a penny on entering into and going out of a tenancy.

in periculo constitutus (in pə-**rik**-yə-loh kon-sti-**t[y]oo**-təs). [Latin] Standing in danger.

in perpetuam commendam (in pər-**pech**-oo-əm kə-**men**-dəm). [Law Latin] In perpetual trust. • Something given *in perpetuam commendam* was equivalent to a gift.

in perpetuam rei memoriam (in pər-**pech**-oo-əm [*or* pər-**pe**-tyoo-əm] **ree**-ı mə-**mor**-ee-əm), *adv.* [Latin] In perpetual memory of a matter. • This phrase refers to a deposition taken to preserve the deponent's testimony.

in perpetuity (in pər-pə-**t[y]oo**-ə-tee). (14c) Forever; without end. See PERPETUITY.

in perpetuum (in pər-**pech**-oo-əm *or* pər-**pe**-tyoo-əm), *adv.* [Latin] (17c) Forever; perpetually. — Sometimes spelled *imperpetuum.*

in perpetuum rei testimonium (in pər-**pech**-oo-əm [*or* pər-**pe**-tyoo-əm] **ree**-ı tes-ti-**moh**-nee-əm), *adv.* [Law Latin] In perpetual testimony of a matter. • This phrase refers to a statute that confirms existing common law.

"Statutes also are either *declaratory* of the common law, or *remedial* of some defects therein. Declaratory, where the old custom of the kingdom is almost fallen into disuse, or become disputable; in which case the parliament has thought proper, *in perpetuum rei testimonium*, and for avoiding all doubts and difficulties, to declare what the common law is and ever hath been." 1 William Blackstone, *Commentaries on the Laws of England* 86 (1765).

in personam (in pər-**soh**-nəm), *adj.* [Latin "against a person"] (18c) **1.** Involving or determining the personal rights and obligations of the parties. **2.** *Civil procedure.* (Of a legal action) brought against a person rather than property. — Also termed *personal.* See *action in personam* under ACTION (4). Cf. IN REM. — **in personam,** *adv.*

"An action is said to be *in personam* when its object is to determine the rights and interests of the parties themselves in the subject-matter of the action, however the action may arise, and the effect of a judgment in such an action is merely to bind the parties to it. A normal action brought by one person against another for breach of contract is a common example of an action *in personam*." R.H. Graveson, *Conflict of Laws* 98 (7th ed. 1974).

in personam judgment. See *personal judgment* under JUDGMENT (2).

in personam jurisdiction. See *personal jurisdiction* under JURISDICTION.

in pessima fide (in **pes**-ə-mə **fɪ**-dee). [Latin] In the worst faith; dishonestly.

in petitorio (in pet-ə-**tor**-ee-oh). [Latin] In a petitory action.

in pios usus (in **pɪ**-əs **yoo**-səs), *adv.* [Law Latin] For pious uses; for religious purposes. • This phrase referred to property used by, or claimed by, the church, such as the property of an intestate who had no known heirs.

in placito (in **plas**-ə-toh). [Law Latin] In a suit.

in plena vita (in **plee**-nə **vɪ**-tə), *adv.* & *adj.* [Law Latin] In full life.

in pleno comitatu (in **plee**-noh kahm-i-**tay**-t[y]oo), *adv.* & *adj.* [Law Latin] In full county court.

in pleno lumine (in **plee**-noh **loo**-mə-nee), *adv.* & *adj.* [Law Latin] In the light of day; in common knowledge; in public.

in poenam (in **pee**-nəm). [Latin] As a penalty; as a punishment.

in point. See ON POINT.

in posse (in **pos**-ee). [Latin] Not currently existing, but ready to come into existence under certain conditions in the future; potential <the will contemplated both living children and children *in posse*>. Cf. IN ESSE.

in possessorio (in pah-ses-**sor**-ee-oh). [Law Latin] In a possessory suit.

in potestate parentis (in poh-tes-**tay**-tee pə-**ren**-tis), *adv.* & *adj.* [Latin] In the power of a parent. See *patria potestas* under POTESTAS.

in potestate patris (in poh-tes-**tay**-tee **pay**-tris *or* **pa**-tris). [Latin] *Roman law.* Under the power of the father. • The phrase appeared in reference to the position of a child in power. See *patria potestas* under POTESTAS; SUB POTESTATE. Cf. SUI JURIS.

in potestate viri (in poh-tes-**tay**-tee **veer**-ɪ). [Latin] Under the power of the husband. • Formerly, this phrase appeared in reference to the position of a wife in legal matters because the husband was the guardian of the wife.

in praemissorum fidem (in pree-mə-**sor**-əm [*or* prem-ə-] **fɪ**-dəm), *adv.* & *adj.* [Law Latin] In confirmation or attestation of the premises. • This phrase commonly appeared in notarized documents.

in praesenti (in pri-**zen**-tɪ *or* pree-). [Latin] At present; right now. Cf. IN FUTURO.

in praesentia dominorum (in pri-**zen**-shee-ə dom-ə-**nor**-əm). [Latin] In presence of the lords. • The phrase was added to the presiding judge's signature to indicate that the remaining judges did not have to sign the document because the presiding judge had signed the writing in their presence. — Abbr. IPD.

in prender (in **pren**-dər), *adj.* [Law French "in taking"] *Hist.* (Of a right) consisting in property taken to fulfill a claim to it, such as an incorporeal hereditament (as a *heriot custom*) that a lord had to seize in order to exercise the right to it. Cf. IN RENDER.

in-presence rule. (1967) *Criminal procedure.* The principle that a police officer may make a warrantless arrest of a person who commits a misdemeanor offense not only in the officer's actual presence but also within the officer's immediate vicinity.

"The common law rule with respect to misdemeanors was quite different; a warrant was required except when a breach of the peace occurred in the presence of the arresting officer. . . . Though the 'in presence' rule might be construed as requiring that the misdemeanor *in fact* have occurred in the officer's presence, the modern view is that the officer may arrest if he has probable cause to believe the offense is being committed in his presence." Wayne R. LaFave & Jerold H. Israel, *Criminal Procedure* § 3.5, at 169-70 (2d ed. 1992).

in primis (in **prɪ**-mis). See IMPRIMIS.

in principio (in prin-**sip**-ee-oh), *adv.* [Latin] At the beginning.

in privato patrimonio (in prɪ-**vay**-toh pa-trə-**moh**-nee-oh). [Latin] Among private property.

inprocessing, *n.* (1972) The procedures by which a person is initially examined and prepared for admittance to a facility (such as a school, refuge, or prison). — **inprocess,** *vb.*

in promptu (in **promp**-t[y]oo), *adv.* & *adj.* [Latin "at hand"] *Archaic.* Impromptu.

in propria persona (in **proh**-pree-ə pər-**soh**-nə). [Latin "in one's own person"] See PRO SE.

in proximo gradu (in **prok**-sə-moh **gray**-d[y]oo). [Latin] *Roman law.* In the nearest degree. • The phrase appeared in reference to a child's relationship to the father or to a grandchild's relation to a grandfather if the grandchild represented his or her deceased father. See PER STIRPES.

in publica custodia (in **pəb**-li-kə kəs-**toh**-dee-ə). [Latin] In the public custody. • The phrase appeared in reference to public records.

in publicam vindictam (in **pəb**-li-kəm vin-**dik**-təm). [Latin] For vindicating public right.

in puram eleemosynam (in **pyoor**-əm el-ə-**mos**-ə-nəm). [Law Latin] In pure charity. • Gifts were sometimes made to churches *in puram eleemosynam*, requiring nothing but prayers for the grantor in return.

in quantum locupletiores facti sumus ex damno alterius (in **kwon**-təm lok-yoo-plee-shee-**or**-eez **fak**-tɪ **s[y]oo**-məs eks **dam**-noh al-**teer**-ee-əs). [Latin] *Roman law.* Insofar as we have been enriched to the loss or by the damage of another. • The phrase appeared in reference to the rule by which certain persons were bound in restitution to the extent of their enrichment. See NEGOTIORUM GESTIO.

in quantum lucratus est (in **kwon**-təm loo-**kray**-təs est). [Latin] Insofar as he has gained or profited.

in quantum valeat (in **kwon**-təm **vay**-lee-at *or* -ət). [Latin] For what it is worth.

inquest. (13c) **1.** An inquiry by a coroner or medical examiner, sometimes with the aid of a jury, into the manner of death of a person who has died under suspicious circumstances, or who has died in prison. — Also termed *coroner's inquest*; *inquisition after death*. **2.** An inquiry into a certain matter by a jury empaneled for that purpose. **3.** The finding of such a specially empaneled jury. **4.** A proceeding, usu. ex parte, to determine, after the defendant has defaulted, the amount of the plaintiff's damages. Cf. INQUISITION.

▸ **grand inquest.** (16c) **1.** An impeachment proceeding. **2.** *Hist.* (*cap.*) The survey of the lands of England in 1085–1086, by order of William the Conqueror, and resulting in the Domesday Book — Also termed *Great Inquest*; *Grand Survey*; *Great Survey*. See DOMESDAY BOOK. **3.** *Hist.* Grand jury.

▸ **inquest of office.** (16c) *Hist.* An inquest conducted by a coroner, sheriff, or other royal officer into the Crown's right to property by reason of escheat, treason, or other ground of forfeiture.

5. WARDMOTE.

inquest jury. See JURY.

in quibus infitiando lis crescit (in **kwib**-əs in-fish-ee-**an**-doh lis **kres**-it). [Latin] *Roman law.* In which the suit increases by denial. • The phrase appeared in reference to the measure of damages in a legal action when, if the defendant wrongfully denied a claim for damages, the defendant could be penalized by a multiple of the original claimed amount, usu. double, triple, or quadruple. — Also spelled *inficiando*.

inquilinus (in-kwə-**lɪ**-nəs), *n.* [Latin] *Roman law.* Someone who leases or lives in another's house or apartment; esp., an urban tenant.

inquirendo (in-kwə-**ren**-doh). [Latin] (17c) *Hist.* An inquiry or investigation; esp., an inquiry into a matter concerning the Crown's interests, such as lands that are forfeited to the Crown.

inquiry. (15c) **1.** *Int'l law.* FACT-FINDING (2). **2.** *Parliamentary law.* A request for information, either procedural or substantive. See REQUEST; POINT (2).

▸ **parliamentary inquiry.** (18c) An inquiry that asks a question about procedure.

3. *Hist.* A writ to assess damages by the sheriff or sheriff's deputies.

inquiry notice. See NOTICE (3).

inquisitio (in-kwə-**zish**-ee-oh). [Latin] Inquisition or inquest. See INQUISITION (1).

▸ ***inquisitio post mortem*** (in-kwə-**zish**-ee-oh pohst **mor**-təm). [Latin] See *inquest of office* under INQUEST (4).

inquisition. (14c) **1.** The record of the finding of the jury sworn by the coroner to inquire into a person's death. **2.** A judicial inquiry, esp. in a derogatory sense. **3.** *Hist. Eccles. law.* A persistent, grueling examination conducted without regard for the examinee's dignity or civil rights. Cf. INQUEST.

inquisition after death. See INQUEST (1).

inquisitor. (16c) **1.** An officer who examines and inquires, such as a coroner or sheriff. **2.** Someone who inquires; esp., one who examines another in a harsh or hostile manner. **3.** *Hist. Eccles. law.* An officer authorized to inquire into heresies; esp., an officer of the Spanish Inquisition.

inquisitorial court. See COURT.

inquisitorial system. (18c) A system of proof-taking used in civil law, whereby the judge conducts the trial, determines what questions to ask, and defines the scope and the extent of the inquiry. • This system prevails in most of continental Europe, in Japan, and in Central and South America. Cf. ADVERSARY SYSTEM.

INR. *abbr.* BUREAU OF INTELLIGENCE AND RESEARCH.

in re (in **ree** *or* **ray**). [Latin "in the matter of"] (1877) (Of a judicial proceeding) not formally including adverse parties, but rather involving something (such as an estate). • The term is often used in case citations, esp. in uncontested proceedings <*In re Butler's Estate*>. — Also termed *matter of* <*Matter of Butler's Estate*>.

in rebus (in **ree**-bəs), *adv.* [Latin] In things, cases, or matters.

in rebus litigiosis (in **ree**-bəs li-tij-ee-**oh**-sis). [Latin] In things subject to litigation.

in rem (in **rem**), *adj.* [Latin "against a thing"] (18c) Involving or determining the status of a thing, and therefore the rights of persons generally with respect to that thing. — Also termed (archaically) *impersonal*. See *action in rem* under ACTION (4). Cf. IN PERSONAM. — **in rem,** *adv.*

> "An action *in rem* is one in which the judgment of the court determines the title to property and the rights of the parties, not merely as between themselves, but also as against all persons at any time dealing with them or with the property upon which the court had adjudicated." R.H. Graveson, *Conflict of Laws* 98 (7th ed. 1974).

▸ **quasi in rem** (**kway**-sɪ in **rem** *or* **kway**-zɪ). [Latin "as if against a thing"] (1804) Involving or determining the rights of a person having an interest in property located within the court's jurisdiction. See *action quasi in rem* under ACTION (4).

in re mercatoria (in **ree** mər-kə-**tor**-ee-ə). [Latin] *Scots law.* In a mercantile transaction. • Documents made in or connected with a mercantile transaction did not require the typical formalities in order to be binding.

> "All writings *in re mercatoria* are privileged, and are held valid and binding, although wanting the solemnities common and necessary to ordinary deeds . . . . This privilege has been given to these documents, because of the rapidity with which, in most cases, they have to be prepared, and the immediate use to which they have to be put, and also because, from the necessity of the case, they are generally prepared by those who are not supposed to be acquainted with the formalities and solemnities of deeds." John Trayner, *Trayner's Latin Maxims* 273 (4th ed. 1894).

in rem judgment. See *judgment in rem* under JUDGMENT (2).

in rem jurisdiction. See JURISDICTION.

in rem suam (in **rem** s[y]**oo**-əm). [Latin] Regarding one's own property; for one's own advantage.

in rem versum (in **rem vər**-səm). [Latin] *Roman law.* Employed in one's own matter; used to one's own advantage. See ACTION DE IN REM VERSO.

in render (in **ren**-dər), *adj.* [Law French "in yielding or paying"] (Of property) required to be given or rendered. Cf. IN PRENDER.

in re propria (in **ree proh**-pree-ə). [Latin] In one's own affairs.

in rerum natura (in **reer**-əm nə-**tyuur**-ə), *adv.* & *adj.* [Law Latin] In the nature of things; in existence. • This phrase was used in a dilatory plea alleging that the plaintiff was a fictitious person, and therefore not capable of bringing the action.

in retentis (in ri-**ten**-tis). [Law Latin "among things withheld"] *Scots law.* Subject to reservation. • Evidence might be taken *in retentis* if, for example, the witness were mortally ill, and then be set aside until the proper time to produce it.

in rigore juris (in **rig**-ər-ee **joor**-is). [Latin] According to strict law.

in rixa (in **rik**-sə). [Latin] *Scots law.* In an altercation or brawl. • Words spoken *in rixa* were usu. not actionable as defamation.

in rixa per plures commissa (in **rik**-sə pər **pluur**-eez [or **ploo**-reez] kə-**mis**-ə). [Latin] *Scots law.* An offense committed in the course of a quarrel involving several persons.

inroll, *vb.* See ENROLL (1).

inrollment. See ENROLLMENT.

INS. *abbr.* IMMIGRATION AND NATURALIZATION SERVICE.

in sacris (in **say**-kris). [Latin] *Scots law.* In sacred matters. • The phrase appeared in reference to the supremacy of ecclesiastical-court jurisdiction in certain matters, esp. those involving church doctrine and discipline.

insane, *adj.* (16c) Mentally deranged; suffering from one or more delusions or false beliefs that (1) have no foundation in reason or reality, (2) are not credible to any reasonable person of sound mind, and (3) cannot be overcome in a sufferer's mind by any amount of evidence or argument. See INSANITY.

insane asylum. See ASYLUM (3).

insane automatism. See AUTOMATISM.

insane delusion. (1838) An irrational, persistent belief in an imaginary state of facts resulting in a lack of capacity to undertake acts of legal consequence, such as making a will. See CAPACITY (2).

insanity, *n.* (16c) Any mental disorder severe enough that it prevents a person from having legal capacity and excuses the person from criminal or civil responsibility. • Insanity is a legal, not a medical, standard. — Also termed *legal insanity*; *lunacy.* Cf. SANITY; *diminished capacity* under CAPACITY (3).

> "The lawyers refer to 'insanity.' This is a legal term only, and one that is not used by the psychiatrist; the latter prefers to speak of mental disorder, mental illness, or of psychosis or neurosis." Winfred Overholser, *Psychiatry and the Law*, 38 Mental Hygiene 243, 244 (1954).

> "The word 'insanity' is commonly used in discussions of this problem although some other term would seem to be preferable such as 'mental disease or defect,' — which may be shortened to 'mental disorder' in general discussions if this is clearly understood to include disease of the mind, congenital lack, and damage resulting from traumatic injury, but to exclude excitement or stupefaction resulting from liquor or drugs. Apart from its uses in the law 'insanity' is usually employed to indicate mental disorder resulting from deterioration or damage as distinguished from congenital deficiency. Criminal incapacity may result as readily from one as from the other, but while the earlier authorities spoke of the 'idiot' and the 'madman,' . . . the more recent tendency in the law has been to include both under the 'insanity' label." Rollin M. Perkins & Ronald N. Boyce, *Criminal Law* 952 (3d ed. 1982).

> "Another objection to the word 'insanity' is the unwarranted assumption that it refers to a very definite mental condition, seldom put into words but apparent in many discussions of the problem." *Id.*

▸ **emotional insanity.** (1872) Insanity produced by a violent excitement of the emotions or passions, although reasoning faculties may remain unimpaired; a passion that for a period creates complete derangement of intellect. • Emotional insanity is sometimes described as an irresistible impulse to do an act. See IRRESISTIBLE-IMPULSE TEST.

▸ **partial insanity.** See *diminished capacity* under CAPACITY (3).

▸ **temporary insanity.** (18c) Insanity that exists only at the time of a criminal act.

insanity defense. *Criminal law.* (1912) An affirmative defense alleging that a mental disorder caused the accused to commit the crime. *See* 18 USCA § 17; Fed. R. Crim. P. 12.2. • Unlike other defenses, a successful insanity defense may not result in an acquittal but instead in a special verdict ("not guilty by reason of insanity") that usu. leads to the defendant's commitment to a mental institution. — Also termed *insanity plea.* See MCNAGHTEN RULES; SUBSTANTIAL-CAPACITY TEST; IRRESISTIBLE-IMPULSE TEST; DURHAM RULE; APPRECIATION TEST.

▸ **black-rage insanity defense.** (1995) An insanity defense based on an African-American's violent eruption of anger induced at least partly by racial tensions. • This defense was first used in the mid-1990s.

Insanity Defense Reform Act of 1984 test. See APPRECIATION TEST.

insanity plea. See INSANITY DEFENSE.

inscribed stock. See STOCK.

inscriptio (in-**skrip**-shee-oh), *n.* [Latin] *Roman law.* A written accusation detailed in an official register. • The accuser was liable to punishment if the accused was acquitted. See INSCRIPTION (3). Pl. ***inscriptiones*** (in-skrip-shee-**oh**-neez). — ***inscribere,*** *vb.*

inscription, *n.* (14c) **1.** The act of entering a fact or name on a list, register, or other record. **2.** An entry so recorded. **3.** *Civil law.* An agreement whereby an accuser must, if the accusation is false, receive the same punishment that the accused would have been given if found guilty. — **inscribe,** *vb.* — **inscriptive,** *adj.*

inscriptiones (in-skrip-shee-**oh**-neez). [Latin] *Hist.* Title deeds; written instruments by which rights or interests are granted.

inscrutable fault. See FAULT.

insecure, *adj.* (17c) Having a good-faith belief that the possibility of receiving payment or performance from another party to a contract is unlikely.

insecurity clause. (1872) A loan-agreement provision that allows the creditor to demand immediate and full payment of the loan balance if the creditor has reason to believe that the debtor is about to default, as when the debtor suddenly loses a significant source of income. Cf. ACCELERATION CLAUSE.

in separali (in sep-ə-**ray**-lɪ), *adv.* & *adj.* [Law Latin] In several; in severalty.

insert, *vb. Parliamentary law.* To amend a motion by placing (specified new wording) within or around the current wording. • Some authorities distinguish amendment by adding, which places new wording after the current wording, from amendment by inserting. See ADD; AMENDMENT (3).

in severalty. See SEVERALTY (2).

inside counsel. See *in-house counsel* under COUNSEL.

inside director. See DIRECTOR.

inside information. (1898) *Securities.* Information about a company's financial or market situation obtained not from public disclosure, but from a source within the company or a source that owes the company a duty to keep the information confidential. — Also termed *insider information.* See INSIDER TRADING.

insider. (1848) **1.** *Securities.* Someone who has knowledge of facts not available to the general public.

▸ **temporary insider.** (1983) A person or firm that receives inside information in the course of performing professional duties for a client. • Generally, that person or firm is subject to the same proscriptions as an insider.

2. Someone who takes part in the control of a corporation, such as an officer or director, or one who owns 10% or more of the corporation's stock. **3.** *Bankruptcy.* An entity or person who is so closely related to a debtor that any deal between them will not be considered an arm's-length transaction and will be subject to close scrutiny.

insider dealing. See INSIDER TRADING.

insider information. See INSIDE INFORMATION.

insider preference. See PREFERENCE.

insider report. See REPORT (1).

insider trading. (1940) *Securities.* The use of material, nonpublic information in trading the shares of a company by a corporate insider or other person who owes a fiduciary duty to the company. • This is the classic definition. The Supreme Court has also approved a broader definition, known as the "misappropriation theory": the deceitful acquisition and misuse of information that properly belongs to persons to whom one owes a duty. Thus, under the misappropriation theory, it is insider trading for a lawyer to trade in the stock of XYZ Corp. after learning that a client of the lawyer's firm is planning a takeover of XYZ. But under the classic definition, that is not insider trading because the lawyer owed no duty to XYZ itself. See BLACKOUT POLICY. — Also termed *insider dealing.*

"'What is insider trading?' The term is probably best defined, to the extent any definition is adequate, as 'the purchase or sale of securities on the basis of material, non-public information.' What counts as 'non-public information'? What non-public information can be deemed 'material'? When is a trader who is in possession of material, non- public information trading 'on the basis of' that information? Must the information be about the company whose securities are being purchased or sold? What characteristics establish 'insider' status sufficient to warrant legal proscriptions of trading? These are all questions that are derived from the definition of insider trading just offered . . . ." C. Edward Fletcher, *Materials on the Law of Insider Trading* 3 (1991).

"A number of different parties may be subject to a variety of monetary penalties under the federal securities laws for engaging in illegal insider trading. These parties may include actual traders, their tippers, as well as broker-dealers and investment advisors (when they fail to take appropriate steps to prevent the insider trading violation(s) or fail to maintain and enforce policies and procedures reasonably designed to prevent the occurrence of such trading). Measures that may be ordered include (1) requiring the subject party to 'disgorge' the ill-gotten profits (or loss avoided) in an SEC enforcement action, (2) subjecting individuals to a maximum criminal fine of $1 million and 10 years imprisonment, and (3) in an SEC enforcement action, within a court's discretion, ordering the subject party to pay into the U.S. Treasury a treble damage penalty amounting to three times the profit gained or loss avoided." Marc I. Steinberg, *Understanding Securities Law* 277–78 (2d ed. 1996).

insidiatio viarum (in-sid-ee-**ay**-shee-oh vɪ-**air**-əm). [Latin "ambush on the highway"] *Hist.* The crime of waylaying someone along the roadway. See LATROCINATION; HIGHWAYMAN.

insilium (in-**sil**-ee-əm). [Law Latin] *Hist.* Pernicious advice or counsel.

in simili materia (in **sim**-ə-lɪ mə-**teer**-ee-ə), *adv.* & *adj.* [Law Latin] Of the same or a similar subject matter.

insimul (in-**sim**-əl *or* **in**-si-məl), *adv.* [Latin] Together, jointly.

insimul computassent (in-**sim**-əl *or* **in**-si-məl kahm-pyoo-**tas**-ənt). [Law Latin "they accounted together"] (18c) *Hist.* A count in an assumpsit action asserting that the parties had reviewed their accounts and that the defendant voluntarily agreed to pay the amount sought by the plaintiff. • This term derives from the initial words of the count.

insimul tenuit (in-**sim**-əl *or* **in**-si-məl **ten**-yoo-it). [Law Latin "he held together"] (17c) *Hist.* A writ brought by a coparcener to recover a fee tail alienated by an earlier tenant; a type of *formedon in the descender.* See *formedon in the descender* under FORMEDON.

insinuare (in-sin-yoo-**air**-ee), *vb.* [Latin] *Roman & civil law.* To register; to deposit (an instrument) with a public registry.

insinuatio (in-sin-yoo-**ay**-shee-oh). [Law Latin] *Hist.* Information or suggestion. • This term sometimes appeared in the phrase *ex insinuatione* ("on the information"), which is the precursor to the modern *on information and belief.* See INFORMATION AND BELIEF.

insinuation (in-sin-yoo-**ay**-shən). (16c) *Civil law.* **1.** The act of depositing (an instrument) with a public registry for recording. **2.** A document that evidences a donation of property.

insinuation of a will. (1913) *Civil law.* The first production of a will for probate.

insist, *vb.* (Of a house in a bicameral legislature) to reaffirm (an amendment) that the other house has considered but in which it has not concurred, or to reaffirm nonconcurrence in an amendment from which the other house has not receded. • An insistence often results in a request for a conference. See CONCUR (3); CONFERENCE (2); RECEDE. Cf. ADHERE (1). — **insistence,** *n.*

"When one house refuses to recede from its amendments, the bill is not thereby lost, because the house may vote to insist upon its amendments. A message is sent to the other house stating that the house has insisted upon its amendments and is usually accompanied by a request for conference. When one house insists upon its amendments, the other house may then insist upon its nonconcurrence in the amendments and request a conference or recede from its nonconcurrence and concur in the amendments, which would constitute a final passage of the bill with the amendments." National Conference of State Legislatures, *Mason's Manual of Legislative Procedure* § 768, at 556–57 (2000).

in situ (in **si**-t[y]oo), *adv.* [Latin] In place.

insofar as, *conj.* (1896) To the degree or extent that.

in solido (in **sol**-ə-doh). [Latin "as a whole"] (1809) (Of an obligation) creating joint and several liability. • The term is used in most civil-law jurisdictions, but no longer in Louisiana. — Also termed *in solidum.* See SOLIDARY.

in solidum (in **sol**-ə-dəm). See IN SOLIDO.

in solo (in **soh**-loh), *adv. & adj.* [Latin] In the soil or ground.

in solo alieno (in **soh**-loh ay-lee-**ee**-noh *or* al-ee-), *adv. & adj.* [Latin] In another's ground.

in solo proprio (in **soh**-loh **proh**-pree-oh), *adv. & adj.* [Latin] In one's own ground.

in solutum (in sə-**loo**-təm). [Latin] In payment.

insolvency, *n.* (17c) **1.** The condition of being unable to pay debts as they fall due or in the usual course of business. **2.** The inability to pay debts as they mature. — Also termed *failure to meet obligations; failing circumstances.* See BANKRUPTCY (1). Cf. SOLVENCY.

▸ **balance-sheet insolvency.** (1966) Insolvency created when the debtor's liabilities exceed its assets. • Under some state laws, balance-sheet insolvency prevents a corporation from making a distribution to its shareholders. — Also termed *balance-sheet test.*

▸ **equity insolvency.** (1918) Insolvency created when the debtor cannot meet its obligations as they fall due. • Under most state laws, equity insolvency prevents a corporation from making a distribution to its shareholders.

▸ **notorious insolvency.** (1802) *Scots law.* A bankruptcy; the stage of insolvency in which the debtor has publicly acknowledged insolvency under the statute. • This stage is usu. followed by sequestration, which is notorious insolvency coupled with the appointment of a trustee for creditors. — Also termed *public insolvency; notour bankruptcy.*

"Bankruptcy, according to the law of Scotland, is public or notorious insolvency. When a debtor in an obligation cannot fulfil his obligation as undertaken . . . a position which constitutes insolvency — and makes public acknowledgment, in manner determined by statute, of his inability, the status or condition of bankruptcy has arisen, and the insolvent debtor is, in the language of the statutes, a 'notour' bankrupt . . . . The law of notour bankruptcy is mainly statutory. Legislation has fixed the circumstances which constitute the status, and determined all the most important results." George Watson, *Bell's Dictionary and Digest of the Law of Scotland* 78 (3d ed. 1882).

▸ **public insolvency.** See *notorious insolvency.*

insolvency law. (1833) A statute that provides relief to a debtor who lacks the means to pay creditors. • The term is sometimes used interchangeably with *bankruptcy law* because legislative drafting may not produce a bright-line distinction. — Also termed *insolvent law.* Cf. BANKRUPTCY LAW (2).

insolvency proceeding. (1846) *Archaic.* A bankruptcy proceeding to liquidate or rehabilitate an estate. See BANKRUPTCY (2).

insolvent, *adj.* (16c) (Of a debtor) having liabilities that exceed the value of assets; having stopped paying debts in the ordinary course of business or being unable to pay them as they fall due. — **insolvent,** *n.*

insolvent estate. See ESTATE (3).

insolvent law. See INSOLVENCY LAW.

in spe (in **spee**). [Latin] In hope.

in specie (in **spee**-shee-ee *or* **spee**-shee). [Latin "in kind"] (16c) In the same or like form; IN KIND <the partners were prepared to return the borrowed items *in specie*>.

inspectator. (16c) *Archaic.* A prosecutor, adversary, or inspector.

inspectio corporis (in-**spek**-shee-oh **kor**-pər-is). [Latin] (1860) *Hist.* An inspection of the person. • An *inspectio corporis* was an actual physical examination, the performance of which was rarely allowed except in extreme cases, such as one involving the concealment of pregnancy.

inspection. (14c) A careful examination of something, such as goods (to determine their fitness for purchase) or items produced in response to a discovery request (to determine their relevance to a lawsuit).

inspection right. (1898) The legal entitlement in certain circumstances to examine articles or documents, such as a consumer's right to inspect goods before paying for them.

inspection search. See *administrative search* under SEARCH (1).

inspector. (17c) **1.** A person authorized to inspect something. See WEAPONS INSPECTOR. **2.** A police officer who ranks below a superintendent or deputy superintendent, and who is in charge of several precincts.

inspectorate (in-**spek**-tə-rət), *n.* (18c) **1.** The group of inspectors who examine and report on schools, factories, etc. **2.** The district under the supervision of an inspector. **3.** The office of an inspector.

inspector general. (*often cap.*) (18c) **1.** One of several federal officials charged with supervising a particular agency's audits or investigations. **2.** A governor-appointed state official who oversees internal review within executive agencies to ensure that there is no waste or abuse of resources.

inspector of taxes. See TAX INSPECTOR.

inspeximus (in-**spek**-si-məs), *vb.* [Latin "we have inspected"] (17c) *Hist.* A charter in which the grantor confirms an earlier charter. • *Inspeximus* was the opening word of the charter. — Also termed *vidimus.*

install, *vb.* (16c) To induct (a person) into an office or a rank <the newly elected governor was soon installed in office>.

installment, *n.* (18c) A periodic partial payment of a debt. Cf. *lump sum* under SUM.

installment accounting method. See ACCOUNTING METHOD.

installment contract. See CONTRACT.

installment credit. See CREDIT (4).

installment debt. See DEBT.

installment land contract. See CONTRACT.

installment loan. See LOAN.

installment note. See NOTE (1).

installment payment. See PAYMENT (2).

installment plan. (1876) **1.** A method or system of paying for goods or services by a series of usu. modest regular payments. — Also termed (BrE) *hire purchase.* **2.** INSTALLMENT SALE.

installment sale. (1893) A conditional sale in which the buyer makes a down payment followed by periodic payments and the seller retains title or a security interest until all payments have been received. — Also termed *installment plan; retail installment sale.*

▸ **disguised installment sale.** (1950) *Bankruptcy.* A debtor's leasing ploy to try to keep property outside the bankruptcy estate, whereby a lease either presents the lessee-debtor with a bargain purchase option or transfers title to the lessee-debtor at the end of the lease term. • When such a lease is discovered, the property is treated as part of the bankruptcy estate, meaning that to defeat competing creditors, the lessor must have perfected a security interest.

instance, *n.* (14c) **1.** An example or occurrence <there were 55 instances of reported auto theft in this small community last year>. **2.** The act of instituting legal proceedings <court of first instance>. **3.** Urgent solicitation or insistence <she applied for the job at the instance of her friend>.

instance, *vb.* (17c) To illustrate by example; to cite <counsel instanced three cases for the court to consider>.

instance court. See COURT.

instant, *adj.* (16c) This; the present (case, judgment, order, etc.); now being discussed <the instant order is not appealable>.

instantaneous crime. See CRIME.

instantaneous death. See DEATH.

instantaneous offense. See *instantaneous crime* under CRIME.

instant case. See *case at bar* under CASE (1).

instanter (in-**stan**-tər), *adv.* (17c) Instantly; at once <the defendant was ordered to file its motion instanter>.

instant-runoff voting. See VOTING.

instar (**in**-stahr). [Latin] *Hist.* Likeness; the equivalent of a thing. • This term appeared in phrases such as *instar omnium* ("equivalent or tantamount to all").

in statu quo (in **stay**-t[y]oo **kwoh**). [Latin "in the state in which"] (17c) In the same condition as previously <Johnson, as a minor, can recover the whole of what he paid if he puts the other party *in statu quo* by returning all the value received>. — Also termed *in statu quo ante.* See STATUS QUO.

instigate, *vb.* (16c) To goad or incite (someone) to take some action or course.

instinct, *adj.* (1803) *Archaic.* Imbued or charged <the contract is instinct with an obligation of good faith>.

in stirpes (in **stər**-peez). See PER STIRPES.

institor (**in**-sti-tor *or* -tər), *n.* [Latin] (17c) *Roman law.* A person, often but not always a son or slave, to whom the transaction of any particular business is committed; esp., a shopkeeper or other person in charge of a commercial business. See *actio institoria* under ACTIO.

institorial power. See POWER (3).

institute, *n.* (16c) **1.** A legal treatise or commentary, such as Coke's *Institutes* in four volumes (first published in 1628). **2.** (*cap.* & *pl.*) An elementary treatise on Roman law in four books. • This treatise is one of the four component parts of the *Corpus Juris Civilis.* — Also termed *Institutes of Justinian; Justinian's Institutes.* See CORPUS JURIS CIVILIS. **3.** (*cap.* & *pl.*) An elementary treatise written by the Roman jurist Gaius. • The *Institutes,* written in the second century A.D., served as a foundation for the *Institutes of Justinian.* — Also termed *Institutes of Gaius.* **4.** (*cap.* & *pl.*) A paraphrase of Justinian's *Institutes* written in Greek by Theophilus, a law professor at Constantinople who helped prepare the *Institutes of Justinian.* • This work was prepared in the sixth century A.D. — Also termed *Paraphrase of Theophilus; Institutes of Theophilus.* **5.** *Civil law.* A person named in a will as heir, but under directions to pass the estate on to some other specified person (called the *substitute*). See SUBSTITUTE (2). — Also termed *institutus.*

▸ **constructive conditional institute.** (1908) *Scots law.* A person not first named in the destination of a *causa mortis* undelivered deed, but who first takes under it because the person or persons named before him or her have predeceased the maker of the destination. • For example, in "to B, and his heirs male, whom failing, to C," the son of B takes as a constructive conditional institute if B predeceases leaving a son. See DESTINATION (3).

▸ **proper conditional institute.** (1826) *Scots law.* The person first named in a destination, but who is to take only if a condition is satisfied. • For example, in "to B, on condition of A's (the grantor's) leaving no issue, whom failing, to C," B is a proper conditional institute. See DESTINATION (3).

6. An organization devoted to the study and improvement of the law. See AMERICAN LAW INSTITUTE.

institute, *vb.* (14c) To begin or start; commence <institute legal proceedings against the manufacturer>.

institute cargo clause. See CARGO CLAUSE.

instituted heir. See *testamentary heir* under HEIR.

Institute for Telecommunication Sciences. See NATIONAL TELECOMMUNICATIONS AND INFORMATION ADMINISTRATION. — Abbr. ITS.

Institute of Museum and Library Services. An independent federal agency that makes grants to support libraries and museums. • It was established within the National Foundation on the Arts and the Humanities in 1996. — Abbr. IMLS. See NATIONAL FOUNDATION ON THE ARTS AND THE HUMANITIES.

Institutes of Gaius. See INSTITUTE (3).

Institutes of Justinian. See INSTITUTE (2).

Institutes of Theophilus. See INSTITUTE (4).

institutio heredis (in-sti-**t**[y]**oo**-shee-oh hə-**ree**-dis). [Latin] (1911) *Roman law.* The naming of an heir, which was essential to the validity of a will; specif., the designation in a will of a person as the testator's heir. — Also termed *heredis institutio.*

institution. (14c) **1.** The commencement of something, such as a civil or criminal action. **2.** An elementary rule, principle, or practice. **3.** An established organization, esp. one of a public character, such as a facility for the treatment of mentally disabled persons. — Also termed *public institution.* **4.** *Civil law.* A testator's appointment of an heir; the designation of an institute. See INSTITUTE (5). **5.** *Eccles. law.* The investiture of a cleric with a benefice, by which the cleric becomes responsible for the spiritual needs of the members of a parish. Cf. PRESENTATION (2); ADVOWSON.

institutional broker. See BROKER.

institutional gerrymandering. See GERRYMANDERING.

institutional investor. See INVESTOR.

institutionalize, *vb.* (1865) **1.** To place (a person) in an institution. **2.** To give (a rule or practice) official sanction.

institutionalized discrimination. See *systemic discrimination* under DISCRIMINATION (3).

institutional lender. (1956) A business, esp. a bank, that routinely makes loans to the general public.

institutional litigant. (1858) An organized group that brings lawsuits not merely to win but also to bring about a change in the law or to defend an existing law.

> "Our second observation relates to what has been called the 'institutional litigant.' There are organized groups, such as labour unions or trade associations, that have a continuing interest in the development of the common law. A group of this sort may take a case to litigation, not so much for the sake of a determination of the case itself, but for the purpose of bringing about a change in the law or of defending an existing rule against a change sought by some other group. When such groups are involved, the usual arguments against prospective changes in the law through judicial decisions lose much of their force. Indeed, when the litigants have this sort of long-term interest, a judicial proceeding may take on, with the assent of all involved, something of the nature of a legislative hearing." Lon L. Fuller, *Anatomy of the Law* 163 (1968).

institutional market. See MARKET.

institutional stare decisis. See STARE DECISIS.

institutiones (in-sti-t[y]oo-shee-**oh**-neez), *n.* [Latin] *Roman law.* Elementary works of law; institutes. See INSTITUTE.

institutus. See INSTITUTE (5).

instruct, *vb.* See JURY CHARGE (3).

instruct down. *Missouri law.* (Of a court) to give jurors an instruction on a lesser included offense. • A court must instruct down only if the jury could find the defendant not guilty of the higher offense but guilty of the lesser one.

instructed delegate. See DELEGATE.

instructed verdict. See *directed verdict* under VERDICT (1).

instruction. See JURY INSTRUCTION.

instructional text. (1981) *Copyright.* A literary, graphic, or pictorial work designed and prepared for use in ordinary teaching activities. *See* 17 USCA § 101.

instruction directive. (1985) A document that contains specific directions concerning the declarant's wishes for healthcare decisions. Cf. ADVANCE DIRECTIVE; LIVING WILL; PROXY DIRECTIVE.

instrument. (15c) **1.** A written legal document that defines rights, duties, entitlements, or liabilities, such as a statute, contract, will, promissory note, or share certificate. — Also termed *legal instrument.*

> "An 'instrument' seems to embrace contracts, deeds, statutes, wills, Orders in Council, orders, warrants, schemes, letters patent, rules, regulations, bye-laws, whether in writing or in print, or partly in both; in fact, any written or printed document that may have to be interpreted by the Courts." Edward Beal, *Cardinal Rules of Legal Interpretation* 55 (A.E. Randall ed., 3d ed. 1924).

2. *Commercial law.* An unconditional promise or order to pay a fixed amount of money, with or without interest or other fixed charges described in the promise or order; esp., commercial paper or a security or any other writing that evidences a right to the payment of money and that is not itself a security agreement or lease but that is of a type that in the ordinary course of business is transferred by delivery with any necessary indorsement or assignment. • Under the UCC, a promise or order must meet several other specifically listed requirements to qualify as an instrument. UCC § 3-104(a). See NEGOTIABLE INSTRUMENT.

▸ **false instrument. 1.** An instrument that contains untrue information or an erroneous statement. **2.** A forged document.

▸ **financing instrument.** See *investment instrument.*

▸ **inchoate instrument.** (1834) An unrecorded instrument that must, by law, be recorded to serve as effective notice to third parties. • Until the instrument is recorded, it is effective only between the parties to the instrument.

▸ **incomplete instrument.** (1822) A paper that, although intended to be a negotiable instrument, lacks an essential element. • An incomplete instrument may be enforced if it is subsequently completed. UCC § 3-115.

▸ **indispensable instrument.** The formal written evidence of an interest in intangibles, so necessary to represent the intangible that the enjoyment, transfer, or enforcement of the intangible depends on possession of the instrument.

▸ **instrument under hand.** (17c) A written instrument that is signed by or on behalf of the maker or the parties.

▸ **instrument under seal.** See *sealed instrument.*

▸ **investment instrument.** (1929) A legal document, such as a bond, share certificate, or promissory note, used to acquire capital through a loan or by selling equity. — Also termed *financing instrument.*

▸ **perfect instrument.** (18c) An instrument (such as a deed or mortgage) that is executed and filed with a public registry.

▸ **sealed instrument.** (17c) At common law and under some statutes, an instrument to which the bound party has affixed a personal seal, usu. recognized as providing indisputable evidence of the validity of the underlying obligations. • Many states have abolished the common-law distinction between sealed and unsealed instruments. The UCC provides that the laws applicable to sealed instruments do not apply to negotiable instruments or contracts for the sale of goods. UCC § 2-203. — Also termed *instrument under seal; sealed document.* Cf. *contract under seal* under CONTRACT.

"At common law, the seal served to render documents indisputable as to the terms of the underlying obligation, thereby dispensing with the necessity of witnesses; the sealed instrument was considered such reliable evidence that it actually became the contract itself — called a 'specialty' — the loss of which meant loss of all rights of the obligee against the obligor. The seal also had many other consequences at common law, some of which have been retained in jurisdictions which still recognize the seal. . . . In states where the seal is still recognized, its primary legal significance is often the application of a longer statute of limitations to actions on sealed instruments." 69 Am. Jur. 2d *Seals* § 2, at 617–18 (1993).

"In medieval England a wax seal may have performed [the functions of a formality] tolerably well. But in the United States few people owned or used a seal and the ritual deteriorated to the point that wax was dispensed with and printing houses decorated the signature lines of their standard forms with the printed letters 'L.S.' for *locus sigilli* (place of the seal). Perfunctory invocation of the rules for sealed documents called into question the seal's utility in making promises enforceable." E. Allan Farnsworth, *Changing Your Mind: The Law of Regretted Decisions* 46 (1998).

▸ **statutory instrument.** See STATUTORY INSTRUMENT.

▸ **testamentary instrument.** See WILL.

3. A means by which something is achieved, performed, or furthered <an instrument of social equality>.

▸ **unconscious instrument.** An instrument that has no volition.

"If the wrongdoer has set in motion an unconscious instrument, and the original force imparted to it has not spent itself at the time of the injury, or if the instrument has been made effective by his negligence, which continued to be operative at the time the injury occurred, responsibility as in the case of the intervention by an irresponsible individual will remain existent. Thus one who unlawfully frightens a horse, causing it to run away and inflict injury upon a third party, will be liable to the latter; and where a cow, thrown by an engine, struck the ground, bounced, and fell against plaintiff, it was held that the bounce and fall of the cow was not so far the proximate cause of the injury as to isolate the negligence of the engineer. Again, where a passenger on defendant's train is jolted to the track through the negligence of the engineer, and while lying there is run over and killed by an engine belonging to another railroad, the negligence of the defendant was held to have made effective the immediate cause of the death, which did not operate as an intervening cause. So, too, where defendant's locomotive set fire to a fence, which was burned, and cattle got into plaintiff's field and damaged the crop, the burning of the fence is to be regarded as the proximate cause." H. Gerald Chapin, *Handbook of the Law of Torts* 93–94 (1917).

instrumental crime. See CRIME.

instrumentality, *n.* (17c) **1.** A thing used to achieve an end or purpose. **2.** A means or agency through which a function of another entity is accomplished, such as a branch of a governing body.

▸ **federal instrumentality.** See FEDERAL INSTRUMENTALITY.

instrumentality rule. (1936) *Corporations.* The principle that a corporation is treated as a subsidiary if it is controlled to a great extent by another corporation. — Also termed *instrumentality theory.*

instrumentality theory. See INSTRUMENTALITY RULE.

instrumental offense. See *instrumental crime* under CRIME.

instrumenta noviter reperta (in-strə-**men**-tə **noh**-və-tər ri-**pər**-tə). [Law Latin] *Hist.* Instruments newly discovered. See EX INSTRUMENTIS DE NOVO REPERTIS.

instrument of accession. (1924) *Int'l law.* A document formally acknowledging the issuing state's consent to an existing treaty, and exchanged with the treaty parties or deposited with a designated state or international organization. See ACCESSION (3).

instrument of appeal. (18c) *Hist. English law.* A document used to appeal a judgment of divorce rendered by a trial judge of the Probate, Divorce and Admiralty Division to the full panel of the court. • The use of the instrument of appeal ended in 1881, when appeals were taken to the Court of Appeal rather than the full panel of the Probate, Divorce and Admiralty Division.

instrument of crime. See CRIMINAL INSTRUMENT.

instrument of ratification. (1908) *Int'l law.* A document formally acknowledging the issuing state's confirmation and acceptance of a treaty, and exchanged by the treaty parties or deposited with a designated state or international organization. See RATIFICATION (4).

instrumentum (in-stroo-**men**-təm). [Latin] *Hist.* A document, deed, or instrument; esp., a document that is not under seal, such as a court roll.

instrument under hand. See INSTRUMENT (2).

instrument under seal. See *sealed instrument* under INSTRUMENT (2).

insubordination. (18c) **1.** A willful disregard of an employer's instructions, esp. behavior that gives the employer cause to terminate a worker's employment. **2.** An act of disobedience to proper authority; esp., a refusal to obey an order that a superior officer is authorized to give.

in subsidium (in səb-**sid**-ee-əm). [Latin] In aid of.

insufficient evidence. See EVIDENCE.

insufficient funds. See NOT SUFFICIENT FUNDS.

insula (**in**-s[y]ə-lə), *n.* [Latin] (1832) *Roman law.* **1.** An island. **2.** A detached house or block of apartments leased to tenants.

insular, *adj.* (17c) **1.** Of, relating to, from, or constituting an island <insular origin>. **2.** Isolated from, uninterested in, or ignorant of things outside a limited scope <insular viewpoint>.

insular area. A territory or commonwealth. • This phrase is used by some writers to denote the genus of which the terms *territory* and *commonwealth* are species. See COMMONWEALTH (2); TERRITORY (1).

insular court. See COURT.

insular possession. See POSSESSION.

in suo (in s[y]**oo**-oh). [Latin] In reference to one's own affairs.

in suo genere (in s[y]oo-oh **jen**-ər-ee). [Latin] Of their own kind. • The phrase usu. referred to certain writings that were binding even though they lacked the formal requirements. See SUI GENERIS.

in suo ordine (in s[y]oo-oh **or**-də-nee). [Latin] In his order.

"In suo ordine . . . . A cautioner who is entitled to the benefit of discussion can only be called upon, for fulfilment of the obligation which he guaranteed, in his order — that is, after the principal creditor has been discussed. So, also, an heir can only be made liable for the moveable debts of his ancestor, after the executor who succeeded to the moveable estate has been discussed, and where the moveable estate has proved insufficient to meet those debts." John Trayner, *Trayner's Latin Maxims* 277 (4th ed. 1894).

insurable, *adj.* (1813) Able to be insured <an insurable risk>. — **insurability,** *n.*

insurable interest. See INTEREST (2).

insurable value. See VALUE.

insurance. (17c) **1.** A contract by which one party (the *insurer*) undertakes to indemnify another party (the *insured*) against risk of loss, damage, or liability arising from the occurrence of some specified contingency. • An insured party usu. pays a premium to the insurer in exchange for the insurer's assumption of the insured's risk. Although indemnification provisions are most common in insurance policies, parties to any type of contract may agree on indemnification arrangements. **2.** The amount for which someone or something is covered by such an agreement. — **insure,** *vb.*

"Insurance, or as it is sometimes called, assurance, is a contract by which one party, for a consideration, which is usually paid in money either in one sum or at different times during the continuance of the risk, promises to make a certain payment of money upon the destruction or injury of something in which the other party has an interest. In fire insurance and in marine insurance the thing insured is property; in life or accident insurance it is the life or health of the person." 1 George J. Couch, *Couch on Insurance* § 1.2, at 4–5 (2d ed. 1984).

▸ **accident and health insurance.** See *health insurance.*

▸ **accident insurance.** (1862) A type of business or personal insurance that indemnifies against loss resulting directly from accidental bodily injuries sustained during the policy term. • Covered losses may include expenses, time, suffering, or death. Cf. *casualty insurance.*

"Accident insurance is similar in most respects to life insurance, of which it is properly a branch. . . . [A]ccident insurance is the most recently developed of all the important branches of insurance, being derived from the practice of life insurance. Most of the conditions existing in connection with contracts of life insurance are found present also in the writing of accident policies . . . . Accident insurance is so closely akin to life insurance that it is generally held that statutes which have been enacted for the regulation of the business of life insurance, or for the purpose of fixing the rights of parties under contracts of life insurance, apply equally well to those of accident insurance." William Reynolds Vance, *Handbook of the Law of Insurance* § 230, at 564 (1904).

▸ **accounts-receivable insurance.** (1942) **1.** Insurance against losses resulting from the insured's inability to collect outstanding accounts receivable because of damage to or destruction of records. **2.** See *credit insurance.*

▸ **additional insurance.** (1849) Insurance added to an existing policy.

▸ **all-risk insurance.** (1927) Insurance that covers every kind of insurable loss except what is specifically excluded. Cf. *limited-policy insurance.*

▸ **annuity insurance.** (1863) An agreement to pay the insured (or *annuitant*) for a stated period or for life.

▸ **assessable insurance.** (1967) **1.** Insurance in which the insured is liable for additional premiums if a loss is unusually large. **2.** See *assessable policy* (1) under INSURANCE POLICY.

▸ **assessment insurance.** (1887) A type of mutual insurance in which the policyholders are assessed as losses are incurred; a policy in which payments to an insured are not unalterably fixed, but are dependent on the collection of assessments necessary to pay the amount insured.

▸ **automobile insurance.** (1912) An agreement to indemnify against one or more kinds of loss associated with the use of an automobile, including damage to a vehicle and liability for personal injury.

▸ **aviation insurance.** (1919) Insurance that protects the insured against a loss connected with the use of an aircraft. • This type of insurance can be written to cover a variety of risks, including bodily injury, property damage, and hangarkeepers' liability.

▸ **bailee insurance.** (1938) A type of floating insurance that covers goods in a bailee's possession but does not particularly describe the covered goods.

▸ **broad-form insurance.** (1959) Comprehensive insurance. • This type of insurance usu. takes the form of an endorsement to a liability or property policy, broadening the coverage that is typically available.

▸ **bumbershoot insurance.** (1984) **1.** Marine insurance that provides broad coverage for ocean marine risks. **2.** See *umbrella insurance.* • This term derives from the British slang term for *umbrella.* The term applies esp. to a policy insured through the London insurance market. See *umbrella policy* under INSURANCE POLICY.

▸ **burial insurance.** (1903) Insurance that pays for the holder's burial and funeral expenses.

▸ **business-interruption insurance.** (1928) An agreement to protect against one or more kinds of loss from the interruption of an ongoing business, such as a loss of profits while the business is shut down to repair fire damage.

▸ **business-partner insurance.** See *partnership insurance.*

▸ **captive insurance.** (1955) **1.** Insurance that provides coverage for the group or business that established it. **2.** Insurance that a subsidiary provides to its parent company, usu. so that the parent company can deduct the premiums set aside as loss reserves.

▸ **cargo insurance.** (1873) An agreement to pay for damage to freight damaged in transit.

▸ **casualty insurance.** (1870) An agreement to indemnify against loss resulting from a broad group of causes such as legal liability, theft, accident, property damage, and workers' compensation. • The meaning of casualty insurance has become blurred because of the rapid increase in different types of insurance coverage. Cf. *accident insurance.*

▸ **claims-made insurance.** (1974) Insurance that indemnifies against all claims made during a specified period, regardless of when the incidents that gave rise to the claims occurred. — Also termed *discovery policy.*

▸ **coinsurance.** (1889) **1.** Insurance provided jointly by two or more insurers. **2.** Insurance under which the insurer and insured jointly bear responsibility. • An example is commercial insurance under which only a portion of a property's value is covered, and the property owner assumes liability for any loss in excess of the policy limits.

▸ **collision insurance.** (1921) Automobile insurance that covers damage to the insured's vehicle resulting from a rollover or collision with any object, but does not cover a personal injury or damage to other property. See *convertible collision insurance.*

▸ **commercial general-liability insurance.** (1977) Insurance that broadly covers an insured's liability exposure, including products liability, tort liability, certain forms of contractual liability, and premises liability. — Formerly called *comprehensive general-liability insurance.* — Abbr. CGL insurance.

▸ **commercial insurance.** (1832) **1.** An indemnity agreement in the form of a deed or bond to protect against a loss caused by a party's breach of contract. **2.** A form of coverage that allows an insurer to adjust the premium rates at will, and doesn't require the insured to accept the premium or renew the coverage from period to period.

> "Commercial insurance is a popular and very elastic term, having reference to indemnity agreements issued in the form of an insurance bond or policy, whereby parties to commercial contracts are, to a designated extent, guaranteed against loss by reason of a breach of contractual obligations on the part of the other contracting party. To this class belong policies of 'contract,' 'credit,' and 'title' insurances." Thomas Gold Frost, *A Treatise on Guaranty Insurance* § 3, at 14 (2d ed. 1909).

▸ **completed-operations insurance.** (1957) Insurance purchased usu. by a building contractor to cover accidents arising out of a job or an operation that the contractor has completed.

▸ **comprehensive general-liability insurance.** (1949) See *commercial general-liability insurance.*

▸ **comprehensive insurance.** (1924) Insurance that combines coverage against many kinds of losses that may also be insured separately. • This is commonly used, for example, in an automobile-insurance policy.

▸ **compulsory insurance.** (1887) Statutorily required insurance; esp., motor-vehicle liability insurance that a state requires as a condition to register the vehicle.

▸ **consequential-loss insurance.** (1952) Insurance that protects the insured against losses that, though resulting from a property loss occasioned by an insured risk, are not covered by ordinary insurance — as when the losses relate to a period in which a business is not operating as a result of loss or damage caused by an insured risk.

▸ **consumer-credit insurance.** (1951) Insurance for the repayment of a loan if the insured borrower dies or becomes involuntarily disabled or unemployed.

▸ **convertible collision insurance.** (1936) Collision insurance that carries a low premium until a claim is made against the policy. See *collision insurance.*

▸ **convertible insurance.** (1926) Insurance that can be changed to another form without further evidence of insurability, usu. referring to a term-life-insurance policy that can be changed to permanent insurance without a medical examination.

▸ **credit accident and health insurance.** See *credit disability insurance.*

▸ **credit-card insurance.** (1958) An agreement to indemnify against unauthorized use of a credit card. — Also termed *fraudulent-use insurance.*

▸ **credit disability insurance.** (1956) An agreement to pay a specified number of periodic payments on a specific loan or credit-card account if the borrower becomes disabled during the term of coverage. — Also termed *credit accident and health insurance.*

▸ **credit insurance.** (1859) An agreement to indemnify against loss that may result from the death, disability, or insolvency of someone to whom credit is extended. • A debtor typically purchases this type of insurance to ensure the repayment of the loan. — Also termed *accounts-receivable insurance.*

▸ **credit involuntary-unemployment insurance.** (1992) An agreement to pay a specified number of periodic payments on a specified loan or credit-card account if the borrower is fired, laid off, or otherwise terminated as an employee during the term of coverage.

▸ **credit life insurance.** See LIFE INSURANCE.

▸ **credit property insurance.** (1969) An agreement to pay to repair or replace property bought with the loan or credit proceeds if the property is lost, damaged, or stolen. • This insurance may serve as collateral for the credit. Unlike most other types of credit insurance, credit property insurance is not directly related to an event affecting a consumer's ability to repay a debt.

▸ **crime insurance.** (1931) Insurance covering losses occasioned by a crime committed by someone other than the insured.

▸ **crop insurance.** (1892) Insurance that protects against loss to growing crops from natural perils such as hail and fire. See FEDERAL CROP INSURANCE CORPORATION.

▸ **D&O insurance.** See *directors' and officers' liability insurance.*

▸ **decreasing term insurance.** (1938) Insurance that declines in value during the term; esp., life insurance that lessens in value to zero by the end of the term.

▸ **deposit insurance.** (1933) *Banking law.* A federally sponsored indemnification program to protect depositors against the loss of their money, up to a specified maximum, if the bank or savings-and-loan association fails or defaults. See FEDERAL DEPOSIT INSURANCE CORPORATION.

▸ **directors and officers' liability insurance.** (1965) *Corporations.* An agreement to indemnify corporate directors and officers against judgments, settlements, and fines arising from negligence suits, shareholder actions, and other business-related suits. • A D&O policy may additionally require reimbursement by the insurer to the corporation of amounts expended to indemnify corporate personnel against litigation-related costs that they incur. — Often shortened to *D&O liability insurance; D&O insurance.*

▸ **disability insurance.** (1959) Coverage purchased to protect a person from a loss of income during a period of incapacity for work. See *general-disability insurance; occupational-disability insurance.* Cf. WORKERS' COMPENSATION.

▸ **discovery policy.** See *claims-made insurance.*

▸ **double insurance.** (18c) Insurance coverage by more than one insurer for the same interest and for the same insured. • Except with life insurance, the insured is entitled to only a single indemnity from a loss, and to recover this, the insured may either (1) sue each insurer for its share of the loss, or (2) sue one or more of the insurers for the entire amount, leaving any paying insurers to recover from the others their respective shares of the loss.

▸ **dread-disease insurance.** (1972) Health insurance that covers medical expenses arising from the treatment of any of several specified catastrophic diseases such as cancer.

▸ **drummer floater insurance.** (1907) *Hist.* Insurance that covered the goods carried by a commercial salesperson while traveling.

▸ **earthquake insurance.** Insurance that covers a building and its contents for damages resulting from an earthquake. • Earthquake damage is usu. excluded from most standard homeowner's and business policies.

▸ **e-commerce insurance.** (2000) Insurance that covers a business's computer-related damages and losses caused by computer hackers and Internet viruses. • Covered damages usu. include physical destruction or harm to computer circuitry, loss of access, loss of use, loss of functionality, and business interruption.

▸ **employers'-liability insurance.** (1886) **1.** An agreement to indemnify an employer against an employee's claim not covered under the workers'-compensation system. **2.** An agreement to indemnify against liability imposed on an employer for an employee's negligence that injures a third party. — Abbr. ELI.

▸ **employment-practices liability insurance.** (1994) Insurance that provides coverage for claims arising from an insured's injury-causing employment practice, such as discrimination, defamation, or sexual harassment. — Abbr. *EPL insurance.*

▸ **endowment insurance.** (1871) A type of life insurance that is payable either to the insured at the end of the policy period or to the insured's beneficiary if the insured dies before the period ends. See *endowment life insurance* under LIFE INSURANCE.

▸ **errors-and-omissions insurance.** (1938) An agreement to indemnify for loss sustained because of a mistake or oversight by the insured — though not for loss due to the insured's intentional wrongdoing. • For example, lawyers often carry this insurance as part of their malpractice coverage to protect them in suits for damages resulting from inadvertent mistakes (such as missing a procedural deadline). While this insurance does not cover the insured's intentional wrongdoing, it may cover an employee's intentional, but unauthorized, wrongdoing. — Often shortened to *E&O insurance.*

▸ **excess insurance.** (1916) An agreement to indemnify against any loss that exceeds the amount of coverage under another policy. — Also termed *excess policy.* See EXCESS CLAUSE. Cf. *primary insurance.*

▸ **excess-lines insurance.** See *surplus-lines insurance.*

▸ **extended insurance.** (1883) Insurance that continues in force beyond the date that the last premium was paid by drawing on its cash value.

▸ **extended-term insurance.** (1925) Insurance that remains in effect after a default in paying premiums, as long as the policy has cash value to pay premiums. • Many life-insurance policies provide this feature to protect against forfeiture of the policy if the insured falls behind in premium payments.

▸ **family-income insurance.** (1925) An agreement to pay benefits for a stated period following the death of the insured. • At the end of the payment period, the face value is paid to the designated beneficiary.

▸ **fidelity insurance.** (1889) An agreement to indemnify an employer against a loss arising from the lack of integrity or honesty of an employee or of a person holding a position of trust, such as a loss from embezzlement. — Also termed *fidelity guaranty insurance; fidelity and guaranty insurance; surety and fidelity insurance.*

> "A contract of fidelity and guaranty insurance is one whereby the insurer, for a valuable consideration, agrees, subject to certain conditions, to indemnify the insured against loss consequent upon the dishonesty or default of a designated employé. The contract partakes of the nature both of insurance and of suretyship. Hence, even in the absence of contract stipulations to such effect, the contract is avoided by the failure of the insured to disclose to the insurer, at the time of making the contract, any known previous acts of dishonesty on the part of the employé, or any dishonest practices that may occur during the currency of the policy. . . . The term 'fidelity and guaranty insurance' . . . is sometimes held to include contracts guarantying titles to real estate and the solvency of debtors, as well as those granting indemnity for losses suffered by reason of the infidelity or dishonesty of employés." William Reynolds Vance, *Handbook of the Law of Insurance* §§ 247–48, at 595 (1904).

▸ **fire insurance.** (1822) An agreement to indemnify against property damage caused by fire, wind, rain, or other similar disaster.

▸ **first-party insurance.** (1953) A policy that applies to an insured or the insured's own property, such as life insurance, health insurance, disability insurance, and fire insurance. — Also termed *indemnity insurance; self-insurance.* Cf. *third-party insurance.*

▸ **fleet insurance.** (1932) Insurance that covers a number of vehicles owned by the same entity.

▸ **floater insurance.** (1916) An agreement to indemnify against a loss sustained to movable property, wherever its location within the territorial limit set by the policy.

▸ **flood insurance.** (1937) Insurance that indemnifies against a loss caused by a flood. • This type of insurance is often sold privately but subsidized by the federal government.

▸ **fraternal insurance.** (1892) Life or health insurance issued by a fraternal benefit society to its members.

▸ **fraudulent-use insurance.** See *credit-card insurance.*

▸ **gambling insurance.** See *wager insurance.*

▸ **GAP insurance.** Guaranteed-asset-protection insurance; that is, a type of insurance that covers the difference between what an asset (such as a car) is worth and what one owes on the asset • This insurance typically springs into effect when an asset is stolen or seriously damaged.

▸ **general-disability insurance.** (1933) Disability insurance that provides benefits to a person who cannot perform any job that the person is qualified for. — Also termed *total-disability insurance.* Cf. *occupational-disability insurance.*

▸ **government insurance.** (1872) Life insurance underwritten by the federal government to military personnel, veterans, and government employees.

▸ **graveyard insurance.** See *wager insurance.*

▸ **group insurance.** (1913) A form of insurance offered to a member of a group, such as the employees of a business, as long as that person remains a member of the group. • Group insurance is typically health or life (usu. term life) insurance issued under a master policy between the insurer and the employer, who usu. pays all or part of the premium for the insured person. Other groups, such as unions and associations, often offer group insurance to their members.

▸ **guaranty insurance** (**gar**-ən-tee). (1895) An agreement to cover a loss resulting from another's default, insolvency, or specified misconduct. — Also termed *surety insurance.*

> "The term 'guaranty insurance' is generic in its scope and signification, and embraces within it those subsidiary species of insurance contracts known as 'fidelity,' 'commercial,' and 'judicial' insurances . . . . In legal acceptation guaranty insurance is an agreement whereby one party (called the 'insurer') for a valuable consideration (termed the 'premium') agrees to indemnify another (called the 'insured') in a stipulated amount against loss or damage arising through dishonesty, fraud, unfaithful performance of duty or breach of contract on the part of a third person . . . sustaining a contractual relationship to the party thus indemnified." Thomas Gold Frost, *A Treatise on Guaranty Insurance* § 1, at 11 (2d ed. 1909).

▸ **health insurance.** (1901) Insurance covering medical expenses resulting from sickness or injury. — Also termed *accident and health insurance*; *sickness and accident insurance.*

▸ **homeowner's insurance.** (1964) Insurance that covers both damage to the insured's residence and liability claims made against the insured (esp. those arising from the insured's negligence).

▸ **indemnity insurance.** See *first-party insurance.*

▸ **industrial life insurance.** See LIFE INSURANCE.

▸ **inland marine insurance.** (1853) An agreement to indemnify against losses arising from the transport of goods on domestic waters (i.e., rivers, canals, and lakes). Cf. *ocean marine insurance.*

▸ **insurance of the person.** (1898) Insurance intended to protect the person, such as life, accident, and disability insurance.

▸ **interinsurance.** See *reciprocal insurance.*

▸ **joint life insurance.** See LIFE INSURANCE.

▸ **judicial insurance.** (1902) Insurance intended to protect litigants and others involved in the court system.

> "By judicial insurance reference is had to insurance bonds or policies issued, in connection with the regular course of judicial or administrative procedure, for the purpose of securing the faithful performance of duty on the part of court appointees, to guarantee due compliance with the terms of undertakings entered into by parties litigant before the courts, and to secure proper administration of statute law." Thomas Gold Frost, *A Treatise on Guaranty Insurance* § 3, at 14 (2d ed. 1909).

▸ **key-employee insurance.** See *key-employee life insurance* under LIFE INSURANCE.

▸ **last-survivor insurance.** See *last-survivor life insurance* under LIFE INSURANCE.

▸ **lease insurance.** (1976) An agreement to indemnify a leaseholder for the loss of a favorable lease terminated by damage to the property from a peril covered by the policy. • The amount payable is the difference between the rent and the actual rental value of the property, multiplied by the remaining term of the lease.

▸ **legal-protection insurance.** (1973) Insurance that covers the costs of a lawsuit brought against the policyholder by another person or entity. — Also termed *legal insurance*; *legal-expenses insurance.*

▸ **level-premium insurance.** (1893) Insurance whose premiums remain constant throughout the life of the agreement. • Most whole life policies are set up this way.

▸ **liability insurance.** (1898) An agreement to cover a loss resulting from the insured's liability to a third party, such as a loss incurred by a driver who injures a pedestrian, and usu. to defend the insured or to pay for a defense regardless of whether the insured is ultimately found liable. • The insured's claim under the policy arises once the insured's liability to a third party has been asserted. — Also termed *third-party insurance*; *public-liability insurance.*

▸ **life insurance.** See LIFE INSURANCE.

▸ **limited-policy insurance.** (1989) Insurance that covers only specified perils; esp., health insurance that covers a specific type of illness (such as dread-disease insurance) or a risk relating to a stated activity (such as travel-accident insurance). Cf. *all-risk insurance*; *open-perils policy* under INSURANCE POLICY.

▸ **Lloyd's insurance.** (1897) Insurance provided by insurers as individuals, rather than as a corporation. • The insurers' liability is several but not joint. Most states either prohibit or strictly regulate this type of insurance. See LLOYD'S OF LONDON.

▸ **loss insurance.** (1961) Insurance purchased by a person who may suffer a loss at the hands of another. • This is the converse of *liability insurance*, which is purchased by potential defendants.

▸ **malpractice insurance** (mal-**prak**-tis). (1943) An agreement to indemnify a professional person, such as a doctor or lawyer, against negligence claims. • While the Model Rules of Professional Responsibility and most states do not require lawyers to carry malpractice insurance, most prudent lawyers do. See *errors-and-omissions insurance.*

> "Most contemporary lawyers regard malpractice insurance as an expensive, but essential, part of law practice. Its cost, along with other costs of the lawyer's trade, is ultimately borne by the consumer, the client who pays the lawyer's fees. . . . Neither the ABA Code nor the ABA Model Rules impose an ethical obligation to carry adequate malpractice insurance. But contemporary lawyers have found it prudent to do so, both to protect their personal assets and to promote their public image as reliable professionals who are financially responsible." Mortimer D. Schwartz & Richard C. Wydick, *Problems in Legal Ethics* 127–28 (2d ed. 1988).

▸ **manual-rating insurance.** A type of insurance whereby the premium is set using a book that classifies certain risks on a general basis, rather than evaluating each individual case.

▸ **marine insurance.** (18c) An agreement to indemnify against injury to a ship, cargo, or profits involved in a certain voyage or for a specific vessel during a fixed period, or to protect other marine interests.

▸ **medigap insurance.** See MEDIGAP INSURANCE.

▸ **mortgage insurance.** (1876) **1.** An agreement to pay off a mortgage if the insured dies or becomes disabled. **2.** An agreement to provide money to the lender if the mortgagor defaults on the mortgage payments. — Also termed *private mortgage insurance* (PMI).

▸ **mutual insurance.** (1827) A system of insurance (esp. life insurance) whereby the policyholders become members of the insurance company, each paying premiums into a common fund from which each can draw in the event of a loss.

▸ **national-service life insurance.** See LIFE INSURANCE.

▸ **no-fault auto insurance.** (1968) *Automobile insurance.* An agreement to indemnify for a loss due to personal injury or property damage arising from the use of an automobile, regardless of who caused the accident.

▸ **nonassessable insurance.** (1969) Insurance in which the premium is set and the insurer is barred from demanding additional payments from the insured.

▸ **occupational-disability insurance.** (1966) Disability insurance that provides benefits to a person who cannot perform his or her regular job. See *disability insurance.*

▸ **occurrence-based liability insurance.** (1975) Insurance that covers bodily injuries or property damage suffered during the policy period. • Each instance of injury or damage is an "occurrence" that may trigger an insured's entitlement to benefits. The terms of occurrence-based liability insurance policies are usu. broad, limited only by specific exclusions. — Also termed *accident-based insurance.*

▸ **ocean marine insurance.** (1842) Insurance that covers risks arising from the transport of goods by sea. Cf. *inland marine insurance.*

▸ **old-age and survivors' insurance.** See OLD-AGE AND SURVIVORS' INSURANCE.

▸ **ordinary insurance.** See *ordinary life insurance* under LIFE INSURANCE.

▸ **ordinary life insurance.** See LIFE INSURANCE.

▸ **overinsurance.** See OVERINSURANCE.

▸ **paid-up insurance.** (1871) Insurance that remains in effect even though no more premiums are due.

▸ **participating insurance.** (1917) A type of insurance that allows a policyholder to receive dividends. • This insurance is invariably issued by a mutual company.

▸ **partnership insurance.** (1876) **1.** Life insurance on the life of a partner, purchased to ensure the remaining partners' ability to buy out a deceased partner's interest. — Also termed *partnership life insurance.* **2.** Health insurance for a partner, payable to the partnership to allow it to continue to operate while the partner is unable to work because of illness or injury. — Also termed (in both senses) *business-partner insurance.*

▸ **patent insurance** (**pat**-ənt). (1924) *Patents.* **1.** Insurance against loss from an infringement of the insured's patent. **2.** Insurance against a claim that the insured has infringed another's patent. **3.** Insurance that funds a claim against a third party for infringing the insured's patent.

▸ **port-risk insurance.** (1932) *Marine insurance.* Insurance on a vessel lying in port. Cf. *time insurance*; *voyage insurance.*

▸ **primary insurance.** (1900) Insurance that attaches immediately on the happening of a loss; insurance that is not contingent on the exhaustion of an underlying policy. Cf. *excess insurance.*

▸ **private mortgage insurance.** See *mortgage insurance.*

▸ **products-liability insurance.** (1937) An agreement to indemnify a manufacturer, supplier, or retailer for a loss arising from the insured's liability to a user who is harmed by any product manufactured or sold by the insured. — Abbr. PLI.

▸ **profit insurance.** (1916) Insurance that reimburses the insured for profits lost because of a specified peril.

▸ **property insurance.** (1887) An agreement to indemnify against property damage or destruction. — Also termed *property-damage insurance.*

▸ **public-liability insurance.** See *liability insurance.*

▸ **reciprocal insurance.** (1913) A system whereby several individuals or businesses act through an agent to underwrite one another's risks, making each insured an insurer of the other members of the group. — Also termed *interinsurance.*

▸ **reinsurance.** See REINSURANCE.

▸ **renewable term insurance.** (1902) Insurance that the insured may continue at the end of a term, but generally at a higher premium. • The insured usu. has the right to renew for additional terms without a medical examination.

▸ **renter's insurance.** Insurance that covers an insured's personal property in leased premises against certain perils or losses as well as liability to a third party.

▸ **replacement insurance.** (1938) Insurance under which the value of the loss is measured by the current cost of replacing the insured property. See *replacement cost* under COST.

▸ **retirement-income insurance.** (1943) An agreement whereby the insurance company agrees to pay an annuity beginning at a certain age if the insured survives beyond that age, or the value of the policy if the insured dies before reaching that age.

▸ **self-insurance.** (1905) A plan under which a business maintains its own special fund to cover any loss. • Unlike other forms of insurance, there is no contract with an insurance company. — Also termed *first-party insurance.*

▸ **sickness and accident insurance.** See *health insurance.*

▸ **single-premium insurance.** See *single-premium life insurance* under LIFE INSURANCE.

▸ **social insurance.** (1890) Insurance provided by a government to persons facing particular perils (such as unemployment or disability) or to persons who have a certain status (such as the elderly or the blind). • Social insurance — such as that created by the Social Security Act of 1935 — is usu. part of a government's broader social policy. See WELFARE STATE.

▸ **split-dollar insurance.** See *split-dollar life insurance* under LIFE INSURANCE.

▸ **step-rate-premium insurance.** Insurance whose premiums increase at times specified in the policy.

▸ **stop-loss insurance.** (1938) Insurance that protects a self-insured employer from catastrophic losses or unusually large health costs of covered employees. • Stop-loss insurance essentially provides excess coverage for a self-insured employer. The employer and the insurance carrier agree to the amount the employer will cover, and the stop-loss insurance will cover claims exceeding that amount.

▸ **straight life insurance.** See *whole life insurance* under LIFE INSURANCE.

▸ **surety and fidelity insurance.** See *fidelity insurance.*

▸ **surety insurance.** See *guaranty insurance.*

▸ **surplus-lines insurance.** (1937) Insurance with an insurer that is not licensed to transact business within the state where the risk is located. — Also termed *excess-lines insurance.*

▸ **term life insurance.** See LIFE INSURANCE.

▸ **terrorism insurance.** (1982) Insurance that indemnifies against losses sustained because of an act of terrorism. • Terrorism insurance has been available since the 1970s; it was (and is) required for U.S. airports of almost all sizes. In the mid-1980s, terrorism insurance was offered to individuals, originally as a form of travel insurance that provided compensation for terrorism-related cancellations or changes in itinerary when traveling to or in certain countries. See TERRORISM.

▸ **third-party insurance.** See *liability insurance.* Cf. *first-party insurance.*

▸ **time insurance.** (1841) *Marine insurance.* Insurance covering the insured for a specified period. Cf. *voyage insurance.*

▸ **title insurance.** (1889) *Real estate.* An agreement to indemnify against loss arising from a defect in title to real property, usu. issued to the buyer of the property by the title company that conducted the title search. Cf. GUARANTEE OF TITLE.

> "Title insurance is normally written by specialized companies that maintain tract indexes: companies involved in writing life or casualty usually are not involved in title insurance. Title insurance is an unusual type of insurance in a few respects. For one thing, it is not a recurring policy: There is only a single premium, and a title insurance policy written on behalf of an owner theoretically remains outstanding forever to protect him or her from claims asserted by others. It is more similar to an indemnification agreement than to an insurance policy. For another, title insurance companies generally do not take risks that they know about. If the title search shows that a risk exists, the company will exclude that risk from the coverage of the policy." Robert W. Hamilton, *Fundamentals of Modern Business* 84 (1989).

▸ **total-disability insurance.** See *general-disability insurance.*

▸ **travel-accident insurance.** (1929) Health insurance limited to injuries sustained while traveling.

▸ **umbrella insurance.** (1957) Insurance that is supplemental, providing coverage that exceeds the basic or usual limits of liability. — Also termed *bumbershoot insurance.*

▸ **underinsurance.** See UNDERINSURANCE.

▸ **unemployment insurance.** (1897) A type of social insurance that pays money to workers who are unemployed for reasons unrelated to job performance. • Individual states administer unemployment insurance, which is funded by payroll taxes. — Also termed *unemployment compensation.*

▸ **universal life insurance.** See LIFE INSURANCE.

▸ **valuable-papers insurance.** (1956) Insurance covering the cost of research, labor, and materials necessary to reconstruct damaged or lost documents and records — written, printed, or otherwise inscribed — including books, maps, manuscripts, legal documents, drawings, and films. • This insurance does not cover cash or securities.

▸ **variable life insurance.** See LIFE INSURANCE.

▸ **voyage insurance.** (1917) *Marine insurance.* **1.** Insurance covering the insured between destinations. Cf. *time insurance.* **2.** See *voyage policy* under INSURANCE POLICY.

▸ **wager insurance.** (18c) Insurance issued to a person who is shown to have no insurable interest in the person or property covered by the policy. • Wager policies are illegal in most states. — Also termed *wager policy; gambling insurance; graveyard insurance.* See *insurable interest* under INTEREST (2).

▸ **war-risk insurance.** (1915) **1.** Insurance covering damage caused by war. • Ocean marine policies are often written to cover this type of risk. **2.** Life and accident insurance provided by the federal government to members of the armed forces. • This type of insurance is offered because the hazardous nature of military service often prevents military personnel from obtaining private insurance.

▸ **whole life insurance.** See LIFE INSURANCE.

insurance adjuster. (1934) See ADJUSTER.

insurance agent. (1866) A person authorized by an insurance company to sell its insurance policies. — Also termed *producer*; (in property insurance) *recording agent*; *record agent.*

▸ **general agent.** An agent with the general power of making insurance contracts on behalf of an insurer.

▸ **special agent.** An agent whose powers are usu. confined to soliciting applications for insurance, taking initial premiums, and delivering policies when issued. — Also termed *local agent*; *solicitor.*

insurance bond. See BOND (3).

insurance broker. See BROKER.

insurance certificate. (1865) **1.** A document issued by an insurer as evidence of insurance or membership in an insurance or pension plan. **2.** *Marine insurance.* A document issued by an insurer to a shipper as evidence that a shipment of goods is covered by a marine insurance policy.

insurance commissioner. (1889) A public official who supervises the insurance business conducted in a state.

insurance company. (18c) A corporation or association that issues insurance policies.

▸ **captive insurance company.** (1967) A company that insures the liabilities of its owner. • The insured is usu. the sole shareholder and the only customer of the captive insurer. — Also termed *captive insurer.* See *captive insurance* under INSURANCE.

▸ **mixed insurance company.** (1987) An insurance company having characteristics of both stock and mutual companies in that it distributes part of the profits to stockholders and also makes distributions to the insureds.

▸ **mutual insurance company.** (1836) An insurance company whose policyholders are both insurers and insureds because they pay premiums into a common fund, from which claims are paid; an insurer whose policyholders are its owners, as opposed to a stock insurance company owned by outside shareholders. Cf. *stock insurance company.*

> "Mutual insurance companies are organized by a number of persons for the purpose of transacting some particular insurance business . . . . A company is a mutual one when the persons constituting the company contribute either cash or assessable premium notes, or both, to a common fund, out of which each is entitled to indemnity in case of loss. The distinguishing feature is mutuality, evidenced by the co-operation of members, uniting for that purpose, each taking a proportionate part in the management of its affairs and being at once insurer and insured, contributing to a fund from which all losses are paid . . . . Democratic ownership and control is a fundamental characteristic of a mutual insurance company." 18 John Alan Appleman, *Insurance Law and Practice* § 10041, at 79–80 (1945).

▸ **stock insurance company.** (1851) An insurance company operated as a private corporation and owned by stockholders who share in the company's profits and losses.

▸ **stock life-insurance company.** (1847) A stock insurance company that does life-insurance business.

insurance contract. See INSURANCE POLICY.

insurance fraud. See FRAUD.

insurance of the person. See INSURANCE.

insurance policy. (1869) **1.** A contract of insurance. **2.** A document detailing such a contract. — Often shortened to *policy.* — Also termed *policy of insurance*; *insurance contract*; *contract of insurance.*

▸ **assessable policy.** (1906) **1.** An insurance policy under which a policyholder may be held liable for losses of the insurance company beyond its reserves. — Also termed *assessable insurance.* **2.** See *assessable insurance* (1) under INSURANCE.

▸ **bailee policy.** (1938) A floating insurance policy that covers goods in a bailee's possession but does not particularly describe the covered goods.

▸ **basic-form policy.** (1997) An insurance policy that offers limited coverage against loss. • A basic-form policy generally covers damages from fire, windstorm, explosion, riot, aircraft, vehicles, theft, or vandalism. — Also termed *limited policy*; *specific policy.*

▸ **blanket policy.** (1894) An insurance policy that indemnifies against all property loss, regardless of location. — Also termed *compound policy*; *floating policy.*

▸ **block policy.** (1928) An all-risk insurance policy that covers groups of property (such as property held in bailment or a business's merchandise) against most perils. See *all-risk insurance* under INSURANCE.

▸ **broad-form policy.** (1950) An insurance policy that offers broad protection with few limitations. • This policy offers greater coverage than a basic-form policy, but less than an open-perils policy.

▸ **closed policy.** (1932) An insurance policy whose terms cannot be changed. • A fraternal benefit society is not permitted to write closed policies. — Also termed *closed insurance contract.*

▸ **compound policy.** See *blanket policy.*

▸ **concurrent policy.** (1937) One of two or more insurance policies that cover the same risk. • Concurrent insurance policies are stated in almost identical terms so that liability can be apportioned between the insurers.

▸ **continuous policy.** See *perpetual policy.*

▸ **corrected policy.** (1874) An insurance policy issued after a redetermination of risk to correct a misstatement in the original policy.

▸ **deferred-dividend policy.** (1905) *Hist.* A life-insurance policy that accumulated a fixed percentage of the insurer's surplus profits, payable as a lump sum on a certain date or at the insured's death, whichever came first.

▸ **discovery policy.** See *claims-made insurance* under INSURANCE.

▸ **endowment policy.** (1871) **1.** A life-insurance policy payable at the end of a specified period, if the insured survives that period, or upon the insured's death if death occurs before the end of the period. **2.** Any insurance arrangement that pays the policyholder a sum of money after an agreed-on period.

▸ **excess policy.** See *excess insurance* under INSURANCE.

▸ **extended policy.** (1903) An insurance policy that remains in effect beyond the time when premiums are no longer paid.

▸ **flier policy.** (1998) An insurance policy issued at a very low rate near the end of the year for the purpose of swelling the insurance agent's annual-sales figures. — Also spelled *flyer policy.*

▸ **floating policy.** (1836) An insurance policy covering property that frequently changes in quantity or location, such as jewelry. — Also termed *running policy*; *blanket policy.*

▸ **following-form policy.** (1982) An insurance policy that adopts the terms and conditions of another insurance policy.

▸ **gambling policy.** See *wager insurance* under INSURANCE.

▸ **graveyard policy.** See *wager insurance* under INSURANCE.

▸ **group policy.** See *master policy.*

▸ **homeowner's policy.** (1959) A multiperil insurance policy providing coverage for a variety of risks, including loss by fire, water, burglary, and the homeowner's negligent conduct.

▸ **incontestable policy.** (1897) An insurance policy containing a provision that prohibits the insurer from contesting or canceling the policy on the basis of statements made in the application.

▸ **interest policy.** An insurance policy whose terms indicate that the insured has an interest in the subject matter of the insurance. Cf. *wager insurance* under INSURANCE.

▸ **joint life policy.** (1927) A life-insurance policy that matures and becomes due upon the death of any of those jointly insured.

▸ **lapsed policy.** (1873) **1.** An insurance policy on which there has been a default in premium payments. **2.** An insurance policy that, because of statutory provisions, remains in force after a default in premium payments. • Statutes normally provide a 30- or 31-day grace period after nonpayment of premiums. Cf. *extended policy.*

▸ **level-rate legal-reserve policy.** (1934) An insurance policy that seeks to build a reserve equal to the policy's face value by the end of the insured's life.

▸ **life policy.** (1834) A life-insurance policy that requires lifetime annual fixed premiums and that becomes payable only on the death of the insured. — Also termed *regular life policy.*

▸ **limited policy.** (1884) **1.** An insurance policy that specifically excludes certain classes or types of loss. **2.** See *basic-form policy.*

▸ **manuscript policy.** (1962) An insurance policy containing nonstandard provisions that have been negotiated between the insurer and the insured.

▸ **master policy.** (1926) An insurance policy that covers multiple insureds under a group-insurance plan. — Also termed *group policy.* See *group insurance* under INSURANCE.

▸ **mixed policy.** (1853) *Marine insurance.* An insurance policy combining aspects of both a voyage policy and a time policy.

▸ **multiperil policy.** (1951) An insurance policy that covers several types of losses, such as a homeowner's policy that covers losses from fire, theft, and personal injury. — Also termed *named-perils policy.*

▸ **nonmedical policy.** (1929) An insurance policy issued without a prior medical examination of the applicant.

▸ **occurrence policy.** (1944) An insurance policy to indemnify for any loss from an event that occurs within the policy period, regardless of when the claim is made.

▸ **open-perils policy.** (1997) A property-insurance policy covering all risks against loss except those specifically excluded from coverage. Cf. *limited-policy insurance* under INSURANCE.

▸ **open policy.** See *unvalued policy.*

▸ **package policy.** (1943) An insurance policy providing protection against multiple perils and losses of both the insured and third parties. • A homeowner's policy is usu. a package policy.

▸ **paid-up policy.** (1872) An insurance policy that remains in effect after premiums are no longer due.

▸ **participating policy.** (1872) An insurance policy that allows the holder a right to dividends or rebates from future premiums. • This type of policy is issued by a mutual company.

▸ **permanent policy.** A renewable insurance policy that is effective for a specified period and is terminable by either the insurer or the insured after giving express notice.

▸ **perpetual policy.** (1879) An insurance policy that remains effective without renewal until one of the parties terminates it according to its terms. — Also termed *continuous policy.*

▸ **regular life policy.** See *life policy.*

▸ **running policy.** See *floating policy.*

▸ **specific policy.** See *basic-form policy.*

▸ **standard policy.** (1893) **1.** An insurance policy providing insurance that is recommended or required by state law, usu. regulated by a state agency. **2.** An insurance policy that contains standard terms used for similar insurance policies nationwide, usu. drafted by an insurance industrial association such as Insurance Services Office.

▸ **survivorship policy.** (1860) A joint life-insurance policy that is payable after all the insureds have died.

▸ **term policy.** (1896) A life-insurance policy that gives protection for a specified period, but that does not have a cash value or reserve value.

▸ **time policy.** (1852) An insurance policy that is effective only during a specified period.

▸ **tontine policy (tahn-teen** *or* tahn-**teen).** (1873) An insurance policy in which a group of participants share advantages so that upon the default or death of any participant, his or her advantages are distributed among the remaining participants until only one remains, whereupon the whole goes to that sole participant. • Under the tontine plan of insurance, no accumulation or earnings are credited to the policy unless it remains in force for the tontine period of a specified number of years. Thus, those who survive the period and keep their policies in force share in the accumulated funds, and those who die or permit their policies to lapse during the period do not. This type of policy takes its name from Lorenzo Tonti, an Italian who invented it in the 17th century. Today, newer and more ingenious forms of insurance have largely made tontine policies defunct. See TONTINE.

▸ **umbrella policy.** (1958) An insurance policy covering losses that exceed the basic or usual limits of liability provided by other policies. See *umbrella insurance* under INSURANCE.

▸ **unvalued policy.** (1887) An insurance policy that does not state a value of the insured property but that, upon loss, requires proof of the property's worth. — Also termed *open policy.*

▸ **valued policy.** (18c) An insurance policy in which the sum to be paid when a loss occurs is fixed by the terms of the contract. • The value agreed on is conclusive for a total loss and provides a basis for determining recovery in cases of partial loss. This value is in the nature of liquidated damages.

▸ **voyage policy.** (1845) *Marine insurance.* A marine-insurance policy that insures a vessel or its cargo during a specified voyage. See *voyage insurance* under INSURANCE.

▸ **wager policy.** See *wager insurance* under INSURANCE.

insurance pool. (1935) A group of several insurers that, to spread the risk, combine and share premiums and losses.

insurance premium. See PREMIUM (1).

insurance rating. (1905) The process by which an insurer arrives at a policy premium for a particular risk. — Often shortened to *rating.*

Insurance Services Office. A nonprofit organization that provides analytical and decision-support services and tools to the insurance industry, including statistical, actuarial, underwriting, and claims data, and drafts of model insurance policy forms and coverage provisions. • The organization is composed of member insurers. It provides data and information to its members and also to nonmember subscribers, such as risk managers, insurance regulators, and self-insureds. — Abbr. ISO.

insurance trust. See TRUST (3).

insurance underwriter. See UNDERWRITER.

insurant, *n.* (1853) Someone who obtains insurance or to whom an insurance policy is issued. • This term is much less common than the attributive noun *insured.*

insure, *vb.* (17c) **1.** To secure, by payment of a premium, the payment of a sum of money in the event of a loss. **2.** To issue or procure an insurance policy on or for (someone or something).

insured, *n.* (17c) Someone who is covered or protected by an insurance policy. — Also termed *assured.*

▸ **additional insured.** (1929) Someone who is covered by an insurance policy but who is not the primary insured. • An additional insured may, or may not, be specifically named in the policy. If the person is named, then the term is sometimes *named additional insured.* — Also termed *secondary insured.*

▸ **class-one insured.** (1982) In a motor-vehicle policy, the named insured and any relative residing with the named insured.

▸ **class-two insured.** (1985) In a motor-vehicle policy, a person lawfully occupying a vehicle at the time of an accident.

▸ **first-named insured.** See *primary insured.*

▸ **named insured.** (1899) A person designated in an insurance policy as the one covered by the policy.

▸ **primary insured.** (1948) The individual or entity whose name appears first in the declarations of an insurance policy. — Also termed *first-named insured.*

insurer. (17c) Someone who agrees, by contract, to assume the risk of another's loss and to compensate for that loss. — Also termed *underwriter; insurance underwriter; carrier; assurer* (for life insurance).

▸ **excess insurer.** (1936) An insurer who is liable for settling any part of a claim not covered by an insured's primary insurer. — Also termed *secondary insurer.* See *primary insurer.*

▸ **primary insurer.** (1901) An insurer who is contractually committed to settling a claim up to the applicable policy limit before any other insurer becomes liable for any part of the same claim. See *excess insurer.*

▸ **quasi-insurer.** (1830) A service provider who is held to strict liability in the provision of services, such as an innkeeper or a common carrier.

▸ **secondary insurer.** See *excess insurer.*

insurgent, *n.* (18c) Someone who, for political purposes, engages in armed hostility against an established government. — **insurgent,** *adj.* — **insurgency,** *n.*

insuring agreement. See INSURING CLAUSE.

insuring clause. (1873) A provision in an insurance policy or bond reciting the risk assumed by the insurer or establishing the scope of the coverage. — Also termed *insuring agreement.*

insurrection. (15c) A violent revolt against an oppressive authority, usu. a government.

> "A popular tumult is a disorderly gathering of people who refuse to listen to the voice of their superiors, whether they be disaffected towards their superiors themselves or merely towards certain private individuals. These violent movements occur when the people believe themselves harassed, and they are more often caused by tax-collectors than by any other class of public officers. If the anger of the people is directed particularly against the magistrates or other officers invested with the public authority, and if it is carried so far as to result in positive disobedience or acts of violence, the movement is called a *sedition.* And when the evil extends and wins over the majority of the citizens in a town or province, and gains such strength that the sovereign is no longer obeyed, it is usual to distinguish such an uprising more particularly by the name of an *insurrection.*" Charles G. Fenwick, *The Law of Nations or the Principles of Natural Law* 336 (1916).

> "Insurrection is distinguished from rout, riot, and offense connected with mob violence by the fact that in insurrection there is an organized and armed uprising against authority or operations of government, while crimes growing out of mob violence, however serious they may be and however numerous the participants, are simply unlawful acts in disturbance of the peace which do not threaten the stability of the government or the existence of political society." 77 C.J.S. *Riot; Insurrection* § 29, at 579 (1994).

intact family. See FAMILY.

in tail. See TAIL.

intake, *n.* (1943) **1.** The official screening of a juvenile charged with an offense in order to determine where to determine where to place the juvenile pending formal adjudication or informal disposition. **2.** The body of officers who conduct this screening. **3.** *Hist. English law.* A piece of land temporarily taken from a common or moorland by a tenant to raise a crop.

intake day. (1985) The day on which new cases are assigned to the courts.

intaker. *Hist.* See FENCE (1).

intangible, *adj.* (17c) Not capable of being touched; impalpable; INCORPOREAL.

intangible, *n.* (1914) Something that lacks a physical form; an abstraction, such as responsibility; esp., an asset that is not corporeal, such as intellectual property.

▸ **general intangible.** (1935) Any personal property other than accounts, chattel paper, commercial tort claims, deposit accounts, documents, goods, instruments, investment property, letter-of-credit rights, letters of credit, money, and oil, gas, or other minerals before extraction. • Some examples are goodwill, things in action, and literary rights. UCC § 9-102(a)(42). See *intangible property* under PROPERTY.

▸ **payment intangible.** (1996) A general intangible under which the account debtor's principal obligation is a monetary obligation. UCC § 9-102(a)(61).

intangible asset. 1. See ASSET. **2.** See *intangible trade value* under VALUE (2).

intangible drilling cost. (1932) *Oil & gas.* An expense that is incident to and necessary for drilling and completing an oil or gas well and that has no salvage value. • Intangible drilling costs may be deducted in the year they are incurred rather than capitalized and depreciated. 26 USCA § 612. — Abbr. IDC.

intangible loss. See LOSS.

intangible movable. See MOVABLE (1).

intangible property. See PROPERTY.

intangible-rights doctrine. (1980) The rule that a person is entitled to receive honest services from those in the public sector or in the private sector who have fiduciary duties to the person. • Public-sector intangible rights derive from public officials' implied fiduciary duty to make governmental decisions in the public interest. Private-sector intangible rights arise out of fiduciary relationships. The intangible-rights doctrine is codified at 18 USCA § 1346. — Also termed *honest-services doctrine.*

intangible tax. See TAX.

intangible thing. See *incorporeal thing* under THING.

intangible trade property. See *intangible trade value* under VALUE (2).

intangible trade value. See VALUE (2).

in tantum (in **tan**-təm). [Latin] To that extent; insofar. Cf. PRO TANTO.

integer (**in**-tə-jər), *adj.* [Latin] (16c) *Archaic.* Whole; untouched. See RES NOVA.

integrated agreement. See INTEGRATED CONTRACT.

integrated bar. See *integrated bar association* under BAR ASSOCIATION.

integrated bar association. See *integrated bar association* under BAR ASSOCIATION.

integrated contract. (1930) One or more writings constituting a final expression of one or more terms of an agreement. — Also termed *integrated agreement*; *integrated writing.* See INTEGRATION (2).

▸ **completely integrated contract.** (1950) An integrated agreement adopted by the parties as a full and exclusive statement of the terms of the agreement. • The parties are therefore prohibited from varying or supplementing the contractual terms through parol (extrinsic) evidence.

▸ **partially integrated contract.** (1958) An agreement in which some, but not all, of the terms are integrated; any agreement other than a completely integrated agreement.

integrated property settlement. See PROPERTY SETTLEMENT (2).

integrated writing. See INTEGRATED CONTRACT.

integration. (17c) **1.** The process of making whole or combining into one. **2.** *Contracts.* The full expression of the parties' agreement, so that all earlier agreements are superseded, the effect being that neither party may later contradict or add to the contractual terms. — Also termed *merger.* See PAROL-EVIDENCE RULE.

▸ **complete integration.** (1930) The quality, state, or condition of fully expressing the intent of the parties. • Parol evidence is therefore inadmissible.

▸ **partial integration.** (1910) The quality, state, or condition of not fully expressing the parties' intent. • Parol (extrinsic) evidence is admissible to clear up ambiguities with respect to the terms that are not integrated.

3. *Wills & estates.* The combining of more than one writing into a single document to form the testator's last will and testament. • The other writing must be present at the time of execution and intended to be included in the will. The issue of integration is more complicated when it concerns a holographic will, which may be composed of more than one document written at different times. **4.** The incorporation of different races into existing institutions (such as public schools) for the purpose of reversing the historical effects of racial discrimination. Cf. DESEGREGATION. **5.** *Antitrust.* A firm's performance of a function that it could have obtained on the open market. • A firm can achieve integration by entering a new market on its own, by acquiring a firm that operates in a secondary market, or by entering into a contract with a firm that operates in a secondary market. — Also termed *vertical integration.* See *vertical merger* under MERGER.

▸ **backward integration.** (1925) A firm's acquisition of ownership of facilities that produce raw materials or parts for the firm's products.

6. *Securities.* The requirement that all security offerings over a given period are to be considered a single offering for purposes of determining an exemption from registration. • The Securities and Exchange Commission and the courts apply five criteria to determine whether two or more transactions are part of the same offering of securities: (1) whether the offerings are part of a single plan of financing, (2) whether the offerings involve issuance of the same class of securities, (3) whether the offerings are made at or about the same time, (4) whether the same type of consideration is received, and (5) whether the offerings are made for the same general purpose. 17 CFR § 230.502.

integration clause. (1941) A contractual provision stating that the contract represents the parties' complete and final agreement and supersedes all informal understandings and oral agreements relating to the subject matter of the contract. — Also termed *merger clause*; *entire-agreement clause.* See INTEGRATION (2); PAROL-EVIDENCE RULE.

integration rule. (1899) The rule that if the parties to a contract have embodied their agreement in a final document, any other action or statement is without effect and is immaterial in determining the terms of the contract. See PAROL-EVIDENCE RULE.

integrity. [fr. Latin *integritas* "unimpaired condition, wholeness, purity"] **1.** Freedom from corruption or impurity; soundness; purity. **2.** Moral soundness; the quality, state, or condition of being honest and upright.

integrity right. (1963) *Copyright.* The right of authors and artists to insist that their creative works not be changed without their authorization. • Integrity is one of the moral rights of artists recognized in civil-law countries, including much of Europe, but largely unavailable in the United States. Cf. MORAL RIGHT; ATTRIBUTION RIGHT.

intellectual disability. **1.** See *developmental disability* under DISABILITY (2). **2.** MENTAL RETARDATION.

intellectual impairment. See *developmental disability* under DISABILITY (2).

intellectual property. (1808) **1.** A category of intangible rights protecting commercially valuable products of the human intellect. • The category comprises primarily trademark, copyright, and patent rights, but also includes trade-secret rights, publicity rights, moral rights, and rights against unfair competition. **2.** A commercially valuable product of the human intellect, in a concrete or abstract form, such as a copyrightable work, a protectable trademark, a patentable invention, or a trade secret. — Abbr. IP.

> "While there is a close relationship between intangible property and the tangible objects in which they are embodied, intellectual property rights are distinct and separate from property rights in tangible goods. For example, when a person posts a letter to someone, the personal property in the ink and parchment is transferred to the recipient. . . . [T]he sender (as author) retains intellectual property rights in the letter." Lionel Bently & Brad Sherman, *Intellectual Property Law* 1-2 (2001).

▸ **hard intellectual property.** Intellectual property, such as a patent, that excludes others from using the invention without the holder's consent even if others find the innovation independently.

▸ **soft intellectual property.** Intellectual property, such as a copyright, that does not preclude independent creation by third parties.

intellectual-property crime. (1998) The offense of illegally copying and selling someone else's intellectual property. — Abbr. IPC.

intellectual-property offense. See INTELLECTUAL-PROPERTY CRIME.

intemperance. (15c) A lack of moderation or temperance; esp., habitual or excessive drinking of alcoholic beverages.

in tempus indebitum (in **tem**-pəs in-**deb**-i-təm). [Law Latin] At an undue time.

intend, *vb.* (14c) **1.** To have in mind a fixed purpose to reach a desired objective; to have as one's purpose <Daniel intended to become a lawyer>. **2.** To contemplate that the usual consequences of one's act will probably or necessarily follow from the act, whether or not those consequences are desired for their own sake <although he activated the theater's fire alarm only on a dare, the jury found that Wilbur intended to cause a panic>. **3.** To signify or mean <the parties intended for the writing to supersede their earlier handshake deal>.

intendant (in-**ten**-dənt). (17c) A director of a government agency, esp. (as used in 17th- and 18th-century France) a royal official charged with the administration of justice or finance.

intended beneficiary. See BENEFICIARY.

intended child. See CHILD.

intended parent. See *intentional parent* under PARENT (1).

intended to be recorded. (18c) (Of a deed or other instrument) not yet filed with a public registry, but forming a link in a chain of title.

intended-use doctrine. (1967) *Products liability.* The rule imposing a duty on a manufacturer to develop a product so that it is reasonably safe for its intended or foreseeable uses. • In determining the scope of responsibility, the court considers the defendant's marketing scheme and the foreseeability of the harm.

intendment (in-**tend**-mənt). (14c) **1.** The sense in which the law understands something <the intendment of a contract is that the contract is legally enforceable>. — Also termed *intendment of law.* **2.** A decision-maker's inference about the true meaning or intention of a legal instrument <there is no need for intendment, the court reasoned, when the text of the statute is clear>. — Formerly also spelled *entendment.*

▸ **common intendment.** (16c) The natural or common meaning in legal interpretation.

3. A person's expectations when interacting with others within the legal sphere.

> "Our institutions and our formalized interactions with one another are accompanied by certain interlocking expectations that may be called intendments, even though there is seldom occasion to bring these underlying expectations across the threshold of consciousness. In a very real sense when I cast my vote in an election my conduct is directed and conditioned by an anticipation that my ballot will be counted in favor of the candidate I actually vote for. This is true even though the possibility that my ballot will be thrown in the wastebasket, or counted for the wrong man, may never enter my mind as an object of conscious attention. In this sense the institution of elections may be said to contain an intendment that the votes cast will be faithfully tallied, though I might hesitate to say, except in a mood of rhetoric, that the election authorities had entered a contract with me to count my vote as I had cast it." Lon L. Fuller, *The Morality of Law* 217 (rev. ed. 1969).

intent. (13c) **1.** The state of mind accompanying an act, esp. a forbidden act. • While motive is the inducement to do some act, intent is the mental resolution or determination to do it. When the intent to do an act that violates the law exists, motive becomes immaterial. Cf. MOTIVE; SCIENTER.

> "The persistence of the word 'intent' in complex social problems where conscious intent is either irrelevant or indeterminable probably retards legal progress. The cloudy ethical atmosphere that hovers about this term tends to make [analysis] difficult." Edward Stevens Robinson, *Law and the Lawyers* 230 (1935).

> "The phrase 'with intent to,' or its equivalents, may mean any one of at least four different things: — (1) That the intent referred to must be the sole or exclusive intent; (2) that it is sufficient if it is one of several concurrent intents; (3) that it must be the chief or dominant intent, any others being subordinate or incidental; (4) that it must be a determining intent, that is to say, an intent in the absence of which the act would not have been done, the remaining purposes being insufficient motives by themselves. It is a question of construction which of those meanings is the true one in the particular case." John Salmond, *Jurisprudence* 383-84 (Glanville L. Williams ed., 10th ed. 1947).

▸ **constructive intent.** (1864) A legal principle that actual intent will be presumed when an act leading to the result could have been reasonably expected to cause that result.

> "Constructive intent is a fiction which permits lip service to the notion that intention is essential to criminality, while recognizing that unintended consequences of an act may sometimes be sufficient for guilt of some offenses." Rollin M. Perkins & Ronald N. Boyce, *Criminal Law* 835 (3d ed. 1982).

▸ **criminal intent.** (17c) **1.** MENS REA. **2.** An intent to commit an actus reus without any justification, excuse, or other defense. — Also termed *felonious intent.* See *specific intent.*

"The phrase 'criminal intent' is one that has been bandied about with various meanings not carefully distinguished. At times it has been used in the sense of the 'intent to do wrong' (the *outline* of the mental pattern which is necessary for crime in general), — as, for example, in the phrase 'the mental element commonly called criminal intent.' At times it has been used in the sense of mens rea as the mental element requisite for guilt of the very offense charged, 'a varying state of mind which is the contrary of an innocent state of mind, whatever may be pointed out by the nature of the crime as an innocent state of mind.' Often it is used to include criminal negligence as well as an actual intent to do the harmful deed, although at other times such negligence is referred to as a substitute, so to speak, for criminal intent in connection with certain offenses. Occasionally it is found in the sense of an intent to violate the law, — implying a knowledge of the law violated. On the other hand, as such knowledge is a factor not ordinarily required for conviction it has been pointed out that to establish ignorance of the law does not disprove criminal intent. Thus it has been said (assuming the absence of any circumstance of exculpation) 'whenever an act is criminal, the party doing the act is chargeable with criminal intent.' . . . This suggests a helpful guide for the use of the phrase 'criminal intent.' Some other term such as mens rea or guilty mind should be employed for more general purposes, and 'criminal intent' be restricted to those situations in which there is (1) an intent to do the *actus reus,* and (2) no circumstance of exculpation." Rollin M. Perkins & Ronald N. Boyce, *Criminal Law* 832–34 (3d ed. 1982).

▸ **donative intent.** (1899) The intent to surrender dominion and control over the gift that is being made.

▸ **felonious intent.** See *criminal intent.*

▸ **general intent.** (17c) The intent to perform an act even though the actor does not desire the consequences that result. • This is the state of mind required for the commission of certain common-law crimes not requiring a specific intent or not imposing strict liability. General intent usu. takes the form of recklessness (involving actual awareness of a risk and the culpable taking of that risk) or negligence (involving blameworthy inadvertence). — Also termed *general criminal intent; general mens rea.*

▸ **hostile intent.** See HOSTILE INTENT.

▸ **immediate intent.** (18c) The intent relating to a wrongful act; the part of the total intent coincident with the wrongful act itself.

▸ **implied intent.** (18c) A person's state of mind that can be inferred from speech or conduct, or from language used in an instrument to which the person is a party.

▸ **intent to kill.** (16c) An intent to cause the death of another; esp., a state of mind that, if found to exist during an assault, can serve as the basis for an aggravated-assault charge.

▸ **larcenous intent.** (1832) A state of mind existing when a person (1) knowingly takes away the goods of another without any claim or pretense of a right to do so, and (2) intends to permanently deprive the owner of them or to convert the goods to personal use. See LARCENY.

▸ **manifest intent.** (17c) Intent that is apparent or obvious based on the available circumstantial evidence, even if direct evidence of intent is not available. • For example, some fidelity bonds cover an employer's losses caused by an employee's dishonest or fraudulent acts committed with a manifest intent to cause a loss to the employer and to obtain a benefit for the employee. Establishing manifest intent sufficient to trigger coverage does not require direct evidence that the employee intended the employer's loss. Even if the employee did not actively want that result, but the result was substantially certain to follow from the employee's conduct, the requisite intent will be inferred.

▸ **predatory intent.** (1957) *Antitrust.* A business's intent to injure a competitor by unfair means, esp. by sacrificing revenues to drive a competitor out of business.

▸ **specific intent.** (18c) The intent to accomplish the precise criminal act that one is later charged with. • At common law, the specific-intent crimes were robbery, assault, larceny, burglary, forgery, false pretenses, embezzlement, attempt, solicitation, and conspiracy. — Also termed *criminal intent.* See SPECIFIC-INTENT DEFENSE.

▸ **testamentary intent.** (1830) A testator's intent that a particular instrument function as his or her last will and testament. • Testamentary intent is required for a will to be valid.

▸ **transferred intent.** (1932) Intent that the law may shift from an originally intended wrongful act to a wrongful act actually committed. • For example, if a person intends to kill one person but kills another inadvertently, the intent may be transferred to the actual act. See TRANSFERRED-INTENT DOCTRINE.

▸ **ulterior intent.** (1848) The intent that passes beyond a wrongful act and relates to the objective for the sake of which the act is done; MOTIVE. • For example, a thief's immediate intent may be to steal another's money, but the ulterior intent may be to buy food with that money.

2. A lawmaker's state of mind and purpose in drafting or voting for a measure.

▸ **legislative intent.** See LEGISLATIVE INTENT.

▸ **original intent.** (17c) The subjective intention of the drafters or ratifiers of an authoritative text. • Original intent denotes a legal fiction, since the idea of a collective but identical intent is something that cannot be said to exist in the preparation or adoption of a text. Cf. ORIGINAL MEANING.

intentio (in-**ten**-shee-oh), *n.* [Latin] **1.** *Roman law.* The part of a formula in which the plaintiff's claim against the defendant is stated. See FORMULA (1). **2.** *Hist.* A count or declaration in a real action. • *Intentio* was an earlier name for *narratio.* See NARRATIO. Pl. ***intentiones*** (in-ten-shee-**oh**-neez).

intention, *n.* (14c) The willingness to bring about something planned or foreseen; the quality, state, or condition of being set to do something. — **intentional,** *adj.*

"Intention is the purpose or design with which an act is done. It is the foreknowledge of the act, coupled with the desire of it, such foreknowledge and desire being the cause of the act, inasmuch as they fulfil themselves through the operation of the will. An act is intentional if, and in so far as, it exists in idea before it exists in fact, the idea realising itself in the fact because of the desire by which it is accompanied." John Salmond, *Jurisprudence* 378 (Glanville L. Williams ed., 10th ed. 1947).

"*Intention.* — This signifies full advertence in the mind of the defendant to his conduct, which is in question, and to its consequences, together with a desire for those consequences." P.H. Winfield, *A Textbook of the Law of Tort* § 10, at 19 (5th ed. 1950).

- ▸ **express intention.** The actual or plainly evident purpose behind an act or statement.
- ▸ **implied intention.** Intention that may be deduced from circumstances and the interpretation of words and actions.

intentional, *adj.* (17c) Done with the aim of carrying out the act.

intentional act. See ACT (2).

intentional father. See *intentional parent* under PARENT (1).

intentional fraud. See FRAUD (1).

intentional infliction of emotional distress. (1958) The tort of intentionally or recklessly causing another person severe emotional distress through one's extreme or outrageous acts. • In a few jurisdictions, a physical manifestation of the mental suffering is required for the plaintiff to recover. — Abbr. IIED. — Also termed (in some states) *outrage.* See *emotional distress* under DISTRESS (4). Cf. NEGLIGENT INFLICTION OF EMOTIONAL DISTRESS.

intentional-injury exclusion. See *expected/intended exclusion* under EXCLUSION (3).

intentional interference with prospective economic advantage. See TORTIOUS INTERFERENCE WITH PROSPECTIVE ADVANTAGE.

intentional invasion. See INVASION (1).

intentionalism. See ORIGINALISM (2).

intentional manslaughter. See *voluntary manslaughter* under MANSLAUGHTER.

intentional mother. See *intentional parent* under PARENT.

intentional parent. See PARENT.

intentional tort. See TORT.

intentional wrong. See WRONG.

intent of the legislature. See LEGISLATIVE INTENT.

intent to kill. See INTENT (1).

intent to publish. *Defamation.* The intent to communicate (defamatory words, etc.) to a third person or with knowledge that the communication will probably reach third persons. See PUBLISH (2).

intent to use. See BONA FIDE INTENT TO USE.

intent-to-use application. See TRADEMARK APPLICATION.

inter (**in**-tər), *prep.* [Latin] (17c) Among.

inter alia (**in**-tər **ay**-lee-ə *or* **ah**-lee-ə), *adv.* [Latin] (17c) Among other things.

inter alios (**in**-tər **ay**-lee-əs *or* **ah**-lee-əs), *adv.* [Latin] (17c) Among other persons.

Inter-American Bar Association. An organization of lawyers from North America, Central America, and South America whose purpose is to promote education, cooperation, and professional exchanges among lawyers from different American countries. — Abbr. IABA.

Inter-American Foundation. An independent federal foundation that supports social and economic development in Latin America and the Caribbean by making grants to private, indigenous organizations that carry out self-help projects benefiting poor people. • The agency is governed by a nine-member board — six from the private sector and three from the government. It was created in 1969 as an experimental foreign-assistance program. 22 USCA § 290f. — Abbr. IAF.

inter apices juris (**in**-tər **ay**-pə-seez [*or* **ap**-ə-seez] **joor**-is), *adv.* [Law Latin] Among the subtleties of the law. See APEX JURIS.

intercalare (in-tər-kə-**lair**-ee), *vb.* [Latin] *Civil law.* To introduce or insert among others; esp., to introduce a day or month into the calendar. • From this Latin term derives the rare English verb *intercalate,* roughly synonymous with *interpolate.*

intercede (in-tər-**seed**), *vb.* [fr. Latin *intercedere* "to interpose"] **1.** *Roman law.* (Of a magistrate, esp. a tribune) to veto. **2.** *Roman law.* To assume another's debt; esp., to act as surety for another. **3.** To go, come, or act between as a peacemaker, in an attempt to reconcile parties at variance; to mediate. **4.** To plead in favor of another; to urge on behalf of a contestant. **5.** To go, come, or pass between (things).

intercept, *n. Family law.* A mechanism by which a portion of an obligor's unemployment benefits, disability income, income-tax refund, or lottery winnings is automatically diverted to a child-support-enforcement agency to satisfy past-due support obligations.

intercept, *vb.* (15c) **1.** To divert (money) from a payee to satisfy a financial obligation of the payee. **2.** To covertly receive or listen to (a communication). • The term usu. refers to covert reception by a law-enforcement agency. See WIRETAPPING. — **interception,** *n.*

intercession. 1. *Roman law.* The assumption of liability for another's debt, esp. by agreeing to act as surety. **2.** *Roman law.* A magistrate's veto. **3.** Solicitation, interposition, or entreaty between parties at variance in an attempt to reconcile them.

intercessor (in-tər-**ses**-ər). Someone who interposes between parties at variance, in an attempt to reconcile them; esp., one who makes intercession with the stronger on behalf of the weaker.

interchangeable bond. See BOND (3).

interchange fee. See FEE (1).

intercircuit assignment. See ASSIGNMENT (5).

intercommon, *vb.* (15c) **1.** To share in the rights to a common. **2.** *Hist. Scots law.* To communicate or deal with (criminals or others). **3.** *Hist. Scots law.* To prohibit (a person) from communicating or dealing with a criminal.

inter conjuges (**in**-tər **kon**-jə-geez), *adv.* & *adj.* [Law Latin] Between husband and wife.

inter conjunctas personas (**in**-tər kən-**jəngk**-təs pər-**soh**-nəs). [Latin] Between conjoined persons, esp. family members. • Generally, conveyances between certain family members were void if designed to defraud.

intercountry adoption. See *international adoption* under ADOPTION (1).

intercourse. (15c) **1.** Dealings or communications, esp. between businesses, governmental entities, or the like.

- ▸ **common intercourse.** (16c) The normal, day-to-day interactions and dealings that people, esp. those in the same community, have with one another.

2. Physical sexual contact, esp. involving the penetration of the vagina by the penis. — Also termed *sexual intercourse.*

interdependence. *Int'l law.* The reliance of countries on each other to ensure their mutual subsistence and advancement.

interdict (**in**-tər-dikt), *n.* (15c) *Roman & civil law.* **1.** An injunction or other prohibitory, exhibitory, or restitutory decree.

▸ **decretal interdict** (di-**kreet**-əl). An interdict that signified the praetor's order or decree by applying the remedy in a pending case.

▸ **edictal interdict** (ee-**dik**-təl). An interdict that declared the praetor's intention to give a remedy in certain cases, usu. in a way that preserves or restores possession.

▸ **exhibitory interdict.** (1874) An interdict by which a praetor compelled a person or thing to be produced.

▸ **possessory interdict.** (1838) An interdict that protected a person whose possession was disturbed without due process. • A possessor in bad faith could obtain a possessory interdict because the interdict did not depend on title. It would, however, establish whether the possessor would be the defendant or the plaintiff in any subsequent claim. See INTERDICTUM.

▸ **prohibitory interdict.** (17c) An interdict by which a praetor forbade something to be done.

▸ **restitutory interdict** (ri-**stich**-ə-tor-ee *or* res-ti-**t[y]oo**-tə-ree). (1969) An interdict by which a praetor directed something to be restored to someone who had been dispossessed of it.

2. *Civil law.* Someone who has been interdicted; a natural person who, because of an infirmity, cannot make reasoned decisions about personal care or property or communicate those decisions; a person deprived of the capacity to make juridical acts. La. Civ. Code arts. 389, 390, 394.

▸ **limited interdict.** (1984) A person whose right to care for himself or herself is restricted by a court decision because of mental incapacity; a person subject to limited interdiction. La. Civ. Code art. 390.

interdict (in-tər-**dikt**), *vb.* (15c) **1.** To forbid or restrain. **2.** To intercept and seize (contraband, etc.). **3.** *Civil law.* To remove a person's right to handle personal affairs because of mental incapacity. **4.** *Roman law.* INTERDICTUM.

interdiction. (16c) **1.** The act of forbidding or restraining. **2.** The interception and seizure of something, esp. contraband. **3.** *Civil law.* The act of depriving a person of the right to handle his or her own affairs because of mental incapacity. See EX CAPITE INTERDICTIONIS. Cf. GUARDIANSHIP (1); CURATORSHIP; CURATOR (2).

> "Interdiction, now scarcely known in practice, was a means formerly adopted for the protection of those who were weak, facile, and easily imposed upon, and also for the protection of those who, being reckless and profuse, were unable to manage their estate with care and prudence. Interdiction was either judicial or voluntary: and in whichever of these modes the interdiction was effected and imposed, any disposition of heritage thereafter by the interdicted, without the consent of his interdictors, was liable to reduction on the ground of interdiction, except where the conveyances were onerous and rational." John Trayner, *Trayner's Latin Maxims* 193 (4th ed. 1894).

▸ **complete interdiction.** See *full interdiction.*

▸ **full interdiction.** (1986) The complete removal of one's right to care for oneself and one's affairs or estate because of mental incapacity. La. Civ. Code art. 389. — Also termed *complete interdiction.*

▸ **interdiction of commercial intercourse.** (1869) *Int'l law.* A governmental prohibition of commercial trade.

▸ **limited interdiction.** See *partial interdiction.*

▸ **partial interdiction.** (1998) The partial removal of one's right to care for oneself and one's affairs or estate because of mental incapacity. — Also termed *limited interdiction.*

interdictory (in-tər-**dik**-tər-ee), *adj.* (18c) **1.** Of, relating to, or involving an interdiction. **2.** Having the power to interdict. — Also termed *interdictive.*

interdictum (in-tər-**dik**-təm), *n.* [Latin] *Roman law.* A summary order to secure the applicant's rights by preventing something from being done (prohibitory interdict) or requiring property to be produced (exhibitory interdict) or restored (restitutory interdict). • A party might apply for an *interdictum* when some wrong had been done, or was likely to be done, and it was necessary either to redress or to prevent the wrong at once, without waiting for the ordinary legal processes; often it was a preliminary to an ordinary action (e.g., by settling which party was entitled to be defendant in the action). — Also termed *interdict.* Pl. ***interdicta.***

interdictum quod vi aut clam (in-tər-**dik**-təm kwod **vɪ** awt **klam**). [Latin "interdict because of force or stealth"] (1922) *Roman law.* An interdict issued against a person who forcibly (*vi*) or secretly (*clam*) altered or occupied the claimant's property. • The interdict required the defendant (the *prohibitus*) to restore the property to its previous condition.—Sometimes shortened to *interdictum quod vi.* Cf. *actio vi bonorum raptorum* under ACTIO.

> "If any person interested in the land forbade another from altering its condition, and the 'prohibitus' notwithstanding persevered, the 'interdictum quod vi' obliged him to restore everything to the state in which it was when the prohibition was signified to him." John George Phillimore, *Private Law Among the Romans* 178 (1863).

inter eosdem (**in**-tər ee-**ahs**-dəm). [Latin] Between the same persons.

interesse (in-tər-**es**-ee). [Latin] (15c) **1.** Monetary interest. **2.** A legal interest in property.

interessee (in-tə-re-**see**). See *real party in interest* under PARTY (2).

interesse termini (in-tər-**es**-ee **tər**-mə-nɪ). [Latin "interest of term or end"] (17c) *Archaic.* A lessee's right of entry onto the leased property; esp., a lessee's interest in real property before taking possession. • An *interesse termini* is not an estate; it is an interest for the term. It gives the lessee a claim against any person who prevents the lessee from entering or accepting delivery of the property.

> "[The *interesse termini's*] essential qualities, as a mere interest, in contradistinction to a term in possession, seems to arise from a want of possession. It is a right or interest only, and not an estate, and it has the properties of a right. It may be extinguished by a release to the lessor, and it may be assigned or granted away, but it cannot, technically considered, be surrendered; for there is no reversion before entry, in which the interest may drown. Nor will a release from the lessor operate by way of enlargement, for the lessee has no estate before entry." 4 James Kent, *Commentaries on American Law* *97 (George Comstock ed., 11th ed. 1866).

"There was a troublesome doctrine of the common law which established, in the case of a lease not operating under the Statute of Uses, that the lessee acquired no estate in the land until he actually entered into possession. Until that time he was said to have a mere right to take possession, and this right was called an *interesse termini*. This requisite of entry to perfect a lease has, however, been swept away by the Law of Property Act, 1925, and all terms of years absolute, whether created before or after the commencement of the Act, can take effect from the date fixed for the commencement of the term without actual entry." G.C. Cheshire, *Modern Law of Real Property* 128–29 (3d ed. 1933).

interest, *n.* (15c) **1.** The object of any human desire; esp., advantage or profit of a financial nature <conflict of interest>. **2.** A legal share in something; all or part of a legal or equitable claim to or right in property <right, title, and interest>. • Collectively, the word includes any aggregation of rights, privileges, powers, and immunities; distributively, it refers to any one right, privilege, power, or immunity.

▸ **absolute interest.** (18c) An interest that is not subject to any condition.

▸ **beneficial interest.** (18c) A right or expectancy in something (such as a trust or an estate), as opposed to legal title to that thing. • For example, a person with a beneficial interest in a trust receives income from the trust but does not hold legal title to the trust property.

▸ **carried interest. 1.** The share of any profits produced by a partnership's investment, paid to the general partner as compensation for managing the investment. • The general partner often contributes little or no capital to acquire the investment but gains an interest in it by providing time and skill. The general partner's interest in the property is "carried" with the property until it is liquidated. **2.** *Oil & gas.* In an oil-and-gas lease, a fractional interest that is free of some or all costs of exploring, drilling, and completing the well. • The owner of a carried lease may earn royalties on production but does not have a working interest, at least until all costs are recouped by the working-interest owner or owners, and often until some multiple of those costs are paid.

▸ **concurrent interest.** See *concurrent estate* under ESTATE (1).

▸ **contingent interest.** (18c) An interest that the holder may enjoy only upon the occurrence of a condition precedent. Cf. *vested interest.*

▸ **controlling interest.** (1842) Sufficient ownership of stock in a company to control policy and management; esp., a greater-than-50% ownership interest in an enterprise.

▸ **defeasible interest.** (18c) An interest that the holder may enjoy until the occurrence of a condition.

▸ **direct interest.** (17c) A certain, absolute interest <the juror was disqualified because she had a direct interest in the lawsuit>.

▸ **entailed interest.** (1846) An interest that devolves through lineal descendants only as a result of a fee tail.

▸ **entire interest.** (17c) A whole interest or right, without diminution. See FEE SIMPLE.

▸ **equitable interest.** (17c) An interest held by virtue of an equitable title or claimed on equitable grounds, such as the interest held by a trust beneficiary.

▸ **executory interest.** See EXECUTORY INTEREST.

▸ **expectant interest.** See *future interest.*

▸ **expectation interest.** (1836) The interest of a nonbreaching party in being put in the position that would have resulted if the contract had been performed. See *expectation damages* under DAMAGES; BENEFIT-OF-THE-BARGAIN RULE.

▸ **financial interest.** (1846) An interest involving money or its equivalent; esp., an interest in the nature of an investment. — Also termed *pecuniary interest.*

▸ **fractional interest.** See *undivided interest.*

▸ **future interest.** (17c) A property interest in which the privilege of possession or of other enjoyment is future and not present. • A future interest can exist in either the grantor (as with a reversion) or the grantee (as with a remainder or executory interest). Today, most future interests are equitable interests in stocks and debt securities, with power of sale in a trustee. — Also termed *future estate; expectant estate; expectant interest; nonpossessory estate; estate in expectancy.* Cf. *present interest.*

"[T]he interest is an existing interest from the time of its creation, and is looked upon as a part of the total ownership of the land or other thing [that] is its subject matter. In that sense, future interest is somewhat misleading, and it is applied only to indicate that the possession or enjoyment of the subject matter is to take place in the future." Lewis M. Simes & Allan F. Smith, *The Law of Future Interests* § 1, at 2–3 (2d ed. 1956).

"To own a future interest *now* means not only to be entitled now to judicial protection of one's possible future possession, but also (in most cases) to be able to make transfers now of that right of possible future possession." Thomas F. Bergin & Paul G. Haskell, *Preface to Estates in Land and Future Interests* 56 (2d ed. 1984). "When O transfers today 'to A for five years,' we can say *either* that O has a future interest *or* that he has a 'present' estate subject to a term for years in A. Similarly, when O transfers today his entire estate in fee simple absolute by a conveyance 'to A for five years, then to B and his heirs,' we can say *either* that B has a future interest *or* that he has a 'present' estate subject to a term for years in A. Unhappily, the fact that we have two locutions available to us can be a source of confusion. . . ." *Id.* at 42.

▸ **inalienable interest.** (1848) An interest that cannot be sold or traded.

▸ **inchoate interest.** (1800) A property interest that has not yet vested.

▸ **insurable interest.** (18c) A legal interest in another person's life or health or in the protection of property from injury, loss, destruction, or pecuniary damage. • To take out an insurance policy, the purchaser or the potential insured's beneficiary must have an insurable interest. If a policy does not have an insurable interest as its basis, it will usu. be considered a form of wagering and thus be held unenforceable. See *wager insurance* under INSURANCE.

▸ **interest in the use and enjoyment of land.** (1834) The pleasure, comfort, and advantage that a person may derive from the occupancy of land. • The term includes not only the interests that a person may have for residential, agricultural, commercial, industrial, and other purposes, but also interests in having the present-use value of the land unimpaired by changes in its physical condition.

▸ **joint interest.** (16c) An interest that is acquired at the same time and by the same title as another person's. See *joint tenancy* under TENANCY.

▸ **junior interest.** (1906) An interest that is subordinate to a senior interest.

▸ **legal interest.** (17c) **1.** An interest that has its origin in the principles, standards, and rules developed by courts of law as opposed to courts of chancery. **2.** An interest recognized by law, such as legal title.

▸ **legally protected interest.** (1925) A property interest that the law will protect against impairment or destruction, whether in law or in equity.

▸ **liberty interest.** (1960) An interest protected by the due-process clauses of state and federal constitutions. See FUNDAMENTAL RIGHT (2).

▸ **multiple interest.** A property interest that is good against an indefinitely large number of people.

▸ **ownership interest.** See *property interest.*

▸ **pecuniary interest.** See *financial interest.*

▸ **possessory interest.** See POSSESSORY INTEREST.

▸ **present interest.** (17c) **1.** A property interest in which the privilege of possession or enjoyment is present and not merely future; an interest entitling the holder to immediate possession. — Also termed *present estate.* Cf. *future interest.* **2.** A trust interest in which the beneficiary has the immediate beneficial enjoyment of the trust's proceeds. **3.** A trust interest in which the trustee has the immediate right to control and manage the property in trust.

▸ **property interest. 1.** *Property law.* An interest, perhaps including rights of possession and control, held by an owner, beneficiary, or remainderman in land, real estate, business, or other tangible items. **2.** *Constitutional law.* A legitimate claim of entitlement to some legal or contractual benefit that cannot be taken away without due process. — Also termed *proprietary interest*; *ownership interest*; *interest in property.*

▸ **proprietary interest.** (17c) **1.** A property right; specif., the interest held by a property owner together with all appurtenant rights, such as a stockholder's right to vote the shares. • Contingent fees and attorney's liens are exceptions to the rule that a lawyer may not have a proprietary interest in a client's claim or the subject matter of the litigation. **2.** See *property interest.*

▸ **reliance interest.** (1936) The interest of a nonbreaching party in being put in the position that would have resulted if the contract had not been made, including out-of-pocket costs.

▸ **restitution interest.** (1936) A nonbreaching party's interest in preventing the breaching party from retaining a benefit received under the contract and thus being unjustly enriched. • The benefit may have been received from the nonbreaching party or from a third party.

▸ **reversionary interest.** (18c) A future interest left in the transferor or successor in interest. See REVERSION.

▸ **senior interest.** (1937) An interest that takes precedence over others; esp., a debt security or preferred share that has a higher claim on a corporation's assets and earnings than that of a junior obligation or common share.

▸ **terminable interest.** (1883) An interest that may be terminated upon the lapse of time or upon the occurrence of some condition.

▸ **undivided interest.** (18c) An interest held under the same title by two or more persons, whether their rights are equal or unequal in value or quantity. — Also termed *undivided right*; *undivided title*; *fractional interest.* See *joint tenancy* and *tenancy in common* under TENANCY.

▸ **vested interest.** (18c) An interest for which the right to its enjoyment, either present or future, is not subject to the happening of a condition precedent. Cf. *contingent interest.*

▸ **working interest.** See WORKING INTEREST.

3. The compensation fixed by agreement or allowed by law for the use or detention of money, or for the loss of money by one who is entitled to its use; esp., the amount owed to a lender in return for the use of borrowed money. — Also termed *finance charge.* See USURY.

▸ **accrued interest.** (18c) Interest that is earned but not yet paid, such as interest that accrues on real estate and that will be paid when the property is sold if, in the meantime, the rental income does not cover the mortgage payments.

▸ **add-on interest.** (1952) Interest that is computed on the original face amount of a loan and that remains the same even as the principal declines. • A $10,000 loan with add-on interest at 8% payable over three years would require equal annual interest payments of $800 for three years, regardless of the unpaid principal amount. With add-on interest, the effective rate of interest is typically about twice the stated add-on interest rate. In the example just cited, then, the effective rate of interest would be about 16%. — Also termed *block interest.* See *add-on loan* under LOAN.

▸ **Boston interest.** (1985) Interest computed by using a 30-day month rather than the exact number of days in the month. — Also termed *New York interest.*

▸ **capped interest.** (1979) Interest that is calculated according to a variable interest rate, as with an adjustable-rate mortgage, but that cannot exceed an upper limit either for a specified period of time or for the entire duration of the period when the interest applies.

▸ **compound interest.** (17c) Interest paid on both the principal and the previously accumulated interest. Cf. *simple interest.*

▸ **conventional interest.** (1878) Interest at a rate agreed to by the parties themselves, as distinguished from that prescribed by law. Cf. *interest as damages.*

▸ **discount interest.** The interest that accrues on a discounted investment instrument (such as a government bond) as it matures. • The investor receives the interest when the instrument is redeemed.

▸ **gross interest.** (1884) A borrower's interest payment that includes administrative, service, and insurance charges.

▸ **illegal interest.** See USURY.

▸ **imputed interest.** (1968) Interest income that the IRS attributes to a lender regardless of whether the lender actually receives interest from the borrower. • This is common esp. in loans between family members.

▸ **interest as damages.** (1841) Interest allowed by law in the absence of a promise to pay it, as compensation for a delay in paying a fixed sum or a delay in assessing and paying damages. Cf. *conventional interest.*

▸ **lawful interest.** (16c) **1.** A rate of interest that is less than or equal to the statutory maximum. **2.** See *legal interest.*

▸ **legal interest.** (17c) **1.** Interest at a rate usu. prescribed by statute. • Courts often order monetary judgments to accumulate legal interest until paid. Cf. *legal rate* under INTEREST RATE. **2.** See *lawful interest.*

▸ **moratory interest.** See *prejudgment interest.*

▸ **New York interest.** See *Boston interest.*

▸ **prejudgment interest.** (1953) Statutorily prescribed interest accrued either from the date of the loss or from the date when the complaint was filed up to the date the final judgment is entered. • Prejudgment interest is usu. calculated only for liquidated sums. Depending on the statute, it may or may not be an element of damages. — Also termed *moratory interest.*

▸ **prepaid interest.** (1887) Interest paid before it is earned.

▸ **qualified residence interest.** (1993) *Tax.* Interest paid on debt that is secured by one's home and that was incurred to purchase, build, improve, or refinance the home. • This type of interest is deductible from adjusted gross income. — Abbr. QRI.

▸ **simple interest.** (17c) Interest paid on the principal only and not on accumulated interest. • Interest accrues only on the principal balance regardless of how often interest is paid. — Also termed *straight-line interest.* Cf. *compound interest.*

▸ **straight-line interest.** See *simple interest.*

▸ **unearned interest.** (1880) Interest received by a financial institution before it is earned.

▸ **unlawful interest.** See USURY.

interest-analysis technique. (1964) *Conflict of laws.* A method of resolving choice-of-law questions by reviewing a state's laws and the state's interests in enforcing those laws to determine whether that state's laws or those of another state should apply. — Also termed *governmental-interest-analysis technique.*

interest arbitration. See ARBITRATION.

interest as damages. See INTEREST (3).

interest-based quorum. See QUORUM.

interest bond. See BOND (3).

interest coupon. See COUPON.

interest-coverage ratio. (1960) The ratio between a company's pretax earnings and the annual interest payable on bonds and loans.

interested party. See PARTY (2).

interested person. See PERSON (1).

interested shareholder. See SHAREHOLDER.

interested stockholder. See *interested shareholder* under SHAREHOLDER.

interested witness. See WITNESS.

interest-equalization tax. See TAX.

interest factor. (1894) *Insurance.* In life-insurance ratemaking, an estimate of the interest or rate of return that the insurer will earn on premium payments over the life of a policy. • The interest factor is one element that a life insurer uses to calculate premium rates. See PREMIUM RATE; *gross premium* (1) under PREMIUM (1). Cf. MORTALITY FACTOR; RISK FACTOR.

interest-free, *adj.* (1943) Involving no charge of extra money that a borrower must pay back in addition to the principal amount.

interest-free loan. See LOAN.

interest group, *n.* (1908) An association of people who join together to try to influence popular opinion or government action. Cf. PRESSURE GROUP.

▸ **special-interest group.** (1920) An organization that seeks to influence legislation or government policy in favor of a particular interest or issue, esp. by lobbying. — Abbr. SIG. — Also termed *special interest.*

interest in property. See PROPERTY INTEREST.

Interest on Lawyers' Trust Accounts. A program that allows a lawyer or law firm to deposit a client's retained funds into an interest-bearing account that designates the interest payments to charitable, law-related purposes, such as providing legal aid to the poor. • Almost all states have either a voluntary or mandatory IOLTA program. — Abbr. IOLTA.

interest-only loan. See LOAN.

interest-only mortgage. See MORTGAGE.

interest policy. See INSURANCE POLICY.

interest rate. (1886) The percentage that a borrower of money must pay to the lender in return for the use of the money, usu. expressed as a percentage of the principal payable for a one-year period. — Often shortened to *rate.* — Also termed *rate of interest.*

▸ **annual percentage rate.** (1941) The actual cost of borrowing money, expressed in the form of an annualized interest rate. — Abbr. APR.

▸ **bank rate.** (1913) The rate of interest at which the Federal Reserve lends funds to member banks.

▸ **base rate.** (1970) The standard rate of interest, set by the Federal Reserve, Bank of England, etc., on which all the banks of a country set their charges.

▸ **contract rate.** (1856) The interest rate printed on the face of a bond certificate.

▸ **coupon rate.** (1962) **1.** The specific interest rate for a coupon bond. — Also termed *coupon interest rate.* See *coupon bond* under BOND (3). **2.** See *nominal rate.*

▸ **discount rate.** (1913) **1.** The interest rate at which a member bank may borrow money from the Federal Reserve. • This rate controls the supply of money available to banks for lending. Cf. *rediscount rate.* **2.** The percentage of a commercial paper's face value paid by an issuer who sells the instrument to a financial institution. **3.** The interest rate used in calculating present value.

▸ **effective rate.** (1912) The actual annual interest rate, which incorporates compounding when calculating interest, rather than the stated rate or coupon rate.

▸ **face rate.** See *nominal rate.*

▸ **fixed interest rate.** An interest rate that is specified and is not subject to change.

▸ **floating rate.** (1921) A varying interest rate that is tied to a financial index such as the prime rate.

▸ **illegal rate.** (1867) An interest rate higher than the rate allowed by law. See USURY.

▸ **legal rate.** (1857) **1.** The interest rate imposed as a matter of law when none is provided by contract. **2.** The maximum interest rate, set by statute, that may be charged on a loan. See *legal interest* under INTEREST (3). Cf. USURY.

▸ **lock rate.** (2000) A mortgage-application interest rate that is established and guaranteed for a specified period. — Also termed *locked-in rate*.

▸ **nominal rate.** (1872) The interest rate stated in a loan agreement or on a bond, with no adjustment made for inflation. — Also termed *coupon rate; face rate; stated rate; stated interest rate*.

▸ **prime rate.** (1952) The interest rate that a commercial bank holds out as its lowest rate for a short-term loan to its most creditworthy borrowers, usu. large corporations. • This rate, which can vary slightly from bank to bank, often dictates other interest rates for various personal and commercial loans. — Often shortened to *prime*. — Also termed *prime lending rate*.

▸ **real rate.** (1895) An interest rate that has been adjusted for inflation over time.

▸ **rediscount rate.** (1913) The interest rate at which a member bank may borrow from the Federal Reserve on a loan secured by commercial paper that has already been resold by the bank. Cf. *discount rate* (1).

▸ **stated rate.** See *nominal rate*.

▸ **variable rate.** (1970) An interest rate that varies at preset intervals in relation to the current market rate (usu. the prime rate).

interest-rate swap. (1982) An agreement to exchange interest receipts or interest-payment obligations, usu. to adjust one's risk exposure, to speculate on interest-rate changes, or to convert an instrument or obligation from a fixed to a floating rate — or from a floating to a fixed rate. • The parties to such an agreement are termed "counterparties."

▸ **generic swap.** See *plain-vanilla swap*.

▸ **hara-kiri swap.** An interest-rate swap made without any profit to the party offering the transaction.

▸ **plain-vanilla swap.** (1981) A typical interest-rate swap that involves one counterparty's paying a fixed interest rate while the other assumes a floating interest rate based on the amount of the principal of the underlying debt. • The underlying debt, called the "notional" amount of the swap, does not change hands — only the interest payments are exchanged. — Also termed *generic swap*.

interests of justice. (17c) The proper view of what is fair and right in a matter in which the decision-maker has been granted discretion. — Also termed (less traditionally) *interest of justice*.

interest suit. See SUIT.

interest unity. See *unity of interest* under UNITY.

interest warrant. See WARRANT (2).

interferant. (1899) **1.** Something that interferes with the proper function of a chemical analysis; specif., a chemical contaminant that renders the results of a blood, breath, or urine test unreliable. **2.** *Patents.* A party to an interference proceeding in the U.S. Patent and Trademark Office. • This term declined in use after the 1960s; today the PTO and courts use the term "contestant." — Also termed (in sense 2) *contestant*. See CONTESTANT (3).

interference, *n.* (18c) **1.** The act of meddling in another's affairs. **2.** An obstruction or hindrance. **3.** *Patents.* An administrative proceeding in the U.S. Patent and Trademark Office to determine who is entitled to the patent when two or more applicants claim the same invention, or when an application interferes with an existing patent. • This proceeding occurs when the same invention is claimed (1) in two pending applications, or (2) in one pending application and a patent issued within a year of the pending application's filing date. — Also termed *priority contest*. **4.** *Trademarks.* An administrative proceeding in the U.S. Patent and Trademark Office to determine whether a mark one party wants to register will cause confusion among consumers with another party's mark. • An administrative hearing may be held to determine whose mark prevails, but applicants usu. withdraw their applications and devise new marks instead. — **interfere,** *vb.*

interference-estoppel rejection. See REJECTION.

interference with a business relationship. See TORTIOUS INTERFERENCE WITH PROSPECTIVE ADVANTAGE.

interference with a contractual relationship. See TORTIOUS INTERFERENCE WITH CONTRACTUAL RELATIONS.

interference with contract. See TORTIOUS INTERFERENCE WITH CONTRACTUAL RELATIONS.

interfering with the administration of justice. See PERVERTING THE COURSE OF JUSTICE.

intergenerational love. (1990) **1.** Affection between adults and children. • This sense usu. refers to interfamilial affection, as between grandparents and grandchildren, and does not include sexual feelings. **2.** Romance or sexual contact between a child below the age of consent and an adult. • Pedophiles often use the term as a euphemism to assert that sexual contact between adults and children is consensual.

intergovernmental, *adj.* (1927) Between or involving governments of different jurisdictional entities, esp. different countries.

intergovernmental immunity. See IMMUNITY (1).

intergovernmental-immunity doctrine. (1939) *Constitutional law.* The principle that both the federal government and the states are independent sovereigns, and that neither sovereign may intrude on the other in certain political spheres. Cf. PREEMPTION (5).

Intergovernmental Maritime Consultative Organization. A unit of the United Nations charged with setting international standards for vessel safety and personnel training for shipping on the open seas. — Abbr. IMCO.

interim, *adj.* (16c) Done, made, or occurring for an intervening time; temporary or provisional <an interim director>.

interim award. See AWARD.

interim bond. See BOND (2).

interim certificate. (1893) A negotiable instrument payable by statute in some states in stocks or bonds and given before the issuance of stocks or bonds in which they are payable.

interim committitur. See COMMITTITUR.

interim curator. See CURATOR (2).

interim dominus (**in**-tər-im **dom**-ə-nəs). [Law Latin] (18c) *Hist.* Proprietor in the meantime. • The feminine form is *domina.*

> "A widow is *interim domina* of terce lands after her service, and in virtue thereof may either possess them herself, or let them out to tenants." John Trayner, *Trayner's Latin Maxims* 286 (4th ed. 1894).

interim financing. See FINANCING.

interim measure of protection. (1928) *Int'l law.* An international tribunal's order to prevent a litigant from prejudicing the final outcome of a lawsuit by arbitrary action before a judgment has been reached. • This measure is comparable to a temporary injunction in national law.

interim-occupancy agreement. (1962) A contract governing an arrangement (called a *leaseback*) whereby the seller rents back property from the buyer. See LEASEBACK.

interim order. See ORDER (2).

interim payment. See *installment payment* under PAYMENT.

interim preservation order. See PRESERVATION ORDER.

interim receipt. See RECEIPT (2).

interim relief. See RELIEF (3).

interim statement. *Accounting.* A periodic financial report issued during the fiscal year (usu. quarterly) that indicates the company's current performance. • The SEC requires the company to file such a statement if it is distributed to the company's shareholders. — Also termed *interim report.*

interim trustee. See TRUSTEE (2).

interim zoning. See ZONING.

interinsurance. See *reciprocal insurance* under INSURANCE.

interinsurance exchange. See RECIPROCAL EXCHANGE.

Interior Department. See DEPARTMENT OF THE INTERIOR.

interlineation (in-tər-lin-ee-**ay**-shən), *n.* (15c) **1.** The act of writing something between the lines of an earlier writing. **2.** Something written between the lines of an earlier writing. Cf. INTERPOLATION (1). — **interline,** *vb.*

interline waybill. See WAYBILL.

interlining. (1970) A carrier's practice of transferring a shipment to another carrier to reach a destination not served by the transferring carrier.

interlocking companies. See COMPANY.

interlocking confessions. See CONFESSION (1).

interlocking director. See DIRECTOR.

interlocking directorships. See DIRECTORSHIP.

interlocutor (in-tər-**lok**-yə-tər). (16c) *Scots law.* A nonfinal judicial order disposing of any part of a case.

interlocutory (in-tər-**lok**-yə-tor-ee), *adj.* (15c) (Of an order, judgment, appeal, etc.) interim or temporary; not constituting a final resolution of the whole controversy. — Also termed *medial.*

interlocutory appeal. See APPEAL (2).

Interlocutory Appeals Act. A 1958 federal statute that grants discretion to a U.S. court of appeals to review an interlocutory order in a civil case if the trial judge states in writing that the order involves a controlling question of law on which there is substantial ground for difference of opinion, and that an immediate appeal from the order may materially advance the termination of the litigation. 28 USCA § 1292(b). Cf. FINALITY DOCTRINE; FINAL-JUDGMENT RULE.

interlocutory application. See APPLICATION.

interlocutory costs. See COSTS (3).

interlocutory decision. See *interlocutory order* under ORDER (2).

interlocutory decree. See *interlocutory judgment* under JUDGMENT (2).

interlocutory injunction. See *preliminary injunction* under INJUNCTION.

interlocutory judgment. See JUDGMENT (2).

interlocutory order. See ORDER (2).

interloper, *n.* (16c) **1.** Someone who interferes without justification. **2.** Someone who trades illegally. — **interlope,** *vb.*

intermeddler. See OFFICIOUS INTERMEDDLER.

intermeddling, *n.* (16c) Officious interference in the affairs of others.

intermediary (in-tər-**mee**-dee-er-ee), *n.* (18c) A mediator or go-between; a third-party negotiator. Cf. FINDER (1). — **intermediate** (in-tər-**mee**-dee-ayt), *vb.*

▸ **informed intermediary.** (1979) *Products liability.* Someone who is in the chain of distribution from the manufacturer to the consumer and who knows the risks of the product. — Also termed *learned intermediary.*

intermediary bank. See BANK.

intermediate account. See ACCOUNT.

intermediate casing. See CASING.

intermediate court. See COURT.

intermediate fact. See FACT.

intermediate order. See *interlocutory order* under ORDER (2).

intermediate scrutiny. (1974) *Constitutional law.* A standard lying between the extremes of rational-basis review and strict scrutiny. • Under the standard, if a statute contains a quasi-suspect classification (such as gender or legitimacy), the classification must be substantially related to the achievement of an important governmental objective. — Also termed *middle-level scrutiny*; *mid-level scrutiny*; *heightened scrutiny.* Cf. STRICT SCRUTINY; RATIONAL-BASIS TEST.

intermediation. (17c) **1.** Any process involving an intermediary. **2.** The placing of funds with a financial intermediary that reinvests the funds, such as a bank that lends the funds to others or a mutual fund that invests the funds in stocks, bonds, or other instruments.

in terminis (in **tər**-mə-nis). [Law Latin] (17c) In express terms; expressly.

in terminis terminantibus (in tər-mə-nis tər-mə-**nan**-ti-bəs), *adv.* & *adj.* [Law Latin] In terms of determination; in express or determinate terms.

intermittent easement. See EASEMENT.

intermittent sentence. See SENTENCE.

intermixture of goods. See CONFUSION OF GOODS.

intermodal transport. See MULTIMODAL SHIPPING.

in terms, *adv. Archaic.* Expressly; in explicit words <Lord Kenyon laid it down in terms that the proprietor of a libelous paper was answerable criminally>.

intermunicipal law. See *private international law* under INTERNATIONAL LAW.

intern, *n.* (1889) An advanced student or recent graduate who is apprenticing to gain practical experience before entering a specific profession. See CLERK (4). — **internship,** *n.*

intern, *vb.* (1866) **1.** To segregate and confine a person or group, esp. those suspected of hostile sympathies in time of war. See INTERNMENT. **2.** To work in an internship.

internal act. See ACT (2).

internal affairs. A division or bureau within a department, usu. one in charge of investigating allegations of misconduct or the mishandling of bureaucratic matters.

internal-affairs doctrine. (1947) *Conflict of laws.* The rule that in disputes involving a corporation and its relationships with its shareholders, directors, officers, or agents, the law to be applied is the law of the state of incorporation. • This doctrine applies in the majority of states. In a few states, notably California and New York, foreign corporations must meet state-law requirements in specified circumstances.

> "Broadly speaking, 'corporate internal affairs' refers to the powers and obligations of a corporation's manager vis-a-vis the corporation and its shareholders, and the rights and duties of the corporation's shareholders vis-a-vis the corporation, its management and the other shareholders. Put differently, corporate internal affairs pretty much encompass the subject matter of those state laws typically referred to as corporate law. In dealing with a corporation's internal affairs, courts . . . have looked to the law of the state of incorporation for the governing rule. Courts often refer to this choice of law principle as the 'internal affairs doctrine.'" Franklin A. Gevurtz, *Corporation Law* 36 (2000).

internal affairs of a foreign corporation. (1856) *Conflict of laws.* Matters that involve only the inner workings of a corporation, such as dividend declarations and the selection of officers.

> "The old statement that a court will not hear cases involving the internal affairs of a foreign corporation has been practically dropped from the law today, and the result when appropriate is achieved under the forum non conveniens rule. Modern courts recognize their jurisdiction to entertain such suits, and insist only upon a discretionary power to refuse to exercise the existent jurisdiction when the facts make it both feasible and more desirable for the case to be heard by a court of the state of incorporation." Robert A. Leflar, *American Conflicts Law* § 255, at 512-13 (3d ed. 1977).

internal attack. A beneficiary's questioning of the propriety of a trust's continuance, the purpose being to terminate the trust and receive from the trustee the interests held for the beneficiary's benefit.

internal audit. See AUDIT.

internal commerce. See *intrastate commerce* under COMMERCE.

internal financing. See FINANCING.

internal law. See LAW.

internal litigation-hold letter. See LITIGATION-HOLD LETTER.

internally displaced person. See *displaced person* under PERSON (1).

internal rate of return. See RATE OF RETURN.

internal revenue. (18c) Governmental revenue derived from domestic taxes rather than from customs or import duties. — Also termed (outside the United States) *inland revenue.*

Internal Revenue Code. Title 26 of the U.S. Code, containing all current federal tax laws. — Abbr. IRC. — Also termed *tax law.*

Internal Revenue Service. A unit in the U.S. Department of the Treasury responsible for enforcing and administering the internal-revenue laws and other tax laws except those relating to alcohol, tobacco, firearms, and explosives. — Abbr. IRS.

internal review. (1916) An assessment performed within an organization where employees or members participate in collecting evidence and provide critical information to the organization's decision-makers.

internal security. (17c) The field of law dealing with measures taken to protect a country from subversive activities.

internal-security act. (1950) A statute illegalizing and controlling subversive activities of organizations whose purpose is believed to be to overthrow or disrupt the government. • In the United States, many provisions in such statutes have been declared unconstitutional. One such law was repealed in 1993. *See* 50 USCA § 781.

internal sovereignty. See SOVEREIGNTY (3).

internal waters. (1840) Any natural or artificial body or stream of water within the territorial limits of a country, such as a bay, gulf, river mouth, creek, harbor, port, lake, or canal. — Also termed *inland waters.*

> "Waters on the landward side of the baseline of the territorial sea form part of the internal waters of a State." Geneva Convention on the Territorial Sea and the Contiguous Zone, Apr. 29, 1958, art. 5, ¶ 1.

international administrative law. See ADMINISTRATIVE LAW.

international adoption. See ADOPTION (1).

international agreement. (1871) A treaty or other contract between different countries, such as GATT or NAFTA. See GENERAL AGREEMENT ON TARIFFS AND TRADE; NORTH AMERICAN FREE TRADE AGREEMENT.

> "Though international agreements are known by a variety of titles, such as treaties, conventions, pacts, acts, declarations, protocols, accords, arrangements, concordats, and *modi vivendi*, none of these terms has an absolutely fixed meaning. The more formal political agreements, however, are usually called *treaties* or *conventions*." Oscar Svarlien, *An Introduction to the Law of Nations* 261 (1955).

international application. See PATENT APPLICATION.

international application designating the United States. See PATENT APPLICATION.

international application originating in the United States. See PATENT APPLICATION.

International Association. See L'ASSOCIATION LITTERAIRE ET ARTISTIQUE INTERNATIONALE.

International Association of Defense Counsel. An invitation-only organization founded in 1920 to foster cooperation between corporate and insurance defense attorneys.

International Bank for Reconstruction and Development. See WORLD BANK.

international bill of exchange. See *foreign draft* under DRAFT (1).

International Bureau for the Protection of Intellectual Property. *Copyright.* A predecessor of the World Intellectual Property Organization. • The bureau was created by combining the Paris Convention's Secretariat (the International Bureau for the Paris Convention) with the Berne Copyright Convention of 1886. It was supervised by the Swiss government until 1970, when the bureau became part of WIPO. — Also termed *Bureaux Internationaux Reunis pour la Protection de la Propriete Intellectuelle*; *BIRPI.*

International Centre for Settlement of Investment Disputes. An autonomous division of the World Bank consisting of an international three-member tribunal that presides over arbitrations affecting the rights of foreign investors. • The center was created in 1966 under the Convention on the Settlement of Investment Disputes Between States and Nationals of Other States. It provides services for the conciliation and arbitration of international investment and trade disputes. — Abbr. ICSID.

international commerce. See COMMERCE.

international commodity agreement. (1941) An undertaking among producing and consuming countries to improve the global market's functioning for a particular commodity. • The purpose of such an agreement is to stabilize trade, supplies, and prices for the benefit of participating countries. — Abbr. ICA. — Often shortened to *commodity agreement.*

international control. (1883) *Int'l law.* The supervision over countries and their subdivisions for the purpose of ensuring the conformity of their conduct with international law.

> "[S]upervision is exercised increasingly not only over the conduct of governmental and intergovernmental institutions, but also over the acts and omissions of individuals to establish their conformity with requirements of public international law. Yet even where supranational entities, notably the European Communities, exercise international control over the conduct of individuals and corporate bodies, generally the supervision is destined to verify or secure conformity of governmental measures with relevant rules of law." Hugo J. Hahn, "International Controls," in 2 *Encyclopedia of Public International Law* 1079–80 (1995).

International Convention for the Protection of Performers, Producers of Phonograms and Broadcasting Organizations. See ROME CONVENTION ON RELATED RIGHTS.

international court. See COURT.

International Court of Justice. The 15-member permanent tribunal that is the principal judicial organ of the United Nations. • The Court sits in the Hague, Netherlands. It has jurisdiction to decide disputes submitted to it by countries, and to render advisory opinions requested by the United Nations and its specialized agencies. The U.N. Security Council has the express power to enforce the Court's judgments. — Abbr. ICJ. — Also termed *World Court.* See STATUTE OF THE INTERNATIONAL COURT OF JUSTICE.

international crime. (1891) *Int'l law.* A grave breach of international law, such as genocide or a crime against humanity, made a punishable offense by treaties or applicable rules of customary international law. • An international crime occurs when three conditions are satisfied: (1) the criminal norm must derive either from a treaty concluded under international law or from customary international law, and must have direct binding force on individuals without intermediate provisions of municipal law, (2) the provision must be made for the prosecution of acts penalized by international law in accordance with the principle of universal jurisdiction, so that the international character of the crime might show in the mode of prosecution itself (e.g., before the International Criminal Court), and (3) a treaty establishing liability for the act must bind the great majority of countries. — Also termed *international offense.*

International Criminal Court. A court established by a treaty known as the Statute of the International Criminal Court (effective 2002), with jurisdiction over genocides, crimes against humanity, war crimes, and aggression. It sits in The Hague, Netherlands. — Abbr. ICC.

International Criminal Police Organization. An international law-enforcement group founded in 1923 and headquartered in Lyons, France. • The organization gathers and shares information on transnational criminals for more than 180 member countries. — Also termed *Interpol.*

> "Interpol is something of a legal curiosity: it engages in intergovernmental activities and yet is not based on any treaty, convention, or other similar instrument. Its founding document is a constitution, drawn up by a group of police officers, that has neither been submitted for diplomatic signatures nor ratified by governments. Nevertheless, the organization received de facto recognition from the outset. . . . Interpol was formally granted the status of an 'intergovernmental agency' by the Economic and Social Council of the United Nations in 1971, and this is regarded as a form of de jure legitimization." Michael Fooner, "Interpol," in 3 *Encyclopedia of Crime and Justice* 910, 910 (Sanford H. Kadish ed., 1983).

international custom. See CUSTOM (1).

International Date Line. (1910) An imaginary line stretching from the North Pole to the South Pole to the east of which the date is one day later than it is to the west.

international economic law. (1939) International law relating to investment, economic relations, economic development, economic institutions, and regional economic integration.

international enclave. See ENCLAVE.

international extradition. See EXTRADITION.

international filing date. See PCT FILING DATE.

international fund. See MUTUAL FUND.

internationalization. (1871) The act or process of bringing a territory of one country under the protection or control of another or of several countries.

> "[T]he concept of internationalization is characterized by three elements: the abolition or limitation of the sovereignty of a specific State; the serving of community interests or at least the interests of a group of States; and the

establishment of an international institutional framework, not necessarily involving an international organization." Rüdiger Wolfrum, "Internationalization," in 2 *Encyclopedia of Public International Law* 1395 (1995).

international jurisdiction. See JURISDICTION.

international jurisprudence. See JURISPRUDENCE.

international law. (1786) The legal system governing the relationships between countries; more modernly, the law of international relations, embracing not only countries but also such participants as international organizations and individuals (such as those who invoke their human rights or commit war crimes). — Also termed *public international law; law of nations; law of nature and nations; jus gentium; jus gentium publicum; jus inter gentes; foreign-relations law; interstate law; law between states* (the word *state*, in the latter two phrases, being equivalent to *nation* or *country*). Cf. TRANSNATIONAL LAW.

"[I]nternational law or the law of nations must be defined as law applicable to states in their mutual relations and to individuals in their relations with states. International law may also, under this hypothesis, be applicable to certain interrelationships of individuals themselves, where such interrelationships involve matters of international concern." Philip C. Jessup, *A Modern Law of Nations* 17 (1948).

"International law is the legal order which is meant to structure the interaction between entities participating in and shaping international relations. This rather wide definition deliberately avoids a reference to States. Although States play a significant role in today's international relations, they are not the only actors. International organizations and other international law subjects, as well as groups of individuals, non-governmental organizations, and even individuals, contribute to the development of international relations. The development that groups of individuals and individuals participate in international relations acting on their own and not on behalf of States is a recent one." Rüdiger Wolfrum, "International Law," in 5 *The Max Planck Encyclopedia of Public International Law* 820, 821 (Rüdiger Wolfrum ed., 2012) (citations omitted).

▸ **customary international law.** (1905) International law that derives from the practice of states and is accepted by them as legally binding. • This is one of the principal sources or building blocks of the international legal system.

▸ **private international law.** (1834) International conflict of laws. • Legal scholars frequently lament the name "private international law" because it misleadingly suggests a body of law somehow parallel to public international law, when in fact it is merely a part of each legal system's private law. — Also termed *international private law; jus gentium privatum; intermunicipal law; comity; extraterritorial recognition of rights.* See CONFLICT OF LAWS (2).

"The expression 'international private law' is no doubt a slight improvement on 'private international law,' as it points out that the rules which the name denotes belong to the domain of private law. But the name, improve it as you will, has the insuperable fault of giving to the adjective 'international' a meaning different from the sense in which it is generally and correctly employed." A.V. Dicey & A. Berriedale Keith, *A Digest of the Law of England with Reference to the Conflict of Laws* 14 (3d ed. 1922).

"[A] word must be said about the name or title of the subject. No name commands universal approval. The expression 'Private International Law,' coined by Story in 1834 [Joseph Story, *Commentaries on the Conflict of Laws* § 9 (1834)], and used on the Continent by [Jean Jacques Gaspard] Foelix in 1838, has been adopted by Westlake and Foote and most French authors. The chief criticism directed against its use is its tendency to confuse private international law with the law of nations or public international law, as it is usually called. There are obvious differences between the two. The latter primarily governs the relations between sovereign states and it may perhaps be regarded as the common law of mankind in an early state of development; the former is designed to regulate disputes of a private nature, notwithstanding that one of the parties may be a private state. There is, at any rate in theory, one common system of public international law . . . ; but . . . there are as many systems of private international law as there are systems of municipal law." G.C. Cheshire, *Private International Law* 15 (6th ed. 1961).

International Law Commission. A body created in 1947 by the United Nations for the purpose of encouraging the progressive development and codification of international law. • The Commission is composed of experts in international law. It has drafted many important treaties that have become binding treaty law, including the Vienna Convention on the Law on Treaties. — Abbr. ILC.

international legal community. (1928) **1.** The collective body of countries whose mutual legal relations are based on sovereign equality. **2.** More broadly, all organized entities having the capacity to take part in international legal relations. **3.** An integrated organization on which a group of countries, by international treaty, confer part of their powers for amalgamated enterprise. • In this sense, the European Union is a prime example.

international legislation. (1836) *Int'l law.* **1.** Law-making among countries or intergovernmental organizations, displaying structural and procedural characteristics that are the same as national legislation. **2.** The product of any concerted effort to change international law by statute. **3.** The process of trying to change international law by statute. **4.** Loosely, the adoption by international bodies of binding decisions, other than judicial and arbitral decisions, concerning specific situations or disputes.

International Monetary Fund. A U.N. specialized agency established to stabilize international exchange rates and promote balanced trade. — Abbr. IMF.

"The International Monetary Fund (IMF) is a central pillar of the postwar economic order established at the Bretton Woods Conference of 1944. It was designed to oversee the global rules governing money in general and adherence to orderly currency relations among the industrial countries in particular. It also was intended to be a lender of last resort for rich and poor countries alike. But the world for which the IMF was created has long ceased to exist and the IMF has found itself thrust into roles that were neither planned nor expected. Its primary mission has become to minister prescriptions to financially distressed economies, especially among the developing countries. In the process, it has acquired immense influence over the economic destinies of many countries. It has also acquired a reputation as an unrelenting disciplinarian whose programs and policies produce economic austerity, social unrest, and political instability. In its proclivity for becoming enmeshed in controversy, the IMF indeed is without peer among international organizations. According to one claim, the IMF has overthrown more governments than Marx and Lenin combined." Don Babai, "International Monetary Fund," in *The Oxford Companion to Politics of the World* 412 (Joel Kreiger ed. 2001).

international offense. See INTERNATIONAL CRIME.

international organization. (1907) *Int'l law.* **1.** An intergovernmental association of countries, established by and operated according to multilateral treaty, whose purpose is to pursue the common aims of those countries. • Examples include the World Health Organization, the International Civil Aviation Organization, and the Organization of Petroleum Exporting Countries. **2.** Loosely, an intergovernmental or nongovernmental international association.

International Parental Kidnapping Crime Act of 1993. A federal statute that implemented the Hague Convention on the Civil Aspects of International Child Abduction. 18 USCA § 1204. — Abbr. IPKCA. See HAGUE CONVENTION ON THE CIVIL ASPECTS OF INTERNATIONAL CHILD ABDUCTION.

international person. *Int'l law.* An entity having a legal personality in international law; one who, being a subject of international law, enjoys rights, duties, and powers established in international law and has the ability to act on the international plane.

International Prisoner Transfer Program. See TREATY TRANSFER.

international private law. **1.** See *private international law* under INTERNATIONAL LAW. **2.** See CONFLICT OF LAWS (2).

international regime. See REGIME.

International Regulations for Preventing Collisions at Sea. See INTERNATIONAL RULES OF THE ROAD.

international relations. (1880) **1.** World politics. **2.** Global political interaction, primarily among sovereign countries. **3.** The academic discipline devoted to studying world politics, embracing international law, international economics, and the history and art of diplomacy.

international river. See RIVER.

International Rules of the Road. *Maritime law.* A set of statutes designed to promote navigational safety. • The International Rules were formalized at the convention on the International Regulations for Preventing Collisions at Sea, 1972. The rules set requirements for navigation lights, day shapes, steering and sailing rules, sound signals in good and restricted visibility condition, and distress signals, among other things. Congress adopted the rules and enacted them in statutory form. 33 USCA § 1602. — Also termed *72 COLREGS*; *International Regulations for Preventing Collisions at Sea, 1972.*

International Schedule of Classes of Goods and Services. *Trademarks.* A nearly worldwide classification system that enhances organization and retrieval of registered marks within a category of goods or services. — Abbr. ISCGS.

international seabed. (1969) The seabed and ocean floor, as well as the subsoil, lying beyond the territorial limits of countries. — Also termed *international seabed area.*

international terrorism. See TERRORISM.

International Trade Administration. A unit in the U.S. Department of Commerce responsible for promoting world trade and strengthening the international trade and investment position of the United States. • Created in 1980, the agency operates through three offices: the Office of the Assistant Secretary for Import Services, the Office of the Assistant Secretary for Market Access and Compliance, and the Office of the Assistant Secretary for Trade Development. — Abbr. ITA.

International Trade Commission. See UNITED STATES INTERNATIONAL TRADE COMMISSION.

International Trade Court. See UNITED STATES COURT OF INTERNATIONAL TRADE.

international union. See UNION.

international will. See WILL.

inter naturalia feudi (**in**-tər nach-ə-**ray**-lee-ə [**fyoo**-dɪ]). [Law Latin] *Scots law.* Among the things naturally arising from a feu. • Such items include payment of duties and stipulated services to be performed for the superior. — Sometimes shortened to *inter naturalia.*

internecine (in-tər-**nee**-sin *or* in-tər-**nee**-sɪn *or* in-tər-**nes**-een), *adj.* (17c) **1.** Deadly; characterized by mass slaughter. **2.** Mutually deadly; destructive of both parties <an internecine civil war>. **3.** Loosely, of, relating to, or involving conflict within a group <internecine faculty politics>.

internee, *n.* (1918) Someone who is put into prison during a war or for political reasons, usu. without trial.

Internet. (1974) A global network connecting countless information networks and computing devices from schools, libraries, businesses, private homes, etc., using a common set of communication protocols. Cf. WORLD WIDE WEB.

> "'The internet' comprises physically the entirety of the global interconnected computer networks, which colloquially is equated with the information, communication, and other services available therein. The term 'internet' is likewise used synonymously for its most famous and widely used service, the world wide web." Johann-Christoph Woltag, "Internet," in 6 *The Max Planck Encyclopedia of Public International Law* 227, 228 (Rüdiger Wolfrum ed., 2012).

> "What is the Internet? The Internet is a global network connection of computers. It is a public network, neither controlled nor owned by any single person or entity. There is no central storage location of information transmitted via the Internet, nor is there a universal channel of communication. Instead, each separate computer or network 'independently . . . exchange[s] communications and information with other computers.' Essentially, it is 'a vast collection of computer networks which form and act as a single huge network for transport of data and messages.'" Daniel B. Garrie & Francis M. Allegra, *Plugged In: Guidebook to Software and the Law* § 3.1, at 89–90 (2013).

Internet Corporation for Assigned Names and Numbers. A nonprofit corporation established in 1998 to assign and manage the system of Internet domain names and to allocate Internet-protocol (IP) address space. — Abbr. ICANN.

Internet luring. (1998) *Criminal law.* The use of the Internet in some way, as by e-mail, to induce a minor to engage in illegal sexual activity. 18 USCA § 2422(b).

Internet patent. See PATENT (3).

Internet payment. See CYBERPAYMENT.

Internet payment service. (1994) An enterprise that offers electronic transfers of money.

Internet-protocol address. (1989) The 10-digit identification tag used by computers to locate specific websites. — Abbr. IP address.

Internet scrip. See SCRIP.

Internet service provider. (1991) A business or other organization that offers Internet access, typically for a fee. — Abbr. ISP.

internment (in-**tərn**-mənt), *n.* (1870) The government-ordered detention of people suspected of disloyalty to the government, such as the confinement of Japanese Americans during World War II. — **intern,** *vb.*

internuncio (in-tər-**nən**-shee-oh), *n.* [fr. Latin *internuntius*] (17c) **1.** A messenger between two parties. **2.** A broker who serves as agent of both parties to a transaction. — Also termed *internuncius*. **3.** A papal representative at a foreign court, ranking below a nuncio. Cf. NUNCIO (1); LEGATE (3). — **internuncial,** *adj.*

inter pares (**in**-tər **pair**-eez), *adv.* & *adj.* [Latin] Between peers; between people in an equal position.

inter partes (in-tər **pahr**-teez), *adv.* [Latin "between parties"] (1816) Between two or more parties; with two or more parties in a transaction. — ***inter partes,*** *adj.*

***inter partes* reexamination.** See REEXAMINATION.

inter partes review. *Patents.* An administrative procedure in the U.S. Patent and Trademark Office whereby the validity of an issued or reissued patent may be challenged on the basis of prior-art patents and printed publications. • For patents filed on or after March 16, 2013, inter partes review cannot be initiated until the time for post-grant review has expired. Cf. POST-GRANT REVIEW.

interpel. See INTERPELLATE.

interpellate (in-tər-**pel**-ayt), *vb.* (16c) **1.** (Of a judge) to interrupt, with a question, a lawyer's argument. **2.** (Of a legislator) to interrupt a legislature's calendar by bringing into question a ministerial policy, esp. in the legislature of France, Italy, or Germany. — Also termed (in Scots law) *interpel* (in-tər-**pel**). — **interpellation,** *n.*

interpellatio (in-tər-pə-**lay**-shee-oh), *n.* [Latin "a demand, interruption"] *Roman law.* **1.** A demand for payment of a debt or for desistance from a course of action. **2.** The interruption of a process, e.g., of the acquisition of title by possession. **3.** The institution of a legal process or appeal. Pl. ***interpellationes*** (in-tər-pə-lay-shee-**oh**-neez).

interplea. (17c) A pleading by which a stakeholder places the disputed property into the court's registry; the plea made by an interpleader. See INTERPLEADER.

interplead, *vb.* (16c) **1.** (Of a claimant) to assert one's own claim regarding property or an issue already before the court. **2.** (Of a stakeholder) to institute an interpleader action, usu. by depositing disputed property into the court's registry to abide the court's decision about who is entitled to the property. Cf. IMPLEAD.

interpleader, *n.* (16c) **1.** A suit to determine a right to property held by a usu. disinterested third party (called a *stakeholder*) who is in doubt about ownership and who therefore deposits the property with the court to permit interested parties to litigate ownership. • Typically, a stakeholder initiates an interpleader both to determine who should receive the property and to avoid multiple liability. Fed. R. Civ. P. 22. See STAKEHOLDER (1). Cf. IMPLEADER; INTERVENTION (1); IMPLEADING. **2.** Loosely, a party who interpleads. — Also termed (in civil law) *concursus.*

> "Interpleader is a form of joinder open to one who does not know to which of several claimants he or she is liable, if liable at all. It permits him or her to bring the claimants into a single action, and to require them to litigate among themselves to determine which, if any, has a valid claim. Although the earliest records of a procedure similar to interpleader were at common law, it soon became an equitable rather than a legal procedure." Charles Alan Wright, *The Law of Federal Courts* § 74, at 531 (5th ed. 1994).

Interpol (**in**-tər-pohl). See INTERNATIONAL CRIMINAL POLICE ORGANIZATION.

interpolation (in-tər-pə-**lay**-shən), *n.* (17c) **1.** The act of inserting words into a document to change or clarify the meaning. • In a negative sense, interpolation can refer to putting extraneous or false words into a document to change its meaning. Cf. INTERLINEATION. **2.** (*often pl.*) *Roman law.* An editorial change made by one of the compilers of the Digests and the Justinian Code. • The compilers made insertions, deletions, and juxtapositions in the texts, but made few real changes to the substantive law. — **interpolate,** *vb.* — **interpolative,** *adj.* — **interpolator,** *n.*

interposition, *n.* (14c) **1.** The act of submitting something (such as a pleading or motion) as a defense to an opponent's claim. **2.** *Archaic.* The action of a state, while exercising its sovereignty, in rejecting a federal mandate that it believes is unconstitutional or overreaching. • The Supreme Court has declared that interposition is an illegal defiance of constitutional authority. — **interpose,** *vb.*

interpret, *vb.* To ascertain the meaning and significance of thoughts expressed in words.

interpretatio (in-tər-pri-**tay**-shee-oh), *n.* [Latin] **1.** *Roman law.* An opinion of a Roman jurist (an interpreter of the law, not an advocate) who did not usu. appear in court. • Such an opinion was not originally binding, but by the Law of Citations (A.D. 426), the opinions of five jurists acquired binding force. See CITATIONS, LAW OF. Pl. ***interpretationes*** (in-tər-pri-tay-shee-**oh**-neez). **2.** INTERPRETATION (1).

- ▸ ***interpretatio authentica.*** See *authentic interpretation* under INTERPRETATION (1).
- ▸ ***interpretatio declarativa.*** See *declarative interpretation* under INTERPRETATION (1).
- ▸ ***interpretatio doctrinalis.*** **1.** Scientific interpretation. **2.** See *doctrinal interpretation* under INTERPRETATION (1).
- ▸ ***interpretatio excedens.*** See *extravagant interpretation* under INTERPRETATION (1).
- ▸ ***interpretatio extensiva.*** See *liberal interpretation* (1) under INTERPRETATION (1).
- ▸ ***interpretatio grammatica.*** See *grammatical interpretation* under INTERPRETATION (1).
- ▸ ***interpretatio historica.*** See *historical interpretation* under INTERPRETATION (1).
- ▸ ***interpretatio historico-grammatica.*** See *historico-grammatical interpretation* under INTERPRETATION (1).
- ▸ ***interpretatio lata.*** See *liberal interpretation* (1) under INTERPRETATION (1).
- ▸ ***interpretatio limitata.*** See *restrictive interpretation* under INTERPRETATION (1).
- ▸ ***interpretatio logica.*** See *logical interpretation* under INTERPRETATION (1).
- ▸ ***interpretatio predestinata.*** See *predestined interpretation* under INTERPRETATION (1).
- ▸ ***interpretatio restricta.*** See *strict interpretation* under INTERPRETATION (1).
- ▸ ***interpretatio soluta.*** See *free interpretation* under INTERPRETATION (1).
- ▸ ***interpretatio stricta.*** See *strict interpretation* under INTERPRETATION (1).

▸ ***interpretatio usualis.*** See *usual interpretation* under INTERPRETATION (1).

▸ ***interpretatio vafer.*** See *artful interpretation* under INTERPRETATION (1).

▸ ***interpretatio verbalis.*** See *strict interpretation* under INTERPRETATION (1).

▸ ***interpretatio viperina*** (in-tər-pri-**tay**-shee-oh vɪ-pə-**rɪ**-nə). [Law Latin "a viper's interpretation"] (18c) *Hist.* A disapproved method of construction, by which ambiguous documents are interpreted in a way that destroys their effectiveness. — Also termed *viperine interpretation.*

interpretation, *n.* (14c) **1.** The ascertainment of a text's meaning; specif., the determination of how a text most fittingly applies to particular facts. Cf. APPLICATION (4).

> "Interpretation, as applied to written law, is the art or process of discovering and expounding the intended signification of the language used, that is, the meaning which the authors of the law designed it to convey to others." Henry Campbell Black, *Handbook on the Construction and Interpretation of the Laws* 1 (1896).

> "There is more to interpretation in general than the discovery of the meaning attached by the author to his words. Even if, in a particular case, that meaning is discoverable with a high degree of certitude from external sources, the question whether it has been adequately expressed remains." Rupert Cross, *Statutory Interpretation* 149 (1976).

▸ **administrative interpretation.** (1863) An interpretation given to a law or regulation by an administrative agency.

▸ **artful interpretation.** A type of predestined interpretation involving cunning attempts to show that the text means something that was not, even by the interpreter's own knowledge, the true meaning. — Also termed *interpretatio vafer.*

▸ **authentic interpretation.** (1967) An interpretation arrived at by asking the drafter or drafting body what the intended meaning was. — Also termed *interpretatio authentica.*

> "The procedure of referring the doubtful statute to its author has acquired a name in the literature of jurisprudence. It is called 'authentic interpretation.' . . . [Although] this device has been tried in . . . recent times in certain European countries, . . . [it] has always failed, and no thoughtful adviser would recommend it to any government today." Lon L. Fuller, *Anatomy of the Law* 29–30 (1968).

▸ **broad interpretation.** See *liberal interpretation.*

▸ **close interpretation.** See *strict interpretation.*

▸ **comparative interpretation.** (1933) A method of statutory construction by which parts of the statute are compared to each other, and the statute as a whole is compared to other documents from the same source on a similar subject.

▸ **comprehensive interpretation.** See *extensive interpretation.*

▸ **contemporaneous interpretation.** See LIVING CONSTITUTIONALISM.

▸ **customary interpretation.** (1902) Interpretation based on earlier rulings on the same subject.

▸ **declarative interpretation.** An interpretation that is thought to settle the meaning of a term that is vague or ambiguous. • An example is an interpretation that settles which specific animals are and are not covered by the term *game.* — Also termed *interpretatio declarativa.*

▸ **doctrinal interpretation.** An interpretation that is based on some doctrine other than fairly deriving the meaning from the text. — Also termed *interpretatio doctrinalis.*

▸ **dynamic interpretation.** An interpretation based on a consideration of evolving societal, legal, and constitutional circumstances or needs as time has passed since the creation or adoption of a governing text. — Also termed *progressive interpretation.* — **dynamicist,** *n.*

▸ **extensive interpretation.** (17c) A liberal interpretation that applies a legal provision, esp. in a statute, to a case not falling within its literal words. • This term is a close synonym of *liberal interpretation.* — Also termed *comprehensive interpretation.*

> "Extensive interpretation (interpretatio extensiva), likewise called liberal interpretation, is that which inclines towards adopting the more or most comprehensive signification of the word. Extensive or comprehensive interpretation seems to be a better term than liberal interpretation. The latter sounds as if a disposition of the interpreter were to be indicated, while his true object is to ascertain the exact meaning; at least the term ought to be reserved for those cases where we actually strive, for some reason or other, to give the most liberal sense to a set of words, for instance in a case which strongly calls for mercy, though the law is distinct and demands punishment." Francis Lieber, *Legal and Political Hermeneutics* 58–59 (William G. Hammond ed., 3d ed. 1880).

▸ **extravagant interpretation.** A mode of interpretation that replaces the true meaning of a text with something clearly beyond it. — Also termed *interpretatio excedens.*

▸ **fair interpretation.** See FAIR READING.

▸ **free interpretation.** An interpretation not based on any specific principle or doctrine other than what the interpreter decides is most desirable. • An early statement of this unconstrained approach is as follows: "Nay, whoever hath an absolute authority to *interpret* any written or spoken laws, it is *he* who is truly the Law Giver to all intents and purposes, and not the Person who first wrote or spoke them." Benjamin Hoadly, *Sixteen Sermons* 291 (1754). — Also termed *unrestricted interpretation; interpretatio soluta.*

▸ **grammatical interpretation.** (1830) **1.** Interpretation that is based exclusively on the words themselves. **2.** An interpretation based on text and context. — Also termed *interpretatio grammatica.* See TEXTUALISM.

▸ **historical interpretation.** **1.** An interpretation based on original meaning; ORIGINALISM. **2.** In the civil-law tradition, interpretation derived from regarding the precept as the culmination of a course of historical development disclosing its idea. — Also termed *interpretatio historica.*

▸ **historico-grammatical interpretation.** An interpretation based on an analysis of history and grammar. — Also termed *interpretatio historico-grammatica.*

▸ **intentional interpretation.** An interpretation based on the intentions (and not necessarily on the words) of a governing text's creators or enactors.

▸ **interpretation contra legem** (**kon**-trə **leg**-əm). An interpretation contrary to the words of the text, usu. arrived at for consequentialist (extratextual) reasons.

▸ ***interpretio* restrictive.** See *strict interpretation.*

▸ **large interpretation.** See *liberal interpretation.*

▸ **liberal interpretation.** (17c) **1.** A broad interpretation of a text in light of the situation presented and possibly beyond the language's permissible meanings, usu. with the object of effectuating the spirit and broad purpose of the text or producing the result that the interpreter thinks desirable. — Also termed *liberal construction; equitable construction; loose interpretation; loose construction; broad interpretation; broad construction; interpretatio extensiva; interpretatio lata.* **2.** Interpretation according to what the reader believes the author reasonably intended, even if, through inadvertence, the author failed to think of it. — Also termed *large interpretation; mixed interpretation.* Cf. *strict interpretation.*

"Liberal construction . . . expands the meaning of the statute to embrace cases which are clearly within the spirit or reason of the law, or within the evil which it was designed to remedy, provided such an interpretation is not inconsistent with the language used. It resolves all reasonable doubts in favor of the applicability of the statute to the particular case." William M. Lile et al., *Brief Making and the Use of Law Books* 343 (Roger W. Cooley & Charles Lesley Ames eds., 3d ed. 1914).

3. In constitutional doctrine, an interpretation that allows the federal government to do something that the Constitution does not say it may do.

▸ **limited interpretation.** See *restrictive interpretation.*

▸ **literal interpretation.** See *strict interpretation.*

▸ **logical interpretation.** (1870) Interpretation that departs from the literal words on the ground that there may be other, more satisfactory evidence of the author's true intention; an interpretation based on reasoning about the lawmaker's meaning. — Also termed *interpretatio logica; rational interpretation.*

▸ **loose interpretation.** See *liberal interpretation.*

▸ **mixed interpretation.** See *liberal interpretation* (2).

▸ **practical interpretation.** **1.** See *contemporaneous construction* under CONSTRUCTION (2). **2.** PRAGMATISM.

▸ **pragmatic interpretation.** See PRAGMATISM.

▸ **predestined interpretation.** An interpretation that is consciously or unconsciously influenced by a strong bias of the mind that makes the text subservient to the interpreter's preconceived views. — Also termed *interpretatio predestinata.*

"Finally, interpretation may be predestined (interpretatio predestinata), if the interpreter, either consciously or unknown to himself, yet laboring under a strong bias of mind, makes the text subservient to his preconceived views, or some object he desires to arrive at. Luther, in his work, De Papatu, charges the catholics with what is called here predestined interpretation of the bible, inasmuch as in his view they do not seek for the true meaning of the bible, but strive to make it subservient to their preconceived dogmas. This peculiar species of interpretation would not have been mentioned here, for it is not genuine interpretation, were it not so common in all branches, in sciences and common life, in law and politics not less than in religion, with protestants as habitually as with catholics, so that none of us can be too watchful against being betrayed into it. It corresponds to what might be called in ratiocination, *ex post facto* reasoning." Francis Lieber, *Legal and Political Hermeneutics* 60–61 (William G. Hammond ed., 3d ed. 1880).

▸ **progressive interpretation.** See *dynamic interpretation.*

▸ **purposive interpretation.** **1.** An interpretation that looks to the "evil" that the statute is trying to correct (i.e., the statute's purpose). **2.** See *teleological interpretation.* — Also termed *purposive construction.*

▸ **rational interpretation.** See *logical interpretation.*

▸ **reasonable interpretation.** An interpretation that is neither strict nor large, but that keeps the words of a text within their common and natural sense and arrives at a fair and just exposition of the text.

"By a reasonable interpretation, we mean, that in case the words are susceptible of two different senses, the one strict, the other more enlarged, that should be adopted, which is most consonant with the apparent objects and intent of the constitution; that, which will give efficacy and force, as a *government*, rather than that, which will impair its operations, and reduce it to a state of imbecility." 1 Joseph Story, *Commentaries on the Constitution of the United States* 298 (3d ed. 1858).

▸ **restricted interpretation.** **1.** See *restrictive interpretation.* **2.** See *strict interpretation.*

▸ **restrictive interpretation.** (17c) An interpretation that is bound by a principle or principles existing outside the interpreted text. — Also termed *restricted interpretation; limited interpretation; interpretatio limitata.* Cf. *unrestrictive interpretation.*

▸ **spurious interpretation.** An interpretation that makes, unmakes, or remakes meaning rather than discovering it. • According to Roscoe Pound, spurious interpretation "puts a meaning into the text as a juggler puts coins, or what not, into a dummy's hair, to be pulled forth presently with an air of discovery." 3 Roscoe Pound, *Jurisprudence* 479–80 (1959).

▸ **statutory interpretation.** See STATUTORY CONSTRUCTION.

▸ **strict interpretation.** (16c) **1.** An interpretation according to the narrowest, most literal meaning of the words without regard for context and other permissible meanings. **2.** An interpretation according to what the interpreter narrowly believes to have been the specific intentions or understandings of the text's authors or ratifiers, and no more. — Also termed (in senses 1 & 2) *strict construction; literal interpretation; literal construction; restricted interpretation; interpretatio stricta; interpretatio restricta; interpretatio verbalis.* **3.** The philosophy underlying strict interpretation of statutes. — Also termed *close interpretation; interpretatio restrictive.* See *strict constructionism* under CONSTRUCTIONISM. Cf. *large interpretation; liberal interpretation* (2).

"Strict construction of a statute is that which refuses to expand the law by implications or equitable considerations, but confines its operation to cases which are clearly within the letter of the statute, as well as within its spirit or reason, not so as to defeat the manifest purpose of the Legislature, but so as to resolve all reasonable doubts against the applicability of the statute to the particular case." William M. Lile et al., *Brief Making and the Use of Law Books* 343 (Roger W. Cooley & Charles Lesley Ames eds., 3d ed. 1914).

"Strict interpretation is an equivocal expression, for it means either literal or narrow. When a provision is ambiguous, one of its meanings may be wider than the other, and the strict (i.e., narrow) sense is not necessarily the strict (i.e., literal) sense." John Salmond, *Jurisprudence* 171 n.(t) (Glanville L. Williams ed., 10th ed. 1947).

4. In constitutional doctrine, an interpretation based on the idea that the federal government cannot do anything that the Constitution does not expressly say it may do.

▸ **systematic interpretation.** In the civil-law tradition, an interpretation derived from analysis of the legal system and fitting the precept into that system.

▸ **teleological interpretation.** An interpretation arrived at through imaginative reconstruction, whereby the judge attempts to read the text as he or she believes the drafter would have wished to phrase it in order to achieve the drafter's desired end. — Also termed *purposive interpretation.* See IMAGINATIVE RECONSTRUCTION.

▸ **textual interpretation.** See TEXTUALISM.

▸ **unrestricted interpretation.** See *free interpretation.*

▸ **unrestrictive interpretation.** (1968) Interpretation in good faith, without reference to any specific principle. Cf. *restrictive interpretation.*

▸ **usual interpretation.** An interpretation on grounds of custom and usage. — Also termed *interpretatio usualis.*

▸ **viperine interpretation.** See *interpretatio viperina* under INTERPRETATIO (2).

2. Loosely, the imputation or creation of meaning that is absent from a text.

"Current legislative terminology, by implying a single concept of 'statutory interpretation,' tends to obscure the important difference between the finding of meaning, on the one hand, and the imputation of meaning or the judicial creation of law, on the other." Reed Dickerson, *Introduction to Symposium on Judicial Law Making in Relation to Statutes*, 36 Ind. L.J. 411, 413 (1961).

3. A translation, esp. oral, from one language to another. 4. CHARACTERIZATION (1). See CONSTRUCTION (2). — **interpret,** *vb.* — **interpretative, interpretive,** *adj.*

interpretation act. (1855) A statute that directs courts on how to uniformly construe the language of other statutes. — Also termed *interpretation statute.*

Interpretation Act of 1850. See BROUGHAM'S ACT.

interpretation clause. (1827) A legislative or contractual provision giving the meaning of frequently used words or explaining how the document as a whole is to be construed. Cf. *construction statute* under STATUTE.

"An 'interpretation clause' is a section sometimes incorporated in a statute, prescribing rules for its construction, or defining the meaning to be attached to certain words and phrases frequently occurring in the other parts of the act. When a statute contains such a clause, the courts are bound to adopt the construction which it prescribes, and to understand the words in the sense in which they are therein defined, although otherwise the language might have been held to mean something different. A definition incorporated in a statute is as much a part of the act as any other portion. It is imperative. . . . An interpretation clause may have the effect to repeal one or more of the settled and accepted rules of statutory construction, either with reference to the particular act in which it is found, or, if inserted in a code or body of compiled laws, generally for the entire statute law of the state." Henry Campbell Black, *Handbook on the Construction and Interpretation of the Laws* § 89, at 269–70 (2d ed. 1911).

interpretation principle. The doctrine that every application of a legal text to particular circumstances entails interpretation.

interpretation statute. See INTERPRETATION ACT.

***interpretatio* restrictive.** See *strict interpretation* under INTERPRETATION (1).

interpretatio viperina. See INTERPRETATIO.

interpretative canon. See *canon of construction* under CANON (1).

interpretative rule. See INTERPRETIVE RULE.

interpreted testimony. See TESTIMONY.

interpreter, *n.* (14c) **1.** Someone who translates, esp. orally, from one language to another, esp. as a vocation; specif., a person who is sworn at a trial to accurately translate the testimony of a witness who is deaf or mute, or who speaks a foreign language. Cf. TRANSLATOR. **2.** Someone who reads and applies a text to a given circumstance; esp., one who engages in construing a governing legal text to determine its proper application to a particular set of facts. **3.** A person who performs a piece of music or a dramatic role. **4.** A computer program that transforms the instructions in another program into a form that can be more easily understood by a given computer.

interpretive canon. See *canon of construction* under CANON (1).

interpretive-direction canon. The doctrine that definition sections and interpretation sections in legal instruments are to be carefully followed. See DEFINED TERM.

interpretive method. A system or approach to reading legal documents, esp. legal instruments. — Also termed *interpretive methodology.*

interpretive rule. *Administrative law.* **1.** The requirement that an administrative agency explain the statutes under which it operates. **2.** An administrative rule explaining an agency's interpretation of a statute. — Also termed *interpretative rule.* Cf. LEGISLATIVE RULE.

interpretive theory of law. (1984) The theory that in a controversial case there is a correct answer that the court must find, as opposed to using its discretion to decide it. • Ronald Dworkin proposed this theory in *Law's Empire* (1987).

interpretivism. (1978) The doctrinal view that the only norms in constitutional adjudication are those stated or closely inferable from the text, and that it cannot be left to the judiciary to give moral content from age to age to such concepts as "fundamental liberties," "fair procedure," and "decency." See ORIGINALISM. Cf. NONINTERPRETIVISM; NONORIGINALISM; LIVING CONSTITUTIONALISM; LIVING-TREE DOCTRINE.

"A long-standing dispute in constitutional theory has gone under different names at different times, but today's terminology seems as helpful as any. Today we are likely to call the contending sides 'interpretivism' and 'noninterpretivism' — the former indicating that judges deciding constitutional issues should confine themselves to enforcing norms that are stated or clearly implicit in the written Constitution, the latter the contrary view that courts should go beyond that set of references and enforce norms that cannot be discovered within the four corners of the instrument." John Hart Ely, *Democracy and Distrust* 1 (1980).

inter quattuor parietes (**in**-tər **kwah**-too-ər pə-**rɪ**-ə-teez), *adv.* & *adj.* [Law Latin] Within the four walls.

interracial, *adj.* (1888) Between different races of people.

interracial adoption. See *transracial adoption* under ADOPTION (1).

interracial marriage. See MISCEGENATION.

inter regalia (**in**-tər ri-**gay**-lee-ə), *adj.* [Latin] Included in the royal powers or prerogatives; among other things belonging to the sovereign. — Also termed *in patrimonio principis.* See REGALIA.

interregnum (in-tə-**reg**-nəm). (16c) **1.** An interval between reigns; the time when a throne is vacant between the reign of a sovereign and the accession of a successor. **2.** A period when a country or organization has no ruler or leader, a new one being awaited. **3.** *Archaic.* Authority exercised during a temporary vacancy of the throne or a suspension of the regular government. **4.** A break or pause in a continuous event.

interrogatee (in-ter-ə-gə-**tee**). (1816) Someone who is interrogated. — Also termed *interrogee* (in-ter-ə-**gee**).

interrogation, *n.* (15c) The formal or systematic questioning of a person; esp., intensive questioning by the police, usu. of a person arrested for or suspected of committing a crime. • The Supreme Court has held that, for purposes of the Fifth Amendment right against self-incrimination, interrogation includes not only express questioning but also words or actions that the police should know are reasonably likely to elicit an incriminating response. *Rhode Island v. Innis,* 446 U.S. 291, 100 S.Ct. 1082 (1980). — **interrogate,** *vb.* — **interrogative,** *adj.*

▸ **custodial interrogation.** (1966) Police questioning of a detained person about the crime that he or she is suspected of having committed. • *Miranda* warnings must be given before a custodial interrogation.

▸ **investigatory interrogation.** (1962) Routine, nonaccusatory questioning by the police of a person who is not in custody.

▸ **noncustodial interrogation.** (1966) Police questioning of a suspect who has not been detained and can leave at will. • *Miranda* warnings are usu. not given before a noncustodial interrogation.

interrogative question. (1940) *Civil law.* In a criminal trial, a question asked of a witness to elicit inadmissible evidence relating to the crime at issue in the case. Cf. ASSERTIVE QUESTION.

interrogator (in-**ter**-ə-gay-tər). (18c) Someone who poses questions to another.

interrogatory (in-tə-**rog**-ə-tor-ee), *n.* (16c) A written question (usu. in a set of questions) submitted to an opposing party in a lawsuit as part of discovery. *See* Fed. R. Civ. P. 33.

▸ **adjusted interrogatory.** *Scots law.* One of a series of questions devised and modified by the parties, or, if they cannot agree on them, by the court, to be posed to witnesses examined on commission. • Adjusted interrogatories are often necessary in commissions to take evidence at distant locations.

▸ **contention interrogatory.** (1975) An interrogatory designed to discover the factual basis of the allegations in a complaint, answer, or counterclaim, or to determine the theory of the opposing party's case.

▸ **cross-interrogatory.** (17c) An interrogatory from a party who has received a set of interrogatories.

▸ **fact interrogatory.** See *identification interrogatory.*

▸ **identification interrogatory.** (1993) A request for the responding party to identify relevant documents, tangible objects, or individuals who have knowledge of facts relating to the lawsuit. — Also termed *fact interrogatory; state-all-facts interrogatory.*

▸ **special interrogatory.** (18c) A written jury question whose answer is required to supplement a general verdict. • This term is not properly used in federal practice, which authorizes interrogatories and special verdicts, but not special interrogatories. Fed. R. Civ. P. 49. The term is properly used, however, in the courts of some states. — Also termed *special issue.*

▸ **state-all-facts interrogatory.** See *identification interrogatory.*

interrogee. See INTERROGATEE.

in terrorem (in te-**ror**-əm), *adv.* & *adj.* [Latin "in order to frighten"] (17c) By way of threat; as a warning <the demand letter was sent *in terrorem*; the client has no intention of actually suing>.

***in terrorem* clause.** See NO-CONTEST CLAUSE.

in terrorem populi (in te-**ror**-əm **pop**-yə-lɪ), *adv.* [Latin] To the terror of the people. • At common law, this phrase was necessary in an indictment for riot.

interruptio (in-tər-**rəp**-shee-oh). [Latin] Interruption. • This word refers to a break in the possession of land that ends a prescriptive claim.

interruption. (15c) A break in the period of possession of land, possibly ending a claim to ownership by prescriptive right.

▸ **legal interruption.** *Louisiana law.* A break in the running of prescription that occurs when the property's possessor acknowledges another person's ownership rights, or the owner (or obligor) sues the possessor (or obligor). La. Civ. Code arts. 3462, 3464. — Also termed *legal interruption of prescription.*

▸ **natural interruption.** *Louisiana law.* A break of more than one year in a possessor's period of possession after a rightful owner or a third person seizes the real property. La. Civ. Code art. 3465. — Also termed *natural interruption of prescription.*

inter rusticos (**in**-tər **rəs**-ti-kohs), *adv.* [Latin] Among the unlearned.

inter se (**in**-tər **see** *or* **say**). [Latin "between or among themselves"] (1845) (Of a right or duty) owed between the parties rather than to others. — Also termed *inter sese* (**in**-tər **see**-see).

> "[T]he law of nations is, or at least includes, a branch of natural law, namely, the rules of natural justice as applicable to the relations of states *inter se.*" John Salmond, *Jurisprudence* 32 (Glanville L. Williams ed., 10th ed. 1947).

intersection. (16c) A place where two roads meet or form a junction.

***inter se* doctrine.** (1927) *Int'l law.* The now-defunct doctrine that relations between members of the British Commonwealth were in no circumstances international and were incapable of giving rights and duties under international law.

inter sese. See INTER SE.

intersex, *n.* (1917) A person whose reproductive system has characteristics of both males and females, or who is genetically mosaic, with some cells that possess XX chromosomes and others that are XY. — Also termed *hermaphrodite.*

interspousal, *adj.* (1906) Between husband and wife.

interspousal immunity. See *husband-wife immunity* under IMMUNITY (2).

interspousal tort immunity. See *husband-wife immunity* under IMMUNITY (2).

interstate, *adj.* (1838) Between two or more states or residents of different states; involving different states, esp. in the United States.

interstate adoption. See ADOPTION (1).

interstate agreement. (1876) An agreement between states. Cf. *interstate compact* under COMPACT.

Interstate Agreement on Detainers Act. A 1956 federal statute allowing the federal government, certain states, and the District of Columbia to temporarily obtain custody of a prisoner for trial even though the prisoner is already incarcerated elsewhere. • Under the Act, if a prisoner makes a written request for a disposition of the untried charges in the second forum, the government obtaining custody must try the prisoner within 180 days of the request. 18 USCA app. 2, § 2. — Abbr. IADA; IAD. See UNIFORM MANDATORY DISPOSITION OF DETAINERS ACT.

interstate commerce. See COMMERCE.

Interstate Commerce Commission. The now-defunct federal agency established by the Interstate Commerce Act in 1887 to regulate surface transportation between states by certifying carriers and pipelines and by monitoring quality and pricing. • In December 1995, when Congress eliminated this agency, the Surface Transportation Board (STB) — a three-member board that is a division of the Department of Transportation — assumed most of the agency's duties. — Abbr. ICC. See SURFACE TRANSPORTATION BOARD.

interstate compact. See COMPACT.

Interstate Compact on the Placement of Children. An agreement whose purpose is to ensure that when states are involved in the placement or adoption of children across state lines, the states cooperate with each other to facilitate the process and to protect the children. • This compact is intended to secure states' cooperation in investigating the suitability of proposed adoptive homes in an interstate adoption and also to alleviate conflicts that often occur when the agencies and courts of more than one state are involved. The compact has been enacted in almost identical form in all 50 states as well as in the District of Columbia and the Virgin Islands. — Abbr. ICPC. — Often shortened to *Interstate Compact.*

interstate contract. See CONTRACT.

interstate extradition. See EXTRADITION.

interstate income-withholding order. (1994) A court order entered to enforce a support order of a court of another state by withholding income of the defaulting person.

interstate law. (1866) **1.** INTERNATIONAL LAW. **2.** The rules and principles used to determine controversies between residents of different states.

interstate rendition. See RENDITION (2).

interstate trade. See *interstate commerce* under COMMERCE.

interstice (in-**tuur**-stis). (17c) **1.** A break or gap in something, esp. something continuous. **2.** An intervening space, esp. between the parts of something. **3.** A short time between events.

intersubjective zap. (1984) In critical legal studies, a so-called spontaneous moment of shared intuition. — Also termed *zap.*

intertwining doctrine. (1981) The principle that if arbitrable and nonarbitrable claims arise from a single transaction and the claims are factually and legally mingled, a court can refuse to compel arbitration of any claims. • This doctrine is of limited effect because the Federal Arbitration Act usu. preempts it.

intervener. See INTERVENOR.

intervening act. See *intervening cause* under CAUSE (1).

intervening agency. See *intervening cause* under CAUSE (1).

intervening cause. See CAUSE (1).

intervening damages. See DAMAGES.

intervening force. 1. See FORCE. **2.** See *intervening cause* under CAUSE (1).

intervening rights. (1874) *Patents.* An infringement defense based on the right of a person to continue practicing an invention even though the patent owner has obtained a reissue patent with broader claims to cover the invention. *See* 35 USCA § 252, ¶ 2. — Also termed *doctrine of intervening rights.*

intervenor. (17c) Someone who voluntarily enters a pending lawsuit because of a personal stake in it. — Also spelled *intervener.*

intervention, *n.* (1860) **1.** The entry into a lawsuit by a third party who, despite not being named a party to the action, has a personal stake in the outcome. *See* Fed. R. Civ. P. 24. • The intervenor sometimes joins the plaintiff in claiming what is sought, sometimes joins the defendant in resisting what is sought, and sometimes takes a position adverse to both the plaintiff and the defendant. Cf. IMPLEADER; INTERPLEADER; IMPLEADING. **2.** The legal procedure by which such a third party is allowed to become a party to the litigation. — Formerly also termed (in senses 1 & 2) *trial of right of property.* **3.** *Int'l law.* One country's interference by force, or threat of force, in another country's internal affairs or in questions arising between other countries. — **intervene,** *vb.* — **interventionary,** *adj.*

> "Intervention may or may not involve the use of force. It is frequently possible for a powerful state to impair the political independence of another weaker state without actually utilizing its armed forces. This result may be accomplished by lending open approval, as by the relaxation of an arms embargo, to a revolutionary group headed by individuals ready to accept the political or economic dominance of the intervening state. It may be accomplished by the withholding of recognition of a new government, combined with various forms of economic and financial pressure until the will of the stronger state prevails through the resignation or overthrow of the government disapproved." Philip C. Jessup, *A Modern Law of Nations* 172–73 (1948).

▸ **humanitarian intervention.** (1906) An intervention by the international community to curb abuses of human rights within a country, even if the intervention infringes the country's sovereignty.

> "[O]ne might distinguish between forcible and non-forcible 'humanitarian' intervention. There are non-forcible actions, such as the provision of humanitarian aid (food, medicine, and the like), that could constitute 'humanitarian

intervention.' Since, however, intervention in its classical incarnation is generally considered to involve the use of force, these non-forcible actions are better described as 'humanitarian assistance' . . . . Humanitarian intervention can then be loosely defined as a threat or use of armed force against another State that is motivated by humanitarian considerations. This broad definition is not technical and does not imply any distinct legal justification for the forcible action. Many legal justifications for the use of force may involve a humanitarian component or motivation: for example, authorization by the Security Council, self-defence, the protection of nationals abroad (itself connected to self-defence arguments), and armed action upon invitation or with the consent of the target State . . . . 'Humanitarian intervention' also has a narrower meaning as an autonomous justification for the use of armed force in another State distinct from other legal justifications. Humanitarian intervention in this narrower sense can be defined as the use of force to protect people in another State from gross and systematic human rights violations committed against them, or more generally to avert a humanitarian catastrophe, when the target State is unwilling or unable to act. This is still a broad definition, which could be applied to almost any instance of use of military force that has been claimed to have a humanitarian objective or to have been based on humanitarian considerations. The term is not one of art, however: it does not appear in any international treaties; and it cannot be said that its boundaries are yet clearly delineated." Vaughan Lowe & Antonios Tzanakopoulos, "Humanitarian Intervention," in 5 *The Max Planck Encyclopedia of Public International Law* 47, 47–48 (Rüdiger Wolfrum ed., 2012).

intervention duty. (1994) *Maritime law.* A shipowner's obligation to remedy hazardous working conditions for longshore workers, even though the shipowner did not create the condition, when the shipowner knows of a nonobvious condition arising in an area that cannot be avoided by the longshore workers in performing their duties. Cf. ACTIVE-OPERATIONS DUTY; TURNOVER DUTY.

interventionist, *adj.* (1915) Based on or committed to the belief that a government or organization should take action or spend money to influence political or financial developments in other countries. — **interventionism,** *n.*

intervertere possessionem (in-tər-**vər**-tər-ee pə-zes[h]-ee-**oh**-nəm). [Latin] *Scots law.* To intercept possession; to alter the possession. • If a bailee received an item under a bailment and then stole the item, the bailee changed the nature of the possession.

interview-summary form. (1994) *Patents.* A U.S. Patent and Trademark Office form for noting in the record the contents of a conversation, by phone or in person, between a patent examiner and an applicant.

inter virum et uxorem (**in**-tər **vɪ**-rəm et ək-**sor**-əm), *adv.* & *adj.* [Latin] Between husband and wife.

inter vivos (**in**-tər **vɪ**-vohs *or* **vee**-vohs), *adj.* & *adv.* [Latin "between the living"] (1837) Of, relating to, or involving property conveyed not by will or in contemplation of an imminent death, but during the conveyor's lifetime.

inter vivos gift. See GIFT.

inter vivos transfer. See TRANSFER.

inter vivos trust. See TRUST (3).

interwar, *adj.* (1939) Occurring in or relating to a period between two wars, esp. that between World War I and World War II.

intestabilis (in-tes-**tay**-bə-lis), *adj.* [Latin] Disqualified from being a witness.

intestable, *adj.* (16c) **1.** Not capable of being tested <an intestable DNA sample>. **2.** Legally incapable of making a will or of benefitting under a will <an insane person is intestable in all states> <the slaying-statute makes killers intestable in relation to their victims>. **3.** Disqualified from giving evidence, esp. testifying <the witness is intestable because of extreme youth>.

intestacy (in-**tes**-tə-see). (18c) The quality, state, or condition of a person's having died without a valid will. Cf. TESTACY.

intestate (in-**tes**-tayt), *adj.* (14c) **1.** Of, relating to, or involving a person who has died without a valid will <having revoked her will without making a new one, she was intestate when she died>. **2.** Of, relating to, or involving the property owned by a person who died without a valid will <an intestate estate>. **3.** Of, relating to, or involving intestacy <a spouse's intestate share>. Cf. TESTATE, *adj.* **4.** *Archaic.* (Of a person) not qualified to testify <the witness could not testify after being found intestate>.

intestate, *n.* (17c) Someone who has died without a valid will. Cf. TESTATOR.

▸ **partial intestate.** (1905) Someone who has died with a valid will that does not dispose of all of his or her net probate estate.

intestate death. See DEATH.

intestate law. (18c) The relevant statute governing succession to estates of those who die without a valid will.

intestate share. See SHARE (1).

intestate succession. See SUCCESSION (2).

intestato (in-tes-**tay**-toh), *adv.* [Latin] *Roman law.* (Of a succession) without a will.

intestatus (in-tes-**tay**-təs), *n.* & *adj.* [Latin] *Roman law.* An intestate; a person who dies without a will. • This term had the same meaning in early English law.

in testimonium (in tes-tə-**moh**-nee-əm), *adv.* & *adj.* [Latin] In witness; in evidence of which. • This phrase sometimes opens attestation clauses.

in the course of employment. (1911) *Workers' compensation.* (Of an accident) having happened to an on-the-job employee within the scope of employment.

in-the-money option. See OPTION (5).

in thesi (in **thee**-sɪ). [Latin] *Hist.* In the particular case, which has occurred. Cf. IN HYPOTHESI.

in the year of Our Lord. See ANNO DOMINI.

intimate association, freedom of. See FREEDOM OF ASSOCIATION.

intimation. (17c) *Scots law.* Notice of a legal obligation coupled with a warning of the penalties for failure to comply.

intimidation, *n.* (17c) Unlawful coercion; extortion. • In England, intimidation was established as a tort in the 1964 case of *Rookes v. Barnard*, 1964 App. Cas. 1129 (P.C. 1964) (appeal taken from B.C.). — **intimidate,** *vb.* — **intimidatory,** *adj.* — **intimidator,** *n.*

"The wrong of intimidation includes all those cases in which harm is inflicted by the use of unlawful threats whereby the lawful liberty of others to do as they please is interfered with. This wrong is of two distinct kinds, for the liberty of action so interfered with may be either that of the plaintiff himself, or that of other persons with resulting damage to the plaintiff." R.F.V. Heuston, *Salmond on the Law of Torts* 364 (17th ed. 1977).

intitle, *vb. Archaic.* See ENTITLE.

in toto (in **toh**-toh), *adv.* [Latin "in whole"] (18c) Completely; as a whole <the company rejected the offer *in toto*>.

intoxicant, *n.* (1863) A substance (esp. liquor) that deprives a person of the ordinary use of the senses or of reason.

intoxicated, *adj.* (16c) Having the brain affected by the presence in the body of a drug or alcohol. — Also termed *inebriated.*

intoxicating liquor. See LIQUOR.

intoxication, *n.* (15c) A diminished ability to act with full mental and physical capabilities because of alcohol or drug consumption; drunkenness. See Model Penal Code § 2.08. — **intoxicate,** *vb.*

▸ **culpable intoxication.** See *voluntary intoxication.*

▸ **involuntary intoxication.** (1870) The quality, state, or condition of having ingested alcohol or drugs against one's will or without one's knowledge. • Involuntary intoxication is an affirmative defense to a criminal or negligence charge.

▸ **pathological intoxication.** (1947) An extremely exaggerated response to an intoxicant. • This may be treated as involuntary intoxication if it is unforeseeable.

▸ **public intoxication.** (1885) The quality, state, or condition of a person who is under the influence of drugs or alcohol in a place open to the general public. • In most American jurisdictions, public intoxication is considered a misdemeanor. In some states, alcoholism is a defense if the offender agrees to attend a treatment program.

▸ **self-induced intoxication.** See *voluntary intoxication.*

▸ **voluntary intoxication.** (18c) The quality, state, or condition of having willingly ingested alcohol or drugs to the point of impairment done with the knowledge that one's physical and mental capabilities would be impaired. • Voluntary intoxication is not a defense to a general-intent crime, but may be admitted to refute the existence of a particular state of mind for a specific-intent crime. — Also termed *culpable intoxication; self-induced intoxication.*

intoxication assault. See ASSAULT.

intoxication defense. See DEFENSE (1).

intoxication manslaughter. See MANSLAUGHTER.

intoxilyzer (in-**tok**-si-lɪ-zər). See BREATHALYZER.

intoximeter (in-tok-**sim**-ə-tər). See BREATHALYZER.

intra (**in**-trə), *adv.* & *adj.* [Latin] Within. Cf. INFRA.

"The use of *infra* (below) in the sense and place of *intra* (within) is a corruption of very ancient date. . . . The expression 'under age' (the correct literal translation of *infra aetatem*) indeed, is of more common occurrence than 'within age.' But the use of *infra* in the sense of *intra*, as expressive of *place*, is an undoubted barbarism." 2 Alexander M. Burrill, *A Law Dictionary and Glossary* 75 (2d ed. 1867).

intra anni spatium (**in**-trə **an**-ɪ **spay**-shee-əm), *adv.* & *adj.* [Latin] Within the space of a year.

intracameral, *adj.* (1974) Of, relating to, or involving actions taken within a chamber, such as a legislative chamber or a judge's chambers; IN CAMERA. Cf. EXTRACAMERAL.

intracircuit assignment. See ASSIGNMENT (5).

intracorporate conspiracy. See CONSPIRACY.

intraday (**in**-trə-day), *adj.* (1972) Occurring within a single day.

intraday account. See *concentration account* under ACCOUNT.

intra-enterprise conspiracy. See CONSPIRACY.

intra familiam (**in**-trə fə-**mil**-ee-əm). [Latin] Within the family. • The phrase appeared in reference to the status of a child before being liberated from the father's tutelage (forisfamiliation). Cf. EXTRA FAMILIAM.

intra fidem (**in**-trə **fɪ**-dəm), *adj.* [Latin] Within belief; credible.

intra fines commissi (**in**-trə **fɪ**-neez kə-**mis**-ɪ). [Law Latin] Within the limits of the trust. • The phrase appeared in reference to an agent's actions committed within the limits of the agency.

intragovernmental, *adj.* (1964) Within a government; between a single government's departments or officials.

intra legem. See EQUITY INTRA LEGEM.

intraliminal right (in-trə-**lim**-ə-nəl). (1967) *Mining law.* The privilege to mine ore in areas within the boundaries of a mineral claim. • In contrast to an extralateral right, an intraliminal right does not give the holder the right to mine a vein of ore outside the lease even if the vein lies mostly within the lease. Cf. APEX RULE.

intra luctus tempus (**in**-trə **lək**-təs **tem**-pəs), *adv.* & *adj.* [Latin] Within the time of mourning.

intra maenia (**in**-trə **mee**-nee-ə), *adv.* & *adj.* [Latin] Within the walls (of a house). • This term was used most commonly in reference to domestic servants.

in transit, *adj.* & *adv.* (1918) (Of people, goods, etc.) being conveyed by a carrier.

intransitive covenant. See COVENANT (1).

in transitu (in **tran**-si-t[y]oo *or* **tranz**-i-t[y]oo). [Latin "in transit; on the journey"] (17c) *Archaic.* Being conveyed from one place to another.

intra parietes (**in**-trə pə-**rɪ**-ə-teez), *adv.* [Latin] Within one's own walls (i.e., in private). • This phrase appeared most commonly in reference to matters settled out of court.

intra paternam familiam (**in**-trə pə-**tər**-nəm fə-**mil**-ee-əm). [Law Latin] Within the father's family. Cf. EXTRA PATERNAM FAMILIAM.

intrapreneur (in-trə-prə-**nər** or **-noor**), *n.* (1978) An employee for a large company whose job is to develop innovative ideas or ways of doing business for that company. Cf. ENTREPRENEUR.

intra quattuor maria (**in**-tər **kwah**-too-ər **mar**-ee-ə), *adv.* & *adj.* [Latin] Within the four seas.

intrastate commerce. See COMMERCE.

intra trajectum (**in**-trə trə-**jek**-təm), *adv.* & *adj.* [Latin] In the passage over; on the voyage over. — Also spelled *in traiectu.*

intra triduum (**in**-trə **trij**-[y]oo-əm). [Latin] Within three days.

intra vires (**in**-trə **vɪ**-reez), *adj.* [Latin "within the powers (of)"] (1877) Of, relating to, or involving an action taken within a corporation's or person's scope of authority <calling a shareholders' meeting is an *intra vires* function of the board of directors>. Cf. ULTRA VIRES. — **intra vires,** *adv.*

intrinsec service (in-**trin**-zik *or* -sik). *Hist.* The feudal services owed by a tenant to an immediate lord; the services arising from an agreement between the tenant and the lord. — Also termed *intrinsecum servitium* (in-**trin**-si-kəm sər-**vish**-ee-əm).

intrinsic (in-**trin**-zik *or* -sik), *adj.* (17c) Belonging to a thing by its very nature; not dependent on external circumstances; inherent; essential.

intrinsic ambiguity. See *patent ambiguity* under AMBIGUITY (1).

intrinsic evidence. See EVIDENCE.

intrinsic fraud. See FRAUD.

intrinsic test. (1861) *Copyright.* A subjective, fact-driven test for infringement whereby the fact-trier gauges whether a reasonable person would perceive substantial similarities between two expressions. Cf. EXTRINSIC TEST.

intrinsic value. See VALUE.

introduced species. See *alien species* under SPECIES (1).

introduce into evidence. (18c) To have (a fact or object) admitted into the trial record, allowing it to be considered by the jury or the court in reaching a decision.

introducta (in-trə-**dək**-tə), *n.* [Latin] *Roman law.* Personal property brought into a leased apartment by the tenant. • The lessor held a tacit mortgage over *introducta* to ensure payment of rent. Cf. INVECTA ET ILLATA.

introductory clause. The first paragraph of a contract, which typically begins with words such as "This Agreement is made on [date] between [parties' names]." — Also termed *commencement; exordium.* See EXORDIUM.

introductory recital. See RECITAL.

intromission (in-trə-**mish**-ən). (16c) **1.** The transactions of an employee or agent with funds provided by an employer or principal; loosely, dealing in the funds of another. **2.** *Scots law.* The act of handling or dealing with the affairs or property of another; the possession of another's property, with or without legal authority.

- ▸ **legal intromission.** (18c) *Scots law.* An authorized intromission, such as a creditor's enforcement of a debt.
- ▸ **necessary intromission.** (17c) *Scots law.* The intromission occurring when a spouse continues in possession of the deceased spouse's goods, for preservation.
- ▸ **vitious intromission** (**vish**-əs). (17c) *Scots law.* Unauthorized dealing with the property of another person, esp. a deceased person. — Also spelled *vicious intromission.*

> "The effect of vitious intromission is to render the heir who is guilty of it liable, under the passive title of vitious intromission, for the debts of the ancestor universally — the severity of this passive title being intended to prevent the carrying off of moveables, which are, from their nature, so liable to embezzlement." William Bell, *Bell's Dictionary and Digest of the Law of Scotland* 521 (George Watson ed., 1882).

3. Penile penetration into the vagina. See PENETRATION (1).

intruder. (15c) Someone who enters, remains on, uses, or touches land or chattels in another's possession without the possessor's consent.

intrusion, *n.* (15c) **1.** A person's entering without permission. See TRESPASS. **2.** In an action for invasion of privacy, a highly offensive invasion of another person's seclusion or private life. — **intrude,** *vb.* — **intrusive,** *adj.*

intrust, *vb. Archaic.* See ENTRUST.

intuitu matrimonii (in-t[y]oo-ə-t[y]oo ma-trə-**moh**-nee-ɪ). [Latin] *Hist.* In the prospect of marriage.

intuitu mortis (in-**t[y]oo**-ə-t[y]oo **mor**-tis). [Latin] *Hist.* In the prospect of death.

intus habet (**in**-təs **hay**-bət). [Law Latin] *Hist.* Has in his own hands. • The phrase appeared in reference to the presumption that the pupil's money that is unaccounted for and held by the tutor is sufficient to offset any claim that the tutor may have against the pupil.

in tuto (in **t[y]oo**-toh). [Law Latin] *Hist.* In safety.

inundate. (16c) To overflow or overwhelm; esp., to flood with water.

inure (in-**yoor**), *vb.* (15c) **1.** To take effect; to come into use <the settlement proceeds must inure to the benefit of the widow and children>. **2.** To make accustomed to something unpleasant; to habituate <abused children become inured to violence>. — Also spelled *enure.* — **inurement,** *n.*

inurement. 1. A benefit; something that is useful or beneficial <a taxable inurement to the benefit of a private person>.

- ▸ **private inurement.** (1976) *Tax.* An inurement consisting in the use by a private shareholder or an individual who has an insider relationship with a tax-exempt organization of the organization's earnings or assets for personal gain other than reasonable and adequate compensation. • Such a benefit is prohibited. See IRC (26 USCA) § 501(c)(3).

2. *Patents.* An inventor's claim that, as a matter of law, another's acts should accrue to the inventor's benefit. • To prove inurement, an inventor must show, among other things, that another person was working, either explicitly or implicitly, at the inventor's request. Experiments conducted at the request of an inventor by another, for example, may inure to the benefit of the inventor for purposes of establishing a reduction to practice. Similarly, acts by an inventor's attorney may inure to the benefit of the inventor in establishing diligence.

inurit labem realem (in-**yuur**-it **lay**-bəm ree-**ay**-ləm). [Law Latin] *Scots law.* It brands (a thing) with a real defect. See LABES REALIS.

in utero (in **yoo**-tə-roh). [Latin "in the uterus"] (18c) In the womb; during gestation or before birth <child *in utero*>.

in utroque jure (in yuu-**troh**-kwee **joor**-ee), *adv.* & *adj.* [Latin] In both laws — that is, civil law and canon law.

invade (in-**vayd**), *vb.* (15c) **1.** To enter (a country, city, or area) using military force, usu. in order to take control of it <the Romans invaded Britain some 2,000 years ago>. **2.** To go into (a place) in large numbers, esp. when unwanted; to engage in a massive intrusion <*Sound of Music* fans invade Salzburg each summer>. **3.** To become involved in (something) in an undesirable way <judges should not invade the province of the jury>. — **invader,** *n.*

invadiare (in-vay-dee-**air**-ee), *vb.* [Law Latin] *Hist.* To pledge or mortgage land.

invadiatio (in-vay-dee-**ay**-shee-oh). [Law Latin] *Hist.* A pledge or mortgage. Cf. VADIATIO.

invadiatus (in-vay-dee-**ay**-təs). [Law Latin] *Hist.* Someone who is under a pledge.

invalid (in-**val**-id), *adj.* (17c) **1.** Not legally binding <an invalid contract>. **2.** Without basis in fact <invalid allegations>.

invalid (**in**-və-lid), *n.* (18c) Someone who, because of serious illness or other disability, lacks the physical or mental capability of managing his or her day-to-day life.

invalid agreement. See *invalid contract* under CONTRACT.

invalid contract. See CONTRACT.

invalidity, *n.* (16c) **1.** The quality, state, or condition of being legally or officially unacceptable; lacking legal support. **2.** The quality, state, or condition of being too old, ill, or injured to work; infirmity.

invalid will. See WILL.

invasion. (17c) **1.** A hostile or forcible encroachment on the rights of another.

▸ **intentional invasion.** (1829) A hostile or forcible encroachment on another's interest in the use or enjoyment of property, esp. real property, though not necessarily inspired by malice or ill will.

2. The incursion of an army for conquest or plunder. **3.** *Trusts.* A withdrawal from principal. • In the third sense, the term is used as a metaphor. — **invade,** *vb.*

invasion of privacy. (1862) An unjustified exploitation of one's personality or intrusion into one's personal activities, actionable under tort law and sometimes under constitutional law. See RIGHT OF PRIVACY.

▸ **invasion of privacy by appropriation.** (1978) The use of another's name or likeness for one's own benefit, esp. commercial gain. • This misappropriation tort protects one's property right to the economic benefits flowing from the commercial use of one's face or name.

▸ **invasion of privacy by false light.** (1983) The use of publicity to place another in a false light in the public eye. • The false light may or may not be defamatory or fictional, but the public use must be one that a reasonable person would object to under the circumstances. See FALSE LIGHT (1).

▸ **invasion of privacy by intrusion.** (1970) An offensive, intentional interference with a person's seclusion or private affairs.

▸ **invasion of privacy by public disclosure of private facts.** (1972) The public revelation of private information about another in an objectionable manner. • Even if the information is true and nondefamatory, a cause of action may arise.

invasive exotics. See *invasive species* under SPECIES (1).

invasive species. See SPECIES (1).

invecta et illata (in-**vek**-tə et i-**lay**-tə). [Latin "(things) carried in and (things) brought in"] *Roman law.* Goods brought onto a rural or urban leasehold by the lessee. • The lessor held a tacit mortgage over the goods to ensure payment of rent. Cf. INTRODUCTA.

invective, *n.* Abusive or haranguing speech.

inveigle (in-**vay**-gəl), *vb.* (16c) To lure or entice through deceit or insincerity <she blamed her friend for inveigling her into making the investment>. — **inveiglement,** *n.*

invent, *vb.* (15c) To create (something) for the first time; esp., to conceive of (an idea) and reduce it to practice.

invented consideration. See CONSIDERATION (1).

inventio (in-**ven**-shee-oh), *n.* [Latin] *Roman law.* A thing found; a finding. • Beginning in the reign of Hadrian, the finder of treasure either acquired title to the property or shared it with the landowner on whose land it was found. See TREASURE TROVE; THESAURI INVENTIO. Pl. ***inventiones*** (in-ven-shee-**oh**-neez).

invention, *n.* (14c) *Patents.* **1.** A useful and patentable process, machine, manufacture, or composition of matter, or any improvement to one of those, created through independent effort and characterized by an extraordinary degree of skill or ingenuity; a newly discovered art or operation. • *Invention* embraces the concept of nonobviousness. See NONOBVIOUSNESS. **2.** The act or process of creating such a device or process. Cf. DISCOVERY (1). **3.** Generally, anything that is created or devised. — **invent,** *vb.*

> "The truth is, the word cannot be defined in such manner as to afford any substantial aid in determining whether a particular device involves an exercise of the inventive faculty or not. In a given case we may be able to say that there is present invention of a very high order. In another we can see that there is lacking that impalpable something that distinguishes invention from simple mechanical skill. Courts, adopting fixed principles as a guide, have by a process of exclusion determined that certain variations in old devices do or do not involve invention; but whether the variation relied upon in a particular case is anything more than ordinary mechanical skill is a question which cannot be answered by applying the test of any general definition." *McClain v. Ortmayer,* 141 U.S. 419, 427, 12 S.Ct. 76, 78 (1891).

> "An 'invention' is any art, machine, manufacture, design, or composition of matter, or any new and useful improvement thereof, or any variety of plant, which is or may be patentable under the patent laws. 37 C.F.R. § 501.3(d)." 60 Am. Jur. 2d *Patents* § 894, at 601 n.98 (1987).

▸ **abandoned invention.** (1874) An invention that an inventor has either deliberately stopped trying to exploit, or has otherwise treated in a way that precludes claiming the invention in a later patent. • Under § 102(c) of the Patent Act, abandonment bars a patent on that invention. But abandonment of an imperfect form of an invention does not bar a patent on a later-perfected form. Unless publicly known, an abandoned invention is not prior art to a later inventor. Under § 102(g) of the Patent Act, abandonment of the same invention by a first inventor also prevents the first inventor from blocking the second inventor's patent application in an interference. Cf. ABANDONED APPLICATION.

▸ **distinct invention.** (1823) One part of an invention that can be used on its own, and the absence of which will not prevent the remainder of the invention from working. • When the subject matter of a patent application is found to be multiple distinct inventions, the examiner requires the inventor to restrict the application to a single invention. See RESTRICTION (4). Cf. *independent invention.*

▸ **improvement invention.** (1936) A nontrivial and nonobvious betterment of an existing device or process. • The improvement may be patented, but the protection applies only to the improvement, not to the invention improved on.

▸ **independent invention.** (1840) An invention that bears no relation to another invention, esp. to another invention covered in the same patent application. • A single patent may not cover multiple independent inventions; the applicant must elect one and drop any others from the application. See RESTRICTION (4). Cf. *distinct invention.*

▸ **new-use invention.** (1969) Discovery of a new use for an existing invention. • As long as the new use is nonobvious — and actually useful — it may be patented. 35 USCA §§ 101–103.

▸ **small invention.** See UTILITY MODEL.

▸ **software-based invention.** (1996) A device or machine that uses innovative software to achieve results. • A software-based invention, process, or method may qualify for a patent, but the physical components and the underlying software are usu. not separately patentable.

inventively new. (1911) *Patents.* Original in any way. • The phrase is sometimes used to distinguish "new" in the usual sense from the term of art in patent law.

inventive step. (1919) *Patents.* In an invention, some advancement that is not obvious to a person reasonably skilled in the art. • The European Patent Convention requires an inventive step to qualify for a patent. The term is roughly equivalent to *nonobviousness* in American patent practice.

inventory, *n.* (15c) **1.** A detailed list of assets; esp., an executor's or administrator's detailed list of the probate-estate assets <make an inventory of the estate>. • The term also sometimes denotes a divorcing spouse's detailed list of all his or her marital and separate assets and liabilities. — Also termed *inventory and appraisement.* See PROBATE ESTATE; ACCOUNTING. **2.** *Accounting.* The portion of a financial statement reflecting the value of a business's raw materials, works-in-progress, and finished products <the company's reported inventory was suspiciously low>. **3.** Raw materials or goods in stock <the dealership held a sale to clear out its October inventory>. **4.** *Bankruptcy.* Personal property leased or furnished, held for sale or lease, or to be furnished under a contract for service; raw materials, work in process, or materials used or consumed in a business, including farm products such as crops or livestock <the debtor was found to have inventory that was valued at $300,000>. — **inventory,** *vb.*

> "Section 547 itself defines 'inventory' and 'receivable.' Do not use the U.C.C. definitions of these terms, or the definitions of them learned in business law classes. It is especially important to note that, for purposes of section 547, 'inventory' includes 'farm products such as crops or livestock . . . .'" David G. Epstein et al., *Bankruptcy* § 6-35, at 351 (1993).

inventory fee. (1977) A probate court's fee for services rendered to a decedent's estate.

inventory search. See SEARCH (1).

inventory-turnover ratio. (1938) *Accounting.* The result of dividing the cost of goods sold by the average value of inventory. • This calculation is used to determine the effectiveness of the company's inventory-management policy.

in ventre sa mere (in **ven**-tree sa **mer**). See EN VENTRE SA MERE.

inventus (in-**ven**-təs), *p.pl.* [Latin] Found. • This word appears in various phrases, such as *thesaurus inventus* ("treasure trove") and *non est inventus* ("he is not found").

inveritare (in-ve-rə-**tair**-ee), *vb.* [Law Latin] To make proof of (something).

inverse condemnation. See CONDEMNATION (2).

inverse-Erie doctrine. See REVERSE-ERIE DOCTRINE.

inverse floater. See *inverse-floating-rate note* under NOTE (1).

inverse-floating-rate note. See NOTE (1).

inverse-order-of-alienation doctrine. (1935) The principle that a purchaser of a parcel of encumbered property may require a secured creditor to collect on a debt first from any parcel still held by the original owner, then from the parcel sold last, then next to last, and so on until the debt has been satisfied. — Also termed *rule of marshaling liens.*

inverse zoning. See ZONING.

inverso ordine (in-**vər**-soh **or**-də-nee). [Latin] Contrary to rule.

inverted market. See BACKWARDATION.

invest, *vb.* (17c) **1.** To supply with authority or power <the U.S. Constitution invests the President with the power to conduct foreign affairs>. See INVESTITURE (1). **2.** To apply (money) for profit <Jillson invested her entire savings in the mutual fund>. **3.** To make an outlay of money for profit <Baird invested in stocks>.

investigate, *vb.* (16c) **1.** To inquire into (a matter) systematically; to make (a suspect) the subject of a criminal inquiry <the police investigated the suspect's involvement in the murder>. **2.** To make an official inquiry <after the judge dismissed the case, the police refused to investigate further>.

investigating bureau. See CREDIT-REPORTING BUREAU.

investigating magistrate. See MAGISTRATE.

investigation, *n.* The activity of trying to find out the truth about something, such as a crime, accident, or historical issue; esp., either an authoritative inquiry into certain facts, as by a legislative committee, or a systematic examination of some intellectual problem or empirical question, as by mathematical treatment or use of the scientific method.

investigative detention. See DETENTION (1).

investigative grand jury. See GRAND JURY.

investigative search. See SEARCH (1).

investigatory detention. See STOP-AND-FRISK.

investigatory interrogation. See INTERROGATION.

investigatory power. See POWER (3).

investigatory stop. See STOP-AND-FRISK.

investitive fact. See FACT.

investitive publication. See PUBLICATION (2).

investiture (in-ves-tə-chuur). (14c) **1.** A formal ceremony at which someone is given an official title; the act of formally installing a person in a ceremony in which the person is clothed in the insignia of the office's position or rank. **2.** The installation of a cleric in office. — Also termed *investment*. **3.** LIVERY OF SEISIN.

investment. (16c) **1.** An expenditure to acquire property or assets to produce revenue; a capital outlay.

▸ **fixed-dollar investment.** (1952) An investment whose face value is the same when sold as it was when purchased. • Examples are bonds held to maturity, certain government securities, and savings accounts.

▸ **fixed-income investment.** (1929) An investment (including preferred stock) that pays a fixed dividend throughout its life and is not redeemable unless the corporation makes a special call.

▸ **inward investment.** (1962) Investment by foreign sources in a country's industry or businesses.

▸ **net investment.** (1891) **1.** The net cash required to start a new project. **2.** The gross investment in capital goods less capital consumption, including depreciation.

2. The asset acquired or the sum invested. **3.** INVESTITURE (1). **4.** LIVERY OF SEISIN.

investment adviser. (1930) Someone who, for pay, advises others, either directly or through publications or writings, about the value of securities or the advisability of investing in, purchasing, or selling securities, or who is in the business of issuing reports on securities. • The term generally excludes an employee of an investment adviser; a depository institution, such as a bank; lawyers, accountants, engineers, and teachers whose investment advice is solely incidental to the practice of their profession; a broker-dealer whose advice is incidental to the conduct of business and who receives no special compensation for that advice; and publishers of bona fide newspapers, newsmagazines, or business or financial publications of general, regular, or paid circulation.

Investment Advisers Act. A 1940 federal statute — administered by the Securities and Exchange Commission — that regulates investment advisers. 15 USCA §§ 80b-1 et seq. — Abbr. IAA.

investment bank. See BANK.

investment banker. (1886) A person or institution that underwrites, sells, or assists in raising capital for businesses, esp. for new issues of stocks or bonds; a trader at an investment bank. See *investment bank* under BANK. — Often shortened to *banker*.

investment banking. (1893) The business of underwriting or selling securities; esp., the marketing of new stocks or bonds.

> "The term 'investment banking' can be used to encompass [underwriting, and acting as a dealer, broker, and market maker], and any person in a firm performing any of those functions could be called an investment banker. By convention, however, those terms are used less broadly. In large securities firms, for example, there are a number of departments. The one most visible to the public handles trades for individuals. The technical term for the persons working with customers in that department is 'registered representative,' but those persons are often called brokers or stockbrokers. Insiders would not call them investment bankers. A department almost invisible to the public handles underwritings and performs a wide range of services primarily for client companies. Among those are: (1) assisting companies in the sale of securities, almost always in large amounts, to such private purchasers as insurance companies; (2) finding acquisition partners for companies that wish to acquire or be acquired by others; and (3) giving financial advice of various sorts to client companies. That department is likely to be called the investment banking department. In any case, its functions are at the heart of the insiders' conception of investment banking." Larry D. Soderquist & Theresa A. Gabaldon, *Securities Law* 30 (1998).

investment bill. See BILL (6).

investment company. See COMPANY.

Investment Company Act. A 1940 federal statute enacted to curb financial malpractices and abuses by regulating investment-company activities and transactions — specifically, by requiring registration of investment companies and prohibiting transactions by unregistered companies; by making certain persons ineligible as affiliated persons or underwriters; by regulating affiliations of directors, officers, and employees; by barring changes in investment policy without shareholder approval; and by regulating contracts of advisers and underwriters. 15 USCA §§ 80a-1 et seq. — Abbr. ICA.

investment contract. (1893) **1.** A contract in which money is invested in a common enterprise with profits to come solely from the efforts of others; an agreement or transaction in which a party invests money in expectation of profits derived from the efforts of a promoter or other third party. **2.** A transaction in which an investor furnishes initial value or risk capital to an enterprise, a portion of that amount being subjected to the risks of the enterprise. • In such an arrangement, the investor typically does not receive the right to exercise control over the managerial decisions of the enterprise.

> "[A]n investment contract for purposes of the Securities Act means a contract, transaction or scheme whereby a person invests his money in a common enterprise and is led to expect profits solely from the efforts of the promoter or a third party. . . . It embodies a flexible rather than a static principle, one that is capable of adaptation to meet the countless and variable schemes devised by those who seek the use of the money of others on the promise of profits." *SEC v. Howey Co.*, 328 U.S. 293, 298–99, 66 S.Ct. 1100, 1103 (1946).

▸ **guaranteed investment contract.** (1982) An investment contract under which an institutional investor invests a lump sum (such as a pension fund) with an insurer that promises to return the principal (the lump sum) and a certain amount of interest at the contract's end. — Abbr. GIC.

investment-direction agreement. (1998) A contract by which a trustee agrees not to diversify the trust's assets, even though the trustee has the legal right to do so, and the beneficiary agrees to hold the trustee harmless for any losses resulting from not diversifying. — Abbr. IDA.

investment discretion. (1934) The ability of a person to (1) determine what will be purchased or sold by or for another person's account, (2) decide what will be purchased or sold by or for the account even though another may have the responsibility, or (3) influence the purchase or sale of securities or property in a way that, according to an administrative agency such as the Securities and Exchange Commission, should be subject to the agency's governing rules and regulations.

investment-grade bond. See BOND (3).

investment-grade rating. (1972) Any of the top four scores given to a bond after an appraisal of its quality by a securities-evaluation agency such as Moody's. • The rating indicates the degree of risk in an investment in the bond. See A (8).

investment income. See *unearned income* (1) under INCOME.

investment indebtedness. (1969) *Tax.* Debt incurred by a taxpayer to acquire or carry assets that may produce income. • The Internal Revenue Code limits the amount of deductible interest on this type of debt.

investment instrument. See INSTRUMENT (2).

investment property. (1880) Any asset purchased to produce a profit, whether from income or resale.

investment security. See SECURITY (4).

investment tax credit. See TAX CREDIT.

investment trust. See *investment company* under COMPANY.

investor. (17c) **1.** A buyer of a security or other property who seeks to profit from it without exhausting the principal. **2.** Broadly, a person who spends money with an expectation of earning a profit.

▸ **accredited investor.** (1979) An investor treated under the Securities Act of 1933 as being knowledgeable and sophisticated about financial matters, esp. because of the investor's large net worth. • In a securities offering that is exempt from registration, an accredited investor (either a person or an entity) is not entitled to protection under the Act's disclosure provisions, although the investor does keep its remedies for fraud.

▸ **angel investor.** (1993) A person — usu. an experienced and successful entrepreneur, professional, or entity — that provides start-up or growth financing to a promising company, often together with advice and contacts. — Also termed *business angel.*

▸ **institutional investor.** (1934) Someone who trades large volumes of securities, usu. by investing other people's money into large managed funds. • Institutional investors are often pension funds, investment companies, trust managers, or insurance companies. See MUTUAL FUND.

▸ **qualified investor.** (1966) *Securities.* An investor who is an individual and has an investment portfolio worth at least $5 million, or a company that owns or manages investments worth at least $25 million.

▸ **sophisticated investor.** (1937) *Securities.* An investor who has sufficient knowledge and experience of financial matters to be capable of evaluating a security's qualities. • Sophisticated investors do not require the full protection of securities laws.

invidious discrimination (in-**vid**-ee-əs di-skrim-ə-**nay**-shən). See DISCRIMINATION (3).

in vinculis (in **ving**-kyə-lis). [Latin "in chains"] (18c) In actual custody.

> "The engagement of a magistrate to an accomplice, that if he will give his evidence, he will experience favor, is merely in the nature of a recommendation to mercy, for no authority is given to a justice of the peace to pardon an offender, and to tell him that he shall be a witness against others. He is not therefore assured of his pardon, but gives his evidence *in vinculis*, in custody: and it depends on his behaviour, whether he shall or shall not be admitted to mercy." 1 Joseph Chitty, *A Practical Treatise on the Criminal Law* 82–83 (2d ed. 1826).

inviolability (in-vɪ-ə-lə-**bil**-ə-tee), *n.* (18c) The quality, state, or condition of being safe from violation.

inviolable (in-**vɪ**-ə-lə-bəl), *adj.* (15c) Safe from violation; incapable of being violated. — **inviolability,** *n.*

inviolate (in-**vɪ**-ə-lit), *adj.* (15c) Free from violation; not broken, infringed, or impaired.

in viridi observantia (in **vir**-ə-dɪ ob-zər-**van**-shee-ə), *adj.* [Latin "in fresh observance"] Present to the minds of people, and in full force and operation.

invisible, *adj. Accounting.* Not reported in a financial statement <invisible earnings>.

invitation, *n. Torts.* In the law of negligence, the enticement of others to enter, remain on, or use property or its structures; conduct that justifies others in believing that the possessor wants them to enter. Cf. PERMISSION (3). — **invite,** *vb.*

invitation seeking offers. INVITATION TO NEGOTIATE.

invitation to bid. INVITATION TO NEGOTIATE.

invitation to negotiate. (1902) *Contracts.* A solicitation for one or more offers, usu. as a preliminary step to forming a contract. — Also termed *invitation seeking offers*; *invitation to bid*; *invitation to treat*; *solicitation for bids*; *preliminary letter*; *offer to chaffer.* Cf. OFFER.

invitation to tender. (1900) The process of soliciting proposals from qualified suppliers or contractors for goods and for work on a project with specific requirements during a specified time frame. — Also termed *request for tenders.*

invitation to treat. INVITATION TO NEGOTIATE.

invited error. See ERROR (2).

invited-error doctrine. (1947) The rule that a litigant cannot complain on appeal of an error at trial that he himself caused or provoked.

invitee (in-vɪ-**tee**). (1837) Someone who has an express or implied invitation to enter or use another's premises, such as a business visitor or a member of the public to whom the premises are held open. • The occupier has a duty to inspect the premises and to warn the invitee of dangerous conditions. — Also termed *licensee with an interest.* Cf. LICENSEE (2); TRESPASSER; BUSINESS VISITOR (1).

▸ **public invitee.** (1937) An invitee who is invited to enter and remain on property for a purpose for which the property is held open to the public.

inviter. (16c) Someone who expressly or impliedly invites another onto the premises for business purposes. — Also spelled *invitor.* Cf. INVITEE.

invito debitore (in-**vɪ**-toh deb-i-**tor**-ee). [Latin] *Roman law.* Without the debtor's consent. • A creditor could assign and a third party could pay a debt *invito debitore.*

invito domino (in-**vɪ**-toh **dom**-ə-noh). [Latin] *Roman law.* Against the owner's consent. • The common-law doctrine of theft was that the taking must be *invito domino.*

invitor. See INVITER.

invito superiore (in-**vɪ**-toh s[y]oo-peer-ee-**or**-ee). [Law Latin] *Scots law.* Without the superior's consent. • Ordinarily, a vassal could not renounce a fee without the superior's consent.

in vitro (in **vee**-troh). [Latin "in glass"] (1894) In an artificial environment rather inside a living body.

in vitro fertilization. (1944) A procedure by which an egg is fertilized outside a woman's body and then inserted into the womb for gestation. — Abbr. IVF. Cf. ARTIFICIAL INSEMINATION; GAMETE INTRAFALLOPIAN TRANSFER; IN VIVO FERTILIZATION; ZYGOTE INTRAFALLOPIAN TRANSFER.

in vivo (in **vee**-voh), *adj.* (1901) Taking place in the body.

in vivo fertilization. (1959) The process by which an egg is fertilized inside a woman's body. Cf. ARTIFICIAL INSEMINATION; GAMETE INTRAFALLOPIAN TRANSFER; IN VITRO FERTILIZATION; ZYGOTE INTRAFALLOPIAN TRANSFER.

invocation. (14c) **1.** The act of calling on for authority or justification. **2.** The act of enforcing or using a legal right <an invocation of the contract clause>.

invoice, *n.* (16c) An itemized list of goods or services furnished by a seller to a buyer, usu. specifying the price and terms of sale; a bill of costs. — **invoice,** *vb.*

▸ **consular invoice.** (1880) An invoice used to hasten the entry of goods into a country by bearing the signature of the country's consul as assurance that the shipment's contents have been preverified for quantity and value.

▸ **pro forma invoice.** (1836) A bill-like document that is sent to a customer to show what the price would be if the customer placed an order.

▸ **sales invoice.** (1939) A document showing details of a purchase or sale, including price and quantity of merchandise.

invoice book. (1829) A journal into which invoices are copied.

involuntary, *adj.* (15c) Not resulting from a free and unrestrained choice; not subject to control by the will. — **involuntariness,** *n.*

> "[T]he law, like everyday thought, usually confines the notion of *involuntary* to that subclass of cases which involve purely physical, physiological, or psychological movements of our limbs, like reflexes and convulsions, movements in sleep, during sleepwalking, or under hypnosis, or due to some disease of the brain, lunacy, or automatism." Alan R. White, *Grounds of Liability* 60–61 (1985).

involuntary alienation. See ALIENATION (1).

involuntary bailment. See BAILMENT (1).

involuntary bankruptcy. See BANKRUPTCY (2).

involuntary conduct. See CONDUCT.

involuntary confession. See CONFESSION (1).

involuntary confinement. See CIVIL COMMITMENT (1).

involuntary conversion. See CONVERSION (2).

involuntary conveyance. See *involuntary alienation* under ALIENATION (1).

involuntary deposit. 1. See DEPOSIT (5). **2.** See *involuntary bailment* under BAILMENT (1).

involuntary dismissal. See DISMISSAL (1).

involuntary dissolution. See DISSOLUTION (3).

involuntary euthanasia. See EUTHANASIA.

involuntary gap claim. See CLAIM (5).

involuntary intoxication. See INTOXICATION.

involuntary lien. See LIEN.

involuntary liquidation. See LIQUIDATION (4).

involuntary manslaughter. See MANSLAUGHTER.

involuntary nonsuit. See NONSUIT (2).

involuntary partition. See PARTITION (2).

involuntary payment. See PAYMENT (2).

involuntary petition. See PETITION (1).

involuntary plaintiff. See PLAINTIFF.

involuntary proceeding. See *involuntary bankruptcy* under BANKRUPTCY.

involuntary protective custody. See CUSTODY (1).

involuntary servitude. See SERVITUDE (5).

involuntary stranding. See *accidental stranding* under STRANDING.

involuntary suretyship. See SURETYSHIP.

involuntary trust. See *constructive trust* under TRUST (3).

involuntary winding up. See WINDING UP.

inward investment. See INVESTMENT (1).

in witness whereof. (16c) The traditional beginning of the concluding clause (termed the *testimonium clause*) of a will or contract, esp. a deed. See TESTIMONIUM CLAUSE.

IO. *abbr.* BUREAU OF INTERNATIONAL ORGANIZATION AFFAIRS.

IOLTA (I-**ohl**-tə). *abbr.* INTEREST ON LAWYERS' TRUST ACCOUNTS.

IO mortgage. See *interest-only mortgage* under MORTGAGE.

IOU (I-oh-**yoo**). [abbr. "I owe you"] (17c) **1.** A memorandum acknowledging a debt; specif., a signed note saying that the signator owes money to someone else to whom the note is directed. **2.** The debt itself. — Also termed *due-bill.*

IP. *abbr.* (1979) **1.** INTELLECTUAL PROPERTY. **2.** See *interested party* under PARTY (2). **3.** See *interested person* under PERSON (1). **4.** Internet protocol.

IPA. *abbr.* INDEPENDENT-PRACTICE ASSOCIATION.

IP address. *abbr.* (1997) INTERNET-PROTOCOL ADDRESS.

IPC. *abbr.* **1.** See *involuntary protective custody* under CUSTODY (1). **2.** INTELLECTUAL-PROPERTY CRIME.

IPD. *abbr.* IN PRAESENTIA DOMINORUM.

IPKCA. *abbr.* INTERNATIONAL PARENTAL KIDNAPPING CRIME ACT OF 1993.

IPO. See *initial public offering* under OFFERING.

IPS. *abbr.* Interim probation supervision.

ipse (**ip**-see). [Latin "he himself"] (16c) The same; the very person.

ipse dixit (**ip**-see **dik**-sit). [Latin "he himself said it"] (15c) Something asserted but not proved <his testimony that she was a liar was nothing more than an *ipse dixit*>. • The phrase is commonly used in court decisions analyzing the admissibility of expert testimony. A court may reject expert-opinion evidence that is connected to existing data only by the expert's "ipse dixit."

ipsissima verba (ip-**sis**-ə-mə **vər**-bə). [Latin "the very (same) words"] (1807) The exact words used by somebody being quoted <on its face, the *ipsissima verba* of the statute supports the plaintiff's position on the ownership issue>.

ipso facto (**ip**-soh **fak**-toh). [Latin "by the fact itself"] (16c) By the very nature of the situation <if 25% of all contractual litigation is caused by faulty drafting, then, *ipso facto*, the profession needs to improve its drafting skills>.

ipso facto clause. (1934) *Bankruptcy.* A contract clause that specifies the consequences of a party's bankruptcy. • The Bankruptcy Code prohibits enforcement of such clauses. — Also termed *bankruptcy clause.*

ipso jure (**ip**-soh **joor**-ee). [Latin "by the law itself"] (1909) By the operation of the law itself <despite the parties' actions, the property will revert to the state, *ipso jure*, on May 1>.

IP spoofing. See SPOOFING.

ipsum corpus (**ip**-səm **kor**-pəs). [Latin] *Roman law.* The thing itself. • The phrase typically referred to a specific item that had to be delivered to a purchaser or legatee.

IRA (I-ahr-**ay** *or* I-rə). *abbr.* (1974) INDIVIDUAL RETIREMENT ACCOUNT.

IRAC (I-rak). A mnemonic acronym used mostly by law students and their legal-writing professors, esp. as a method of answering essay questions on law exams, the letters being commonly said to stand for either (1) issue, rule, application, conclusion, or (2) issue, rule, analysis, conclusion. Cf. CRAC; CREAC.

ira motus (I-rə **moh**-təs), *adj.* [Latin] Moved or excited by anger or passion. • This term was formerly used in the plea of *son assault demesne.*

IRC. *abbr.* **1.** INTERNAL REVENUE CODE. **2.** INMATE RECORD COORDINATOR.

IRD. See *income in respect of a decedent* under INCOME.

ire ad largum (I-ree ad **lahr**-gəm), *vb.* [Latin] To go at large; i.e., to be released from judicial restraint.

iris scan. (1995) A computer image made as a high-quality photograph of a person's iris (i.e., the round colored part of the center of the eye) generated for purposes of identification. • The police often use iris scans to check the information on a passport or ID.

iron-safe clause. (1886) A provision in a fire-insurance policy requiring the insured to preserve the books and inventory records of a business in a fireproof safe.

IRR. See *internal rate of return* under RATE OF RETURN.

irrational, *adj.* (16c) Not guided by reason or by a fair consideration of the facts <an irrational ruling>. See ARBITRARY.

irrebuttable presumption. See *conclusive presumption* under PRESUMPTION.

irreclaimable, *adj.* Incapable of being reclaimed, restored, or redeemed <an irreclaimable criminal> <irreclaimable land>.

irreconcilability canon. The doctrine that if a legal instrument contains truly irreconcilable provisions at the same level of generality, and they have been simultaneously adopted, neither provision should be given effect.

irreconcilable, *adj.* **1.** Not capable of reconciliation; not subject to harmonization; incurably incompatible. **2.** (Of persons, parties, etc.) incapable of being appeased or pacified; implacable.

irreconcilable, *n.* Someone who refuses reconciliation or compromise; specif., a legislator who cannot or does not work in harmony with fellow legislators, esp. because of adherence to a hopeless political program.

irreconcilable differences. (1975) *Family law.* Differences between spouses so strong as to give rise to grounds for divorce; persistent and unresolvable disagreements between spouses, leading to the breakdown of the marriage. • These differences may be cited — without specifics — as grounds for no-fault divorce. At least 33 states have provided that irreconcilable differences are a basis for divorce. — Abbr. ID. Cf. IRRETRIEVABLE BREAKDOWN OF THE MARRIAGE; INCOMPATIBILITY.

irreconcilable-differences divorce. See DIVORCE.

irrecoverable, *adj.* **1.** (Of something taken, lost, or destroyed) incapable of being gotten back <an irrecoverable loss>. **2.** (Of a debt) incapable of being recouped <an irrecoverable loan>. **3.** (Of a disease, danger, etc.) irremediable; that cannot be recovered from.

irrecusable, *adj.* (18c) (Of an obligation) that cannot be avoided, although made without one's consent, as with the obligation to not strike another without some lawful excuse. Cf. RECUSABLE (1).

irredeemable, *adj.* **1.** Beyond the power of redemption; irreclaimable <irredeemable felons>. **2.** That cannot be made good by payment or restitution <an irredeemable loss>. **3.** Not able to be exchanged for money or goods <expired stamps are irredeemable>.

irredeemable bond. See *annuity bond* under BOND (3).

irredeemable ground rent. See *ground rent* (2) under RENT (1).

irredentism (i-ri-**dent**-iz-əm). *Int'l law.* The political policy or program of a party or group that seeks to adjust national boundaries so as to reincorporate its people with the country with which the party or group is most closely associated, without having to move people from one geographic area to another. — **irredentist,** *n.*

irrefragable (i-**ref**-rə-gə-bəl), *adj.* (16c) Unanswerable; not to be controverted; impossible to refute <the defense feebly responded to the prosecution's irrefragable arguments>. — **irrefragability,** *n.*

irrefutable (i-**ref**-yə-tə-bəl *or* ir-ə-**fyoo**-tə-bəl), *adj.* Incapable of being disproved or countered effectively.

irregular, *adj.* (14c) Not in accordance with law, method, or usage; not regular.

irregular endorsement. See *irregular indorsement* under INDORSEMENT.

irregular heir. See HEIR.

irregular indorsement. See INDORSEMENT.

irregularity. (14c) **1.** Something irregular; esp., an act or practice that varies from the normal conduct of an action. **2.** *Eccles. law.* An impediment to clerical office.

irregular judgment. See JUDGMENT (2).

irregular process. See PROCESS (2).

irregular succession. See SUCCESSION (2).

irrelevance, *n.* (1847) **1.** The quality, state, or condition of being inapplicable to a matter under consideration. — Also termed *irrelevancy.* **2.** IRRELEVANCY (1).

irrelevancy, *n.* (16c) **1.** Something not relevant. — Also termed *irrelevance.* **2.** IRRELEVANCE (1).

irrelevant (i-**rel**-ə-vənt), *adj.* (16c) **1.** (Of evidence) having no probative value; not tending to prove or disprove a matter in issue. — Also termed *impertinent.* Cf. IMMATERIAL. **2.** (Of a pleaded allegation) having no substantial relation to the action, and will not affect the court's decision. — **irrelevance,** *n.*

irrelevant consideration. See CONSIDERATION (3).

irrelevant evidence. See EVIDENCE.

irrelevant question. See QUESTION (1).

irremediable (i-ri-**meed**-ee-ə-bəl), *adj.* Incapable of being cured, corrected, or redressed <irremediable errors in the trial>.

irremediable breakdown of the marriage. See IRRETRIEVABLE BREAKDOWN OF THE MARRIAGE.

irremissible (i-ri-**mis**-ə-bəl), *adj.* Incapable of being pardoned or forgiven <irremissible crimes>. — Also termed *irremittable.*

irremittable, *adj.* See IRREMISSIBLE.

irreparable (i-**rep**-ə-rə-bəl), *adj.* Incapable of being rectified, restored, remedied, cured, regained, or repaired; that cannot be made right or good. — **irreparability,** *n.*

irreparable damages. See DAMAGES.

irreparable harm. See *irreparable injury* under INJURY.

irreparable injury. See INJURY.

irreparable-injury rule (i-**rep**-ə-rə-bəl). (1969) The principle that equitable relief (such as an injunction) is available only when no adequate legal remedy (such as monetary damages) exists. • Although courts continue to cite this rule, they do not usu. follow it literally in practice. — Also termed *adequacy test.*

> "The irreparable injury rule has received considerable scholarly attention. In 1978, Owen Fiss examined the possible reasons for the rule and found them wanting. A vigorous debate over the economic wisdom of applying the rule to specific performance of contracts began about the same time, and soon came to center on the transaction costs of administering the two remedies. Both Fiss and Dan Dobbs have noted that the rule does not seem to be taken very seriously, and in a review of Fiss's book, I argued that the definition of adequacy pulls most of the rule's teeth. The Restatement (Second) of Torts dropped the rule from the blackletter and condemned it as misleading, but replaced it only with a long and unstructured list of factors to be considered. . . . [M]any sophisticated lawyers believe that the rule continues to reflect a serious preference for legal over equitable remedies." Douglas Laycock, *The Death of the Irreparable Injury Rule* 9 (1991).

irrepealable (i-ri-**peel**-ə-bəl), *adj.* Incapable of being repealed, annulled, or otherwise nullified <no statutes are irrepealable>. — **irrepealability,** *n.*

irrepleviable (i-rə-**plev**-ee-ə-bəl), *adj.* (16c) (Of property) not capable of being replevied. — Formerly also termed *irreplevisable.* Cf. REPLEVIABLE.

irreproachable, *adj.* **1.** Free from blame; blameless and innocent. **2.** Not open to criticism or reproach.

irreprovable (i-ri-**proov**-ə-bəl), *adj.* Not liable to reproof; IRREPROACHABLE.

irresistible force. See FORCE.

irresistible-impulse test. (1892) *Criminal law.* A test for insanity, holding that a person is not criminally responsible for an act if mental disease prevented that person from controlling potentially criminal conduct. • The few jurisdictions that have adopted this test have combined it with the *McNaghten* rules. — Also termed *control test; volitional test.* See INSANITY DEFENSE; MCNAGHTEN RULES.

> "The first reaction of the legal profession to the irresistible impulse defense, when it was introduced to the law many years ago, was inclined to be favorable. Then a change set in and for many years the prevailing view was strongly against its recognition. Present indications are that the tide is changing again. There seems to be a growing belief to the effect that ignoring the possibility of such a defense fails to give full recognition to the fundamental concept of mens rea." Rollin M. Perkins & Ronald N. Boyce, *Criminal Law* 975 (3d ed. 1982).

irresistible superhuman cause. See ACT OF GOD.

irresistible violence. *Archaic.* See VIS MAJOR.

irresponsible, *adj.* **1.** *Archaic.* Not chargeable with responsibility; not subject to legal obligation <an irresponsible infant>. **2.** Not to be held accountable or called into question <an irresponsible, repressive government>. **3.** Unable to answer for consequences; not able to render satisfaction, esp. because of insolvency <an irresponsible, serially bankrupt debtor>. **4.** (Of a person) doing potentially harmful things without considering the likely results <an irresponsible spendthrift>.

irretrievable breakdown of the marriage. (1973) *Family law.* A ground for divorce that is based on incompatibility between marriage partners and in many states is the sole ground for no-fault divorce. — Abbr. IBM. — Also termed *irretrievable breakdown; irremediable breakdown of the marriage; irremediable breakdown.* Cf. IRRECONCILABLE DIFFERENCES; INCOMPATIBILITY.

irreversible, *adj.* **1.** Incapable of being recalled, repealed, or nullified; IRREVOCABLE. **2.** (Of change, damage, etc.) so extensive or so great as to make it impossible to revert to an earlier state or condition. **3.** (Of an illness or poor physical condition) persistent and incurable.

irrevocable (i-**rev**-ə-kə-bəl), *adj.* (14c) Unalterable; committed beyond recall. — **irrevocability,** *n.*

irrevocable guaranty. See GUARANTY (1).

irrevocable letter of credit. See LETTER OF CREDIT.

irrevocable license. See LICENSE.

irrevocable offer. See OFFER (2).

irrevocable power of attorney. See POWER OF ATTORNEY.

irrevocable proxy. See PROXY.

irrevocable trust. See TRUST (3).

irrigation district. (1879) *Water law.* A quasi-political subdivision or agency established to develop, preserve, and conserve water for the benefit and use of the district's residents.

irritancy, *n.* (17c) *Civil law.* The action of rendering void or the quality, state, or condition of being rendered void.

irritant, *adj.* (16c) *Civil law.* Rendering void.

irritant clause. (1830) *Civil law.* A deed term providing that if the deed's holder performs an act specifically prohibited by the deed, the act or deed is automatically nullified.

irrogare (i-rə-**gair**-ee), *vb.* [Latin] *Civil law.* To inflict a penalty; to make or ordain, as a law.

irrotulatio (i-rah-chə-**lay**-shee-oh). [Law Latin] An enrollment; an entry on a record.

IRS. *abbr.* (1963) INTERNAL REVENUE SERVICE.

IRV. See *instant-runoff voting* under VOTING.

ISCGS. *abbr.* INTERNATIONAL SCHEDULE OF CLASSES OF GOODS AND SERVICES.

ISD. *abbr.* INFORMATION SOCIETY DIRECTIVE.

ish. (15c) *Scots law.* **1.** An exit. • This appears in the phrase "ish and entry," often used in a lease, license, etc., to give someone the right to use necessary ways and passages to pass through another's property, esp. to reach a church or marketplace. **2.** The expiration of a lease, license, etc.; the end of a period of time.

island. (bef. 12c) A tract of land surrounded by water but smaller than a continent; esp., land that is continually surrounded by water and not submerged except during abnormal circumstances.

island rule. (1970) The doctrine that an island that was once within the confines of a state's boundaries remains part of the state's territory regardless of later gradual changes in the location of the thalweg — that is, the center of the main downstream navigation channel. • The island rule is an exception to the rule of thalweg. See RULE OF THALWEG; THALWEG.

ISO. *abbr.* **1.** Incentive stock option. See STOCK OPTION (2). **2.** INSURANCE SERVICES OFFICE.

isolated sale. See SALE.

isolating, *n. Family law.* A parent's or caregiver's pattern of cutting a child off from normal social experiences, preventing the child from forming friendships, or making the child believe that he or she is alone in the world. Cf. IGNORING; REJECTING.

isolationism (I-sə-**lay**-shən-iz-əm), *n.* (1922) Beliefs or actions that are based on the political principle that one's own country should not be involved in the affairs of other countries. — **isolationist,** *adj.* & *n.*

ISP. *abbr.* (1992) INTERNET SERVICE PROVIDER.

is qui cognoscit (is KWI cog-**nos**-it). [Latin "he who recognizes"] The cognizor in a fine. See COGNIZOR; FINE (1).

is qui cognoscitur (is KWI cog-**nos**-ə-tər). [Latin "he who is recognized"] The cognizee in a fine. See COGNIZEE; FINE (1).

is qui omnino desipit (is KWI om-**NI**-noh dee-**sip**-it). [Latin] *Hist.* Someone who is completely void of reason. • The phrase appeared in reference to an insane person, not an idiot.

issuable, *adj.* (16c) **1.** Capable of being issued <an issuable writ>. **2.** Open to dispute or contention <an issuable argument>. **3.** Possible as an outcome <an award as high as $5 million is issuable in this case>.

issuable defense. See DEFENSE (1).

issuable plea. See PLEA (3).

issue, *n.* (16c) **1.** A point in dispute between two or more parties. • In an appeal, an issue may take the form of a separate and discrete question of law or fact, or a combination of both.

> "In federal civil procedure, an issue is a single, certain, and material point arising out of the allegations and contentions of the parties; it is matter affirmed on one side and denied on the other, and when a fact is alleged in the complaint and denied in the answer, the matter is then put in issue between the parties." 35A C.J.S. *Federal Civil Procedure* § 357, at 541 (1960).

▸ **collateral issue.** (18c) A question or issue not directly connected with the matter in dispute.

▸ **deep issue.** (1944) The fundamental issue to be decided by a court in ruling on a point of law. • A deep issue is usu. briefly phrased in separate sentences, with facts interwoven (in chronological order) to show precisely what problem is to be addressed. Cf. *surface issue.*

> "Essentially, a deep issue is the ultimate, concrete question that a court needs to answer to decide a point your way. *Deep* refers to the deep structure of the case — not to deep thinking. The deep issue is the final question you pose when you can no longer usefully ask the follow-up question, 'And what does *that* turn on?'" Bryan A. Garner, *The Winning Brief* 56 (2d ed. 2004).

▸ **fact issue.** See *issue of fact.*

▸ **factual issue.** See *issue of fact.*

▸ **general issue.** (16c) **1.** A plea (often a general denial) by which a party denies the truth of every material allegation in an opposing party's pleading. **2.** The issue arising from such a plea.

> "The general issue is a denial of the legal conclusion sought to be drawn from the declaration. It denies by a general form of expression the defendant's liability, and enables the defendant to contest, without specific averments of the defense to be asserted, most of the allegations which the plaintiff may be required to prove to sustain his action, and in some actions to raise also various affirmative defenses. It fails to perform the functions of pleading, either in giving notice or in reducing the case to specific issues." Benjamin J. Shipman, *Handbook of Common-Law Pleading* § 169, at 304 (Henry Winthrop Ballantine ed., 3d ed. 1923).

▸ **immaterial issue.** (18c) An issue not necessary to decide the point of law. Cf. *material issue.*

▸ **informal issue.** (18c) *Rare.* An issue that arises when a defendant does not properly or fully plead in answer to a material allegation.

▸ **issue of fact.** (17c) A point supported by one party's evidence and controverted by another's. — Also termed *fact issue; question of fact; factual issue.*

▸ **issue of law.** (18c) A point on which the evidence is undisputed, the outcome depending on the court's interpretation of the law; esp., QUESTION OF LAW (3). — Also termed *legal issue.*

▸ **legal issue.** (17c) **1.** A legal question, usu. at the foundation of a case and requiring a court's decision; QUESTION OF LAW (1). — Also termed *issue of law; question of law.* **2.** See *issue of law.*

▸ **material issue.** (17c) An issue that must be decided in order to resolve a controversy. • The existence of a material issue of disputed fact precludes summary judgment. Cf. *immaterial issue.*

▸ **multifarious issue.** (1848) An issue that inquires about several different points (esp. facts) when each one should be inquired about in a separate issue.

▸ **rights issue.** See *rights offering* under OFFERING.

▸ **scrip issue.** See *rights offering* under OFFERING.

▸ **special issue.** (17c) **1.** At common law, an issue arising from a specific allegation in a pleading. • Special issues are no longer used in most jurisdictions. **2.** See *special interrogatory* under INTERROGATORY.

▸ **surface issue.** (1938) A superficially stated issue phrased in a single sentence, without many facts, and usu. beginning with the word *whether.* Cf. *deep issue.*

▸ **ultimate issue.** (17c) A not-yet-decided point that is sufficient either in itself or in connection with other points to resolve the entire case. — Also termed *ultimate question.*

2. *Securities.* A class or series of securities that are simultaneously offered for sale. — Also termed *bond issue; stock issue.* See OFFERING.

▸ **bonus stock issue.** (1903) An issue of free shares to existing members of a corporation. • The power to issue these shares is normally granted in the corporate charter or constitution.

▸ **hot issue.** (1962) A security that, after an initial or secondary offering, is traded in the open market at a substantially higher price. — Also termed *hot stock.*

▸ **new issue.** A stock or bond sold by a corporation for the first time, often to raise working capital. See BLUE-SKY LAW.

▸ **original issue.** The first issue of securities of a particular type or series.

▸ **shelf issue.** (1985) An issue of securities that were previously registered but not released at the time of registration.

3. *Wills & estates.* Lineal descendants; offspring.

▸ **issue female.** (16c) **1.** Female descendants. **2.** A female whose descent from a specified ancestor is traceable through the direct female line. See *tail female* under TAIL.

▸ **issue male.** (16c) **1.** Male descendants. **2.** A male whose descent from a specified ancestor is traceable through the direct male line. See *tail male* under TAIL.

▸ **lawful issue.** (16c) Descendants, including descendants more remote than children. • At common law, the term included only those who were children of legally recognized subsisting marriages. See DESCENDANT; HEIR.

4. *Commercial law.* The first delivery of a negotiable instrument by its maker or holder.

issue, *vb.* (14c) **1.** To accrue <rents issuing from land> **2.** To be put forth officially <without probable cause, the search warrant will not issue> **3.** To send out or distribute officially <issue process> <issue stock>. — **issuance,** *n.*

issued capital. See *subscribed capital* under CAPITAL.

issued-share capital. See *subscribed capital* under CAPITAL.

issued stock. See STOCK.

issue estoppel. See COLLATERAL ESTOPPEL.

issue fee. (1932) *Patents.* The charge that an inventor must pay the U.S. Patent and Trademark Office before an allowed patent application can be issued as a patent.

issue pleading. See PLEADING (2).

issue preclusion. See COLLATERAL ESTOPPEL.

issuer. (18c) **1.** A person or entity (such as a corporation or bank) that issues securities, negotiable instruments, or letters of credit. **2.** A bailee that issues negotiable or nonnegotiable documents of title.

▸ **nonreporting issuer.** (1975) An issuer not subject to the reporting requirements of the Exchange Act because it (1) has not voluntarily become subject to the reporting requirements, (2) has not had an effective registration statement under the Securities Act within the fiscal year, and (3) did not, at the end of its last fiscal year, meet the shareholder or asset tests under the Exchange Act registration requirements.

issue roll. (17c) *Hist. English law.* A court record on which the issues in contested matters are briefly noted. • This practice was abolished in 1834. See INCIPITUR.

issuing bank. See BANK.

ITA. *abbr.* INTERNATIONAL TRADE ADMINISTRATION.

ita lex scripta est (I-tə leks **skrip**-tə est). [Latin] (18c) So the law is written. • This expression means that the law must be obeyed despite the apparent rigor of its application. The idea is that we must be content with the law as it stands, without inquiring into its reasons. — Sometimes shortened to *ita scripta est* ["so it is written"].

> "If practice be the whole he is taught, practice must also be the whole he will ever know: if he be uninstructed in the elements and first principles upon which the rule of practice is founded, the least variation from established precedents will totally distract and bewilder him: *ita lex scripta est* is the utmost his knowledge will arrive at; he must never aspire to form, and seldom expect to comprehend, any arguments drawn *a priori*, from the spirit of the laws and the natural foundations of justice." 1 William Blackstone, *Commentaries on the Laws of England* 32 (1765).

Italian lottery. See NUMBERS GAME.

ita te Deus adjuvet (I-tə tee **dee**-əs **aj**-ə-vet). [Latin] *English law.* So help you God. • An old form of administering an oath in England, usu. in connection with other words, such as: *Ita te Deus adjuvet, et sacrosancta Dei Evangelia* ("So help you God, and God's holy gospels"), and *Ita te Deus adjuvet et omnes sancti* ("So help you God and all the saints").

ITC. See *investment tax credit* under TAX CREDIT.

item. (16c) **1.** A piece of a whole, not necessarily separated. **2.** *Commercial law.* A negotiable instrument or a promise or order to pay money handled by a bank for collection or payment. • The term does not include a payment order governed by Article 4A of the UCC or a credit- or debit-card slip. UCC 4-104(a)(9).

▸ **line item.** (1924) *Accounting.* In a financial statement, a single entry or notation to which a particular dollar amount is attached.

▸ **par item.** An item that a drawee bank will remit to another bank without charge.

3. In drafting, a subpart of text that is the next smaller unit than a subparagraph. • In federal drafting, for example, "(4)" is the item in the following citation: Rule 19(a)(1)(B)(4). — Also termed (in sense 3) *clause.*

itemize, *vb.* (1864) To list in detail; to state by items <an itemized bill>.

itemized deduction. See DEDUCTION (2).

item veto. See *line-item veto* under VETO.

item-veto clause. See VETO CLAUSE (1).

iter (I-tər *or* **it**-ər), *n.* [Latin] (17c) **1.** *Roman law.* A rural servitude that allowed the holder to walk or ride on horseback (but not drive a draft animal) through another's land. — Also termed *servitus itineris* (sər-vi-təs I-**tin**-ər-is). Cf. ACTUS (4); VIA (2). **2.** *Hist.* A journey; esp., a circuit made by an eyre justice. See EYRE.

ITIN. *abbr.* Individual taxpayer identification number; a nine-digit number issued to someone, such as an immigrant, who cannot obtain a Social Security number.

itinerant vendor. See VENDOR.

itinerate (ɪ-**tin**-ə-rayt), *vb.* (17c) (Of a judge) to travel on a circuit for the purpose of holding court. See CIRCUIT. — **itineration,** *n.* — **itinerant,** *adj.* & *n.*

ITS. *abbr.* Institute for Telecommunication Sciences. See NATIONAL TELECOMMUNICATIONS AND INFORMATION ADMINISTRATION.

ITSP. *abbr.* Interstate transportation of stolen property.

iudex (**yoo**-deks). [Latin] See JUDEX.

iudicum reiectio. See JUDICUM REJECTIO.

iudicum sortitio. See JUDICUM SORTITIO.

iudicum subsortitio. See JUDICUM SUBSORTITIO.

ius (yəs *or* yoos). [Latin "law, right"] See JUS.

ius praetorium. See LEX PRAETORIUM.

ius primae noctis. See DROIT DU SEIGNEUR; MARCHET.

ius provocationis. See JUS PROVOCATIONIS.

iustae nuptiae. See JUSTAE NUPTIAE.

IVA. *abbr.* INDIVIDUAL VOLUNTARY ARRANGEMENT.

IVF. *abbr.* (1978) IN VITRO FERTILIZATION.

IWO. *abbr.* INCOME-WITHHOLDING ORDER.

J

J. *abbr.* **1.** JUDGE. **2.** JUSTICE (5). **3.** JUDGMENT (2). **4.** JUS. **5.** JOURNAL.

JA. *abbr.* **1.** JUDGE ADVOCATE. **2.** See *joint account* under ACCOUNT.

jabot (zhə-**boh** *or* **zhab**-oh). [French "bird's crop"] A frill of lace, tulle, chiffon, or the like fastened at the neck and worn over the front of a shirt or costume, today esp. over judicial robes by some judges. • In the United States, jabots were popularized by Justice Ruth Bader Ginsburg. They are common in some parts of the Western world in the attire of male and female judges alike. In jurisdictions where barristers wear robes, jabots are sometimes a part of the prescribed dress. — Also termed (more specif.) *judicial collar*; (slang) *neck doily.*

Jac. *abbr.* Jacobus — the Latin form of the name *James*, used principally in citing statutes enacted during the reigns of English kings of that name (e.g., "St. 1, Jac. 2").

jacens (**jay**-senz). [Latin] Lying; fallen; in abeyance. See *hereditas jacens* under HEREDITAS.

jackpot justice. (1959) *Slang.* The awarding of enormous and apparently arbitrary damages to plaintiffs, thereby making the plaintiffs wealthy and encouraging others to file lawsuits seeking excessive damages for even minor actual harm.

***Jackson–Denno* hearing.** (1965) A court proceeding, held outside the jury's presence to determine whether the defendant's confession was voluntary and therefore admissible as evidence. *Jackson v. Denno*, 378 U.S. 368, 84 S.Ct. 1774 (1964). — Also termed *Jackson v. Denno hearing.*

***Jackson* motion.** (2011) *Criminal law.* A request to have a judge convert the defendant's detention into a civil commitment on grounds that the defendant is incompetent to stand trial. *Jackson v. Indiana*, 406 U.S. 715 (1972).

***Jackson* standard.** (1980) *Criminal law.* The principle that the standard of review on appeal — when a criminal defendant claims that there is insufficient evidence to support the conviction — is to determine whether, after considering the evidence in the light most favorable to the prosecution, any rational trier of fact could have found the essential elements of the crime beyond a reasonable doubt. *Jackson v. Virginia*, 443 U.S. 307, 99 S.Ct. 2781 (1979).

***Jackson v. Denno* hearing.** See JACKSON–DENNO HEARING.

jactitation (jak-ti-**tay**-shən). (17c) **1.** A false boasting or claim that causes injury to another. **2.** *Civil law.* SLANDER OF TITLE.

jactitation of marriage. (16c) *Hist.* **1.** False and actionable boasting or claiming that one is married to another. **2.** An action against a person who falsely boasts of being married to the complainant.

> "Jactitation of marriage is a cause of action which arises when a person falsely alleges that he or she is married to the petitioner, and the remedy sought is a perpetual injunction against the respondent to cease making such allegations. The cause is now uncommon in English municipal law and almost unknown in the conflict of laws." R.H. Graveson, *Conflict of Laws* 349 (7th ed. 1974).

jactitation of title. See SLANDER OF TITLE.

jactura (jak-**t[y]oor**-ə), *n.* [Latin] *Civil law.* **1.** A throwing of goods overboard to lighten or save a vessel; JETTISON. **2.** A loss incurred from this; general average. See *general average* under AVERAGE. — Also termed *jactus.*

jactus lapilli (**jak**-təs lə-**pil**-ɪ). [Latin "the throwing down of a stone"] *Roman law.* A landowner's throwing of a small stone onto a neighbor's land to symbolically protest construction that could threaten the thrower's interest. Cf. NOVI OPERIS NUNTIATIO.

jactus mercium navis levandae causa (**jak**-təs **mər**-shee-əm **nay**-vis lə-**van**-dee **kaw**-zə). [Latin "the throwing of goods into the sea for the purpose of lightening the ship"] *Roman law.* JETTISON. See LEX RHODIA.

jactus retis (**jak**-təs **ree**-tis). [Latin] (17c) *Roman law.* The casting of a net in the context of *emptio spei.* See *emptio spei* under EMPTIO.

JAG. *abbr.* JUDGE ADVOCATE GENERAL.

JAG Department. Judge Advocate General's Department.

JAG Manual. See MANUAL OF THE JUDGE ADVOCATE GENERAL.

jail, *n.* (13c) A prison; esp., a local government's detention center where persons awaiting trial or those convicted of misdemeanors are confined. — Also spelled (esp. BrE) *gaol.* — Also termed *holding cell*; *lockup*; *jailhouse*; *house of detention*; *community correctional center.* Cf. PRISON. — **jail,** *vb.*

jailage (**jayl**-ij). *Hist.* **1.** A jailer's compensation. **2.** A monetary exaction by a jailer.

jailbait, *n.* (1925) *Slang.* A girl or boy who is below the age statutorily established as the minimum age for engaging in sexual relations as an adult. See *statutory rape* under RAPE (2).

jailbird, *n. Slang.* Someone who is in prison or has spent time there.

jail break, *n.* (1910) An escape or attempted escape from prison, esp. by two or more people, often by use of force.

jail credit. (1950) Time spent by a criminal defendant in confinement while awaiting trial. • This time is usu. deducted from the defendant's final sentence (if convicted). — Also termed *jail-credit time.*

jail delivery. (1806) **1.** An escape by several prisoners from a jail. **2.** *Archaic.* A clearing procedure by which all prisoners at a given jail are tried for the offenses that they are accused of having committed.

- ▸ **general jail delivery.** (16c) Collectively, acquittals in high numbers as a result of either lax or reckless administration of the law or defects in the law.

3. *Archaic.* The commission issued to judges of assize, directing them to clear a jail by trying — and either acquitting or condemning — all the inmates. **4.** *Archaic.* The court charged with the trial of all ordinary criminal cases. — Also spelled (BrE) *gaol delivery.* See COMMISSION OF GAOL DELIVERY.

jailer. (13c) A keeper, guard, or warden of a prison or jail; one who is in charge of a jail, or part of it, and of the prisoners confined there. — Also spelled (esp. BrE) *gaoler.*

jailhouse. See JAIL.

jailhouse lawyer. (1951) A prison inmate who seeks release through legal procedures or who gives legal advice to other inmates. — Also termed *guardhouse lawyer.*

jail liberties. (1802) Bounds within which a jail or prison lies and throughout which certain prisoners are allowed to move freely, usu. after giving bond for the liberties. • The bounds are considered an extension of the prison walls. Historically, jail liberties were given in England to those imprisoned for debt. The prisoners were allowed to move freely within the city in which the prison was located. — Also spelled (esp. BrE) *gaol liberties.* — Also termed *jail limits.* See BOUND (2).

> "[S]tatutes were from time to time passed enlarging the gaol liberties, in order to mitigate the hardships of imprisonment: thus, the whole city of Boston was held the 'gaol liberties' of its county gaol. And so with a large part of New York City. . . . The prisoner, while within the limits, is considered as within the walls of the prison." 1 John Bouvier, *Bouvier's Law Dictionary* 1333–34 (Francis Rawle ed., 8th ed. 1914).

jail mail. *Slang.* Correspondence sent by or to an incarcerated person. • It is often screened by prison personnel.

Jamaican switch. (1985) An illegal scheme whereby one conspirator convinces the victim of a need for help in handling a large sum of money, usu. by claiming to have found the money or by claiming to be an unsophisticated foreigner, and promises to share part of the money with the victim or asks the victim for help in finding a suitable charity to donate to, at which time the other conspirator appears and promises to assist if both the victim and first conspirator provide good-faith money, the intent being for the two conspirators to leave with all the money, including the victim's. • The name given to this scheme is likely to be considered offensive by some. — Also termed *pigeon drop.*

***James* hearing.** (1981) A court proceeding held to determine whether the out-of-court statements of a coconspirator should be admitted into evidence, by analyzing whether there was a conspiracy, whether the declarant and the defendant were part of the conspiracy, and whether the statement was made in furtherance of the conspiracy. *U.S. v. James,* 590 F.2d 575 (5th Cir. 1979); Fed. R. Evid. 801(d)(2)(E).

Jane Doe. (18c) A fictitious name for a female party to a legal proceeding, used because the party's true identity is unknown or because her real name is being withheld. — Also termed *Jane Roe; Mary Major.* Cf. JOHN DOE.

Janus-faced (**jay**-nəs fayst), *adj.* (17c) Having two contrasting or contradictory aspects; two-faced <a Janus-faced plea>.

***Jason* clause.** (1926) *Maritime law.* A bill-of-lading clause requiring contribution in general average even when the peril that justified the sacrifice was the result of the carrier's negligence, for which the carrier is otherwise exempt from liability by statute. • The clause is named after the Supreme Court case that upheld its enforceability, *The Jason,* 225 U.S. 32, 32 S.Ct. 560 (1912). See *general average* under AVERAGE.

jaywalking, *n.* (1919) The act or an instance of a pedestrian's crossing a street without heeding traffic regulations, as by crossing between intersections or at a place other than a crosswalk. — **jaywalker,** *n.* — **jaywalk,** *vb.*

JCP. *abbr.* Justice of the Common Pleas. See COURT OF COMMON PLEAS.

JCPC. *abbr.* JUDICIAL COMMITTEE OF THE PRIVY COUNCIL.

JCUS. *abbr.* JUDICIAL CONFERENCE OF THE UNITED STATES.

JD. *abbr.* JUVENILE DELINQUENT.

J.D. *abbr.* JURIS DOCTOR.

JDP. *abbr.* JUDICIAL-DIVERSION PROGRAM.

Jedburgh justice (**jed**-bər-ə). See JUSTICE (4).

Jeddart justice (**jed**-ərt). See *Jedburgh justice* under JUSTICE (4).

jedge and warrant (jej). (18c) *Scots law.* The authority formerly given by the Dean of Guild of a burgh to rebuild or repair a dilapidated house or tenement.

Jedwood justice (**jed**-wəd). See *Jedburgh justice* under JUSTICE (4).

***Jencks* material.** (1961) *Criminal procedure.* A prosecution witness's written or recorded pretrial statement that a criminal defendant, upon filing a motion after the witness has testified, is entitled to have in preparing to cross-examine the witness. • The defense may use a statement of this kind for impeachment purposes. *Jencks v. U.S.,* 353 U.S. 657, 77 S.Ct. 1007 (1957); Jencks Act, 18 USCA § 3500. Cf. BRADY MATERIAL.

▸ **reverse *Jencks* material.** (1990) *Criminal procedure.* A defense witness's written or recorded pretrial statement that a prosecutor is entitled to have in preparing to cross-examine the witness. • Reverse *Jencks* material may be obtained during pretrial discovery. Discoverable statements include a witness's signed or adopted written statement, and transcripts or recordings of the witness's oral statements, including grand-jury testimony. *U.S. v. Nobles,* 422 U.S. 225, 231–34, 95 S.Ct. 2160, 2166–68 (1975); Fed. R. Crim. P. 26.2. — Also termed *reverse Jencks; reverse discovery; reciprocal discovery.*

***Jensen* doctrine.** (1942) *Maritime law.* The principle that a state statute may not apply in a maritime case if to do so would "work material prejudice to the characteristic features of the general maritime law or interfere with the proper harmony and uniformity of that law." *Southern Pac. Co. v. Jensen,* 244 U.S. 205, 37 S.Ct. 524 (1917).

jeofail (jə-**fayl** *or* **jef**-ayl), *n.* [fr. French *j'ay faillé* "I have made an error"] (16c) *Archaic.* **1.** A pleading error or oversight that results in a misjoined issue and requires a repleader. **2.** The acknowledgment of such an error. — Also spelled *jeofaile.*

jeopardy. (14c) The risk of conviction and punishment that a criminal defendant faces at trial. • Jeopardy attaches in a jury trial when the jury is empaneled, and in a bench trial when the first witness is sworn. — Also termed *legal jeopardy.* See DOUBLE JEOPARDY.

jeopardy assessment. See ASSESSMENT (2).

***Jepson* claim.** See PATENT CLAIM.

jerk note. (1854) *Hist. Maritime law.* A permit, issued by a customs collector to the ship's master, authorizing the master to receive cargo for an outbound voyage. Cf. STIFFENING NOTE.

jetsam (**jet**-səm). (16c) The portion of a ship's cargo and equipment that is (1) thrown overboard in an effort to save the ship from a perilous condition, and that (2) either sinks beneath the surface or is washed ashore. — Also termed *jettison*. Cf. FLOTSAM; LAGAN (1); WAVESON.

jettison (**jet**-ə-sən), *n*. (15c) *Maritime law.* **1.** The act of voluntarily throwing cargo overboard to lighten or stabilize a ship that is in immediate danger. — Also termed *equitable jettison; jactura; jactus mercium navis levandae causa.* See *general average* under AVERAGE. **2.** JETSAM. — **jettison,** *vb.*

> "The goods must not be swept away by the violence of the waves, for then the loss falls entirely upon the merchant or his insurer, but they must be intentionally sacrificed by the mind and agency of man, for the safety of the ship and the residue of the cargo. The jettison must be made for sufficient cause, and not from groundless timidity. It must be made in a case of extremity, when the ship is in danger of perishing by the fury of a storm, or is laboring upon rocks or shallows, or is closely pursued by pirates or enemies; and then if the ship and the residue of the cargo be saved by means of the sacrifice, nothing can be more reasonable than that the property saved should bear its proportion of the loss." 3 James Kent, *Commentaries on American Law* 232–33 (George Comstock ed., 11th ed. 1866).

jeux de bourse (**zhoo** də **bərs**), *n*. [French "games of the stock exchange"] Speculation in stocks or bonds, as by dealing in options or futures.

***Jewell* instruction** (**joo**-wəl). (1977) *Criminal procedure.* A court's instruction to the jury that the defendant can be found to have the requisite criminal mental state despite being deliberately ignorant of some of the facts surrounding the crime. • If a defendant claims ignorance of some fact essential to the crime, such as not knowing that a particular bag contained drugs, but the surrounding circumstances would put a reasonable person on notice that there was a high probability of illegality, as when the defendant has taken the bag from a known drug-dealer and has noticed the smell of marijuana coming from the bag, then the court may instruct the jury that it is entitled to infer the defendant's guilty knowledge if the defendant deliberately avoided knowledge of the critical facts. *U.S. v. Jewell*, 532 F.2d 697 (9th Cir. 1976). — Also termed *deliberate-indifference instruction; deliberate-indifference direction.* Cf. *willful-blindness instruction* under JURY INSTRUCTION.

Jim Crow law. (1891) *Hist.* A law enacted or purposely interpreted to discriminate against blacks, such as a law requiring separate restrooms for blacks and whites. • Jim Crow laws are unconstitutional under the 14th Amendment.

> "At the same time that the caricature of blacks as 'Jim Crow' was perpetuated through popular culture, barriers to legal and social advancement were maintained through rigid policies of segregation, enforced by custom in the North and by law in the South. The Supreme Court gave its blessing to all such laws and customs in 1896 when it formally approved a state law restricting blacks to separate cars on trains, popularly referred to as Jim Crow cars. . . . From then on more and more laws were passed throughout the South consigning blacks to separate (and inevitably inferior) 'Jim Crow' facilities; naturally these were referred to as Jim Crow laws. By the 1920s this systematic segregation of blacks was being referred to as Jim Crowism, and finally, in the 1940s, the term completed its evolution, with the entire system of subjection of blacks to white control being referred to simply as Jim Crow." James E. Clapp et al., *Lawtalk: The Unknown Stories Behind Familiar Legal Expressions* 142–43 (2011).

jingle rule. See DUAL-PRIORITIES RULE.

JJ. *abbr.* **1.** Judges. **2.** Justices.

JJDPA. *abbr.* JUVENILE JUSTICE AND DELINQUENCY PREVENTION ACT.

J.N. *abbr.* JOHN-A-NOKES.

JNOV. *abbr.* Judgment *non obstante veredicto.* See *judgment notwithstanding the verdict* under JUDGMENT (2).

JO. *abbr.* Juvenile offender. See JUVENILE DELINQUENT.

JOA. *abbr.* Judgment of acquittal.

job action. (1938) *Labor law.* **1.** A concerted, temporary action by employees (such as a sickout or work slowdown), intended to pressure management to concede to the employees' demands without resorting to a strike. — Also termed *industrial action.* See STRIKE (1). **2.** ADVERSE EMPLOYMENT ACTION.

jobber, *n*. (17c) **1.** Someone who buys from a manufacturer and sells to a retailer; a wholesaler or middleman. **2.** A middleman in the exchange of securities among brokers; specif., one who works on a stock exchange by buying shares, etc., from brokers and selling them to other brokers. — Also termed *stockjobber; stock-jobber.* **3.** Someone who works by the job; a contractor. — **job,** *vb.*

jobber's agreement. See HAZANTOWN AGREEMENT.

jobbery, *n*. (1837) The practice or act of perverting a public service in a way that serves private ends; unfair means to serve private interests.

job description. (1920) An official listing of the responsibilities required of someone holding a particular employment position.

job market. See LABOR MARKET.

job security. (1925) Protection of an employee's job, often through a union contract.

job-targeting program. (1993) An initiative by a labor union to maintain or improve its share of the labor in a particular market by financing or backing contractors who bid on targeted projects. — Also termed *market-recovery program.*

jocus partitus (**joh**-kəs pahr-**tɪ**-təs), *n*. [Law Latin "divided game"] *Hist.* A gambling arrangement made by the parties on a lawsuit's outcome.

john. *Slang.* A customer or prospective customer of a prostitute.

John-a-Nokes. (16c) *Archaic.* A fictitious name for an unknown party to a legal proceeding, esp. the first party. • The name is short for "John who dwells at an oak." — Abbr. J.N. — Also spelled *John-a-Noakes.*

John-a-Stiles. (16c) *Archaic.* A fictitious name for an unknown party to a legal proceeding, esp. the second party. • The name is short for "John who dwells at a stile" — that is, at a set of steps that help people climb over a fence or go through a gate in a field. — Abbr. J.S. — Also spelled *John-a-Styles.*

John Doe. (16c) A fictitious name used in a legal proceeding to designate a person whose identity is unknown, to protect a person's known identity, or to indicate that a true defendant does not exist. • In England, "William Styles" was also used. Cf. JANE DOE; RICHARD ROE.

> "Sheriffs in time growing remiss in their duty, allowed of any persons as *pledges*, sometimes returning the names of fictitious persons as *pledges*, at others, neglecting to require or return any at all. . . . And the legislature, to supply the want of real persons as *pledges*, and recompense the defendant where he has been unjustly or vexatiously sued, has by various statutes, either given him the costs he has incurred in making his defence; or else deprived the plaintiff of recovering those costs he is entitled to by law, in cases of obtaining a verdict, by leaving it to the judge at the trial to certify on the record, that he had little or no cause of action. Since these statutes for allowing the defendant his costs, where the plaintiff fails, or is nonsuited, the writ to the coroner to affeer the *pledges* has fallen into disuse, and two good-natured personages, *John Doe* and *Richard Roe*, from their universal acquaintance and peculiar longevity, have become the ready and common *pledges* of every suitor." 1 George Crompton, *Rules and Cases of Practice in the Courts of King's Bench and Common Pleas* xlvii (3d ed. 1787).

> "The fictitious names *John Doe* and *Richard Roe* regularly appeared in actions of ejectment at common law. *Doe* was the nominal plaintiff, who by a fiction was said to have entered land under a valid lease; *Roe* was said to have ejected *Doe*, and the lawsuit took the title *Doe v. Roe*. These fictional allegations disappeared upon the enactment of the Common Law Procedure Act of 1852. . . . Beyond actions of ejectment, and esp. in the U.S., *John Doe*, *Jane Doe*, *Richard Roe*, *Jane Roe*, and *Peter Poe* have come to identify a party to a lawsuit whose true name is either unknown or purposely shielded." Bryan A. Garner, *Garner's Dictionary of Legal Usage* 292–93 (3d ed. 2011).

John Doe defendant. See DEFENDANT.

John Doe summons. See SUMMONS.

John Doe warrant. See WARRANT (1).

joinder, *n.* (17c) The uniting of parties or claims in a single lawsuit. Cf. CONSOLIDATION (3). — **join,** *vb.*

▸ **collusive joinder.** (1883) Joinder of a defendant, usu. a nonresident, in order to have a case removed to federal court. See *manufactured diversity* under DIVERSITY OF CITIZENSHIP.

▸ **compulsory joinder.** (1901) The necessary joinder of a party if either of the following is true: (1) in that party's absence, those already involved in the lawsuit cannot receive complete relief; or (2) the absent party claims an interest in the subject of an action, so that party's absence might either impair the protection of that interest or leave some other party subject to multiple or inconsistent obligations. Fed. R. Civ. P. 19(a). — Also termed *mandatory joinder.*

▸ **fraudulent joinder.** (1836) The bad-faith joinder of a party, usu. a resident of the state, to prevent removal of a case to federal court.

▸ **joinder in demurrer.** (17c) *Common-law pleading.* A set form of words by which either party accepts or joins in a legal issue; esp., the plaintiff's acceptance of the defendant's issue of law. See PLEADING (quot.).

▸ **joinder in issue.** See *joinder of issue.*

▸ **joinder in pleading.** (1852) *Common-law pleading.* One party's acceptance of the opposing party's proposed issue and mode of trial.

▸ **joinder of documents.** See JOINDER OF DOCUMENTS.

▸ **joinder of error.** (1822) A written denial of the errors alleged in an assignment of errors in a criminal case.

▸ **joinder of issue.** (18c) **1.** The submission of an issue jointly for decision. **2.** The acceptance or adoption of a disputed point as the basis of argument in a controversy. — Also termed *joinder in issue*; *similiter.* **3.** The taking up of the opposite side of a case, or of the contrary view on a question.

▸ **joinder of offenses.** (1836) The charging of an accused with two or more crimes as multiple counts in a single indictment or information. • Unless later severed, joined offenses are tried together at a single trial. Fed. R. Crim. P. 8(a).

▸ **joinder of parties.** (1802) The combination of two or more persons or entities as plaintiffs or defendants in a civil lawsuit.

▸ **joinder of remedies.** (1881) The joinder of alternative claims, such as breach of contract and quantum meruit, or of one claim with another prospective claim, such as a creditor's claim against a debtor to recover on a loan and the creditor's claim against a third party to set aside the transfer of the loan's collateral.

▸ **mandatory joinder.** See *compulsory joinder.*

▸ **misjoinder.** See MISJOINDER.

▸ **nonjoinder.** See NONJOINDER.

▸ **permissive joinder.** (1903) The optional joinder of parties if (1) their claims or the claims asserted against them are asserted jointly, severally, or in respect of the same transaction or occurrence, and (2) any legal or factual question common to all of them will arise. Fed. R. Civ. P. 20.

▸ **pretensive joinder.** (1972) Joinder of defendants solely to obtain venue in a jurisdiction in which the action could not otherwise be tried.

joinder in demurrer. See JOINDER.

joinder in issue. See *joinder of issue* under JOINDER.

joinder in pleading. See JOINDER.

joinder of documents. (1968) The reading together of two or more documents that jointly meet statutory requirements even though one or some of the documents alone would be insufficient.

joinder of error. See JOINDER.

joinder of issue. See JOINDER.

joinder of offenses. See JOINDER.

joinder of parties. See JOINDER.

joinder of remedies. See JOINDER.

joint, *adj.* (14c) **1.** (Of a thing) common to or shared by two or more persons or entities <joint bank account>. **2.** (Of a person or entity) combined, united, or sharing with another <joint heirs>.

joint account. See ACCOUNT.

joint action. See ACTION (4).

joint activity. See JOINT PARTICIPATION.

joint administration. (1826) *Bankruptcy.* The management of two or more bankruptcy estates, usu. involving related debtors, under one docket for purposes of handling various administrative matters, including notices to creditors, to conclude the cases more efficiently. • A bankruptcy court can order a joint administration when there are two or more cases pending involving a husband and wife, a partnership and at least one partner, two or more business partners, or a business and an affiliate. The intent should be to increase the administrative efficiency of administering the two cases; the substantive rights of creditors should not ordinarily be affected. Fed. R. Bankr. P. 1015. — Also termed *procedural consolidation.* See ADMINISTRATION (3). Cf. *substantive consolidation* under CONSOLIDATION.

joint adoption. See ADOPTION (1).

joint adventure. 1. See *common adventure* under ADVENTURE. **2.** JOINT VENTURE.

joint agreement. See AGREEMENT.

joint and mutual will. See WILL.

joint and reciprocal will. See *joint and mutual will* under WILL.

joint and several, *adj.* (17c) (Of liability, responsibility, etc.) apportionable at an adversary's discretion either among two or more parties or to only one or a few select members of the group; together and in separation. See JOINT; SEVERAL.

joint and several bond. See BOND (3).

joint and several liability. See LIABILITY.

joint-and-several liability doctrine. (1970) The principle that when two or more persons cause an injury, each is liable for the full amount of damages.

joint and several note. See NOTE (1).

joint-and-several promise. See PROMISE.

joint-and-survivorship account. See *joint account* under ACCOUNT.

joint annuity. See ANNUITY.

joint authors. (17c) *Copyright.* Two or more authors who collaborate in producing a copyrightable work, each author intending to merge his or her respective contributions into a single work, and each being able to exploit the work as desired while remaining accountable for a pro rata share of the profits to the coauthor or coauthors.

joint ballot. See BALLOT (2).

joint board. *Labor law.* A committee — usu. made up of an equal number of representatives from management and the union — established to conduct grievance proceedings or resolve grievances.

joint bond. See BOND (3).

joint-check rule. (1977) The principle that when an owner or general contractor issues a check that is made jointly payable to a subcontractor and the subcontractor's materialman supplier, the materialman's indorsement on the check certifies that all amounts due to the materialman, up to the amount of the check, have been paid. • This rule protects the owner or general contractor from lien foreclosure by a materialman who was not paid by the subcontractor. By issuing a joint check, the owner or general contractor is not left merely to hope that the subcontractor pays all the materialmen. And the materialman is protected because it can refuse to indorse the check until it is satisfied that the subcontractor will pay it the appropriate amount.

joint committee. See COMMITTEE (1).

joint contract. See CONTRACT.

joint covenant. See COVENANT (1).

joint creditor. See CREDITOR.

joint custody. See CUSTODY (2).

joint debtor. See DEBTOR.

joint defendant. See CODEFENDANT.

joint-defense privilege. See PRIVILEGE (3).

joint demise. See DEMISE.

joint employment. See EMPLOYMENT.

joint enterprise. (17c) **1.** *Criminal law.* An undertaking by two or more persons who set out to commit an offense they have conspired to. See CONSPIRACY. **2.** *Torts.* An undertaking by two or more persons with an equal right to direct and benefit from the endeavor, as a result of which one participant's negligence may be imputed to the others. — Also termed (in senses 1 & 2) *common enterprise.* **3.** JOINT VENTURE. **4.** A joint venture for noncommercial purposes.

> "A business relationship is needed for a joint venture but not for a joint enterprise. Thus, a joint enterprise may be defined as a non-commercial joint venture." 46 Am. Jur. 2d *Joint Ventures* § 6, at 27 (1994).

joint estate. See ESTATE (1).

joint executor. See EXECUTOR (2).

joint heir. See HEIR.

joint indictment. See INDICTMENT.

joint interest. See INTEREST (2).

joint-interest purchase. See SPLIT-INTEREST PURCHASE OF PROPERTY.

joint inventor. (1813) *Patents.* Someone who collaborates with another or others in developing an invention. • All joint inventors must be identified on a patent application.

> "Employing a friend, mechanic, model maker or other person to do work for one on an idea does not, as a rule, make him a joint inventor with the originator. One has a right to employ someone else to do one's work. There are conditions, however, where such person would become a joint inventor, or even sole inventor. It is best to play safe and consult an experienced patent lawyer, laying before him all of the facts." Richard B. Owen, *Patents, Trademarks, Copyrights, Departmental Practice* 7 (1925).

joint judgment. See JUDGMENT (2).

joint legal custody. See *joint custody* under CUSTODY (2).

joint liability. See LIABILITY.

joint life insurance. See LIFE INSURANCE.

joint life policy. See INSURANCE POLICY.

joint managing conservatorship. See *joint custody* under CUSTODY (2).

joint mortgage. See MORTGAGE.

joint negligence. See NEGLIGENCE.

joint note. See NOTE (1).

joint obligation. See OBLIGATION.

joint offense. See OFFENSE (2).

joint ownership. See OWNERSHIP.

joint participation. (1971) *Civil-rights law.* A pursuit undertaken by a private person in concert with a governmental entity or state official, resulting in the private person's performing public functions and thereby being subject to claims under the civil-rights laws. — Also termed *joint activity.* See SYMBIOTIC-RELATIONSHIP TEST; NEXUS TEST.

joint party. See COPARTY.

joint physical custody. See *joint custody* under CUSTODY (2).

joint plaintiff. See COPLAINTIFF.

joint possession. See POSSESSION.

joint-powers agreement. (1949) A contract between a special district and a city or county in which the city or county agrees to cooperate with and lend its powers to or perform services for the special district.

joint promise. See PROMISE.

joint-promise rule. (1967) The principle that when a promise is made jointly to or by two or more persons, the promise is enforceable by or against any one or all of the persons.

joint property. See PROPERTY.

joint rate. See RATE (2).

joint representation. See *concurrent representation* under REPRESENTATION (2).

joint resolution. See RESOLUTION (1).

jointress. (17c) *Hist.* A woman who has a jointure. — Also termed *jointuress.* See JOINTURE (1).

joint return. See TAX RETURN.

joint rule. See RULE (3).

joint session. See SESSION (1).

joint stock. See STOCK.

joint-stock association. See *joint-stock company* under COMPANY.

joint-stock company. See COMPANY.

joint tariff. See TARIFF (5).

joint tenancy. See TENANCY.

joint tenant. See *joint tenancy* under TENANCY.

joint tortfeasors. See TORTFEASOR.

joint trespass. See TRESPASS.

joint trial. See TRIAL.

joint trustee. See COTRUSTEE.

jointure (**joyn**-chər). (15c) **1.** *Archaic.* A woman's freehold life estate in land, made in consideration of marriage in lieu of dower and to be enjoyed by her only after her husband's death; a settlement under which a wife receives such an estate. • The four essential elements are that (1) the jointure must take effect immediately upon the husband's death, (2) it must be for the wife's own life, and not for another's life or for a term of years, (3) it must be held by her in her own right and not in trust for her, and (4) it must be in lieu of her entire dower. See DOWER.

▸ **equitable jointure.** (1803) A premarital arrangement for a woman to enjoy a jointure, accepted by the woman in lieu of dower. — Also termed *equitable dower.*

2. A settlement under which a wife receives such an estate. — Also termed *legal jointure.* **3.** An estate in lands given jointly to a husband and wife before they marry. See JOINTRESS.

jointuress. See JOINTRESS.

joint venture. (18c) A business undertaking by two or more persons engaged in a single defined project. • The necessary elements are (1) an express or implied agreement; (2) a common purpose that the group intends to carry out; (3) shared profits and losses; and (4) each member's equal voice in controlling the project. — Also termed *joint adventure; joint enterprise.* Cf. PARTNERSHIP; STRATEGIC ALLIANCE; VENTURE.

> "There is some difficulty in determining when the legal relationship of joint venture exists, with authorities disagreeing as to the essential elements. . . . The joint venture is not as much of an entity as is a partnership." Henry G. Henn & John R. Alexander, *Laws of Corporations* § 49, at 106 (3d ed. 1983).

joint-venture corporation. See CORPORATION.

joint verdict. See VERDICT (1).

joint welfare fund. See FUND (1).

joint will. See WILL.

joint work. See WORK (2).

joker. (1904) **1.** An ambiguous clause inserted in a legislative bill to render it inoperative or uncertain in some respect without arousing opposition at the time of passage. **2.** A rider or amendment that is extraneous to the subject of the bill.

Jones Act. *Maritime law.* A federal statute that allows a seaman injured during the course of employment to recover damages for the injuries in a negligence action against the employer. • If a seaman dies from such injuries, the seaman's personal representative may maintain an action against the employer. 46 USCA § 30104.

Jones Act vessel. See VESSEL.

jour (zhoor), *n.* [French] (15c) Day <*jour en banc*>.

journal. (15c) **1.** A book or record kept, usu. daily, as of the proceedings of a legislature or the events of a ship's voyage. — Also termed *log; logbook.* See MINUTES (2). **2.** *Accounting.* In double-entry bookkeeping, a book in which original entries are recorded before being transferred to a ledger. **3.** A periodical or magazine, esp. one published for a scholarly or professional group. — Abbr. J.

journal entry. See ENTRY (2).

journalist's privilege. See PRIVILEGE (3).

journal of notarial acts (noh-**tair**-ee-əl). (2007) The notary public's sequential record of notarial transactions, usu. a bound book listing the date, time, and type of each official act, the type of instrument acknowledged or verified before the notary, the signature of each person whose signature is notarized, the type of information used to verify the identity of parties whose signatures are notarized, and the fee charged. • This journal, required by law in many states, provides a record that may be used as evidence in court. — Also termed *notarial record; notarial register; notary record book; sequential journal.*

journeys accounts. (17c) *Hist.* The number of days (usu. 15) after the abatement of a writ within which a new writ could be obtained. • This number was based on how many days it took for the plaintiff to travel (or *journey*) to the court.

joyriding, *n.* (1909) The illegal driving of someone else's automobile without permission, but usu. with no intent to deprive the owner of it permanently; the crime of stealing a car and driving it for pleasure, often recklessly. • Under the Model Penal Code, the offender's reasonable belief that the owner would have consented is an affirmative defense. See Model Penal Code § 223.9. — Also termed *unauthorized use of a vehicle*. — **joyride,** *vb.* — **joyrider,** *n.*

> "When the automobile began to appear and was limited to the possession of a few of the more fortunate members of the community, many persons who ordinarily respected the property rights of others, yielded to the temptation to drive one of these new contrivances without the consent of the owner. This became so common that the term 'joyrider' was coined to refer to the person who indulged in such unpermitted use of another's car. For the most part it was a relatively harmless type of trespass . . . ." Rollin M. Perkins & Ronald N. Boyce, *Criminal Law* 333 (3d ed. 1982).

JP. *abbr.* (18c) JUSTICE OF THE PEACE.

J.P. court. See *justice court* under COURT.

JPML. *abbr.* JUDICIAL PANEL ON MULTIDISTRICT LITIGATION.

JPO. *abbr.* Japanese Patent Office.

***J.P. Stevens* test.** (1988) *Patents.* A two-part test to determine whether a patent-applicant's conduct amounted to inequitable conduct before the Patent and Trademark Office, by deciding (1) whether the threshold levels of materiality and intent are met, and (2) whether, on balance, the facts show inequitable conduct as a matter of law. *J.P. Stevens v. Lex Tex Ltd.*, 747 F.2d 1553 (Fed. Cir. 1984). • In the balance, information that is clearly material or conduct that is clearly deceptive can decide the outcome.

J.S. *abbr.* JOHN-A-STILES.

JSC. *abbr.* Justice of Supreme Court.

JSD. [Law Latin *juris scientiae doctor*] *abbr.* DOCTOR OF JURIDICAL SCIENCE.

JSL. *abbr.* See *joint and several liability* under LIABILITY.

JTC. *abbr.* JUDICIAL-TENURE COMMISSION.

jubere (juu-**beer**-ee), *vb.* [Latin] *Civil law.* **1.** To order, direct, or command. **2.** To assure or promise.

JUD. [Law Latin *juris utriusque doctor* "doctor of both laws"] *abbr.* A doctor of both civil and canon law.

judex (**joo**-deks), *n.* [Latin] **1.** *Roman law.* A private person appointed by a praetor or other magistrate to hear and decide a case. • The Roman judex was originally drawn from a panel of qualified persons of standing but was later himself a magistrate. **2.** *Roman & civil law.* A judge. **3.** *Hist.* A juror. — Also spelled *iudex.* Pl. **judices** (**joo**-di-seez).

▸ ***judex ad quem*** (ad **kwem**). (17c) *Civil law.* A judge to whom an appeal is taken.

▸ ***judex a quo*** (ay **kwoh**). (18c) *Civil law.* A judge from whom an appeal is taken.

▸ ***judex datus*** (**day**-təs). *Roman law.* A judex assigned by a magistrate or provincial governor to try a case under *cognitio extraordinaria.* See COGNITIO EXTRAORDINARIA.

▸ ***judex delegatus*** (del-ə-**gay**-təs). (16c) *Roman & civil law.* A delegated judge under *cognitio extraordinaria*; a special judge. See COGNITIO EXTRAORDINARIA.

▸ ***judex fiscalis*** (fis-**kay**-lis). (17c) *Roman law.* A judex having jurisdiction of matters relating to the *fiscus.* See FISCUS (1).

▸ ***judex ordinarius*** (or-də-**nair**-ee-əs). (16c) *Civil law.* A judge having jurisdiction in his own right rather than by delegated authority. • The judge was typically a provincial governor.

▸ ***judex pedaneus*** (pə-**day**-nee-əs). (18c) *Roman law.* A judex to whom petty cases are delegated; an inferior or deputy judge under *cognitio extraordinaria.* — Also termed *judex specialis.*

▸ ***judex quaestionis*** (kwes-chee-**oh**-nis *or* kwes-tee-). (17c) *Roman law.* The chairman of the jury in a criminal case, either a praetor or a magistrate of lower rank.

▸ ***judex selectus*** (sə-**lek**-təs). (1908) *Civil law.* A judge selected to hear the facts in a criminal case.

▸ ***judex specialis*** (spesh-ee-**ay**-lis). *Roman law.* See *judex pedaneus.*

judge, *n.* (14c) A public official appointed or elected to hear and decide legal matters in court; a judicial officer who has the authority to administer justice. • The term is sometimes held to include all officers appointed to decide litigated questions, including a justice of the peace and even jurors (who are judges of the facts). But in ordinary legal usage, the term is limited to the sense of an officer who (1) is so named in his or her commission, and (2) presides in a court. *Judge* is often used interchangeably with *court.* See COURT (2). — Abbr. J. (and, in plural, JJ.)

▸ **administrative-law judge.** See ADMINISTRATIVE-LAW JUDGE.

▸ **administrative patent judge.** (1994) *Patents.* A U.S. Patent and Trademark Office adjudicator charged with conducting interference and appeal proceedings. — Abbr. APJ.

▸ **associate judge.** (18c) An appellate judge who is neither a chief judge nor a presiding judge. — Also termed *puisne judge.*

▸ **bankruptcy judge.** (1873) A judicial officer appointed by a U.S. Court of Appeals to preside over cases filed under the Bankruptcy Code and proceedings related to bankruptcy cases that are referred by the U.S. district court. • A bankruptcy judge is appointed for a term of 14 years. 28 USCA §§ 151 et seq. See ARTICLE I JUDGE.

▸ **chief administrative patent judge.** (1997) *Patents.* The supervisor of administrative patent judges at the U.S. Patent and Trademark Office. — Abbr. CAPJ.

▸ **chief judge.** (15c) The judge who presides over the sessions and deliberations of a court, while also overseeing the administration of the court. — Abbr. C.J.

▸ **circuit judge.** (18c) **1.** A judge who sits on a circuit court; esp., a federal judge who sits on a U.S. court of appeals. **2.** *Hist.* A special judge added to a court for the purpose of holding trials, but without being a regular member of the court. — Abbr. C.J.

▸ **city judge.** See *municipal judge.*

▸ **continuing part-time judge.** (1992) A judge who serves repeatedly on a part-time basis by election or under a continuing appointment.

▸ **county judge.** (18c) A local judge having criminal or civil jurisdiction, or sometimes both, within a county.

▸ **criminal-court judge.** (1845) A judge who sits on a court with jurisdiction only over criminal matters.

▸ **de facto judge** (di **fak**-toh). (1829) A judge operating under color of law but whose authority is procedurally defective, such as a judge appointed under an unconstitutional statute. — Also termed *judge de facto.*

▸ **district judge.** (18c) **1.** A judge in a federal or state judicial district. **2.** See *metropolitan stipendiary magistrate* under MAGISTRATE. — Abbr. D.J.

▸ **duty judge.** A judge responsible for setting an arrestee's bail, usu. by telephone or videoconference.

▸ **family-court judge.** (1937) A judge who sits on a court that has jurisdiction exclusively over matters involving domestic relations, such as divorce and child-custody matters.

▸ **feeder judge.** See FEEDER JUDGE.

▸ **general-duty judge.** A judge serving on a multijudge court who is assigned, usu. on a rotating basis, to a variety of tasks such as late-night search warrants, hospital applications for emergency operations and blood transfusions, management of judicial functions relating to a grand jury, and ex parte and emergency matters.

▸ **grab-bag judge.** (1958) *Slang.* A judge who has not been regularly assigned to a particular court or to particular types of cases but who instead handles cases ad hoc as assignments are made from time to time.

▸ **hanging judge.** (18c) *Slang.* A judge who is harsh (sometimes corruptly so) with defendants, esp. those accused of capital crimes.

▸ **inferior judge.** (16c) A judge who sits on a lower court.

▸ **judge de facto.** See *de facto judge.*

▸ **judge delegate.** (16c) A judge who acts under delegated authority.

▸ **judge of probate.** See *probate judge.*

▸ **judge ordinary.** (1858) *Hist.* The judge of the English Court for Divorce and Matrimonial Causes from 1857-1875.

▸ **judge pro tempore** (proh **tem**-pə-ree). See *visiting judge.*

▸ **juvenile-court judge.** (1912) A judge who sits on a court that has jurisdiction exclusively over matters involving juveniles, such as suits involving child abuse and neglect, matters involving status offenses, and, sometimes, suits to terminate parental rights.

▸ **lay judge.** (16c) A judge who is not a lawyer.

▸ **mentor judge.** An experienced judge who helps a new judge by sharing knowledge and offering guidance.

▸ **midnight judge.** See MIDNIGHT JUDGE.

▸ **military judge.** (17c) A commissioned officer of the armed forces who is on active duty and is a member of a bar of a federal court or of the highest court of a state. • The Judge Advocate General of the particular service must certify a military judge as qualified for duty. A military judge of a general court-martial must also be a member of an independent judiciary. A military judge is detailed to every general court-martial and usu. to a special court-martial.

▸ **municipal judge.** (18c) A local judge having criminal or civil jurisdiction, or sometimes both, within a city. — Also termed *city judge.*

▸ **presiding judge.** (18c) **1.** A judge in charge of a particular court or judicial district; esp., the senior active judge on a three-member panel that hears and decides cases. **2.** A chief judge. — Abbr. P.J. — Also termed *president judge.*

▸ **probate judge.** (18c) A judge having jurisdiction over probate, inheritance, guardianships, and the like. — Also termed *judge of probate; surrogate; register; registry.*

▸ **puisne judge** (**pyoo**-nee). [Law French *puisné* "later born"] (17c) **1.** A junior judge; a judge without distinction or title. • This was the title formerly used in English common-law courts for a judge other than the chief judge. Today *puisne judge* refers to any judge of the English High Court, apart from the Chief Justice. **2.** See *associate judge.*

▸ **senior administrative patent judge.** (2007) *Patents.* A semiretired administrative patent judge who remains active in hearing interferences in the U.S. Patent and Trademark Office. — Abbr. SAPJ.

▸ **senior judge.** (18c) **1.** The judge who has served for the longest time on a given court. **2.** A federal or state judge who qualifies for senior status and chooses this status over retirement. See SENIOR STATUS.

▸ **side judge.** (1830) *Archaic.* A judge — or one of two judges — of inferior rank, associated with a judge of a higher rank for the purpose of constituting a court.

▸ **special judge.** (17c) A judge appointed or selected to sit, usu. in a specific case, in the absence or disqualification of the regular judge or otherwise as provided by statute.

> "Many, if not all, jurisdictions have made provision for the selection of a substitute or special judge to serve in place of the regular judge in the event of disqualification, voluntary recusal, disability, or other absence of the regular judge. The circumstances under which a special or substitute judge may act in place of the regular judge, and the manner in which such a judge may be chosen, are matters of purely local regulation, entirely dependent on local constitutions and statutes." 46 Am. Jur. 2d *Judges* § 248, at 331 (1994).

▸ **temporary judge.** See *visiting judge.*

▸ **three-hat judge.** (2008) *Slang.* A judge who is authorized to perform in any of three judicial capacities; esp., in New York, a superior-court judge who may act as a family-court judge, a surrogate, or a county-court judge. • Three-hat judges are particularly common in rural areas.

▸ **trial judge.** (17c) The judge before whom a case is tried. • This term is used most commonly on appeal from the judge's rulings.

▸ **United States Magistrate Judge.** See UNITED STATES MAGISTRATE JUDGE.

▸ **visiting judge.** (1888) A judge appointed by the presiding judge of an administrative region to sit temporarily on a given court, usu. in the regular judge's absence. — Also termed *temporary judge; judge pro tempore.*

judge advocate. (17c) *Military law.* **1.** An officer of a court-martial who acts as a prosecutor. **2.** A legal adviser on a military commander's staff. **3.** Any officer in the Judge

Advocate General's Corps or in a department of a U.S. military branch. — Abbr. JA.

▸ **staff judge advocate.** (1934) A certified military lawyer with the staff of a convening or supervisory authority that exercises general court-martial jurisdiction.

▸ **judge advocate general.** (*often cap.*) The senior legal officer and chief legal adviser within a branch of the armed services. — Abbr. JAG.

judgeless, *adj.* (Of a situation, a group of people, or a place) lacking the guidance of a judge; not having the benefit of a judge's presence.

Judge Lynch. See LYNCH LAW.

judge-made law. (1817) **1.** The law established by judicial precedent rather than by statute. See COMMON LAW. **2.** The law that results when judges construe statutes contrary to legislative intent. — Also termed (in sense 2) *judicial legislation*; *bench legislation*; *judicial law*. See JUDICIAL ACTIVISM.

judgement. See JUDGMENT (2).

judge-proof, *adj.* (Of a legal instrument) so well drafted that even the most willful judge cannot conceivably misinterpret the words; impervious to judicial misreading.

judge's chamber. See CHAMBER.

judgeship. (17c) **1.** The position, office, or authority of a judge. **2.** The period of a judge's incumbency.

judge-shopping. (1962) The practice of filing several lawsuits asserting the same claims — in a court or a district with multiple judges — with the hope of having one of the lawsuits assigned to a favorable judge and of nonsuiting or voluntarily dismissing the others. Cf. FORUM-SHOPPING.

Judges' Rules. *Hist. English law.* A set of rules issued by the Queen's Bench Division to govern the taking of statements by the police. • They were superseded in 1984 by the Police and Criminal Evidence Act.

> "England has a concise and authoritative statement of some of the essentials of police conduct in the 'Judges' Rules.' These regulate police interrogation by outlining the circumstances in which suspects must be cautioned as to their rights before being questioned, and those in which they may not be questioned at all. They were first promulgated in 1912 when conflicting judicial decisions led the police to ask the Queen's Bench judges to agree on proper methods of interrogation which would insure the admission into evidence of confessions legitimately obtained. They were added to in 1918, revised in 1930 and again in 1964, and they are issued with the approval of the Home Office, thus making them in effect administrative regulations for all police forces in England. While they do not purport to cover police activity in general and while they are not entirely free of ambiguity, they provide in compact and generally clear form a practical guide to police conduct in one of its central and crucial aspects.
>
> "No close equivalent to the Judges' Rules exists anywhere in the United States. Instead, the rules governing police conduct are scattered through statutes, administrative regulations, judicial decisions, and official and unofficial manuals of bewildering variety and complexity and awesome bulk. The result is that police officers in the front line of law enforcement are too often unsure of what the law is with respect to their duties and responsibilities." Delmar Karlen, *Anglo-American Criminal Justice* 101 (1967).

judge trial. See *bench trial* under TRIAL.

judgey, *adj.* (1974) Characteristic of or like a judge, esp. in a bad sense; judgmental.

judgitis (jə-jɪt-əs). (1956) An emotional disequilibrium that results when a judge confuses the trappings of judicial office with his or her own personal grandeur; the self-important condescension to which certain emotionally insecure judges are susceptible. See JUDICIAL DIVA (2).

judgment. (13c) **1.** The mental faculty that causes one to do or say certain things at certain times, such as exercising one's own discretion or advising others; the mental faculty of decision-making.

▸ **bad judgment.** The failure to exercise good judgment; esp., a tendency to do or say the wrong thing or exercising discretion unwisely. — Also termed *unsound judgment*.

▸ **good judgment.** The mental faculty that causes one to do or say the right thing at the right time. — Also termed *sound judgment*.

▸ **sound judgment.** See *good judgment*.

▸ **unsound judgment.** See *bad judgment*.

▸ **value judgment.** See VALUE JUDGMENT.

2. A court's final determination of the rights and obligations of the parties in a case. • The term *judgment* includes an equitable decree and any order from which an appeal lies. Fed. R. Civ. P. 54. — Also spelled (esp. BrE) *judgement*. — Abbr. J. — Also termed (historically) *judgment ex cathedra*. Cf. RULING (2); OPINION (1).

> "An action is instituted for the enforcement of a right or the redress of an injury. Hence a judgment, as the culmination of the action declares the existence of the right, recognizes the commission of the injury, or negatives the allegation of one or the other. But as no right can exist without a correlative duty, nor any invasion of it without a corresponding obligation to make amends, the judgment necessarily affirms, or else denies, that such a duty or such a liability rests upon the person against whom the aid of the law is invoked." 1 Henry Campbell Black, *A Treatise on the Law of Judgments* § 1, at 2 (2d ed. 1902).

▸ **accumulative judgment.** (1921) A second or additional judgment against a person who has already been convicted, the execution of which is postponed until the completion of any prior sentence.

▸ **agreed judgment.** (1945) A settlement that becomes a court judgment when the judge sanctions it. • In effect, an agreed judgment is merely a contract acknowledged in open court and ordered to be recorded, but it binds the parties as fully as other judgments. — Also termed *consent judgment*; *stipulated judgment*; *judgment by consent*.

▸ **alternative judgment.** A determination that gives the losing party options for satisfying that party's duties.

▸ **cognovit judgment** (kog-**noh**-vit). (1857) A debtor's confession of judgment; judgment entered in accordance with a cognovit. See CONFESSION OF JUDGMENT; COGNOVIT.

▸ **conditional judgment.** (1822) A judgment whose force depends on the performance of certain acts to be done in the future by one of the parties. • For example, a conditional judgment may order the sale of mortgaged property in a foreclosure proceeding unless the mortgagor pays the amount decreed within the time specified. — Also termed *common order*.

▸ **confession of judgment.** See CONFESSION OF JUDGMENT.

▸ **consent judgment.** See *agreed judgment*.

▸ **contradictory judgment.** *Civil law.* A judgment that has been given after the court has heard the parties make their claims and defenses. • In Louisiana, this term is opposed to *default judgment.* Cf. *contradictory motion* under MOTION (1).

▸ **declaratory judgment.** (1886) A binding adjudication that establishes the rights and other legal relations of the parties without providing for or ordering enforcement. • Declaratory judgments are often sought, for example, by insurance companies in determining whether a policy covers a given insured or peril. — Also termed *declaratory decree; declaration.*

▸ **default judgment.** See DEFAULT JUDGMENT.

▸ **deferred judgment.** (1896) A conditional judgment placing a convicted defendant on probation, the successful completion of which will prevent entry of the underlying judgment of conviction. • This type of probation is common with minor traffic offenses. — Also termed *deferred adjudication; deferred-adjudication probation; deferred prosecution; probation before judgment; probation without judgment; pretrial intervention; adjudication withheld.* Cf. DEFERRED PROSECUTION.

▸ **deficiency judgment.** (1865) A judgment against a debtor for the unpaid balance of the debt if a foreclosure sale or a sale of repossessed personal property fails to yield the full amount of the debt due. — Also termed *deficiency decree.*

▸ **definitive judgment.** See *final judgment.*

▸ **determinative judgment.** See *final judgment.*

▸ **discretionary judgment.** An independent and necessary decision made in the absence of express instructions or guidance.

▸ **domestic judgment.** A judgment rendered by the courts of the state or country where the judgment or its effect is at issue.

▸ **dormant judgment.** (18c) A judgment that has not been executed or enforced within the statutory time limit. • As a result, any judgment lien may have been lost and execution cannot be issued unless the judgment creditor first revives the judgment. See REVIVAL (1).

▸ **erroneous judgment.** (17c) A judgment issued by a court with jurisdiction to issue it, but containing an improper application of law. • This type of judgment is not void, but can be corrected by a trial court while the court retains plenary jurisdiction, or in a direct appeal. — Also termed *judgment in error.* See ERROR (2).

▸ **excess judgment.** *Insurance.* A judgment that exceeds all of the defendant's insurance coverage.

▸ **executory judgment** (eg-**zek**-yə-tor-ee). (18c) A judgment that has not been carried out, such as a yet-to-be fulfilled order for the defendant to pay the plaintiff.

▸ **final appealable judgment.** See *final judgment.*

▸ **final judgment.** (18c) A court's last action that settles the rights of the parties and disposes of all issues in controversy, except for the award of costs (and, sometimes, attorney's fees) and enforcement of the judgment. — Also termed *final appealable judgment; final decision; final decree; definitive judgment; determinative judgment; final appealable order.* See FINAL-JUDGMENT RULE.

▸ **foreign judgment.** A decree, judgment, or order of a court in a state, country, or judicial system different from that where the judgment or its effect is at issue.

▸ **in personam judgment.** See *personal judgment.*

▸ **in rem judgment.** See *judgment in rem.*

▸ **interlocutory judgment** (in-tər-**lok**-[y]ə-tor-ee). (17c) An intermediate judgment that determines a preliminary or subordinate point or plea but does not finally decide the case. • A judgment or order given on a provisional or accessory claim or contention is generally interlocutory. — Also termed *interlocutory decree.*

▸ **irregular judgment.** A judgment that may be set aside because of some irregularity in the way it was rendered, such as a clerk's failure to send a defendant notice that a default judgment has been rendered.

▸ **joint judgment.** (17c) A judgment under which each of two or more defendants is held liable for all the damages.

> "A joint judgment creates a joint judgment liability which has some of the characteristics of a joint contratual [sic] liability. For instance, it seems that on the death of one of the joint judgment debtors the whole liability survives to the others. It has been held in the United States that a joint judgment is released as to all by the release of one, even though the creditor's original right was several as well as joint, so that he might have obtained, had he so chosen, separate judgments against each of the defendants." Glanville Williams, *Joint Obligations* 83 (1949).

▸ **judgment as a matter of law.** (1873) A judgment rendered during a jury trial — either before or after the jury's verdict — against a party on a given issue when there is no legally sufficient basis for a jury to find for that party on that issue. • In federal practice, the term *judgment as a matter of law* has replaced both the directed verdict and the judgment notwithstanding the verdict. Fed. R. Civ. P. 50. Cf. SUMMARY JUDGMENT.

▸ **judgment by confession.** See CONFESSION OF JUDGMENT.

▸ **judgment by consent.** See *agreed judgment.*

▸ **judgment by default.** See DEFAULT JUDGMENT.

▸ **judgment by *nil dicit.*** See *nil dicit default judgment* under DEFAULT JUDGMENT.

▸ **judgment by *non sum informatus.*** See NON SUM INFORMATUS.

▸ **judgment for money.** See *money judgment.*

▸ **judgment homologating the tableau** (hə-**mahl**-ə-gay-ting / ta-**bloh** *or* **tab**-loh). (1834) *Civil law.* A judgment approving a plan for distributing property of a decedent's estate. • The distribution plan is known as the tableau of distribution. La. Code Civ. Proc. art. 3307. See HOMOLOGATION.

▸ **judgment in error.** See *erroneous judgment.*

▸ **judgment in personam.** See *personal judgment.*

▸ **judgment in rem** (in **rem**). (18c) A judgment that determines the status or condition of property and that operates directly on the property itself. • The phrase denotes a judgment that affects not only interests in a thing but also all persons' interest in the thing. — Also termed *in rem judgment.*

▸ **judgment in retraxit.** See *judgment of retraxit.*

▸ **judgment *inter partes.*** See *personal judgment.*

▸ **judgment *nil capiat per billa*** (nil **kap**-ee-ət pər **bil**-ə). (1816) Judgment that the plaintiff take nothing by the bill; a take-nothing judgment in a case instituted by a bill.

▸ **judgment *nil capiat per breve*** (nil **kap**-ee-ət pər **breev** *or* **bree**-vee). (1916) Judgment that the plaintiff take nothing by the writ; a take-nothing judgment in a case instituted by a writ.

▸ **judgment *nisi*** (**nI**-sI). (18c) A provisional judgment that, while not final or absolute, may become final on a party's motion. See NISI.

▸ **judgment notwithstanding the verdict.** (18c) A judgment entered for one party even though a jury verdict has been rendered for the opposing party. — Also termed *judgment non obstante veredicto* (non ahb-**stan**-tee ver-ə-**dik**-toh). — Abbr. JNOV; judgment N.O.V. See *judgment as a matter of law.*

> "At common law the judgment non obstante veredicto is rendered when the plea confesses a cause of action and the matter relied upon in avoidance is insufficient, although found true, to constitute either a defense or a bar to the action. It can be entered only on the application of the plaintiff, made after the verdict, and before the entry of judgment thereon. The defendant was not, at the common law, entitled to this judgment under any circumstances. If a verdict for the plaintiff was not supported by the pleadings, the remedy of the defendant was to move to arrest the judgment. But the practice with respect to judgment notwithstanding or contrary to the verdict has been regulated by statute in many states, and in some of them broadened to permit such a judgment in favor of either party under certain circumstances." 1 A.C. Freeman, *A Treatise of the Law of Judgments* 17–19 (Edward W. Tuttle ed., 5th ed. 1925).

▸ **judgment nunc pro tunc** (**nəngk** proh **təngk**). (17c) A judgment entered on a day after the time when it should have been entered, replacing that entered on the earlier date; specif., a procedural device by which the record of a judgment is amended to accord with what the judge actually said and did, so that the record will be accurate. • This device is often used to correct defects in real-estate titles. — Also termed *decree nunc pro tunc*; *nunc pro tunc judgment.* See NUNC PRO TUNC.

▸ **judgment of acquittal.** (17c) A judgment, rendered on the defendant's motion or court's own motion, that acquits the defendant of the offense charged when the evidence is insufficient. Fed. R. Crim. P. 29. See *directed verdict* under VERDICT (1).

▸ **judgment of blood.** See *death sentence* under SENTENCE.

▸ **judgment of *cassetur billa.*** See CASSETUR BILLA.

▸ **judgment of *cassetur breve.*** See CASSETUR BREVE.

▸ **judgment of conviction.** (1806) **1.** The written record of a criminal judgment, consisting of the plea, the verdict or findings, the adjudication, and the sentence. Fed. R. Crim. P. 32(d)(1). **2.** A sentence in a criminal case. See SENTENCE.

▸ **judgment of discontinuance.** (18c) **1.** A judgment dismissing a plaintiff's action based on interruption in the proceedings occasioned by the plaintiff's failure to continue the suit at the appointed time or times. **2.** NONSUIT (1). — Often shortened to *discontinuance.* See DISCONTINUANCE.

▸ **judgment of dismissal.** (1809) A final determination of a case (against the plaintiff in a civil action or the government in a criminal action) without a trial on its merits. See DISMISSAL.

▸ **judgment of nolle prosequi** (**nahl**-ee **prahs**-ə-kwI). (1869) A judgment entered against a plaintiff who, after appearance but before judgment on the merits, has decided to abandon prosecution of the lawsuit. See NOLLE PROSEQUI.

▸ **judgment of nonsuit.** (18c) **1.** *Hist.* The judgment given against a plaintiff who fails to be present in court to hear the jury render its verdict or who, after issue is joined, fails to bring the issue to be tried in due time. • This judgment does not prevent the plaintiff from filing the same case again. **2.** NONSUIT (2).

▸ **judgment of repleader.** See REPLEADER.

▸ **judgment of retraxit** (ri-**trak**-sit). (1846) *Hist.* A judgment against a plaintiff who has voluntarily retracted the claim. • Such a judgment bars the plaintiff from relitigating the claim. — Also termed *judgment in retraxit.* See RETRAXIT.

▸ **judgment on the merits.** (18c) A judgment based on the evidence rather than on technical or procedural grounds. — Also termed *decision on the merits.*

▸ **judgment on the pleadings.** (18c) A judgment based solely on the allegations and information contained in the pleadings, and not on any outside matters. Fed. R. Civ. P. 12(c). Cf. SUMMARY JUDGMENT.

▸ **judgment on the verdict.** (17c) A judgment for the party receiving a favorable jury verdict.

▸ **judgment quasi in rem** (**kway**-sI [*or* -zI] in **rem**). (1905) A judgment based on the court's jurisdiction over the defendant's interest in property rather than on its jurisdiction over the defendant or the property. • Such a judgment affects only particular persons' interests in a thing — that is, only the persons who are named or described in the proceeding.

▸ **judgment *quod billa cassetur*** (kwod **bil**-ə kə-**see**-tər). (18c) Judgment that the bill be quashed. • This is a judgment for the defendant.

▸ **judgment *quod breve cassetur*** (kwod **breev** *or* **bree**-vee kə-**see**-tər). Judgment that the writ be quashed. • This is a judgment for the defendant.

▸ **judgment *quod computet.*** See QUOD COMPUTET.

▸ **judgment *quod recuperet*** (kwod ri-**kyoo**-pər-it). (17c) Judgment that the plaintiff recover.

▸ **judgment *respondeat ouster*** (ri-**spon**-dee-at **ows**-tər). (1805) *Hist.* An interlocutory judgment requiring the defendant who has made a dilatory plea to give a more substantial defense; RESPONDEAT OUSTER.

▸ **junior judgment.** (1815) A judgment rendered or entered after the rendition or entry of another judgment, on a different claim, against the same defendant.

▸ **money judgment.** (1869) A judgment for damages subject to immediate execution, as distinguished from equitable or injunctive relief. — Also termed *judgment for money.*

▸ **nunc pro tunc judgment.** See *judgment nunc pro tunc.*

▸ **personal judgment.** (1829) **1.** A judgment that imposes personal liability on a defendant and that may therefore be satisfied out of any of the defendant's property within judicial reach. **2.** A judgment resulting from an action in which a court has personal jurisdiction over the parties. **3.** A judgment against a person as distinguished from a judgment against a thing, right, or status. — Also termed *judgment in personam* (in pər-**soh**-nəm); *in personam judgment*; *judgment inter partes* (**in**-tər **pahr**-teez).

▸ **several judgment.** (16c) A judgment under which each of two or more defendants is held proportionately liable for damages.

▸ **simulated judgment.** (1903) *Civil law.* A judgment that, although founded on an actual debt and intended for collection by the usual legal processes, is actually entered into by the parties to give one of them an undeserving advantage or to defraud third parties.

▸ **stipulated judgment.** See *agreed judgment.*

▸ **summary judgment.** See SUMMARY JUDGMENT.

▸ **suspension of judgment.** See STAY.

▸ **take-nothing judgment.** (1938) A judgment for the defendant providing that the plaintiff recover nothing in damages or other relief. — Also termed (in some states) *no cause of action.*

▸ **valid judgment. 1.** A judgment that will be recognized by common-law states as long as it is in force in the state where the judgment was rendered. **2.** A judicial act rendered by a court having jurisdiction over the parties and over the subject matter in a proceeding in which the parties have had a reasonable opportunity to be heard.

▸ **voidable judgment.** (17c) A judgment that, although seemingly valid, is defective in some material way; esp., a judgment that, although rendered by a court having jurisdiction, is irregular or erroneous.

▸ **void judgment.** (18c) A judgment that has no legal force or effect, the invalidity of which may be asserted by any party whose rights are affected at any time and any place, whether directly or collaterally. • From its inception, a void judgment continues to be absolutely null. It is incapable of being confirmed, ratified, or enforced in any manner or to any degree. One source of a void judgment is the lack of subject-matter jurisdiction.

3. *English law.* An opinion delivered by a member of the appellate committee of the House of Lords; a Law Lord's judicial opinion. — Also termed (in sense 3) *speech.*

judgmental immunity. See ERROR-OF-JUDGMENT RULE.

judgment book. See *judgment docket* under DOCKET (1).

judgment by comparison. (1941) *Patents.* Allowance of a patent claim because a similar claim has been allowed before. • There is no stare decisis doctrine in patent prosecutions, but examiners may consider allowance of similar claims as a decision-making aid.

judgment creditor. (18c) A person having a legal right to enforce execution of a judgment for a specific sum of money. *See U.S. v. Gilbert Assocs., Inc.*, 345 U.S. 361, 365, 73 S.Ct. 701, 704 (1953).

▸ **bona fide judgment creditor.** (1806) Someone who recovers a judgment without engaging in fraud or collusion.

judgment debt. See DEBT.

judgment debtor. (18c) A person against whom a money judgment has been entered but not yet satisfied.

judgment docket. See DOCKET (1).

judgment ex cathedra. 1. EX CATHEDRA. **2.** JUDGMENT (2).

judgment execution. 1. EXECUTION (3). **2.** EXECUTION (4).

judgment file. See *judgment docket* under DOCKET (1).

judgment lien. See LIEN.

judgment *non obstante veredicto*. See *judgment notwithstanding the verdict* under JUDGMENT (2).

judgment note. (1845) **1.** A nonnegotiable promissory note, illegal in most states, containing a power of attorney to appear and confess judgment for a specified sum. **2.** COGNOVIT NOTE.

judgment N.O.V. See *judgment notwithstanding the verdict* under JUDGMENT (2).

judgment of blood. See *death sentence* under SENTENCE.

judgment of cassetur billa. See CASSETUR BILLA.

judgment of cassetur breve. See CASSETUR BREVE.

judgment of repleader. See REPLEADER.

Judgment of Solomon. A decision that is extremely difficult to make. • The reference is to the biblical story in which King Solomon gives a wise judgment to two women who both claimed to be the mother of a baby — the order being to split the baby in half. The woman who objected on the baby's behalf, preferring instead to relinquish her claim, was found to be the mother. See SPLIT THE BABY.

judgment-proof, *adj.* (18c) (Of an actual or potential judgment debtor) unable to satisfy a judgment for money damages because the person has no property, does not own enough property within the court's jurisdiction to satisfy the judgment, or claims the benefit of statutorily exempt property. — Also termed *execution-proof.*

judgment *quod computet*. See QUOD COMPUTET.

judgment receiver. See RECEIVER (1).

judgment record. See *judgment docket* under DOCKET (1).

judgment roll. See *judgment docket* under DOCKET (1).

> "As the pleadings constitute part of the record, it is indispensable that they be filed. In some of the codes they must be filed at the institution of the action; in others, by or before the first day of the term; in others, at or before the trial. They must be used in making the 'judgment roll,' and in the practice of each State (not here considered) procedure is provided to procure filing." Edwin E. Bryant, *The Law of Pleading Under the Codes of Civil Procedure* 179 (2d ed. 1899).

judgment-roll appeal. See APPEAL (2).

judgment sale. See *execution sale* under SALE.

judgment seat. (16c) **1.** The bench on which a judge sits. **2.** By extension, a court or tribunal.

judgment summons. See SUMMONS.

judicable (**joo**-di-kə-bəl), *adj.* (17c) *Rare.* Capable of being adjudicated; triable; justiciable. — Also termed *judiciable* (joo-**dish**-ə-bəl).

judicare (joo-di-**kair**-ee), *vb.* [Latin] *Civil law.* To judge; to decide or determine judicially; to give judgment or sentence.

judicate, *vb.* See ADJUDICATE.

judicative (**joo**-di-kay-tiv *or* -kə-tiv), *adj. Rare.* See ADJUDICATIVE.

judicator (**joo**-di-kay-tər), *n.* (18c) *Rare.* A person authorized to act or serve as a judge.

judicatory (**joo**-di-kə-tor-ee), *adj.* (17c) **1.** Of, relating to, or involving judgment. **2.** Allowing a judgment to be made; giving a decisive indication.

judicatory (**joo**-di-kə-tor-ee), *n.* (16c) **1.** A court; any tribunal with judicial authority <a church judicatory>. **2.** The administration of justice <working toward a more efficient judicatory>.

judicatum solvi (joo-di-**kay**-təm **sol**-vi). [Latin "that the judgment will be paid"] (17c) **1.** *Roman law.* The payment of the sum awarded by way of judgment. **2.** *Roman law.* Security for the payment of the sum awarded by way of judgment. • This applied when a representative appeared on the defendant's behalf at the trial. **3.** *Civil law.* A court-ordered caution given by the defendant in a maritime case. See CAUTION.

> "Judicatum solvi . . . . The cautioner in such an obligation is bound in payment or fulfilment of whatever may be decerned for, and he is not liberated from the obligation by the death of the principal debtor. It is a kind of caution not infrequently required. Under the civil law this caution was required of any defender who remained in possession, during the suit, of the subject which gave rise to the dispute." John Trayner, *Trayner's Latin Maxims* 292–93 (4th ed. 1894).

judicature (**joo**-di-kə-chər). (16c) **1.** The action of judging or of administering justice through duly constituted courts. **2.** JUDICIARY (3). **3.** A judge's office, function, or authority. **4.** The system by which courts, trials, and other aspects of the administration of justice are organized in a country. — Also termed (in sense 4) *judicial system.*

Judicature Acts. A series of statutes that reorganized the superior courts of England in 1875. • The Judicature Acts were superseded by the Supreme Court Act of 1981.

judices (**joo**-di-seez). [Latin] *pl.* JUDEX.

judicia (joo-**dish**-ee-ə). [Latin] *pl.* JUDICIUM.

judiciable, *adj.* See JUDICABLE.

judicial (joo-**dish**-əl), *adj.* (14c) **1.** Of, relating to, or by the court or a judge <judicial duty> <judicial demeanor>. **2.** In court <the witness's judicial confession>. **3.** Legal <the Attorney General took no judicial action>. **4.** Of, relating to, or involving a judgment <an award of judicial interest at the legal rate>. Cf. JUDICIOUS.

▸ **quasi-judicial.** See QUASI-JUDICIAL.

judicial act. See ACT (2).

judicial activism, *n.* (1947) A philosophy of judicial decision-making whereby judges allow their personal views about public policy, among other factors, to guide their decisions, usu. with the suggestion that adherents of this philosophy tend to find constitutional violations and are willing to ignore governing texts and precedents. Cf. JUDICIAL RESTRAINT (3). — **judicial activist,** *n.*

judicial activity report. (1978) A regularly issued memo, usu. monthly or quarterly, on caseload and caseflow within a given court or court system.

judicial administration. (17c) The process of doing justice through a system of courts.

judicial admission. See ADMISSION (1).

judicial arbitration. See *court-annexed arbitration* under ARBITRATION.

Judicial Article. (1881) *Constitutional law.* Article III of the U.S. Constitution, which creates the Supreme Court, vests in Congress the right to create inferior courts, provides for life tenure for federal judges, and specifies the powers and jurisdiction of the federal courts.

judicial assize. See ASSIZE (6).

judicial-authority justification. See JUSTIFICATION (2).

judicial bias. See BIAS.

judicial bond. See BOND (2).

judicial branch. (18c) The division of government consisting of the courts, whose function is to ensure justice by interpreting, applying, and generally administering the laws; JUDICIARY (1). Cf. LEGISLATIVE BRANCH; EXECUTIVE BRANCH.

judicial bypass. (1977) A procedure permitting a person to obtain a court's approval for an act that would ordinarily require the approval of someone else, such as a law that requires a minor to notify a parent before obtaining an abortion but allows an appropriately qualified minor to obtain a court order permitting the abortion without parental notice.

judicial-bypass provision. (1988) *Family law.* **1.** A statutory provision that allows a court to assume a parental role when the parent or guardian cannot or will not act on behalf of a minor or an incompetent. **2.** A statutory provision that allows a minor to circumvent the necessity of obtaining parental consent by obtaining judicial consent.

judicial cognizance. See JUDICIAL NOTICE.

judicial collar. See JABOT.

judicial combat. See TRIAL BY COMBAT.

judicial comity. See COMITY.

Judicial Committee of the Privy Council. *English law.* A United Kingdom tribunal, created in 1833, with jurisdiction to hear certain admiralty and ecclesiastical appeals, and certain appeals from the Commonwealth. • From the 16th century until the 19th, the Court of Delegates was the final court of appeal in England for ecclesiastical suits. During the reign of William IV, the power to hear final appeals was transferred to the Privy Council, and then to the Judicial Committee of the Privy Council. The committee consists entirely of lay people; ecclesiastics become members of the court only if an appeal is brought under the Church Discipline Act. Even then the ecclesiastics must be episcopal privy counselors. The Judicial Committee's decisions are not treated as binding precedent in the United Kingdom, but they are influential because of the overlapping composition of members of the Privy Council and the House of Lords in its judicial capacity. — Abbr. JCPC. — Also termed *Court of Final Appeal.*

judicial compensation. 1. The remuneration that judges receive for their work. **2.** *Civil law.* A court's judgment finding that two parties are mutually obligated to one another and crafting the amount of the judgment in accordance with the amount that each party owes. • A claim for compensation is usu. contained in a reconventional demand. La. Code Civ. Proc. 1902. See *reconventional demand* under DEMAND (1).

Judicial Conference of the United States. The policy-making body of the federal judiciary, responsible for surveying the business of the federal courts, making recommendations to Congress on matters affecting the judiciary, and supervising the work of the Administrative Office of the United States Courts. • The Conference was originally established in 1923 as the Conference of Senior Circuit Judges. 28 USCA § 331. — Abbr. JCUS. See ADMINISTRATIVE OFFICE OF THE UNITED STATES COURTS.

judicial confession. See CONFESSION (1).

judicial contempt. See CONTEMPT (2).

judicial control. *Civil law.* A doctrine by which a court can deny cancellation of a lease if the lessee's breach is of minor importance, is not caused by the lessee, or is based on a good-faith mistake of fact.

judicial council. (1925) A regularly assembled group of judges whose mission is to increase the efficiency and effectiveness of the courts on which they sit; esp., a semi-annual assembly of a federal circuit's judges called by the circuit's chief judge. 28 USCA § 332.

judicial day. See *juridical day* under DAY.

judicial declaration. See DECLARATION (1).

judicial dictum. See DICTUM.

judicial discretion. See DISCRETION (4).

judicial diva. (1991) *Slang.* **1.** A particularly confident, skilled, and physically attractive female judge. • The term was coined by assistant U.S. attorney David B. Lat, who is also responsible for the related terms *litigatrix* and *benchslap* (a practice said to be favored by judicial divas and aggressive judges generally). See BENCHSLAP; LITIGATRIX. **2.** By considerable extension, any egotistical judge who seems to crave attention and sycophancy. • In both senses, the word is likely to be considered derogatory and offensive. — Also termed *judicial prima donna.* See JUDGITIS.

judicial-diversion program. (1994) *Criminal law.* A plan or system whereby a defendant charged with a certain class of felony (not the most serious types) may, usu. after a guilty plea, undergo drug-abuse or alcohol-abuse treatment and, upon successful completion, have his or her conviction conditionally sealed. — Abbr. JDP.

judicial document. A court-filed paper that is subject to the right of public access because it is or has been both relevant to the judicial function and useful in the judicial process. *See Lugosch v. Pyramid Co. of Onandaga*, 435 F.3d 110, 119 (2d Cir. 2006).

judicial economy. (1942) Efficiency in the operation of the courts and the judicial system; esp., the efficient management of litigation so as to minimize duplication of effort and to avoid wasting the judiciary's time and resources. • A court can enter a variety of orders to promote judicial economy. For instance, a court may consolidate two cases for trial to save the court and the parties from having two trials, or it may order a separate trial on certain issues if doing so would provide the opportunity to avoid a later trial that would be more complex and time-consuming.

judicial-economy exception. (1981) An exemption from the final-judgment rule, by which a party may seek immediate appellate review of a nonfinal order if doing so might establish a final or nearly final disposition of the entire suit. See FINAL-JUDGMENT RULE.

judicial estoppel. See ESTOPPEL.

judicial evidence. See EVIDENCE.

judicial exclusion. See EXCLUSION (2).

judicial fact. See *judicially noticed fact* under FACT.

judicial factor. See FACTOR.

judicial foreclosure. See FORECLOSURE.

judicial hearing. See HEARING (1).

judicial House of Lords. See HOUSE OF LORDS.

judicialia brevia. See *brevia judicialia* under BREVE.

judicial immunity. See IMMUNITY (1).

judicial independence. (1775) The structural separation of the judiciary from the political branches of government so that judges remain free from improper influences, partisan interests, and the pressures of interest groups.

judicial inquiry. (17c) An official in-court investigation of events, facts, and actions to address a question of law and render an opinion.

judicial insurance. See INSURANCE.

judicialize, *vb.* (1877) **1.** To pattern (procedures, etc.) after a court of law <these administrative hearings have been judicialized>. **2.** To bring (something not traditionally within the judicial system) into the judicial system <political questions are gradually becoming judicialized>. — **judicialization,** *n.*

judicial jurisdiction. See JURISDICTION.

judicial knowledge. See JUDICIAL NOTICE.

judicial law. See JUDGE-MADE LAW.

judicial legislation. **1.** See JUDGE-MADE LAW (2). **2.** See LEGISLATION (3).

judicial lien. See LIEN.

judicially created double patenting. See DOUBLE PATENTING.

judicially created double-patenting rejection. See REJECTION.

judicially noticed fact. See FACT.

judicial morsel. See *ordeal of the morsel* under ORDEAL.

judicial mortgage. See MORTGAGE.

judicial notice. (17c) A court's acceptance, for purposes of convenience and without requiring a party's proof, of a well-known and indisputable fact; the court's power to accept such a fact <the trial court took judicial notice of the fact that water freezes at 32 degrees Fahrenheit>. Fed R. Evid. 201. — Also termed *judicial cognizance; judicial knowledge.* See *judicially noticed fact* under FACT.

▸ **judicial notice of prior art.** (1908) *Patents.* Acknowledgment by the U.S. Patent and Trademark Office of all materials in its possession as prior art, for settling questions of novelty and priority. • Patents, applications, and records of interferences and appeals may be submitted by citation alone.

judicial novation. See *compulsory novation* under NOVATION.

judicial oath. See OATH.

judicial officer. See OFFICER (1).

judicial opinion. See OPINION (1).

judicial order. See ORDER (2).

Judicial Panel on Multidistrict Litigation. A panel of federal judges responsible for transferring civil actions having common questions of fact from one district court to another to consolidate pretrial proceedings. • The panel was created in 1968. The Chief Justice appoints its members. 28 USCA § 1407. — Abbr. JPML.

judicial partition. See *equitable partition* under PARTITION (2).

judicial power. (16c) **1.** The authority vested in courts and judges to hear and decide cases and to make binding judgments on them; the power to construe and apply the law when controversies arise over what has been done or not done under it. • Under federal law, this power is vested in the U.S. Supreme Court and in whatever inferior courts Congress establishes. The other two great powers of government are the legislative power and the executive power.

> "The exercise of judicial power by the Supreme Court is provided for, in part, by the Constitution, but Congress is authorized to ordain and establish inferior courts, — which means to define their respective jurisdictions; to bestow upon a court so much judicial power; and to make such restrictions, rules, and regulations as Congress itself may deem proper. Thus Congress establishes such courts and defines their several jurisdictions, but whatsoever judicial power a court possesses, by act of Congress, the court derives from the Constitution in its grant of such power. The jurisdiction of any inferior court of the United States, thus defined by Congress, may vary, from time to time, by act of Congress, but every case arising in the court must be shown, by the record of the court, to be within its jurisdiction. The reason for this important rule (and seeming restriction) conforms to the essential principle in all judicial proceeding: the principle of authority. No court acts without authority and, as judicial examination has for its ultimate purpose the settlement of controversy in a legal manner, the jurisdiction of the court is of primary importance. One of the purposes of the Union is 'to establish justice,' and precision in the whole matter of exercise of judicial power is essential." Francis Newton Thorpe, *The Essentials of American Constitutional Law* § 101, at 118–19 (1917).

2. A power conferred on a public officer involving the exercise of judgment and discretion in deciding questions of right in specific cases affecting personal and proprietary interests. • In this sense, the phrase is contrasted with *ministerial power.*

judicial prima donna. See JUDICIAL DIVA.

judicial privilege. 1. See PRIVILEGE (1). **2.** See *litigation privilege* under PRIVILEGE (1).

judicial proceeding. See PROCEEDING.

judicial-proceedings privilege. See *litigation privilege* under PRIVILEGE (1).

judicial process. See PROCESS.

judicial question. (18c) A question that is proper for determination by the courts, as opposed to a moot question or one properly decided by the executive or legislative branch. Cf. POLITICAL QUESTION.

judicial record. See DOCKET (1).

judicial remedy. See REMEDY.

judicial restraint. (18c) **1.** A restraint imposed by a court, as by a restraining order, injunction, or judgment. **2.** The principle that when a court can resolve a case based on a particular issue, it should do so without reaching unnecessary issues. **3.** A philosophy of judicial decision-making whereby judges avoid indulging their personal beliefs about the public good and instead try merely to interpret the law as legislated and according to precedent; esp., the idea that judges should not try to change a law that is not unconstitutional. — Also termed (in senses 2 & 3) *judicial self-restraint.* Cf. JUDICIAL ACTIVISM.

judicial review. (1851) **1.** A court's power to review the actions of other branches or levels of government; esp., the courts' power to invalidate legislative and executive actions as being unconstitutional. **2.** The constitutional doctrine providing for this power. **3.** A court's review of a lower court's or an administrative body's factual or legal findings. See REVIEW (2). Cf. DEPARTMENTALISM; JUDICIAL SUPREMACY; POPULAR CONSTITUTIONALISM.

> "The original idea of judicial review seems to have been conceived primarily to preserve the integrity and uphold the independence of the courts as against the other departments, and to preserve and protect certain personal and private rights, such as the right of trial by jury, which were thought to be natural and inalienable." Charles Grove Haines, *Judicial Review of Legislation in the United States and the Doctrines of Vested Rights and of Implied Limitations on Legislatures*, 2 Tex. L. Rev. 257, 270 (1924).

▸ **de novo review.** (1955) A court's nondeferential review of an administrative decision, usu. through a review of the administrative record plus any additional evidence the parties present. — Also termed *de novo review.*

▸ **plenary review.** (1936) Appellate review by all the members of a court rather than a panel.

judicial robe. See ROBE (1).

judicial sale. See SALE.

judicial self-restraint. 1. See JUDICIAL RESTRAINT (2). **2.** See JUDICIAL RESTRAINT (3).

judicial separation. 1. See SEPARATION (1). **2.** See SEPARATION (2). **3.** See *divorce a mensa et thoro* under DIVORCE.

judicial sequestration. See SEQUESTRATION (5).

judicial settlement. See SETTLEMENT (2).

judicial stacking. See STACKING (1).

judicial supremacy. *Constitutional law.* The doctrine that interpretations of the Constitution by the federal judiciary in the exercise of judicial review, esp. U.S. Supreme Court interpretations, are binding on the coordinate branches of the federal government and the states. • The doctrine usu. applies to judicial determinations that some legislation or other action is unconstitutional. Proponents of judicial supremacy frequently acknowledge that, when the courts determine that some action is constitutional, nonjudicial actors may legitimately act on their contrary judgment that the action is unconstitutional. See DEPARTMENTALISM; JUDICIAL REVIEW; POPULAR CONSTITUTIONALISM. Cf. LEGISLATIVE SUPREMACY.

judicial system. See JUDICATURE (4).

judicial tender. See TENDER (3).

judicial-tenure commission. (1968) A commission that reviews complaints against judges, investigates those complaints, and makes recommendations about appropriate measures to the highest court in the jurisdiction. — Abbr. JTC.

judicial trustee. See TRUSTEE (1).

judicial writ. See WRIT.

judicia populi (joo-**dish**-ee-ə **pop**-yə-lɪ). [Latin] (1892) *Roman law.* The criminal jurisdiction of the comitia. See COMITIA.

judicia publica (joo-**dish**-ee-ə **pəb**-li-kə). [Latin] (17c) *Roman law.* The jurisdiction of the *quaestiones perpetuae.* See QUAESTIO PERPETUA.

judiciary (joo-**dish**-ee-er-ee *or* joo-**dish**-ə-ree), *n.* (18c) **1.** The branch of government responsible for interpreting the laws and administering justice. Cf. EXECUTIVE (1); LEGISLATURE. **2.** A system of courts. **3.** A body of judges. — Also termed (in sense 3) *judicature.* — **judiciary,** *adj.*

▸ **career judiciary.** A body of judges whose jobs have been selected early in their working lives and who enjoy a relative stability in position, with possibilities of steady advancement.

> "Once we recognize that barristers are a form of judge, and then add to that the fact that almost all the higher-court judges in England are former barristers, and the further fact that almost all barristers have been barristers ever since they completed their education, we can see that in actuality England has a career judiciary. In this respect England is like the Continent and decidedly unlike the United Sates, where most entry into the judiciary still is lateral, though this is changing slowly. The careerist character of the English judiciary is confirmed by the promotion ladder (with its many rungs — assistant recorder, recorder, Queen's Counsel, deputy High Court judge, High Court judge, Court of Appeal judge, law lord) and reinforced by the virtual abolition of the civil jury, for the civil jury brings into the ranks of the American judiciary (jurors are lay judges) a host of complete amateurs. Moreover, most American judges — indeed, almost all except federal judges, and they are fewer than 10 per cent of the total even of judges who have a general jurisdiction — are elected rather than appointed. Elections are a method of selection inimical to the emergence of a competent career judiciary." Richard A. Posner, *Law and Legal Theory in England and America* 30–31 (1996).

judicia summaria (joo-**dish**-ee-ə sə-**mair**-ee-ə). [Law Latin "summary proceedings"] *Scots law.* Actions that can be summarily disposed of.

judicio de amparo. See AMPARO.

judicio sisti (joo-**dish**-ee-oh **sis**-tɪ). [Latin "to be present in court"] (16c) **1.** *Roman law.* Appearance in court. **2.** *Roman law.* Security for appearance in court; VADIMONIUM. **3.** *Scots law.* A type of caution requiring a claimant or the principal debtor to appear in court whenever the opponent demanded it. • This type of caution was used in some criminal cases and in cases involving defendants who were foreigners or posed a flight risk. See CAUTION.

judicious (joo-**dish**-əs), *adj.* (16c) Well-considered; discreet; wisely circumspect <the court's judicious application of the rules of evidence>. Cf. JUDICIAL. — **judiciousness,** *n.*

judicium (joo-**dish**-ee-əm), *n.* [Latin] *Hist.* **1.** A judgment. **2.** A judicial proceeding; a trial. **3.** A court or tribunal. • In Roman law, the plural *judicia* refers to criminal courts. Pl. ***judicia.***

▸ ***judicium capitale*** (kap-i-**tay**-lee). [Latin] *Hist.* A judgment of death; a capital sentence.

▸ ***judicium parium*** (**par**-ee-əm). [Latin] (1851) *Hist.* A judgment of one's peers; a jury trial or verdict.

▸ ***judicium publicum*** (**pəb**-li-kəm). [Latin "public trial"] (17c) A criminal proceeding under a public statute. • The term derived from the Roman rule allowing any member of the public to initiate a prosecution. See COMITIA.

> "*Judicium publicum* may have originally meant trial by or before the actual popular assembly, though it is doubtful whether the phrase existed at all before the 'people' had come to be replaced by *quaestores*. There is much to be said, in spite of Justinian's explanation [*Inst.* 4.18.1], for the view that these criminal trials were called 'public' as being 'of public interest,' because, to use Blackstone's words, their subject-matter affects the whole community." 2 E.C. Clark, *History of Roman Private Law* § 10, at 441 (1914).

judicium Dei (joo-**dish**-ee-əm **dee**-ɪ). *Hist.* God's supposed judgment on the merits of the case, made manifest by the outcome of an observable event. • Examples dating from Norman times were the trial by combat and the ordeal. See ORDEAL; TRIAL BY COMBAT.

> "[T]he ordeal will give an answer, but it is useless for us to ask by what process it had arrived at that conclusion. It would be hazardous to doubt the correctness of that answer — Henry II had asked questions and received, through his officers and the ordeals, divers answers as to which he received some disquieting conclusions (which he published); most people would possibly have felt that there was something blasphemous about it. After all, the most solemn mode of referring to the ordeal in the liturgical books was by the title they habitually gave it: '*Judicium Dei*,' the 'Judgement of God.' . . . [I]t would be impertinence to ask too many questions, and it would be inviting trouble to be at all free in criticizing a time-honoured institution which both Church and State had openly approved." Theodore F.T. Plucknett, *Edward I and Criminal Law* 71 (1960).

judicium ecclesiasticum. See FORUM ECCLESIASTICUM.

judicium parium. See JUDICIUM.

judicium per pares. [Law Latin "judgment by peers"] (16c) *Hist.* The medieval doctrine by which a vassal could demand to be tried by the special law of his fief in a proceeding at which the lord presided and the other men of the fief acted as judges (not jurors) who would declare the law or rule of the fief — leaving the facts to be settled by some formal process. • Although this doctrine differs significantly from the modern jury trial, it is commonly thought to be its medieval precursor.

judicium publica. See JUDICIUM.

judicum rejectio (**joo**-di-kəm ri-**jek**-shee-oh). [Latin] *Roman law.* A litigant's right to exercise peremptory challenges against a judge or a certain number of jurors.

judicum sortitio (**joo**-di-kəm sor-**tish**-ee-oh). [Latin] *Roman law.* The practice of choosing jurors by drawing from an urn the names of eligible participants. • The English word *sortition* (meaning "the drawing or casting of lots") derives from the Latin *sortitio.*

judicum subsortitio (**joo**-di-kəm səb-sor-**tish**-ee-oh). [Latin] *Roman law.* The practice of choosing supplemental jurors (when necessary after peremptory challenges have been exercised) by drawing from an urn the names of eligible participants.

judiocracy. See JURISTOCRACY.

juge (zhoozh), *n.* [French] (1882) *French law.* A judge.

▸ ***juge de paix*** (**zhoozh** də **pe** *or* **pay**). An inferior judge; esp., a police magistrate.

▸ ***juge d'instruction*** (**zhoozh** da*n*-strook-**syawn**). (1882) A magistrate who conducts preliminary criminal proceedings, as by taking complaints, interrogating parties and witnesses, and formulating charges.

juicio (**hwee**-syoh). *Spanish law.* **1.** A trial or suit; litigation. **2.** Wisdom; prudence. **3.** The capacity to distinguish right from wrong and truth from falsehood.

juise (juu-**IZ**) (14c) *Hist.* **1.** A judgment, sentence, or penalty. **2.** By extension, the instrument of punishment, esp. a gibbet.

Julian calendar. See OLD STYLE.

jumbo. See *jumbo certificate* under CERTIFICATE OF DEPOSIT.

jumbo certificate. See CERTIFICATE OF DEPOSIT.

jumbo mortgage. See MORTGAGE.

jump bail, *vb.* (1889) (Of an accused) to fail to appear in court at the appointed time after promising to appear and posting a bail bond. — Also termed *skip bail.* See BAIL-JUMPING.

jump citation. See *pinpoint citation* under CITATION (3).

jumping a claim. (1854) *Hist.* The act of taking possession of public land to which another has previously acquired a claim. • The first occupant has the right to the land both under squatter law and custom and under preemption laws of the United States.

Junian Latin, *n.* See LATINI JUNIANI.

junior, *adj.* (13c) Lower in rank or standing; subordinate <a junior interest>.

junior bond. See BOND (3).

junior counsel. See COUNSEL.

junior creditor. See CREDITOR.

junior debt. See *subordinate debt* under DEBT.

junior execution. See EXECUTION (4).

junior interest. See INTEREST (2).

junior judgment. See JUDGMENT (2).

junior lien. See LIEN.

junior mortgage. See MORTGAGE.

junior partner. See PARTNER.

junior party. (1897) *Patents.* In an interference proceeding, the party or parties who did not file the patent application first. • A junior party has the burden of proving that he or she is the first inventor. Cf. SENIOR PARTY.

junior security. See SECURITY (4).

junior user. (1911) *Trademarks.* A person other than the first person to use a trademark. • A junior user may be permitted to continue using a mark in areas where the senior user's mark is not used, if the junior user did not know about the other user, and was the first user to register the mark. — Also termed *second user*; *latecomer.* See INNOCENT JUNIOR USER. Cf. SENIOR USER.

▸ **innocent junior user.** (1949) *Trademarks.* Someone who, without actual or constructive knowledge, uses a trademark that has previously been used in a geographically distant market, and who may continue to use the trademark in a limited geographic area as long as the senior user does not use the mark there.

junior writ. See WRIT.

junk asset. See *troubled asset* under ASSET.

junk bond. See BOND (3).

junkie. *Slang.* Someone who often takes illegal drugs; a drug addict or habitual user. — Also termed *druggie.*

junta (**huun**-tə *or* **juun**-tə), *n.* (1714) A military government that has come into power by use of force.

jura (**joor**-ə), *n. pl.* [Latin] Rights. See JUS.

▸ ***jura fiscalia*** (fis-**kay**-lee-ə). *Hist.* Fiscal rights; rights of the Exchequer.

▸ ***jura fixa*** (**joor**-ə **fik**-sə). (17c) *Hist.* Immovable rights.

▸ ***jura in personam.*** (1887) A right to enforce a particular person's obligation to another. See JUS IN PERSONAM.

▸ ***jura in rem.*** See JUS IN RE.

▸ ***jura majestatis*** (maj-ə-**stay**-tis). (17c) *Hist.* Rights of sovereignty or majesty.

▸ ***jura mixti dominii*** (**miks**-tI də-**min**-ee-I). *Hist.* Rights of mixed dominion; the king's or queen's right or power of jurisdiction.

▸ ***jura personarum*** (pər-sə-**nair**-əm). (18c) Rights of persons. See JUS PERSONARUM.

▸ ***jura praediorum*** (pree-dee-**or**-əm). *Hist.* The rights of estates.

▸ ***jura regalia*** (ri-**gay**-lee-ə). (16c) *Hist.* Royal rights; the prerogatives of the Crown. See REGALIA (1).

▸ ***jura rerum*** (**reer**-əm). (18c) Rights of things. See JUS RERUM.

▸ ***jura summi imperii*** (**səm**-I im-**peer**-ee-I). (1881) *Hist.* Rights of supreme dominion; rights of sovereignty.

jural (**joor**-əl), *adj.* (17c) **1.** Of, relating to, or involving law or jurisprudence; legal <jural and equitable rules>. **2.** Of, relating to, or involving rights and obligations <jural relations>.

jural act. See ACT (2).

jural activity. See *jural act* under ACT (2).

jural agent. (2004) An official — someone who has the appropriate authoritative status in society to enforce or affect the society's legal system — who engages in a jural act. • Common examples include judges, legislators, and police officers acting in their official capacities. See *jural act* under ACT (2).

jural cause. See *proximate cause* under CAUSE (1).

jura majestatis. See JURA.

juramentum (joor-ə-**men**-təm), *n.* [Latin] *Civil law.* An oath. Pl. ***juramenta*** (joor-ə-**men**-tə).

▸ ***juramentum calumniae*** (kə-**ləm**-nee-ee). (16c) An oath of calumny. See *oath of calumny* under OATH.

▸ ***juramentum corporalis*** (kor-pə-**ray**-lis). A corporal oath. See *corporal oath* under OATH.

▸ ***juramentum in litem*** (in **lI**-tem *or* -təm). (16c) An oath in litem. See *oath in litem* under OATH.

▸ ***juramentum judiciale*** (joo-dish-ee-**ay**-lee). An oath by which the judge defers the decision of the case to either of the parties.

▸ ***juramentum necessarium*** (nes-ə-**sair**-ee-əm). (1892) A necessary or compulsory oath.

▸ ***juramentum voluntarium*** (vol-ən-**tair**-ee-əm). (1893) A voluntary oath.

jura mixti dominii. See JURA.

jurant (**joor**-ənt), *n.* (16c) *Archaic.* Someone who takes an oath. — **jurant,** *n.*

jura personarum. See JURA.

jura praediorum. See JURA.

jura regalia. See JURA.

jura rerum. See JURA.

jura summi imperii. See JURA.

jurat (**joor**-at). (18c) **1.** [fr. Latin *jurare* "to swear"] A certification added to an affidavit or deposition stating when and before what authority the affidavit or deposition was made. • A jurat typically says "Subscribed and sworn to before me this _____ day of [month], [year]," and the officer (usu. a notary public) thereby certifies three things: (1) that the person signing the document did so in the officer's presence, (2) that the signer appeared before the officer on the date indicated, and (3) that the officer administered an oath or affirmation to the signer, who swore to or affirmed the contents of the document. — Also termed *jurata.* Cf. VERIFICATION.

▸ **witness jurat.** (1992) A subscribing witness's certificate acknowledging the act of witnessing. • Even though this certificate is technically an acknowledgment and not a true jurat, the phrase *witness jurat* is commonly used. See ACKNOWLEDGMENT.

2. [fr. Latin *juratus* "one sworn"] In France and the Channel Islands, a municipal officer or magistrate.

jurata (juu-**ray**-tə), *n.* **1.** *Hist.* A jury of 12 persons; esp., a jury existing at common law. **2.** JURAT (1).

juration (juu-**ray**-shən). (17c) *Archaic.* **1.** The act of administering an oath. **2.** The act of swearing on oath.

jurative. See JURATORY.

jurator (juu-**ray**-tər). *Archaic.* See JUROR.

juratorial (joor-ə-**toh**-ri-əl) *adj.* (1865) Of, relating to, or involving a jury.

juratory (**joor**-ə-tor-ee), *adj.* (16c) Of, relating to, or containing an oath. — Also termed *jurative.*

juratory caution. (16c) **1.** *Maritime law.* A court's permission for an indigent to disregard filing fees and court costs. • A suit on a juratory caution is the equivalent of a suit in forma pauperis. The right was first recognized in United States admiralty courts in *Bradford v. Bradford*, 3 F. Cas. 1129 (1878). See IN FORMA PAUPERIS. **2.** *Scots law.* A security given on oath, such as a bond.

jure (**joor**-ee), *adv.* [Latin] (17c) **1.** By right; in right. **2.** By law. See DE JURE.

▸ ***jure accessionis*** (**joor**-ee ak-sesh-ee-**oh**-nis). (1823) By the law of natural accession. • For example, the fruits of trees on one's land are one's property *jure accessionis.*

▸ ***jure accretionis*** (ə-kree-shee-**oh**-nis). (18c) By right of accretion.

▸ ***jure belli*** (**bel**-ɪ). (16c) By the right or law of war.

▸ ***jure civili*** (sə-**vɪ**-lɪ). (16c) By the civil law.

▸ ***jure coronae*** (kə-**roh**-nee). (17c) In right of the Crown.

▸ ***jure devolutionis*** (dev-ə-loo-shee-**oh**-nis). By right of devolution.

▸ ***jure divino*** (di-**vɪ**-noh). (16c) By divine right.

▸ ***jure ecclesiae*** (e-**klee**-z[h]ee-ee). (16c) By right of the church.

▸ ***jure gentium*** (**jen**-shee-əm). (16c) By the law of nations.

▸ ***jure officii*** (ə-**fish**-ee-ɪ). (17c) By right of office.

▸ ***jure proprietatis*** (prə-prɪ-ə-**tay**-tis). (17c) By right of property.

▸ ***jure proprio*** (**proh**-pree-oh). (17c) By one's own proper right.

▸ ***jure repraesentationis*** (rep-rə-zen-tay-shee-**oh**-nis). (17c) By right of representation; in the right of another person.

▸ ***jure sanguinis*** (**sang**-gwi-nis). (17c) By right of blood.

▸ ***jure uxoris*** (ək-**sor**-is). (17c) In right of a wife.

jure gestionis (**joor**-ee jes-chee-**oh**-nis), *n.* [Latin "by way of doing business"] (1918) A country's acts that are essentially commercial or private, in contrast to its public or governmental acts. • Under the Foreign Sovereign Immunities Act, a foreign country's immunity is limited to claims involving its public acts. The statutory immunity does not extend to claims arising from the private or commercial acts of a foreign state. 28 USCA § 1605. Cf. JURE IMPERII. See COMMERCIAL-ACTIVITY EXCEPTION; RESTRICTIVE PRINCIPLE OF SOVEREIGN IMMUNITY.

jure imperii (**joor**-ee im-**peer**-ee-ɪ), *n.* [Latin "by right of sovereignty"] (1908) The public acts that a country undertakes as a sovereign state, for which the sovereign is usu. immune from suit or liability in a foreign country. Cf. JURE GESTIONIS; COMMERCIAL-ACTIVITY EXCEPTION. See RESTRICTIVE PRINCIPLE OF SOVEREIGN IMMUNITY.

jure naturae. **1.** See EX JURE NATURAE. **2.** See NATURAL LAW.

juridical (juu-**rid**-i-kəl), *adj.* (16c) **1.** Of, relating to, or involving judicial proceedings or to the administration of justice. **2.** Of, relating to, or involving law; legal. — Also termed *juridic.* Cf. NONJURIDICAL.

juridical act. See ACT (2).

juridical day. See DAY.

juridical double taxation. See *double taxation* (3) under TAXATION (1).

juridical fact. See *legal fact* (1) under FACT.

juridical link. (1947) A legal relationship between members of a group, such as those in a potential class action, sufficient to make a single suit more efficient or effective than multiple suits. — Also termed *juridical relationship.*

juridical person. See *artificial person* under PERSON (3).

juridical relationship. JURIDICAL LINK.

juridification (joor-id-i-fi-**kay**-shən), *n.* [loan translation fr. German *Verrechtlichung*] (1984) The gradual transformation of social relations into legal relations and, accordingly, social conflicts into legal conflicts, mostly as a result of legislation and judicial decisions.

jurimetrics (joor-ə-**me**-triks), *n.* (1949) The use of scientific or empirical methods, including measurement, in the study or analysis of legal matters. — **jurimetrician** (joor-ə-me-**trish**-ən), **jurimetricist** (joor-ə-**me**-trə-sist), *n.*

> "A variety of contextual frames of reference have been employed by commentators to explain and clarify the basis for judicial decision-making, the most fundamental aspect of the judge's job. These range from exploration of the judge's personality to the employment of small group theory, game theory and Guttman scaling to measure and apprehend the nature of judicial decision-making. Indeed, the disciplined effort to identify with mathematical precision the decision process has been dubiously termed

'jurimetrics.'" Alexander B. Smith & Abraham S. Blumberg, "The Problem of Objectivity," in 2 *Crime and Justice* 485–86 (Leon Radzinowicz & Marvin E. Wolfgang eds., 1971).

juris (**joor**-is), *adj.* [Latin] **1.** Of law. **2.** Of right.

▸ ***juris divini*** (di-**vi**-ni). (16c) *Roman law.* Of divine right; subject to divine law. • The phrase appeared in reference to churches or to religious items that could not be privately sold.

▸ ***juris positivii.*** Of positive law.

▸ ***juris privati*** (pri-**vay**-ti). (17c) Of private right; relating to private property or private law.

▸ ***juris publici*** (**pəb**-li-si). (17c) Of public right; relating to common or public use, or to public law.

juriscenter (**joor**-ə-sen-tər *or* joor-ə-**sen**-tər), *n.* (1966) *Conflict of laws.* The jurisdiction that is most appropriately considered a couple's domestic center of gravity for matrimonial purposes.

jurisconsult (joor-is-**kon**-səlt *or* -kən-**səlt**). (17c) Someone who is learned in the law, esp. in civil or international law; JURIST.

jurisdictio contentiosa (joor-is-**dik**-shee-oh kən-ten-shee-**oh**-sə). [Latin] *Roman law.* Contentious as opposed to voluntary jurisdiction. See *contentious jurisdiction* (1) under JURISDICTION.

jurisdictio emanata (joor-is-**dik**-shee-oh em-ə-**nay**-tə). [Law Latin "a jurisdiction emanating from the court"] *Hist.* A court's inherent jurisdiction, esp. to punish a contemner. See CONTEMNER.

jurisdictio in consentientes (joor-is-**dik**-shee-oh in kən-sen-shee-**en**-teez). [Law Latin "jurisdiction over parties by virtue of their consent"] (1828) *Scots law.* Consensual jurisdiction. See *consent jurisdiction* under JURISDICTION.

jurisdiction, *n.* (14c) **1.** A government's general power to exercise authority over all persons and things within its territory; esp., a state's power to create interests that will be recognized under common-law principles as valid in other states <New Jersey's jurisdiction>. **2.** A court's power to decide a case or issue a decree <the constitutional grant of federal-question jurisdiction>. — Also termed (in sense 2) *competent jurisdiction*; (in both senses) *coram judice*; *adjudicatory jurisdiction.*

"Rules of jurisdiction in a sense speak from a position outside the court system and prescribe the authority of the courts within the system. They are to a large extent constitutional rules. The provisions of the U.S. Constitution specify the outer limits of the subject-matter jurisdiction of the federal courts and authorize Congress, within those limits, to establish by statute the organization and jurisdiction of the federal courts. Thus, Article III of the Constitution defines the judicial power of the United States to include cases arising under federal law and cases between parties of diverse state citizenship as well as other categories. The U.S. Constitution, particularly the Due Process Clause, also establishes limits on the jurisdiction of the state courts. These due process limitations traditionally operate in two areas: jurisdiction of the subject matter and jurisdiction over persons. Within each state, the court system is established by state constitutional provisions or by a combination of such provisions and implementing legislation, which together define the authority of the various courts within the system." Fleming James Jr., Geoffrey C. Hazard Jr. & John Leubsdorf, *Civil Procedure* § 2.1, at 55 (5th ed. 2001).

3. A geographic area within which political or judicial authority may be exercised <the accused fled to another jurisdiction>. **4.** A political or judicial subdivision within such an area <other jurisdictions have decided the issue differently>. Cf. VENUE (1), (2). — **jurisdictional,** *adj.*

▸ **agency jurisdiction.** The regulatory or adjudicative power of a government administrative agency over a subject matter or matters.

▸ **ancillary jurisdiction.** (1835) A court's jurisdiction to adjudicate claims and proceedings related to a claim that is properly before the court. • For example, if a plaintiff brings a lawsuit in federal court based on a federal question (such as a claim under Title VII), the defendant may assert a counterclaim over which the court would not otherwise have jurisdiction (such as a state-law claim of stealing company property). The concept of ancillary jurisdiction has now been codified, along with the concept of pendent jurisdiction, in the supplemental-jurisdiction statute. 28 USCA § 1367. See *supplemental jurisdiction.* Cf. *pendent jurisdiction.*

▸ **anomalous jurisdiction.** (1864) **1.** Jurisdiction that is not granted to a court by statute, but that is inherent in the court's authority to govern lawyers and other officers of the court, such as the power to issue a preindictment order suppressing illegally seized property. **2.** An appellate court's provisional jurisdiction to review the denial of a motion to intervene in a lower-court case, so that if the court finds that the denial was correct, then its jurisdiction disappears — and it must dismiss the appeal for want of jurisdiction — because an order denying a motion to intervene is not a final, appealable order. See ANOMALOUS-JURISDICTION RULE.

▸ **appellate jurisdiction.** (18c) The power of a court to review and revise a lower court's decision. • For example, U.S. Const. art. III, § 2 vests appellate jurisdiction in the Supreme Court, while 28 USCA §§ 1291–1295 grant appellate jurisdiction to lower federal courts of appeals. Cf. *original jurisdiction.*

▸ **arising-in jurisdiction.** (1992) A bankruptcy court's jurisdiction over issues relating to the administration of the bankruptcy estate, and matters that occur only in a bankruptcy case. 28 USCA §§ 157, 1334.

▸ **assistant jurisdiction.** (1829) The incidental aid provided by an equity court to a court of law when justice requires both legal and equitable processes and remedies. — Also termed *auxiliary jurisdiction.*

▸ **common-law jurisdiction. 1.** A place where the legal system derives fundamentally from the English common-law system <England, the United States, Australia, and other common-law jurisdictions>. **2.** A court's jurisdiction to try such cases as were cognizable under the English common law <in the absence of a controlling statute, the court exercised common-law jurisdiction over those claims>.

▸ **complete jurisdiction.** (17c) A court's power to decide matters presented to it and to enforce its decisions.

▸ **concurrent jurisdiction.** (17c) **1.** Jurisdiction that might be exercised simultaneously by more than one court over the same subject matter and within the same territory, a litigant having the right to choose the court in which to file the action. **2.** Jurisdiction shared by two or more states, esp. over the physical boundaries (such as rivers or other bodies of water) between them. — Also termed *coordinate jurisdiction; overlapping jurisdiction.* Cf. *exclusive jurisdiction.*

"In several cases, two States divided by a river exercise concurrent jurisdiction over the river, no matter where the inter-state boundary may be; in some cases by the Ordinance of 1787 for organizing Territories northwest of the Ohio River, in some cases by Acts of Congress organizing Territories or admitting States, and in some cases by agreements between the States concerned." 1 Joseph H. Beale, *A Treatise on the Conflict of Laws* § 44.3, at 279 (1935).

▸ **consent jurisdiction.** (1855) Jurisdiction that parties have agreed to, either by accord, by contract, or by general appearance. • Parties may not, by agreement, confer subject-matter jurisdiction on a federal court that would not otherwise have it.

▸ **contentious jurisdiction.** (17c) **1.** A court's jurisdiction exercised over disputed matters. **2.** *Eccles. law.* The branch of ecclesiastical-court jurisdiction that deals with contested proceedings.

▸ **continuing jurisdiction.** (1855) A court's power to retain jurisdiction over a matter after entering a judgment, allowing the court to modify its previous rulings or orders. See CONTINUING-JURISDICTION DOCTRINE.

▸ **coordinate jurisdiction.** See *concurrent jurisdiction.*

▸ **criminal jurisdiction.** (16c) A court's power to hear criminal cases.

▸ **default jurisdiction.** (1986) *Family law.* In a child-custody matter, jurisdiction conferred when it is in the best interests of the child and either (1) there is no other basis for jurisdiction under the Uniform Child Custody Jurisdiction Act or the Parental Kidnapping Prevention Act, or (2) when another state has declined jurisdiction in favor of default jurisdiction. • Jurisdiction is rarely based on default because either home-state jurisdiction or significant-connection jurisdiction almost always applies, or else emergency jurisdiction is invoked. Default jurisdiction arises only if none of those three applies, or a state with jurisdiction on any of those bases declines to exercise it and default jurisdiction serves the best interests of the child.

▸ **delinquency jurisdiction.** (1931) The power of the court to hear matters regarding juvenile acts that, if committed by an adult, would be criminal. Cf. *status-offense jurisdiction.*

▸ **diversity jurisdiction.** (1927) A federal court's exercise of authority over a case involving parties who are citizens of different states and an amount in controversy greater than a statutory minimum. 28 USCA § 1332. See DIVERSITY OF CITIZENSHIP; AMOUNT IN CONTROVERSY.

▸ **emergency jurisdiction.** *Family law.* A court's ability to take jurisdiction of a child who is physically present in the state when that child has been abandoned or when necessary to protect the child from abuse. • Section 3(a)(3) of the Uniform Child Custody Jurisdiction Act allows for emergency jurisdiction. It is usu. temporary, lasting only as long as is necessary to protect the child.

▸ **equitable jurisdiction.** See *equity jurisdiction.*

▸ **equity jurisdiction.** (18c) In a common-law judicial system, the power to hear certain civil actions according to the procedure of the court of chancery, and to resolve them according to equitable rules. — Also termed *equitable jurisdiction.*

"[T]he term equity jurisdiction does not refer to jurisdiction in the sense of the power conferred by the sovereign on the court over specified subject-matters or to jurisdiction over the res or the persons of the parties in a particular proceeding but refers rather to the merits. The want of equity jurisdiction does not mean that the court has no power to act but that it should not act, as on the ground, for example, that there is an adequate remedy at law." William Q. de Funiak, *Handbook of Modern Equity* 38 (2d ed. 1956).

▸ **exclusive jurisdiction.** (18c) A court's power to adjudicate an action or class of actions to the exclusion of all other courts <federal district courts have exclusive jurisdiction over actions brought under the Securities Exchange Act>. Cf. *concurrent jurisdiction.*

▸ **extended jurisdiction.** **1.** The power of a court to exercise or retain jurisdiction over a particular person or matter on its own authority or by request, as in a guardianship, or by statute. **2.** *Family law.* In a case of abuse and neglect, a court's retention of jurisdiction beyond the point when the child reaches the age of majority.

▸ **extended juvenile jurisdiction.** *Criminal law.* The authority of a juvenile court to retain jurisdiction over a youthful offender who receives both a juvenile sentence and an adult sentence even after the offender reaches the age at which the juvenile court's jurisdiction would normally end. — Abbr. EJJ.

▸ **extraterritorial jurisdiction.** (1818) A court's ability to exercise power beyond its territorial limits. See LONG-ARM STATUTE.

▸ **federal jurisdiction.** (1800) **1.** The exercise of federal-court authority. **2.** The area of study dealing with the jurisdiction of federal courts.

▸ **federal-juvenile-delinquency jurisdiction.** A federal court's power to hear a case in which a person under the age of 18 violates federal law. • In such a case, the federal court derives its jurisdictional power from 18 USCA §§ 5031 et seq. The Act severely limits the scope of federal-juvenile-delinquency jurisdiction because Congress recognizes that juvenile delinquency is essentially a state issue. The acts that typically invoke federal jurisdiction are (1) acts committed on federal lands (military bases, national parks, Indian reservations), and (2) acts that violate federal drug laws or other federal criminal statutes.

▸ **federal-question jurisdiction.** (1941) *Constitutional law.* The exercise of federal-court power over claims arising under the U.S. Constitution, an act of Congress, or a treaty. 28 USCA § 1331.

▸ **foreign jurisdiction.** (16c) **1.** The powers of a court of a sister state or foreign country. **2.** Extraterritorial process, such as long-arm service of process.

▸ **general jurisdiction.** (16c) **1.** A court's authority to hear a wide range of cases, civil or criminal, that arise within its geographic area. **2.** A court's authority to hear all claims against a defendant, at the place of the defendant's domicile or the place of service, without any showing that a connection exists between the claims and the forum state. Cf. *limited jurisdiction; specific jurisdiction.*

▸ **general personal jurisdiction.** (1938) Jurisdiction arising when a person's continuous and systematic contacts with a forum state enable the forum state's courts to adjudicate a claim against the person, even when the claim is not related to the person's contacts with the forum state. Cf. *personal jurisdiction*; *specific personal jurisdiction*.

▸ **home-state jurisdiction.** (1969) *Family law.* In interstate child-custody disputes governed by the Uniform Child Custody Jurisdiction and Enforcement Act, jurisdiction based on the child's having been a resident of the state for at least six consecutive months immediately before the commencement of the suit. See HOME STATE.

▸ **inherent jurisdiction.** (17c) **1.** The legal authority vested in a court to hear any matter that comes before it unless a statute or rule limits that authority. **2.** The jurisdiction derived by a governmental entity from a fundamental government instrument, such as a constitution.

▸ **in personam jurisdiction.** See *personal jurisdiction*.

▸ **in rem jurisdiction** (in rem). (1930) A court's power to adjudicate the rights to a given piece of property, including the power to seize and hold it. — Also termed *jurisdiction in rem*. See IN REM. Cf. *personal jurisdiction*; *subject-matter jurisdiction*.

▸ **international jurisdiction.** (1868) A court's power to hear and determine matters between different countries or persons of different countries.

▸ **judicial jurisdiction.** (17c) The legal power and authority of a court to make a decision that binds the parties to any matter properly brought before it.

▸ **jurisdiction in personam.** See *personal jurisdiction*.

▸ **jurisdiction in rem.** See *in rem jurisdiction*.

▸ **jurisdiction *loci*.** See *spatial jurisdiction*.

▸ **jurisdiction of the person.** See *personal jurisdiction*.

▸ **jurisdiction over the person.** See *personal jurisdiction*.

▸ **jurisdiction quasi in rem.** See *quasi-in-rem jurisdiction*.

▸ **jurisdiction *ratione materiae*.** See *subject-matter jurisdiction*.

▸ **jurisdiction *ratione personae*.** See *personal jurisdiction*.

▸ **jurisdiction *ratione temporis*.** See *temporal jurisdiction*.

▸ **legislative jurisdiction.** (17c) A legislature's general sphere of authority to enact laws and conduct all business related to that authority, such as holding hearings.

▸ **limited jurisdiction.** (16c) Jurisdiction that is confined to a particular type of case or that may be exercised only under statutory limits and prescriptions. — Also termed *special jurisdiction*. Cf. *general jurisdiction*.

> "It is a principle of first importance that the federal courts are courts of limited jurisdiction. . . . The federal courts . . . cannot be courts of general jurisdiction. They are empowered to hear only such cases as are within the judicial power of the United States, as defined in the Constitution, and have been entrusted to them by a jurisdictional grant by Congress." Charles Alan Wright, *The Law of Federal Courts* § 7, at 27 (5th ed. 1994).

▸ **long-arm jurisdiction.** (1962) Jurisdiction over a nonresident defendant who has had some contact with the jurisdiction in which the petition is filed.

▸ **original jurisdiction.** (17c) A court's power to hear and decide a matter before any other court can review the matter. Cf. *appellate jurisdiction*.

▸ **overlapping jurisdiction.** See *concurrent jurisdiction*.

▸ **pendent jurisdiction** (**pen**-dənt). (1942) A court's jurisdiction to hear and determine a claim over which it would not otherwise have jurisdiction, because the claim arises from the same transaction or occurrence as another claim that is properly before the court. • For example, if a plaintiff brings suit in federal court claiming that the defendant, in one transaction, violated both a federal and a state law, the federal court has jurisdiction over the federal claim (under federal-question jurisdiction) and also has jurisdiction over the state claim that is pendent to the federal claim. Pendent jurisdiction has now been codified as supplemental jurisdiction. 28 USCA § 1367. — Also termed *pendent-claim jurisdiction*. See *supplemental jurisdiction*. Cf. *ancillary jurisdiction*.

▸ **pendent-party jurisdiction.** (1973) A court's jurisdiction to adjudicate a claim against a party who is not otherwise subject to the court's jurisdiction, because the claim by or against that party arises from the same transaction or occurrence as another claim that is properly before the court. • Pendent-party jurisdiction has been a hotly debated subject, and was severely limited by the U.S. Supreme Court in *Finley v. U.S.*, 490 U.S. 545, 109 S.Ct. 2003 (1990). The concept is now codified in the supplemental-jurisdiction statute, and it applies to federal-question cases but not to diversity-jurisdiction cases. 28 USCA § 1367. Neither pendent-party jurisdiction nor supplemental jurisdiction may be used to circumvent the complete-diversity requirement in cases founded on diversity jurisdiction. See *supplemental jurisdiction*.

▸ **personal jurisdiction.** (1820) A court's power to bring a person into its adjudicative process; jurisdiction over a defendant's personal rights, rather than merely over property interests. — Also termed *in personam jurisdiction*; *jurisdiction in personam*; *jurisdiction of the person*; *jurisdiction over the person*; *jurisdiction ratione personae*. See IN PERSONAM. Cf. *in rem jurisdiction*; *general personal jurisdiction*; *specific personal jurisdiction*.

▸ **plenary jurisdiction** (**plee**-nə-ree *or* **plen**-ə-ree). (1833) A court's full and absolute power over the subject matter and the parties in a case.

▸ **prescriptive jurisdiction.** See PRESCRIPTIVE JURISDICTION.

▸ **primary jurisdiction. 1.** The power of an agency to decide an issue in the first instance when a court, having concurrent jurisdiction with the agency, determines that it would be more pragmatic for the agency to handle the case initially. See PRIMARY-JURISDICTION DOCTRINE.

> "The doctrine of primary jurisdiction typically is raised, not in a proceeding before an administrative agency, but in litigation before a court. Agency and court jurisdiction to resolve disputes and issues frequently overlap. Primary jurisdiction is a concept used by courts to allocate initial decision-making responsibility between agencies and courts where such overlaps exist. . . . A holding that an agency has primary jurisdiction to resolve an issue raised in a judicial proceeding has two important consequences. First, it transfers some of the power to resolve that issue to the agency. . . . Second, if the issues referred to the

agency as within its primary jurisdiction are critical to judicial resolution of the underlying dispute, the court cannot proceed with the trial of the case until the agency has resolved those issues and the agency's decision has been either affirmed or reversed by a reviewing court." Richard J. Pierce Jr. et al., *Administrative Law and Process* 206, 207–08 (3d ed. 1999).

2. The power that a court has over a criminal defendant who is being criminally charged elsewhere on the same or different charges, when that court (e.g., state or federal) was the first in which the defendant appeared. • Primary jurisdiction may affect how a defendant's time in custody is credited to any sentences ultimately imposed, as well as where the defendant will first serve prison time. — Also termed *primary custody.*

▸ **probate jurisdiction.** (1823) Jurisdiction over matters relating to wills, settlement of decedents' estates, and (in some states) guardianship and the adoption of minors.

▸ **prorogated jurisdiction.** (1862) *Civil law.* Jurisdiction conferred by the express consent of all the parties on a judge who would otherwise be disqualified. Cf. *tacit prorogation* under PROROGATION.

▸ **quasi-in-rem jurisdiction** (**kway**-sı in **rem** *or* **kway**-zı). (1918) Jurisdiction over a person but based on that person's interest in property located within the court's territory. — Also termed *jurisdiction quasi in rem.* See *quasi in rem* under IN REM.

▸ **removal jurisdiction.** Jurisdiction exercised by a federal court after a defendant properly moves a lawsuit from state court under 28 USCA § 1441. See REMOVAL (2).

▸ **significant-connection jurisdiction.** (1977) *Family law.* In a child-custody matter, jurisdiction based on (1) the best interests of the child, (2) at least one parent's (or litigant's) significant connection to the state, and (3) the presence in the state of substantial evidence about the child's present or future care, protection, training, and personal relationships. • This type of jurisdiction is conferred by both the Uniform Child Custody Jurisdiction Act and the Parental Kidnapping Prevention Act. Generally, the home state will also be the state with significant connections and substantial evidence. Jurisdiction based on a significant connection or substantial evidence alone is conferred only when the child has no home state. — Also termed *significant-connection/substantial-evidence jurisdiction; significant connection–substantial evidence jurisdiction; substantial-evidence jurisdiction.* See HOME STATE.

▸ **spatial jurisdiction.** (1938) Jurisdiction based on the physical territory that an entity's authority covers. — Also termed *jurisdiction loci.*

▸ **special jurisdiction.** See *limited jurisdiction.*

▸ **specific jurisdiction.** (1828) Jurisdiction that stems from the defendant's having certain minimum contacts with the forum state so that the court may hear a case whose issues arise from those minimum contacts. Cf. *general jurisdiction.*

▸ **specific personal jurisdiction.** (1967) Jurisdiction based on a person's minimum contacts with the forum state when the claim arises out of or is related to those contacts. See MINIMUM CONTACTS. Cf. *personal jurisdiction; general personal jurisdiction.*

▸ **state jurisdiction.** (18c) **1.** The exercise of state-court authority. **2.** A court's power to hear all matters, both civil and criminal, arising within its territorial boundaries.

▸ **status-offense jurisdiction.** (1975) The power of the court to hear matters regarding noncriminal conduct committed by a juvenile. See *status offense* under OFFENSE (2). Cf. *delinquency jurisdiction.*

▸ **subject-matter jurisdiction.** (1936) Jurisdiction over the nature of the case and the type of relief sought; the extent to which a court can rule on the conduct of persons or the status of things. — Also termed *jurisdiction of the subject matter; jurisdiction of the cause; jurisdiction over the action; jurisdiction ratione materiae.* Cf. *personal jurisdiction.*

▸ **summary jurisdiction.** (18c) **1.** A court's jurisdiction in a summary proceeding. **2.** The court's authority to issue a judgment or order (such as a finding of contempt) without the necessity of a trial or other process. **3.** *English law.* A court's power to make an order immediately, without obtaining authority or referral, as in a magistrate's power to dispose of a criminal case without referring it to the Crown Court for a formal trial or without drawing a jury.

▸ **supplemental jurisdiction.** (1836) Jurisdiction over a claim that is part of the same case or controversy as another claim over which the court has original jurisdiction. • Since 1990, federal district courts have had supplemental jurisdiction which includes jurisdiction over both ancillary and pendent claims. 28 USCA § 1367. See *ancillary jurisdiction; pendent jurisdiction.*

▸ **temporal jurisdiction.** Jurisdiction based on the court's having authority to adjudicate a matter when the underlying event occurred. — Also termed *jurisdiction ratione temporis.*

▸ **territorial jurisdiction.** (17c) **1.** Jurisdiction over cases arising in or involving persons residing within a defined territory. **2.** Territory over which a government, one of its courts, or one of its subdivisions has jurisdiction.

▸ **transient jurisdiction** (**tran**-shənt). (1956) Personal jurisdiction over a defendant who is served with process while in the forum state only temporarily (such as during travel).

▸ **voluntary jurisdiction.** (16c) **1.** Jurisdiction exercised over unopposed matters. **2.** *Eccles. law.* Jurisdiction that does not require a judicial proceeding, as with granting a license or installing a nominee to a benefice.

jurisdictional amount. See AMOUNT IN CONTROVERSY.

jurisdictional discovery. See DISCOVERY.

jurisdictional error. See ERROR (2).

jurisdictional fact. See FACT.

jurisdictional-fact doctrine. (1932) *Administrative law.* The principle that if evidence is presented challenging the factual findings that triggered an agency's action, then a court will review the facts to determine whether the agency had authority to act in the first place. • This doctrine is generally no longer applied. Cf. CONSTITUTIONAL-FACT DOCTRINE.

jurisdictional gerrymandering. See GERRYMANDERING (2).

jurisdictional limits. (1800) The geographic boundaries or the constitutional or statutory limits within which a court's authority may be exercised.

jurisdictional-ouster canon. The canon that a statute cannot oust courts of jurisdiction unless it does so expressly. • Some legal commentators view this canon as false.

jurisdictional plea. See PLEA (3).

jurisdictional statement. See JURISDICTION CLAUSE (1).

jurisdictional strike. See STRIKE (1).

jurisdiction clause. (1861) **1.** At law, a statement in a pleading that sets forth the court's jurisdiction to act in the case. — Also termed *jurisdictional statement.* **2.** *Equity practice.* The part of the bill intended to show that the court has jurisdiction, usu. by an averment that adequate relief is unavailable outside equitable channels.

jurisdiction in personam. See *personal jurisdiction* under JURISDICTION.

jurisdiction in rem. See *in rem jurisdiction* under JURISDICTION.

jurisdictionis fundandae (joor-is-dik-shee-**oh**-nis fən-**dan**-dee). [Law Latin] *Scots law.* For the purpose of founding jurisdiction. See ARRESTUM JURISDICTIONIS FUNDANDAE CAUSA.

jurisdictionless, *adj.* (1887) (Of a tribunal, court, etc.) having no jurisdiction.

jurisdiction *loci.* See *spatial jurisdiction* under JURISDICTION.

jurisdiction of the cause. See *subject-matter jurisdiction* under JURISDICTION.

jurisdiction of the person. See *personal jurisdiction* under JURISDICTION.

jurisdiction of the subject matter. See *subject-matter jurisdiction* under JURISDICTION.

jurisdiction over the action. See *subject-matter jurisdiction* under JURISDICTION.

jurisdiction over the person. See *personal jurisdiction* under JURISDICTION.

jurisdiction-prorogation clause. See FORUM-SELECTION CLAUSE.

jurisdiction quasi in rem. See *quasi-in-rem jurisdiction* under JURISDICTION.

jurisdiction *ratione materiae.* See *subject-matter jurisdiction* under JURISDICTION.

jurisdiction *ratione personae.* See *personal jurisdiction* under JURISDICTION.

jurisdiction *ratione temporis.* See *temporal jurisdiction* under JURISDICTION.

jurisdiction to prescribe. See PRESCRIPTIVE JURISDICTION.

jurisdictio voluntaria (joor-is-**dik**-shee-oh vol-ən-**tair**-ee-ə). [Latin] (17c) *Roman law.* Voluntary jurisdiction. See *voluntary jurisdiction* under JURISDICTION.

Juris Doctor (**joor**-is **dok**-tər). (1895) Doctor of law — the law degree most commonly conferred by an American law school. — Abbr. J.D. — Also termed *Doctor of Jurisprudence; Doctor of Law; law degree.* Cf. MASTER OF LAWS; LL.B.; DOCTOR OF LAWS.

juris et de jure (**joor**-is et dee **joor**-ee). [Latin] Of law and of right <a presumption *juris et de jure* cannot be rebutted>.

jurisinceptor (joor-is-in-**sep**-tər). [Latin] *Hist.* A student of the civil law.

jurisperitus (joor-is-pə-**rɪ**-təs), *adj.* [Latin] (Of a person) skilled or learned in law. See LEGISPERITUS.

juris positivii. See JURIS.

juris privati. See JURIS.

jurisprude (**joor**-is-prood), *n.* (1937) **1.** Someone who makes a pretentious display of legal knowledge or who is overzealous about the importance of legal doctrine. **2.** JURISPRUDENT.

jurisprudence (joor-is-**prood**-ənts), *n.* (17c) **1.** Originally (in the 18th century), the study of the first principles of the natural law, the civil law, or the law of nations. — Also termed *jurisprudentia naturalis* (joor-is-proo-**den**-shee-ə nach-ə-**ray**-lis). **2.** More modernly, the study of the general or fundamental elements of a particular legal system, as opposed to its practical and concrete details. **3.** The study of legal systems in general. **4.** Judicial precedents considered collectively. **5.** In German literature, the whole of legal knowledge. **6.** A system, body, or division of law. **7.** CASELAW.

> "Jurisprudence addresses the questions about law that an intelligent layperson of speculative bent — not a lawyer — might think particularly interesting. What is law? . . . Where does law come from? . . . Is law an autonomous discipline? . . . What is the purpose of law? . . . Is law a science, a humanity, or neither? . . . A practicing lawyer or a judge is apt to think questions of this sort at best irrelevant to what he does, at worst naive, impractical, even childlike (how high is up?)." Richard A. Posner, *The Problems of Jurisprudence* 1 (1990).

▸ **analytical jurisprudence.** (1876) **1.** A method of legal study that concentrates on the logical structure of law, the meanings and uses of its concepts, and the formal terms and the modes of its operation. **2.** See *expository jurisprudence.* — Also termed *analytic jurisprudence.*

▸ **censorial jurisprudence.** See LAW REFORM.

▸ **civil jurisprudence.** See *municipal jurisprudence.*

▸ **comparative jurisprudence.** See COMPARATIVE LAW.

▸ **critical jurisprudence.** The branch of legal philosophy concerned with estimating the value of existing legal institutions and deducing from that analysis what reforms in the law might be desirable. —Also termed *deontological jurisprudence.*

▸ **deontological jurisprudence.** See *critical jurisprudence.*

▸ **economic jurisprudence.** A philosophical approach to law stressing the economic effects of legal institutions, doctrines, and practices.

▸ **equity jurisprudence.** (1826) **1.** The legal science treating the rules, principles, and maxims that govern the decisions of a court of equity. **2.** The cases and controversies that are considered proper subjects of equity. **3.** The nature and form of the remedies that equity grants.

▸ **ethical jurisprudence.** (1826) The branch of legal philosophy concerned with the law from the viewpoint of its ethical significance and adequacy. • This area of study brings together moral and legal philosophy. — Also termed (in German) *Rechtsphilosophie;* (in French) *philosophie du droit.*

▸ **ethnological jurisprudence.** The scholarly study of the interactions between legal institutions and tribal or national organizations, as modified by the environment.

▸ **expository jurisprudence.** (18c) The scholarly exposition of the contents of an actual legal system as it now exists or once existed. — Also termed *systematic jurisprudence*; *analytical jurisprudence*.

▸ **feminist jurisprudence.** (1978) A branch of jurisprudence that examines the relationship between women and law, including the history of legal and social biases against women, the elimination of those biases in modern law, and the enhancement of women's legal rights and recognition in society.

> "The first published use of the phrase 'feminist jurisprudence' occurred in 1978 when Professor Ann Scales published an article called *Toward a Feminist Jurisprudence*. Feminist legal theory is diverse, and anything but monolithic. Many feminists believe that it is difficult to generalize about feminist jurisprudence. It is, however, possible to understand feminist legal theory as a reaction to the jurisprudence of modern legal scholars (primarily male scholars) who tend to see law as a process for interpreting and perpetuating a universal, gender-neutral public morality. Feminist legal scholars, despite their differences, appear united in claiming that 'masculine' jurisprudence of 'all stripes' fails to acknowledge, let alone respond to, the interests, values, fears, and harms experienced by women." Gary Minda, *Postmodern Legal Movements* 129–30 (1995).

▸ **general jurisprudence.** (18c) **1.** The scholarly study of the fundamental elements of a given legal system. — Also termed *jurisprudentia generalis*.

> "The term 'general jurisprudence' involves the misleading suggestion that this branch of legal science is that which relates not to any single system of law, but to those conceptions and principles that are to be found in all developed legal systems, and which are therefore in this sense general. It is true that a great part of the matter with which it is concerned is common to all mature systems of law. All of these have the same essential nature and purposes, and therefore agree to a large extent in their first principles. But it is not because of universal reception that any principles pertain to the theory or philosophy of law. For this purpose such reception is neither sufficient nor necessary. Even if no system in the world save that of England recognised the legislative efficacy of judicial precedents, the theory of case-law would none the less be a fit and proper subject of general jurisprudence. *Jurisprudentia generalis* is not the study of legal systems in general, but the study of the general or fundamental elements of a particular legal system." John Salmond, *Jurisprudence* 3 n.(b) (Glanville L. Williams ed., 10th ed. 1947).

2. The scholarly study of the law, legal theory, and legal systems generally; the scholarly comparison of all the legal systems of the world. — Also termed *jurisprudentia universalis*; *philosophy of law*; *legal philosophy*.

> "According to Austin (1790–1859), general jurisprudence is the study of the 'principles, notions and distinctions' common to the maturer systems of law." Rupert Cross & J.W. Harris, *Precedent in English Law* 2 (4th ed. 1991).

3. A method of legal study that seeks to identify those legal rules that are common to all systems of law. **4.** A method of legal study that seeks to identify the most fundamental legal principles and institutions as they occur in civilized countries.

▸ **historical jurisprudence.** (1823) The branch of legal philosophy concerned with the history of the first principles and conceptions of a legal system, dealing with (1) the general principles governing the origin and development of law, and (2) the origin and development of the legal system's first principles.

> "Historical jurisprudence was a passive restraining mode of thought on legal subjects by way of reaction from the active creative thought of the era of philosophy. It was a reaction, too, from the confident disregard of traditional legal institutions and conditions of time and place which characterized the French Revolution. We were not ready for it in the fore part of the last century. But we accepted it eagerly toward the end of that century when it was already moribund in Europe." Roscoe Pound, *The Formative Era of American Law* 113 (1938).

▸ **international jurisprudence.** The scholarly study of the principles on which the law existing between states and other entities to whom personality is based.

▸ **jurisprudence *constante*** (kən-**stan**-tee). (1898) *Civil law.* The doctrine that a court should give great weight to a rule of law that is accepted and applied in a long line of cases, and should not overrule or modify its own decisions unless clear error is shown and injustice will arise from continuation of a particular rule of law. • Civil-law courts are not bound by the common-law doctrine of stare decisis. But they do recognize the doctrine of *jurisprudence constante*, which is similar to stare decisis, one exception being that *jurisprudence constante* does not command strict adherence to a legal principle applied on one occasion in the past. Cf. STARE DECISIS.

▸ **jurisprudence of conceptions.** (1908) The extension of a maxim or definition, usu. to a logical extreme, with relentless disregard for the consequences. • The phrase appears to have been invented by Roscoe Pound. See *Mechanical Jurisprudence*, 8 Colum. L. Rev. 605, 608 (1908).

▸ **jurisprudence of difference.** An approach to law that focuses on social disparities and variations, such as those reflecting feminist, gay, lesbian, transsexual, religious, and other cultural viewpoints.

> "What has been the relation of the new jurisprudence of difference to lawyers' professionalism, the self-identity of lawyers as a professional group? In an important sense the effects have been largely negative. The aim of these new movements in thought about law has been, in part, to undermine lawyers' satisfaction with their familiar practices and to declare the unacceptable moral arbitrariness of these practices." Roger Cotterrell, *The Politics of Jurisprudence: A Critical Introduction to Legal Philosophy* 234 (2d ed. 2003).

▸ **municipal jurisprudence.** The scholarly study of the internal law of a definite political community or state. — Also termed *civil jurisprudence*. Cf. *international jurisprudence*.

▸ **normative jurisprudence.** See NATURAL LAW (2).

▸ **outsider jurisprudence.** (1989) A branch of jurisprudence that examines the ways in which law is thought to be structured so as to promote the interests of white males and to exclude females and persons of color. Cf. *feminist jurisprudence*.

▸ **particular jurisprudence.** (18c) The scholarly study of the legal system within one specific jurisdiction, the focus being on the fundamental assumptions of that system only.

▸ **positivist jurisprudence.** (1931) A theory that denies validity to any law that is not derived from or sanctioned by a sovereign or some other determinate source. — Also termed *positivistic jurisprudence.*

▸ **psychological jurisprudence. 1.** The study of effects of the law on the minds of those on whom it operates. **2.** The use of psychology and psychoanalysis as a means of predicting the behavior of legal decision-makers, esp. judges.

▸ **sociological jurisprudence.** (1906) A philosophical approach to law stressing the actual social effects of legal institutions, doctrines, and practices. • This influential approach was started by Roscoe Pound in 1906 and became a precursor to legal realism. — Also termed *sociology of law.* See LEGAL REALISM.

▸ **systematic jurisprudence.** See *expository jurisprudence.*

▸ **therapeutic jurisprudence.** (1989) The study of the effects of law and the legal system on the behavior, emotions, and mental health of people; esp., a multidisciplinary examination of how law and mental health interact. • This discipline originated in the late 1980s as an academic approach to mental-health law.

jurisprudence *constante.* See JURISPRUDENCE.

jurisprudence of conceptions. See JURISPRUDENCE.

jurisprudence of difference. See JURISPRUDENCE.

jurisprudent, *n.* (17c) A person learned in the law; a specialist in jurisprudence. — Also termed *jurisprude.*

jurisprudentia generalis. See *general jurisprudence* (1) under JURISPRUDENCE.

jurisprudential (joor-is-proo-**den**-shəl), *adj.* (18c) Of, relating to, or involving jurisprudence.

jurisprudentia naturalis. See JURISPRUDENCE (1).

jurisprudentia universalis. See *general jurisprudence* (2) under JURISPRUDENCE.

juris publici. See JURIS.

jurist. (15c) **1.** Someone who has thorough knowledge of the law; esp., a judge or an eminent legal scholar. — Also termed *legist.* **2.** JURISPRUDENT.

juristic, *adj.* (1831) **1.** Of, relating to, or involving a jurist <juristic literature>. **2.** Of, relating to, or involving law <a corporation is a typical example of a juristic person>. — Also termed *juristical.*

juristic act. See *act in the law* under ACT (2).

juristic concept. An undefined category of legal phenomena systematized and expounded by jurists so as to become part of the body of authoritative grounds or guides to decision in support of the operation of the judicial process.—Also termed *juristic conception.* Cf. LEGAL CONCEPT.

juristic person. See *artificial person* under PERSON (3).

juristocracy (joor-is-**tok**-rə-see), *n.* (1923) Government by the judiciary; esp., a judicial system in which judicial activists are prevalent. — Also termed *jurocracy; judiocracy.* See JUDICIAL ACTIVISM. — **juristocratic,** *adj.*

Juris utriusque Doctor. See J.U.D.

jurocracy. See JURISTOCRACY.

juror (**joor**-ər *also* **joor**-or). (14c) A member of a jury; a person serving on a jury panel. — Also formerly termed *layperson.*

▸ **grand juror.** (16c) A person serving on a grand jury.

▸ **petit juror** (**pet**-ee). (18c) A trial juror, as opposed to a grand juror.

▸ **presiding juror.** (1982) The juror who chairs the jury during deliberations and speaks for the jury in court by announcing the verdict. • The presiding juror is usu. elected by the jury at the start of deliberations. — Also termed *foreman; foreperson;*(in Scots law) *jury chancellor.*

▸ **stealth juror.** (1997) A juror, esp. one in a high-profile case, who deliberately fails to disclose a relevant bias in order to qualify as a juror and bases a decision on that bias rather than on the facts and law. • Although a stealth juror may be fined or prosecuted for perjury based on a lie or omission, the usual penalty is only removal from the jury.

▸ **tales-juror** (**tay**-leez- *or* **taylz**-joor-ər). See TALESMAN.

juror misconduct. See MISCONDUCT (1).

jury, *n.* (15c) A group of persons selected according to law and given the power to decide questions of fact and return a verdict in the case submitted to them. • In certain contexts, *jury* embraces any fact-trier, including an arbitrator or a trial judge sitting in a nonjury proceeding. — Also termed *empaneled jury; impaneled jury.*

▸ **advisory jury.** (1892) A jury empaneled to hear a case when the parties have no right to a jury trial. *See* Fed. R. Civ. P. 39(c). • The judge may accept or reject the advisory jury's verdict.

▸ **anonymous jury.** (1979) *Criminal law.* A jury whose identities cannot be disclosed because, for example, the individual jurors may be subjected to intimidation or violence. • Although anonymous juries are allowed in federal court, some states do not permit them.

▸ **blue-ribbon jury.** (1940) A jury consisting of jurors who are selected for their special qualities, such as advanced education or special training, sometimes used in a complex civil case (usu. by stipulation of the parties) and sometimes also for a grand jury (esp. one investigating governmental corruption). • A blue-ribbon jury is not allowed in criminal trials because it would violate the defendant's right to trial by a jury of peers. An even more elite group of jurors, involving specialists in a technical field, is called a *blue-blue-ribbon jury.*

▸ **common jury.** See *petit jury.*

▸ **coroner's jury.** (17c) A jury summoned by a coroner to investigate the cause of death.

▸ **deadlocked jury.** See *hung jury.*

▸ **death-qualified jury.** (1961) *Criminal law.* A jury that is fit to decide a case involving the death penalty because the jurors have no absolute ideological bias against capital punishment. Cf. *life-qualified jury.*

▸ **dual juries.** Two separately impaneled juries for two (or two sets of) defendants in a single trial — some evidence being common to both defendants, and some not — in which each jury renders a separate verdict.

▸ **fair and impartial jury.** See *impartial jury.*

▸ **foreign jury.** (17c) A jury obtained from a jurisdiction other than that in which the case is brought.

▸ **good jury.** See *special jury.*

▸ **grand jury.** See GRAND JURY.

▸ **homage jury.** (18c) *Hist.* A jury in a court baron, consisting of tenants who made homage to the lord. See COURT BARON.

▸ **hung jury.** (1854) A jury that cannot reach a verdict by the required voting margin. — Also termed *deadlocked jury.*

▸ **impartial jury.** (17c) A jury that has no opinion about the case at the start of the trial and that bases its verdict on competent legal evidence. — Also termed *fair and impartial jury.*

▸ **inquest jury.** (1873) A jury summoned from a particular district to appear before a sheriff, coroner, or other ministerial officer and inquire about the facts concerning a death. See INQUEST (4). — Also termed *jury of inquest.*

▸ **jury *de medietate linguae*** (dee mee-dee-ə-**tay**-tee **ling**-gwee). [Latin "jury of halfness of language"] (18c) *Hist.* A jury made up of half natives and half aliens, allowed when one of the parties is an alien.

▸ **jury of indictment.** See GRAND JURY.

▸ **jury of inquest.** See *inquest jury.*

▸ **jury of matrons.** (17c) *Hist.* A jury of "discreet and lawful women" impaneled to try a question of pregnancy, as when a woman sentenced to death pleads, in stay of execution, that she is pregnant.

▸ **jury of the vicinage** (**vis**-ə-nij). (17c) **1.** At common law, a jury from the county where the crime occurred. **2.** A jury from the county where the court is held. See VICINAGE.

▸ **life-qualified jury.** (1983) *Criminal law.* In a case involving a capital crime, a jury selected from a venire from which the judge has excluded anyone unable or unwilling to consider a sentence of life imprisonment, instead of the death penalty, if the defendant is found guilty. Cf. *death-qualified jury.*

▸ **mixed jury.** (1878) A jury composed of both men and women or persons of different races.

▸ **petit jury** (**pet**-ee). (15c) A jury (usu. consisting of 6 or 12 persons) summoned and empaneled in the trial of a specific case. — Also termed *petty jury*; *trial jury*; *common jury*; *traverse jury.* Cf. GRAND JURY.

▸ **police jury.** See POLICE JURY.

▸ **presenting jury.** See GRAND JURY.

▸ **rogue jury.** (1975) A jury that ignores the law and evidence in reaching a capricious verdict. • Rogue juries include those that base their verdicts on unrevealed, deeply held prejudices; on undue sympathy or antipathy toward a party; or on chance (as by tossing a coin). The verdicts often result in inappropriate awards, punishments, convictions, or acquittals. Unlike jury nullification, a rogue jury's verdict is not based on a desire to achieve a just, fair, or moral outcome. Cf. JURY NULLIFICATION.

▸ **shadow jury.** (1974) A group of mock jurors paid to observe a trial and report their reactions to a jury consultant hired by one of the litigants. • The shadow jurors, who are matched as closely as possible to the real jurors, provide counsel with information about the jury's likely reactions to the trial. — Also termed *phantom jury.*

▸ **sheriff's jury.** (18c) *Hist.* A jury selected and summoned by a sheriff to hold inquests for various purposes, such as assessing damages in an action in which the defendant makes no defense or ascertaining the mental condition of an alleged lunatic.

▸ **special jury.** (17c) **1.** A jury chosen from a panel that is drawn specifically for that case. • Such a jury is usu. empaneled at a party's request in an unusually important or complicated case. — Also termed *struck jury.* See STRIKING A JURY. **2.** At common law, a jury composed of persons above the rank of ordinary freeholders, usu. summoned to try more important questions than those heard by ordinary juries. — Also termed *good jury.*

▸ **struck jury.** (18c) **1.** A jury selected by allowing the parties to alternate in striking from a list any person whom a given party does not wish to have on the jury, until the number is reduced to the appropriate number (traditionally 12). See STRIKING A JURY. **2.** See *special jury* (1).

▸ **traverse jury.** See *petit jury.*

▸ **trial jury.** See *petit jury.*

jury address. See JURY SPEECH.

jury box. (1826) The enclosed part of a courtroom where the jury sits. — Also spelled *jury-box.*

jury challenge. See CHALLENGE (2).

jury chancellor. See *presiding juror* under JUROR.

jury charge. (1883) **1.** JURY INSTRUCTION. **2.** A set of jury instructions. — Often shortened to *charge.*

jury commissioner. See COMMISSIONER.

jury direction. See JURY INSTRUCTION.

jury duty. (1829) **1.** The obligation to serve on a jury. **2.** Actual service on a jury. **3.** A period of time spent or to be spent as a member of a jury in court. — Also termed *jury service.*

jury fee. See FEE (1).

jury-fixing. (1887) The act or an instance of illegally procuring the cooperation of one or more jurors who actually influence the outcome of the trial. — Also termed *fixing a jury.* Cf. EMBRACERY; JURY-PACKING. — **jury-fixer,** *n.*

jury instruction. (*usu. pl.*) (1943) A direction or guideline that a judge gives a jury concerning the law of the case. — Often shortened to *instruction.* — Also termed *jury charge*; *charge*; *jury direction*; *direction.*

▸ **acquit-first instruction.** (1994) *Criminal procedure.* A jury instruction requiring jurors to consider a lesser charge only after acquitting the defendant of the more serious charge. • Generally speaking, a deadlocked jury may not consider a lesser offense. — Also termed *acquittal-first instruction*; *sequential instruction.*

▸ **additional instruction.** (1821) A jury charge, beyond the original instructions, that is usu. given in response to the jury's question about the evidence or some point of law. — Also termed *additional direction*; *further instruction*; *further direction.*

▸ **adverse-inference instruction.** (1973) *Criminal procedure.* A court's instruction to the jury that a negative conclusion may be drawn against a party based on evidence that was or was not produced at trial, as when a crucial witness (other than the defendant) did not testify, crucial evidence was not presented, or the defendant refused to take a breath test to measure blood alcohol content after being stopped for reckless or erratic driving. — Also termed *adverse-inference charge*. Cf. *no-adverse-inference instruction*.

▸ **affirmative converse instruction.** (1966) An instruction presenting a hypothetical that, if true, commands a verdict in favor of the defendant. • An affirmative converse instruction usu. begins with language such as "your verdict must be for the defendant if you believe ...." — Also termed *affirmative converse direction*.

▸ **affirmative instruction.** (1835) An instruction that removes an issue from the jury's consideration, such as an instruction that whatever the evidence, the defendant cannot be convicted under the indictment count to which the charge is directed. — Also termed *affirmative charge; affirmative direction*.

▸ **argumentative instruction.** (1888) An instruction that assumes facts not in evidence, that singles out or unduly emphasizes a particular issue, theory, or defense, or that otherwise invades the jury's province regarding the weight, probative value, or sufficiency of the evidence. — Also termed *argumentative direction*.

▸ **binding instruction.** See *mandatory instruction*.

▸ **cautionary instruction.** (1881) **1.** A judge's instruction to the jurors to disregard certain evidence or consider it for specific purposes only. **2.** A judge's instruction for the jury not to be influenced by outside factors and not to talk to anyone about the case while the trial is in progress. — Also termed *cautionary direction; prophylactic jury instruction*.

▸ **conscious-avoidance instruction.** See *willful-blindness instruction*.

▸ **curative instruction.** (1890) A court's instruction to the jury to disregard something that should not have happened in court, such as an improper outburst, misconduct by a lawyer, or testimony that flouts an order in limine. — Also termed *curative direction*.

▸ **deliberate-indifference instruction.** See JEWELL INSTRUCTION.

▸ **disparaging instruction.** (1907) A jury charge that discredits or defames a party to a lawsuit. — Also termed *disparaging direction*.

▸ **eyewitness-identification instruction.** See *identification instruction*.

▸ **formula instruction.** (1927) A jury charge derived from a standardized statement of the law on which the jury must base its verdict. — Also termed *formula direction*.

▸ **further instruction.** See *additional instruction*.

▸ **general instruction.** Any jury instruction that does not present a question or issue to be answered. — Also termed *general direction*.

▸ **identification instruction.** (1964) An instruction cautioning jurors about the reliability of testimony as to a perpetrator's appearance. — Also termed *eyewitness-identification instruction; mistaken-identification instruction; identification direction; eyewitness-identification direction; mistaken-identification direction*.

▸ ***Jewell* instruction.** See JEWELL INSTRUCTION.

▸ **mandatory instruction.** (1895) An instruction requiring a jury to find for one party and against the other if the jury determines that, based on a preponderance of the evidence, a given set of facts exists. — Also termed *binding instruction; mandatory direction; binding direction*.

▸ **mistaken-identification instruction.** See *identification instruction*.

▸ **model jury instruction.** (1964) A form jury charge usu. approved by a state bar association or similar group regarding matters arising in a typical case. • Courts usu. accept model jury instructions as authoritative. — Also termed *pattern jury instruction; pattern jury charge; model jury charge; model jury direction; pattern jury direction*.

▸ **no-adverse-inference instruction.** (1978) *Criminal law*. A jury instruction, granted at the request of the defense, that no negative conclusions are to be drawn from the fact that the defendant has not testified at trial. — Also termed *no-adverse-inference charge*. Cf. *adverse-inference instruction*.

▸ **ostrich instruction.** (1966) *Slang*. See *willful-blindness instruction*.

▸ **pattern jury instruction.** See *model jury instruction*.

▸ **peremptory instruction.** (1829) A court's explicit direction that a jury must obey, such as an instruction to return a verdict for a particular party. — Also termed *peremptory direction*. See *directed verdict* under VERDICT (1).

▸ **sequential instruction.** (1991) See *acquit-first instruction*.

▸ **single-juror instruction.** (1980) An instruction stating that if any juror is not reasonably satisfied with the plaintiff's evidence, then the jury cannot render a verdict for the plaintiff. — Also termed *single-juror direction*.

▸ **special instruction.** (1807) An instruction on some particular point or question involved in the case, usu. in response to counsel's request for such an instruction. — Also termed *special charge; special direction*.

▸ **standard instruction.** (1914) A jury instruction that has been regularly used in a given jurisdiction. — Also termed *standard direction*.

▸ **theory-of-defense instruction.** (1958) A jury instruction whose purpose is to explain a defense theory that is not clearly or adequately explained by pattern or standard jury instructions.

▸ **willful-blindness instruction.** (1980) An instruction that an otherwise culpable defendant may be held accountable for a crime if the defendant deliberately avoided finding out about the crime. — Also termed *conscious-avoidance instruction; willful-blindness direction; conscious-avoidance direction; ostrich instruction; ostrich direction*. Cf. JEWELL INSTRUCTION.

juryless, *adj.* (1808) (Of a court or proceeding) having no jury.

jury list. (1801) **1.** A roster of all the people within a given jurisdiction who possess the necessary legal qualifications for jury duty. **2.** A list of people summoned for jury selection.

juryman. *Archaic.* See JUROR.

jury nullification. (1982) A jury's knowing and deliberate rejection of the evidence or refusal to apply the law either because the jury wants to send a message about some social issue that is larger than the case itself or because the result dictated by law is contrary to the jury's sense of justice, morality, or fairness. Cf. *verdict contrary to law* under VERDICT (1); *rogue jury* under JURY.

jury of indictment. See GRAND JURY.

jury-packing. (1887) The act or an instance of contriving to have a jury composed of persons who are predisposed toward one side or the other. — Also termed *packing a jury.* Cf. EMBRACERY; JURY-FIXING.

jury panel. See VENIRE (1).

jury pardon. (1974) A rule that permits a jury to convict a defendant of a lesser offense than the offense charged if sufficient evidence exists to convict the defendant of either offense.

jury pool. See VENIRE (1).

jury process. (18c) **1.** The procedure by which jurors are summoned and their attendance is enforced. **2.** The papers served on or mailed to potential jurors to compel their attendance.

jury question. (18c) **1.** An issue of fact that a jury decides. See QUESTION OF FACT. **2.** A special question that a court may ask a jury that will deliver a special verdict. See *special interrogatory* under INTERROGATORY.

jury sequestration. See SEQUESTRATION (8).

jury service. See JURY DUTY.

jury shuffle. (1974) *Texas law.* A process for rearranging a venire whereby the cards with the veniremembers' names on them are shuffled so that the veniremembers will be seated in a different order. • The prosecution and the defense may each request a jury shuffle once before voir dire begins. No reason for the request need be given. After voir dire begins, neither party may request a shuffle.

jury speech. (1859) The opening or closing statement of counsel in a jury trial. See OPENING STATEMENT; CLOSING ARGUMENT. — Also termed *jury address.*

jury summation. See CLOSING ARGUMENT.

jury-tampering. See EMBRACERY.

jury trial. See TRIAL.

jury verdict form. (1952) A document announcing the judgment or verdict of the jury.

jury waiver. See WAIVER (3).

jury wheel. (1873) A physical device or electronic system used for storing and randomly selecting names of potential jurors.

jurywoman. (1805) *Archaic.* A female juror; esp., a member of a jury of matrons. See *jury of matrons* under JURY.

jus (jəs *also* joos *or* yoos), *n.* [Latin "law, right"] **1.** Law in the abstract. **2.** A system of law. **3.** A legal right, power, or principle. **4.** *Roman law.* Man-made law. • The term usu. refers to a right rather than a statute. — Abbr. J. — Also spelled *ius.* Cf. FAS. Pl. ***jura*** (**joor**-ə *also* **yoor**-ə).

> "*Ius,* when used in a general sense, answers to our word *Law* in its widest acceptation. It denotes, not one particular law nor collection of laws, but the entire body of principles, rules, and statutes, whether written or unwritten, by which the public and the private rights, the duties and the obligations of men, as members of a community, are defined, inculcated, protected and enforced." William Ramsay, *A Manual of Roman Antiquities* 285–86 (Rodolfo Lanciani ed., 15th ed. 1894).

jus abstinendi (jəs ab-stə-**nen**-dɪ), *n.* [Law Latin "right of abstaining"] *Roman & civil law.* The right of an heir to renounce or decline an inheritance, as when it would require taking on debt.

jus abutendi (jəs ab-yə-**ten**-dɪ), *n.* [Latin "right of abusing"] (18c) *Roman & civil law.* The right to make full use of property, even to the extent of wasting or destroying it. Cf. JUS UTENDI.

> "In a world of discovery and colonizing activity, in a society of pioneers engaged in discovering, appropriating and exploiting the resources of nature, this interest [conservation] seemed negligible. In the crowded world of today the law is constantly taking account of it and the *jus abutendi* as an incident of ownership is becoming obsolete." Roscoe Pound, *The Spirit of the Common Law* 209 (1921).

jus accrescendi (jəs ak-rə-**sen**-dɪ), *n.* [Latin "right of accretion"] (17c) A right of accrual; esp., the right of survivorship that a joint tenant enjoys. See RIGHT OF SURVIVORSHIP. Cf. JUS NON DECRESCENDI.

jus actionis (jəs ak-shee-**oh**-nis). [Latin] *Scots law.* A right of action.

jus actus (jəs **ak**-təs). [Latin] *Roman law.* A rural servitude giving a person the right of passage for a carriage or cattle. See ACTUS (4).

jus ad bellum. [Latin "right to war"] (1916) Criteria to be considered before deciding whether engaging in a war is just. See BELLUM JUSTUM; JUS BELLI. Cf. JUS IN BELLO.

jus administrationes (jəs ad-mi-ni-stray-shee-**oh**-neez). [Latin] *Scots law. Hist.* The outmoded right by which a husband had unfettered control of his wife's heritable property.

jus ad rem (jəs ad rem), *n.* [Law Latin "right to a thing"] (17c) A right in specific property arising from another person's duty and valid only against that person; an inchoate or incomplete right to a thing. Cf. JUS IN RE.

jus aedilium (jəs ee-**dil**-ee-əm). [Latin "law of the aediles"] *Roman law.* The body of law developed through the edicts of aediles. — Also termed *jus aedilicium* (jəs ee-dɪ-**lish**-ee-əm). See AEDILE; JUS HONORARIUM.

Jus Aelianum (jəs ee-lee-**ay**-nəm). [Latin] *Roman law.* A manual of laws drawn up in the second century B.C. by the consul Sextus Aelius, consisting of three parts: (1) the laws of the Twelve Tables; (2) a commentary on them; and (3) the forms of procedure. See TWELVE TABLES.

jus aequum (jəs **ee**-kwəm). [Latin "law that is equal or fair"] (17c) *Roman law.* Law characterized by equity, flexibility, and adaptation to the circumstances of a particular case. Cf. JUS STRICTUM.

jus aesneciae (jəs ees-**neesh**-ee-ee). [Latin] *Hist.* The right of primogeniture. — Also spelled *esneciae.*

jus agendi (jəs ə-**jen**-dɪ). [Latin] (17c) *Scots law.* One's power to take action to pursue one's rights.

jus albanagii (jəs al-bə-**nay**-jee-ɪ), *n.* [Law Latin "confiscating the goods of aliens"] See DROIT D'AUBAINE.

jus albinatus (jəs al-bi-**nay**-təs), *n.* [Law Latin "right of alien confiscation"] See DROIT D'AUBAINE.

jus angariae (jəs ang-**gair**-ee-ee), *n.* [Latin "right of angary"] See ANGARY.

jus antiquum (jəs an-**tɪ**-kwəm). [Latin] (17c) *Roman law.* The old law. — Also termed *jus vetus.* Cf. JUS NOVUM.

> "In the later Empire (which dates from the fourth century) there were two groups of sources of law: first, the 'jus vetus,' or 'jus' simply, i.e. the old traditional law, the development of which was completed in the classical period of Roman jurisprudence (in the course of the second and the beginning of the third century); secondly, the 'leges' or 'jus novum,' i.e. the later law which had sprung from imperial legislation. These two classes of law, 'jus' and 'leges,' mutually supplementing each other, constituted the whole body of law as it existed at the time, and, taken together, represented the result of the entire development of Roman law from the earliest times down to . . . the epoch of the later Empire." Rudolph Sohm, *The Institutes: A Textbook of the History and System of Roman Private Law* 116–17 (James Crawford Ledlie trans., 3d ed. 1907).

jus apparentiae (jəs ap-ə-**ren**-shee-ee). [Law Latin] (17c) *Scots law.* The right of apparency. • An heir who was open to a succession but not fully vested in title had the right of apparency, a right that allowed the heir to take certain actions on behalf of the estate, such as defending the ancestor's title.

jus aquaeductus (jəs ak-wə-**dək**-təs), *n.* [Latin] *Roman & civil law.* A servitude that gives a landowner the right to conduct water from another's land through pipes or channels.

jus aquaehaustus (jəs **ak**-wee **haws**-təs). [Latin] *Roman law.* See AQUAEHAUSTUS.

jus asyli (jəs ə-**sɪ**-lɪ). [Latin] *Hist.* Right of asylum.

jus aucupandi (jəs awk-yuu-**pan**-dɪ). [Latin] *Scots law.* The right of catching birds; the right of fowling.

jus banci (jəs **ban**-sɪ), *n.* [Law Latin "right of bench"] (17c) *Hist.* The right or privilege of having an elevated and separate seat of judgment, formerly allowed only to the king's judges, who administered what was from then on called "high justice."

jus belli (jəs **bel**-ɪ), *n.* [Latin "law of war"] (17c) The law of nations as applied during wartime, defining in particular the rights and duties of the belligerent powers and of neutral countries.

jus bellum dicendi (jəs **bel**-əm di-**sen**-dɪ), *n.* [Latin] The right of proclaiming war.

jus canonicum (jəs kə-**non**-i-kəm), *n.* [Law Latin] See CANON LAW (1).

jus capiendi (jəs kap-ee-**en**-dɪ). [Latin "the right to take or receive"] *Roman law.* The right of taking property under a will.

jus civile (jəs si-**vɪ**-lee). [Latin] (16c) *Roman law.* The traditional law of the city of Rome, beginning with the Twelve Tables and developed by juristic interpretation. • It covered areas of law restricted to Roman citizens, such as the formalities of making a will. Over time, the *jus civile* was modified by, for example, the *jus honorarium* (which modified the requisites for a valid will) and the *jus sentium* (which modified the stipulation). The original *jus civile* was eventually absorbed into a general Roman law. See CIVIL LAW (1); JUS QUIRITIUM.

jus civitatis (jəs siv-i-**tay**-təs). [Latin] (17c) *Roman law.* The right of citizenship; the right of a Roman citizen.

jus cloacae (jəs kloh-**ay**-see), *n.* [Latin "right of sewer or drain"] *Civil law.* An easement consisting in the right of having a sewer or conducting surface water over or through the land of one's neighbor.

jus cogens (jəs **koh**-jenz), *n.* [Latin "compelling law"] (1895) **1.** *Int'l law.* A mandatory or peremptory norm of general international law accepted and recognized by the international community as a norm from which no derogation is permitted. • A peremptory norm can be modified only by a later norm that has the same character. Cf. JUS DISPOSITIVUM. **2.** *Civil law.* A mandatory rule of law that is not subject to the disposition of the parties, such as an absolute limitation on the legal capacity of minors below a certain age. — Also termed (in sense 2) *peremptory norm.*

jus commercii (jəs kə-**mər**-shee-ɪ), *n.* [Latin "right of commerce"] (17c) *Roman & civil law.* The right to make contracts, acquire and transfer property, and conduct business transactions.

jus commune (jəs kə-**myoo**-nee), *n.* (17c) **1.** *Roman & civil law.* The common or public law or right, as opposed to a law or right established for special purposes. Cf. JUS SINGULARE. **2.** The common law of England. See COMMON LAW (3). — Also termed (in senses 1 & 2) *lex communis.* See LEX COMMUNIS. **3.** The shared law of much of continental Western Europe during the Middle Ages, consisting of a blend of canon law and rediscovered Roman law.

> "[J]us commune is a phrase well known to the canonists. They use it to distinguish the general and ordinary law of the universal church both from any rules peculiar to this or that provincial church, and from those papal *privilegia* which are always giving rise to ecclesiastical litigation." 1 Frederick Pollock & Frederic W. Maitland, *History of English Law Before the Time of Edward I* 176 (2d ed. 1898).

jus compascuum (jəs kəm-**pas**-kyoo-əm), *n.* [Latin "the right to feed together"] (17c) *Hist.* The right of common pasture. Cf. COMMON (1).

jus condendum (jəs kən-**den**-dəm). [Latin] *Hist.* Law needing to be made.

jus conditum (jəs kən-**dɪt**-əm). [Latin] *Hist.* Established law.

jus connubii (jəs kə-**n[y]oo**-bee-ɪ), *n.* [Latin "right of marriage"] See CONNUBIUM.

jus coronae (jəs kə-**roh**-nee), *n.* [Latin "right of the Crown"] (17c) The right of succession to the English throne.

jus crediti (jəs **kred**-i-tɪ). [Latin "the right of credit"] (18c) *Roman & Scots law.* A creditor's right to a debt; a creditor's right to recover a debt through legal process. Cf. JUS EXIGENDI.

> "[T]he term is frequently used in contradistinction to a mere *spes*, or defeasible expectancy. This *jus crediti* is often of great importance; for although a person may not be entitled to be put in immediate possession of a subject, yet the obligation to deliver it to him at some future time creates in him a vested right, which forms part of his estate." William Bell, *Bell's Dictionary and Digest of the Law of Scotland* 620 (George Watson ed., 7th ed. 1890).

jus cudendae monetae (jəs kyoo-**den**-dee mə-**nee**-tee), *n.* [Law Latin] *Hist.* The right of coining money.

jus curialitatis (jəs kyoor-ee-al-ə-**tay**-tis), *n.* [Law Latin] *Hist.* The right of curtesy.

jus dare (jəs **dair**-ee), *vb.* [Latin] To give or make the law. • This is the function and prerogative of the legislature. Cf. JUS DICERE.

jus delatum (jəs di-**lay**-təm). [Law Latin] (17c) *Scots law.* A transferred right.

jus deliberandi (jəs di-lib-ə-**ran**-dɪ), *n.* [Latin "right of deliberating"] (18c) *Roman & civil law.* A right granted to an heir to take time to consider whether to accept or reject an inheritance. Cf. *tempus deliberandi* under TEMPUS.

jus denegandi (jəs den-i-**gan**-dɪ). [Latin] *Hist.* Right to refuse.

jus de non appellando (jəs dee non ap-ə-**lan**-doh). [Latin] (18c) *Hist.* The supreme judicial power.

jus detractus (jəs di-**trak**-təs). [Latin] *Hist.* Right of taking away.

jus devolutum (jəs dev-ə-**loo**-təm). [Law Latin "a devolved right"] (17c) *Scots law.* The right of the presbytery to appoint a minister to a vacant church if a patron failed to present a fit minister within six months of the vacancy. Cf. TANQUAM JURE DEVOLUTO.

jus dicere (jəs **dɪ**-sər-ee), *vb.* [Latin] *Hist.* To declare or decide the law. • This is the function and prerogative of the judiciary. Cf. JUS DARE.

jus disponendi (jəs dis-pə-**nen**-dɪ), *n.* [Latin "right of disposing"] (17c) The right to dispose of property; the power of alienation.

jus dispositivum (jəs dis-poz-ə-**tɪ**-vəm), *n.* [Latin "law subject to the disposition of the parties"] (1926) *Int'l law.* A norm that is created by the consent of participating countries, as by an international agreement, and is binding only on the countries that agree to be bound by it. Cf. JUS COGENS (1).

jus distrahendi (jəs dis-trə-**hen**-dɪ), *n.* [Latin "right of distraining"] The right to sell pledged goods upon default.

jus dividendi (jəs div-i-**den**-dɪ), *n.* [Latin "right of dividing"] The right to dispose of real property by will.

jus divinum (jəs di-**vɪ**-nəm). **1.** See DIVINE LAW. **2.** See NATURAL LAW.

jus domino proximum (jəs **dom**-ə-noh **prok**-sə-məm). [Law Latin] *Scots law.* A right nearly equal to that of absolute property; a feuholder's right. See FEU.

> "Jus domino proximum . . . . Such a right is enjoyed by one who holds lands in feu, for he is entitled to sell the subjects, or alter or use them in any way he thinks proper. And yet the property is not absolutely his — that is, he does not hold the property so absolutely as did the superior from whom he acquired, because the land is burdened with the feu-duty payable to the superior, and to this extent the absolute right of property is restricted. Similar to the right of a feuar under our law, was that of the *emphyteuta* under the civil law." John Trayner, *Trayner's Latin Maxims* 304–05 (4th ed. 1894).

jus duplicatum (jəs d[y]oo-pli-**kay**-təm). See DROIT-DROIT.

jus ecclesiasticum (jəs e-klee-z[h]ee-**as**-ti-kəm). [Law Latin] See ECCLESIASTICAL LAW.

jus edicendi (jəs ed-i-**sen**-dɪ *or* ee-di-). [Latin "right of decreeing"] *Roman law.* The right (esp. of the praetors) to issue edicts. See JUS PRAETORIUM.

> "High-ranking magistrates had the *ius edicendi*, the right to issue edicts, i.e. legally binding directives within their appropriate sphere of jurisdiction. The edicts of the praetors can be fairly said to have revolutionized Roman civil law in the late Republic, forming a body of law later described as the *ius honorarium* — 'the law laid down by the magistrates.'" Paul du Plessis, *Borkowski's Textbook on Roman Law* 33 (4th ed. 2010).

jus et consuetudo regni. [Latin] (1897) The law and custom of the realm.

jus et norma loquendi (jəs et **nor**-mə loh-**kwen**-dɪ). [Latin "the law and rule of speech"] Idiomatic language, including speech and pronunciation, as established by the custom of a particular country.

jus excludendi (jəs ek-skloo-**den**-dɪ). [Latin] *Hist.* Right of exclusion.

jus exigendi (jəs ek-si-**jen**-dɪ). [Latin] (18c) *Scots law.* A creditor's right to enforce immediate payment of a debt. Cf. JUS CREDITI.

> "For example, where a testator directs his testamentary trustees to pay a certain legacy, which he has unconditionally bequeathed to the legatee, six months after his (the testator's) death, the legacy vests on the death of the testator, and the legatee acquires then the *jus crediti*, but he cannot enforce payment of the legacy until after the expiry of the six months; he acquires the *jus exigendi* when the debt has become prestable." John Trayner, *Trayner's Latin Maxims* 305 (4th ed. 1894).

jus ex non scripto (jəs eks non **skrip**-toh). See *unwritten law* under LAW.

jus falcandi (jəs fal-**kan**-dɪ), *n.* [Latin] *Hist.* The right of mowing or cutting.

jus fetiale (jəs fee-shee-**ay**-lee), *n.* [Latin] (1877) **1.** FETIAL LAW. **2.** The law of negotiation and diplomacy. • This phrase captured the classical notion of international law. — Also spelled *jus feciale.*

jus fiduciarium (jəs fi-d[y]oo-shee-**air**-əm), *n.* [Latin] (18c) *Civil law.* A right in trust. Cf. JUS LEGITIMUM.

jus fluminum (jəs **floo**-mə-nəm), *n.* [Latin] *Civil law.* The right to use rivers.

jus fodiendi (jəs foh-dee-**en**-dɪ), *n.* [Latin] *Civil law.* The right to dig on another's land.

jus fruendi (jəs froo-**en**-dɪ), *n.* [Latin "right of enjoying"] (18c) *Roman & civil law.* The right to use and enjoy another's property without damaging or diminishing it. See USUFRUCT.

jus futurum (jəs fyoo-**t[y]oor**-əm), *n.* [Latin "future right"] *Civil law.* A right that has not fully vested; an inchoate or expectant right.

jus gentium (jəs **jen**-shee-əm). [Latin "law of nations"] (16c) **1.** INTERNATIONAL LAW. **2.** *Roman law.* The body of law, taken to be common to all civilized peoples, and applied in dealing with the relations between Roman citizens and foreigners. — Also termed *jus inter gentes.*

> "The early Roman law (the *jus civile*) applied only to Roman citizens. It was formalistic and hard and reflected the status of a small, unsophisticated society rooted in the soil. It was totally unable to provide a relevant background for an expanding, developing nation. This need was served by the creation and progressive augmentation of the *jus gentium*. This provided simplified rules to govern the relations between foreigners, and between foreigners and citizens. . . . The progressive rules of the *jus gentium* gradually overrode the narrow *jus civile* until the latter system ceased to exist. Thus, the *jus gentium* became the common law of the Roman Empire and was deemed to be of universal application." Malcolm N. Shaw, *International Law* 15 (4th ed. 1997).

jus gentium privatum (jəs **jen**-shee-əm prɪ-**vay**-təm). See *private international law* under INTERNATIONAL LAW.

jus gentium publicum (jəs **jen**-shee-əm **pəb**-li-kəm). See INTERNATIONAL LAW.

jus gladii (jəs **glad**-ee-ɪ). [Latin "right of the sword"] (16c) *Roman law.* The executory power of the law, esp. for provincial governors; the power or right to inflict the death penalty. • This term took on a similar meaning under English law. — Also termed *potestas gladii.*

> "And the prosecution of these offences is always at the suit and in the name of the king, in whom, by the texture of our constitution, the *jus gladii*, or executory power of the law, entirely resides." 4 William Blackstone, *Commentaries on the Laws of England* 177 (1765).

jus habendi (jəs hə-**ben**-dɪ), *n.* [Latin] (17c) *Civil law.* The right to have a thing; the right to be put in actual possession of property.

jus haereditatis (jəs hə-red-ə-**tay**-tis), *n.* [Latin] (17c) *Civil law.* The right of inheritance.

jus hauriendi (jəs haw-ree-**en**-dɪ), *n.* [Latin] *Civil law.* The right of drawing water.

jus honorarium (jəs [h]on-ə-**rair**-ee-əm). [Latin "magisterial law"] (17c) *Roman law.* The body of law established by the edicts of magistrates, esp. the praetors (*jus praetorium*) and the aediles (*jus aedilium*). • In the Roman Republic, the term sometimes referred collectively to all the proclamations of magistrates of the Roman Republic, such as the consuls, praetors, aediles, quaestors, censors, provincial governors, and pontifices. Although these magistrates were not legislators, they were entitled and indeed bound to declare by edict how they proposed to administer justice, and their edicts were a supplementary source of law. — Also termed *edicta magistratuum.*

jus honorum (jəs [h]ə-**nor**-əm). [Latin] (17c) *Roman law.* The right of a citizen to hold public office, whether civil, military, or sacred. Cf. JUS SUFFRAGII.

jus imaginis (jəs ə-**maj**-ə-nis). [Latin] (17c) *Roman law.* The right to use or display pictures or statues of ancestors. • The right was restricted to upper-class Roman citizens.

jus immunitatis (jəs i-myoo-nə-**tay**-tis), *n.* [Latin "law of immunity"] *Civil law.* Exemption from the burden of public office.

jus in bello. [Latin "law in waging war"] (1916) The criteria for determining whether the conduct of an ongoing war is just. See BELLUM JUSTUM; JUS BELLI. Cf. JUS AD BELLUM.

jus incognitum (jəs in-**kog**-nə-təm), *n.* [Latin] *Civil law.* An unknown or obsolete law.

jus incorporale (jəs in-kor-pə-**ray**-lee). [Latin] (17c) *Hist.* An incorporeal right. See INCORPOREAL.

jus individuum (jəs in-də-**vij**-oo-əm), *n.* [Latin] An individual or indivisible right; a right that cannot be divided.

jus in personam (jəs in pər-**soh**-nəm), *n.* [Latin "right against a person"] (1803) A right of action against a particular person to enforce that person's obligation. — Also termed *jura in personam.* See *right in personam* under RIGHT.

jus in re (jəs in ree), *n.* [Law Latin "right in or over a thing"] (17c) A right in property valid against anyone in the world; a complete and perfect right to a thing. — Also termed *jus in rem; jura in rem.* Cf. JUS AD REM.

jus in re aliena (jəs in ree ay-lee-**ee**-nə *or* al-ee-), *n.* [Latin] An easement or right in or over another's property; ENCUMBRANCE. — Also termed *right in re aliena.*

jus in rem (jəs in rem), *n.* [Latin "right to a thing"] See JUS IN RE.

jus in re propria (jəs in ree **proh**-pree-ə), *n.* [Latin] The right of enjoyment that is incident to full ownership of property; full ownership itself. — Also termed *right in re propria.*

jus inter gentes (jəs **in**-tər **jen**-teez), *n.* [Latin "law among nations"] See JUS GENTIUM.

jus Italicum (jəs ɪ-**tal**-ə-kəm). [Latin] (17c) *Roman law.* A privilege granted by the emperor to cities outside Italy, giving them the status of communities within Italy. • This privilege included the right to own land by quiritarian title.

jus itineris (jəs ɪ-**tin**-ə-ris). [Latin] *Roman law.* A rustic praedial servitude granting the right to pass over an adjoining property on foot or horseback.

jusjurandum (jəs-juu-**ran**-dəm), *n.* [Latin] An oath. See JURAMENTUM.

jus Latii (jəs **lay**-shee-ɪ). [Latin] (17c) *Roman law.* Rights granted to a citizen of a Roman colony. • The colonial citizen's status was midway between *peregrine* and full citizen of Rome. — Also termed *jus Latium.*

jus legationis (jəs li-gay-shee-**oh**-nis). [Latin] *Hist.* Law of legation.

jus legitimum (jəs lə-**jit**-ə-məm), *n.* [Latin] (18c) *Civil law.* A right enforceable in law. Cf. JUS FIDUCIARIUM.

jus liberorum (jəs lib-ə-**ror**-əm). [Latin "right of children"] (17c) *Roman law.* A privilege conferred on a parent who has several children; esp., the immunity from compulsory guardianship (*tutela*) given to a woman with three or more children. — Also termed *jus trium liberorum.*

jus liquidissimum (jəs lik-wi-**dis**-i-məm). [Latin] (1838) *Maritime law.* The principle that a salvager is entitled to a reward for saving life or property imperiled at sea.

jus mariti (jəs mah-**ree**-tɪ *or* mə-**rɪ**-tɪ). [Law Latin] (17c) *Hist. Scots law.* The outmoded right under which a husband acquired ownership of all his wife's movable property. • The husband had a right of administration, or power of management, not only of the movable estate but also of the wife's heritable estate, so that all her deeds required his consent. An 1881 statute abolished the *jus mariti* for marriages contracted after the statute took effect, as well as the right of administration for the income and produce of the wife's heritable estate in such marriages.

jus merae facultatis (jəs **meer**-ee fak-əl-**tay**-tis). [Law Latin] *Hist.* A right of mere power; a right of power merely to act.

jus merum (jəs **meer**-əm). See MERE RIGHT.

jus moribus constitutum (jəs **mor**-ə-bəs kon-stə-**t[y]oo**-təm). [Latin] See *unwritten law* under LAW.

jus naturae (jəs nə-**t[y]oor**-ee). [Latin] See NATURAL LAW.

jus naturale (jəs nach-ə-**ray**-lee). [Latin] See NATURAL LAW.

jus navigandi (jəs nav-ə-**gan**-dɪ), *n.* [Latin] (17c) *Civil law.* The right of navigation; the right of commerce by sea.

jus necessitatis (jəs nə-ses-i-**tay**-tis), *n.* [Latin] A person's right to do what is required for which no threat of legal punishment is a dissuasion. • This idea implicates the proverb that necessity knows no law (*necessitas non habet legem*), so that an act that would be objectively understood as necessary is not wrongful even if done with full and deliberate intention.

jus nobilius (jəs noh-**bil**-ee-əs). [Law Latin] (17c) *Hist.* A superior right.

jus non decrescendi (jəs non dee-kre-**sen**-dɪ). [Law Latin] (17c) *Scots law.* The right of not suffering diminution. Cf. JUS ACCRESCENDI.

jus non sacrum (jəs non **say**-krəm). [Latin "nonsacred law"] *Hist.* The body of law regulating the duties of a civil magistrate in preserving the public order. Cf. JUS SACRUM.

jus non scriptum (jəs non **skrip**-təm). See *unwritten law* under LAW.

jus novum (jəs **noh**-vəm). [Latin] (17c) *Roman law.* The new law; the law of the later Roman Empire. — Also termed *leges.* See LEX. Cf. JUS ANTIQUUM.

jus obligationis (jəs ob-li-gay-shee-**oh**-nis). [Law Latin "a right of obligation"] *Hist.* A personal right. See JUS AD REM.

jus offerendi (jəs ahf- *or* awf-ə-**ren**-dɪ). [Latin] *Roman law.* The right of subrogation; the right to succeed to a senior creditor's lien and priority upon tendering the amount due to that creditor. — Also termed *jus offerendae pecuniae.*

jus oneris ferendi (jəs **on**-ə-ris fə-**ren**-dɪ). [Latin] *Roman law.* An urban praedial servitude granting the right for one's own house to be supported by a neighbor's. • The servitude was exceptional in requiring a positive duty of the servient owner.

jus pascendi (jəs pə-**sen**-dɪ). See *servitus pascendi* under SERVITUS.

jus patronatus (jəs pa-trə-**nay**-təs), *n.* [Latin] (16c) *Eccles. law.* The right of patronage; the right to present a clerk to a benefice.

jus persequendi in judicio quod sibi debetur (jəs pər-sə-**kwen**-dɪ in joo-**dish**-ee-oh kwod **sib**-ɪ **deb**-ə-tər). [Latin] *Roman law.* The right of suing before a court for that which is due to us. • The phrase is Justinian's definition of an action.

jus personarum (jəs pər-sə-**nair**-əm), *n.* [Latin "law of persons"] (17c) *Civil law.* The law governing the rights of persons having special relations with one another (such as parents and children or guardians and wards) or having limited rights (such as aliens or incompetent persons). See LAW OF PERSONS. Cf. JUS RERUM.

jus pignoris (jəs **pig**-nə-ris). [Latin "the right of pledge"] (18c) *Roman law.* A creditor's right in the property that a debtor pledges to secure a debt.

jus poenitendi (jəs pen-i-**ten**-dɪ), *n.* [Latin] The right to rescind or revoke an executory contract when the other party defaults.

jus portus (jəs **por**-təs), *n.* [Latin] *Civil & maritime law.* The right of port or harbor.

jus positivum (jəs poz-i-**tiv**-əm). See POSITIVE LAW.

jus possessionis (jəs pə-zes[h]-ee-**oh**-nis), *n.* [Latin] (17c) *Civil law.* A right of which possession is the source or title; a possessor's right to continue in possession. Cf. JUS PROPRIETATIS.

jus possidendi (jəs pos-ə-**den**-dɪ), *n.* [Latin] (17c) *Civil law.* A person's right to acquire or to retain possession; an owner's right to possess.

jus post bellum (jəs pohst **bel**-əm). [Latin] *Hist.* Law after war.

jus postliminii (jəs pohst-lə-**min**-ee-ɪ). [Latin] See POSTLIMINIUM.

jus praeminens (jəs **pree**-mi-nenz). [Latin] *Hist.* Preeminent right.

jus praesens (jəs **pree**-senz *or* -zenz), *n.* [Latin "present right"] *Civil law.* A right that has been completely acquired; a vested right.

jus praetorium (jəs pri-**tor**-ee-əm). [Latin "law of the praetors"] (17c) *Roman law.* The body of law developed through the edicts of the praetors. • This was the mainspring of Republican reform. See PRAETOR; EDICTUM PRAETORIS; JUS HONORARIUM. — Also termed *praetorian law.*

> "[Remember] the great contribution which the *Jus praetorium* made to Roman equity. Papinian's famous definition of Praetorian Law assigns to it a threefold function: 'To give fuller effect to, to supplement, and to reform the *Jus civile* with a view to the public advantage.' That is the view of a great lawyer looking back upon the whole course of its development during some centuries, and summing up its characteristics in the light of the results actually achieved in the end. But it would be an entire mistake to believe that the early praetors attempted so ambitious a flight." James Mackintosh, *Roman Law in Modern Practice* 54–55 (1934).

jus praeventionis (jəs pree-ven-shee-**oh**-nis). [Law Latin "a right of preference"] (17c) *Scots law.* A court's jurisdictional superiority by virtue of being the first court to exercise its jurisdiction in a case.

jus precarium (jəs pri-**kair**-ee-əm), *n.* [Latin] (17c) *Civil law.* A right to a thing held for another, for which there was no remedy by legal action but only by entreaty or request.

jus presentationis (jəs prez-ən-tay-shee-**oh**-nis), *n.* [Latin] (17c) *Civil law.* The right to present a clerk to a church.

jus primae noctis (jəs **prɪ**-mee **nok**-tis). [Latin "right of first night"] See DROIT DU SEIGNEUR; MARCHET.

jus privatum (jəs prɪ-**vay**-təm), *n.* [Latin "private law"] (18c) **1.** *Roman & civil law.* Private law, consisting of all the branches of law that regulate the relations of citizens to one another, including family law, property, obligations, and testate and intestate succession. **2.** The right, title, or dominion of private ownership. See PRIVATE LAW. Cf. JUS PUBLICUM.

jus projiciendi (jəs prə-jish-ee-**en**-dɪ), *n.* [Latin] *Civil law.* A servitude granting the right to build a projection (such as a balcony) from one's house in the open space belonging to a neighbor.

jus proprietatis (jəs prə-prɪ-ə-**tay**-tis), *n.* [Latin] (17c) *Civil law.* A right in property based on ownership rather than actual possession. Cf. JUS POSSESSIONIS.

jus protectionis (jəs prə-tek-shee-**oh**-nis). [Latin] *Hist.* Right of protection.

jus protegendi (jəs proh-tə-**jen**-dɪ), *n.* [Latin] *Civil law.* A servitude granting the right to make the roof or tiling of one's house extend over a neighbor's house.

jus provocationis (jəs prov-ə-kay-shee-**oh**-nis). [Latin] *Roman law.* The right possessed by every Roman citizen to appeal to the people in their Comitia, or later the emperor, from the infliction of summary punishment by a magistrate (*coercitio*). • Modern romanists disagree about the precise meaning of this term. — Also termed *jus provocatio.*

jus publicum (jəs **pəb**-li-kəm), *n.* [Latin "public law"] (16c) **1.** *Roman & civil law.* Public law, consisting of constitutional law, administrative law, criminal law and procedure, and the law relating to sacred rites (*jus sacrum*). **2.** The right, title, or dominion of public ownership; esp., the government's right to own real property in trust for the public benefit. See PUBLIC LAW. Cf. JUS PRIVATUM.

jus puniendi (jəs pyoo-nee-**en**-dɪ). [Latin] *Hist.* Right to punish.

jus quaesitum (jəs kwi-**sɪ**-təm *or* -**zɪ**-təm), *n.* [Latin] (17c) *Civil law.* **1.** A right to ask or recover, as from one who is under an obligation. **2.** An acquired right.

jus quaesitum tertio (jəs kwi-**sɪ**-təm **tər**-shee-oh). [Law Latin] (17c) *Scots law.* A contractual right conferred on a third party. • A third-party right may be conferred on a specified individual or on an identifiable class of people.

> "Where, in a contract between two parties, a stipulation is introduced in favour of a third, who is not a contracting party, the right thus created is said to be *jus quaesitum tertio.* Such a right, generally speaking, cannot be recalled by the contracting parties, and the third party, so far as he is concerned, may require exhibition and implement of the contract." William Bell, *Bell's Dictionary and Digest of the Laws of Scotland* 622 (George Watson ed., 7th ed. 1890).

jus quiritium (jəs kwi-**rɪ**-shee-əm). [Latin] (17c) *Roman law.* The ancient, primitive law of the Romans before the development of the *jus praetorium* and the *jus gentium*; the original *jus civile.*

jus recuperandi (jəs ri-k[y]oo-pə-**ran**-dɪ), *n.* [Latin] (17c) *Civil law.* The right of recovering, esp. lands.

jus regale (jəs ri-**gay**-lee). [Law Latin] (17c) *Scots law.* A royal right; a sovereign's right.

jus regendi (jəs ri-**jen**-dɪ), *n.* [Law Latin] (17c) A proprietary right vested in a sovereign.

jus relictae (jəs ri-**lik**-tee), *n.* [Law Latin "right of a widow"] (17c) *Civil & Scots law.* A widow's claim to her share of her deceased husband's movable estate. • If the widow has children, her share is one-third; if not, her share is one-half.

jus relicti (jəs ri-**lik**-tɪ), *n.* [Law Latin "right of a widower"] *Civil & Scots law.* A widower's right in his deceased wife's separate movable estate, historically two-thirds if there were surviving children, and otherwise one-half. Under the Married Women's Property Act of 1881, the amount became one-third in the case of surviving children, and otherwise one-half.

jus repraesentationis (jəs rep-ri-zen-tay-shee-**oh**-nis), *n.* [Latin] (17c) *Civil law.* The right to represent or be represented by another.

jus rerum (jəs **reer**-əm), *n.* [Latin "law of things"] (1880) *Civil law.* The law regulating the rights and powers of persons over things, as how property is acquired, enjoyed, and transferred. See LAW OF THINGS. Cf. JUS PERSONARUM.

jus resistendi (jəs rez-i-**sten**-dɪ). [Latin] *Hist.* Right to resist.

jus respondendi (jəs ree-spon-**den**-dɪ). [Latin "the right of responding"] *Roman law.* The authority conferred on certain jurists when delivering legal opinions. • Modern romanists disagree about the precise meaning of this term. In any event, *jus respondendi* was defunct by A.D. 305.

jus retentionis (jəs ri-ten-shee-**oh**-nis), *n.* [Latin] (18c) *Civil law.* The right to retain a thing until the delivery of something else that the person retaining the thing is entitled to.

jus retinendi et insistendi (jəs ret-i-**nen**-dɪ et in-sis-**ten**-dɪ). [Law Latin] *Scots law.* A right of retention and of insisting. • The phrase usu. referred to a seaman's right to recover wages both by taking a lien against the ship and by proceeding against the owner for payment.

jus retractus (jəs ri-**trak**-təs), *n.* [Latin "the right of retraction"] (1847) *Civil law.* **1.** The right of certain relatives of one who has sold immovable property to repurchase it. **2.** A debtor's right, upon sale of the debt by the creditor, to have a third person redeem it within a year for the price paid by the purchaser.

jus rusticorum praediorum. See *rural servitude* under SERVITUDE (3).

jus sacrum (jəs **say**-krəm). [Latin "sacred law"] (18c) *Roman law.* The body of law regulating matters of public worship, such as sacrifices and the appointment of priests. Cf. JUS NON SACRUM.

jus sanguinis (jəs **sang**-gwə-nis), *n.* [Latin "right of blood"] (16c) The rule that a child's citizenship is determined by the parents' citizenship. • Most countries follow this rule. Cf. JUS SOLI.

jus scriptum (jəs **skrip**-təm). [Latin] See *written law* under LAW.

jus sibi dicere (jəs **sib**-ɪ **dɪ**-sər-ee). [Latin] (17c) *Hist.* To declare the law for oneself; to take the law into one's own hand.

jus singulare (jəs sing-gyə-**lair**-ee), *n.* [Latin "individual law"] (17c) *Roman & civil law.* A law or right established for special purposes, as opposed to the common or public law or right. Cf. JUS COMMUNE (1).

jus soli (jəs **soh**-lɪ), *n.* [Latin "right of the soil"] (1884) The rule that a child's citizenship is determined by place of birth. • This is the U.S. rule, as affirmed by the 14th Amendment to the Constitution. Cf. JUS SANGUINIS.

jus spatiandi (jəs spay-shee-**an**-dɪ), *n.* [Latin "right of walking about"] *Civil law.* The public's right-of-way over specific land for purposes of recreation and instruction.

jus spatiandi et manendi. [Latin "the right to stray and remain"] (2001) A rite of passage and enjoyment of land granted to the public only for purposes of recreation and education.

jus standi (jəs **stan**-dɪ). [Latin] *Hist.* Right of standing.

jus stapulae (jəs **stay**-pyə-lee), *n.* [Law Latin "right of staple"] *Civil law.* A town's right or privilege of stopping imported merchandise and forcing it to be offered for sale in its own market. See STAPLE.

jus strictum (jəs **strik**-təm). [Latin "strict law"] (17c) *Roman law.* Law rigorously interpreted according to the letter. — Also termed *strictum jus.* See STRICTI JURIS. Cf. JUS AEQUUM.

jus suffragii (jəs sə-**fray**-jee-ɪ). [Latin] (17c) *Roman law.* The right of a citizen to vote. Cf. JUS HONORUM.

just, *adj.* (14c) Legally right; lawful; equitable.

justa causa (**jəs**-tə **kaw**-zə), *n.* [Latin] (15c) *Civil law.* A just cause; a lawful ground. — Also termed *causa justa.* See *good cause* under CAUSE (2).

justae nuptiae (**jəs**-tee **nəp**-shee-ee). [Latin "legal marriage"] (1869) *Roman law.* A marriage between two persons who had the legal capacity to wed. • *Justae nuptiae* was the only union that created the familial relationship known as *patria potestas.* — Also termed *justum matrimonium.* See *patria potestas* under POTESTAS. Cf. CONCUBINATUS.

> "*Iustae nuptiae* is such a marriage as satisfies all the rules of civil law. Any marriage between two persons who had the capacity of civil marriage with each other (*conubium*) was necessarily *iustae nuptiae,* for if the union was defective in any other respect it was no marriage at all. On the other hand, if there was no *conubium* between the parties it might still be actually a marriage (*nuptiae, nuptiae non iustae*), the wife being *uxor non iusta,* the children *liberi non iusti.* Such a marriage, in which one party at least would not be a *civis,* did not produce *patria potestas* over children . . . ." W.W. Buckland, *A Manual of Roman Private Law* 63–64 (2d ed. 1939).

jus talionis. See LEX TALIONIS.

just-as-probable rule. (1982) *Workers' compensation.* A doctrine whereby a workers'-compensation claim will be denied if it is equally likely that the injury resulted from a non-work-related cause as from a work-related cause.

just cause. See *good cause* under CAUSE (2).

just compensation. See COMPENSATION.

Just Compensation Clause. See TAKINGS CLAUSE.

just deserts (di-**zərts**). (16c) What one really deserves; esp., the punishment that a person deserves for having committed a crime. — Also termed *deserts.*

jus tertii (jəs **tər**-shee-ɪ), *n.* [Latin "right of a third party"] (17c) **1.** Against a claim of an interest in property, the defense that a third party has a better right than the claimant.

> "[N]o defendant in an action of trespass can plead the *jus tertii* — the right of possession outstanding in some third person — as against the fact of possession in the plaintiff." R.F.V. Heuston, *Salmond on the Law of Torts* 46 (17th ed. 1977).

2. The doctrine that, particularly in constitutional law, courts do not decide what they do not need to decide.

> "Jus tertii . . . says nothing about the nature of legal argument on the merits of a case once formed, but as a symbol for the separability of cases is a useful term of art. Translated, however, it reads 'right of a third person.' It may once have been associated with a presumption of common-law jurisprudence that one cannot be harmed by an action that achieves its effect through effects upon others, cannot be 'indirectly' harmed." Joseph Vining, *Legal Identity* 120 (1978).

3. *Trademarks.* A trademark-infringement defense based on the claim that a third party has trademark rights superior to those of the plaintiff. • The defense may not be successful if the alleged infringer is found to have competed unfairly against the plaintiff even though the third party has superior trademark rights.

justice. (17c) **1.** The fair treatment of people. **2.** The quality of being fair or reasonable. **3.** The legal system by which people and their causes are judged; esp., the system used to punish people who have committed crimes. **4.** The fair and proper administration of laws.

> "[I]t is certain that law cannot be divorced from morality in so far as it clearly contains, as one of its elements, the notion of right to which the moral quality of justice corresponds. This principle was recognized by the great Roman jurist, Ulpian, in his famous definition of justice: 'To live honourably, not to harm your neighbor, to give every one his due.' [*Honeste vivere, alterum non laeere, suum cuique tribuere.*] All three rules are, of course, moral precepts, but they can all be made to apply to law in one way or another. The first, for instance, which seems pre-eminently ethical, inasmuch as it lays down rules for individual conduct, implies some legal connotation. A man has to shape his life in an honourable and dignified manner—one might add, as a truthful and law-abiding citizen. The juridical counterparts of ethical rules are still more noticeable in the last two rules of the definition. The command not to harm one's fellow-men may be taken to be a general maxim for the law of crime and tort, while the command to give every one his due may be considered as the basis of private law. And this last precept is certainly not concerned with morals alone: the individual is not required merely to confer a benefit upon his neighbour, but to render to him that which belongs to him as a matter of right." Paul Vinogradoff, *Common Sense in Law* 19–20 (H.G. Hanbury ed., 2d ed. 1946).

> "Justice in one sense is identical with the ethics of who should receive benefits and burdens, good or bad things of many sorts, given that others might receive these things. Although discourse about justice is often influenced by models of law, the ethics of justice is a subject in itself. To 'receive' a benefit or burden is to have any of a large number of more concrete relations to it: not only legal ownership or other entitlement may be relevant, but also nonlegal matters. Enjoyment of an experience, having access to many opportunities, getting protection from or exposure to a risk, and so on may be relevant. The 'others' relevant to justice may be those living in a person's community, those in other communities, or even those dead, those yet to live, or perhaps possible persons who will never live. Central cases of justice, however, usually involve persons living at the same time in the same community (although the community may be very narrowly or broadly defined). Here intuitions and arguments seem better grounded." Edward Sankowski, "Justice," in *The Oxford Companion to Philosophy* 463, 463–64 (Ted Honderich ed., 2d ed. 2005).

▸ **commutative justice** (kə-**myoo**-tə-tiv *or* **kom**-yə-tay-tiv). (1856) Justice concerned with the relations between persons and esp. with fairness in the exchange of goods and the fulfillment of contractual obligations.

▸ **condign justice.** (16c) An outcome according to what the litigants deserve; esp., justice based on the kind and degree of punishment that is appropriate for a given offense.

▸ **corrective justice.** (18c) The Aristotelian notion that the exclusive function of law is to require those who have caused harm to remedy the consequences of their fault.

▸ **distributive justice.** (16c) Justice owed by a community to its members, including the fair allocation of common advantages and sharing of common burdens.

▸ **Jedburgh justice** (**jed**-bər-ə). (1847) A brand of justice involving punishment (esp. execution) first and trial afterward. • The term alludes to Jedburgh, a Scottish border town where in the 17th century raiders were said to have been hanged without the formality of a trial. Jedburgh justice differs from lynch law in that the former was administered by an established court (albeit after the fact). — Also termed *Jeddart justice; Jedwood justice.* Cf. LIDFORD LAW; LYNCH LAW.

▸ **justice in personam.** See *personal justice.*

▸ **justice in rem.** See *social justice.*

▸ **natural justice.** (17c) Justice as defined in a moral, as opposed to a legal, sense. — Also termed *justitia naturalis*. Cf. NATURAL LAW.

"Although the judges have frequently asserted that a foreign judgment which contravenes the principles of natural justice cannot be enforced in England, it is extremely difficult to fix with precision the exact cases in which the contravention is sufficiently serious to justify a refusal of enforcement. Shadwell V.-C. once said that 'whenever it is manifest that justice has been disregarded, the court is bound to treat the decision as a matter of no value and no substance.' [*Price v. Dewhurst*, 8 Sim 279, 302 (1837).] But this goes too far. . . . The expression 'contrary to natural justice' has, however, figured so prominently in judicial statements that it is essential to fix, if possible, its exact scope. The only statement that can be made with any approach to accuracy is that in the present context, the expression is confined to something glaringly defective in the procedural rules of the foreign law. . . . In other words, what the courts are vigilant to watch is that the defendant has not been deprived of an opportunity to present his side of the case." G.C. Cheshire, *Private International Law* 675 (6th ed. 1961).

▸ **personal justice.** (16c) Justice between parties to a dispute, regardless of any larger principles that might be involved. — Also termed *justice in personam*; *popular justice*; *social justice*.

▸ **poetic justice.** A situation in which a bad person or evildoer suffers in such a way that people consider the suffering deserved payback or condign punishment.

▸ **popular justice.** (17c) Demotic justice, which is usu. considered less than fully fair and proper even though it satisfies prevailing public opinion in a particular case. Cf. *social justice*.

"Nothing is more treacherous than popular justice in many of its manifestations, subject as it is to passion, to fallacy, and to the inability to grasp general notions or to distinguish the essential from the inessential." Carleton K. Allen, *Law in the Making* 387 (7th ed. 1964).

▸ **positive justice.** (17c) Justice as it is conceived, recognized, and incompletely expressed by the civil law or some other form of human law. Cf. POSITIVE LAW.

▸ **preventive justice.** (17c) Justice intended to protect against probable future misbehavior. • Specific types of preventive justice include appointing a receiver or administrator, issuing a restraining order or injunction, and binding over to keep the peace.

▸ **rough justice.** Unfair treatment of a person or cause.

▸ **social justice.** (1902) **1.** Justice that conforms to a moral principle, such as that all people are equal. **2.** One or more equitable resolutions sought on behalf of individuals and communities who are disenfranchised, underrepresented, or otherwise excluded from meaningful participation in legal, economic, cultural, and social structures, with the ultimate goal of removing barriers to participation and effecting social change. — Also termed *justice in rem*. Cf. *personal justice*; CAUSE LAWYERING.

▸ **substantial justice.** (17c) Justice fairly administered according to rules of substantive law, regardless of any procedural errors not affecting the litigant's substantive rights; a fair trial on the merits.

5. A judge, esp. of an appellate court or a court of last resort. — Abbr. J. (and, in plural, JJ.).

▸ **associate justice.** (18c) An appellate-court justice other than the chief justice.

▸ **chief justice.** (15c) The presiding justice of an appellate court, usu. the highest appellate court in a jurisdiction and esp. the U.S. Supreme Court. — Abbr. C.J.

▸ **circuit justice.** (18c) **1.** A justice who sits on a circuit court. **2.** A U.S. Supreme Court justice who has jurisdiction over one or more of the federal circuits, with power to issue injunctions, grant bail, or stay execution in those circuits.

▸ **circuit-riding justice.** (1928) *Hist.* A U.S. Supreme Court justice who, under the Judiciary Act of 1789, was required to travel within a circuit to preside over trials. • In each of three circuits that then existed, two justices sat with one district judge. See CIRCUIT-RIDING.

6. *Hist.* Judicial cognizance of causes or offenses; jurisdiction.

▸ **high justice.** *Hist.* Jurisdiction over crimes of every kind, including high crimes.

▸ **low justice.** *Hist.* Jurisdiction over petty offenses.

justice-broker. (17c) *Archaic.* A judge who sells judicial decisions.

justice court. See COURT.

justice ejectment. See EJECTMENT.

justice foncière. [French] (1892) *French law.* Land court. See *land court* under COURT.

justice in eyre (air). (16c) *Hist.* One of the itinerant judges who, in medieval times, investigated allegations of wrongdoing, tried cases, and levied fines. — Also termed *justicia errante*; *justiciar in itinere*. See EYRE.

justicement. (17c) *Archaic.* **1.** The administration of justice. **2.** (*pl.*) All things relating to justice.

justice of the peace. (15c) A local judicial officer having jurisdiction over minor criminal offenses and minor civil disputes, and authority to perform routine civil functions (such as administering oaths and performing marriage ceremonies). — Abbr. J.P. Cf. MAGISTRATE (3).

justice-of-the-peace court. See *justice court* under COURT.

justice of the quorum. (16c) **1.** A judge on a panel designated to hear appeals. • In Massachusetts, the panel is sometimes called a *quorum*. **2.** *Hist.* A county justice or justice of the peace, designated by the governor in a commission of peace, who had to be present or else a court could not sit. **3.** *Hist.* A distinction conferred on a justice of the peace by directing — in the commission authorizing the holding of quarter sessions — that from among those holding court must be two or more specially so named. • The distinction was conferred on some, or occasionally all, of the justices of the peace of a county in England. **4.** *Hist.* A keeper of the peace to whom a royal special commission granted the power to try felonies and misdemeanors, and in whose absence a court could not do business. • The words of the commission granting the judicial power were *quorum aliquem vestrum* [person's name] *unum esse volumus*, which gave rise to the term *justice of the quorum*. The number of justices of the quorum necessary for court business was set by statute and varied in different places and times.

"These justices are appointed . . . jointly and severally, to keep the peace, and any two or more of them to enquire of and determine felonies and other misdemeanors in which number some particular justices, or one of them, are directed to be always included, and no business is to be done without their presence; the words of the commission running thus, "quorum aliquem vestrum a.b.c.d., etc. unum esse volumus," whence the persons so named are usually called justices of the quorum. And formerly it was customary to appoint only a select number of justices eminent for their skill and discretion to be of the quorum, but now the practice is to advance almost all of them to that dignity, etc." 1 William Blackstone, *Commentaries on the Laws of England* 40 (1765).

justicer, *n.* (14c) *Archaic.* Someone who administers justice; a judge.

justice *seigneuriale.* (1897) *Hist. French law.* A local court presided over by the local lord or lords, who were empowered to deliver justice, sometimes including the death penalty. • Such courts originated under feudal law and were initially designed for landlords to deliver justice to their tenants. These courts were abolished in France and its North American colonies in 1789. — Also termed *seigneurial justice.*

justiceship. (16c) **1.** The position, office, or authority of a justice. **2.** The period of a justice's incumbency.

justice's warrant. See *peace warrant* under WARRANT (1).

justiciability (jə-stish-ee-ə-**bil**-ə-tee *or* jə-stish-ə-**bil**-ə-tee), *n.* (15c) The quality, state, or condition of being appropriate or suitable for adjudication by a court. See MOOTNESS DOCTRINE; RIPENESS. Cf. STANDING.

"Concepts of justiciability have been developed to identify appropriate occasions for judicial action. . . . The central concepts often are elaborated into more specific categories of justiciability — advisory opinions, feigned and collusive cases, standing, ripeness, mootness, political questions, and administrative questions." 13 Charles Alan Wright et al., *Federal Practice and Procedure* § 3529, at 278–79 (2d ed. 1984).

justiciable (jə-**stish**-ee-ə-bəl *or* jəs-**tish**-ə-bəl), *adj.* (17c) (Of a case or dispute) properly brought before a court of justice; capable of being disposed of judicially <a justiciable controversy>.

justicia errante. See JUSTICE IN EYRE.

justicial (jəs-**tish**-əl), *adj.* (15c) **1.** Of, relating to, or involving justice or its administration. **2.** Of, relating to, or involving one or more justices or their offices.

justiciar (jə-**stish**-ee-ər), *n.* (15c) **1.** *Hist.* A royal judicial officer in medieval England; esp., a justice presiding over a superior court. **2.** JUSTICIARY (2). — Also spelled *justicier.*

justiciarii itinerantes (jəs-tish-ee-**air**-ee-I I-tin-ə-**ran**-teez), *n.* [Latin "itinerant justices"] (17c) Justices in eyre. See JUSTICE IN EYRE.

justiciarii residentes (jəs-tish-ee-**air**-ee-I rez-i-**den**-teez), *n.* [Latin "resident justices"] *Hist.* Justices who usu. held court in Westminster, as opposed to traveling with the eyre. Cf. EYRE.

justiciar in itinere. See JUSTICE IN EYRE.

justiciary (jə-**stish**-ee-er-ee), *adj.* Of, relating to, or involving the administration of justice; pertaining to the law.

justiciary (jə-**stish**-ee-er-ee), *n.* (15c) **1.** A justice or judge. **2.** *Hist.* The chief administrator of both government and justice. • From the time of the Norman Conquest in 1066 until the reign of Henry III (1216–1272), the justiciary presided in the King's Court and in the Exchequer, supervising all governmental departments and serving as regent in the king's absence. These functions were later divided among several officials such as the Lord Chancellor, the Chief Justice, and the Lord High Treasurer. — Also termed *justiciar*; *chief justiciar*; *capitalis justiciarius.* **3.** *Scots law.* The administration of justice, esp. of criminal law; the process by which the legal system operates. See HIGH COURT OF JUSTICIARY.

justicias facere. (17c) To exercise judicial functions.

justicier. See JUSTICIAR.

justicies (jə-**stish**-ee-eez). (17c) *Hist.* A writ empowering the sheriff to allow certain debt cases in a county court. • The writ was so called because of the significant word in the writ's opening clause, which stated in Latin, "We command you that you do justice to [a person named]."

justicing room. (1873) *Hist.* A room in which cases are heard and justice is administered; esp., such a room in the house of a justice of the peace.

justifiable, *adj.* (16c) Legally or morally acceptable for one or more good reasons; excusable; defensible.

justifiable homicide. See HOMICIDE.

justifiable war. See BELLUM JUSTUM.

justification, *n.* (14c) **1.** A lawful or sufficient reason for one's acts or omissions; any fact that prevents an act from being wrongful. **2.** A showing, in court, of a sufficient reason why a defendant acted in a way that, in the absence of the reason, would constitute the offense with which the defendant is charged. • Under the Model Penal Code, the defendant must believe that the action was necessary to avoid a harm or evil, and reasonable persons must agree that the harm or evil expected to result from taking the action is one that is less than the harm or evil that the law creating the offense charged seeks to prevent. If the defendant's belief that his action was necessary is mistaken, the defense is not available when the mistaken belief is the result of the defendant's negligence or recklessness and the required mental state of the offense charged is also negligence or recklessness. Model Penal Code § 3.02. — Also termed *justification defense*; *necessity defense*; *lawful justification.* — See *lesser-evils defense* under DEFENSE (1); NECESSITY (1), (4). Cf. JUSTIFICATION DEFENSE; EXCUSE (2).

"A little bit of history: the term 'justification' was formerly used for cases where the aim of the law was not frustrated, while 'excuse' was used for cases where it was not thought proper to punish. Killing a dangerous criminal who had tried to avoid arrest was *justified*, since the law (if one may personify) wished this to happen, whereas killing in self-defence was merely *excused*. The distinction was important because justification was a defence to the criminal charge while an excuse was not, being merely the occasion for a royal pardon. By the end of the middle ages (it is difficult to assign a fixed date) even excuses were recognised by the courts, since when there has been no reason to distinguish between justification and excuse." Glanville Williams, *Textbook of Criminal Law* 39 (1978).

"The prison-break situation illustrates why it is important to distinguish between claims of excuse and of justification. . . . If the escape were deemed justified, one would be inclined to think of the attempted escape as lawful (or, at least, not unlawful). After all a valid claim of justification renders conduct right and proper. If the escape is not unlawful, the guards have no right to resist. Not so with an excuse: an excuse does not challenge the wrongfulness or unlawfulness of the conduct, but merely denies the personal accountability of the actor for the wrongful act. The guards retain the right to resist escapes excused on grounds of insanity, voluntary intoxication, duress, or personal necessity." George P. Fletcher, "Excuse: Theory," in *Encyclopedia of Crime & Justice* 637, 638 (Joshua Dressler ed., 2d ed. 2002).

▸ **defensive-force justification.** (1982) A justification defense available when an aggressor has threatened harm to the particular interest that is the subject of the defense — usu. to the actor (self-defense), to other persons (defense of others), or to property (defense of property).

▸ **imperfect justification.** (1853) A reason or cause that is insufficient to completely justify a defendant's behavior but that can be used to mitigate criminal punishment.

▸ **judicial-authority justification.** A justification defense available when an actor has engaged in conduct constituting an offense in order to comply with a court order.

▸ **public-authority justification.** (1982) A justification defense available when an actor has been specifically authorized to engage in the conduct constituting an offense in order to protect or further a public interest.

3. A surety's proof of having enough money or credit to provide security for the party for whom it is required. — **justify,** *vb.* — **justificatory** (jəs-**tif**-i-kə-tor-ee), *adj.*

justification defense. *Criminal & tort law.* A defense that arises when the defendant has acted in a way that the law does not seek to prevent. • Traditionally, the following defenses were justifications: consent, self-defense, defense of others, defense of property, necessity (choice of evils), the use of force to make an arrest, and the use of force by public authority. — Sometimes shortened to *justification.* Cf. EXCUSE (2); JUSTIFICATION (2).

justificator (**jəs**-tə-fi-kay-tər). *Hist.* (17c) **1.** A compurgator; a person who testifies under oath in defense of an accused person. **2.** A juror.

Justinian Code (jəs-**tin**-ee-ən). *Roman law.* A collection of imperial constitutions drawn up by a commission of ten persons appointed by the Roman emperor Justinian, and published in A.D. 529. • Ten jurists, headed by Tribonian, carried out the project beginning in February A.D. 528 and ending in April 529. It replaced all prior imperial law, but was in force only until A.D. 534, when it was supplanted by a revision, the *Codex Repetitae Praelectionis.* The precise contents of the first work are unknown. But the second work, containing the 12 books of the revised code, includes the imperial constitutions of the Gregorian, Hermogenian, and Theodosian Codes, together with later legislation, revised and harmonized into one systematic whole. It deals with ecclesiastical law, criminal law, administrative law, and private law. In modern writings, the A.D. 534 version is the work referred to as the Justinian Code. — Also termed *Justinianean Code* (jəs-tin-ee-**an**-ee-ən); *Code of Justinian*; *Codex Justinianus* (**koh**-deks-jəs-tin-ee-**ay**-nəs); *Codex Vetus* ("Old Code"); *Codex Iustinianus Repetitae Praelectionis.*

> "By the time when the *Digest* and *Institutes* had been completed it was obvious that the *Codex*, published little more than four years earlier, was incomplete, since in the interval Justinian . . . had promulgated other new constitutions. Tribonian, therefore, was appointed to revise the Code, so as to bring it fully up to date, and at the end of the year A.D. 534 this new Code, known as the *Codex Repetitae Praelectionis*, was promulgated, and is the only Code which survives to the present day. Justinian seem to have laboured under the erroneous impression that the system he had framed would be adequate for all time. But as there is nothing static about law, further legislative enactments, termed *Novellae Constitutiones*, were issued during his reign. . . . In modern times Justinian's various compilations came to be called collectively the *Corpus Juris Civilis*: the *Corpus* being regarded as a single work, made up of the *Institutes*, the *Digest*, the *Codex Repetitae Praelectionis*, and the *Novels*." R.W. Leage, *Roman Private Law* 44 (C.H. Ziegler ed., 2d ed. 1930).

Justinianist (jə-**stin**-ee-ə-nist), *n.* (17c) **1.** Someone who is knowledgeable about the Institutes of Justinian. **2.** Someone who has been trained in civil law.

Justinian's Digest. See DIGEST (2).

Justinian's Institutes. See INSTITUTE.

justitia (jəs-**tish**-ee-ə), *n.* [Latin] Justice.

justitia denegata (jəs-**tish**-ee-ə dee-nə-**gay**-tə). See DENIAL OF JUSTICE.

justitia naturalis (jəs-**tish**-ee-ə nach-ə-**ray**-lis). See *natural justice* under JUSTICE (4).

justitium (jəs-**tish**-ee-əm), *n.* [Latin] (17c) *Civil law.* A suspension or intermission of the administration of justice in the courts, as for vacation time.

justo tempore (**jəs**-toh **tem**-pə-ree). [Latin "at the right time"] *Hist.* In due time.

jus tripertitum (jəs trɪ-pər-**tɪ**-təm). [Latin "law in three parts"] *Roman law.* The law of wills in the time of Justinian, deriving from the praetorian edicts, from the civil law, and from the imperial constitutions. See *testamentum tripertitum* under TESTAMENTUM.

jus trium liberorum (jəs **trɪ**-əm lib-ə-**ror**-əm). [Latin] See JUS LIBERORUM.

just title. See TITLE (2).

justum matrimonium. See JUSTAE NUPTIAE.

justus titulus (jəs-təs **tich**-ə-ləs). [Latin] *Hist.* Just title. See *just title* under TITLE (2).

just value. See *fair value* under VALUE (2).

just war. (15c) **1.** BELLUM JUSTUM. **2.** See JUST-WAR DOCTRINE.

just-war doctrine. (1943) *Int'l law.* The principle that a war should have a morally and legally sufficient cause, and must be conducted with restraint. • Precisely what is morally or legally sufficient depends on the norms of a time and place. Over the centuries the doctrine has been invoked to justify wars waged in self- defense, to avenge injuries and punish wrongs, and over religious differences. Restraint means that the least amount of force possible under the circumstances should be used and only when necessary. — Also termed *just-war theory.* See BELLUM JUSTUM.

jus urbanorum praediorum. See *urban servitude* (2) under SERVITUDE (2).

jus utendi (jəs yoo-**ten**-dɪ), *n.* [Latin "right of using"] (17c) *Roman & civil law.* The right to use another's property without consuming it or destroying its substance. See USUFRUCT. Cf. JUS ABUTENDI.

jus vindicandi (jəs vin-di-**kan**-dɪ). *Roman law.* An owner's right to recover lost possession even from a bona fide possessor who has given value. • This right, which generally does not exist under modern law, had many exceptions. See R.W. Lee, *An Introduction to Roman–Dutch Law* 433 (4th ed. 1946).

jus vitae necisque (jəs **vɪ**-tee ni-**sis**-kwee). [Latin "right of life and death"] *Roman law.* The power held by the head of the household over persons under his paternal power and over his slaves. • This right was greatly diminished under later Roman law. See *patria potestas* under POTESTAS.

jus voluntarium (jəs vol-ən-**tair**-ee-əm). [Latin] *Hist.* Optional law.

juvenile (**joo**-və-nəl *or* -nɪl), *n.* (18c) Someone who has not reached the age (usu. 18) at which one should be treated as an adult by the criminal-justice system; MINOR. — **juvenile,** *adj.* — **juvenility** (joo-və-**nil**-ə-tee), *n.*

▸ **certified juvenile.** (1971) A juvenile who has been certified to be tried as an adult.

juvenile court. See COURT.

juvenile-court counselor. (1951) A social worker who, as part of a court program, provides guidance and advice to youth who have committed criminal offenses, often performing detention-center intake responsibilities to determine the appropriate level of custody and working as part of the team of workers who supervise youth in confinement. — Also termed *juvenile probation officer.*

juvenile-court judge. See JUDGE.

juvenile delinquency. (1816) **1.** Serious antisocial behavior by a minor, such as vandalism, theft, or joyriding; esp., behavior that would be criminally punishable if the actor were an adult, but instead is usu. punished by special laws applying only to minors. See DELINQUENCY. Cf. INCORRIGIBILITY.

> "'Juvenile delinquency,' when employed as a technical term rather than merely a descriptive phrase, is entirely a legislative product . . . ." Rollin M. Perkins & Ronald N. Boyce, *Criminal Law* 940 (3d ed. 1982).

2. More broadly, a juvenile's violation of the law.

Juvenile Delinquency Prevention Act. A federal statute whose purpose is (1) to help states and local communities provide preventive services to youths who are in danger of becoming delinquent, (2) to help in training personnel employed in or preparing for employment in occupations that involve the provision of those services, and (3) to give technical assistance in this field. 42 USCA §§ 3801 et seq.

juvenile delinquent. (1816) A minor, often 7–15 years of age, who has committed an act that, if the minor had been an adult, would constitute a crime. • Juvenile offenses may be punishable by special laws not applicable to adults. — Abbr. JD. — Sometimes shortened to *delinquent.* — Also termed *juvenile offender*; *youthful offender*; *delinquent minor.* See OFFENDER. Cf. *delinquent child* under CHILD.

Juvenile Justice and Delinquency Prevention Act. A federal statute that provides funding, assistance, training, and support to state-operated juvenile-justice programs, initiatives, and court systems. 42 USCA §§ 5601–5785. — Abbr. JJDPA.

juvenile-justice system. (1962) The collective institutions through which a youthful offender passes until any charges have been disposed of or the assessed punishment has been concluded. • The system comprises juvenile courts (judges and lawyers), law enforcement (police), and corrections (probation officers and social workers).

juvenile offender. (1819) See JUVENILE DELINQUENT.

juvenile officer. See OFFICER (1).

juvenile parole. See PAROLE.

juvenile petition. See PETITION (1).

juvenile probation officer. See JUVENILE-COURT COUNSELOR.

juvie (**joo**-vee), *n. Slang.* **1.** A juvenile delinquent. **2.** A facility such as a detention home for juvenile delinquents. — Also spelled *juvey.*

juxta (**jəks**-tə). [Latin] Near; following; according to.

juxta conventionem (**jəks**-tə kən-ven-shee-**oh**-nəm). [Latin] According to the covenant.

juxta formam statuti (**jəks**-tə **for**-məm stə-**t**[y]**oo**-tɪ). [Latin] According to the form of the statute.

juxtaposition (jəks-tə-pə-**zish**-ən), *n.* (17c) **1.** The act or an instance of placing two or more things side by side or near one another. **2.** *Patents.* See AGGREGATION (3). — **juxtapose** (jəks-tə-**pohz**), *vb.* — **juxtapositional,** *adj.*

juxta ratam (**jəks**-tə **ray**-təm). [Latin] At or after the rate.

juxta tenorem sequentem (**jəks**-tə tə-**nor**-əm sə-**kwen**-təm). [Latin] According to the tenor following.

juzgado (hoos-**gah**-doh). [Spanish "court"] **1.** A court of law, esp. one presided over by a single judge. **2.** A courthouse.

K

K. *abbr.* Contract.

K-9 dog. See *police dog* under DOG (1).— Also spelled *K9 dog.*

K-9 officer. See *police dog* under DOG (1).— Also spelled *K9 officer.*

k/a. *abbr.* Known as.

kakistocracy. Government by the worst people.

Kaldor-Hicks efficiency. See WEALTH MAXIMIZATION.

kalendar. *Archaic.* See CALENDAR.

kalendarium (kal-ən-**dair**-ee-əm). [Latin] *Roman law.* **1.** A book of accounts in which a moneylender recorded the names of debtors and the principal and interest due. **2.** A written register of births, recorded daily.

Kalends. See CALENDS.

kangaroo court. See COURT.

Karolingian, *adj.* See CAROLINGIAN.

***Kastigar* hearing.** See HEARING.

***Katz* test.** (1969) *Criminal law.* A two-pronged means of assessing whether a person had a reasonable expectation of privacy at the time of a search, the standard being that (1) the person had a subjective expectation of privacy, and (2) society would recognize that expectation as reasonable. *Katz v. U.S.*, 389 U.S. 347, 88 S.Ct. 507 (1967).

K.B. *abbr.* (1818) KING'S BENCH.

K.C. *abbr.* (1898) KING'S COUNSEL.

k.d., *adj. abbr.* (In a bill of lading) knocked down; not assembled or set up. • When goods, equipment, or the like are shipped in disassembled form, the bill of lading is marked "k.d."

keelage (**keel**-ij). (17c) *Hist.* **1.** The right to demand payment of a toll by a ship entering or anchoring in a harbor. **2.** The toll so paid.

keelhaul (**keel**-hawl), *vb.* (17c) **1.** *Hist.* To drag (a person) through the water under the bottom of a ship as punishment or torture. **2.** To rebuke or reprimand harshly.

Keeling Schedule. (1948) *English law.* A device that shows how an existing statute will read if a proposed amendment is adopted. • A Keeling Schedule is usu. included as an appendix to the proposed amendment. The schedule is named for E.H. Keeling, a member of Parliament who began promoting the use of schedules in 1938 as a way to avoid amending legislation by reference. Although Keeling Schedules can be a great aid to legislators, they are rarely used today.

keeper. (15c) Someone who has the care, custody, or management of something and who usu. is legally responsible for it <a dog's keeper> <a keeper of lost property>.

Keeper of the Briefs. See CUSTOS BREVIUM.

Keeper of the Broad Seal. See KEEPER OF THE GREAT SEAL.

Keeper of the Great Seal. *English & Scots law.* In England and Scotland, an officer who has custody of the Great Seal and who authenticates state documents of the highest importance. • In England, the duties of the Keeper of the Great Seal are now discharged by the Lord Chancellor. — Also termed *Lord Keeper of the Great Seal; Lord Keeper; Keeper of the Broad Seal; Custos Sigilli.*

Keeper of the Hanaper. *Hist. English law.* The head of the receiving and accounting department in Chancery. • The Hanaper received fees collected on charters and letters granted under the Great Seal and fines for Chancery writs, paid Chancery staff wages, purchased office supplies, and accounted for the Chancery's revenues and expenses.

Keeper of the King's Conscience. See LORD CHANCELLOR.

Keeper of the Privy Seal (**priv**-ee). **1.** LORD PRIVY SEAL. **2.** In Scotland and Cornwall, an officer similar to the English Lord Privy Seal.

Keeper of the Rolls. See CUSTOS ROTULORUM.

keeping house. (18c) *English law. Bankruptcy.* (Of a debtor) shutting oneself in the home to avoid contact with creditors.

keeping in repair. (17c) To take necessary actions to maintain something in good, usable condition.

keeping the peace. (16c) To maintain law and order or to refrain from disturbing it.

Kellogg–Briand Pact. *Int'l law.* A 1928 treaty under which the United States, France, and (by 1933) 63 other countries purported to outlaw war and pledged to settle future differences through diplomacy. • Among the signatories were Germany, Japan, and Italy — countries whose acts of aggression lead to World War II. 46 Stat. 2343, T.S. No. 796. — Also termed *Pact of Paris.*

kenning to a terce. (18c) *Hist. Scots law.* The sheriff's determination of which tracts or parts of a decedent's land belong to a widow; esp., a sheriff's assignment of dower.

Keogh plan (**kee**-oh). (1952) A tax-deferred retirement program developed for the self-employed. • This plan is also known as an *H.R. 10 plan*, after the House of Representatives bill that established the plan. — Also termed *self-employed retirement plan.* Cf. INDIVIDUAL RETIREMENT ACCOUNT.

kerb-crawling. See CURB-CRAWLING.

***Kercheval* rule.** (1984) *Criminal law.* The doctrine that evidence of a defendant's withdrawn guilty plea is not admissible at trial. *Kercheval v. U.S.*, 274 U.S. 220 (1927).

***Ker–Frisbie* rule.** (1974) The principle that the government's power to try a criminal defendant is not impaired by the defendant's having been brought back illegally to the United States from a foreign country. *Ker v. Illinois*, 119 U.S. 436, 7 S.Ct. 225 (1886); *Frisbie v. Collins*, 342 U.S. 519, 72 S.Ct. 509 (1952). — Also termed *Ker–Frisbie doctrine.*

Ketubah (ke-**too**-vah), *n.* (1841) *Jewish law.* A prenuptial agreement, signed by at least two independent witnesses, in which a husband promises to support his wife and to pay her a certain sum of money if the couple divorces.

• If the couple is still married when the husband dies, the sum promised upon divorce becomes the primary debt to be paid out of the husband's estate. The terms of a Ketubah are often enforceable in secular courts under general contract-law principles.

keyage (**kee**-əj). See QUAYAGE.

KeyCite, *vb.* (1997) To determine the subsequent history of (a case, statute, etc.) by using the online citator of the same name to establish that the point being researched is still good law. — **KeyCiting,** *n.*

key-employee life insurance. See LIFE INSURANCE.

key encryption. (1989) A software-cryptography system that generates and employs a secure key pair, one public key and one private key, to verify a digital signature and decipher a secure, coded document. • While the public key is known to all possible recipients of a message, the private key is known only to the message's sender. Key encryption transforms the message's characters into an indecipherable "hash." A person who has the signer's public key can decipher the message and detect whether it has been altered and whether it was transmitted using the sender's private key. It does not necessarily identify the sender; identity is verified using a digital certificate. — Also termed *public-key encryption*. — Abbr. PKE. See DIGITAL CERTIFICATE; HASH.

key-executive insurance. See *key-employee insurance* under INSURANCE.

key man. See KEY PERSON.

key-man insurance. See *key-employee life insurance* under LIFE INSURANCE.

key money. (1948) **1.** Payment (as rent or security) required from a new tenant in exchange for a key to the leased property. **2.** Payment made (usu. secretly) by a prospective tenant to a landlord or current tenant to increase the chance of obtaining a lease in an area where there is a housing shortage. • Key money in the first sense is a legal transaction; key money in the second sense is usu. an illegal bribe that violates housing laws.

key-number system. (1909) A legal-research indexing system developed by West Publishing Company (now the West Group) to catalogue American caselaw with headnotes. • In this system, a number designates a point of law, allowing a researcher to find all reported cases addressing a particular point by referring to its number.

key person. (1938) An important officer or employee; a person primarily responsible for a business's success. — Also termed *key man*.

key-person insurance. See *key-employee insurance* under INSURANCE.

keys-to-the-jailhouse doctrine. *Slang.* A means of determining whether incarceration for contempt of court is civil contempt or criminal contempt, the pivotal factor being whether imprisonment ends upon the person's performing some act that the court has ordered (civil) or upon the running of some finite term of imprisonment (criminal).

keyword, *n.* (1997) **1.** A word or phrase typed into a computer so that it will search for that word on the Internet or in a particular database. **2.** A term assigned to a document, webpage, or the like so that it may be found by such a search.

kickback, *n.* (1920) A sum of money illegally paid to someone in authority, esp. for arranging for a company to receive a lucrative contract; esp., a return of a portion of a monetary sum received, usu. as a result of coercion or a secret agreement <the contractor paid the city official a 5% kickback on the government contract>. — Also termed *payoff*. Cf. BRIBERY.

kicker. 1. An extra charge or penalty, esp. a charge added to a loan in addition to interest. **2.** An equity participation that a lender seeks as a condition for lending money, so that the lender may participate in rentals, profits, or extra interest.

kickout clause. (1983) A contractual provision allowing a party to end or modify the contract if a specified event occurs <under the kickout clause, the company could refuse to sell the land if it were unable to complete its acquisition of the new headquarters>.

kiddie tax. See TAX.

kidnap, *n.* See KIDNAPPING.

kidnap, *vb.* (17c) To seize and take away (a person) by force or fraud, often with a demand for ransom. — **kidnapper,** *n.*

kidnapping. (17c) **1.** At common law, the crime of forcibly abducting a person from his or her own country and sending the person to another. • This offense amounted to false imprisonment aggravated by moving the victim to another country. **2.** The crime of seizing and taking away a person by force or fraud, usu. to hold the person prisoner in order to demand something from his or her family, employer, or government. — Also termed *kidnap*; *simple kidnapping*; (loosely) *abduction*; (archaically) *manstealing*. See ABDUCTION.

▸ **aggravated kidnapping.** (1943) Kidnapping accompanied by some aggravating factor (such as a demand for ransom or injury of the victim).

▸ **child-kidnapping.** (1978) The kidnapping of a minor, often without the element of force or fraud (as when someone walks off with another's baby). — Also termed *child-stealing*; *baby-snatching*; *childnapping*.

▸ **kidnapping by cesarean.** (2004) The kidnapping of a baby by a person who causes the unlawful and forcible delivery of the baby by cesarean section without the mother's consent. • The kidnapper is usu. a woman of childbearing age who has lost a baby or is unable to bear one. — Also termed *newborn kidnapping by cesarean section*.

▸ **kidnapping for ransom.** (1909) The offense of unlawfully seizing a person and then confining the person, usu. in a secret place, while attempting to extort ransom. • This grave crime is sometimes made a capital offense. In addition to the abductor, a person who acts as a go-between to collect the ransom is generally considered guilty of the crime.

▸ **newborn-kidnapping by cesarean section.** See *kidnapping by cesarean*.

▸ **parental kidnapping.** (1984) The kidnapping of a child by one parent in violation of the other parent's custody or visitation rights. See PARENTAL KIDNAPPING PREVENTION ACT.

▸ **simple kidnapping.** (1943) Kidnapping not accompanied by an aggravating factor.

kidnapping by cesarean. See KIDNAPPING.

kill, *vb.* (14c) To end life; to cause physical death. • The word is also used figuratively in putting an end to something <opponents were able to kill the proposed amendment>.

killer amendment. See AMENDMENT (3).

killing by misadventure. See ACCIDENTAL KILLING.

killing with malice. See MALICIOUS KILLING.

kin, *n.* (bef. 12c) **1.** One's relatives; family. — Also termed *kindred.* **2.** A relative by blood, marriage, or adoption, though usu. by blood only; a kinsman or kinswoman. See NEXT OF KIN.

kinbote. See *manbote* under BOTE (3).

kind arbitrage. See *convertible arbitrage* under ARBITRAGE.

kindlie (**kɪnd**-lee). *Scots law.* A tenant's right to a lease's renewal.

kindred. 1. See KIN. **2.** See KINSHIP.

kinfolk (**kin**-foh[l]k), *n.* (15c) A person's extended family; relatives. See RELATIVE. — Also termed (BrE) *kinsfolk.*

king. (bef. 12c) **1.** A man who possesses, in his own right, the sovereignty and royal power in a monarchy. Cf. QUEEN (1). **2.** (*cap.*) *English law.* The British government; the Crown. See CROWN. — **kingship,** *n.*

> "In modern times it has become usual to speak of the Crown rather than of the King, when we refer to the King in his public capacity as a body politic. We speak of the property of the Crown, when we mean the property which the King holds in right of his Crown. So we speak of the debts due by the Crown, of legal proceedings by and against the Crown, and so on. The usage is one of great convenience, because it avoids a difficulty which is inherent in all speech and thought concerning corporations sole, the difficulty, namely, of distinguishing adequately between the body politic and the human being by whom it is represented and whose name it bears." John Salmond, *Jurisprudence* 341–42 (Glanville L. Williams ed., 10th ed. 1947).

kingpin, *n.* The most important person involved in an organization, esp. one that carries out illegal activities.

King's Advocate. See LORD ADVOCATE.

King's Bench. *English law.* Historically, the highest common-law court in England, presided over by the reigning monarch. • When a queen begins to reign, the name automatically changes to *Queen's Bench.* In 1873, during Queen Victoria's reign, the court's jurisdiction was transferred to the Queen's Bench Division of the High Court of Justice. — Abbr. K.B. — Also termed *Court of King's Bench*; *Coram Rege Court*; *banc le roy.* Cf. QUEEN'S BENCH; QUEEN'S BENCH DIVISION.

> "The court of *King's Bench* is the highest court of ordinary justice in criminal cases within the realm, and paramount to the authority of justices of gaol delivery, and commissions of oyer and terminer. It has jurisdiction over all criminal causes, from high treason down to the most trivial misdemeanor or breach of the peace." 1 Joseph Chitty, *A Practical Treatise on the Criminal Law* 156 (2d ed. 1826).

King's Chambers. In the United Kingdom, waters lying within an imaginary line drawn from headland to headland around the coast of Great Britain.

King's Counsel. In the United Kingdom, Canada, and territories that have retained the rank, an elite, senior-level barrister or advocate. • Originally, a King's Counsel was appointed to serve as counsel to the reigning monarch. — Also termed *senior counsel.* — Abbr. K.C. Cf. QUEEN'S COUNSEL.

King's Court. See CURIA REGIS (1).

King's evidence. See *Queen's evidence* under EVIDENCE.

King's Great Sessions in Wales. See COURT OF GREAT SESSIONS IN WALES.

King's peace. (15c) *Hist.* A royal subject's right to be protected from crime (to "have peace") in certain areas subject to the king's immediate control, such as the king's palace or highway. • A breach of the peace in one of these areas subjected the offender to punishment in the King's Court. Over time, the area subject to the King's peace grew, which in turn increased the jurisdiction of the royal courts. — Also written *King's Peace.* — Also termed *pax regis*; *grith.* Cf. AGAINST THE PEACE AND DIGNITY OF THE STATE.

> "A breach of the King's Peace was at one time the most comprehensive of all offences against the Crown; it indeed included, and still includes, all the more serious crimes. At one time, in fact, every indictment charged the accused with an offence 'against the peace of our Sovereign Lord the King'; and, though this form is no longer employed, that is mainly because the imperative duty of not disturbing the King's Peace has by now evolved into an elaborate system of Criminal Law." Edward Jenks, *The Book of English Law* 134 (P.B. Fairest ed., 6th ed. 1967).

King's proctor. See QUEEN'S PROCTOR.

King's silver. (17c) *Hist.* Money paid in the Court of Common Pleas for a license to levy a feudal fine; an amount due on granting a *congé d'accorder* in levying a fine of lands. • It amounted to three-twentieths of the supposed annual value of the land, or ten shillings for every five marks of land. — Also termed *post-fine.* See CONGÉ D'ACCORDER; FINE (1).

kinship. (1833) **1.** Relationship by blood, marriage, or adoption. **2.** By extension, any strong connection between people. — Also termed *kindred.*

kinsman. See RELATIVE.

kintal. See QUINTAL.

kirkinbelkœr. [Norwegian "church books"] In medieval Norwegian law, church books that contained ecclesiastical legislation.

kissing the Book. *Hist. English law.* The practice of touching one's lips to a copy of the Bible (esp. the New Testament) after taking an oath in court. • This practice, formerly used in England, was replaced by the practice of placing one's hand on the Bible while swearing.

kitchen cabinet. See CABINET.

kiting. (1872) **1.** CHECK-KITING. **2.** *Commercial law. Slang.* Raising money on credit, often by using accommodation paper. **3.** *Criminal law. Slang.* The act or practice of prisoners' corresponding with each other by misaddressing an envelope so that it will be returned as undeliverable — but returned to the intended recipient. • This practice typically violates prison rules.

***Klaxon* doctrine** (**klak**-sən). (1966) *Conflict of laws.* The principle that a federal court exercising diversity jurisdiction must apply the choice-of-law rules of the state where the court sits. • In *Klaxon Co. v. Stentor Elec. Mfg. Co.*, the Supreme Court extended the rule of *Erie v. Tompkins* to choice-of-law issues. 313 U.S. 487, 61 S.Ct. 1020 (1941). — Also termed *Erie/Klaxon doctrine.* See ERIE DOCTRINE.

kleptomania (klep-tə-**may**-nee-ə), *n.* (1830) A compulsive urge to steal, esp. without economic motive. — **kleptomaniac,** *n.* & *adj.*

knifeman (**nɪf**-mən), *n.* Someone who attacks or kills someone else with a knife. Pl. **knifemen.**

knight. (bef. 12c) **1.** *Hist.* In the Middle Ages, a person of noble birth who, having been trained in arms and chivalry, was bound to follow an earl, baron, or other superior lord into battle. **2.** In the United Kingdom, a man on whom the monarch has bestowed an honorary dignity (knighthood) as a reward for personal merit of some kind. • The status of knighthood no longer relates to birth or possessions and does not involve military service.

knight bachelor. See BACHELOR (3).

knight of the post. *Hist.* A hired perjurer.

knight-service. See SERVICE (6).

knight's fee. (14c) *Hist.* The amount of land that gave rise to the obligation of knight-service. • The amount varied from less than a hide to more than six hides. See HIDE.

knight's service. See *knight-service* under SERVICE (6).

knobstick. See SCAB.

knock-and-announce rule. (1969) *Criminal procedure.* The requirement that the police knock at the door and announce their identity, authority, and purpose before entering a residence to execute an arrest or search warrant. — Also termed *knock-and-notice rule.* Cf. *no-knock search warrant* under SEARCH WARRANT; *no-knock search* under SEARCH (1).

knock-for-knock agreement. (1949) **1.** An arrangement between insurers whereby each will pay the claim of its insured without claiming against the other party's insurance. **2.** A contract in which the parties mutually indemnify each other for any injuries suffered by a party's employees or for damages to a party's property. — Also termed (in sense 2) *knock-for-knock indemnity agreement.*

knock in, *vb.* To rap on the courtroom door to announce the entry of (one or more judges) <the law clerk, acting as bailiff, knocked in the judges>.

knockoff, *n.* (1966) *Intellectual property.* An unauthorized counterfeit and usu. inferior copy of another's product, esp. one protected by patent, trademark, trade dress, or copyright, usu. passed off at a substantially lower price than the original.

knock off, *vb.* (1879) **1.** To make an unauthorized copy of (another's product), usu. for sale at a substantially lower price than the original <the infringer knocked off popular dress designs>. **2.** *Slang.* To murder <the gang leader was knocked off by one of his lieutenants>. **3.** *Slang.* To rob or burglarize <the thieves knocked off the jewelry store in broad daylight>.

knock-out auction. See AUCTION.

knock-out game. *Slang.* A criminal assault in which an attacker targets a stranger and attempts to render the victim unconscious with a single punch to the head.

knockout rule. *Contracts.* The principle that even if a form acceptance that is sent in response to a form offer varies the terms of the offer in nonmaterial ways, a contract is nevertheless formed, the nonmaterial varying terms in the two forms being void and replaceable by the rules of the UCC.

know all men by these presents. (16c) Take note. • This archaic form of address — a loan translation of the Latin *noverint universi per praesentes* — was traditionally used to begin certain legal documents such as bonds and powers of attorney, but in modern drafting style the phrase is generally considered deadwood. See NOVERINT UNIVERSI PER PRAESENTES. Cf. PATEAT UNIVERSIS PER PRAESENTES.

know-how. (1838) The learning, ability, and technique to do something; specif., the information, practical knowledge, techniques, and skill required to achieve some practical end, esp. in industry or technology. • Know-how is considered intangible property in which rights may be bought and sold. See TRADE SECRET.

knowing, *adj.* (14c) **1.** Having or showing awareness or understanding; well-informed <a knowing waiver of the right to counsel>. **2.** Deliberate; conscious <a knowing attempt to commit fraud>. — **knowingly,** *adv.*

knowing consent. See *informed consent* under CONSENT (1).

knowingly, *adv.* (15c) In such a manner that the actor engaged in prohibited conduct with the knowledge that the social harm that the law was designed to prevent was practically certain to result; deliberately. • Under the Model Penal Code, *knowingly* describes to the mental state resulting in the second-highest level of criminal culpability. A person who acts *purposely* wants to cause the social harm, while a person who acts *knowingly* understands that the social harm will almost certainly be a consequence of the action, but acts with other motives and does not care whether the social harm occurs. See CULPABILITY; MENS REA. Cf. PURPOSELY.

> "'Knowingly' or 'knowledge' has a broad sweep when used in connection with the element of a crime, and an untrue representation has been 'knowingly' made if by one who knows it is untrue, believes it is untrue or is quite aware that he has not the slightest notion whether it is true or not." Rollin M. Perkins & Ronald N. Boyce, *Criminal Law* 379 (3d ed. 1982).

> "A person acts knowingly with respect to a material element of an offense when: (i) if the element involves the nature of his conduct or the attendant circumstances, he is aware that his conduct is of that nature or that such circumstances exist; and (ii) if the element involves an element of his conduct, he is aware that it is practically certain that his conduct will cause such a result." Model Penal Code § 2.02(2)(b).

knowledge. (14c) **1.** An awareness or understanding of a fact or circumstance; a state of mind in which a person has no substantial doubt about the existence of a fact. Cf. INTENT (1); NOTICE (1), (2); SCIENTER (1).

> "It is necessary . . . to distinguish between producing a result intentionally and producing it knowingly. Intention and knowledge commonly go together, for he who intends a result usually knows that it will follow, and he who knows the consequences of his act usually intends them. But there may be intention without knowledge, the consequence being desired but not foreknown as certain or even probable. Conversely, there may be knowledge without intention, the consequence being foreknown as the inevitable concomitant of that which is desired, but being itself an object of repugnance rather than desire, and therefore not intended. When King David ordered Uriah the Hittite to be set in the forefront of the hottest battle, he intended the death of Uriah only, yet he knew for a certainty that many others of his men would fall at the same time and place." John Salmond, *Jurisprudence* 380–81 (Glanville L. Williams ed., 10th ed. 1947).

"[B]ecause there are several areas of the criminal law in which there may be good reason for distinguishing between one's objectives and [one's] knowledge, the modern approach is to define separately the mental states of knowledge and intent . . . . This is the approach taken in the Model Penal Code [§ 2.02(2)(a) & (b)]." Wayne R. LaFave & Austin W. Scott Jr., *Criminal Law* 218 (2d ed. 1986).

▸ **actual knowledge.** (16c) **1.** Direct and clear knowledge, as distinguished from constructive knowledge <the employer, having witnessed the accident, had actual knowledge of the worker's injury>. — Also termed *express actual knowledge.* **2.** Knowledge of information that would lead a reasonable person to inquire further <under the discovery rule, the limitations period begins to run once the plaintiff has actual knowledge of the injury>. — Also termed (in sense 2) *implied actual knowledge.*

"The third issue in section 523(a)(3) is the meaning of 'notice or actual knowledge.' Under the Uniform Commercial Code knowledge means actually knowing something; notice means having received information from which one could infer the existence of the relevant fact. What the adjective 'actual' adds to the idea of 'knowledge' is unclear." David G. Epstein et al., *Bankruptcy* § 7-27, at 516 (1993).

▸ **common knowledge.** See COMMON KNOWLEDGE.

▸ **constructive knowledge.** (18c) Knowledge that one using reasonable care or diligence should have, and therefore that is attributed by law to a given person <the court held that the partners had constructive knowledge of the partnership agreement even though none of them had read it>.

▸ **express actual knowledge.** See *actual knowledge* (1).

▸ **firsthand knowledge.** See *personal knowledge.*

▸ **general knowledge.** (17c) **1.** Knowledge of facts about many different subjects; the cumulative knowledge that someone possesses, expansive or paltry as it may be, as a result of a lifetime of learning. **2.** Widely known facts that a significant segment of the population would be familiar with.

▸ **implied actual knowledge.** See *actual knowledge* (2).

▸ **imputed knowledge.** (18c) Knowledge attributed to a given person, esp. because of the person's legal responsibility for another's conduct <the principal's imputed knowledge of its agent's dealings>.

▸ **personal knowledge.** (17c) Knowledge gained through firsthand observation or experience, as distinguished from a belief based on what someone else has said. • Rule 602 of the Federal Rules of Evidence requires lay witnesses to have personal knowledge of the matters they testify about. An affidavit must also be based on personal knowledge, unless the affiant makes it clear that a statement relies on "information and belief." — Also termed *firsthand knowledge.*

▸ **reckless knowledge.** (1911) A person's awareness that a prohibited circumstance may exist, regardless of which the person accepts the risk and goes on to act.

▸ **scientific knowledge.** (17c) *Evidence.* Knowledge that is grounded on scientific methods that have been supported by adequate validation. • Four primary factors are used to determine whether evidence amounts to scientific knowledge: (1) whether it has been tested; (2) whether it has been subjected to peer review and publication; (3) the known or potential rate of error; and (4) the degree of acceptance within the scientific community. See DAUBERT TEST; SCIENTIFIC METHOD.

▸ **superior knowledge.** (17c) Knowledge greater than that of another person, esp. so as to adversely affect that person <in its fraud claim, the subcontractor alleged that the general contractor had superior knowledge of the equipment shortage>.

2. Information, understanding, or skill that one gains through education or experience. **3.** *Archaic.* CARNAL KNOWLEDGE.

knowledge-of-falsity exclusion. See EXCLUSION (3).

known creditor. See CREDITOR.

known heir. See HEIR.

known-loss doctrine. (1992) *Insurance.* A principle denying insurance coverage when the insured knows before the policy takes effect that a specific loss has already happened or is substantially certain to happen. — Also termed *known-risk doctrine*; *known-loss rule.*

known person. See PERSON (1).

knuckleduster, *n.* (1858) See BRASS KNUCKLES.

***Kolstad* defense.** (1999) In an employment-discrimination case, an affirmative defense that bars a court from imposing punitive damages against an employer who makes a good-faith effort to comply with antidiscrimination laws, esp. Title VII of the Civil Rights Act of 1964. • Under this defense, if successful, an employer whose manager acts contrary to the employer's good-faith antidiscrimination efforts may not be subject to punitive damages. *Kolstad v. Am. Dental Ass'n*, 527 U.S. 526, 119 S.Ct. 2118 (1999). *See* TITLE VII OF THE CIVIL RIGHTS ACT OF 1964.

Kompetenz-Kompetenz. See COMPETENCE-COMPETENCE DOCTRINE.

koop (**kə**-wəp), *n.* [Dutch] *Dutch law.* Purchase; bargain.

koopbrief (**kə**-wəp-breef). [Dutch] *Dutch law.* A deed of sale.

***Kovel* letter.** (1981) An attorney's letter to an expert, esp. an accountant, memorializing that the expert has been hired by the attorney and that their communications, together with the expert's work product, are privileged. *U.S. v. Kovel*, 306 F.3d 40 (2d Cir. 2002).

Kutak Commission. The American Bar Association's Commission of the Evaluation of Professional Standards (1977–1983), created after the Watergate scandal and charged with drafting the Model Rules of Professional Conduct. • The commission is named for its chair, Robert J. Kutak of Omaha, Nebraska.

L

L. *abbr.* **1.** LAW (5). **2.** LORD (1). **3.** LOCUS. **4.** LATIN.

L. A measure of the money supply, including M3 items plus banker's acceptances, T-bills, and similar long-term investments. See M3.

label, *n.* (17c) **1.** *Trademarks.* An informative display of written or graphic matter, such as a logo, title, or similar marking, affixed to goods or services to identify their source <manufacturer's label>. • A label may be put on the packaging or container of a manufactured product, or on the packaging or surface of a natural substance. **2.** Any writing (such as a codicil) attached to a larger writing <the addendum appeared on a label stapled to the contract>. **3.** A narrow slip of paper or parchment attached to a deed or writ in order to hold a seal <several dangling labels attached to the deed>. **4.** A pejorative word, phrase, or moniker that is used to describe a person, group, or thing, esp. unfairly or incorrectly <he unjustly acquired the "troublemaker" label>. — **label,** *vb.*

label-and-significant-characteristics test. (1993) *Securities.* The rule that an instrument will be governed by the securities laws if it is labeled a stock and has the significant characteristics typically associated with shares of stock.

labeling. Under the Federal Food, Drug, and Cosmetic Act, any label or other written, printed, or graphic matter that is on a product or its container, or that accompanies the product. • To come within the Act, the labeling does not need to accompany the product. It may be sent before or after delivery of the product, as long as delivery of the product and the written material are part of the same distribution program.

label license. See LICENSE.

labes realis quae rei inhaeret (**lay**-beez ree-**ay**-lis kwee **ree**-I in-**heer**-it). [Latin] *Scots law.* A real defect that attaches to the thing. Cf. VITIUM REALE.

> "Theft, also, constitutes a *labes realis* in the title of any one holding the subject stolen, no matter how honestly he may have acquired it; and on this defect, which attaches to it until it return to his possession, the true owner may vindicate his right, and recover his subject wherever it can be found." John Trayner, *Trayner's Latin Maxims* 312 (4th ed. 1894).

labina (lə-**bI**-nə), *n. Archaic.* Land covered by water; swampland.

la bomba (lə **bom**-bə). *(sometimes cap.)* An incendiary device consisting of a plastic bag filled with fuel and placed inside a paper bag stuffed with tissue and rigged with a fuse. • A person who uses such a device to start a fire violates the federal arson statute. *See* 18 USCA § 844(j).

labor, *n.* (13c) **1.** Work of any type, including mental exertion <the fruits of one's labor>. • The term usu. refers to work for wages as opposed to profits.

▸ **child labor.** See CHILD LABOR.

▸ **hard labor.** See HARD LABOR.

▸ **spousal labor.** See SPOUSAL LABOR.

2. Workers considered as an economic unit or a political element <a dispute between management and labor over retirement benefits>. **3.** A Spanish land measure equal to $177^{1}/_{7}$ acres. • This measure has been used in Mexico and was once used in Texas.

labor, *vb.* (14c) **1.** To work, esp. with great exertion <David labored long and hard to finish the brief on time>. **2.** *Archaic.* To tamper with or improperly attempt to influence (a jury). • This sense derives from the idea that the tamperer "endeavors" to influence the jury's verdict. See EMBRACERY. — **laborer,** *n.*

labor agreement. See COLLECTIVE-BARGAINING AGREEMENT.

laborariis (lay-bə-**rair**-ee-is), *n.* [Latin "about laborers"] *Hist.* An ancient writ against a person who had no other means of support but refused to work throughout the year.

laboratory conditions. *Labor law.* The ideal conditions for a union election, in which the employees may exercise free choice without interference from the employer, the union, or anyone else.

labor camp. A type of prison where the prisoners are required to do hard physical work, usu. outdoors.

labor contract. See COLLECTIVE-BARGAINING AGREEMENT.

Labor Day. (1886) A public holiday set aside in honor esp. of blue-collar workers and organized labor. • Although in many countries the designated day is May 1, in the United States and Canada it is the first Monday in September.

labor–desert model. The view that the inventive process results from the inventor's labor to create something of added value to society, and that this added value justifies some social reward ("just deserts") to the inventor. — Also termed *value-added model.* Cf. EUREKA MODEL; LABOR MODEL.

labor dispute. (1907) A controversy between an employer and its employees concerning the terms or conditions of employment, or concerning the association or representation of those who negotiate or seek to negotiate the terms or conditions of employment. — Also termed *industrial dispute.*

Labor Disputes Act. See NORRIS–LAGUARDIA ACT.

laborer. (14c) **1.** Someone who makes a living by physical labor. **2.** WORKER.

laborer's lien. See *mechanic's lien* under LIEN.

labor force. Collectively, all the people who work either for a company or in a specified region, field, or industrial segment. Cf. LABOR (2).

laboring a jury. See EMBRACERY.

labor law. The field of law governing the relationship between employers and employees, esp. law governing the dealings of employers and the unions that represent employees. — Also termed *employment law*; *industrial law*. See NATIONAL LABOR RELATIONS ACT.

labor–management relations. (1947) The broad spectrum of activities concerning the relationship between employers and employees, both union and nonunion. See FAIR LABOR STANDARDS ACT; NATIONAL LABOR RELATIONS ACT; NATIONAL LABOR RELATIONS BOARD.

Labor–Management Relations Act. A 1947 federal statute that regulates certain union activities, permits suits against unions for proscribed acts, prohibits certain strikes and boycotts, and provides steps for settling strikes involving national emergencies. 29 USCA §§ 141 et seq. — Abbr. LMRA. — Also termed *Taft-Hartley Act*. See NATIONAL LABOR RELATIONS BOARD.

labor market. The number of people available for work in a specified region in comparison with the number of jobs available there. — Also termed *job market*.

labor model. (1988) The view that the inventive process is the product of the inventor's labor, and the invention is therefore the property of the inventor by natural right. See LOCKEAN LABOR THEORY. Cf. EUREKA MODEL, LABOR–DESERT MODEL.

labor organization. See UNION.

labor practice. See UNFAIR LABOR PRACTICE.

labor relations. (1858) The relationship between workers and employers. — Also termed *industrial relations*.

labor-relations act. (1935) A statute regulating relations between employers and employees. • Although the Labor–Management Relations Act is the chief federal labor-relations act, various states have enacted these statutes as well.

Labor Relations Board. See NATIONAL LABOR RELATIONS BOARD.

labor theory. See LOCKEAN LABOR THEORY.

labor union. See UNION.

labor-unionism. See TRADE-UNIONISM.

lacca. See LACTA.

Lacey Act. A 1900 federal statute that permits states to enforce their own game laws prohibiting the importation of animals from other states or countries. 16 USCA §§ 661 et seq. See GAME LAW.

la chambre des esteilles (lə **shahm**-brə də zes-**tay**), *n.* [French] *Hist.* The Star Chamber. See STAR CHAMBER, COURT OF.

laches (**lach**-iz *or* [incorrectly] **lach**-eez). [Law French "remissness; slackness"] (14c) **1.** Unreasonable delay in pursuing a right or claim — almost always an equitable one — in a way that prejudices the party against whom relief is sought. — Also termed *sleeping on rights*.

▸ **prosecution laches.** (1997) *Patents.* In a claim for patent-infringement, the equitable defense that the patentee did not timely enforce the patent rights.

2. The equitable doctrine by which a court denies relief to a claimant who has unreasonably delayed in asserting the claim, when that delay has prejudiced the party against whom relief is sought. Cf. LIMITATION (3).

> "The doctrine of laches . . . is an instance of the exercise of the reserved power of equity to withhold relief otherwise regularly given where in the particular case the granting of such relief would be unfair or unjust." William F. Walsh, *A Treatise on Equity* 472 (1930).

laches, estoppel by. See *estoppel by laches* under ESTOPPEL.

***Lackey* claim.** (1995) A prisoner's assertion that incarceration on death row for a protracted period is cruel and unusual punishment. *Lackey v. Texas*, 514 U.S. 1045, 115 S.Ct. 1421 (1995) (denying cert.).

lack-of-antecedent-basis rejection. See REJECTION.

lack of capacity. The disability of a person to create or enter into a contract of other legal relation because of some special characteristic. See CAPACITY (2).

lack of enablement. See NONENABLEMENT.

lack-of-enablement rejection. See *nonenablement rejection* under REJECTION (3).

lack-of-fair-warning challenge. See FAIR-WARNING CHALLENGE.

lack of jurisdiction. See WANT OF JURISDICTION.

lack of prosecution. See WANT OF PROSECUTION.

lack-of-utility rejection. See REJECTION.

La Codi (lah **koh**-dɪ). A 12th-century summary of the Justinian Code compiled for the use of the judges of Provence. • It was the first treatise on Roman law in a native dialect.

> "*Lo Codi* stands already under the influence of the glossators. It follows closely a summary of the *Codex* extant in a MS. of Troyes (*Summa Trecensis*) and attributed by Fitting to Irnerius himself. The authorship of Irnerius cannot be proved, but the *Summa Trecensis* is, in any case, a fair sample of an early glossator's work. The compilers of the *Codex* have also utilized a *Summa Codicis* of Rogerius, a glossator of the third generation. It seems, in fact, that Rogerius personally took part in the compilation of the *Codi*. Yet the *Codi* has distinctive features which on the one hand distinguish it from the Bolognese books, and on the other hand connect it with the tradition of the *Exceptiones Petri*. It is written not for academic use, but for the courts, and more particularly for laymen acting as presiding judges or arbitrators; it is absolutely free from pedantry or abstruse argument; it aims chiefly at clearness, and at easy access in case of reference. Cases likely to occur in common practice are constantly put. *Lo Codi* is, in short, a manual for immediate use, somewhat resembling the books of reference of modern justices of the peace." Paul Vinogradoff, *Roman Law in Medieval Europe* 73–74 (1929).

lacta (**lak**-tə), *n.* [Law Latin] *Hist.* Lack of or defect in the weight of money. — Also termed *lacca*.

l'acte de l'état civil. See ACTE (1).

lacuna. (17c) A missing part of something; a blank space; a gap. Pl. **lacunae.**

lada (**lay**-də), *n.* [Law Latin] **1.** *Hist.* A court of justice. **2.** A canal for draining marshy ground; a watercourse; a lade.

lade (layd), *n.* (18c) *Hist.* The mouth of a river. — Also spelled *lode*.

laden in bulk, *adj.* (1882) *Maritime law.* (Of a vessel) loaded with a cargo that lies loose in the hold instead of packaged. • Cargoes of corn, salt, and similar items are usu. shipped in bulk.

lading, bill of. See BILL OF LADING.

lady. (bef. 12c) In the United Kingdom, a title belonging to the wife of a peer, (by courtesy) the wife of a baronet or knight, or any single or married woman whose father was a nobleman carrying a rank of earl or higher.

Lady Bird deed. See DEED.

lady-court. (1830) *Hist.* The court of a lady of the manor.

Lady Day. See *quarter day* under DAY.

lady's friend. (1845) *Hist.* The title of an officer in the English House of Commons, whose duty was to secure a suitable provision for a wife when her husband sought a parliamentary divorce. • In 1857, parliamentary divorces and the office of lady's friend were abolished by statute.

laenland. See LOANLAND.

laesa majestas (**lee**-zə mə-**jes**-tas). See LESE MAJESTY.

laesio enormis (**lee**-shee-oh i-**nor**-mis). [Law Latin "excessive loss" or "abnormal loss of more than half"] (1834) *Roman & civil law.* **1.** The sale of a thing for which the buyer paid less than half of its real value. • The seller could rescind the sale, but the buyer could keep the item purchased by paying the full value. Generally, this doctrine was limited to land sales. **2.** The injury sustained by one party to an onerous contract when the overreaching party receives twice the value of that party's money or property, such as a purchaser who pays less than half of the value of the property sold, or a seller who receives more than double the property's value. • If coowner coheirs partition or sell property, *laesio enormis* may exist when the purchaser pays less than one-fourth of the value rather than one-half. See La. Civ. Code arts. 824, 1406. — Also spelled *lesio enormis.* — Also termed *lesion*; *enorm lesion*; (in full) *laesio enormis vel ultra dimidium* (**lee**-shee-oh i-**nor**-mis vel **əl**-trə di-**mid**-ee-əm); (in Louisiana) *lesion beyond moiety.*

> "Lesion (*laesio enormis*) was the rule, established very late, that a seller could rescind a contract if he had received less than half its real value .... [I]n spite of its imperfections, lesion not only was adopted in all modern civilian systems (French Code Civil 1674–1683), but became the means of testing the validity of contracts generally by their fairness, a principle embodied in the German Civil Code (section 138) and the Swiss Code of Obligations (section 21). Such a test is no more difficult to apply in law than in equity, where it has long been established in our system. As the Romans applied it, it was a clumsy and inadequate way of reaching this result. In modern courts, in civil-law countries, it invests judges with a discretion not very likely to be abused, but sufficient to act as a deterrent to the grosser forms of economic exploitation." Max Radin, *Handbook of Roman Law* 233–34 (1927).

laesio ultra dimidium vel enormis. See LAESIO ENORMIS.

laesiwerp (**lee**-zə-wərp), *n.* [Saxon fr. *laisus* "bosom" + *werpire* "to surrender"] *Hist.* A thing surrendered to another's hands or power; a thing given or delivered.

laet (layt), *n.* (bef. 12c) *Hist.* A person of a class between servile and free.

lag, *n.* (1811) *Archaic. Slang.* **1.** A convict. • The term *old lag* refers to a repeat offender. See RECIDIVIST. **2.** An ex-convict. **3.** A term of imprisonment; a prison sentence.

lag, *vb.* (1819) *Archaic. Slang.* **1.** To arrest for a crime. **2.** To imprison or jail.

laga. See LAGE.

lagan (**lag**-ən), *n.* (17c) **1.** Goods that are abandoned at sea but attached to a buoy so that they may be recovered. — Also termed *lagend*; *lagon*; *ligan*; *ligen*; *logan.* Cf. FLOTSAM; JETSAM; WAVESON. **2.** *Archaic.* Wreckage or cargo lying on the seabed.

lage (law *or* lay), *n.* [fr. Saxon *lag* "law"] (bef. 12c) *Hist.* **1.** Law. **2.** The territory in which certain law was in force, such as danelage, mercenlage, and West-Saxon lage. • This term is essentially an obsolete form of the word *law.* — Also termed *lagh*; *laga*; *lagu.* See DANELAW; MERCENLAGE; WEST-SAXON LAW.

lage day (**law** day). A law day; a juridical day; a day of open court. — Also termed *lagh day.*

lageman (**law**-mən *or* **lay**-mən). See LEGALIS HOMO.

lagemannus. See LAHMAN.

lagend (**lag**-ənd). See LAGAN.

lagging economic indicator. See ECONOMIC INDICATOR.

lagging indicator. See INDICATOR.

lagh day. See LAGE DAY.

lagon (**lag**-ən). See LAGAN.

lagu. See LAGE.

lahman (**law**-mən *or* **lay**-mən), *n.* [Saxon fr. *lah* "law"] *Archaic.* A lawyer. — Also termed *lagemannus.*

laicus (**lay**-ə-kəs), *n.* [Law Latin] *Hist.* A layman; one who is not in the ministry.

***Laidlaw* vacancy.** (1991) Under the National Labor Relations Act, a genuine opening in an employer's workforce, resulting from the employer's expanding its workforce or discharging a particular employee, or from an employee's resigning or otherwise leaving the employment. • The opening must be offered to striking workers, in order of seniority, after a strike has been resolved. *Laidlaw Corp. v. NLRB*, 414 F.2d 99 (7th Cir. 1969).

lairwite (**lair**-wɪt), *n.* [fr. Saxon *lagan* "to lie" + *wite* "a fine"] (13c) *Hist.* A fine for adultery or fornication paid to the lord of the manor; esp., a lord's privilege of receiving a fine for fornication with the lord's female villeins. — Also termed *lairesite*; *lecherwite* (**lech**-ər-wɪt); *legerwite*; *leirwita*; *leyerwite*; *legenita* (lə-**jen**-ə-tə); *legruita* (lə-**groo**-ə-tə).

lais gents (**lay** zhon[ts]), *n. pl.* [Law French] *Hist.* Laymen; a jury.

laissez-faire (les-ay-**fair**), *n.* [French "let (people) do (as they choose)"] (1825) **1.** Governmental abstention from interfering in economic or commercial affairs. **2.** The doctrine favoring such abstention. — **laissez-faire,** *adj.*

laissez passer (les-ay pah-**say**), n. [French "let (people) pass"] (1914) **1.** A single-use, one-way travel document issued to an applicant, usu. one who has lost or cannot obtain a passport. **2.** A document given by a host government to foreign diplomatic personnel to permit them free passage across the host country's border. — Also termed *laisser passer.*

laity (**lay**-ə-tee). (15c) Collectively, persons who are not members of the clergy.

lake, *n.* (12c) **1.** A large body of standing water in a depression of land or basin supplied from the drainage of an extended area; esp., a natural depression in the surface of the earth containing a reasonably permanent body of water that is substantially at rest. **2.** A widened or expanded part of a river.

Lambeth degree (**lam**-bəth). (1859) *Hist.* A degree conferred by the Archbishop of Canterbury, rather than by a university, as authorized under the Ecclesiastical Licenses

Act of 1533 (25 Hen. 8, ch. 21). • The degrees were conferred in music, theology, law, and medicine.

***Lamb-Weston* rule.** (1968) *Insurance.* The doctrine that, when two insurance policies provide coverage for a loss, and each of them contains an other-insurance clause — creating a conflict in the order or apportionment of coverage — both of the other-insurance clauses will be disregarded and liability will be prorated between the insurers. *Lamb-Weston, Inc. v. Oregon Auto. Ins. Co.*, 341 P.2d 110 (Or. 1959).

lame duck. (1910) **1.** An official, esp. an elected one, whose power has waned because his or her term of office will end soon; esp., an elected official serving out a term after a successor has been elected. **2.** A person, business, institution, etc. that is having serious problems and needs help.

lame-duck amendment. See TWENTIETH AMENDMENT.

lame-duck session. See SESSION (1).

Lammas. See *quarter day* under DAY.

lammas land. See LAND.

land, *n.* (bef. 12c) **1.** An immovable and indestructible three-dimensional area consisting of a portion of the earth's surface, the space above and below the surface, and everything growing on or permanently affixed to it. **2.** An estate or interest in real property. See LANDS.

> "In its legal significance, 'land' is not restricted to the earth's surface, but extends below and above the surface. Nor is it confined to solids, but may encompass within its bounds such things as gases and liquids. A definition of 'land' along the lines of 'a mass of physical matter occupying space' also is not sufficient, for an owner of land may remove part or all of that physical matter, as by digging up and carrying away the soil, but would nevertheless retain as part of his 'land' the space that remains. Ultimately, as a juristic concept, 'land' is simply an area of three-dimensional space, its position being identified by natural or imaginary points located by reference to the earth's surface. 'Land' is not the fixed contents of that space, although, as we shall see, the owner of that space may well own those fixed contents. Land is immoveable, as distinct from chattels, which are moveable; it is also, in its legal significance, indestructible. The contents of the space may be physically severed, destroyed or consumed, but the space itself, and so the 'land,' remains immutable." Peter Butt, *Land Law* 9 (2d ed. 1988).

▸ **accommodation land.** (1843) Land that is bought by a builder or speculator who erects houses or improvements on it and then leases it at an increased rent.

▸ **acquired federal land.** (*usu. pl.*) (2003) Federal land that was never in the public domain. See *federal land.*

▸ **acquired land.** Land acquired by the government from private hands or from another governmental entity; esp., property acquired by the federal government from private or state ownership. • This term is frequently contrasted with *public domain.* — Also termed *acquired lands.* See PUBLIC DOMAIN (1).

> "'Acquired lands' are lands the United States acquired from private or state owners by gift, purchase, exchange, or condemnation. In most but not all cases, such lands actually have been 'reacquired,' because the United States previously had purchased or won them from foreign and Indian sovereigns. Distinguishing between lands because of ownership origins that go back over a century is a policy with little to recommend it, but some statutes and judicial opinions maintain the distinction." George Cameron Coggins, *Public Natural Resources Law* § 1.02[1] (1990).

▸ **arable land** (**ar**-ə-bəl). (16c) Land fit for cultivation. — Formerly also termed *araturia; aralia; aratia.*

▸ **bounty land.** A portion of public land given or donated as a reward, esp. for military service. See MILITARY BOUNTY LAND.

▸ **certificate land.** Land in the western part of Pennsylvania set apart after the American Revolution to be bought with certificates that the soldiers received in lieu of pay. Cf. *donation land.*

▸ **Crown land.** (17c) Demesne land of the Crown; esp., in England and Canada, land belonging to the sovereign personally, or to the government, as distinguished from land held under private ownership. — Also termed *demesne land of the Crown.* See *demesne land.*

▸ **demesne land** (di-**mayn** *or* di-**meen**). (15c) *Hist.* Land reserved by a lord for personal use.

▸ **donation land.** Land granted from the public domain to an individual as a gift, usu. as a reward for services or to encourage settlement in a remote area. • The term was initially used in Pennsylvania to reward Revolutionary War soldiers. Cf. *certificate land.*

▸ **earned land.** Public land that is conveyed by a land patent to a private person who has performed a certain condition, usu. one spelled out in an earlier grant. See PATENT (2).

▸ **enclosed land.** (17c) Land that is actually enclosed and surrounded with fences.

▸ **fabric land.** (17c) *Hist.* Land given toward the maintenance, repair, or rebuilding of a cathedral or other church. • This term derives from funds given *ad fabricam ecclesiae reparandam* ("to repair the fabric of the church").

> "Fabrick-Lands are lands given towards the maintenance, rebuilding, or repair of Cathedrals or other churches . . . . In antient time almost every one gave by his Will more or less to the *Fabrick* of the Cathedral or Parish-Church where he liv'd." Thomas Blount, *Nomo-Lexicon: A Law-Dictionary* (1670).

▸ **fast land.** (*often pl.*) (16c) Land that is above the high-water mark and that, when flooded by a government project, is subjected to a governmental taking. • Owners of fast lands are entitled to just compensation for the taking. See TAKING (2).

▸ **federal land.** (*usu. pl.*) (1889) Land owned by the United States government. • Federal lands are classified as public lands (also termed "lands in the public domain") or acquired federal lands, depending on how the land was obtained. See *acquired federal land.*

▸ **government land.** See *public land.*

▸ **hide land.** *Hist.* See HIDE.

▸ **improved land.** (17c) Land that has been developed; esp., land occupied by buildings and structures. • The improvements may or may not enhance the value of the land.

▸ **indemnity land.** See INDEMNITY LAND.

▸ **lammas land** (**lam**-əs). (17c) *Hist.* Land over which persons other than the owner have the right of pasturage during winter, from lammas (reaping time) until sowing time.

▸ **lieu land** (loo). (1918) Public land within indemnity limits granted in lieu of those lost within place limits.

▸ **life land.** (1858) *Hist.* Land leased for a term measured by the life of one or more persons. — Also termed *lifehold.*

▸ **made land.** Artificially formed land, usu. land that has been reclaimed by filling or created by dredging.

▸ **mineral land.** (18c) Land that contains deposits of valuable minerals in quantities justifying the costs of extraction and using the land for mining, rather than agricultural or other purposes.

▸ **place land.** See INDEMNITY LAND.

▸ **public land.** (17c) Lands or land interests held by the government, without regard to how the government acquired ownership; unappropriated land belonging to the federal or state government. — Also termed *public lands*; *government land*; *public ground.*

"The terms 'public lands' and 'federal lands' may . . . include less than full fee interests, such as severed mineral estates. They usually do not, however, refer to submerged lands off the seacoasts (over which the United States asserts jurisdiction but not title), or lands held in trust for Indians." George Cameron Coggins et al., *Federal Public Land and Resources Law* 3 (3d ed. 1993).

▸ **reserved land.** See RESERVATION (3).

▸ **riparian land.** (1866) **1.** Land that includes part of the bed of a watercourse or lake. **2.** Land that borders on a public watercourse or public lake whose bed is owned by the public.

▸ **school land.** (18c) Public real estate set apart for sale or exploitation by a state to establish and fund public schools.

▸ **seated land.** (1822) Land that is occupied, cultivated, improved, reclaimed, farmed, or used as a place of residence, with or without cultivation.

▸ **settled land.** Any land — or any interest in it — that is the subject of any document limiting it to, or putting it into trust for, a person by way of succession.

▸ **swamp and overflowed land.** (1853) Land that, because of its boggy, marshy, fenlike character, is unfit for cultivation, requiring drainage or reclamation to render it available for beneficial use. • Such lands were granted out of the U.S. public domain to the littoral states by acts of Congress in 1850 and thereafter. 43 USCA §§ 981 et seq.

▸ **tideland.** See TIDELAND.

▸ **unimproved land.** (18c) **1.** Raw land that has never been developed, and usu. that lacks utilities. **2.** Land that was formerly developed but has now been cleared of all buildings and structures.

▸ **withdrawn land.** See RESERVATION (3).

land, law of. See LAW OF THE LAND.

land agent. **1.** Someone who controls or manages a landed estate for the owner by seeing to the production, advancement, and value of the land; esp., one whose job is to attend to someone else's land, buildings, farm, cattle, etc. — Also termed *land manager*; *land steward.* **2.** LANDMAN (1).

land bank. (1921) **1.** A bank created under the Federal Farm Loan Act to make loans at low interest rates secured by farmland. **2.** A program in which land is retired from agricultural production for conservation or tree-cultivation purposes. — Also termed *soil bank.* See FEDERAL HOME LOAN BANK.

land boundary. See BOUNDARY (1).

land certificate. A document entitling a person to receive from the government a certain amount of land by following prescribed legal steps. • It contains an official description of the land, as well as the name and address of the person receiving the entitlement, and is prima facie evidence of the truth of the matters it contains. — Also termed *land warrant.*

landcheap. (bef. 12c) *Hist.* A customary fine paid in money or cattle when any real property within a manor or borough was transferred.

land-conservation agreement. See *land-conservation easement* under EASEMENT.

land-conservation easement. See EASEMENT.

land contract. See *installment land contract* under CONTRACT.

land cop. *Hist.* The sale of land evidenced by the transfer in court of a rod or festuca as a symbol of possession. • The seller handed the rod to the reeve and the reeve handed it to the purchaser. The conveyance occurred in court to provide better evidence of the transfer and to bar the claims of expected heirs.

land court. See COURT.

land-customs zone. See CUSTOMS ZONE.

land damages. See *just compensation* under COMPENSATION.

land department. (1837) A federal or state bureau that determines factual matters regarding the control and transfer of public land. • The federal land department includes the General Land Office headed by the Secretary of the Interior. See DEPARTMENT OF THE INTERIOR.

land description. See LEGAL DESCRIPTION.

land developer. See DEVELOPER (1).

land district. See DISTRICT.

landed, *adj.* (15c) **1.** (Of a person) having an estate in land; possessing real estate <landed proprietor>. **2.** (Of an estate, etc.) consisting of land <landed property>.

landed estate. See ESTATE (1).

landed-estates court. See COURT.

landed property. See *landed estate* under ESTATE (1).

landed security. See SECURITY (4).

landed servitude. See *servitude appurtenant* under SERVITUDE (3).

landefricus (lan-də-**frɪ**-kəs). *Hist.* A landlord or lord of the soil.

landegandman (lan-də-**gand**-mən *or* **lan**-də-gənd-mən). *Hist.* A customary or inferior tenant of a manor.

land-end, *n.* (16c) *Hist.* **1.** In an English parish without enclosures during the Middle Ages, a small parcel of ground severed from the rest by a road or pathway. **2.** In traditional farming, the part of an open field where plow horses or oxen turn and the furrow is transverse to that of the rest of the field.

landfall, *n.* (17c) **1.** The first land spotted after a nautical voyage. **2.** The sudden transfer of substantial land upon the death of a rich person. Cf. WINDFALL.

land flip. (1988) *Real estate.* A transaction in which a piece of property is purchased for one price and immediately sold, usu. to a fictitious entity, for a much higher price, to dupe a lender or later purchaser into thinking that the property is more valuable than it actually is.

land forces. See UNITED STATES ARMY.

land-gavel (**land**-gav-əl). (bef. 12c) *Hist.* A tax or rent issuing from land; tax calculated according to the Domesday Book. — Also spelled *landgable*; *land-gabel*; *land-gafol.* See GAVEL (1), (2); DOMESDAY BOOK.

***Landgraf* doctrine.** See PRESUMPTION AGAINST RETROACTIVITY.

land grant. (1862) A donation of public land to an individual, a corporation, or a subordinate government.

▸ **private land grant.** (1861) A land grant to a natural person. See *land patent* under PATENT (2).

landhlaford (**land**-[h]lav-ərd). *Hist.* A proprietor of land; a lord of the soil.

landholder. (17c) Someone who possesses or owns land. Cf. LANDOWNER.

landholding, *n.* (1876) **1.** The fact or practice of possessing or owning real estate; landownership. **2.** The land that someone possesses or owns.

land improvement. See IMPROVEMENT.

landing. (15c) **1.** A place on a river or other navigable water for loading and unloading goods, or receiving and delivering passengers and watercraft. **2.** The termination point on a river or other navigable water for these purposes. **3.** The act or process of coming back to land after a voyage or flight.

landing law. (1976) A law prohibiting the possession or sale of fish or game that have been taken illegally.

landing waiter. See LAND WAITER.

land lease. See *ground lease* under LEASE.

landlocked, *adj.* (17c) **1.** Surrounded by land, with no way to get in or out except by crossing the land of another <because the tract was landlocked, the buyer claimed an easement of necessity across the seller's property>. **2.** (Of a country) surrounded by other countries, with no access to major navigable waterways; having no coast or easy access to the sea by reason of being surrounded by masses of land <the landlocked country had always been at a mercantile disadvantage to its seafaring neighbors>.

landlord. (bef. 12c) **1.** At common law, the feudal lord who retained the fee of the land. — Sometimes shortened to *lord.* **2.** Someone who rents a room, building, or piece of land to someone else. — Also termed (in sense 2) *lessor.*

▸ **absentee landlord.** (1822) A landlord who does not live on the leased premises; usu., one who lives far away. — Also termed *absentee management.*

landlord-and-tenant relationship. See LANDLORD–TENANT RELATIONSHIP.

landlordism, *n.* (1844) The collective behavior of landlords; esp., the overreaching tactics of callous and abusive landlords, such as slumlords. • The term is invariably pejorative.

landlordry, *n.* (16c) **1.** The quality, state, or condition of a landlord. **2.** Landlords collectively.

landlord's hypothec. See HYPOTHEC.

landlord's lien. See LIEN.

landlord's warrant. See WARRANT (1).

landlord–tenant relationship. (1921) The legal relationship between the lessor and lessee of real estate. • The relationship is contractual, created by a lease (or agreement for lease) for a term of years, from year to year, for life, or at will, and exists when one person occupies the premises of another with the lessor's permission or consent, subordinated to the lessor's title or rights. There must be a landlord's reversion, a tenant's estate, transfer of possession and control of the premises, and (generally) an express or implied contract. — Also termed *landlord-and-tenant relationship.* See LEASE.

landman. (1923) *Oil & gas.* **1.** A person responsible for acquiring oil and gas leases, negotiating arrangements for development of leases, and managing leased properties. • In this field, both men and women are commonly known as *landmen.* — Also termed *land agent*; *exploration manager.* **2.** Someone who lives or works on the land — as opposed to *seaman.* — Also termed (in sense 2 only) *landsman.* **3.** TERRE-TENANT (1).

land manager. 1. LANDMAN (1). **2.** LAND AGENT (1).

landmark. (bef. 12c) **1.** A feature of land (such as a natural object, or a monument or marker) that demarcates the boundary of the land <according to the 1891 survey, the crooked oak tree is the correct landmark at the property's northeast corner>. **2.** A historically significant building or site <the schoolhouse built in 1898 is the county's most famous landmark>. See MONUMENT.

landmark decision. (1913) A judicial decision that significantly changes existing law. • Examples are *Brown v. Board of Educ.*, 347 U.S. 483, 74 S.Ct. 686 (1954) (holding that segregation in public schools violates the Equal Protection Clause), and *Palsgraf v. Long Island R.R.*, 162 N.E. 99 (N.Y. 1928) (establishing that a defendant's duty in a negligence action is limited to plaintiffs within the apparent zone of danger — that is, plaintiffs to whom damage could be reasonably foreseen). — Also termed *landmark case.* Cf. LEADING CASE (1).

land-measurer. (17c) See SURVEYOR.

land-measuring, *n.* (16c) The art and science of surveying parcels of land and expressing the dimensions in acres, hectares, rods, perches, or the like. Cf. LAND-SURVEYING.

land office. (17c) A government office that keeps records about sales of land by systematically documenting real-estate conveyances, showing sellers, buyers, dates of transactions, and evidence of titles. — Also termed (BrE) *land registry.*

landowner. (18c) Someone who owns land. Cf. LANDHOLDER. — **landownership,** *n.*

landowner's royalty. See ROYALTY (2).

land patent. See PATENT (2).

land pollution. See POLLUTION.

land-poor, *adj.* (1873) (Of a person) owning a substantial amount of unprofitable or encumbered land, but lacking the money to improve or maintain the land or to pay the charges due on it.

land-preservation agreement. See *land-conservation easement* under EASEMENT.

landreeve. (1842) *Hist.* A person charged with (1) overseeing certain parts of a farm or estate, (2) attending to the timber, fences, gates, buildings, private roads, and watercourses, (3) stocking the commons, (4) watching for encroachments of all kinds, (5) preventing and detecting waste and spoliation by tenants and others, and (6) reporting on findings to the manager or land steward.

land registration. (1853) The statutory system for recording rights in land with a public agency.

land registry. See LAND OFFICE.

land-rent. See RENT (1).

land revenue. See REVENUE.

Landrum–Griffin Act. A federal law, originally enacted in 1959 as the Labor–Management Reporting and Disclosure Act, designed to (1) curb corruption in union leadership and undemocratic conduct in internal union affairs, (2) outlaw certain types of secondary boycotts, and (3) prevent so-called hot-cargo provisions in collective-bargaining agreements. See HOT CARGO.

lands, *n. pl.* (14c) **1.** At common law, real property less extensive than either tenements or hereditaments. **2.** By statute in some states, real property including tenements and hereditaments. See HEREDITAMENT (2); TENEMENT.

land sales contract. See *installment land contract* under CONTRACT.

land scrip. (1834) **1.** A negotiable instrument entitling the holder, usu. a person or company engaged in public service, to possess specified areas of public land. See SCRIP (1). **2.** A certificate given to someone who purchases public land stating that the purchase price has been duly paid.

landsman. See LANDMAN.

lands, tenements, and hereditaments. (16c) Real property. • The term was traditionally used in wills, deeds, and other instruments.

land steward. See LAND AGENT (1).

land-surveying, *n.* (18c) The art and science of determining the boundaries of and improvements on any portion of land, as of an estate, farm, ranch, township, or the like, and of preparing an accurate map of it. Cf. LAND-MEASURING.

land tax. See *property tax* under TAX.

land-tenant. See TERRE-TENANT.

Land Titles and Transfer Act. *Hist.* An 1875 English statute establishing a registry for titles to real property, and providing for the transfer of lands and recording of those transfers. 38 & 39 Vict., ch. 87. • The act is analogous in some respects to American recording laws, such as those providing for a registry of deeds. A system of title registration superseded this registry system in 1925.

land trust. See TRUST (3).

land-trust certificate. (1927) An instrument granting the holder a share of the benefits of property ownership, while the trustee retains legal title. See *land trust* under TRUST (3).

land-use exaction. See EXACTION (3).

land-use planning. (1939) The deliberate, systematic development of real estate through methods such as zoning, environmental-impact studies, and the like. — Also spelled *landuse planning.* — Also termed *urban planning.*

land-use regulation. (1938) An ordinance or other legislative enactment governing the development or use of real estate. — Also spelled *landuse regulation.*

> "Public regulation of the use and development of land comes in a variety of forms which generally focus on four aspects of land use: (1) the type of use, such as whether it will be used for agricultural, commercial, industrial, or residential purposes; (2) the density of use, manifested in concerns over the height, width, bulk, or environmental impact of the physical structures on the land; (3) the aesthetic impact of the use, which may include the design and placement of structures on the land; and (4) the effect of the particular use of the land on the cultural and social values of the community, illustrated by community conflicts over adult entertainment, housing for service-dependent groups such as low-income families and developmentally disabled persons, and whether the term *family* should be defined in land use regulations to include persons who are not related by blood or marriage." Peter W. Salsich Jr., *Land Use Regulation* 1 (1991).

land-use zone. See ZONE (2).

land waiter. (18c) *English law.* A customhouse officer with the responsibility of examining, tasting, weighing, measuring, and accounting for merchandise landing at any port. —Also termed *landing waiter.*

land warfare. See WARFARE.

land warrant. See LAND CERTIFICATE.

Langdell method. See CASEBOOK METHOD.

Langdell system. See CASEBOOK METHOD.

langeman (**lan**-jə-mən), *n. Hist.* A lord of a manor. Pl. **langemanni** (lan-jə-**man**-I).

language. (14c) **1.** Any organized means of conveying or communicating ideas, esp. by human speech, written characters, or sign language <what language did they speak?>. **2.** The letter or grammatical import of a document or instrument, as distinguished from its spirit <the language of the statute>.

languidus (**lang**-gwi-dəs), *n.* [Law Latin "sick"] *Hist.* At common law, a return of process made by the sheriff when a defendant whom the sheriff had taken into custody was too sick to be removed.

Lanham Act (**lan**-əm). A 1946 federal statute that provides for a national system of trademark registration and protects the owner of a federally registered mark against the use of similar marks if any confusion might result or if the strength of a strong mark would be diluted. • The Lanham Act's scope is independent of and concurrent with state common law. 15 USCA §§ 1051 et seq. — Also termed *Federal Trademark Act; Trademark Act of 1946.*

lapidation (lap-ə-**day**-shən), *n.* (17c) An execution by stoning a person to death. — **lapidate** (**lap**-ə-dayt), *vb.*

lappage (**lap**-ij). (1836) Interference; lap and overlap; conflict. • Lappage applies when two different owners claim under deeds or grants that, in part, cover the same land.

lapping. (1939) An embezzlement technique by which an employee takes funds from one customer's accounts receivable and covers it by using a second customer's payment to pay the first account, then a third customer's payment to pay the second account, and so on.

lapse, *n.* (16c) **1.** The termination of a right or privilege because of a failure to exercise it within some time limit or because a contingency has occurred or not occurred. **2.** *Wills & estates.* The failure of a testamentary gift, esp. when the beneficiary dies before the testator. See ANTI-LAPSE STATUTE. Cf. ADEMPTION.

lapse, *vb.* (18c) **1.** (Of an estate or right) to pass away or revert to someone else because conditions have not been fulfilled or because a person entitled to possession has failed in some duty. See *lapsed policy* under INSURANCE POLICY. **2.** (Of a devise, grant, etc.) to become void.

lapsed devise. See DEVISE.

lapsed legacy. See LEGACY (1).

lapsed policy. See INSURANCE POLICY.

lapse patent. See PATENT (2).

lapse statute. See ANTILAPSE STATUTE.

lapsus bonis (lap-səs **boh**-nis). [Latin] (17c) *Scots law.* Reduced in worldly circumstances. • The phrase appeared in reference to a person who was having temporary financial difficulties.

LAPS value test. (1988) A measure based on a community's values by which a court determines the literary, artistic, political, or scientific worth or merit of an allegedly obscene work. • The test originated in *Miller v. California*, 413 U.S. 15, 93 S.Ct. 2607 (1973). See MILLER TEST.

larcenable (**lahr**-sə-nə-bəl), *adj.* (1920) Subject to larceny <because it cannot be carried away, real estate is not larcenable>.

larcenist, *n.* (1803) Someone who commits larceny. See LARCENY.

larcenous (**lahr**-sə-nəs), *adj.* (18c) **1.** Of, relating to, or characterized by larceny <a larcenous taking>. **2.** (Of a person) contemplating or tainted with larceny; thievish <a larcenous purpose>.

larcenous intent. See INTENT (1).

larceny (**lahr**-sə-nee), *n.* (15c) The unlawful taking and carrying away of someone else's tangible personal property with the intent to deprive the possessor of it permanently. • Common-law larceny has been broadened by some statutes to include embezzlement and false pretenses, all three of which are often subsumed under the statutory crime of "theft. Cf. ROBBERY.

> "The criminal offence of larceny or theft in the Common Law was intimately connected with the civil wrong of trespass. 'Where there has been no trespass,' said Lord Coleridge, 'there can at law common be no larceny.' Larceny, in other words, is merely a particular kind of trespass to goods which, by virtue of the trespasser's intent, is converted into a crime. Trespass is a wrong, not to ownership but to *possession*, and theft, therefore, is not the violation of a person's right to ownership, but the infringement of his possession, accompanied with a particular criminal intent." 4 *Stephen's Commentaries on the Laws of England* 72–73 (L. Crispin Warmington ed., 21st ed. 1950).

> "[T]he distinctions between larceny, embezzlement and false pretenses serve no useful purpose in the criminal law but are useless handicaps from the standpoint of the administration of criminal justice. One solution has been to combine all three in one section of the code under the name of 'larceny.' This has one disadvantage, however, because it frequently becomes necessary to add a modifier to make clear whether the reference is to common-law larceny or to statutory larceny." Rollin M. Perkins & Ronald N. Boyce, *Criminal Law* 389 (3d ed. 1982).

▸ **aggravated larceny.** (1831) Larceny accompanied by some aggravating factor (as when the theft is from someone's house or person). — Also termed *compound larceny.*

▸ **complicated larceny.** See *mixed larceny.*

▸ **compound larceny. 1.** See *aggravated larceny.* **2.** See *mixed larceny.*

▸ **constructive larceny.** (1827) Larceny in which the perpetrator's felonious intent to appropriate the goods is construed from the defendant's conduct at the time of asportation, although a felonious intent was not present before that time.

▸ **grand larceny.** (1828) Larceny of property worth more than a statutory cutoff amount, usu. $100. Cf. *petit larceny.*

> "The English law, as the result of an early statute [the Statute of Westminster I, ch. 15 (1275)], classified this offense [larceny] as either (1) grand larceny or (2) petit larceny (now frequently written petty larceny), the former being a capital offense and the latter punishable by forfeiture of goods and whipping, but not death. Both, as mentioned earlier, were felonies. The offense was grand larceny if the value of the property stolen exceeded twelve pence and petit larceny if it did not. Modern statutes very generally retain this same classification (sometimes without using these labels) but with different penalties and different values set as the dividing line." Rollin M. Perkins & Ronald N. Boyce, *Criminal Law* 335 (3d ed. 1982).

▸ **larceny by a constructive trespass.** (1992) Larceny that occurs when a property owner mistakenly gives another person more property than is due, and the recipient knows about the error but does not disclose it before taking the excess property with the intent of converting it to his or her own use.

▸ **larceny by bailee.** (1858) Larceny committed by a bailee who converts the property to personal use or to the use of a third party.

▸ **larceny by extortion.** See *theft by extortion* under THEFT.

▸ **larceny by false pretenses.** See FALSE PRETENSES.

▸ **larceny by false promise.** (1967) The crime of obtaining property by representing that a future act will be carried out when the person making the representation has no intent to personally perform or to have another person perform. See *false promise* under PROMISE.

▸ **larceny by finding.** (1849) The act of taking permanent possession of a possibly abandoned object under circumstances that require an attempt to discover whether the object was actually lost or unattended. Also termed *theft by finding; stealing by finding.*

▸ **larceny by fraud and deception.** See *larceny by trick.*

▸ **larcency by mistake.** (1886) The act of taking control of another's property with the knowledge that the person delivering it made an error in the amount or nature of the property or in determining the identity of the recipient.

▸ **larceny by trick.** (1898) Larceny in which the taker misleads the rightful possessor, by misrepresentation of fact, into giving up possession of (but not title to) the goods. — Also termed *larceny by trick and deception; larceny by trick and device; larceny by fraud and deception; larceny by false pretense.* Cf. FALSE PRETENSES; *cheating by false pretenses* under CHEATING.

▸ **larceny from the person.** (18c) Larceny in which the goods are taken directly from the person, but without violence or intimidation, the victim usu. being unaware of the taking. • Pickpocketing is a typical example. This offense is similar to robbery except that violence or intimidation is not involved. Cf. ROBBERY.

▸ **larceny of property lost, mislaid, or delivered by mistake.** See *theft of property lost, mislaid, or delivered by mistake* under THEFT.

▸ **mixed larceny.** (18c) **1.** Larceny accompanied by aggravation or violence to the person. Cf. *simple larceny.* **2.** Larceny involving a taking from a house. — Also termed *compound larceny; complicated larceny.*

▸ **petit larceny.** (16c) Larceny of property worth less than an amount fixed by statute, usu. $100. — Also spelled *petty larceny.* Cf. *grand larceny.*

▸ **simple larceny.** (18c) Larceny unaccompanied by aggravating factors; larceny of personal goods unattended by an act of violence. Cf. *mixed larceny* (1).

large interpretation. See *liberal interpretation* under INTERPRETATION (1).

larger parcel. (1895) *Eminent domain.* A portion of land that is not a complete parcel, but is the greater part of a bigger tract, entitling the owner to damages both for the parcel taken and for its severance from the larger tract. • To grant both kinds of damages, a court generally requires the owner to show unity of ownership, unity of use, and contiguity of the land. But some states and the federal courts do not require contiguity when there is strong evidence of unity of use. See ECONOMIC UNIT.

laron (**lar**-ən), *n.* [Law French] (14c) *Hist.* A thief.

***Larrison* rule** (**lar**-ə-sən). (1952) *Criminal law.* The doctrine that a defendant may be entitled to a new trial on the basis of newly discovered evidence of false testimony by a government witness if the jury might have reached a different conclusion without the evidence and it unfairly surprised the defendant at trial. *Larrison v. U.S.*, 24 F.2d 82 (7th Cir. 1928). • Beginning in the late 1970s (well after the Wright quotation below), a majority of federal circuits repudiated the rule — including the Seventh Circuit itself. *See U.S. v. Mitrione*, 357 F.3d 712 (7th Cir. 2004).

> "The most usual rule in cases in which it is claimed that there was false testimony at the trial or that the witness has since recanted is the 'Larrison rule,' taking its name from the Seventh Circuit case in which it was announced. This is that three requirements must be met before a new trial will be granted on this ground: '(a) [That the] the court is reasonably well satisfied that the testimony given by a material witness [was] false. (b) That without it the jury *might* have reached a different conclusion. (c) That the party seeking the new trial was taken by surprise when the false testimony was given and was unable to meet it for it did not know of its falsity until after the trial.'" 3 Charles Alan Wright, *Federal Practice and Procedure* § 557.1, at 343 (2d ed. 1982) (quoting *Larrison*, 24 F.2d at 87–88).

lascivious (lə-**siv**-ee-əs), *adj.* (15c) (Of conduct) tending to excite lust; lewd; indecent; obscene.

lascivious cohabitation. See *illicit cohabitation* under COHABITATION.

L'Association Litteraire et Artistique Internationale. *Copyright.* An organization of authors, artists, and other supporters of international copyright protection. • In 1878, the Association drafted five resolutions that would become the starting point for the Berne Convention. In 1883, the organization called the first meeting in Berne, Switzerland for the purpose of creating a union to enforce international copyrights. — Often shortened to the *International Association.* — Abbr. ALAI.

last, *n.* (bef. 12c) *Hist.* **1.** A burden. **2.** A measure of weight used for bulky commodities.

last antecedent, rule of the. See RULE OF THE LAST ANTECEDENT.

last-antecedent canon. RULE OF THE LAST ANTECEDENT.

last-clear-chance doctrine. (1904) *Torts.* The rule that a plaintiff who was contributorily negligent may nonetheless recover from the defendant if the defendant had the last opportunity to prevent the harm but failed to use reasonable care to do so (in other words, if the defendant's negligence is later in time than the plaintiff's). • This doctrine allows the plaintiff to rebut the contributory-negligence defense in the few jurisdictions where contributory negligence completely bars recovery. — Also termed *discovered-peril doctrine; humanitarian doctrine; last-opportunity doctrine; subsequent-negligence doctrine; supervening-negligence doctrine; doctrine of ultimate negligence; doctrine of discovered peril; doctrine of subsequent negligence.*

last-employer rule. (1979) The doctrine that liability for an occupational injury or illness falls to the employer who exposed the worker to the injurious substance just before the first onset of the disease or injury. — Also termed *last-injurious-exposure rule.*

last heir. See HEIR.

last illness. (1904) The sickness ending in the person's death. — Also termed *last sickness.*

last-in, first-out. (1934) An accounting method that assumes that the most recent purchases are sold or used first, matching current costs against current revenues. — Abbr. LIFO. Cf. FIRST-IN, FIRST-OUT; NEXT-IN, FIRST-OUT.

last-injurious-exposure rule. See LAST-EMPLOYER RULE.

last-in-time-marriage presumption. (1983) *Family law.* A presumption that the most recently contracted marriage is valid. • This presumption generally arises in a situation similar to this: A person, believing himself or herself to be divorced, remarries. This person dies, and the new spouse makes a claim for the decedent's pension benefits. Then a former spouse, claiming that there was never a valid divorce, also claims the right to receive the benefits. The last-in-time-marriage presumption operates so that the former spouse bears the burden of proving that there was no valid divorce.

last-link doctrine. (1985) The rule that an attorney need not divulge nonprivileged information if doing so would reveal information protected by the attorney–client privilege, particularly if the information would provide essential evidence to support indicting or convicting the client of a crime. • This doctrine is often relied on as an exception to the rule that a client's identity is not privileged. For example, if divulging the client's name would supply the last link of evidence to indict or convict that client, the attorney need not disclose the client's name.

last-opportunity doctrine. See LAST-CLEAR-CHANCE DOCTRINE.

last-proximate-act test. (1961) *Criminal law.* A common-law test for the crime of attempt, based on whether the defendant does the final act necessary to commit an offense (such as pulling the trigger of a gun, not merely aiming it). • Most courts have rejected this test as being too lenient. See ATTEMPT (2).

last resort, court of. See *court of last resort* under COURT.

last-shot doctrine. *Contracts.* The principle that in a battle of the forms, the terms in the last contract form sent from one party to the other are the ones that constitute the agreement.

last sickness. See LAST ILLNESS.

last-straw doctrine. (1966) *Employment law.* The rule that the termination of employment may be justified by a series of incidents of poor performance, not one of which alone would justify termination, followed by a final incident showing a blatant disregard for the employer's interests.

last-survivor life insurance. See LIFE INSURANCE.

last-treatment rule. (1961) The doctrine that, for an ongoing physician–patient relationship, the statute of limitations on a medical-malpractice claim begins to run when the treatment stops or the relationship ends.

last will. See WILL.

last will and testament. See *last will* under WILL.

last word. The final say as between advocates who await a decision from those they seek to persuade; the opportunity to speak at the very end.

> "The prosecution necessarily has the right to open its case to the jury, and this opportunity to present its own point of view while the minds of the jury are still fresh is a considerable advantage. It might seem to be only fair that the defence should have the last word before the jury, or, rather, the last word before the judge sums up. This is conceded by our law if the defending counsel calls no evidence other than (if he wishes) the accused person himself. In this case, the Crown counsel addresses the jury after the close of the evidence, and the defending counsel puts his argument last. But, by a surprising and wholly indefensible rule, the order is reversed if the defending counsel finds it necessary to call any witness other than the defendant himself. In that case, the prosecution has the last word before the jury. As a result, the defence is sometimes in an unhappy and puzzling dilemma: whether to call a witness whose evidence may or may not be of some assistance, and forfeit the last word, or whether to do without the evidence for the sake of preserving the last word." Glanville Williams, *The Proof of Guilt* 84–85 (3d ed. 1963).

last-wrongdoer rule. (1919) *Torts.* The principle that when two or more people not acting in concert injure the same victim, the person who acted nearest to or at the time of the final injury is responsible for the damage and relieves any prior wrongdoers, including the plaintiff, from liability. • This rule of causation has been criticized and rejected by courts. — Also termed *nearest-wrongdoer rule.*

lata culpa. See CULPA.

lata neglegentia (**lay**-tə neg-lə-**jen**-shee-ə). See NEGLEGENTIA.

latching. A survey of a mine; an underground survey.

late, *adj.* (bef. 12c) **1.** Tardy; coming after an appointed or expected time <a late filing>. **2.** (Of a person) only recently having died <the late Secretary of State>.

late charge. See CHARGE (7).

latecomer. See JUNIOR USER.

latens (**lay**-tenz), *adj.* [Latin] Hidden or unapparent.

latent (**lay**-tənt), *adj.* (15c) Concealed; dormant <a latent defect>. Cf. PATENT, *adj.*

latent ambiguity. See AMBIGUITY (1).

latent danger. See DANGER.

latent deed. See DEED.

latent defect. See *hidden defect* under DEFECT.

latent defect in title. See DEFECT IN TITLE (2).

latent equity. See EQUITY (5).

latent intent. See *dormant legislative intent* under LEGISLATIVE INTENT.

latent intention. See *dormant legislative intent* under LEGISLATIVE INTENT.

lateral departure. See DEPARTURE (1).

lateral sentencing. See *lateral departure* under DEPARTURE (1).

lateral support. See SUPPORT (4).

laterare (lat-ə-**rair**-ee). [Law Latin] *Hist.* To lie sideways, rather than endways. • This term was formerly used in land descriptions.

late-term abortion. See ABORTION.

latifundium (lat-ə-**fən**-dee-əm), *n.* [Latin fr. *latus* "broad" + *fundus* "land"] (17c) *Roman law.* A large private estate, common in the late Republic.

Latin. (bef. 12c) The language of the ancient Romans and a primary language of the civil and canon law, and formerly of the common law.

> "The value of the Latin has always consisted in its peculiar expressiveness as a language of law terms, in its superior conciseness which has made it the appropriate language of law maxims, and in its almost unlimited capacity of condensation by means of abbreviations and contractions, many of which are retained in popular use at the present day." 2 Alexander M. Burrill, *A Law Dictionary and Glossary* 131 (2d ed. 1867).
>
> "The Latin maxims have largely disappeared from arguments and opinions. In their original phraseology they convey no idea that cannot be well expressed in modern English." William C. Anderson, *Law Dictionaries*, 28 Am. L. Rev. 531, 532 (1894).

latinarius (lat-ə-**nair**-ee-əs), *n.* [Latin] *Hist.* An interpreter of Latin.

Latini Juniani (lə-**tI**-nI joo-nee-**ay**-nI), *n. pl.* [Latin "Junian Latins"] (17c) *Roman law.* Informally manumitted slaves who acquired some rights and privileges as free people, but not Roman citizenship. • They were a special class of freedmen (*libertini*) who could become citizens. If a *Latinus Junianus* did not become a citizen, then upon death that person's status reverted to slavery, and his or her patron acquired all the decedent's property. — Also termed *libertine Junian Latins.* See LEX JUNIA NORBANA. Cf. INGENUUS; SERVUS (1).

> "Upon all these persons . . . a new and definite status was conferred; they were henceforth to be known as *Latini Juniani*, their position being based upon *Latinitas*, a status which had been enjoyed by certain Latin colonists. A *Latinus Junianus* had no public rights . . . . But he had part of the *commercium*, i.e. he could acquire proprietary and other rights *inter vivos*, but not *mortis causâ*. A *Latinus Junianus*, therefore, could neither take under a will . . . nor could he make one . . . . But, subject to these disabilities, a *Latinus Junianus* was a free man, and his children, though not, like the children of citizens, under his *potestas*, were

free-born citizens." R.W. Leage, *Roman Private Law* 68–69 (C.H. Ziegler ed., 2d ed. 1930).

latitat (**lat**-ə-tat), *n.* [Law Latin "he lurks"] (16c) *Hist.* A writ issued in a personal action after the sheriff returned a bill of Middlesex with the notation that the defendant could not be found. • The writ was called *latitat* because of its fictitious recital that the defendant lurks about in the county. It was abolished by the Process in Courts of Law at Westminster Act of 1832 (St. 2, Will. 4, ch. 39). See BILL OF MIDDLESEX; TESTATUM.

> "Latitat is a writ by which all men in personal actions are originally called in the king's bench to answer. And it is called latitat, because it is supposed by the writ that the defendant cannot be found in the county of Middlesex, as it appears by the return of the sheriff of that county, but that he lurks in another county: and therefore to the sheriff of that county is this writ directed to apprehend him." *Termes de la Ley* 277 (1st Am. ed. 1812).

latitatio (lat-ə-**tay**-shee-oh), *n.* [Law Latin] *Civil law.* A lurking; a hiding; a concealment, esp. to avoid a trial.

Latium majus (**lay**-shee-əm **may**-jəs). [Latin] *Roman law.* The greater rights conferred on the inhabitants of Latium and, later, of colonies outside Italy, giving citizenship to all members of the local curia or town council and their children. Cf. LATIUM MINUS.

> "Under the Principate there is a distinction between *Latium maius* and *Latium minus*. The former referred to the rights granted to colonies founded as a *coloniae Latinae* outside Italy, combined with the concession of Roman citizenship to a larger group of individuals than *Latium minus*, in which only the municipal magistrates and members of the municipal council . . . were rewarded with Roman citizenship." Adolf Berger, *Encyclopedic Dictionary of Roman Law* 537–38 (1953).

Latium minus (**lay**-shee-əm **mı**-nəs). [Latin] *Roman law.* The right of citizenship granted to the superior magistrates of provincial colonies. — Also termed *minus Latium*. Cf. LATIUM MAIUS.

lator (**lay**-tər), *n.* [Latin "a bearer, proposer"] (16c) *Civil law.* **1.** A bearer; a messenger. **2.** A maker or giver of laws.

latori praesentium (lay-**tor**-ı *or* lə-**tor**-ı pri-**sen**-shee-əm). [Law Latin] *Scots law.* To the bearer of these presents. • The phrase appeared in reference to written notes or bonds made payable to an unnamed creditor.

lato sensu (**lay**-toh **sen**-s[y]oo). [Latin] *Hist.* In a wide sense; in a broad sense.

latro (**la**-troh), *n.* [Latin] *Roman law.* A robber; a brigand.

latrocination (la-trə-sə-**nay**-shən). [fr. Latin *latrocinium* "highway robbery"] (17c) *Archaic.* The act of robbing; a depredation; a theft. — Also termed *latrociny*; *latrocinium*. See LARCENY; THEFT.

latrocinium (la-trə-**sin**-ee-əm), *n.* [Latin fr. *latro* "a robber"] (1810) *Hist.* **1.** LATROCINATION. **2.** Something stolen. **3.** The right to judge and execute thieves.

latrociny (**la**-trə-sə-nee). See LATROCINATION.

laudamentum (law-də-**men**-təm), *n. Hist.* A jury award.

laudare (law-**dair**-ee), *vb.* [Latin] **1.** *Civil law.* To name; to cite or quote as authority. **2.** *Hist.* To determine or pass on (a case, etc.) judicially.

laudare auctorem (law-**dair**-ee awk-**tor**-əm). See NOMINATIO AUCTORIS.

laudatio (law-**day**-shee-oh), *n.* [Latin] *Roman law.* Court testimony concerning an accused person's good behavior and integrity of life. • This testimony resembles the practice in modern criminal trials of calling persons to speak favorably about a defendant's character. Pl. ***laudationes*** (law-day-shee-**oh**-neez).

laudator (law-**day**-tər), *n.* [Latin] **1.** *Roman law.* A character witness in a criminal trial. **2.** *Hist.* An arbitrator. Pl. ***laudatores*** (law-də-**tor**-eez).

laudatory words. *Patents.* In a patent claim, descriptive but self-serving and conclusory words about the invention's quality or features, such as "faster" or "more effective." • Laudatory words are usu. not allowed in the claims of utility-patent applications, but they are allowed in plant-patent applications.

laudemium (law-**dee**-mee-əm), *n.* [Law Latin] *Hist.* A sum paid to a landowner by a person succeeding to a particular form of land contract by gift, devise, exchange, or sale; HERIOT. • The payment equaled 2% of the purchase money, and was paid to the landowner for acceptance of the successor. — Also termed (in old English law) *acknowledgment money*. See EMPHYTEUSIS.

laudum (**law**-dəm), *n.* [Law Latin] *Hist.* An arbitrament. See ARBITRAMENT.

laughe, *n.* See FRANKPLEDGE.

laughing heir. See HEIR.

launch, *n.* (18c) **1.** The movement of a vessel from the land into the water, esp. by sliding along ways from the stocks on which the vessel was built. **2.** A large open boat used in any service; LIGHTER.

laundering, *n.* See MONEY-LAUNDERING.

laundry list. (1958) *Slang.* An enumeration of items, as in a statute or court opinion <Texas's consumer-protection law contains a laundry list of deceptive trade practices>.

laureate (**lor**-ee-it), *n.* (16c) **1.** *Hist.* An officer of the sovereign's household, who composed odes annually on the sovereign's birthday, on the new year, and occasionally on the occurrence of a remarkable victory. **2.** A person honored for great achievement in the arts and sciences, and esp. in poetry.

laus Deo (**laws dee**-oh *or* **lows day**-oh). [Latin] *Archaic.* Praise be to God. • This was a heading to a bill of exchange.

law. (bef. 12c) **1.** The regime that orders human activities and relations through systematic application of the force of politically organized society, or through social pressure, backed by force, in such a society; the legal system <respect and obey the law>. **2.** The aggregate of legislation, judicial precedents, and accepted legal principles; the body of authoritative grounds of judicial and administrative action; esp., the body of rules, standards, and principles that the courts of a particular jurisdiction apply in deciding controversies brought before them <the law of the land>. **3.** The set of rules or principles dealing with a specific area of a legal system <copyright law>. **4.** The judicial and administrative process; legal action and proceedings <when settlement negotiations failed, they submitted their dispute to the law>. **5.** A statute <Congress passed a law>. — Abbr. L. **6.** COMMON LAW <law but not equity>. **7.** The legal profession <she spent her entire career in law>.

> "Some twenty years ago I pointed out two ideas running through definitions of law: one an imperative idea, an idea

of a rule laid down by the lawmaking organ of a politically organized society, deriving its force from the authority of the sovereign; and the other a rational or ethical idea, an idea of a rule of right and justice deriving its authority from its intrinsic reasonableness or conformity to ideals of right and merely recognized, not made, by the sovereign." Roscoe Pound, "More About the Nature of Law," in *Legal Essays in Tribute to Orrin Kip McMurray* at 513, 515 (Max Radin & Alexander M. Kidd eds., 1935).

"All law is the law of a group of individuals or of groups made up of individuals. No one can make a law purely for himself. He may form a resolution, frame an ambition, or adopt a rule, but these are private prescriptions, not laws." Tony Honoré, *Making Law Bind: Essays Legal and Philosophical* 33 (1987).

"It will help to distinguish three senses of the word 'law.' The first is law as a distinctive social institution; that is the sense invoked when we ask whether primitive law is really law. The second is law as a collection of sets of propositions — the sets we refer to as antitrust law, the law of torts, the Statute of Frauds, and so on. The third is law as a source of rights, duties, and powers, as in the sentence 'The law forbids the murdering heir to inherit.'" Richard A. Posner, *The Problems of Jurisprudence* 220–21 (1990).

▸ **adjective law.** See ADJECTIVE LAW.

▸ **canon law.** See CANON LAW.

▸ **caselaw.** See CASELAW.

▸ **civil law.** See CIVIL LAW.

▸ **common law.** See COMMON LAW.

▸ **consuetudinary law** (kon-swə-**t[y]oo**-də-ner-ee). [fr. Latin *consuetudo* "custom"] (18c) *Hist.* Ancient customary law that is based on an oral tradition. See CUSTOMARY LAW.

"Great as may be the difficulty experienced by philosophical jurists in defining the ground of the authority of consuetudinary law, there is no room to dispute the importance of its contributions to every system of jurisprudence, ancient or modern. The men who first drew, accepted, and endorsed a bill of exchange did as much for the law as any lawgiver has ever accomplished. They may or may not have acted on the advice of jurists; but, whether or not, they began a practice which grew into custom, and as such was recognized by the tribunals as a law-creating one, — one conferring rights and imposing obligations. There is much of this — far more probably than is commonly imagined — in the history of every system of law." James Muirhead, *Historical Introduction to the Private Law of Rome* 243 (Henry Goudy ed., 1899).

▸ **conventional law.** See CONVENTIONAL LAW.

▸ **customary law.** See CUSTOMARY LAW.

▸ **divine law.** See DIVINE LAW.

▸ **elementary law.** See ELEMENTARY LAW.

▸ **enacted law.** Law that has its source in legislation; WRITTEN LAW.

▸ **federal law.** See FEDERAL LAW.

▸ **fundamental law.** See FUNDAMENTAL LAW.

▸ **general law.** (16c) **1.** Law that is neither local nor confined in application to particular persons. • Even if there is only one person or entity to which a given law applies when enacted, it is general law if it purports to apply to all persons or places of a specified class throughout the jurisdiction. — Also termed *general statute*; *law of a general nature*. Cf. *special law*. **2.** A statute that relates to a subject of a broad nature.

▸ **imperative law.** (17c) A rule in the form of a command; a rule of action imposed on people by some authority that enforces obedience.

"Strictly speaking, it is not possible to say that imperative law is a command in the ordinary sense of the word. A 'command' in the ordinary meaning of the word is an expression of a wish by a person or body as to the conduct of another person, communicated to that other person. But (1) in the case of the law there is no determinate person who as a matter of psychological fact commands all the law. We are all born into a community in which law already exists, and at no time in our lives do any of us command the whole law. The most that we do is to play our part in enforcing or altering particular portions of it. (2) Ignorance of the law is no excuse; thus a rule of law is binding even though not communicated to the subject of the law." John Salmond, *Jurisprudence* 21 n.(c) (Glanville L. Williams ed., 10th ed. 1947).

▸ **imperfect law.** Law that is neither imperative nor arising from a definite text, examples being customary law and early international law. Cf. *perfect law*.

▸ **internal law. 1.** Law that regulates the domestic affairs of a country. Cf. INTERNATIONAL LAW. **2.** LOCAL LAW (3).

▸ **international law.** See INTERNATIONAL LAW.

▸ **local law.** See LOCAL LAW.

▸ **moral law.** See MORAL LAW.

▸ **municipal law.** See MUNICIPAL LAW.

▸ **natural law.** See NATURAL LAW.

▸ **partial law.** (16c) A statute designed (usu. intentionally) to affect the rights of only one particular person or only certain classes of people, rather than all people.

▸ **perfect law.** Law that is imperative and definite, such as the positive law within a jurisdiction. Cf. *imperfect law*.

▸ **permanent law.** (17c) A statute that continues in force for an indefinite time.

▸ **positive law.** See POSITIVE LAW.

▸ **procedural law.** See PROCEDURAL LAW.

▸ **prospective law.** See *prospective statute* under STATUTE.

▸ **public law.** See PUBLIC LAW.

▸ **special law.** (16c) A statute that pertains to and affects a particular case, person, place, or thing, as opposed to the general public. — Also termed *special act*; *private law*. Cf. *general law* (1); *private bill* under BILL (3).

▸ **state law.** See STATE LAW.

▸ **sumptuary law.** See SUMPTUARY LAW.

▸ **tacit law.** Law that derives its authority from the people's consent, without a positive enactment.

▸ **unenacted law.** (1882) Law that does not have its source in legislation. See *unwritten law*.

▸ **unwritten law.** (16c) A rule, custom, or practice that has not been enacted in the form of a statute or ordinance. • The term traditionally includes caselaw. Hence there certainly is a written memorial of the "unwritten law." The phrase simply denotes that this law does not originate in a writing such as a statute. — Also termed *jus non scriptum*; *jus ex non scripto*; *lex non scripta*; *jus moribus constitutum*; *unenacted law*. See CASELAW. Cf. *written law*.

"[T]he very words of the court promulgating the opinion and making the decision do not determine absolutely the rule of law but . . . the rule of law is ascertained by discovering what general proposition was essential to the result reached, and by using the words of the opinion as a mere aid in the ascertaining of that rule, so that, although opinions are written, the authoritative rules derived from them are sometimes not written, but are ascertained by the use of reason, causing case law to be classed as unwritten law — *lex non scripta*, to use the Latin phrase." William M. Lile et al., *Brief Making and the Use of Law Books* 335 (Roger W. Cooley & Charles Lesley Ames eds., 3d ed. 1914).

"In the common law it is not too much to say that the judges are always ready to look behind the words of a precedent to what the previous court was trying to say, or to what it would have said if it could have foreseen the nature of the cases that were later to arise, or if its perception of the relevant factors in the case before it had been more acute. There is, then, a real sense in which the written words of the reported decisions are merely the gateway to something lying behind them that may be called, without any excess of poetic license, 'unwritten law.'" Lon L. Fuller, *Anatomy of the Law* 145 (1968).

▸ **written law.** (16c) Statutory law, together with constitutions and treaties, as opposed to judge-made law. — Also termed *jus scriptum*; *lex scripta*. Cf. *unwritten law*.

law-abiding, *adj.* (1839) Respectful of and obedient to the law; observant of the law. — **law-abidingness,** *n.*

law agent. *Scots law.* See SOLICITOR (4).

law and economics. (*often cap.*) (1979) **1.** A discipline advocating the economic analysis of the law, whereby legal rules are subjected to a cost-benefit analysis to determine whether a change from one legal rule to another will increase or decrease allocative efficiency and social wealth. • Originally developed as an approach to antitrust policy, law and economics is today used by its proponents to explain and interpret a variety of legal subjects. **2.** The field or movement in which scholars devote themselves to this discipline. **3.** The body of work produced by these scholars.

law and literature. (*often cap.*) (1789) **1.** Traditionally, the study of how lawyers and legal institutions are depicted in literature; esp., the examination of law-related fiction as sociological evidence of how a given culture, at a given time, views law. — Also termed *law in literature*. **2.** More modernly, the application of literary theory to legal texts, focusing esp. on lawyers' rhetoric, logic, and style, as well as legal syntax and semantics. — Also termed *law as literature*. **3.** The field or movement in which scholars devote themselves to this study or application. **4.** The body of work produced by these scholars.

law arbitrary. A law not found in the nature of things, but imposed by the legislature's mere will; a bill not immutable.

law as integrity. An interpretive method that calls on judges to read legal texts according to the principles that, in the judges' eyes, portray them in their best moral light. *See* Scott J. Shapiro, *Legality* 304 (2011).

law as literature. See LAW AND LITERATURE (2).

law between states. See INTERNATIONAL LAW.

law-binding, *n.* (18c) A style of tan hardcover bookcovering, usu. calf or sheep, traditionally used for lawbooks. — Also termed *law-calf*.

lawbook. (16c) A book, usu. a technical one, about the law; esp., a primary legal text such as a statute book or a book that reports caselaw. — Also written *law book*.

law-breach, *n.* (bef. 12c) A violation of the law; an infraction or more serious misdeed.

lawbreaker, *n.* (15c) Someone who violates or has violated the law; someone who does something illegal.

lawburrows (**law**-bər-ohz). (15c) *Scots law.* **1.** An action requiring security for the peaceable behavior of a party. **2.** Security obtained by a party apprehensive of danger to safeguard the peace; specif., a writ in the name of the sovereign commanding a person to give security against committing violence on another.

law-calf. See LAW-BINDING.

law clerk. 1. See CLERK (4). **2.** See PARALEGAL (2).

law commission. (*often cap.*) An official or quasi-official body of people formed to propose legal reforms intended to improve the administration of justice. • Such a body is often charged with the task of reviewing the law with an eye toward systematic development and reform, esp. through codification.

law court. 1. See COURT (1). **2.** See COURT (2). — Also written *law-court*.

law court of appeals. *Hist.* An appellate tribunal, formerly existing in South Carolina, for hearing appeals from the courts of law.

law-craft, *n.* (16c) The practice of law.

"This quest for ever-broader empirical understanding must, of course, be kept under reasonable control in practical law-craft, lest it delay necessary decisions in a continually expanding and pointlessly expensive fact-finding spiral." Bruce A. Ackerman, *Reconstructing American Law* 30 (1984).

law day. (13c) **1.** *Archaic.* The yearly or twice-yearly meeting of one of the early common-law courts. **2.** *Archaic.* The day appointed for a debtor to discharge a mortgage or else forfeit the property to the lender. **3.** (*cap.*) A day on which American schools, public assemblies, and courts draw attention to the importance of law in modern society. • Since 1958, the ABA has sponsored Law Day on May 1 of each year.

law degree. See JURIS DOCTOR.

law department. (1849) A branch of a corporation, government agency, university, or the like charged with handling the entity's legal affairs.

law enforcement. (1895) **1.** The detection and punishment of violations of the law. • This term is not limited to the enforcement of criminal laws. For example, the Freedom of Information Act contains an exemption from disclosure for information compiled for law-enforcement purposes and furnished in confidence. That exemption is valid for the enforcement of a variety of noncriminal laws (such as national-security laws) as well as criminal laws. See 5 USCA § 552(b)(7). **2.** CRIMINAL JUSTICE (2). **3.** Police officers and other members of the executive branch of government charged with carrying out and enforcing the criminal law.

law-enforcement agent. See LAW-ENFORCEMENT OFFICER.

Law Enforcement Assistance Administration. A former federal agency (part of the Department of Justice) that was responsible for administering law-enforcement grants under the Omnibus Crime Control and Safe Streets Act of 1968. • It has been replaced by a variety of federal agencies, including the National Institute of Corrections and National Institute of Justice. — Abbr. LEAA.

Law Enforcement Information Network. A computerized communications system that some states use to document driver's-license records, automobile registrations, wanted-persons' files, and the like. — Abbr. LEIN.

law-enforcement officer. (1919) A person whose duty is to enforce the laws and preserve the peace. — Sometimes shortened to *law officer.* — Also termed *law-enforcement agent.* See PEACE OFFICER; SHERIFF.

law-enforcement system. See CRIMINAL-JUSTICE SYSTEM.

law firm. (1852) An association of lawyers who practice law together, usu. sharing clients and profits, in a business organized traditionally as a partnership but often today as either a professional corporation or a limited-liability company. • Many law firms have a hierarchical structure in which the partners (or shareholders) supervise junior lawyers known as "associates," who are usu. employed on a track to partnership.

▸ **captive law firm.** (1993) A law firm staffed by employees of an insurance company. • These lawyers typically defend insureds in lawsuits covered under the insurer's liability policies. The insurer's use of a captive firm to defend an insured raises ethical questions about whether the lawyers will act in the insured's best interests. — Often shortened to *captive firm.*

Law French. (17c) The corrupted form of the Norman French language that arose in England after William the Conqueror invaded England in 1066 and that was used for several centuries as the primary language of the English legal system; the Anglo-French used in medieval England in judicial proceedings, pleadings, and lawbooks. — Also written *law French.* — Abbr. L.F. See NORMAN FRENCH.

> "That Law French was barbarous in its decrepitude does not in the least diminish the value of it to our law when it was full of vitality. It helped to make English law one of the four indigenous systems of the civilized world, for it exactly expressed legal ideas in a technical language which had no precise equivalent." Percy H. Winfield, *The Chief Sources of English Legal History* 14 (1925).

> "To the linguist, law French is a corrupt dialect by definition. Anglo-French was in steady decline after 1300. Lawyers such as Fortescue, on the other hand, were probably serious in maintaining that it was the vernacular of France which was deteriorating by comparison with the pristine Norman of the English courts. That Fortescue could make such a claim, while living in France, is in itself a clear demonstration that by the middle of the fifteenth century there was a marked difference between the French of English lawyers and the French of France." J.H. Baker, *A Manual of Law French* 11 (1979).

> "Law French refers to the Anglo-Norman patois used in legal documents and all judicial proceedings from the 1260s to the reign of Edward III (1327–1377), and used with frequency in legal literature up to the early 18th century. When first introduced into England, this brand of French was the standard language used in Normandy; by the 1300s, through linguistic isolation, it became a corrupted language — by French standards, at any rate." Bryan A. Garner, *Garner's Dictionary of Legal Usage* 520 (3d ed. 2011).

lawful, *adj.* (13c) Not contrary to law; permitted or recognized by law; rightful <the police officer conducted a lawful search of the premises>. See LEGAL. — **lawfulness,** *n.*

lawful admission. (1899) *Immigration.* Legal entry into the country, including under a valid immigrant visa. • Lawful admission is one of the requirements for an immigrant to receive a naturalization order and certificate. 8 USCA §§ 1101(a)(20), 1427(a)(1), 1429.

lawful age. (16c) **1.** See *age of capacity* under AGE. **2.** See *age of majority* (1) under AGE.

lawful arrest. See ARREST (2).

lawful authorities. (16c) Those persons (such as the police) with the right to exercise public power, to require obedience to their lawful commands, and to command or act in the public name.

lawful cause. See *good cause* under CAUSE (2).

lawful condition. See CONDITION (2).

lawful correction. The appropriate and moderate discipline of a child for misbehavior. • Factors in determining whether correction is lawful or excessive include the child's age, sex, condition, and disposition, as well as the surrounding circumstances.

lawful damages. See DAMAGES.

lawful deed. See *good deed* under DEED.

lawful dependent. See DEPENDENT (1).

lawful discrimination. See DISCRIMINATION (3).

lawful entry. See ENTRY (1).

lawful excuse. See EXCUSE (2).

lawful fence. (17c) A strong, substantial, and well-suited barrier that is sufficient to prevent animals from escaping property and to protect the property from trespassers. — Also termed *legal fence; good and lawful fence.* Cf. SPITE FENCE.

lawful goods. (16c) Property that one may legally hold, sell, or export; property that is not contraband.

lawful heir. See HEIR (1).

lawful interest. See INTEREST (3).

lawful issue. See ISSUE (3).

lawful justification. See JUSTIFICATION (2).

lawful man. See LEGALIS HOMO.

lawful money. See MONEY.

lawful noncitizen. See NONCITIZEN.

lawful-orders defense. See NUREMBERG DEFENSE (2).

lawful possession. See POSSESSION.

lawful process. See *legal process* under PROCESS.

lawful representative. See REPRESENTATIVE (1).

lawgiver. (14c) **1.** A legislator, esp. one who promulgates an entire code of laws; LAWMAKER. **2.** A judge with the power to interpret law. — **lawgiving,** *adj.* & *n.*

> "John Chipman Gray in his *The Nature and Sources of the Law* (1921) repeats a number of times a quotation from Bishop Hoadley [1676–1761]: 'Whoever hath an *absolute authority to interpret* any written or spoken laws, it is *he* who is truly the *Law-giver* to all intents and purposes, and not the person who first wrote or spoke them.'" Lon L. Fuller, *Anatomy of the Law* 23–24 (1968).

law guardian. See *guardian ad litem* under GUARDIAN (1).

law-hand. (18c) *Hist.* An outmoded rococo method of handwriting once used by scribes in preparing legal documents.

law in action. (1909) The law as applied in the day-to-day workings of the legal system, as opposed to the law found in books. — Sometimes written *law-in-action.* — Also termed *functionalism.* See LEGAL REALISM. Cf. LAW IN BOOKS.

law in books. (1909) The legal rules to be found in texts; esp., sterile, oft-repeated rules that seem to depart from the way in which the law actually operates in the day-to-day workings of the legal system. — Sometimes written *law-in-books*. Cf. LAW IN ACTION.

law in literature. See LAW AND LITERATURE (1).

law journal. (1803) **1.** A legal periodical or magazine, esp. one published by a bar association. — Abbr. L.J. **2.** LAW REVIEW (1).

law language. See LEGALESE.

Law Latin. (16c) A corrupted form of Latin formerly used in law and legal documents, including judicial writs, royal charters, and private deeds. • It primarily consists of a mixture of Latin, French, and English words used in English sentence structures. — Abbr. L.L.; L. Lat. — Also written *law Latin*.

> "LAW LATIN. A technical kind of Latin, in which the pleadings and proceedings of the English courts were enrolled and recorded from a very early period to the reign of George II . . . . The principal peculiarities of this language consist first, in its construction, which is adapted so closely to the English idiom as to answer to it sometimes word for word; and, secondly, in the use of numerous words 'not allowed by grammarians nor having any countenance of Latin,' but framed from the English by merely adding a Latin termination, as *murdrum* from murder . . . ." 2 Alexander M. Burrill, *A Law Dictionary and Glossary* 135 (2d ed. 1867).

> "Law Latin, formerly sometimes called 'dog Latin,' is the bastardized or debased Latin formerly used in law and legal documents. For the most part, we have escaped from its clutches. In 1730, Parliament abolished Law Latin in legal proceedings, but two years later found it necessary to allow Latin phrases that had previously been in common use, such as *fieri facias, habeas corpus, ne exeat,* and *nisi prius*. As Blackstone would later say, some Latinisms were 'not . . . capable of an English dress with any degree of seriousness.' 3 William Blackstone, *Commentaries on the Laws of England* 323 (1768)." Bryan A. Garner, *Garner's Dictionary of Legal Usage* 521 (3d ed. 2011).

lawless, *adj.* **1.** Not obeying the law; not controlled by the law <lawless hoodlums>. **2.** Having no laws <lawless frontier>.

law list. (18c) **1.** A published compilation of the names and addresses of practicing lawyers and other information of interest to the profession, such as legal organizations, court calendars, rosters of specialists, court reporters, and the like. **2.** A legal directory that provides biographical information about lawyers, such as Martindale-Hubbell. • Many states and large cities have law lists or directories. See MARTINDALE-HUBBELL LAW DIRECTORY.

Law Lord. (18c) *Hist.* A member of the appellate committee of the House of Lords, consisting of the Lord Chancellor, the salaried Lords of Appeal in Ordinary, and any peer who holds or has held high judicial office. — Also written *law lord*.

law lore. (1812) Knowledge of legal history; the collective traditions that are passed down from generation to generation of lawyers.

lawmaker. An elected official responsible for making laws; LEGISLATOR.

lawmaking. See LEGISLATION (1).

lawman (**law**-mən), *n.* A male law-enforcement officer; a police or other officer who is responsible for ensuring that the law is not violated with impunity.

law martial. See MARTIAL LAW.

law merchant. (15c) A system of customary law that developed in Europe during the Middle Ages and regulated the dealings of mariners and merchants in the commercial countries of the world until the 17th century. • Many of the law merchant's principles came to be incorporated into the common law, which in turn formed the basis of the Uniform Commercial Code. — Also termed *commercial law; lex mercatoria*. Pl. **laws merchant.**

> "The term *lex mercatoria* or law merchant is used to designate the concept of an anational body of legal rules and principles, which are developed primarily by the international business community itself based on custom, industry practice, and general principles of law that are applied in commercial arbitrations . . . in order to govern transactions between private parties, as well as between private parties and States, in transborder trade, commerce, and finance. It is a reaction to the increased complexities of modern international commerce . . . and the inability of domestic law to provide adequate solutions that stabilize the parties' mutual rights and obligations. The notion of *lex mercatoria* is mainly used in scholarly writings in private international law; decisions by arbitral tribunals, domestic courts, and commercial contracts use the notion less frequently, even though the concept of an anational body of rules for international commerce is increasingly recognized in legal practice . . . ." Stephan W. Schill, "Lex Mercatoria," in 6 *The Max Planck Encyclopedia of Public International Law* 823, 823 (Rüdiger Wolfrum ed., 2012).

lawmonger, *n.* (17c) A low or disreputable lawyer; a pettifogger or shyster. See PETTIFOGGER; SHYSTER.

lawnote. See NOTE (2).

law of a general nature. See *general law* under LAW.

law of arms. See ARMS, LAW OF.

law of capture. See RULE OF CAPTURE.

law of Citations. See CITATIONS, LAW OF.

law of competence. A law establishing and defining the powers of a government official, including the circumstances under which the official's pronouncements constitute laws. — Also termed *power-delegating law*. See *jural act* under ACT (2); JURAL AGENT.

law of deceit. (1881) *Hist.* The body of 19th-century common-law torts that developed into the modern laws of trademark, securities fraud, deceptive trade practices, and unfair competition.

law of evidence. See EVIDENCE (4).

law officer. (18c) **1.** A person that the law invests with a position of trust, authority, or command, such as an attorney general or solicitor general. **2.** LAW-ENFORCEMENT OFFICER. **3.** OFFICER OF THE COURT.

law of Langobardi. See LOMBARD LAW.

law of Lombardy. See LOMBARD LAW.

law of marque (mahrk). (17c) A rule of reprisal allowing one who has been wronged but cannot obtain justice to take the goods of the wrongdoer found within the wronged person's precinct, in satisfaction of the wrong.

law of Moses. See MOSAIC LAW.

law of nations. See INTERNATIONAL LAW.

law of nature. See NATURAL LAW.

law of nature and nations. See INTERNATIONAL LAW.

law of obligations. (17c) The category of law dealing with proprietary rights in personam — namely, the relations between obligor and obligee. • It is one of the three departments into which civil law was traditionally divided. See IN PERSONAM. Cf. LAW OF PROPERTY; LAW OF STATUS.

law of persons. (17c) The law relating to persons; the law that pertains to the different statuses of persons. • This is also commonly known as the *jus personarum*, a shortened form of *jus quod ad personas pertinet* ("the law that pertains to persons"). See JUS PERSONARUM.

law of property. (17c) The category of law dealing with proprietary rights in rem, such as personal servitudes, predial servitudes, and rights of real security. • It is one of the three departments into which civil law was traditionally divided: persons, property, and modes of acquiring property (obligations). In modern civil codes that follow the model of the German Civil Code, civil law is divided into five books: general principles, obligations, family law, property, and succession. See IN REM. Cf. LAW OF OBLIGATIONS; LAW OF STATUS.

law of remedy. See REMEDY.

law of shipping. (18c) The part of maritime law relating to the building, equipping, registering, owning, inspecting, transporting, and employing of ships, along with the laws applicable to shipmasters, agents, crews, and cargoes; the maritime law relating to ships. — Also termed *shipping law*. See MARITIME LAW; JONES ACT.

law of status. (1846) The category of law dealing with personal or nonproprietary rights, whether in rem or in personam. • It is one of the three departments into which civil law is divided. Cf. LAW OF OBLIGATIONS; LAW OF PROPERTY.

law of the apex. (1886) *Mining law.* The principle that title to a given tract of mineral land, with defined mining rights, goes to the person who locates the surface covering the outcrop or apex.

law of the case. (18c) **1.** The doctrine holding that a decision rendered in a former appeal of a case is binding in a later appeal. **2.** An earlier decision giving rise to the application of this doctrine. Cf. LAW OF THE TRIAL; RES JUDICATA; STARE DECISIS.

law of the circuit. (1861) **1.** The law as announced and followed by a U.S. Circuit Court of Appeals. **2.** The rule that one panel of judges on a U.S. Circuit Court of Appeals should not overrule a decision of another panel of judges on the same court. **3.** The rule that an opinion of one U.S. Circuit Court of Appeals is not binding on another circuit but may be considered persuasive.

law of the flag. (1865) *Maritime law.* The law of the country whose flag is flown by a particular vessel where it is registered. • That country's laws govern the ship's internal affairs. *See McCulloch v. Sociedad de Marineros de Honduras*, 372 U.S. 10 (1963).

law of the forum. See LEX FORI.

Law of The Hague. The first widely accepted body of international law of war, as approved by conventions in The Hague in 1899 and 1907. • The Law of The Hague set up procedures for mediation and arbitration of disputes to avoid war, and attempted to regulate the type and use of weapons in warfare. See LIEBER CODE.

law of the land. (15c) The law in effect in a country and applicable to its members, whether the law is statutory, administrative, or case-made. — Also termed *lex terrae*; *ley de terre*.

> "[As for] the effect of the Norman Conquest on the history of Law . . . [,] it converted the law of England into a *lex terrae*, a true local law. There is to be no longer a law of the Mercians, another of the West Saxons, and another of the Danes, not even a law for the English and a law for the Normans, but a law of the land. It took about a century to accomplish this result, which we doubtless owe to feudal principles." Edward Jenks, *Law and Politics in the Middle Ages* 35 (1898).

law of the partnership. The rule that the parties' agreement controls the features of a partnership.

law of the place. (1947) Under the Federal Tort Claims Act, the state law applicable to the place where the injury occurred. • Under the Act, the federal government waives its sovereign immunity for specified injuries, including certain wrongful acts or omissions of a government employee causing injury that the United States, if it were a private person, would be liable for under the law of the state where the incident occurred. 28 USCA § 1346(b).

law of the road. (1836) The collective statutes, ordinances, rules, and customs that regulate travel on public highways and streets.

law of the sea. (1831) The body of international law governing how countries use and control the sea and its resources. Cf. GENERAL MARITIME LAW; MARITIME LAW.

law of the staple. (16c) *Hist.* The law administered in the court of the mayor of the staple; the law merchant. See STAPLE (1), (2).

law of the trial. (1879) A legal theory or court ruling that is not objected to and is used or relied on in a trial <neither party objected to the court's jury instruction, so it became the law of the trial>. Cf. LAW OF THE CASE.

law of things. (17c) The law relating to things; the law that is determined by changes in the nature of things. • This is also commonly known as the *jus rerum*, a shortened form of *jus quod ad res pertinet* ("the law that pertains to things"). See JUS RERUM.

law practice. (17c) An attorney's professional business, including the relationships that the attorney has with clients and the goodwill associated with those relationships. Cf. PRACTICE OF LAW.

law question. See QUESTION OF LAW.

law reform. (1846) The process of, or a movement dedicated to, streamlining, modernizing, or otherwise improving a body of law generally or the code governing a particular branch of the law; specif., the investigation and discussion of the law on a topic (e.g., bankruptcy), usu. by a commission or expert committee, with the goal of formulating proposals for change to improve the operation of the law. — Also termed *science of legislation*; *censorial jurisprudence*.

> "A first point is what is commonly meant by law reform. A vast number of matters are contained in legislation, including, for example, speed limits, the rate of income tax, school leaving age and the hours when we can go to pubs. Alteration of the law about these matters and of a whole range of other regulations of our conduct and activities is not regarded as 'law reform:' all these things are regarded as part of regulation of the way we live, of the policy that is to be applied. There are many fields which 'law' controls but in which lawyers have no particular standing. The field of law reform is pre-eminently that of the law with which lawyers are concerned in their ordinary practice, which of course includes conveyancing, drawing wills, contracts and so on as well as litigation. Whilst law reform is primarily concerned with 'lawyers law' there is

no clear-cut boundary." R.M. Jackson, *The Machinery of Justice in England* 439 (5th ed. 1967).

law report. See REPORT (3).

law reporter. 1. *Hist.* A lawyer who attended judicial sessions to summarize proceedings and transcribe judicial pronouncements. — Often shortened to *reporter.*

"The sixteenth century was a time when to become a recognized law-reporter was the mark of the successful practitioner, when a lawyer's reputation usually governed the value attached to any cases he collected. Yet no survey of these men and their work can be properly undertaken without preliminary consideration of the Tudor Yearbooks which lasted intermittently until 1535. In common with those of previous reigns, these tattered remnants of a great medieval tradition stand as a monument to the articulate, if nameless, reporters of the early common law. So much has been written over the last hundred years by so many eminent scholars on the origins, maturity and decline of the Yearbooks that further comment may seem sterile, if not presumptuous. Nonetheless, it is hardly possible to appreciate the development of 'private' reporting without endeavoring to place it against the background of the Yearbook tradition. The picture which emerges is not so much that of one system ending and another taking its place; rather, what we see is the slow decline of the one and the parallel growth of the other, both unpremeditated and probably unrelated." L.W. Abbott, *Law Reporting in England 1485–1585* 9 (1973).

2. See REPORT (3).

law review. (1845) **1.** A journal containing scholarly articles, essays, and other commentary on legal topics by professors, judges, law students, and practitioners. • Law reviews are usu. published at law schools and edited by law students <law reviews are often grossly overburdened with substantive footnotes>. **2.** The law-student staff and editorial board of such a journal <she made law review>. — Abbr. L. Rev. — Also termed *law journal.* See LAW JOURNAL.

law Salique (sə-**leek**). See SALIC LAW.

law school. (17c) An institution for formal legal education and training, usu. a graduate department or school in a university but sometimes a stand-alone school for graduate studies in law. • Graduates who complete the standard program, usu. three years in length, receive a Juris Doctor (or, formerly, a Bachelor of Laws).

▸ **accredited law school.** (1905) A law school approved by the state and the Association of American Law Schools, or by the state and the American Bar Association. • In all states except California, only graduates of an accredited law school may take the bar examination.

Law School Admissions Test. A standardized examination purporting to measure the likelihood of success in law school. • Most American law schools use the results of this examination in admissions decisions. — Abbr. LSAT (**el**-sat).

law society. (1821) **1.** An organization whose membership is open to lawyers and law students and offers benefits such as resources for professional contacts and education. **2.** (*cap.*) *English law.* A professional organization in England, chartered in 1845, governing the education, practice, and conduct of articled clerks and solicitors. • A clerk or solicitor must be enrolled with the Law Society to be admitted to the legal profession.

Law Society of Scotland. A professional organization established by statute in 1949, governing the admission, conduct, and practice of solicitors enrolled to practice in Scotland.

Laws of Amalfi (ah-**mahl**-fee). See AMALPHITAN CODE.

laws of Oléron (**oh**-lə-ron *or* aw-lay-**ron**). The oldest collection of maritime laws, thought to be a code existing at Oléron (an island off the coast of France) during the 12th century. • It was introduced into England, with certain additions, in the reign of Richard I (1189–1199).

Laws of the Barbarians. See LEGES BARBARORUM.

laws of the several states. (1814) State statutes and state-court decisions on questions of general law.

laws of Visby (**vis**-bee). A code of maritime customs and decisions adopted on the island of Gothland (in the Baltic Sea), where Visby was the principal port. • Most scholars believe that this code postdates the laws of Oléron. The code was influential throughout northern Europe. In recognition of the ancient code, the Visby Protocol to amend the Hague Rules was signed in Visby. The Hague–Visby Rules govern most of the world's liner trade. — Also spelled *laws of Wisby.* — Also termed *Gothland sea laws.*

laws of war. (16c) *Int'l law.* The rules and principles agreed on by most countries for regulating matters inherent in or incident to the conduct of a public war, such as the relations of neutrals and belligerents, blockades, captures, prizes, truces and armistices, capitulations, prisoners, and declarations of war and peace. Cf. GENEVA CONVENTIONS OF 1949.

laws of Wisby. See LAWS OF VISBY.

law spiritual. See ECCLESIASTICAL LAW.

lawsuit, *n.* See SUIT.

lawsuit, *vb. Archaic.* To proceed against (an adversary) in a lawsuit; to sue.

law-talk, *n.* (1867) **1.** LEGALESE. **2.** Discussion that is heavily laced with lawyers' concerns and legal references.

law-way, *n.* (1965) A legal norm that characterizes a society or family of related societies with a shared heritage; a traditional pattern of legal doctrine common to a people. • The term is used in Geoffrey Sawer's *Law in* Society (1965). Cf. FOLKWAY.

law-worthy, *adj.* (1818) *Hist.* Entitled to or deserving the benefit and protection of the law. — Also termed *law-worth.* See LIBERAM LEGEM AMITTERE; LEGALIS HOMO; LIBERA LEX.

law writer. (1852) Someone who writes on legal subjects, usu. from a technical, nonpopular point of view.

lawyer, *n.* (14c) Someone who, having been licensed to practice law, is qualified to advise people about legal matters, prepare contracts and other legal instruments, and represent people in court. Cf. ATTORNEY. — **lawyerly, lawyerlike,** *adj.* — **lawyerdom,** *n.*

▸ **certified military lawyer.** A person qualified to act as counsel in a general court-martial. • To be qualified, the person must be (1) a judge advocate of the Army, Navy, Air Force, or Marine Corps, or a law specialist of the Coast Guard, (2) a graduate of an accredited law school, or a member of a federal-court bar or the bar of the highest court of a state, and (3) certified as competent to perform such duties by the Judge Advocate General of the armed force that the person is a member of.

▸ **cowboy lawyer.** See *Rambo lawyer.*

▸ **criminal lawyer.** (18c) A lawyer whose primary work is to represent criminal defendants. • This term is rarely if ever applied to prosecutors despite their integral involvement in the criminal-justice system.

▸ **guardhouse lawyer.** See JAILHOUSE LAWYER.

▸ **headnote lawyer.** *Slang.* A lawyer who relies on the headnotes of judicial opinions rather than taking the time to read the opinions themselves.

▸ **jailhouse lawyer.** See JAILHOUSE LAWYER.

▸ **prudent lawyer.** A lawyer whose judgment is good; esp., a careful and discreet lawyer possessing practical knowledge. See *good judgment* under JUDGMENT (1).

▸ **public-interest lawyer.** (1969) An attorney whose practice is devoted to advocacy on behalf of a public institution or nongovernmental organization, or to advising and representing indigent clients and others who have limited access to legal aid. • Public-interest lawyers often practice in fields such as civil rights and immigration law.

▸ **Rambo lawyer.** (1989) *Slang.* A lawyer, esp. a litigator, who uses aggressive, unethical, or illegal tactics in representing a client and who lacks courtesy and professionalism in dealing with other lawyers. — Often shortened to *Rambo.* — Also termed *cowboy lawyer.*

▸ **transactional lawyer.** (1990) A lawyer who works primarily on transactions such as licensing agreements, mergers, acquisitions, joint ventures, and the like. See OFFICE PRACTITIONER.

lawyer, *vb.* (18c) **1.** To practice as a lawyer <associates often spend their days and nights lawyering, with little time for recreation>. **2.** To supply with lawyers <the large law-school class will certainly help lawyer the state>. See LAWYER UP.

lawyer autonomy. See AUTONOMY.

lawyer–client privilege. See *attorney–client privilege* under PRIVILEGE (3).

lawyering, *n.* (1842) **1.** The work or skill of a duly licensed attorney at law, esp. as it involves representing a client to invoke and pursue legal procedures to resolve disputes, to effect transactions that require some degree of sophistication, or to change or preserve the client's status. • In modern usage, the term is used in many collocations, such as *collaborative lawyering, comparative lawyering, cross-cultural lawyering,* and *preventive lawyering.* By extension, it appears in phrases such as *jailhouse lawyering, lay lawyering,* and *pro se lawyering,* in each of which the activity is attributed to someone other than an attorney at law. *See* Josiah M. Daniel, *A Proposed Definition of the Term* Lawyering, 101 Law Lib. J. 207 (2009). **2.** *Archaic.* The activity or practice of arguing, quarreling, or wrangling.

lawyer-referral service. (1947) A program, usu. offered by a bar association, that helps nonindigent clients clarify their legal problems and provides either contact information for lawyers who practice in the appropriate field or information about government agencies or consumer organizations that may be able to provide services. • Under the Model Rules of Professional Conduct, a lawyer may pay only the usual charges of a not-for-profit or qualified lawyer-referral service. A qualified-lawyer referral service is one that is approved by a regulatory authority as affording adequate protections for prospective clients. — Also termed *lawyer referral and information service.*

lawyer up, *vb. Slang.* To retain one or more lawyers in preparation for legal, esp. criminal, action.

lawyer–witness. See WITNESS.

lawyer–witness rule. (1982) The principle that an attorney who will likely be called as a fact witness at trial may not participate as an advocate in the case unless the testimony will be about an uncontested matter or the amount of attorney's fees in the case, or if disqualifying the attorney would create a substantial hardship for the client. • The rule permits an attorney actively participating in the case to be a witness on merely formal matters but discourages testimony on other matters on behalf of a client. The rule may apply when another member of the attorney's firm may be called as a witness. Model Rule of Professional Conduct 3.7 (1983). — Also termed *advocate–witness rule; attorney–witness rule.*

lay, *adj.* (14c) **1.** Not ecclesiastical; not of the clergy. **2.** Not trained in or knowing much about a particular profession or subject; not expert, esp. with reference to law or medicine; nonprofessional.

lay, *n.* (1850) *Maritime law.* A share of the profits of a fishing or whaling trip, akin to wages, allotted to the officers and seamen.

lay, *vb.* (14c) To allege or assert.

> "The Laying of Damages. — At common law the declaration must 'lay damages.'" Edwin E. Bryant, *The Law of Pleading Under the Codes of Civil Procedure* 209 (2d ed. 1899).

layaway. (1961) **1.** A method of buying goods by having the seller, usu. for a deposit, keep the goods until the full price can be paid by a predetermined date. **2.** An agreement between a retail seller and a consumer to hold goods for future sale. • The seller sets the goods aside and agrees to sell them to the consumer at an agreed price in the future. The consumer deposits with the seller some portion of the price of the goods, and may agree to other conditions with the seller, such as progress payments. The consumer ordinarily receives the goods once the full purchase price has been paid.

lay corporation. See CORPORATION.

lay damages, *vb.* (1880) To allege damages, esp. in the complaint. See AD DAMNUM CLAUSE.

layday. (1842) *Maritime law.* A day allowed by a voyage charterparty for the charterer to load or unload cargo. • If more time is used, the vessel's owner is entitled to compensation for the delay, usu. in the form of demurrage. If less time is used, the owner may pay dispatch. — Also written *lay day.* See DEMURRAGE; DISPATCH; LAYTIME; READY-BERTH CLAUSE. Cf. *day of demurrage* under DAY.

lay fee. See FEE (2).

lay impropriator (im-**proh**-pree-ay-tər). (17c) *Eccles. law.* A layperson holding a benefice or other spiritual impropriation.

laying a foundation. *Evidence.* Introducing evidence of certain facts needed to render later evidence relevant, material, or competent. • For example, propounding a hypothetical question to an expert is necessary before the expert may render an opinion.

laying of the venue. (18c) A statement in a complaint naming the district or county in which the plaintiff proposes that any trial of the matter should occur. See VENUE.

lay investiture. (1924) *Eccles. law.* The ceremony by which a layperson places a bishop in possession of lands, money revenues, and other diocesan temporalities.

lay judge. See JUDGE.

layman. (15c) **1.** Someone who is not a member of the clergy. **2.** Someone who is not a member of a profession or an expert on a particular subject, esp. by comparison with someone who is. — Also termed *layperson.*

layoff. (1868) The termination of employment at the employer's instigation, usu. through no fault of the employee; esp., the termination — either temporary or permanent — of many employees in a short time for financial reasons. — Also termed *reduction in force.* — **lay off,** *vb.*

▸ **mass layoff.** (1989) *Labor law.* Under the Worker Adjustment and Retraining Notification Act, a reduction in force that results in the loss of work at a single site, of 30 days or more, for at least 500 full-time employees, or 50 or more full-time employees if they make up at least 33%of the employees at that site. 29 USCA § 2101(a)(3). See WORKER ADJUSTMENT AND RETRAINING NOTIFICATION ACT.

layoff bet. See BET (1).

layoff bettor. (1974) A bookmaker who accepts layoff bets from other bookmakers. See *layoff bet* under BET (1).

lay on the table. (1822) *Parliamentary law.* **1.** To temporarily set aside (a matter before a deliberative assembly); TABLE (1). • Some parliamentary writers prefer the form "to lay on the table" and disapprove of the form "to table." Cf. TAKE FROM THE TABLE. **2.** *British English.* To schedule for consideration.

lay opinion testimony. See TESTIMONY.

layperson. 1. See LAYMAN. **2.** *Hist.* See JUROR.

lay system. (1945) *Maritime law.* A system in which a fishing vessel's catch is sold by contract or at auction, and after costs are paid and the shipowner is compensated, the net profits are divided among the crew members according to agreed-on percentages.

lay tenure. See TENURE.

laytime. (1951) *Maritime law.* Time allowed by a voyage charterparty for the charterer to load or unload cargo. • If more time is used, the vessel's owner is entitled to compensation for the delay, usu. in the form of demurrage. If less time is used, the owner may pay dispatch. — See DEMURRAGE; DISPATCH; LAYDAY.

lay witness. See WITNESS.

lazaretto. See QUARANTINE (4) (quot.).

LBO. See *leveraged buyout* under BUYOUT.

LC. *abbr.* **1.** LETTER OF CREDIT. **2.** LETTER OF CREDENCE. — Also written L/C.

L-Claim proceeding. (1997) A hearing under the Racketeer Influenced and Corrupt Organizations Act, intended to ensure that property ordered to be forfeited belongs solely to the defendant. • A petition for an L-Claim proceeding is filed by a third party who claims an interest in the property. The purpose is not to divide the assets among competing claimants, and general creditors of the defendant are not be allowed to maintain an L-Claim petition. The name refers to its legal basis in subsection *l* of RICO's penalty provision. 18 USCA § 1963(*l*)(2).

LCM method. *abbr.* LOWER-OF-COST-OR-MARKET METHOD.

LEAA. *abbr.* LAW ENFORCEMENT ASSISTANCE ADMINISTRATION.

leaching (leech-ing). (18c) The process by which moving fluid separates the soluble components of a material. • Under CERCLA, leaching is considered a release of contaminants. The term is sometimes used to describe the migration of contaminating materials, by rain or groundwater, from a fixed source, such as a landfill. 42 USCA § 9601(22).

lead counsel. See COUNSEL.

leader. See LOSS LEADER.

leading case. (17c) **1.** A judicial decision that first definitively settled an important legal rule or principle and that has since been often and consistently followed. • An example is *Miranda v. Arizona*, 384 U.S. 436, 86 S.Ct. 1602 (1966) (creating the exclusionary rule for evidence improperly obtained from a suspect being interrogated while in police custody). Cf. LANDMARK DECISION. **2.** An important, often the most important, judicial precedent on a particular legal issue. **3.** Loosely, a reported case that is cited as the dispositive authority on an issue being litigated. — Also termed (in sense 3) *ruling case.*

> "A leading case is one which first definitely settled an important rule or principle of law, and has since been often and consistently followed. The authority of such cases is of the very highest." Henry Campbell Black, *Handbook on the Law of Judicial Precedents* § 31, at 95 (1912).

leading counsel. See *lead counsel* under COUNSEL.

leading economic indicator. See ECONOMIC INDICATOR.

leading indicator. See INDICATOR.

leading-object rule. See MAIN-PURPOSE RULE.

leading of a use. (18c) *Hist.* In a deed, the specification, before the levy of a fine of land, of the person to whose use the fine will inure. • If the deed is executed after the fine, it "declares" the use.

> "As if A., tenant in tail, with reversion to himself in fee, would settle his estate on B. for life, remainder to C. in tail, remainder to D. in fee . . . . He therefore usually, after making the settlement proposed, covenants to levy a fine . . . and directs that the same shall enure to the uses in such settlement mentioned. This is now a deed to *lead* the uses of the fine or recovery, and the fine when levied, or recovery when suffered, shall enure to the uses so specified, and no other." 2 William Blackstone, *Commentaries on the Laws of England* 363 (1766).

leading question. (1824) A question that suggests the answer to the person being interrogated; esp., a question that may be answered by a mere "yes" or "no." • Leading questions are generally allowed only in cross-examination. — Also termed *categorical question*; *suggestive question*; *suggestive interrogation.*

> "**Leading questions.** Questions suggesting the answer which the person putting the question wishes or expects to receive, or suggesting disputed facts as to which the witness is to testify, must not, if objected to by the adverse party, be asked in an examination in chief, or a re-examination, except with the permission of the Court, but such questions may be asked in cross-examination." James Fitzjames Stephen, *A Digest of the Law of Evidence* 124 (4th ed. 1892).

"A leading question is one which puts the answer (which the attorney desires) into the mouth of the witness, or which suggests the answer to him. It is called leading because it virtually 'leads' the witness into the desired answer. Not only are such questions objectionable in law, but they make a bad impression on the jury, and they may suspect that the lawyer is the witness instead of the person on the stand; or they may feel that the lawyer is acting improperly in coaching the witness." Samuel Weiss, *How to Try a Case* 53–54 (1930).

"[W]hat is a leading question? 'What were you doing at 10 p.m. yesterday?' Has one not heard some such reply as, 'Ah! that's a leading question' or, 'I'm not going to be cross-examined'? Of course it is *not* a leading question, nor is it an example of cross-examination. On the other hand, 'Were you in Trafalgar Square at 10 p.m. yesterday?' *is* a leading question, and one that, in legal proceedings *may* be asked in cross-examination. As this elementary example shows, a leading question is one that suggests the answer; and since it is from the witness, and not from counsel, that the facts are to be elicited, the reason for the prohibition referred to is obvious." *Notable Cross-Examinations* xiii–xiv (Edward Wilfrid Fordham ed., 1951).

lead-lag study. (1974) A survey used to determine the amount of working capital that a utility company must reserve and include in its rate base, by comparing the time the company has to pay its bills and the time taken by its customers to pay for service. • The term comes from the phrases "lead time" and "lag time." Lead time is the average number of days between the company's receipt and payment of invoices it receives. Lag time is the average number of days between the company's billing of its customers and its receipt of payment. By analyzing the difference in timing between inward cash flow and outward cash flow, the company can calculate the amount of necessary reserves.

leads doctrine. (1972) *Tax.* In a tax-evasion case, the rule that the government must investigate all the taxpayer's leads that are reasonably accessible and that, if true, would establish the taxpayer's innocence, or the government risks having the trial judge presume that any leads not investigated are true and exonerating.

league. (15c) **1.** A covenant made by countries, groups, or individuals for promoting common interests or ensuring mutual protection. **2.** An alliance or association of countries, groups, or individuals formed by such a covenant. **3.** A unit of distance, usu. measuring about three miles (or some 4,828 meters on land, or three nautical miles or some 5,556 meters at sea).

▸ **marine league.** (17c) A geographical measure of distance equal to one-twentieth part of a degree of latitude, or three nautical miles.

League of Nations. An organization of countries formed in 1919 to promote international cooperation and peace. • President Woodrow Wilson endorsed the League in an address to Congress, but the United States never joined. The League dissolved in 1946 and turned its assets over to the United Nations.

leakage. (15c) **1.** The waste of a liquid caused by its leaking from a storage container. **2.** An allowance against duties granted by customs to an importer of liquids for losses sustained by this waste. **3.** *Intellectual property.* Loss in value of a piece of intellectual property because of unauthorized copying. • The types of intellectual property most susceptible to leakage are recordable media such as compact discs and videotapes.

leal (leel), *adj.* [Law French] (13c) *Hist.* Loyal.

lean, *vb.* (bef. 12c) **1.** To incline or tend in opinion or preference. • A court is sometimes said to "lean toward" or "lean against" an advocate's position, meaning that the court regards that position favorably or unfavorably. **2.** To yield; to submit.

leapfrog development. (1976) An improvement of land that requires the extension of public facilities from their current stopping point, through undeveloped land that may be scheduled for future development, to the site of the improvement.

leap year. See YEAR.

learned (lər-nid), *adj.* (14c) **1.** Having a great deal of learning; erudite. • A lawyer might refer to an adversary as a "learned colleague" or "learned opponent" — a comment that, depending on the situation and tone of voice, may be either a genuine compliment or a sarcastic slight. **2.** Well-versed in the law and its history. • Statutes sometimes require that judges be "learned in the law," a phrase commonly construed as meaning that they must have earned a law degree and been admitted to the bar.

learned friend. (17c) A fellow member of the legal profession, usu. one of the same rank such as a fellow lawyer or a fellow judge.

Learned Hand formula. See HAND FORMULA.

Learned Hand test. See HAND FORMULA.

learned intermediary. See *informed intermediary* under INTERMEDIARY.

learned-intermediary doctrine. (1984) The principle that a prescription-drug manufacturer fulfills its duty to warn of a drug's potentially harmful effects by informing the prescribing physician, rather than the end-user, of those effects.

learned-treatise rule. (1946) *Evidence.* An exception to the hearsay rule, by which a published text may be established as authoritative, either by expert testimony or by judicial notice. • Under the Federal Rules of Evidence, a statement in a published treatise, periodical, or pamphlet on sciences or arts (such as history or medicine) can be established as authoritative — and thereby admitted into evidence for the purpose of examining or cross-examining an expert witness — by expert testimony or by the court's taking judicial notice of the authoritative nature or reliability of the text. If the statement is admitted into evidence, it may be read into the trial record, but it may not be received as an exhibit. Fed. R. Evid. 803(18).

learner's permit. See *provisional driver's license* under DRIVER'S LICENSE.

learning, *n.* (bef. 12c) **1.** *Hist.* Legal doctrine. **2.** The act of acquiring knowledge.

lease, *n.* (14c) **1.** A contract by which a rightful possessor of real property conveys the right to use and occupy the property in exchange for consideration, usu. rent. • The lease term can be for life, for a fixed period, or for a period terminable at will. **2.** Such a conveyance plus all covenants attached to it. **3.** The written instrument memorializing such a conveyance and its covenants. — Also termed (redundantly) *lease agreement*; *lease contract.* **4.** The piece of real property so conveyed. **5.** A contract by which the rightful possessor of personal property conveys the right to use that property in exchange for consideration. — Also termed *tenancy agreement*. **6.** LOCATIO.

▸ **assignable lease.** (1915) A lease that the lessee can transfer to a successor. See SUBLEASE.

▸ **building lease.** (17c) A long-term lease of land that includes a covenant to erect or alter a building or other improvement. Cf. *ground lease*.

▸ **capital lease.** See LEASE-PURCHASE AGREEMENT.

▸ **commercial lease.** (1909) A lease for business purposes.

▸ **community lease.** (1919) A lease in which a number of lessors owning interests in separate tracts execute a lease in favor of a single lessee.

▸ **concurrent lease.** (1946) A lease that begins before a previous lease ends, entitling the new lessee to be paid all rents that accrue on the previous lease after the new lease begins, and to remedies against the holding tenant.

"A landlord who has granted a lease may nevertheless grant another lease of the same land for all or some of the period of the first lease. The second lease does not deprive the lessee under the first lease of the right to possession of the property, but is, in reality, a lease of the reversion. Because the two leases operate concurrently during at least some part of their respective durations, they are known as 'concurrent leases.'" Peter Butt, *Land Law* 233 (2d ed. 1988).

▸ **consumer lease.** (1972) **1.** A lease of goods by a person who is in the business of selling or leasing a product primarily for the lessee's personal or household use. UCC § 2A-103(1)(e). **2.** A residential — rather than commercial — lease.

▸ **derivative lease.** See SUBLEASE.

▸ **durable lease.** (1816) A lease that reserves a rent payable annually, usu. with a right of reentry for nonpayment.

▸ **edge lease.** (1939) *Oil & gas.* A lease located on the edge of a field.

▸ **finance lease.** (1966) A fixed-term lease used by a business to finance capital equipment. • The lessor's service is usu. limited to financing the asset, and the lessee pays maintenance costs and taxes and has the option of purchasing the asset at lease-end for a nominal price. Finance leases strongly resemble security agreements and are written almost exclusively by financial institutions as a way to help a commercial customer obtain an expensive capital item that the customer might not otherwise be able to afford. UCC § 2A-103(1)(g). — Also termed *full payout lease*; *tripartite lease*.

"By carving out the 'finance lease' for special treatment, the drafters of Article 2A have recognized a distinct species of lease that is written almost exclusively by financial institutions and — although treated as a true lease — does not normally carry with it certain of the responsibilities that the typical lessor bears under Article 2A." 2 James J. White & Robert S. Summers, *Uniform Commercial Code* § 13-3, at 4 (4th ed. 1995).

"A finance lease is the product of a three-party transaction. The supplier manufactures or supplies the goods pursuant to the lessee's specification, perhaps even pursuant to a purchase order, sales agreement or lease agreement between the supplier and the lessee. After the prospective finance lease is negotiated, a purchase order, sales agreement, or lease agreement is entered into by the lessor (as buyer or prime lessee) or an existing order, agreement or lease is assigned by the lessee to the lessor, and the lessor and the lessee then enter into a lease or sublease of the goods. Due to the limited function usually performed by the lessor, the lessee looks almost entirely to the supplier for representations, covenants and warranties. If a manufacturer's warranty carries through, the lessee may also look to that. Yet, this definition does not restrict the lessor's function solely to the supply of funds; if the lessor undertakes or performs other functions, express warranties, covenants, and the common law will protect the lessee." UCC § 2A-103 cmt. (g).

▸ **full-service lease.** (1967) A lease in which the lessor agrees to pay all maintenance expenses, insurance premiums, and property taxes.

▸ **graduated lease.** (1930) A lease in which rent varies depending on future contingencies, such as operating expenses or gross income.

▸ **gross lease.** (1939) A lease in which the lessee pays a flat amount for rent, out of which the lessor pays all the expenses (such as fuel, water, and electricity).

▸ **ground lease.** (1840) A long-term (usu. 99-year) lease of land only. • Such a lease typically involves commercial property, and any improvements built by the lessee usu. revert to the lessor. — Also termed *ground-rent lease*; *land lease*.

▸ **headlease.** See HEADLEASE.

▸ **hereditary lease.** (18c) A lease that gives a tenant and the tenant's successors a perpetual right to lease property and that binds the landlord to accept a deceased tenant's appointed successor or statutory heir as the new tenant. • The landlord cannot choose the tenant or increase the rent. Historically, the lease often remained in a family as long as ownership remained in the landlord's family. The landlord could terminate the lease only if the tenant failed to pay rent, or else neglected or seriously damaged the property. India and the Isle of Jersey, as well as some civil-law countries, still recognize hereditary leases. — Occas. shortened to *hereditary*.

▸ **index lease.** (1951) A lease that provides for increases in rent according to the increases in the consumer price index.

▸ **land lease.** See *ground lease*.

▸ **lease by estoppel.** (17c) A lease granted by a person who does not have an interest in the premises when leased but later acquires an interest.

▸ **leveraged lease.** (1972) A lease that is collateral for the loan through which the lessor acquired the leased asset, and that provides the lender's only recourse for nonpayment of the debt; a lease in which a creditor provides nonrecourse financing to the lessor (who has substantial leverage in the property) and in which the lessor's net investment in the lease, apart from nonrecourse financing, declines during the early years and increases in later years. — Also termed *third-party equity lease*; *tax lease*.

▸ **master lease.** (1935) A contract that establishes a leasehold's basic terms and conditions applicable to all related contracts for rental properties.

▸ **mineral lease.** (1846) A lease in which the lessee has the right to explore for and extract oil, gas, or other minerals. • The rent usu. is based on the amount or value of the minerals extracted.

▸ **mining lease.** (1846) A lease of a mine or mining claim, in which the lessee has the right to work the mine or claim, usu. with conditions on the amount and type of work to be done. • The lessor is compensated with either fixed rent or royalties based on the amount of ore mined.

▸ **month-to-month lease.** (1914) A tenancy with no written contract. • Rent is paid monthly, and usu. one month's notice by the landlord or tenant is required to terminate the tenancy. — Also termed *monthly lease.* See *periodic tenancy* under TENANCY.

▸ **net lease.** (1923) A lease in which the lessee pays rent plus property expenses (such as taxes and insurance).

▸ **net-net-net lease.** (1962) A lease in which the lessee pays all the expenses, including mortgage interest and amortization, leaving the lessor with an amount free of all claims. — Also termed *triple net lease.*

▸ **no-term lease.** (1919) *Oil & gas.* A mineral lease with a drilling-delay rental clause that allows the lessee to extend the primary term indefinitely by paying delay rentals. • No-term leases were common at the end of the 19th century. Some courts refused to enforce them on the ground that they created a mere estate at will, terminable at the will of either the lessor or the lessee. Other courts upheld them, but with the stipulation that the lessee had an obligation to either test or release the lease within a reasonable time.

▸ **oil-and-gas lease.** (1892) A lease granting the right to extract oil and gas from a specified piece of land. • Although called a "lease," this interest is typically considered a determinable fee in the minerals rather than a grant of possession for a term of years.

▸ **operating lease.** (1913) A lease of property (esp. equipment) for a term that is shorter than the property's useful life. • Under an operating lease, the lessor is typically responsible for paying taxes and other expenses on the property. Cf. LEASE-PURCHASE AGREEMENT.

▸ **"or" lease.** *Oil & gas.* A mineral lease with a drilling-delay rental clause structured so that the lessee promises to start drilling operations or to pay delay rentals from time to time during the primary term. • If the lessee fails to do one or the other, the lease does not automatically terminate, but the lessee is liable for the delay-rental amount.

▸ **parol lease** (pə-**rohl** *or* **par**-əl). (17c) A lease based on an oral agreement; an unwritten lease.

▸ **percentage lease.** (1938) A lease in which the rent is based on a percentage of gross (or net) sales or profits, typically with a set minimum rent.

▸ **perpetual lease.** (17c) **1.** An ongoing lease not limited in duration. **2.** A grant of lands in fee with a reservation of a rent in fee; a fee farm.

▸ **perpetually renewable lease.** (1907) *Hist.* A lease that a tenant may renew for another period as often as it expires, usu. by making a payment upon exercising the right. • In 1922, this type of lease was effectively abolished in England by the Law of Property Act, which provided for the conversion of existing and future perpetually renewable leases to term-of-years leases, and set the maximum term at 2,000 years.

▸ **proprietary lease.** (1926) A lease between a cooperative apartment association and a tenant.

▸ **reversionary lease.** (18c) A lease that will take effect when a prior lease terminates.

▸ **sandwich lease.** (1976) A lease in which the lessee subleases the property to a third party, esp. for more rent than under the original lease.

▸ **short lease.** (17c) A lease of brief duration, often less than six months.

▸ **sublease.** See SUBLEASE.

▸ **synthetic lease.** (1996) A method for financing the purchase of real estate, whereby the lender creates a special-purpose entity that buys the property and then leases it to the ultimate user (usu. a corporation). • A synthetic lease is treated as a loan for tax purposes and as an operating lease for accounting purposes, so that the "lessee" can deduct the property's depreciation and the loan's interest yet keep both the asset and the debt off its balance sheet.

▸ **tax lease.** (1875) **1.** The instrument or estate given to the purchaser of land at a tax sale when the law does not permit the sale of an estate in fee for nonpayment of taxes but instead directs the sale of an estate for years. **2.** See *leveraged lease.*

▸ **third-party equity lease.** See *leveraged lease.*

▸ **timber lease.** (1853) A real-property lease that contemplates that the lessee will cut timber on the leased premises.

▸ **top lease.** (1930) *Oil & gas.* A lease granted on property already subject to an oil-and-gas lease. • Generally, any rights granted by a top lease grants are valid only if the existing lease ends.

▸ **tripartite lease.** See *finance lease.*

▸ **triple net lease.** See *net-net-net lease.*

▸ **"unless" lease.** (1920) *Oil & gas.* An oil-and-gas lease with a drilling-delay rental clause structured as a special limitation to the primary term. • Unless delay rentals are paid or drilling operations are started from time to time as specified, an "unless" lease automatically terminates, and the lessee has no liability for its failure to perform.

lease, *vb.* (16c) **1.** To grant the possession and use of (land, buildings, rooms, movable property, etc.) to another in return for rent or other consideration <the city leased the stadium to the football team>. **2.** To take a lease of; to hold by a lease <Carol leased the townhouse from her uncle>.

lease agreement. See LEASE (3).

lease and release. (17c) *Hist.* A method of transferring seisin without livery, whereby the owner and the transferee would enter into a lease for a term of years, to take effect only when the transferee entered the property, whereupon the owner would release all interest in the property to the transferee by written instrument. • Once the transferee owned both the term and the freehold interest, the two interests would merge to form one estate in fee simple. This lease-and-release procedure was fully acceptable to the courts, on the theory that livery of seisin to one already occupying the land was unnecessary.

leaseback, *n.* (1947) The sale of property on the understanding, or with the express option, that the seller may lease the property from the buyer, usu. immediately after the sale. — Also termed *sale and leaseback*; *sale-leaseback.*

lease by estoppel. See LEASE.

lease contract. See LEASE (3).

lease for life. (16c) *Hist.* A lease of land for the duration of a specified number of lives instead of for a specified term of years. • Unlike a tenant for a term of years, a lessee for life could recover the land if dispossessed.

> "The rent payable was usually fairly small, but a fine was paid when the lease was granted; a further fine was payable when, on the termination of the lives, the tenant exercised the right the lease gave him to replace them and so extend the lease. If the lessor was a corporation such as a monastery or college, the fines were treated as income by the then members of the corporation, to the disadvantage of their successors. Leases for life finally lost their popularity when legislation in the first half of the nineteenth century compelled corporations to add such fines to their capital." Robert E. Megarry & M.P. Thompson, *A Manual of the Law of Real Property* 306 (6th ed. 1993).

lease for years. See *tenancy for a term* under TENANCY.

leasehold, *n.* (18c) A tenant's possessory estate in land or premises, the four types being the tenancy for years, the periodic tenancy, the tenancy at will, and the tenancy at sufferance. • Although a leasehold has some of the characteristics of real property, it has historically been classified as a chattel real. — Also termed *leasehold estate*; *leasehold interest.* See TENANCY. Cf. FREEHOLD.

leaseholder. (1858) A tenant who has a possessory estate in realty; esp., someone who lives in a leasehold house, apartment, etc.

leaseholder royalty. See *landowner's royalty* under ROYALTY (2).

leasehold improvements. (1845) Beneficial changes to leased property (such as a parking lot or driveway) made by or for the benefit of the lessee. • The phrase is used in a condemnation proceeding to determine the share of compensation to be allocated to the lessee.

leasehold interest. (18c) **1.** LEASEHOLD; esp., for purposes of eminent domain, the lessee's interest in the lease itself, measured by the difference between the total remaining rent and the rent the lessee would pay for similar space for the same period. **2.** A lessor's or lessee's interest under a lease contract. UCC § 2A-103(1)(m). **3.** WORKING INTEREST.

leasehold mortgage. See MORTGAGE.

leasehold-mortgage bond. See BOND (3).

leasehold reversion. See REVERSION.

leasehold royalty. See *landowner's royalty* under ROYALTY (2).

leasehold value. (1885) The value of a leasehold interest. • This term usu. applies to a long-term lease when the rent paid under the lease is lower than current market rates. Some states permit the lessee to claim the leasehold interest from the landlord in a condemnation proceeding, unless the lease prohibits such a claim. Other states prohibit these claims by statute. See LEASEHOLD INTEREST; NO-BONUS CLAUSE.

lease insurance. See INSURANCE.

lease-lend. See LEND-LEASE.

lease option. See OPTION (5).

lease-purchase agreement. (1939) A rent-to-own purchase plan under which the buyer takes possession of the goods with the first payment and takes ownership with the final payment; a lease of property (esp. equipment) by which ownership of the property is transferred to the lessee at the end of the lease term. • Such a lease is usu. treated as an installment sale. Under a capital lease, the lessee is responsible for paying taxes and other expenses on the property. — Also termed *lease-to-purchase agreement*; *hire-purchase agreement*; *capital lease.* Cf. *operating lease* under LEASE.

lease with an option to purchase. See *lease option* under OPTION (5).

leasing-making. (18c) *Hist. Scots law.* Oral sedition.

least-intrusive-means doctrine. (1978) A doctrine requiring the government to exhaust all other investigatory means before seeking sensitive testimony, as by compelling an attorney to testify before a grand jury on matters that may be protected by the attorney–client privilege.

least-intrusive-remedy doctrine. (1989) The rule that a legal remedy should provide the damaged party with appropriate relief, without unduly penalizing the opposing party or the jurisdiction's legal system, as by striking only the unconstitutional portion of a challenged statute while leaving the rest intact.

least-restrictive educational environment. See LEAST-RESTRICTIVE ENVIRONMENT.

least-restrictive environment. (1975) Under the Individuals with Disabilities Education Act, the school setting that, to the greatest extent appropriate, educates a disabled child together with children who are not disabled. 20 USCA § 1412(5). — Also termed *least-restrictive-educational environment.* Cf. MAINSTREAMING.

least-restrictive-means test. (1972) The rule that a law or governmental regulation should be crafted in a way that will protect individual civil liberties as much as possible and should be only as restrictive as necessary to accomplish a legitimate governmental purpose.

leaute (**low**-tay), *n.* [Law French "legality"] *Hist.* Legality; the condition of a lawful man (*legalis homo*). See LEGALIS HOMO.

leave, *n.* (bef. 12c) **1.** Permission <by leave of court>. **2.** Departure; the act of going away <took his leave>. **3.** Extended absence for which someone, often an employee, has authorization; esp., a voluntary vacation from military duties with the chance to visit home; furlough <on a three-month leave from the army>.

▸ **adoption leave.** (1967) A period of usu. paid leave granted to an employee who is adopting a child to allow time to settling into the new family arrangement.

▸ **bereavement leave.** (1956) A period of paid leave granted to an employee upon the death of a defined class of the employee's relatives or household members.

▸ **compassionate leave.** (1917) **1.** A period of usu. paid leave granted to an employee upon the onset of a serious illness or injury to a defined class of the employee's relatives or household members, esp. for the care of the family member's health needs. **2.** Special permission to have time away from work because a relative has died or is very ill.

▸ **family leave.** (1981) An unpaid leave of absence taken from work to have or care for a baby or to care for a sick family member. See FAMILY AND MEDICAL LEAVE ACT.

▸ **family medical leave.** (1987) **1.** A period of paid leave granted to an employee to take time off for major family-related medical issues. • The Family Medical Leave Act of 1993 (FMLA), 29 USCA §§ 2601 et seq., allows employees to take up to 12 weeks of unpaid leave each year for family illness, childbirth, or adoption. It requires employers to maintain the employees' insurance benefits and to keep their positions for them pending their return. The statute applies to all businesses and government agencies having 50 or more employees. **2.** A usu. short period of paid or unpaid leave granted at an employer's discretion for any humane reason not otherwise covered by a company's written policies.

▸ **family-responsibility leave.** (1991) A period of usu. paid leave granted to an employee to attend to important domestic concerns, such as a wedding, a household emergency, or educational appointments for children.

▸ **garden leave.** (1990) *English law.* **1.** A period during which a person whose employment will terminate on a set date is ordered to stay away from the workplace but remains on the payroll. **2.** An employee's suspension pending an investigation or disciplinary proceedings related to alleged misconduct. — Also termed *gardening leave.*

▸ **leave without pay.** (1909) A period of time when the employee who is not at work will not be compensated. • The employer usually retains the employee's job so that the employee may return to it. — Also termed *unpaid leave.*

▸ **maternity leave.** (1919) A period of usu. paid leave granted to an employee who is about to give birth or has recently given birth to a child, or to a mother who is going through an adoption. See *parental leave.* Cf. *paternity leave.*

▸ **military leave.** See MILITARY LEAVE.

▸ **paid leave.** (1921) A period of time when the employee who is not at work will nevertheless be compensated, usu. at the employer's discretion, as when an employee has been suspended during an investigation of an incident in which the employee was involved.

▸ **parental leave.** (1972) A period of usu. paid leave granted to an employee to care for a child or make arrangements for the child's welfare. • Minimum benefits may be stipulated by law, and they vary from jurisdiction to jurisdiction. The term *parental leave* may encompass *maternity leave, paternity leave,* and *adoption leave.*

▸ **paternity leave.** (1973) A period of usu. paid leave granted to an employee who is about to become or has recently become a father, through either birth or adoption.

▸ **sick leave.** (1820) A period of paid leave that an employee can use to stay home and recuperate during a period of temporary illness. — Also termed *paid sick days.*

▸ **unpaid leave.** See *leave without pay.*

leave, *vb.* (bef. 12c) **1.** To depart; voluntarily go away; quit (a place). **2.** To depart willfully with the intent not to return <Nelson left Texas and became a resident of Massachusetts>. **3.** To deliver (a summons, money, an article, etc.) by dropping off at a certain place, esp. to await the return of someone; esp., to post (a copy of a writ, etc.). **4.** To give by will; to bequeath or devise <she left her ranch to her stepson>. • This usage has historically been considered loose by the courts, and it is not always given testamentary effect. **5.** To be survived by <he left no brothers or sisters>.

leave and license. In an action for trespass to land, the defense that the plaintiff consented to the defendant's presence.

leave no issue, *vb.* (16c) To die without any surviving child or other descendant. • The spouse of a deceased child is usu. not issue. See FAILURE OF ISSUE.

leave of absence. (18c) A worker's temporary absence from employment or duty with the intention to return. • Salary level and seniority typically are unaffected by a leave of absence.

leave of court. (18c) Judicial permission to follow a nonroutine procedure <the defense sought leave of court to allow the defendant to exit the courtroom when the autopsy photographs are shown>. — Often shortened to *leave.*

leave to appeal. (16c) Permission asked for or granted to file for review in an appellate court. Cf. APPLICATION FOR LEAVE TO APPEAL; MOTION FOR LEAVE TO APPEAL.

leave to sit. *Parliamentary law.* Permission from a deliberative assembly for a committee or other subordinate body to meet while the assembly is meeting.

leave without pay. See LEAVE.

LEC. *abbr.* LOCAL-EXCHANGE CARRIER.

leccator (lə-**kay**-tər). [Latin] *Archaic.* A debauched person; a lecher. — Also spelled *lecator.*

lecherwite (**lech**-ər-wɪt). See LAIRWITE.

lecture method. See HORNBOOK METHOD.

ledger (**lej**-ər). (16c) **1.** A book or series of books used for recording financial transactions in the form of debits and credits; esp., a book in which a business or bank records how much money it receives and spends. — Also termed *general ledger.* **2.** *Archaic.* A resident ambassador or agent. — Also termed (in sense 2) *leger; lieger.*

ledo (**lee**-doh), *n.* [Latin] *Hist.* The rising water of the sea; neap tide. See *neap tide* under TIDE.

leet (leet). (13c) *Hist.* A criminal court. • The last leets were abolished in England in 1977.

> "Leet is a court derived out of the sheriff's turn, and inquires of all offences under the degree of high treason that are committed against the crown and dignity of the king. But those offences which are to be punished with loss of life or member, are only inquirable there, and to be certified over to the justices of assise. See stat. 1 E. 3, c. 17." *Termes de la Ley* 278–79 (1st Am. ed. 1812).

left-handed marriage. See *morganatic marriage* under MARRIAGE (1).

legabilis (lə-**gay**-bə-lis), *n.* [Latin] *Hist.* Property or goods that may be given by will. • As an adjective, the term also meant "bequeathable."

legable, *adj.* (18c) **1.** (Of property) capable of being bequeathed; bequeathable.

legacy (**leg**-ə-see), *n.* (15c) A gift by will, esp. of personal property and often of money. Cf. BEQUEST; DEVISE.

▸ **absolute legacy.** (17c) A legacy given without condition and intended to vest immediately. Cf. *vested legacy.*

▸ **accumulated legacy.** (1898) A legacy that has not yet been paid to a legatee.

▸ **accumulative legacy.** See *additional legacy.*

▸ **additional legacy.** A second legacy given to a legatee in the same will (or in a codicil to the same will) that gave another legacy. • An additional legacy is supplementary to another and is not considered merely a repeated expression of the same gift. — Also termed *accumulative legacy; cumulative legacy.*

▸ **alternate legacy.** (1983) A legacy by which the testator allows the legatee to choose one of two or more items.

▸ **conditional legacy.** (17c) A legacy that will take effect or be defeated subject to the occurrence or nonoccurrence of an event.

▸ **contingent legacy.** (18c) A legacy that depends on an uncertain event and thus has not vested. • An example is a legacy given to one's granddaughter "if she attains the age of 21.

▸ **cumulative legacy. 1.** See *accumulative legacy.* **2.** See *additional legacy.*

▸ **demonstrative legacy** (di-**mon**-strə-tiv). (18c) A legacy paid from a particular source if that source has enough money. • If it does not, the amount of the legacy not paid from that source is taken from the estate's general assets.

▸ **failed legacy.** See *lapsed legacy.*

▸ **general legacy.** (18c) **1.** A gift of personal property that the testator intends to come from the estate's general assets, payable in money or items indistinguishable from each other, such as shares of publicly traded stock. **2.** *Civil law.* A testator's gift of a fraction or proportion of the estate remaining after particular legacies have been satisfied. **3.** *Civil law.* A testator's gift of all, a fraction, or a proportion of one of certain categories of property, as specified by statute. See La. Civ. Code arts. 1586, 3506(28). — Also termed *legacy under a general title.* Cf. *particular legacy; universal legacy.*

▸ **lapsed legacy.** (18c) A legacy to a legatee who dies either before the testator dies or before the legacy is payable. • It falls into the residual estate unless the jurisdiction has an antilapse statute. — Also termed *failed legacy; failed gift.* See ANTILAPSE STATUTE.

▸ **legacy under a general title.** See *general legacy.*

▸ **legacy under a particular title.** See *particular legacy.*

▸ **legacy under a universal title.** (1846) *Louisiana law.* A testamentary disposition of all immovable property, or all movable property, or a fixed proportion of all immovable property or of all movable property. La. Civ. Code art. 1612. Cf. *general legacy; particular legacy; universal legacy.*

▸ **modal legacy** (**moh**-dəl). (1878) A legacy accompanied by directions about the manner in which it will be applied to the legatee's benefit <a modal legacy for the purchase of a business>.

▸ **particular legacy.** (17c) *Civil law.* A testamentary gift that is not expressed as a fraction or proportion and is less than all the estate; any testamentary gift that does not meet the definition of a general legacy or a universal legacy. *See* La. Civ. Code arts. 1587, 3506(28). — Also termed *legacy under a particular title.* Cf. *general legacy; universal legacy.*

▸ **pecuniary legacy** (pi-**kyoo**-nee-er-ee). (18c) A legacy of a sum of money.

▸ **prelegacy.** (1941) *Roman & civil law.* **1.** A legacy that is given to one of several heirs in addition to that heir's share of the estate. See HEIR (4). **2.** A legacy that the testator directs to be paid before other legacies or given some other form of priority.

▸ **residuary legacy** (ri-**zij**-oo-er-ee). (18c) A legacy of the estate remaining after the satisfaction of all claims and all specific, general, and demonstrative legacies.

▸ **special legacy.** See *specific legacy.*

▸ **specific legacy.** (18c) A legacy of a specific or unique item of property, such as any real estate or a particular piece of furniture. — Also termed *special legacy.*

▸ **substitutional legacy.** (1894) A legacy that replaces a different legacy already given to a legatee.

▸ **trust legacy.** (1861) A legacy of personal property to trustees to be held in trust, with the income usu. paid to a specified beneficiary.

▸ **universal legacy.** (1831) *Louisiana law.* A testamentary disposition of all property, movable and immovable, to one or more persons. La. Civ. Code art. 1585. Cf. *general legacy; legacy under a universal title; particular legacy.*

▸ **vested legacy.** (18c) A legacy given in such a way that the legatee has a fixed, indefeasible right to its payment. • A legacy is said to be vested when the testator's words making the bequest convey a transmissible interest, whether present or future, to the legatee. Thus, a legacy to be paid when the legatee reaches the age of 21 is a vested legacy because it is given unconditionally and absolutely. Although the legacy is vested, the legatee's enjoyment of it is deferred. Cf. *absolute legacy; contingent legacy.*

▸ **void legacy.** (18c) A legacy that never had any legal existence. • The subject matter of such a legacy is treated as a part of the estate and passes under the residuary clause of a will or (in the absence of a residuary clause) under the rules for intestate succession.

2. *Roman & civil law.* An obligation imposed by a testator in his or her will to perform a material service for a legatee. • If it is unclear who is to perform the service, the legacy burdens the heir.

▸ **sublegacy.** (1883) *Roman & civil law.* An obligation imposed by a testator on a legatee to perform a material service for the testator's heir.

legacy data. (1990) Old information that an organization has, whether stored in computers or in paper records.

legacy duty. See *legacy tax* under TAX.

legacy tax. See TAX.

legal, *adj.* (15c) **1.** Of, relating to, or involving law generally; falling within the province of law <pro bono legal services>. **2.** Established, required, or permitted by law; LAWFUL <it is legal to carry a concealed handgun in some states>. **3.** Of, relating to, or involving law as opposed to equity.

legal act. (15c) **1.** Any act not condemned as illegal. • For example, a surgeon's incision is a legal act, while stabbing is an illegal one. **2.** An action or undertaking that creates a legally recognized obligation; an act that binds a person in some way.

> "A lunatic, though capable of holding property, was in Roman law incapable of any legal act." Thomas E. Holland, *The Elements of Jurisprudence* 354 (13th ed. 1924).

3. See *act in the law* under ACT (2). 4. See *act of the law* under ACT (2).

legal-acumen doctrine (**lee**-gəl ə-**kyoo**-mən). (1905) The principle that if a defect in, or the invalidity of, a claim to land cannot be discovered without legal expertise, then equity may be invoked to remove the cloud created by the defect or invalidity.

legal advice. See ADVICE OF COUNSEL (1).

legal-advice exception. (1983) **1.** The rule that an attorney may withhold as privileged the client's identity and information regarding fees if there is a strong probability that disclosing the information would implicate the client in the criminal activity for which the attorney was consulted. See ADVICE OF COUNSEL (1). Cf. ADVICE OF COUNSEL (2). **2.** An exemption contained in open-meetings legislation, permitting a governmental body to meet in closed session to consult with its attorney about certain matters.

legal age. (18c) **1.** See *age of capacity* under AGE. **2.** See *age of majority* (1) under AGE.

legal aid. (1890) **1.** A system in which government subsidizes the provision of legal services to the poor. **2.** Free or inexpensive legal services provided to those who cannot afford to pay the normal fees. • Legal aid is usu. administered locally by a specially established organization. See LEGAL SERVICES CORPORATION.

> "In the 1870's and 1880's the only substantial move toward improvement was the limited beginnings of legal aid work. The common law, and in some states a few early statutes, held out to the poor the help of counsel assigned by the court. But by the later nineteenth century this practice had long fallen into disuse in civil cases. In criminal cases, the glaring unfairness of lack of counsel had kept the practice alive. However, it was limited, in practice if not in law, to the offenses that carried the most serious penalties; and in the great cities it was often the means by which police-court hangers-on victimized the families or relatives of the accused. The roots of modern legal aid work were in the service first tendered by a German immigrant aid society in New York in 1876, and during the slow growth of the movement over the next thirty years this limited origin was characteristic. The founding of the Detroit legal aid unit in 1909, by the city bar association, marked the first recognition by the organized bar that it had some responsibility to do something to make justice more available to the poor. As late as 1910 there were still but fourteen legal aid societies in operation. But here, as in so many other respects, 1910 was a threshold year. In the next three years the number of legal aid organizations doubled. The lead now passed from the single-mission or proprietary groups which had done most of the work theretofore, to the unorganized charities, which now saw legal aid as one phase of their broad programs. By 1918 there were forty-one societies and four public defender offices." James Willard Hurst, *The Growth of American Law* 152–53 (1950).

legal analyst. See PARALEGAL.

legal argot. See LEGALESE.

legal asset. See ASSET.

legal assignment. See ASSIGNMENT (2).

legal assistant. (1939) **1.** PARALEGAL. **2.** A legal secretary.

legal benefit. See BENEFIT (2).

legal brief. See BRIEF (1).

legal capital. See CAPITAL.

legal cause. See *proximate cause* under CAUSE (1).

legal centralism. (1970) The theory suggesting that state-constructed legal entities form the center of legal life and control lesser normative systems (such as the family or business networks) that define appropriate behavior and social relationships. — Also termed *legal centrism*; *legocentrism* (lee-goh-**sen**-triz-əm).

legal certainty. See CERTAINTY.

legal-certainty test. (1964) *Civil procedure.* A test designed to determine whether the amount in controversy satisfies the minimum needed to establish the court's jurisdiction, the rule being that the amount claimed in the complaint will control unless there is a "legal certainty" that the claim is actually less than the minimum amount. See AMOUNT IN CONTROVERSY.

legal chemistry. See FORENSIC CHEMISTRY.

legal citology (sɪ-**tol**-ə-jee). (1996) The study of citations (esp. in footnotes) and their effect on legal scholarship. — Often shortened to *citology.* — **legal citologist** (sɪ-**tol**-ə-jist), *n.*

Legal Code. See CODE (2).

legal concept. A legally defined category into which facts can be put so that a series of rules, principles and standards become legally applicable. — Also termed *legal conception.* Cf. JURISTIC CONCEPT.

legal conclusion. (17c) A statement that expresses a legal duty or result but omits the facts creating or supporting the duty or result. Cf. CONCLUSION OF LAW; CONCLUSION OF FACT; FINDING OF FACT.

legal consideration. See *valuable consideration* under CONSIDERATION (1).

legal correlative. (1953) A legal status that has a corresponding or reciprocal status, such as a right that corresponds to a duty. • Wesley Newcomb Hohfeld of Yale Law School first introduced the bases for the concept of legal correlatives in two articles published in the *Yale Law Journal* in 1913 and 1917. He polished the concept in the book *Fundamental Legal Conceptions, as Applied in Judicial Reasoning and Other Legal Essays*, published posthumously in 1919.

> "Rights and duties have a distinct relationship and are called legal correlatives by Hohfeld. In terms of intellectual property, the right is a right to do certain things, such as making copies of a work of copyright, making articles to a design covered by a design right, or making products in accordance with a patented invention. The correlative duty is a duty owed by all others not to infringe the right. This duty exists even if the person infringing the right does not know of it. Looking at Hohfeld's scheme again, it can be seen that there are associated privileges and 'no rights.' The right resulting from the operation of intellectual property gives the owner of that right a corresponding privilege, that is the privilege to exploit the work. The correlative 'no right' is to the effect that persons other than the owner do not have this privilege." David Bainbridge, *Intellectual Property* 11 (5th ed. 2002).

legal costs. **1.** See COST (2). **2.** See COST (3).

legal cruelty. See CRUELTY.

legal culture. A society's attitudes toward and expectations of its system of laws.

legal custody. **1.** See CUSTODY (2). **2.** See CUSTODY (3). **3.** See DECISION-MAKING RESPONSIBILITY.

legal custom. See CUSTOM (1).

legal death. **1.** See *brain death* under DEATH. **2.** See *civil death* (2) under DEATH. **3.** See *civil death* (3) under DEATH.

legal debt. See DEBT.

legal defense. See DEFENSE (1).

legal demand. See DEMAND (1).

legal dependent. See DEPENDENT (1).

legal description. (18c) A formal description of real property, including a description of any part subject to an easement or reservation, complete enough that a particular piece of land can be located and identified. • The description can be made by reference to a government survey, metes and bounds, or lot numbers of a recorded plat. — Also termed *land description*.

legal detriment. See DETRIMENT (2).

legal disability. See DISABILITY (2).

legal discretion. See *judicial discretion* under DISCRETION (4).

legal distributee. See DISTRIBUTEE.

legal drafting. See DRAFTING.

legal duty. See DUTY (1).

legaldygook. (1990) Complicated legal language, esp. of the willfully obscure type, usu. found in various types of poor legal writing, including bad law reviews, bad treatises, bad regulations, and bad statutes, all of which are sometimes prepared by inexpert writers whose purpose seems to be something other than clear and easy communication. See LEGALESE. Cf. GOBBLEDYGOOK. — Also spelled *legaldegook*.

legal efficacy. See EFFICACY.

legal-elements test. (1980) *Criminal law.* A method of determining whether one crime is a lesser included offense in relation to another crime, by examining the components of the greater crime to analyze whether a person who commits the greater crime necessarily commits the lesser one too. — Also termed *same-elements test*.

legal entity. (18c) A body, other than a natural person, that can function legally, sue or be sued, and make decisions through agents. • A typical example is a corporation. Cf. *artificial person* under PERSON (3).

legalese (lee-gə-**leez**). (1914) The peculiar language of lawyers; esp., the speech and writing of lawyers at their communicative worst, characterized by antique jargon, pomposity, affected displays of precision, ponderous abstractions, and hocus-pocus incantations. — Also termed (more neutrally) *law-talk*; *law language*; *legal jargon*; *legal argot*. See PLAIN-LANGUAGE MOVEMENT; LEGALDYGOOK. Cf. OFFICIALESE.

legal estate. See ESTATE (1).

legal estoppel. See ESTOPPEL.

legal ethics. (1828) **1.** The standards of professional conduct applicable to members of the legal profession within a given jurisdiction. • Ethical rules consist primarily of the ABA Model Rules of Professional Conduct and the earlier ABA Model Code of Professional Responsibility, together with related regulatory judgments and opinions. The Model Rules of Professional Conduct have been enacted into law, often in a modified form, in most states. **2.** The study of such standards. **3.** A lawyer's practical observance of or conformity to established standards of professional conduct. See MODEL RULES OF PROFESSIONAL CONDUCT.

> "In one sense, the term 'legal ethics' refers narrowly to the system of professional regulations governing the conduct of lawyers. In a broader sense, however, legal ethics is simply a special case of ethics in general, as ethics is understood in the central traditions of philosophy and religion. From this broader perspective, legal ethics cuts more deeply than legal regulation: it concerns the fundamentals of our moral lives as lawyers." Deborah L. Rhode & David Luban, *Legal Ethics* 3 (1992).

legal etiquette. (1830) Collectively, the professional courtesies that lawyers have traditionally observed in their professional conduct, shown through civility and a strong sense of honor. — Also termed *etiquette of the profession*.

legal evidence. See EVIDENCE.

legal excuse. See EXCUSE (2).

legal-expenses insurance. See *legal-protection insurance* under INSURANCE.

legal fact. See FACT.

legal family. *Comparative law.* One of several large groups of national legal systems that comparative lawyers identify in order to present the systems comprehensibly and to analyze them methodically.

> "Different legal systems can only be treated as belonging to the same legal family if they are sufficiently 'similar,' 'affiliated,' or 'close' to each other. It is therefore of paramount importance to establish convincing criteria that would be helpful in concluding whether or not there is a sufficient degree of proximity. It comes as no surprise that comparative lawyers have not produced a uniform solution to the problem." Hein Kötz, "Legal Families," in 2 *The Max Planck Encyclopedia of European Private Law* 1063, 1063 (Jürgen Basedow et al. eds., 2012).

legal father. See FATHER.

legal fence. See LAWFUL FENCE.

legal fiction. (17c) An assumption that something is true even though it may be untrue, made esp. in judicial reasoning to alter how a legal rule operates; specif., a device by which a legal rule or institution is diverted from its original purpose to accomplish indirectly some other object. • The constructive trust is an example of a legal fiction. — Often shortened to *fiction*. — Also termed *fiction of law*; *fictio juris*.

> "I . . . employ the expression 'Legal Fiction' to signify any assumption which conceals, or affects to conceal, the fact that a rule of law has undergone alteration, its letter remaining unchanged, its operation being modified. . . . It is not difficult to understand why fictions in all their forms are particularly congenial to the infancy of society. They satisfy the desire for improvement, which is not quite wanting, at the same time that they do not offend the superstitious disrelish for change which is always present." Henry S. Maine, *Ancient Law* 21–22 (17th ed. 1901).

> "Legal fiction is the mask that progress must wear to pass the faithful but blear-eyed watchers of our ancient legal treasures. But though legal fictions are useful in thus mitigating or absorbing the shock of innovation, they work havoc in the form of intellectual confusion." Morris R. Cohen, *Law and the Social Order* 126 (1933).

legal force. See *reasonable force* under FORCE.

legal formalism, *n.* (1895) **1.** The theory that law is a set of rules and principles independent of other political and social institutions. • Legal formalism was espoused by such scholars as Christopher Columbus Langdell and Lon Fuller. See FORMALISM. Cf. LEGAL REALISM. **2.** The use of deductive logic to derive the outcome of a legal problem from premises accepted as authoritative. — **legal formalist,** *n.*

legal fraud. See *constructive fraud* (1) under FRAUD.

legal heir. See HEIR (1).

legal history. (18c) **1.** The branch of knowledge that records and explains the events within a system of law, or within systems of law generally, as steps in the progress of civilization. **2.** The events that form the subject matter of this branch of knowledge. **3.** A treatise that systematically presents these events, usu. together with a philosophical explanation of them.

legal holiday. (1867) **1.** A day designated by law as exempt from court proceedings, issuance of process, and the like. • Legal holidays vary from state to state. — Also termed *nonjudicial day*. **2.** An official holiday on which most government offices and banks are closed. — Sometimes shortened to *holiday*.

legal hybrid. (1960) *Property.* A cooperative housing unit in which the same person holds a lease and also owns stock in the cooperative association that owns or leases the unit.

legal impossibility. See IMPOSSIBILITY.

legal incapacity. See INCAPACITY (2).

legal incompetence. See INCOMPETENCY.

legal incompetency. See INCOMPETENCY.

legal inconsistency. See *legally inconsistent verdict* under VERDICT (1).

legal injury. See INJURY.

legal-injury rule. (1956) The doctrine that the statute of limitations on a claim does not begin to run until the claimant has sustained some legally actionable damage. • Under this rule, the limitations period is tolled until the plaintiff has actually been injured. — Also termed *damage rule*.

legal innocence. See INNOCENCE.

legal insanity. See INSANITY.

legal instrument. See INSTRUMENT (1).

legal insurance. See *legal-protection insurance* under INSURANCE.

legal interest. 1. See INTEREST (2). **2.** See INTEREST (3).

legal interruption. See INTERRUPTION.

legal intromission. See INTROMISSION (2).

legal investments. See LEGAL LIST.

legalis homo (lə-**gay**-lis **hoh**-moh). [Latin "lawful man"] (17c) *Hist.* Someone who has full legal capacity and full legal rights; one who has not been deprived of any rights in court by outlawry, excommunication, or infamy. • A *legalis homo* was said to stand *rectus in curia* ("right in court"). A lawful man was able to serve as a juror and to swear an oath. — Also termed *legal man*; *lawful man*; *lageman*; *liber et legalis homo*. See RECTUS IN CURIA. Pl. ***legales homines*** (lə-**gay**-leez **hom**-ə-neez).

legalism, *n.* (1928) **1.** Formalism carried to an extreme; an inclination to exalt the importance of law or formulated rules in any area of action. See FORMALISM.

> "What is legalism? It is the ethical attitude that holds moral conduct to be a matter of rule following, and moral relationships to consist of duties and rights determined by rules." Judith N. Shklar, *Legalism: Law, Morals, and Political Trials* 1 (1964).

> "If . . . the law and the lawyer are to make a socially valuable contribution to the operation of the social security system, there must be abandoned old-established habits of thought as to the nature of law and the whole gamut of practices summed up in the layman's word of deadly insult, 'legalism' — his word for rigid attachment to legal precedent, the substitution of legal rule for policy, the fettering of discretion, the adversary style, the taking of technical points, formality." Leslie Scarman, *English Law — The New Dimension* 43 (1974).

2. A mode of expression characteristic of lawyers; a jargonistic phrase frequently adopted by lawyers, such as "pursuant to."

legalis moneta Angliae (lə-**gay**-lis mə-**nee**-tə **ang**-glee-ee), *n.* [Latin] Lawful money of England.

legal issue. See ISSUE (1).

legalist, *n.* (1829) Someone who views things from a legal or formalistic standpoint; esp., one who believes in strict adherence to the letter of the law rather than its spirit.

legalistic, *adj.* (17c) Characterized by legalism; unduly concerned with small legal details <a legalistic argument>.

legality. (15c) **1.** The quality, state, or condition of being allowed by law. **2.** Strict adherence to law, prescription, or doctrine. **3.** A formality required by law <they have sold the house but are waiting to complete the legalities>. **4.** The principle that a person may not be prosecuted under a criminal statute that has not been previously published. — Also termed (in sense 4) *principle of legality*.

legalize, *vb.* (18c) **1.** To make lawful; to authorize or justify by legal sanction <the bill to legalize marijuana never made it to the Senate floor>. **2.** To imbue with the spirit of the law; to make legalistic <as religions age, they tend to become legalized>. — Also spelled (BrE) *legalise*. — **legalization,** *n.*

legalized nuisance. See NUISANCE.

legal jargon. See LEGALESE.

legal jeopardy. See JEOPARDY.

legal jointure. See JOINTURE (2).

legal lexicography (lek-si-**kog**-rə-fee), *n.* The art of compiling and writing law glossaries, law dictionaries, or the like by marshaling the potential headwords, researching their history and development, recording and arranging the senses, illustrating usage, and producing this information for use in either a traditional book or an electronic format.

legal liability. See LIABILITY (1).

legal liberty. See LIBERTY (2).

legal life estate. See *life estate* under ESTATE (1).

legal life tenant. See LIFE TENANT.

legal list. A group of investments in which institutions and fiduciaries (such as banks and insurance companies) may legally invest according to state statutes. • States usu. restrict the legal list to low-risk securities meeting certain specifications. — Also termed *approved list*; *legal investments*.

legally, *adv.* (16c) **1.** In a lawful way; in a manner that accords with the law <may legally sell the books>. **2.** According to the law <still legally married>.

legally determined, *adj.* (17c) (Of a claim, issue, etc.) decided by legal process <liability for the accident was legally determined>.

legally incapacitated person. (1919) A person, other than a minor, who is temporarily or permanently impaired by mental illness, mental deficiency, physical illness or disability, or alcohol or drug use to the extent that the person lacks sufficient understanding to make or communicate responsible personal decisions or to enter into contracts. — Abbr. LIP. — Also termed *legally incompetent person; incompetent.*

legally incompetent person. LEGALLY INCAPACITATED PERSON.

legally inconsistent verdict. See VERDICT (1).

legally liable. LIABLE (2).

legally protected interest. See INTEREST (2).

legally sufficient consideration. See *sufficient consideration* under CONSIDERATION (1).

legal malice. See *implied malice* under MALICE.

legal malpractice. See MALPRACTICE.

legal man. See LEGALIS HOMO.

legal maxim. See MAXIM.

legal memory. (1882) The period during which a legal right or custom can be determined or established. • Traditionally, common-law legal memory began in the year 1189, but in 1540 it became a steadily moving period of 60 years. Cf. TIME IMMEMORIAL (2).

> "Because of the importance to feudal landholders of seisin and of real property in general, the writ of right has been called 'the most solemn of all actions.' Nevertheless, it was believed that the time within which such a complainant would be allowed to prove an ancestor to have been seised of the estate in question must be limited. At first this was done by selecting an arbitrary date in the past, before which 'legal memory' would not run. The date initially was Dec. 1, 1135 (the death of Henry I); in 1236 it was changed by statute to Dec. 19, 1154 (the coronation of Henry II); and in 1275 it became Sept. 3, 1189 (the coronation of Richard I). Finally, in 1540, an arbitrary period of sixty years was set as the period of 'legal memory.' The latter change was probably made because it was felt that a 350-year statute of limitations was somewhat awkward." Thomas F. Bergin & Paul G. Haskell, *Preface to Estates in Land and Future Interests* 45 n.65 (2d ed. 1984).

legal mind. (18c) The intellect, legal capacities, and attitudes of a well-trained lawyer — often used as an anthropomorphic conception <although this distinction occurs naturally to the legal mind, it is too technical to be satisfactory>.

legal monopoly. See MONOPOLY (2).

legal moralism. (1963) The theory that a government or legal system may prohibit conduct that is considered immoral.

legal mortgage. See MORTGAGE.

legal name. See NAME.

legal negligence. See *negligence per se* under NEGLIGENCE.

legal newspaper. See NEWSPAPER.

legal notice. 1. See *constructive notice* under NOTICE (3). **2.** See *due notice* under NOTICE (3).

legal obligation. See OBLIGATION.

legal officer. See OFFICER (2).

legal ontology. A branch of philosophical study dealing with the very existence of law and the nature of that existence.

legal opinion. See OPINION (2).

legal order. (16c) **1.** Traditionally, a set of regulations governing a society and those responsible for enforcing them. **2.** Modernly, such regulations and officials plus the processes involved in creating, interpreting, and applying the regulations; LEGAL SYSTEM.

legal owner. See OWNER.

legal pad. A usu. 8½″×14″ notepad containing sheets of yellow writing paper with lines on it for composition or notetaking.

legal parent. See PARENT (1).

legal paternalism. (1913) The theory that a government or legal system is justified in controlling the individual and private affairs of citizens. • This theory is often associated with legal positivists. See PATERNALISM; LEGAL POSITIVISM.

legal person. See *artificial person* under PERSON (3).

legal personality. See PERSONALITY (1).

legal-personal representative. See REPRESENTATIVE (1).

legal philosophy. See *general jurisprudence* (2) under JURISPRUDENCE.

legal pneumoconiosis. See PNEUMOCONIOSIS.

legal portion. See LEGITIME.

legal positivism, *n.* (1939) The theory that legal rules are valid only because they are enacted by an existing political authority or accepted as binding in a given society, not because they are grounded in morality or in natural law. • Legal positivism has been espoused by such scholars as H.L.A. Hart. See POSITIVE LAW. Cf. LOGICAL POSITIVISM. — **legal positivist,** *n.*

> "[I]t will be helpful to offer some comparisons between legal positivism and its counterpart in science. Scientific positivism condemns any inquiry projecting itself beyond observable phenomena; it abjures metaphysics, it renounces in advance any explanation in terms of ultimate causes. Its program of research is to chart the regularities discernible in the phenomena of nature at the point where they become open to human observation, without asking — as it were — how they got there. In the setting of limits to inquiry there is an obvious parallel between scientific and legal positivism. The legal positivist concentrates his attention on law at the point where it emerges from the institutional processes that brought it into being. It is the finally made law itself that furnishes the subject of his inquiries. How it was made and what directions of human effort went into its creation are for him irrelevancies." Lon L. Fuller, *Anatomy of the Law* 177–78 (1968).

▸ **inclusive legal positivism.** The theory that it is possible for a society's rule of recognition to incorporate moral constraints on the content of law. — Also termed *soft legal positivism; incorporationism.*

▸ **soft legal positivism.** See *inclusive legal positivism.*

legal possessor. See POSSESSOR.

legal practice. See PRACTICE OF LAW.

legal practitioner. (1830) **1.** A lawyer. **2.** In the traditional English system, a member of one of the recognized branches of practice.

> "Legal practitioners may be either barristers, special pleaders not at the bar, certified conveyancers, or solicitors. The three latter may recover their fees, but the first may not, their acting being deemed of a voluntary nature, and their fees merely in the light of honorary payments; and it follows from this, that no action lies against them for negligence or unskilfulness." John Indermaur, *Principles*

of the Common Law 169 (Edmund H. Bennett ed., 1st Am. ed. 1878).

legal prejudice. See PREJUDICE (1).

legal presumption. See *presumption of law* under PRESUMPTION.

legal proceeding. See PROCEEDING.

legal process. See PROCESS (2).

legal-protection insurance. See INSURANCE.

legal question. See QUESTION OF LAW.

legal rate. See INTEREST RATE.

legal realism, *n.* (1930) **1.** The theory that law is based not on formal rules or principles but instead on judicial decisions deriving from social interests and public policy as conceived by individual judges. • American legal realism — which flourished in the early 20th century — was espoused by such scholars as John Chipman Gray, Jerome Frank, and Karl Llewellyn. **2.** The use of policy analysis to resolve a legal problem based on what best promotes public welfare. — Often shortened to *realism.* See FUNCTIONALISM. Cf. LEGAL FORMALISM. — **legal realist,** *n.*

▸ **constructive juristic realism.** The view, first announced by Roscoe Pound, that the various realist schools might establish a "constructive program" of understanding law by (1) empirically isolating the subject elements of legal decision-making so as to reach general conclusions about where and how it operates in the legal order; (2) comparing administrative and judicial processes to understand how they interact; (3) recognizing the relative place of individual cases within the general scheme of the legal order; (4) accepting the plurality of influences in all situations and relinquishing the idea of necessary sequence from a single cause to a single effect in a straight line; and (5) recognizing that there is no one approach for arriving at juristic truth. See 1 Roscoe Pound, *Jurisprudence* 284–87 (1959).

▸ **logical-positive realism.** A brand of legal realism that seeks to study decision-making scientifically by objectively investigating lawyers' and judges' modes of thought and problem-solving methods without preconceived postulates. See 1 Roscoe Pound, *Jurisprudence* 269–76 (1959).

▸ **psychological realism.** The theory that law is only what judges and officials actually do, as motivated by their individual inclinations and prejudices, and that the "rational" element in law is an illusion.

> "In its extreme form, psychological realism conceives of each item of the judicial process as shaped wholly and inexorably by the psychological determinants of the behavior of the individual judge. It thinks of the judicial process in terms of 'the judge' and is largely taken up with consideration of the abstract psychology of the abstract judge as it is dogmatically assumed to dictate every item of concrete judicial behavior." 1 Roscoe Pound, *Jurisprudence* 266–67 (1959).

▸ **skeptical realism.** A brand of legal realism that rejects the idea of law in any other sense than that of aggregate items of judicial and official action, in the belief that the existence and consistent application of precedent has little to do with the actual course of judicial or administrative determination. See 1 Roscoe Pound, *Jurisprudence* 295–96 (1959).

legal regime. See REGIME.

legal relation. (17c) The connection in law between one person or entity and another; VINCULUM JURIS.

legal release. See *general release* under RELEASE (8).

legal remedy. See REMEDY.

legal representative. See REPRESENTATIVE (1).

legal rescission. See RESCISSION.

legal research. (18c) **1.** The finding and assembling of authorities that bear on a question of law. **2.** The field of study concerned with the effective marshaling of authorities that bear on a question of law.

legal reserve. See RESERVE (1).

legal residence. See DOMICILE (2).

legal right. See RIGHT.

legal ruling. See RULING (2).

legal science. (18c) **1.** The field of study that, as one of the social sciences, deals with the institutions and principles that particular societies have developed (1) for defining the claims and liabilities of persons against one another in various circumstances, and (2) for peaceably resolving disputes and controversies in accordance with principles accepted as fair and right in the particular community at a given time.

> "Legal science is . . . the systematised body of knowledge concerned with law in the most general sense of that word, the systematic examination and exposition of matters legal, institution, offices, doctrines, principles and rules, concepts and techniques." David M. Walker, *The Scottish Legal System* 19 (6th ed. 1992).

2. A scientific study of legal principles that supposedly leads to predictable results.

> "[S]ince most persons consider that a true science makes predictions possible, we ought to put an end to notions of a 'legal science' or a 'science of law,' unless we so define 'legal' or 'law' as to exclude much of what must be included in the judicial administration of justice, because no formula for predicting most trial-court decisions can be devised which does not contain hopelessly numerous variables that cannot be pinned down or correlated." Jerome Frank, *Courts on Trial: Myth and Reality in American Justice* 190 (1950).

legal secretary. (1897) An employee in a law office whose responsibilities include typing legal documents and correspondence, keeping records and files, and performing other duties supportive of the employer's law practice. • Legal secretaries are usu. more highly skilled, and therefore more highly compensated, than secretaries in general business.

legal seisin. See *seisin in law* under SEISIN.

legal separation. 1. See SEPARATION (1). **2.** See SEPARATION (2). **3.** See *divorce a mensa et thoro* under DIVORCE.

Legal Services Corporation. A nonprofit federal corporation that provides financial aid in civil cases to those who cannot afford legal assistance through grants to legal-aid and other organizations and by contracting with individuals, firms, corporations, and organizations to provide legal services. • The agency was created by the Legal Services Corporation Act of 1974. 42 USCA § 2996. — Abbr. LSC.

legal servitude. See SERVITUDE (2).

legal setoff. See SETOFF.

legal signature. See SIGNATURE.

legal subdivision. See SUBDIVISION.

legal subrogation. See *equitable subrogation* under SUBROGATION.

legal succession. 1. See SUCCESSION (2). **2.** See DESCENT.

legal system. (18c) The laws and the way they work in a particular jurisdiction.

"Modern jurists have paid increasing attention to the general concept and minimum requirements of a 'legal system' as distinct from the individual legal norm. A legal system 'constitutes an individual system determined by "an inner coherence of meaning", . . . an integrated body of rules . . . .' [Alf Ross, *On Law and Justice* 32, 34 (1958).] A multitude of individual legal norms may not amount to a legal system unless they are linked with each other in an integrated structure. . . . The awareness of a legal system as a structure in which the different organs, participants, and substantive prescriptions of the legal order react upon each other, is essentially the corollary to the increasing complexity of modern society, in which millions of individuals depend on the functioning of a complicated network of legal rules of many different types, and the interplay of public authorities of many different levels." W. Friedmann, *Legal Theory* 16 (5th ed. 1967).

"Among the many problems of legal theory of major importance are those which center around the concept of 'legal system.' The term 'legal system' is often used very broadly, as when we speak, for example, of the Anglo-American legal system. The late Hermann Kantorowicz, in his recently published *Definition of Law*, called any body of legal rules which had the same spatial or temporal origin a legal system. But although such broad uses are intelligible and legitimate, it is clear that legal theory requires also a more exact use of the term, a more exact concept, which will focus upon the *systematic* character of legal systems. Of course, it may be possible for a legal system to be 'systematic' in a variety of ways, and it is important to recognize that there is no privileged sense of the term 'system.' But in the last analysis legal theory will concentrate upon those senses which prove the most fruitful for the understanding and description of legal phenomena. Accordingly, we must reject any formulation of the concept of 'legal system' which would force us to distort the very phenomena which we seek to understand." M.P. Golding, "Kelsen and the Concept of 'Legal System,'" in *More Essays in Legal Philosophy* 69, 69 (Robert S. Summers ed., 1971).

legal tender. (18c) The money (bills and coins) approved in a country for the payment of debts, the purchase of goods, and other exchanges for value. See TENDER (4); THEORY OF LAW (2).

legal theory. (1804) **1.** See *general jurisprudence* under JURISPRUDENCE. **2.** The principle under which a litigant proceeds, or on which a litigant bases its claims or defenses in a case.

legal title. See TITLE (2).

legal tutorship. See TUTORSHIP.

legal-unities doctrine. (1998) *Hist.* The common-law rule that a wife had no separate existence from her husband. — Also termed *doctrine of legal unities*; *unities doctrine of marriage*. See MARRIED WOMEN'S PROPERTY ACTS; SPOUSAL-UNITY DOCTRINE.

legal usufruct. See USUFRUCT.

legal value. See BENEFIT (2).

legal vote. See VOTE (1).

legal voter. See VOTER (2).

legal willfulness. See WILLFULNESS.

Legal Writing Institute. A nonprofit corporation founded in 1984 to promote the exchange of information and ideas about the teaching of legal writing. • It is composed mainly of legal-writing teachers at American law schools. Like its sister organization, the Association of Legal Writing Directors, it seeks to improve the teaching of legal writing through research and scholarship, a biennial conference, an annual survey of legal-writing programs, an active listserv, and publications that include a journal called *Legal Writing*. — Abbr. LWI.

legal wrong. See WRONG.

legantine. See LEGATINE.

legare (lə-**gair**-ee), *vb.* [Latin] *Roman law.* To bequeath one or more specified items to some person other than an heir, or to make such a bequest to an heir in advance of the estate's division between the heirs.

legatarius (leg-ə-**tair**-ee-əs), *n.* [Latin] **1.** *Roman law.* The person to whom property is bequeathed; the named recipient of a *legatum*; LEGATEE. **2.** *Hist.* A legate; a messenger or envoy. See LEGATE. Pl. ***legatarii.***

legatary (leg-ə-ter-ee), *n. Archaic.* See LEGATEE.

legate (leg-it), *n.* [fr. Latin *legare* "to send as an envoy"] (12c) **1.** *Roman law.* An official who undertakes a special mission for the emperor, or an official or body such as a municipality. **2.** *Roman law.* A person deputed to assist or act for the emperor, a governor, or a general in a military or administrative activity. **3.** A papal representative who may or may not have both diplomatic and ecclesiastical status; a diplomatic agent of the Vatican. Cf. NUNCIO (1); INTERNUNCIO (3).

▸ ***legate a latere*** (ay **lat**-ə-ree). See *legatus a latere* under LEGATUS.

▸ ***legate missus*** (**mis**-əs). See *legatus missus* under LEGATUS.

▸ ***legate natus*** (**nay**-təs). See *legatus natus* under LEGATUS.

4. A representative of a state or the highest authority in a state; an ambassador; a person commissioned to represent a country in a foreign country. — Also termed *legatus*. — **legatine,** *adj.*

legate (lə-**gayt**), *vb.* (16c) To give or leave as a legacy; to make a testamentary gift of (property); BEQUEATH.

legatee (leg-ə-**tee**). (17c) **1.** Someone who is named in a will to take personal property; one who has received a legacy or bequest. **2.** Loosely, one to whom a devise of real property is given. — Also termed (archaically) *legatary*. Cf. DEVISEE.

▸ **general legatee.** (18c) A person whose bequest is of a specified quantity to be paid out of the estate's personal assets.

▸ **prelegatee.** (1837) *Roman & civil law.* An heir who receives a legacy in addition to the heir's share of the estate. See HEIR (4).

▸ **residuary legatee** (ri-**zij**-oo-er-ee). (18c) A person designated to receive the residue of a decedent's estate. See *residuary estate* under ESTATE (3).

▸ **specific legatee.** (18c) The recipient, under a will, of designated property that is transferred by the owner's death.

▸ **universal legatee.** (17c) A residuary legatee that receives the entire residuary estate.

legatine (**leg**-ə-teen *or* -tɪn), *adj.* (17c) Of, relating to, or involving a legate. — Also termed (erroneously) *legantine.*

legatine constitution. (17c) *Hist. Eccles. law.* A code of ecclesiastical laws issued with the authority of a papal legate, such as those enacted in English national synods in 1220 and 1268.

legatine court. See COURT.

legation (lə-**gay**-shən). (14c) *Int'l law.* **1.** The act or practice of sending a diplomat to another country; a diplomatic mission. **2.** A body of diplomats sent to a foreign country and headed by an envoy extraordinary or a minister plenipotentiary. **3.** The building or office where a legation works; esp., official residence of a diplomatic minister in a foreign country. Cf. EMBASSY. — **legationary,** *adj.*

legative (**leg**-ə-tiv), *adj.* Of, relating to, or involving a legate or deputy.

legator (lə-**gay**-tər *or* leg-ə-**tor**), *n.* (17c) *Rare.* Someone who bequeaths a legacy; TESTATOR. — **legatorial,** *adj.*

legatory (**leg**-ə-tor-ee), *n. Hist.* The one-third portion of a freeman's estate in land that he could dispose of by will. • The other two portions of the estate were subject to claims of the wife and children.

legatum (lə-**gay**-təm), *n.* [Latin fr. *legare* "to bequeath"] **1.** *Roman law.* A special bequest; a gift left by a deceased person to be paid from the estate by the heir. • Unlike an heir, a legatee acquired a benefit and no duties attached. **2.** *Hist.* A legacy or bequest to the church, esp. for tithes not paid while the donor lived. See MORTUARY.

▸ ***legatum debiti*** (lə-**gay**-təm **deb**-ə-tɪ). [Latin "legacy of debt"] *Roman law.* A legacy to the decedent's creditor of what the decedent owes. • This type of legacy was void unless it bettered the creditor's position in some way, as by removing a valid defense that the debtor had to the creditor's claim.

▸ ***legatum dotis*** (lə-**gay**-təm **doh**-tis). [Latin] *Roman law.* A legacy of dowry. • A husband might bequeath a dowry back to his wife, the result being that the husband's heirs were not entitled to retain the usual deductions for children, and the widow could receive her dowry immediately.

▸ ***legatum generis*** (lə-**gay**-təm **jen**-ə-ris). [Latin "legacy of a genus"] (1861) *Roman law.* A legacy of a subject of a general class; a legacy of a kind of thing, rather than a specifically named item. • For example, the testator might make a gift of a horse without specifically naming which one of ten horses in the estate.

> "Legatum generis . . . . Normally the testator set in his testament who had to make the choice from among the things of the same kind (slaves, horses) belonging to the estate: the heir, the legatee or a third person. The jurists did not agree about the solution [when] . . . the testator did not entitle any person to make the selection. Apparently the rules varied according to the form in which such a legacy (*legatum*) was left. The Justinian law favored the choice by the legatee." Adolf Berger, *Encyclopedic Dictionary of Roman Law* 540 (1953).

▸ ***legatum liberationis*** (lə-**gay**-təm lib-ə-ray-shee-**oh**-nis). [Latin "legacy of a discharge"] (17c) *Roman law.* A legacy by which a testator released the indebted legatee from a debt. — Also termed *liberatio legata* (lib-ə-**ray**-shee-oh lə-**gay**-tə).

▸ ***legatum nominis*** (lə-**gay**-təm **nahm**-ə-nis). [Latin "legacy of a name"] (1826) *Roman law.* A legacy by which a testator willed to the legatee a debt owed to the testator from a third party. • The heir was obliged to hand over the relevant documents and cede any rights of action on them.

▸ ***legatum optionis*** (lə-**gay**-təm op-shee-**oh**-nis). [Latin "legacy of an option"] *Roman law.* A legacy of one of several items that the designated beneficiary chooses from the testator's estate. • Originally, if the legatee died after the testator but before making the selection, the legacy failed. Justinian later changed the law to make selection by the legatee's representative under these circumstances valid.

▸ ***legatum peculii*** (lə-**gay**-təm pi-**kyoo**-lee-ɪ). [Latin] *Roman law.* A legacy of a *peculium* to a free person or to a manumitted slave; a legacy of a slave's *peculium* with or without the slave. See PECULIUM.

▸ ***legatum quantitatis*** (lə-**gay**-təm kwon-ti-**tay**-tis). [Latin "a legacy of quantity"] *Roman law.* A general legacy of a certain amount, such as a legacy of two horses.

▸ ***legatum rei alienae*** (lə-**gay**-təm **ree**-ɪ ay-lee-**ee**-nee *or* al-ee-). [Latin "a legacy of something belonging to another"] (17c) *Roman law.* A legacy of an item that belongs to a third party. • The heir was obliged to purchase the item from the third party, if that was possible, and give it to the legatee or otherwise pay its value to the legatee.

▸ ***legatum universitatis*** (lə-**gay**-təm yoo-ni-vər-sə-**tay**-tis). [Latin "a universal legacy"] *Hist.* A legacy of the testator's entire estate.

legatus (lə-**gay**-təs), *n.* A legate. See LEGATE. Pl. ***legati*** (lə-**gay**-tɪ).

▸ ***legatus a latere*** (ay **lat**-ə-ree). [Latin "legate from the (Pope's) side"] (16c) A papal legate (esp. a cardinal) appointed for a special diplomatic mission and not as a permanent representative. • This is a type of *legatus missus.* — Also termed *legate a latere.* Cf. NUNCIO.

▸ ***legatus datus*** (**day**-təs). See *legatus missus.*

▸ ***legatus missus*** (**mis**-əs). [Latin "legate sent"] (17c) A legate sent on a special mission. — Also termed *legate missus; legatus datus* (**day**-təs).

▸ ***legatus natus*** (**nay**-təs). [Latin "legate born"] (16c) A bishop or archbishop who claims to be a legate by virtue of office in an important see, such as Canterbury. — Also termed *legate natus.*

legem amittere (**lee**-jəm ə-**mit**-ə-ree), *vb.* [Latin "to lose one's law"] *Hist.* To lose the privilege of taking an oath, usu. because of a criminal conviction.

legem facere (**lee**-jəm **fay**-sə-ree), *vb.* [Law Latin] *Hist.* To make an oath; to wage law.

legem ferre (**lee**-jəm **fer**-ee), *vb.* [Latin "to carry the proposal"] *Roman law.* **1.** To propose a law to the popular assembly. **2.** To enact a law.

legem habere (**lee**-jəm hə-**beer**-ee), *vb.* [Latin] *Hist.* To be able to testify under oath. • In England, witnesses with criminal convictions were unable to testify until the 19th century, by the Evidence Act of 1843 (6 & 7 Vict., ch. 85).

legem jubere (**lee**-jəm jə-**beer**-ee), *vb.* [Latin] *Roman law.* To pass a proposed law.

legem ponere (**lee**-jəm **poh**-nə-ree), *vb.* [Latin] *Hist.* **1.** To propound a law. **2.** To pay in cash.

legem sciscere (**lee**-jəm **sis**-ə-ree), *vb.* [Latin] *Roman law.* (Of the people) to consent to a proposed law.

legem vadiare (**lee**-jəm vad-ee-**air**-ee), *vb.* [Latin] *Hist.* To wage law; to offer to make a sworn defense to an action for debt, accompanied by 11 neighbors as character witnesses. See COMPURGATION.

legenita. See LAIRWITE.

leger, *n. Archaic.* See LEDGER (2).

legerwite. See LAIRWITE.

leges (**lee**-jeez), *n. pl.* [Latin] **1.** See LEX. **2.** See LEGES PUBLICAE. **3.** JUS NOVUM.

leges Angliae (**lee**-jeez **ang**-glee-ee). [Latin] (17c) *Hist.* The laws of England, as distinguished from the civil law and other legal systems.

leges barbarorum (**lee**-jeez bahr-bə-**ror**-əm). [Latin "laws of the barbarians"] (1833) *Hist.* The customary laws of medieval European law; esp., the customary laws of Germanic tribes during the Middle Ages. • These include the *lex romana Visigothorum*, the *lex Burgundionum*, and the *lex Salica*. — Also termed *folk laws*; *Laws of the Barbarians*; *barbarian laws*. See SALIC LAW.

> "Many of the conquering Germanic tribes sought to state their own tribal customs in writing. Several of these so-called codes or *leges barbarorum* were published from time to time shortly after the fall of the Western Empire in the middle of the fifth century until about the time of Charlemagne, 800. The most famous is a Frankish one, the *Lex Salica*, which probably dates from the second half of the fifth century." W.J.V. Windeyer, *Lectures on Legal History* 1 (2d ed. 1949).

leges centuriatae. See LEX CENTURIATA.

leges curiatae. See LEX CURIATA.

leges de imperio. See LEGES IMPERII.

leges Edwardi Confessoris (**lee**-jeez ed-**wahr**-dɪ kon-fə-**sor**-is), *n.* [Latin "Laws of Edward the Confessor"] *Hist.* A legal treatise written between 1130 and 1135, of dubious authority, compiling English law as it stood at the end of the reign of Henry I. — Also termed *Leges Edward*; (in ancient texts) *Leges Eadward*.

> "[W]e have a book [*leges Edwardi Confessoris*] written in Latin which expressly purports to give us the law of Edward as it was stated to the Conqueror in the fourth year of his reign by juries representing the various parts of England . . . . It is a private work of a bad and untrustworthy kind. It has about it something of the political pamphlet and is adorned with pious legends. The author, perhaps a secular clerk of French parentage, writes in the interest of the churches, and, it is to be feared, tells lies for them." 1 Frederick Pollock & Frederic W. Maitland, *The History of English Law Before the Time of Edward I* 103 (2d ed. 1898).

leges et consuetudines regni (**lee**-jeez et kon-swə-**t[y]oo**-də-neez **reg**-nɪ), *n.* [Latin "laws and customs of the kingdom"] *Hist.* The common law. • This was the accepted term for the common law since at least the late 12th century.

leges Henrici (**lee**-jeez hen-**rɪ**-sɪ), *n.* [Latin] *Hist. English law.* A book anonymously written between 1114 and 1118 containing Anglo-Saxon and Norman laws. • The book lends insight to the period before the full development of Norman law in England. — Also termed *leges Henrici Primi*.

> "Closely connected with the *Quadripartitus* is a far more important book, the so-called *Leges Henrici*. It seems to have been compiled shortly before the year 1118. After a brief preface, it gives us Henry's coronation charter (this accounts for the name which has unfortunately been given in modern days to the whole book), and then the author makes a gallant, if forlorn, attempt to state the law of England. At first sight the outcome seems to be a mere jumble of fragments . . . . But the more closely we examine the book, the more thoroughly convinced we shall be that its author has undertaken a serious task in a serious spirit; he means to state the existing law of the land . . . ." 1 Frederick Pollock & Frederic W. Maitland, *The History of English Law Before the Time of Edward I* 99 (2d ed. 1898).

leges imperfectae (**lee**-jeez im-pər-**fek**-tee). [Latin] *Hist.* Incomplete laws.

leges imperii (**lee**-jeez im-**peer**-ee-ɪ). [Latin] (18c) *Roman law.* Laws conferring lawmaking and other powers on the emperor. — Also termed *leges de imperio*.

leges Juliae (**lee**-jeez **joo**-lee-ee). See *lex Julia judiciorum publicorum* under LEX JULIA.

leges non scriptae (**lee**-jeez non **skrip**-tee). [Latin] (17c) *Hist.* Unwritten or customary laws, including ancient acts of Parliament. Cf. LEGES SCRIPTAE.

leges perfectae (**lee**-jeez pər-**fek**-tee). [Latin] *Hist.* Complete laws.

leges publicae (**lee**-jeez **pəb**-lə-see). [Latin] *Roman law.* Statutes passed by the vote of the Roman people in popular assemblies. • Most *leges publicae* were of temporary political interest but some, such as the *lex Aquilia* or the *lex Falcidia*, had a long life. — Often shortened to *leges*.

leges regiae (**lee**-jeez **ree**-ji-ee). [Latin "laws of the kings"] (17c) *Roman law.* (*often cap.*) Fragments of customary law relating mostly to religious rites and traditionally attributed to Roman kings.

leges sacratae (**lee**-jeez sə-**kray**-tee). [Latin] (17c) *Roman law.* Laws whose violation was punished by devoting the offender to the infernal gods.

leges scriptae (**lee**-jeez **skrip**-tee), *n.* [Latin] (17c) *Hist.* Written laws; esp., statutory laws or acts of Parliament that are reduced to writing before becoming binding. Cf. LEGES NON SCRIPTAE.

leges sub graviori lege (**lee**-jeez səb grav-ee-**or**-ɪ **lee**-jee). [Latin] (18c) Laws under a weightier law.

leges tabellariae (**lee**-jeez tab-ə-**lair**-ee-ee). [Latin] *Roman law.* (17c) Laws that regulated voting by ballot.

leges tributae (**lee**-jeez tri-**byoo**-tee). [Latin] *Roman law.* Laws passed in the comitia tributa. See *comitia tributa* under COMITIA.

legibus solutus (**lee**-jə-bəs sə-**loo**-təs), *adj.* [Latin "released from the laws"] (17c) *Roman law.* (Of the emperor or other designated person) not bound by the law.

legiosus (lee-jee-**oh**-səs), *adj.* [Law Latin] *Hist.* Litigious.

leg irons. Metal chains that are shackled to a prisoner's legs.

legis actio (**lee**-jis **ak**-shee-oh). (17c) *Roman law.* A legal or lawful action; an action at law requiring the use of a fixed form of words. • These actions were abolished by the *leges Juliae*. — Also termed *actio legis*. Pl. ***legis actiones*** (**lee**-jis ak-shee-**oh**-neez).

legis actio sacramento. See SACRAMENTO.

legislate, *vb.* (18c) **1.** To make or enact law <the role of our lawmakers is to legislate, not to adjudicate>. **2.** To bring (something) into or out of existence by making laws; to attempt to control (something) by legislation <virtually every attempt to legislate morality has failed>.

legislation. (17c) **1.** The process of making or enacting a positive law in written form, according to some type of formal procedure, by a branch of government constituted to perform this process. — Also termed *lawmaking*; *statute-making*. **2.** The law so enacted; collectively, the formal utterances of the legislative organs of government. **3.** The whole body of enacted laws.

"'Legislation' has not always meant what we understand by it today, or even what Coke understood by it in the seventeenth century, as that which has received the 'threefold assent' of King, Lords and Commons. It did not reach that state of development until the reign of Edward III. Throughout the greater part of the Middle Ages it was by no means easy to say what a 'statute' was, whence it proceeded and what authority it wielded. Indeed, 'statute' was not a term in very common use, and at least seven other names were applied to different kinds of instruments for 'laying down the law.' Sometimes they seem to have proceeded from the monarch himself and sometimes they were the solemn act of the King on the advice of his Council; they might be imperative or declaratory, general or local, or even in the form of a grant, confirmation or resolution rather than that of a sovereign command. They were, in short, simply decrees of the central government, undoubtedly of great force and authority, but of no uniform pattern and of no clearly defined scope; nor could they be otherwise, for there was at this period no mature conception of a distribution of powers and a monarch had to keep order in his realm as best he could. . . . Judges did not consider themselves 'bound' by statutes as they do today, for they very naturally wished to be assured of the origin and authority of the instrument before they were ready to bow to it; they were the servants and mouthpieces of the common law, not of parchments and edicts; and the scant respect which they sometimes paid to 'statutes' has led to a theory that in the Middle Ages the position was the converse of that which exists today and that all enacted law was subordinate in the last resort to a supreme, overriding common law. This is an exaggeration, but not a very serious one, for some traces of this doctrine linger on even in Coke, who cannot be said to have undervalued the authority of statute. Indeed, even in Blackstone there remain some supposed limitations on the scope of Acts of Parliament, not the least being a Law of God, which is only the old Law of Nature in theological guise; and it was not until the nineteenth century that his last restraint was explicitly renounced by the judges . . . ." Carleton Kemp Allen, *Law and Orders: An Inquiry into the Nature and Scope of Delegated Legislation and Executive Powers in English Law* 23-24 (2d ed. 1956).

"[L]aw as communication, as an institutionalized way to regulate and direct human behavior, is best served by legislation. Some features of legislation should be noted. First, legislation until modern times was relatively rare. Second, although legislation may break with the past, it does so only at the time when it is promulgated. It is a feature of legislation, especially marked perhaps in codification, that once it is in place it tends to remain unaltered, possibly for centuries. The courts may reinterpret it away from its original purpose, but then the resulting law is as difficult to find and know as any judge-made law. Third, very little statute law and very few codes are original in the sense that they are made fresh for the territory in which they operate, without a great dependence on law from elsewhere. . . . Fourth, even 'original' legislation has roots, usually hidden, in the (often distant) past that are not present in the consciousness of the legislator and that affect the attempt to direct behavior. Fifth, apart from topics of consuming passion to them, legislators are generally not interested in law reform, especially in the field of private law. Change by legislation may be a long time coming." Alan Watson, "Law and Communication," in 2 *International Encyclopedia of Communications* 408, 409-10 (Erik Barnouw ed., 1989).

▸ **ancillary legislation.** (1860) Legislation that is auxiliary to principal legislation.

▸ **antideficiency legislation.** (1964) **1.** Legislation enacted to provide revenue to cover a budget deficiency. **2.** Legislation enacted to limit the rights of secured creditors to recover in excess of the security. — Also termed (in sense 2) *antideficiency statute*.

▸ **barebones legislation.** See *skeletal legislation*.

▸ **class legislation.** See *local and special legislation*.

▸ **delegated legislation.** In some legal systems, legislation that consists of detailed agency and departmental regulations implementing general legislative provisions.

▸ **entrenched legislation.** Legislation that may be amended or repealed only by following certain prescribed procedures, such as a referendum or special majority. See REPEALABILITY CANON.

▸ **general legislation.** (18c) Legislation that applies to the community at large.

▸ **judicial legislation.** (18c) The making of new legal rules by judges; JUDGE-MADE LAW (2). See MAKE LAW (2).

"It has been said to be 'merely misleading' to speak of judicial legislation, and it must be admitted that to do so is to use highly metaphorical language. There is no equivalent to the authoritative text of a statute, and, even when they are not bound by a statute or indistinguishable precedent, the judges' power to innovate is limited by what they cannot consider as well as by what they must consider. They cannot conduct those extensive examinations of empirical data and considerations of social policy which precede, or should precede, much legislation." Rupert Cross & J.W. Harris, *Precedent in English Law* 34 (4th ed. 1991).

▸ **local and special legislation.** (1853) Legislation that affects only a specific geographic area or a particular class of persons. • Such legislation is unconstitutional if it arbitrarily or capriciously distinguishes between members of the same class. — Also termed *class legislation*.

▸ **pork-barrel legislation.** (1961) Legislation that favors a particular local district by allocating funds or resources to projects (such as constructing a highway or a post office) of economic value to the district and of political advantage to the district's legislator.

▸ **referential legislation.** Legislation that incorporates one or more other statutes by reference or is incorporated into other statutes by reference. — Also termed *legislation by reference*.

"*Referential Legislation.* Legislation by reference, that is to say, the incorporation of the provisions of one Act in another Act, has been subjected to much criticism. Some of it is, no doubt, deserved, but referential legislation is useful and necessary. The *Interpretation Act*, for example, is incorporated in every other Act, and if this were not so, it would be necessary to repeat most of its provisions in every statute. Indeed, before the *Interpretation Act* appeared, it was customary to repeat the same savings clause over and over again in repealing Acts. The principal purposes of an *Interpretation Act* — purposes universally approved — are to avoid repetition, secure uniformity and save some of the time and expense involved in preparing, printing and passing bills and publishing statutes." Elmer A. Driedger, *The Composition of Legislation* 152 (1957).

▸ **ripper legislation.** Legislation passed in violation (esp. in flagrant violation) of the established principles of separation of powers or federalism.

"The desire of the politician, lobbyist, and boss to give powers to officers or boards which they feel able to control, is at the bottom of that unsettling and dismembering of institutions which is effected by the so-called 'ripper' legislation. The term 'ripper' bill designates a measure which, in disregard of constitutional practice and rational principles of administration, tears to pieces constitutional and legal arrangements and distributes administrative powers among willing tools. 'Ripper' legislation is the fruit of 'ripper' practice in legislative procedure. The total disregard of constitutional and parliamentary rules naturally leads to legislation in which all principles of a sane and settled polity are ignored. As the party machinery grew more and more invincible in Pennsylvania, the constitutional restrictions of 1873 were gradually set at naught. Only upon rare occasion was the political conscience successfully appealed to, as when in 1889 Governor Beaver asked for the enforcement of Article 17 of the Constitution. The Pennsylvania machine has been an adept in 'ripper' legislation; among striking examples of such measures are the following: An act depriving district attorneys of the right to challenge jurors in certain cases, an act taking the power to grant liquor licenses from the judiciary and giving it to a state excise board, an act granting away water power belonging to the state, and a law which gave final power in matters of assessment of property in Philadelphia to the Board of Tax Revision. In 1905, the machine politicians propounded a new constitutional doctrine to the effect that inasmuch as a majority of all registered voters had not voted for a certain constitutional amendment but only a majority of those actually voting upon it, the legislature was not bound to enforce it. As this amendment required the personal registration of voters, its enforcement would have touched a most sensitive point of practical politics in Pennsylvania." Paul S. Reinsch, *American Legislatures and Legislative Methods* 266–67 (1907).

▸ **skeletal legislation.** Basic legislation that broadly states objectives and standards rather than prescribing precise and definite rules, usu. with the expectation that it will be amplified by a body other than the legislature. • Administrative and regulatory agencies are usu. authorized to interpret the legislation and create rules and regulations for its application and enforcement. But the executive branch may also be called on to flesh out the law. — Also termed *skeleton legislation*; *barebones legislation*.

▸ **spent legislation.** Legislation that does nothing more than amend a principal statute. • The amendment is said to be "spent legislation" because its operative language has been fully incorporated into the principal statute.

▸ **subordinate legislation.** (18c) **1.** Legislation that derives from any authority other than the sovereign power in a state and that therefore depends for its continued existence and validity on some superior or supreme authority. **2.** REGULATION (3).

▸ **supreme legislation.** (17c) Legislation that derives directly from the supreme or sovereign power in a state and is therefore incapable of being repealed, annulled, or controlled by any other legislative authority.

4. A proposed law being considered by a legislature <gun-control legislation was debated in the House>. **5.** The field of study concentrating on statutes.

legislative, *adj.* (17c) Of, relating to, or involving lawmaking or to the power to enact laws; concerned with making laws.

legislative act. See ACT (2).

legislative apportionment. See APPORTIONMENT (3).

legislative assembly. 1. LEGISLATURE. **2.** The lower house of a bicameral legislature. **3.** The single legislative body in many of the British colonies. **4.** *Hist.* In France, the legislative body of 1791–1792 or 1849–1851, as opposed to the "constituent assemblies" that preceded them. See NATIONAL ASSEMBLY.

legislative authority. See AUTHORITY (1).

legislative branch. (18c) The division of government responsible for enacting laws; LEGISLATURE. Cf. EXECUTIVE BRANCH; JUDICIAL BRANCH.

legislative committee. See COMMITTEE (1).

legislative council. (17c) **1.** A state agency that studies legislative problems and plans legislative strategy between regular legislative sessions. **2.** In some English-speaking jurisdictions, the upper house of a legislature (corresponding to an American Senate). **3.** In some English-speaking jurisdictions, the lower house of a legislature (corresponding to an American House of Representatives).

legislative counsel. (1839) A person or group charged with helping legislators fulfill their legislative duties, such as by performing research, drafting bills, and the like.

legislative court. See COURT.

legislative day. See DAY.

legislative district. See DISTRICT.

legislative districting. (1962) The process of dividing a state into territorial districts to be represented in the state or federal legislature. See APPORTIONMENT (3); REAPPORTIONMENT; GERRYMANDERING. Cf. MALAPPORTIONMENT.

legislative divorce. See DIVORCE.

legislative-equivalency doctrine. (2003) The rule that a law should be amended or repealed only by the same procedures that were used to enact it.

legislative exclusion. See STATUTORY EXCLUSION.

legislative fact. See FACT.

legislative free-riding. A legislature's passive reliance on the judiciary to ameliorate poor legal drafting by "interpreting" statutory provisions by means other than a fair reading of the words in context, as by creating equitable exceptions to plainly worded mandates or by filling *casus omissi* with judicially fabricated gap-fillers. — Also termed *free-riding*.

legislative function. (1808) **1.** The duty to determine legislative policy. **2.** The duty to form and determine future rights and duties. See LEGISLATIVE POWER.

legislative history. (1844) The proceedings leading to the enactment of a statute, including hearings, committee reports, and floor debates. • Legislative history is sometimes recorded so that it can later be used to aid in or influence interpretations of the statute. Cf. STATUTORY HISTORY.

▸ **subsequent legislative history.** Legislative history that postdates the statute in question; esp., self-created legislative history by legislators who seek to achieve a result they were unable to obtain during the legislative process. *See Gott v. Walters*, 756 F.2d 902 (D.C. Cir. 1985).

legislative immunity. See IMMUNITY (1).

legislative intent. (1812) The collective design or plan that the enacting legislature is posited to have had for the application of a statute to specific situations that might arise. — Also termed *intention of the legislature*; *intent of the legislature*; *congressional intent*; *parliamentary intent*.

"'Intention of the Legislature' is a common but very slippery phrase, which, popularly understood, may signify anything from intention embodied in positive enactment to speculative opinion as to what the Legislature probably would have meant, although there has been an omission to enact it. In a Court of Law or Equity, what the Legislature intended to be done or not to be done can only be legitimately ascertained from that which it has chosen to enact, either in express words or by reasonable and necessary implication." *Saloman v. Saloman & Co.*, [1897] A.C. 22, 38.

▸ **dormant legislative intent.** The intent that the legislature would have had if a given ambiguity, inconsistency, or omission had been called to the legislators' minds. — Sometimes shortened to *dormant intent.* — Also termed *latent intent; latent intention.*

legislative-intent theory. A traditional doctrine of interpretation declaring that the judicial interpreter's goal is to discover the legislature's presumed intent. • A major critic of this theory was John Chipman Gray, who wrote: "[I]n almost all [cases of statutory interpretation], it is probable, and . . . in most of them it is perfectly evident, that the makers of the statutes had no real intention, one way or another, on the point in question; that if they had, they would have made their meaning clear; and that when the judges are professing to declare what the Legislature meant, they are, in truth, themselves legislating to fill up *casus omissi.*" John Chipman Gray, *The Nature and Sources of the Law* § 370, at 165 (1909).

legislative investigation. A formal inquiry conducted by a legislative body incident to its legislative authority. • A legislature has many of the same powers as a court to support a legislative inquiry, including the power to subpoena and cross-examine a witness and to hold a witness in contempt.

legislative jurisdiction. See JURISDICTION.

legislative law. See STATUTORY LAW.

legislative officer. See OFFICER (1).

legislative power. (17c) *Constitutional law.* The power to make laws and to alter them; a legislative body's exclusive authority to make, amend, and repeal laws. • Under federal law, this power is vested in Congress, consisting of the House of Representatives and the Senate. A legislative body may delegate a portion of its lawmaking authority to agencies within the executive branch for purposes of rulemaking and regulation. But a legislative body may not delegate its authority to the judicial branch, and the judicial branch may not encroach on legislative duties.

legislative privilege. See PRIVILEGE (1).

Legislative Reference Service. *Hist.* See CONGRESSIONAL RESEARCH SERVICE.

legislative rule. (17c) An administrative rule created by an agency's exercise of delegated quasi-legislative authority. • A legislative rule has the force of law. — Also termed *substantive rule.* Cf. INTERPRETATIVE RULE.

legislative scheme. See SCHEME (1).

legislative supremacy. The doctrine that in their role as interpreters of statutes, courts are subordinate to legislatures except when exercising the power of declaring a statute unconstitutional. Cf. JUDICIAL SUPREMACY.

legislative veto. See VETO.

legislator, *n.* (17c) Someone who makes laws within a given jurisdiction; a member of a legislative body. — Also termed *lawmaker.* — **legislatorial** (lej-is-lə-**tor**-ee-əl), *adj.*

legislature. (17c) The branch of government responsible for making or changing statutory laws. • The federal government and most states have bicameral legislatures, usu. consisting of a house of representatives and a senate. — Also termed *legislative assembly.* Cf. EXECUTIVE (1); JUDICIARY (1).

legisperitus (lee-jis-**per**-ə-təs), *n.* [Law Latin] *Hist.* A lawyer or advocate; one skilled in the law. Cf. JURISPERITUS.

legisprudence (lee-jis-**proo**-dənts). (1950) The systematic analysis of statutes within the framework of jurisprudential philosophies about the role and nature of law.

legist (**lee**-jist). (15c) **1.** One learned or skilled in the law; an expert lawyer. **2.** JURIST. — Formerly also termed *legister.*

legitim. *Scots law.* The right of any surviving lawful issue to share in the movable estate of the father. • The legitim comprised third of the estate if there was a surviving spouse, or one-half otherwise. — Also termed *bairn's part.* Cf. LEGITIME.

legitimacy. (17c) **1.** Lawfulness. **2.** The status of a person who is born within a lawful marriage or who acquires that status by later action of the parents; legal kinship between a child and its parent or parents. Cf. ILLEGITIMACY.

"In this age of equality, the question might fairly be asked whether a discussion of child support should even be concerned about 'legitimacy' and 'illegitimacy.' The answer is 'yes,' for several reasons. Most rules regarding child support were fashioned at a time when legitimacy was the precondition to full support entitlement and illegitimate paternity had only limited legal consequences. True, by U.S. Supreme Court doctrine, distinctions between 'legitimate' and 'illegitimate' children should no longer be maintainable, but many state statutes have not yet been adapted to this view. Distinctions on the basis of legitimacy, however unconstitutional, continue to be made." Harry D. Krause, *Child Support in America* 103 (1981).

legitimacy presumption. See PRESUMPTION OF PATERNITY.

legitima gubernatio (lə-**jit**-ə-mə g[y]oo-bər-**nay**-shee-oh). [Latin "lawful government"] See RECTA GUBERNATIO.

legitima portio. See LEGITIME; PORTIO LEGITIMA.

legitima potestas (lə-**jit**-ə-mə pə-**tes**-təs *or* -tas). [Latin] *Scots law.* The lawful power, esp. to dispose of one's property. Cf. LIEGE POUSTIE.

legitima remedia (lə-**jit**-ə-mə ri-**mee**-dee-ə). [Law Latin] *Scots law.* Lawful remedies.

legitima successio (lə-**jit**-ə-mə sək-**ses**-ee-oh). [Latin] *Scots law.* Legal succession.

legitimate (lə-**jit**-ə-mət), *adj.* (15c) **1.** Complying with the law; lawful <a legitimate business>. **2.** Genuine; valid <a legitimate complaint>. **3.** Born of legally married parents <a legitimate child>.

legitimate child. See CHILD.

legitimate expectation. See EXPECTATION.

legitimate heir. See HEIR (1).

legitimate portion. See LEGITIME.

legitimation, *n.* (16c) **1.** The act of making something lawful; authorization. **2.** The act or process of authoritatively declaring a person legitimate, esp. a child whose parentage has been unclear. Cf. ADOPTION (1). **3.** *Hist.*

Proof of a person's identity and of legal permission to reside in a certain place or engage in a certain occupation. — **legitimate** (lə-**jit**-ə-mayt), *vb.*

▸ **legitimation *per subsequens matrimonium*** (pər səb-**see**-kwenz ma-trə-**moh**-nee-əm), *n.* [Latin] The legitimation of a child born outside wedlock by the later marriage of the parents.

> "Legitimation 'per subsequens matrimonium.' From the time of Constantine, the rule of Roman law was that children born before marriage were made legitimate by the subsequent marriage of their parents. This rule became part of canon law about the twelfth century, and was later adopted by practically all the legal systems on the Continent, and in South America. It has received statutory recognition in most of the North American States. Until the Legitimacy Act of 1926, however, it formed no part of the law of England or of Wales or of Ireland, though it obtained in Scotland, the Isle of Man and the Channel Islands." G.C. Cheshire, *Private International Law* 427–28 (6th ed. 1961).

legitime (**lej**-ə-tim), *n.* (18c) *Civil law.* The part of a testator's property that his or her children (and occasionally other heirs) are legally entitled to regardless of the will's terms; esp., the part of a decedent's estate reserved, by law, individually to a forced heir. See La. Civ. Code arts. 1494, 1495. • The legitime cannot be denied the children without legal cause. In Roman law, the amount of the legitime was one-fourth of the claimant's share on intestacy. — Also spelled (esp. in Scotland) *legitim.* — Also termed *legal portion*; *legitimate portion*; *legitima portio*; *forced portion.* See *forced heir* under HEIR; (for Scots law) LEGITIM; REDUCTION. Cf. PORTIO LEGITIMA.

legitimi heredes (lə-**jit**-ə-mɪ hə-**ree**-deez), *n. pl.* [Latin] *Roman law.* Heirs on intestacy, as determined by the Twelve Tables; specif., the Praetor's second rank of claimants to an intestate's estate, comprising the agnates of the Twelve Tables order and some others, such as the decedent's patron. See TWELVE TABLES.

legitimo modo (lə-**jit**-ə-mə **moh**-doh). [Latin] (17c) *Scots law.* In legal form.

legitimum tempus restitutionis (lə-**jit**-ə-məm **tem**-pəs res-ti-t[y]oo-shee-**oh**-nis). [Law Latin "the legal period for restitution"] *Hist.* The time during which a claim can be made for restitution.

legitimus (lə-**jit**-ə-məs), *adj.* [Latin] *Roman law.* (Of a person) legitimate; lawful.

legit vel non (**lee**-jit vel **non**). [Latin] *Eccles. law.* Does he read or not. • This was the formal question propounded by a secular court to an ordinary (an ecclesiastical official) when an accused person claimed exemption from the court's jurisdiction by benefit of clergy. If the ordinary found that the accused was entitled to exemption, he responded "*legit ut clericus,*" or, "he reads like a clerk." See BENEFIT OF CLERGY.

lego (**lee**-goh), *vb.* [Latin] *Roman law.* I bequeath. • This was a common term for designating a legacy in a will.

legocentrism. See LEGAL CENTRALISM.

lego-literary (lee-goh-**lit**-ər-er-ee), *adj.* (1826) *Rare.* Of, relating to, or involving law and literature. See LAW AND LITERATURE.

legruita. See LAIRWITE.

leguleian (leg-yə-**lee**-ən), *n.* (17c) *Rare.* A pettifogging lawyer. — Also termed *leguleius* (leg-yoo-**lee**-əs). — **leguleian,** *adj.*

legum baccalaurens. See LL.B.

LEIN. *abbr.* LAW ENFORCEMENT INFORMATION NETWORK.

leipa (**lɪ**-pə), *n.* [Law Latin] *Hist.* A runaway or fugitive.

leirwita. See LAIRWITE.

Leistungsschutzrecht. [German] NEIGHBORING RIGHT.

lemon law. (18c) **1.** A statute designed to protect a consumer who buys a substandard automobile, usu. by requiring the manufacturer or dealer either to replace the vehicle or to refund the full purchase price. • Almost all states have lemon laws in effect. — Also termed *lemon protection.* **2.** By extension, a statute designed to protect a consumer who buys any product of inferior quality. — Also termed (in sense 2) *quality-of-products legislation.*

***Lemon* test.** (1971) A legal standard for judging the state's violation of the Establishment Clause of the First Amendment. • The *Lemon* test has most often been used in school-related cases. It employs a three-pronged test to determine the state's action: (1) Does the state's action have a religious purpose? (2) Does the state's action have the primary effect of either promoting or inhibiting religion? (3) Does the state's action create an "excessive entanglement" between church and state? *Lemon v. Kurtzman*, 403 U.S. 602, 91 S.Ct. 2105 (1971). In recent years, the Court has not overturned *Lemon* but has declined to apply it when deciding Establishment Clause cases.

***le mort saisit le vif* doctrine** (lə **mor** se-**zee** lə **veef**). [French "the dead seizes the living"] The principle requiring that there be no gap in the possession of a freehold estate in land, so that legal title vests immediately in the heirs upon the death of the person through whom they claim title. • The doctrine does not exclude unknown heirs or heirs absent at the date of death.

lend, *vb.* (bef. 12c) **1.** To allow the temporary use of (something), sometimes in exchange for compensation, on condition that the thing or its equivalent be returned. **2.** To provide (money) temporarily on condition of repayment, usu. with interest.

lender. (bef. 12c) A person or entity from which something (esp. money) is borrowed.

lending right. (1960) *Copyright.* The power of a copyright owner to control the use of copies of the work beyond the first sale, when that use involves offering the copy to the public for temporary use with no consideration required. • Lending rights are recognized among members of the European Union.

lend-lease. (1941) A mutually beneficial exchange made between friendly parties; esp., an arrangement made in 1941, under the Lend-Lease Act, whereby U.S. destroyers were lent to Great Britain in exchange for Britain's leasing of land to the United States for military bases. — Also termed *lease-lend.*

leniency. (18c) **1.** The quality or fact of being more tolerant or merciful than expected. **2.** The judicial act of reducing a penalty or excusing minor wrongful conduct.

lenient, *adj.* (17c) Tolerant; mild; merciful <lenient sentence>.

lenient test. (1996) The principle that the attorney–client privilege applicable to a document or other communication will be waived only by a knowing or intentional disclosure, and will not usu. be waived by an inadvertent disclosure. Cf. STRICT TEST; HYDRAFLOW TEST.

lenity (**len**-ə-tee). (16c) The quality, state, or condition of being lenient; mercy or clemency. See RULE OF LENITY.

lenity rule. See RULE OF LENITY.

lenocinium (lee-noh-**sin**-ee-əm), *n.* [Latin "pandering, brothel-keeping"] **1.** *Roman law.* The crime of prostituting for gain. **2.** *Roman & Scots law.* A husband's scheming in his wife's adultery, as by encouraging another man to seduce her. • The wife could assert this claim as a defense in a divorce action brought by the husband.

leodes (lee-**oh**-deez), *n.* [Law Latin] *Hist.* **1.** A vassal. **2.** Service to be provided to another. **3.** Compensation to be paid by one who killed or seriously injured a vassal, divided among the sovereign, the vassal's lord, and the vassal's next of kin; WERGILD.

leonina societas (lee-ə-**nɪ**-nə sə-**sɪ**-ə-tas). See SOCIETAS LEONINA.

leonine contract (**lee**-ə-nɪn). See *adhesion contract* under CONTRACT.

***Leon* rule.** (1984) The doctrine that evidence from a search is not to be suppressed if an officer, acting in good faith, has obtained a search warrant from a judge or magistrate judge and has acted within its scope. *See U.S. v. Leon*, 468 U.S. 897 (1984).

leproso amovendo (lep-**roh**-soh ay-moh-**ven**-doh), *n.* [Latin "for removing a leper"] (16c) *Hist.* A writ to remove a leper who participated in public gatherings, such as church or meetings.

le roy (lər **wah** *or* lə **roy**), *n.* [Law French] The king. — Also spelled *le roi*.

le roy le veut (lər **wah** lə **voo**). [Law French] *Hist.* The king (or the queen) wills it. • This is the form of the king's or queen's approval to a public bill passed by Parliament. For a queen, the sentence is *la reine le veut.*

> "If the king consents to a public bill, the clerk usually declares, '*le roy le veut*, the king wills it so to be:' if to a private bill, '*soit fait comme il est desiré*, be it as it is desired.' If the king refuses his assent, it is in the gentle language of '*le roy s'avisera*, the king will advise upon it.'" 1 William Blackstone, *Commentaries on the Laws of England* 184 (1765).

le roy remercie ses loyal sujets, accepte leur benevolence, et ainsi le veut (lər **wah** ruu-mair-**see** say lwɪ-**ahl** soo-**zhay**, ak-**sept** luu[r] bay-nay-voh-**lawns**, ay an-**see** lə **vuu**). [Law French] *Hist.* The king thanks his loyal subjects, accepts their benevolence, and therefore wills it to be so. • This is a form of the royal assent to a bill of supply, authorizing money for public purposes. For a queen, the sentence was *la reine remercie ses loyal sujets . . . .*

le roy s'avisera (lər **wah** sa-veez-**rah**). [Law French] The king will advise on it. • This is a form of the refusal of royal assent to a public bill in Parliament (not exercised since 1713). It corresponds to the judicial phrase *curia advisari vult*. For a queen, the sentence was *la reine s'avisera.* See CURIA ADVISARI VULT.

lese majesty (leez **maj**-əs-tee). [Law French "injured majesty"] (16c) **1.** A crime against the state, esp. against the ruler. — Also termed *laesa majestas*; *crimen laesae majestatis*; *crimen majestatis.* See *crimen majestatis* under CRIMEN; TREASON. **2.** An attack on a custom or traditional belief. — Also spelled *lèse-majesté*; *lèse majesty*; *leze majesty.*

lesio enormis. See LAESIO ENORMIS.

lesion (**lee**-zhən). (15c) **1.** An injury or wound; esp., an area of wounded tissue. **2.** *Civil law.* Loss from another's failure to perform a contract; the injury suffered by one who did not receive the equivalent value of what was bargained for. La. Civ. Code art. 2589. — Also spelled (in sense 2) *lésion.* **3.** See LAESIO ENORMIS.

> "The concept of *lésion*, unknown as such to the common law, may be defined as a detriment to one of the parties to a contract which results from an imbalance or disparity between the performance promised on the two sides. Down through the ages, civilians have differed over whether it gave the injured party a right of avoidance or rescission. Classical Roman law, designed for a society whose members were strong enough to protect their own interests, denied the right, but by the time of the French Revolution the right had come to be recognized, particularly by the canonists and Pothier. But the Revolution, both because of its emphasis on individual will and because of economic reasons, was hostile to the concept of *lésion* and the Civil Code provided that it did not affect the validity of a contract except in certain prescribed instances, most notably the case of the vendor of real property. The number of exceptions was enlarged both by subsequent legislation and, at least indirectly, by judicial decision, and this raised a question of the reversal of the general principle that rejected the concept." Allan Farnsworth, "The Development of the Civil Law of Obligations in New States: Senegal, Madagascar, and Ethiopia," in *Essays on the Civil Law of Obligations* 64 (Joseph Dainow ed., 1969).

lesion beyond moiety. See LAESIO ENORMIS.

less-developed country. See DEVELOPING COUNTRY.

lessee (le-**see**). (15c) Someone who has a possessory interest in real or personal property under a lease; TENANT.

- ▸ **lessee in the ordinary course of business.** (1996) A person who, in good faith and without knowledge that the lease is in violation of a third party's ownership rights, security interest, or leasehold interest, leases in the ordinary course from a person in the business of selling or leasing goods of that kind. UCC § 2A-103(1)(o). • The UCC specifically excludes pawnbrokers from the definition.
- ▸ **merchant lessee.** (1814) A lessee who is a merchant of goods similar to those being leased. UCC § 2A-103(1)(t).

lessee's interest. (1812) The appraised value of leased property from the lessee's perspective for purposes of assignment or sale. • The value is usu. the property's market value minus the lessor's interest. Cf. LESSOR'S INTEREST.

lesser-evils defense. See DEFENSE (1).

lesser included offense. See OFFENSE (2).

lesser-interest clause. (1948) *Oil & gas.* A provision in an oil-and-gas lease allowing the lessee to reduce payments proportionately if the lessor turns out to own less than 100% of the mineral interest. — Also termed *proportionate-reduction clause.*

lesser offense. See *lesser included offense* under OFFENSE (2).

less-lethal, *n. Jargon.* A weapon that inflicts pain or discomfort short of death, as by firing bean bags or rubber bullets, or by discharging electromagnetic, acoustic, or other energy so that the target may be incapacitated but usu. not seriously injured. — Also termed *less-lethal force*; *nonlethal weapon*; *nondeadly weapon.*

less-lethal force. See LESS-LETHAL.

lessor (**les**-or *or* le-**sor**). (14c) Someone who conveys real or personal property by lease; esp., LANDLORD.

lessor of the plaintiff. (17c) *Hist.* The true party in interest prosecuting an action for ejectment. • At common law, an ejectment action theoretically was only for the recovery of the unexpired term of the lease. Conventions of pleadings at the time required the true plaintiff to grant a fictitious lease, thereby becoming a lessor, to an equally fictitious plaintiff in whose name the action would be prosecuted.

lessor's interest. (1821) The present value of the future income under a lease, plus the present value of the property after the lease expires. Cf. LESSEE'S INTEREST.

let, *n.* (12c) An impediment or obstruction <free to act without let or hindrance>.

let, *vb.* (bef. 12c) **1.** To allow or permit <the court, refusing to issue an injunction, let the nuisance continue>. **2.** To offer (property) for lease; to rent out <the hospital let office space to several doctors>. **3.** To award (a contract), esp. after bids have been submitted <the federal agency let the project to the lowest bidder>.

lethal, *adj.* (16c) **1.** Deadly; fatal <the lethal blow>. **2.** Capable of causing death <a lethal drug>.

lethal injection. (1898) An injection of a substance or substances into a prisoner to carry out a sentence of capital punishment. • Now the most widely used method of execution in the United States, lethal injection was first adopted by Oklahoma in 1977 because it was considered cheaper and more humane than either electrocution or lethal gas. A typical lethal injection consists of three chemicals that are administered into one or more parts of the inmate's body (usu. the arms) in the following order: (1) sodium thiopental, a barbiturate anesthetic, which induces deep unconsciousness; (2) pancuronium bromide, which paralyzes all voluntary muscles and causes suffocation; and (3) potassium chloride, which induces irreversible cardiac arrest. If all goes as planned, the entire execution takes about five minutes, death usually occurring less than two minutes after the final administration.

lethal weapon. See *deadly weapon* under WEAPON.

letter. (13c) **1.** A written communication that is usu. enclosed in an envelope, sealed, stamped, and delivered (esp., an official written communication) <an opinion letter>. **2.** (*usu. pl.*) A written instrument containing or affirming a grant of some power or right <letters testamentary>. **3.** Strict or literal meaning <the letter of the law>. • This sense is based on the sense of a letter of the alphabet. Cf. SPIRIT.

letter bomb. See BOMB.

letter-book. (18c) A merchant's book for holding correspondence.

letter contract. See CONTRACT.

letter dimissory. LETTER MISSIVE.

letter immunity. See IMMUNITY (3).

letter missive. (15c) **1.** *Hist.* A letter from the king (or queen) to the dean and chapter of a cathedral, containing the name of the person whom the king wants elected as bishop. **2.** *Hist.* After a lawsuit is filed against a peer, peeress, or lord of Parliament, a request sent to the defendant to appear and answer the suit. **3.** *Civil law.* The appellate record sent by a lower court to a superior court. — Often shortened to *missive.* — Also termed *letter dimissory.*

letter of advice. *Int'l commercial law.* A notice that a draft has been sent by the drawer to the drawee. UCC § 3-701.

letter of advocation. *Hist. Scots law.* A warrant, issued by the Court of Session, discharging an inferior court from further proceedings in a matter and transferring the action to the issuing superior court. • In a criminal case, the High Court of Justiciary could issue a letter to call up a case for review from an inferior court. The letter of advocation was abolished in 1868 and replaced by appeal.

letter of allotment. (1844) A document detailing and confirming how many shares have been allotted to an applicant for shares in a new issue or a rights offering. — Also termed *allotment letter.* See *rights offering* under OFFERING.

letter of attorney. 1. See POWER OF ATTORNEY (1). **2.** See ATTORNEY (1).

letter of attornment. (1978) A grantor's letter to a tenant, stating that the leased property has been sold and directing the tenant to pay rent to the new owner. See ATTORNMENT (1).

letter of censure. See CENSURE, *n.*

letter of comfort. See COMFORT LETTER.

letter of comment. See DEFICIENCY LETTER.

letter of commitment. See COMMITMENT LETTER (1).

letter of credence. (16c) *Int'l law.* A document that accredits a diplomat to the government of the country to which he or she is sent. — Abbr. LC; L/C. — Also termed *letters of credence.*

letter of credit. (17c) *Commercial law.* An instrument under which the issuer (usu. a bank), at a customer's request, agrees to honor a draft or other demand for payment made by a third party (the *beneficiary*), as long as the draft or demand complies with specified conditions, and regardless of whether any underlying agreement between the customer and the beneficiary is satisfied. • Letters of credit are governed by Article 5 of the UCC. — Abbr. LC; L/C. — Often shortened to *credit.* — Also termed *circular letter of credit; circular note; bill of credit.*

> "There is some confusion over the exact nature of credits. They resemble a number of commercial devices that are not credits. Often, there is confusion between letters of credit and guaranties, and occasionally between letters of credit and lines of credit. In the credit transaction itself, it is important to distinguish the credit from other contracts and from the acceptance. Generally, the broad credit transaction consists of three separate relationships. These include those that are (1) between the issuer and the beneficiary; (2) between the beneficiary and the account party; and (3) between the account party and the issuer. The first is the letter-of-credit engagement. The second is usually called the underlying contract, and the third is called the application agreement." John F. Dolan, *The Law of Letters of Credit* ¶ 2.01, at 2-2 (1984).

> "A seller hesitates to give up possession of its goods before it is paid. But a buyer wishes to have control of the goods before parting with its money. To relieve this simple tension, merchants developed the device known as the 'letter of credit' or simply the 'credit' or the 'letter.' Today, letters of credit come in two broad varieties. The 'commercial' letter dates back at least 700 years. It is a mode of payment in the purchase of goods, mostly in international

sales. The 'standby' letter of credit is a much more recent mutant. It 'backs up' obligations in a myriad of settings. In the most common standby a bank promises to pay a creditor upon documentary certification of the applicant's default." 3 James J. White & Robert S. Summers, *Uniform Commercial Code* § 26-1, at 105 (4th ed. 1995).

▸ **clean letter of credit.** (1921) A letter of credit that is payable on its presentation. • No document needs to be presented along with it. — Also termed *suicide letter of credit.* Cf. *documentary letter of credit.*

▸ **commercial letter of credit.** (1908) A letter of credit used as a method of payment in a sale of goods (esp. in an international transaction), with the buyer being the issuer's customer and the seller being the beneficiary, so that the seller can obtain payment directly from the issuer instead of from the buyer.

▸ **confirmed letter of credit.** (1918) A letter of credit that directly obligates a financing agency (such as a bank) doing business in the seller's financial market to a contract of sale. UCC § 2-325(3).

▸ **documentary letter of credit.** (1921) A letter of credit that is payable when presented with another document, such as a certificate of title or invoice. — Abbr. DL/C. Cf. *clean letter of credit.*

▸ **export letter of credit.** (1921) A commercial letter of credit issued by a foreign bank, at a foreign buyer's request, in favor of a domestic exporter.

▸ **general letter of credit.** (1836) A letter of credit addressed to any and all persons without naming anyone in particular. Cf. *special letter of credit.*

▸ **guaranty letter of credit.** See *standby letter of credit.*

▸ **import letter of credit.** (1921) A commercial letter of credit issued by a domestic bank, at an importer's request, in favor of a foreign seller.

▸ **irrevocable letter of credit** (i-rev-ə-kə-bəl). (1918) **1.** A letter of credit that the issuing bank guarantees will not be withdrawn or canceled before the expiration date. **2.** A letter of credit that cannot be modified or revoked without the customer's consent. **3.** A letter of credit that cannot be modified or canceled without the consent of all parties. — Abbr. ILC.

▸ **negotiation letter of credit.** (1984) A letter of credit in which the issuer's engagement runs to drawers and indorsers under a standard negotiation clause.

"Letter-of-credit law has long distinguished the straight credit from the negotiation credit. The engagement of the former runs to the beneficiary; the engagement of the latter runs to 'drawers, endorsers, and bona fide holders.' This quoted phrase is the traditional negotiation clause. The significance of it is that it obviously extends the credit engagement to parties other than the person with whom the account party is doing business." John F. Dolan, *The Law of Letters of Credit* ¶ 8.02[6], at 8-11 (1984).

▸ **open letter of credit.** (1843) A letter of credit that can be paid on a simple draft without the need for documentary title.

▸ **revocable letter of credit** (rev-ə-kə-bəl). (1921) A letter of credit in which the issuing bank reserves the right to cancel and withdraw from the transaction upon appropriate notice. • The letter cannot be revoked if the credit has already been paid by a third party.

▸ **revolving letter of credit.** (1967) A letter of credit that self-renews by providing for a continuing line of credit that the beneficiary periodically draws on and the bank customer periodically repays. • A revolving letter of credit is used when there will be multiple drafts under a single transaction or multiple transactions under a single credit. — Abbr. RL/C.

▸ **special letter of credit.** (1843) A letter of credit addressed to a particular individual, firm, or corporation. Cf. *general letter of credit.*

▸ **standby letter of credit.** (1974) A letter of credit used to guarantee either a monetary or a nonmonetary obligation (such as the performance of construction work), whereby the issuing bank agrees to pay the beneficiary if the bank customer defaults on its obligation. — Abbr. SLC; SL/C. — Also termed *guaranty letter of credit.*

▸ **straight letter of credit.** (1937) A letter of credit requiring that drafts drawn under it be presented to a specified party.

▸ **suicide letter of credit.** See *clean letter of credit.*

▸ **time letter of credit.** (1949) A letter of credit that is duly honored by the issuer accepting drafts drawn under it. — Also termed *acceptance credit; usance credit.*

▸ **transferable letter of credit.** (1965) A letter of credit that authorizes the beneficiary to assign the right to draw under it.

▸ **traveler's letter of credit.** (1922) **1.** A letter of credit addressed to a correspondent bank, from which one can draw credit by identifying oneself as the person in whose favor the credit is drawn. **2.** A letter of credit used by a person traveling abroad, by which the issuing bank authorizes payment of funds to the holder in the local currency by a local bank. • The holder signs a check on the issuing bank, and the local bank forwards it to the issuing bank for its credit.

letter of exchange. See DRAFT (1).

letter of hypothecation. (1858) A written agreement for a loan to pay for imported goods that are also pledged as collateral and that the lender is authorized to sell if the debtor refuses to accept them or fails to pay for them.

letter of intent. (1942) A written statement detailing the preliminary understanding of parties who plan to enter into a contract or some other agreement; a noncommittal writing preliminary to a contract. • A letter of intent is not meant to be binding and does not hinder the parties from bargaining with a third party. Business people typically mean not to be bound by a letter of intent, and courts ordinarily do not enforce one; but courts occasionally find that a commitment has been made. — Abbr. LOI. — Also termed *memorandum of intent; memorandum of understanding; term sheet; commitment letter.* Cf. *precontract* under CONTRACT.

"[T]he parties may have agreed to postpone the creation of the contract to some future date, which may never arise. The 'subject to contract' cases are one example of this. Another is the 'letter of intent.' This is a very commonly employed commercial device by which one party indicates to another that he is very likely to place a contract with him. A typical situation would involve a contractor who is proposing to tender for a large building contract and who would need to subcontract, for example, the plumbing and electrical work. He would need to obtain estimates from the subcontractors on which his own tender would, in part, be based but he would not wish to enter into a firm contract with them unless and until his tender was successful. Often he would send a 'letter of intent' to his chosen subcontractors to tell them of their selection. More often than not such letters are so worded as not to create any obligation on either side but in some cases they may contain an invitation to commence preliminary work which at least creates an obligation to pay for that work." M.P. Furmston, *Cheshire, Fifoot and Furmston's Law of Contract* 58 (16th ed., 2012).

letter of license. (17c) *English law.* An agreement signed by all the creditors of a financially troubled business that does the following: (1) grants the debtor more time to pay debts, (2) permits the debtor to continue business in the hope of overcoming its financial distress, and (3) protects the debtor from arrest, lawsuit, or other interference while the letter is in effect. See ARRANGEMENT WITH CREDITORS.

letter of recall. (1840) **1.** A document sent from one country's executive to that of another, summoning a minister back to his or her own country. **2.** A manufacturer's letter to a buyer of a particular product, asking the buyer to bring the product back to the dealer for repair or replacement. — Also termed *recall letter.*

letter of recredentials (ree-krə-**den**-shəlz). A formal letter from a host country's diplomatic secretary of state to a minister or ambassador who has been recalled by his or her own country. • The letter officially accredits the foreign minister back to his or her home country.

letter of request. 1. A document issued by one court to a foreign court, requesting that the foreign court (1) take evidence from a specific person within the foreign jurisdiction or serve process on an individual or corporation within the foreign jurisdiction and (2) return the testimony or proof of service for use in a pending case. *See* Fed. R. Civ. P. 28. — Also termed *letter rogatory* (**rog**-ə-tor-ee); *rogatory letter*; *requisitory letter* (ri-**kwiz**-ə-tor-ee). Cf. COMMISSION TO EXAMINE A WITNESS. **2.** An instrument by which an inferior court withdraws or waives jurisdiction so that a matter can be heard in the court immediately above. — Abbr. LOR. Pl. **letters of request.**

letter of the law. (17c) The strictly literal meaning of the law, rather than the intention or policy behind it. — Also termed *litera legis.* Cf. SPIRIT.

letter of undertaking. An agreement by which a shipowner — to avoid having creditors seize the ship and release it on bond — agrees to post security on the ship, and to enter an appearance, acknowledge ownership, and pay any final decree entered against the vessel whether it is lost or not. • A letter of undertaking is often issued by the shipowner's liability insurer. — Abbr. LOU.

"Such informal or extra-legal agreements save court costs and the marshal's fees, avoid the annoyance of having the vessel even temporarily arrested and may well be cheaper than the usual surety bond . . . . In *Continental Grain Co. v. Federal Barge Lines, Inc.*, [268 F.2d 240 (5th Cir. 1959), *aff'd*, 364 U.S. 19, 80 S.Ct. 1470 (1960)], Judge Brown commented that a letter of undertaking given by a shipowner would be treated 'as though, upon the libel being filed, the vessel had actually been seized, a claim filed, a stipulation to abide decrees with sureties executed and filed by claimant, and the vessel formally released. Any other course would imperil the desirable avoidance of needless cost, time and inconvenience to litigants, counsel, ships, clerks, marshals, keepers and court personnel through the ready acceptance of such letters of undertakings.' [268 F.2d at 243]. If, as Judge Brown suggests, the informal agreement is treated as having the same effect as a formal release under bond or stipulation, few questions relating to their use will ever have to be litigated." Grant Gilmore & Charles L. Black Jr., *The Law of Admiralty* § 9-89, at 800-01 (2d ed. 1975).

letter rogatory. See LETTER OF REQUEST.

letter ruling. (1950) *Tax.* A written statement issued by the IRS to an inquiring taxpayer, explaining the tax implications of a particular transaction. — Also termed *private letter ruling.*

letters. (16c) *Wills & estates.* A court order giving official authority to a fiduciary to conduct appointed tasks. • Examples are letters of administration, letters of conservatorship, letters of guardianship, and letters testamentary. Unif. Probate Code § 1-201(23). See LETTER (2).

letters *ad colligendum bona defuncti* (ad kol-ə-**jen**-dəm **boh**-nə di-**fungk**-tī), *n.* [Law Latin] (17c) *Hist.* An authorization from a judicial officer to an approved person to collect and maintain the goods of a person who died intestate. • These letters were issued only if no representative or creditor existed to exercise this function.

letters close. See LETTERS SECRET.

letter security. See *restricted security* under SECURITY (4).

letters of absolution. (16c) *Hist.* Letters issued by an abbot releasing a member of his order from his vows of obedience to that order, thus permitting entry into another order.

letters of administration. (16c) A formal document issued by a probate court to appoint the administrator of an estate. • Letters of administration originated in the Probate of Testaments Act of 1357 (31 Edw. 3, ch. 4), which provided that in case of intestacy the ordinary (a high-ranking ecclesiastical official within a territory) should depute the decedent's closest friends to administer the estate; a later statute, the Executors Act of 1529 (21 Hen. 8, ch. 4), authorized the ordinary to grant administration to the surviving spouse, to next of kin, or to both of them jointly. — Also termed *administration letters.* See ADMINISTRATION (4). Cf. LETTERS TESTAMENTARY.

▸ **letters of administration c.t.a.** (1894) Letters of administration appointing an administrator *cum testamento annexo* (with the will annexed) either because the will does not name an executor or because the named executor does not qualify. See *administration cum testamento annexo* under ADMINISTRATION.

▸ **letters of administration d.b.n.** (1877) Letters of administration appointing an administrator *de bonis non* (concerning goods not yet administered) because the named executor failed to complete the estate's probate. See *administration de bonis non* under ADMINISTRATION.

letters of credence. See LETTER OF CREDENCE.

letters of guardianship. (18c) A court order appointing a guardian to care for the well-being, property, and affairs of a minor or an incapacitated adult. • It defines the scope of the guardian's rights and duties, including the extent of control over the ward's education and medical issues. See GUARDIAN (1).

letters of horning. (17c) *Hist. Scots law.* An execution process in which the creditor holding a decree obtained royal letters commanding the debtor to either perform or be outlawed. See HORNING.

letters of marque (mahrk). (16c) A license authorizing a private citizen to engage in reprisals against citizens or vessels of another country. • Congress has the exclusive power to grant letters of marque (U.S. Const. art. I, § 8, cl. 11), but it has done so only once since the 19th century. — Also termed *letters of marque and reprisal.*

> "[F]ormerly it was not uncommon for a state to issue 'letters of marque' to one of its own subjects, who had met with a denial of justice in another state, authorizing him to redress the wrong for himself by forcible action, such as the seizure of the property of subjects of the delinquent state." J.L. Brierly, *The Law of Nations* 321 (5th ed. 1955).

letters of safe conduct. (16c) *Hist.* Formal written permission from the English sovereign to a citizen of a country at war with England, permitting that person to travel and ship goods, to England or on the high seas, without risk of seizure. • Passports or licenses from foreign ambassadors now may serve the same purpose. See SAFE CONDUCT.

letters of slains. (17c) *Hist.* Letters to the Crown from the relatives of a slain person concurring with the offender's application for a royal pardon. • A pardon could not be granted without the family's concurrence. — Also spelled *letters of slanes.*

Letters of the Holy Sepulcher. See ASSIZES DE JERUSALEM.

letters patent. (15c) **1.** *Hist.* A document granting some right or privilege, issued under governmental seal but open to public inspection. — Also termed *literae patentes* (**lit**-ər-ee pə-**ten**-teez). Cf. LETTERS SECRET. **2.** A governmental grant of the exclusive right to use an invention or design. — Also termed (in both senses) *patent deed.* See PATENT (2).

letters rogatory. See LETTER OF REQUEST.

letters secret. *Hist.* A governmental document that is issued to a private person, closed and sealed, and thus not made available for public inspection. — Also termed *letters close.* Cf. LETTERS PATENT (1).

letters testamentary. (17c) A probate-court order approving the appointment of an executor under a will and authorizing the executor to administer the estate. Cf. LETTERS OF ADMINISTRATION.

▸ **ancillary letters testamentary.** (1882) Letters testamentary issued at a place where the testator owned property but did not have a domicile. • The executor or administrator is not authorized to act outside the issuing court's territorial jurisdiction.

▸ **domiciliary letters testamentary.** (1957) Letters testamentary issued at the place where the testator was domiciled.

letter stock. See *restricted security* under SECURITY (4).

lettre (**le**-trə), *n.* [French "letter"] (18c) *Hist.* A formal instrument granting some authority.

lettre de cachet (**le**-trə də ka-**shay**). [French "letter with a seal"] (18c) A royal warrant issued for the imprisonment of a person without trial.

leuca (**loo**-kə), *n.* [Law Latin] *Hist.* **1.** *French law.* A league, consisting of 1,500 paces. **2.** A league, consisting of 1,000 paces. **3.** A privileged space of one mile around a monastery.

levance and couchance (**lev**-ənts / **kow**-chənts). (1886) *Hist.* The quality, state, or condition of being levant and couchant. See LEVANT AND COUCHANT.

levandae navis causa (lə-**van**-dee **nay**-vis **kaw**-zə), *n.* [Latin "for the sake of lightening the ship"] *Maritime law.* The practice of throwing goods overboard to avoid total loss, entitling the owner to compensation from other participants in the maritime venture. See JETTISON; *general average* under AVERAGE.

levant and couchant (**lev**-ənt / **kow**-chənt), *adj.* [Law French *couchant et levant* "lying down and rising up"] (16c) *Hist.* (Of cattle and other beasts) trespassing on land for a period long enough to have lain down to rest and risen to feed (usu. at least one night and one day). • This period was the minimum required as grounds for distraint. — Also termed *couchant and levant.*

levari facias (lə-**vair**-ɪ **fay**-shee-əs). [Law Latin "that you cause to be levied"] (17c) A writ of execution ordering a sheriff to seize a judgment debtor's goods and income from lands until the judgment debt is satisfied. • This writ is now used chiefly in Delaware. Cf. FIERI FACIAS.

▸ ***levari facias damna de disseisitoribus*** (lə-**vair**-ɪ **fay**-shee-əs **dam**-nə dee dis-see-zə-**tor**-ə-bəs), *n.* [Law Latin "that you cause to be levied the damages from the disseisors"] (17c) *Hist.* A writ directing the sheriff to levy property to pay damages owed to one wrongfully dispossessed of a freehold estate. See DISSEISIN.

▸ ***levari facias quando vicecomes returnavit quod non habuit emptores*** (lə-**vair**-ɪ **fay**-shee-əs **kwon**-doh vɪ-see-**koh**-meez ree-tər-**nay**-vit kwod non **hay**-byoo-it emp-**tor**-eez), *n.* [Law Latin "that you cause to be levied when the sheriff has returned that it had no buyers"] (17c) *Hist.* A writ directing a sheriff, who had already seized some of the debtor's property and found it unsalable, to sell as much additional property as necessary to pay the entire debt.

▸ ***levari facias residuum debiti*** (lə-**vair**-ɪ **fay**-shee-əs ri-**zij**-oo-əm **deb**-ə-tɪ), *n.* [Law Latin "that you cause to be levied the rest of the debt"] (17c) *Hist.* A writ directing the sheriff to levy on a debtor's lands or goods to pay the remainder of a partially satisfied debt.

levato velo (lə-**vay**-toh **vee**-loh). [Latin "with the curtain raised"] (17c) *Roman law.* The principle, applied to cases of wreck and salvage, and later to all maritime matters, that cases should be heard in public. • Although commentators disagree about the origin of the expression, it probably refers to the place where causes were heard. A sail was spread before the door, and when the cases were heard, the sail was raised, allowing the proceedings to be open to the public.

levee (**lev**-ee), *n.* (17c) **1.** An embankment constructed along the edge of a river to prevent flooding. **2.** A landing place on a body of navigable water for loading and unloading goods or receiving and delivering passengers and boats.

levee district. See DISTRICT.

levée en masse. See LEVY EN MASSE.

level of abstraction. *Copyright.* The degree to which a work describes an idea or process in a general rather than concrete way. • Judge Learned Hand posited that from any work one can restate the idea in more and more abstract ways, omitting more and more details, until one is left with an uncopyrightable idea rather than a protectable work of originality. See *Nichols v. Universal Pictures Corp.*, 45 F.2d 119 (1930).

level-premium insurance. See INSURANCE.

level-rate legal-reserve policy. See INSURANCE POLICY.

leverage, *n.* (1830) **1.** Positional advantage that may well help a person get what he or she wants from others; effectiveness. **2.** The use of credit or borrowed funds (such as buying on margin) to improve one's speculative ability and to increase an investment's rate of return. **3.** The advantage obtained from using credit or borrowed funds rather than equity capital. **4.** The ratio between a corporation's debt and its equity capital. — Also termed *leverage ratio.* **5.** The effect of this ratio on common-stock prices.

leverage, *vb.* (1957) **1.** To provide (a borrower or investor) with credit or funds to improve speculative ability and to seek a high rate of return. **2.** To supplement (available capital) with credit or outside funds. **3.** To fund (a company) with debt as well as shareholder equity. **4.** *Antitrust.* To use power in one market to gain an unfair advantage in another market. **5.** *Insurance.* To manipulate two coverages, as by an insurer's withholding settlement of one claim to influence a claim arising under another source of coverage.

leverage contract. (1975) An agreement for the purchase or sale of a contract for the future delivery of a specified commodity, usu. silver, gold, or another precious metal, in a standard unit and quantity, for a particular price, with no right to a particular lot of the commodity. • A leverage contract operates much like a futures contract, except that there is no designated contract market for leverage contracts. The market sets the uniform terms of a futures contract. But in a leverage contract, the individual merchant sets the terms, does not guarantee a repurchase market, and does not guarantee to continue serving or acting as the broker for the purchaser. Leverage contracts are generally forbidden for agricultural commodities. 7 USCA § 23(a). Cf. FUTURES CONTRACT.

leveraged buyout. See BUYOUT.

leveraged lease. See LEASE.

leveraged recapitalization. See RECAPITALIZATION.

leverage fund. See *dual fund* under MUTUAL FUND.

leverage ratio. See LEVERAGE (4).

leveraging up. See *leveraged recapitalization* under RECAPITALIZATION.

leviable (**lev**-ee-ə-bəl), *adj.* (15c) **1.** Able to be levied; assessable <the fine is leviable on each offense>. **2.** Able to be levied on; seizable in execution of a judgment <leviable goods>.

leviora delicta (lev-ee-**or**-ə də-**lik**-tə). [Latin "the less serious delicts"] *Scots law.* Lesser crimes (such as breach of the peace) that can be summarily tried.

levir (**lee**-vər), *n.* [Latin] (1865) *Roman law.* **1.** A husband's brother. **2.** A wife's brother-in-law.

levirate marriage. See MARRIAGE (1).

levis (**lee**-vis), *adj.* [Latin] *Hist.* Light; trifling.

levis culpa. See CULPA.

levis nota (**lee**-vis **noh**-tə), *n.* [Latin] *Hist.* Slight mark or brand.

levissima culpa. See CULPA.

Levitical degrees. See *prohibited degree* under DEGREE.

levy (**lev**-ee), *n.* (13c) **1.** The imposition of a fine or tax; the fine or tax so imposed. — Also termed *tax levy.* **2.** The enlistment of soldiers into the military; the soldiers so enlisted. **3.** The legally sanctioned seizure and sale of property; the money obtained from such a sale. — Also termed (in sense 3) *levy of execution.*

▸ **capital levy.** (1885) A tax on private or industrial wealth.

▸ **wrongful levy.** (18c) A levy on a third party's property that is not subject to a writ of execution.

levy, *vb.* (14c) **1.** To impose or assess (a fine or a tax) by legal authority <levy a tax on gasoline>. **2.** To enlist for service in the military <the troops were quickly levied>. **3.** To declare or wage (a war) <the rival clans levied war against each other>. **4.** To take or seize property in execution of a judgment <the judgment creditor may levy on the debtor's assets>.

levy court. See COURT.

levy en masse. (1807) A large conscription or mobilization of troops, esp. in response to a threatened invasion. — Also spelled *levée en masse; levy in mass.*

levy of execution. See LEVY (3).

lewd, *adj.* (14c) Obscene or indecent; tending to moral impurity or wantonness <lewd behavior>.

lewd and lascivious cohabitation. See *illicit cohabitation* under COHABITATION.

lewd house. See DISORDERLY HOUSE (2).

lewdness. (16c) Gross, wanton, and public indecency that is outlawed by many state statutes; a sexual act that the actor knows will likely be observed by someone who will be affronted or alarmed by it. See Model Penal Code § 251.1. — Also termed *open lewdness.* Cf. INDECENT EXPOSURE; OBSCENITY.

lex (leks), *n.* [Latin "law"] **1.** Law, esp. statutory law. **2.** Positive law, as opposed to natural law. • Strictly speaking, *lex* is a statute, whereas *jus* is law in general (as well as a right). **3.** A system or body of laws, written or unwritten, that are peculiar to a jurisdiction or to a field of human activity. **4.** A collection of uncodified laws within a jurisdiction. **5.** LEX PUBLICA. **6.** LEX PRIVATA. **7.** *Civil law.* A legislative bill. Cf. JUS. Pl. ***leges*** (**lee**-jeez). **8.** The acquisition of property under some specific law, when the property is made over by a magistrate to the claimant. **9.** A term of a contract, treaty, or other agreement.

lex abrogata (leks ab-rə-**gay**-tə). [Latin] *Hist.* An abrogated law.

lex actus (leks **ak**-təs). See *lex loci actus* under LEX LOCI.

lex Aebutia (leks i-**byoo**-shee-ə). [Latin] *Roman law.* A statute that introduced simplified forms of pleading and procedure. • This was probably enacted in the later part of the second century B.C. See *lex Julia judiciorum publicorum* under LEX JULIA.

lex Aelia Sentia (leks ee-**lee**-ə **sen**-tee-ə). *Roman law.* A statute that set minimum age requirements for an owner and a slave in a valid manumission, voided manumissions made to defraud creditors, and created the status of *dediticii* for some manumitted slaves, esp. criminals. See DEDITICII; LATINI JUNIANI.

lex aeterna (leks ee-**tər**-nə). [Latin] (1895) Eternal law. See NATURAL LAW (1).

lex Anastasiana (leks an-ə-stay-shee-**ay**-nə). [Latin] *Roman law.* **1.** A law establishing that emancipated brothers and sisters receive an intestate inheritance equal to those not emancipated. See AGNATI. **2.** A law providing that a person purchasing a debt from the original creditor for less than its nominal value was not entitled to recover from the debtor more than the amount paid with lawful interest.

lex Angliae (leks **ang**-glee-ee), *n.* [Latin] (17c) *Hist.* The law of England; the common law.

lex annua. See *edictum perpetuum* under EDICTUM.

lex anterior (leks an-**teer**-ee-or). [Latin] *Hist.* Prior law.

lex apparens (leks ə-**par**-enz), *n.* [Law Latin "apparent law"] (17c) *Hist.* The legal processes of trial by ordeal or wager of battle. • The plaintiff could not summon the defendant for trial by these processes before establishing a clear or apparent right through testimony. See ORDEAL.

lex Apuleia (leks ap-yə-**lee**-ə). [Latin] *Roman law.* A law giving a coguarantor, who had paid more than the proper share of debt, an action of reimbursement against the remaining guarantors. — Also spelled *lex Appuleia.*

lex Aquilia (leks ə-**kwil**-ee-ə). [Latin "Aquilian law"] (17c) *Roman law.* A Roman statute imposing liability for pecuniary loss tortiously caused and generally regulating loss caused by damage to property, including compensation to be paid for injury to another's slave or livestock. • A loss had to be financially measurable and caused wrongfully. If the liable party denied liability, then damages were doubled. This law applied to negligence as well as *dolus.* Enacted about 287 B.C., the statute superseded the earlier provisions of the Twelve Tables. — Also termed *Aquilian law.* See DAMNUM INJURIA DATUM; DOLUS. See *actio legis Aquiliae* under ACTIO.

lex arbitri (leks **ahr**-bi-trɪ), *n.* [Latin] (1967) *Hist.* The law governing how an arbitration is to be conducted and the relationship between the arbitration and the courts.

> "Usually by virtue of choosing the arbitral seat, the parties will simultaneously have chosen the procedural law or '*lex arbitri*' of the arbitral seat to govern the arbitral proceedings and the courts of the arbitral seat to exercise supervisory authority over the arbitration." 1 Gary B. Born, *International Commercial Arbitration* 1243 (2009).

lex Atilia (leks ə-**til**-ee-ə). [Latin] *Roman law.* A law granting to magistrates the right to appoint guardians. • The law is named after the person who proposed it, perhaps the tribune L. Atilius Regulus. It was enacted about 210 B.C. — Also termed *Atilian law.*

lex Atinia (leks ə-**tin**-ee-ə). [Latin] *Roman law.* A law declaring that a prescriptive right cannot be acquired in stolen property. • It was enacted in the late third or early second century B.C. — Also termed *Atinian law.*

lex Baiuvariorum (leks bay-ə-vair-ee-**or**-əm). [Latin] (17c) *Hist.* The law of Bavaria, a barbarian country in the Early Middle Ages, first collected (together with the law of the Franks and Alemanni) by Theodoric (ca. 454–526), and finally completed and promulgated by Dagobert (ca. 612–639). — Also termed *lex Baioriorum; lex Boiorum.*

lex barbara (leks **bahr**-bə-rə). [Latin] (17c) *Roman law.* The law of barbarian countries, i.e., those that were not subject to the Roman Empire.

lex Boiorum. See LEX BAIUVARIORUM.

lex Brehonia (leks bri-**hoh**-nee-ə), *n.* [Law Latin] *Hist.* The Brehon or Irish law.

lex Bretoisa (leks bre-**toy**-sə), *n.* [Latin] *Hist.* The law of ancient Britons; the law of Marches of Wales.

lex Burgundionum (leks bər-gən-dee-**oh**-nəm), *n.* [Law Latin] *Hist.* The law of the Burgundians, first published about A.D. 495. — Also termed *lex Romana Burgundonium.*

lex Calpurnia (leks kal-**pər**-nee-ə). [Latin] *Roman law.* A law extending the *lex Silia* by establishing procedures to recover goods other than money. • This affected the *actiones legis.* See LEX SILIA; LEGIS ACTIO.

lex Canuleia (leks kan-yoo-**lee**-ə). [Latin] *Roman law.* A law of 445 B.C. granting plebeians the right to marry patricians.

lex causae (leks **kaw**-zee). [Latin] (1935) The legal system that governs a dispute.

lex centuriata (leks **lee**-jeez sen-tyoor-ee-**ay**-tee). [Latin] (17c) *Roman law.* A law passed in the comitia centuriata. See *comitia centuriata* under COMITIA. Pl. ***leges centuriatae.***

lex Cincia (leks **sin**-shee-ə). [Latin] *Roman law.* A law of 204 B.C. prohibiting certain types of gifts and all gifts or donations of property beyond a certain measure, except to a near relative.

lex Claudia (leks **klaw**-dee-ə). [Latin] (17c) *Roman law.* A statute that abolished the ancient guardianship of adult women by their male agnate relatives. • This became effective in the first century A.D. — Also termed *lex Claudia de tutela.*

lex comitatus (leks kom-ə-**tay**-təs), *n.* [Law Latin] *Hist.* The law of the county; the law administered in the county court before the earl and his deputies.

lex commercii (leks kə-**mər**-shee-ɪ), *n.* [Latin] The law of business or commerce; commercial law. — Also termed *lex commissoria* (leks kom-ə-**sor**-ee-ə). See LEX COMMISSORIA.

lex commissoria (leks kom-i-**sor**-ee-a). [Latin "forfeiture clause" or "cancellation clause"] (1897) *Roman law.* **1.** A term in a contract of sale allowing the seller to rescind the sale if the price was not paid by the agreed time. **2.** A clause by which, in a pledge agreement, a debtor and creditor could agree that if the debtor fails to timely pay the debt, the creditor obtains absolute title of the pledged property.

> "By the *lex commissoria* at Rome, the debtor and creditor might agree that if the debtor did not pay at the day, the pledge should become the absolute property of the creditor. But a law of Constantine abolished this power, as unjust and oppressive, and having a growing asperity in practice." 2 James Kent, *Commentaries on American Law* *583 (George Comstock ed., 11th ed. 1866).

3. An agreement in which such a failure-to-timely-pay clause appears. — Also written *commissoria lex.* **3.** LEX COMMERCII.

> "But the position of the seller was a good deal more awkward, especially if he had sold a unique object, such as a piece of land, for, apart from express agreement, he would have to retain the land or other object in case the buyer later came along with the price and demanded delivery. The difficulty could be avoided by the insertion of a term known as *lex commissoria,* which gave the seller an option of declaring the contract at an end if the buyer did not pay within the agreed time. This term probably became common form in Roman law, but was never implied. It always had to be expressly inserted in the contract . . . . Not until the time of Lord Mansfield was a similar development complete in English law, though in the end we carried it much further than the Romans." W.W. Buckland & Arnold

D. McNair, *Roman Law & Common Law: A Comparison in Outline* 231 (F.H. Lawson ed., 2d ed. 1952).

lex communis (leks kə-**myoo**-nis), *n.* [Latin] (17c) The common law. See JUS COMMUNE.

lex contractus (leks kən-**trak**-təs). See *lex loci contractus* under LEX LOCI.

lex Cornelia (leks kor-**nee**-lee-ə *or* kor-**neel**-yə). [Latin] *Roman law.* One of several laws passed by the dictator L. Cornelius Sulla in 82–81 B.C. — Also termed *Cornelian law.*

▸ ***lex Cornelia de edictis*** (leks kor-**nee**-lee-ə dee ee-**dik**-təs). See *lex Cornelia de jurisdictione.*

▸ ***lex Cornelia de falsis*** (leks kor-**nee**-lee-ə dee **fal**-soh *or* **fawl**-sis). [Latin] *Roman law.* See *lex cornelia nummaria testamentaria.*

▸ ***lex Cornelia de injuriis*** (leks kor-**nee**-lee-ə dee in-**joor**-ee-is). [Latin] *Roman law.* The Cornelian law providing a civil action for the recovery of a penalty in certain cases of bodily injury and violent invasion of property. • The precise boundary between the crime and the delict is not clear. But the two procedures probably existed side by side.

"Lex Cornelia de iniuriis . . . . Punished three kinds of injury committed by violence: *pulsare* (beating), *verberare* (striking, causing pains) and *domum introire* (forcible invasion of another's domicile)." Adolf Berger, *Encyclopedic Dictionary of Roman Law* 549 (1953).

▸ ***lex Cornelia de jurisdictione*** (leks kor-**nee**-lee-ə dee joor-is-**dik**-shee-oh-nee). [Latin] *Roman law.* The law forbidding a praetor from departing, during his term of office, from the edict he had promulgated at the term's commencement. • It did not, however, forbid the offer of new remedies. — Also termed *lex Cornelia de edictis.*

▸ ***lex Cornelia de sicariis et veneficis*** (leks kor-**nee**-lee-ə dee si-**kair**-ee-is et və-**nee**-fə-sis). [Latin] *Roman law.* A law combining jurisdiction over gangster-type killings and poisoning, or attempts at such crimes, and addressing the bringing of false witness and bribery of a judge or juror, if those actions brought about a person's death. • The statute was soon extended to cover murder generally when committed within or close to Rome. Emperor Antoninus Pius added a provision for murder to include a slaveowner who deliberately killed his own slave.

▸ ***lex Cornelia de sponsu*** (leks kor-**nee**-lee-ə dee **spon**-s[y]oo). [Latin] *Roman law.* A law prohibiting a person from acting as surety for the same debtor to the same creditor in the same year for more than a specified amount.

▸ ***lex Cornelia nummaria testamentaria*** (leks kor-**nee**-lee-ə nə-**mair**-ee-ə tes-tə-men-**tair**-ee-ə). *Roman law.* A statute making forgery (*falsum*) a crime, and creating a special court to try forgery cases. • Until the later Roman Empire, *falsum* included both coining and document forgery. — Also termed *lex Cornelia de falsis* (leks kor-**nee**-lee-ə dee **fal**-soh *or* **fawl**-sis). See FALSUM (2).

"It is not absolutely clear whether Sulla passed two laws, one on forging wills and the other on forging money, or whether the one *lex Cornelia nummaria testamentaria* provided for both sorts of offence to be heard by the *quaestio de falsis* which it created." O.F. Robinson, *The Criminal Law of Ancient Rome* 36 (1995).

lex curiata (lex kyoor-ee-**ay**-tə). [Latin] (17c) *Roman law.* Laws passed in the comitia curiata. See *comitia curiata* under COMITIA. Pl. ***leges curiatae*** (**lee**-jeez kyoor-ee-**ay**-tee).

lex Danorum (leks dan-**or**-əm). See DANELAW.

lex delicti (leks də-**lik**-tɪ). See *lex loci delicti* under LEX LOCI.

lex deraisnia (leks də-**rayn**-ee-ə), *n.* [Law Latin] (17c) *Hist.* A law by which a party denies an accusation, showing it to be against reason or probability.

lex de responsis prudentium (leks dee ri-**spon**-sis proo-**den**-shee-əm). [Latin "law on the replies of the jurisprudents"] See CITATIONS, LAW OF.

lex domicilii (leks dom-ə-**sil**-ee-ɪ). [Latin] (18c) **1.** The law of the country where a person is domiciled. **2.** The determination of a person's rights by establishing where, in law, that person is domiciled. *See* Restatement (Second) of Conflict of Laws §§ 11 et seq. (1971).

Lex Duodecim Tabularum (leks d[y]oo-ə-**des**-əm tab-yə-**lair**-əm). See TWELVE TABLES.

lex et consuetudo parliamenti (leks et kon-swə-**t[y]oo**-doh parl-[y]ə-**men**-tɪ), *n.* [Latin] (17c) *Hist.* The law and custom (or usage) of Parliament.

lex et consuetudo regni (leks et kon-swə-**t[y]oo**-do **reg**-nɪ), *n.* [Latin] (1917) *Hist.* The law and custom of the realm; the common law.

lex Fabia de plagiariis (leks **fay**-bee-ə dee plaj-ee-**air**-ee-əs), *n.* [Latin] (18c) *Hist.* A law directed against kidnapping and harboring of slaves.

lex Falcidia (leks fal-**sid**-ee-ə). See FALCIDIAN LAW.

lex ferenda (leks fə-**ren**-də). [Latin] (1893) *Hist.* Law proposed for enactment. — Also termed *de lege ferenda.*

lex feudi (leks **fyoo**-dɪ). [Law Latin] (1848) *Scots law.* The law of the feu; the law relating to feudal title.

lex fori (leks **for**-ɪ). [Latin] (1803) The law of the forum; the law of the jurisdiction where the case is pending <the *lex fori* governs whether the death penalty is a possible punishment for a first-degree-murder conviction>. — Also termed *lex ordinandi.* Cf. LEX LOCI (1).

lex Francorum (leks frang-**kor**-əm), *n.* [Law Latin] (17c) The law of the Franks, promulgated by Theodoric I, son of Clovis I, at the same time as the law of Alemanni and Bavaria.

lex Frisionum (leks frizh-ee-**oh**-nəm), *n.* [Law Latin] (1898) The law of the Frisians, promulgated in the middle of the eighth century.

lex Fufia Caninia (leks **foof**-ee-ə kə-**nɪ**-nee-ə). [Latin] *Roman law.* A law prohibiting owners from freeing by will more than a certain number or proportion of their slaves. • Justinian later abrogated this law. — Also termed *Fufian Caninian law.*

lex Furia testamentaria (leks **fyoor**-ee-ə tes-tə-men-**tair**-ee-ə. [Latin] *Roman law.* A law prohibiting a testator from bequeathing more than 1,000 asses (i.e., 722 pounds) of copper or the equivalent. • This law, dating from the middle of the republic, was one of the first to restrict legacies. It was passed between 204 and 169 B.C.

"The *lex Furia* . . . provided that no one except [close] relatives . . . should take by will or gift in view of death more than 1000 asses [copper coins]. It did not rescind the disposition, but enacted a penalty of four times the amount, recoverable by a stringent procedure from anyone who took such a legacy or gift, contrary to the law. But this law left it open to a testator to leave nothing to the heir, supposing he made a sufficient number of legatees up to the statutable limit." 1 Henry John Roby, *Roman Private Law in the Times of Cicero and of the Antonines* 344–45 (1902).

lex Fusia Caninia. See LEX FUFIA CANINIA.

lex Gabinia (leks gə-**bin**-ee-ə). [Latin] (18c) *Roman law.* A law introducing popular election by secret ballot. • Secret ballots were also used in judicial meetings. — Also termed *lex Gabinia tabellaria* (leks gə-**bin**-ee-ə tab-ə-**lair**-ee-ə). ***lex generalis*** (leks jen-ə-**ray**-lis). (1919) A law of general application, as opposed to one that affects only a particular person or a small group of people.

lex Genucia (leks jə-**n**[y]**oo**-shee-ə). [Latin] *Roman law.* A law prohibiting the charging of interest on loans between Roman citizens. • The statute was proposed in the 4th century B.C., but it is uncertain when, if ever, it was enacted. If enacted, it was not enforced.

lex Gothica (leks **goth**-ik-ə), *n.* [Law Latin] *Hist.* The law of the Goths. • It was first promulgated in writing in A.D. 466.

lex Horatia Valeria. See LEX VALERIA HORATIA.

lex Hortensia (leks hor-**ten**-s[h]ee-ə). [Latin] *Roman law.* A law extending to the plebeians full participation in public laws of government and worship; specif., an important constitutional law that made laws passed by the assemblies of the common people (the plebeians) binding on all citizens. • Previously, plebeian assemblies could not bind the patrician class. This statute put enactments of the *concilium plebis* on the same footing as *leges.* See JUS PUBLICUM; JUS SACRUM.

lex Hostilia de furtis (leks hos-**til**-ee-ə dee **fər**-tis). [Latin] *Roman law.* A law of the early Republic providing that the state could prosecute a person for theft on behalf of an owner when the owner was captive or abroad. • This affected the *actiones legis.* See LEGIS ACTIO.

lexical definition. See DEFINITION.

lex imperatoria (leks im-pər-ə-**tor**-ee-ə). [Latin] Imperial law.

lex incorporationis. [Latin] (1939) The law of the state where incorporation takes place. See INTERNAL-AFFAIRS DOCTRINE.

lex Irnitana. (1984) *Roman law.* A Roman charter that detailed the municipal structure, laws, and judicial system for a small town in the province of Seville, Spain. • This charter was recorded on bronze tablets and is one version of a model document (called the *Flavian municipal law*) used as a basis for individual town charters in the Roman Empire. The *lex Irnitana* is the longest version found to date. — Also termed *Flavian municipal law.*

LEXIS (**lek**-sis). A proprietary online computer service that provides access to databases of legal information, including federal and state caselaw, statutes, and secondary materials.

lex judicialis (leks joo-dish-ee-**ay**-lis), *n.* [Latin "judicial law"] An ordeal. See ORDEAL.

lex Julia (leks **joo**-lee-ə). [Latin] *Roman law.* One of several Roman statutes dating from the reign of the Emperor Augustus (27 B.C.–A.D. 14) or sometimes from Julius Caesar (47–44 B.C.).

▸ ***lex Julia de adulteriis coercerendis*** (leks **joo**-lee-ə dee ə-**dəl**-tər-ee-is koh-ər-sə-**ren**-dəs). [Latin] *Roman law.* A statute of 18 B.C. making adultery a public crime, justiciable before a *quaestio perpetua.* — Sometimes shortened to *lex Julia de adulteriis.*

▸ ***lex Julia de ambitu*** (leks **joo**-lee-ə dee **am**-bi-t[y]oo). [Latin] *Roman law.* A law of 18 B.C. discouraging electoral corruption by a would-be magistrate.

▸ ***lex Julia de annona*** (leks **joo**-lee-ə dee ə-**noh**-nə). [Latin] *Roman law.* A law against business combinations that negatively affected the grain supply, esp. attempts to raise the price of corn.

▸ ***lex Julia de cessione bonorum*** (leks **joo**-lee-ə dee ses[h]-ee-**oh**-nee bə-**nor**-əm). [Latin] *Roman law.* A law governing bankruptcies allowing a debtor to avoid further adverse action by ceding all the debtor's property to the creditors.

▸ ***lex Julia de majestate*** (leks **joo**-lee-ə dee maj-ə-**stay**-tee. [Latin] *Roman law.* A treason law imposing capital punishment on a person acting against the emperor or state. • Enacted about 8 B.C., this was the last specific law on treason.

▸ ***lex Julia de maritandis ordinibus*** (leks **joo**-lee-ə dee mar-ə-**tan**-dis or-**din**-ə-bəs). [Latin] *Roman law.* A law regulating marriages, imposing a duty to be married on all men between 25 and 60, and on all women between 20 and 50, and forbidding marriages between senators and freedwomen, and forbidding senators and all other freeborn citizens from marrying actresses, prostitutes, and the like. • This 18 B.C. statute is usu. considered as one law with the *lex Papia Poppea* of A.D. 9, which exempted women with three children or more from being placed under guardianship.

▸ ***lex Julia de peculatu*** (leks **joo**-lee-ə dee pek-yə-**lay**-t[y]oo). [Latin] *Roman law.* A law punishing the embezzlement of public funds. • Originally a magistrate determined the punishment. The same court had jurisdiction for transgressions under *lex Julia de residius* and for sacrilege, the wrongful taking of money dedicated to sacred or religious purposes. See *lex Julia de residuis.*

▸ ***lex Julia de residuis*** (leks **joo**-lee-ə dee ri-**zij**-oo-is). [Latin] *Roman law.* A law punishing persons who could not account for public funds lawfully in their charge. See *lex Julia de peculatu.*

▸ ***lex Julia judiciorum privatorum*** (leks **joo**-lee-ə joo-dish-ee-**or**-əm prɪ-və-**tor**-əm). See *lex Julia judiciorum publicorum.*

▸ ***lex Julia judiciorum publicorum*** (leks **joo**-lee-ə joo-dish-ee-**or**-əm pə-bli-**kor**-əm). [Latin] *Roman law.* An Augustan statute that, with the *lex Julia judiciorum privatorum*, reformed various aspects of civil procedure. • The two laws are often referred to together as *leges Juliae*, or *duae Juliae.* Together with the *lex Aebutia*, the *leges Julia* largely abolished the *legis actiones*, the ancient form of Roman civil procedure that relied on fixed oral forms.

lex Junia Norbana (leks **joo**-nee-ə nor-**bay**-nə). [Latin] *Roman law.* A law creating the status of Junian Latin for informally manumitted slaves. — Often shortened to *lex Junia.* See LATINI JUNIANI.

"After the *lex Junia Norbana*, we find the following classes of persons, under the division of the law of persons into free men or slaves: 1. *Ingenui*, or persons born free. 2. *Libertini* . . . ex-slaves who, on gaining their freedom, became *cives.* 3. *Latini Juniani* . . . ex-slaves who, on manumission and by reason of some defect therein, became something short of full citizens. 4. *Dediticii* . . . . 5. Slaves proper." R.W. Leage, *Roman Private Law* 70 (C.H. Ziegler ed., 2d ed. 1930).

lex Junia Velleia (leks **joo**-nee-ə və-**lee**-yə). [Latin] *Roman law.* A law providing that certain kinds of descendants must be treated as posthumously born children of a decedent for purposes of heirship. • This probably was enacted in A.D. 26.

lex Kantiae (leks **kan**-shee-ee). [Law Latin] *Hist.* A body of customs, mainly concerning land tenure, prevailing in Kent during the time of Edward I.

lex Langobardorum. See LEX LONGOBARDORUM.

lex lata (leks **lat**-tə). [Latin] (17c) *Hist.* The law as it exists; enacted law.

lex ligeantiae (leks lij-ee-**an**-shee-ee). [Law Latin] (1901) *Hist.* The law of the country to which a person owes national allegiance. • Some jurists have thought that this law ought to decide many of the questions that have usu. been determined by the *lex domicilii.*

lex loci (leks **loh**-sɪ). [Latin] (18c) **1.** The law of the place; local law. Cf. LEX FORI. **2.** See *lex loci contractus.*

▸ ***lex loci actus*** (leks **loh**-sɪ **ak**-təs). [Law Latin] (1848) The law of the place where an act is done or a transaction is completed. — Often shortened to *lex actus.*

▸ ***lex loci celebrationis*** (leks **loh**-sɪ sel-ə-bray-shee-**oh**-nis). [Latin "law of the place of the ceremony"] (1882) The law of the place where a contract, esp. of marriage, is made. • This law usu. governs when the validity of a marriage is at issue. Restatement (Second) of Conflict of Laws § 283(2) (1971).

▸ ***lex loci contractus*** (leks **loh**-sɪ kən-**trak**-təs). [Latin] (18c) The law of the place where a contract is executed or to be performed. • *Lex loci contractus* is often the proper law by which to decide contractual disputes. — Often shortened to *lex loci; lex contractus.*

"The *lex loci contractus* controls the nature, construction, and validity of the contract; and on this broad foundation the law of contracts, founded on necessity and commercial convenience, is said to have been originally established. If the rule were otherwise, the citizens of one country could not safely contract, or carry on commerce, in the territories of another." 2 James Kent, *Commentaries on American Law* *454 (George Comstock ed., 11th ed. 1866).

▸ ***lex loci delicti*** (leks **loh**-sɪ də-**lik**-tɪ). [Latin] (1847) The law of the place where the tort or other wrong was committed. — Often shortened to *lex delicti.* — Also termed *lex loci delictus; lex loci delicti commissi; place-of-wrong rule; place-of-wrong law.* Cf. LOCUS DELICTI.

▸ ***lex loci protectionis*** (leks **loh**-sɪ prə-tek-shee-**oh**-nis). [Latin] *Hist.* The law of the place of protection.

▸ ***lex loci rei sitae*** (leks **loh**-sɪ **ree**-ɪ **sɪ**-tee). [Latin] (1849) LEX SITUS.

▸ ***lex loci solutionis*** (leks **loh**-sɪ sə-loo-shee-**oh**-nis). [Latin "law of the place of solution"] (1838) The law of the place where a contract is to be performed (esp. by payment). — Often shortened to *lex solutionis.*

lex Longobardorum (leks long-goh-bahr-**dor**-əm). [Latin "law of the Lombards"] (1846) *Hist.* An ancient legal code developed between the fifth and eighth centuries, in force until the reign of Charlemagne; the laws of the Lombards, seen cumulatively from the Edict of Rothari in A.D. 643, and added to by Liutprand. • It was a subject of study in the early law school at Pavia. — Also spelled *lex Langobardorum; lex Langobardica.*

lex majoris partis [Latin "law of the major party"] (18c) Majority rule. See MAJORITY RULE.

"The voice of the majority decides. For the lex majoris partis is the law of all councils, elections, &c. where not otherwise expressly provided. But if the house be equally divided, 'semper presumatur pro negante:' that is, the former law is not to be changed but by a majority." Thomas Jefferson, *A Manual of Parliamentary Practice* 105 (1801) (citation omitted).

lex manifesta (leks man-ə-**fes**-tə). [Law Latin] (17c) *Hist.* **1.** Open law; manifest law. **2.** Trial by duel or ordeal. — Also termed *manifest law.*

lex marityma. *Hist.* The body of customs, usage, and local rules governing seagoing commerce that developed in the maritime countries of medieval Europe.

lex mercatoria (leks mər-kə-**tor**-ee-ə). [Latin "mercantile law"] **1.** LAW MERCHANT. **2.** A modern system of customary law governing international transactions and having its history in common commercial practices in international trade as well as in awards of international arbitrators in commercial cases. • Although the origin of this modern *lex mercatoria* is subject to debate, it is often traced to the medieval version. — Also termed *new law merchant; transnational commercial law.*

"Lex mercatoria seems to mean different things to different people. . . . The various notions may usefully be distinguished and grouped under three headings. First, the most ambitious concept of lex mercatoria is that of an autonomous legal order, created spontaneously by parties involved in international economic relations and existing independently of national legal orders. Second, lex mercatoria has been viewed as a body of rules sufficient to decide a dispute, operating as an alternative to an otherwise applicable national law. Third, it may be considered as a complement to otherwise applicable law, viewed as nothing more than the gradual consolidation of usage and settled expectations in international trade." Laurence Craig et al., *International Chamber of Commerce Arbitration* § 35.01, at 623 (3d ed. 2000).

lex merciorum (leks mər-shee-**or**-əm). See MERCENLAGE.

lex mitior (leks **mit**-ee-or). [Latin] *Hist.* A more lenient law.

lex monetae (leks mə-**nee**-tee). [Latin] (1945) The law of the country whose money is in question.

lex naturae (leks nə-**tyoor**-ee). See NATURAL LAW.

lex naturale (leks nach-ə-**ray**-lee). [Law Latin] See NATURAL LAW.

lex non scripta (leks non **skrip**-tə). [Latin "unwritten law"] See *unwritten law* under LAW. Pl. ***leges non scriptae.***

"One of the most remarkable designations of the common law was that of *lex non scripta,* which it derives from its own nature, because there are no records extant to show its legislative enactment, it being one of its peculiar perfections, that it has been in use time out of mind, or, in the solemn language of the law, time whereof the memory of man runneth not to the contrary." George Crabb, *A History of English Law* 2 (1st Am. ed. 1831).

lex ordinandi (leks or-də-**nan**-dɪ). See LEX FORI.

lex originis (leks ə-**rij**-i-nis). [Latin] *Hist.* The law of the origin (of a person, institution, etc.).

lex Papia Poppea (leks **pay**-pee-ə pah-**pee**-ə). [Latin] *Roman law.* A law proposed by the consuls Papius and

Poppeus at the request of Augustus. • It is usu. considered with the *lex Julia de maritandis ordinibus* as one law. — Also termed *Papian law*; *Poppean law*. See *lex Julia de maritandis ordinibus* under LEX JULIA.

lex patriae (leks **pay**-tree-ee *or* **pa**-tree-ee). [Latin] (17c) National law; the law of one's country. See PERSONAL LAW.

lex patrimonii (leks pat-ri-**moh**-nee-ɪ). [Latin] *Hist.* The law of the patrimony (e.g., of an ecclesiastical endowment).

lex Petronia (leks pə-**troh**-nee-ə). [Latin] *Roman law.* A law forbidding masters from sending their slaves to fight wild beasts in the arena without a magistrate's authorization. • This law was enacted sometime before A.D. 79.

lex Plaetoria (leks pli- *or* plee-**tor**-ee-ə). [Latin] (1836) *Roman law.* A law protecting minors against frauds and permitting them to apply for a guardian or curator to assist them.

lex Poetelia (leks poh-ə-**tee**-lee-ə). [Latin] *Roman law.* A law abolishing a creditor's right to reduce his debtor to slave-like treatment. • This law was enacted sometime before 300 B.C.

lex Pompeia de parricidiis (leks pom-**pee**-ə dee par-ə-**sɪ**-dee-is). [Latin] *Roman law.* A law of 70 or 55 B.C. defining what murders amounted to parricide and establishing a special expiatory punishment, in which the offender was executed by being sewn up in a sack with a dog, a rooster, a viper, and a monkey, and thrown into the sea or a river. See PARRICIDE.

lex posterior derogat priori (leks pah-**steer**-ee-ər **der**-ə-gat prɪ-**or**-ɪ). [Latin "a later law prevails over an earlier one"] (1919) The principle that a later statute negates the effect of a prior one if the later statute expressly repeals, or is obviously repugnant to, the earlier law.

lex praetoria (leks pri- *or* pree-**tor**-ee-ə). [Latin "praetorian law"] (1836) **1.** *Roman law.* Law laid down in the praetor's edict. Cf. JUS PRAETORIUM. **2.** *Hist.* The applicable rules in a court of equity.

lex privata (leks prɪ-**vay**-tə). [Latin "private law"] (17c) *Roman law.* A term in a private contract. — Sometimes shortened to *lex*.

lex publica (leks **pəb**-li-kə). [Latin "public law"] (1897) *Roman law.* **1.** A law passed by a popular assembly and binding on all people. **2.** A written law. — Sometimes shortened to *lex*.

lex Publilia (leks p[y]oo-**blil**-ee-ə). [Latin "Publilian law"] *Roman law.* A law dispensing with senatorial approval for the enactments of the *plebs* (common citizens). • In 339 B.C. these laws strengthened the force of the *plebiscita* and indirectly weakened the patrician element in the Senate by permitting *auctoritas patrum* to be given in advance for some legislation, and requiring one of the censors to be a plebeian. — Also termed *leges Publiliae Philonis*.

lex regia (leks **ree**-jee-ə). [Latin "royal law"] (17c) *Roman law.* A law ostensibly enacted by the Roman people granting wide legislative and executive powers to the emperor, later interpreted as providing that the emperor was a source of law, the emperor had full legislative powers, and the emperor's will or pleasure had the full force of law. See LEX IMPERII.

lex rei sitae (leks **ree**-ɪ **sɪ**-tee). [Law Latin] (1836) *Scots law.* The law of the place where the property is situated.

lex Rhodia (leks **roh**-dee-ə). [Latin] (17c) *Roman law.* The Rhodian law governing the subject of jettison. • This began as the common law of the ancient Mediterranean Sea. It required that all consignors and the shipmaster share losses equally. — Also termed *lex Rhodia de jactu*. See RHODIAN LAW.

Lex Ribuaria. A mid-7th-century code of Franco-Germanic law. • The name comes from the Ribuarian Franks, who lived in the area of what is now Cologne, Germany. — Also termed *Lex Ripuaria*; *Lex Ribuariorum*.

lex Romana (leks rə-**man**-ə). [Latin] (17c) ROMAN LAW.

lex Romana Burgundonium. See LEX BURGUNDONIUM.

Lex Romana Canonice Compta (leks roh-**man**-ə kə-**non**-see **komp**-tə). *Eccles. law.* A 9th-century compilation of Roman laws intended to provide members of the Roman Catholic Church with the rules of Roman law that were relevant to them.

lex romana curiensis (leks roh-**man**-ə kyoor-ee-**en**-sis). [Latin] *Hist.* **1.** The law of the papal Curia. **2.** (*cap.*) An 8th-century law drafted for the Romance population of Eastern Switzerland, Tyrol, and Northern Italy, based on a flawed abstract of the *Lex Romana Visigothorum*.

lex Romana Visigothorum. See LEX VISIGOTHORUM.

lex Salica (leks **sal**-ə-kə). [Latin] See SALIC LAW.

lex Scribonia (leks skri-**boh**-nee-ə). [Latin] *Roman law.* A law of the late Republic abolishing the acquisition of praedial servitudes through prescription.

lex scripta (leks **skrip**-tə). [Latin "written law"] See *written law* under LAW. Pl. ***leges scriptae.***

lex Sempronia (leks sem-**proh**-nee-ə). [Latin] *Roman law.* A law of 122 B.C. transferring the duty of jury service from the senators to the equestrians (knights). • The control of the juries in the *quaestiones perpetuae*, particularly in extortion (*repetundae*) trials, was one of the key areas of political conflict in the late Republic.

lex Silia (leks **sil**-ee-ə). [Latin] (1883) *Roman law.* A law providing for personal actions for a fixed sum of money; specif., a law from perhaps 250 B.C. introducing the *legis actio per condictionem* to claim a fixed sum of money.

lex situs (leks **sɪ**-təs. [Law Latin] (1848) The law of the place where property is located. — Also termed *lex loci rei sitae*. *See* Restatement (Second) of Conflict of Laws §§ 222 et seq. (1971).

lex solutionis. See *lexi loci solutionis* under LEX LOCI.

lex sportiva internationalis (leks spor-**tɪ**-və in-tər-nay-shee-ə-**nal**-is). [Modern Latin] *Hist.* The international law of sports.

> "*Lex sportiva (internationalis). . . . Neo.* 'The (international) law of sports.' (1) The international laws and regulations relating to athletic contests, such as the Olympic Games or World Cup. (2) The jurisprudence of international tribunals on matters relating to sports, especially that of the Court of Arbitration for Sport. *See* Gérald Simon, *Puissance Sportive et Ordre Juridique Étatique* (Paris: Librairie générale de droit et de jurisprudence ed., 1990)." Aaron X. Fellmeth & Maurice Horwitz, *Guide to Latin in International Law* 177 (2009).

lex talionis (leks tal-ee-**oh**-nis). [Law Latin] (16c) The law of retaliation, under which punishment should be in kind — an eye for an eye, a tooth for a tooth, and so on — but no more. — Also termed *eye for an eye*; *jus talionis*; *principle of retribution*.

"Kant, for example, expresses the opinion that punishment cannot rightly be inflicted for the sake of any benefit to be derived from it either by the criminal himself or by society, and that the sole and sufficient reason and justification of it lies in the fact that evil has been done by him who suffers it. Consistently with this view, he derives the measure of punishment, not from any elaborate considerations as to the amount needed for the repression of crime, but from the simple principle of *lex talionis*: 'Thine eye shall not pity; but life shall go for life, eye for eye, tooth for tooth, hand for hand, foot for foot" [*Deuteronomy*, xix 21]. No such principle, indeed, is capable of literal interpretation; but subject to metaphorical and symbolical applications it is in Kant's view the guiding rule of the ideal scheme of criminal justice." John Salmond, *Jurisprudence* 118 (Glanville L. Williams ed., 10th ed. 1947).

"But if the old form of the *lex talionis*, an eye for an eye or a tooth for a tooth, sounds too barbaric today, may we not reformulate the retributive theory and put it thus: Everyone is to be punished alike in proportion to the gravity of his offense or to the extent to which he has made others suffer?" Morris R. Cohen, *Reason and Law* 53 (1961).

lex terrae (leks **ter**-ee). [Law Latin] See LAW OF THE LAND.

lex Theodosiana (leks thee-ə-doh-see-**an**-ə). See THEODOSIAN CODE.

lex Valeria Horatia (leks və-**leer**-ee-ə hə-**ray**-shee-ə). [Latin] *Roman law.* A law making enactments by the assembly of the people in tribes binding on all citizens. • Several laws of this name were enacted in 449 B.C. One was aimed at strengthening the force of *plebiscita*. Another protected plebeian tribunes with sacrosanctity. A third, more dubious, law falls between the lex Valeria of 509 B.C. and the lex Valeria of 300 B.C. in granting the right of *provocatio* to the Roman citizen oppressed by a magistrate. — Also termed *lex Horatia Valeria*. Cf. LEX HORTENSIA.

lex validitatis (leks val-ə-**day**-tis. [Latin] *Conflict of laws.* The presumption of validity given to marriages, contracts, and other matters.

lex Visigothorum (leks viz-ə-gah-**thor**-əm). [Latin "law of the Visigoths"] (1846) An early 6th-century code of Roman law that applied to Hispano-Roman and Gallo-Roman peoples ruled by the Visigoths, a German tribe that conquered Spain in the 5th century. • Its primary source is the *Breviary of Alaric*, prepared for Alaric II, the Visigoth king who ordered Roman law collected into this code. In the late 7th century, Kings Recceswinth and Erwig imposed a Visigothic common law, and it is to this law that the phrase *lex Visigothorum* usu. applies. — Also spelled *lex Wisigothorum*. — Sometimes written *lex Romana Wisigothorum* — Also termed *lex Romana Visigothorum; liber judiciorum*. See BREVIARIUM ALARICIANUM.

lex Voconia (leks və-**koh**-nee-ə). [Latin] *Roman law.* A law enacted in 169 B.C. to regulate inheritance (esp. by women) by capping the amount receivable by anyone as legacy or gift in view of death at no more than the heirs took. • The Falcidian law superseded the *lex Voconia*. — Also termed *Voconian law*. See FALCIDIAN LAW.

"Lex Voconia . . . . Contained several provisions concerned with the law of succession: (1) No woman could be heir . . . to an estate having a value greater than a fixed amount . . . . (2) Admitted among female agnates only the sisters of the deceased to intestate succession. (3) No one person — male or female — could receive by legacy more than the heir (or all heirs together) instituted in the last will." Adolf Berger, *Encyclopedic Dictionary of Roman Law* 561 (1953).

lex Wallensica (leks wawl-**en**-zə-kə), *n.* [Latin] Welsh law.

ley (lay), *n.* [Law French] *Hist.* Law.

ley civile (lay see- *or* sə-**veel**), *n.* [Law French] *Hist.* **1.** The civil law. **2.** The Roman law. — Also termed *ley escripte*.

ley de terre (lay də tair). [Law French] See LAW OF THE LAND.

leyerwite. See LAIRWITE.

ley escripte (lay **es**-kript). See LEY CIVILE.

ley gager (lay **gay**-jər), *n.* [Law French] *Hist.* Wager of law; the defendant's giving of security to make law on a particular day. See WAGER OF LAW.

leze majesty. See LESE MAJESTY.

L.F. *abbr.* LAW FRENCH.

LHWCA. *abbr.* LONGSHORE AND HARBOR WORKERS' COMPENSATION ACT.

liability, *n.* (18c) **1.** The quality, state, or condition of being legally obligated or accountable; legal responsibility to another or to society, enforceable by civil remedy or criminal punishment <liability for injuries caused by negligence>. — Also termed *legal liability; subjection; responsibility*. Cf. FAULT. **2.** (*often pl.*) A financial or pecuniary obligation in a specified amount; DEBT <tax liability> <assets and liabilities>.

"The term 'liability' is one of at least double signification. In one sense it is the synonym of *duty*, the correlative of *right*; in this sense it is the opposite of *privilege* or *liberty*. If a duty rests upon a party, society is now commanding performance by him and threatening penalties. In a second sense, the term 'liability' is the correlative of *power* and the opposite of *immunity*. In this case society is not yet commanding performance, but it will so command if the possessor of the power does some operative act. If one has a power, the other has a liability. It would be wise to adopt the second sense exclusively. Accurate legal thinking is difficult when the fundamental terms have shifting senses." William R. Anson, *Principles of the Law of Contract* 9 (Arthur L. Corbin ed., 3d Am. ed. 1919).

"Liability or responsibility is the bond of necessity that exists between the wrongdoer and the remedy of the wrong. This *vinculum juris* is not one of mere duty or obligation; it pertains not to the sphere of *ought* but to that of *must*." John Salmond, *Jurisprudence* 364 (Glanville L. Williams ed., 10th ed. 1947).

▸ **absolute liability. 1.** *Archaic.* See *strict liability*. **2.** A type of strict liability based on causation alone, without any other limiting factors. • Absolute liability is often distinguished from strict products liability, which limits strict liability to injuries caused by a product defect. Cf. PRODUCTS LIABILITY.

"No one wants absolute liability where all the article has to do is to cause injury." *Phillips v. Kimwood Mach. Co.*, 525 P.2d 1033, 1036 (Or. 1974).

3. *Int'l law.* A state's liability or responsibility that arises even in the absence of any intention or negligence imputable to the state. — Also termed *absolute responsibility*.

▸ **accomplice liability.** (1958) Criminal responsibility of one who acts with another before, during, or (in some jurisdictions) after a crime. *See* 18 USCA § 2.

▸ **accrued liability.** (1877) A debt or obligation that is properly chargeable in a given accounting period but that is not yet paid.

▸ **aiding-and-abetting liability.** (1972) Civil or, more typically, criminal liability imposed on one who assists in or facilitates the commission of an act that results in harm or loss, or who otherwise promotes the act's accomplishment. See AID AND ABET. Cf. *causer liability.*

▸ **alternative liability.** (1929) Liability arising from the tortious acts of two or more parties — when the plaintiff proves that one of the defendants has caused harm but cannot prove which one caused it — resulting in a shifting of the burden of proof to each defendant. Restatement (Second) of Torts § 433B(3) (1965).

▸ **causer liability.** (1984) Civil or criminal liability imposed on the person whose acts resulted in harm or loss. Cf. *aiding-and-abetting liability.*

▸ **civil liability.** (1817) **1.** Liability imposed under the civil, as opposed to the criminal, law. **2.** The quality, state, or condition of being legally obligated for civil damages.

▸ **contingent liability.** (18c) A liability that will occur only if a specific event happens; a liability that depends on the occurrence of a future and uncertain event. • In financial statements, contingent liabilities are usu. stated in footnotes.

▸ **coordinate liability.** (2003) A common liability shared equally by two or more persons for one debt or sum, discharge of the debt by one giving rise to contribution rights.

▸ **corporate liability.** (1821) Liability incurred by a company as a result of certain acts of its members or officers.

▸ **current liability.** (1889) A business liability that will be paid or otherwise discharged with current assets or by creating other current liabilities within the next year (or operating cycle). — Also termed *short-term debt.*

▸ **derivative liability.** (1886) Liability for a wrong that a person other than the one wronged has a right to redress. • Examples include liability to a widow in a wrongful-death action and liability to a corporation in a shareholder's derivative suit.

▸ **enterprise liability.** (1941) **1.** A type of liability, inspired by workers' compensation, holding that business enterprises should be responsible for the injuries caused by their activities, regardless of fault or blameworthiness. *See, e.g.,* Howard C. Klemme, "The Enterprise Theory of Torts," 47 Colo. L. Rev. 153, 158 (1976) ("In its broadest terms the theory of enterprise liability in torts is that losses to society created or caused by an enterprise or, more precisely, by an activity, ought to be borne by that enterprise or activity."). **2.** The first collective theory of products liability, making each member of a small industry jointly liable when each is aware of the risks and has jointly controlled those risks. *See Hall v. E.I. DuPont De Neumours & Co.*, 345 F.Supp. 353 (E.D.N.Y. 1972). Cf. *market-share liability.* **3.** Liability imposed on each member of an industry responsible for manufacturing a harmful or defective product, allotted by each manufacturer's market share of the industry. — Also termed (in senses 1–3) *industry-wide liability.* See *market-share liability.* **4.** Criminal liability imposed on a business (such as a corporation or partnership) for certain offenses, such as public-welfare offenses or offenses for which the legislature specifically intended to impose criminal sanctions. *See* Model Penal Code § 2.07. See *public-welfare offense* under OFFENSE (2).

▸ **fault liability.** (1930) Liability based on some degree of blameworthiness. — Also termed *fault-based liability.* Cf. *strict liability.*

▸ **independent liability.** (1823) Liability arising from an individual's actions, unrelated to any other sources of liability.

▸ **industry-wide liability.** See *enterprise liability* (1)–(3).

▸ **innkeeper's liability.** (1828) The liability of a hotelier for loss of or damage to a guest's property when the loss is not caused by the guest, an act of nature, or civil unrest.

▸ **joint and several liability.** (1819) Liability that may be apportioned either among two or more parties or to only one or a few select members of the group, at the adversary's discretion. • Thus, each liable party is individually responsible for the entire obligation, but a paying party may have a right of contribution or indemnity from nonpaying parties. — Abbr. JSL. See *solidary liability.*

▸ **joint liability.** (18c) Liability shared by two or more parties.

▸ **liability in solido.** See *solidary liability.*

▸ **liability without fault.** See *strict liability.*

▸ **limited liability.** (1833) Liability restricted by law or contract; esp., the liability of a company's owners for nothing more than the capital they have invested in the business.

▸ **manufacturer liability.** See PRODUCTS LIABILITY.

▸ **market-share liability.** (1980) Liability that is imposed, usu. severally, on each member of an industry, based on each member's share of the market or respective percentage of the product that is placed on the market.

▸ **official liability.** Liability of an officer or receiver for a breach of contract or a tort committed during the officer's or receiver's tenure, but not involving any personal liability.

▸ **penal liability.** (1832) Liability arising from a proceeding intended at least partly to penalize a wrongdoer. Cf. *remedial liability.*

▸ **personal liability.** (18c) Liability for which one is personally accountable and for which a wronged party can seek satisfaction out of the wrongdoer's personal assets.

▸ **premises liability.** See PREMISES LIABILITY.

▸ **primary liability.** (1834) Liability for which one is directly responsible, as opposed to secondary liability.

▸ **products liability.** See PRODUCTS LIABILITY.

▸ **remedial liability.** (1919) Liability arising from a proceeding whose object contains no penal element. • The two types of proceedings giving rise to this liability are specific enforcement and restitution. Cf. *penal liability.*

▸ **secondary liability.** (1830) Liability that does not arise unless the primarily liable party fails to honor its obligation.

▸ **several liability.** (1819) Liability that is separate and distinct from another's liability, so that the plaintiff may bring a separate action against one defendant without joining the other liable parties.

▸ **shareholder's liability.** (1886) **1.** The statutory, added, or double liability of a shareholder for a corporation's debts, despite full payment for the stock. **2.** The liability of a shareholder for any unpaid stock listed as fully owned on the stock certificate, usu. occurring either when the shareholder agrees to pay full par value for the stock and obtains the certificate before the stock is paid for, or when partially paid-for stock is intentionally issued by a corporation as fully paid, the consideration for it being entirely fictitious. — Also termed *stockholder's liability.*

▸ **solidary liability** (**sol**-ə-dair-ee). (1921) *Civil law.* The liability of any one debtor among two or more joint debtors to pay the entire debt if the creditor so chooses. La. Civ. Code art. 1794. • This is equivalent to joint and several liability in the common law. — Also termed *liability in solido.* See *joint and several liability.*

▸ **statutory liability.** (1821) Liability that is created by a statute (or regulation) as opposed to common law.

▸ **stockholder's liability.** See *shareholder's liability.*

▸ **strict liability.** (1844) Liability that does not depend on proof of negligence or intent to do harm but that is based instead on a duty to compensate the harms proximately caused by the activity or behavior subject to the liability rule. • Prominent examples of strict liability involve the rules governing abnormally dangerous activities and the commercial distribution of defective products. — Also termed *liability without fault.* See *strict products liability* under PRODUCTS LIABILITY. Cf. *absolute liability*; *fault liability*; OUTCOME RESPONSIBILITY.

▸ **tortious liability.** (1894) Liability that arises from the breach of a duty that (1) is fixed by the law, (2) is categorical in nature and owed to any person who is within the scope of the duty, and (3) when breached, is redressable by an action for compensatory, unliquidated damages. • In some cases, tortious liability can also be redressed by extracompensatory or punitive damages.

▸ **vicarious liability** (vɪ-**kair**-ee-əs). (1875) Liability that a supervisory party (such as an employer) bears for the actionable conduct of a subordinate or associate (such as an employee) based on the relationship between the two parties. — Also termed *imputed liability.* See RESPONDEAT SUPERIOR.

"The vicarious liability of an employer for torts committed by employees should not be confused with the liability an employer has for his own torts. An employer whose employee commits a tort may be liable in his own right for negligence in hiring or supervising the employee. If in my business I hire a truck driver who has a record of drunk driving and on whom one day I detect the smell of bourbon, I (along with my employee) may be held liable for negligence if his driving causes injury. But that is not 'vicarious' liability—I am held liable for my own negligence in hiring that employee or letting him drive after I know he has been drinking." Kenneth S. Abraham, *The Forms and Functions of Tort Law* 166 (2002).

liability bond. See BOND (2).

liability dividend. See *scrip dividend* under DIVIDEND.

liability in solido. See *solidary liability* under LIABILITY.

liability insurance. See INSURANCE.

liability limit. (1915) *Insurance.* The maximum amount of coverage that an insurance company will provide on a single claim under an insurance policy. — Also termed *limit of liability*; *policy limits.*

liability release. See *general release* under RELEASE (8).

liability without fault. See *strict liability* under LIABILITY.

liable (**lɪ**-ə-bəl *also* **lɪ**-bəl), *adj.* (15c) **1.** Responsible or answerable in law; legally obligated. **2.** (Of a person) subject to or likely to incur (a fine, penalty, etc.). — Also termed *legally liable.* See LIABILITY. **3.** Likely to do or say something or to behave in a particular way, esp. because of a fault or natural tendency. **4.** Likely to be affected by a particular kind of problem.

liar's loan. See LOAN.

libel (**lɪ**-bəl), *n.* (14c) **1.** A defamatory statement expressed in a fixed medium, esp. writing but also a picture, sign, or electronic broadcast. • Libel is classified as both a crime and a tort but is no longer prosecuted as a crime. — Also termed *defamatory libel.* **2.** The act of making such a statement; the unprivileged publication of defamatory matter by written or printed words, by its embodiment in physical form or by any other form of communication that has the potentially harmful qualities characteristic of written or printed words. — Also termed (in senses 1 & 2) *written defamation.* See DEFAMATION. Cf. SLANDER.

"Everything printed or written which reflects on the character of another, and is published without lawful justification or excuse, is a libel, whatever the intention may have been. The words need not necessarily impute disgraceful conduct to the plaintiff; it is sufficient if they render him contemptible or ridiculous. Any written words are defamatory which impute to the plaintiff that he has been guilty of any crime, fraud, dishonesty, immorality, vice or dishonorable conduct, or has been accused or suspected of any such misconduct; or which suggest that the plaintiff is suffering from any infectious disorder; or which have a tendency to injure him in his office, profession, calling or trade. And so, too, are all words which hold the plaintiff up to contempt, hatred, scorn or ridicule, and which, by thus engendering an evil opinion of him in the minds of right-thinking men, tend to deprive him of friendly intercourse and society. It need not necessarily be in writing or printing. Any caricature or scandalous painting or effigy will constitute a libel; but it must be something permanent in its nature — not fleeting, as are spoken words." Martin L. Newell, *The Law of Defamation, Libel and Slander in Civil and Criminal Cases* 43 (1890).

"The distinction itself between libel and slander is not free from difficulty and uncertainty. As it took form in the seventeenth century, it was one between written and oral words. But later on libel was extended to include pictures, signs, statues, motion pictures, and even conduct carrying a defamatory imputation, such as hanging the plaintiff in effigy, erecting a gallows before his door, dishonoring his valid check drawn upon the defendant's bank, or even . . . following him over a considerable period in a conspicuous manner. From this it has been concluded that libel is that which is communicated by the sense of sight, or perhaps also by touch or smell, while slander is that which is conveyed by the sense of hearing." W. Page Keeton et al., *Prosser and Keeton on the Law of Torts* § 112, at 786 (5th ed. 1984).

"Libel is written or visual defamation; slander is oral or aural defamation." Robert D. Sack & Sandra S. Baron, *Libel, Slander, and Related Problems* § 2.3, at 67 (2d ed. 1994).

▸ **blasphemous libel.** (17c) *Hist. Criminal law.* The obsolete offense committed by one who vilified Jesus Christ, the Bible, the Christian religion, the Book of Common Prayer, or the Christian deity.

▸ **criminal libel.** (17c) At common law, a malicious libel that is designed to expose a person to hatred, contempt, or ridicule and that may subject the author to criminal sanctions. • Because of constitutional protections of free speech, libel is no longer criminally prosecuted.

▸ **false-implication libel.** Libel that creates a false implication or impression even though each statement in the article, taken separately, is true. See FALSE LIGHT; INVASION OF PRIVACY.

▸ **group libel.** (1940) Libel that defames a class of persons, esp. because of their race, sex, national origin, religious belief, or the like. • Civil liability for group libel is rare because the plaintiff must prove that the statement applied particularly to him or her. Cf. *hate speech* under COMMITTEE (1).

▸ **libel per quod** (pər **kwod**). (1927) **1.** Libel that is actionable only on allegation and proof of special damages. • Most jurisdictions do not recognize libel per quod, holding instead that general damages from libel are presumed. **2.** Libel in which the defamatory meaning is not apparent from the statement on its face but rather must be proved from extrinsic circumstances. See INNUENDO (2).

▸ **libel per se** (pər **say**). (1843) **1.** Libel that is actionable in itself, requiring no proof of special damages. • Most jurisdictions do not distinguish between libel per se and libel per quod, holding instead that general damages from libel are presumed. **2.** Libel that is defamatory on its face, such as the statement "Frank is a thief."

▸ **obscene libel.** (18c) *Hist.* **1.** The common-law crime of publishing, with the intent to corrupt, material (esp. sexual words or pictures) that tends to deprave or corrupt those whose minds are open to immoral influences. **2.** A writing, book, picture, or print that is so obscene that it shocks the public sense of decency.

▸ **seditious libel.** (16c) Libel made with the intent of inciting sedition. • Like other forms of criminal libel, seditious libel is no longer prosecuted. See SEDITION.

▸ **trade libel.** (1880) Trade defamation that is written or recorded. See *trade defamation* under DEFAMATION; DISPARAGEMENT (3). Cf. *trade slander* under SLANDER.

3. The complaint or initial pleading in an admiralty or ecclesiastical case. — Also termed (in sense 3) *libel of information.*

libel, *vb.* (16c) **1.** To defame (someone) in a permanent medium, esp. in writing. **2.** *Hist. Maritime law.* To sue in admiralty or ecclesiastical court. • This use of the term was eliminated with the merging of the Admiralty Rules into the Federal Rules of Civil Procedure in 1986.

libelant (**lɪ**-bəl-ənt). (16c) **1.** The party who institutes a suit in admiralty or ecclesiastical court by filing a libel. **2.** LIBELER. — Also spelled *libellant.*

libelee (lɪ-bəl-**ee**). (1856) The party against whom a libel has been filed in admiralty or ecclesiastical court. — Also spelled *libellee.*

libeler. (16c) Someone who publishes a written defamatory statement. — Also spelled *libeller.* — Also termed *libelant.*

libellary procedure (**lɪ**-bəl-er-ee). (1915) *Roman law.* The preliminary proceedings in a lawsuit, initiated by a plaintiff's written claims (in a *libellus*) to the magistrate.

libellos agere (lə-**bel**-əs **aj**-ə-ree), *vb.* [Latin] *Roman law.* To assist the emperor in responding to petitions. — Also termed *libellum agere.*

libellous, *adj.* See LIBELOUS.

libellus (lə-**bel**-əs), *n.* [Latin] **1.** *Roman law.* A small book; a written statement to a court; a petition. **2.** *Hist.* An instrument conveying all or part of land. **3.** Any one of a number of legal petitions or documents, such as a bill of complaint.

libellus accusatorius (lə-**bel**-əs ə-kyoo-zə-**tor**-ee-əs). [Latin] *Roman law.* A criminal accusation in writing.

libellus appellatorius (lə-**bel**-əs ə-pel-ə-**tor**-ee-əs). [Latin] *Roman law.* A written appeal in *cognitio* proceedings.

libellus conventionis (lə-**bel**-əs kən-ven-shee-**oh**-nis). [Latin] (1871) *Roman law.* The statement of a plaintiff's claim in a petition sent to the magistrate, who directs its delivery to the defendant.

> "The *libellus conventionis* was very like the *intentio* of the formulary system, and the modern statement of claim, since it set forth in a succinct manner the nature of the plaintiff's right and the circumstances attending its alleged violation." R.W. Leage, *Roman Private Law* 417 (C.H. Ziegler ed., 2d ed. 1930).

libellus divortii (lə-**bel**-əs di-**vor**-shee-ɪ). [Latin] *Roman law.* A bill of divorce. — In the later Roman Empire, also termed *libellus repudii.*

libellus famosus (lə-**bel**-əs fə-**moh**-səs). [Latin] (17c) *Roman law.* A defamatory publication.

> "Libellus famosus . . . . According to the *Lex Cornelia de iniuriis* punishment was inflicted on the person who wrote (*scripserit*), composed (*composuerit*) or edited (*ediderit*) such a lampoon, even if the publication was made under another name or anonymously (*sine nomine*)." Adolf Berger, *Encyclopedic Dictionary of Roman Law* 562 (1953).

libellus repudii (lə-**bel**-əs ri-**pyoo**-dee-ɪ). See LIBELLUS DIVORTII.

libellus rerum (lə-**bel**-əs **reer**-əm), *n.* [Latin] *Hist.* An inventory.

libellus supplex (lə-**bel**-əs **səp**-leks). [Latin] (1941) *Roman law.* A petition, esp. to the emperor. • All petitions to the emperor had to be in writing.

libel of accusation. (16c) *Scots law.* The instrument stating the criminal charge against an accused person.

libel of information. *Maritime law.* See LIBEL (3).

libel of review. (1839) *Maritime law.* A new proceeding attacking a final decree after the right to appeal has expired. See LIBEL (3).

libelous, *adj.* (17c) Constituting or involving libel; defamatory <a libelous newspaper story>. — Also spelled *libellous.*

libel per quod. See LIBEL.

libel per se. See LIBEL.

libel-proof, *adj.* (Of a reputation) so badly damaged as to be impervious to further harm from false statements.

libel tourism. (2004) The practice of evading media-friendly jurisdictions by suing for defamation in foreign courts in which plaintiffs are more likely to prevail.

liber (**lɪ**-bər), *adj.* [Latin "free"] **1.** (Of courts, public places, etc.) open and accessible. **2.** (Of a person) having the quality, state, or condition of a freeman. **3.** (Of a person) free from another's service or authority.

liber (**lɪ**-bər), *n.* [Latin "book"] **1.** A book of records, esp. of deeds. **2.** A main division of a literary or professional work.

libera batella (**lib**-ər-ə bə-**tel**-ə), *n.* [Latin "free boat"] (17c) *Hist.* The right to have a boat fish in certain waters; free fishery.

libera chasea habenda (**lib**-ər-ə **chay**-see-ə hə-**ben**-də), *n.* [Law Latin] (17c) *Hist.* A judicial writ granting a person the right to a free chase after game belonging to the person's manor, after the jury's verdict granting that right. See CHASE.

libera eleemosyna (**lib**-ər-ə el-ə-**mos**-ə-nə). See FRANKALMOIN.

libera falda (**lib**-ər-ə **fal**-də *or* **fawl**-də). See DE LIBERA FALDA.

liberal, *adj.* (14c) **1.** (Of a condition, state, opinion, etc.) not restricted; expansive; tolerant <liberal policies>. **2.** (Of a person or entity) advocating greater levels of social welfare through increased government spending, modern reforms in social policy, leniency toward the underprivileged, nontraditional individual rights, and moderate redistributions of wealth <liberal politicos>. Cf. CONSERVATIVE (1); PROGRESSIVE (1). **3.** (Of an act, etc.) generous <a liberal gift>. **4.** (Of an interpretation, construction, etc.) not strict or literal; loose <a liberal reading of the statute>.

liberal construction. See *liberal interpretation* under INTERPRETATION (1).

liberal constructionism. See CONSTRUCTIONISM.

liberal constructionist. See CONSTRUCTIONIST.

libera lex (**lib**-ər-ə **leks**), *n.* [Latin "free law"] (17c) *Hist.* Free law; the law of the land. • This phrase referred to the law enjoyed by free and lawful men, as opposed to men who had lost the benefit and protection of the law as a result of committing crimes. See LIBERAM LEGEM AMITTERE.

liberal interpretation. See INTERPRETATION (1).

liberalism. 1. Collectively, the principles or theories of those who are not bound by orthodox tenets, by established ideas in politics and religion, or by received opinion. **2.** The doctrine espoused by a liberal party, esp. on social and political issues. Cf. CONSERVATISM.

liberality, *n.* (14c) **1.** Formal understanding of and respect for other people's opinions; catholicity. **2.** The quality, state, or condition of being magnanimous and generous in giving, granting, or yielding; generosity. **3.** A gift or gratuity.

liberalize (**lib**-ə-rə-lɪz), *vb.* To make a system, laws, policies, or moral attitudes less strict, censorious, and rhadamanthine.

liberam legem amittere (**lib**-ər-əm **lee**-jəm ə-**mit**-ə-ree). [Latin] *Hist.* To lose one's free law. • This phrase refers to falling, by crime or infamy, from the status of *libera lex.* By what was known as a "villenous judgment," a person would be discredited as juror and witness, would forfeit goods and chattels and lands for life, would have his houses razed and trees uprooted, and would go to prison. This was the ancient punishment of a conspirator and of a party involved in a wager of battle who cried "craven." — Also termed *amittere liberam legem*; *amittere legem terrae* ("to lose the law of the land"). See VILLENOUS JUDGMENT.

libera piscaria (**lib**-ər-ə pis-**kair**-ee-ə). See *free fishery* under FISHERY (1).

liberare (lib-ə-**rair**-ee), *vb.* **1.** *Civil law.* To set (a person) free. **2.** *Hist.* To deliver or transfer (a writ, etc.).

liberari facias (lib-ə-**rair**-ee **fay**-shee-əs). [Law Latin "that you cause to be delivered"] (18c) *Hist.* A writ of execution ordering a sheriff to seize the debtor's unsalable real property and deliver it to the creditor to satisfy the creditor's claim. Cf. LEVARI FACIAS; FIERI FACIAS.

Liber Assisarum (**lɪ**-bər as-ɪ-**zair**-əm), *n.* [Law Latin "Book of Assizes"] *Hist.* A collection of cases arising in assizes and other country trials. • It was the fourth volume of the reports of the reign of Edward III.

liberate (lib-ə-**ray**-tee), *n.* [Law Latin] (15c) *Hist.* **1.** A chancery writ to the Exchequer ordering the payment of an annual pension or other sum. **2.** A writ to the sheriff authorizing delivery of any property given as bond and then taken when a defendant forfeited a recognizance. **3.** A writ to a jailer ordering delivery of a prisoner who had paid bail. **4.** A writ to a sheriff commanding him to deliver to the plaintiff lands or goods pledged as part of a commercial trade loan arrangement (a statute staple) available in certain merchant towns in England. • If a debtor defaulted on this obligation, the creditor could obtain a writ of extent, which directed the sheriff to take an inventory and entitled the creditor to keep the debtor's property for a time until the rentals on the property equaled the amount due. The writ of *liberate* was issued after the inventory had been performed under the writ of extent. See EXTENT; STAPLE (1), (2).

liberate, *vb.* (17c) To free (prisoners, a city, a country, etc.) from someone's control; esp., to set (a person) free, as from slavery, bondage, or hostile control.

liberatio (lib-ə-**ray**-shee-oh), *n.* [Law Latin] *Hist.* Money paid for the delivery or use of a thing; a payment.

liberatio legata (lib-ə-**ray**-shee-oh lə-**gay**-tə). See LEGATUM LIBERATIONIS.

liberation. (15c) **1.** The act or an instance of freeing someone or something. **2.** *Civil law.* Final payment under a contract, thereby extinguishing the debt.

liberation movement. (1843) *Int'l law.* An organized effort to achieve the political independence of a particular country or people.

liberatio nominis (lib-ə-**ray**-shee-oh **nahm**-ə-nis). [Latin] *Roman law.* The discharge of a debt.

liberative, *adj.* (18c) Serving or tending to free or release.

liberative prescription. See PRESCRIPTION.

Liber Authenticae. See AUTHENTICUM (2).

Liber Authenticorum (**lɪ**-bər aw-then-tə-**kor**-əm). [Latin] *Roman law.* A translated, unabridged collection of Justinian's Greek Novels, assembled between A.D. 535 and 556. • This collection is distinguished from the similar work, the *Epitome Juliani.* — Also termed *Authenticum.*

libera warrena (**lib**-ər-ə wor-**ee**-nə). See *free warren* under WARREN.

liber bancus (**lɪ**-bər **bang**-kəs). See FREE BENCH.

liber et legalis homo (**lɪ**-bər et lə-**gay**-lis). See LEGALIS HOMO.

liberi (**lib**-ər-ɪ), *n. pl.* [Latin] *Roman law.* **1.** Children. **2.** Descendants. • In the praetorian rules of intestate succession, *liberi* were the first rank of claimants, comprising the *sui heredes* of the Twelve Tables, and some others, such as emancipated children. Cf. LEGITIMI HEREDES.

liberis nascituris (**lib**-ər-is nas-ə-**t[y]uur**-is). [Latin] *Hist.* To children yet to be born. • The phrase usu. referred to designations made in marriage contracts.

liber iudiciorum. See LEX VISIGOTHORUM.

liber judicialis of Alfred (lɪ-bər joo-dish-ee-**ay**-lis), *n.* [Law Latin] See DOOMBOOK.

liber niger (**lɪ**-bər **nɪ**-jər), *n.* [Latin "black book"] (17c) *Hist.* An ancient record, such as the register in the Exchequer and the register of charters of abbeys and cathedrals.

Liber Niger Parvus (**lɪ**-bər **nɪ**-jər **pahr**-vəs). See BLACK BOOK OF THE EXCHEQUER.

liber ruber scaccarii (**lɪ**-bər **roo**-bər skə-**kair**-ee-ɪ), *n.* [Law Latin] (18c) *Hist.* Red book of the Exchequer. • This was an ancient register of the names of those holding land *per baroniam* during the reign of Henry II.

libertarian, *n.* Someone who strongly believes that people should be free to do and think as they please without any governmental interference. — **libertarian,** *adj.*

libertas (li-**bər**-tas *or* **lib**-ər-tas), *n.* [Latin "liberty, freedom"] *Hist.* A privilege or franchise.

libertas ecclesiastica (li-**bər**-tas e-klee-z[h]ee-**as**-ti-kə), *n.* [Law Latin "church liberty"] *Hist.* Immunity from secular law, enjoyed by the church and the clergy, who are subject to ecclesiastical law. • This immunity was created in Magna Carta (1215).

libertatibus allocandis (lib-ər-**tay**-tə-bəs al-ə-**kan**-dis). See DE LIBERTATIBUS ALLOCANDIS.

libertatibus exigendis in itinere (lib-ər-**tay**-tə-bəs ek-sə-**jen**-dis in ɪ-**tin**-ə-ree), *n.* [Latin] (17c) *Hist.* A writ from the king to one of a panel of itinerant judges (the justices in eyre) ordering them to admit an attorney to represent a criminal defendant. See EYRE.

liberti (li-**bər**-tɪ), *n. pl.* [Latin] *Roman law.* Manumitted slaves, considered in their relation with their former masters, who were known as *patrons.* Cf. INGENUUS; LIBERTINI.

liberticide (lə-**bər**-tə-sɪd), *n.* (18c) **1.** The destruction of liberty. **2.** A destroyer of liberty. — **liberticidal,** *adj.*

liberties. (15c) *Hist.* **1.** Privileged districts exempt from the sheriff's jurisdiction. **2.** In American colonial times, laws. **3.** Political subdivisions of Philadelphia.

libertini (lib-ər-**tɪ**-nɪ), *n. pl.* [Latin] *Roman law.* See LATINI JUNIANI.

liberty. (14c) **1.** Freedom from arbitrary or undue external restraint, esp. by a government <give me liberty or give me death>. **2.** A right, privilege, or immunity enjoyed by prescription or by grant; the absence of a legal duty imposed on a person <the liberties protected by the Constitution>. — Also termed *legal liberty.*

"[Liberty] denotes not merely freedom from bodily restraint but also the right of the individual to contract, to engage in any of the common occupations of life, to acquire useful knowledge, to marry, establish a home and bring up children, to worship God according to the dictates of his own conscience, and generally to enjoy those privileges long recognized at common law as essential to the orderly pursuit of happiness by free men." *Meyer v. Nebraska,* 262 U.S. 390, 399, 43 S.Ct. 625, 626 (1923).

"The word *liberty* has become a symbol around which have clung some of the most generous human emotions. We have been brought up to thrill with admiration at the men who say, Give me liberty or give me death. But the philosopher asks whether all those who are devoted to liberty mean the same thing. Does liberty or freedom, for instance, involve free trade? Does it involve freedom to preach race hatred or the overthrow of all that we regard as sacred? Many who believe in liberty characterize the freedom which they are not willing to grant, as license, and they do it so often that one may be inclined to think that what we really need is less liberty and more license. Moreover, there is a confusion between the absence of legal restraint and the presence of real freedom as positive power to do what we want. The legal freedom to earn a million dollars is not worth a cent to one who has no real opportunity. It is fashionable to assert that men want freedom above all other things, but a strong case may be made out for the direct contrary. Absolute freedom is just what people do not want . . . ." Morris R. Cohen, *Reason and Law* 101–02 (1961).

"A liberty, as that word will be used in the following discussion, means any occasion on which an act or omission is not a breach of duty. When I get up in the morning, dress, take breakfast, and so on, I am exercising liberties, because I do not commit legal wrongs. Since the commission of legal wrongs is relatively infrequent, almost every act is the exercise of a liberty. An example of a liberty appearing in legal works is the defense of privilege in defamation; also the (more or less) general defenses in tort, such as consent, necessity, private defense, and statutory authority. When a person has a substantive defense in law to an action or prosecution, that is to say a legal defense on the merits, he has a liberty, i.e., the conduct of which complaint is made is not a breach of duty. This is not necessarily true of a merely procedural or adjectival defense. The defense under statutes of limitation, for example, generally does not deny the duty, but alleges that the duty has become unenforceable through lapse of time. Several other unenforceable duties are known to the law. Except in the case of these unenforceable duties or other procedural objections it is true to say that a successful objection in point of law to a claim involves the assertion of a liberty." Glanville Williams, "The Concept of Legal Liberty," in *Essays in Legal Philosophy* 121, 121–22 (Robert S. Summers ed., 1968).

▸ **civil liberty.** See CIVIL LIBERTY.

▸ **individual liberty.** See *personal liberty.*

▸ **natural liberty.** (16c) The power to act as one wishes, without any restraint or control, unless by nature.

"This natural liberty . . . being a right inherent in us by birth . . . . But every man, when he enters into society, gives up a part of his natural liberty, as the price of so valuable a purchase; and, in consideration of receiving the advantages of mutual commerce, obliges himself to conform to those laws, which the community has thought proper to establish." 1 William Blackstone, *Commentaries on the Laws of England* 121 (1765).

▸ **personal liberty.** (16c) One's freedom to do as one pleases, limited only by the government's right to regulate the public health, safety, and welfare. — Also termed *individual liberty.*

"[T]here is another invention . . . also peculiar to the Anglo-Saxon people; that is, the invention or the idea of personal liberty; which is understood, and has always been understood, by Anglo-Saxons in a sense in which it never existed before, so far as I know, in any people in the history of the world. It is that notion of personal liberty which was the cause of representative government, not representative government that was the cause of personal liberty. In other words, the people did not get up a parliament for the sake of having that parliament enact laws securing personal liberty. It was the result of a condition of personal liberty which prevailed among them and in their laws that resulted in representative government, and in the institution of a legislature, making, as we now would say, the laws; though a thousand years ago they never said that a legislature *made* laws, they only said that it *told what the laws were.*" Frederic Jesup Stimson, *Popular Law-Making* 3 (1910).

"The right of personal liberty consists in the power of locomotion, of changing situation, or moving one's person to whatsoever place one's own inclination may direct, without imprisonment or restraint, unless by due course of law." Harvey Cortlandt Voorhees, *The Law of Arrest in Civil and Criminal Actions* 1 (2d ed. 1915).

▸ **political liberty.** (17c) A person's freedom to participate in the operation of government, esp. in elections and in the making and administration of laws.

▸ **religious liberty.** (17c) Freedom — as guaranteed by the First Amendment — to express, without external control other than one's own conscience, any or no system of religious opinion and to engage in or refrain from any form of religious observance or public or private religious worship, as long as it is consistent with the peace and order of society.

"A thing that we forget is that political liberty is a product, almost a by-product, of religious liberty. The theory of civil rights that we know is common to the history of Europe and America, and found its political expression in the 1581 Proclamation of the States-General of the Netherlands deposing Philip II of Spain, in the English Declaration of Right of 1689 and in the American Declaration of Independence of 1776. Yet this theory is the direct outcome of the religious struggles of the seventeenth century. It is not that, even if there had never been those struggles, men would not have had just the same their bitter controversies as to the seat and distribution of political power. For certain they would have. But it is not likely that such controversies would then have taken the same direction." Lord Radcliffe, *The Law and Its Compass* 70–71 (1960).

"There has always been a degree of tension in the American formula for religious liberty. It stems, in part, from two seemingly contrary notions: on the one hand, the civil equality of all religions, and, on the other hand, the belief that the state has a vested interest in a religiously based society. The seeds of this ambiguity were evident throughout the greater part of the colonial era." H. Frank Way, "Religious Liberty," in 3 *Encyclopedia of the American Judicial System* 1212 (Robert J. Janosik ed., 1987).

Liberty Clause. (1971) *Constitutional law.* The Due Process Clause in the 14th Amendment to the U.S. Constitution. See DUE PROCESS CLAUSE.

liberty interest. See INTEREST (2).

liberty not. See NO-DUTY.

liberty of a port. (1842) *Marine insurance.* A license incorporated in a marine policy allowing the vessel to dock and trade at a designated port other than the principal port of destination.

liberty of contract. See FREEDOM OF CONTRACT.

liberty of speech. See FREEDOM OF SPEECH.

liberty of the globe. (1844) *Marine insurance.* A license incorporated in a marine policy authorizing the vessel to go to any part of the world, rather than be confined to a particular port of destination.

liberty of the press. See FREEDOM OF THE PRESS.

liberum maritagium (**lib**-ər-əm mar-ə-**tay**-jee-əm). See FRANKMARRIAGE.

liberum servitium (**lib**-ər-əm sər-**vish**-ee-əm), *n.* [Law Latin] See SERVITIUM LIBERUM.

liberum socagium (**lib**-ər-əm sok-**ay**-jee-əm), *n.* [Law Latin] See *free socage* under SOCAGE.

liberum tenementum (**lib**-ər-əm ten-ə-**men**-təm), *n.* [Law Latin] (17c) *Hist.* **1.** A plea of freehold; a defensive common-law pleading in an action for trespass to lands. • The defendant pleaded either ownership of the land in question or authorization from the freehold owner. **2.** FREEHOLD.

liberum veto (**lib**-ər-əm **vee**-toh). [Latin] *Hist.* Free veto. See VETO.

LIBOR. *abbr.* LONDON INTERBANK OFFERED RATE.

libra (**lɪ**-brə), *n.* [Latin] (14c) *Hist.* An English pound; a sum of money equal to a pound sterling. Pl. ***librae.***

▸ ***libra arsa*** (**lɪ**-brə **ahr**-sə), *n.* [Law Latin] *Hist.* A pound melted to test its purity.

▸ ***libra numerata*** (**lɪ**-brə n[y]oo-mə-**ray**-tə), *n.* [Law Latin] *Hist.* A pound of money that has been counted.

▸ ***libra pensa*** (**lɪ**-brə **pen**-sə), *n.* [Law Latin] *Hist.* A pound of money by weight.

librarian. *Parliamentary law.* An officer charged with custody of an organization's books, periodicals, and other published matter, and sometimes of the organization's own archives and files as well.

Library of Congress. A library on the U.S. Capitol grounds responsible for conducting research for members of Congress and congressional committees. • The Library maintains collections of materials that in many areas are the world's most extensive. Headed by a librarian appointed by the President with the advice and consent of the Senate, it was established in 1860. 2 USCA §§ 131 et seq. — Abbr. LOC.

Libri Feudorum. A 12th-century compilation of the feudal customs that governed fiefs in Lombardy, northern Italy. • The text was supplemented in later centuries by scholars who wrote commentaries, interpretations, and glosses. Cf. LOMBARD LAW.

libripens (**lib**-rə-penz), *n.* [Latin] *Roman law.* Someone who holds a bronze balance during actual or ritual sales, such as the ceremonies of emancipating a son from his father or conveying important property; a scale-holder. • The purchaser strikes the balance with a piece of bronze to symbolize completion of the sale. The seller then receives the bronze as a sign of the purchase money. See MANCIPATION.

liceity. (lI-**say**-ə-tee or li-) *Eccles. law.* The legality of an act, esp. of a sacrament. • Liceity is distinguished from validity in ecclesiastical law. Although an act or some part of it may be illegal, its performance or effects may be valid. For example, Roman Catholic law requires that the Eucharist be celebrated with unleavened wheat bread. If leavened bread is used, the bread would be an illegal substance, but the sacrament's validity would not be affected.

license, *n.* (15c) **1.** A privilege granted by a state or city upon the payment of a fee, the recipient of the privilege then being authorized to do some act or series of acts that would otherwise be impermissible. • A license in this sense is a method of governmental regulation exercised under the police power, as with a license to drive a car, operate a taxi service, keep a dog in the city, or sell crafts as a street vendor. — Also termed *permit.* **2.** A permission, usu. revocable, to commit some act that would otherwise be unlawful; esp., an agreement (not amounting to a lease or profit à prendre) that it is lawful for the licensee to enter the licensor's land to do some act that would otherwise be illegal, such as hunting game. See SERVITUDE (1).

"[A] license is an authority to do a particular act, or series of acts, upon another's land, without possessing any estate therein. It is founded in personal confidence, and is not assignable, nor within the statute of frauds." 2 James Kent, *Commentaries on American Law* *452–53 (George Comstock ed., 11th ed. 1866).

3. The certificate or document evidencing such permission. — **license,** *vb.*

▸ **artistic license.** (1998) An open-source license that prohibits the sale of modified software unless it is included in a package with other software.

▸ **bare license.** (17c) A license in which no property interest passes to the licensee, who is merely not a trespasser. • It is revocable at will. — Also termed *naked license*; *mere license*.

▸ **blanket license.** (1929) *Copyright.* A license granted by a performing-rights society, such as ASCAP or BMI, to use all works in the society's portfolio in exchange for a fixed percentage of the user's revenues.

▸ **box-top license.** See *shrinkwrap license*.

▸ **broadcast license.** (1931) A government-issued license granting the licensee permission to use part of the radio-frequency spectrum in a given geographical area for purposes of providing radio or television programs. — Also termed *broadcasting license*.

▸ **BSD license.** (1993) A form of open-source license that allows users to incorporate the source code into proprietary products as long as the names of the original creator or contributors are not used to endorse or promote the products without permission. • It was originally created for the Berkeley Software Distribution operating system developed at the University of California. — Also termed *BSD-style license*.

▸ **clickwrap license.** See POINT-AND-CLICK AGREEMENT.

▸ **compulsory license.** (1908) **1.** *Copyright.* A statutorily created license that allows certain parties to use copyrighted material without the explicit permission of the copyright owner in exchange for a specified royalty. — Also termed *equitable remuneration.* **2.** *Patents.* A statutorily created license that allows certain people to pay a royalty and use an invention without the patentee's permission. • While some countries currently recognize compulsory licenses, the United States never has.

▸ **conditional license.** See *provisional license* (1).

▸ **cross-license.** (1899) *Patents.* An agreement between two or more patentees to exchange licenses for their mutual benefit and use of the licensed products.

▸ **distribution license.** (1941) A marketing license, usu. limited by geography.

▸ **exclusive license.** (18c) A license that gives the licensee the sole right to perform the licensed act, often in a defined territory, and that prohibits the licensor from performing the licensed act and from granting the right to anyone else; esp., such a license of a copyright, patent, or trademark right.

▸ **general-public license.** See *open-source license*.

▸ **implied license.** (1815) A royalty-free license arising from a property owner's conduct regarding another person's use of the property even though the owner has not expressly consented to the property's use. • In a patent context, for example, the circumstances surrounding the conduct give rise to an affirmative grant of consent or permission to infringe a patent's claims. For example, the conduct of a patentee who encourages the manufacture of infringing products may be construed as an implied license to use the patent. An implied license may also arise when a patentee authorizes the sale or express grant of a license to a buyer, who then resells the license to a third party; the third party is the patentee's implied licensee.

▸ **implied license by acquiescence.** (1943) An implied license that arises from the patentee's tacit or passive acceptance of or implied consent to an otherwise infringing act.

▸ **implied license by conduct.** (1998) An implied license based on the patentee's course of conduct, including language, from which another person could properly infer that the patentee consented to the other's use of the patent. See *implied license by equitable estoppel*; *implied license by legal estoppel*.

▸ **implied license by equitable estoppel.** (1975) An implied license usu. based on the patentee's failure to take timely action to enforce patent rights against an infringer after objecting to the infringer's actions, thereby misleading the infringer to believe that the patentee will not act. *See A.C. Aukerman Co. v. R.L. Chaides Constr. Co.*, 960 F.2d 1020, 1042–43 (Fed. Cir.1992).

▸ **implied license by legal estoppel.** (1993) An implied license usu. based on the patentee's broadcast grant of a right or interest that cannot be derogated by the patentee's later acts.

▸ **irrevocable license.** (1836) A license that cannot be terminated for any reason.

▸ **label license.** (1969) A notice on an item's package granting the purchaser a license to practice the process by using the item without additional payments to the licensor.

▸ **license coupled with an interest.** (1836) An irrevocable license in real estate that confers the right (not the mere permission) to perform an act or acts on the property; esp., a license incidental to the ownership of an interest in a chattel located on the land with respect to which the license exists. • This type of license is considered an interest in the land itself. An injunction may be obtained to prevent the wrongful revocation of such a license. — Also termed *license coupled with the grant of an interest*.

"A licence may be coupled with some interest in the land or chattels thereon. Thus the right to enter another man's land to hunt and take away the deer killed, or to cut down a tree and remove it, involves the grant of an interest in the deer or tree and also a licence annexed to it to come on the land. The interest must be a recognised interest in the property, and it must have been validly created. Thus at law a right to take game or minerals, being a *profit à prendre*, must have been created by deed or prescription, whereas no formalities are required for the grant of a right to take away chattels, such as felled or cut hay. Equity will give effect to a specifically enforceable agreement to grant an interest, so that a licence coupled with a *profit à prendre* granted merely in writing but for value may be protected by injunction." Robert E. Megarry & M.P. Thompson, *A Manual of the Law of Real Property* 428 (6th ed. 1993).

▸ **limited license.** (1902) A license that is narrow in scope or narrower than another license granted for the same purpose, or a license subject to conditions or limitations.

▸ **mechanical license.** (1949) A grant of the right to produce and release a copyrighted work in exchange for a royalty based on the number of units manufactured and sold.

▸ **mere license.** See *bare license.*

▸ **Mozilla public license.** (1998) An open-source license that allows software users to modify and publicly distribute the software, but requires users to release the changed software under the same copyright as the original source code, and to release all claims to patent rights. • The Mozilla public license was developed for the Netscape and Netscape Communicator browsers but is not limited to use with them. — Abbr. MPL.

▸ **naked license.** (1831) **1.** A license allowing a licensee to use a trademark on any goods and services the licensee chooses. **2.** See *bare license.*

▸ **nonexclusive license.** (1890) A license of intellectual-property rights that gives the licensee a right to use, make, or sell the licensed item on a shared basis with the licensor and possibly other licensees.

▸ **nonmetered license.** (2012) *Patents.* An agreement to allow a patent's use in exchange for a flat percentage of sales, regardless of how much the patent is actually used. • The Supreme Court rejected a nonmetered license as patent misuse, saying that the buyer has a right to insist on paying only for actual use. *Zenith Radio Co. v. Hazeltine Research, Inc.*, 395 U.S. 100, 89 S.Ct. 1562 (1969). See PATENT-MISUSE DOCTRINE.

▸ **off-sale license.** (1933) A state-issued permit to sell alcoholic beverages that, usu. while in their sealed containers, may be taken away from and consumed off the premises. — Also termed *off-premises license.* Cf. *on-sale license.*

▸ **on-sale license.** (1946) A state-issued permit to sell alcoholic beverages to be consumed on the premises only. — Also termed *on-premises license.* Cf. *off-sale license.*

▸ **open-source license.** (1998) A license that allows open-source software users to copy, distribute, or modify the source code, and publicly distribute derived works based on the source code. • Open-source licenses usu. do not require royalty or other fees on distribution. The license typically requires a user who redistributes original or modified software that was received under an open-source license to provide the original license terms, including all disclaimers, to all future users, and to distribute the source code with any machine-executable software. It is unclear who has the right or power to enforce the terms of an open-source license. — Sometimes termed *general-public license.*

▸ **proprietary license.** (1985) A license that restricts a software user's ability to copy, distribute, or modify the software.

▸ **provisional license. 1.** A license granted only with express restrictions or conditions. **2.** LEARNER'S PERMIT.

▸ **shrinkwrap license.** (1984) A license printed on the outside of a package wrapper, esp. a software package, to advise the buyer that by opening the package, the buyer becomes legally bound to abide by the terms of the license. • Shrink-wrap licenses usu. seek to (1) prohibit users from making unauthorized copies of the software, (2) prohibit modifications to the software, (3) limit use of the software to one computer, (4) limit the manufacturer's liability, and (5) disclaim warranties. — Also written *shrink-wrap license.* — Also termed *box-top license*; *tear-me-open license*; *shrinkwrap agreement.* See POINT-AND-CLICK AGREEMENT.

▸ **site license.** (1982) *Copyright.* A software license that allows a company to install a set number of copies on individual computers within the company.

▸ **synchronization license.** (1981) A license to reproduce and synchronize a copyrighted musical composition with visual images that are not covered by the musical work's copyright. • Synchronization rights are commonly associated with audiovisual productions, such as music videos or movies.

▸ **tear-me-open license.** See *shrinkwrap license.*

▸ **use-based license.** (1998) An open-source software license to which the user assents by acting according to the license's terms, namely by using, modifying, or distributing the licensed software. • Unlike a point-and-click agreement, the user does not have to expressly declare acceptance of the license terms before using the software.

license bond. See BOND (2).

license coupled with the grant of an interest. See *license coupled with an interest* under LICENSE.

licensed, *adj.* Having official permission to do something, usu. as evidenced by a written certificate.

licensee. (1864) **1.** One to whom a license is granted; someone who has official permission to do something. **2.** Someone who has permission to enter or use another's premises, but only for one's own purposes and not for the occupier's benefit. • The occupier has a duty to warn the licensee of any dangerous conditions known to the occupier but unknown to the licensee. An example of a licensee is a social guest. Cf. INVITEE; TRESPASSER.

▸ **bare licensee.** (1864) A licensee whose presence on the premises the occupier tolerates but does not necessarily approve, such as one who takes a shortcut across another's land. — Also termed *naked licensee*; *mere licensee.*

▸ **licensee by invitation.** (1894) Someone who is expressly or impliedly permitted to enter another's premises to transact business with the owner or occupant or to perform an act benefiting the owner or occupant.

▸ **licensee by permission.** (1894) Someone who has the owner's permission or passive consent to enter the owner's premises for one's own convenience, curiosity, or entertainment.

▸ **licensee with an interest.** See INVITEE.

▸ **mere licensee.** See *bare licensee.*

▸ **naked licensee.** See *bare licensee.*

license fee. (1836) **1.** A monetary charge imposed by a governmental authority for the privilege of pursuing a particular occupation, business, or activity. — Also termed *license tax.* **2.** A charge of this type accompanied by a requirement that the licensee take some action, or be subjected to regulations or restrictions.

license in amortization. *Hist.* A license authorizing the conveyance of property otherwise invalid under the statutes of mortmain. See MORTMAIN.

license plate. 1. A sign with numbers on it at the front and back of a car. — Also termed (BrE) *number plate.* **2.** LICENCE-PLATE NUMBER.

license-plate number. (1917) The official set of numbers and letters shown on the front and back of a vehicle on the license plate. — Also termed (BrE) *registration number.*

licenser. See LICENSOR.

license tax. See LICENSE FEE (1).

licensing. (15c) **1.** The sale of a license authorizing another to use something (such as computer software) protected by copyright, patent, or trademark. **2.** A governmental body's process of issuing a license. — Also termed *licensure.*

licensing laws. The laws that state where and when people or businesses can sell alcohol.

licensor. (17c) Someone who grants a license to another. — Also spelled *licenser.*

licensure. See LICENSING (2).

licentia (li-**sen**-shee-ə), *n.* [fr. Latin *licere* "to be lawful"] *Hist.* License; permission.

licentia concordandi (li-**sen**-shee-ə kon-kor-**dan**-dɪ), *n.* [Law Latin "license to agree"] (17c) *Hist.* One of the proceedings on levying a fine of lands. See CONGÉ D'ACCORDER.

> "The *licentia concordandi*, or leave to agree the suit. For, as soon as the action is brought, the defendant knowing himself to be in the wrong, is supposed to make overtures of peace and accommodation to the plaintiff. Who, accepting them, but having, upon suing out the writ, given pledges to prosecute his suit, which he endangers if he now deserts it without license, he therefore applies to the court for leave to make the matter up." 2 William Blackstone, *Commentaries on the Laws of England* 350 (1766).

licentia loquendi (li-**sen**-shee-ə loh-**kwen**-dɪ). [Latin "license to speak"] See IMPARLANCE.

licentia surgendi (li-**sen**-shee-ə sər-**jen**-dɪ), *n.* [Law Latin "license to arise"] (17c) *Hist.* Permission or writ from the court to a tenant in a real action to get out of bed and appear in court, following the tenant's earlier plea of inability to appear because of illness that confined the tenant to bed. • The tenant could lose the case by default for falsely claiming illness. See DE MALO; ESSOIN.

licentiate (lɪ-**sen**-shee-ət), *n.* (16c) Someone who has obtained a license or authoritative permission to exercise some function, esp. to practice a profession <a licentiate in law should be held to high ethical standards>.

licentia transfretandi. See DE LICENTIA TRANSFRETANDI.

licentious (lɪ-**sen**-shəs), *adj.* (16c) Lacking or ignoring moral or legal restraint, esp. in sexual activity; lewd; lascivious. — **licentiousness,** *n.*

licere (li-**seer**-ee), *vb.* [Latin] *Roman law.* To be allowed by law. • The stipulation *habere licere* guaranteed the buyer indemnity from eviction.

liceri. See LICITARI.

licet (**lɪ**-set *or* **lis**-ət). [Latin] *Hist.* **1.** It is permitted; it is lawful. **2.** It is conceded; it is granted.

licit (**lis**-it), *adj.* (15c) Not forbidden by law; permitted; legal. — **licitly,** *adv.*

licitari (lis-ə-**tair**-ee), *vb.* [Latin] *Roman law.* To bid for an item, esp. repeatedly during the same sale. — Also termed *liceri.*

licitation (lis-ə-**tay**-shən). (17c) **1.** The offering for sale or bidding for purchase at an auction; esp., in civil law, a judicial sale of property held in common. See La. Civ. Code art. 811. **2.** CANT.

licitator (lis-ə-**tay**-tər), *n.* [Latin] (17c) *Roman law.* The bidder at a sale.

lictor (**lik**-tər), *n.* [Latin] (14c) *Roman law.* An officer who accompanied a magistrate having *imperium* and traditionally carried a bundle of rods and an ax, symbolizing the magistrate's powers of life and death and of corporal punishment over citizens. See IMPERIUM.

Lidford law (**lid**-fərd). (17c) *Hist.* A form of lynch law permitting a person to be punished first and tried later. • The term took its name from the English town of Lidford (now Lydford) where this type of action supposedly took place. See LYNCH LAW. Cf. *Jedburgh justice* under JUSTICE (4).

lie, *n.* A false statement or other indication that is made with knowledge of its falsity; an untruthful communication intended to deceive. See FIB.

> "To tell a lie is to address a false statement to another person knowing that it is false or not believing that it is true, or being reckless as to its truth or falsity. The circumstances must be such that the other person regards the statement as seriously made (not in jest, or in a game of 'let's pretend' or in the context of some form of openly acknowledged fiction, or in a context in which the addressee's interest in the matter is wholly illegitimate). Indeed, the speaker must intend the statement seriously, or at least realize that the addressee or addressees will reasonably assume that it is being made seriously." Neil MacCormick, *Practical Reason in Law and Morality* 69 (2008).

▸ **baldfaced lie.** An outright lie of some seriousness told with no sense of hesitation or reluctance, but instead with a conviction intended to induce belief among listeners or readers. — Often erroneously termed *boldfaced lie; boldface lie.*

▸ **proleptic lie.** (2009) A false statement that one has already done what ought to have been done or what one intends shortly to do.

▸ **white lie.** A harmless falsehood, esp. one uttered to avoid doing harm (such as offending or embarrassing someone).

lie, *vb.* (bef. 12c) **1.** To tell an untruth; to speak or write falsely <she lied on the witness stand>. See PERJURY. Cf. FABRICATE. **2.** To have foundation in the law; to be legally supportable, sustainable, or proper <in such a situation, an action lies in tort>. **3.** To exist; to reside <final appeal lies with the Supreme Court>.

lie-and-buy, *n.* (1995) *Criminal law. Slang.* The making of a false statement during, or in relation to, the purchase of something, esp. a firearm.

Lieber Code. A codification of rules and customs of warfare, which set out the humane and ethical treatment of persons. • It was first developed by Francis Lieber during the American Revolution, formally adopted as law by Abraham Lincoln during the Civil War, and used as the basis for the first codified international rules of law at The Hague Peace Conference of 1899. The rules were extended and refined in another Hague convention in

1907, and became known as the Law of The Hague. See GENEVA CONVENTIONS OF 1949; LAW OF THE HAGUE.

lie detector. See POLYGRAPH.

liege (leej), *adj.* (14c) *Hist.* **1.** Entitled to feudal allegiance and service. **2.** Bound by feudal tenure to a lord paramount; owing allegiance and service. **3.** Loyal; faithful. — Also termed *ligius.*

liege, *n.* (14c) *Hist.* **1.** A vassal bound to feudal allegiance. — Also termed *liege man; liege woman.* **2.** A loyal subject of a monarch or other sovereign. **3.** A feudal lord entitled to allegiance and service; a sovereign or superior lord. — Also termed (in sense 3) *liege lord.*

liegeance. See LIGEANCE.

liege homage, *n.* (14c) *Hist.* Homage paid by one sovereign to another, including pledges of loyalty and services.

liege lord, *n. Hist.* See LIEGE (3).

liege man, *n. Hist.* See LIEGE (1).

liege poustie (leej pow-stee). [Law French "liege power" fr. Latin *legitima potestas* "lawful power"] (17c) *Scots law.* The lawful power of one in good health, as a result of which the person might dispose of heritable property. • The phrase often appeared attributively, as in *liege poustie conveyance.* See IN LECTO AEGRITUDINIS. Cf. LEGITIMA POTESTAS.

> "LIEGE POUSTIE; is that state of health which gives a person full power to dispose *mortis causa,* or otherwise, of his heritable property. The term, according to our institutional writers, is derived from the words *legitima potestas,* signifying the lawful power of disposing of property at pleasure. It is used in contradistinction to *deathbed* — a *liege poustie* conveyance being a conveyance not challengeable on the head of deathbed . . . . The tests of *liege poustie,* opposed to the presumption of deathbed, are survivance during sixty days, and going to kirk or market unsupported." William Bell, *Bell's Dictionary and Digest of the Law of Scotland* 662 (George Watson ed., 7th ed. 1890).

> "[A] *liege poustie* conveyance being one not challengeable by the heir on the ground of death-bed. This condition of health the granter of a deed was held to have enjoyed, if at the time of granting it he was not affected by the disease of which he died, or if, after executing it, he attended kirk or market, unsupported, or survived for sixty days." John Trayner, *Trayner's Latin Maxims* 329 (4th ed. 1894).

lieger, *n. Archaic.* See LEDGER (2).

liege subject. See *natural-born subject* under SUBJECT (1).

liege woman, *n. Hist.* See LIEGE (1).

lie in franchise, *vb.* (18c) *Hist.* (Of wrecks, waifs, strays, etc.) to be seizable without judicial action.

lie in grant, *vb.* (17c) *Hist.* (Of incorporeal hereditaments) to be passable by deed or charter without the ceremony of livery of seisin.

lie in livery, *vb.* (17c) *Hist.* (Of corporeal hereditaments) to be passable by livery of seisin rather than by deed.

lien (leen *or* **lee**-ən), *n.* (16c) A legal right or interest that a creditor has in another's property, lasting usu. until a debt or duty that it secures is satisfied. • Typically, the creditor does not take possession of the property on which the lien has been obtained. Cf. PLEDGE (3). — **lien,** *vb.* — **lienable, liened,** *adj.*

▸ **accountant's lien.** (1851) The right of an accountant to retain a client's papers until the accountant's fees have been paid.

▸ **agent's lien.** (1834) A lien against property of the estate, in favor of an agent, to secure the agent's compensation as well as all necessary expenses incurred under the agent's power.

▸ **agister's lien** (ə-**jis**-tərz). (1875) A lien on the animals under an agister's care, to secure payment of the agister's fee. See AGISTER; AGISTMENT.

▸ **agricultural lien.** (1876) **1.** A statutory lien that protects a seller of farming equipment by giving the seller a lien on crops grown with the equipment. **2.** *Secured transactions.* An interest (other than a security interest) in farm products having three characteristics: (1) it must secure payment or performance of an obligation for goods or services furnished in connection with a debtor's farming operation, or of an obligation for rent on real property leased by a debtor in connection with farming; (2) it must be created by statute in favor of a person either who in the ordinary course of business furnished goods or services to a debtor in connection with the debtor's farming, or who leased real property to a debtor in connection with the debtor's farming; and (3) the effectiveness of the interest must not depend on the person's possession of the personal property. UCC § 9-102(a)(5).

▸ **architect's lien.** (1901) A statutory lien on real property in favor of an architect who has drawn the plans for and supervised the construction of improvements on the property.

▸ **artisan's lien.** See *mechanic's lien.*

▸ **attachment lien.** (1842) A lien on property seized by prejudgment attachment. • Such a lien is initially inchoate but becomes final and perfected upon entry of a judgment for the attaching creditor and relates back to the date when the lien first arose. — Also termed *lien of attachment.* See ATTACHMENT.

▸ **attorney's lien.** (1828) The right of an attorney to hold or retain a client's money or property (a *retaining lien*) or to encumber money payable to the client (a *charging lien*) until the attorney's fees have been properly determined and paid.

▸ **auctioneer's lien.** (1895) The right of an auctioneer to retain property, goods, and documents held on the seller's behalf until the winning bidder has paid all that is owed for what has been sold, including the buyer's premium and any expenses or liabilities properly incurred.

▸ **bailee's lien.** See BAILEE'S LIEN.

▸ **banker's lien.** (1843) The right of a bank to satisfy a customer's matured debt by seizing the customer's money or property in the bank's possession.

▸ **blanket lien.** (1876) A lien that gives a creditor the entitlement to take possession of any or all of the debtor's real property to cover a delinquent loan.

▸ **carrier's lien.** (1855) A carrier's right to retain possession of cargo until the owner of the cargo pays its shipping costs.

▸ **charging lien.** (1861) **1.** An attorney's lien on a claim that the attorney has helped the client perfect, as through a judgment or settlement. **2.** A lien on specified property in the debtor's possession.

▸ **chattel lien.** See *mechanic's lien.*

▸ **choate lien (koh-**it). (1882) A lien in which the lienholder, the property, and the monetary amount are established so that the lien is perfected and nothing else needs to be done to make it enforceable.

▸ **common-law lien.** (1828) **1.** A lien granted by the common law, rather than by statute, equity, or agreement by the parties. **2.** The right of one person to retain possession of property belonging to another until certain demands of the possessing party are met. • This type of lien, unlike an equitable lien, cannot exist without possession.

▸ **concurrent lien.** (1876) One of two or more liens of equal priority attaching to the same property.

▸ **construction lien.** See *mechanic's lien.*

▸ **consummate lien** (kən-**səm**-it). (1867) A judgment lien arising after the denial of a motion for a new trial. Cf. *inchoate lien.*

▸ **conventional lien.** (1826) A lien that is created by the express agreement of the parties, in circumstances in which the law would not create a lien.

▸ **deferred lien.** (1875) A lien effective at a future date, as distinguished from a present lien that is currently possessory.

▸ **demurrage lien** (di-**mər**-ij). (1918) A carrier's lien on goods for any unpaid demurrage charges. See DEMURRAGE.

▸ **dragnet lien.** (1980) A lien that is enlarged to cover any additional credit extended to the debtor by the same creditor.

▸ **equitable lien.** (18c) A right, enforceable only in equity, to have a demand satisfied from a particular fund or specific property, without having possession of the fund or property. • It arises mainly in four circumstances: (1) when an occupant of land, believing in good faith to be the owner of that land, makes improvements, repairs, or other expenditures that permanently increase the land's value, (2) when one of two or more joint owners makes expenditures of that kind, (3) when a tenant for life completes permanent and beneficial improvements to the estate begun earlier by the testator, and (4) when land or other property is transferred subject to the payment of debts, legacies, portions, or annuities to third persons. — Also termed *equitable levy.*

▸ **execution lien.** (1859) A lien on property seized by a levy of execution. • Such a lien gives the execution creditor priority over later transferees of the property and over prior unrecorded conveyances of interests in the property. See EXECUTION (3).

▸ **factor's lien.** (1830) A lien, usu. statutory, on property held on consignment by a factor. • It allows the factor to keep possession of the property until the account has been settled. See FACTOR (2).

▸ **first lien.** (18c) A lien that takes priority over all other charges or encumbrances on the same property and that must be satisfied before other charges may share in proceeds from the property's sale. — Also termed *first security; first security interest.*

▸ **fixed and floating lien.** See *fixed and floating charge* under CHARGE (7).

▸ **floating lien.** (1923) **1.** A lien that is expanded to cover any additional property obtained by the debtor while the debt is outstanding. **2.** A lien that continues to exist even when the collateral changes in character, classification, or location. — Also termed *floating charge.*

▸ **garnishment lien.** (1897) A lien on a debtor's property held by a garnishee. • Such a lien attaches in favor of the garnishing creditor when a garnishment summons is served and also impounds any credits the garnishee owes the debtor so that they must be paid to the garnishing creditor. — Also termed *lien of garnishment.* See GARNISHMENT.

▸ **general lien.** (18c) A possessory lien by which the lienholder may retain any of the debtor's goods in the lienholder's possession until any debt due from the debtor, whether in connection with the retained goods or otherwise, has been paid. • Factors, insurance brokers, packers, stockbrokers, and bankers have a general lien over the property of their clients or customers. Cf. *particular lien.*

> "The usage of any trade sufficient to establish a general lien, must . . . have been so uniform and notorious, as to warrant the inference that the party against whom the right is claimed had knowledge of it. This general lien may also be created by express agreement; as, where one or more persons give notice that they will not receive any property for the purpose of their trade or business, except on condition that they shall have a lien upon it, not only in respect to the charges arising on the particular goods, but for the general balance of account. All persons who afterwards deal with them, with the knowledge of such notice, will be deemed to have acceded to that agreement." 2 James Kent, *Commentaries on American Law* *637 (George Comstock ed., 11th ed. 1866).

▸ **grantor's lien.** See *vendor's lien* (1).

▸ **healthcare lien.** (1997) A statutory lien asserted by an HMO, insurer, medical group, or independent practice association against those liable to the patient for damages, to recover money paid or claim money payable for healthcare services provided under a healthcare service plan or a disability insurance policy. — Also termed *medical lien.* Cf. *hospital lien; workers'-compensation lien.*

▸ **hospital lien.** (1934) A statutory lien asserted by a hospital to recover the costs of emergency and ongoing medical and other services. • The lien applies against any judgment, compromise, or settlement received by a hospital patient either from a third person who caused the patient's injuries or from the third person's insurer. See *healthcare lien.*

▸ **hotelkeeper's lien.** (1875) A possessory or statutory lien allowing an innkeeper to hold, as security for payment, personal property that a guest brought into the hotel. — Also termed *innkeeper's lien.*

▸ **inchoate lien** (in-**koh**-it). (1838) A judgment lien that may be defeated if the judgment is vacated or a motion for new trial is granted. Cf. *consummate lien.*

▸ **innkeeper's lien.** See *hotelkeeper's lien.*

▸ **involuntary lien.** (1889) A lien arising without the debtor's consent.

▸ **judgment lien.** (1831) A lien imposed on a judgment debtor's nonexempt property. • This lien gives the judgment creditor the right to attach the judgment debtor's property. — Also termed *lien of judgment*. See EXEMPT PROPERTY.

▸ **judicial lien.** (1890) A lien obtained by judgment, levy, sequestration, or other legal or equitable process or proceeding. • If a debtor is adjudged to owe money to a creditor and the judgment has not been satisfied, the creditor can ask the court to impose a lien on specific property owned and possessed by the debtor. After the court imposes the lien, it usu. issues a writ directing the local sheriff to seize the property, sell it, and turn over the proceeds to the creditor.

▸ **junior lien.** (1858) A lien that is subordinate to one or more other liens on the same property.

▸ **laborer's lien.** See *mechanic's lien*.

▸ **landlord's lien.** (1844) **1.** At common law, a lien that gave a landlord the right to seize a tenant's property and sell it publicly to satisfy overdue rent. See DISTRESS. **2.** Generally, a statutory lien on a tenant's personal property at the leased premises in favor of a landlord who receives preferred-creditor status on that property. • Such a lien usu. secures the payment of overdue rent or compensation for damage to the premises.

▸ **lien of attachment.** See *attachment lien*.

▸ **lien of factor at common law.** *Hist.* A lien not created by statute; a common-law lien.

▸ **lien of garnishment.** See *garnishment lien*.

▸ **lien of judgment.** See *judgment lien*.

▸ **lien of partners.** See *partner's lien*.

▸ **manufacturer's lien.** (1860) A statutory lien that secures payment for labor or materials expended in producing goods for another.

▸ **maritime lien.** (1831) A lien on a vessel, given to secure the claim of a creditor who provided maritime services to the vessel or who suffered an injury from the vessel's use. — Also termed *tacit hypothecation*.

> "The maritime lien has been described as one of the most striking peculiarities of Admiralty law, constituting a charge upon ships of a nature unknown alike to common law and equity. It arises by operation of law and exists as a claim upon the property, secret and invisible. A maritime lien may be defined as: (1) a privileged claim, (2) upon maritime property, (3) for service done to it or injury caused by it, (4) accruing from the moment when the claim attaches, (5) travelling with the property unconditionally, (6) enforced by means of an action in rem." Griffith Price, *The Law of Maritime Liens* 1 (1940).

▸ **mechanic's lien.** (1821) A statutory lien that secures payment for labor or materials supplied in improving, repairing, or maintaining real or personal property, such as a building, an automobile, or the like. — Also termed *lien of the mechanic*; *artisan's lien*; *chattel lien* (for personal property); *construction lien* (for labor); *garageman's lien* (for repaired vehicles); *laborer's lien* (for labor); *materialman's lien* (for materials).

> "The lien of the mechanic, here treated of, is a remedy in the nature of a charge on land, given by statute to the persons named therein, to secure a priority or preference of payment for the performance of labor or supply of materials to buildings or other improvements, to be enforced against the particular property in which they have become incorporated, in the manner and under the limitations therein expressly provided. It is exclusively the creature of statute, deriving its existence only from positive enactment, and not arising out of, or of the essence of, the contract for labor, or dependent on the motives which suggest its being enforced. It is a mere incidental accompaniment as a means of enforcing payment, — a remedy given by law, which secures the preference provided for, but which does not exist, however equitable the claim may be, unless the party brings himself within the provisions of the statute, and shows a substantial compliance with all its essential requirements. It is not a judgment, and does not give the mechanic a right to his debt, which arises out of the performance of contract, and exists without the aid of statute. It does not confer an independent right, or create an estate in the property itself, or give any interest which would support an action of ejectment. It has, however, been held to confer an insurable interest. The absolute ownership of land and powers incident to property are not in the slightest degree suspended by its operation; nor are prior encumbrances interfered with. It does not give any right of possession to the property, as against the owner; nor a right to have a receiver of rents and profits appointed pending the suit. The owner's free enjoyment of the property will be interfered with only when his use of it tends to its injury to such an extent as to impair its value as a security. It does not create, even after being judicially established by judgment or decree, any privity of estate, or right of entry thereunder, but is in the nature of a legal charge, running with the land, encumbering it in every change of ownership, and preventing subsequent alienations or encumbrances only by making them subordinate to the rights of the lien-holder." Samuel Phillips, *A Treatise on the Law of Mechanics' Liens on Real and Personal Property* § 9, at 15–16 (1874).

▸ **medical lien.** See *healthcare lien*.

▸ **mortgage lien.** (1846) A lien on the mortgagor's property securing the mortgage.

▸ **municipal lien.** (1851) A lien by a municipal corporation against a property owner for the owner's proportionate share of a public improvement that specially and individually benefits the owner.

▸ **particular lien.** (1833) A possessory lien by which the possessor of goods has the right to retain specific goods until a debt incurred in connection with those goods has been paid. — Also termed *special lien*. Cf. *general lien*.

> "A general lien is the right to retain the property of another, for a general balance of accounts; but a *particular* lien is a right to retain it only for a charge on account of labor employed or expenses bestowed upon the identical property detained. The former is taken strictly, but the latter is favored in law. The right rests on principles of natural equity and commercial necessity, and it prevents circuitry of action, and gives security and confidence . . . ." 2 James Kent, *Commentaries on American Law* *634 (George Comstock ed., 11th ed. 1866).

▸ **partner's lien.** (1870) A partner's equitable lien on partnership property as security for the application of that property to partnership purposes; esp., a right to have the partnership property applied in payment of the partnership's debts and to have whatever is due the firm from fellow partners deducted from what would otherwise be payable to them for their shares — Also termed *lien of partners*.

> "The lien of the partners is intended to secure whatever is due to or from the firm by or to the members thereof as such. It does not extend to debts incurred between the firm and its members otherwise than in their capacity as partners, and in case of the bankruptcy of a partner his assignees may claim his share without regard to such a debt; as, for example, a debt for money borrowed by one partner from another for a purely private purpose of his own." Floyd R. Mechem, *Elements of the Law of Partnership* 373–74 (2d ed. 1920).

▸ **possessory garageman's lien.** (1975) A lien on a vehicle in the amount of the repairs performed by the garage.

▸ **possessory lien.** (1840) A lien allowing the creditor to keep possession of the encumbered property until the debt is satisfied. • A power of sale may or may not be combined with this right of possession. Examples include pledges of chattels, the liens of innkeepers, garageman's liens, and vendor's liens. See PLEDGE.

▸ **prime lien.** (1903) A lien that arises and attaches after another validly recorded lien in such a way that the lien has equal or superior rights in the same collateral.

▸ **prior lien.** (18c) A lien that is superior to one or more other liens on the same property, usu. because it was perfected first. — Also termed *priority lien.*

▸ **retaining lien.** (1861) An attorney's right to keep a client's papers until the client has paid for the attorney's services. • The attorney's retaining lien is not recognized in some states.

▸ **second lien.** (1830) A lien that is next in rank after a first lien on the same property and therefore is next entitled to satisfaction out of the proceeds from the property's sale.

▸ **secret lien.** (1830) A lien not appearing of record and unknown to purchasers; a lien reserved by the vendor and kept hidden from third parties, to secure the payment of goods after delivery.

▸ **senior lien.** (1851) A lien that has priority over other liens on the same property.

▸ **special lien.** See *particular lien.*

▸ **specific lien.** (18c) A lien secured on a particular thing by a contract or by a judgment, execution, attachment, or other legal proceeding.

▸ **statutory lien.** (1827) **1.** A lien arising solely by force of statute, not by agreement of the parties. • Examples are federal tax liens and mechanic's liens. **2.** *Bankruptcy.* Either of two types of liens: (1) a lien arising solely by force of a statute on specified circumstances or conditions, or (2) a lien of distress for rent, whether or not statutory. • For bankruptcy purposes, a statutory lien does not include a security interest or judicial lien, whether or not the interest or lien arises from or is made effective by a statute.

▸ **superlien.** See SUPERLIEN.

▸ **tax lien.** (1852) **1.** A lien on property, and all rights to property, imposed by the federal government for unpaid federal taxes. **2.** A lien on real estate in favor of a state or local government that may be foreclosed for nonpayment of taxes. • A majority of states have adopted the Uniform Federal Tax Lien Registration Act.

▸ **vendee's lien.** (1859) *Real estate.* A buyer's lien on the purchased land as security for repayment of purchase money paid in, enforceable if the seller does not or cannot convey good title.

▸ **vendor's lien.** (1830) **1.** *Real estate.* A seller's lien on land as security for the purchase price. • This lien may be foreclosed in the same way as a mortgage: the buyer usu. has a redemption period within which to pay the full purchase price. — Also termed *grantor's lien.* **2.** A lien held by a seller of goods, who retains possession of the goods until the buyer has paid in full.

▸ **voluntary lien.** (1900) A lien created with the debtor's consent.

▸ **warehouser's lien.** (1986) A lien covering storage charges for goods stored with a bailee. — Also termed *warehouseman's lien.*

▸ **workers'-compensation lien.** (1976) **1.** A statutory lien, asserted by a healthcare provider, to recover the costs of emergency and ongoing medical and other services. • The lien applies against any workers'-compensation benefits paid to a patient. **2.** A statutory lien, asserted by a workers'-compensation insurance carrier, against an insured worker's recovery from a third-party tortfeasor, to recover benefits paid to the injured worker. — Also termed *workers'-compensation subrogation lien.* Cf. *healthcare lien.*

lienable, *adj.* (1855) (Of property) legally amenable to a lien; capable of being subject to a lien.

lien account. See ACCOUNT.

lien avoidance. (1957) *Bankruptcy.* A debtor's depriving a creditor of a security interest in an asset of the bankruptcy estate. 11 USCA §§ 506(d), 522(f).

lien creditor. See CREDITOR.

lienee (leen-**ee** *or* lee-ən-**ee**). (1853) **1.** One whose property is subject to a lien. **2.** An encumbrancer who holds a lien; LIENHOLDER. Because the word is a "contronym" with opposite senses, it is best avoided — along with its correlative *lienor.*

> "[A] mortgagee is the owner of the property, while a pledgee or other lienee is merely an encumbrancer of it." John Salmond, *Jurisprudence* 440 (Glanville L. Williams ed., 10th ed. 1947).

lienholder. (1830) A person having or owning a lien. — Also termed *lienor; lienee.*

lien of a covenant. (1916) The beginning portion of a covenant, stating the names of the parties and the character of the covenant.

lien of attachment. See *attachment lien* under LIEN.

lien of factor at common law. See LIEN.

lien of garnishment. See *garnishment lien* under LIEN.

lien of judgment. See *judgment lien* under LIEN.

lien of partners. See *partner's lien* under LIEN.

lienor. See LIENHOLDER.

lien-stripping. (1987) *Bankruptcy.* The practice of splitting a mortgagee's secured claim into secured and unsecured components and reducing the claim to the market value of the debtor's residence, thereby allowing the debtor to modify the terms of the mortgage and reduce the amount of the debt. • The U.S. Supreme Court has prohibited lien-stripping in all Chapter 7 cases (*Nobelman v. American Savs. Bank*, 508 U.S. 324, 113 S.Ct. 2106 (1993)) and in Chapter 13 cases involving a debtor's principal residence (*Dewsnup v. Timm*, 502 U.S. 410, 112 S.Ct. 773 (1992)), and the Bankruptcy Reform Act of 1994 modified the Bankruptcy Code to prohibit lien-stripping in Chapter 11 cases involving an individual's principal residence.

lien theory. (1882) The idea that a mortgage resembles a lien, so that the mortgagee acquires only a lien on the property and the mortgagor retains both legal and equitable title unless a valid foreclosure occurs. • Most American states — commonly called *lien states, lien jurisdictions,* or *lien-theory jurisdictions* — have adopted this theory. Cf. TITLE THEORY.

lien waiver. See WAIVER (3).

lieu conus (l[y]oo **kon**-yoo), *n.* [Law French] *Hist.* A place generally known and noticed by those in the area of it, such as a castle or manor.

lieu land. See LAND.

lieutenancy. (15c) The rank, office, or commission of a lieutenant. See COMMISSION OF LIEUTENANCY.

lieutenant. (14c) **1.** A deputy of or substitute for another; one acting by vicarious authority <he sent his chief lieutenant to the meeting>. **2.** A composite part of the title of many government and military officials who are subordinate to others, esp. when the duties of the higher official may devolve to the subordinate <lieutenant governor>. **3.** In the U.S. Army, a commissioned officer next below captain. **4.** In the U.S. Navy, an officer next below lieutenant commander.

lieutenant colonel. (16c) In the U.S. military, an officer next below colonel and above major.

lieutenant commander. (1839) In the U.S. Navy, an officer next below commander and above lieutenant.

lieutenant general. (16c) In the U.S. Army, an officer next below four-star general and above major general.

lieutenant governor. (16c) A deputy or subordinate governor, sometimes charged with such duties as presiding over the state legislature, but esp. important as the governor's successor if the governor dies, resigns, or becomes disabled.

life, *n.* **1.** The period within which a plant or animal exists as a vibrant, growing, or even subsisting organism before it dies — a period that mere objects never have. **2.** The state of being alive as a human; an individual person's existence. **3.** See *life imprisonment* under IMPRISONMENT.

life annuity. See ANNUITY.

life assurance. See LIFE INSURANCE.

life beneficiary. See BENEFICIARY.

life-care contract. (1950) An agreement in which one party is assured of care and maintenance for life in exchange for transferring property to the other party. Cf. CORODY.

life estate. See ESTATE (1).

life estate pur autre vie. See ESTATE (1).

life expectancy. (1848) **1.** The period that a person of a given age and sex is expected to live, according to actuarial tables. **2.** The period that a given person is expected to live, taking into account individualized characteristics such as heredity, past and present diseases, and other relevant medical data. See ACTUARIAL TABLE; LIFE TABLE.

life-hold. See *life land* under LAND.

life imprisonment. See IMPRISONMENT.

life in being. (1836) Under the rule against perpetuities, anyone alive when a future interest is created, whether or not the person has an interest in the estate. See IN BEING; RULE AGAINST PERPETUITIES. Cf. MEASURING LIFE.

life-income period-certain annuity. See ANNUITY.

life in prison. See *life imprisonment* under IMPRISONMENT.

life insurance. (1809) An agreement between an insurance company and the policyholder to pay a specified amount to a designated beneficiary on the insured's death. — Also termed (BrE) *life assurance.* See ASSURANCE (2).

> "Life and accident insurance has been defined as a contract whereby one party, for a stipulated consideration, agrees to indemnify another against injury by accident or death from any cause not excepted in the contract. Strictly speaking, however, a contract of life insurance is not one of indemnity, but is an absolute engagement to pay a certain sum at the end of a definite or indefinite time." 43 Am. Jur. 2d *Insurance* § 3 (1982).

▸ **corporate-owned life insurance.** (1954) A life-insurance policy bought by a company on an employee's life, naming the company as beneficiary. — Abbr. COLI.

▸ **credit life insurance.** (1949) Life insurance on a borrower, usu. in a consumer installment loan, in which the amount due is paid if the borrower dies.

▸ **decreasing-term life insurance.** See *decreasing term insurance* under INSURANCE.

▸ **endowment life insurance.** (1877) Life insurance that is payable either to the insured at the end of the policy period or to the insured's beneficiary if the insured dies before the period ends. — Also termed *endowment insurance.*

▸ **industrial life insurance.** (1900) Life insurance characterized by (1) a small death benefit (usu. $2,000 or less), (2) premium payments that are due weekly, biweekly, or monthly and that are collected at home by the insurer's representative, and (3) no required medical examination of the insured. — Sometimes shortened to *industrial insurance.*

▸ **joint life insurance.** (1920) Life insurance on two or more persons, payable to the survivor or survivors when one of the policyholders dies.

▸ **key-employee life insurance.** (1983) Life insurance taken out by a company on an essential or valuable employee, with the company as beneficiary. — Also termed *key-employee insurance*; *key-man insurance*; *key-person insurance*; *key-executive insurance.*

▸ **last-survivor life insurance.** (1990) Life insurance on two or more persons, payable after all the insureds have died. — Also termed *last-survivor insurance.*

▸ **limited-payment life insurance.** (1928) Life insurance that requires premium payments for less than the life of the agreement.

▸ **national-service life insurance.** (1940) Life insurance available to a person in active U.S. military service on or after October 8, 1940, and issuable at favorable rates. • This insurance was established by the National Service Life Insurance Act of 1940, and is regulated by the Administrator of Veterans Affairs. 38 USCA §§ 1901–1929. — Abbr. NSLI.

▸ **ordinary life insurance.** (1878) **1.** Life insurance having an investment-sensitive cash value, such as whole life insurance or universal life insurance. • Ordinary insurance is one of three main categories of life insurance. — Often shortened to *ordinary insurance.* Cf. *group insurance* under INSURANCE; *industrial life insurance.* **2.** See *whole life insurance.*

▸ **partnership life insurance.** See *partnership insurance* (1) under INSURANCE.

▸ **single-premium life insurance.** (1936) Life insurance that is paid for in one installment rather than a series of premiums over time. — Also termed *single-premium insurance.*

▸ **split-dollar life insurance.** (1956) An arrangement between two people (often an employer and employee) by which life insurance is written on the life of one, though both share the premium payments. • On the insured's death or other event terminating the plan, the noninsured person receives the cash value of the insurance as reimbursement, and the beneficiary named by the insured is entitled to the remainder. — Also termed *split-dollar insurance.*

▸ **straight life insurance.** See *whole life insurance.*

▸ **term life insurance.** (1894) Life insurance that covers the insured for only a specified period. • It pays a fixed benefit to a named beneficiary upon the insured's death but is not redeemable for a cash value during the insured's life. Cf. *whole life insurance.*

▸ **universal life insurance.** (1868) Term life insurance in which the premiums are paid from the insured's earnings from a money-market fund.

▸ **variable life insurance.** (1956) Life insurance in which the premiums are invested in securities and whose death benefits thus depend on the securities' performance, though there is a minimum guaranteed death benefit. — Abbr. VLI.

▸ **whole life insurance.** (1917) Life insurance that covers an insured for life, during which the insured pays fixed premiums, accumulates savings from an invested portion of the premiums, and receives a guaranteed benefit upon death, to be paid to a named beneficiary. • Such a policy may provide that at a stated time, premiums will end or benefits will increase. — Also termed *ordinary life insurance*; *straight life insurance.* Cf. *term life insurance.*

life-insurance trust. See TRUST (3).

life interest. (18c) An interest in real or personal property measured by the duration of the holder's or another named person's life. See *life estate* under ESTATE (1).

life land. See LAND.

lifelode. See LIVELODE.

life of a writ. (1942) The effective period during which a writ may be levied. • That period usu. ends on the day that the law or the writ itself provides that it must be returned to court.

life-owner. See LIFE TENANT.

life peerage. (18c) *English law.* The grant of the noble title of baron to a person for life, offered through letters patent. • The Life Peerages Act of 1958 first allowed this and removed the disqualifications of women from serving in the House of Lords. See PEER.

life policy. See INSURANCE POLICY.

life-prolonging procedure. See LIFE-SUSTAINING PROCEDURE.

life-qualified jury. See JURY.

lifer. See NONREMOVABLE INMATE.

liferent. (15c) *Scots law.* The right to use and enjoy during a lifetime the property of another (the fiar) without consuming its substance. — Also spelled *life-rent.* See USUFRUCT.

liferentrix. (16c) *Archaic.* A woman who has a liferent.

life sentence. See SENTENCE.

life settlement. See *viatical settlement* under SETTLEMENT (3).

lifestyle evidence. (1984) Evidence relating to a person's affiliations, allegiances, and choices, esp. as regards household arrangements, gang membership, politics, and church membership.

life-sustaining procedure. (1976) A medical procedure that uses mechanical or artificial means to sustain, restore, or substitute for a vital function and that serves only or mainly to postpone death. — Also termed *life-prolonging procedure*; *life-support system.*

life table. (1825) An actuarial table that gives the probable proportions of people who will live to different ages. Cf. ACTUARIAL TABLE.

life tenancy. See *life estate* under ESTATE (1).

life tenant. (16c) Someone who, until death, is beneficially entitled to property; the holder of a life estate. — Also termed *tenant for life*; *life-owner.* See *life estate* under ESTATE (1).

▸ **equitable life tenant.** (1880) A life tenant not automatically entitled to possession but who makes an election allowed by law to a person of that status — such as a spouse — and to whom a court will normally grant possession if security or an undertaking is given.

▸ **legal life tenant.** (1886) A life tenant who is automatically entitled to possession by virtue of a legal estate.

life-threatening, *adj.* Of, relating to, or involving illness, injury, or danger that could cause a person to die.

lifetime gift. See *inter vivos gift* under GIFT.

life without parole. (1931) *Criminal law.* Lifetime imprisonment without the possibility of early release.

LIFO (lɪ-foh). *abbr.* (1945) LAST-IN, FIRST-OUT.

lift, *vb.* (16c) **1.** To stop or put an end to; to revoke or rescind <lift the stay>. **2.** To discharge or pay off (a debt or obligation) <lift a mortgage>. **3.** *Slang.* To steal <lift a purse>.

lifting costs. (1921) *Oil & gas.* The cost of producing oil and gas after drilling is complete but before the oil and gas is removed from the property, including transportation costs, labor, costs of supervision, supplies, costs of operating the pumps, electricity, repairs, depreciation, certain royalties payable to the lessor, gross-production taxes, and other incidental expenses.

lifting the corporate veil. See PIERCING THE CORPORATE VEIL.

liga (**lee**-gə), *n.* [Law Latin] *Hist.* A league or confederation.

ligan (lɪ-gən), *n.* See LAGAN.

ligare (lə-**gair**-ee), *vb.* [Latin] *Hist.* **1.** To tie or bind. **2.** To enter into a treaty or league.

ligea (**lee**-jee-ə), *n.* [Law Latin] *Hist.* A female subject; a liege woman. See LIEGE (1).

ligeance (lɪ-jənts *or* **lee**-jənts). (14c) *Hist.* **1.** The obedience of a citizen to the citizen's sovereign or government; allegiance. **2.** The territory of a state or sovereign. — Also spelled *liegeance.* See LIEGE.

> "Liegeance is a true and faithful obedience of the subject due to his sovereign; and this liegeance, which is an incident inseparable to every subject, is in four manners; the first is natural, the second acquired, the third local, and the fourth legal." *Termes de la Ley* 280 (1st Am. ed. 1812).

ligen, *n.* See LAGAN.

ligeus (**lee**-jee-əs), *n.* [Law Latin] *Hist.* A male subject; a liege man. See LIEGE (1).

light-and-air easement. See EASEMENT.

light-duty work. See *light work* under WORK (1).

lighterage (**lɪ**-tər-ij). (15c) **1.** The loading and unloading of goods between a ship and a smaller vessel, called a lighter, that is able to use a restricted port or dock. **2.** The compensation paid for this service. **3.** The loading and unloading of freight between a railroad car and a ship's side.

light most favorable. (1861) The standard of scrutinizing or interpreting a verdict by accepting as true all evidence and inferences that support it and disregarding all contrary evidence and inferences <in reviewing the defendant's motion for judgment notwithstanding the verdict, the court reviewed the evidence in the light most favorable to the verdict>. — Also termed *most favorable light.*

lights, ancient. See ANCIENT-LIGHTS DOCTRINE.

light work. See WORK (1).

ligia et non ligia (**lij**-ee-ə et non **lij**-ee-ə). [Law Latin] *Scots law.* Liege and nonliege. • A liege fee was held under the Crown while a nonliege fee was held under a vassal of the Crown. See LIEGE.

ligius (**lee**-jee-əs), *n.* [Law Latin] *Hist.* A person bound to another by solemn relationship, as between subject and sovereign. See LIEGE.

lignagium (lig-**nay**-jee-əm), *n.* [Law Latin] *Hist.* **1.** A right to cut firewood. **2.** The payment for this right.

ligula (**lig**-yə-lə), *n.* [Law Latin] *Hist.* A copy or transcript of a court roll or deed.

like, *adj.* (12c) **1.** Equal in quantity, quality, or degree; corresponding exactly <like copies>. **2.** Similar or substantially similar <like character>.

like-kind exchange. (1963) An exchange of trade, business, or investment property (except inventory or securities) for property of the same kind, class, or character. • Such an exchange is not taxable unless cash or other property is received. IRC (26 USCA) § 1031. — Abbr. LKE.

like-kind property. (1946) *Tax.* Property that is of such a similar kind, class, or character to other property that a gain from an exchange of the property is not recognized for federal income-tax purposes. See LIKE-KIND EXCHANGE.

likelihood-of-confusion test. (1942) *Trademarks.* A test for trademark infringement, based on the probability that a substantial number of ordinarily prudent buyers will be misled or confused about the source of a product.

likelihood-of-success-on-the-merits test. (1981) *Civil procedure.* The rule that a litigant who seeks a preliminary injunction, or seeks to forestall the effects of a judgment during appeal, must show a reasonable probability of success in the litigation or appeal.

likely, *adj.* **1.** Apparently true or real; probable <the likely outcome>. • In this oldest sense, the term is sometimes used ironically to express incredulity, as in the phrase *a likely story.* **2.** Showing a strong tendency; reasonably expected <likely to snow>. **3.** Well adapted for a given purpose; suitable <a likely place for settling a new community>.

limbo time. (1992) The period when an employee is neither on duty nor off duty, as a railroad worker awaiting transportation from a duty assignment to the place of final release. 49 USCA § 21103(b)(4); *Brotherhood of Locomotive Eng'rs v. Atchison, Topeka & Santa Fe R.R.*, 516 U.S. 152, 116 S.Ct. 595 (1996).

limenarcha (lim-ən-**ahr**-kə), *n.* [Latin] (17c) *Roman law.* An officer in charge of a harbor or frontier post.

limine. See IN LIMINE.

limine out (**lim**-ə-nee), *vb.* (1997) (Of a court) to exclude (evidence) by granting a motion in limine <the trial judge limined out most of the plaintiff's medical records>.

limit, *n.* (14c) **1.** A restriction or restraint. **2.** A boundary or defining line. **3.** The extent of power, right, or authority. — **limit,** *vb.* — **limited,** *adj.*

limitation. (14c) **1.** The act of limiting; the quality, state, or condition of being limited. **2.** A restriction. **3.** A statutory period after which a lawsuit or prosecution cannot be brought in court. — Also termed *limitations period; limitation period; limitation of action* See STATUTE OF LIMITATIONS. Cf. LACHES. **4.** *Property.* The restriction of the extent of an estate; the creation by deed or devise of a lesser estate out of a fee simple. See WORDS OF LIMITATION.

▸ **collateral limitation.** (18c) *Hist.* A limitation that makes the duration of an estate dependent on another event (other than the life of the grantee), such as an estate to A until B turns 21.

▸ **conditional limitation.** (18c) **1.** See *executory limitation.* **2.** A lease provision that automatically terminates the lease if a specified event occurs, such as if the lessee defaults.

▸ **executory limitation.** (18c) A restriction that causes an estate to automatically end and revest in a third party upon the happening of a specified event. • This type of limitation, which was not recognized at common law, can be created only as a shifting use or an executory devise. It is a condition subsequent in favor of someone other than the transferor. — Also termed *conditional limitation.* See *fee simple subject to an executory limitation* under FEE SIMPLE.

> "When a condition subsequent is created in favor of someone other than the transferor, the *Restatement of Property* calls the condition subsequent an *executory limitation.* It calls A's estate an *estate in fee simple subject to an executory limitation.*" Thomas F. Bergin & Paul G. Haskell, *Preface to Estates in Land and Future Interests* 52 (2d ed. 1984).

▸ **limitation over.** (17c) An additional estate created or contemplated in a conveyance, to be enjoyed after the first estate expires or is exhausted. • An example of language giving rise to a limitation over is "to A for life, remainder to B.

▸ **special limitation.** (17c) A restriction that causes an estate to end automatically and revert to the grantor upon the happening of a specified event. See *fee simple determinable* under FEE SIMPLE.

> "[I]f a deed or will uses such words as 'for so long as,' 'while,' 'during,' or 'until' to introduce the circumstances under which an estate may end prior to its running its maximum course, it is generally assumed that a special limitation was intended." Thomas F. Bergin & Paul G. Haskell, *Preface to Estates in Land and Future Interests* 50 (2d ed. 1984).

▸ **supplanting limitation.** (1942) A limitation involving a secondary gift that is expressed in a clause following the original gift and that is typically introduced by the words "but if," "and if," or "in case."

5. *Patents.* ELEMENT (2).

▸ **negative limitation.** See NEGATIVE LIMITATION.

limitation clause. (18c) A contract term that restricts the rights of the parties, esp. for the types of remedies or damages available.

limitation of action. See LIMITATION (3).

limitation of assize. (17c) *Hist.* A period prescribed by statute within which a person is required to allege that the person was properly seised of lands sued for under a writ of assize.

limitation-of-damages clause. (1933) A contractual provision by which the parties agree on a maximum amount of damages recoverable for a future breach of the agreement. Cf. LIQUIDATED-DAMAGES CLAUSE.

limitation of liability. (1836) **1.** A written statement, esp. a clause in a contract, that restricts the conditions under which a party may be responsible for loss or damages. **2.** *Corporations.* A contract clause specif. stating that each shareholder's liability for the corporation's debts and other obligations is no more than the par value of the shareholder's fully paid-up shares.

limitation-of-liability act. (1897) A federal or state statute that limits the type of damages that may be recovered, the liability of particular persons or groups, or the time during which an action may be brought. — Abbr. LLA. See FEDERAL TORT CLAIMS ACT; *sovereign immunity* under IMMUNITY (1).

limitation-of-liability clause. A contract provision specifying the amount of exposure that a party will have if sued on a claim arising out of the contract by another party. • The limit may apply to only certain types of claims or to all claims. Cf. EXCULPATORY CLAUSE.

limitation-of-remedies clause. (1974) A contractual provision that restricts the remedies available to the parties if a party defaults. • Under the UCC, such a clause is valid unless it fails of its essential purpose or it unconscionably limits consequential damages. Cf. LIQUIDATED-DAMAGES CLAUSE; PENALTY CLAUSE.

limitation on indebtedness. See DEBT LIMITATION.

limitation over. See LIMITATION (4).

limitation period. See LIMITATION (3).

limitations, statute of. See STATUTE OF LIMITATIONS.

limitations period. 1. See LIMITATION (3). **2.** See STATUTE OF LIMITATIONS.

limit debate. (1828) *Parliamentary law.* To set a limit on how long debate may continue, or on the number and length of speeches. See DEBATE. Cf. CLOSE DEBATE; EXTEND DEBATE.

limited administration. See ADMINISTRATION.

limited admissibility. See ADMISSIBILITY.

limited appeal. See APPEAL (2).

limited appearance. See *special appearance* under APPEARANCE.

limited-capacity well. See WELL.

limited certiorari. See *narrow certiorari* under CERTIORARI.

limited company. See COMPANY.

limited court. See COURT.

limited debate. See DEBATE.

limited defense. See *personal defense* under DEFENSE (4).

limited-dividend housing association. (1976) An independent entity formed by housing developers and used for borrowing funds from a public agency. • The developers invest in the association, agree to limit the return on their investment to a prescribed percentage, and rent a defined portion of the housing units to persons of low and moderate income. In exchange the government lender charges a below-market interest rate, subsidizes rents or interest rates, and may grant other tax benefits.

limited divorce. See DIVORCE.

limited exclusion order. See EXCLUSION ORDER (3).

limited executor. See EXECUTOR (2).

limited fee. See *base fee* under FEE (2).

limited guaranty. See GUARANTY (1).

limited interdict. See INTERDICT (2).

limited interdiction. See *partial interdiction* under INTERDICTION (3).

limited interpretation. See *restrictive interpretation* under INTERPRETATION (1).

limited jurisdiction. See JURISDICTION.

limited liability. See LIABILITY.

limited-liability company. See COMPANY.

limited-liability corporation. See *limited-liability company* under COMPANY.

limited-liability limited partnership. See PARTNERSHIP.

limited-liability partnership. See PARTNERSHIP.

limited license. See LICENSE.

limited-market property. See *special-purpose property* under PROPERTY.

limited member. See *nonvoting member* under MEMBER (1).

limited monarchy. See MONARCHY.

limited owner. See OWNER.

limited partner. See PARTNER.

limited partnership. See PARTNERSHIP.

limited partnership association. See PARTNERSHIP ASSOCIATION.

limited-payment life insurance. See LIFE INSURANCE.

limited policy. See INSURANCE POLICY.

limited-policy insurance. See INSURANCE.

limited power of appointment. See POWER OF APPOINTMENT.

limited publication. See PUBLICATION.

limited public forum. See *designated public forum* under PUBLIC FORUM.

limited-purpose marriage. See MARRIAGE (1).

limited-purpose public figure. See PUBLIC FIGURE.

limited release. See RELEASE.

limited severance. See *partial severance* under SEVERANCE (1).

limited trust. See TRUST (3).

limited veto. See *qualified veto* under VETO.

limited voting. See VOTING.

limited waiver. See WAIVER (1).

limited warranty. See WARRANTY (2).

limiting instruction. See JURY INSTRUCTION.

limit of liability. See LIABILITY LIMIT.

limit order. See ORDER (8).

Lincoln Law. See FALSE CLAIMS ACT.

Lincoln's Inn. One of the Inns of Court in London. See INN OF COURT (1).

Lindbergh Act. See FEDERAL KIDNAPPING ACT.

line, *n.* (14c) **1.** A demarcation, border, or limit <the line between right and wrong>. See MEANDER LINE. **2.** A person's occupation or business <what line of business is Watson in?>. **3.** In manufacturing, a series of closely related products. **4.** The ancestry of a person; lineage <the Fergusons came from a long line of wheat farmers>.

▸ **collateral line.** (16c) A line of descent connecting persons who are not directly related to each other as ascendants or descendants, but who are descendants of a common ancestor.

▸ **direct line.** (17c) A line of descent traced through only those persons who are related to each other directly as ascendants or descendants.

▸ **maternal line.** (17c) A person's ancestry or relationship with another traced through the mother.

▸ **paternal line.** (17c) A person's ancestry or relationship with another traced through the father.

linea (**lin**-ee-ə), *n.* [Latin "line"] *Hist.* A line of descent.

▸ ***linea directa*** (**lin**-ee-ə də-**rek**-tə). [Latin "direct line"] (17c) *Roman law.* The relationship among persons in the direct line of ascent and descent, such as grandfather, father, and son. — Also termed *linea recta.*

▸ ***linea transversa*** (**lin**-ee-ə trans-**vər**-s-ə). [Latin "transverse line"] *Roman law.* The relationship between persons in collateral lines of descent, such as uncle and nephew. — Also termed *linea obliqua.*

lineage (**lin**-ee-əj). (14c) Ancestry and progeny; family, ascending or descending.

lineal (**lin**-ee-əl), *adj.* (15c) Derived from or relating to common ancestors, esp. in a direct line; hereditary. Cf. COLLATERAL (2).

lineal, *n.* (18c) A lineal descendant; a direct blood relative.

lineal ascendant. See ASCENDANT.

lineal consanguinity. See CONSANGUINITY.

lineal descendant. See DESCENDANT.

lineal descent. See DESCENT.

lineal heir. See HEIR.

lineal warranty. See WARRANTY (1).

linea obliqua. See *linea transversa* under LINEA.

linea recta. See *linea directa* under LINEA.

line-cutting. See QUEUE-JUMPING.

line item. See ITEM (2).

line-item veto. See VETO.

line management. See MANAGEMENT (2).

line manager. See MANAGER (1).

line of credit. (1917) The maximum amount of borrowing power extended to a borrower by a given lender, to be drawn on by the borrower as needed. — Also termed *credit line.*

line of demarcation. See DEMARCATION LINE.

line officer. See OFFICER (1).

line-of-sight test. (1975) *Wills & estates.* A criterion for determining whether a testator could have seen the witnesses attesting the testator's will, the gauge being whether, without changing his or her position, the testator could have looked directly at them. • This test applies to the will-execution requirement that the witnesses be in the testator's presence when they sign the will. It does not require proof that the testator actually saw the act. — Also termed *line-of-vision test.* Cf. CONSCIOUS-PRESENCE TEST; PRESENCE-OF-THE-TESTATOR RULE.

line of title. See CHAIN OF TITLE (1).

line-of-vision test. See LINE-OF-SIGHT TEST.

lines and corners. See METES AND BOUNDS.

line slip. (1978) An insurance document written by a broker and describing the prospective risk to be insured, based on which the underwriters then decide what fraction of the risk they are willing to insure. — Also termed *broker's slip; broker's placing slip.*

lineup. (1915) *Criminal law.* A police identification procedure in which physically similar persons, one of whom may be the suspect, are shown to the victim, usu. simultaneously, or a witness to determine whether the suspect can be identified as the perpetrator of the crime. — Also termed *police lineup*; (BrE) *identity parade*; *identification parade.* Cf. SHOWUP; PHOTO ARRAY.

▸ **blank lineup.** (1971) *Criminal law.* A lineup in which the suspect or defendant does not appear, as one of two lineups, the other of which includes the suspect or defendant.

▸ **conventional lineup.** (1968) A lineup in which the witness can view all the persons simultaneously and look at each one repeatedly before identifying the culprit or declaring that no one in the lineup is the culprit. • This technique allows a witness to compare the members of the lineup to each other as well as to the witness's memory. — Also termed *simultaneous identification procedure.*

▸ **double-blind sequential lineup.** (2001) A lineup in which the law-enforcement officer or officers conducting the procedure do not know which participant is the suspect.

▸ **sequential lineup.** (1974) A lineup in which each person is shown separately to the witness, who must decide whether or not a person is the culprit before the next person is shown. • Under this technique, the witness can compare a person only to the witness's memory of the suspect's appearance.

▸ **simultaneous lineup.** (2000) A lineup in which the witness views all members of the lineup at the same time.

***Lingle* test.** (1989) *Labor law.* A test for determining whether a union member's state-law claim against the employer is preempted by the Labor–Management Relations Act, the controlling principle being that if the state-law claim can be resolved without interpreting the collective-bargaining agreement, then there is no preemption. *Lingle v. Norge Division of Magic Chef, Inc.*, 486 U.S. 399, 108 S.Ct. 1877 (1988). See MARCUS MODEL; WHITE MODEL.

linguistic profiling. (2001) Profiling based on vocal characteristics that suggest a speaker's race, sex, or national, ethnic, or regional origin. • This type of profiling occurs when the speaker is not visible but can be heard, as in a telephone conversation or voice message. Cf. RACIAL PROFILING.

link, *n.* (15c) **1.** A unit in a connected series; something that binds separate things <link in the chain of title>. **2.** A unit of land measurement <one link equals 7.92 inches>. See CHAIN; ROD. **3.** See HYPERLINK.

link financing. See FINANCING.

link-in-chain principle. (1962) *Criminal procedure.* The principle that a criminal defendant's Fifth Amendment right against self-incrimination protects the defendant not only from answering directly incriminating questions but also from giving answers that might connect the defendant to criminal activity in the chain of evidence.

LIO. *abbr.* See *lesser included offense* under OFFENSE.

LIP. *abbr.* LEGALLY INCAPACITATED PERSON.

liquere (li-**kweer**-ee), *vb.* [Latin] *Roman law.* To be clear, evident, or apparent. • When a judex appointed to try a civil case swore under oath *sibi non liquere* ("that it was not clear to him"), he would be discharged from deciding the case. See NON LIQUET.

liquid, *adj.* (1879) **1.** (Of an asset) capable of being readily converted into cash. **2.** (Of a person or entity) possessing assets that can be readily converted into cash.

liquid asset. See *current asset* under ASSET.

liquidate, *vb.* (16c) **1.** To settle (an obligation) by payment or other adjustment; to extinguish (a debt). **2.** To ascertain the precise amount of (debt, damages, etc.) by litigation or agreement. **3.** To determine the liabilities and distribute the assets of (an entity), esp. in bankruptcy or dissolution. **4.** To convert (a nonliquid asset) into cash. **5.** To wind up the affairs of (a corporation, business, etc.). **6.** *Slang.* To get rid of (a person), esp. by killing.

liquidated, *adj.* (18c) **1.** (Of an amount or debt) settled or determined, esp. by agreement. **2.** (Of an asset or assets) converted into cash.

liquidated account. See ACCOUNT.

liquidated amount. (18c) A figure readily computed, based on an agreement's terms. — Also termed *liquidated sum.*

liquidated claim. See CLAIM (3).

liquidated damages. See DAMAGES.

liquidated-damages clause. (1873) A contractual provision that determines in advance the measure of damages if a party breaches the agreement. • Traditionally, courts have upheld such a clause unless the agreed-on sum is deemed a penalty for one of the following reasons: (1) the sum grossly exceeds the probable damages on breach, (2) the same sum is made payable for any variety of different breaches (some major, some minor), or (3) a mere delay in payment has been listed among the events of default. — Also termed *agreed-damages clause.* Cf. LIMITATION-OF-REMEDIES CLAUSE; PENALTY CLAUSE.

liquidated debt. See DEBT.

liquidated demand. See *liquidated claim* under CLAIM (3).

liquidated sum. See LIQUIDATED AMOUNT.

liquidating distribution. See DISTRIBUTION.

liquidating dividend. See *liquidation dividend* under DIVIDEND.

liquidating partner. See PARTNER.

liquidating price. See *redemption price* under PRICE.

liquidating trust. See TRUST (3).

liquidation, *n.* (16c) **1.** The act of determining by agreement or by litigation the exact amount of something (as a debt or damages) that before was uncertain. **2.** The act of settling a debt by payment or other satisfaction. **3.** The act or process of converting assets into cash, esp. to settle debts.

▸ **one-month liquidation.** (1960) A special election, available to certain shareholders, that determines how the distributions received in liquidation by electing shareholders will be treated for federal income-tax purposes. • To qualify for the election, the corporation must be completely liquidated within one month. IRC § 333.

▸ **partial liquidation.** (1832) A liquidation that does not completely dispose of a company's assets; esp., a liquidation occurring when some corporate assets are distributed to shareholders (usu. on a pro rata basis) and the corporation continues to operate in a restricted form.

▸ **twelve-month liquidation.** (1964) A liquidation occurring within 12 months from adoption of the liquidation plan to complete liquidation, subject to a tax law prohibiting the company from recognizing any gains or losses on property sold within that time frame. • Generally, inventory will not be included unless a bulk sale occurs. IRC § 337.

4. *Bankruptcy.* The process — under Chapter 7 of the Bankruptcy Code — of collecting a debtor's nonexempt property, converting that property to cash, and distributing the cash to the various creditors. • Upon liquidation, the debtor hopes to obtain a discharge, which releases the debtor from any further personal liability for prebankruptcy debts. See CHAPTER 7. Cf. REHABILITATION (3).

▸ **involuntary liquidation.** (1856) A liquidation initiated by creditors against the debtor.

▸ **voluntary liquidation.** (1844) A liquidation approved and initiated by the debtor.

liquidation bankruptcy. See CHAPTER 7 (2).

liquidation court. See COURT.

liquidation dividend. See DIVIDEND.

liquidation preference. See PREFERENCE.

liquidation price. See PRICE.

liquidation right. (1937) *Securities law.* A right of common stockholders to a pro rata distribution of a corporation's net assets on dissolution. • The right is usu. subordinate to other classes of securities, such as preferred stock, that have priority of payment.

liquidation value. 1. See VALUE (2). **2.** See *liquidation price* under PRICE.

liquidator. (1858) A person appointed to wind up a business's affairs, esp. by selling off its assets. See LIQUIDATION (3), (4). Cf. RECEIVER.

liquid debt. See DEBT.

liquidity. (1923) **1.** The quality, state, or condition of being readily convertible to cash. **2.** *Securities.* The characteristic of having enough units in the market that large transactions can occur without substantial price variations. • Most stocks traded on the New York Stock Exchange, for example, have liquidity.

liquidity ratio. (1930) The ratio between a person's or entity's assets that are held in cash or liquid form and the amount of the person's or entity's current liabilities, indicating the ability to pay current debts as they come due.

liquor. (14c) An alcoholic or intoxicating liquid, esp. one of a spirituous nature as distinguished from beer and wine. See SPIRITUOUS. Cf. ALCOHOL.

> "*Liquor, or Liquors.* Either of these terms, standing alone, is too wide to have a precise legal signification, unless explained by the context or by necessary inferences from the subject-matter of the statute. When thus explained, however, the word 'liquor' or 'liquors' is commonly understood as including all varieties of intoxicating beverages, whether spirituous, vinous, or malt. Thus it is held that this word, as used in a federal statute providing that 'there shall be no allowance for breakage, leakage, or damage on wines, liquors, cordials, or distilled spirits,' includes fermented as well as distilled liquors, and covers lager beer. So, under a statute forbidding a credit of more than ten dollars for 'liquors' sold, it is held that champagne wine is included." Henry Campbell Black, *A Treatise on the Laws Regulating the Manufacture and Sale of Intoxicating Liquors* § 7, at 8 (1892).

▸ **intoxicating liquor.** (17c) **1.** An ardent, spirituous, distilled, or vinous liquid or compound containing a minimum statutory percentage of alcohol and consumed as a beverage. **2.** Any distilled or fermented alcoholic beverage containing a minimum statutory percentage of alcohol and capable of causing drunkenness when consumed in sufficient quantities. See SPIRITUOUS. Cf. ALCOHOL.

liquor offense. See OFFENSE (2).

lis (lis). [Latin] (17c) A piece of litigation; a controversy or dispute.

lis alibi pendens (lis **al**-ə-bɪ **pen**-dənz). [Latin] (18c) **1.** A lawsuit pending elsewhere. **2.** *Hist.* A preliminary defense that a case involving the same parties and the same subject is pending in another court. See LIS PENDENS.

lis est sopita (**lis** est sə-**pɪ**-tə). [Latin] *Hist.* The suit is concluded; the issues in a case are decided. — Also termed *lis est finita* (**lis** est fi-**nɪ**-tə).

lis mota (lis **moh**-tə), *n.* [Latin "a lawsuit moved"] (1833) *Hist.* A dispute that has begun and later forms the basis of a lawsuit.

lis pendens (lis **pen**-dənz). [Latin] (17c) **1.** A pending lawsuit. **2.** The jurisdiction, power, or control acquired by a court over property while a legal action is pending. **3.** A notice, recorded in the chain of title to real property, required or permitted in some jurisdictions to warn all persons that certain property is the subject matter of litigation, and that any interests acquired during the pendency of the suit are subject to its outcome. — Also termed (in sense 3) *notice of lis pendens*; *notice of pendency.* Cf. PENDENTE LITE.

> "The particular property involved in the suit must be so definitely described and identified in the pleading that any one reading it can learn thereby what property is intended to be made the subject of litigation. It is, perhaps, not necessary that the land be described by metes and bounds. Reasonable certainty as to the intent would be sufficient. A lis pendens, and its consequent notice, begins to operate when the suit is properly commenced by the service of process, and continues to operate until the rendition of final judgment. A purchaser, pendente lite, of the subject of the litigation, if he buys in good faith, and without notice of the rights and interest of the litigants, is not affected by the suit pending, or by notice of its pendency, unless the suit has been prosecuted with due diligence. Where the suit abates the death of a party, the lis pendens will not lose its force as a notice, if it be revived without unreasonable delay. The lis pendens may be operative after the rendition of the judgment if an appeal is taken, and diligently prosecuted. The abandonment or voluntary dismissal of the suit prevents the application of this doctrine." James W. Eaton, *Handbook of Equity Jurisprudence*, § 55, at 152–53 (1901).

lis sub judice (lis səb **joo**-di-see). [Latin] *Hist.* Lawsuit before the court; the present case.

list, *n.* (13c) **1.** A roll or register, as of names. **2.** A docket of cases ready for hearing or trial. See CALENDAR (2); DOCKET.

list, *vb.* (bef. 12c) **1.** To set down or enter (information) in a list. **2.** To register (a security) on an exchange so that it may be publicly traded. **3.** To place (property) for sale under an agreement with a real-estate agent or broker.

listed security. See SECURITY (4).

listed security exchange. (2002) An organized secondary security market operating at a designated location, such as the New York Stock Exchange.

listed species. See *candidate species* under SPECIES (1).

listed stock. See *listed security* under SECURITY (4).

listening device. (1940) An electronic means, such as a miniature radio transmitter with a microphone, used to intercept, overhear, or record, usu. covertly, sounds and voices; an electronic tool used for eavesdropping. — Also termed *covert-listening device*; *wire*; (slang) *bug.*

lister. (18c) A person authorized to compile lists of taxable property for assessment and appraisal; an assessor.

listing. (1891) **1.** *Real estate.* An agreement between a property owner and an agent, whereby the agent agrees to try to secure a buyer or tenant for a specific property at a certain price and terms in return for a fee or commission. — Also termed *listing agreement*; *authorization to sell.*

▸ **exclusive-agency listing.** (1952) A listing providing that one agent has the right to be the only person, other than the owner, to sell the property during a specified period. — Also termed *exclusive listing*; *exclusive-authorization-to-sell listing.*

▸ **general listing.** See *open listing.*

▸ **multiple listing.** (1927) A listing providing that the agent will allow other agents to try to sell the property. • Under this agreement, the original agent gives the selling agent a percentage of the commission or some other stipulated amount.

▸ **net listing.** (1949) A listing providing that the agent agrees to sell the owner's property for a set minimum price, any amount over the minimum being retained by the agent as commission. — Also termed *net sale contract.*

▸ **open listing.** (1949) A listing that allows selling rights to be given to more than one agent at a time, obligates the owner to pay a commission when a specified broker makes a sale, and reserves the owner's right to personally sell the property without paying a commission. — Also termed *nonexclusive listing; general listing; simple listing.*

2. *Securities.* The contract between a firm and a stock exchange by which the trading of the firm's securities on the exchange is handled. See *listed security* under SECURITY (4).

▸ **dual listing.** (1965) The listing of a security on more than one exchange.

3. *Tax.* The creation of a schedule or inventory of a person's taxable property; the list of a person's taxable property.

listing agent. See AGENT.

listing agreement. See LISTING (1).

list of creditors. (1818) A schedule giving the names and addresses of creditors, along with amounts owed them. • This list is required in a bankruptcy proceeding.

list price. See PRICE.

litem (**lɪ**-tem *or* -təm). See AD LITEM.

litem denuntiare (**lɪ**-tem də-nən-shee-**air**-ee). [Latin "to announce a suit"] *Roman law.* **1.** The summoning of a defendant by a magistrate exercising *cognitio* in the late classical period. **2.** The notification by a buyer to the seller of a claim by a third party to the things sold. — Also spelled *litem denunciare.* Cf. LITIS DENUNTIATIO.

litem suam facere (**lɪ**-tem **s[y]oo**-əm **fay**-sə-ree). [Latin "to make a suit one's own"] (16c) *Roman law.* (Of a judex) to fail in his official duty through imprudence, such as not adhering to the formula, or not following due procedure. • This failure amounted to misconduct in the judex's duties, and a litigant was given a private action against him. The scope of actionable misconduct is not certain. It included not obeying the formula and not adjourning the trial properly, but it may also have included overt acts of corruption, such as accepting bribes.

lite pendente (**lɪ**-tee pen-**den**-tee). [Latin] See PENDENTE LITE.

litera (**lit**-ər-ə), *n.* [Latin "letter"] *Hist.* **1.** A letter. **2.** The letter of a law, as distinguished from its spirit. — Also spelled *littera.* See LETTER (3). Pl. ***literae.***

literacy test. (1915) *Hist.* A test of one's ability to read and write, formerly required in some states as a condition for registering to vote. • Literacy tests were abused at various times in United States history to preclude minorities from exercising the right to vote. This practice was prohibited by the Voting Rights Act of 1965. 42 USCA §§ 1971–1974. *See South Carolina v. Katzenbach,* 383 U.S. 301, 86 S.Ct. 8 (1966).

literae mortuae (**lit**-ər-ee **mor**-choo-ee), *n.* [Latin] (17c) *Hist.* Dead letters; filler words in a statute.

literae patentes (**lit**-ər-ee pə-**ten**-teez), *n.* [Latin "open letters"] (17c) *Hist.* A public grant from the sovereign to a subject, conferring the right to land, a franchise, a title, liberty, or some other endowment. • The modern "patent" and, more closely, "letters patent" derive from this term. See LETTERS PATENT (1).

> "The term 'patent' is short for 'letters patent,' derived from the Latin *literae patentes*, meaning open letters. Generally, letters patent were letters addressed by the sovereign 'to all whom these presents shall come,' reciting a grant of some dignity, office, franchise, or other privilege that has been given by the sovereign to the patentee.'" Donald S. Chisum et al., *Principles of Patent Law* 2 (1998).

literae procuratoriae (**lit**-ər-ee prok-yə-rə-**tor**-ee-ee), *n.* [Law Latin] *Hist.* Letters of procuration; letters of attorney; power of attorney. See POWER OF ATTORNEY.

literae recognitionis (**lit**-ər-ee rek-əg-nish-ee-**oh**-nis), *n.* [Latin] *Hist.* A bill of lading. See BILL OF LADING.

literae sigillatae (**lit**-ər-ee sij-ə-**lay**-tee), *n.* [Latin] *Hist.* Sealed letters. • A sheriff's return on a writ was often called *literae sigillatae.*

literal, *adj.* (16c) According to expressed language. • Literal performance of a condition requires exact compliance with its terms.

literal canon. See *strict constructionism* under CONSTRUCTIONISM.

literal construction. See *strict interpretation* under INTERPRETATION (1).

literal contract. See CONTRACT.

litera legis. See LETTER OF THE LAW.

literal infringement. See INFRINGEMENT.

literal interpretation. See *strict construction* under CONSTRUCTION.

literalism. An interpretive doctrine that reads words according to their literal senses — never figuratively — and that applies meaning whatever the result. • *Literal* here bears a clinical sense, not a pejorative one: "A sensible literal meaning of a statute must always be followed if there is no other meaning that the words can reasonably bear." Frederick J. de Sloovère, *Textual Interpretation of Statutes,* 11 N.Y.U. L.Q. Rev. 538, 543 (1934). Correspondingly: "If there is but a single sensible meaning, it is nearly always the literal meaning." *Id.* at 547. Cf. HYPERLITERALISM.

literal proof. See PROOF.

literal rule. 1. See *strict constructionism* under CONSTRUCTIONISM. **2.** The doctrine that effect must be given to the words of a legal instrument, esp. a statute, regardless of the consequences, however ridiculous or contrary to the known objects of the instrument those consequences may be. • Of this rule, which has been called "[t]he first and predominant rule of statutory interpretation," one commentator states: "It is productive of certainty in the sense that it renders the decision of a court easier to predict than would be the case if the judges assumed that they have a roving commission to carry out the object of legislation, irrespective of the words used." Rupert Cross, *Precedent in English Law* 179 (1961).

literal translation. See TRANSLATION (1).

literary, *adj.* (17c) Of, relating to, or involving literature or other written forms of expression.

literary composition. (18c) A written expression involving mental effort, arranged in a purposeful order. Cf. *literary work* under WORK (2).

literary executor. See EXECUTOR (2).

literary property. (18c) **1.** The physical property in which an intellectual production is embodied, such as a book, screenplay, or lecture. **2.** An owner's exclusive right to possess, use, and dispose of such a production. See COPYRIGHT; INTELLECTUAL PROPERTY.

literary work. See WORK (2).

literate, *adj.* (15c) **1.** Able to read and write a language. **2.** Knowledgeable and educated. — **literacy,** *n.*

literatura (lit-ər-ə-**t[y]uur**-ə), *n.* [Latin fr. *litera* "a letter"] *Hist.* Education. • *Ad literaturam ponere* means the right to educate one's children, esp. male children. During feudal times, servile tenants could not educate their children without the lord's consent.

litigable (**lit**-ə-gə-bəl), *adj.* (18c) Able to be contested or disputed in court <litigable claims>. — **litigability,** *n.*

litigant. (17c) A party to a lawsuit; the plaintiff or defendant in a court action, whether an individual, firm, corporation, or other entity.

▸ **institutional litigant.** See INSTITUTIONAL LITIGANT.

▸ **self-represented litigant.** See PRO SE.

▸ **vexatious litigant.** (1831) A litigant who repeatedly files frivolous lawsuits. • Many jurisdictions have statutes or local rules requiring a vexatious litigant to obtain the court's permission to file any further lawsuits or pleadings. The litigant may also be subject to sanctions.

litigate (**lit**-ə-gayt), *vb.* To take or defend against a claim or a complaint in a court of law.

litigation, *n.* (17c) **1.** The process of carrying on a lawsuit <the attorney advised his client to make a generous settlement offer in order to avoid litigation>. **2.** A lawsuit itself <several litigations pending before the court>. — **litigatory, litigational,** *adj.*

> "In litigation you either take the initiative or you stand on the defensive, and your attack or defense must be supported upon one or both of these two elements. The aim of an intelligent preparation is to secure for your client a superior advantage over his adversary on the law, or on the facts, or on both. If by prudent provision you can be stronger on the facts under the law, you will win, or if your case be in the proper construction of the law, which you can show, it may be by great research and exhaustiveness of presentation to be for you, again you have the preponderance. But if you can present superior combinations, both of law and fact, then you are doubly safe. The right preparation of a case is scientific, and its object is to present for the client at the trial, on those points of controversy, which are cardinal or controlling, the ascendency as already explained. A little observance of trials and arguments will give the reader a clearer insight into the subject than many more pages, however plainly written and filled it might be to overflowing, with illustrations. As the student observes the argument after the evidence is all in, he will often detect for himself, the preponderance of the prevailing party, and he will likewise, while hearing discussion of legal questions, begin to see before the judge delivers his opinion, who will win it and how. Napoleon's saying, that the art of war consisted all in being the stronger on a certain point, is accepted as a maxim. So in litigation, there are turning points, either of law or fact, where superiority will win for the party who has it." John C. Reed, *Practical Suggestions for the Management of Law-suits* 20–21 (1876).

▸ **complex litigation.** Litigation involving several parties who are separately represented, and usu. involving multifarious factual and legal issues.

> "What exactly is 'complex litigation'? The problem is that no one really knows — or, more accurately perhaps, various definitions don't agree. Complex civil litigation has an 'I-know-it-when-I-see-it' quality. Nearly everyone agrees that matters like the massive asbestos litigation, the AT&T antitrust suit, or the remedial phase of a school desegregation case are complex. But trying to find a common thread that both describes these cases and distinguishes them from the run-of-the-mill car crash is difficult." Jay Tidmarsh & Roger H. Transgrud, *Complex Litigation* 1 (2002).

▸ **imported litigation.** (1927) One or more lawsuits brought in a state that has no interest in the dispute.

▸ **megalitigation.** (1985) Civil, usu. commercial, litigation that is extraordinarily complex, time-consuming, and expensive. — Also written *mega-litigation.*

litigation costs. See COST (3).

litigation guardian. See *guardian ad litem* under GUARDIAN (1).

litigation hold. See HOLD (1).

litigation-hold letter. (2008) A writing that orders the segregation and retention of certain documents and data that are or may be relevant to a threatened or pending litigation or an official investigation.

▸ **internal litigation-hold letter.** (2008) A litigation-hold letter sent by a company, directly or through its attorneys, to its own employees.

litigation privilege. See PRIVILEGE (1).

litigator. (16c) **1.** A trial lawyer. **2.** A lawyer who prepares cases for trial, as by conducting discovery and pretrial motions, trying cases, and handling appeals. **3.** *Archaic.* A party to a lawsuit; a litigant.

litigatrix (lit-i-**gay**-triks). [Latin fem. form of *litigator*] (1771) **1.** *Hist.* A female litigant. **2.** *Slang.* An assertive and successful female attorney; esp., one who is particularly intimidating or ruthless, or shows a habitual animosity toward men. • In sense 2, the word is supposedly a portmanteau word from *litigator* and *dominatrix.* The sense was coined in 1991 by assistant U.S. attorney David B. Lat. Some regard the term as objectionable on grounds of sexism.

litigious (li-**tij**-əs), *adj.* (14c) **1.** Prone to legal disputes; eager to take disagreements into a court of law <our litigious society>. **2.** *Archaic.* Of, relating to, or involving the subject of a lawsuit <the litigious property>. **3.** *Archaic.* Of, relating to, or involving lawsuits; litigatory <they couldn't settle the litigious dispute>. — **litigiousness, litigiosity** (li-tij-ee-**os**-ə-tee), *n.*

litigious right. (1817) *Civil law.* A right that cannot be exercised without first being determined in a lawsuit. La. Civ. Code art. 2652. • If the right is sold, it must be in litigation at the time of sale to be considered a litigious right.

litis aestimatio (**lɪ**-tis es-tə-**may**-shee-oh). [Latin] (17c) *Roman law.* The judicial estimate of the measure of damages.

litis contestatio (**lɪ**-tis kon-tes-**tay**-shee-oh). [Latin] (16c) **1.** *Roman law.* The final agreement of the parties to a suit on the formula the praetor would issue to the judex. — Also termed *contestatio litis.* See FORMULA.

> "Both parties being present, or represented, before the praetor, the plaintiff stated the nature of his claim and asked for an action. It lay in the discretion of the praetor to give or to refuse it. . . . If, in the event, the praetor refused any action at all, or any action which the plaintiff

was willing to accept, the matter was at an end . . . . If, on the other hand, subject to the direction and approval of the praetor, the parties agreed upon the issues to be referred . . . [a] document framed in identical terms was issued to the judex by the praetor as his authority to act. This ceremonial in which three persons concurred (plaintiff, defendant, praetor) was the litis contestatio." R.W. Lee, *The Elements of Roman Law* 179–80 (4th ed. 1956).

2. *Hist.* A contested point in a lawsuit; a litigable issue developed by the litigants' alternating statements. **3.** CONTESTATION OF SUIT.

litis denuntiatio (lɪ-tis də-nən-s[h]ee-**ay**-shee-oh), *n.* [Latin] (1923) *Civil law.* The process by which a land purchaser, sued for possession of the land by a third party, notified the land seller and demanded aid in defending the suit under the seller's warranty of title. — Also spelled *litis denunciatio.* Cf. LITEM DENUNTIARE.

litis dominium (lɪ-tis də-**min**-ee-əm), *n.* [Latin] See DOMINUS LITIS.

litis ordinatio (lɪ-tis or-di-**nay**-shee-oh). [Latin "the order or regulation of a lawsuit"] (1863) *Scots law.* The form under which a lawsuit is conducted.

litispendence (lɪ-tis-**pen**-dənts). (17c) *Archaic.* The time during which a lawsuit is pending.

litter, *n.* (18c) Wastepaper, cans, and other refuse that people have discarded and left on the ground in a public place.

litteris obligatio (**lit**-ər-is ob-lə-**gay**-shee-oh). [Latin] *Roman law.* An obligation arising from formal, written entries in account books; an obligation arising from a literal contract. See *literal contract* under CONTRACT.

Little FTC Acts. See UNFAIR TRADE PRACTICES AND CONSUMER PROTECTION LAW.

littoral (**lit**-ər-əl), *adj.* (17c) Of, relating to, or involving the coast or shore of an ocean, sea, or lake <the littoral right to limit others' consumption of the water>. Cf. RIPARIAN. — **littoral,** *n.*

littoral erosion. See EROSION.

littoral state. See STATE (1).

littus maris (lit-əs **mar**-is) [Law Latin "shore of the sea"] (1855) **1.** Ordinary tides or neap tides that occur between the full moon and dark of the moon. **2.** The shore between the normal high-water and low-water marks.

litura (li-**t[y]oor**-ə), *n.* [Latin] *Roman law.* A blot or erasure in a will or other instrument.

livelihood. (15c) A means of supporting one's existence, esp. financially.

livelode. (16c) *Archaic.* Livelihood; maintenance. — Also termed *lifelode.*

livery (**liv**-ə-ree *or* **liv**-ree). (15c) **1.** The delivery of the possession of real property. Cf. DELIVERY. **2.** *Hist.* An heir's writ, upon reaching the age of majority, to obtain seisin of his lands from the king. **3.** The boarding and care of horses for a fee. **4.** A business that rents vehicles.

livery in chivalry. (18c) *Hist.* The delivery of possession of real property from a guardian to a ward in chivalry when the ward reached majority.

livery office. (18c) An office designated for the delivery of lands.

livery of seisin. (15c) *Hist.* The ceremony by which a grantor conveyed land to a grantee. • Livery of seisin involved either (1) going on the land and having the grantor symbolically deliver possession of the land to the grantee by handing over a twig, a clod of dirt, or a piece of turf (called *livery in deed*) or (2) going within sight of the land and having the grantor tell the grantee that possession was being given, followed by the grantee's entering the land (called *livery in law*). See INVESTITURE; SEISIN.

"[W]e may now pause to wonder how transfer of these potentially infinite interests was accomplished. Without a modern system of land records, it would be desirable that the transfer be effected with sufficient ceremony not only to mark itself indelibly in the memories of the participants, but also to give notice to interested persons such as the mesne lord above the transferor. The central idea was to make ritual *livery* (meaning 'delivery,' from the Old French *livrer*) of *seisin* (meaning, roughly, 'possession,' from the Old French *saisir* or *seisir*). The transferor and transferee would go to the land to be transferred, and the transferor would then hand to the transferee a lump of soil or a twig from a tree — all the while intoning the appropriate words of grant, together with the magical words 'and his heirs' if the interest transferred was to be a potentially infinite one." Thomas F. Bergin & Paul G. Haskell, *Preface to Estates in Land and Future Interests* 10–11 (2d ed. 1984).

lives in being. See LIFE IN BEING.

livestock, *n.* (18c) Domestic animals and fowls that (1) are kept for profit or pleasure, (2) can normally be confined within boundaries without seriously impairing their utility, and (3) do not normally intrude on others' land in such a way as to harm the land or growing crops.

live storage. (1919) The storage of cars in active daily use, rather than cars put away for an extended period. • A garage owner's responsibility sometimes depends on whether a car is in live or dead storage. Cf. DEAD STORAGE.

live thalweg. See THALWEG.

living, *n.* (14c) One's source of monetary support or resources; esp., one's employment.

living constitutionalism. *Constitutional law.* The doctrine that the Constitution should be interpreted and applied in accordance with changing circumstances and, in particular, with changes in social values. • While many authorities use the terms *living constitutionalism* and *nonoriginalism* interchangeably, others view living constitutionalism as a form of nonoriginalism that values interpretive conformity with changed circumstances and norms more greatly than do other forms of nonoriginalism. See NONORIGINALISM. Cf. ORIGINALISM; INTERPRETIVISM; NONINTERPRETIVISM; LIVING-TREE DOCTRINE. — Also termed *contemporaneous interpretation.* — **living constitutionalist,** *n.*

living probate. See *antemortem probate* under PROBATE (1).

living separate and apart. (18c) (Of spouses) living away from each other, along with at least one spouse's intent to dissolve the marriage. • One basis for no-fault divorce in many states exists if the spouses have lived apart for a specified period. — Sometimes shortened to *separate and apart.*

living-together agreement. See COHABITATION AGREEMENT.

living-tree doctrine. *Canadian law.* A doctrine of constitutional interpretation characterizing the Canadian Constitution as "a living tree capable of growth and expansion" and mandating that it be given "a large and liberal interpretation." • This doctrine, which does not apply to legislation, was first announced in a 1930 decision of the Judicial Committee of the Privy Council. *See Edwards v. A.G. for Canada*, [1930] A.C. 124. Cf. ORIGINALISM; NONORIGINALISM; INTERPRETIVISM; NONINTERPRETIVISM; LIVING CONSTITUTIONALISM.

living trust. See *inter vivos trust* under TRUST (3).

living wage. See WAGE.

living will. (1972) An instrument, signed with the formalities statutorily required for a will, by which a person directs that his or her life not be artificially prolonged by extraordinary measures when there is no reasonable expectation of recovery from extreme physical or mental disability. • Most states have living-will legislation. — Also termed *declaration of a desire for a natural death*; *directive to physicians*. See NATURAL-DEATH ACT; UNIFORM HEALTH-CARE DECISIONS ACT. Cf. ADVANCE DIRECTIVE (1), (2); INSTRUCTION DIRECTIVE.

L.J. *abbr.* (1866) **1.** Law Judge. **2.** LAW JOURNAL. **3.** LORD JUSTICE OF APPEAL.

L.JJ. *abbr.* Lords justices. See LORD JUSTICE OF APPEAL.

LKE. *abbr.* LIKE-KIND EXCHANGE.

L.L. *abbr.* LAW LATIN.

LLA. *abbr.* LIMITATION-OF-LIABILITY ACT.

L.Lat. *abbr.* LAW LATIN.

LL.B. *abbr.* (18c) Legum baccalaurens; bachelor of Laws. • This was formerly the law degree ordinarily conferred by American law schools. It is still the normal degree in British law schools. Cf. JURIS DOCTOR.

L.L.C. See *limited-liability company* under COMPANY.

LL.D. *abbr.* (18c) DOCTOR OF LAWS.

LL.J. *abbr.* Lords justices. See LORD JUSTICE OF APPEAL.

L.L.L.P. *abbr.* See *limited-liability limited partnership* under PARTNERSHIP.

LL.M. *abbr.* (18c) MASTER OF LAWS.

Lloyd's. See LLOYD'S OF LONDON.

Lloyd's association. See LLOYD'S UNDERWRITERS.

Lloyd's bond. See BOND (3).

Lloyd's insurance. See INSURANCE.

Lloyd's of London. *Insurance.* **1.** A London insurance mart where individual underwriters gather to quote rates and write insurance on a wide variety of risks. **2.** A voluntary association of merchants, shipowners, underwriters, and brokers formed not to write policies but instead to issue a notice of an endeavor to members who may individually underwrite a policy by assuming shares of the total risk of insuring a client. • The names of the bound underwriters and the attorney-in-fact appear on the policy. — Also termed *Lloyd's*; *London Lloyd's*.

> "[I]t is not the corporation of Lloyd's which undertakes insurance risks and enters into policies of insurance; that is done by the individual members of Lloyd's, acting usually in groups or 'syndicates,' which are not partnerships or companies but merely fortuitous aggregations of, say, five, ten, or more members represented in common by one *underwriting agent* having power to bind them each individually and separately to contracts of insurance. These members are frequently referred to as 'names'; and their agent is said to 'write' for them. If, as is commonly the case, he also is a member of Lloyd's, then he will 'write' for himself, too." 2 *Stephen's Commentaries on the Laws of England* 237 (L. Crispin Warmington ed., 21st ed. 1950).

Lloyd's underwriters. An unincorporated association of underwriters who, under a common name, engage in the insurance business through an attorney-in-fact having authority to obligate the underwriters severally, within specified limits, on insurance contracts that the attorney makes or issues in the common name. — Also termed *Lloyd's association*; *American Lloyd's*.

L.L.P. See *limited-liability partnership* under PARTNERSHIP.

LMRA. *abbr.* LABOR–MANAGEMENT RELATIONS ACT.

load, *n.* An amount added to a security's price or to an insurance premium in order to cover the sales commission and expenses <the mutual fund had a high front-end load>. — Also termed *sales load*; *acquisition cost*.

load factor. (1902) **1.** The ratio of a utility customer's usage levels during a given period compared to the customer's demand during peak periods. **2.** An analysis of the number of passengers on an airplane or other common carrier compared to available capacity.

load fund. See MUTUAL FUND.

load house. (1987) A place used to harbor and shield illegal aliens after they have been smuggled across the border while awaiting further transportation.

loading. (1867) *Insurance.* An amount added to a life-insurance premium to cover the insurer's business expenses and contingencies. — Also termed *expense loading*. See *gross premium* (1) under PREMIUM (1).

load line. (1884) *Maritime law.* **1.** The depth to which a safely loaded ship will sink in salt water. **2.** One of a set of graduated marks on the side of a ship, indicating the depth to which the ship can be loaded in varying waters (such as salt water or freshwater) and weather conditions. • Load lines must, by law in most maritime countries, be cut and painted amidships. — Also termed (in sense 2) *load-line marks*; *Plimsoll marks*.

> "The interest of shipowners led them, in early times, to load vessels to a point beyond safety; the greater the weight of the vessel's load, of course, the lower she rides in the water, and the more vulnerable she is to heavy seas. Many seamen consequently lost their lives. Britain led the way in establishing standards of depth in the water believed to be safe; Samuel Plimsoll, M.P., was the moving spirit, and gave his name to the Plimsoll mark, now seen on the side of all large vessels, which marks the limits of safety for different seas and seasons. Since 1929, the United States has made mandatory the placing of and compliance with loadline marks . . . ." Grant Gilmore & Charles L. Black Jr., *The Law of Admiralty* § 11-12, at 987 (2d ed. 1975).

loadmanage. (15c) *Hist.* **1.** The fee paid to loadsmen, who sail in small vessels acting as pilots for larger ships. **2.** The hiring of a pilot for a vessel. **3.** A pilot's or loadsman's skill. — Also spelled *lodemanage*; *lode manage*.

loadsman. (14c) *Hist.* **1.** Someone who directs a ship's course from a small boat traveling in front of the larger ship rather than from the ship itself. • The loadsmen had a monopoly on piloting in the cinque ports. See CINQUE PORTS. **2.** Someone who took the ship to a berth after a pilot had brought it into port. — Also spelled *loadman*; *lodeman*; *lodesman*.

loan, *n.* (12c) **1.** An act of lending; a grant of something for temporary use <Turner gave the laptop as a loan, not a gift>. **2.** A thing lent for the borrower's temporary use;

esp., a sum of money lent at interest <Hull applied for a car loan>.

▸ **accommodation loan.** (1834) A loan for which the lender receives no consideration in return. See ACCOMMODATION.

▸ **add-on loan.** (1972) A loan in which the interest is calculated at the stated rate for the loan agreement's full term for the full principal amount, and then the interest is added to the principal before installment payments are calculated, resulting in an interest amount higher than if it were calculated on the monthly unpaid balance. • Consumer loans are typically add-on loans. — Also termed *contract loan*. See *add-on interest* under INTEREST (3).

▸ **amortized loan.** (1930) A loan calling for periodic payments that are applied first to interest and then to principal, as provided by the terms of the note. See AMORTIZATION (1).

▸ **back-to-back loan.** (1978) A loan arrangement by which two firms lend each other funds denominated in different currencies for a specified period. • The purpose is usu. to protect against fluctuations in the currencies' exchange rates.

▸ **balloon loan.** (1975) An installment loan in which one or more of the later repayments are much larger than earlier payments; esp., a loan featuring a string of payments that are too small to amortize the entire loan within the loan period, coupled with a large final lump-sum payment of the outstanding balance.

▸ **below-market loan.** See *interest-free loan*.

▸ **bridge loan.** (1975) A short-term loan that is used to cover costs until more permanent financing is arranged or to cover a portion of costs that are expected to be covered by an imminent sale. — Also termed *bridge financing*; *swing loan*.

▸ **broker call loan.** See *call loan*.

▸ **building loan.** (1851) A type of bridge loan used primarily for erecting a building. • The loan is typically advanced in parts as work progresses and is used to pay the contractor, subcontractors, and material suppliers. — Also termed *construction loan*. See *interim financing* under FINANCING.

▸ **call loan.** (1869) A loan for which the lender can demand payment at any time, usu. with 24 hours' notice, because there is no fixed maturity date. — Also termed *broker call loan*; *demand loan*. Cf. *term loan*.

▸ **cash-advance loan.** See *payday loan*.

▸ **character loan.** (1936) A loan made in reliance on the borrower's character and stable earnings. • Character loans are usu. secured by a mortgage or by other property, but sometimes they are unsecured.

▸ **check-advance loan.** See *payday loan*.

▸ **clearing loan.** (1960) A loan made to a bond dealer pending the sale of a bond issue.

▸ **collateral loan.** See *secured loan*.

▸ **commercial loan.** (1875) A loan that a financial institution gives to a business, generally for 30 to 90 days.

▸ **commodity loan.** (1923) A loan secured by a commodity (such as cotton or wool) in the form of a warehouse receipt or other negotiable instrument.

▸ **consolidation loan.** (1875) A loan whose proceeds are used to pay off other individual loans, thereby creating a more manageable debt.

▸ **construction loan.** See *building loan*.

▸ **consumer loan.** (1957) A loan that is given to an individual for family, household, personal, or agricultural purposes and that is generally governed by truth-in-lending statutes and regulations.

▸ **contract loan.** See *add-on loan*.

▸ **Crown loan.** (1979) *Tax*. An interest-free demand loan, usu. from parent to child, in which the borrowed funds are invested and the income from the investment is taxed at the child's rate. • This type of loan is named for one Harry Crown of Chicago, reputedly one of the first persons to use it. See *kiddie tax* under TAX.

▸ **day loan.** (1932) A short-term loan to a broker to finance daily transactions.

▸ **deferred-deposit loan.** See *payday loan*.

▸ **demand loan.** See *call loan*.

▸ **discount loan.** (1943) A loan in which interest is deducted in advance, at the time the loan is made.

▸ **doorstep loan.** A loan offered by a door-to-door solicitor, usu. for home repairs at a high interest rate and under misleading or fraudulent terms. • The term is used primarily in the United Kingdom.

▸ **GI loan.** See *veteran's loan*.

▸ **home-equity loan.** (1984) A line of bank credit given to a homeowner, using as collateral the homeowner's equity in the home. — Often shortened to *equity loan*. — Also termed *home-equity line of credit*. See EQUITY (7).

▸ **installment loan.** (1916) A loan that is to be repaid in usu. equal portions over a specified period.

▸ **interest-free loan.** (1946) Money loaned to a borrower at no charge or, under the Internal Revenue Code, with a charge that is lower than the market rate. IRC (26 USCA) § 7872. — Also termed (in the IRC) *below-market loan*.

▸ **interest-only loan.** (1978) A loan for which the borrower pays only the interest on the principal balance of the loan for a stated period, usu. a few years. • At the end of the stated period, the principal balance is unchanged. An interest-only loan features low initial payments in return for significantly larger payments later or a balloon payment at the end of the term.

▸ **liar's loan.** (2007) **1.** A loan that involves no background check and can be obtained by claiming that one meets the lender's income and other requirements. **2.** See *no-doc loan* (1). **3.** See *stated-income loan* (1). Cf. *NINJA loan*.

▸ **maritime loan.** (1810) A loan providing that a lender will not be repaid if the cargo is damaged or lost because of a navigational peril, but that the lender will be repaid plus interest if the cargo arrives safely or is damaged because of the carrier's negligence. — Also termed *marine loan*.

▸ **mortgage loan.** (1846) A loan secured by a mortgage or deed of trust on real property.

▸ **NINJA loan.** *abbr.* (2007) No-income, no-job, no-assets loan. Cf. *liar's loan* (1); *no-doc loan* (1); *stated-income loan* (1).

▸ **no-doc loan.** (1987) **1.** A loan for which a borrower provides only minimal proof of ability to repay. • The name is short for "no documentation." **2.** See *liar's loan* (1). Cf. *NINJA loan.*

▸ **nonperforming loan.** (1984) An outstanding loan that is not being repaid.

▸ **nonrecourse loan.** (1941) A secured loan that allows the lender to attach only the collateral, not the borrower's personal assets, if the loan is not repaid.

▸ **participation loan.** (1928) A loan issued by two or more lenders. See LOAN PARTICIPATION.

▸ **payday loan.** (1937) A small, short-term, unsecured loan with a very high annual interest rate. • Typically, a borrower gives a lender a postdated personal check for the borrowed amount (usu. between $100 and $2,000), plus a fee. In exchange, the lender gives the borrower cash or electronically transfers money to the borrower's account (less the fee). The lender then waits to cash the check until a stipulated date, usu. the borrower's next payday. Some states ban payday lending outright, while others place few restrictions on the practice. — Also termed *payday advance*; *cash-advance loan*; *check-advance loan*; *postdated-check loan*; *deferred-deposit loan.*

▸ **policy loan.** (1906) An insurer's loan to an insured, secured by the policy's cash reserve.

▸ **postdated-check loan.** See *payday loan.*

▸ **precarious loan.** (1934) **1.** A loan that may be recalled at any time. **2.** A loan in danger of not being repaid.

▸ **premium loan.** (1884) A loan made to an insured by the insurer to enable the insured to pay further premiums. • The reserve value of the policy serves as collateral.

▸ **recourse loan.** (1970) A loan that allows the lender, if the borrower defaults, not only to attach the collateral but also to seek judgment against the borrower's (or guarantor's) personal assets.

▸ **refund-anticipation loan.** (1976) A short-term high-interest loan repaid with a person's federal-income-tax refund. • Marketed by retail income-tax preparers, these loans (sometimes spanning only one or two days) were discontinued in the 2013 tax season after federal regulators found widespread noncompliance with state and federal lending laws. — Abbr. RAL. See *refund-anticipation check* under CHECK.

▸ **revolver loan.** (1985) A single loan that a debtor takes out in lieu of several lines of credit or other loans from various creditors, and that is subject to review and approval at certain intervals. • A revolver loan is usu. taken out in an attempt to resolve problems with creditors. Cf. *revolving credit* under CREDIT (4).

▸ **revolving loan.** (1927) A loan that is renewed at maturity.

▸ **scratch-and-dent loan.** (2007) A loan made to a borrower who was able to repay when the loan was made but has since fallen behind on payments.

▸ **secured loan.** (1862) A loan that is secured by property or securities. — Also termed *collateral loan.*

▸ **short-term loan.** (1902) A loan with a due date of less than one year, usu. evidenced by a note.

▸ **signature loan.** (1963) An unsecured loan based solely on the borrower's promise or signature. • To obtain such a loan, the borrower must usu. be highly creditworthy.

▸ **stated-income loan.** (2007) **1.** A loan extended to a borrower who claimed a certain income but has not verified the claim. **2.** See *liar's loan* (1). Cf. *NINJA loan.*

▸ **subprime loan.** (1993) A loan, esp. a mortgage or home-equity loan, made to one whose financial condition and creditworthiness are poor, creating a high risk of default. • A subprime loan usu. has an adjustable interest rate that is low at inception, to help a financially weak borrower qualify, then rises over the life of the loan.

▸ **swing loan.** See *bridge loan.*

▸ **term loan.** (18c) A loan with a specified due date, usu. of more than one year. • Such a loan typically cannot be repaid before maturity without incurring a penalty. — Also termed *time loan.* Cf. *call loan.*

▸ **title loan.** A short-term high-interest loan secured by the borrower's car or other motor vehicle. • In exchange for cash, the lender places a lien on the vehicle; the borrower surrenders the title document (which must be in the borrower's name) as collateral. If the borrower defaults on the loan, the lender may repossess and sell the vehicle to recoup the loan amount. — Also termed *auto-title loan; car-title loan.*

▸ **veteran's loan.** (1944) A federally guaranteed loan extended to armed-forces veterans for the purchase of a home. — Also written *veterans' loan*; *veteran loan.* — Also termed *VA loan*; *GI loan.*

loan, *vb.* (12c) To lend, esp. money.

loan-amortization schedule. (1958) A schedule that divides each loan payment into an interest component and a principal component. • Typically, the interest component begins as the largest part of each payment and declines over time. See AMORTIZATION (1).

loan association. See SAVINGS-AND-LOAN ASSOCIATION.

loan broker. See BROKER.

loan-brokerage fee. See MORTGAGE DISCOUNT.

loan certificate. See CERTIFICATE.

loan commitment. (1940) A lender's binding promise to a borrower to lend a specified amount of money at a certain interest rate, usu. within a specified period and for a specified purpose (such as buying real estate). See MORTGAGE COMMITMENT.

loan-disclosure statement. See DISCLOSURE STATEMENT.

loaned employee. See *borrowed employee* under EMPLOYEE.

loaned servant. See *borrowed employee* under EMPLOYEE.

loan for consumption. (1840) An agreement by which a lender delivers goods to a borrower who consumes them and who is obligated to return goods of the same quantity, type, and quality.

loan for exchange. (1915) A contract by which a lender delivers personal property to a borrower who agrees to return similar property, usu. without compensation for its use.

loan for use. (1837) An agreement by which a lender delivers an asset to a borrower who must use it according to its normal function or according to the agreement, and who must return it when finished using it. • No interest is charged.

loanland. *Hist.* A tenancy involving the loan of land by one person to another. — Also spelled *laenland.* Cf. BOOKLAND; FOLKLAND.

> "Laenlands were loaned lands, that is, lands granted for a period, either the life of the grantee or some longer time such as three lives. In return the grantees performed services, usually of an agricultural nature, or made payments in kind to their landlords. Laenlands, like boclands, were usually held under a written instrument, and they are therefore sometimes included in the boclands. But strictly, laenland and bocland differed. Bocland, we may say, was held directly as a result of a charter from the king, whereas laenland was temporarily held by grant from some great landlord." W.J.V. Windeyer, *Lectures on Legal History* 28 (2d ed. 1949).

loan-origination fee. See FEE (1).

loan participation. (1934) The coming together of multiple lenders to issue a large loan (called a *participation loan*) to one borrower, thereby reducing each lender's individual risk.

loan ratio. See LOAN-TO-VALUE RATIO.

loan-receipt agreement. (1943) *Torts.* A settlement agreement by which the defendant lends money to the plaintiff interest-free, the plaintiff not being obligated to repay the loan unless he or she recovers money from other tortfeasors responsible for the same injury.

loansharking, *n.* (1914) The practice of lending money at excessive and esp. usurious rates, and often using threats or extortion to enforce repayment. — Also termed *extortionate credit transaction.* — **loan-shark,** *vb.* — **loan shark,** *n.*

loan society. (1841) *English law.* A club organized to collect deposits from and make loans to industrial workers. • The loan societies were forerunners of the American savings-and-loan associations.

loan-to-value ratio. (1938) The ratio, usu. expressed as a percentage, between the amount of a mortgage loan and the value of the property pledged as security for the mortgage. • For example, an $80,000 loan on property worth $100,000 results in a loan-to-value ratio of 80% — which is usu. the highest ratio that lenders will agree to without requiring the debtor to buy mortgage insurance. — Often shortened to *LTV ratio.* — Also termed *loan ratio.*

loan value. (1902) *Insurance.* **1.** The maximum amount that may be lent safely on property or life insurance without jeopardizing the lender's need for protection from the borrower's default. **2.** The amount of money an insured can borrow against the cash value of his or her life-insurance policy.

lobby, *vb.* (1837) **1.** To talk with or curry favor with a legislator, usu. repeatedly or frequently, in an attempt to influence the legislator's vote <she routinely lobbies for tort reform in the state legislature>. **2.** To support or oppose (a measure) by working to influence a legislator's vote <the organization lobbied the bill through the Senate>. **3.** To try to influence (a political decision-maker) <the counsel for legislative affairs lobbied Senator Smith to bury the bill>. — **lobbying,** *n.* — **lobbyist,** *n.*

lobbying act. (1948) A federal or state law governing the conduct of lobbyists, usu. by requiring them to register and file activity reports. • An example is the Federal Regulation of Lobbying Act, 12 USCA § 261.

lobby vote. See VOTE (4).

LOC. *abbr.* LIBRARY OF CONGRESS.

local act. 1. See LOCAL LAW (1). **2.** See LOCAL LAW (2).

local action. See ACTION (4).

local administrator. See ADMINISTRATOR (1).

local agency. See AGENCY (3).

local agent. See AGENT.

local allegiance. See *actual allegiance* under ALLEGIANCE (1).

local and special legislation. See LEGISLATION (3).

local assessment. See ASSESSMENT (2).

local authority. See AUTHORITY (3).

local bar. See *local bar association* under BAR ASSOCIATION.

local bar association. See BAR ASSOCIATION.

local chattel. See CHATTEL.

local concern. (1833) An activity conducted by a municipality in its proprietary capacity.

local council. *English law.* A group of people responsible for providing houses, schools, parks, etc. in a small area such as a village or town.

local counsel. See COUNSEL.

local-counsel rule. A local rule requiring a lawyer admitted pro hac vice to engage counsel admitted to practice within the jurisdiction. • The primary purpose of such a rule is to ensure that local rules of procedure are followed. See PRO HAC VICE.

local court. See COURT.

local custom. See CUSTOM (1).

local-exchange carrier. (1981) *Telecommunications law.* An entity that provides telephone service, usu. on a local basis, through a local-exchange network. 47 USCA § 153(26). — Abbr. LEC. See LOCAL-EXCHANGE NETWORK.

local-exchange network. (1975) *Telecommunications law.* A system for providing telephone service on a local basis. • A local-exchange network usu. consists of such elements as switches, local loops, and transport trunks, and capabilities such as billing databases and operator services. Switches are pieces of equipment that direct calls to the appropriate destination. Local loops are the wires that connect telephones to the switches. Transport trunks are the wires that carry calls from switch to switch. All the elements of a local-exchange network are often referred to as a bundle, and there are federal requirements that a local-exchange carrier who controls a local-exchange network permit competition by selling some access, including unbundled access, to its local-exchange network. 47 USCA § 251(c). See LOCAL-EXCHANGE CARRIER; UNBUNDLING RULES.

local government. See GOVERNMENT (3).

local improvement. See IMPROVEMENT (3).

local-improvement assessment. See *local assessment* under ASSESSMENT (2).

locality, *n.* (17c) **1.** A definite region; vicinity; neighborhood; community. **2.** *Hist. Scots law.* The land held by a widow in usufruct under the terms of her marriage contract. • If a widow has locality lands, she cannot assert her statutory claim to a one-third share of her husband's real property.

locality of a lawsuit. (1939) The place where a court may exercise judicial authority.

locality-plus test. (1967) *Maritime law.* The requirement that, for a federal court to exercise admiralty tort jurisdiction, not only must the alleged wrong occur on navigable waters, it must also relate to a traditional maritime activity *Executive Jet Aviation, Inc. v. Cleveland*, 409 U.S. 249, 93 S.Ct. 493 (1972). — Also termed *locality-plus rule*; *maritime-connection doctrine.*

locality rule. (1941) **1.** The doctrine that, in a professional-malpractice suit, the standard of care applicable to the professional's conduct is the reasonable care exercised by similar professionals in the same vicinity and professional community. **2.** The doctrine that, in determining the appropriate amount of attorney's fees to be awarded in a suit, the proper basis is the rate charged by similar attorneys for similar work in the vicinity. **3.** LOCALITY TEST.

locality test. (1974) *Maritime law.* The requirement that, for a federal court to exercise admiralty tort jurisdiction, the alleged wrong must have occurred on navigable waters. • The test was replaced by the locality-plus test in *Executive Jet Aviation, Inc. v. Cleveland*, 409 U.S. 249, 93 S.Ct. 493 (1972). — Also termed *locality rule.* See LOCALITY-PLUS TEST.

localization doctrine. (1941) The doctrine that a foreign corporation, by doing sufficient business in a state, will subject itself to that state's laws.

local law. (17c) **1.** A statute that relates to or operates in a particular locality rather than the entire state. **2.** A statute that applies to particular persons or things rather than an entire class of persons or things. — Also termed (in senses 1 & 2) *local act*; *local statute.* **3.** The law of a particular jurisdiction, as opposed to the law of a foreign state. — Also termed *internal law.* **4.** *Conflict of laws.* The body of standards, principles, and rules — excluding conflict-of-laws rules — that the state courts apply to controversies before them. Restatement (Second) of Conflict of Laws § 4(1) (1971).

local-law theory. (1926) *Conflict of laws.* The view that, although a court of the forum recognizes and enforces a local right (that is, one created under its own law), in a foreign-element case it does not necessarily apply the rule that would govern an analogous case of a purely domestic character, but instead takes into account the law of the foreign country by fashioning a local right as nearly as possible on the law of the country in which the decisive facts have occurred. • This theory is credited to Walter Wheeler Cook, who expounded it in the first chapter of his *Logical and Legal Bases of the Conflict of Laws* (1949).

> "Since the court of the forum adopts the view that the chosen law would have taken not of the actual case, but of an equivalent domestic case, it does not necessarily recognize the right that would have been vested in the plaintiff according to that law. . . . It is scarcely deniable, however, that this local law theory is little more than what a learned writer has stigmatized as a sterile truism — sterile because it affords no basis for the systematic development of private international law. To remind an English judge, about to try a case containing a foreign element, that whatever decision he gives he must enforce only the *lex fori*, is a technical quibble that explains nothing and solves nothing. It provides no guidance whatever upon the limits within which he must have regard to the foreign law." G.C. Cheshire, *Private International Law* 35 (6th ed. 1961).

local option. An option that allows a municipality or other governmental unit to determine a particular course of action without the specific approval of state officials. — Also termed *local veto.* Cf. HOME RULE.

local patent rules. See LOCAL RULE.

local receiver. See RECEIVER (1).

local-remedies rule. See EXHAUSTION-OF-LOCAL-REMEDIES RULE.

local rule. (1819) **1.** A rule based on the physical conditions of a state and the character, customs, and beliefs of its people. **2.** A rule by which an individual court supplements the procedural rules applying generally to all courts within the jurisdiction. • Local rules deal with a variety of matters, such as requiring extra copies of motions to be filed with the court or prohibiting the reading of newspapers in the courtroom. Fed. R. Civ. P. 83.

▸ **local patent rules.** *Patents.* A set of rules adopted by a federal district court to deal specifically with pretrial procedure and trial of patent-infringement cases.

local stare decisis. See STARE DECISIS.

local statute. 1. See LOCAL LAW (1). **2.** See LOCAL LAW (2).

local union. See UNION.

local usage. See USAGE (1).

local veto. See LOCAL OPTION.

locare (lə-**kair**-ee), *vb.* [Latin] *Roman law.* To let or hire out. See LOCATOR.

locare aliquid faciendum (lə-**kair**-ee **al**-i-kwid fay-shee-**en**-dəm). [Latin] *Roman law.* To contract to have someone perform work for remuneration. Cf. CONDUCERE ALIQUID FACIENDUM.

locare aliquid utendum (lə-**kair**-ee **al**-i-kwid yoo-**ten**-dəm). [Latin] *Roman law.* To let something on hire for the use of the lessee; to accept consideration for the use of an object. Cf. CONDUCERE ALIQUID UTENDUM.

locarium (lə-**kair**-ee-əm), *n.* [Law Latin] *Hist.* Rent.

locatarius (loh-kə-**tair**-ee-əs), *n.* [Latin] *Hist.* A person with whom something is deposited; a depositee.

locatio (lə-**kay**-shee-oh), *n.* [Latin] *Roman & civil law.* Any contract by which the use of the thing bailed, or the use of the labor or services, is agreed to be given for a compensation. • This type of contract benefits both parties. — Also termed *lease*; *hiring.* Cf. ABLOCATION; DEPOSITUM. Pl. ***locationes*** (lə-kay-shee-**oh**-neez).

▸ ***locatio conductio*** (lə-**kay**-shee-oh kən-**duk**-shee-oh). [Latin] (18c) *Roman law.* A letting for hire; specif., a contract by which one person agreed to give to another the use, or the use and enjoyment, of a thing or of services or labor in return for remuneration, usu. money. • In Roman law, it covered a broad range of circumstances in return for a *merces* or rent.

▸ ***locatio custodiae*** (lə-**kay**-shee-oh kəs-**toh**-dee-ee). [Latin] *Roman law.* The hiring of care or service, as when the bailee is to protect the thing bailed.

▸ ***locatio mercium vehendarum.*** See *locatio operis mercium vehendarum.*

▸ ***locatio operarum*** (lə-**kay**-shee-oh op-ə-**rair**-əm). [Latin "the letting of services"] (17c) *Roman & civil law.* A contract of employment; specif., contract in which someone, usu. a day laborer, hires out his services for a specified price. — Also termed *locatio operis faciendi.* Cf. REDEMPTIO OPERIS.

▸ ***locatio operis faciendi*** (lə-**kay**-shee-oh **op**-ə-ris fay-shee-**en**-dɪ). [Latin "the letting of a job to be done"] (18c) *Roman law.* A contract by which someone hires a contractor (*conductor*) to undertake work (e.g., to build a home or teach a slave to read) on behalf of the hirer. — Sometimes shortened to *locatio operis.* See *locatio operarum.*

▸ ***locatio operis mercium vehendarum*** (lə-**kay**-shee-oh **op**-ə-ris **mər**-shee-əm vee-hən-**dair**-əm). [Latin "the letting of the job of carrying goods"] (18c) *Roman law.* A bailment in which goods are delivered to the bailee for transport elsewhere, esp. by sea. — Also termed *locatio mercium vehendarum.*

▸ ***locatio rei*** (lə-**kay**-shee-oh **ree**-ɪ). [Latin "letting of a thing"] (18c) *Roman law.* The hiring of a thing for use, by which the hirer gains the temporary use of the thing for a fee.

> "*Locatio rei* was the letting of a *res* for hire. Roman law differed in several aspects from the relevant rules of English law. Firstly, there was not in Roman law a fundamental distinction between the hiring of personal property and the lease of real property: *locatio rei* applied both to land and movables. Secondly, in Roman law the hirer did not obtain possession. Thirdly, the locatio was a mere contract and even the tenant of land did not have a right to be restored if he were [wrongfully] ejected, his sole remedy being an action for breach of contract. Fourthly, the Roman contract gave more consideration to the tenant or hirer than does English law." G.W. Paton, *Bailment in the Common Law* 53 (1952).

location. (16c) **1.** The specific place or position of a person or thing. **2.** The act or process of locating. **3.** *Real estate.* The designation of the boundaries of a particular piece of land, either on the record or on the land itself. **4.** *Mining law.* The act of appropriating a mining claim. — Also termed *mining location.* See MINING CLAIM. **5.** The claim so appropriated. **6.** *Civil law.* A contract for the temporary use of something for hire; a leasing for hire. See LOCATIO.

location-damage clause. See SURFACE-DAMAGE CLAUSE.

locative calls (**lok**-ə-tiv). (1807) *Property.* In land descriptions, specific descriptions that fix the boundaries of the land. • Locative calls may be marks of location, landmarks, or other physical objects. If calls in a description conflict, locative calls control over those indicating a general area of a boundary. See CALL (5); DIRECTORY CALLS.

locator (loh-**kay**-tər), *n.* [Latin] (17c) **1.** *Roman law.* (usu. ital.) Someone who lets out property or services for reward, or who contracts to have another person (the *conductor*) perform work for reward; a lessor or landlord. See CONDUCTOR (2).

▸ ***locator operarum,*** *n.* (18c) Someone who offers one's labor for hire, esp. as a day laborer.

▸ ***locator operas faciendi,*** *n.* Someone who employs contract labor.

▸ ***locator rei,*** *n.* (18c) A lessor or landlord.

2. Someone who is entitled to locate land or set the boundaries of a mining claim.

locatum (lə-**kay**-təm), *n.* [Latin] *Hist.* A hiring. See BAILMENT.

Lochnerize (**lok**-nər-ɪz), *vb.* (1976) (Of a court) to scrutinize and strike down economic legislation under the guise of enforcing the Due Process Clause, esp. in the manner of the U.S. Supreme Court during the early 20th century. • The term takes its name from the decision in *Lochner v. New York,* 198 U.S. 45, 25 S.Ct. 539 (1905), in which the Court invalidated New York's maximum-hours law for bakers. — **Lochnerization,** *n.*

lockbox. (1872) **1.** A secure box, such as a post-office box, strongbox, or safe-deposit box. **2.** A facility offered by a financial institution for quickly collecting and consolidating checks and other funds from a party's customers.

lockdown. (1977) The temporary confinement of prisoners in their cells during a state of heightened alert caused by an escape, riot, or other emergency.

lockdown order. (1982) A court order imposing restrictions on an incarcerated person — beyond the normal restrictions.

Lockeanism. See LOCKEAN LABOR THEORY.

Lockean labor theory. (1979) The philosopher John Locke's justification of private property, based on the natural right of one's ownership of one's own labor, and the right to nature's common property to the extent that one's labor can make use of it. • Locke's theory, from the fifth chapter of his *Second Treatise on Civil Government,* is often used to analyze the natural rights of inventors, authors, and artists in their own creations. — Also termed *labor theory; Lockeanism.* Cf. PERSONALITY THEORY; UTILITARIANISM.

locked in, *adj.* **1.** (Of a person) unable to sell appreciated securities and realize the gain because of liability for capital gains taxes <my accountant advised me not to sell the stock because I am locked in>. **2.** (Of a price, rate, etc.) staying the same for a given period <the 7% mortgage rate is locked in for 30 days>.

locked-in rate. See *lock rate* under INTEREST RATE.

lockout. (1854) **1.** An employer's withholding of work and closing of a business because of a labor dispute.

▸ **defensive lockout.** (1963) A lockout that is called to prevent imminent and irreparable financial harm to the company or to protect a legal right. • Defensive lockouts were legal, but the U.S. Supreme Court abolished the distinction between defensive and offensive lockouts in favor of a balancing test. *American Ship Bldg. Co. v. NLRB,* 380 U.S. 300, 85 S.Ct. 955 (1965).

▸ **offensive lockout.** (1969) A lockout called by management to assert economic pressure on workers and thereby gain a bargaining advantage over a union. • Offensive lockouts were illegal before the U.S. Supreme Court abolished the legal distinction between offensive and defensive lockouts in favor of a balancing test. *American Ship Bldg. Co. v. NLRB,* 380 U.S. 300, 85 S.Ct. 955 (1965).

2. Loosely, an employee's refusal to work because the employer unreasonably refuses to abide by an expired employment contract while a new one is being negotiated. Cf. STRIKE; BOYCOTT; PICKETING.

lock rate. See INTEREST RATE.

lockup, *n.* **1.** A small prison where a criminal or someone accused of a crime can be kept for a short time; JAIL. **2.** See LOCKUP OPTION.

lockup agreement. (1983) *Securities.* A contract between an underwriter and a corporation's insiders that prohibits the insiders from selling any personal stockholdings for a specified time after the corporation makes a public offering of securities. Cf. MARKET STAND-OFF AGREEMENT.

lockup option. (1987) A defense against a corporate takeover, in which a friendly party is entitled to buy parts of a corporation for a set price when a person or group acquires a certain percentage of the corporation's shares. • An agreement of this kind may be illegal, to the extent it is not undertaken to serve the best interests of the shareholders. — Often shortened to *lockup.*

loco parentis. See IN LOCO PARENTIS.

loco rerum immobilium (**loh**-koh **reer**-əm im-ə-**bil**-ee-əm). [Latin] *Scots law.* Treated as immovable things. • The phrase appeared in reference to a determination of whether certain items (such as shares of stock) should be treated as movable or immovable property.

loco tutoris (**loh**-koh t[y]oo-**tor**-is). [Latin] *Scots law.* In the place of a tutor.

> "The Court of Session is in the practice of appointing, on application made for such appointment, a factor *loco tutoris* on the estates of pupils not having tutors. Such an appointment places the factor in the same position towards the pupil, both as regards his person and the administration of his estate, as if he held the office by virtue of relationship and was tutor-at-law, or had received the appointment of tutor from the pupil's father under his testamentary settlement, the only difference being that the office of a tutor appointed by the Court is not gratuitous." John Trayner, *Trayner's Latin Maxims* 336–37 (4th ed. 1894).

locum tenens (**loh**-kəm **tee**-nenz *or* **ten**-ənz), *n.* [Law Latin "holding the place"] (17c) *Hist.* A deputy; a substitute; a representative.

locuples (**lok**-yə-pleez), *adj.* [Latin] (17c) *Civil law.* Having the means to pay any amount that the plaintiff might recover. — Also termed *locuplete.*

locupletari cum damno alterius (lok-yuu-plə-**tair**-ɪ kəm **dam**-noh al-**teer**-ee-əs). [Latin] To be enriched through the damage sustained by another.

locus (**loh**-kəs). [Latin "place"] (18c) The place or position where something is done or exists. — Abbr. L. See SITUS.

locus actus (**loh**-kəs **ak**-təs). [Latin "place of the act"] (1861) The place where an act was done; the place of performance.

locus celebrationis. [Latin] (1860) The place where a contract is entered into.

locus classicus. [Latin "a source belonging to the highest class"] (1853) An authoritative passage from a standard or classic work, cited as an instance or illustration of a point.

locus contractus (**loh**-kəs kən-**trak**-təs). [Latin "place of the contract"] (17c) The place where a contract was made. Cf. *lex loci contractus* under LEX LOCI.

locus criminis (**loh**-kəs **krim**-ə-nis), *n.* [Latin] (1894) The place where a crime was committed.

locus damni (**loh**-kəs **dam**-nɪ). [Latin] *Hist.* The place of injury.

locus delicti (**loh**-kəs də-**lik**-tɪ). [Latin "place of the wrong"] (18c) The place where an offense was committed; the place where the last event necessary to make the actor liable occurred. Cf. *lex loci delicti* under LEX LOCI.

> "When a statute does not indicate where Congress considered the place of committing the crime to be, the site or *locus delicti* must be determined from the nature of the crime and the location of the acts or omissions constituting the offense." *U.S. v. Clinton,* 574 F.2d 464, 465 (9th Cir. 1978).

locus in quo (**loh**-kəs in **kwoh**). [Latin "place in which"] (18c) The place where something is alleged to have occurred.

locus partitus (**loh**-kəs pahr-**tɪ**-təs), *n.* [Latin "a place divided"] (17c) *Hist.* The act of dividing two towns or counties to determine which of them contains the land or place in question.

locus poenitentiae (**loh**-kəs pen-ə-**ten**-shee-ee). [Latin "place of repentance"] (17c) **1.** A point at which it is not too late for one to change one's legal position; the possibility of withdrawing from a contemplated course of action, esp. a wrong, before being committed to it.

> "The requirement of an overt act before conspirators can be prosecuted and punished exists . . . to provide a *locus poenitentiae* — an opportunity for the conspirators to reconsider, terminate the agreement, and thereby avoid punishment." *People v. Zamora,* 557 P.2d 75, 82 n.8 (Cal. 1976).

2. The opportunity to withdraw from a negotiation before finally concluding the contract.

locus publicus (**loh**-kəs **pəb**-li-kəs). [Latin] (1841) *Roman law.* A public place.

> "Locus publicus . . . . A parcel of public land. It is property of the Roman people and is protected by various interdicts . . . against violation by private individuals who might endanger its public character or its use by the people." Adolf Berger, *Encyclopedic Dictionary of Roman Law* 568 (1953).

locus regit actum (**loh**-kəs **ree**-jit **ak**-təm), *n.* [Latin "the place rules the act"] (1847) *Int'l law.* The rule that a transaction complying with the legal formalities of the country where it is created will be considered valid in the country where it is to be effective, even if that country requires additional formalities.

locus rei sitae (**loh**-kəs **ree**-ɪ **sɪ**-tee), *n.* [Latin "place where a thing is situated"] (1855) *Civil law.* The rule that the place where the land is located is the proper forum in a case involving real estate.

locus sigilli (**loh**-kəs si-**jil**-ɪ), *n.* [Latin] (17c) The place of the seal. • Today this phrase is almost always abbreviated "L.S." These are the traditional letters appearing on many notarial certificates to indicate where the notary public's embossed seal should be placed. If a rubber-stamp seal is used, it should be placed near but not over this abbreviation. See NOTARY SEAL.

> "For some period in history seals were required to consist of wax affixed to the parchment or paper on which the terms of the instrument were written. The wax was required to have an identifiable impression made upon it. Usually this was made by a signet ring. In time when ordinary people, who did not have signet rings, learned to read and write, it was to be expected that substitutes for the traditional seal would be accepted by the law. Thus, today it would be generally accurate to say that a seal may consist of wax, a gummed wafer, an impression on the paper, the word 'seal,' the letters 'L.S.' (locus sigilli) or even a pen scratch." John

D. Calamari & Joseph M. Perillo, *The Law of Contracts* § 7-3, at 296 (3d ed. 1987).

locus solutionis (**loh**-kəs sə-loo-shee-**oh**-nis). [Latin] (1831) *Hist.* The place of performance.

locus standi (**loh**-kəs **stan**-dɪ *or* -dee). [Latin "place of standing"] (1835) The right to bring an action or to be heard in a given forum; STANDING.

lode, *n.* (16c) **1.** MINERAL LODE. **2.** LADE.

lode claim. See MINING CLAIM.

lodeman. See LOADSMAN.

lodemanage, *n.* See LOADMANAGE.

lodesman. See LOADSMAN.

lodestar. (14c) [lit. "a guiding star"] **1.** A principle or fact that guides someone's actions; an inspiration or model. **2.** A reasonable amount of attorney's fees in a given case, usu. calculated by multiplying a reasonable number of hours worked by the prevailing hourly rate in the community for similar work, and often considering such additional factors as the degree of skill and difficulty involved in the case, the degree of its urgency, its novelty, and the like. • Most statutes that authorize an award of attorney's fees use the lodestar method for computing the award. — Also termed *lodestar amount.*

lodge, *vb.* See FILE (1).

lodger. (16c) **1.** Someone who rents and occupies a room in another's house. **2.** Someone who occupies a designated area in another's house but acquires no property interest in that area, which remains in the owner's legal possession.

log, *n.* (1825) **1.** ARREST RECORD (2). **2.** JOURNAL (1).

logan. See LAGAN.

logbook. (17c) **1.** A ship's or aircraft's journal containing an account of each trip, often with a history of events during the voyage; JOURNAL (1). **2.** Any journal or record of events.

logia (**loj**-ee-ə), *n.* [Latin] *Hist.* A small house or cottage.

logical-cause doctrine. (1980) The principle that, if the plaintiff proves that an injury occurred and proves a logical cause of it, a party desiring to defeat the claim cannot succeed merely by showing that there is another imaginable cause, but must also show that the alternative cause is more probable than the cause shown by the plaintiff.

logical interpretation. See INTERPRETATION (1).

logical-positive realism. See LEGAL REALISM.

logical positivism. (1931) A philosophical system or movement requiring that meaningful statements be in principle verifiable. Cf. LEGAL POSITIVISM.

logical realism. See LEGAL REALISM.

logical-relationship standard. (1976) *Civil procedure.* A test applied to determine whether a defendant's counterclaim is compulsory, by examining whether both claims are based on the same operative facts or whether those facts activate additional rights, otherwise dormant, for the defendant. • One of the most important factors considered is whether hearing the claims together would promote judicial economy and efficiency. Fed. R. Civ. P. 13(a).

"[U]nder the fourth test — frequently referred to as the 'logical relationship' standard — the principal consideration in determining whether a counterclaim is compulsory rests on the efficiency or economy of trying the counterclaim in the same litigation as the main claim. As a result, the convenience of the court, rather than solely the counterclaim's relationship to the facts or issues of the opposing claim, is controlling. The hallmark of this approach is flexibility. Although the fourth test has been criticized for being overly broad in scope and uncertain in application, it has by far the widest acceptance among the courts." Jack H. Friedenthal et al., *Civil Procedure* § 6.7, at 352 (2d ed. 1993).

logic bomb. (1978) Destructive or disruptive computer software that is planted on a computer, server, or network and waits until a certain time to activate itself.

logium (**loj**-ee-əm), *n.* [Latin] *Hist.* A lodge, hovel, or outhouse.

logographus (log-ə-**graf**-əs), *n.* [Latin fr. Greek] *Roman law.* A bookkeeper or public clerk.

logomachy (loh-**gom**-ə-kee), *n.* **1.** Wordy strife; a war of words. **2.** An argument about words. — **logomachist,** *n.*

logorrhea (leg-ə-**ree**-ə), *n.* Pathological garrulity; incessant talkativeness.

logrolling, *n.* (1812) **1.** The exchanging of political favors; esp., the trading of votes among legislators to gain support of measures that are beneficial to each legislator's constituency. **2.** The legislative practice of including several propositions in one measure or proposed constitutional amendment so that the legislature or voters will pass all of them, even though these propositions might not have passed if they had been submitted separately. • Many state constitutions have single-subject clauses that prohibit this practice. — **logroll,** *vb.*

LOI. *abbr.* LETTER OF INTENT.

loitering, *n.* (14c) The criminal offense of remaining in a certain place (such as a public street) for no apparent reason. • Loitering statutes are generally held to be unconstitutionally vague. Cf. VAGRANCY. — **loiter,** *vb.*

▸ **gang loitering.** Loitering by two or more people, at least one of whom is a suspected or known gang member. — Also termed *gang-related loitering.*

LoJack. 1. A radio-signal transmitter used esp. to track stolen vehicles. • It is manufactured by the LoJack Corporation in Canton, Massachusetts. The term is trademarked. **2.** An electronic ankle-bracelet monitoring device. — Also termed (in sense 2) *ankle bracelet.*

lollipop syndrome. (1986) *Family law.* A situation in which one or both parents, often in a custody battle, manipulate the child with gifts, fun, good times, and minimal discipline in an attempt to win over the child. See *Disneyland parent* under PARENT. Cf. RESCUE SYNDROME.

Lombard law. (16c) A Germanic customary law based primarily on a code called the Edict of Rothar, published in A.D. 643. • Rothar was the King of the Lombards at the time (A.D. 636–652), and his code (written in Latin) was more complete than the Germanic *leges barbarorum.* — Also termed *law of Lombardy; laws of the Langobards; laws of Langobardis.* Cf. LEGES BARBARORUM; LIBRI FEUDORUM.

Lombard League. *Hist.* A 12th- and 13th-century alliance of city-states in northern Italy, formed to resist the efforts of the Holy Roman emperors to curtail the city-states' liberties and jurisdiction in Lombardy.

London commodity option. (1972) An agreement to buy or sell a futures contract for a commodity traded on the London markets, for a particular price and within a particular time.

London Interbank Offered Rate. A daily compilation by the British Bankers Association of the rates that major international banks charge each other for large-volume, short-term loans of Eurodollars, with monthly maturity rates calculated out to one year. • These daily rates are used as the underlying interest rates for derivative contracts in currencies other than the euro. — Abbr. LIBOR. Cf. EURO INTERBANK OFFERED RATE.

London Lloyd's. See LLOYD'S OF LONDON.

***Lone Pine* order.** (1995) A case-management order in a toxic-tort lawsuit involving many plaintiffs, establishing procedures and deadlines for discovery, including requiring the plaintiffs to timely produce evidence and expert opinions to substantiate each plaintiff's exposure to the hazardous substance, the injury suffered, and the cause of the injury. *Lore v. Lone Pine Corp.*, No. L-33606-85 (N.J. Super. Ct. Nov. 18, 1986). • Although the *Lone Pine* opinion is unreported, it has become famous for the kind of case-management order involved, in part because the plaintiffs' claims were dismissed for failure to timely provide expert opinions.

long, *adj.* (1859) **1.** Holding a security or commodity in anticipation of a rise in price <a buyer long on pharmaceutical stock>. **2.** Of, relating to, or involving a purchase of securities or commodities in anticipation of rising prices <a long position>. Cf. SHORT.

long, *adv.* By a long purchase; into or in a long position <bought the wheat long>.

long account. See ACCOUNT.

longa manu (**long**-gə **man**-yoo), *adv.* [Latin "with a long hand"] *Roman & civil law.* Indirectly; by the longest route. • This described the transfer of ownership by pointing out, at some distance, the thing to the transferee and authorizing its taking. This could be done, for example, by handing over the keys at the door of a warehouse, or by pointing out the boundaries of land. See CONSTITUTUM POSSESSORIUM. Cf. BREVI MANU.

long-arm, *adj.* Of, relating to, or arising from a long-arm statute <long-arm jurisdiction>.

long-arm jurisdiction. See JURISDICTION.

long-arm statute. (1951) A statute providing for jurisdiction over a nonresident defendant who has had contacts with the territory where the statute is in effect. • Most state long-arm statutes extend this jurisdiction to its constitutional limits. — Also termed *single-act statute.* See *long-arm jurisdiction* under JURISDICTION.

long-firm fraud. See FRAUD.

long-form bill of lading. See BILL OF LADING.

longi temporis praescriptio (**long**-gɪ **tem**-pə-ris pri-**skrip**-shee-oh). [Latin] (1921) *Roman law.* The prescriptive period after which a possessor of property could defeat any challenge to his title. See USUCAPIO.

Long Parliament. *Hist.* **1.** The English Parliament of Charles I meeting between 1640 and 1653, dissolved by Oliver Cromwell in 1653, then recalled and finally dissolved in 1660. **2.** The English Parliament that met between 1661 and 1678, after the restoration of the monarchy. • This Parliament is sometimes called the "Long Parliament of Charles II" to distinguish it from that of sense 1.

long robe. (17c) *Hist.* The legal profession <gentlemen of the long robe>. See ROBE.

long-run incremental cost. (1953) **1.** *Antitrust.* A cost threshold for determining whether predatory pricing has occurred, consisting of all costs that, over a several-year period, would not be incurred if the product in question were not offered. • It differs from average variable cost because it includes some costs that do not vary in the short run but that do vary over a longer period, depending on whether a particular product is offered. — Abbr. LRIC. Cf. *average variable cost* under COST (1). **2.** See *indirect cost* under COST (1),

Longshore and Harbor Workers' Compensation Act. A federal law designed to provide workers'-compensation benefits to persons, other than seamen, who work in maritime occupations, esp. stevedoring and ship service. 33 USCA § 901–950. — Abbr. LHWCA.

longshoreman. (1811) A maritime laborer who works on the wharves in a port; esp., a person who loads and unloads ships. Cf. STEVEDORE.

long-term capital gain. See CAPITAL GAIN.

long-term capital loss. See LOSS.

long-term debt. See DEBT.

long-term foster care. See FOSTER CARE (1).

long-term security. See SECURITY (4).

long title. See TITLE (3).

long ton. See TON.

look and feel. See TRADE DRESS.

look-and-feel protection. (1987) Copyright protection of the images generated or revealed when one activates a computer program.

lookout, *n.* (17c) A careful, vigilant watching <the motorist's statutory duty of proper lookout>.

look-through principle. (1993) *Tax.* A doctrine for allocating transfer-gains taxes on real estate by looking beyond the entity possessing legal title to identify the beneficial owners of the property.

LOOP. *abbr.* Limited order of protection.

loophole. (17c) An ambiguity, omission, or exception (as in a law or other legal document) that provides a way to avoid a rule without violating its literal requirements; esp., a tax-code provision that allows a taxpayer to legally avoid or reduce income taxes.

loopification, *n.* (1982) In critical legal studies, the collapse of a legal distinction resulting when the two ends of a continuum become so similar that they become indistinguishable <it may be impossible to distinguish "public" from "private" because of loopification>. — **loopify,** *vb.*

loose construction. See *liberal interpretation* under INTERPRETATION (1).

loose constructionism. See *liberal constructionism* under CONSTRUCTIONISM.

loose constructionist. See *liberal constructionist* under CONSTRUCTIONIST.

looseleaf service. (1927) A type of lawbook having pages that are periodically replaced with updated pages, designed to cope with constant change and increasing bulk.

> "The first loose leaf service covered the federal income tax, and was published in 1913 shortly after the Federal Income Tax Law of 1913 went into effect. It was followed in 1914 by a service reporting on the activities of the Federal Trade Commission, which had just been established. The loose leaf method was, therefore, first used as a means of reporting new tax and business laws which were to be subject to administrative interpretation . . . . These first loose leaf services were designed . . . not to reprint just the bare text of the revenue and commission acts, but to follow up and report each new development on these new laws as it occurred." Arthur Sydney Beardsley, *Legal Bibliography and the Use of Law Books* § 185, at 313–14 (1937).

loquela (lə-**kwee**-lə), *n.* [Law Latin "talk"] *Hist.* **1.** The oral discussions between the parties to a lawsuit leading to the issue, now called the pleadings. **2.** Settlement discussions.

loquela sine die (lə-**kwee**-lə **sɪ**-nee **dɪ**-ee *or* **sin**-ay **dee**-ay), *n.* [Law Latin] *Hist.* Indefinite postponement of an action.

LOR. *abbr.* LETTER OF REQUEST.

lord. (bef. 12c) **1.** A title of honor or nobility belonging properly to a baron but applied also to anyone who attains the rank of a peer; PEER (2). — Abbr. L. **2.** (*cap.* & *pl.*) HOUSE OF LORDS. **3.** A property owner whose land is in a tenant's possession; LANDLORD (1).

▸ **temporal lord** (**tem**-pə-rəl). (15c) One of the English peers (other than ecclesiastical) who sit in Parliament.

Lord Advocate. *Scots law.* An important political functionary in Scottish affairs who acts as the principal Crown counsel in civil cases, the chief public prosecutor of crimes, and legal adviser to the Scottish government on matters of Scots law. — Formerly also termed *King's Advocate.* Cf. ADVOCATE GENERAL.

lord-and-master rule. See HEAD-AND-MASTER RULE.

Lord Brougham's Act. See BROUGHAM'S ACT.

Lord Campbell's Act. See CAMPBELL'S ACT.

Lord Chamberlain. *English law.* The second officer of the royal household in England, who serves as a peer, a privy councilor, and a member of the ruling government. — Also termed *Lord Chamberlain of the Household.*

Lord Chancellor. *English law.* The highest judicial officer in England. • The Lord Chancellor sits as speaker of the House of Lords, is a member of the Cabinet, and presides at appellate judicial proceedings. — Also termed *Lord High Chancellor; Keeper of the King's Conscience.*

Lord Chief Justice of England. *English law.* The chief judge of the Queen's Bench Division of the High Court of Justice. • The Lord Chief Justice also serves on the Court of Appeal, and ranks second only to the Lord Chancellor in the English judicial hierarchy. — Formerly termed *Chief Justice of England.* Cf. CHIEF JUSTICE OF THE COMMON PLEAS.

Lord Clerk Register. *Scots law.* The officer who, from 1288 to 1879, was keeper of the rolls of court and records of Scotland. • These functions were later discharged by the Keeper of the Registers of Scotland and the Keeper of the Records of Scotland.

Lord Denman's Act. See DENMAN'S ACT (1).

Lord Ellenborough's Act. See ELLENBOROUGH'S ACT.

Lord High Chancellor. See LORD CHANCELLOR.

Lord High Steward. *Hist. English law.* The speaker *pro tempore* and presiding officer in the House of Lords during a criminal trial of a peer for a felony or for treason. • The privilege of peerage in criminal proceedings was abolished in 1948.

Lord High Treasurer. *Hist. English law.* An officer in charge of the royal revenues and customs duties, and of leasing the Crown lands. • The functions of the Lord High Treasurer are now vested in the lords commissioners of the treasury.

lord in gross. (17c) *Hist.* A lord holding the title not by virtue of a manor; a lord without a manor.

Lord Justice. See LORD JUSTICE OF APPEAL.

Lord Justice-Clerk. *Scots law.* The second highest judicial officer in Scotland, historically with special responsibility for criminal law. • The Lord Justice-Clerk presides over the Second Division of the Inner House of the Court of Session.

Lord Justice General. *Scots law.* The highest judicial officer in Scotland, and head of the High Court of Justiciary. • The Lord Justice General also holds the office of Lord President of the Court of Session.

Lord Justice of Appeal. *English law.* A judge of the English Court of Appeal. — Often shortened to *lord justice.* — Abbr. L.J. (or, in pl., either LL.J. or L.JJ.).

Lord Keeper. See KEEPER OF THE GREAT SEAL.

Lord Keeper of the Great Seal. See KEEPER OF THE GREAT SEAL.

Lord Keeper of the Privy Seal. See LORD PRIVY SEAL.

Lord Langdale's Act. See WILLS ACT (2).

Lord Lieutenant. *English law.* **1.** An honorary officeholder who is the Queen's representative in a county and the principal military officer there, originally appointed to muster the inhabitants to defend the country. **2.** *Hist.* The former viceroy of the Crown in Ireland.

Lord Lyndhurst's Act. See LYNDHURST'S ACT.

Lord Lyon King at Arms. *Scots law.* The monarch's representative who grants arms to suitable applicants, oversees the use of armorial bearings, holds court to determine rights to arms and chieftainship, and supervises messengers-at-arms.

Lord Mansfield's rule. (1924) The principle that neither spouse may testify about whether the husband had access to the wife at the time of a child's conception. • In effect, this rule — which has been abandoned by most states — made it impossible to bastardize a child born during a marriage.

Lord Mayor. 1. *Hist. English law.* The chief officer of the corporation of the city of London, so called because the fourth charter of Edward III conferred on that officer the honor of having maces carried before him by the sergeants. **2.** The title of the principal magistrate of a city, the office of which has been conferred by letters patent.

lord mayor's court. See COURT.

Lord of Appeal. *English law.* A member of the House of Lords, of whom at least three must be present for the hearing and determination of appeals, and including the Lord Chancellor, the Lords of Appeal in Ordinary, and the peers that have held high judicial offices, such as ex-chancellors and judges of the superior court in the United Kingdom and Ireland.

Lord of Appeal in Ordinary. *Hist. English law.* A person appointed and salaried to aid the House of Lords in the hearing of appeals. • These lords ranked as barons for life, and sat and voted in the House of Lords even after retirement. Cf. LAW LORD.

Lord of Parliament. A member of the House of Lords.

Lord of Session. *Scots law.* Any judge of the Court of Session. — Also termed *Senator of the College of Justice.* See COURT OF SESSION (1).

Lord Ordinary. *Scots law.* A judge of the Court of Session, sitting alone at first instance in the Outer House. See COURT OF SESSION (1).

Lord President. *Scots law.* The highest judicial officer in Scotland, heading the Court of Session and the First Division of the Upper House. • The Lord President also holds the office of Lord Justice-General of Scotland.

Lord Privy Seal (priv-ee). *English law.* An officer who has custody of the privy seal and who authenticates either a state document before it passes to receive the Great Seal or a document that does not require the Great Seal because of its minor importance. • The Lord Privy Seal has nominal official duties but is often made a member of the British cabinet. — Also termed *Keeper of the Privy Seal; Lord Keeper of the Privy Seal; Privy Seal.*

Lords. See HOUSE OF LORDS.

Lord's Day Act. See BLUE LAW.

lordship. (bef. 12c) *English law.* **1.** Dominion. **2.** An honorary title used for a nobleman other than a duke. **3.** A customary title for a judge or some other public official.

Lords Marchers. See MARCHERS.

lord spiritual. (15c) *English law.* An archbishop or bishop who is a member of the House of Lords.

lord temporal. (15c) *English law.* A House of Lords member who is not an ecclesiastic.

Lord Tenterden's Act. See TENTERDEN'S ACT.

Lord Tenterden's rule. See EJUSDEM GENERIS.

Lord Thurlow's rule. (18c) *Wills & estates.* The traditional doctrine that whether extinction by ademption of a specific devise has occurred depends solely on whether the subject matter of the specific devise exists as part of the testator's estate at death and that the testator's intent regarding the devise's further viability is irrelevant. • The rule takes its name from the judge who decided (1786) *Ashburner v. Macguire*, 29 Eng. Rep. 62 (Ch.), the case in which the rule originated.

loser-pays rule. See ENGLISH RULE.

loss. (bef. 12c) **1.** An undesirable outcome of a risk; the disappearance or diminution of value, usu. in an unexpected or relatively unpredictable way. • When the loss is a decrease in value, the usual method of calculating the loss is to ascertain the amount by which a thing's original cost exceeds its later selling price. **2.** *Tax.* The excess of a property's adjusted value over the amount realized from its sale or other disposition. IRC (26 USCA) § 1001. — Also termed *realized loss.* See AMOUNT REALIZED. Cf. GAIN (3). **3.** *Insurance.* The amount of financial detriment caused by an insured person's death or an insured property's damage, for which the insurer becomes liable. **4.** The failure to maintain possession of a thing.

▸ **actual loss.** (18c) A loss resulting from the real and substantial destruction of insured property.

▸ **actual total loss.** (1808) **1.** See *total loss.* **2.** *Marine insurance.* The total loss of a vessel covered by an insurance policy (1) by its real and substantive destruction, (2) by injuries that destroy its existence as a distinct individual of a particular class, (3) by its being reduced to a wreck irretrievably beyond repair, or (4) by its being placed beyond the insured's control and beyond the insured's power of recovery.

▸ **business loss.** See *ordinary loss.*

▸ **capital loss.** (1921) The loss realized upon selling or exchanging a capital asset. Cf. CAPITAL GAIN.

▸ **casualty loss.** (1934) For tax purposes, the total or partial destruction of an asset resulting from an unexpected or unusual event, such as an automobile accident or a tornado.

▸ **consequential loss.** (1829) A loss arising from the results of damage rather than from the damage itself. • A consequential loss is proximate when the natural and probable effect of the wrongful conduct, under the circumstances, is to set in operation the intervening cause from which the loss directly results. When the loss is not the natural and probable effect of the wrongful conduct, the loss is remote. — Also termed *indirect loss; consequential injury.* Cf. *direct loss.*

▸ **constructive total loss.** (1805) **1.** Such serious damage to the insured property that the cost of repairs would exceed the value of the thing repaired. — Also termed *constructive loss.* **2.** *Marine underwriting.* According to the traditional American rule, such serious damage to the insured property that the cost of repairs would exceed half the value of the thing repaired. — Abbr. CTL. See *total loss.*

▸ **deductible loss.** (1905) A taxpayer's loss that may be deducted in computing net taxable income, as when the loss occurred as a result of embezzlement or theft. *See Alison v. U.S.*, 344 U.S. 167, 170, 73 S.Ct. 191, 192 (1952).

▸ **direct loss.** (18c) A loss that results immediately and proximately from an event. Cf. *consequential loss.*

▸ **disaster loss.** (1968) A casualty loss sustained in a geographic area that the President designates as a disaster area. • It may be treated as having occurred during the previous tax year so that a victim may receive immediate tax benefits.

▸ **economic loss.** See ECONOMIC LOSS.

▸ **expectation loss.** See *benefit-of-the-bargain damages* under DAMAGES.

▸ **extraordinary loss.** (17c) A loss that is both unusual and infrequent, such as a loss resulting from a natural disaster.

▸ **general average loss.** (18c) *Marine underwriting.* A loss at sea usu. incurred when cargo is thrown overboard to save the ship; a loss due to the voluntary and intentional sacrifice of part of a venture (usu. cargo) to save the rest of the venture from imminent peril. • Such a loss is borne equally by all the interests concerned in the venture. See AVERAGE (3).

▸ **hobby loss.** (1946) A nondeductible loss arising from a personal hobby, as contrasted with an activity engaged in for profit. • The law generally presumes that an activity is engaged in for profit if profits are earned during at least three of the last five years. IRC (26 USCA) § 183.

▸ **indirect loss.** See *consequential loss.*

▸ **intangible loss.** (1928) The damage caused by the disruption of an intangible right or benefit.

▸ **long-term capital loss.** (1938) A loss on a capital asset held for an extended period, usu. at least 12 months.

▸ **net loss.** (18c) The excess of all expenses and losses over all revenues and gains.

▸ **net operating loss.** (1921) The excess of operating expenses over revenues, the amount of which can be deducted from gross income if other deductions do not exceed gross income. — Abbr. NOL.

▸ **nonpecuniary loss.** (1909) *Civil law.* A loss resulting from emotional or sentimental loss. *See* La. Civ. Code art. 1998. — Also termed *emotional-distress damages*; *dommage moral* (French law).

▸ **ordinary loss.** (1850) *Tax.* A loss incurred from the sale or exchange of an item that is used in a trade or business. • The loss is deductible from ordinary income, and thus is more beneficial to the taxpayer than a capital loss. — Also termed *business loss.*

▸ **out-of-pocket loss.** (1921) The difference between the value of what the buyer paid and the market value of what was received in return. • In breach-of-contract cases, out-of-pocket loss is used to measure restitution damages.

▸ **paper loss.** (1924) A loss that is realized only by selling something (such as a security) that has decreased in market value. — Also termed *unrealized loss.*

▸ **partial loss.** (18c) A loss of part of the insured property; damage not amounting to a total loss. Cf. *total loss.*

▸ **particular average loss.** (1814) *Marine underwriting.* A loss suffered by and borne alone by particular interests in a maritime venture. • Such a loss is usu. a partial loss.

▸ **passive loss.** (1986) A loss, with limited tax deductibility, from an activity in which the taxpayer does not materially participate, from a rental activity, or from a tax-shelter activity.

▸ **pecuniary loss.** (17c) A loss of money or of something having monetary value.

▸ **products-liability loss.** (1978) The total of a taxpayer's products-liability expenses up to the amount of the taxpayer's net operating loss. IRC (26 USCA) § 172(j)(1). — Abbr. PLL. See *net operating loss.*

▸ **progressive loss.** (1847) **1.** Loss that spreads or becomes more expensive to repair over time. **2.** Late-manifesting harm that is related to an event that caused immediate harm, worsens over time, and is not catalyzed by any additional causative agent. • A classic example is asbestosis, a disease that manifests long after exposure to asbestos fibers.

▸ **recognized loss.** (1939) *Tax.* The portion of a loss that is subject to income taxation. IRC (26 USCA) § 1001(c).

▸ **salvage loss.** (1831) **1.** Generally, a loss that presumptively would have been a total loss if certain services had not been rendered. **2.** *Marine underwriting.* The difference between the salvage value, less the salvage charges, and the original value of the insured property.

▸ **temporal loss.** (17c) A specific pecuniary loss.

> "When shall a man be said to have suffered a *temporal loss* from a communication concerning him? Since the remedy sought to be recovered by a personal action in a court of law is of a pecuniary admeasurement. The term *temporal,* used as descriptive of the loss upon which a suit may be supported, seems particularly opposed to *spiritual grievances,* which cannot be estimated in money, and for which a remedy must be found, if at all, under a constitution very differently constituted; and so, a mere injury to the feelings without actual deterioration of person or property, cannot form an independent and substantive ground of proceeding, though in other cases it may materially influence a jury in their assessment of damages." Thomas Starkie, *A Treatise on the Law of Slander, Libel, Scandalum Magnatum, and False Rumours* 9 (Edward D. Ingraham ed., 1st Am. ed. 1826).

▸ **total loss.** (1924) The complete destruction of insured property so that nothing of value remains and the subject matter no longer exists in its original form. • Generally, a loss is total if, after the damage occurs, no substantial remnant remains standing that a reasonably prudent uninsured owner, desiring to rebuild, would use as a basis to restore the property to its original condition. — Also termed *actual total loss.* Cf. *partial loss*; *constructive total loss.*

▸ **unrealized loss.** See *paper loss.*

loss adjuster. See ADJUSTER.

loss assessor. (1896) Someone employed by a private person to ascertain, arrange, or settle a matter, esp. one employed by an insurance policyholder to prepare a claim and negotiate a settlement with the insurer. Cf. ADJUSTER.

loss carryback. See CARRYBACK.

loss carryforward. See CARRYOVER.

loss carryover. See CARRYOVER.

loss insurance. See INSURANCE.

loss leader. (1922) A good or commodity sold at a very low price, usu. below cost, to attract customers to buy other items. — Sometimes shortened to *leader.* See BAIT AND SWITCH (1).

loss-making, *adj.* (Of a product or business) not making a profit; unprofitable.

loss of amenities. (1898) Substantial deprivation of some or all of life's pleasures.

loss-of-bargain damages. See *benefit-of-the-bargain damages* under DAMAGES.

loss-of-bargain rule. (1903) The doctrine that damages for a breach of a contract should put the injured party in the position it would have been in if both parties had performed their contractual duties.

loss-of-chance doctrine. (1987) A rule in some states providing a claim against a doctor who has engaged in medical malpractice that, although it does not result in a particular injury, decreases or eliminates the chance of surviving or recovering from the preexisting condition for which the doctor was consulted. — Also termed *lost-chance doctrine*; *increased-risk-of-harm doctrine.*

loss of consortium (kən-**sor**-shee-əm). (1878) **1.** A loss of the benefits that one spouse is entitled to receive from the other, including companionship, cooperation, aid, affection, and sexual relations. • Loss of consortium can be recoverable as damages from a tortfeasor in a personal-injury or wrongful-death action. Originally, only the husband could sue for loss of consortium. But in 1950, nearly a century after the enactment of the married women's property acts, a wife's action for negligent impairment of consortium was first recognized. *Hitaffer v. Argonne Co.*, 183 F.2d 811 (D.C. Cir. 1950). Today 48 states and the District of Columbia recognize both a husband's and a wife's right to sue for loss of consortium (Utah and Virginia do not). **2.** A similar loss of benefits (minus sexual relations) that one is entitled to receive from a parent or child. See CONSORTIUM.

loss of earning capacity. (1890) See LOST EARNING CAPACITY.

loss of enjoyment. (1858) Detrimental changes in a person's life, lifestyle, or ability to participate in previously enjoyed activities and pleasures of life. — Also termed *loss of enjoyment of life.*

loss of enjoyment of life. See LOSS OF ENJOYMENT.

loss of expectation of life. See LOSS OF LIFE EXPECTANCY.

loss of life expectancy. (1927) The period by which an injured person's projected life span is shortened because of an injury. — Also termed *loss of expectation of life.* See LIFE EXPECTANCY.

loss-of-use exclusion. See *failure-to-perform exclusion* under EXCLUSION (3).

loss-payable clause. (1895) *Insurance.* An insurance-policy provision that authorizes the payment of proceeds to someone other than the named insured, esp. to someone who has a security interest in the insured property. • Typically, a loss-payable clause either designates the person as a beneficiary of the proceeds or assigns to the person a claim against the insurer, but the clause usu. does not treat the person as an additional insured. See MORTGAGE CLAUSE.

loss payee. (1925) *Insurance.* A person or entity named in an insurance policy (under a loss-payable clause) to be paid if the insured property suffers a loss.

loss ratio. (1898) **1.** *Insurance.* The ratio between premiums paid and losses incurred during a given period. **2.** A bank's loan losses compared to its loan assets; a business's receivable losses compared to its receivables.

loss reserve. See RESERVE (1).

lost, *adj.* (16c) **1.** (Of property) beyond the possession and custody of its owner and not locatable by diligent search <lost at sea> <lost papers>. **2.** (Of a person) missing <lost child>. **3.** *Parliamentary law.* (Of a motion) rejected; not adopted <the motion is lost>.

lost-and-found, *n.* **1.** A place where things that are lost, mislaid, or accidentally left in a public place are kept until someone comes to claim them. **2.** The things so left. — Also termed (BrE in both senses) *lost property.*

lost boundary. See BOUNDARY (1).

lost-chance doctrine. (1985) **1.** LOSS-OF-CHANCE DOCTRINE. **2.** A rule permitting a claim, in limited circumstances, against someone who fails to come to the aid of a person who is in imminent danger of being injured or killed. Cf. GOOD SAMARITAN DOCTRINE.

lost corner. See CORNER (1).

lost earning capacity. (1908) A person's diminished earning power resulting from an injury. • This impairment is recoverable as an element of damages in a tort action. Cf. *lost earnings* under EARNINGS.

> "To some extent the phrases 'loss of earnings' and 'loss of earning capacity' are used interchangeably. But the preferred view is that they are different concepts. The former covers real loss which can be proved at the trial; the latter covers loss of the chances of getting equivalent work in the future." R.F.V. Heuston, *Salmond on the Law of Torts* 572 (17th ed. 1977).

lost earnings. See EARNINGS.

lost-expectation damages. See *expectation damages* under DAMAGES.

lost or not lost. (1832) *Marine insurance.* A policy provision fixing the effective date of the policy to a time preceding the policy date, even if the insured ship has already been lost when the policy takes effect, as long as neither party then knows, or has means of knowing, that the ship has been lost.

lost profits. (1852) **1.** *Contracts.* A measure of damages that allows a seller to collect the profits that would have been made on the sale if the buyer had not breached. UCC § 2-708(2). **2.** *Patents.* A measure of damages set by estimating the net amount not realized by a plaintiff-inventor because of the infringing defendant's actions. • The plaintiff can ask for a lost-profits recovery by showing that the patent is in demand, that the plaintiff is able to meet the demand, and that there are no acceptable noninfringing alternatives on the market. — Also termed (redundantly) *lost-profits damages.*

lost-profits damages. See LOST PROFITS.

lost property. 1. See PROPERTY. **2.** LOST-AND-FOUND.

lost-sales-of-unpatented-items theory. *Patents.* A theory of lost-profits remedy whereby compensation is sought for sales of unpatented items that the plaintiff would have sold along with patented items but for the defendant's infringement.

lost-volume damages. See DAMAGES.

lost-volume seller. (1974) A seller of goods who, after a buyer has breached a sales contract, resells the goods to a different buyer who would have bought identical goods from the seller's inventory even if the original buyer had not breached. • Such a seller is entitled to lost profits, rather than contract price less market price, as damages from the original buyer's breach. UCC § 2-708(2).

lost wages. See WAGE.

lost will. See WILL.

lot. (bef. 12c) **1.** A tract of land, esp. one having specific boundaries or being used for a given purpose.

- ▸ **minimum lot.** (1933) A lot that has the least amount of square footage allowed by a local zoning law.
- ▸ **nonconforming lot.** (1952) A previously lawful lot that now violates an amended or newly adopted zoning ordinance.

2. An article that is the subject of a separate sale, lease, or delivery, whether or not it is sufficient to perform the contract. UCC §§ 2-105(5); 2A-103(1)(s). **3.** A specified number of shares or a specific quantity of a commodity designated for trading.

▸ **odd lot.** (1870) A number of shares of stock or the value of a bond that is less than a round lot.

▸ **round lot.** (1837) The established unit of trading for stocks and bonds. • A round lot of stock is usu. 100 shares, and a round lot of bonds is usu. $1,000 or $5,000 par value. — Also termed *even lot*; *board lot.*

lot and scot. (16c) *Hist.* A collection of duties paid by voters before voting in certain cities and boroughs.

lot line. (1829) A land boundary that separates one tract from another <from the street to the alley, the lot line is 150 feet>.

lottery. (16c) **1.** A system of deciding who will get something by choosing people's names by chance. **2.** A method of raising revenues, esp. state-government revenues, by selling tickets and giving prizes (usu. cash prizes) to those who hold tickets with winning numbers that are drawn at random. — Also termed *lotto.*

▸ **Dutch lottery.** (18c) A lottery in which tickets are drawn from classes, and the number and value of prizes are fixed and increasing with each class. • This type of lottery originated in Holland in the 16th century. — Also termed *class lottery.*

▸ **Genoese lottery** (jen-oh-**eez** *or* -**ees**). (1835) A lottery in which, out of 90 consecutive numbers, five are drawn by lot, each player wagering that one or more of the numbers they have chosen will be drawn. • This type of lottery originated in Genoa in about 1530. — Also termed *number lottery*; *numerical lottery*; *numbers game.* See NUMBERS GAME.

▸ **Italian lottery.** See NUMBERS GAME.

LOU. *abbr.* LETTER OF UNDERTAKING.

***Loudermill* right.** A public employee's right to procedures that ensure the satisfaction of due-process requirements before the government can dismiss the employee from a job. *Cleveland Bd. of Educ. v. Loudermill*, 470 U.S. 532, 105 S.Ct. 1487 (1985). • Generally, the employer must meet with the employee to discuss the grounds for termination before the dismissal. This right applies only to public-sector employees.

love. 1. A strong feeling of deep affection for someone or something, esp. a family member or close friend. **2.** A strong feeling of affection for someone to whom one is sexually attracted. **3.** An intense feeling of enjoyment that something arouses in a person.

love day. See DAY.

Lovely claim. (1839) *Hist. Property.* An entitlement to settle on and take ownership of public land in Arkansas, created by the federal government for Lovely County settlers who were displaced by an 1828 treaty that gave the settlers' land to the Cherokee nation. • The term gets its name from Lovely County in the Arkansas territory, which straddled what is now the Oklahoma–Arkansas border. The treaty divided the county, granted the portion west of the Mississippi River to the Cherokee nation, and required the settlers in that territory to relocate. On May 24, 1828, Congress passed an act granting relief to Lovely County settlers who were forced to leave the Cherokee land and granted them land on the eastern side of the river. *Lovely claims* are found in chains of title in Arkansas.

lowbote. See BOTE (3).

low diligence. See *slight diligence* under DILIGENCE (2).

lower chamber. See LOWER HOUSE.

lower court. 1. See *court below* under COURT. **2.** See *inferior court* under COURT.

lower estate. See *servient estate* under ESTATE (4).

lower house. (1885) (*usu. cap.*) A group of elected representatives who make laws in a country, usu. as part of the more populous chamber in a bicameral legislature, as with the House of Representatives in Congress or the House of Commons in the United Kingdom. — Also termed *lower chamber.* Cf. UPPER HOUSE.

lower low tide. See TIDE.

lower-of-cost-or-market method. (1958) A means of pricing or costing inventory by which inventory value is set at either acquisition cost or market cost, whichever is lower. — Abbr. LCM method.

lower-of-cost-or-market rule. (1950) The principle that the measure of a legal remedy is determined by the acquisition cost or market cost, whichever is lower.

lower scale. See SCALE.

lowest-intermediate-balance rule. (1941) A principle that establishes limits on a claimant's ability to trace assets through a commingled fund — used typically when a creditor's money has been deposited into a wrongdoer's bank account and commingled with money that belongs to the wrongdoer — the creditor's recovery never to exceed the lowest balance that the account had between the time when the creditor's money was added to it and the time when withdrawals were stopped.

> "Trust law applies the lowest intermediate balance rule when, after commingling the beneficiary's money with her own, the trustee draws out funds and dissipates them. . . . For example, T is trustee for B of $1000. T deposits B's money together with $1000 of her own money in a bank. T then withdraws all but $500 and spends it. T later deposits $1000 of her own money back into the account. B is entitled to $500, the lowest intermediate balance." *Bombardier Capital, Inc. v. Key Bank of Maine*, 639 A.2d 1065, 1067 (Me. 1994).

lowest responsible bidder. (1844) A bidder who has the lowest price conforming to the contract specifications and who is financially able and competent to complete the work, as shown by the bidder's prior performance.

low-grade security. See SECURITY (4).

low-IQ defense. See *Atkins defense* under DEFENSE (1).

low justice. See JUSTICE (6).

low-tide elevation. (1951) An offshore natural feature, such as a rock, mudflat, sandbar, reef, or shoal, that is exposed when the tide is low and submerged when high.

low-total voting. See VOTING.

low-water mark. See WATERMARK (1).

loyalty, *n.* (15c) Faithfulness or allegiance to a person, cause, duty, or government. — **loyal,** *adj.*

loyalty oath. See *oath of allegiance* under OATH.

L.P. See *limited partnership* under PARTNERSHIP.

L.R. *abbr.* Law Reports. See REPORT (3).

LRIC. *abbr.* LONG-RUN INCREMENTAL COST.

L.S. *abbr.* LOCUS SIGILLI.

LSAT. *abbr.* LAW SCHOOL ADMISSIONS TEST.

LSC. *abbr.* LEGAL SERVICES CORPORATION.

Ltd. *abbr.* (1900) Limited — used in company names to indicate limited liability.

LTV ratio. See LOAN-TO-VALUE RATIO.

luce clarius (**loo**-see **klair**-ee-əs). [Latin] *Scots law.* Clearer than light. • The phrase expresses the idea that the evidence is very clear, usu. in circumstances necessary to support a conviction in a criminal case. — Also termed *luce meridiana clariores.*

luce meridiana clariores. LUCE CLARIUS.

lucid, *adj.* (16c) **1.** Understandable. **2.** Rational. **3.** Sane.

lucid interval. (17c) **1.** A brief period during which an insane person regains sanity sufficient to have the legal capacity to contract and act on his or her own behalf. **2.** A period during which a person has enough mental capacity to understand the concept of marriage and the duties and obligations it imposes. **3.** A period during which an otherwise incompetent person regains sufficient testamentary capacity to execute a valid will. — Also termed *lucid moment.*

lucid moment. See LUCID INTERVAL.

lucra nuptialia (**loo**-krə nəp-shee-**ay**-lə). [Latin] (1906) *Roman law.* The property that one spouse receives from another, whether by gift, marriage-gift, *dos*, or testamentary disposition. See POENAE SECUNDARUM NUPTIARUM.

lucrativa causa (loo-krə-**tɪ**-və **kaw**-zə). [Latin] *Roman law.* Enrichment for which the acquirer pays nothing (e.g., a bequest). — Also termed *causa lucrativa.*

lucrativa usucapio pro herede (loo-krə-**tɪ**-və yoo-z[y]oo-**kay**-pee-oh *or* -**kap**-ee-oh). [Latin] *Roman law.* A means of acquiring title to land that an heir has not possessed and excluding the rightful heirs by holding it for one year after the death of the landowner. • There was no requirement that the possessor act in good faith. This practice survived from primitive law. — Also termed *lucrativa uscapio pro herede.* See USUCAPIO.

lucrative (**loo**-krə-tiv), *adj.* (15c) **1.** Profitable; remunerative <a lucrative business>. **2.** *Civil law.* Acquired or held without accepting burdensome conditions or giving consideration <lucrative ownership>.

lucrative bailment. See *bailment for hire* under BAILMENT (1).

lucrative office. See OFFICE.

lucrative succession. See PRAECEPTIO HAEREDITATIS.

lucrative title. See TITLE (2).

lucre (**loo**-kər), *n.* (14c) Monetary gain; profit.

lucri causa (**loo**-krɪ **kaw**-zə). [Latin] For the sake of gain. • *Lucri causa* was formerly an essential element of larceny, but today the thief's intent to deprive the possessor of property is generally sufficient. See LARCENY.

> "'*Lucri causa*' literally means for the sake of gain. On rare occasions the suggestion has been made that no taking is with intent to steal unless the thief is motivated by some purpose of gain or advantage. Even those advancing this suggestion have not insisted upon an intent to gain a *pecuniary* advantage. An intent to take away property and destroy it for the purpose of destroying evidence has been held to be sufficient even by those who have been inclined to insist upon *lucri causa* as essential to an intent to steal. The generally accepted view does not include this element at all. It regards intent to deprive the owner of his property permanently, or an intent to deal with another's property unlawfully in such a manner as to create an obviously unreasonable risk of permanent deprivation, as all that is required to constitute the *animus furandi* — or intent to steal." Rollin M. Perkins & Ronald N. Boyce, *Criminal Law* 332–33 (3d ed. 1982).

lucro captando. **1.** See CERTANS DE LUCRO CAPTANDO. **2.** IN LUCRO CAPTANDO.

lucrum (**loo**-krəm), *n.* [Latin] **1.** *Roman law.* Gain; profit. **2.** *Hist.* A small parcel of land.

lucrum cessans (**loo**-krəm **ses**-anz). [Law Latin "ceasing gain"] (17c) *Hist.* Damages awarded to include a loss of anticipated profit in addition to an actual realizable loss. — Also termed *lucrum interceptum.* See DAMNUM EMERGENS.

lucrum interceptum (**loo**-krəm in-tər-**sep**-təm). See LUCRUM CESSANS.

luctuosa hereditas (lək-choo-**oh**-sə hə-**red**-i-tas), *n.* [Latin "mournful inheritance"] See *hereditas luctuosa* under HEREDITAS.

luctus (**lək**-təs), *n.* [Latin] *Roman law.* Mourning. — Also termed *tempus lugendi.*

ludere in extremis (**loo**-də-ree in ek-**stree**-mis). [Latin] *Hist.* To make sport on deathbed. • A person was presumed never to trifle at the point of death.

lukewarm bench. See BENCH.

lumi-lite (**loo**-mee lɪt), *n.* (2001) *Criminal law.* In a crime investigation, a chemical spray that can be used to cause blood and semen to glow in the dark and therefore be much more easily detectable.

luminar (loo-mə-**nair**-ee), *n.* [Latin "lamp"] *Hist.* A small lamp or candle set burning on a church altar, the maintenance of which was provided by lands and rents. Pl. ***luminaria.***

lumping. *Criminal procedure.* The imposition of a general sentence on a criminal defendant. See *general sentence* under SENTENCE.

lumping sale. See SALE.

lump sum. (1867) See SUM.

lump-sum agreement. (1948) *Int'l law.* An agreement for one country that caused injuries to another country's citizens to make a single payment to the other country to settle outstanding claims for those injuries. • The recipient country has the power to decide how the settlement funds should be distributed. This method of settling claims has become increasingly common since the mid-20th century as an alternative to submitting the claims to an international tribunal.

lump-sum alimony. See *alimony in gross* under ALIMONY (1).

lump-sum payment. See PAYMENT (2).

lunacy. See INSANITY.

lunar month. See MONTH (3).

lunatic, *n.* (14c) *Archaic & derogatory.* An insane person; one who is mentally ill. See INSANE.

- ▸ **dangerous lunatic.** (18c) A mentally incompetent person who seems reasonably likely to harm himself or herself, another person, or property.

lunch-hour rule. (1944) The doctrine that an employer is not responsible for injuries suffered or caused by an employee who takes a lunch break off work premises and, during the break, is not performing tasks in the course of the employment.

Luxembourgish sandwich. See DOUBLE IRISH.

luxury tax. See TAX.

LWI. *abbr.* LEGAL WRITING INSTITUTE.

lying by. The act or an instance of being present at a transaction affecting one's interests but remaining silent. • Courts often treat a person who was "lying by" at a transaction as having agreed to it and as being prevented from objecting to it.

lying in wait. (16c) *Criminal law.* The series of acts involved in watching, waiting for, and hiding from someone, with the intent of killing or inflicting serious bodily injury on that person. • Because lying in wait shows premeditation and deliberation, it can result in an increased sentence.

lynch, *vb.* (1836) (Of a mob) to kill (somebody) without legal authority, usu. by hanging.

lynching law. See ANTILYNCHING LAW.

lynch law. (1811) The administration of summary punishment, esp. death, for an alleged crime, without legal authority. — Also termed (through personification) *Judge Lynch.*

lynch mob. A group of people who kill someone, esp. by hanging, without a legal trial.

Lyndhurst's Act. *Hist.* An English statute that rendered marriages within certain degrees of kinship null and void. Marriage Act of 1835, 5 & 6 Will. 4, ch. 54. — Also termed *Lord Lyndhurst's Act.*

lytae (**lI-tee**), *n.* [Latin, fr. Greek] *Roman law.* Civil-law students in their fourth year of study.

M

M. 1. *abbr.* MORTGAGE. **2.** *Hist.* A letter engraved on a treasury note to show that the note bears interest at the rate of one mill per centum. **3.** *Hist.* A brand placed on the left thumb of a person convicted of manslaughter who claimed the benefit of clergy.

M1. A measure of the money supply including cash, checking accounts, and travelers' checks.

M2. A measure of the money supply including M1 items, plus savings and time deposits, money-market accounts, and overnight-repurchase agreements.

M3. A measure of the money supply including M2 items, plus large time deposits and money-market funds held by institutions.

mace. (14c) **1.** *Hist.* A weapon used in warfare, consisting of a staff topped by a heavy head, usu. of metal. **2.** A scepter; an ornamental form of weapon used as an emblem of the dignity of an office, as in Parliament and the U.S. House of Representatives. • In the House of Commons, it is laid on the table when the Speaker is in the chair. In the U.S. House of Representatives, it is usu. placed to the right of the Speaker and is borne upright by the sergeant-at-arms on extraordinary occasions, as when necessary to quell a disturbance or bring refractory members to order. **3.** (*cap.*) The trademarked name of a chemical liquid that can be sprayed in a person's face to cause dizziness and temporary immobilization.

mace-bearer. (16c) Someone who carries a mace before an official, usu. one of high rank. See MACE (2).

Macedonian Decree. See SENATUS CONSULTUM MACEDONIAUM.

mace-greff (**mays**-gref). (15c) *Hist.* A purchaser of stolen goods; esp., a person who knowingly buys stolen food. — Also spelled *mace-griefe.*

mace-proof, *vb.* To exempt from an arrest; to secure against an arrest.

macer. *Scots law.* See BAILIFF (1).

machination (mak-ə-**nay**-shən). (15c) (*usu. pl.*) **1.** An act of planning a scheme, esp. for an evil purpose. **2.** The scheme so planned.

machine. (16c) *Patents.* A device or apparatus consisting of fixed and moving parts that work together to perform some function. • Machines are one of the statutory categories of inventions that can be patented. — Also termed *apparatus; device.* Cf. MANUFACTURE; PROCESS (3).

***Machinists* preemption.** See PREEMPTION.

MACRS. *abbr.* Modified Accelerated Cost Recovery System. See ACCELERATED COST RECOVERY SYSTEM.

mactator (mak-**tay**-tər), *n.* [Law Latin "slaughterer"] (17c) *Hist.* A murderer.

maculare (mak-yə-**lair**-ee), *vb.* [Law Latin] *Hist.* To wound (a person).

made land. See LAND.

made law. See POSITIVE LAW.

Madison Amendment. See TWENTY-SEVENTH AMENDMENT.

Mad Parliament. In 1258, a commission of 24 barons summoned to Oxford by Henry III to carry out certain reforms and settle differences between the king and the barons. • The assembly was called the Mad Parliament because it ultimately abridged the king's power and gave unprecedented powers to the barons. The commission produced the Provisions of Oxford. — Also termed *parliamentum insanum.* See PROVISIONS OF OXFORD.

Madrid Agreement. *Trademarks.* **1.** An 1890 treaty establishing a system for the international registration of trademarks. • The agreement's official name is the Madrid Arrangement Concerning the International Registration of Marks. A product of the Madrid Revision Conference of the Paris Convention in 1890, it was last revised in 1967. Under this treaty's registration system, called the *Madrid Union,* a mark registered in a treaty country that is also registered (in French) with the World Intellectual Property Organization receives equal protection in all signatory countries. The United States ratified the treaty in 2002. **2.** An 1890 treaty designed to discourage false indications of geographic source by permitting member countries to seize falsely marked imported goods. — Also termed *Madrid Arrangement; Madrid Registration of Marks Treaty; Madrid Union.* • Also a product of the Madrid Revision Conference of the Paris Convention in 1890, the treaty bears the official name the Madrid Arrangement Concerning the Prevention of False or Deceptive Indications of Source. It applies to manufactured and handmade goods, and agricultural products. — Also termed (in sense 2) *Madrid Agreement for the Repression of False or Deceptive Indications of Source of Goods.*

Madrid Protocol. *Trademarks.* **1.** A 1996 international agreement that allows citizens of a Madrid Agreement signatory country to apply for a single international trademark through the World Intellectual Property Organization instead of registering the trademark in each individual country. • An applicant must apply for the trademark's registration in a treaty-member country before applying for international trademark protection. **2.** A 1989 international trademark-registration agreement that supplements the Madrid Agreement on trademark registration, harmonizes the Agreement's registration system with that of the European Union, and allows citizens of nonmember countries to apply for international trademark registration without first registering the trademark in a member country. • When referred to along with the Madrid Registration of Marks Treaty, it is sometimes also termed *Madrid System.* See MADRID AGREEMENT (1).

Madrid Registration of Marks Treaty. See MADRID AGREEMENT (1).

Madrid System. See MADRID PROTOCOL (2).

Madrid Union. See MADRID AGREEMENT (1).

maegbote. See BOTE (3).

Mafia (**mah**-fee-ə *or* **maf**-ee-ə). [fr. the secret society in Sicily known for exacting blackmail and protection money, as well as carrying out vengeance against anyone who injures its members; old Sicilian adj. *mafiusu*, rooted in Arabic *mayhas* "aggressive boasting or braggadocio"] **1.** A secret organization of criminals active esp. in Italy and the United States. **2.** Any group involved in organized crime. See ORGANIZED CRIME.

magister (mə-**jis**-tər), *n.* [fr. Latin *magis* "more"] (15c) *Roman law.* **1.** A master; a superior, esp. by office or position. **2.** A teacher; esp., one who has obtained eminence in a particular field of learning.

▸ ***magister ad facultates*** (mə-**jis**-tər ad fak-əl-**tay**-teez), *n.* [Latin "master for permissions"] (17c) *Eccles. law.* **1.** An officer who grants dispensations, as to marry or to eat meat on prohibited days. **2.** MASTER OF THE FACULTIES.

▸ ***magister bonorum vendendorum*** (mə-**jis**-tər bə-**nor**-əm ven-den-**dor**-əm). [Law Latin "master for sale of goods"] *Roman law.* A master appointed by the creditors of an insolvent debtor to direct the sale of the debtor's entire estate at auction.

▸ ***magister cancellariae*** (mə-**jis**-tər kan-sə-**lair**-ee-ee), *n.* [Law Latin "master in chancery"] *Hist.* A master in chancery — so called because the officer was a priest.

▸ ***magister libellorum*** (mə-**jis**-tər lɪ-bə-**lor**-əm). [Latin "master of written petitions"] (1844) *Roman law.* The chief of the imperial chancery bureau that handled petitions to the emperor.

▸ ***magister litis*** (mə-**jis**-tər **lɪ**-tis), *n.* [Latin "master of a lawsuit"] *Roman law.* Someone who directs or controls a lawsuit.

▸ ***magister navis*** (mə-**jis**-tər **nay**-vis). [Latin "master of a ship"] (17c) *Roman law.* The master of a trading vessel. • The master's trading debts, including the ship's maintenance expenses, gave rise to an *actio exercitoria.* See *actio exercitoria* under ACTIO.

▸ ***magister palatii*** (mə-**jis**-tər pə-**lay**-shee-ɪ), *n.* [Latin "master of the palace"] *Civil law.* A master of the palace, similar to the English Lord Chamberlain.

▸ ***magister societatis*** (mə-**jis**-tər sə-sɪ-ə-**tay**-tis). [Latin "master of partnership"] *Roman law.* A person appointed to administer a partnership's business; a managing partner or an employee.

magisterial (maj-ə-**steer**-ee-əl), *adj.* (17c) Of, relating to, or involving the character, office, powers, or duties of a magistrate. — Also termed *magistral; magistratic.*

magisterial district. See *magisterial precinct* under PRECINCT.

magisterial precinct. See PRECINCT.

magistracy (**maj**-ə-strə-see). (16c) **1.** The office, district, or power of a magistrate. **2.** A body of magistrates.

magistral, *adj.* (16c) **1.** Of, relating to, or involving a master or masters <an absolutely magistral work>. **2.** Formulated by a physician <a magistral ointment>. **3.** MAGISTERIAL.

magistralia brevia (maj-ə-**stray**-lee-ə **bree**-vee-ə), *n.* [Law Latin "magisterial writs"] *Hist.* Magisterial writs, which were drafted by clerks of the chancery for use in special matters.

magistrate (**maj**-ə-strayt), *n.* (14c) **1.** The highest-ranking official in a government, such as the king in a monarchy, the president in a republic, or the governor in a state. — Also termed *chief magistrate; first magistrate.* **2.** A local official who possesses whatever power is specified in the appointment or statutory grant of authority. **3.** A judicial officer with strictly limited jurisdiction and authority, often on the local level and often restricted to criminal cases. Cf. JUSTICE OF THE PEACE. **4.** See *judicial officer* (3) under OFFICER. — **magisterial** (maj-ə-**stir**-ee-əl), *adj.*

▸ **chamber magistrate.** (1965) *Australian law.* **1.** An assistant judge who rules on mostly minor matters not in open court but instead in chambers. **2.** A person, usu. a lawyer, who advises members of the public on legal matters, esp. procedural matters relating to a local court.

▸ **committing magistrate.** (18c) A judicial officer who conducts preliminary criminal hearings and may order that a defendant be released for lack of evidence, sent to jail to await trial, or released on bail. See *examining court* under COURT.

▸ **district-court magistrate.** (1932) In some states, a quasi-judicial officer given the power to set bail, accept bond, accept guilty pleas, impose sentences for traffic violations and similar offenses, and conduct informal hearings on civil infractions.

▸ **federal magistrate.** See UNITED STATES MAGISTRATE JUDGE.

▸ **investigating magistrate.** (1908) A quasi-judicial officer responsible for examining and sometimes ruling on certain aspects of a criminal proceeding before it comes before a judge.

> "The institution of the *investigating magistrate* is another measure for preserving the integrity of the law at the level of enforcement. In this case the measure is directed not toward curing the evils of a lax or sporadic enforcement, but toward the evils of an opposite nature, those resulting from an excess of zeal on the part of the prosecutor. Under the system in question, before a criminal charge may be brought before the regular courts it must be investigated by a special official and, in effect, certified as deserving trial in court. The investigating magistrate is thus a kind of quasi-judge standing halfway between the prosecutor and the regular court. The danger of the institution lies precisely in this twilight zone of function which it occupies. The certification of a case for trial inevitably tends to confirm the criminal charge against the suspect, thus creating what may amount in practice to a strong presumption of guilt. The element of prejudgment involved constitutes a threat to the integrity of the trial in open court; the accused has, in effect, had a kind of half-trial in advance of the real trial, and this half-trial is conducted, not *before* but *by* a kind of half-judge who acts essentially as an inquisitorial court. In those countries where it is a part of the legal system, the role of the investigating magistrate continues to be a subject of some debate, and even where it is generally accepted, there is always some lingering concern lest it become the subject of inconspicuous abuse." Lon L. Fuller, *Anatomy of the Law* 38–39 (1968).

▸ **metropolitan stipendiary magistrate** (stɪ-**pen**-dee-er-ee). (1952) *English law.* A stipendiary magistrate with jurisdiction in inner London areas. • Under the Access to Justice Act 1999, these magistrates have been renamed *district judges (magistrates' courts).* See *stipendiary magistrate.*

▸ **police magistrate.** (18c) A judicial officer who has jurisdiction to try minor criminal offenses, breaches of police regulations, and similar violations. — Also termed *police justice.*

▸ **stipendiary magistrate** (stɪ-**pen**-dee-er-ee). (1835) *English law.* A salaried magistrate who performs either in the place of or along with Justices of the Peace, and is appointed from barristers and solicitors of seven years standing. — Often shortened to *stipendiary.*

▸ **U.S. Magistrate.** See UNITED STATES MAGISTRATE JUDGE.

Magistrate Judge, U.S. See UNITED STATES MAGISTRATE JUDGE.

magistrate's court. See COURT.

magistratic, *adj.* See MAGISTERIAL.

magistratus (maj-ə-**stray**-təs), *n.* [fr. Latin *magister* "a master"] *Roman law.* **1.** A magistrate. **2.** A magistrate's office.

> "Magistratus. Denotes both the public office and the official himself. Magistracy was a Republican institution; under the Principate some *magistratus* continued to exist but with gradually diminishing importance; in the post-Diocletian Empire some former magistracies still exist but reduced nearly completely to an honorific title . . . . The most characteristic features of the Republican magistracy were the limited duration (one year) and colleagueship since each magistracy was covered by at least two persons . . . with equal power . . . . Magistrates were elected by the people . . . . During his year of service a *magistratus* could not be removed. Misdemeanor in office could be prosecuted only after the term, hence the tenure of an office for two consecutive years was prohibited . . . . The tenure of a public office was considered an honor; for that reason the magistrates did not receive any compensation. Their political influence was, however, of greatest importance . . . ." Adolf Berger, *Encyclopedic Dictionary of Roman Law* 571–72 (1953).

magistratus majores (maj-ə-**stray**-təs mə-**jor**-eez). [Latin "superior magistrates"] (17c) *Roman law.* Magistrates with superior powers, including the power to review their own judgments. Cf. MAGISTRATUS MINORES.

magistratus minores (maj-ə-**stray**-təs mi-**nor**-eez). [Latin "lesser magistrates"] (17c) *Roman law.* Magistrates with limited powers. Cf. MAGISTRATUS MAJORES.

> "The *magistratus minores* were officials of minor importance, they had no *imperium* and were vested with a restricted jurisdiction and some functions in specific fields . . . . The tenure of a minor magistracy opened the way for the quaestorship, the first step in the career of *magistratus maiores.*" Adolf Berger, *Encyclopedic Dictionary of Roman Law* 572 (1953).

magna assisa (**mag**-nə ə-**sɪ**-zə), *n.* [Law Latin] (1852) *Hist.* The grand assize. See *grand assize* under ASSIZE (5).

magna assisa eligenda (**mag**-nə ə-**sɪ**-zə el-ə-**jen**-də). See DE MAGNA ASSISA ELIGENDA.

Magna Carta (**mag**-nə **kahr**-tə). [Latin "great charter"] The English charter that King John granted to the barons in 1215 and that Henry III and Edward I later confirmed. • It is generally regarded as one of the great common-law documents and as the foundation of constitutional liberties. The other three great charters of English liberty are the Petition of Right (3 Car. (1628)), the Habeas Corpus Act (31 Car. 2 (1679)), and the Bill of Rights (1 Will. & M. (1689)). — Also spelled *Magna Charta.* — Also termed *Great Charter.*

> "The history of Magna Carta is the history not only of a document but also of an argument. The history of the document is a history of repeated re-interpretation. But the history of the argument is a history of a continuous element of political thinking. In this light there is no inherent reason why an assertion of law originally conceived in aristocratic interests should not be applied on a wider scale." J.C. Holt, *Magna Carta* 16 (1965).

> "Magna Carta came to be reckoned as the beginning of English statute law; it was printed as the first of the statutes of the realm. But to explain this we have first to remark that of Magna Carta there are several editions. We have four versions of the charter, that of 1215, that of 1216, that of 1217 and that of 1225, and between them there are important differences. Several clauses which were contained in the charter of 1215 were omitted in that of 1216 and were never again inserted. It seems to have been thought unadvisable to bind the young king to some of the more stringent conditions to which John had been subjected. The charter of 1217 again differs from that of 1216. Substantially it is in 1217 that the charter takes its final form; still it is the charter of 1225 which is the Magna Carta of all future times. That there were four versions is a fact to be carefully remembered; it is never enough to refer to Magna Carta without saying which edition you mean." F.W. Maitland, *The Constitutional History of England* 15 (1908; repr. 1955).

magna centum (**mag**-nə **sen**-təm), *n.* [Law Latin "great hundred"] Six score, or 120.

magna culpa (**mag**-nə **kəl**-pə). [Latin "great fault"] (1885) *Roman law.* Gross fault. • This is sometimes equivalent to *dolus.* See DOLUS.

magna neglegentia. See *gross negligence* under NEGLIGENCE.

magnetic-ink-character-recognition check. See CHECK.

magnum cape. See *cape magnum* under CAPE.

Magnuson–Moss Warranty Act (**mag**-nə-sən–**maws** *or* –**mos**). A federal statute requiring that a written warranty of a consumer product fully and conspicuously disclose, in plain language, the terms and conditions of the warranty, including whether the warranty is full or limited, according to standards given in the statute. 15 USCA §§ 2301–2312. — Abbr. MMWA.

magnus rotulus statutorum (**mag**-nəs **roch**-ə-ləs stach-ə-**tor**-əm). [Law Latin "the great statute roll"] The first of the English statute rolls, beginning with Magna Carta and ending with Edward III.

mahr, *n.* (18c) *Islamic law.* A gift of money or property that must be made by a man to the woman he marries. • The parties agree to the mahr's amount and time of payment before marrying. If the time of payment is indefinite or if the mahr's outstanding balance is not paid sooner, the agreed amount or outstanding balance becomes due on divorce or the husband's death. Despite the religious basis for a mahr, secular courts may uphold the agreement if its secular terms are enforceable as a prenuptial contract. — Also termed *sadaq.* Cf. NIKAH.

maiden. (bef. 12c) **1.** A young unmarried woman. **2.** *Scots law.* An instrument used to behead criminals. • The Earl of Morton, who had introduced the instrument to Scotland, was the first to be executed by it, in 1581. It was the prototype of the guillotine. Hence, "*to kiss the maiden* was to be put to death." H. Percy Smith, *Glossary of Terms and Phrases* 307 (1883).

maiden assize. See ASSIZE (1).

maiden name. See NAME.

maiden rent. See MARCHET.

maiestas (mə-**yes**-tas). See MAJESTAS.

maihem. See MAIM.

maihematus (may-hə-**may**-təs), *p.pl.* [Law Latin] Maimed; wounded.

maihemium. See MAIM.

mail, *n.* (13c) **1.** One or more items that have been properly addressed, stamped with postage, and deposited for delivery in the postal system. **2.** An official system for delivering such items; the postal system. **3.** One or more written or oral messages sent electronically (e.g., through e-mail or voicemail).

▸ **certified mail.** (1955) Mail for which the sender requests proof of delivery in the form of a receipt signed by the addressee. • The receipt (a green card, which is usu. referred to as such) must be signed before the mail will be delivered. — Also termed *certified mail, return receipt requested;* (BrE) *registered post; recorded delivery.*

▸ **registered mail.** (1921) Mail that the U.S. Postal Service records at the time of mailing and at each point on its route so as to guarantee safe delivery.

mail, *vb.* (1827) **1.** To deposit (a letter, package, etc.) with the U.S. Postal Service; to ensure that a letter, package, etc. is properly addressed, stamped, and placed into a receptacle for mail pickup. **2.** To deliver (a letter, package, etc.) to a private courier service that undertakes delivery to a third person, often within a specified time.

mailable, *adj.* (1845) (Of a letter or package) lawful to send through a postal service.

mail bomb. See *letter bomb* under BOMB.

mailbox rule. (1975) **1.** *Contracts.* The principle that an acceptance becomes effective — and binds the offeror — once it has been properly mailed. • The mailbox rule does not apply, however, if the offer specifies that an acceptance is not effective until received. **2.** The principle that when a pleading or other document is filed or served by mail, filing or service is deemed to have occurred on the date of mailing. • The mailbox rule varies from jurisdiction to jurisdiction. It may apply only to certain types of filings, or it may apply to the use of an overnight courier instead of the U.S. mail. — Also termed *dispatch rule.*

mail cover. (1959) A process by which the U.S. Postal Service provides a government agency with information on the face of an envelope or package (such as a postmark) for the agency's use in locating a fugitive, identifying a coconspirator, or obtaining other evidence necessary to solve a crime.

mail fraud. See FRAUD.

mail order. (1867) A method of buying and selling whereby the buyer chooses goods from a catalogue and orders them from a company that sends them by post or courier.

mail-order divorce. See DIVORCE.

maim, *n.* (14c) *Archaic.* The type of strength-diminishing injury required to support a charge of mayhem, usu. involving a wound or injury that is both severe and permanent; esp., serious injury to a body part that is necessary for fighting. — Also termed *maihem; maihemium.* See MAYHEM. — **maim,** *vb.*

> "Maim is such a hurt of any part of a man's body, whereby he is rendered less able in fighting, either to defend himself, or annoy his adversary. . . . The cutting off, or disabling, or weakening a man's hand or finger, or striking out his eye, or foretooth, or castrating him, are said to be maims, but the cutting off his ear, or nose, were not esteemed maims at the common law, because they do not weaken but only disfigure." Edward Bullingbrooke, *The Duty and Authority of Justices of the Peace and Parish Officers for Ireland* 541 (rev. ed. 1788).

> "Maihem or maim is where by the wrongful act of another any member is hurt or taken away, whereby the party is made unperfect to fight: as if a bone be taken out of the hand . . . . But the cutting of an ear or nose, or breaking of the hinder teeth, or such like, is no maihem, because it is rather a deformity of body than diminishing of strength; and that is commonly tried by the justices beholding the party. And if the justices stand in doubt whether the hurt be a maihem or not, they use and will of their own discretion take the help and opinion of some skilful chirurgeon [surgeon], to consider thereof, before they determine upon the cause." *Termes de la Ley* 283–84 (1st Am. ed. 1812).

> "'Maim' is the modern equivalent of the old word 'mayhem,' and some have long been inclined to abandon the earlier word entirely. There is a tendency, on the other hand, to retain 'mayhem' for the offense and to use 'maim' for the type of injury originally required for such a crime. This usage has a distinct advantage because statutory enlargements have included another type of injury within the scope of this offense, and today mayhem (the offense) may involve something other than *maim* (the injury)." Rollin M. Perkins & Ronald N. Boyce, *Criminal Law* 239 (3d ed. 1982).

mainad (**may**-nəd). [fr. Saxon *manath* "a deceitful oath"] *Hist.* Perjury.

main-a-main (may-nah-**mayn**), *adv.* [Law French] *Hist.* Immediately.

main channel. See CHANNEL (1).

main demand. See DEMAND (1).

maine-port. *Hist.* A small tribute (such as loaves of bread) that parishioners pay to the rector in lieu of tithes.

main motion. See MOTION (2).

main opinion. See *majority opinion* under OPINION (1).

mainour (**may**-nər), *n.* [fr. Law French *manier* "to handle"] (15c) *Hist.* A stolen article found in the hands of a thief. • At common law, the thief could be arraigned and tried without an indictment. — Also spelled *manour; meinour.* — Also termed *mannopus; manuopus.*

mainovre (mə-**noo**-vər), *n.* [fr. Law French *main* "hand" + *oeuvre* "work"] *Hist.* **1.** A trespass committed by hand. **2.** Manual labor. — Also spelled *mainoeuvre.*

mainpernable (**mayn**-pər-nə-bəl), *adj.* (15c) Capable of being bailed (mainprised); bailable. See MAINPRISE (2).

mainpernor (**mayn**-pər-nər), *n.* [Law French, fr. Old French *main* "hand" + *pernor* "taker"] (14c) *Hist.* **1.** A surety for a prisoner's appearance; one who gives mainprise for another. — Also termed *mainpriser.*

> "Mainpernors differ from bail, in that a man's bail may imprison or surrender him up before the stipulated day of appearance; mainpernors can do neither, but are barely sureties for his appearance at the day: bail are only sureties, that the party be answerable for the special matter for which they stipulate; mainpernors are bound to produce him to answer all charges whatsoever." 3 William Blackstone, *Commentaries on the Laws of England* 128 (1768).

2. A form of bail taken under a writ of mainprise. — Also termed *manucaptor* (man-yoo-**kap**-tər). See MAINPRISE.

main pot. *Tax.* A step in evaluating tax liability in which qualified transactions are compared to determine whether a net gain or loss has occurred. IRC (26 USCA) § 1231. — Also termed *big pot; hotchpot; hodgepodge.* Cf. CASUALTY POT.

mainprise (**mayn**-prɪz), *n.* [Law French, fr. Old French *main* "hand" + *prise* "taking"] (14c) *Hist.* **1.** Delivery of a prisoner to the mainpernor. **2.** A suretyship undertaking that makes the surety responsible for a prisoner's appearance in court on a specified date and time. **3.** A writ ordering the sheriff to take the security of a mainpernor for the prisoner's appearance and release the prisoner. — Also spelled *mainprize.* — Also termed *writ of mainprise; manucaption* (man-yoo-**kap**-shən). See DE HOMINE REPLEGIANDO.

mainprise, *vb.* (14c) *Hist.* To release (a prisoner) on the surety of a mainpernor.

main-purpose rule. (1915) *Contracts.* The doctrine that if a promise to guarantee another's debt is made primarily for the promisor's own benefit, then the statute of frauds does not apply and the promise need not be in writing to be enforceable. — Also termed *main-purpose doctrine; leading-object rule.*

main-relief rule. (1956) A doctrine by which venue for a lawsuit may be founded on the primary relief sought by the plaintiff, even if other claims, which alone would not support venue, are included in the suit.

main-rent. See VASSALAGE (2).

main sea. See SEA.

main seas. See *high seas* under SEA.

mainstreaming. (1973) The practice of educating a disabled student in classes with students who are not disabled, in a regular-education setting, as opposed to a special-education class. Cf. LEAST-RESTRICTIVE ENVIRONMENT.

mainsworn (**mayn**-sworn), *p.pl. Hist.* Forsworn, by making a false oath with a hand on a book. • This was used primarily in north England.

maintain, *vb.* (14c) **1.** To continue (something). **2.** To continue in possession of (property, etc.). **3.** To assert (a position or opinion); to uphold (a position or opinion) in argument. **4.** To care for (property) for purposes of operational productivity or appearance; to engage in general repair and upkeep. **5.** To support (someone) financially; esp., to pay alimony to. **6.** (Of a third party to a lawsuit) to assist a litigant in prosecuting or defending a lawsuit; to meddle in someone else's litigation.

maintainor. (15c) *Criminal law.* Someone who meddles in someone else's litigation by providing money or other assistance; a person who is guilty of maintenance. — Also spelled *maintainer.* See MAINTENANCE (8).

maintenance, *n.* (14c) **1.** The continuation of something, such as a lawsuit. **2.** The continuing possession of something, such as property. **3.** The assertion of a position or opinion; the act of upholding a position in argument. **4.** The care and work put into property to keep it operating and productive; general repair and upkeep. **5.** Financial support given by one person to another, usu. paid as a result of a legal separation or divorce; esp., ALIMONY (1). • Maintenance may end after a specified time or upon the death, cohabitation, or remarriage of the receiving party.

▸ **child maintenance. 1.** A parent's regular furnishing of necessaries to his or her child, including food, clothes, lodging, and school supplies. **2.** A parent's regular monetary contribution sufficient to furnish such necessaries, esp. when made in accordance with a court order.

▸ **maintenance in gross.** (1914) A fixed amount of money to be paid upon divorce by one former spouse to the other, in a lump sum or in installments. • Typically, the total amount is unmodifiable regardless of any change in either person's circumstances.

▸ **separate maintenance.** (17c) Money paid by one married person to another for support if they are no longer living together as husband and wife. • This type of maintenance is often mandated by a court order. An action for separate maintenance is not maintainable after the marriage has been dissolved. — Also termed *separate support.*

6. An amount advanced from an estate to support a decedent's dependents until the estate is settled. — Also termed (if applicable to only one person) *personal maintenance;* (if applicable to a group) *family maintenance.* **7.** *English law.* A statutory scheme that empowers a chancery court to revise the dispositive provisions in a will (and intestate shares, if any) to benefit the decedent's dependent relatives, including the surviving spouse until remarriage. • Australia, New Zealand, and most Canadian provinces have similar laws. — Also termed *testator's-family maintenance.* **8.** Improper assistance in prosecuting or defending a lawsuit given to a litigant by someone who has no bona fide interest in the case; meddling in someone else's litigation. Cf. CHAMPERTY.

maintenance and cure. (1905) *Maritime law.* Compensation provided to a sailor who becomes sick or injured while a member of a vessel's crew. • The obligation is broader than what would be covered under workers' compensation, as it applies to illness or injury whether or not arising out of shipboard duties. See CURE (2).

maintenance assessment. See MAINTENANCE FEE (2).

maintenance bond. See BOND (2).

maintenance call. See *margin call* under CALL (2).

maintenance fee. (1887) **1.** A periodic payment required to maintain a privilege, such as a license. **2.** A charge for keeping an improvement in working condition or a residential property in habitable condition. — Also termed *maintenance assessment.* **3.** A fee charged for reinvesting earnings and dividends in mutual funds. **4.** *Patents.* The periodic charge a patentee must pay the U.S. Patent and Trademark Office in order to keep the patent in force. • U.S. maintenance fees are due 3½, 7, and 11½ years from the date the patent is issued.

maintenance in gross. See MAINTENANCE (5).

maintenance margin requirement. See MARGIN REQUIREMENT.

maintenance of capital. (1875) *Corporations.* The retention of a shareholder's investments within the company to finance the company's business. • When a company receives share capital, it does not return the capital to the shareholders until the company is wound up. — Also termed *capital maintenance.*

maintenance order. See SUPPORT ORDER.

maior (**may**-ər). See MAJOR.

maister (**may**-stər). *Archaic.* A master.

maître (**may**-trə *or* **mayt**-ər), *n.* [French] *French law.* A master, esp. of a vessel.

maius Latium. See LATIUM MAIUS.

majestas (mə-**jes**-tas), *n.* [Latin "supreme power"] *Roman law.* **1.** The majesty, sovereign authority, or supreme prerogative of the state or sovereign; the supreme power of the people, esp. as represented by their highest representatives, the consuls, or the emperor. **2.** The crime of high treason. See *crimen majestatis* under CRIMEN.

> "*Majestas* . . . . From being an attribute of the *princeps*, the word 'majesty' came to be an honorific title confined, at first, to the Roman emperors of the West but later extended to all kings. From the time of Henry II, it has been used in England, the full form being 'Her Most Gracious Majesty.' The usual form is 'Her Majesty.'" David M. Walker, *The Oxford Companion to Law* 798 (1980).

major (**may**-jər). [Latin] (17c) **1.** *Roman law.* An older person, esp. one older than 25 and hence of full capacity. **2.** *Roman law.* An ascendant; an ancestor. **3.** *Hist.* A mayor. **4.** ADULT. **5.** In the U.S. Army, U.S. Air Force, or U.S. Marine Corps, a commissioned officer who ranks above a captain and below a lieutenant-colonel.

major action. *Environmental law.* An undertaking that may have a significant impact on the environment, triggering the need for an environmental assessment under the National Environmental Policy Act and some state laws. Cf. MAJOR-FEDERAL ACTION.

major-and-minor fault rule. See MAJOR-MINOR FAULT RULE.

major annus (**may**-jər **an**-əs). [Latin "the greater year"] A leap year, made up of 366 days.

majora regalia (mə-**jor**-ee ri-**gay**-lee-ə). See *regalia majora* under REGALIA.

major crime. See FELONY (1).

major disaster. A catastrophe, such as a hurricane, tornado, storm, flood, earthquake, drought, or fire, so severe that it warrants disaster assistance from the federal government. • When the President declares a major disaster, the federal government supplements the efforts and resources of states, local governments, and relief organizations to alleviate the damage, loss, hardship, and suffering caused by the catastrophe. 40 CFR § 109.

major dispute. See DISPUTE.

majorennitati proximus (may-jər-en-ə-**tay**-tɪ **prok**-sə-məs). [Law Latin] (18c) *Scots law.* Near majority. • Minors who were near the age of majority had difficulty arguing that a contracting party had taken advantage of their age and inexperience. See IN CONFINIO MAJORIS AETATIS.

majores (mə-**jor**-eez), *n.* [Latin "greater persons"] **1.** *Roman law.* Ancestors; forebears. **2.** *Hist.* Greater persons; persons of a higher status.

major federal action. *Environmental law.* An undertaking, either carried out by a federal agency or approved by a federal agency, that may have a significant impact on the environment. • Examples include constructing an aqueduct or dam, constructing a highway through wetlands, or adopting certain agency regulations. • Under the National Environmental Policy Act, a federal agency that plans to take a major federal action that may significantly affect the environment is required to prepare and file an environmental-impact statement, along with any public comments, with the Environmental Protection Agency. 40 CFR §§ 1506.9, 1508. — Abbr. MFA.

majori minus inest (mə-**jor**-ɪ **mɪ**-nəs **in**-est). [Latin] *Scots law.* The greater includes the less. • The phrase refers to the principle that any conveyance of a primary right to property includes any lesser rights to that property.

majority. (16c) **1.** The status of one who has attained the age (usu. 18) at which one is entitled to full civic rights and considered legally capable of handling one's own affairs. See *age of majority* under AGE. Cf. MINORITY (1). **2.** A number that is more than half of a total; a group of more than 50 percent <the candidate received 50.4 percent of the votes — barely a majority>. • A majority always refers to more than half of some defined or assumed set. In parliamentary law, that set may be all the members or some subset, such as all members present or all members voting on a particular question. A "majority" without further qualification usu. means a simple majority. See *simple majority.* Cf. PLURALITY; MINORITY (2); HALF PLUS ONE.

▸ **absolute majority.** (18c) A majority of all those who are entitled to vote in a particular election, regardless of how many voters actually cast ballots. See QUORUM.

▸ **constitutional majority.** See *majority of all the members.*

▸ **extraordinary majority.** See *supermajority.*

▸ **majority of all the members.** (1817) A majority of all the actual members, disregarding vacancies. — Also termed *constitutional majority; majority of the entire membership; majority of the membership.*

▸ **majority of all the memberships.** A majority of all the possible memberships, including vacancies. — Also termed *majority of the fixed membership.*

▸ **majority of the entire membership.** See *majority of all the members.*

▸ **majority of the fixed membership.** See *majority of all the memberships.*

▸ **majority of the membership.** See *majority of all the members.*

▸ **ordinary majority.** See *simple majority.*

▸ **overall majority.** (1918) **1.** A majority over all other candidates combined. **2.** The difference between the number of votes gained by the winner and the total votes gained by all the other contenders or political factions.

▸ **plural majority.** See PLURALITY.

▸ **simple majority.** (17c) A numerical majority of those actually voting. • Absent members, members who are present but do not vote, blanks, and abstentions are not counted. — Also termed *ordinary majority.*

▸ **supermajority.** (1958) A fixed proportion greater than half (often two-thirds or a percentage greater than 50%), required for a measure to pass. • Such a majority is needed for certain extraordinary actions, such as ratifying a constitutional amendment or approving a fundamental corporate change. — Also termed *extraordinary majority.*

▸ **veto-proof majority.** (1980) A legislative majority large enough that it can override an executive veto.

majority-consent procedure. (1988) *Corporations.* A statutory provision allowing shareholders to avoid a shareholders' meeting and to act instead by written consent of the holders of a majority of shares. • Delaware and a few other states have enacted such procedures.

majority leader. (1898) The legislator in charge of the legislative caucus that has the most members, as in the U.S. Senate or House of Representatives. Cf. MINORITY LEADER.

majority-minority district. See DISTRICT.

majority opinion. See OPINION (1).

majority principle. See MAJORITY RULE (1).

majority report. See REPORT (1).

majority rule. (1848) **1.** The principle that a majority of a group has the power to make decisions that bind the group; the principle that in the choice of alternatives, the one preferred by the greater number is selected. • It is governance by the majority of those who actually participate, regardless of the number entitled to participate. — Also termed *majority principle.*

> "There is much discussion about the ethical basis of majority rule — whether, for example, it rests on the force or coercion which is applied by sheer weight of numbers. I think the answer is that the will of the majority is the only practical means by which any association of human beings can be made to work, and I should not be afraid of the principle that, in the last resort, it is made to work by superior might. That would be an alarming thought if it meant that the will of the majority must in all cases be imposed on minorities by the Big Stick; but it is the essence of democracy that this does not normally happen, since, as we shall see, the will of the majority is not merely arbitrary domination, but, as nearly as possible, major opinion qualified by a great variety of minor dissents. If, however, difference of view is, on any essential principle, irreconcilable, then there is no course open but resort to coercion, and either rebellion or civil war is the result. It is a testimony to the average efficacy of the democratic method that this *ultima ratio* has been rare, and it is perhaps not without significance that its most conspicuous and most tragic example in the nineteenth century — the American Civil War — arose out of a principle fundamental to the whole fibre of democracy, that of human liberty." Carleton Kemp Allen, *Democracy and the Individual* 43–44 (1943).

2. The constitutional principle "that a majority of the people of a State . . . elect a majority of that State's legislators," *Reynolds v. Sims*, 377 U.S. 533, 583–84, 84 S.Ct. 1362, 1393 (1964), from which it follows that each voter is entitled to a share of the franchise equal to that of each other voter. See ONE-PERSON, ONE-VOTE RULE. **3.** *Corporations.* The common-law principle that a director or officer owes no fiduciary duty to a shareholder with respect to a stock transaction. • This rule has been restricted by both federal insider-trading rules and state-law doctrine. Cf. SPECIAL-FACTS RULE.

majority shareholder. See SHAREHOLDER.

majority verdict. See VERDICT (1).

majority vote. See MAJORITY (2).

majority voting. See VOTING.

majority whip. See WHIP.

major life activity. (1979) A basic activity that an average person in the general population can perform with little or no difficulty, such as seeing, hearing, sleeping, eating, walking, traveling, or working. • A person who is substantially limited in a major life activity is protected from discrimination under a variety of disability laws, most significantly the Americans with Disabilities Act and the Rehabilitation Act. 42 USCA § 12102(2); 29 USCA § 705(9)(B). — Abbr. MLA. See AMERICANS WITH DISABILITIES ACT.

major-minor fault rule. (1948) *Maritime law.* The principle that if the fault of one vessel in a collision is uncontradicted and sufficient to account for the accident, then the other vessel is presumed not to have been at fault and therefore not to have contributed to the accident. • The elimination of the divided-damages rule has made this rule obsolete. — Also termed *major-and-minor fault rule.*

major offense. **1.** See OFFENSE (2). **2.** See FELONY (1).

major party. See PARTY (2).

major trend. See TREND.

majus jus **(may-jəs jəs).** [Law Latin "a greater right"] (1926) *Hist.* A greater right. • This was a plea in a real action.

make, *vb.* (bef. 12c) **1.** To cause (something) to exist <to make a record>. **2.** To enact (something) <to make law>. **3.** To acquire (something) <to make money on execution>. **4.** To legally perform, as by executing, signing, or delivering (a document) <to make a contract>.

make default. **1.** DEFAULT (1). **2.** DEFAULT (2).

make law. (15c) **1.** To legislate. **2.** To issue a legal precedent, esp. a judicial decision, that establishes a new rule of law on a particular subject.

> "It seems true to say that the often hot but always arid controversy over whether or not judges do can or should 'make law' or 'legislate' is in essence a verbal or terminological question. In the last resort it is a matter of *fiat* whether we should use a different word to describe the process of enactment of statutes by Parliaments, after political debates in which it is irrelevant to the justification of the enactment that it conflicts with the previous rules or principles of law (for that is often the purpose of such enactments) and the process of judicial rule-making justified by reference to analogies and principles in the existing law so far as these promote 'commonsense' values. Of course, there is a sense in which decisions and rulings so justified only make explicit what was implicit in the preexisting law; and that is an important difference between the two processes. But equally it is true that the law is changed the moment after a great 'leading case' is decided from what it was the moment before; and that is an important similarity. What is important is to see both the difference and the similarity. The terminology is a good deal less important, though there is much to be said for reserving 'legislation' and 'legislate' to describe the former process, and to find some other term, for the latter — why not the much derided eighteenth-century usage of 'declaring' the law? At least such a distinction helps us to see the point of the doctrine of separation of powers, and to perceive the reality of the limits upon judicial powers of legal innovation." Neil MacCormick, *Legal Reasoning and Legal Theory* 188 (1978).

3. *Hist.* To deny a plaintiff's charge under oath, in open court, with compurgators.

make purpart **(pər-pahrt),** *vb.* (1831) To divide and apportion property formerly held in common. See PURPART.

maker. (14c) **1.** Someone who frames, promulgates, or ordains (as in *lawmaker*). **2.** Someone who signs a promissory note. See NOTE (1). Cf. COMAKER. **3.** DRAWER.

▸ **accommodation maker.** (1829) Someone who signs a note as a surety. See ACCOMMODATION (2); *accommodation indorser* under INDORSER.

▸ **prime maker.** (1972) The person who is primarily liable on a note or other negotiable instrument.

maker's mark. See MERCHANT'S MARK.

makeup gas. (1970) *Oil & gas.* Natural gas that has been paid for by the purchaser, usu. under a take-or-pay contract, but that is to be delivered in the years following payment. See *take-or-pay contract* under CONTRACT.

make-whole doctrine. (1991) *Insurance.* The principle that, unless the insurance policy provides otherwise, an insurer will not receive any of the proceeds from the settlement of a claim, except to the extent that the settlement funds exceed the amount necessary to fully compensate the insured for the loss suffered.

mal (mal), *adj.* [Law French "bad; wrong; against"] Bad; wrong. • In Law French, *mal* was a separable word, equivalent to the Latin *male* ("badly"). In its modern uses, *mal-* is a prefix in terms such as *maladministration* and *malpractice.*

mala antiqua (**mal**-ə an-**tɪ**-kwə). (1971) Old crimes; offenses that date back to antiquity.

mala demonstratio (**mal**-ə dem-ən-**stray**-shee-oh). [Latin] *Hist.* Erroneous description.

maladminister, *vb.* To manage (a company, government department, organization, etc.) badly; specif., to administer in a faulty, inefficient way, esp. in matters involving public affairs. — **maladministrator,** *n.*

maladministration. (17c) Poor management or regulation by a public officer; specif., an official's abuse of power. — Also termed *misadministration; breach of trust.*

mala fide (**mal**-ə **fɪd**-ee), *adv.* [Latin] In or with bad faith. Cf. BONA FIDE.

mala fides (**mal**-ə **fɪ**-deez), *n.* See BAD FAITH (1). Cf. BONA FIDE.

mala in se (**mal**-ə in **say** *or* **see**). See MALUM IN SE.

malandrinus (mal-ən-**drɪ**-nəs), *n.* [Law Latin "brigand"] *Hist.* A thief; a pirate.

malapportionment, *n.* (1959) The improper or unconstitutional apportionment of a legislative district. See APPORTIONMENT (3); GERRYMANDERING; LEGISLATIVE DISTRICTING. — **malapportion,** *vb.*

mala praxis (**mal**-ə **prak**-sis). [Law Latin] (17c) *Hist.* Malpractice; unskillful treatment, esp. by a doctor.

> "Injuries, affecting a man's *health,* are where by any unwholesome practices of another a man sustains any apparent damage in his vigor or constitution. As by selling him bad provisions or wine . . . or by the neglect or unskilful management of his physician, surgeon, or apothecary. For it hath been solemnly resolved . . . that *mala praxis* is a great misdemeanor and offence at common law, whether it be for curiosity and experiment, or by neglect; because it breaks the trust which the party had placed in his physician, and tends to the patient's destruction." 3 William Blackstone, *Commentaries on the Laws of England* 122 (1768).

mala prohibita (**mal**-ə proh-**hib**-i-tə). See MALUM PROHIBITUM.

malconduct (mal-**kon**-dəkt), *n.* Improper, faulty, or wrongful conduct, esp. through maladministering public affairs. Cf. MISCONDUCT.

malconduct in office. See *official misconduct* under MISCONDUCT.

male creditus (**mal**-ee **kred**-ə-təs). [Law Latin] *Hist.* (Of a person) in bad repute; untrusted.

malediction (mal-ə-**dik**-shən). (15c) *Hist.* A curse placed on property donated to a church to protect it against anyone attempting to violate the church's rights.

malefaction (mal-ə-**fak**-shən), *n.* [Latin *malefacere* "to do evil"] (15c) *Archaic.* An evil deed; a crime or offense. — Also termed *maleficium.* — **malefactory,** *adj.*

malefactor (**mal**-ə-fak-tər), *n.* [Latin] (15c) Someone who does bad or illegal things; WRONGDOER.

maleficium (mal-ə-**fish**-ee-əm), *n.* [Latin "a misdeed"] (1830) *Roman law.* A delict. See MALEFACTION.

maleson. See MALISON.

malesworn (**mayl**-sworn), *p.pl.* Forsworn. — Also spelled *malsworn.*

malfeasance (mal-**fee**-zənts), *n.* (17c) A wrongful, unlawful, or dishonest act; esp., wrongdoing or misconduct by a public official; MISFEASANCE IN PUBLIC OFFICE. Cf. MISFEASANCE; NONFEASANCE. — **malfeasant** (mal-**fee**-zənt), *adj.* — **malfeasor** (mal-**fee**-zər), *n.*

malfunction, *n.* A fault in the way something works, as with a machine, a piece of one's wardrobe, or a part of one's body.

malfunction theory. (1979) *Products-liability law.* A principle permitting a products-liability plaintiff to prove that a product was defective by proving that the product malfunctioned, instead of requiring the plaintiff to prove a specific defect. • A plaintiff relying on the malfunction theory usu. must also prove that the product was not misused, and must disprove all reasonable explanations for the occurrence other than a defect.

malgovernment. Bad government; misgovernment. Cf. KAKISTOCRACY.

mal gree (mal **gree**). [Law French "against the will"] *Hist.* Against the will; without consent.

malice, *n.* (14c) **1.** The intent, without justification or excuse, to commit a wrongful act. **2.** Reckless disregard of the law or of a person's legal rights. **3.** Ill will; wickedness of heart. • This sense is most typical in nonlegal contexts. — Also termed (in sense 2) *abandoned and malignant heart; abandoned heart; malignant and abandoned heart.*

> "Malice means in law wrongful intention. It includes any intent which the law deems wrongful, and which therefore serves as a ground of liability. Any act done with such an intent is, in the language of the law, malicious, and this legal usage has etymology in its favour. The Latin *malitia* means badness, physical or moral — wickedness in disposition or in conduct — not specifically or exclusively ill-will or malevolence; hence the malice of English law, including all forms of evil purpose, design, intent, or motive. [But] intent is of two kinds, being either immediate or ulterior, the ulterior intent being commonly distinguished as the motive. The term malice is applied in law to both these forms of intent, and the result is a somewhat puzzling ambiguity which requires careful notice. When we say that an act is done maliciously, we mean one of two distinct things. We mean either that it is done intentionally, or that it is done with some wrongful motive." John Salmond, *Jurisprudence* 384 (Glanville L. Williams ed., 10th ed. 1947).

> "[M]alice in the legal sense imports (1) the absence of all elements of justification, excuse or recognized mitigation, and (2) the presence of either (a) an actual intent to cause the particular harm which is produced or harm of the same general nature, or (b) the wanton and wilful doing of an act with awareness of a plain and strong likelihood that such harm may result. . . . The Model Penal Code does not use 'malice' because those who formulated the Code had a blind prejudice against the word. This is very regrettable because it represents a useful concept despite some unfortunate language employed at times in the effort to express

it." Rollin M. Perkins & Ronald N. Boyce, *Criminal Law* 860 (3d ed. 1982).

▸ **actual malice.** (18c) **1.** The deliberate intent to commit an injury, as evidenced by external circumstances. — Also termed *express malice; malice in fact.* Cf. *implied malice.* **2.** *Defamation.* Knowledge (by the person who utters or publishes a defamatory statement) that a statement is false, or reckless disregard about whether the statement is true. • To recover for defamation, a plaintiff who is a public official or public figure must overcome the defendant's qualified privilege by proving the defendant's actual malice. And for certain other types of claims, a plaintiff must prove actual malice to recover presumed or punitive damages. — Also termed *New York Times malice; constitutional malice; common-law malice.*

▸ **common-law malice.** See *actual malice* (2).

▸ **constructive malice.** See *implied malice.*

▸ **express malice.** (17c) **1.** *Criminal law.* The intent to kill or seriously injure arising from a deliberate, rational mind. **2.** See *actual malice* (1). **3.** *Defamation.* The bad-faith publication of defamatory material.

▸ **general malice.** (17c) Malice that is necessary for any criminal conduct; malice that is not directed at a specific person. Cf. *particular malice.*

▸ **implied malice.** (17c) Malice inferred from a person's conduct. — Also termed *constructive malice; legal malice; presumed malice; malice in law.* Cf. *actual malice* (1).

▸ **malice in fact.** See *actual malice* (1).

▸ **murderous malice.** Any one of seven types of malice: (1) the intent to kill the person actually killed; (2) the intent to kill A, but causing death to B; (3) the intent to kill someone, but not any particular victim (see *universal malice*); (4) the intent to do an act intrinsically likely to kill, though without the intent of killing and with the intent to hurt; (5) intent to do an act intrinsically likely to kill, though without the intention of hurting anyone (for example, dropping a concretè block from an overpass without looking to see whether cars are passing underneath); (6) the intent to commit a felonious act of violence against an unwilling victim; or (7) formerly, the intent to commit an act not likely to kill, with the intent of opposing a police officer who is trying to arrest a suspect.

▸ **particular malice.** (16c) Malice that is directed at a particular person. — Also termed *special malice.*

▸ **transferred malice.** (1961) Malice directed to one person or object but instead harming another in the way intended for the first.

> "[I]f A shoots at B intending to kill him, but the shot actually kills C, this is held to be murder of C. So also if A throws a stone at one window and breaks another, it is held to be malicious damage to the window actually broken. This doctrine, which is known as the doctrine of transferred malice, applies only where the harm intended and the harm done are of the same kind. If A throws a stone at a human being and unintentionally breaks a window, he cannot be convicted of malicious damage to the window." John Salmond, *Jurisprudence* 382 (Glanville L. Williams ed., 10th ed. 1947).

▸ **universal malice.** (17c) The state of mind of a person who determines to take a life on slight provocation, without knowing or caring who may be the victim.

malice aforethought. (17c) The requisite mental state for common-law murder, encompassing any one of the following: (1) the intent to kill, (2) the intent to inflict grievous bodily harm, (3) extremely reckless indifference to the value of human life (the so-called "abandoned and malignant heart"), or (4) the intent to commit a dangerous felony (which leads to culpability under the felony-murder rule). — Also termed *premeditated malice; preconceived malice; malice prepense; malitia praecogitata.*

> "Malice aforethought is the term which came into use during medieval times to indicate the mental element necessary in the felony of murder. It has been the subject of voluminous jurisprudential enquiry . . . ." J.W. Cecil Turner, *Kenny's Outlines of Criminal Law* 27 (16th ed. 1952).

> "Every intentional killing is with malice aforethought unless under circumstances sufficient to constitute (1) justification, (2) excuse, or (3) mitigation." Rollin M. Perkins & Ronald N. Boyce, *Criminal Law* 58 (3d ed. 1982).

malice exception. (1977) A limitation on a public official's qualified immunity, by which the official can face civil liability for willfully exercising discretion in a way that violates a known or well-established right. See *qualified immunity* under IMMUNITY (1).

malice in fact. See *actual malice* (1) under MALICE.

malice in law. See *implied malice* under MALICE.

malice prepense. See MALICE AFORETHOUGHT.

malicious, *adj.* (13c) **1.** Substantially certain to cause injury. **2.** Without just cause or excuse.

malicious abandonment. See ABANDONMENT (4).

malicious abuse of legal process. See ABUSE OF PROCESS.

malicious abuse of process. See ABUSE OF PROCESS.

malicious accusation. See ACCUSATION.

malicious act. (17c) An intentional, wrongful act done willfully or intentionally against another without legal justification or excuse.

malicious arrest. See ARREST (2).

malicious assault with a deadly weapon. See ASSAULT.

malicious bankruptcy. See BANKRUPTCY (2).

malicious damage. See MALICIOUS MISCHIEF.

malicious defense. See DEFENSE (2).

malicious execution. See EXECUTION (4).

malicious injury. See INJURY.

malicious institution of civil proceedings. See MALICIOUS PROSECUTION.

malicious killing. (17c) An intentional killing without legal justification or excuse. — Also termed *killing with malice.* Cf. ACCIDENTAL KILLING.

maliciously, *adv.* (14c) **1.** In a spirit of ill will. **2.** With malice aforethought. See MALICE AFORETHOUGHT.

maliciously damaging the property of another. See MALICIOUS MISCHIEF.

malicious mischief. (18c) The common-law misdemeanor of intentionally destroying or damaging another's property. • Although modern statutes predominantly make this offense a misdemeanor, a few make it a felony (depending on the nature of the property or its value). *See* Model Penal Code § 220.3. — Also termed *malicious mischief and trespass*; *malicious injury*; *malicious trespass*; *malicious damage*; *maliciously damaging the property of another*; (in the Model Penal Code) *criminal mischief*. See MISCHIEF.

> "Such phrases as 'malicious mischief and trespass,' 'malicious injury,' and 'maliciously damaging the property of another,' are merely additional labels used at times to indicate the same offense. It was a misdemeanor according to the common law of England, although some confusion has resulted from Blackstone's statement that it was 'only a trespass at common law.' Before the word 'misdemeanor' became well established the old writers tended to use the word 'trespass' to indicate an offense below the grade of felony. And it was used at times by Blackstone for this purpose, as in the phrase 'treason, felony, or trespass.'" Rollin M. Perkins & Ronald N. Boyce, *Criminal Law* 405 (3d ed. 1982).

malicious motive. See MOTIVE.

malicious prosecution. (17c) **1.** The institution of a criminal or civil proceeding for an improper purpose and without probable cause. • The tort requires proof of four elements: (1) the initiation or continuation of a lawsuit; (2) lack of probable cause for the lawsuit's initiation; (3) malice; and (4) favorable termination of the original lawsuit. Restatement (Second) of Torts §§ 674–81B (1977). **2.** The tort claim resulting from the institution of such a proceeding. • Once a wrongful prosecution has ended in the defendant's favor, he or she may sue for tort damages. — Also termed (in the context of civil proceedings) *malicious use of process*; (archaically) *malicious institution of civil proceedings*. Cf. ABUSE OF PROCESS; VEXATIOUS SUIT; *malicious defense* under DEFENSE (2).

> "**Malicious prosecution — The action of, defined.** — A judicial proceeding, instituted by one person against another from wrongful or improper motives, and without probable cause to sustain it. It is usually called a malicious prosecution; and an action for damages for being subjected to such a suit is called an action for malicious prosecution. In strictness, the prosecution might be malicious, that is, brought from unlawful motives, although founded on good cause. But it is well established that unless want of probable cause and malice concur no damages are recoverable. However blameworthy was the prosecutor's motives, he cannot be cast in damages if there was probable cause for the complaint he made. Hence, the term usually imports a causeless as well as an ill-intended prosecution. It commonly, but not necessarily, means a prosecution on some charge of crime." Martin L. Newell, *A Treatise on the Law of Malicious Prosecution, False Imprisonment, and the Abuse of Legal Process* 6 (1892).

> "The mental element which is requisite to found liability for malicious prosecution is similar to that which is sufficient to destroy qualified privilege in libel: it amounts to an abuse of the right to prosecute which is based on the public interest in bringing criminals to book. The abuse here arises from the fact that the prosecution is animated by a desire to use the criminal law for some purpose for which it is not intended. It is particularly unfortunate that the word 'malice' was ever used in this context for it is quite possible for a prosecutor to have been inspired by personal dislike of the plaintiff and by a desire for vengeance against him and yet not be liable for malicious prosecution; and this may happen even where the proceedings were instituted without reasonable and probable cause, if the prosecutor honestly believed that he had a good case and that he could therefore satisfy his animosity against the plaintiff by obtaining his conviction." J.F. Lever, "Means, Motives and Interests in the Law of Torts," in *Oxford Essays in Jurisprudence* 62–63 (A.G. Guest ed., 1961).

> "The distinction between an action for malicious prosecution and an action for abuse of process is that a malicious prosecution consists in maliciously causing process to be issued, whereas an abuse of process is the employment of legal process for some purpose other than that which it was intended by the law to effect — the improper use of a regularly issued process. For instance, the initiation of vexatious civil proceedings known to be groundless is not abuse of process, but is governed by substantially the same rules as the malicious prosecution of criminal proceedings." 52 Am. Jur. 2d *Malicious Prosecution* § 2, at 187 (1970).

Malicious Shooting or Stabbing Act. See ELLENBOROUGH'S ACT.

malicious technology. Any electronic or mechanical means, esp. software, used to monitor or gain access to another's computer system without authorization for the purpose of impairing or disabling the system. • Examples of malicious technology are Trojan horses, time-outs, keystroke logging, and data-scrambling devices. — Also termed *malware*.

malicious trespass. See MALICIOUS MISCHIEF.

malicious use of process. See MALICIOUS PROSECUTION.

malign (mə-**lɪn**), *vb.* (15c) To defame; to slander or libel. See CALUMNIATE. — **malign,** *adj.*

malignancy (mə-**lig**-nən-see), *n.* **1.** A feeling of intense hatred. **2.** *Medical.* A cancerous growth. — **malignant,** *adj.*

malignant and abandoned heart. See ABANDONED AND MALIGNANT HEART.

malignare (mal-əg-**nair**-ee), *vb.* [Latin] *Hist.* **1.** To malign; to slander. **2.** To maim.

malinger, *vb.* (1820) To feign illness or disability, esp. in an attempt to avoid an obligation or to continue receiving disability benefits.

malison (**mal**-ə-zən *or* -sən). [fr. Latin *malum* "evil" + *sonus* "a sound"] (13c) *Hist.* A curse. — Also spelled *maleson.*

malitia (mə-**lish**-ee-ə). [Latin "malice"] *Hist.* An actual evil design; express malice. • *Malitia* originally signified general wrongdoing, and did not describe a wrongdoer's state of mind; *malitia praecogitata*, for example, indicated only the seriousness of the offense, though it was eventually rendered *malice aforethought.*

▸ ***malitia capitalis*** (mə-**lish**-ee-ə kap-i-**tay**-lis). [Latin] *Hist.* Deadly malice.

▸ ***malitia excogitata*** (eks-koj-ə-**tay**-tə). See *malitia praecogitata.*

▸ ***malitia praecogitata*** (pree-koj-ə-**tay**-tə). See MALICE AFORETHOUGHT. — Also termed *malitia excogitata.*

> "[T]he word *felony* is often coupled with what will in the future be another troublesome term of art, to wit, *malice aforethought* or *malice prepense* (*malitia excogitata, praecogitata*). . . . When it first came into use, it hardly signified a state of mind; some qualifying adjective such as *praemeditata* or *excogitata* was needed if much note was to be taken of intention or of any other psychical fact. When we first meet with *malice prepense* it seems to mean little more than intentional wrong-doing; but the somewhat weighty adjectives which are coupled with *malitia* in its commonest context — adjectives such as *excogitata* — are, if we mistake not, traces of the time when *forsteal, guetapens,* waylaying, the setting of ambush, was (what few crimes were) a specially reserved plea of the crown to be emended, if indeed it was emendable, by a heavy *wite.*" 2 Frederick Pollock & Frederic W. Maitland, *The History of English Law Before the Time of Edward I* 468-69 (2d ed. 1899).

malleable, *adj.* (14c) **1.** (Of an object) capable of extension by hammering <the metal was malleable>. **2.** (Of a person) capable of being influenced <the young student was malleable>.

Malleus Maleficarum (**mal**-ee-əs mal-ə-fi-**kair**-əm). [Latin "Hammer of Witches"] *Hist.* An encyclopedic work of demonology and witchcraft, prepared in 1486 by two Dominican friars (Heinrich Kraemer and Johann Sprenger) as part of their efforts to eradicate witchcraft in Germany. • The *Malleus Maleficarum* was based largely on folk beliefs, but it was relied on for several centuries as an authoritative source on how to detect, extract confessions from, and prosecute witches.

***Mallory* rule.** See MCNABB–MALLORY RULE.

mallum (**mal**-əm), *n.* [Law Latin] (1844) *Hist.* **1.** A superior court among the Salian Franks, with criminal jurisdiction; a high court that handles important business. **2.** A public national assembly. — Also termed *mallus.*

mallus. See MALLUM.

malo animo (**mal**-oh **an**-ə-moh), *adv.* [Latin] With evil intent; with malice.

malo grato (**mal**-oh **gray**-toh), *adv.* [Latin] Unwillingly.

Maloney Act. A 1938 amendment to the Securities Exchange Act of 1934, providing for broker registration in over-the-counter markets.

malpractice (mal-**prak**-tis). (17c) An instance of negligence or incompetence on the part of a professional. • To succeed in a malpractice claim, a plaintiff must also prove proximate cause and damages. — Also termed *professional negligence.*

▸ **legal malpractice.** (1875) A lawyer's failure to render professional services with the skill, prudence, and diligence that an ordinary and reasonable lawyer would use under similar circumstances. — Also termed *attorney malpractice.*

▸ **medical malpractice.** (1834) A doctor's failure to exercise the degree of care and skill that a physician or surgeon of the same medical specialty would use under similar circumstances. — Often shortened to *med. mal.*

malpractice insurance. See INSURANCE.

malsworn. See MALESWORN.

maltreat, *vb.* (17c) To treat (a person or animal) cruelly. Cf. ABUSE, *vb.*; MISTREAT.

maltreatment. (18c) Bad or cruel treatment whether resulting from ignorance, neglect, or willfulness; esp., improper treatment by a surgeon. See MALPRACTICE.

malum (**mal**-əm *also* **may**-ləm), *n.* [Latin] Something bad or evil. Pl. ***mala.***

malum in se (**mal**-əm in **say** *or* **see**), *n.* [Latin "evil in itself"] (17c) A crime or an act that is inherently immoral, such as murder, arson, or rape. — Also termed *malum per se.* Cf. MALUM PROHIBITUM. Pl. ***mala in se.*** — ***malum in se,*** *adj.*

> "The basis for the distinction between *mala in se* and *mala prohibita*, between what one might call a crime and an offence — or between what one might call a felony and a misdemeanour, if one could modernize those terms so that the latter was given its natural meaning — is that crime means to the ordinary man something that is sinful or immoral, and an offence at worst a piece of misbehaviour." Patrick Devlin, *The Enforcement of Morals* 33 (1968).

> "The distinction between offenses *mala in se* and offenses *mala prohibita* was recognized at least as early as the fifteenth century. It has been criticized repeatedly. About a century and a half ago the distinction was said to be one 'not founded upon any sound principle' and which had 'long since been exploded.' [Quoting *Bensley v. Bignold*, 5 B. & A. 335, 341, 106 Eng. Rep. 1214, 1216 (1822); other citations omitted.] The Supreme Court, however, has shown that it is just as firmly entrenched today as it was in 1495." Rollin M. Perkins & Ronald N. Boyce, *Criminal Law* 880 (3d ed. 1982).

malum per se. See MALUM IN SE.

malum prohibitum (**mal**-əm proh-**hib**-i-təm), *n.* [Latin "prohibited evil"] (18c) An act that is a crime merely because it is prohibited by statute, although the act itself is not necessarily immoral. • Misdemeanors such as jaywalking and running a stoplight are *mala prohibita*, as are many regulatory violations. Cf. MALUM IN SE. Pl. **mala prohibita.** — **malum prohibitum,** *adj.*

> "Much of the criminal law that is regulatory in character — the part of it that deals with *malum prohibitum* rather than *malum in se* — is based upon the . . . principle . . . that the choice of the individual must give way to the convenience of the many." Patrick Devlin, *The Enforcement of Morals* 16 (1968).

> "As customarily used these phrases are mutually exclusive. An offense *malum prohibitum* is not a wrong which is prohibited, but something which is wrong *only* in the sense that it is against the law. This is emphasized at times by such phrases as '*malum prohibitum* only' or 'but *malum prohibitum*,' although it is understood without any such qualification. A failure to understand this usage of the terms has led some to assume that all statutory additions to the common law of crimes are *mala prohibita*. One writer emphasized his confusion by speaking of embezzlement as *malum prohibitum*. This assumption is utterly without foundation. An act may be *malum in se* although no punishment is provided by law. If this defect is corrected by appropriate legislation, what previously was *malum in se* does not cease to be so by reason of having been defined and made punishable by law." Rollin M. Perkins & Ronald N. Boyce, *Criminal Law* 884–85 (3d ed. 1982).

malum regimen (**mal**-əm **rej**-ə-men). [Law Latin] (1858) *Scots law.* Bad medical treatment. • A defendant in a homicide case may assert as a defense that the decedent actually died as a result of bad medical treatment, not the defendant's actions.

malus animus (**mal**-əs **an**-ə-məs). [Latin] *Scots law.* Bad intention. • This intention, coupled with a prohibited act carrying it out, resulted in a crime. See DOLE; MENS REA.

malveilles (mal-**vay** *also* mal-**vayls**), *n.* [French "misdemeanors"] *Hist.* **1.** Ill will. **2.** Crimes; misdemeanors; malicious acts.

malveis procurors (**mal**-vay prə-**kyoor**-ərz). [Law French "defective procurers"] *Hist.* Persons who pack juries, as by nomination or other practice.

malversation (mal-vər-**say**-shən), *n.* [French "ill behavior"] (16c) Official corruption; misbehavior by an official in the exercise of the duties of the office. — **malverse,** *vb.*

malware. (1990) *Slang.* See MALICIOUS TECHNOLOGY.

man. (bef. 12c) **1.** An adult male. **2.** Humankind. — Also termed *mankind.* **3.** A human being. **4.** *Hist.* A vassal; a feudal tenant.

manacle (**man**-ə-kəl). (14c) (*oft. pl.*) An iron ring that is clasped to a prisoner's wrist or ankle and attached to a chain; a shackle or metal fetter. Cf. HANDCUFF.

manage, *vb.* (16c) **1.** To exercise executive, administrative, and supervisory powers. **2.** To conduct, control, carry on, or supervise. **3.** To regulate or administer a use or expenditure.

managed care. (1982) A system of comprehensive healthcare provided by a health-maintenance organization, a preferred-provider organization, or a similar group.

managed-care organization. (1989) An association of professional healthcare providers that offers healthcare-service plans to subscribers. — Abbr. MCO. Cf. HEALTH-MAINTENANCE ORGANIZATION; PREFERRED-PROVIDER ORGANIZATION.

management. (16c) **1.** The people in an organization who are vested with a certain amount of discretion and independent judgment in managing its affairs.

▸ **c-level management.** (2001) Collectively, the officers of an organization holding titles prefixed by "chief"; the upper tier of top management <she was promoted from senior vice president to the c-level>. — Also termed *c-board.*

▸ **middle management.** (1941) Company employees who exercise some discretion and independent judgment in carrying out top management's directives.

▸ **top management.** (1937) A high level of company management at which major policy decisions and long-term business plans are made. — Also termed *upper management.*

2. The act or system of controlling and making decisions for a business, department, etc.

▸ **line management.** A system of management in which information and instructions are passed from one person to someone immediately higher or lower in rank and to no one else.

management buyout. See BUYOUT.

management company. See COMPANY.

Management Directorate. The division of the Department of Homeland Security responsible for handling the Department's financial and personnel affairs.

management fee. See FEE (1).

management prerogative. See *managerial prerogative* under PREROGATIVE.

manager. (16c) **1.** Someone who administers or supervises the affairs of a business, office, or other organization.

▸ **general manager.** (18c) A manager who has overall control of a business, office, or other organization, including authority over other managers. • A general manager is usu. equivalent to a president or chief executive officer of a corporation.

▸ **line manager. 1.** A corporate manager who is responsible for the main activities of production, sales, etc. **2.** Someone who is one level higher in rank than another and is in charge of that person's work.

2. A legislator appointed to a conference committee charged with adjusting differences in a bill passed by both houses in different versions. — Also termed *conferee*; *manager of a conference.* **3.** *Parliamentary law.* A member who displays the evidence against another member who is charged with misconduct and faces possible disciplinary action. **4.** A representative appointed by the House of Representatives to prosecute an impeachment before the Senate. **5.** A member of a board of managers; DIRECTOR (2). See BOARD OF DIRECTORS. **6.** A court-of-equity appointee responsible for carrying on a business for the benefit of creditors or other beneficiaries.

managerial prerogative. See PREROGATIVE.

manager of a conference. See MANAGER (2).

manager's privilege. See PRIVILEGE (3).

managing agent. See AGENT.

managing conservator. See CONSERVATOR.

managing conservatorship. See CUSTODY (2).

managing director. See DIRECTOR.

managium (mə-**nay**-jee-əm), *n.* [Law Latin, fr. Law French *manage* "a dwelling"] *Hist.* A dwelling; a mansion house. — Also termed *mensa* (**men**-sə).

***Manahan*-type carried interest.** (1985) *Oil & gas.* A transaction in which the owner of a lease assigns all the working interest to someone else — who takes on specified costs of drilling and development — and the assignor retains a reversionary interest in part of the working interest, which reverts to the assignor once the assignee has recovered the specified costs during the payout period. *Manahan Oil Co. v. Commissioner*, 8 T.C. 1159 (1947).

manbote. See BOTE (3).

manceps (**man**-seps), *n.* [Latin "an agent"] **1.** *Roman law.* A purchaser of something at a state auction, esp. a right or advantage, as in the right to farm taxes. See CONDUCTOR (2).

> "Manceps. One who at a public auction, conducted by a magistrate, through the highest bid obtained the right to collect taxes (a tax farmer) or custom duties, the lease of public land (*ager publicus*) or other advantages (a monopoly). — In postal organization *manceps* was a post-station master." Adolf Berger, *Encyclopedic Dictionary of Roman Law* 573 (1953).

2. Someone who undertakes to perform a task and gives security for the performance. **3.** *Roman law.* A state postmaster.

manche-present (mah*n*sh-pray-**zon**). [Law French "a present from the donor's own hand"] A bribe.

mancipable (**man**-si-pə-bəl), *adj.* (1875) Capable of mancipation.

mancipant (**man**-si-pənt), *n.* (1880) Someone who transfers property by mancipation.

mancipare (man-sə-**pair**-ee), *vb.* [fr. Latin *manus* "hand" + *capere* "to take"] *Roman law.* **1.** To alienate (a thing) through mancipation. **2.** To sell (esp. a person) fictitiously as part of the emancipation process. See MANCIPATION.

mancipatio (man-sə-**pay**-shee-oh), *n.* [Latin] See MANCIPATION.

mancipation (man-si-**pay**-shən), *n.* [fr. Latin *mancipatio* "hand-grasp"] (16c) **1.** *Roman law.* A legal formality for transferring property by either an actual or a simulated purchase; a formal conveyance in the guise of a sale. • The formality required the presence of the thing being conveyed (*res mancipi*), and of five adult male citizens acting as witnesses. Another person (the *libripens*) held the bronze scales with which the purchase price had been weighed out. The buyer made an assertion of ownership, struck the scales with a piece of bronze or copper, then gave the metal piece to the seller as a symbolic price. In Roman classical law, either this procedure or *cessio in jure* was necessary to pass legal title. This form of sale was abolished by Justinian. **2.** A similar form used for making a will, adoption, emancipation of children, etc. — Also termed *mancipatio.* See RES MANCIPI. Cf. EMANCIPATION. — **mancipate,** *vb.* — **mancipatory (man-si-pə-tor-ee),** *adj.*

> "Mancipatio is the solemn sale per aes et libram. In the presence of five witnesses (cives Romani puberes) a skilled weighmaster (libripens) weighs out to the vendor a certain amount of uncoined copper (aes, raudus, rauduscuIum) which is the purchase-money, and the purchaser, with solemn words, takes possession with his hand — hence the description of the act as 'hand-grasp' — of the thing purchased as being his property." Rudolph Sohm, *The Institutes: A Textbook of the History and System of Roman Private Law* 48 (James Crawford Ledlie trans., 3d ed. 1907).

mancipatory will. See WILL.

mancipi res (**man**-sə-pɪ **reez**). See RES MANCIPI.

mancipium (man-**sip**-ee-əm), *n.* [Latin "a slave"] *Roman law.* **1.** A slave, esp. by virtue of being captured by an enemy in war. **2.** A temporary quasi-servile status, necessarily occurring in an emancipation, and also when a master or father noxally surrendered a slave or son to an injured party to answer for an offense committed by the slave or son against that party. See EMANCIPATION; NOXAL ACTION (1).

> "But if the *patria potestas* could be created, it could also be terminated, by an artificial process . . . . The father could not by a simple act of his own will release the son from his control. For this purpose he must sell him out of his own hands into that state of *mancipium* or qualified slavery of which we have spoken. Even then the father's power was not destroyed: it was suspended during the existence of the *mancipium;* but if the *mancipium* ceased, if the son was set free by the person who held him in that condition, the father's right revived . . . . It was not until he had sold him three times over, that he used up his right of control beyond the possibility of a revival. This, then, was the form by which the son was liberated from the *patria potestas.*" James Hadley, *Introduction to Roman Law* 126–27 (1881).

3. MANCIPATION (1).

M & A. *abbr.* Mergers and acquisitions. See MERGER.

mandamus (man-**day**-məs), *n.* [Latin "we command"] (16c) A writ issued by a court to compel performance of a particular act by a lower court or a governmental officer or body, usu. to correct a prior action or failure to act. — Also termed *writ of mandamus; mandate;* (BrE) *order.* Pl. **mandamuses.** — **mandamus,** *vb.*

> "The modern writ of mandamus may be defined as a command issuing from a common-law court of competent jurisdiction, in the name of the state or sovereign, directed to some corporation, officer, or inferior court, requiring the performance of a particular duty therein specified, which duty results from the official station of the party to whom the writ is directed, or from operation of law. In the specific relief which it affords, a mandamus operates much in the nature of a bill in chancery for specific performance, the principal difference being that the latter remedy is resorted to for the redress of purely private wrongs, or the enforcement of contract rights, while the former generally has for its object the performance of obligations arising out of official station, or specially imposed by law upon the respondent. The object of a mandamus is to prevent disorder from a failure of justice and a defect of police, and it should be granted in all cases where the law has established no specific remedy and where in justice there should be one. And the value of the matter in issue, or the degree of its importance to the public, should not be too scrupulously weighed.
>
> . . .
>
> "The writ of mandamus is of very ancient origin, so ancient indeed that its early history is involved in obscurity, and has been the cause of much curious research and of many conflicting opinions. It seems, originally, to have been one of that large class of writs or mandates, by which the sovereign of England directed the performance of any desired act by his subjects, the word '*mandamus*' in such writs or letters missive having doubtless given rise to the present name of the writ. These letters missive or mandates, to which the generic name mandamus was applied, were in no sense judicial writs, being merely commands issuing directly from the sovereign to the subject, without the intervention of the courts, and they have now become entirely obsolete. The term mandamus, derived from these letters missive, seems gradually to have been confined in its application to the judicial writ issued by the kings bench, which has by a steady growth developed into the present writ of mandamus." James L. High, *A Treatise on Extraordinary Legal Remedies* § 2, at 5–6 (1884).

▸ **alternative mandamus.** (1809) A writ issued upon the first application for relief, commanding the defendant either to perform the act demanded or to appear before the court at a specified time to show cause for not performing it.

▸ **peremptory mandamus.** (17c) An absolute and unqualified command to the defendant to do the act in question. • It is issued when the defendant defaults on, or fails to show sufficient cause in answer to, an alternative mandamus.

mandans (**man**-danz), *n.* [Latin] *Roman law.* The principal for whom a mandated person undertakes to perform a gratuitous service. See MANDATOR (2).

mandant (**man**-dənt), *n.* [French] (17c) *French & Scots law.* The principal in a contract of mandate, such as a bailor in a bailment. See MANDATOR.

mandatary (**man**-də-ter-ee), *n.* (15c) **1.** A person to whom a mandate is given. See MANDATE (4). **2.** An agent, esp. one who acts gratuitously but is entitled to be indemnified for expenses incurred in carrying out the mandate. — Also termed (in Roman law) *mandatarius.* **3.** *Civil law.* The person who is employed to a mandator in a gratuitous agency. — Also termed *mandatee; mandatarius.* See MANDATE (4). — **mandatary,** *adj.*

mandate, *n.* (16c) **1.** An order from an appellate court directing a lower court to take a specified action. — Also termed (BrE) *order.* See MANDAMUS. **2.** A judicial command directed to an officer of the court to enforce a court order. **3.** In politics, the electorate's overwhelming show of approval for a given political candidate or platform. **4.** *Roman & civil law.* A written command given by a principal to an agent; specif., a commission or contract by which one person (the *mandator*) requests someone (the *mandatary*) to perform some service gratuitously, the commission becoming effective when the mandatary agrees. La. Civ. Code art. 2989. • In this type of contract, no liability is created until the service requested has begun. The mandatary is bound to use reasonable care in performance, while the mandator is bound to indemnify against loss incurred in performing the service. — Also termed *mandatum.* **5.** *Louisiana law.* A contract by which one person, the principal, confers authority on another person, the mandatary, to transact one or more affairs for the principal. La. Civ. Code arts. 2989 et seq. • The contract of mandate may be either onerous or gratuitous. It is gratuitous if the parties do not state otherwise. **6.** *Hist. Int'l law.* An authority given by the League of Nations to certain governments to take over the administration and development of designated territories. Cf. TRUSTEESHIP (2). — **mandate,** *vb.*

mandated reporter. (1977) A person who is statutorily required to inform authorities about known or suspected unlawful conduct, such as child or elder abuse or neglect.

mandatee. See MANDATARY.

mandate rule. (1958) The doctrine that, after an appellate court has remanded a case to a lower court, the lower court must follow the decision that the appellate court has made in the case, unless new evidence or an intervening change in the law dictates a different result.

mandator (man-**day**-tər *or* **man**-day-tər). (17c) **1.** Someone who delegates the performance of a mandate to another. **2.** *Civil law.* The person who employs another (called a *mandatary* or *mandatarius*) in a gratuitous agency. See MANDATE (4). — Also termed *mandant.* **3.** BAILOR (1).

mandatory, *adj.* (15c) Of, relating to, or constituting a command; required; preemptory.

> "A provision in a statute is said to be mandatory when disobedience to it, or want of exact compliance with it, will make the act done under the statute absolutely void." Henry Campbell Black, *Handbook on the Construction and Interpretation of the Laws* 334 (1896).

mandatory abstention. See ABSTENTION.

mandatory arbitration. See ARBITRATION.

mandatory class action. See CLASS ACTION.

mandatory commitment. See COMMITMENT.

mandatory direction. See *mandatory instruction* under JURY INSTRUCTION.

mandatory injunction. See INJUNCTION.

mandatory instruction. See JURY INSTRUCTION.

mandatory joinder. See *compulsory joinder* under JOINDER.

mandatory penalty. See *mandatory sentence* under SENTENCE.

mandatory/permissive canon. The doctrine that mandatory words (such as *must* and *shall*) in a legal instrument impose a duty and that permissive words (such as *may*) grant discretion.

mandatory power. See POWER (5).

mandatory presumption. See *conclusive presumption* under PRESUMPTION.

mandatory punishment. See *mandatory sentence* under SENTENCE.

mandatory reporting. (1966) The statutory duty of certain people to inform an authority about certain activities that are or may be unlawful, such as financial, sexual, or other types of abuse.

mandatory rule. See RULE (1).

mandatory sentence. See SENTENCE.

mandatory sentencing. See SENTENCING.

mandatory statute. See STATUTE.

mandatory subject of bargaining. (1955) *Labor law.* A topic that is required by the National Labor Relations Act to be discussed in good faith by the parties during labor negotiations; an essential employment matter, including wages, hours, and other terms and conditions of employment, about which management and the union are required to negotiate in good faith, and that can lawfully form the basis of a collective-bargaining impasse. 29 USCA § 158(d). — Often shortened to *mandatory subject.* Cf. PERMISSIVE SUBJECT OF BARGAINING.

mandatory trust. See TRUST (3).

mandatory waiver. The mandatory transfer, without judicial discretion, of a case from juvenile court to criminal court once the prosecutor has charged a juvenile with one of certain statutorily enumerated serious crimes. See TRANSFER STATUTE. Cf. STATUTORY EXCLUSION.

mandatum (man-**day**-təm). (16c) *Roman & civil law.* A bailment in which the bailee will, without recompense, perform some service relating to the goods; MANDATE (4). • This type of bailment is for the sole benefit of the bailor.

mandavi ballivo (man-**day**-vɪ bə-**lɪ**-voh). [Law Latin "I have commanded the bailiff"] *Hist.* A sheriff's return stating that the sheriff ordered a bailiff to execute a writ.

man-endangering state of mind. See PERSON-ENDANGERING STATE OF MIND.

manerium (mə-**neer**-ee-əm), *n.* [Law Latin, fr. Latin *manere* "to remain"] *Hist.* A manor.

> "The term *manerium* seems to have come in with the Conqueror, though other derivatives from the Latin verb *manere*, in particular *mansa, mansio, mansiuncula* had been freely employed by the scribes of the land-books. But these had as a rule been used as representatives of the English *hide*, and just for this reason they were incapable of expressing the notion that the Normans desired to express by the word *manerium*. In its origin that word is but one more name for a house. Throughout the Exeter Domesday the word *mansio* is used instead of the *manerium* of the Exchequer record, and even in the Exchequer record we may find these two terms used interchangeably . . . ." Frederic W. Maitland, *Domesday Book and Beyond* 108–09 (1921).

mangonare (mang-gə-**nair**-ee), *vb.* [Late Latin] To buy in a market; to deal.

manhood. (13c) **1.** A male person's majority. **2.** *Hist.* A ceremony of a vassal paying homage to the vassal's lord. — Also termed *homagium.*

> "Besides an oath of *fealty*, or profession of faith to the lord, which was the parent of our oath of allegiance, the vassal or tenant upon investiture did usually *homage* to his lord; openly and humbly kneeling, being ungirt, uncovered, and holding up his hands both together between those of the lord, who sate before him; and there professing that 'he did become his *man*, from that day forth, of life and limb and earthly honour:' and then he received a kiss from his lord. Which ceremony was denominated *homagium*, or *manhood*, by the feudists." 2 William Blackstone, *Commentaries on the Laws of England* 53 (1766).

mania a potu. See DELIRIUM TREMENS.

mania transitoria. (1871) *Hist.* Insanity of brief duration, experienced while committing a criminal act. • In a memorandum opinion, the Supreme Court used the term to mean *emotional insanity.* See *Mutual Life Ins. Co. v. Terry*, 82 U.S. 580, 583–84 (1872). But other courts have applied the literal meaning (temporary insanity). *See, e.g., Rush v. Megee*, 36 Ind. 69 (1871). Cf. *emotional insanity* and *temporary insanity* under INSANITY.

manifest, *adj.* Clear; obvious; unquestionable.

manifest, *n.* (16c) A document listing the cargo or passengers carried on a ship, airplane, or other vehicle; esp., a shipping or warehousing document containing a list of the contents, value, origin, carrier, and destination of the goods. Cf. CONTENT.

manifestation, *n.* (15c) **1.** A clear sign or indication that a particular situation or feeling exists; that which exhibits, displays, or reveals. **2.** The act of appearing or becoming clear. **3.** A public demonstration or display of power or purpose, as by a despot or dictatorship.

manifestation of intention. (1826) *Wills & estates.* The external expression of the testator's intention, as distinguished from an undisclosed intention. — Also termed *manifestation of intent.*

manifestation theory. (1977) *Insurance.* The doctrine that coverage for an injury or disease falls to the policy in effect when the symptoms of the covered injury or disease first appear. Cf. EXPOSURE THEORY; ACTUAL-INJURY TRIGGER; TRIPLE TRIGGER.

> "Some injuries do not manifest themselves until a period of time has elapsed between the occurrence of the event that produces the harm and the time when it becomes apparent. Particularly when these claims result from what often were not recognized as dangerous products or chemicals when the exposure occurred, such as asbestos or dioxin, the consequences are referred to as 'delayed manifestation' injuries . . . . [Under the] '[m]anifestation' theory . . . [some] courts have concluded that coverage is provided by the insurance policy in place at the time the injury becomes apparent, that is, when the injury is manifested." Robert E. Keeton & Alan I. Widiss, *Insurance Law: A Guide to Fundamental Principles, Legal Doctrines, and Commercial Practices* § 5.10(d)(3), at 598 (1988).

manifest constitutional error. See ERROR (2).

manifest-disregard doctrine. (1983) The principle that an arbitration award will be vacated if the arbitrator knows the applicable law and deliberately chooses to disregard it, but will not be vacated for a mere error or misunderstanding of the law.

manifest disregard of the law. (1855) A decision-maker's, esp. an arbitrator's, plainly apparent decision to ignore a governing legal standard, as a result of which the decision may be subject to being vacated or reversed. • A mere error in applying the law or a misunderstanding of the law is not enough to constitute a manifest disregard of the law.

manifest error. See ERROR (2).

manifest-error-or-clearly-wrong rule. (1981) In some jurisdictions, the doctrine that an appellate court cannot set aside a trial court's finding of fact unless a review of the entire record reveals that the finding has no reasonable basis.

manifest injustice. A direct, obvious, and observable error in a trial court, such as a defendant's guilty plea that is involuntary or is based on a plea agreement that the prosecution has rescinded.

manifest intent. See INTENT (1).

manifest law. See LEX MANIFESTA.

manifestly excessive sentence. See SENTENCE.

manifest necessity. See NECESSITY (5).

manifest-necessity rule. (1953) *Criminal law.* The doctrine that double jeopardy bars retrial of a defendant after a mistrial unless the trial court finds that there was a manifest necessity to grant the mistrial over an objection by the defense.

manifesto. (17c) A written statement publicly declaring the issuer's principles, policies, or intentions; esp., a formal document explaining why a state or country declared war or took some other significant international action.

manifest thief. See FUR MANIFESTUS.

manifest weight of the evidence. See WEIGHT OF THE EVIDENCE.

manipulation. *Securities.* (1888) The illegal practice of raising or lowering a security's price by creating the appearance of active trading. • Manipulation is prohibited by section 10(b) of the Securities Exchange Act of 1934. 15 USCA § 78j(b). — Also termed *market manipulation; stock manipulation.*

mankind. See MAN (2).

Mann Act. A 1910 federal law making it illegal to transport an individual in interstate or foreign commerce for prostitution or other criminal sexual activity. • It is named for its sponsor, Rep. James Robert Mann (1856–1922). 18 USCA §§ 2421–2424. — Also termed *White Slave Traffic Act.*

manner and form. See MODO ET FORMA.

manner of death. (16c) The circumstances under which the cause of death arose.

manner of service. (18c) The way or means by which service of process was made.

mannire (mə-**nI**-ree), *vb.* [Law Latin] *Hist.* To summon (an adverse party) to court; to prosecute (a case).

mannopus (man-**oh**-pəs). [fr. Latin *manus* "hand" + *opus* "work"] *Hist.* **1.** Manual labor. **2.** A day's work. **3.** Goods taken from the hands of an apprehended thief; MAINOUR.

manor. (14c) **1.** A feudal estate, usu. granted by the king to a lord or other high person and cultivated as a unit. • In more ancient times, the lord's manor included a village community, usu. composed of serfs.

> "[T]o ask for a definition of a manor is to ask for what can not be given. We may however draw a picture of a typical manor, and, this done, we may discuss the deviations from this type . . . . [W]e may regard the typical manor (1) as being, *qua* vill, a unit of public law, of police and fiscal law, (2) as being a unit in the system of agriculture, (3) as being a unit in the management of property, (4) as being a jurisdictional unit. But we . . . see that hardly one of these traits can be considered as absolutely essential. The most important is the connection between the manor and the vill . . . ." 1 Frederick Pollock & Frederic W. Maitland, *The History of English Law Before the Time of Edward I* 596–97 (2d ed. 1898).

> "The term [*manor*] applied, after the Norman conquest, to estates organized under knights, ecclesiastical corporations, or otherwise, and managed and cultivated as units. By the end of the 11th century, the main element was the feudal lord, and soon he came to be regarded as the owner of the manor, and to have authority over the tenants, and the right to hold a court for them . . . . In the thirteenth and fourteenth centuries, a manor also implied a right of jurisdiction exercised through a court baron, attended by both freeholders and villein tenants . . . . In the eighteenth century the manorial court decayed rapidly, cases being generally brought in the King's courts, the only surviving business being copyhold conveyancing." David M. Walker, *The Oxford Companion to Law* 803 (1980).

▸ **reputed manor.** (17c) A manor in which the lands not granted in tenancy but reserved for the lord's own use (demesne lands) and services become absolutely separated. • The manor is no longer a manor in actuality, only in reputation. — Also termed *seigniory in gross.*

2. A jurisdictional right over tenants of an estate, usu. exercised through a court baron. 3. *Hist.* In the United States, a tract of land occupied by tenants who pay rent to a proprietor. 4. A mansion on an estate.

manorial extent. (1834) *Hist.* A survey of a manor by a jury of tenants, giving the numbers and names of tenants, the size of their holdings, the kind of tenure, and the kind and amount of the tenants' services.

manorial system. (1867) The medieval system of land ownership in which serfs and some freemen cultivated the soil of a manor in return for a lord's protection. See MANOR (1).

manprice. See WERGILD.

manse (mans), *n.* [Law Latin] (15c) *Hist.* **1.** A portion of land large enough to maintain one family.; a sufficient amount of land to be worked by a yoke of oxen for a year. **2.** A house without land; MESSUAGE. **3.** The residence of a minister, esp. a Presbyterian minister. **4.** A large, imposing residence. — Also termed *mansus.*

manser (**man**-sər), *n.* [Law Latin] *Hist.* A bastard.

Mansfield rule. (1968) The doctrine that a juror's testimony or affidavit about juror misconduct may not be used to challenge the verdict. • This Mansfield rule is intended to ensure that jurors are heard through their verdict, not through their postverdict testimony. In practice, the rule lessens the possibility that losing parties will seek to penetrate the secrets of the jury room. The rule was first announced in *Vaise v. Delaval*, 99 Eng. Rep. 944 (K.B. 1785), in an opinion by William Murray, first Earl of Mansfield, the Lord Chief Justice of the Court of King's Bench.

mansio (**man**-shee-oh), *n.* [Law Latin] *Hist.* **1.** An inn. **2.** A house.

mansion-house. (16c) **1.** *Hist.* The residence of the lord of a manor. **2.** DWELLING-HOUSE.

mansion-house rule. (1985) The doctrine that a tract of land lying in two counties will be assessed, for property-tax purposes, in the county in which the house is located.

manslaughter, *n.* (15c) The unlawful killing of a human being without malice aforethought. — Also termed (in some jurisdictions) *culpable homicide.* Cf. MURDER. — **manslaughter,** *vb.*

> "[M]anslaughter is very difficult to define precisely, because it includes so many different types of culpability. The main line of division is between voluntary and involuntary manslaughter, the first occurring where there is an intention to do some illegal harm to a person, the second where there is no such intention. . . . Manslaughter . . . may not be the result of intent at all. It may be the consequence of negligence. This, indeed, is one of the principal causes of involuntary manslaughter, and it has long been clear that a different degree of negligence, sometimes termed 'gross,' 'criminal,' or 'complete,' is a necessary prerequisite of criminal liability, but these epithets have not added much from the standpoint of legal clarity." G.W. Keeton, *The Elementary Principles of Jurisprudence* 315–16 (2d ed. 1949).

▸ **first-degree manslaughter.** See *voluntary manslaughter.*

▸ **intentional manslaughter.** See *voluntary manslaughter.*

▸ **intoxication manslaughter.** (1993) An unintentional homicide committed by an intoxicated person while operating a vehicle or some other type of machinery.

▸ **involuntary manslaughter.** (18c) Homicide in which there is no intention to kill or do grievous bodily harm, but that is committed with criminal negligence or during the commission of a crime not included within the felony-murder rule. — Also termed *negligent manslaughter; second-degree manslaughter; manslaughter in the second degree.* Cf. ACCIDENTAL KILLING.

> "Involuntary manslaughter is a 'catch-all' concept. It includes all manslaughter not characterized as voluntary." Rollin M. Perkins & Ronald N. Boyce, *Criminal Law* 104 (3d ed. 1982).

> "The only differences between the legal use and the everyday use of 'voluntary,' 'not voluntary,' and 'involuntary' seem to be (a) a more frequent use of 'involuntary' as a synonym of 'not voluntary' and (b) a technical use of 'involuntary' in the crime of 'involuntary manslaughter,' where it seems to have the meaning of 'unintentional.' Thus, as contrasted with 'voluntary manslaughter,' there is no suggestion that death, as contrasted with harm, was intended or foreseen. Though it is often confined to cases of assault and battery where death results, for example either from the withholding of food or from excessive chastisement of a child, some jurists say that it can be due to any unlawful and dangerous action causing death." Alan R. White, *Grounds of Liability* 61–62 (1985).

▸ **manslaughter in the first degree.** See *voluntary manslaughter.*

▸ **manslaughter in the second degree.** See *involuntary manslaughter.*

▸ **manslaughter with a motor vehicle.** (1935) Criminal negligence in which the driver knew of the danger of collision and recklessly or wantonly collided with a person who died as a result, the driver's not having used reasonable means that were within his or her control to prevent the accident. — Also termed *manslaughter with an automobile.*

▸ **misdemeanor manslaughter.** (1947) Unintentional homicide that occurs during the commission of a misdemeanor (such as a traffic violation).

▸ **negligent manslaughter.** See *involuntary manslaughter.*

▸ **second-degree manslaughter.** See *involuntary manslaughter.*

▸ **voluntary manslaughter.** (18c) An act of murder reduced to manslaughter because of extenuating circumstances such as adequate provocation (arousing the "heat of passion") or diminished capacity. — Also termed *intentional manslaughter; first-degree manslaughter; manslaughter in the first degree; unintentional murder.*

manstealing. See KIDNAPPING.

mansuetae naturae (man-**swee**-tee nə-**tyoor**-ee), *adj.* [Latin "of a tamable nature"] (1855) *Civil law.* (Of animals) tame or tamable.

mansuetae naturae (man-**swee**-tee nə-**tyoor**-ee), *n.* (1896) *Civil law.* Tame, domesticated animals. See *domestic animal* under ANIMAL. Cf. FERAE NATURAE.

mansuetus (man-**swee**-təs), *adj.* [Latin] *Roman law.* Tame; tamed.

mansus. See MANSE.

manticulate (man-**tik**-yə-layt), *vb.* To pick pockets. — **manticulation,** *n.*

mantle child. See CHILD.

mantrap. See TRAP (1).

manual, *adj.* (15c) Used or performed by hand <manual labor>.

manual body-cavity search. See SEARCH (1).

manual delivery. (1816) Delivery of personal property by actual and corporeal change in possession.

Manual for Courts-Martial. A manual that implements the Uniform Code of Military Justice. • It was adopted in 1969 by presidential executive order. — Abbr. MCM.

manual gift. See GIFT.

manu aliena (**man**-yoo ay-lee-**ee**-nə *or* al-ee-). [Latin] *Scots law.* By the hand of another. • The phrase was contained in a notary's docket and was attached to the end of an instrument of seisin, as a means for the notary to indicate that the instrument was written by another person. See DOCKET (5).

manualis obedientia (man-yoo-**ay**-lis ə-bee-dee-**en**-shee-ə). [Latin "obedience by (taking or kissing) hand"] Sworn obedience on an oath.

manual labor. (15c) Work performed chiefly through muscular exertion, with or without tools or machinery.

Manual of Classification. *Patents.* The U.S. Patent and Trademark Office's official looseleaf publication describing the patent classification system and giving brief explanations of each class and subclass within the system. — Abbr. MOC.

Manual of Patent Examining Procedure. The book of substantive law (judicial and administrative-law precedents) and procedural rules for patent examiners at the U.S. Patent and Trademark Office. • The MPEP is the primary resource that patent examiners use to process patent applications. — Abbr. MPEP.

Manual of the Judge Advocate General. The Secretary of the Navy's directive on military justice, with minor variations between rules applicable to the Navy and those applicable to the Marine Corps. — Also termed *JAG Manual.*

manual-rating insurance. See INSURANCE.

manu brevi (**man**-yoo **bree**-vɪ). See BREVI MANU.

manucaptio (man-yə-**kap**-shee-oh), *n.* [Law Latin] *Hist.* **1.** Surety; security; bail. **2.** A writ allowing a person to be admitted to bail, when the person had been arrested for a felony but could not be admitted to bail by the sheriff. See MAINPRISE.

manucaption (man-yoo-**kap**-shən), *n.* (16c) *Hist.* **1.** MAINPRISE. **2.** A writ ordering someone to produce an alleged felon in court.

manucaptor. See MAINPERNOR (2).

manufacture, *n.* (16c) *Patents.* A thing that is made or built by a human being (or by a machine), as distinguished from something that is a product of nature; esp., any material form produced by a machine from an unshaped composition of matter. • Manufactures are one of the statutory categories of inventions that can be patented. Examples of manufactures are chairs and tires. 35 USCA § 101. — Also termed *article of manufacture; fabrication.* Cf. MACHINE; PROCESS (3).

▸ ***defective manufacture.*** See *defective product* under PRODUCT.

manufactured diversity. See DIVERSITY OF CITIZENSHIP.

manufactured home. See HOME.

manufacturer. (17c) A person or entity engaged in producing or assembling new products. • A federal law has broadened the definition to include those who act for (or are controlled by) any such person or entity in the distribution of new products, as well as those who import new products for resale. 42 USCA § 4902(6).

manufacturer's liability. See PRODUCTS LIABILITY.

manufacturer's lien. See LIEN.

manufacturer-suggested retail price. See *suggested retail price* under PRICE.

manufacturer's warranty. See WARRANTY (1).

manufacturing clause. (1976) *Hist.* **1.** A component of the Copyright Act of 1976 prohibiting imports of more than 2,000 copies of a nondramatic English-language literary work by an American author, unless the material was manufactured in Canada or the U.S. • The manufacturing clause expired in 1986. **2.** A component of the Copyright Act of 1909 limiting copyright protection for English-language books and periodicals to those printed in the U.S.

manufacturing cost. See COST (1).

manufacturing defect. See DEFECT.

manu forti (**man**-yoo **for**-tɪ). [Latin] With strong hand. • This term was used in old writs of trespass to allege forcible entry, as in *manu forti et cum multitudine gentium* ("with strong hand and multitude of people").

manu longa (**man**-yoo **long**-gə). See LONGA MANU.

manu militari (**man**-yoo mil-ə-**tair**-ɪ). [Latin] *Hist.* By military force.

manumission (man-yə-**mish**-ən), *n.* [Latin *manumissio* "I send out of hand"] (15c) *Roman law.* The granting of freedom to a slave. • In the Republic and early Empire, there were three usual methods, all of which made the freed slave a citizen. These were (1) *manumission vindicta* (by the rod), a fictitious lawsuit in which a liberator touched the slave with a wand or rod in the presence of the praetor and alleged that he was free; (2) *manumission censu*, by which the slave's name was enrolled in the census as a citizen; and (3) *manumission testamento*, by will. Under Justinian, a grant of freedom in any form (except in fraud of creditors) made the slave free and a citizen. — Also termed *manumissio.*

> "Manumission is a kind of new birth. The master (patronus) therefore stands to his freedman in a relation analogous to the relation between father and son. The patron, as such, is entitled, as against his libertus, to a father's rights of succession and guardianship. He has the right of moderate chastisement (levis coercitio). He has the same claim to be treated with respect as he has against his son. He can claim to be supported by the libertus, if he falls into poverty. He is, lastly, entitled to certain services on the part of the freedman, which he can, if necessary, enforce by action, provided only the freedman had promised them after his manumission and in a manner not derogatory to his liberty." Rudolph Sohm, *The Institutes: A Textbook of the History and System of Roman Private Law* 170 (James Crawford Ledlie trans., 3d ed. 1907).

▸ **manumission *censu.*** (1946) The freeing of a slave by having the censor enter the slave's name on the census roll, the slave professing to be a freeman in the presence of the master. • Once the censor entered the slave's name on the census roll, the slave became a freeman and a citizen — by a simple stroke of the pen. — Also termed *manumissio censu; manumission by census.*

▸ **manumission *sacrorum causa.*** (1889) The freeing of a slave by the master's solemnly declaring that the slave was to be free while holding a limb of the slave and promising to pay a sum of money if the freedman later departs from the *sacra* (family rites). • The master then turned around and released the slave, who became free but was bound to perform the family rites. — Also termed *manumissio sacrorum causa.*

▸ **manumission *testamento.*** (1906) The freeing of a slave by will in either of two ways: (1) the master's granting the slave freedom outright in the will, or (2) the master's imposing on an heir the obligation of freeing the slave, in which case the slave became the freedman of the heir. — Also termed *manumissio testamento; manumission by will.*

▸ **manumission *vindicta.*** (1909) The ceremonial freeing of a slave whereby a third party, in the presence of the praetor, placed a rod (*vindicta*) on the slave while claiming that the slave was a freedman, whereupon the master admitted the slave's freedom and the praetor then declared the slave to be free. • This ceremony was actually a fictitious action at law. — Also termed *manumissio vindicta.*

manumit (man-yə-**mit**), *vb.* (15c) To free (a slave). — **manumitter,** *n.*

manung (**man**-əng). *Hist.* An official's jurisdictional district. — Also spelled *monung.*

manuopus (man-yoo-**oh**-pəs). See MAINOUR.

manupes (**man**-yə-peez), *n.* [Law Latin] *Hist.* A full 12-inch foot as a legal measure.

manupretium (man-yə-**pree**-shee-əm), *n.* [Latin] *Roman law.* Wages for performed labor or services.

manu propria (**man**-yoo **proh**-pree-ə). [Latin] *Hist.* By one's own hand.

manurable (mə-**n[y]oor**-ə-bəl), *adj.* [Law French fr. Old French *main* "hand"] (17c) *Hist.* (Of a thing) capable of being held in hand; capable of being touched.

manure (mə-**nyoor**), *vb.* [Law French fr. Old French *main* "hand"] *Hist.* To use (something) manually; to perform manual labor on (something).

manus (**may**-nəs), *n.* [Latin "hand"] (1854) **1.** *Roman law.* The power exercised by the head of a family over all its members and slaves; esp., a husband's power over his wife; marital subordination, which accompanied most marriages in early Rome. **2.** *Hist.* A compurgator, or the oath taken. • This usage of *manus* may stem from the affiant's placing a hand on the Bible while taking the oath. See COMPURGATOR.

manuscript. (16c) An unpublished writing; an author's typescript or written work product that is proposed for publication.

manuscript policy. See INSURANCE POLICY.

manus mortua (**may**-nəs **mor**-choo-ə). [Latin "dead hand"] See MORTMAIN.

manutenentia (man-yə-tə-**nen**-shee-ə), *n.* [Law Latin] *Hist.* The old writ of maintenance. See MAINTENANCE.

manworth. *Hist.* The value of a person's life.

MAP. *abbr.* MUTUAL-AGREEMENT PROGRAM.

***Mapp* hearing.** (1971) *Criminal procedure.* A hearing held to determine whether evidence implicating the accused was obtained as the result of an illegal search and seizure, and should therefore be suppressed. *Mapp v. Ohio,* 367 U.S. 643, 81 S.Ct. 1684 (1961).

maprince. See WERGILD.

maquiladora (mah-kee-lə-**dor**-ə), *n.* [fr. Spanish *maquilar* "gristmill"] (1976) A Mexican corporation, esp. one that holds a permit to operate under a special customs regime that temporarily allows the corporation to import duty-free into Mexico various raw materials, equipment, machinery, replacement parts, and other items needed for the assembly or manufacture of finished goods for export. — Often shortened to *maquila.*

mara (**mair**-ə), *n.* [Law Latin] *Hist.* A lake; a pool; a body of water that cannot be drained.

MARAD. *abbr.* MARITIME ADMINISTRATION.

maraud (mə-**rawd**), *vb.* (18c) To rove about to pillage or plunder; to loot. — **marauder,** *n.*

marcatus (mahr-**kay**-təs), *n.* [Law Latin] *Hist.* The yearly rent of a tract of land.

march. (13c) *Hist.* A boundary between countries or territories, esp. the border between England and Wales or between England and Scotland.

Marchers. (15c) *Hist. English law.* Lords who lived on the borders of Scotland and Wales, and operated, with the permission of the English sovereigns, under their own private laws. • Their laws were eventually abolished by the Acts of Union in the mid-16th century. — Also termed *Lords Marchers; Marcher Lords.*

> "Thus the Lords Marchers were practically independent potentates of a kind very unusual in England. From this two consequences flowed. In the first place there grew up in their jurisdictions a mixture of Welsh custom and English law known as the custom of the Marches. In the second place, although they held of the king, their allegiance sat so lightly upon them that it was necessary to declare in 1354 that 'all the Lords of the Marches of Wales shall be perpetually attending and annexed to the crown of England, and not to the principality of Wales, in whose hands so ever the same principality be.'" 1 William Holdsworth, *A History of English Law* 121 (7th ed. 1956).

marchet (**mahr**-chet). *Hist.* A fee paid by a feudal tenant to the lord so that the tenant's daughter could marry someone outside the lord's jurisdiction or so that the lord would waive the *droit du seigneur.* — Also termed *marcheta; marchetum; merchet; mercheta; merchetum; maiden rent.* See DROIT DU SEIGNEUR.

> "Any service which stamps the tenant as an unfree man, stamps his tenure as unfree; and in common opinion such services there are, notably the *merchetum.* Now among the thousands of entries in English documents relating to this payment, it would we believe be utterly impossible to find one which gave any sanction to the tales of a *ius primae noctis.* The context in which this duty is usually mentioned explains at least one of the reasons which underlie it. The tenant may not give his daughter (in some cases his son or daughter) in marriage — at least not outside the manor . . . . No doubt a subjection to this restraint was regarded as very base, and sometimes it is described in vigourous words which express a free man's loathing for servility: — 'he must buy, he must make ransom for, his flesh and blood.'" 1 Frederick Pollock & Frederic W. Maitland, *The History of English Law Before the Time of Edward I* 372 (2d ed. 1898).

march-in rights. (1992) *Patents.* The government's right to step in and grant a new license or revoke an existing license if the owner of a federally funded invention (or the owner's licensee) has not adequately developed or applied the invention within a reasonable time. 35 USCA § 203.

marchioness (**mahr**-shə-nis *or* mahr-shə-**nes**), *n.* [fr. Law Latin *marchionissa*, the feminine counterpart to *marchio* "marquess"] (16c) A female dignity, equivalent to a marquis, conferred by creation or by marriage with a marquis. See MARQUIS.

Marcus model. (1992) *Labor law.* A method for determining whether a union member's state-law claim against the employer is preempted by federal law, by focusing on whether the state-law claim can be maintained independently of an interpretation of the collective-bargaining agreement. • In *Lingle v. Norge Div. of Magic Chef, Inc.*, 486 U.S. 399, 108 S.Ct. 1877 (1988), the Supreme Court held that a union member's state-law retaliatory-discharge claim was not preempted by the Labor-Management Relations Act because the claim could be resolved without interpreting the collective-bargaining agreement. There are at least two models for applying the *Lingle* test: the White model, which focuses on whether the claim is negotiable or nonnegotiable (that is, whether state law allows the claim to be waived by a private contract), and the Marcus model, which focuses on the independence of the claim in relation to the collective-bargaining agreement. Under the Marcus model, if the claim can be maintained separately from an interpretation of the collective-bargaining agreement, it is not preempted regardless of whether the claim is generally waivable in contract. The Marcus model is named for the author of the law-review note in which it was proposed. Stephanie R. Marcus, Note, *The Need for a New Approach to Federal Preemption of Union Members' State Law Claims*, 99 Yale L.J. 209 (1989). See LINGLE TEST. Cf. WHITE MODEL.

mare (**mair**-ee *or* **mahr**-ee), *n. Hist.* [Latin] The sea. See SEA.

▸ ***mare clausum*** (**mair**-ee *or* **mahr**-ee **klaw**-zəm). [Latin "closed sea"] (17c) A sea or other body of navigable water that is under the jurisdiction of a particular country and is closed to other countries.

▸ ***mare liberum*** (**mair**-ee *or* **mahr**-ee **lib**-ər-əm *or* **lɪ**-bər-əm). [Latin "free sea"] (17c) **1.** A sea or other body of navigable water that is open to all countries. **2.** FREEDOM OF THE SEAS.

marescallus (mar-ə-**skal**-əs), *n.* [Law Latin] **1.** A marshal; a high royal officer. — Also termed *mareschal.* **2.** A master of the stables. **3.** A military officer, similar to a constable, who acted as quartermaster. **4.** An officer of the Court of Exchequer. **5.** A state officer. **6.** An officer of a manor.

marettum (mə-**ret**-əm), *n.* [fr. Latin *mare* "the sea" + *tegere* "to cover"] *Hist.* Marshy ground flooded by the sea.

margin, *n.* (14c) **1.** A boundary or edge. **2.** A measure or degree of difference. **3.** PROFIT MARGIN. **4.** The difference between a loan's face value and the market value of the collateral that secures the loan. **5.** Cash or collateral required to be paid to a securities broker by an investor to protect the broker against losses from securities bought on credit. **6.** The amount of an investor's equity in securities bought on credit through the broker. — **margin,** *vb.* — **marginal, margined,** *adj.*

▸ **good-faith margin.** (1983) The amount of margin that a creditor exercising good judgment would customarily require for a specified security position. • This amount is established without regard to the customer's other assets or securities positions held with respect to unrelated transactions.

▸ **gross margin.** (1888) The difference between what something costs to produce and what it is sold for.

marginable security. See SECURITY (4).

margin account. See ACCOUNT.

marginal cost. See COST (1).

marginal note. A brief notation, in the nature of a subheading, placed in the margin of a printed statute to give a brief indication of the matters dealt with in the section or subsection beside which it appears. • For ease of reference, marginal notes are usu. in distinctive print. Many jurisdictions hold that notes of this kind cannot be used as the basis for an argument about the interpretation of a statute. — Also termed *sidenote.*

marginal release. See RELEASE (8).

marginal revenue. See REVENUE.

marginal tax rate. See TAX RATE.

margin call. See CALL (2).

margin deficiency. (1975) *Securities.* The extent to which the amount of the required margin exceeds the equity in a margin account.

margined security. See SECURITY (4).

margin list. (1970) A Federal Reserve Board list limiting the loan value of a particular bank's stock to a certain percentage (e.g., 50%) of its market value. • When a bank is not on the list, no limit is placed on the loan value of stock used as collateral.

margin requirement. (1921) *Securities.* The percentage of the purchase price that a buyer must deposit with a broker to buy a security on margin. • This percentage of the purchase price is set and adjusted by the Federal Reserve Board.

> "Margin requirements are the statutory and administrative restrictions placed upon the percentage of the value of securities that may be borrowed for the purpose of the purchase of such securities, the term 'margin' referring to the percentage of the value that must be paid in cash by the purchaser. Such requirements have been implemented for the purposes of preventing the excessive use of credit for the purchase or carrying of securities, and of reducing the aggregate amount of the national credit resources, which are directed by speculation into the stock market, and of achieving a more balanced use of such resources." 69 Am. Jur. 2d *Securities Regulation — Federal* § 481 (1993).

▸ **initial margin requirement.** (1946) The minimum percentage of the purchase price that a buyer must deposit with a broker. • The Federal Reserve Board establishes minimum margin requirements to prevent excessive speculation and price volatility.

▸ **maintenance margin requirement.** (1972) The minimum equity that a buyer must keep in a margin account, expressed as a percentage of the account value.

margin stock. See *marginable security* under SECURITY (4).

margin transaction. (1908) A securities or commodities transaction made through a broker on a margin account. — Also termed *buying on margin.* See MARGIN (5).

mariage de convenance. See *marriage of convenience* under MARRIAGE (1).

marinarius (mar-ə-**nair**-ee-əs), *n.* [Law Latin] *Hist.* A seaman; a mariner. • *Marinarius capitaneus* (kap-ə-**tay**-nee-əs) was the admiral or warden of the ports.

marine, *adj.* (15c) **1.** Of, relating to, or involving the sea <marine life>. **2.** Of, relating to, or involving sea navigation, sea commerce, or the navy <marine insurance> <marine interest>.

marine belt. See *territorial waters* under WATER.

marine carrier. See CARRIER (1).

marine contract. See *maritime contract* under CONTRACT.

Marine Court in the City of New York. The New York City court, originally created to resolve seamen's disputes, that was the predecessor of the City Court of New York.

marine insurance. See INSURANCE.

marine interest. See MARITIME INTEREST.

marine league. See LEAGUE.

marine loan. See *maritime loan* under LOAN.

marine peril. See PERIL OF THE SEA.

marine pollution. See POLLUTION.

marine protest. (1822) A writing attested by a justice of the peace, a notary public, or a consul, made or verified by the master of a vessel, stating that the vessel has suffered a severe voyage and that the master has engaged in neither misconduct nor negligence. See PROTEST.

mariner. (14c) A person employed on a vessel in sea navigation; SEAMAN.

marine-rescue doctrine. (1995) The rule that when a person on a ship goes overboard, the ship must use all reasonable means to retrieve the person from the water if the person can be seen, and, if the person cannot be seen, must search for the person as long as it is reasonably possible that the person is still alive.

marine risk. See PERIL OF THE SEA.

mariner's hypothec. See HYPOTHEC.

mariner's will. See *soldier's will* under WILL.

marine rule. The doctrine that if the cost of restoring damaged property would exceed one-half the value of the property before the damage, then the property is deemed to be totally destroyed. • The marine rule developed in the context of applying marine insurance to damaged ships, but it has also been applied to other property, including buildings.

marine service. See MARITIME SERVICE.

maritage (**ma**-ri-tij), *n.* See DOWRY.

maritagium (mar-ə-**tay**-jee-əm), *n.* [Law Latin] *Hist.* **1.** A lord's right to arrange a marriage for his infant ward; specif., the power of a feudal lord to give his infant ward or a vassal's heiress, minor heir, or widow in marriage, or to extract a fine from a vassal upon the vassal's marriage. **2.** *Hist.* The income derived from fines paid by vassals for the lord's permission to marry. **3.** DOWER. **4.** A marriage gift; DOWRY. See DOS. — Also termed (in sense 4) *maritage.*

> "*Maritagium,* which answered to the *dos* of the Romans, signified the portion which a man gave with his daughter in marriage . . . . When a man received lands with his wife in *maritagium* or as a marriage portion, and had an heir by her, male or female, that was heard to cry within four walls, the maritagium remained to the husband during his life, whether the heir lived or not, but after his death it went to the original owner." George Crabb, *A History of English Law* 86 (1st Am. ed. 1831).

> "[W]hile to the common lawyer *dos* meant dower, in other systems it meant dowry: a gift to the wife, or to husband and wife, by the bride's parents or other relatives. In England this was called the 'marriage-gift' or *maritagium*. Marriage-gifts were commonly made either to establish a cadet branch of a family or to assist a daughter who was not an heiress to make a good match." J.H. Baker, *An Introduction to English Legal History* 310 (3d ed. 1990).

maritagium habere (mar-ə-**tay**-jee-əm hə-**beer**-ee). [Law Latin] To have the right of arranging a woman's marriage. • This was a privilege granted by the Crown to favored subjects. See MARITAGIUM.

marital, *adj.* (17c) Of, relating to, or involving the marriage relationship <marital property>.

marital agreement. (1866) An agreement between spouses or two people engaged to be married concerning the division and ownership of marital property during marriage or upon dissolution by death or divorce; esp., a premarital contract or separation agreement primarily concerned with dividing marital property in the event of divorce. — Also termed *marriage settlement*; *property settlement.* See PRENUPTIAL AGREEMENT; POSTNUPTIAL AGREEMENT.

marital annulment. See ANNULMENT (2).

marital coercion. See COERCION (3).

marital-communications privilege. See *marital privilege* (1) under PRIVILEGE (3).

marital deduction. See DEDUCTION (2).

marital-deduction trust. See TRUST (3).

marital dissolution. See DIVORCE.

marital domicile. See *matrimonial domicile* under DOMICILE.

marital estate. See *marital property* under PROPERTY.

marital home. See HOME.

marital immunity. See *husband–wife immunity* under IMMUNITY (2).

marital life-estate trust. See *bypass trust* under TRUST (3).

marital misconduct. (1891) Any of the various statutory grounds for a fault divorce, such as adultery or cruelty. See *fault divorce* under DIVORCE.

marital portion. (1813) **1.** *Civil law.* The portion of a deceased spouse's estate to which the surviving spouse is entitled. **2.** *Louisiana law.* The portion of a deceased spouse's estate to which the surviving spouse is entitled if the spouse died "rich in comparison with the surviving spouse." La. Civ. Code art. 2432.

marital-privacy doctrine. (1973) A principle that limits governmental intrusion into private family matters, such as those involving sexual relations between married persons. • The marital-privacy doctrine was first recognized in *Griswold v. Connecticut*, 381 U.S. 479, 85 S.Ct. 1678 (1965). The doctrine formerly deterred state intervention into incidents involving domestic violence. Today, with the trend toward individual privacy rights, the doctrine does not discourage governmental protection from domestic violence. — Also termed *doctrine of marital privacy.*

marital privilege. See PRIVILEGE (3).

marital property. See PROPERTY.

marital rape. See RAPE (2).

marital relationship. See RELATIONSHIP.

marital residence. See HOME.

marital rights. (18c) Rights and incidents (such as property or cohabitation rights) arising from the marriage contract.

marital settlement agreement. See DIVORCE AGREEMENT.

marital status. (1882) The condition of being single, married, legally separated, divorced, or widowed.

marital tort. See TORT.

maritare (mar-ə-**tair**-ee), *vb. Hist.* To marry.

mariticide. (1992) **1.** The murder of one's husband. **2.** A woman who murders her husband. Cf. UXORICIDE. — **mariticidal,** *adj.*

maritima Angliae (mə-**rit**-ə-mə **ang**-glee-ee). [Law Latin] (17c) *Hist.* **1.** The seacoast. **2.** The Crown's sea revenue, as from wreckage and from whales or sturgeons cast ashore. • The revenue was formerly collected by sheriffs and later by the Lord High Admiral.

maritima incrementa (mə-**rit**-ə-mə in-krə-**men**-tə). [Latin "marine increases"] (18c) *Hist.* Alluvion caused by the sea; land gained from the sea.

maritime (**mar**-i-tɪm), *adj.* (16c) **1.** Connected with or situated near the sea. **2.** Of, relating to, or involving sea navigation or commerce.

> "The word 'maritime' has in the Constitution its appropriate meaning, i.e., relating to the sea, and 'sea' is a word of wide extension and application . . . . Its classical and scriptural equivalents are applied to all sorts of navigable waters. It is not restricted, even in common speech, to waters where the tide ebbs and flows, for the Baltic Sea, the Black Sea, the Sea of Azof, the Sea of Marmora, the Mediterranean Sea, the great scenes of early maritime enterprise, have no visible tide." 1 Steven F. Friedell, *Benedict on Admiralty* § 103, at 7-5 (7th ed. 1996).

Maritime Administration. A unit in the U.S. Department of Transportation responsible for subsidizing certain costs of operating ships under the U.S. flag; constructing or supervising the construction of merchant-type ships for the U.S. government; administering the War Risk Insurance Program; and operating the Merchant Marine Academy, which trains merchant-marine officers. — Abbr. MARAD.

maritime belt. See *territorial waters* under WATER.

maritime boundary. See *territorial waters* under WATER.

maritime claim. See CLAIM (4).

Maritime Commission. See FEDERAL MARITIME COMMISSION.

maritime-connection doctrine. See LOCALITY-PLUS TEST.

maritime contract. See CONTRACT.

maritime court. See ADMIRALTY (1).

maritime crime. See CRIME.

maritime employment. (1929) Under the Longshoremen's and Harbor Workers' Compensation Act, a job that is related to the loading, unloading, construction, or repair of a vessel. 33 USCA § 902(3).

maritime flag. See FLAG.

maritime flavor. (1917) The relation of a given case to shipping concerns. • This is a factor used in determining federal admiralty jurisdiction over a particular matter by analyzing whether the matter sufficiently relates to marine and shipping concerns and whether there is need for a federal response.

maritime interest. Interest charged on a loan secured by a sea vessel or its cargo, or both. • Because of the lender's considerable risk, the interest rate may be extraordinarily high. — Also termed *marine interest.*

maritime jurisdiction. See ADMIRALTY AND MARITIME JURISDICTION.

maritime law. (17c) The body of law governing marine commerce and navigation, the carriage at sea of persons and property, and marine affairs in general; the rules governing contract, tort, and workers'-compensation claims or relating to commerce on or over water. — Also termed *admiralty; admiralty law; sea law.* Cf. GENERAL MARITIME LAW; LAW OF THE SEA.

maritime lien. See LIEN.

maritime loan. See LOAN.

maritime peril. (1866) A danger or risk arising from navigating or being at sea.

maritime service. *Maritime law.* Work performed in connection with a ship or commerce on navigable waters, such as service to preserve a ship's crew, cargo, or equipment. — Also termed *marine service.*

maritime state. (18c) *Hist.* The collective officers and mariners of the British navy.

maritime tort. See TORT.

maritus (mə-**rɪ**-təs), *n.* [Latin] A husband; a married man.

mark, *n.* (bef. 12c) **1.** A symbol, impression, or feature on something, usu. to identify it or distinguish it from something else. **2.** TRADEMARK (1). **3.** SERVICEMARK.

▸ **benchmark.** See BENCHMARK.

▸ **certification mark.** See *certification trademark* under TRADEMARK.

▸ **collective mark.** See *collective trademark* under TRADEMARK.

markdown. (1897) A reduction in a selling price.

marked money. (1883) Money that bears a telltale mark so that the money can be traced, usu. to a perpetrator of a crime, as when marked money is given to a kidnapper as ransom.

market, *n.* (bef. 12c) **1.** A place of commercial activity in which goods or services are bought and sold <the farmers' market>. — Also termed *mart.* **2.** A geographic area or demographic segment considered as a place of demand for particular goods or services; esp., prospective purchasers of goods, wherever they are <the foreign market for microchips>. **3.** *Hist.* The privilege of having a public market. **4.** The opportunity for buying and selling goods or services; the extent of economic demand <a strong job market for accountants>. **5.** A securities or commodities exchange <the stock market closed early because of the blizzard>. **6.** The business of such an exchange; the enterprise of buying and selling securities or commodities <the stock market is approaching an all-time high>. **7.** The price at which the buyer and seller of a security or commodity agree <the market for wheat is $8 per bushel>.

▸ **advancing market.** See *bull market.*

▸ **aftermarket.** See *secondary market.*

▸ **auction market.** A market (such as the New York Stock Exchange) in which securities are bought and sold by competitive bidding through brokers. Cf. *negotiated market.*

▸ **bear market.** (1903) A securities market characterized by falling prices over a prolonged period. — Also termed *down market; receding market.* See BEAR.

▸ **black market.** (1931) An illegal market for goods that are controlled or prohibited by the government, such as the underground market for prescription drugs.

▸ **bull market.** (1891) A securities market characterized by rising prices over a prolonged period. — Also termed *advancing market; strong market.* See BULL (3).

▸ **buyer's market.** (1926) A market in which supply significantly exceeds demand, resulting in lower prices.

▸ **capital market.** (1848) A securities market in which stocks and bonds with long-term maturities are traded. See *financial market.*

▸ **common market.** (1954) An economic association formed by several countries to reduce or eliminate trade barriers among them, and to establish uniform trade barriers against nonmembers; esp. (*usu. cap.*), EUROPEAN UNION.

▸ **currency market.** See *foreign-exchange market.*

▸ **derivative market.** (1981) A market for the exchange of derivative instruments. — Also termed *paper market.* See DERIVATIVE.

▸ **discount market.** The portion of the money market in which banks and other financial institutions trade commercial paper.

▸ **down market.** See *bear market.*

▸ **financial market.** (1873) A market for the exchange of capital and debt instruments. See *capital market; money market.*

▸ **foreign-exchange market.** (1848) A market where various currencies are traded internationally. • Foreign-exchange markets take the form of spot, futures, and options markets. — Also termed *currency market.* See *futures market; spot market.*

▸ **forward market.** See *futures market.*

▸ **free market.** See *open market.*

▸ **Friday market.** The normal tendency for stock-prices to decline on Fridays. • The tendency occurs because many investors balance their accounts before the weekend to avoid any adverse changes in market prices over the weekend.

▸ **futures market.** A commodity exchange in which futures contracts are traded; a market for a trade (e.g., commodities futures contracts and stock options) that is negotiated at the current price but calls for delivery at a future time. — Also termed *forward market.* See FUTURES CONTRACT.

▸ **geographic market.** (1951) *Antitrust.* The part of a relevant market that identifies the regions in which a firm might compete. • If a firm can raise prices or cut production without causing a quick influx of supply to the area from outside sources, that firm is operating in a distinct geographic market.

> "For purposes of [the Sherman Act], the relevant geographic market comprises the area in which the defendant effectively competes with other individuals or businesses for distribution of the relevant product. Stated differently, the relevant geographic market consists of the area from which the sellers of a particular product derive their customers, and the area within which the purchasers of the product can practically seek the product." 54 Am. Jur. 2d *Monopolies, Restraints of Trade, and Unfair Trade Practices* § 57, at 119–20 (1996).

▸ **gray market.** (1946) A market in which the seller uses legal but sometimes unethical methods to avoid a manufacturer's distribution chain and thereby sell goods (esp. imported goods) at prices lower than those envisioned by the manufacturer. See PARALLEL IMPORTS.

> "One of the most controversial areas of customs law concerns 'gray market goods,' goods produced abroad with authorization and payment but which are imported into unauthorized markets. Trade in gray market goods has increased dramatically in recent years, in part because fluctuating currency exchange rates create opportunities to import and sell such goods at a discount rate from local price levels." Ralph H. Folsom & Michael W. Gordon, *International Business Transactions* § 20.8 (1995).

▸ **institutional market.** The demand among large investors and corporations for short-term funds and commercial paper.

▸ **labor market.** See LABOR MARKET.

▸ **market overt.** (17c) An open, legally regulated public market where buyers, with some exceptions, acquire good title to products regardless of any defects in the seller's title. Cf. FAIR, *n.*

▸ **money market.** (18c) **1.** Collectively, the banks and other institutions that buy, sell, lend, or borrow money, esp. foreign currencies, for a profit. **2.** The financial market for dealing in short-term negotiable instruments such as commercial paper, certificates of deposit, banker's acceptances, and U.S. Treasury securities. See *financial market.*

▸ **negotiated market.** (1956) A market (such as an over-the-counter securities market) in which buyers and sellers seek each other out and negotiate prices. Cf. *auction market.*

▸ **open market.** (18c) A market in which any buyer or seller may trade and in which prices and product availability are determined by free competition. — Also termed *free market.*

▸ **original market.** See *primary market.*

▸ **over-the-counter market.** See OVER-THE-COUNTER MARKET.

▸ **paper market.** See *derivative market.*

▸ **primary market.** The market for goods or services that are newly available for buying and selling; esp., the securities market in which new securities are issued by corporations to raise capital. — Also termed *original market.*

▸ **product market.** (1944) *Antitrust.* The part of a relevant market that applies to a firm's particular product by identifying all reasonable substitutes for the product and by determining whether these substitutes limit the firm's ability to affect prices.

"For purposes of an antitrust claim under . . . the Sherman Act, the relevant product market includes those services or commodities which are reasonably interchangeable by consumers for the same purposes. In order to establish the relevant product market, therefore, a plaintiff must sufficiently identify what types of products are reasonably interchangeable substitutes for the defendant's product within the appropriate area of competition." 54 Am. Jur. 2d *Monopolies, Restraints of Trade, and Unfair Trade Practices* § 58, at 121 (1996).

▸ **public market.** A market open to both buyers and sellers.

▸ **receding market.** See *bear market.*

▸ **recognized market.** A market where the items bought and sold are numerous and similar, where competitive bidding and bartering are not prevalent, and where prices paid in sales of comparable items are publicly quoted. • Examples of recognized markets include stock and commodities exchanges. Under the UCC, a secured creditor may, upon the debtor's default, sell the collateral in a recognized market without notifying the debtor. Such a sale is presumed to be commercially reasonable.

▸ **relevant market.** (1948) *Antitrust.* A market that is capable of being monopolized — that is, a market in which a firm can raise prices above the competitive level without losing so many sales that the price increase would be unprofitable. • The relevant market includes both the *product market* and the *geographic market.*

▸ **secondary market.** The market for goods or services that have previously been available for buying and selling; esp., the securities market in which previously issued securities are traded among investors. — Also termed *aftermarket.*

▸ **seller's market.** (1934) A market in which demand exceeds (or approaches) supply, resulting in raised prices.

▸ **soft market.** (1949) A market (esp. a stock market) characterized by falling or drifting prices and low volume.

▸ **spot market.** (1939) A market (esp. in commodities) in which payment or delivery is immediate <the spot market in oil>.

▸ **strong market.** See *bull market.*

▸ **thin market.** (1930) A market in which the number of bids or offerings is relatively low.

▸ **underground market. 1.** A market located in a basement or otherwise below ground level. **2.** See *black market.*

marketability. (1877) Salability; the probability of selling property, goods, securities, or services at specified times, prices, and terms.

marketability test. (1968) *Mining law.* The principle that, for someone to obtain a patent on a mining claim on federal land, there must be a showing that a reasonably prudent person could extract and market the claimed mineral at a profit, and that at the time of discovery, a large enough market for the mineral existed to attract the efforts of a reasonably prudent person.

marketable, *adj.* (16c) Of commercially acceptable quality; fit for sale and in demand by buyers. — Also termed *merchantable.*

marketable-product rule. (1957) *Oil & gas.* For royalty-calculation purposes, the doctrine that "production" occurs when oil or gas is pumped up, stored, and made marketable through processing. • Until producing a marketable product, the lessee bears all costs of capturing and handling oil and gas. Cf. CAPTURE-AND-HOLD RULE.

marketable security. See SECURITY (4).

marketable title. See TITLE (2).

marketable-title act. (1957) A state statute providing that a person can establish good title to land by searching the public records only back to a specified time (such as 40 years). See *marketable title* under TITLE (2).

market activity. See MARKET VOLUME.

market approach. (1958) A method of appraising real property, by surveying the market and comparing the property to similar pieces of property that have been recently sold, and making appropriate adjustments for differences between the properties, including location, size of the property, and the dates of sale. — Also termed *comparative-sales approach; market-comparison approach; market-data approach; market-comparables analysis; comparable-sales approach; comparables analysis.* Cf. COST APPROACH; INCOME APPROACH.

market average. A price level for a specific group of stocks.

market bid. See *bid price* under PRICE.

market-comparables analysis. See MARKET APPROACH.

market-comparison approach. See MARKET APPROACH.

market correction. See DOWN REVERSAL.

market-data approach. See MARKET APPROACH.

market-driven, *adj.* Influenced directly by consumer demand; subject to fluctuations resulting from what the public wants or does not want.

market economy. See ECONOMY.

market equity. (1938) The percentage of the total market value that a particular company's securities account for, represented by each class of security. Cf. BOOK EQUITY.

market forces. (1942) (*pl.*) The ways in which the collective behavior of buyers and sellers affects the levels of prices and wages, esp. in the relative absence of government influence.

marketing, *n.* (16c) **1.** The act or process of promoting and selling, leasing, or licensing products or services. **2.** The part of a business concerned with meeting customers' needs. **3.** The area of study concerned with the promotion and selling of products or services.

marketing contract. See CONTRACT.

marketing covenant. (1962) *Oil & gas.* In a mineral lease, the implied promise that the lessee will market the production from the lease within a reasonable time and at a reasonable price. See REASONABLY-PRUDENT-OPERATOR STANDARD.

marketing defect. See DEFECT.

market intermediary. (1957) *Securities.* A person whose business is to enter into transactions on both sides of the market. Investment Company Act, 15 USCA § 80a-3(c)(2)(B)(i).

market leader. (1937) **1.** The business that sells the most of a particular type of product. **2.** The product or service that is the most successful one of its type.

market-maker. (1962) *Securities.* Someone who helps establish a market for securities by reporting bid-and-asked quotations. • A market-maker is typically a specialist permitted to act as a dealer, a dealer acting in the capacity of block positioner, or a dealer who, with respect to a security, routinely enters quotations in an interdealer communication system or otherwise and is willing to buy and sell securities for the dealer's own account. — Also spelled *marketmaker.*

market-making, *n.* (1902) The practice of establishing prices for over-the-counter securities by reporting bid-and-asked quotations. • A broker-dealer engaged in this practice, which is regulated by both the NASD and the SEC, buys and sells securities as a principal for its own account, and thus accepts two-way bids (both to buy and to sell). See BID AND ASKED.

market manipulation. See MANIPULATION.

market order. See ORDER (8).

market-out clause. (1953) *Oil & gas.* A contract provision permitting a pipeline-purchaser of natural gas to lower the purchase price if market conditions make it uneconomical to continue buying at the contract price, and permitting the well owner to respond by accepting the lower price or by rejecting it and canceling the contract. • Market-out clauses often refer to competing fuels such as fuel oil. — Also termed *economic-out clause.*

market overt. See MARKET.

market-participant doctrine. (1983) The principle that, under the Commerce Clause, a state does not discriminate against interstate commerce by acting as a buyer or seller in the market, by operating a proprietary enterprise, or by subsidizing private business. • Under the Dormant Commerce Clause principle, the Commerce Clause — art. I, § 8, cl. 3 of the U.S. Constitution — disallows most state regulation of, or discrimination against, interstate commerce. But if the state is participating in the market instead of regulating it, the Dormant Commerce Clause analysis does not apply, and the state activity will generally stand. See *Dormant Commerce Clause* under COMMERCE CLAUSE.

marketplace, *n.* (14c) **1.** An open area in a town or city where a market is held; esp., a town square where public sales are held. **2.** The business environment in which goods and services are sold in competition with other suppliers.

marketplace of ideas. (1949) A forum in which expressions of opinion can freely compete for acceptance without governmental restraint. • Although Justice Oliver Wendell Holmes was the first jurist to discuss the concept as a metaphor for explaining freedom of speech, the phrase *marketplace of ideas* dates in American caselaw only from 1954.

market portfolio. See PORTFOLIO (1).

market power. (1915) The ability to reduce output and raise prices above the competitive level — specif., above marginal cost — for a sustained period, and to make a profit by doing so. • In antitrust law, a large amount of market power may constitute monopoly power. See MONOPOLIZATION. Cf. MARKET SHARE.

> "In economic terms, market power is the ability to raise prices without a total loss of sales; without market power, consumers shop around to find a rival offering a better deal." 54 Am. Jur. 2d *Monopolies, Restraints of Trade, and Unfair Trade Practices* § 49, at 110 n.87 (1996).

market price. See PRICE.

market quotation. See QUOTATION (2).

market-recovery program. See JOB-TARGETING PROGRAM.

market rent. See *open-market rent* under RENT (1).

market reputation. See *business reputation* under REPUTATION (2).

market-rigging. (1851) **1.** The practice of illegally or unfairly controlling the price or sale of goods in order to gain an unfair advantage. **2.** *Securities.* The practice of inflating the price of a stock through a system of pretended purchases.

market share. (1954) The percentage of the market for a product that a firm supplies, usu. calculated by dividing the firm's output by the total market output. • In antitrust law, market share is used to measure a firm's market power, and if the share is high enough — generally 70% or more — then the firm may be guilty of monopolization. See MONOPOLIZATION. Cf. MARKET POWER.

market-share liability. See LIABILITY.

market-share theory. (1973) *Antitrust.* **1.** A method of determining damages for lost profits by calculating the impact of the defendant's violation on the plaintiff's output or market share. Cf. BEFORE-AND-AFTER THEORY; YARDSTICK THEORY. **2.** *Patents.* A theory of lost-profits remedy offered when the patentee and the infringer share the market with a noninfringing competitor. • Using this method, the court assumes that the percentage of the market that the patentee holds is the same as the percentage of the infringer's market that the patentee would have captured but for the infringement.

markets-in-financial-instruments directive. See DIRECTIVE ON MARKETS IN FINANCIAL INSTRUMENTS.

market stand-off agreement. (1999) *Securities.* A provision in a stock-purchase contract in which the stockholder promises not to sell or otherwise transfer any securities during a specified period after the corporation makes a public stock offering. Cf. LOCKUP AGREEMENT.

market structure. The broad organizational characteristics of a particular market, including seller concentration, product differentiation, and barriers to entry.

market trend. See TREND.

market value. See *fair market value* under VALUE (2).

market value at the well. (1929) *Oil & gas.* The value of oil or gas at the place where it is sold, minus the reasonable cost of transporting it and processing it to make it marketable.

market-value rule. (1873) **1.** ENTIRE-MARKET-VALUE RULE. **2.** The principle that the measure of a legal remedy is determined by how much the thing lost would have commanded in an exchange. — Also termed (in sense 2) *fair-market-value rule.*

market volume. 1. The total number of shares traded on one day on a stock exchange. **2.** The total number of shares of one stock traded on one day. — Also termed *market activity.*

***Mark Hopkins* doctrine.** (1969) The principle that when an employee leaves a job because of a labor dispute, any later employment the employee has must be bona fide and intended as permanent for the employee to avoid a labor-dispute disqualification from unemployment benefits if the employee leaves the later job. *Mark Hopkins, Inc. v. Employment Comm'n*, 151 P.2d 229 (Cal. 1944).

marking. 1. PATENT MARKING. **2.** *Trademarks.* The requirement that the owner of a registered trademark must affix to each product a notice that it is sold under a registered trademark. • In the United States, a trademark owner who fails to give notice that its products are sold under a registered trademark cannot recover damages for infringement unless the defendant has had actual notice of the registration.

▸ **false marking.** *Patents.* The false marking or advertising of a product as patented or covered by a pending application when in fact it is not. • The false-marking statute, 35 USCA § 292, provides for a statutory fine or a private claim to redress false marking. Under current law, false-marking claims may be brought only by the U.S. Government or by competitors who can prove actual damages. — Also termed *false patent marking.*

marking estoppel. See ESTOPPEL.

marking statute. 1. *Patents.* The federal statute containing the patent-marking requirement. 35 USCA § 287. See PATENT MARKING. **2.** *Trademarks.* The federal statute containing the marking requirement for registered trademarks. 15 USCA § 1111. See MARKING (2).

***Markman* hearing.** (1996) *Patents.* A hearing at which the court receives evidence and argument concerning the construction to be given to terms in a patent claim at issue. *Markman v. Westview Instruments, Inc.*, 52 F.3d 967, 984-85 (Fed. Cir. 1995) (*en banc*), *aff'd*, 517 U.S. 370, 116 S.Ct.1384 (1996). • In the namesake decision, the Federal Circuit Court of Appeals held that the construction of patent claims — and therefore the scope of the patentee's rights — is a question of law. In a *Markman* hearing, the court interprets the claims before the question of infringement is submitted to the fact-finder.

markmoot (mahrk-moot), *n.* (1849) *Hist.* An early English or Scottish court that held hearings on a territorial border (i.e., a march or mark) between counties, hundreds, or countries. — Also spelled *markmote.*

markon. An amount (usu. expressed as a percentage) initially added to a product's cost to obtain the list price. • Further increases or decreases in price are called *markups* or *markdowns*, respectively.

marksman. (17c) **1.** Someone who signs documents with some kind of character or symbol instead of writing his or her name. **2.** A highly skilled shooter.

***Marks* rule.** The doctrine that, when the U.S. Supreme Court issues a fractured, plurality opinion, the opinion of the justices concurring in the judgment on the narrowest grounds — that is, the legal standard with which a majority of the Court would agree — is considered the Court's holding. *Marks v. U.S.*, 430 U.S. 188, 97 S.Ct. 990 (1977).

mark-to-market accounting method. See *fair-value accounting method* under ACCOUNTING METHOD.

markup, *n.* (1916) **1.** An amount added to an item's cost to determine its selling price. See PROFIT MARGIN. **2.** A session of a congressional committee during which a bill is revised and put into final form before it is reported to the appropriate house.

mark up, *vb.* (1868) **1.** To increase (the price of goods, etc.) **2.** To revise or amend (a legislative bill, a rule, etc.). **3.** To place (a case) on the trial calendar.

***Markush* claim.** See PATENT CLAIM.

***Markush* doctrine (mahr-kəsh).** (1942) *Patents.* An exception to the policy against the use of alternative language in claims, by which in certain claims (esp. those involving chemical components) a claimant can use an alternative, subgeneric phrase when there is no applicable, commonly accepted generic expression. • Characterized by a phrase such as "selected from the group consisting of," the claim includes a group of substances any one of which could serve the same function in the process. The term *Markush* comes from Dr. Eugene A. Markush, who was granted a dye-preparation patent in 1923. *Ex parte Markush*, 1925 Dec. Comm'r Pat. 126. See MARKUSH GROUP.

> "The Patent Office early adopted a policy against use of alternative language in claims. Thus, a claimant could not use the specific alternative phrase 'glass or plastic' but could use a generic phrase (such as 'impervious transparent material') that would cover effectively the desired alternatives. The *Markush* doctrine developed as an exception . . . . With chemical compounds there may be no suitable phrase to cover the alternatives. Under limited circumstances a claimant could use an artificial or coined subgeneric group in the form of 'material selected from the group consisting of X, Y, and Z.'" 2 Donald S. Chisum, *Patents* § 8.06[2], at 8-119 to 8-120 (1992).

***Markush* group.** (1942) *Patents.* A limited form of generic claim that recites an element, states the element is a member of a group, and names the other group members, any of which could substitute for the first recited element. • All *Markush* group members must have at least one common property that is mainly responsible for their function in the claimed relationship. Although each material in the group is different, each must be able to serve the same function. See MARKUSH DOCTRINE.

marque (mahrk). (15c) *Archaic.* Reprisal. See LETTERS OF MARQUE.

marque, law of. (17c) *Archaic.* A reprisal entitling one who has been wronged and is unable to receive ordinary justice to take the goods of the wrongdoer (if they can be found within one's own precinct) in satisfaction for the wrong. See LETTERS OF MARQUE.

marquis (mahr-kwis *or* **mahr-kee).** (14c) An English nobleman below and next in order to a duke. — Also spelled *marquess.*

marquisate (mahr-kwi-sit *or* **-zit),** *n.* [Law Latin] (16c) *Hist.* The seigniory of a marquis.

marriage, *n.* (13c) **1.** The legal union of a couple as spouses. • The essentials of a valid marriage are (1) parties legally capable of contracting to marry, (2) mutual consent or agreement, and (3) an actual contracting in the form prescribed by law. Marriage has important consequences in many areas of the law, such as torts, criminal law, evidence, debtor–creditor relations, property, and contracts. — Also termed *matrimony; conjugal union.*

> "It has frequently been said by courts, and even by Legislatures, that marriage is a 'civil contract.' But to conclude from these statements that marriage . . . has all, or even many, of the incidents of an ordinary private contract, would be a grave error. In fact, these statements to the effect that marriage is a 'civil contract' will be found, upon examination, to have been used only for the purpose of expressing the idea that marriage, in the American states, is a civil, and not a religious institution, or that . . . in some

> states mutual consent alone without formal celebration is sufficient to constitute a valid marriage known as a common law marriage, or that, as is true in all states, the mutual consent of the parties is essential, even in the case of a ceremonial marriage." Joseph W. Madden, *Handbook of the Law of Persons and Domestic Relations* § 1-3, at 2–3 (1931).

▸ **arranged marriage.** (1878) A marriage in which one's parents choose one's spouse.

▸ **attempted marriage.** See *void marriage.*

▸ **civil marriage.** (17c) A marriage solemnized as a civil contract, as distinguished from one solemnized as a religious sacrament. Cf. *ecclesiastical marriage.*

▸ **clandestine marriage** (klan-**des**-tin). (16c) **1.** A marriage that rests merely on the agreement of the parties. **2.** A marriage entered into in a secret way, as one solemnized by an unauthorized person or without all required formalities. See *Fleet marriage.*

▸ **common-law marriage.** (17c) A marriage that takes legal effect, without license or ceremony, when two people capable of marrying live together as husband and wife, intend to be married, and hold themselves out to others as a married couple. • The common-law marriage traces its roots to the English ecclesiastical courts, which until 1753 recognized a kind of informal marriage known as *sponsalia per verba de praesenti,* which was entered into without ceremony. Today a common-law marriage, which is the full equivalent of a ceremonial marriage, is authorized in 11 states and in the District of Columbia. If a common-law marriage is established in a state that recognizes such marriages, other states, even those that do not authorize common-law marriage, must give full faith and credit to the marriage. A common-law marriage can be dissolved only by annulment, divorce, or death. — Also termed *consensual marriage; informal marriage.* See *common-law husband* under HUSBAND; *common-law wife* under WIFE; PER VERBA DE FUTURO CUM COPULA; SPONSALIA PER VERBA DE PRAESENTI.

▸ **confidential marriage.** In some jurisdictions (such as California), a marriage between a man and a woman in which only the two parties and the officiant are present at the ceremony. • Confidential marriages are neither witnessed nor recorded in public records. They are recorded in nonpublic records. Although rarely performed, they are generally legal. To obtain a confidential marriage, the parties must each be at least 18, must be of the opposite sex, and usu. must have lived together for an extended period. In ecclesiastical law, such a marriage is termed an *occult marriage* or, if performed in the strictest secrecy, a *marriage of conscience.*

> "A few states provide for confidential marriages. This allows parties to go through all the formalities but have the records of the marriage, including the license, remain confidential. . . . A key practical effect of confidential marriage is to allow parties who have been living as husband and wife in a jurisdiction that does not recognize informal marriages to achieve marital status without publicity. However, it does not relate back to the time when the parties started holding themselves out as a married couple and thus it can have consequences in determining the extent of marital or community property or various other rights." Walter Wadlington & Raymond C. O'Brien, *Family Law in Perspective* 26 (2001).

▸ **consensual marriage.** Marriage by consent alone, without any formal process. See *common-law marriage.*

▸ **consular marriage.** (1876) A marriage solemnized in a foreign country by a consul or diplomatic official of the United States, esp. at an embassy, consulate, or other diplomatic property. • Consular marriages are recognized in some jurisdictions. — Also termed *diplomatic marriage; marriage of state.*

▸ **covenant marriage.** (1990) A special type of marriage in which the parties agree to more stringent requirements for marriage and divorce than are otherwise imposed by state law for ordinary marriages. • In the late 1990s, several states (beginning with Louisiana: see Acts 1997, No. 1380, § 5) passed laws providing for covenant marriages. The requirements vary, but most of these laws require couples who opt for covenant marriage to undergo premarital counseling. A divorce will be granted only after the couple has undergone marital counseling and has been separated for a specified period (usu. at least 18 months). The divorce prerequisites typically can be waived with proof that a spouse has committed adultery, been convicted of a felony, abandoned the family for at least one year, or physically or sexually abused the other spouse or a child. — Also termed (in slang) *high-test marriage.*

▸ **cross-marriage.** (16c) A marriage by a brother and sister to two people who are also brother and sister.

▸ **dead marriage.** (1861) A marriage whose substance has disintegrated; a marriage that has irretrievably broken down.

▸ **de facto marriage** (di **fak**-toh). (1861) **1.** A marriage that, despite the parties' living as husband and wife, is defective for some reason. **2.** In some legal systems, the union of a couple unprotected by any legal formalities.

▸ **defunct marriage.** (1954) A marriage in which both parties, by their conduct, indicate their intent to no longer be married.

▸ **diplomatic marriage.** See *consular marriage.*

▸ **ecclesiastical marriage.** (1866) A marriage solemnized as a religious sacrament, as distinguished from one solemnized merely as a civil contract. Cf. *civil marriage.*

▸ **fixed-term marriage.** See *temporary marriage.*

▸ **Fleet marriage.** (18c) *Hist.* **1.** A clandestine ceremonial marriage performed in the 17th or 18th century in the Fleet prison in London by a chaplain who had been imprisoned for debt. **2.** A clandestine ceremonial marriage performed by an unscrupulous itinerant clergymen in the area in London near the Fleet Prison. • Parliament attempted to stop the practice, but it was not until the statute of 26 George 2, ch. 33, declaring marriages performed outside public chapels or churches to be void and punishable as a felony, that the practice ceased.

▸ **fraudulent marriage.** (1831) A marriage based on a misrepresentation regarding some issue of fundamental importance to the innocent party, who relies on the misrepresentation in the decision to marry. • The misrepresentation must concern something of fundamental importance to a marriage, such as religious beliefs, the ability to have sexual relations, or the ability or desire to have children. Cf. *sham marriage.*

▸ **green-card marriage.** (1988) *Slang.* A sham marriage in which a U.S. citizen marries a foreign citizen for the sole purpose of allowing the foreign citizen to become a permanent U.S. resident. • The Marriage Fraud Amendments were enacted to regulate marriages entered into for the purpose of circumventing U.S. immigration laws. 8 USCA §§ 1154 (h), 1255(e). See *sham marriage.*

▸ **Gretna-Green marriage.** (1835) A marriage entered into in a jurisdiction other than where the parties reside to avoid some legal impediment that exists where they live; a runaway marriage. • Gretna Green, a Scottish village close to the English border, served as a convenient place for eloping English couples to wed since in Scots law parties over 16 did not need parental consent.

"A 'Gretna-Green marriage' was a marriage solemnized in Scotland by parties who went there to avoid the delay and formalities required in England. . . . In the United States, the term describes marriages celebrated between residents of a State who go to a place beyond and yet near to the boundary line of an adjoining State, on account of some advantage afforded by the law of that State." William C. Anderson, *A Dictionary of Law* 496 (1889).

▸ **handfast marriage.** (1945) **1.** *Hist.* A marriage, often lacking only solemnization by clergy, characterized by the couple's joining of hands to conclude a marriage contract. **2.** *Hist.* A betrothal with all the binding effects of a marriage, including conjugal rights and cohabitation, followed by a later formal ceremony. **3.** A trial or probationary marriage wherein the couple agrees to cohabit and behave as spouses for a definite period, usu. one year, at the end of which they will mutually decide to separate or go through a permanently binding marriage. • The legal status of such a marriage is unsettled, as many such trial marriages are initiated with a ritual ceremony including an exchange of vows before a presiding officer legally empowered to perform marriages, yet the couple intends to remain free to end the relationship without legal proceedings. Cf. *marriage in jest*; *common-law marriage.* **4.** A binding form of marriage practiced by some modern pagan religions. • Unlike in sense 3, such marriages are entered into with the expectation of permanent duration. — Also termed (in senses 3 & 4) *handfasting.*

▸ **high-test marriage.** See *covenant marriage.*

▸ **homosexual marriage.** See *same-sex marriage.*

▸ **informal marriage.** See *common-law marriage.*

▸ **in-marriage.** Marriage between relatives; in-breeding.

▸ **left-handed marriage.** See *morganatic marriage.*

▸ **levirate marriage** (**lev**-i-rət). A compulsory marriage between a widow and a brother of her deceased husband.

▸ **limited-purpose marriage.** (1953) A marriage in which the parties agree to be married only for certain reasons. • An example is a marriage in which the parties agree to marry so that a child will not be born illegitimate but agree not to live together or to have any duties toward each other. Courts have usu. found these marriages to be binding for all purposes. Cf. *sham marriage*; *green card-marriage.*

▸ **marriage by habit and repute.** (18c) *Scots law.* An irregular marriage created by cohabitation that implies a mutual agreement to be married, followed by a general reputation within the community. • This type of marriage is still recognized in Scotland. See *Scotch marriage.*

▸ **marriage in jest.** (1930) A voidable marriage in which the parties lack the requisite intent to marry.

▸ **marriage of conscience.** *Eccles. law.* See *confidential marriage.*

▸ **marriage of convenience.** (18c) **1.** A marriage entered into for social or financial advantages rather than out of mutual love. — Also termed *mariage de convenance.* **2.** Loosely, an ill-considered marriage that, at the time, is convenient for the parties involved.

▸ **marriage of state.** See *consular marriage.*

▸ **marriage of the left hand.** See *morganatic marriage.*

▸ **marriage *per verba de futuro subsequente copula.*** *Scots law. Hist.* An irregular marriage created by a promise to marry in the future followed by an act of sexual intercourse. • Originally medieval canon law, this type of marriage was recognized in Scotland until 1940. See *Scotch marriage.*

▸ **marriage *per verba de praesenti.*** (17c) *Scots law. Hist.* An irregular marriage created at the time of a mutual agreement to be married. • Originally medieval canon law, this type of marriage was recognized in Scotland until 1940. See *Scotch marriage.*

▸ **mixed marriage.** (17c) **1.** A marriage between people adhering to different religions or sects; esp., a marriage between a Catholic and a non-Catholic Christian. **2.** A marriage between persons of different races or nationalities. Cf. MISCEGENATION. **3.** Jocularly, marriage between people of different political beliefs or affiliations.

▸ **morganatic marriage** (mor-gə-**nat**-ik). (1827) *Hist.* A marriage between a man of superior status to a woman of inferior status, with the stipulation that the wife and her children have no claims to the husband's title or possessions. • By extension, the term later referred to the marriage of a woman of superior status to a man of inferior status. The concept is now limited to royal marriages. — Also termed *left-handed marriage*; *marriage of the left hand*; *salic marriage.*

▸ **occult marriage.** *Eccles. law.* See *confidential marriage.*

▸ **open marriage.** (1970) A marriage in which both partners accept that they, or at least one of them, will have sex with other people.

▸ **opposite-sex marriage.** (ca. 2005) A marriage between a man and a woman. • This term arose as a "retronym" to provide a contrast to same-sex marriage.

▸ **pleasure marriage.** See *temporary marriage.*

▸ **plural marriage.** (1862) A marriage in which one spouse is already married to someone else; a bigamous or polygamous union; POLYGAMY.

▸ **putative marriage** (**pyoo**-tə-tiv). (1811) A marriage in which either the husband or the wife believes in good faith that the two are married, but for some technical reason they are not formally married (as when the ceremonial official was not authorized to perform a marriage). • A putative marriage is typically treated as valid to protect the innocent spouse. The concept of a putative marriage was adopted from the Napoleonic Code in those states having a civil-law tradition, such as California, Louisiana, and Texas. This type of marriage is also recognized in the Uniform Marriage and Divorce

Act. The legal rule by which putative marriages exist is sometimes referred to as the *putative-spouse doctrine.* — Also termed *putative matrimony.*

▸ **salic marriage.** See *morganatic marriage.*

▸ **same-sex marriage.** (1972) The ceremonial union of two people of the same sex; a marriage between two women or two men. • *See U.S. v. Windsor,* 133 S.Ct. 2675 (2013). — Also termed *gay marriage*; *homosexual marriage.* Cf. CIVIL COMMITMENT (2); CIVIL UNION; DOMESTIC PARTNERSHIP.

▸ **Scotch marriage.** (18c) *Scots law.* A marriage by consensual contract, without the necessity of a formal ceremony. • Until 1940, Scots law retained the medieval canon-law forms of marriage *per verba de praesenti* and *per verba de futuro subsequente copula.* These promises constituted irregular but valid marriages. Scots law still retains the irregular marriage by cohabitation with habit and repute. No ceremony needs to be proved but, after the death of one spouse, the surviving spouse or any child can obtain a court's confirmation that a marriage existed, based on the general belief of neighbors, friends, and family.

▸ **sham marriage.** (18c) A purported marriage in which all the formal requirements are met or seemingly met, but in which the parties go through the ceremony with no intent of living together as husband and wife. Cf. *green-card marriage*; *fraudulent marriage*; *limited-purpose marriage.*

▸ **temporary marriage.** *Islamic law.* A short fixed-term marriage agreed to privately and orally between a man and an unmarried woman. — Also termed *fixed-term marriage*; *pleasure marriage.*

> "Temporary marriage (*mut'a*), recognized by the 'Twelver' Shiites, is not admitted by the Sunnis, but actual conditions are hardly different on both sides, because of the facility of divorce, the stability of most *mut'a* marriages among the Shiites, and the possibility of concubinage; among the Sunnis, too, the effect of a *mut'a* marriage can be achieved by an informal agreement outside the contract of marriage." Joseph Schacht, *An Introduction to Islamic Law* 163 (1982).

▸ **valid marriage.** See MARRIAGE (1).

▸ **voidable marriage.** (1845) A marriage that is initially invalid but that remains in effect unless terminated by court order. • For example, a marriage is voidable if either party is underage or otherwise legally incompetent, or if one party used fraud, duress, or force to induce the other party to enter the marriage. The legal imperfection in such a marriage can be inquired into only during the lives of both spouses, in a proceeding to obtain a judgment declaring it void. A voidable marriage can be ratified once the impediment to a legal marriage has been removed.

▸ **void marriage.** (17c) A marriage that is invalid from its inception, that cannot be made valid, and that can be terminated by either party without obtaining a divorce or annulment. • For example, a marriage is void if the parties are too closely related or if either party is already married. A void marriage does not exist, has never existed, and needs no formal act to be dissolved — although a judicial declaration may be obtained. — Also termed *attempted marriage.* See NULLITY OF MARRIAGE (1).

2. *Roman law.* A consensual agreement between a man and a woman to be married. • The consent of both parties and of any paterfamilias was necessary. Other requirements were the attainment of puberty and legal capacity (*conubium*). If either or both withdrew consent to be married, the marriage ended in divorce; no specific grounds were necessary. In the Christian empire, divorce without adequate grounds was penalized. **3.** MARRIAGE CEREMONY. — **marital,** *adj.*

▸ **ceremonial marriage.** (1876) A wedding that follows all the statutory requirements and that has been solemnized before a religious or civil official.

▸ **civil marriage.** (17c) A wedding ceremony conducted by an official, such as a judge, or by some other authorized person — as distinguished from one solemnized by a member of the clergy.

▸ **double-proxy marriage.** (2011) A wedding in which both parties to a marriage are absent but represented by stand-ins. • Only Montana allows this type of marriage.

▸ **proxy marriage.** (1924) A wedding in which someone stands in for an absent bride or groom, as when one party is stationed overseas in the military. • Proxy marriages are prohibited in most states.

marriageable, *adj.* (16c) (Of a person) suitable for contracting a marriage as judged by age, physical condition, and mental capacity, and being under no legal disability that would prevent marriage. See *marriageable age* under AGE. — **marriageability,** *n.*

marriageable age. See *marriageable age* under AGE.

marriage act. (*often cap.*) (18c) A statute that governs legal marriages.

marriage article. (1831) A premarital stipulation between spouses who intend to incorporate the stipulation in a postnuptial agreement.

marriage bonus. (1938) *Tax.* The difference between the reduced income-tax liability owed by a married couple filing a joint income-tax return and the greater amount they would have owed had they been single and filed individually. — Also termed *singles' penalty.* Cf. MARRIAGE PENALTY.

marriage broker. (17c) Someone who arranges or negotiates marriages in exchange for consideration. • A marriage broker may be subject to criminal liability.

marriage brokerage. (1847) **1.** A business that arranges or negotiates a marriage contract on behalf of one or both parties. **2.** *Archaic.* The compensation received by a marriage broker for arranging a marriage. — Also termed *marriage-brokerage.*

marriage-brokerage contract. (1847) *Archaic.* An agreement under which a person, acting for compensation, procures someone for a marriage. • Traditionally, these contracts have been void as being against public policy.

marriage celebrant. See CIVIL-MARRIAGE CELEBRANT.

marriage ceremony. (17c) The religious or civil proceeding that solemnizes a marriage. — Sometimes shortened to *marriage.* — Also termed *wedding.*

marriage certificate. (1821) A document that is executed by the religious or civil official presiding at a marriage ceremony and filed with a public authority (usu. the county clerk) as evidence of the marriage. — Also termed *certificate of marriage*; (BrE) *marriage lines*. Cf. MARRIAGE LICENSE.

marriage contract. See CONTRACT.

marriage license. (17c) A document, issued by a public authority, that grants a couple permission to marry. Cf. MARRIAGE CERTIFICATE.

marriage mill. (1930) A place that facilitates hasty, often secret, marriages by requiring few or no legal formalities. • Marriage-mill unions may be voidable but are rarely void in the absence of absolute impediments to marriage.

marriage-notice book. (1836) An English registry of marriage applications and licenses.

marriage officer. (1839) A diplomatic agent, consul, or other person authorized to officiate at a wedding of a given country's citizens who are in a foreign country.

marriage of state. See *consular marriage* under MARRIAGE (1).

marriage penalty. (1942) *Tax.* The difference between the greater income-tax liability owed by a married couple filing a joint income-tax return and the lesser amount they would owe had they been single and filed individually. • A marriage penalty exists whenever a married couple is treated disadvantageously under a tax code in comparison with an unmarried couple. Cf. MARRIAGE BONUS.

marriage portion. See DOWRY.

marriage power. See POWER (3).

marriage promise. See PROMISE.

marriage records. (1878) Government or church records containing information on prospective couples (such as a woman's maiden name and address) and on wedding services performed.

marriage settlement. **1.** See MARITAL AGREEMENT. **2.** See PRENUPTIAL AGREEMENT.

married, *adj.* (14c) **1.** Having a spouse; united with another by matrimony <a married woman>. **2.** Of, relating to, or involving marriage; CONNUBIAL; CONJUGAL <the married state>.

married woman's separate estate in equity. (1875) *Hist.* At common law, a trust that a rich family could set up for a daughter so that she would not lose control of her own money and property to her husband. • The daughter could escape the severe limits of coverture by having her family establish a separate estate in equity, allowing her the benefit of income that was not controlled by her husband even if the husband was named as trustee. See COVERTURE; MARRIED WOMEN'S PROPERTY ACTS.

married women's property acts. (*sometimes cap.*) (1869) Statutes enacted to remove a married woman's legal disabilities; esp., statutes that abolished the common-law prohibitions against a married woman's contracting, suing and being sued, or acquiring, holding, and conveying property in her own right, free from any restrictions by her husband. • In addition, these acts abolished the spousal-unity doctrine. In actual usage, the term almost always appears in the plural form (*acts*, not *act*), except when referring to a particular statute. — Also termed *married women's acts; married woman's property acts; married woman's acts; emancipation acts; married women's emancipation acts.* See MERGER DOCTRINE (3); SPOUSAL-UNITY DOCTRINE; LEGAL-UNITIES DOCTRINE.

> "About fifty years ago the legislatures in this country commenced enacting what are known as Married Women's Acts. These have been extended from time to time, and to-day throughout the entire Union it may be said, speaking generally, that married women have been secured in all their just rights of property. Our example spread at length to England, and Parliament passed the Married Women's Property Acts of 1870 and 1882, based upon the principles of the American legislation. I may have dwelt upon this subject at a tedious length. I cannot, however, but regard legislation which emancipates the wife from the shackles of the common law, which enlarges her rights far beyond those which Equity recognized, and places them upon an assured statutory basis, — legislation whose considerate beneficence penetrates every household in the land, and whose blessings will be the most felt where most needed, — as meriting unqualified approval, and which the future historian of our laws will place to the lasting credit of our own era." John F. Dillon, *The Laws and Jurisprudence of England and America* 364–65 (1895)

> "The women's rights movement existed throughout the nineteenth century. It succeeded in partially reducing the legal disabilities of married women during the second half of that century by bringing about the enactment in all states of Married Women's Property Acts. The purpose of these Acts was to place married women on an equal footing with their husbands with respect to contracts, earnings, the ownership of property and the right to sue or be sued, but as they were construed by the courts they frequently failed to accomplish the intended reforms." Homer H. Clark Jr. & Ann Laquer Estin, *Domestic Relations: Cases and Problems* 8 (6th ed. 2000).

***Marsden* motion.** (1983) A criminal defendant's request that a court dismiss or replace a court-appointed attorney on grounds that the attorney is not completely or adequately representing the defendant. *People v. Marsden*, 465 P.2d 44 (Cal. 1970).

marshal, *n.* (13c) **1.** A law-enforcement officer with duties similar to those of a sheriff. **2.** A judicial officer who provides court security, executes process, and performs other tasks for the court. — **marshalship,** *n.*

▸ **United States Marshal.** (1816) A federal official who carries out the orders of a federal court. • U.S. Marshals are employees of the executive branch of government.

marshal, *vb.* (15c) **1.** To arrange or rank in order <the brief effectively marshaled the appellant's arguments>. **2.** To arrange (assets, etc.) according to their liability or availability for payment of debts. **3.** To fix the order of (creditors) according to their priority; to rank.

marshaling assets, rule of. See RULE OF MARSHALING ASSETS.

marshaling doctrine. (1929) The principle that, when a senior creditor has recourse to two or more funds to satisfy its debt, and a junior creditor has recourse to only one fund to satisfy its debt, the senior creditor must satisfy its debt out of the funds in which the junior creditor has no interest. See RULE OF MARSHALING ASSETS.

marshaling the evidence. (1892) **1.** Arranging all of a party's evidence in the order that it will be presented at trial. **2.** The practice of formulating a jury charge so that it arranges the evidence to give more credence to a particular interpretation.

Marshal of the Queen's Bench. *Hist.* A custodial officer of the Queen's Bench prison. • The position was abolished by the Queen's Prison Act of 1842 (St. 5 & 6 Vict., ch. 22).

Marshalsea (**mahr**-shəl-see), *n.* [fr. Law Latin *marescallia*] *Hist.* **1.** The court or seat of the marshal of the royal household. **2.** A debtor's prison in London under the jurisdiction of the Court of Marshalsea. See COURT OF MARSHALSEA.

mart. See MARKET (1).

marte suo decurrere (**mahr**-tee s[y]**oo**-oh də-**kər**-ər-ee). [Latin] *Hist.* To run its course by its own force. • In the civil law, this term was applied to a suit that ran its course without obstruction.

martial law (**mahr**-shəl). (1933) **1.** The law by which during wartime the army, instead of civil authority, governs the country because of a perceived need for military security or public safety. • The military assumes control purportedly until civil authority can be restored. **2.** A body of firm, strictly enforced rules that are imposed because of a perception by the country's rulers that civil government has failed, or might fail, to function. • Martial law is usu. imposed when the rulers foresee an invasion, insurrection, economic collapse, or other breakdown of the rulers' desired social order.

> "Martial law is the public law of necessity. Necessity calls it forth, necessity justifies its exercise, and necessity measures the extent and degree to which it may be employed. That necessity is no formal, artificial, legalistic concept but an actual and factual one: it is the necessity of taking action to safeguard the state against insurrection, riot, disorder, or public calamity. What constitutes necessity is a question of fact in each case." Frederick B. Wiener, *A Practical Manual of Martial Law* 16 (1940).

> "[T]he term 'martial law' carries no precise meaning. The Constitution does not refer to 'martial law' at all and no Act of Congress has defined the term. It has been employed in various ways by different people and at different times. By some it has been identified as 'military law' limited to members of, and those connected with, the armed forces. Others have said that the term does not imply a system of established rules but denotes simply some kind of day to day expression of a General's will dictated by what he considers the imperious necessity of the moment. See *U.S. v. Diekelman*, 92 U.S. 520, 526, 23 L.Ed. 742. In 1857 the confusion as to the meaning of the phrase was so great that the Attorney General in an official opinion had this to say about it: 'The Common Law authorities and commentators afford no clue to what martial law, as understood in England, really is. . . . In this country it is still worse.' 8 Op.Atty.Gen. 365, 367. What was true in 1857 remains true today." *Duncan v. Kahanamoku*, 327 U.S. 304, 315, 66 S.Ct. 606, 611 (1946).

▸ **absolute martial law.** (1914) The execution of government functions entirely by military agencies, as a result of which the authority of civil agencies is superseded.

▸ **qualified martial law.** (1903) The execution of government functions partly by military agencies, as a result of which the authority of some civil agencies is superseded.

3. The law by which the army in wartime governs foreign territory that it occupies. **4.** Loosely, MILITARY LAW.

Martindale-Hubbell Law Directory. A set of books, traditionally published annually, and a website containing a roster and ratings of lawyers and law firms in most cities of the United States, corporate legal departments, government lawyers, foreign lawyers, and lawyer-support providers, as well as a digest of the laws of the states, the District of Columbia, and territories of the United States, and a digest of the laws of many foreign jurisdictions, including Canada and its provinces.

***Martinez* report.** (1983) A report that a court may require a pro se party to file in order to clarify a vague or incomprehensible complaint. *Martinez v. Aaron*, 570 F.2d 317 (10th Cir. 1978).

Martinmas. See *quarter day* under DAY.

Mary Carter agreement. (1972) A contract, usu. secret, by which one or more, but not all, codefendants settle with the plaintiff and obtain a release, along with a provision granting them a portion of any recovery from the nonparticipating codefendants. • In a Mary Carter agreement, the participating codefendants agree to remain parties to the lawsuit and, if no recovery is awarded against the nonparticipating codefendants, to pay the plaintiff a settled amount. Such an agreement is void as against public policy in some states but is valid in others if disclosed to the jury. *Booth v. Mary Carter Paint Co.*, 202 So. 2d 8 (Fla. Dist. Ct. App. 1967). — Abbr. MCA. Cf. GALLAGHER AGREEMENT.

Mary Major. See JANE DOE.

masking, *n.* **1.** *Criminal law.* The act or practice of a defendant's agreeing by plea bargain to plead guilty to a less serious offense than the one originally charged, as by pleading guilty to parking on the curb when one has been charged with speeding in a school zone. **2.** In critical legal studies, the act or an instance of concealing something's true nature <being a crit, Max contends that the legal system is merely an elaborate masking of social injustices>. — **mask,** *vb.*

mask work. (1983) *Copyright.* A three-dimensional pattern of metallic insulation or semiconducting material present or removed from the layers of a computer chip. • Mark works are protected under the Semiconductor Chip Protection Act of 1984. 17 USCA §§ 902 et seq.

massa (**mas**-ə), *n.* [Latin] A mass or lump of metal, esp. of gold and silver before it is made into a cup or other useful or ornamental object.

Massachusetts ballot. See BALLOT (4).

Massachusetts trust. See *business trust* under TRUST (4).

massacre, *n.* (16c) The violent killing of a great many people, esp. defenseless people, as a single atrocity or a series of closely related atrocities. Cf. *mass murder* under MURDER. — **massacre,** *vb.*

mass-action theory. (1974) The principle that, as long as a labor union functions, it is vicariously liable for the joint acts of its members.

mass-appraisal method. (1972) A technique for valuing large areas of land by studying market data to determine the price that similar property would sell for, without engaging in a parcel-by-parcel analysis.

mass asset. See ASSET.

***Massiah* rule.** (1964) The principle that an attempt to elicit incriminating statements (usu. not during a formal interrogation) from a suspect whose right to counsel has attached but who has not waived that right violates the Sixth Amendment. *Massiah v. U.S.*, 377 U.S. 201, 84 S.Ct. 1199 (1964). See DELIBERATE ELICITATION.

mass layoff. See LAYOFF.

mass meeting. See MEETING.

mass murder. See MURDER.

mass rape. **1.** See *gang rape* under RAPE (2). **2.** See *war rape* under RAPE (2).

mass tort. See TORT.

mast. (17c) **1.** *Military law.* A Navy disciplinary proceeding at which the commanding officer of a unit considers minor offenses charged against enlisted personnel. • The charges may be dismissed, the accused person may receive a punishment prescribed by military law, or the matter may be referred to a court-martial. The proceeding is not officially a trial, and no conviction or acquittal results. Traditionally, when a ship's captain disciplines crew members at sea, the hearing is held and the discipline announced (and sometimes carried out) at the ship's mainmast or *at the mast.* Depending on the rank of the presiding officer, it may be also termed *captain's mast, admiral's mast,* or (for an admiral) *flag mast.* **2.** On board a ship, the usual place of assembly for a court hearing, public sale, etc. • On sailing ships, the place is the mainmast. On all other vessels, the captain designates a place as the "mast." Cf. (in sense 2) MAST SELLING.

mast, at the. See MAST (1).

master, *n.* (bef. 12c) **1.** Someone who has personal authority over another's services; specif., a principal who employs another to perform one or more services and who controls or has the right to control the physical conduct of the other in the performance of the services; EMPLOYER <the law of master and servant>.

> "[A] master is a species of principal. All masters are principals, but all principals are not necessarily masters. A principal becomes a master only if his control of the agent's physical conduct is sufficient." William A. Gregory, *The Law of Agency and Partnership* 5 (3d ed. 2001).

2. A parajudicial officer (such as a referee, an auditor, an examiner, or an assessor) specially appointed to help a court with its proceedings. • A master may take testimony, hear and rule on discovery disputes, enter temporary orders, and handle other pretrial matters, as well as computing interest, valuing annuities, investigating encumbrances on land titles, and the like — usu. with a written report to the court. Fed. R. Civ. P. 53. — Also termed (in sense 2) *special master.*

▸ **special master.** (1833) A master appointed to assist the court with a particular matter or case.

▸ **standing master.** (1848) A master appointed to assist the court on an ongoing basis.

3. Someone in command of a vessel or aircraft.

master agreement. (1941) *Labor law.* An agreement between a union and industry leaders, the terms of which serve as a model for agreements between the union and individual companies within the industry.

master and servant. (16c) The relation between two persons, one of whom (the master) has authority over the other (the servant), with the power to direct the time, manner, and place of the services provided. • This relationship is similar to that of principal and agent, but that terminology applies to employments in which the employee has some discretion, whereas the servant is almost completely under the control of the master. Also, an agent usu. acts for the principal in business relations with third parties, whereas a servant does not. See *master–servant relationship* under RELATIONSHIP. Cf. PRINCIPAL AND AGENT.

> "Torts are the chief subject-matter of the law of master and servant. A servant is employed to perform mechanical or operative acts for his master. While so engaged he may negligently or wilfully injure third persons. In such case it is held that the master is liable for every wrong committed by the servant in the course of the employment and for the master's benefit. And it is immaterial whether the master authorized or directed the act; the first inquiry is whether it was within the course of the employment, and a secondary inquiry may be whether it was for the master's benefit. . . . Contract is the chief subject-matter of the law of principal and agent because an agent is employed mainly to influence third persons to enter into new legal relations with the principal. But an agent may have authority, real or ostensible, to make representations to third persons which when acted upon involve the principal in a tort liability. Accordingly we have to discuss here such torts as may be committed by an agent as agent, namely, torts arising from representations made by the agent to a third person in order to induce him to act. These torts differ from those committed by a servant in this, that a servant injures a person by acting upon him or his property, while an agent injures a person by inducing the injured person to act to his own prejudice; and this the agent does by making representations calculated to influence the conduct of the injured person." Ernest W. Huffcut, *The Law of Agency* 193–94 (1901).

master-at-arms. (18c) An officer with police duties on a ship.

Master at Common Law. An officer of an English superior court of common law, appointed to record court proceedings, supervise the issuance of writs, and receive and account for fees paid into the court.

Master-General of the Ordnance. See MASTER OF THE ORDNANCE.

master in chancery. (17c) **1.** An officer appointed by a court of equity to assist the court. **2.** *English law.* (*usu. cap.*) A senior official or clerk of a court of chancery who assists the Chancellor in various duties such as inquiring into matters referred by the court, examining cases, taking oaths and affidavits, hearing testimony, and computing damages. • There were many Masters in Chancery at the same time. The office was abolished in 1897 and was replaced by the office of Master of the Supreme Court. — Also termed *master of the chancery.* See MASTER OF THE SUPREME COURT.

> "[I]t seems proper to notice one class of [officers of the courts of equity], as they constitute one of the means by which such courts take testimony and settle facts in questions which come before them; and that is Masters in chancery. When such courts feel themselves incompetent to grant relief without some preliminary information, a reference of the matters is made to a master, who has power to procure such information for the purpose of satisfying the conscience of the court. To this end, he is authorized to examine witnesses or the parties themselves; and, after a hearing upon the matters referred to him, he reports the results at which he arrives to the court." Emory Washburn, *Lectures on the Study and Practice of the Law* 272–73 (1874).

Master in Lunacy. *Hist. English law.* A judicial officer appointed by the Lord Chancellor to conduct inquiries into the state of mind of people alleged to be lunatics incapable of handling their own affairs and to ensure in each case that the lunatic's property is properly managed for his or her benefit.

master lease. See LEASE.

master limited partnership. See *publicly traded partnership* under PARTNERSHIP.

mastermind. (1872) Someone who plans and organizes a complicated enterprise, esp. one involving a crime.

master of a ship. (16c) *Maritime law.* A commander of a merchant vessel; a captain of a ship. • The master is responsible for the vessel's navigation and the safety and care of the crew and cargo. — Also termed *shipmaster.*

Master of Laws. A law degree conferred on those completing graduate-level legal study, beyond the J.D. or LL.B. — Abbr. LL.M. Cf. JURIS DOCTOR; LL.B.; DOCTOR OF LAWS.

Master of Requests. *Hist. English law.* A judge of the Court of Requests. See COURT OF REQUESTS.

master of the chancery. See MASTER IN CHANCERY.

Master of the Crown Office. *English law.* A Supreme Court officer who is appointed by the Lord Chief Justice. • Formerly, the Master was appointed by the Lord Chancellor to prosecute criminal cases in the name of the Crown.

Master of the Faculties. *Eccles. law.* An officer in the province of Canterbury who heads the Court of Faculties, grants licenses, and admits or removes notaries public. — Also termed *magister ad facultates.* See COURT OF FACULTIES.

Master of the Horse. *Hist. English law.* A peer who as third officer of the royal household, next to the lord steward and lord chamberlain, attends the sovereign on state occasions. • The official was originally in charge of the royal stables, but that duty is now entrusted to the Crown Equerry.

Master of the Mint. *Hist. English law.* A salaried warden who supervised all activities of the royal mint. • The office was abolished under the Coinage Act of 1870 and replaced with Master Worker and Warden of Her Majesty's Royal Mint.

Master of the Ordnance. *Hist. English law.* Beginning with the reign of Henry VIII, a superior officer responsible for royal artillery and weapons. • The more modern representative is the Master-General of the Ordnance, a military officer and member of the Army Council. — Also termed *Master-General of the Ordnance.*

Master of the Pells. See CLERK OF THE PELLS.

Master of the Rolls. *English law.* The president of the Court of Appeal in England. • Formerly, the Master of the Rolls was an assistant judge to a court of chancery, responsible for keeping the rolls and chancery records. In recent times, the most famous Master of the Rolls was Lord Denning (who lived from 1899 to 1999).

> "Since 1875, the Master of the Rolls has been president of the Court of Appeal. Until 1958 he had the general responsibility for the public records (a responsibility then transferred to the Lord Chancellor) and is still responsible for the records of the Chancery of England. He admits persons as solicitors of the Supreme Court." David M. Walker, *The Oxford Companion to Law* 816 (1980).

Master of the Supreme Court. *English law.* An official of the Queen's Bench and Chancery Divisions of the Supreme Court who fills the several positions of master in the common-law courts, the Queen's Coroner and Attorney, the Master of the Crown Office, record and writ clerks, and associates.

master plan. (1914) *Land-use planning.* A municipal plan for housing, industry, and recreation facilities, including their projected environmental impact. See PLANNED-UNIT DEVELOPMENT.

master policy. See INSURANCE POLICY.

master's deed. See *special master's deed* under DEED.

master's draft. (1839) *Maritime law.* A contract for money loaned to a ship's master to cover necessary disbursements, payable from the first freight the ship receives, and secured by the vessel and freight. See BOTTOMRY BOND.

master–servant relationship. See RELATIONSHIP.

master–servant rule. See RESPONDEAT SUPERIOR.

master's in chancery deed. See *special master's deed* under DEED.

master's report. A master's formal report to a court, usu. containing a recommended decision in a case as well as findings of fact and conclusions of law.

mast selling. *Hist.* The practice of selling the goods of a dead seaman at the mast. See MAST (2).

matched order. See ORDER (8).

matching-acceptance rule. See MIRROR-IMAGE RULE.

matching principle. (1979) *Tax.* A method for handling expense deductions, by which the depreciation in a given year is matched by the associated tax benefit.

mate. (14c) **1.** A spouse or other long-term life partner. **2.** A second-in-command officer on a merchant vessel. **3.** A petty officer who assists a warrant officer. **4.** A friend or companion.

materfamilias (may-tər-fə-**mil**-ee-əs), *n.* [Latin] (18c) *Roman law.* **1.** The wife of a paterfamilias, or the mistress of a family. **2.** A respectable woman, either married or single.

materia (mə-**teer**-ee-ə), *n.* [Latin] **1.** Materials, esp. for building, as distinguished from the form given to something by the exercise of labor or skill. **2.** Matter; substance.

material, *adj.* (14c) **1.** Of, relating to, or involving matter; physical <material goods>. **2.** Having some logical connection with the consequential facts <material evidence>. **3.** Of such a nature that knowledge of the item would affect a person's decision-making; significant; essential <material alteration of the document>. Cf. RELEVANT. — **materiality,** *n.*

material, *n.* (*often pl.*) **1.** A solid substance such as wood, plastic, metal, or paper. **2.** The things that are used for making or doing something. **3.** Information, ideas, data, documents, or other things that are used in reports, books, films, studies, etc.

▸ **extrinsic material.** Information that is not included in a statute or document subject to interpretation but that may be helpful to understanding its meaning.

▸ **waste material.** An unwanted material that is discarded as defective, worthless, or useless.

material adverse information. See MATERIAL INFORMATION.

material allegation. See ALLEGATION.

material alteration. See ALTERATION (2).

material breach. See BREACH OF CONTRACT.

material change in circumstances. See CHANGE IN CIRCUMSTANCES.

material evidence. See EVIDENCE.

material fact. See FACT.

material fallacy. See FALLACY.

material information. *Securities.* Information that would be important to a reasonable investor in making an investment decision. • In an "efficient" market, materiality translates into information that alters the price of a firm's stock. *See* 15 USCA § 78j(b), 17 CFR § 240.10b-5.

▸ **material adverse information.** (1963) *Securities.* Material information that is likely to make an investment less attractive.

material issue. See ISSUE (1).

materialman. (18c) Someone who supplies materials used in constructing or repairing a structure or vehicle. — Also termed *material supplier.*

materialman's lien. See *mechanic's lien* under LIEN.

material misrepresentation. See MISREPRESENTATION.

material omission. See OMISSION.

material reciprocity. See *conditional national treatment* under NATIONAL TREATMENT.

material representation. See REPRESENTATION (1).

material risk. See RISK.

material supplier. See MATERIALMAN.

material term. See TERM (2).

material witness. See WITNESS.

material-witness arrest. See ARREST (2).

material-witness proceeding. (1956) A hearing in which a party to a criminal action seeks to require someone to testify, and perhaps to be arrested for this purpose, on grounds that the person has relevant knowledge about which he or she could usefully testify.

maternal, *adj.* (15c) Of, relating to, or coming from one's mother <maternal property>. Cf. PATERNAL.

maternal line. See LINE.

maternal-line descent. See DESCENT.

maternal-preference presumption. (1975) *Family law.* The belief that custody of a child, regardless of age, should be awarded to the mother in a divorce unless she is found to be unfit. • Most jurisdictions no longer adhere to the maternal-preference presumption. — Also termed *maternal-preference doctrine.* Cf. PRIMARY-CAREGIVER DOCTRINE; TENDER-YEARS DOCTRINE.

maternal property. See PROPERTY.

materna maternis (mə-**tər**-nə mə-**tər**-nis). (17c) Goods acquired through the mother descend to those connected with her. • The phrase invoked the distinction between the succession of consanguineous half-brothers and uterine half-brothers. Cf. PATERNA PATERNIS.

maternity (mə-**tər**-ni-tee). (17c) **1.** The quality, state, or condition of being a mother, esp. a biological one; motherhood. Cf. FILIATION. **2.** The section of a hospital devoted to the care of mothers and infants during and after childbirth. **3.** ATTRIBUTION RIGHT.

maternity leave. See LEAVE.

maternity presumption. See PRESUMPTION OF MATERNITY.

matertera (mə-**tər**-tər-ə), *n.* [Latin] (16c) *Roman law.* A maternal aunt.

matertera magna (mə-**tər**-tər-ə **mag**-nə). [Latin] (17c) *Roman law.* A great-aunt; the sister of one's grandmother.

matertera major (mə-**tər**-tər-ə **may**-jər). [Latin] *Roman law.* A greater aunt; the sister of one's great-grandmother.

matertera maxima (mə-**tər**-tər-ə **maks**-ə-mə). [Latin] *Roman law.* A great-great-great aunt; the sister of one's great-great-grandmother. — Also termed *abmatertera.*

mathematical-algorithm exception. See ALGORITHM EXCEPTION.

mathematical evidence. See EVIDENCE.

***Mathews v. Eldridge* test.** (1980) *Constitutional law.* The principle for determining whether an administrative procedure provides due-process protection, by analyzing (1) the nature of the private interest that will be affected by governmental action, (2) the risk of an erroneous deprivation through the procedure used, (3) the probable value of additional or substitute procedural safeguards, (4) the governmental function involved, and (5) the administrative burden and expense that would be created by requiring additional or substitute procedural safeguards. *Mathews v. Eldridge*, 424 U.S. 319, 96 S.Ct. 893 (1976).

matima (**mat**-i-mə), *n.* [Law Latin] *Hist.* A godmother.

matriarch. (17c) A woman who rules or dominates a social or political group. Cf. PATRIARCH.

matriarchate. (1884) **1.** The title, office, or position of a matriarch. **2.** The geopolitical area ruled by a matriarch. See MATRIARCH; MATRIARCHY.

matriarchy (**may**-tree-ahr-kee), *n.* (1885) **1.** A social system in which the oldest woman in a family controls the family and its possessions. **2.** A social system in which descent and inheritance are traced through the female line. **3.** A society in which women hold most of the power. Cf. GYNECOCRACY; PATRIARCHY. — **matriarchal,** *adj.*

matricide (**ma**-trə-sɪd), *n.* (16c) **1.** The act of killing one's own mother. **2.** Someone who kills his or her mother. — **matricidal,** *adj.*

matricula (mə-**trik**-yə-lə), *n.* [Latin] (16c) **1.** *Roman law.* A register of public officials. **2.** *Hist.* A register or certificate of enrollment in any organized group or society.

matriculate, *vb.* (16c) To enroll or register (in a university, college, etc.) — **matriculation,** *n.*

matrilineal (mat-ri-**lin**-ee-əl), *adj.* (1904) **1.** Of, relating to, or involving the maternal family line <matrilineal ancestry>. **2.** (Of a legal system) tracing descent through the maternal line <matrilineal system>. — Also termed *matrilinear.*

matrilineal descendant. See DESCENDANT.

matrilinealism. See MATRILINY.

matrilinear. See MATRILINEAL.

matrilinearism. See MATRILINY.

matriliny (**mat**-ri-lɪ-nee), *n.* (1906) The practice of tracing lineage or descent matrilineally. — Also termed *matrilinealism; matrilinearism.*

matrimonial action. See ACTION (4).

matrimonial case. See CASE (1).

matrimonial cause. See *matrimonial case* under CASE (1).

matrimonial cohabitation. See COHABITATION.

matrimonial domicile. See DOMICILE.

matrimonial home. See *matrimonial domicile* under DOMICILE.

matrimonial proceedings. (17c) A lawsuit related to the effective termination of a marriage, including divorce, nullity, and judicial separation.

matrimonial property. See *marital property* under PROPERTY.

matrimonial res. (1893) **1.** The marriage estate. **2.** The state of marriage; the legal relationship between married persons, as opposed to the property and support obligations arising from the marriage.

matrimonium (ma-trə-**moh**-nee-əm), *n.* [Latin] *Roman law.* Marriage. — Also termed *nuptiae* (**nəp**-shee-ee).

▸ ***matrimonium ipsum*** (ma-trə-**moh**-nee-əm **ip**-səm). [Latin] (1901) *Hist.* Marriage itself.

▸ ***matrimonium non justum*** (ma-trə-**moh**-nee-əm non **jəs**-təm). [Latin] (1914) *Roman law.* A marriage between two persons one or both of whom do not have the legal capacity to wed (*conubium*). • Children resulting from such a marriage were legitimate but were not considered in *potestas*.

matrimony, *n.* (14c) **1.** The ceremony in which two people become married; MARRIAGE (1). **2.** The quality, state, or condition of being married. — **matrimonial,** *adj.*

matrix (**may**-triks), *n.* [Latin] **1.** *Hist.* Mother. **2.** *Civil law.* The original legal instrument, from which all copies must be made. **3.** A list of the parties to a lawsuit, including the addresses at which pleadings and notices can be served. • A matrix is commonly used to list the names and addresses of creditors and other parties in a bankruptcy case. Many bankruptcy courts have specific rules on how to prepare the matrix.

matrix ecclesia (**may**-triks e-**klee**-z[h]ee-ə). [Latin] (17c) *Eccles. law.* A mother church; a cathedral church in relation to parochial churches in the same diocese, or a parish church in relation to dependent chapels.

matter, *n.* (13c) **1.** A subject under consideration, esp. involving a dispute or litigation; CASE (1) <this is the only matter on the court's docket today>. **2.** Something that is to be tried or proved; an allegation forming the basis of a claim or defense <the matters raised in the plaintiff's complaint are not actionable under state law>. **3.** Any physical or tangible expression of a thought.

▸ **matter in deed.** (16c) **1.** A matter that can be proved by a writing under seal. **2.** See *matter of fact*.

▸ **matter in pais** (in pay). (17c) A matter of fact that has not been recorded in writing and that must therefore be proved by parol evidence.

▸ **matter of fact.** (16c) A matter involving a judicial inquiry into the truth of alleged facts. — Also termed *matter in deed*.

▸ **matter of form.** (16c) A matter concerned only with formalities or noncritical characteristics <the objection that the motion was incorrectly titled related to a matter of form>. Cf. *matter of substance*.

▸ **matter of law.** (16c) A matter involving a judicial inquiry into the applicable law.

▸ **matter of record.** (16c) A matter that has been entered on a judicial or other public record and can therefore be proved by producing that record.

▸ **matter of substance.** (16c) A matter concerning the merits or critical elements, rather than mere formalities <the party objected because the motion was based on a repealed statute that related to a matter of substance>. Cf. *matter of form*.

▸ **new matter. 1.** A litigant's claim or defense that goes beyond the issues raised in the original litigation, either by raising a new issue with new facts to be proved or by raising a defense that does not implicate an element of the original claims. • A typical example of new matter is an affirmative defense. **2.** See NEW MATTER (2).

▸ **special matter.** *Common-law pleading.* Out-of-the-ordinary evidence that a defendant is allowed to enter, after notice to the plaintiff, under a plea of the general issue.

matter in controversy. See AMOUNT IN CONTROVERSY.

matter of. See IN RE.

matter of course. (17c) Something done as a part of a routine process or procedure.

mature, *vb.* (1861) (Of a debt or obligation) to become due <the bond matures in ten years>. — **maturity,** *n.* — **mature,** *adj.*

matured claim. See CLAIM (3).

mature-minor doctrine. (1977) *Family law.* A rule holding that an adolescent, though not having reached the age of majority, may make decisions about his or her health and welfare if the adolescent demonstrates an ability to articulate reasoned preferences on those matters. • The mature-minor doctrine was recognized as constitutionally protected in medical decisions (abortion rights) in *Planned Parenthood of Cent. Missouri v. Danforth*, 428 U.S. 52, 96 S.Ct. 2831 (1976). Not all states recognize the common-law mature-minor doctrine. Cf. PARENTAL-CONSENT STATUTE.

maturity date. See *date of maturity* under DATE.

maturity value. (1902) The amount that is due and payable on an obligation's maturity date. — Also termed *terminal value*.

maugre (**maw**-gər), *prep.* (13c) *Archaic.* Despite <the witness may testify maugre counsel's objection>.

maxim (**mak**-sim). (16c) A traditional legal principle that has been frozen into a concise expression. • Examples are "possession is nine-tenths of the law" and *caveat emptor* ("let the buyer beware"). — Also termed *legal maxim*. For a thorough compilation of maxims, see Appendix B.

> "Maxims have had a chequered career in the law. Once lauded and often quoted, today's shrinking Latinity has encouraged their move into the shadows, both in Academe and in the courts." Robert E. Megarry, *A New Miscellany-at Law* 211 (Bryan A. Garner ed., 2005).

▸ **equitable maxim.** (17c) A traditional principle of fairness stated in a concise expression and applied by a court of equity. • Examples are "equity will not suffer a wrong to be without a remedy" and "equity requires clean hands." — Also termed *maxim of equity*.

maximalist retributivism. See RETRIBUTIVISM.

maximum cure. (1940) *Maritime law.* The point at which a seaman who is injured or sick has stabilized, after which no additional medical treatment will improve the seaman's condition. • A shipowner's obligation to provide maintenance and cure to a sick or injured seaman usu. continues until the seaman has reached maximum cure.

Farrell v. U.S., 336 U.S. 511, 69 S.Ct. 707 (1949); *Vella v. Ford Motor Co.*, 421 U.S. 1, 95 S.Ct. 1381 (1975). See CURE (2); MAINTENANCE AND CURE.

maximum expiration date. (1950) *Criminal law. Slang.* The final date on which a prisoner or parolee might serve a custodial sentence or period of parole supervision, assuming the worst from the prisoner's or parolee's viewpoint.

maximum medical improvement. (1955) The point at which an injured person's condition stabilizes, and no further recovery or improvement is expected, even with additional medical intervention. • This term is most often used in the context of a workers'-compensation claim. An injured employee usu. receives temporary benefits until reaching maximum medical improvement, at which time a determination can be made about any permanent disability the employee has suffered and any corresponding benefits the employee should receive. — Abbr. MMI.

maximum penalty. See PENALTY (1).

maximum-security prison. See PRISON.

maximum sentence. See SENTENCE.

may, *vb.* (bef. 12c) **1.** To be permitted to <the plaintiff may close>. **2.** To be a possibility <we may win on appeal>. Cf. CAN. **3.** Loosely, is required to; shall; must <if two or more defendants are jointly indicted, any defendant who so requests may be tried separately>. • In dozens of cases, courts have held *may* to be synonymous with *shall* or *must*, usu. in an effort to effectuate what is said to be legislative intent.

Mayflower Compact. (1620) A social covenant signed by 41 the first settlers of Plymouth Plantation in 1620. • Signing aboard the Mayflower at Cape Cod, the religious pilgrims covenanted to "combine [themselves] togeather into a civill body politick" (in the spelling of their day), enabling them to "enacte, constitute, and frame such just & equall laws, ordinances, acts, constitutions, & offices, from time to time, as shall be thought most meete & convenient for the general good of the Colonie."

> "The Mayflower Compact was rediscovered in the mid-eighteenth century by historians who idealized it as the foundation of American liberties and the first written constitution. In fact, it was neither. Jefferson did not consult it in drafting the Declaration of Independence, and there is no record of its being mentioned at the Constitutional Convention. Nor was the Mayflower Compact a constitution. The Pilgrim constitution, the Great Fundamentals, was not drafted until 1636. The Compact was rather a social contract." 1 Ralph C. Chandler, Richard A. Enslen & Peter G. Renstrom, *The Constitutional Law Dictionary* 50 (1985).

mayhem (**may**-hem), *n.* (15c) **1.** The crime of maliciously injuring a person's body, esp. to impair or destroy the victim's capacity for self-defense. • Modern statutes usu. treat this as a form of aggravated battery. See BATTERY. Cf. *serious bodily injury* under INJURY.

> "Mayhem, according to the English common law, is maliciously depriving another of the use of such of his members as may render him less able, in fighting, either to defend himself or to annoy his adversary. It is a felony." Rollin M. Perkins & Ronald N. Boyce, *Criminal Law* 239 (3d ed. 1982).

2. Violent destruction. **3.** Rowdy confusion or disruption. — **maim** (in sense 1), *vb.*

May it please the court. (17c) An introductory phrase that lawyers use when first addressing a court, esp. when presenting oral argument to an appellate court.

mayn (mayn), *n.* [Law French] *Hist.* A hand; handwriting.

maynover (mə-**noo**-vər *or* may-**noh**-vər), *n.* [Law French] *Hist.* A work by hand; something produced by manual labor.

mayor, *n.* (14c) An official elected or appointed as the chief executive of a city, town, or other municipality. — **mayoral** (**may**-ər-əl), *adj.*

mayoralty (**may**-ər-əl-tee). (14c) **1.** The office or dignity of a mayor. **2.** The period during which someone serves as mayor. — Also termed *mayorship.*

mayor of the staple. (16c) *Hist.* A person appointed to take recognizances of debt between staple merchants, and to hear disputes arising between merchants. See STAPLE (1), (2).

mayor's court. See COURT.

mayorship. See MAYORALTY.

MBDA. *abbr.* MINORITY BUSINESS DEVELOPMENT AGENCY.

MBE. See *Multistate Bar Examination* under BAR EXAMINATION.

MBO. See *management buyout* under BUYOUT.

MC. *abbr.* MEMBER OF CONGRESS.

MCA. *abbr.* **1.** MARY CARTER AGREEMENT. **2.** MOTOR CARRIER ACT.

MCC. *abbr.* Metropolitan correction center.

McCain–Feingold. See BIPARTISAN CAMPAIGN REFORM ACT.

McCarran Act. A 1950 federal statute requiring, among other things, members of the Communist party to register with the Attorney General and requiring Communist organizations to provide the government with a list of its members. • The Act was passed during the Cold War. Over the years, the U.S. Supreme Court declared various portions of the Act unconstitutional, but it was not fully repealed until 1993. *See, e.g., U.S. v. Spector*, 343 U.S. 169, 72 S.Ct. 591 (1952); *Aptheker v. Secretary of State*, 378 U.S. 500, 84 S.Ct. 1659 (1964); *U.S. v. Robel*, 389 U.S. 258, 88 S.Ct. 419 (1967). — Also termed *McCarran Internal Security Act; Subversive Activities Control Act of 1950.*

McCarran–Ferguson Act. *Insurance.* A federal law allowing a state to regulate insurance companies doing business in that state, and also to levy a tax on them. 15 USCA §§ 1011–1015. — Abbr. MFA.

McCarran Internal Security Act. See MCCARRAN ACT.

***McClanahan* presumption.** (1992) The presumption that the states do not have jurisdiction to tax members of an American Indian tribe who live or work on tribal land. • The presumption is not limited to tribal members who live or work on a formal reservation. Instead, it includes those who live or work on informal reservations, in dependent tribal communities, and on tribal allotments. *McClanahan v. Arizona Tax Comm'n*, 411 U.S. 164, 93 S.Ct. 1257 (1973).

***McDonnell Douglas* test.** (1975) *Employment law.* The principle for applying a shifting burden of proof in employment-discrimination cases, essentially requiring the plaintiff to come forward with evidence of discrimination and the defendant to come forward with evidence showing that the employment action at issue was taken for nondiscriminatory reasons. • Under this test, the plaintiff must first establish a prima facie case of discrimination, as by showing that the plaintiff is a member of a protected group and has suffered an adverse employment action. If the plaintiff satisfies that burden, then the defendant must articulate a legitimate, nondiscriminatory reason for the employment action at issue. If the defendant satisfies that burden, then the plaintiff must prove that the defendant's stated reason is just a pretext for discrimination and that discrimination was the real reason for the employment action. *McDonnell Douglas Corp. v. Green*, 411 U.S. 792, 93 S.Ct. 1817 (1973). Cf. BURDEN-SHIFTING ANALYSIS.

mcf. *abbr. Oil & gas.* One thousand cubic feet, one of the standard units for measuring natural gas.

***McKenzie* friend.** (1978) *English law.* An assistant, lay or professional, who attends court with a litigant to assist in the case. • The term comes from *McKenzie v. McKenzie*, [1970] 3 All ER 1034, a divorce case in which the husband appeared pro se. An Australian barrister volunteered to sit with him in court and quietly assist him to present his case by taking notes and suggesting questions for cross-examination.

MCM. *abbr.* MANUAL FOR COURTS-MARTIAL.

***McNabb–Mallory* rule.** (1958) *Criminal procedure.* The doctrine that a confession is inadmissible if obtained during an unreasonably long detention period between arrest and a preliminary hearing. • Because of the broader protections afforded under the *Miranda* rule, the *McNabb–Mallory* rule is rarely applied in modern cases. *McNabb v. U.S.*, 318 U.S. 332, 63 S.Ct. 608 (1943); *Mallory v. U.S.*, 354 U.S. 449, 77 S.Ct. 1356 (1957). — Often shortened to *Mallory rule.*

***McNaghten* rules** (mik-**nawt**-ən). (1917) *Criminal law.* The doctrine that a person is not criminally responsible for an act when a mental disability prevented the person from knowing either (1) the nature and quality of the act or (2) whether the act was right or wrong. • The federal courts and most states have adopted this test in some form. *McNaghten's Case*, 8 Eng. Rep. 718 (H.L. 1843). — Also spelled *McNaughten rules*; *M'Naghten rules*; *M'Naughten rules.* — Also termed *right-and-wrong test*; *right-wrong test.* See INSANITY DEFENSE.

> "Four points stand out and should be understood whenever reference to M'Naghten is made other than in regard to procedure. (1) It applies only in case of 'a defect of reason, from disease of the mind' and without this the following do not apply except that 'disease' as so used will be interpreted to include congenital defect or traumatic injury. (2) If, because of this 'defect of reason,' the defendant did not know what he was doing he is not guilty of crime. (3) Even if the defendant knew what he was doing he is not guilty of crime if, because of this 'defect of reason,' he did not know he was doing wrong. (4) If the defendant acted under an insane delusion, and was not otherwise insane, his accountability to the criminal law is the same as if the facts were as they seemed to him to be." Rollin M. Perkins & Ronald N. Boyce, *Criminal Law* 959–60 (3d ed. 1982).

***McNary* comity.** (1995) The principle that a U.S. district court should not hear a taxpayer's civil-rights challenge to the administration of a state's tax system. *Fair Assessment in Real Estate Ass'n v. McNary*, 454 U.S. 100, 102 S.Ct. 177 (1981).

MCO. *abbr.* MANAGED-CARE ORGANIZATION.

m-commerce. See MOBILE COMMERCE.

MCP. *abbr.* Misdemeanor conference part.

MCPR. *abbr.* MODEL CODE OF PROFESSIONAL RESPONSIBILITY.

M.D. *abbr.* (15c) **1.** Middle District, usu. in reference to U.S. judicial districts. **2.** Doctor of medicine.

MDA. *abbr.* MISSILE DEFENSE AGENCY.

MDC. *abbr.* Metropolitan detention center.

MDL. *abbr.* MULTIDISTRICT LITIGATION.

MDP. *abbr.* MULTIDISCIPLINARY PRACTICE.

MDV. *abbr.* MOTION FOR DIRECTED VERDICT.

mea culpa. [Latin] (16c) An acknowledgment of one's mistake or fault.

mean, *adj.* (14c) **1.** Of, relating to, or involving an intermediate point between two points or extremes <a mean position>. **2.** Medium in size <a mean height>. **3.** (Of a value, etc.) average <a mean score>. Cf. MEDIAN.

meander line (mee-**an**-dər). (1865) A survey line (not a boundary line) on a portion of land, usu. following the course of a river or stream.

mean high tide. See TIDE.

meaning. (14c) The sense of anything, but esp. of words; that which is conveyed (or intended to be conveyed) by a written or oral statement or other communicative act. • The word ordinarily includes a mistaken but reasonable understanding of a communication. Cf. AMBIGUITY.

> "A particular legal norm (rule, principle, standard . . .) is not the text (whether type or token) whose promulgation or pronouncement is the norm's formal source. More proximate to the norm is the text's meaning. But no meaning can correctly be said to be the norm unless it is the meaning which the text has when taken in conjunction with all the norms or meanings which properly affect its legally sound interpretation and its validity and authority as law." John Finnis, *Intention and Identity* 100 (2011).

▸ **natural and ordinary meaning.** See *plain meaning.*

▸ **objective meaning.** The meaning that would be attributed to an unambiguous document (or portion of a document) by a disinterested reasonable person who is familiar with the surrounding circumstances. • A party to a contract is often held to its objective meaning, which it is considered to have had reason to know, even if the party subjectively understood or intended something else.

▸ **plain and ordinary meaning. 1.** See *plain meaning.* **2.** *Patents.* The usual, customary meaning given to a term in a patent claim by those of ordinary skill in the art at the time of the invention. • In the construction of patent claims, words in the claim must be given their plain and ordinary meaning unless that is inconsistent with the patent's specification. — Also termed *natural and ordinary meaning.*

▸ **plain meaning.** The meaning attributed to a document (usu. by a court) by giving the words their ordinary sense, without referring to extrinsic indications of the author's intent. — Also termed *ordinary meaning*; *plain and ordinary meaning.* See PLAIN-MEANING RULE.

▸ **subjective meaning.** The meaning that a party to a legal document attributes to it when the document is written, executed, or otherwise adopted.

mean lower low tide. See TIDE.

mean low tide. See TIDE.

mean reserve. See RESERVE (1).

means, *n.* (14c) **1.** Available resources, esp. for the payment of debt; income. — Also termed *means of support.* **2.** Something that helps to attain an end; an instrument; a cause.

means-combination claim. See PATENT CLAIM.

means of support. See MEANS (1).

means-plus-function clause. (1967) *Patents.* An element in a patent claim, usu. in a claim for an apparatus patent, asserting that the claim element is a way to perform a given function or is a step in the process of performing a given function. • The claim will be interpreted as including the structure or means stated in the patent specification and equivalents at the time of interpretation or infringement, but not all possible means of achieving the same function. 35 USCA § 112, ¶ 6. — Abbr. MPF clause. — Also termed *means-plus-function element*; *means-plus-function claim.* See *combination patent* under PATENT (3).

> "Identifying a means plus function clause. Whenever a court confronts a claim element calling for a 'means' to perform a stated function, the court must first determine whether this clause is subject to § 112 ¶ 6. The court determines this question as a matter of law, as part of its claim construction. The inquiry is a three-part analysis. First, it is not necessary to use the word 'means' in order to fall under the statute. If a claim element uses a general, nonstructural noun followed by recitation of a performed function, then the statute may be triggered. The courts apply a presumption that if the applicant used the word 'means' in the clause, he intended to trigger the statutory provision. This presumption is rebuttable by showing that the clause contains structural language or that it does not recite a true function. Thus, use of the word 'means' followed by a function being performed will not trigger the statute if the claim element also provides some description of structure to perform the function. Although the statutory language suggests that the claim element must be devoid of structure in order for the statute to apply, the courts have held that the claim must identify substantial structure in order to avoid § 112 ¶ 6, but sometimes just one or two words connoting structure will meet this test. Many patents have multiple elements using means plus function language, and the court will approach these claims by analyzing each means clause separately in light of the patent and prosecution history." 2 Stuart B. Soffer & Robert C. Kahrl, *Thesaurus of Claim Construction* 1101-02 (2d ed. 2013).

means test. (1925) **1.** An official check to ascertain whether someone is truly poor enough to qualify for certain benefits, esp. welfare. **2.** *Bankruptcy.* A test to determine whether an individual debtor's Chapter 7 filing is presumed to be an abuse of the Bankruptcy Code requiring dismissal or conversion of the case to Chapter 13 or otherwise. • Abuse is presumed if the debtor's aggregate current monthly income exceeds (1) $10,000 (net of statutorily allowed expenses), or (2) 25% of the debtor's nonpriority unsecured debt if that amount is at least $6,000. A showing of special circumstances justifying additional expenses or adjustments of current monthly income may rebut the presumption. 11 USCA § 707(b)(2). — **means-tested,** *adj.*

mean trading price. See PRICE.

mearstone. See MERESTONE.

measurable damages. See DAMAGES.

measure of damages. (18c) The basis for calculating damages to be awarded to someone who has suffered an injury; the test by which the amount of damages is ascertained. • For example, the measure of damages in an action on a penal bond is compensation for the actual loss, not exceeding the established penalty.

measuring life. (1922) Under the rule against perpetuities, the last beneficiary to die who was alive at the testator's death and who usu. holds a preceding interest. • A measuring life is used to determine whether an interest will vest under the rule against perpetuities. See RULE AGAINST PERPETUITIES. Cf. LIFE IN BEING.

measuring money. *Hist.* An extra duty collected on cloth. • It was abolished during the reign of Henry IV.

mechanical license. See LICENSE.

mechanical rights. (1914) *Copyright.* The right to reproduce a song in a phonorecord form, such as audiotape or compact disc. • The right is obtained by paying a statutory royalty; it is not necessary to obtain the songwriter's express permission. See MECHANICAL ROYALTY. Cf. PERFORMANCE RIGHT.

mechanical royalty. (1931) *Copyright.* The payment to which a songwriter is entitled each time a mechanical-right holder reproduces a song on a phonorecord. • Mechanical-royalty rates are statutory, and payable per song or per minute (whichever is higher). If an artist is willing to pay the statutory rate, the songwriter's permission is not needed before a recording is made. If they choose to, artists and songwriters may negotiate lower royalty rates. 37 CFR § 255. — Also termed *statutory rate.*

mechanic's lien. See LIEN.

MED. *abbr.* OFFICE OF MEDICAL SERVICES.

medfee (**med**-fee). (17c) *Hist.* A bribe or reward; compensation given for things exchanged of unequal value.

media concludendi (**mee**-dee-ə kon-kloo-**den**-dɪ). [Latin] (17c) *Hist.* The steps of an argument.

medial, *adj.* See INTERLOCUTORY.

median, *adj.* (15c) Located in or related to the precise midpoint in a range of values or quantities, such that half of them fall above the midpoint and half below. Cf. MEAN.

media nox (**mee**-dee-ə **noks**), *n.* [Latin] (16c) *Hist.* Midnight.

medianus homo (mee-dee-**ay**-nəs **hoh**-moh). [Latin] *Hist.* A man of middle fortune.

media sententia (**mee**-dee-ə sen-**ten**-shee-ə). [Latin] (1870) *Roman law.* A middle view.

> "The Proculeians held that specification, by changing the form of the raw material, changed its nature, and replaced it by something quite new, and that, therefore, the maker of the new article was the owner of it, and not the person to whom belonged the material of which it was made. The Sabinians, on the other hand, were of opinion that the material retained its original nature, and continued to subsist, notwithstanding its change of form, and that, accordingly, the new article belonged to the proprietor of the material. Neither of these extreme views were adopted by Justinian, who followed a middle opinion, based on this distinction: 'If the thing made can be reduced to its former rude materials, then the owner of the materials is also considered the owner of the thing made; but if the thing cannot be so reduced, then he who made it is the owner of it.' (Just. Inst. B. 2, T. 1, § 25.)" John Trayner, *Trayner's Latin Maxims* 349 (4th ed. 1894).

mediate, *vb.* **1.** *Archaic.* To occupy an intermediate place or position; to be in the middle <the fourth hole on the course physically mediates between the third and the seventh>. **2.** To serve as a connection between other things; to be a transition from one to another <accumulating knowledge is nothing but a mediating process>. **3.** To intercede between disputants in order to harmonize or reconcile them; to intervene for the purpose of settlement or reconciliation <she mediated between her feuding friends>. **4.** To accomplish by beneficial intercession; to effect through mediation <the Vatican mediated the peace>. **5.** To settle (a dispute) by intervention; to resolve (discord) between clashing factions <no friends could mediate their strife>. **6.** To change the effect or influence of (something), esp. by mitigation <to mediate the effects of a lack of exercise>. **7.** To be a party or to serve as an advocate or mediator in a mediation that seeks to prevent or settle a lawsuit <the retired judge mediated two lawsuits last month> <because the parties have already gone through two unsuccessful mediations, they are unlikely to mediate again>.

mediate datum (mee-dee-**ay**-tee **day**-təm). [Latin] (1944) An intermediate fact whose existence implies the existence of ultimate facts.

mediate descent. See DESCENT.

mediated settlement agreement. See SETTLEMENT (2).

mediate evidence. See *secondary evidence* under EVIDENCE.

mediate possession. See POSSESSION.

mediate powers (**mee**-dee-it). (1820) Subordinate powers incidental to primary powers, esp. as given by a principal to an agent; powers necessary to accomplish the principal task <adjusting debt is a mediate power to collecting debt>. Cf. PRIMARY POWERS.

mediate testimony. See *secondary evidence* under EVIDENCE.

mediation (mee-dee-**ay**-shən), *n.* (14c) **1.** A method of nonbinding dispute resolution involving a neutral third party who tries to help the disputing parties reach a mutually agreeable solution; CONCILIATION. — Also termed *case evaluation; facilitated negotiation.* Cf. COLLABORATIVE LAW; COOPERATIVE LAW; ARBITRATION. **2.** *Int'l law.* A process whereby a neutral country helps other countries peacefully resolve disputes between them. — **mediate** (**mee**-dee-ayt), *vb.* — **mediatory** (**mee**-dee-ə-tor-ee), *adj.*

> "Simply stated, mediation does not resolve a dispute, it merely helps the parties do so. In contrast, the FAA presumes that the arbitration process itself will produce a resolution independent of the parties' acquiescence — an award which declares the parties' rights and which may be confirmed with the force of a judgment. . . . In short, because the mediation process does not purport to adjudicate or resolve a case in any way, it is not 'arbitration' within the meaning of the FAA." *Advanced Bodycare Solutions, LLC v. Thione Int'l Inc.*, 524 F.3d 1235, 1240 (11th Cir. 2008) (internal citations omitted).

> "The distinction between *mediation* and *conciliation* is widely debated among those interested in alternative dispute resolution, arbitration, and international diplomacy. Some suggest that *conciliation* is 'a nonbinding arbitration,' whereas *mediation* is merely 'assisted negotiation.' Others put it nearly the opposite way: *conciliation* involves a third party's trying to bring together disputing parties to help them reconcile their differences, whereas *mediation* goes further by allowing the third party to suggest terms on which the dispute might be resolved. Still others reject these attempts at differentiation and contend that there is no consensus about what the two words mean — that they are generally interchangeable. Though a distinction would be convenient, those who argue that usage indicates a broad synonymy are most accurate." Bryan A. Garner, *Garner's Dictionary of Legal Usage* 570 (3d ed. 2011).

▸ **evaluative mediation.** (1982) Mediation in which the mediator may direct the parties' thinking and communications to some extent by evaluating the merits, strengths, and weaknesses of each party's position.

▸ **facilitative mediation.** (1986) Mediation in which the mediator helps the parties communicate and negotiate but does not offer advice or comments on the merits or otherwise intervene in the dispute.

Mediation and Conciliation Service. A federal agency that tries to prevent the interruption of commerce resulting from labor disputes, by assisting parties in settling their disputes through mediation and conciliation. • The agency can intervene on its own motion or on the motion of a party to the dispute. — Also termed *Federal Mediation and Conciliation Service.* 29 USCA §§ 172–173.

mediation–arbitration. An alternative-dispute-resolution process in which the parties first attempt to reach an agreement with the assistance of a mediator, and proceed to binding arbitration if they cannot.

mediator (**mee**-dee-ay-tər), *n.* (14c) A neutral person who tries to help disputing parties reach an agreement. Cf. ARBITRATOR.

mediators of questions. (18c) *Hist.* Six persons authorized by 27 Edw. 3, St. 2, ch. 24 to settle disputes between merchants.

Medicaid. (1966) A cooperative federal–state program that pays for medical expenses for qualifying individuals who cannot afford private medical services. • The program is authorized under the Social Security Act. — Also termed *Medical Assistance*; (in California) *MediCal.* Cf. MEDICARE.

Medicaid fraud. See *healthcare fraud* under FRAUD.

Medicaid-qualifying trust. See TRUST (3).

MediCal. See MEDICAID.

medical abandonment. See ABANDONMENT (2).

medical abuse. See ABUSE.

Medical Assistance. See MEDICAID.

medical directive. See ADVANCE DIRECTIVE (2).

medical-emergency exception. (1975) *Criminal law.* The principle that a police officer does not need a warrant to enter a person's home if the entrance is made to render aid to someone whom the officer reasonably believes to be in need of immediate assistance.

medical evidence. See EVIDENCE.

medical examination. An inspection of or investigation into the state of a person's health, or of part of the body, often involving the testing of fluids, tissues, and motor responses, as well as the gathering of information about lifestyle and health history.

▸ **independent medical examination.** (1910) A medical examination made by an impartial healthcare professional, usu. a physician. — Abbr. IME.

medical examiner. (1820) A public official who investigates deaths, conducts autopsies, and helps the state prosecute homicide cases. • Medical examiners have replaced coroners in many states. — Sometimes shortened to *examiner.* See CORONER.

medical expense. See EXPENSE.

medical-expense reimbursement plan. See EMPLOYEE BENEFIT PLAN.

medical history. See MEDICAL RECORDS.

medical jurisprudence. See FORENSIC MEDICINE.

medical lien. See *healthcare lien* under LIEN.

medically necessary abortion. See ABORTION.

medical malpractice. See MALPRACTICE.

medical neglect. See NEGLECT.

medical parole. See PAROLE.

medical privilege. See PRIVILEGE (3).

medical probability. See REASONABLE MEDICAL PROBABILITY.

medical records. (1905) The documents that compose a medical patient's healthcare history. — Also termed *medical history.*

medicals. See *medical expense* (2) under EXPENSE.

medical statement. (1897) A written declaration about some aspect of a person's health, whether by the declarant or by a healthcare professional.

Medicare. (1953) A federal program — established under the Social Security Act — that provides health insurance for the elderly and the disabled. Cf. MEDICAID; MEDIGAP INSURANCE.

> "The Medicare Program is really three programs, Parts A, B, and C. Part A, the Hospital Insurance program, covers inpatient hospital, skilled nursing, home health, and hospice services. . . . Part B (Supplemental Medical Insurance) benefits help pay for physician's services, outpatient hospital services, renal dialysis, speech and physical therapy, ambulatory surgery, home health services, durable medical equipment, rural health clinic services, comprehensive outpatient rehabilitation facility services, and some diagnostic tests. . . . Part C, the Medicare + Choice managed care program, was established by the Balanced Budget Act of 1997. Under the Medicare + Choice program, Medicare contracts with a wide variety of prepaid health plans on a risk basis to provide care to its beneficiaries." Barry R. Furrow et al., *Health Law* § 11-1, at 538 (2d ed. 2000).

Medicare fraud. See *healthcare fraud* under FRAUD.

medication abortion. See ABORTION.

medicine. 1. A substance possessing or thought by professionals to possess curative or remedial properties; a preparation used in treating disease or other illness. **2.** The scientific study and practice of preserving health and treating disease or injury; the science and art of preventing, curing, and alleviating sickness or affliction; HEALTHCARE.

medicolegal (med-i-koh-**lee**-gəl), *adj.* (1835) Involving the application of medical science to law <the coroner's medicolegal functions>. See FORENSIC MEDICINE.

medietas linguae (mi-**dɪ**-ə-tas **ling**-gwee), *n.* [Law Latin] (17c) *Hist.* Half-tongue. • The term was applied to a jury equally divided between natives and aliens. See DE MEDIETATE LINGUAE.

mediety. See MOIETY (1).

medigap insurance. (1975) *Slang.* A private insurance policy for Medicare patients to cover costs not covered by Medicare. Cf. MEDICARE.

medio. See DE MEDIO.

medio tempore (**mee**-dee-oh **tem**-pə-ree). [Latin] *Hist.* In the meantime.

meditatio fugae (med-i-**tay**-shee-oh **fyoo**-jee). [Latin] (17c) *Scots law.* The intention of absconding.

> "When a creditor is in circumstances to make oath or affirmation that his debtor, whether native or foreigner, is *in meditatione fugae*, in order to avoid the payment of his debt, or where he has reasonable ground for apprehending that the debtor has such an intention, it is competent for the creditor to apply to a magistrate, who, on inquiring into the circumstances, and finding reason to believe that the creditor's application is well founded, will grant a warrant for apprehending the debtor for examination; and may afterwards grant warrant to imprison him until he find caution *judicio sisti.*" William Bell, *Bell's Dictionary and Digest of the Law of Scotland* 711–12 (George Watson ed., 7th ed. 1890).

medium concludendi (**mee**-dee-əm kon-kloo-**den**-dɪ). [Law Latin] (17c) *Hist.* The ground of action; the cause of action.

medium filum. See *filum aquae* under FILUM.

medium impedimentum (**mee**-dee-əm im-ped-ə-**men**-təm). [Law Latin "a mid-impediment"] (17c) *Hist.* An intervening circumstance that prevents a second event from occurring as a result of the first one.

medium-neutral citation. See CITATION (3).

medium of exchange. (18c) Anything generally accepted as payment in a transaction and recognized as a standard of value <money is a medium of exchange>. Cf. EXCHANGE (2); CURRENCY; LEGAL TENDER.

medium-security prison. See PRISON.

medium tempus (**mee**-dee-əm **tem**-pəs). [Latin "intermediate period"] *Hist.* See *mesne profits* under PROFIT (1).

medium work. See WORK (1).

medletum (med-**lee**-təm), *n.* [Law Latin fr. French *mesler* "to mingle"] *Hist.* **1.** A mixing together of something. **2.** An affray or sudden encounter; a melee. **3.** Interference in a business matter.

medley (**med**-lee). (14c) A sudden or casual instance of fighting; AFFRAY. Cf. CHANCE-MEDLEY.

med. mal. See *medical malpractice* under MALPRACTICE.

meer dreit (meer drayt *or* dreet). See MERE RIGHT.

meeting, *n.* (14c) *Parliamentary law.* A single official gathering of people to discuss or act on matters in which they have a common interest; esp., the convening of a deliberative assembly to transact business. • A deliberative assembly's meeting begins with a call to order and continues (aside from recesses) until the assembly adjourns. See *call to order* under CALL (1); ADJOURN; RECESS (2). Cf. SESSION. — **meet,** *vb.*

> "The distinction should be noted between the *assembly* (that is, the body of people who assemble) and the *meeting* (which is the event of their being assembled to transact business)." Henry M. Robert, *Robert's Rules of Order Newly Revised* § 1, at 2 (10th ed. 2000).

▸ **adjourned meeting.** (18c) **1.** A meeting that continues the session of a regular or special meeting. —Also termed *adjournment.* See *continued meeting.* **2.** A meeting that has adjourned. • These two senses are opposite in meaning, so the term "continued meeting" is preferable for sense 1.

▸ **annual meeting.** (17c) A yearly meeting to elect or install officers or directors and to conduct other routine organizational business as prescribed in bylaws. • An organization's governing documents usu. specify the time and place of such a meeting.

▸ **business meeting.** (1838) A formal meeting called for considering business, as opposed to a purely educational or social event. • A business meeting may fall within a program that also includes social and informational events. See PROGRAM (1).

▸ **called meeting.** See *special meeting.*

▸ **continued meeting.** (1830) A meeting that is part of a session that will be or has been resumed after an adjournment (sometimes called a *recess*, although technically a recess is a break within a single meeting); *adjourned meeting* (1). • This terms is sometimes used in an attempt to avoid confusion about the term *adjourned meeting.*" See RECESS (2).

▸ **creditors' meeting.** (1874) *Bankruptcy.* The first meeting of a debtor's creditors and equity security holders, presided over by the U.S. Trustee and at which a bankruptcy trustee may be elected and the debtor may be examined under oath. 11 USCA § 341. — Also termed *meeting of creditors; 341 meeting; first meeting of creditors.*

▸ **extraordinary general meeting.** A special meeting of an organization's members or a company's shareholders, usu. on short notice, to discuss and resolve an urgent matter. — Abbr. EGM.

▸ **general meeting.** See *regular meeting.*

▸ **mass meeting.** (18c) A meeting of an unorganized body called to discuss a particular issue or to organize for a particular purpose and usu. open to anyone interested in that issue or purpose.

▸ **organizational meeting.** (1935) **1.** A mass meeting that establishes a permanent or ongoing organization. **2.** A meeting that begins an ongoing organization's proceedings under its regular order, such as adopting governing documents and electing officers, usu. following a mass meeting and an interval when the organization operates under provisional officers while its governing documents are drafted. • If the organizational meeting is for a corporation and the articles of incorporation name the initial directors, the directors hold the meeting. Otherwise, the incorporator holds the meeting. **3.** The first meeting after a dissolution, at which a newly reconstituted deliberative assembly — such as a legislative body or a convention whose members are assuming the seats to which they have been elected or re-elected for a new term — elects officers, adopts rules, and otherwise organizes for the new session.

▸ **premeeting meeting.** A private gathering of decision-makers held before a public meeting to discuss business to be decided at the public meeting. • Premeeting meetings generally violate open-meetings laws, especially if the public is not allowed to attend or if the informal meetings are held routinely.

▸ **regular meeting.** (18c) A periodic meeting held at a time set in an organization's governing documents or under a standing rule or schedule that the deliberative assembly has adopted. — Also termed *stated meeting; general meeting.* Cf. *special meeting.*

▸ **special meeting.** (18c) A meeting that is not a regular meeting; a meeting called for a particular purpose, usu. between regular meetings, as authorized by statute or bylaw. — Also termed *called meeting.* Cf. *regular meeting.*

▸ **stated meeting.** See *regular meeting.*

▸ **telephone meeting.** A public meeting in which some or all of the officials are not physically present but take part by electronic communications such as telephone, closed-circuit television, or Internet text, audio, or audiovisual means. — Also termed *telephonic meeting, telemeeting, teleconference.*

▸ **341 meeting.** See *creditors' meeting.*

meeting-competition defense. (1961) *Antitrust.* A defense to a charge of price discrimination whereby the defendant shows that the lower price was a good-faith attempt to match what it believed to be a competitor's equally low offer.

meeting of creditors. See *creditors' meeting* under MEETING.

meeting of the minds. (1830) *Contracts.* Actual assent by both parties to the formation of a contract, meaning that they agree on the same terms, conditions, and subject matter. • Although a meeting of the minds was required under the traditional subjective theory of assent, modern contract doctrine requires only objective manifestations of assent. — Also termed *mutuality of assent; aggregatio mentium; assensio mentium.* See *mutual assent* under ASSENT.

megalitigation. See LITIGATION.

megalopolis (meg-ə-**lop**-ə-lis). (1828) A heavily populated, continuous urban area that is one vast city or composed of several cities and towns.

Megan's law (**meg**-ənz *or* **may**-gənz). (1994) A statute that requires sex offenders who are released from prison to register with a local board and that provides the means to disseminate information about the registrants to the community where they live. • Although many of these statutes were enacted in the late 1980s, they took their popular name from Megan Kanka of New Jersey, a seven-year-old who in 1994 was raped and murdered by a twice-convicted sex offender who lived across the street from her house. All states have these laws, but only some require community notification (as by publishing offenders' pictures in local newspapers); in others, people must call a state hotline or submit names of persons they suspect. The federal version of Megan's law may be found at 42 USCA § 14071. — Also termed *registration and community-notification law; community-notification law.*

meigne (mayn), *n.* [Law French] *Hist.* See MEINY.

meindre age (**min**-dər **ayj** *or* **azh**), *n.* [Law French] *Hist.* Lesser age; minority. See MINORITY (1).

meiny (**may**-nee), *n.* [Law French] (13c) *Hist.* A family, esp. a royal household. — Also spelled *meine; meinie; meigne.*

melior (**mee**-lee-ər), *adj.* [Latin] Better; the better, as in *melior res* ("the better thing or chattel").

meliorating waste. See AMELIORATING WASTE.

meliorations (meel-yə-**ray**-shənz). (17c) **1.** *Scots law.* Improvements — other than repairs — made to an estate by a tenant or liferenter. • The cost of meliorations is not recoverable from the landlord or fiar. **2.** Lasting improvements.

melioribus damnis. See DE MELIORIBUS DAMNIS.

melius inquirendum (**mee**-lee-əs in-kwə-**ren**-dəm), *n.* [Law Latin "to be better inquired into"] (16c) *Hist.* A writ ordering the escheator to investigate a matter further, as by inquiring who is the next heir of a party who died seised of lands.

Melson formula. (1979) *Family law.* A method of calculating a noncustodial parent's child-support obligation to ensure that (1) neither parent falls below the poverty level in meeting child-support obligations, and (2) a child of a wealthier noncustodial parent shares in that parent's higher standard of living. • Named for Judge Elwood F. Melson of Delaware Family Court, the formula has been adopted in several states, such as Delaware, Hawaii, Montana, and West Virginia. The formula works as follows. A self-support reserve is first deducted from the parent-obligor's net income. Next, a primary support amount per child is calculated at an established subsistence level, added to actual work-related child-care expenses, and allocated between the parents. After deducting the support obligor's self-support reserve and pro rata share of the child's adjusted primary support amount, a percentage of the obligor's remaining income is allocated to additional child support as a cost-of-living adjustment. Total child support is determined by adding together the noncustodial parent's share of primary support and the standard-of-living allowance.

member. (14c) **1.** *Parliamentary law.* One of the individuals of whom an organization or a deliberative assembly consists, and who enjoys the full rights of participating in the organization — including the rights of making, debating, and voting on motions — except to the extent that the organization reserves those rights to certain classes of membership.

▸ **charter member.** (1887) A member who was a member when the charter was granted or adopted; a founder.

▸ **full member.** See *voting member.*

▸ **informational member.** See *nonvoting member.*

▸ **limited member.** See *nonvoting member.*

▸ **member ex officio.** (18c) A member who serves on a board or committee by virtue of holding an office, and whose membership will therefore pass with the office to his or her successor. — Also termed *ex officio member.* See EX OFFICIO.

▸ **nonvoting member.** (1881) A member whose rights do not include the right of voting on the organization's or assembly's business. — Also termed *informational member; limited member.*

▸ **voting member.** (1847) A fully enfranchised member, as distinguished from a nonvoting member. — Also termed *full member.*

2. *Military law.* A person assigned to a court-martial to determine guilt and punishment. **3.** *English law.* A district or section; an outlying part of a parish, port, estate, or manor. **4.** A limb or other functional organ of an animal body, such as an arm or leg.

member bank. See BANK.

member corporation. See MEMBER FIRM.

member firm. (1936) *Securities.* A brokerage firm with at least one director, officer, or general partner who holds a seat in an organized securities exchange. — Also termed (if organized as a corporation) *member corporation.*

member of a crew. See SEAMAN.

member of Congress. (18c) An elected official who sits in either the U.S. Senate or the House of Representatives. • The official may be appointed to fill an unexpired term. — Abbr. MC.

member of Parliament. (17c) A person with the right to sit in one of the two houses of Parliament. — Abbr. MP.

membership committee. See COMMITTEE (1).

members' scheme of arrangement. See SCHEME OF ARRANGEMENT.

members' voluntary winding up. See *voluntary winding up* under WINDING UP.

membrana (mem-**bray**-nə), *n.* [Latin "parchment"] *Hist.* **1.** A skin of parchment. **2.** A notebook of leaves of parchment. • The English rolls were made of several types of parchment and the term *membrana* was used in referring to them.

membrum (**mem**-brəm), *n.* [Latin "limb"] A division of something, esp. a slip or small piece of land.

memdispo (**mem**-dis-poh). *Slang.* See *memorandum opinion* under OPINION (1).

memorandum. (15c) **1.** An informal written note or record outlining the terms of a transaction or contract <the memorandum indicated the developer's intent to buy the property at its appraised value>. • To satisfy the statute of frauds, a memorandum can be written in any form, but it must (1) identify the parties to the contract, (2) indicate the contract's subject matter, (3) contain the contract's essential terms, and (4) contain the signature of the party against whom enforcement is sought. — Also termed *memorandum bill; memorial; note.* See STATUTE OF FRAUDS. **2.** A party's written statement of its legal arguments presented to the court, usu. in the form of a brief <memorandum of law>.

▸ **analytical memorandum.** See *research memorandum.*

▸ **closed memorandum.** (1978) A memorandum prepared by a law student using only given facts and the materials, usu. a collection of cases, in a packet provided to the student. — Also termed *closed memo; closed-universe memo.*

▸ **open memorandum.** (1978) A memorandum prepared by a law student based on a given set of facts and using any available resources for research. — Also termed *open memo.*

▸ **persuasive memorandum.** A memorandum written to sway the reader to accept the writer's position on a stated problem.

▸ **research memorandum.** (1937) A memorandum whose purpose is analyze a legal issue and inform the reader about possible approaches and outcomes. • This type of memorandum is usu. an in-house document. — Also termed *analytical memorandum.*

3. An informal written communication used esp. in offices <the firm sent a memorandum reminding all lawyers to turn in their timesheets>. **4.** MEMORANDUM

CLAUSE. — Often shortened to *memo*. Pl. **memoranda, memorandums.**

memorandum articles. (1805) *Marine insurance.* Goods described in the memorandum clause. See MEMORANDUM CLAUSE.

memorandum check. See CHECK.

memorandum clause. (1840) A marine-insurance clause protecting underwriters from liability for injury to goods that are particularly perishable, or for minor damages. — Often shortened to *memorandum*.

> "This clause was first introduced into the English [marine-insurance] policies about the year 1749. Before that time the insurer was liable for every injury, however small, that happened to the thing insured. . . . The memorandum clause . . . usually declares that the enumerated articles, and any other articles that are perishable in their own nature, shall be free from average under a given rate, unless general, or the ship be stranded. In consequence of this exception, all small partial losses, however inconsiderable, are to be borne by a general average, provided they were incurred in a case proper for such an average . . . ." 3 James Kent, *Commentaries on American Law* *294–95 (George Comstock ed., 11th ed. 1866).

memorandum decision. See *memorandum opinion* under OPINION (1).

memorandum disposition. See *memorandum opinion* under OPINION (1).

memorandum in error. (2008) A document alleging a factual error, usu. accompanied by an affidavit of proof.

memorandum of alteration. (1843) *English law.* A patentee's disclaimer of certain rights — such as rights to part of an invention that is not new and useful — to avoid losing the whole patent. • Until the mid-19th century, if a single patent was granted for two inventions, one of which was not new and useful, the entire patent would be defective.

memorandum of association. (1856) *English law.* A legal document setting up a corporation — either with or without limited liability — and including the company's name, purpose, and duration. See ARTICLES OF INCORPORATION.

memorandum of intent. See LETTER OF INTENT.

memorandum of understanding. See LETTER OF INTENT. — Abbr. MOU.

memorandum opinion. See OPINION (1).

memorandum package. (1918) The goods sent from a consigner to a consignee.

memorandum sale. See SALE.

memorial, *n.* (17c) **1.** An abstract of a legal record, esp. a deed; MEMORANDUM (1). **2.** A written statement of facts presented to a legislature or executive as a petition.

memoriter (mə-**mor**-ə-tər), *adv.* [Latin "with an accurate memory"] From memory; by recollection. • *Memoriter* proof of a written instrument is furnished by the recollection of a witness who knew the instrument.

memory corruption. (1989) The alteration, esp. when subconscious, of an individual's memory over time. • Memory is subject to considerable change over time, including (1) the loss of details or modification of memory so as to make it consistent with underlying knowledge; (2) changes in the content of memory based on exposure to postevent information before or during questioning; and even (3) the creation of firsthand memories when someone only reads about the event or discusses it with others. Memory is based on perception, which is an interpretive process taking into account an individual's "experience, learning, preferences, biases, and expectations." Sensory overload can occur when a person is bombarded with too much information in too short a time. Because of our ability to process only a small fraction of incoming data, even in conditions good for observation, we focus only on certain stimuli. Further, people are poor perceivers of duration, time, speed, distance, height, and weight. The issue of memory corruption is therefore often an issue in the accuracy of eyewitness identification. See EYEWITNESS IDENTIFICATION.

menacing, *n.* (14c) An attempt to commit common-law assault. • The term is used esp. in jurisdictions that have defined assault to include battery. See ASSAULT.

mendacity (men-**das**-ə-tee), *n.* (16c) **1.** The quality of being untruthful. **2.** A lie; falsehood. **3.** The habitual use of deceit, falsehood, or, misdirection. See FALSEHOOD (2). Cf. PERJURY. — **mendacious** (men-**day**-shəs), *adj.*

mendicatorie (men-di-kə-**tor**-ee-ee). [Law Latin] *Hist.* As a supplicant or beggar.

mend-the-hold doctrine. (1990) The principle that a nonperforming party's defense in a breach-of-contract action must be raised before the close of evidence. • A minority of courts limit a defendant to the first defense raised after litigation begins, unless the defendant can show a good-faith basis for a new defense. Most courts allow the defendant to raise several defenses as long as each defense is based on the reason given for nonperformance when the breach occurred. The term comes from 19-century wrestling jargon, "mend the hold" meaning "get a better grip on your opponent."

men of straw. *Hist.* False witnesses who wandered around courts and were paid to give untrue testimony. • They stuffed straw into their shoes so that advocates could recognize them. See STRAW MAN (4).

mens (menz), *n.* [Latin] Mind; intention; will.

mensa. See MANAGIUM.

mensa et thoro (**men**-sə et **thor**-oh). [Latin] (18c) Bed and board. See A MENSA ET THORO; *divorce a mensa et thoro* under DIVORCE.

mensalia (men-**say**-lee-ə), *n.* [fr. Latin *mensa* "a table"] *Hist.* Parsonages; spiritual livings. — Also termed *mensal benefices.*

mensis (**men**-sis), *n.* [Latin] *Roman law.* A month.

mens legis (menz **lee**-jis). [Latin "the mind of the law"] (1933) The spirit or purpose of a law.

mens legislatoris (menz lej-is-lə-**tor**-is). [Latin "the intention of the lawmaker"] (1943) Legislative intent.

mensor (**men**-sor), *n.* [fr. Latin *metiri* "to measure"] *Roman law.* A measurer of land; a surveyor.

mens rea (menz **ray**-ə). [Law Latin "guilty mind"] (18c) The state of mind that the prosecution, to secure a conviction, must prove that a defendant had when committing a crime <the mens rea for theft is the intent to deprive the rightful owner of the property>. • Mens rea is the second of two essential elements of every crime at common law, the other being the actus reus. Under the Model Penal

Code, the required levels of mens rea — expressed by the adverbs *purposely, knowingly, recklessly,* and *negligently* — are termed "culpability requirements." — Also termed *mental element; criminal intent; guilty mind.* See CULPABILITY; PURPOSELY; RECKLESSLY. Cf. ACTUS REUS. Pl. ***mentes reae*** (**men**-teez **ree**-ee).

> "Most English lawyers would however now agree with Sir James Fitzjames Stephen that the expression *mens rea* is unfortunate, though too firmly established to be expelled, just because it misleadingly suggests that, in general, moral culpability is essential to a crime, and they would assent to the criticism expressed by a later judge that the true translation of *mens rea* is 'an intention to do the act which is made penal by statute or by the common law.' [*Allard v. Selfridge,* (1925) 1 K.B. at 137]." H.L.A. Hart, "Legal Responsibility and Excuses," in *Punishment and Responsibility* 28, 36 (1968).

> "Some years ago the mens-rea doctrine was criticized on the ground that the Latin phrase is 'misleading.' If the words 'mens rea' were to be regarded as self-explanatory they would be open to this objection, but they are to be considered merely as a convenient label which may be attached to any psychical fact sufficient for criminal guilt (in connection with socially harmful conduct). This includes a field too complex for any brief self-explanatory phrase, and since it is important to have some sort of dialectic shorthand to express the idea, this time-honored label will do as well as any." Rollin M. Perkins & Ronald N. Boyce, *Criminal Law* 826–27 (3d ed. 1982).

> "For a phrase so central to criminal law, 'mens rea' suffers from a surprising degree of confusion in its meaning. One source of confusion arises from the two distinct ways in which the phrase is used, in a broad sense and in a narrow sense. In its broad sense, 'mens rea' is synonymous with a person's blameworthiness, or more precisely, those conditions that make a person's violation sufficiently blameworthy to merit the condemnation of criminal conviction. In this broad sense, the phrase includes all criminal law doctrines of blameworthiness — mental requirements of an offense as well as excuse defenses such as insanity, immaturity, and duress, to name a few. This was a frequent usage of 'mens rea' at common law. It remains common among nonlegal disciplines such as philosophy and psychology, perhaps because it captures in a single phrase criminal law's focus on personal culpability. The modern meaning of mens rea, and the one common in legal usage today, is more narrow: Mens rea describes the state of mind or inattention that, together with its accompanying conduct, the criminal law defines as an offense. In more technical terms, the mens rea of an offense consists of those elements of the offense definition that describe the required mental state of the defendant at the time of the offense, but does not include excuse defenses or other doctrines outside the offense definition. To help distinguish this more narrow conception from the broader, the Model Penal Code drafters substitute the term 'culpability' for 'mens rea.' Thus, Model Penal Code section 2.02, governing the Code's offense mental states, is titled 'General Requirements of Culpability' and subsection (2), defining the offense mental elements employed by the Code, is titled 'Kinds of Culpability.' Unfortunately, the term 'culpability' has come to suffer some of the same confusion between broad and narrow meanings as the term 'mens rea.' While most frequently used in its narrow sense, as interchangeable with 'blameworthiness,' the meaning of both 'mens rea' and 'culpability' must often be determined from their context." Paul H. Robinson, "Mens Rea," in *Encyclopedia of Crime & Justice* 995, 995–96 (Joshua Dressler ed., 2d ed. 2002).

mens rea canon. The doctrine that a statute creating a criminal offense whose elements are similar to those of a common-law crime will be presumed to require a culpable state of mind (mens rea) in its commission.

mens rea defense. See *state-of-mind defense* under DEFENSE (1).

mensularius (men-sə-**lair**-ee-əs), *n.* [fr. Latin *mensa* "a table"] *Roman law.* A dealer in money; a moneychanger; a banker.

mensura (men-**s[y]oor**-ə), *n.* [Latin] *Hist.* A measure.

mensura domini regis (men-**s[y]oor**-ə **dom**-ə-nɪ **ree**-jis). [Law Latin "the measure of our lord the king"] (18c) *Hist.* The standard weights and measures established under Richard I, in his Parliament at Westminster in 1197.

> "Thus, under king Richard I, in his parliament holden at Westminster, A.D. 1197, it was ordained that there shall be only one weight and one measure throughout the kingdom, and that the custody of the assise or standard of weights and measures shall be committed to certain persons in every city and borough . . . . In king John's time this ordinance of king Richard was frequently dispensed with for money which occasioned a provision to be made for enforcing it . . . . These original standards were called *pondus regis,* and *mensura domini regis;* and are directed by a variety of subsequent statutes to be kept in the exchequer, and all weights and measures to be made conformable thereto." 1 William Blackstone, *Commentaries on the Laws of England* 265–66 (1765).

mental abuse. See *emotional abuse* under ABUSE.

mental anguish. See *emotional distress* under DISTRESS (4).

mental capacity. See CAPACITY (3).

mental cruelty. See CRUELTY.

mental defective, *n.* Someone who, as a result of marked intellectual disability, or mental illness, incompetency, condition, or disease, is a danger to self or to others, or lacks the mental capacity to contract or manage his or her own affairs. *See* 27 CFR § 478.11. — Sometimes shortened to *defective* (considered a callous, derogatory usage). See DEFECTIVE (3).

mental disease. See MENTAL ILLNESS (2).

mental disorder. See MENTAL ILLNESS (1).

mental distress. See *emotional distress* under DISTRESS (4).

mental disturbance. See EXTREME MENTAL OR EMOTIONAL DISTURBANCE.

mental dysfunction. See MENTAL ILLNESS (1).

mental element. See MENS REA.

mental evaluation. 1. See INDEPENDENT MENTAL EVALUATION. **2.** See *mental examination* under EXAMINATION (8).

mental examination. See EXAMINATION (8).

mental harm. (1889) Any impairment of the functioning of a person's mind, esp. when the impairment has resulted from something external, such as an injury.

▸ **consequential mental harm.** Mental harm resulting from physical personal injury.

mental-hygiene arrest. See ARREST (2).

mental illness. (1847) **1.** A disorder in thought or mood so substantial that it impairs judgment, behavior, perceptions of reality, or the ability to cope with the ordinary demands of life. — Also termed *mental disorder; mental dysfunction.* **2.** Mental disease that is severe enough to necessitate care and treatment for the afflicted person's own welfare or the welfare of others in the community. — Abbr. MI. — Also termed *mental disease.*

mental impairment. (1850) **1.** A mental or psychological disability, such as an intellectual disability, emotional or mental illness, organic brain syndrome, or specific learning disability. **2.** *English law.* The state of arrested or incomplete mental development, including significant impairment of intelligence and social functioning, and abnormally aggressive or seriously irresponsible behavior.

mental incompetence. See INCOMPETENCY.

mental infirmity. (18c) Intellectual and memory impairment due to disease, usu. associated with old age.

mentally disordered person. (1913) A person whose behavior is irrational and presents a danger of serious physical harm to the person or to others.

mental-process privilege. See *deliberative-process privilege* (1) under PRIVILEGE (1).

mental reservation. (17c) One party's silent understanding or exception to the meaning of a contractual provision.

mental retardation. Congenital below-average intellectual ability thought to equate to an IQ of 70 or under, marked by significant deficits in cognitive functioning, abnormal development, and social maladjustment. — Abbr. MR. — Also termed *intellectual disability.*

mental shock. See SHOCK.

mental state. (18c) **1.** The condition of a person's mental health or capacity, as determined by an expert who examines the person. **2.** The condition of a person's mind based on thoughts and feelings.

▸ **culpable mental state.** (1934) Having the state of mind to act intentionally, knowingly, recklessly, or with criminal negligence.

mental suffering. See *emotional distress* under DISTRESS (4).

mente captus (**men**-tee **kap**-təs). [Latin "captured in mind"] (16c) Persons who are habitually insane.

mentes reae (**men**-teez **ree**-ee). *pl.* (1932) MENS REA.

mentiri (men-**tɪ**-rɪ), *vb.* [Latin] To lie.

mentition (men-**tish**-ən), *n.* [fr. Latin *mentitio* "lying"] (17c) The act of lying.

mentor judge. See JUDGE.

MEPA. *abbr.* MULTIETHNIC-PLACEMENT ACT OF 1994.

mera facta quae in meris faciendi finibus consistunt (**meer**-ə **fak**-tə kwee in **meer**-is fay-shee-**en**-dɪ **fin**-ə-bəs kən-**sis**-tənt). [Latin] *Hist.* Mere acts consisting in bare performance.

mera noctis (**meer**-ə **nok**-tis), *n.* [Latin "middle of the night"] Midnight.

mercantile (**mər**-kən-teel *or* -tɪl *or* -til), *adj.* (17c) Of, relating to, or involving merchants or trading; commercial <the mercantile system>.

mercantile agency. See CREDIT BUREAU.

mercantile agent. See AGENT; FACTOR (3).

mercantile law. See COMMERCIAL LAW (1).

Mercantile Law Amendment Acts. The Mercantile Law Amendment Act of 1856 (19 & 20 Vict., chs. 60, 97) and the Mercantile Law Amendment Act (Scotland) of 1856, passed primarily to reconcile parts of the mercantile laws of England, Scotland, and Ireland.

mercantile paper. See *commercial paper* (1) under PAPER.

mercative (mər-**kay**-tiv), *adj.* [fr. Latin *mercatum* "a market"] (17c) *Scots law.* Belonging to trade.

mercatum (mər-**kay**-təm), *n.* [Law Latin] A market; a contract of sale; a bargain.

mercedary (mər-sə-**der**-ee), *n.* [Latin] (17c) An employer; one who hires.

mercenarius (mər-sə-**nair**-ee-əs), *n.* [Latin] **1.** An employee; a servant. **2.** A soldier of fortune. — Also spelled *mercennarius.*

mercenary (**mər**-sə-ner-ee). (14c) *Int'l law.* A professional soldier hired by someone other than his or her own government to fight in a foreign country.

mercenlage (**mər**-sən-law). [fr. Saxon *myrcnalag*] (17c) *English law.* The law of the Mercians. • This was one of the three principal legal systems prevailing in England at the beginning of the 11th century. It was observed in many midland counties and those bordering on Wales. — Also spelled *merchenlage* (**mər**-shən-law). — Also termed *lex merciorum* (**leks** mər-shee-**or**-əm); *Mercian law* (**mər**-shee-ən *or* **mər**-shən). See DANELAW; WEST SAXON LAW.

> "[A]bout the beginning of the eleventh century there were three principal systems of laws prevailing in different districts . . . . The *Mercen-Lage*, or Mercian laws, which were observed in many of the midland counties, and those bordering on the principality of Wales; the retreat of the ancient Britons; and therefore very probably intermixed with the British or Druidical customs." 1 William Blackstone, *Commentaries on the Laws of England* 65 (1765).

merces (**mər**-seez), *n.* [Latin] *Roman law.* **1.** An agreed payment for a thing or services specifically contracted for; rent, hire.

> "There must be consent, a thing let, and an agreed payment (*merces*) . . . . The *merces* must be certain and Justinian's texts say that, as in sale, it must be money. But there is not the same difficulty here, and Gaius does not state such a rule. It is possible that it did not exist in classical law and, even under Justinian, some cases cannot be reconciled with the rule. The rent of land might be in produce and even a fraction of the crop. This last conflicts with the rule of Gaius that it must be certain: it is held by some writers that the text is interpolated, by others that the relation was not really *locatio conductio*, but *societas* (partnership). The *merces* was not usually a lump sum: more often it was a series of periodical payments." W.W. Buckland, *A Manual of Roman Private Law* 289–90 (2d ed. 1939).

2. A reward, esp. for a gratuitous service. Cf. HONORARIUM.

> "A recompense paid for any kind of services, without a preceding agreement (e.g., for saving one's life) is also called *merces.*" Adolf Berger, *Encyclopedic Dictionary of Roman Law* 581 (1953).

merchandise (**mər**-chən-dɪz *also* -dɪs). (13c) **1.** In general, a movable object involved in trade or traffic; that which is passed from one person to another by purchase and sale. **2.** In particular, that which is dealt in by merchants; an article of trading or the class of objects in which trade is carried on by physical transfer; collectively, mercantile goods, wares or commodities, or any subjects of regular trade, animate as well as inanimate. • This definition generally excludes real estate, ships, intangibles such as software, and the like, and does not apply to money, stocks, bonds, notes, or other mere representatives or measures of actual commodities or values. — Also termed (in senses 1 & 2) *article of merchandise.* **3.** Purchase and sale; trade; traffic, dealing, or advantage from dealing.

merchandise broker. See BROKER.

Merchandise Marks Acts. *Hist.* An 1887 statute (50 & 51 Vict., ch. 28) making it a misdemeanor to fraudulently mark merchandise for sale or to sell merchandise so marked. • This statute was repealed in 1968.

merchant. (13c) One whose business is buying and selling goods for profit; esp., a person or entity that holds itself out as having expertise peculiar to the goods in which it deals and is therefore held by the law to a higher standard of expertise than that of a nonmerchant. • Because the term relates solely to goods, a supplier of services is not considered a merchant.

> "The definition of 'merchant' in [UCC] Section 2-104(1) identifies two separate but often interrelated criteria: Does the seller 'deal in goods' of that kind, or does the seller 'otherwise by his occupation' hold himself out as having special knowledge with respect to the goods? It should be emphasized that the drafters have placed these two criteria in the alternative by use of the word 'or.' Thus, the definition clearly catches all those who regularly sell inventory even though they may have no expertise regarding the particular product. This would include distributors, wholesalers, and retail dealers. Dealers who sell prepackaged goods containing a defect over which they have no control might be surprised to learn that they have given an implied warranty of merchantability with respect to the goods, but such is the law." Barkley Clark & Christopher Smith, *The Law of Product Warranties* § 5.02[1], at 5-25 (1984).

merchantable (**mər**-chənt-ə-bəl), *adj.* (15c) Fit for sale in the usual course of trade at the usual selling prices; MARKETABLE. — Also termed *salable.* See *implied warranty of merchantability* under WARRANTY (2). — **merchantability,** *n.*

merchantable quality. (18c) The character of goods that are fit for sale in the usual course of trade at the usual selling prices.

merchantable title. See *marketable title* under TITLE (2).

merchant appraiser. (1840) An expert appointed by a customs officer to reexamine and revalue imported goods for customs purposes. • The appraiser is usu. an experienced merchant who deals in or has dealt in goods of the character and quality of those at issue. An appraiser is appointed only when an importer requests one.

merchant bank. See BANK.

merchant exception. (1973) *Contracts.* In a sale of goods, an exemption from the statute of frauds whereby a contract between merchants is enforceable if, within a reasonable time after they reach an oral agreement, a written confirmation of the terms is sent, to which the recipient does not object within ten days of receiving it. • The only effect of failing to object to the written confirmation is that the recipient will be precluded from relying on the statute of frauds — or the lack of a formal, written agreement — as a defense to a breach-of-contract claim. The party seeking to enforce an agreement must still prove that an agreement was reached. UCC § 2-201.

merchant lessee. See LESSEE.

merchantman. (17c) *Archaic.* A vessel employed in foreign or interstate commerce or in the merchant service.

merchant marine. (18c) **1.** All of a country's ships that are used for trade, as opposed to military ships. **2.** All the personnel who work on a country's trade ships. **3.** Any one such person. — Also termed (in sense 3) *merchant mariner; merchant seaman.* — Also termed (in senses 1 & 2, esp. BrE) *merchant navy.*

merchant's accounts. (1835) Current, mutual accounts between merchants showing debits and credits for merchandise.

merchant's defense. (1972) The principle that a store owner will not be held liable for reasonably detaining a suspected shoplifter, to facilitate an investigation by a law-enforcement officer, if probable cause exists to suspect the detained person of wrongfully removing merchandise from the store.

merchant seaman. See SEAMAN.

merchant's firm offer. See *irrevocable offer* under OFFER.

Merchant Shipping Acts. English statutes to improve shipping conditions by, among other things, vesting the supervision of merchant shipping in the board of trade.

merchant's mark. (16c) *Hist.* A distinguishing mark that manufacturers or traders used to designate goods that they exclusively manufactured or sold. • The merchant's mark was a precursor to the modern trademark. — Also termed *maker's mark.* See TRADEMARK.

merchet (**mər**-chet). See MARCHET.

mercheta. See MARCHET.

merchetum. See MARCHET.

merciament (**mər**-see-ə-mənt). *Archaic.* See AMERCEMENT.

Mercian law. See MERCENLAGE.

Mercimoniatus Angliae (mər-sə-moh-nee-**ay**-təs **ang**-glee-ee). [Law Latin] (17c) *Hist.* English customs duties on merchandise brought into the country.

Mercosur. A common market of South American countries created to facilitate free trade among members. • The entity was created by the Treaty of Asunción in 1991. The charter countries were Argentina, Brazil, Paraguay, and Uruguay. — Also termed *Southern Common Market.*

mercy. (13c) Compassionate treatment, as of criminal offenders or of those in distress; esp., imprisonment, rather than death, imposed as punishment for capital murder. See CLEMENCY.

mercy killing. See EUTHANASIA.

mercy rule. (1981) *Evidence.* The principle that a defendant is entitled to offer character evidence as a defense to a criminal charge. • This type of evidence is often offered by the defendant's friends and relatives. Fed. R. Evid. 404(a)(1).

mere (mair *or* mer), *n.* [Law French] (13c) Mother, as in the phrase *en ventre sa mere* ("in its mother's womb").

mere-continuation doctrine. (1984) A principle under which a successor corporation will be held liable for the acts of a predecessor corporation, if only one corporation remains after the transfer of assets, and both corporations share an identity of stock, shareholders, and directors. — Also termed *continuity-of-entity doctrine.* Cf. SUBSTANTIAL-CONTINUITY DOCTRINE.

mere-evidence rule. (1962) *Criminal procedure.* The former doctrine that a search warrant allows seizure of the instrumentalities of the crime (such as a murder weapon) or the fruits of the crime (such as stolen goods), but does not permit the seizure of items that have evidentiary value only (such as incriminating documents). • The Supreme Court has abolished this rule, and today warrants may be issued to search for and seize all evidence of a crime.

Warden v. Hayden, 387 U.S. 294, 87 S.Ct. 1642 (1967); Fed. R. Crim. P. 41(b).

mere license. See *bare license* under LICENSE.

mere licensee. See *bare licensee* under LICENSEE.

mere motu. See EX MERE MOTU.

mere-presence defense. (1979) *Criminal law.* A criminal defendant's claim that his or her mere presence at the scene of a crime, without more, does not in itself constitute a crime. Cf. WIFFEM DEFENSE.

mere representation. See REPRESENTATION (1).

mere right. An abstract right in property, without possession or even the right of possession. — Also termed *jus merum; merum jus; meer dreit.*

> "The mere *right of property*, the *jus proprietatis*, without either possession or even the right of possession. This is frequently spoken of in our books under the name of the *mere right, jus merum*; and the estate of the owner is in such cases said to be totally devested, and *put to a right*. A person in this situation may have the true ultimate property of the lands in himself: but by the intervention of certain circumstances, either by his own negligence, the solemn act of his ancestor, or the determination of a court of justice, the presumptive evidence of that right is strongly in favour of his antagonist; who has thereby obtained the absolute right of possession . . . . The heir therefore in this case has only a *mere right*, and must be strictly held to the proof of it, in order to recover the lands." 2 William Blackstone, *Commentaries on the Laws of England* 197–98 (1766).

merestone (**meer**-stohn). (bef. 12c) *Archaic.* A stone that marks land boundaries. — Also spelled *mearstone.*

meretricious (mer-ə-**trish**-əs), *adj.* (17c) **1.** Involving prostitution <a meretricious encounter>. **2.** (Of a romantic relationship) involving either unlawful sexual connection or lack of capacity on the part of one party <a meretricious marriage>. **3.** Superficially attractive but fake nonetheless; alluring by false show <meretricious advertising claims>.

meretricious relationship. (1892) *Archaic.* A stable, marriage-like relationship in which the parties cohabit knowing that a lawful marriage between them does not exist.

mere volunteer. See VOLUNTEER (4).

mergee (mər-**jee**). (1955) A participant in a corporate merger.

merger. (18c) **1.** The act or an instance of combining or uniting. **2.** *Contracts.* The substitution of a superior form of contract for an inferior form, as when a written contract supersedes all oral agreements and prior understandings. See INTEGRATION (2).

> "Where two parties have made a simple contract for any purpose, and afterwards have entered into an identical engagement by deed, the simple contract is *merged* in the deed and becomes extinct. This extinction of a lesser in a higher security, like the extinction of a lesser in a greater interest in lands, is called *merger*." William R. Anson, *Principles of the Law of Contract* 85 (Arthur L. Corbin ed., 3d Am. ed. 1919).

3. *Contracts.* The replacement of a contractual duty or of a duty to compensate with a new duty between the same parties, based on different operative facts, for the same performance or for a performance differing only in liquidating a duty that was previously unliquidated. **4.** *Property.* The absorption of a lesser estate into a greater estate when both become the same person's property. — Also termed *merger of estates.* Cf. SURRENDER (3).

> "[I]t would be absurd to allow a person to have two distinct estates, immediately expectant on each other, while one of them includes the time of both . . . . There would be an absolute incompatibility in a person filling, at the same time, the characters of tenant and reversioner in one and the same estate; and hence the reasonableness, and even necessity, of the doctrine of merger." 3 James Kent, *Commentaries on American Law* *99 (George Comstock ed., 11th ed. 1866).

5. *Criminal law.* The absorption of a lesser included offense into a more serious offense when a person is charged with both crimes, so that the person is not subject to double jeopardy. • For example, a defendant cannot be convicted of both attempt (or solicitation) and the completed crime — though merger does not apply to conspiracy and the completed crime. — Also termed *merger of offenses; merger of charges.*

> "As a rule, at common law, where a person by the same act commits two crimes, one a felony and the other a misdemeanor, the misdemeanor merges in the felony; but if the crimes are of the same degree, both felonies or misdemeanors, there is no merger. In some states this doctrine has not been recognized, while in most states it has been abolished by statutes allowing conviction of a less offense than is charged in the indictment if it is included in the offense charged." William. L. Clark, *Handbook of Criminal Law* 43 (Francis B. Tiffany ed., 2d ed. 1902).

6. *Civil procedure.* The effect of a judgment for the plaintiff, which absorbs any claim that was the subject of the lawsuit into the judgment, so that the plaintiff's rights are confined to enforcing the judgment. Cf. BAR (5). **7.** The joining of the procedural aspects of law and equity. **8.** The absorption of one organization (esp. a corporation) that ceases to exist into another that retains its own name and identity and acquires the assets and liabilities of the former. • Corporate mergers must conform to statutory formalities and usu. must be approved by a majority of the outstanding shares. — Also termed *corporate merger.* Cf. CONSOLIDATION (5); BUYOUT.

▸ **bust-up merger.** (1991) A merger in which the acquiring corporation sells off lines of business owned by the target corporation to repay the loans used in the acquisition.

▸ **cash merger.** (1966) A merger in which shareholders of the target company must accept cash for their shares. — Also termed *cash-out merger; freeze-out merger.*

▸ **conglomerate merger.** (1953) A merger between unrelated businesses that are neither competitors nor customers or suppliers of each other.

> "A merger which is neither vertical nor horizontal is a conglomerate merger. A pure conglomerate merger is one in which there are no economic relationships between the acquiring and the acquired firm. Mixed conglomerate mergers involve horizontal or vertical relationships, such as the acquisition of a firm producing the same product as the acquirer but selling it in a different geographical market, which is not a horizontal merger because the merging companies are not competitors . . . ." 54 Am. Jur. 2d *Monopolies, Restraints of Trade, and Unfair Trade Practices* § 169, at 226 (1996).

▸ **de facto merger** (di **fak**-toh). (1973) A transaction that has the economic effect of a statutory merger but that is cast in the form of an acquisition or sale of assets or voting stock. • Although such a transaction does not meet the statutory requirements for a merger, a court will generally treat it as a statutory merger for purposes of the appraisal remedy.

▸ **downstream merger.** (1949) A merger of a parent corporation into its subsidiary.

▸ **forward triangular merger.** See *triangular merger.*

▸ **freeze-out merger.** See *cash merger.*

▸ **horizontal merger.** (1938) A merger between two or more businesses that are on the same market level because they manufacture similar products in the same geographic region; a merger of direct competitors. — Also termed *horizontal integration.*

▸ **product-extension merger.** (1964) A merger in which the products of the acquired company are complementary to those of the acquiring company and may be produced with similar facilities, marketed through the same channels, and advertised by the same media.

▸ **reverse triangular merger.** (1972) A merger in which the acquiring corporation's subsidiary is absorbed into the target corporation, which becomes a new subsidiary of the acquiring corporation. (FTM). — Abbr. RTM. — Also termed *reverse subsidiary merger.*

▸ **short-form merger.** (1938) A statutory merger that is less expensive and time-consuming than an ordinary statutory merger, usu. permitted when a subsidiary merges into a parent that already owns most of the subsidiary's shares. • Such a merger is generally accomplished when the parent adopts a merger resolution, mails a copy of the plan to the subsidiary's record shareholders, and files the executed articles of merger with the secretary of state, who issues a certificate of merger.

▸ **statutory merger.** (1933) A merger provided by and conducted according to statutory requirements.

▸ **stock merger.** (1961) A merger involving one company's purchase of another company's capital stock.

▸ **triangular merger.** (1969) A merger in which the target corporation is absorbed into the acquiring corporation's subsidiary, with the target's shareholders receiving stock in the parent corporation. — Abbr. TM. — Also termed *subsidiary merger; forward triangular merger* (FTM).

▸ **upstream merger.** (1959) A merger of a subsidiary corporation into its parent.

▸ **vertical merger.** (1942) A merger between businesses occupying different levels of operation for the same product, such as between a manufacturer and a retailer; a merger of buyer and seller.

9. The merger of rights and duties in the same person, resulting in the extinction of obligations; esp., the blending of the rights of a creditor and debtor, resulting in the extinguishment of the creditor's right to collect the debt. • As originally developed in Roman law, a merger resulted from the marriage of a debtor and creditor, or when a debtor became the creditor's heir. — Also termed *confusion; confusion of debts; confusion of rights.* Cf. CONFUSION OF TITLES. **10.** The absorption of a contract into a court order, so that an agreement between the parties (often a marital agreement incident to a divorce or separation) loses its separate identity as an enforceable contract when it is incorporated into a court order.

merger clause. See INTEGRATION CLAUSE.

merger doctrine. (1987) **1.** *Copyright.* The principle that since an idea cannot be copyrighted, neither can an expression that must inevitably be used in order to express the idea. • When the idea and expression are very difficult to separate, they are said to merge. For example, courts have refused copyright protection for business-ledger forms (*Baker v. Selden*, 101 U.S. 99 (1879)), and for contest rules that were copied almost verbatim (*Morrissey v. Procter & Gamble*, 379 F.2d 675 (1st Cir. 1967)). — Also termed *Baker v. Selden doctrine.* **2.** DEED-MERGER DOCTRINE. **3.** *Hist. Family law.* The common-law principle that, upon marriage, the husband and wife combined to form one legal entity. — Often shortened to *merger.* See SPOUSAL-UNITY DOCTRINE; LEGAL-UNITIES DOCTRINE.

merger guidelines. (1965) A set of rules promulgated and applied by the Antitrust Division of the U.S. Department of Justice and the Federal Trade Commission in examining and challenging proposed corporate mergers that could adversely affect the marketplace.

merger of charges. See MERGER (5).

merger of deed and contract. See DEED-MERGER DOCTRINE.

merger of estates. See MERGER (4).

merger of offenses. See MERGER (5).

meritorious (mer-ə-**tor**-ee-əs), *adj.* (15c) **1.** (Of an act, etc.) deserving of esteem or reward <meritorious trial performance>. **2.** (Of a case, etc.) worthy of legal victory; having enough legal value to prevail in a dispute <meritorious claim>.

meritorious consideration. See *good consideration* under CONSIDERATION (1).

meritorious defense. See DEFENSE (1).

merit-plan election. See MISSOURI PLAN.

merit regulation. (1958) Under state blue-sky laws, the practice of requiring securities offerings not only to be accompanied by a full and adequate disclosure but also to be substantively fair, just, and equitable.

merits. (18c) **1.** The elements or grounds of a claim or defense; the substantive considerations to be taken into account in deciding a case, as opposed to extraneous or technical points, esp. of procedure <trial on the merits>. **2.** EQUITY (3) <on questions of euthanasia, the Supreme Court has begun to concern itself with the merits as well as the law>.

merits brief. See *brief on the merits* under BRIEF (1).

merits discovery. See DISCOVERY.

merit selection. A method of choosing judges through the scrutiny and recommendation of a nonpartisan commission of lawyers and nonlawyers who identify, recruit, investigate, and evaluate applicants for judgeships and then submit names, usu. three, to the appointing authority, most often a governor. • Merit selection is intended to minimize political influence by eliminating the need for aspiring judges to raise money, advertise, and make campaign promises, all of which can weaken judicial independence and credibility. See JUDICIAL INDEPENDENCE. Cf. MISSOURI PLAN.

merits review. See *appeal de novo* under APPEAL.

merit system. (1879) The practice of hiring and promoting employees, esp. government employees, based on their competence rather than political favoritism. Cf. SPOILS SYSTEM.

Merit Systems Protection Board. The independent federal agency that oversees personnel practices of the federal government and hears and decides appeals from adverse personnel actions taken against federal employees. • It has five regional offices and five field offices. Its functions were transferred from the former Civil Service Commission under Reorganization Plan No. 2 of 1978. — Abbr. MSPB. See CIVIL SERVICE COMMISSION.

MERP. *abbr.* Medical-expense reimbursement plan. See EMPLOYEE BENEFIT PLAN.

Merrill Act. 1. An 1862 federal statute that provided for the maintenance of at least one college in each state, the chief object being instruction in the branches of learning related to agriculture and the mechanical arts, though other scientific and classical studies, as well as military studies, were not excluded. • For this purpose a federal grant was made of 30,000 acres of public land for each senator and representative, from the sale of which an endowment was to be invested. **2.** An 1890 federal statute providing for an annual appropriation (from the proceeds of selling public lands) to these colleges, the income to be applied only to facilities and instruction in agriculture, the mechanical arts, the English language, and other branches of knowledge relating directly to industrial life.

***Merrill* doctrine.** (1990) The principle that the government cannot be estopped from disavowing an agent's unauthorized act. *Federal Crop Ins. Corp. v. Merrill*, 332 U.S. 380, 68 S.Ct. 1 (1947).

merum (**meer**-əm). [Latin] *Hist.* Mere; naked.

merum jus (**meer**-əm **jəs**). See MERE RIGHT.

merx (mərks). [Latin] *Hist.* Trade articles; merchandise.

merx et pretium (**mərks** et **pree**-shee-əm). [Law Latin] *Roman & Scots law.* Goods and a price. • These components are two essential items for a sales contract.

mescreaunt (mes-kree-**awnt** *or* **mis**-kree-ənt). [Law French] *Hist.* MISCREANT. — Also spelled *mescroyant.*

mese (meez *or* mees), *n.* [Law French] (15c) *Hist.* A house. — Also spelled *mees*; *meas.*

mesnalty (**meen**-əl-tee), *n.* [fr. Law French and English mesne "middle"] (16c) *Hist.* **1.** The estate or manor held by a mesne lord. **2.** The right of the mesne; the tenure of the mesne lord. — Also spelled *mesnality.* See MESNE LORD.

mesne (meen), *adj.* (16c) **1.** Occupying a middle position; intermediate or intervening, esp. in time of occurrence or performance <the mesne encumbrance has priority over the third mortgage, but is subordinate to the first mortgage>. **2.** *Hist.* Of, relating to, or involving a lord who holds land of a superior while himself having a tenant.

mesne, writ of. See DE MEDIO.

mesne agreement. (1954) A transfer of intellectual-property rights through an intermediary, usu. an assignee, rather than directly from the property's creator.

mesne assignment. See ASSIGNMENT (2).

mesne conveyance. See CONVEYANCE (1).

mesne encumbrance. See ENCUMBRANCE.

mesne estate. See ESTATE (1).

mesne lord. (17c) *Hist.* A feudal lord who stood between a tenant and the chief lord, and held land from a superior lord. See LORD (3).

> "A person who, being himself a tenant, is lord of under tenants, is called a mesne lord. These under-tenures were constantly multiplying [in the Middle Ages], and not only tithes became complicated, but the interests of the superior lords were gravely affected." Frederick Pollock, *The Land Laws* 70 (3d ed. 1896).

mesne process. See PROCESS (2).

mesne profits. 1. See *mesne profit* under PROFIT. **2.** ACTION FOR MESNE PROFITS.

mesonomic (mes-ə-**nom**-ik *also* mee-zə), *adj.* (1927) Of, relating to, or involving an act that, although it does not affect a person's physical freedom, has legal consequences in its evolution. • This term was coined by the philosopher Albert Kocourek in his book *Jural Relations* (1927). Cf. ZYGNOMIC.

message. (14c) A written or oral communication, often sent through a messenger or other agent, or electronically (e.g., through e-mail or voicemail).

- ▸ **annual message.** A message from the President or a governor given at the opening of an annual legislative session.
- ▸ **Presidential message.** (1822) A communication from the President to the U.S. Congress on a matter relating to the state of the union, esp. one requiring legislative consideration. U.S. Const. art. II, § 3. — Also termed *State of the Union.*

> "Under the first two Presidents of the Republic it was the custom for the chief executive to meet the two houses of Congress in person, at the opening of each session, and address them upon the state of the Union, recommending at the same time such acts of legislation as he deemed important or necessary, and this custom was revived by President Wilson. But with this exception it has been the practice for the President to make all his communications to Congress, under this clause of the Constitution, in writing. An annual message is prepared by the President and delivered to Congress by his private secretary. And from time to time he sends to Congress special messages relating to particular topics of national interest, often accompanied by correspondence or other documents. It is also usual for Congress to request the President to communicate to it facts or papers in his possession or knowledge which bear upon any subject to which the attention of Congress is addressed, either by way of contemplated legislation or of investigation. These requests are always complied with, unless in the judgment of the executive the interests of the nation require that such facts or documents, or the dealings of the executive department with the subject in hand, should for the present be kept secret." Henry Campbell Black, *Handbook of American Constitutional Law* 137 (4th ed. 1927).

- ▸ **special message.** A message from the President or a governor relating to a particular matter.
- ▸ **veto message.** See VETO MESSAGE.

message from the Crown. (18c) An official communication from the sovereign to Parliament.

messarius (mə-**sair**-ee-əs), *n.* [fr. Latin *messis*] *Hist.* A chief servant; a bailiff; an overseer of the harvest.

messenger. (14c) **1.** Someone who conveys a communication; esp., one employed to deliver parcels or other communications. **2.** *Hist.* An officer who performs certain ministerial duties, such as taking temporary charge of assets of an insolvent estate.

messuage (**mes**-wij). (14c) A dwelling house together with the curtilage, including any outbuildings. See CURTILAGE.

meta (**mee**-tə), *n.* [Latin] (16c) **1.** *Roman law.* The mark where a racecourse ends or around which chariots turn; by extension, a limit in space or time. **2.** *Hist.* A boundary; a border.

metadata. (1970) Secondary data that organize, manage, and facilitate the use and understanding of primary data. • Metadata are evaluated when conducting and responding to electronic discovery. If privileged documents or final versions of computer files may contain metadata, they might be "scrubbed" before release. *See* Fed. R. Civ. P. 26(b)(2)(B).

metalaw (**met**-ə-law). (1956) A hypothetical set of legal principles based on the rules of existing legal systems and designed to provide a framework of agreement for these different systems.

> "[T]he Constitution controls the deployment of governmental power and defines the rules for how such power may be structured and applied. The Constitution, therefore, is not a body of rules about ordinary private actions, but a collection of rules about the rules and uses of law: in a word, *metalaw*." Laurence H. Tribe, *Constitutional Choices* 246 (1985).

metallum (mə-**tal**-əm), *n.* (18c) *Roman law.* **1.** Metal; a mine. **2.** Labor in the mines as punishment for a crime. • Metallum was one of the most severe punishments short of death.

metatag. (1996) In HTML computer code, a word or phrase that usu. identifies the subject of a webpage and acts as a hidden keyword for Internet search engines. • A person who uses a trademark as a metatag without permission may infringe on the trademark owner's rights.

metatus (mə-**tay**-təs), *n.* [Law Latin] *Hist.* A dwelling; quarters; a seat.

metayer system (me-**tay**-yər *or* met-ə-**yay**). (1848) An agricultural system in which land is divided into small farms among single families who pay a landlord a fixed portion — usu. half — of the produce and the landlord provides the stock. • The system was formerly prevalent in parts of France and Italy, and in the southern part of the United States. — Also written *métayer system.*

metecorn (**meet**-korn). *Archaic.* A portion of grain a lord pays a tenant for labor.

metegavel (**meet**-gav-əl). *Archaic.* A rent or tribute paid in supplies of food.

metelotage (me-te-loh-**tahzh**). [French] **1.** *French law.* The leasing of a ship. **2.** A seaman's wages.

mete out, *vb.* (bef. 15c) To dispense or measure out (justice, punishment, etc.) <shortly after the jury returned its verdict, the judge meted out an appropriate punishment>.

meter. (18c) **1.** A metric unit of length equal to 39.368 inches. **2.** An instrument of measurement used to measure use or consumption, esp. used by a utility company to measure utility consumption <a gas meter> <a water meter> <a parking meter>.

meter rate. (1889) A rate that a utility company applies to determine a charge for service <meter rate based on kilowatt-hours of electricity>.

metes and bounds (meets). (15c) The territorial limits of real property as measured by distances and angles from designated landmarks and in relation to adjoining properties. • Metes and bounds are usu. described in deeds and surveys to establish the boundary lines of land. — Also termed *running description; butts and bounds; lines and corners.* See CALL (5).

metewand (**meet**-wahnd). (15c) *Archaic.* A measuring staff of varying lengths.

meteyard (**meet**-yahrd). (bef. 12c) *Archaic.* A metewand that is one yard long.

meth house. (1988) *Slang.* A drug house where methamphetamines, particularly crystal methamphetamine, are sold. See DRUG HOUSE; CRYSTAL METH.

method. (15c) A mode of organizing, operating, or performing something, esp. to achieve a goal <method of election> <method of performing a job>.

method claim. See PATENT CLAIM.

method patent. See PATENT (3).

methods of unfair competition. See UNFAIR ACTS.

metric system. (1864) A decimal system for measuring length, weight, area, or volume, based on the meter as a unit length and the kilogram as a unit mass.

metropolitan, *adj.* (14c) Of, relating to, or involving a city or metropolis.

metropolitan, *n.* (14c) *Eccles. law.* An archbishop; the head of a province <the Archbishop of Canterbury is a metropolitan>.

metropolitan council. (1924) An official or quasi-official body appointed or elected by voters of a metropolitan area to provide for the unified administration of services (such as sewage disposal or public transportation) to the cities and towns within the metropolitan area.

metropolitan district. See DISTRICT.

metropolitan magistrate. See *metropolitan stipendiary magistrate* under MAGISTRATE.

metteshep (**meet**-shəp). (18c) *Hist.* **1.** An acknowledgment paid in a measure of corn. **2.** A penalty imposed on a tenant for neglect of duty, such as failing to cut the lord's corn. — Also spelled *mettenschep.*

metus (**mee**-təs), *n.* [Latin] *Roman law.* **1.** Fear of imminent danger; apprehension of serious danger, esp. in the form of duress to force a person to do something; the use of threats to bring about some end. • *Metus* was more comprehensive than duress is in Anglo-American law. It included fear of any evil that was serious enough to affect a reasonable person.

> "Fear (metus) had the same effect as fraud as regards the avoidance of the contract. It might be set up by way of defence (exceptio metus) or be the ground of restitutio in integrum, or give rise to an action (actio metus) .... It was not any kind of fear which grounded this action. The evil threatened must be of a serious character ...." R.W. Lee, *The Elements of Roman Law* 352 (4th ed. 1956).

2. A threat that diminishes the value of another's property. • In both senses, a victim was allowed to seek fourfold damages against the perpetrator. Cf. DOLUS.

metus perjurii (**mee**-təs pər-**joor**-ee-ɪ). [Law Latin] (18c) *Scots law.* The fear of perjury.

> "On this ground the evidence of the parties to a cause, and that of their relatives, was formerly excluded. It was feared that their own, or their relatives,' interest in the result of the cause might lead them to give false evidence, in order

to bring about a favourable decision. This, however, is no longer law. The desire to obtain all the light possible on the facts in dispute, has overcome the *metus perjurii*." John Trayner, *Trayner's Latin Maxims* 353–54 (4th ed. 1894).

meubles (**muu**-bəl *or* **myoo**-blə), *n.* [Law French] (18c) Movables, such as household utensils. See MOVABLE.

Mexican divorce. See DIVORCE.

MFA. *abbr.* **1.** MAJOR FEDERAL ACTION. **2.** MCCARRAN–FERGUSON ACT.

MFN. *abbr.* MOST FAVORED NATION.

MFN clause. See MOST-FAVORED-NATION CLAUSE.

MFN treatment. *abbr.* MOST-FAVORED-NATION TREATMENT.

MFR. *abbr.* **1.** MOTION FOR REHEARING. **2.** Motion for reconsideration. See MOTION FOR REHEARING.

MHA. *abbr.* Mental-hygiene arrest.

MI. *abbr.* MENTAL ILLNESS.

MICA. *abbr.* Mentally ill, chemically addicted.

Michaelmas. See *quarter day* under DAY.

Michaelmas sittings (mik-əl-məs). (18c) *English law.* In England, a term of court running from November 2 to November 25. • Until 1875, this was also called the *Michaelmas term.* The division of the legal year into terms was abolished by the Judicature Act of 1873. — Also termed *Michaelmas term.* Cf. EASTER SITTINGS; HILARY SITTINGS; TRINITY SITTINGS.

Michaelmas term. See MICHAELMAS SITTINGS.

miche (mich), *vb. Hist.* To hide; to sneak; to play truant. — Also spelled *mitch.*

michery (mich-ər-ee). (14c) *Hist.* Theft; cheating.

Michigan v. Long **presumption.** (1986) The doctrine that the United States Supreme Court has no jurisdiction over an appeal from a state court of last resort if the ruling is based on independent and adequate state grounds. *Michigan v. Long*, 463 U.S. 1032, 103 S.Ct. 3469 (1983).

Mickey Mouse Protection Act. See SONNY BONO COPYRIGHT TERM EXTENSION ACT.

MICR check. See *magnetic-ink-character-recognition check* under CHECK.

microstate. See STATE (1).

MID. *abbr.* See *miscellaneous itemized deduction* under DEDUCTION (2).

Midcal **test.** (1981) *Antitrust.* The doctrine that the anticompetitive acts of a private party will be considered state acts — and thereby protected from liability under the antitrust laws — if the acts are within a clearly articulated and affirmatively expressed policy of the state, and if the conduct is actively supervised by the state. *California Retail Liquor Dealers Ass'n v. Midcal Aluminum, Inc.*, 445 U.S. 97, 100 S.Ct. 937 (1980). See STATE-ACTION DOCTRINE; ACTIVE SUPERVISION.

mid-channel. See MIDDLE LINE OF MAIN CHANNEL.

middle burden of proof. See BURDEN OF PROOF.

middle-level scrutiny. See INTERMEDIATE SCRUTINY.

middle line of main channel. (1888) The equidistant point in the main channel of the river between the well-defined banks on either shore; the middle thread of a river's current. — Also termed *mid-channel; middle of the river.*

middleman. (17c) An intermediary or agent between two parties; esp., a dealer (such as a wholesaler) who buys from producers and sells to retailers or consumers.

middle management. See MANAGEMENT (1).

middle of the river. See MIDDLE LINE OF MAIN CHANNEL.

middle-of-the-road test. See HYDRAFLOW TEST.

middle thread. (1841) The center line of something; esp., an imaginary line drawn lengthwise through the middle of a stream's current.

mid-level scrutiny. See INTERMEDIATE SCRUTINY.

midnight deadline. (1957) A time limit for doing something, ending at midnight on a particular day. • For a bank, the midnight deadline is midnight on the next banking day following the day on which the bank receives the relevant item or from which the time for taking action begins to run, whichever is later. UCC § 4-104(a)(10).

midnight judge. (1936) *Hist.* A federal judicial nominee appointed by President John Adams just before his term expired, in an effort to pack the judiciary with Federalist Party sympathizers. • The Judiciary Act of 1801, passed and signed into law a few weeks before Adams's term expired, led to the appointment of 84 federal judges and countless marshals, clerks, attorneys, registers of wills, and justices of the peace, all of whom were affiliated with the Federalists. The Senate approved nominations and granted commissions up until its final adjournment just before Thomas Jefferson's inauguration. More than half of the commissions had not been delivered by the end of inauguration day. Secretary of State James Madison, acting at Jefferson's direction, barred their delivery and treated them as void. This led William Marbury to seek a federal court order to compel Madison to deliver Marbury's commission as justice of the peace. *See Marbury v. Madison*, 5 U.S. 137 (1803).

midshipman. (17c) A naval cadet; a student at the U.S. Naval Academy.

Midsummer Day. See *quarter day* under DAY.

midterm election. See *off-year election* under ELECTION (3).

midway. See THALWEG.

Midwest Piping **rule.** (1953) *Labor law.* The doctrine that an employer may not recognize multiple unions during a period in which there are conflicting claims of representation. *Midwest Piping & Supply Co.*, 63 NLRB Dec. (CCH) 1060 (1945).

MiFID. *abbr.* DIRECTIVE ON MARKETS IN FINANCIAL INSTRUMENTS.

migrant, *n.* (18c) **1.** A person who moves from place to place, esp. to find work.

▸ **economic migrant.** (1956) See *economic refugee* under REFUGEE.

2. An animal or bird that travels from one place to another in certain seasons.

migrant worker. See WORKER.

migration. (17c) Movement (of people or animals) from one country or region to another.

migratory corporation. See CORPORATION.

migratory divorce. See DIVORCE.

***Mike O'Connor* rule.** (1981) *Labor law.* The doctrine that unilateral changes that an employer makes after a union victory in an initial-representation election — but before the employer's objections have been resolved — are automatic violations of the National Labor Relations Act if the employer's objections are rejected. • If the employer's objections are sustained, any failure-to-bargain charge will be dismissed because the employer had no duty to bargain. But if the employer's objections are rejected, the employer is considered to have been under a duty to bargain as of the date of the election, which is why the unilateral changes are automatic violations of the Act. *Mike O'Connor Chevrolet-Buick-GMC Co.*, 209 NLRB Dec. (CCH) 701 (1974).

mild exigency. (1984) A circumstance that justifies a law-enforcement officer's departure from the knock-and-announce rule, such as the likelihood that the building's occupants will try to escape, resist arrest, or destroy evidence. See KNOCK-AND-ANNOUNCE RULE.

mile. (bef. 12c) **1.** A measure of distance equal to 5,280 feet. — Also termed *statute mile.* **2.** NAUTICAL MILE.

mileage. (18c) **1.** The distance in miles between two points. **2.** The distance a vehicle has traveled as reflected by an odometer. **3.** An allowance paid for travel expenses, as of a witness or public employee.

miles (MI-leez), *n.* [Latin] **1.** *Roman law.* A soldier. **2.** *Hist.* A knight.

militant democracy. See DEMOCRACY.

militare (mil-ə-**tair**-ee), *vb.* [Latin] **1.** *Roman law.* To serve as a soldier. • This verb later referred to serving in public office, civil or military. **2.** *Hist.* To be knighted.

military, *adj.* (15c) **1.** Of, relating to, or involving the armed forces <military base>. **2.** Of, relating to, or involving war <military action>.

military, *n.* (18c) The armed forces.

military allotment. (1945) *Family law.* A child-support deduction from the salary of an obligor parent on active duty in the United States military and paid to the obligee parent. See *attachment of wages* under ATTACHMENT (1).

military board. (18c) A group of persons appointed to act as a fact-finding agency or as an advisory body to the appointing military authority.

military bounty land. (1803) Land offered to members of the military as a reward for services. See *donation land, bounty land* under LAND; BOUNTY-LAND WARRANT.

military commission. A court, usu. composed of both civilians and military officers, that is modeled after a court-martial and that tries and decides cases concerning martial-law violations. See COURT-MARTIAL (2).

military-contract defense. See GOVERNMENT-CONTRACTOR DEFENSE.

military-contractor defense. See GOVERNMENT-CONTRACTOR DEFENSE.

military court. See COURT.

military court of inquiry. See COURT.

military desertion. See DESERTION.

military draft. See DRAFT (2).

military government. (17c) *Int'l law.* The control of all or most public functions within a country, or the assumption and exercise of governmental functions, by military forces or individual members of those forces; government exercised by a military commander under the direction of the executive or sovereign, either externally during a foreign war or internally during a civil war. • A military government's actions supersede all local law. See MARTIAL LAW.

military judge. See JUDGE.

military judge alone. (1969) *Military law.* A court-martial presided over by a single judge with no other court-martial members present.

military jurisdiction. (1821) The three types of governmental power given the military by the U.S. Constitution — specif., jurisdiction under military law, jurisdiction under military government, and jurisdiction under martial law.

military justice. (16c) A structure of punitive measures designed to foster order, morale, and discipline within the military. See MILITARY LAW.

military law. (17c) **1.** The branch of public law governing military discipline and other rules regarding service in the armed forces. • It is exercised both in peacetime and in war, is recognized by civil courts, and includes rules far broader than for the punishment of offenders. — Also termed *military justice.* — Sometimes loosely termed *martial law.* Cf. MARTIAL LAW.

> "Military Law . . . is largely, but not exclusively, statutory in character, and prescribes the rights of, and imposes duties and obligations upon, the several classes of persons composing its military establishment; it creates military tribunals, endows them with appropriate jurisdiction and regulates their procedure; it also defines military offenses and, by the imposition of adequate penalties, endeavors to prevent their occurrence." George B. Davis, *A Treatise on the Military Law of the United States* 1 (3d ed. 1915).

2. More broadly, the administrative as well as the disciplinary rules for the armed forces — as, for example, the rules of enlistment and billeting.

military leave. (1918) A policy contained in employment policies or collective-bargaining agreements allowing a long-term leave of absence — without an accompanying loss of benefits — for a person in active service in the U.S. armed forces.

military necessity. (1864) *Int'l law.* A principle of warfare allowing coercive force, subject to the laws of war, to achieve a desired end, as long as the force used is not more than is called for by the situation. • This principle dates from the Hague Convention on Laws and Customs of War on Land of October 18, 1907, which prohibits the destruction or seizure of enemy property "unless such destruction or seizure be imperatively demanded by the necessities of war."

> "In the final analysis, the law of international armed conflict is a product of reconciliation between demands of military necessity and humanitarian considerations. If military necessity were to prevail completely, belligerent parties would have full freedom of action, with a view to winning a war. If humanitarian considerations were the only guide to the conduct of hostilities, the waging of war would become impossible by dint of the death, injury, and suffering that unavoidably accompany it. The law of international armed conflict therefore takes a middle road, rendering unto military necessity what is due to it, while protecting and respecting at least a minimal level of humanitarianism even in the midst of hostilities." Yoram Dinstein, "Military

Necessity," in 7 *The Max Planck Encyclopedia of Public International Law* 201, 201 (Rüdiger Wolfrum ed., 2012).

military objective. *Int'l law.* An object that by its nature, location, or use contributes to military action, and is thus susceptible to attack. • Under Geneva Convention Protocol 1 (1977), only military — rather than civilian — objects are proper targets.

military occupation. (18c) **1.** A job in the armed forces. **2.** The seizure and control of territory by military force; OCCUPATION (3).

military offense. (16c) An offense, such as desertion, that lies within the jurisdiction of a military court. See COURT-MARTIAL.

military officer. See OFFICER (2).

military rank. See RANK.

Military Rules of Evidence. The rules of evidence applicable to military law and courts-martial. — Abbr. MRE.

military salvage. See SALVAGE (1).

military tenure. See TENURE.

military testament. See *soldier's will* under WILL.

militate (**mil**-ə-tayt), *vb.* (16c) To exert a strong influence <the evidence of police impropriety militates against a conviction>. Cf. MITIGATE.

milites (**mil**-ə-teez), *n.* **1.** *Roman law.* Members of the military; soldiers. **2.** *Hist.* Knights who are part of the royal army, by virtue of feudal tenure.

> "[Knights] are also called in our law *milites*, because they formed a part of the royal army, in virtue of their feodal tenures; one condition of which was, that every one who held a knight's fee immediately under the crown . . . was obliged to be knighted and attend the king in his wars, or fine for his non-compliance." 1 William Blackstone, *Commentaries on the Laws of England* 404 (1765).

3. *Scots law.* Freeholders holding estates from barons for military service.

militia (mə-**lish**-ə), *n.* (16c) **1.** A body of citizens armed and trained, esp. by a state, for military service apart from the regular armed forces. • The Constitution recognizes a state's right to form a "well-regulated militia" but also grants Congress the power to activate, organize, and govern a federal militia. U.S. Const. amend. II; U.S. Const. art. I, § 8, cl. 15–16. See NATIONAL GUARD.

▸ **reserve militia.** (1861) All persons who are not exempt from military service and not actively serving in the armed forces or national guard.

2. *Roman law.* Military service.

> "The term 'Militia' has had at least two different meanings. One refers to all citizens and resident aliens who may be called in an emergency. These comprise the unorganized militia which is a reservoir of all able-bodied manpower without individual classification. The second meaning is the modern-day sense most commonly considered in the United States. It refers to those male citizens and/or resident aliens, generally 18–45 years, who are individually enrolled in regularly organized, uniformed, equipped, and trained National Guard units. A majority of the State Constitutions or general statutes embody this distinction." William L. Shaw, *The Interrelationship of the United States Army and the National Guard,* 31 Mil. L. Rev. 39, 44 (1966).

Militia Clause. (1918) *Constitutional law.* One of two clauses of the U.S. Constitution giving Congress the power to call forth, arm, and maintain a military force to enforce compliance with its laws, suppress insurrections, and repel invasions. U.S. Const. art. I, § 8, cls. 15 and 16. Cf. ARMY CLAUSE.

mill. (bef. 12c) **1.** A machine that grinds corn, grain, or other substances, esp. using a wheel and circular motion. • The substance ground in a mill is sometimes called grist, esp. when it is a grain. Courts sometimes refer to the grinding process as a metaphor for the judicial process <suits to collect on promissory notes are grist for the summary-judgment mill because the material facts in such cases are often undisputed>. **2.** The building in which the grinding is performed, along with the site, dam, or other items connected with the mill. **3.** A monetary unit equal to one-tenth of a cent. • Mills are a money of account used in the United States and Canada, esp. to reckon tax rates.

millage rate. See MILL RATE.

Miller Act. A federal law requiring the posting of performance and payment bonds before an award is made for a contract for construction, alteration, or repair of a public work or building. 40 USCA §§ 270a–270d-1.

***Miller* test.** (1973) The three-pronged test, set forth in *Miller v. California*, 413 U.S. 15, 93 S.Ct. 2607 (1973), used to determine whether material is legally obscene. — Also termed *Miller standard.* See OBSCENE; LAPS VALUE TEST.

***Miller* trust.** See TRUST (3).

Miller–Tydings Act. A 1937 federal statute enacted to amend the Sherman Act by exempting fair-trade laws from the Act and legalizing resale-price-maintenance agreements between producers and retailers of products. • The Act was repealed by the Consumer Goods Pricing Act of 1975.

***Miller v. Shugart* agreement.** (1989) A settlement in which an insured consents to a judgment in favor of the plaintiff, on the condition that the plaintiff will satisfy the judgment only out of proceeds from the insured's policy, and will not seek recovery against the insured personally. • Although the phrase takes its name from a Minnesota case, it is used in other jurisdictions as well. *Miller v. Shugart*, 316 N.W.2d 729 (Minn. 1982).

milling in transit. (1887) An arrangement in which a shipment is temporarily detained at an intermediate point, usu. for the application of some manufacturing process, with or without an increase of a freight charge by the carrier.

mill power. (1833) A unit of water power used in defining quantities and weights of water available to a lessee.

mill privilege. (18c) The right of a mill-site owner to construct a mill and to use power from a stream to operate it, with due regard to the rights of other owners along the stream's path.

mill rate. (1921) A tax applied to real property whereby each mill represents $1 of tax assessment per $1,000 of the property's assessed value <the mill rate for taxes in this county is 10 mills, so for a home valued at $100,000, the owner will pay $1,000 in property taxes>. — Also termed *millage rate.*

mill site. (1816) **1.** A small tract of land on or contiguous to a watercourse, suitable for the erection and operation of a mill. **2.** *Mining law.* A small parcel of nonmineral public land (not exceeding five acres) claimed and occupied by an owner of a mining claim because the extra space is needed for mining or ore-reduction operations. 30 USCA § 42.

***Mimms* order.** (1993) *Criminal law.* A police officer's command for a motorist or passenger to get out of the vehicle. • A *Mimms* order need not be independently justified if the initial stop was lawful.

***Mimms* rule.** (1979) *Criminal law.* The doctrine that police may order the driver of a vehicle that has been lawfully stopped, together with all its passengers, to get out of it. *Pennsylvania v. Mimms*, 434 U.S. 106, 98 S.Ct. 330 (1977).

mina (**mɪ**-nə), *n.* [Law Latin] *Hist.* A measure of grain or corn.

minage (**mɪ**-nij), *n.* [Law French] *Hist.* A toll for selling grain or corn by the *mina.*

minare (mi-**nair**-ee), *vb.* [Law Latin] *Hist.* To mine.

mind. (bef. 12c) **1.** The source of thought and intellect; the seat of mental faculties. **2.** The ability to will, direct, or assent. — Also termed *sound mind.* **3.** Memory.

mind and memory. (15c) *Archaic.* A testator's mental capacity to make a will <she argued that her uncle was not of sound mind and memory when executing the will because he had Alzheimer's disease>. • This phrase was generally used as part of the phrase *of sound mind and memory*, referring to the capacity of a testator to make a will. See BONA MEMORIA; CAPACITY (2).

mine. (14c) **1.** An underground excavation used to obtain minerals, ores, or other substances. **2.** A mineral deposit; a place containing a mineral deposit.

mineral, *n.* (15c) **1.** Any natural inorganic matter that has a definite chemical composition and specific physical properties that give it value <most minerals are crystalline solids>. **2.** A subsurface material that is explored for, mined, and exploited for its useful properties and commercial value. **3.** Any natural material that is defined as a mineral by statute or caselaw.

▸ **mineral *ferae naturae*** (**feer**-ee nə-**tyoor**-ee) (1900) A mineral in liquid or gaseous form that is capable of migrating from one place to another and that one must reduce to possession to acquire ownership of. • Oil, gas, and water are most often referred to as *mineral ferae naturae.*

mineral acre. (1938) *Oil & gas.* The full mineral interest in one acre of land.

mineral deed. See DEED.

mineral district. See DISTRICT.

mineral easement. See EASEMENT.

mineral entry. (1882) The right of entry on public land to mine valuable mineral deposits.

> "It is the policy of the United States, as expressed in Acts of Congress, to make public lands available to the people for the purpose of mining valuable mineral deposits, and to encourage exploration for, and development of, mineral resources on public lands. Accordingly, the United States has reserved all lands 'valuable for minerals' . . . from disposition under the nonmineral statutes, and has made them open to entry for mining purposes, under regulations prescribed by law . . . . In other words . . . where statute authorizes the Federal Government to acquire lands, without indicating that lands are to be acquired for a particular purpose, lands so acquired are public lands subject to mineral entry." 53A Am. Jur. 2d *Mines and Minerals* § 23, at 274 (1996).

mineral *ferae naturae*. See MINERAL.

mineral interest. (1846) *Oil & gas.* The right to search for, develop, and remove minerals from land or to receive a royalty based on the production of minerals. • Mineral interests are granted by an oil-and-gas lease. — Also termed *mineral right.* See FEE INTEREST; SUBSURFACE INTEREST; SURFACE INTEREST.

mineral land. See LAND.

mineral lease. See LEASE.

mineral lode. (1870) A mineral bed of rock with definite boundaries in a general mass of a mountain; any belt of mineralized rock lying within boundaries that clearly separate it from neighboring rock. — Also termed *lode.*

> "Typically, a lode is a concentration of valuable mineral with boundaries sufficiently distinct to import such a definite trend, continuity, and apartness to the formation that it can be traced through the enclosing mass of rock." 1 *American Law of Mining* § 32.02(2), at 32-7 (2d ed. 1998).

mineral right. See MINERAL INTEREST.

mineral royalty. See ROYALTY (2).

mineral servitude. See SERVITUDE (2).

Minerals Management Service. A unit in the U.S. Department of the Interior responsible for entering into and managing leases for the recovery of minerals on the outer continental shelf and for collecting and distributing royalty and other payments due the U.S. and Indian tribes from mineral production. — Abbr. MMS.

minerator (**min**-ər-ay-tər). [Law Latin] A miner.

miner's inch. (1865) A measurement of water discharge, equaling nine-gallons per minute from a one-inch square pipe. • The precise measurement of a miner's inch varies in different localities.

Mine Safety and Health Administration. A unit in the U.S. Department of Labor responsible for preventing mine accidents and occupational diseases in the country's mining industry. • It sets mandatory safety and health standards, assesses fines for their violation, and investigates mine accidents. Its programs are operated through regional administrators located in the country's mining regions. — Abbr. MSHA.

minimal contacts. See MINIMUM CONTACTS.

minimalist retributivism. See RETRIBUTIVISM.

minimal participant. (1987) *Criminal law.* Under the federal sentencing guidelines, a defendant who is among the least culpable of a group of criminal actors, as when the defendant does not understand the scope or structure of the criminal enterprise or the actions of the other members of the group. • The offense level for a crime of a minimal participant can be decreased by four levels. U.S. Sentencing Guidelines Manual § 3B1.2(a). Cf. MINOR PARTICIPANT.

minimal scrutiny. See RATIONAL-BASIS TEST.

mini-maxi, *n.* An underwriting arrangement for a securities transaction, whereby a broker is required to sell the minimum number of securities on an all-or-none basis and the balance on a best-efforts basis. See UNDERWRITING (2).

miniment (**min**-ə-mənt). See MUNIMENT.

mini-*Miranda* requirement. (2007) *Debtor–creditor law.* A debt collector's obligation when communicating with a debtor to inform the debtor that (1) the communication is from a debt collector seeking to collect a debt and (2) any information received will be used for that purpose. • This disclosure is required by the Fair Debt Collection Practices Act.

minimization requirement. (1972) *Criminal law.* The mandate that police officers acting under an eavesdropping warrant must use the wiretap in a way that will intercept the fewest possible conversations that are not subject to the warrant.—Also termed *duty of minimization.*

minimum, *adj.* (17c) Of, relating to, or constituting the smallest acceptable or possible quantity in a given case <minimum charge to a customer of a public utility>.

minimum contacts. (1945) A nonresident defendant's forum-state connections, such as business activity or actions foreseeably leading to business activity, that are substantial enough to bring the defendant within the forum-state court's personal jurisdiction without offending traditional notions of fair play and substantial justice. *International Shoe Co. v. Washington*, 326 U.S. 310, 66 S.Ct. 154 (1945). — Also termed *minimal contacts.* See PURPOSEFUL-AVAILMENT DOCTRINE.

minimum-fee schedule. (1937) *Hist.* A list of the lowest fees that a lawyer may charge, set by a state bar association. • The courts held that minimum-fee schedules, now defunct, violated antitrust laws.

minimum-holding buyback. See REDEMPTION (3).

minimum lot. See LOT (1).

minimum-royalty clause. (1903) *Patents.* A royalty-agreement provision that prescribes a fixed payment by the licensee to the patentee, regardless of whether the invention is actually used.

minimum sale. See EXHIBITION VALUE.

minimum scrutiny. See RATIONAL-BASIS TEST.

minimum-security prison. See PRISON.

minimum sentence. See SENTENCE.

minimum tax. See *alternative minimum tax* under TAX.

minimum wage. See WAGE.

mining. (14c) The process of extracting ore or minerals from the ground; the working of a mine. • This term also encompasses oil and gas drilling.

mining claim. (1852) A parcel of land that contains precious metal in its soil or rock and that is appropriated by a person according to established rules and customs known as the process of *location.* See LOCATION (4), (5).

▸ **lode claim.** (1874) A mining claim (on public land) to a well-defined vein embedded in rock; a mining claim to a mineral lode.

▸ **placer claim.** (1851) A mining claim that is not a lode claim; a claim where the minerals are not located in veins or lodes within rock, but are usu. in softer ground near the earth's surface.

> "It has long been recognized that the distinction between lode and placer claims must be tempered by scientific findings as to the nature of the mineral deposits under consideration, and the practicalities of modern mining methods, which may permit the use of surface mining methods to remove certain lodes or veins of minerals previously only reached by underground methods." 53A Am. Jur. 2d *Mines and Minerals* § 21, at 273 (1996).

mining lease. See LEASE.

mining location. **1.** See LOCATION (4). **2.** See LOCATION (5).

mining partnership. (1845) An association of persons to jointly share a mining business, including the profits, expenses, and losses. • The partnership has features of both a tenancy in common and an ordinary commercial partnership.

> "It has generally been held that the law governing ordinary commercial or trading partnerships applies, with a few exceptions, to mining partnerships. The principal exception and the main distinction between mining partnerships and commercial partnerships generally is based on the fact that the principle of delectus personae, meaning the right of a partner to exercise choice and preference as to the admission of any new members to the firm, and as to the persons to be so admitted, does not apply to mining partnerships . . . ." 58 C.J.S. *Mines and Minerals* § 387, at 380 (1998).

mining rent. (1902) Consideration given for a mining lease, whether the lease creates a tenancy, conveys a fee, or grants a mere license or incorporeal right.

minister, *n.* (14c) **1.** A person acting under another's authority; an agent. **2.** A prominent government officer appointed to manage an executive or administrative department. **3.** A diplomatic representative, esp. one ranking below an ambassador.

▸ **foreign minister.** (17c) **1.** A minister of foreign affairs, who in many countries is equivalent to the U.S. Secretary of State. **2.** An ambassador, minister, or envoy from a foreign government.

▸ **minister plenipotentiary** (plen-ə-pə-**ten**-shee-er-ee). (17c) A minister ranking below an ambassador but possessing full power and authority as a governmental representative, esp. as an envoy of a sovereign ruler. • This officer is often regarded as the personal representative of a head of state.

▸ **public minister.** A high diplomatic representative such as an ambassador, envoy, or resident, but not including a commercial representative such as a consul.

4. A person authorized by a Christian church to perform religious functions.

ministerial, *adj.* (16c) Of, relating to, or involving an act that involves obedience to instructions or laws instead of discretion, judgment, or skill; of, relating to, or involving a duty that is so plain in point of law and so clear in matter of fact that no element of discretion is left to the precise mode of its performance <the court clerk's ministerial duties include recording judgments on the docket>.

ministerial act. See ACT (2).

ministerial duty. **1.** See *ministerial act* under ACT (2). **2.** See DUTY (2).

ministerial-function test. (1990) The principle that the First Amendment bars judicial resolution of a Title VII employment-discrimination claim based on a religious preference, if the employee's responsibilities are religious in nature, as in spreading faith, supervising a religious order, and the like. 42 USCA § 2000e-1(a). See TITLE VII OF THE CIVIL RIGHTS ACT OF 1964.

ministerial office. See OFFICE.

ministerial officer. See OFFICER (1).

ministerial trust. See *passive trust* under TRUST (3).

minister plenipotentiary. **1.** See MINISTER (3). **2.** See *ambassador plenipotentiary* under AMBASSADOR.

minister's privilege. See PRIEST–PENITENT PRIVILEGE.

ministrant (**min**-ə-strənt). (1818) **1.** Someone who ministers; a dispenser. **2.** *Hist. Eccles. law.* A party who cross-examines a witness.

ministri regis (mi-**nis**-trɪ **ree**-jis). [Latin] (17c) *Hist.* Ministers of the king. • This term was applied to judges and ministerial officers.

minitrial. (1990) A private, voluntary, and informal form of dispute resolution in which each party's attorney presents an abbreviated version of its case to a neutral third party and to the opponent's representatives, who have settlement authority. • The third party may render an advisory opinion on the anticipated outcome of litigation. Cf. *summary jury trial* under TRIAL.

> "The idea behind the minitrial is that the parties can resolve a dispute on their own more efficiently if litigant representatives with settling authority are educated about the strengths and weaknesses of each side, giving summary presentations of their best cases under the eye of a jointly selected neutral advisor. After each case is presented, the parties meet privately to negotiate an agreement. The minitrial is confidential and nonbinding. Usually, no transcript is made of the proceeding. Minitrials have had some success in saving both time and money." Alfred C. Aman Jr. & William T. Mayton, *Administrative Law* 291 (2d ed. 2001).

minor, *n.* (16c) **1.** Someone who has not reached full legal age; a child or juvenile. — Also termed *infant.* Cf. ADULT.

▸ **emancipated minor.** (1817) A minor who is self-supporting and independent of parental control, usu. as a result of a court order. See EMANCIPATION.

▸ **minor in need of supervision.** See *child in need of supervision* under CHILD. — Abbr. MINS.

2. *Roman law.* Someone who is past puberty but less than 25 years old. — Also termed *minor quam 25 annis.*

minor aetas (**mɪ**-nər **ee**-tas). [Latin] *Hist.* Lesser age; minority; infancy.

minora regalia (mi-**nor**-ə ri-**gay**-lee-ə). See *regalia minora* under REGALIA.

minor crime. See MISDEMEANOR.

minor dispute. See DISPUTE.

minor fact. See FACT.

minority. (15c) **1.** The quality, state, or condition of being under legal age. • Although at common law minority lasted until the age of 21, today by statute the age is generally 18. In Scots law, legal minority begins at the end of puberty; until then, a person is a *pupil.* — Also termed *infancy; nonage; immaturity.* Cf. MAJORITY (1). **2.** A group having fewer than a controlling number of votes or similar rights. Cf. MAJORITY (2). **3.** A group that is different in some respect (such as race or religious belief) from the majority and that is sometimes treated differently as a result; a member of such a group. • Some courts have held that the term *minority,* in this sense, is not limited to a group that is outnumbered. It may also be applied to a group that has been traditionally discriminated against or socially suppressed, even if its members are in the numerical majority in an area.

▸ **discrete and insular minority.** (1938) A minority group that cannot be easily joined or left, that is defined by a characteristic that cannot be easily changed, and that lacks both ordinary protections of the political process and the power to obtain them. • Legislation aimed at discrete and insular minorities are subject to a heightened standard of review for constitutionality. See *discrete and insular class* under CLASS (1).

▸ **ethnic minority.** (1945) A racially distinct group of people who are different from the main group in a region or country.

▸ **religious minority.** (1829) A distinct group of people whose basic religious beliefs differ from those of the main group in a region or country.

Minority Business Development Agency. A unit in the U.S. Department of Commerce responsible for developing and coordinating a national program for minority business enterprise. — Abbr. MBDA.

minority discount. (1962) A reduction in the value of a closely held business's shares that are owned by someone who has only a minority interest in the business. • The concept underlying a minority discount is recognition that controlling shares — those owned by someone who can control the business — are worth more in the market than noncontrolling shares. But when dissenting shareholders object to a corporate act, such as a merger, and become entitled to have their shares appraised and bought by the corporation, many courts hold that incorporating a minority discount into the valuation of the dissenters' shares is inequitable and is not permitted. See APPRAISAL REMEDY.

minority government. See GOVERNMENT (3).

minority leader. (1898) The legislator in charge of the legislative caucus that does not constitute a majority of the members, as in the U.S. Senate or House of Representatives. Cf. MAJORITY LEADER.

minority opinion. See *dissenting opinion* under OPINION (1).

minority report. See REPORT (1).

minority right. See RIGHT.

minority shareholder. See SHAREHOLDER.

minority whip. See WHIP.

minor participant. (1960) *Criminal law.* Under the federal sentencing guidelines, a defendant who is less culpable for a crime than the other members of the group committing the crime, but who has more culpability than a minimal participant. • A defendant who is a minor participant can have the offense level for the crime decreased by two levels. U.S. Sentencing Guidelines Manual § 3B1.2(b). Cf. MINIMAL PARTICIPANT.

minor quam 25 annis (**mɪ**-nər kwam 25 **an**-is). [Latin]. See MINOR (2).

minor's estate. See ESTATE (1).

minor's trust. See *2503(c) trust* under TRUST (3).

MINS. *abbr.* Minor in need of supervision. See *child in need of supervision* under CHILD.

mint, *adj.* Appearing to be new and in perfect condition <a mint-condition dustjacket>.

mint, *n.* (15c) **1.** A government-authorized place for coining money. **2.** A large supply, esp. of money. **3.** The source of a fabrication or invention. — **mint,** *vb.*

mintage. (16c) **1.** The mint's charge for coining money. **2.** The product of minting; money.

mint-mark. (18c) An authorized mark on a coin showing where it was minted.

minuend (**min**-yoo-end). (18c) In a mathematical equation, the number from which another number (the subtrahend) is subtracted to arrive at a remainder or balance. • The term is used in law in a variety of accounting and mathematical contexts. Cf. SUBTRAHEND.

minus (**mɪ**-nəs), *adj.* & *adv.* [Latin] *Roman law.* Less; less than; not at all. • A debt remaining wholly unpaid was called *minus solutum.*

minus Latium. See LATIUM MINUS.

minute. (14c) **1.** One-sixtieth of an hour; 60 seconds. **2.** Loosely, a very short time. **3.** An item of business listed in a minute book or in minutes. See MINUTE BOOK; MINUTES (1), (2).

minute book. (16c) **1.** A book in which a court clerk enters minutes of court proceedings. **2.** A record of the subjects discussed and actions taken at a corporate directors' or shareholders' meeting. — Also termed *minutes book.*

minute entry. See *minute order* (1) under ORDER (2).

minute order. See ORDER (2).

minutes. (15c) **1.** Memoranda or notes of a transaction, proceeding, or meeting. **2.** *Parliamentary law.* The formal record of a deliberative assembly's proceedings, approved (as corrected, if necessary) by the assembly. — Also termed *journal*; *record*; *report.* See DISPENSE WITH THE READING OF THE MINUTES; SPREAD UPON THE MINUTES.

> "The *minutes* of an organization include a record of all official actions taken, the presiding officer, the presence of a quorum, and information showing that the meeting was duly called and thus legal. The other contents of the minutes will depend upon the degree of detail desired. . . . The minutes should be an *official record of actions taken* by the organization, not a transcript of what individuals say in meetings." Ray E. Keesey, *Modern Parliamentary Procedure* 84 (1994).

> "The official record of the proceedings of a deliberative assembly is usually called the *minutes*, or sometimes — particularly in legislative bodies — the *journal.* In an ordinary society, the minutes should contain mainly a record of what was *done* at the meeting, not what was *said* by the members. The minutes should never reflect the secretary's opinion, favorable or otherwise, on anything said or done." Henry M. Robert III et al., *Robert's Rules of Order Newly Revised* § 48, at 468 (11th ed. 2011).

3. *Scots law.* Written forms for preserving evidence.

> "When it is necessary to preserve evidence of any incidental judicial act or statement, this is done in the Court of Session, and also in the inferior courts, by a minute. Thus, where the pursuer restricts his libel, or makes a reference to the defender's oath . . . this is done by a minute. Strictly speaking, those minutes ought to be prepared by the clerk of court, as their form imports. They commence with the name of the counsel . . . and purport to be a statement made by him . . . ." William Bell, *Bell's Dictionary and Digest of the Law of Scotland* 721 (George Watson ed., 7th ed. 1890).

minutes book. See MINUTE BOOK.

minutio (mi-**n**[**y**]**oo**-shee-oh), *n.* [Latin] *Roman law.* A lessening or reduction. See DEMINUTIO.

***Miranda* hearing** (mə-**ran**-də). (1966) A pretrial proceeding held to determine whether the *Miranda* rule has been followed and thus whether the prosecutor may introduce into evidence the defendant's statements to the police made after arrest. See MIRANDA RULE.

***Miranda* rule.** (1966) The doctrine that a criminal suspect in police custody must be informed of certain constitutional rights before being interrogated. • The suspect must be advised of the right to remain silent, the right to have an attorney present during questioning, and the right to have an attorney appointed if the suspect cannot afford one. If the suspect is not advised of these rights or does not validly waive them, any evidence obtained during the interrogation cannot be used against the suspect at trial (except for impeachment purposes). *Miranda v. Arizona*, 384 U.S. 436, 86 S.Ct. 1602 (1966).

***Miranda* warning.** See MIRANDA RULE.

Mirandize (mə-**ran**-dɪz), *vb.* (1971) *Slang.* To read or recite (to an arrestee) rights under the *Miranda* rule <the suspect was arrested, Mirandized, and interrogated>. See MIRANDA RULE.

mirror-image rule. (1972) *Contracts.* The doctrine that the acceptance of a contractual offer must be positive, unconditional, unequivocal, and unambiguous, and must not change, add to, or qualify the terms of the offer; the common-law principle that for a contract to be formed, the terms of an acceptance must correspond exactly with those of the offer. • In modern commercial contexts, the mirror-image rule has been replaced by a UCC provision that allows parties to enforce their agreement despite minor discrepancies between the offer and the acceptance. The rule still applies to international sales contracts governed by the UN Convention on Contracts for the International Sales of Goods (article 19). — Also termed *matching-acceptance rule*; *ribbon-matching rule.* See BATTLE OF THE FORMS.

> "If an offeree purports to accept an offer but in doing so adds various conditions and qualifications of his own, is the acceptance binding on the offeror, at least in part? Generally speaking, the answer is no: the common law rule, reflected in Restatement Section 59, is that a statement of acceptance is effective only if it is a mirror image of the offer and expresses unconditional assent to all of the terms and conditions imposed by the offeror." Marvin A. Chirelstein, *Concepts and Case Analysis in the Law of Contracts* 54 (1990).

misa (**mɪ**-zə). [Law Latin] *Hist.* **1.** The issue in a writ of right; a mise. **2.** An agreement; a compromise.

misadministration. See MALADMINISTRATION.

misadventure. (13c) **1.** A mischance or misfortune; MISHAP. **2.** Homicide committed accidentally by a person doing a lawful act and having no intent to injure; ACCIDENTAL KILLING.

misallege, *vb.* (16c) To erroneously assert (a fact, a claim, etc.).

misapplication, *n.* (17c) The improper or illegal use of funds or property lawfully held. — **misapply,** *vb.*

misappropriation, *n.* (18c) **1.** The application of another's property or money dishonestly to one's own use. See EMBEZZLEMENT. Cf. APPROPRIATION (1); EXPROPRIATION (1). **2.** *Intellectual property.* The common-law tort of using the noncopyrightable information or ideas that an organization collects and disseminates for a profit to compete unfairly against that organization, or copying a work whose creator has not yet claimed or been granted exclusive rights in the work. *Int'l News Serv. v. Associated Press*, 248 U.S. 215, 29 S.Ct. 68 (1918). • The elements of misappropriation are (1) the plaintiff must have invested time, money, or effort to extract the information, (2) the defendant must have taken the information with no similar investment, and (3) the plaintiff must have suffered a competitive injury because of the taking. **3.** The doctrine giving rise to such a tort claim. — **misappropriate,** *vb.*

> "The doctrine of 'misappropriation,' which is a distinct branch of unfair competition, . . . has been applied to a variety of situations in which the courts have sensed that one party was dealing 'unfairly' with another, but which were not covered by the three established statutory systems protecting intellectual property: copyright, patent, and trademark/deception as to origin." *U.S. Golf Ass'n v. St. Andrews Systems, Data-Max, Inc.* 749 F.2d 1028, 1034–35 (3d Cir. 1984).

misappropriation theory. (1980) *Securities.* The doctrine that a person who wrongfully uses confidential information to buy or sell securities in violation of a duty owed to the one who is the information source is guilty of securities fraud.

misbehavior, *n.* (15c) One or more bad acts that are unacceptable in the eyes of the law or of other people in general; MISCONDUCT (1). — **misbehave,** *vb.*

misbehavior in office. See *official misconduct* under MISCONDUCT.

misbranding, *n.* (1890) The act or an instance of labeling one's product falsely or in a misleading way. • Misbranding is prohibited by federal and state law. — **misbrand,** *vb.*

miscarriage. (16c) **1.** Spontaneous and involuntary premature expulsion of a nonviable fetus. — Also termed *spontaneous abortion.* **2.** A failure to reach a hoped-for conclusion or expected result; a failure in one's plans. **3.** A failure to transport something properly to an intended destination. — **miscarry,** *vb.*

▸ **criminal miscarriage.** *Hist.* See ABORTION (1).

miscarriage of justice. (1862) A grossly unfair outcome in a judicial proceeding, as when a defendant is convicted despite a lack of evidence on an essential element of the crime. — Also termed *failure of justice.*

miscegenation (mi-sej-ə-**nay**-shən). (1863) *Archaic.* Sexual relations between races; esp., the production of offspring by parents of different races, usu. when and where considered illegal. • In 1967, the U.S. Supreme Court held that laws banning interracial marriages are unconstitutional. *Loving v. Virginia,* 388 U.S. 1, 87 S.Ct. 1817 (1967). But for years, such laws technically remained on the books in some states. The last remaining state-law ban on interracial marriages was a provision in the Alabama constitution. The Alabama legislature voted to repeal the ban, subject to a vote of the state's citizens, in 1999; the repeal became effective in 2000. See *mixed marriage* under MARRIAGE (1). — **miscegenetic,** *adj.*— **miscegenationist, miscegenator,** *n.* — **miscegenate,** *vb.*

miscellaneous itemized deduction. See DEDUCTION (2).

mischarge. (1939) An erroneous jury instruction that may be grounds for reversing a verdict. — Also termed *misdirection.*

mischief (**mis**-chəf). (14c) **1.** A condition in which a person suffers a wrong or is under some hardship, esp. one that a statute seeks to remove or for which equity provides a remedy <this legislation seeks to eliminate the mischief of racially restrictive deed covenants>. **2.** Injury or damage caused by a specific person or thing <the vandals were convicted of criminal mischief>. **3.** The act causing such injury or damage <their mischief damaged the abbey>. See MALICIOUS MISCHIEF.

mischief rule. (1861) In statutory construction, the doctrine that a statute should be interpreted by first identifying the problem (or "mischief") that the statute was designed to remedy and then adopting a construction that will suppress the problem and advance the remedy. • This is a primarily British name for purposivism (see PURPOSIVISM). Under this approach, "the words of the text are expanded or contracted from their usual meaning to carry out the legislative purpose," and "[t]here is no need to first find the text ambiguous or uncertain before obtaining from other sources an understanding of the purpose of the statute." Unif. Statute & Rule Construction Act § 18 cmt. (1995). Originally, however, the rule was to be applied only in cases of ambiguity — that is, when the literal rule was inapplicable. *See* Rupert Cross, *Precedent in English Law* 183 (1961). The classic and most ancient statement of the rule occurred in *Heydon's Case*:

> "For the sure and true interpretation of all statutes in general (be they penal or beneficial, restrictive or enlarging of the common law) four things are to be discerned and considered: first, what was the common law before the making of the act. Second, what was the mischief and defect for which the common law did not provide. Third, what remedy the Parliament hath resolved and appointed to cure the disease of the Commonwealth. And fourth, the true reason of the remedy; and then the offence of all the judges is always to make such construction as shall suppress the mischief, and advance the remedy, and to suppress subtle inventions and evasions for continuance of the mischief, and *pro privato commodo,* and to add force and life to the cure and remedy, according to the true intent of the makers of the act, *pro bono publico.*" *Heydon's Case,* 3 Rep. 7a (1584).

The prevailing scholarly view today is that the mischief rule represents "the last remnant of the equity of a statute." J.H. Baker, *An Introduction to English Legal History* 212 (4th ed. 2002). — Also termed *rule in Heydon's Case; purpose approach.* See PURPOSIVISM. Cf. GOLDEN RULE; PLAIN-MEANING RULE; EQUITY-OF-THE-STATUTE RULE.

misconduct (mis-**kon**-dəkt). (17c) **1.** A dereliction of duty; unlawful, dishonest, or improper behavior, esp. by someone in a position of authority or trust. See MISBEHAVIOR.

▸ **affirmative misconduct.** (1897) **1.** An affirmative act of misrepresentation or concealment of a material fact; intentional wrongful behavior. • Some courts hold that there must be an ongoing pattern of misrepresentation or false promises, as opposed to an isolated act of providing misinformation. **2.** With respect to a claim of estoppel against the federal government, a misrepresentation or concealment of a material fact by a government employee — beyond a merely innocent or negligent misrepresentation.

▸ **employee misconduct.** Misconduct engaged in by an employee esp. while on the job, but also possibly off the job (if the conduct harms the company in some way). • Employee misconduct could cover a broad range of behaviors, from minor infractions of company rules to criminal conduct.

▸ **gross misconduct in the workplace.** Intentional or reckless behavior that might harm someone, esp. a fellow employee, or the employer. • Gross misconduct may include acts in disregard of the safety of others, unlawful discrimination, libel, harassment, and various criminal offenses.

▸ **juror misconduct.** (1954) A juror's violation of the court's charge or the law, committed either during trial or in deliberations after trial, such as (1) communicating about the case with outsiders, witnesses, attorneys, bailiffs, or judges, (2) bringing into the jury room information relating to the case but not in evidence, and (3) conducting experiments regarding theories of the case outside the court's presence.

▸ **misconduct in office.** See *official misconduct.*

▸ **official misconduct.** (1830) A public officer's corrupt violation of assigned duties by malfeasance, misfeasance, or nonfeasance. — Also termed *misconduct in office; misbehavior in office; malconduct in office; misdemeanor in office; corruption in office; official corruption; political corruption.*

▸ **serious and willful misconduct.** See SERIOUS AND WILLFUL MISCONDUCT.

▸ **wanton misconduct.** (1844) An act, or a failure to act when there is a duty to do so, in reckless disregard of another's rights, coupled with the knowledge that injury will probably result. — Also termed *wanton and reckless misconduct.*

▸ **willful and wanton misconduct.** (1866) Conduct committed with an intentional or reckless disregard for the safety of others, as by failing to exercise ordinary care to prevent a known danger or to discover a danger. See *gross negligence* under NEGLIGENCE. — Also termed *willful indifference to the safety of others.*

▸ **willful misconduct.** (1804) Misconduct committed voluntarily and intentionally.

▸ **willful misconduct of an employee.** (1884) The deliberate disregard by an employee of the employer's interests, including its work rules and standards of conduct, justifying a denial of unemployment compensation if the employee is terminated for the misconduct.

2. An attorney's dishonesty or attempt to persuade a court or jury by using deceptive or reprehensible methods.

misconduct in office. See *official misconduct* under MISCONDUCT (1).

misconstruction. (16c) An incorrect or mistaken interpretation of a statute, contract, etc.; a false understanding.

miscontinuance. (16c) A continuance erroneously ordered by a court. See CONTINUANCE (3).

misconviction. (1888) The wrongful conviction of an innocent person, usu. as a result of erroneous or fraudulent forensic evidence or mistaken eyewitness identification.

miscreant (**mis**-kree-ənt). (14c) **1.** A wrongdoer; a bad person who causes trouble for people or hurts others. **2.** An apostate; an unbeliever.

misdate. (16c) To erroneously date (a document, etc.).

misdeed. (bef. 12c) A wrong or illegal action; OFFENSE (2).

misdelivery. (1867) Delivery not according to contractual specifications; esp., delivery to the wrong person or delivery of goods in a damaged condition. • This concept applies to contracts of carriage and contracts of sale, lease, etc., requiring delivery in some form.

misdemeanant (mis-də-**mee**-nənt), *n.* (1819) Someone who has been convicted of a misdemeanor.

misdemeanor (mis-di-**mee**-nər). (16c) **1.** A crime that is less serious than a felony and is usu. punishable by fine, penalty, forfeiture, or confinement (usu. for a brief term) in a place other than prison (such as a county jail). — Also spelled (BrE) *misdemeanour.* — Also termed *minor crime; summary offense.* Cf. FELONY (1).

> "'Misdemeanor' was the label ultimately adopted to apply to all offenses other than treason or felony. The term included a wide variety of wrongs and misprisions. Many of the substantive legal principles and procedures applicable to felonies were not applied in the case of misdemeanors. The difference in treatment between felonies and misdemeanors has carried over from common law to current practice, and today misdemeanors are often treated differently than felonies [in] the procedures employed in trying such cases as well as [in] the consequences of a conviction. The traditional distinction between felonies and misdemeanors has been abolished in England." Rollin M. Perkins & Ronald N. Boyce, *Criminal Law* 15 (3d ed. 1982).

▸ **gross misdemeanor.** (18c) A serious misdemeanor, though not a felony. — Also termed *high misdemeanor.*

▸ **high misdemeanor.** (17c) **1.** *Hist. English law.* A crime that ranked just below high treason in seriousness. • In English law, the term was essentially synonymous with crime. Examples of crimes called high misdemeanors are riot and conspiracy. In early American law, the term had the same meaning as in English law and was used in defining crimes such as sedition. **2.** See *gross misdemeanor.* **3.** See *serious misdemeanor.*

▸ **serious misdemeanor.** (1893) One of a class of misdemeanors having more severe penalties than most other misdemeanors. • Conduct rising to the level of a serious misdemeanor can, in some jurisdictions, be charged as either a felony or a misdemeanor. — Also termed *high misdemeanor; indictable misdemeanor; penitentiary misdemeanor; aggravated misdemeanor.*

▸ **treasonable misdemeanor.** See TREASONABLE MISDEMEANOR.

2. *Archaic.* Any crime, including a felony.

> "A crime, or misdemeanor, is an act committed, or omitted, in violation of a public law, either forbidding or commanding it. This general definition comprehends both crimes and misdemeanors; which, properly speaking, are mere synonymous terms: though, in common usage, the word, 'crimes,' is made to denote such offences as are of a deeper and more atrocious dye; while smaller faults, and omissions of less consequence, are comprised under the gentler name of 'misdemeanors' only." 4 William Blackstone, *Commentaries on the Laws of England* 5 (1769).

misdemeanor in office. See *official misconduct* under MISCONDUCT.

misdemeanor manslaughter. See MANSLAUGHTER.

misdemeanor-manslaughter rule. (1967) The doctrine that a death occurring during the commission of a misdemeanor (or sometimes a nondangerous felony) is involuntary manslaughter. • Many states and the Model Penal Code have abolished this rule. Cf. FELONY-MURDER RULE.

> "Companion to the felony-murder rule is the so-called misdemeanor-manslaughter rule[:] . . . Homicide resulting from the perpetration or attempted perpetration of an unlawful act, less than a dangerous felony, is manslaughter if the unlawful act is malum in se." Rollin M. Perkins & Ronald N. Boyce, *Criminal Law* 108 (3d ed. 1982).

misdescription. (1848) **1.** A contractual error or falsity that deceives, injures, or materially misleads one of the contracting parties. **2.** A bailee's inaccurate identification, in a document of title, of goods received from the bailor. **3.** An inaccurate legal description of land in a deed.

misdirection. See MISCHARGE.

mise (meez *or* mɪz), *n.* [Law French] (15c) *Hist.* **1.** Expenses incurred in litigation. **2.** The general issue in a writ of right. • When a tenant pleads superior title to the plaintiff, the tenant is said to join the *mise* on the mere right. **3.** A settlement; a compromise, as in the *Mise of Lewes* between Henry III and the rebelling barons.

mise money. (17c) *Hist.* Money paid by contract to purchase a privilege.

miserabile depositum (miz-ə-**rab**-ə-lee di-**poz**-ə-təm). [Law Latin "a pitiful deposit"] *Civil law.* A deposit or bailment made in an emergency, as in a shipwreck, fire, or insurrection.

miserere (miz-ə-**reer**-ee). [Latin] (13c) *Hist.* Have mercy. • This is the first phrase of the 51st psalm ("Miserere mei, Deus," or "Have mercy on me, O God"), used to test a person claiming benefit of clergy. See NECK VERSE.

misericordia (miz-ə-ri-**kor**-dee-ə). [Law Latin] *Hist.* **1.** Mercy. **2.** An arbitrary fine as a punishment. **3.** An exemption from a fine.

misericordia communis (miz-ə-ri-**kor**-dee-ə kə-**myoo**-nis). [Law Latin] *Hist.* A fine levied on a whole county.

misfeasance (mis-**fee**-zənts), *n.* (16c) **1.** A lawful act performed in a wrongful manner. **2.** More broadly, a transgression or trespass; MALFEASANCE. Cf. NONFEASANCE. — **misfeasant,** *adj.* — **misfeasor,** *n.*

misfeasance in public office. (1880) The tort of excessive, malicious, or negligent exercise of statutory powers by a public officer. — Also termed *malfeasance.*

mishap (**mis**-hap), *n.* (14c) A small accident or mistake, esp. when the consequences are not severe; a relatively trivial instance of bad luck; mischance.

mishering. See MISKERING.

mishersing. See MISKERING.

misidentification. (1902) An erroneous affirmative declaration or other indication, usu. based on memory, that an innocent person was the perpetrator of a crime or an object or place was connected with a crime.

misjoinder (mis-**joyn**-dər). (18c) **1.** The improper union of parties in a civil case. See JOINDER. Cf. DISJOINDER; NONJOINDER (1). **2.** The improper union of offenses in a criminal case.

miskenning (mis-**ken**-ing). [fr. French *misw* "wrong" + Saxon *cennan* "to declare"] (bef. 12c) *Hist.* **1.** A wrongful summons. **2.** A pleading mistake or irregularity.

> "But every defeated plaintiff could be amerced 'for a false claim.' Incidentally too any falsehood . . . that is, any fraudulent misuse of the machinery of the law, would be punished by imprisonment. Then again every default in appearance brought an amercement on the defaulter and his pledges. Every mistake in pleading, every *miskenning* . . . brought an amercement on the pleader if the mistake was to be retrieved. A litigant who hoped to get to the end of his suit without an amercement must have been a sanguine man; for he was playing a game of forfeits." 2 Frederick Pollock & Frederic W. Maitland, *The History of English Law Before the Time of Edward I* 519 (2d ed. 1899).

miskering (**mis**-kər-ing). (17c) *Hist.* Freedom or immunity from amercement. — Also termed *abishering; abishersing; mishering; mishersing.* See AMERCEMENT.

mislaid property. See PROPERTY.

mislay, *vb.* (15c) To deposit (property, etc.) in a place not afterward recollected; to lose (property, etc.) by forgetting where it was placed. See *mislaid property* under PROPERTY.

mislead, *vb.* To cause (another person) to believe something that is not so, whether by words or silence, action or inaction; to deceive. • Although the misleading may be inadvertent, the term usu. implies willful deceit.

misleading, *adj.* (16c) (Of an instruction, direction, etc.) delusive; calculated to be misunderstood.

misnomer (mis-**noh**-mər). (15c) A mistake in naming a person, place, or thing, esp. in a legal instrument. • In federal pleading — as well as in most states — misnomer of a party can be corrected by an amendment, which will relate back to the date of the original pleading. Fed. R. Civ. P. 15(c)(3).

misperformance. (17c) A faulty attempt to discharge an obligation (esp. a contractual one). Cf. PERFORMANCE; NONPERFORMANCE.

mispleading. (16c) Pleading incorrectly. • A party who realizes that its pleading is incorrect can usu. amend the pleading, as a matter of right, within a certain period, and can thereafter amend with the court's permission.

misprision (mis-**prizh**-ən). (15c) **1.** Concealment or nondisclosure of a serious crime by one who did not participate in the crime.

> "Misprision of felony, that is, the concealment of the commission of a felony, is a criminal act. A similar neglect to prevent or disclose the commission of a treason is misprision of treason. All misprisions are misdemeanors, and a misprision of a misdemeanor is too trifling an offence for the criminal law to take cognizance of." John Wilder May, *The Law of Crimes* § 19, at 15 (Harry Augustus Bigelow ed., 1905).

▸ **clerical misprision.** (18c) A court clerk's mistake or fraud that is apparent from the record.

▸ **misprision of felony.** (16c) Concealment or nondisclosure of someone else's felony. *See* 18 USCA § 4.

▸ **misprision of treason.** (16c) Concealment or nondisclosure of someone else's treason.

▸ **negative misprision.** (18c) The wrongful concealment of something that should be revealed <misprision of treason>.

▸ **positive misprision.** (18c) The active commission of a wrongful act <seditious conduct against the government is positive misprision>.

2. Seditious conduct against the government. **3.** An official's failure to perform the duties of public office. **4.** Misunderstanding; mistake.

> "The word 'misprision' has been employed with different meanings. While Blackstone thought of it as referring to a grave misdemeanor, it seems to have been used earlier to indicate the entire field of crime below the grade of treason or felony before the word 'misdemeanor' became the generally accepted label for this purpose. More recently it has been said: 'Misprision is nothing more than a word used to describe a misdemeanor which does not possess a specific name.' [*U.S. v. Perlstein*, 126 F.2d 789, 798 (3d Cir. 1942).] It has been associated with two specific offenses, and only these, from the earliest times. They are misprision of treason and misprision of felony, which consist of the criminal default of one in regard to the crime of another." Rollin M. Perkins & Ronald N. Boyce, *Criminal Law* 572 (3d ed. 1982).

misprisor (mis-prɪ-zər). (1941) Someone who commits misprision of felony.

misreading. An act of fraud in which a person incorrectly reads the contents of an instrument to an illiterate or blind person with the intent to deceitfully obtain that person's signature.

misrecital. (16c) An incorrect statement of a factual matter in a contract, deed, pleading, or other instrument.

misrepresentation, *n.* (17c) **1.** The act or an instance of making a false or misleading assertion about something, usu. with the intent to deceive. • The word denotes not just written or spoken words but also any other conduct that amounts to a false assertion. **2.** The assertion so made; an incorrect, unfair, or false statement; an assertion that does not accord with the facts. — Also termed *false representation*; (redundantly) *false misrepresentation*. Cf. REPRESENTATION (1). — **misrepresent,** *vb.*

"A misrepresentation, being a false assertion of fact, commonly takes the form of spoken or written words. Whether a statement is false depends on the meaning of the words in all the circumstances, including what may fairly be inferred from them. An assertion may also be inferred from conduct other than words. Concealment or even nondisclosure may have the effect of a misrepresentation . . . . [A]n assertion need not be fraudulent to be a misrepresentation. Thus a statement intended to be truthful may be a misrepresentation because of ignorance or carelessness, as when the word 'not' is inadvertently omitted or when inaccurate language is used. But a misrepresentation that is not fraudulent has no consequences . . . unless it is material." Restatement (Second) of Contracts § 159 cmt. a (1979).

▸ **active misrepresentation.** (1832) See *affirmative misrepresentation.*

▸ **affirmative misrepresentation.** Misrepresentation by overt action or communication rather than by failing to act or communicate. — Also termed *active misrepresentation.*

▸ **assisted misrepresentation.** (1899) The act of contributing by word or conduct to another's misrepresentation so as to give an impression of credibility. • For example, a person who receives and acknowledges a mortgage for $200,000 even though a lesser amount was actually loaned assists a misrepresentation if the mortgage is later sold for $200,000.

▸ **fraudulent misrepresentation.** (18c) A false statement that is known to be false or is made recklessly — without knowing or caring whether it is true or false — and that is intended to induce a party to detrimentally rely on it. — Also termed *fraudulent representation*; *deceit.*

"A misrepresentation is fraudulent if the maker intends his assertion to induce a party to manifest his assent and the maker (a) knows or believes that the assertion is not in accord with the facts, or (b) does not have the confidence that he states or implies in the truth of the assertion, or (c) knows that he does not have the basis that he states or implies for the assertion." Restatement (Second) of Contracts § 162(1) (1979).

▸ **innocent misrepresentation.** (1809) A false statement that the speaker or writer does not know is false; a misrepresentation that, though false, was not made fraudulently.

"[I]t is not at all necessary for relief that the misrepresentation should be fraudulent. An innocent misrepresentation is just as disastrous to the person deceived as one tainted with falsehood; and it is equally a ground for estoppel." John S. Ewart, *An Exposition of the Principles of Estoppel by Misrepresentation* 79 (1900).

▸ **material misrepresentation.** (18c) **1.** *Contracts.* A false statement that is likely to induce a reasonable person to assent or that the maker knows is likely to induce the recipient to assent. **2.** *Torts.* A false statement to which a reasonable person would attach importance in deciding how to act in the transaction in question or to which the maker knows or has reason to know that the recipient attaches some importance. *See* Restatement (Second) of Torts § 538 (1979).

"The materiality of a misrepresentation is determined from the viewpoint of the maker, while the justification of reliance is determined from the viewpoint of the recipient. . . . The requirement of materiality may be met in either of two ways. First, a misrepresentation is material if it would be likely to induce a reasonable person to manifest his assent. Second, it is material if the maker knows that for some special reason it is likely to induce the particular recipient to manifest his assent. There may be personal considerations that the recipient regards as important even though they would not be expected to affect others in his situation, and if the maker is aware of this the misrepresentation may be material even though it would not be expected to induce a reasonable person to make the proposed contract. One who preys upon another's known idiosyncrasies cannot complain if the contract is held voidable when he succeeds in what he is endeavoring to accomplish. . . . Although a nonfraudulent misrepresentation that is not material does not make the contract voidable under the rules stated in this Chapter, the recipient may have a claim to relief under other rules, such as those relating to breach of warranty." Restatement (Second) of Contracts § 162 cmt. c (1979).

▸ **misrepresentation by silence.** (1900) **1.** See *passive misrepresentation* (1). **2.** The act of failing to make required disclosures or corrections to previous statements when there is a duty to do so.

▸ **misrepresentation of fact.** (18c) A false statement about the occurrence, existence, or quality of an act, circumstance, event, or thing, tangible or intangible.

▸ **misrepresentation of law.** (1838) A false statement about common or statutory law applicable to given facts.

▸ **misrepresentation of source.** See PASSING OFF.

▸ **negligent misrepresentation.** (1888) A careless or inadvertent false statement in circumstances where care should have been taken.

▸ **passive misrepresentation.** (1901) **1.** The act of remaining silent under circumstances that make the silence seem to support a false statement's validity. — Also termed *silent misrepresentation*; *misrepresentation by silence.* **2.** The act of leading a person to believe something that isn't true without actually making any false statements.

▸ **personal misrepresentation.** (1849) A false statement made or authorized by an individual with knowledge of the falsity.

▸ **silent misrepresentation.** See *passive misrepresentation* (1).

misrepresentee. (1936) Someone to whom something has been misrepresented.

misrepresenter. (17c) Someone who misrepresents something to another. — Also spelled *misrepresentor.*

misrule, *n.* (14c) **1.** Bad government; misgovernment. **2.** Disorder; anarchy.

Missile Defense Agency. A unit in the U.S. Department of Defense responsible for developing and deploying a missile-defense system capable of protecting the United States, its armed forces, and others from missile attack. — Abbr. MDA.

missilia (mi-**sɪ**-lee-ə), *n. pl.* [fr. Latin *mittere* "to throw"] *Roman law.* Money that the praetors, consuls, or wealthy individuals throw as gifts to people on the street; largesse.

missing-evidence rule. (1981) The doctrine that, when a party fails at trial to present evidence that the party controls and that would have been proper to present, the jury is entitled to infer that the evidence would have been unfavorable to that party.

missing person. (18c) **1.** Someone whose whereabouts are unknown and, after a reasonable time, seem to be unascertainable. **2.** Someone who has disappeared and whose family has asked the police for help in finding the person. **3.** Someone whose continuous and unexplained absence entitles the heirs to petition a court to declare the person dead and to divide up the person's property. See SEVEN-YEARS'-ABSENCE RULE. Cf. DISAPPEARED PERSON.

missing ship. *Maritime law.* A vessel that has been gone for an unreasonably long time, leading to the presumption that it is lost at sea; esp., a vessel that has been gone longer than the average time it takes a vessel to make a similar voyage in the same season.

missing-witness instruction. (1958) A jury instruction that allows a jury to infer that a witness who is known, friendly, and available to a party, but is not called by that party to testify, would have testified unfavorably against that party. • This is an exception to the instruction that a jury may not draw an inference from evidence not produced. — Also termed *absent-witness instruction*; *missing-witness charge*. See MISSING-WITNESS RULE.

missing-witness rule. (1961) The doctrine that, when a party fails at trial to present a witness who is available only to that party and whose testimony would have been admissible, the jury is entitled to infer that the witness's testimony would have been unfavorable to that party.

missio in bona (**mis**[**h**]-ee-oh in **boh**-nə). [Latin] (1887) *Roman law.* **1.** A praetor's grant to a creditor of individual items of the judgment debtor's property already in the creditor's possession. **2.** A praetor's grant to a creditor in possession of the debtor's whole estate, as a form of execution of judgment.

missio in possessionem (**mis**[**h**]-ee-oh in pə-zes[h]-ee-**oh**-nəm). [Latin] (17c) *Roman law.* A praetor's grant to a creditor of the debtor's entire estate as a form of execution of judgment.

mission. (17c) An important, official task that an individual or group carries out.

▸ **covert mission.** (1826) An operation planned and executed to create a political or military effect without revealing who sponsored or carried out the operation. — Also termed *covert operation*; *covert action*; *secret mission*.

missive. See LETTER MISSIVE.

Missouri Nonpartisan Court Plan. See MISSOURI PLAN.

Missouri plan. A system for the merit selection of judges whereby a nonpartisan commission screens candidates for a judicial vacancy and sends a list of the best-qualified candidates to the governor, who then has 60 days within which to select a nominee, in default of which the commission makes the selection. • At the next general election after the judge completes one year of service, the judge must stand for a nonpartisan retention election. If not reelected, the judge is removed from office and the process begins anew. See MERIT SELECTION. — Also termed *Missouri Nonpartisan Court Plan*; *merit-plan election*.

mistake, *n.* (17c) **1.** An error, misconception, or misunderstanding; an erroneous belief. See ERROR. **2.** *Contracts.* The situation in which either (1) the parties to a contract did not mean the same thing, or (2) at least one party had a belief that did not correspond to the facts or law. • As a result, the contract may be voidable.

> "In this Restatement the word 'mistake' is used to refer to an erroneous belief. A party's erroneous belief is therefore said to be a 'mistake' of that party. The belief need not be an articulated one, and a party may have a belief as to a fact when he merely makes an assumption with respect to it, without being aware of alternatives. The word 'mistake' is not used here, as it is sometimes used in common speech, to refer to an improvident act, including the making of a contract, that is the result of such an erroneous belief. This usage is avoided here for the sake of clarity and consistency. Furthermore, the erroneous belief must relate to the facts as they exist at the time of the making of the contract. A party's prediction or judgment as to events to occur in the future, even if erroneous, is not a 'mistake' as that word is defined here. An erroneous belief as to the contents or effect of a writing that expresses the agreement is, however, a mistake. Mistake alone, in the sense in which the word is used here, has no legal consequences. The legal consequences of mistake in connection with the creation of contractual liability are determined by [substantive rules]." Restatement (Second) of Contracts § 151 cmt. a (1979).

> "The word *mistake* is generally used in the law of contracts to refer to an erroneous perception — what the Restatement Second calls 'a belief that is not in accord with the facts.' To avoid confusion, it should not be used, as it sometimes is in common speech, to refer to an improvident act, such as the making of a contract, that results from such a perception. Nor should it be used, as it sometimes is by courts and writers, to refer to what is more properly called a misunderstanding, a situation in which two parties attach different meanings to their language." 2 E. Allan Farnsworth, *Farnsworth on Contracts* § 9.2, at 589–90 (3d ed. 2004) (quoting Restatement (Second) of Contracts § 151 (3d ed. 1979)).

▸ **basic mistake.** (1925) A mistake of fact or of law constituting the basis on which a transaction rests.

▸ **bilateral mistake.** See *mutual mistake* (1).

▸ **collateral mistake.** See *unessential mistake*.

▸ **common mistake.** See *mutual mistake* (2).

▸ **essential mistake.** (1818) *Contracts.* A mistake serious enough that no real consent could have existed, so that there was no real agreement.

▸ **fundamental mistake.** (17c) A mistake that prevents an act from having legal effect because the required intent was absent.

▸ **honest mistake.** (17c) A mistake made unintentionally.

▸ **inessential mistake.** See *unessential mistake*.

▸ **mistake of fact.** (1808) **1.** A mistake about a fact that is material to a transaction; any mistake other than a mistake of law. — Also termed *error in fact*; *error of fact*. **2.** The defense asserting that a criminal defendant acted from an innocent misunderstanding of fact rather than from a criminal purpose.

▸ **mistake of law.** (18c) **1.** A mistake about the legal effect of a known fact or situation. — Also termed *error in law; error of law.* **2.** The defense asserting that a defendant did not understand the criminal consequences of certain conduct. • This defense is generally not as effective as a mistake of fact.

▸ **mutual mistake.** (18c) **1.** A mistake in which each party misunderstands the other's intent. — Also termed *bilateral mistake.* **2.** A mistake that is shared and relied on by both parties to a contract. • A court will often revise or nullify a contract based on a mutual mistake about a material term. — Also termed (in sense 2) *common mistake.*

> "The term 'common mistake' is more usually, but less grammatically, referred to as 'mutual mistake.' Cheshire and Fifoot on *Contract* have made a heroic effort to introduce and establish the more correct term, and it does seem to be gaining ground. However, the beginner is warned that the term 'mutual mistake' is nearly always used by the Courts to mean what we here call 'common mistake.'" P.S. Atiyah, *An Introduction to the Law of Contract* 190 n.7 (3d ed. 1981).

▸ **nonessential mistake.** See *unessential mistake.*

▸ **unessential mistake.** (1928) *Contracts.* A mistake that does not relate to the nature of the contents of an agreement, but only to some external circumstance, so that the mistake has no effect on the validity of the agreement. — Also termed *inessential mistake; nonessential mistake; collateral mistake.*

▸ **unilateral mistake.** (1885) A mistake by only one party to a contract. • A unilateral mistake is generally not as likely to be a ground for voiding the contract as is a mutual mistake.

mistaken-identification direction. See *identification instruction* under JURY INSTRUCTION.

mistaken-identification instruction. See *identification instruction* under JURY INSTRUCTION.

mistaken identity. (18c) A situation in which someone believes, and esp. has reported to authorities, that he or she has seen a particular person when in fact it was someone else <a case of mistaken identity>. See IDENTITY (5).

mistakenly induced revocation. See DEPENDENT RELATIVE REVOCATION.

mistake-of-fact defense. (1936) *Criminal law.* A criminal defendant's claim that some factual error negates the mens rea necessary for a guilty verdict.

mistery (**mis**-tər-ee). *Hist.* A business; a trade. — Also spelled *mystery.*

mistreat. (15c) To treat (a person or animal) badly, esp. to the level of cruelty; to abuse. Cf. ABUSE, *vb.*; MALTREAT.

mistrial. (17c) **1.** A trial that the judge brings to an end without a determination on the merits because of a procedural error or serious misconduct occurring during the proceedings. **2.** A trial that ends inconclusively because the jury cannot agree on a verdict. — Also termed *abortive trial.*

misunderstanding. (13c) **1.** A flawed interpretation of meaning or significance. **2.** A situation in which the words or acts of two people suggest assent, but one or both of them in fact intend something different from what the words or acts express. **3.** A quarrel; an instance of usu. mild wrangling.

misuse, *n.* (14c) **1.** *Products liability.* A defense alleging that the plaintiff used the product in an improper, unintended, or unforeseeable manner. **2.** *Patents.* The use of a patent either to improperly extend the granted monopoly to nonpatented goods or to violate antitrust laws.

misuser. (17c) An abuse of a right or office, as a result of which the person having the right might lose it <it is an act of misuser to accept a bribe>. Cf. USER.

mitigate (**mit**-ə-gayt), *vb.* (15c) To make less severe or intense; to make less harmful, unpleasant, or seriously bad <the fired employee mitigated her damages for wrongful termination by accepting a new job>. Cf. MILITATE. — **mitigatory** (**mit**-ə-gə-tor-ee), *adj.*

mitigating circumstance. See CIRCUMSTANCE.

mitigating defense. See DEFENSE (1).

mitigation. (14c) **1.** A reduction in how harmful, unpleasant, or seriously bad a situation is; a lessening in severity or intensity.

▸ **environmental mitigation.** See ENVIRONMENTAL MITIGATION.

2. The portrayal of a crime, mistake, or misjudgment as being less than complete, as by pointing to other contributory causes or to the person's own background of adversity as a factor.

mitigation banking. See ENVIRONMENTAL MITIGATION.

mitigation cost. See COST (1).

mitigation-of-damages doctrine. (1978) The principle inducing a plaintiff, after an injury or breach of contract, to make reasonable efforts to alleviate the effects of the injury or breach. • If the defendant can show that the plaintiff failed to mitigate damages, the plaintiff's recovery may be reduced. — Also termed *avoidable-consequences doctrine.* Cf. DOCTRINE OF CONSTRUCTIVE SERVICE (2).

mitigation of punishment. (18c) *Criminal law.* A reduction in punishment due to mitigating circumstances that reduce the criminal's level of culpability, such as the existence of no prior convictions. See *mitigating circumstance* under CIRCUMSTANCE.

mitigator. A factor tending to show that a criminal defendant, though guilty, is less culpable than the act alone would indicate <the fact that he was coerced into taking part in the robbery may have been a mitigator in the minds of the jurors>. Cf. AGGRAVATOR.

mitiori sensu. See IN MITIORI SENSU.

mitter avant (**mit**-ər ə-**vant**), *vb.* [Law French] *Hist.* To present or produce (evidence, etc.) to a court.

mittimus (**mit**-ə-məs). [Law Latin "we send"] (15c) *Hist.* **1.** A court order or warrant directing a jailer to detain a person until ordered otherwise; COMMITMENT (4). **2.** A certified transcript of a prisoner's conviction or sentencing proceedings. **3.** A writ directing the transfer of records from one court to another. Pl. **mittimuses.**

mixed action. See ACTION (4).

mixed blood. See BLOOD.

mixed cognation. See COGNATION (2).

mixed condition. See CONDITION (2).

mixed contract. See CONTRACT.

mixed cost. See COST (1).

mixed government. See GOVERNMENT (3).

mixed insurance company. See INSURANCE COMPANY.

mixed interpretation. See *liberal interpretation* under INTERPRETATION (1).

mixed jury. See JURY.

mixed larceny. See LARCENY.

mixed law. (15c) A law concerning both persons and property.

mixed marriage. See MARRIAGE (1).

mixed-motive doctrine. (1985) *Employment law.* The principle that, when the evidence in an employment-discrimination case shows that the complained-of employment action was based in part on a nondiscriminatory reason and in part on a discriminatory reason, the plaintiff must show that discrimination was a motivating factor for the employment action and, if the plaintiff makes that showing, then the defendant must show that it would have taken the same action without regard to the discriminatory reason.

mixed nuisance. See NUISANCE.

mixed policy. See INSURANCE POLICY.

mixed presumption. See PRESUMPTION.

mixed property. See PROPERTY.

mixed question. (18c) **1.** MIXED QUESTION OF LAW AND FACT. **2.** An issue involving conflicts of foreign and domestic law.

mixed question of law and fact. (1805) An issue that is neither a pure question of fact nor a pure question of law. • Mixed questions of law and fact are typically resolved by juries. See *intermediate fact* under FACT. — Often shortened to *mixed question.* — Also termed *mixed question of fact and law; mixed issue of law and fact.*

> "Many issues in a lawsuit involve elements of both law and fact. Whether these be referred to as mixed questions of law and fact, or legal inferences from the facts, or the application of law to the facts, there is substantial authority that they are not protected by the 'clearly erroneous' rule and are freely reviewable. This principle has been applied to antitrust violations, bankruptcy, contracts, copyright, taxation, and to other areas of the law." 9A Charles Alan Wright & Arthur R. Miller, *Federal Practice and Procedure* § 2589, at 608–11 (2d ed. 1995).

mixed theory of punishment. (1978) Any of a number of theories of punishment that include consequentialist and retributivist elements, the most familiar being negative retributivism. Cf. CONSEQUENTIALISM (3); UTILITARIAN-DETERRENCE THEORY; *hedonistic utilitarianism* under UTILITARIANISM; RETRIBUTIVISM; *negative retributivism* under RETRIBUTIVISM.

mixed tithes. See TITHE.

mixed treaty. See TREATY (1).

mixed trust. See TRUST (3).

mixed war. See WAR (1).

mixtion (**miks**-chən). (14c) *Archaic.* **1.** The process of mixing products together so that they can no longer be separated. **2.** The product of mixing.

mixtum imperium (**miks**-təm im-**peer**-ee-əm). [Latin] (16c) *Hist.* Mixed authority; mixed jurisdiction. • This term refers to the power of subordinate civil magistrates.

MJOA. *abbr.* MOTION FOR JUDGMENT OF ACQUITTAL.

MLA. *abbr.* **1.** MOTION FOR LEAVE TO APPEAL. **2.** MAJOR LIFE ACTIVITY.

MMBtu. *abbr. Oil & gas.* One million British thermal units, one of the standard units for measuring a quantity of natural gas.

MMF. *abbr.* See *money-market fund* under MUTUAL FUND.

MMI. *abbr.* MAXIMUM MEDICAL IMPROVEMENT.

MMS. *abbr.* MINERALS MANAGEMENT SERVICE.

MMWA. *abbr.* MAGNUSON–MOSS WARRANTY ACT.

***M'Naghten* rules.** See MCNAGHTEN RULES.

***M'Naughten* rules.** See MCNAGHTEN RULES.

M.O. *abbr.* (1955) MODUS OPERANDI.

mobile commerce. (2005) The practice of using wireless handheld devices to buy and sell goods and services and to conduct financial and other transactions through services on the Internet. — Also termed *m-commerce.*

mobile goods. See GOODS.

mobile money. (1996) The use of a mobile device, usu. a phone, to transfer money between bank accounts, to make a deposit or withdrawal, to pay a bill, or to buy something. — Also termed *mobile payment; mobile transfer.*

***Mobile–Sierra* doctrine.** (1974) The principle that the Federal Energy Regulatory Commission may not grant a rate increase to a natural-gas producer unless the producer's contract authorizes a rate increase, or unless the existing rate is so low that it may adversely affect the public interest (as by threatening the continued viability of the public utility to continue its service). *United Gas Pipe Line Co. v. Mobile Gas Serv. Corp.*, 350 U.S. 332, 76 S.Ct. 373 (1956); *Federal Power Comm'n v. Sierra Pac. Power Co.*, 350 U.S. 348, 76 S.Ct. 368 (1956). — Also termed *Sierra–Mobile doctrine.*

mobilia (moh-**bil**-ee-ə), *n. pl.* [Latin "movables"] *Roman law.* Movable things. • The term primarily refers to inanimate objects but sometimes also refers to slaves and animals (these more properly called *moventia*).

> "*Mobilia*, is strictly such goods as are passively moveable, or removeable: and *Moventia*, such as actively and by their own accord do move themselves, as live goods. Yet regularly moveables are indifferently understood of both, and will pass them in a devise." Lord Chief Baron Gilbert, *A Treatise of Equity* 101 (3d ed. 1792).

mobiliary (moh-**bil**-ee-air-ee), *adj.* **1.** Of, relating to, or involving movable property. **2.** More narrowly, of, relating to, or involving household furniture. **3.** Of, relating to, or involving the mobilization of troops, equipment, etc.

mobilia sequuntur personam (moh-**bil**-ee-ə si-**kwən**-tər pər-**soh**-nəm). [Latin] (1844) *Int'l law.* Movables follow the person — i.e., the law of the person. • This is the general principle that rights of ownership and transfer of movable property are determined by the law of the owner's domicile. Cf. IMMOBILIA SITUM SEQUUNTUR.

> "The maxim *mobilia sequuntur personam* is the exception rather than the rule, and is probably to be confined to certain special classes of general assignments such as marriage settlements and devolutions on death and bankruptcy." *Handel v. Slatford*, 1953 Q.B. 248, 257 (Eng. C.A.).

"Under the influence of Savigny many Continental systems in the mid-nineteenth century led the way for Anglo-American law in limiting the operation of the doctrine of *mobilia sequuntur personam* to universal assignments of movables, adopting for particular assignments the single principle of the *lex situs* of the movable." R.H. Graveson, *Conflict of Laws* 457 (7th ed. 1974).

mob-madness. The unrestrained, frenetic emotionalism of an overexcited crowd.

MOC. *abbr.* MANUAL OF CLASSIFICATION.

mock trial. (18c) **1.** A fictitious trial organized to allow law students, or sometimes lawyers, to practice the techniques of trial advocacy. **2.** A fictitious trial, arranged by a litigant's attorney, to assess trial strategy, to estimate the case's value or risk, and to evaluate the case's strengths and weaknesses. • In this procedure, people from the relevant jury pool are hired to sit as mock jurors who, after a condensed presentation of both sides, deliberate and reach a verdict (often while being observed by the participants behind a one-way glass). The jurors may later be asked specific questions about various arguments, techniques, and other issues. Because the mock jurors usu. do not know which side has hired them, their candid views are thought to be helpful in formulating trial strategies. Cf. MOOT COURT.

modal legacy. See LEGACY (1).

mode. (17c) **1.** A manner of behaving, living, or doing something <mode of proceeding> <mode of process>. **2.** A particular way that a machine, device, or piece of equipment can operate <put your cellphone on airplane mode>. **3.** The mood of a verb; specif., the manner in which the action, being, or state of verb is expressed or conceived <imperative mode>. — Also termed *mood*. **4.** The arrangement of prepositions in a syllogism; esp., the style of the connection between the major and minor premises. **5.** Collectively, the qualities, attributes, or relations of any existing things, esp. when considered independently.

model act. (1931) A statute drafted by the National Conference of Commissioners on Uniform State Laws and proposed as guideline legislation for the states to borrow from or adapt to suit their individual needs. • Examples of model acts include the Model Employment Termination Act and the Model Punitive Damages Act. Cf. UNIFORM LAW; UNIFORM ACT.

Model Code of Professional Responsibility. A set of guidelines for lawyers, organized in the form of canons, disciplinary rules, and ethical considerations. • Published by the ABA in 1969, this code has been replaced in most states by the Model Rules of Professional Conduct as the ethical standards by which lawyers are regulated and disciplined, although the Model Code continues to be used to interpret and apply the Model Rules. — Abbr. MCPR.

model jury charge. See *model jury instruction* under JURY INSTRUCTION.

model jury direction. See *model jury instruction* under JURY INSTRUCTION.

model jury instruction. See JURY INSTRUCTION.

Model Marriage and Divorce Act. See UNIFORM MARRIAGE AND DIVORCE ACT.

Model Penal Code. A criminal code drafted and proposed by the American Law Institute, adopted in 1962, and used as the basis for criminal-law revision by many states. — Abbr. MPC.

"[T]he [Model Penal] Code stimulated a movement for legislative criminal law reform of unprecedented scope. The latest Annual Report of the American Law Institute reveals that over thirty states have adopted revised criminal codes since the Model Penal Code started reporting its drafts; six states and Congress have revisions completed awaiting enactment; and three states have revisions under way. In very few instances has any jurisdiction adopted the Code substantially whole. But in virtually no case has the revision escaped the impact of the Code's formulations. As a result the Model Penal Code has by now permeated and transformed the criminal law of the country." Sanford H. Kadish, *Codifiers of the Criminal Law: Wechsler's Predecessors*, 78 Colum. L. Rev. 1098, 1144 (1978).

Model Penal Code test. See SUBSTANTIAL-CAPACITY TEST.

Model Putative Fathers Act. See UNIFORM PUTATIVE AND UNKNOWN FATHERS ACT.

Model Rules of Professional Conduct. A set of ethical guidelines for lawyers, organized in the form of 59 rules — some mandatory, some discretionary — together with explanatory comments. • Published by the ABA in 1983, these rules generally replaced the Model Code of Professional Responsibility and have been adopted as law, sometimes with modifications, by most states. The Model Code of Professional Responsibility is sometimes used to interpret and apply the Model Rules. — Abbr. MRPC.

Model State Trademark Bill. A proposed statute intended to standardize trademark laws among the states. • The bill was first promulgated by the International Trademark Association (then called the United States Trademark Association) in 1949. — Abbr. MSTB.

model statute. See *uniform statute* under STATUTE.

moderamen inculpatae tutelae (moh-də-**ray**-mən in-kəl-**pay**-tee t[y]oo-**tee**-lee). [Law Latin] (17c) *Hist.* **1.** The degree of force justified in self-defense. **2.** A plea of justifiable self-defense. — Also termed *inculpatae tutelae moderatio* (mod-ə-**ray**-shee-oh).

moderate castigavit (mod-ə-**ray**-tee kas-tə-**gay**-vit). [Latin "he moderately chastised"] (1877) *Hist.* A plea justifying a trespass because it is really a chastisement that the defendant is legally entitled to inflict on the plaintiff because of their relationship.

moderate force. See *nondeadly force* under FORCE.

moderator. (16c) **1.** Someone who presides at a meeting or assembly. See CHAIR (1). **2.** *Scots law.* The person who presides in a public assembly; specif., the elected chair of the General Assembly of the Church of Scotland or another Presbyterian church, of a presbytery, or of a kirk session.

modiatio (moh-dee-**ay**-shee-oh), *n.* [Latin] *Hist.* A duty paid for every tierce of wine. See PRISAGE.

modica differentia (**mod**-i-kə dif-ə-**ren**-shee-ə). [Latin] (17c) *Scots law.* A moderate difference, esp. in price.

modicum. (14c) A small amount.

▸ **modicum of evidence.** (1861) A small but sufficient amount of evidence.

modification. (17c) **1.** A change to something; an alteration or amendment <a contract modification>. **2.** A qualification or limitation of something <a modification of drinking habits>. **3.** *Parliamentary law.* A change in a motion that its mover initiates or accepts, usu. before the chair has stated the motion. • The mover controls a motion only until the chair states the question, after which the motion belongs to the assembly and the mover cannot modify it without the assembly's permission. See *request for permission to modify a motion* under REQUEST.

modification order. (1936) *Family law.* A post-divorce order that changes the terms of child support, custody, visitation, or alimony. • A modification order may be agreed to by the parties or may be ordered by the court. The party wishing to modify an existing order must show a material change in circumstances from the time when the order sought to be modified was entered. See CHANGE IN CIRCUMSTANCES.

Modified Accelerated Cost Recovery System. See ACCELERATED COST RECOVERY SYSTEM.

modified-comparative-negligence doctrine. See 50-PERCENT RULE.

modify, *vb.* **1.** To make somewhat different; to make small changes to (something) by way of improvement, suitability, or effectiveness <the focus group helped the inventors modify their invention>. **2.** To make more moderate or less sweeping; to reduce in degree or extent; to limit, qualify, or moderate <the judge modified the punishment, reducing the prison term to two years>. **3.** (Of an adjective or adverb) to describe or limit the meaning of (a noun or verb) <in the phrase *drive recklessly,* the adverb *recklessly* modifies the verb *drive*>. **4.** *Scots law.* To decide on or determine (the stipend of a parish, etc.) <the decision-makers modified the stipend at £45 per week>.

modius (**moh**-dee-əs), *n.* [Latin "a measure"] (14c) *Hist.* **1.** A bushel. **2.** An uncertain measure, as of land.

modo et forma (**moh**-doh et **for**-mə). [Latin] In manner and form. • In common-law pleading, this phrase began the conclusion of a traverse. Its object was to put the burden on the party whose pleading was being traversed not only to prove the allegations of fact but also to establish as correct the manner and form of the pleading. — Also termed *manner and form.*

modus (**moh**-dəs), *n.* [Latin "mode"] (16c) **1.** *Criminal procedure.* The part of a charging instrument describing the manner in which an offense was committed. **2.** *Roman & civil law.* Mode; manner; consideration, esp. the manner in which a gift, bequest, servitude, etc. is to be employed. See SUB MODO. **3.** *Eccles. law.* See DE MODO DECIMANDI. Cf. MODUS OPERANDI.

modus decimandi (**moh**-dəs des-ə-**man**-dɪ). See DE MODO DECIMANDI.

modus de non decimando (**moh**-dəs dee non des-ə-**man**-doh). See DE NON DECIMANDO.

modus habilis (**moh**-dəs **hab**-ə-lis). [Latin] (18c) A valid manner (in proving a debt, etc.).

modus operandi (**moh**-dəs op-ə-**ran**-dɪ *or* -dee). [Latin "a manner of operating"] (17c) A method of operating or a manner of procedure; esp., a pattern of criminal behavior so distinctive that investigators attribute it to the work of the same person <staging a fight at the train station was part of the pickpocket's modus operandi>. — Abbr. M.O. Pl. **modi operandi.**

modus procedendi (**moh**-dəs proh-sə-**den**-dɪ). [Latin] *Hist.* Manner of proceeding.

modus tenendi (**moh**-dəs tə-**nen**-dɪ). [Latin] *Hist.* The manner of holding. • This phrase referred to the different types of tenures by which estates were held.

Modus Tenendi Parliamentum (moh-dəs tə-**nen**-dɪ pahr-lə-**men**-təm). [Law Latin "the manner of holding Parliament"] *Hist.* A 14th-century writing on the powers of Parliament, translated in the 17th century and edited by T.D. Hardy in 1846.

modus transferendi (**moh**-dəs trans-fə-**ren**-dɪ). [Law Latin] (17c) *Hist.* The manner of transferring. — Also spelled *modus transferrendi.* Cf. TITULUS TRANSFERENDI.

modus vacandi (**moh**-dəs və-**kan**-dɪ). [Law Latin] (17c) *Hist.* The manner of vacating. • This term was often used in determining the circumstances under which a vassal surrendered an estate to a lord.

modus vivendi (**moh**-dəs vi-**ven**-dɪ or -dee). [Latin "means of living (together)"] (1882) *Int'l law.* A temporary, provisional arrangement concluded between subjects of international law and giving rise to binding obligations on the parties.

> "[Modus vivendi] is an instrument of toleration looking towards a settlement, by preparing for or laying down the basis of a method of living together with a problem or by bridging over some difficulty pending a permanent settlement. Normally it is used for provisional and interim arrangements which ultimately are to be replaced by a formal agreement of a more permanent and detailed character. There is no clear distinction of a *modus vivendi* from other treaties. The most distinguishing feature is its provisional character; nevertheless a *modus vivendi* may be exercised for an indefinite period of time if it is prolonged *sine die* or if a definitive solution to the problem cannot be reached by treaty. Some 'temporary' arrangements have actually turned out to be quite durable." Walter Rudolf, "Modus Vivendi,'" in 3 *Encyclopedia of Public International Law* 443 (1997).

moeble (**myoo**-bəl), *adj.* [Law French] *Hist.* Movable, as in the phrase *biens moebles* ("movable goods").

moiety (**moy**-ə-tee). (15c) **1.** A half of something (such as an estate). — Also termed *mediety.* **2.** A portion less than half; a small segment. **3.** In federal customs law, a payment made to an informant who assists in the seizure of contraband, the payment being no more than 25% of the contraband's net value (up to a maximum of $250,000). 19 USCA § 1619.

moiety act. (1875) *Criminal law.* A statute providing that a portion (such as half) of an imposed fine will inure to the benefit of an informant whose information leads to a conviction.

mole. (1922) Someone who uses a long affiliation with an organization to gain access to and betray confidential information.

molestation. (15c) **1.** The persecution or harassment of someone <molestation of a witness>. **2.** The act of making unwanted and indecent advances to or on someone, esp. for sexual gratification <sexual molestation>. — **molest,** *vb.* — **molester,** *n.*

▸ **child molestation.** (1951) Any indecent or sexual activity with, involving, or surrounding a child, usu. under the age of 14. *See* Fed. R. Evid. 414(d).

***Molineux* rule.** (1959) *New York law.* The principle that evidence of prior crimes is inadmissible when offered to prove the defendant's bad character and to show that the defendant is therefore more likely than not to have committed the crime charged. • The evidence is admissible if offered to prove something other than criminal propensity, such as motive, identity, absence of mistake or accident, intent, or the existence of a common scheme or plan. The rule was first handed down in *People v. Molineux*, 61 N.E. 286 (N.Y. 1901).

moliturae (mol-i-**t[y]uur**-ee *or* -**chuur**-ee). [Law Latin] *Scots law*. Tolls for grinding grain; multures. See CUM ASTRICTIS MULTURIS.

molliter manus imposuit (**mol**-ə-tər **man**-əs im-**poz**-[y]ə-wit). [Latin] *Hist*. He gently laid hands on. • This phrase was used in actions of trespass and assault to justify a defendant's use of force as reasonable, as when it was necessary to keep the peace.

Molotov cocktail. A simple bomb consisting of a bottle filled with gasoline and a lighted cloth. — Also termed (BrE) *petrol bomb*.

mommy track. (1988) *Employment law. Slang*. A career path that allows a mother to work under less stringent performance requirements with the understanding that she will probably have a more limited salary and less opportunity for advancement.

monandry, *n*. (1855) The condition or practice of a woman's having only one husband at a time. — **monandrous,** *adj*.

monarchy, *n*. (14c) A government in which a single person rules, with powers varying from absolute dictatorship to the merely ceremonial.

▸ **limited monarchy.** (17c) A monarchical form of government in which the monarch's power is subject to constitutional or other restraints. — Also termed *constitutional monarchy*.

> "Ours is now, as has been seen, a 'constitutional' or 'limited' monarchy. The Queen and the Crown (which represents not only the Queen herself, but also her Government) are symbolic of the whole might and unity of the State; but, for all practical purposes, the Queen is herself powerless. The business of government which is carried on in her name is done by her Ministers. Her Majesty only acts upon the 'advice' of her Ministers and they are . . . responsible to Parliament for their acts." Philip S. James, *Introduction to English Law* 111 (9th ed. 1976).

moneta (mə-**nee**-tə), *n*. [Latin] Money.

monetagium (mon-ə-**tay**-jee-əm), *n*. [Law Latin "mintage"] *Hist*. **1.** The right to coin money; mintage. **2.** A tribute paid by s tenant to persuade a lord not to change coinage.

monetarism (**mon**-i-tə-riz-əm). (1963) An economic theory claiming that the money supply is the basic influence on the economy. • The theory was originated by Milton Friedman in the late 1960s. — **monetarist,** *adj*.

monetary, *adj*. (17c) **1.** Of, relating to, or involving money <monetary value> <monetary damages>. **2.** Financial <monetary services> <monetary investments>.

monetary bequest. See *pecuniary bequest* under BEQUEST.

monetization, *n*. (1867) **1.** The process of establishing something as a nation's legal tender. **2.** The production of coins and banknotes. **3.** The conversion of investments to cash. **4.** Revenue generation, such as by selling non-income-producing possessions or charging for services that were previously free.

monetize. (1879) **1.** To convert (a metal) into coins. **2.** To give a standard value to (a valuable commodity, such as gold or silver) as a basis for a national currency. **3.** To use (a thing, esp. a business model) in commerce so as to make money; esp., to convert (something of value) into cash. **4.** To purchase (debt) so as to make available money that would otherwise be used in servicing the debt.

money. (14c) **1.** The medium of exchange authorized or adopted by a government as part of its currency; esp., domestic currency <coins and currency are money>. UCC § 1-201(24). **2.** Assets that can be easily converted to cash <demand deposits are money>. **3.** Capital that is invested or traded as a commodity <the money market> **4.** (*pl*.) Funds; sums of money <investment moneys>. — Also spelled (in sense 4) *monies*. See MEDIUM OF EXCHANGE; LEGAL TENDER.

▸ **current money.** (17c) Money that circulates throughout a country; currency.

▸ **earnest money.** See EARNEST MONEY.

▸ **e-money.** (1993) Money or a money substitute that is transformed into information stored on a computer or computer chip so that it can be transferred over information systems such as the Internet. Cf. *e-check* under CHECK. — Also termed *digital cash*; *electronic cash*; *electronic currency*; *Internet scrip*; *on-line scrip*.

▸ **fiat money.** (1880) Paper money that, in contrast to hard currency, is not backed by reserves but instead derives its value from government regulation or law declaring it legal tender. — Also termed *fiat currency*; *flat money; soft money; soft currency*. See *soft currency* under CURRENCY. Cf. *real money* (1); *hard currency* under CURRENCY.

▸ **hand money.** See HAND MONEY.

▸ **hard money.** (18c) **1.** See *real money* (1); *hard currency* under CURRENCY. **2.** Cash. **3.** *Campaign-finance law*. Direct political-campaign contributions that are subject to legal limits, public disclosure, and regulation by the Federal Election Commission. Cf. *soft money* (3). **4.** Permanent or long-term funding issued by a government or other entity at regular intervals, providing a steady source of financial support to the beneficiary.

▸ **head money.** See HEAD MONEY.

▸ **hush money.** See HUSH MONEY.

▸ **imprest money.** See IMPREST MONEY.

▸ **key money.** See KEY MONEY.

▸ **lawful money.** (16c) Money that is legal tender for the payment of debts.

▸ **mobile money.** See MOBILE MONEY.

▸ **money of necessity.** An irregular type of money issued in exigent circumstances, as during a siege.

▸ **nonfederal money.** See *soft money* (3).

▸ **paper money.** (17c) **1.** Paper documents that circulate as currency. — Also termed *soft money*. Cf. *real money* (1). **2.** Bills drawn by a government against its own credit.

▸ **real money.** (17c) **1.** Money that has metallic or other intrinsic value, as distinguished from paper currency, checks, and drafts. — Also termed *hard money*. See *hard currency* under CURRENCY. Cf. *paper money* (1). **2.** Current cash, as opposed to money on account.

▸ **smart money.** (1926) **1.** Funds held by sophisticated, usu. large investors who are considered capable of minimizing risks and maximizing profits <the smart money

has now left this market>. **2.** See *punitive damages* under DAMAGES <although the jury awarded only $7,000 in actual damages, it also awarded $500,000 in smart money>.

▸ **soft money.** (1878) **1.** See *paper money* (1). **2.** See *fiat money; soft currency* under CURRENCY. **3.** *Campaign-finance law.* The collective political-campaign contributions that are not regulated by federal campaign-finance laws, as they are ostensibly used not for supporting federal candidates but for generic party-building activities such as increasing voter turnout or party membership. • Because it is often difficult in practice to determine how soft money is spent, such donations are often used as a means of avoiding federal campaign-finance regulations. — Also termed *nonfederal money.* Cf. *hard money* (3).

money bequest. See *pecuniary bequest* under BEQUEST.

money bill. See *revenue bill* under BILL (3).

money broker. See BROKER.

money changer. (14c) One whose primary business is exchanging currencies.

money claim. (1844) *Hist.* Under the English Judicature Act of 1875, money claimed as damages, as for breaches of contract and rent arrearages.

money count. See COUNT (2).

money demand. (1821) A claim for a fixed, liquidated sum, as opposed to a damage claim that must be assessed by a jury.

moneyed capital. See CAPITAL.

moneyed corporation. See CORPORATION.

money had and received. See *action for money had and received* under ACTION (4).

money judgment. See JUDGMENT (2).

money land. (1826) Money held in a trust providing for its conversion into land.

money-laundering, *n.* (1974) The act of transferring illegally obtained money through legitimate people or accounts so that its original source cannot be traced. • Money-laundering is a federal crime. 18 USCA § 1956. It is also addressed by state governments, e.g., through the Uniform Money Services Act. Because some money-laundering is conducted across national borders, enforcement of money-laundering laws often requires international cooperation, fostered by organizations such as Interpol. — Also termed *laundering of monetary instruments.*

moneylender. (16c) **1.** Someone whose business is to make monetary loans to people at interest. **2.** PAWNBROKER.

money made. A sheriff's return on a writ of execution signifying that the sum stated on the writ was collected.

money market. See MARKET.

money-market account. (1979) An interest-bearing account at a bank or other financial institution. • Such an account usu. pays interest competitive with money-market funds but allows a limited number of transactions per month. See *money market* under MARKET.

money-market fund. See MUTUAL FUND.

money of necessity. See MONEY.

money order. (1802) A negotiable draft issued by an authorized entity (such as a bank, telegraph company, post office, etc.) to a purchaser, in lieu of a check, to be used to pay a debt or otherwise transmit funds on the credit of the issuer.

money paid. See *action for money paid* under ACTION (4).

money-purchase plan. See EMPLOYEE BENEFIT PLAN.

money scrivener. (17c) A money broker; one who obtains money for mortgages or other loans.

money service business, *n.* (1997) A nonbank entity that provides mechanisms for people to make payments or to obtain currency or cash in exchange for payment instruments. • Money service businesses do not accept deposits or make loans. They include money transmitters, payment instrument sellers, stored-value providers, check cashers, and currency exchangers. — Abbr. MSB. — Also termed *nonbank financial institution* (NBFI); *nondepository provider of financial services* (NDP).

money supply. (1871) All the money that exists in a country's economic system at a particular time; the total amount of money in circulation in the economy. See M1; M2; M3.

monger (**məng**-gər). (bef. 12c) A seller of goods; a trader or dealer <moneymonger>. • The term has pejorative connotations. It appears most frequently today in a combination form, as in *bribemonger, fishmonger, loanmonger, pardonmonger, perjurymonger, rulemonger, scandalmonger,* and *warmonger.*

monier (moh-**nyair** *or* **mən**-ee-ər), *n.* [fr. Law Latin *monetarius* "a moneyer"] *Hist.* **1.** A minister of the mint. **2.** A banker; a dealer in money. — Also spelled *moneyer.*

monies. See MONEY (4).

moniment. (16c) *Archaic.* A memorial; a monument.

monism. *Int'l law.* The doctrine that domestic and international law combine to form one body of law, international law being automatically incorporated into domestic law. Cf. DUALISM.

monition (mə-**nish**-ən), *n.* (14c) **1.** Generally, a warning or caution; ADMONITION. **2.** *Civil & maritime law.* A summons to appear in court as a defendant or to answer contempt charges. **3.** *Eccles. law.* A formal notice from a bishop demanding that an offense within the clergy be corrected or avoided. — **monish** (**mon**-ish), *vb.* — **monitory** (**mon**-ə-tor-ee), *adj.*

monitory letter. (17c) *Eccles. law.* Admonitory communications sent from an ecclesiastical judge to staff members in response to reported abuses or scandals.

monocracy (mə-**nok**-rə-see). (17c) A government by one person. See DICTATORSHIP (1).

monocrat (**mon**-ə-krat). (1848) A monarch who governs alone.

monogamy (mə-**nog**-ə-mee), *n.* (18c) **1.** The custom prevalent in most modern cultures restricting a person to one spouse at a time. **2.** The state or condition of being married to only one spouse. Cf. BIGAMY; POLYGAMY. **3.** The state or condition of being in a relationship and having only one sexual partner during that time. — **monogamous,** *adj.* — **monogamist,** *n.*

▸ **serial monogamy.** (1974) Sexual exclusivity at any given time through a series of sexual relationships, as opposed to one long relationship or several simultaneous relationships.

monomachy (mə-**nom**-ə-kee). *Hist.* See DUEL (2).

monomania (mon-ə-**may**-nee-ə). (1823) Insanity about some particular subject or class of subjects, usu. manifested by a single insane delusion. • A will made by someone suffering from this condition is usu. held valid unless the evidence shows that particular provisions in the will were influenced by the insane delusion. — **monomaniacal,** *adj.* — **monomaniac,** *n.*

monopolist (mə-**nop**-ə-list), *n.* (17c) **1.** Someone who has a monopoly; specif., a seller or combination of sellers who can alter the price of a product in the market by changing the quantity sold. • By reducing output, a monopolist can raise the price above the cost of supplying the market. **2.** A proponent of a monopoly.

monopolium (mon-ə-**poh**-lee-əm). [Latin fr. Greek *monopolion* "a selling alone"] *Hist.* The sole power of sale; a monopoly.

monopolization, *n.* (18c) The activity or process of obtaining a monopoly. • In federal antitrust law, monopolization is an offense with two elements: (1) the possession of monopoly power — that is, the power to fix prices and exclude competitors — within the relevant market, and (2) the willful acquisition or maintenance of that power, as distinguished from growth or development as a consequence of a superior product, business acumen, or historical accident. *U.S. v. Grinnell Corp.*, 384 U.S. 563, 86 S.Ct. 1698 (1966). — **monopolize,** *vb.*

▸ **attempted monopolization.** (1897) The effort to monopolize any part of interstate or foreign commerce, consisting in (1) a specific intent to control prices or destroy competition in the relevant market, (2) predatory or anticompetitive conduct, and (3) a "dangerous probability" of success in achieving monopoly in the relevant market.

monopoly, *n.* (16c) **1.** Control or advantage obtained by one supplier or producer over the commercial market within a given region. Cf. OLIGOPOLY. **2.** The market condition existing when only one economic entity produces a particular product or provides a particular service. • The term is now commonly applied also to situations that approach but do not strictly meet this definition. — **monopolistic,** *adj.* — **monopolist,** *n.*

> "[Ninety per cent] is enough to constitute a monopoly; it is doubtful whether sixty or sixty-four per cent is enough; and certainly thirty-three per cent is not." *U.S. v. Aluminum Co. of Am.*, 148 F.2d 416, 424 (2d Cir. 1945).

> "In the modern sense, a monopoly exists when all, or so nearly all, of an article of trade or commerce within a community or district, is brought within the hands of one person or set of persons, as practically to bring the handling or production of the commodity or thing within such single control to the exclusion of competition or free traffic therein. A monopoly is created when, as the result of efforts to that end, previously competing businesses are so concentrated in the hands of a single person or corporation, or a few persons or corporations acting together, that they have power, for all practical purposes, to control the prices of a commodity and thus to suppress competition. In brief, a monopoly is the practical suppression of effective business competition which thereby creates a power to control prices to the public harm." 54A Am. Jur. 2d *Monopolies, Restraints of Trade, and Unfair Trade Practices* § 781, at 107 (1996).

▸ **bilateral monopoly.** (1906) A hypothetical market condition in which there is only one buyer and one seller, resulting in transactional delays because either party can hold out for a better deal without fearing that the other party will turn to a third party.

▸ **legal monopoly.** (18c) The exclusive right granted by government to business to provide utility services that are, in turn, regulated by the government.

▸ **natural monopoly.** (17c) A monopoly resulting from a circumstance over which the monopolist has no power, as when the market for a product is so limited that only one plant is needed to meet demand.

3. *Patents.* The exclusive right of a patentee to make, use, sell, offer for sale, or import an invention for a certain period of time, subject to the rights of the owners of other patents that would be infringed.

> "[T]he statute of monopolies, 21 Jac. I. c. 3, allows a royal patent of privilege to be granted for fourteen years to any inventor of a new manufacture, for the sole working or making of the same; by virtue whereof a temporary property becomes vested in the patentee." William Blackstone, 2 *Commentaries on the Laws of England* 407 (1766).

monopoly leveraging. (1982) A theory of liability holding that a party violates the antitrust laws when it exploits its monopoly power in one market to gain a competitive advantage in another market.

monopoly power. (1954) The power to control prices or to exclude competition. • The size of the market share is a primary determinant of whether monopoly power exists.

monopsony (mə-**nop**-sə-nee), *n.* (1933) A market situation in which one buyer controls the market. — **monopsonistic,** *adj.*

> "Monopsony is often thought of as the flip side of monopoly. A monopolist is a seller with no rivals; a monopsonist is a buyer with no rivals. A monopolist has power over price exercised by limiting output. A monopsonist also has power over price, but this power is exercised by limiting aggregate purchases. Monopsony injures efficient allocation by reducing the quantity of the input product or service below the efficient level." Lawrence A. Sullivan & Warren S. Grimes, *The Law of Antitrust: An Integrated Handbook* 137–38 (2000).

Monroe Doctrine. (1850) The principle that the United States will allow no intervention or domination in the Western Hemisphere by any non-American country. • This principle, which has some recognition in international law (though not as a formal doctrine), was first announced by President James Monroe in 1823. Cf. POLK DOCTRINE.

> "The Monroe doctrine is a policy which the United States has followed in her own interest more or less consistently for more than a century, and in itself is not contrary to international law, though possible applications of it might easily be so. But it certainly is not a *rule* of international law. It is comparable to policies such as the 'balance of power' in Europe, or the British policies of maintaining the independence of Belgium or the security of our sea-routes to the East, or the former Japanese claim to something like a paramount influence over developments in the Far East. Apart from other objections, it is impossible to regard as a rule of law a doctrine which the United States claims the sole right to interpret, which she interprets in different senses at different times, and which she applies only as and when she chooses. Nor is the doctrine, as Article 21 of the Covenant described it, a 'regional understanding,' for the other states of the region concerned, that is to say, the Continent of America, have never been parties to it and indeed have often resented it." J.L. Brierly, *The Law of Nations* 314 (5th ed. 1955).

monstrans de droit (**mon**-strənz də **droyt**). [Law French] *Hist.* A manifestation of right as a method of obtaining restitution from the Crown. • It was replaced by the writ of right. Currently, restitution is obtained by an ordinary action against the government.

monstrans de faits (**mon**-strənz də **fay[ts]**). [Law French] *Hist.* A showing of deeds; a profert.

monstraverunt (mon-strə-**veer**-ənt). [Latin "they have showed"] *Hist.* A writ of relief for tenants of ancient demesne who were distrained by their lord to do more than the tenure required. — Also termed *writ of monstraverunt.*

> "The little writ serves the turn of a man who claims land according to the custom of the manor; but the tenants of whom we are speaking are protected, and protected collectively, against any increase of their services. This is very plain when the manor is in the hands of a mesne lord. If he attempts to increase the customary services, some of the tenants, acting on behalf of all, will go to the royal chancery and obtain a writ against him. Such a writ begins with the word *Monstraverunt*. The king addresses the lord: — 'A, B and C, men of your manor of X, which is of the ancient demesne of the crown of England, have shown us that you exact from them other customs and services than those which they owe, and which their ancestors did in the time when that manor was in the hands of our predecessors, kings of England; therefore we command you to cease from such exactions, otherwise we shall order our sheriff to interfere." 1 Frederick Pollock & Frederic W. Maitland, *The History of English Law Before the Time of Edward I* 388 (2d ed. 1898).

montes pietatis (**mon**-teez pɪ-ə-**tay**-tis). [Latin "mountains of piety"] (16c) *Hist.* Institutions established to lend money upon pledges of goods.

Montevideo Treaty. *Copyright.* An 1889 copyright treaty among Western Hemisphere countries, based on the Berne Convention but affording less copyright protection.

month. (18c) (bef. 12c) **1.** One of the twelve periods of time in which the calendar is divided <the month of March>. — Also termed *calendar month*; *civil month.* **2.** Any time period approximating 30 days <due one month from today>. **3.** At common law, a period of 28 days; the period of one revolution of the moon <a lunar month>. — Also termed *lunar month.* **4.** One-twelfth of a tropical year; the time it takes the sun to pass through one sign of the zodiac, usu. approximating 30 days <a solar month> — Also termed *solar month.*

monthly lease. See *month-to-month lease* under LEASE.

month-to-month lease. See LEASE.

month-to-month tenancy. See *periodic tenancy* under TENANCY.

Montreal Agreement. A private agreement, signed by most international airlines, waiving both the Warsaw Convention's limitation on liability for death and personal-injury cases (currently about $20,000) and the airline's due-care defenses, raising the liability limit per passenger to $75,000, and providing for absolute liability on the part of the carrier (in the absence of passenger negligence) for all flights originating, stopping, or terminating in the United States. • The Montreal Agreement was the result of negotiations in 1965 and 1966 following the United States' denunciation of the Warsaw Convention, based primarily on its low liability limits. — Also termed *Agreement Relating to Liability Limitation of the Warsaw Convention and the Hague Protocol.*

monument, *n.* (15c) **1.** A written document or record, esp. a legal one. **2.** Any natural or artificial object that is fixed permanently in land and referred to in a legal description of the land. — **monumental,** *adj.*

▸ **mural monument.** (18c) A monument set into or otherwise made part of a wall.

▸ **natural monument.** (1801) A nonartificial permanent thing on land, such as a tree, river, or beach. — Also termed *natural object.*

Moody's Investor's Service. An investment-analysis and advisory service. • Moody's rates the financial strength of businesses from Aaa (strongest) to Aa, A, Baa, and so on to C. The grade may also be modified with a 1, 2, or 3 according to the business's relative strength among similar companies. — Often shortened to *Moody's.*

Mooney-Napue violation. See NAPUE VIOLATION.

moonlighting. (1957) The fact or practice of working at a second job after the hours of a regular job. — Also termed *dual employment*; *multiple job-holding.*

moonshine. (18c) *Slang.* A distilled alcoholic beverage, esp. whiskey, that is illegally manufactured.

moorage. (17c) **1.** An act of mooring a vessel at a wharf. **2.** A mooring charge.

moored in safety. (18c) *Marine insurance.* (Of a vessel) located in a usual place for landing or loading cargo, free from any imminent peril insured against.

moot, *adj.* (16c) **1.** *Archaic.* Open to argument; debatable. **2.** Having no practical significance; hypothetical or academic <the question on appeal became moot once the parties settled their case>. — **mootness,** *n.*

moot, *n.* [Middle English *moot* fr. A.S. *gemot*] **1.** *Hist.* A meeting; a formal assembly. **2.** *Hist.* The hall or place where such a meeting takes place. — Also termed *moot-hall.* **3.** *Hist.* A court formed by assembling the men of the village or tun, the hundred, or the kingdom, or their representatives. **4.** An argument on a hypothetical case by way of practice; a dispute, debate, or contested discussion.

> "The Word *Moot* (as derived from the *Saxon, Motian,* to Plead) is a Term used in the *Inns of Court,* and signifies that Exercise or Arguing of Cases, which young *Barristers* and Students have been used to perform at certain Times, the better to qualify them for Practice, and Defence of Clients [sic] Causes." Giles Jacob, *A Law Grammar* 184 (1744).

moot, *vb.* (bef. 12c) **1.** *Archaic.* To raise or bring forward (a point or question) for discussion. **2.** To render (a question) moot or of no practical significance.

moot case. (16c) A matter in which a controversy no longer exists; a case that presents only an abstract question that does not arise from existing facts or rights.

moot court. (18c) **1.** A fictitious court held usu. in a law school to argue moot or hypothetical cases, esp. at the appellate level. **2.** A practice session for an appellate argument in which a lawyer presents the argument to other lawyers, who first act as judges by asking questions and who later provide criticism on the argument. — Also termed *practice court.* Cf. MOCK TRIAL.

mooted, *adj.* **1.** Unsettled; disputed; agreed so as to subject to different points of view. **2.** Made irrelevant; (of a pending lawsuit) rendered no longer a true case or controversy.

moot man. (17c) *Hist.* Someone who argued cases in the Inns of Court.

mootness doctrine. (1963) The principle that American courts will not decide moot cases — that is, cases in which there is no longer any actual controversy. Cf. RIPENESS.

mop fair. See STATUTE FAIR.

mora (**mor**-ə), *n.* [Latin] (16c) *Roman law.* Willful delay or default in fulfilling a legal obligation. • A creditor or debtor in *mora* could be required to pay interest on any money owed.

> "*Mora.* This was wrongful failure to discharge a legal obligation on demand made at a fitting time and place. It must be wilful: failure to appear, by mistake, or in a *bona fide* belief that there was no *obligatio*, or doubt about it, or by mishap, did not suffice to put a debtor *in mora*." W.W. Buckland, *A Manual of Roman Private Law* 338 (2d ed. 1939).

> "The word *mora* means delay or default. In its technical sense it means a culpable delay in making or accepting performance. . . . The definition includes both *mora debitoris* and *mora creditoris*. In French law and other civil law systems mora debitoris seems (sometimes, if not always) to occur as a mean term between failure to perform a duty timeously and liability for breach. . . . *Mora* usually attaches to a debtor, but it may also attach to a creditor who fails to accept performance duly tendered . . . ." R.W. Lee, *An Introduction to Roman-Dutch Law* 445 (4th ed. 1946).

mora (**mor**-ə), *n.* [Law Latin] *Hist.* A moor; unprofitable ground.

moral, *adj.* **1.** Of, relating to, or involving the study or doctrine of human conduct, of right and wrong behavior, of virtues and vices, of good and evil, and of the universal principles of what it means to live a good life; dealing with principles of good and bad conduct <a moral issue>. **2.** Of, relating to, or involving an ethical view of character, conduct, intentions, and social relations <moral conviction>. **3.** Establishing or disseminating principles of right and wrong behavior <moral values>. **4.** Characterized by excellence in personal conduct; acting in accordance with what is good, right, and honest, esp. in sexual matters <a moral person>. **5.** Subject to a law that enjoins acceptable behavior; capable of understanding the difference between right and wrong <a moral agent>. **6.** Appealing to people's sense of right, whether through the intellect or emotions, but usu. not through practical help <moral support>. **7.** Of, relating to, involving, or operating on one's conscience or ethical judgment <to feel a moral obligation>. **8.** Serving to inculcate lessons about right and wrong <moral writings>. **9.** Virtual or near, though not completely demonstrable <a moral certainty>.

moral absolutism. (1919) The view that a person's action can always properly be seen as right or wrong, regardless of the situation or the consequences. — Also termed *ethical absolutism; objective ethics.* See ABSOLUTISM. Cf. MORAL RELATIVISM. — **moral absolutist,** *n.*

moral certainty. (17c) Absolute certainty. • Moral certainty is not required to sustain a criminal conviction. See REASONABLE DOUBT; *proof beyond a reasonable doubt* under PROOF.

moral coercion. See UNDUE INFLUENCE (1).

moral consideration. See *good consideration* (1) under CONSIDERATION (1).

moral depravity. See MORAL TURPITUDE (1).

moral duress. See DURESS (3).

moral duty. See DUTY (1).

moral evidence. See EVIDENCE.

moral fraud. See *actual fraud* under FRAUD.

moral hazard. See HAZARD (2).

moralistic fallacy. See FALLACY.

morality. (14c) **1.** The doctrine of right and wrong in human conduct; ethics; moral philosophy. — Also termed *moral law.* **2.** Conformity with recognized rules of correct conduct; behavior that accords with what is true and honorable.

> "Morality is concerned with the question as to what is good and bad, right and wrong, in the conduct of human beings." Edgar Bodenheimer, *Treatise on Justice* § 4, at 17 (1967).

▸ **private morality.** (18c) A person's ideals, character, and private conduct, which are not valid governmental concerns if the individual is to be considered sovereign over body and mind and if the need to protect the individual's physical or moral well-being is insufficient to justify governmental intrusion. • In his essay *On Liberty* (1859), John Stuart Mill distinguished between conduct or ideals that affect only the individual from conduct that may do harm to others. Mill argued that governmental intrusion is justified only to prevent harm to others, not to influence a person's private morality.

▸ **public morality.** (18c) **1.** The ideals or general moral beliefs of a society. **2.** The ideals or actions of an individual to the extent that they affect others.

3. The character of being virtuous, esp. in sexual matters.

> "[T]he terms 'morality' and 'immorality' . . . are understood to have a sexual connotation. In fact, the terms 'ethics' and 'morals' are no longer interchangeable in everyday speech. A governmental official arraigned on a 'morals charge' will be accused of something quite different from one accused of an 'ethics violation.'" William P. Golding, *Philosophy of Law* 55 (1975).

moral law. (15c) Collectively, the principles defining right and wrong conduct; one or more standards to which an action must conform to be right or virtuous. See MORALITY.

> "It quite often happens that the moral law disapproves of something which the secular permits as a concession to human frailty." Patrick Devlin, *The Enforcement of Morals* 78 (1968).

moral necessity. See NECESSITY (5).

moral obligation. See OBLIGATION.

moral person. See *artificial person* under PERSON (3).

moral relativism. (1917) The view that there are no absolute or constant standards of right and wrong. — Also termed *ethical relativism; subjective ethics.* Cf. MORAL ABSOLUTISM. — **moral relativist,** *n.*

moral right. (*usu. pl.*) (1980) *Copyright.* The right of an author or artist, based on natural-law principles, to guarantee the integrity of a creation despite any copyright or property-law right of its owner. • Moral rights include rights of (1) attribution (also termed "paternity"): the right to be given credit and to claim credit for a work, and to deny credit if the work is changed; (2) integrity: the right to ensure that the work is not changed without the artist's consent; (3) publication: the right not to reveal a work before its creator is satisfied with it; and (4) retraction: the right to renounce a work and withdraw it from sale or display. Moral rights are recognized by law in much of Europe. Limited moral rights are recognized in the United States in 17 USCA § 106A. Cf. INTEGRITY RIGHT; ATTRIBUTION RIGHT.

> "The recognition of moral rights is founded in the notion that works of art belong to their creators in a way that transcends the sale or transfer of the work to a new owner, because the artist has imbued the work with her personality." Eric M. Brooks, *"Titled" Justice: Site-Specific Art and Moral Rights After U.S. Adherence to the Berne Convention*, 77 Cal. L. Rev. 1431, 1434 (1989).

> "Moral rights protect an author's non-pecuniary or non-economic interests. The 1988 [Copyright] Act provides authors and directors with the right to be named when a work is copied or communicated (the right of attribution), the right *not* to be named as the author of a work which one did not create (the right to object against false attribution), and the right to control the form of the work (the right of integrity)." Lionel Bently & Brad Sherman, *Intellectual Property Law* 233 (2001).

moral suasion. (17c) The act or effort of persuading by appeal to principles of morality.

moral turpitude. (17c) **1.** Conduct that is contrary to justice, honesty, or morality; esp., an act that demonstrates depravity. • In the area of legal ethics, offenses involving moral turpitude — such as fraud or breach of trust — traditionally make a person unfit to practice law. — Also termed *moral depravity*. **2.** *Military law.* Any conduct for which the applicable punishment is a dishonorable discharge or confinement not less than one year.

> "Moral turpitude means, in general, shameful wickedness — so extreme a departure from ordinary standards of honest, good morals, justice, or ethics as to be shocking to the moral sense of the community. It has also been defined as an act of baseness, vileness, or depravity in the private and social duties which one person owes to another, or to society in general, contrary to the accepted and customary rule of right and duty between people." 50 Am. Jur. 2d *Libel and Slander* § 165, at 454 (1995).

moral wrong. See WRONG.

moral-wrong doctrine. (1962) The doctrine that if a wrongdoer acts on a mistaken understanding of the facts, the law will not exempt the wrongdoer from culpability when, if the facts had been as the actor believed them to be, his or her conduct would nevertheless be immoral.

morandae solutionis causa (mə-**ran**-dee sə-loo-shee-**oh**-nis **kaw**-zə). [Latin] *Hist.* For the purpose of delaying payment.

moratorium (mor-ə-**tor**-ee-əm). (1875) **1.** An authorized postponement, usu. a lengthy one, in the deadline for paying a debt or performing an obligation. **2.** The period of this delay. **3.** The suspension of a specific activity. Pl. **moratoriums, moratoria.**

moratory (**mor**-ə-tor-ee), *adj.* (1891) Of, relating to, or involving a delay; esp., pertaining to a moratorium.

moratory damages. See DAMAGES.

moratory interest. See *prejudgment interest* under INTEREST (3).

more burgi (**mor**-ee **bər**-jɪ). [Law Latin] *Hist.* According to the custom in burgage-tenure. See BURGAGE-TENURE (2).

more or less. (16c) (Of a quantity) larger or smaller. • This phrase often appears in deeds <the property contains 120 acres, more or less> and sometimes in contracts <seller's wheat field will produce 50 bushels per acre, more or less>. It qualifies a good-faith representation of quantity. By using the phrase, the parties mutually acknowledge that the true circumstances may differ from what the parties believe they are when the contract is made, and accept a risk that the true quantity will be slightly different. When the qualifying phrase is present, neither party can recover for a surplus or deficiency.

morganatic marriage. See MARRIAGE (1).

morgangiva (mor-**gan**-jə-və), *n.* [Law Latin "morning gift" from Old Norse] (18c) *Hist.* A gift made to the bride on the morning after the wedding; a type of dowry. — Also spelled *morgangina*.

Morgan Nick Alert. See AMBER ALERT.

Morgan presumption. (1948) A presumption that shifts the burden of proof by requiring the person against whom it operates to produce sufficient evidence to outweigh the evidence that supports the presumed fact, as in requiring a criminal defendant who was arrested while in possession of an illegal substance — and is thereby presumed to have knowingly possessed it — to produce sufficient evidence to entitle the jury to find that the defendant's evidence outweighs the evidence of knowing possession. *See* Edmund M. Morgan, *Instructing the Jury Upon Presumptions and Burdens of Proof*, 47 Harv. L. Rev. 59, 82–83 (1933). Cf. THAYER PRESUMPTION.

morning-after pill. See EMERGENCY CONTRACEPTIVE PILL.

mors (morz), *n.* [Latin "death"] *Roman law.* **1.** Death. **2.** The punishment of death.

morsellum terrae (mor-**sel**-əm **ter**-ee). [Law Latin "a morsel of earth"] *Hist.* A small parcel of land.

morsel of execration. See *ordeal of the morsel* under ORDEAL.

mors naturalis (**morz** nach-ə-**ray**-lis). See *natural death* under DEATH.

mortality factor. *Insurance.* In life-insurance ratemaking, an estimate of the average number of deaths that will occur each year at each specific age, calculated by using an actuarial table. • The mortality factor is one element that a life insurer uses to calculate premium rates. See ACTUARIAL TABLE; PREMIUM RATE. Cf. INTEREST FACTOR; RISK FACTOR.

mortality table. See ACTUARIAL TABLE.

mort civile (mor[t] see-**veel**). [Law French] See CIVIL DEATH (1).

mort d'ancestor (mor[t] **dan**-ses-tər). [Law French "death of an ancestor"] *Hist.* An assize founded on the death of an ancestor. — Also termed (in Scots law) *brieve of mortancestry*.

> "Another of the petty assizes was that of mort d'ancestor, founded on the Assize of Northhampton 1176. The question in this assize was whether the plaintiff's father (or other close ancestor) had been seised in fee — that is, of an inheritable estate — on the day he died, and whether the plaintiff was his next heir; if both questions were answered in the affirmative, the plaintiff was entitled to be put in seisin." J.H. Baker, *An Introduction to English Legal History* 267–68 (3d ed. 1990).

mortgage (**mor**-gij), *n.* (15c) **1.** A conveyance of title to property that is given as security for the payment of a debt or the performance of a duty and that will become void upon payment or performance according to the stipulated terms. — Also termed (archaically) *dead pledge*. **2.** A lien against property that is granted to secure an obligation (such as a debt) and that is extinguished upon payment or performance according to stipulated terms. **3.** An instrument (such as a deed or contract) specifying the terms of such a transaction. **4.** Loosely, the loan on which such a transaction is based. **5.** The mortgagee's rights conferred by such a transaction. **6.** Loosely, any real-property security transaction, including a deed of trust. — Abbr. M. — **mortgage,** *vb.*

> "The chief distinction between a mortgage and a pledge is that by a mortgage the general title is transferred to the mortgagee, subject to be revested by performance of the condition; while by a pledge the pledgor retains the general title in himself, and parts with the possession for a special purpose. By a mortgage the title is transferred; by a pledge, the possession." Leonard A. Jones, *A Treatise on the Law of Mortgages* § 4, at 5–6 (5th ed. 1908).

▸ **adjustable-rate mortgage.** (1975) A mortgage in which the lender can periodically adjust the mortgage's interest rate in accordance with fluctuations in some external market index. — Abbr. ARM. — Also termed *variable-rate mortgage; flexible-rate mortgage.* Cf. *exploding adjustable-rate mortgage.*

▸ **all-inclusive mortgage.** See *wraparound mortgage.*

▸ **amortized mortgage.** (1913) A mortgage in which the mortgagor pays the interest as well as a portion of the principal in the periodic payment. • At maturity, the periodic payments will have completely repaid the loan. — Also termed *self-liquidating mortgage.* See AMORTIZATION (1). Cf. *straight mortgage.*

▸ **balloon-payment mortgage.** (1978) A mortgage requiring periodic payments for a specified time and a lump-sum payment of the outstanding balance at maturity.

▸ **blanket mortgage.** (1878) A mortgage that covers an aggregation of property or that secures or provides for indebtedness previously existing in various forms; esp., a mortgage covering two or more properties that are pledged to support a debt.

▸ **bulk mortgage.** (1919) **1.** A mortgage of personal property in bulk; a pledge of an aggregate of goods in one location. **2.** A mortgage of more than one real-estate parcel.

▸ **chattel mortgage (chat-əl).** (1841) A mortgage on goods purchased on installment, whereby the seller transfers title to the buyer but retains a lien securing the unpaid balance. • Chattel mortgages have generally been replaced by security agreements, which are governed by Article 9 of the UCC. Cf. *retail installment contract* under CONTRACT.

▸ **closed-end mortgage.** (1954) A mortgage that does not permit either prepayment or additional borrowing against the collateral. Cf. *open-end mortgage.* — Also termed *closed mortgage.*

▸ **closed mortgage.** See *closed-end mortgage.*

▸ **collateral mortgage.** (1853) *Civil law.* A mortgage securing a promissory note pledged as collateral security for a principal obligation.

▸ **common-law mortgage.** See *deed of trust* under DEED.

▸ **consolidated mortgage.** (1874) A mortgage created by combining two or more mortgages.

▸ **construction mortgage.** (1893) A mortgage used to finance a construction project.

▸ **contingent-interest mortgage.** (1983) A mortgage whose interest rate is directly related to the economic performance of the pledged property.

▸ **contribution mortgage.** (1928) **1.** A mortgage in which the land secured is developed using the money raised from investors. **2.** A mortgage in which the money secured is advanced by more than one lender in separate amounts.

▸ **contributory mortgage.** (1878) A mortgage for which there is more than one lender. See *participation mortgage* (2).

▸ **conventional mortgage.** (1822) A mortgage, not backed by government insurance, by which the borrower transfers a lien or title to the lending bank or other financial institution. • These mortgages, which feature a fixed periodic payment of principal and interest throughout the mortgage term, are typically used for home financing. — Also termed *conventional loan.*

▸ **current-account mortgage.** See *offset mortgage.*

▸ **direct-reduction mortgage.** (1935) An amortized mortgage in which the principal and interest payments are paid at the same time — usu. monthly in equal amounts — with interest being computed on the remaining balance. — Abbr. DRM.

▸ **dry mortgage.** (1974) A mortgage that creates a lien on property but does not impose on the mortgagor any personal liability for any amount that exceeds the value of the premises.

▸ **equitable mortgage.** (1827) A transaction that has the intent but not the form of a mortgage, and that a court of equity will treat as a mortgage. Cf. *technical mortgage.*

> "Courts of equity are not governed by the same principles as courts of law in determining whether a mortgage has been created, and generally, whenever a transaction resolves itself into a security, or an offer or attempt to pledge land as security for a debtor liability, equity will treat it as a mortgage, without regard to the form it may assume, or the name the parties may choose to give it. The threshold issue in an action seeking imposition of an equitable mortgage is whether the plaintiff has an adequate remedy at law. In applying the doctrine of equitable mortgages doubts are resolved in favor of the transaction being a mortgage." 59 C.J.S. *Mortgages* § 12, at 62 (1998).

▸ **exploding adjustable-rate mortgage.** (2007) An adjustable-rate mortgage for which the lender resets the interest rate so high that the borrower can no longer make payments. — Sometimes shortened to *exploding ARM.* Cf. *adjustable-rate mortgage.*

▸ **extended first mortgage.** See *wraparound mortgage.*

▸ **FHA mortgage.** (1938) A mortgage that is insured fully or partially by the Federal Housing Administration.

▸ **first mortgage.** A mortgage that is senior to all other mortgages on the same property.

▸ **fixed-rate mortgage.** (1971) A mortgage with an interest rate that remains the same over the life of the mortgage regardless of market conditions. — Abbr. FRM.

▸ **flexible-rate mortgage.** **1.** See *adjustable-rate mortgage.* **2.** See *renegotiable-rate mortgage.*

▸ **flip mortgage.** (1987) A graduated-payment mortgage allowing the borrower to place all or some of the down payment in a savings account and to use the principal and interest to supplement lower mortgage payments in the loan's early years.

▸ **future-advances mortgage.** (1967) A mortgage in which part of the loan proceeds will not be paid until a future date.

▸ **general mortgage.** (1822) *Civil law.* A blanket mortgage against all the mortgagor's present and future property. La. Civ. Code art. 3285.

▸ **graduated mortgage.** See *graduated-payment mortgage.*

▸ **graduated-payment adjustable-rate mortgage.** (1983) A mortgage combining features of the graduated-payment mortgage and the adjustable-rate mortgage. — Abbr. GPARM. — Also termed *graduated mortgage.*

▸ **graduated-payment mortgage.** (1977) A mortgage whose initial payments are lower than its later payments. • The payments are intended to gradually increase, as the borrower's income increases over time.

▸ **growing-equity mortgage.** (1982) A mortgage that is fully amortized over a significantly shorter term than the traditional 25- to 30-year mortgage, with increasing payments each year. — Abbr. GEM.

▸ **indemnity mortgage.** See *deed of trust* under DEED.

▸ **interest-only mortgage.** (1971) A balloon-payment mortgage on which the borrower must at first make only interest payments, but must make a lump-sum payment of the full principal at maturity. — Abbr. IO mortgage. — Also termed *standing mortgage*; *straight-term mortgage.*

▸ **joint mortgage.** (1846) A mortgage given to two or more mortgagees jointly.

▸ **judicial mortgage.** (1822) *Civil law.* A judgment lien created by a recorded legal judgment.

▸ **jumbo mortgage.** (1983) A mortgage loan in a principal amount that exceeds the dollar limits for a government guarantee.

▸ **junior mortgage.** (1851) A mortgage that is subordinate to another mortgage on the same property. — Also termed *puisne mortgage.*

▸ **leasehold mortgage.** (1908) A mortgage secured by a lessee's leasehold interest.

▸ **legal mortgage.** (1822) *Civil law.* A creditor's mortgage arising by operation of law on the debtor's property. — Also termed *tacit mortgage.*

▸ **offset mortgage.** (1989) *English law.* A flexible mortgage, common in the United Kingdom, in which the interest payment is reduced by offsetting against the mortgage debt the balance of the borrower's savings or other deposit accounts at the same institution. • For example, if the mortgage principal is $200,000 and the borrower has $30,000 in a savings account, the mortgage interest would be calculated based on $170,000. — Also termed *current-account mortgage.*

▸ **open-end mortgage.** (1927) A mortgage that allows the mortgagor to borrow additional funds against the same property. Cf. *closed-end mortgage.*

▸ **package mortgage.** (1948) A mortgage that includes both real and incidental personal property, such as a refrigerator or stove.

▸ **participation mortgage.** (1917) **1.** A mortgage that permits the lender to receive profits of the venture in addition to the normal interest payments. **2.** A mortgage held by more than one lender. — Also termed (in sense 2) *participating mortgage*; *contributory mortgage.*

▸ **price-level-adjusted mortgage.** (1978) A mortgage with a fixed interest rate but the principal balance of which is adjusted to reflect inflation. — Abbr. PLAM.

▸ **puisne mortgage.** See *junior mortgage.*

▸ **purchase-money mortgage.** (1858) A mortgage that a buyer gives the seller, when the property is conveyed, to secure the unpaid balance of the purchase price. — Abbr. PMM. See SECURITY AGREEMENT.

▸ **reincarnated mortgage.** *Slang.* See *zombie mortgage.*

▸ **renegotiable-rate mortgage.** (1980) A government-sponsored mortgage that requires the mortgagee to renegotiate its terms every three to five years, based on market conditions. — Also termed *flexible-rate mortgage*; *rollover mortgage.*

▸ **reverse annuity mortgage.** (1978) A mortgage in which the lender disburses money over a long period to provide regular income to the (usu. elderly) borrower, and in which the loan is repaid in a lump sum when the borrower dies or when the property is sold. — Abbr. RAM. — Also termed *reverse mortgage.*

▸ **rollover mortgage.** See *renegotiable-rate mortgage.*

▸ **second mortgage.** (1959) A mortgage that is junior to a first mortgage on the same property, but that is senior to any later mortgage.

> "A landowner who already holds land subject to a mortgage may wish to hypothecate his equity. He does this by taking out a '*second mortgage*.' Should the mortgagor default in his obligation on the first mortgage, the first mortgagee may foreclose. If there is a deficiency upon sale, the second mortgagee loses his security in the equity because there is no equity. If the mortgagee does not default on the first mortgage, but does on the second, the second mortgagee can foreclose on the mortgagor's equity. Such a foreclosure would not affect the first mortgagee's rights." Edward H. Rabin, *Fundamentals of Modern Real Property Law* 1087 (1974).

▸ **self-liquidating mortgage.** See *amortized mortgage.*

▸ **senior mortgage.** (1856) A mortgage that has priority over another mortgage (a junior mortgage) on the same property.

▸ **shared-appreciation mortgage.** (1981) A mortgage giving the lender the right to recover (as contingent interest) an agreed percentage of the property's appreciation in value when it is sold or at some other specified, future date. — Abbr. SAM.

▸ **shared-equity mortgage.** (1981) A mortgage in which the lender shares in the profits from the property's resale. • The lender must usu. first purchase a portion of the property's equity by providing a portion of the down payment.

▸ **special mortgage.** (1822) *Civil law.* A mortgage burdening only particular, specified property of the mortgagor. La. Civ. Code art. 3285.

▸ **standing mortgage.** See *interest-only mortgage.*

▸ **straight mortgage.** (1906) A mortgage in which the mortgagor is obligated to pay interest during the mortgage term along with a final payment of principal at the end of the term. Cf. *amortized mortgage.*

▸ **straight-term mortgage.** See *interest-only mortgage.*

▸ **submortgage.** (1825) A mortgage created when a person holding a mortgage as security for a loan procures another loan from a third party and pledges the mortgage as security; a loan to a mortgagee who puts up the mortgage as collateral or security for the loan.

▸ **tacit mortgage.** See *legal mortgage.*

▸ **technical mortgage.** (1848) A traditional, formal mortgage, as distinguished from an instrument having the character of an equitable mortgage. Cf. *equitable mortgage.*

▸ **VA mortgage.** (1950) A veteran's mortgage that is guaranteed by the Veterans Administration.

▸ **variable-rate mortgage.** See *adjustable-rate mortgage.*

▸ **Welsh mortgage.** (1829) A type of mortgage, formerly common in Wales and Ireland, by which the mortgagor, without promising to pay the debt, transfers title and possession of the property to the mortgagee, who takes the rents and profits and applies them to the interest, often with a stipulation that any surplus will reduce the principal. • The mortgagee cannot compel the mortgagor to redeem, and cannot foreclose the right to redeem, because no time is fixed for payment. The mortgagor is never in default, but may redeem at any time.

▸ **wraparound mortgage.** (1967) A second mortgage issued when a lender assumes the payments on the borrower's low-interest first mortgage (usu. issued through a different lender) and lends additional funds. • Such a mortgage covers both the outstanding balance of the first mortgage and the additional funds loaned. 12 CFR § 226.17 cmt. 6. — Also termed *extended first mortgage*; *all-inclusive mortgage.*

▸ **zero-rate mortgage.** (1981) A mortgage with a large down payment but no interest payments, with the balance paid in equal installments.

▸ **zombie mortgage.** *Slang.* A mortgage that has been paid in full but remains active because there is no record that it was paid off. — Also termed *reincarnated mortgage.*

mortgage-backed security. See SECURITY (4).

mortgage banker. (1897) An individual or organization that originates real-estate loans for a fee, resells them to other parties, and services the monthly payments.

mortgage bond. See BOND (3).

mortgage broker. See BROKER.

mortgage certificate. (1843) A document evidencing part ownership of a mortgage.

mortgage clause. (1851) An insurance-policy provision that protects the rights of a mortgagee when the insured property is subject to a mortgage. • Such a clause usu. provides that any insurance proceeds must be allocated between the named insured and the mortgagee "as their interests may appear." — Also termed *mortgagee clause.* See LOSS-PAYABLE CLAUSE; ATIMA.

▸ **open mortgage clause.** (1902) A mortgage clause that does not protect the mortgagee if the insured mortgagor does something to invalidate the policy (such as committing fraud). • This type of clause has been largely superseded by the mortgage-loss clause, which affords the mortgagee more protection. — Also termed *simple mortgage clause.* Cf. MORTGAGE-LOSS CLAUSE.

▸ **standard mortgage clause.** (1895) A mortgage clause that protects the mortgagee's interest even if the insured mortgagor does something to invalidate the policy. • In effect, this clause creates a separate contract between the insurer and the mortgagee. — Also termed *union mortgage clause.*

mortgage commitment. (1939) A lender's written agreement with a borrower stating the terms on which it will lend money for the purchase of specified real property, usu. with a time limitation.

mortgage company. (1873) A company that makes mortgage loans and then sells or assigns them to investors.

mortgage-contingency clause. (1965) A real-estate-sale provision that conditions the buyer's performance on obtaining a mortgage loan.

mortgage deed. See DEED.

mortgage discount. (1928) The difference between the mortgage principal and the amount the mortgage actually sells for; the up-front charge by a lender at a real-estate closing for the costs of financing. • Although usu. paid by the buyer, the discount is sometimes paid by the seller when required by law, as with a VA mortgage. — Also termed *point*; *mortgage point*; *loan-brokerage fee*; *new-loan fee.*

mortgagee (mor-gə-**jee**). (16c) One to whom property is mortgaged; the mortgage creditor, or lender. — Also termed *mortgage-holder.*

▸ **mortgagee in possession.** (18c) A mortgagee who takes control of mortgaged land by agreement with the mortgagor, usu. upon default of the loan secured by the mortgage.

mortgagee clause. See MORTGAGE CLAUSE.

mortgagee policy. (1909) A title-insurance policy that covers only the mortgagee's title and not the owner's title. Cf. OWNER'S POLICY.

mortgage foreclosure. See FORECLOSURE.

mortgage-guarantee insurance. (1952) Insurance provided by the Mortgage Guarantee Insurance Company to mortgage lenders that grant mortgages to parties having less than a 20% down payment. • The cost of the insurance is included in the closing costs.

mortgage-holder. See MORTGAGEE.

mortgage insurance. See INSURANCE.

mortgage lien. See LIEN.

mortgage loan. See LOAN.

mortgage-loss clause. (1924) A mortgage clause providing that title insurance will not be invalidated by the mortgagor's acts. • Thus, even if the mortgagor does an act that would otherwise make the policy void, the act merely voids the policy as against the mortgagor, but it remains in full force for the benefit of the mortgagee. — Also termed *New York standard clause*; *union-loss clause.* Cf. *open mortgage clause* under MORTGAGE CLAUSE.

mortgage market. (1909) The conditions that provide the demand for new mortgage loans and the later resale of those loans in the secondary mortgage market.

▸ **primary mortgage market.** (1965) The national market in which mortgages are originated.

▸ **secondary mortgage market.** (1948) The national market in which existing mortgages are bought and sold, usu. on a package basis.

mortgage note. See NOTE (1).

mortgage point. 1. See POINT (3). **2.** See MORTGAGE DISCOUNT.

mortgager. See MORTGAGOR.

mortgage servicing. (1935) The administration of a mortgage loan, including the collection of payments, release of liens, and payment of property insurance and taxes. • Servicing is usu. performed by the lender or the lender's agent, for a fee.

mortgage warehousing. (1947) An arrangement in which a mortgage company holds loans for later resale at a discount.

mortgaging out. (1952) The purchase of real property by financing 100% of the purchase price.

mortgagor (mor-gə-**jor** *or* **mor**-gə-jər). (16c) Someone who mortgages property; the mortgage-debtor, or borrower. — Also spelled *mortgager; mortgageor.* See CHARGER.

mortification. (14c) The act of disposing of or contributing property for religious, charitable, or public purposes.

mortis causa (**mor**-tis **kaw**-zə). See *gift causa mortis* under GIFT.

mortmain (**mort**-mayn). [French "deadhand"] (15c) The condition of lands or tenements held in perpetuity by an ecclesiastical or other corporation. • Land alienated in mortmain is not inalienable, but it will never escheat or pass by inheritance (and thus no inheritance taxes will ever be paid) because a corporation does not die. See AMORTIZE (3); DEADHAND CONTROL.

mortmain statute. (1839) A law that limits gifts and other dispositions of land to corporations (esp. charitable ones) and that prohibits corporations from holding land in perpetuity. • In England, laws such as the Provisions of Westminster and Magna Carta essentially required the Crown's authorization before land could vest in a corporation. The object was to prevent lands from being held by religious corporations in perpetuity. Although this type of restriction was not generally part of the common law in the United States, it influenced the enactment of certain state laws restricting the amount of property that a corporation could hold for religious or charitable purposes. — Also termed *mortmain act; statute of mortmain.*

mortua manus. See DEADHAND CONTROL.

mortuary. (16c) **1.** A place where cadavers are prepared for burial; a place where dead bodies are held before burial. **2.** A burial place. **3.** *Hist.* A customary gift left by a deceased to a parish church for past tithes owed. — Also termed (in sense 3) *soul scot.*

mortuary table. See ACTUARIAL TABLE.

mortuum vadium (**mor**-choo-əm **vay**-dee-əm). See *vadium mortuum* under VADIUM.

mortuus (**mor**-choo-əs), *adj.* [Latin] *Hist.* **1.** Dead. **2.** A sheriff's return that the named party is dead.

mortuus civiliter. See *civiliter mortuus* under CIVILITER.

mortuus sine prole (**mor**-choo-əs **sɪ**-nee **proh**-lee). [Latin] Dead without issue. — Abbr. *m.s.p.*

Mosaic law. (17c) Ancient Hebrew law as reflected in the Pentateuch (the first five books of the Hebrew Bible), also known collectively as the Torah, the foremost part consisting of the Ten Commandments. • This body of moral and ceremonial law is traditionally attributed to Moses. — Also termed *law of Moses.* — Sometimes written *Mosaic Law* and *Law of Moses.*

most favorable light. See LIGHT MOST FAVORABLE.

most favored nation. (18c) A treaty status granted to a country, usu. in international trade, allowing it to enjoy the privileges that the other party accords to other countries under similar circumstances. • The primary effect of most-favored-nation status is lower trade tariffs. — Sometimes shortened to *favored nation.* Abbr. MFN. — Also termed *most-favored-nation status.*

most-favored-nation clause. (1846) **1.** A clause in an agreement between two countries providing that each will treat the other as well as it treats any other country that is given preferential treatment. **2.** By extension, such a clause in any contract, but esp. an oil-and-gas contract. — Often shortened to *favored-nation clause; MFN clause.* — Also termed *most-favored-nations clause.* Cf. *preferential tariff* under TARIFF (2).

> "Special difficulties have arisen in connection with the interpretation of the 'most-favored-nation' clause frequently inserted in commercial treaties. The purpose of this clause is to provide for an equality of treatment in commercial relations on the part of a particular state toward other states, and with this in view to provide that any subsequent privileges that may be granted to any one state shall be automatically extended to other states with which such treaties have been concluded. Disputes have arisen, as between the United States and Great Britain, whether, after concluding such an agreement, a state is precluded from entering into individual arrangements with a third state known as 'reciprocity treaties,' by which particular privileges are granted in return for reciprocal concessions from the other party. The United States has claimed that these latter agreements are based upon special advantages, which form the consideration of a contract quite distinct from the mere general commercial treaty. On the other hand, Great Britain, France, and Germany have insisted that such reciprocity treaties do not form a class by themselves, and that the concessions made in them should be extended, in accordance with the most-favored-nation clause, to all other states with which the agreement has been made." Charles G. Fenwick, *International Law* 335 (1924).

most-favored-nation status. See MOST FAVORED NATION.

most-favored-nation treatment. *Intellectual property.* The practice or policy of automatically and unconditionally granting any intellectual-property protection, advantage, favor, privilege, or immunity that by treaty is extended to nationals of any member country to the nationals of all member countries. • This treatment is incorporated into the TRIPs agreement. — Abbr. MFN treatment.

most-favored-tenant clause. (1962) A commercial-lease provision ensuring that the tenant will be given the benefit of any negotiating concessions given to other tenants.

Most Honorable. See HONORABLE.

most-significant-contacts test. See MOST-SIGNIFICANT-RELATIONSHIP TEST.

most-significant-relationship test. (1968) *Conflict of laws.* The doctrine that, to determine the state law to apply to a dispute, the court should determine which state has the most substantial connection to the occurrence and the parties. • For example, in a tort case, the court should consider where the injury occurred, where the conduct that caused the injury occurred, the residence, place of business, or place of incorporation of the parties, and the place where the relationship between the parties, if any, is centered. Restatement (Second) of Conflict of Laws § 145 (1971). In a case involving a contract, the court should consider where the contract was made, where the contract was negotiated, where the contract was to be performed, and the domicile, place of business, or place of incorporation of the parties. *Id.* § 188. — Also termed *most-significant-contacts test.*

most suitable use. See *highest and best use* under USE (1).

most-suitable-use value. See *optimal-use value* under VALUE (2).

moteer (**moh**-teer). (18c) *Hist.* A customary payment or service made at the lord's court.

mother. (bef. 12c) A woman who has given birth to, provided the egg for, or legally adopted a child. • The term is sometimes interpreted as including a pregnant woman who has not yet given birth.

▸ **adoptive mother.** See *adoptive parent* under PARENT.

▸ **biological mother.** (1965) The woman who provides the egg that develops into an embryo. • With today's genetic-engineering techniques, the biological mother may not be the birth mother, but she is usu. the legal mother. — Also termed *genetic mother; natural mother.*

▸ **birth mother.** (1958) The woman who carries an embryo during the gestational period and who delivers the child. • When a child is conceived through artificial insemination, the birth mother may not be the genetic or biological mother. And she may not be the legal mother. — Also termed *gestational mother.* See *surrogate mother; natural mother; biological mother.*

▸ **de facto mother.** See *de facto parent* under PARENT.

▸ **foster mother .** See *foster parent* under PARENT.

▸ **genetic mother.** See *biological mother.*

▸ **gestational mother.** See *birth mother.*

▸ **godmother.** See GODPARENT.

▸ **intentional mother.** See *intentional parent* under PARENT.

▸ **natural mother. 1.** See *birth mother.* **2.** See *biological mother.*

▸ **psychological mother.** See *psychological parent* under PARENT.

▸ **stepmother.** (bef. 12c) The wife of one's father by a later marriage. — Formerly also termed *mother-in-law.*

▸ **surrogate mother.** (1914) **1.** A woman who carries out the gestational function and gives birth to a child for another; esp., a woman who agrees to provide her uterus to carry an embryo throughout pregnancy, typically on behalf of an infertile couple, and who relinquishes any parental rights she may have upon the birth of the child. • A surrogate mother may or may not be the genetic mother of a child. — Often shortened to *surrogate.* — Also termed *surrogate parent; gestational surrogate; gestational carrier; surrogate carrier.* **2.** Someone who performs the role of a mother.

mother country. (18c) A colonizing country; a colonial power. See COLONY.

Mother Hubbard clause. (1939) **1.** A clause stating that a mortgage secures all the debts that the mortgagor may at any time owe to the mortgagee. — Also termed *anaconda clause; dragnet clause.* **2.** *Oil & gas.* A provision in an oil-and-gas lease protecting the lessee against errors in the description of the property by providing that the lease covers all the land owned by the lessor in the area. • A Mother Hubbard clause is sometimes combined with an after-acquired-title clause. — Also termed *cover-all clause.* **3.** A court's written declaration that any relief not expressly granted in a specific ruling or judgment is denied.

> "*Mother Hubbard* suggests that the mortgagor goes to great lengths to satisfy the mortgagee, just as Mother Hubbard (in the popular nursery rhyme) is absurdly solicitous toward her dog. E.g.: 'Amerada . . . invokes the "coverall" (sometimes called the "*Mother Hubbard*") clause in an oil and gas lease from Koch, dated January 19, 1945.' *Gardner v. Amerada Petroleum Corp.*, 91 F.Supp. 134, 135 (S.D. Tex. 1950). *Anaconda* suggests that the unsuspecting debtor may get wrapped up in the serpentine clutches of indebtedness. The *dragnet* metaphor suggests a broadly cast net that sweeps in all past and future debts. Today, *Mother Hubbard clause* is the most usual phrase." Bryan A. Garner, *Garner's Dictionary of Legal Usage* 591 (3d ed. 2011).

mother-in-law. (14c) **1.** The mother of a person's spouse. **2.** See *stepmother* under MOTHER.

motion. (18c) **1.** A written or oral application requesting a court to make a specified ruling or order.

> "Frequently, in the progress of litigation, it is desired to have the court take some action which is incidental to the main proceeding, as appointing an auditor, or entering a survey of land, etc. Such action is invoked by an application usually less formal than the pleadings, and called a motion. These are either oral or in writing. Sometimes great particularity is required, and the truth of the matters presented must be supported by affidavit. Each kind of motion is dealt with as justice and expediency seem to require." John C. Townes, *Studies in American Elementary Law* 621 (1911).

▸ **calendar motion.** (1930) A motion relating to the time of a court appearance • Examples include motions to continue, motions to advance, and motions to reset.

▸ **contradictory motion.** (1895) *Civil law.* A motion that is likely to be contested or that the nonmoving side should have an opportunity to contest. Cf. *contradictory judgment* under JUDGMENT (2).

▸ ***coram nobis* motion.** (1944) A motion to vacate an allegedly unlawful conviction.

▸ **cross-motion.** (1827) A competing request for relief or orders similar to that requested by another party against the cross-moving party, such as a motion for summary judgment or for sanctions.

▸ **dilatory motion** (**dil**-ə-tor-ee). (18c) **1.** A motion made solely for the purpose of delay or obstruction. **2.** A motion that delays the proceedings.

▸ **dispositive motion.** (1939) A motion for a trial-court order to decide a claim or case in favor of the movant without further proceedings.

▸ **enumerated motion.** (1822) *Archaic.* A motion directly related to the proceeding or the merits of the case.

▸ **ex parte motion** (eks **pahr**-tee). (1831) A motion made to the court without notice to the adverse party; a motion that a court considers and rules on without hearing from all sides. — Also termed *ex parte application*.

▸ **motion for reduction.** (1973) *Family law.* A motion to lessen the amount of child-support payments. • This is a type of motion to modify.

▸ **motion for resettlement.** (1924) A request to clarify or correct the form of an order or judgment that does not correctly state the court's decision. • The motion cannot be used to request a substantial change to or amplification of the court's decision.

▸ **motion of course.** (1828) A party's request that the court may grant as a matter of routine, without investigating or inquiring further.

▸ **motion to modify.** (1869) A post-final-decree motion asking the court to change one of its earlier orders; esp., a request to change child support or visitation. — Also termed *complaint for modification*; *motion for modification*.

▸ **omnibus motion.** (1889) A motion that makes several requests or asks for multiple forms of relief; esp., in criminal law, a defense pretrial motion requesting a hearing on various in limine motions as well as on suppression issues.

▸ **posttrial motion.** (1889) A motion made after judgment is entered, such as a motion for new trial.

▸ **show-cause motion.** (1876) A motion filed with the court requesting that a litigant be required to appear and explain why that litigant has failed to comply with a legal requirement.

▸ **speaking motion.** (1935) A motion that addresses matters not raised in the pleadings.

▸ **special motion.** (16c) A motion specifically requiring the court's discretion upon hearing, as distinguished from one granted as a matter of course.

2. *Parliamentary law.* A proposal made in a meeting, in a form suitable for its consideration and action, that the meeting (or the organization for which the meeting is acting) take a certain action or view. • A motion may be a *main motion*, a *secondary motion*, or a *restorative motion*. A motion technically becomes a "question" when the chair states it for the meeting's consideration. But for most purposes, the parliamentary terms "motion" and "question" are interchangeable. Cf. REQUEST.

▸ **coexisting motion.** (1969) *Parliamentary law.* A main motion, such as one raising a question of privilege, that is pending at the same time as another main motion of lower precedence.

▸ **immediately pending motion.** The pending motion directly under consideration; the pending motion last stated by the chair and next in line for a vote. See *pending motion*; PRECEDENCE (4).

▸ **improper motion.** (18c) A motion that is out of order. See OUT OF ORDER.

▸ **incidental main motion.** A main motion that relates to a procedural rather than a substantive matter, or relates to action previously taken; often, an otherwise secondary motion made when no main motion is pending.— Also termed *procedural main motion*; *quasi-main motion*; *specific main motion*. See *main motion*. Cf. *original main motion*.

▸ **incidental motion.** (18c) A secondary motion that relates to the procedure under which other business is considered. See *secondary motion*.

▸ **main motion.** (18c) A motion that brings business before a meeting. • A main motion may be an *original main motion* or an *incidental main motion*. The practical distinction is that consideration of an incidental main motion cannot be objected to, and such a motion is usually not referred to a resolutions committee. See OBJECTION (2); *resolutions committee* under COMMITTEE (1). — Also termed *principal motion*; *proposition*.

▸ **motion that brings a question again before the assembly.** See *restorative motion*.

▸ **motion to divide the question.** See divide the question.

▸ **ordinary main motion.** See *original main motion*.

▸ **original main motion.** A main motion that relates to a substantive rather than a procedural matter; a main motion that is not an incidental main motion. — Also termed *ordinary main motion*; *substantive main motion*; *substantive motion*. See *main motion*. Cf. *incidental main motion*.

▸ **parliamentary motion.** (1808) **1.** Any motion that is not an original main motion. **2.** A motion under parliamentary law; MOTION (2).

▸ **pending motion.** (1837) A motion under consideration, even though other pending motions of higher rank may have taken precedence over it. Cf. *immediately pending motion*.

▸ **principal motion.** See *main motion*.

▸ **privileged motion.** (1827) A secondary motion that does not relate to other business, but rather to the organization, the meeting, its members, and their rights and privileges, and is thus entitled to prompt attention in preference over other pending business. See *secondary motion*; PRIVILEGE (5).

▸ **procedural main motion.** See *incidental main motion*.

▸ **procedural motion.** (1944) A motion that relates to the manner in which a meeting conducts its business, rather than to the business itself.

▸ **quasi-main motion.** See *incidental main motion*.

▸ **restorative motion.** (1993) A motion that reintroduces a question already disposed of. • Restorative motions may resemble, or be specific types of, main motions or secondary motions; they may bring up main motions, secondary motions, or other restorative motions for consideration; a motion that brings a question again before the assembly. — Also termed *restoratory motion*.

▸ **restoratory motion.** See *restorative motion*.

▸ **Rule 12(b)(6) motion.** (1952) A motion to dismiss a case because the plaintiff has not stated a claim on which relief can be granted. — Often shortened to *12(b)(6) motion*. See MOTION TO DISMISS.

▸ **secondary motion.** (18c) A motion that does not itself bring business before the meeting, and is therefore in order when a main motion is pending. • A secondary motion may be an *incidental motion* (although not an *incidental main motion*), a *privileged motion*, or a *subsidiary motion*. Cf. *main motion*; *restorative motion*.

▸ **specific main motion.** See *incidental main motion*.

▸ **subsidiary motion.** A secondary motion that directly affects the main motion's form or consideration. See *secondary motion.*

▸ **substantive main motion.** See *original main motion.*

▸ **substantive motion.** See *original main motion.*

motion day. (1809) A day regularly scheduled by courts or commissions to hear all motions, such as every Tuesday or the third Monday of the month.

motion for a directed verdict. See MOTION FOR DIRECTED VERDICT.

motion for a more definite statement. See MOTION FOR MORE DEFINITE STATEMENT.

motion for a new trial. See MOTION FOR NEW TRIAL.

motion for a protective order. See MOTION FOR PROTECTIVE ORDER.

motion for directed verdict. (1904) A party's request that the court enter judgment in its favor before submitting the case to the jury because there is no legally sufficient evidentiary foundation on which a reasonable jury could find for the other party. • Under the Federal Rules of Civil Procedure, the equivalent court paper is known as a motion for judgment as a matter of law. — Abbr. MDV. — Also termed *motion for a directed verdict; motion for a trial order of dismissal; TOD motion.* See MOTION FOR JUDGMENT AS A MATTER OF LAW; *directed verdict* under VERDICT (1).

motion for j.n.o.v. See MOTION FOR JUDGMENT NOTWITHSTANDING THE VERDICT.

motion for judgment as a matter of law. (1956) A party's request that the court enter a judgment in its favor before the case is submitted to the jury, or after a contrary jury verdict, because there is no legally sufficient evidentiary basis on which a jury could find for the other party. • Under the Federal Rules of Civil Procedure, a party may move for judgment as a matter of law anytime before the case has been submitted to the jury. This kind of motion was formerly known as a *motion for directed verdict* (and still is in many jurisdictions). If the motion is denied and the case is submitted to the jury, resulting in an unfavorable verdict, the motion may be renewed within ten days after entry of the judgment. This aspect of the motion replaces the court paper formerly known as a *motion for judgment notwithstanding the verdict.* Fed. R. Civ. P. 50.

motion for judgment notwithstanding the verdict. (1822) A party's request that the court enter a judgment in its favor despite the jury's contrary verdict because there is no legally sufficient evidentiary basis for a jury to find for the other party. • Under the Federal Rules of Civil Procedure, this procedure has been replaced by the provision for a motion for judgment as a matter of law, which must be presented before the case has been submitted to the jury but can be reasserted if it is denied and the jury returns an unfavorable verdict. Fed. R. Civ. P. 50. — Also termed *motion for j.n.o.v.* See MOTION FOR JUDGMENT AS A MATTER OF LAW.

motion for judgment of acquittal. (1923) A criminal defendant's request, at the close of the government's case or the close of all evidence, to be acquitted because there is no legally sufficient evidentiary basis on which a reasonable jury could return a guilty verdict. • If the motion is granted, the government has no right of appeal. Fed. R. Crim. P. 29(a). — Abbr. MJOA.

motion for judgment on the pleadings. (1923) A party's request that the court rule in its favor based on the pleadings on file, without accepting evidence, as when the outcome of the case rests on the court's interpretation of the law. Fed. R. Civ. P. 12(c).

motion for leave to appeal. (1874) A request that an appellate court review an interlocutory order that meets the standards of the collateral-order doctrine. — Abbr. MLA. See COLLATERAL-ORDER DOCTRINE. Cf. LEAVE TO APPEAL.

motion for modification. See *motion to modify* under MOTION (1).

motion for more definite statement. (1904) A party's request that the court require an opponent to amend a vague or ambiguous pleading to which the party cannot reasonably be required to respond. Fed. R. Civ. P. 12(e). — Also termed *motion for a more definite statement.*

> "Another disfavored motion is the motion for a more definite statement. By a 1948 amendment to the rules, the old bill of particulars was abolished. The motion for more definite statement, which serves much the same function, is to be granted only where a pleading to which a responsive pleading is permitted is so vague or ambiguous that the party cannot reasonably be required to frame a responsive pleading. If the pleading is sufficiently definite that the opponent can reply to it, the motion for more definite statement should be denied and any particulars that the opponent needs to prepare for trial obtained by depositions, interrogatories, and similar discovery procedures. The motion is never proper where no responsive pleading is permitted, nor should it be used to force the plaintiff to include additional particulars that may make the complaint vulnerable to a motion to dismiss." Charles Alan Wright, *The Law of Federal Courts* § 66, at 461–62 (5th ed. 1994).

motion for new trial. (18c) A party's postjudgment request that the court vacate the judgment and order a new trial for such reasons as factually insufficient evidence, newly discovered evidence, and jury misconduct. • In many jurisdictions, this motion is required before a party can raise such a matter on appeal. — Also termed *motion for a new trial.*

motion for protective order. (1948) A party's request that the court protect it from potentially abusive action by the other party, usu. relating to discovery, as when one party seeks discovery of the other party's trade secrets. • A court will sometimes craft a protective order to protect one party's trade secrets by ordering that any secret information exchanged in discovery be used only for purposes of the pending suit and not be publicized. — Also termed *motion for a protective order.*

motion for reconsideration. See MOTION FOR REHEARING.

motion for reduction. See MOTION (1).

motion for rehearing. A party's request that the court allow another hearing of a case, motion, or appeal, usu. to consider an alleged error or omission in the court's judgment or opinion. — Abbr. MFR. — Also termed *motion for reconsideration.*

motion for relief from stay. See MOTION TO LIFT THE STAY.

motion for relief from the judgment. (1867) A party's request that the court correct a clerical mistake in the judgment — that is, a mistake that results in the judgment's incorrectly reflecting the court's intentions — or relieve the party from the judgment because of such matters as (1) inadvertence, surprise, or excusable neglect, (2) newly discovered evidence that could not have been discovered through diligence in time for a motion for new trial, (3) the judgment's being the result of fraud, misrepresentation, or misconduct by the other party, or (4) the judgment's being void or having been satisfied or released. Fed. R. Civ. P. 60. Cf. MOTION TO ALTER OR AMEND THE JUDGMENT.

motion for repleader. (18c) *Common-law pleading.* An unsuccessful party's posttrial motion asking that the pleadings begin anew because the issue was joined on an immaterial point. • The court never awards a repleader to the party who tendered the immaterial issue. Cf. REPLEADER.

motion for resettlement. See MOTION (1).

motion for severance. See MOTION TO SEVER.

motion for summary judgment. (1842) A request that the court enter judgment without a trial because there is no genuine issue of material fact to be decided by a fact-finder — that is, because the evidence is legally insufficient to support a verdict in the nonmovant's favor. • In federal court and in most state courts, the movant-defendant must point out in its motion the absence of evidence on an essential element of the plaintiff's claim, after which the burden shifts to the nonmovant-plaintiff to produce evidence raising a genuine fact issue. But if a party moves for summary judgment on its own claim or defense, then it must establish each element of the claim or defense as a matter of law. Fed. R. Civ. P. 56. — Abbr. MSJ. — Also termed *summary-judgment motion*; *motion for summary disposition.* See SUMMARY JUDGMENT.

motion in arrest of judgment. (17c) **1.** A defendant's motion claiming that a substantial error appearing on the face of the record vitiates the whole proceeding and the judgment. **2.** A postjudgment motion in a criminal case claiming that the indictment is insufficient to sustain a judgment or that the verdict is somehow insufficient.

motion in limine (in **lim**-ə-nee). (18c) A pretrial request that certain inadmissible evidence not be referred to or offered at trial. • Typically, a party makes this motion when it believes that mere mention of the evidence during trial would be highly prejudicial and could not be remedied by an instruction to disregard. If, after the motion is granted, the opposing party mentions or attempts to offer the evidence in the jury's presence, a mistrial may be ordered. A ruling on a motion in limine does not always preserve evidentiary error for appellate purposes. To raise such an error on appeal, a party may be required to formally object when the evidence is actually admitted or excluded during trial.

motion of course. See MOTION (1).

motion to alter or amend the judgment. (1950) A party's request that the court correct a substantive error in the judgment, such as a manifest error of law or fact. • Under the Federal Rules of Civil Procedure, a motion to alter or amend the judgment must be filed within ten days after the judgment is entered. It should not ordinarily be used to correct clerical errors in a judgment. Those types of errors — that is, errors that result in the judgment not reflecting the court's intention — may be brought in a motion for relief from the judgment, which does not have the ten-day deadline. A motion to alter or amend the judgment is usu. directed to substantive issues regarding the judgment, such as an intervening change in the law or newly discovered evidence that was not available at trial. Fed. R. Civ. P. 59(e). Cf. MOTION FOR RELIEF FROM THE JUDGMENT.

motion to compel discovery. (1960) A party's request that the court force the party's opponent to respond to the party's discovery request (as to answer interrogatories or produce documents). Fed. R. Civ. P. 37(a). — Often shortened to *motion to compel.* — Also termed *motion to enforce discovery.*

motion to correct inventorship. (1983) *Patents.* A request in an interference proceeding to add one or more unnamed coinventors to the patent application. • The motion will be granted unless the unnamed coinventor acted with the intent to deceive.

motion to dismiss. (18c) A request that the court dismiss the case because of settlement, voluntary withdrawal, or a procedural defect. • Under the Federal Rules of Civil Procedure, a plaintiff may voluntarily dismiss the case (under Rule 41(a)) or the defendant may ask the court to dismiss the case, usu. based on one of the defenses listed in Rule 12(b). These defenses include lack of personal or subject-matter jurisdiction, improper venue, insufficiency of process, the plaintiff's failure to state a claim on which relief can be granted, and the failure to join an indispensable party. A defendant will frequently file a motion to dismiss for failure to state a claim, which is governed by Rule 12(b)(6), claiming that even if all the plaintiff's allegations are true, they would not be legally sufficient to state a claim on which relief might be granted. — Abbr. MTD. See DEMURRER.

motion to dismiss for failure to prosecute. (1889) *Criminal procedure.* A criminal defendant's motion, usu. oral, made at the appointed time of trial if the prosecution cannot proceed, as when a critical witness or crucial evidence is missing — typically proper only when a speedy-trial deadline has passed.

motion to dissolve interference. (1883) *Patents.* A request by the senior party to dismiss challenges to its priority as the first inventor.

motion to divide the question. See DIVIDE THE QUESTION.

motion to enforce discovery. See MOTION TO COMPEL DISCOVERY.

motion to lift the stay. (1969) *Bankruptcy.* A party's request that the bankruptcy court alter the automatic bankruptcy stay to allow the movant to act against the debtor or the debtor's property, as when a creditor seeks permission to foreclose on a lien because its security interest is not adequately protected. — Also termed *motion for relief from stay*; *motion to modify the stay.*

motion to modify. See MOTION (1).

motion to modify the stay. See MOTION TO LIFT THE STAY.

motion to quash (kwahsh). (18c) A party's request that the court nullify process or an act instituted by the other party, as in seeking to nullify a subpoena.

motion to remand. (1816) In a case that has been removed from state court to federal court, a party's request that the federal court return the case to state court, usu. because the federal court lacks jurisdiction or because the procedures for removal were not properly followed. 28 USCA § 1447(c).

motion to sever. (1877) **1.** *Civil procedure.* A party's or defendant's request to have all or some of its claims or defenses tried separately from those of coparties or codefendants. • Common grounds for the motion are that the claims and counterclaims are so different that they should logically be heard separately, that the case involves different causes of action that should logically be tried separately, that prejudice to a party will result from trying the claims together, or that a party has been improperly joined.

> "A motion to sever is made to separate parties or issues included in a single cause of action. Typically, such a motion is made where severance will result in a more efficient disposition of the case. For example, one party or claim may be subject to a jurisdictional defense not applicable to the remainder of the action. A party moving for severance should be prepared to demonstrate with particularity the grounds supporting the motion. . . . A motion to sever is favored by the court when it allows one significant issue in a multi-issue case to be resolved by the court in a manner that encourages settlement of the remainder of the case. For example, where the resolution of a statute of limitations issue or other jurisdictional question as a preliminary matter can reduce the likelihood of further trial on the substantive issues, the motion should be favorably considered. Conversely, where the parties are unable to represent that resolution of a single issue may significantly affect the resolution of the remaining issues, a motion to sever will be less favorably considered." Gerald A. Kafka & Rita A. Cavanagh, *Litigation of Federal Civil Tax Controversies* § 7.04 (2012).

2. *Criminal procedure.* A defendant's request to have all or part of the case against the defendant tried separately from that of the codefendants. — Also termed (in both senses) *motion for severance.*

> "A motion to sever is a motion by one of two or more joint accused to be tried separately from the other or others. . . . The more common grounds of motions for severance are that the mover desired to avail himself on his trial of the testimony of one or more of his coaccused, or of the testimony of the wife of one, or that the defenses of the other accused are antagonistic to his own, or that the evidence as to them will in some manner prejudice his defense." United States War Department, *A Manual for Courts-Martial* 127 (1920).

motion to strike. (1806) **1.** *Civil procedure.* A party's request that the court delete insufficient defenses or immaterial, redundant, impertinent, or scandalous statements from an opponent's pleading. Fed. R. Civ. P. 12(f). **2.** *Evidence.* A request that inadmissible evidence be deleted from the record and that the jury be instructed to disregard it.

motion to suppress. (18c) *Criminal law.* A request that the court prohibit the introduction of illegally obtained evidence at a criminal trial. — Also termed *suppression motion.*

motion to transfer venue. (1934) A request that the court transfer the case to another district or county, usu. because the original venue is improper under the applicable venue rules or because of local prejudice. See VENUE; CHANGE OF VENUE.

motion to withdraw. (1831) **1.** An attorney's request for a court's permission to cease representing a client in a lawsuit. **2.** A defendant's formal request for a court's permission to change the defendant's plea or strike an admission. — Also termed (in sense 2) *motion to withdraw a plea.*

motion to withdraw a plea. See MOTION TO WITHDRAW (2).

motive. (14c) Something, esp. willful desire, that leads one to act. — Also termed *ulterior intent.* Cf. INTENT.

> "The term 'motive' is unfortunately ambiguous. That feeling which internally urges or pushes a person to do or refrain from doing an act is an emotion, and is of course evidential towards his doing or not doing the act. But when that evidential fact comes in turn to be evidenced, we must rely on two sorts of data, (a) the person's own expressions of that emotion, e.g., 'I hate M,' or 'I wish I owned that necklace'; and (b) external circumstances likely in human experience to arouse the emotion, e.g., a slander on D may be evidence that D became angry; a purse of money left in sight of D may be evidence that D's desire to have it was aroused. Now this second sort of evidential circumstance (b) is loosely referred to as 'motive,' — though in reality it is only evidential of the emotion, which itself is evidential of the act." John H. Wigmore, *A Students' Textbook of the Law of Evidence* 76 (1935).

▸ **bad motive.** (18c) A person's knowledge that an act is wrongful while the person commits the act.

> "**Motive.** — A bad motive is not an essential element of any crime. The existence of a motive is a circumstance to be considered with all the other evidence by the jury in reaching a conclusion of guilt or innocence and the lack of proof of it may be a circumstance tending to show innocence; but proof of motive is not necessary to convict, nor is its absence ground for acquittal; for crimes may be thoroughly established and no motive appear. Indeed, the very absence of known motive may aggravate the offense. On the other hand, a good motive is no defense. A wilful wrong inflicted on others, unwarranted by law, is malicious, though committed in pursuance of a general good purpose and sincere design to bring about some altruistic end. The fact that a person has conscientious scruples against being vaccinated is no defense in an action against him for refusing to be vaccinated where a penal statute requires it to be done." T.W. Hughes, *A Treatise on Criminal Law and Procedure* § 106, at 67–68 (1919).

▸ **dual motive.** *Labor law.* An employer's mixed lawful and unlawful reasons for an adverse employment action. • For example, an employer may be motivated to fire an employee for violating rules and also for protected union activity or for belonging to a certain race or religion.

▸ **malicious motive.** (18c) A motive for bringing a prosecution, other than to do justice.

Motor Carrier Act. A 1935 federal statute subjecting commercial motor carriers of freight and passengers in interstate commerce to the regulations of the Interstate Commerce Commission, now the U.S. Department of Transportation. • The Act was repealed in the 1980s. — Abbr. MCA.

motor vehicle. See VEHICLE.

motor-vehicle accident. See *car accident* under ACCIDENT (2).

MOU. *abbr.* MEMORANDUM OF UNDERSTANDING.

movable, *n.* (*usu. pl.*) (15c) **1.** Property that can be moved or displaced, such as personal goods; a tangible or intangible thing in which an interest constitutes personal property; specif., anything that is not so attached to land as to be regarded as a part of it as determined by local law. — Also spelled (BrE) *moveable.* — Also termed *movable property; movable thing.*

> "Movables and immovables. The main distinction drawn in later Roman law and modern systems based thereon between kinds of things subject to ownership and possession. While basically the distinction corresponds to everyday conceptions, assigning animals and vehicles to the former and land and buildings to the latter category,

particular things may be assigned to one category rather than the other for reasons of convenience. Thus, in French law, farm implements and animals are immovables. The distinction is also important in international private law, more so than that between real and personal . . . . Thus, land held on lease is personal property by English law for historical reason, but in international private law it is a right in immovable property." David M. Walker, *The Oxford Companion to Law* 858 (1980).

▸ **intangible movable.** (1931) A physical thing that can be moved but that cannot be touched in the usual sense. • Examples are light and electricity.

"'Intangible movables' is a term of art in the common law which has been applied more widely than its meaning literally justifies, which is merely to those things that have physical existence and can be moved, though cannot be touched in the normal sense, such as light, electricity and radioactive waves. In English law the term has been generally applied to interests created by law which have only a legal, not a physical existence, and are accordingly capable only of legal, not physical, movement. It is convenient, however, to retain a term which is generally accepted and understood in this special legal meaning." R.H. Graveson, *Conflict of Laws* 470 (7th ed. 1974).

2. *Scots law.* A nonheritable right. — Also spelled (BrE) *moveable.* Cf. IMMOVABLE. — **movable,** *adj.*

"Moveables are, in the phraseology of the law of Scotland, opposed to heritage; so that every species of property, and every right a person can hold, is by that law either heritable or moveable. Hence, moveables are not merely corporeal subjects capable of being moved, but every species of property, corporeal or incorporeal, which does not descend to the heir in heritage." William Bell, *Bell's Dictionary and Digest of the Law of Scotland* 662 (George Watson ed., 1882).

movable estate. See *personal property* (1) under PROPERTY.

movable fixture. See *tenant's fixture* under FIXTURE.

movable freehold. See FREEHOLD.

movable property. See MOVABLE (1).

movable thing. See MOVABLE (1).

movant (**moov**-ənt). (1875) Someone who makes a motion to the court or a deliberative body. — Formerly also spelled *movent.* — Also termed *moving party*; *mover.*

move, *vb.* (15c) **1.** To make an application (to a court) for a ruling, order, or some other judicial action <the appellant moved the court for a new trial>. **2.** To make a motion <the senator moved that a vote be taken>. See MOTION (2).

moveable. See MOVABLE (2).

movent. See MOVANT.

moventia. See quot. at MOBILIA.

mover, *n.* (1988) **1.** *Slang.* A stock that experiences spectacular market price changes; a very unstable stock. **2.** MOVANT.

moving expense. See EXPENSE.

moving papers. (1859) The papers that constitute or support a motion in a court proceeding. — Also termed *motion papers.*

moving part. (1825) *Patents.* A separate component of an apparatus that works together with another to produce the intended useful result. • Moving parts and a rule of operation generally distinguish an apparatus from an article of manufacture.

moving party. See MOVANT.

moving violation. (1954) An infraction of a traffic law while the vehicle is in motion.

Mozilla public license. See LICENSE.

MP. *abbr.* (18c) Member of Parliament. See PARLIAMENT.

MPC. *abbr.* MODEL PENAL CODE.

MPC test. See SUBSTANTIAL-CAPACITY TEST.

MPEP. *abbr.* MANUAL OF PATENT EXAMINING PROCEDURE.

MPF clause. *abbr.* MEANS-PLUS-FUNCTION CLAUSE.

MPI. *abbr.* Minimum period of imprisonment.

MPL. *abbr.* See *Mozilla public license* under LICENSE.

MPRE. *abbr.* MULTISTATE PROFESSIONAL RESPONSIBILITY EXAM.

MQT. *abbr.* See *Medicaid-qualifying trust* under TRUST (3).

MR. *abbr.* MENTAL RETARDATION.

Mr. Denman's Act. See DENMAN'S ACT (2).

MRE. *abbr.* MILITARY RULES OF EVIDENCE.

Mr. Green. *Slang.* Money, esp. as a criminal-defense lawyer's retainer <we haven't yet seen Mr. Green>.

MRPC. *abbr.* MODEL RULES OF PROFESSIONAL CONDUCT.

MSA. *abbr.* See *mediated settlement agreement* under SETTLEMENT (2).

MSB. *abbr.* MONEY SERVICE BUSINESS.

MSHA. *abbr.* MINE SAFETY AND HEALTH ADMINISTRATION.

MSJ. *abbr.* MOTION FOR SUMMARY JUDGMENT.

MSOP. *abbr.* Mandatory sex-offender program.

m.s.p. *abbr.* MORTUUS SINE PROLE.

MSP. *abbr.* MUNCHAUSEN SYNDROME BY PROXY.

MSPB. *abbr.* MERIT SYSTEMS PROTECTION BOARD.

MSRP. *abbr.* Manufacturer-suggested retail price. See *suggested retail price* under PRICE.

MSTB. *abbr.* MODEL STATE TRADEMARK BILL.

MTA. abbr. MULTILATERAL TRADE AGREEMENT.

MTD. *abbr.* MOTION TO DISMISS.

MTR. *abbr.* See *marginal tax rate* under TAX RATE.

MUD. *abbr.* See *municipal utility district* under DISTRICT.

mug book. (1947) A collection of mug shots of criminal suspects maintained by law-enforcement agencies (such as the FBI and police departments) to be used in identifying criminal offenders.

mugshot. (1950) A photograph of a person's face, esp. one taken after the person has been arrested and booked. — Also written *mug shot.*

mulct (məlkt), *n.* (16c) A fine or penalty.

mulct, *vb.* (17c) **1.** To punish by a fine. **2.** To deprive or divest of, esp. fraudulently.

mulct law. (1894) *Hist.* An Iowa statute that allowed some saloons to pay the state a sum of money and continue to operate despite a statewide prohibition against alcohol sales. • While the money paid was called a mulct, it was effectively a licensing tax rather than a criminal penalty because continuing violations of the liquor law were not prosecuted.

mule. (1922) *Slang.* A person hired to smuggle contraband, esp. a controlled substance, and deliver it to the distributor at a destination point. • For example, a drug mule might carry cocaine through a security checkpoint by concealing it beneath a suitcase's false bottom. Cf. DRUG RUNNER.

mulier (**myoo**-lee-ər), *n.* [Latin] **1.** *Roman law.* A woman. • This term at various times referred to a marriageable virgin, a woman not a virgin, a wife, or a mistress. **2.** *Hist. & Scots law.* A legitimate son; the son of a *mulier* ("lawful wife").

mulieratus filius (myoo-lee-**er**-ə-təs **fil**-ee-əs). (17c) *Hist. & Scots law.* A legitimate son or daughter; the son of a *mulier* ("lawful wife").

mulier puisne (**myoo**-lee-ər **pyoo**-nee). [Law Latin] (17c) *Hist.* The younger lawful son, usu. distinguished from the *bastard eigné* ("the elder bastard son").

> "The common law developed one exception to its harsh doctrine of bastardy. Where the eldest son was born out of wedlock (the *bastard eigné*) and the next son was born to the same parents after the marriage (the *mulier puisné*), and upon the ancestor's death the *bastard eigné* entered as heir and remained in undisturbed possession until his own death, the *bastard eigné* was treated as if he had been legitimate with respect to the inheritance of that land. The reason given by Littleton was that a person who was legitimate by the Canon law could not be bastardised posthumously, when he no longer had the opportunity to contest the issue." J.H. Baker, *An Introduction to English Legal History* 559 (3d ed. 1990).

mulierty (**myoo**-lee-ər-tee). (17c) *Hist.* The condition of a legitimate child, as distinguished from a bastard.

multa (**məl**-tə), *n.* [Latin "a fine"] *Hist. Eccles. law.* A fine the bishops paid to the king so that they could make and probate wills and administer estates. — Also termed *multura episcopi* (məl-**t[y]oor**-ə i-**pis**-kə-pɪ).

multicraft union. See UNION.

multidisciplinary practice. (1987) A fee-sharing association of lawyers and nonlawyers in a firm that delivers both legal and nonlegal services. • Rule 5.4 of the Model Rules of Professional Conduct effectively bars multidisciplinary practice. Under this rule, a lawyer cannot (1) share legal fees with nonlawyers, (2) form a partnership involving the practice of law with nonlawyers, (3) form a law firm in which a nonlawyer has an interest, or (4) allow a nonlawyer to direct the lawyer's professional judgment. — Abbr. MDP. — Sometimes termed *multidisciplinary practice of law.*

multidistrict litigation. (1966) *Civil procedure.* Federal-court litigation in which civil actions pending in different districts and involving common fact questions are transferred to a single district for coordinated pretrial proceedings, after which the actions are returned to their original districts for trial. • Multidistrict litigation is governed by the Judicial Panel on Multidistrict Litigation, which is composed of seven circuit and district judges appointed by the Chief Justice of the United States. 28 USCA § 1407. — Abbr. MDL.

Multiethnic Placement Act of 1994. A model statute intended to (1) decrease the length of time that a child awaits adoption, (2) identify and recruit adoptive and foster parents who can meet the needs of available children, and (3) eliminate adoption discrimination based on race, color, or national origin of the child or the adoptive parents. — Abbr. MEPA.

multifarious (məl-tə-**fair**-ee-əs), *adj.* (16c) **1.** (Of a single pleading) improperly joining distinct matters or causes of action, and thereby confounding them. **2.** Improperly joining parties in a lawsuit. **3.** Diverse; many and various. — **multifariousness,** *n.*

multifarious issue. See ISSUE (1).

multilateral, *adj.* (1827) Involving more than two parties <a multilateral agreement>.

multilateral advance pricing agreement. See ADVANCE PRICING AGREEMENT.

multilateral trade agreement. A treaty that regulates international commerce, such as TRIPs, GATT, or GATS. — Abbr. MTA.

multilevel-distribution program. See PYRAMID SCHEME.

multimaturity bond. See *put bond* under BOND (3).

multimodal shipping. (1996) The transportation of freight using more than one means of carriage and usu. more than one carrier. • For example, a cargo may be carried first by air or sea, then by rail or truck to its destination. — Also termed *intermodal transport; multimodal carriage.*

multinational corporation. See CORPORATION.

multipartite, *adj.* (17c) (Of a document, etc.) divided into many parts.

multiperil policy. See INSURANCE POLICY.

multiple access. See ACCESS (3).

multiple admissibility. See ADMISSIBILITY.

multiple-class application. See *combined application* under TRADEMARK APPLICATION.

multiple counts. See COUNT (2).

multiple damages. See DAMAGES.

multiple-dependent claim. See PATENT CLAIM.

multiple evidence. See EVIDENCE.

multiple hearsay. See *double hearsay* under HEARSAY.

multiple interest. See INTEREST (2).

multiple job-holding. See MOONLIGHTING.

multiple listing. See LISTING (1).

multiple offense. See OFFENSE (2).

multiple-party account. See ACCOUNT.

multiple sentences. See SENTENCE.

multiplicity (məl-tə-**plis**-i-tee), *n. Criminal procedure.* The improper charging of the same offense in more than one count of a single indictment or information. • Multiplicity violates the Fifth Amendment protection against double jeopardy. — **multiplicitous** (məl-tə-**plis**-i-təs), *adj.*

multiplicity of actions. (17c) The existence of two or more lawsuits litigating the same issue against the same defendant. — Also termed *multiplicity of suits; multiplicity of proceedings.* See PIECEMEAL LITIGATION.

multiplicity of claims. See AGGREGATION OF CLAIMS.

multiplied damages. See *multiple damages* under DAMAGES.

Multistate Bar Examination. See BAR EXAMINATION.

multistate corporation. See CORPORATION.

Multistate Professional Responsibility Exam. A test based on the ABA Model Rules of Professional Conduct, the

ABA Code of Judicial Conduct, and caselaw bearing on legal ethics. • The test is administered by ACT for the National Conference of Bar Examiners, and is a requirement for admission to the bar in most states. — Abbr. MPRE.

multital (**məl**-ti-təl), *adj.* (1917) **1.** Of, relating to, or involving legal relations that exist among three or more people, esp. a multitude of people. Cf. UNITAL.

> "Tort and breach of contract are alike breaches of *duty*, but in the case of tort the pre-existing duty of the wrong-doer was one that was shared by every other member of society; and the injured party whose right was violated had not merely one right, he had a multitude of rights. His rights and the correlative duties of others were 'multital.' The secondary right and duty, however, arising from the tort, are relations that exist between the two persons only. They are 'unital.' In the case of a breach of contract, both the primary right and duty and the secondary right and duty are 'unital.'" William R. Anson, *Principles of the Law of Contract* 11 (Arthur L. Corbin ed., 3d Am. ed. 1919).

2. *Rare.* See IN REM.

multura episcopi. See MULTA.

multure. (13c) *Hist.* **1.** A quantity of grain that was paid to a mill's owner or tenant in exchange for grinding the remaining grain. **2.** A miller's right to payment in grain for milling services rendered.

Munchausen syndrome by proxy (**mən**-chow-zən). (1977) A condition in which a caregiver, usu. a parent, fabricates or induces a child's medical condition and seeks medical treatment for the child on the basis of the fabrications or induced condition. • This syndrome is a kind of child abuse, esp. when the victim is subjected to repeated medical examinations and treatment, often of an invasive nature, and sometimes even to physical injuries that induce symptoms consistent with the falsified medical condition. The parent is usu. emotionally deprived and fabricates or causes the child's illness or medical condition as an attention-getting device. — Abbr. MSP.

mund (mənd *or* muund). [Old English "hand"] (bef. 12c) *Hist.* A right to protection or guardianship; a guardian. Cf. MANUS (1).

> "Once more we see prerogatival rights growing, while feudal claims fall into the background; and in the case of lunacy we see a guardianship, a *mund*, which is not profitable to the guardian, and this at present is a novel and noteworthy thing." 1 Frederick Pollock & Frederic W. Maitland, *The History of English Law Before the Time of Edward I* 481 (2d ed. 1898).

mundium (**mən**-dee-əm). [Law Latin] The legal protection and representation granted to a person who is socially and physically weak.

> "In a society of persons in which the authority to maintain the law was in the hands of its members, and of which the membership rested on the ability to bear arms and defend oneself ('weer'), those who, for want of strength or some other reason, were unable to do so, could not play an active part, and were necessarily placed under the authority of those whose protection they needed. Originally, *mundium* was not limited to family law. Gradually it lost its wider meaning, and in its restricted sense it received different applications, as family relations became classified into separate groups, and the conception of *mundium* appeared under different forms, with special rules and special names — e.g., marital power, parental power, guardianship, and curatorship." Alexander Wood Renton & George Grenville Phillimore, *The Comparative Law of Marriage and Divorce* 10 (1910).

munera (**myoo**-nər-ə), *n.* [Law Latin "graces"] *Hist.* Tenancies at will; tenancies made at the grantor's pleasure.

munera publica (**myoo**-nər-ə **pəb**-li-kə). [Latin] (18c) *Roman law.* Public duties, such as performing the offices of tutor and curator, and of *index privatus.* Sing. ***munus publicum.***

> "Among the Romans there were certain offices regarded as public duties, which no citizen (unless he could plead certain specified excuses) could refuse to accept of and fulfil; and among these were included the offices of tutor and curator. These offices are voluntary by the law of Scotland, and their acceptance, as well as the performance of the attendant duties, cannot be imposed upon any one against his own wish. But if the office has been once accepted and acted upon, the tutor or curator cannot resign it. He must perform the duties of his office until it expires through the death, attainment of minority or majority, as the case may be, or it may be through the marriage of the ward, and he will be liable for the consequences of his neglect, as well as the consequences of his actings and intromissions." John Trayner, *Trayner's Latin Maxims* 364 (4th ed. 1894).

muni (**myoo**-nee), *n.* See *municipal bond* under BOND (3).

municeps (**myoo**-nə-seps), *n.* [fr. Latin *munus* "office" + *capere* "to take"] *Roman law.* **1.** A citizen of a municipality (*municipium*). **2.** A member of the council of a *municipium.* Pl. ***municipes*** (myoo-ni-**sip**-eez).

municipal, *adj.* (16c) **1.** Of, relating to, or involving a city, town, or local governmental unit. **2.** Of, relating to, or involving the internal government of a state or country (as contrasted with *international*).

municipal, *n.* See *municipal bond* under BOND (3).

municipal action. (1853) Any authorized exercise of governmental power by a municipal officer, board, agency, or other municipal body.

municipal affairs. (1825) The matters relating to the local government of a municipality.

municipal aid. (1869) Financial or other assistance provided by a municipality to a private business, usu. to encourage it to relocate to the municipality.

municipal attorney. See CITY ATTORNEY.

municipal bond. See BOND (3).

municipal borough. See BOROUGH (3).

municipal charter. See CHARTER (2).

municipal corporation. (1833) A city, town, or other local political entity formed by charter from the state and having the autonomous authority to administer the state's local affairs; esp., a public corporation created for political purposes and endowed with political powers to be exercised for the public good in the administration of local civil government. — Also termed *municipality.* Cf. *quasi-corporation* under CORPORATION.

> "A municipal corporation is perfect as contradistinguished from the imperfect quasi corporation, the county, district, or township, loosely organized under general law into a governmental agency for local administration of the state authority within a subdivision of the state, which in strictness cannot be said to be incorporated, though the statutes of many states declare them to be corporations. The municipal corporation is duly incorporated not primarily to enforce state laws, but chiefly to regulate the local affairs of the city, town, or district incorporated by proper legislation and administration. It is lawfully and fully empowered so to do. Practically it may fall far short of perfection, but in the eye of the law it is the only ideal of a complete public corporation. Its object is public, thought incidents

connected with it may be of private nature, and so far forth it is subject to the rules of liability controlling private corporations in the ownership of property, while the quasi public corporation is of a private nature and object, with incidents only that are public. The municipal is the only corporation standing as the representative of the purely public corporation." Roger W. Cooley, *Handbook of the Law of Municipal Corporations* 15-16 (1914).

▸ **municipal corporation de facto.** (1868) A corporation recognized to exist, although it has not fully complied with statutory requirements, when there is (1) a valid law authorizing its incorporation, (2) a colorable and bona fide attempt to organize under that law, and (3) an assumption of powers conferred under that law.

municipal court. See COURT.

municipal domicile. See DOMICILE.

municipal election. See ELECTION (3).

municipal function. (1842) The duties and responsibilities that a municipality owes its members.

municipal government. See *local government* under GOVERNMENT (3).

municipality. (18c) **1.** A city, town, or other local political entity with the powers of self-government; MUNICIPAL CORPORATION. **2.** The governing body of a municipal corporation. **3.** The community under the jurisdiction of a city's or township's government.

municipalize, *vb.* **1.** To make into a municipality; to render municipal in character <after the train bypassed the village, population dwindled and the place was never municipalized>. **2.** To transfer from private ownership to municipal ownership; (of a city or town) to take over the ownership and management of (water, gas, and electricity works; streetcars, docks, ferries, etc.) <the city municipalized the ferries decades ago>.

municipal judge. See JUDGE.

municipal law. (16c) **1.** The ordinances and other laws applicable within a city, town, or other local governmental entity. **2.** The internal law of a country, as opposed to international law.

municipal lien. See LIEN.

municipal officer. See OFFICER (1).

municipal ordinance. See ORDINANCE.

municipal security. See *municipal bond* under BOND (3).

municipal utility district. (1921) A publicly owned corporation, or a political subdivision, that provides the public with a service or services, such as water, electricity, gas, transportation, or telecommunications. — Abbr. MUD. — Also termed *public utility district* (PUD).

municipal warrant. See WARRANT (2).

municipium (myoo-nə-**sip**-ee-əm), *n.* [Latin "free town"] (18c) *Roman law.* A self-governing town; specif., any community allied with or conquered by Rome and allowed to maintain certain privileges (such as maintaining separate laws called *leges municipales*). • The members of a *municipium* were also Roman citizens. Pl. ***municipia*** (myoo-ni-**sip**-ee-ə).

muniment (**myoo**-nə-mənt). (15c) A document (such as a deed or charter) evidencing the rights or privileges of a person, family, or corporation. — Also termed (archaically) *miniment.*

muniment house. (17c) *Hist.* A place (such as a room in a castle or cathedral) where titles, deeds, and other evidences of title are stored.

muniment of title. (1806) Documentary evidence of title, such as a deed or a judgment regarding the ownership of property. — Also termed *common assurance.* See CHAIN OF TITLE.

mural monument. See MONUMENT.

murder, *n.* (bef. 12c) The killing of a human being with malice aforethought. • At common law, the crime of murder was not subdivided, but many state statutes have adopted the degree structure outlined below, though the Model Penal Code has not. Model Penal Code § 210.2. See MALICE AFORETHOUGHT. Cf. MANSLAUGHTER. — **murder,** *vb.* — **murderous,** *adj.*

"The word 'murder' has . . . had a devious history. Its original sense is the particularly heinous crime of secret slaying. After the conquest it was observed that Normans were frequently found dead under mysterious circumstances, and so William I enacted that if anyone were found slain and the slayer were not caught, then the hundred should pay a fine; this fine is a *murdrum.* The practice soon grew up to taking inquests and if it were presented that the dead man was English, then the fine was not due. In 1267 it was enacted that accidental deaths should not give rise to *murdrum,* and finally in 1340 presentment of Englishry and *murdrum* were abolished. Henceforth the word slowly tends to get linked up with 'malice aforethought' and so we get the classical formulae describing the crime of murder." Theodore F.T. Plucknett, *A Concise History of the Common Law* 445 (5th ed. 1956).

▸ **constructive murder.** See *felony murder.*

▸ **depraved-heart murder.** (1975) A murder resulting from an act so reckless and careless of the safety of others that it demonstrates the perpetrator's complete lack of regard for human life. — Also termed *depraved-indifference murder*; *unintentional murder*; *extreme-indifference murder*; *depraved-mind murder.*

▸ **extreme-indifference murder.** See *depraved-heart murder.*

▸ **felony murder.** (1926) Murder that occurs during the commission of a dangerous felony (often limited to rape, kidnapping, robbery, burglary, and arson). — Also termed *unintentional murder*; (in English law) *constructive murder.* See FELONY-MURDER RULE.

▸ **first-degree murder.** (1895) Murder that is willful, deliberate, or premeditated, or that is committed during the course of another dangerous felony. • All murder perpetrated by poisoning or by lying in wait is considered first-degree murder. All types of murder not involving willful, deliberate, and premeditated killing are usu. considered second-degree murder. — Also termed *murder of the first degree*; *murder one.*

▸ **mass murder.** (1917) A murderous act or series of acts by which a criminal kills many victims at or near the same time, usu. as part of one act or plan. Cf. *serial murder*; MASSACRE.

▸ **murder by torture.** (1901) A murder preceded by the intentional infliction of pain and suffering on the victim.

"In some jurisdictions, a murder by torture may constitute murder in the first degree. It occurs when a defendant intentionally inflicts pain and suffering upon his victim for the purpose of revenge, extortion, or persuasion." 2 Charles

E. Torcia, *Wharton's Criminal Law* § 144, at 281 (15th ed. 1994).

▸ **murder of the first degree.** See *first-degree murder.*

▸ **murder of the second degree.** See *second-degree murder.*

▸ **murder of the third degree.** See *third-degree murder.*

▸ **murder one.** See *first-degree murder.*

▸ **murder three.** See *third-degree murder.*

▸ **murder two.** See *second-degree murder.*

▸ **open murder.** See OPEN MURDER.

▸ **second-degree murder.** (1909) Murder that is not aggravated by any of the circumstances of first-degree murder. — Also termed *murder of the second degree; murder two.*

▸ **serial murder.** (1977) A murder in which a criminal kills one of many victims over time, often as part of a pattern in which the criminal targets victims who have some similar characteristics. Cf. *mass murder.*

▸ **third-degree murder.** (1933) A wrong that did not constitute murder at common law. • Only a few states have added to their murder statutes a third degree of murder. The other states classify all murders in two degrees. Manslaughter is not a degree of the crime of murder, but instead is a distinct offense. — Also termed *murder of the third degree; murder three.*

▸ **unintended murder.** See *unintentional murder* (1).

▸ **unintentional murder.** (18c) **1.** A killing for which malice is implied because the person acted with intent to cause serious physical injury or knew that the conduct was substantially certain to cause death or serious physical injury. • In some jurisdictions, this term is applied generally to several grades of killings without express intent. — Also termed *unintended murder.* **2.** See *depraved-heart murder.* **3.** See *felony murder.* **4.** See *voluntary manslaughter* under MANSLAUGHTER.

▸ **willful murder.** (16c) The unlawful and intentional killing of another without excuse or mitigating circumstances.

murder clause. A contract provision that imposes onerous — often unreasonable — obligations on one party. • Murder clauses are usu. found in construction contracts.

murderous malice. See MALICE.

murdrum (**mər**-drəm). [Law Latin] (13c) *Hist.* **1.** The secret killing of someone. **2.** A fine against the tithing where the secret and unsolved homicide took place.

> "The readiness with which the Norman administrators seized on this Anglo-Saxon system was probably due to its effectiveness in collecting the *murdrum,* the murder fine. In ordinary cases of homicide, the whole district — except the kin of the suspect — would be zealous to bring the malefactor to justice. But we can readily see that, if the person killed was a Norman, every effort would be made to shield the murderer. The Norman rulers had recourse to the device . . . of imposing a group responsibility. The tithing within which the murdered Norman was found was compelled to pay a fine or to discover and surrender the homicide. The word *murdrum* is a word of uncertain etymology, and has given us our term for willful homicide." Max Radin, *Handbook of Anglo-American Legal History* 175–76 (1936).

3. Murder; specif., murder with malice aforethought. See MALICE AFORETHOUGHT.

murorum operatio (myuur-**or**-əm op-ə-**ray**-shee-oh). [Latin] *Hist.* Repair work to the fortifications of buildings, cities, or castles, performed by their inhabitants.

must-carry rule. (1981) A federal regulation requiring cable-television providers to make a portion of their signal capacity available to local commercial- and public-television stations. *See* 47 CFR § 76.56 (2011).

muster, *vb.* (14c) *Military law.* **1.** To assemble (troops) in one place for inspection or service. **2.** To assemble (potential troops) in one place for enlistment.

muster roll. (1809) *Maritime law.* A shipmaster's account listing the name, age, national character, and quality of every employee on the ship. • In wartime, it is used in ascertaining a ship's neutrality.

must-pass bill. See BILL (3).

mutatio libelli (myoo-**tay**-shee-oh lɪ-**bel**-ɪ). [Latin] *Hist.* Modification of the complaint.

mutation, *n.* (14c) A significant and basic alteration; esp., in property law, the alteration of a thing's status, such as from separate property to community property. — **mutate,** *vb.* — **mutational,** *adj.*

mutation of libel. (1888) *Maritime law.* An amendment to a complaint. See LIBEL (3).

mutatio nominis (myoo-**tay**-shee-oh **nom**-ə-nis). [Latin] (17c) *Roman law.* Change of name. • It was allowed provided that no prejudice was thereby caused to others. The related phrase *mutato nomine* (myoo-**tay**-toh **nom**-ə-nee) means "the name having been changed."

mutatis mutandis (myoo-**tay**-tis myoo-**tan**-dis). [Latin] (16c) All necessary changes having been made; with the necessary changes <what was said regarding the first contract applies *mutatis mutandis* to all later ones>.

mute, *n.* (17c) **1.** Someone who cannot speak. **2.** A person (esp. a prisoner) who stands silent when required to answer or plead. • Formerly, if a prisoner stood mute, a jury was empaneled to determine whether the prisoner was intentionally mute or mute by an act of God. By the Criminal Law Act of 1827 (7 & 8 Geo. 4, ch. 28), if a prisoner was mute by malice, the officer automatically entered a plea of not guilty and the trial proceeded. If adjudicated to be insane, the prisoner was kept in custody until the Crown determined what should be done. See STAND MUTE.

mute by visitation of God. (1897) *Hist.* The condition of a criminal defendant who remains silent rather than entering a plea at arraignment or trial for physical or psychological reasons beyond his or her control, such as deafness, muteness, or insanity. Cf. MUTE OF MALICE.

mute of malice. (16c) *Hist.* The condition of a criminal defendant who remains silent rather than entering a plea at arraignment or trial by his or her own deliberate choice. See STAND MUTE. Cf. MUTE BY VISITATION OF GOD.

mutilate, *vb.* **1.** To severely and violently damage; esp., to cut off or cut out an essential part of; to maim or cripple <some of the prisoners of war had been mutilated>. **2.** To damage or change (something) so much that it is utterly spoiled; to render seriously defective by destroying or removing a material part of <the editors mutilated the essay beyond recognition>.

mutilation, *n.* (16c) **1.** The act or an instance of rendering a document legally ineffective by subtracting or altering — but not completely destroying — an essential part through cutting, tearing, burning, or erasing. **2.** *Criminal law.* The act of cutting off or permanently damaging a body part, esp. an essential one. See MAYHEM. — **mutilator,** *n.*

mutineer. (17c) A participant in a mutiny; esp., a mutinous soldier or sailor.

mutiny (myoo-tə-nee), *n.* (16c) **1.** An insubordination or insurrection of armed forces, esp. sailors, against the authority of their commanders; a forcible revolt by members of the military against constituted authority, usu. their commanding officers. See REVOLT (2). **2.** Loosely, any uprising against authority. — Also termed (in both senses) *inciting revolt.* — **mutinous,** *adj.*

Mutiny Act. *Hist.* An English statute enacted annually from 1689 to 1879 to provide for a standing army and to punish mutiny, desertion, and other military offenses. • It was merged into the Army Discipline and Regulation Act of 1879 (ch. 33).

mutual, *adj.* (16c) **1.** Generally, directed by each toward the other or others; reciprocal. **2.** (Of a condition, credit covenant, promise, etc.) reciprocally given, received, or exchanged. **3.** (Of a right, etc.) belonging to two parties; common. — **mutuality,** *n.*

mutual account. See ACCOUNT.

mutual affray. See MUTUAL COMBAT.

mutual-agreement program. (1978) A prisoner-rehabilitation plan in which the prisoner agrees to take part in certain self-improvement activities to receive a definite parole date. — Abbr. MAP.

mutual assent. See ASSENT.

mutual association. A cooperatively owned savings and loan association whose deposits are shares of the association. • A mutual association is not allowed to issue stock and is usu. regulated by the Office of Thrift Supervision, an agency of the U.S. Treasury Department. — See SAVINGS-AND-LOAN ASSOCIATION.

mutual-benefit association. (1848) A fraternal or social organization that provides benefits for its members, usu. on an assessment basis.

> "In the absence of . . . statutory definition, the question of the extent to which mutual benefit, fraternal beneficiary, and like associations or societies, are within the meaning of the insurance laws must depend upon the terms of the different statutes, and the various circumstances of each particular case . . . . Broadly speaking, when a company, society, or association, either voluntary or incorporated, and whether known as a relief, benevolent, or benefit society, or by some similar name, contracts for a consideration to pay a sum of money upon the happening of a certain contingency, and the prevalent purpose and nature of the organization is that of insurance, it will be regarded as an insurance company and its contracts as insurance contracts . . . ." 2A George J. Couch, *Couch on Insurance* § 20:2, at 11 (rev. 2d ed. 1984).

mutual-benefit insurance. (1852) Benefits provided by a mutual-benefit association upon the occurrence of a loss.

mutual combat. (17c) A consensual fight on equal terms — arising from a moment of passion but not in self-defense — between two persons armed with deadly weapons. • A murder charge may be reduced to voluntary manslaughter if death occurred by mutual combat. — Also termed *mutual affray.* Cf. DUEL.

mutual company. See COMPANY.

mutual contract. See *bilateral contract* under CONTRACT.

mutual debts. See DEBT.

mutual demands. (17c) Countering demands between two parties at the same time <a claim and counterclaim in a lawsuit are mutual demands>.

mutual fund. (1934) **1.** An investment company that invests its shareholders' money in a usu. diversified selection of securities. — Often shortened to *fund.* **2.** Loosely, a share in such a company.

▸ **balanced fund.** (1959) A mutual fund that maintains a balanced investment in stocks and bonds, investing a certain percentage in senior securities.

▸ **bond fund.** (1961) A mutual fund that invests primarily in specialized corporate bonds or municipal bonds.

▸ **closed-end fund.** (1961) A mutual fund having a fixed number of shares that are traded on a major securities exchange or an over-the-counter market.

▸ **common-stock fund.** (1956) A mutual fund that invests only in common stock.

▸ **dual fund.** (1968) A closed-end mutual fund that invests in two classes of stock — stock that pays dividends and stock that increases in investment value without dividends. • A dual fund combines characteristics of an income fund and a growth fund. — Also termed *dual-purpose fund; leverage fund; split fund.*

▸ **fully managed fund.** (1989) A mutual fund whose policy allows reasonable discretion in trading securities in combination or quantity.

▸ **global fund.** (1985) A mutual fund that invests in stocks and bonds throughout the world, including the U.S. — Also termed *world fund.* Cf. *single-country fund; international fund.*

▸ **growth fund.** (1961) A mutual fund that typically invests in well-established companies whose earnings are expected to increase. • Growth funds usu. pay small dividends but offer the potential for large share-price increases.

▸ **hedge fund.** See HEDGE FUND.

▸ **income fund.** (1967) A mutual fund that typically invests in securities that consistently produce a steady income, such as bonds or dividend-paying stocks.

▸ **index fund.** (1973) A mutual fund that invests in the stock of companies constituting a specific market index, such as Standard & Poor's 500 stocks, and thereby tracks the stock average.

▸ **international fund.** (1965) A mutual fund that invests in stocks and bonds of companies outside the U.S., but not those within. Cf. *global fund; single-country fund.*

▸ **leverage fund.** See *dual fund.*

▸ **load fund.** A mutual fund that charges a commission, usu. ranging from 4 to 9%, either when shares are purchased (a *front-end load*) or when they are redeemed (a *back-end load*).

▸ **money-market fund.** (1982) A mutual fund that invests in low-risk government securities and short-term notes. — Abbr. MMF.

▸ **no-load fund.** (1962) A mutual fund that does not charge any sales commission (although it may charge fees to cover operating costs).

▸ **open-end fund.** (1961) A mutual fund that continually offers new shares and buys back existing shares on demand. • An open-end fund will continue to grow as more shareholders invest because it does not have a fixed number of shares outstanding.

▸ **performance fund.** (1967) A mutual fund characterized by an aggressive purchase of stocks expected to show near-term growth.

▸ **regional fund.** A mutual fund that concentrates its investments in a specific geographic area or a particular economic area.

▸ **single-country fund.** (1986) A mutual fund that invests in an individual country outside the U.S. Cf. *global fund*; *international fund*.

▸ **split fund.** See *dual fund*.

▸ **utility fund.** (1982) A mutual fund that invests only in public-utility securities.

▸ **value fund.** A mutual fund that invests in stocks that its manager believes to be priced below their true market value.

▸ **vulture fund.** (1991) An investment company that purchases bankrupt or insolvent companies to reorganize them in hopes of reselling them at a profit.

▸ **world fund.** See *global fund*.

mutual-fund wrap account. See ACCOUNT.

mutual insurance. See INSURANCE.

mutual insurance company. See INSURANCE COMPANY.

mutuality. (16c) The state of sharing or exchanging something; a reciprocation; an interchange <mutuality of obligation>.

mutuality doctrine. (1926) The collateral-estoppel requirement that, to bar a party from relitigating an issue determined against that party in an earlier action, both parties must have been in privity with one another in the earlier proceeding. — Also termed *mutuality of parties*.

mutuality of assent. See MEETING OF THE MINDS.

mutuality of benefits. See RECIPROCITY (2).

mutuality of contract. See MUTUALITY OF OBLIGATION.

mutuality of debts. (1901) *Bankruptcy.* For purposes of setoff, the condition in which debts are owed between parties acting in the same capacity, even though the debts are not of the same character and did not arise out of the same transaction.

mutuality of estoppel. (1852) The collateral-estoppel principle that a judgment is not conclusively in favor of someone unless the opposite decision would also be conclusively against that person.

mutuality of obligation. (1838) The agreement of both parties to a contract to be bound in some way. — Also termed *mutuality of contract*. See *mutual assent* under ASSENT.

> "[The] so-called doctrine of 'mutuality of obligation' in bilateral contracts . . . unfortunately has been the cause of no little confusion. This confusion is evident from the fact that, while it is commonly admitted there is such a doctrine, there is a lack of unanimity, both in the statement of it and in regard to its application. The most common mode of statement is: 'In a bilateral agreement both promises must be binding or neither is binding.' This statement is obviously ambiguous, since it does not indicate in what sense the promises must be binding. The fact is that it has been variously interpreted and applied by the courts with results that have sometimes been inconsistent with other well settled principles of the law of consideration. Usually it has been held to mean that a promise that is not legally obligatory cannot be consideration in spite of the fact that it may satisfy all the usual requirements of consideration. However, at times it has in effect been held to involve the requirement that the undertaking of the promise relied upon as a consideration must be reasonably commensurate with, or equivalent to, the undertaking of the promise which it supports, before it can constitute consideration — a kind of doctrine of mutuality of undertaking." John Edward Murray Jr., *Murray on Contracts* § 90, at 190–91 (2d ed. 1974).

> "The doctrine of mutuality of obligation is commonly expressed in the phrase that in a bilateral contract 'both parties must be bound or neither is bound.' But this phrase is over-generalization because the doctrine is not one of mutuality of obligation but rather one of mutuality of consideration. Phrasing the rule in terms of mutuality of obligation rather than in terms of consideration has led to so-called exceptions and judicial circumventions . . . . It has been suggested that the term 'mutuality of obligation' should be abandoned and we must agree in the light of the confusion that this term has engendered." John D. Calamari & Joseph M. Perillo, *The Law of Contracts* § 4-12, at 226 (3d ed. 1987).

mutuality of parties. See MUTUALITY DOCTRINE.

mutuality of remedy. (1819) The availability of a remedy, esp. equitable relief, to both parties to a transaction, sometimes required before either party can be granted specific performance. See SPECIFIC PERFORMANCE.

mutual mistake. See MISTAKE.

mutual promises. See PROMISE.

mutual release. See RELEASE (8).

mutual rescission. See RESCISSION (2).

mutual running account. See *mutual account* under ACCOUNT.

mutual savings bank. See BANK.

mutual testament. See *mutual will* under WILL.

mutual will. See WILL.

mutuant (**myoo**-choo-ənt). The provider of property in a mutuum. See MUTUUM. Cf. MUTUARY.

mutua petitio (**myoo**-choo-ə pə-**tish**-ee-oh). [Latin] (18c) *Scots law.* A counterclaim. See COUNTERCLAIM. Pl. ***mutuae petitiones.***

mutuari (myoo-choo-**air**-ɪ), *vb.* [Latin] To borrow.

mutuary (**myoo**-choo-er-ee). (1839) The recipient of property in a mutuum. See MUTUUM. Cf. MUTUANT.

mutuatus (myoo-choo-**ay**-təs), *n.* [Latin] A borrowing; a loan of money.

mutui datio (**myoo**-choo-ɪ **day**-shee-oh). [Latin] *Roman law.* The lending of objects that can be weighed, measured, or counted (such as bullion, corn, wine, oil, and coined money), on the understanding that the borrower will repay by restoring an equal amount of the object borrowed. See MUTUUM (2).

mutus et surdus (**myoo**-təs et **sər**-dəs). [Latin] *Hist.* Deaf and dumb.

mutuum (**myoo**-choo-əm), *n.* (15c) **1.** A transaction (sometimes referred to as a bailment) in which goods are delivered but, instead of being returned, are replaced by other goods of the same kind. • At common law such a transaction is regarded as a sale or exchange, not as a bailment, because the particular goods are not returned. **2.** *Roman law.* A real contract in which money or fungible goods were delivered from the lender to the borrower, who was strictly liable to return an equivalent amount. • Because the contract was gratuitous, any interest had to be demanded by stipulation. This was one of the real contracts, along with the loan for use (*commodatum* (kom-ə-**day**-təm)), deposit (*depositum* (di-**poz**-i-təm)), and pledge (*pignoratio* (pig-nə-**ray**-shee-oh)). See MUTUI DATIO.

> "Mutuum is a contract . . . completed by delivery, according to which a thing for use and in commercio is delivered by the creditor to the debtor, to be his property, subject to the restitution to the creditor at his demand, of a thing not the same, but identically the same in kind and in measure. The mutuum must consist of things that can be weighed and numbered, as wine, corn, money, and that are consumed by use." John George Phillimore, *Private Law Among the Romans* 238 (1863).

mutuus dissensus (**myoo**-choo-əs di-**sen**-səs). [Latin] *Hist.* Mutual disagreement.

MVA. *abbr.* Motor-vehicle accident.

mysterious disappearance. A loss of property under unknown or baffling circumstances that are difficult to understand or explain. • The term is used in insurance policies covering theft.

> "Under a policy insuring against loss of property by 'mysterious disappearance' recovery is generally allowed where the article disappears from the place the insured left it, while recovery is ordinarily disallowed where the insured has no recollection of when he last had possession of the article and cannot say when or from what place it disappeared. Thus the addition of the words 'mysterious disappearance' to a theft policy does not transform it to an 'all loss' policy covering lost or mislaid articles, but it remains a theft policy." 43 Am. Jur. 2d *Insurance* § 501, at 575–76 (1982).

mystic testament. See *mystic will* under WILL.

mystic will. See WILL.

N

n.a. *abbr.* (1947) **1.** (*cap.*) National Association. See *national bank* under BANK. **2.** Not applicable. **3.** Not available. **4.** Not allowed.

NAA. *abbr.* NEUTRON-ACTIVATION ANALYSIS.

NAACP. *abbr.* (1910) NATIONAL ASSOCIATION FOR THE ADVANCEMENT OF COLORED PEOPLE.

NAFTA (**naf**-tə). *abbr.* (1990) NORTH AMERICAN FREE TRADE AGREEMENT.

nail-and-mail service. See SERVICE (7).

naked, *adj.* (14c) (Of a legal act or instrument) lacking confirmation or validation <naked ownership of property>. — **nakedness,** *n.*

naked assignment. See *assignment in gross* under ASSIGNMENT (2).

naked authority. See AUTHORITY (1).

naked bailment. See *gratuitous bailment* under BAILMENT (1).

naked confession. See CONFESSION (1).

naked contract. See NUDUM PACTUM.

naked debenture. See DEBENTURE (3).

naked deposit. 1. See *gratuitous bailment* under BAILMENT (1). **2.** See DEPOSIT (5).

naked expectancy. See *naked possibility* under POSSIBILITY.

naked land trust. See *land trust* (1) under TRUST (3).

naked license. See LICENSE.

naked licensee. See *bare licensee* under LICENSEE.

naked option. See OPTION (5).

naked owner. See OWNER.

naked ownership. See *imperfect ownership* under OWNERSHIP.

naked possession. See POSSESSION.

naked possibility. See POSSIBILITY.

naked power. See POWER (3).

naked promise. See *gratuitous promise* under PROMISE.

naked trust. See *passive trust* under TRUST (3).

nam (nam), *n.* [Old English *naam*] *Hist.* The act of distraining property.

nam (nam *or* nahm), *prep.* [Latin] For.

> "Nam . . . . This particle is frequently used as introductory to the quotation of a maxim, and sometimes erroneously treated as a part of the maxim quoted." 2 Alexander M. Burrill, *A Law Dictionary and Glossary* 219 (2d ed. 1867).

namare (nə-**mair**-ee), *vb.* [Law Latin] *Hist.* To distrain property.

namation (nə-**may**-shən), *n.* [fr. Old English *nam*] (18c) *Hist.* **1.** The act of distraining property. **2.** *Scots law.* The impounding of property. — Also termed *namatio.*

name, *n.* (bef. 12c) A word or phrase identifying or designating a person or thing and distinguishing that person or thing from others.

▸ **alias.** See ALIAS.

▸ **assumed name.** (17c) **1.** ALIAS (1). **2.** The name under which a business operates or by which it is commonly known <Antex Corporation's assumed name is Computer Warehouse>. • Many states require an individual or business operating under an assumed name to file an assumed-name certificate, usu. in the secretary of state's office or the county clerk's office where the principal place of business is located. — Also termed *fictitious name.* See D/B/A. Cf. *corporate name.*

▸ **brand name.** See TRADENAME.

▸ **business name.** (1835) The name by which people identify a business, its products, or its services; esp., the name under which a sole proprietorship conducts its commercial activities. — Cf. TRADENAME.

▸ **Christian name.** See *personal name.*

▸ **corporate name.** (1855) The registered name under which a corporation conducts legal affairs such as suing, being sued, and paying taxes; the name that a corporation files with a state authority (usu. the secretary of state) as the name under which the corporation will conduct its affairs. • A corporate name usu. includes, and in many states is required to include, the word "corporation," "incorporated," or "company," or an abbreviation of one of those words. Cf. *assumed name.*

▸ **distinctive name.** (17c) A name, esp. a tradename, that clearly distinguishes one thing from another. • To maintain an action for tradename infringement, the plaintiff must prove, among other things, that it owns a distinctive name.

▸ **family name.** See SURNAME.

▸ **fictitious name. 1.** See *assumed name.* **2.** See ALIAS. **3.** See JOHN DOE.

▸ **first name.** See *personal name.*

▸ **full name.** (16c) An individual's personal name, second or middle names or initials (if any), and surname arranged in a customary order. • In Western cultures, the traditional order is usu. personal name, middle names or initials, and surname. In many other cultures, the order is surname first, followed by one or more personal names.

▸ **generic name.** See GENERIC NAME.

▸ **geographic name.** (1883) A name that designates a geographic location or area. — Also termed *geographical name.*

▸ **given name.** See *personal name.*

▸ **legal name.** (17c) A person's full name as recognized in law. • A legal name is usu. acquired at birth or through a court order. There are no rules governing a legal name's length or constitution; it may be a single name (e.g.,

Prince) or include words not generally used in human names (e.g., Moon Unit).

▸ **maiden name.** (17c) A woman's childhood surname (which may or may not remain her surname for life). • Normally the term is used only in reference to a woman who has married and changed her last name.

▸ **nickname.** See NICKNAME.

▸ **personal name.** (17c) An individual's name or names given at birth, as distinguished from a family name. — Also termed *given name*; (in the Western tradition) *first name*; (in the Christian tradition) *Christian name*. Cf. *surname*.

▸ **proprietary name.** (1898) *Trademarks.* A nondescriptive name that may be owned and registered as a trademark.

▸ **street name.** See STREET NAME.

▸ **surname.** (14c) The family name automatically bestowed at birth, acquired by marriage, or adopted by choice. • Although in many cultures a person's surname is traditionally the father's surname, a person may take the mother's surname or a combination of the parents' surnames. — Also termed *family name*.

▸ **tradename.** See TRADENAME.

name-and-arms clause. (1843) *Hist.* A clause (usu. in a will or settlement transferring property) providing that the property's recipient must assume and continue using the testator's or settlor's surname and coat-of-arms, or else the property will pass to another person.

named additional insured. See *additional insured* under INSURED.

named insured. See INSURED.

named-insured exclusion. See EXCLUSION (3).

named partner. See *name partner* under PARTNER.

named-perils policy. See *multiperil policy* under INSURANCE POLICY.

named plaintiff. See *class representative* under REPRESENTATIVE.

namely, *adv.* (14c) By name or particular mention; that is to say <the plaintiff asserted two claims, namely wrongful termination and slander>. • The term indicates what is to be included by name. By contrast, *including* implies a partial list and indicates that something is not listed. See INCLUDE.

name partner. See PARTNER.

namium (**nay**-mee-əm), *n.* [Law Latin] *Hist.* The act of distraining property.

namium vetitum (**nay**-mee-əm **vet**-ə-təm), *n.* [Law Latin "taking prohibited"] (18c) *Hist.* A refused or prohibited taking or redelivery. • This term is most often associated with the circumstance in which a lord's bailiff distrained animals or goods, and was ordered by the lord to take them to an unknown place or otherwise not to redeliver them when the sheriff came to replevy them. — Also termed *vetitum namium*.

nanny state. (1965) *Pejorative.* A government that overregulates its citizens by interfering with individual choice. • This term is a politically charged label for a government that coddles its citizens through intrusive legislation, such as bans on selling sodas in oversized containers, limits on portions of fried foods, and the like.

nanny tax. See TAX.

nantissement (non-tis-**mahn**), *n.* [French] *French law.* A security or pledge. • If it involves movable property, it is called *gage*. If it involves immovable property such as real estate, it is called *antichrèse*.

NAPABA. *abbr.* NATIONAL ASIAN PACIFIC AMERICAN BAR ASSOCIATION.

Napoleonic Code. 1. (*usu. pl.*) The codification of French law commissioned by Napoleon in the 19th century, including the *Code civil* (1804), the *Code de procédure civil* (1806), the *Code de commerce* (1807), the *Code pénal* (1810), and the *Code d'instruction crimenelle* (1811). — Sometimes shortened to *Napoléon*. — Also termed *Code Napoléon* (CN). **2.** Loosely, CIVIL CODE (2).

***Napue* violation** (**nap**-yoo *or* **nay**-pyoo). (1967) Uncorrected false testimony by a prosecution witness where there is a reasonable possibility that it could have affected the jury's judgment. — Also termed *Mooney–Napue violation*. See *Napue v. Illinois*, 360 U.S. 264, 79 S.Ct. 1173 (1959); *Mooney v. Holohan*, 294 U.S. 103, 55 S.Ct. 340 (1935).

NAR. *abbr.* NATIONAL ASSOCIATION OF REALTORS.

NARA. *abbr.* NATIONAL ARCHIVES AND RECORDS ADMINISTRATION.

narcoanalysis (nahr-koh-ə-**nal**-ə-sis). (1936) The process of injecting a "truth-serum" drug into a patient to induce semiconsciousness, and then interrogating the patient. • This process has been utilized to enhance the memory of a witness.

narcotic, *n.* (14c) **1.** An addictive drug, esp. an opiate, that dulls the senses and induces sleep. **2.** (*usu. pl.*) A drug that is controlled or prohibited by law. — **narcotic,** *adj.*

narr. *abbr.* NARRATIO.

narr-and-cognovit law (nahr-and-kahg-**noh**-vit). [Latin *narratio* "declaration" and *cognovit* "the person has conceded"] (1929) *Hist.* A law providing that a plaintiff will be granted judgment on a note through an attorney's confession that the amount shown on the note, together with interest and costs, constitutes a legal and just claim. Cf. *cognovit judgment* under JUDGMENT (2); CONFESSION OF JUDGMENT.

narratio (nə-**ray**-shee-oh), *n.* [Latin "narrative"] *Hist.* A declaration, complaint, or petition in which the plaintiff sets out the facts of a case; an oral narrative by the plaintiff of the facts and legal arguments on which the claim is based. • The term has also been called the *conte* or *tale*. — Abbr. *narr.* See INTENTIO; DECLARATION (7).

> "[T]he making of the count, in Latin the *narratio*, was the very centre of the legal process. We do not know how it came about that the litigant was allowed to speak through the mouth of another, though it has been suggested that it was not to prevent mistakes being made but to prevent them being fatal. Certainly the litigant could disavow what was said on his behalf; and perhaps it was only 'said' by him when he formally adopted it. If this is right, our modern barrister began as one who could harmlessly blunder." S.F.C. Milsom, *Historical Foundations of the Common Law* 28 (1969).

narrative recital. See RECITAL.

narrative verdict. See VERDICT (3).

narrator (na-**ray**-tor *or* na-**ray**-tər), *n.* [Law Latin] *Hist.* A pleader or counter; a person who prepares pleadings (i.e., *narrs*). • For example, a serjeant-at-law was also known as *serviens narrator.* Pl. **narratores** (na-rə-**tor**-eez).

> "The Latin *narrator* and its French equivalent *contour* became technical terms. If an English term was in use, it was perhaps *forspeaker.*" 1 Frederick Pollock & Frederic W. Maitland, *The History of English Law Before the Time of Edward I* 215 n.1 (2d ed. 1898).

narrow certiorari. See CERTIORARI.

narrow-channel rule. (1901) The navigational requirement that a vessel traveling down a slim fairway must keep as near to the fairway wall on the vessel's starboard side as is safe and practicable. 33 USCA § 2009(a)(i).

narrowly tailored, *adj.* (1972) (Of a content-neutral restriction on the time, place, or manner of speech in a designated public forum) being only as broad as is reasonably necessary to promote a substantial governmental interest that would be achieved less effectively without the restriction; no broader than absolutely necessary. See *designated public forum* under PUBLIC FORUM.

narrow sea. (*often pl.*) (16c) A sea running between two coasts that are close to each other. • The English Channel, for example, is a narrow sea.

narrow ultra vires. See ULTRA VIRES.

NASA. *abbr.* (1958) NATIONAL AERONAUTICS AND SPACE ADMINISTRATION.

NASD. *abbr.* (1940) NATIONAL ASSOCIATION OF SECURITIES DEALERS.

NASDAQ (**naz**-dak). *abbr.* NATIONAL ASSOCIATION OF SECURITIES DEALERS AUTOMATED QUOTATIONS.

NASS. *abbr.* NATIONAL AGRICULTURAL STATISTICS SERVICE.

NASS test. *abbr.* NECESSARY-AND-SUFFICIENT SET TEST.

natale (nə-**tay**-lee), *n.* [Latin "of or belonging to birth"] *Hist.* The status a person acquires by birth. • For example, if one or both parents of a child were serfs, the child was generally regarded as a serf, and a child born free rarely became a serf. See NATIVUS.

nati et nascituri (**nay**-tɪ et nas-ə-**t[y]oor**-ɪ *or* -**t[y]ər**-ɪ), *n. pl.* [Latin "born and to be born"] (1853) *Hist.* A person's heirs, near and remote.

natio (**nay**-shee-oh), *n.* [Latin] *Hist.* **1.** A nation. **2.** A group of students. **3.** A native place.

nation, *n.* (14c) **1.** A large group of people having a common origin, language, and tradition and usu. constituting a political entity. • When a nation is coincident with a state, the term *nation-state* is often used. — Also termed *nationality.* See NATION-STATE.

> "The word Nation, in the fullest adaptation of the term, means, in modern times, a numerous and homogeneous population (having long emerged from the hunter's and nomadic state), permanently inhabiting and cultivating a coherent territory, with a well-defined geographic outline, and a name of its own — the inhabitants speaking their own language, having their own literature and common institutions, which distinguish them clearly from other and similar groups of people; being citizens or subjects of a unitary government, however subdivided it may be, and feeling an organic unity with one another, as well as being conscious of a common destiny. Organic intellectual and political internal unity, with proportionate strength, and a distinct and obvious demarcation from similar groups, are notable elements of the idea of a modern nation in its fullest sense. A nation is a nation only when there is but one nationality; and the attempt at establishing a nationality within a nationality is more inconsistent and mischievous even than the establishment of 'an empire within an empire.'" 2 Francis Lieber, *The Miscellaneous Writings of Francis Lieber* 227–28 (1880).

> "The nearest we can get to a definition is to say that a nation is a group of people bound together by common history, common sentiment and traditions, and, usually (though not always, as, for example, Belgium or Switzerland) by common heritage. A state, on the other hand, is a society of men united under one government. These two forms of society are not necessarily coincident. A single nation may be divided into several states, and conversely a single state may comprise several nations or parts of nations." John Salmond, *Jurisprudence* 136 (Glanville L. Williams ed., 10th ed. 1947).

2. A community of people inhabiting a defined territory and organized under an independent government; a sovereign political state. Cf. STATE (1).

national, *adj.* (16c) **1.** Of, relating to, or involving a country <national anthem>. **2.** Nationwide in scope <national emergency>.

national, *n.* (17c) **1.** A member of a nation. **2.** A person owing permanent allegiance to and under the protection of a state. 8 USCA § 1101(a)(21).

▸ **national of the United States.** (1921) A citizen of the United States or a noncitizen who owes permanent allegiance to the United States. 8 USCA § 1101(a)(22). — Also termed *U.S. national; U.S. citizen.*

National Aeronautics and Space Act. A 1958 federal statute that created the National Aeronautics and Space Administration (NASA). 42 USCA §§ 2451–2484.

National Aeronautics and Space Administration. The independent federal agency that conducts research into space flight and that builds and flies space vehicles. • NASA was created by the National Aeronautics and Space Act of 1958. 42 USCA §§ 2451–2484. — Abbr. NASA.

National Agricultural Statistics Service. An agency in the U.S. Department of Agriculture responsible for compiling statistical information and estimating agricultural production, supply, price, chemical use, and other related statistics. • Most of the data come from farmers, ranchers, and agribusinesses. — Abbr. NASS.

national airspace. See AIRSPACE.

National Archives and Records Administration. An independent federal agency that sets procedures for preserving governmental records that are important for legal and historical reasons; helps federal agencies manage their records; provides record-storage access; and manages the Presidential Libraries system. • The agency, run by the Archivist of the United States, retains only a small percentage of the federal records produced each year. It publishes the *United States Statutes at Large,* the *Federal Register,* the *Code of Federal Regulations,* the weekly *Compilation of Presidential Documents,* the annual *Public Papers of the President,* and the *United States Government Manual.* It is a successor to the National Archives Establishment, created in 1934, that was made a unit of the General Services Administration in 1949. It became an independent agency in 1984. — Abbr. NARA. See FEDERAL REGISTER.

National Asian Pacific American Bar Association. A professional association of Asian Pacific American attorneys, judges, law professors, and law students, emphasizing civil rights and immigration issues. — Abbr. NAPABA.

National Assembly. *Hist.* In France, the first of the revolutionary assemblies, existing from 1789 to 1791. • Its chief work was the formation of the constitution, as a result of which it was also known as the "Constituent Assembly." The legislatures organized in France in 1848 (after the February revolution) and in 1871 (after the overthrow of the second empire) were also known as *National Assemblies.* Cf. LEGISLATIVE ASSEMBLY (4).

national association. See *national bank* under BANK.

National Association for the Advancement of Colored People. An organization that strives to ensure equal political, educational, social, and economic rights for black Americans and others, with a special focus on eliminating race-based discrimination. • Founded in 1909, the NAACP uses primarily the legal system and public awareness to further its goals. — Abbr. NAACP.

National Association of Realtors. An association of real-estate brokers and agents promoting education, professional standards, and modernization in areas of real estate such as brokerage, appraisal, and property management. — Abbr. NAR.

National Association of Securities Dealers. Formerly, a group of brokers and dealers that was empowered by the SEC to regulate the over-the-counter securities market. • The association merged in 2007 with the regulatory committee of the New York Stock Exchange to form the Financial Industry Regulatory Authority. — Abbr. NASD.

National Association of Securities Dealers Automated Quotations. A computerized system for recording transactions and displaying price quotations for a group of actively traded securities on the over-the-counter market. — Abbr. NASDAQ.

National Association of Women Lawyers. An organization, formed in 1899, devoted to the interests of female lawyers and their families. — Abbr. NAWL.

national bank. See BANK.

National Bar Association. An organization of primarily African-American lawyers, founded in 1925 to promote education, professionalism, and the protection of civil rights. — Abbr. NBA.

National Capital Parks Commission. See NATIONAL CAPITAL PLANNING COMMISSION.

National Capital Planning Commission. A 12-member federal commission that plans the development of federal lands and facilities in the National Capital region, an area that includes the District of Columbia and six nearby counties — two in Maryland and four in Virginia. • The Commission was originally established as the National Capital Park Commission, a park-planning agency, in 1924. — Abbr. NCPC.

National Capital Region. The District of Columbia and six nearby counties: Montgomery and Prince George's in Maryland. and Fairfax, Loudoun, Prince William, and Arlington in Virginia. — Abbr. NCR.

National Cemetery Administration. A unit in the U.S. Department of Veterans Affairs responsible for operating national cemeteries, providing headstones for unmarked graves of veterans worldwide, and making grants to states for establishing and caring for veterans' cemeteries. — Abbr. NCA.

National Conference of Black Lawyers. An organization of African American attorneys formed in 1969, active esp. in civil rights. — Abbr. NCBL.

National Conference of Commissioners on Uniform State Laws. An organization that drafts and proposes statutes for adoption by individual states, with the goal of making the laws on various subjects uniform among the states. • Founded in 1892 and composed of representatives from all 50 states, the Conference has drafted more than 200 uniform laws, including the Uniform Commercial Code. In 2007, the Conference adopted an informal name for itself: the Uniform Law Commission. — Abbr. NCCUSL. — Also termed *Uniform Law Commissioners* (ULC). See UNIFORM LAW COMMISSION; UNIFORM ACT; MODEL ACT; UNIFORM LAW.

National Council of Juvenile and Family Court Judges. An organization of judges and hearing officers who exercise jurisdiction over abuse, neglect, divorce, custody and visitation, support, domestic-violence, and other family-law cases. • Founded in 1937, the Council has an educational and support facility located near Reno, Nevada. It provides training, technical support, and professional assistance in improving courtroom operations. — Abbr. NCJFCJ.

National Credit Union Administration. An independent federal agency that charters, insures, supervises, and examines federal credit unions; administers the National Credit Union Share Insurance Fund and the Community Development Revolving Loan Fund; and manages the Central Liquidity Facility, a separate mixed-ownership government corporation that supplies emergency loans to member credit unions. • The agency was established in 1970 and reorganized in 1978. — Abbr. NCUA.

national currency. See CURRENCY.

National Daily Quotation Service. See PINK SHEET.

national debt. (18c) The total amount owed by the government of a country; esp., the total financial obligation of the federal government, including such instruments as Treasury bills, notes, and bonds, as well as foreign debt.

national defense. (18c) **1.** All measures taken by a country to protect itself against its enemies. • A country's protection of its collective ideals and values is included in the concept of national defense. **2.** A country's military establishment.

National Disaster Medical System. A unit of the Federal Emergency Management Agency in the U.S. Department of Homeland Security responsible for training, equipping, and deploying teams of emergency medical responders and for coordinating the transportation of people affected by emergencies. • The agency was transferred from the U.S. Department of Health and Human Services in 2003. — Abbr. NDMS.

national domicile. See DOMICILE.

National Economic Council. See OFFICE OF POLICY DEVELOPMENT.

national emergency. (18c) A state of national crisis or a situation requiring immediate and extraordinary national action.

National Endowment for the Arts. An independent federal agency that promotes involvement in the arts by making grants to organizations, honoring artists for their achievements, expanding artistic resources, preserving cultural heritage, and funding projects that educate children and adults in the arts. — Abbr. NEA. See NATIONAL FOUNDATION ON THE ARTS AND THE HUMANITIES.

National Endowment for the Humanities. An independent federal agency that supports research, education, and public programs in the humanities through grants to individuals, groups, and institutions. — Abbr. NEH. See NATIONAL FOUNDATION ON THE ARTS AND THE HUMANITIES.

National Environmental Policy Act. A 1969 federal statute establishing U.S. environmental policy. • The statute requires federal agencies to submit an environmental-impact statement with every proposal for a program or law that would affect the environment. 42 USCA §§ 4321–4347 — Abbr. NEPA. See ENVIRONMENTAL-IMPACT STATEMENT.

> "One should not assume that NEPA's emphasis upon procedural consideration of environmental consequences somehow diminishes its stature. To the contrary, NEPA is the key environmental statute to be reckoned with in lawsuits challenging agency action on NEPA grounds. As a result of the popularity of NEPA in court, federal agencies have become extremely sensitive to NEPA's procedural commands. They have not only sought to articulate the environmental impacts of their decisions before-the-fact, they have also either abandoned projects or mitigated their adverse environmental consequences after performing NEPA studies." Jan G. Laitos, *Natural Resources Law* § 4.01, at 119 (2002).

National Environmental Satellite, Data, and Information Service. See NATIONAL OCEANIC AND ATMOSPHERIC ADMINISTRATION.

National Firearms Act. A 1934 federal statute that governs the manufacture, possession, and transfer of certain types of firearms and other weapons. • In its original form, the act banned gangster-type weapons, such as machine guns and sawn-off shotguns. It has been expanded by amendments to cover most rifles and handguns, and also "destructive devices" such as grenades and land mines. 26 USCA §§ 5801 et seq. — Abbr. NFA.

National Foundation on the Arts and the Humanities. An independent federal foundation that encourages and supports progress in the humanities and the arts by supporting the National Endowment for the Arts, the National Endowment for the Humanities, and the Institute of Museum and Library Services. • The agency was created by act of Congress in 1965. — Abbr. NFAH. See NATIONAL ENDOWMENT FOR THE ARTS; NATIONAL ENDOWMENT FOR THE HUMANITIES; INSTITUTE OF MUSEUM AND LIBRARY SERVICES.

national government. (17c) The government of an entire country, as distinguished from that of a province, state, subdivision, or territory of the country and as distinguished from an international organization. See *federal government* (2) under GOVERNMENT (3).

national guard. 1. (*usu. cap.*) The U.S. militia, which is maintained as a reserve for the U.S. Army and Air Force. • Its members are volunteers, recruited and trained on a statewide basis and equipped by the federal government. A state may request the National Guard's assistance in quelling disturbances, and the federal government may order the National Guard into active service in times of war or other national emergency. See MILITIA. **2.** Any military establishment that serves as a country-wide constabulary and defense force. — **National Guardsman,** *n.*

National Highway Traffic Safety Administration. A unit in the U.S. Department of Transportation responsible for regulating the safety of motor vehicles and their equipment. • The agency's work focuses on matters such as theft prevention, speed limits, truthful odometer readings, and fuel consumption. It was established by the Highway Safety Act of 1970. 23 USCA §§ 101 et seq. — Abbr. NHTSA.

National Imaging and Mapping Agency. A unit in the U.S. Department of Defense responsible for providing the armed forces and intelligence officers with up-to-date and accurate geospatial information, esp. in the form of photographs, maps, and charts. — Abbr. NIMA.

national income. (18c) The collective earnings from a nation's current production, including all individuals' compensation, interest, rental income, and after-tax profits.

National Indian Gaming Association. A nonprofit organization dedicated to advancing the economic, social, and political welfare of American Indian peoples, and to protecting tribes that remain self-sufficient through gaming enterprises. • NIGA works with the federal government to develop and implement gaming policies and practices. — Abbr. NIGA. Cf. NATIONAL INDIAN GAMING COMMISSION.

National Indian Gaming Commission. An independent federal agency established to regulate and maintain the integrity of gaming activities on Indian lands by promoting tribal economic development and self-sufficiency and by ensuring that the tribes receive the primary benefits of the gaming activities. • The Commission was created by the Indian Gaming Regulatory Act of 1988 as a unit of the U.S. Department of the Interior. — Abbr. NIGC. Cf. NATIONAL INDIAN GAMING ASSOCIATION.

National Industrial Recovery Act. A 1933 federal statute — a centerpiece of President Franklin Delano Roosevelt's New Deal — providing for temporary federal control of industry, as by establishing codes of fair practices for trade unions and collective bargaining, abolishing child labor, and developing public works as a means of creating employment. • In 1935, the U.S. Supreme Court unanimously held Title I of the statute unconstitutional in *A.L.A. Schechter Poultry Corp. v. U.S.*, 295 U.S. 495, 55 S.Ct. 837 (1935).

National Institute for Literacy. A federally aided institute that leads national efforts to achieve universal literacy. — Abbr. NIFL.

National Institute of Corrections. A federal organization (established within the Bureau of Prisons) whose responsibilities include helping federal, state, and local authorities improve correctional programs, conducting research on correctional issues such as crime prevention, and conducting workshops for law-enforcement personnel, social workers, judges, and others involved in treating and rehabilitating offenders. 18 USCA §§ 4351–4353. — Abbr. NIC. See BUREAU OF PRISONS.

National Institute of Standards and Technology. See TECHNOLOGY ADMINISTRATION.

nationalism, *n.* **1.** Devotion to a whole country rather than to certain sections of it. **2.** The desire for national independence and home rule; specif., the reified urge of a group of people of the same race, origin, language, etc. to form an independent country. See HOME RULE. **3.** The advocacy of greater centralization and broadening of federal power in order to deal more effectively with the concentration of corporate wealth. **4.** A late form of socialism claiming that all industry must be conducted by the government on the basis of a common obligation to work and a general guarantee of livelihood, all workers being entitled to the same pay. — **nationalist,** *n.* & *adj.*

"The term *nationalism* is of recent coinage. Like most of the 'isms' that have entered the political language during the last two hundred years, it signifies a tendency, attitude, or general quality closely related to the term and concept of *nation*. It signifies a political theory of the relations between the state and society and of the source of political power, obligation, and cohesion. It may indicate a comprehensive ideology that sees in the nation the primary or even exclusive framework of social existence and belonging. It may relate to political convictions and beliefs that hold loyalty and dedicated service to the nation as the highest virtue and obligation. Moreover, *nationalism* has come to designate a historical concept describing a fundamental trend and motive power in modern history that have shaped the world in the image of the national state." Yehoshua Arieli, "Nationalism," in 2 *Encyclopedia of American Political History* 841, 841 (Jack P. Greene ed., 1984).

nationality. (17c) **1.** NATION (1). **2.** The relationship between a citizen of a country and the country itself, customarily involving allegiance by the citizen and protection by the state; membership in a country. • This term is often used synonymously with *citizenship*. See CITIZENSHIP. **3.** The formal relationship between a ship and the country under whose flag the ship sails. See FLAG STATE.

Nationality Act. See IMMIGRATION AND NATIONALITY ACT.

nationality theory. (1878) The jurisdictional principle that citizens are subject to the laws of their country, no matter where the citizens are.

nationalization, *n.* (1847) **1.** The act of bringing an industry under governmental control or ownership. **2.** The act of giving a person the status of a citizen. See NATURALIZATION.

nationalize, *vb.* (1809) **1.** To bring (an industry) under governmental control or ownership. **2.** To give (a person) the status of a citizen; NATURALIZE.

National Labor Relations Act. A federal statute regulating the relations between employers and employees and establishing the National Labor Relations Board. 29 USCA §§ 151–169. • The statute is also known as the Wagner Act of 1935. It was amended by the Taft–Hartley Act of 1947 and the Landrum–Griffin Act of 1959. — Abbr. NLRA. — Also termed *Wagner Act*.

National Labor Relations Board. An independent five-member federal board created to prevent and remedy unfair labor practices and to safeguard employees' rights to organize into labor unions. • The board hears complaints of unfair labor practices and issues orders that can be reviewed or enforced by a U.S. court of appeals. The agency was created by the National Labor Relations Act of 1935. 29 USCA § 153. — Abbr. NLRB. — Often shortened to *Labor Relations Board*.

National Lawyers Guild. An association of lawyers, law students, and legal workers dedicated to promoting a left-wing political and social agenda. • Founded in 1937, it now comprises some 4,000 members. — Abbr. NLG. Cf. FEDERALIST SOCIETY.

National Marine Fisheries Service. — Abbr. NMFS. See NATIONAL OCEANIC AND ATMOSPHERIC ADMINISTRATION.

National Mediation Board. An independent federal board that mediates labor–management disputes in the airline and railroad industries and provides administrative and financial support in adjusting grievances in the railroad industry. • The agency was created by the Railway Labor Act of 1934 to prevent interruptions in service. 45 USCA §§ 154–163. — Abbr. NMB. Cf. FEDERAL MEDIATION AND CONCILIATION SERVICE.

national minimum wage. See WAGE.

national monument. (1879) A building, landmark, wilderness area, special feature of the land, archaeological site, etc. that is kept and protected by a country's government for people to visit; specif., an object or structure and the land on which it is situated, publicly proclaimed by the U.S. President to be of cultural, historic, or scientific interest. *See* 16 USCA § 341.

National Motor Vehicle Theft Act. See DYER ACT.

National Oceanic and Atmospheric Administration. A unit in the U.S. Department of Commerce responsible for monitoring the environment in order to make accurate and timely weather forecasts and to protect life, property, and the environment. • It was established in 1970 under Reorganization Plan No. 4 of 1970 and operates through several agencies: the National Weather Service (NWS); the National Environmental Satellite, Data, and Information Service (NESDIS); the National Marine Fisheries Service (NMFS); the National Ocean Service (NOS); and the Office of Oceanic and Atmospheric Research (OAR). It also maintains a fleet of ships and aircraft for research. — Abbr. NOAA.

National Ocean Service. See NATIONAL OCEANIC AND ATMOSPHERIC ADMINISTRATION.

national of the United States. See NATIONAL.

National Organ Transplant Act. A 1984 federal law banning the sale of human organs. 42 USCA §§ 273–274. — Abbr. NOTA.

national origin. (1880) The country in which a person was born, or from which the person's ancestors came. • This term is used in several antidiscrimination statutes, including Title VII of the Civil Rights Act of 1964, which prohibits discrimination because of an individual's "race, color, religion, sex, or national origin." 42 USCA § 2000e-2.

national-origin discrimination. See DISCRIMINATION (3).

national park. (1868) A scenic, natural, historic, and recreational area owned by the United States and set aside for permanent protection. • Yellowstone National Park was declared the first national park in 1872. *See* 16 USCA § 1a-1.

National Park Service. A unit in the U.S. Department of the Interior responsible for managing the country's national parks, monuments, scenic parkways, preserves, trails, river ways, seashores, lakeshores, recreational areas, and historic sites commemorating movements, events, and personalities of America's past. • The Service was established in 1916. 16 USCA § 1. — Abbr. NPS.

National Priorities List. *Environmental law.* The Environmental Protection Agency's list of the most serious uncontrolled or abandoned hazardous-waste sites that are identified for possible long-term remediation as Superfund sites. 40 CFR § 35.6015. — Abbr. NPL.

National Quotation Bureau. A company that publishes daily price quotations (*pink sheets*) of over-the-counter securities. — Abbr. NQB.

National Railroad Passenger Corporation. A federally chartered corporation created by the Rail Passenger Service Act of 1970 to provide intercity rail passenger service. • The corporation owns or leases railroad stations and operates passenger trains over tracks that are almost entirely owned by others. — Abbr. NRPC. — Usu. termed *Amtrak.*

National Reporter System. A series of lawbooks, published by the West Group, containing every published appellate decision of the federal and state courts in the United States. • For federal courts, the system includes the *Supreme Court Reporter, Federal Reporter, Federal Claims Reporter, Federal Supplement, Federal Rules Decisions, Bankruptcy Reporter, Military Justice Reporter,* and *Veterans Appeals Reporter.* For state courts, the system includes the *Atlantic Reporter, California Reporter, New York Supplement, North Eastern Reporter, North Western Reporter, Pacific Reporter, South Eastern Reporter, Southern Reporter,* and *South Western Reporter.* — Abbr. NRS.

> "In 1879, the first unit of the National Reporter System was published. In it there was combined in one publication the current supreme court decisions of a group of neighboring states. Later the scope was extended to include the decisions of the intermediate appellate courts. This provided the lawyer with not only the decisions of his own courts but also with the decisions of courts in neighboring states where similar conditions prevailed and similar problems were likely to arise. Combining the decisions of several states in one publication also permitted prompt publication instead of being compelled to wait one or more years until sufficient material had accumulated in one jurisdiction to make a bound volume. The large circulation reduced the cost while uniformity in format and compactness of type reduced the bulk and required less shelf-space. This plan was extended until, by 1888, the entire country was embraced in the series of Reporters comprising the National Reporter System." Carlton B. Putnam, *How to Find the Law* § 4, at 88 (1949).

National Response Center. *Environmental law.* A nationwide communication center located in Washington, D.C., responsible for receiving, and relaying to appropriate federal officials, all notices of oil discharges and other releases of hazardous substances. 40 CFR § 310.11. — Abbr. NRC.

national river. See RIVER.

National Science Foundation. An independent federal foundation that promotes progress in science and engineering through grants, contracts, and other agreements awarded to universities, colleges, academic consortia, and nonprofit and small-business institutions. • It was created by the National Science Foundation Act of 1950. — Abbr. NSF.

national seashore. (1962) An area abutting a seacoast and maintained by a country's government for recreational purposes.

national security. (18c) The safety of a country and its governmental secrets, together with the strength and integrity of its military, seen as being necessary to the protection of its citizens.

National Security Agency. A unit in the U.S. Department of Defense responsible for protecting U.S. information systems as well as producing foreign intelligence information. • The agency uses code makers and code breakers. — Abbr. NSA.

National Security Council. An agency in the Executive Office of the President responsible for advising the President on national-security matters. • It was created by the National Security Act of 1947. 50 USCA § 402. — Abbr. NSC.

national-security letter. (1994) A document that is issued by an FBI official, or by a senior official of another federal agency, and that functions as a subpoena requiring the recipient, usu. a business, to turn over specific business documents. • The Department of Justice provides guidelines for the issuance of a national-security letter, which is not typically reviewed by a court or magistrate. Federal law prohibits the letter's recipient from disclosing the existence of the letter, except to an attorney. One use of the directives has been to allow Internet service providers to confidentially disclose user information upon certification that records are relevant to an investigation of terrorism or to clandestine intelligence activities. *See* 18 USCA § 2709. — Abbr. NSL.

national-security privilege. See *state-secrets privilege* under PRIVILEGE (3).

national-service life insurance. See LIFE INSURANCE.

National Stolen Property Act. A federal statute that makes it a crime to transport, transmit, or transfer in interstate or foreign commerce goods or money worth $5,000 or more if the person knows that the money or goods were obtained unlawfully. 18 USCA §§ 2311 et seq. — Abbr. NSPA.

national synod. See SYNOD.

National Technical Information Service. See TECHNOLOGY ADMINISTRATION.

National Technical Institute for the Deaf. A federally aided institute, located in Rochester, New York, responsible for educating large numbers of deaf students on a college campus designed primarily for students who can hear. • Established by Congress in 1965, the institute is a part of the Rochester Institute for Technology. — Abbr. NTID.

National Telecommunications and Information Administration. A unit in the U.S. Department of Commerce responsible for advising the President on telecommunications and information policy; conducting research through its Institute for Telecommunications Sciences; and making grants to support advanced infrastructures and to increase ownership by women and minorities. — Abbr. NTIA.

National Transportation Safety Board. An independent five-member federal board that investigates air, rail, water, highway, pipeline, and hazardous-waste accidents; conducts studies; and makes recommendations to government agencies, the transportation industry, and others on safety measures and practices. • The agency was created in 1966. 49 USCA §§ 1101–1155. — Abbr. NTSB.

national treatment. (1886) *Intellectual property.* The policy or practice of a country that accords the citizens of other countries the same intellectual-property protection as it gives its own citizens, no formal treaty of reciprocity being in place. • The principle of national treatment underlay the first international intellectual-property treaties in the 19th century, the Paris and Berne Conventions. It is also embodied in the TRIPs Agreement. Cf. RECIPROCITY; UNIVERSALITY.

"The beauty of the principle of national treatment is that it allows countries the autonomy to develop and enforce their own laws, while meeting the demands for international protection. Effectively, national treatment is a mechanism of international protection without harmonization." Lionel Bently & Brad Sherman, *Intellectual Property Law* 5 (2001).

▸ **conditional national treatment.** The policy or practice of a country that accords national treatment to persons (or products) from foreign countries, but only with the stipulation that the foreign countries provide a level of protection equivalent to that of the first country. — Also termed *material reciprocity.*

national-treatment clause. (1927) A provision contained in some treaties, usu. commercial ones, according foreigners the same rights, in certain respects, as those accorded to nationals.

national union. See UNION.

National Weather Service. See NATIONAL OCEANIC AND ATMOSPHERIC ADMINISTRATION.

nationhood. (1843) **1.** National character. **2.** National status; the quality, state, or condition of being a nation, whereby a legal relationship exists between the individual, who owes allegiance, and the state, which owes protection. **3.** Political independence or existence as a discrete sovereign political state.

nations, law of. See INTERNATIONAL LAW.

nation-state. (1895) **1.** A country that contains one as opposed to several nationalities. **2.** A type of political organization under which relatively homogeneous people populate a country. **3.** *Hist.* Any one of several European countries, such as England, France, or Spain, that between 1500 and 1900 developed a compact, independent government from the small or weak feudal units of the Middle Ages. Cf. NATION (1).

natis et nascituris (**nay**-tis et nas-i-**t[y]uur**-is). [Latin] *Hist.* To children born and to be born. • This was a common destination used to convey an inheritance.

native, *n.* (16c) **1.** Someone who is a citizen of a particular place, region, or country by virtue of having been born there. **2.** A person whose national origin derives from having been born within a particular place. **3.** Loosely, a person born abroad whose parents are citizens of the country and are not permanently residing abroad. **4.** Loosely, a person or thing belonging to a group indigenous to a particular place. • The term *Native American* is sometimes shortened to *native.*

Native American law. (1949) See INDIAN LAW (1).

native-born, *adj.* (18c) **1.** Born within the territorial jurisdiction of a country. **2.** Born of parents who convey rights of citizenship to their offspring, regardless of the place of birth.

native title. See *aboriginal title* (1) under TITLE (2).

nativi conventionarii (nə-**tɪ**-vɪ kən-ven-shee-ə-**nair**-ee-ɪ), *n. pl.* [Law Latin] (18c) *Hist.* Villeins by contract.

nativi de stipite (nə-**tɪ**-vɪ dee **stip**-ə-tee), *n. pl.* [Law Latin] (18c) *Hist.* Villeins by birth. See NATIVUS; NATALE.

nativitas (nə-**tiv**-ə-tas), *n.* [Law Latin] *Hist.* The servitude or bondage of serfs.

nativo habendo (nə-**tɪ**-voh hə-**ben**-doh), *n.* DE NATIVO HABENDO.

nativus (nə-**tɪ**-vəs), *n.* [Law Latin] *Hist.* Someone who is born a villein or serf.

"Having seen what serfdom means, we may ask how men become serfs. The answer is that almost always the serf is a born serf; *nativus* and *villanus* were commonly used as interchangeable terms . . . ." 1 Frederick Pollock & Frederic W. Maitland, *The History of English Law Before the Time of Edward I* 422 (2d ed. 1898).

NATO. *abbr.* (1949) NORTH ATLANTIC TREATY ORGANIZATION.

natural, *adj.* (14c) **1.** In accord with the regular course of things in the universe and without accidental or purposeful interference <a natural death as opposed to murder>. **2.** Normal; proceeding from the regular character of a person or thing <it is natural for a duck to fly south in the winter>. **3.** Brought about by nature as opposed to artificial means <a natural lake>. **4.** Inherent; not acquired or assumed <natural talent>. **5.** Indigenous; native <the original or natural inhabitants of a country>. **6.** Of, relating to, or involving a birth <natural child as distinguished from adopted child>. **7.** Untouched by civilization; wild <only a small part of the forest remains in its natural state>. — **naturally,** *adv.*

natural, *n.* (16c) **1.** Someone who is native to a place. See NATIVE; *natural-born citizen* under CITIZEN (1). **2.** A person or thing well suited for a particular endeavor.

natural-accumulation doctrine. (1984) The rule that a governmental entity or other landowner is not required to remove naturally occurring ice or snow from public property, such as a highway, unless the entity has, by taking some affirmative action (such as highway construction), increased the travel hazard to the public.

natural affection. (16c) The love naturally existing between close relatives, such as parent and child. • Natural affection is not consideration for a contract. See CONSIDERATION (1); *executory contract* under CONTRACT.

natural allegiance. See ALLEGIANCE (1).

natural and ordinary meaning. See *plain meaning* under MEANING.

natural and probable consequence. See *natural consequence* under CONSEQUENCE.

natural and probable result. See *natural consequence* under CONSEQUENCE.

natural-born citizen. See CITIZEN (1).

Natural Born Citizen Clause. (1988) *Constitutional law.* The clause of the U.S. Constitution barring persons not born in the United States from the presidency. U.S. Const. art. II, § 1, cl. 5.

natural-born subject. See SUBJECT (1).

natural boundary. See BOUNDARY (1).

natural channel. See CHANNEL (1).

natural child. See CHILD.

natural cognation. See COGNATION (2).

natural consequence. See CONSEQUENCE.

natural day. See DAY.

natural death. See DEATH.

natural-death act. (1977) A statute that allows a person to prepare a living will instructing a physician to withhold life-sustaining procedures if the person should become terminally ill. See ADVANCE DIRECTIVE; LIVING WILL.

natural domicile. See *domicile of origin* under DOMICILE.

natural duty. See *moral duty* under DUTY (1).

natural equity. See EQUITY (3).

natural father. See *biological father* under FATHER.

natural flood channel. See CHANNEL (1).

natural fool. (16c) *Hist.* Someone who is mentally challenged from birth. See INCOMPETENCY.

natural fruit. See FRUIT (2).

natural gas. See DISTILLATE (1).

natural guardian. See GUARDIAN (1).

natural heir. See HEIR.

naturalia (nach-ə-**ray**-lee-ə). [Latin] *Roman & civil law.* The natural ingredients of a contract that the law automatically imports into it, such as the inability of a testator to bind himself contractually not to change his testament.

naturalia feudi (nach-ə-**ray**-lee-ə **fyoo**-dɪ). [Law Latin] *Scots law.* Those things that naturally belong to a feu grant. • The phrase included the grantor's warranty against eviction of the grantee.

natural infancy. See INFANCY (2).

natural interruption. See INTERRUPTION.

naturalis possessio (nach-ə-**ray**-lis pə-**zes**[**h**]-ee-oh). See *possessio naturalis* under POSSESSIO.

naturalistic fallacy. See FALLACY.

naturalization. (16c) The granting of citizenship to a foreign-born person under statutory authority.

naturalization certificate. (1834) A government-issued document certifying that a person is a naturalized citizen, bestowed usu. after the oath-taking ceremony at which the person takes an oath of allegiance. *See* 8 CFR § 338.1. — Also termed *certificate of naturalization.*

Naturalization Clause. (1849) *Constitutional law.* The constitutional provision stating that every person born or naturalized in the United States is a citizen of the United States and of the state of residence. U.S. Const. amend. XIV, § 1. See JUS SOLI.

naturalization court. (1911) A court having jurisdiction to hear and decide naturalization petitions. • Naturalization courts were abolished as a result of the Immigration Act of 1990. Under current U.S. law, the Attorney General has the sole authority to naturalize citizens. But after a hearing before an immigration officer, an applicant may seek review of the denial of an application for naturalization in the federal district court for the district in which the applicant resides. If an applicant is certified to be eligible for naturalization, the oath of allegiance may be administered by the Attorney General, a federal district court, or a state court of record. See *oath of allegiance* under OATH.

naturalization deposition. See DEPOSITION (2).

naturalization petition. (1887) A formal application by which an alien seeks to become a naturalized citizen of a country. See *naturalization deposition* under DEPOSITION (2).

naturalize, *vb.* (16c) To grant the rights, privileges, and duties of citizenship to (one previously a noncitizen); to make (a noncitizen) a citizen under statutory authority. — **naturalization,** *n.*

naturalized citizen. See CITIZEN (1).

natural justice. See JUSTICE (4).

natural law. (15c) **1.** A physical law of nature <gravitation is a natural law>. **2.** A philosophical system of legal and moral principles purportedly deriving from a universalized conception of human nature or divine justice rather than from legislative or judicial action; moral law embodied in principles of right and wrong <many ethical teachings are based on natural law>. — Also termed *law of nature; natural justice; lex aeterna; eternal law; lex naturae; lex naturalae; divine law; jus divinum; jus naturale; jus naturae;* (in sense 2) *normative jurisprudence; jure naturae.* Cf. FUNDAMENTAL LAW; POSITIVE LAW; DIVINE LAW.

> "Natural law, as it is revived today, seeks to organize the ideal element in law, to furnish a critique of old received ideals and give a basis for formulating new ones, and to yield a reasoned canon of values and a technique of applying it. I should prefer to call it philosophical jurisprudence. But one can well sympathize with those who would salvage the good will of the old name as an asset of the science of law." Roscoe Pound, *The Formative Era of American Law* 29 (1938).

> "It is true that when medieval writers spoke of natural law as being discoverable by reason, they meant that the best human reasoning could discover it, and not, of course, that the results to which any and every individual's reasoning led him was natural law. The foolish criticism of Jeremy Bentham: 'a great multitude of people are continually talking of the law of nature; and then they go on giving you their sentiments about what is right and what is wrong; and these sentiments, you are to understand, are so many chapters and sections of the law of nature,' merely showed a contempt for a great conception which Bentham had not taken the trouble to understand." J.L. Brierly, *The Law of Nations* 20–21 (5th ed. 1955).

> "[N]atural law is often an idealization of the opposite to that which prevails. Where inequality or privilege exists, natural law demands its abolition." Morris R. Cohen, *Reason and Law* 96 (1961).

> "As for the term 'law,' as understood in the phrase 'natural law,' it does not connote that the relevant principles and norms have their directive force precisely as the commands, imperatives, or dictates of a superior will. Even those natural law theorists who argue (as most do) that the most ultimate explanation of those principles and norms (as of all other realities) is a transcendent, creative, divine source of existence, meaning, and value, will also argue that the principles and norms are inherently fitting and obligatory (not fitting or obligatory because commanded), or that the source of their obligation is rather divine wisdom than divine will. Instead, the term 'law' in the phrase 'natural law' refers to standards of right choosing, standards which are normative (that is, rationally directive and 'obligatory') because they are true and choosing otherwise than in accordance with them is unreasonable. And the term 'natural' (and related uses of 'by nature,' 'in accordance with nature,' and 'of nature') in this context signifies any one or more of the following: (a) that the relevant standards (principles and norms) are not 'positive,' that is, are directive prior to any positing by individual decision or group choice or convention; (b) that the relevant standards are

'higher' than positive laws, conventions, and practices, that is, provide the premises for critical evaluation and endorsement or justified rejection of or disobedience to such laws, conventions, or practices; (c) that the relevant standards conform to the most demanding requirements of critical reason and are objective, in the sense that a person who fails to accept them as standards for judgment is in error; (d) that adherence to the relevant standards tends systematically to promote human flourishing, the fulfillment of human individuals and communities." John Finnis, *Reason in Action* 200-01 (2011).

natural liberty. See LIBERTY.

natural life. (15c) A person's physical life span.

natural monopoly. See MONOPOLY (2).

natural monument. See MONUMENT.

natural mother. **1.** See *birth mother* under MOTHER. **2.** See *biological mother* under MOTHER.

natural object. **1.** A person likely to receive a portion of another person's estate based on the nature and circumstances of their relationship. — Also termed *natural object of bounty*; *natural object of one's bounty*; *natural object of testator's bounty.* **2.** See *natural boundary* under BOUNDARY (1). **3.** See *natural monument* under MONUMENT.

natural obligation. See OBLIGATION.

natural person. See PERSON (1).

natural possession. See POSSESSION.

natural premium. See PREMIUM (1).

natural presumption. See PRESUMPTION.

natural resource. (1870) **1.** Any material from nature having potential economic value or providing for the sustenance of life, such as timber, minerals, oil, water, and wildlife. **2.** Environmental features that serve a community's well-being or recreational interests, such as parks.

Natural Resources Conservation Service. An agency in the U.S. Department of Agriculture responsible for providing information and financial assistance to farmers and ranchers for voluntary conservation programs. • The Service was formerly known as the Soil Conservation Service. — Abbr. NRCS.

natural right. See RIGHT.

natural servitude. See SERVITUDE (2).

natural succession. See SUCCESSION (2).

natural wastage. (1944) A reduction in the number of people employed by an organization when replacements are not assigned to those who die, retire, or leave employment by reason of illness or disability.

natural watercourse. See WATERCOURSE.

natural wear and tear. See WEAR AND TEAR.

natural wrong. See *moral wrong* under WRONG.

natural year. See YEAR.

natura negotii (nə-**tyoor**-ə ni-**goh**-shee-I). [Latin] (18c) *Hist.* The nature of the transaction.

nature. (14c) **1.** A fundamental quality that distinguishes one thing from another; the essence of something. **2.** A wild condition, untouched by civilization. **3.** A disposition or personality of someone or something. **4.** Something pure or true as distinguished from something artificial or contrived. **5.** The basic instincts or impulses of someone or something. **6.** The elements of the universe, such as mountains, plants, planets, and stars.

nauclerus (naw-**kleer**-əs), *n.* [Latin fr. Greek *naus* "ship" + *klēros* "allotment"] *Roman law.* A shipmaster; a skipper.

naulage (**naw**-lij), *n.* [Old French fr. Law Latin *naulagium* "passage money"] (17c) The fare for passengers or goods traveling by ship. See NAULUM.

naulum (**naw**-ləm), *n.* [Latin fr. Greek] (16c) *Roman law.* Fare; freights; a shipowner's fee for carrying people or goods from one place to another.

nauta (**naw**-tə), *n.* [Latin fr. Greek *naus* "ship"] *Roman law.* A sailor.

nautae, caupones, stabularii (**naw**-tee, kaw-**poh**-neez, stab-yə-**lair**-ee-I). [Latin] *Roman law.* Carriers by sea, innkeepers, stablers. • The phrase was used in an edict holding shippers, innkeepers, and stablers liable for damages to goods entrusted to them for safekeeping (*receptum*). Members of this group were also vicariously liable for the torts of their employees and slaves.

"The edict is in these terms: 'NAUTAE, CAUPONES, STABULARII, QUOD CUJUSQUE SALVUM FORE RECEPERINT, NISI RESTITUENT, IN EOS JUDICIUM DABO.' This rule, from its expediency, has been, with some variations, received into the law of Scotland. Persons of this description are liable for their servants, or even for the acts of guests and passengers; and the extent of the damage may be proved by the oath of the claimant." William Bell, *Bell's Dictionary and Digest of the Law of Scotland* 737 (George Watson ed., 7th ed. 1890).

nautical, *adj.* (16c) Of, relating to, or involving ships or shipping, carriage by sea, or navigation.

nautical assessor. (1866) A person skilled in maritime matters who is summoned in an admiralty case to assist the judge on points requiring special expertise.

nautical mile. (1834) A measure of distance for air and sea navigation, equal to one minute of arc of a great circle of the earth. • Different measures have been used by different countries because the earth is not a perfect sphere. Since 1959, however, the United States has used an international measure for a nautical mile, set by the Hydrographic Bureau, equal to 6,076.11549 feet, or 1,852 meters.

nauticum fenus (**naw**-ti-kəm **fee**-nəs), *n.* [Greek *nautikon* "nautical" + Latin *fenus* "interest"] *Roman & civil law.* A loan to finance the transport of goods by sea; specif., a loan on bottomry made to a transporter of merchandise by ship. • The loan is subject to an extremely high rate of interest because it does not have to be repaid unless the ship safely reaches its destination. The *nauticum fenus* is both a loan and marine insurance. The rate, originally unlimited because of the risks of sea travel, was eventually fixed at 12%. The money loaned is *pecunia trajecticia* (money conveyed overseas). — Also spelled *nauticum foenus.* — Also termed *fenus nauticum*; *nautica pecunia*; *foenus nauticum.*

NAV. *abbr.* NET ASSET VALUE.

navagium (na-**vay**-jee-əm), *n.* [Latin "ship; voyage"] *Hist.* A tenant's duty to transport the lord's goods by ship.

naval, *adj.* (15c) **1.** Of, relating to, or involving ships or shipping. **2.** Of, relating to, or involving a navy. See NAVY.

naval law. (1816) A system of regulations governing naval forces. See CODE OF MILITARY JUSTICE.

navarch (**nay**-vahrk), *n.* [fr. Greek *naus* "ship" + *archos* "chief"] (1808) *Hist.* A master of an armed ship. — Also termed *navarchus.* Cf. NAVICULARIUS.

navicularius (nə-vik-yə-**lair**-ee-əs), *n.* [Latin "shipowner"] *Hist.* A person engaged in the shipping business.

navigable (**nav**-i-gə-bəl), *adj.* (15c) **1.** Capable of allowing vessels or vehicles to pass, and thereby usable for travel or commerce <the channel was barely navigable because it was so narrow>.

▸ **navigable in fact,** *adj.* (1842) Naturally usable for travel or commerce in the present condition. • A stream is navigable in fact if, in its natural and ordinary state, it can be used for travel or commerce. For admiralty jurisdiction, the water must be capable of being used as a route in interstate or international commerce in customary modes of travel.

2. Capable of being steered <navigable aircraft>. — Also termed *boatable.* See NAVIGABLE WATER.

navigable airspace. See AIRSPACE.

navigable sea. (16c) *Int'l law.* The ocean waters divided into three zones of control among countries: (1) the inland waters, which are near a country's shores and over which a country has complete sovereignty; (2) territorial waters, which are measured from the seaward edge of the inland waters, over which a country has extensive control but over which innocent parties must be allowed to travel to other countries; and (3) the high seas, which are international waters not subject to the domain of any single country.

navigable water. (16c) **1.** At early common law, any body of water affected by the ebb and flow of the tide. • This test was first adopted in England because most of England's in-fact navigable waters are influenced by the tide, unlike the large inland rivers that are capable of supporting commerce in the United States. — Also termed *boatable water.*

> "In addition to its bearing on admiralty jurisdictional inquiries, the navigable waters issue comes up in cases involving the scope of Congress's regulatory authority under the commerce clause; the validity and interpretation of a variety of statutes and regulations administered by the Coast Guard; the powers of the Corps of Engineers over waterways, dams, marinas, etc., under the Rivers & Harbors Act and other statutes; the Federal Power Commission's authority to inspect and license electricity-generating dams; the existence and exercise of a servitude of navigation, which affects both public access to waterways on private land and governmental regulatory authority over such waters; and disputes over the ownership of stream beds. The foregoing is not an exhaustive listing. Well over a thousand federal statutes use the term 'navigable waters.'" David W. Robertson, Steven F. Friedell & Michael F. Sturley, *Admiralty and Maritime Law in the United States* 53 n.1 (2001).

2. (*usu. pl.*) A body of water that is used, or typically can be used, as a highway for commerce with ordinary modes of trade and travel on water. • Under the Commerce Clause, Congress has broad jurisdiction over all navigable waters of the United States.

▸ **navigable water of the United States.** (1812) Navigable water that alone — or in combination with other waters — forms a continuous highway for commerce with other states or foreign countries.

navigate, *vb.* (16c) **1.** To travel or sail in a vessel on water <to navigate from New York to Bermuda>. **2.** To steer <to navigate the plane>. **3.** To make way through, on, or about something <the plaintiff was unable to navigate the stairs in the dark>. — **navigator,** *n.*

navigation. (16c) **1.** The act of sailing vessels on water. **2.** The process and business of directing the course of a vessel from one place to another. See RULES OF NAVIGATION.

navigation easement. See EASEMENT.

navigation servitude. See SERVITUDE (2).

navis (**nay**-vis), *n.* [Latin] A ship; a vessel.

navy. (14c) **1.** A fleet of ships. **2.** The military sea force of a country, including its collective ships and its corps of officers and enlisted personnel; esp. (*usu. cap.*), the division of the U.S. armed services responsible primarily for seagoing forces. • The U.S. Constitution gives Congress the power to establish a navy and make laws governing the naval forces. U.S. Const. art. I, § 8, cl. 13–14.

Navy Department. A division of the Department of Defense that oversees the operation and efficiency of the Navy, including the Marine Corps component (and the U.S. Coast Guard when operating as a naval service). • Established in 1798, the Department is headed by the Secretary of the Navy, who is appointed by the President and reports to the Secretary of Defense. — Also termed *Department of the Navy.*

navy yard. (18c) The land on which ships are built for the U.S. Navy and the contiguous waters that are necessary to float the ships.

NAWL. *abbr.* NATIONAL ASSOCIATION OF WOMEN LAWYERS.

nay, *n.* (14c) *Parliamentary law.* A negative vote. See YEAS AND NAYS. Cf. YEA.

nazeranna (naz-ə-**ran**-ə). *Hist.* The amount that a person paid to the government as an acknowledgment for public office or a grant of public lands.

N.B. *abbr.* [Latin *nota bene*] (17c) Note well; take notice — used in documents to call attention to something important.

NBA. *abbr.* NATIONAL BAR ASSOCIATION.

NBFI. *abbr.* Nonbank financial institution. See MONEY SERVICE BUSINESS.

NCA. *abbr.* NATIONAL CEMETERY ADMINISTRATION.

NCBL. *abbr.* NATIONAL CONFERENCE OF BLACK LAWYERS.

NCCUSL (nə-**k[y]oo**-səl). *abbr.* NATIONAL CONFERENCE OF COMMISSIONERS ON UNIFORM STATE LAWS.

n.c.d. *abbr.* NEMINE CONTRADICENTE.

NCF. *abbr.* See *net cash flow* under CASH FLOW.

NCJFCJ. *abbr.* NATIONAL COUNCIL OF JUVENILE AND FAMILY COURT JUDGES.

NCO. *abbr.* See *noncommissioned officer* under OFFICER.

NCPC. *abbr.* NATIONAL CAPITAL PLANNING COMMISSION.

NCR. *abbr.* NATIONAL CAPITAL REGION.

NCUA. *abbr.* NATIONAL CREDIT UNION ADMINISTRATION.

N.D. *abbr.* **1.** Northern District, in reference to a U.S. judicial district. **2.** NEMINE DISSENTIENTER.

NDMS. *abbr.* NATIONAL DISASTER MEDICAL SYSTEM.

NDP. *abbr.* Nondepository provider of financial services. See MONEY SERVICE BUSINESS.

N.E. *abbr.* NORTH EASTERN REPORTER.

N/E. See NOTICE OF ALLOWABILITY/EXAMINER'S AMENDMENT.

NEA. *abbr.* (1970) NATIONAL ENDOWMENT FOR THE ARTS.

ne admittas (nee ad-**mit**-əs), *n.* [Latin "that you admit not"] (16c) *Eccles. law.* A writ prohibiting a bishop, usu. in a *quare impedit* action, from admitting the other party's clerk to be a parson of a church. • After a party institutes a *quare impedit* action to enforce a right to propose a clerk to the position of parson of a vacant church (right of advowson), that party can resort to the *ne admittas* writ if it is believed that the bishop will admit another person's proposed clerk before the *quare impedit* action concludes. See QUARE IMPEDIT.

neap tide. See TIDE.

near, *adv.* & *adj.* (13c) **1.** Close to; not far away, as a measure of distance <the neighbors' houses are near one another>. **2.** Almost; close in degree <a near miss>. **3.** Closely tied by blood <my brother is a near relative>. **4.** Familiar; intimate <a near friend>.

nearest-reasonable-referent canon. The doctrine that when the syntax in a legal instrument involves something other than a parallel series of nouns or verbs, a prepositive or postpositive modifier normally applies only to the nearest reasonable referent. See RULE OF THE LAST ANTECEDENT.

> "Although this principle is often given the misnomer *last-antecedent canon* . . . , it is more accurate to consider it separately and to call it the *nearest-reasonable-referent canon.* Strictly speaking, only pronouns have antecedents, and the canon here under consideration also applies to adjectives, adverbs, and adverbial or adjectival phrases — and it applies not just to words that precede the modifier, but also to words that follow it. Most commonly, the syntax at issue involves an adverbial phrase that follows the referent." Antonin Scalia & Bryan A. Garner, *Reading Law: The Interpretation of Legal Texts* 152 (2012).

nearest-wrongdoer rule. See LAST-WRONGDOER RULE.

nearly closed-ended claim. See PATENT CLAIM.

near money. See *current asset* under ASSET.

neat, *adj.* (bef. 12c) **1.** Clean; pure. **2.** Free from extraneous matter.

neat weight. See *net weight* under WEIGHT (1).

ne baila pas (nə **bay**-lə **pah**), *n.* [Law French "he or she did not deliver"] In an action for detinue, a defendant's plea denying the receipt of the property in question.

***Nebbia* hearing.** See BAIL-SOURCE HEARING.

ne bis in idem. See NON BIS IN IDEM.

necation (ni-**kay**-shən), *n.* [fr. Latin *necare* "to kill"] (18c) *Hist.* The act of killing.

necessaries. (14c) **1.** Things that are indispensable to living <an infant's necessaries include food, shelter, and clothing>. • Necessaries include whatever food, medicine, clothing, shelter, and personal services are usu. considered reasonably essential for the preservation and enjoyment of life, to the extent that a person having a duty of protection must furnish them. — Also termed *necessities*; *necessities of life.* **2.** Things that are essential to maintaining the lifestyle to which one is accustomed <a multimillionaire's necessaries may include a chauffeured limousine and a private chef>. • The term includes whatever is reasonably needed for subsistence, health, comfort, and education, considering the person's age, station in life, and medical condition, but it excludes (1) anything purely ornamental, (2) anything solely for pleasure, (3) what the person is already supplied with, (4) anything that concerns someone's estate or business as opposed to personal needs, and (5) borrowed money. Under the common law, a husband was required to pay debts incurred by his wife or children for necessaries. Beginning in the late 1960s, most states began to change their statutes regarding the obligation to provide necessaries to include both husband and wife. See DOCTRINE OF NECESSARIES; FAMILY-EXPENSE STATUTE.

> "Things may be of a useful character, but the quality or quantity supplied may take them out of the character of necessaries. Elementary textbooks might be a necessary to a student of law, but not a rare edition of 'Littleton's Tenures,' or eight or ten copies of 'Stephen's Commentaries.' Necessaries also vary according to the station in life of the infant or his peculiar circumstances at the time. The quality of clothing suitable to an Eton boy would be unnecessary for a telegraph clerk; the medical attendance and diet required by an invalid would be unnecessary to one in ordinary health. It does not follow therefore that because a thing is of a useful class, a judge is bound to allow a jury to say whether or no it is a necessary." William R. Anson, *Principles of the Law of Contract* 172 (Arthur L. Corbin ed., 3d Am. ed. 1919).

3. *Maritime law.* Supplies and services needed for the maintenance and operation of a vessel, including repairs, tow fees, and the costs of loading and unloading. • Authorized provision of necessaries automatically confers a maritime lien to the provider under the Federal Maritime Lien Act, 42 USCA § 971–973.

> "The case law is clear that 'necessaries' does not mean absolutely indispensable; rather, the term refers to what is reasonably needed in the ship's business." Thomas J. Schoenbaum, *Admiralty and Maritime Law* 256 (1987).

necessarily included offense. See *lesser included offense* under OFFENSE (2).

necessarius (ne-sə-**sair**-ee-əs), *adj.* [Latin] **1.** Necessary; essential. **2.** Unavoidable; obligatory; compelling.

necessary, *adj.* **1.** That is needed for some purpose or reason; essential <three elements necessary to meet standing requirements>. **2.** That must exist or happen and cannot be avoided; inevitable <necessary evil>.

necessary and proper, *adj.* (16c) Being appropriate and well adapted to fulfilling an objective.

Necessary and Proper Clause. (1926) *Constitutional law.* The clause of the U.S. Constitution permitting Congress to make laws "necessary and proper" for the execution of its enumerated powers. U.S. Const. art. I, § 8, cl. 18. • The Supreme Court has broadly interpreted this clause to grant Congress the implied power to enact any law reasonably designed to achieve an express constitutional power. *McCulloch v. Maryland*, 17 U.S. (4 Wheat.) 316 (1819). — Also termed *Basket Clause*; *Coefficient Clause*; *Elastic Clause*; *Sweeping Clause.*

necessary-and-sufficient set test. *Torts.* A test designed to identify actual causes in cases of overdetermined causation, whereby a particular condition is held to have caused a specific consequence if and only if it was a necessary element of a set of antecedent actual conditions that were sufficient for the occurrence of the consequence. — Abbr. NASS test. Cf. *but-for cause*, *concurrent cause* under CAUSE (1); *overdetermined causation* under CAUSATION.

necessary damages. See *general damages* under DAMAGES.

necessary deposit. See DEPOSIT (5).

necessary diligence. See DILIGENCE (2).

necessary domicile. See DOMICILE.

necessary implication. See IMPLICATION.

necessary improvement. See IMPROVEMENT.

necessary inference. (17c) A conclusion that is unavoidable if the premise on which it is based is taken to be true.

necessary intromission. See INTROMISSION (2).

necessary party. See PARTY (2).

necessary repair. (16c) An improvement to property that is both needed to prevent deterioration and proper under the circumstances.

necessary way. See *easement by necessity* under EASEMENT.

necessitas (nə-**ses**-i-tas), *n.* [Latin] *Roman law.* **1.** Necessity. **2.** A force or influence that compels an unwilling person to act. • The term refers to a lack of free will to do a legal act, as opposed to *libera voluntas* ("free will").

necessitas culpabilis (nə-**ses**-i-tas kəl-**pay**-bə-lis). [Latin "culpable necessity"] (17c) *Hist.* An unfortunate necessity that, while essentially excusing the act done under its compulsion, does not necessarily relieve the actor from blame.

> "And as to the necessity which excuses a man who kills another *se defendendo* lord Bacon entitles it *necessitas culpabilis* . . . . For the law intends that the quarrel or assault arose from some unknown wrong . . . and since in quarrels both parties may be, and usually are, in some fault; and it scarce can be tried who was originally in the wrong; the law will not hold the survivor entirely guiltless. But it is clear, in the other case, that where I kill a thief that breaks into my house, the original default can never be upon my side." 4 William Blackstone, *Commentaries on the Laws of England* 186–87 (1769).

necessitate juris (nə-ses-i-**tay**-tee **joor**-is). [Latin] *Hist.* By necessity of law. • That phrase appeared in reference to acts necessarily arising from the effect of a legal rule.

necessities. (14c) **1.** Indispensable things of any kind. **2.** NECESSARIES (1).

necessities of life. See NECESSARIES (1).

necessitous, *adj.* (17c) Living in a state of extreme want; hard up.

necessitous circumstances. (17c) The situation of one who is very poor; extreme want.

necessitudo (nə-ses-i-**t[y]oo**-doh), *n.* [Latin "need"] *Hist.* **1.** An obligation. **2.** A close connection or relationship between persons, such as a family relationship.

necessity. 1. Something that must be done or accomplished for any one of various reasons, ranging from the continuation of life itself to a legal requirement of some kind to an intense personal desire; a requirement. • Context normally supplies a sense of the degree of urgency. **2.** The quality, state, or condition of being necessary. **3.** Physical or moral compulsion; the pressure of circumstance. **4.** *Criminal law.* A justification defense for a person who acts in an emergency that he or she did not create and who commits a harm that is less severe than the harm that would have occurred but for the person's actions. • For example, a mountain climber lost in a blizzard can assert necessity as a defense to theft of food and blankets from another's cabin. — Also termed *emergency defense; choice of evils; duress of circumstances; lesser-evils defense.* See JUSTIFICATION DEFENSE; *lesser-evils defense* under DEFENSE (1). **5.** *Torts.* A privilege that may relieve a person from liability for trespass or conversion if that person, having no alternative, harms another's property in an effort to protect life or health.

> "[T]he defense of necessity . . . is the strongest possible form of compulsion. It is a question which, in fact, is hardly ever raised, and which, when it is raised, is always, as it ought to be, dealt with exceptionally. The only case of the kind of which I am aware was the case of R. *v.* Dudley and Stephens, in which certain sailors in danger of death by starvation killed one of their number and ate him. This was held to be murder on grounds which appear from the judgment. . . I think, on the whole, the judgment was right, but I disagree with part of it, which appears to me to 'base a legal conclusion upon a questionable moral' and 'theological foundation, and to be rhetorically expressed.' There is not, and I think there cannot be, any principle involved in cases of this kind. It is, in my judgment, one of the very few cases in which a pardon might properly have been granted before trial. I can imagine somewhat similar cases, in which, notwithstanding R. *v.* Dudley, necessity might be an excuse. Suppose a man is so situated that he must either leave two persons to die, or kill one. You must either run over a boat, or have a fatal collision with a ship. You must leave both mother and child to die, or effect the delivery in such a way as to sacrifice at least one life. The subject is one on which it is useless to argue." James Fitzjames Stephen, *A General View of the Criminal Law of England* 76–77 (2d ed. 1890).

> "In some cases even damage intentionally done may not involve the defendant in liability when he is acting under necessity to prevent a greater evil. The precise limits of the defence are not clear, for it has affinities with certain other defences, such as act of God, self-help, duress, or inevitable accident. It is distinguishable from self-defence on the ground that this presupposes that the plaintiff is prima facie a wrongdoer: the defence of necessity contemplates the infliction of harm on an innocent plaintiff. The defence, if it exists, enables a defendant to escape liability for the intentional interference with the security of another's person or property on the ground that the acts complained of were necessary to prevent greater damage to the commonwealth or to another or to the defendant himself, or to their or his property. The use of the term necessity serves to conceal the fact that the defendant always has a choice between two evils. This is what distinguishes the defence of necessity from that of impossibility." R.F.V. Heuston, *Salmond on the Law of Torts* 493 (17th ed. 1977).

▸ **manifest necessity.** (17c) A sudden and overwhelming emergency, beyond the court's and parties' control, that makes conducting a trial or reaching a fair result impossible and that therefore authorizes the granting of a mistrial. • The standard of manifest necessity must be met to preclude a defendant from successfully raising a plea of former jeopardy after a mistrial.

▸ **military necessity.** See MILITARY NECESSITY.

▸ **moral necessity.** (17c) A necessity arising from a duty incumbent on a person to act in a particular way.

▸ **physical necessity.** (17c) A necessity involving an actual, tangible force that compels a person to act in a particular way.

▸ **private necessity.** (16c) *Torts.* A necessity that involves only the defendant's personal interest and thus provides only a limited privilege. • For example, if the defendant harms the plaintiff's dock by keeping a boat moored to the dock during a hurricane, the defendant can assert private necessity but must compensate the plaintiff for the dock's damage.

▸ **public necessity.** (16c) *Torts.* A necessity that involves the public interest and thus completely excuses the defendant's liability. • For example, if the defendant destroys the plaintiff's house to stop the spread of a fire that threatens the town, the defendant can assert public necessity.

6. RULE OF NECESSITY.

necessity defense. 1. JUSTIFICATION (2). **2.** See *lesser-evils defense* under DEFENSE (1).

neck doily. See JABOT.

neck verse. (15c) *Hist.* A verse, usu. consisting of the opening verse of Psalm 51 (*Miserere mei, Deus* "Have mercy on me, O God"), that was used as a literacy test for an accused who claimed benefit of clergy. • An accused who read the passage satisfactorily would not receive the maximum sentence (the person's neck would be saved). Although judges could assign any passage, they usu. chose Psalm 51, so that for many years criminals memorized this verse and pretended to read it. Still, the records show that many accused persons failed the test. The reading of the neck verse was abolished in 1707. See BENEFIT OF CLERGY.

> "During the fourteenth and fifteenth centuries the judges' attitudes to benefit of clergy changed completely, and they came to see it as a regular means of escape from the mandatory death penalty. Physical appearance was disregarded, and reading became the sole test of clerical status. When a man was convicted of a felony, he would fall on his knees and 'pray the book'; he would then be tendered a passage from the psalter, known as the neck-verse, and if he could read or recite it satisfactorily his clergy was taken to be proved . . . . Strictly speaking, the decision whether the convict read 'as a clerk' was for the ordinary; but he was subject to the control of the judges, and could be fined for refusing to accept someone. By the end of the sixteenth century as many as half of all men convicted of felony were recorded as having successfully claimed benefit of clergy." J.H. Baker, *An Introduction to English Legal History* 587 (3d ed. 1990).

nec manifestum (**nek** man-i-**fes**-təm). [Latin] *Civil law.* Not manifest. • The phrase usu. referred to a theft in which the thief was not caught in the act.

ne conjuges mutuo amore se invicem spolient (nee kən-**joo**-jeez **myoo**-choo-oh ə-**mor**-ee see in-**vɪ**-səm **spoh**-lee-ənt). [Latin] *Roman & civil law.* Lest spouses through their mutual love should impoverish one another. • The phrase appeared in reference to the rationale for holding that donations between husband and wife were invalid. A similar phrase, *ne mutuato amore invicem spoliarentur* ("lest they should be impoverished by each other through their mutual affection"), was also used.

necropsy (**nek**-rop-see). See AUTOPSY (1).

ne disturba pas (nə di-**stər**-bə **pah**), *n.* [Law French "did not disturb"] *Eccles. law.* A defendant's general denial (plea of the general issue) in a *quare impedit* action. See QUARE IMPEDIT.

ne dominia rerum sint incerta, neve lites sint perpetuae (nee də-**min**-ee-ə **reer**-əm sint in-**sər**-tə, **nee**-vee **lɪ**-teez sint pər-**pech**-oo-ee). [Latin] *Hist.* Lest the ownership of things should remain uncertain or lawsuits never come to an end. • The phrase appeared in reference to the principle on which all actions prescribed after (usu.) 30 years. See PRESCRIPTION.

ne dona pas (nə **doh**-nə **pah**), *n.* [Law French "did not give"] *Hist.* A defendant's general denial (plea of the general issue) in a formedon action, alleging that the plaintiff was given the right to land under a gift of tail. — Also termed *non dedit.* See FORMEDON.

née (nay), *adj.* [French] (17c) (Of a woman) born. • This term is sometimes used after a married woman's name to indicate her maiden name <Mrs. Robert Jones, née Thatcher>. The masculine form (not common in English) is *né.* — Also spelled *nee.*

need, *n.* (bef. 12c) **1.** The lack of something important; a requirement. **2.** Indigence. **3.** An opportunity or condition for growth or other positive change. — **need,** *vb.*

need-to-know basis. (1953) A justification for restricting access to information to only those with a clear and approved reason for requiring access — used as a means of protecting confidential information that affects a range of interests, from national security to trade secrets to the attorney–client privilege.

needy, *adj.* (12c) **1.** Needful; necessary. **2.** Indigent; very poor. • *Needy* implies a more permanent and less urgent condition than *necessitous.* See NECESSITOUS.

ne exeat (nee **ek**-see-ət [*or* **ek**-see-at]). [Latin "that he not depart"]. (17c) **1.** A writ restraining a person from leaving the republic; specif., an equitable writ ordering the person to whom it is addressed not to leave the jurisdiction of the court or the state. • *Ne exeat* writs are usu. issued to ensure the satisfaction of a claim against the defendant. The full phrase is *ne exeat republica* (nee **ek**-see-ət [*or* **ek**-see-at] ri-**pəb**-li-kəh) [Latin "let him not go out of the republic"]. **2.** *Family law.* An equitable writ restraining a person from leaving, or removing a child or property from, the jurisdiction. • A *ne exeat* is often issued to prohibit a person from removing a child or property from the jurisdiction — and sometimes from leaving the jurisdiction. — Also termed *writ of ne exeat; ne exeat republica; ne exeat regno.*

> "The district courts of the United States . . . shall have such jurisdiction to make and issue in civil actions, writs and orders of injunction, and of *ne exeat republica*, orders appointing receivers, and such other orders and processes . . . as may be necessary or appropriate for the enforcement of the internal revenue laws." IRC (26 USCA) § 7402(a).

> "Such a writ [*ne exeat*] might be issued upon the commencement of the suit for equitable relief, during the pendency of the suit, or upon issuance of the final decree to secure its enforcement. But such writ related primarily to the person of the defendant and issued only upon satisfactory proof that he planned or intended to remove himself beyond the court's jurisdiction so that he might escape obedience to such command as might be or had been laid upon him. The writ has been frequently termed an equitable bail. It involves taking and keeping the defendant in custody until he gives bail or bond in a designated amount, conditioned upon his keeping himself amenable to the effective processes of the court." William Q. de Funiak, *Handbook of Modern Equity* 21 (2d ed. 1956).

ne exeat regno. See NE EXEAT.

ne exeat republica. See NE EXEAT.

nefas (**nee**-fas), *n.* [Latin *ne* "not" + *fas* "right"] **1.** *Roman law.* Something that the gods forbid. **2.** *Roman law.* Something against the law or custom. **3.** *Hist.* Something that is wicked. Cf. FAS.

nefastus (ni-**fas**-təs), *n.* [Latin *ne* "not" + *fastus* "lawful for public business"] *Roman law.* A day when it is unlawful to open the courts, administer justice, or hold public assemblies. • The priests in charge of supervising the laws and religious observances established an official calendar, on which certain days, marked "*nefasti*," were to be devoted to religious or public ceremonies. — Also termed *dies nefasti*. Cf. *dies fasti* under DIES.

negate, *vb.* (17c) **1.** To deny. **2.** To nullify; to render ineffective.

negative, *adj.* (15c) **1.** Of, relating to, or involving something bad; not positive <a negative attitude>. **2.** Of, relating to, or involving refusal of consent; not affirmative <a negative answer>.

negative, *n.* (16c) **1.** A word or phrase of denial or refusal <"no" and "not" are negatives>. **2.** A word expressing the opposite of the positive <two negatives and one positive>. **3.** The original plate or film of a photograph, on which light and shadows are the opposite of the positive images later created and printed <not only the pictures, but also the negatives, were required to be returned>. **4.** *Archaic.* The power of veto <the king's negative has eroded>.

negative, *vb.* (18c) To negate; to deny, nullify, or render ineffective <the jury negatived fraud>.

negative act. See ACT (2).

negative amortization. See AMORTIZATION (1).

negative averment. See AVERMENT.

negative cash flow. See CASH FLOW.

negative causation. See CAUSATION.

Negative Commerce Clause. See *Dormant Commerce Clause* under COMMERCE CLAUSE.

negative condition. See CONDITION (2).

negative contingent fee. See *reverse contingent fee* under CONTINGENT FEE.

negative covenant. See COVENANT (1).

negative defense. See DEFENSE (1).

negative disinheritance. See DISINHERITANCE.

negative duty. See DUTY (1).

negative easement. See EASEMENT.

negative equity. See EQUITY (7).

negative evidence. See EVIDENCE.

negative externality. See EXTERNALITY.

negative fact. See FACT.

negative identification. The accurate refusal to identify anyone in one or more arrays of supposed suspects, none of whom is thought by police to have any connection with the crime at issue — esp. when the photographs or lineups include people close in appearance to the actual suspect. • A negative identification may be admissible if the reliability of a positive identification is at issue.

negative-implication canon. See EXPRESSIO UNIUS EST EXCLUSIO ALTERIUS.

negative limitation. (1919) *Patents.* In a patent application, a claim that describes what the element is not or does not do, rather than what it is or does. • Although older caselaw held that a negative limitation rendered a claim indefinite, more recent decisions allow those that define a clear alternative as long as the claim is not overbroad.

negative misprision. See MISPRISION (1).

negative plea. See PLEA (3).

negative-pledge clause. (1935) **1.** A provision requiring a borrower, who borrows funds without giving security, to refrain from giving future lenders any security without the consent of the first lender. **2.** A provision, usu. in a bond indenture, stating that the issuing entity will not pledge its assets if it will result in less security to the bondholders under the indenture agreement.

negative pregnant. (17c) A denial implying its affirmative opposite by seeming to deny only a qualification of the allegation and not the allegation itself. • An example is the statement, "I didn't steal the money last Tuesday," the implication being that the theft might have happened on another day. — Also termed *negative pregnant with an affirmative*. Cf. AFFIRMATIVE PREGNANT.

negative prescription. See PRESCRIPTION (4).

negative proof. See PROOF.

negative reprisal. See REPRISAL (1).

negative retributivism. See RETRIBUTIVISM.

negative right. See RIGHT.

negative servitude. See SERVITUDE (3).

negative statute. See STATUTE.

negative testimony. See *negative evidence* under EVIDENCE.

negative veto. See *qualified veto* under VETO.

neglect, *n.* (16c) **1.** The omission of proper attention to a person or thing, whether inadvertent, negligent, or willful; the act of treating someone or something heedlessly or inattentively. **2.** *Family law.* The failure to give proper attention, supervision, or necessities, esp. to a child, to such an extent that harm results or is likely to result. Cf. ABUSE. — **neglect,** *vb.*

> "'Neglect' is not the same thing as 'negligence.' In the present connection the word 'neglect' indicates, as a purely objective fact, that a person has not done that which it was his duty to do; it does not indicate the *reason* for this failure. 'Negligence,' on the other hand, is a subjective state of mind, and it indicates a particular reason why the man has failed to do his duty, namely because he has not kept the performance of the duty in his mind as he ought to have done. A man can 'neglect' his duty either intentionally or negligently." J.W. Cecil Turner, *Kenny's Outlines of Criminal Law* 108 n.1 (16th ed. 1952).

▸ **child neglect.** (1930) The failure of a person responsible for a minor to care for the minor's emotional or physical needs. • Child neglect is a form of child abuse. Local child-welfare departments investigate reports of child neglect. In a severe case, criminal charges may be filed against a person suspected of child neglect.

▸ **culpable neglect.** (18c) Censurable or blameworthy neglect; neglect that is less than gross carelessness but more than the failure to use ordinary care.

▸ **developmental neglect.** (1984) Failure to provide necessary emotional nurturing and physical or cognitive stimulation, as a result of which a child could suffer from serious developmental delays.

▸ **educational neglect.** (1853) Failure to ensure that a child attends school in accordance with state law.

▸ **excusable neglect.** (1855) A failure — which the law will excuse — to take some proper step at the proper time (esp. in neglecting to answer a lawsuit) not because of the party's own carelessness, inattention, or willful disregard of the court's process, but because of some unexpected or unavoidable hindrance or accident or because of reliance on the care and vigilance of the party's counsel or on a promise made by the adverse party.

▸ **inexcusable neglect.** (18c) Unjustifiable neglect; neglect that implies more than unintentional inadvertence. • A finding of inexcusable neglect in, for example, failing to file an answer to a complaint will prevent the setting aside of a default judgment.

▸ **medical neglect.** (1818) Failure to provide medical, dental, or psychiatric care that is necessary to prevent or to treat serious physical or emotional injury or illness. • In determining whether a parent's refusal to consent to medical treatment is neglectful, courts use any of three approaches: (1) an ad hoc test, (2) a best-interests-of-the-child test, or (3) a balancing test that weighs the interests of the parents, the child, and the state. Cf. FAITH-HEALING EXEMPTION.

▸ **physical neglect.** (1873) Failure to provide necessaries, the lack of which has caused or could cause serious injury or illness.

▸ **willful neglect.** (18c) Intentional or reckless failure to carry out a legal duty, esp. in caring for a child.

neglected child. See CHILD.

neglectful, *adj.* (16c) Not looking after someone or something properly; not giving enough attention; CARELESS (1).

neglect hearing. See HEARING.

neglegentia (neg-li-**jen**-shee-ə), *n.* [Latin] *Roman law.* Carelessness; inattentive omission. • *Neglegentia* can be of varying degrees, which may or may not result in actionable liability. — Also spelled *negligentia.* See CULPA (1). Cf. DILIGENTIA.

> "In the sources *negligentia* is tantamount to *culpa*, and similarly graduated (*magna, lata negligentia*). Precision in terminology is no more to be found here than in the field of *culpa*. One text declares . . . 'gross negligence (*magna negligentia*) is *culpa, magna culpa* is *dolus*'; another says: 'gross negligence (*dissoluta negligentia*) is near to *dolus* (*prope dolum*).' In the saying '*lata culpa* is exorbitant (extreme) negligence, i.e., not to understand (*intelligere*) what all understand' . . . *negligentia* is identified with ignorance." Adolf Berger, *Encyclopedic Dictionary of Roman Law* 593 (1953).

▸ ***lata neglegentia*** (**lay**-tə neg-li-**jen**-shee-ə). Extreme negligence resulting from an unawareness of something that the actor should have known.

▸ ***magna neglegentia*** (**mag**-nə neg-li-**jen**-shee-ə). See *gross negligence* under NEGLIGENCE.

negligence, *n.* (14c) **1.** The failure to exercise the standard of care that a reasonably prudent person would have exercised in a similar situation; any conduct that falls below the legal standard established to protect others against unreasonable risk of harm, except for conduct that is intentionally, wantonly, or willfully disregardful of others' rights; the doing of what a reasonable and prudent person would not do under the particular circumstances, or the failure to do what such a person would do under the circumstances. • The elements necessary to recover damages for negligence are (1) the existence of a duty on the part of the defendant to protect the plaintiff from the injury complained of, and (2) an injury to the plaintiff from the defendant's failure. The term denotes culpable carelessness. The Roman-law equivalents are *culpa* and *neglegentia*, as contrasted with *dolus* (wrongful intention). — Also termed *actionable negligence; ordinary negligence; simple negligence.* See BREACH OF DUTY OF CARE. **2.** A tort grounded in this failure, usu. expressed in terms of the following elements: duty, breach of duty, causation, and damages.

> "Negligence in law ranges from inadvertence that is hardly more than accidental to sinful disregard of the safety of others." Patrick Devlin, *The Enforcement of Morals* 36 (1968).

> "During the first half of the nineteenth century, negligence began to gain recognition as a separate and independent basis of tort liability. Its rise coincided in a marked degree with the Industrial Revolution; and it very probably was stimulated by the rapid increase in the number of accidents caused by industrial machinery, and in particular by the invention of railways. It was greatly encouraged by the disintegration of the old forms of action, and the disappearance of the distinction between direct and indirect injuries, found in trespass and case . . . . Intentional injuries, whether direct or indirect, began to be grouped as a distinct field of liability, and negligence remained as the main basis for unintended torts. Negligence thus developed into the dominant cause of action for accidental injury in this nation today." W. Page Keeton et al., *Prosser and Keeton on the Law of Torts* § 28, at 161 (5th ed. 1984).

> "Negligence is a matter of risk — that is to say, of recognizable danger of injury . . . . In most instances, it is caused by heedlessness or inadvertence, by which the negligent party is unaware of the results which may follow from his act. But it may also arise where the negligent party has considered the possible consequences carefully, and has exercised his own best judgment. The almost universal use of the phrase 'due care' to describe conduct which is not negligent should not obscure the fact that the essence of negligence is not necessarily the absence of solicitude for those who may be adversely affected by one's actions but is instead behavior which should be recognized as involving unreasonable danger to others." *Id.* at 169.

▸ **active negligence.** (1875) Negligence resulting from an affirmative or positive act, such as driving through a barrier. Cf. *passive negligence.*

▸ **advertent negligence.** (1909) Negligence in which the actor is aware of the unreasonable risk that he or she is creating; RECKLESSNESS. — Also termed *willful negligence; supine negligence.*

▸ **casual negligence.** (1812) A plaintiff's failure to (1) pay reasonable attention to his or her surroundings, so as to discover the danger created by the defendant's negligence, (2) exercise reasonable competence, care, diligence, and skill to avoid the danger once it is perceived, or (3) prepare as a reasonable person would to avoid future dangers.

▸ **collateral negligence.** (1874) An independent contractor's negligence, for which the employer is generally not liable. See COLLATERAL-NEGLIGENCE DOCTRINE.

▸ **comparative negligence.** (1862) A plaintiff's own negligence that proportionally reduces the damages recoverable from a defendant. — Also termed *comparative fault.* See COMPARATIVE-NEGLIGENCE DOCTRINE.

▸ **concurrent negligence.** (1831) The negligence of two or more parties acting independently but causing the same damage. Cf. *joint negligence.*

▸ **contributory negligence.** (1822) **1.** A plaintiff's own negligence that played a part in causing the plaintiff's injury and that is significant enough (in a few jurisdictions) to bar the plaintiff from recovering damages. • While *assumption of the risk* denotes the voluntary incurring of the chance of an accident, *contributory* *negligence* denotes negligence that contributes to a particular accident that actually occurs. In some circumstances the two concepts can be difficult to distinguish. **2.** A negligence-based legal defense that constitutes a bar to liability. • In most jurisdictions, this defense has been superseded by comparative negligence. See CONTRIBUTORY-NEGLIGENCE DOCTRINE; DISTRACTION DOCTRINE. **3.** *Rare.* The negligence of a third party — neither the plaintiff nor the defendant — whose act or omission played a part in causing the plaintiff's injury.

"The contributory negligence of a third party is no excuse for the negligence of the defendant." Thomas E. Holland, *The Elements of Jurisprudence* 154 (13th ed. 1924).

▸ **criminal negligence.** (1838) **1.** Gross negligence so extreme that it is punishable as a crime. • For example, involuntary manslaughter or other negligent homicide can be based on criminal negligence, as when an extremely careless automobile driver kills someone. — Also termed *culpable negligence*; *gross negligence.*

"Though the legislatures and the courts have often made it clear that criminal liability generally requires more fault than the ordinary negligence which will do for tort liability, they have not so often made it plain just what is required in addition to tort negligence — greater risk, subjective awareness of the risk, or both. Statutes are sometimes worded in terms of 'gross negligence' or 'culpable negligence' or 'criminal negligence,' without any further definition of these terms. . . . The courts thus have had to do their best with little guidance from the legislature, with varying results." Wayne R. LaFave & Austin W. Scott Jr., *Criminal Law* § 3.7, at 235–37 (2d ed. 1986).

2. The objectively assessed mental state of an actor who should know that there is a substantial and unjustifiable risk that the social harm that the law is designed to prevent will occur but who nevertheless engages in the prohibited action. • Under the Model Penal Code, this mental state represents the minimum level of culpability required for criminal liability except when the offense carries absolute liability. Cf. CULPABILITY; MENS REA; RECKLESSLY.

"Though the legislatures and the courts have often made it clear that criminal liability generally requires more fault than the ordinary negligence which will do for tort liability, they have not so often made it plain just what is required in addition to tort negligence — greater risk, subjective awareness of the risk, or both. Statutes are sometimes worded in terms of 'gross negligence' or 'culpable negligence' or 'criminal negligence,' without any further definition of these terms. . . . The courts thus have had to do their best with little guidance from the legislature, with varying results." Wayne R. LaFave & Austin W. Scott Jr., *Criminal Law* § 3.7, at 235–37 (2d ed. 1986).

▸ **culpable negligence.** (17c) **1.** Negligent conduct that, while not intentional, involves a disregard of the consequences likely to result from one's actions. **2.** See *criminal negligence.*

"'Culpable negligence,' while variously defined, has been held incapable of exact definition; it means something more than negligence . . . . In connection with negligence, the word 'culpable' is sometimes used in the sense of 'blamable,' and it has been regarded as expressing the thought of a breach of a duty or the commission of a fault; but culpable negligence has been held to amount to more than 'blameworthy' conduct . . . . It does not involve the element of intent . . . . On the other hand, it has been said to be intentional conduct which the actor may not intend to be harmful but which an ordinary and reasonably prudent man would recognize as involving a strong probability of injury to others." 65 C.J.S. *Negligence* § 1(13) (1966).

▸ **gross negligence.** (16c) **1.** A lack of even slight diligence or care. • The difference between *gross negligence* and *ordinary negligence* is one of degree and not of quality. Gross negligence is traditionally said to be the omission of even such diligence as habitually careless and inattentive people do actually exercise in avoiding danger to their own person or property. — Also termed *willful and wanton misconduct.* **2.** A conscious, voluntary act or omission in reckless disregard of a legal duty and of the consequences to another party, who may typically recover exemplary damages. — Also termed *reckless negligence*; *wanton negligence*; *willful negligence*; *willful and wanton negligence*; *willful and wanton misconduct*; *hazardous negligence*; *magna neglegentia.* **3.** See *criminal negligence.*

"Negligence is gross if the precautions to be taken against harm are very simple, such as persons who are but poorly endowed with physical and mental capacities can easily take." H.L.A. Hart, "Negligence, *Mens Rea* and Criminal Responsibility," in *Punishment and Responsibility* 136, 149 (1968).

"*Gross Negligence.* As it originally appeared, this was very great negligence, or the want of even slight or scant care. It has been described as a failure to exercise even that care which a careless person would use. Several courts, however, dissatisfied with a term so nebulous . . . have construed gross negligence as requiring willful, wanton, or reckless misconduct, or such utter lack of all care as will be evidence thereof . . . . But it is still true that most courts consider that 'gross negligence' falls short of a reckless disregard of the consequences, and differs from ordinary negligence only in degree, and not in kind." W. Page Keeton et al., *Prosser and Keeton on the Law of Torts* § 34, at 211–12 (5th ed. 1984).

▸ **hazardous negligence.** (1904) **1.** Careless or reckless conduct that exposes someone to extreme danger of injury or to imminent peril. **2.** See *gross negligence* (2).

▸ **hybrid comparative negligence.** (1980) A plaintiff's own negligence that proportionately reduces damages recoverable from defendant and, if great enough, bars any recovery from that defendant. See 50-PERCENT RULE.

▸ **imputed contributory negligence.** (1880) Contributory negligence that can be vicariously transferred between parties, such as employee and employer.

▸ **imputed negligence.** (18c) Negligence of one person charged to another; negligence resulting from a party's special relationship with another party who is originally negligent — so that, for example, a parent might be held responsible for some acts of a child.

▸ **inadvertent negligence.** (18c) Negligence in which the actor is not aware of the unreasonable risk that he or she is creating, but should have foreseen and avoided it. — Also termed *simple negligence.*

▸ **joint negligence.** (18c) The negligence of two or more persons acting together to cause an accident. Cf. *concurrent negligence.*

▸ **legal negligence.** See *negligence per se.*

▸ **negligence in law.** (1843) Failure to observe a duty imposed by law. See *negligence per se*; *legal negligence.*

▸ **negligence per se.** (1841) Negligence established as a matter of law, so that breach of the duty is not a jury question. • Negligence per se usu. arises from a statutory violation. — Also termed *legal negligence.*

▸ **ordinary negligence.** (16c) **1.** Lack of ordinary diligence; the failure to use ordinary care. • The term is most commonly used to differentiate between *negligence* and *gross negligence*. **2.** NEGLIGENCE (1).

▸ **passive negligence.** (18c) Negligence resulting from a person's failure or omission in acting, such as failing to remove hazardous conditions from public property. Cf. *active negligence*.

▸ **professional negligence.** See MALPRACTICE.

▸ **reckless negligence.** See *gross negligence*.

▸ **simple negligence. 1.** See *inadvertent negligence*. **2.** See NEGLIGENCE (1).

▸ **slight negligence.** (18c) The failure to exercise the great care of an extraordinarily prudent person, resulting in liability in special circumstances (esp. those involving bailments or carriers) in which lack of ordinary care would not result in liability; lack of great diligence.

> "[T]he best test of whether an act is culpably negligent in the particular case is to inquire whether there was a duty to exercise ordinary care, or something more or less than ordinary care, incumbent upon the party, and whether he had reasonably fulfilled that duty; if he has, he is not negligent; if he has not, he is negligent. The words 'ordinary' and 'reasonably' are no doubt vague, but the subject is only further obscured by the introduction of the words 'gross' and 'slight' because nobody can really say what they mean, though anybody may easily give to them some peculiar or exaggerated meaning." Horace Smith, *A Treatise on the Law of Negligence* 8 (1st Am. ed. fr. 2d English ed. 1887).

▸ **subsequent negligence.** (1827) The negligence of the defendant when, after the defendant's initial negligence and the plaintiff's contributory negligence, the defendant discovers — or should have discovered — that the plaintiff was in a position of danger and fails to exercise due care in preventing the plaintiff's injuries. — Also termed *supervening negligence*. See LAST-CLEAR-CHANCE DOCTRINE.

▸ **supine negligence.** See *advertent negligence*.

▸ **tax negligence.** (1956) Negligence arising out of the disregard of tax-payment laws, for which the Internal Revenue Service may impose a penalty — 5% of the amount underpaid. IRC (26 USCA) § 6651(a).

▸ **wanton negligence.** See *gross negligence*.

▸ **willful and wanton negligence.** See *gross negligence*.

▸ **willful negligence. 1.** See *advertent negligence*. **2.** See *gross negligence*.

negligence rule. (1914) *Commercial law.* The principle that if a party's negligence contributes to an unauthorized signing or a material alteration in a negotiable instrument, that party is estopped from raising this issue against later parties who transfer or pay the instrument in good faith. • Examples of negligence include leaving blanks or spaces on the amount line of the instrument, erroneously mailing the instrument to a person with the same name as the payee, and failing to follow internal procedures designed to prevent forgeries.

negligent, *adj.* (14c) Characterized by a person's failure to exercise the degree of care that someone of ordinary prudence would have exercised in the same circumstance <the negligent driver went through the stop sign> <negligent construction caused the bridge to collapse>. — **negligently,** *adv.*

> "[A] careful consideration is needed of the differences between the meaning of expressions like 'inadvertently' and 'while his mind was a blank' on the one hand, and 'negligently' on the other. In ordinary English, and also in lawyers' English, when harm has resulted from someone's negligence, if we say of that person that he has acted negligently we are not thereby *merely* describing the frame of mind in which he acted. 'He negligently broke a saucer' is not the same *kind* of expression as 'he inadvertently broke a saucer.' The point of the adverb 'inadvertently' *is* merely to inform us of the agent's psychological state, whereas if we say 'He broke it negligently' we are not merely adding to this an element of blame or reproach, but something quite specific, viz. we are referring to the fact that the agent failed to comply with a standard of conduct with which any ordinary reasonable man *could* and *would* have complied: a standard requiring him to take precautions against harm. The word 'negligently,' both in legal and in non-legal contexts, makes an essential reference to an omission to do what is thus required: it is not a flatly descriptive psychological expression like 'his mind was a blank.'" H.L.A. Hart, "Negligence, *Mens Rea* and Criminal Responsibility," in *Punishment and Responsibility* 136, 147–48 (1968).

negligent act. See ACT (2).

negligent conversion. See *technical conversion* under CONVERSION (2).

negligent entrustment. (1944) The act of leaving a dangerous article (such as a gun or car) with a person who the lender knows, or should know, is likely to use it in an unreasonably risky manner.

negligent escape. See ESCAPE (3).

negligent hiring. (1915) *Torts.* An employer's lack of care in selecting an employee who the employer knew or should have known was unfit for the position, thereby creating an unreasonable risk that another person would be harmed.

negligent homicide. See HOMICIDE.

negligentia (neg-li-**jen**-shee-ə), *n.* [Latin] *Roman law.* See NEGLEGENTIA.

negligent infliction of emotional distress. (1970) The tort of causing another severe emotional distress through one's negligent conduct. • Most courts will allow a plaintiff to recover damages for emotional distress if the defendant's conduct results in physical contact with the plaintiff or, when no contact occurs, if the plaintiff is in the zone of danger. — Abbr. NIED. See *emotional distress* under DISTRESS (4); ZONE-OF-DANGER RULE. Cf. INTENTIONAL INFLICTION OF EMOTIONAL DISTRESS.

negligent manslaughter. See *involuntary manslaughter* under MANSLAUGHTER.

negligent misrepresentation. See MISREPRESENTATION.

negligent nondisclosure. See NONDISCLOSURE.

negligent offense. See OFFENSE (2).

negligent tort. See TORT.

négoce (ni-**gohs**), *n.* [French] Trade; business.

negotiability. (18c) **1.** At common law, the capability of commercial paper to have its title transferred by indorsement and delivery, or by delivery alone, so that the transferee has a rightful claim on it. • Negotiability (which pertains to commercial paper) differs from assignability (which pertains to contracts in general) because an assignee traditionally takes title subject to all equities, and an assignment is not complete without notice to the debtor, whereas an indorsee takes free of all equities and without any notice to the debtor. **2.** A written instrument's capability of being transferred by delivery or indorsement when the transferee takes the instrument for value, in good faith, and without notice of conflicting title claims or defenses.

"Use of terms — 'negotiability' — 'transferability.' — The student should observe carefully the distinction between the terms *negotiability* and *transferability.* The one is exclusively the language of the Law Merchant, and the other of the Common Law. Substantially every property right, existing in contract or non-contract, in writing or not, possesses by the modern Common Law the quality of 'transferability.' But 'negotiability' is alone a characteristic of instruments of the Law Merchant. . . . Negotiability . . . endows [instruments] with the privilege of passing from hand to hand like money, free of the defenses which an earlier party might have asserted, and free of the claims of earlier owners, so that transfer before maturity to a new and honest holder for value carries complete legal title to him, with the right to recover the face value thereof, in his own name and behalf, regardless of previous infirmities or equities in the instrument." Melville M. Bigelow, *The Law of Bills, Notes, and Checks* 32 (William Minor Lile ed., 3d ed. 1928).

negotiable, *adj.* (18c) **1.** (Of a written instrument at common law) capable of being transferred by delivery or indorsement when the transferee takes the instrument for value, in good faith, and without notice of conflicting title claims or defenses.

"The truth is that 'negotiable' has an original and an acquired signification. Originally it meant transferable; but afterwards it was used to indicate the supposed effects of transfer, namely, that the transferee (1) took free from equities, and (2) could sue in his own name. And thus we say that certain choses are transferable, although not negotiable — meaning that they are transferable, but that certain effects do not accompany their transfer. According to primary meaning, then, a 'negotiable' instrument is a transferable instrument; and in that sense the word truly indicated, at one time, a real distinction among choses in action. The secondary meaning, however — that in which it is taken as indicating the existence of peculiar effects of transfer — was always inaccurate and unscientific; for as to the transferee bringing an action in his own name, that is the normal result or effect of all transferability; and as to honest acquisition conferring title, this secondary meaning arrogates to the transfer of bills and notes alone, an effect (1) which existed sometimes in the case of other property, and (2) which sometimes was absent from bills themselves. In other words, 'negotiable' was used (in the secondary sense) to mark off bills and notes from other choses in action, by a peculiarity of which they not only had no exclusive possession, but which frequently was altogether absent. However dubious to some lawyers this assertion may appear to be, there is at least no doubt (1) that at the present day all choses in action arising out of contract are transferable; and (2) that any rule as to transferees of choses in action taking free from equities is by no means confined to bills and notes, but is, as we have seen, 'a rule which must yield when it appears, from the nature or terms of the contract, that it must have been intended to be assignable free from and unaffected by such equities.'" John S. Ewart, *An Exposition of the Principles of Estoppel by Misrepresentation* 384 (1900) (citation omitted).

"The term 'negotiable,' in its enlarged signification, is used to describe any written security which may be transferred by indorsement and delivery, or by delivery merely, so as to vest in the indorsee the legal title, and thus enable him to bring a suit thereon in his own name. But in a strictly commercial classification, and as the term is technically used, it applies only to those instruments which, like bills of exchange, not only carry the legal title with them by indorsement, or delivery, but carry as well, when transferred before maturity, the right of the transferee to demand the full amounts which their faces call for. 'Assignable' is the more appropriate term to describe bonds, and ordinary notes, or notes of hand as they are most commonly called; as 'negotiable' is the more fitting term to describe the peculiar instruments of commerce." 1 John W. Daniel, *A Treatise on the Law of Negotiable Instruments* § 2, at 3 (Thomas H. Calvert ed., 7th ed. 1933).

2. (Of a written instrument under modern law) capable of being transferred by transfer of possession, or by indorsement and transfer of possession, to a person who thereby becomes the holder. • An instrument is negotiable if the transferee thereby becomes a holder, regardless of whether the transferee meets the additional due-course requirements. *See* UCC § 3-201. Negotiation does not always require voluntary delivery. It can take place by an involuntary transfer of possession, as through a thief. **3.** (Of a deal, agreement, etc.) capable of being accomplished. **4.** (Of a price or deal) subject to further bargaining and possible change. Cf. NONNEGOTIABLE; ASSIGNABLE.

negotiable bill of lading. See BILL OF LADING.

negotiable bond. See BOND (2).

negotiable certificate of deposit. See CERTIFICATE OF DEPOSIT.

negotiable document of title. See DOCUMENT OF TITLE.

negotiable instrument. (18c) A written instrument that (1) is signed by the maker or drawer, (2) includes an unconditional promise or order to pay a specified sum of money, (3) is payable on demand or at a definite time, and (4) is payable to order or to bearer. UCC § 3-104(a). • Among the various types of negotiable instruments are bills of exchange, promissory notes, bank checks, certificates of deposit, and other negotiable securities. — Also termed *negotiable paper; negotiable note.*

"What are called 'negotiable instruments,' or 'paper to bearer,' such as bills of exchange, or promissory notes, do really pass from hand to hand, either by delivery or indorsement, giving to each successive recipient a right against the debtor, to which no notice to the debtor is essential, and which, if the paper is held bona fide and for value, is unaffected by flaws in the title of intermediate assignors." Thomas E. Holland, *The Elements of Jurisprudence* 315–16 (13th ed. 1924).

"One must first understand that a negotiable instrument is a peculiar animal and that many animals calling for the payment of money and others loosely called 'commercial paper' are not negotiable instruments and not subject to the rules of Article 3." James J. White & Robert S. Summers, 2 *Uniform Commercial Code* § 16-1, at 70 (4th ed. 1995).

negotiable note. See NEGOTIABLE INSTRUMENT.

negotiable order of withdrawal. (1973) A negotiable instrument (such as a check) payable on demand and issued against funds deposited with a financial institution. — Abbr. NOW.

negotiable-order-of-withdrawal account. See *NOW account* under ACCOUNT.

negotiable paper. See NEGOTIABLE INSTRUMENT.

negotiable words. (1819) The terms and phrases that make a document a negotiable instrument. — Also termed *words of negotiability.* See NEGOTIABLE INSTRUMENT.

"The instrument must contain express words of negotiability, although there is no set form of such expression. It is enough if the intention of the parties to make it negotiable can be fairly construed from the terms of the contract. The usual form of making an instrument negotiable is making it payable either (a) To order, or (b) To bearer." Charles P. Norton, *Handbook of the Law of Bills and Notes* 20–21 (4th ed. 1914).

negotiate, *vb.* (16c) **1.** To communicate with another party for the purpose of reaching an understanding <they

negotiated with their counterparts for weeks on end>. **2.** To bring about by discussion or bargaining <she negotiated a software license agreement>. **3.** At common law, to transfer (an instrument) by delivery or indorsement, whereby the transferee takes the instrument for value, in good faith, and without notice of conflicting title claims or defenses <Jones negotiated the check at the neighborhood bank>. **4.** Under the UCC, to transfer possession of an instrument, usu. by delivery or indorsement and delivery, whereby the transferee becomes its holder. • Transfer of possession may be involuntary (as through theft), and the transferee does not have to meet any additional due-course requirements. UCC § 3-201.

negotiated agreement. A settlement that disputing parties reach between themselves, usu. with the help of their attorneys, but without benefit of formal mediation. — Also termed *negotiated settlement.*

negotiated market. See MARKET.

negotiated offering. See OFFERING.

negotiated plea. See PLEA (1).

negotiated settlement. See NEGOTIATED AGREEMENT.

negotiating bank. See BANK.

negotiation, *n.* (16c) **1.** A consensual bargaining process in which the parties attempt to reach agreement on a disputed or potentially disputed matter. • Negotiation usu. involves complete autonomy for the parties involved, without the intervention of third parties.

> "Negotiation, we may say, ought strictly to be viewed simply as a means to an end; it is the road the parties must travel to arrive at their goal of mutually satisfactory settlement. But like other means, negotiation is easily converted into an end in itself; it readily becomes a game played for its own sake and a game played with so little reserve by those taken up with it that they will sacrifice their own ultimate interests in order to win it." Lon L. Fuller, *Anatomy of the Law* 128 (1968).

2. (*usu. pl.*) Dealings conducted between two or more parties for the purpose of reaching an understanding. **3.** At common law, the transfer of an instrument by delivery or indorsement whereby the transferee takes it for value, in good faith, and without notice of conflicting title claims or defenses. See HOLDER IN DUE COURSE. **4.** The transfer of possession of an instrument, whether voluntary or involuntary, by a person other than the issuer to a person who thereby becomes its holder. • Transfer of possession may be involuntary (as through theft), and the transferee does not have to meet any additional due-course requirements. UCC § 3-201(a). — **negotiate,** *vb.* — **negotiable,** *adj.* — **negotiability,** *n.*

▸ **due negotiation.** The transfer of a negotiable document of title so that the transferee takes it free of certain claims enforceable against the transferor. • This is the good-faith-purchase exception to the doctrine of derivative title. UCC §§ 7-501(a)(5); 7-502(a).

negotiation letter of credit. See LETTER OF CREDIT.

negotiator, *n.* (17c) **1.** Someone who takes part in discussions aimed at reaching an agreement, esp. in business or politics. **2.** One who transfers an instrument such as a bill of exchange by delivery or indorsement.

negotiorum gestio (ni-goh-shee-**or**-əm **jes**-chee-oh), *n.* [Latin "management of another's affairs"] (1830) *Roman & civil law.* A quasi-contractual situation in which an actor (*negotiorum gestor*) manages or interferes in the business transaction of another person (*dominus negotii*) in that person's absence, without authority but out of concern or friendship. La. Civ. Code art. 2292. • By such conduct, the actor is bound to conduct the matter to a conclusion and to deliver the transaction's proceeds to the person, who likewise must reimburse the actor for any expenses incurred. La. Civ. Code art. 2297. A *negotiorum gestio* does not exist if the *gestor* acted self-interestedly or if the owner expressly forbade the *gestor* from acting on the owner's behalf. See *actio negotiorum gestorum* under ACTIO.

> "The *negotiorum gestio,* according to the civilians, is a species of spontaneous agency, or an interference by one in the affairs of another, in his absence, from benevolence or friendship, and without authority. The *negotiorum gestor* acquires no right of property by means of the interference, and he is strictly bound not only to good faith, but to ordinary care and diligence; and in some cases he is held responsible for the slightest neglect." 2 James Kent, *Commentaries on American Law* *616 n.(c) (George Comstock ed., 11th ed. 1866).

negotiorum gestor (ni-goh-shee-**or**-əm **jes**-tor), *n.* [Latin "a manager of another's affairs"] (17c) *Roman & civil law.* Someone who acts without authority to protect another person's interests, in the reasonable belief that the owner would approve the action if made aware of the circumstances. La. Civ. Code art. 2292. • The actor has a claim to be compensated by the owner for the trouble taken, and the owner has a claim for any loss that results from the *negotiorum gestor*'s fault. — Sometimes shortened to *gestor.* See NEGOTIORUM GESTIO. Pl. ***negotiorum gestores.***

negotium (ni-**goh**-shee-əm), *n.* [Latin] *Roman law.* **1.** A matter; an affair, as in *negotium absentis*, a matter concerning an absent person. **2.** A transaction; an agreement. **3.** A trade; a business. **4.** A civil or criminal trial. Pl. ***negotia.***

NEH. *abbr.* NATIONAL ENDOWMENT FOR THE HUMANITIES.

n.e.i. *abbr.* NON EST INVENTUS.

neife (neef), *n.* [Law French] (16c) *Hist.* A person born into bondage or serfdom; specif., a female serf. — Also spelled *naif; neif; niefe.*

> "For the children of villeins were also in the same state of bondage with their parents; whence they were called in Latin, *nativi*, which gave rise to the female appellation of a villein, who was called a *neife*." 2 William Blackstone, *Commentaries on the Laws of England* 93–94 (1766).

neighbor, *n.* (bef. 12c) **1.** Someone who lives near another <Jensen's neighbor spotted the fire>. **2.** A person or thing situated near something <Canada is the United States' neighbor to the north>. **3.** A person in relation to humankind <love thy neighbor>.

neighborhood. (15c) **1.** The immediate vicinity; the area near or next to a specified place. **2.** People living in a particular vicinity, usu. forming a community within a larger group and having similar economic statuses and social interests. **3.** The condition of being close together.

neighborhood effect. See EXTERNALITY.

neighborhood watch. (1972) A system organized by those who dwell in a discrete area of a city or town whereby members of the group routinely watch each other's houses so as to help prevent crime.

neighboring right. (*usu. pl.*) (1967) *Copyright.* An intellectual-property right of a performer or of an entrepreneur such as a publisher, broadcaster, or producer, as distinguished from a moral right belonging to an author or artist as the work's creator. • In civil-law systems, neighboring rights and moral rights are typically protected by different laws, while in common-law systems both are typically protected by the same copyright laws. — Also termed *related right*; *entrepreneurial right*; (in French) *droit voisins*; (in German) *Leistungsschutzrecht*; (in Italian) *diritto connessi*. Cf. MORAL RIGHT.

> "Civil law countries have generally, but not consistently, consigned protection of collaborative technological productions to regimes of neighboring rights. Common law countries, with their utilitarian emphasis on the products rather than the processes of creative work, have generally, but not consistently, included these productions in the subject matter of copyright, alongside such traditional objects as novels and musical works." Paul Goldstein, *International Copyright: Principles, Law, and Practice* 157 (2001).

neighbor principle. (1963) The doctrine that one must take reasonable care to avoid acts or omissions that one can reasonably foresee will be likely to injure one's neighbor. • According to this principle, *neighbor* includes all persons who are so closely and directly affected by the act that the actor should reasonably think of them when engaging in the act or omission in question.

ne injuste vexes (nee in-**jəs**-tee **vek**-seez), *n.* [Law Latin "do not trouble unjustly"] (16c) *Hist.* A writ prohibiting a lord from demanding more services from a tenant than the tenure allowed.

> "The writ of *ne injuste vexes* . . . which prohibits distresses for greater services than are really due to the lord; being itself of the prohibitory kind, and yet in the nature of a writ of right. It lies, where the tenant in fee-simple and his ancestors have held of the lord by certain services; and the lord hath obtained seisin of more or greater services, by the inadvertent payment or performance of them by the tenant himself. Here the tenant cannot . . . avoid the lord's possessory right, because of the seisin given by his own hands; but is driven to this writ, to devest the lord's possession, and establish the mere right of property, by ascertaining the services, and reducing them to their proper standard." 3 William Blackstone, *Commentaries on the Laws of England* 234 (1768).

neither party. A docket entry reflecting the parties' agreement not to continue to appear to prosecute and defend a lawsuit. • This entry is equivalent to a dismissal.

Nelson Act. See BANKRUPTCY ACT.

ne luminibus officiatur (nee loo-**min**-i-bəs ə-fish-ee-**ay**-tər). [Latin "that lights be not impeded"] (18c) *Roman law.* An urban praedial servitude restraining a homeowner from constructing anything that blocks light to an adjoining house.

nem. con. *abbr.* NEMINE CONTRADICENTE.

nem. dis. *abbr.* NEMINE DISSENTIENTE.

nemine contradicente (**nem**-i-nee kon-trə-di-**sen**-tee). [fr. Latin *nemo* "nobody" + *contradicere* "contradict"] Without opposition or dissent. • This phrase expresses the lack of opposition by members of a court, legislative body, or other group to a resolution or vote <the motion passed *nemine contradicente*>. It is used in the British House of Commons. — Abbr. *nem. con.*; *n.c.d.* — Also termed *nemine dissentiente*. Cf. NEMINE DISSENTIENTE.

nemine dissentiente (**nem**-i-nee di-sen-shee-**en**-tee). [fr. Latin *nemo* "nobody" + *dissentio* "dissents"] Without opposition or dissent; NEMINE CONTRADICENTE. • This phrase is used in the British House of Lords. — Abbr. *nem dis.*; *n.d.* Cf. NEMINE CONTRADICENTE.

nemo (**nee**-moh), *n.* [Latin] No one; no man. • This term is the first word of many Latin maxims, such as *nemo est supra leges* ("no one is above the law").

ne mutuato amore invicem spoliarentur (nee myoo-choo-**ay**-toh ə-**mor**-ee in-**VI**-səm spoh-lee-ə-**ren**-tər). [Latin] See NE CONJUGES MUTUO AMORE SE INVICEM SPOLIENT.

neocolonialism. See COLONIALISM (1).

neonatal (nee-oh-**nayt**-əl), *adj.* (1902) Of, relating to, or involving the first four weeks of life. Cf. PERINATAL. — **neonate** (**nee**-oh-nayt *or* **nee**-ə-nayt), *n.*

neonaticide. See INFANTICIDE (1).

neonatology (nee-oh-nay-**tol**-ə-jee *or* nee-ə-nə-**tol**-ə-jee), *n.* (1960) The branch of medicine dealing with the development of newborn children, as well as various disorders of early infancy. — **neonatological** (nee-oh-nay-tə-**loj**-i-kəl *or* nee-ə-), *adj.* — **neonatologist** (nee-oh-nay-**tol**-ə-jist *or* nee-ə-nə-**tol**-ə-jist), *n.*

NEPA (**nee**-pə). *abbr.* NATIONAL ENVIRONMENTAL POLICY ACT.

nephew. (14c) **1.** The son of a person's brother or sister; sometimes understood to include the son of a person's brother-in-law or sister-in-law. • This term is extended in some wills to include a grandnephew. Cf. NIECE.

▸ **half nephew.** (1824) The son of one's half brother or half sister.

2. *Hist.* A grandchild. **3.** *Hist.* A descendant.

> "[*N*]*ephew* . . . a son's or daughter's son, a grandson (also . . . a granddaughter), later also a brother's or sister's son, a nephew, in general a descendant . . . . The application, as with all other terms denoting relationship beyond the first degree, formerly varied ('grandson,' 'nephew,' 'cousin,' 'kinsman,' etc.); its final exclusive use for 'nephew' instead of 'grandson' is prob. due in part to the fact that, by reason of the great difference in age, a person has comparatively little to do with his grandsons, if he has any, while nephews are proverbially present and attentive, if their uncle is of any importance." 5 *The Century Dictionary and Cyclopedia* 3968 (1895).

nepos (**nep**-ohs), *n.* [Latin] (16c) **1.** *Roman law.* A grandson. **2.** *Hist.* A nephew. • The term *nepos* later became *neveu* and then "nephew." See NEPHEW.

nepotism (**nep**-ə-tiz-əm), *n.* (17c) Bestowal of official favors on one's relatives, esp. in hiring; specif., the practice of unfairly giving the best jobs to members of one's family when one is in a position of power. Cf. CRONYISM. — **nepotistic** (nep-ə-**tis**-tik), *adj.*

neptis (**nep**-tis), *n.* [Latin] *Hist.* **1.** A granddaughter. **2.** A female descendant.

ne relessa pas (nə rə-**les**-ə **pah**), *n.* [Law French "did not release"] A plaintiff's reply to a defendant's plea of release as a defense to liability in a case.

nerve-center test. (1961) A method courts sometimes use to determine the location of a company's principal place of business by examining where the company's central decision-making authority lies. • Factors include the locations where the corporate officers, directors, and (sometimes) shareholders reside, and where they direct and control the corporation's activities.

NESDIS. *abbr.* National Environmental Satellite, Data, and Information Service. See NATIONAL OCEANIC AND ATMOSPHERIC ADMINISTRATION.

net, *n.* (15c) **1.** An amount of money remaining after a sale, minus any deductions for expenses, commissions, and taxes. **2.** The gain or loss from a sale of stock. **3.** See *net weight* under WEIGHT (1).

net assets. See *net worth* under WORTH (3).

net asset value. (1957) The market value of a share in a mutual fund, computed by deducting any liabilities of the fund from its total assets and dividing the difference by the number of outstanding fund shares. — Abbr. NAV. — Also termed *asset value.* See MUTUAL FUND.

net balance. See *net proceeds* under PROCEEDS.

net book cost. See COST (1).

net book value. See OWNERS' EQUITY.

net-capital rules. (1957) *Securities.* Basic financial-responsibility standards adopted by the Securities and Exchange Commission under the Securities Exchange Act of 1934. • Under these rules, securities brokers are required to maintain a minimum level of capitalization and to maintain aggregate indebtedness at a level less than a specified multiple of the broker's net capital. 15 USCA § 78o(c)(3); SEC Rule 15c3-1 (17 CFR § 240.15c3-1.

net cash flow. See CASH FLOW.

net cost. See COST (1).

net earnings. See *net income* under INCOME.

net estate. See *net probate estate* under PROBATE ESTATE.

net gain. See GAIN (3).

nether house of Parliament. (16c) *Hist.* The lower house of Parliament; the English House of Commons. • This name was given to the House of Commons at the time of Henry VIII.

net income. See INCOME.

net investment. See INVESTMENT (1).

net lease. See LEASE.

net level annual premium. See PREMIUM (1).

net listing. See LISTING (1).

net loss. See LOSS.

net margin. See *net profit margin* under PROFIT MARGIN.

net national product. (1937) The total value of goods and services produced in a country during a specific period, after deducting capital replacement costs.

net-net-net lease. See LEASE.

net operating asset. See ASSET.

net operating income. See INCOME.

net operating loss. See LOSS.

net position. **1.** The difference between long and short contracts held by a securities or commodities trader. **2.** The amount gained or lost because of a change in the value of a stock or commodity.

net premium. See PREMIUM (1).

net present value. See PRESENT VALUE.

net price. See PRICE.

net probate estate. See PROBATE ESTATE.

net proceeds. See PROCEEDS.

net profit. See PROFIT (1).

net profit margin. See PROFIT MARGIN.

net-profits interest. (1938) *Oil & gas.* A share of production free of the costs of production. • Like a royalty, the interest is expressed as a fraction or a percentage of production. But unlike a royalty, it is payable only if there is a net profit, and the costs that are used to calculate the net profit depend on what is negotiated. — Abbr. NPI.

net quick assets. **1.** See ASSET. **2.** See QUICK-ASSET RATIO.

net realizable value. (1930) **1.** For a receivable, the amount of cash expected from the collection of present customer balances. **2.** For inventory, the selling price less the completion and disposal costs. **3.** An accounting method requiring the value of scrap or by-products to be treated as a reduction in the cost of the primary products. — Abbr. NRV.

net rent. See RENT (1).

net rental. See RENTAL (1).

net return. See RETURN.

net revenue. See *net profit* under PROFIT (1).

net sale. See SALE.

net sale contract. See *net listing* under LISTING (1).

net single premium. See PREMIUM (1).

netspionage. [fr. (Inter)net + espionage] (1999) *Slang.* Spying that is enabled by and carried out through computer networks, esp. for the purpose of appropriating or misappropriating data.

net tangible worth. See WORTH (3).

net tonnage. See TONNAGE (1).

net valuation premium. See *net premium* under PREMIUM (1).

net value. See VALUE (2).

net weight. See WEIGHT (1).

network element. *Telecommunications.* A facility or piece of equipment used to provide telecommunications service, as by a local-exchange network, and each feature, function, or capability of the service. 47 USCA § 153(29).

net worth. See WORTH (3).

net-worth method. (1948) The procedure the Internal Revenue Service uses to determine the taxable income of a taxpayer who does not keep adequate records. • The change in net worth for the year determines the taxpayer's gross income, after taking into account nontaxable receipts and nondeductible expenses.

net yield. See YIELD.

ne unques (nee **əng**-kweez). [Law French] Never.

ne unques accouple (nee **əng**-kweez ə-**kəp**-əl), *n.* [Law French "never married"] In a dower action by a widow to recover the estate of her deceased husband, a tenant's plea denying the woman's marriage to the decedent. — Also termed *ne unques accouple en loiall matrimonies.* See DOWER.

ne unques executor (nee **əng**-kweez ig-**zek**-yə-tər), *n.* [Law French "never executor"] A plea that the defendant or plaintiff is not an executor as alleged.

ne unques seise que dower (nee əng-kweez see-zee kə dow-ər), *n.* [Law French "never seised of a dowable estate"] *Hist.* In a dower action, the tenant's general denial (plea of general issue) that the widow's husband was never seised of a dowable estate of inheritance.

ne unques son receiver (nee əng-kweez sawn ri-see-vər), *n.* [Law French "never a receiver"] In an action for an accounting, the defendant's plea denying the receipt of anything from the plaintiff. — Also termed *ne unques receivour.*

ne urbs ruinis deformetur (nee ərbz roo-ɪ-nis di-for-mə-tər). [Latin] *Scots law.* Lest the city should be disfigured by ruinous houses. • The phrase appeared in reference to the jurisdiction of the Dean of Guild, who presided over construction projects, to order repairs to or demolition of unsafe buildings.

neutral, *adj.* (15c) **1.** Not supporting any of the people or groups involved in an argument or disagreement; indifferent to the outcome of a dispute. **2.** (Of a judge, mediator, arbitrator, or actor) refraining from taking sides in a dispute; impartial; unbiased. **3.** (Of a policy, interpretation, language, etc.) not inherently favoring any particular faction or point of view; couched so as not to express a predisposition or preference. • The term frequently applies to statutes that regulate or restrict speech.

▸ **content-neutral.** (1965) (Of a regulation or discrimination) applicable to all speech, regardless of viewpoint and subject matter. See TIME-PLACE-OR-MANNER RESTRICTION. Cf. *subject-matter-neutral*; *viewpoint-neutral.*

▸ **subject-matter-neutral.** (1985) (Of a regulation or discrimination) not based on the topic or subject of speech. See TIME-PLACE-OR-MANNER RESTRICTION. Cf. *content-neutral*; *viewpoint-neutral.*

▸ **viewpoint-neutral.** (1978) (Of a regulation or discrimination) not based on a point of view or an ideology. • Viewpoint neutrality was first addressed in *Rosenberger v. Visitors of Univ. of Va.*, 515 U.S. 819, 115 S.Ct. 2510 (1989). See TIME-PLACE-OR-MANNER RESTRICTION. Cf. *content-neutral*; *subject-matter-neutral.*

neutral, *n.* (15c) **1.** A person or country taking no side in a dispute; esp., a country that is at peace and is committed to aid neither of two or more belligerents. Cf. BELLIGERENT, *n.*

> "The rights of neutrals have grown up to be an important part of international law in modern times. . . . Now, when a war arises between two states, the interests of all neutrals are more affected than formerly; or, in other words, neutral power has increased more than war power, and the tendency is more and more towards such alterations of the code of war as will favor neutral commerce . . . ." Theodore D. Woolsey, *Introduction to the Study of International Law* § 163, at 276 (5th ed. 1878).

2. A nonpartisan arbitrator typically selected by two other arbitrators — one of whom has been selected by each side in the dispute.

neutral forum. See FORUM.

neutralism, *n.* (16c) Any doctrine favoring neutrality, esp. in international matters. — **neutralist,** *n.*

neutrality, *n.* (15c) **1.** The quality, state, or condition of being impartial or unbiased. **2.** The condition of a country that in time of war takes no part in the dispute but continues peaceful dealings with the belligerents. — **neutral,** *adj.*

▸ **armed neutrality.** (18c) A condition of neutrality that the neutral state is willing to maintain by military force.

neutrality law. (1838) *Int'l law.* An act that prohibits a country from militarily aiding either of two or more belligerent powers with which the country is at peace; esp., a federal statute forbidding acts — such as the equipping of armed vessels or the enlisting of troops — designed to assist either of two belligerents that are at peace with the United States. 22 USCA §§ 441–457.

neutrality proclamation. (1877) *Int'l law.* At the outbreak of a war between two countries, an announcement by the President that the United States is neutral and that its citizens may not violate the neutrality laws, as in the Neutrality Proclamation of 1793, issued during the war between France and Great Britain.

neutralization. (1817) **1.** The act of making something ineffective. **2.** *Int'l law.* The process by which a country's integrity has been permanently guaranteed by international treaty, conditionally on its maintaining a perpetual neutrality except in its own defense. • Switzerland is the only remaining example, having been neutralized by the Treaty of Vienna in 1815 — a provision reaffirmed by the Treaty of Versailles in 1919. **3.** The act of declaring certain persons or property neutral and safe from capture. See NEUTRAL PROPERTY. **4.** *Evidence.* The cancellation of unexpected harmful testimony from a witness by showing, usu. by cross-examination, that the witness has made conflicting statements. • For example, a prosecutor may attempt to neutralize testimony of a state witness who offers unexpected adverse testimony. See IMPEACHMENT (2).

neutral principles. (1959) *Constitutional law.* Rules grounded in law, as opposed to rules based on personal interests or beliefs. • In this context, the phrase was popularized by Herbert Wechsler. See *Toward Neutral Principles of Constitutional Law*, 73 Harv. L. Rev. 1 (1959).

neutral property. (18c) Things belonging to citizens of a country that is not a party to a war, as long as the things are properly used and labeled. • For example, harmless neutral property aboard a captured belligerent ship would not normally be subject to seizure. But the hiding of explosives in otherwise neutral property could allow the property to be seized as contraband.

neutral reportage. (1977) The accurate and disinterested reporting of serious charges made by a responsible, prominent organization against a public figure.

neutral-reportage defense. See NEUTRAL-REPORTAGE PRIVILEGE.

neutral-reportage privilege. (1977) The protection extended to impartial and accurate news reporting of false accusations made against public figures. • The privilege, first developed in the 1970s, is usu. invoked as a defense against charges of libel. It is accepted in the U.K. but generally not in the U.S. — Also termed *neutral-reportage defense.* Cf. WIRE-SERVICE DEFENSE.

neutron-activation analysis. (1951) A method of identifying and analyzing physical evidence by measuring gamma rays emitted by a sample of material after that material has been bombarded with neutrons in a nuclear reactor. • This technique can be used, for example, to detect gunshot residue on the hand of someone who recently fired a gun. The analysis is usu. expensive to perform, but most courts allow the results into evidence. — Abbr. NAA.

Nevada trust. See *asset-protection trust* (1) under TRUST (3).

ne varietur (nee vair-ee-**ee**-tər), *n.* [Latin "it must not be altered"] (1807) A notation of identity that a person, usu. a notary, places on documents or translations of documents. • In Louisiana, this notation is typically placed on a collateral mortgage note to bind and identify the note with the collateral mortgage.

never indebted, plea of. (1880) A common-law traverse — or denial — by which the defendant in an action on a contract debt denies that an express or implied contract existed. — Also termed *non debit.* See TRAVERSE.

new, *adj.* (bef. 12c) **1.** (Of a person, animal or thing) recently come into being <the new car was shipped from the factory this morning>. **2.** (Of any thing) recently discovered <a new cure for cancer>. **3.** (Of a person or condition) changed from the former state <she has a new state of mind>. **4.** Unfamiliar; unaccustomed <she asked for directions because she was new to the area>. **5.** Beginning afresh <a new day in court>.

new acquisition. See ACQUISITION.

new and useful. *Patents.* Both novel and having practical utility. • This phrase expresses two of the requirements for an invention to be patentable. 35 USCA § 101. See PATENT (3).

new asset. See ASSET.

new assignment. See ASSIGNMENT (7).

newborn-kidnapping by cesarean section. See *kidnapping by cesarean* under KIDNAPPING.

new business. See BUSINESS (5).

new-business rule. (1964) The principle precluding an award of damages for lost profits to a business with no recent record of profitability, because the damages would be too speculative.

new cause of action. See CAUSE OF ACTION (2).

new-contract dispute. See *major dispute* under DISPUTE.

new court commitment. See COMMITMENT.

new debtor. See DEBTOR.

new-debtor syndrome. (1981) Conduct showing a debtor's bad faith in filing for bankruptcy, as a result of which the court may dismiss the bankruptcy petition. • An example is the debtor's formation of a corporation, immediately before the bankruptcy filing, solely to take advantage of the bankruptcy laws.

new drug. See DRUG.

new-for-old. 1. *Marine insurance.* In adjusting a partial marine-insurance loss, the principle that old materials apply toward payment of the new, so that the old material's value is deducted from the total repair expenses, and then from that balance one-third of the cost of repairs (one-third of the new materials for the old on the balance) is deducted and charged against the insured shipowner. — Also termed *deduction for new.* **2.** The principle that a party whose property has been damaged is entitled to recover only the amount necessary to restore the property to the condition it was in before the damage, instead of acquiring a new item to replace one that was old and depreciated.

New Inn. *Hist. English law.* One of the Inns of Chancery (collegiate houses) in which law students were placed before entering the Inns of Court. • This practice continued until approximately 1650, when the buildings began to be used only by barristers and solicitors. See INN OF CHANCERY. Cf. INN OF COURT.

new issue. See ISSUE (2).

new law merchant. See LEX MERCATORIA.

new-loan fee. See MORTGAGE DISCOUNT.

newly discovered evidence. See EVIDENCE.

new matter. 1. See MATTER. **2.** *Patents.* Additional information in an amended patent application that adds to the original disclosure. • Since the new matter was reduced to practice after the application was filed, it cannot carry the same filing date. Rather, it must be included in a continuation-in-part application. — Also termed *disconformity.*

new-matter rejection. See REJECTION.

new promise. See PROMISE.

new-rule principle. (1989) *Criminal procedure.* A doctrine barring federal courts from granting habeas corpus relief to a state prisoner because of a rule, not dictated by existing precedent, announced after the prisoner's conviction and sentence became final. — Also termed *nonretroactivity principle.* See HABEAS CORPUS.

New Rules. See HILARY RULES.

new ruling. (1931) *Criminal procedure.* A Supreme Court ruling not dictated by precedent existing when the defendant's conviction became final and thus not applicable retroactively to habeas cases. • For example, when the Court in *Ford v. Wainwright,* 477 U.S. 399, 106 S.Ct. 2595 (1986), ruled that the Eighth Amendment prohibits execution of insane prisoners, this new ruling was nonretroactive because it departed so widely from prior doctrine. *Teague v. Lane,* 489 U.S. 288, 109 S.Ct. 1060 (1989). See HABEAS CORPUS.

new series. See N.S.

newsman's privilege. See *journalist's privilege* (1) under PRIVILEGE (3).

newspaper. (17c) A publication for general circulation, usu. in sheet form, appearing at regular intervals, usu. daily or weekly, and containing matters of general public interest, such as current events.

▸ **daily newspaper.** (18c) A newspaper customarily published five to seven days every week. — Often shortened to *daily.*

▸ **legal newspaper.** (1862) A newspaper containing matters of legal interest including summaries of cases, legal advertisements, legislative or regulatory changes, and local bankruptcy notices.

▸ **newspaper of general circulation.** (1838) A newspaper that contains news and information of interest to the general public, rather than to a particular segment, that is available to the public within a certain geographic area, that is circulated mostly to paid subscribers, and that has been continuously serving the same readership area for a specified time. • Legal notices (such as class-action notices, notices of elections, and calls for bids on public-works projects) are often required by law to be published in a newspaper of general circulation.

"The phrase 'newspaper of general circulation' is a term of art in most States and does not necessarily mean the newspaper best calculated to reach interested persons." 1 Ann Taylor Schwing, *Open Meeting Laws* § 5.28, at 316 (3d ed. 2011).

▸ **official newspaper.** A newspaper designated to contain all the public notices, resolves, acts, and advertisements of a state or municipal legislative body.

newspaper prospectus. See PROSPECTUS.

new style. (17c) The modern system for ordering time according to the Gregorian method, introduced by Pope Gregory XIII in 1582 and adopted in England and the American colonies in 1752. • Because the Julian calendar year was slightly longer than the astronomical year, the vernal equinox over time had been displaced by ten days. Pope Gregory reformed the calendar by announcing that October 5, 1582 would be called October 15. And, while generally retaining a leap year for years divisible by 4, he skipped leap years in years divisible by 100 (such as 1800 and 1900), but retained leap years for years divisible by 400 (such as 2000). Thus, the years 2000, 2004, 2008, etc. are leap years, but 2100 is not. — Abbr. n.s. — Also termed *Gregorian calendar.* Cf. OLD STYLE.

new trial. See TRIAL.

new-use claim. See PATENT CLAIM.

new-use invention. See INVENTION.

new value. See VALUE (2).

new-value defense. See DEFENSE (1).

new works. See WORKS.

New York Arbitration Convention. See NEW YORK CONVENTION.

New York Convention. The Convention on the Recognition and Enforcement of Foreign Arbitral Awards, under which member states commit to enforce arbitration agreements and to recognize and enforce arbitration awards that are subject to the Convention. 10 June 1958, 21 U.S.T. 2517, 330 U.N.T.S. 38. — Also termed *New York Arbitration Convention.*

New York interest. See *Boston interest* under INTEREST (3).

New York standard clause. See MORTGAGE-LOSS CLAUSE.

New York Stock Exchange. An association of member firms that handle the purchase and sale of securities both for themselves and for customers. • This exchange, the dominant one in the United States, trades in only large companies having at least one million outstanding shares. — Abbr. NYSE.

New York Supplement. A set of regional lawbooks, part of the West Group's National Reporter System, containing every published appellate decision from intermediate and lower courts of record in New York, from 1888 to date. • The first series ran from 1888 to 1937; the second series is the current one. — Abbr. N.Y.S.; N.Y.S.2d.

***New York Times* malice.** See *actual malice* (2) under MALICE.

***New York Times* rule.** A commonsense rule of ethical conduct holding that one should not do anything arguably newsworthy — in public or in private — that one would mind having reported on the front page of a major newspaper. • In various communities, a local newspaper is substituted for the *Times.* — Also termed *New York Times test; New York Times v. Sullivan* rule. See *actual malice* (2) under MALICE.

nexi (**nek**-sɪ), *n. pl.* [Latin] *Roman law.* Debtors given in bondage to creditors until their debts have been paid. See NEXUM.

next devisee. See DEVISEE.

next eventual estate. See ESTATE (1).

next friend. (16c) Someone who appears in a lawsuit to act for the benefit of an incompetent or minor plaintiff, but who is not a party to the lawsuit and is not appointed as a guardian. — Also termed *prochein ami.* Cf. *guardian ad litem* under GUARDIAN (1).

next-in, first-out. (1949) A method of inventory valuation (but not a generally accepted accounting principle) whereby the cost of goods is based on their replacement cost rather than their actual cost. — Abbr. NIFO. Cf. FIRST-IN, FIRST-OUT; LAST-IN, FIRST-OUT.

next of kin. (18c) **1.** The person or persons most closely related to a decedent by blood or affinity. Cf. RELATIVE. **2.** An intestate's heirs — that is, the person or persons entitled to inherit personal property from a decedent who has not left a will. See HEIR.

next presentation. See PRESENTATION.

nexum (**nek**-səm), *n.* [Latin] (1886) *Roman law.* A transaction or practice of early Roman law under which a debtor, upon a failure to repay the debt, could be seized and held in bondage until the debt was repaid. • This practice was allowed in very early Roman law.

"*Nexum.* This highly controversial matter will be briefly dealt with as *nexum* had long been obsolete in classical law. Little is really known of it: it has been doubted whether there ever was such an institution. No text tells us that there was a contract called nexum . . . . But we have texts which speak of *nexum* as creative of obligation . . . and many literary texts dealing with debtors who were *nexi,* so that it may be taken as certain that there was such a transaction . . . which in some way reduced debtors to a sort of slavery, that great hardships resulted and that a *l. Poetelia* . . . practically ended this state of things, presumably by requiring an actual judgment before seizure. The effect was not to abolish *nexum,* but, by depriving it of its chief value, the power of seizure . . . to leave it with no advantages to counterbalance its clumsiness, so that it went out of use." W.W. Buckland, *A Text-book of Roman Law from Augustus to Justinian* 429–30 (Peter Stein ed., 3d ed. 1963).

nexus, *n.* (17c) **1.** A connection or link, often a causal one <cigarette packages must inform consumers of the nexus between smoking and lung cancer>. Pl. **nexuses; nexus. 2.** *Roman law.* (*ital.*) In very early times, a debtor given in bondage to creditors until the debts have been paid. See NEXUM. Pl. ***nexi.***

nexus realis (**nek**-səs ree-**ay**-lis). [Latin "a real fetter"] (18c) *Scots law.* An encumbrance to property, such as a servitude.

nexus test. (1975) The standard by which a private person's act is considered state action — and may give rise to liability for violating someone's constitutional rights — if the conduct is so closely related to the government's conduct that the choice to undertake it may fairly be said to be that of the state. • While similar to the symbiotic-relationship test, the nexus test focuses on the particular act complained of, instead of on the overall relationship of the parties. Still, some courts use the terms and analyses interchangeably. — Also termed *close-nexus test.* Cf. SYMBIOTIC-RELATIONSHIP TEST. See JOINT PARTICIPATION; STATE-COMPULSION TEST.

> "The complaining party must . . . show that there is a sufficiently close nexus between the State and the challenged action of the regulated entity so that the action of the latter may be fairly treated as that of the State itself. The purpose of this requirement is to assure that constitutional standards are invoked only when it can be said that the State is responsible for the specific conduct of which the plaintiff complains. . . . [O]ur precedents indicate that a State normally can be held responsible for a private decision only when it has exercised coercive power or has provided such significant encouragement, either overt or covert, that the choice must in law be deemed to be that of the State." *Blum v. Yaretsky*, 457 U.S. 991, 1004, 102 S.Ct. 2777, 2786 (1982).

NFA. *abbr.* NATIONAL FIREARMS ACT.

NFAH. *abbr.* NATIONAL FOUNDATION ON THE ARTS AND THE HUMANITIES.

NGO. *abbr.* (1946) NONGOVERNMENTAL ORGANIZATION.

NGRI. See *not guilty by reason of insanity* under NOT GUILTY.

NHTSA. *abbr.* NATIONAL HIGHWAY TRAFFIC SAFETY ADMINISTRATION.

NIC. *abbr.* NATIONAL INSTITUTE OF CORRECTIONS.

nichil (**nich**-əl), *n.* [Old French *nichil* fr. Latin *nihil* "nothing"] (16c) *Hist. English law.* A debt owed to the Exchequer's office but nihiled by sheriffs as nonleviable. • Once a year, an officer of the Clerk of Nichils enrolled these amounts and sent them to the treasurer's remembrancer's office from which process was issued for their recovery. Both offices were abolished in 1833. — Also spelled *nichill; nichel.*

nichil, *vb.* (17c) (Of a sheriff) to make return that a debt is worthless, because the debtor either cannot be found or is unable to pay.

Nickerson letter. (1998) In New York City, a document issued by the Board of Education offering to pay the tuition of a disabled child who has been admitted to a state-approved private school and whose educational needs cannot be met in a public school. • Nickerson letters are named for Judge Eugene P. Nickerson, who presided over the class-action suit that led to their creation. *See Jose P. v. Ambach*, 669 F.2d 865 (2d Cir. 1982); *see also Jose P. v. Ambach*, 557 F. Supp. 1230 (E.D.N.Y. 1983).

nickname, *n.* (15c) **1.** A shortened version of a person's name <"Bill" is William's nickname>. **2.** A descriptive or alternative name, in addition to or instead of the actual name <David Smith's nickname is "Red">.

niece. (14c) The daughter of a person's brother or sister; sometimes understood to include the daughter of a person's brother-in-law or sister-in-law. • This term is extended in some wills to include a grandniece. Cf. NEPHEW.

▸ **half niece.** (1824) The daughter of one's half brother or half sister.

NIED. *abbr.* NEGLIGENT INFLICTION OF EMOTIONAL DISTRESS.

nient (nee-**ent**). [Law French] Not; nothing.

nient culpable (nee-**ent kəl**-pə-bəl), *n.* [Law French] *Hist.* A general plea of "not guilty" in a tort or criminal action.

> "When the prisoner hath thus pleaded not guilty, *non culpabilis*, or *nient culpable*; which was formerly used to be abbreviated upon the minutes, thus, '*non* (or *nient*) *cul.*' the clerk of the assise, or clerk of the arraigns, on behalf of the crown replies, that the prisoner is guilty, and that he is ready to prove him so." 4 William Blackstone, *Commentaries on the Laws of England* 333 (1769).

nient dedire (nee-**ent** də-**deer**), *vb.* [Law French] *Hist.* To deny nothing; to be subject to a default judgment.

nient le fait (nee-**ent** lə **fay**). [Law French] *Hist.* Not the deed. • This term was the earlier version of *non est factum.* See NON EST FACTUM.

nient seisi (nee-**ent see**-zee), *n.* [Law French "not seised"] *Hist.* The general denial in a writ to recover an annuity.

NIFL. *abbr.* NATIONAL INSTITUTE FOR LITERACY.

NIFO (**nɪ**-foh). *abbr.* NEXT-IN, FIRST-OUT.

NIGA. *abbr.* NATIONAL INDIAN GAMING ASSOCIATION.

NIGC. *abbr.* NATIONAL INDIAN GAMING COMMISSION.

night. (bef. 12c) **1.** The time from sunset to sunrise. **2.** Darkness; the time when a person's face is not discernible. • This definition was used in the common-law definition of certain offenses, such as burglary.

> "The definition of a burglar, as given by Sir Edward Coke, is, 'he that by night breaketh and entereth into a mansion-house, with intent to commit a felony.' . . . The *time* must be by night, and not by day; for in the daytime there is no burglary . . . . As to what is reckoned night, and what day, for this purpose anciently the day was accounted to begin only at sunrising, and to end immediately upon sunset; but the better opinion seems to be, that if there be daylight . . . enough, begun or left, to discern a man's face withal, it is no burglary. But this does not extend to moonlight; for then many midnight burglaries would go unpunished: and besides, the malignity of the offence does not so properly arise from its being done in the dark, as at the dead of night when all the creation, except beasts of prey, are at rest; when sleep has disarmed the owner, and rendered his castle defenceless." 4 William Blackstone, *Commentaries on the Laws of England* 224 (1769).

3. Thirty minutes after sunset and thirty minutes before sunrise, or a similar definition as set forth by statute, as in a statute requiring specific authorization for night searches. **4.** Evening. — Also termed *nighttime.* Cf. DAY.

nightwalker. (15c) **1.** *Hist.* Someone who suspiciously wanders about at night and who might disturb the peace. • Nightwalking was an example of a "common" offense requiring no specific facts to be asserted in the indictment. **2.** A prostitute who walks the streets at night; streetwalker. **3.** A sleepwalker.

nihil. See NIHIL EST.

nihil ad rem (**nɪ**-hil ad **rem**). [Latin] Not to the point.

nihil capiat per breve (**nɪ**-hil **kap**-ee-ət pər **bree**-vee *or* breev), *n.* [Latin "Let him take nothing by his writ"] (17c) A judgment against the plaintiff in an action at bar or in abatement. — Also termed *nihil capiat per billam* ("let him take nothing by his bill").

nihil dicit (**nɪ**-hil **dɪ**-sit), *n.* [Latin "he says nothing"] (16c) **1.** The failure of a defendant to answer a lawsuit. **2.** See *nil dicit default judgment* under DEFAULT JUDGMENT.

***nihil dicit* default judgment.** See *nil dicit default judgment* under DEFAULT JUDGMENT.

nihil est (**nɪ**-hil est). [Latin "there is nothing"] A form of return by a sheriff or constable who was unable to serve a writ because nothing was found to levy on. — Often shortened to *nihil.* Cf. NULLA BONA.

nihil habet (**nɪ**-hil **hay**-bət). [Latin "he has nothing"] A form of return by a sheriff or constable who was unable to serve a scire facias or other writ on the defendant. See SCIRE FACIAS.

nihilism (**nɪ**-əl-iz-əm *or* **nee**-). (1812) **1.** A doctrine maintaining that there is no rational justification for moral principles and that there is no objective truth. **2.** The view that traditional beliefs are unfounded and that life is meaningless and useless. **3.** A theory that the existing economic, social, or political institutions should be destroyed, regardless of the result, because of the basic undesirability of those institutions. • This theory, featured by Ivan Turgenev in his 1861 novel *Fathers and Sons,* was popular among Russian extremists until the collapse of the czarist government.

nihilist, *n.* (1854) Someone who advocates nihilism. See NIHILISM.

nihil novit (**nɪ**-hil **noh**-vit). [Law Latin] *Scots law.* He knew nothing. • The phrase appeared in reference to a defendant's oath denying any knowledge of the matter in issue.

> "[A] defender may swear that he knows nothing of the matter referred, and so obtain absolvitor; but such an answer would not avail any defender in regard to a *factum proprium.* In regard to such a matter, an answer of *nihil novit* would, in the general case, be regarded as simply an evasion, and be treated as an admission of the debt." John Trayner, *Trayner's Latin Maxims* 387 (4th ed. 1894).

nikah. *Islamic law.* A prenuptial contract, witnessed by at least two men, recording the parties' mutual agreement to marry, the husband's promise to give his wife a certain sum of money or property, and possibly other terms about the parties' rights in and expectations from the marriage. • The contract may be enforceable under general contract-law principles. — Also termed *nikah nama.* Cf. MAHR.

nil (nil). [Latin] (16c) Nothing. • This word is a contracted form of *nihil.* See NIHIL EST.

nil debet (nil **deb**-ət). [Latin "he owes nothing"] (17c) *Hist.* A general denial in a debt action on a simple contract.

> "The proper general issue in debt on simple contracts and statutes is 'nil debet,' which is a formal denial of the debt. It denies not only the existence of any contract, but under it any matters in excuse or in discharge may also be shown." Benjamin J. Shipman, *Handbook of Common-Law Pleading* § 184, at 327 (Henry Winthrop Ballantine ed., 3d ed. 1923).

***nil dicit* default judgment.** See DEFAULT JUDGMENT.

nil habuit in tenementis (nil **hab**-yoo-it in ten-ə-**men**-tis), *n.* [Law Latin "he has nothing in the tenements"] (17c) *Hist.* In an action to recover rent on a lease, the defendant's plea that the landlord has no title or interest in the property at issue.

nil ligatum (nil li-**gay**-təm). [Latin "nothing is bound"] No obligation has been incurred.

NIMA. *abbr.* NATIONAL IMAGING AND MAPPING AGENCY.

nimble dividend. See DIVIDEND.

nimmer. (14c) A petty thief; pilferer; pickpocket.

1908 Berlin Act. See BERLIN ACT.

1909 Copyright Act. See COPYRIGHT ACT OF 1909.

1971 Paris Act of the Berne Convention. See BERNE PARIS ACT.

1976 Copyright Act. See COPYRIGHT ACT OF 1976.

1933 Act. See SECURITIES ACT OF 1933.

1934 Act. See SECURITIES EXCHANGE ACT OF 1934.

Nineteenth Amendment. The constitutional amendment, ratified in 1920, providing that a citizen's right to vote cannot be denied or abridged by the United States, or by any state within it, on the basis of sex. — Also termed *Women's Suffrage Amendment.*

1928 Rome Act. See ROME ACT.

ninety-day letter. (1933) *Tax.* Statutory notice of a tax deficiency sent by the IRS to a taxpayer. • During the 90 days after receiving the notice, the taxpayer must pay the taxes (and, if desired, seek a refund) or challenge the deficiency in tax court. IRC (26 USCA) §§ 6212–6213. — Also written *ninety-day letter.* — Also termed *notice of deficiency*; *deficiency notice*; *tax-deficiency notice.* Cf. THIRTY-DAY LETTER.

NINJA loan. See LOAN.

Ninth Amendment. The constitutional amendment, ratified with the Bill of Rights in 1791, providing that rights listed in the Constitution must not be construed in a way that denies or disparages unlisted rights, which are retained by the people.

nisi (**nɪ**-sɪ), *adj.* [Latin "unless"] (18c) (Of a court's ex parte ruling or grant of relief) having validity unless the adversely affected party appears and shows cause why it should be withdrawn <a decree *nisi*>. See *decree nisi* under DECREE.

nisi aliud convenerit (**nɪ**-sɪ **ay**-lee-əd kən-**ven**-ər-it). [Latin] *Hist.* Unless it has been otherwise agreed; unless something else has been agreed to.

nisi decree. See *decree nisi* under DECREE.

nisi feceris (**nɪ**-sɪ **fee**-sə-ris), *n.* [Law Latin "unless you have done so"] *Hist.* A clause in a manorial writ providing that the king's court or officer will do justice if the lords fail. • This provision allowed royal courts to usurp the jurisdiction of manorial courts.

nisi malitia suppleat aetatem (**nɪ**-sɪ mə-**lish**-ee-ə **səp**-lee-at ee-**tay**-təm). [Latin] *Roman & Scots law.* Unless malice supplies want of age. • A child under the age of puberty was presumed to lack the necessary intent to commit a crime unless an evil intent was specifically shown.

nisi prius (**nɪ**-sɪ **prɪ**-əs). [Latin "unless before then"] (16c) A civil trial court in which, unlike in an appellate court, issues are tried before a jury. • The term is obsolete in the United States except in New York and Oklahoma. — Abbr. n.p. — Also termed *nisi prius court.*

nisi prius clause. (1823) An entry to the record authorizing a jury trial in the designated county. See NISI PRIUS.

nisi prius court. See NISI PRIUS.

nisi prius record. (1804) A civil-trial record. See RECORD (4).

nisi prius roll. (18c) The transcript of a case at nisi prius. — Also termed *nisi prius record.*

NIST. *abbr.* National Institute of Standards and Technology. See TECHNOLOGY ADMINISTRATION.

nitroglycerine charge. See ALLEN CHARGE.

nixie. [fr. German *nichts* "nothing"] (1890) **1.** A piece of mail that cannot be delivered, usu. because the addressee is fictitious or the address is incorrect. **2.** *Hist.* An undeliverable piece of mail created by a postal inspector for the purpose of discovering interference with mail processing and delivery. — Also termed *nix*; *nixey*.

n.l. *abbr.* NON LIQUET.

NLG. *abbr.* NATIONAL LAWYERS GUILD.

NLRA. *abbr.* NATIONAL LABOR RELATIONS ACT.

NLRB. *abbr.* NATIONAL LABOR RELATIONS BOARD.

NMB. *abbr.* NATIONAL MEDIATION BOARD.

NMFS. *abbr.* NATIONAL MARINE FISHERIES SERVICE.

NMI. *abbr.* No middle initial.

NMN. *abbr.* No middle name.

NOA. *abbr. Slang.* **1.** No oral argument. • This notation is used esp. in an appellate case in which oral argument is not granted <since the case was NOA, the court relied exclusively on the briefs>. **2.** NOTICE OF ALLOWANCE. **3.** NOTICE OF APPEAL. **4.** NOTICE OF APPEARANCE.

NOAA. *abbr.* NATIONAL OCEANIC AND ATMOSPHERIC ADMINISTRATION.

no-action clause. (1916) An insurance-policy provision that bars suit against the insurer until the liability of the insured has been determined by a judgment.

no-action letter. (1959) A letter from the staff of a governmental agency stating that if the facts are as represented in a person's request for an agency ruling, the staff will advise the agency not to take action against the person. • Typically, a no-action letter is requested from the SEC on such matters as shareholder proposals, resales of stock, and marketing techniques.

no actus reus (noh **ak**-təs **ree**-əs). (1964) A plea in which a criminal defendant either denies involvement with a crime or asserts that the harm suffered is too remote from the criminal act to be imputable to the defendant.

no-adverse-inference instruction. See JURY INSTRUCTION.

no-answer default judgment. See DEFAULT JUDGMENT.

no arrival, no sale. (1875) A delivery term, included in some sales contracts, by which the seller assumes the duty to deliver the goods to a specified place, and assumes the risk of loss for the goods while they are in transit. • If the goods arrive damaged or late, the buyer can either avoid the contract or accept the goods at a discount.

no-asset case. *Bankruptcy.* A Chapter 7 case in which no assets are available to satisfy any part of the creditors' unsecured claims.

no award. In an action to enforce an award, the defendant's plea denying that an award was made.

nobile officium (**noh**-bə-lee ə-**fish**-ee-əm), *n.* [Latin "noble office or privilege"] (17c) *Scots law.* The power of a superior court, the Court of Session, or the High Court to give equitable relief when none is possible under law. Cf. EX NOBILI OFFICIO.

nobility, *n. pl.* (14c) **1.** Persons of social or political preeminence, usu. derived by inheritance or from the sovereign. • In English law, there are various degrees of nobility, or peerage, such as dukes, marquises, earls, viscounts, and barons, and their female counterparts. Nobility is generally created either by a writ of summons to sit in Parliament or by a royal grant through letters patent, and was once usu. accompanied by a large land grant. Nobility by writ descended to a person's bodily heirs. The modern practice is to grant nobility by letters patent, which provide limitations as to future heirs. The U.S. Constitution prohibits granting a title of nobility. U.S. Const. art. I, § 9, cl. 8.

> "In England nobility is apt to be confounded with the peculiar institution of the British peerage. Yet nobility, in some shape or another, has existed in most places and times or the world's history, while the British peerage is an institution purely local, and one which has actually hindered the existence of a nobility in the sense which the word bears in most other countries. . . . . Nobility, then, in the strict sense of the word, is the hereditary handing on from generation to generation of some acknowledged pre-eminence, a pre-eminence founded on hereditary succession, and on nothing else. . . . . The pre-eminence so handed on may be of any kind, from substantial political power to mere social respect and precedence." 17 *Encyclopaedia Britannica* 538 (9th ed. 1907).

2. Persons of high or noble character. **3.** The collective body of persons making up the noble class.

no bill, *n.* (18c) A grand jury's notation that insufficient evidence exists for an indictment on a criminal charge <the grand jury returned a no bill instead of the indictment the prosecutors expected>. <the grand jury no-billed three of the charges>. Cf. TRUE BILL. — **no-bill,** *vb.*

noblesse (noh-**bles**), *n.* [French "nobility"] (15c) Collectively, the titled nobles of a foreign country.

noblesse oblige (noh-**bles** ə-**bleezh**), *n.* [French "the duty of nobility"] (1837) The responsibility of a society's privileged class toward those less privileged. • Privilege is traditionally thought to entail responsibility.

no-bonus clause. *Landlord–tenant law.* A lease provision that takes effect upon governmental condemnation, limiting the lessee's damages to the value of any improvements to the property and preventing the lessee from recovering the difference between the lease's fixed rent and the property's market rental value. See CONDEMNATION.

NOC. *abbr.* NOTICE OF COMPLETION.

no case to answer. (1886) *English law.* The prosecution's or plaintiff's failure to adduce sufficient evidence to prove a case. • The defense may assert "no case to answer" when the prosecution or plaintiff rests its case. See HALF-TIME SUBMISSION.

no cause of action. See *take-nothing judgment* under JUDGMENT (2).

nocent (**noh**-sənt), *adj.* [fr. Latin *nocere* "harm"] *Archaic.* (15c) **1.** Injurious; harmful. **2.** Guilty; criminal. • This word is the little-used antonym of *innocent*.

nocent (**noh**-sənt), *n.* [fr. Latin *nocere* "harm"] (15c) *Hist.* Someone who is guilty.

no-claim, *n.* (1921) The lack of a claim. • Legal philosophers devised this term to denote the opposite of a claim. As one jurisprudent has said apologetically, "there is no word in English which expresses the lack of a claim and therefore the rather barbarous 'no-claim' has been suggested." George Whitecross Paton, *A Textbook of Jurisprudence* 291 (G.W. Paton & David P. Derham eds., 4th ed. 1972).

no-confidence vote. (1840) The formal legal method by which a legislative body, by a majority vote, forces the resignation of a cabinet or ministry. — Also termed *vote of no confidence*.

no-constitutional-doubt canon. See CONSTITUTIONAL-DOUBT CANON.

no-contact order. See STAY-AWAY ORDER.

no contest. (1931) A criminal defendant's plea that, while not admitting guilt, the defendant will not dispute the charge. • This plea is often preferable to a guilty plea, which can be used against the defendant in a later civil lawsuit. — Also termed *no-contest plea; nolo contendere; non vult contendere.*

no-contest clause. (1929) A provision designed to threaten one into action or inaction; esp., a testamentary provision that threatens to dispossess any beneficiary who challenges the terms of the will. — Also termed *in terrorem clause; noncontest clause; terrorem clause; anticontest clause; forfeiture clause.*

noctanter (nok-**tan**-tər), *n.* [Latin "by night"] *Hist.* A chancery writ issued to a sheriff as a first step in the recovery of damages for destroying a ditch or hedge. • The neighboring villagers (vills) were held liable for the damages unless they indicted the offender.

noctem de firma (**nok**-təm dee **fər**-mə), *n.* [Law Latin "night of duty (payable)"] (17c) *Hist.* The duty or custom of providing entertainment or provisions for a night. • At the time of the Norman Conquest, this was the duty or custom of entertaining the king for one night. — Also termed *noctes; firma noctis.*

nocumentum (nok-yə-**men**-təm). [fr. Latin *nocere* "to harm"] *Hist.* A nuisance. • There was no remedy at law for a nuisance causing only property damage, but there was a remedy for a nuisance causing injury.

no cure, no pay. (1846) *Maritime law.* The common-law principle that compensation for salvage must come from the material salvaged, and that if no material is salvaged there can be no compensation. • By contrast, civil-law tradition awards compensation even for a failed effort. Cf. ASSISTANCE.

no-doc loan. See LOAN.

no-duty, *n.* (1919) Liberty not to do an act. — Also termed *liberty not.*

no-duty doctrine. (1966) *Torts.* **1.** The rule that a defendant who owes no duty to the plaintiff is not liable for the plaintiff's injury. **2.** The rule that the owner or possessor of property has no duty to warn or protect an invitee from known or obvious hazards.

***Noerr–Pennington* doctrine.** (1967) The principle that the First Amendment shields from liability (esp. under antitrust laws) companies that join together to lobby the government. • The doctrine derives from a line of Supreme Court cases beginning with *Eastern R.R. Presidents Conference v. Noerr Motor Freight, Inc.*, 365 U.S. 127, 81 S.Ct. 523 (1961), and *United Mine Workers v. Pennington*, 381 U.S. 657, 85 S.Ct. 1585 (1965).

no evidence. (15c) **1.** The lack of a legally sufficient evidentiary basis for a reasonable fact-finder to rule in favor of the party who bears the burden of proof <there is no evidence in the record about his whereabouts at midnight>. • Under the Federal Rules of Civil Procedure, a party can move for judgment as a matter of law to claim that the other party — who bears the burden of proof — has been fully heard and has not offered sufficient evidence to prove one or more essential elements of the suit or defense. Fed. R. Civ. P. 50. Though such a contention is usu. referred to as a no-evidence motion, the issue is not whether there was actually no evidence, but rather whether the evidence was sufficient for the fact-finder to be able to reasonably rule in favor of the other party.

> "Since judgment as a matter of law deprives the party opposing the motion of a determination of the facts by a jury, it should be granted cautiously and sparingly. Nevertheless, the federal courts do not follow the rule that a scintilla of evidence is enough to create an issue for the jury. The question is not whether there is literally no evidence upon which the jury properly could find a verdict for that party." 9A Charles Alan Wright & Arthur Miller, *Federal Practice and Procedure* § 2524, at 252–54 (2d ed. 1995).

2. Evidence that has no value in an attempt to prove a matter in issue <that testimony is no evidence of an alibi>.

no-eyewitness rule. (1956) *Torts.* The largely defunct principle that if no direct evidence shows what a dead person did to avoid an accident, the jury may infer that the person acted with ordinary care for his or her own safety. • In a jurisdiction where the rule persists, a plaintiff in a survival or wrongful-death action can assert the rule to counter a defense of contributory negligence.

no-fault, *adj.* (1967) Of, relating to, or involving a claim that is adjudicated without any determination that a party is blameworthy <no-fault divorce>.

no-fault auto insurance. See INSURANCE.

no-fault divorce. See DIVORCE.

no funds. An indorsement marked on a check when there are insufficient funds in the account to cover the check.

no-further-representation clause. (2005) A contractual provision, usu. in a settlement agreement, prohibiting the plaintiff's attorney from representing future clients who have the same or a similar claim against the defendant. • Such a clause is thought to be void as against public policy.

> "If your standard settlement papers include a clause prohibiting opposing counsel from representing future clients with the same claim, you're violating ethics rules. Typically a defendant's tool, this provision — known as a no-further-representation clause — is popular in class action and mass product-liability settlements. But a little-known ethics rule prohibits lawyers from agreeing, or even offering to agree, to a restriction on an attorney's right to practice law." Leslie A. Gordon, *Prohibited Provisions: No-Further-Representation Clauses May Be Advantageous, but They're Also Unethical*, 91 ABA J. 18, 18 (Apr. 2005).

no goods. See NULLA BONA.

NOIBN. *abbr.* NOT OTHERWISE INDEXED BY NAME.

noise easement. See EASEMENT.

noisy withdrawal. A lawyer's publicly announced abandonment of legal representation coupled with a renunciation of work product and sometimes the informing of authorities about the client's wrongdoing. See WITHDRAWAL (2).

no-knock search. See SEARCH (1).

no-knock search warrant. See SEARCH WARRANT.

NOL. See *net operating loss* under LOSS.

Nolan Act. *Hist. Patents.* A post-World War I statute that extended the U.S. patenting deadlines for citizens of former enemy countries. • A similar measure, the Boykin Act, was passed after World War II.

no-legislative-history rule. See NO-RECOURSE RULE.

nolens volens (**noh**-lenz **voh**-lenz), *adv.* & *adj.* [Latin] (16c) Willing or unwilling <*nolens volens*, the school district must comply with the court's injunction>.

no-limit order. See ORDER (8).

nolissement (nə-lis-**mahn**), *n.* [French] *French law.* The chartering of a ship; AFFREIGHTMENT.

nolition (noh-**lish**-ən). (17c) The absence of volition; unwillingness.

nolle prosequi (**nahl**-ee **prahs**-ə-kwɪ), *n.* [Latin "not to wish to prosecute"] (17c) **1.** A legal notice that a lawsuit or prosecution has been abandoned. **2.** A docket entry showing that the plaintiff or the prosecution has abandoned the action. — Often shortened to *nolle.*

"In America the term [*nolle prosequi*] bears the same meaning as in England, with one exception. The attorney-general has not the same discretion with which English law invests him. Although in some States the prosecuting officer may enter a *nolle prosequi* at his discretion, in others the leave of the court must be obtained." 17 *Encyclopaedia Britannica* 546 (9th ed. 1907).

"Nolle prosequi is a formal entry on the record by the prosecuting officer by which he declares that he will not prosecute the case further, either as to some of the counts of the indictment, or as to part of a divisible count, or as to some of the persons accused, or altogether. It is a judicial determination in favor of accused and against his conviction, but it is not an acquittal, nor is it equivalent to a pardon." 22A C.J.S. *Criminal Law* § 419, at 1 (1989).

nolle prosequi (**nahl**-ee **prahs**-ə-kwɪ), *vb.* (1875) To abandon (a suit or prosecution); to have (a case) dismissed by a nolle prosequi <the state nolle prosequied the charges against Johnson>. — Often shortened to *nolle pros*; *nol-pros*; *nol-pro.*

no-load fund. See MUTUAL FUND.

nolo contendere (**noh**-loh kən-**ten**-də-ree). [Latin "I do not wish to contend"] (1829) NO CONTEST. — Often shortened to *nolo.*

nolo plea. See PLEA (1).

no man's land. *Labor law.* The lack of clear jurisdiction between a state government and the federal government over labor disputes. • This term was common in the 1950s, but its use has declined as later laws have clarified jurisdictional issues.

NOM clause. *abbr.* NO-ORAL-MODIFICATION CLAUSE.

nomen (**noh**-men or -mən), *n.* [Latin] (17c) **1.** *Roman law.* A personal name. • A Roman citizen generally had three names: a *praenomen* ("first name"), a *nomen* ("the name of the family group"), and *cognomen* ("a surname"). **2.** *Hist.* A person's first name. **3.** More broadly, any name. See AGNOMEN. Pl. **nomina.**

▸ ***nomen collectivum*** (**noh**-men kol-ək-**tɪ**-vəm). [Latin] (17c) A collective name; a name of a class of things.

▸ ***nomen generale*** (**noh**-men jen-ə-**ray**-lee). [Latin] (1856) A general name; a *genus.*

▸ ***nomen generalissimum*** (**noh**-men jen-ə-rə-**lis**-i-məm). [Law Latin] (1826) A name with the most general meaning.

"*Nomen generalissimum.* A very general name: a comprehensive term. Such are the terms crime, demand, draft, estate, goods, grant, heir, house, instrument, interest, land, merchandise, obligation, offense." William C. Anderson, *A Dictionary of Law* 711 (1889).

▸ ***nomen juris*** (**noh**-men **joor**-is). [Latin] (17c) A legal name or designation.

▸ ***nomen universitatis*** (**noh**-men yoo-ni-vər-sə-**tay**-tis). [Latin] (17c) *Hist.* The name of the whole together.

"Thus the name Barony is, in our law, a *nomen universitatis*, for it includes not only the lands over which the rights of barony extend, but also the rights competent to the owner of the barony themselves." John Trayner, *Trayner's Latin Maxims* 390 (4th ed. 1894).

nomen transcripticium (**noh**-men tran-skrip-**tish**-ee-əm). [Latin "entry (in an account) transferred"] *Roman law.* A creditor's entry of a money debt into a new account (*expensilatio*) after closing another account, thereby creating, with the debtor's permission, a literal contract from an existing obligation, which may or may not have been enforceable. Pl. ***nomina transcripticia.***

"The subject will, perhaps, become clearer by examples: . . . A has in the past had dealings by way of sale, exchange, etc., with B, of which an account appears in his *codex* showing a balance against B for 500 *aurei*. A, with B's consent, closes this account by a statement on the opposite page (contrary to fact) that B has paid the *aurei* . . . and opens a new account with the statement (contrary to strict fact) that he has advanced to B the sum of 500 *aurei*. Hence the *expensilatio* represents a *nomen transcripticium*; a *nomen* (debt) has been transferred from one account to another . . . . In effect the old contracts between A and B have been novated, i.e. extinguished, one single obligation having been substituted in their place; obviously a course which offered many advantages to both parties, as it simplified the accounts, and saved disputes about the previous transactions." R.W. Leage, *Roman Private Law* 317–18 (C.H. Ziegler ed., 2d ed. 1930).

no-merit brief. See *Anders brief* under BRIEF (1).

nomina debitorum (**nahm**-ə-nə deb-i-**tor**-əm). [Latin "entries (in a ledger) of names of debtors"] (17c) *Roman law.* Records of debt. See NOMEN TRANSCRIPTICIUM.

nominal (**nahm**-ə-nəl), *adj.* (17c) **1.** Existing in name only <he was the nominal leader but had no real authority>. **2.** (Of a price or amount) trifling, esp. as compared to what would be expected <the lamp sold for a nominal price of ten cents>. **3.** Of, relating to, or involving a name or term <a nominal definition>. — **nominally,** *adv.*

nominal account. See ACCOUNT.

nominal asset. See ASSET.

nominal capital. See CAPITAL.

nominal consideration. See CONSIDERATION (1).

nominal damages. See DAMAGES.

nominal defendant. See *nominal party* under PARTY (2).

nominal director. See *dummy director* under DIRECTOR.

nominal partner. See PARTNER.

nominal party. See PARTY (2).

nominal-payee rule. (1976) *Commercial law.* The rule that validates any person's indorsement of an instrument (such as a check) when the instrument's drawer intended for the payee to have no interest in the instrument. UCC § 3-404(b).

nominal plaintiff. See *nominal party* under PARTY (2).

nominal rate. See INTEREST RATE.

nominal sentence. See SENTENCE.

nominal trust. See *passive trust* under TRUST (3).

nominal value. See PAR VALUE.

nominal yield. See *coupon yield* under YIELD.

nominandus (nahm-ə-**nan**-dəs). [Latin] *Scots law.* To be named. • The phrase usu. referred to an heir whom the entailer had the right to name if that right was reserved in the deed of entail. See ENTAIL.

nominate (**nom**-ə-nət), *adj.* (1818) *Civil law.* Classified; having a special name or designation. See *nominate contract* under CONTRACT.

nominate, *vb.* (16c) **1.** To propose (a person) for election or appointment <Steven nominated Jane for president>. **2.** To name or designate (a person) for a position <the testator nominated an executor, who later withdrew because he couldn't perform his duties>.

nominate action. See ACTION (4).

nominate contract. See CONTRACT.

nominatim (nah-mi-**nay**-təm), *adv.* [fr. Latin *nomen* "name"] (1819) *Roman law.* By name. • This term refers to mentioning someone or something expressly by name or by specific description, so that (for example) to disinherit persons *nominatim* means that there is no doubt who is meant to be excluded.

nominating and reducing. (18c) *Hist.* A method used, esp. in London, to obtain special jurors from which to select a jury panel. • Under this method, a number representing each person on a sheriff's list is drawn from a box until 48 unchallenged people have been nominated. Each party then strikes 12 people and the remaining 24 constitute the panel.

nominating committee. See COMMITTEE (1).

nominatio auctoris (nah-mi-**nay**-shee-oh awk-**tor**-is). [Latin "naming of the originator (or seller)"] **1.** In an action for the recovery of something, such as real estate, the defendant's plea that the property is actually owned by another party. • The true owner is then required to defend the action. **2.** *Roman law.* In an action alleging ownership of an item, the defendant's plea naming the seller, who then must assist in the defense of the action against the plaintiff. — Also termed *laudare auctorem.*

nomination. (15c) **1.** The act of proposing a person for election or appointment. **2.** The act of naming or designating a person for an office, membership, award, or like title or status. • Under parliamentary law, each nomination is effectively a proposal for filling the blank in the question, "*Resolved,* That ——— be elected." See BLANK (2). See CLOSE NOMINATIONS; OPEN NOMINATIONS.

nomination borough. See *pocket borough* under BOROUGH.

nomination paper. (*usu. pl.*) (1837) A document filed by an independent political group — usu. one not qualifying as a political party or able to hold primary elections — to place one or more nominees on a general-election ballot.

nomination to a living. (18c) *Eccles. law.* The right of an advowson owner to present a clerk to the bishop for induction to a benefice. • The owner of an advowson can grant the right to another but is then bound to present whomever the grantee chooses.

nominative absolute. See NOMINATIVUS PENDENS.

nominativus pendens (nahm-ə-nə-**tɪ**-vəs **pen**-denz), *n.* [Latin "nominative hanging"] (1872) In a sentence, a nominative phrase that is not grammatically connected with the rest of the sentence. — Also termed *nominative absolute.*

> "Nominativus pendens . . . . The opening words in the form of a deed *inter partes* ('This deed,' etc., down to 'whereas'), though an intelligible and convenient part of the deed, having regard to the predicate 'witnesseth' or 'nor this deed witnesseth,' are sometimes of this kind." William A. Jowitt, *The Dictionary of English Law* 1230 (Clifford Walsh ed., 1959).

nomina villarum (**nahm**-ə-nə vi-**lair**-əm), *n.* [Latin "names of the villages"] (17c) *Hist.* In the reign of Edward II, a list compiled by sheriffs of the names of the villages and possessors in their respective counties.

nomine (**nahm**-ə-nee), *adv.* [fr. Latin *nomen* "name"] *Roman law.* **1.** By name; under the name of, as in *sine nomine edere librum* ("to publish [a book] anonymously"). **2.** On behalf of, as in *proprio (suo) nomine* ("on one's own behalf").

nomine albae firmae (**nahm**-ə-nee **al**-bee **fər**-mee), *adv.* [Law Latin] *Scots law.* In name of blench farm. • The phrase appeared in reference to one of the tenures by which lands were held for only a nominal sum (such as a penny) from the superior.

nomine damni (**nahm**-ə-nee **dam**-nɪ), *adv.* [Latin] *Scots law.* By way of damage. • A person was required to pay interest *nomine damni.*

nomine dotis (**nahm**-ə-nee **doh**-tis), *adv.* [Latin] *Scots law.* By way of dowry.

nominee (nom-i-**nee**), *n.* (17c) **1.** Someone who is proposed for an office, membership, award, or like title or status. • An individual seeking nomination, election, or appointment is a *candidate.* A candidate for election becomes a *nominee* after being formally nominated. See CANDIDATE. **2.** A person designated to act in place of another, usu. in a very limited way. **3.** A party who holds bare legal title for the benefit of others or who receives and distributes funds for the benefit of others.

nominee account. See ACCOUNT.

nominee trust. See TRUST (3).

nomine feudifirmae (**nahm**-ə-nee fyoo-di-**fər**-mee). [Law Latin] *Scots law.* In name of feu-farm; on account of lands held in feu. See FEU.

nomine poenae (**nahm**-ə-nee **pee**-nee), *n.* [Latin "in the name of penalty"] (17c) **1.** *Civil law.* A clause in a testament requiring the heir to do something by way of penalty. **2.** At common law, a penalty for nonperformance, such as additional rent to be paid by a tenant to a landlord for failing to perform certain conditions in a lease.

nominis receptio (**nahm**-ə-nis ri-**sep**-shee-oh). [Latin] *Roman law.* A presiding judge's registering of an accused person's name in the rolls of a criminal court. • This registration was essential for the case to be tried. The day fixed for a criminal trial was ordinarily ten days after the *nominis receptio.*

nomocanon (nə-**mok**-ə-non *or* noh-mə-**kan**-ən). (1908) **1.** A collection of canon and imperial laws applicable to ecclesiastical matters in the orthodox churches. • The first nomocanon is falsely ascribed to Johannes Scholasticus, patriarch of Constantinople, in 553. Later canons consist primarily of the canons of the Quinisext and the ecclesiastical laws of Justinian. **2.** A collection of the ancient canons of the apostles, councils, and fathers, without regard to imperial constitutions.

nomogenetics. See COMPARATIVE NOMOGENETICS.

nomographer (nə-**mog**-rə-fər). (17c) **1.** Someone who drafts laws. **2.** A person skilled in nomography.

nomography (nə-**mog**-rə-fee). (1832) **1.** The art of drafting laws, with special emphasis on style as opposed to content; the techniques of framing readable, workable, and unambiguous statutes. **2.** A treatise on the drafting of laws. — **nomographic,** *adj.* — **nomographer,** *n.*

> "In the present work, the term nomography will be employed to distinguish that part of the art of legislation which has relation to the *form* given, or proper to be given, to the *matter* of which the body of the law and its several parts are composed: — the *form,* in contradistinction to the *matter,* and in so far as the one object is capable of being held in contemplation apart from the other." Jeremy Bentham, "Of Nomography," in 3 *The Works of Jeremy Bentham* 231, 233 (John Bowring ed., 1843).

nomoscopy. See COMPARATIVE NOMOSCOPY.

nomothete (**noh**-mə-theet), *n.* [fr. Greek *nomos* "law" + *thetes* "a person who prescribes"] (16c) *Hist.* A lawgiver. — Also spelled *nomotheta.*

> "It was [in ancient Greek law] provided that all motions to repeal or amend an existing law should be brought before the ecclesia or general meeting of citizens, at the beginning of the year. They might be then and there rejected; but if a motion was received favorably, the ecclesia appointed a body of nomothetes, sometimes as many as a thousand in number, before whom the proposal was put on trial according to the regular forms of Athenian judicial procedure. A majority vote of the nomothetes was decisive for acceptance or rejection." 5 *Century Dictionary and Cyclopedia* 4011 (1895).

nomothetics. See COMPARATIVE NOMOTHETICS.

non (non). [Latin] (14c) Not; no. • This term negates, sometimes as a separate word and sometimes as a prefix.

nonability. (17c) **1.** The lack of legal capacity, esp. to sue on one's own behalf. **2.** A plea or exception raising a lack of legal capacity.

nonacceptance. (17c) **1.** The refusal or rejection of something, such as a contract offer; REJECTION (1). **2.** A buyer's rejection of goods because they fail to conform to contractual specifications. *See* UCC § 2-601(a). **3.** A drawee's failure or refusal to receive and pay a negotiable instrument.

non acceptavit (non ak-sep-**tay**-vit). [Latin "he did not accept"] In an assumpsit action against the acceptor of a bill of exchange, the defendant's plea denying acceptance of the bill.

nonaccess. *Family law.* (17c) Absence of opportunity for sexual intercourse. • Nonaccess is often used as a defense by the alleged father in paternity cases. See ACCESS (3). Cf. *multiple access* under ACCESS (3).

non accrevit infra sex annos (non ə-**kree**-vit **in**-frə **seks an**-ohs), *n.* [Latin "it did not accrue in six years"] *Hist.* The general pleading form for the statute-of-limitations defense.

nonacquiescence (non-ak-wee-**es**-ənts). *Administrative law.* An agency's policy of declining to be bound by lower-court precedent that is contrary to the agency's interpretation of its organic statute, but only until the Supreme Court has ruled on the issue.

nonactionable, *adj.* (1840) Not providing legal grounds for a claim or other legal action.

nonactuarially sound retirement system. A retirement plan that uses current contributions and assets to pay current benefit obligations, instead of investing contributions to pay future benefits. Cf. ACTUARIALLY SOUND RETIREMENT SYSTEM.

non adimpletus contractus (non ad-im-**plee**-təs kən-**trak**-təs). [Latin] *Hist.* An unfulfilled contract.

nonadmission. (16c) **1.** The failure to acknowledge something. **2.** The refusal to allow something, such as evidence in a legal proceeding.

nonadmitted asset. See ASSET.

nonae et decimae (**noh**-nee et **des**-ə-mee), *n. pl.* [Law Latin "ninths and tenths"] *Hist.* Two payments that church-farm tenants make to the church, the first being rent for the land and the second being a tithe.

nonage (non-ij). (14c) **1.** MINORITY (1). **2.** NONAGIUM.

nonaggression pact. (1923) *Int'l law.* A treaty in which two or more countries agree not to engage in hostile military operations against one another. — Also termed *nonaggression treaty.*

nonagium (noh-**nay**-jee-əm). [Latin "a ninth"] (1848) *Hist.* The ninth part of a decedent's personal property, sometimes payable to the parish clergy for pious uses. — Also termed *nonage.*

nonalienation pact. See PACT DE NON ALIENANDO.

nonaligned state. (1962) *Int'l law.* A (usu. less developed) country that has banded together with other similarly situated countries to enhance its political and economic position in the world. • The movement of nonaligned states formally began at a summit in 1961, and during the Cold War these countries declared their independence from both the western and the Soviet blocs.

nonancestral estate. See ESTATE (1).

nonancestral property. See *nonancestral estate* under ESTATE (1).

nonapparent easement. See *discontinuous easement* under EASEMENT.

nonapparent servitude. See SERVITUDE (3).

nonappearance. (15c) A party's unexplained and unexcused absence from a proceeding before a tribunal despite being summoned, esp. to prosecute or defend a lawsuit. — Also termed *failure to appear; failure to appear in court.* See DEFAULT; NONSUIT.

nonapportionment rule. (1956) *Oil & gas.* The majority doctrine that royalties accrued under a mineral lease on land that is later subdivided during the lease term are not shared by the owners of the subdivisions, but belong exclusively to the owner of the land where the producing well is located. • For example, if Grey granted a lease to Wainwright, then sold one-half of the land to Svenson, and a well on Wainwright's half began producing minerals, only Wainwright would be entitled to the royalty. Cf. APPORTIONMENT RULE.

nonart rejection. See *formal rejection* under REJECTION.

nonassertion letter. (1949) *Patents.* A patentee's written declaration that the holder does not intend to enforce the right to exclude others from practicing specified claims of a patent. • The patentee may choose to waive the right entirely or specify a time limit for the waiver.

nonassertive conduct. See CONDUCT.

nonassessable insurance. See INSURANCE.

nonassessable stock. See STOCK.

nonassignable, *adj.* (1835) (Of a right, duty, or ownership) not transferable. — **nonassignability,** *n.*

non assumpsit (non ə-**səm[p]**-sit). [Latin "he did not undertake"] (17c) *Hist.* A general denial in an action of assumpsit. See ASSUMPSIT.

> "'Non assumpsit' is the general issue in assumpsit, whether special or general, and is in effect a formal denial of liability on the promise or contract alleged. It denies not only the inducement or statement of the plaintiff's right, but also the breach, and allows any defense tending to show that there was no debt or cause of action at the time of commencing suit." Benjamin J. Shipman, *Handbook of Common-Law Pleading* § 182, at 322 (Henry Winthrop Ballantine ed., 3d ed. 1923).

▸ ***non assumpsit infra sex annos*** (non ə-**səm[p]**-sit **in**-frə **seks an**-ohs), *n.* [Latin "he did not undertake within six years"] *Hist.* The specific pleading form for the statute-of-limitations defense in an action of assumpsit.

nonbailable, *adj.* (1811) **1.** (Of a person) not entitled to bail <the defendant was nonbailable because of a charge of first-degree murder>. **2.** (Of an offense) not admitting of bail <murder is a nonbailable offense>.

nonbank, *adj.* (1929) Of, relating to, or being an entity other than a bank <a nonbank depositor> <a nonbank creditor>.

nonbank bank. See BANK.

nonbank financial institution. See MONEY SERVICE BUSINESS.

nonbeliever. See ATHEIST.

nonbillable time. (1947) An attorney's or paralegal's time that is not chargeable to a client. Cf. BILLABLE TIME.

nonbinding arbitration. See ARBITRATION.

nonbinding minitrial. See *summary jury trial* under TRIAL.

nonbinding summary jury trial. See *summary jury trial* under TRIAL.

non bis idem. See NON BIS IN IDEM.

non bis in idem (non **bis** in **ɪ**-dem). [Latin] *Scots law.* Not twice for the same thing. • The phrase usu. referred to the law forbidding more than one trial for the same offense. It essentially refers to the double-jeopardy bar. — Also termed *non bis idem; non bis in eodem; ne bis in idem* (nee **bis** in **ɪ**-dəm). See DOUBLE JEOPARDY.

noncallable bond. See *noncallable security* under SECURITY (4).

noncallable security. See SECURITY (4).

noncancelability clause. (1972) An insurance-policy provision that prevents the insurer from canceling the policy after an insured's loss, as long as the premium has been paid.

noncapital, *adj.* (1865) (Of a crime) not involving or deserving of the death penalty <noncapital murder>.

noncareer vice-consul. See VICE-CONSUL.

noncash charge. See CHARGE (7).

noncash proceeds. See PROCEEDS (2).

non cepit (non **see**-pit). [Latin "he did not take"] (17c) *Hist.* A general denial in a replevin action that puts at issue both the taking and the place of taking. — Also termed *non cepit modo et forma.* See REPLEVIN.

> "'Non cepit' is the general issue in replevin, and is a formal denial both of the fact and the place of the alleged taking. It denies the taking only, and not the plaintiff's right of possession. Where replevin may be and is brought for goods lawfully obtained, but unlawfully detained, the general issue is 'non detinet,' which is a denial of the detention. It denies the detention only, and not the plaintiff's right." Benjamin J. Shipman, *Handbook of Common-Law Pleading* § 178, at 318 (Henry Winthrop Ballantine ed., 3d ed. 1923).

noncircumvention agreement. (1986) A contractual provision or separate contract containing mutual promises to use confidential information only for certain purposes and only while the contract is in force. — Also termed *noncircumvent agreement.*

noncitable, *adj.* (1975) Not authorized by a court to be used as legal precedent. • In general, unpublished opinions are noncitable, although court rules vary. — Also termed *uncitable.* Cf. CITABLE.

noncitizen. (1850) Someone who is not a citizen of a particular place. See ALIEN.

▸ **lawful noncitizen.** (1924) A noncitizen who is present in a country and possesses a valid visa or has been granted permanent residency.

nonclaim. (15c) A person's failure to pursue a right within the legal time limit, resulting in that person's being barred from asserting the right. See STATUTE OF LIMITATIONS.

nonclaim statute. See STATUTE.

nonclergyable, *adj.* (1828) **1.** *Hist.* (Of an offense) punishable without benefit of clergy. • At one time, an offender who qualified for benefit of clergy could escape trial in the secular courts regardless of the crime. The benefit was applied so broadly by the end of the 16th century that Parliament declared certain crimes, such as murder, robbery, arson, and piracy, nonclergyable. Over time, more crimes and misdemeanors were added to the list until the benefit was finally abolished in the 19th century. **2.** *Archaic.* (Of a person) not eligible to claim benefit of clergy. See BENEFIT OF CLERGY (1).

noncode state. (1926) *Hist.* A state that, at a given time, had not procedurally merged law and equity, so that equity was still administered as a separate system. • The term was current primarily in the early to mid-20th century. — Also termed *common-law state.* Cf. CODE STATE.

noncombatant, *adj.* (1826) **1.** Not serving in a fighting capacity <noncombatant personnel>. **2.** Not designed for combat <noncombatant vehicle>.

noncombatant, *n.* (1811) **1.** An armed-service member who serves in a nonfighting capacity, such as an army doctor. **2.** A civilian in wartime.

noncommercial partnership. See *nontrading partnership* under PARTNERSHIP.

noncommercial use. See USE (1).

noncommissioned officer. See OFFICER (2).

noncompensable (non-kəm-**pen**-sə-bəl), *adj.* (1892) Incapable of being compensated for; not entitled to recompense <noncompensable wrongs>. • For an obsolete synonym, see BOTELESS.

noncompete covenant. See *covenant not to compete* under COVENANT (1).

noncompetition agreement. See *covenant not to compete* under COVENANT (1).

noncompetition covenant. See *covenant not to compete* under COVENANT (1).

non compos mentis (non **kom**-pəs **men**-tis), *adj.* [Latin "not master of one's mind"] (17c) **1.** Insane. **2.** Incompetent. Cf. COMPOS MENTIS.

non concessit (non kən-**ses**-it), *n.* [Law Latin "he did not grant"] (17c) *Hist.* **1.** *English law.* The plea by which the defendant denies that certain rights were given by letters patent to the plaintiff. • For example, if a plaintiff sues for the infringement of a patent right, the defendant can deny that the Crown granted the plaintiff that right as alleged in the plaintiff's declaration. **2.** A plea by a stranger to a deed, by which the title and operation of the deed are placed in issue.

nonconcur, *vb.* (18c) To fail or refuse to agree or acquiesce to. — **nonconcurrence,** *n.*

nonconformance. See NONCONFORMITY.

nonconforming goods. See GOODS.

nonconforming lot. See LOT (1).

nonconforming use. See USE (1).

nonconformist. (17c) Someone who refuses to follow established customs, practices, beliefs, or ideas; esp., an English Protestant who refuses to adhere to the Church of England.

nonconformity. (17c) The failure to comply with something, such as a contract specification. — Also termed *nonconformance.*

nonconsensual, *adj.* (1920) Not occurring by mutual consent <nonconsensual sexual relations>.

nonconsent. (1844) **1.** Lack of voluntary agreement. **2.** *Criminal law.* In the law of rape, the refusal to engage willingly in sexual intercourse. See CONSENT.

non constat (non **kon**-stat). [Latin "it is not settled"] (17c) It is not certain or agreed. • The phrase is generally used to state that some conclusion does not necessarily follow although it might appear on its face to follow. Cf. NON SEQUITUR.

> "Non Constat . . . . Words frequently used, particularly in argument, to express dissatisfaction with the conclusions of the other party: as, it was moved in arrest of judgment that the declaration was not good, because *non constat* whether AB was seventeen years of age when the action was commenced." 3 John Bouvier, *Bouvier's Law Dictionary* 2355 (Francis Rawle ed., 8th ed. 1914).

nonconstitutional, *adj.* (1879) *Constitutional law.* Of, relating to, or involving some legal basis or principle other than those of the U.S. Constitution or a state constitution <the appellate court refused — on nonconstitutional procedural grounds — to hear the defendant's argument about cruel and unusual punishment>. Cf. UNCONSTITUTIONAL.

nonconsumable, *n.* (1902) A thing (such as land, a vehicle, or a share of stock) that can be enjoyed without any change to its substance other than a natural diminution over time; NONFUNGIBLE. Cf. CONSUMABLE. — **nonconsumable,** *adj.*

noncontestability clause. See INCONTESTABILITY CLAUSE.

noncontest clause. See NO-CONTEST CLAUSE.

noncontinuing guaranty. See *limited guaranty* under GUARANTY (1).

noncontinuous easement. See *discontinuous easement* under EASEMENT.

noncontract, *adj.* See NONCONTRACTUAL.

noncontract demurrage. See DEMURRAGE (1).

noncontractual, *adj.* (1883) Not relating to or arising from a contract <a noncontractual obligation>. — Also termed *noncontract.*

noncontractual duty. See DUTY (1).

noncontribution clause. (1932) A fire-insurance-policy provision stating that only the interests of the property owner and the first mortgagee are protected under the policy.

noncontributory, *adj.* (1907) **1.** Not involved in something; esp., not being one of the causes of a particular event. **2.** (Of an employee benefit plan) funded solely by the employer. Cf. CONTRIBUTORY.

noncontributory pension plan. See PENSION PLAN.

noncooperation, *n.* (18c) **1.** The refusal to work with someone else to achieve some mutually beneficial result or to do as someone else requests. **2.** The refusal through civil disobedience to comply with governmental directives.

noncore proceeding. See RELATED PROCEEDING.

noncovered wages. See WAGE.

non culpabilis (non kəl-**pay**-bə-ləs). [Latin] (17c) Not guilty. — Abbr. *non cul.*

noncumul. (1956) *French law.* A rule prohibiting parties to a contract from suing each other in tort (delict) if the loss arises because of contractual fault. Cf. CONTORT.

noncumulative approach. See DUALITY OF ART.

noncumulative dividend. See DIVIDEND.

noncumulative preferred stock. See STOCK.

noncumulative stock. See *noncumulative preferred stock* under STOCK.

noncumulative voting. See VOTING.

noncustodial, *adj.* (1960) **1.** (Of an interrogation, etc.) taking place while a person is not in custody. **2.** (Of a criminal sentence or other punishment) not involving prison time. **3.** Of, relating to, or involving someone, esp. a parent, who does not have sole or primary custody.

noncustodial interrogation. See INTERROGATION.

noncustodial parent. See PARENT (1).

noncustodial sentence. See SENTENCE.

non damnificatus (non dam-nə-fə-**kay**-təs). [Latin "he is not damaged"] (17c) In an action of debt on a bond that holds the plaintiff harmless, the defendant's plea that the plaintiff has not been damaged.

nondeadly force. See FORCE.

nondeadly weapon. See LESS-LETHAL.

non debit. See NEVER INDEBTED, PLEA OF.

non decimando (non des-ə-**man**-doh). See DE NON DECIMANDO.

non dedit (non **dee**-dit), *n.* [Latin "he did not grant"] (17c) NE DONA PAS.

non deficit jus sed probatio (non **def**-ə-sit jəst sed proh-**bay**-shee-oh). [Latin] *Scots law.* The right is not lacking, but the proof of it. • The phrase appeared in reference to the principle that many rights, both disputed and sometimes undisputed, require a special mode of proof, such as a written document.

nondelegable (non-**del**-ə-gə-bəl), *adj.* (1902) (Of a power, function, etc.) not capable of being entrusted to another's care <the duty to maintain the premises is a nondelegable duty>.

nondelegable duty. See DUTY (1).

nondelegation doctrine. See DELEGATION DOCTRINE.

nondelivery. (18c) A failure to transfer or convey something, such as goods. See *failure to make delivery* under FAILURE. Cf. DELIVERY.

nondemise charter. See *voyage charter* under CHARTER (8).

nondemise charterparty. See *voyage charter* under CHARTER (8).

non demiset (non də-**mɪ**-zit). [Latin "he did not demise"] (1840) *Hist.* **1.** A defensive plea in an action for rent when the plaintiff failed to plead that the demise was by indenture. • It could not be used if the plaintiff alleged an indenture. **2.** In a replevin action, a plea in bar to an avowry for arrears of rent.

nondepository provider of financial services. See MONEY SERVICE BUSINESS.

non detinet (non **det**-i-net *or* **det**-ə-nət). [Latin "he does not detain"] (17c) *Hist.* **1.** The pleading form of a general denial in a detinue action for recovery of goods detained by the defendant. • A *non detinet* denies both the detention and the plaintiff's right of possession or property in the goods claimed. See DETINUE. **2.** Loosely, NON CEPIT.

nondirection. (18c) The failure of a judge to properly instruct a jury on a necessary point of law.

nondischargeable debt. See DEBT.

nondisclosure. (1908) **1.** The failure or refusal to reveal something that either might be or is required to be revealed. Cf. CONCEALMENT.

▸ **deliberate nondisclosure.** *Insurance.* The intentional or reckless failure to disclose correct, relevant information to an insurer.

▸ **innocent nondisclosure.** (1896) *Insurance.* An inadvertent failure to disclose something although the customer acted honestly and reasonably under the circumstances.

▸ **negligent nondisclosure.** (1990) *Insurance.* The failure to exercise reasonable care to disclose relevant information or correct mistakes in relevant information.

2. NONDISCLOSURE AGREEMENT.

nondisclosure agreement. (1958) *Trade secrets.* A contract or contractual provision containing a person's promise not to disclose any information shared by or discovered from a holder of confidential information, including all information about trade secrets, procedures, or other internal or proprietary matters. • Employees and some nonemployees, such as beta-testers and contractors, are frequently required to sign nondisclosure agreements. — Abbr. NDA. — Often shortened to *nondisclosure.* — Also termed *confidentiality agreement.*

nondisclosure clause. See *confidentiality clause* under CLAUSE.

nondiscretionary account. See ACCOUNT.

nondiscretionary trust. See *fixed trust* under TRUST (3).

nondisparagement clause. See CLAUSE.

non distringendo (non di-strin-**jen**-doh). [Law Latin "not to be distrained"] (17c) A writ to prevent the distraint of something.

nondiverse, *adj.* (1947) **1.** Of, relating to, or involving similar types <the attorney's practice is nondiverse: she handles only criminal matters>. **2.** (Of a person or entity) having the same citizenship as the party or parties on the other side of a lawsuit <the parties are nondiverse because both plaintiff and defendant are California citizens>. See *diversity jurisdiction* under JURISDICTION.

nondomestic arbitration award. See ARBITRATION AWARD.

noneconomic damages. See *nonpecuniary damages* under DAMAGES.

nonelected claim. See PATENT CLAIM.

nonenablement. (1973) *Patents.* In a patent application's specification, the quality of not being clear or complete enough to teach a of ordinary person skill in the art how to make and use the invention without undue experimentation. — Also termed *lack of enablement.*

nonenablement rejection. See REJECTION.

nonengagement letter. A letter from a lawyer declining to represent a potential client in some legal matter and formally disclaiming any attorney–client relationship.

non entia (non **en**-shee-ə). [Law Latin] (16c) *Hist.* Nonentities; things not existing.

nonentrenchment doctrine. See REPEALABILITY CANON.

nones (nohnz), *n.* [fr. Latin *nonus* "ninth"] (bef. 12c) **1.** *Roman law.* In the Roman calendar, the ninth day before the Ides, being the 7th of March, May, July, and October, and the 5th of the other months. **2.** *Eccles. law.* In the Roman Catholic church, one of the seven daily canonical hours (about 3:00 p.m.) for prayer and devotion. **3.** *Archaic.* The ninth hour after sunrise, usu. about 3:00 p.m. Cf. CALENDS; IDES.

nonessential mistake. See *unessential mistake* under MISTAKE.

nonessential term. See *nonfundamental term* under TERM (2).

non est. See NON EST INVENTUS.

non est factum (non est **fak**-təm). [Latin "it is not his deed"] (16c) *Hist.* A denial of the execution of an instrument sued on.

> "The general issue in covenant is 'non est factum,' which is a formal denial that the deed is the deed of the defendant." Benjamin J. Shipman, *Handbook of Common-Law Pleading* § 187, at 331 (Henry Winthrop Ballantine ed., 3d ed. 1923).

▸ **general *non est factum.*** (18c) *Hist.* A broad, nonspecific denial that an instrument was executed or executed properly.

▸ **particular *non est factum.*** See *special non est factum.*

▸ **special *non est factum*.** (18c) *Hist.* A pleading that specifies the grounds on which an instrument's execution is invalid or nonbinding. — Also termed *particular non est factum.*

▸ **verified *non est factum*.** (1862) *Hist.* A sworn denial that puts the validity of the instrument as well as the signature in question.

non est inventus (non est in-**ven**-təs). [Latin "he is not found"] (16c) *Hist.* A statement in a sheriff's return indicating that the person ordered arrested could not be found in the sheriff's jurisdiction. — Abbr. *n.e.i.* — Sometimes shortened to *non est.*

> "If *non est inventus* was returned to the bill, and the plaintiff had reason to think that the defendant was still in the same county, he might have another *bill*, and after that a third, and so on till the defendant was caught . . . ." 1 George Crompton, *Practice Common-Placed: Rules and Cases of Practice in the Courts of King's Bench and Common Pleas* xxxv (3d ed. 1787).

non-Euclidean zoning. See ZONING.

nonexclusive easement. See *common easement* under EASEMENT.

nonexclusive-jurisdiction clause. A contract provision specifying the courts in which the parties may bring claims arising out of the contract but not limiting the parties to those courts.

nonexclusive license. See LICENSE.

nonexclusive listing. See *open listing* under LISTING (1).

nonexecutive right. (1984) *Oil & gas.* A mineral interest that does not confer the right to lease. • Nonexclusive rights include royalty interests and nonexecutive mineral interests.

nonexempt assets. (1878) A debtor's holdings and possessions that can be liquidated in bankruptcy to satisfy creditors' claims. — Also termed *nonexempt property.* Cf. EXEMPT PROPERTY (1).

nonexempt property. See NONEXEMPT ASSETS.

nonfeasance (non-**feez**-ənts), *n.* (16c) The failure to act when a duty to act exists. Cf. MALFEASANCE; MISFEASANCE; FEASANCE. — **nonfeasant,** *adj.* — **nonfeasor,** *n.*

> "Hence there arose very early a difference, still deeply rooted in the law of negligence, between 'misfeasance' and 'nonfeasance' — that is to say, between active misconduct working positive injury to others and passive inaction or a failure to take steps to protect them from harm." W. Page Keeton et al., *Prosser and Keeton on the Law of Torts* § 56, at 374 (5th ed. 1984).

non fecit (non **fee**-sit). [Latin "he did not make it"] (1877) A denial in an assumpsit action on a promissory note.

non fecit vastum contra prohibitionem (non **fee**-sit **vas**-təm **kon**-trə proh-[h]ə-bish-ee-**oh**-nəm). [Latin "he did not commit waste against the prohibition"] In an estrepement action, a tenant's denial of any destruction to lands after an adverse judgment but before the sheriff has delivered possession of the lands to the plaintiff. See ESTREPEMENT.

nonfederal money. See *soft money* (3) under MONEY.

nonfelonious homicide. See HOMICIDE.

nonfiler. *Tax.* See *illegal tax protester* under TAX PROTESTER.

nonforfeitable, *adj.* (1871) Not subject to forfeiture. See FORFEITURE.

nonforfeiture option. See OPTION (5).

nonfreehold estate. See ESTATE (1).

nonfulfillment. The failure to carry through on a promise, commitment, plan, order, etc.

nonfunctional, *n.* (1908) *Trademarks.* A feature of a good that, although it might identify or distinguish the good from others, is unrelated to the product's use.

nonfundamental term. See TERM (2).

nonfunded deferred-compensation plan. See *nonqualified deferred-compensation plan* under EMPLOYEE BENEFIT PLAN.

nonfungible (non-**fən**-jə-bəl), *adj.* (1897) Not commercially interchangeable with other property of the same kind <a piece of land is regarded as nonfungible>. — **nonfungible,** *n.*

nongermane amendment. See AMENDMENT (3).

nongovernmental, *adj.* (1853) **1.** Not involving the government <nongovernmental purposes>. **2.** (Of an organization) independent of and not controlled by a government <nongovernmental relief organizations>.

nongovernmental organization. (1919) *Int'l law.* Any scientific, professional, business, or public-interest organization that is neither affiliated with nor under the direction of a government; an international organization that is not the creation of an agreement among countries, but rather is composed of private individuals or organizations. • Examples of nongovernmental organizations, which are often granted consultative status with the United Nations, include Amnesty International, Greenpeace, and the International Committee of the Red Cross. — Abbr. NGO. — Also termed *private voluntary organization.*

nongrantor-owner trust. See TRUST (3).

non grata (non **grah**-də), *adj.* (1925) Unapproved; unwelcome. See PERSONA NON GRATA.

non haec in foedera veni. [Latin "I did not promise that."] (1809) A plea or claim that a contractual performance now demanded exceeds the original undertaking and that the demand should not be allowed. • Aeneas replies with these words to Dido's disappointed expectation of marriage. Virgil, *Aeneid* 4.337–39. A defendant may reply as Aeneas did if presented with a claimed obligation to do more than he undertook, as when asked to pay for something other than what was promised, or when performance of a contract has become so onerous that it is a materially different thing from what either side anticipated when the contract was formed.

> "There is an obvious and critical difference between the plea *non haec in foedera veni* — denying one's obligation to perform under the circumstances prevailing — and the claim that the risk of the disparity in question was allocated by contract to the other party. The former entitles a party not to proceed; it takes the latter, however, to found a claim in restitution based on one's performance or part performance of a mistaken or frustrated contract." Andrew Kull, *Mistake, Frustration, and the Windfall Principle of Contract Remedies*, 43 Hastings L.J. 1, 39 (1991).

nonimmigrant visa. See VISA.

non impedivit (non im-pə-**dɪ**-vit), *n.* [Latin "he did not impede"] (17c) *Hist.* The defendant's general denial in a *quare impedit* action. • This is the Latin form equivalent to *ne disturba pas*. See NE DISTURBA PAS; QUARE IMPEDIT.

non implacitando aliquem de libero tenemento sine brevi (non im-plas-ə-**tan**-doh **al**-ə-kwem dee **lib**-ər-oh ten-ə-**men**-toh SI-nee **bree**-VI) [Latin "not impleading anyone of his free tenement without a breve"] (17c) *Hist.* A writ that, without a writ from the king, prohibited bailiffs or others from distraining anyone from touching their freehold estates.

noninfamous crime. See CRIME.

noninfamous offense. See *noninfamous crime* under CRIME.

non infregit conventionem (non in-**free**-jit kən-ven-shee-**oh**-nəm). [Latin "he committed no breach of covenant"] (1834) *Hist.* A defensive plea in an action for breach of covenant.

noninstallment credit. See CREDIT (4).

noninsurable risk. See RISK.

nonintercourse. (18c) **1.** The refusal of one country to deal commercially with another. • For example, the Non-Intercourse Act of 1809, a congressional act, prohibited the importation of British or French goods. **2.** The lack of access, communication, or sexual relations between husband and wife. Cf. NONACCESS.

nonintercourse act. (1804) *Int'l law.* A statute that suspends commercial or other relations between countries.

non-interest-bearing bond. See *discount bond* under BOND (3).

non interfui (non in-**tər**-fyoo-I). [Latin "I was not present"] *Hist.* A reporter's note.

noninterpretivism, *n.* (1978) The doctrine that the meaning of a legal instrument adopted in the past is subject to historical development and must be ascertained at any given time by recourse to insights and values then and there prevailing; esp., the doctrinal view that constitutional adjudication should not be confined to the text and that courts are justified in resorting instead to modern moral and political ideals that represent the judges' views of sound public policy. Cf. INTERPRETIVISM; ORIGINALISM; NONORIGINALISM; LIVING CONSTITUTIONALISM; LIVING-TREE DOCTRINE. — **noninterpretivist,** *n.*

> "**Noninterpretivism.** This ungainly name was invented as a counterpart of interpretivism, the view that courts, in deciding on the meaning of the Constitution, should find their authoritative sources only in the constitutional text and the clearly established inventions of those who adopted the text. A noninterpretivist, then, was one who believed that courts might properly go beyond these sources, enforcing constitutional norms not readily discernible in the text or the Framers' intentions, narrowly conceived. These terms lost their vogue fairly quickly because few commentators (and no judges) wanted to admit that their views were anything other than interpretations of the Constitution." Kenneth L. Karst, "Noninterpretivism," in *Encyclopedia of the American Constitution* 341 (1st Supp., Leonard W. Levy ed., 1991).

nonintervention. (1831) *Int'l law.* The principle that a country should not interfere in the internal affairs of another country. • The U.N. Charter binds it from intervening "in matters which are essentially within the domestic jurisdiction of any state . . . ." U.N. Charter art. 2(7). — Also termed *principle of nonintervention.*

nonintervention executor. See *independent executor* under EXECUTOR (2).

nonintervention will. See WILL.

non intromittendo, quando breve praecipe in capite subdole impetratur (non in-troh-mi-**ten**-doh, **kwon**-doh **bree**-vee **pree**-sə-pee [*or* **pres**-ə-pee] in **kap**-ə-tee **səb**-də-lee im-pə-**tray**-tər), *n.* [Latin "not interfering, when the writ praecipe in capite was obtained by deceit"] *Hist.* A writ issued to the King's Bench or Eyre, commanding them not to aid a person who obtained a praecipe in capite for lands from the king because that person likely obtained the writ deceitfully, and ordering them to put that person to the writ of right.

nonintromittent clause (non-in-troh-**mit**-ənt). (1855) *English law.* A clause in the charter of a borough exempting it from the jurisdiction of the justices of the peace appointed for the borough's county.

nonissuable plea. See PLEA (3).

nonjoinder. (1823) **1.** The failure to bring a person who is a necessary party into a lawsuit. Fed. R. Civ. P. 12(b)(7), 19. See JOINDER. Cf. MISJOINDER (1); DISJOINDER. **2.** *Patents.* Failure to name a coinventor in a patent application.

nonjudicial day. See DAY.

nonjudicial foreclosure. See FORECLOSURE.

nonjudicial oath. See OATH.

nonjudicial punishment. See PUNISHMENT (1).

nonjuridical (non-juu-**rid**-i-kəl), *adj.* (1853) **1.** Not involving judicial proceedings or the administration of justice <the dispute was nonjuridical>. **2.** Not involving the law; not legal <a natural person is a nonjuridical entity>. Cf. JURIDICAL.

non juridicus (non juu-**rid**-i-kəs), *adj.* [Latin "not judicial"] (17c) Of, relating to, or involving a day when courts do not sit or when legal proceedings cannot be conducted, such as a Sunday.

nonjuring, *adj.* (17c) Not swearing allegiance; specif., not willing to declare fealty to the British Crown after the Glorious Revolution of 1688, when William and Mary assumed the throne. See FEALTY.

nonjuror. (17c) **1.** Someone who is not serving as a juror. **2.** *Hist.* Someone who refused to pledge allegiance to the sovereign; specif., in England and Scotland, a clergyman who, after 1688, refused to break the oath to James II and his heirs and successors by refusing to recognize William of Orange as king. • In Scotland, a nonjuror was also recognized by the Presbyterian Church as a clergyman who refused to renounce the Episcopal Church when it was disestablished in 1690 in favor of Presbyterianism.

nonjury, *adj.* (1897) Of, relating to, or involving a matter determined by a judicial officer, such as a judge, rather than a jury <the plaintiff asked for a nonjury trial>.

nonjury trial. See *bench trial* under TRIAL.

nonjusticiable (non-jəs-**tish**-ee-ə-bəl *or* non-jəs-**tish**-ə-bəl), *adj.* (1915) Not proper for judicial determination <the controversy was nonjusticiable because none of the parties had suffered any harm>.

nonjusticiable question. See POLITICAL QUESTION.

nonlapse statute. See ANTILAPSE STATUTE.

nonlawyer. (1808) Someone who is not a lawyer; specif., one who has neither earned a law degree nor passed a bar examination.

nonlethal weapon. See LESS-LETHAL.

nonleviable (non-**lev**-ee-ə-bəl), *adj.* (1860) (Of property or assets) exempt from execution, seizure, forfeiture, or sale, as in bankruptcy. See HOMESTEAD LAW.

non liquet (non **lɪ**-kwet *or* **li**-kwet). [Latin "it is not clear"] (16c) **1.** *Civil law.* The principle that a decision-maker may decline to decide a dispute on the ground that the matter is unclear. • Even British judges formerly sometimes said *Non liquet* and found for the defendant. **2.** *Int'l law.* A tribunal's nondecision resulting from the unclarity of the law applicable to the dispute at hand. • In modern usage, the phrase appears almost always in passages stating what a court must not do: tribunals are routinely disallowed from declaring a *non liquet.* — Abbr. *n.l.*

nonliquidating distribution. See DISTRIBUTION.

nonliteral infringement. See DOCTRINE OF EQUIVALENTS.

nonmailable, *adj.* (1878) Of, relating to, or involving a letter or parcel that cannot be transported by mail for a particular reason such as the package's size, contents, or obscene label.

nonmarital child. See *illegitimate child* under CHILD.

nonmarketable security. See SECURITY (4).

nonmedical policy. See INSURANCE POLICY.

nonmember, *n.* (17c) A person or entity that does not belong to a particular club or organization.

nonmember bank. See BANK.

non memini (non **mem**-ə-nɪ). [Law Latin] (18c) *Scots law.* I do not remember. • The phrase appeared in reference to an oath in which one person swore no remembrance of a transaction.

> "Where a party to whose oath the resting-owing of a debt, or a payment, is referred, swears that he does not remember receiving the goods charged for, or of his incurring the debt, or of receiving the alleged payment, such oath, as not being evidence of the point referred, may result in decree of absolvitor in his favour, where the whole circumstances tend to the conclusion that the *non memini* is not only an honest answer, but a reasonable one. But if the fact referred is so recent that the deponent cannot be believed to be ignorant of it, or to have forgotten it, he is considered as concealing the truth, and will be decerned against in the same manner as if he had refused to depone." John Trayner, *Trayner's Latin Maxims* 397 (4th ed. 1894).

non merchandizanda victualia (non mər-chən-di-**zan**-də vik-choo-**ay**-lee-ə), *n.* [Law Latin "not to merchandise victuals"] *Hist.* A writ directing justices of assize to investigate and punish town magistrates who retailed victuals while in office.

nonmerchantable title. See *unmarketable title* under TITLE (2).

nonmetered license. See LICENSE.

non molestando (non moh-lə-**stan**-doh), *n.* [Law Latin "by not molesting"] (17c) *Hist.* A writ available to a person whose possession of land has been disturbed, contrary to the Crown's protection.

nonmonetary item. (1965) An asset or liability whose price fluctuates over time (such as land, equipment, inventory, and warranty obligations).

nonmoral, *adj.* (1838) Not within the realm of morality or ethics; outside the bonds of moral or ethical considerations.

nonmovant (non-**moov**-ənt). (1955) A litigating party other than the one that has filed the motion currently under consideration <the court, in ruling on the plaintiff's motion for summary judgment, properly resolved all doubts in the nonmovant's favor>.

nonmutual collateral estoppel. See COLLATERAL ESTOPPEL.

nonnative species. See *alien species* under SPECIES (1).

nonnavigable, *adj.* (1824) **1.** (Of a body of water) unaffected by the tide. **2.** (Of a body of water) incapable of allowing vessels to pass for travel or commerce. **3.** (Of any vessel) incapable of being steered. Cf. NAVIGABLE.

nonnegotiable, *adj.* (1859) **1.** (Of an agreement or term) not subject to change or even discussion <the kidnapper's demands were nonnegotiable>. **2.** (Of an instrument or note) incapable of transferring by indorsement or delivery. Cf. NEGOTIABLE.

nonnegotiable bill of lading. See *straight bill of lading* under BILL OF LADING.

nonnegotiable document of title. See DOCUMENT OF TITLE.

non numeratae pecuniae (non n[y]oo-mə-**ray**-tee pi-**kyoo**-nee-ee). [Latin] (17c) *Hist.* (Defense) of money not paid.

non obstante (non ahb-**stan**-tee *or* əb-**stan**-tee), *n.* [Latin "notwithstanding"]. **1.** *Hist.* A doctrine used by the Crown of England to give effect to certain documents, such as grants or letters patent, despite any laws to the contrary. • This doctrine was abolished by the Bill of Rights. **2.** A phrase used in documents to preclude any interpretation contrary to the stated object or purpose. **3.** NON OBSTANTE VEREDICTO.

non obstante veredicto (non ahb-**stan**-tee [*or* əb-**stan**-tee] ver-ə-**dik**-toh). [Latin] (15c) Notwithstanding the verdict. — Abbr. n.o.v.; NOV. — Often shortened to *non obstante.* — Often misspelled *non obstante verdicto.* See *judgment notwithstanding the verdict* under JUDGMENT (2).

nonobviousness. (1928) *Patents.* **1.** An invention's quality of being sufficiently different from the prior art that, at the time the invention was made, it would not have been obvious to a person having ordinary skill in the art relevant to the invention. **2.** The requirement that this quality must be demonstrated for an invention to be patentable. • Nonobviousness may be demonstrated with evidence concerning prior art or with other objective evidence, such as commercial success or professional approval. The test of obviousness involves examining the scope and content of the prior art, the differences between the prior art and the patent claims, and the level of ordinary skill in the art. 35 USCA § 103. See GRAHAM FACTORS. Cf. NOVELTY.

nonoccupant visitor. (1996) *Criminal procedure.* Someone who owns, coowns, is employed by, or is a patron of a business enterprise where a search is being conducted in accordance with a search warrant.

nonoccupational, *adj.* (1918) **1.** Not relating to one's job. **2.** Of, relating to, or involving a general-disability policy providing benefits to an individual whose disability prevents that individual from working at any occupation.

nonoccupier. (1958) Someone who does not occupy a particular piece of land; esp., an entrant on land who is either an invitee or a licensee. See INVITEE; LICENSEE (2).

non omittas propter liberatem (non ə-**mit**-əs **prop**-tər lib-ə-**ray**-təm). [Latin "do not omit because of any liberty"] *Hist.* A clause, usu. contained in writs of execution, directing the sheriff to execute the writ regardless of whether the sheriff had been granted the requisite special authority from a franchise (liberty) or district.

nonoperating income. See INCOME.

nonoperative performance bond. See PERFORMANCE BOND.

nonoriginal bill. See BILL (2).

nonoriginalism. *Constitutional law.* A family of approaches to constitutional interpretation united in maintaining that the Constitution need not be interpreted in accordance with the text's original meaning or the intentions or understandings of its framers or ratifiers; more broadly, the view that a text need not be interpreted in accordance with its original meaning (that is, the understanding of informed readers at the time of its adoption), but rather may be given new meanings to accord with the times. See ORIGINAL MEANING; LIVING CONSTITUTIONALISM. Cf. ORIGINALISM; INTERPRETIVISM; NONINTERPRETIVISM; LIVING-TREE DOCTRINE.

nonownership theory. (1922) *Oil & gas.* A characterization of oil-and-gas rights used in a minority of jurisdictions, holding that the owner of a severed mineral interest does not have a present right to possess the oil and gas in place, but only to search for, develop, and produce it. • Because there is no right to present possession, the interest of such an owner in a nonownership-theory state is akin to a profit a prendre: a right to use the land and remove items of value from it. This theory is used in California, Wyoming, Louisiana, and Oklahoma. Cf. OWNERSHIP-IN-PLACE THEORY.

non pars substantiae sive fundi, sed accidens (non parz səb-**stan**-shee-ee **sɪ**-vee **fən**-dɪ, sed **ak**-si-denz). [Law Latin] *Scots law.* Not a part of the substance or the land, but an accident. • The phrase appeared in reference to servitudes, among other things.

nonparticipating, *adj.* (1859) Not taking part in something; specif., not sharing or having the right to share in profits or surpluses. — Often shortened to *nonpar.*

nonparticipating preferred stock. See STOCK.

nonparticipating royalty. See ROYALTY (2).

nonpartisan, *adj.* (1843) Not involving, representing, or supporting the ideas of any political party or group; free from party affiliation or designation <nonpartisan election of judges>.

nonparty witness. See WITNESS.

nonpayment. (15c) Failure to deliver money or other valuables, esp. when due, in discharge of an obligation. Cf. PAYMENT (1).

nonpecuniary damages. See DAMAGES.

nonpecuniary injury. See *irreparable injury* under INJURY.

nonpecuniary loss. See LOSS.

nonperformance. (16c) Failure to discharge an obligation (esp. a contractual one). Cf. PERFORMANCE; MISPERFORMANCE.

nonperforming loan. See LOAN.

nonperson, *n.* (1876) **1.** A person who is regarded as having no legal or social status; one who has undergone civil death. See *civil death* (1) under DEATH. **2.** UNPERSON.

nonpersonal action. See ACTION (4).

non placet (non **play**-sət), *n.* [Latin "it does not please] (16c) A vote against some proposed measure; a negative vote.

non plevin (non **plev**-in). [Latin] (16c) *Hist.* The failure to timely replevy land after it is taken by the Crown on a default.

non ponendis in assisis et juratis (non pə-**nen**-dis in ə-**sɪ**-zis et juu-**ray**-tis), *n.* [Law Latin "not to be put in assizes and juries"] (18c) *Hist.* A writ discharging a person from jury duty.

nonpossessory estate. See *future interest* under INTEREST (2).

non possumus (non **pahs**-ə-məs), *n.* [Latin "we cannot"] (1875) A statement of inability to accomplish something. • The popes have traditionally used this phrase in denying requests.

nonpracticing entity. (2006) *Patents.* A person or company that acquires patents with no intent to use, further develop, produce, or market the patented invention. • When a nonpracticing entity focuses on aggressively or opportunistically enforcing the patent against alleged infringers, it is also termed (pejoratively) a *patent troll.*

nonprivity (non-**priv**-ə-tee). (1902) The quality, state, or condition of not being in privity of contract with another; lack of privity. See PRIVITY (1).

▸ **horizontal nonprivity.** (1982) The lack of privity occurring when the plaintiff is not a buyer within the distributive chain, but one who consumes, uses, or is otherwise affected by the goods. • For example, a houseguest who becomes ill after eating meat that her host bought from the local deli is in horizontal nonprivity with the deli.

▸ **vertical nonprivity.** (1982) The lack of privity occurring when the plaintiff is a buyer within the distributive chain who did not buy directly from the defendant. • For example, someone who buys a drill from a local hardware store and later sues the drill's manufacturer is in vertical nonprivity with the manufacturer.

nonprobate, *adj.* (1919) **1.** Of, relating to, or involving some method of transmitting property at death other than by a gift by will <nonprobate distribution>. **2.** Of, relating to, or involving the property so disposed <nonprobate assets>. See *nonprobate asset* under ASSET.

nonprobate asset. See ASSET.

nonprobate property. See *nonprobate asset* under ASSET.

non procedendo ad assisam (non proh-sə-**den**-doh ad ə-**sɪ**-zəm). See DE NON PROCEDENDO AD ASSISAM.

non procedendo ad assisam rege inconsulto (non proh-sə-**den**-doh ad ə-**sɪ**-zəm **ree**-jee in-kən-**səl**-toh). [Latin] (17c) *Hist.* A writ to put a stop to the trial of a case relating to someone who is in the king's service, esp. when the king has not been consulted.

nonprofit, *adj.* (1896) Using whatever money is earned to help people, esp. through charitable causes, and not to generate any private financial advantage <nonprofit corporation>. Cf. PROFITLESS.

nonprofit association. See ASSOCIATION.

nonprofit corporation. See CORPORATION.

nonproliferation, *n.* (1962) *Int'l law.* The effort to limit the number of nuclear, chemical, and biological weapons in the world, esp. by stopping countries that do not yet have them from developing them.

Nonproliferation Bureau. See BUREAU OF NONPROLIFERATION.

nonproliferation treaty. See TREATY (1).

non pros (**non** prahs), *n. abbr.* (17c) NON PROSEQUITUR.

nonpros (**non**-prahs), *vb.* (18c) To enter a non prosequitur against. See NON PROSEQUITUR.

nonprosecution, affidavit of. See *affidavit of nonprosecution* under AFFIDAVIT.

non prosequitur (non prə-**sek**-wə-tər *or* proh-). [Latin "he does not prosecute"] (18c) The judgment rendered against a plaintiff who has not pursued the case. — Often shortened to *non pros.* See NONPROS.

nonpublic forum. (1978) *Constitutional law.* Public property that is not designated or traditionally considered an arena for public communication, such as a jail or a military base. • The government's means of regulating a nonpublic forum need only be reasonable and viewpoint-neutral to be constitutional. Cf. PUBLIC FORUM.

non-purchase-money, *adj.* (1941) Not relating to or involving an obligation secured by property obtained by a loan <non-purchase-money mortgage>. Cf. *purchase-money mortgage* under MORTGAGE.

nonqualified deferred-compensation plan. See EMPLOYEE BENEFIT PLAN.

nonqualified executive-compensation plan. See *nonqualified deferred-compensation plan* under EMPLOYEE BENEFIT PLAN.

nonqualified pension plan. See PENSION PLAN.

nonqualified stock option. See STOCK OPTION.

non quieta movere (non kwɪ-**ee**-tə moh-**veer**-ee), *n.* [Latin "not to disturb what is settled"] (18c) Stare decisis. • *Non quieta movere* expresses the same principle as *stare decisis.* It is part of the longer phrase *stare decisis et non quieta movere* ("to adhere to precedents, and not to unsettle things that are established"). See STARE DECISIS.

nonrecognition. (1932) *Int'l law.* The refusal of one government to recognize the legitimacy of another government. Cf. RECOGNITION (6).

nonrecognition provision. (1932) *Tax.* A statutory rule that allows all or part of a realized gain or loss not to be recognized for tax purposes. • Generally, this type of provision only postpones the recognition of the gain or loss. See RECOGNITION (4).

nonrecourse, *adj.* (1926) Of, relating to, or involving an obligation that can be satisfied only out of the collateral securing the obligation and not out of the debtor's other assets.

nonrecourse loan. See LOAN.

nonrecourse note. See NOTE (1).

nonrecourse rule. See NO-RECOURSE RULE.

nonrecurring dividend. See *extraordinary dividend* under DIVIDEND.

nonrefoulement (non-ri-**fowl**-mənt). [French] (1960) A refugee's right not to be expelled from one state to another, esp. to one where his or her life or liberty would be threatened. Cf. REFOULEMENT.

> "The most critical of all refugee rights is protection against *refoulement*. Article 33, paragraph 1, of the Convention reads: 'No Contracting State shall expel or return ("*refouler*") a refugee in any manner whatsoever to the frontiers of territories where his life or freedom would be threatened on account of his race, religion, nationality, membership of a particular social group or political opinion.' A contracting state's duty of *nonrefoulement* in Article 33 is owed to all persons within its jurisdiction who, in fact, meet the criteria of a refugee in the Convention, regardless of whether this person has been formally recognized as such pursuant to a national determination procedure. On the other hand, only persons who, in fact, meet the Convention's definition of a refugee are entitled to protection under Article 33. It has been argued that a contracting state's duty of *nonrefoulement* applies only to refugees and asylum-seekers who have managed to enter its territory (whether lawfully or unlawfully), but not to those who present themselves at its borders. However, the prevailing international interpretation is that the duty of *nonrefoulement* also covers rejections at the border. This means that if a state refuses a refugee admission to its territory and as a result of this act the refugee is pushed back to a territory in which she risks persecution, the state is in violation of its obligation under Article 33. In practice, this means that a contracting state must either admit the person to its territory and process her claim for protection or send the person to a safe third state." Mark Gibney, "Refugees," in 4 *Encyclopedia of Human Rights* 315, 318 (David P. Forsythe ed., 2009).

nonrefundable, *adj.* (1924) Incapable of being paid back; (of a sum of money) not returnable for any reason. See NONRETURNABLE (2).

nonrefund annuity. See ANNUITY.

nonremovable inmate. (1999) An alien who, having been detained, would ordinarily be deportable but cannot be deported because the United States does not maintain diplomatic ties with the alien's country of origin. — Also termed *indefinite detainee; lifer.*

nonrenewal. (1819) A failure to renew something, such as a lease or an insurance policy.

nonreporting issuer. See ISSUER.

non repugnantia (non ree-pəg-**nan**-shee-ə). [Law Latin] (17c) *Scots law.* An absence of opposition, as to a claim.

nonresidence, *n.* (16c) **1.** The status of living outside the limits of a particular place. **2.** *Eccles. law.* The absence of a spiritual person from the benefice. • This was an offense punishable by sequestering the benefice and forfeiting part of its income.

nonresident, *n.* (16c) **1.** Someone who does not live within a particular jurisdiction. **2.** Someone who is not staying in a particular hotel, living in a particular apartment building, etc. — Abbr. n.r. — **nonresident,** *adj.*

nonresident alien. See ALIEN.

nonresident decedent. See DECEDENT.

non residentia clerici regis (non rez-i-**den**-shee-ə **kler**-ə-sɪ **ree**-jis). See DE NON RESIDENTIA CLERICI REGIS.

nonresidential, *adj.* (1898) **1.** (Of an area, building, etc.) not being a place where people live. **2.** (Of an educational course, activity, etc.) not providing participants with lodging arrangements.

nonresidential parent. See *noncustodial parent* under PARENT (1).

non residentio pro clerico regis (non rez-i-**den**-shee-oh proh **kler**-ə-koh **ree**-jis). [Latin "by nonresidence for a royal clerk"] *Hist.* A writ ordering a bishop not to harass a clerk who, being employed in the royal service, has become a nonresident.

nonresident-motorist statute. (1928) A state law governing the liabilities and obligations of nonresidents who use the state's highways.

nonresponsive, *adj.* (1886) **1.** (Of a reply to a question, esp. from a witness under oath) not directly answering the question asked. **2.** *Patents.* (Of a patent applicant's answer) not addressing every rejection, objection, and requirement contained in a patent examiner's office action. • A nonresponsive reply may render an application abandoned. 37 CFR 1.111.

nonresponsive answer. See *unresponsive answer* under ANSWER (2).

nonretroactivity principle. See NEW-RULE PRINCIPLE.

nonreturnable, *adj.* (1885) **1.** (Of purchased items) not subject to being taken back for a refund, for use again, etc. <nonreturnable bottles>. **2.** (Of a sum of money) not subject to being paid back; NONREFUNDABLE <a nonreturnable deposit>.

nonrun time. See *dead time* under TIME.

non sanae mentis (non **say**-nee **men**-tis), *adj.* [Latin] (17c) Not of sound mind.

nonsectarian, *adj.* (1831) Not affiliated with or limited to any particular religious group or its beliefs.

non-self-governing territory. See TERRITORY (1).

non sequitur (non **sek**-wə-tər). [Latin "it does not follow"] (16c) **1.** An inference or conclusion that does not logically follow from the premises. **2.** A remark or response that does not logically follow from what was previously said. Cf. NON CONSTAT.

nonservant agent. See AGENT.

nonservice. (18c) The failure to serve a summons, warrant, or other process in a civil or criminal case.

nonshareholder constituency. (1984) A group of nonstockholders, such as employees or the public, who have an interest in the corporation's business — an interest that the corporation may legally consider, in addition to shareholders' interests, in making major policy decisions. — Also termed *alternative constituency.*

nonskip person. (1988) *Tax.* Someone who is not a skip person for purposes of the generation-skipping transfer tax. IRC (26 USCA) § 2613(b). See SKIP PERSON.

nonsolicitation agreement. (1969) A promise, usu. in a contract for the sale of a business, a partnership agreement, or an employment contract, to refrain, for a specified time, from either (1) enticing employees to leave the company, or (2) trying to lure customers away. — Also termed *nonsolicit agreement.* — Sometimes shortened to *nonsolicit.*

non solvendo pecuniam ad quam clericus mulctatur pro non-residentia (non sol-**ven**-doh pi-**kyoo**-nee-əm ad kwam **kler**-ə-kəs məlk-**tay**-tər proh non-rez-ə-**den**-shee-ə). [Latin] *Hist.* A writ prohibiting an ordinary from taking a pecuniary mulct imposed on a clerk of the sovereign for nonresidence.

nonsovereign state. See STATE (1).

nonstaple. (1957) *Patents.* An unpatented thing or material that is a component of a patented product or is used in a patented process, but that has little or no other practical use. • Patentees have a limited right to control the market for nonstaples through tying agreements. But if the thing supplied is a staple, the tying agreement is restraint of trade. 35 USCA § 271(d). Cf. STAPLE (3).

nonstatutory, *adj.* (1852) **1.** Enforceable by some legal precept other than enacted law, such as precedent or trade custom. **2.** *Patents.* Unpatentable for not meeting some statutory requirement, e.g., novelty, utility, nonobviousness, or enabling description. **3.** *Patents.* Of, relating to, or involving an equitable defense to an infringement claim, esp. estoppel, inequitable conduct, or laches.

nonstatutory bond. See *voluntary bond* under BOND (3).

nonstatutory claim. See *omnibus claim* under PATENT CLAIM.

nonstatutory subject matter. (1950) *Patents.* A thing that does not fit into any of the categories of things that by law can be patented. • Examples include works of nature, abstract ideas, human movements. 35 USCA § 101.

nonstock corporation. See CORPORATION.

non submissit (non səb-**mis**-it). [Latin "he did not submit"] In a debt action on a bond to perform an arbitration award, a defendant's denial that he or she submitted to the arbitration.

non sui juris (non **s[y]oo**-I *or* **soo**-ee **joor**-is), *adj.* [Latin "not of one's own right"] (17c) Lacking legal age or capacity. Cf. SUI JURIS.

nonsuit, *n.* (15c) **1.** A plaintiff's voluntary dismissal of a case or of a defendant, without a decision on the merits. • Under the Federal Rules of Civil Procedure, a voluntary dismissal is equivalent to a nonsuit. Fed. R. Civ. P. 41(a). — Also termed *voluntary discontinuance.* **2.** A court's dismissal of a case or of a defendant because the plaintiff has failed to make out a legal case or to bring forward sufficient evidence. — Also termed *involuntary nonsuit; compulsory nonsuit.* See *judgment of nonsuit* under JUDGMENT (2). — **nonsuit,** *vb.*

> "It did not follow [in the 15th–18th centuries], of course, that the issue in a trial at *nisi prius* would ever get to the jury at all, for it might be that the plaintiff would be 'nonsuited' on the ground that he had failed to prove something which was essential to his case or that the case which he had proved was different from that which he had pleaded." Geoffrey Radcliffe & Geoffrey Cross, *The English Legal System* 184 (G.J. Hand & D.J. Bentley eds., 6th ed. 1977).

> "Nonsuit . . . is equivalent to a demurrer to the evidence in that, even if all facts that plaintiff presents are true, the evidence is not, as a matter of law, sufficient to entitle plaintiff to a judgment. However, a voluntary nonsuit, unlike a demurrer or a directed verdict which resolves the action on its merits, may result in another trial of the cause." 75A Am. Jur. 2d *Trial* § 853 (1991).

non sum informatus (non səm in-fər-**may**-təs), *n.* [Latin "I am not informed"] (17c) *Hist.* A type of default judgment based on a defense attorney's statement that the client gave no instructions to answer the lawsuit.

nonsupport. (1909) *Family law.* The failure to support a person for whom one is legally obliged to provide, such as a child, spouse, or other dependent. • Nonsupport is a crime in most states. — Also termed *criminal nonsupport; criminal neglect of family; abandonment of minor children; abandonment of children.* Cf. SUPPORT.

nontariff barrier. (1965) An official policy, other than a tariff, that restricts international trade, esp. by limiting imports or exports. — Abbr. NTB. Cf. NONTARIFF MEASURE.

nontariff measure. (1979) An official policy, other than a tariff, that affects international-trade conditions, including a policy that increases trade as well as one that restricts it. — Abbr. NTM. Cf. NONTARIFF BARRIER.

non tenent insimul (non **ten**-ənt **in**-sim-əl), *n.* [Latin "they do not hold together"] (17c) *Hist.* In a partition action, the defendant's plea denying a joint tenancy with the plaintiff in the estate at issue.

non tenuit (non **ten**-yuu-wit). [Latin] (17c) In an action of replevin, the plaintiff's plea in bar to the defendant's assertion of a rightful taking of property (avowry), whereby the plaintiff denies holding the property in the manner and form alleged.

nontenure (non **ten**-yər). (16c) *Hist.* A general denial in a real action, whereby the defendant denies holding some or all of the land in question.

nonterm. See NON TERMINUS.

non terminus (non **ter**-mi-nəs), *n.* [Law Latin "not the end"] (16c) *Hist.* The vacation between two terms of a court. • In England, it was also called "the time of days of the king's peace." — Also termed *nonterm*; *non term.*

nontestifying expert. See *consulting expert* under EXPERT.

nontoxic, *adj.* (1862) Not poisonous or harmful to one's health. Cf. TOXIC.

nontrading partnership. See PARTNERSHIP.

nontraditional public forum. See *designated public forum* under PUBLIC FORUM.

non ultra petita partium (non **əl**-trə pə-**tɪ**-tə **pahr**-shee-əm). [Latin] Not beyond the pleadings of the parties.

nonunion, *adj.* (1863) **1.** (Of a person or thing) not belonging to or affiliated with a labor union <a nonunion worker> <a nonunion contract>. **2.** (Of a position or belief) not favoring labor unions <she will not alter her nonunion stance>. **3.** (Of a product) not made by labor-union members <the equipment was of nonunion manufacture>. — Also termed *nonunionized.*

nonuse. (16c) **1.** The failure to exercise a right <nonuse of the easement>. **2.** The condition of not being put into service <the equipment was in nonuse>. **3.** *Intellectual property.* See ABANDONMENT (9)&(11).

nonuser. (16c) **1.** The failure to exercise a right (such as a franchise or easement), as a result of which the person having the right might lose it <the government may not revoke a citizen's voting right because of nonuser>. Cf. USER (1). **2.** Someone who does not make use of something.

non usurpavit (non yoo-sər-**pay**-vit). [Latin "he has not usurped"] (1836) A defendant's denial of an alleged usurpation of an office or franchise.

non utendo (non yoo-**ten**-do). [Latin] (18c) *Roman & Scots law.* By nonuse. • Certain rights (such as some servitudes) could be lost through neglect of use.

non valentia agere (non və-**len**-shee-ə **aj**-ə-ree). [Latin] (18c) Inability to sue. See NONABILITY.

nonverbal, *adj.* (1846) Not using or even involving words <nonverbal forms of communication>.

nonverbal testimony. See TESTIMONY.

non-vessel-operating common carrier. See CARRIER (1).

nonviolence, *n.* (1831) The abstention as a matter of principle from any behavior that is intended to hurt other people physically; esp., the practice of opposing a government without using any kind of force, as by passively disobeying the law. Cf. CIVIL DISOBEDIENCE.

nonvital term. See *nonfundamental term* under TERM (2).

nonvoluntary euthanasia. See EUTHANASIA.

nonvoting member. See MEMBER (1).

nonvoting stock. See STOCK.

non vult contendere (non vəlt kən-**ten**-də-ree). [Latin "he will not contest it"] (1901) NO CONTEST.

nonwaiver agreement. (1898) *Insurance.* A contract (supplementing a liability-insurance policy) in which the insured acknowledges that the insurer's investigation or defense of a claim against the insured does not waive the insurer's right to contest coverage later. Cf. RESERVATION-OF-RIGHTS LETTER.

nook. (16c) *Hist.* A variable quantity of land, often 12.5 acres.

no-oral-modification clause. (1969) A contractual provision stating that the parties cannot make any oral modifications or alterations to the agreement. — Abbr. NOM clause. See INTEGRATION CLAUSE; ZIPPER CLAUSE.

no par. See *no-par stock* under STOCK.

no-par stock. See STOCK.

no-par-value stock. See *no-par stock* under STOCK.

no-pass, no-play rule. (1984) A state law requiring public-school students who participate in extracurricular activities (such as sports or band) to maintain a minimum grade-point average or else lose the privilege to participate.

no progress. See WANT OF PROSECUTION.

no-prosecution letter. (1957) A written communication from a prosecutor, esp. a federal prosecutor, to the effect that the government does not intend to prosecute possible charges. • Such a letter is commonly sought from a federal prosecutor before a defendant pleads guilty in a state case where there is overlapping federal jurisdiction, esp. in drug cases, weapon cases, and child-pornography cases.

NOR. *abbr.* **1.** NOTICE OF REMOVAL. **2.** NOTICE OF RESPONSIBILITY.

no recourse. (17c) **1.** The lack of means by which to obtain reimbursement from, or a judgment against, a person or entity <the bank had no recourse against the individual executive for collection of the corporation's debts>. **2.** A notation indicating that such means are lacking <the bill was indorsed "no recourse">. See *nonrecourse loan* under LOAN; WITHOUT RECOURSE.

no-recourse rule. The traditional common-law rule barring recourse to legislative history as an aid in statutory interpretation. • The rule was first announced in the famous copyright case of *Millar v. Taylor*: "The sense and meaning of an Act of Parliament must be collected from what it says when passed into a law; and not from the history of changes it underwent in the house where it took its rise. That history is not known to the other house, or to the Sovereign." [1769] 4 Burr. 2303, 2332, 98 Eng. Rep. 201, 217 (K.B.). The no-recourse rule was well accepted in 18th-century America and was not seriously eroded until the mid-20th century. *See* Hans W. Baade, *"Original Intent" in Historical Perspective: Some Critical Glosses*, 69 Tex. L. Rev. 1001, 1010–11 (1991). — Also termed *nonrecourse rule*; *no-legislative-history rule*; (BrE) *exclusionary rule*.

No Religious Test Clause. See RELIGIOUS TEST CLAUSE.

no-retreat rule. (1973) *Criminal law.* A doctrine in many states allowing the victim of a threat to use force, sometimes including lethal force, against an invader or attacker even if the victim could avoid the need for it by running away or otherwise retreating. • Some versions of the rule allow victims this privilege when in their homes; some allow it whenever a victim is threatened with an assault. See STAND-YOUR-GROUND LAW. Cf. RETREAT RULE.

> "California belongs to the majority of jurisdictions with a '[n]o [r]etreat [r]ule,' under which the victim of an assault is under no obligation to 'retreat to the wall' before exercising the right of self-defense, but is entitled to 'stand his ground.'" *People v. Ross*, 155 Cal. App. 4th 1033, 1044 (2007) (citations omitted).

no-right, *n.* (1913) The absence of right against another in some particular respect. • A no-right is the correlative of a privilege. — Also termed *liability*.

> "A says to B, 'If you will agree to pay me $100 for this horse you may have him and you may indicate your agreement by taking him.' This is a physical fact, called an offer, consisting of certain muscular acts of A having certain physical results in B. The legal relations immediately following are (in part) as follows: B now has the *privilege* of taking the horse and A has *no-right* that he shall not . . . ." William R. Anson, *Principles of the Law of Contract* 321 (Arthur L. Corbin ed., 3d Am. ed. 1919).

> "'No-right' is sometimes derided as being a purely negative concept. If a no-right is something that is not a right, the class of no-rights must, it is said, include elephants. The answer is that negative terms are often useful as alternative ways of stating propositions involving negatives. For instance, the terms 'alien,' 'cold,' and 'dark' are all negative or privative, because their meaning includes the idea of the absence of something else. The proposition that A is an alien means that A is not a British subject; in the one mode of statement the negative is incorporated in the noun, whereas in the other it is expressed as a separate word. Similarly the word 'liberty' is negative, and critics who attack the concept of no-right should logically attack the concept of liberty also. . . . [L]iberty means 'no-duty not.' . . . [F]or the sake of clear thinking it is necessary to give each of the four meanings [of right] a separate name. Words like 'no-right' and 'no-duty' may seem uncouth at first sight, but it is surely a clear and useful statement to say that 'right' sometimes means 'no-duty not.'" John Salmond, *Jurisprudence* 240–41 n.(u) (Glanville L. Williams ed., 10th ed. 1947).

norm. (1821) **1.** A model or standard accepted (voluntarily or involuntarily) by society or other large group, against which society judges someone or something. • An example of a norm is the standard for right or wrong behavior. **2.** An actual or set standard determined by the typical or most frequent behavior of a group.

> "It is hardly surprising that being the fundamental concept of jurisprudence which it is, discussion about the concept of a norm seems endless. Every definition of this concept includes decisions about the content and method of the discipline, and hence about its character. What one is concerned with, and how one justifies it, depends on whether a norm is understood as the objective 'meaning of an act by which a certain behavior is commanded, permitted, or authorised,' or as 'counter-factually stabilised behavioural expectations,' or as a command, or as a model of behaviour which is either followed, or if not followed has a social reaction as a consequence, or as an expression having a certain form, or as a social rule. The problems raised by this list of definitions are significant . . . ." Robert Alexy, *A Theory of Constitutional Rights* 20–21 (Julian Rivers trans., 2002) (citations omitted).

▸ **basic norm.** (1934) In the legal theory of Hans Kelsen, the law from which all the other laws in a society derive. • Kelsen's "pure theory of law" maintains that laws are norms. Therefore, a society's legal system is made up of its norms, and each legal norm derives its validity from other legal norms. Ultimately, the validity of all laws is tested against the "basic norm," which may be as simple as the concept that all pronouncements of the monarch are to be obeyed. Or it may be an elaborate system of lawmaking, such as a constitution. — Also termed *grundnorm*. See GRUNDNORM; PURE THEORY.

normal, *adj.* (15c) **1.** According to a regular pattern; natural <it is normal to be nervous in court>. • The term describes not just forces that are constantly and habitually operating but also forces that operate periodically or with some degree of frequency. In this sense, its common antonyms are *unusual* and *extraordinary*. **2.** According to an established rule or norm <it is not normal to deface statues>. **3.** Setting a standard or norm <a normal curriculum was established in the schools>. **4.** Of, relating to, or involving conformity to the behaviors and customs typical for a person's reference group or culture. — **normality,** *n.*

normal balance. A type of debit or credit balance that is usu. found in ledger accounts. • For example, assets usu. have debit balances and liabilities usu. have credit balances.

normal college. See NORMAL SCHOOL.

normalized earnings. See EARNINGS.

normalized financial statement. See FINANCIAL STATEMENT (1).

normal law. (1904) The law as it applies to persons who are free from legal disabilities.

normal market. See CONTANGO (1).

normal mind. (1887) A mental capacity that is similar to that of the majority of people who can handle life's ordinary responsibilities.

normal school. (1826) A training school for public-school teachers. • Normal schools first appeared in the United States in the 1800s and were two-year post-high-school training programs for elementary-school teachers. At the turn of the century, normal schools expanded into four-year teaching colleges. Most of these institutions have developed into liberal arts colleges offering a wider variety of education and teaching programs. — Also termed *normal college*.

Norman French. (17c) A language that was spoken by the Normans and became the official language of English courts after the Norman Conquest in 1066. • The language deteriorated into Law French and continued to be used until the late 17th century. English became the official language of the courts in 1731.

normative, *adj.* (1852) Establishing or conforming to a norm or standard; prescribing a set of rules or standards of behavior <Rawls's theory describes normative principles of justice>.

normative canon. See CANON (1).

normative jurisprudence. See NATURAL LAW (2).

Norris–La Guardia Act (**nor**-is lə-**gwahr**-dee-ə). A 1932 federal statute that forbids federal courts from ruling on labor policy and that severely limits their power to issue injunctions in labor disputes. • The statute was passed to curb what were seen as federal-court abuses of the injunctive process, to declare the government's neutrality on labor policy, to curtail employers' widespread use of injunctions to thwart union activity, and to promote the use of collective bargaining to resolve disputes. 29 USCA §§ 101–115. — Also termed *Labor Disputes Act*; *Anti-Injunction Act*.

Norroy (**nor**-oy). (15c) *English law.* The third of the three Kings at Arms (and the chief herald), whose province lies on the north side of the river Trent. • The Norroy's duties have included the supervision of weddings and funerals of nobility. See HERALD.

North American Free Trade Agreement. A 1994 agreement between the United States, Canada, and Mexico, designed to phase out all tariffs and eliminate many nontariff barriers (such as quotas) inhibiting the free trade of goods between the participating countries. • Among other provisions, it set minimum standards for intellectual-property protection afforded other members' citizens. Negotiated at the same time as the GATT talks that produced TRIPs, NAFTA borrowed from many TRIPs provisions on intellectual-property protection, as by as protecting computer software and databases by copyright. While NAFTA incorporates by reference the Berne Convention standards of intellectual-property rights, it exempts the U.S. from recognizing Berne's moral rights. — Abbr. NAFTA.

North Atlantic Treaty Organization. A military alliance by which the member countries (there are now 26) have agreed that an armed attack against any of them is to be considered an attack on all, so that if any such attack occurs, each member country will assist the party attacked as an act of collective self-defense, the purpose being to restore and maintain security in the North Atlantic region. • The alliance was established by the North Atlantic Treaty of 1949. Cf. ANZUS TREATY. — Abbr. NATO.

North Eastern Reporter. A set of regional lawbooks, part of the West Group's National Reporter System, containing every published appellate decision from Illinois, Indiana, Massachusetts, New York, and Ohio, from 1885 to date. • The first series ran from 1885 to 1936; the second series is the current one. — Abbr. N.E.; N.E.2d.

North Western Reporter. A set of regional lawbooks, part of the West Group's National Reporter System, containing every published appellate decision from Iowa, Michigan, Minnesota, Nebraska, North Dakota, South Dakota, and Wisconsin, from 1879 to date. • The first series ran from 1879 to 1941; the second series is the current one. — Abbr. N.W.; N.W.2d.

Northwest Territory. *Hist.* The first possession of the United States, being the geographical region south of the Great Lakes, north of the Ohio River, and east of the Mississippi River, as designated by the Continental Congress in the late 1700s. • This area includes the present states of Ohio, Indiana, Illinois, Michigan, Wisconsin, and the eastern part of Minnesota.

NOS. *abbr.* National Ocean Service. See NATIONAL OCEANIC AND ATMOSPHERIC ADMINISTRATION.

noscitur a sociis (**nos**-ə-tər ay [*or* ah] **soh**-shee-is). [Latin "it is known by its associates"] (18c) A canon of construction holding that the meaning of an unclear word or phrase, esp. one in a list, should be determined by the words immediately surrounding it. — Also termed *associated-words canon.* Cf. EJUSDEM GENERIS; EXPRESSIO UNIUS EST EXCLUSIO ALTERIUS; RULE OF RANK.

> "The *ejusdem generis* rule is an example of a broader linguistic rule or practice to which reference is made by the Latin tag *noscitur a sociis*. Words, even if they are not general words like 'whatsoever' or 'otherwise' preceded by specific words, are liable to be affected by other words with which they are associated." Rupert Cross, *Statutory Interpretation* 118 (1976).

nose coverage. See PRIOR-ACTS COVERAGE.

no-setoff certificate. See WAIVER OF DEFENSES.

no-shop provision. (1985) A stipulation prohibiting one or more parties to a commercial contract from pursuing or entering into a more favorable agreement with a third party.

nosocomus (nos-ə-**koh**-məs), *n.* [Greek "an attendant on the side"] *Hist.* Someone who manages a hospital that cares for paupers.

nostra sponte. See SUA SPONTE.

no-strike clause. (1923) A labor-agreement provision that prohibits employees from striking for any reason and establishes instead an arbitration system for resolving labor disputes.

NOTA. *abbr.* NATIONAL ORGAN TRANSPLANT ACT.

nota (**noh**-tə), *n.* [Latin "mark"] (18c) *Hist.* **1.** A promissory note. **2.** A brand placed on a person by law.

nota bene (**noh**-tə **ben**-ee *or* **bee**-nee *or* **ben**-ay). See N.B.

notabilis excessus (noh-**tab**-ə-lis ek-**ses**-əs). [Law Latin] (17c) *Hist.* A very great excess.

notae (**noh**-tee), *n. pl.* [Latin] (18c) *Hist.* Shorthand characters. See NOTARIUS.

no-talk provision. See *confidentiality clause* under CLAUSE.

notarial, *adj.* (15c) Of, relating to, or involving the official acts of a notary public <a notarial seal>. — Also spelled (in Scots law) *notorial.* See NOTARY PUBLIC.

notarial act. (18c) An official function of a notary public, such as placing a seal on an affidavit. See NOTARY PUBLIC.

notarial protest certificate. See PROTEST CERTIFICATE.

notarial record. See JOURNAL OF NOTARIAL ACTS.

notarial register. See JOURNAL OF NOTARIAL ACTS.

notarial seal. See NOTARY SEAL.

notarial will. See WILL.

notario publico. (1956) *Mexican law.* An attorney who has been licensed for at least three years and is empowered to issue judicial opinions, make binding judgments in minor cases, mediate disputes, and perform marriages. • There is no equivalent professional status in the American legal system, and no direct translation of the term. The status and duties of an American notary public are not comparable to those of a *notario publico.* — Often shortened to *notario.* Cf. NOTARY PUBLIC.

notarius (noh-**tair**-ee-əs), *n.* [fr. Latin *nota* "a character or mark"] **1.** *Roman law.* A writer (sometimes a slave) who takes dictation or records proceedings by shorthand. • A *notarius* was later also called a *scriba.* **2.** *Roman law.* An officer of the court who takes a magistrate's dictation by shorthand. Cf. SCRIBA. **3.** *Hist.* An officer who prepares deeds and other contracts. **4.** A notary or a scribe.

notarize, *vb.* (1922) (Of a notary public) to attest to the authenticity of (a signature, mark, etc.).

notary public (**noh**-tə-ree), *n.* (16c) A person authorized by a state to administer oaths, certify documents, attest to the authenticity of signatures, and perform official acts in commercial matters, such as protesting negotiable instruments. — Often shortened to *notary.* — Abbr. n.p. Cf. NOTARIO PUBLICO. Pl. **notaries public.** — **notarize,** *vb.* — **notarial,** *adj.*

> "A notary public is an officer long known to the civil law, and designated as *registrarius, actuarius,* or *scrivarius.*" John Proffatt, *A Treatise on the Law Relating to the Office and Duties of Notaries Public* § 1, at 1 (John F. Tyler & John J. Stephens eds., 2d ed. 1892).

> "The notary public, or notary, is an official known in nearly all civilized countries. The office is of ancient origin. In Rome, during the republic, it existed, the title being *tabelliones forenses,* or *personae publicae*; and there are records of the appointment of notaries by the Frankish kings and the Popes as early as the ninth century. They were chiefly employed in drawing up legal documents; as scribes or scriveners they took minutes and made short drafts of writings, either of a public or a private nature. In modern times their more characteristic duty is to attest the genuineness of any deeds or writings, in order to render the same available as evidence of the facts therein contained." Benjamin F. Rex, *The Notaries' Manual* § 1, at 1–2 (J.H. McMillan ed., 6th ed. 1913).

> "In jurisdictions where the civilian law prevails, such as in the countries of continental Europe, a notary public is a public official who serves as a public witness of facts transacted by private parties . . . and also serves as impartial legal advisor for the parties involved. . . . In colonial Louisiana, the notary public had the same rank and dignity as his continental civilian ancestor. . . . Although notaries still constitute a protected profession in present-day Louisiana, holding office for life provided they renew their bonds periodically in compliance with the governing statute, the importance of their function has diminished over the years to the point that it has been said that a Louisiana notary is no longer a truly civilian notary. Indeed, the trained lawyer is nowadays the Louisiana, and American, counterpart of the continental civilian notary." Saul Litvinoff, 5 *Louisiana Civil Law Treatise: The Law of Obligations* 296–97 (2d ed. 2001).

notary record book. See JOURNAL OF NOTARIAL ACTS.

notary's certificate. (18c) A notary's signed and sealed or stamped statement attesting to the time and place that the specified acts and documents were authenticated.

notary seal. (18c) **1.** The imprint or embossment made by a notary public's seal. **2.** A device, usu. a stamp or embosser, that makes an imprint on a notarized document. — Also termed *notarial seal.*

▸ **embossed seal.** (1959) **1.** A notary seal that is impressed onto a document, raising the impression above the surface. • An embossed seal clearly identifies the original document because the seal is only faintly reproducible. For this reason, this type of seal is required in some states and on some documents notarized for federal purposes. **2.** The embossment made by this seal.

▸ **rubber-stamp seal.** (1948) **1.** In most states, a notary public's official seal, which is ink-stamped onto documents and is therefore photographically reproducible. • It typically includes the notary's name, the state seal, the words "Notary Public," the name of the county where the notary's bond is filed, and the expiration date of the notary's commission. **2.** The imprint made by this seal.

notation credit. (1956) A letter of credit specifying that anyone purchasing or paying a draft or demand for payment made under it must note the amount of the draft or demand on the letter. See LETTER OF CREDIT.

note, *n.* (17c) **1.** A written promise by one party (the *maker*) to pay money to another party (the *payee*) or to bearer. • A note is a two-party negotiable instrument, unlike a draft (which is a three-party instrument). — Also termed *promissory note.* Cf. DRAFT (1).

▸ **accommodation note.** (18c) A note that an accommodating party has signed and thereby assumed secondary liability for; ACCOMMODATION PAPER.

▸ **approved indorsed note.** (1826) A note indorsed by a person other than the maker to provide additional security.

▸ **balloon note.** (1938) A note requiring small periodic payments but a very large final payment. • The periodic payments usu. cover only interest, while the final payment (the balloon payment) represents the entire principal.

▸ **banker's note.** (18c) A promissory note given by a private banker or an unincorporated banking institution.

▸ **banknote.** See BANKNOTE.

▸ **blue note.** (1908) A note that maintains a life-insurance policy in effect until the note becomes due.

▸ **bought note.** (1857) A written memorandum of a sale delivered to the buyer by the broker responsible for the sale.

▸ **circular note.** See LETTER OF CREDIT.

▸ **coal note.** (1818) *Hist.* A promissory note written according to a statute that required payment for coal out of any vessel in the port of London to be in cash or by promissory note containing the words "value received in coal." • Noncompliance with the statute resulted in a fine of £100.

▸ **cognovit note.** See COGNOVIT NOTE.

▸ **collateral note.** See *secured note.*

▸ **coupon note.** (1873) A note with attached interest coupons that the holder may present for payment as each coupon matures.

▸ **demand note.** (1862) A note payable whenever the creditor wants to be paid. See *call loan* under LOAN.

▸ **executed note.** (1875) A note that has been signed and delivered.

▸ **floating-rate note.** (1974) A note carrying a variable interest rate that is periodically adjusted within a predetermined range, usu. every six months, in relation to an index, such as Treasury bill rates. — Abbr. FRN. — Also termed *floater.*

▸ **foreign note.** (1817) A note made by a person or entity in another country.

▸ **hand note.** A note that is secured by a collateral note.

▸ **installment note.** (1848) A note payable at regular intervals. — Also termed *serial note.*

▸ **inverse-floating-rate note.** (1992) A note structured in such a way that its interest rate moves in the opposite direction from the underlying index (such as the London Interbank Offer Rate). • Many such notes are risky investments because if interest rates rise, the securities lose their value and their coupon earnings fall. — Also termed *inverse floater.*

▸ **joint and several note.** (18c) A note for which multiple makers are jointly and severally liable for repayment, meaning that the payee may legally look to all the makers, or any one of them, for payment of the entire debt. See *joint and several liability* under LIABILITY.

▸ **joint note.** (18c) A note for which multiple makers are jointly, but not severally, liable for repayment, meaning that the payee must legally look to all the makers together for payment of the debt. See *joint liability* under LIABILITY.

▸ **mortgage note.** (1841) A note evidencing a loan for which real property has been offered as security.

▸ **negotiable note.** See NEGOTIABLE INSTRUMENT.

▸ **nonrecourse note.** (1955) A note that may be satisfied upon default only by means of the collateral securing the note, not by the debtor's other assets. Cf. *recourse note.*

▸ **note of hand.** See *promissory note.*

▸ **post note. 1.** See *time note.* **2.** POST NOTE.

▸ **premium note.** (1804) A promissory note given by an insured to an insurance company for part or all of the premium.

▸ **promissory note.** (18c) An unconditional written promise, signed by the maker, to pay absolutely and in any event a certain sum of money either to, or to the order of, the bearer or a designated person. — Also termed *note of hand.*

"A promissory note may be defined to be a written engagement by one person to pay another person, therein named, absolutely and unconditionally, a certain sum of money at a time specified therein. The definition given by Mr. Justice Blackstone is, that Promissory Notes, or notes of hand, are a plain and direct engagement in writing to pay a sum specified at a time limited therein, to a person therein named, or sometimes to his order, or often to the bearer at large. Perhaps this definition may be thought faulty in not stating that the engagement is to be absolute and unconditional. Mr. Justice Bayley more succinctly states that a Promissory Note is a written promise for the payment of money at all events. Mr. Chancellor Kent follows the definition of Mr. Justice Bayley; and, perhaps, each is open to the objection, that while it seeks brevity it is incomplete, as it does not state that the promise is made by one person to pay the money to another person specified." Joseph Story, *Commentaries on the Law of Promissory Notes* § 1, at 1–2 (6th ed. 1868).

▸ **recourse note.** (1954) A note that may be satisfied upon default by pursuing the debtor's other assets in addition to the collateral securing the note. Cf. *nonrecourse note.*

▸ **reissuable note.** (2004) A note that may again be put into circulation after having once been paid.

▸ **renewal note.** (1825) A note that continues an obligation that was due under a prior note.

▸ **sale note.** (18c) A broker's memorandum on the terms of a sale, given to the buyer and seller.

▸ **savings note.** (1949) A short-term, interest-bearing paper issued by a bank or the U.S. government.

▸ **secured note.** (1847) A note backed by a pledge of real or personal property as collateral. — Also termed *collateral note.*

▸ **self-canceling installment note.** (1981) A debt obligation that is automatically extinguished at the creditor's death. • Any remaining balance on the note becomes uncollectible. Self-canceling notes are typically used in estate planning. — Abbr. SCIN.

▸ **serial note.** See *installment note.*

▸ **sold note.** (1827) A written memorandum of sale delivered to the seller by the broker responsible for the sale, and usu. outlining the terms of the sale. See CONFIRMATION SLIP.

▸ **stock note.** (1818) A note that is secured by securities, such as stocks or bonds.

▸ **tax-anticipation note.** (1928) A short-term obligation issued by state or local governments to finance current expenditures and that usu. matures once the local government receives individual and corporate tax payments. — Abbr. TAN.

▸ **time note.** A note payable only at a specified time and not on demand. — Also termed *post note.*

▸ **treasury note.** See TREASURY NOTE.

▸ **unsecured note.** (1844) A note not backed by collateral.

2. A scholarly legal essay shorter than an article and restricted in scope, explaining or criticizing a particular set of cases or a general area of the law, and usu. written by a law student for publication in a law review. — Also termed *comment*; *lawnote.* Cf. ANNOTATION. **3.** A minute or memorandum intended for later reference; MEMORANDUM (1).

▸ **broker's note.** (1830) A memorandum, usu. one authorizing a broker to act as a principal's agent, that is prepared by the broker and a copy given to the principal.

note, *vb.* (13c) **1.** To observe carefully or with particularity <the defendant noted that the plaintiff seemed nervous>. **2.** To put down in writing <the court reporter noted the objection in the record>. **3.** *Archaic.* To brand <as punishment, the criminal was noted>. See NOTA.

note broker. See BROKER.

note of a fine. (17c) *Hist. English law.* A step in the judicial process for conveying land, consisting of a chirographer's brief of the proceedings before the documents of conveyance are engrossed. — Also termed *abstract of a fine.* See FINE (1).

note of allowance. (1829) *English law.* A master's note, upon receiving a party's memorandum of an error of law in a case, allowing error to be asserted.

note of hand. See *promissory note* under NOTE (1). Pl. **notes of hand.**

note of protest. A notary's preliminary memo, to be formalized at a later time, stating that a negotiable instrument was neither paid nor accepted upon presentment. See PROTEST.

note payable. See *account payable* under ACCOUNT.

note receivable. See *account receivable* under ACCOUNT.

no-term lease. See LEASE.

note verbal (noht **vər**-bəl). (1945) *Int'l law.* An unsigned diplomatic note, usu. written in the third person, that sometimes accompanies a diplomatic message or note of protest to further explain the country's position or to request certain action. — Also spelled *note verbale* (vair-**bahl**).

not-for-profit corporation. See *nonprofit corporation* under CORPORATION.

not found. Words placed on a bill of indictment, meaning that the grand jury has insufficient evidence to support a true bill. See IGNORAMUS; NO BILL. Cf. TRUE BILL.

not guilty. (15c) **1.** A defendant's plea denying the crime charged. **2.** A jury verdict acquitting the defendant because the prosecution failed to prove the defendant's guilt beyond a reasonable doubt. — Also termed *not-guilty verdict.* Cf. INNOCENT.

▸ **not guilty by reason of insanity.** (1844) **1.** A not-guilty verdict, based on mental illness, that usu. does not release the defendant but instead results in commitment to a mental institution. **2.** A criminal defendant's plea of not guilty that is based on the insanity defense. — Abbr. NGRI. — Also termed *not guilty on the ground of insanity.* See INSANITY DEFENSE.

3. *Common-law pleading.* A defendant's plea denying both an act of trespass alleged in a plaintiff's declaration and the plaintiff's right to possess the property at issue.

> "In trespass, whether to person or property, the general issue is 'not guilty.' It operates in the first place as a denial that the defendant committed the act of trespass alleged, to wit, the application of force to the plaintiff's person, the entry on his land, or the taking or damages of his goods. It also denies the plaintiff's possession, title, or right of possession of the land or goods." Benjamin J. Shipman, *Handbook of Common-Law Pleading* § 170, at 307–08 (Henry Winthrop Ballantine ed., 3d ed. 1923).

▸ **not guilty by statute.** (1841) *Hist.* Under certain acts of Parliament, the pleading form for a defendant's general denial in a civil action. • This pleading form allowed a public officer to indicate action under a statute. The officer had to write the words "by statute" in the margin along with the year, chapter, and section of the applicable statute, and the defendant could not file any other defense without leave of court. The right to plead "not guilty by statute" was essentially removed by the Public Authorities Protection Act of 1893.

4. A general denial in an ejectment action.

> "The general issue in ejectment is not guilty. This plea operates as follows: (1) As a denial of the unlawfulness of the withholding; i.e., of the plaintiff's title and right of possession. (2) All defenses in excuse or discharge, including the statute of limitations, are available under the general issue in ejectment." Benjamin J. Shipman, *Handbook of Common-Law Pleading* § 188, at 333 (Henry Winthrop Ballantine ed., 3d ed. 1923).

not-guilty plea. See PLEA (1).

not-guilty verdict. 1. ACQUITTAL (1). **2.** NOT GUILTY (2).

nothous (**noh**-thəs), *adj.* (18c) *Archaic.* Spurious; illegitimate.

nothus (**noh**-thəs), *n.* [Latin fr. Greek *nothos* "false"] *Roman law.* An illegitimate child; one of base birth. • If the child's mother was a Roman citizen, the child was also a Roman citizen. — Also termed *spurius.*

notice, *n.* (16c) **1.** Legal notification required by law or agreement, or imparted by operation of law as a result of some fact (such as the recording of an instrument); definite legal cognizance, actual or constructive, of an existing right or title <under the lease, the tenant must give the landlord written notice 30 days before vacating the premises>. • A person has notice of a fact or condition if that person (1) has actual knowledge of it; (2) has received information about it; (3) has reason to know about it; (4) knows about a related fact; or (5) is considered as having been able to ascertain it by checking an official filing or recording. **2.** The condition of being so notified, whether or not actual awareness exists <all prospective buyers were on notice of the judgment lien>. Cf. KNOWLEDGE. **3.** A written or printed announcement <the notice of sale was posted on the courthouse bulletin board>.

▸ **actual notice.** (18c) **1.** Notice given directly to, or received personally by, a party. — Also termed *express notice.* **2.** *Property.* Notice given by open possession and occupancy of real property.

▸ **adequate notice.** See *due notice.*

▸ **advance notice.** Notice given beforehand, usu. by a specified amount of time. — Sometimes (erroneously) written *advanced notice.*

▸ **commercial-law notice.** (1982) Under the UCC, notice of a fact arising either as a result of actual knowledge or notification of the fact, or as a result of circumstances under which a person would have reason to know of the fact. UCC § 1-202(a).

▸ **constructive notice.** (18c) Notice arising by presumption of law from the existence of facts and circumstances that a party had a duty to take notice of, such as a registered deed or a pending lawsuit; notice presumed by law to have been acquired by a person and thus imputed to that person. — Also termed *legal notice.*

▸ **direct notice.** (17c) Actual notice of a fact that is brought directly to a party's attention. — Also termed *positive notice.*

▸ **due notice.** (17c) Sufficient and proper notice that is intended to and likely to reach a particular person or the public; notice that is legally adequate given the particular circumstance. — Also termed *adequate notice; legal notice.*

▸ **enforcement notice.** See ENFORCEMENT NOTICE.

▸ **express notice.** (18c) Actual knowledge or notice given to a party directly, not arising from any inference, duty, or inquiry. See *actual notice.*

▸ **fair notice.** (17c) **1.** Sufficient notice apprising a litigant of the opposing party's claim. **2.** The requirement that a pleading adequately apprise the opposing party of a claim. • A pleading must be drafted so that an opposing attorney of reasonable competence would be able to ascertain the nature and basic issues of the controversy and the evidence probably relevant to those issues. **3.** FAIR WARNING.

▸ **immediate notice.** (17c) **1.** Notice given as soon as possible. **2.** More commonly, and esp. on notice of an insurance claim, notice that is reasonable under the circumstances.

▸ **implied notice.** (18c) Notice that is inferred from facts that a person had a means of knowing and that is thus imputed to that person; actual notice of facts or circumstances that, if properly followed up, would have led to a knowledge of the particular fact in question. — Also termed *indirect notice*; *presumptive notice.*

▸ **imputed notice.** (1831) Information attributed to a person whose agent, having received actual notice of the information, has a duty to disclose it to that person. • For example, notice of a hearing may be imputed to a witness because it was actually disclosed to that witness's attorney of record.

▸ **indirect notice.** See *implied notice.*

▸ **inquiry notice.** (1945) Notice attributed to a person when the information would lead an ordinarily prudent person to investigate the matter further; esp., the time at which the victim of an alleged securities fraud became aware of facts that would have prompted a reasonable person to investigate.

▸ **judicial notice.** See JUDICIAL NOTICE.

▸ **legal notice. 1.** See *constructive notice.* **2.** See *due notice.*

▸ **notice by publication.** See *public notice.*

▸ **personal notice.** (17c) Oral or written notice, according to the circumstances, given directly to the affected person.

▸ **positive notice.** See *direct notice.*

▸ **presumptive notice.** See *implied notice.*

▸ **public notice.** (16c) Notice given to the public or persons affected, usu. by publishing in a newspaper of general circulation. • This notice is usu. required, for example, in matters of public concern. — Also termed *notice by publication.*

▸ **reasonable notice.** (17c) Notice that is fairly to be expected or required under the particular circumstances.

▸ **record notice.** (1855) Constructive notice of the contents of an instrument, such as a deed or mortgage, that has been properly recorded.

▸ **short notice.** (17c) Notice that is inadequate or not timely under the circumstances.

4. *Intellectual property.* A formal sign attached to items that embody or reproduce an intellectual property right. • Notice of patent is made by placing the word "patent" (or its abbreviation, "pat.") and the item's patent number on an item made by a patentee or licensee. There are three statutory notice forms for U.S. trademark and servicemark registration. The most common is the symbol with the letter R (®) but "Reg. U.S. Pat. & Tm. Off." or "Registered in U.S. Patent and Trademark Office" affords the same legal protection. A copyright notice also takes several forms. The first part may be the symbol with the letter C in a circle (©), or the word "Copr." or "Copyright." It must be followed by the copyright owner's name and the year that the work was first published. Informal signs, such as "Brand," "TM," "Trademark," "SM," and "Service Mark," adjacent to words or other symbols considered to be protectable marks are not legal notices of exclusive rights. **5.** *Parliamentary law.* A meeting's published call. See *call of a meeting* under CALL (1). **6.** *Parliamentary law.* A formal statement that certain business may come before a meeting, usu. made at an earlier meeting or published with the call of the meeting that will consider the business, and made as a prerequisite to the business's consideration. See *call of a meeting* under CALL (1). — Also termed *previous notice.*

notice, *vb.* (15c) **1.** To give legal notice to or of <the plaintiff's lawyer noticed depositions of all the experts that the defendant listed>. **2.** To realize or give attention to <the lawyer noticed that the witness was leaving>.

notice act. See NOTICE STATUTE.

notice-and-comment period. (1974) *Administrative law.* The statutory time frame during which an administrative agency publishes a proposed regulation and receives public comment on the regulation. • The regulation cannot take effect until after this period expires. — Often shortened to *comment period.*

notice-and-comment rulemaking. See *informal rulemaking* under RULEMAKING.

notice-based quorum. See QUORUM.

notice by publication. See *public notice* under NOTICE (3).

notice doctrine. (1924) The equitable doctrine that when a new owner takes an estate with notice that someone else had a claim on it at the time of the transfer, that claim may still be asserted against the new owner even if it might have been disregarded at law. — Also termed *doctrine of notice.*

notice filing. (1948) The perfection of a security interest under Article 9 of the UCC by filing only a financing statement, as opposed to a copy or abstract of the security agreement. • The financing statement must contain (1) the debtor's signature, (2) the secured party's name and address, (3) the debtor's name and mailing address, and (4) a description of the types of, or items of, collateral.

notice of abandonment. (18c) **1.** The formal notification that an action will no longer be pursued, such as notice from a plaintiff to a defendant that litigation will be nonsuited. **2.** *Property.* A formal announcement, usu. in writing and recorded, that a person is relinquishing a claim to personal or real property. **3.** *Patents.* A written declaration from the U.S. Patent Office to a patent applicant that the application has been terminated because the applicant failed to pursue prosecution. **4.** *Construction law.* A builder's or contractor's announcement that work on unfinished property is being discontinued. See ABANDONMENT. **5.** *Bankruptcy.* A bankruptcy trustee's announcement that he or she intends to abandon property of the bankruptcy estate.

notice-of-alibi rule. (1969) The principle that, upon written demand from the government, a criminal defendant who intends to call an alibi witness at trial must give notice of who that witness is and where the defendant claims to have been at the time of the alleged offense. • The government is, in turn, obligated to give notice to the defendant of any witness it intends to call to rebut the alibi testimony. *See* Fed. R. Crim. P. 12.1.

notice of allowability. (1980) *Patents.* Notification from the U.S. Patent and Trademark Office that at least one claim in a patent application has been approved on their merits. • This notice is followed by the Notice of Allowance. The notice may also be issued if at least one claim is allowable but the application is under a secrecy order. It may include examiner's amendments incorporating some formal changes.

notice of allowance. (1888) **1.** *Patents.* The formal notification from the U.S. Patent and Trademark Office that a patent application has been approved and that a patent can be issued. • The patent itself is not issued until the applicant has paid the issue fee. **2.** *Trademarks.* The formal notification from the U.S. Patent and Trademark Office that a trademark may be placed on the Principal Register if it is actually used in commerce. — Abbr. NOA.

notice of appeal. (18c) A document filed with a court and served on the other parties, stating an intention to appeal a trial court's judgment or order. • In most jurisdictions, filing a notice of appeal is the act by which the appeal is perfected. For instance, the Federal Rules of Appellate Procedure provide that an appeal is taken by filing a notice of appeal with the clerk of the district court from which the appeal is taken, and that the clerk is to send copies of the notice to all the other parties' attorneys, as well as the court of appeals. Fed. R. App. P. 3(a), (d). — Abbr. NOA. — Also termed *claim of appeal.* See APPEAL.

notice of appearance. (1844) **1.** *Procedure.* A party's written notice filed with the court or oral announcement on the record informing the court and the other parties that the party wants to participate in the case. **2.** *Bankruptcy.* A written notice filed with the court or oral announcement in open court by a person who wants to receive all pleadings in a particular case. • This notice is usu. filed by an attorney for a creditor who wants to be added to the official service list. **3.** A pleading filed by an attorney to notify the court and the other parties that he or she represents one or more parties in the lawsuit. — Abbr. NOA.

notice of completion. (1868) *Construction law.* A written and recorded announcement that a building project is finished, thereby limiting the time for filing mechanic's liens against the property. • The time for filing a lien begins to run when the notice of completion is filed. — Abbr. NOC.

notice of copyright. See COPYRIGHT NOTICE.

notice of deficiency. See NINETY-DAY LETTER.

notice of dishonor. (1804) Notice to the indorser of an instrument that acceptance or payment has been refused. • This notice — along with presentment and actual dishonor — is a condition of an indorser's secondary liability. UCC § 3-503(a). — Also termed *certificate of protest; certificate of dishonor.*

notice of incomplete application. (1959) *Patents.* A notice sent to the applicant by the U.S. Patent and Trademark Office when a patent application lacks a required document or the filing fee. • The applicant generally has two months to complete the application, with an extension available upon payment of a surcharge.

notice of lis pendens. See LIS PENDENS (3).

notice of motion. (18c) Written certification that a party to a lawsuit has filed a motion or that a motion will be heard or considered by the court at a particular time. • Under the Federal Rules of Civil Procedure, the requirement that a motion be made in writing is fulfilled if the motion is stated in a written notice of the hearing on the motion. Also, the courts in most jurisdictions require all motions to include a certificate, usu. referred to as a certificate of service, indicating that the other parties to the suit have been given notice of the motion's filing. Notice of any hearing or other submission of the motion must usu. be provided to all parties by the party requesting the hearing or submission. Fed. R. Civ. P. 5(d), 7(b)(1); Fed. R. Civ. P. Form 19.

notice of nonresponsibility. (1912) *Construction law.* A written disclaimer that, if posted conspicuously and recorded, relieves a property owner from liability for work or materials used on the property without the owner's authorization. • It protects an owner against mechanic's liens that could arise when repairs or improvements are made by a tenant or other person in possession.

notice of orders or judgments. (1854) Written notice of the entry of an order or judgment, provided by the court clerk or one of the parties. • Notice of a judgment is usu. provided by the clerk of the court in which the judgment was entered. If the court does not provide notice, a party is usu. required to provide it. Under the Federal Rules of Civil Procedure and the Federal Rules of Criminal Procedure, the clerk is required to provide immediate notice of any order or judgment to any party to the case who is not in default. Fed. R. Civ. P. 77(d); Fed. R. Crim. P. 49(c).

notice of pendency. See LIS PENDENS (3).

notice of prior-art references. (2001) *Patents.* Notification from a patent examiner of the previously issued patents used in rejecting one or more of the applicant's claims.

notice of protest. (18c) **1.** A statement, given usu. by a notary public to a drawer or indorser of a negotiable instrument, that the instrument was neither paid nor accepted; information provided to the drawer or indorser that protest was made for nonacceptance or nonpayment of a note or bill. See PROTEST (2). **2.** A shipowner's or crew's declaration under oath that damages to their vessel or cargo were the result of perils of the sea and that the shipowner is not liable for the damages. See PERIL OF THE SEA.

notice of removal. (1892) The pleading by which the defendant removes a case from state court to federal court. • A notice of removal is filed in the federal district court in the district and division in which the suit is pending. The notice must contain a short and plain statement of the grounds for removal and must include a copy of all process, pleadings, and orders that have been served on the removing party while the case has been pending. The removing party must also notify the state court and other parties to the suit that the notice of removal has been filed. A notice of removal must be filed, if at all, within 30 days after the defendant is served with process in the suit. 28 USCA § 1446; *Murphy Bros., Inc. v. Michetti Pipe Stringing, Inc.*, 526 U.S. 344, 119 S.Ct. 1322 (1999). — Abbr. NOR.

notice of responsibility. A written notification by a government agency informing the recipient of a time-sensitive obligation to take some specified action, such as controlling noxious weeds, remediating a contaminated area, refraining from bringing alcohol to a space rented from the government (such as a community center), reimbursing court-appointed counsel in dependency proceedings, or any other such requirement. — Abbr. NOR.

notice of trial. (17c) A document issued by a court informing the parties of the date on which the lawsuit is set for trial. • While the court typically provides the notice to all parties, it may instead instruct one party to send the notice to all the others.

notice pleading. See PLEADING (2).

notice-prejudice rule. (1988) A doctrine barring an insurer from using late notice as a reason to deny an insured's claim unless the insurer can show that it was prejudiced by the untimely notice.

notice-race statute. See RACE-NOTICE STATUTE.

notice statute. (1864) A recording act providing that the person with the most recent valid claim, and who purchased without notice of an earlier, unrecorded claim, has priority. • About half the states have notice statutes. — Also termed *notice act.* Cf. RACE STATUTE; RACE-NOTICE STATUTE.

notice to admit. See REQUEST FOR ADMISSION.

notice to all the world. (17c) A general public announcement regarding a lawsuit, esp. to persons within the jurisdiction where a lawsuit is pending.

notice to appear. (17c) A summons or writ by which a person is cited to appear in court. • This is an informal phrase sometimes used to refer to the summons or other initial process by which a person is notified of a lawsuit. The Federal Rules of Civil Procedure require the summons to state that the defendant must appear and defend within a given time and that failure to do so will result in a default judgment. Fed. R. Civ. P. 4(a). — Abbr. NTA. See PROCESS; SUMMONS; DEFAULT JUDGMENT; NOTICE TO PLEAD.

notice to creditors. (17c) *Bankruptcy.* A formal notice to creditors that a creditors' meeting will be held, that proofs of claim must be filed, or that an order for relief has been granted. — Also termed *bankruptcy notice.* See BANKRUPTCY NOTICE.

notice to pay rent or quit. See NOTICE TO QUIT.

notice to plead. (18c) A warning to a defendant, stating that failure to file a responsive pleading within a prescribed time will result in a default judgment. • The Federal Rules of Civil Procedure require the summons to notify the defendant that failure to appear and defend within a prescribed time will result in a default judgment. Fed. R. Civ. P. 4(a). See PROCESS; SUMMONS; DEFAULT JUDGMENT; NOTICE TO APPEAR.

notice to produce. See REQUEST FOR PRODUCTION.

notice to quit. (18c) **1.** A landlord's written notice demanding that a tenant surrender and vacate the leased property, thereby terminating the tenancy. **2.** A landlord's notice to a tenant to pay any back rent within a specified period (often seven days) or else vacate the leased premises. — Also termed *notice to pay rent or quit.*

notice to treat. (1840) *English law.* In the exercise of its compulsory-purchase power, an authority's invitation to negotiate given to the owner of an interest in the land that the authority seeks to acquire. • A notice to treat has the effect of a concluded contract of sale, leaving only the price to be fixed.

notification. (15c) **1.** *Int'l law.* A formal announcement of a legally relevant fact, action, or intent, such as notice of an intent to withdraw from a treaty. **2.** NOTICE. • A person receives notification if someone else (1) informs the person of the fact or of other facts from which the person has reason to know or should know the fact, or (2) does an act that, under the rules applicable to the transaction, has the same effect on the legal relations of the parties as the acquisition of knowledge. *See* Restatement of Agency § 9(2).

notify, *vb.* (14c) **1.** To inform (a person or group) in writing or by any method that is understood <I notified the court of the change in address>. **2.** *Archaic.* To give notice of; to make known <to notify the lawsuit to all the defendants>. See NOTICE.

noting protest. See PROTEST (2).

not in order. See OUT OF ORDER (1).

notio (**noh**-shee-oh), *n.* [fr. Latin *noscere* "to know"] **1.** *Roman law.* An investigation of a case by a magistrate. **2.** *Hist.* The authority of a judge to try a case. Pl. ***notiones*** (noh-shee-**oh**-neez).

notitia (noh-**tish**-ee-ə), *n.* [Latin "knowledge"] (18c) **1.** *Roman law.* Knowledge; information. • This term carried over for a time into English practice. **2.** *Roman law.* A list; register; catalogue. • The *Notitia Dignitatum* (dig-ni-**tay**-təm) was a list of the high offices in the Eastern and Western parts of the empire, complied in the late fourth or early fifth century A.D. **3.** *Hist.* Notice. **4.** A list of ecclesiastical sees.

not law. (16c) A judicial decision regarded as wrong by the legal profession.

> "Even when it is not possible to point out any decision that affects the point in question in any one of the ways enumerated, it sometimes happens that the profession has grown to ignore the old decision as wrong or obsolete; and though this does not happen often, when it does happen, the old decision is very likely not to be followed in case the point is squarely raised again. This is one of the instances in which lawyers rather mystically, though soundly, say that a decision is 'not law.'" William M. Lile et al., *Brief Making and the Use of Law Books* 329 (Roger W. Cooley & Charles Lesley Ames eds., 3d ed. 1914).

notorial. See NOTARIAL.

notoriety. (16c) **1.** The quality, state, or condition of being generally, and often unfavorably, known and spoken of <the company executive achieved notoriety when she fled the country to avoid paying taxes>. **2.** A person in such a state <the notoriety gave a rare interview>.

notorious, *adj.* (15c) **1.** Generally known and spoken of, usu. unfavorably. **2.** (Of the possession of property) so conspicuous as to impute notice to the true owner. — Also termed (in sense 2) *open and notorious.* See ADVERSE POSSESSION.

notorious cohabitation. See COHABITATION.

notorious insolvency. See INSOLVENCY.

notorious possession. See POSSESSION.

not otherwise indexed by name. (1918) A phrase used in shipping and tariff construction, usu. to show a classification of something generally rather than specifically. • For example, a shipment of aircraft and boat engines merely labeled "other articles" is *not otherwise indexed by name.* — Abbr. NOIBN.

notour bankruptcy. See *notorious insolvency* under INSOLVENCY.

not possessed. *Common-law pleading.* In an action in trover, the defendant's plea denying possession of the articles allegedly converted. See TROVER.

not proven. (17c) An archaic jury verdict — now used only in Scots criminal law — equivalent in result to not guilty, but carrying with it a strong suspicion of guilt not fully proved. — Also termed *Scotch verdict.*

not satisfied. A form of return by a sheriff or constable, on a writ of execution, indicating only that the amount due on a judgment was not paid. • A general return of this type is usu. viewed as technically deficient because it does not state why the writ was not satisfied. Cf. NULLA BONA.

not sufficient funds. (1845) The notation of dishonor (of a check) indicating that the drawer's account does not contain enough money to cover payment. — Abbr. NSF. — Also termed *insufficient funds.*

notwithstanding, *prep.* [loan translation of Latin *non obstante*] (15c) **1.** Despite; in spite of <notwithstanding the conditions listed above, the landlord can terminate the lease if the tenant defaults>. **2.** Not opposing; not availing to the contrary <her riches notwithstanding>.

n.o.v. *abbr.* NON OBSTANTE VEREDICTO.

nova causa interveniens. See *intervening cause* under CAUSE (1).

nova causa obligationis (**noh**-və **kaw**-zə ahb-li-gay-shee-**oh**-nis). [Latin] *Hist.* A new ground of obligation.

nova custuma (**noh**-və **kəs**-t[y]ə-mə), *n.* [Law Latin "new custom"] (17c) *Hist.* A tax; an imposition. Cf. ANTIQUA CUSTUMA.

nova debita (**noh**-və **deb**-i-tə). [Latin] (18c) *Scots law.* New debts, as distinguished from preexisting ones.

> "A security granted by a debtor within sixty days of his bankruptcy for a debt contracted before that period is reducible as a fraudulent preference. But security or payment granted in consideration of a *novum debitum* — a debt presently contracted — is not reducible although granted within the sixty days." John Trayner, *Trayner's Latin Maxims* 402 (4th ed. 1894).

novae narrationes (**noh**-vee nə-ray-shee-**oh**-neez), *n.* [Law Latin "new counts or tales"] (17c) *Hist.* A collection of pleading forms published during the reign of Edward III.

novalia (noh-**vay**-lee-ə). [Law Latin "new lands" or "newly tilled land"] (1838) *Scots law.* Land newly cultivated. • Exemptions from paying teinds, or tithes, were sometimes granted for *novalia.*

nova statuta (**noh**-və stə-**t[y]oo**-tə), *n. pl.* [Law Latin] (18c) *Hist.* New statutes. • This term refers to the statutes passed beginning with the reign of Edward III. Cf. VETERA STATUTA.

novation (noh-**vay**-shən), *n.* (16c) **1.** The act of substituting for an old obligation a new one that either replaces an existing obligation with a new obligation or replaces an original party with a new party. • A novation may substitute (1) a new obligation between the same parties, (2) a new debtor, or (3) a new creditor. **2.** A contract that (1) immediately discharges either a previous contractual duty or a duty to make compensation, (2) creates a new contractual duty, and (3) includes as a party one who neither owed the previous duty nor was entitled to its performance. • A novation rests on a contract, which must be clearly shown. It cannot be made binding by later acquiescence or ratification without a new consideration or the existence of facts that constitute an estoppel. If the novation involves the original debtor's discharge, it must be contemporaneous with and must result from the consummation of an arrangement with the new debtor. — Also termed *substituted agreement*; (Scots law) *innovation*; (Roman law) *novatio* (noh-**vay**-shee-oh). See STIPULATIO AQUILIANA; *substituted contract* under CONTRACT; ACCORD (2). — **novate** (noh-**vayt** *or* **noh**-vayt), *vb.* — **novatory** (**noh**-və-tor-ee), *adj.*

> "Novation is the emerging and transfer of a prior debt into another obligation either civil or natural, that is, the constitution of a new obligation in such a way as to destroy a prior one." Ulpian, *D.* 46.2.1 *pr.*

> "The only way in which it is possible to transfer contractual duties to a third party is by the process of novation, which requires the consent of the other party to the contract. In fact novation really amounts to the extinction of the old obligation, and the creation of a new one, rather than to the transfer of the obligation from one person to another. Thus if B owes A £100, and C owes B the same amount, B cannot transfer to C the legal duty of paying his debt to A without A's consent. But if A agrees to accept C as a debtor in place of B, and if C agrees to accept A as his creditor in place of B, the three parties may make a tripartite agreement to this effect, known as novation. The effect of this is to extinguish B's liability to A and create a new liability on the part of C." P.S. Atiyah, *An Introduction to the Law of Contract* 283 (3d ed. 1981).

> "The word 'novation' is used in a variety of senses. Courts frequently use it as synonymous with 'substituted contract.' Most academic writers and both contracts restatements, however, restrict its use to describe a substituted contract involving at least one obligor or obligee who was not a party to the original contract. . . . The development of a separate category under the rubric 'novation' is doubtless traceable to problems of consideration formerly thought to be present in such contracts because of the former common law rule that consideration must be supplied by the promisee. This rule has long been laid to rest almost everywhere." John D. Calamari & Joseph M. Perillo, *The Law of Contracts* § 11-8, at 444–45 (3d ed. 1987).

▸ **compulsory novation.** (1875) Novation that results from a judgment imposing an obligation. — Also termed *judicial novation.*

> "Compulsory novation occurs upon a judgment, which displaces the prior rights and obligations of the respective parties to the suit in which the judgment has been decreed, in so far as those rights and obligations depend upon the issues which constitute the subject of the judgment. The parties are deemed to bind themselves to each other to fulfill the judgment of the Court." L.R. Caney, *A Treatise on the Law Relating to Novation* 3 (1938).

▸ **judicial novation.** See *compulsory novation.*

▸ **objective novation.** (1978) *Civil law.* A novation involving the substitution of a new obligation for an old one.

▸ **subjective novation.** (1983) *Civil law.* A novation involving the substitution of a new obligor for a previous obligor who has been discharged by the obligee.

novel assignment. See *new assignment* under ASSIGNMENT (7).

novel disseisin (**nov**-əl dis-**see**-zin), *n.* (16c) A recent disseisin. See DISSEISIN; *assize of novel disseisin* under ASSIZE (8).

Novellae (nə-**vel**-ee). See NOVELS.

Novellae Constitutiones. See NOVELS.

Novellae Leonis (nə-**vel**-ee lee-**oh**-nis), *n.* [Latin "novels of Leo"] A collection of 113 ordinances issued by Emperor Leo from A.D. 887–893.

Novels. A collection of 168 constitutions issued by the Roman emperor Justinian and his immediate successors. • Taken together, the Novels make up one of four component parts of the *Corpus Juris Civilis.* — Also termed *Novellae; Novellae Constitutiones.* See CORPUS JURIS CIVILIS.

novelty. (14c) **1.** *Trade secrets.* The newness of information that is generally unused or unknown and that gives its owner a competitive advantage in a business field. • In the law of trade secrets, novelty does not require independent conception or even originality. A rediscovered technique with marketable applications can qualify as a novelty and be protected as a trade secret. **2.** *Patents.* Newness of an invention both in form and in function or performance; the strict statutory requirement that this originality be demonstrated before an invention is patentable. • Proving novelty is one purpose of the rigorous and expensive examination process. If the invention has been previously patented, described in a publication, known or used by others, or sold, it is not novel. 35 USCA § 102. Cf. NONOBVIOUSNESS.

> "Although the statute uses the words 'not *known*,' these are not to be taken literally. Novelty consists primarily in the invention not having been used by others in the United States or patented or described in any printed publication in this or any foreign country." Roger Sherman Hoar, *Patent Tactics and Law* 36–37 (3d ed. 1950).

▸ **absolute novelty.** (1851) *Patents.* The rule in most countries, but not in the United States, that an inventor must always file a patent application before the invention is publicly used, placed on sale, or disclosed. • Under U.S. law, an inventor is given a one-year grace period — beginning on the date of any public use, sale, offer of sale, or publication by the inventor or the inventor's agent — in which to file a patent application. After that, the patent is barred. Canada and Mexico also give the first inventor or the inventor's assignees a one-year grace period for filing, but they bar a patent for the first inventor if the invention is independently developed and disclosed by someone else during that time. — Also termed *absolute-novelty requirement.* Cf. BAR DATE.

noverca (nə-**vər**-kə), *n.* [Latin] A stepmother.

noverint, *n.* [fr. the traditional words that began a release, namely *Noverint universi per praesentes*] A writ.

noverint universi per praesentes (**noh**-və-rənt yoo-ni-**vər**-sɪ pər pri-**zen**-teez). [Latin] Know all men by these presents. • This is a formal phrase once found at the beginning of writs and deeds of release. In translation, the phrase still sometimes appears on various types of legal documents. See KNOW ALL MEN BY THESE PRESENTS; PATEAT UNIVERSIS PER PRAESENTES.

novigild (**noh**-və-gild), *n.* [fr. Latin *novem* "nine" + Anglo-Saxon *gid* or *geld* "a payment"] *Hist.* The money a person must pay for damaging another person's property, the amount equaling nine times the purchase price of the property damaged.

novi operis nuntiatio (**noh**-vɪ **ahp**-ə-ris nən-shee-**ay**-shee-oh). [Latin "new work protest"] *Roman law.* A protest against an *opus novum* ("new work"). • A person whose rights were impaired by the building of a new structure could protest to the praetor. The praetor could order the builder to give the protestor a security against any loss caused by the construction (*edictum de novi operis nuntiatione*). If the builder refused, the praetor could prohibit further construction with a prohibitory interdict (*interdictum de novi operis nuntiatione*). — Also written *operis novi nuntiatio.* Cf. JACTUS LAPILLI.

> "The 'operis novi nuntiatio' is the extrajudicial act by which anyone apprehensive of injury from walls newly begun may prevent their continuance, till his right has been decided, with the privilege of compelling his adversary, who perseveres after such a notice, to restore everything to the state in which it was at the time the 'nuntiatio' was given, however the question of right may be decided." John George Phillimore, *Private Law Among the Romans* 173 (1863).

noviter perventa (**noh**-və-tər pər-**ven**-tə), *n. pl.* [Law Latin "newly known"] (1840) *Eccles. law.* Newly discovered facts, which are usu. allowed to be introduced in a case even after the pleadings are closed.

novodamus (noh-və-**day**-məs), *n.* [Latin *novo damus* "we grant anew"] (17c) *Scots law.* **1.** A clause in a charter that progressively grants certain rights anew. • The phrase appeared in reference to any charter by which a superior renewed a previous land grant to a vassal. **2.** A charter containing such a clause.

> "This clause is subjoined to the dispositive clause; and by it the superior, whether the Crown or a subject, grants *de novo* the subjects, rights, or privileges therein described. Such a clause is usually inserted where the vassal is sensible of some defect or flaw in the former right . . . . This was also the correct form of proceeding . . . when the vassal wished to get free of burdens chargeable upon the subject for casualties due to the superior; for a charter of *novodamus* is accounted in law an original right, which imports a discharge of all prior burdens." William Bell, *Bell's Dictionary and Digest of the Law of Scotland* 747 (George Watson ed., 7th ed. 1890).

novus actus interveniens (**noh**-vəs **ak**-təs in-tər-**vee**-nee-ənz). See *intervening cause* under CAUSE (1).

novus homo (**noh**-vəs **hoh**-moh), *n.* [Latin "new man"] *Hist.* A man who has been pardoned for a crime.

NOW. *abbr.* (1966) **1.** NEGOTIABLE ORDER OF WITHDRAWAL. **2.** National Organization for Women.

NOW account. See ACCOUNT.

now comes. See COMES NOW.

noxa (**nok**-sə), *n.* [Latin "injury"] (1872) *Hist.* **1.** *Roman law.* A harm done or an offense committed such as injury to a person or property, esp. by a slave or son. • This gave rise to noxal liability. **2.** *Roman law.* The obligation to pay for damage committed by a son, slave, or animal. • The father or owner generally had to pay damages or else surrender the tortfeasor offending person or animal to the injured party (*noxal surrender*). — Also termed *noxal liability.* See NOXAL ACTION. **3.** An offense, generally. **4.** The punishment for an offense. **5.** Something that exerts a harmful effect on the body.

noxal (**nok**-səl), *adj.* (18c) *Archaic.* Of, relating to, or involving a claim against a father or owner for damage done by a son, a slave, or an animal.

noxal action. [fr. Latin *actio noxalis* "injurious action"] (18c) **1.** *Roman law.* The claim against an owner or father for a tort committed by a son, a slave, or an animal. • The head of the family could be sued either to pay a penalty due or to surrender the tortfeasor to the injured party. Roman law also provided for the surrender of animals that caused damage under the *actio de pauperie.* See *actio de pauperie* under ACTIO. **2.** *Hist.* A person's claim to recover for damages committed by a person's son, slave, or animal.

noxal liability. See NOXA (2).

noxal surrender. See NOXA (2).

noxious (**nok**-shəs), *adj.* (15c) **1.** Harmful to health; injurious. **2.** Unwholesome; corruptive. **3.** *Archaic.* Guilty.

n.p. *abbr.* (16c) **1.** NISI PRIUS. **2.** NOTARY PUBLIC.

NPI. *abbr.* NET-PROFITS INTEREST.

NPL. *abbr.* NATIONAL PRIORITIES LIST.

NPS. *abbr.* NATIONAL PARK SERVICE.

NPV. See *net present value* under PRESENT VALUE.

NQB. *abbr.* NATIONAL QUOTATION BUREAU.

NQDC. *abbr.* See *nonqualified deferred-compensation plan* under EMPLOYEE BENEFIT PLAN.

NQSO. *abbr.* See *nonqualified stock option* under STOCK OPTION.

n.r. *abbr.* **1.** New reports. **2.** Not reported. **3.** NONRESIDENT.

NRC. *abbr.* (1974) **1.** NUCLEAR REGULATORY COMMISSION. **2.** NATIONAL RESPONSE CENTER.

NRCS. *abbr.* NATURAL RESOURCES CONSERVATION SERVICE.

NRPC. *abbr.* NATIONAL RAILROAD PASSENGER CORPORATION.

NRS. *abbr.* NATIONAL REPORTER SYSTEM.

NRV. *abbr.* NET REALIZABLE VALUE.

n.s. *abbr.* (17c) **1.** New series. • This citation form indicates that a periodical has been renumbered in a new series. **2.** NEW STYLE.

NSA. *abbr.* (1952) NATIONAL SECURITY AGENCY.

NSC. *abbr.* (1948) NATIONAL SECURITY COUNCIL.

NSF. *abbr.* (1950) **1.** NATIONAL SCIENCE FOUNDATION. **2.** NOT SUFFICIENT FUNDS.

NSL. *abbr.* NATIONAL-SECURITY LETTER.

NSLI. *abbr.* NATIONAL-SERVICE LIFE INSURANCE.

NSPA. *abbr.* NATIONAL STOLEN PROPERTY ACT.

NTA. *abbr.* NOTICE TO APPEAR.

NTB. *abbr.* NONTARIFF BARRIER.

NTIA. *abbr.* NATIONAL TELECOMMUNICATIONS AND INFORMATION ADMINISTRATION.

NTID. *abbr.* NATIONAL TECHNICAL INSTITUTE FOR THE DEAF.

NTIS. *abbr.* National Technical Information Service. See TECHNOLOGY ADMINISTRATION.

NTM. *abbr.* NONTARIFF MEASURE.

NTSB. *abbr.* NATIONAL TRANSPORTATION SAFETY BOARD.

nubilis (**n[y]oo**-bə-lis), *n.* [Latin "marriageable"] *Civil law.* A person, esp. a girl, who is old enough to be married.

nuclear-nonproliferation treaty. See *nonproliferation treaty* under TREATY (1).

nuclear option. *Slang.* The decision of the presiding officer of the U.S. Senate that the validity of a Senate rule or precedent is a constitutional question that requires an immediate vote of the full Senate. • The issue underlying the rule, most commonly a filibuster of an executive appointment, is decided by simple majority vote without regard for any conflicting rules. Formerly termed *constitutional option*, the current term is an analogy to the extreme measure of a nuclear weapon.

Nuclear Regulatory Commission. An independent federal agency that licenses and regulates civilian use of nuclear energy. • The agency was created by the Energy Reorganization Act of 1974. Executive Order 11834 of 1975 gave it additional functions previously performed by the Atomic Energy Commission. — Abbr. NRC.

nuclear waste. See WASTE (2).

nuda detentio (n[y]**oo**-də di-**ten**-shee-oh). [Latin] See *possessio naturalis* under POSSESSIO.

nuda patientia (**n[y]oo**-də pash-ee-**en**-shee-ə). [Latin] Mere sufferance. • In a servitude, the servient estate owner's obligation is one of mere sufferance because, while the owner has to submit to the dominant estate, the owner does not have to take any positive steps (such as fixing a sidewalk) to enhance the exercise of the dominant servitude.

nuda possessio (**n[y]oo**-də pə-**zes[h]**-ee-oh). [Latin] Mere possession.

nude, *adj.* (15c) **1.** Naked; unclothed. **2.** Lacking in consideration or in some essential particular. See NUDUM PACTUM. **3.** Mere; lacking in description or specification.

nude contract. See NUDUM PACTUM.

nude matter. (17c) A mere allegation.

> "[N]ude matter is not of so high nature, as either a mater of Record or a speciality, otherwise there called mater in deede; which maketh mee to thinke, that nude mater is a naked allegation of a thing done, to be proved only by witnesses, and not either by Record, or other speciality in writing vnder seale." John Cowell, *The Interpreter* (1607).

nude pact. See NUDUM PACTUM.

nudity. The state of not wearing any clothes.

▸ **public nudity.** The state of not wearing any clothes in a nonprivate place where one is likely to encounter others.

nudum dominium (**n[y]oo**-dəm də-**min**-ee-əm). See DOMINIUM (1).

nudum officium (**n[y]oo**-dəm ə-**fish**-ee-əm). [Latin] *Scots law.* The bare office, without the usual emoluments. Pl. ***nuda officia.***

nudum pactum (**n[y]oo**-dəm **pak**-təm). [Latin "bare agreement"] (17c) **1.** *Roman law.* An informal agreement that is not legally enforceable, because it does not fall within the specific classes of agreements that can support a legal action. • But a *pactum* could create an exception to or modification of an existing obligation. **2.** An agreement that is unenforceable as a contract because it is not "clothed" with consideration. — Also termed *naked contract*; *nude contract*; *nude pact.*

nugatory (**n[y]oo**-gə-tor-ee), *adj.* (17c) Of no force or effect; useless; invalid <the Supreme Court rendered the statute nugatory by declaring it unconstitutional>.

nugatory contract. See CONTRACT.

nuisance. (14c) **1.** A condition, activity, or situation (such as a loud noise or foul odor) that interferes with the use or enjoyment of property; esp., a nontransitory condition or persistent activity that either injures the physical condition of adjacent land or interferes with its use or with the enjoyment of easements on the land or of public highways.

• Liability might or might not arise from the condition or situation. — Formerly also termed *annoyance.*

"It is not practicable to give other than a general definition of what constitutes a nuisance. A precise, technical definition, applicable to all cases, cannot be given, because of the varying circumstances upon which the decisions are based. To this there is the exception generally of what is designated as a nuisance *per se.* The only approximately accurate method of determining the meaning of the term nuisance is to examine the cases adjudicating what are and are not nuisances. . . . It is also true that one of the great difficulties in defining a nuisance technically is to describe the degree of annoyance necessary to cause the actionable injury. . . . A nuisance may generally be defined as anything that works or causes injury, damage, hurt, inconvenience, annoyance, or discomfort to one in the enjoyment of his legitimate and reasonable rights of person or property; or that which is unauthorized, immoral, indecent, offensive to the senses, noxious, unwholesome, unreasonable, tortious, or unwarranted, and which injures, endangers, or damages one in an essential or material degree in, or which materially interferes with, his legitimate rights to the enjoyment of life, health, comfort, or property, real or personal. A nuisance may exist not only by reason of doing an act, but also by omitting to perform a duty." Joseph A. Joyce & Howard C. Joyce, *Treatise on the Law Governing Nuisances* 22 (1906).

"A nuisance may be merely a right thing in the wrong place, like a pig in the parlor instead of the barnyard." *Village of Euclid v. Amber Realty Co.*, 272 U.S. 365, 388, 47 S.Ct. 114, 118 (1926).

"A 'nuisance' is a state of affairs. To conduct a nuisance is a tort. In torts, the word 'nuisance' has had an extremely elastic meaning; sometimes it is little more than a pejorative term, a weasel word used as a substitute for reasoning. . . . The general distinction between a nuisance and a trespass is that the trespass flows from a physical invasion and the nuisance does not." Roger A. Cunningham et al., *The Law of Property* § 7.2, at 417 (2d ed. 1993).

2. Loosely, an act or failure to act resulting in an interference with the use or enjoyment of property. • In this sense, the term denotes the action causing the interference, rather than the resulting condition <the Slocums' playing electric guitars in their yard constituted a nuisance to their neighbors>.

"There is perhaps no more impenetrable jungle in the entire law than that which surrounds the word 'nuisance.' It has meant all things to all people, and has been applied indiscriminately to everything from an alarming advertisement to a cockroach baked in a pie." W. Page Keeton et al., *Prosser and Keeton on the Law of Torts* § 86, at 616 (5th ed. 1984).

3. The class of torts arising from such conditions, acts, or failures to act when they occur unreasonably. — Also termed *actionable nuisance.*

"Nuisance is really a field of tortious liability rather than a single type of tortious conduct: the feature which gives it unity is the interest invaded — that of the use and enjoyment of land. The tort emphasises the harm to the plaintiff rather than the conduct of the defendant." R.F.V. Heuston, *Salmond on the Law of Torts* 50–51 (17th ed. 1977).

▸ **abatable nuisance.** (1871) **1.** A nuisance so easily removable that the aggrieved party may lawfully cure the problem without notice to the liable party, such as overhanging tree branches. **2.** A nuisance that reasonable persons would regard as being removable by reasonable means.

▸ **absolute nuisance.** (18c) **1.** Interference with a property right that a court considers fixed or invariable, such as a riparian owner's right to use a stream in its natural condition. **2.** See *nuisance per se.* **3.** Interference in a place where it does not reasonably belong, even if the interfering party is careful. **4.** Interference for which a defendant is held strictly liable for resulting harm, esp. in the nature of pollution. Cf. *qualified nuisance.*

Sense 4 has been disapproved: "[T]he use of the term 'nuisance' to describe the tort liability that sometimes results from accidental invasions produces too much confusion." W. Page Keeton et al., *Prosser and Keeton on the Law of Torts* § 89, at 637 (5th ed. 1984).

▸ **anticipatory nuisance.** (1930) A condition that, although not yet at the level of a nuisance, is very likely to become one, so that a party may obtain an injunction prohibiting the condition. — Also termed *prospective nuisance.*

▸ **attractive nuisance.** (1901) A dangerous condition that may attract children onto land, thereby causing a risk to their safety. See ATTRACTIVE-NUISANCE DOCTRINE. Cf. ALLUREMENT; *dangerous condition* (2) under CONDITION (5).

▸ **cognate nuisance.** (1906) *Rare.* Interference with an easement.

"The term nuisance is applied to torts of two distinct groups, first, acts of wrongful user by an owner or possessor of land resulting in an unreasonable interference with the rights of enjoyment of the owner or possessor of neighboring land, and, second, wrongful interferences with easements or other incorporeal rights." William F. Walsh, *A Treatise on Equity* 170 (1930).

"When an easement was interfered with, an action on the case lay as a matter of course. . . . Such an interference is sometimes called 'cognate nuisance' to distinguish it from interferences with the personal enjoyment of the incidents of occupying the land." J.H. Baker, *An Introduction to English Legal History* 486 (3d ed. 1990).

▸ **common nuisance.** See *public nuisance.*

▸ **continuing nuisance.** (1837) A nuisance that is either uninterrupted or frequently recurring. • It need not be constant or unceasing, but it must occur often enough that it is almost continuous.

▸ **legalized nuisance.** (1878) A nuisance sanctioned by legislative, executive, or other official action and therefore immune from liability, such as a city park.

▸ **mixed nuisance.** (1894) A condition that is both a private nuisance and a public nuisance, so that it is dangerous to the community at large but also causes particular harm to private individuals.

▸ **nuisance at law.** See *nuisance per se.*

▸ **nuisance dependent on negligence.** See *qualified nuisance.*

▸ **nuisance in fact.** (1855) A nuisance existing because of the circumstances of the use or the particular location. • For example, a machine emitting high-frequency sound may be a nuisance only if a person's dog lives near enough to the noise to be disturbed by it. — Also termed *nuisance per accidens.*

▸ **nuisance per se** (pər say). (1860) Interference so severe that it would constitute a nuisance under any circumstances; a nuisance regardless of location or circumstances of use, such as a leaky nuclear-waste storage facility. — Also termed *nuisance at law; absolute nuisance.*

"A nuisance per se, as the term implies, is a nuisance in itself, and which, therefore, cannot be so conducted or maintained as to be lawfully carried on or permitted to exist. Such a nuisance is a disorderly house, or an obstruction to a highway or to a navigable stream. Again, 'Nuisances per se have been defined to be such things as are nuisances at all times and under all circumstances, irrespective of location or surroundings.' [*Hundley v. Harrison*, 26 So. 294, 294 (Ala. 1899).]" Joseph A. Joyce & Howard C. Joyce, *Treatise on the Law Governing Nuisances* 20 (1906).

▸ **permanent nuisance.** (18c) A nuisance that cannot readily be abated at reasonable expense. Cf. *temporary nuisance.*

▸ **private nuisance.** (17c) **1.** A nuisance that affects a private right not common to the public or that causes a special injury to person or to property of a single person or a determinate number of people. **2.** A condition that interferes with a person's enjoyment of property; esp., a structure or other condition erected or put on nearby land, creating or continuing an invasion of the actor's land and amounting to a trespass to it. • The condition constitutes a tort for which the adversely affected person may recover damages or obtain an injunction.

"Trespass and private nuisance are alike in that each is a field of tort liability rather than a single type of tortious conduct. In each, liability may arise from an intentional or an unintentional invasion. For an intentional trespass, there is liability without harm; for a private nuisance, there is no liability without significant harm. . . . In private nuisance an intentional interference with the plaintiff's use or enjoyment is not of itself a tort, and unreasonableness of the interference is necessary for liability." Restatement (Second) of Torts § 821D cmt. d (1979).

"The different ways and combinations of ways in which the interest in the use or enjoyment of land may be invaded are infinitely variable. A private nuisance may consist of an interference with the physical condition of the land itself, as by vibration or blasting which damages a house, the destruction of crops, flooding, raising the water table, or the pollution of a stream or of an underground water supply." W. Page Keeton et al., *Prosser and Keeton on the Law of Torts* § 87, at 619 (5th ed. 1984).

▸ **prospective nuisance.** See *anticipatory nuisance.*

▸ **public nuisance.** (17c) An unreasonable interference with a right common to the general public, such as a condition dangerous to health, offensive to community moral standards, or unlawfully obstructing the public in the free use of public property. • Such a nuisance may lead to a civil injunction or criminal prosecution. — Also termed *common nuisance.*

"A public or common nuisance is an offense against the public order and economy of the State, by unlawfully doing any act or by omitting to perform any duty which the common good, public decency or morals, or the public right to life, health, and the use of property requires, and which at the same time annoys, injures, endangers, renders insecure, interferes with, or obstructs the rights or property of the whole community, or neighborhood, or of any considerable number of persons; even though the extent of the annoyance, injury, or damage may be unequal or may vary in its effect upon individuals." Joseph A. Joyce & Howard C. Joyce, *Treatise on the Law Governing Nuisances* 10 (1906).

"Public and private nuisances are not in reality two species of the same genus at all. There is no generic conception which includes the crime of keeping a common gaming-house and the tort of allowing one's trees to overhang the land of a neighbour. A public nuisance falls within the law of torts only in so far as it may in the particular case constitute some form of tort also. Thus the obstruction of a highway is a public nuisance; but if it causes any special and peculiar damage to an individual, it is also a tort actionable at his suit." R.F.V. Heuston, *Salmond on the Law of Torts* 49–50 (17th ed. 1977).

"[P]ublic nuisance . . . is an amorphous and unsatisfactory area of the law covering an ill-assorted collection of wrongs, some of which have little or no association with tort and only appear to fill a gap in criminal law. Others cover what could be generally described as 'noisome trade,' which could be dealt with under some form of statutory nuisance. Yet a third group deals with what we would generally describe as 'abuses of the highway' . . . ." R.W.M. Dias & B.S. Markesinis, *Tort Law* 254 (1984).

▸ **qualified nuisance.** (1944) A condition that, though lawful in itself, is so negligently permitted to exist that it creates an unreasonable risk of harm and, in due course, actually results in injury to another. • It involves neither an intentional act nor a hazardous activity. — Also termed *nuisance dependent on negligence.* Cf. *absolute nuisance.*

▸ **recurrent nuisance.** (1905) A nuisance that occurs from time to time with distinct intervals between occurrences, rather than being continuous or only briefly interrupted.

▸ **temporary nuisance.** (1879) A nuisance that can be corrected by a reasonable expenditure of money or labor. Cf. *permanent nuisance.*

nuisance money. See *nuisance settlement* under SETTLEMENT (2).

nuisance per accidens. See *nuisance in fact* under NUISANCE.

nuisance prior art. See ART (3).

nuisance settlement. See SETTLEMENT (2).

nuke. *Slang.* See DENIAL-OF-SERVICE ATTACK.

nul (nəl). [Law French] No; none. • This negative particle begins many phrases, such as *nul tiel.*

nul agard (**nəl** ə-**gahrd**), *n.* [Law French "no award"] (18c) In an action to enforce an arbitration award on an arbitration bond, a plea denying the existence of the award. Cf. AGARD.

nul disseisin (**nəl** dis-**see**-zin). [Law French "no disseisin"] (17c) In a real action, a defendant's plea that the plaintiff was not deprived of the possession of any land and tenements. See DISSEISIN.

nul fait agard (nəl **fay** ə-**gahrd**). [Law French] No award was made. Cf. AGARD.

null, *adj.* (16c) Having no legal effect; without binding force; VOID <the contract was declared null and void>. • The phrase *null and void* is a common redundancy.

nulla bona (**nəl**-ə **boh**-nə). [Latin "no goods"] (18c) A form of return by a sheriff or constable upon an execution when the judgment debtor has no seizable property within the jurisdiction. Cf. NIHIL EST.

nulla persona (**nəl**-ə pər-**soh**-nə). [Latin] (17c) *Hist.* No person. • The phrase appeared in reference to the status of one who essentially has no legal rights usu. because of that person's actions, such as committing a crime, or that person's status, such as being a minor.

nulla poena sine lege (**nəl**-ə **pee**-nə **sɪ**-nee **lee**-jee *or* **sin**-ay **lay**-gay). [Latin] (1929) No punishment without a law authorizing it.

nulla sasina, nulla terra (**nəl**-ə **say**-si-nə [*or* **say**-zi-], **nəl**-ə **ter**-ə). [Law Latin] (17c) *Scots law.* No seisin (or enfeoffment), no land. • The phrase appeared in reference to the principle that there could be no indefeasible right in land until an enfeoffment was taken.

nullification (nəl-i-fi-**kay**-shən), *n.* (18c) **1.** The act of making something void; specif., the action of a state in abrogating a federal law, on the basis of state sovereignty. **2.** The quality, state, or condition of being void. See JURY NULLIFICATION.

nullification doctrine. (1830) The theory — espoused by southern states before the Civil War — advocating a state's right to declare a federal law unconstitutional and therefore void.

nullify, *vb.* (17c) To make void; to render invalid.

nullity (**nəl**-ə-tee). (16c) **1.** Something that is legally void <the forged commercial transfer is a nullity>. **2.** The fact of being legally void <she filed a petition for nullity of marriage>.

▸ **absolute nullity.** (17c) *Civil law.* **1.** An act that is incurably void because it is against public policy, law, or order. • Absolute nullity can be invoked by any party or by the court. *See* La. Civ. Code arts 7, 2030. **2.** The quality, state, or condition of such a nullity. See NULLITY OF MARRIAGE.

▸ **relative nullity.** (1821) *Civil law.* **1.** A legal nullity that can be cured by confirmation because the object of the nullity is valid. • Relative nullity may be invoked only by those parties for whose interest it was established. *See* La. Civ. Code art. 2031. **2.** The quality, state, or condition of such a nullity.

nullity of marriage. (16c) **1.** The invalidity of a presumed or supposed marriage because it is void on its face or has been voided by court order. • A void marriage, such as an incestuous marriage, is invalid on its face and requires no formality to end. — Often shortened to *nullity.* See *void marriage* under MARRIAGE (1).

> "The declaration of nullity is appropriate if the marriage is relatively null or absolutely null yet one or both spouses were in good faith. If the marriage is relatively null, civil effects flow until the declaration of nullity. On the other hand, the marriage that is absolutely null generally produces civil effects only if one or both of the spouses were in good faith and only so long as good faith lasts." 16 Katherine S. Spaht & W. Lee Hargrave, *Louisiana Civil Law Treatise: Matrimonial Regimes* § 7.6, at 348 (2d ed. 1997).

2. A suit brought to nullify a marriage. — Also termed *nullity suit.* See ANNULMENT.

nullity suit. See NULLITY OF MARRIAGE (2).

nullius filius (nə-**lɪ**-əs **fil**-ee-əs), *n.* [Latin "son of no one"] (16c) An illegitimate child.

nullius in bonis (nə-**lɪ**-əs in **boh**-nis), *adj.* [Latin "among the property of no person"] (16c) *Hist.* Belonging to no one. • Wild animals were considered to be *nullius in bonis.* — Also termed *in nullius bonis.*

nullius juris (nə-**lɪ**-əs **joor**-is). [Latin] *Hist.* Of no legal force.

nullum arbitrium (**nəl**-əm ahr-**bi**-tree-əm), *n.* [Law Latin "no decision"] (17c) *Hist.* In an action to enforce an arbitration bond, a plea denying the existence of an arbitration award.

nullum crimen sine lege (**nəl**-əm **krɪ**-mən **sɪ**-nee **lee**-jee). [Latin] *Hist.* No crime without law.

nullum est erratum (**nəl**-əm est ə-**ray**-təm), *n.* [Latin "there is no error in the record"] In response to an assignment of error, the common plea that there is no error in the record. • The effect of the plea is essentially to admit well-pleaded facts.

nullum fecerunt arbitrium (**nəl**-əm fə-**see**-rənt ahr-**bi**-tree-əm). [Latin "they never submitted to arbitration"] (17c) *Hist.* In an action to enforce an arbitration award, the defendant's plea denying that there had been an arbitration.

Nullum Tempus Act (**nəl**-əm **tem**-pəs akt), *n.* [Latin] *Hist. English law.* The Crown Suits Act of 1769 (amended in 1862) that limited the Crown's time to sue, in land and other specified matters, to 60 years. • The statute altered the common-law rule of *nullum tempus aut locus occurrit regi* ("no time or place affects the Crown"), which was based on the idea that the Crown was too busy with governmental affairs to timely attend to its legal affairs.

nullum tempus occurrit reipublicae (**nəl**-əm **tem**-pəs ə-**kər**-it ree-ɪ-**pəb**-lə-see), *n.* [Latin "no time runs against the state"] The principle that a statute of limitations does not apply to a commonwealth or state unless a statute specifically provides that it does. • The purpose of the rule is to fully protect public rights and property from injury.

nul tiel (nəl teel). [Law Latin] (17c) No such. • This phrase typically denotes a plea that denies the existence of something.

***nul tiel* corporation,** *n.* [Law French "no such corporation exists"] (1823) A plea denying the existence of an alleged corporation. • The defense of *nul tiel corporation* must usu. be affirmatively pleaded by a defendant before a plaintiff is required to prove its corporate existence.

***nul tiel* record,** *n.* [Law French "no such record"] (17c) A plea denying the existence of the record on which the plaintiff bases a claim. • Evidence may generally be introduced to invalidate the record only, not the statements in the record. See *trial by record* under TRIAL.

> "The proper general issue in debt on judgments is 'nul tiel record,' which denies the existence of the record alleged. Nul tiel record sets up: (1) the defense either that there is no record at all in existence; or (2) one different from that which the defendant has declared of; or (3) that the judgment is void on the face of the record." Benjamin J. Shipman, *Handbook of Common-Law Pleading* § 186, at 330 (Henry Winthrop Ballantine ed., 3d ed. 1923).

nul tort (nəl tort), *n.* [Law French "no wrong"] (17c) *Hist.* A type of general denial in an action to recover lands and tenements, by which the defendant claims that no wrong was done. See NUL DISSEISIN.

> "The *general* issue, or general plea, is what traverses, thwarts, and denies at once the whole declaration; without offering any special matter whereby to evade it . . . . [I]n real actions, *nul tort*, no wrong done; *nul disseisin*, no disseisin; and in a writ of right, that the tenant has more right to hold than the demandant has to demand. These pleas are called the general issue, because, by importing an absolute and general denial of what is alleged in the declaration, they amount at once to an issue; by which we mean a fact affirmed on one side and denied on the other." 3 William Blackstone, *Commentaries on the Laws of England* 305 (1768).

nul waste (nəl wayst), *n.* [Law French "no waste"] (17c) *Hist.* The defendant's general denial in an action to recover damages for the destruction of lands and tenements. See NUL TORT.

number lottery. See *Genoese lottery* under LOTTERY.

number plate. See LICENSE PLATE (1).

numbers game. (1935) **1.** A traditionally illegal lottery in which the players typically choose a series of numbers, usu. three, and win if their chosen numbers match a series of numbers drawn randomly, often the following day. • Numbers games have historically been operated in poor neighborhoods and have permitted players to bet small amounts or even to bet on credit. An additional element of their historical attraction was the players' avoidance of paying income tax on winnings. Numbers games are traditionally associated with organized crime, and because of their odds (about 1:1,000), they are noted for being rigged and making large profits for racketeers. Some states today offer similar numbers games as lotteries. — Also termed *numbers racket*; *policy racket*; *Italian lottery*. **2.** See *Genoese lottery* under LOTTERY.

numerata pecunia (n[y]oo-mə-**ray**-tə pi-**kyoo**-nee-ə), *n.* [Latin] *Hist.* Money counted or paid.

numerical lottery. See *Genoese lottery* under LOTTERY.

numerosity (n[y]oo-mər-**ahs**-ə-tee). (1958) The requirement in U.S. district courts that, for a case to be certified as a class action, the party applying for certification must show, among other things, that the class of potential plaintiffs is so large that the joinder of all of them into the suit is impracticable. See CLASS ACTION.

nummata (nə-**may**-tə), *n.* [Law Latin "money"] The monetary price of something.

nummata terrae (nə-**may**-tə **ter**-ee), *n.* [Law Latin] (17c) *Hist.* An acre of land.

nummi pupillares (**nəm**-ɪ pyoo-pə-**lair**-eez). [Latin] *Scots law.* Money belonging to a pupil.

nunciato (nən-shee-**ay**-toh). See NUNTIATIO.

nuncio (**nən**-shee-oh), *n.* [Italian, fr. Latin *nunciare* "to announce"] (16c) **1.** A papal ambassador to a foreign court or government; a representative of the Vatican in a country that maintains diplomatic relations with it. — Also termed *nuncius*; *nuntio*. Cf. *legatus a latere* under LEGATUS; INTERNUNCIO (3); LEGATE (3). **2.** *Archaic.* A messenger.

nunc pro tunc (**nəngk** proh **təngk** *or* **nuungk** proh **tuungk**). [Latin "now for then"] (17c) Having retroactive legal effect through a court's inherent power <the court entered a *nunc pro tunc* order to correct a clerical error in the record>.

> "It sometimes happens that an order made, or a judgment rendered, or other thing done in the progress of a case, and that should be entered upon the record, is inadvertently omitted therefrom. To cure such omission, the court may, upon motion, make what is called an entry *nunc pro tunc*; that is, the court may cause to be made *now*, an entry that shall have the same legal force and effect as if made at the time when it should have been made. The power of the court to correct such omissions in this way rests upon the maxim *actus curiae neminem gravabit*—an act of the court shall prejudice no one." George L. Phillips, *An Exposition of the Principles of Pleading Under the Codes of Civil Procedure* § 529, at 560 (1896).

nunc pro tunc amendment. See AMENDMENT (2).

nunc pro tunc judgment. See *judgment nunc pro tunc* under JUDGMENT (2).

nuncupare (nəng-kyuu-**pair**-ee), *vb.* [Latin "call by name"] *Hist.* To name or pronounce orally. • *Nuncupare heredem* means to name an heir before public witnesses.

nuncupate (**nəng**-kyə-payt), *vb.* [fr. Latin *nuncupare* "call by name"] (16c) **1.** *Hist.* To designate or name. **2.** To vow or declare publicly and solemnly. **3.** To declare orally, as a will. **4.** To dedicate or inscribe (a work).

nuncupative (**nəng**-kyə-pay-tiv *or* nəng-**kyoo**-pə-tiv), *adj.* [fr. Latin *nuncupare* "to name"] (15c) Stated by spoken word; declared orally.

nuncupative testament by public act. See *nuncupative will by public act* under WILL.

nuncupative will. See WILL.

nuncupative will by public act. See WILL.

nunc valent et quantum valuerunt tempore pacis (nəngk **vay**-lent et **kwon**-təm val-yoo-**er**-ənt **tem**-pə-ree **pay**-sis). [Latin] *Scots law.* The value (of the lands) now, and their value in time of peace. • This was the object of an inquiry formerly made in an inquest to assess the value of lands for taxation purposes.

nundinae (**nən**-də-nee), *n.* [fr. Latin *novem* "nine" + *dies* "day"] **1.** *Roman law.* A fair or market. **2.** *Roman law.* The period between two consecutive markets (usu. eight days), including the market days. • This period was often fixed for the payment of debts.

nundination (nən-di-**nay**-shən), *n.* [fr. Latin *nundinatio* "the holding of a market or fair"] (16c) *Hist.* The act of buying or selling at a fair.

nunquam indebitatus (**nən[g]**-kwam in-deb-i-**tay**-təs), *n.* [Latin "never indebted"] (1836) *Hist.* A defensive plea in a debt action, by which the defendant denies any indebtedness to the plaintiff. Cf. CONCESSIT SOLVERE.

nuntiatio (nən-shee-**ay**-shee-oh), *n.* [Latin "a declaration"] *Hist.* A formal declaration or protest. • A *nuntiatio novi operiis* was an injunction placed on the construction of a new building by the person protesting the construction. — Also spelled *nunciato*.

nuntio. See NUNCIO.

nuntius (**nən**-shee-əs), *n.* [Latin] "bearer of news"] (16c) **1.** *Roman law.* A messenger. • Declarations through a messenger were usu. as valid as those by letter. **2.** *Hist.* A messenger sent to make an excuse for a party's absence in court. **3.** *Hist.* An officer of the court. — Also termed *summoner*; *beadle*. **4.** *Eccles. law.* NUNCIO (1).

nuper obiit (**n[y]oo**-pər **oh**-bee-it), *n.* [Latin "lately died"] (16c) *Hist.* A writ available to an heir to establish the equal division of land when, on the death of an ancestor who held the estate in fee simple, a coheir took the land and prevented the other heirs from possessing it. The writ was abolished in 1833. See COPARCENER.

nuptiae (**nəp**-shee-ee). See MATRIMONIUM.

nuptiae secundae (**nəp**-shee-ee sə-**kən**-dee), *n.* [Latin] *Eccles. law.* A second or subsequent marriage. • In canon law, second or subsequent marriages were frowned on, and priests would not officiate at those ceremonies.

nuptial (**nəp**-shəl), *adj.* (15c) Of, relating to, or involving marriage.

nuptiales tabulae (nəp-shee-**ay**-leez **tab**-yə-lee). [Latin] (1939) *Roman law.* Marriage tablets — i.e., documents recording a marriage and the terms on which it was entered into. • These writings were not essential to the validity of a marriage.

Nuremberg defense (n[y]ər-əm-bərg). (1954) **1.** The supposed defense that one is not liable for acts done at the request of a superior; specif., a person's claim that he or she was "just following orders" and therefore should not be held responsible for actions taken. • The term comes from the Nuremberg war-crimes trials after World War II (1945–1946). — Also termed *superior orders; superior-orders defense; following-orders defense; good-soldier defense.* Cf. SERGEANT SCHULTZ DEFENSE. **2.** The defense asserted by a member of the military who has been charged with the crime of failing to obey an order and who claims that the order was illegal, esp. that the order would result in a violation of international law. • The term is sometimes used more broadly to describe situations in which citizens accused of committing domestic crimes, such as degradation of government property, claim that their crimes were justified or mandated by international law. *See Hinzman and Hughey v. Canada (Citizenship and Immigration),* 2007 FCA 171, Canada: Federal Court of Appeal, 30 April 2007. — Also termed *lawful-orders defense.*

nurture, *vb.* (14c) **1.** To supply with nourishment. **2.** To train, educate, or develop.

nurturing-parent doctrine. (1982) *Family law.* The principle that, although a court deciding on child support generally disregards a parent's motive in failing to maximize earning capacity, the court will not impute income to a custodial parent who remains at home or works less than full-time in order to provide a better environment for a child. • The doctrine is fact-specific; courts apply it case by case.

nurus (**n[y]oor**-əs), *n.* [Latin] A daughter-in-law.

NVOCC. *abbr.* See *non-vessel-operating common carrier* under CARRIER (1).

N.W. *abbr.* NORTH WESTERN REPORTER.

NWS. *abbr.* National Weather Service. See NATIONAL OCEANIC AND ATMOSPHERIC ADMINISTRATION.

nychthemeron (nik-**thee**-mər-ahn), *n.* [Greek] (17c) An entire day and night; a 24-hour period.

NYS. *abbr.* NEW YORK SUPPLEMENT.

NYSE. *abbr.* (1939) NEW YORK STOCK EXCHANGE.

nystagmus (ni-**stag**-məs). (18c) A rapid, involuntary jerking or twitching of the eyes, sometimes caused by ingesting drugs or alcohol. See HORIZONTAL-GAZE NYSTAGMUS TEST.

O

OAG. *abbr.* Office of the Attorney General. See ATTORNEY GENERAL.

OAR. *abbr.* Office of Oceanic and Atmospheric Research. See NATIONAL OCEANIC AND ATMOSPHERIC ADMINISTRATION.

OASDHI. *abbr.* Old Age, Survivors, Disability, and Health Insurance. See OLD-AGE AND SURVIVORS' INSURANCE.

OASDI. *abbr.* Old Age, Survivors, and Disability Insurance. See OLD-AGE AND SURVIVORS' INSURANCE.

OASI. *abbr.* OLD-AGE AND SURVIVORS' INSURANCE.

oath. (bef. 12c) **1.** A solemn declaration, accompanied by a swearing to God or a revered person or thing, that one's statement is true or that one will be bound to a promise. • The person making the oath implicitly invites punishment if the statement is untrue or the promise is broken. The legal effect of an oath is to subject the person to penalties for perjury if the testimony is false. **2.** The statement or promise made in such a declaration. **3.** The form of words used for such a declaration. **4.** A formal declaration made solemn without a swearing to God or a revered person or thing; AFFIRMATION. Cf. PLEDGE (1).

> "The word 'oath' (apart from its use to indicate a profane expression) has two very different meanings: (1) a solemn appeal to God in attestation of the truth of a statement or the binding character of such a promise; (2) a statement or promise made under the sanction of such an appeal." Rollin M. Perkins & Ronald N. Boyce, *Criminal Law* 515 (3d ed. 1982).

▸ **assertory oath** (ə-**sər**-tə-ree). (18c) An oath or affirmation by which one attests to some factual matter, rather than making a promise about one's future conduct. • A courtroom witness typically takes such an oath.

▸ **corporal oath** (**kor**-pər-əl). (16c) An oath made solemn by touching a sacred object, esp. the Bible. — Also termed *solemn oath*; *corporale sacramentum*.

> "*Oath* (*Juramentum*) Is a calling Almighty God to witness that the Testimony is true; therefore it is aptly termed *Sacramentum*, a Holy Band, a Sacred Tye, or Godly Vow. And it is called a *Corporal Oath*, because the party when he swears, toucheth with his right hand the *Holy Evangelists* or Book of the *New Testament*." Thomas Blount, *Nomo-Lexicon: A Law-Dictionary* (1670).

▸ **decisive oath.** (18c) *Civil law.* An oath or affirmation by a party in a lawsuit, used to decide the case because the party's adversary, not being able to furnish adequate proof, offered to refer the decision of the case to the party. — Also termed *decisory oath*.

▸ **expurgatory oath.** (1831) A prospective juror's declaration of unequivocal assurance that the juror can render an impartial verdict based solely on the evidence. • An expurgatory oath occurs especially after the juror's impartiality has been called into question.

▸ **extrajudicial oath.** (17c) An oath or affirmation that, although formally sworn, is taken outside a legal proceeding or outside the authority of law. — Also termed *nonjudicial oath*.

▸ **false oath.** See PERJURY.

▸ **judicial oath.** (17c) An oath or affirmation taken in the course of a judicial proceeding, esp. in open court.

▸ **loyalty oath.** See *oath of allegiance*.

▸ **nonjudicial oath.** (1885) **1.** An oath or affirmation taken out of court, esp. before an officer ex parte. — Also termed *voluntary oath*. **2.** See *extrajudicial oath*.

▸ **oath *de calumnia*.** See *oath of calumny*.

▸ **oath ex officio** (eks ə-**fish**-ee-oh). (16c) *Hist.* At common law, an oath under which a person accused of a crime swore to answer questions before an ecclesiastical court. — Also termed *oath de veritate dicenda*.

> "The oath *de veritate dicenda* has a slightly sinister reputation in English and American histories. It is the canonical name for what is known to students of constitutional history as the *ex officio* oath. In the hands of the Court of High Commission, created by the Tudor and Stuart monarchs to enforce religious uniformity, the oath became a tool of despotism, used against opponents of king and church during the seventeenth century. It required defendants to agree, under penalties of contempt, to answer questions that would be put to them, and this before they knew what the charges against them were. Not without reason, defendants were reluctant to take it. Its subsequent repudiation and statutory prohibition have been one source of the modern privilege against self-incrimination, the right accorded to all persons accused of a crime not to be compelled to give evidence against themselves." R.H. Helmholz, *The Spirit of Classical Canon Law* 155 (1996).

▸ **oath in litem** (**lɪ**-tem *or* -təm). (17c) *Civil law.* An oath or affirmation taken by a plaintiff in testifying to the value of the thing in dispute when there is no evidence of value or when the defendant has fraudulently suppressed evidence of value.

▸ **oath of abjuration.** (17c) *Hist. English law.* An oath renouncing any and all right of descendants of a pretender to the Crown.

▸ **oath of allegiance.** (16c) An oath or affirmation by which one promises to maintain fidelity to a particular sovereign or government. • This oath is most often administered to a high public officer, to a soldier or sailor, or to an alien applying for naturalization. When taken in naturalization proceedings, the oath often includes the forswearing of all allegiance to other sovereigns — Also termed *loyalty oath*; *test oath*.

▸ **oath of calumny** (**kal**-əm-nee). (17c) *Hist.* An oath that a plaintiff or defendant took to attest to that party's good faith and to the party's belief that there was a bona fide claim. — Also termed *oath de calumnia*. See CALUMNY.

▸ **oath of office.** (16c) An oath or affirmation taken by a person about to enter into the duties of public office, by which the person promises to perform the duties of that office in good faith.

▸ **oath of supremacy.** (16c) *Hist. English law.* An oath required of those taking office, along with the oaths of allegiance and abjuration, declaring that the sovereign is superior to the church in ecclesiastical matters.

▸ **oath purgatory.** See *purgatory oath*.

▸ **oath suppletory.** See *suppletory oath.*

▸ **pauper's oath.** (1844) An affidavit or verification of poverty by a person requesting public funds or services. See *poverty affidavit* under AFFIDAVIT; IN FORMA PAUPERIS.

▸ **promissory oath.** (15c) An oath or affirmation that binds the party to observe a specified course of conduct in the future. • Both the oath of office and the oath of allegiance are types of promissory oaths.

▸ **purgatory oath.** (16c) An oath or affirmation taken to clear oneself of a charge or suspicion. — Also termed *oath purgatory.*

▸ **solemn oath.** See *corporal oath.*

▸ **suppletory oath** (**səp**-lə-tor-ee). (17c) **1.** *Civil law.* An oath or affirmation administered to a party, rather than a witness, in a case in which a fact has been proved by only one witness. • In a civil-law case, two witnesses are needed to constitute full proof. See HALF-PROOF. **2.** An oath or affirmation administered to a party to authenticate or support some piece of documentary evidence offered by the party. — Also termed *oath suppletory.*

▸ **test oath.** See *oath of allegiance.*

▸ **voluntary oath.** See *nonjudicial oath* (1).

oathable. See OATHWORTHY.

oath against an oath. See SWEARING MATCH.

oath de veritate dicenda. See *oath ex officio* under OATH.

oath-helper. See COMPURGATOR.

oath of abjuration. See ABJURATION.

Oath or Affirmation Clause. (1974) *Constitutional law.* The clause of the U.S. Constitution requiring members of Congress and the state legislatures, and all members of the executive or judicial branches — state or local — to pledge by oath or affirmation to support the Constitution. U.S. Const. art. VI, cl. 3. — Also termed *Oaths Clause.*

oath-rite. (17c) The form or ceremony used when taking an oath.

Oaths Clause. OATH OR AFFIRMATION CLAUSE.

oathworthy, *adj.* (bef. 12c) Legally capable of making an oath. — Also termed *oathable.*

obaeratus (oh-bə-**ray**-təs), *adj.* [Latin] *Roman law.* Burdened with debt.

obaeratus, *n.* [Latin] *Roman law.* A debtor.

Obamacare. (2007) AFFORDABLE CARE ACT. • Often used pejoratively by the Act's opponents and sometimes reclaimed by its supporters, the name is a portmanteau of the surname of President Barack Obama, who signed the law, and *healthcare.*

ob continentiam delicti (ob kon-tə-**nen**-shee-əm də-**lik**-tɪ). [Latin] (1826) On account of contiguity to the offense; being contaminated by association with something illegal.

ob contingentiam (ob kon-tin-**jen**-shee-əm). [Latin] (18c) *Hist.* **1.** On account of connection; by reason of similarity. • This phrase appeared when there was a close enough connection between two or more lawsuits to consolidate them. **2.** In case of contingency.

ob defectum haeredis (ob di-**fek**-təm hə-**ree**-dis). [Law Latin] (1874) *Hist.* On account of a failure of heirs.

obedience. (13c) Compliance with a law, command, or authority.

obediential obligation. See OBLIGATION.

ob favorem mercatorum (ob fə-**vor**-əm mər-kə-**tor**-əm). [Latin] In favor of merchants.

obiit (**oh**-bee-it). [Latin] He died; she died.

obiit sine prole (**oh**-bee-it **sɪ**-nee **proh**-lee *also* **sin**-ay **prohl**). [Latin] He died without issue. — Abbr. *o.s.p.*

obit. (14c) **1.** *Archaic.* A memorial service on the anniversary of a person's death. **2.** A record or notice of a person's death; an obituary.

obiter (**oh**-bit-ər), *adv.* [Latin "by the way"] (16c) Incidentally; in passing <the judge said, obiter, that a nominal sentence would be inappropriate>.

obiter, *n.* See OBITER DICTUM.

obiter dictum (**ob**-i-tər **dik**-təm). [Latin "something said in passing"] (18c) A judicial comment made while delivering a judicial opinion, but one that is unnecessary to the decision in the case and therefore not precedential (although it may be considered persuasive). — Often shortened to *dictum* or, less commonly, *obiter.* See DICTUM. Cf. HOLDING (1); *judicial dictum* under DICTUM; RATIO DECIDENDI. Pl. **obiter dicta.**

> "Strictly speaking an 'obiter dictum' is a remark made or opinion expressed by a judge, in his decision upon a cause, 'by the way' — that is, incidentally or collaterally, and not directly upon the question before the court; or it is any statement of law enunciated by the judge or court merely by way of illustration, argument, analogy, or suggestion. . . . In the common speech of lawyers, all such extrajudicial expressions of legal opinion are referred to as 'dicta,' or 'obiter dicta,' these two terms being used interchangeably." William M. Lile et al., *Brief Making and the Use of Law Books* 304 (Roger W. Cooley & Charles Lesley Ames eds., 3d ed. 1914).

obiter ex post facto (**ob**-i-tər eks post **fak**-toh). A court's holding that, according to a later court, was expressed in unnecessarily broad terms. • Some authorities suggest that this is not, properly speaking, a type of obiter dictum at all.

object (**ob**-jekt), *n.* (15c) **1.** A person or thing to which thought, feeling, or action is directed <the natural object of one's bounty>. See NATURAL OBJECT.

▸ **object of a power.** (1829) A person appointable by a donee. See POWER OF APPOINTMENT.

2. Something sought to be attained or accomplished; an end, goal, or purpose <the financial objects of the joint venture>.

▸ **object of an action.** (1836) The legal relief that a plaintiff seeks; the remedy demanded or relief sought in a lawsuit. Cf. SUBJECT OF AN ACTION.

▸ **object of a statute.** (18c) The aim or purpose of legislation; the end or design that a statute is meant to accomplish.

object (əb-**jekt**), *vb.* (15c) **1.** To state in opposition; to put forward as an objection <the prosecution objected that the defendant's discovery requests were untimely>. **2.** To state or put forward an objection, esp. to something in a judicial proceeding <the defense objected to the testimony on the ground that it was privileged>. — **objector,** *n.*

objectant. See CONTESTANT (1).

object code. (1961) *Copyright.* The machine-readable language compiled from a computer programmer's source code. • Object code is difficult to reverse-engineer, so publicly available software is always in this form. Object code is protected by copyright law and may also be protected by patent law. Because people cannot read or understand it, object code is deposited with the U.S. Copyright Office more often than source code. Cf. SOURCE CODE.

objection, *n.* (18c) **1.** A formal statement opposing something that has occurred, or is about to occur, in court and seeking the judge's immediate ruling on the point. • The party objecting must usu. state the basis for the objection to preserve the right to appeal an adverse ruling. See PLEADING (quot.).

▸ **continuing objection.** (1940) A single objection to all the questions in a given line of questioning. • A judge may allow a lawyer to make a continuing objection when the judge has overruled an objection applicable to many questions, and the lawyer wants to preserve the objection for the appellate record. — Also termed *running objection.*

▸ **frivolous objection.** (18c) A petty, often baseless, objection.

▸ **general objection.** (18c) An objection made without specifying any grounds in support of the objection. • A general objection preserves only the issue of relevancy. — Also termed *broadside objection.*

▸ **speaking objection.** (1958) An objection that contains more information (often in the form of argument) than needed by the judge to sustain or overrule it. • Many judges prohibit lawyers from using speaking objections, and sometimes even from stating the grounds for objections, because of the potential for influencing the jury.

▸ **specific objection.** (1894) An objection that is accompanied by a statement of one or more grounds in support of the objection.

▸ **standing objection.** (1907) An objection to an opposing lawyer's entire line of questioning, made instead of repeating question-by-question objections.

▸ **vexatious objection.** (1822) An objection made to delay, annoy, or otherwise impede a proceeding solely for tactical reasons.

2. *Parliamentary law.* A motion that suppresses a main motion, esp. one that will or may inflame controversy, immediately and without debate. • The motion, because it disposes of the main motion without any debate, usu. requires a supermajority. — Also termed *question of consideration; objection to consideration of a question.*

> "Objection to the consideration of a question is used when an original main motion is of a delicate or personal nature, or is contentious or inflammatory (such as sectarian, political, racial, etc.), or is irrelevant, unprofitable, or otherwise objectionable or discriminatory. The motion can be avoided altogether by instantly objecting to the consideration of the question." George Demeter, *Demeter's Manual of Parliamentary Law and Procedure* 141 (1969).

3. *Parliamentary law.* A negative vote, esp. one that defeats a request for general consent. **4.** *Patents.* An examiner's action identifying a defect in the form of a patent application, usu. in the specification or a drawing. • An objection does not raise questions about the merit of the claims. An examiner might object, for instance, to a defective oath or to a trademark appearing on the drawings. Cf. REJECTION (4).

objectionable, *adj.* (18c) Open to opposition, esp. adverse reason or contrary argument. — Also termed *exceptionable.*

objection in point of law. (17c) A defensive pleading by which the defendant admits the facts alleged by the plaintiff but objects that they do not make out a legal claim.

objection to consideration of a question. See OBJECTION (2).

objective, *adj.* (17c) **1.** Of, relating to, or based on externally verifiable phenomena, as opposed to an individual's perceptions, feelings, or intentions <the objective facts>. **2.** Without bias or prejudice; disinterested <because her son was involved, she felt she could not be objective>. **3.** Existing outside the mind as something real, not only as an idea <objective reality>. Cf. SUBJECTIVE.

objective but-for test. See BUT-FOR MATERIALITY.

objective entrapment. See ENTRAPMENT.

objective ethics. See MORAL ABSOLUTISM.

objective impossibility. See IMPOSSIBILITY.

objective meaning. See MEANING.

objective method. See HYPOTHETICAL-PERSON DEFENSE.

objective novation. See NOVATION.

objective standard. See STANDARD.

objective theory of contract. (1904) The doctrine that a contract is not an agreement in the sense of a subjective meeting of the minds but is instead a series of external acts giving the objective semblance of agreement. — Often shortened to *objective theory.* Cf. SUBJECTIVE THEORY OF CONTRACT; MEETING OF THE MINDS.

object of a power. See *permissible appointee* under APPOINTEE.

object of a right. (1880) The thing in respect of which a right exists; the subject matter of a right. — Also termed *subject of a right.* See SUBJECT OF A RIGHT.

object offense. See OFFENSE (2).

object of the power. See *permissible appointee* under APPOINTEE.

object of the power of appointment. See *permissible appointee* under APPOINTEE.

objurgatrix (ob-jər-**gay**-triks). (16c) *Hist.* A common scold. See SCOLD.

oblatio (ah-**blay**-shee-oh), *n.* [Latin] (1880) *Roman law.* A tender of payment or performance due. Pl. ***oblationes*** (ah-blay-shee-**oh**-neez).

oblation (ah-**blay**-shən). (15c) **1.** An offering or sacrifice, esp. one in a religious or ritualistic ceremony. **2.** The act of offering the gift or sacrifice itself. — **oblatory,** *adj.*

obligant (**ob**-lə-gənt). (16c) *Scots law.* A debtor in an obligation; OBLIGOR.

obligate, *vb.* (16c) **1.** To bind by legal or moral duty; to make (someone) have to do something because it is the law or has become that person's duty. **2.** To commit (funds, property, etc.) to meet or secure an obligation.

obligatio (ah-blə-**gay**-shee-oh), *n.* [Latin] *Roman law.* An obligation; a legal bond. Pl. ***obligationes*** (ah-blə-gay-shee-**oh**-neez).

▸ ***obligatio civilis*** (ah-blə-**gay**-shee-oh sə-**VI**-lis). [Latin "civil obligation"] *Roman law.* **1.** An obligation recognized under *jus civile* as opposed to one recognized only under *jus honorarium.* **2.** A legally enforceable obligation, such as one by contract.

▸ ***obligatio ex contractu*** (ah-blə-**gay**-shee-oh eks kən-**trak**-t[y]oo). (1878) *Roman law.* [Latin "contractual obligation"] A contractual obligation.

▸ ***obligatio ex delicto*** (ah-blə-**gay**-shee-oh eks də-**lik**-toh). [Latin "tortious obligation"] (17c) *Roman law.* An obligation arising from a wrongdoing against the person or property of another; an obligation enforceable in tort. — Also termed *obligatio ex maleficio* (mal-ə-**fish**-ee-oh).

▸ ***obligatio ex maleficio.*** See *obligatio ex delicto.*

▸ ***obligatio ex pacto*** (ob-li-**gay**-shee-oh eks **pak**-toh). [Latin "obligation from a treaty"] *Hist.* A treaty obligation.

▸ ***obligatio honoraria*** (ah-blə-**gay**-shee-oh [h]on-ə-**rair**-ee-ə). (1936) *Roman law.* An obligation that the praetor or an aedile declares actionable.

▸ ***obligatio litteris*** (ah-blə-**gay**-shee-oh **lit**-ər-is). [Latin "written obligation"] (1895) **1.** *Hist.* A written contract. — Also termed *obligatio litterarum.* **2.** *Scots law.* A contract that must be constituted in formal writing. — Also spelled *obligatio literis.* **3.** *Roman law.* Literal contract, strictly comprising only the *nomen transcripticium.* See NOMEN TRANSCRIPTICIUM.

▸ ***obligatio naturalis*** (ah-blə-**gay**-shee-oh nach-ə-**ray**-lis). [Latin "natural obligation"] (17c) *Roman law.* An obligation that is not legally enforceable, although it may produce legal effects; an obligation deriving only from the law of nature.

▸ ***obligatio quasi ex contractu*** (ah-blə-**gay**-shee-oh **kway**-SI [*or* -ZI] eks kən-**trak**-t[y]oo). [Latin "obligation from quasi-contract"] (1915) *Roman law.* An obligation arising between two persons who have not contracted with each other but have formed a relationship similar to a contractual one, or where a payment is made in error; a quasi-contractual obligation. See *implied-in-law contract* under CONTRACT.

▸ ***obligatio quasi ex delicto*** (ah-blə-**gay**-shee-oh **kway**-SI [*or* -ZI] eks də-**lik**-toh). [Latin "obligation from something resembling a tort"] (1878) *Roman law.* An obligation arising from a wrong that is not covered by an *obligatio ex delicto* but that nonetheless creates liability. — Also termed *obligatio quasi ex maleficio* (mal-ə-**fish**-ee-oh).

▸ ***obligatio verborum*** (ah-blə-**gay**-shee-oh vər-**bor**-əm). [Latin "a verbal obligation"] (1886) *Roman law.* An obligation arising from a solemn question and answer using specific words.

obligation, *n.* (18c) **1.** A legal or moral duty to do or not do something. • The word has many wide and varied meanings. It may refer to anything that a person is bound to do or forbear from doing, whether the duty is imposed by law, contract, promise, social relations, courtesy, kindness, or morality. **2.** A formal, binding agreement or acknowledgment of a liability to pay a certain amount or to do a certain thing for a particular person or set of persons; esp., a duty arising by contract. — Also termed (in sense 2) *civil obligation.* See DUTY (1); LIABILITY (1). **3.** *Civil law.* A legal relationship in which one person, the obligor, is bound to render a performance in favor of another, the obligee. La. Civ. Code art. 1756.

> "[I]n English-speaking countries an unfortunate habit has arisen of using 'obligation' in a lax manner as co-extensive with duties of every kind." Frederick Pollock, *A First Book of Jurisprudence* 82 (1896).

> "Obligation in its popular sense is merely a synonym for duty. Its legal sense, derived from Roman law, differs from this in several respects. In the first place, obligations are merely one class of duties, namely, those which are the correlatives of rights *in personam.* An obligation is the *vinculum juris,* or bond of legal necessity, which binds together two or more determinate individuals. . . . Secondly, the term obligatio is in law the name, not merely of the duty, but also of the correlative right. It denotes the legal relation or *vinculum juris* in its entirety, including the right of the one party, no less than the liability of the other. Looked at from the point of view of the person entitled, an obligation is a right; looked at from the point of view of the person bound, it is a duty. . . . An obligation, therefore, may be defined as a proprietary right *in personam* or a duty which corresponds to such a right." John Salmond, *Jurisprudence* 460 (Glanville L. Williams ed., 10th ed. 1947).

> "[I]n its more general acceptation, the word 'obligation' means something that the law or morals command a person to do, a command that is made effective by the imposition of a sanction if the person fails to obey or comply. When given that reference, the word 'obligation' is made synonymous with the word 'duty.' In that sense it is said, for example, that all citizens of a certain age are under an obligation to fulfill their military duties . . . .
> "In another sense, the word 'obligation' means an instrument in writing, however informal, whereby one party contracts with another for the payment of a sum of money. In commercial law, for example, the word 'obligation' may mean a negotiable instrument . . . .
> "In the technical terminology of the civil codes, however, the word 'obligation' means a legal bond that binds two persons in such a way that one of them, the creditor or obligee, is entitled to demand from the other, the debtor or obligor, a certain performance." Saul Litvinoff, 5 *Louisiana Civil Law Treatise: The Law of Obligations* 1–2 (2d ed. 2001).

▸ **absolute obligation.** (17c) An obligation requiring strict fulfillment according to the terms of the engagement, without any alternatives to the obligor.

▸ **accessorial obligation.** See *secondary obligation.*

▸ **accessory obligation.** (17c) See *secondary obligation.*

▸ **alternative obligation.** (18c) An obligation that can be satisfied in at least two different ways, at the choice of the obligor. — Also termed *disjunctive obligation.* Cf. *facultative obligation.*

▸ **bifactoral obligation** (bI-**fak**-tər-əl). (1896) An obligation created by two parties.

▸ **civil obligation.** (17c) **1.** See *conventional obligation.* **2.** OBLIGATION (2).

▸ **community obligation.** (1893) A debt or other obligation incurred by either spouse after marriage in a community-property state. • Such an obligation is presumed to be an obligation of the community and not of the individual spouse.

▸ **conditional obligation.** (17c) An obligation that depends on an uncertain event. — Also termed *dependent obligation.*

▸ **conjunctive obligation.** (1842) An obligation composed of multiple performances that can be separately rendered or enforced; esp., an obligation in which several objects are connected by *and* (not *or*) or are in some other way clearly meant to be separately included in the contract. • For example, a loan agreement's conjunctive obligation may require payment of four loan installments and delivery of a deed of trust. Each loan installment and the deed's delivery is a separate, enforceable performance.

▸ **contractual obligation.** (1869) An obligation arising from a contract or agreement.

▸ **conventional obligation.** (18c) An obligation that results from agreement of the parties; a contractual obligation. — Also termed *express obligation; civil obligation.* Cf. *obediential obligation.*

▸ **correal obligation (kor-ee-əl *or* kə-ree-əl).** (1871) *Roman & civil law.* A joint and several obligation.

"A correal obligation means a plurality of obligations based on a community of obligation: a joint liability in respect of the whole of the same debt or a joint right in respect of the whole of the same claim." Rudolph Sohm, *The Institutes: A Textbook of the History and System of Roman Private Law* 361 (James Crawford Ledlie trans., 3d ed. 1907).

▸ **current obligation.** (18c) An obligation that is presently enforceable, but not past due.

▸ **dependent obligation.** See *conditional obligation.*

▸ **determinate obligation.** (18c) An obligation that has a specific thing as its object. • For example, an obligation to deliver the 1491 Venice edition of *Vocabularium Iuris* that once belonged to H.L.A. Hart can be discharged only by delivering the specified book. Cf. *indeterminate obligation.*

▸ **disjunctive obligation.** See *alternative obligation.*

▸ **divisible obligation.** (18c) An obligation that can be divided without the consent of the parties. • Either the performing party or the receiving party may unilaterally divide the obligation.

▸ **express obligation.** See *conventional obligation.*

▸ **facultative obligation.** (1894) *Civil law.* An obligation by which the debtor owes a single thing but may discharge the obligation by furnishing another specified thing in place of the one that is due. Cf. *alternative obligation.*

▸ **heritable obligation.** (18c) An obligation that may be enforced by a successor of the creditor or against a successor of the debtor. — Also termed *inheritable obligation.*

▸ **imperfect obligation.** See *moral obligation.*

▸ **implied obligation.** See *obediential obligation.*

▸ **implied obligation of cooperation.** (1961) *Contracts.* An understood duty to refrain from interfering with the other party's performance. — Also termed *obligation of noninterference.*

▸ **independent obligation.** (18c) An obligation whose performance does not rely on performance by another person or another's readiness and willingness to perform.

▸ **indeterminate obligation.** (1802) **1.** An obligation by which the obligor is bound to deliver one of a certain species of items. • For example, an obligation to deliver a pre-1509 edition of *Vocabularium Iuris* can be discharged by delivering any edition published before that date. **2.** An obligation that is not specific in amount or form, or is subject to being changed by a third party. Cf. *determinate obligation.*

▸ **inheritable obligation.** See *heritable obligation.*

▸ **joint obligation.** (18c) **1.** An obligation that binds two or more debtors to a single performance for one creditor. **2.** An obligation that binds one debtor to a single performance for two or more creditors.

▸ **moral obligation.** (18c) **1.** An ethical imperative arising not from the law (and not legally enforceable) but from a universal or nearly universal view of what is good and right. See MORAL. **2.** A previously existing duty that has become inoperative by positive law, such as a statute of limitations. • In the law of contracts, a moral obligation in sense 2 is sufficient to support an express promise as valuable consideration because it amounts to the voluntary revival or creation of a duty that existed once before but had been dispensed with. — Also termed *imperfect obligation; natural obligation.*

▸ **natural obligation.** (16c) **1.** *Civil law.* A moral duty that is not enforceable by judicial action. • Natural obligations are recognized in civil-law jurisdictions. While they are not enforceable by judicial action, something that has been performed under a natural obligation may not be reclaimed. For example, if an indigent patient in a hospital has no legal obligation to pay for the treatment but does so anyway, that person cannot later reclaim the payments voluntarily made. — Also termed *obligatio naturalis.* **2.** See *moral obligation.*

▸ **obediential obligation** (ə-bee-dee-**en**-shəl). (18c) An obligation imposed on a person because of a situation or relationship, such as an obligation of parents to care for their children. — Also termed *implied obligation.* Cf. *conventional obligation.*

▸ **obligation of cooperation.** (1932) **1.** *Int'l law.* A nation's responsibility to participate in concert with other nations to protect common interests. **2.** *Contracts.* The responsibility to work with the other party to carry out the terms of an agreement.

▸ **obligation of noninterference.** See *implied obligation of cooperation.*

▸ **perfect obligation.** (17c) A legally enforceable obligation; one that is recognized and sanctioned by positive law.

▸ **personal obligation.** (17c) **1.** An obligation performable only by the obligor, not by the obligor's heirs or representatives. **2.** An obligation in which the obligor is bound to perform without encumbering his or her property for its performance.

▸ **primary obligation.** (17c) **1.** An obligation that arises from the essential purpose of the transaction between the parties. • For an attempt to distinguish two sets of correlative obligations — *principal* vs. *accessorial* as opposed to *primary* vs. *secondary* — *see* Herschel W. Arant, *Handbook of the Law of Suretyship and Guaranty* §§ 2–3, at 3–5 (1931). Cf. *secondary obligation.* **2.** A fundamental contractual term imposing a requirement on a contracting party from which other obligations may arise. — Also termed *principal obligation.*

"The term primary obligation indicates the existence of an accessorial promise that is conditioned on the primary obligor's nonperformance of his duty. The terms principal and accessorial obligations and the terms primary and secondary obligations are not mutually exclusive. For example, where B signs a note with A to enable him to borrow money, A and B each assume a primary obligation, though B's obligation is accessory. As to the creditor, whether he knows that A signs to enable B to obtain the loan or not, each owes him a similar duty. The duty of neither is conditioned on nonperformance of the other's duty. Each is equally a debtor and the creditor's remedy against each is the same; each is referred to as a primary debtor or a primary obligor; the promise of each is characterized in the cases as 'direct,' 'original,' 'unconditional,' or 'primary.'" Herschel W. Arant, *Handbook of the Law of Suretyship and Guaranty* 4 (1931).

▸ **primitive obligation.** (17c) The obligation designated as the first to be satisfied.

▸ **principal obligation.** See *primary obligation* (2).

▸ **pure obligation.** (17c) *Scots law.* An absolute obligation already due and immediately enforceable. — Also termed *pure debt.*

▸ **secondary obligation.** (17c) A duty, promise, or undertaking that is incident to a primary obligation; esp., a duty to make reparation upon a breach of contract. • For example, a mortgage to secure payment of a bond is a secondary obligation. The primary obligation is to pay the bond itself. — Also termed *accessory obligation*; *accessorial obligation.*

▸ **several obligation.** (17c) **1.** An obligation that binds two or more debtors to separate performances for one creditor. **2.** An obligation that binds one debtor to separate performances for two or more creditors.

▸ **simple obligation.** (17c) An obligation that does not depend on an outside event; an unconditional obligation. — Also termed *independent obligation.*

▸ **single obligation.** (17c) An obligation with no penalty attached for nonperformance, as when one party simply promises to pay 20 dollars to another.

▸ **solidary obligation** (**sol**-ə-der-ee). (1818) *Roman & civil law.* An obligation that binds each of two or more debtors for the entire performance at the option of the creditor. • Solidary obligations are analogous to common-law joint and several obligations.

"A solidary obligation means the *separate* liability of several persons in respect of one and the same object. The normal case of a solidary obligation is a joint delict, as when two or more persons, acting jointly, do damage to property or commit a theft. So far as the obligation creates a duty to pay damages, it is solidary. Each of the co-delinquents is liable to make good the whole of the same damage." Rudolph Sohm, *The Institutes: A Textbook of the History and System of Roman Private Law* 361–62 (James Crawford Ledlie trans., 3d ed. 1907).

▸ **statutory obligation.** (18c) An obligation — whether to pay money, perform certain acts, or discharge duties — that is created by or arises out of a statute, rather than based on an independent contractual or legal relationship.

▸ **substitute obligation.** (1946) *Civil law.* An obligation that takes the place of an extinguished obligation by novation. See NOVATION.

▸ **unifactoral obligation** (yoo-nə-**fak**-tər-əl). (1896) An obligation created by one party.

obligation, mutuality of. See MUTUALITY OF OBLIGATION.

obligational. See OBLIGATORY.

obligatio naturalis. See OBLIGATIO.

obligation bond. See *general obligation bond* under BOND (3).

obligationes innominati. See INNOMINATE OBLIGATIONS.

obligation of contract. (18c) A duty, or more generally the collective duties, imposed by a legally enforceable agreement, esp. as considered against the constitutional prohibition of a state law that impairs such a duty or duties. See CONTRACT CLAUSE.

Obligation of Contracts Clause. See CONTRACTS CLAUSE.

obligation of cooperation. See OBLIGATION.

obligation of noninterference. See *implied obligation of cooperation* under OBLIGATION.

obligations, law of. See LAW OF OBLIGATIONS.

obligations *erga omnes* [Latin "duties toward all"] *Int'l law.* A country's duties that concern issues affecting the international community at large, not just the country's neighboring states. — Also termed *erga omnes obligations*; *erga omnes partes obligations.*

obligatio quasi ex contractu. See OBLIGATIO.

obligatio quasi ex delicto. See OBLIGATIO.

obligatio quasi ex maleficio. See *obligatio quasi ex delicto* under OBLIGATIO.

obligatory (ə-**blig**-ə-tor-ee), *adj.* (14c) **1.** Legally or morally binding <an obligatory promise>. **2.** Required by a law, a rule, etc.; mandatory <attendance is not obligatory>. **3.** Creating or recording an obligation <a writing obligatory>. — Also termed (rarely) *obligational.*

oblige (ə-**blɪj**), *vb.* (14c) **1.** To bind by legal or moral duty; OBLIGATE. **2.** To bind by doing a favor or service.

obligee (ob-lə-**jee**). (16c) **1.** One to whom an obligation is owed; a promisee, creditor, or donor beneficiary. **2.** Under the Uniform Interstate Family Support Act, any person to whom a duty of support is owed. **3.** *Archaic.* Someone who is obliged to do something; OBLIGOR (1).

"Several dictionaries, such as *The Random House College Dictionary* (rev. ed. 1995) and *Webster's New World Dictionary* (4th ed. 2007), define *obligee* in its etymological sense ['obliged'], as if it were synonymous with *obligor. Random House*, for example, defines *obligee* as 'a person who is obligated to another,' but that meaning ought to be reserved for *obligor.* An *obligee*, in modern usage, is one to whom an obligation is owed." Bryan A. Garner, *Garner's Dictionary of Legal Usage* 624 (3d ed. 2011).

obligor (ob-lə-**gor** *or* **ob**-lə-gor). (16c) **1.** Someone who has undertaken an obligation; a promisor or debtor. UCC § 9-102(a)(59). **2.** Under the Uniform Interstate Family Support Act, any person who owes a duty of support. **3.** *Archaic.* Someone who obliges another to do something; OBLIGEE (1).

▸ **principal obligor.** (18c) Someone who is under a duty of indemnity.

oblique (oh-**bleek** *or* ə-**bleek**), *adj.* (15c) **1.** Not direct in descent; collateral <an oblique heir>. **2.** Indirect; circumstantial <oblique evidence>.

oblique evidence. See *circumstantial evidence* (1) under EVIDENCE.

obliquus (ob-**lɪ**-kwəs). [Latin "oblique"] *Hist.* (Of a line of descent) collateral; indirect. Cf. RECTUS.

obliterate, *vb.* (16c) **1.** To wipe out, rub off, or erase (a writing or other markings). **2.** To remove from existence; to destroy all traces of. — **obliteration,** *n.*

obliterated corner. See CORNER (1).

oblivion. (14c) **1.** The act or an instance of forgetting or having forgotten <the oblivion of sleep>. **2.** The quality, state, or condition of being completely forgotten or unknown <a once-famous politician now in oblivion>. **3.** An official disregard of an offense; pardon; amnesty <an act of oblivion by Parliament>.

obloquy (**ob**-lə-kwee). (15c) **1.** Abusive or defamatory language; CALUMNY. **2.** The quality, state, or condition of being ill spoken of; disgrace, bad repute, and loss of respect.

ob majorem cautelam (ob mə-**jor**-əm kaw-**tee**-ləm). [Law Latin] (18c) *Hist.* For greater security.

ob metum perjurii (ob **mee**-təm pər-**joor**-ee-ı). [Law Latin] (18c) *Scots law.* On account of the fear of perjury. See METUS PERJURII.

ob non solutum canonem (ob non sə-**loo**-təm kə-**noh**-nəm). [Law Latin] (17c) *Scots law.* On account of unpaid canon or feu duty. • A vassal could forfeit land if the vassal failed to pay the feu duty for two (later five) years. See FEU.

obnoxious, *adj.* (16c) **1.** Offensive; objectionable <obnoxious behavior>. **2.** Contrary; opposed <a practice obnoxious to the principle of equal protection under the law>. **3.** *Archaic.* Exposed to harm; liable to something undesirable <actions obnoxious to criticism>.

ob pias causas (ob **pı**-əs **kaw**-zəs). [Latin] (17c) *Hist.* On account of religious or charitable reasons; for dutiful considerations.

> "Provisions made by a son to his father *ob pias causas* are those which proceed from the affectionate regard and natural duty which the son is bound morally to render to his father." John Trayner, *Trayner's Latin Maxims* 412 (4th ed. 1894).

ob poenam negligentiae (ob **pee**-nəm neg-li-**jen**-shee-ee). [Law Latin] *Hist.* On account of punishment for negligence. • The law punished those who were negligent in protecting their own interests.

ob publicam utilitatem (ob **pəb**-li-kəm yoo-til-ə-**tay**-təm). [Latin] *Hist.* On account of public utility; for the public advantage.

obreption (ob-**rep**-shən). (15c) The fraudulent obtaining of a gift or dispensation, esp. from a sovereign or ecclesiastical authority. Cf. SUBREPTIO.

obreptione (ob-rep-shee-**oh**-nee). [Latin] *Hist.* By surprise; by deceit.

ob reverentiam personae et metum perjurii (ob rev-ə-**ren**-shee-əm pər-**soh**-nee et **mee**-təm pər-**joor**-ee-ı). [Law Latin] (18c) *Hist.* On account of reverence to the person and the fear of perjury. • On this basis, certain witnesses could be excluded or could decline to answer certain questions that might cause them to commit perjury rather than admit to some act. This principle is essentially the forerunner to the Fifth Amendment privilege against self-incrimination. See METUS PERJURII.

***O'Brien* test.** (1969) A test to determine whether a statute that regulates speech (1) is supported by an important government interest in regulating the speech that is unrelated to suppressing the message and (2) affects First Amendment rights only so much as is essential to achieve the government interest. • The test was devised in *U.S. v. O'Brien*, 391 U.S. 367, 88 S.Ct. 1673 (1968). In that case, the U.S. Supreme Court held that a statute prohibiting the burning of draft cards was constitutional because the government had an important interest, unrelated to regulating speech, in administering the draft and draft cards were necessary to achieve that government interest.

obrogate (**ob**-rə-gayt), *vb.* (17c) *Civil law.* To modify or repeal (a law) in whole or in part by passing a new law. Cf. ABROGATE. — **obrogation,** *n.*

obscene, *adj.* (16c) Extremely offensive under contemporary community standards of morality and decency; grossly repugnant to the generally accepted notions of what is appropriate. • Under the Supreme Court's three-part test, material is legally obscene — and therefore not protected under the First Amendment — if, taken as a whole, the material (1) appeals to the prurient interest in sex, as determined by the average person applying contemporary community standards; (2) portrays sexual conduct, as specifically defined by the applicable state law, in a patently offensive way; and (3) lacks serious literary, artistic, political, or scientific value. *Miller v. California*, 413 U.S. 15, 93 S.Ct. 2607 (1973).

> "If there be no abstract definition, . . . should not the word 'obscene' be allowed to indicate the present critical point in the compromise between candor and shame at which the community may have arrived here and now?" *U.S. v. Kennerley*, 209 F. 119, 121 (S.D.N.Y. 1913).

> "Throughout the ages 'obscenity' appears to have included that which was 'sexually impure' or that which produced 'lustful thoughts' although these concepts seem to have had no precise content. Originally, 'obscene' also included that which was blasphemous or sacrilegious; but currently the Supreme Court of the United States has said that 'under the First and Eleventh Amendments a state may not ban a film on the basis of a censor's conclusion that it is sacrilegious.'" Frank E. Horack Jr., *Cases and Materials on Legislation* 25 (2d ed. 1940) (citations omitted).

obscene libel. See LIBEL (2).

obscenity, *n.* (16c) **1.** The quality, state, or condition of being morally abhorrent or socially taboo, esp. as a result of referring to or depicting sexual or excretory functions. **2.** Something (such as an expression or act) that has this characteristic. See CONTEMPORARY COMMUNITY STANDARDS. Cf. INDECENCY.

> "Obscenity is not deemed to be protected by the First Amendment, and the operative legal tests for obscenity are spongy and leave much to the vagaries of juries asked to evaluate expert testimony on literary merit, offensiveness, and other unmeasurables." Richard A. Posner, *Law and Literature: A Misunderstood Relation* 329 (1988).

▸ **commercialized obscenity.** (1956) Obscenity produced and marketed for sale to the public.

▸ **obscenity as to minors.** See *variable obscenity.*

▸ **variable obscenity.** (1960) Obscenity that may legally be accessible by or distributed to adults but not children. — Also termed *obscenity as to minors.*

obsequies (**ahb**-si-kweez), *n.* (14c) A funeral ceremony. • Though plural in form, and taking a plural verb (the obsequies were held later that week>, this noun normally denotes a single event. It can also, however, denote several such rites. The singular noun *obsequy* is rare.

observance, *n.* (13c) **1.** An act or an instance of following a law, rule, custom, etc.; a careful heeding <observance of flag rules>. **2.** A rule governing members of a society, club, or religious order <obeying sectarian observances>. **3.** A customary rite, procedure, or ceremony; esp., something one does as part of a ceremony <baptismal observances>.

observation post. (1909) A position from which an enemy or potential enemy can be watched.

observation tower. (1888) A tall structure designed so that a guard, police officer, forest ranger, etc. can see a long way to watch prisoners, detect lawbreaking, spot forest fires, etc.

observe, *vb.* (14c) **1.** To watch carefully <the police observed his movements for two hours>. **2.** To see and notice <criminologists have observed a decrease in the crime rate>. **3.** To adhere to or abide by (a law, rule, or custom) <a traffic citation for failing to observe the speed limit>.

observer. (1925) **1.** Someone who routinely watches or pays attention to particular things. **2.** Someone who sees or looks at something. **3.** Someone who attends a meeting, class, or other event to see what takes place. **4.** *Int'l law.* A representative of a country or international organization who attends a meeting of an international body (such as the United Nations) to which the observer's country does not belong in order to watch what happens there. • Observers do not vote or sign documents, but they are sometimes allowed to participate in discussions.

obses (**ob**-seez), *n.* [Latin] A hostage in wartime. Pl. ***obsides.***

obsignare (ob-sig-**nair**-ee), *vb.* [Latin] *Civil law.* To seal up, as with money that has been tendered and refused.

obsignation, *n.* (16c) A formal ratification or confirmation, esp. by an official seal. — **obsignatory** (ob-**sig**-nə-tor-ee), *adj.*

obsignator (ahb-sig-**nay**-tor *or* -tər), *n.* [Latin] *Roman law.* Someone who affixes a seal, esp. as a witness, to a will or other document. Pl. ***obsignatores*** (ahb-sig-nə-**tor**-eez).

obsolescence (ob-sə-**les**-ənts). (1832) **1.** The process, quality, state, or condition of falling into disuse or gradually becoming obsolete. **2.** A diminution in the value or usefulness of property, esp. as a result of technological advances. • For tax purposes, obsolescence is usu. distinguished from physical deterioration. Cf. DEPRECIATION.

- ▸ **economic obsolescence.** (1930) Obsolescence that results from external economic factors, such as decreased demand or changed governmental regulations. — Also termed *external obsolescence.* Cf. *functional obsolescence.*
- ▸ **external obsolescence.** See *economic obsolescence.*
- ▸ **functional obsolescence.** (1945) Obsolescence that results either from inherent deficiencies in the property, such as inadequate equipment or design, or from technological improvements available after the use began. Cf. *economic obsolescence.*
- ▸ **planned obsolescence.** (1932) A system or policy of deliberately producing consumer goods that will wear out or become outdated after limited use, thus inducing consumers to buy new items more frequently. — Also termed *built-in obsolescence.*

obsolescent, *adj.* (18c) Going out of use; becoming obsolete.

obsolete, *adj.* (17c) No longer in general use; out-of-date.

obstacle preemption. See PREEMPTION.

obstante (ob-**stan**-tee *or* əb-). [Latin] Withstanding; hindering. See NON OBSTANTE VEREDICTO.

obsta principiis (**ob**-stə prin-**sip**-ee-is). [Latin] Withstand beginnings; resist the first approaches or encroachments.

obstinate desertion. See DESERTION.

obstrict (əb-**strikt**), *vb.* (16c) To coerce. — **obstrictive,** *adj.* — **obstrictiveness,** *n.*

> "*The element of coercion or obstrictiveness.* The contrast here is between voluntary and obstricted (or coerced) conduct. The coercion need not be actual (objective), but may be merely potential (subjective) by fear of the possible force; as, when the faithful canine, Towser, susceptible to the sight of a feline enemy, is tempted to pursue, but upon his owner's stern voice and a shake of the stick, Towser turns humbly back and crushes his impulse." John Henry Wigmore, *Problems of Law* 7–8 (1920).

obstriction. (17c) *Archaic.* Obligation; bond.

obstruct (əb-**strəkt**), *vb.* (16c) **1.** To block or stop up (a road, passageway, etc.); to close up or close off, esp. by obstacle <obstruct the runway>. **2.** To make difficult or impossible; to keep from happening; hinder <to obstruct the peace process>. **3.** To cut off a line of vision; to shut out <the new construction obstructs our view of the road>.

obstructing justice. See PERVERTING THE COURSE OF JUSTICE.

obstructing process. See OBSTRUCTION OF PROCESS.

obstructing public justice. See PERVERTING THE COURSE OF JUSTICE.

obstructing the administration of justice. See PERVERTING THE COURSE OF JUSTICE.

obstructing the course of justice. See PERVERTING THE COURSE OF JUSTICE.

obstruction. (16c) **1.** Something that impedes or hinders, as in a street, river, design, flight path, etc.; an obstacle. **2.** The act of impeding or hindering something; interference. **3.** *Oil & gas.* A common-law doctrine that suspends the running of time under an oil-and-gas lease or extends the lease for a reasonable period of time if rights granted under the lease are interfered with by the lessor or someone claiming through the lessor. — **obstructive,** *adj.*

obstructionism (əb-**strək**-shə-niz-əm), *n.* (1879) The act or practice of purposely preventing or delaying a legal or political process; deliberate interference with the normal course of work, esp. in a legislative body. — **obstructionist,** *adj.* & *n.*

obstruction of justice. (1854) Interference with the orderly administration of law and justice, as by giving false information to or withholding evidence from a police officer or prosecutor, or by harming or intimidating a witness or juror. • Obstruction of justice is a crime in most jurisdictions. — Also termed *obstructing justice*; *obstructing public justice.* See PERVERTING THE COURSE OF JUSTICE.

> "The goal, — to proscribe every wilful act of corruption, intimidation or force which tends in any way to distort or impede the administration of law either civil or criminal — has been very largely attained, partly by aid of legislation. And any punishable misdeed of such a nature which is not recognized as a distinct crime, is usually called 'obstruction of justice,' or 'obstructing justice,' — a common-law misdemeanor." Rollin M. Perkins & Ronald N. Boyce, *Criminal Law* 552 (3d ed. 1982).

obstruction of process. (18c) Interference of any kind with the lawful service or execution of a writ, warrant, or other process. • Most jurisdictions make this offense a crime. — Also termed *obstructing process*; *resisting process.*

obtain, *vb.* **1.** To bring into one's own possession; to procure, esp. through effort <to obtain wealth>. **2.** To succeed either in accomplishing (something) or in having it be accomplished; to attain by effort <to obtain a loan>. **3.** To be established by law or custom; to be prevalent or general <the same rule obtains in Arkansas>.

obtaining property by false pretenses. See FALSE PRETENSES.

obtain the floor. (1820) *Parliamentary law.* To receive recognition from the chair as being entitled to speak after claiming the floor. See FLOOR (1).

obtest (ob- *or* əb-**test**), *vb.* (16c) **1.** To call to or invoke as a witness. **2.** To ask for earnestly; beseech; implore. **3.** To protest.

obtorto collo (ob-**tor**-toh **kah**-loh). [Latin] (16c) *Roman law.* Dragged by the neck. • Because a plaintiff could not sue an absent defendant, the plaintiff was sometimes said to have to drag a defendant *obtorto collo* to court.

obtulit se (**ob**-t[y]ə-lit **see**). [Latin] Offered himself. • In old English practice, these words were entered on the record when one party appeared ("offered himself") in court against an opposing party who did not appear.

ob turpem causam (ob **tər**-pəm [*or* -pem] **kaw**-zəm). [Latin] (17c) For an immoral consideration; on account of disgraceful consideration. • An obligation *ob turpem causam* (i.e., founded on what was termed *turpis causa*) could not be enforced.

obvention (ob- *or* əb-**ven**-shən). (15c) *Eccles. law.* An incoming fee or revenue, esp. one that comes occasionally or incidentally.

obviate (**ob**-vee-ayt), *vb.* (16c) **1.** To dispose of or do away with (a thing); to anticipate and prevent from arising <they obviated the growing problem through legislation>. **2.** To make unnecessary <the movant obviated the all-night drafting session by getting the opponent to agree to an extension>. — **obviation,** *n.* — **obviator,** *n.*

obvious error. A standard of review that applies to unobjected-to actions and omissions at trial that are so seriously prejudicial as to result in manifest injustice.

obviousness, *n.* (1921) *Patents.* The quality, state, or condition of being easily apparent to a person with ordinary skill in a given art, considering the scope and content of the prior art, so that the person could reasonably believe that, at the time it was conceived, the invention was to be expected. • An invention that is determined to be obvious cannot be patented. Although an obviousness inquiry is rife with questions of fact, the ultimate conclusion is a question of law. *See* 35 USCA 5103. Cf. NONOBVIOUSNESS. — **obvious,** *adj.*

▸ **prima facie obviousness.** *Patents.* A procedural tool used in the examination of U.S. patent applications in which the patent examiner must make an initial showing of obviousness before the applicant must produce evidence of nonobviousness. • The patent examiner bears the initial burden of establishing obviousness. A prima facie case of obviousness is established when the examiner articulates nonconclusory, explicit reasons for obviousness that are rationally supported by the factual record.

obviousness double patenting. See DOUBLE PATENTING.

obviousness-type double patenting. (1967) **1.** DOUBLE PATENTING (2). **2.** See *judicially created double patenting* under DOUBLE PATENTING (2).

obviousness-type double-patenting rejection. See *judicially created double-patenting rejection* under REJECTION.

o.c. *abbr.* **1.** Ope consilio. See OPE ET CONSILIO. **2.** Orphan's court. See *probate court* under COURT. **3.** (*cap.*) ORGANIZED CRIME.

OCC. *abbr.* OFFICE OF THE COMPTROLLER OF THE CURRENCY.

occasio (ə-**kay**-zhee-oh). [Law Latin] *Hist.* **1.** A tax that a lord imposed on his vassals or tenants for his necessity. **2.** Hindrance or trouble; esp., vexatious litigation.

occasional sale. See SALE.

occision (ok-**sizh**-ən), *n.* (15c) *Hist.* A slaying, esp. of more than one person.

occultatio thesauri inventi (ok-əl-**tay**-shee-oh thə-**saw**-rɪ in-**ven**-tɪ). [Law Latin] (1829) *Hist.* The concealment of found treasure.

occult marriage. See *confidential marriage* under MARRIAGE (1).

occupancy. (16c) **1.** The act, state, or condition of holding, possessing, or residing in or on something; actual possession, residence, or tenancy, esp. of a dwelling or land. • In this sense, the term denotes whatever acts are done on the land to manifest a claim of exclusive control and to indicate to the public that the actor has appropriated the land. Hence, erecting and maintaining a substantial enclosure around a tract of land usu. constitutes occupancy of the whole tract.

▸ **constructive occupancy.** (1814) A manifest intent to occupy property physically, followed within a reasonable time by actual occupancy.

2. The act of taking possession of something that has no owner (such as abandoned property) so as to acquire legal ownership. See ADVERSE POSSESSION. **3.** The period or term during which one owns, rents, or otherwise occupies property. **4.** The quality, state, or condition of being occupied. **5.** The use to which property is put. **6.** The number of people who stay, work, or live in a room or building at the same time.

occupant. (16c) **1.** Someone who has possessory rights in, or control over, certain property or premises. **2.** Someone who acquires title by occupancy. — Also termed *occupier.*

▸ **general occupant.** (18c) Someone who occupies land in the interim arising after the death of a *pur autre vie* tenant but before the death of the person who serves as the measuring life for the estate. • The *pur autre vie* tenant does not state who may occupy the land after the death of the first tenant; the land can be occupied by the first possessor of the land. — Also termed *common occupant.* Cf. CESTUI QUE VIE.

▸ **special occupant.** (18c) A person specifically designated in a conveyance as being entitled to a life estate if the conveyee dies before the end of the life estate; specif., a *pur autre vie* tenant's heir who occupies land in the interim between the death of the tenant and the death of the person who serves as the measuring life for the estate. • A special occupancy can arise when the grant to the *pur autre vie* tenant provides that possession is for the life of the tenant, then to the tenant's heirs.

occupant statute. See BETTERMENT ACT.

occupare (ok-yə-**pair**-ee), *vb.* [Latin] *Civil law.* To seize or take possession of (property); to enter (land) upon a vacant possession.

occupatile (**ok**-yə-pə-tɪl). *Hist.* Property that has been left by its rightful owner and is now possessed by another.

occupatio (ok-yə-**pay**-shee-oh), *n. Roman law.* A mode of acquisition by which a person obtains absolute title by first possessing a thing that previously belonged to no one, such as a wild bird or pearls on the shore. Cf. RULE OF CAPTURE (2).

occupation. (14c) **1.** An activity or pursuit in which a person engages; esp., a person's usual or principal work or business.

▸ **dangerous occupation.** (18c) An occupation that involves an appreciable risk of death or serious bodily injury.

2. The possession, control, or use of real property; OCCUPANCY. **3.** The seizure and control of territory by military force; the condition of territory that has been placed under the authority of an army, esp. a hostile one. — Also termed *military occupation.*

▸ **belligerent occupation.** (1864) The seizure and control of territory by hostile forces. • Adding the adjective *belligerent* to the noun *occupation* makes the phrase more unambiguously pejorative.

4. The period during which territory seized by military force is held.

occupational crime. See CRIME.

occupational-disability insurance. See INSURANCE.

occupational disease. (1901) A disease that is contracted as a result of exposure to debilitating conditions or substances in the course of employment. • Employees who suffer from occupational diseases are eligible for workers' compensation. Courts have construed the term to include a variety of ailments, including lung conditions (such as asbestosis or black lung), hearing loss, and carpal tunnel syndrome. — Also termed *industrial disease.*

> "Certain diseases and infirmities which develop gradually and imperceptibly as a result of engaging in particular employments and which are generally known and understood to be usual incidents or hazards thereof, are distinguished from those having a traumatic origin, or otherwise developing suddenly and unexpectedly, by the terms 'occupational,' and 'industrial.'" 82 Am. Jur. 2d *Workers' Compensation* § 326 (1992).

occupational driver's license. See *conditional driver's license* under DRIVER'S LICENSE.

occupational hazard. See HAZARD (1).

occupational offense. See *occupational crime* under CRIME.

Occupational Safety and Health Act of 1970. A federal statute that requires employers to (1) keep the workplace free from recognized hazards that cause or are likely to cause death or serious physical harm to employees, and (2) comply with standards promulgated by the Secretary of Labor. 29 USCA §§ 651–678. — Abbr. OSHA (**oh**-shə).

> "Although OSHA has been one of the most controversial pieces of protective legislation ever enacted, Congress has not passed any substantive amendments to the Act. There have been, however, some limitations on OSHA enforcement activity attached to appropriations bills. In addition, OSHA has been affected by newer laws such as the Criminal Fine Enforcement Act, the Equal Access to Justice Act, and the Surface Transportation Assistance Act. . . . The Act covers employment in every state, the District of Columbia, Puerto Rico, and all American territories, an estimated 5 million workplaces and 75 million employees." Mark A. Rothstein, *Occupational Safety and Health Law* 7 (1990).

Occupational Safety and Health Administration. A unit in the U.S. Department of Labor responsible for setting and enforcing workplace safety and health standards and for helping employers comply with them. • It was created under the Occupational Safety and Health Act of 1970. There are ten regional offices. — Abbr. OSHA.

Occupational Safety and Health Review Commission. An independent, quasi-judicial commission that resolves allegations of unsafe or unhealthy working conditions. • It was established by the Occupational Safety and Health Act of 1970. — Abbr. OSHRC.

occupational tax. See *occupation tax* under TAX.

occupation tax. See TAX.

occupatio pacifica (ok-yə-**pay**-shee-oh pə-**sif**-i-kə). [Latin] *Hist.* A peaceful seizure of territory.

occupavit (ok-yə-**pay**-vit). [Law Latin] *Hist.* A writ to regain possession to land or a tenement from which one was ejected in time of war.

occupied territory. See TERRITORY (1).

occupier. See OCCUPANT.

occupy, *vb.* **1.** To seize or take possession of; esp., to enter and take control of (a place) <the Iraqis briefly occupied Kuwait>. **2.** To take up the extent, space, room, or time of <the company's headquarters occupy 20 acres>. **3.** To hold possession of; to be in actual possession of <Queen Elizabeth II occupies the throne>. **4.** To employ; to possess or use the time or capacity of <the computer industry occupies millions of workers>. **5.** To use (money) in commerce; to invest; to employ for profit <to occupy $10 million in the venture>. **6.** To live or stay in (a place) <he occupies the apartment without paying rent>.

occupying claimant. (1801) Someone who claims the right under a statute to recover for the cost of improvements done to land that is later found not to belong to the person.

occupying-claimant act. See BETTERMENT ACT.

occurrence. (1978) Something that happens or takes place; specif., an accident, event, or continuing condition that results in personal injury or property damage that is neither expected nor intended from the standpoint of an insured party. • This specific sense is the standard definition of the term under most liability policies.

occurrence-based liability insurance. See INSURANCE.

occurrence policy. See INSURANCE POLICY.

occurrence rule. (1977) *Civil procedure.* The rule that a limitations period begins to run when the alleged wrongful act or omission occurs, rather than when the plaintiff discovers the injury. • This rule applies, for example, to most breach-of-contract claims. See STATUTE OF LIMITATIONS. Cf. DISCOVERY RULE.

ocean. (14c) **1.** The continuous body of salt water that covers more than 70% of the earth's surface; the high seas; the open sea. Cf. SEA. **2.** Any of the principal geographic divisions of this body. • There are generally considered to be five oceans: Atlantic, Pacific, Indian, Arctic, and Antarctic.

ocean bill of lading. See BILL OF LADING.

ocean marine insurance. See INSURANCE.

OCHAMPUS. *abbr.* OFFICE OF CIVILIAN HEALTH AND MEDICAL PROGRAMS OF THE UNIFORMED SERVICES.

ochlocracy (ah-**klah**-krə-see). (16c) Government by the lowest classes; mob-rule.

octo tales (**ok**-toh **tay**-leez *or* **taylz**). [Latin "eight such"] (17c) **1.** A supply of eight additional jurors for a trial. **2.** A writ commanding a sheriff to summon eight more jurors for a trial. See TALES.

octroi (**ok**-troy *or* ahk-**trwah**), *n.* [French] (16c) **1.** *Hist.* A grant or privilege of a charter by a sovereign. **2.** A local tax levied on certain goods that are brought into a city (esp. in some European countries). **3.** The place where such a tax is collected. **4.** The agency for collecting such a tax.

octroy (**ok**-troy), *vb.* (15c) (Of a sovereign) to grant or concede as a privilege.

o/d. *abbr.* **1.** OVERDRAFT (1). **2.** OVERDRAFT (2).

OD. *abbr.* (1959) **1.** Overdose. **2.** OVERDRAFT (1). **3.** OVERDRAFT (2). **4.** See *ordinary seaman* under SEAMAN.

odal (**oh**-dəl), *n.* (18c) *Hist.* Land not subject to feudal duties or burdens; ALLODIUM. — Also termed *odel*; *odhal*; *odhall*. — **odal,** *adj.* <an odal right>.

odd lot. See LOT (3).

odd-lot, *adj.* (1955) Of, relating to, or designating a worker who is so substantially disabled as to be unable to find stable employment in the ordinary labor market, and thus is considered totally disabled and entitled to workers'-compensation benefits under the odd-lot doctrine <an odd-lot worker who could find only sporadic employment>.

odd-lot doctrine. (1953) *Workers' compensation.* The doctrine that permits a finding of total disability for an injured claimant who, though able to work sporadically, cannot obtain regular employment and steady income and is thus considered an "odd lot" in the labor market.

odel. See ODAL.

odhal. See ODAL.

odhall. See ODAL.

odio et atia. See DE ODIO ET ATIA.

odium (**oh**-dee-əm). (17c) **1.** The quality, state, or condition of being hated. **2.** A state of disgrace, usu. resulting from detestable conduct. **3.** Hatred or strong aversion accompanied by loathing or contempt. — **odious,** *adj.*

ODP. *abbr.* OFFICE OF DOMESTIC PREPAREDNESS.

oeconomicus (ee-kə-**nom**-ə-kəs). [Law Latin fr. Greek] *Hist.* An executor of a will.

oeconomus (ee-**kon**-ə-məs). [Latin fr. Greek] (16c) *Civil law.* A manager or administrator.

OEQ. *abbr.* OFFICE OF ENVIRONMENTAL QUALITY.

OES. *abbr.* BUREAU OF OCEANS AND INTERNATIONAL ENVIRONMENTAL AND SCIENTIFIC AFFAIRS.

OFCCP. *abbr.* OFFICE OF FEDERAL CONTRACT COMPLIANCE PROGRAMS.

of counsel. See COUNSEL.

of course. (16c) **1.** Following the ordinary procedure <the writ was issued as a matter of course>. **2.** Naturally; obviously; clearly <we'll appeal that ruling, of course>.

OFD. *abbr.* OPEN-FILE DISCOVERY.

off-board, *adj.* (1943) Outside a major exchange; over-the-counter or between private parties <an off-board securities transaction>. — Also termed *off-the-board*. See OVER-THE-COUNTER.

off-calendar, *adj.* Postponed; (of a case or hearing) removed from the court's schedule pending further action.

offend, *vb.* (14c) **1.** To commit a crime or crimes; to do wrong <many released prisoners are likely to offend again>. **2.** To transgress moral law; to commit one or more sins <though carefully instructed about the code's requirement of truth-telling, he offended>. **3.** To cause difficulty or injury <the court struck the offending provision>. **4.** To cause ire or consternation; to be against people's feelings of what is morally or socially acceptable <stray comments that needlessly offend>. **5.** To make (a person) angry or upset by saying or doing something considered rude, unkind, or tasteless <we were offended by that language>.

offender. (15c) Someone who has committed a crime; esp., one who has been convicted of a crime.

▸ **adult offender.** (1831) **1.** Someone who has committed a crime after reaching the age of majority. **2.** Someone who, having committed a crime while a minor, has been convicted after reaching the age of majority. **3.** A juvenile who has committed a crime and is tried as an adult rather than as a juvenile.

▸ **career offender.** (1965) Under the federal-sentencing guidelines, an adult who, after being convicted of two violent felonies or controlled-substance felonies, commits another such felony. U.S. Sentencing Guidelines Manual § 4B1.1.

▸ **first offender.** (1884) Someone who authorities believe has committed a crime but who has never before been convicted of a crime. • First offenders are often treated leniently at sentencing or in plea negotiations.

▸ **habitual offender.** (18c) **1.** Someone who commits the same or a similar offense a certain number of times in a certain period, as set by statute, and is therefore eligible for an enhanced sentence. **2.** RECIDIVIST.

▸ **persistent felony offender.** (1964) Someone who has at least thrice been convicted of felonies usu. of a specified level of seriousness and often within a specified period, as a result of which the criminal sentence is to be enhanced.

▸ **persistent violent felony offender.** (1978) Someone who has at least thrice been convicted of a violent felony, as a result of which the criminal sentence is to be enhanced. — Abbr. PVFO.

▸ **predicate felony offender.** (1978) Someone who has at least twice been convicted of felonies usu. of a specified level of seriousness and often within a specified period, as a result of which the criminal sentence is to be enhanced. — Also termed *second felony offender*.

▸ **prior and persistent offender.** *Missouri law.* See RECIDIVIST.

▸ **repeat offender.** (1956) Someone who has been convicted of a crime more than once; RECIDIVIST.

▸ **second felony offender.** See *predicate felony offender*.

▸ **situational offender.** (1945) A first-time offender who is unlikely to commit future crimes.

▸ **status offender.** (1967) A youth who engages in conduct that — though not criminal by adult standards — is considered inappropriate enough to bring a charge against the youth in juvenile court; a juvenile who commits a status offense. Cf. *youthful offender*; JUVENILE DELINQUENT.

▸ **youthful offender.** (1885) **1.** A person in late adolescence or early adulthood who has been convicted of a crime. • A youthful offender is often eligible for special programs not available to older offenders, including community supervision, the successful completion of which may lead to erasing the conviction from the offender's record. **2.** JUVENILE DELINQUENT. — Also termed *young offender*; *youth offender*. Cf. *status offender*.

offense (ə-fents). (14c) **1.** A violation of the law; a crime, often a minor one. See CRIME. Cf. MISBEHAVIOR. — Also termed *criminal offense*.

> "The terms 'crime,' 'offense,' and 'criminal offense' are all said to be synonymous, and ordinarily used interchangeably. 'Offense' may comprehend every crime and misdemeanor, or may be used in a specific sense as synonymous with 'felony' or with 'misdemeanor,' as the case may be, or as signifying a crime of lesser grade, or an act not indictable, but punishable summarily or by the forfeiture of a penalty." 22 C.J.S. *Criminal Law* § 3, at 4 (1989).

▸ **acquisitive offense.** (1981) An offense characterized by the unlawful appropriation of another's property. • This is a generic term that refers to a variety of crimes (such as larceny) rather than a particular one.

▸ **administrative offense.** See *administrative crime* under CRIME.

▸ **allied offense.** (1896) A crime with elements so similar to those of another that the commission of the one is automatically the commission of the other.

▸ **antecedent offense.** See *antecedent crime* under CRIME.

▸ **anticipatory offense.** See *inchoate offense*.

▸ **arrestable offense.** (1967) *English law.* An offense for which the punishment is fixed by law or for which a statute authorizes imprisonment for five years, or an attempt to commit such an offense. • This statutory category, created in 1967, abolished the traditional distinction between felonies and misdemeanors. — Also spelled (esp. BrE) *arrestable offence*.

▸ **bailable offense.** (18c) A criminal charge for which a defendant may be released from custody after providing proper security <misdemeanor theft is a bailable offense>.

▸ **capital offense.** (16c) A crime for which the death penalty may be imposed. — Also termed *capital crime*.

▸ **civil offense.** See *public tort* under TORT.

▸ **cognate offense.** (1866) A lesser offense that is related to the greater offense because it shares several of the elements of the greater offense and is of the same class or category. • For example, shoplifting is a cognate offense of larceny because both crimes require the element of taking property with the intent to deprive the rightful owner of that property. Cf. *lesser included offense*.

▸ **commercial offense.** See *commercial crime* under CRIME.

▸ **common-law offense.** See *common-law crime* under CRIME.

▸ **complainantless offense.** See *victimless crime* under CRIME.

▸ **compound offense.** (1838) An offense composed of one or more separate offenses. • For example, robbery is a compound offense composed of larceny and assault.

▸ **computer offense.** See *computer crime* under CRIME.

▸ **consensual offense.** See *victimless crime* under CRIME.

▸ **constructive offense.** See *constructive crime* under CRIME.

▸ **continuing offense.** (18c) A crime (such as a conspiracy) that is committed over a period of time, so that the last act of the crime controls when the statute of limitations begins to run.

▸ **continuous offense.** See *continuous crime* under CRIME.

▸ **corporate offense.** See *corporate crime* under CRIME.

▸ **credit-card offense.** See CREDIT-CARD CRIME.

▸ **cumulative offense.** (1833) An offense committed by repeating the same act at different times.

▸ **cyberoffense.** See *computer crime* under CRIME.

▸ **divisible offense.** (1847) A crime that includes one or more crimes of lesser grade. • For example, murder is a divisible offense comprising assault, battery, and assault with intent to kill.

▸ **economic offense.** See *economic crime* under CRIME.

▸ **enhanced offense.** See *enhanced crime* under CRIME.

▸ **environmental offense.** See ENVIRONMENTAL CRIME.

▸ **expressive offense.** See *expressive crime* under CRIME.

▸ **extraneous offense.** (1881) An offense beyond or unrelated to the offense for which a defendant is on trial.

▸ **federal offense.** See FEDERAL CRIME.

▸ **general-intent offense.** See *general-intent crime* under CRIME.

▸ **graded offense.** (1891) A crime that is divided into various degrees of severity with corresponding levels of punishment, such as murder (first-degree and second-degree) or assault (simple and aggravated). See DEGREE (2); DEGREE OF CRIME; GRADE.

▸ **hate offense.** See *hate crime* under CRIME.

▸ **high offense.** See *high crime* under CRIME.

▸ **honor offense.** See *honor crime* under CRIME.

▸ **impeachable offense.** See IMPEACHABLE OFFENSE.

▸ **implied offense.** See *constructive crime* under CRIME.

▸ **inchoate offense.** (1809) A step toward the commission of another crime, the step in itself being serious enough to merit punishment. • The three inchoate offenses are attempt, conspiracy, and solicitation. The term is sometimes criticized (see quot. below). — Also termed *anticipatory offense*; *inchoate crime*; *preliminary crime*.

> "These preliminary crimes have sometimes been erroneously described as 'inchoate' offences. This is misleading because the word 'inchoate' connotes something which is not yet completed, and it is therefore not accurately used to denote something which is itself complete, even though it be a link in a chain of events leading to some object which is not yet attained. The offence of incitement is fully performed even though the person incited immediately

repudiates the suggested deed, a conspiracy is committed although the conspirators have not yet moved to execute their purposed crime, and the performance of a criminal attempt must always have been reached before the end is gained. In all these instances it is the ultimate crime which is inchoate and not the preliminary crime, the position indeed being just the same as in the example imagined above of a man who stole a revolver and committed other crimes in order to effect his purpose of murder. There the murder was inchoate, but the larceny and other crimes (including the attempt) were completed." J.W. Cecil Turner, *Kenny's Outlines of Criminal Law* 77 (16th ed. 1952).

▸ **included offense.** See *lesser included offense.*

▸ **index offense.** (1980) One of eight classes of crimes reported annually by the FBI in the Uniform Crime Report. • The eight classes are murder (and nonnegligent homicide), rape, robbery, aggravated assault, burglary, larceny-theft, arson, and auto theft. — Also termed *index crime.*

▸ **indictable offense.** (18c) A crime that can be prosecuted only by indictment. • In federal court, such an offense is one punishable by death or by imprisonment for more than one year or at hard labor. Fed. R. Crim. P. 7(a). See INDICTMENT.

"[I]t is impossible to take the distinction between indictable and non-indictable offences as corresponding with any great accuracy to our actual sense of their importance to the community. Thus we find amongst the list of indictable offences many that are obsolete or comparatively venial (though no doubt blameworthy!) — such as cheating at play, corruptly taking a reward for restoring a stolen dog, destroying hop-binds, Jesuits and monks coming into the realm, killing hares and rabbits by night in a warren, or 'Depraving the Book of Common Prayer.' On the other hand amongst non-indictable offences are classed many acts of the utmost importance: Assaulting constables in the execution of their duty, aggravated and common assaults, brothel-keeping, and cruelty to animals." Howard League for Penal Reform, *Counsel for the Defence: An Enquiry into the Question of Legal Aid for Poor Prisoners* 4 (1926).

▸ **infamous offense.** See *infamous crime* under CRIME.

▸ **instantaneous offense.** See *instantaneous crime* under CRIME.

▸ **instrumental offense.** See *instrumental crime* under CRIME.

▸ **intellectual-property offense.** See INTELLECTUAL-PROPERTY CRIME.

▸ **international offense.** See INTERNATIONAL CRIME.

▸ **joint offense.** (18c) An offense (such as conspiracy) committed by the participation of two or more persons.

▸ **lesser included offense.** (1908) A crime that is composed of some, but not all, of the elements of a more serious crime and that is necessarily committed in carrying out the greater crime <battery is a lesser included offense of murder>. • For double-jeopardy purposes, a lesser included offense is considered the "same offense" as the greater offense, so that acquittal or conviction of either offense precludes a separate trial for the other. — Abbr. LIO. — Also termed *included offense; necessarily included offense; predicate offense; predicate act;* (esp. in English law) *alternative verdict.* Cf. *cognate offense.*

▸ **liquor offense.** (1874) Any crime involving the inappropriate use or sale of intoxicating liquor. See DRAM-SHOP LIABILITY; DRIVING WHILE INTOXICATED.

▸ **major offense.** (1853) **1.** An offense the commission of which involves one or more lesser included offenses, as murder may include assault and battery. **2.** See *major crime* under CRIME.

▸ **military offense.** See MILITARY OFFENSE.

▸ **multiple offense.** (1908) An offense that violates more than one law but that may require different proof so that an acquittal or conviction under one statute does not exempt the defendant from prosecution under another.

▸ **necessarily included offense.** See *lesser included offense.*

▸ **negligent offense.** (1879) A violation of law arising from a defective discharge of duty or from criminal negligence. See *criminal negligence* under NEGLIGENCE.

▸ **noninfamous offense.** See *noninfamous crime* under CRIME.

▸ **object offense.** (1943) The crime that is the object of the defendant's attempt, solicitation, conspiracy, or complicity. • For example, murder is the object offense in a charge of attempted murder. — Also termed *target offense.*

▸ **occupational offense.** See *occupational crime* under CRIME.

▸ **offense against humanity.** See CRIME AGAINST HUMANITY.

▸ **offense against international law.** See CRIME AGAINST THE LAW OF NATIONS.

▸ **offense against nature.** See CRIME AGAINST NATURE.

▸ **offense against peace.** See CRIME AGAINST PEACE.

▸ **offense against property.** (1837) A crime against another's personal property. • The common-law offenses against property were larceny, embezzlement, cheating, cheating by false pretenses, robbery, receiving stolen goods, malicious mischief, forgery, and uttering forged instruments. Although the term *crimes against property,* a common term in modern usage, includes crimes against real property, the term *offense against property* is traditionally restricted to personal property. Cf. CRIMES AGAINST PROPERTY.

▸ **offense against public justice and authority.** (1917) A crime that impairs the administration of justice. • The common-law offenses of this type were obstruction of justice, barratry, maintenance, champerty, embracery, escape, prison breach, rescue, misprision of felony, compounding a crime, subornation of perjury, bribery, and misconduct in office.

▸ **offense against the environment.** See ENVIRONMENTAL CRIME.

▸ **offense against the habitation.** (1849) A crime against another's house — traditionally either arson or burglary.

▸ **offense against the law of nations.** See CRIME AGAINST THE LAW OF NATIONS.

▸ **offense against the person.** (1854) A crime against the body of another human being. • The common-law offenses against the person were murder, manslaughter, mayhem, rape, assault, battery, robbery, false imprisonment, abortion, seduction, kidnapping, and abduction. Cf. CRIMES AGAINST PERSONS.

▸ **offense against the public health, safety, comfort, and morals.** (1976) A crime traditionally viewed as endangering the whole of society. • The common-law offenses of this type were nuisance, bigamy, adultery, fornication, lewdness, illicit cohabitation, incest, miscegenation, sodomy, bestiality, buggery, abortion, and seduction.

▸ **offense against the public peace.** (18c) A crime that tends to disturb the peace. • The common-law offenses of this type were riot, unlawful assembly, dueling, rout, affray, forcible entry and detainer, and libel on a private person.

▸ **offense malum in se.** See MALUM IN SE.

▸ **offense malum prohibitum.** See MALUM PROHIBITUM.

▸ **offense of omission.** See *crime of omission* under CRIME.

▸ **offense of passion.** See *crime of passion* under CRIME.

▸ **offense of violence.** See *violent crime* under CRIME.

▸ **offense without victims.** See *victimless crime* under CRIME.

▸ **organizational offense.** See *organizational crime* under CRIME.

▸ **organized offense.** See ORGANIZED CRIME.

▸ **personal-condition offense.** See *status crime* under CRIME.

▸ **petty offense.** (17c) A minor or insignificant crime. 18 USCA § 19. Cf. *serious offense.*

> "[W]e find . . . an apparent implication that a 'petty offense' is not a 'crime.' Much could be said for such a position but it is not the law at the present time. In the federal penal code, for example, it is provided that any misdemeanor 'the penalty for which does not exceed imprisonment for a period of six months or a fine of not more than $500, or both, is a petty offense.'" Rollin M. Perkins & Ronald N. Boyce, *Criminal Law* 22 (3d ed. 1982) (quoting 18 USCA § 1(3)).

▸ **political offense.** See POLITICAL OFFENSE.

▸ **predatory offense.** See *predatory crime* under CRIME.

▸ **predicate offense.** (1969) **1.** An earlier offense that can be used to enhance a sentence levied for a later conviction. • Predicate offences are defined by statute and are not uniform from state to state. **2.** See *lesser included offense.*

▸ **preliminary offense.** See *inchoate offense* under OFFENSE.

▸ **presumed offense.** See *constructive crime* under CRIME.

▸ **prior offense.** See PRIOR CONVICTION.

▸ **public offense.** (16c) An act or omission forbidden by law.

▸ **public-welfare offense.** (1933) A minor offense that does not involve moral delinquency and is prohibited only to secure the effective regulation of conduct in the interest of the community. • An example is driving a car with one brake-light missing. — Also termed *regulatory offense*; *contravention.*

▸ **quasi-offense.** See *quasi-crime* under CRIME.

▸ **regulatory offense.** (1929) **1.** A statutory crime, as opposed to a common-law crime. — Also termed *status offense.* **2.** See *public-welfare offense.*

▸ **same offense.** (18c) **1.** For double-jeopardy purposes, the same criminal act, omission, or transaction for which the person has already stood trial. See DOUBLE JEOPARDY. **2.** For sentencing and enhancement-of-punishment purposes, an offense that is quite similar to a previous one.

▸ **second offense.** (18c) An offense committed after conviction for a first offense. • The previous conviction, not the indictment, forms the basis of the charge of a second offense.

▸ **separate offense.** (18c) **1.** An offense arising out of the same event as another offense but containing some differences in elements of proof. • A person may be tried, convicted, and sentenced for each separate offense. **2.** An offense arising out of a different event entirely from another offense under consideration.

▸ **serious offense.** (18c) An offense not classified as a petty offense and usu. carrying at least a six-month sentence. — Also termed *serious crime.* See FELONY (1). Cf. *petty offense.*

▸ **sexual offense.** (1885) An offense involving unlawful sexual conduct, such as prostitution, indecent exposure, incest, pederasty, and bestiality.

▸ **signature offense.** See *signature crime* under CRIME.

▸ **spontaneous offense.** See *spontaneous crime* under CRIME.

▸ **status offense.** (1957) **1.** See *status crime* under CRIME. **2.** A minor's violation of the juvenile code by doing some act that would not be considered illegal if an adult did it, but that indicates that the minor is beyond parental control. • Examples include running away from home, truancy, and incorrigibility. See JUVENILE DELINQUENCY. **3.** An offense that only a certain category of people can be charged with, such as felon in possession of a firearm. **4.** An offense in which motive is not a consideration in determining guilt, such as a traffic violation. — Also termed (in sense 4) *regulatory offense.*

▸ **statutory offense.** See *statutory crime* under CRIME.

▸ **street offense.** See *street crime* under CRIME.

▸ **strict-liability offense.** (1957) See *strict-liability crime* under CRIME.

▸ **substantive offense** (səb-stən-tiv). (18c) A crime that is complete in itself and is not dependent on another crime for one of its elements. — Also termed *substantive crime*; *substantive felony.*

▸ **summary offense.** (1928) An offense (such as a petty misdemeanor) that can be prosecuted without an indictment. Cf. *indictable offense.*

▸ **target offense.** See *object offense.*

▸ **unnatural offense.** See SODOMY.

▸ **unrelated offense.** (1896) A crime that is independent from the charged offense.

▸ **vice offense.** See *vice crime* under CRIME.

▸ **victimless offense.** See *victimless crime* under CRIME.

▸ **violent offense.** (1965) A crime characterized by extreme physical force, such as murder, forcible rape, and assault and battery with a dangerous weapon. — Abbr. VF (violent felony); VFO (violent felony offense). — Also termed *violent felony*; *violent felony offense.* See *violent crime* under CRIME.

▸ **visible offense.** See *street crime* under CRIME.

▸ **war offense.** See WAR CRIME.

▸ **white-collar offense.** See WHITE-COLLAR CRIME.

2. *Civil law.* An intentional unlawful act that causes injury or loss to another and that gives rise to a claim for damages. La. Civ. Code art. 2315. • This sense of *offense* is essentially the same as the common-law intentional tort.

▸ **quasi-offense.** (1820) *Civil law.* A negligent unlawful act that causes injury or loss to another and that gives rise to a claim for damages. • This is equivalent to the common-law tort of negligence. — Also termed *quasi-delict.*

3. *Parliamentary law.* A breach of order or other misconduct for which the applicable rules subject a member to a penalty.

offense against humanity. See CRIME AGAINST HUMANITY.

offense against international law. See CRIME AGAINST THE LAW OF NATIONS.

offense against nature. See CRIME AGAINST NATURE.

offense against peace. See CRIME AGAINST PEACE.

offense against the environment. See ENVIRONMENTAL CRIME.

offense against the law of nations. See CRIME AGAINST THE LAW OF NATIONS.

offense malum in se. See MALUM IN SE.

offense malum prohibitum. See MALUM PROHIBITUM.

offense of omission. See *crime of omission* under CRIME.

offense of passion. See *crime of passion* under CRIME.

offense of violence. See *violent crime* under CRIME.

offense principle. (1979) In legal philosophy, the view that a proposed criminal prohibition is sound if it (1) would probably prevent acts that would induce a seriously unpleasant mental state in persons other than the actors, and (2) is probably a necessary means to this end.

offense without victims. See *victimless crime* under CRIME.

offensive (ə-**fen**-siv), *adj.* (16c) **1.** Making attack; aggressive <offensive tactics>. **2.** Of, relating to, or designed for attack <an offensive weapon>. **3.** Unpleasant or disagreeable to the senses; obnoxious <an offensive odor>. **4.** Causing displeasure, anger, or resentment; esp., repugnant to the prevailing sense of what is decent or moral <patently offensive language and photographs>. See OBSCENE.

offensive and defensive league. (1889) *Int'l law.* A league binding the parties not only to aid one another when attacked but also to support one another when attacking in offensive warfare. See LEAGUE (2).

offensive collateral estoppel. See COLLATERAL ESTOPPEL.

offensive lockout. See LOCKOUT (1).

offensive strike. See STRIKE (1).

offensive treaty. See TREATY (1).

offensive-use waiver. See WAIVER (1).

offer, *n.* (15c) **1.** The act or an instance of presenting something for acceptance; specif., a statement that one is willing to do something for another person or to give that person something <the prosecutor's offer of immunity>.

▸ **settlement offer.** See SETTLEMENT OFFER.

2. A promise to do or refrain from doing some specified thing in the future, conditioned on an act, forbearance, or return promise being given in exchange for the promise or its performance; a display of willingness to enter into a contract on specified terms, made in a way that would lead a reasonable person to understand that an acceptance, having been sought, will result in a binding contract <she accepted the $750 offer on the Victorian armoire>. Cf. ACCEPTANCE (1).

> "[A]n offer is, in effect, a promise by the offeror to do or abstain from doing something, provided that the offeree will accept the offer and pay or promise to pay the 'price' of the offer. The price, of course, need not be a monetary one. In fact, in bilateral contracts, as we explained earlier, the mere promise of payment of the price suffices to conclude the contract, while in a unilateral contract it is the actual payment of the price which is required." P.S. Atiyah, *An Introduction to the Law of Contract* 44 (3d ed. 1981).

▸ **conditional offer.** (16c) An offer made on the stipulation that it will not take effect until some contingent prerequisite has been satisfied; an offer that comes into effect only upon the occurrence of some specified event.

▸ **irrevocable offer** (i-rev-ə-kə-bəl). (1885) An offer that includes a promise to keep it open for a specified period, during which the offer cannot be withdrawn without the offeror's becoming subject to liability for breach of contract. • Traditionally, this type of promise must be supported by consideration to be enforceable, but under UCC § 2-205, a merchant's signed, written offer giving assurances that it will be held open — but lacking consideration — is nonetheless irrevocable for the stated period (or, if not stated, for a reasonable time not exceeding three months). — Also termed (in the UCC) *firm offer*; (specif.) *merchant's firm offer.*

> "It has sometimes been asserted that an irrevocable offer is 'a legal impossibility.' See Langdell, Summary of the Law of Contracts, § 178, also § 4; Wormser, 'The True Conception of Unilateral Contracts,' 26 *Yale Law Journal*, 137, note; Lee, Title Contracts, in Jenks' Dig. of Eng. Civ. Law, § 195; Ashley, Contracts, § 13. A close analysis shows that there is nothing impossible either in the conception itself or in its application. If we define 'offer' as an *act* on the part of the offeror . . . , then no offer can ever be revoked, for it is of yesterday — it is indeed *factum*. But if we mean by 'offer' the legal relation that results from the offeror's act, the *power* then given to the offeree of creating contractual relations by doing certain voluntary acts on his part, then the offer may be either revocable or irrevocable according to the circumstances. The idea of an irrevocable power is not at all an unfamiliar one." William R. Anson, *Principles of the Law of Contract* 53–54 n.3 (Arthur L. Corbin ed., 3d Am. ed. 1919).

▸ **offer to all the world.** (1861) An offer, by way of advertisement, of a reward for the rendering of specified services, addressed to the public at large. • As soon as someone renders the services, a contract is made. — Also termed *public offer.*

▸ **offer to chaffer.** See INVITATION TO NEGOTIATE.

▸ **open offer.** An opportunity for a company's current shareholders to buy new shares at a price usu. lower than the current market price, usu. for the purpose of raising money for the company. • The shareholders may not sell this right to buy new shares; it is simply an entitlement that will expire if not used. — Also termed *entitlement issue.* Cf. *rights offering* under OFFERING; TENDER OFFER.

▸ **public-exchange offer.** (1966) A takeover attempt in which the bidder corporation offers to exchange some of its securities for a specified number of the target corporation's voting shares. Cf. TENDER OFFER.

▸ **public offer.** See *offer to all the world.*

▸ **standing offer.** (1842) An offer that is in effect a whole series of offers, each of which is capable of being converted into a contract by a distinct acceptance.

▸ **tender offer.** See TENDER OFFER.

▸ **two-tier offer.** See TWO-TIER OFFER.

3. A price at which one is ready to buy or sell; an amount of money that one is willing to pay or accept for something <she lowered her offer to $200>. **4.** *Archaic.* ATTEMPT (2) <an offer to commit battery>. — **offer,** *vb.* — **offeror,** *n.*

> "Where criminal assault has been given this dual scope, a definition in terms of 'an attempt or offer' to commit a battery is assumed to represent both grounds. The word 'offer,' it is said, signifies a threat that places the other in reasonable apprehension of receiving an immediate battery. It would be a mistake, however, to assume that the word carried any such significance when it first appeared in the definition of this offense. In one of its meanings, 'offer' is a synonym of 'attempt.'" Rollin M. Perkins & Ronald N. Boyce, *Criminal Law* 163 (3d ed. 1982).

offeree (ah-fər-**ee**). (1882) One to whom an offer is made.

offer for sale by tender. See *Dutch auction* (4) under AUCTION.

offer in compromise. See SETTLEMENT OFFER.

offering, *n.* (15c) **1.** The act of making an offer; something offered for sale. **2.** The sale of an issue of securities. — Also termed (BrE) *flotation.* See ISSUE (2).

▸ **all-or-none offering.** (1975) An offering that allows the issuer to terminate the distribution if the entire block of offered securities is not sold.

▸ **exempt offering.** (1957) An offering of securities that are not subject to the registration requirements of the Securities Act of 1933.

▸ **initial public offering.** (1920) A company's first public sale of stock; the first offering of an issuer's equity securities to the public through a registration statement. — Abbr. IPO.

▸ **negotiated offering.** (1974) A securities offering in which the terms (including the underwriters' compensation) have been negotiated between the issuer and the underwriters.

▸ **primary offering.** (1938) An offering of newly issued securities.

▸ **private offering.** (1857) An offering made only to a small group of interested buyers. — Also termed *private placement.*

▸ **public offering.** (1850) An offering made to the general public.

▸ **registered offering.** (1945) A public offering of securities registered with the SEC and with appropriate state securities commissions. — Also termed *registered public offering.*

▸ **rights offering.** (1950) An issue of stock-purchase rights allowing shareholders to buy newly issued stock at a fixed price, usu. below market value, and in proportion to the number of shares they already own. — Also termed *privileged subscription*; *rights issue*; *scrip issue.* Cf. PREEMPTIVE RIGHT.

▸ **secondary offering.** (1940) **1.** Any offering by an issuer of securities after its initial public offering. **2.** An offering of previously issued securities by persons other than the issuer. See *secondary distribution* (1) under DISTRIBUTION.

▸ **special offering.** (1946) An offering of a large block of stock that, because of its size and the market in the particular issue, is specially handled on the floor of the stock exchange.

▸ **undigested offering.** (2006) A public offering of securities that remain unsold because there is insufficient demand at the offered price.

offering circular. (1933) A document, similar to a prospectus, that provides information about a private securities offering. — Also termed *offering statement.*

offering price. See *asking price* under PRICE.

offering statement. See OFFERING CIRCULAR.

offer of compromise. See SETTLEMENT OFFER.

offer of judgment. (1971) A settlement offer by one party to allow a specified judgment to be taken against the party. • In federal procedure (and in many states), if the adverse party rejects the offer, and if a judgment finally obtained by that party is not more favorable than the offer, then that party must pay the costs incurred after the offer was made. Fed. R. Civ. P. 68.

offer of performance. (18c) *Contracts.* One party's reasonable assurance to the other, through words or conduct, of a present ability to fulfill contractual obligations. • When performances are to be exchanged simultaneously, each party is entitled to refuse to proceed with the exchange until the other party makes an appropriate offer of performance. Cf. TENDER (1).

> "The requirement of an offer of performance is to be applied in the light of what is reasonably to be expected by the parties in view of the practical difficulties of absolute simultaneity and is subject to the agreement of the parties, as supplemented or qualified by usage and course of dealing." Restatement (Second) of Contracts § 238 cmt. b (1979).

offer of proof. (17c) *Procedure.* A presentation of evidence for the record (but outside the jury's presence) usu. made after the judge has sustained an objection to the admissibility of that evidence, so that the evidence can be preserved on the record for an appeal of the judge's ruling. • An offer of proof, which may also be used to persuade the court to admit the evidence, consists of three parts: (1) the evidence itself, (2) an explanation of the purpose for which it is offered (its relevance), and (3) an argument supporting admissibility. Such an offer may include tangible evidence or testimony (through questions and answers, a lawyer's narrative description, or an affidavit). Fed. R. Evid. 103(a)(2). — Also termed *avowal.*

offer of settlement. See SETTLEMENT OFFER.

offeror (ah-fər-**or**). (1882) Someone who makes an offer.

offer to all the world. See OFFER.

offer to chaffer. See INVITATION TO NEGOTIATE.

office. (13c) **1.** A position of duty, trust, or authority, esp. one conferred by a governmental authority for a public purpose <the office of attorney general>. **2.** (*often cap.*) A division of the U.S. government ranking immediately below a department <the Patent and Trademark Office>. **3.** A place where business is conducted or services are performed <a law office>. • In sense 3, an office may be a building, a suite of rooms in the building, or an individual room within the building or suite. Context usually clarifies the precise sense.

▸ **alienation office.** (17c) See ALIENATION OFFICE.

▸ **lucrative office.** (18c) **1.** A position that produces fee revenue or a salary to the officeholder. **2.** A position that yields a salary adequate to the services rendered and exceeding incidental expenses; a position whose pay is tied to the performance of the office's duties.

▸ **ministerial office.** (16c) An office that does not include authority to exercise judgment, only to carry out orders given by a superior office, or to perform duties or acts required by rules, statutes, or regulations.

▸ **office of honor.** (16c) An uncompensated public position of considerable dignity and importance to which public trusts or interests are confided.

▸ **public office.** See PUBLIC OFFICE.

▸ **registered office.** (1846) A company's office to which all letters and official documents should be sent.

office action. *Patents & Trademarks.* A patent examiner's communication with a patent applicant, usu. to state the reasons for denying an application.

▸ **advisory office action.** (1999) An office action in which the patent examiner replies to an applicant's response following final rejection of the application. • An advisory action addresses the status of an amendment made in the applicant's response to the final rejection, indicates the status of the claims for appeal, addresses an affidavit or exhibit, or responds to a request for reconsideration. — Also termed *advisory action.*

▸ **final office action.** (1953) A patent examiner's determination that an application is not allowable. • The applicant may file a continuation application, appeal the decision, or request continued prosecution. Cf. *first office action.*

▸ **first office action.** (1904) A patent examiner's initial reply to a patent application. • If the examiner's first report is a rejection of all or most of the application's claims, it is termed a *shotgun rejection.* To avoid abandoning the prosecution, the applicant must respond by answering the examiner's reasons for rejection, amending the claims, or both. Cf. *final office action.*

office audit. See AUDIT.

office-block ballot. See BALLOT (4).

office classification. See CLASSIFICATION OF PATENTS.

office expense. See OVERHEAD.

office grant. See GRANT (4).

officeholder, *n.* (18c) Someone who has an official position, esp. in government.

office hours. *Military law.* See *nonjudicial punishment* under PUNISHMENT.

office lawyer. See OFFICE PRACTITIONER.

office of child-support enforcement. (1974) *Family law.* A state or federal agency established under Title IV(D) of the Social Security Act to help custodial parents collect child support. 42 USCA §§ 651 et seq. • State offices of child-support enforcement generally come under the aegis of the Department of Human Resources. The federal Office of Child Support Enforcement has established the Parent-Locator Service.

Office of Civilian Health and Medical Programs of the Uniformed Services. A unit in the U.S. Department of Defense responsible for administering a civilian health and medical care program for the spouses and dependent children of active members of the armed forces and for retired military personnel, their spouses and children. — Abbr. OCHAMPUS.

Office of Community Planning and Development. A unit in the U.S. Department of Housing and Urban Development responsible for administering grant programs to help communities plan and finance their growth and development, increase their capacity to govern, and provide shelter and services for homeless people. — Abbr. CPD.

Office of Counterintelligence. An office in the U.S. Department of Energy responsible for conducting counterintelligence programs involving industrial intelligence activities of foreigners and foreign governments.

Office of Domestic Preparedness. A unit in the U.S. Department of Homeland Security responsible for helping state and local governments train and equip emergency responders, plan and conduct disaster drills, and offer other technical assistance to prevent, plan for, and respond to acts of terrorism. • The Office was transferred from the U.S. Department of Justice in 2003. — Abbr. ODP.

Office of Enrollment and Discipline. *Patents.* The division of the U.S. Patent and Trademark Office charged with licensing patent attorneys and patent agents, and with hearing complaints involving their misconduct. • The office is authorized to sanction practitioners, and to suspend or disbar them from practice before the PTO. Its authority is concurrent with state disciplinary procedures. — Abbr. OED.

Office of Environmental Quality. An office in the Executive Office of the President responsible for supporting the Council on Environmental Quality. — Abbr. OEQ. See COUNCIL ON ENVIRONMENTAL QUALITY.

Office of Fair Housing and Equal Opportunity. A unit in the U.S. Department of Housing and Urban Development responsible for administering the fair-housing laws and regulations that prohibit discrimination in public and private housing. — Abbr. FHEO.

Office of Federal Contract Compliance Programs. The division of the Employment Standards Administration in the U.S. Department of Labor responsible for enforcing contractors' compliance with Executive Order 11246, which prohibits job discrimination on the basis of race, color, gender, religion, or national origin. — Abbr. OFCCP. See EMPLOYMENT STANDARDS ADMINISTRATION; DEPARTMENT OF LABOR.

Office of Federal Housing Enterprise Oversight. A unit in the U.S. Department of Housing and Urban Development responsible for overseeing the financial safety and soundness of the Federal National Mortgage Association (Fannie Mae) and the Federal Home Loan Mortgage Corporation (Freddie Mac). — Abbr. OFHEO.

Office of Government Ethics. An independent federal agency in the executive branch responsible for issuing rules and regulations about ethical conduct and financial disclosure, providing training in ethics, monitoring the ethics of practices in departments and agencies, and giving guidance on matters of ethics. • The agency was established under the Ethics in Government Act of 1978 and became a separate agency in 1988. — Abbr. OGE.

Office of Healthy Homes and Lead Hazard Control. A unit office in the U.S. Department of Housing and Urban Development responsible for informing the public about the dangers of lead poisoning, esp. by lead-based paint; developing methods of detection and abatement; encouraging states and local governments to develop prevention programs; and implementing the Department's Healthy Home Initiative to warn the public of other potential household hazards. — Abbr. OHHLHC.

office of honor. See OFFICE.

Office of Housing. A unit in the U.S. Department of Housing and Urban Development responsible for administering aid for building and financing new and rehabilitated housing and for preserving existing housing.

Office of Initial Patent Examination. The section of the U.S. Patent and Trademark Office that determines whether a new patent application is in the correct form, whether the claims are dependent or independent, how much the application fee should be, and to which examining group the application should be assigned. — Abbr. OIPE.

Office of Labor-Management Standards. The division of the Employment Standards Administration in the U.S. Department of Labor responsible for enforcing the Labor–Management Reporting and Disclosure Act of 1959, which establishes standards for labor-union management and financial operations. • The Act sets out a list of union-members' rights, including the right to fair elections of union leaders, the right to know about the union's administrative policies and financial transactions, and the right to have union funds safeguarded. — Abbr. OLMS. See EMPLOYMENT STANDARDS ADMINISTRATION.

Office of Management and Budget. An office in the Executive Office of the President responsible for helping the President prepare the annual federal budget and supervising its administration. • It was originally established by Reorganization Plan No.1 of 1939 as the Bureau of the Budget. — Abbr. OMB.

Office of Medical Services. A unit in the U.S. Department of State responsible for providing primary healthcare services for the Department's overseas employees and their eligible family members. — Abbr. MED.

Office of National Drug Control Policy. An office in the Executive Office of the President responsible for coordinating efforts at federal, state, and local levels to control illegal drug abuse and for devising national antidrug activities. • The office was created by the National Narcotics Leadership Act of 1988. 21 USCA §§ 1701–1713. — Abbr. ONDCP.

Office of Oceanic and Atmospheric Research. See NATIONAL OCEANIC AND ATMOSPHERIC ADMINISTRATION.

Office of Passport Services. See BUREAU OF CONSULAR AFFAIRS.

Office of Personnel Management. The independent federal agency that administers the personnel system of the government by helping agencies recruit and evaluate employees; manage retirement and health-benefit systems; coordinate temporary assignments; conduct investigations; and develop leadership in the federal executive service. • The agency was established by Reorganization Plan No. 2 of 1978 and given various functions of the former U.S. Civil Service Commission by Executive Order 12107 of 1978. — Abbr. OPM. See CIVIL SERVICE COMMISSION.

Office of Policy Development. An office in the Executive Office of the President comprising the Domestic Policy Council and the National Economic Council. • It was established in 1993 by Executive Order 12859. — Abbr. OPD.

Office of Private Sector Liaison. A unit in the U.S. Department of Homeland Security responsible for working with individual businesses through trade associations and other nongovernmental organizations on matters of security.

Office of Protocol. A unit in the U.S. Department of State responsible for advising the President, the Vice President, the Secretary of State, and other U.S. officials on matters of custom and decorum, and for planning and hosting state dinners and other affairs, esp. involving foreign heads of state and other diplomats. • The Office also manages the Blair House, where diplomatic visitors often stay. It is run by the Chief of Protocol.

Office of Public and Indian Housing. A unit in the U.S. Department of Housing and Urban Development responsible for providing technical assistance and operating subsidies to public-housing agencies and Indian housing authorities in developing low-income housing. — Abbr. PIH.

Office of Science and Technology Policy. An office in the Executive Office of the President responsible for advising the President on scientific, engineering, and technological development and for coordinating research and development programs. • The office was created by the National Science and Technology Policy, Organization, and Priorities Act of 1976. — Abbr. OSTP.

Office of Special Counsel. An independent federal agency that investigates activities prohibited by the civil-service laws, rules, and regulations and, if the investigation warrants it, litigates the matter before the Merit Systems Protection Board. • The agency was established by Reorganization Plan No. 2 of 1978. — Abbr. OSC.

Office of Special Investigations. A component of the criminal division of the Department of Justice that identifies and investigates suspected perpetrators of human-rights violations abroad, after the suspects have entered, or tried to enter, the United States. • Originally created in 1948 to seek out Nazi and Axis persecutors, the Office's mission has since been expanded to include other transgressors of human rights. — Abbr. OSI.

Office of State and Local Government Coordination. A unit in the U.S. Department of Homeland Security responsible for coordinating security matters with state and local governments. — Abbr. OSLGC.

Office of Surface Mining Reclamation and Enforcement. A unit in the U.S. Department of the Interior responsible for protecting against the adverse effects of surface coal mining by enforcing laws relating to surface mining and restoration and by assisting states and local governments, which have primary responsibility in this area. — Abbr. OSM.

Office of Tax-Shelter Analysis. An office in the U.S. Internal Revenue Service responsible for identifying and investigating questionable tax shelters. • The office was created in 2000. — Abbr. OTSA.

Office of Technology Assessment. A former office in the legislative branch of the federal government responsible for analyzing public-policy issues relating to science and technology. • The Office was active from 1972 to 1995. — Abbr. OTA.

Office of Technology Policy. See TECHNOLOGY ADMINISTRATION.

Office of the Comptroller of the Currency. An office in the U.S. Department of the Treasury responsible for regulating approximately 2,600 national banks by examining them; approving or denying applications for bank charters, branches, or mergers; closing banks that fail to follow rules and regulations; and regulating banking practices. — Abbr. OCC.

Office of the Pettybag. See PETTYBAG.

Office of the United States Trade Representative. An office in the Executive Office of the President responsible for setting and administering overall trade policy. • It was established under Reorganization Plan No. 3 of 1979. 19 USCA § 2171. — Abbr. OUSTR.

Office of Thrift Supervision. An office in the U.S. Department of the Treasury responsible for regulating and examining thrift institutions to ensure that they are financially sound. — Abbr. OTS.

Office of Workers' Compensation Programs. The division of the Employment Standards Administration in the U.S. Department of Labor responsible for processing and adjudicating claims under the Federal Employees' Compensation Act, the Longshore and Harbor Workers' Compensation Act, the Black Lung Benefits Reform Act, and similar worker-benefits statutes and regulations. — Abbr. OWCP. See EMPLOYMENT STANDARDS ADMINISTRATION.

office practice. (1872) A law practice that primarily involves handling matters outside court, such as negotiating and drafting contracts, preparing wills and trusts, setting up corporations and partnerships, and advising on tax or employment issues; a transactional-law practice.

office practitioner. (1933) A lawyer who does not litigate; an attorney whose work is accomplished primarily in the office, without court appearances. — Also termed *office lawyer*; *transactional lawyer.*

officer. (14c) **1.** Someone who holds an office of trust, authority, or command. • In public affairs, the term refers esp. to a person holding public office under a national, state, or local government, and authorized by that government to exercise some specific function. In corporate law, the term refers esp. to a person elected or appointed by the board of directors to manage the daily operations of a corporation, such as a CEO, president, secretary, or treasurer. Cf. DIRECTOR (2).

▸ **acting officer.** (18c) One performing the duties of an office — usu. temporarily — but who has no claim of title to the office.

▸ **administrative officer.** (1834) **1.** An officer of the executive department of government, usu. of inferior rank. **2.** A ministerial or executive officer, as distinguished from a judicial officer. **3.** *Family law.* An official, other than a judge, who is appointed to preside over child-support matters. See CHILD-SUPPORT-ENFORCEMENT AGENCY. Cf. MASTER (2); JUDGE.

▸ **attendance officer.** See TRUANCY OFFICER.

▸ **authorized officer.** (18c) An officer who has the authority to carry out some act, such as signing forms on behalf of an organization; esp., a member of a business entity who has been formally empowered to conduct business on its behalf, such as a general manager, general partner, president, vice president, or treasurer.

▸ **chief executive officer.** See CHIEF EXECUTIVE OFFICER.

▸ **city officer.** See *municipal officer.*

▸ **constitutional officer.** (18c) A government official whose office is created by a constitution, rather than by a statute; one whose term of office is fixed and defined by a constitution.

▸ **corporate officer.** (18c) An officer of a corporation, such as a CEO, president, secretary, or treasurer.

▸ **county officer.** (18c) An officer whose authority and jurisdiction are confined to the limits of the county served.

▸ **court officer.** See OFFICER OF THE COURT.

▸ **de facto officer.** See *officer de facto.*

▸ **de jure officer.** See *officer de jure.*

▸ **escrow officer.** See ESCROW AGENT.

▸ **executive officer.** See EXECUTIVE (2).

▸ **federal officer.** (18c) **1.** A sworn law-enforcement officer employed by a federal agency or entity. **2.** A person elected or appointed to an office in the federal government or any agency or entity.

▸ **fiscal officer.** (18c) **1.** The person (such as a state or county treasurer) charged with the collection and distribution of public money. **2.** The person (such as a chief financial officer) whose duties are to oversee the financial matters of a corporation or business.

▸ **health officer.** See HEALTH OFFICER.

▸ **hearing officer.** (1925) **1.** ADMINISTRATIVE-LAW JUDGE. **2.** See *judicial officer* (3).

▸ **inferior officer.** (16c) **1.** An officer who is subordinate to another officer. **2.** A United States officer appointed by the President, by a court, or by the head of a federal department. • Senate confirmation is not required. See *United States officer.*

▸ **judicial officer.** (17c) **1.** A judge or magistrate. **2.** Any officer of the court, such as a bailiff or court reporter. **3.** A person, usu. an attorney, who serves in an appointive capacity at the pleasure of an appointing judge, and whose actions and decisions are reviewed by that judge. — Also termed *magistrate*; *referee*; *special master*; *commissioner*; *hearing officer.*

▸ **juvenile officer.** (1911) A juvenile-court employee, sometimes a social worker or probation officer, who works with the judge to direct and develop the court's child-welfare work. — Also termed *county agent.*

▸ **law-enforcement officer.** See LAW-ENFORCEMENT OFFICER.

▸ **legislative officer.** (1821) **1.** A member of a federal, state, or municipal legislative body. **2.** A government official whose duties relate primarily to the enactment of laws, such as a federal or state senator, representative, or assembly member. • State and federal constitutions generally restrict legislative officers' duties to the enactment of legislation. But legislative officers occasionally exercise judicial functions, such as presenting or hearing cases of impeachment of other government officers.

▸ **line officer.** A military officer assigned to the line of the army or navy.

▸ **ministerial officer.** (17c) An officer who primarily executes mandates issued by the officer's superiors; one who performs specified legal duties when the appropriate conditions have been met, but who does not exercise personal judgment or discretion in performing those duties.

▸ **municipal officer.** (18c) An officer for a city, town, or borough; an officer of a municipality. — Also termed *city officer; town officer.*

▸ **officer de facto** (di **fak**-toh). (18c) **1.** An officer who exercises the duties of an office under color of an appointment or election, but who has failed to qualify for office for any one of various reasons, as by being under the required age, having failed to take the oath, having not furnished a required bond, or having taken office under a statute later declared unconstitutional. **2.** *Corporations.* Someone who is acting under color of right and with apparent authority, but who is not legally a corporate officer. • The corporation is bound by all acts and contracts of an officer de facto in the same way as it is with those of an officer de jure. — Also termed *de facto officer.*

▸ **officer de jure** (di **joor**-ee). (18c) **1.** An officer who exercises the duties of an office for which the holder has fulfilled all the qualifications. **2.** A duly authorized corporate officer. — Also termed *de jure officer.*

▸ **peace officer.** See PEACE OFFICER.

▸ **police officer.** See POLICE OFFICER.

▸ **presiding officer.** An officer who presides, esp. over a civilian court or deliberative assembly. See CHAIR (1); PRESIDE.

▸ **principal officer.** (16c) **1.** An officer with the most authority of the officers being considered for some purpose. **2.** A United States officer appointed by the President with the advice and consent of the Senate. — Also termed *primary officer.* See *United States officer.*

▸ **probation officer.** (1880) A government officer who supervises the conduct of a probationer.

▸ **recording officer.** See SECRETARY (3).

▸ **safety officer.** (1860) **1.** Someone within an organization who is responsible for the safety of the people who work there. **2.** An OSHA employee responsible for investigating the safety practices and procedures at a place of business. See OCCUPATIONAL SAFETY AND HEALTH ACT OF 1970.

▸ **staff officer.** A military officer whose job is to help an officer of higher rank.

▸ **state officer.** (17c) **1.** A person whose authority or jurisdiction extends to the general public or state as a whole, as distinguished from an officer whose authority and jurisdiction are confined to the limits of a particular political subdivision. **2.** An officer exercising authority under a state — rather than the federal — government.

▸ **subordinate officer.** (17c) **1.** An officer ranking below and performing under the direction of another officer. **2.** An independent officer subject only to statutory direction.

▸ **town officer.** See *municipal officer.*

▸ **truancy officer.** See TRUANCY OFFICER.

▸ **trust officer.** (1905) A trust-company official responsible for administering funds held by the company as a trustee.

▸ **United States officer.** (1813) An officer appointed under the authority of the federal government; specif., an officer appointed in the manner described in Article II, section 2, of the U.S. Constitution.

2. *Military law.* Someone who holds a commission in the armed forces, or a military post higher than that of the lowest ranks; a person who holds a position of authority within the military. — Also termed *military officer.*

▸ **brevet officer** (brə-**vet** *or* **brev**-it). (18c) A military officer who holds a nominal rank above that for which the person is paid.

▸ **commissioned officer.** (18c) An officer in the armed forces who holds grade and office under a presidential commission.

▸ **general officer.** (17c) A military officer whose command extends to a body of forces composed of several regiments. • Examples are generals, lieutenant-generals, major-generals, and brigadiers.

▸ **legal officer.** (17c) **1.** The officer responsible for handling military justice within a command. **2.** The adviser and assistant to a commanding officer on military-law matters. **3.** Any commissioned officer of the Navy, Marine Corps, or Coast Guard who has been designated to perform legal duties for a command.

▸ **noncommissioned officer.** (18c) An enlisted person in the Army, Air Force, or Marine Corps in certain pay grades above the lowest pay grade. • Examples are sergeants and corporals. — Abbr. NCO.

▸ **officer of the day.** (18c) An officer who has charge, for the time being, of the guard, prisoners, and police of a military force or camp. — Also termed *orderly officer.*

▸ **officer of the guard.** (16c) A commissioned officer whose detail is to command the guard of a military force or camp. • The officer of the guard is under the command of the officer of the day.

▸ **orderly officer.** See *officer of the day.*

▸ **petty officer.** (18c) An enlisted person in the Navy or Coast Guard with a pay-grade of E-4 or higher.

▸ **preliminary-inquiry officer.** (1965) The person, usu. an officer, who conducts a preliminary inquiry.

▸ **presiding officer.** (18c) **1.** The president of the court in a special court-martial that does not have a military judge. **2.** In a court-martial with a military judge, the military judge.

▸ **superior commissioned officer.** (1915) A commissioned officer who is superior in command or rank.

▸ **warrant officer.** (17c) **1.** Someone who holds a commission or warrant in a warrant-officer grade. • A warrant officer's rank is below a second lieutenant or ensign but above cadets, midshipmen, and enlisted personnel. **2.** See SERGEANT-AT-ARMS (4).

officer of the court. (16c) Someone who is charged with upholding the law and administering the judicial system. • Typically, *officer of the court* refers to a judge, clerk, bailiff, sheriff, or the like, but the term also applies to a lawyer, who is obliged to obey court rules and who owes a duty of candor to the court. — Also termed *court officer.*

officer of the peace. See PEACE OFFICER.

officer's report. See REPORT.

official (ə-**fish**-əl), *adj.* (16c) **1.** Of, relating to, or involving an office or position of trust or authority <official duties>. **2.** Authorized or approved by a proper authority <a company's official policy>.

official, *n.* (14c) **1.** Someone who holds or is invested with a public office; a person elected or appointed to carry out some portion of a government's sovereign powers. — Also termed *public official.*

> "'Who is a legal official?' might now seem like a question with one obvious answer, but there is little agreement about it among theorists. In part, this is because the definition can be manipulated like other variables in a theory to provide more or less support for different theories about the law." Stephen Michael Sheppard, *I Do Solemnly Swear: The Moral Obligations of Legal Officials* 18 (2009).

2. One authorized to act for a corporation or organization, esp. in a subordinate capacity. **3.** (*usu. cap.*) OFFICIAL PRINCIPAL.

official bond. See BOND (2).

official-capacity suit. See SUIT.

official corruption. See *official misconduct* under MISCONDUCT.

officialese (ə-fish-ə-**leez**), *n.* (1884) The peculiar language of government officials at their worst, characterized esp. by the use of high-sounding words for commonplace ideas, circumlocutions, equivocation, doublespeak, hair-splitting pedantry, logorrhea, and pervasive opacity. Cf. LEGALESE.

Official Gazette. *Patents & Trademarks.* Either of two weekly publications of the U.S. Patent and Trademark Office: one for patents, publishing abstracts of new patents; and one for trademarks, publishing samples of trademarks proposed for registration. — Abbr. OG.

official liability. See LIABILITY.

official misconduct. See MISCONDUCT (1).

official newspaper. See NEWSPAPER.

official principal. (*usu. cap.*) (16c) *Eccles. law.* A person appointed by an archbishop, bishop, or archdeacon to exercise jurisdiction in and preside over an ecclesiastical court. — Sometimes shortened to *official.*

official privilege. See PRIVILEGE (1).

official record. See RECORD.

official religion. See *state religion* under RELIGION.

official report. See REPORT (3).

official shorthand writer. See COURT REPORTER (1).

official use. See USE (4).

officiis belli (ə-**fish**-ee-is **bel**-ɪ). [Latin] By the duties of war.

officina brevium (aw-fə-**sɪ**-nə **bree**-vee-əm). [Latin "workshop of writs"] (17c) *Hist.* OFFICINA JUSTITIAE.

officina justitiae (aw-fə-**sɪ**-nə jəs-**tish**-ee-ee). [Latin "workshop of justice"] (17c) *Hist.* The court of chancery, where the king's writs were issued. — Also termed *officina brevium.* See CHANCERY.

officio. See EX OFFICIO.

officious guarantor. See GUARANTOR.

officious intermeddler (ə-**fish**-əs). (18c) Someone who confers a benefit on another without being requested or having a legal duty to do so, and who therefore has no legal grounds to demand restitution for the benefit conferred. — Sometimes shortened to *intermeddler.* — Also termed (archaically) *volunteer.* See *benefit officiously conferred* under BENEFIT (2); VOLUNTEER (4).

officiousness (ə-**fish**-əs-nəs), *n.* (16c) Interference in the affairs of others without justification under the circumstances. — **officious,** *adj.*

officious testament. See TESTAMENT.

officious will. See *officious testament* under TESTAMENT.

officium virile (ə-**fish**-ee-əm və-**rɪ**-lee). [Latin] (18c) *Roman law.* A man's office. • Certain offices, such as tutor and curator, could be discharged only by men.

off-label use. (1987) Use of prescription medicine or medical products for conditions and in circumstances not approved by the Food and Drug Administration.

off point. (1951) Not discussing the precise issue at hand; irrelevant. Cf. ON POINT.

off-premises license. See *off-sale license* under LICENSE.

off-sale license. See LICENSE.

offset, *n.* (18c) Something (such as an amount or claim) that balances or compensates for something else; SETOFF (3).

> "Both setoff and recoupment existed at common law, but their scope has been modified, expanded, and ultimately merged by subsequent statutory and decisional law. The final equitable concept of 'offset' recognizes that the debtor may satisfy a creditor's claim by acquiring a claim that serves to counterbalance or to compensate for the creditor's claim. . . . [C]ourts use the terms 'offset' and 'setoff' interchangeably, often switching between them from sentence to sentence, supporting the conclusion that there is no substantive difference between them." 4 Ann Taylor Schwing, *California Affirmative Defenses* § 44:1, at 4-5 (2d ed. 1996).

offset, *vb.* (17c) To balance or calculate against; to compensate for <the gains offset the losses>.

offset account. See ACCOUNT.

offshore asset-protection trust. See *asset-protection trust* (1) under TRUST (3).

offshore trust. See *foreign-situs trust* under TRUST (3).

offspring. (bef. 12c) Children; issue; progeny.

off-the-board, *adj.* See OFF-BOARD.

off the record. (1920) **1.** (Of a statement, comment, or testimony) not recorded as official evidence of a proceeding, such as a trial or deposition. **2.** (Of a statement) not intended for quotation or attribution. • In either sense, whenever the phrase appears before the noun it modifies, it should be hyphenated <off-the-record comments>. Cf. ON THE RECORD.

off-year election. See ELECTION (3).

OFHEO. *abbr.* OFFICE OF FEDERAL HOUSING ENTERPRISE OVERSIGHT.

OFR. *abbr.* Office of Federal Register. See FEDERAL REGISTER.

of record. (16c) **1.** Recorded in the appropriate records <counsel of record>. See *attorney of record* under ATTORNEY. **2.** (Of a court) that has proceedings taken down stenographically or otherwise documented <court of record>. See *court of record* under COURT.

of the essence. (18c) (Of a contractual requirement) so important that if the requirement is not met, the promisor will be held to have breached the contract and a rescission by the promisee will be justified <time is of the essence>.

OG. *abbr.* OFFICIAL GAZETTE.

OGE. See OFFICE OF GOVERNMENT ETHICS.

OHHLHC. *abbr.* OFFICE OF HEALTHY HOMES AND LEAD HAZARD CONTROL.

OID. *abbr.* ORIGINAL-ISSUE DISCOUNT.

oil-and-gas lease. See LEASE.

oil fingerprinting. (1971) The chemical analysis of oil to identify its source. • This is usu. done to trace the source of an oil spill.

OIPE. *abbr.* OFFICE OF INITIAL PATENT EXAMINATION.

Oireachtas (**air**-ək-thəs *or* **eer**-ək-təs). The Parliament of the Republic of Ireland.

Old-Age and Survivors' Insurance. (1935) A system of insurance, subsidized by the federal government, that provides retirement benefits for persons who reach retirement age and payments to survivors upon the death of the insured. • This was the original name for the retirement and death benefits established by the Social Security Act of 1935. As the scope of these benefits expanded, the name changed to Old Age, Survivors, and Disability Insurance (OASDI), and then to Old Age, Survivors, Disability, and Health Insurance (OASDHI). Today, the system is most often referred to as *Social Security.* — Abbr. OASI. See SOCIAL SECURITY ACT.

old-age pension. See PENSION.

old business. See *unfinished business* under BUSINESS (5).

old combination. See COMBINATION.

old-combination rejection. See REJECTION.

old lag. See RECIDIVIST.

Old *Natura Brevium* (nə-t[y]**oor**-ə **bree**-vee-əm). *Hist.* A treatise on the writs in use during the reign of Edward III. — Abbr. O.N.B. See BREVE.

old-soldier's rule. See EGGSHELL-SKULL RULE.

old style. (17c) The system of ordering time according to the Julian method, introduced by Julius Caesar in 46 B.C., by which all years have 365 days except the years divisible by 4, which have 366 days. • This differs from the modern calendar in that it assumes that there are exactly 365.25 days in a year. But there are actually slightly less than 365.25 days in a solar year, so the old-style calendar adds too many days over time. The Julian calendar was reformed by Pope Gregory XIII in 1582. — Abbr. o.s. — Also termed *Julian calendar.* Cf. NEW STYLE.

Oléron, laws of (**oh**-lə-ron *or* aw-lay-**ron**). See LAWS OF OLÉRON.

oligarchy (**ol**-ə-gahr-kee), *n.* (16c) A government in which a small group of persons exercises control; the persons who constitute such a government. — **oligarchic, oligarchical,** *adj.*

oligopolistic price coordination. See CONSCIOUS PARALLELISM.

oligopoly (ol-ə-**gop**-ə-lee), *n.* (1895) Control or domination of a market by a few large sellers, creating high prices and low output similar to those found in a monopoly. Cf. MONOPOLY. — **oligopolistic,** *adj.* — **oligopolist,** *n.*

> "One reason for the difficulty in describing and delimiting oligopoly power is the large number of variables that confront any theorist building an oligopoly model. Pure monopoly is akin to a single player game, such as solitaire, but the oligopoly model may be more like a multihand poker game. . . . Unlike poker, where for any hand one player will win all of the money bet, the players in an oligopolistic market can actually increase the returns that all of them receive through disciplined pricing." Lawrence A. Sullivan & Warren S. Grimes, *The Law of Antitrust: An Integrated Handbook* 38–39 (2000).

oligopsony (ol-ə-**gop**-sə-nee), *n.* (1937) Control or domination of a market by a few large buyers or customers. — **oligopsonistic,** *adj.* — **oligopsonist,** *n.*

OLMS. *abbr.* OFFICE OF LABOR-MANAGEMENT STANDARDS.

olograph, *n.* See HOLOGRAPH. — **olographic,** *adj.*

olographic will. See *holographic will* under WILL.

OMB. *abbr.* OFFICE OF MANAGEMENT AND BUDGET.

ombudsman (**om**-bədz-mən). (1872) **1.** An official appointed to receive, investigate, and report on private citizens' complaints about the government. **2.** A similar appointee in a nongovernmental organization (such as a company or university). — Often shortened to *ombuds.*

> "An ombudsman serves as an alternative to the adversary system for resolving disputes, especially between citizens and government agencies . . . . An ombudsman is . . . (1) an independent and nonpartisan officer of the legislature who supervises the administration; (2) one who deals with specific complaints from the public against administrative injustice and maladministration; and (3) one who has the power to investigate, criticize and publicize, but not to reverse administration action." 4 Am. Jur. 2d *Alternative Dispute Resolution* § 23 (1995).

omissa et male appretiata (ə-**mis**-ə et **mal**-ee ə-pree-shee-**ay**-tə). [Law Latin] (1808) *Hist.* Things omitted and erroneously valued.

> "When an executor confirms and omits in the inventory part of the defunct's effects, he may have the mistake corrected. But if he do not take steps for this purpose, any one interested in the succession may apply, either to have the executor compelled to confirm the omission, or himself to confirm it. Ordinary executors *ad omissa et male appretiata* ought to call the principal executor to their confirmation, or it will be null; but this rule does not hold in the case of executors-creditors." William Bell, *Bell's Dictionary and Digest of the Law of Scotland* 753 (George Watson ed., 7th ed. 1890).

omission, *n.* (14c) **1.** A failure to do something; esp., a neglect of duty <the complaint alleged that the driver had committed various negligent acts and omissions>. **2.** The act of leaving something out <the contractor's omission of the sales price rendered the contract void>. **3.** The state of having been left out or of not having been done <his omission from the roster caused no harm>. **4.** Something that is left out, left undone, or otherwise neglected <the many omissions from the list were

unintentional>. — Formerly also termed *omittance.* — **omit,** *vb.* — **omissive, omissible,** *adj.*

▸ **material omission.** (17c) An omission that significantly affects a person's decision-making.

omittance. (17c) *Archaic.* OMISSION.

omitted-case canon. The doctrine that nothing is to be added to what a legal instrument states or reasonably implies; the principle that a matter not covered is to be treated as not covered. — Also termed *casus omissus canon.* See CASUS OMISSUS.

omne jus reale (**om**-nee jəs ree-**ay**-lee). [Law Latin] *Hist.* Every real right.

omne quod in se erat (**om**-nee kwod in see **er**-at). [Latin] (17c) *Hist.* All that one had in his power.

omnibus (**om**-ni-bəs), *adj.* (1842) Of, relating to, or involving numerous objects or items at once; including many things or having various purposes.

omnibus account. See *concentration account* under ACCOUNT.

omnibus bill. See BILL (3).

omnibus claim. See PATENT CLAIM.

omnibus clause. (1880) **1.** A provision in an automobile-insurance policy that extends coverage to all drivers operating the insured vehicle with the owner's permission.

▸ **statutory omnibus clause.** (1949) *Insurance.* An omnibus clause provided by statute.

2. RESIDUARY CLAUSE.

omnibus count. See COUNT (2).

omnibus hearing. See HEARING.

omnibus motion. See MOTION (1).

omni exceptione major (**om**-nee ek-sep-shee-**oh**-nee **may**-jor). [Law Latin] (17c) *Scots law.* Beyond all exception. • The phrase often referred to witnesses of such exceptional character that their testimony was above suspicion.

omnium (**om**-nee-əm), *n.* (18c) The total amount or value of the items in a combined fund or stock. • The term is used primarily in British mercantile law.

omnium bonorum (**om**-nee-əm bə-**nor**-əm). [Latin] (18c) *Roman & Scots law.* Of all goods. • The phrase appeared in reference to a conveyance of or partnership in one's entire estate.

OMVI. *abbr.* Operating a motor vehicle while intoxicated. See DRIVING UNDER THE INFLUENCE.

OMVUI. *abbr.* Operating a motor vehicle while under the influence. See DRIVING UNDER THE INFLUENCE.

on all fours. (1914) (Of a law case) squarely on point (with a precedent) on both facts and law; nearly identical in all material ways <our client's case is on all fours with the Supreme Court's most recent opinion>. Cf. WHITE-HORSE CASE.

> "The courts, nowadays, are governed largely by precedent, and this imposes on the advocate the necessity of supporting his client's cause by concrete authorities — cases 'on all fours' with, or at least analogous to, the case at bar." William M. Lile et al., *Brief Making and the Use of Law Books* 98 (Roger W. Cooley & Charles Lesley Ames eds., 3d ed. 1914).

O.N.B. *abbr.* OLD NATURA BREVIUM.

onboard bill of lading. See BILL OF LADING.

on call. See ON DEMAND.

on-call district attorney. See DISTRICT ATTORNEY.

ONDCP. See OFFICE OF NATIONAL DRUG CONTROL POLICY.

on demand. (17c) When presented or upon request for payment <this note is payable on demand>. — Also termed *on call.* See PAYABLE.

one-action rule. (1943) In debtor-creditor law, the principle that when a debt is secured by real property, the creditor must foreclose on the collateral before proceeding against the debtor's unsecured assets.

one-bite rule. (1911) **1.** The principle that a person or entity gets only one chance to assert the same rights or bring the same claims. — Also termed *one-bite-at-the-apple rule.* See RES JUDICATA. **2.** A common-law rule or statutory provision holding a dog-owner responsible for any harm or injury caused by the dog only if the owner knows or has reason to know that the dog is dangerous. • Some states have modified this common-law rule by statute, while other states have adopted this rule as is in their state codes. — Also termed *first-bite rule*; *one-free-bite rule.*

> "The phrase *one bite* or *one-bite rule* has two primary uses in the legal context. One refers to the liability of the owner of an animal for the damage done when that animal attacks someone. Under the traditional rule, a dog owner is not liable to a person bitten by the dog unless the dog has previously demonstrated vicious tendencies — usually by biting someone else — so that the owner should have been aware of the need to take precautions to avoid further attacks. This leads judges to say that the dog is entitled to 'one bite,' or 'one free bite.' The rule both protects the owner the first time and imposes liability for repeat offenses. The first bite may be free, but after that the owner had better get out the checkbook. Although some states retain this rule, others have replaced it with statutes that take away the free bite, making owners strictly liable for all injuries caused by their pets. The second use of the phrase *one-bite rule* in law is more metaphorical (no actual biting here), but it too refers to a single chance. In this context *one bite* precludes repeated assertions of the same legal claim." James E. Clapp et al., *Lawtalk: The Unknown Stories Behind Familiar Legal Expressions* 166 (2011).

3. *Administrative law.* A principle requiring an administrative agency to use the notice-and-comment rulemaking framework to issue interpretations that contradict a regulation. See *informal rulemaking* under RULEMAKING.

one-book rule. (1992) *Criminal procedure.* The doctrine that the revised edition of federal sentencing guidelines will apply if a criminal defendant is convicted of two crimes, the first of which is committed before the effective date of the revision and the second after. *See U.S. v. Kumar,* 617 F.3d 612 (2d Cir. 2010).

one-court-of-justice doctrine. (1972) A principle in some states holding that there is but a single court in the state and that this court is composed of several divisions, such as the supreme court, the courts of appeals, and district courts, probate courts, and any other legislatively created courts. • Michigan, for example, has embodied this doctrine in its constitution (art. VI, § 1). — Also termed *one court of justice.*

one-day, one-trial method. (1976) A system of summoning and using jurors whereby a person answers a jury summons and participates in the venire for one day only, unless the person is actually empaneled for a trial, in which event the juror's service lasts for the entire length of the trial. • This system, which is used in several states, reduces the average term of service and expands the number of individual jurors called.

one-free-bite rule. See ONE-BITE RULE (2).

one-half plus one. See HALF PLUS ONE.

180-day rule. (1966) *Criminal procedure.* **1.** A rule that, in some jurisdictions, allows a person charged with a felony to be released on personal recognizance if the person has been in jail for 180 days without being brought to trial, and if the delay has not resulted from the defendant's own actions. **2.** A rule requiring all pending charges against a prison inmate to be brought to trial in 180 days or to be dismissed with prejudice.

one-man, one-vote rule. See ONE-PERSON, ONE-VOTE RULE.

one-month liquidation. See LIQUIDATION (3).

one-party consent rule. (1980) The principle that one party to a telephone or other conversation may secretly record the conversation. • This principle applies in most but not all states.

one-party-consent state. (1991) *Criminal law.* A state in which the law makes it lawful to record a wire, oral, or electronic conversation as long as one person in the conversation has consented to the recording. Cf. TWO-PARTY-CONSENT STATE.

one-person, one-vote rule. (1965) *Constitutional law.* The principle that the Equal Protection Clause requires legislative voting districts to have about the same population. *Reynolds v. Sims*, 377 U.S. 533, 84 S.Ct. 1362 (1964). — Also termed *one-man, one-vote rule.* See APPORTIONMENT.

onerando pro rata portione. See DE ONERANDO PRO RATA PORTIONE.

onerare (on-ə-**rair**-ee), *vb.* [Latin] *Hist.* To burden or load.

onera realia (**on**-ər-ə ree-**ay**-lee-ə). [Law Latin] (18c) *Scots law.* Real burdens.

> "Onera realia . . . are burdens or encumbrances affecting land, and exigible from it. They are distinguished from personal burdens, which only affect and are exigible from the person upon whom they lie. A single example may illustrate the nature of both. It is a common enough practice, when lands are sold, for the seller not to insist on payment of the full price at the time of the sale, but to allow a part of the price to remain on the lands as a burden. If the balance so left be declared . . . to be a real lien . . . it is a burden for which the lands may be attached and sold, into whose possession soever they may come. But if the burden of payment of the remainder of the price be laid upon the purchaser alone, and not upon the lands, then the burden is personal, and a subsequent purchaser from him incurs no liability therefor, the lands not being affected." John Trayner, *Trayner's Latin Maxims* 423 (4th ed. 1894).

onerari non (on-ə-**rair**-I non). [Law Latin] *Hist.* Ought not to be charged. • In pleading, these words were used by a defendant to begin a plea in a debt action. Cf. ACTIO NON.

oneratio (on-ə-**ray**-shee-oh). [Law Latin] *Hist.* A cargo or lading.

oneris ferendi (**on**-ə-ris fə-**ren**-dI). [Latin] (17c) *Roman law.* Of bearing a weight or burden. See *servitus oneris ferendi* under SERVITUS; JUS ONERIS FERENDI; PARIES ONERI FERENDO, UTI NUNC EST, ITA SIT.

onerous (**oh**-nər-əs *or* **on**-ər-əs), *adj.* (14c) **1.** Excessively burdensome or troublesome; causing hardship <onerous discovery requests>. **2.** Having or involving obligations that outweigh the advantages <onerous property>. **3.** *Civil law.* Done or given in return for something of equivalent value; supported by consideration <an onerous contract>. Cf. GRATUITOUS (1). — **onerousness,** *n.*

onerous cause. (1829) *Civil law.* An advantage obtained in exchange for a contractual obligation. See. La. Civ. Code arts. 1909, 1967.

onerous contract. See CONTRACT.

onerous deed. See DEED.

onerous donation. See DONATION (1).

onerous gift. See GIFT.

onerous title. See TITLE (2).

onerous trust. See TRUST (3).

one-satisfaction rule. (1965) The principle that a plaintiff is only entitled to only one recovery for a particular harm, and that the plaintiff must elect a single remedy if the jury has awarded more than one. • This rule is, for example, one of the foundations of a defendant's right to have a jury verdict reduced by the amount of any settlements the plaintiff has received from other entities for the same injury. — Also termed *single-recovery rule.*

one-subject rule. (1929) The principle that a statute should embrace only one topic, which should be stated in its title.

one-time charge. See *special charge* under CHARGE (7).

one-way ratchet theory. See RATCHET THEORY.

one-witness rule. (1921) **1.** Any requirement that a single witness to the signing of a legal document is sufficient to make the instrument effective. **2.** *Criminal law.* A (largely rejected) doctrine that if a crime has been established by only a single witness who provides inherently contradictory testimony, the witness's testimony is held to be unreliable as a matter of law.

one-year rule. (1920) *Patents.* The statutory requirement that a patent application must be filed within one year after any publication, public use, sale, or offer for sale of the invention. • If an inventor waits longer than a year, the patent is blocked by this "statutory bar." *See* 35 USCA § 102(b).

ongoing earnings. See *operating earnings* under EARNINGS.

online scrip. See *Internet scrip* under SCRIP.

onomastic (on-ə-**mas**-tik), *adj.* (16c) **1.** Of, relating to, or involving names or nomenclature. **2.** (Of a signature on an instrument) in a handwriting different from that of the body of the document; esp., designating an autograph signature alone, as distinguished from the main text in a different hand or in typewriting. Cf. HOLOGRAPH; SYMBOLIC. — **onomastics** (in sense 1), *n.*

on or about. (17c) Approximately; at or around the time specified. • This language is used in pleading to prevent a variance between the pleading and the proof, usu. when there is any uncertainty about the exact date of a pivotal event. When used in nonpleading contexts, the phrase is mere jargon.

on pain of. (14c) Or else suffer punishment for noncompliance. • This phrase usu. follows a command or condition <ordered to cease operations on pain of a $2,000 fine>.

on point. (1927) Discussing the precise issue now at hand; apposite <this opinion is not on point as authority in our case>. — Also termed *in point.* Cf. OFF POINT.

on-premises license. See *on-sale license* under LICENSE.

on-sale bar. (1965) *Patents.* A statutory bar prohibiting patent eligibility if an invention was sold or offered for sale more than one year before the patent application is filed. 35 USCA § 102(b).

on-sale license. See LICENSE.

onset date. (1966) The beginning of a period of disability for purposes of disability payments by the Social Security Administration.

on the brief. (Of a lawyer) having participated in preparing a given brief. • The names of all the lawyers on the brief are typically listed on the front cover.

on the floor. *Parliamentary law.* **1.** (Of a motion) under consideration; PENDING (2) <the motion is on the floor>. **2.** (Of a member) physically present at a meeting and attending to its deliberations <the senator is on the floor>.

on the merits. (18c) (Of a judgment) delivered after the court has heard and evaluated the evidence and the parties' substantive arguments.

on the pleadings. (18c) (Of a judgment) rendered for reasons that are apparent from the faces of the complaint and answer, without hearing or evaluating the evidence or the substantive arguments. See SUMMARY JUDGMENT.

on the record. (18c) **1.** (Of a statement, comment, or testimony) recorded as official evidence of a proceeding, such as a trial or deposition. **2.** (Of a statement) intended for quotation or attribution. • In either sense, whenever the phrase appears before the noun it modifies, it should be hyphenated <an on-the-record statement>. Cf. OFF THE RECORD.

onus (**oh**-nəs). (17c) **1.** A burden; a load. **2.** A disagreeable responsibility; an obligation. **3.** ONUS PROBANDI.

onus probandi (**oh**-nəs prə-**ban**-dɪ). [Latin] (18c) BURDEN OF PROOF. — Often shortened to *onus.*

OOH-DNR. *abbr.* See *out-of-hospital do-not-resuscitate order* under DO-NOT-RESUSCITATE ORDER.

op. *abbr.* (*often cap.*) **1.** OPINION (1). **2.** Opinions.

OPD. *abbr.* OFFICE OF POLICY DEVELOPMENT.

OPEC (**oh**-pek). *abbr.* (1960) Organization of Petroleum Exporting Countries.

ope et consilio (**oh**-pee et kən-**sil**-ee-oh). [Latin] *Civil law.* By aid and counsel. • The term is usu. applied to accessories to crimes. It is analogous to the common-law concept of aiding and abetting. — Abbr. o.c. — Sometimes shortened to *ope consilio.* Cf. ART AND PART.

ope exceptionis (**oh**-pee ek-sep-shee-**oh**-nis). [Latin "by force of exception"] (17c) *Hist.* In a civil case, a plea asserting a peremptory exception that a document on which the action is based is void.

open, *adj.* (bef. 12c) **1.** Manifest; apparent; notorious. **2.** Visible; exposed to public view; not clandestine. **3.** Not closed, settled, fixed, or terminated.

open account. See ACCOUNT.

open adoption. See ADOPTION (1).

open and notorious. (16c) **1.** NOTORIOUS (2). **2.** (Of adultery) known and recognized by the public and flouting the accepted standards of morality in the community.

open and notorious adultery. See ADULTERY.

open and notorious cohabitation. See *notorious cohabitation* under COHABITATION.

open and notorious possession. See *notorious possession* under POSSESSION.

open-and-public-meeting law. See OPEN-MEETING LAW.

open bid. See BID (2).

open brief. See BRIEF (1).

open check. See CHECK.

open closed shop. See SHOP.

open court. (15c) **1.** A court that is in session, presided over by a judge, attended by the parties and their attorneys, and engaged in judicial business. • *Open court* usu. refers to a proceeding in which formal entries are made on the record. The term is distinguished from a court that is hearing evidence in camera or from a judge that is exercising merely magisterial powers. **2.** A court session that the public is free to attend. • Most state constitutions have open-court provisions guaranteeing the public's right to attend trials.

open credit. See *revolving credit* under CREDIT (4).

open diplomacy. See DIPLOMACY (1).

open-door law. See OPEN-MEETING LAW.

open-end, *adj.* (1931) **1.** Allowing for future changes or additions <open-end credit plan>. **2.** Continually issuing or redeeming shares on demand at the current net asset value <open-end investment company>. — Also termed *open-ended.*

open-end credit plan. See CREDIT PLAN.

open-ended claim. See PATENT CLAIM.

open-end fund. See MUTUAL FUND.

open-end mortgage. See MORTGAGE.

open-end mortgage bond. See BOND (3).

open entry. See ENTRY (1).

open-fields doctrine. (1963) *Criminal procedure.* The rule permitting a warrantless search of the area outside a property owner's curtilage; the principle that no one has a reasonable expectation of privacy in anything in plain sight. • Unless there is some other legal basis for the search, it must exclude the home and any adjoining land (such as a yard) that is within an enclosure or otherwise protected from public scrutiny. — Also termed *open-field doctrine*; *open-fields rule.* Cf. PLAIN-VIEW DOCTRINE.

open-file discovery. (1971) *Criminal law.* A case-specific policy in which prosecutors allow defense counsel to see (but not always to obtain copies of) all the documents in their file relating to the defendant. — Abbr. OFD.

open forum. (17c) **1.** GOOD OF THE ORDER. **2.** PUBLIC FORUM.

open-governmental-proceedings law. See OPEN-MEETING LAW.

open guaranty. See *continuing guaranty* under GUARANTY (1).

opening address. See OPENING STATEMENT.

opening a judgment. A court's grant of a motion for a rehearing on the merits but keeping the court's decision in effect.

opening argument. See OPENING STATEMENT.

opening bidding. See OPENING THE BIDDING.

opening brief. See BRIEF (1).

opening brief on the merits. See *opening brief* under BRIEF (1).

opening statement. (1848) At the outset of a trial, an advocate's statement giving the fact-finder a preview of the case and of the evidence to be presented. • Although the opening statement is not supposed to be argumentative, lawyers — purposefully or not — often include some form of argument. The term is thus sometimes referred to as *opening argument.* — Also termed *opening address.*

opening the bidding. In a sheriff's sale of real property, the unethical practice of setting aside the concluded sale to accept a better post-sale offer. — Also termed *opening bidding.*

opening the door. An attorney's conduct or questions that render otherwise inadmissible evidence or objectionable questions admissible.

open letter of credit. See LETTER OF CREDIT.

open lewdness. See LEWDNESS.

open listing. See LISTING (1).

open market. See MARKET.

open-market rent. See RENT (1).

open marriage. See MARRIAGE (1).

open-meeting law. (1972) A statute requiring a governmental department or agency to open its meetings or its records to public access. — Also termed *sunshine law; public-meeting law; open-door law; freedom-of-access law; right-to-know law; open-governmental-proceedings law; open-and-public-meeting law* (together with variations replacing *law* with *act* or *statute* or *legislation*).

> "Various States lay claim to the first open meeting law. Unlike the broadly applicable open meeting laws now common in the United States, early laws imposed open meeting requirements on specific public entities. A Kansas statute governing school board meetings was enacted in 1868. A Michigan court has identified an open meeting law passed in 1895, requiring public city council meetings. Oklahoma enacted a law governing meetings of county commissioners in 1897. Utah's first law, governing city councils, was passed in 1898. Florida enacted its first law in 1905. Similar provisions requiring particular public bodies to meet in public predated the enactment of comprehensive open meeting laws in many States. Alabama enacted what some consider the first comprehensive open meeting law in 1915. Even in 1950, Alabama was the only State with a comprehensive statute. By 1959, twenty States had open meeting laws. Fifteen years later, only four States were without some form of open meeting law. Since the enactment of the New York and Rhode Island open meeting laws in 1976, every State has had a generally applicable law requiring open meetings of at least a significant number of governmental bodies." 1 Ann Taylor Schwing, *Open Meeting Laws* § 1.1, at 3–4 (3d ed. 2011).

open memorandum. See MEMORANDUM (2).

open microphone. See GOOD OF THE ORDER.

open-mine doctrine. (1950) *Wills & estates.* The principle that minerals produced from a mine, well, or quarry that was open when a life estate began and the royalties and bonuses related to them belong to the life tenant rather than the remainderman.

open mortgage clause. See MORTGAGE CLAUSE.

open murder. 1. An unsolved homicide. See HOMICIDE. **2.** A charge presenting the elements of both first- and second-degree murder. • The jury must decide whether to convict of either first- or second-degree murder (but not both) based on the evidence.

open nominations, *vb.* (1942) *Parliamentary law.* To begin taking nominations from the floor upon passage of a motion.

open offer. See OFFER (2).

open order. See ORDER (8).

open-perils policy. See INSURANCE POLICY.

open policy. See *unvalued policy* under INSURANCE POLICY.

open possession. See *notorious possession* under POSSESSION.

open price. See PRICE.

open-public-records act. See OPEN-RECORDS ACT.

open-records act. (1969) A statute providing for public access to view and copy government records maintained by public agencies. — Also termed *open-public-records act.*

open seas. See *high seas* under SEA.

open season. (1846) A specific time of year when it is legal to hunt or catch game or fish.

open session. See SESSION (1).

open shop. See SHOP.

open-shop–closed-shop operation. See DOUBLE-BREASTED OPERATION.

open source, *adj.* (1998) Of or related to software that includes human-readable source code and can be freely revised.

open-source license. See LICENSE.

open-source software. (1998) Software that is usu. not sold for profit, includes both human-readable source code and machine-readable object code, and allows users to freely copy, modify, or distribute the software. • Even though open-source software is made widely available for free, it may be protected by federal trademark law. *See Planetary Motion Inc. v. Techplosion Inc.*, 261 F.3d 1188 (11th Cir. 2001).

open space. (17c) Undeveloped (or mostly undeveloped) urban or suburban land that is set aside and permanently restricted to agricultural, recreational, or conservational uses. • The land may be publicly or privately owned. Access may be restricted or unrestricted. Open spaces are not necessarily in a natural state: the term includes land used for public parks, gardens, farms, and pastures. But it does not include structures such as parking lots, swimming pools, or tennis courts.

open-space preserve. In urban planning, an area of land or water that is intentionally left undeveloped to protect or conserve it. — Also termed *open-space reserve; open-space reservation; greenspace.*

open town. (18c) *Int'l law.* An undefended city in a combat zone that is laid open to the grasp of the attacking forces.

open union. See UNION.

open verdict. See VERDICT (3).

operability (op-ər-ə-**bil**-i-tee), *n.* (1917). **1.** The ability (of a thing) to work more or less as intended <the operability of a weapon>. **2.** *Patents.* The ability of an invention to work as described in the patent application. • A patent examiner may challenge the operability of an invention and require some proof, such as a demonstration of a working model.

operating agreement. (1967) **1.** *Oil & gas.* A contract among owners of the working interest in a producing oil or gas well setting forth the parties' agreements about drilling, development, operations, and accounting. **2.** *Corporations.* A limited-liability company's governing document that sets out the financial and managerial rights of the company's members.

operating a motor vehicle under the influence. See DRIVING UNDER THE INFLUENCE.

operating a motor vehicle while intoxicated. See DRIVING UNDER THE INFLUENCE.

operating a vehicle while intoxicated. See DRIVING WHILE INTOXICATED.

operating-cost ratio. (1934) The ratio between the net sales of a business and its operating costs.

operating earnings. See EARNINGS.

operating expense. See EXPENSE.

operating income. See *ordinary income* (1) under INCOME.

operating interest. See WORKING INTEREST.

operating lease. See LEASE.

operating profit. See PROFIT (1).

operating under the influence. See DRIVING UNDER THE INFLUENCE.

operating while intoxicated. See DRIVING UNDER THE INFLUENCE.

operational, *adj.* (1922) **1.** Engaged in operation; able to function. **2.** Ministerial.

operational efficiency. See BUSINESS EFFICACY.

operation of law. (17c) The means by which a right or a liability is created for a party regardless of the party's actual intent <because the court didn't rule on the motion for rehearing within 30 days, it was overruled by operation of law>.

operations clause. (1923) *Oil & gas.* A provision in an oil-and-gas lease specifying that the lease will not expire as long as oil-and-gas development continues on the leased property. See CONTINUOUS-OPERATIONS CLAUSE; WELL-COMPLETION CLAUSE.

operative, *adj.* (15c) **1.** Being in or having force or effect; esp., designating the part of a legal instrument that gives effect to the transaction involved <the operative provision of the contract>. **2.** Having principal relevance; essential to the meaning of the whole <*may* is the operative word of the statute>.

operative clause. See CLAUSE.

operative construction. (1822) **1.** The interpretation of a writing or agreement, esp. a contract, statute, or regulation, that is being relied on by the parties, a court, or an administrative agency. **2.** *Patents.* A working embodiment of an invention, usu. used to conceptualize the invention and how it will work rather than to create a working model. **3.** The doctrine that the interpretation of a statute or regulation made by an administrative agency charged with enforcing it is entitled to judicial deference unless it is arbitrary and capricious.

operative fact. See FACT.

operative part. The principal provision in a legal instrument dealing with the creation or transfer of rights by which the object of the instrument is given effect.

operative performance bond. See PERFORMANCE BOND.

operative trust. See *active trust* under TRUST (3).

operative words. (17c) In a transactional document, the words that actually effect the transaction; the particular phraseology by which the object of a legal instrument is given effect. • For example, in a conveyance, the operative words are those that pass title.

operis novi nuntiatio. See NOVI OPERIS NUNTIATIO.

OPIC. *abbr.* OVERSEAS PRIVATE INVESTMENT CORPORATION.

opinio juris sive necessitatis (ə-**pin**-ee-oh **joor**-is **sɪ**-vee nə-ses-i-**tay**-tis). [Latin "opinion that an act is necessary by rule of law"] (1937) *Int'l law.* The principle that for conduct or a practice to become a rule of customary international law, it must be shown that countries believe that international law (rather than moral obligation) mandates the conduct or practice. — Also termed *opinio juris.*

opinion. (14c) **1.** A court's written statement explaining its decision in a given case, usu. including the statement of facts, points of law, rationale, and dicta. — Abbr. op. — Also termed *judicial opinion.* See DECISION (1). Cf. JUDGMENT (2); RULING (2).

▸ **advisory opinion.** (1837) **1.** A nonbinding statement by a court of its interpretation of the law on a matter submitted for that purpose. • Federal courts are constitutionally prohibited from issuing advisory opinions by the case-or-controversy requirement, but other courts, such as the International Court of Justice, render them routinely. See CASE-OR-CONTROVERSY REQUIREMENT. **2.** A written statement, issued only by an administrator of an employee benefit plan, that interprets ERISA and applies it to a specific factual situation. • Only the parties named in the request for the opinion can rely on it, and its reliability depends on the accuracy and completeness of all material facts.

▸ **bench opinion.** (1914) **1.** A court's oral opinion delivered in open court. **2.** The text of a U.S. Supreme Court opinion disseminated to the public immediately after the Court announces the opinion in open court. • A bench opinion is distributed in a printed pamphlet prepared by the Court's Public Information Office and electronically through Project Hermes, the Court's system for distributing opinions to subscribers, usu. universities and media groups. A bench opinion may be corrected or amended by a slip opinion. See PROJECT HERMES. Cf. *slip opinion.*

▸ **concurring opinion.** See CONCURRENCE (3).

▸ **depublished opinion.** (1983) An intermediate appellate court's opinion that has been struck from the official reports, esp. by the highest court.

▸ **dissenting opinion.** (1817) An opinion by one or more judges who disagree with the decision reached by the majority. — Often shortened to *dissent.* — Also termed *minority opinion.*

▸ **extrajudicial opinion.** (17c) **1.** An opinion that is beyond the court's authority to render. • Such opinions are void. **2.** A judge's personal or scholarly opinion expressed in a medium other than a judicial opinion.

▸ **majority opinion.** (1882) An opinion joined in by more than half the judges considering a given case. — Also termed *main opinion*.

▸ **memorandum opinion.** (1912) A unanimous appellate opinion that succinctly states the decision of the court; an opinion that briefly reports the court's conclusion, usu. without elaboration because the decision follows a well-established legal principle or does not relate to any point of law. — Also termed *memorandum decision*; *memorandum disposition*; (slang) *memdispo*.

▸ **minority opinion.** See *dissenting opinion*.

▸ **per curiam opinion** (pər **kyoor**-ee-əm). (1860) An opinion handed down by an appellate court without identifying the individual judge who wrote the opinion. — Sometimes shortened to *per curiam* (per cur).

> "The most controversial form of summary disposition is a *per curiam* opinion that simultaneously grants certiorari and disposes of the merits at some length, discussing both the facts and the issues involved. The result is usually a reversal of the judgment below . . . . The parties are given no opportunity to file briefs on the merits or to argue orally before the Court. Indeed, they are given no formal notice whatever of the Court's intention to dispose of the certiorari papers in this manner . . . ." Robert L. Stern et al., *Supreme Court Practice* 320 (8th ed. 2002).

▸ **plurality opinion.** (1908) An opinion lacking enough judges' votes to constitute a majority, but receiving more votes than any other opinion.

▸ **qualified opinion.** See QUALIFIED OPINION.

▸ **seriatim opinions** (seer-ee-**ay**-tim). (1832) A series of opinions written individually by each judge on the bench, as opposed to a single opinion speaking for the court as a whole.

▸ **slip opinion.** (1940) **1.** An appellate-court opinion that is published individually after being rendered and then collectively in advance sheets before being released for publication in a reporter. • Unlike an unpublished opinion, a slip opinion can usu. be cited as authority. A slip opinion may be a corrected or amended version of a bench opinion. — Also termed *slipsheet*. Cf. *bench opinion*; ADVANCE SHEETS. **2.** *Archaic*. A preliminary draft of a court opinion not yet ready for publication. — Also termed *slip decision*. Cf. *unpublished opinion*.

▸ **unpublished opinion.** (1849) An opinion that the court has specifically designated as not for publication. • Court rules usu. prohibit citing an unpublished opinion as authority. Such an opinion is considered binding only on the parties to the particular case in which it is issued. Cf. *slip opinion*.

2. A formal expression of judgment or advice based on an expert's special knowledge; esp., a document, usu. prepared at a client's request, containing a lawyer's understanding of the law that applies to a particular case. — Also termed *opinion letter*.

> "The essence of a lawyer's job is to obtain the facts and the law with due diligence and then to give advice. But, strangely, no controlling definition has evolved for what is an 'opinion.' The lack of a definition is not crucial for some purposes. On the other hand, a definition is vital in other areas; for example, to determine within a law firm when peer review is necessary . . . ." 8 Arnold S. Jacobs, *Opinion Letters in Securities Matters* § 3, at Intro-12 (1998).

▸ **adverse opinion.** An outside auditor's opinion that a company's financial statements do not conform with generally accepted accounting principles or do not accurately reflect the company's financial position.

▸ **audit opinion.** (1973) A certified public accountant's opinion regarding the audited financial statements of an entity.

▸ **comfort opinion.** (1974) *Securities*. An attorney's written opinion that there is no reason to believe that the registration statement contains any material misrepresentations or omissions that would violate section 11 of the Securities Act of 1933. • The attorney usu. participates in the registration statement's preparation and confers with the securities issuer's representatives, underwriters, and public accountants before writing the opinion. The comfort opinion's purpose is to reassure the parties that the registration statement complies with securities laws; it is not part of the statement and is usu. not included.

▸ **coverage opinion.** (1934) A lawyer's opinion on whether a particular event is covered by a given insurance policy.

▸ **fairness opinion.** (1975) *Securities*. A professional assessment by an investment bank or other financial or legal expert about whether the terms of a merger, acquisition, or other corporate deal are fair.

▸ **infringement opinion.** (1949) *Patents*. A patent attorney's opinion about the probable outcome of an infringement hearing or trial on whether a particular product or process infringes one or more claims of another's patent.

▸ **legal opinion.** (18c) A written document in which an attorney provides his or her understanding of the law as applied to assumed facts. • The attorney may be a private attorney or attorney representing the state or other governmental entity. Private attorneys frequently render legal opinions on the ownership of real estate or minerals, insurance coverage, and corporate transactions. A party may be entitled to rely on a legal opinion, depending on factors such as the identity of the parties to whom the opinion was addressed, the nature of the opinion, and the law governing the opinion. See *coverage opinion*.

▸ **patentability opinion.** (1970) *Patents*. A patent attorney's or patent agent's opinion on the patent office's probable holding about the allowability of a patent application's claims. • The opinion is almost a mini-examination report because it is based on consideration of the invention's subject matter, prior art, etc.

▸ **title opinion.** (1927) A lawyer's or title company's opinion on the state of title for a given piece of real property, usu. describing whether the title is clear and marketable or whether it is encumbered. See TITLE SEARCH.

▸ **unqualified opinion.** An audit opinion given by an accountant who is satisfied that the financial statements reviewed were fairly presented and consistent with the previous year, and that the audit was performed in accordance with generally accepted auditing standards.

▸ **validity opinion.** (1973) *Patents*. A patent attorney's opinion about the likelihood that a patent or patent claim will be invalidated in light of evidence suggesting obviousness, lack of invention, unenforceability, etc.

3. A person's thought, belief, or inference, esp. a witness's view about a facts in dispute, as opposed to personal knowledge of the facts themselves. — Also termed (in sense 3) *conclusion.* See *opinion evidence* under EVIDENCE.

▸ **expert opinion.** (1866) An opinion offered by a witness whose knowledge, skill, experience, training, and education qualify the witness to help a fact-finder understand the evidence or decide a factual dispute. See *expert witness* under WITNESS.

▸ **fixed opinion.** (1807) A bias or prejudice that disqualifies a potential juror.

opinion evidence. See EVIDENCE.

opinion letter. See OPINION (2).

opinion rule. (1896) *Evidence.* The principle that a witness should testify to facts, not opinions, and that a nonexpert witness's opinions are often excludable from evidence. • Traditionally, this principle is regarded as one of the important exclusionary rules in evidence law. It is based on the idea that a witness who has observed data should provide the most factual evidence possible, leaving the jury to draw inferences and conclusions from the evidence. Under this system, the witness's opinion is unnecessary. Today, opinions are admissible if rationally based on a witness's perceptions and helpful to the fact-finder.

> "This rule [the opinion rule] is an historical blunder, for the early cases excluding 'opinion' meant a belief by a person who had personally seen and known nothing, and was therefore not qualified to speak; whereas the modern rule applies it to witnesses who have had personal observation as a basis for their inference. Moreover, it is a senseless rule, for not once in a thousand times can the observed data be exactly and fully reproduced in words. Still further, no harm could be done by letting the witness offer his inference, except perhaps the waste of a moment's time, whereas the application of the rule wastes vastly more time. And finally the rule is so pedantically applied by most courts that it excludes the most valuable testimony, such as would be used in all affairs of life outside a court room." John H. Wigmore, *A Students' Textbook of the Law of Evidence* 156 (1935).

> "The [opinion] rule in its stark simplicity might be interpreted as excluding all value judgments, that is to say all statements not being factual propositions susceptible of some sort of empirical proof or disproof. The rule, if it is to be given any purely logical meaning at all, must be interpreted as excluding at least all inferences drawn from perceived data. Even if value judgments are saved by construing the rule as having application only to factual propositions, the rule would seem to purport to exclude all such propositions in the formulation of which inference by the witness has played some part." Zelman Cowen, *Essays on the Law of Evidence* 162 (1956).

opinion testimony. See TESTIMONY.

opinion work product. See WORK PRODUCT.

OPM. *abbr.* OFFICE OF PERSONNEL MANAGEMENT.

oppignorate (ə-**pig**-nə-rayt), *vb.* (17c) *Archaic.* To pawn or pledge. — Also spelled *oppignerate.* Cf. PIGNORATE.

opponent. (16c) **1.** An adverse party in a contested matter. **2.** A party that is challenging the admissibility of evidence. • In this sense, the word is an antonym of *proponent.* **3.** *Parliamentary law.* A member who speaks against a pending motion. Cf. PROPONENT (3).

opportunity. The fact that the alleged doer of an act was present at the time and place of the act.

opportunity cost. See COST (1).

opportunity to be heard. (17c) The chance to appear in a court or other tribunal and present evidence and argument before being deprived of a right by governmental authority. • The opportunity to be heard is a fundamental requirement of procedural due process. It ordinarily includes the right to receive fair notice of the hearing, to secure the assistance of counsel, and to cross-examine adverse witnesses. See *procedural due process* under DUE PROCESS.

opposer. (15c) **1.** *Intellectual property.* Someone who formally seeks to prevent the grant of a patent or the registration of a trademark. **2.** *Hist.* APPOSER.

opposing counsel. See COUNSEL.

opposite-sex marriage. See MARRIAGE (1).

opposition. 1. Strong disagreement with or protest against a plan, law, system, etc. **2.** The relation between two things that are as different as possible from each other. **3.** One or more people that someone is striving or competing against; ADVERSARY. **4.** *Patents.* An action or procedure by which a third party can request a patent application's refusal or an issued patent's annulment. • Most countries allow opposition in some form. **5.** *Trademarks.* A procedure by which a third party can contest a trademark after it has been approved but before it has been placed on the Principal Register. Cf. CANCELLATION.

oppression. (14c) **1.** The act or an instance of unjustly exercising authority or power so that one or more people are unfairly or cruelly prevented from enjoying the same rights that other people have.

> "Oppression such as to justify intervention may be defined as the abusive denial to a people under the control of a sovereign state of a reasonable degree of autonomy and the right to the retention of their language and racial and religious institutions." Ellery C. Stowell, *International Law: A Restatement of Principles in Conformity with Actual Practice* 354 (Edward S. Corwin ed., 1931).

2. An offense consisting in the abuse of discretionary authority by a public officer who has an improper motive, as a result of which a person is injured. • This offense does not include extortion, which is typically a more serious crime.

> "**Extortion and Oppression by Public Officers.** Every public officer commits a misdemeanor who, in the exercise, or under colour of exercising the duties of his office, does any legal act, or abuses any discretionary power with which he is invested by law from an improper motive, the existence of which motive may be inferred either from the nature of the act, or from the circumstances of the case. But an illegal exercise of authority, caused by a mistake as to the law, made in good faith, is not a misdemeanor within this Article.
>
> "If the illegal act consists in taking under colour of office from any person any money or valuable thing which is not due from him at the time when it is taken, the offense is called 'extortion.'
>
> "If it consists in inflicting upon any person any bodily harm, imprisonment, or other injury, not being extortion, the offence is called 'oppression.'" James Fitzjames Stephen, *A Digest of the Criminal Law* 88 (5th ed. 1894).

3. *Contracts.* Coercion to enter into an illegal contract. • Oppression is grounds for the recovery of money paid or property transferred under an illegal contract. See DURESS; UNCONSCIONABILITY. **4.** *Corporations.* Unfair treatment of minority shareholders (esp. in a close corporation) by the directors or those in control of the corporation. — Also termed (in sense 4) *shareholder oppression.* See FREEZE-OUT. — **oppress,** *vb.* — **oppressive,** *adj.*

oppressive child labor. See CHILD LABOR.

oppressor. (14c) A person or group that treats certain people unfairly or cruelly, preventing them from enjoying the same rights that other people in society have; esp., a public official who unlawfully or wrongfully exercises power under color of authority in a way that causes one or more people harm.

opprobrium (ə-**proh**-bree-əm), *n.* (17c) **1.** The disgrace that traditionally follows from, or is attached to, wrongdoing, esp. after its public revelation; infamy. **2.** Strong criticism or disapproval, esp. when expressed publicly; esp., a contemptuous reproach. — **opprobrious,** *adj.*

OPRA. *abbr.* OPTIONS PRICE REPORTING AUTHORITY.

optima fide (**op**-ti-mə **fı**-dee). [Latin] (16c) *Hist.* In the best faith.

optimal-use value. See VALUE (2).

opt in, *vb.* (1966) To choose to participate in (something); to decide to join a group or system <when the choice of settling or not settling came, the Joneses opted in, hoping to avoid a lengthy trial>.

option, *n.* (17c) **1.** The right or power to choose; something that may be chosen <the lawyer was running out of options for settlement>. **2.** An offer that is included in a formal or informal contract; esp., a contractual obligation to keep an offer open for a specified period, so that the offeror cannot revoke the offer during that period <the option is valid because it is supported by consideration>. — Also termed *option contract*; (redundantly) *time option.* See *irrevocable offer* under OFFER; OPTION AGREEMENT. **3.** The right conveyed by such a contract <Pitts declined to exercise his option to buy the house>. **4.** A contract by which a property owner agrees with another party that the latter may buy the property at a fixed price within a specified time; the right or privilege to buy property at the election of the purchaser. **5.** The right (but not the obligation) to buy or sell a given quantity of securities, commodities, or other assets at a fixed price within a specified time <trading stock options is a speculative business>. Cf. FUTURES CONTRACT.

▸ **American option.** (1975) An option that can be exercised on any day, including its expiration date. — Also termed *American-style option.* Cf. *European option.*

▸ **at-the-money option.** (1976) An option whose exercise price is the same as the price of the underlying stock.

▸ **bonus option.** (1968) *Securities.* An option to receive unissued shares as a bonus.

▸ **buyer's option.** (1842) **1.** A time-bound privilege to purchase something on specified terms at a given price. **2.** *Contracts.* A seller's agreement that a buyer may choose to buy a greater or smaller quantity of a specified product at a fixed price. **3.** *Securities.* An option accorded to allow a buyer of stocks to acquire them at a certain future date at a specified price and to demand their delivery (with notice) at any time.

▸ **call option.** (1914) An option to buy something (esp. securities) at a fixed price even if the market rises; the right to require another to sell. — Often shortened to *call.* — Also termed *option call.*

▸ **cash-value option.** (1902) The right of a life-insurance policyholder to surrender the policy for its cash value at a specified time or at any time.

▸ **commodity option.** (1969) An option to buy or sell a commodity.

▸ **European option.** (1973) An option that can be exercised only on its expiration date. — Also termed *European-style option.* Cf. *American option.*

▸ **futures option.** (1978) An option to buy or sell a futures contract.

▸ **in-the-money option.** (1975) An option that has value because selling or buying the underlying stock at the current market price would result in greater profit or less cost than exercising the option.

▸ **lease option.** (1935) In a contract for rental property, a clause that gives the renter the right to buy the property at a fixed price, usu. at or after a fixed time. — Also termed *lease with an option to purchase.*

▸ **naked option.** (1904) A call option that grants another the right to buy stock even though the option-giver does not own the stock to back up that commitment. — Also termed *uncovered option.*

▸ **nonforfeiture option.** (1923) A policyholder's option, upon the lapse of premium payments, to continue an insurance policy for a shorter period than the original term, to surrender the policy for its cash value, to continue the policy for a reduced amount, or to take some other action rather than forfeit the policy.

▸ **option call.** See *call option.*

▸ **option to purchase real property.** (1912) A contractual provision by which an owner of realty enters an agreement with another allowing the latter to buy the property at a specified price within a specified time, or within a reasonable time in the future, but without imposing an obligation to purchase on the person to whom it is given. — Often shortened to *option to purchase.* — Also termed *purchase option.*

▸ **out-of-the-money option.** (1975) An option that has no value because the current market price of the underlying stock would result in a loss on a purchase or sale.

▸ **put option.** (1881) An option to sell something (esp. securities) at a fixed price even if the market declines; the right to require another to buy. — Often shortened to *put.*

▸ **seller's option.** A special stock-exchange transaction that gives the seller the right to deliver the security within a specified period, usu. 5 to 60 days.

▸ **settlement option.** (1908) *Insurance.* A life-insurance-policy clause providing choices in the method of paying benefits to a beneficiary, as by lump-sum payment or periodic installments.

▸ **stock option.** See STOCK OPTION.

▸ **uncovered option.** See *naked option.*

6. *Hist. Eccles. law.* The requirement that a newly elected bishop convey to the archbishop the right to fill the next vacant ecclesiastical benefice in the new bishop's see.

option, *vb.* (1888) To grant or take an option to buy or acquire rights to (something) <Ward optioned his first screenplay to the studio for $50,000>.

option agreement. (1903) *Corporations.* A share-transfer restriction that commits the shareholder to sell, but not the corporation or other shareholders to buy, the shareholder's shares at a fixed price when a specified event occurs. Cf. BUY–SELL AGREEMENT (2); OPTION (2).

optional bond. See BOND (3).

optional completeness, rule of. See RULE OF OPTIONAL COMPLETENESS.

optional-completeness doctrine. See RULE OF OPTIONAL COMPLETENESS.

optional writ. See WRIT.

option call. See *call option* under OPTION (5).

option contract. See OPTION (2).

optionee (op-shə-**nee**). (1904) Someone who receives an option from another. — Also termed *option-holder.*

option-giver. See OPTIONOR.

option-holder. See OPTIONEE.

optionor (**op**-shə-nər *or* op-shə-**nor**). (1904) Someone who grants an option to another. — Also spelled *optioner.* — Also termed *option-giver.*

option premium. See PREMIUM (4).

option spread. (1989) *Securities.* The difference between the option price and the market price of the underlying stock when the option is exercised. See SPREAD.

Options Price Reporting Authority. A national market-system plan approved by the SEC for collecting and disseminating last-sale and quotation information on options traded on a five-member exchange consisting of the American Stock Exchange, the Chicago Board of Options Exchange, the New York Stock Exchange, the Pacific Stock Exchange, and the Philadelphia Stock Exchange. — Abbr. OPRA.

option tender bond. See *put bond* under BOND (3).

option to purchase real property. See OPTION (5).

opt out, *vb.* (1922) To choose not to participate in (something); to decide not to be part of a group or system <with so many plaintiffs opting out of the class, the defendant braced itself for multiplicitous lawsuits>.

opt-out class. See CLASS (4).

opt-out statute. (1981) *Bankruptcy.* A state law that limits the exemptions that a debtor who has filed for bankruptcy can claim to those provided by state and local bankruptcy laws, and nonbankruptcy federal law. • The federal bankruptcy code includes an "opt-out" provision that allows states to choose not to adopt the federal exemptions. 11 USCA § 522(b). — Also termed *opt-out legislation.*

opus (**oh**-pəs), *n.* [Latin "work"] (18c) A product of work or labor; esp., an artistic, literary, or musical work or composition. Pl. **opuses, opera** (**ah**-pə-rə *or* **oh**-pə-rə).

opus manufactum (**oh**-pəs man-yə-**fak**-təm). [Latin] (1834) *Civil law.* An artifact; an artificial work, as distinguished from what is natural. Pl. ***opera manufacta.***

opus novum (**oh**-pəs **noh**-vəm). [Latin "new work"] (1956) *Civil law.* A structure newly built on land. Pl. ***opera nova.*** See NOVI OPERIS NUNTIATIO.

O.R. *abbr.* Own recognizance; on one's own recognizance; on recognizance <the prosecutor agreed not to object to releasing the suspect O.R.>. See RECOGNIZANCE; RELEASE ON RECOGNIZANCE.

oraculum (ə-**rak**-yə-ləm), *n.* [Latin "a solemn declaration"] *Roman law.* In the later empire, an order or decision by the emperor.

oral, *adj.* (17c) Spoken or uttered; not expressed in writing. Cf. PAROL.

oral argument. (1823) An advocate's spoken presentation before a court (esp. an appellate court) supporting or opposing the legal relief at issue. — Also termed (BrE) *hearing.* Cf. ADDRESS TO THE COURT.

> "[T]he oral argument is the one chance for *you* (not for some chance-assigned mere judge) to answer any questions you can stir any member of the court into being bothered about and into bothering with, and the one chance to sew up each such question into a remembered point in favor. . . . In any but freak situations, oral argument is a must." Karl N. Llewellyn, *The Common Law Tradition: Deciding Appeals* 240 (1960).

oral confession. See CONFESSION (1).

oral contract. See *parol contract* (1) under CONTRACT.

oral defamation. See SLANDER.

oral deposition. See DEPOSITION (2).

oral evidence. See *testimonial evidence* under EVIDENCE.

oral trust. See TRUST (3).

oral will. See WILL.

Orange Book. *Patents.* A list of patents on drugs or drug products for which generic-drug applications may be submitted to the Food and Drug Administration. • The expiration dates of the patents are also listed. An applicant may submit a generic-drug application at any time, but the applicant must either accept deferral of FDA approval until the patent expires or contest the validity of the patent. The Orange Book's official title is *Approved Drug Products With Therapeutic Equivalence Evaluations.*

oratio consultoria (or-**ay**-shee-oh kon-səl-**tor**-ee-ə). See LIBELLUS CONSULTORIA.

orator (**or**-ə-tər), *n.* (15c) **1.** *Roman law.* (*ital.*) An advocate or pleader. **2.** *Hist.* A plaintiff or petitioner in an action in chancery. **3.** Someone who engages in persuasive public speaking; esp., someone who is good at persuasive public speaking.

oratory (**or**-ə-tor-ee), *n.* (16c) The skill of persuasive speech-making; the exercise of eloquence in public speaking.

▸ **deliberative oratory.** Speech-making within a general assembly.

▸ **display oratory.** See *epideictic oratory.*

▸ **epideictic oratory** (ep-i-**dɪk**-tik). Any type of speech-making other than deliberative or forensic oratory. — Also termed *display oratory.*

▸ **forensic oratory.** Speech-making in a court of law.

▸ **political oratory.** Collectively, deliberative oratory and forensic oratory.

oratrix (**or**-ə-triks). (16c) *Hist.* A female orator.

orbation (or-**bay**-shən). (17c) *Hist.* Bereavement or deprivation of one's parents or children.

ordeal. (bef. 12c) *Hist.* A primitive form of trial in which an accused person was subjected to a usu. dangerous or painful physical test, the result being considered a divine revelation of the person's guilt or innocence. • The participants believed that God would reveal a person's culpability by protecting an innocent person from some or all consequences of the ordeal. The ordeal was commonly used in Europe until the 13th century, but only sporadically after 1215, when the Fourth Lateran Council forbade the clergy from participating in ordeals. — Also termed *trial by ordeal; judicium Dei* ("judgment of God"); *vulgaris purgatio.* Cf. CANFARA.

> "Ordeals involved an appeal to God to reveal the truth in human disputes, and they required priestly participation to achieve this rapport with the Deity. Several forms of ordeal were recognised by the early Christian Church, but in England they usually took the form of fire or water. In the former, a piece of iron was put into a fire and then in the party's hand; the hand was bound, and inspected a few days later: if the burn had festered, God was taken to have decided against the party. The ordeal of cold water required the party to be trussed and lowered into a pond; if he sank, the water was deemed to have 'received him' with God's blessing, and so he was quickly fished out. . . . In 1215, the Lateran Council . . . took the decisive step of forbidding clergy to participate any more in ordeals. This led in England to the introduction of the criminal trial jury." J.H. Baker, *An Introduction to English Legal History* 5–6 (3d ed. 1990).

▸ **bread-and-cheese ordeal.** See *ordeal of the morsel.*

▸ **ordeal by fire.** (17c) An ordeal in which the accused person was forced to hold a piece of hot metal or to walk barefoot across a hot surface, the judgment of guilt or innocence depending on how quickly and cleanly the person's hands or feet healed. • Typically the person's hand was bandaged and, upon the bandage's removal three days later, was examined for festers (indicating guilt). — Also termed *fire ordeal; ordeal by hot iron; ordeal of fire.*

> "Such evidence as we have seems to show that the ordeal of hot iron was so arranged as to give the accused a considerable chance of escape." 2 Frederick Pollock & Frederic W. Maitland, *History of English Law Before the Time of Edward I* 599 (2d ed. 1899).

▸ **ordeal by hot iron.** See *ordeal by fire.*

▸ **ordeal by water.** (18c) **1.** An ordeal in which guilt or innocence depended on whether the accused person floated or sank after being submerged in cold water. • A priest would first consecrate the pool of water, adjuring it to receive the innocent but reject the guilty. An accused who sank was declared innocent; one who floated was adjudged guilty because floating revealed the water's (and therefore God's) rejection of the person. This type of ordeal was used esp. in witchcraft trials. — Also termed *ordeal by cold water; cold-water ordeal; ordeal of cold water;* (in ecclesiastical law) *aquae frigidae judicium.* **2.** An ordeal in which guilt or innocence was determined by how quickly the accused person's arm healed after being placed in boiling water. • Often the person was forced to retrieve a stone from the bottom of a pot of boiling water. The person's hand and arm were then bandaged and, upon the bandage's removal three days later, were examined for festers (indicating guilt). — Also termed (in sense 2) *ordeal by hot water; hot-water ordeal; ordeal of hot water;* (in both senses) *water ordeal; ordeal of water;* (in ecclesiastical law) *aquae ferventis judicium; aenum.*

> "The ordeal of water was a very singular institution. Sinking was the sign of innocence, floating the sign of guilt. As any one would sink unless he understood how to float, and intentionally did so, it is difficult to see how any one could ever be convicted by this means. Is it possible that this ordeal may have been an honourable form of suicide, like the Japanese happy despatch? In nearly every case the accused would sink. This would prove his innocence, indeed, but there would be no need to take him out. He would thus die honourably. If by any accident he floated, he would be put to death disgracefully." 1 James Fitzjames Stephen, *A History of the Criminal Law of England* 73 (1883).

▸ **ordeal of the morsel.** (1876) An ordeal in which the person who was to make the proof was given a one-ounce piece of bread or cheese that a priest had solemnly charged to stick in the throat of the guilty. • A person who choked was declared guilty; a person who did not was declared innocent. — Also termed *corsnaed; corsned; trial by corsnaed; judicial morsel; morsel of execration.*

▸ **single ordeal.** (17c) An ordeal prescribed for someone accused of a less serious crime and involving less risk or torture than a triple ordeal. • For example, a single ordeal by fire required the accused to pick up a red-hot piece of iron weighing one pound, while a triple ordeal involved a piece of iron weighing three pounds.

▸ **triple ordeal.** (18c) An ordeal prescribed for someone accused of a more serious crime and involving more risk or torture than a single ordeal. • For example, a triple ordeal by water required the accused to submerge an arm into boiling water up to the elbow, while a single ordeal required the arm to be submerged only to the wrist. — Also termed *threefold ordeal.*

ordelf (**or**-delf). See OREDELF.

ordels (or-**deelz**). (17c) *Hist. English law.* The right to conduct trials by ordeal within a given jurisdiction.

order, *n.* (16c) **1.** A command, direction, or instruction. See MANDATE (1). **2.** A written direction or command delivered by a government official, esp. a court or judge. • The word generally embraces final decrees as well as interlocutory directions or commands. — Also termed *court order; judicial order.* See MANDAMUS.

> "An order is the mandate or determination of the court upon some subsidiary or collateral matter arising in an action, not disposing of the merits, but adjudicating a preliminary point or directing some step in the proceedings." 1 Henry Campbell Black, *A Treatise on the Law of Judgments* § 1, at 5 (2d ed. 1902).

> "While an order may under some circumstances amount to a judgment, they must be distinguished, owing to the different consequences flowing from them, not only in the matter of enforcement and appeal but in other respects, as, for instance, the time within which proceedings to annul them must be taken. Rulings on motions are ordinarily orders rather than judgments. The class of judgments and of decrees formerly called interlocutory is included in the definition given in [modern codes] of the word 'order.'" 1 A.C. Freeman, *A Treatise of the Law of Judgments* § 19, at 28 (Edward W. Tuttle ed., 5th ed. 1925).

▸ **administrative order.** (1894) **1.** An order issued by a government agency after an adjudicatory hearing. **2.** An agency regulation that interprets or applies a statutory provision.

▸ **affiliation order.** See *filiation order.*

▸ **alternative order.** (1836) An order commanding the party to whom it is directed either to do or stop doing a specific thing or to show cause why the court should not enter the order.

▸ **antiharassment order.** (1991) A type of restraining order available to victims of harassment or stalking, usu. forbidding a person to contact, surveil, or approach the victim.

▸ **blanket order.** See BLANKET ORDER (1).

▸ **collateral order.** (1817) An order separable from and collateral to the main claim, issued when the right involved would be irreparably lost if postponed until final judgment in the case. See COLLATERAL-ORDER DOCTRINE.

▸ **common order.** See *conditional judgment* under JUDGMENT (2).

▸ **decretal order** (di-**kree**-təl). (17c) A court of chancery's interlocutory order that is issued on motion of a party and has the effect of a final decree. See *decree nisi* under DECREE.

▸ **departure order.** *Immigration* law. An order to leave the country issued to a noncitizen who has agreed to leave voluntarily by a certain date at the person's own expense. — Also termed *voluntary-departure order.*

▸ **deportation order.** *Immigration law.* An order for the person named to be involuntarily removed from the country and sent back to the country of origin.

▸ **dismissal order.** (1886) A court order ending a lawsuit without a decision on the merits. — Also termed *order of dismissal.*

▸ **divestiture order.** (1943) An order transferring a case from a local court of limited jurisdiction to a more superior court of general jurisdiction.

▸ **docket order.** (1896) A court order memorialized only as an entry on the docket sheet.

▸ **enforcement order.** A court's order issued to compel a person or entity to comply with a statute, regulation, contract provision, previous court order, or other binding authority.

▸ **ex parte order** (eks **pahr**-tee). (18c) An order made by the court upon the application of one party to an action without notice to the other.

▸ **filiation order.** (1842) *Family law.* A court's determination of paternity, usu. including a direction to pay child support. • Governments usu. seek filiation orders so that some or all of the public funds spent on the child's welfare can be recovered from a nonmarital child's father. Until the early 20th century, municipalities, not the state, had the legal duty to support the poor, including unwed mothers and their children. In some states, two judges had to determine who an unacknowledged child's father was before the municipality could recover its expenditures. — Also termed *affiliation order; order of filiation.*

▸ **final order.** (16c) An order that is dispositive of the entire case. See *final judgment* under JUDGMENT (2).

▸ **foreign support order.** See SUPPORT ORDER.

▸ **health-insurance order.** See HEALTH-INSURANCE ORDER.

▸ **income-withholding order.** See INCOME-WITHHOLDING ORDER.

▸ **interim order.** (18c) **1.** A temporary court decree that remains in effect for a specified time or until a specified event occurs. **2.** See *interlocutory order.*

▸ **interlocutory order** (in-tər-**lok**-yə-tor-ee). (17c) An order that relates to some intermediate matter in the case; any order other than a final order. • Most interlocutory orders are not appealable until the case is fully resolved. But by rule or statute, most jurisdictions allow some types of interlocutory orders (such as preliminary injunctions and class-certification orders) to be immediately appealed. — Also termed *interlocutory decision; interim order; intermediate order.* See *appealable decision* under DECISION (1); COLLATERAL-ORDER DOCTRINE.

▸ **maintenance order.** See SUPPORT ORDER.

▸ **minute order.** (1918) **1.** An order recorded in the minutes of the court rather than directly on a case docket. • Although practice varies, traditionally when a trial judge is sitting officially, with or without a court reporter, a clerk or deputy clerk keeps minutes. When the judge makes an oral order, the only record of that order may be in the minutes. It is therefore referred to as a minute order. — Also termed *minute entry.* **2.** A court order not directly relating to a case, such as an order adopting a local rule of court. • In this sense, the court is not a single judge acting in an adjudicatory capacity, but a chief judge, or a group of two or more judges, acting for a court in an administrative or some other nonadjudicatory capacity.

▸ **modification order.** See MODIFICATION ORDER.

▸ **order of dismissal.** See *dismissal order.*

▸ **order to pay. 1.** *Commercial law.* A written order to a person to deliver money, usu. out of funds on deposit with that person, to a third party on demand. **2.** A court order directing a person to deliver money that the person owes or for which the person is responsible.

▸ **order to produce.** *Criminal procedure.* A notice to law-enforcement personnel to bring a prisoner into court for a judicial proceeding. — Abbr. OTP.

▸ **preclusion order.** (1921) An order barring a litigant from presenting or opposing certain claims or defenses for failing to comply with a discovery order.

▸ **pretrial order.** See PRETRIAL ORDER.

▸ **protective order.** See PROTECTIVE ORDER.

▸ **provisional order.** See PROVISIONAL ORDER.

▸ **qualified domestic-relations order.** See QUALIFIED DOMESTIC-RELATIONS ORDER.

▸ **receiving order.** (1883) A court's direction to a bankruptcy receiver or trustee to take some action.

▸ **restraining order.** See RESTRAINING ORDER.

▸ **scheduling order.** (1959) A court's order that sets the time deadlines for different procedural actions in a case, such as amending pleadings, filing motions, and completing discovery.

▸ **self-executing order.** (1926) An order that is immediately effective, usu. for injunctive or prohibitive purposes or to fix the status of a party until a hearing can be held.

▸ **separation order.** (1882) A court order granting a married person's request for a legal separation. See SEPARATION AGREEMENT (1).

▸ **sessional order.** (1823) A resolution adopted by both houses of a legislature at the beginning of each session to regulate the order and handling of business for that session.

▸ **show-cause order.** (1925) An order directing a party to appear in court and explain why the party took (or failed to take) some action or why the court should or should not impose some sanction or grant some relief. — Abbr. SCO. — Also termed *order to show cause* (OSC; OTSC); *rule to show cause; show-cause rule.*

▸ **standing order. 1.** A prospective omnibus court order that applies to all cases pending before a court. • Some individual judges issue a standing order on a subject when there is no local rule bearing on it, often because a rule would not be acceptable to the other judges on the court. Standing orders are frequently criticized because they undermine uniformity of procedural rules, esp. at the local level. Cf. *standing rule* under RULE (3). **2.** *Banking.* An arrangement whereby a bank pays a fixed amount from one's account at regular intervals because one has specified that the payments are to be recurrent. **3.** See *split order* under ORDER (8).

▸ **supervision order.** (1938) *Family law.* A court's order placing a child or young person under the supervision of a child-welfare agency or a probation officer in a case of neglect, abuse, or delinquency.

▸ **support order.** See SUPPORT ORDER.

▸ **temporary order.** (1808) A court order issued during the pendency of a suit, before the final order or judgment has been entered.

▸ **temporary restraining order.** See TEMPORARY RESTRAINING ORDER.

▸ **turnover order.** (1918) An order by which the court commands a judgment debtor to surrender certain property to a judgment creditor, or to the sheriff or constable on the creditor's behalf. • Such an order is usu. directed to property that is difficult to acquire by the ordinary judgment-collection process, such as share certificates and accounts receivable.

▸ **umbrella order.** See BLANKET ORDER (1).

▸ **visitation order.** See VISITATION ORDER.

▸ **voluntary-departure order.** See *departure order.*

3. *Parliamentary law.* The principles and practices of parliamentary law; the conduct of business according to those principles and practices; DECORUM. See IN ORDER; OUT OF ORDER. **4.** *Parliamentary law.* An item of business, or an agenda or series of such items <call for the orders of the day>. See AGENDA.

▸ **general order.** An order of the day other than a special order. See *order of the day* (1). Cf. *special order.*

▸ **order of business.** (18c) **1.** AGENDA. **2.** The sequence in which a meeting considers its business.

> "A settled order of business is, however, necessary for the government of the presiding person, and to restrain individual members from calling up favorite measures, or matters under their special patronage, out of their just turn. It is useful also for directing the discretion of the house, when they are moved to take up a particular matter, to the prejudice of others having priority of right to their attention in the general order of business." Thomas Jefferson, *A Manual of Parliamentary Practice* 30 (1801).

▸ **order of the day.** (17c) **1.** An item of business scheduled for consideration at a certain upcoming meeting, at a certain time, or in a certain order. • An order of the day is either a *general order* or a *special order.* **2.** The daily order of business. See *order of business.*

▸ **special order.** An order of the day scheduled for consideration at a certain time, and which outranks and interrupts any other business except another special order scheduled earlier for the same time. See TIME CERTAIN.

5. *Parliamentary law.* A vote that assigns a duty to an officer, employee, or other agent, customarily in the form, "*Ordered,* That ...." **6.** *Parliamentary law.* RULE (3). **7.** *Commercial law.* The words in a draft (such as a check) directing one person to pay money to or deliver something to a designated person. • An order should appear to be the demand of a right as opposed to the request for a favor. See *order paper* under PAPER. **8.** *Securities.* A customer's long-standing standard instructions to a financial institution, esp. to a broker about how and when to buy or sell securities.

▸ **all-or-none order.** (1979) An order to buy a security to be executed either in its entirety or not at all.

▸ **alternative order.** (1979) An order to buy a security by either of two alternatives (e.g., buy a stock at a limited price or buy on a stop order). — Also termed *either-or order.*

▸ **buy order.** (1931) An investor's instruction to purchase stock.

▸ **day order.** (1969) An order to buy or sell on one particular day only. Cf. *open order.*

▸ **discretionary order.** (1934) An order to buy or sell at any price acceptable to the broker.

▸ **either-or order.** See *alternative order.*

▸ **fill-or-kill order.** (1979) An order that must be executed as soon as it reaches the trading floor. • If the order is not filled immediately, it is canceled.

▸ **limit order.** (1932) An order to buy or sell at a specified price, regardless of market price. Cf. *no-limit order.*

▸ **market order.** (1934) An order to buy or sell at the best price immediately available on the market. — Also termed *order at the market.*

▸ **matched order.** (1934) An order to buy and sell the same security, at about the same time, in about the same quantity, and at about the same price.

▸ **no-limit order.** (1988) An order to buy or sell securities with no limits on price. Cf. *limit order.*

▸ **open order.** (1931) An order that remains in effect until filled by the broker or canceled by the customer. Cf. *day order.*

▸ **order at the market.** See *market order.*

▸ **percentage order.** (1979) An order to buy or sell a stated amount of a certain stock after a fixed number of shares of the stock have traded.

▸ **scale order.** (1930) An order to buy or sell a security at varying price ranges.

▸ **sell order.** (1931) An investor's instruction to sell stock.

▸ **split order.** (1989) An order directing a broker to sell some stock at one price and some stock at another price. — Also termed *standing order.*

▸ **stop order.** (1954) An order to buy or sell when the security's price reaches a specified level (the *stop price*) on the market. • By fixing the price beforehand, the investor is cushioned against stock fluctuations. — Also termed *stop-loss order*; *stop-limit order*.

▸ **time order.** (1979) An order that becomes a market or limited-price order at a specified time.

order absolute. See *decree absolute* under DECREE.

order assigning residue. (1876) A probate court's order naming the persons entitled to receive parts of an estate and allotting that share to each.

order at the market. See *market order* under ORDER (8).

order bill of lading. See BILL OF LADING.

order check. See CHECK.

order document. See *order paper* under PAPER.

order draft. See *order check* under CHECK.

ordered, adjudged, and decreed. (17c) The traditional words used to introduce a court decision <It is therefore ordered, adjudged, and decreed that Martin must return the overpayment to Hurley>.

> "The usual style of a decree is 'it is ordered, adjudged, and decreed'; and of an order or rule, 'it is ordered,' etc." 1 Henry Campbell Black, *A Treatise on the Law of Judgments* § 2, at 6–7 (2d ed. 1902).

order instrument. See *order paper* under PAPER.

orderly officer. See *officer of the day* under OFFICER (2).

order nisi. See *decree nisi* under DECREE.

order of business. See ORDER (4).

order of dismissal. See *dismissal order* under ORDER.

order of filiation. See *filiation order* under ORDER (2).

order of proof. The sequence in which litigants are allowed to present evidence to a tribunal, including rebuttal evidence.

> "Generally the order of proof rests in the sound discretion of the trial court, and the exercise of this discretion is not reviewable except for manifest abuse. Statutes controlling the order of proof almost uniformly permit the statutory order to be varied in the court's discretion. As a general rule he who has the opening ought to introduce all his evidence to make out his side of the issue, except that which merely serves to answer the adversary's case; then the evidence of the adversary is heard, and, finally, the party who had the opening may introduce rebutting evidence which merely serves to answer or qualify his adversary's case. Rebutting evidence within this rule means not all evidence whatever which contradicts defendant's witnesses and corroborates plaintiff's, but evidence in denial of some affirmative case or fact which defendant has attempted to prove. Neither side ought to be permitted to give evidence by piecemeal." Austin Abbott, *A Brief for the Trial of Civil Issues Before a Jury* 114–16 (2d ed. 1900).

> "In no event should counsel enter the trial without a definite order of proof. Know in advance the order in which you will call your witnesses, the substance of their testimony and the order in which the documentary evidence such as maps, diagrams, surveys, will be presented and at what times. Do not wander from pillar to post in unfolding your case, relying upon the cumulative effect of the testimony to somehow pop forth a specific act of negligence." 3 Sydney C. Schweitzer, *Trial Guide* 1167 (1948).

order of protection. See RESTRAINING ORDER; SPECIAL ORDER OF CONDITIONS.

Order of the Coif (koyf). **1.** Formerly, the order of serjeants-at-law, the highest order of counsel at the English Bar. • The last serjeant was appointed to the Order in 1875. **2.** An honorary legal organization whose members are selected on the basis of their law-school grades. See COIF.

order of the day. See ORDER (4).

order paper. See PAPER.

Order, Resolution, or Vote Clause. (2009) *Constitutional law.* U.S. Const., art. I, § 7, cl. 3.

order to pay. See ORDER (2).

order to produce. See *order to produce* under ORDER (2).

order to show cause. See *show-cause order* under ORDER (2).

ordinance (**or**-də-nənts). (14c) An authoritative law or decree; specif., a municipal regulation, esp. one that forbids or restricts an activity. • Municipal governments can pass ordinances on matters that the state government allows to be regulated at the local level. A municipal ordinance carries the state's authority and has the same effect within the municipality's limits as a state statute. — Also termed *bylaw*; *municipal ordinance*.

> "Local laws of a municipal corporation, duly enacted by the proper authorities, prescribing general, uniform and permanent rules of conduct, relating to the corporate affairs of the municipality, are, in this country, generally designated as ordinances. 'By-laws' or 'bye-laws' was the original designation. In England and in a few states such local laws are so named, the prefix 'by' or 'bye' signifying the place of habitation or local community with defined limits. The words 'by-laws' and 'ordinances' are often used interchangeably in statutes and charters, as that upon 'the passage of any by-law or ordinance,' the yeas and nays shall be called and recorded. Occasionally the general term ordinance is used in a broad sense, so as to embrace municipal charters and statutes relating to the government of the municipality. However, such use is inaccurate, for ordinances are not, in the constitutional sense, public laws, but mere local regulations or by-laws, operating in a particular locality." Eugene McQuillin, *A Treatise on the Law of Municipal Ordinances* 2–3 (1904) (citation omitted).

> "An ordinance . . . may be purely administrative in nature, establishing offices, prescribing duties, or setting salaries; it may have to do with the routine or procedure of the governing body. Or it may be a governmental exercise of the power to control the conduct of the public — establishing rules which must be complied with, or prohibiting certain actions or conduct. In any event it is the determination of the sovereign power of the state as delegated to the municipality. It is a legislative enactment, within its sphere, as much as an act of the state legislature." 1 Judith O'Gallagher, *Municipal Ordinances* § 1A.01, at 3 (2d ed. 1998).

ordinandi lex (or-də-**nan**-dɪ **leks**). [Latin] The law of procedure, as distinguished from substantive law.

ordinarily prudent person. See REASONABLE PERSON.

ordinary, *adj.* (15c) **1.** Occurring in the regular course of events; normal; usual. Cf. EXTRAORDINARY. **2.** (Of a judge) having jurisdiction by right of office rather than by delegation. **3.** (Of jurisdiction) original or immediate, as opposed to delegated.

ordinary, *n.* (14c) **1.** *Eccles. law.* A high-ranking official who has immediate jurisdiction over a specified territory, such as an archbishop over a province or a bishop over a diocese. **2.** *Civil law.* A judge having jurisdiction by right of office rather than by delegation. **3.** A probate judge. • The term is used in this sense only in some U.S. states.

ordinary ambassador. See *resident ambassador* under AMBASSADOR.

ordinary and necessary business expense. See *ordinary and necessary expense* under EXPENSE.

ordinary and necessary expense. See EXPENSE.

ordinary annuity. See ANNUITY.

ordinary assembly. See ASSEMBLY (1).

ordinary care. See *reasonable care* under CARE (2).

ordinary committee. See COMMITTEE (1).

ordinary course of business. See COURSE OF BUSINESS.

ordinary diligence. See DILIGENCE (2).

ordinary gain. See GAIN (3).

ordinary goods. See GOODS.

ordinary high tide. See *mean high tide* under TIDE.

ordinary income. See INCOME.

ordinary insurance. See *ordinary life insurance* under LIFE INSURANCE.

ordinary law. See STATUTORY LAW.

ordinary-lay-observer test. See AUDIENCE TEST.

ordinary life insurance. 1. See LIFE INSURANCE. **2.** See *whole life insurance* under LIFE INSURANCE.

ordinary loss. See LOSS.

ordinary main motion. See *original main motion* under MOTION (2).

ordinary majority. See *simple majority* under MAJORITY.

ordinary meaning. See *plain meaning* under MEANING.

ordinary-meaning canon. 1. The doctrine that words in a legal instrument are to be understood in their ordinary, everyday meanings unless the context indicates that they bear a technical sense or are otherwise defined in the text. **2.** Loosely, PLAIN-MEANING RULE.

ordinary negligence. See NEGLIGENCE.

ordinary-observer test. See AUDIENCE TEST.

ordinary's court. See *probate court* under COURT.

ordinary seaman. See SEAMAN.

ordinary shares. See *common stock* under STOCK.

ordinary skill. 1. See SKILL. **2.** See ORDINARY SKILL IN THE ART.

ordinary skill in the art. (1847) *Patents.* The level of technical knowledge, experience, and expertise possessed by a typical engineer, scientist, designer, etc. in a technology that is relevant to an invention.

ordinary standing rule. See *standing rule* (1) under RULE (3).

ordinary wear and tear. See WEAR AND TEAR.

ordinary witness. See WITNESS.

ordinary work product. See *fact work product* under WORK PRODUCT.

ordinatio forestae (or-di-**nay**-shee-oh for-**es**-tee), *n.* See ASSISA DE FORESTA.

ordinatum est (or-də-**nay**-təm est). [Law Latin] *Hist.* It is ordered. • These were the usual first words of a court order entered in Latin.

ordinis beneficium (**or**-də-nis ben-ə-**fish**-ee-əm). [Latin "the benefit of order"] *Civil law.* The privilege of a surety to require the creditor to exhaust the principal debtor's property before having recourse against the surety. See DISCUSSION.

ordo. (1849) **1.** *Eccles. law.* A book containing the rules and directions for devotionals and the liturgy; a directory of religious services. **2.** *Hist.* In a classical textbook, the arrangement of words necessary for making a translation into English. **3.** *Hist.* A lawbook setting forth the forms of action and various rules, such as those on pleading.

ordo attachiamentorum (**or**-doh ə-tach-ee-ə-men-**tor**-əm). [Law Latin] *Hist.* The order in which attachments are arranged.

ordo judiciorum (**or**-doh joo-dish-ee-**or**-əm). [Latin] (18c) *Eccles. law.* **1.** The sequential order of judgments. **2.** The rule by which the course of hearing each case was prescribed.

ordonnance (**or**-də-nənts *or* or-doh-**nahns**). [French] (18c) **1.** *Archaic.* A law, decree, or ordinance. **2.** A compilation of a body of law on a particular subject, esp. prizes and captures at sea. **3.** The arrangement or composition of elements or parts, esp. in art, architecture, or literature. **4.** An optimal arrangement that produces the best possible effect; the proper disposition of several parts in relation to the whole.

oredelf (**or**-delf). (16c) *Hist.* The right to dig for mineral ore on one's own land. — Also spelled *oredelfe*; *ordelf.*

ore tenus (**or**-ee **tee**-nəs *or* **ten**-əs), *adv.* & *adj.* [Latin "by word of mouth"] (17c) **1.** Orally; by word of mouth; VIVA VOCE <pleading carried on ore tenus>.

> "Pleadings are the mutual altercations between the plaintiff and defendant; which at present are set down and delivered into the proper office in writing, though formerly they were usually put in by their counsel *ore tenus*, or *viva voce*, in court, and then minuted down by the chief clerks, or prothonotaries; whence in our old law French the pleadings are frequently denominated the *parol*." 3 William Blackstone, *Commentaries on the Laws of England* 293 (1768).

2. Made or presented orally <ore tenus evidence>.

ore tenus rule. (1964) The presumption that a trial court's findings of fact are correct and should not be disturbed unless clearly wrong or unjust.

orfgild. (17c) *Hist.* **1.** Restitution given by the hundred or county to a person whose property was stolen. — Also termed *cheapgild.* **2.** A payment in or restoration of cattle.

organ-donor card. (1972) A card that one carries to show that, upon death, a doctor may take parts of one's body to use in the medical treatment of someone else. — Often shortened to *donor card.*

organic act. See *organic statute* under STATUTE.

organic disease. See DISEASE.

organic law. (1831) **1.** The body of laws (as in a constitution) that define and establish a government; FUNDAMENTAL LAW. **2.** *Civil law.* Decisional law; CASELAW.

organic statute. See STATUTE.

organization. (15c) **1.** A body of persons (such as a union or corporation) formed for a common purpose. — Also termed *society.* **2.** See UNION.

organizational crime. See *corporate crime* under CRIME.

organizational expense. See EXPENSE.

organizational meeting. See MEETING.

organizational offense. See *organizational crime* under CRIME.

organizational picketing. See PICKETING.

organizational standing. See *associational standing* under STANDING.

organizational strike. See *recognition strike* under STRIKE (1).

organized crime. (1867) **1.** Widespread criminal activities that are coordinated and controlled through a central syndicate. See RACKETEERING. **2.** Persons involved in these criminal activities; a syndicate of criminals who rely on their unlawful activities for income. — Abbr. OC. See SYNDICATE.

organized labor. (1848) **1.** Workers who are affiliated by membership in a union. **2.** A union, or unions collectively, considered as a political force.

organized offense. See ORGANIZED CRIME.

organ trafficking. See TRAFFICKING.

original, *adj.* See ORIGINALITY; *original writ* under WRIT.

original acquisition. See ACQUISITION.

original administration. See ADMINISTRATION.

original bill. See BILL (2).

original contractor. See *general contractor* under CONTRACTOR.

original conveyance. See *primary conveyance* under CONVEYANCE (1).

original cost. See *acquisition cost* (1) under COST (1).

original-document rule. See BEST-EVIDENCE RULE.

original domicile. See *domicile of origin* under DOMICILE.

original drawing. See DRAWING.

original estate. See ESTATE (1).

original evidence. See EVIDENCE.

originalia (ə-rij-ə-**nay**-lee-ə *or* -**nayl**-yə). (17c) *Hist.* Records compiled in the Chancery and transmitted to the Remembrancer's office in the Exchequer. • These records were kept from 1236 to 1837. Cf. RECORDA.

original intent. See INTENT (2).

originalism. (1980) **1.** The doctrine that words of a legal instrument are to be given the meanings they had when they were adopted; specif., the canon that a legal text should be interpreted through the historical ascertainment of the meaning that it would have conveyed to a fully informed observer at the time when the text first took effect. — Also termed *doctrine of original public meaning*; *original-meaning doctrine*; *original public meaning.* **2.** The doctrine that a legal instrument should be interpreted to effectuate the intent of those who prepared it or made it legally binding. • Sense 1 is an objective test. Sense 2 embodies a subjective test. — Also termed (in both senses) *historical interpretation*; *historicism*; *fixed-meaning canon.* — Also termed (in sense 2) *intentionalism.* See INTERPRETIVISM. Cf. NONORIGINALISM; NONINTERPRETIVISM; LIVING CONSTITUTIONALISM; LIVING-TREE DOCTRINE.

original issue. See ISSUE (2).

original-issue discount. (1954) The difference between a bond's face value and the price at which it is initially sold. — Abbr. OID.

originality. (18c) *Copyright.* **1.** The quality, state, or condition of being the product of independent creation and having a minimum degree of creativity. • Originality is a requirement for copyright protection. But this is a lesser standard than that of novelty in patent law: to be original, a work does not have to be novel or unique. Cf. NOVELTY. **2.** The degree to which a product claimed for copyright is the result of an author's independent efforts. Cf. CREATIVITY.

> "'Original' in reference to a copyrighted work means that the particular work 'owes its origin' to the 'author.' No large measure of novelty is necessary." *Alfred Bell & Co. v. Catalda Fine Arts, Inc.*, 191 F.2d 99, 102 (2d Cir. 1951).

> "The *sine qua non* of copyright is originality. To qualify for copyright protection, a work must be original to the author. . . . To be sure, the requisite level of creativity is extremely low; even a slight amount will suffice. The vast majority of works make the grade quite easily, as they possess some creative spark, 'no matter how crude, humble or obvious' it might be." *Feist Publ'ns v. Rural Tel. Serv. Co.*, 499 U.S. 340, 345, 111 S.Ct. 1282, 1287 (1991).

original jurisdiction. See JURISDICTION.

original main motion. See MOTION (2).

original market. See *primary market* under MARKET.

original meaning. The understanding of a text, esp. an important legal instrument such as the U.S. Constitution, reflecting what an informed, reasonable member of the community would have understood at the time of adoption according to then-prevailing linguistic meanings and interpretive principles. • This term is contrasted, in originalist theory, with the original intent of the framers, or the original understanding of the ratifiers, both of which may or may not be the same as public meaning. — Also termed *original public meaning.* See FIXED-MEANING CANON; ORIGINAL UNDERSTANDING.

original-meaning doctrine. See ORIGINALISM (1).

original-package doctrine. (1893) *Constitutional law.* The principle that imported goods are exempt from state taxation as long as they are unsold and remain in the original packaging. • The Supreme Court abolished this doctrine in 1976, holding that states can tax imported goods if the tax is nondiscriminatory. See IMPORT-EXPORT CLAUSE.

original precedent. See PRECEDENT (2).

original process. See PROCESS (2).

original promise. See PROMISE.

original public meaning. **1.** See ORIGINALISM (1). **2.** See ORIGINAL MEANING.

original receiver. See *principal receiver* under RECEIVER.

original source. The person or persons who first disclosed fraud to the government, derived from direct and indirect information on which a qui tam complaint is based under the False Claims Act or a similar state law.

original taking. See TAKING (1).

original title. See TITLE (2).

original understanding. The collective perceptions and understandings of the informed public at the time of a legal instrument's adoption. Cf. ORIGINAL MEANING.

original writ. See WRIT.

original-writing rule. See BEST-EVIDENCE RULE.

origination clause. (*often cap.*) (1984) *Constitutional law.* **1.** The constitutional provision that all bills for increasing taxes and raising revenue must originate in the House of Representatives, not the Senate (U.S. Const. art. I, § 7, cl. 1). • The Senate may, however, amend revenue bills. **2.** A provision in a state constitution requiring that revenue bills originate in the lower house of the state legislature.

origination fee. See FEE (1).

originator. 1. Someone who conceives of something and starts it. **2.** The entity that initiates a funds transfer subject to UCC article 4A. UCC § 4A-104(c).

"or" lease. See LEASE.

ornamental fixture. See FIXTURE.

ornest. *Hist.* See TRIAL BY COMBAT.

ORP. *abbr.* Ordinary, reasonable, and prudent — the standard on which negligence cases are based.

orphan, *n.* (15c) **1.** A child whose parents are both dead. **2.** A child with one dead parent and one living parent. — More properly termed *half orphan.* **3.** A child who has been deprived of parental care and has not been legally adopted; a child without a parent or guardian.

orphan drug. See DRUG.

orphan's business. (1881) *Hist.* A probate court's jurisdiction over the allotment of distributive shares of an estate to the decedent's family, esp. the children.

orphan's court. See *probate court* under COURT.

o.s. *abbr.* (18c) OLD STYLE.

OS. See *ordinary seaman* under SEAMAN.

OSC. *abbr.* **1.** OFFICE OF SPECIAL COUNSEL. **2.** Order to show cause. See *show-cause order* under ORDER (2).

OSHA (oh-shə). *abbr.* (1971) **1.** OCCUPATIONAL SAFETY AND HEALTH ACT OF 1970. **2.** OCCUPATIONAL SAFETY AND HEALTH ADMINISTRATION.

OSHRC. *abbr.* OCCUPATIONAL SAFETY AND HEALTH REVIEW COMMISSION.

OSI. *abbr.* OFFICE OF SPECIAL INVESTIGATIONS.

OSM. *abbr.* OFFICE OF SURFACE MINING RECLAMATION AND ENFORCEMENT.

o.s.p. *abbr.* OBIIT SINE PROLE.

OST. *abbr.* OUTER SPACE TREATY.

ostendit vobis (os-**ten**-dit **voh**-bis). [Latin] *Hist.* Shows to you. • In old pleading, these words were used by a demandant to begin a count.

ostensible (ah-**sten**-sə-bəl), *adj.* (18c) Open to view; declared or professed; apparent.

ostensible agency. See *agency by estoppel* under AGENCY (1).

ostensible agent. See *apparent agent* under AGENT.

ostensible authority. See *apparent authority* under AUTHORITY (1).

ostensible partner. See *nominal partner* under PARTNER.

OSTP. See OFFICE OF SCIENCE AND TECHNOLOGY POLICY.

ostrich defense. See DEFENSE (1).

ostrich direction. See *willful-blindness instruction* under JURY INSTRUCTION.

ostrich instruction. See *willful-blindness instruction* under JURY INSTRUCTION.

OTA. *abbr.* OFFICE OF TECHNOLOGY ASSESSMENT.

OTC. *abbr.* (1965) OVER-THE-COUNTER.

OTC market. *abbr.* OVER-THE-COUNTER MARKET.

other consideration. See CONSIDERATION (1).

other good and valuable consideration. See *other consideration* under CONSIDERATION (1).

other income. See INCOME.

other-insurance clause. (1901) An insurance-policy provision that attempts to limit coverage if the insured has other coverage for the same loss. • The three major other-insurance clauses are the pro rata clause, the excess clause, and the escape clause. See ESCAPE CLAUSE; EXCESS CLAUSE; PRO RATA CLAUSE.

other-property rule. (1966) The principle that tort recovery is unavailable if the only damage caused by a product defect is to the product itself. *See East River S.S. Corp. v. Transamerica Delaval, Inc.*, 476 U.S. 858, 106 S.Ct. 2295 (1986).

otherwise, *adv.* **1.** In a different way; in another manner <David Berkowitz, otherwise known as Son of Sam>. **2.** By other causes or means <to succeed by hard work and otherwise>. **3.** In other conditions or circumstances <to know him otherwise than through law practice>. **4.** Except for what has just been mentioned <page 99 was illegible; otherwise, the records were easy to decipher>. **5.** Busy doing something else <she was otherwise engaged that day>. **6.** To the contrary; differently <although the economists say that legal markets are soft, many law-firm leaders think otherwise>. • The term *otherwise* tends to be quite broad in scope.

OTP. *abbr.* **1.** Office of Technology Policy. See TECHNOLOGY ADMINISTRATION. **2.** See *order to produce* under ORDER (2).

OTS. *abbr.* OFFICE OF THRIFT SUPERVISION.

OTSA. *abbr.* OFFICE OF TAX-SHELTER ANALYSIS.

OTSC. *abbr.* Order to show cause. See *show-cause order* under ORDER (2).

OUI. *abbr.* Operating under the influence. See DRIVING UNDER THE INFLUENCE.

our federalism. (*often cap.*) (1971) The doctrine holding that a federal court must refrain from hearing a constitutional challenge to state action if federal adjudication would be considered an improper intrusion into the state's right to enforce its own laws in its own courts. — Also termed *doctrine of our federalism.* Cf. ABSTENTION; FEDERALISM.

oust, *vb.* (15c) **1.** To put out of possession; to deprive of a right or inheritance. **2.** To force (a person) from a position of power for the purpose of serving as a replacement.

ouster. (16c) **1.** The wrongful dispossession or exclusion of someone (esp. a cotenant) from property (esp. real property); DISPOSSESSION. **2.** Removal from a position of power; esp., the removal of a public or corporate officer from office. Cf. EJECTMENT.

ouster le main (**ow**-stər lə **mayn**). [Law French "remove the hand"] (16c) *Hist.* **1.** A delivery of land out of the monarch's hands because the monarch has no right or title to hold it. **2.** A judgment or writ granting such a delivery. **3.** A delivery of land from a guardian to a ward once the ward attains legal age. — Also written *ouster-le-main.*

outbid, *vb.* (16c) To offer a higher price than (someone else), esp. at an auction.

outbuilding. (17c) A detached building (such as a shed or garage) within the grounds of a main building.

outcome-determinative test. (1959) *Civil procedure.* A test used to determine whether an issue is substantive for purposes of the *Erie* doctrine by examining the issue's potential effect on the outcome of the litigation. See ERIE DOCTRINE.

outcome responsibility. (1988) The view that those who cause harm are responsible for it even in the absence of fault. Cf. *strict liability* under LIABILITY.

> "Outcome responsibility serves to foster a sense of identity because it does not stretch indefinitely into the future but enables each of us to claim for ourselves, or to share with a few others, outcomes of limited extent, whether successes or failures. Yet outcome responsibility for harm to another does not by itself create a duty to compensate. The form that our responsibility for an outcome should take remains an open question. An apology or telephone call will often be enough. But outcome responsibility is a basis on which the law can erect a duty to compensate if there is reason to do so. There will be some reason to do so if the conduct in question is socially undesirable and if there is also reason to treat the harm suffered as the infringement of a right." Tony Honoré, *Responsibility and Fault* 77–78 (1999).

outcry. (14c) **1.** A victim's out-of-court statement about the facts of a crime, usu. made very soon after the crime was committed. • An outcry need not be made soon after the crime was committed if the victim is a child or is incapable of immediately making a statement. **2.** An uproar or loud clamor; a strong protest or objection.

outcry witness. See WITNESS.

outer bar. (1851) *English law.* A group of junior barristers who sit outside the dividing bar in the court. • These barristers rank below the King's Counsel or Queen's Counsel. — Also termed *utter bar.* Cf. INNER BAR.

outer barrister. See BARRISTER.

Outer House. *Scots law.* The first-instance jurisdiction of the Court of Session. See COURT OF SESSION (1).

outer space. (1842) **1.** The known and unknown areas of the universe beyond Earth's airspace. • The boundary between airspace and outer space is not fixed or precise. Cf. AIRSPACE. **2.** *Int'l law.* The space surrounding the planet that by United Nations treaty is not subject to claim of appropriation by any national sovereignty. • The treaty does not expressly define *outer space.* See OUTER SPACE TREATY.

Outer Space Treaty. *Int'l law.* The short title of the United Nations Treaty on Principles Governing the Activities of States in the Exploration and Use of Outer Space, Including the Moon and Other Celestial Bodies, 18 U.S.T. pt. 3, at 2410 (Jan. 27, 1967). • This treaty stipulates that, because space exploration is in the interest of all humanity, no country may claim territory, establish military bases, or station weapons on any other planet or a moon. The treaty also declares that international law and the United Nations charter apply in space. — Abbr. OST. See OUTER SPACE.

outfangthief (**owt**-fang-theef). [fr. Old English *ut* "out" + *fangen* "taken" + *theof* "thief"] (bef. 12c) *Hist.* The right of a lord of a manor to pursue a thief outside the manor's jurisdiction and to bring the thief back for trial and punishment; a lord's right to punish all thefts committed within his territories, wherever the thief might be caught. — Also spelled *outfangthef*; *utfangthief*; *utfangthef.* Cf. INFANGTHIEF.

outlaw, *n.* (bef. 12c) **1.** Someone who has been deprived of the benefit and protection of the law; a person under a sentence of outlawry. **2.** A lawless person or habitual criminal; esp., a fugitive from the law. **3.** *Int'l law.* A person, organization, or country under a ban or restriction because it is considered to be in violation of international law or custom.

outlaw, *vb.* (18c) **1.** To deprive (someone) of the benefit and protection of the law; to declare an outlaw <outlaw the fugitive>. **2.** To make illegal <outlaw fireworks within city limits>. **3.** To remove from legal jurisdiction or enforcement; to deprive of legal force <outlaw a claim under the statute>.

outlawry. (14c) **1.** *Hist.* The act or process of depriving someone of the benefit and protection of the law. **2.** The quality, state, or condition of being outlawed; the status of an outlaw. **3.** Disregard or disobedience of the law. See SACER; CONSECRATIO CAPITIS.

outlaw strike. See *wildcat strike* under STRIKE (1).

outline form. (1963) *Patents.* A style of writing patent claims that uses a numbered or lettered subparagraph for each element. Cf. COLON-SEMICOLON FORM; SINGLE-PARAGRAPH FORM; SUBPARAGRAPH FORM.

out-of-court, *adj.* (1950) Not done or made as part of a judicial proceeding <an out-of-court settlement> <an out-of-court statement that was not under oath>. See EXTRAJUDICIAL.

out-of-court settlement. See SETTLEMENT (2).

out-of-home placement. (1972) *Family law.* The placing of a child in a living arrangement outside the child's home (as in foster care or institutional care), usu. as the result of abuse or neglect; specif., in a child-abuse or child-neglect case, state action that removes a child from a parent's or custodian's home and places the child in foster care or with a relative, either temporarily or for an extended period. Cf. FOSTER-CARE PLACEMENT.

out-of-hospital do-not-resuscitate order. See DO-NOT-RESUSCITATE ORDER.

out of order. (18c) **1.** (Of a motion) not in order <the motion is out of order because it conflicts with the bylaws>. • A motion may be "out of order" because it is inherently inappropriate for the deliberative assembly's consideration at any time (e.g., because it proposes an unlawful action). A motion that is not appropriate simply because it is brought before the meeting at the wrong time but that may be appropriate for consideration at another time is more precisely referred to as "not in order." See IN ORDER.

> "Motions that conflict with the corporate charter, constitution or bylaws of a society, or with procedural rules prescribed by national, state, or local laws, are out of order, and if any motion of this kind is adopted, it is null and void. Likewise, motions are out of order if they conflict

with a motion that has been adopted by the society and has been neither rescinded, nor reconsidered and rejected after adoption. Such conflicting motions, if adopted, are null and void unless adopted by the vote required to rescind or amend the motion previously adopted." Henry M. Robert, *Robert's Rules of Order Newly Revised* § 39, at 332 (10th ed. 2000).

2. (Of a person) guilty of a breach of decorum or other misconduct during a meeting <the member is out of order>.

out-of-pocket expense. See EXPENSE.

out-of-pocket loss. See LOSS.

out-of-pocket rule. (1940) The principle that a defrauded buyer may recover from the seller as damages the difference between the amount paid for the property and the actual value received. Cf. BENEFIT-OF-THE-BARGAIN RULE (2).

out of the money, *adj.* (Of a creditor) unpaid because a debtor has insufficient assets to pay the claim.

out-of-the-money option. See OPTION (5).

out of the state. See BEYOND SEAS (2).

out of time. After a deadline; too late <because the statute of limitations expired before the action's filing, this lawsuit is out of time and should be dismissed>.

outplacement. (1948) *Employment law.* An employer's service of helping unwanted or unneeded workers, esp. executives, find new jobs when the employer has decided to employ them no longer.

output, *n.* (1841) **1.** The quantity of goods or work produced by a person, machine, factor, business, etc. **2.** The activity or process of producing goods or materials. **3.** The amount of electricity produced by a generator.

output contract. See CONTRACT.

outrage, *n.* See INTENTIONAL INFLICTION OF EMOTIONAL DISTRESS.

outrageous, *adj.* (14c) Exceeding all reasonable bounds of human decency; extremely shocking, offensive, or unfair.

outrageous conduct. See CONDUCT.

outrageous-conduct defense. See DEFENSE (1).

outside director. See DIRECTOR.

outside financing. See FINANCING.

outside influence. See INFLUENCE.

outside party. See THIRD PARTY.

outsider jurisprudence. See JURISPRUDENCE.

outsourcing, *n.* (1981) **1.** The procuring of products or services from an outside manufacturer or supplier, usu. on grounds of economizing; esp., the recourse to foreign labor for cost-cutting purposes. **2.** *Employment law.* A business's or organization's procurement of goods or services by contract with an outside supplier; specif., the use of workers outside the business or organization to do a job. See BUSINESS-PRODUCT OUTSOURCING.

outsourcing agreement. (1984) An agreement between a business and a service provider in which the service provider promises to provide necessary services, esp. data processing and information management, using its own staff and equipment, and usu. at its own facilities. See OUTSOURCING.

outstanding, *adj.* (18c) **1.** Unpaid; uncollected <outstanding debts>. **2.** Publicly issued and sold <outstanding shares>.

outstanding capital stock. See *outstanding stock* under STOCK.

outstanding security. See SECURITY (4).

outstanding stock. See STOCK.

outstanding warrant. See WARRANT (1).

outvote, *vb.* (17c) To defeat (a candidate, measure, proposition, etc.) by winning more votes.

outweigh, *vb.* (16c) To be of more importance or value than (something else).

over, *adj.* (bef. 12c) (Of a property interest) intended to take effect after the failure or termination of a prior estate; preceded by some other possessory interest <a limitation over> <a gift over>.

overage (oh-və-rij), *adj.* (1857) Too old for a particular purpose or activity.

overage (oh-vər-ayj), *n.* (1909) **1.** An excess or surplus, esp. of goods or merchandise. **2.** A percentage of retail sales paid to a store's landlord in addition to fixed rent.

overall majority. See MAJORITY.

overbid. See BID, *vb.*

overbreadth doctrine. (1970) *Constitutional law.* The doctrine holding that if a statute is so broadly written that it deters free expression, then it can be struck down on its face because of its chilling effect — even if it also prohibits acts that may legitimately be forbidden. • The Supreme Court has used this doctrine to invalidate a number of laws, including those that would disallow peaceful picketing or require loyalty oaths. Cf. VAGUENESS DOCTRINE.

overdetermined causation. See CAUSATION.

overdraft. (1843) **1.** A withdrawal of money from a bank in excess of the balance on deposit. **2.** The amount of money so withdrawn; specif., the amount of money that a bank customer owes to the bank after spending more money than the customer has in the account on which the payment is drawn. — Abbr. (in senses 1 & 2) OD; o/d. **3.** A line of credit extended by a bank to a customer (esp. an established or institutional customer) who might overdraw on an account.

overdraw, *vb.* (18c) To draw on (an account) in excess of the balance on deposit; to make an overdraft.

overdue, *adj.* (1805) **1.** Not paid by the appointed time; unpaid beyond the proper time of payment <overdue bills>. **2.** Delayed beyond the scheduled time <an overdue flight>. **3.** Too great; excessive <overdue profits>. **4.** Having ought to have occurred already, esp. long before now <an overdue honor>.

overhead, *n.* (1907) Business expenses (such as rent, utilities, or support-staff salaries) that cannot be allocated to a particular product or service; fixed or ordinary operating costs. • Under § 38 of the Restatement of the Law Governing Lawyers (2000), a lawyer may not charge a client separately for general overhead expenses. — Also termed *administrative expense*; *office expense.*

overheated economy. See ECONOMY.

overinclusive, *adj.* (1949) (Of legislation) extending beyond the class of persons intended to be protected or regulated;

burdening more persons than necessary to cure the problem <an overinclusive classification>.

overinsurance. (18c) **1.** Insurance (esp. from the purchase of multiple policies) that exceeds the value of the thing insured. **2.** Excessive or needlessly duplicative insurance.

overissue, *n.* (1803) An issue of securities beyond the authorized amount of capital or credit.

overlapping jurisdiction. See *concurrent jurisdiction* under JURISDICTION.

overpayment. See PAYMENT (2).

overplus. See SURPLUS.

overreaching, *n.* (16c) **1.** The act or an instance of taking unfair commercial advantage of another, esp. by fraudulent means. **2.** The act or an instance of defeating one's own purpose by going too far. — **overreach,** *vb.*

overridden veto. See VETO.

override (**oh**-vər-rɪd), *n.* (1931) **1.** A commission paid to a manager on a sale made by a subordinate; ROYALTY (2). **2.** A commission paid to a real-estate broker who listed a property when, within a reasonable amount of time after the expiration of the listing, the owner sells that property directly to a buyer with whom the broker had negotiated during the term of the listing.

override (oh-vər-**rɪd**), *vb.* (14c) To prevail over; to nullify or set aside <Congress mustered enough votes to override the President's veto>.

overriding royalty. See ROYALTY (2).

overrule, *vb.* (16c) **1.** To rule against; to reject <the judge overruled all of the defendant's objections>. **2.** (Of a court) to overturn or set aside (a precedent) by expressly deciding that it should no longer be controlling law <in *Brown v. Board of Education*, the Supreme Court overruled *Plessy v. Ferguson*>. Cf. VACATE (1).

> "If a decision is not a recent one, and especially if it seems to be very poor, it should not be relied upon without ascertaining whether it may not have been expressly or impliedly overruled by some subsequent one; that is, whether the court may not have laid down a contrary principle in a later case." Frank Hall Childs, *Where and How to Find the Law* 94 (1922).

> "Overruling is an act of superior jurisdiction. A precedent overruled is definitely and formally deprived of all authority. It becomes null and void, like a repealed statute, and a new principle is authoritatively substituted for the old." John Salmond, *Jurisprudence* 189 (Glanville L. Williams ed., 10th ed. 1947).

overseas bill of lading. See BILL OF LADING.

Overseas Private Investment Corporation. A federally chartered corporation that promotes private investment in developing countries by making or guaranteeing loans; supporting private funds that invest in foreign countries; insuring investments against political risks; and engaging in outreach activities. • It was established as an independent agency by the Foreign Affairs Reform and Restructuring Act of 1998. The agency is self-sustaining. — Abbr. OPIC.

overseer of the poor. *Hist.* See GUARDIAN OF THE POOR.

oversman. See UMPIRE.

oversubscription. (1896) A situation in which there are more people who want to have or use something than actually can; esp., the predicament of having more subscribers to a new issue of securities than there are securities available for purchase.

overt, *adj.* (14c) Open and observable; not concealed or secret <the conspirators' overt acts>.

overt act. (16c) *Criminal law.* **1.** (16c) *Criminal law.* An outward, physical manifestation of the will performed esp. by a conspirator. • An overt act can constitute evidence of participation in a conspiracy even if the act itself is not a crime and is merely preparatory. **2.** An act that indicates an intent to kill or seriously harm another person and thus gives that person a justification to use self-defense. **3.** An outward act, however innocent in itself, done in furtherance of a conspiracy, treason, or criminal attempt. • An overt act is usu. a required element of these crimes. **4.** ACTUS REUS. — Also termed *positive act.*

overtax, *vb.* (17c) To make (people) pay too much in taxes; to engage in confiscatory taxation. • The perennial question, of course, is how much is "too much." To some, overtaxing is almost synonymous with taxing. To others, overtaxing is an impossibility when it comes to "the wealthy."

over-the-counter, *adj.* (1921) **1.** Not listed or traded on an organized securities exchange; traded between brokers and dealers who negotiate directly <over-the-counter stocks>. **2.** (Of drugs) sold legally without a doctor's prescription <over-the-counter cough medicine>. — Abbr. OTC.

over-the-counter market. (1931) The market for securities that are not traded on an organized exchange. • Over-the-counter (OTC) trading usu. occurs through telephone or computer negotiations between buyers and sellers. Many of the more actively traded OTC stocks are listed on NASDAQ. — Abbr. OTC market.

overtime. (18c) **1.** The hours worked by an employee in excess of a standard day or week. • Under the Fair Labor Standards Act, employers must pay extra wages (usu. 1½ times the regular hourly rate) to certain employees (usu. nonsalaried ones) for each hour worked in excess of 40 hours per week. **2.** The extra wages paid for excess hours worked.

overtry, *vb.* (1911) (Of a trial lawyer) to try a lawsuit by expending excessive time, effort, and other resources to explore minutiae, esp. to present more evidence than the fact-trier can assimilate, the result often being that the adversary gains arguing points by disputing the minutiae.

overturn, *vb.* (1842) To overrule or reverse <the court overturned a long-established precedent>.

OWCP. *abbr.* OFFICE OF WORKERS' COMPENSATION PROGRAMS.

owelty (**oh**-əl-tee). (16c) **1.** Equality as achieved by a compensatory sum of money given after an exchange of parcels of land having different values or after an unequal partition of real property. **2.** The sum of money so paid.

OWI. *abbr.* Operating while intoxicated. See DRIVING UNDER THE INFLUENCE.

owing, *adj.* (15c) That is yet to be paid; owed; due <a balance of $5,000 is still owing>.

owling. (17c) *Hist. English law.* The smuggling of wool or sheep out of England. • The term usu. refers to nighttime smuggling.

own, *vb.* (bef. 12c) To rightfully have or possess as property; to have legal title to.

owned-property exclusion. See EXCLUSION (3).

owner. (bef. 12c) Someone who has the right to possess, use, and convey something; a person in whom one or more interests are vested. • An owner may have complete property in the thing or may have parted with some interests in it (as by granting an easement or making a lease). See OWNERSHIP.

▸ **adjoining owner.** (18c) Someone who owns land abutting another's; ABUTTER. — Also termed *adjoiner.*

▸ **beneficial owner.** (18c) **1.** One recognized in equity as the owner of something because use and title belong to that person, even though legal title may belong to someone else; esp., one for whom property is held in trust. — Also termed *equitable owner.* **2.** A corporate shareholder who has the power to buy or sell the shares, but who is not registered on the corporation's books as the owner. **3.** *Intellectual property.* A person or entity who is entitled to enjoy the rights in a patent, trademark, or copyright even though legal title is vested in someone else. • The beneficial owner has standing to sue for infringement. A corporation is typically a beneficial owner if it has a contractual right to the assignment of the patent but the employee who owns the patent has failed to assign it. Similarly, a patent or copyright owner who has transferred title as collateral to secure a loan would be a beneficial owner entitled to sue for infringement.

▸ **copyright owner.** See COPYRIGHT OWNER.

▸ **disponent owner.** (1958) *Scots law.* The conveying owner; SELLER (2).

▸ **equitable owner.** See *beneficial owner* (1).

▸ **general owner.** (18c) Someone who has the primary or residuary title to property; one who has the ultimate ownership of property. Cf. *special owner.*

▸ **innocent owner.** (18c) The owner of property that another person uses without the owner's knowledge or consent while committing a wrongful act or omission. See *innocent-owner defense* under DEFENSE (1).

▸ **legal owner.** (17c) One recognized by law as the owner of something; esp., one who holds legal title to property for the benefit of another. See TRUSTEE (1).

▸ **limited owner.** (1836) A tenant for life; the owner of a life estate. See *life estate* under ESTATE (1).

▸ **naked owner.** (1882) *Civil law.* A person whose property is burdened by a usufruct. • The naked owner has the right to dispose of the property subject to the usufruct, but not to derive its fruits. See USUFRUCT.

▸ **owner of record.** See *record owner.*

▸ **owner pro hac vice** (proh hahk **vee**-chay). See *bareboat charter* under CHARTER (8).

▸ **record owner.** (1863) **1.** A property owner in whose name the title appears in the public records. **2.** STOCKHOLDER OF RECORD.

▸ **sole and unconditional owner.** (1871) *Insurance.* The owner who has full equitable title to, and exclusive interest in, the insured property.

▸ **special owner.** (18c) One (such as a bailee) with a qualified interest in property. Cf. *general owner.*

owners' association. (1968) **1.** The basic governing entity for a condominium or planned unit developments. • It is usu. an unincorporated association or a nonprofit corporation. — Also termed *homeowners' association.* **2.** See *homeowners' association* under ASSOCIATION.

owners' equity. (1935) The aggregate of the owners' financial interests in the assets of a business entity; the capital contributed by the owners plus any retained earnings. • Owners' equity is calculated as the difference in value between a business entity's assets and its liabilities. — Also termed *owner's equity; book value; net book value;* (in a corporation) *shareholders' equity; stockholders' equity.*

ownership. (16c) The bundle of rights allowing one to use, manage, and enjoy property, including the right to convey it to others. • Ownership implies the right to possess a thing, regardless of any actual or constructive control. Ownership rights are general, permanent, and heritable. Cf. POSSESSION; TITLE (1).

> "Ownership does not always mean absolute dominion. The more an owner, for his advantage, opens up his property for use by the public in general, the more do his rights become circumscribed by the statutory and constitutional powers of those who use it." *Marsh v. Alabama,* 326 U.S. 501, 506, 66 S.Ct. 276, 278 (1946).

> "Possession is the *de facto* exercise of a claim; ownership is the *de jure* recognition of one. A thing is owned by me when my claim to it is maintained by the will of the state as expressed in the law; it is possessed by me, when my claim to it is maintained by my own self-assertive will. Ownership is the guarantee of the law; possession is the guarantee of the facts. It is well to have both forms if possible; and indeed they normally co-exist." John Salmond, *Jurisprudence* 311 (Glanville L. Williams ed., 10th ed. 1947).

▸ **bare ownership.** See *trust ownership.*

▸ **beneficial ownership.** (18c) **1.** A beneficiary's interest in trust property. — Also termed *equitable ownership.* **2.** A corporate shareholder's power to buy or sell the shares, though the shareholder is not registered on the corporation's books as the owner.

▸ **bonitary ownership** (bahn-ə-**tair**-ee). (1875) *Roman law.* A type of equitable ownership recognized by the praetor when the property was conveyed by an informal transfer, or by a formal transfer by one not the true owner. — Also termed *bonitarian ownership; in bonis habere.*

▸ **complete ownership.** *Hist. Louisiana law.* See *perfect ownership.*

▸ **contingent ownership.** (1886) Ownership in which title is imperfect but is capable of becoming perfect on the fulfillment of some condition; conditional ownership. Cf. *vested ownership.*

▸ **corporeal ownership.** (1894) The actual and complete ownership of land or chattels with the right to use and control.

▸ **cross-ownership.** (1940) Ownership by a single person or entity of two or more related businesses such that the owner can control competition.

▸ **equitable ownership.** See *beneficial ownership* (1).

▸ **full ownership.** *Hist. Louisiana law.* See *perfect ownership.*

▸ **imperfect ownership.** (1846) *Louisiana law.* Ownership of property subject to a usufruct interest held by another. See La. Civ. Code art. 478. — Also termed *naked ownership.*

▸ **incorporeal ownership.** (1931) An ownership interest in land or chattels without the right to use or control, as with mineral rights.

▸ **joint ownership.** (18c) Undivided ownership shared by two or more persons. • Typically, an owner's interest, at death, passes to the surviving owner or owners by virtue of the right of survivorship.

▸ **naked ownership.** *Louisiana law.* See *imperfect ownership.*

▸ **ownership in common.** (1838) Ownership shared by two or more persons whose interests are divisible. • Typically their interests, at death, pass to the dead owner's heirs or successors.

▸ **perfect ownership.** (1847) *Hist. Louisiana law.* The complete bundle of rights to use, enjoy, and dispose of property without limitation. — Also termed *full ownership; complete ownership.*

▸ **public ownership.** (1846) Government ownership.

▸ **qualified ownership.** (18c) Ownership that is shared, restricted to a particular use, or limited in the extent of its enjoyment.

▸ **trust ownership.** (1893) A trustee's interest in trust property. — Also termed *bare ownership.*

▸ **unqualified ownership.** (1829) Absolute ownership.

▸ **vested ownership.** (1867) Ownership in which title is perfect; absolute ownership. Cf. *contingent ownership.*

ownership-in-place theory. (1928) *Oil & gas.* A characterization of oil-and-gas rights used in a majority of jurisdictions, holding that the owner has the right to present possession of the oil and gas in place as well as the right to use the land surface to search, develop, and produce from the property, but that the interest in the minerals terminates if the oil and gas flows out from under the owner's land. • This theory is used in Texas, New Mexico, Kansas, Mississippi, and other major producing states. The rights of a severed-mineral-interest owner to oil and gas in these states are often described as an estate in fee simple absolute, but ownership of specific oil-and-gas molecules is subject to the rule of capture. See also NONOWNERSHIP THEORY.

owner's policy. *Real estate.* A title-insurance policy covering the owner's title as well as the mortgagee's interest. Cf. MORTGAGEE POLICY.

own-product exclusion. See EXCLUSION (3).

own-work exclusion. See EXCLUSION (3).

oxfild (**oks**-fild). *Hist.* A restitution made by a county or hundred for a wrong done by someone within that region.

oxgang (**oks**-gang). (14c) *Hist.* An indefinite quantity of land equal to what an ox plows in one year, usu. 12 to 15 acres. • An oxgang, equaling one-eighth of a carucate, was used to assess land for tax purposes. — Also termed *oxgate; bovate; bovata terrae.* Cf. CARUCATE.

oyer (**oy**-ər *or* **oh**-yər). [fr. Old French *oïr* "to hear"] (15c) *Hist.* **1.** A criminal trial held under a commission of oyer and terminer. See COMMISSION OF OYER AND TERMINER. **2.** The reading in open court of a document (esp. a deed) that is demanded by one party and read by the other. **3.** *Common-law pleading.* A prayer to the court by a party opposing a profert, asking to have the instrument on which the opponent relies read aloud. • Oyer can be demanded only when a profert has been properly made, but it is disallowed for a private writing under seal.

> "A party having a right to demand oyer is yet not obliged, in all cases, to exercise that right; nor is he obliged, in all cases, after demanding it, to notice it in the pleading he afterwards files or delivers. Sometimes, however, he is obliged to do both, namely, where he has occasion to found his answer upon any matter contained in the deed of which profert is made, and not set forth by his adversary. In these cases the only admissible method of making such matter appear to the court is to demand oyer, and, from the copy given, set forth the whole deed verbatim in his pleading." Benjamin J. Shipman, *Handbook of Common-Law Pleading* § 289, at 483 (Henry Winthrop Ballantine ed., 3d ed. 1923).

oyer, demand of. See DEMAND OF OYER.

oyer and terminer (**oy**-ər an[d] **tər**-mə-nər). [Law French *oyer et terminer* "to hear and determine"] (15c) **1.** See COMMISSION OF OYER AND TERMINER. **2.** COURT OF OYER AND TERMINER (2).

oyez (**oh**-yay *or* **oh**-yez *or* **oh**-yes). [Law French] (15c) Hear ye. • The utterance *oyez, oyez, oyez* is usu. used in court by the public crier to call the courtroom to order when a session begins or when a proclamation is about to be made.

P

P. *abbr.* PACIFIC REPORTER.

P.2d. *abbr. Pacific Reporter Second Series.* See PACIFIC REPORTER.

P.A. *abbr.* See *professional association* under ASSOCIATION.

paage (**pay**-ij). See PEDAGE.

PAC (pak). *abbr.* (1939) POLITICAL-ACTION COMMITTEE.

pacare (pə-**kair**-ee), *vb.* [Law Latin] *Hist.* To pay.

PACER. *abbr.* Public Access to Court Electronic Records — an Internet service providing access to federal-court records (pacer@pse.uscourts.gov).

pacification (pas-ə-fi-**kay**-shən), *n.* (15c) *Int'l law.* The act of making peace between two belligerent countries. — **pacify** (**pas**-ə-fɪ), *vb.*

pacific blockade. See BLOCKADE.

pacificist. See PACIFIST.

Pacific Reporter. A set of regional lawbooks, part of the West Group's National Reporter System, containing every officially published appellate decision from Alaska, Arizona, California, Colorado, Hawaii, Idaho, Kansas, Montana, Nevada, New Mexico, Oklahoma, Oregon, Utah, Washington, and Wyoming, from 1883 to date. • The first series ran from 1883 to 1931. The second series ran from 1931 to 2000. The third series is the current one. — Abbr. P.; P.2d; P.3d.

pacifism (**pas**-ə-fiz-əm). (1902) *Int'l law.* The advocacy of peaceful methods rather than war as a means of solving disputes.

pacifist (**pas**-ə-fist), *n.* (1906) Someone who is opposed to war; a person who believes in pacifism. — Also termed *pacificist.* Cf. CONSCIENTIOUS OBJECTOR.

pack, *vb.* (16c) To choose or arrange (a tribunal, jurors, etc.) to accomplish a desired result <pack a jury>.

package. *Criminal law. Slang.* A guilty plea resulting from plea-bargaining.

package mortgage. See MORTGAGE.

package policy. See INSURANCE POLICY.

packing, *n.* A gerrymandering technique in which a dominant political or racial group minimizes minority representation by concentrating the minority into as few districts as possible. Cf. CRACKING; STACKING (2).

packing a jury. See JURY-PACKING.

Pac-Man defense (**pak**-man). (1983) An aggressive antitakeover defense by which the target company attempts to take over the bidder company by making a cash tender offer for the bidder company's shares. • The name derives from a video game popular in the 1980s, the object of which was to gobble up the enemy. This defense is seldom used today. Cf. CROWN-JEWEL DEFENSE; SCORCHED-EARTH DEFENSE.

pact. (15c) A formal agreement between two or more parties; esp., a solemn agreement (such as a treaty) between two or more countries or governmental entities, esp. one to provide mutual aid or to cease hostilities.

> "Popular understanding notwithstanding, there is no legal difference between various kinds of international instruments because of the name they are given. In other words, 'treaties,' 'pacts,' 'protocols,' 'conventions,' 'covenants,' and 'declarations' are all terms to convey international agreements. Some of these terms may connote more or less solemnity or formality, but it does not matter for purposes of characterizing an accord as an international agreement, binding under international law." David J. Bederman, *International Law Frameworks* 25 (2001).

pacta in favorem tertii (**pak**-tə in fə-**vor**-əm **tər**-shee-ɪ). [Latin] *Hist.* Agreements in favor of a third party.

pacta sunt servanda (**pak**-tə sənt sər-**van**-də). [Latin "agreements must be kept"] (1847) The rule that agreements and stipulations, esp. those contained in treaties, must be observed <the Quebec courts have been faithful to the *pacta sunt servanda* principle>.

> "The *pacta sunt servanda* rule embodies an elementary and universally agreed principle fundamental to all legal systems . . . . Although its good faith (bona fide) element runs through many aspects of international law — and the legal effect of certain unilateral statements rests on good faith — it is of prime importance for the stability of treaty relations . . . . The oft-quoted Latin phrase means no more than that agreements which are legally binding must be performed. The third preamble to the Vienna Convention on the Law of Treaties (1969) ('VCLT') notes that 'the principles of free consent and of good faith and the pacta sunt servanda rule are universally recognised.' The rule is stated in the one sentence of Art. 26, entitled *pacta sunt servanda*: 'Every treaty in force is binding upon the parties to it and must be performed in good faith.'" Anthony Aust, "*Pacta Sunt Servanda,*" in 8 *The Max Planck Encyclopedia of Public International Law* 15, 15 (Rüdiger Wolfrum ed., 2012).

pact de non alienando (**pakt** dee **non** ay-lee-ə-**nan**-doh). [Latin] (1830) *Civil law.* An agreement not to alienate encumbered (esp. mortgaged) property. • This stipulation will not void a sale to a third party, but it does allow the mortgagee to proceed directly against the mortgaged property without notice to the purchaser. — Also termed *nonalienation pact.*

pactio (**pak**-shee-oh). [Latin] *Civil law.* **1.** The negotiating process that results in a *pactum.* **2.** The *pactum* arrived at; an agreement. Pl. ***pactiones.***

paction (**pak**-shən). (15c) **1.** PACTIO. **2.** *Int'l law.* An agreement between two countries to be performed by a single act, as opposed to one mandating ongoing obligations or acts.

pactional, *adj.* (17c) Of, relating to, or involving an agreement. — **pactionally,** *adv.*

Pact of Paris. See KELLOGG–BRIAND PACT.

pactum (**pak**-təm), *n.* [Latin] *Roman & civil law.* An agreement or convention, usu. falling short of a contract; a pact. — Also termed *pactum conventum.* Pl. ***pacta.***

▸ ***pactum constitutae pecuniae*** (**pak**-təm kon-stə-**t[y]oo**-tee pi-**kyoo**-nee-ee). [Latin "agreement for a fixed sum of money"] See *pactum de consituto.*

▸ ***pactum corvinum de hereditate viventis*** (**pak**-təm kor-**vɪ**-nəm dee hə-red-i-**tay**-tee vɪ-**ven**-tis). [Latin "a raven-like contract on the inheritance of the living"] An agreement concerning the succession of one still living. — Also termed *pactum de successione viventis*; *pactum super hereditate viventis*.

> "It is supposed that the Romans called this a corvine agreement (*pactum corvinum*) on account of the eager rapacity of ravens, which prompts them to attack and commence to devour animals weakened and dying before death has actually taken place." John Trayner, *Trayner's Latin Maxims* 429 (4th ed. 1894).

▸ ***pactum de compromittendo*** (**pak**-təm dee kom-prə-mi-**ten**-doh). [Latin] *Hist.* Agreement on submission to arbitration.

▸ ***pactum de constituto*** (**pak**-təm dee kon-sti-**t[y]oo**-toh). [Latin "an agreement"] (1880) An informal agreement to pay an existing debt, one's own or another's, at a fixed time. • The agreement was enforceable by a praetor. Justinian extended the *pactum de constituto* from money to debts of any kind. The *pactum* could also be used to give security; it differs from fidejussion mainly in its informality. — Also termed *pactum constitutae pecuniae*. See CONSTITUTUM. Cf. FIDEJUSSION.

▸ ***pactum de contrahendo*** (**pak**-təm dee kon-trə-**hen**-doh). [Latin] *Hist.* Agreement to bargain.

▸ ***pactum de negotiando*** (**pak**-təm dee nə-goh-shee-**an**-doh). [Latin] *Hist.* Agreement on conducting business.

▸ ***pactum de non petendo*** (**pak**-təm dee non pə-**ten**-doh). [Latin "agreement not to sue"] (17c) An informal agreement of release; specif., an agreement in which a creditor promises not to enforce the debt. — Also termed *pactum ne petatur*.

▸ ***pactum de quota litis*** (**pak**-təm dee **kwoh**-tə **lɪ**-tis). [Latin "agreement about a portion of the amount in issue"] (17c) An agreement in which a creditor promises to pay a portion of a difficult-to-collect debt to a person attempting to collect it; an agreement to share the proceeds of a litigation.

▸ ***pactum de retroemendo.*** [Latin] (19c) An agreement that under certain circumstances a buyer may require the seller to buy back the item sold.

> "*Pactum de retroemendo*. This is a clause entitling the buyer to make the seller take the thing back in certain events. Its operation was similar to that of a *pactum de retrovendendo*." F. De Zulueta, *The Roman Law of Sale* 58 (1945).

▸ ***pactum de retrovendendo*** (**pak**-təm dee re-troh-ven-**den**-doh). [Latin] (1863) An agreement concerning the selling back of an object. • This agreement gave the seller the right to repurchase the item sold within a certain period and at a fixed price.

> "*Pactum de retrovendendo*. Such a clause entitled the seller in certain events — it might be on demand within a certain period — to buy back at an agreed price. There is no ground for regarding it as creating a condition affecting the principal contract or as operating *in rem*; it was enforceable by action on the contract." F. De Zulueta, *The Roman Law of Sale* 58 (1945).

▸ ***pactum de successione viventis*** (**pak**-təm dee sək-ses[h]-ee-**oh**-nee vɪ-**ven**-tis). [Latin] See *pactum corvinum de hereditate viventis*.

▸ ***pactum displicentiae*** (**pak**-təm dis-pli-**sen**-shee-ɪ). (1929) *Roman law.* A sale on approval. • The buyer had the property on trial and could reject it.

▸ ***pactum donationis*** (**pak**-təm doh-nay-shee-**oh**-nis). [Latin] (1921) An agreement to make a gift. • Justinian made such agreements enforceable. If informal, the agreement would be valid up to a fix sum (500 *solidi*).

▸ ***pactum illicitum*** (**pak**-təm i-**lis**-ə-təm). [Latin] (18c) An illegal agreement.

▸ ***pactum legis commissoriae*** (**pak**-təm **lee**-jis kom-i-**sor**-ee-ee). [Latin] (17c) An agreement under which the seller received the benefit of the *lex commissoria*. See LEX COMMISSORIA.

▸ ***pactum legis commissoriae in pignoribus*** (**pak**-təm **lee**-jis kom-i-**sor**-ee-ee in pig-**nor**-ə-bəs). [Law Latin] (17c) An agreement giving the pledgee the benefit of a forfeiture clause. See LEX COMMISSORIA.

> "The *pactum legis commissoriae in pignoribus* was . . . a Roman law paction, sometimes adjected to a redeemable right, whereby it was provided, that, if the subject were not redeemed against a determinate day, the right of reversion should be irritated, and the subject should become the irredeemable property of him to whom it was impledged. Such stipulations were held in the Roman law to be *contra bonos mores*; but, by the law of Scotland, irritant clauses in contracts, obligations, infeftments, and the like, are effectual." William Bell, *Bell's Dictionary and Digest of the Law of Scotland* 758 (George Watson ed., 7th ed. 1890).

▸ ***pactum liberatorium*** (**pak**-təm lib-ər-ə-**tor**-ee-əm). [Law Latin "a liberating agreement"] (17c) An agreement liberating parties from honoring a real right. • This type of agreement appears to have been long defunct.

▸ ***pactum super hereditate viventis*** (**pak**-təm s[y]**oo**-pər hə-red-i-**tay**-tee vɪ-**ven**-tis). [Law Latin] See *pactum corvinum de hereditate viventis*.

pact with the devil. See DEVIL'S BARGAIN.

pad, *vb.* (1831) *Slang.* (Of a lawyer, paralegal, etc.) to overstate the number of (billable hours worked). See BILLABLE HOUR. — **padding,** *n.*

padded-payroll rule. See FICTITIOUS-PAYEE RULE.

***Padilla* claim.** (2010) *Criminal law.* A criminal defendant's assertion that his or her counsel was ineffective by reason of failing to inform the client of the adverse effects of a criminal conviction on immigration status. *See Padilla v. Kentucky*, 559 U.S. 356, 130 S.Ct. 1473 (2010).

paedophile. See PEDOPHILE.

paedophilia. See PEDOPHILIA.

paid-in capital. See CAPITAL.

paid-in fund. See FUND (1).

paid-in surplus. See SURPLUS.

paid leave. See LEAVE.

paid sick days. See *sick leave* under LEAVE.

paid-up insurance. See INSURANCE.

paid-up lease. (1926) *Oil & gas.* A mineral lease that does not provide for delay-rental payments and does not subject the lessor to any covenant to drill. • In effect, the lessor makes all delay-rental payments, and perhaps a bonus, when the lease is signed. A paid-up lease may be used to lease a small area or a fractional interest, or for a short primary term or for small delay rentals. The lease is effective through the primary term.

paid-up policy. See INSURANCE POLICY.

paid-up stock. See *full-paid stock* under STOCK.

PAIMI Act. *abbr.* PROTECTION AND ADVOCACY FOR INDIVIDUALS WITH MENTAL ILLNESS ACT.

pain and suffering. (1825) Physical discomfort or emotional distress compensable as an element of noneconomic damages in torts. See DAMAGES.

pain of, on. See ON PAIN OF.

pains and penalties, bill of. See BILL OF PAINS AND PENALTIES.

pair. (1819) *Parliamentary law.* Two voters, usu. legislators, on opposite sides of an issue who agree that they will abstain if either cannot vote on the issue. • A pair is usu. announced and recorded.

> "In a legislative body it is a rule that no member can vote who is not present when the question is put, but 'pairing,' which is a type of absentee voting by which a member agrees with a member who would have voted opposite to the first member not to vote, has long been used in Congress and some of the states and has been recognized by the courts. Each house of the legislature, under the authority to make rules for its own governance, has power to recognize what are called 'pairs.'" National Conference of State Legislatures, *Mason's Manual of Legislative Procedure* § 538, at 385 (2000).

paired vote. See VOTE (1).

pais (pay *or* pays). See IN PAIS.

Palace Court. *Hist.* A court having jurisdiction over all personal actions arising within 12 miles of Whitehall, the City of London excepted. • This court was created by James I in response to complaints about the inconvenience of using the itinerant Court of the Marshalsea; its jurisdiction was similar to that of the Marshalsea, but the court remained in Whitehall. It was abolished along with the Court of the Marshalsea in 1849. — Formerly also termed *curia palatii.* See COURT OF THE MARSHALSEA.

> "The court of the *marshalsea,* and the *palace court* at Westminster, though two distinct courts, are frequently confounded together. The former was originally holden before the steward and marshal of the king's house, and was instituted to administer justice between the king's domestic servants, that they might not be drawn into other courts, and thereby the king lose their service. . . . But this court being ambulatory, and obliged to follow the king in all his progresses, so that by the removal of the household, actions were frequently discontinued, and doubts having arisen as to the extent of its jurisdiction . . . [the king] erected a new court of record, called the *curia palatii,* or *palace-court,* to be held before the steward of the household and knight marshal, and the steward of the court, or his deputy; with jurisdiction to hold plea of all manner of personal actions whatsoever, which shall arise between any parties within twelve miles of his majesty's palace at Whitehall." 3 William Blackstone, *Commentaries on the Laws of England* 76 (1768).

palimony (pal-ə-moh-nee). [Portmanteau word from *pal* + *alimony*] (1977) **1.** A court's award of post-relationship support or compensation for services, money, and goods contributed during a long-term nonmarital relationship, esp. where a common-law marriage cannot be established. • Though not recognized under most state statutes, caselaw in some jurisdictions authorizes palimony claims. The term originated in the press coverage of *Marvin v. Marvin,* 557 P.2d 106 (Cal. 1976). Cf. ALIMONY. **2.** Loosely, child support. • This sense is esp. common in the United Kingdom.

pallio cooperire (pal-ee-oh koh-op-ə-RI-ree). [Latin "to cover with a pallium"] (1847) *Hist.* A marriage of persons who have already had a child together. • The pallium (a rectangular woolen wrap) was a veil or cover over either the bride or both the bride and groom, and it would be extended to cover the bastard child. Its removal at the wedding legitimized the child.

Palmer's Act. An 1856 English statute giving a person accused of a crime outside the jurisdiction of the Central Criminal Court the right to have the case tried in that court. St. 19 & 20 Vict., ch. 16. — Also termed *Central Criminal Court Act.* See CENTRAL CRIMINAL COURT.

palming off. See PASSING OFF.

***Palsgraf* rule** (pawlz-graf). (1932) *Torts.* The principle that negligent conduct resulting in injury will lead to liability only if the actor could have reasonably foreseen that his or her conduct would cause the injury. • In *Palsgraf v. Long Island R.R.,* 162 N.E. 99 (N.Y. 1928), two railroad attendants negligently dislodged a package of fireworks from a man they were helping board a train. The package exploded on impact and knocked over some scales that fell on Mrs. Palsgraf. The New York Court of Appeals, in a 4–3 majority opinion written by Chief Justice Benjamin Cardozo, held that the attendants could not have foreseen the possibility of injury to Palsgraf and therefore did not breach any duty to her. In the dissenting opinion, Justice William S. Andrews asserted that the duty to exercise care is owed to all, and thus a negligent act will subject the actor to liability to all persons proximately harmed by it, whether or not the harm is foreseeable. Both opinions have been widely cited to support the two views expressed in them.

Pan-American Convention. *Copyright.* One of a series of copyright conventions held among Western Hemisphere countries to negotiate treaties patterned after the Berne Convention. • The first Convention was held in 1902, the last in 1946. The largest was the 1910 Pan American Convention in Buenos Aires.

pandect (pan-dekt). (16c) **1.** A complete legal code, esp. of a country or a system of law, together with commentary. **2.** (*cap.* & *pl.*) The 50 books constituting Justinian's *Digest* (one of the four works making up the *Corpus Juris Civilis*), first published in A.D. 533. • The substance of 2,000 treatises was distilled into this abridgment. One estimate is that 3 million lines were reduced to 150,000. This prodigious amount of work was carried out in three short years (A.D. 530–533) by a commission of 17 jurists headed by Tribonian. — Also termed (in sense 2) *Digest.* — Also spelled (in reference to German law) *pandekt.* See CORPUS JURIS CIVILIS. Pl. **pandects, pandectae.**

pander, *n.* [fr. *Pandare,* a character in Chaucer, or, earlier, *Pandarus,* in Boccaccio] (15c) Someone who engages in pandering. — Also termed *panderer.* See PIMP.

pandering (pan-dər-ing), *n.* (17c) **1.** The act or offense of recruiting a prostitute, finding a place of business for a prostitute, or soliciting customers for a prostitute. — Also termed *promoting prostitution.* **2.** The act or offense of selling or distributing textual or visual material (such as magazines or videotapes) openly advertised to appeal to the recipient's sexual interest. • Although the concept of pandering was invoked by the U.S. Supreme Court in *Ginzburg v. U.S.,* 383 U.S. 463, 86 S.Ct. 942 (1966), it has seldom been discussed by the Court since then. — **pander,** *vb.*

***Panduit* test.** (1983) *Patents.* A four-factor test for measuring profits lost because of patent infringement. • The patentee must prove that (1) there was a demand for the product; (2) the patentee had the manufacturing and marketing capacity to meet that demand; (3) there were no acceptable noninfringing alternatives on the market; and (4) an ascertainable amount of money was lost in profits. *Panduit Corp. v. Stahlin Bros. Fibre Works, Inc.*, 575 F.2d 1152 (6th Cir. 1978).

P & L. *abbr.* Profit and loss. See INCOME STATEMENT.

panel. (14c) **1.** A list of persons summoned as potential jurors; VENIRE. **2.** A group of persons selected to serve on a jury; JURY. **3.** A set of judges selected from a complete court to decide a specific case; esp., a group of three judges designated to sit for an appellate court. **4.** *Scots law.* A person indicted in a crime; the accused. — Also spelled (in sense 4) *pannel.*

panelation (pan-əl-**ay**-shən). (2003) The act of empaneling a jury. — Also spelled *panellation.*

panel attorney. See ATTORNEY.

panel-shopping. (1974) The practice of choosing the most favorable group of judges to hear an appeal.

panhandling. (1885) The act or practice of approaching or stopping strangers and begging for money or food. — **panhandler,** *n.* — **panhandle,** *vb.*

pannage (**pan**-ij). (14c) *Hist.* **1.** The right to feed animals, esp. swine, on the windfallen nuts, etc. in a forest. **2.** The payment made to a forest's owner in exchange for the right.

papal law (**pay**-pəl). See CANON LAW (1).

paper. (14c) **1.** Any written or printed document or instrument. **2.** A negotiable document or instrument evidencing a debt; esp., commercial documents or negotiable instruments considered as a group. See NEGOTIABLE INSTRUMENT. **3.** (*pl.*) COURT PAPERS.

▸ **accommodation paper.** See ACCOMMODATION PAPER.

▸ **bankable paper.** (1825) Notes, checks, bank bills, drafts, and other instruments received as cash by banks.

▸ **bearer paper.** (1892) An instrument payable to the person who holds it rather than to the order of a specific person. • Bearer paper is negotiated simply by delivering the instrument to a transferee. — Also termed *bearer document*; *bearer instrument.*

▸ **chattel paper** (**chat**-əl). See CHATTEL PAPER.

▸ **commercial paper.** (1785) **1.** An instrument, other than cash, for the payment of money. • Commercial paper — typically existing in the form of a draft (such as a check) or a note (such as a certificate of deposit) — is governed by Article 3 of the UCC. But even though the UCC uses the term *commercial paper* when referring to negotiable instruments of a particular kind (drafts, checks, certificates of deposit, and notes as defined by Article 3), the term long predates the UCC as a business and legal term in common use. Before the UCC, it was generally viewed as synonymous with *negotiable paper* or *bills and notes.* It was sometimes applied even to nonnegotiable instruments. — Also termed *mercantile paper*; *company's paper.* See NEGOTIABLE INSTRUMENT.

> "'Commercial paper' is rather a popular than a technical expression, often used, however, both in statutes and in decisions of courts, to designate those simple forms of contract long recognized in the world's commerce and governed by the law merchant." 1 Joseph F. Randolph, *A Treatise on the Law of Commercial Paper* § 1, at 1 (2d ed. 1899).

2. Such instruments collectively. — Also termed *bills and notes.* **3.** Loosely, a short-term unsecured promissory note, usu. issued and sold by one company to meet another company's immediate cash needs.

▸ **commodity paper.** (1915) An instrument representing a loan secured by a bill of lading or warehouse receipt.

▸ **order paper.** (1890) An instrument payable to a specific payee or to any person that the payee designates. • In an unrelated sense, *order paper* is used in English law to refer to the list of subjects to be discussed in Parliament on a given day. — Also termed (in the main sense) *order document*; *order instrument.*

paper barrister. See BARRISTER.

paper-hanger. (1914) *Criminal law. Slang.* Someone who writes bad checks.

paper loss. See LOSS.

paper market. See *derivative market* under MARKET.

paper money. See MONEY.

paper patent. See PATENT (3).

paper profit. See PROFIT (1).

papers. See COURT PAPERS.

paper standard. (1810) A monetary system based entirely on paper; a system of currency that is not convertible into gold or other precious metal. Cf. GOLD STANDARD.

paper street. See STREET.

paper terrorism. See TERRORISM.

paper title. See *record title* under TITLE (2).

Papian law. See LEX PAPIA POPPEA.

par. See PAR VALUE.

parade of horribles. (1941) A litany of detrimental or retrograde consequences that will, in the view of an opponent of some proposed action, occur if the action is taken. Cf. SLIPPERY SLOPE; WEDGE PRINCIPLE.

parade-of-horrors objection. See WEDGE PRINCIPLE.

paradox of blackmail. (1981) Encapsulation of the idea that criminalization of blackmail is puzzling or hard to explain in light of the twin facts that the act a blackmailer threatens to perform typically is legal and that it is generally lawful to negotiate payment to refrain from exercising a legal right. See BLACKMAIL.

parage (**par**-ij), *n.* [Law French] (13c) *Hist.* Equality of condition, blood, or dignity; esp., the equal tenure in land existing among the nobility who inherit from a common ancestor. — Also termed *paragium.* Cf. DISPARAGARE (2).

paragium (pə-**ray**-jee-əm). [Law Latin] PARAGE.

parajudge. 1. See UNITED STATES MAGISTRATE JUDGE. **2.** A staff attorney within a court or a judge's chambers. — **parajudicial,** *adj.*

paralegal, *n.* (1967) **1.** Someone who has some education in law and assists a lawyer in duties related to the practice of law but who is not a licensed attorney. — Also termed *legal assistant*; *legal analyst.* **2.** *Canadian law.* A nonlawyer who is legally qualified through experience or special training and is licensed to provide limited legal services in certain fields. • Paralegals may assist in representing clients in both civil and criminal matters. — Also termed (in sense 2) *law clerk*. — **paralegal,** *adj.*

paralegalize, *vb.* (1977) *Slang.* To proofread, cite-check, and otherwise double-check the details in (a legal document).

parallel citation. See CITATION (3).

parallel imports. (1952) Goods bearing valid trademarks that are manufactured abroad and imported into the United States to compete with domestically manufactured goods bearing the same valid trademarks. • Domestic parties commonly complain that parallel imports compete unfairly in the U.S. market. But U.S. trademark law does not prohibit the sale of most parallel imports. — Also termed *gray-market goods*. See *gray market* under MARKET.

parallel parenting. See PARENTING.

parallel-parenting plan. See PARENTING PLAN.

parallel proceeding. See PROCEEDING.

parallel research. (1958) *Intellectual property.* The coincident but independent development of similar information or ideas by more than one person. • Parallel research may be offered to establish an independent-conception defense. If more than one person independently reaches the same result, each may protect the product as a trade secret.

paramilitary, *adj.* (1935) **1.** Of, relating to, or involving the provision of help to a military organization; of, pertaining to, or typical of a force that is organized on the model of a military organization, esp. as an auxiliary force. **2.** Of, relating to, or involving an illegal group that is organized like a militia.

paramount consideration. An overriding goal; a factor of superordinate importance. • Unless the evidence about it is inconclusive, a paramount consideration usu. has a decisive effect on a point to be determined. See CONSIDERATION (3).

paramount title. See TITLE (2).

paraph (par-əf), *n.* (16c) **1.** *Hist.* A flourish that follows a signature, intended as a safeguard against forgery. **2.** *Civil law.* A signature itself; esp., a notary public's signature on a document, followed by the date, names of the parties, and seal.

paraph (par-əf), *vb.* (1856) *Civil law.* To add a paraph to <paraphed the contract>.

parapherna (par-ə-**fər**-nə), *n.* [Greek "things brought on the side"] (18c) **1.** *Roman law.* Property of a wife not forming part of her dowry. See DOS (1). **2.** *Scots law.* A married woman's personal property, such as clothing, jewelry, and intimate possessions, which a husband did not acquire by virtue of marriage. See JUS MARITI.

paraphernalia (par-ə-fər-**nay**-lee-ə). (17c) *Hist.* Property that a wife was allowed to keep, in addition to her dowry, on the death of her husband.

> "[I]n one particular instance the wife may acquire a property in some of her husband's goods: which shall remain to her after his death and not go to the executors. These are called her *paraphernalia,* which is a term borrowed from the civil law . . . signifying something over and above her dower." 2 William Blackstone, *Commentaries on the Laws of England* 435–36 (1765).

paraphernal property. See *extradotal property* under PROPERTY.

Paraphrase of Theophilus. See INSTITUTE (4).

parata executio (pə-**ray**-tə ek-sə-**kyoo**-shee-oh). [Law Latin "a prepared diligence"] (18c) *Scots law.* A creditor's completed diligence allowing the creditor to proceed to obtain payment of a debt.

paratitla (par-ə-**tɪt**-lə), *n. pl.* [Law Latin "next to the title"] *Roman & civil law.* Notes or abstracts prefixed to titles of law, giving a summary of their contents.

paratum habeo (pə-**ray**-təm **hay**-bee-oh). [Law Latin "I have him in readiness"] (17c) *Hist.* A sheriff's return of a *capias ad respondendum,* signifying that the defendant is ready to be brought to court.

paratus est verificare (pə-**ray**-təs est ver-ə-fi-**kair**-ee). [Law Latin] He is ready to verify. • This phrase formerly concluded a verified pleading.

paravail (par-ə-**vayl** *or* **par**-ə-vayl), *adj.* [Law French "at the bottom"] (16c) *Hist.* (Of a tenant) holding of another tenant.

parcel, *n.* (15c) **1.** A small package or bundle. **2.** A tract of land; esp., a continuous tract or plot of land in one possession, no part of which is separated from the rest by intervening land in another's possession.

parcel, *vb.* (15c) To divide and distribute (goods, land, etc.) • This verb is often used with *out* <the land is parceled out in allotments> or, rarely, *off* <the father arranged to have a 10.474-acre tract of his farm parceled off and retitled to his children as joint tenants>.

parcel bomb. See *letter bomb* under BOMB.

parcenary (**pahr**-sə-ner-ee). See COPARCENARY.

parcener (**pahr**-sə-nər). See COPARCENER.

parco fracto (**pahr**-koh **frak**-toh). See DE PARCO FRACTO.

par delictum (pahr di-**lik**-təm). [Latin] (1824) Equal guilt; equal wrong.

pardon, *n.* (14c) **1.** The act or an instance of officially nullifying punishment or other legal consequences of a crime. • A pardon is usu. granted by the chief executive of a government. The President has the sole power to issue pardons for federal offenses, and state governors have the power to issue pardons for state crimes. — Also termed *executive pardon; free pardon.* See CLEMENCY. Cf. COMMUTATION (2); REPRIEVE. — **pardon,** *vb.*

> "The term *pardon* is first found in early French law and derives from the Late Latin *perdonare* ('to grant freely'), suggesting a gift bestowed by the sovereign. It has thus come to be associated with a somewhat personal concession by a head of state to the perpetrator of an offense, in mitigation or remission of the full punishment that he has merited." Leslie Sebba, "Amnesty and Pardon," in 1 *Encyclopedia of Crime and Justice* 59, 59 (Sanford H. Kadish ed., 1983).

▸ **absolute pardon.** (17c) A pardon that releases the wrongdoer from punishment and restores the offender's civil rights without qualification. — Also termed *full pardon; unconditional pardon.*

▸ **conditional pardon.** (17c) A pardon that does not become effective until the wrongdoer satisfies a prerequisite or that will be revoked upon the occurrence of some specified act.

▸ **faultless pardon.** (17c) A pardon granted because the act for which the person was convicted was not a crime.

▸ **general pardon.** See AMNESTY.

▸ **partial pardon.** (17c) A pardon that exonerates the offender from some but not all of the punishment or legal consequences of a crime.

▸ **unconditional pardon.** See *absolute pardon.*

2. *Eccles. law.* An indulgence; a remission of temporal punishment by divine justice through the sacrament of penance. **3.** PLEA OF PARDON.

pardon attorney. (1906) A Justice Department lawyer who considers applications for federal pardons and makes recommendations for review by the President.

parens binubus (**par**-enz bɪ-**n**[**y**]**oo**-bəs). [Latin "twice-married parent"] *Roman law.* A parent who has remarried. • In Roman law, the children from the previous marriage acquired all property that the *parens binubus* acquired gratuitously in the previous marriage.

parens patriae (**par**-enz **pay**-tree-ee *or* **pa**-tree-ɪ). [Latin "parent of his or her country"] (18c) **1.** *Roman law.* The emperor as the embodiment of the state. **2.** The state regarded as a sovereign; the state in its capacity as provider of protection to those unable to care for themselves <the attorney general acted as *parens patriae* in the administrative hearing>. **3.** A doctrine by which a government has standing to prosecute a lawsuit on behalf of a citizen, esp. on behalf of someone who is under a legal disability to prosecute the suit <*parens patriae* allowed the state to institute proceedings>. • The state ordinarily has no standing to sue on behalf of its citizens, unless a separate, sovereign interest will be served by the suit. — Also termed *doctrine of parens patriae.*

parent. (15c) **1.** The lawful father or mother of someone. • In ordinary usage, the term denotes more than responsibility for conception and birth. The term commonly includes (1) either the natural father or the natural mother of a child, (2) either the adoptive father or the adoptive mother of a child, (3) a child's putative blood parent who has expressly acknowledged paternity, and (4) an individual or agency whose status as guardian has been established by judicial decree. In law, parental status based on any criterion may be terminated by judicial decree. In other words, a person ceases to be a legal parent if that person's status as a parent has been terminated in a legal proceeding. — Also termed *legal parent.*

▸ **absent parent.** See *noncustodial parent.*

▸ **adoptive parent.** (18c) A parent by virtue of legal adoption. See ADOPTION (1).

▸ **biological parent.** (1932) The woman who provides the egg or the man who provides the sperm to form the zygote that grows into an embryo. — Also termed *genetic parent.*

▸ **birth parent.** (1977) Either the biological father or the mother who gives birth to a child. — Sometimes written *birthparent.*

▸ **constructive parent.** See *equitable parent.*

▸ **custodial parent.** (1933) The parent awarded physical custody of a child in a divorce. See PHYSICAL CUSTODY (2). Cf. *noncustodial parent.*

▸ **de facto parent.** (1944) An adult who (1) is not the child's legal parent, (2) has, with consent of the child's legal parent, resided with the child for a significant period, (3) has routinely performed a share of the caretaking functions at least as great as that of the parent who has been the child's primary caregiver without any expectation of compensation for this care, and (4) has established a parental role with the child. • Because the status of de facto parent is subordinate to that of legal parent, a person who expects to be afforded the status of parent should, if possible, adopt the child. The primary function of this conceptual status is to provide courts with a means for maintaining a relationship between a child and an adult who has functioned as a parent when that adult is prohibited from legally adopting the child. The status is usu. limited to a person who has assumed the role of parent with the knowledge and consent, either express or implied, of the legal parent. But it may also arise when there is a total failure or inability of the legal parent to perform parental duties. Cf. *equitable parent; psychological parent.*

▸ **Disneyland parent.** (1982) A noncustodial parent who indulges his or her child with gifts and good times during visitation and leaves most or all disciplinary responsibilities to the other parent; esp., a noncustodial parent who provides luxuries that the custodial parent cannot afford but performs no disciplinary duties, in an effort to gain or retain the child's affection. — Also termed *Santa Claus dad.* See LOLLIPOP SYNDROME.

▸ **domiciliary parent.** (1966) A parent with whom a child lives.

▸ **dual-residential parent.** (1998) A parent who shares primary residential responsibility for a child with the other parent when each provides a residence that is substantially a primary residence. • In many jurisdictions, dual residence is referred to as joint physical custody. See RESIDENTIAL RESPONSIBILITY; CUSTODY (2). Cf. *residential parent.*

▸ **equitable parent.** (1979) **1.** A husband who, though not the biological father, is treated by the court as the father in an action for custody or visitation, usu. when the husband (1) has treated the child as his own while married to the child's mother, (2) is the only father the child has ever known, and (3) seeks the rights of fatherhood. **2.** A mother or father, not by blood or adoption, but by virtue of the close parent-like relationship that exists between that person and a child. • The status of equitable parent is a legal fiction that is used as an equitable remedy. Most commonly, the status of equitable parent arises when a person, living with the child and one of his or her legal or natural parents, forms a close bond with the child and assumes the duties and responsibilities of a parent. — Also termed *constructive parent.* See *adoption by estoppel* under ADOPTION (1). Cf. *psychological parent; de facto parent.*

▸ **foster parent.** (17c) An adult who, though without blood ties or legal ties, cares for and rears a child, esp. an orphaned or neglected child who might otherwise be deprived of nurture, usu. under the auspices and direction of an agency and for some compensation or benefit. • Foster parents sometimes give care and support temporarily until a child is legally adopted by others. See FOSTER CARE. Cf. *foster child* under CHILD.

▸ **genetic parent.** See *biological parent.*

▸ **godparent.** See GODPARENT.

▸ **intended parent.** See *intentional parent.*

▸ **intentional parent.** (1995) The person whose idea it is to have and raise a child and who (1) enters into a surrogacy contract with a surrogate mother, and (2) is the legal parent of the child regardless of any genetic link to the child. — Also termed *intended parent.* See *intended child* under CHILD.

▸ **noncustodial parent.** (1949) In the child-custody laws of some states, a parent without the primary custody rights of a child; esp., the parent not awarded physical custody of a child in a divorce. • The noncustodial parent is typically awarded visitation with the child. — Also termed *nonresidential parent; possessory conservator; absent parent.* See PHYSICAL CUSTODY (2). Cf. *custodial parent.*

▸ **nonresidential parent.** See *noncustodial parent.*

▸ **parent by estoppel.** (1983) A man who, though not a child's legal father, is estopped from denying liability for child support. • This estoppel usu. arises when the man (1) has lived with the child for at least two years, (2) has believed in good faith that he was the child's father, (3) has accepted parental responsibilities, and (4) has entered into a coparenting agreement with the child's mother — and when the court finds that recognition of the status of parent is in the child's best interests. See ESTOPPEL.

▸ **primary domiciliary parent.** (1988) In a joint-custody arrangement, the parent who exercises primary physical custody. See *joint custody* under CUSTODY (2).

▸ **psychological parent.** (1963) Someone who, on a continuing and regular basis, provides for a child's emotional and physical needs. • The psychological parent may be the biological parent, a foster parent, a guardian, a common-law parent, or some other person unrelated to the child.

▸ **residential parent.** (1978) A parent who has primary residential responsibility for a child and who is not a dual-residential parent. See RESIDENTIAL RESPONSIBILITY. Cf. *dual-residential parent.*

▸ **stepparent.** (1840) The spouse of one's mother or father by a later marriage.

▸ **surrogate parent.** (1972) **1.** Someone who carries out the role of a parent by court appointment or the voluntary assumption of parental responsibilities. **2.** See *surrogate mother* (2) under MOTHER.

2. See *parent corporation* under CORPORATION.

parentage (**pair**-ən-tij *or* **par**-). (15c) The quality, state, or condition of being a parent; kindred in the direct ascending line.

parentage action. See PATERNITY SUIT.

parental access. See VISITATION (2).

parental-alienation syndrome. See PARENT-ALIENATION SYNDROME.

parental-autonomy doctrine. (1980) The principle that a parent has a fundamental right to raise his or her child and to make all decisions regarding that child free from governmental intervention, unless (1) the child's health and welfare are jeopardized by the parent's decisions, or (2) public health, welfare, safety, and order are threatened by the parent's decisions. • The Supreme Court first recognized the doctrine of parental autonomy over the family in *Meyer v. Nebraska,* 262 U.S. 390, 43 S.Ct. 625 (1923). — Also termed *family-autonomy doctrine.* Cf. PARENTAL-PRIVILEGE DOCTRINE.

parental consent. See CONSENT (1).

parental-consent statute. (1953) A statute that requires a minor to obtain his or her parent's consent before receiving elective medical treatment, such as an abortion. • Without parental consent, a physician or other medical professional commits a battery on a child when giving nonemergency medical treatment. To pass constitutional muster, a parental-consent statute must include a judicial-bypass provision. *Planned Parenthood of Southeastern Pa. v. Casey,* 505 U.S. 833, 112 S.Ct. 2791 (1992). — Also termed *parental-consent treatment statute.* See JUDICIAL-BYPASS PROVISION. Cf. PARENTAL-NOTIFICATION STATUTE; MATURE-MINOR DOCTRINE.

parental-consent treatment statute. See PARENTAL-CONSENT STATUTE.

parental consortium. See CONSORTIUM (1).

parental-discipline privilege. (1972) A parent's right to use reasonable force or to impose reasonable punishment on a child in a way that is necessary to control, train, and educate. • Several factors are used to determine the reasonableness of the action, including whether the actor is the parent; the child's age, sex, and physical and mental state; the severity and foreseeable consequences of the punishment; and the nature of the misconduct. Cf. PARENTAL-PRIVILEGE DOCTRINE.

parental functions. See PARENTING FUNCTIONS.

parent-alienation syndrome. (1990) A situation in which one parent has manipulated a child to fear or hate the other parent; a condition resulting from a parent's actions that are designed to poison a child's relationship with the other parent. • Some mental-health specialists deny that this phenomenon amounts to a "psychological syndrome." — Abbr. PAS. — Also termed *parental-alienation syndrome.*

parental immunity. See IMMUNITY (2).

parental-immunity doctrine. See *parental immunity* (1) under IMMUNITY (2).

parental kidnapping. See KIDNAPPING.

Parental Kidnapping Prevention Act. A 1980 federal statute providing a penalty for child-kidnapping by a noncustodial parent and requiring states to recognize and enforce a child-custody order rendered by a court of another state. 28 USCA § 1738A; 42 USCA §§ 654–655, 663. — Abbr. PKPA. Cf. UNIFORM CHILD CUSTODY JURISDICTION ACT; FEDERAL KIDNAPPING ACT.

parental leave. See LEAVE.

parental-liability statute. (1963) A law obliging parents to pay damages for torts (esp. intentional ones) committed by their minor children. • All states have these laws, but most limit the parents' monetary liability to about $3,000 per tort. Parents can also be held criminally liable for the acts of their children. One group of laws is aimed at contributing to the delinquency and endangering the welfare of a minor. More recently, the laws have been directed at improper supervision and failure to supervise. The first law aimed at punishing parents for the acts of their children was enacted in Colorado in 1903. By 1961 all but two states had enacted similar laws. At least five states make it a felony for a parent to intentionally, knowingly, and recklessly provide a firearm to a child, or permit the child to handle a firearm, when the parent is aware of a substantial risk that the child will use the weapon to commit a crime. — Also termed *parental-responsibility statute; failure-to-supervise statute.* Cf. PARENTAL-RESPONSIBILITY STATUTE.

parental-notification statute. (1979) A law that requires a physician to notify a minor's parent of her intention to have an abortion. Cf. PARENTAL-CONSENT STATUTE.

parental-preference doctrine. (1974) The principle that custody of a minor child should ordinarily be granted to a fit parent rather than another person. • The preference can be rebutted by proof that the child's best interests are to the contrary. — Also termed *parental-rights doctrine; parental-superior-rights doctrine; parental-presumption rule.* Cf. BEST INTERESTS OF THE CHILD.

parental-presumption rule. See PARENTAL-PREFERENCE DOCTRINE.

parental-privilege doctrine. (2004) The parent's right to discipline his or her child reasonably, to use reasonable child-rearing practices free of governmental interference, and to exercise decision-making authority over the child. Cf. PARENTAL-AUTONOMY DOCTRINE; PARENTAL-DISCIPLINE PRIVILEGE.

parental-responsibility statute. (1956) **1.** A law imposing criminal sanctions (such as fines) on parents whose minor children commit crimes as a result of the parents' failure to exercise sufficient control over them. — Also termed *control-your-kid law.* **2.** PARENTAL-LIABILITY STATUTE.

parental rights. (18c) A parent's rights to make all decisions concerning his or her child, including the right to determine the child's care and custody, the right to educate and discipline the child, and the right to control the child's earnings and property. See TERMINATION OF PARENTAL RIGHTS.

parental-rights doctrine. See PARENTAL-PREFERENCE DOCTRINE.

parental-superior-rights doctrine. See PARENTAL-PREFERENCE DOCTRINE.

parent application. See PATENT APPLICATION.

parent by estoppel. See PARENT.

parent–child immunity. See *parental immunity* (1) under IMMUNITY (2).

parent–child relationship. See RELATIONSHIP.

parent committee. See COMMITTEE (1).

parent company. See *parent corporation* under CORPORATION.

parent corporation. See CORPORATION.

parentela (par-ən-tee-lə), *n. pl.* [Law Latin] (15c) Persons who can trace descent from a common ancestor.

parentelic method (par-ən-**tee**-lik *or* -**tel**-ik). (1935) A scheme of computation used to determine the paternal or maternal collaterals entitled to inherit when a childless intestate decedent is not survived by parents or their issue. • Under this method, the estate passes to grandparents and their issue; if there are none, to great-grandparents and their issue; and so on down each line until an heir is found. The Uniform Probate Code uses a limited parentelic system: it looks first to the grandparents and their issue, but if no heir is found in that line, the search ends and the estate escheats to the state. See DEGREE (6). Cf. GRADUAL METHOD.

parent filing date. See *effective filing date* under DATE.

parenticide (pə-**ren**-tə-sɪd). (17c) **1.** The act of murdering one's parent. **2.** Someone who murders his or her parent. — **parenticidal,** *adj.*

parenting, *n.* (1918) **1.** Performance of the functions of a parent. **2.** One or more methods of child-rearing.

▸ **parallel parenting.** (1989) A situation in which divorced parents, although disagreeing on some aspects of child-rearing, allow each other to handle discipline and daily regimens in their own individual ways when with the child.

▸ **shared parenting.** (1978) Cooperation between divorced parents in child-rearing.

parenting agreement. See PARENTING PLAN.

parenting function. (1978) **1.** A task that serves the direct or day-to-day needs of a child or of a child's family. • Parenting functions include providing necessaries, making decisions about the child's welfare, and maintaining the family residence. Cf. CARETAKING FUNCTIONS. **2.** CUSTODY (2).

parenting plan. (1982) A plan that allocates custodial responsibility and decision-making authority for what serves the child's best interests and that provides a mechanism for resolving any later disputes between parents. — Also termed *parenting agreement.* See CUSTODY (2); CUSTODIAL RESPONSIBILITY; DECISION-MAKING RESPONSIBILITY.

▸ **parallel-parenting plan.** *Family law.* A written agreement between parents providing for matters relating to their child's maintenance and welfare; esp., a specific and inflexible plan designed to minimize parental interaction and conflict and to allow each parent to make most decisions independently when that parent has physical custody of the child. — Also termed *child agreement.*

parenting time. See VISITATION.

parents-in-law. (1852) The parents of one's spouse.

parent–subsidiary freezeout. See FREEZEOUT.

pares curiae (par-eez **kyoor**-ee-ee). [Law Latin "peers of the court"] (16c) *Hist.* A lord's tenants who sat in judgment of a fellow tenant.

pares curtis (par-eez **kər**-tis). [Law Latin] (17c) *Hist.* The peers of the court. — Also termed *pares curiae.*

> "The lord was, in early times, the legislator and judge over all his feudatories: and therefore the vassals of the inferior lords were bound by their fealty to attend their domestic courts baron, (which were instituted in every manor or barony, for doing speedy and effectual justice to all the tenants) in order as well to answer such complaints as might be alleged against themselves, as to form a jury or homage for the trial of their fellow-tenants; and upon this account, in all the feodal institutions both here and on the continent, they are distinguished by the appellation of the peers of the court; *pares curtis,* or *pares curiae.*" 2 William Blackstone, *Commentaries on the Laws of England* 54 (1766).

pares regni (**par**-eez **reg**-nɪ). [Law Latin] (17c) *Hist.* Peers of the realm.

Pareto optimality (pə-**ray**-toh *or* pə-**ret**-oh), *n.* (1952) An economic situation in which no person can be made better off without making someone else worse off. • The term derives from the work of Vilfredo Pareto (1848–1923), an Italian economist and sociologist. — **Pareto-optimal,** *adj.*

Pareto superiority, *n.* (1962) An economic situation in which an exchange can be made that benefits someone and injures no one. • When such an exchange can no longer be made, the situation becomes one of Pareto optimality. — **Pareto-superior,** *adj.*

pari causa, in. See IN PARI CAUSA.

pari delicto, in. See IN PARI DELICTO.

paries communis (**pair**-ee-eez kə-**myoo**-nis). [Latin] A common wall; a party wall.

paries oneri ferendo, uti nunc est, ita sit (**pair**-ee-eez **on**-ər-ɪ fə-**ren**-doh, **yoo**-tɪ **nəngk** est, ɪ-tə **sit**). [Latin] *Roman law.* The wall for bearing the burden, as it now is, so let it be. • The phrase constituted the urban servitude *oneris ferendi.* See ONERIS FERENDI; JUS ONERIS FERENDI; *servitus oneris ferendi* under SERVITUS.

pari materia, in. See IN PARI MATERIA.

parimutuel betting (par-i-**myoo**-choo-əl). (1906) A system of gambling in which bets placed on a race are pooled and then paid (less a management fee and taxes) to those holding winning tickets.

pari passu (**pahr**-ee **pahs**-oo *or* **pair**-ɪ, **pair**-ee, *or* **par**-ee **pas**-[y]oo). [Latin "by equal step"] (16c) Proportionally; at an equal pace; without preference <creditors of a bankrupt estate will receive distributions *pari passu*>.

pari ratione (**pair**-ɪ ray-shee-**oh**-nee *or* rash-ee-**oh**-nee). [Latin] *Roman & civil law.* For the like reason; by like mode of reasoning.

Paris Additional Act. *Copyright.* An 1896 amendment to the Berne Convention extending copyright protection to photographs as derivative works.

Paris Convention. See PARIS CONVENTION FOR THE PROTECTION OF INDUSTRIAL PROPERTY.

Paris Convention for the Protection of Industrial Property. A treaty designed to unify and streamline patent prosecutions and trademark applications among the signatories. • The Convention eased the harsh effects of the first-to-file priority rule by allowing an applicant in any member country one year in which to apply in other member countries while maintaining the application's original priority date. It also banned patent-protection discrimination against residents of other member countries. Now administered by the World Intellectual Property Organization, an agency of the United Nations, the Convention was first signed in 1883, revised most recently in 1967, and amended in 1970. — Often shortened to *Paris Convention.* — Also termed *Paris Industrial Property Convention.*

> "The 1883 Paris Convention for the Protection of Industrial Property is the cornerstone of the international patent granting system. It represents the first efforts of several countries to adopt a common approach to industrial property. The fundamental principles of 'right of priority' and 'national treatment' set out by the Convention have been of capital importance to the internationalization of intellectual property rights over the last century." Marta Pertegás Sender, *Cross-Border Enforcement of Patent Rights* 4 (2002).

parish. (14c) **1.** In Louisiana, a governmental subdivision analogous to a county in other U.S. states. **2.** *Eccles. law.* A division of a town or district, subject to the ministry of one pastor.

▸ **district parish.** (1818) *Eccles. law.* A geographical division of an English parish made by the Crown's commissioners for the building of new churches for worship, celebration of marriages, christenings, and burials.

parish court. See *county court* (1) under COURT.

Paris Industrial Property Convention. See PARIS CONVENTION FOR THE PROTECTION OF INDUSTRIAL PROPERTY.

par item. See ITEM (2).

parity (**pair**-i-tee). (16c) **1.** The quality, state, or condition of being equal, esp. in pay, rights, or power. **2.** Equality between the monetary units from two different countries; equivalence between foreign currencies.

parium judicium (**pair**-ee-əm joo-**dish**-ee-əm). [Law Latin "the decision of equals"] The judgment of peers; trial by a jury of one's peers or equals.

***Parker* doctrine.** See STATE-ACTION DOCTRINE.

parking. (1983) **1.** The sale of securities subject to an agreement that the seller will buy them back at a later time for a similar price. • Parking is illegal if done to circumvent securities regulations or tax laws. It is often a method of evading the net-capital requirements of the Financial Industry Regulatory Authority (FIRA), which requires a brokerage firm to discount the value of any stock it holds in its own account when it files its monthly report about its net-capital condition. To reach technical compliance with the FIRA's net-capital requirements, a brokerage firm "sells" stock from its own account to a customer at market price, thereby avoiding the discount for reporting purposes. Having filed its report, it can then "buy" the shares back from the customer, usu. at the same price at which it "sold" the stock, plus interest. **2.** The placement of assets in a safe, short-term investment while other investment opportunities are being considered. — Also termed (in sense 1) *stock-parking.*

parking-lot rule. (1974) The principle that workers'-compensation insurance covers the injuries suffered by an employee on the employer's premises when the employee is arriving at or leaving work. — Also termed *premises rule.*

parliament. (12c) **1.** The supreme legislative body of some countries; esp. (*cap.*), in the United Kingdom, the national legislature consisting of the monarch, the House of Lords, and the House of Commons <a majority in Parliament>.

▸ **hung parliament.** A parliament in which no political party has more elected representatives than all the others combined.

2. The period during which a parliament meets <during the present parliament>.

parliamentarian. (17c) **1.** A member of parliament. **2.** *Parliamentary law.* A consultant trained in parliamentary law who advises the chair and others on matters of parliamentary law and procedure. • The parliamentarian, who is often a professional, only advises and never "rules" on procedural issues. See PARLIAMENTARY LAW; PARLIAMENTARY PROCEDURE.

"The parliamentarian is a consultant, commonly a professional, who advises the president and other officers, committees, and members on matters of parliamentary procedure. The parliamentarian's role during a meeting is purely an advisory and consultative one — since parliamentary law gives to the chair alone the power to rule on questions of order or to answer parliamentary inquiries. . . . After the parliamentarian has expressed an opinion on a point, the chair has the duty to make the final ruling and, in doing so, has the right to follow the advice of the parliamentarian or to disregard it." Henry M. Robert, *Robert's Rules of Order Newly Revised* § 47, at 449–50 (10th ed. 2002).

parliamentary, *adj.* (17c) **1.** Of, relating to, or governed by a parliament. **2.** *Parliamentary law.* Of, relating to, or involving rules of order for the conduct of business in deliberative assemblies.

parliamentary authority. A parliamentary manual that an organization has adopted for its deliberations, and whose provisions govern the organization in every case to which they apply, as long as they are consistent with law and with the organization's governing documents. See PARLIAMENTARY MANUAL.

parliamentary borough. See BOROUGH (3).

parliamentary diplomacy. See DIPLOMACY (1).

parliamentary divorce. See *legislative divorce* under DIVORCE.

parliamentary inquiry. See INQUIRY (2).

parliamentary intent. See LEGISLATIVE INTENT.

parliamentary law. (18c) The body of rules and precedents governing the proceedings of legislative bodies and other deliberative assemblies. — Also termed *parliamentary procedure.*

"Thomas Jefferson speaks of 'the Parliamentary branch of the law.' From this country's beginning, it has been an underlying assumption of our culture that what has been authoritatively established as parliamentary law is in the nature of a body of law — in the sense of being binding within all assemblies except as they may adopt special rules varying from the general parliamentary law." Henry M. Robert III et al., *Robert's Rules of Order Newly Revised* xxx (11th ed. 2011).

▸ **common parliamentary law.** (1848) **1.** See *general parliamentary law.* **2.** The common law as applied to parliamentary law; parliamentary law as it is found in judicial decisions. • Except as dictated by constitutional, statutory, or other legally binding provisions, or the rules of an assembly or organization to which it is subordinate, a deliberative assembly transacts business in accordance with its own rules, precedents, and customs.

▸ **general parliamentary law.** (1845) The basic principles and practices of parliamentary law, as commonly understood among a meeting's members based on their experience in other deliberative assemblies or as explicated in a recognized parliamentary manual, that apply in the absence of adopted rules of order. — Also termed *common parliamentary law.*

"A deliberative assembly that has not adopted any rules is commonly understood to hold itself bound by the rules and customs of the *general parliamentary law* — or *common parliamentary law* . . . — to the extent that there is agreement in the meeting body as to what these rules and practices are." Henry M. Robert III et al., *Robert's Rules of Order Newly Revised* § 1, at 3 (11th ed. 2011).

parliamentary manual. (1838) A code or reference, usu. a commercially published book, that contains parliamentary rules and is offered for adoption by organizations as their parliamentary authority. • The leading parliamentary manuals in print in the United States are *Robert's Rules of Order Newly Revised* for nonlegislative bodies, and *Mason's Manual of Legislative Procedure* for state legislatures. Cf. PARLIAMENTARY AUTHORITY.

parliamentary motion. See MOTION (2).

parliamentary practice. See PARLIAMENTARY PROCEDURE.

parliamentary privilege. 1. See PRIVILEGE (1). **2.** See PRIVILEGE (5).

parliamentary procedure. (18c) **1.** PARLIAMENTARY LAW. **2.** Parliamentary law as applied in a particular organization, including the parliamentary authority and other rules that the organization adopts. — Also termed *parliamentary practice.*

parliamentary will. See WILL.

Parliament House. *Scots law.* The building in Edinburgh that is the site of the Court of Session, the High Court of Justiciary, the attendant offices of both courts, and the library of the Faculty of Advocates.

parliamentum insanum. See MAD PARLIAMENT.

parloir aux Bourgeois. [French] Guildhall; town hall. Pl. ***parloirs aux Bourgeois.***

Parmenides' fallacy. See FALLACY.

parody. (16c) *Intellectual property.* A transformative use of a well-known work for purposes of satirizing, ridiculing, critiquing, or commenting on the original work, as opposed to merely alluding to the original to draw attention to the later work. • In constitutional law, a parody is protected as free speech. In copyright law, a parody must satisfy the four-factor test for fair use of the copyrighted material, or else it may constitute infringement. See FAIR USE.

"Trademark parodies, even when offensive, do convey a message. The message may be simply that business and product images need not always be taken too seriously; a trademark parody reminds us that we are free to laugh at the images and associations linked with the mark." *L.L. Bean, Inc. v. Drake Publishers, Inc.*, 811 F.2d 26, 34 (1st Cir. 1987).

"We do not, of course, suggest that a parody may not harm the market at all, but when a parody, like a scathing theater review, kills demand for the original, it does not produce a harm cognizable under the Copyright Act. Because 'parody may quite legitimately aim at garroting the original, destroying it commercially as well as artistically,' the role of the courts is to distinguish between 'biting criticism [that merely] suppresses demand [and] copyright infringement[, which] usurps it.'" *Campbell v. Acuff-Rose Music, Inc.* 510 U.S. 569, 591, 114 S.Ct. 1164, 1178 (1994) (citations omitted).

par of exchange. (17c) The recognized standard value of one country's currency expressed in terms of that of another.

parol (pə-**rohl** *or* **par**-əl), *adj.* (16c) **1.** Oral; unwritten <parol evidence>. **2.** Not under seal <parol contract>.

parol (pə-**rohl** *or* **par**-əl), *n.* (15c) **1.** An oral statement or declaration. **2.** *Hist.* The oral pleadings in a case.

"Anciently pleadings were conducted in court orally, and the whole pleadings were called the parol; but for centuries the pleadings in civil actions have been required to be in writing." Edwin E. Bryant, *The Law of Pleading Under the Codes of Civil Procedure* 178–79 (2d ed. 1899).

parolable (pə-**rohl**-ə-bəl), *adj.* (1916) *Criminal law.* **1.** (Of a person) eligible for release on parole <parolable offender>. **2.** (Of a criminal offense) being of such a nature as to allow the offender at some point to become eligible for release on parole <parolable offense>.

parol agreement. See *parol contract* (1) under CONTRACT.

parol arrest. See ARREST (2).

parol contract. See CONTRACT.

parol demurrer. See DEMURRER.

parole (pə-**rohl**), *n.* (17c) *Criminal law.* The conditional release of a prisoner from imprisonment before the full sentence has been served. • Although not available under some sentences, parole is usu. granted for good behavior on the condition that the parolee regularly report to a supervising officer for a specified period. Cf. PARDON; PROBATION (1). — **parole,** *vb.*

> "The essence of parole is release from prison, before completion of the sentence, on condition that the prisoner abide by certain rules during the balance of the sentence. Parole is not freedom." 59 Am. Jur. 2d *Pardon and Parole* § 6 (1987).

▸ **bench parole.** See *bench probation* under PROBATION.

▸ **juvenile parole.** (1910) The conditional release of a juvenile offender from confinement. — Also termed *aftercare.*

▸ **medical parole.** (1961) The release of a terminally ill prisoner to a hospital, hospice, or other healthcare facility. — Also termed *compassionate release.*

parole board. (1898) *Criminal law.* A governmental body that decides whether prisoners may be released from prison before completing their sentences. — Also termed *board of parole; parole commission.*

parolee (pə-roh-**lee**). (1903) *Criminal law.* A prisoner who is released on parole.

parole-eligibility date. (1942) *Criminal law.* The date on which a prisoner, given his or her current circumstances, might first become a candidate for release on parole.

parole revocation. (1930) *Criminal law.* The administrative or judicial act of returning a parolee to prison because of the parolee's failure to abide by the conditions of parole (as by committing a new offense).

parol evidence. See EVIDENCE.

parol-evidence rule. (1893) *Contracts.* The common-law principle that a writing intended by the parties to be a final embodiment of their agreement cannot be modified by evidence of earlier or contemporaneous agreements that might add to, vary, or contradict the writing. • This rule usu. operates to prevent a party from introducing extrinsic evidence of negotiations that occurred before or while the agreement was being reduced to its final written form. See INTEGRATION (2); MERGER (2). Cf. FOUR-CORNERS RULE.

> "The basic principle is often called the 'parol evidence rule,' and according to this rule evidence is not admissible to contradict or qualify a complete written contract. The rule is usually stated in the form of a rule of evidence, but it is probably best regarded as a rule of substantive law. The question is not really whether evidence can be admitted which might vary the written document, but whether, if the evidence is admitted, it will have the legal effect of varying the document." P.S. Atiyah, *An Introduction to the Law of Contract* 161–62 (3d ed. 1981).

> "The parol evidence rule assumes that the formal writing reflects the parties' minds at a point of maximum resolution and, hence, that duties and restrictions that do not appear in the written document, even though apparently accepted at an earlier stage, were not intended by the parties to survive. In addition, and quite apart from the survival of matters discarded in the course of negotiations, there is the obvious danger of outright fraud." Marvin A. Chirelstein, *Concepts and Case Analysis in the Law of Contracts* 82–83 (1990).

parole violation. (1916) *Criminal law.* A parolee's breaching the terms of release in some material respect, as a result of which a hearing may be held and reincarceration imposed if warranted. — Also termed *violation of parole.*

parole warrant. See WARRANT.

parol lease. See LEASE.

parols de ley (pə-**rohlz** də **lay**). [Law French] Words of law; technical words.

parol term. See *supplementary term* under TERM (2).

parol trust. See *oral trust* (1) under TRUST (3).

Parratt–Hudson **doctrine.** (1986) The principle that a state actor's random, unauthorized deprivation of someone's property does not amount to a due-process violation if the state provides an adequate postdeprivation remedy. *Parratt v. Taylor,* 451 U.S. 527, 101 S.Ct. 1908 (1984); *Hudson v. Palmer,* 468 U.S. 517, 104 S.Ct. 3194 (1984).

parricide (**par**-ə-sɪd), *n.* (16c) **1.** The act of killing a close relative, esp. a parent. **2.** Someone who kills such a relative. Cf. PATRICIDE. — **parricidal,** *adj.*

parricidium (par-ə-**sid**-ee-əm), *n.* [Latin] (16c) *Roman law.* **1.** The murder of a near relative, esp. a parent. **2.** In ancient law, the murder of any free citizen. • This ancient, broad sense of *parricidium* gave way in pre-Imperial law to *homicidium* (homicide), which extended to the killing of a slave.

pars (pahrz). [Latin] *Hist.* A party to an action.

pars contractus (**pahrz** kən-**trak**-təs). [Law Latin] (1812) *Hist.* Part of the contract.

> "Verbal consensual contracts are binding upon the contracting parties immediately upon their consents being interchanged, and neither of them can afterwards resile from the transaction . . . . But if it be agreed that their contract shall be reduced to writing, such agreement being *pars contractus,* the contract is not finally entered into, nor does it become binding, until the writing has been executed." John Trayner, *Trayner's Latin Maxims* 436 (4th ed. 1894).

pars ejusdem negotii (**pahrz** ee-**jəs**-dəm ni-**goh**-shee-ɪ). [Latin] (1809) *Hist.* Part of the same transaction. • The phrase refers, for example, to an obligation attached to a condition, both of which must be considered together to constitute one transaction.

pars enitia (**pahrz** i-**ni**-shee-ə). [Law Latin "oldest's part"] *Hist.* An oldest child's portion of lands divided by lot.

pars fundi (**pahrz fən**-dɪ). [Latin] (18c) *Hist.* Part of the ground.

parsimony clause (**pahr**-si-moh-nee klawz). (2006) *Criminal procedure.* A sentencing-statute provision directing the judge to impose a sentence no stiffer than necessary to comply with the enumerated sentencing factors, such as the seriousness of the offense, the likelihood of further criminal conduct by the defendant, and the deterrence of others.

pars judicis (**pahrz joo**-di-sis). [Latin] (18c) *Hist.* The part of the judge. • The phrase *par judicis* referred to the judge's obligation to perform the duties of the office.

parson. See RECTOR (1).

pars rationabilis (pahrz rah-shee-ohn-**ay**-bil-is) See YORK, CUSTOM OF.

pars rea (**pahrz ree**-ə). (17c) A party defendant.

pars viscerum matris (**pahrz vis**-ər-əm **may**-tris). [Latin] (17c) *Hist. Scots law.* Part of the mother's body. • The phrase appeared in reference to a fetus.

part and pertinent. *Scots law.* See APPURTENANT.

parte inaudita (**pahr**-tee in-aw-**dy**-tə *or* in-**aw**-di-tə). [Latin "one side being unheard"] (18c) Of, relating to, or involving action taken ex parte.

parte non comparente (**pahr**-tee non kom-pə-**ren**-tee). (1805) *Hist.* The party not having appeared. • In civil cases, a party's failure to appear usu. resulted in a default judgment against the defendant. But in criminal cases, the accused's failure to appear raised no presumption of guilt; still, the offender was cited for contempt and made an outlaw. See OUTLAW.

partes beneficii (**pahr**-teez ben-ə-**fish**-ee-ɪ). [Law Latin] (17c) *Hist.* Parts of a benefice.

partes finis nihil habuerunt (**pahr**-teez fɪ-nis **nɪ**-hil hab-yoo-**eer**-ənt). [Law Latin "the parties to the fine had nothing"] (17c) *Hist.* A plea to set aside a conveyance of land on grounds that the transferor did not have a sufficient ownership interest in the property to alienate it.

> "Yet where a *stranger* . . . officiously interferes in an estate which in nowise belongs to him, his fine is of no effect; and may at any time be set aside . . . by pleading that '*partes finis nihil habuerunt*.'" 2 William Blackstone, *Commentaries on the Laws of England* 356–57 (1765).

partes soli (**pahr**-teez **soh**-lɪ). [Latin] (1805) *Hist.* Parts of the soil.

part exchange. See TRADE-IN.

partial, *adj.* (14c) **1.** Unfairly supporting one person, group, or organization against another; predisposed to one side of an issue. **2.** Not complete; of, relating to, or involving only a part rather than the whole. Cf. IMPARTIAL.

partial acceptance. See *varying acceptance* under ACCEPTANCE (1).

partial account. See ACCOUNT.

partial arbitration award. See ARBITRATION AWARD.

partial assignment. See ASSIGNMENT (2).

partial average. See *particular average* under AVERAGE (3).

partial award. See *interim award* under AWARD.

partial-birth abortion. See ABORTION.

partial breach. See BREACH OF CONTRACT.

partial defense. See DEFENSE (1).

partial dependent. See DEPENDENT (1).

partial disability. See DISABILITY (2).

partial emancipation. See EMANCIPATION.

partial eviction. See EVICTION.

partial evidence. See EVIDENCE.

partial excuse. See EXCUSE (2).

partial failure of consideration. See FAILURE OF CONSIDERATION.

partial guardian. See GUARDIAN (1).

partial insanity. See *diminished capacity* under CAPACITY (3).

partial integration. See INTEGRATION (2).

partial interdiction. See INTERDICTION (3).

partial intestate. See INTESTATE.

partiality. Bias or favoritism toward one person, side, or thing over others; an undue inclination to favor one side of a dispute over others. — **partial,** *adj.*

partial law. See LAW.

partial limitation. *Insurance.* A policy provision in which the insurer agrees to pay a total loss if the actual loss exceeds a specified amount.

partial liquidation. See LIQUIDATION (3).

partial loss. See LOSS.

partially disclosed principal. See PRINCIPAL (1).

partially integrated contract. See INTEGRATED CONTRACT.

partially undisclosed principal. See *unidentified principal* under PRINCIPAL.

partial pardon. See PARDON (1).

partial-performance doctrine. See PART-PERFORMANCE DOCTRINE.

partial release. See RELEASE (8).

partial-release clause. See CLAUSE.

partial responsibility. See *diminished capacity* under CAPACITY (3).

partial severance. See SEVERANCE (1).

partial summary judgment. See SUMMARY JUDGMENT.

partial truce. See *special truce* under TRUCE.

partial verdict. See VERDICT (1).

partial waiver. See WAIVER (1).

partial zoning. See ZONING.

partiarius (pahr-shee-**air**-ee-əs), *n.* & *adj.* [Latin] *Roman law.* **1.** A legatee entitled to a portion of an inheritance along with the appointed heirs. **2.** A tenant who is bound to hand over a portion of the crop in lieu of rent.

partibus (**pahr**-ti-bəs), *n.* (1829) *Scots law.* A note written in the margin of a summons stating the Lord Ordinary selected by the pursuer.

particeps (**pahr**-tə-seps), *n.* [Latin] **1.** A participant. **2.** A part owner.

particeps criminis (**pahr**-tə-seps **krim**-ə-nis), *n.* [Latin "partner in crime"] (17c) **1.** An accomplice or accessory. See ACCESSORY. Pl. ***participes criminis*** (pahr-**tis**-ə-peez).

> "The courts of justice will allow the objection that the consideration of the contract was immoral or illegal to be made even by the guilty party to the contract, for the allowance is not for the sake of the party who raises the objection, but is grounded on general principles of policy. A *particeps criminis* has been held to be entitled, in equity, on his own application to relief against his own contract, when the contract was illegal, or against the policy of the law, and relief became necessary to prevent injury to others." 2 James Kent, *Commentaries on American Law* *467 (George Comstock ed., 11th ed. 1866).

"Even in felonies but little practical importance now attaches to the distinctions between the first three of these four classes of 'accomplices' — a term which the law applies to all the *participes criminis*, whatever their degree of 'complicity' in the offence, though popular use generally limits it to those who take only a minor part. For the maximum punishment prescribed for any given crime is the same in the case of all three classes." J.W. Cecil Turner, *Kenny's Outlines of Criminal Law* 90 (16th ed. 1952).

2. The doctrine that one participant in an unlawful activity cannot recover in a civil action against another participant in the activity. • This is a civil doctrine only, having nothing to do with criminal responsibility. Cf. IN PARI DELICTO DOCTRINE.

particeps fraudis (pahr-tə-seps **fraw**-dis). [Latin "an accomplice in the fraud"] (17c) *Roman law.* Someone who participates in a fraud, esp. by helping to deceive a debtor's creditors. — Also termed *conscius fraudis.*

participating bond. See BOND (3).

participating insurance. See INSURANCE.

participating policy. See INSURANCE POLICY.

participating preferred stock. See STOCK.

participation, *n.* (14c) **1.** The act of taking part in something, such as a partnership, a crime, or a trial. **2.** The right of an employee to receive part of a business's profits; profit-sharing. See JOINT PARTICIPATION. — **participate,** *vb.*

participation loan. See LOAN.

participation mortgage. See MORTGAGE.

participation stock. See STOCK.

particular average. See AVERAGE (3).

particular average loss. See LOSS.

particular custom. See *local custom* under CUSTOM (1).

particular damages. See *special damages* under DAMAGES.

particular estate. See ESTATE (1).

particularity (pahr-tik-yə-**lair**-i-tee). (16c) **1.** The quality, state, or condition of being both reasonably detailed and exact <the requirement of pleading with particularity>. **2.** A quality that makes something different from all others; a peculiarity <the particularity of this fact situation>. **3.** A minute detail; a very specific fact <the particularities of her description>.

particular jurisprudence. See JURISPRUDENCE.

particular legacy. See LEGACY.

particular lien. See LIEN.

particular malice. See MALICE.

particular *non est factum*. See *special non est factum* under NON EST FACTUM.

particular partnership. See PARTNERSHIP.

particular power. See *special power* under POWER (3).

particular recital. See RECITAL.

particulars, *n. pl.* **1.** The material facts alleged in pleadings, including the specifics of any claim, defense, or other matter pleaded; specif., in a criminal case, the factual allegations of the charging instrument indicating the time, place, and manner of the alleged commission of the offense charged. **2.** The specific facts about a person's background. **3.** In a conveyance of real property, the description of the subject matter of the sale, including the seller's interest and the details of the title, together with the facts of any tenancies, easements, liens, and other encumbrances. — Also termed (in sense 3) *particulars of title.*

particulars, bill of. See BILL OF PARTICULARS.

particulars of sale. (18c) A document that describes the various features of a thing (such as a house) that is for sale.

particular successor. See SUCCESSOR.

particular tenant. See TENANT (1).

particular title. See TITLE (2).

partisan gerrymandering. See GERRYMANDERING (2).

partisanship. See PRINCIPLE OF PARTISANSHIP.

partitio (pahr-**tish**-ee-oh), *n.* [Latin] *Roman law.* Division; partition.

▸ ***partitio legata*** (pahr-**tish**-ee-oh lə-**gay**-tə). [Latin] A directive from a testator to an heir to divide the inheritance and deliver a designated portion to a named legatee; a testamentary partition.

partition, *n.* (15c) **1.** Something that separates one part of a space from another. **2.** The act of dividing; esp., the division of real property held jointly or in common by two or more persons into individually owned interests. — Also termed *partition in kind.*

"Partition is the segregation of property owned in undivided shares, so as to vest in each co-owner exclusive title to a specific portion in lieu of his undivided interest in the whole. The term 'partition' is generally, but not exclusively, applied to real estate. All kinds of property may be partitioned by the voluntary acts of the owners. In the case of real estate, this is usually accomplished by a conveyance or release, to each co-tenant by the others, of the portion which he is entitled to hold in severalty. But, even when no actual conveyance is made, a voluntary written agreement for a partition will be treated as such in equity, and specific performance will be enforced by conveyance. And a parol partition may be made of lands owned by tenants in common, provided each party takes and retains exclusive possession of the portion allotted to him." James W. Eaton, *Handbook of Equity Jurisprudence* 571 (Archibald H. Throckmorton ed., 2d ed. 1923).

▸ **definitive partition.** (1840) A partition that is irrevocable.

▸ **equitable partition.** (18c) A partition ordered by a court to achieve a fair division. — Also termed *judicial partition.*

▸ **involuntary partition.** (1878) A partition made over the objections of at least one owner of the property.

▸ **judicial partition.** See *equitable partition.*

▸ **partition of succession.** (1825) *Louisiana law.* The division of an estate among an intestate's heirs. See La. Civ. Code art. 1293.

▸ **provisional partition.** (1834) A temporary partition, often made before the remainder of the property can be divided.

▸ **statutory partition.** (1840) Partition authorized by and often regulated by a statute.

▸ **voluntary partition.** (1826) A partition agreed to and sought by all the owners of a property.

3. *Oil & gas.* The division of an undivided mineral interest by voluntary agreement or judicial action. — **partition,** *vb.* — **partible,** *adj.*

partition in kind. See PARTITION (2).

partner. (13c) **1.** Someone who shares or takes part with another, esp. in a venture with shared benefits and shared risks; an associate or colleague <partners in crime>. **2.** One of two or more persons who jointly own and carry on a business for profit <the firm and its partners were sued for malpractice>. See PARTNERSHIP. **3.** One of two persons who are married or who live together; a spouse or companion <my partner in life>.

▸ **dormant partner.** See *silent partner.*

▸ **general partner.** (1804) A partner who ordinarily takes part in the daily operations of the business, shares in the profits and losses, and is personally responsible for the partnership's debts and other liabilities. — Also termed *full partner.*

▸ **junior partner.** (18c) A partner whose participation is limited with respect to both profits and management.

▸ **limited partner.** (1822) A partner who receives profits from the business but does not take part in managing the business and is not liable for any amount greater than his or her original investment. — Also termed *special partner*; (in civil law) *partner in commendam.* See *limited partnership* under PARTNERSHIP.

▸ **liquidating partner.** (1825) The partner appointed to settle the accounts, collect the assets, adjust the claims, and pay the debts of a dissolving or insolvent firm.

▸ **name partner.** (1945) A partner whose name appears in the name of the partnership <Mr. Tibbs is a name partner in the accounting firm of Gibbs & Tibbs>. — Also termed *named partner*; *title member.*

▸ **nominal partner.** (18c) Someone who is held out as a partner in a firm or business but who has no actual interest in the partnership. — Also termed *ostensible partner*; *partner by estoppel.*

▸ **ostensible partner.** See *nominal partner.*

▸ **partner by estoppel.** See *nominal partner.*

▸ **partner in commendam** (in kə-**men**-dəm). See *limited partner.*

▸ **quasi-partner.** (1809) Someone who joins others in an enterprise that appears to be, but is not, a partnership. • A joint venturer, for example, is a quasi-partner.

▸ **secret partner.** (18c) A partner whose connection with the firm is concealed from the public. — Also termed *sleeping partner.*

▸ **senior partner.** (18c) A high-ranking partner, as in a law firm.

▸ **silent partner.** (18c) A partner who shares in the profits but who has no active voice in management of the firm and whose existence is often not publicly disclosed. — Also termed *dormant partner.*

> "It is worth emphasizing that control does not necessarily mean active involvement. One of the most interesting figures in partnership law, in fact, is the 'silent' partner — typically a person who has invested in a business in return for a profit share, and who reserves the right to, and to some extent may in fact, participate in routine management decisions, may participate in no decisions at all, and may even be unaware of what is happening in the business for long periods of time. The fact of the person's financial interest in the partnership may be a secret from everyone except the other partners (indeed, such secrecy may be vital). Such a person is nonetheless a partner like any other for purposes, among other things, of personal liability for the debts of the partnership. The law simply does not distinguish between active and passive partners." William A. Klein & John C. Coffee Jr., *Business Organization and Finance* 64 (2002).

▸ **sleeping partner.** See *secret partner.*

▸ **special partner.** See *limited partner.*

▸ **surviving partner.** (17c) The partner who, upon the partnership's dissolution because of another partner's death, serves as a trustee to administer the firm's remaining affairs.

partnership. (16c) A voluntary association of two or more persons who jointly own and carry on a business for profit. • Under the Uniform Partnership Act, a partnership is presumed to exist if the persons agree to share proportionally the business's profits or losses. Cf. JOINT VENTURE; STRATEGIC ALLIANCE.

> "Partnership, often called copartnership, is usually defined to be a voluntary contract between two or more competent persons to place their money, effects, labor, and skill, or some or all of them, in lawful commerce or business, with the understanding, that there shall be a communion of the profits thereof between them. Pufendorf has given a definition substantially the same. '*Contractus societatis est, quo duo pluresve inter se pecuniam, res, aut operas conferunt, eo fine, ut quod inde redit lucri inter singulos pro rata dividatur.*' Potheir says, that partnership is a contract whereby two or more persons put, or contract to put, something in common to make a lawful profit in common, and reciprocally engage with each other to render an account thereof: or, as he has expressed it in another place, '*Societas est contractus de conferendis bona fide rebus aut operis, animo lucri quod honestum sit ac licitum in commune faciendi.*' Domat says, that partnership is a contract between two or more persons, by which they join in common either their whole substance or a part of it, or unite in carrying on some commerce, or some work, or some other business, that they may share among them all the profit or loss, which they may have by the joint stock, which they have put into partnership. Vinnius says: '*Societas est contractus, quo inter aliquos res aut operae communicantur, lucri in commune faciendi gratita.*' The Civil Code of France defines it thus: 'Partnership is a contract, by which two or more persons agree to put something in common, with a view of dividing the benefit which may result from it.' Language nearly equivalent has been adopted by many other foreign writers." Joseph Story, *Commentaries on the Law of Partnership* § 2, at 4–5 (John C. Gray Jr. ed., 6th ed. 1868).

▸ **collapsible partnership.** (1962) *Tax.* A partnership formed by partners who intend to dissolve it before they realize any income. • Any partner's gain resulting from unrealized receivables or inventory that has increased substantially in value will be treated by the IRS as ordinary income rather than as capital gain. IRC (26 USCA) § 751. Cf. *collapsible corporation* under CORPORATION.

▸ **commercial partnership.** See *trading partnership.*

▸ **family partnership.** (1902) A business partnership in which the partners are related. IRC (26 USCA) § 704(e). • In this phrase, the term *family* includes a person's spouse, ancestors, lineal descendants, siblings, and any trusts established primarily for the benefit of those persons. See FAMILY-PARTNERSHIP RULES.

▸ **fixed-term partnership.** A partnership formed for a definite period of time. • When the term expires, the partnership automatically ends. — Also termed *partnership for a fixed term*; *partnership of a fixed term.*

▸ **general partnership.** (18c) A partnership in which all partners participate fully in running the business and share equally in profits and losses (though the partners' monetary contributions may vary).

▸ **implied partnership.** See *partnership by estoppel.*

▸ **limited-liability limited partnership.** (1994) A limited partnership formed under the 2001 Uniform Limited Partnership Act or similar statute whose certificate of limited partnership states that it is a limited-liability limited partnership — all obligations of the LLLP being solely those of the LLLP, whether arising in contract, tort, or otherwise. ULPA § 102(9). • Recognized in about half the states, an LLLP is most commonly found in the real estate industry. A general partner is not personally liable, directly or indirectly, by way of contribution or otherwise for an LLLP obligation solely by reason of being or acting as a general partner. ULPA § 404(c). Earlier LLLP statutes provided a more limited degree of protection for the general partners. — Abbr. LLLP. — Also termed *triple-L P.*

▸ **limited-liability partnership.** (1854) A partnership in which a partner is not liable for a negligent act committed by another partner or by an employee not under the partner's supervision; specif., modernly, a general partnership that has filed a statement of qualification under the 1997 Revised Uniform Partnership Act (RUPA) or similar statute in order to limit the liability of its partners. • An obligation of the partnership incurred while the partnership is an LLP, whether arising in contract, tort, or otherwise, is solely the obligation of the partnership. A partner is not personally liable, directly or indirectly, by way of contribution or otherwise, for such a partnership obligation solely by reason of being or acting as a partner. RUPA §§ 101(5), 306(c). Earlier LLP statutes provided less protection for the partners. — Abbr. LLP.

▸ **limited partnership.** (18c) A partnership composed of one or more persons who control the business and are personally liable for the partnership's debts (called *general partners*), and one or more persons who contribute capital and share profits but who cannot manage the business and are liable only for the amount of their contribution (called *limited partners*). • The chief purpose of a limited partnership is to enable persons to invest their money in a business without taking an active part in managing the business, and without risking more than the sum originally contributed, while securing the cooperation of others who have ability and integrity but insufficient money. — Abbr. L.P. — Also termed *special partnership*; (in civil law) *partnership in commendam.*

> "Unknown at common law, the limited partnership was derived from the *commenda* or *societe en commandite* of continental Europe to permit a person to invest and share in the profits of a partnership business and yet limit one's liability to one's investment. It was first recognized in the United States by a New York statute of 1822. It is now recognized by statute in all American jurisdictions." Henry G. Henn & John R. Alexander, *Laws of Corporations* § 28, at 86 (3d ed. 1983).

> "[T]he two primary characteristics of a limited partnership [are] liability of limited partners only for their agreed contributions, and a hierarchical structure with management in one or more general partners and very little power or authority in the limited partners. Thus, limited partners are typically — although not necessarily — passive contributors of capital. . . . In this respect they resemble shareholders in a corporation, but, depending on the details of the organizational documents, they may have greater or lesser rights." 3 Alan R. Bromberg & Larry E. Ribstein, *Bromberg and Ribstein on Partnership* § 12.01, at 12:5–12:6 (1999).

▸ **master limited partnership.** See *publicly traded partnership.*

▸ **nontrading partnership.** (1853) A partnership that does not buy and sell but instead is a partnership of employment or occupation. — Also termed *noncommercial partnership.* • This type of partnership offers services rather than goods.

▸ **particular partnership.** A partnership in which the members unite to share the benefits of a single transaction or enterprise.

▸ **partnership at will.** (1849) A partnership that any partner may dissolve at any time without thereby incurring liability. Cf. *partnership for a term.*

▸ **partnership by estoppel.** (1872) A partnership implied by law when one or more persons represent themselves as partners to a third party who relies on that representation. • A person who is deemed a partner by estoppel becomes liable for any credit extended to the partnership by the third party. — Also termed *implied partnership.*

▸ **partnership for a fixed term.** See *fixed-term partnership.*

▸ **partnership for a term.** (1845) A partnership that exists for a specified duration or until a specified event occurs. • Such a partnership can be prematurely dissolved by any partner, but that partner may be held liable for breach of the partnership agreement. Cf. *partnership at will.*

▸ **partnership in commendam.** See *limited partnership.*

▸ **publicly traded partnership.** (1982) A partnership whose interests are traded either over-the-counter or on a securities exchange. • These partnerships may be treated as corporations for income-tax purposes. IRC (26 USCA) § 7704(a). — Abbr. PTP. — Also termed *master limited partnership.*

▸ **special partnership.** (18c) **1.** See *limited partnership.* **2.** A partnership formed only for a single venture.

▸ **subpartnership.** (1859) An arrangement between a firm's partner and a nonpartner to share the partner's profits and losses in the firm's business, but without forming a legal partnership between the partner and the nonpartner.

> "[A] 'subpartnership' . . . is sometimes designated a partnership within a partnership, and . . . arises when a partner agrees with an outsider to share with him his profits derived from the business. Such person is not a partner, accurately speaking, nor is he under a partnership liability. The term 'subpartnership' is misleading. The so-called 'subpartner' has no relations whatsoever with the firm, but only with the person with whom he has contracted." Eugene Allen Gilmore, *Handbook on the Law of Partnership* 75 (1911).

▸ **tiered partnership.** (1985) An ownership arrangement consisting of one parent partnership that is a partner in one or more subsidiary partnerships.

▸ **trading partnership.** (1839) A partnership whose usual business involves buying and selling. — Also termed *commercial partnership.*

> "A trading partnership is one engaged in buying and selling as a business. 'The test of the character of the partnership is buying and selling. If it buys and sells, it is

"commercial or trading. If it does not buy or sell, it is one of employment or occupation.' 'Trading,' in its business sense, signifies, as a rule, the buying to sell again; but what are known as trading partnerships include also partnerships formed for manufacturing or mechanical purposes. The importance of the distinction between trading and nontrading partnerships lies in the fact that it is only in the case of trading partnerships that a partner has implied power to borrow money and give firm mercantile paper therefor." William George, *Handbook of the Law of Partnership* § 31, at 91–92 (1897).

▸ **umbrella limited partnership.** (1995) A limited partnership used by a real-estate investment trust to acquire investment properties in exchange for shares in the partnership. See *umbrella-partnership real-estate investment trust* under REAL-ESTATE INVESTMENT TRUST.

▸ **universal partnership.** (1816) A partnership formed by persons who agree to contribute all their individually owned property — and to devote all their skill, labor, and services — to the partnership.

partnership agreement. (1802) A contract defining the partners' rights and duties toward one another — not the partners' relationship with third parties. — Also termed *partnership articles; articles of partnership.*

partnership association. (1812) A business organization that combines the features of a limited partnership and a close corporation. • Partnership associations are statutorily authorized in only a few states. — Also termed *statutory partnership association; limited partnership association.*

partnership at will. See PARTNERSHIP.

partnership capital. The funds or assets contributed by partners toward the operation of a partnership.

partnership certificate. (1880) A document that evidences the participation of the partners in a partnership. • The certificate is often furnished to financial institutions when the partnership borrows money.

partnership distribution. See DISTRIBUTION.

partnership for a fixed term. See *fixed-term partnership* under PARTNERSHIP.

partnership insurance. See INSURANCE.

partnership life insurance. See *partnership insurance* (1) under INSURANCE.

partner's lien. See LIEN.

part payment. See PAYMENT (2).

part performance. 1. See PERFORMANCE (1). **2.** See PART-PERFORMANCE DOCTRINE.

part-performance doctrine. (1935) The equitable principle by which a failure to comply with the statute of frauds is overcome by a party's execution, in reliance on an opposing party's oral promise, of a substantial portion of an oral contract's requirements. — Sometimes shortened to *part performance.* See *part performance* under PERFORMANCE.

"Part performance is not an accurate designation of such acts as taking possession and making improvements when the contract does not provide for such acts, but such acts regularly bring the doctrine into play. The doctrine is contrary to the words of the Statute of Frauds, but it was established by English courts of equity soon after the enactment of the Statute. Payment of purchase-money, without more, was once thought sufficient to justify specific enforcement, but a contrary view now prevails, since in such cases restitution is an adequate remedy. English decisions treated a transfer of possession of the land as sufficient, if unequivocally referable to the oral agreement, apparently on the ground that the promise to transfer had been executed by a common-law conveyance. Such decisions are not generally followed in the United States. Enforcement has instead been justified on the ground that repudiation after 'part performance' amounts to a 'virtual fraud.' A more accurate statement is that courts with equitable powers are vested by tradition with what in substance is a dispensing power based on the promisee's reliance, a discretion to be exercised with caution in the light of all the circumstances." Restatement (Second) of Contracts § 129 cmt. a (1979).

part-sovereign state. See SOVEREIGN STATE.

part-time employee. See EMPLOYEE.

party. (13c) **1.** Someone who takes part in a transaction <a party to the contract>.

"Note, that if an Indenture be made between two as Parties thereto in the Beginning, and in the Deed one of them grants or lets a Thing to another who is not named in the Beginning, he is not Party to the Deed, nor shall take any Thing thereby." John Rastell, *Les Termes de la Ley* 471 (26th ed. 1721).

"A person who takes part in a legal transaction or proceeding is said to be a party to it. Thus, if an agreement, conveyance, lease, or the like, is entered into between A. and B., they are said to be parties to it; and the same expression is often, though not very correctly, applied to the persons named as the grantors or releasors in a deed-poll." 2 Stewart Rapalje & Robert L. Lawrence, *A Dictionary of American and English Law* 930 (1883).

▸ **party of the first part.** (18c) *Archaic.* The party named first in a contract; esp., the owner or seller.

▸ **party of the second part.** (18c) *Archaic.* The party named second in a contract; esp., the buyer.

2. One by or against whom a lawsuit is brought; anyone who both is directly interested in a lawsuit and has a right to control the proceedings, make a defense, or appeal from an adverse judgment; LITIGANT <a party to the lawsuit>. • For purposes of res judicata, a party to a lawsuit is a person who has been named as a party and has a right to control the lawsuit either personally, or, if not fully competent, through someone appointed to protect the person's interests. In law, all nonparties are known as "strangers" to the lawsuit.

"Those persons who institute actions for the recovery of their rights, or the redress of their wrongs, and those against whom the actions are instituted, are the *parties* to the actions. The former are, in actions at common law, called plaintiffs, and the latter, defendants. In real actions, the parties are styled demandant and tenant; in appeals, appellant and respondent; in admiralty practice, libellant and respondent; in equity, plaintiff (or complainant) and defendant; on writs of error, plaintiff in error and defendant in error; on certioraris, relator and defendant; in criminal proceedings, the king, or the people, or state, or commonwealth, and prisoner; (the person on whose complaint the proceedings were instituted being styled the prosecutor;) in the Scotch law, pursuer and defender; and in the civil law, actor and *reus.*" Oliver L. Barbour, *A Summary of the Law of Parties to Actions at Law and Suits in Equity* 18 (1864).

▸ **adverse party.** (15c) A party whose interests in a transaction, dispute, or lawsuit are opposed to another party's interests. Cf. *hostile witness* under WITNESS.

▸ **aggrieved party.** (17c) A party entitled to a remedy; esp., a party whose personal, pecuniary, or property rights have been adversely affected by another person's actions or by a court's decree or judgment. — Also termed *party aggrieved; person aggrieved.*

▸ **coparty.** See COPARTY.

▸ ***de micromis* party.** *Environmental law.* A party that has contributed a very small amount of waste to a polluted site. • A *de micromis* party must contribute some amount to cleanup costs.

▸ ***de minimis* party.** *Environmental law.* A party that has contributed a significant but not large amount of waste to a polluted site. • A *de minimis* party must contribute a substantial amount to cleanup costs.

▸ **fictitious party.** (18c) Someone who is named in a writ, complaint, or record as a party in a suit, but who does not actually exist, or a person who is named as a plaintiff but is unaware of the suit and did not consent to be named.

▸ **formal party.** See *nominal party.*

▸ **improper party.** A party whose involvement in a lawsuit is not permitted under a rule or statute or who has no connection with the subject matter of the suit.

▸ **indispensable party.** (1821) A party who, having interests that would inevitably be affected by a court's judgment, must be included in the case. • If such a party is not included, the case must be dismissed. Fed. R. Civ. P. 19(b). Cf. *necessary party.*

▸ **innocent party.** (16c) A party who did not consciously or intentionally participate in an event or transaction.

▸ **interested party.** (17c) A party who has a recognizable stake (and therefore standing) in a matter. — Abbr. IP.

▸ **joint party.** See COPARTY.

▸ **major party.** *Environmental law.* A party that has contributed a substantial amount or most of the waste to a polluted site, thereby being liable to perform cleanup work there.

▸ **necessary party.** (18c) A party who, being closely connected to a lawsuit, should be included in the case if feasible, but whose absence will not require dismissal of the proceedings. See *compulsory joinder* under JOINDER. Cf. *indispensable party.*

▸ **nominal party.** (18c) A party to an action who has no control over it and no financial interest in its outcome; esp., a party who has some immaterial interest in the subject matter of a lawsuit and who will not be affected by any judgment, but who is nonetheless joined in the lawsuit to avoid procedural defects. • An example is the disinterested stakeholder in a garnishment action. — Also termed *formal party.* Cf. *real party in interest.*

▸ **party aggrieved.** See *aggrieved party.*

▸ **party cast.** (17c) The losing party in a lawsuit.

▸ **party in interest.** See *real party in interest.*

▸ **party opponent.** (18c) An adversary in a legal proceeding. — Sometimes written *party-opponent.*

▸ **party to be charged.** (1923) A defendant in an action to enforce a contract falling within the statute of frauds.

▸ **prevailing party.** (17c) A party in whose favor a judgment is rendered, regardless of the amount of damages awarded <in certain cases, the court will award attorney's fees to the prevailing party>. — Also termed *successful party. See Buckhannon Bd. & Care Home, Inc. v. West Va. Dep't of Health & Human Res.*, 532 U.S. 598, 603, 121 S.Ct. 1835, 1839 (2001) (relying on the seventh edition of *Black's Law Dictionary* [1999]).

▸ **proper party.** (1823) A party who may be joined in a case for reasons of judicial economy but whose presence is not essential to the proceeding. See *permissive joinder* under JOINDER.

▸ **real party in interest.** (1804) A person entitled under the substantive law to enforce the right sued on and who generally, but not necessarily, benefits from the action's final outcome. — Also termed *party in interest*; (archaically) *interessee.* Cf. *nominal party.*

> "[T]he 'real party in interest' is the party who, by the substantive law, possesses the right sought to be enforced, and not necessarily the person who will ultimately benefit from the recovery. . . . The concept of real party in interest should not be confused with the concept of standing. The standing question arises in the realm of public law, when governmental action is attacked on the ground that it violates private rights or some constitutional principle. . . . Unfortunately, . . . confusion between standing on the one hand and real party in interest or capacity on the other has been increasing." Charles Alan Wright, *The Law of Federal Courts* § 70, at 490 & n.2 (5th ed. 1994).

▸ **successful party.** See *prevailing party.*

▸ **third party.** See THIRD PARTY.

3. Any one of two or more groups of people contending for rival opinions or policies within a society or community; POLITICAL PARTY. **4.** Partisanship; party zeal. **5.** A number of people assembled for some purpose, esp. for amusement or entertainment; also, an entertainment to which a number of people are invited. **6.** A detachment within a company of soldiers or other people. See SEARCH PARTY. **7.** Someone concerned in or privy to a matter; esp., someone involved in either of two sides in an affair <he was party to those secrets>.

party affiliation. (1848) An association with a political party, including membership but also sometimes based on vaguer connections such as self-identification or general sentiment in support of the party's values.

party-appointed arbitrator. See ARBITRATOR.

party-column ballot. See BALLOT (4).

party wall. See WALL.

party witness. See WITNESS.

parum cavisse videtur (**par**-əm kə-**vis**-ee VI-**dee**-tər). [Latin] *Hist.* He seems to have taken too little care; he seems to have been incautious. • This expression was used by a judge when pronouncing a death sentence.

par value. (1807) The value of an instrument or security as shown on its face; esp., the arbitrary dollar amount assigned to a stock share by the corporate charter, or the principal of a bond at maturity. — Often shortened to *par.* — Also termed *face value*; *nominal value*; *stated value.*

par-value stock. See STOCK.

parvis (**pahr**-vis). [fr. Old French *pareis* "paradise," fr. Late Latin *paradsus* "garden"] (15c) *Hist.* An academic exercise, such as a moot court. — Also spelled *pervise*; *parvise.*

PAS. *abbr.* PARENT-ALIENATION SYNDROME.

pass, *vb.* (14c) **1.** To pronounce or render an opinion, ruling, sentence, or judgment <the court refused to pass on the constitutional issue, deciding the case instead on

procedural grounds>. **2.** To transfer or be transferred <the woman's will passes title to the house to her nephew, much to her husband's surprise>. **3.** To enact (a legislative bill or resolution); to adopt <Congress has debated whether to pass a balanced-budget amendment to the Constitution>. See ADOPTION (5). **4.** To approve or certify (something) as meeting specified requirements <the mechanic informed her that the car had passed inspection>. **5.** To publish, transfer, or circulate (a thing, often a forgery) <he was found guilty of passing counterfeit bills>. **6.** To forgo or proceed beyond <the case was passed on the court's trial docket because the judge was presiding over a criminal trial>. **7.** ABSTAIN (1).

passage, *n.* (13c) **1.** ADOPTION (5); esp., the passing of a legislative measure into law. **2.** A right, privilege, or permission to cross land or water; an easement to travel through another's property. **3.** The process of traveling, esp. in transit <safe passage>. **4.** The act of coming and going <right of passage>.

pass-along, *adj.* See PASS-THROUGH.

passbook. (1828) A depositor's book in which a bank records all the transactions on an account. — Also termed *bankbook.*

passed dividend. See DIVIDEND.

passim (**pas**-im), *adv.* [Latin] (17c) Here and there; throughout (the cited work). • In modern legal writing, the citation signal *see generally* is preferred to *passim* as a general reference, although *passim* can be useful in a brief's index of authorities to show that a given authority is cited throughout the brief.

passing off, *n.* (1900) *Intellectual property.* The act or an instance of falsely representing one's own product as that of another in an attempt to deceive potential buyers. • Passing off is actionable in tort under the law of unfair competition. It may also be actionable as trademark infringement. — Also termed *palming off; misrepresentation of source.* Cf. MISAPPROPRIATION. — **pass off,** *vb.*

▸ **reverse passing off.** (1981) The act or an instance of falsely representing another's product as one's own in an attempt to deceive potential buyers. — Also termed *reverse palming off.*

passing on. See *pass-on defense* under DEFENSE (1).

passive, *adj.* Not involving active participation; esp., of, relating to, or involving a business enterprise in which an investor does not have immediate control over the activity that produces income.

passive activity. (1962) *Tax.* A business activity in which the taxpayer does not materially participate and therefore does not have immediate control over the income. • A typical example is the ownership and rental of real property by someone not in the real-property business.

passive adoption-registry statute. See ADOPTION-REGISTRY STATUTE.

passive bond. See BOND (3).

passive breach of contract. See BREACH OF CONTRACT.

passive concealment. See CONCEALMENT.

passive conduct. See CONDUCT.

passive covenant. See COVENANT (1).

passive debt. See DEBT.

passive duty. See *negative duty* under DUTY (1).

passive euthanasia. See EUTHANASIA.

passive income. See INCOME.

passive investment income. See INCOME.

passive loss. See LOSS.

passive mercy killing. See DYATHANASIA.

passive misrepresentation. See MISREPRESENTATION.

passive negligence. See NEGLIGENCE.

passive resistance. (18c) Opposition by noncooperation; specif., a method of protesting against something, esp. a government, by refusing to cooperate while using no violence.

passive trust. See TRUST (3).

passive use. See USE (4).

pass-on defense. See DEFENSE (1).

passport. (15c) **1.** A formal document certifying a person's identity and citizenship so that the person may travel to and from a foreign country. **2.** SEA LETTER. **3.** SAFE CONDUCT.

> "A passport is the universally accepted evidence of a person's identity and nationality. It does not give its bearer the right to travel in another country, but it does request that other governments permit him to travel in their territories or within their jurisdictions. It also entitles him to the protection and assistance of his own diplomatic and consular officers abroad." Burdick H. Brittin, *International Law for Seagoing Officers* 183 (4th ed. 1981).

▸ **diplomatic passport. 1.** A passport issued to certain government officials, esp. diplomats and their dependents, for government-work-related international travel, and granting admission without a visa to the holder when entering a country where the holder is or will be accredited as a diplomat. **2.** A passport given to a foreign citizen who has no passport and cannot obtain one for extraordinary reasons, such as legal exile.

passport control. (1919) The checkpoint at which passports and any necessary visas are checked when people leave or enter a country.

passport fraud. (1932) *Criminal law.* The crime of willfully and knowingly making a false statement in applying for or using a passport.

Passport Office. See BUREAU OF CONSULAR AFFAIRS.

pass the witness. See TAKE THE WITNESS.

pass-through, *adj.* (1951) (Of a seller's or lessor's costs) chargeable to the buyer or lessee. — Also termed *pass-along.*

pass-through security. See SECURITY (4).

pass-through taxation. See TAXATION (1).

past consideration. See CONSIDERATION (1).

past recollection recorded. (1904) *Evidence.* A document concerning events that a witness once knew about but can no longer remember. • The document itself is evidence and, despite being hearsay, may be admitted and read into the record if it was prepared or adopted by the witness when the events were fresh in the witness's memory. Fed. R. Evid. 803(5). — Also termed *recorded recollection; past recorded recollection.* Cf. PRESENT RECOLLECTION REFRESHED.

***Pasula–Robinette* test.** (1987) The principle that if a miner establishes a prima facie case of retaliation for filing a claim under the Mine Safety and Health Act, the mine operator can still prevail by proving, as an affirmative defense, that (1) the miner did not engage in a protected activity, (2) the adverse action was based on the miner's unprotected activity, and (3) the mine operator would have taken the same action based solely on the unprotected activity. • To establish a prima facie case of retaliation, the evidence must show that the miner engaged in a protected activity and that an adverse employment action occurred based at least in part on that activity. 30 USCA § 815(c); *Secretary ex rel. Pasula v. Consolidation Coal Co.*, 2 FMSHRC 2786 (1980); *Secretary ex rel. Robinette v. United Coal Co.*, 3 FMSHRC 802 (1981).

pat-down, *n.* See FRISK.

pateat universis per praesentes (**pat**-ee-at yoo-nə-**vər**-sis pər pri-**zen**-teez). [Law Latin] Let it be open to all men by these presents. Cf. KNOW ALL MEN BY THESE PRESENTS; NOVERINT UNIVERSI PER PRAESENTES.

***Pate* hearing.** (1975) A proceeding in which the trial court seeks to determine whether a criminal defendant is competent to stand trial. *Pate v. Robinson*, 383 U.S. 375, 86 S.Ct. 836 (1966); 18 USCA § 4241. — Also termed *competency hearing; incompetency hearing.*

patent (**pay**-tənt), *adj.* (14c) Obvious; apparent <a patent ambiguity>. Cf. LATENT.

patent (**pat**-ənt), *n.* (14c) **1.** The governmental grant of a right, privilege, or authority. **2.** The official document so granting. — Also termed *public grant.* See LETTERS PATENT.

▸ **call patent.** (18c) A land patent in which the corners have been staked but the boundary lines have not been run out at the time of the grant.

▸ **escheat patent.** See *escheat grant* under GRANT (4).

▸ **land patent.** (1821) An instrument by which the government conveys a grant of public land to a private person.

▸ **lapse patent.** (18c) A land patent substituting for an earlier patent to the same land that lapsed because the previous patentee did not claim it.

3. The right to exclude others from making, using, marketing, selling, offering for sale, or importing an invention for a specified period (20 years from the date of filing), granted by the federal government to the inventor if the device or process is novel, useful, and nonobvious. 35 USCA §§ 101–103. • The holding of a patent alone does not by itself grant any right to make, use, or sell anything if that activity would infringe another's blocking patent. — Also termed *patent of invention; patent right; patent grant.*

> "The franchise which the patent grants consists altogether in the right to exclude everyone from making, using or vending the patented article, without the permission of the patentee. This is all he obtains by the patent." *Bloomer v. McQuewan*, 55 U.S. 539, 549 (1852).

> "What, exactly, is a patent and how does it operate to foster the 'progress of the useful arts'? In its simplest terms a patent is an agreement between an inventor and the public, represented by the federal government: in return for a full public disclosure of the invention the inventor is granted the right for a fixed period of time to exclude others from making, using, or selling the defined invention in the United States. It is a limited monopoly, designed not primarily to reward the inventor (this may or may not follow), but to encourage a public disclosure of inventions so that after the monopoly expires, the public is free to take unrestricted advantage of the invention." Earl W. Kintner & Jack L. Lahr, *An Intellectual Property Law Primer* 7-11 (2d ed. 1982).

▸ **basic patent.** See *pioneer patent.*

▸ **blocking patent.** (1964) One of two patents, neither of which can be effectively practiced without infringing the other. • For example, if *A* patents an improvement of *B*'s patented invention, *A* cannot practice the improvement without infringing *B*'s patent. Nor can *B* use the improvement without infringing *A*'s patent. Owners of blocking patents often cross-license each other. See *fencing patent;* DOMINATION.

▸ **broadened reissue patent.** (1939) *Patents.* A patent that is issued again, having broader claims than the original, surrendered patent. • Under 35 USCA § 251, a patent may be reissued, under certain circumstances, with broader claims than the original patent if the reissue application is filed within two years of the grant of the original patent. See INTERVENING RIGHTS.

▸ **business-method patent.** (1998) A U.S. patent that describes and claims a series of process steps that, as a whole, constitutes a method of doing business. • Until 1998, methods for doing business were not expressly recognized as being patentable. In that year, the Federal Circuit Court of Appeals held in *State Street Bank & Trust Co. v. Signature Fin. Group, Inc.*, 140 F.3d 1368 (Fed. Cir. 1998), that business methods are subject to the same legal requirements for patentability as any other process or method. — Abbr. BMP. — Also termed *cyberpatent.*

▸ **combination patent.** (1868) A patent granted for an invention that unites existing components in a novel and nonobvious way.

▸ **Community patent.** (1966) An international patent issued by the European Patent Office. • Community patents are good for 20 years from the application date. They may be registered in any country in the European Union and other EPC signatories.

▸ **copending patent.** (1908) A patent whose application is being prosecuted at or near the same time as another, similar patent. • Continuing applications must be copending with an existing patent application. A copending patent may affect another patent's validity if it discloses the same invention, or discloses some part of the invention that, combined with other prior art, results in anticipation (esp. if the copending patent is issued before the affected patent). A copending patent may be shown to be an unpatentable improvement on another copending patent's invention. 35 USCA § 102(e). See COPENDING.

▸ **cyberpatent. 1.** See *business-method patent.* **2.** See *Internet patent.*

▸ **design patent.** (1875) A patent granted for a new, original, and ornamental design for an article of manufacture; a patent that protects a product's appearance or nonfunctional aspects. • Design patents — which, unlike utility patents, have a term of only 14 years from the date the patent is granted — are similar to copyrights. 36 USCA § 171.

▸ **dominating patent.** See *fencing patent.*

▸ **fencing patent.** (1944) A patent procured for some aspect of an invention that the inventor does not intend to produce but that the inventor wants to prevent competitors from using in making improvements. • By making a claim whose only purpose is to protect other claims, the inventor seeks to "fence in" any such competing improvements. Courts disfavor fencing claims. — Also termed *dominating patent.*

▸ **improvement patent.** (1910) A patent having claims directed to an improvement on a preexisting invention. • If the preexisting invention is patented by another, the owner of the improvement patent may need a license to practice the invention covered by the claims of the improvement patent. Similarly, the owner of the preexisting invention's patent may need a license to practice the invention in the improvement patent. Cf. *pioneer patent.*

▸ **in-force patent.** (1996) A patent that has not expired or been ruled invalid.

▸ **Internet patent.** A type of utility patent granted on an invention that combines business methods and software programs for Internet applications. — Also termed *cyberpatent.*

▸ **method patent.** (1920) A patent having method or process claims that define a series of actions leading to a tangible physical result. — Also termed *process patent.*

▸ **paper patent.** (1907) A patent granted for a discovery or invention that has never been used commercially. • A paper patent may receive less protection under the law than a patent granted for a device that is actually used in industry. As a prior-art reference, a paper patent may carry less weight with examiners than one for an invention that has been commercially exploited, because it may suggest that the invention did not work as claimed.

▸ **pioneer patent.** (1889) A patent covering a function or a major technological advance never before performed, a wholly novel device, or subject matter of such novelty and importance as to mark a distinct step in the progress of the art, as distinguished from a mere improvement or perfection of what had gone before. • Under U.S. law, the claims of a pioneer patent are entitled to broader interpretation and to be given a broader range of equivalents. A pioneer patent is usu. the first one documented by a patent-tracking service, although it may not be the first patent published by a national registry, such as the PTO. — Cf. *improvement patent.*

> "To what liberality of construction these claims are entitled depends to a certain extent upon the character of the invention, and whether it is what is termed on ordinary parlance a 'pioneer.' This word, although used somewhat loosely, is commonly understood to denote a patent covering a function never before performed, a wholly novel device, or one of such novelty and importance as to mark a distinct step in the progress of the art, distinguished from a mere improvement or perfection of what had gone before." *Westinghouse v. Boyden Power Brake Co.*, 170 U.S. 537, 561–62, 18 S.Ct. 707, 718 (1898).

▸ **plant patent.** (1931) A patent granted for the invention or discovery of a new and distinct variety of asexually reproducing plant. 36 USCA § 161.

▸ **process patent.** (1878) A patent for a method of treating specified materials to produce a certain result; a patent outlining a means of producing a physical result independently of the producing mechanism. • The result might be brought about by chemical action, by applying some element or power of nature, by mixing certain substances together, or by heating a substance to a certain temperature. See *method patent.*

▸ **reissue patent.** (1877) A patent that is issued to correct unintentional or unavoidable errors in an original patent, such as to revise the specification or to fix an invalid claim. • A reissue may correct patent defects that might call the validity of the patent into question. It is also used, although rarely, to make the claims broader or narrower. The patentee risks the possibility that previously allowed claims may be rejected. It does not change the term of the patent. 35 USCA § 251. — Sometimes shortened to *reissue.*

▸ **submarine patent.** (1994) *Slang.* A patent that is delayed in prosecution by the applicant in order to let an infringing user continue to develop its business, with the intention of taking in later-invented technology once the patent finally "surfaces" from the U.S. Patent and Trademark Office. • Typically, the patent applicant is aware of the developments and consciously delays the PTO's issuance of a patent, so that the invention's unwitting users will be forced to pay license fees. As of 29 November 2000, most patent applications must be published within 18 months of filing, so submarine patents are relatively rare now. See CONTINUATION-APPLICATION LACHES DOCTRINE.

▸ **utility-model patent.** See UTILITY MODEL.

▸ **utility patent.** (1883) A patent granted for one of the following types of inventions: a process, a machine, a manufacture, or a composition of matter (such as a new chemical). • Utility patents are the most commonly issued patents. 35 USCA § 101.

patentability opinion. See OPINION (2).

patentability search. (1919) An inventor's research into a field's state of the art to determine whether an invention will qualify for patent protection. Cf. INFRINGEMENT SEARCH; VALIDITY SEARCH.

patentable, *adj.* (1817) Capable of being patented <patentable processes>.

patentable combination. (1849) A series of process steps, mechanical elements, or a mixture of materials that produce a desirable result or effect that is not obvious from the qualities of the individual components or steps.

patentable subject matter. (1871) Things that by law can be patented; any machine, process, manufacture, or material composition, or an improvement to such things, that (1) is discovered or invented, (2) is new and useful, and (3) meets the statutory conditions and requirements to qualify for a patent. • Patents may be issued for "any new and useful process, machine, manufacture, or composition of matter, or any new and useful improvement thereof." 35 USCA § 101. Patents may not be issued for laws of nature, naturally occurring materials, physical phenomena, or abstract ideas and formulas. But if a naturally occurring material is processed in a way that gives it a new use, that process may be patentable. — Often shortened to *subject matter.* — Also termed *statutory subject matter.*

Patent Act. *Patents.* The current federal statute governing patent registrations and rights, enacted in 1952. 35 USCA §§ 1 et seq. • The Act reversed several Supreme Court doctrines of patentability by eliminating the synergism and "flash of genius" requirements for combination patents (§ 103), making "means-plus-function" claims valid once again (§ 112), and narrowing the patent-misuse doctrine of contributory infringement (§ 271). — Also termed *Patent Act of 1952*.

Patent Act of 1790. *Hist.* The first U.S. patent statute, establishing a board to examine patent applications, specifications, and drawings to determine whether the invention is "sufficiently useful and important" to justify the granting of a patent. • The examining board, comprising the Secretary of State, the Secretary of War, and the Attorney General, was abolished three years later in favor of a simple registration system.

Patent Act of 1793. *Hist.* An early U.S. patent statute that (1) abandoned the examination process in favor of simple registration (2) established the infringement defenses of invalidity for lack of novelty or public use; and (3) articulated the four categories of patentable subject matter as machine, manufacture, composition of matter, and art (now called *process*). • The State Department handled the registration of patents, and their question of their validity was left up to the courts.

Patent Act of 1836. *Hist.* The U.S. statute that charged the Patent Office with examining patent applications for novelty and utility, and that first required claims in patent applications.

Patent Act of 1870. A U.S. statute that shifted the burden of disclosing the exact nature of an invention to the patent applicant by requiring a rigorous listing of distinct claims. • Before the Act was passed, patent claims were less important than the description and drawings, and the scope of the patent grant was often ambiguous.

Patent Act of 1952. See PATENT ACT.

patent agent. See AGENT.

patent ambiguity. See AMBIGUITY (1).

Patent and Copyright Clause. (1929) *Constitutional law.* The constitutional provision granting Congress the authority to promote the advancement of science and the arts by establishing a national system for patents and copyrights. U.S. Const. art. I, § 8, cl. 8.

Patent and Trademark Depository Library. A library that has been designated by the U.S. Patent and Trademark Office as an official repository for information to aid in a patent or trademark search. — Abbr. PTDL.

Patent and Trademark Law Amendments Act. See BAYH-DOLE ACT.

Patent and Trademark Office. The Department of Commerce agency that examines patent and trademark applications, issues patents, registers trademarks, and furnishes patent and trademark information and services to the public. — Abbr. PTO.

patent application. (1893) *Patents.* An inventor's request for a patent, filed with the U.S. Patent and Trademark Office and accompanied by a specification (ending with at least one claim), drawings, the filing fee, and (except for a provisional patent application) an oath or a declaration.

▸ **allowed application.** (1897) A patent application for which the U.S. Patent and Trademark Office examiner has determined that at least one pending claim meets the conditions for patentability. • When an application is allowed, the PTO notifies the applicant through a Notice of Allowability and a Notice of Allowance. Once a patent application is allowed, a patent normally issues after the applicant has paid the required issue fee.

▸ **application for a reissue patent.** (1901) An application by a patentee to change the scope of a patent that has already been issued, or to correct clerical or technological errors in the issued patent. • The scope of the claims can be broadened only if the application is made within two years of the date the patent was issued. See *reissue patent* under PATENT (3). Cf. *certificate of correction* under CERTIFICATE.

▸ **child application.** (1973) A later-filed application in a chain of continuing applications filed during the pendency of an earlier application and sharing common subject matter. • The first-filed application is called the parent application. Cf. *parent application*.

▸ **continued-prosecution application.** (2000) A request to abandon a patent application after final rejection and reopen a new case with the same file wrapper as the parent application. • CPAs are authorized in 37 CFR § 1.53. — Abbr. CPA. — Also termed *Rule 1.53 application*. Cf. REQUEST FOR CONTINUED EXAMINATION.

▸ **continuing application.** (1870) A patent application that is filed while the parent application is pending and that carries on prosecution of some or all of the original application. • Continuation, continuation-in-part, divisional, and reissue applications are all forms of continuing applications.

▸ **Convention application.** (1927) A patent application filed in accordance with the terms of an international patent treaty such as the Paris Convention or the Patent Cooperation Treaty.

▸ **divisional application.** (1889) A patent application based on the same disclosure as the original application but claiming a different invention. • If an examiner finds that a disclosure reveals two or more distinct inventions, the applicant must restrict the original application to claiming one of the inventions. A divisional application can then be filed on any nonelected invention, and it will keep the same filing date as the parent application. — Often shortened to *divisional*. — Also termed *restriction application*.

▸ **file-wrapper continuation application. 1.** See CONTINUATION. **2.** See CONTINUATION-IN-PART.

▸ **grandparent application.** (1968) The first-filed application in a chain of at least three continuation or continuation-in-part patent applications.

▸ **informal application.** (1876) A patent application that is not in the correct form as required by the U.S. Patent and Trademark Office. • According to the Manual of Patent Examining Procedure, an application is informal if it is printed on both sides of the paper, or is not permanent, legible, or reproducible. An informal application may be corrected and still retain the original filing date.

▸ **international application.** (1967) An application under the Patent Cooperation Treaty for patent protection in specified member countries. • A PCT filing may be added as long as 31 months after the initial filing in a national patent office. It allows for simultaneous patent searches and examinations in multiple countries. — Also termed *PCT application*; *PCT filing*. See PATENT COOPERATION TREATY.

▸ **international application designating the United States.** (1971) An international-patent application that is filed in accordance with the Patent Cooperation Treaty and specifically seeks patent protection in the United States. • The application may be filed in any country, including the United States, that is a party to the treaty.

▸ **international application originating in the United States.** (1971) An international-patent application that is filed in the U.S. Patent and Trademark Office in accordance with the Patent Cooperation Treaty. • Under the treaty, the PTO acts as a receiving office for international applications. The applicant may or may not be seeking patent protection in the United States.

▸ **parent application.** (1905) The first-filed application in a chain of later-filed continuation or continuation-in-part applications. • An application becomes the parent application when another type of application (such as continuation, divisional, or substitute) is filed. The term "parent" is generally not used to refer to a provisional application. Cf. *child application.*

▸ **provisional application.** (1891) An application that can be filed up to a year before the patent application itself, in order to establish a date for prior art and constructive reduction to practice. • The PPA must include a full description of the invention, but claims, drawings and prior-art disclosures are not required. — Also termed *provisional patent application.* — Abbr. PPA.

▸ **restriction application.** See *divisional application.*

▸ **Rule 1.53 application.** See *continued-prosecution application.*

▸ **substitute application.** (1885) A duplicate application filed after the response period for a first office action has expired and the first application has been deemed abandoned. • A substitute application carries some danger for the applicant: the original filing date is lost, and any developments since that date become prior art that the examiner must consider before granting the patent.

patent-application amendment. (1971) *Patents.* A modification to a patent application, usu. narrowing or eliminating some claims in response to an examiner's rejection.

▸ **amendment after allowance.** (1959) An amendment submitted to the U.S. Patent and Trademark Office after the PTO has mailed notice of a patent application's approval. • Once a notice of allowance has been mailed, prosecution of the application is closed on the merits, and the entry of any amendment is within the discretion of the patent examiner. Amendments after allowance commonly address such matters as an amendment to the specification or claims, a change in the drawings or the list of inventors, and the submission of prior art. Amendments that merely correct formal matters in the specification or drawings, change the claims without changing their scope, or cancel a claim are typically approved by the Office. Amendments of greater significance require approval of the supervisory examiner under policies established by the group director. CFR § 1.312. — Also termed *312 amendment*; *Rule 312 amendment.* See *amendment after payment of issue fee.*

▸ **amendment after appeal.** (1909) An amendment made after an appeal is taken from a patent application's final rejection. • Such an amendment is not made as a matter of right but is frequently allowed if it puts the case in better form for consideration on appeal or helps implement an examiner's recommendation.

▸ **amendment after final action.** (1964) An amendment made after final rejection of the patent application. • The amendment may drop claims but not add them. To be entered, it may make changes in form, but may not raise new issues for the examiner. CFR § 1.116. — Also termed *Rule 116 amendment.*

▸ **amendment after payment of issue fee.** (1984) An amendment made by the applicant after the application has been allowed and the issue fee paid. • Such an amendment is not made as a matter of right but is governed by 37 CFR § 1.312. It must be accompanied by a petition to the Commissioner showing good and sufficient reasons why the amendment was not presented earlier. See *amendment after allowance.*

▸ **amendment before first action.** See *preliminary amendment.*

▸ **amendment in excess of filing fee.** An amendment to a patent application that increases the number of claims in the original application and requires payment of an additional fee.

▸ **preliminary amendment.** (1936) An amendment filed before the U.S. Patent and Trademark Office issues an office action on a patent application. • Amendments that are not filed with the original application are not considered part of the original disclosure. — Also termed *amendment before first action.*

▸ **Rule 116 amendment.** See *amendment after final action.*

▸ **Rule 312 amendment.** See *amendment after allowance.*

▸ **312 amendment.** See *amendment after allowance.*

patent attorney. (1870) *Patents.* A lawyer who drafts and prosecutes patent applications, and who represents inventors in infringement suits and interference hearings; esp., a member of the Patent Bar. • In addition to a law license, a patent attorney must have a scientific or technical background, pass the patent bar examination, and be licensed by the U.S. Patent and Trademark Office. Cf. AGENT.

patent claim. (1832) *Patents.* A formal statement describing the novel features of an invention and defining the scope of the patent's protection <claim #3 of the patent describes an electrical means for driving a metal pin>. Cf. SPECIFICATION (3).

> "[The patent] application concludes with one or more 'claims,' which are summaries of the points of novelty of the invention disclosed by the specification, said claims also following certain fixed forms. If they are broad and in general terms, the patentee will be well protected, and will be the possessor of a worth while patent; but if, on the other hand, the claims are limited in scope, if they recite a multiplicity of exactly stated and unimportant elements, or if they are bad in any one of a number of other ways, the chances of success are small, the patent will be full of loopholes of which infringers will be prompt to take advantage, the inventor will not have received all he is entitled to, nor all he has paid for, and, if the claims are very limited, it is more than likely that he will have obtained a patent not worth the paper upon which it is printed." Richard B. Owen, *Patents, Trademarks, Copyrights, Departmental Practice* 14 (1925).

> "The claims of a patent application are the 'legal heart' of the application and are the single most important part of the entire application. The claims define the scope of legal protection granted by the patent which eventually issues from the patent application. The claims define, in technical

terms, the extent of the protection conferred by a patent, or the protection sought in a patent application. The claims are of the utmost importance both during prosecution and litigation, since well over 95 percent of the prosecution will be directed to defining the invention, via the claims, to overcome the prior art, and since the claims of the issued patent will determine whether or not a product infringes on the patent." Morgan D. Rosenberg, *Patent Application Drafting: A Practical Guide* 1 (2012).

▸ **apparatus claim.** (1919) A patent claim on a mechanical device, explaining how the components are connected and function together. • The preamble of an apparatus claim typically states the function of the machine; the body explains its elements and how they work together.

▸ **appendant claim.** See *dependent claim.*

▸ **closed-ended claim.** (1991) A patent claim that expressly limits its scope to a list of elements, typically introduced by the phrase "consisting of." Cf. *nearly closed-ended claim; open-ended claim.*

▸ **coined-name claim.** A chemical-patent claim consisting only of the name of the new material. • A coined-name claim is allowed by the U.S. Patent and Trademark Office only on the rare occasion when the name is established in the field before the patent is applied for. The chemical composition, its physical properties, and the process for making it must still be disclosed in the specification.

▸ **dependent claim.** (1930) A patent claim that refers to and further limits another claim or set of claims in the same patent application. — Also termed *appendant claim.*

▸ **design claim.** (1938) The single claim allowed in an application for a design patent, incorporating by reference the drawing and other specifications. • The brief claim typically starts with "an ornamental design for" and ends with "as shown" or "as shown and described." Cf. *omnibus claim.*

▸ **fingerprint claim.** (1992) A chemical-patent claim that differentiates the material from prior art in terms of some physical feature, such as melting point or spectrum, rather than its chemical composition. • Fingerprint claims are allowed only when the chemical composition cannot be determined or cannot be distinguished from prior art.

▸ **generic claim.** (1879) A claim that encompasses a class of elements, any of which could function as equivalents. • For a generic claim to be valid, the specific elements it encompasses must have a definable feature in common that makes them fit for the purpose. — Also termed *genus claim.* Cf. *species claim.*

▸ **improvement claim.** See *Jepson claim.*

▸ **independent claim.** (1877) A patent claim that does not refer to any other claim.

▸ ***Jepson* claim.** (1943) An improvement-patent claim characterized by a preamble setting forth the current state of the art, followed by the phrase "the improvement comprising" and a description of the claimed patentable improvement. • The name comes from *Ex parte Jepson*, 1917 C.D. 62, 243 O.G. 526 (Ass't Comm'r Pat. 1917), in which this type of claim was first approved and sanctioned by the Commissioner of Patents. — Also termed *improvement claim.*

▸ ***Markush* claim.** (1933) A patent claim that includes elements listing alternative chemicals, materials, or steps in a process. • A *Markush* claim typically has language such as "selected from the group consisting of." The alternatives must all give the same result, rather than patentably distinct products. The name derives from *Ex parte Markush*, 1925 Dec. Comm'r Pat. 126. See MARKUSH DOCTRINE.

▸ **means-combination claim.** (1967) A type of claim in a patent application that includes multiple limitations, at least one of which is in means-plus-function or step-plus-function form. • Means-combination claims are acceptable to examiners.

▸ **means-plus-function claim.** See MEANS-PLUS-FUNCTION CLAUSE.

▸ **method claim.** (1895) A patent claim that describes what is done to a workpiece in order to achieve the useful result claimed. • A method claim is the same thing as a process claim, but "method" is used more often in applications for mechanical and electrical devices.

▸ **multiple-dependent claim.** (1970) A dependent claim that refers to more than one other preceding claim.

▸ **nearly closed-ended claim.** (2004) A patent claim that limits its scope to a list of elements but does not expressly exclude close analogues. The claim is typically introduced by a phrase such as "consisting essentially of." Cf. *closed-ended claim; open-ended claim.*

▸ **new-use claim.** (1976) A method claim for a new way of using an existing invention.

▸ **nonelected claim.** (1960) A claim that has been withdrawn from consideration based on the examiner's finding that the application claims more than one invention. • The applicant must elect to prosecute one invention. Other claims may either be abandoned or else be prosecuted separately under a divisional application. See RESTRICTION (4).

▸ **nonstatutory claim.** See *omnibus claim.*

▸ **omnibus claim.** (1922) A claim in a patent application that does not distinctly narrate a means to carry out a function but rather refers to the drawings or description with phrases such as "as described and shown." • Omnibus claims are rejected in the United States but are accepted elsewhere. — Also termed *nonstatutory claim.* Cf. *design claim.*

▸ **open-ended claim.** (1991) A patent claim that contains a nonexclusive list of elements, typically introduced by the phrase "consisting of." • A later patent applicant cannot avoid infringement by merely adding an analogue to the list. Cf. *closed-ended claim; nearly closed-ended claim.*

▸ **plant-patent claim.** (1933) The single claim in a plant-patent application, describing the principal distinguishing characteristics of the plant.

▸ **process claim.** (1879) A patent claim that describes by steps what is done to the subject matter, usu. a substance, in order to achieve a useful result. • A process claim is the same thing as a method claim, but "process" is used more often in applications for chemical patents.

▸ **product-by-process claim.** (1946) A patent claim defining a product through the process by which it is made. • The product-by-process claim is most often used to define new chemical compounds, such as drugs.

▸ **product claim.** (1919) A patent claim that covers the structure, apparatus, or composition of a product.

▸ **single-means claim.** (1930) A type of claim in a patent application that indicates a process, result, or function but does not describe the method of reaching that end <a method of curing cancer>. • Where no other method is obvious, such an assertion claims rights to all possible ways of achieving the result — ways not specified in the application and even ways that have not yet been invented. Single-means claims are rejected as too broad. — Also termed *single-element means claim.* Cf. MEANS-PLUS-FUNCTION CLAUSE.

▸ **species claim.** (1928) A claim that is limited to a single apparatus, process, composition of matter, or article of manufacture, rather than to a range of similar and related items. Cf. *generic claim.*

▸ ***Squires* claim.** (2009) A utility-patent claim that incorporates a drawing or table by reference. • This claim is allowed by the U.S. Patent and Trademark Office only if there is no practical way to define the invention in words, but the invention is simple to illustrate with the drawing or table. See SQUIRES DOCTRINE.

▸ **subcombination claim.** (1918) A patent claim, usu. on a device, describing a subsystem of a larger combination. • A subcombination may be patented separately if it has its own utility.

Patent Cooperation Treaty. *Patents.* A 1970 treaty that streamlined the process of securing patents in multiple countries by establishing a single filing date and providing for a single preliminary patent search. • An inventor who wants to qualify for patents from several member countries files a standard application in one country, thus preserving the priority date, then submits a PCT filing that designates which other countries' patents are being applied for. WIPO, the United Nations' World Intellectual Property Organization, administers the treaty. — Often shortened to PCT. See *international application* under PATENT APPLICATION.

patent danger. See *apparent danger* (1) under DANGER.

patent deed. See LETTERS PATENT.

patent defect. See DEFECT.

patent defect in title. See DEFECT IN TITLE (1).

patent deposit. See DEPOSIT (6).

patent disclaimer. See *statutory disclaimer* under DISCLAIMER.

patentee (pat-ən-**tee**). (17c) *Patents.* Someone who either has been granted a patent or has succeeded in title to a patent. • Although it might seem helpful to distinguish a patentee as a person to whom a patent is issued and a patent-holder as the owner of a patent, including the original grantee's assigns, the Patent Act explicitly includes all title-holders under the term "patentee." 35 USCA § 100(d). — Also termed *patent-holder; patent-owner.*

patent-exhaustion doctrine. (1977) *Patents.* The rule that the unconditioned sale of a patented article ends the patentee's monopoly right to control its use. • That control may still be exercised by limitations in a contract or license, as long as it does not amount to anticompetitive patent misuse. *Adams v. Burke*, 84 U.S. (17 Wall.) 453 (1874). See FIRST-SALE DOCTRINE.

patent grant. See PATENT (3).

patent-holder. See PATENTEE.

patent infringement. See INFRINGEMENT.

patent in suit. (1846) *Patents.* The patent currently being litigated; the patent at issue in the present lawsuit. — Also written *patent-in-suit.*

patent insurance. See INSURANCE.

patent marking. (1929) *Patents.* The incorporation or affixation of a patent number to a patented article's surface or surrounding packaging. • Affixing the patent number to a product gives constructive notice of patent rights to infringers. Without the number in place, a patentee can not recover losses that occur before the infringer has actual notice of the patent. 35 USCA § 287. See PATENT NUMBER.

▸ **false patent marking.** See *false marking* under MARKING.

patent medicine. (18c) A packaged drug that is protected by trademark and is available without prescription.

patent-misuse doctrine. (1950) *Patents.* An equitable rule that patentees should not be allowed to use their patent to effectively broaden the scope of their monopoly in restraint of trade or otherwise against the public interest. • Two common examples of anticompetitive broadening are (1) using a patent to restrain competition from an unpatented product or process, and (2) employing the patent beyond its lifespan to exclude others from gaining commercial advantages by using the product or process. The practical effect of finding patent misuse is the loss of patent protection. The doctrine operates independently of antitrust law but overlaps it in many ways and arose in the same era, at the turn of the 20th century. It has been described as an application of the equitable rule of "unclean hands." See *nonmetered license* under LICENSE.

patent number. (1868) *Patents.* The unique eight-character number that the U.S. Patent and Trademark Office assigns to a patent upon issuance. See PATENT MARKING.

Patent Office. See UNITED STATES PATENT AND TRADEMARK OFFICE.

Patent Office Reports. *Hist.* The former official publication of the U.S. Patent and Trademark Office. • It was replaced in 1872 by the Official Gazette of the United States Patent and Trademark Office.

patent of invention. See PATENT (3).

patent of precedence. (18c) *Hist.* A royal grant to someone by letters patent of a higher social or professional rank than the person would ordinarily hold or be entitled to. • In the 19th and early 20th centuries, the patent was most often used to give certain barristers more rights and privileges. For example, a King's Counsel could not represent a party against the Crown without a patent of precedence. See PREAUDIENCE.

patentor (**pat**-ən-tər *or* pat-ən-**tor**). (1890) Someone who grants a patent.

patent-owner. See PATENTEE.

patent pending. (1917) *Patents.* The designation given to an invention while the Patent and Trademark Office is processing the patent application. • The phrase warns others that a patent may issue and that if it does, copiers might become infringers. No protection against infringement exists, however, unless an actual patent is granted. — Abbr. pat. pend.

patent pool. *Patents.* **1.** An agreement between two or more patentees to license one or more of their patents to each other or to some other party. **2.** The aggregation of intellectual-property rights that are the subject of cross-licensing, whether they are transferred directly by the patentee to a licensee or to some vehicle specifically established to administer the aggregated interests, such as a joint venture.

patent pooling. (1930) *Patents.* The cross-licensing of patents among patentees. • Patent pooling does not violate antitrust laws unless it is done to suppress competition or control an industry.

patent-prosecution process. See PROSECUTION (4).

patent right. 1. See PATENT (3). **2.** See RIGHT.

patent-right dealer. (1868) Someone who buys and sells or brokers the sale or purchase of patent rights.

Patent Roll. *Hist. English law.* A list of the letters patent issued in the United Kingdom in any given year. • The first Patent Roll was issued in England in 1201. The Rolls were originally used to grant offices, lands, licenses, peerages, and pensions. In later centuries, they included grants of patents for inventions.

patent search. 1. See INFRINGEMENT SEARCH. **2.** See PATENTABILITY SEARCH. **3.** See VALIDITY SEARCH.

patent solicitor. See *patent agent* under AGENT.

patent suppression. (1923) *Patents.* The deliberate nonuse of a patent, esp. in order to deny the public or competitors the benefit of the invention. • Patent suppression is a rich source of urban legend, such as the rumor of oil companies sitting on inventions that would greatly improve gas mileage, or pantyhose companies suppressing a patent on no-run nylon. But the stories are not always fictional: in 1942 Standard Oil admitted trying to delay synthetic-rubber technology in order to protect its market in natural rubber.

patent term. (18c) *Patents.* The period during which a patent is in force. *See* 35 USCA § 154.

patent-term adjustment. (2000) *Patents.* The time enlargement that may be given to a utility or plant patent term if the issue of the original patent is delayed because of the U.S. Patent and Trademark Office's failure to prosecute the patent application. • Upon application by the patentee, the director of USPTO determines the period of any adjustment. The patent-term-adjustment provisions of the American Inventors Protection Act of 1999, as amended by the Intellectual Property and High Technology Technical Amendments Act of 2002, became effective on May 29, 2000 and apply to utility- or plant-patent applications filed on or after that date. 35 USCA § 154. — Abbr. PTA. Cf. PATENT-TERM EXTENSION.

patent-term extension. (1978) *Patents.* A lengthening of the time a patent remains in force, given to compensate inventors for time lost because of administrative delays such as interferences, secrecy orders, or appeals. • The extension applies to original utility and plant patents issued after June 7, 1995 and before May 29, 2000. Its maximum length is five years. — Abbr. PTE. Cf. PATENT-TERM ADJUSTMENT.

patent-term guarantee. (1994) *Patents.* An inventor's statutory right to extend the term of a patent if the application was delayed by the U.S. Patent and Trademark Office. • The term can be extended up to five years if the application was delayed because of an interference proceeding or appellate review, or if the PTO missed a statutory deadline for certain steps in the prosecution, or failed to grant the patent within three years of the filing date. The guarantee took effect May 29, 2000.

patent troll. See NONPRACTICING ENTITY.

patent watch. (1976) *Patents.* A system for continually monitoring published patent applications and newly issued patents in a particular scientific or technological field to detect or ensure against infringements.

patent writ. See WRIT.

pater (**pay**-tər), *n.* [Latin] (16c) Father.

paterfamilias (pay-tər-fə-**mil**-ee-əs *or* pah-tər-), *n.* [Latin] (15c) *Roman law.* The male head of a family or household, the senior ascendant male; esp., one invested with *potestas* (power) over another. — Also termed *homo sui juris.* See *patria potestas* under POTESTAS. Pl. **paterfamiliases** or ***patresfamilias.***

▸ **bonus paterfamilias** (**boh**-nəs). [Latin] *Hist.* Good father of the family.

paternal, *adj.* (15c) Of, relating to, or coming from one's father <paternal property>. Cf. MATERNAL.

paternalism, *n.* (1873) A government's policy or practice of taking responsibility for the individual affairs of its citizens, esp. by supplying their needs or regulating their conduct in a heavy-handed manner. — **paternalistic,** *adj.*

paternal line. See LINE.

paternal-line descent. See DESCENT.

paternal property. See PROPERTY.

paterna paternis (pə-**tər**-nə pə-**tər**-nis). [Law Latin] (17c) *Civil law.* Goods acquired through the father and therefore, in a further succession, descending to his relatives. • In Roman law, the phrase invoked the distinction between the succession of consanguinean half-brothers and uterine half-brothers. Cf. MATERNA MATERNIS.

paternity (pə-**tər**-ni-tee). (15c) **1.** The quality, state, or condition of being a father, esp. a biological one; fatherhood. Cf. FILIATION. **2.** ATTRIBUTION RIGHT.

paternity action. See PATERNITY SUIT.

paternity leave. See LEAVE.

paternity presumption. See PRESUMPTION OF PATERNITY.

paternity suit. (1945) *Family law.* A court proceeding to determine whether a person is the father of a child (esp. one born out of wedlock), usu. initiated by the mother in an effort to obtain child support. — Also termed *paternity action*; *parentage action*; *bastardy proceeding*; *bastardy process.*

paternity test. (1926) *Family law.* A test, usu. involving DNA identification or tissue-typing, for determining whether a given man is the biological father of a particular child. See DNA IDENTIFICATION; HUMAN-LEUKOCYTE ANTIGEN TEST; BLOOD-GROUPING TEST.

pater patriae (**pay**-tər **pay**-tree-ee *or* **pa**-tree-ee). [Latin] (16c) Father of the country. See PARENS PATRIAE.

pat-frisk, *n.* (1969) *Criminal procedure.* The patting down of a person in an attempt to discover something that the person might be carrying, esp. weapons.

pathfinder document. See *preliminary prospectus* under PROSPECTUS.

pathological intoxication. See INTOXICATION.

pathology (pə-**thol**-ə-jee), *n.* (17c) The branch of medical study that examines the origins, symptoms, and nature of diseases. — **pathological** (path-ə-**loj**-i-kəl), *adj.* — **pathologist** (pə-**thol**-ə-jist), *n.*

patiens (**pay**-shee-enz), *n.* [Latin] Someone who suffers or permits; the passive party in a transaction. Cf. AGENS (1).

patient, *n.* (14c) A person under medical or psychiatric care.

patient-dumping. (1966) A hospital's practice, mainly for economic reasons, of prematurely discharging patients, or denying care to women in labor or other emergency patients, or discharging, transferring, or referring unstable emergency patients to other facilities.

patient-litigant exception. (1951) *Torts.* An exemption from the doctor–patient privilege, whereby the patient, or someone claiming through or under the patient, can lose the privilege when the patient's mental or physical condition is brought into issue as the basis of a claim or defense in a lawsuit against the healthcare professional whose interests are adverse to those of the patient.

patient–physician privilege. See *doctor–patient privilege* under PRIVILEGE (3).

Patient Protection and Affordable Care Act. See AFFORDABLE CARE ACT.

patient's bill of rights. (1973) A general statement of patient rights voluntarily adopted by a healthcare provider or mandated by statute, covering such matters as access to care, patient dignity and confidentiality, personal safety, consent to treatment, and explanation of charges.

pat. pend. *abbr.* PATENT PENDING.

patria (**pay**-tree-ə *or* **pa**-tree-ə), *n.* [Latin] (18c) **1.** *Roman law.* The fatherland; a person's home area. **2.** *Hist.* The country or the area within it, such as a county or neighborhood. **3.** *Hist.* A jury, as when a defendant "puts himself upon the country" (*ponit se super patriam*). See CONCLUSION TO THE COUNTRY; GOING TO THE COUNTRY; PAYS.

> "Though our Latin uses *patria*, our French uses *pays*, which descends from Latin *pagus*. The 'country' of this formula is not our father-land but 'the country-side.'" 2 Frederick Pollock & Frederic W. Maitland, *The History of English Law Before the Time of Edward I* 624 n.1 (2d ed. 1899).

patria potestas. See POTESTAS.

patriarch. (bef. 12c) **1.** A man who rules or dominates a social or political group. **2.** *Eccles. law.* The title of the most senior bishop in the Orthodox or Roman Catholic Church. Cf. MATRIARCH.

patriarchate. (17c) **1.** The title, office, or position of a patriarch. **2.** The geopolitical area ruled by a patriarch. See PATRIARCH; PATRIARCHY.

patriarchy. (17c) **1.** A social or political system in which men govern. **2.** A social system in which descent and inheritance are traced through the male line. Cf. GYNECOCRACY; MATRIARCHY.

patriation. (1975) *Canadian law.* The process of transferring constitution-related legislation or documents from a former colonial power to a country that was once a dependency of that power.

> "The word 'patriation' is a Canadian neologism that describes the bringing of the Canadian Constitution to Canada. Although this may sound strange to non-Canadian readers, Canada's formal Constitution was, before 1982, to be found in a U.K. statute. Therefore, only the U.K. Parliament was competent to amend it and to formally terminate its authority over future constitutional amendments. As a U.K. statute, the Canadian Constitution had never been in Canada. Therefore, it could not be 'repatriated.' Hence the use of the word 'patriation.'" Jean-Francois Gaudreault-Desbiens, *The Quebec Secession Reference and the Judicial Arbitration of Conflicting Narratives About Law, Democracy, and Identity*, 23 Vt. L. Rev. 793, 807 n.43 (1999).

patrician (pə-**trish**-ən), *n.* (15c) *Roman law.* One of a privileged class of Roman citizens, as contrasted with plebeians. • Originally probably the rank was only by birth. They monopolized all the priesthoods, and probably their class was defined by religious prerogatives, but senate membership was not confined to patricians. They lost their monopolies by B.C. 300, but one consul continued to be a patrician, and they held at least half the priestly offices. Emperors could and did confer patrician status on favored individuals. The hereditary patricians disappeared in the third century A.D., but later emperors revived the title as a personal honor for faithful service.

patricide (**pa**-trə-sɪd), *n.* (16c) **1.** The act of killing one's own father. **2.** Someone who kills his or her father. Cf. PARRICIDE. — **patricidal,** *adj.*

patrilineal (pat-ri-**lin**-ee-əl), *adj.* (1904) **1.** Of, relating to, or involving the paternal family line <patrilineal ancestry>. **2.** (Of a legal system) tracing descent through the paternal line <patrilineal system>. — Also termed *patrilinear.*

patrilineal descendant. See DESCENDANT.

patrilinealism. See PATRILINY.

patrilinear. See PATRILINEAL.

patrilinearism. See PATRILINY.

patriliny (**pat**-ri-li-nee), *n.* (1906) The practice of tracing lineage or descent patrilineally. — Also termed *patrilinealism; patrilinearism.*

patrimonial (pa-trə-**moh**-nee-əl), *adj.* (16c) Of, relating to, or involving an inheritance, esp. from a male ancestor.

patrimonio ejus abest (pa-trə-**moh**-nee-oh **ee**-jəs **ab**-est). [Latin] (18c) *Hist.* That which is wanting from a person's estate. • The phrase includes items held by one person but due to another, such as stolen goods or money for an unpaid debt.

patrimonium (pa-trə-**moh**-nee-əm), *n.* [Latin] *Roman law.* Property that is capable of being inherited; private property. — Also termed *patrimony.*

patrimony (**pa**-tri-moh-nee). (14c) **1.** An estate inherited from one's father or other ancestor; legacy or heritage. **2.** *Civil law.* All of a person's assets and liabilities that are capable of monetary valuation and subject to execution for a creditor's benefit. **3.** PATRIMONIUM.

Patriot Act. See USA PATRIOT ACT.

patron. (15c) **1.** A customer or client of a business, esp. a regular one. **2.** A licensee invited or permitted to enter leased land for the purpose for which it is leased. **3.** Someone who protects, supports, or champions some person or thing, such as an institution, social function, or cause; a benefactor.

patronage (**pay**-trə-nij). (16c) **1.** The giving of support, sponsorship, or protection. **2.** All the customers of a business; clientele. **3.** The power to appoint persons to governmental positions or to confer other political favors. — Also termed (in sense 3) *political patronage.* See SPOILS SYSTEM.

patronizing a prostitute. (1956) The offense of requesting or securing the performance of a sex act for a fee; PROSTITUTION. Cf. SOLICITATION (3).

patronus (pə-**troh**-nəs), *n.* [Latin] **1.** *Roman law.* Someone who had manumitted a slave, and was therefore entitled to certain services from the slave. **2.** ADVOWEE. Pl. ***patroni*** (pə-**troh**-nı).

patruus (**pa**-troo-əs), *n.* [Latin] *Roman & civil law.* A father's brother; a paternal uncle.

patruus magnus (**pa**-troo-əs **mag**-nəs), *n.* [Latin] (16c) *Roman & civil law.* A grandfather's brother; a great-uncle.

patruus major (**pa**-troo-əs **may**-jər), *n.* [Latin] *Roman law.* A great grandfather's brother.

patruus maximus (**pa**-troo-əs **mak**-sə-məs). See ABPATRUUS.

pattern, *n.* (1883) A mode of behavior or series of acts that are recognizably consistent <a pattern of racial discrimination>.

pattern jury charge. See *model jury instruction* under JURY INSTRUCTION.

pattern jury direction. See *model jury instruction* under JURY INSTRUCTION.

pattern jury instruction. See *model jury instruction* under JURY INSTRUCTION.

pattern of racketeering activity. (1972) Two or more related criminal acts that amount to, or pose a threat of, continued criminal activity. • This phrase derives from the federal Racketeer Influenced and Corrupt Organizations Act. See RACKETEERING.

pattern-or-practice case. (1970) A lawsuit, often a class action, in which the plaintiff attempts to show that the defendant has systematically engaged in discriminatory activities, esp. by means of policies and procedures. • Typically, such a case involves employment discrimination, housing discrimination, or school segregation. A plaintiff must usu. show that a defendant's behavior forms a pattern of actions or is embedded in routine practices but inferences of executive or official complicity may be drawn from a consistent failure to respond to complaints or implement corrective measures.

pattern similarity. See *comprehensive nonliteral similarity* under SIMILARITY.

paucital (**paw**-si-təl), *adj. Rare.* See IN PERSONAM.

Pauline privilege. (1901) *Eccles. law.* The doctrine that a baptized person's marriage to a never-baptized person may be dissolved under certain circumstances, when dissolution is beneficial to the Roman Catholic Church. • The privilege is ordinarily exercised when (1) the marriage was valid, (2) the baptized spouse now wishes to marry a Catholic, and (3) at the time of the marriage, both parties were unbaptized in any faith. Before the privilege can be exercised, four conditions must be satisfied: (1) the unbaptized spouse must have deserted the baptized spouse without just cause, (2) the unbaptized spouse must still be unbaptized, (3) the baptized spouse must make the proper appeals to the Church, and (4) the Church must rule that the privilege is exercisable. There is uncertainty about the extent of the privilege. Cf. PETRINE PRIVILEGE.

pauper. (16c) A very poor person, esp. one who receives aid from charity or public funds; INDIGENT. See IN FORMA PAUPERIS.

pauperies (**paw**-pər-eez), *n.* [Latin "impoverishment"] *Roman law.* Damage done by a domesticated four-footed animal. • The animal's owner was liable for the damage or was required to give the animal to the injured person. For an etymological treatment of the term, see Alan Watson, "The Original Meaning of *Pauperies,*" in *Legal Origins and Legal Change* 129 (1991). See *actio de pauperie* under ACTIO.

pauper's affidavit. See *poverty affidavit* under AFFIDAVIT.

pauper's oath. See OATH.

pawn, *n.* (15c) **1.** An item of personal property deposited as security for a debt; a pledge or guarantee. • In modern usage, the term is usu. restricted to the pledge of jewels and other personal chattels to pawnbrokers as security for a small loan. **2.** The act of depositing personal property in this manner. **3.** The condition of being held on deposit as a pledge. **4.** PIGNUS (1). Cf. BAILMENT (1). — **pawn,** *vb.*

pawnbroker, *n.* (17c) Someone who lends money, usu. at a high interest rate, in exchange for personal property that is deposited as security by the borrower. • If the money is not paid back, the pawnbroker may sell the personal property. Cf. MONEYLENDER. — **pawnbroking,** *n.*

> "Pawnbrokers are those who make a business of loaning money on the security of corporeal property, rather than incorporeal property, such as corporate stock. In many countries, as in France, the business of pawnbroking is carried on as a public institution, so that money may be borrowed by the poor at a reasonable rate of interest. In England and in the United States, however, it is carried on, just as any other enterprise, by individuals; but in almost all of the states of this country the business is to a greater or less degree regulated by special statutes." Armistead M. Dobie, *Handbook on the Law of Bailments and Carriers* 174 (1914).

pawnee. (18c) Someone who receives a deposit of personal property as security for a debt.

pawnor. (1846) Someone who deposits an item of personal property as security for a debt. — Also spelled *pawner.*

pax in maribus (**paks** in **mar**-i-bəs). [Latin] *Hist.* Peace on the seas.

pax in terris (**paks** in **ter**-is). [Latin] *Hist.* Peace on the lands.

pax regis (**paks ree**-jis), *n.* [Latin "the king's peace"] (17c) *Hist.* **1.** The king's guarantee of peace and security of life and property to all within his protection. See KING'S PEACE. **2.** VERGE (1).

pay, *n.* (14c) **1.** Compensation for services performed; salary, wages, stipend, or other remuneration given for work done.

▸ **danger pay.** Additional compensation that a worker is paid for doing dangerous work. — Also termed *damage money.*

▸ **equal pay.** (18c) Pay that is based on kind and quality of work done, such that two or more employees earn the same amount for the same work, and not according to any individual or group characteristic unrelated to ability, qualification, or performance.

▸ **fair pay.** (18c) Pay that is reasonably related to the competitive market value of the employee's skill and job performance.

▸ **deferred pay.** Any type of postponed compensation for services performed.

▸ **half pay. 1.** Fifty percent of the compensation for services performed. **2.** Reduced pay; esp., a reduced allowance paid to an officer when not in actual service or after retirement.

▸ **hazard pay.** (1956) Special compensation for work done under unpleasant or unsafe conditions.

▸ **performance-related pay.** (1982) Compensation that is increased if the worker does an especially effective job; a bonus or other salary enhancement given on grounds of exemplary results on the job.

▸ **redundancy pay.** See SEVERANCE PAY.

2. The act of paying or being paid. **3.** Someone considered from the viewpoint of reliability and promptness in meeting financial obligations. **4.** Metaphorically, retribution or punishment.

pay, *vb.* (13c) **1.** To give money for a good or service that one buys; to make satisfaction <pay by credit card>. **2.** To transfer money that one owes to a person, company, etc. <pay the utility bill>. **3.** To give (someone) money for the job that he or she does; to compensate a person for his or her occupation; COMPENSATE (1) <she gets paid twice a month>. **4.** To give (money) to someone because one has been ordered by a court to do so <pay the damages>. **5.** To be profitable; to bring in a return <the venture paid 9%>.

payable, *adj.* (14c) (Of a sum of money or a negotiable instrument) that is to be paid. • An amount may be payable without being due. Debts are commonly payable long before they fall due. Cf. DUE AND PAYABLE.

▸ **payable after sight.** (18c) Payable after acceptance or protest of nonacceptance. See *sight draft* under DRAFT (1).

▸ **payable at call.** (1860) Payable immediately upon demand.

▸ **payable at sight.** (18c) Payable immediately upon presentation. See *bill payable at sight* under BILL (6).

▸ **payable on demand.** (17c) Payable when presented or upon request for payment; payable at once at any time.

▸ **payable to bearer.** (18c) Payable to anyone holding the instrument.

▸ **payable to order.** (17c) Payable only to a specified payee.

payable, *n.* See *account payable* under ACCOUNT.

payable date. See DATE.

pay any bank. (1902) A draft indorsement that permits only banks to acquire the rights of a holder until the draft is either returned to the customer initiating collection or specially indorsed by a bank to a person who is not a bank. UCC § 4-201(b). • A bank normally endorses an item "Pay any bank" when forwarding it for collection, regardless of the type of indorsement (if any) the item carries at first receipt. The indorsement protects the collecting bank by preventing the item from straying from the regular bank-collection process.

payback. (18c) **1.** The act or an instance of repaying someone. **2.** The return on an investment, esp. an investment of capital. **3.** *Slang.* Revenge or retribution, esp. of a petty nature.

payback method. (1953) An accounting procedure that measures the time required to recover a venture's initial cash investment.

payback period. (1953) The length of time required to recover a venture's initial cash investment, without accounting for the time value of money.

paycheck, *n.* (1864) **1.** A check in payment of a salary or wages. **2.** The amount in wages that someone earns.

payday, *n.* (16c) **1.** A day scheduled for issuance of paychecks. **2.** The day on which stock transfers must be paid for.

payday advance. See *payday loan* under LOAN.

payday loan. See LOAN.

paydown, *n.* (1967) A loan payment in an amount less than the total loan principal.

payee. (18c) One to whom money is paid or payable; esp., a party named in commercial paper as the recipient of the payment. Cf. PAYOR.

payer. See PAYOR.

paygrade, *n.* (1883) The rank of an employee, esp. military personnel, based on a scale of salaries or wages.

pay-if-paid clause. See CLAUSE.

paying quantities. (1873) *Oil & gas.* An amount of mineral production from a single well sufficient to justify a reasonably prudent operator to continue producing from that well. • Most jurisdictions interpret the language "for so long thereafter as oil and gas is produced" in habendum clauses to mean so long as paying quantities are produced. See HABENDUM CLAUSE.

paylist, *n.* See PAYROLL (1).

paymaster, *n.* (16c) A corporate or governmental officer in charge of paying salaries or wages to employees. — **paymastership,** *n.*

payment. (14c) **1.** Performance of an obligation by the delivery of money or some other valuable thing accepted in partial or full discharge of the obligation. **2.** The money or other valuable thing so delivered in satisfaction of an obligation.

▸ **advance payment.** (16c) A payment made in anticipation of a contingent or fixed future liability or obligation.

▸ **balloon payment.** (1935) A final loan payment that is usu. much larger than the preceding regular payments and that discharges the principal balance of the loan. See *balloon note* under NOTE (1).

▸ **benefactor payment.** (1985) The payment of a defense attorney's fees by a third party rather than by the defendant. • Benefactor payments raise ethical questions about who the attorney's loyalty is with (the client or the benefactor) and may produce a conflict of interest. In a criminal case, they may also be considered evidence of a criminal enterprise.

▸ **conditional payment.** (17c) Payment of an obligation only on condition that something be done. • Generally, the payor reserves the right to demand the payment back if the condition is not met.

▸ **constructive payment.** (1827) A payment made by the payor but not yet credited by the payee. • For example, a rent check mailed on the first of the month is a constructive payment even though the landlord does not deposit the check until ten days later.

▸ **direct payment.** (18c) **1.** A payment made directly to the payee, without using an intermediary, such as a child-support payment made directly to the obligee parent rather than through the court. **2.** A payment that is absolute and unconditional on the amount, the due date, and the payee.

▸ **down payment.** (1926) The portion of a purchase price paid in cash (or its equivalent) at the time the sale agreement is executed. Cf. BINDER (2); EARNEST MONEY.

▸ **indefinite payment.** (18c) **1.** A stream of payments with no termination date, or a single payment with no specified due date. **2.** A payment that does not specify to which debt it should be applied when it is made to a single creditor who holds several of the payor's debts.

▸ **installment payment.** (1901) One of a series of periodic payments made under an installment plan. — Also termed *interim payment.* See INSTALLMENT SALE.

▸ **interim payment.** See *installment payment.*

▸ **involuntary payment.** (18c) A payment obtained by fraud or duress.

▸ **lump-sum payment.** (1914) A payment of a large amount all at once, as opposed to a series of smaller payments over time. Cf. *periodic payment.*

▸ **mobile payment.** See MOBILE MONEY.

▸ **overpayment.** (16c) A payment that is more than the amount owed or due. *See Sorenson v. Secretary of Treasury,* 475 U.S. 851, 854–55, 106 S.Ct. 1600, 1603–04 (1986).

▸ **part payment.** (15c) A buyer's delivery of money or other thing of value to the seller, and its acceptance by the seller, when the money or the value of the thing does not equal the full sum owed.

▸ **periodic payment.** (1873) One of a series of payments made over time instead of a one-time payment for the full amount. Cf. *lump-sum payment.*

▸ **two-party payment.** (1985) A single payment made by check to two people, usu. for the sum of the amount due to each person.

▸ **unofficious payment.** (1984) A payment made by a person who has an interest in seeing that it should be made.

3. A disbursement of money. **4.** A dividend; an amount paid out from earnings.

payment bond. See BOND (2).

payment date. See DATE.

payment in due course. (1816) A payment to the holder of a negotiable instrument at or after its maturity date, made by the payor in good faith and without notice of any defect in the holder's title. See HOLDER IN DUE COURSE.

payment intangible. See INTANGIBLE.

payment into court. (1829) A party's money or property deposited with a court for distribution after a proceeding according to the parties' settlement or the court's order. See INTERPLEADER.

payoff, *n.* **1.** The act, instance, or timing of payment. **2.** A reckoning or settlement. **3.** KICKBACK. **4.** *Slang.* A climactic event, esp. an improbable one.

payola (pay-**oh**-lə). (1937) **1.** Money, property, or a favor offered, promised, or given to someone in a position of trust to induce dishonest behavior; a bribe, a fix, or graft. • The term originated in the music industry to refer to a bribe given to a disc jockey to induce the promotion of a particular record. It evolved to include other forms of bribery. **2.** The practice of paying bribes for commercial advantage or special favors.

pay-on-death account. See ACCOUNT.

pay-on-death bank account. See *pay-on-death account* under ACCOUNT.

payor. (16c) Someone who pays; esp., a person responsible for paying a negotiable instrument. — Also spelled *payer.* See DRAWEE; PAYEE.

payor bank. See BANK.

pay-or-play contract. See CONTRACT.

payout period. (1940) **1.** The time required for an asset to produce enough revenue to pay back the initial investment; esp., in oil-and-gas law, the time required for a well to produce a sufficient amount of oil or gas to pay back the investment in the well. **2.** The time during which withdrawals from a retirement account or payments of an annuity are made.

payout ratio. (1951) The ratio between a corporation's dividends per share and its earnings per share. Cf. COMMON-STOCK RATIO.

pay raise. (1938) An increase in the amount of money that someone earns for doing a job. — Often shortened to *raise.* — Also termed (BrE) *pay rise.*

pay rise. See PAY RAISE.

payroll. (18c) **1.** A list of employees to be paid and the amount due to each of them. — Also termed *paylist.* **2.** The total compensation payable to a company's employees for one pay period. **3.** The activity of managing salary payments for workers in a business. **4.** A business's financial records of employees' wages, bonuses, taxes, and net pay.

payroll tax. See TAX.

pays (pay *or* pays), *n.* [Law French] The country; a jury. — Also spelled *pais.* See *trial per pais* under TRIAL; PATRIA.

payslip. See PAY STUB.

pay stub. (1935) A piece of paper that an employee receives on payday showing the amount that he or she has been paid as well as the amounts deducted for taxes, insurance, etc. — Also termed *payslip.*

pay-when-paid bond. See BOND (2).

pay-when-paid clause. See CLAUSE.

PBGC. *abbr.* PENSION BENEFIT GUARANTY CORPORATION.

PBS. *abbr.* (1969) **1.** PUBLIC BUILDINGS SERVICE. **2.** Public Broadcasting Service.

PBT. *abbr.* **1.** See *portable breath test* under BREATH TEST. **2.** See *preliminary breath test* under BREATH TEST.

P.C. *abbr.* (1881) **1.** See *professional corporation* under CORPORATION. **2.** POLITICAL CORRECTNESS. **3.** PRIVY COUNCILLOR.

PCA. *abbr.* POSSE COMITATUS ACT.

PCCL (**pik**-əl), *n. abbr.* Postconviction conditional (driver's) license. — Also termed (in slang) *pickle*.

PCR action. See POSTCONVICTION-RELIEF PROCEEDING.

PCSO. *abbr.* See *police community-support officer* under POLICE OFFICER.

PCT. *abbr.* PATENT COOPERATION TREATY.

PCT application. See *international application* under PATENT APPLICATION.

PCT filing. See *international application* under PATENT APPLICATION.

PCT filing date. (1986) *Patents.* The date of an international application under the Patent Cooperation Treaty. — Also termed *international filing date.* See PATENT COOPERATION TREATY; PCT FILING.

P.D. *abbr.* **1.** PUBLIC DEFENDER. **2.** Police department.

PDA. See PREGNANCY-DISCRIMINATION ACT.

PDR. *abbr.* Prisoner data report.

peace, *n.* (12c) **1.** A state of public tranquility; freedom from civil disturbance or hostility <breach of the peace>.

> "The *peace,* in the most extensive sense of the term, comprehends the whole of the criminal law. 'Against the peace,' all crimes are laid to be committed. Whoever, therefore, had authority to take cognizance of crimes was, from the nature of his office, considered as a conservator of the peace. The king himself was styled its great conservator through all his dominions. His judges and his ministers of justice were also official conservators of the peace. Others were conservators by tenure or prescription. Others, again, were elected in the full county court, in pursuance of a writ directed to the sheriff. Besides all these, extraordinary conservators of the peace were appointed by commission from the king, as occasion required. They were to continue, says my Lord Bacon, for the term of their lives, or at the king's pleasure. For this service, adds the same great authority, choice was made of the best men of calling in the county, and but few in the shire. They might bind any man to keep the peace, and be of the good behaviour; and they might send for the party, directing their warrant to the sheriff or constable to arrest the party and bring him before them." 2 *Collected Works of James Wilson* 912 (Kermit L. Hall and Mark David Hall eds., 2007).

2. The absence of war, fighting, or other hostilities. **3.** The termination or absence of armed conflict between countries. See *peace treaty* under TREATY. — **peaceable,** *adj.* — **peaceful,** *adj.*

▸ **armed peace.** (17c) A situation in which two or more countries, while at peace, are actually armed for possible or probable hostilities.

peace, justice of the. See JUSTICE OF THE PEACE.

peaceable possession. See POSSESSION.

peace bond. See BOND (2).

Peace Corps. An independent federal agency that promotes peace and friendship in the world by sending volunteers to other countries to work in education, agriculture, health, small-business development, urban development, the environment, and information technology. • The agency was established by the Peace Corps Act of 1961 and became independent in 1988. 22 USCA § 2501-1. Its threefold mission is to help people from participating countries in meeting their need for trained men and women; to help promote a better understanding of Americans on the part of people served; and to help promote Americans' understanding of the peoples of the world. The Peace Corps traces its roots to 1960, when then-Senator John F. Kennedy, as a presidential candidate, challenged University of Michigan students to serve their country in the cause of peace by living and working in developing countries.

peace dividend. (1968) The money that a government saves on weapons when it reduces its military strength, as when the risk of hostilities has declined, so that this money is available for other purposes.

peacekeeping troops. (1963) *Int'l law.* A group of soldiers who are sent to a place, usu. a foreign country, to stop or prevent two opposing groups from fighting each other. — Also termed *peacekeeping force.*

peacemaker's court. See COURT.

peace officer. (18c) A civil officer (such as a sheriff or police officer) appointed to maintain public tranquility and order; esp., a person designated by public authority to keep the peace and arrest persons guilty or suspected of crime. • This term may also include a judge who hears criminal cases or another public official (such as a mayor) who may be statutorily designated as a peace officer for limited purposes. — Also termed *officer of the peace; conservator of the peace.*

Peace of God and the church. (17c) *Hist.* The cessation of litigation between terms and on Sundays and holidays.

peacetime. (16c) A period in which a country has declared neither a war nor a national emergency, even if the country is involved in a conflict or quasi-conflict.

peace treaty. See TREATY (1).

peace warrant. See WARRANT (1).

peak demand. (1911) The point (during some specified period) at which customer use results in the highest level of demand for a utility.

peccavi (pe-**kay**-VI *or* pe-**kah**-vee), *n.* [Latin "I have sinned"] (16c) An acknowledgment or confession of guilt.

peculation (pek-yə-**lay**-shən), *n.* (17c) Embezzlement, esp. by a public official. Cf. DEPECULATION. — **peculate** (**pek**-yə-layt), *vb.* — **peculative** (**pek**-yə-lə-tiv), *adj.* — **peculator** (**pek**-yə-lay-tər), *n.*

peculatus (pek-yə-**lay**-təs), *n.* [Latin] *Roman law.* The offense of stealing or embezzling public funds; PECULATION. Cf. FURTUM (1).

peculiar, *adj.* (15c) Different from the norm; special; particular <peculiar benefit>.

peculiar, *n.* (16c) *Hist. Eccles. law.* A district, parish, chapel, or church that was not subject to a bishop's jurisdiction but was independent, with power to probate wills and the like. • Peculiars were created, usu. under papal authority, to limit a bishop's power. There were several types, including royal peculiars (e.g., the Chapel Royal at St. James's Palace or St. George's in Windsor), peculiars of the Archbishop of Canterbury, and peculiars of bishops and deans. The jurisdiction and privileges of the peculiars were abolished by various statutes in the 19th century.

peculiar benefit. See *special benefit* under BENEFIT (2).

peculiar-risk doctrine. (1958) The principle that an employer will be liable for injury caused by an independent contractor if the employer failed to take reasonable precautions against a risk that is peculiar to the contractor's work and that the employer should have recognized. — Also termed *peculiar-risk exception.*

peculium (pi-**kyoo**-lee-əm), *n.* [Latin] (17c) *Roman law.* Property or money given by the head of a household to a son or slave, to be used at that person's discretion for living expenses or business transactions; property at the disposal of the slave or son-in-power.

peculium adventitium. See ADVENTITIOUS PROPERTY.

peculium profectitium. See PROFECTITIUM PECULIUM.

pecune. [Origin unknown] *Hist.* CRIB.

pecunia (pi-**kyoo**-nee-ə), *n.* [Latin] *Hist.* **1.** Money. **2.** Real or personal property.

▸ ***pecunia certa*** (pi-**kyoo**-nee-ə **sər**-tə). [Latin] (1895) *Roman law.* A definite sum of money.

▸ ***pecunia constituta*** (pi-**kyoo**-nee-ə kon-sti-**t[y]oo**-tə). [Latin "fixed sum of money"] *Roman law.* Money owed on a fixed (constituted) day. See *pactum de constituto* under PACTUM.

▸ ***pecunia non numerata*** (pi-**kyoo**-nee-ə non n[y]oo-mə-**ray**-tə). [Latin "money not paid"] *Roman law.* A defense that even though defendant acknowledged receiving money, it had not in fact been paid. Cf. *exceptio pecuniae non numeratae* under EXCEPTIO.

▸ ***pecunia numerata*** (pi-**kyoo**-nee-ə n[y]oo-mə-**ray**-tə). [Latin] (17c) *Hist.* Money numbered or counted out; money given to pay a debt.

▸ ***pecunia trajectitia*** (pi-**kyoo**-nee-ə traj-ek-**tish**-ee-ə). [Latin "money conveyed overseas"] (17c) *Roman law.* Money lent in connection with the transport of goods by ship, the lender bearing the risk of loss until the goods reached their destination. • Although interest on such a loan was originally unlimited, it was later restricted to 12%. See NAUTICUM FENUS.

pecuniary (pi-**kyoo**-nee-er-ee), *adj.* (16c) Of, relating to, or consisting of money; monetary <a pecuniary interest in the lawsuit>.

pecuniary ability. (18c) Income from any source or sources sufficient to meet or pay an obligation, or for some other purpose, such as providing suitable maintenance for a spouse.

pecuniary advantage. See *financial advantage* under ADVANTAGE.

pecuniary benefit. See BENEFIT (2).

pecuniary bequest. See BEQUEST.

pecuniary cause. (16c) *Eccles. law.* A lawsuit maintainable in an ecclesiastical court to redress an injury relating to the church, such as a parishioner's failure to pay a tithe to a parson.

pecuniary damages. See DAMAGES.

pecuniary devise. See DEVISE.

pecuniary gain. See GAIN (1).

pecuniary injury. See INJURY.

pecuniary interest. See *financial interest* under INTEREST (2).

pecuniary legacy. See LEGACY (1).

pecuniary loss. See LOSS.

pecunia trajectitia. See PECUNIA.

PED. *abbr.* Parole eligibility date.

pedage (**ped**-ij). (14c) *Hist.* A toll or tax paid to travel through another's land, entitling the traveler to protection and safe conduct. — Also termed *paage; pedagium.*

pedagium (pi-**day**-jee-əm). [Law Latin] See PEDAGE.

pedal possession. See POSSESSION.

pedaneus (pi-**day**-nee-əs), *n.* & *adj.* [Latin] *Roman law.* A judge who sat at the foot of the tribunal (i.e., in the lowest seat) ready to try minor cases at the command of the magistrate; deputy or assistant judge.

pederasty (**ped**-ər-as-tee), *n.* [fr. Greek *paiderastēs* "a lover of boys"] (17c) Anal intercourse between a man and a boy. • Pederasty is illegal in all states. Cf. SODOMY. — **pederast** (**ped**-ə-rast), *n.*

pedigree. (15c) A history of family succession; ancestry or lineage.

pedigree information. (1971) Background information elicited through routine preliminary questioning of a person — relating, for example, to one's name, address, employment, scars and tattoos, and the like — and not specifically calculated to incriminate the person. • Pedigree information is admissible even if not preceded by *Miranda* warnings.

pedis abscissio (**pee**-dis *or* **ped**-is ab-**sish**-ee-oh). [Latin "cutting off a foot"] *Hist.* Punishment by cutting off the offender's foot.

pedis positio (**pee**-dis *or* **ped**-is pə-**zish**-ee-oh). [Latin "the placement of the foot"] (17c) *Hist.* A putting or placing of the foot; a foothold. • This term denoted possession of land by actual entry.

pedis possessio. See POSSESSIO.

***pedis possessio* doctrine** (**pee**-dis *or* **ped**-is pə-**zes[h]**-ee-o). [Latin "possession-of-a-foot doctrine"] (1958) The principle that a prospector working on land in the public domain is entitled to freedom from fraudulent or forcible intrusions while actually working on the site. • To invoke the doctrine successfully, a prospector must show (1) actual physical occupancy of the ground, (2) diligent bona fide work directed at making a mineral discovery, and (3) the purposeful exclusion of others.

pedophile. (1941) Someone who engages in pedophilia; specif., someone who is sexually attracted to children. — Also spelled (BrE) *paedophile.*

pedophilia. (1906) **1.** A sexual disorder consisting in the desire for sexual gratification by molesting children, esp. prepubescent children. **2.** An adult's act of child molestation. • Pedophilia can but does not necessarily involve intercourse. The American Psychiatric Association applies both senses to perpetrators who are at least 16 years old and at least five years older than their victims. Cf. PEDERASTY. — Also spelled (BrE) *paedophilia.*

peeper. See PEEPING TOM.

peeping Tom. (18c) Someone who spies on another (as through a window), usu. for sexual pleasure; VOYEUR. — Also termed *peeper.*

peer, *n.* (13c) **1.** Someone who is of equal status, rank, or character with another.

"The commonalty, like the nobility, are divided into several degrees; and, as the lords, though different in rank, yet all of them are peers in respect of their nobility, so the commoners, though some are greatly superior to others, yet all are in law peers, in respect of their want of nobility . . . ." 1 William Blackstone, *Commentaries on the Laws of England* 391 (1765).

2. A member of the British nobility (such as a duchess, marquis, earl, viscount, or baroness). — Also termed *lord.* — **peerage** (**peer**-ij), *n.*

"The Crown has power to create any number of peers and of any degree. In modern practice the power is exercised on the advice of the Prime Minister and the honour is most commonly a reward for political services. Peerages can be, and have been, conferred for party political reasons; 12 were created in 1712 to save the government, and 16 to help pass the Reform Bill in 1832. In 1832 and 1911 the Opposition of the House of Lords was overcome by the threat to create enough peers to secure a majority. . . . The main privilege of a peer is to sit and vote in the House of Lords." David M. Walker, *The Oxford Companion to Law* 942 (1980).

peer review. (1967) The critical assessment of manuscripts submitted to a journal by experts who are not part of the editorial staff. • Submission to the scrutiny of peer review increases the likelihood that substantive flaws in method will be detected, esp. in the sciences. *See Daubert v. Merrell Dow Pharm., Inc.*, 509 U.S. 579, 593, 113 S.Ct. 2786, 2797 (1993). In determining reliability of expert evidence, the courts consider whether a researcher's methods have been subjected to peer review. *Id.*

peer-reviewed journal. (1980) A publication whose practice is to forward submitted articles to disinterested experts who screen them for scholarly or scientific reliability so that articles actually published have already withstood expert scrutiny and comment.

peer-review organization. (1978) A governmental agency that monitors health-regulation compliance by private hospitals requesting public funds (such as Medicare and Medicaid payments). 42 USCA §§ 1320c-1, 1320c-3. — Abbr. PRO.

peer-review privilege. See PRIVILEGE (3).

peers of fees. *Hist.* Vassals or tenants of the same lord who judged disputes arising out of fees.

peine forte et dure (**pen for** tay **door** *or* **payn fort** ay **dyoor**). [French "strong and hard punishment"] (18c) *Hist.* The punishment of an alleged felon who refused to plead, consisting of pressing or crushing the person's body under heavy weights until the accused either pleaded or died.

"In all other felonies, however, the punishment of *peine forte et dure* was, until lately, denounced as the consequence of an obstinate silence. The greatest caution and deliberation were indeed to be exercised before it was resorted to; and the prisoner was not only to have '*trina admonitio*,' but a respite of a few hours, and the sentence was to be distinctly read to him, that he might be fully aware of the penalty he was incurring." 1 Joseph Chitty, *A Practical Treatise on the Criminal Law* 425–26 (2d ed. 1826).

"In old English law, a person charged with felony who, refusing to accept jury trial, was pressed to death (*peine forte et dure*), was not regarded as committing suicide, so that he did not forfeit his property." Glanville Williams, *The Sanctity of Life and the Criminal Law* 270 n.4 (1957).

pell. See CLERK OF THE PELLS.

pellex (**pel**-eks), *n.* [Latin] *Roman law.* A concubine.

penal (**pee**-nəl), *adj.* (15c) Of, relating to, or being a penalty or punishment, esp. for a crime.

"The general rule is that penal statutes are to be construed strictly. By the word 'penal' in this connection is meant not only such statutes as in terms impose a fine, or corporal punishment, or forfeiture as a consequence of violating laws, but also all acts which impose by way of punishment damages beyond compensation for the benefit of the injured party, or which impose any special burden, or take away or impair any privilege or right." William M. Lile et al., *Brief Making and the Use of Law Books* 344 (Roger W. Cooley & Charles Lesley Ames eds., 3d ed. 1914).

"The word *penal* connotes some form of punishment imposed on an individual by the authority of the state. Where the primary purpose of a statute is expressly enforceable by fine, imprisonment, or similar punishment the statute is always construed as penal." 3 Norman J. Singer, *Sutherland Statutes and Statutory Construction* § 59.01, at 1 (4th ed. 1986).

penal action. See ACTION (4).

penal bill. See *penal bond* under BOND (2).

penal bond. See BOND (2).

penal clause. See PENALTY CLAUSE.

penal code. (18c) A compilation of criminal laws, usu. defining and categorizing the offenses and setting forth their respective punishments. — Also termed *criminal code.* See MODEL PENAL CODE.

penal colony. (1803) A remote place of detention for convicts and political prisoners, usu. in an isolated part of a country or in a country's extraterritorial holdings, esp. a place from which escape is difficult or impossible. • Historical examples include the Soviet Union's gulags in Siberia and France's penal colony on Devil's Island off the coast of Guiana.

penal custody. See CUSTODY (1).

penal institution. See PRISON.

penalize (**pen**-ə-lɪz or **peen**-), *vb.* (1879) **1.** To impose a penalty; to punish <the student was penalized for infractions of the honor code>. **2.** To treat unfairly <some lawyers at the firm felt penalized for their pro bono activities>.

penal law. 1. See *penal statute* under STATUTE. **2.** See CRIMINAL LAW.

penal liability. See LIABILITY.

penal redress. See REDRESS.

penal sanction. See *criminal sanction* under SANCTION.

penal servitude. (17c) Confinement in prison with hard labor. See HARD LABOR. Cf. IMPRISONMENT.

penal statute. See STATUTE.

penal sum. (17c) The monetary amount specified as a penalty in a penal bond. See *penal bond* under BOND (2).

penalty. (15c) **1.** Punishment imposed on a wrongdoer, usu. in the form of imprisonment or fine; esp., a sum of money exacted as punishment for either a wrong to the state or a civil wrong (as distinguished from compensation for the injured party's loss). • Though usu. for crimes, penalties are also sometimes imposed for civil wrongs.

► **civil penalty.** (17c) A fine assessed for a violation of a statute or regulation <the EPA levied a civil penalty of

$10,000 on the manufacturer for exceeding its pollution limits>.

▸ **maximum penalty.** (1843) The heaviest punishment permitted by law.

▸ **statutory penalty.** (18c) A penalty imposed for a statutory violation; esp., a penalty imposing automatic liability on a wrongdoer for violation of a statute's terms without reference to any actual damages suffered.

2. An extra charge against a party who violates a contractual provision.

▸ **prepayment penalty.** (1948) A charge assessed against a borrower who elects to pay off a loan before it is due.

3. Excessive stipulated damages that a contract purports to impose on a party that breaches. • If the damages are excessive enough to be considered a penalty, a court will usu. not enforce that particular provision of the contract. Some contracts specify that a given sum of damages is intended "as liquidated damages and not as a penalty" — but even that language is not foolproof. **4.** PENALTY CLAUSE.

> "A *penalty* is a sum which a party . . . agrees to pay or forfeit in the event of a breach, but which is fixed, not as a pre-estimate of probable actual damages, but as a *punishment*, the threat of which is designed to prevent the breach, or as *security*, where the sum is deposited or the covenant to pay is joined in by one or more sureties, to insure that the person injured shall collect his actual damages. Penalties . . . are not recoverable or retainable as such by the person in whose favor they are framed . . . ." Charles T. McCormick, *Handbook on the Law of Damages* § 146, at 600 (1935).

penalty clause. (1843) A contractual provision that assesses against a defaulting party an excessive monetary charge unrelated to actual harm. • Penalty clauses are generally unenforceable. — Often shortened to *penalty*. — Also termed *penal clause*. Cf. LIQUIDATED-DAMAGES CLAUSE; LIMITATION-OF-REMEDIES CLAUSE.

> "It not infrequently happens that contracts provide for what is to happen in the event of a breach by the parties, or by one of them. Such provisions may be perfectly simple attempts to avoid future disputes, and to quantify the probable amount of any loss. That is unobjectionable. But sometimes clauses of this kind are not designed to quantify the amount of the probable loss, but are designed to terrorize, or frighten, the party into performance. For example, a contract may provide that the promisor is to pay £5 on a certain event, but if he fails to do so, he must then pay £500. Now a clause of that kind is called a penalty clause by lawyers, and for several hundred years it has been the law that such promises cannot be enforced. The standard justification for the law here is that it is unfair and unconscionable to enforce clauses which are designed to act *in terrorem*." P.S. Atiyah, *Promises, Morals, and Law* 57–58 (1981).

penalty/illegality canon. The interpretive doctrine that a statute penalizing an act makes it unlawful.

penalty phase. (1959) The part of a criminal trial in which the fact-finder determines the punishment for a defendant who has been found guilty. — Also termed *sentencing phase*. Cf. GUILT PHASE.

penalty point. (1957) A punishment levied for a traffic offense and accumulated on the driver's record. • If a driver receives a statutorily set number of points, the driver's license may be restricted, suspended, or terminated.

penance. (13c) **1.** *Eccles. law.* A punishment assessed by an ecclesiastical court for some spiritual offense. **2.** More broadly, something that a person must do to show sorrow or remorse for a transgression, esp. for religious reasons. **3.** In Catholicism, a sacrament in which a priest absolves the sins of one who sorrowfully confesses and promises to make reparations. — Also termed *confession*. See CONFESSOR.

pend, *vb.* (18c) (Of a lawsuit) to be awaiting decision or settlement.

pendency (**pen**-dən-see), *n.* (17c) The quality, state, or condition of being pending or continuing undecided.

pendens. See LIS PENDENS.

pendent (**pen**-dənt), *adj.* (18c) **1.** Not yet decided; pending <a pendent action>. **2.** Of, relating to, or involving pendent jurisdiction or pendent-party jurisdiction <pendent parties>. **3.** Contingent; dependent <pendent on a different claim>.

pendent-claim jurisdiction. See *pendent jurisdiction* under JURISDICTION.

pendente lite (pen-**den**-tee **lɪ**-tee), *adv.* [Latin "while the action is pending"] (18c) During the proceeding or litigation; in a manner contingent on the outcome of litigation. — Also termed *lite pendente*. Cf. LIS PENDENS.

pendente lite administration. See *administration pendente lite* under ADMINISTRATION.

pendente processu (pen-**den**-tee prə-**ses**-[y]oo). [Law Latin] (17c) *Hist.* During the pendency of the process or lawsuit.

pendentes fructus (pen-**den**-teez **frək**-təs). [Latin] *Hist.* Hanging fruits. • These fruits, as distinguished from fruits that have been gathered and remain on the bona fide possessor's property, must be restored to a real owner who defeats the claims of a bona fide possessor. — Sometimes shortened to *pendentes*.

pendente tutela (pen-**den**-tee t[y]oo-**tee**-lə). [Latin] (18c) *Hist.* During the tutory.

pendent jurisdiction. See JURISDICTION.

pendent-party jurisdiction. See JURISDICTION.

pendent-venue doctrine. (1981) The principle that once venue is established for a federal claim, proof of venue for additional federal claims, cross-claims, and counterclaims is unnecessary when the claims arise out of the same operative facts.

pending, *adj.* (17c) **1.** Remaining undecided; awaiting decision <a pending case>. **2.** *Parliamentary law.* (Of a motion) under consideration; moved by a member and stated by the chair as a question for the meeting's consideration. See CONSIDERATION (2); ON THE FLOOR. • A motion may be immediately pending, meaning that it is directly under consideration, being the last motion stated by the chair and next in line for a vote; or it may be pending subject to other motions of higher rank that have taken precedence over it. See *immediately pending motion* and *pending motion* under MOTION (2).

pending, *prep.* (17c) **1.** Throughout the continuance of; during <in escrow pending arbitration>. **2.** While awaiting; until <the injunction was in force pending trial>.

pending-action canon. The doctrine that when statutory law is altered during the pendency of a lawsuit, the courts at every level must apply the new law unless doing so would violate the presumption against retroactivity. — Also termed *pending-lawsuit canon.* See PRESUMPTION AGAINST RETROACTIVITY.

pending motion. See MOTION (2).

pending-ordinance doctrine. (1971) The principle that a municipality may properly deny an application for a property use that, although it would satisfy existing law, would violate a law that is pending when the application is made. • This doctrine was judicially created, mainly to short-circuit landowners' attempts to circumvent a new ordinance by applying for a nonconforming use on the eve of its approval.

penetration, *n.* (15c) **1.** The act of piercing or passing something into or through a body or object. **2.** *Criminal law.* The entry of the penis or some other part of the body or a foreign object into the vagina or other bodily orifice. • This is the typical meaning today in statutes defining sexual offenses. — Also termed *intromission.* See RAPE (1). **3.** The depth reached by a bullet or other projectile in something against which the projectile is fired. — **penetrate,** *vb.*

penetration pricing. (1956) The pricing of a new product below its anticipated market price to enter a market and capture market share by breaking down existing brand loyalties.

penitentiary (pen-ə-**ten**-shə-ree), *n.* (1807) A correctional facility or other place of long-term confinement for convicted criminals; PRISON. — **penitentiary,** *adj.*

penitentiary misdemeanor. See *serious misdemeanor* under MISDEMEANOR.

***Pennoyer* rule** (pə-**noy**-ər). (1968) The principle that a court may not issue a personal judgment against a defendant over whom it has no personal jurisdiction. *Pennoyer v. Neff,* 95 U.S. 714 (1877).

***Pennsylvania* rule.** *Torts.* The principle that a tortfeasor who violates a statute in the process of causing an injury has the burden of showing that the violation did not cause the injury. *The Pennsylvania,* 86 U.S. (19 Wall.) 125, 136 (1874).

penny stock. See STOCK.

penology (pee-**nol**-ə-jee), *n.* (1838) The study of penal institutions, crime prevention, and the punishment and rehabilitation of criminals, including the art of fitting the right treatment to an offender. Cf. CRIMINOLOGY. — **penological** (pee-nə-**loj**-i-kəl), *adj.* — **penologist** (pee-**nol**-ə-jist), *n.*

pen register. (1953) **1.** An electronic device that tracks and records all the numbers dialed from a particular telephone line, as well as all the routing, addressing, or signaling information transmitted by other means of electronic communications. *See* 18 USCA § 3127(3). • Because a pen register does not record the contents of any communication, it may not constitute a Fourth Amendment search requiring a search warrant (though it does need a court order). Some states, however, do consider the use of a pen register invasive enough to require a search warrant. **2.** A similar electronic device that tracks and records Internet communications. Cf. WIRETAPPING.

pensio (**pen**-shee-oh), *n.* [Latin] *Roman & civil law.* A payment for the use of a thing, such as rent for the use of another's house.

pension. (16c) **1.** A regular series of payments made to a person (or the person's representatives or beneficiaries) for past services or some type of meritorious work done; esp., such a series of payments made by the government. **2.** *Hist.* A payment or series of payments made by a noble to a person of some eminence, such as a writer or scientist, to remain in the recipient's good graces. **3.** A fixed sum paid regularly to a person (or to the person's beneficiaries), esp. by an employer as a retirement benefit. Cf. (for senses 1 & 3) ANNUITY (2), (3). **4.** An assemblage of the benchers of one of the English inns of court. **5.** A small annual charge made on each bencher of one of the English inns of court.— Also termed *pension writ.* **6.** *Hist.* A sum paid to a cleric in lieu of tithes.

▸ **old-age pension.** (1856) *Pejorative or jocular.* A pension paid to a retiree of advanced years.

▸ **vested pension.** (1919) A pension in which an employee (or employee's estate) has rights to benefits purchased with the employer's contributions to the plan, even if the employee is no longer employed by this employer at the time of retirement. • The vesting of qualified pension plans is governed by ERISA. See EMPLOYEE RETIREMENT INCOME SECURITY ACT.

pensionable, *adj.* (1869) **1.** Conferring the right to receive a pension <pensionable age>. **2.** Constituting money from which sums are regularly taken for a pension <pensionable pay>.

Pension and Welfare Benefits Administration. *Hist.* A former unit in the U.S. Department of Labor that was responsible for regulating employee pension plans under the Employees Retirement Income Security Act (ERISA) and for enforcing the Act through its field offices. • It has been replaced by the Employee Benefits Security Administration. — Abbr. PWBA.

Pension Benefit Guaranty Corporation. A self-financing federal corporation that guarantees payment of pension benefits in covered benefit pension plans. — Abbr. PBGC.

pensioner. (15c) **1.** A recipient or beneficiary of a pension or pension plan; specif., a retired employee, clerk, or soldier who receives a regular allowance. **2.** A boarder, as in a school or convent. **3.** *Hist.* An official in one of the English inns of court who collected and recorded pensions.

pension plan. (1909) **1.** Under ERISA, any plan, fund, or program established or maintained by an employer or an employee organization to provide retirement income to employees or to defer income by extending it to the termination of employment or beyond. 29 USCA § 1002(2)(A). **2.** Under the Internal Revenue Code, an employer's plan established and maintained primarily to provide systematically for the payment of definitely determinable benefits to employees over a period of years, usu. for life, after retirement. See EMPLOYEE RETIREMENT INCOME SECURITY ACT. Cf. EMPLOYEE BENEFIT PLAN. — Also termed *pension scheme.*

▸ **contributory pension plan.** (1929) A pension plan funded by both employer and employee contributions.

▸ **defined-benefit pension plan.** (1971) A pension plan in which an employer commits to paying an employee a specific benefit for life beginning at retirement. • The amount of the benefit is based on factors such as age, earnings, and years of service.

▸ **defined-contribution pension plan.** See *defined-contribution plan* under EMPLOYEE BENEFIT PLAN.

▸ **defined pension plan.** (1976) A pension plan in which the employer promises specific benefits to each employee. — Also termed *fixed-benefit plan.*

▸ **noncontributory pension plan.** (1918) A pension plan funded solely by the employer's contributions.

▸ **nonqualified pension plan.** (1955) A deferred-compensation plan in which an executive increases retirement benefits by annual additional contributions to the company's basic plan.

▸ **qualified pension plan.** (1945) A pension plan that complies with federal law (ERISA) and thus allows the employee to receive tax benefits for contributions and tax-deferred investment growth. — Often shortened to *qualified plan.*

▸ **top-hat pension plan.** (1973) An unfunded pension plan that is maintained by an employer to provide deferred compensation for a select group of managers or highly paid employees. • Top-hat plans are generally not subject to the broad remedial provisions of ERISA because Congress recognized that certain individuals, by virtue of position or compensation level, can substantially influence the design or operation of their deferred-compensation plans. — Often shortened to *top-hat plan.*

pension trust. See TRUST (3).

pension writ. (16c) *Hist. English law.* A peremptory order to a member of an inn of court delinquent in dues. See PENSION (5).

Pentagon Force Protection Agency. A civilian-defense unit within the U.S. Department of Defense responsible for protecting and safeguarding occupants and visitors of the Pentagon, together with the building's infrastructure, the Navy Annex, and other assigned Pentagon facilities. • The Agency was formed after the Pentagon was attacked on 11 September 2001. — Abbr. PFPA.

penumbra (pi-**nəm**-brə), *n.* [fr. Latin *pene* "almost" + *umbra* "shade"] (18c) A surrounding area or periphery of uncertain extent. • In constitutional law, the Supreme Court has ruled that the specific guarantees in the Bill of Rights have penumbras containing implied rights, esp. the right of privacy. Pl. **penumbras, penumbrae** (pi-**nəm**-bree). — **penumbral** (pi-**nəm**-brəl), *adj.*

> "Problems of fringe meaning are sometimes spoken of as 'problems of the penumbra,' the point being that, in the case of a great many words, there is no doubt about the hard core of their meanings, but different views may well be taken on the question whether the words are applicable to things or situations outside that hard core." Rupert Cross, *Statutory Interpretation* 57 (1976).

penumbral right. See *implied right* under RIGHT.

penuria peritorum (pə-**nyoor**-ee-ə per-i-**tor**-əm). [Latin] (1827) *Hist.* A scarcity of (legally) skilled men. • The phrase appeared in reference to the grantor's lack of proper assistance in preparing and executing a conveyance.

penuria testium (pə-**nyoor**-ee-ə **tes**-tee-əm). [Latin] (17c) *Hist.* A scarcity of witnesses.

> "The disqualifications formerly attaching to witnesses, and especially that of relationship, were sometimes disregarded in occult or private facts, where there must, from the nature of the case, be a scarcity of unexceptionable witnesses . . . . It was not enough in this sense, to constitute a *penuria testium,* to prove that the other evidence was scanty and defective; it had to be shown farther that the *penuria* was necessarily occasioned by the very nature of the question at issue." William Bell, *Bell's Dictionary and Digest of the Law of Scotland* 798 (George Watson ed., 7th ed. 1890).

peonage (**pee**-ə-nij), *n.* (1844) Illegal and involuntary servitude in satisfaction of a debt. — **peon,** *n.*

> "Peonage, which is a term descriptive of a condition that existed in Spanish America, and especially in Mexico, and in the territory of New Mexico, and which may be defined as the status or condition of compulsory service based upon the indebtedness of the peon to the master, the basic fact being the indebtedness, is abolished and prohibited by an act of Congress which further declares that any statute, resolution, regulation, ordinance, or usage of any territory or state designed or operating to establish, maintain, or enforce, directly or indirectly, the voluntary or involuntary service or labor of any persons as peons, in liquidation of any debt or obligation, or otherwise, shall be null and void [42 USCA § 1994]." 45 Am. Jur. 2d *Involuntary Servitude and Peonage* § 10, at 935–36 (1969).

people. (13c) **1.** Men, women, and children generally; persons <55 people were rescued>. **2.** Persons other than oneself, often those of a particular type <the mall was full of theater people>. **3.** The citizens and other permanent residents of a particular country or area <the people of Australia>. **4.** Those of a particular race <people of Chinese descent>. **5.** All the ordinary residents of a country or state, as opposed to the government or ruling class <the people rebelled>. **6.** (*usu. cap.*) The citizens of a state as represented by the prosecution in a criminal case <*People v. Snyder*>. **7.** Those that a monarch or leader rules or governs; subjects generally <the king ordered his people to stay at home>. **8.** Those who work for a person or organization <the manager staffed the project with all her people>. **9.** One's relatives, esp. parents, siblings, and grandparents <my people are from West Texas>.

People's certification. See CERTIFICATION.

people's court. (1912) **1.** A court in which individuals can resolve small disputes. See *small-claims court* under COURT. **2.** *Hist.* (*cap.*) In Nazi Germany, a tribunal that dealt with political offenses such as treason. • In German, *Volksgerichtshof.*

people-smuggling. (1988) The crime of helping a person enter a country illegally in return for a fee. Cf. *human trafficking* under TRAFFICKING; SMUGGLING.

peppercorn. (17c) A small or insignificant thing or amount; nominal consideration <the contract was upheld despite involving mere peppercorn>. See *nominal consideration* under CONSIDERATION (1); *peppercorn rent* under RENT.

peppercorn rent. See RENT (2).

per (pər), *prep.* [Latin] (14c) **1.** Through; by <the dissent, per Justice Thomas>. **2.** For each; for every <55 miles per hour>. **3.** In accordance with the terms of; according to <per the contract>.

per aequipollens (pər ee-kwi-**pol**-enz). [Latin] (17c) *Hist.* By an equivalent.

per aes et libram (pər **ees** et **lɪ**-brəm). [Latin] (18c) *Roman law.* By bronze (or copper) and scales. • The phrase typically referred to the fictitious sale in a *mancipation* during which the purchaser struck the scales with a piece of bronze or copper and then gave it to the seller as a symbol of the price. See MANCIPATION.

per alium stetit (pər **ay**-ee-əm **stet**-it). [Latin] *Hist.* It was owing to (something done by) another.

per ambages (pər am-**bay**-jeez). [Latin] *Hist.* Indirectly; evasively.

perambulation. (15c) The act or custom of walking around the boundaries of a piece of land, either to confirm the boundaries or to preserve evidence of them. — **perambulate,** *vb.*

perambulatione facienda. See DE PERAMBULATIONE FACIENDA.

per annum (pər **an**-əm), *adv.* [Latin] (16c) By, for, or in each year; annually <interest of eight percent per annum>.

P/E ratio. *abbr.* PRICE-EARNINGS RATIO.

per autre vie. See PUR AUTRE VIE.

per aversionem (pər ə-vər-zhee-**oh**-nəm). [Latin "for a lump sum"] (17c) *Roman & civil law.* Of, relating to, or involving a sale in which goods are taken in bulk or land is bought by estimation of the number of acres. • This type of sale is so called because the buyer "turns away" from a careful scrutiny of the things purchased.

> "It is a fundamental principle, pervading everywhere the doctrine of sales of chattels, that if the goods of different value be sold in bulk, and not separately, and for a single price, or *per aversionem*, in the language of the civilians, the sale is perfect, and the risk with the buyer; but if they be sold by number, weight, or measure, the sale is incomplete, and the risk continues with the seller, until the specific property be separated and identified." 2 James Kent, *Commentaries on American Law* *496 (George Comstock ed., 11th ed. 1866).

per bouche (pər **boosh**). [Law French] By the mouth; orally.

per capita (pər **kap**-i-tə), *adj.* [Latin "by the head"] (17c) **1.** Divided equally among all individuals, usu. in the same class <the court will distribute the property to the descendants on a per capita basis>. Cf. PER STIRPES.

> "*Per capita* means taking as an individual and not as a representative of an ancestor. Suppose the testator . . . with three living children and three grandchildren who are the issue of a deceased son, had desired and had so stated in his will that his own children and the children of his deceased son should share equally in the estate. In that event the estate would be divided into six parts and each of the three children and each of the three grandchildren would receive an equal portion of the total estate — namely, one-sixth." Gilbert Thomas Stephenson, *Wills* 30 (1934).

▸ **per capita with representation.** (1935) Divided equally among all members of a class of takers, including those who have predeceased the testator, so that no family stocks are cut off by the prior death of a taker. • For example, if T (the testator) has three children — A, B, and C — and C has two children but predeceases T, C's children will still take C's share when T's estate is distributed.

2. Allocated to each person; possessed by each individual <the average annual per capita income has increased over the last two years>. — **per capita,** *adv.*

per capita tax. See *poll tax* under TAX.

percentage depletion. (1932) *Oil & gas.* A method of allowing a taxpayer who owns an economic interest in a producing oil or gas well to deduct a specified percentage of the gross income from the well in lieu of depleting the actual basis. 26 USCA § 611. Cf. COST DEPLETION.

percentage game. See GAME.

percentage lease. See LEASE.

percentage-of-completion method. See ACCOUNTING METHOD.

percentage order. See ORDER (8).

perception. (14c) **1.** An observation, awareness, or realization, usu. based on physical sensation or experience; appreciation or cognition. • The term includes both the actor's knowledge of the actual circumstances and the actor's erroneous but reasonable belief in the existence of nonexistent circumstances. **2.** *Roman & civil law.* The act of taking into possession (as rents, profits, etc.), esp. by a bona fide possessor or usufructuary. — Also termed (in Roman law) *perceptio* (pər-**sep**-shee-oh).

percepti sed non consumpti (pər-**sep**-tɪ sed non kən-**səmp**-tɪ). [Latin] *Hist.* Fruits gathered but not consumed.

perch, *n.* (13c) **1.** A pole or similar marker planted in the bed of a river, lake, or harbor, to aid navigation. **2.** ROD. **3.** *Property. Archaic.* A measure of area equal to 1/160th of an acre. • This unit is sometimes found in old deeds. Historically, the measurement varied according to local usage, but was standardized by the 19th century. — Also termed (in sense 3) *pole.*

percipient witness. See WITNESS.

percolating water. See WATER.

per collationem bonorum (pər kə-lay-shee-**oh**-nəm bə-**nor**-əm). [Latin] (17c) *Scots law.* By bringing goods received into account (collation). • When heirs-at-law, or heirs who had received from a deceased ancestor during the ancestor's lifetime, wished to share in the legitim fund, they had to bring in (to collate) what they had received before the legitim could be shared out. See COLLATION (2).

per consequens (pər **kon**-sə-kwenz). [Latin] (15c) By consequence; consequently.

per considerationem curiae (pər kən-sid-ə-ray-shee-**oh**-nəm **kyoor**-ee-ee). [Law Latin] (18c) By the consideration of the court.

per contra (pər **kon**-trə). [Latin] (16c) On the other hand; to the contrary; by contrast.

per cur. *abbr.* Per curiam. See *per curiam opinion* under OPINION (1).

per curiam (pər **kyoor**-ee-əm), *adv.* & *adj.* [Latin] (15c) By the court as a whole.

per curiam, *n.* See *per curiam opinion* under OPINION (1).

per curiam opinion. See OPINION (1).

per definitionem (pər def-i-nish-ee-**oh**-nəm). [Latin] By way of definition; by definition.

per diem (pər **dɪ**-əm *or* **dee**-əm), *adv.* [Latin] (15c) By the day; for each day. Cf. IN DIEM.

per diem, *adj.* & *adv.* (18c) Based on or calculated by the day <per diem interest> <paid per diem>.

per diem, *n.* (1812) **1.** A monetary daily allowance, usu. to cover expenses; specif., an amount of money that a worker is allowed to spend daily while on the job, esp. on a business trip. **2.** A daily fee; esp., an amount of money that an employer pays a worker for each day that is worked.

perdonatio utlagariae (pər-də-**nay**-shee-oh ət-lə-**gair**-ee-ee). [Law Latin "pardon of outlawry"] (17c) *Hist.* A pardon given to a person who had been outlawed for failing to obey a court's summons but who then voluntarily surrendered.

perduellio (pər-d[y]oo-**el**-ee-oh), *n.* [Latin "treason"] *Roman law.* The crime of hostility to one's native country; treasonous conduct, such as joining the enemy or deserting the battlefield. • This term corresponds to the English phrase *high treason.* In the Roman republic, several acts might constitute *perduellio,* such as assuming regal power; trying to subvert, by violence, the established form of government, esp. by fomenting internal rebellion; and promoting the designs of external foes. *Perduellio* was later absorbed into a broader category of crimes against the state, the *crimen laesae majestatis.* — Also termed (in English) *perduellion* (pər-d[y]oo-**el**-yən). See *crimen majestatis* under CRIMEN.

perdurable (pər-**d[y]uur**-ə-bəl), *adj.* (15c) (Of an estate in land) lasting or enduring; durable; permanent.

peregrinus (per-i-**grɪ**-nəs), *n. Roman law.* A free person who was not a Roman citizen; a free foreigner. Pl. ***peregrini.*** Cf. INCOLA.

perempt (pə-**rempt**), *n.* (1963) *Slang.* See *peremptory challenge* under CHALLENGE (2).

perempt (pə-**rempt**), *vb.* (18c) **1.** *Slang.* To strike (a prospective juror) by peremptory challenge <prosecutors perempted the defendant's neighbor>. **2.** *Slang.* To exercise a peremptory challenge <both sides had plenty of opportunities to perempt>. • The difference between sense 1 and sense 2 is that sense 1 is transitive, whereas sense 2 is intransitive. This slangy verb, a linguistic back-formation from the adjective *peremptory,* is often mispronounced as if it were *preempt* (pree-**empt**) — an entirely different word. **3.** *Civil law.* To quash, do away with, or extinguish.

peremption (pər-**emp**-shən), *n.* (18c) *Civil law.* A period of time fixed by statute for the existence of a right. • If the right is not exercised during this period, it is extinguished. Whereas prescription simply bars a specific remedy, peremption bars the action itself. See STATUTE OF REPOSE. Cf. PRESCRIPTION (1).

peremptoria litis et causae (pər-emp-**tor**-ee-ə **lɪ**-tis et **kaw**-zee). [Law Latin] *Hist.* Decisive of the suit and cause. • The phrase appeared in reference to peremptory defenses, to which there could be no reply.

peremptory (pər-**emp**-tə-ree), *adj.* (15c) **1.** Final; absolute; conclusive; incontrovertible <the king's peremptory order>. **2.** Not requiring any shown cause; arbitrary <peremptory challenges>. **3.** (Of behavior) abrupt, with neither politeness nor friendliness; indicating an expectation of immediate obedience.

peremptory, *n.* See *peremptory challenge* under CHALLENGE (2).

peremptory challenge. See CHALLENGE (2).

peremptory day. See DAY.

peremptory defense. See DEFENSE (1).

peremptory direction. See *peremptory instruction* under JURY INSTRUCTION.

peremptory exception. See EXCEPTION (1).

peremptory instruction. See JURY INSTRUCTION.

peremptory mandamus. See MANDAMUS.

peremptory norm. See JUS COGENS (2).

peremptory plea. See PLEA (3).

peremptory rule. See RULE (1).

peremptory strike. See *peremptory challenge* under CHALLENGE (2).

peremptory writ. See WRIT.

per eundem (pər ee-**ən**-dəm). [Latin] By the same. • This term often appears in the phrase *per eundem in eadem* ("by the same judge in the same case").

per expressum (pər ek-**spres**-əm). [Latin] (17c) *Hist.* Expressly; explicitly.

per facta concludentia (pər **fak**-tə kon-kloo-**den**-shee-ə). [Latin] By concluding deeds.

per fas aut nefas (pər **fas** awt **nee**-fas). [Latin] (16c) *Hist.* By lawful or unlawful means.

perfect (pər-**fekt**), *vb.* (14c) To take all legal steps needed to complete, secure, or record (a claim, right, or interest); to provide necessary public notice in final conformity with the law <perfect a security interest> <perfect the title>.

perfect attestation clause. (1875) A testamentary provision asserting that all actions required to make a valid testamentary disposition have been performed.

perfect competition. See COMPETITION.

perfect defense. See DEFENSE (1).

perfect duty. See DUTY (1).

perfected security interest. See SECURITY INTEREST.

perfect equity. See EQUITY (5).

perfect grant. See GRANT (4).

perfecting amendment. See AMENDMENT (3).

perfect instrument. See INSTRUMENT (2).

perfection. Validation of a security interest as against other creditors, usu. by filing a statement with some public office or by taking possession of the collateral. Cf. ATTACHMENT (4).

▸ **automatic perfection.** (1968) The self-operative perfection of a purchase-money security interest without filing or without possession of the collateral. • The security interest is perfected simply by the attachment of the security interest, without any additional steps. See *purchase-money security interest* under SECURITY INTEREST.

▸ **temporary perfection.** (1971) The continuous perfection of a security interest for a limited period. • For example, a security interest in proceeds from the original collateral is perfected for 20 days after the debtor receives the proceeds; the interest will become unperfected after this 20-day period unless certain statutory requirements are met. On most instruments, a secured party who advances new value under a written security agreement obtains a 21-day perfection period, even if the secured party does not file a financing statement and the collateral remains with the debtor. UCC §§ 9-312, 9-315.

perfect law. See LAW.

perfect obligation. See OBLIGATION.

perfect ownership. See OWNERSHIP.

perfect right. See RIGHT.

perfect sale. See *emptio perfecta* under EMPTIO.

perfect self-defense. See SELF-DEFENSE (1).

perfect tender. See TENDER (3).

perfect-tender rule. (1970) *Commercial law.* The principle that a buyer may reject a seller's goods if the quality, quantity, or delivery of the goods fails to conform precisely to the contract. • Although the perfect-tender rule was adopted by the UCC (§ 2-601), other Code provisions — such as the seller's right to cure after rejection — have softened the rule's impact. Cf. SUBSTANTIAL-PERFORMANCE DOCTRINE.

> "At common law, a buyer of goods possessed a legal right to insist upon 'perfect tender' by the seller. If the goods failed to conform exactly to the description in the contract — whether as to quality, quantity or manner of delivery — the buyer could reject the goods and rescind the contract, which meant that the parties would be returned to the positions they occupied before the contract was entered into." Marvin A. Chirelstein, *Concepts and Case Analysis in the Law of Contracts* 112 (1990).

perfect title. See TITLE (2).

perfect trial. See TRIAL.

perfect usufruct. See USUFRUCT.

perfect war. See WAR (1).

per feloniam (pər fə-**loh**-nee-əm). [Latin] (16c) *Hist.* With criminal intent.

perficere susceptum munus (pər-**fis**-ər-ee sə-**sep**-təm **myoo**-nəs). [Latin] *Scots law.* To perform the duties of an office undertaken. • One assuming an office could not then capriciously resign from the office. See REBUS INTEGRIS.

perfidy (**pər**-fə-dee). *Int'l law.* A combatant's conduct that creates the impression that an adversary is entitled to, or is obliged to accord, protection under international law, when in fact the conduct is a ruse to gain an advantage. • Acts of perfidy include feigning an intent to negotiate under a flag of truce, or feigning protected status by using signs, emblems, or uniforms of the United Nations or of a neutral country.

performable, *adj.* (16c) (Of an obligation) capable of being or expected to be carried out.

per formam doni (pər **for**-məm **doh**-nɪ). [Law Latin] (17c) By the form of the gift; by the designation of the giver rather than by operation of law.

performance, *n.* (16c) **1.** The successful completion of a contractual duty, usu. resulting in the performer's release from any past or future liability; EXECUTION (2). — Also termed *full performance.* Cf. NONPERFORMANCE; MISPERFORMANCE.

▸ **defective performance.** (1832) A performance that, whether partial or full, does not wholly comply with the contract. • One example is late performance.

▸ **exact performance.** Full performance of an obligation as detailed in the contract.

▸ **future performance.** (17c) Performance in the future of an obligation that will become due under a contract.

▸ **misperformance.** See MISPERFORMANCE.

▸ **nonperformance.** See NONPERFORMANCE.

▸ **part performance.** (18c) **1.** The accomplishment of some but not all of one's contractual obligations. **2.** A party's execution, in reliance on an opposing party's oral promise, of enough of an oral contract's requirements that a court may hold the statute of frauds not to apply. **3.** PART-PERFORMANCE DOCTRINE.

▸ **performance in specie.** See SPECIFIC PERFORMANCE.

▸ **specific performance.** See SPECIFIC PERFORMANCE.

▸ **substantial performance.** (18c) Performance of the primary, necessary terms of an agreement. See SUBSTANTIAL-PERFORMANCE DOCTRINE.

▸ **vicarious performance.** (18c) Performance carried by an employee, agent, or other nominee.

> "It is necessary . . . to distinguish between assignment of a contractual liability and vicarious performance of a contract. Normally a person who contracts to do something must do it himself. But in the case of a duty of performance which involves no personal element, so that it does not matter to the other party who does the promised act, so long as it is done in accordance with the contract, the party liable may do it by a servant or agent or other nominee. This is not an assignment of the contractual liability, for the original contractor remains liable and if the deputy has done the work badly it is not the deputy but the contractor himself who is answerable to the other party." 2 *Stephen's Commentaries on the Laws of England* 76–77 (L. Crispin Warmington ed., 21st ed. 1950).

2. The equitable doctrine by which acts consistent with an intention to fulfill an obligation are construed to be in fulfillment of that obligation, even if the party was silent on the point. **3.** A company's earnings. **4.** The ability of a corporation to maintain or increase earnings.

performance bond. (1918) **1.** A bond given by a surety to ensure the timely performance of a contract. • In major international agreements, performance bonds are typically issued by banks, but sometimes also by insurance companies. The face amount of the bond is typically 2% of the value of performance, but occasionally as much as 5%. **2.** A third party's agreement to guarantee the completion of a construction contract upon the default of the general contractor. — Also termed *completion bond*; *surety bond*; *contract bond.* Cf. *common-law bond* under BOND (2).

▸ **nonoperative performance bond.** (1999) A performance bond that is not currently in effect but is activated upon the issuance of the buyer's letter of credit or other approved financing.

▸ **operative performance bond.** (1999) A performance bond that has been activated by the issuance of the buyer's letter of credit or other approved financing.

▸ **revolving performance bond.** (1980) A performance bond that is in effect on a continuing basis for the duration of the contract, usu. plus an additional number of days (often 45).

▸ **up-front performance bond.** (1998) A performance bond given before the issuance of the buyer's letter of credit or other financing.

performance bonus. See BONUS.

performance contract. See CONTRACT.

performance fund. See MUTUAL FUND.

performance plan. (1982) A bonus compensation plan in which executives are paid according to the company's growth.

performance-related pay. See PAY (1).

performance right. (1941) A copyright holder's exclusive right to recite, play, act, show, or otherwise render the protected work publicly, whether directly or by technological means (as by broadcasting the work on television). • Every public performance of a copyrighted work requires authorization from the copyright owner or its representative, unless a statutory ephemeral-recording exemption applies. — Also termed *public-performance right.*

performance shares. (1973) Stock given to an executive when the corporation meets a performance objective.

performance specification. See STATEMENT OF WORK.

performance stock. See *glamour stock* under STOCK.

per fraudem (pər **fraw**-dəm), *adv.* [Latin] (17c) By fraud; fraudulently.

periculo petentis (pə-**rik**-yə-loh pə-**ten**-tis). [Latin] (17c) *Hist.* At the risk of the person seeking. • A private person was liable in damages for a judicial warrant wrongfully issued at that person's insistence.

> "[A] creditor seeking a warrant for the apprehension of his debtor as *in meditatione fugae*, obtains it *periculo petentis*, and he, not the judge, will be liable in damages if the debtor can show that the obtaining of the warrant and the using of it were illegal." John Trayner, *Trayner's Latin Maxims* 454 (4th ed. 1894).

periculosus (pər-ik-yə-**loh**-səs), *adj.* [Latin] Dangerous; perilous.

periculum (pə-**rik**-yə-ləm), *n.* [Latin] *Civil law.* Peril; danger; risk. Pl. ***pericula.***

peril. (13c) **1.** Exposure to the risk of injury, damage, or loss; a danger or problem in a particular activity or situation <the perils of litigation>.

▸ **inescapable peril.** (1933) A danger that one cannot avoid without another's help. See LAST-CLEAR-CHANCE DOCTRINE.

2. *Insurance.* The cause of a risk of loss to person or property; esp., the cause of a risk such as fire, accident, theft, forgery, earthquake, flood, or illness <insured against all perils>. Cf. RISK (3).

peril of the sea. (1808) An action of the elements at sea having such great force as to overcome the strength of a well-founded ship and the normal precautions of good marine practice. • A peril of the sea may relieve a carrier from liability for the resulting losses. — Also termed *danger of navigation; danger of river; marine peril; marine risk;* (in regard to the Great Lakes) *perils of the lakes; danger of the sea.*

> "Of the marine perils, by far the most important are those 'of the seas.' What is covered is not any loss that may happen *on* the sea, but fortuitous losses occurring through extraordinary action of the elements at sea, or any accident or mishap in navigation. By far the greatest number of claims for marine loss, and of the insurance problems connected with other topics treated in this book arise under this clause. Extraordinary action of the wind and waves is a sea peril. Collision, foundering, stranding, striking on rocks and icebergs, are all covered under these words. Even a swell from a passing ship may be a 'peril of the sea.' On the other hand, ordinary wear and tear are not included under the coverage of this or any other phrase in the clause, nor are losses which are anticipatable as regular incidents of sea carriage in general or of navigation in a particular part of the world." Grant Gilmore & Charles L. Black Jr., *The Law of Admiralty* § 2-9, at 72–73 (2d ed. 1975).

perimere causam (pə-**rim**-ə-ree **kaw**-zəm). [Latin] *Hist.* To put an end to the cause. • The phrase appeared in reference to the legal effect of a peremptory defense. See *peremptory defense* under DEFENSE (1).

perinatal (per-i-**nayt**-əl), *adj.* (1944) At or around the time of birth; esp., of, relating to, or involving the period from about the 12th week of gestation through the 28th day of life. Cf. NEONATAL.

per incuriam (pər in-**kyoor**-ee-əm), *adj.* (17c) (Of a judicial decision) wrongly decided, usu. because the judge or judges were ill-informed about the applicable law.

> "There is at least one exception to the rule of *stare decisis.* I refer to judgments rendered *per incuriam.* A judgment *per incuriam* is one which has been rendered inadvertently. Two examples come to mind: first, where the judge has forgotten to take account of a previous decision to which the doctrine of *stare decisis* applies. For all the care with which attorneys and judges may comb the case law, *errare humanum est,* and sometimes a judgment which clarifies a point to be settled is somehow not indexed, and is forgotten. It is in cases such as these that a judgment rendered in contradiction to a previous judgment that should have been considered binding, and in ignorance of that judgment, with no mention of it, must be deemed rendered *per incuriam;* thus, it has no authority. . . . The same applies to judgments rendered in ignorance of legislation of which they should have taken account. For a judgment to be deemed *per incuriam,* that judgment must show that the legislation was not invoked." Louis-Philippe Pigeon, *Drafting and Interpreting Legislation* 60 (1988).

> "As a general rule the only cases in which decisions should be held to have been given *per incuriam* are those of decisions given in ignorance or forgetfulness of some inconsistent statutory provision or of some authority binding on the court concerned, so that in such cases some features of the decision or some step in the reasoning on which it is based is found on that account to be demonstrably wrong. This definition is not necessarily exhaustive, but cases not strictly within it which can properly be held to have been decided *per incuriam,* must in our judgment, consistently with the *stare decisis* rule which is an essential part of our law, be of the rarest occurrence." Rupert Cross & J.W. Harris, *Precedent in English Law* 149 (4th ed. 1991).

perinde est ac si scriptum non esset (pər-**in**-dee est ak SI **skrip**-təm non **es**-et). [Latin] *Scots law.* It is the same as if it had not been written. • A deed that failed to convey the grantor's meaning adequately could not be supplemented by extrinsic evidence and would be void for uncertainty.

per infortunium (pər in-for-**t[y]oo**-nee-əm), *adj. or adv.* [Latin] (17c) By misadventure. • At common law, when one person killed another *per infortunium,* a conviction and royal pardon were necessary even when there was no fault. See *homicide per infortunium* under HOMICIDE.

> "It may seem strange to modern minds that for centuries it was a rule of our law that a man who killed another either by misadventure (*per infortunium*) or in reasonable self-defence (against an attack not itself felonious), although he did not commit a felony, must yet be held guilty of unlawful homicide and require the King's pardon if he were to escape punishment, and even if granted pardon would still be liable to suffer forfeiture of his property; and that he was exposed to claims for compensation from the family of the deceased." J.W. Cecil Turner, *Kenny's Outlines of Criminal Law* 113 (16th ed. 1952).

per insidias et industriam (pər in-**sid**-ee-əs et in-**dəs**-tree-əm). [Latin] (1829) *Hist.* By stratagem and on purpose; intentionally.

periodic alimony. See *permanent alimony* under ALIMONY (1).

periodic audit. See AUDIT.

periodic estate. See *periodic tenancy* under TENANCY.

periodic payment. See PAYMENT (2).

periodic-payment-plan certificate. See STOCK CERTIFICATE.

periodic tenancy. See TENANCY.

period of prescription. (18c) The period fixed by local law as sufficient for obtaining or extinguishing a right through lapse of time. • In addition to a fixed number of years, the period includes whatever further time is allowed by local law because of infancy, insanity, coverture, and other like circumstances. See PRESCRIPTIVE RIGHT; PRESCRIPTION (3), (4), (5).

peripheral right. See RIGHT.

periphrasis (pə-**rif**-rə-sis), *n.* (16c) A roundabout way of writing or speaking; circumlocution. — **periphrastic** (per-ə-**fras**-tik), *adj.*

perishable-food-disparagement act. See AGRICULTURAL-DISPARAGEMENT LAW.

perjure (**pər**-jər), *vb.* **1.** To make (oneself) culpable of deliberately making material false or misleading statements while under oath. **2.** (In a passive sense) to become involved in, or proved to be guilty of, perjury.

perjured (**pər**-jərd), *adj.* (17c) **1.** Who has perjured himself or herself; guilty of perjury <a perjured witness>. **2.** Suggesting or characterized by perjury <a perjured countenance>. — **perjurious** (pər-**joor**-ee-əs), *adj.*

perjury (**pər**-jər-ee), *n.* (14c) The act or an instance of a person's deliberately making material false or misleading statements while under oath; esp., the willful utterance of untruthful testimony under oath or affirmation, before a competent tribunal, on a point material to the adjudication. — Also termed *false swearing*; *false oath*; *falsehood*; (archaically) *forswearing*. See FALSEHOOD. Cf. MENDACITY. — **perjuror** (**pər**-jər-ər), *n.*

> "Perjury by the common law, seemeth to be *a wilful false oath, by one who being lawfully required to depose the truth in any judicial proceeding, swears absolutely, in a matter material to the point in question, whether he be believed or not.*" Edward Bullingbrooke, *The Duty and Authority of Justices of the Peace and Parish Officers for Ireland* 598 (rev. ed. 1788).

perjury-trap doctrine. (1989) The principle that an indictment for perjury must be dismissed if prosecutors have secured it by haling the defendant before a grand jury as a witness in an attempt to get the evidence necessary for a perjury charge, particularly if the witness's testimony is not materially related to an ongoing grand-jury investigation. • The perjury-trap doctrine does not apply if there was a legitimate basis for an investigation and for particular questions that were answered falsely.

perk, *n.* See PERQUISITE.

per legem terrae (pər **lee**-jəm **ter**-ee). [Law Latin] (17c) By the law of the land; by due process of law.

***Perlman* doctrine.** (1979) The principle that a discovery order directed at a disinterested third party is immediately appealable on the theory that the third party will not risk contempt by refusing to comply. • The doctrine originated in *Perlman v. U.S.*, 247 U.S. 7, 13, 38 S.Ct. 417, 420 (1918). The Court reasoned that the third party's ability to protect his or her rights would be thwarted if the party could not appeal immediately.

permanency hearing. See HEARING.

permanency plan. (1983) A proposed written strategy for the eventual permanent placement of a child who has been removed from his or her parents. • A permanency plan, ideally, provides either for the child's safe return to one or both parents or for the child's adoption. If neither of these alternatives is possible, then the plan will provide for long-term foster care, relative care, or guardianship. Under the Adoption and Safe Families Act, long-term foster care is the choice of last resort. — Also termed *permanent plan*.

permanency-planning hearing. See *permanency hearing* under HEARING.

permanent abode. See DOMICILE (1).

permanent alimony. See ALIMONY (1).

permanent allegiance. See ALLEGIANCE (1).

permanent chargé d'affaires. See CHARGÉ D'AFFAIRES.

permanent committee. See *standing committee* under COMMITTEE (1).

permanent damages. See DAMAGES.

permanent disability. See DISABILITY (2).

permanent employment. See EMPLOYMENT.

permanent exclusion order. See EXCLUSION ORDER (3).

permanent financing. See FINANCING.

permanent fixture. See FIXTURE.

permanent injunction. See INJUNCTION.

permanent injury. See INJURY.

permanent law. See LAW.

permanent nuisance. See NUISANCE.

permanent plan. See PERMANENCY PLAN.

permanent policy. See INSURANCE POLICY.

permanent protective order. See PROTECTIVE ORDER.

permanent statute. See *perpetual statute* under STATUTE.

permanent taking. See TAKING (2).

permanent treaty. See TREATY (1).

permanent trespass. See TRESPASS.

permanent vegetative state. See VEGETATIVE STATE.

permanent ward. See WARD.

per membra curiae (pər **mem**-brə **kyoor**-ee-ee). [Law Latin] (17c) *Hist.* By members of the court.

per metas et bundas (pər **mee**-təs et **bən**-dəs). [Law Latin] (1817) By metes and bounds.

per minas. See *duress per minas* under DURESS (3).

permissible, *adj.* (15c) Allowed by the law or by applicable rules; allowable; admissible. See PERMISSIVE (1).

permissible appointee. See APPOINTEE.

permissible purpose. Under the federal Fair Credit Reporting Act, a circumstance under which a consumer reporting agency may lawfully furnish a consumer report. 15 USCA § 1681b.

permissible-repair doctrine. See REPAIR DOCTRINE.

permission. (15c) **1.** The act of permitting; the official act of allowing someone to do something. **2.** A license or liberty to do something; authorization.

▸ **express permission.** (16c) Permission that is clearly and unmistakably granted by actions or words, oral or written.

▸ **implied permission.** (18c) **1.** Permission that is inferred from words or actions. **2.** See *implied consent* under CONSENT (1).

3. Conduct that justifies others in believing that the possessor of property is willing to have them enter if they want to do so. Cf. INVITATION.

permissive, *adj.* (15c) **1.** PERMISSIBLE <permissive venue>. **2.** Recommending or tolerating, but not compelling or prohibiting; giving power of choice <permissive legislation>. **3.** Not strict; allowing behavior that many others would disapprove of <teachers who are too permissive>.

permissive abstention. See ABSTENTION.

permissive counterclaim. See COUNTERCLAIM.

permissive inference. See *permissive presumption* under PRESUMPTION.

permissive joinder. See JOINDER.

permissive presumption. See PRESUMPTION.

permissive search. See *consent search* under SEARCH (1).

permissive statute. See STATUTE.

permissive subject of bargaining. (1963) *Labor law.* An employment or collective-bargaining issue, other than a basic employment issue, that is not required to be the subject of collective bargaining but that cannot be implemented by management without union approval. • For example, altering the scope of the bargaining unit does not affect a term or condition of employment, so it is a permissive, instead of mandatory, subject of bargaining. Disagreement on a permissive subject of bargaining cannot be used as the basis for an impasse in negotiating a collective-bargaining agreement, unlike a mandatory subject of bargaining. — Often shortened to *permissive subject.* Cf. MANDATORY SUBJECT OF BARGAINING.

permissive tenant. See *tenant at sufferance* under TENANT (1).

permissive use. See USE (4).

permissive waste. See WASTE (1).

permit (**pər**-mit), *n.* (17c) A certificate evidencing permission; an official written statement that someone has the right to do something; LICENSE (1) <a gun permit>.

permit (pər-**mit**), *vb.* (15c) **1.** To consent to formally; to allow (something) to happen, esp. by an official ruling, decision, or law <permit the inspection to be carried out>. **2.** To give opportunity for; to make (something) happen <lax security permitted the escape>. **3.** To allow or admit of <if the law so permits>.

permit bond. See *license bond* under BOND (2).

permit card. (1939) *Labor law.* A document issued by a union to a nonunion member to allow the person to work on a job covered by a union contract.

permittee (pər-mi-**tee**). (1846) Someone who has permission to do something.

▸ **subpermittee.** (1953) Someone who receives permission to act from a permittee.

per mitter le droit (pər **mit**-ər lə **droyt**). [Law French] *Hist.* By passing the right. • This described how releases became effective, as when a person disseised of land released the estate to the disseisor, at which time the right and possession combined to give the disseisor the entire estate.

per mitter l'estate (pər **mit**-ər lə-**stayt**). [Law French] *Hist.* By passing the estate. • This described the manner in which a joint tenant's right to an entire estate arose when the tenant received the remaining estate from the other joint tenant.

per modum exceptionis (pər **moh**-dəm ek-sep-shee-**oh**-nis). [Latin] (1812) *Hist.* By way of exception.

per modum gratiae (pər **moh**-dəm **gray**-shee-ee). [Latin] (17c) *Hist.* By way of favor.

per modum justitiae (pər **moh**-dəm jəs-**tish**-ee-ee). [Latin] (17c) *Hist.* By way of justice.

per modum poenae (pər **moh**-dəm **pee**-nee). [Latin] (17c) *Hist.* By way of penalty.

per modum simplicis querelae (pər **moh**-dəm **sim**-pli-sis kwə-**ree**-lee). [Law Latin] (17c) *Scots law.* By way of simple complaint. • Some actions could be brought by a complaint unaccompanied by formal summons.

permutatio (pər-myoo-**tay**-shee-oh), *n.* [Latin "exchange"] *Roman law.* An agreement for barter or exchange. • The agreement became binding as soon as one party had transferred ownership of his thing to the other. Pl. ***permutationes*** (pər-myoo-tay-shee-**oh**-neez).

permutation. (14c) *Civil law.* Barter; exchange.

per my et per tout (pər **mee** ay pər **too**[**t**]). [Law French] By the half and by the whole. • This phrase described the estate held by joint tenants: *by the half* for purposes of survivorship, *by the whole* for purposes of alienation. Cf. PER TOUT ET NON PER MY.

pernancy (**pər**-nən-see). (17c) *Hist.* A taking or reception, as of the profits of an estate.

pernor of profits (**pər**-nər *or* -nor). (15c) *Hist.* Someone who receives the profits of property; one who has the pernancy of the profits.

peroration (pər-or-**ray**-shən), *n.* (15c) **1.** The concluding part of a speech, usu. in which the main points are summarized. **2.** Erroneously, a long speech that might sound impressive but in fact has little substance. — **perorate,** *vb.*

perp (pərp), *n.* (1968) *Slang.* Perpetrator; a person who has committed a particular crime <the police brought in the perp for questioning>. See PERPETRATOR.

perpars (**pər**-pahrz). [Law Latin, fr. Latin *per partes* "by parts"] See PURPART.

perparts. See PURPART.

perpetrate, *vb.* (16c) To commit or carry out (an act, esp. a crime) <find whoever perpetrated this heinous deed>. — **perpetration,** *n.*

perpetrator. (16c) Someone who commits a crime or offense; one who does something illegal or immoral.

perpetua (pər-**pech**-oo-ə). See *exceptio peremptoria* under EXCEPTIO.

perpetual bond. See *annuity bond* under BOND (3).

perpetual disability. See *absolute disability* under DISABILITY (2).

perpetual edict. See *edictum perpetuum* under EDICTUM.

perpetual freehold. See FREEHOLD.

perpetual injunction. See *permanent injunction* under INJUNCTION.

perpetual lease. See LEASE.

perpetually renewable lease. See LEASE.

perpetual policy. See INSURANCE POLICY.

perpetual statute. See STATUTE.

perpetual succession. See SUCCESSION (4).

perpetual trust. See TRUST (3).

perpetuation of testimony. (1824) The means or procedure for preserving for future use witness testimony that might otherwise be unavailable at trial.

perpetuities, rule against. See RULE AGAINST PERPETUITIES.

perpetuity (pər-pə-**t[y]oo**-ə-tee). (14c) **1.** The state of continuing for all future time; the condition of persisting forever. **2.** *Hist.* An unbarrable entail. **3.** *Hist.* An inalienable interest. **4.** An interest that does not take effect or vest within the period prescribed by law. • In reference to the rule against perpetuities, only sense 4 is now current. See RULE AGAINST PERPETUITIES.

> "A persistent phenomenon in English legal history is the conflict between the vanity of the individual who seeks to cheat mortality by a posthumous direction of his fortunes and the policy of the state to maintain all forms of property in constant circulation. This antagonism, though in the nine centuries of English law it has assumed many forms, is perennial. It evoked the constant reiteration of the judges that they would not countenance the 'monstrous perpetuity.' To this end they destroyed all devices to prevent a tenant in tail from converting his interest into the freely alienable fee simple, they forbade the limitation of estates to two successive unborn generations and, with the help of the legislature, restrained the accumulation of capital beyond reasonable limits." C.H.S. Fifoot, *English Law and Its Background* 121 (1932).

> "A perpetuity is a thing odious in law, and destructive of the Commonwealth; it would put a stop to commerce and prevent the circulation of the riches of the Kingdom, and therefore is not to be countenanced in equity. If in equity you could come nearer to a perpetuity than the rules of Common Law would admit, all men being desirous to continue their estates in their families, would settle their estates by way of trust; which might indeed make well for the jurisdiction of the court, but would be destructive of the commonwealth." (1683) 1 Vern. 163 (per Lord North) (as quoted in George W. Keeton, *English Law: The Judicial Contribution* 118 (1974)).

perpetuity of the king *or* **queen.** (18c) A fiction of English law that for political purposes the king or queen is immortal; that is, a monarch dies, but the office is never vacant.

per procurationem (pər prok-yə-ray-shee-**oh**-nəm). [Latin] By proxy. — Abbr. *per pro.*; *p. proc.*; *p. pro.*; *p.p.* — Also termed *per procuration.*

perp walk. [Truncated fr. *perpetrator walk*] (1986) *Criminal law. Slang.* The police practice of walking an arrestee, esp. one accused of a white-collar crime, in public, usu. before media. • The perp walk, usu. arranged by police, typically occurs at the arrestee's home or workplace shortly after the arrest — or at the courthouse before or after arraignment.

per quae servitia (pər **kwee** sər-**vish**-ee-ə). [Latin "by which services"] (17c) *Hist.* A real action by which the grantee of a landed estate could compel the tenants of the grantor to attorn to him. • This action was abolished in the 19th century.

perquisite (**pər**-kwi-zit). (16c) A privilege or benefit given in addition to one's salary or regular wages. — Often shortened to *perk.*

perquisitor (pər-**kwiz**-ə-tər). [Latin "a seeker out"] (18c) *Hist.* A purchaser; esp., one who first acquires an estate by sale or gift.

per quod (pər **kwod**), *adv.* & *adj.* [Latin "whereby"] (17c) Requiring reference to additional facts; (of libel or slander) actionable only on allegation and proof of special damages. See *actionable per quod* under ACTIONABLE; *libel per quod* under LIBEL; *slander per quod* under SLANDER.

per quod consortium amisit (pər **kwod** kən-**sor**-shee-əm ə-**mɪ**-zit). [Law Latin] (18c) *Hist.* Whereby he lost the company (of his wife). • This phrase was used in a trespass declaration to describe the loss suffered by a husband whose wife had been injured, esp. beaten or otherwise abused.

per quod servitium amisit (pər **kwod** sər-**vish**-ee-əm ə-**mɪ**-zit). [Law Latin] (17c) *Hist.* Whereby he lost the services (of his servant). • This phrase was used in a trespass declaration to describe the loss suffered by a master whose servant had been injured by another. See *actio per quod servitium amisit* under ACTIO.

per rescriptum principis (pər ri-**skrip**-təm **prin**-si-pis). [Latin] (17c) *Roman law.* By the prince's rescript; by an imperial written reply to a petition.

Perringer release. See *Pierringer release* under RELEASE (2).

per saltum (pər **sal**-təm). [Latin] (16c) *Hist.* By a leap; without an intermediate step.

per se (pər **say**), *adv.* & *adj.* [Latin] (16c) **1.** Of, in, or by itself; standing alone, without reference to additional facts. • This phrase denotes that something is being considered alone, not with other collected things. See *actionable per se* under ACTIONABLE; *libel per se* under LIBEL; *slander per se* under SLANDER. **2.** As a matter of law.

persecutio (pər-sə-**kyoo**-shee-oh), *n.* [Latin] *Roman law.* A lawsuit or civil claim under *cognitio extraordinaria.* See COGNITIO EXTRAORDINARIA. Pl. ***persecutiones*** (pər-sə-kyoo-shee-**oh**-neez).

persecution, *n.* (14c) Violent, cruel, and oppressive treatment directed toward a person or group of persons because of their race, religion, sexual orientation, politics, or other beliefs. See *hate crime* under CRIME; WELL-FOUNDED FEAR OF PERSECUTION. — **persecute,** *vb.*

per se deadly weapon. See *deadly weapon per se* under WEAPON.

per se DWI. See DRIVING WHILE INTOXICATED.

persequi (**pər**-sə-kwɪ), *vb.* [Latin] *Roman law.* To claim through a judicial proceeding.

per se rule. (1940) *Antitrust.* The judicial principle that a trade practice violates the Sherman Act simply if the practice is a restraint of trade, regardless of whether it actually harms anyone. See SHERMAN ANTITRUST ACT. Cf. RULE OF REASON.

per se violation. (1928) *Antitrust.* A trade practice (such as price-fixing) that is considered inherently anticompetitive and injurious to the public without any need to determine whether it has actually injured market competition.

persistent felony offender. See OFFENDER.

persistent price discrimination. See PRICE DISCRIMINATION.

persistent-refusal rule. (2004) *Criminal procedure.* In some states, the doctrine that evidence of a motorist's refusal to submit to a chemical test is admissible at trial only if the prosecution meets the burden of showing, by a preponderance of the evidence, that the motorist repeatedly refused the testing. • In an administrative proceeding, as opposed to a judicial proceeding, persistence often need not be shown.

persistent vegetative state. See VEGETATIVE STATE.

persistent violent felony offender. See OFFENDER.

person. (13c) **1.** A human being. — Also termed *natural person.*

▸ **absent person.** *Louisiana law.* Someone who has no representative in the state and whose whereabouts are not known and cannot be ascertained by diligent effort. La. Civ. Code art. 47.

▸ **adult disabled person.** (1978) A child over the age of 18 for whom a parent continues to have a duty of support.

▸ **associated person.** See ASSOCIATED PERSON.

▸ **disabled person.** (1872) Someone who has a mental or physical impairment. See DISABILITY. — Also termed *disabled individual.*

▸ **disadvantaged person.** Someone who experiences deprivation or discrimination because of a disability, inherent trait, or social or economic factors.

▸ **disappeared person.** See DISAPPEARED PERSON.

▸ **displaced person.** (1944) Someone who remains within an internationally recognized state border after being forced to flee a home or place of habitual residence because of armed conflict, internal strife, the government's systematic violations of human rights, or a natural or man-made disaster. — Also termed *internally displaced person.* Cf. EVACUEE; REFUGEE.

▸ **fit and proper person.** Someone who is regarded as honest and trustworthy and has the necessary education, background, experience, or other qualifications for a specific position.

▸ **homeless person.** (1849) Someone who has no accommodation that he or she is entitled to occupy or that it would be reasonable to allow the person to continue occupying; esp., one who habitually stays in a public or private place not designed for or ordinarily used as regular lodging for human beings.

▸ **interested person.** (1844) A person having a property right in or claim against a thing, such as a trust or decedent's estate. • The meaning may expand to include an entity, such as a business that is a creditor of a decedent. — Abbr. IP.

▸ **known person.** (16c) A person whose identity is familiar to others or discoverable from records or other sources of information.

▸ **person in loco parentis** (in **loh**-koh pə-**ren**-tis). (1827) Someone who acts in place of a parent, either temporarily (as a schoolteacher does) or indefinitely (as a stepparent does); a person who has assumed the obligations of a parent without formally adopting the child. See IN LOCO PARENTIS.

▸ **person in need of supervision.** See *child in need of supervision* under CHILD. — Abbr. PINS.

▸ **person not deceased.** (1894) Someone who is either living or has not yet been born.

▸ **person of incidence.** (1880) The person against whom a right is enforceable; a person who owes a legal duty. • The meaning may expand to include an entity, such as an insurance company.

▸ **person of inherence** (in-**heer**-ənts). (1909) The person in whom a legal right is vested; the owner of a right. • The meaning may expand to include an entity.

▸ **person of interest.** (1937) *Police jargon.* Someone who is the subject of a police investigation or wanted for questioning but who has not been identified by investigators as being suspected of committing the crime itself.

▸ **person of opposite sex sharing living quarters.** See POSSLQ.

▸ **person of ordinary skill in the art.** See PERSON SKILLED IN THE ART.

▸ **person skilled in the art.** See PERSON SKILLED IN THE ART.

▸ **person with ordinary skill in the art.** See PERSON SKILLED IN THE ART.

▸ **private person.** (16c) **1.** Someone who does not hold public office or serve in the military. **2.** *Civil law.* An entity such as a corporation or partnership that is governed by private law.

▸ **protected person.** (17c) **1.** A person for whom a conservator has been appointed or other protective order has been made. **2.** *Int'l law.* Someone who is protected by a rule of international law; esp., one who is in the hands of an occupying force during a conflict. • Protected persons are entitled to a standard of treatment (including a prohibition on coercion and corporal punishment) under the Geneva Convention Relative to the Protection of Civilian Persons in Time of War (1949). **3.** *English law.* An inhabitant of a protectorate of the United Kingdom. • Though not a British subject, such a person is given diplomatic protection by the Crown.

▸ **smuggled person.** (1896) *Immigration law.* A person who pays another to help the person illegally cross a border, and is free to go once the border crossing is achieved. Cf. *trafficked person.*

▸ **trafficked person.** (1994) A person who is deceived or forced into illegally entering a country and then forced to work for another. Cf. *smuggled person.*

2. The living body of a human being <contraband found on the smuggler's person>. **3.** An entity (such as a corporation) that is recognized by law as having most of the rights and duties of a human being. • In this sense, the term includes partnerships and other associations, whether incorporated or unincorporated.

> "So far as legal theory is concerned, a person is any being whom the law regards as capable of rights and duties. Any being that is so capable is a person, whether a human being or not, and no being that is not so capable is a person, even though he be a man. Persons are the substances of which rights and duties are the attributes. It is only in this respect that persons possess juridical significance, and

this is the exclusive point of view from which personality receives legal recognition." John Salmond, *Jurisprudence* 318 (Glanville L. Williams ed., 10th ed. 1947).

"The word 'person' is now generally used in English to denote a human being, but the word is also used in a technical legal sense, to denote a subject of legal rights and duties. English law recognizes two categories of persons in this legal sense: 'natural persons' and 'artificial persons.' Natural persons are those animate beings which possess a capacity to own legal rights and to owe legal duties; artificial persons are sometimes also described as 'legal' or 'juristic' persons, but this usage can be confusing, as the latter terms are also used of both animate beings and inanimate entities, to denote the fact that they have an existence as legal actors, rather than the fact that they exist only in the legal, and not in the biological sphere." 1 *English Private Law* § 3.18, at 142–43 (Peter Birks ed., 2000).

▸ **artificial person.** (17c) An entity, such as a corporation, created by law and given certain legal rights and duties of a human being; a being, real or imaginary, who for the purpose of legal reasoning is treated more or less as a human being. • An entity is a person for purposes of the Due Process and Equal Protection Clauses but is not a citizen for purposes of the Privileges and Immunities Clauses in Article IV § 2 and in the Fourteenth Amendment. — Also termed *fictitious person*; *juristic person*; *juridical person*; *legal person*; *moral person*. Cf. LEGAL ENTITY.

▸ **control person.** See CONTROL PERSON.

▸ **fictitious person.** See *artificial person*.

▸ **international person.** See INTERNATIONAL PERSON.

▸ **juridical person.** See *artificial person*.

▸ **juristic person.** See *artificial person*.

▸ **legal person.** See *artificial person*.

▸ **moral person.** See *artificial person*.

▸ **private person.** See *private person* (2) under PERSON (1).

▸ **public person.** A sovereign government, or a body or person delegated authority under it.

persona (pər-**soh**-nə), *n.* [Latin] (1812) *Roman law.* A person; an individual human being.

"By the Roman law, every human being who had rights (other than such as were merely personal), or was subject to obligations or duties (other than such as were merely personal), had two personalities (*personas*), one natural, the other legal, artificial, and fictitious; and it was in the latter that his rights were vested, and upon the latter that his obligations and duties were imposed. It was a peculiarity of the legal personality that, being the creature of law, it continued to exist so long as there was any reason for its existence. It was not affected, therefore, by the death of the natural person, but continued its existence in the natural person's successor or heir." C.C. Langdell, *A Brief Survey of Equity Jurisdiction*, 4 Harv. L. Rev. 99, 101 (1890).

▸ ***persona designata*** (pər-**soh**-nə dez-ig-**nay**-tə). [Latin] (1812) A person considered as an individual (esp. in a legal action) rather than as a member of a class.

▸ ***persona dignior*** (pər-**soh**-nə **dig**-nee-or). [Latin] (18c) *Hist.* The more worthy or respectable person; the more fitting person.

▸ ***persona ficta*** (pər-**soh**-nə **fik**-tə). [Latin "false mask"] (1893) *Hist.* A fictional person, such as a corporation.

"But units other than individual men can be thought of as capable of acts, or of rights and liabilities: such are Corporations and even *Hereditates Iacentes*. Accordingly the way is clear to apply the name of person to these also. The mediaeval lawyers did so, but as they regarded Corporations as endowed with personality by a sort of creative act of the State, and received from the Roman lawyers the conception of the *hereditas iacens* as representing the *persona* of the deceased rather than as itself being a person, they called these things *Personae Fictae*, an expression not used by the Romans." W.W. Buckland, *Elementary Principles of the Roman Private Law* 16 (1912).

▸ **persona grata.** See PERSONA GRATA.

▸ ***persona illustris*** (pər-**soh**-nə i-**ləs**-tris). [Latin] (17c) *Hist.* A person of distinction.

▸ ***persona miserabilis*** (pər-**soh**-nə miz-ə-**rab**-ə-lis). [Latin "a pitiable person"] (17c) *Roman law.* An unfortunate person, esp. because of age, illness, or status. • A *persona miserabilis* received certain privileges in litigation.

▸ ***persona moralis*** (pər-**soh**-nə mə-**ray**-lis). [Latin] (1937) A collective entity that, by law or custom, is recognized as an artificial person (e.g., a church or corporation). See *artificial person* under PERSON (2).

▸ ***persona nasciturus*** (pər-**soh**-nə nas-ə-**t[y]oor**-əs *or* -**t[y]ər**-əs). [fr. Latin *nascor* "to be born"] *Roman law.* An unborn child. — Sometimes shortened to *nasciturus*.

▸ **persona non grata.** See PERSONA NON GRATA.

▸ ***persona praedilecta*** (pər-**soh**-nə pree-də-**lek**-tə). [Law Latin] (1863) *Scots law.* A preferred person.

"This phrase signifies one person who, among others appointed with him as colleagues in some office, enjoys the confidence and esteem of the person appointing, more than those appointed with him. Thus a testator not unfrequently appoints among his trustees one who shall be a *sine qua non* — that is, one whose concurrence and consent shall be indispensable to every act of administration under the trust. Such a trustee falls within the description of a *persona praedilecta*." John Trayner, *Trayner's Latin Maxims* 456 (4th ed. 1894).

▸ ***persona standi in judicio.*** See PERSONA STANDI IN JUDICIO.

personable, *adj.* (16c) Having the status of a legal person (and thus the right to plead in court, enter into contracts, etc.) <a personable entity>.

person aggrieved. See *aggrieved party* under PARTY (2).

persona grata (pər-**soh**-nə **gray**-tə *or* **grah**-tə *or* **grat**-ə), *n.* [Latin] (1851) An acceptable person; esp., a diplomat who is acceptable to a host country. Cf. PERSONA NON GRATA. Pl. **personae gratae** (pər-**soh**-nee **gray**-tee *or* **grah**-tee *or* **grat**-ee).

personal, *adj.* (14c) **1.** Of or affecting a person <personal injury>. **2.** Of or constituting personal property <personal belongings>. See IN PERSONAM.

personal action. See ACTION (4).

personal asset. See ASSET.

personal-attack rule. (1967) The FCC requirement that a broadcaster notify a person whose character or integrity was attacked on-air and offer that person an equal opportunity to respond. • The FCC dropped the rule in 2000 by judicial order. *Repeal of the Personal Attack and Personal Editorial Rules*, 15 FCC Rcd. 20697 (2000).

personal bodily injury. See BODILY INJURY.

personal bond. See BOND (2).

personal-capacity suit. See SUIT.

personal chattel. See *chattel personal* under CHATTEL.

personal check. See CHECK.

personal-comfort doctrine. (1957) The principle that the course of employment is not interrupted by certain acts relating to the employee's personal comfort, typically short breaks for eating, drinking, using the restroom, and the like. — Also termed *personal-comfort rule*.

personal-condition crime. See *status crime* under CRIME.

personal-condition offense. See *status crime* under CRIME.

personal contract. See CONTRACT.

personal covenant. See COVENANT (4).

personal crime. See CRIME.

personal defense. See DEFENSE (4).

personal demand. See DEMAND (3).

personal deterrence. See *specific deterrence* under DETERRENCE.

personal disability. See DISABILITY (2).

personal-editorial rule. See POLITICAL-EDITORIAL RULE.

personal effects. See EFFECTS.

personal estate. See *personal property* (1) under PROPERTY.

personal evidence. See TESTIMONY.

personal exemption. See EXEMPTION (3).

personal expense. See EXPENSE.

personal goodwill. See GOODWILL.

personal history. (17c) An individual's background; the particular experiences and events that shape a person's life.

personal holding company. See COMPANY.

personal-holding-company tax. See *holding-company tax* under TAX.

personal identification number. See PIN.

personali exceptione (pər-sə-**nay**-lɪ ek-sep-shee-**oh**-nee). [Latin] (18c) *Hist.* By personal exception; by an exception based on personal reasons. — Also termed *personali objectione* (əb-jek-shee-**oh**-nee).

personal immunity. See IMMUNITY (1).

personal income. See INCOME.

personal indignity. See INDIGNITY.

personal injury. See INJURY.

personalis actio (pər-sə-**nay**-lis **ak**-shee-oh). [Latin] (1893) *Hist.* A personal action; an action *in personam*.

personaliter (pər-sə-**nay**-lə-tər), *adv.* [Latin] Personally; in person.

personality. (1870) **1.** The legal status of one regarded by the law as a person; the legal conception by which the law regards a human being or an artificial entity as a person. — Also termed *legal personality.*

> "Legal personality . . . refers to the particular device by which the law creates or recognizes units to which it ascribes certain powers and capacities." George Whitecross Paton, *A Textbook of Jurisprudence* 393 (G.W. Paton & David P. Derham eds., 4th ed. 1972).

2. *Parliamentary law.* (*usu. pl.*) An improper reference to a member by name or in his or her personal capacity.

> "No person in speaking, is to mention a member then present by his name; but to describe him by his seat in the house, or who spoke last, or on the other side of the question, nor to digress from the matter to fall upon the person, by speaking, reviling, nipping, or unmannerly words against a particular member. The consequences of a measure may be reprobated in strong terms; but to arraign the motives of those who propose or advocate it, is a personality, and against order." Thomas Jefferson, *A Manual of Parliamentary Practice* 36–37 (1801) (citations omitted).

personality-profile evidence. (1997) Psychological or psychiatric testimony and documentation relating to the general mental makeup of perpetrators of certain types of crimes. • Evidence of this kind, not being tied to a particular defendant, is often held inadmissible.

personality theory. (1982) *Intellectual property.* A rationalization of intellectual-property laws, esp. copyright, drawing on the philosophy of G.W.F. Hegel, whereby personal expression is viewed as a form of self-actualization that gives the creator inalienable moral rights in the creations. • As a way of analyzing intellectual-property rights, personality theory takes the point of view of the individual inventor, author, or artist rather than that of society as a whole. Cf. LOCKEAN LABOR THEORY; UTILITARIANISM.

personal judgment. See JUDGMENT (2).

personal jurisdiction. See JURISDICTION.

personal justice. See JUSTICE (4).

personal knowledge. See KNOWLEDGE (1).

personal law. (18c) The law that governs a person's family matters, usu. regardless of where the person goes. • In common-law systems, personal law refers to the law of the person's domicile. In civil-law systems, it refers to the law of the individual's nationality (and so is sometimes called *lex patriae*). Cf. TERRITORIAL LAW.

> "The idea of the personal law is based on the conception of man as a social being, so that those transactions of his daily life which affect him most closely in a personal sense, such as marriage, divorce, legitimacy, many kinds of capacity, and succession, may be governed universally by that system of law deemed most suitable and adequate for the purpose . . . . [A]lthough the law of the domicile is the chief criterion adopted by English courts for the personal law, it lies within the power of any man of full age and capacity to establish his domicile in any country he chooses, and thereby automatically to make the law of that country his personal law." R.H. Graveson, *Conflict of Laws* 188 (7th ed. 1974).

personal liability. See LIABILITY.

personal liberty. See LIBERTY.

personal maintenance. See MAINTENANCE (6).

personal misrepresentation. See MISREPRESENTATION.

personal name. See NAME.

personal notice. See NOTICE (3).

personal obligation. See OBLIGATION.

personal privilege. See PRIVILEGE (5).

personal property. See PROPERTY.

personal-property tax. See TAX.

personal recognizance. See RECOGNIZANCE (1).

personal replevin. See REPLEVIN.

personal representative. See REPRESENTATIVE (1).

personal reputation. See REPUTATION.

personal-residence trust. See TRUST (3).

Personal Responsibility and Work Opportunity Reconciliation Act. A 1996 federal statute that overhauled the welfare system, as well as requiring states to provide a means for collecting child support by (1) imposing liens on a child-support obligor's assets, and (2) facilitating income-withholding. • The Act did away with Aid to Families with Dependent Children in favor of Temporary Assistance to Needy Families. It also limited the length of time that persons could receive welfare and tied states' receipt of federal child-support funds to their implementing enhanced paternity-establishment services. — Also termed *Welfare Reform Act.* See AID TO FAMILIES WITH DEPENDENT CHILDREN; TEMPORARY ASSISTANCE TO NEEDY FAMILIES. — Abbr. PRWORA.

personal-restraint petition. (1976) A motion filed by a convicted and sentenced prisoner seeking release from custody either on the prisoner's own recognizance or to house arrest with the aid of an electronic monitoring device while the court reconsiders the prisoner's sentence.

personal right. See RIGHT.

personal security. See SECURITY (4).

personal service. (16c) **1.** Actual delivery of the notice or process to the person to whom it is directed. — Also termed *actual service.* See *actual service, personal service* under SERVICE (7). **2.** A beneficial or useful act performed on behalf of another by an individual personally. • In this sense, a personal service is an economic service involving either the intellectual or manual personal effort of an individual, as opposed to the salable product of the person's skill. See SERVICE (2).

personal servitude. See SERVITUDE (3).

personal stare decisis. See STARE DECISIS.

personal statute. See STATUTE.

personal suretyship. See SURETYSHIP.

personal tithe. See TITHE.

personal tort. See TORT.

personal treaty. See TREATY (1).

personal trust. See *private trust* under TRUST (3).

personalty (**pərs**-ən-əl-tee). (16c) Personal property as distinguished from real property. See *personal property* (1) under PROPERTY.

▸ **quasi-personalty.** (1851) Things that are considered movable by the law, though fixed to real property either actually (as with a fixture) or fictitiously (as with a lease for years).

personal union. *Int'l law.* Two countries allied with each other and ruled by a single monarch but retaining wholly separate governmental institutions and not merged into a single political entity.

personal warrandice. See WARRANDICE.

personal warranty. See WARRANTY (2).

personal wrong. See WRONG.

personam. See IN PERSONAM.

persona miserabilis. See PERSONA.

persona moralis. See PERSONA.

persona nasciturus. See PERSONA.

persona non grata (pər-**sohn**-ə non **grah**-də), *n.* [Latin] (1888) An unwanted person; esp., a diplomat who is not acceptable to a host country. See NON GRATA. Cf. PERSONA GRATA. Pl. **personae non gratae.**

> "The right of each State to declare any diplomatic or consular agent *persona non grata* is one of the oldest principles of diplomatic and consular law . . . , echoed as far back as the work of the founding fathers of international law. It is a right that has remained uncontested and is currently enshrined in Art. 9 Vienna Convention on Diplomatic Relations (1961) and Art. 23 Vienna Convention on Consular Relations (1963), which both drew upon the Draft Convention on Diplomatic Privileges and Immunities of 1932 ('Harvard Draft'), enabling similar terms of provision. Considering its long, constant, and undisputed implementation, there is little doubt that these provisions constitute rules of customary international law." Jean d'Aspremont, *"Persona Non Grata,"* in 8 *The Max Planck Encyclopedia of Public International Law* 293, 293 (Rüdiger Wolfrum ed., 2012).

persona non grata letter. (1984) A written notice sent to a person, often a student suspended or expelled from a school or college, not to trespass on property where the person's presence is prohibited. — Also termed *PNG letter.* Cf. TRESPASS NOTICE.

persona praedilecta. See PERSONA.

persona proposita. See PROPOSITUS.

persona standi in judicio (pər-**soh**-nə **stan**-dɪ in joo-**dish**-ee-oh). [Law Latin] (1809) **1.** Capacity of standing in judgment; the right to appear in court. **2.** One with personal standing to vindicate a legal right.

> "What *persona standi* is, may be more easily learned by considering the loss of it by civil death or outlawry . . . . But there are others besides outlaws who have no *persona standi*. A pupil cannot pursue or defend; that must be done by his tutor in his name. And companies, as such, have not a *persona standi* . . . . *Persona standi* applies to the *status* of the person, as qualified to pursue or defend in actions generally; title to pursue applies to particular actions, and requires, in addition to a *persona standi*, that the party have a proper legal interest in the particular action pursued or defended." William Bell, *Bell's Dictionary and Digest of the Law of Scotland* 800 (George Watson ed., 7th ed. 1890).

personation. See IMPERSONATION.

person-endangering state of mind. (1990) An intent to kill, inflict great bodily injury, act in wanton disregard of an unreasonable risk to others, or perpetrate a dangerous felony. — Also termed *man-endangering state of mind.*

person *in loco parentis.* See PERSON (1).

person in need of supervision. See *child in need of supervision* under CHILD. — Abbr. PINS.

personnel (pər-sə-**nel**), *n.* (1819) **1.** Collectively, the people who work in a company, organization, or military force. **2.** A corporate department in charge of hiring and firing staff and dealing with employee problems.

person not deceased. See PERSON (1).

person of incidence. See PERSON (1).

person of inherence. See PERSON (1).

person of interest. See PERSON (1).

person of opposite sex sharing living quarters. See POSSLQ.

person of ordinary skill in the art. See PERSON SKILLED IN THE ART.

person skilled in the art. (1962) *Patents.* A fictional construct of the patent laws, denoting someone who has reasonably developed abilities in the field of the invention at issue. • The patent application must be clear and complete enough to teach a person skilled in the art how to make and use the invention without undue experimentation. — Abbr. POSA (for *person of* [or *with*] *ordinary skill in the art*). — Also termed *person of ordinary skill in the art*; *person with ordinary skill in the art*. See ARTISAN (2).

> "The term 'person skilled in the art . . .' has been interpreted to mean a person having ordinary or fair information in that particular line, not necessarily a person of high scientific attainments. The skill or knowledge to be imputed to such a person will vary with the complexity of the art to which the invention relates." Archie R. McCrady, *Patent Office Practice* 61 (2d ed. 1946).

> "[An] important principle of claim construction is that patents are intended to be read and understood by persons skilled in the art, sometimes also stated as a hypothetical 'person of ordinary skill in the art.' Under this principle, a patent need not contain every detail of a technology needed by laymen to understand an invention. Rather, a patent need only contain information needed by persons skilled in the art to which the patent pertains in order for them to understand the nature of the invention and the boundaries of the claimed invention. Many patents are thus virtually indecipherable to persons not being versed in the relevant scientific discipline, particularly in areas such as polymer chemistry, genetic material, and electromagnetic energy. Just as the adequacy of disclosure of a patent as a whole is measured with reference to a person skilled in the art, so the adequacy and meaning of claim language is measured with respect to persons skilled in the art." 1 Stuart B. Soffer & Robert C. Kahrl, *Thesaurus of Claim Construction* 21 (2d ed. 2013).

person with ordinary skill in the art. See PERSON SKILLED IN THE ART.

per stirpes (pər **stər**-peez), *adv.* & *adj.* [Latin "by roots or stocks"] (17c) Proportionately divided between beneficiaries according to their deceased ancestor's share. — Also termed *in stirpes*; *per stirpem*. Cf. PER CAPITA.

persuade, *vb.* (15c) **1.** To induce (another) to do something; to make someone decide to do something, esp. by giving reasons <Steve persuaded his neighbor to sign the release after the accident>. **2.** To make someone believe something or feel sure about it; to convince <Marten must persuade the jury of his innocence>.

persuaded confession. See CONFESSION (1).

persuasion. (14c) The act of influencing or attempting to influence others by reasoned argument; the act or practice of persuading.

▸ **fair persuasion.** (16c) Argument, exhortation, or persuasion that does not involve harassment, threats, or misrepresentations.

▸ **unfair persuasion.** See UNFAIR PERSUASION.

persuasion burden. See BURDEN OF PERSUASION.

persuasive, *adj.* (15c) Capable of making other people believe or do something; successfully prompting the decision that one wants someone else to make.

persuasive authority. See AUTHORITY (4).

persuasive memorandum. See MEMORANDUM (2).

persuasive precedent. See PRECEDENT (2).

per subsequens matrimonium (pər **səb**-sə-kwenz ma-trə-**moh**-nee-əm). [Latin] (18c) *Roman & civil law.* By subsequent marriage. • The phrase often referred to a child's legitimation by the later marriage of the child's parents.

per tacitam reconventionem (pər **tas**-ə-təm ree-kən-ven-shee-**oh**-nəm). [Latin] (17c) *Hist.* By a tacit renewal of the contract.

per tacitam relocationem (pər **tas**-ə-təm ree-loh-kay-shee-**oh**-nəm). [Latin] (17c) *Hist.* By tacit relocation. See TACIT RELOCATION.

pertain, *vb.* (14c) To relate directly to; to concern <statutes pertaining to environmental cleanups>.

pertinent, *adj.* (15c) Of, relating to, or involving the particular issue at hand; relevant <pertinent testimony>.

pertinent art. 1. See *analogous art* under ART (3). **2.** See *relevant art* under ART (3).

per totam curiam (pər **toh**-təm **kyoor**-ee-əm). [Law Latin] (17c) By the whole court.

per tout et non per my (pər **too[t]** ay **non** pər **mee**). [Law French] By the whole and not by the half. • This phrase described the estate given to a husband and wife — both are seised of the entire estate. Cf. PER MY ET PER TOUT.

perturbator (**pər**-tər-bay-tər). [Law Latin] (16c) *Hist.* A person, esp. a man, who disturbs the peace.

perturbatrix (pər-tər-**bay**-triks), *n.* [Law Latin] (18c) *Hist.* A woman who disturbs the peace.

per universitatem (pər yoo-nə-vər-sə-**tay**-təm). [Latin] (17c) *Civil law.* By an aggregate or whole; as an entirety. • This term describes the acquisition of an entire estate, esp. of an entire inheritance by universal succession.

per venditionis, donationis, cessionis, vel commutationis titulum (pər ven-dish-ee-**oh**-nis, doh-nay-shee-**oh**-nis, sesh-ee-**oh**-nis, vel kom-yə-tay-shee-**oh**-nis **tich**-[y]ə-ləm). [Law Latin] (1838) *Hist.* By the title of sale, donation, cession, or barter.

> "Per venditionis, donationis, cessionis, vel commutationis titulum . . . . These terms were used in the older forms of conveyancing, to distinguish lands so acquired from lands acquired either by inheritance or feudal grant. They signify what is now known by the name of a singular title." John Trayner, *Trayner's Latin Maxims* 452 (4th ed. 1894.).

per verba de futuro. (17c) By words in the future tense.

per verba de futuro cum copula. [Latin] (1845) A promise of marriage in the future given to a person with whom the promisor is currently engaged in a sexual relationship. • A few states recognize the formation of a common-law marriage under these circumstances. See *common-law marriage* under MARRIAGE (1).

per verba de praesenti. (16c) By words in the present tense.

perverse (pər-**vers**), *adj.* (15c) Behaving unreasonably, esp. by deliberately doing the opposite of what a reasonable person might be expected to do.

perverse verdict. See VERDICT (1).

pervert (**per**-vərt), *n.* (1856) A person whose behavior, esp. sexual behavior, is considered abnormal and unacceptable.

perverting the course of justice. (17c) *English law.* The skewing of the disposition of legal proceedings, as by fabricating or destroying evidence, witness-tampering, or threatening or intimidating a judge; OBSTRUCTION OF JUSTICE. — Also termed *interfering with the administration of justice*; *obstructing the administration of justice*; *obstructing the course of justice*; *obstructing justice*; *obstructing public justice*; *defeating the due course of justice*; *defeating the ends of justice*; *attempting to pervert the course of justice*.

per vim legis (pər **vim lee**-jis). [Latin] (1866) *Hist.* By force of law. • The phrase generally referred to persons who succeeded by intestacy to an estate.

pervise. See PARVIS.

per vivam vocem (pər **vɪ**-vəm **voh**-səm). [Law Latin] By the living voice.

per voluntatem hominis (pər vol-ən-**tay**-təm **hom**-ə-nis). [Latin] *Hist.* By the will of man. • The phrase appeared in reference to an act done by the testator's intention.

pessima fides (**pes**-ə-mə **fɪ**-deez). [Latin] *Hist.* The worst faith. • The phrase appeared in reference to moral dishonesty.

pessimi exempli (**pes**-ə-mɪ eg-**zem**-plɪ). [Latin] (17c) *Hist.* Of the worst example.

> "Thus, to acquit a man of a crime because he had committed it under the influence of drink, or to allow any one to take benefit under a contract induced by his fraud, would be *pessimi exempli*, as tending to lead others to be dishonest or unfair in their dealings, or to be careless of their habits or their acts." John Trayner, *Trayner's Latin Maxims* 457 (4th ed. 1894).

petens (**pet**-enz). [Latin] *Hist.* A demandant; a plaintiff in a real action.

peter-pence. (13c) *Hist. English law.* A tax levied on each house in England and paid to the Pope, so called because it was collected on St. Peter's Day. — Also termed *hearth money.*

petit (**pet**-ee *or* **pet**-it), *adj.* [Law French "minor, small"] (15c) See PETTY.

petit cape. See *cape parvum* under CAPE.

petite assize. See ASSIZE (5).

***Petite* policy.** (1971) The Department of Justice rule forbidding a federal prosecution after a previous state or federal prosecution based on the same acts unless (1) a substantial federal interest supports the prosecution, (2) the previous prosecution failed to vindicate the federal interest, (3) there is sufficient evidence to sustain a conviction, and (4) an Assistant Attorney General has approved the prosecution,. United States Attorneys' Manual § 9–2.031 (Sept. 1997); *Petite v. U.S.*, 361 U.S. 529, 80 S.Ct. 450 (1960). — Also termed *dual and successive prosecution policy.*

> "In response to the Court's continuing sensitivity to the fairness implications of the multiple prosecution power, the Justice Department adopted the policy of refusing to bring a federal prosecution following a state prosecution except when necessary to advance compelling interests of federal law enforcement. The *Petite* policy was designed to limit the exercise of the power to bring successive prosecutions for the same offense to situations comporting with the rationale for the existence of that power. Although not constitutionally mandated, this Executive policy serves to protect interests which, but for the 'dual sovereignty' principle inherent in our federal system, would be embraced by the Double Jeopardy Clause. In light of the parallel purposes of the Government's *Petite* policy and the fundamental constitutional guarantee against double jeopardy, the federal courts should be receptive, not circumspect, when the Government seeks leave to implement that policy." *Rinaldi v. U.S.*, 434 U.S. 22, 28–29, 98 S.Ct. 81, 85 (1977) (citation omitted).

> "('Petite Policy') . . . . The purpose of this policy is to vindicate substantial federal interests through appropriate federal prosecutions, to protect persons charged with criminal conduct from the burdens associated with multiple prosecutions and punishments for substantially the same act(s) or transaction(s), to promote efficient utilization of Department resources, and to promote coordination and cooperation between federal and state prosecutors." *United States Attorneys' Manual* § 9-2.031 (Sept. 1997).

petitio (pə-**tish**-ee-oh), *n.* [Latin] (16c) **1.** *Civil law.* A plaintiff's suit, esp. in an action in rem. **2.** *Hist.* A petition or demand; esp., a count in a real action.

petitio principii (pə-**tish**-ee-oh prin-**sip**-ee-ɪ *or* pə-**tit**-ee-oh). [Latin "postulation of the beginning"] (16c) *Hist.* Begging the question; that is, a logical fallacy wherein what is to be proved is implicitly presumed as true in the premise; an argument whose premise is also the conclusion. — Also termed *circular argument.* See BEG THE QUESTION.

petition, *n.* (15c) **1.** A formal written request presented to a court or other official body.

- ▸ **bankruptcy petition.** See *voluntary petition.*
- ▸ **certiorari petition.** (1936) A petition seeking discretionary review from an appellate court. See CERTIORARI.
- ▸ **creditor's petition.** See *involuntary petition.*
- ▸ **debtor's petition.** See *voluntary petition.*
- ▸ **involuntary petition.** (1868) A petition filed in a bankruptcy court by a creditor seeking to declare a debtor bankrupt. • This petition may be filed only under Chapter 7 or Chapter 11 of the Bankruptcy Code. — Also termed *creditor's petition.*
- ▸ **juvenile petition.** (1945) A juvenile-court petition alleging delinquent conduct by the accused. • The accusations made in a juvenile petition are sometimes tried in an adjudication hearing. See *adjudication hearing* (3) under HEARING.
- ▸ **petition for probate.** (1856) A written application by which a party requests that a court admit a will to probate.
- ▸ **petition in error.** See APPEAL (2).
- ▸ **voluntary petition.** (1842) A petition filed with a bankruptcy court by a debtor seeking protection from creditors. — Also termed *bankruptcy petition; debtor's petition.*

2. In some states, the first pleading in a lawsuit; COMPLAINT. **3.** *Patents.* A patent applicant's request to a patent office's administrative head for supervision of a procedural or jurisdictional matter related to the patent application. — **petition,** *vb.*

petition de droit. See PETITION OF RIGHT.

petitioner. (15c) A party who presents a petition to a court or other official body, esp. when seeking relief on appeal. — Also termed (archaically) *plaintiff in error.* Cf. RESPONDENT (2).

petition for access. (1950) *Patents.* Application to inspect a patent application, made by someone who does not usu. have the authority to do so. • The petition must demonstrate a special need for access, and show that the applicant has been notified of the petition. The patent applicant is entitled to a hearing before access is granted.

petition in bankruptcy. (18c) A formal written request, presented to a bankruptcy court, seeking protection for an insolvent debtor. • The debtor (in a voluntary bankruptcy) or the debtor's creditors (in an involuntary bankruptcy) can file such a petition to initiate a bankruptcy proceeding.

petition of right. (17c) *English law.* **1.** (*cap.*) One of the four great charters of English liberty (3 Car. I (1628)), establishing that "no man be compelled to make or yield any gift, loan, benevolence, tax, or such like charge, without common consent by act of parliament." • The other three great charters are Magna Carta, the Habeas Corpus Act (31 Car. 2 (1679)), and the Bill of Rights (1 W. & M. (1689)). — Also termed *Petition of Right of 1628.* **2.** *Hist.* A proceeding in chancery by which a subject claims that a debt is owed by the Crown or that the Crown has broken a contract or wrongfully detained the subject's property. • Although the petition is addressed directly to the Crown, the courts adjudicate the claim just as in an action between private parties. — Also termed *petition de droit.*

> "The Petition of Right reconfirmed Magna Carta's provision that no freeman could be imprisoned but by lawful judgment of his peers or 'by the law of the land.' The Petition also reconfirmed a 1354 reenactment of the great charter which first used the phrase 'by due process of law' instead of 'by the law of the land.' By condemning the military trial of civilians, the Petition invigorated due process and limited martial law. One section of the Petition provided that no one should be compelled to make any loan to the crown to pay any tax 'without common consent by act of parliament.' Americans later relied on this provision in their argument against taxation without representation. Other sections of the act of 1628 provided that no one should be imprisoned or be forced to incriminate himself by having to answer for refusing an exaction not authorized by Parliament. Condemnation of imprisonment without cause or merely on executive authority strengthened the writ of habeas corpus. . . . The Third Amendment of the Constitution derives in part from the Petition of Right." Leonard W. Levy, "Petition of Right," in *Encyclopedia of the American Constitution* 1383, 1383–84 (Leonard W. Levy ed., 1986).

petition to make special. (1934) *Patents.* A petition asking the U.S. Patent and Trademark Office to expedite a patent prosecution. • Special processing is available, for example, in favored areas of science (such as cancer research and energy conservation), where the inventor is sick or elderly, and where infringement is already taking place.

petit juror. See JUROR.

petit jury. See JURY.

petit larceny. See LARCENY.

petitor (pet-ə-tər), *n.* [Latin] (16c) *Roman law.* A plaintiff in a civil action; ACTOR (4).

petitorium (pet-ə-**tor**-ee-əm). See *petitory action* under ACTION (4).

petitory action. See ACTION (4).

petitory suit. See *petitory action* (2) under ACTION (4).

petit serjeanty. See SERJEANTY.

petit treason. See *petty treason* under TREASON.

Petrine privilege. (1944) *Eccles. law.* The Pope's power to dissolve a marriage between a baptized spouse and an unbaptized spouse when the Pauline Privilege is unavailable and the dissolution would be beneficial to the interests of the Church. • The privilege is usu. exercised to dissolve a previous marriage of a Roman Catholic. But sometimes it is applied in the case of a baptized non-Catholics who wishes to marry a Catholic. On rare occasions, the privilege has also been extended to dissolve the marriage of two unbaptized non-Catholics if one of them wishes to marry a Catholic. Cf. PAULINE PRIVILEGE.

petrol bomb. See MOLOTOV COCKTAIL.

petroleum-conservation law. (1980) *Oil & gas.* A state statute that limits the rule of capture and defines the correlative-rights doctrine by regulating the drilling and operation of oil-and-gas wells. • Petroleum-conservation laws are intended to prevent waste and protect correlative rights.

pettifogger (**pet**-i-fog-ər), *n.* (16c) **1.** A lawyer lacking in education, ability, sound judgment, or common sense. **2.** A lawyer who clouds an issue with insignificant details. — **pettifog,** *vb.* — **pettifoggery** (pet-i-**fog**-ər-ee), *n.*

pet trust. See TRUST (3).

petty, *adj.* (16c) Relatively insignificant or minor <a petty crime>. Cf. GRAND.

petty assize. See ASSIZE (6).

petty average. See *particular average* under AVERAGE (3).

Pettybag (**pet**-ee-bag). (14c) *Hist. English law.* A judicial office of the common-law side of the chancery court, with jurisdiction both in suits for and against barristers, solicitors, and other officers of the court and in proceedings involving writs of extent, acknowledgments, recalls of letters patent, recognizances, writs of scire facias, and writs of certiorari. • The court was so called because the original records were kept in a little bag or sack. It existed from Tudor to Victorian times. In the mid-19th century, the Pettybag was shrunk to but one clerk, and it was finally abolished altogether in 1889. — Also written *Petty Bag* or *Petty-Bag.* — Also termed *Office of the Pettybag; Pettybag office.*

petty cash. See CASH.

petty jury. See *petit jury* under JURY.

petty larceny. See *petit larceny* under LARCENY.

petty offense. See OFFENSE (2).

petty officer. See OFFICER (2).

petty patent. See UTILITY MODEL.

petty session. See SESSION (1).

petty theft. See THEFT.

petty treason. See TREASON.

p.fat. *abbr.* PRAEFATUS.

PFPA. *abbr.* PENTAGON FORCE PROTECTION AGENCY.

PGS. *abbr.* See *pictorial, graphic, and sculptural work* under WORK (2).

PH. *abbr.* Preliminary hearing.

phallocracy. (1977) Government by a man or men.

phantom jury. See *shadow jury* under JURY.

phantom stock. See STOCK.

phantom stock plan. (1959) A long-term benefit plan under which a corporate employee is given units having the same characteristics as the employer's stock shares. • It is termed a "phantom" plan because the employee does not actually hold any shares but instead holds the right to the value of those shares. — Abbr. PSP. — Also termed *shadow stock plan.*

phenotype. (1910) *Patents.* A living organism's physical characteristics and behavior. • A patent on living matter must disclose its genetic makeup rather than just describe its phenotype. Cf. GENOTYPE.

Philadelphia lawyer. (1788) A shrewd and learned lawyer. • This term can have positive or negative connotations today, but when it first appeared (in colonial times), it carried only a positive sense deriving from Philadelphia's position as America's center of learning and culture.

philosophie du droit. See *ethical jurisprudence* under JURISPRUDENCE.

philosophy of law. See *general jurisprudence* (2) under JURISPRUDENCE.

phishing, *n.* (1996) *Slang.* The criminal activity of sending of a fraudulent electronic communication that appears to be a genuine message from a legitimate entity or business for the purpose of inducing the recipient to disclose sensitive personal information. Cf. BOILER-ROOM TRANSACTION; TELESCAM.

▸ **spear phishing.** (2005) Phishing that targets selected people, usu. upper management, and that appears to be sent by someone in a trusted authority position close to the recipient, such as the CEO of the recipient's company. — Also termed *whaling.*

phone count. See COUNT (2).

Phonograms Convention. See GENEVA PHONOGRAMS CONVENTION.

phonorecord (foh-noh-rek-ərd). (1968) A physical object (such as a phonographic record, cassette tape, or compact disc) from which fixed sounds can be perceived, reproduced, or otherwise communicated directly or with a machine's aid. • The term is fairly common in copyright contexts since it is defined in the U.S. Copyright Act of 1976 (17 USCA § 101).

photo array. (1971) A series of photographs, often police mug shots, shown sequentially to a witness for the purpose of identifying the perpetrator of a crime. — Often shortened to *array.* — Also termed *photographic array; sequential photo array; six pack.* See ARRAY. Cf. LINEUP.

photofit. See IDENTIKIT.

photo spread. (1943) A group of photographs printed together, usu. in a magazine over several pages.

p.h.v. *abbr.* PRO HAC VICE.

phylacist (fɪ-lə-sist), *n.* (17c) *Archaic.* A jailer. — Also spelled *phylasist.*

physical, *adj.* **1.** Of, relating to, or involving the material universe and its phenomena; relating to the physical sciences <a physical explanation of this phenomenon>. **2.** Of, relating to, or involving material things; pertaining to real, tangible objects <the physical world around us>. **3.** Of, relating to, or involving the properties, forces, and phenomena treated of in physics <the physical characters of a mineral>. **4.** Of, relating to, or involving the natural sciences <physical chemistry>. **5.** Of, relating to, or involving someone's body as opposed to mind <physical main>. **6.** Of, relating to, or involving sex rather than just friendship <a physical relationship>. **7.** Of, relating to, or involving touching people a great deal <she is a very physical person>. **8.** Of, relating to, or involving rough or violent contact <football is a very physical game>.

physical child endangerment. See CHILD ENDANGERMENT.

physical cruelty. See CRUELTY.

physical custody. (1884) **1.** Custody of a person (such as an arrestee) whose freedom is directly controlled and limited. **2.** *Family law.* The right to have the child live with the person awarded custody by the court. — Also termed *residential custody.* **3.** Possession of a child during visitation.

physical diagnosis. See DIAGNOSIS.

physical disability. See DISABILITY (2).

physical endangerment. See *physical child endangerment* under CHILD ENDANGERMENT.

physical evidence. See *real evidence* (1) under EVIDENCE.

physical examination. See EXAMINATION (8).

physical fact. See FACT.

physical-facts rule. (1923) *Evidence.* The principle that oral testimony may be disregarded when it is inconsistent or irreconcilable with the physical evidence in the case. — Also termed *doctrine of incontrovertible physical facts; incontrovertible-physical-facts doctrine.*

physical force. See *actual force* under FORCE.

physical harm. See HARM.

physical hazard. See HAZARD (2).

physical-impact rule. See IMPACT RULE.

physical impossibility. See *factual impossibility* under IMPOSSIBILITY.

physical incapacity. See IMPOTENCE.

physical injury. See *bodily injury* under INJURY.

physical-inventory accounting method. See ACCOUNTING METHOD.

physical necessity. See NECESSITY (5).

physical neglect. See NEGLECT.

physical-proximity test. (1955) *Criminal law.* A common-law test for the crime of attempt, focusing on how much more the defendant would have needed to do to complete the offense. See ATTEMPT (2).

physical shock. See SHOCK.

physical taking. See TAKING (2).

physician-assisted suicide. See *assisted suicide* under SUICIDE (1).

physician–client privilege. See *doctor–patient privilege* under PRIVILEGE (3).

physician–patient privilege. See *doctor–patient privilege* under PRIVILEGE (3).

physician's directive. See ADVANCE DIRECTIVE (2).

P.I. *abbr.* (1953) **1.** See *personal injury* under INJURY. **2.** Private investigator.

PIA. *abbr.* PRACTICABLY IRRIGABLE ACREAGE.

piacle (pɪ-ə-kəl), *n.* (17c) *Archaic.* A serious crime requiring expiation.

pia fraus **(pɪ**-ə **fraws).** [Latin "pious fraud"] (17c) A subterfuge or evasion considered morally justifiable; esp., evasion or disregard of the law in the interests of a religious institution, such as the church's circumventing the mortmain statutes.

picaroon (pik-ə-**roon**). (17c) A robber, plunderer, or pirate.

pickery. (15c) *Hist. Scots law.* Petty theft.

picketing. (1832) The demonstration by one or more persons outside a business or organization to protest the entity's activities or policies and to pressure the entity to meet the protesters' demands; esp., an employees' demonstration aimed at publicizing a labor dispute and influencing the public to withhold business from the employer. • Picketing is usu. considered a form of fair persuasion of third persons if access to the place of business is not materially obstructed. Cf. BOYCOTT; STRIKE.

▸ **common-situs picketing.** (1955) The illegal picketing by union workers of a construction site, stemming from a dispute with one of the subcontractors.

▸ **informational picketing.** (1960) Picketing to inform the public about a matter of concern to the union, such as unfair treatment of workers.

▸ **organizational picketing.** (1952) Picketing by a union in an effort to persuade the employer to accept the union as the collective-bargaining agent of the employees; esp., picketing by members of one union when the employer has already recognized another union as the bargaining agent for the company's employees.— Also termed *recognition picketing.*

▸ **secondary picketing.** (1937) The picketing of an establishment with which the picketing party has no direct dispute in order to pressure the party with which there is a dispute. See *secondary boycott* under BOYCOTT; *secondary strike* under STRIKE (1).

▸ **unlawful picketing.** (1901) Picketing carried on in violation of law, as when the picketers use threats or violence to dissuade other employees from returning to work.

picket line. (1894) A queue of people who stand or march outside a workplace, often chanting and otherwise demonstrating, in an effort to prevent or discourage people from going in or coming out during a strike.

pickle. *Slang.* See PCCL.

pickpocket. (16c) A thief who steals money or property from the person of another, usu. by stealth but sometimes by physical diversion such as bumping into or pushing the victim, esp. in a crowded place.

pickpocketing, *n.* See *larceny from the person* under LARCENY.

pickup tax. See TAX.

pictorial, graphic, and sculptural work. See WORK (2).

piecemeal zoning. See *partial zoning* under ZONING.

piecework. (16c) Work done or paid for by the piece or job.

piepowder court (**pɪ**-pow-dər). (16c) *Hist.* In medieval England, a court having jurisdiction over a fair or market and presided over by the organizer's steward. • These courts had unlimited jurisdiction over disputes between merchants or merchants and purchasers, as well as over allegations of theft and violence. The name is a corruption of two French words (*pied* and *poudre*) meaning "dusty feet." — Also termed *court of piepowder.* — Also spelled *piepoudre; piedpoudre; pipowder; py-powder.*

piercing the corporate veil. (1928) The judicial act of imposing personal liability on otherwise immune corporate officers, directors, or shareholders for the corporation's wrongful acts. — Also termed *disregarding the corporate entity; veil-piercing; lifting the corporate veil.* See CORPORATE VEIL.

> "[C]ourts sometimes apply common law principles to 'pierce the corporate veil' and hold shareholders personally liable for corporate debts or obligations. Unfortunately, despite the enormous volume of litigation in this area, the case law fails to articulate any sensible rationale or policy that explains when corporate existence should be disregarded. Indeed, courts are remarkably prone to rely on labels or characterizations of relationships (such as 'alter ego,' 'instrumentality,' or 'sham') and the decisions offer little in the way of predictability or rational explanation of why enumerated factors should be decisive." Barry R. Furrow et al., *Health Law* § 5-4, at 182 (2d ed. 2000).

***Pierringer* release.** See RELEASE (8).

PIF. *abbr.* POOLED-INCOME FUND.

pigeon drop. See JAMAICAN SWITCH.

piggyback registration rights. See REGISTRATION RIGHTS.

pigneratio. See PIGNORATIO (1).

pigneratitia actio. See *actio pigneratitia* under ACTIO.

pignorate (**pig**-nə-rayt), *vb.* (17c) **1.** To give over as a pledge; to pawn. **2.** To take in pawn. Cf. OPPIGNORATE. — **pignorative,** *adj.*

pignoratio (pig-nə-**ray**-shee-oh), *n.* [Latin] **1.** *Roman law.* The real contract (*pignus*) under which a debtor handed something over to a creditor as security; the act of pawning; depositing as a pledge. — Also spelled *pigneratio.* **2.** *Civil law.* The impounding of another's cattle (or other animals) that have damaged property until the cattle's owner pays for the damage. Pl. ***pignorationes*** (pig-nə-ray-shee-**oh**-neez).

pignoratitia actio (pig-nə-rə-**tish**-ee-ə **ak**-shee-oh). [Latin] *Roman law.* An action founded on a pledge, either by the debtor (an action *directa*) or by a creditor (an action *contraria*). Cf. *cautio pigneratitia* under CAUTIO.

pignorative contract. See CONTRACT.

pignoris capio (**pig**-nə-ris **kap**-ee-oh). [Latin "taking a pledge"] (16c) *Roman law.* A form of extrajudicial execution by which a creditor took a pledge from a debtor's property.

pignus (**pig**-nəs), *n.* [Latin "pledge"] **1.** *Roman & civil law.* (*ital.*) A bailment in which goods are delivered to secure the payment of a debt or performance of an engagement, accompanied by a power of sale in case of default. • This type of bailment is for the benefit of both parties. — Also termed *pawn; pledge.* See PIGNORATIO; IMPIGNORATION.

> "The 'pignus,' pledge, is the right given to a creditor in the admitted property of another for his security; it is also used to signify the thing so given." John George Phillimore, *Private Law Among the Romans* 210 (1863).

2. A lien. Pl. ***pignora*** or ***pignera.***

▸ ***pignus judiciale*** (**pig**-nəs joo-dish-ee-**ay**-lee). [Latin] (1901) *Civil law.* The lien that a judgment creditor has on the property of the judgment debtor.

▸ ***pignus legale*** (**pig**-nəs lə-**gay**-lee). [Latin] *Civil law.* A lien arising by operation of law, such as a landlord's lien on the tenant's property.

▸ ***pignus praetorium*** (**pig**-nəs pri-**tor**-ee-əm). [Latin "a magisterial pledge"] (17c) *Roman law.* A pledge given to a creditor by order of a magistrate.

PIH. *abbr.* OFFICE OF PUBLIC AND INDIAN HOUSING.

PII. *abbr.* See *passive investment income* under INCOME.

pilferage (**pil**-fər-ij), *n.* (18c) **1.** The act or an instance of stealing; esp., theft of items that have little worth. **2.** The item or items stolen. See LARCENY; THEFT. — **pilfer** (**pil**-fər), *vb.*

pill. See POISON PILL.

pillage (**pil**-ij), *n.* (14c) **1.** The forcible seizure of another's property, esp. in war; esp., the wartime plundering of a city or territory. **2.** The property so seized or plundered; BOOTY. — Also termed *plunder.* — **pillage,** *vb.*

pillory (**pil**-ə-ree), *n.* (14c) *Hist.* A punishment instrument consisting of a wooden framework with holes through which an offender's head and hands are placed and secured. • A person put in a pillory usu. had to stand rather than sit (as with the stocks). Cf. STOCKS.

> "In the history of our own and other European countries, the pillory may be traced back to remote times, and its origin is almost lost in the mists of antiquity. Its story is one of tragedy and comedy, and full of historic interest and importance. In England, in bygone ages, the pillory was a familiar object, and perhaps no engine of punishment was more generally employed. Where there was a market, the pillory might be seen, for if the local authorities neglected to have it ready for immediate use, should occasion require it, they ran the risk of forfeiting the right of holding a market, which was a most serious matter in the olden time. Lords of Manors, in addition to having the right of a pillory, usually had a ducking-stool and gallows." William Andrews, *Bygone Punishments* 143 (1899).

▸ **finger pillory.** (1851) *Hist. Eccles. law.* A miniature stock used to confine the fingers of a person who misbehaved during church services.

pilot. (15c) **1.** A person in control of an airplane. **2.** *Maritime law.* A person in control of a vessel.

> "A *pilot* is a person taken on board at a particular place, for the purpose of conducting a ship through a river, road, or channel, or from or into a port. His duty, therefore, is properly the duty to navigate the ship over and through his pilotage limits, or as it is commonly called, his pilotage ground. . . . The office of a pilot is not a public one, unless expressly so constituted. Ordinarily, it is considered as a mere private profession, trade, or calling, which may be, and is in most instances, subjected to certain regulations and restraints, by the interposition of legislative authority." Henry Flanders, *A Treatise on the Law of Shipping* 400–01 (1853).

▸ **bar pilot.** See *branch pilot.*

▸ **branch pilot.** (1864) A pilot, esp. one who is trained and licensed to navigate rivers and their tributaries. • The term originated in England when pilots were licensed to navigate the River Thames and its tributaries. — Also termed *bar pilot.* See TRINITY HOUSE.

▸ **compulsory pilot.** (1874) A ship pilot entitled by law to guide a ship for a particular purpose, such as piloting the ship into harbor. • The compulsory nature of the appointment relieves the vessel's owner of personal liability if the pilot causes a collision. Cf. *voluntary pilot.*

> "In some waters and under certain circumstances the law requires a ship to be placed in charge of, and navigated by, a qualified or licensed pilot; and in such cases it is a statutory offence on the part of the owner or person in charge of the ship not to take a pilot on board. A pilot taken under these circumstances, called a 'compulsory' pilot, is held to be placed in charge of the ship by the law, and to supersede the master in the conduct of the ship so long as she is in pilotage waters. He is not the servant or agent of the owner; and for a collision caused entirely by his negligence neither is the owner answerable at law nor the ship in Admiralty. In such a case the remedy of the injured person is against the pilot alone." Reginald G. Marsden, *A Treatise on the Law of Collisions at Sea* 227 (3d ed. 1891).

▸ **voluntary pilot.** (1922) A ship pilot who controls a ship with the permission of the vessel's owner. • The vessel's owner is personally liable for damage resulting from a collision caused by a voluntary pilot. Cf. *compulsory pilot.*

> "If a vessel is in the hands of a harbor pilot at the time of the collision, the question arises whether the fault of the pilot is imputed to the vessel owner or operator. American law draws an unwarranted distinction between the 'voluntary pilot,' who is taken on voluntarily, and the 'compulsory pilot,' who is mandated by a statute or local regulation. The voluntary pilot is considered to be the same as any crew member, and his fault is fully attributable to the vessel owner. A compulsory pilot's fault, however, cannot be imputed to the shipowner personally; the doctrine of *respondeat superior* does not apply. At most, the vessel is liable *in rem* since the compulsory pilot's negligence is attributable to the ship. The distinction makes little sense in that it throws the loss upon potentially innocent parties and ignores the fact that the vessel owner commonly carries insurance against this liability. In any collision case, therefore, care should be taken to assert a maritime lien and to sue the vessel *in rem* if a compulsory pilot may be involved." Thomas J. Schoenbaum, *Admiralty and Maritime Law* § 13-1, at 450–51 (1987).

pilotage (**pɪ**-lə-tij). (16c) **1.** The navigating of vessels; the business of navigating vessels. **2.** Compensation that a pilot receives for navigating a vessel, esp. into and out of harbor or through a channel or passage.

▸ **compulsory pilotage.** (1868) A requirement, imposed by law in some jurisdictions, that vessels approaching or leaving a harbor must take on a licensed pilot to guide the vessel into or out of the harbor.

> "The compulsory pilot presents a special problem. Statutes that impose a fine or imprisonment for the failure to take a pilot obviously create compulsory pilotage. Some statutes, however, allow the ship to refuse the pilot provided she pays his fee or half of it ('half-pilotage'). The Supreme Court has indicated that it does not regard the tendering of this alternative as amounting to compulsion. It makes a difference, because it is pretty well settled that if the pilotage is 'compulsory' the *respondeat superior* nexus is broken, and the shipowner cannot be held personally liable for the fault of the pilot resulting in collision. The ship's liability *in rem*, however, is unaffected by the fact that the pilotage is compulsory. This is one of the more striking consequences of the endowment of the ship with a juristic personality independent of that of her owner." Grant Gilmore & Charles L. Black Jr., *The Law of Admiralty* § 7-16, at 520–21 (2d ed. 1975).

▸ **half-pilotage.** (1834) Compensation equaling half the value of services that a pilot has offered to perform. • Shipowners can avoid compulsory pilotage in some jurisdictions by payment of half-pilotage.

pimp, *n.* (17c) Someone who solicits customers for a prostitute, usu. in return for a share of the prostitute's earnings. See PANDERING (1). Cf. BAWD. — **pimp,** *vb.* — **pimping,** *n.*

PIN. *abbr.* (1976) Personal identification number; specif., an individually assigned code that a person uses to obtain money from a cash machine, in conjunction with a plastic card, or to engage in other types of credit-card transactions.

pincite. See *pinpoint citation* under CITATION (3).

pinkerton. (1884) *Slang.* A private detective or security guard, usu. one who is armed. • The name comes from the Pinkerton Detective Agency, the first private detective agency in the United States, established in 1852.

***Pinkerton* rule.** (1948) *Criminal law.* The doctrine imposing liability on a conspirator for all reasonably foreseeable offenses committed in furtherance of the conspiracy, even if those offenses are actually performed by coconspirators. *Pinkerton v. U.S.*, 328 U.S. 640, 66 S.Ct. 1180 (1946).

pink sheet. (1959) A daily publication listing over-the-counter stocks, their market-makers, and their prices. • Printed on pink paper, pink sheets are published by the National Quotation Bureau, a private company. — Also termed *National Daily Quotation Service.*

pink slip. (1904) **1.** *Slang.* A notice of employment termination given to an employee by an employer, esp. as the result of a layoff. **2.** An official document that proves ownership of a particular car.

pinpoint citation. See CITATION (3).

PINS. (1963) *abbr.* Person in need of supervision; esp., a juvenile who has been adjudged incorrigible. See *child in need of supervision* under CHILD.

pioneer drug. See DRUG.

pioneer patent. See PATENT (3).

pious gift. See *charitable gift* under GIFT.

pious use. See USE (1).

Pipe Rolls. *Hist.* The Exchequer's records of royal revenue, including revenue from feudal holdings, judicial fees, and tax revenue collected by the sheriffs. • The Pipe Rolls comprise 676 rolls, covering the years 1131 and 1156 to 1833 (except for gaps in 1216 and 1403). — Also termed *Great Rolls of the Exchequer.*

> "The Pipe rolls (so called possibly because of their pipe-like appearance when rolled up and stacked) were the rolls of the Exchequer and consist of parchment skins sewn together. Roger of Salisbury, Henry I's Treasurer, had established a rudimentary national financial system and the Pipe roll recording financial details at the end of Henry's reign is in existence . . . . The rolls contain much information concerning royal debtors, administration, and personnel of the King's government." L.B. Curzon, *English Legal History* 64–65 (2d ed. 1979).

PIR. *abbr.* PRESENTENCE-INVESTIGATION REPORT.

piracy, *n.* (16c) **1.** Robbery, kidnapping, or other criminal violence committed at sea. **2.** A similar crime committed aboard a plane or other vehicle. **3.** HIJACKING.

▸ **air piracy.** (1948) The crime of using force or threat to seize control of an aircraft; the hijacking of an aircraft, esp. one in flight. — Also termed *aircraft piracy.*

4. The unauthorized and illegal reproduction or distribution of materials protected by copyright, patent, or trademark law. See INFRINGEMENT. — **pirate,** *vb.* — **piratical** (pɪ-**rat**-ə-kəl), *adj.* — **pirate,** *n.*

> "[T]he test of piracy [is] not whether the identical language, the same words, are used, but whether the substance of the production is unlawfully appropriated." Eaton S. Drone, *A Treatise on the Law of Property in Intellectual Productions* 97 (1879).

> "[I]n some countries the problem is what might be called the 'cycle of piracy' — legitimate copyright owners refuse to sell in the country because of the piracy problem, which means that the only way the public can obtain the goods it wants is to turn to piracy. This in turn only strengthens the resolve of copyright owners not to do business in the country." *Intellectual Property in the New Technological Age* 514 (Robert P. Merges et al. eds., 1997).

▸ **video piracy.** (1980) The illegal copying and sale or rental of copyrighted motion pictures.

pirate recording. (1972) *Copyright.* An unauthorized copy of the sounds on a copyright-protected recording, including digital duplication made available over the Internet. — Sometimes also termed *bootleg recording.*

piscary. 1. See FISHERY (1). **2.** See *common of piscary* under COMMON (1).

pit and gallows. (17c) *Hist. Scots law.* An ancient form of capital punishment for theft by which a condemned woman was drowned in a pit and a condemned man was hanged on a gallows.

PITI. *abbr.* Principal, interest, taxes, and insurance — the components of a monthly mortgage payment.

P.J. See *presiding judge* under JUDGE.

PKPA. *abbr.* PARENTAL KIDNAPPING PREVENTION ACT.

pl. *abbr.* PLACITUM (8).

P.L. *abbr.* PUBLIC LAW.

placard (plak-ahrd *or* **plak-ərd).** (15c) **1.** *Hist.* An official document, such as a license or permit. **2.** An advertisement posted in a public place.

place land. See INDEMNITY LAND.

placement. (1913) **1.** The act of selling a new issue of securities or arranging a loan or mortgage. **2.** The act of finding employment for a person, esp. as done by an employment agency.

place of abode. (16c) A person's residence or domicile. See ABODE; RESIDENCE; DOMICILE.

place of business. (16c) A location at which one carries on a business. Cf. DOMICILE (2).

▸ **principal place of business.** (1825) The place of a corporation's chief executive offices, which is typically viewed as the "nerve center."

place of contracting. (18c) The country or state in which a contract is entered into. • The place of contracting is not necessarily the place where the document is signed; another location may be designated in the contract.

place of delivery. (17c) The place where goods sold are to be sent by the seller. • If no place is specified in the contract, the seller's place of business is usu. the place of delivery. UCC § 2-308.

place of employment. (17c) The location at which work done in connection with a business is carried out; the place where some process or operation related to the business is conducted.

place of performance. (1829) The place where a promise is to be performed, either by specific provision or by interpretation of the language of the promise.

place of wrong. (1930) The place, esp. the state, where the last event necessary to make an actor liable for an alleged tort takes place.

place-of-wrong law. See *lex loci delicti* under LEX LOCI.

place-of-wrong rule. See *lex loci delicti* under LEX LOCI.

placer claim. See MINING CLAIM.

placet. [Latin] *Obs.* It pleases. • This term was formerly used in registering a vote of assent.

placita **(plas-ə-tə),** *n.* [Latin] *pl.* PLACITUM.

placitabile (plas-ə-**tay**-bə-lee), *adj.* [Law Latin] That may be pleaded; pleadable.

placita communia (**plas**-ə-tə kə-**myoo**-nee-ə). [Latin] (18c) Common pleas; civil actions between subject and subject.

placita coronae (**plas**-ə-tə kə-**roh**-nee). [Latin] (17c) Pleas of the Crown; criminal actions.

placita juris (**plas**-ə-tə **joor**-is). [Law Latin "pleas of law"] (17c) *Hist.* Positive statements or guiding principles of the law, in contrast to legal conclusions or maxims.

placitare (plas-ə-**tair**-ee), *vb.* [Law Latin] To plead; to bring an action in a court of law.

placitory (**plas**-ə-tor-ee), *adj.* [Law Latin] (17c) Of, relating to, or involving pleas or pleading.

placitum (**plas**-ə-təm), *n.* [Latin] (17c) *Hist.* **1.** *Roman law.* An imperial constitution. **2.** A judicial decision. **3.** A court; a judicial tribunal. **4.** A judicial proceeding; a trial. **5.** A fine, mulct, or pecuniary punishment. **6.** A pleading or plea. **7.** A paragraph or section of a title or page where the point decided in a case is set forth separately. — Abbr. (in sense 7) pl. Pl. ***placita.***

placitum et conventio. See *consensus ad idem* under CONSENSUS.

placitum fractum (**plas**-ə-təm **frak**-təm). [Law Latin] (1831) *Hist.* A day past or lost to the defendant.

placitum nominatum (**plas**-ə-təm nom-ə-**nay**-təm). [Law Latin] (1831) *Hist.* The day appointed for a defendant to appear and plead.

placuit regi et concilio suo (**plak**-yoo-it **ree**-jɪ et kən-**sil**-ee-oh s[y]**oo**-oh). [Law Latin] *Hist.* It has pleased the king and his council.

plagiarism. (17c) **1.** The deliberate and knowing presentation of another person's original ideas or creative expressions as one's own; the wrongful appropriation of another's expression of ideas, or of the ideas themselves, by slight variation of expression; specif., the act of stealing passages from someone else's compositions, either verbatim or in substance; literary theft <the candidate was accused of plagiarism>. • Generally, plagiarism is immoral but not illegal. If the expression's creator gives unrestricted permission for its use and the user claims the expression as original, the user commits plagiarism but does not violate copyright laws. If the original expression is copied without permission, the plagiarist may violate copyright laws, even if credit goes to the creator. And if the plagiarism results in material gain, it may be deemed a passing-off activity that violates the Lanham Act. It can also be a criminal act under 17 USCA §§ 5–6. Cf. INFRINGEMENT. — **plagiarist** (**play**-jə-rist), *n.*

> "Plagiarism, which many people commonly think has to do with copyright, is not in fact a legal doctrine. True plagiarism is an ethical, not a legal, offense and is enforceable by academic authorities, not courts. Plagiarism occurs when someone — a hurried student, a neglectful professor, an unscrupulous writer — falsely claims someone else's words, whether copyrighted or not, as his own. Of course, if the plagiarized work is protected by copyright, the unauthorized reproduction is also a copyright infringement." Paul Goldstein, *Copyright's Highway* 12 (1994).

> "That the supporting evidence for the accusation of plagiarism may on occasion be elusive, insufficient, or uncertain, is not the same as thinking that the definition of plagiarism is uncertain. The gray areas may remain resistant to adjudication without being resistant to definition. It may be perfectly clear what constitutes plagiarism ('using the work of another *with an intent to deceive*') without its being clear that what faces us is truly a case of this." Christopher Ricks, "Plagiarism," 97 *Proceedings of the British Academy* 149, 151 (1998).

2. An idea, phrase, or story that has been copied from someone else's work without attribution <it takes close research to detect the plagiarisms>.

plagiarius (play-jee-**air**-ee-əs), *n.* [Latin] *Roman law.* A kidnapper.

plagiarize (**play**-jə-rɪz), *vb.* (17c) To take phrases, sentences, or ideas from someone else's work and use them in one's own work without attribution, as if they were one's own; to use the ideas and expressions of someone else without giving due credit.

plagium (**play**-jee-əm), *n.* [Latin] (16c) *Roman law.* The act of kidnapping, esp. a slave or child, which included harboring another's slave. — Also termed *crimen plagii.*

plaideur (play- *or* ple-**dər**), *n.* [Law French "pleader"] *Archaic.* An attorney at law; an advocate.

plaidoyer (ple-dwah-**yay**), *n.* [French] (17c) *Hist.* An advocate's plea.

plain and ordinary meaning. See MEANING.

plain bond. See DEBENTURE (3).

plainclothes, *adj.* (1908) (Of a police officer) wearing ordinary clothes so as not to be recognized as a police officer while at work. Cf. *undercover officer* under POLICE OFFICER.

plain-English movement. See PLAIN-LANGUAGE MOVEMENT.

plainer, *n.* An advocate of plain language as opposed to gobbledygook, bafflegab, and insider lingo, the idea being that caliginous sesquipedality and other types of inscrutable expression are inefficient, error-prone, unpersuasive, undemocratic, and altogether unpleasant. Cf. LEGALESE; LEGALDYGOOK.

> "The plain language movement includes many plainers (practitioners and campaigners) worldwide. Law is only one aspect of the movement; some plainers promote plain medicine; others plain government, plain technical writing, plain finance, and plain scientific papers. Some legal plainers are linguists, writers, editors, or legal translators. Some are practicing lawyers who write plainly for their clients; they might be private lawyers offering intelligible documents to the public, or government lawyers drafting plain legislation. Other plainers, whether or not they are lawyers, are one step removed from the public; they help lawyers redraft their standard documents and train them to write plainly for themselves; some are academics teaching the next generation of lawyers to communicate plainly." Mark Adler, "The Plain Language Movement," in *The Oxford Handbook of Language and Law* 67, 70 (Peter M. Tiersma & Lawrence B. Solan eds., 2012).

plain error. See ERROR (2).

plain-feel doctrine. (1984) *Criminal procedure.* The principle that a police officer, while conducting a legal pat-down search, may seize any contraband that the officer can immediately and clearly identify, by touch but not by manipulation, as being illegal or incriminating. — Also termed *plain-touch doctrine.*

plain-language law. (1978) Legislation requiring nontechnical, readily comprehensible language in consumer contracts such as residential leases or insurance policies. • Many of these laws have genuinely simplified the needlessly obscure language in which consumer contracts have traditionally been couched.

plain-language movement. (1978) **1.** The loosely organized campaign to encourage legal writers and business writers to write clearly and concisely — without legalese — while preserving accuracy and precision. **2.** The body of persons involved in this campaign. — Also termed *plain-English movement.*

plain meaning. See MEANING.

plain-meaning rule. (1937) **1.** The doctrine that if a legal text is unambiguous it should be applied by its terms without recourse to policy arguments, legislative history, or any other matter extraneous to the text unless doing so would lead to an absurdity. • Though often applied, this rule is often condemned as simplistic because the meaning of words varies with the verbal context and the surrounding circumstances, not to mention the linguistic ability of the users and readers (including judges). Cf. GOLDEN RULE; MISCHIEF RULE; EQUITY-OF-THE STATUTE RULE.

> "[W]here the language of an enactment is clear, and construction according to its terms does not lead to absurd or impracticable consequences, the words employed are to be taken as the final expression of the meaning intended." *U.S. v. Mo. Pac. R.R.*, 278 U.S. 269, 278 (1929).

> "On its positive side, the plain meaning rule states a tautology: Words should be read as saying what they say. The rule tells us to respect meaning but it does so without disclosing what the specific meaning is. At best, it reaffirms the preeminence of the statute over materials extrinsic to it. In its negative aspect, on the other hand, the rule has sometimes been used to read ineptly expressed language out of its proper context, in violation of established principles of meaning and communication. To this extent it is an impediment to interpretation." Reed Dickerson, *The Interpretation and Application of Statutes* 229 (1975).

2. Loosely, ORDINARY-MEANING RULE.

plain-sight rule. See PLAIN-VIEW DOCTRINE.

plaint. (13c) **1.** *Archaic.* A complaint, esp. one filed in a replevin action. See COMPLAINT (1). **2.** *Civil law.* A complaint or petition, esp. one intended to set aside an allegedly invalid testament.

plaintiff. (14c) The party who brings a civil suit in a court of law. — Abbr. pltf. Cf. DEFENDANT.

▸ **abnormal plaintiff.** (1961) Someone who, through some unusual attribute (such as a thin skull or a special susceptibility to bleeding) is injured more readily and more seriously than most other people. — Also termed *unusual plaintiff.* See EGGSHELL-SKULL RULE.

▸ **eggshell-skull plaintiff.** A plaintiff whose physical or mental condition makes the person exceptionally vulnerable to injury. — Also termed *eggshell plaintiff.*

▸ **involuntary plaintiff.** (1929) A plaintiff who is joined in a lawsuit by court order when the party's joinder is imperative for the litigation and the party is subject to the court's jurisdiction but refuses to join the suit voluntarily. • Under Federal Rule of Civil Procedure 19(a), a party is usu. joined as a defendant but may be joined as an involuntary plaintiff in "a proper case."

▸ **unusual plaintiff.** See *abnormal plaintiff.*

▸ **use plaintiff.** See USE PLAINTIFF.

plaintiff in error. (17c) *Archaic.* **1.** See APPELLANT. **2.** See PETITIONER.

plaintiff's-viewpoint rule. (1925) The principle that courts should measure the amount in controversy in a diversity-jurisdiction case by analyzing only the amount of damages claimed by the plaintiff. See *diversity jurisdiction* under JURISDICTION.

plain-touch doctrine. See PLAIN-FEEL DOCTRINE.

plain-vanilla swap. See INTEREST-RATE SWAP.

plain-view doctrine. (1963) *Criminal procedure.* The rule permitting a police officer's warrantless seizure and use as evidence of an item seen in plain view from a lawful position or during a legal search when the officer has probable cause to believe that the item is evidence of a crime. • Although some states hold that the plain-view discovery must be inadvertent, the U.S. Supreme Court has held that the viewing need not be inadvertent. *Horton v. California*, 496 U.S. 128, 110 S.Ct. 2301 (1990). — Also termed *clear-view doctrine*; *plain-sight rule.* Cf. OPEN-FIELDS DOCTRINE.

PLAM. See *price-level-adjusted mortgage* under MORTGAGE.

plan, *n.* **1.** BANKRUPTCY PLAN. **2.** EMPLOYEE BENEFIT PLAN.

planned obsolescence. See OBSOLESCENCE.

planned-unit development. (1962) A land area zoned for a single-community subdivision with flexible restrictions on residential, commercial, and public uses. — Abbr. PUD. Cf. RESIDENTIAL CLUSTER.

> "A PUD is primarily an alternative to traditional zoning since it provides a mixing of uses. The location and identification of the permitted uses are provided on the PUD map or plat, which closely resembles a subdivision plat. Development approval is generally granted for the PUD at one time rather than on a lot by lot basis and in that way closely tracks the subdivision approval process." Julian Conrad Juergensmeyer & Thomas E. Roberts, *Land Use Planning and Development Regulation Law* § 7.15, at 288 (2003).

planning board. (1913) A local government body responsible for approving or rejecting proposed building projects. • In most jurisdictions, the planning board's decisions are subject to the review of the city council. — Also termed *planning commission.*

plan of arrangement. (1847) *Bankruptcy.* An insolvent debtor's written proposal for partially or completely settling outstanding debts.

plan of rehabilitation. See BANKRUPTCY PLAN.

plan of reorganization. See BANKRUPTCY PLAN.

plan-of-the-convention doctrine. (2002) *Constitutional law.* The principle that each U.S. state, by ratifying the U.S. Constitution, has consented to the possibility of being sued by each of the other states, and has no immunity from such a suit under the 11th Amendment.

plant patent. See PATENT (3).

Plant Patent Act. *Patents.* The 1930 federal statute that extended patent protection for developing "any distinct and new" varieties of asexually reproducing plants. • Before passage of the Act, plant patents were rejected because the subject matter was considered naturally occurring and therefore unpatentable. 35 USCA §§ 161–164. — Abbr. PPA.

plant-patent claim. See PATENT CLAIM.

Plant Variety Protection Act. *Patents.* The 1970 federal statute that extended patent-like protection for developing new and distinct varieties of seed-producing plants. • A Certificate of Plant Variety Protection gives the holder exclusive rights to sell, reproduce, and develop further hybrids from the plant. 7 USCA §§ 2321–2582. — Abbr. PVPA.

plat. (15c) **1.** A small piece of land set apart for some special purpose; PLOT (1). **2.** A map or plan of delineated or partitioned ground; esp., a map describing a piece of land and its features, such as boundaries, lots, roads, and easements; PLAT MAP.

platform. (1837) A statement of principles and policies adopted by a political party as the basis of the party's appeal for public support.

platform committee. See COMMITTEE (1).

plat map. (1941) A document showing the legal divisions of land by lot, street, and block number. • A plat map is usu. drawn after the property has been described by some other means, such as a government survey. Once a plat map is prepared, property descriptions are defined by referring to the map. Plat maps are usu. recorded by a government agency. — Often shortened to *plat*.

plausibility test. See TWOMBLY TEST.

plausible, *adj.* (16c) **1.** Conceivably true or successful; possibly correct or even likely; REASONABLE (2) <a plausible account>. **2.** (Of a person) reasonably convincing and seemingly truthful, though possibly mendacious <a plausible liar>.

plea, *n.* (13c) **1.** *Criminal law.* An accused person's formal response of "guilty," "not guilty," or "no contest" to a criminal charge. — Also termed *criminal plea.*

▸ ***Alford* plea.** See ALFORD PLEA.

▸ **blind plea.** (1972) A guilty plea made without the promise of a concession from either the judge or the prosecutor. Cf. *negotiated plea.*

▸ **conditional plea.** (1924) A plea of guilty or nolo contendere entered with the court's approval and the government's consent, the defendant reserving the right to appeal any adverse determinations on one or more pretrial motions. • If an appeal is successful, the plea is withdrawn and a new one entered. Fed. R. Crim. P. 11(a)(2).

▸ **connected plea.** (1993) A criminal defendant's plea that the prosecution has conditioned on a codefendant's also pleading guilty. — Also termed *wired plea.*

▸ **guilty plea.** (1942) An accused person's formal admission in court of having committed the charged offense. • A guilty plea must be made voluntarily and only after the accused has been informed of and understands his or her rights. It ordinarily has the same effect as a guilty verdict and conviction after a trial on the merits. A guilty plea is usu. part of a plea bargain.

▸ **insanity plea.** See INSANITY DEFENSE.

▸ **negotiated plea.** (1956) The plea agreed to by a criminal defendant and the prosecutor in a plea bargain. See PLEA BARGAIN. Cf. *blind plea.*

▸ **no-contest plea.** See NO CONTEST.

▸ **nolo plea.** (1942) A plea by which the defendant does not contest or admit guilt. *See* Fed. R. Crim. P. 11(b); NOLO CONTENDERE.

▸ **not-guilty plea.** (1912) An accused person's formal denial in court of having committed the charged offense. • The prosecution must then prove all elements of the charged offense beyond a reasonable doubt if the defendant is to be convicted.

▸ **provident plea.** (1952) *Military law.* A plea that is entered knowingly, intelligently, and consciously, and is legally and factually consistent and accurate.

▸ **wired plea.** See *connected plea.*

2. At common law, the defendant's responsive pleading in a civil action. Cf. DECLARATION (7). **3.** A factual allegation offered in a case; a pleading. See DEMURRER; PLEADING (quot.).

▸ **affirmative plea.** See *pure plea.*

▸ **anomalous plea.** (1851) An equitable plea in which a party states new facts and negates some of the opponent's stated facts. • Partly confession and avoidance and partly traverse, the plea is appropriate when the plaintiff, in the bill, has anticipated the plea, and the defendant then traverses the anticipatory matters. — Also termed *plea not pure.* Cf. *pure plea.*

▸ **common plea.** (17c) **1.** A common-law plea in a civil action as opposed to a criminal prosecution. — Also termed *common cause*; *common suit.* **2.** *Hist.* A plea made by a commoner.

> "By 'common pleas' Magna Carta meant no more than ordinary pleas between commoners." Alan Harding, *A Social History of English Law* 51 (1966).

▸ **dilatory plea** (**dil**-ə-tor-ee). (16c) A plea that does not challenge the merits of a case but that seeks to delay or defeat the action on procedural grounds.

> "Dilatory pleas are those which do not answer the general right of the plaintiff, either by denial or in confession and avoidance, but assert matter tending to defeat the particular action by resisting the plaintiff's present right of recovery. They may be divided into two main classes: (1) Pleas to the jurisdiction and venue. (2) Pleas in abatement. A minor class, sometimes recognized, is pleas in suspension of the action." Benjamin J. Shipman, *Handbook of Common-Law Pleading* § 220, at 382 (Henry Winthrop Ballantine ed., 3d ed. 1923).

▸ **double plea.** (16c) A plea consisting in two or more distinct grounds of complaint or defense for the same issue. Cf. *alternative pleading* under PLEADING (2); DUPLICITY (3).

▸ **equivocal plea.** A plea of guilty qualified by terms that, if true, indicate the defendant is in fact not guilty, or may not understand the effects of the plea, or is not acting voluntarily. • A refusal to admit actual guilt does not make a plea equivocal.

▸ **general plea.** See *general denial* under DENIAL (3).

▸ **issuable plea.** (17c) A plea on the merits presenting a cognizable complaint to the court. Cf. *issuable defense* under DEFENSE (1).

▸ **jurisdictional plea.** (1900) A plea asserting that the court lacks jurisdiction either over the defendant or over the subject matter of the case. — Also termed *plea to the jurisdiction.*

▸ **negative plea.** (16c) A plea that traverses some material fact or facts stated in the bill. — Also termed *plea to the action.*

▸ **nonissuable plea.** (1841) A plea on which a court ruling will not decide the case on the merits, such as a plea in abatement.

▸ **peremptory plea.** (18c) A plea that responds to the merits of the plaintiff's claim or prosecutor's charge; PLEA IN BAR. • At common law, the peremptory pleas set forth special reasons why a trial could not proceed. They were the plea of autrefois acquit, the plea of autrefois convict, the plea of autrefois attaint, and the plea of pardon. See AUTREFOIS; PLEA OF PARDON.

▸ **plea in abatement.** (17c) A plea that objects to the place, time, or method of asserting the plaintiff's claim but does not dispute the claim's merits. • A defendant who successfully asserts a plea in abatement leaves the claim open for continuation in the current action or reassertion in a later action if the defect is cured. — Also termed *abater.*

▸ **plea in bar.** See PLEA IN BAR.

▸ **plea in confession and avoidance.** See CONFESSION AND AVOIDANCE.

▸ **plea in discharge.** (18c) A plea that the defendant has previously satisfied and discharged the plaintiff's claim.

▸ **plea in equity.** (17c) A special defense relying on one or more reasons why the suit should be dismissed, delayed, or barred. • The various kinds are (1) pleas to the jurisdiction, (2) pleas to the person, (3) pleas to the form of the bill, and (4) pleas in bar of the bill. Pleas in equity generally fall into two classes: *pure pleas* and *anomalous pleas.*

▸ **plea in error.** See SPECIAL PLEA IN ERROR.

▸ **plea in estoppel.** (1831) *Common-law pleading.* A plea that neither confesses nor avoids but rather pleads a previous inconsistent act, allegation, or denial on the part of the adverse party to preclude that party from maintaining an action or defense.

▸ **plea in reconvention.** (1826) *Civil law.* A plea that sets up a new matter, not as a defense, but as a cross-complaint, setoff, or counterclaim.

▸ **plea in suspension.** (1875) A plea that shows some ground for not proceeding in the suit at the present time and prays that the proceedings be stayed until that ground is removed, such as a party's being a minor or the plaintiff's being an alien enemy.

▸ **plea not pure.** See *anomalous plea.*

▸ **plea of confession and avoidance.** See CONFESSION AND AVOIDANCE.

▸ **plea of privilege.** (17c) A plea that raises an objection to the venue of an action. See CHANGE OF VENUE.

▸ **plea of release.** (18c) A plea that admits the claim but sets forth a written discharge executed by a party authorized to release the claim. See RELEASE (2).

▸ **plea puis darrein continuance** (**pwis dar**-ayn kən-**tin**-yoo-ənts). [Law French "plea since the last continuance"] (18c) A plea that alleges new defensive matter that has arisen during a continuance of the case and that did not exist at the time of the defendant's last pleading.

▸ **plea to further maintenance to the action.** (1830) *Hist.* A defensive plea asserting that events occurring after the commencement of the action necessitate its dismissal. • The plea is obsolete because of the pleading requirements in federal and state rules of civil procedure.

▸ **plea to the action.** See *negative plea.*

▸ **plea to the declaration.** (1820) A plea in abatement that objects to the declaration and applies immediately to it. — Also termed *plea to the count.*

▸ **plea to the jurisdiction.** See *jurisdictional plea.*

▸ **plea to the person of the defendant.** (1872) A plea in abatement alleging that the defendant has a legal disability to be sued.

▸ **plea to the person of the plaintiff.** (1821) A plea in abatement alleging that the plaintiff has a legal disability to sue.

▸ **plea to the writ.** (17c) A plea in abatement that objects to the writ (summons) and applies (1) to the form of the writ for a matter either apparent on the writ's face or outside the writ, or (2) to the way in which the writ was executed or acted on.

▸ **pure plea.** (18c) An equitable plea that affirmatively alleges new matters that are outside the bill. • If proved, the effect is to end the controversy by dismissing, delaying, or barring the suit. A pure plea must track the allegations of the bill, not evade it or mistake its purpose. Originally, this was the only plea known in equity. — Also termed *affirmative plea.* Cf. *anomalous plea.*

▸ **rolled-up plea.** (1929) *Defamation.* A defendant's plea claiming that the statements complained of are factual and that, to the extent that they consist of comment, they are fair comment on a matter of public interest. See FAIR COMMENT.

▸ **special plea.** (16c) A plea alleging one or more new facts rather than merely disputing the legal grounds of the action or charge. • All pleas other than general issues are special pleas. See *general issue* under ISSUE (1).

▸ **verified plea.** (1831) A plea that is proved true or legitimate by supporting evidence.

plea affidavit. (1991) *Criminal procedure.* A sworn and notarized written guilty plea to a misdemeanor, traffic violation, or other similarly nonserious criminal infraction, usu. submitted in absentia.

plea bargain, *n.* (1963) A negotiated agreement between a prosecutor and a criminal defendant whereby the defendant pleads guilty or no contest to a lesser offense or to one of multiple charges in exchange for some concession by the prosecutor, usu. a more lenient sentence or a dismissal of the other charges. — Also termed *plea agreement; negotiated plea; sentence bargain.* — **plea-bargain,** *vb.* — **plea-bargaining,** *n.*

▸ **charge bargain.** (1890) **1.** *Criminal law.* A plea bargain whereby a prosecutor agrees to drop some of the counts or reduce the charge to a less serious offense in exchange for a plea of either guilty or no contest from the defendant. **2.** An agreement made before criminal charges are filed whereby a prosecutor allows a defendant to plead guilty to a lesser charge or only some of the charges in exchange for dismissal of the higher or remaining charges. *See Bousley v. U.S.*, 523 U.S. 614, 635, 118 S.Ct. 1604, 1612 (1998). — Also termed *count bargain.* See COP A PLEA. Cf. *sentence bargain;* FACT BARGAIN.

▸ **sentence bargain.** (1972) An agreement between a prosecutor and a defendant whereby the defendant promises to plead guilty or no contest to the stated charge in return for a lighter sentence. • Usu. a judge must approve the bargain. See PLEA BARGAIN. Cf. *charge bargain*; FACT BARGAIN.

plea colloquy. (1969) *Criminal procedure.* An open-court dialogue between the judge and a criminal defendant, usu. just before the defendant enters a plea, to establish that the defendant understands the consequences of the plea. Cf. ALLOCUTION.

plead, *vb.* (13c) **1.** To make a specific plea, esp. in response to a criminal charge <he pleaded not guilty>. **2.** To assert or allege in a pleading <fraud claims must be pleaded with particularity>. **3.** To file or deliver a pleading <the plaintiff hasn't pleaded yet>.

pleader. (13c) **1.** A party who asserts a particular pleading. **2.** Someone who pleads in court on behalf of another. **3.** *Hist.* At common law, a person who (though not an attorney) specialized in preparing pleadings for others. — Also termed *special pleader.* **4.** *Hist.* NARRATOR.

pleading, *n.* (16c) **1.** A formal document in which a party to a legal proceeding (esp. a civil lawsuit) sets forth or responds to allegations, claims, denials, or defenses. • In federal civil procedure, the main pleadings are the plaintiff's complaint and the defendant's answer.

> "The [common-law] pleadings in a cause are commenced, on the part of the plaintiff, with the *declaration*, which is a statement in writing of his cause of action, in legal form. This declaration, as every other pleading in the cause, is required to be framed agreeably to the established rules and forms of pleading, and if defective in any particular, either in substance or form, may be objected to, as insufficient in law, by *demurrer*, on the part of defendant; or he may allege some matter in abatement of the action, or may deny the declaration to be true in point of fact, or may set up matter in avoidance of it — such answer on the part of the defendant being technically denominated his *plea*. To the defense thus made, the plaintiff may again, in his turn, *reply*, either, in case of a demurrer, by reasserting his declaration to be sufficient in law to support his action, and referring that question to the judgment of the court, which is termed a *joinder in demurrer*; or, in case of a special plea, he may on his part demur to such plea, as insufficient in law to constitute a defense; or he may deny it to be true in point of fact, or allege some new matter in avoidance of it, according to the circumstances — such answer being styled a *replication*. To the replication the defendant may either *demur* upon the law, or oppose a *rejoinder* as to the fact; and to the rejoinder the plaintiff may demur, or oppose a *surrejoinder*; and so the parties may proceed, by a system of alternate *allegation* and *objection*, *denial* or *evasion*, technically termed the pleadings, until they arrive at an issue, that is, some specific point of law, or fact, affirmed on one side and denied on the other, and presenting the exact question for the court or jury to determine." Sabin D. Puterbaugh, *Puterbaugh's Common Law Pleading and Practice* 36–37 (3d ed. 1873).

▸ **accusatory pleading.** (1908) An indictment, information, or complaint by which the government begins a criminal prosecution.

▸ **amended pleading.** (1809) A pleading that replaces an earlier pleading and that contains matters omitted from or not known at the time of the earlier pleading. Cf. *supplemental pleading.*

> "An amendment is the correction of an error or the supplying of an omission in the process or pleadings. An amended pleading differs from a supplemental pleading in that the true function of the latter is to spread upon the record matter material to the issue which has arisen *subsequent* to the filing of a pleading, while matter of amendment purely is matter that might *well have been pleaded at the time the pleading sought to be amended was filed*, but which through error or inadvertence was omitted or misstated. It has been declared that the allowance of amendments is incidental to the exercise of all judicial power and is indispensable to the ends of justice." Eugene A. Jones, *Manual of Equity Pleading and Practice* 68 (1916).

▸ **anomalous pleading.** (1845) A pleading that is partly affirmative and partly negative in its allegations.

▸ **argumentative pleading.** (1814) A pleading that states allegations rather than facts, and thus forces the court to infer or hunt for supporting facts. • Conclusory statements in court papers are a form of argumentative pleading. — Also termed *inferential pleading.*

▸ **articulated pleading.** (1953) A pleading that states each allegation in a separately numbered paragraph.

▸ **defective pleading.** (17c) A pleading that fails to meet minimum standards of sufficiency or accuracy in form or substance.

▸ **hypothetical pleading.** (1852) A pleading asserting that if a certain fact is true, then a certain result must follow. • Hypothetical pleadings are generally improper.

▸ **inferential pleading.** See *argumentative pleading.*

▸ **pleading to the merits.** (1891) A responsive pleading that addresses the plaintiff's cause of action, in whole or in part.

▸ **responsive pleading.** (1833) A pleading that replies to an opponent's earlier pleading. See ANSWER.

▸ **sham pleading.** (1825) An obviously frivolous or absurd pleading that is made only for purposes of vexation or delay. — Also termed *sham plea*; *false plea*; (archaically) *deceitful plea.*

▸ **shotgun pleading.** (1964) A pleading that encompasses a wide range of contentions, usu. supported by vague factual allegations.

▸ **supplemental pleading.** (1841) A pleading that either corrects a defect in an earlier pleading or addresses facts arising since the earlier pleading was filed. • Unlike an amended pleading, a supplemental pleading merely adds to the earlier pleading and does not replace it. Cf. *amended pleading.*

2. A system of defining and narrowing the issues in a lawsuit whereby the parties file formal documents alleging their respective positions.

> "The principal objects of pleading are, firstly, to define the issues of fact and questions of law to be decided between the parties; secondly, to give to each of them distinct notice of the case intended to be set up by the other, and thus to prevent either party from being taken by surprise at the trial; and, thirdly, to provide a brief summary of the case of each party, which is readily available for reference, and from which the nature of the claim and defence may be easily apprehended, and constitute a permanent record of the questions raised in the action, and of the issues decided therein, so as to prevent future litigation upon matters already adjudicated upon between the litigants." Edward Bullen & Stephen Leake, *Bullen and Leake's Precedents of Pleadings* 1 (Alfred Thompson Denning and Arthur Grattan-Bellew eds., 9th ed. 1935).

▸ **alternative pleading.** (1868) A form of pleading whereby the pleader alleges two or more independent claims or defenses that are not necessarily consistent with each other, such as alleging both intentional infliction of emotional distress and negligent infliction of emotional distress based on the same conduct. Fed. R. Civ. P. 8(e)(2). — Also termed *pleading in the alternative*. Cf. DUPLICITY (3); *double plea* under PLEA (3).

▸ **artful pleading.** (1950) A plaintiff's disguised phrasing of a federal claim as solely a state-law claim in order to prevent a defendant from removing the case from state court to federal court.

▸ **code pleading.** (1860) A procedural system requiring that the pleader allege merely the facts of the case giving rise to the claim or defense, not the legal conclusions necessary to sustain the claim or establish the defense. — Also termed *fact pleading*. Cf. *issue pleading*.

"In this country the movement for pleading reform resulted in the adoption of the New York Code of 1848, the model and forerunner of all the practice codes in states which have adopted code pleading. By this act a single combined system of law and equity administered through the form of the one civil action was substituted for the two separate law and equity systems previously existing, and the forms of action at law and the separate suit in equity were abolished. It was further provided that the pleadings should state the facts, and the forming of the issue was less stressed. In addition to the fusion of law and equity and the substitution of fact pleading for issue pleading, the code adopted for all actions various equity principles such as freer joinder of parties and the split judgment, in part for the plaintiff, in part for the defendant." Charles E. Clark, *Handbook of the Law of Code Pleading* § 7, at 21 (2d ed. 1947).

▸ **common-law pleading.** (1822) The system of pleading historically used in the three common-law courts of England (the King's Bench, the Common Pleas, and the Exchequer) up to 1873.

▸ **equity pleading.** (18c) The system of pleading used in courts of equity. • In most jurisdictions, rules unique to equity practice have been largely supplanted by one set of rules of court, esp. where law courts and equity courts have merged.

▸ **fact pleading.** See *code pleading*.

▸ **issue pleading.** (1916) The common-law method of pleading, the main purpose of which was to frame an issue. Cf. *code pleading*.

▸ **notice pleading.** (1918) A procedural system requiring that the pleader give only a short and plain statement of the claim showing that the pleader is entitled to relief, and not a complete detailing of all the facts. Fed. R. Civ. P. 8(a).

▸ **pleading in the alternative.** See *alternative pleading*.

▸ **special pleading.** See SPECIAL PLEADING.

3. The legal rules regulating the statement of the plaintiff's claims and the defendant's defenses <today, pleading is a much simpler subject than it was in former years>.

pleading the baby act. See BABY ACT, PLEADING THE.

pleading the Fifth. See TAKE THE FIFTH; RIGHT AGAINST SELF-INCRIMINATION.

plead (one's) belly. (1857) *Hist. Slang.* (Of a female defendant) to claim pregnancy as a defense, usu. to postpone or avoid a court's sentence of capital punishment or transportation. • A woman who pleaded that she was pregnant was treated with suspicion. The judge would appoint a jury of matrons (often consisting of 12 married mothers) to examine the claimant (under the writ *de ventre inspiciendo*). If the woman was declared to be "quick with child" (in an advanced state of pregnancy rather than "barely with child" or only newly or just possibly pregnant), she enjoyed a reprieve from execution or transportation until after the child's birth (or miscarriage). Because juries of matrons often declared barren defendants to be pregnant, a court would keep track of a reprieved woman to see if the delay was justified or if she should be made to suffer the sentence ("called down") at the next session. Although the plea and the special jury are no longer in use, the prohibition against executing a pregnant woman persists in modern law. 18 USCA § 3596(b).

plead over, *vb.* (17c) **1.** To fail to notice a defective allegation in an opponent's pleading before responding to the pleading. **2.** *Hist.* To plead the general issue after a defendant has had a dilatory plea overruled. See AIDER BY PLEADING OVER.

plead the Fifth. See TAKE THE FIFTH.

plea in abatement. See PLEA (3).

plea in avoidance. See *affirmative defense* under DEFENSE (1).

plea in bar. (17c) A plea that seeks to defeat the plaintiff's or prosecutor's action completely and permanently. — Also termed *peremptory plea*.

▸ **general plea in bar.** (18c) A criminal defendant's plea of not guilty by which the defendant denies every fact and circumstance necessary to be convicted of the crime charged.

▸ **special plea in bar.** (17c) A plea that, rather than addressing the merits and denying the facts alleged, sets up some extrinsic fact showing why a criminal defendant cannot be tried for the offense charged. • Examples include the plea of *autrefois acquit* and the plea of pardon.

plea in confession and avoidance. See CONFESSION AND AVOIDANCE.

plea in discharge. See PLEA (3).

plea in equity. See PLEA (3).

plea in error. See SPECIAL PLEA IN ERROR.

plea in estoppel. See PLEA (3).

plea in justification. See *affirmative defense* under DEFENSE (1).

plea in reconvention. See PLEA (3).

plea in suspension. See PLEA (3).

plea not pure. See *anomalous plea* under PLEA (3).

plea of confession and avoidance. See CONFESSION AND AVOIDANCE.

plea of pardon. *Criminal law.* A peremptory plea in which a criminal defendant asserts that he or she has already been pardoned for the offense and therefore cannot be tried for it. See *peremptory plea* under PLEA (1).

plea of pregnancy. (18c) *Hist.* A plea of a woman convicted of a capital crime to stay her execution until she gives birth. See PLEAD (ONE'S) BELLY.

plea of privilege. See PLEA (3).

plea of release. See PLEA (3).

plea of sanctuary. See DECLINATORY PLEA.

plea of tender. (18c) At common law, a pleading asserting that the defendant has consistently been willing to pay the debt demanded, has offered it to the plaintiff, and has brought the money into court ready to pay the plaintiff. See TENDER.

plea puis darrein continuance. See PLEA (3).

pleasure appointment. See APPOINTMENT (1).

pleasure marriage. See *temporary marriage* under MARRIAGE (1).

plea to further maintenance to the action. See PLEA (3).

plea to the action. See *negative plea* under PLEA (3).

plea to the count. See *plea to the declaration* under PLEA (3).

plea to the declaration. See PLEA (3).

plea to the jurisdiction. See *jurisdictional plea* under PLEA (3).

plea to the person of the defendant. See PLEA (3).

plea to the person of the plaintiff. See PLEA (3).

plea to the writ. See PLEA (3).

plebeian (pli-**bee**-ən), *n.* (16c) *Roman law.* A member of the Roman plebs; an ordinary citizen, not a member of the upper class (patricians).

plebiscite (**pleb**-ə-SIT *or* **pleb**-ə-sit), *n.* (1860) **1.** A binding or nonbinding referendum on a proposed law, constitutional amendment, or significant public issue. Cf. REFERENDUM; INITIATIVE. **2.** *Int'l law.* A direct vote of a country's electorate to decide a question of public importance, such as union with another country or a proposed change to the constitution. — **plebiscitary** (plə-**bi**-sə-ter-ee), *adj.*

plebiscitum (pleb-ə-SI-təm), *n.* [Latin] (16c) *Roman law.* An enactment passed at the request of a tribune by the assembly of the common people (the *concilium plebis*). See CONCILIUM PLEBIS. Pl. ***plebiscita.***

plebs (plebz), *n.* [Latin] (16c) *Roman law.* The common people in ancient Rome; the general body of citizens, excluding the patricians. Pl. **plebes** (**plee**-beez).

pledge, *n.* (14c) **1.** A formal promise or undertaking. Cf. OATH. **2.** The act of providing something as security for a debt or obligation. **3.** A bailment or other deposit of personal property to a creditor as security for a debt or obligation; PAWN (2). See *contract to pledge* under CONTRACT. Cf. LIEN (1). **4.** The item of personal property so deposited; PAWN (1). **5.** The thing so provided. — Formerly also termed *safe-pledge.* **6.** A security interest in personal property represented by an indispensable instrument, the interest being created by a bailment or other deposit of personal property for the purpose of securing the payment of a debt or the performance of some other duty. **7.** *Hist.* Someone who acts as a surety for the prosecution of a lawsuit. • In early practice, pledges were listed at the end of the declaration. Over time the listing of pledges became a formality, and fictitious names (such as "John Doe" or "Richard Roe") were allowed. — **pledge,** *vb.* — **pledgeable,** *adj.*

> "A pledge is something more than a mere lien and something less than a mortgage. In an early English case Chief Justice Gibbs said: 'Undoubtedly, as a general proposition, a right of lien gives no right to sell the goods. But when goods are deposited, by way of security, to indemnify a party against a loan of money, it is more than a lien. The lender's rights are more extensive than such as accrue under an ordinary lien in the way of trade.' [*Pothonier & Hodgson v. Dawson*, (1816) Holt 383, 385.] Both in a pledge and in a lien the general property remains in the debtor and the creditor has only a special property. But the nature and extent of this special property in the two cases is quite different. A lien gives only a personal right to retain possession. The creditor holding this security cannot transfer it to any other person, nor can he himself enforce it by sale of his own motion, without the aid of judicial proceedings. A creditor holding a pledge may, on the other hand, transfer his interest to another, and he may himself enforce his security by sale without the aid of a court.
>
> . . .
>
> "A pledge differs from a chattel mortgage in three essential characteristics. 1. It may be constituted without any contract in writing, merely by delivery of the thing pledged. 2. It is constituted by a delivery of the thing pledged, and is continued only so long as the possession remains with the creditor. 3. It does not generally pass the title to the thing pledged, but gives only a lien to the creditor, while the debtor retains the general property. While the distinction between these two forms of security is well defined, yet, owing to the haste with which transactions are often made, and to the meagerness or abbreviations of the written papers which accompany them, it is not easy always to determine what character is properly to be attributed to them." Leonard A. Jones, *A Treatise on the Law of Collateral Securities and Pledges* 4–5, 6–7 (Edward M. White ed., 3d ed. 1912).

> "A pledge is a bailment of personal property to secure an obligation of the bailor. If the purpose of the transaction is to transfer property for security only, then the courts will hold the transaction a pledge, even though in form it may be a sale or other out-and-out transfer." Ray Andrews Brown, *The Law of Personal Property* § 128, at 622 (2d ed. 1936).

> "The pledge is as old as recorded history and is still in use, as the presence of pawnbrokers attests. In this transaction the debtor borrows money by physically transferring to a secured party the possession of the property to be used as security, and the property will be returned if the debt is repaid. Since the debtor does not retain the use of pledged goods, this security device has obvious disadvantages from the debtor's point of view." Ray D. Henson, *Handbook on Secured Transactions Under the Uniform Commercial Code* § 3-1, at 17 (3d ed. 1983).

pledged account. See ACCOUNT.

pledgee. (18c) One with whom a pledge is deposited.

pledgery. *Archaic.* See SURETYSHIP.

pledgor. (18c) Someone who gives a pledge to another. — Also spelled *pledger.*

plegiis acquietandis. See DE PLEGIIS ACQUIETANDIS.

plena aetas (**plee**-nə **ee**-tas). [Latin] (17c) Full age. See *age of majority* under AGE.

plena forisfactura (**plee**-nə for-is-**fak**-chər-ə). [Latin "complete forfeiture"] (17c) A forfeiture of all that one possesses.

plena probatio. See *probatio plena* under PROBATIO.

plenarty (**plee**-nər-tee *or* **plen**-ər-tee), *n.* (15c) *Hist.* The condition of being full or occupied; esp., the state of a benefice that is lawfully occupied by an incumbent.

plenary (**plee**-nə-ree *or* **plen**-ə-ree), *adj.* (15c) **1.** Full; complete; entire <plenary authority>. **2.** (Of an assembly) intended to have the attendance of all members or participants <plenary session>.

plenary action. See ACTION (4).

plenary confession. See CONFESSION (1).

plenary guardianship. See GUARDIANSHIP.

plenary jurisdiction. See JURISDICTION.

plenary power. See POWER (3).

plenary review. See JUDICIAL REVIEW.

plenary session. See SESSION (1).

plenary suit. See SUIT.

plene (**plee**-nee), *adv.* [Latin] Fully; completely; sufficiently.

plene administravit (**plee**-nee ad-min-ə-**stray**-vit). [Law Latin "he has fully administered"] (17c) *Hist.* A defensive plea in which an executor or administrator asserts that no assets remain in the estate to satisfy the plaintiff's demand.

plene administravit praeter (**plee**-nee ad-min-ə-**stray**-vit **pree**-tər). [Law Latin "he has fully administered, except"] (1809) *Hist.* A defensive plea in which an executor or administrator asserts that no assets remain in the estate, except a stated few that are insufficient to satisfy the plaintiff's demand.

plene computavit (**plee**-nee kom-pyoo-**tay**-vit). [Law Latin "he has fully accounted"] (17c) *Hist.* A plea in an action of account render, alleging that the defendant has fully accounted. See ACCOUNTING (3).

plenipotentiary (plen-ə-pə-**ten**-shee-er-ee). (17c) Someone who has full power to take action or make decisions, esp. as a representative of a government in a foreign country; a person fully commissioned to act for another. See *minister plenipotentiary* under MINISTER.

plenitudo potestatis (plen-i-**tyoo**-doh poh-tes-**tay**-tis). [Latin] *Hist.* Fullness of power.

pleno jure (**plee**-noh **joor**-ee). [Latin] *Hist.* With full right. • The phrase usu. referred to a conveyance of the full rights to property.

plenum dominium. See *dominium plenum* under DOMINIUM (1).

plevin (**plev**-in), *n.* (14c) *Archaic.* An assurance or warrant; a pledge.

PLI. *abbr.* See *products-liability insurance* under INSURANCE.

Plimsoll marks. See LOAD LINE (2).

PLL. *abbr.* See *products-liability loss* under LOSS.

plot, *n.* (bef. 12c) **1.** A measured piece of land; LOT (1). Cf. PLAT (1). **2.** A plan forming the basis of a conspiracy.

plot plan. (1925) A plan that shows a proposed or present use of a plot of land, esp. of a residential area.

plottage. (1916) The increase in value achieved by combining small, undeveloped tracts of land into larger tracts.

plow back, *vb.* (1912) To reinvest earnings and profits into a business instead of paying them out as dividends or withdrawals.

plowbote. See BOTE (2).

plowland. See CARUCATE.

plowman's fee. See FEE (2).

PLR. *abbr.* (1969) PUBLIC-LENDING RIGHT.

PLRA. *abbr.* PRISON LITIGATION REFORM ACT.

pltf. *abbr.* PLAINTIFF.

plunder, *n.* (17c) **1.** Movable property that has been taken by violence, robbery, or pillaging. **2.** The act of robbing or pillaging.

plunder, *vb.* See PILLAGE.

plunderage. (17c) *Maritime law.* The embezzling of goods on a ship.

plurality. (1803) The greatest number (esp. of votes), regardless of whether it is a simple or an absolute majority <a four-member plurality of the Supreme Court agreed with this view, which received more votes than any other>. — Also termed *plural majority.* Cf. MAJORITY (2).

plurality opinion. See OPINION (1).

plurality vote. See PLURALITY.

plurality voting. 1. See PLURALITY. **2.** See VOTING.

plural majority. See PLURALITY.

plural marriage. 1. See MARRIAGE (1). **2.** See POLYGAMY.

plural wife. See WIFE.

pluries (**pluur**-ee-eez), *n.* [Latin "many times"] (15c) A third or subsequent writ issued when the previous writs have been ineffective; a writ issued after an alias writ. — Also termed *pluries writ.*

plurinational administrative institution. (2004) *Int'l law.* An entity designed to perform transnational administrative activities when politically oriented international organizations and traditional international agreements are unsuitable. • These institutions usu. arise in fields where transnational arrangements are necessary (such as natural-resource management, transportation, or utilities), and they are often organized as international corporations, national agencies, or private corporations.

***plurium* defense.** See *multiple access* under ACCESS (3).

plus factor. (1943) A fact that supports finding that a specified legal test has been satisfied.

plus petere tempore (pləs pə-**ten**-dɪ **tem**-pə-ree). [Latin "to overclaim in point of time"] *Roman law.* To claim before payment was due.

plus petitio (pləs-pə-**tish**-ee-oh). [Latin "overclaim" or "claiming too much"] (17c) *Roman law.* A claim for more than is due; esp., the mistake of claiming more in one's pleadings than is due. • This was fatal to the action under classical law. Under *cognitio extraordinaria*, however, a claimant could continue the action, but could be liable for treble damages to any person injured by the overstated claim. — Also spelled (erroneously) *pluspetitio.* — Also termed *pluris petitio.*

> "A plaintiff may overclaim . . . in substance (*re*) when he claims a bigger amount than is due to him; in time (*tempore*) when he claims before the payment is due; in place (*loco*), when he claims at a place (in a city) other than that where the payment had to be performed . . . or in cause (*causa*) when he claims a certain thing although the debtor had the right to choose between two or more things . . . . After the abolition of the formula-regime the *pluspetitio* lost its actuality. Imperial legislation modified the severe provisions against overclaims . . . . In Justinian's law the plaintiff lost the case only if he maliciously persisted during the whole trial in his overclaim." Adolf Berger, *Encyclopedic Dictionary of Roman Law* 633 (1953).

plus quam tolerabile (pləs kwam tol-ə-**rab**-ə-lee). [Latin] (1839) *Hist.* More than can be endured. • The phrase appeared in reference to damage to crops from unavoidable causes (*vis major*).

plutocracy. (18c) Government by the wealthy. — Also termed *tumocracy.*

p.m. *abbr.* (17c) POST MERIDIEM.

PM. *abbr.* (1907) **1.** POSTMASTER. **2.** PRIME MINISTER. **3.** BUREAU OF POLITICAL–MILITARY AFFAIRS.

PMI. *abbr.* Private mortgage insurance. See *mortgage insurance* under INSURANCE.

PMM. *abbr.* See *purchase-money mortgage* under MORTGAGE.

PMRT. *abbr.* See *purchase-money resulting trust* under TRUST (3).

PMSI. *abbr.* See *purchase-money security interest* under SECURITY INTEREST.

pneumoconiosis. (1881) Chronic lung disease and related conditions characterized by respiratory and pulmonary impairments and caused or aggravated by coal-dust exposure during coal-mine employment.• The disease is usu. latent and often does not manifest until after coal-dust exposure has ended. 20 CFR § 718.201. — Also termed *black-lung disease.*

▸ **clinical pneumoconiosis.** (1980) Any medically recognized condition caused by coal-dust exposure while working in a coal mine and characterized by large, permanent deposits of particulate matter in the lungs, coupled with the lung tissue's fibrotic reaction. • Some examples of clinical pneumoconioses are silicosis or silicotuberculosis, massive pulmonary fibrosis, and anthrosilicosis. Cf. *legal pneumoconiosis.*

▸ **legal pneumoconiosis.** (1982) Any chronic restrictive or obstructive pulmonary disease or impairment and related conditions arising out of coal-mine employment. Cf. *clinical pneumoconiosis.*

PNG letter. See PERSONA NON GRATA LETTER.

P.O. *abbr.* (1824) **1.** Post office. **2.** PURCHASE ORDER.

POA. *abbr.* **1.** POWER OF APPOINTMENT. **2.** POWER OF ATTORNEY.

poaching, *n.* (17c) The illegal taking or killing of fish or game on another's land. — **poach,** *vb.*

POC. *abbr.* PROOF OF CLAIM.

pocket borough. See BOROUGH (3).

pocket immunity. See IMMUNITY (3).

pocket judgment. *Hist.* See STATUTE MERCHANT (1).

pocket money. See HAT MONEY.

pocket part. (1931) A supplemental pamphlet inserted usu. into the back inside cover of a lawbook, esp. a treatise or code, to update the material in the main text until the publisher issues a new edition of the entire work. • Legal publishers frequently leave a little extra room inside their hardcover books so that pocket parts may later be added. — Also termed *cumulative supplement.*

pocket veto. See VETO.

pocket-veto clause. See VETO CLAUSE (1).

P.O.D. *abbr.* (1859) Pay on delivery.

POD account. See *pay-on-death account* under ACCOUNT.

poena (**pee**-nə). [Latin] (1859) Punishment; penalty.

poena arbitraria (**pee**-nə ahr-bi-**trair**-ee-ə). [Law Latin] *Hist.* Arbitrary punishment; punishment left to a judge's discretion.

poena corporalis (**pee**-nə kor-pə-**ray**-lis). [Latin] *Hist.* Corporal punishment.

poena ordinaria (**pee**-nə or-di-**nair**-ee-ə). [Law Latin] (17c) *Hist.* Ordinary punishment; punishment fixed by law.

poena pecuniary. A fine.

poenae secundarum nuptiarum (**pee**-nee sek-ən-**dair**-əm nəp-shee-**air**-əm). [Latin "penalties of second marriages"] *Roman law.* Disabilities that, for the protection of children of a first marriage, are imposed on a parent who remarries.

> "If either parent re-married, the interests of the children of the first marriage were protected (in the later Roman Empire) by a number of legal rules the effect of which was to confer certain benefits on the children and to impose certain disabilities — the so-called poenae secundarum nuptiarum — on the parens binubus. The most important of these rules was that which declared that all the property which the parens binubus had acquired gratuitously from his or her deceased spouse, whether by way of gift, dos, donatio propter nuptias, or testamentary disposition — the so-called lucra nuptialia — should become ipso jure the property of the children of the first marriage at the moment of the conclusion of the second marriage, and that only a usufruct should be reserved for the parens binubus." Rudolph Sohm, *The Institutes: A Textbook of the History and System of Roman Private Law* 477 (James Crawford Ledlie trans., 3d ed. 1907).

poenalis (pi-**nay**-lis), *adj.* [Latin] *Roman law.* Imposing a penalty; penal.

poena pilloralis (**pee**-nə pil-ə-**ray**-lis). [Latin] *Hist.* Punishment of the pillory.

poenitentia (pee-nə-**ten**-shee-ə *or* pen-ə), *n.* [Latin "repentance"] *Roman law.* Reconsideration; changing one's mind.

poetic justice. See JUSTICE (4).

POF. *abbr.* Preliminary order of forfeiture.

pogrom (**poh**-grəm), *n.* (ca. 1900) A systematic massacre of a large number of helpless people, usu. for reasons of race or religion. Cf. GENOCIDE.

poinding (**pin**-ding), *n.* (15c) *Scots law.* A judgment creditor's seizing of a debtor's corporeal movable property to satisfy the debt. — **poind,** *vb.*

point, *n.* (13c) **1.** A pertinent and distinct legal proposition, issue, or argument <point of error>. **2.** *Parliamentary law.* Any of several kinds of requests made in a deliberative body. See REQUEST.

▸ **point of clarification.** (1958) A question about procedure or substance.

▸ **point of information.** (1915) An inquiry asking a question about a motion's merits or effect. • A point of information can be made only to seek information, not to volunteer information. It may request an objective fact or an expert opinion, but may not request anyone — including the chair or the mover — to speculate about how he or she expects or intends that the present or future leadership will interpret or apply a motion. See INQUIRY (2). — Also termed *question of information; request for information.*

▸ **point of order.** (18c) A request suggesting that the meeting or a member is not following the applicable rules and asking the chair enforce the rules. • Some organizations use the term "point of order" as a generic term that also includes a parliamentary inquiry and a question of privilege. — Also termed *question of order.* See *parliamentary inquiry* under INQUIRY; *question of privilege* under QUESTION (3).

▸ **point of privilege.** (17c) A motion that raises a question of privilege. See *question of privilege* under QUESTION (3); RAISE A QUESTION OF PRIVILEGE.

▸ **procedural point.** (1907) A request that raises a personal privilege relating to a member's ability to participate effectively in the meeting, such as the member's ability to see or hear the proceedings. See *personal privilege* under PRIVILEGE (5).

3. One percent of the face value of a loan (esp. a mortgage loan), paid up front to the lender as a service charge or placement fee <the borrower hoped for only a two-point fee on the mortgage>. — Also termed *mortgage point.* See MORTGAGE DISCOUNT. **4.** A unit used for quoting stock, bond, or commodity prices <the stock closed up a few points today>. **5.** A payment to secure a loan, stated as a percentage of the loan's face amount.

point-and-click agreement. (2000) An electronic version of a shrinkwrap license in which a computer user agrees to the terms of an electronically displayed agreement by pointing the cursor to a particular location on the screen and then clicking. • Point-and-click agreements usu. require express acceptance only once but may include a clause providing for a user's ongoing-acceptance of any changes to the agreement's terms, whether or not the user is notified of the changes. See *shrinkwrap license* under LICENSE. — Also termed *e-contract; clickwrap license; clickwrap agreement; user agreement; website-user agreement; web-wrap agreement.* Cf. E-CONTRACT.

point-of-arrest testing. See *preliminary breath test* under BREATH TEST.

point of attachment. (1967) *Copyright.* A connection with a copyright-convention member country sufficient to make a work eligible for protection under that convention. • For example, a work is eligible for Berne Convention protection if the author is a citizen of a Berne member country or if the work originated in a Berne member country. — Also termed *connecting factor.*

point of error. (18c) An alleged mistake by a lower court asserted as a ground for appeal. See ERROR (2); WRIT OF ERROR.

point of fact. (17c) A discrete factual proposition at issue in a case.

point of law. (16c) A discrete legal proposition at issue in a case.

▸ **reserved point of law.** (1821) An important or difficult point of law that arises during trial but that the judge sets aside for future argument or decision so that testimony can continue. — Also termed *point reserved.*

point of sale. (1844) The place or shop where a product is sold. — Also termed *point of purchase.*

point reserved. See *reserved point of law* under POINT OF LAW.

points-and-authorities brief. See *brief on the merits* under BRIEF (1).

point source. (1971) *Environmental law.* The discernible and identifiable source from which pollutants are discharged.

point system. (1955) *Criminal law.* A system that assigns incremental units to traffic violations, the accumulation of a certain number within a year resulting in the automatic suspension of a person's driving privileges.

poisonous-tree doctrine. See FRUIT-OF-THE-POISONOUS-TREE DOCTRINE.

poison pill. (1963) Something in a company's financial or legal structure that is intended to make it difficult for another company or for a group of shareholders to take control of it; esp., a corporation's defense against an unwanted takeover bid whereby shareholders are granted the right to acquire equity or debt securities at a favorable price to increase the bidder's acquisition costs. — Often shortened to *pill.* See TAKEOVER DEFENSE; SHARK REPELLENT. Cf. PORCUPINE PROVISION.

> "Another recent defensive tactic is the 'poison pill,' which is a conditional stock right that is triggered by a hostile takeover and makes the takeover prohibitively expensive. The poison pill is a variation of the scorched earth defense . . . ." 2 Thomas Lee Hazen, *Treatise on the Law of Securities Regulation* § 11.20, at 338–39 (3d ed. 1995).

poison-pill amendment. See AMENDMENT (3).

***Polaroid* test.** (1964) *Trademarks.* A judicial test for trademark infringement, analyzing eight factors: (1) strength of the mark, (2) similarity between the marks, (3) proximity of the products' markets, (4) effects on market expansion (ability to "bridge the gap"), (5) actual confusion, (6) the defendant's good or bad faith, (7) quality of the products, and (8) sophistication of the buyer. *Polaroid Corp. v. Polarad Electronics Corp.*, 287 F.2d 492, 495 (2d Cir. 1961).

pole. 1. ROD. **2.** PERCH (3).

police, *n.* (18c) **1.** The governmental department charged with the preservation of public order, the promotion of public safety, and the prevention and detection of crime. **2.** The officers or members of this department. — **police,** *vb.*

police action. See ARMED CONFLICT.

police-assisted suicide. See *suicide-by-cop* under SUICIDE (1).

police blotter. See ARREST RECORD.

police chief. (1831) The head of a police department.

police commissioner. See COMMISSIONER.

police community-support officer. See POLICE OFFICER.

police constable. See CONSTABLE.

police court. See *magistrate's court* (1) under COURT.

police department. (18c) **1.** The official local law-enforcement organization in a particular town, city, or area. **2.** The building in which this organization has its headquarters or a satellite office.

police dog. See DOG (1).

police jury. (1811) *Louisiana law.* The governing body of a parish.

police justice. See *police magistrate* under MAGISTRATE.

police lab. See CRIME LABORATORY.

police lineup. See LINEUP.

police magistrate. See MAGISTRATE.

police officer. (18c) A law-enforcement officer responsible for preserving public order, promoting public safety, and preventing and detecting crime. Cf. PEACE OFFICER.

▸ **ghost officer.** (1990) An undercover police officer who trails another undercover officer, observes from a distance, and notifies a backup team if the undercover officer appears to be in danger. • The ghost officer does not have direct contact with suspects.

▸ **police community-support officer.** (1999) A police officer whose job is to patrol an area to improve the safety and security of people who live and work there and to monitor criminal activity in the area. — Abbr. PCSO.

▸ **undercover officer.** (1946) A police officer whose appearance is that of an ordinary person and who, in order to carry out an investigation, displays nothing to indicate that he or she is a police officer. • The undercover officer's job is to gather enough information about a suspect and criminal activity to enable a successful prosecution. — Also termed *undercover police officer.* Cf. PLAINCLOTHES.

police power. (1821) **1.** The inherent and plenary power of a sovereign to make all laws necessary and proper to preserve the public security, order, health, morality, and justice. • It is a fundamental power essential to government, and it cannot be surrendered by the legislature or irrevocably transferred away from government.

> "[I]t is possible to evolve at least two main attributes or characteristics which differentiate the police power: it aims directly to secure and promote the public welfare, and it does so by restraint or compulsion." Ernst Freund, *The Police Power* § 3, at 3 (1904).

> "The whole theory of police power is a judicial invention. The term does not appear in our constitutions, and not one man in ten thousand knows its precise limitations." Morris R. Cohen, *Law and the Social Order* 138 (1933).

2. A state's Tenth Amendment right, subject to due-process and other limitations, to establish and enforce laws protecting the public's health, safety, and general welfare, or to delegate this right to local governments. **3.** Loosely, the power of the government to intervene in the use of privately owned property, as by subjecting it to eminent domain. See EMINENT DOMAIN.

police regulation. See REGULATION (3).

police science. See CRIMINAL JUSTICE (2).

police state. See STATE (1).

policy. (14c) **1.** A standard course of action that has been officially established by an organization, business, political party, etc. See PUBLIC POLICY. **2.** A document containing a contract of insurance; INSURANCE POLICY. **3.** A type of lottery in which bettors select numbers to bet on and place the bet with a "policy writer."

policy analysis. See REALISM.

policy court. See COURT.

policyholder. (1818) Someone who owns an insurance policy, regardless of whether that person is the insured party. — Also termed *policyowner.*

policy limits. See LIABILITY LIMIT.

policy loan. See LOAN.

policy of insurance. See INSURANCE POLICY.

policy of the law. See PUBLIC POLICY (1).

policyowner. See POLICYHOLDER.

policy proof of interest. (1891) *Insurance.* Evidence — shown by possession of a policy — that a person making a claim has an insurable interest in the loss. — Abbr. PPI.

policy racket. See NUMBERS GAME.

policy reserve. See RESERVE (1).

policy rider. See RIDER.

policy stacking. See STACKING (1).

policy value. (1863) *Insurance.* The amount of cash available to a policyholder on the surrender or cancellation of the insurance policy.

policy year. (1872) *Insurance.* The year beginning on the date that a policy becomes effective. Cf. ANNIVERSARY DATE.

political, *adj.* (16c) Of, relating to, or involving politics; pertaining to the conduct of government.

political-action committee. (1839) An organization formed by a special-interest group to raise and contribute money to the campaigns of political candidates who seem likely to promote its interests; a group formed by a business, union, or interest group to help raise money for politicians who support the group's public-policy interests. — Abbr. PAC. See INTEREST GROUP.

> "To the degree that PACs resemble other organized interest groups, their emergence should not be cause for alarm. Like the AFL-CIO, the Business Roundtable, the NAACP, the AARP, or Greenpeace, any single political action committee is a collection of individuals (in most cases) with shared interests who have decided to unite in an effort to effect desirable political outcomes. But what is particularly interesting about PACs—and troubling to some—is the precise nature of their efforts to achieve their goals. Whereas lobbyists are increasingly limited in what they can provide for legislators in an attempt to influence the policy-making process, the essence of PACs is to provide financial resources to aid election campaigns. The direct provision of money to lawmakers conjures up images of influence peddling, vote buying, and power brokering, all of which are anathema to representative government. Thus, although PACs fall under the general rubric of 'interest groups,' it is the financial nature of their relationship to members of Congress that makes them subject to close scrutiny." Daniel S. Ward, "PACs and Congressional Decisions," in 2 *Encyclopedia of the American Legislative System* 1092 (Joel H. Silbey ed., 1994).

political assessment. See ASSESSMENT (2).

political asylum. See ASYLUM (2).

political corporation. See *public corporation* (2) under CORPORATION.

political correctness, *n.* (1979) **1.** The inclination to avoid language and practices that might offend anyone's political sensibilities, esp. in social, racial, or sexual matters. **2.** An instance in which a person conforms to this inclination; euphemistic language, innocuous behavior, and nonjudgmental attitudes that are self-consciously adopted so as not to offend or insult anyone. — Abbr. P.C. — **politically correct,** *adj.*

political corruption. See *official misconduct* under MISCONDUCT.

political crime. See POLITICAL OFFENSE.

political economy. See ECONOMY.

political-editorial rule. (1968) The former FCC requirement that a broadcaster who has endorsed a candidate must notify the candidate's opponents and offer them equal opportunities to respond. • The FCC dropped the rule in 2000 by judicial order. *Repeal of the Personal Attack and Personal Editorial Rules*, 15 FCC Rcd. 20697 (2000). — Also termed *political-editorializing rule*; *personal-editorial rule*.

political equality. See EQUALITY.

political gerrymandering. See GERRYMANDERING (1).

political law. See POLITICAL SCIENCE.

political liberty. 1. See LIBERTY. **2.** See *political right* under RIGHT.

Political–Military Affairs Bureau. See BUREAU OF POLITICAL–MILITARY AFFAIRS.

political offense. (18c) A crime directed against the security or government of a country, such as treason, sedition, or espionage. • Under principles of international law, the perpetrator of a political offense cannot be extradited. — Also termed *political crime*.

political oratory. See ORATORY.

political party. (18c) An organization of voters formed to influence the government's conduct and policies by nominating and electing candidates to public office. • The United States has traditionally maintained a two-party system, which today comprises the Democratic and Republican parties. — Often shortened to *party*.

political patronage. See PATRONAGE (3).

political power. (16c) The power vested in a person or body of persons exercising any function of the state; the capacity to influence the activities of the body politic. — Also termed *civil power*.

▸ **sovereign political power.** (1882) Power that is absolute and uncontrolled within its own sphere. • Within its designated limits, its exercise and effective operation do not depend on, and are not subject to, the power of any other person and cannot be prevented or annulled by any other power recognized within the constitutional system. — Often shortened to *sovereign power*. — Also termed *supreme power*.

▸ **subordinate political power.** (1975) Power that, within its own sphere of operation, is subject in some degree to external control because there exists some superior constitutional power that can prevent, restrict, direct, or annul its operation. — Often shortened to *subordinate power*.

political prisoner. See PRISONER (3).

political question. (1808) A question that a court will not consider because it involves the exercise of discretionary power by the executive or legislative branch of government. — Also termed *nonjusticiable question*. Cf. JUDICIAL QUESTION.

political-question doctrine. (1935) The judicial principle that a court should refuse to decide an issue involving the exercise of discretionary power by the executive or legislative branch of government.

political right. See RIGHT.

political science. (17c) The branch of learning concerned with the study of the principles and conduct of government. — Also termed *political law*.

political society. See STATE (1).

political subdivision. (1827) A division of a state that exists primarily to discharge some function of local government.

political trial. See TRIAL.

political-vote privilege. See PRIVILEGE (3).

political warfare. See WARFARE.

politicide. 1. The systematic elimination of a political or social entity. **2.** The mass-killing or elimination of a group on political grounds. • Politicide differs from genocide in that the animus is not based on race, religion, or ethnicity. **3.** The act or commission of a blunder that results in the end of one's own political career.

politicking, *n.* (1886) Engagement in political activities to gain support for oneself or for a particular political group.

politics. (16c) **1.** The science of the organization and administration of the state. **2.** The activity or profession of engaging in political affairs.

polity (pol-ə-tee). (16c) **1.** The total governmental organization as based on its goals and policies. **2.** A politically organized body or community.

polity approach. (1975) A method of resolving church-property disputes by which a court examines the structure of the church to determine whether the church is independent or hierarchical, and then resolves the dispute in accordance with the decision of the proper church-governing body.

Polk Doctrine. *Int'l law.* The principle announced by President James K. Polk that the Monroe Doctrine (dating from 1823) remained sound and that the United States would oppose any European interference in North America. Cf. MONROE DOCTRINE.

> "In his annual message of December 2, 1845, President Polk, referring to our dispute with Great Britain as to the Oregon territory, and to the possible intervention of European powers in consequence of our annexation of Texas and possibly of other territory southward, sought to give President Monroe's announcement on the subject of colonization the meaning popularly but erroneously conveyed by the expression 'no more European colonies on this continent.' But, in so doing, he restricted its application to North America, saying that 'it should be distinctly announced to the world as our settled policy, that no future European colony or dominion shall, with our consent, be planted or established on any part of the North American continent.' It is obvious that President Polk, in pronouncing against the establishment of any 'dominion' by a European power—a term which includes the acquisition by voluntary transfer or by conquest of territory already occupied—asserted something quite different from Monroe's declaration against 'colonization.' He asserted something which should be called the Polk doctrine rather than the Monroe doctrine; and it was, perhaps, the consciousness of this fact that led him to restrict the new doctrine, which was to be maintained by us without regard to other American powers, and not merely by each of those powers 'by its own means,' to the North American continent." John Bassett Moore, "The Monroe Doctrine: Its Origin and Meaning," in 1 *The Collected Papers of John Bassett Moore* 334, 338–39 (1944).

poll, *n.* (18c) **1.** A sampling of opinions on a given topic, conducted randomly or obtained from a specified group. **2.** The act or process of voting at an election. **3.** The result of the counting of votes. **4.** (*usu. pl.*) The place where votes are cast.

poll, *vb.* (17c) **1.** To ask how each member of (a group) individually voted <after the verdict was read, the judge polled the jury>. **2.** To question (people) so as to elicit votes, opinions, or preferences <the committee polled 500 citizens about their views>. **3.** To receive (a given number of votes) in an election <the third-party candidate polled only 250 votes in the county>. —**polling,** *n.*

pollicitation. *Contracts.* (15c) The offer of a promise.

> "By a *promise* we mean an accepted offer as opposed to an offer of a promise, or, as Austin called it, a *pollicitation*." William R. Anson, *Principles of the Law of Contract* 6 (Arthur L. Corbin ed., 3d Am. ed. 1919).

polling booth. (1805) A small, partly enclosed space in a polling place where a person can vote in an election.

polling place. (18c) The location where people go to vote in an election. — Also termed *polling booth; voting station.*

poll tax. See TAX.

pollutant. (1892) A poisonous or noxious substance that contaminates the environment, esp. the air and water.

▸ **criteria pollutants.** (1974) Pollutants, esp. air pollutants, that are known to be hazardous to health, such as smog and acid rain. — Also termed *criteria contaminants.*

pollute, *vb.* (14c) To corrupt or defile; esp., to contaminate the soil, air, or water with noxious substances. — **pollution,** *n.* — **polluter,** *n.*

polluter-pays principle. (1972) *Int'l law.* The doctrine that the costs of cleaning up damage caused by pollution should be borne by the person responsible for causing the pollution.

pollution. (14c) **1.** The harmful addition of a substance or thing into an environment; esp., the introduction of man-made products, esp. waste products, into a natural area <further increases in fertilizer use will lead to nitrate pollution>. **2.** The state or condition of being polluted.

▸ **land pollution.** (1909) The disposal of solid or liquid wastes on the surface of land or underground, producing nuisances, soil and water contamination, and threats to public health.

▸ **marine pollution.** (1952) The introduction of harmful substances and products, such as toxins, chemicals, and solid waste, into the ocean.

▸ **water pollution.** (1865) The contamination of a body of water by directly or indirectly discharging into it substances that were inadequately treated to remove harmful materials.

pollution exclusion. See EXCLUSION (3).

po. lo. suo. *abbr.* PONIT LOCO SUO.

polyandry (**pol**-ee-an-dree). (17c) The condition or practice of a woman's having more than one husband at the same time. Cf. POLYGYNY; MONANDRY.

polyarchy (**pol**-ee-ahr-kee). (17c) Government by many persons. — Also termed *polygarchy* (**pol**-ə-gahr-kee). Cf. MONARCHY. — **polyarchal,** *adj.*

polygamist (pə-**lig**-ə-məst). (17c) **1.** Someone who has several spouses simultaneously. **2.** An advocate of polygamy.

polygamy (pə-**lig**-ə-mee), *n.* (16c) **1.** The state or practice of having more than one spouse simultaneously. — Also termed *simultaneous polygamy; plural marriage.* **2.** *Hist.* The fact or practice of having more than one spouse during one's lifetime, though never simultaneously. • Until the third century, polygamy included remarriage after a spouse's death because a valid marriage bond was considered indissoluble. — Also termed *successive polygamy; serial polygamy; sequential marriage.* Cf. BIGAMY; MONOGAMY. — **polygamous,** *adj.* — **polygamist,** *n.*

> "Polygamy (many marriages) is employed at times as a synonym of bigamy and at other times to indicate the simultaneous marriage of two or more spouses." Rollin M. Perkins & Ronald N. Boyce, *Criminal Law* 458 (3d ed. 1982).

> "[T]his one-marriage-at-a-time rule behind which the legal systems of the West have seemingly thrown so much weight is not what a sociologist would call a general prohibition of polygamy. Polygamy can be simultaneous (if more than one spouse is simultaneously present) or successive (if spouses are married one after the other). Only simultaneous polygamy is prohibited by the laws with which we are here concerned. These statutes reserve the use of the word *polygamy* for that kind which is not very common among us. They do not affect the serial form, which is so very popular in the United States and Western Europe that . . . the law is fast changing to adapt to it." Mary Ann Glendon, *The Transformation of Family Law* 52 (1989).

polygarchy. See POLYARCHY.

polygraph, *n.* (1923) A piece of equipment used to determine whether someone is lying by measuring and recording involuntary physiological changes in the human body, esp. sudden changes in the heart rate, during interrogation. • Polygraph results are inadmissible as evidence in most states but are commonly used by the police as an investigative tool. — Also termed *lie detector.* — **polygraphic,** *adj.* — **polygraphy,** *n.*

polygyny (pə-**lij**-ə-nee). (18c) The condition or practice of having more than one wife at the same time. Cf. POLYANDRY.

POMIC. *abbr.* Post-offense manipulation of investigative communications — that is, a perpetrator's or another's conduct intended to skew the course of a criminal investigation.

pondere, numero, et mensura (**pon**-dər-ee, **n[y]oo**-mər-oh, et men-**s[y]uur**-ə). [Latin] (1828) *Hist.* By weight, number, and measure. • The phrase appeared in reference to methods for determining fungibles.

> "Pondere, numero, et mensura . . . . These are the tests proposed by our law, by which to ascertain whether a certain subject falls within that class of subjects known as fungibles, which class includes all those things which perish in the using, and which can be estimated generally by weight, number and measure; such, for example, are corn, wine, money, &c." John Trayner, *Trayner's Latin Maxims* 462 (4th ed. 1894).

pone (**poh**-nee). [Latin "put"] (14c) *Hist.* An original writ used to remove an action from an inferior court (such as a manorial court or county court) to a superior court. • The writ was so called from the initial words of its mandate, which required the recipient to "put" the matter before the court issuing the writ.

ponendis in assisis (pə-**nen**-dis in ə-**SI**-zis). [Latin "to be placed in assizes"] (17c) *Hist.* A writ directing the sheriff to empanel a jury for an assize or real action.

ponendo sigillum ad exceptionem. See DE PONENDO SIGILLUM AD EXCEPTIONEM.

ponendum in ballium (pə-**nen**-dəm in **bal**-ee-əm). [Latin "to be placed in bail"] (18c) *Hist.* A writ commanding that a prisoner be bailed in a bailable matter.

pone per vadium (**poh**-nee pər **vay**-dee-əm). [Latin] (17c) *Hist.* A writ commanding the sheriff to summon a defendant who has failed to appear in response to an initial writ by attaching some of the defendant's property and requiring the defendant to find sureties. • It was so called from the words of the writ, *pone per vadium et salvos plegios* ("put by gage and safe pledges").

ponit loco suo (**poh**-nit **loh**-ko s[y]**oo**-oh). [Latin] (18c) Puts in his place. • This phrase was formerly used in a power of attorney. — Abbr. *po. lo. suo.*

ponit se super patriam (**poh**-nit see s[y]**oo**-pər **pay**-tree-əm *or* **pa**-tree-əm). [Latin "he puts himself upon the country"] (17c) *Hist.* A defendant's plea of not guilty in a criminal action. — Abbr. *po. se.* See GOING TO THE COUNTRY; PATRIA (3).

pontifex (**pon**-ti-feks), *n.* (16c) *Roman law.* A member of the college of pontiffs, one of several groups of priests, who had control of religion in Rome. — Also termed *pontiff.* Pl. **pontifices** (pon-**tif**-i-seez).

pontiff. (16c) **1.** *Roman law.* A member of the council of priests in ancient Rome. — Also termed *pontifex.*

> "The specialists who interpreted the Twelve Tables and the unwritten part of the law were called *pontiffs*. At first they dealt with both sacred law (how to appease the gods) and secular law (how to secure peace among men). Some of them later confined themselves to secular law. As an example of how they interpreted the law, the Twelve Tables said that if a father sells his son three times (into bondage, to pay off debts) the son is to be free from his father's power. The Twelve Tables said nothing about a daughter. The pontiffs held that if a father sold his daughter once, she was free." Tony Honoré, *About Law* 13 (1995).

2. The leader of the Catholic Church; the Pope. See PONTIFEX.

pony homestead. See *constitutional homestead* under HOMESTEAD (1).

Ponzi scheme (**pon**-zee). (1920) A fraudulent investment scheme in which money contributed by later investors generates artificially high dividends or returns for the original investors, whose example attracts even larger investments. • Money from the new investors is used directly to repay or pay interest to earlier investors, usu. without any operation or revenue-producing activity other than the continual raising of new funds. This scheme takes its name from Charles Ponzi, who in the late 1920s was convicted for fraudulent schemes he conducted in Boston. See GIFTING CLUB. Cf. PYRAMID SCHEME.

pool, *n.* (1868) **1.** An association of individuals or entities who share resources and funds to promote their joint undertaking; esp., an association of persons engaged in buying or selling commodities. • If such an association is formed to eliminate competition throughout a single industry, it is a restraint of trade that violates federal antitrust laws. **2.** A gambling scheme in which numerous persons contribute stakes for betting on a particular event (such as a sporting event).

pool agreement. *Maritime law.* A contract between shipowners or others having rights in vessels to cooperate in the management and operation of all vessels controlled by the group whereby each ship earns from the pool a share in net pool income proportionately with the ship's agreed theoretical earning capacity, as opposed to its actual earnings in the pool.

pool clerk. See CLERK (5).

pooled-income fund. (1970) A trust created and maintained by a public charity rather than a private person, whereby (1) the donor creates an irrevocable, vested remainder in the charitable organization that maintains the trust, (2) the property transferred by each donor is commingled with property transferred by other donors, (3) the fund cannot invest in tax-exempt securities, (4) no donor or income beneficiary can be a trustee, (5) the donor retains (either personally or for one or more named income beneficiaries) a life income interest, and (6) each income beneficiary is entitled to and receives a proportional share of the annual income based on the rate of return earned by the fund. IRC (26 USCA) § 642(c)(5). — Abbr. PIF.

pooled-information privilege. See *joint-defense privilege* under PRIVILEGE (3).

pooled trust. See TRUST (3).

pooling, *n. Oil & gas.* The bringing together of small tracts of land or fractional mineral interests over a producing reservoir for the purpose of drilling an oil or gas well. • Pooling is usu. associated with collecting a large enough tract to meet well-spacing regulations. — Also termed *communitization.* Cf. UNITIZATION.

> "In general, the term 'pooling' is used here to refer to small units, usually of the one-well drilling unit variety, while the term 'unitization' is used in reference to units covering large land areas, particularly the fieldwide or poolwide unit. In some of the articles and cases these terms have gradually come to have the meanings ascribed to them in the preceding sentence and it is convenient to preserve that distinction here in so far as possible. However, it will be observed that the bulk of the comments in this volume relates generally to any type of voluntary combination or consolidation of ownership interests for development and production purposes, regardless of the size of the area that may be involved. Hence, no attempt is made here to use these terms and to distinguish between them with any degree of scientific accuracy, except where the text itself indicates that one type of consolidation or the other is particularly referred to." Leo J. Hoffman, *Voluntary Pooling and Unitization: Oil and Gas* 6-7 (1954).

▸ **compulsory pooling.** (1952) Pooling done by order of a regulatory agency. — Also termed *forced pooling.*

▸ **forced pooling.** See *compulsory pooling.*

▸ **voluntary pooling.** (1942) Pooling arranged by agreement of the owners of mineral interests.

pooling agreement. (1907)A contractual arrangement by which corporate shareholders agree that their shares will be voted as a unit. — Also termed *voting agreement; shareholder voting agreement; shareholder-control agreement.*

pooling clause. (1938) *Oil & gas.* A provision found in most oil-and-gas leases granting the lessee the right to combine part or all of the leased acreage with other properties for development or operation.

pooling of interests. A method of accounting used in mergers, whereby the acquired company's assets are recorded on the acquiring company's books at their cost when originally acquired. • No goodwill account is created under the pooling method.

Poor Law. *Hist.* The British statute that provided relief to paupers, originally on the parish level and supported by property taxes. • The Poor Law was supplanted in 1948 by the National Assistance Act.

poor man's court. See RUSTICUM FORUM.

poor-person motion. See IN FORMA PAUPERIS MOTION.

poor relief. See WELFARE (2).

POP. *abbr.* PROBLEM-ORIENTED POLICING.

pop, *n. Telecommunications.* A calculation of the potential customer base for a mobile-phone-service provider, calculated by the number of people living in the area multiplied by the company's percentage ownership of the area's cellular service.

Poppean law. See LEX PAPIA POPPEA.

popular action. See QUI TAM ACTION.

popular constitutionalism. *Constitutional law.* An interpretive approach or descriptive account that gives an engaged and active citizenry significant, and possibly ultimate, authority in constitutional interpretation. See CONSTITUTIONALISM. Cf. DEPARTMENTALISM; JUDICIAL SUPREMACY; JUDICIAL REVIEW.

popular election. See ELECTION (3).

popularis (pop-yə-**lair**-is), *adj.* [Latin] *Roman law.* (Of an action) available to any male member of the public. See *actio popularis* under ACTIO.

popular justice. See JUSTICE (4).

popular sovereignty. See SOVEREIGNTY (1).

popular use. See USE (1).

populus (**pop**-yə-ləs), *n.* & *adj.* [Latin] *Roman law.* The people; the whole body of Roman citizens, patricians, and plebeians.

porcupine provision. (1982) A clause in a corporation's charter or bylaws designed to prevent a takeover without the consent of the board of directors. Cf. SHARK REPELLENT; POISON PILL.

pork-barrel legislation. See LEGISLATION (3).

pornography, *n.* (1842) Material (such as writings, photographs, or movies) depicting sexual activity or erotic behavior in a way that is designed to arouse sexual excitement. • Pornography is protected speech under the First Amendment unless it is determined to be legally obscene. — Often shortened to *porn.* See OBSCENITY. — **pornographic,** *adj.* — **pornographer,** *n.*

▸ **child pornography.** (1967) Material depicting a person under the age of 18 engaged in sexual activity. • Child pornography is not protected by the First Amendment, even if it falls short of the legal standard for obscenity, and those directly involved in its distribution can be criminally punished.

▸ **virtual child pornography.** (1996) Material that includes a computer-generated image that appears to be a minor engaged in sexual activity but that in reality does not involve a person under the age of 18.

port. (bef. 12c) **1.** A harbor where ships load and unload cargo. **2.** Any place where persons and cargo are allowed to enter a country and where customs officials are stationed. — Also termed (in sense 2) *port of entry.*

▸ **foreign port.** (17c) **1.** One exclusively within the jurisdiction of another country or state. **2.** A port other than a home port.

▸ **free port.** (16c) A designated location created by countries for temporarily holding commodities and manufactured goods that are in transit internationally; specif., a port located outside a country's customs frontier, so that goods may be delivered usu. free of import duties or taxes, without being subjected to customs-control procedures; FREE-TRADE ZONE. • While in a free port, the items are not subject to customs taxes. Other tax advantages may be extended to them. — Also written *freeport.* — Also termed *bonded area.*

▸ **home port.** (18c) The port that is either where a vessel is registered or where its owner resides.

▸ **port of call.** (1838) A port at which a ship stops during a voyage.

▸ **port of delivery.** (17c) The port that is the terminus of any particular voyage and where the ship unloads its cargo.

▸ **port of departure.** (18c) The port from which a vessel departs on the start of a voyage.

▸ **port of destination.** (18c) The port at which a voyage is to end. • This term generally includes any stopping places at which the ship receives or unloads cargo.

▸ **port of discharge.** (17c) The place where a substantial part of the cargo is discharged.

portable breath test. See BREATH TEST.

portable business. (1983) A portfolio of legal business that an attorney can take from one firm or geographic location to another, with little loss in client relationships. — Also termed *portable practice.*

port authority. (1870) A state or federal agency that regulates traffic through a port or that establishes and maintains airports, bridges, tollways, and public transportation.

port charter. See CHARTER (8).

portfolio. (1848) **1.** The various securities or other investments held by an investor at any given time. • An investor will often hold several different types of investments in a portfolio for the purpose of diversifying risk.

▸ **market portfolio.** (1930) A value-weighted portfolio of every asset in a particular market.

2. The role within the government of a high official <minister without portfolio>.

portfolio income. See INCOME.

portfolio-pumping. (1998) *Securities.* The practice of purchasing additional shares of a stock near the end of a fiscal period in an attempt to improve an investment fund's apparent performance. — Also termed *window dressing.*

portio legitima (**por**-shee-oh lə-**jit**-i-mə). [Latin "lawful portion"] (18c) *Roman & civil law.* The portion of an estate required by law to be left to close relatives; specif., the portion of an inheritance that a given heir is entitled to, and of which the heir cannot be deprived by the testator without special cause. Cf. LEGITIME. Pl. ***portiones legitimae.***

portion. (14c) A share or allotted part (as of an estate).

portioner (**por**-shə-nər), *n.* (15c) **1.** *Scots law.* Someone who owns a portion of a decedent's estate.

▸ **heir portioner.** (17c) **1.** One of two or more female heirs who, in the absence of male heirs, inherit equal shares of an estate. **2.** One of two or more usu. female heirs in the same degree who take equal shares per capita.

2. The proprietor of a small fee. **3.** *Hist.* A minister who serves a benefice with others. • The person was called a *portioner* because he had only a portion of the tithes or allowance that a vicar commonly has out of a rectory or impropriation.

portionibus haereditariis (por-shee-**oh**-nə-bəs hə-red-i-**tair**-ee-is). [Law Latin] *Hist.* In hereditary portions.

port of call. See PORT.

port of delivery. See PORT.

port of departure. See PORT.

port of destination. See PORT.

port of discharge. See PORT.

port of entry. See PORT (2).

portorium (por-**tor**-ee-əm). [Law Latin] *Hist.* **1.** A tax or toll levied at a port or at the gates of a city. **2.** A toll for passing over a bridge.

port-risk insurance. See INSURANCE.

portsale. (16c) *Hist.* A public sale of goods to the highest bidder; an auction.

port-state control. (1977) *Maritime law.* The exercise of authority under international conventions for a state to stop, board, inspect, and when necessary detain vessels sailing under foreign flags while they are navigating in the port state's territorial waters or are in one of its ports. • The purpose is to ensure the safety of the vessels as well as to enforce environmental regulations. Cf. COASTAL-STATE CONTROL; FLAG-STATE CONTROL.

port toll. (1808) A duty paid for bringing goods into a port.

portwarden. (18c) An official responsible for the administration of a port.

POSA. *abbr.* Person with ordinary skill in the art. See PERSON SKILLED IN THE ART.

po. se. *abbr.* PONIT SE SUPER PATRIAM.

posit, *vb.* (17c) **1.** To presume true or to offer as true. **2.** To present as an explanation.

position. (1960) The extent of a person's investment in a particular security or market.

positional-risk doctrine. (1953) The principle by which the workers'-compensation requirement that the injury arise out of employment is satisfied if the injured worker's employment required the worker to be at the place where the injury occurred at the time it occurred. — Also termed *positional-risk analysis; positional-risk test.*

position of the United States. (1981) The legal position of the federal government in a lawsuit, esp. in a case involving the Equal Access to Justice Act. • Under the EAJA, the reasonableness of the position in light of precedent determines whether the government will be liable for the opposing party's attorney's fees.

positive act. (17c) **1.** OVERT ACT. **2.** ACT (2).

positive condition. See CONDITION (2).

positive covenant. See COVENANT (1).

positive discrimination. See AFFIRMATIVE ACTION.

positive duty. See DUTY (1).

positive easement. See *affirmative easement* under EASEMENT.

positive evidence. See *direct evidence* (1) under EVIDENCE.

positive externality. See EXTERNALITY.

positive fact. See FACT.

positive fraud. See *actual fraud* under FRAUD.

positive justice. See JUSTICE (4).

positive law. (14c) A system of law promulgated and implemented within a particular political community by political superiors, as distinct from moral law or law existing in an ideal community or in some nonpolitical community. • Positive law typically consists of enacted law — the codes, statutes, and regulations that are applied and enforced in the courts. The term derives from the medieval use of *positum* (Latin "established"), so that the phrase *positive law* literally means law established by human authority. — Also termed *jus positivum; made law.* Cf. NATURAL LAW.

> "A judge is tethered to the positive law but should not be shackled to it." Patrick Devlin, *The Enforcement of Morals* 94 (1968).

positive misprision. See MISPRISION (1).

positive notice. See *direct notice* under NOTICE (3).

positive prescription. See PRESCRIPTION (5).

positive proof. See PROOF.

positive reprisal. See REPRISAL (1).

positive right. See RIGHT.

positive servitude. See SERVITUDE (3).

positive testimony. See *affirmative testimony* under TESTIMONY.

positive wrong. See WRONG.

positivi juris (poz-ə-**tI**-vI **joor**-is). [Law Latin] (17c) Of positive law. See POSITIVE LAW.

positivism. (1846) **1.** The doctrine that all true knowledge is derived from observable phenomena, rather than speculation or reasoning. See LEGAL POSITIVISM; LOGICAL POSITIVISM; *positivist jurisprudence* under JURISPRUDENCE. **2.** An approach to philosophy grounded in empirical facts that can be scientifically verified, as opposed to unverifiable assumptions. — **positivist,** *adj.* & *n.*

> "The French mathematician and philosopher Auguste Comte (1798–1857), who may be regarded as the philosophical founder of modern positivism, distinguished three great stages in the evolution of human thinking. The first stage, in his system, is the theological stage, in which all phenomena are explained by reference to supernatural causes and the intervention of a divine being. The second is the metaphysical stage, in which thought has recourse to ultimate principles and ideas, which are conceived as existing beneath the surface of things and as constituting the real moving forces in the evolution of mankind. The third and last stage is the positivistic stage, which rejects all hypothetical constructions in philosophy, history, and science and confines itself to the empirical observation and connection of facts under the guidance of methods used in the natural sciences." Edgar Bodenheimer, *Jurisprudence: The Philosophy and Method of the Law* 91 (rev. ed. 1974).

positivistic, *adj.* (1859) Of, relating to, or involving legal positivism. See LEGAL POSITIVISM.

positivistic jurisprudence. See *positivist jurisprudence* under JURISPRUDENCE.

positivist jurisprudence. See JURISPRUDENCE.

posse (**pos**-ee). [Latin] (16c) **1.** A possibility. See IN POSSE. Cf. IN ESSE. **2.** Power; ability. **3.** POSSE COMITATUS.

posse comitatus (**pos**-ee kom-ə-**tay**-təs), *n.* [Latin "power of the county"] (16c) A group of citizens who are called together to help the sheriff keep the peace or conduct rescue operations. — Often shortened to *posse*.

Posse Comitatus Act. An 1878 federal statute that, with a few exceptions, prohibits the Army or Air Force from directly participating in civilian law-enforcement operations, as by making arrests, conducting searches, or seizing evidence. • The Act does not usu. apply to members of the Navy, the National Guard, or the Coast Guard. 18 USCA § 1385. — Abbr. PCA.

possess, *vb.* (14c) **1.** To have in one's actual control; to have possession of. **2.** To have (a quality, ability, etc.).

possessio (pə-**zes**[**h**]-ee-oh), *n.* [Latin] The de facto control of a thing that the holder intends to control.

▸ ***pedis possessio*** (**pee**-dis *or* **ped**-is pə-**zes**[**h**]-ee-oh). [Latin] (1816) A foothold; an actual possession of real property, implying either actual occupancy or enclosure or use. — Also termed *substantial possession*; *possessio pedis*. See PEDIS POSSESSIO DOCTRINE.

▸ ***possessio ad interdicta*** (pə-**zes**[**h**]-ee-oh ad in-tər-**dik**-tə). [Latin] *Hist.* Possession for the purpose of an interdict.

▸ ***possessio ad usucapionem*** (pə-**zes**[**h**]-ee-oh ad yoo-zə-kay-pee-**oh**-nəm). [Latin] *Hist.* Possession for the purpose of acquiring ownership.

▸ ***possessio bonorum*** (pə-**zes**[**h**]-ee-oh bə-**nor**-əm). [Latin] (1846) *Roman law.* Possession of goods.

▸ ***possessio civilis*** (pə-**zes**[**h**]-ee-oh sə-**vɪ**-lis). [Latin] (17c) *Roman law.* Legal possession; that is, possession accompanied by an intent to hold it as one's own. — Also termed *possession in law*. See *possessory interdict* under INTERDICT (1); USUCAPIO; *possession in law* under POSSESSION. Cf. *possessio naturalis*.

▸ ***possessio corporis.*** See *corporeal possession* under POSSESSION.

▸ ***possessio fictitia.*** See *constructive possession* under POSSESSION.

▸ ***possessio fratris*** (pə-**zes**[**h**]-ee-oh **fray**-tris *or* **fra**-tris). [Latin] (16c) *Hist.* The possession or seisin of a brother; that is, a possession of an estate by a brother that would entitle his full sister to succeed him as heir, to the exclusion of a half-brother.

▸ ***possessio juris.*** See *incorporeal possession* under POSSESSION.

▸ ***possessio longi temporis*** (pə-**zes**[**h**]-ee-oh long-gɪ **tem**-pə-ris). [Latin] *Hist.* Possession for a long period of time.

▸ ***possessio mala fide*** (pə-**zes**[**h**]-ee-oh **mal**-ə **fɪ**-dee). [Latin] Possession in bad faith, as by a thief. Cf. *bona fide possession* under POSSESSION.

▸ ***possessio naturalis*** (pə-**zes**[**h**]-ee-oh nach-ə-**ray**-lis). [Latin "natural possession"] (1838) *Roman law.* The simple holding of a thing, often under a contract, with no intent of keeping it permanently. • This type of possession exists when the possessor's holding of the object is limited by a recognition of another person's outstanding right. The holder may be a usufructuary, a bailee, or a servant. — Also termed *naturalis possessio*; *nuda detentio*; *detentio*; *possession in fact*. See *natural possession* under POSSESSION. Cf. *possessio civilis*.

▸ ***possessio nec vi nec clam nec precario*** (pə-**zes**[**h**]-ee-oh nek **vɪ** nek **klam** nek pri-**kair**-ee-oh). [Latin] *Hist.* Possession not by force, nor by secret, nor by entreaty.

▸ ***possessio pedis.*** See *pedis possessio*.

possession. (14c) **1.** The fact of having or holding property in one's power; the exercise of dominion over property. **2.** The right under which one may exercise control over something to the exclusion of all others; the continuing exercise of a claim to the exclusive use of a material object. **3.** *Civil law.* The detention or use of a physical thing with the intent to hold it as one's own. La. Civ. Code art. 3421(1). **4.** (*usu. pl.*) Something that a person owns or controls; PROPERTY (2). Cf. OWNERSHIP; TITLE (1). **5.** A territorial dominion of a state or country.

> "[A]s the name of Possession is . . . one of the most important in our books, so it is one of the most ambiguous. Its legal senses (for they are several) overlap the popular sense, and even the popular sense includes the assumption of matters of fact which are not always easy to verify. In common speech a man is said to possess or to be in possession of anything of which he has the apparent control, or from the use of which he has the apparent power of excluding others. . . . [A]ny of the usual outward marks of ownership may suffice, in the absence of manifest power in some one else, to denote as having possession the person to whom they attach. Law takes this popular conception as a provisional groundwork, and builds up on it the notion of possession in a technical sense, as a definite legal relation to something capable of having an owner, which relation is distinct and separable both from real and from apparent ownership, though often concurrent with one or both of them." Frederick Pollock & Robert Samuel Wright, *An Essay on Possession in the Common Law* 1–2 (1888).

> "In the whole range of legal theory there is no conception more difficult than that of possession. The Roman lawyers brought their usual acumen to the analysis of it, and since their day the problem has formed the subject of a voluminous literature, while it still continues to tax the ingenuity of jurists. Nor is the question one of mere curiosity or scientific interest, for its practical importance is not less than its difficulty. The legal consequences which flow from the acquisition and loss of possession are many and serious. Possession, for example, is evidence of ownership; the possessor of a thing is presumed to be the owner of it, and may put all other claimants to proof of their title." John Salmond, *Jurisprudence* 285 (Glanville L. Williams ed., 10th ed. 1947).

▸ **actual possession.** (16c) Physical occupancy or control over property. Cf. *constructive possession*.

▸ **adverse possession.** See ADVERSE POSSESSION.

▸ **bona fide possession.** (1815) Possession of property by a person who in good faith does not know that the property's ownership is disputed.

▸ **civil possession.** (17c) **1.** *Civil law.* Possession existing by virtue of a person's intent to own property even though the person no longer occupies or has physical control of it. **2.** *Louisiana law.* The continuation of possession through the possessor's presumed intent to continue holding the thing as his or her own, after the possessor' ceases to possess the thing corporeally. La. Civ. Code arts. 3431–32. • Civil possession may be evidenced by such things as paying taxes on the property or granting rights of interest in it.

▸ **constructive possession.** (18c) **1.** Control or dominion over a property without actual possession or custody of it. — Also termed *effective possession*. **2.** *Civil law.* Possession by operation of law of an entirety by virtue of corporeal possession of a part. • When a possessor holds title to a property and physically possesses part of it, the law will deem the possessor to hold constructive possession of the rest of the property described in the title. La. Civ. Code art. 3426. — Also termed *possessio fictitia*; *possession in law*. Cf. *actual possession*.

▸ **corporeal possession.** (18c) Possession of a material object, such as a farm or a coin. — Also termed *natural possession*; *possessio corporis*; (Ger.) *Sachenbesitz*.

▸ **criminal possession.** (1811) The unlawful possession of certain prohibited articles, such as illegal drugs or drug paraphernalia, firearms, or stolen property.

▸ **derivative possession.** (1851) Lawful possession by one (such as a tenant) who does not hold title.

▸ **direct possession.** See *immediate possession*.

▸ **double possession.** (1952) The doctrine that, in a bailment, both the bailor and the bailee have possession of the item that has been bailed. • This doctrine does not apply in most Anglo-American jurisdictions.

> "It has been suggested that the essence of bailment is that the bailee secures possession and therefore that the bailor loses possession. This elementary proposition is sometimes obscured by the fact that some dicta treat the possession of the bailee as the possession of the bailor. The theoretical justification for this is the doctrine of 'double possession' — a principal may have possession through the possession of an agent. This view is in accord with some foreign systems, but it does not suit the basic principles of English law which treats possession as exclusive." G.W. Paton, *Bailment in the Common Law* 6 (1952).

▸ **effective possession.** See *constructive possession*.

▸ **exclusive possession.** (18c) The exercise of exclusive dominion over property, including the use and benefit of the property.

▸ **hostile possession.** (1812) Possession asserted against the claims of all others, esp. the record owner. See ADVERSE POSSESSION.

▸ **immediate possession.** (17c) Possession that is acquired or retained directly or personally. — Also termed *direct possession*.

▸ **immemorial possession.** (17c) Possession that began so long ago that no one still living witnessed its beginning.

▸ **incorporeal possession.** (1964) Possession of something other than a material object, such as an easement over a neighbor's land, or the access of light to the windows of a house. — Also termed *possessio juris*; *quasi-possession*.

> "It is a question much debated whether incorporeal possession is in reality true possession at all. Some are of opinion that all genuine possession is corporeal, and that the other is related to it by way of analogy merely. They maintain that there is no single generic conception which includes *possessio corporis* and *possessio juris* as its two specific forms. The Roman lawyers speak with hesitation and even inconsistency on the point. They sometimes include both forms under the title of *possessio*, while at other times they are careful to qualify incorporeal possession as *quasi possessio* — something which is not true possession, but is analogous to it. The question is one of no little difficulty, but the opinion here accepted is that the two forms do in truth belong to a single genus. The true idea of possession is wider than that of corporeal possession, just as the true idea of ownership is wider than that of corporeal ownership." John Salmond, *Jurisprudence* 288–89 (Glanville L. Williams ed., 10th ed. 1947).

▸ **indirect possession.** See *mediate possession*.

▸ **insular possession.** (1898) An island territory of the United States, such as Guam.

▸ **joint possession.** (17c) Possession shared by two or more persons.

▸ **lawful possession.** (16c) **1.** Possession based on a good-faith belief in and claim of ownership. **2.** Possession granted by the property owner to the possessor.

▸ **mediate possession** (mee-dee-it). (1947) Possession of a thing through someone else, such as an agent. • In every instance of mediate possession, there is a direct possessor (such as an agent) as well as a mediate possessor (the principal). — Also termed *indirect possession*.

> "If I go myself to purchase a book, I acquire direct possession of it; but if I send my servant to buy it for me, I acquire mediate possession of it through him, until he has brought it to me, when my possession becomes immediate." John Salmond, *Jurisprudence* 300 (Glanville L. Williams ed., 10th ed. 1947).

▸ **naked possession.** (16c) The mere possession of something, esp. real estate, without any apparent right or colorable title to it.

▸ **natural possession.** (16c) *Civil law.* The exercise of physical detention or control over a thing, as by occupying a building or cultivating farmland. • Natural possession may be had without title, and may give rise to a claim of unlawful possession or a claim of ownership by acquisitive prescription. The term "natural possession" has been replaced by the term "corporeal possession" in the Louisiana Civil Code, by virtue of a 1982 revision. La. Civ. Code Ann. art. 3425. See *corporeal possession*; PRESCRIPTION (5). Cf. *possessio naturalis* under POSSESSIO.

▸ **notorious possession.** (18c) Possession or control that is evident to others; possession of property that, because it is generally known by people in the area where the property is located, gives rise to a presumption that the actual owner has notice of it. • Notorious possession is one element of adverse possession. — Also termed *open possession*; *open and notorious possession*. See ADVERSE POSSESSION.

▸ **open and notorious possession.** See *notorious possession*.

▸ **open possession.** See *notorious possession*.

▸ **peaceable possession.** (16c) Possession (as of real property) not disturbed by another's hostile or legal attempts to recover possession; esp., wrongful possession that the rightful possessor has appeared to tolerate. Cf. *scrambling possession* (1); ADVERSE POSSESSION.

▸ **pedal possession.** (1839) Actual possession, as by living on the land or by improving it. • This term usu. appears in adverse-possession contexts.

▸ **possession animo domini.** (1830) *Civil law.* Possession with the intent to own a thing, movable or immovable; possession as an owner. *See* La. Civ. Code art. 3427.

▸ **possession by relation of law.** (1830) A person's legally recognized possession of land despite the person's not having actual possession after being improperly or unlawfully dispossessed by another.

▸ **possession in fact.** (17c) Actual possession that may or may not be recognized by law. • For example, an employee's possession of an employer's property is for some purposes not legally considered possession, the term *detention* or *custody* being used instead. — Also termed *possessio naturalis*.

▸ **possession in law.** (16c) **1.** Possession that is recognized by the law either because it is a specific type of possession in fact or because the law for some special reason attributes the advantages and results of possession to someone who does not in fact possess. **2.** See *constructive possession.* — Also termed *possessio civilis.*

> "There is no conception which will include all that amounts to possession in law, and will include nothing else, and it is impossible to frame any definition from which the concrete law of possession can be logically deduced." John Salmond, *Jurisprudence* 287 (Glanville L. Williams ed., 10th ed. 1947).

▸ **possession of a right.** (17c) The continuing exercise and enjoyment of a right. • This type of possession is often unrelated to an ownership interest in property. For example, a criminal defendant possesses the right to demand a trial by jury. — Also termed *possessio juris;* (Ger.) *Rechtsbesitz.*

▸ **precarious possession.** (1831) *Civil law.* Detention of property by someone other than the owner or possessor on behalf of or with permission of the owner or possessor. • A lessee has precarious possession of the leased property.

> "[Article 3437 of the Louisiana Civil Code defines precarious possession as] 'exercise of possession over a thing with the permission of or on behalf of the owner or possessor.' The definition indicates the difference between *possession* in the proper sense of the word and precarious possession, that is, *detention.* A possessor is one who possesses as owner, whereas a precarious possessor or detainer is one who exercises factual authority over a thing with the permission of or on behalf of another person." A.N. Yiannopoulos, *Property: The Law of Things — Real Rights — Real Actions* § 319, at 629 (4th ed. 2001).

▸ **quasi-possession.** See *incorporeal possession.*

▸ **scrambling possession.** (1823) **1.** A wrongful possession that the rightful possessor has not appeared to tolerate. Cf. *peaceable possession.* **2.** Possession that is uncertain because it is in dispute. • With scrambling possession, the dispute is over who actually has possession — not over whether a party's possession is lawful.

▸ **simple possession.** (1959) *Criminal law.* The possession of a controlled substance with no aggravating circumstances such as intent to sell.

▸ **substantial possession.** See *pedis possessio* under POSSESSIO.

▸ **temporary innocent possession.** (1975) The inadvertent possession of something prohibited, such as contraband, esp. when, upon discovery, the possessor intended to turn it over to the police.

possession unity. See *unity of possession* under UNITY.

possessio pedis. See *pedis possessio* under POSSESSIO.

possessor. (15c) Someone who has possession of real or personal property; esp., a person who is in occupancy of land with the intent to control it or has been but no longer is in that position, but no one else has gained occupancy or has a right to gain it. — **possessorial** (pos-ə-**sor**-ee-əl), *adj.*

▸ **legal possessor.** (17c) One with the legal right to possess property, such as a buyer under a conditional sales contract, as contrasted with the legal owner who holds legal title. See *legal owner* under OWNER.

▸ **possessor bona fide** (**boh**-nə **fɪ**-dee). (17c) A possessor who believes that no other person has a better right to the possession.

▸ **possessor mala fide** (**mal**-ə **fɪ**-dee). (1852) A possessor who knows that someone else has a better right to the possession.

possessorium (pos-ə-**sor**-ee-əm). See *possessory action* (1) under ACTION (4).

possessory (pə-**zes**-ə-ree), *adj.* (15c) Of, relating to, or having possession.

possessory action. See ACTION (4).

possessory claim. (1833) Title to public land held by a claimant who has filed a declaratory statement but has not paid for the land.

possessory conservator. See *noncustodial parent* under PARENT.

possessory estate. 1. ESTATE (1). **2.** POSSESSORY INTEREST.

possessory garageman's lien. See LIEN.

possessory interdict. See INTERDICT (1).

possessory interest. (18c) **1.** The present right to control property, including the right to exclude others, by a person who is not necessarily the owner. **2.** A present or future right to the exclusive use and possession of property. — Also termed *present possessory interest; possessory estate; present estate.*

> "We shall use the term 'possessory interest' to include both present and future interests, and to exclude such interests as easements and profits. The reader should note that the Restatement of Property uses the term 'possessory' to refer only to interests that entitle the owner to *present* possession. *See* Restatement, Property §§ 7, 9, 153 (1936)." Thomas F. Bergin & Paul G. Haskell, *Preface to Estates in Land and Future Interests* 19–20 n.1 (2d ed. 1984).

possessory lien. See LIEN.

possessory warrant. See WARRANT (1).

possibilitas (pos-ə-**bil**-ə-tas). [Latin] Possibility; a possibility.

possibility. (14c) **1.** The quality, state, or condition of being conceivable in theory or in practice; the character of perhaps being, of perhaps existing, or of comporting with physical laws or the laws of reason <the possibility of miracles>. • In this sense, the word often (but not always) conveys a sense of uncertainty or improbability. **2.** The chance that something is or might be true, or that something might or will happen <the possibility of a terrorist attack>. **3.** (*often pl.*) An opportunity to do something; something that can be done or tried <possibilities for reducing costs>. **4.** The relative likelihood that something can be successfully done or tried <explore the possibilities of restoring diplomatic relations>. **5.** An event that may or may not happen; something that might plausibly occur or take place <a remote possibility of a peace settlement>. **6.** A contingency either proximate or remote; esp., a contingent interest in real or personal property <possibility of reverter>.

▸ **bare possibility. 1.** See *naked possibility.* **2.** A chance of damage or injury that might result from a defendant's conduct but that is so remote as to provide insufficient grounds for liability in tort.

▸ **naked possibility.** (18c) A mere chance or expectation that a person will acquire future property. • A conveyance of a naked possibility is usu. void for lack of subject matter, as in a deed conveying all rights to a future estate not yet in existence. — Also termed *bare possibility*; *naked expectancy*. Cf. EXPECTANCY (2).

▸ **possibility coupled with an interest.** (18c) An expectation recognized in law as an estate or interest, as occurs in an executory devise or in a shifting or springing use. • This type of possibility may be sold or assigned. See *shifting use*, *springing use* under USE.

▸ **possibility on a possibility.** See *remote possibility*.

▸ **remote possibility.** (17c) A limitation dependent on two or more facts or events that are contingent and uncertain; a double possibility. — Also termed *possibility on a possibility*.

possibility of reverter. (18c) A reversionary interest that is subject to a condition precedent; specif., a future interest retained by a grantor after conveying a fee simple determinable, so that the grantee's estate terminates automatically and reverts to the grantor if the terminating event ever occurs. • In this type of interest, the grantor transfers an estate whose maximum potential duration equals that of the grantor's own estate and attaches a special limitation that operates in the grantor's favor. — Often shortened to *reverter*. See *fee simple determinable* under FEE SIMPLE. Cf. REMAINDER (1); REVERSION.

> "Most treatise-writers define the possibility of reverter as the interest a transferor keeps when he transfers a fee simple determinable or a fee simple conditional. See, e.g., 1 American Law of Property § 4.12; Simes & Smith § 281. Although this definition is all right as far as it goes, it fails to provide for interests less than the fee simple that are granted on special limitation. . . . Although we call the possibility of reverter an 'estate,' the courts of an earlier era would probably have called it a 'possibility of becoming an estate.'" Thomas F. Bergin & Paul G. Haskell, *Preface to Estates in Land and Future Interests* 58 n.5 (2d ed. 1984).

possibility on a possibility. See *remote possibility* under POSSIBILITY.

possidere (pos-ə-**dee**-ree). [Latin fr. *potis* "having power" + *sedere* "to sit"] *Hist.* To possess (a thing), esp. as a person with an interest protected by law (e.g., an owner or mortgagee) rather than a mere custodian.

> "A distinction was made in the civil law, and adopted by Bracton, between *possidere*, (to possess,) and *esse in possessione*, (to be in possession.) . . . . Thus, a guardian, holding in demesne though not in fee, was said to be *in possession*, though he did not *possess*. The same language was applied to a bailiff, . . . a domestic, . . . a fermor or lessee, . . . and a tenant at will from day to day, and from year to year." 2 Alexander M. Burrill, *A Law Dictionary and Glossary* 314 (2d ed. 1867).

POSSLQ (**pahs**-əl-kyoo). *abbr.* (1978) A person of opposite sex sharing living quarters. • Although this term (which is used by the Census Bureau) is intended to include only a person's roommate of the opposite sex to whom the person is not married, the phrase literally includes those who are married. This overbreadth has occasionally been criticized. See CUPOS.

> "In the 1980 census, the United States Census Bureau — recognizing a societal change with numerous persons living together without being 'officially' married — counted not only persons who were 'Single' and 'Married,' but also 'Persons of the Opposite Sex Sharing Living Quarters.' The acronym is *POSSLQ* — and, of course, is pronounced *posslekew*. It has been suggested that, although the source was stunningly unlikely, it was the Very Word that society has been looking for to describe these relationships: POSSLQ. Precise, businesslike, nonjudgmental. And, in its own way, sort of poetic, too . . . ." *Fischer v. Dallas Federal Savings and Loan Ass'n*, 106 F.R.D. 465 (N.D. Tex. 1985).

post. [Latin] (14c) After. Cf. ANTE.

post, *vb.* (17c) **1.** To publicize or announce by affixing a notice in a public place <foreclosure notice was posted at the county courthouse>. **2.** To transfer (accounting entries) from an original record to a ledger <post debits and credits>. **3.** To place in the mail <post a letter>. **4.** To make a payment or deposit; to put up <post bail>.

postage (**pohs**-tij). (16c) The fee charged for mailing a letter or package.

postage and handling. (1900) The charge for packing and sending something, usu. an item that someone has purchased. — Also termed (BrE) *postage and packing*.

postage and packing. See POSTAGE AND HANDLING.

postage currency. See *postal currency* under CURRENCY.

postage-paid envelope. (1867) An envelope that one can send back to its sender without a stamp because the sender has already paid for the return. — Also termed *reply-paid envelope*.

postal currency. See CURRENCY.

Postal Rate Commission. An independent federal agency that recommends changes in postage rates, fees, and mail classifications to the governors of the United States Postal Service. • It was created by the Postal Reorganization Act. 39 USCA §§ 3601–3604. — Abbr. PRC.

post-answer default judgment. See DEFAULT JUDGMENT.

post audit. See AUDIT.

post bail, *vb.* See GIVE BAIL.

post causam cognitam (pohst **kaw**-zəm **kog**-ni-təm). [Latin] (1812) *Hist.* After investigation. Cf. CAUSA COGNITA.

post contractum debitum (pohst kən-**trak**-təm **deb**-i-təm). [Latin] (17c) *Hist.* After debt has been contracted.

postconviction conditional (driver's) license. See PCCL.

postconviction-relief proceeding. (1964) A state or federal procedure for a prisoner to request a court to vacate or correct a conviction or sentence. — Also termed *postconviction-remedy proceeding*; *PCR action*; *postconviction proceeding*.

postdate, *vb.* (17c) **1.** To put a date on (an instrument, such as a check) that is later than the actual date. Cf. BACKDATE (1). **2.** To occur, live, or be made later in history than something else. Cf. ANTEDATE.

postdated check. See CHECK.

postdated-check loan. See *payday loan* under LOAN.

post diem (pohst **dɪ**-əm). [Latin] (1848) After the day. • A plea of payment *post diem* is made after the day when the money becomes due.

postdispute arbitration agreement. See ARBITRATION AGREEMENT.

post disseisina. See DE POST DISSEISINA.

postea (**poh**-stee-ə), *n.* [Latin "afterward"] (17c) *Hist.* A formal statement, endorsed on the trial record, giving an account of the proceedings at trial; a record of what occurred at nisi prius after the issue had been joined.

"With the verdict of the jury [in the 15th–18th centuries] . . . the proceedings at *nisi prius* closed, and the case was sent back to the court at Westminster from which it issued for judgment, after a statement of the holding of the trial and of the verdict had been added to the record. This statement, from the fact that it began with the Latin word 'postea,' or 'afterwards,' was known as the 'postea' and was in fact drafted by the party in whose favour the verdict had gone, whence the phrase 'postea to the plaintiff' or 'the defendant,' which is found in the old reports." Geoffrey Radcliffe & Geoffrey Cross, *The English Legal System* 185 (G.J. Hand & D.J. Bentley eds., 6th ed. 1977).

posted water. See WATER.

poste restante. See GENERAL DELIVERY.

posteriores (pah-steer-ee-**or**-eez), *n. pl.* [Latin] *Roman law.* Descendants in a direct line beyond the sixth degree.

posteriority (pah-steer-ee-**or**-ə-tee). (16c) The quality, state, or condition of being subsequent. • This word was formerly used to describe the relationships existing between a tenant and the two or more lords the tenant held of; the tenant held the older tenancy "by priority" and the more recent one "by posteriority."

posterity, *n.* (14c) **1.** Future generations collectively. **2.** All the descendants of a person to the furthest generation.

post-expiration-sales theory. (2004) *Patents.* A theory of lost-profits remedy by which compensation is sought for sales lost after a patent has expired, on the basis that infringement gave the competitor a head start on entering the market. — Also termed *accelerated-reentry theory.*

post facto (pohst **fak**-toh). [Latin] (16c) After the fact. See EX POST FACTO.

post-factum (pohst-**fak**-təm). [Latin] An after-act; an act done afterward. — Also termed *postfactum.*

postfine. *Hist. English law.* A duty paid to the crown for the royal license to levy a fine, esp. at the conclusion of the judicial process of fine and recovery. See ALIENATION OFFICE.

post-fine. See KING'S SILVER.

postglossators (pohst-glah-**say**-tərz), *n. pl.* (*often cap.*) (1915) A group of mainly Italian jurists who were active during the 13th through the 15th centuries writing commentaries and treatises that related Roman law to feudal and Germanic law, canon law, and other contemporary bodies of law. • The postglossators constituted the second wave of Roman-law study after its revival in the 11th century, the first being that of the glossators. — Also termed *commentators.* See GLOSSATORS.

"[The] jurists who were said to be the successors of the Glossators [were] . . . the Post-Glossators or Commentators. It is only in an external and literal sense that the work initiated by the Glossators was continued by the Commentators, but different style, technique, interpretative conceptions, and originality in the tackling of legal problems resulted in achievements substantially distinct from those of the Glossators. The merely legal interpretation of the Roman texts was completed and concluded by the Glossators. The task which remained, therefore, was the philosophic interpretation of the Roman law, the penetration into the intricate mechanism behind the law, and the exposition of universally valid, general principles. With this aim in view, the Commentators extended the sphere of legal science and studies from the mere interpretation of individual legal rules to the investigation and presentation of the fundamental principles, notions, and sources of the law. The apprehension of the legal problems as a coherent whole, the systematization of the huge body of law, and the conception that the individual jural precept is merely the legal expression and enforceable verification of an idea behind the law, is the great achievement of the Post-Glossators." Walter Ullmann, *The Medieval Idea of Law* 1–2 (1946).

postgrant opposition. See POSTGRANT REVIEW.

postgrant review. *Patents.* An administrative proceeding in the U.S. Patent and Trademark Office in which the validity of a patent is challenged within the first year of the patent's issuance or reissuance on the basis of prior-art patents or printed publications. • The procedure can be initiated only for patents issuing on applications filed on or after March 16, 2013. — Also termed *postgrant opposition.* Cf. INTER PARTES REVIEW.

post hoc (pohst hok). [Latin fr. *post hoc, ergo propter hoc* "after this, therefore because of this"] (1844) **1.** *adv.* After this; subsequently. **2.** *adj.* Of, relating to, or involving the fallacy of assuming causality from temporal sequence; confusing sequence with consequence.

post hoc ergo propter hoc. [Latin "after this, therefore resulting from it"] (17c) The logical fallacy of assuming that a causal relationship exists when acts or events are merely sequential.

posthumous (**pos**-chə-məs), *adj.* (17c) Occurring or existing after death; esp., (of a child) born after the father's death.

posthumous adoption. See ADOPTION (1).

posthumous child. See CHILD.

posthumous work. See WORK (2).

posting. (17c) **1.** *Accounting.* The act of transferring an original entry to a ledger. **2.** The act of mailing a letter. **3.** A method of substituted service of process by displaying the process in a prominent place (such as the courthouse door) when other forms of service have failed. See SERVICE (1). **4.** A publication method, as by displaying municipal ordinances in designated localities. **5.** The act of providing legal notice, as by affixing notices of judicial sales at or on the courthouse door. **6.** The procedure for processing a check, including one or more of the following steps: (1) verifying any signature, (2) ascertaining that sufficient funds are available, (3) affixing a "paid" or other stamp, (4) entering a charge or entry to a customer's account, and (5) correcting or reversing an entry or erroneous action concerning the check.

post-issue activity. (2004) *Patents.* Any acts done during a patent's term, including making, using, or selling a patented invention or process, esp. without authorization.

postjudgment discovery. See DISCOVERY.

postliminium (pohst-lə-**min**-ee-əm), *n.* [fr. Latin *post* "after" + *limen* "threshold"] (17c) **1.** *Roman & civil law.* The reentering of one's residence. **2.** *Roman & civil law.* The doctrine that a restoration of a person's lost rights or status relates back to the time of the original loss or deprivation, esp. in regard to the restoration of the status of a prisoner of war.

"[A] person who is taken captive and comes back within the limits of the Empire is correctly described as returning by postliminium. By 'limen' (threshold) we mean the frontier of a house, and the old lawyers applied the word to the frontier of the Roman State; so that the word postliminium conveys the idea of recrossing the frontier. If a prisoner is recovered from a beaten foe he is deemed to have come back by postliminium." R.W. Lee, *The Elements of Roman Law* 85–86 (4th ed. 1956).

3. *Int'l law.* The act of invalidating all of an occupying force's illegal acts, and the post-occupation revival of all illegitimately modified legal relations to their former condition, esp. the restoration of property to its rightful owner. — Also termed *postliminy; jus postliminii.*

post litem motam (pohst **lɪ**-təm **moh**-təm). [Law Latin] (1816) After suit commenced. • Depositions held after litigation had begun were formerly sometimes so called.

postman (**pohst**-mən). (18c) **1.** *Hist.* A barrister in the Court of Exchequer who had precedence in motions. • The postman was so called because of the post he stood next to when making motions. Cf. TUBMAN.

> "The postman was an experienced member of the junior Bar who had a place in the Court of Exchequer by the post anciently used as a measure of length in excise cases. He had precedence in motions over all other juniors . . . ." Sir Robert Megarry, *A Second Miscellany-at-Law* 122 (1973).

2. Someone whose job is to collect and deliver mail.

postmarital, *adj.* (1836) **1.** Of, relating to, or occurring after marriage. Cf. PREMARITAL. **2.** Of, relating to, or occurring after divorce.

postmark. (17c) An official mark put by the post office on an item of mail to cancel the stamp and to indicate the place and date of sending or receipt.

postmaster. (16c) A U.S. Postal Service official responsible for a local branch of the post office • The archaic female counterpart to this traditionally male position is *postmistress.* — Abbr. PM.

Postmaster General. The head of the U.S. Postal Service.

post meridiem (pohst mə-**rid**-ee-əm). [Latin] (17c) After noon. — Abbr. p.m.; PM.

postmortem, *adj.* (1824) Done or occurring after death <a postmortem examination>.

postmortem, *n.* See AUTOPSY (1).

postmortem annulment. See ANNULMENT (2).

postmortem examination. See AUTOPSY (1).

postnatus (pohst **nay**-təs). [Latin] (17c) A person born after a certain political event that affected the person's political rights; esp., a person born after the Declaration of Independence. Cf. ANTENATUS. Pl. ***postnati.***

post note. (18c) A banknote payable at a future time rather than on demand. See *time note* under NOTE (1).

postnup, *n. Slang.* See POSTNUPTIAL AGREEMENT.

postnuptial (pohst-**nəp**-shəl), *adj.* (1807) Made or occurring during marriage <a postnuptial contract>. Cf. PRENUPTIAL.

postnuptial agreement (pohst-**nəp**-shəl). (1834) An agreement entered into during marriage to define each spouse's property rights in the event of death or divorce. • The term commonly refers to an agreement between spouses during the marriage at a time when separation or divorce is not imminent. When dissolution is intended as the result, it is more properly called a *property settlement* or *marital agreement.* — Often shortened to *postnup.* — Also termed *postnuptial settlement.* Cf. PRENUPTIAL AGREEMENT.

postnuptial settlement. See POSTNUPTIAL AGREEMENT.

postnuptial will. See WILL.

post-obit agreement. See BOND (3).

post-obit bond. See BOND (3).

postpone, *vb.* (15c) **1.** To put off to a later time; to change the date or time for (a planned event or action) to a later one. **2.** To place lower in precedence or importance; esp., to subordinate (a lien) to a later one. **3.** *Parliamentary law.* To temporarily or permanently suppress a main motion. — **postponement,** *n.*

▸ **postpone definitely.** To delay a main motion's consideration to a specified time or until a specified condition occurs, usu. no later than the following morning. — Also termed *postpone to a certain time; postpone to a definite time; postpone to a time certain.* See TIME CERTAIN.

▸ **postpone indefinitely.** (1818) To dispose of a main motion without taking a view on its merits while preventing its further consideration during the same session. • This motion's ancient form in the English Parliament was to postpone consideration until "this day six months" (or "three months") — that is, some time beyond the current session, sufficiently remote that the body expected not to consider the matter again. — Also termed *indefinite postponement.* See INDEFINITELY.

▸ **postpone temporarily.** See TABLE.

▸ **postpone to a certain time.** See *postpone definitely.*

▸ **postpone to a definite time.** See *postpone definitely.*

▸ **postpone to a time certain.** See *postpone definitely.*

post prolem suscitatam (pohst **proh**-ləm səs-ə-**tay**-təm). [Law Latin] (17c) After issue born.

postrelease supervision. (1938) *Criminal procedure.* In some jurisdictions, a part of a criminal sentence whereby a felon serving a determinate sentence is required to undergo a specified period of police monitoring after the completion of a prison term.

postremogeniture. See BOROUGH ENGLISH.

post-revocation conditional license. See DRIVER'S LICENSE.

post tantum temporis (pohst **tan**-təm **tem**-pə-ris). [Latin] (18c) *Hist.* After so long a time.

post-terminal sitting. (1979) A court session held after the normal term.

post terminum (pohst **tər**-mə-nəm). [Law Latin] (17c) After term, as a writ returned after the ending of a judicial term.

post-traumatic stress disorder. (1980) A severe anxiety disorder triggered by a traumatic event and characterized by all-pervading fear, anxiety, depression, intrusive thoughts, memories, flashbacks, mood swings, feelings of helplessness, and confusion. — Abbr. PTSD.

posttrial discovery. See *postjudgment discovery* under DISCOVERY.

posttrial motion. See MOTION (1).

posttrial proceeding. See PROCEEDING.

postulate, *vb.* (16c) **1.** *Eccles. law.* To name someone to an ecclesiastical position, subject to approval by a higher authority. **2.** To suggest as having happened or as being true.

postulatio (pos-chə-**lay**-shee-oh). [Latin] **1.** *Roman law.* The act of naming or accusing another of a crime before the praetor. **2.** *Hist. Eccles. law.* A petition requesting the naming or transfer of a bishop. **3.** POSTULATIO ACTIONIS.

postulatio actionis (pos-chə-**lay**-shee-oh ak-shee-**oh**-nis). [Latin] (17c) *Roman law.* A request to a magistrate having jurisdiction for permission to bring an action. — Often shortened to *postulatio.*

potency (**poht**-ən-see). (15c) **1.** General efficiency or capability; the power or energy to effect a certain result. **2.** The strength of something, esp. a drug. **3.** The power that something has to influence people; efficacy. **4.** The ability of a man to achieve an erection and have sex. Cf. IMPOTENCE.

potentate (**poh**-tən-tayt). (15c) A ruler who possesses great power or sway; a monarch whose power is not limited by a parliament; DESPOT (1).

potentia (pə-**ten**-shee-ə). [Latin] Possibility; power.

potential, *adj.* (14c) Capable of coming into being; possible if the necessary conditions exist <things having a potential existence may be the subject of mortgage, assignment, or sale>.

potential-elective forfeiture. See FORFEITURE.

potentially responsible party. (1983) *Environmental law.* A person or entity that may be required to clean up a polluted site because the person or entity (1) owns or operates on the site, (2) arranged for the disposal of a hazardous substance on the site, (3) transported a hazardous substance to the site, or (4) contributed in any other way to contaminate the site. — Abbr. PRP. See SUPERFUND.

potential Pareto superiority. See WEALTH MAXIMIZATION.

potentia propinqua (pə-**ten**-shee-ə prə-**ping**-kwə). [Latin] (17c) Common possibility.

potestas (pə-**tes**-təs *or* -tas), *n.* [Latin "power"] (1816) *Roman law.* Authority or power, such as the power of a magistrate to enforce the law, or the authority of an owner over a slave.

▸ ***patria potestas*** (**pay**-tree-ə *or* **pa**-tree-ə). [Latin "paternal power"] (17c) The authority held by the male head of a family (the paterfamilias) over his legitimate and adopted children, as well as further descendants in the male line, unless emancipated. • Initially, the father had extensive powers over the family, including the power of life and death; until Justinian's time, the father alone in his *familia* had proprietary capacity but he could give a son or slave a *peculium.* Over time, the broad nature of the *patria potestas* gradually became more in the nature of a responsibility to support and maintain family members. But except in early Roman history, a wife did not fall into her husband's power but remained in her father's until she became *sui juris* by his death. — Also termed *fatherly power.*

> "The power of the father continued ordinarily to the close of his life, and included not only his own children, but also the children of his sons, and those of his sons' sons, if any such were born during his lifetime. . . . Originally and for a long time the *patria potestas* had a terribly despotic character. Not only was the father entitled to all the service and all the acquisitions of his child, as much as to those of a slave, but he had the same absolute control over his person. He could inflict upon him any punishment however severe." James Hadley, *Introduction to Roman Law* 119–21 (1881).

> "Nature and Extent of Patria Potestas. — From the most remote ages the power of a Roman father over his children, including those by adoption as well as by blood, was unlimited. A father might, without violating any law, scourge or imprison his son, or sell him for a slave, or put him to death, even after that son had risen to the highest honours in the state. This jurisdiction was not merely nominal, but, in early times, was not infrequently exercised to its full extent, and was confirmed by the laws of the XII Tables. . . . By degrees the right of putting a child to death (*ius vitae et necis*) fell into desuetude; and long before the close of the republic, the execution of a son by order of his father, although not forbidden by any positive statute, was regarded as something strange, and, unless under extraordinary circumstances, monstrous. But the right continued to exist in theory . . . after the establishment of the empire. [In the Christian empire, these extreme punishments were forbidden and disciplinary powers were reduced to those of reasonable chastisement. — Ed.]" William Ramsay, *A Manual of Roman Antiquities* 291–92 (Rodolfo Lanciani ed., 15th ed. 1894).

▸ ***potestas gladii*** (pə-**tes**-təs [*or* -tas] **glad**-ee-ɪ). [Latin "the power of the sword"] *Roman law.* See JUS GLADII.

▸ ***potestas maritalis*** (pə-**tes**-təs [*or* -tas] mar-ə-**tay**-lis). [Latin] (17c) *Hist.* The marital power. • In Roman law, this was an institution, one that was decaying by the end of the Republic.

potestative condition. See CONDITION (2).

POTUS. *abbr.* (1895) PRESIDENT OF THE UNITED STATES.

pound, *n.* (12c) **1.** A place where impounded property is held until redeemed. **2.** A place for the detention of stray animals. **3.** A measure of weight equal to 16 avoirdupois ounces or 7,000 grains. **4.** The basic monetary unit of the United Kingdom, equal to 100 pence. • A pound was worth 20 shillings until decimalization in 1968. — Also termed (in sense 4) *pound sterling.*

poundage, *n. Criminal procedure.* A surcharge (such as 3%) deducted from returned bail when a defendant receives an unfavorable result (that is, a conviction).

poundage fee. (18c) A percentage commission awarded to a sheriff for moneys recovered under judicial process, such as execution or attachment.

pound-breach. (13c) *Hist.* The offense of breaking a pound for the purpose of taking out something that has been impounded.

pound of land. (16c) An uncertain quantity of land, usu. thought to be about 52 acres.

pound sterling. See POUND (4).

pour acquit (**poor** a-**kee**), *n.* [French "for acquittance"] *French law.* The formula that a creditor adds when signing a receipt.

pour appuyer (**poor** a-poo-**yay**). [Law French] For the support of; in the support of.

pour autre vie. [Law French] For another's life.

pour autrui (**poor** oh-troo-**ee**). [Law French] For others.

***pour faire* proclaimer** (**poor fair** prə-**klay**-mər), *n.* [Law French "for making a proclamation"] *Hist.* A writ addressed to the mayor or bailiff of a city or town, requiring that official to make a proclamation about some matter, such as a nuisance.

pour out, *vb.* (1978) *Slang.* To deny (a claimant) damages or relief in a lawsuit <the plaintiff was poured out of court by the jury's verdict of no liability>.

pourover trust. See TRUST (3).

pourover will. See WILL.

pourparler (poor-pahr-**lər**), *vb.* [French] (1900) To informally discuss before actual negotiating begins. — **pourparler,** *n.*

pourparty (**poor**-pahr-tee). [Law French] See PURPART.

pourpresture (poor-**pres**-chər). [Law French] See PURPRESTURE.

pour seisir terres (poor SI-zər **ter**-eez). [Law French "for seizing the lands"] *Hist.* A writ by which the Crown could seize land that the wife of its deceased tenant, who held *in capite,* had for her dower if she married without leave.

poverty. (13c) **1.** The condition of being indigent; the scarcity of the means of subsistence <war on poverty>. **2.** Dearth of something desirable <a poverty of ideas>. **3.** A level of income below the threshold considered necessary to achieve a sufficient standard of living.

poverty affidavit. See AFFIDAVIT.

POW. *abbr.* (1919) PRISONER OF WAR.

***Powell* doctrine.** See CORRUPT-MOTIVE DOCTRINE.

power. (13c) **1.** The ability to act or not act; esp., a person's capacity for acting in such a manner as to control someone else's responses. **2.** Dominance, control, or influence over another; control over one's subordinates. **3.** The legal right or authorization to act or not act; a person's or organization's ability to alter, by an act of will, the rights, duties, liabilities, or other legal relations either of that person or of another.

> "A *power* is the capacity to change a legal relationship. In this terminology the offeree has, before the contract is made, a *power* to create a contract by means of acceptance." E. Allan Farnsworth, *Contracts* § 3.4, at 114 n.3 (3d ed. 1999).

▸ **agent's power.** (18c) The ability of an agent or apparent agent to act on behalf of the principal in matters connected with the agency or apparent agency.

▸ **concurrent power.** (1812) A political power independently exercisable by both federal and state governments in the same field of legislation.

▸ **congressional power.** (1808) *Constitutional law.* The authority vested in the U.S. Senate and House of Representatives to enact laws and take other constitutionally permitted actions. U.S. Const. art. I.

▸ **constitutional power.** See CONSTITUTIONAL POWER.

▸ **delegated power.** (17c) Power normally exercised by an authority that has temporarily conferred the power on a lower authority.

▸ **derivative power.** (17c) Power that arises only from a grant of authority. • Power may be derived, for example, by an agent from a principal, or by a head of state from constitutional or statutory provisions.

▸ **discretionary power.** (17c) A power that a person may choose to exercise or not, based on the person's judgment.

▸ **emergency power.** A power granted to or used by a public authority to deal with the circumstances of a particular emergency.

▸ **enumerated power.** (1805) A political power specifically delegated to a governmental branch by a constitution. — Also termed *express power.*

▸ **exclusive power.** A power held by only one person or authoritative body.

▸ **express power. 1.** A power explicitly granted by a legal instrument. See ENUMERATED POWER. **2.** A power that is granted to all corporations alike by statute, whether inserted in the charter or not. **3.** A power statutorily allowed to corporations whose incorporators take advantage of it by reserving it in the corporate charter.

> "Express powers relate not only to the right to engage in a special line of business as set forth in the statement in the articles of the object or purposes for which the corporation is formed, but they relate as well to other powers which are here termed 'express,' inasmuch as they depend upon the existence of specific statutes authorizing their exercise by such corporations as desire to avail themselves thereof. These express powers may be divided into twenty-eight classes, enumerated as follows: (1) power to purchase its own capital stock; (2) power to subscribe for, purchase, and hold stock in other corporations; (3) power to consolidate with other corporations; (4) power to transact all or any part of its business outside of the State of its origin; (5) power to extend its corporate existence; (6) power to change its corporate name; (7) power to increase or decrease its capital stock; (8) power to issue preferred stock; (9) power to change the corporate purposes; (10) power to change the number of directors; (11) power to change its domiciliary office or place for the transaction of its business; (12) power to acquire and enforce a lien upon stock of the corporation to secure the payment of debts due the corporation from stockholders; (13) power to levy assessments against the stockholders with the right to forfeit the stock for non-payment thereof; (14) power to authorize voting at stockholders' meetings by proxy; (15) power to allow cumulative voting at the election of directors; (16) power to issue stock as full paid and non-assessable in exchange for property or services; (17) power to sell the corporate assets; (18) power to voluntarily dissolve the corporation without recourse to the courts; (19) power to insert in the charter provisions for the regulation of the internal affairs of the corporation; (20) power to authorize directors to adopt by-laws; (21) power to authorize appointment of executive committee from board of directors; (22) power to enlarge or diminish corporate powers; (23) power to change par value of shares; (24) power of bondholders to vote at elections of directors; (25) power to classify directors; (26) power to amend articles before organization; (27) power to surrender charter before organization; (28) power given to minority stockholders to compel purchase of their holdings upon consolidation." Thomas Gold Frost, *A Treatise on the Incorporation and Organization of Corporations* 34–35 (2d ed. 1906).

▸ **fatherly power.** See *patria potestas* under POTESTAS.

▸ **fiscal power.** A governmental body's powers to finance government operations and public obligations, such as by taxation, borrowing, and levying fines, and to spend the money raised for public purposes.

▸ **implied power.** (1807) A political power that is not enumerated but that nonetheless exists because it is needed to carry out an express power.

▸ **incident power.** (17c) A power that, although not expressly granted, must exist because it is necessary to the accomplishment of an express purpose. — Also termed *incidental power.*

▸ **inherent power.** (17c) A power that necessarily derives from an office, position, or status.

▸ **institorial power** (in-stə-**tor**-ee-əl). (1819) *Civil law.* The power given by a business owner to an agent to act in the owner's behalf.

▸ **investigatory power** (in-**ves**-tə-gə-tor-ee). (*usu. pl.*) (1825) The authority conferred on a governmental agency to inspect and compel disclosure of facts germane to an investigation.

▸ **judicial power.** See JUDICIAL POWER.

▸ **marriage power.** (17c) The power of a governmental body to define and regulate marriage.

▸ **mediate powers.** See MEDIATE POWERS.

▸ **naked power.** (18c) The power to exercise rights over something (such as a trust) without having a corresponding interest in that thing. Cf. *power coupled with an interest.*

▸ **particular power.** See *special power.*

▸ **plenary power** (**plee**-nə-ree *or* **plen**-ə-ree). (16c) Power that is broadly construed; esp., a court's power to dispose of any matter properly before it.

▸ **police power.** See POLICE POWER.

▸ **power coupled with an interest.** (18c) A power to do some act, conveyed along with an interest in the subject matter of the power. • A power coupled with an interest is not held for the benefit of the principal, and it is irrevocable because of the agent's interest in the subject property. For this reason, some authorities assert that it is not a true agency power. — Also termed *power given as security*; *proprietary power.* See *irrevocable power of attorney* under POWER OF ATTORNEY. Cf. *naked power.*

> "[S]uppose that the principal borrows money from the agent and by way of security authorizes the agent to sell Blackacre if the loan is not repaid and pay himself out of the proceeds. In such case there is no more reason why the principal should be permitted to revoke than if he had formally conveyed or mortgaged Blackacre to the agent. Hence it would be highly unfair to the agent to allow his principal to revoke. The reason why such a case is not properly governed by the considerations usually making an agency revocable is that this is in reality not a case of agency at all. In a normal agency case the power is conferred upon the agent to enable him to do something for the principal while here it is given to him to enable him to do something for himself. Coupled with an interest means that the agent must have a present interest in the property upon which the power is to operate." Harold Gill Reuschlein & William A. Gregory, *The Law of Agency and Partnership* § 47, at 99 (1990).

▸ **power given as security.** See *power coupled with an interest.*

▸ **power of acceptance.** (1848) An offeree's power to bind an offeror to a contract by accepting the offer.

▸ **power of revocation** (rev-ə-**kay**-shən). (17c) A power that a person reserves in an instrument (such as a trust) to revoke the legal relationship that the person has created.

▸ **power of sale.** (18c) A power granted to sell the property that the power relates to. • The power's exercise is often conditioned on the occurrence of a specific event, such as the nonpayment of a debt.

▸ **power of the purse.** See *spending power.*

▸ **power over oneself.** See CAPACITY (2).

▸ **power over other persons.** See AUTHORITY (1).

▸ **primary powers.** See PRIMARY POWERS.

▸ **private power.** (16c) A power vested in a person to be exercised for personal ends and not as an agent for the state.

▸ **proprietary power.** See *power coupled with an interest.*

▸ **public power.** (16c) A power vested in a person as an agent or instrument of the functions of the state. • Public powers comprise the various forms of legislative, judicial, and executive authority.

▸ **quasi-judicial power.** (1927) An administrative agency's power to adjudicate the rights of those who appear before it. 5 USCA § 554.

▸ **quasi-legislative power.** (1864) An administrative agency's power to engage in rulemaking. 5 USCA § 553.

▸ **reserved power.** (1831) A political power that is not enumerated or prohibited by a constitution, but instead is reserved by the constitution for a specified political authority, such as a state government. See TENTH AMENDMENT.

▸ **restraining power.** (17c) A power to restrict the acts of others.

▸ **resulting power.** A political power derived from the aggregate powers expressly or impliedly granted by a constitution.

▸ **special power.** (18c) **1.** An agent's limited authority to perform only specific acts or to perform under specific restrictions. — Also termed *particular power.* **2.** See *limited power of appointment* under POWER OF APPOINTMENT.

▸ **spending power.** (1923) *Constitutional law.* The power granted to a governmental body to spend public funds; esp., the congressional power to spend money for the payment of debt and provision of the common defense and general welfare of the United States. U.S. Const. art. I, § 8, cl. 1. — Also termed *power of the purse.*

> "**Spending Power.** The power to spend public funds is so much a sine qua non of government that ordinarily it needs no express authorization in constitutions, including those of the several states. However, because the U.S. Constitution was designed to give the federal government specified powers, particularly the fiscal power lacking under the Articles of Confederation, Article 1, section 8, begins its enumeration of powers of Congress with the power to 'lay and collect taxes, duties, imposts, and excises, to pay the debts and provide for the common defense and general welfare of the United States.' The list continues with specified objects of lawmaking, such as commerce, bankruptcy, coinage, war and military and naval forces, and (in Article IV, section 3) the territory or other property of the United States. From the start, there was controversy whether the implicit power to spend revenues for the 'general welfare of the United States' extended beyond the enumerated objects of congressional law-making powers." Hans A. Linde, "Spending Power," in *Encyclopedia of the American Constitution* 507 (1st Supp., Leonard W. Levy ed., 1991).

▸ **taxing power.** (18c) *Constitutional law.* The power granted to a governmental body to levy a tax; esp., the congressional power to levy and collect taxes as a means of effectuating Congress's delegated powers. U.S. Const. art. I, § 8, cl. 1. See SIXTEENTH AMENDMENT. — Also termed *taxation power*; *power to tax.*

> "Unavowed purposes of legislation are not always intrinsically objectionable or contrary to public interest. Under systems of limited powers, such as American constitutions have established, it has happened now and then that a generally desired object could be attained only by indirection. Thus the United States has occasionally resorted to the taxing power for the purpose of accomplishing objects not otherwise within the general legislative power of Congress. In the last instance of this kind, the suppression of the white phosphorus match industry by a prohibitive tax, there was no pretense that the law was in any sense a revenue measure. Such instances of perversion of power are regrettable, and yet we have to take cognizance of the fact that

legal development now and then takes this devious course." Ernst Freund, *Standards of American Legislation* 103 (1917).

▸ **temporal power.** (16c) Power in civil, political, or secular affairs, as contrasted with purely spiritual or ecclesiastical authority.

▸ **trust power.** See *beneficial power.*

▸ **visitatorial power.** (17c) The power to inspect or make decisions about an entity's operations. — Also termed *visitorial power.*

4. A document granting legal authorization. See AUTHORITY. **5.** An authority to affect an estate in land by (1) creating some estate independently of any estate that the holder of the authority possesses, (2) imposing a charge on the estate, or (3) revoking an existing estate. See POWER OF APPOINTMENT; PERMIT.

"The word 'power' is normally used in the sense of an authority given to a person to dispose of property which is not his. The person giving the power is called the donor and the person to whom it is given the donee." Robert E. Megarry & P.V. Baker, *A Manual of the Law of Real Property* 253 (4th ed. 1969).

▸ **appendant power** (ə-**pen**-dənt). (17c) **1.** A power that gives the donee a right to appoint estates that attach to the donee's own interest. **2.** A power held by a donee who owns the property interest in the assets subject to the power, and whose interest can be divested by the exercise of the power. • The appendant power is generally viewed as adding nothing to the ownership and thus is not now generally recognized as a true power. — Also termed *power appendant*; *power appurtenant.*

▸ **avoiding power.** (1955) *Bankruptcy.* The power of a bankruptcy trustee or debtor in possession to void certain transfers made or obligations incurred by a debtor, including fraudulent conveyances, preferences transferred to creditors, unperfected security interests in personal property, and unrecorded mortgages. 11 USCA §§ 544–553.

▸ **beneficial power.** (18c) A power that is executed for the benefit of the power's donee, as distinguished from a *trust power,* which is executed for the benefit of someone other than the power's donee (i.e., a trust beneficiary).

▸ **collateral power.** (17c) A power created when the donee has no estate in the land, but simply the authority to appoint.

▸ **general power.** See POWER OF APPOINTMENT.

▸ **limited power.** See POWER OF APPOINTMENT.

▸ **mandatory power.** (17c) A power that the donee must exercise and must do so only as instructed, without discretion.

▸ **power appendant.** See *appendant power.*

▸ **power appurtenant.** See *appendant power.*

▸ **power collateral.** See *power in gross.*

▸ **power in gross.** (18c) A power held by a donee who has an interest in the assets subject to the power but whose interest cannot be affected by the exercise of the power. • An example is a life tenant with a power over the remainder. — Also termed *power collateral.*

▸ **power of appointment.** See POWER OF APPOINTMENT.

▸ **relative power.** A power that relates directly to land, as distinguished from a collateral power.

▸ **testamentary power.** See POWER OF APPOINTMENT.

6. Physical strength. **7.** Moral or intellectual force. **8.** A person of influence <a power in the community>. **9.** One of the great countries of the world <one of the world's two great powers>. See PROTECTING POWER. **10.** The military or unit of it, such as a troop of soldiers.

power-delegating law. See LAW OF COMPETENCE.

power given as security. See *power coupled with an interest* under POWER (3).

power of alienation. (16c) The capacity to sell, transfer, assign, or otherwise dispose of property.

power of appointment. (18c) A power created or reserved by a person having property subject to disposition, enabling the donee of the power to designate transferees of the property or shares in which it will be received; esp., a power conferred on a donee by will or deed to select and determine one or more recipients of the donor's estate or income. • If the power is exercisable before the donee's death, it is exercisable wholly in favor of the donee. If the power is testamentary, it is exercisable wholly in favor of the donee's estate. — Abbr. POA. — Often shortened to *power.* — Also termed *enabling power.*

▸ **general power of appointment.** (18c) A power of appointment by which the donee can appoint — that is, dispose of the donor's property — in favor of anyone at all, including oneself or one's own estate; esp., a power that authorizes the alienation of a fee to any alienee. — Often shortened to *general power.*

▸ **hybrid power of appointment.** (1959) A power of appointment that has some but not all qualities in common with a general (and sometimes special) power of appointment.

▸ **limited power of appointment.** (1830) A power of appointment that either does not allow the entire estate to be conveyed or restricts to whom the estate may be conveyed; esp., a power by which the donee can appoint to only the person or class specified in the instrument creating the power, but cannot appoint to oneself or one's own estate. — Often shortened to *limited power.* — Also termed *special power of appointment.*

▸ **special power of appointment.** See *limited power of appointment.*

▸ **testamentary power of appointment** (tes-tə-**men**-tə-ree *or* -tree). (1858) A power of appointment created by a will. — Often shortened to *testamentary power.*

power-of-appointment trust. See TRUST (3).

power of attorney. (18c) **1.** An instrument granting someone authority to act as agent or attorney-in-fact for the grantor. • An ordinary power of attorney is revocable and automatically terminates upon the death or incapacity of the principal. — Also termed *letter of attorney*; *warrant of attorney.* See ATTORNEY (1). **2.** The authority so granted; specif., the legal ability to produce a change in legal relations by doing whatever acts are authorized. — Abbr. POA. Pl. **powers of attorney.**

▸ **durable power of attorney.** (1980) A power of attorney that remains in effect during the grantor's incompetency. • Such instruments commonly allow an agent to make healthcare decisions for a patient who has become incompetent.

▸ **general power of attorney.** (18c) A power of attorney that authorizes an agent to transact business for the principal. Cf. *special power of attorney.*

▸ **irrevocable power of attorney** (i-rev-ə-kə-bəl). (18c) A power of attorney that the principal cannot revoke. — Also termed *power of attorney coupled with an interest.* See *power coupled with an interest* under POWER (3).

▸ **power of attorney coupled with an interest.** See *irrevocable power of attorney.*

▸ **power of attorney for healthcare.** See ADVANCE DIRECTIVE (1).

▸ **special power of attorney.** (18c) A power of attorney that limits the agent's authority to only a specified matter. Cf. *general power of attorney.*

▸ **springing power of attorney.** (1980) A power of attorney that becomes effective only when needed, at some future date or upon some future occurrence, usu. upon the principal's incapacity. — Also termed *springing durable power of attorney.* See *durable power of attorney;* ADVANCE DIRECTIVE.

power of revocation (rev-ə-**kay**-shən). See POWER (3).

power of sale. See POWER (3).

power-of-sale clause. (1883) A provision in a mortgage or deed of trust permitting the mortgagee or trustee to sell the property without court authority if the payments are not made.

power-of-sale foreclosure. See FORECLOSURE.

power of termination. (1919) A future interest retained by a grantor after conveying a fee simple subject to a condition subsequent, so that the grantee's estate terminates (upon breach of the condition) only if the grantor exercises the right to retake it. — Also termed *right of entry; right of reentry; right of entry for breach of condition; right of entry for condition broken.* See *fee simple subject to a condition subsequent* under FEE SIMPLE. Cf. POSSIBILITY OF REVERTER.

power of the purse. See *spending power* under POWER (3).

power over oneself. See CAPACITY (2).

power over other persons. See AUTHORITY (1).

power politics. (1901) *Int'l law.* **1.** An approach to foreign policy that encourages a country to use its economic and military strength to enlarge its own power as an end in itself; a system in which a country is willing to bring its economic and (esp.) military strength to bear in an effort to increase its own power. **2.** The threat or use of military force to end an international disagreement.

power-sharing, *n.* (1950) An arrangement in which different groups, such as political parties, share authority in decision-making.

power structure. (1938) The way in which the people who control an organization, society, or country are organized.

power to inspect. (1948) *Patents.* The authority of a third party to review a patent application. • The power may be given by the applicant or an assignee, often to a potential buyer. It must specify which application the person is authorized to see, and it becomes part of the record of the application. See ACCESS (4), (6).

p.p. *abbr.* **1.** PER PROCURATIONEM. **2.** PROPRIA PERSONA.

PPA. *abbr.* **1.** See *provisional application* under PATENT APPLICATION. **2.** PLANT PATENT ACT.

PPACA. *abbr.* Patient Protection and Affordable Care Act. — Usu. shortened to *Affordable Care Act.* See AFFORDABLE CARE ACT. Cf. OBAMACARE.

PPI. *abbr.* **1.** POLICY PROOF OF INTEREST. **2. PPI.** *abbr.* Pre-plea investigation.

PPIR. *abbr.* PRE-PLEA INVESTIGATION REPORT.

PPO. *abbr.* **1.** PREFERRED-PROVIDER ORGANIZATION. **2.** See *permanent protective order* under PROTECTIVE ORDER.

PPR. *abbr.* Pre-plea report. See PRE-PLEA INVESTIGATION REPORT.

p. pro. *abbr.* PER PROCURATIONEM.

p. proc. *abbr.* PER PROCURATIONEM.

PR. *abbr.* (1942) **1.** PUBLIC RELATIONS. **2.** PRESENTENCE-INVESTIGATION REPORT.

practicable, *adj.* (16c) **1.** (Of a thing) reasonably capable of being accomplished; feasible in a particular situation <a practicable plan> **2.** Capable of being used; usable <practicable technology>.

practicably irrigable acreage. (1963) Land that is susceptible to prolonged irrigation, at reasonable cost. — Abbr. PIA.

practical, *adj.* (15c) **1.** Real as opposed to theoretical; of, relating to, or involving real situations and events rather than ideas, emotions, or idealized situations <for practical purposes>. **2.** Likely to succeed or be effective <a practical alternative>. **3.** Useful or suitable for a particular purpose or situation <a well-drafted indemnity clause may be the most practical solution>. **4.** (Of a person) good at dealing with problems and making decisions based on what is possible and will actually work <she tried to be practical and figure out a solution>.

practical construction. **1.** See *contemporaneous construction* under CONSTRUCTION (2). **2.** See PRAGMATISM (2).

practical finality. (1899) The situation in which a court order directs immediate delivery of physical property, subjecting the losing party to irreparable harm if an immediate appeal were not possible. • Practical finality provides an exception to the usual rule that interlocutory orders are not appealable. — Also termed *Forgay-Conrad doctrine; Forgay rule.* See FINALITY DOCTRINE.

practical interpretation. **1.** See *contemporaneous construction* under CONSTRUCTION (2). **2.** PRAGMATISM.

practically avoidable. See AVOIDABLE.

practical obscurity. (1989) (Of a document) the quality of being exempt from disclosure to a third party because the document's subject is a private person whose privacy interest is paramount and the public interest in the information is minimal. • The term was coined in *U.S. Dep't of Justice v. Reporters Committee for Freedom of the Press,* 489 U.S. 749, 109 S.Ct. 1468 (1989), in which the Court held that information about a private person that is in the government's control for compilation purposes only, not as a record of government acts, is exempt from Freedom of Information Act requests when the person's privacy interest outweighs a third party's interest in disclosure.

practical reasoning. See REALISM.

practice, *n.* (15c) **1.** The procedural methods and rules used in a court of law <local practice requires that an extra copy of each motion be filed with the clerk>. **2.** PRACTICE OF LAW <where is your practice?>.

practice, *vb. Patents.* **1.** To make and use (a patented invention) <the employer had a shop right to practice the patent, but not to sell it>. **2.** To build a physical embodiment of an invention. See REDUCTION TO PRACTICE.

practice act. (1881) A statute governing practice and procedure in courts. • Practice acts are usu. supplemented with court rules such as the Federal Rules of Civil Procedure.

practice book. (1873) A volume devoted to the procedures in a particular court or category of courts, usu. including court rules, court forms, and practice directions.

practice court. (1831) **1.** MOOT COURT. **2.** (*cap.*) BAIL COURT.

practice goodwill. See GOODWILL.

practice guide. (1937) A written explanation of how to proceed in a particular area of law or in a particular court or locality.

practice of law. (17c) The professional work of a lawyer, encompassing a broad range of services such as conducting cases in court, preparing papers necessary to bring about various transactions from conveying land to effecting corporate mergers, preparing legal opinions on various points of law, drafting wills and other estate-planning documents, and advising clients on legal questions. • The term also includes activities that comparatively few lawyers engage in but that require legal expertise, such as drafting legislation and court rules. — Also termed *legal practice.* Cf. LAW PRACTICE.

▸ **multidisciplinary practice of law.** See MULTIDISCIPLINARY PRACTICE.

▸ **unauthorized practice of law.** (1928) The practice of law by a person, typically a nonlawyer, who has not been licensed or admitted to practice law in a given jurisdiction. — Abbr. UPL.

"The definitions and tests employed by courts to delineate unauthorized practice by non-lawyers have been vague or conclusory, while jurisdictions have differed significantly in describing what constitutes unauthorized practice in particular areas.

"Certain activities, such as the representation of another person in litigation, are generally proscribed. Even in that area, many jurisdictions recognize exceptions for such matters as small-claims and landlord-tenant tribunals and certain proceedings in administrative agencies. Moreover, many jurisdictions have authorized law students and others not locally admitted to represent indigent persons or others as part of clinical legal education programs.

"Controversy has surrounded many out-of-court activities such as advising on estate planning by bank trust officers, advising on estate planning by insurance agents, stock brokers, or benefit-plan and similar consultants, filling out or providing guidance on forms for property transactions by real estate agents, title companies, and closing-service companies, and selling books or individual forms containing instructions on self-help legal services accompanied by personal, non-lawyer assistance on filling them out in connection with legal procedures such as obtaining a marriage dissolution. The position of bar associations has traditionally been that non-lawyer provisions of such services denies the person served the benefit of such legal measures as the attorney-client privilege, the benefits of such extraordinary duties as that of confidentiality of client information and the protection against conflicts of interest, and the protection of such measures as those regulating lawyer trust accounts and requiring lawyers to supervise non-lawyer personnel. Several jurisdictions recognize that many such services can be provided by non-lawyers without significant risk of incompetent service, that actual experience in several states with extensive non-lawyer provision of traditional legal services indicates no significant risk of harm to consumers of such services, that persons in need of legal services may be significantly aided in obtaining assistance at a much lower price than would be entailed by segregating out a portion of a transaction to be handled by a lawyer for a fee, and that many persons can ill afford, and most persons are at least inconvenienced by, the typically higher cost of lawyer services." Restatement (Third) of the Law Governing Lawyers § 4 cmt. c (1998).

practicks (**prak**-tiks). (*usu. pl.*) (16c) *Hist. Scots law.* An old collection of notes about points of practice, decisions of the Court of Sessions, statutes, and forms, compiled by members of the court. • An example is Balfour's *Practicks* (1469–1579). A precursor of law reports, the notes remain historical legal literature of some authority.

practitioner. (16c) A person engaged in the practice of a profession, esp. law or medicine.

praebentes causam mortis (pri-**ben**-teez **kaw**-zəm **mor**-tis). [Latin] *Hist.* (Persons) occasioning the cause of death.

praeceptio haereditatis (pri-**sep**-shee-oh hə-red-i-**tay**-tis). [Law Latin] (17c) *Scots law.* A taking of the inheritance in advance. — Also termed *lucrative succession.*

"Praeceptio haereditatis . . . . This is one of the passive titles known in law, which, if incurred by the heir, renders him in some measure liable for his ancestor's debts. It was introduced to prevent an heir from receiving and enjoying, under a gratuitous disposition *inter vivos* from his ancestor, that heritable estate to which he would be entitled to succeed on the ancestor's death, and of thus avoiding responsibility for his ancestor's debts and other obligations." John Trayner, *Trayner's Latin Maxims* 466–67 (4th ed. 1894).

praeceptores (pree-sep-**tor**-eez). [Law Latin "masters"] *Hist.* The chief clerks of Chancery, responsible for preparing remedial writs.

praecipe (**pree**-sə-pee *or* **pres**-ə-pee), *n.* [Latin "command"] (15c) **1.** At common law, a writ ordering a defendant to do some act or to explain why inaction is appropriate. — Also termed *writ of praecipe.* **2.** A written motion or request seeking some court action, esp. a trial setting or an entry of judgment. — Also spelled *precipe.* — **praecipe,** *vb.*

▸ ***praecipe quod reddat*** (**pree**-sə-pee or **pres**-ə-pee kwod **red**-at). [Latin "command that he render"] (16c) *Hist.* A writ directing the defendant to return certain property. • An action for common recovery was often begun with this writ. When the writ was brought to recover land, it was termed *ingressu.* See COMMON RECOVERY.

"The *praecipe quod reddat* was the proper writ when the plaintiff's action was for a specifick thing; as for the recovery of a debt certain, or for the restoration of such a chattel, or for giving up such a house, or so much land, specifying the nature and quantity of it. By this writ the sheriff was commanded to summon the tenant or defendant to appear at *Westminster,* at such a day in term." 1 George Crompton, *Rules and Cases of Practice in the Courts of King's Bench and Common Pleas* xxxix (3d ed. 1787).

praecipitium (pree-sə-**pish**-ee-əm *or* pres-ə-), *n.* [Latin "headlong fall"] *Roman law.* The punishment of casting a criminal from the Tarpeian rock.

praecipuum (pri-**sip**-yoo-əm), *n.* [Latin] *Hist.* The estate portion that is not subject to rules of division; the part of an estate that one claimant (usu. the eldest heir-portioner) receives to the exclusion of all others.

praeco (**pree**-koh), *n.* [Latin] *Roman law.* A herald or crier.

praedia (**pree**-dee-ə), *n.* [Latin] The plural of *praedium* (land; an estate). See PRAEDIUM.

▸ ***praedia bellica*** (**pree**-dee-ə **bel**-ə-kə). [Latin] Property seized in war; booty.

▸ ***praedia stipendiaria*** (**pree**-dee-ə stɪ-pen-dee-**air**-ee-ə). [Latin] Provincial lands belonging to the *res publicae*; the senatorial provinces.

▸ ***praedia tributaria*** (**pree**-dee-ə trib-yoo-**tair**-ee-ə). [Latin] Provincial lands belonging to the emperor; the imperial provinces.

praedial (**pree**-dee-əl), *adj.* See PREDIAL.

praedial tithe. See *predial tithe* under TITHE.

praedictus (pri-**dik**-təs), *adj.* [Law Latin] *Hist.* Aforesaid. • In pleading, *praedictus* usu. referred to a defendant, a town, or lands, *idem* to a plaintiff, and *praefatus* to a person other than a party. Cf. PRAEFATUS.

praedium (**pree**-dee-əm), *n.* [Latin] *Roman law.* Land; an estate. Pl. ***praedia.***

▸ ***praedium dominans*** (**pree**-dee-əm **dom**-ə-nanz). [Latin] (17c) A dominant estate; an estate benefiting from a servitude. See SERVITUDE. Cf. *dominant estate* under ESTATE (4). — Also termed *dominant praedium.*

▸ ***praedium rusticum*** (**pree**-dee-əm **rəs**-ti-kəm). [Latin] (1987) An estate used for agricultural purposes. See *rural servitude* under SERVITUDE (3).

▸ ***praedium serviens*** (**pree**-dee-əm **sər**-vee-enz). [Latin] (17c) An estate burdened by a servitude; a servient estate. See SERVITUDE. Cf. *servient estate* under ESTATE (4). — Also termed *servient praedium.*

▸ ***praedium urbanum*** (**pree**-dee-əm ər-**bay**-nəm). [Latin] (1915) An estate used for business or for dwelling; any estate other than a *praedium rusticum.* See *urban servitude* (2) under SERVITUDE (3).

praedo (**pree**-doh), *n.* [Latin] *Roman law.* A robber. Pl. ***praedones.***

praefatus (pri-**fay**-təs), *adj.* [Latin] Aforesaid. — Abbr. *praefat; p. fat.* Cf. PRAEDICTUS.

praefectura (pri-**fek**-chər-ə), *n.* [Latin] *Roman law.* **1.** The office of prefect. **2.** A town or territory administered by a prefect.

praefectus urbi (pri-**fek**-təs ər-bɪ). [Latin "prefect of the city"] (16c) *Roman law.* A senator charged with keeping law and order in the city of Rome. • This duty originated in the early Empire. The *praefectus* had both criminal and civil jurisdiction; the latter was gradually taken over from the praetor, although the *praefectus*'s civil jurisdiction was always *cognitio.* — Also termed *urban prefect; prefect of the city.*

> "*Praefectus urbi.* The prefect of the city was originally a mere delegate appointed in case of the temporary absence of the emperor, but the office became a permanency owing to Tiberius' continued residence away from Rome in the latter part of his reign, and under subsequent emperors the prefect remained in office even when the emperor was present. His duties included generally the maintenance of order in the city, and he had under his command the urban cohorts, in effect a police force numbering between 4,000 and 6,000 men. He early assumed criminal jurisdiction, and in the end became the chief criminal court not only for Rome but for the district within 100 miles." H.F. Jolowicz, *Historical Introduction to the Study of Roman Law* 345–46 (1952).

praefectus vigilum (pri-**fek**-təs vi-**jil**-əm). [Latin "prefect of the watch"] (17c) *Roman law.* An officer, immediately subordinate to the *praefectus urbi,* with police and fire-prevention duties. • This officer had the authority to punish offenses relating to the public peace. See PRAEFECTUS URBI.

praefectus villae (pri-**fek**-təs **vil**-ee). [Latin] *Hist.* The mayor of a town.

praefine (**pree**-fɪn). See PRIMER FINE.

praejuramentum (pree-joor-ə-**men**-təm), *n.* [Law Latin] *Hist.* A preparatory oath.

praelegatum (pree-lə-**gay**-təm), *n.* [Latin] *Roman law.* A legacy to one of several heirs whereby the legatee was entitled to the legacy before the estate was divided. • This was similar to an advancement.

praelibatio matrimonii (pree-lɪ-**bay**-shee-oh ma-trə-**moh**-nee-ɪ). [Law Latin] *Hist.* A foretaste of marriage.

praematura diligentia (pree-mə-**t[y]uur**-ə [*or* -**chuur**-ə] dil-ə-**jen**-shee-ə). [Law Latin] *Scots law.* Premature execution of a judgment.

praemium emancipationis (**pree**-mee-əm i-man-sə-pay-shee-**oh**-nis). [Latin "reward for emancipation"] *Roman law.* A compensation allowed by Constantine to a father on the emancipation of his child, consisting of one-third of the property that came to the child from his mother's side. • Justinian replaced this with the usufruct of half the child's separate property.

praemium pudicitiae (**pree**-mee-əm pyoo-də-**sish**-ee-ee. [Latin "the price of chastity"] *Hist.* Compensation paid by a man who seduced a chaste woman. — Also written *premium pudicitiae.* — Also termed *praemium pudoris.*

praemunire (pree-myoo-**nɪ**-ree), *n.* [Latin *praemoneri* "to be forewarned"] (16c) *Hist. English law.* The criminal offense of obeying an authority other than the king. • *Praemunire* stems from the efforts of Edward I (1272–1307) to counter papal influence in England, and takes its name from the writ's initial words: *praemunire facias* ("that you cause to be forewarned"). One type of *praemunire* was to appeal to the pope rather than the monarch. Another was to bring a suit in a temporal court instead of a royal court, in part because the monarch wanted all fines levied as punishment to go to the royal coffers, not those of the church. — Also spelled *premunire; praemonere.*

praenomen (pree-**noh**-mən), *n.* [Latin] (17c) *Roman law.* The first of a person's three names, given to distinguish the person from family members. • The full name of the man known to history as Julius Caesar is Gaius Julius Caesar — Gaius being his praenomen.

praeposita negotiis vel rebus domesticis (pri-**poz**-ə-tə ni-**goh**-shee-is vel **ree**-bəs də-**mes**-ti-sis). [Latin] *Hist.* Set over domestic affairs. • The phrase usu. referred to a wife's status.

praepositor (pri-**poz**-ə-tər *or* -tor), *n.* [Law Latin "supervisor, reeve"] (17c) *Hist.* Someone who delegates duties (esp. of a business's management) to another; one who places (another) in a position over others.

praepositura (pri-poz-ə-**t[y]uur**-ə), *n.* [Latin "management" or "supervisory office"] *Hist.* **1.** One to whom management duties are delegated. **2.** The area of responsibility delegated to a person to manage, esp. a wife's authority to manage the household. • In Scots law, a wife's *praepositura* was her implied mandate to bind her husband in any trade that she superintended with his acquiescence, and in the management of household affairs.

praepositus (pree-**poz**-ə-təs), *n.* [Latin] (17c) *Hist.* **1.** An officer next in authority to the alderman of a hundred. **2.** A steward or bailiff of an estate.

praepositus negotiis (pri-**poz**-ə-təs ni-**goh**-shee-is). [Latin] *Hist.* Put in charge of another's business.

praepositus negotiis societatis (pri-**poz**-ə-təs ni-**goh**-shee-is sə-sɪ-ə-**tay**-tis). [Latin] (1830) *Hist.* Put in charge of a partnership's business.

praepositus villae (pree-**poz**-ə-təs **vil**-ee). [Latin] (17c) *Hist.* A constable of a town; a petty constable.

praerogativa regis (pree-rog-ə-**tɪ**-və **ree**-jis). [Law Latin "of the Crown's prerogative"] *Hist.* A declaration made at the time of Edward I (1272–1307) defining certain feudal and political rights of the Crown, including the right to wardship of an idiot's lands to protect the idiot's heirs from disinheritance or alienation. — Also termed *de praerogativa regis* (dee pree-rog-ə-**tɪ**-və **ree**-jis).

> "The king's right is distinctly stated in the document known as *praerogativa Regis*, which we believe to come from the early years of Edward I. The same document seems to be the oldest that gives us any clear information about a wardship of lunatics. The king is to provide that the lunatic and his family are properly maintained out of the income of his estate, and the residue is to be handed over to him upon his restoration to sanity, or, should he die without having recovered his wits, is to be administered by the ordinary for the good of his soul; but the king is to take nothing to his own use." 1 Frederick Pollock & Frederic W. Maitland, *The History of English Law Before the Time of Edward I* 481 (2d ed. 1898).

praescriptio (pri-**skrip**-shee-oh), *n.* [Latin] *Roman law.* **1.** A preliminary portion of a *formula* that defines the scope of action. **2.** A defensive plea in an action to recover land by which the defendant asserts ownership based on continuous possession for a prescribed time. — Also termed (in sense 2) *praescriptio longi temporis.* Pl. ***praescriptiones*** (pri-skrip-shee-**oh**-neez).

praescriptio fori (pri-**skrip**-shee-oh **for**-ɪ). [Latin] (1933) *Roman law.* An objection on the ground that the person objecting is not subject to the court's jurisdiction.

praescriptis verbis (pri-**skrip**-tis **vər**-bis). [Latin "in the words before written"] (1863) **1.** *Roman law.* An action on a bilateral agreement under which one party had performed and required the other to perform in turn. **2.** *Roman law.* The grounds given for the existence of a contract that falls into the class later described as innominate. • Innominate contracts were developed and recognized late in classical law. See *innominate contract* under CONTRACT. **3.** *Hist.* (Of a clause) restricted in scope by introductory words — esp., in a pleading, words defining the issue.

praeses (**pree**-seez), *n.* [Latin] (17c) **1.** *Roman law.* A governor of a province. **2.** The president of a college or university.

praestare (pree-**stair**-ee), *vb.* [Latin] *Roman law.* **1.** To perform an obligation. **2.** To undertake liability.

praestatio culpae levis (pri-**stay**-shee-oh **kəl**-pee **lee**-vis). [Law Latin] *Hist.* An obligation for the middle degree of diligence — that is, the diligence and care required by a person of ordinary prudence. • This phrase was a forerunner of the modern terms *reasonable care* and *reasonable person.*

praesumitur pro negante (pri-**zyoo**-mə-tər proh ni-**gan**-tee). [Latin] It is presumed for the negative. • This is the rule of the House of Lords when the votes are equal on a motion.

praesumptio (pri-**zəmp**-shee-oh), *n.* [Latin] A presumption. Pl. ***praesumptiones*** (pri-zəmp-shee-**oh**-neez).

▸***praesumptio fortior*** (pri-**zəmp**-shee-oh **for**-shee-ər *or* -or). [Latin] (1960) A strong presumption (of fact); a presumption strong enough to shift the burden of proof to the opposing party.

▸***praesumptio hominis*** (pri-**zəmp**-shee-oh **hom**-ə-nis). [Latin] (17c) The presumption of an individual; that is, a natural presumption unfettered by rules.

▸***praesumptio juris*** (pri-**zəmp**-shee-oh **joor**-is). [Latin] (16c) A presumption of law; that is, one in which the law assumes the existence of something until it is disproved. See *presumption of law* and *rebuttable presumption* under PRESUMPTION.

▸***praesumptio juris et de jure.*** [Latin "presumption of law and of right"] An irrebuttable presumption of law concerning a right.

▸***praesumptio Muciana*** (pri-**zəmp**-shee-oh myoo-shee-**ay**-nə). [Latin] (1953) *Roman law.* The rebuttable presumption that in case of doubt a thing possessed by a married woman had been given to her by her husband. • The presumption was named after the jurist Quintus Mucius.

praeter dotem (**pree**-tər **doh**-təm *or* -tem). [Latin] *Hist.* Over and above the dowry.

praeteritio (pree-tə- *or* pret-ə-**rish**-ee-oh), *n.* [Latin] *Roman law.* A testator's exclusion of an heir by passing the heir over. • In Roman law, passing over *sui heredes* usu. invalidated the will. See SUI HEREDES.

praeter legem. See EQUITY PRAETER LEGEM.

praetor (**pree**-tər), *n.* [Latin] (15c) *Roman law.* The magistrate responsible for identifying and framing the legal issues in a case and for ordering a lay judge (judex) to hear evidence and decide the case in accordance with the formula. See FORMULA (1). — Also spelled *pretor.*

▸***praetor aerarius*** (ay-**rair**-ee-əs). [Latin] (1828) A praetor connected with the treasury. — Also termed *praetor aerarium.*

▸***praetor fideicommissarius*** (fɪ-dee-ɪ-kom-ə-**sair**-ee-əs). [Latin] (1896) A special praetor having jurisdiction over cases involving trusts.

▸***praetor peregrinus*** (per-ə-**grɪ**-nəs). [Latin] (17c) A praetor who decided cases between citizens and foreigners and cases between foreigners.

▸***praetor tutelaris*** (t[y]oo-tə-**lair**-is). [Latin] (17c) A praetor who dealt with the affairs of minors.

▸***praetor urbanus*** (ər-**bay**-nəs). [Latin] (17c) A praetor who decided cases between citizens.

praetorian edict. See *edictum praetoris* under EDICTUM.

praetorian law. See JUS PRAETORIUM.

praetorium (pree-**tor**-ee-əm), *n.* (16c) *Roman law.* **1.** A building where lawsuits were adjudicated by one or more praetors. **2.** The official residence of a Roman governor in the provinces. —Also spelled *pretorium*.

praevaricatio (pri-var-ə-**kay**-shee-oh), *n.* [Latin "collusion with an opponent"] *Roman law.* An accuser's colluding with the defense in such a way that the accused will be acquitted. • An accuser might do this in various ways, as by deemphasizing the most important charges, refraining from calling the most important witnesses, or refraining from exercising peremptory challenges against jurors who would tend to favor the accused. See CALUMNIA. Cf. TERGIVERSATIO.

praevaricator (pree-var-ə-**kay**-tər). See PREVARICATOR.

praevento termino (pri-**ven**-toh **tər**-mə-noh). [Law Latin "by anticipating the term"] (1874) *Scots law.* An action in the Court of Session to prevent a delay in a suspension or an appeal. See SUSPENSION (6).

pragmatic, *adj.* **1.** Of, relating to, or involving the practical side of something; matter-of-fact. **2.** Businesslike. **3.** *Archaic.* Energetic; effectual. **4.** Handling problems one by one as they arise without following some strict or rigid set of ideas.

> "I have reflected on the use of the word 'pragmatic' to describe the method of treating each problem as it arises and in its particular context, instead of approaching them all on the basis of some single general principle. It seems to me that it would probably convey this meaning to contemporary English or American readers as well as, or better than, any other one word." Leon Radzinowicz, *Ideology and Crime* 101 (1966).

pragmatic construction. See PRAGMATISM.

pragmatism. 1. A commonsense, practical, nonideological way of dealing with problems and affairs generally. **2.** In judging, an approach to statutory construction seeking to adjudicate disputes without being overly constrained by the text of statutes or contracts, esp. if the result is thought to produce socially optimal results. • This approach is considered a relatively unstructured problem-solving process involving common sense, a respect for stare decisis, and a sense of social needs. *See* Frank B. Cross, *The Theory and Practice of Statutory Interpretation* 13 (2009); William N. Eskridge Jr. & Philip Frickey, *Statutory Interpretation as Practical Reasoning*, 42 Stan. L. Rev. 321, 345–53 (1990); William N. Eskridge Jr., *No Frills Textualism*, 119 Harv. L. Rev. 2041, 2041–43, 2055 (2006) (book rev.). — Also termed *pragmatic construction; pragmatic interpretation*; *practical interpretation*; *practical construction.*

pratique (pra-**teek** *or* **prat**-ik). (17c) *Maritime law.* A license allowing a vessel to trade in a particular country or port after complying with quarantine requirements or presenting a clean bill of health.

praxis (**prak**-sis). [Greek "doing; action"] (1933) In critical legal studies, practical action; the practice of living the ethical life in conjunction and in cooperation with others.

prayer conference. See CHARGE CONFERENCE.

prayer for relief. (18c) A request addressed to the court and appearing at the end of a pleading; esp., a request for specific relief or damages. — Often shortened to *prayer.* — Also termed *demand for relief*; *request for relief.* See AD DAMNUM CLAUSE.

> "*The prayer for relief.* The plaintiff prays in his bill for the relief to which he supposes himself entitled on the case made out in the bill. This is called the *special* prayer. He then prays for general relief, usually in these words: 'And the plaintiff (*or* your orator) prays for such further or other relief as the nature of the case may require, and as may be agreeable to equity and good conscience.' Both prayers are generally inserted in the bill, — the special prayer first, the general following." Edwin E. Bryant, *The Law of Pleading Under the Codes of Civil Procedure* 69 (2d ed. 1899).

▸ **general prayer.** (18c) A prayer for additional unspecified relief, traditionally using language such as, "Plaintiff additionally prays for such other and further relief to which she may show herself to be justly entitled." • The general prayer typically follows a special prayer.

▸ **special prayer.** (18c) A prayer for the particular relief to which a plaintiff claims to be entitled.

prayer in aid. See AID PRAYER.

prayer of process. (18c) A conclusion in a bill in equity requesting the issuance of a subpoena if the defendant fails to answer the bill.

pray tales. See TALES.

PRC. *abbr.* POSTAL RATE COMMISSION.

PRCL. *abbr.* Postrevocation conditional license.

preamble (**pree**-am-bəl), *n.* (14c) **1.** An introductory statement in a constitution, statute, or other document explaining the document's basis and objective; esp., a statutory recital of the inconveniences for which the statute is designed to provide a remedy. • A preamble often consists of a series of clauses introduced by the conjunction *whereas.* Such a preamble is sometimes called the *whereas clauses.* See PREFATORY-MATERIALS CANON.

> "The preamble cannot control the enacting part of the statute, in cases where the enacting part is expressed in clear, unambiguous terms; but in case any doubt arises on the enacting part, the preamble may be resorted to to explain it, and show the intention of the law maker." *Den v. Urison*, 2 N.J.L. 212 (1807).

> "The importance of examining the preamble, for the purpose of expounding the language of a statute, has been long felt, and universally conceded in all juridical discussions. It is an admitted maxim in the ordinary course of the administration of justice, that the preamble of a statute is a key to open the mind of the makers, as to the mischiefs, which are to be remedied, and the objects, which are to be accomplished by the provisions of the statute." 1 Joseph Story, *Commentaries on the Constitution of the United States* § 459, at 326 (3d ed. 1858).

2. *Patents.* The first words of a patent claim, often a single phrase indicating the field of art. • The preamble is typically nonlimiting unless it "breathes life and meaning into the claims." *Corning Glass Works v. Sumitomo Elec. U.S.A., Inc.*, 868 F.2d 1251, 1257 (Fed. Cir. 1989). Elements, the later parts of the claim, narrow this broad identification more and more specifically. Cf. BODY OF A CLAIM; TRANSITION PHRASE. — **preambulary** (pree-**am**-byə-ler-ee), **preambular** (pree-**am**-byə-lər), *adj.*

preappointed evidence. See EVIDENCE.

preargument-conference attorney. See CIRCUIT MEDIATOR.

preaudience. (18c) *English law.* The right of a senior barrister, esp. a Queen's Counsel or King's Counsel, to be heard in court before other barristers.

prebankruptcy, *adj.* (1926) Occurring before the filing of a bankruptcy petition; PREPETITION <prebankruptcy transactions>.

prebankruptcy planning. *Bankruptcy.* The arrangement of a debtor's property so that the debtor can take maximum advantage of exemptions, commonly converting nonexempt assets into exempt ones.

prebend (**preb**-ənd), *n.* (15c) **1.** A stipend granted in a cathedral church for the support of the members of the chapter. **2.** The property from which the stipend comes.

prebendary (**preb**-ən-der-ee). (15c) A person serving on the staff of a cathedral who receives a stipend from the cathedral's endowment.

prebut (pree-bət), *vb.* (2002) *Slang.* To rebut an argument in advance of an opponent's making it; to engage in anticipatory refutation. — **prebuttal,** *n.*

precariae (pri-**kair**-ee-ee). [Law Latin "favors"] *Hist.* Day labor that tenants of certain manors were bound to give their lords at harvest time. — Also termed *preces.*

precarious, *adj.* (17c) **1.** Dependent on the will or pleasure of another; uncertain <precarious privileges>. **2.** Of the nature of a precarium <a precarious grant of property>. **3.** (Of a situation) likely to become worse easily or quickly <precarious financial position>. **4.** Likely to fall or to cause someone to fall <a precarious mountain trail>.

precarious loan. See LOAN.

precarious possession. See POSSESSION.

precarious right. See RIGHT.

precarious trade. See TRADE (1).

precarium (pri-**kair**-ee-əm), *n.* [Latin] (17c) **1.** *Roman law.* The gratuitous grant of the enjoyment of property, revocable at will. **2.** The property so granted. **3.** *Hist.* An estate or tenure arising from a precarious grant, and usu. characterized by uncertainty or arduous conditions of tenure. — Also termed *precary.*

precatory (**prek**-ə-tor-ee), *adj.* (17c) (Of words) requesting, recommending, or expressing a desire rather than a command. • An example of precatory language is "it is my wish and desire to . . . ."

precatory trust. See TRUST (3).

precatory word. (*usu. pl.*) (18c) Collectively, expressions of requests, desires, or recommendations, as distinguished from commands, esp. in a will or deed. • Generally, precatory words are not recognized as legally enforceable instructions.

precautionary appeal. See *protective appeal* under APPEAL (2).

precautionary principle. (1988) *Int'l law.* The doctrine that when there are threats of serious or irreversible damage to the environment, a lack of full scientific certainty is not a reason for postponing measures to prevent the damage.

precede, *vb.* **1.** To go before in rank, dignity, or importance; to outrank or take precedence over <high-court justices precede intermediate judges in all questions of seating preference>. **2.** To be or go before in arrangement or sequence <in our filing system, new correspondence precedes older>. **3.** To go before in order of time; to occur earlier than <the phone call preceded the e-mail>. **4.** To preface or introduce; to supply with a prelude or preface <to precede the main text with an editor's note>. **5.** To go or walk before (someone else); to go somewhere before (another person) <Vice Chancellor David Williams preceded the Duke of Edinburgh in the procession>.

precedence (**pres**-ə-dənts *or* prə-**seed**-ənts), *n.* (16c) **1.** The order or priority in place or time observed by or for persons of different statuses (such as political dignitaries) on the basis of rank during ceremonial events. — Also termed *diplomatic precedence.* **2.** Generally, the quality, state, or condition of going before something else according to some system of priorities. **3.** *Parliamentary law.* The ranked priority that determines whether a motion is in order while another motion is pending, or whether a pending motion yields to another motion.

> "There is a principle that determines the precedence of motions. The closer a motion is to final disposition of the matter under consideration, the lower it is in the order of precedence. The further removed the motion is from final disposition of the matter, the higher it is in the order of precedence." National Conference of State Legislatures, *Mason's Manual of Legislative Procedure* 6 (2000).

4. *Parliamentary law.* The priority in which a member is entitled to the floor. — Also termed *precedence in recognition; preference in being recognized.* **5.** The order in which persons may claim the right to administer an intestate's estate. • The traditional order is (1) surviving spouse, (2) next of kin, (3) creditors, and (4) public administrator.

precedent (prə-**seed**-ənt *also* **pres**-ə-dənt), *adj.* (14c) Preceding in time or order <condition precedent>.

precedent (**pres**-ə-dənt), *n.* (16c) **1.** Something of the same type that has occurred or existed before. **2.** An action or official decision that can be used as support for later actions or decisions; esp., a decided case that furnishes a basis for determining later cases involving similar facts or issues. See STARE DECISIS.

> "In law a precedent is an adjudged case or decision of a court of justice, considered as furnishing a rule or authority for the determination of an identical or similar case afterwards arising, or of a similar question of law. The only theory on which it is possible for one decision to be an authority for another is that the facts are alike, or, if the facts are different, that the principle which governed the first case is applicable to the variant facts." William M. Lile et al., *Brief Making and the Use of Law Books* 288 (Roger W. Cooley & Charles Lesley Ames eds., 3d ed. 1914).

> "A precedent . . . is a judicial decision which contains in itself a principle. The underlying principle which thus forms its authoritative element is often termed the *ratio decidendi.* The concrete decision is binding between the parties to it, but it is the abstract *ratio decidendi* which alone has the force of law as regards the world at large." John Salmond, *Jurisprudence* 191 (Glanville L. Williams ed., 10th ed. 1947).

> "One may say, roughly, that a case becomes a precedent only for such a general rule as is necessary to the actual decision reached, when shorn of unessential circumstances." 1 James Parker Hall, Introduction, *American Law and Procedure* xlviii (1948).

> "One may often accord respect to a precedent not by embracing it with a frozen logic but by drawing from its thought the elements of a new pattern of decision." Lon L. Fuller, *Anatomy of the Law* 151 (1968).

▸ **binding precedent.** (17c) A precedent that a court must follow. • For example, a lower court is bound by an applicable holding of a higher court in the same jurisdiction. — Also termed *authoritative precedent; binding authority.* Cf. *imperative authority* under AUTHORITY (4).

▸ **declaratory precedent.** (1900) A precedent that is merely the application of an already existing legal rule.

▸ **original precedent.** (17c) A precedent that creates and applies a new legal rule. • An original precedent is usu. created when the court distinguishes the matter to be decided from older cases.

▸ **persuasive precedent.** (1905) A precedent that is not binding on a court, but that is entitled to respect and careful consideration. • For example, if the case was decided in a neighboring jurisdiction, the court might evaluate the earlier court's reasoning without being bound to decide the same way.

▸ **precedent sub silentio** (səb sə-**len**-shee-oh). (1825) A legal question that was neither argued nor explicitly discussed in a judicial decision but that seems to have been silently ruled on and might therefore be treated as a precedent.

▸ **superprecedent.** (1976) **1.** A precedent that defines the law and its requirements so effectively that it prevents divergent holdings in later legal decisions on similar facts or induces disputants to settle their claims without litigation. • This sense was posited by W. Landes and Richard A. Posner in *Legal Precedent: A Theoretical and Empirical Analysis*, 19 J. Law & Econ. 249, 251 (1976). **2.** A precedent that has become so well established in the law by a long line of reaffirmations that it is very difficult to overturn it; specif., a precedent that has been reaffirmed many times and whose rationale has been extended to cover cases in which the facts are dissimilar, even wholly unrelated, to those of the precedent. • For example, *Roe v. Wade* has been called a superprecedent because it has survived more than three dozen attempts to overturn it and has been relied on in decisions protecting gay rights and the right to die. Cf. *super stare decisis* under STARE DECISIS.

> "Super precedents are not unique to the courts, but rather are constitutional decisions in which public institutions have heavily invested, repeatedly relied, and consistently approved over significant periods of time. These are decisions which have been so repeatedly and widely cited for so long that their meaning and value have increased to the point of being secured by enduring networks. They are deeply and irrevocably embedded into our culture and national consciousness, so much so that it seems un-American to attack, much less to formally reconsider them. These decisions are the clearest instances in which the institutional values promoted by fidelity to precedent — consistency, stability, predictability, and social reliance — are compelling." Michael J. Gerhardt, *The Power of Precedent* 178 (2008).

3. DOCTRINE OF PRECEDENT. **4.** A form of pleading or property-conveyancing instrument. • Precedents are often compiled in book form and used by lawyers as guides for preparing similar documents.

> "Collections of Precedents have existed from very early times. In this connection precedents must not be confused with judicial precedents or case law. We refer here simply to common-form instruments compiled for use in practice, whereby the lawyer can be more or less certain that he is using the correct phraseology for the particular case before him. They were used both in conveyancing and litigation. . . . It is interesting to note that these precedents were apparently among the first legal works to be published after printing was introduced. Collections of conveyancing precedents continued to be brought up to date or new volumes issued . . . ." A.K.R. Kiralfy, *Potter's Outlines of English Legal History* 42–43 (5th ed. 1958).

precedented (**pres**-i-den-tid), *adj.* (17c) Having the support, justification, or sanction of an earlier example of like kind. Cf. UNPRECEDENTED.

precedential (pres-i-**den**-shəl), *adj.* (17c) **1.** Of, relating to, or constituting a precedent; having force or providing support as an example for imitation. **2.** Taking precedence; antecedent. **3.** Of, relating to, or involving official or social precedence.

precedent sub silentio. See PRECEDENT (2).

prece partium (**pree**-see **pahr**-shee-əm). [Law Latin] (17c) On the prayer of the parties.

precept (**pree**-sept). (14c) **1.** A standard or rule of conduct; a command or principle that governs thinking or behavior <several legal precepts govern here>. **2.** A writ or warrant issued by an authorized person demanding another's action, such as a judge's order to an officer to bring a party before the court <the sheriff executed the precept immediately>.

preceptive statute. See STATUTE.

precept of *clare constat*. See CLARE CONSTAT.

preceptum amissionis superioritatis (pri-**sep**-təm ə-mis[h]-ee-**oh**-nis suu-peer-ee-or-ə-**tay**-tis). [Law Latin "a precept of a lost superiority"] (1835) *Hist.* A precept to force a superior to give a vassal's disponee entry to the land.

preces (**pree**-seez), *n.* [Latin "prayers"] **1.** *Roman law.* A petition, esp. one addressed to the emperor by a private person. Cf. RESCRIPT (3). **2.** PRECARIAE.

preces primariae (**pree**-seez prɪ-**mair**-ee-ee). [Latin] *Hist.* The right of the sovereign to appoint a person to fill a vacant prebendary office after the sovereign's accession. • This right was exercised during the reign of Edward I. — Also termed *primae preces.* See PREBENDARY.

precinct. (15c) A geographical unit of government, such as an election district, a police district, or a judicial district.

▸ **magisterial precinct.** (1894) A county subdivision that defines the territorial jurisdiction of a magistrate, constable, or justice of the peace. — Also termed *magisterial district.*

precipe (**pre**-sə-pee). See PRAECIPE.

précis (pray-**see** *or* **pray**-see), *n.* [French] (18c) A concise summary of a text's essential points; an abstract. Pl. **précis** (pray-**seez** *or* **pray**-seez).

precision. (17c) **1.** The quality, state, or condition of being minutely exact and correct; exactness. **2.** The accuracy with which a proposition is stated, an operation performed, or a measurement completed. — **precise,** *adj.*

preclude, *vb.* [fr. Latin *praecludere* "to foreclose"] (16c) To prevent or make impossible; to rule out beforehand by necessary consequence.

precludi non debet (pri-**kloo**-dɪ non **dee**-bet *or* **deb**-et). [Latin "he ought not to be barred"] *Hist.* The beginning of a plaintiff's reply to a plea in bar in which the plaintiff objects to being barred from maintaining the action. — Sometimes shortened to *precludi non.*

preclusion. (1868) **1.** The foreclosure of some eventuality before it can happen. **2.** Issue preclusion. See COLLATERAL ESTOPPEL. **3.** Claim preclusion. See RES JUDICATA. **4.** The exclusion of evidence from a hearing or trial, esp. because of a party's failure to provide proper discovery or adequate notice.

preclusion order. See ORDER (2).

precognition (pree-kog-**nish**-ən). (17c) *Scots law.* **1.** A preliminary examination under oath of persons believed to have knowledge about the facts of a case; esp., in a criminal case, to determine whether there is sufficient evidence for a trial. **2.** The written record of the statement that a prospective witness can give as evidence.

precompounded prescription drug. See DRUG.

preconceived malice. See MALICE AFORETHOUGHT.

preconception. (17c) A belief or opinion that someone has already formed before knowing the facts; PREJUDICE (2).

precondition. See CONDITION (2).

precontract. See CONTRACT.

preconviction conditional license. See HARDSHIP PRIVILEGE.

predate, *vb.* See ANTEDATE.

predation. See PREDATORY PRICING.

predator. See SEXUAL PREDATOR.

predatory crime. See CRIME.

predatory intent. See INTENT (1).

predatory offense. See *predatory crime* under CRIME.

predatory pricing. (1952) Unlawful below-cost pricing intended to eliminate specific competitors and reduce overall competition; pricing below an appropriate measure of cost for the purpose of eliminating competitors in the short run and reducing competition in the long run. — Also termed *predation.* See ANTITRUST.

> "In its most orthodox form, 'predatory pricing' refers to a practice of driving rivals out of business by selling at a price below cost. The predator's intent — and the only intent that can make predatory pricing rational, profit-maximizing behavior — is to charge monopoly prices after rivals have been dispatched or disciplined. Predatory pricing is analyzed under the antitrust laws as illegal monopolization or attempt to monopolize under § 2 of the Sherman Act, or sometimes as a violation of the Clayton Act § 2, generally called the Robinson-Patman Act." Herbert Hovenkamp, *Federal Antitrust Policy* 335 (2d ed. 1999).

predecease, *vb.* (16c) To die before (another) <she predeceased her husband>.

predecessor. (14c) **1.** Someone who precedes another, esp. in an office or position. **2.** An ancestor.

predecisional, *adj.* (1950) Of, relating to, or occurring during the time before a decision.

predetermined, *adj.* (17c) Decided or arranged beforehand; foreordained.

predial (**pree**-dee-əl), *adj.* (15c) Of, consisting of, relating to, or attached to land <predial servitude>. — Also spelled *praedial.*

predial servitude. See *servitude appurtenant* under SERVITUDE (3).

predial tithe. See TITHE.

predicate acquittal. See ACQUITTAL (1).

predicate act. (1977) **1.** See *predicate offense* under OFFENSE (2). **2.** See *lesser included offense* under OFFENSE (2). **3.** Under RICO, one of two or more related acts of racketeering necessary to establish a pattern. See RACKETEER INFLUENCED AND CORRUPT ORGANIZATIONS ACT. **4.** An act that must be completed before legal consequences can attach either to it or to another act or before further action can be taken. • A predicate act itself may be criminalized if it is followed by or performed in tandem with another prohibited act. In statutes, words such as "if" often precede a description of a predicate act.

predicate-act canon. The doctrine that authorization of an act also authorizes a necessary predicate act. See PREDICATE ACT (4).

predicate fact. See FACT.

predicate felony offender. See OFFENDER.

predicate offense. See *lesser included offense* under OFFENSE (2).

predicted tide. See TIDE.

prediction. (16c) **1.** A statement about what someone thinks will happen; a forecast <predictions of an acquittal>. **2.** The act of making such a statement; a foretelling <the very fact of this prediction showed a lack of circumspection>.

predictions of future dangerousness. See FUTURE DANGEROUSNESS, PREDICTIONS OF.

prediction theory. 1. See BAD-MAN THEORY. **2.** See PREDICTIVE THEORY OF LAW.

predictive theory of law. (1956) The view that the law is nothing more than a set of predictions about what the courts will decide in given circumstances. • This theory is embodied in Holmes's famous pronouncement, "The prophecies of what the courts will do in fact, and nothing more pretentious, are what I mean by the law." Oliver Wendell Holmes, *The Path of the Law,* 10 Harv. L. Rev. 457, 460–61 (1897). — Also termed *prediction theory.* Cf. BAD-MAN THEORY.

predictor. (17c) **1.** Something that indicates what will possibly or probably happen in the future. **2.** Someone who makes a prediction.

predilection (pred-i-**lek**-shən). (17c) An established partiality toward something; a distinct preference.

predisposition. (17c) A person's inclination to engage in a particular activity; esp., an inclination that vitiates a criminal defendant's claim of entrapment. — **predispose,** *vb.* — **predisposed,** *adj.*

predispute, *adj.* Of, relating to, or occurring before dispute, case, or controversy arises.

predispute arbitration agreement. See ARBITRATION AGREEMENT.

predispute mediation clause. (2000) A contractual provision requiring the parties to mediate any disagreements arising after the contract is executed.

predominant, *adj.* (16c) More powerful, more common, or more noticeable than others; having superior strength, influence, and pervasiveness. — **predominance,** *n.*

predominant-aspect test. See PREDOMINANT-PURPOSE TEST.

predominant-purpose test. (1980) An assessment of whether Article 2 of the UCC applies to an exchange, conducted by considering whether the exchange's chief aspect, viewed in light of all the circumstances, is the sale of goods. • If goods account for most of the exchange's value, it is probably a sale; if services account for most of the value, it probably is not. The leading case is *Bonebrake v. Cox,* 499 F.2d 951, 960 (8th Cir. 1974). — Also termed *predominant-aspect test.*

preembryo. See ZYGOTE.

preemption (pree-**emp**-shən), *n.* (18c) **1.** The right to buy before others. See RIGHT OF PREEMPTION. **2.** The purchase of something under this right. **3.** An earlier seizure or appropriation. **4.** The occupation of public land so as to establish a preemptive title. **5.** *Constitutional law.* The principle (derived from the Supremacy Clause) that a federal law can supersede or supplant any inconsistent state law or regulation. — Also termed (in sense 5) *federal preemption.* See COMPLETE-PREEMPTION DOCTRINE. — **preempt,** *vb.* — **preemptive,** *adj.*

▸ **conflict preemption.** See *obstacle preemption.*

▸ ***Garmon* preemption.** (1963) *Labor law.* A doctrine prohibiting state and local regulation of activities that are actually or arguably (1) protected by the National Labor Relations Act's rules relating to the right of employees to organize and bargain collectively, or (2) prohibited by the National Labor Relations Act's provision that governs unfair labor practices. *San Diego Bldg. Trades Council v. Garmon,* 359 U.S. 236, 79 S.Ct. 773 (1959). — Also termed *Garmon doctrine.* See COLLECTIVE BARGAINING; UNFAIR LABOR PRACTICE.

▸ ***Machinists* preemption.** (1984) *Labor law.* The doctrine prohibiting state regulation of an area of labor activity or management-union relations that Congress has intentionally left unregulated. *Lodge 76, Int'l Ass'n of Machinists v. Wisconsin Employment Relations Comm'n,* 427 U.S. 132, 96 S.Ct. 2548 (1976).

▸ **obstacle preemption.** (1979) The principle that federal or state statute can supersede or supplant state or local law that stands as an obstacle to accomplishing the full purposes and objectives of the overriding federal or state law. — Also termed *conflict preemption.*

preemption claimant. (1824) Someone who has settled on land subject to preemption, intending in good faith to acquire title to it.

preemption right. (18c) The privilege to take priority over others in claiming land subject to preemption. • The privilege arises from the holder's actual settlement of the land. See PREEMPTION (3).

preemptive right. (1897) A shareholder's privilege to purchase newly issued stock — before the shares are offered to the public — in an amount proportionate to the shareholder's current holdings in order to prevent dilution of the shareholder's ownership interest. • This right must be exercised within a fixed period, usu. 30 to 60 days. — Also termed *subscription privilege.* See SUBSCRIPTION RIGHT. Cf. *rights offering* under OFFERING.

preemptive self-defense. See SELF-DEFENSE (2).

preexisting condition. See CONDITION (2).

preexisting duty. See DUTY (1).

preexisting-duty rule. (1990) *Contracts.* The rule that if a party does or promises to do what the party is already legally obligated to do — or refrains or promises to refrain from doing what the party is already legally obligated to refrain from doing — the party has not incurred detriment. • This rule's result is that the promise does not constitute adequate consideration for contractual purposes. For example, if a builder agrees to construct a building for a specified price but later threatens to walk off the job unless the owner promises to pay an additional sum, the owner's new promise is not enforceable because, under the preexisting-duty rule, there is no consideration for that promise. — Also termed *preexisting-legal-duty rule.*

prefatory-materials canon. The doctrine that a preamble, purpose clause, or recital is a permissible indicator of meaning. See PREAMBLE (1).

prefect (**pree**-fekt), *n.* (14c) **1.** A high official or magistrate put in charge of a particular command, department, or region. **2.** In New Mexico, a probate judge.

prefect of the city. See PRAEFECTUS URBI.

prefer, *vb.* (14c) **1.** To put forward or present for consideration; esp., (of a grand jury), to bring (a charge or indictment) against a criminal suspect <the defendant claimed he was innocent of the charges preferred against him>. **2.** To give priority to, such as to one creditor over another <the statute prefers creditors who are first to file their claims>.

preference. (15c) **1.** The favoring of one person or thing over another. **2.** The person or thing so favored. **3.** The quality, state, or condition of treating some persons or things more advantageously than others. **4.** Priority of payment given to one or more creditors by a debtor; a creditor's right to receive such priority. **5.** *Bankruptcy.* PREFERENTIAL TRANSFER.

▸ **insider preference.** (1981) A transfer of property by a bankruptcy debtor to an insider more than 90 days before but within one year after the filing of the bankruptcy petition.

▸ **liquidation preference.** (1936) A preferred shareholder's right, once the corporation is liquidated, to receive a specified distribution before common shareholders receive anything.

▸ **voidable preference.** See PREFERENTIAL TRANSFER.

preference case. See *preferred cause* under CAUSE (3).

preference cause. See *preferred cause* under CAUSE (3).

preference elicitation. A largely rejected approach to statutory construction whereby the court seeks to decide cases in the manner preferred by the current legislature or in a manner best able to elicit the preferences of the current legislature via statutory modification. • This theory "has not been explicitly embraced by the [Supreme] Court or by most of the commenters." Frank B. Cross, *The Theory and Practice of Statutory Interpretation* 16 (2009). Cf. IMAGINATIVE RECONSTRUCTION.

preference in being recognized. See PRECEDENCE (4).

preference shares. See *preferred stock* under STOCK.

preferential (pref-ə-**ren**-shəl), *adj.* (18c) **1.** Giving advantage to one or more over others; favoring some people or things over others <preferential treatment>. **2.** Creating or using a favorable standard or treatment in trade relations <preferential exchange rates>. **3.** Designed to elicit decision-makers' relative likes and dislikes, esp. in an election <preferential primaries>.

preferential assignment. See PREFERENTIAL TRANSFER.

preferential ballot. See *preferential vote* under VOTE (1).

preferential debt. See DEBT.

preferential debt payment. See PREFERENTIAL TRANSFER.

preferential nonunion shop. See SHOP.

preferential rule. (1959) *Evidence.* A rule that prefers one kind of evidence to another. • It may work provisionally, as when a tribunal refuses to consider one kind of evidence until another kind (presumably better) is shown to be unavailable, or it may work absolutely, as when the tribunal refuses to consider anything but the better kind of evidence.

> "There are only three or four . . . sets of [preferential] rules. There is a rule preferring the production of the *original of a document*, in preference to a copy. There is a rule requiring the *attesting witness* to a will to be summoned to evidence its execution. And there is a rule preferring the magistrate's *official report* of testimony taken before him. Then there are a few miscellaneous rules, such as the officially certified enrollment of a statute, etc." John H. Wigmore, *A Students' Textbook of the Law of Evidence* 219 (1935).

preferential shop. See *preferential union shop* under SHOP.

preferential tariff. See TARIFF (2).

preferential transfer. (1874) *Bankruptcy.* A prebankruptcy transfer made by an insolvent debtor to or for the benefit of a creditor, thereby allowing the creditor to receive more than its proportionate share of the debtor's assets; specif., an insolvent debtor's transfer of a property interest for the benefit of a creditor who is owed on an earlier debt, when the transfer occurs no more than 90 days before the date when the bankruptcy petition is filed or (if the creditor is an insider) within one year of the filing, so that the creditor receives more than it would otherwise receive through the distribution of the bankruptcy estate. • Under the circumstances described in 11 USCA § 547, the bankruptcy trustee may, for the estate's benefit, recover a preferential transfer from the transferee. — Also termed *preference*; *voidable preference*; *voidable transfer*; *preferential assignment*; *preferential debt payment.* Cf. FRAUDULENT CONVEYANCE (2).

preferential union shop. See SHOP.

preferential vote. See VOTE (1).

preferential voting. See VOTING.

preferred, *adj.* (15c) Possessing or accorded a priority or privilege; favored <a preferred claim>.

preferred cause. See CAUSE (3).

preferred creditor. See CREDITOR.

preferred dividend. See DIVIDEND.

preferred docket. See DOCKET (2).

preferred-provider organization. (1984) A group of healthcare providers (such as doctors, hospitals, and pharmacies) that contract with a third party, such as an insurer, to provide healthcare services at a discounted cost to covered persons in a given geographic area. — Abbr. PPO. Cf. HEALTH-MAINTENANCE ORGANIZATION; MANAGED-CARE ORGANIZATION.

preferred stock. See STOCK.

preferring of charges. (1905) **1.** The bringing of a criminal complaint or other formal allegations before an adjudicator for trial, usu. by a prosecutor. **2.** *Military law.* The formal completion of a charge sheet, which includes signing and swearing to the charges and specifications. • Only a person subject to the Uniform Code of Military Justice can prefer charges. Cf. INITIATION OF CHARGES.

prefiled bill. See BILL (3).

prefine. *Hist. English law.* A fee paid beforehand by one resorting to the judicial process of fine and recovery for the conveyance of land. See ALIENATION OFFICE.

pregnancy, *n.* The period during which a woman or female animal has a fetus growing inside her body. — **pregnant,** *adj.*

Pregnancy-Discrimination Act. A federal statute that prohibits workplace discrimination against a pregnant woman or against a woman affected by childbirth or a related medical condition. 42 USCA § 2000e. • The Pregnancy-Discrimination Act is part of Title VII of the Civil Rights Act of 1964. — Abbr. PDA.

pregnant chad. See *dimpled chad* under CHAD.

prehearing conference. (1946) An optional conference for the discussion of procedural and substantive matters on appeal, usu. held in complex civil, criminal, tax, and agency cases. • Those attending are typically the attorneys involved in the case as well as a court representative such as a judge, staff attorney, or deputy clerk. Fed. R. App. P. 33.

> "The prehearing conference, if held, generally is scheduled after the time for appeal and cross-appeal has passed, and as soon as it becomes apparent that the case is complex due to the legal issues, the length of the record, or the number of parties. In a complex or multiparty case, the conference provides a forum in which to discuss briefing responsibilities, timing, and handling the record and joint appendix. There may be some discussion of the amount of oral argument the parties desire and how that argument will be divided . . . ." Michael E. Tigar, *Federal Appeals: Jurisdiction and Practice* § 8.06, at 309–10 (2d ed. 1993).

preheritance. See ADVANCEMENT (1).

prehire agreement. (1959) An employment contract between a union and an employer, in which the employer agrees to hire union members. See *closed shop* under SHOP.

prejudgment attachment. See ATTACHMENT (1).

prejudgment interest. See INTEREST (3).

prejudice, *n.* (14c) **1.** Damage or detriment to one's legal rights or claims. See *dismissal with prejudice* and *dismissal without prejudice* under DISMISSAL.

▸ **legal prejudice.** (18c) A condition that, if shown by a party, will usu. defeat the opposing party's action; esp., a condition that, if shown by the defendant, will defeat a plaintiff's motion to dismiss a case without prejudice. • The defendant may show that dismissal will deprive the defendant of a substantive property right or preclude the defendant from raising a defense that will be unavailable or endangered in a second suit.

▸ **undue prejudice.** (17c) The harm resulting from a fact-trier's being exposed to evidence that is persuasive but inadmissible (such as evidence of prior criminal conduct) or that so arouses the emotions that calm and logical reasoning is abandoned.

2. A preconceived judgment or opinion formed with little or no factual basis; a strong and unreasonable dislike or distrust. — Also termed *preconception.* — **prejudice,** *vb.*

prejudicial error. See *reversible error* under ERROR (2).

prejudicial publicity. (1935) Extensive media attention devoted to an upcoming civil or criminal trial, esp. when it tends to make potential jurors form opinions before they have heard the evidence. • Under the Due Process Clause, extensive coverage of a criminal trial may deprive the defendant of a fair trial.

prelegacy. See LEGACY (1).

prelegatee. See LEGATEE.

preliminary, *adj.* (17c) Coming before and usu. leading up to the main part of something happening before something that is more important, often in preparation for it <preliminary negotiations>.

preliminary alcohol screening. See *preliminary breath test* under BREATH TEST.

preliminary amendment. See PATENT-APPLICATION AMENDMENT.

preliminary availability search. (2004) *Trademarks.* A cursory or moderate search of registered trademarks and common-law uses of proposed-trademark names or phrases, done to narrow the list of names phrases before conducting a thorough search.

preliminary award. See *interim award* under AWARD.

preliminary complaint. See COMPLAINT.

preliminary crime. See *inchoate offense* under OFFENSE (2).

preliminary evidence. See EVIDENCE.

preliminary examination. 1. See EXAMINATION (3). **2.** See PRELIMINARY HEARING.

preliminary hearing. (1842) *Criminal procedure.* A criminal hearing (often conducted by a magistrate) to determine whether there is sufficient evidence to prosecute an accused person; specif., a proceeding before a judge or magistrate judge held soon after a criminal defendant is taken into custody, usu. on felony charges, the typical prosecution having the burden to establish reasonable cause to believe that the defendant has committed a felony. • If sufficient evidence exists, the case will be set for trial or bound over for grand-jury review, or an information will be filed in the trial court. — Also termed *preliminary examination; probable-cause hearing; bindover hearing; examining trial; felony hearing.* Cf. ARRAIGNMENT.

preliminary injunction. See INJUNCTION.

preliminary inquiry. (1952) *Military law.* The initial investigation of a reported or suspected violation of the Uniform Code of Military Justice. Cf. PRETRIAL INVESTIGATION.

preliminary-inquiry officer. See OFFICER (2).

preliminary letter. See INVITATION TO NEGOTIATE.

preliminary objection. *Int'l law.* In a case before an international tribunal, an objection that, if upheld, would render further proceedings before the tribunal impossible or unnecessary. • An objection to the court's jurisdiction is an example of a preliminary objection.

preliminary offense. See *inchoate offense* under OFFENSE.

preliminary proof. See PROOF.

preliminary prospectus. See PROSPECTUS.

preliminary protective hearing. See *shelter hearing* under HEARING.

preliminary statement. (1834) The introductory part of a brief or memorandum in support of a motion, in which the advocate summarizes the essence of what follows. • In at least two jurisdictions, New York and New Jersey, the preliminary statement is a standard part of court papers. In many other jurisdictions, advocates do not routinely include it. But preliminary statements are typically allowed, even welcomed, though not required. — Also termed *summary of argument.*

preliminary warrant. See WARRANT (1).

premarital, *adj.* (1878) Of, relating to, or occurring before marriage; existing before a marriage takes place. Cf. POSTMARITAL.

premarital agreement. See PRENUPTIAL AGREEMENT.

premarital asset. See ASSET.

prematurity. 1. The circumstance existing when the facts underlying a plaintiff's complaint do not yet create a live claim. Cf. RIPENESS. **2.** The affirmative defense based on this circumstance.

premeditated, *adj.* (16c) Done with willful deliberation and planning; consciously considered beforehand; plotted in advance <a premeditated killing>.

premeditated malice. See MALICE AFORETHOUGHT.

premeditation, *n.* (15c) Conscious consideration and planning that precedes an act (such as committing a crime); the pondering of an action before carrying it out. See FORETHOUGHT. — **premeditate,** *vb.*

premier. See PRIME MINISTER.

premier serjeant. See SERJEANT-AT-LAW.

premiership. (18c) The period during which a person serves as prime minister. See PRIME MINISTER.

premise (**prem**-is), *n.* (14c) A previous statement or contention from which a conclusion is deduced; a statement or idea that one accepts as true and uses as a basis for developing other ideas. — Also spelled (BrE) *premiss.* — **premise** (**prem**-is *or* pri-**mız**), *vb.*

premises (**prem**-ə-siz). (15c) **1.** Matters (usu. preliminary facts or statements) previously referred to in the same instrument <wherefore, premises considered, the plaintiff prays for the following relief>. **2.** The part of a deed that describes the land being conveyed, as well as naming the parties and identifying relevant facts or explaining the reasons for the deed. **3.** A house or building, along with its grounds; esp., the buildings and land that a shop, restaurant, company, etc. uses <smoking is not allowed on these premises>.

> "*Premises* (= a house or building) has a curious history in legal usage. Originally, in the sense of things mentioned previously, it denoted the part of a deed that sets forth the names of the grantor and grantee, as well as the things granted and the consideration. Then, through hypallage in the early 18th century, it was extended to refer to the subject of a conveyance or bequest as specified in the premises of the deed. Finally, it was extended to refer to a house or building along with its grounds. In short, someone who says, "No alcohol is allowed on these premises," is engaging unconsciously in a popularized legal technicality." Bryan A. Garner, *Garner's Dictionary of Legal Usage* 700 (3d ed. 2011).

▸ **demised premises.** (17c) Leased property. — Also termed *premises demised.*

premises liability. (1950) A landowner's or landholder's tort liability for conditions or activities on the premises.

premises rule. See PARKING-LOT RULE.

premium, *n.* (17c) **1.** The amount paid at designated intervals for insurance; esp., the periodic payment required to keep an insurance policy in effect. — Also termed *insurance premium.*

▸ **advance premium.** (1863) A payment made before the start of the period covered by the insurance policy.

▸ **earned premium.** (1876) The portion of an insurance premium applicable to the coverage period that has already expired. • For example, if the total premium for a one-year insurance policy is $1,200, the earned premium after three months is $300.

▸ **experience-rated premium.** A premium that is based on the prior claims experience of the policyholder.

▸ **gross premium.** (1852) **1.** The net premium plus expenses (i.e., the loading), less the interest factor. See LOADING; INTEREST FACTOR. **2.** The premium for participating life insurance. See *participating insurance* under INSURANCE.

▸ **natural premium.** (1883) The actual cost of life insurance based solely on mortality rates. • This amount will be less than a net premium. See *net premium*.

▸ **net level annual premium.** (1899) A net premium that stays the same each year.

▸ **net premium.** (1841) **1.** Generally, the premium amount for an insurance policy less agent commissions. **2.** The portion of the premium that covers the estimated cost of claims. **3.** The money needed to provide benefits under an insurance policy. • The net premium in a life-insurance policy is calculated by using an assumed interest and mortality-table rate; it does not include additional expense amounts that will be charged to the policyholder. — Also termed *net valuation premium*.

▸ **net single premium.** (1859) The money that must be collected from a policyholder at one time to guarantee enough money to pay claims made on an insurance policy. • This amount assumes that interest accrues at an expected rate and is based on a prediction of the likelihood of certain claims.

▸ **net valuation premium.** See *net premium*.

▸ **unearned premium.** (1870) The portion of an insurance premium applicable to the coverage period that has not yet occurred. • In the same example as above under *earned premium*, the unearned premium after three months is $900.

2. A sum of money paid in addition to a regular price, salary, or other amount; a supplemental amount of money above the normal or standard rate. **3.** The amount by which a security's market value exceeds its face value. — Also termed (specif.) *bond premium*. Cf. DISCOUNT (3).

▸ **call premium.** (1936) The percentage amount of a bond's face value that a company pays, along with the face value, to redeem a callable bond; the difference between a bond's call price and its par value.

▸ **control premium.** (1957) A premium paid for shares carrying the power to control a corporation. • The control premium is often computed by comparing the aggregate value of the controlling block of shares with the cost that would be incurred if the shares could be acquired at the going market price per share.

4. The amount paid to buy a securities option. — Also termed (in sense 4) *option premium*.

premium bond. See BOND (3).

premium loan. See LOAN.

premium note. See NOTE (1).

premium on capital stock. See *paid-in surplus* under SURPLUS.

premium *pudoris*. See PRAEMIUM PUDICITIAE.

premium rate. (1872) **1.** *Insurance.* The price per unit of life insurance. • It is usu. expressed as a cost per thousands of dollars of coverage. Life insurers use three factors — the interest factor, the mortality factor, and the risk factor — to calculate premium rates. — Sometimes shortened to *rate*. See INTEREST FACTOR; MORTALITY FACTOR; RISK FACTOR. **2.** A higher-than-normal amount that one pays for a service, usu. because demand is particularly high at that specific time.

premium stock. See STOCK.

premium tax. See TAX.

premunire. See PRAEMUNIRE.

prenatal injury. (1907) Harm to a fetus or an embryo. Cf. BIRTH INJURY.

prenatal tort. See TORT.

prender, *n.* (16c) The right to take a thing before it is offered. — Also spelled *prendré*.

prender de baron (**pren**-dər də **bar**-ən). [Law French "a taking of husband"] (17c) *Hist.* A plea asserting that the former wife of a murder victim should not be allowed to appeal a murder case against the alleged killer because she has since remarried.

prendré. See PRENDER.

prenup, *n. Slang.* See PRENUPTIAL AGREEMENT.

prenuptial (pree-**nəp**-shəl), *adj.* (1857) Made or occurring before marriage; premarital. — Also termed *antenuptial* (an-tee-**nəp**-shəl). Cf. POSTNUPTIAL.

prenuptial agreement. (1882) An agreement made before marriage usu. to resolve issues of support and property division if the marriage ends in divorce or by the death of a spouse. — Also termed *antenuptial agreement*; *antenuptial contract*; *premarital agreement*; *premarital contract*; *marriage settlement*. — Sometimes shortened to *prenup*. Cf. POSTNUPTIAL AGREEMENT; COHABITATION AGREEMENT.

prenuptial gift. See GIFT.

prenuptial will. See WILL.

prepaid card. See STORED-VALUE CARD.

prepaid expense. See EXPENSE.

prepaid income. See INCOME.

prepaid interest. See INTEREST (3).

prepaid legal services. (1963) An arrangement — usu. serving as an employee benefit — that enables a person to make advance payments for future legal services.

preparation. *Criminal law.* The act or process of devising the means necessary to commit a crime. Cf. ATTEMPT.

preparatory work. See TRAVAUX PRÉPARATOIRES.

prepayment clause. (1935) A loan-document provision that permits a borrower to satisfy a debt before its due date. • Although any interest not yet due is waived, the lender may impose a penalty for prepayment.

prepayment penalty. See PENALTY (2).

prepense (**pree**-pens), *adj.* (17c) *Rare.* Planned; deliberate <malice prepense>.

prepetition (pree-pə-**tish**-ən), *adj.* (1938) Occurring before the filing of a petition (esp. in bankruptcy) <prepetition debts>. — Also termed (in bankruptcy) *prebankruptcy.*

pre-plea investigation report. (1972) A memorandum report prepared by a state or county probation department, usu. with the consent of both the prosecution and the defense, for the court's consideration in whether to accept a guilty plea. — Abbr. PPIR; PPI; PPR. —Often shortened to *pre-plea investigation.* — Also termed *pre-plea report.* Cf. PRESENTENCE-INVESTIGATION REPORT.

preponderance (pri-**pon**-dər-ənts), *n.* (17c) Superiority in weight, importance, or influence; the quality of having a greater number or quantity of something. — **preponderate** (pri-**pon**-dər-ayt), *vb.* — **preponderant** (pri-**pon**-dər-ənt), *adj.*

preponderance of the evidence. (18c) The greater weight of the evidence, not necessarily established by the greater number of witnesses testifying to a fact but by evidence that has the most convincing force; superior evidentiary weight that, though not sufficient to free the mind wholly from all reasonable doubt, is still sufficient to incline a fair and impartial mind to one side of the issue rather than the other. • This is the burden of proof in most civil trials, in which the jury is instructed to find for the party that, on the whole, has the stronger evidence, however slight the edge may be. — Also termed *preponderance of proof; balance of probability; greater weight of the evidence.* See REASONABLE DOUBT. Cf. *clear and convincing evidence* under EVIDENCE; BURDEN OF PROOF.

> "Criminal convictions are so serious in their consequences that it is felt that an accused person should be freed, if there is any fair or reasonable doubt about his guilt, even though there seems to be considerable likelihood that he did commit the crime. . . . In civil cases, however, the consequence of losing a case, although serious enough in many cases, is not considered to be such as to require so stringent a rule. Accordingly the plaintiff is entitled to a verdict if he proves the case 'by the preponderance of the evidence.' In other words, he is entitled to a verdict even though there may be a reasonable doubt as to the liability of the accused, if the jury is satisfied nevertheless that the plaintiff has proved his case." Charles Herman Kinnane, *A First Book on Anglo-American Law* 562 (2d ed. 1952).

prepositive/postpositive-modifier canon. See SERIES-QUALIFIER CANON.

prepositive/postpositive-qualifier canon. See SERIES-QUALIFIER CANON.

prerequisite (pri-**rek**-wi-zit), *n.* (17c) Something that is necessary before something else can take place or be done.

prerogative (pri-**rog**-ə-tiv), *n.* (15c) An exclusive right, power, privilege, or immunity, usu. acquired by virtue of office. — **prerogative,** *adj.*

▸ **managerial prerogative.** (1946) A manager's discretionary power to make decisions affecting the business or organization, esp. day-to-day operational issues. — Also termed *management prerogative.*

▸ **prerogative of mercy.** (17c) The discretionary power of a supreme authority, such as a state governor, national president, or sovereign, to commute a death sentence, change the method of execution, or issue a pardon.

prerogative court. See COURT.

prerogative of mercy. See PREROGATIVE.

prerogative writ. See *extraordinary writ* under WRIT.

pres (pray). [Law French] (15c) Near. See CY PRES.

presale. (1938) The sale of real property (such as condominium units) before construction has begun.

prescribable (pri-**skrɪb**-ə-bəl), *adj.* (1890) (Of a right) that can be acquired or extinguished by prescription.

prescribe, *vb.* (15c) **1.** To dictate, ordain, or direct; to establish authoritatively (as a rule or guideline). **2.** To claim ownership through prescription. **3.** To invalidate or otherwise make unenforceable through prescription. **4.** To become invalid or otherwise unenforceable through prescription.

prescript, *adj.* (15c) Having the nature of a rule or command.

prescript, *n.* (16c) *Archaic.* A rule, law, command, or ordinance; PRESCRIPTION (2). • A general term, *prescript* may also apply to an edict, a regulation, or any instructive guideline.

prescription, *n.* (15c) **1.** The act of establishing authoritative rules. Cf. PROSCRIPTION (1). **2.** A rule so established. — Also termed (archaically) *prescript.* **3.** The effect of the lapse of time in creating and destroying rights. **4.** The extinction of a title or right by failure to claim or exercise it over a long period. — Also termed *negative prescription; extinctive prescription.* **5.** The acquisition of title to a thing (esp. an intangible thing such as the use of real property) by open and continuous possession over a statutory period. — Also termed *positive prescription; acquisitive prescription.* Cf. ADVERSE POSSESSION. See (for senses 3–5) PERIOD OF PRESCRIPTION.

> "*Prescription*—which originally signified any exception, but came latterly to be especially identified with the *exceptio ratione temporis*—is a plea which may be employed for the purpose either of extinguishing or of establishing a right of property. The manifest desirability of 'fixing and ascertaining property,' and of preventing forgeries, has procured it a place in the municipal code of all human societies." J.H. Millar, *A Handbook of Prescription* 1 (1893).

6. *Int'l law.* The acquisition of a territory through a continuous and undisputed exercise of sovereignty over it. **7.** *Oil & gas.* A Louisiana doctrine that extinguishes unused mineral servitudes after ten years if there is no effort to discover or produce on the land or the land pooled with it.

▸ **acquisitive prescription** (ə-**kwiz**-ə-tiv). (1854) **1.** PRESCRIPTION (5). **2.** *Civil law.* A mode of acquiring ownership or other legal rights through possession for a specified period of time.

▸ **liberative prescription** (**lib**-ə-rə-tiv). (1882) *Civil law.* A bar to a lawsuit resulting from its untimely filing. La. Civ. Code art. 3447. • This term is essentially the civil-law equivalent of a statute of limitations. See STATUTE OF LIMITATIONS.

▸ **prescription in a que estate** (ah **kee**). [Law French "prescription in whose estate"] (1825) A claim of prescription based on the immemorial enjoyment of the right by the claimant and the former owners whose estate the claimant has succeeded to.

▸ **prescription of nonuse.** (1882) *Civil law.* A mode of extinction of a real right other than ownership (such as a servitude) as a result of failure to exercise the right for a specified period of time.

▸ **quinquinnial prescription.** (17c) Prescription after a period of five years; a bar that arises upon the passage of a lustrum.

prescriptive, *adj.* (17c) **1.** Expressing what must or should be done <prescriptive legal instruments>. **2.** Based on or determined by ancient custom or long-standing use; having existed for so long as to have become a matter of right <prescriptive easement>.

prescriptive easement. See EASEMENT.

prescriptive jurisdiction. (1960) *Int'l law.* The ability of a government to prescribe law relating to certain activity that has an effect within its sovereign territory. • Section 18 of the Restatement (Second) of Foreign Relations Law of the United States notes that a nation may prescribe legal rules relating to extraterritorial activities having an effect within the territory of the legislating nation because (1) "the conduct and its effect are generally recognized as constituent elements of a crime or tort," or (2) the effect within the nation is both substantial and the "direct and foreseeable result of the conduct."

prescriptive right. (17c) A right obtained by prescription <after a nuisance has been continuously in existence for 20 years, a prescriptive right to continue it is acquired as an easement appurtenant to the land on which it exists>.

presence, *n.* (14c) **1.** The quality, state, or condition of being in a particular time and place, particularly with reference to some act that was done then and there <his presence at the scene saved two lives>. **2.** Close physical proximity coupled with awareness <the agent was in the presence of the principal>.

▸ **constructive presence.** (1807) **1.** *Criminal law.* Legal imputation of having been at a crime scene, based on having been close enough to the scene to have aided and abetted the crime's commission. See CONSPIRACY. **2.** *Wills & estates.* Legal imputation of a witness's having been in the room when a will was signed, based on the fact that the testator and the witness were able to see each other at the time of the signing. • This principle was commonly employed until the 20th century, when the presence-of-the-testator rule became dominant. See PRESENCE-OF-THE-TESTATOR RULE.

presence-of-defendant rule. (1999) The principle that a felony defendant is entitled to be present at every major stage of the criminal proceeding. Fed. R. Crim. P. 43.

presence of the court. (18c) The company or proximity of the judge or other courtroom official. • For purposes of contempt, an action is in the presence of the court if it is committed within the view of the judge or other person in court and is intended to disrupt the court's business. See *direct contempt* under CONTEMPT.

> "Some decisions indicate that the term 'in the presence of the court' is to be given a liberal interpretation, that 'the court' consists not of the judge, the courtroom, the jury, or the jury room individually, but of all of these combined, and that the court is present wherever any of its constituent parts is engaged in the prosecution of the business of the court according to law." 17 Am. Jur. 2d *Contempt* § 19 (1990).

presence-of-the-testator rule. (1999) The principle that a testator must be aware (through sight or other sense) that the witnesses are signing the will. • Many jurisdictions interpret this requirement liberally, and the Uniform Probate Code has dispensed with it. See CONSCIOUS-PRESENCE TEST. Cf. LINE-OF-SIGHT TEST.

present, *adj.* (14c) **1.** Now existing; at hand <a present right to the property>. **2.** Being considered; now under discussion <the present appeal does not deal with that issue>. **3.** In attendance; not elsewhere <all present voted for him>.

present ability. See ABILITY.

present and voting. (17c) *Parliamentary law.* (Of a member) casting a vote. • The result of a vote is ordinarily determined with reference to the members voting (often termed, somewhat redundantly, as "present and voting"). An answer of "present" when casting a vote amounts to an abstention because the voter is indicating that he or she is present but not voting. See ABSTAIN (1).

presentation. (15c) **1.** The delivery of a document to an issuer or named person for the purpose of initiating action under a letter of credit; PRESENTMENT (3). **2.** *Hist. Eccles. law.* A benefice patron's nomination of a person to fill a vacant benefice. • If the bishop rejected the appointee, the patron could enforce the right to fill the vacancy by writ of *quare impedit* in the Court of Common Pleas. See QUARE IMPEDIT. Cf. ADVOWSON; INSTITUTION (5).

▸ **next presentation.** (17c) *Hist. Eccles. law.* In the law of advowsons, the right to present to the bishop a clerk to fill the first vacancy that arises in a church or other ecclesiastical office.

present case. See *case at bar* under CASE (1).

present conveyance. See CONVEYANCE (1).

present covenant. See COVENANT (4).

presentence hearing. (1940) A proceeding at which a judge or jury receives and examines all relevant information regarding a convicted criminal and the related offense before passing sentence. — Also termed sentencing hearing.

presentence-investigation report. (1943) A probation officer's detailed account of a convicted defendant's educational, criminal, family, and social background, conducted at the court's request as an aid in passing sentence. *See* Fed. R. Crim. P. 32(c). — Abbr. PSI; PR; PSR; PIR; PSIR. — Often shortened to *presentence investigation* or *presentence report.* Cf. PRE-PLEA INVESTIGATION REPORT.

▸ **face-sheet PSI.** *Criminal law. Slang.* A brief presentence-investigation report, usu. prepared by the probation department, consisting of minimal information on a cover sheet with court-related information.

presentence report. See PRESENTENCE-INVESTIGATION REPORT.

present enjoyment. See ENJOYMENT.

presenter. *Commercial law.* Any person presenting a document (such as a draft) to an issuer for honor. UCC § 5-102(a)(13).

present estate. 1. ESTATE (1). **2.** See *present interest* under INTEREST. **3.** See POSSESSORY INTEREST.

presenting bank. See BANK.

presenting jury. See GRAND JURY.

present interest. See INTEREST (2).

presentment (pri-**zent**-mənt). (15c) **1.** The act of presenting or laying before a court or other tribunal a formal statement about a matter to be dealt with legally. **2.** *Criminal procedure.* A formal written accusation returned by a grand jury on its own initiative, without a prosecutor's previous indictment request. • Presentments are obsolete in the federal courts. See CHARGING INSTRUMENT.

> "A grand jury has only two functions, either to indict or to return a 'no bill.' The Constitution speaks also of a 'presentment,' but this is a term with a distinct historical meaning now not well understood. Historically presentment was the process by which a grand jury initiated an independent investigation and asked that a charge be drawn to cover the facts should they constitute a crime. With United States attorneys now always available to advise grand juries, proceeding by presentment is an outmoded practice." 1 Charles Alan Wright, *Federal Practice and Procedure* § 110, at 459 (3d ed. 1999).

3. The formal production of a negotiable instrument for acceptance or payment; esp., a demand for acceptance or payment made on the maker, acceptor, drawee, or other payor by or on behalf of the holder. — Also termed (in sense 3) *presentation.*

> "Presentment and dishonor occur, for instance, when the holder of a check attempts to cash it at the drawee bank, but payment is refused because the drawer lacks sufficient funds on deposit. The demand for payment is presentment. The bank's refusal to pay is dishonor." 2 James J. White & Robert S. Summers, *Uniform Commercial Code* § 16-8, at 100 (4th ed. 1995).

▸ **presentment for acceptance.** (18c) Production of an instrument to the drawee, acceptor, or maker for acceptance. • This type of presentment may be made anytime before maturity, except that with bills payable at sight, after demand, or after sight, presentment must be made within a reasonable time.

▸ **presentment for payment.** (18c) Production of an instrument to the drawee, acceptor, or maker for payment. • This type of presentment must be made on the date when the instrument is due.

presentment agency. (1983) *Criminal law.* In some jurisdictions, a state agency that conducts juvenile-delinquency prosecutions. — Also termed *presentment office.*

presentment of Englishry. (1857) *Hist.* The offering of proof that a slain person was English rather than (before the Conquest) a Dane or (after the Conquest) a Norman. • This requirement was issued first by the conquering Danes and then by the Normans to protect these groups from the English by the threat of a village- or hundred-wide amercement if the inhabitants failed to prove that a dead person found among them was English.

presentment office. See PRESENTMENT AGENCY.

presentment warranty. See WARRANTY (2).

present recollection refreshed. (1908) *Evidence.* A witness's memory that has been enhanced by showing the witness a document that describes the relevant events. • The document itself is merely a memory stimulus and is not admitted in evidence. Fed. R. Evid. 612. — Also termed *refreshing recollection; refreshing memory; present recollection revived.* Cf. PAST RECOLLECTION RECORDED.

presents, *n. pl.* (14c) *Archaic.* The instrument under consideration. • This is usu. part of the phrase *these presents,* which is part of the longer phrase *know all men by these presents* (itself a loan translation from the Latin *noverint universi per praesentes*). See KNOW ALL MEN BY THESE PRESENTS.

present sale. See SALE.

present sense impression. (1942) *Evidence.* One's perception of an event or condition, formed during or immediately after the fact. • A statement containing a present sense impression is admissible even if it is hearsay. Fed. R. Evid. 803(1). Cf. EXCITED UTTERANCE.

present use. See USE (4).

present value. (17c) The sum of money that, with compound interest, would amount to a specified sum at a specified future date; future value discounted to its value today. — Also termed *present worth.*

▸ **actuarial present value.** See ACTUARIAL PRESENT VALUE.

▸ **adjusted present value.** (1957) An asset's value determined by adding together its present value and the value added by capital-structure effects. — Abbr. APV.

▸ **net present value.** (1851) The present value of net cash flow from a project, discounted by the cost of capital. • This value is used to evaluate the project's investment potential. — Abbr. NPV.

present worth. See PRESENT VALUE.

preservationist. (1927) Someone who works to prevent artifacts, historical places, or archaeologically significant sites from being harmed.

preservation of error. (1903) The taking of all steps necessary under the rules of procedure or at common law in bringing an improper act or statement to the trial court's attention so that, if not corrected, the mistake can be reviewed on appeal.

preservation order. (1913) A direction to a property owner to maintain a historic building or conserve a natural habitat.

▸ **interim preservation order.** (1974) An order prohibiting a property owner from taking action that would alter a historic building or natural habitat before the court makes a final order.

preservation rule. The doctrine that a party must raise each question of law in the trial court if the party hopes to have an appellate court review the point.

preside, *vb.* (15c) **1.** To be in charge of a formal event, organization, or company; specif., to occupy the place of authority, esp. as a judge during a hearing or trial <preside over the proceedings>. **2.** To exercise management or control <preside over the estate>.

presidency. 1. The function or action of one who presides; superintendence.

▸ **unitary presidency.** The degree to which a president may act in the absence of legislative approval.

2. The office of a president, esp. that of the President of the United States. **3.** The term during which a president holds office; the period when someone is president.

president, *n.* (14c) **1.** The chief political executive of a government that does not have a monarch; the head of state. **2.** The chief executive officer of a corporation or other organization. **3.** CHAIR (1). **4.** CHAIR (3). See (in senses 3 & 4) *presiding officer* under OFFICER (1). — **presidential,** *adj.*

▸ **immediate past president.** (1888) The last president who held office before the incumbent. See EMERITUS.

▸ **president-elect.** (18c) Someone who has been elected as a new president but has not yet taken office; an officer who automatically succeeds to the presidency when the incumbent president's term expires. • If the organization's governing documents so provide, the president-elect may act as president in the incumbent president's absence, or may assume the presidency early if the incumbent does not finish the term.

president emeritus. See EMERITUS.

presidential, *adj.* (17c) **1.** Of, relating to, or involving a presidency or president. **2.** Having the stereotypical characteristics of a good president.

presidential elector. See ELECTOR (1).

presidential message. See MESSAGE.

presidential succession. (1816) The order of precedence in assuming the presidency in the event of a president's death or disability.

president judge. See *presiding judge* under JUDGE.

president of a court-martial. (18c) *Military law.* The senior member in rank present at a court-martial trial.

President of the United States. The highest executive officer of the federal government of the United States. • The President is elected to a four-year term by a majority of the presidential electors chosen by popular vote from each of the states. The President must be a natural citizen, must be at least 35 years old, and must have been a resident for 14 years within the United States. U.S. Const. art. II, § 1. — Abbr. POTUS.

presiding arbitrator. See ARBITRATOR.

presiding judge. See JUDGE.

presiding juror. See JUROR.

presiding officer. 1. See OFFICER (1). **2.** See OFFICER (2). **3.** See CHAIR (1).

presidium (pri-**zid**-ee-əm). (1858) **1.** A nongovernmental executive committee. **2.** An executive committee chosen to represent a large political organization, esp. in a communist country.

press, *n.* (15c) **1.** The news media; print and broadcast news organizations collectively.

> "The Constitution specifically selected the press, which includes not only newspapers, books, and magazines, but also humble leaflets and circulars, to play an important role in the discussion of public affairs." *Mills v. Alabama*, 384 U.S. 214, 219, 86 S.Ct. 1434, 1437 (1966).

> "'Press' could refer to one or more subsets of media, defined either by function or form. To the extent that existing law defines 'the press' at all, it does so mostly in terms of specific media forms. The Supreme Court has addressed the matter only obliquely . . . . [I]t has never had to decide whether a particular litigant was 'press.' In most cases the question does not arise because the claimed right would be protected as fully by the Speech Clause as by the Press Clause. The cases in which the Court seems to rely on the Press Clause have involved newspapers or magazines whose status as press was unquestioned. The Court on other occasions has mentioned 'publishers and broadcasters,' 'the media,' 'editorial judgment,' 'editorial control,' 'journalistic discretion,' and 'newsgathering' as possible objects of protection. The most famous discussion of the meaning of the Press Clause, a 1974 speech by Justice Stewart, identified its beneficiaries as 'the daily newspapers and other established media,' or 'newspapers, television, and magazines.'" David A. Anderson, *Freedom of the Press*, 80 Texas L. Rev. 429, 436 (2002).

2. *Hist.* A piece of parchment, as one sewed together to make up a roll or record of judicial proceedings.

Press Clause. (1924) *Constitutional law.* The First Amendment provision that "Congress shall make no law . . . abridging the freedom . . . of the press." U.S. Const. amend I. — Also termed *Freedom of the Press Clause.*

pressure group. (1924) An interest group or an organization that engages in a campaign to sway public opinion and change government policy. Cf. INTEREST GROUP.

prest (prest). (14c) *Hist.* A duty to be paid by the sheriff upon his account in the Exchequer or for money remaining in his custody.

prestable (**pres**-tə-bəl), *adj.* (17c) *Scots law.* **1.** Payable. **2.** Enforceable; exigible. • This term appears generally in reference to a debt. Cf. EXIGIBLE.

prestation (pre-**stay**-shən). (15c) *Hist.* **1.** A payment (or *presting*) of money. **2.** The rendering of a service.

prest money. (16c) *Hist.* A monetary payment made to a soldier or sailor on enlistment.

presume, *vb.* (14c) **1.** To accept something as true until it is shown not to be true. **2.** To assume beforehand; to suppose to be true in the absence of proof.

presumed bias. See *implied bias* under BIAS.

presumed crime. See *constructive crime* under CRIME.

presumed fact. See FACT.

presumed father. See FATHER.

presumed malice. See *implied malice* under MALICE.

presumed offense. See *constructive crime* under CRIME.

presumed-seller test. (1999) A method of imposing product liability on a manufacturer if the manufacturer, having full knowledge of the product's dangerous propensities, would be negligent in placing the product on the market.

presumption. (15c) **1.** Something that is thought to be true because it is highly probable. **2.** A legal inference or assumption that a fact exists because of the known or proven existence of some other fact or group of facts. • Most presumptions are rules of evidence calling for a certain result in a given case unless the adversely affected party overcomes it with other evidence. A presumption shifts the burden of production or persuasion to the opposing party, who can then attempt to overcome the presumption. See BURDEN OF PRODUCTION.

> "It is essential to a just view of the subject that our notions of the nature of PRESUMPTIONS be precise and distinct. A PRESUMPTION is a probable consequence, drawn from facts, (either certain, or proved by direct testimony,) as to the truth of a fact alleged, but of which there is no direct proof. It follows, therefore, that a presumption of any fact is an inference of that fact from others that are known. The word presumption, therefore, inherently imports a conclusion of the judgment; and it is applied to denote such facts or moral phaenomena, as from experience we know to be invariably or commonly connected with some other related fact. A wounded and bleeding body is discovered; it has been plundered; wide and deep footmarks are found in a direction proceeding from the body; or a person is seen running from the spot. In the one case are observed marks of flight, in the other is seen the fugitive, and we know that guilt naturally endeavors to escape detection. These circumstances induce the presumption that crime has been committed; the presumption is a conclusion or consequence from the circumstances. The antecedent circumstances therefore are one thing, the presumption from

them another and different one. Of presumptions afforded by moral phaenomena, a memorable instance is recorded in the judgment of Solomon, whose knowledge of the all-powerful force of maternal love supplied him with an infallible criterion of truth. So, when Aristippus, who had been cast away on an unknown shore, saw certain geometrical figures traced in the sand, his inference that the country was inhabited by people conversant with mathematics was a presumption of the same nature. It is evident, that this kind of reasoning, is not peculiar to legal science, but is a logical process common to every subject of human investigations." William Wills, *An Essay on the Principles of Circumstantial Evidence* 13–14 (1st Am. ed. fr. 3d London ed. 1852).

"A 'presumption' is a rule of law that courts or juries shall or may draw a particular inference from a particular fact or from particular evidence, unless and until the truth of such inference is disproved." John D. Lawson, *The Law of Presumptive Evidence* 639 (2d ed. 1899).

"A presumption may be defined to be an inference as to the existence of one fact from the existence of some other fact founded upon a previous experience of their connection." William P. Richardson, *The Law of Evidence* § 53, at 25 (3d ed. 1928).

▸ **absolute presumption.** See *conclusive presumption.*

▸ **adverse presumption.** See *adverse inference* under INFERENCE (1).

▸ **artificial presumption.** See *presumption of law.*

▸ **competing presumption.** See *conflicting presumption.*

▸ **conclusive presumption.** (18c) A presumption that cannot be overcome by any additional evidence or argument because it is accepted as irrefutable proof that establishes a fact beyond dispute <it is a conclusive presumption that a child under the age of seven is incapable of committing a felony>. — Also termed *absolute presumption*; *irrebuttable presumption*; *mandatory presumption*; *presumption juris et de jure.* Cf. *rebuttable presumption.*

"'Conclusive presumptions' or 'irrebuttable presumptions' are usually mere fictions, to disguise a rule of substantive law (e.g., the conclusive presumption of malice from an unexcused defamation); and when they are not fictions, they are usually repudiated by modern courts." John H. Wigmore, *A Students' Textbook of the Law of Evidence* 454 (1935).

"Conclusive presumptions, sometimes called irrebuttable presumptions of law, are really rules of law. Thus it is said that a child under the age of fourteen years is conclusively presumed to be incapable of committing rape. This is only another way of saying that such a child cannot be found guilty of rape." Richard Eggleston, *Evidence, Proof and Probability* 92 (1978).

▸ **conditional presumption.** See *rebuttable presumption.*

▸ **conflicting presumption.** (1830) One of two or more presumptions that would lead to opposite results. — Also termed *inconsistent presumption*; *competing presumption.*

"'Conflicting presumptions' are simply two ordinary presumptions that would give opposite results; usually they are really successive presumptions. E.g., where A proves himself to be the son of N, wife of M, but M and N were already separated, and later M married P, and had a son B, the later marriage of M might presume a prior divorce from N before separation to make it valid, and yet the birth of A from a married mother might be presumed legitimate, and thus the question whether A or B was the legitimate son would be attended by opposing presumptions. But in this aspect the doctrine of presumptions is clouded with difficulties and leads to much vain speculation and logical unrealism." John H. Wigmore, *A Students' Textbook of the Law of Evidence* 454 (1935).

▸ **disputable presumption.** See *rebuttable presumption.*

▸ **dry presumption.** (1899) A presumption that has no probative value unless the party with the burden of proof presents evidence to support the presumption.

▸ **factual presumption.** See *presumption of fact.*

▸ **heeding presumption.** (1990) A rebuttable presumption that an injured product user would have followed a warning label had the product manufacturer provided one.

▸ **inconsistent presumption.** See *conflicting presumption.*

▸ **irrebuttable presumption.** See *conclusive presumption.*

▸ **legal presumption.** See *presumption of law.*

▸ **mandatory presumption.** See *conclusive presumption.*

▸ ***McClanahan* presumption.** See MCCLANAHAN PRESUMPTION.

▸ **mixed presumption.** (1838) A presumption containing elements of both law and fact.

▸ **Morgan presumption.** See MORGAN PRESUMPTION.

▸ **natural presumption.** (16c) A deduction of one fact from another, based on common experience.

▸ **permissive presumption.** (1827) A presumption that a trier of fact is free to accept or reject from a given set of facts. — Also termed *permissive inference.*

▸ **presumption juris et de jure.** See *conclusive presumption.*

▸ **presumption of a quorum.** (1891) *Parliamentary law.* The presumption that a quorum, once established, is present until the chair or a member notices otherwise.

▸ **presumption of fact.** (17c) A type of rebuttable presumption that may be, but as a matter of law need not be, drawn from another established fact or group of facts <the possessor of recently stolen goods is, by presumption of fact, considered the thief>. — Also termed *factual presumption.*

▸ **presumption of financial ability.** The rebuttable conclusion, derived from legal implication, that each party to a contract has access to the money necessary to perform the obligations undertaken.

▸ **presumption of general application.** (1965) A presumption that applies across the board to all legislation, as a result of which lawmakers need not list each such presumption in all bills.

"One function of the word 'presumption' in the context of statutory interpretation is to state the result of this legislative reliance (real or assumed) on firmly established legal principles. There is a 'presumption' that *mens rea* is required in the case of statutory crimes, and a 'presumption' that statutory powers must be exercised reasonably. These presumptions apply although there is no question of linguistic ambiguity in the statutory wording under construction, and they may be described as 'presumptions of general application.' At the level of interpretation, their function is the promotion of brevity on the part of the draftsman. Statutes make dreary enough reading as it is, and it would be ridiculous to insist in each instance upon an enumeration of the general principles taken for granted." Rupert Cross, *Statutory Interpretation* 142–43 (1976).

▸ **presumption of innocence.** See PRESUMPTION OF INNOCENCE.

▸ **presumption of intent.** (18c) A permissive presumption that a criminal defendant who intended to commit an act did so.

▸ **presumption of law.** (16c) A legal assumption that a court is required to make if certain facts are established and no contradictory evidence is produced <by presumption of law, a criminal defendant is considered innocent until proven guilty beyond a reasonable doubt>. — Also termed *legal presumption; artificial presumption; praesumptio juris; pseudopresumption of law.*

▸ **presumption of maternity.** See PRESUMPTION OF MATERNITY.

▸ **presumption of natural and probable consequences.** See PRESUMPTION OF NATURAL AND PROBABLE CONSEQUENCES.

▸ **presumption of paternity.** See PRESUMPTION OF PATERNITY.

▸ **presumption of regularity.** See PRESUMPTION OF REGULARITY.

▸ **presumption of survivorship.** See PRESUMPTION OF SURVIVORSHIP.

▸ **presumption of validity.** See PRESUMPTION OF VALIDITY.

▸ **prima facie presumption.** See *rebuttable presumption.*

▸ **procedural presumption.** (1931) A presumption that may be rebutted by credible evidence.

▸ **pseudopresumption of law.** See *presumption of law.*

▸ **rebuttable presumption.** (1852) An inference drawn from certain facts that establish a prima facie case, which may be overcome by the introduction of contrary evidence. — Also termed *prima facie presumption; disputable presumption; conditional presumption; praesumptio juris.* Cf. *conclusive presumption.*

> "A rebuttable presumption of law being contested by proof of facts showing otherwise, which are denied, the presumption loses its value, unless the evidence is equal on both sides, in which case it should turn the scale." John D. Lawson, *The Law of Presumptive Evidence* 660 (2d ed. 1899).

▸ **statutory presumption.** (1819) A rebuttable or conclusive presumption that is created by statute.

▸ **Thayer presumption.** See THAYER PRESUMPTION.

presumption against absurdity. See ABSURDITY DOCTRINE.

presumption against change in common law. The doctrine that a statute will be construed to alter the common law only when that disposition is clear.

presumption against extraterritoriality. See EXTRATERRITORIALITY CANON.

presumption against federal preemption. The doctrine that a federal statute is presumed to supplement rather than displace state law. See PREEMPTION (5).

presumption against implied repeal. The doctrine that repeal of a statute by implication is disfavored.

presumption against implied right of action. The doctrine that a statute's mere prohibition of a certain act does not imply creation of a private right of action for its violation. See RIGHT OF ACTION.

presumption against inconsistency. See PRESUMPTION OF CONSISTENT USAGE.

presumption against ineffectiveness. The doctrine that a textually permissible interpretation that furthers rather than obstructs the document's purpose should be favored. See PRESUMPTION OF VALIDITY; CONSTITUTIONAL-DOUBT CANON; UT RES MAGIS VALEAT QUAM PEREAT (2).

presumption against retroactivity. The doctrine that a statute presumptively has no retroactive application. — Also termed *Landgraf doctrine* [*Landgraf v. USI Film Prods.*, 511 U.S. 244, 114 S.Ct. 1483 (1994)]. See RETROACTIVE LAW. Cf. PENDING-ACTION CANON.

presumption against superfluities. See SURPLUSAGE CANON.

presumption against surplusage. See SURPLUSAGE CANON.

presumption against unconstitutionality. See CONSTITUTIONAL-DOUBT CANON.

presumption against waiver of sovereign immunity. The doctrine that a statute does not waive sovereign immunity, and a federal statute does not eliminate state sovereign immunity, unless that disposition is unequivocally clear.

presumption of consistency. See PRESUMPTION OF CONSISTENT USAGE.

presumption of consistent usage. The doctrine that a word or phrase is presumed to bear the same meaning throughout a text, esp. a statute, unless a material variation in terms suggests a variation in meaning. — Also termed *presumption against inconsistency; consistent-meaning canon; presumption of consistency; identical-words presumption; golden rule.*

presumption of death. (18c) A presumption that arises on the unexpected disappearance and continued absence of a person for an extended period, commonly seven years.

presumption-of-fertility rule. See FERTILE-OCTOGENARIAN RULE.

presumption of financial ability. See PRESUMPTION.

presumption-of-identity rule. (1994) The common-law rule that unless there is a specific, applicable statute in another state, a court will presume that the common law has developed elsewhere identically with how it has developed in the court's own state, so that the court may apply its own state's law. • Today this rule applies primarily in Georgia. *See Shorewood Packaging Corp. v. Commercial Union Ins.*, 865 F. Supp. 1577 (N.D. Ga. 1994).

presumption of innocence. (18c) *Criminal law.* The fundamental principle that a person may not be convicted of a crime unless the government proves guilt beyond a reasonable doubt, without any burden placed on the accused to prove innocence. • For a classic essay on the development of the presumption — and its elevation to a kind of cliché — see Carleton K. Allen, "The Presumption of Innocence," in *Legal Duties and Other Essays in Jurisprudence* 253–94 (1931).

presumption of legislative knowledge. The doctrine that the legislature is knowledgeable about all existing law relating to its pending bills.

presumption of legitimacy. See PRESUMPTION OF PATERNITY.

presumption of malice. (18c) **1.** *Criminal law.* A rebuttable presumption that a wrongdoer acted without justification, excuse, or reason to deliberately cause harm to another.

2. *Libel law.* The presumption that an unprivileged publication of defamation per se was made with ill will and unjustifiable motive.

presumption of maternity. (1966) *Family law.* The presumption that the woman who has given birth to a child is both the genetic mother and the legal mother of the child. — Also termed *maternity presumption.* Cf. PRESUMPTION OF PATERNITY.

presumption of natural and probable consequences. (1980) *Criminal law.* The presumption that mens rea may be derived from proof of the defendant's conduct.

presumption of paternity. (1829) *Family law.* The presumption that the father of a child is the man who (1) is married to the child's mother when the child was conceived or born (even though the marriage may have been invalid), (2) married the mother after the child's birth and agreed either to have his name on the birth certificate or to support the child, or (3) welcomed the child into his home and later held out the child as his own. — Also termed *paternity presumption*; *presumption of legitimacy*; *legitimacy presumption.* See *presumed father* under FATHER.

presumption of regularity. (1826) The law's robust assumption that, unless there is a clear showing to the contrary, all official actions have taken place in the ordinary course of governmental administration and according to lawful authority.

presumption of survivorship. (1844) The presumption that one of two or more victims of a common disaster survived the others, based on the supposed survivor's youth, good health, or other reason rendering survivorship likely.

presumption of validity. (1873) **1.** The doctrine that an interpretation that validates outweighs one that invalidates. See UT RES MAGIS VALEAT QUAM PEREAT (2); PRESUMPTION AGAINST INEFFECTIVENESS. **2.** Broadly, CONSTITUTIONAL-DOUBT CANON. **3.** *Patents.* The doctrine that the holder of a patent is entitled to a statutory presumption that the patent is valid and that the burden is on a challenger to prove invalidity. See BORN VALID.

presumptive (pri-**zəmp**-tiv), *adj.* (15c) **1.** Giving reasonable grounds for belief; based on reasonable thoughts about what is likely to be true. **2.** Based on a legal presumption. — **presumptively,** *adv.*

presumptive authority. See *implied authority* under AUTHORITY (1).

presumptive damages. See *punitive damages* under DAMAGES.

presumptive death. See DEATH.

presumptive evidence. See EVIDENCE.

presumptive heir. See *heir presumptive* under HEIR.

presumptive notice. See *implied notice* under NOTICE (3).

presumptive proof. See *conditional proof* under PROOF.

presumptive release date. (1975) The projected date on which a prisoner serving an indeterminate sentence might be paroled in the absence of complicating factors (such as a poor disciplinary record), esp. when the sentence is for a nonviolent felony and the prisoner has no history of violence.

presumptive sentence. See SENTENCE.

presumptive sentencing. See SENTENCING.

presumptive taker. See TAKER.

presumptive title. See TITLE (2).

presumptive trust. See *resulting trust* under TRUST (3).

presuppose, *vb.* (15c) **1.** To depend on something that is believed to exist or to be true <the idea that he is innocent presupposes that the gloves could not have been a good fit>. **2.** To have to happen if something is true <litigation presupposes that there will be winners and losers>.

presupposition (pree-səp-i-**zish**-ən), *n.* (16c) **1.** The act of taking something for granted or of implying or involving as a necessary condition. **2.** That which is taken for granted or implied or involved as a necessary condition. **3.** The belief or inference that something previously existed. — **presuppose,** *vb.*

pret a usage. *Civil law.* A gratuitous loan for use.

pretax, *adj.* (1917) Existing or occurring before the assessment or deduction of taxes <pretax income>.

pretax earnings. See EARNINGS.

prête-nom (pret-**nohm**). [French] (1882) Someone who lends his name.

pretense, *n.* (15c) **1.** A way of behaving that is calculated to make people believe something untrue <the pretense of being ill>. **2.** A claim made but not supported by fact <his pretense to royalty proved false>. **3.** A professed rather than real purpose <false pretenses>. **4.** A false show; an instance of dissembling <the jury saw through his pretense of surprise>. — Also spelled (BrE) *pretence.*

pretensive joinder. See JOINDER.

preterlegal (pree-tər-**lee**-gəl), *adj.* (17c) *Rare.* Beyond the range of what is legal; not according to law <preterlegal customs>.

pretermission (pree-tər-**mish**-ən). (18c) **1.** The condition of one who is pretermitted, as an heir of a testator. **2.** The act of omitting an heir from a will.

pretermission statute. See PRETERMITTED-HEIR STATUTE.

pretermit (pree-tər-**mit**), *vb.* (15c) **1.** To ignore or disregard purposely <the court pretermitted the constitutional question by deciding the case on procedural grounds>. **2.** To neglect, overlook, or omit accidentally; esp., to fail to include through inadvertence <the third child was pretermitted in the will>. • Although in ordinary usage sense 1 prevails, in legal contexts (esp. involving heirs) sense 2 is usual.

pretermitted child. See *pretermitted heir* under HEIR.

pretermitted defense. See DEFENSE (1).

pretermitted heir. See HEIR.

pretermitted-heir statute. (1955) A state law that, under certain circumstances, grants an omitted heir the right to inherit a share of the testator's estate, usu. by treating the heir as though the testator had died intestate. • Most states have a pretermitted-heir statute, under which an omitted child or spouse receives the same share of the estate as if the testator had died intestate, unless the omission was intentional. The majority rule, and that found in the Uniform Probate Code, is that only afterborn children — that is, children born after the execution of a will — receive protection as pretermitted heirs. Under that circumstance, an inference arises that their omission was inadvertent rather than purposeful. — Also termed *pretermission statute.*

pretermitted spouse. See *pretermitted heir* under HEIR.

pretext (**pree**-tekst), *n.* (16c) A false or weak reason or motive advanced to hide the actual or strong reason or motive. — **pretextual** (pree-**teks**-choo-əl), *adj.*

pretext arrest. See *pretextual arrest* under ARREST (2).

pretext stop. See *pretextual stop* under STOP.

pretextual arrest. See ARREST (2).

pretextual search. See SEARCH (1).

pretextual stop. See STOP.

pretextus (pree-**teks**-təs). [Latin] A pretext.

pretium (**pree**-shee-əm). [Latin] Price; value; worth.

- ▸ ***pretium affectionis*** (**pree**-shee-əm ə-fek-shee-**oh**-nis). (17c) An enhanced value placed on a thing by the fancy of its owner, growing out of an attachment for the specific article and its associations; sentimental value. • This value is usu. not taken as a basis for measuring damages.
- ▸ ***pretium doloris*** (**pree**-shee-əm də-**lor**-is). [Latin] *Hist.* Price or damages for the infliction of pain.
- ▸ ***pretium periculi*** (**pree**-shee-əm pə-**rik**-yə-lı). (1830) The price of the risk, such as the premium paid on an insurance policy.

pretorial court (pri-**tor**-ee-əl). See COURT.

pretorium. See PRAETORIUM.

pretrial conference. (1938) An informal meeting at which opposing attorneys confer, usu. with the judge, to work toward the disposition of the case by discussing matters of evidence and narrowing the issues that will be tried. *See* Fed. R. Civ. P. 16; Fed. R. Crim. P. 17.1. • The conference takes place shortly before trial and ordinarily results in a pretrial order. — Often shortened to *pretrial.* — Also termed *pretrial hearing.*

pretrial detention. See DETENTION (1).

pretrial disclosure. See DISCLOSURE (2).

pretrial discovery. See DISCOVERY.

pretrial diversion. See DIVERSION PROGRAM (1).

pretrial hearing. See PRETRIAL CONFERENCE.

pretrial intervention. (1974) **1.** DIVERSION PROGRAM (1). **2.** See DEFERRED PROSECUTION (1). **3.** See *deferred judgment* under JUDGMENT (2).

pretrial investigation. (1946) *Military law.* An investigation to decide whether a case should be recommended for forwarding to a general court-martial.

pretrial order. (1939) A court order setting out the claims and defenses to be tried, the stipulations of the parties, and the case's procedural rules, as agreed to by the parties or mandated by the court at a pretrial conference. *See* Fed. R. Civ. P. 16(e). • In federal court, a pretrial order supersedes the pleadings.

pretrial services. An investigation of a federal criminal defendant's background, conducted after the defendant has been arrested and charged but before trial, to help the court determine whether to release or detain the defendant pending trial. • If the court orders release, a pretrial-services officer supervises the defendant on release.

prevail, *vb.* (17c) **1.** To obtain the relief sought in an action; to win a lawsuit <the plaintiff prevailed in the Supreme Court>. **2.** To be commonly accepted or predominant; to achieve general currency <it's unclear which line of precedent will prevail>.

prevailing party. See PARTY (2).

prevarication (pri-var-ə-**kay**-shən), *n.* (16c) The act or an instance of avoiding the truth, esp. by not answering questions directly; deviation from honest expression; EQUIVOCATION (1). — **prevaricate** (pri-**var**-ə-kayt), *vb.*

prevaricator (pri-**var**-ə-kay-tər), *n.* [Latin] (15c) **1.** A liar; an equivocator. **2.** *Roman law.* Someone who betrays another's trust, such as an advocate who aids the opposing party by betraying the client. — Also spelled (in sense 2) *praevaricator.*

prevent, *vb.* (15c) To stop from happening; to hinder or impede <a gag order to prevent further leaks to the press>.

preventative law. See PREVENTIVE LAW.

prevention. 1. The stopping of something, esp. something bad, from happening. **2.** *Civil law.* The right of one of several judges having concurrent jurisdiction to exercise that jurisdiction over a case that the judge is first to hear.

prevention doctrine. (1979) *Contracts.* The principle that each contracting party has an implied duty to not do anything that prevents the other party from performing its obligation. — Also termed *prevention-of-performance doctrine.*

preventive custody. See CUSTODY (1).

preventive detention. See DETENTION (1).

preventive injunction. See INJUNCTION.

preventive justice. See JUSTICE (4).

preventive law. Law practice that seeks to minimize a client's risk of litigation or secure more certainty with regard to the client's legal rights and duties. • Emphasizing planning, counseling, and the nonadversarial resolution of disputes, preventive law focuses on the lawyer's role as adviser and negotiator. — Also termed (less correctly) *preventative law.*

preventive punishment. See PUNISHMENT (1).

preventive self-defense. See *preemptive self-defense* under SELF-DEFENSE (1).

previous-construction canon. See PRIOR-CONSTRUCTION CANON.

previously taxed income. See INCOME.

previous notice. See NOTICE (6).

previous question. See CLOSE DEBATE.

price. (14c) The amount of money or other consideration asked for or given in exchange for something else; the cost at which something is bought or sold.

- ▸ **agreed price.** (18c) The price for a sale, esp. of goods, arrived at by mutual agreement. Cf. *open price.*
- ▸ **arm's-length price.** (1945) The price at which two unrelated, unaffiliated, and nondesperate parties would freely agree to do business. See *arm's-length transaction* under TRANSACTION; *fair market value* under VALUE.
- ▸ **asked price.** (1864) The lowest price at which a seller is willing to sell a security at a given time. See SPREAD (2).

▸ **asking price.** (18c) The price at which a seller lists property for sale, often implying a willingness to sell for less. — Also termed *ask price; offering price.*

▸ **at-the-market price.** The price at which a good or service is offered, or will fetch, within a specified area; esp., the retail price that store owners in the same vicinity generally charge for a particular thing or its equivalent. — Abbr. ATM price.

▸ **bid price.** (1915) The highest price that a prospective buyer is willing to pay for a security at a given time. — Also termed *market bid.* See SPREAD (2).

▸ **call price.** (1907) **1.** The price at which a bond may be retired before its maturity. **2.** See *strike price.*

▸ **ceiling price.** (1941) **1.** The highest price at which a buyer is willing to buy. **2.** The highest price allowed by a government agency or by some other regulatory institution.

▸ **closing price.** (1834) The price of a security at the end of a given trading day. — Also termed *close.*

▸ **cost price.** (1836) The price that a seller pays for something to be sold.

▸ **de-escalating price.** (1969) The decreasing market price for a unit or a good or service caused by intense competition between vendors.

▸ **discriminatory price.** (1913) The variable market price of a unit of a good or service offered by competing vendors who incurred the same marginal cost to produce the good.

▸ **excessive price.** A price that has no reasonable relation to the value of a good or service and is higher than that value.

▸ **exercise price.** See *strike price.*

▸ **ex-works price.** (1950) The price of goods as they leave the factory. See EX WORKS.

▸ **fixed price.** A price that is agreed on by a wholesaler and a retailer for the later sale or resale of an item. • Agreements to fix prices are generally prohibited by state and federal statutes.

▸ **floor price.** (1940) The lowest price at which a seller is willing to sell.

▸ **hammer price.** (1857) The final price at an auction, where the auctioneer traditionally knocks the lectern with a gavel to announce that the item up for auction has been sold to a certain bidder at a specified price.

▸ **liquidating price.** See *redemption price.*

▸ **liquidation price.** (1926) A price that is paid for property sold to liquidate a debt. • Liquidation price is usu. below market price. — Also termed *liquidation value.*

▸ **list price.** (1871) A published or advertised price of goods; retail price; esp., a price suggested for a product by those who make it.

▸ **manufacturer-suggested retail price.** See *suggested retail price.*

▸ **market price.** (15c) The prevailing price at which something is sold in a specific market. See *at-the-market price; fair market value* under VALUE (2).

▸ **mean trading price.** (1985) *Securities.* The average of the daily trading price of a security determined at the close of the market each day during a 90-day period.

▸ **net price.** (18c) The price of something, after deducting cash discounts.

▸ **offering price.** See *asking price.*

▸ **open price.** (1906) The price for a sale, esp. of goods, that has not been settled at the time of a sale's conclusion. UCC § 2-305. Cf. *agreed price.*

▸ **predatory price.** See PREDATORY PRICING.

▸ **purchase price.** (18c) The price actually paid for something, esp. a house.

▸ **put price.** See *strike price.*

▸ **redemption price.** (1870) **1.** The price of a bond that has not reached maturity, purchased at the issuer's option. **2.** The price of shares when a mutual-fund shareholder sells shares back to the fund. — Also termed *liquidating price; repurchase price.*

▸ **reserve price.** (1866) In an auction, the amount that a seller of goods stipulates as the lowest acceptable offer. • The reserve price may or may not be announced. See WITH RESERVE; WITHOUT RESERVE.

▸ **sales price.** (18c) The total amount for which property is sold, often including the costs of any services that are a part of the sale. • Under sales-tax statutes, the amount is typically valued in money even if the value is not received in money. — Also termed *selling price.*

▸ **spot price.** (1882) The amount for which a commodity is sold in a spot market.

▸ **strike price.** (1980) *Securities.* The price for which a security will be bought or sold under an option contract if the option is exercised. — Also termed *striking price; exercise price; call price; put price.* See OPTION (5).

▸ **subscription price.** See SUBSCRIPTION PRICE.

▸ **suggested retail price.** (1913) The sales price recommended to a retailer by a manufacturer of the product. — Abbr. SRP. — Also termed *manufacturer-suggested retail price* (MSRP).

▸ **support price.** (1943) A minimum price set by the federal government for a particular agricultural commodity.

▸ **target price.** (1954) A price set by the federal government for particular agricultural commodities. • If the market price falls below the target price, farmers receive a subsidy from the government for the difference.

▸ **trade price.** (18c) The price at which a manufacturer or wholesaler sells to others in the same business or industry.

▸ **transfer price.** (1969) The price charged by one segment of an organization for a product or service supplied to another segment of the same organization; esp., the charge assigned to an exchange of goods or services between a corporation's organizational units.

▸ **uniform price.** (17c) The single, unchanging market price for all units of a good or service regardless of supplier.

▸ **unit price.** (1908) A price of a product expressed as per-item cost or in a well-known measure such as ounces or pounds.

▸ **upset price.** (18c) The lowest amount that a seller is willing to accept for property or goods sold at auction.

▸ **wholesale price.** (18c) The price that a retailer pays for goods purchased (usu. in bulk) from a wholesaler for resale to consumers at a higher price.

price amendment. (1941) *Securities.* A change in a registration statement, prospectus, or prospectus supplement affecting the offering price, the underwriting and selling discounts or commissions, the amount of proceeds, the conversion rates, the call prices, or some other matter relating to the offering price.

price control. (*often pl.*) (18c) A system in which the government sets the prices of things. — Also termed *price-fixing.*

price/cost analysis. (1986) A technique of determining, for antitrust purposes, whether predatory pricing has occurred by examining the relationship between a defendant's prices and either its average variable cost or its average total cost.

price discrimination. (1915) The practice of offering identical or similar goods to different buyers at different prices when the costs of producing the goods are the same. • Price discrimination can violate antitrust laws if it reduces competition. It may be either direct, as when a seller charges different prices to different buyers, or indirect, as when a seller offers special concessions (such as favorable credit terms) to some but not all buyers.

▸ **persistent price discrimination.** (1955) A monopolist's systematic policy of obtaining different rates of return from different sales groupings.

price-earnings ratio. (1929) The ratio between a stock's current share price and the corporation's earnings per share for the last year. • Some investors avoid stocks with high price-earnings ratios because those stocks may be overpriced. — Abbr. P/E ratio. Cf. *earnings yield* under YIELD.

price-erosion theory. (1990) *Patents.* A theory of lost-profits remedy that measures the difference between what an item could have sold for with patent protection and what it actually sold for while having to compete against an infringing item.

price expectancy. See EXHIBITION VALUE.

price-fixing. (1889) **1.** PRICE CONTROL. **2.** *Antitrust.* The artificial setting or maintenance of prices at a certain level, contrary to the workings of the free market; an agreement between producers and sellers of a product to set prices at a high level. • Price-fixing is usu. illegal per se under antitrust law. See FIX (3); PRICE CONTROL. — Also termed *fixing prices.*

> "Price-fixing agreements may or may not be aimed at complete elimination of price competition. The group making those agreements may or may not have the power to control the market. But the fact that the group cannot control the market prices does not necessarily mean that the agreement as to prices has no utility to the members of the combination. The effectiveness of price-fixing agreements is dependent on many factors, such as competitive tactics, position in the industry, the formula underlying price policies. Whatever economic justification particular price-fixing agreements may be thought to have, the law does not permit an inquiry into their reasonableness. They are all banned because of their actual or potential threat to the central nervous system of the economy." *U.S. v. Socony-Vacuum Oil Co.*, 310 U.S. 150, 225-26 n.59, 60 S.Ct. 811, 845 n.59 (1940).

▸ **horizontal price-fixing.** (1935) Price-fixing among competitors on the same level, such as retailers throughout an industry.

▸ **vertical price-fixing.** (1936) Price-fixing among parties in the same chain of distribution, such as manufacturers and retailers attempting to control an item's resale price.

price-gouging. See GOUGING.

price index. (1886) **1.** An index of average prices as a percentage of the average prevailing at some other time (such as a base year). **2.** A list of particular goods and services and how much their prices periodically change (e.g., monthly). See CONSUMER PRICE INDEX; PRODUCER PRICE INDEX.

price leadership. (1942) A market condition in which an industry leader establishes a price that others in the field adopt as their own. • Price leadership alone does not violate antitrust laws without other evidence of an intent to create a monopoly.

price-level-adjusted mortgage. See MORTGAGE.

price memorandum. (1998) *Securities.* A document created by an underwriter to explain how securities are priced for a public offering and, typically, to show estimates and appraisals that are not allowed as part of the offering documents.

price-renegotiation clause. (1965) *Oil & gas.* A provision in a gas contract allowing for price renegotiation from time to time or upon election of one of the parties.

price squeeze. (1941) *Antitrust.* Discriminatory pricing practiced by a manufacturer or distributor who also supplies materials or products to a competitor, and charges a high wholesale price in an attempt to reduce or eliminate a competitor's ability to make a retail profit.

price support. (1927) The artificial maintenance of prices (as of a particular commodity) at a certain level, esp. by governmental action (as by subsidy); esp., a system in which the government keeps the price of a product at a particular level by giving the producer money or by buying the product itself.

price war. (1895) A period of sustained or repeated price-cutting in an industry (esp. among retailers), designed to undersell competitors or force them out of business.

priest–penitent privilege. See PRIVILEGE (3).

primae impressionis (**prɪ**-mee im-pres[h]-ee-**oh**-nis). (17c) [Law Latin] Of the first impression. See *case of first impression* under CASE (1).

primae preces. See PRECES PRIMARIAE.

prima facie (**prɪ**-mə **fay**-shə *or* **fay**-shee), *adj.* (18c) Sufficient to establish a fact or raise a presumption unless disproved or rebutted; based on what seems to be true on first examination, even though it may later be proved to be untrue <a prima facie showing>.

prima facie, *adv.* [Latin] (15c) At first sight; on first appearance but subject to further evidence or information <the agreement is prima facie valid>.

prima facie case. (1805) **1.** The establishment of a legally required rebuttable presumption. **2.** A party's production of enough evidence to allow the fact-trier to infer the fact at issue and rule in the party's favor.

prima facie evidence. See EVIDENCE.

prima facie obviousness. See OBVIOUSNESS.

prima facie presumption. See *rebuttable presumption* under PRESUMPTION.

prima facie privilege. See *qualified immunity* under IMMUNITY (1).

prima facie tort. See TORT.

primage (prɪ-mij). See HAT MONEY.

primary, *n.* See *primary election* under ELECTION (3).

primary activity. (1938) *Labor law.* Concerted action (such as a strike or picketing) directed against an employer with which a union has a dispute. Cf. SECONDARY ACTIVITY.

primary agent. See AGENT.

primary allegation. See ALLEGATION.

primary amendment. See AMENDMENT (3).

primary assumption of risk. See ASSUMPTION OF THE RISK.

primary assumption of the risk. See ASSUMPTION OF THE RISK.

primary authority. See AUTHORITY (4).

primary beneficiary. See BENEFICIARY.

primary boycott. See BOYCOTT.

primary caregiver. (1975) *Family law.* **1.** The parent who has had the greatest responsibility for the daily care and rearing of a child. See TENDER-YEARS DOCTRINE; PRIMARY-CAREGIVER DOCTRINE. **2.** The person (including a nonparent) who has had the greatest responsibility for the daily care and rearing of a child. — Also termed *primary caretaker.*

primary-caregiver doctrine. (1987) *Family law.* The presumption that, in a custody dispute, the parent who is a child's main caregiver will be the child's custodian, assuming that he or she is a fit parent. • This doctrine includes the quality and the quantity of care that a parent gives a child — but excludes supervisory care by others while the child is in the parent's custody. Under this doctrine, courts sometimes divide children into three age groups: those under the age of 6, those 6 to 14, and those 14 and older. For children under the age of 6, an absolute presumption exists in favor of the primary caretaker as custodian. For those 6 to 14, the trial court may hear the child's preference on the record but without the parents being present. For those 14 and older, the child may be allowed to choose which parent will be the custodian, assuming that both parents are fit. — Also termed *primary-caretaker doctrine*; *primary-caregiver presumption*; *primary-caretaker presumption*; *primary-caregiver preference.* Cf. MATERNAL-PREFERENCE PRESUMPTION; TENDER-YEARS DOCTRINE.

primary caretaker. See PRIMARY CAREGIVER.

primary cause. See *proximate cause* under CAUSE (1).

primary committee. (2004) *Bankruptcy.* A group of creditors organized to help the debtor draw up a reorganization plan.

primary conveyance. See CONVEYANCE (1).

primary custody. See *primary jurisdiction* under JURISDICTION.

primary devise. See DEVISE.

primary domiciliary parent. See PARENT (1).

primary-duty doctrine. (1952) *Maritime law.* The principle that a seaman cannot recover damages if the injury arose from an unseaworthy condition created by the seaman's breach of duty.

primary election. See ELECTION (3).

primary evidence. See EVIDENCE.

primary-evidence rule. The doctrine that when evidence sought in an illegal search is seized during that search, the inevitable-discovery doctrine does not apply. See INEVITABLE-DISCOVERY DOCTRINE.

primary fact. See FACT.

primary insurance. See INSURANCE.

primary insured. See INSURED.

primary insurer. See INSURER.

primary jurisdiction. See JURISDICTION.

primary-jurisdiction doctrine. (1935) A judicial doctrine whereby a court tends to favor allowing an agency an initial opportunity to decide an issue in a case in which the court and the agency have concurrent jurisdiction. See *primary jurisdiction* under JURISDICTION.

primary lease. See HEADLEASE.

primary liability. See LIABILITY.

primary-line competition. See *horizontal competition* under COMPETITION.

primary-line injury. (1954) *Antitrust.* Under the price-discrimination provisions of the Robinson–Patman Act, the practice of charging below-cost, predatory prices in an attempt to eliminate the seller's competition in the market. 15 USCA § 13(a). • A primary-line injury, which hinders or seeks to hinder competition among the seller's competitors, is distinguishable from a secondary-line injury, which refers to discriminatory pricing that hinders or seeks to hinder competition among the seller's customers, by favoring one customer over another in the prices the seller charges. Cf. SECONDARY-LINE INJURY.

> "Liggett contends that Brown & Williamson's discriminatory volume rebates to wholesalers threatened substantial competitive injury by furthering a predatory pricing scheme designed to purge competition from the economy segment of the cigarette market. This type of injury, which harms direct competitors of the discriminating seller, is known as a primary-line injury." *Brooke Group Ltd. v. Brown & Williamson Tobacco Corp.*, 509 U.S. 209, 220, 113 S.Ct. 2578, 2586 (1993).

primary market. See MARKET.

primary mortgage market. See MORTGAGE MARKET.

primary obligation. See OBLIGATION.

primary offering. See OFFERING.

primary officer. See *principal officer* under OFFICER (1).

primary plea. See *primary allegation* (2) under ALLEGATION.

primary powers. (1864) The chief powers given by a principal to an agent to accomplish the agent's tasks. Cf. MEDIATE POWERS.

primary purpose or effect. (1988) *Copyright.* The main reason for or consequence of using a product, as a test for whether its sale amounts to contributory infringement. • The Supreme Court rejected the test in a landmark copyright case, but four justices said that if the primary purpose or effect of the product's sale or use infringes the copyrights of others, its manufacturer could be enjoined from selling the product or required to pay a reasonable royalty to the copyright owners. *Sony Corp. of Am. v. Universal City Studios, Inc.*, 464 U.S. 417, 457–500, 104 S.Ct. 774, 796–818 (1984) (Blackmun, J., dissenting). Cf. COMMERCIALLY SIGNIFICANT NONINFRINGING USE.

primary-purpose test. (2004) A standard for assessing whether an out-of-court statement is testimonial for purposes of the Confrontation Clause, the primary criterion being whether the police interrogated the suspect to help in an emergency (permissible) or to establish past facts for a potential prosecution in the future (impermissible). *See Davis v. Washington*, 547 U.S. 813, 126 S.Ct. 2266 (2006).

primary receiver. See *principal receiver* under RECEIVER (1).

primary reserve ratio. See RESERVE RATIO.

primary residential responsibility. See RESIDENTIAL RESPONSIBILITY.

primary right. See RIGHT.

primary term. (1915) *Oil & gas.* The option period — set by the habendum clause in an oil-and-gas lease — during which the lessee has the right to search, develop, and produce from the property. • The primary term should be long enough to allow the lessee to evaluate the property and make arrangements to drill. In practice, the primary term may extend for 24 hours or 25 years, depending on how much competition there is for leases in the area. See HABENDUM CLAUSE. Cf. SECONDARY TERM.

primate (**prɪ**-mit). (13c) A chief ecclesiastic; an archbishop or bishop having jurisdiction over other bishops within a province.

prime, *n.* See *prime rate* under INTEREST RATE.

prime, *vb.* To take priority over <Watson's preferred mortgage primed Moriarty's lien>.

prime contractor. See *general contractor* under CONTRACTOR.

prime cost. See COST (1).

prime lending rate. See *prime rate* under INTEREST RATE.

prime lien. See LIEN.

prime maker. See MAKER.

prime minister. (*often cap.*) (17c) The chief executive of a parliamentary government; the head of a cabinet. — Abbr. PM. — Also termed *premier.* See PREMIER; PREMIERSHIP.

primer (**prim**-ər *or* **prɪ**-mər). [Law French] (15c) First; primary <primer seisin>.

prime rate. See INTEREST RATE.

primer election. (18c) A first choice; esp., the eldest coparcener's pick of land on division of the estate. See ELECTION.

primer fine (**prim**-ər *or* **prɪ**-mər **fɪn**). [Latin] (17c) *Hist.* A fee payable to the Crown on the suing out of a writ of praecipe to begin a conveyance by fine. See FINE (1). — Also termed *praefine.*

primer seisin. 1. See SEISIN. **2.** FIRST FRUITS (1).

prime serjeant. See *premier serjeant* under SERJEANT-AT-LAW.

prime tenant. See TENANT (1).

primitiae (pri-**mish**-ee-ee). [fr. Latin *primus* "first"] See FIRST FRUITS (2). — **primitial** (pri-**mish**-əl), *adj.*

primitive obligation. See OBLIGATION.

primo fronte (**prɪ**-moh **fron**-tee). [Latin] *Hist.* At first sight.

primo prosequi, secundo dedere (**prɪ**-moh **prahs**-i-kwɪ si-**kən**-do **ded**-ə-ree). [Latin] *Hist.* First to prosecute, second to deliver.

primogeniture (prɪ-mə-**jen**-ə-chər). (15c) **1.** The quality, state, or condition of being the firstborn child among siblings. **2.** The common-law right of the firstborn son to inherit his ancestor's estate, usu. to the exclusion of younger siblings. — Also termed (in sense 2) *primogenitureship.* See BIRTHRIGHT; BOROUGH ENGLISH. **3.** An estate or possession so inherited. Cf. SECUNDOGENITURE.

> "If by primogeniture we only mean 'that the male issue shall be admitted before the female, and that, when there are two or more males in equal degrees, the eldest only shall inherit, but the females "all together"' [Blackstone's definition], then ancient records may indeed contain but scant references. But primogeniture embraces all the cases of single inheritance, and may indeed be defined as the prerogative enjoyed by an eldest son or occasionally an eldest daughter, through law or custom, to succeed to their ancestor's inheritance in preference to younger children. Nay, we might even make it more comprehensive, extending it to all cases of single succession depending upon priority in birth." Radhabinod Pal, *The History of the Law of Primogeniture* 11 (1929).

> "We might note here, parenthetically, that the English preference for single-file male descent — that is, the system of descent known as *primogeniture* — was never cordially received in this country. Our statutes of descent and distribution uniformly provide for sons' and daughters' sharing the inheritance equally. Although this seems a fairer method than primogeniture, which was finally abolished in Britain with the 1925 reforms, the descent of property to an ever-expanding group of heirs can seriously complicate the clearing of old titles." Thomas F. Bergin & Paul G. Haskell, *Preface to Estates in Land and Future Interests* 9 (2d ed. 1984).

primogenitureship. See PRIMOGENITURE (2).

primo loco (**prɪ**-moh **loh**-koh). [Latin] *Hist.* In the first place.

primo venienti (**prɪ**-moh ven-ee-**en**-tɪ). [Latin] (18c) To the one first coming. • This refers to the former practice by estate executors of paying debts as they were presented without regard to whether the estate had enough assets to pay all the debts.

primum decretum (**prɪ**-məm di-**kree**-təm). [Latin "first decree"] (17c) **1.** *Hist. Eccles. law.* A preliminary decree granted in favor of the plaintiff on the nonappearance of a defendant. **2.** *Maritime law.* A provisional decree.

prince consort. (18c) The husband of a ruling queen, if he is not king.

princeps (**prin**-seps), *n.* [Latin] (17c) *Roman law.* A leading person, esp. the emperor.

principal, *adj.* (13c) Chief; primary; most important.

principal, *n.* (14c) **1.** Someone who authorizes another to act on his or her behalf as an agent. Cf. AGENT.

▸ **apparent principal.** (1847) Someone who, by outward manifestations, has made it reasonably appear to a third person that another is authorized to act as the person's agent.

▸ **disclosed principal.** (1856) A principal of whose identity a third party has knowledge or notice at the time an agent interacts with the third party on behalf of the principal. • A disclosed principal is always liable on a contract entered into by the agent with the principal's authority, but the agent is usu. not liable.

▸ **partially disclosed principal.** (1934) A principal whose existence — but not actual identity — is revealed by the agent to a third party.

▸ **undisclosed principal.** (1835) A principal whose identity is kept secret by the agent; a principal for whom the other party has no notice that the agent is acting. • An undisclosed principal and the agent are both liable on a contract entered into by the agent with the principal's authority. This doctrine is unique to common-law agency and is not recognized by civil-law doctrine. Cf. *undisclosed agent* under AGENT.

> "In the cases of undisclosed principal, T. has dealt with A., believing A. to be the principal and intending to contract with A., the person before him. Later it is discovered that A. was really intending to act as agent of P. What are the liabilities and rights of P., A., and T. under these circumstances? Between the cases of disclosed and undisclosed principal there is an intermediate group of cases which may be called those of 'unnamed' principal. In these T. knows that A. represents some one, but does not know the identity of P. It can readily be seen that the rules applicable to this intermediate group of cases will differ from those applicable to either of the other groups. The conferring of rights and liabilities upon the 'undisclosed' or 'unnamed' principal is one of the unique features of the law of principal and agent. In a suit by P. against A., or by A. against P., there is no change of legal relation because P. was undisclosed or unnamed to T." Francis B. Tiffany, *Handbook of the Law of Principal and Agent* § 90, at 251–52 (Richard R.B. Powell ed., 2d ed. 1924).

▸ **unidentified principal.** (1926) A principal whose identity is unknown to a third party when the agent and the third party interact. • An agent for an unidentified principal who makes a contract on the principal's behalf is subject to liability on the contract, as is the principal. — Also termed *partially undisclosed principal*; *unnamed principal*.

> "The terms 'partially undisclosed principal' and 'unnamed principal' are synonyms for 'unidentified principal.' The terminology 'unidentified principal' is preferable. 'Partially disclosed' misleadingly suggests that some portion of the principal's identity is known to the third party. 'Unnamed principal' is too restrictive because a third party may know the principal's identity but not know the principal's name." Restatement (Third) of Agency § 1.04 cmt. b (2006).

2. Someone who commits or participates in a crime. — Also termed *criminal principal*. Cf. ACCESSORY (2); ACCOMPLICE (2).

> "The student should notice that in criminal law the word 'principal' suggests the very converse of the idea which it represents in mercantile law. In the former, as we have seen, an accessory proposes an act, and the 'principal' carries it out. But in the law of contract, and in that of tort, the 'principal' only authorizes an act, and the 'agent' carries it out. Where the same transaction is both a tort and a crime, this double use of the word may cause confusion. For example, if, by an innkeeper's directions, his chamber-maid steals jewels out of a guest's portmanteau, the maid is the 'principal' in a *crime*, wherein her master is an accessory before the fact; whilst she is also the agent in a *tort*, wherein her master is the 'principal.'" J.W. Cecil Turner, *Kenny's Outlines of Criminal Law* 89 (16th ed. 1952).

▸ **principal in the first degree.** (18c) The perpetrator of a crime. — Also termed *first-degree principal*.

> "By a principal in the first degree, we mean the actual offender — the man in whose guilty mind lay the latest blamable mental cause of the criminal act. Almost always, of course, he will be the man by whom this act itself was done. But occasionally this will not be so; for the felony may have been committed by the hand of an innocent agent who, having no blamable intentions in what he did, incurred no criminal liability by doing it. In such a case the man who instigates this agent is the real offender; his was the last *mens rea* that preceded the crime, though it did not cause it immediately but mediately." J.W. Cecil Turner, *Kenny's Outlines of Criminal Law* 85–86 (16th ed. 1952).

▸ **principal in the second degree.** (18c) Someone who helped the perpetrator at the time of the crime. — Also termed *accessory at the fact*; *second-degree principal*. See ABETTOR.

> "The distinction between principals in the first and second degrees is a distinction without a difference except in those rare instances in which some unusual statute has provided a different penalty for one of these than for the other. A principal in the first degree is the immediate perpetrator of the crime while a principal in the second degree is one who did not commit the crime with his own hands but was present and abetting the principal. It may be added, in the words of Mr. Justice Miller, that one may perpetrate a crime, not only with his own hands, but 'through the agency of mechanical or chemical means, as by instruments, poison or powder, or by an animal, child, or other innocent agent' acting under his direction." Rollin M. Perkins & Ronald N. Boyce, *Criminal Law* 736 (3d ed. 1982) (quoting *Beausoliel v. U.S.*, 107 F.2d 292, 297 (D.C. Cir. 1939)).

3. Someone who has primary responsibility on an obligation, as opposed to a surety or indorser. **4.** The corpus of an estate or trust. **5.** The amount of a debt, investment, or other fund, not including interest, earnings, or profits.

principal action. See *main demand* under DEMAND (1).

principal and agent. (17c) The relation between two persons, one of whom (the principal) hires the other (the agent), whose tasks involve primarily the creation of new legal relations between the hirer and third persons. • This relationship is similar to that of master and servant, but that terminology applies to employments in which the employee has little or no discretion, whereas the agent has considerable latitude. Cf. MASTER AND SERVANT.

> "The law of principal and agent is modern in origin, provides the background for the law of partnerships and corporations, is instructive as to the close interrelation of business and law, and presents a fertile field for constructive work." Francis B. Tiffany, *Handbook of the Law of Principal and Agent* § 3, at 5 (Richard R.B. Powell ed., 2d ed. 1924).

principal challenge. See CHALLENGE (2).

principal contract. See CONTRACT.

principal covenant. See COVENANT (1).

principal creditor. See CREDITOR.

principal demand. See *main demand* under DEMAND (1).

principal fact. 1. See *fact in issue* under FACT. **2.** See *ultimate fact* under FACT.

principal in the first degree. See PRINCIPAL (2).

principal in the second degree. See PRINCIPAL (2).

principalis (prin-sə-**pay**-lis), *adj.* [Latin] Principal, as in *principalis debitor* ("principal debtor").

principal motion. See *main motion* under MOTION (2).

principal obligation. See *primary obligation* (2) under OBLIGATION.

principal obligor. See OBLIGOR.

principal officer. See OFFICER (1).

principal place of business. See PLACE OF BUSINESS.

principal receiver. See RECEIVER.

Principal Register. *Trademarks.* The list of distinctive marks approved for federal trademark registration. • The register is maintained by the U.S. Patent and Trademark Office. Only marks that are strong, distinctive, and famous are listed. 15 USCA § 1052. Cf. SUPPLEMENTAL REGISTER.

principal right. See RIGHT.

principle, *n.* (14c) A basic rule, law, or doctrine; esp., one of the fundamental tenets of a system.

principled, *adj.* (17c) **1.** Having strong, unshakable opinions about what is morally right and wrong <he took a principled stand against recovery>. **2.** Based on clear, definite, logical, and consistent ideas <litigation doesn't yet impose punitive damages in a principled way>.

principle of finality. See FINALITY DOCTRINE.

principle of interpretation. See *canon of construction* under CANON (1).

principle of interrelating canons. The doctrine that no canon of interpretation is absolute and that each may be overcome by the strength of differing principles that point in other directions.

principle of legality. See LEGALITY (4).

principle of nonintervention. See NONINTERVENTION.

principle of partisanship. The doctrine that a lawyer acting as an advocate must, within the established bonds of legal ethics, maximize the changes that his or her client will have a favorable outcome. — Also termed *doctrine of zealous advocacy.*

principle of retribution. See LEX TALIONIS.

print. (13c) **1.** *Copyright.* The impression made in a material by a die, mold, stamp, or the like; a distinctive stamped or printed mark or design. **2.** FINGERPRINT.

printed-matter doctrine. (1950) *Patents.* The rule that printed matter may not be patented unless it is a physical part of a patentable invention. • For example, the doctrine has been used to deny patents for systems of representing sheet music and for methods of compiling directories. But it cannot be used to deny a patent for computer software.

Printers Ink Statute. A model statute drafted in 1911 and adopted in a number of states making it a misdemeanor to print an advertisement that contains a false or deceptive statement.

prior, *adj.* (17c) **1.** Preceding in time or order <under this court's prior order>. **2.** Taking precedence <a prior lien>.

prior, *n.* (1919) *Criminal law. Slang.* A previous conviction <because the defendant had two priors, the judge automatically enhanced his sentence>. See PRIOR CONVICTION.

prior-acts coverage. (1973) *Insurance.* A claims-made professional-liability policy indorsement that makes the effective date retroactive and extends the policy's protection to claims made and lawsuits filed during the policy period for negligent acts that occurred before the policy was actually purchased. — Also termed *nose coverage.* Cf. TAIL COVERAGE.

prior and persistent offender. See RECIDIVIST.

prior-appropriation doctrine. (1959) The rule that, among the persons whose properties border on a waterway, the earliest users of the water have the right to take all they can use before anyone else has a right to it. Cf. RIPARIAN-RIGHTS DOCTRINE.

prior art. See ART (3).

prior-claim rule. (1989) The principle that before suing for a tax refund or abatement, a taxpayer must first assert the claim to the Internal Revenue Service.

prior consistent statement. See STATEMENT.

prior-construction canon. The doctrine that if a statute uses words or phrases that have already received authoritative construction by the jurisdiction's court of last resort, or even uniform construction by inferior courts or a responsible administrative agency, they are to be understood according to that construction. — Also termed *previous-construction canon; rule in Ex parte Campbell;* (loosely) *reenactment canon.* Cf. BORROWED-STATUTE DOCTRINE.

> "Perhaps the best explanation for the prior-construction canon is this: The word or phrase at issue is a statutory term used in a particular field of law (to which the statute at issue belongs). When that term has been authoritatively interpreted by a high court, or has been given uniform interpretation by the lower courts or the responsible agency, the members of the bar practicing in that field reasonably enough assume that, in statutes pertaining to that field, the term bears this same meaning. The term has acquired, in other words, a technical legal sense . . . that should be given effect in the construction of later-enacted statutes. This footing is sounder than the fanciful presumption of legislative knowledge." Antonin Scalia & Bryan A. Garner, *Reading Law: The Interpretation of Legal Texts* 324 (2012).

prior conviction. A punishable offense already on a criminal defendant's record. — Often shortened (in slang) to *prior.* — Also termed *prior offense; prior crime; antecedent crime.*

prior creditor. See CREDITOR.

prior crime. See PRIOR CONVICTION.

prior-exclusive-jurisdiction doctrine. (1994) The rule that a court will not assume in rem jurisdiction over property that is already under the jurisdiction of another court of concurrent jurisdiction.

prior inconsistent statement. See STATEMENT.

priori petenti (prɪ-**or**-ɪ pə-**ten**-tɪ). [Latin "to the first person applying"] (1859) *Wills & estates.* The principle that when two or more persons are equally entitled to administer an estate, the court will appoint the person who applies first.

priority. (15c) **1.** The status of being earlier in time or higher in degree or rank; precedence. **2.** *Commercial law.* An established right to such precedence; esp., a creditor's right to have a claim paid before other creditors of the same debtor receive payment. **3.** The doctrine that, as between two courts, jurisdiction should be accorded the court in which proceedings are first begun. **4.** *Patents & Trademarks.* The status of being first to invent something (and therefore be potentially eligible for patent protection) or to use a mark in trade (and therefore be potentially eligible for trademark registration).

▸ **priority of adoption.** (1878) *Trademarks.* Priority in designing or creating a trademark. • Priority of adoption does not in itself confer the right to exclusive use of a mark if someone else was first to use it in commerce. — Also termed *priority of appropriation*; *priority of invention*. Cf. *priority of use*.

▸ **priority of appropriation.** *Trademarks.* See *priority of adoption.*

▸ **priority of invention.** (1817) **1.** *Patents.* The determination that one among several patent applications, for substantially the same invention, should receive the patent when the U.S. Patent and Trademark Office has declared interference. • This determination depends on the date of conception, the date of reduction to practice, and diligence. **2.** *Trademarks.* See *priority of adoption.*

▸ **priority of use.** (1880) *Trademarks.* Priority in using a mark in actual commerce. • The priority of use, not the priority of adoption, determines who has the right to protection. Cf. *priority of adoption.*

priority award. (1939) *Patents.* A final judgment by the U.S. Patent and Trademark Office designating one party in an interference contest as the first inventor. — Also termed *award in interference.*

priority claim. See CLAIM (5).

priority contest. See INTERFERENCE (3).

priority date. See DATE.

priority-jurisdiction rule. See FIRST-TO-FILE RULE.

priority lien. See *prior lien* under LIEN.

priority of liens. (1813) The ranking of liens in the order in which they are perfected.

prior laesit (**prɪ**-ər **lee**-sit). [Law Latin] (17c) *Scots law.* He (or she) first injured. • The phrase usu. referred to the provocation for an assault.

prior lien. See LIEN.

prior offense. See PRIOR CONVICTION.

prior petens (**prɪ**-ər **pet**-enz). [Latin] (1824) The person first applying.

prior preferred stock. See STOCK.

prior publication. (1851) *Patents.* Public disclosure of the basis for or existence of an invention, made before filing a patent application for the invention. • If the publication was made more than a year before the application is filed, the patent is barred by statute. Publication occurs when the information is made available to any member of the general public. See *limited publication* under PUBLICATION.

prior-relationship rape. See *relationship rape* under RAPE (2).

prior restraint. (1833) A governmental restriction on speech or publication before its actual expression. • Prior restraints violate the First Amendment unless the speech is obscene, is defamatory, or creates a clear and present danger to society. — Also termed *prior restraint of speech.*

> "The legal doctrine of prior restraint (or formal censorship before publication) is probably the oldest form of press control. Certainly it is one of the most efficient, since one censor, working in the watershed, can create a drought of information and ideas long before they reach the fertile plain of people's minds. In the United States, the doctrine of prior restraint has been firmly opposed by the First Amendment to the Constitution, and by the Supreme Court, perhaps most notably in the case of *Near v. Minnesota*, decided in 1931. But the philosophy behind that doctrine lives zestfully on, and shows no signs of infirmities of age." David G. Clark & Earl R. Hutchinson, *Mass Media and the Law* 11 (1970).

prior sale. *Patents.* Sale or offer of sale of an invention before a patent is applied for. • If the sale occurred more than one year before the application is filed, the patent is barred by statute. 35 USCA § 102(b).

prior sentence. See SENTENCE.

prior-use bar. See PUBLIC-USE BAR.

prior-use doctrine. (1856) The principle that, without legislative authorization, a government agency may not appropriate property already devoted to a public use.

prior-use easement. See EASEMENT.

prior-user right. (1969) *Patents.* The right of a first inventor to continue using an invention after someone else has patented it. • This right protects first inventors in most countries from the harsh effects of a first-to-file system. See PRIVATE-USE EXCEPTION.

prisage (**prɪ**-zij). (16c) *Hist.* A royal duty on wine imported into England. • Prisage was replaced by butlerage in the reign of Edward I. Cf. BUTLERAGE.

prisel en auter lieu (**prɪ**-zəl awn **oh**-tayl-yoo). [Law French "a taking in another place"] (1804) A plea in abatement in a replevin action.

prison. (bef. 12c) A building or complex where people are kept in long-term confinement as punishment for a crime, or in short-term detention while waiting to go to court as criminal defendants; specif., a state or federal facility of confinement for convicted criminals, esp. felons. — Also termed *penitentiary*; *penal institution*; *adult correctional institution.* Cf. JAIL.

▸ **close-security prison.** A prison or prison-unit in which inmates are usu. kept in one- to two-person cells, which they may occasionally leave for work assignments, correctional programs, or exercise.

▸ **federal prison.** (1838) A prison that is operated and managed by a national or federal government; esp., in the United States, one run by the Federal Bureau of Prisons for incarcerating those convicted of federal crimes.

▸ **maximum-security prison.** A prison or prison-unit in which inmates are tightly restricted and closely monitored at all times.

▸ **medium-security prison.** A prison or prison-unit in which groups of inmates stay in communal cells, often resembling dormitories with bunk beds and lockers.

▸ **minimum-security prison.** A prison or prison-unit in which inmates, who are only light supervised or monitored, have only slight restrictions on their movements and activities.

▸ **private prison.** (1865) A prison that is managed by a private company, not by a governmental agency.

▸ **state prison.** (17c) **1.** A prison that is operated and managed by state correctional authorities, usu. for incarcerating those convicted of more serious crimes such as felonies. **2.** In some countries, a prison run by a government usu. to confine those found guilty of political offenses. — Also termed *state's prison.* See *political prisoner* under PRISONER.

▸ **supermax prison.** A prison or prison-unit for heavily supervised single-cell confinement of inmates who are particularly violent or disruptive. • Supermax prisons can be stand-alone facilities or part of another facility and are designed to hold the most troublesome prisoners in solitary confinement, typically for a three-year or indefinite term. Inmates are usu. allowed only one hour to 90 minutes outside of their cell per day.

"A 'super-max' prison is designed and designated as a prison for the most difficult prisoners. . . . The 'super-max' candidate is a federal prisoner, often due to having committed multiple-jurisdiction crimes causing him (it is nearly always a male who achieves this notoriety) to become a fugitive under federal law. Also, the dim-witted inmates who commit heinous crimes often are more or less model prisoners and make little trouble. The super-max candidate is an inmate who is extremely dangerous to staff and to other inmates, who is a known troublemaker, who has had escapes or escape attempts, and who would be highly dangerous to the public if he did escape. Such prisoners are described by the BOP as 'extremely violent, predatory, disruptive and/or escape prone.' A few such prisoners are sent immediately to super-max prisons on conviction of a federal crime, but most serve time in more ordinary prisons and are then transferred to a super-max." Vergil L. Williams, *Dictionary of American Penology* 215 (rev. ed. 1996).

prison breach. (17c) A prisoner's forcible breaking and departure from a place of lawful confinement; the offense of escaping from confinement in a prison or jail. • *Prison breach* has traditionally been distinguished from *escape* by the presence of force, but some jurisdictions have abandoned this distinction. — Also termed *prison break*; *prisoner escape*; *prison breaking*; *breach of prison*. Cf. ESCAPE (2); *escape from custody* under ESCAPE (2).

"Breach of prison by the offender himself, when committed for *any* cause, was felony at the common law: or even conspiring to break it. But this severity is mitigated by the statute *de frangentibus prisonam*, I Edw. II, which enacts that no person shall have judgment of life or member, for breaking prison, unless committed for some capital offence. So that to break prison, when lawfully committed for any treason or felony, remains still a felony as at the common law; and to break prison, when lawfully confined upon any other inferior charge, is still punishable as a high misdemeanor by fine and imprisonment." 4 William Blackstone, *Commentaries on the Laws of England* 130–31 (1769).

prison camp. (1864) **1.** A guarded place where prisoners, esp. prisoners of war or political prisoners, are kept. **2.** A usu. minimum-security camp for the detention of trustworthy prisoners who are often employed on government projects. Cf. BOOT CAMP (2). **3.** A special facility where prisoners of war are kept.

prisoner. (14c) **1.** Someone who is being confined in prison. **2.** Someone who has been apprehended by a law-enforcement officer and is in custody, regardless of whether the person has yet been put in prison; specif., a person who is kept in prison as legal punishment or who is kept there while awaiting trial as a criminal defendant. **3.** Someone who is taken by force and kept somewhere.

"While breach of prison, or prison breach, means breaking out of or away from prison, it is important to have clearly in mind the meaning of the word 'prison.' If an officer arrests an offender and takes him to jail the layman does not think of the offender as being 'in prison' until he is safely behind locked doors, but no one hesitates to speak of him as a 'prisoner' from the moment of apprehension. He is a prisoner because he is 'in prison . . . whether he were actually in the walls of a prison, or only in the stocks, or in the custody of any person who had lawfully arrested him . . . .'" Rollin M. Perkins & Ronald N. Boyce, *Criminal Law* 566 (3d ed. 1982) (quoting 2 Hawk. P.C. ch. 18, § 1 (6th ed. 1788)).

▸ **federal prisoner.** (1832) A prisoner confined in a federal prison.

▸ **political prisoner.** (1828) A prisoner incarcerated for engaging in political activity against his or her government. — Also termed *state prisoner*. See PRISONER OF CONSCIENCE.

▸ **state prisoner.** (17c) **1.** A prisoner confined in a state prison. **2.** See *political prisoner*.

4. A person who has been captured by an enemy and is being kept somewhere. Cf. CAPTIVE (1); DETAINEE; PRISONER OF WAR.

prisoner at the bar. (16c) *Archaic*. An accused person who is on trial.

prisoner escape. 1. See ESCAPE. **2.** See PRISON BREACH.

prisoner of conscience. (1961) *Human-rights law*. Someone who is imprisoned because of his or her beliefs, race, sex, ethnic origin, language, or religion. • The range of "beliefs" that fall within this definition is not settled but may include political ideologies and objections to military service, esp. in wartime. See *political prisoner* under PRISONER.

prisoner of war. (17c) A person, usu. a soldier, who is captured by or surrenders to the enemy in wartime. — Also termed *captive*. — Abbr. POW.

prisoner's dilemma. (1957) A logic problem — often used by law-and-economics scholars to illustrate the effect of cooperative behavior — involving two prisoners who are being separately questioned about their participation in a crime, so that something like the following situation arises (1) if both confess, they will each receive a 5-year sentence; (2) if neither confesses, they will each receive a 3-year sentence; and (3) if one confesses but the other does not, the confessing prisoner will receive a 1-year sentence while the silent prisoner will receive a 10-year sentence. • Each prisoner, reasoning only for himself, will thus find it in his interest to confess, though this causes both of them to receive longer sentences than they would have received if neither had talked. The problem is said to illustrate how rational decisions by each member of a group can make the group as a whole worse off. See EXTERNALITY.

"In a merger vote, stockholders can vote no and still receive the transactional consideration if the merger prevails. In a tender offer, however, a non-tendering shareholder individually faces an uncertain fate. That stockholder could be one of the few who hold out, leaving herself in an even more thinly traded stock with little hope of liquidity. . . . For these reasons, some view tender offers as creating a prisoner's dilemma — distorting choice and creating incentives for stockholders to tender into offers that they believe are inadequate in order to avoid a worse fate." *In re Pure Res., Inc. S'holders Litig.*, 808 A.2d 421 (Del. Ch. 2002).

prison-gate arrest. See ARREST (2).

Prison Litigation Reform Act. A federal statute designed to reduce the number of frivolous lawsuits and petitions filed by prisoners and to reduce the power of federal courts over state prison systems. 110 Stat. 1321-66–1321-77 (1996). — Abbr. PLRA.

prison-mailbox rule. (1989) The doctrine that for purposes of computing a legal deadline, a prisoner's court filing is considered filed when it is deposited in the prison's internal mail system.

prison visitor. (1837) Someone who visits a prisoner, usu. to provide advice or solace.

prist (prist). [Law French] *Hist.* Ready. • In oral pleading, this term was used to express a joinder of issue.

privacy. (16c) The quality, state, or condition of being free from public attention to intrusion into or interference with one's acts or decisions.

▸ **autonomy privacy.** (1974) An individual's right to control his or her personal activities or intimate personal decisions without outside interference, observation, or intrusion. • If the individual's interest in an activity or decision is fundamental, the state must show a compelling public interest before the private interest can be overcome. If the individual's interest is acknowledged to be less than fundamental or is disputed, then a court must apply a balancing test. *Hill v. NCAA*, 865 P.2d 633, 653, 654 (Cal. 1994).

▸ **informational privacy.** (1968) *Tort.* A private person's right to choose to determine whether, how, and to what extent information about oneself is communicated to others, esp. sensitive and confidential information.

▸ **personal privacy.** (1894) A person's interest in nondisclosure or selective disclosure of confidential or private information or matters relating to his or her person. *See U.S. Dep't of Justice v. Reporters Comm. for Freedom of the Press*, 489 U.S. 749, 762–63, 109 S.Ct. 1468, 1476–77 (1989).

privacy, invasion of. See INVASION OF PRIVACY.

privacy, right of. See RIGHT OF PRIVACY.

privacy act. See PRIVACY LAW (1).

Privacy Act of 1974. An act that regulates the government's creation, collection, use, and dissemination of records that can identify an individual by name, as well as other personal information. 18 USCA § 552a.

privacy law. (1936) **1.** A federal or state statute that protects a person's right to be left alone or that restricts public access to personal information such as tax returns and medical records. — Also termed *privacy act.* **2.** The area of legal studies dealing with a person's right to be left alone and with restricting public access to personal information such as tax returns and medical records.

privacy privilege. See PRIVILEGE (3).

privata delicta (prɪ-**vay**-tə di-**lik**-tə). [Latin] (16c) *Roman law.* Private wrongs; torts. See DELICT. Cf. PUBLICA DELICTA.

privatae leges (prɪ-**vay**-tee **lee**-jeez). [Law Latin] *Scots law.* Personal laws. • These were laws, such as a pardon, that affected a single individual, not a class of people.

private, *adj.* (14c) **1.** Of, relating to, or involving an individual, as opposed to the public or the government. **2.** (Of a company) not having shares that are freely available on an open market. **3.** Confidential; secret.

private act. See *special statute* under STATUTE.

private action. See *civil action* under ACTION (4).

private adoption. See ADOPTION (1).

private agent. See AGENT.

private annuity. See ANNUITY.

private attorney. See ATTORNEY (1).

private-attorney-general doctrine. (1966) The equitable principle that allows the recovery of attorney's fees to a party who brings a lawsuit that benefits a significant number of people, requires private enforcement, and is important to society as a whole.

private bank. See BANK.

private benefit. *Tax.* The use of a tax-exempt organization's assets primarily to further the interests of a private individual or entity, rather than for a public interest. • Under most circumstances, this type of benefit is prohibited. *See* IRC (26 USCA) § 501(c)(3). Cf. *private inurement* under INUREMENT.

▸ **qualitatively incidental private benefit.** (2009) A permissible private benefit arising from circumstances under which a benefit to the public cannot be achieved without necessarily also benefiting a private interest.

▸ **quantitatively incidental private benefit.** (2009) A permissible private benefit that is a necessary but insubstantial concomitant to a public benefit.

private bill. See BILL (3).

private boundary. See BOUNDARY (1).

private brand. See BRAND.

private carrier. See CARRIER (1).

private contract. See CONTRACT.

private corporation. See CORPORATION.

private delict. See DELICT (1).

private detective. See PRIVATE INVESTIGATOR.

private easement. See EASEMENT.

private enterprise. (18c) An economic system in which private businesses compete freely with one another in an environment of minimal government regulation.

private equity. See EQUITY (8).

privateer (prɪ-və-**teer**), *n.* (17c) **1.** A vessel owned and operated by private persons, but authorized by a country on certain conditions to damage the commerce of the enemy by acts of piracy. **2.** A sailor on such a vessel.

privateering, *n.* (17c) *Int'l law.* The practice of arming privately owned merchant ships for the purpose of attacking enemy trading ships. • Before the practice was outlawed, governments commissioned privateers by issuing letters of marque to their merchant fleets. Privateering was prohibited by the Declaration of Paris Concerning Naval Warfare of 1856, which has been observed by nearly all countries since that time. — **privateer,** *vb.*

private fact. See FACT.

private foundation. See FOUNDATION.

private fund. See FUND.

private grant. See GRANT (4).

private-hands exception. (1988) *Postal law.* An exception under the Private Express Statute permitting the sending or carrying of letters or packages over postal routes as long as the private carrier earns no compensation. *See* 18 § USCA 1696(c); *see also University of Cal. v. Public Emp't Relations Bd.*, 485 U.S. 589, 594–95, 108 S.Ct. 1404, 1409 (1988).

private income. See INCOME.

private injury. See *personal injury* (2) under INJURY.

private international law. See INTERNATIONAL LAW.

private inurement. See INUREMENT (1).

private investigator. (1908) Someone whose job is to find information, esp. on missing people and similar problems, by gathering intelligence through surveillance and research, and reporting on relevant findings. — Abbr. P.I. — Also termed *private detective.*

private judging. (1979) A type of alternative dispute resolution whereby the parties hire a private individual to hear and decide a case. • This process may occur as a matter of contract between the parties or in connection with a statute authorizing such a process. — Also termed *rent-a-judging.*

> "In contrast [to arbitration], private judging is a less contractual, less privatized process. Party agreement, usually formed post-dispute, does send a case to private judging. And the parties have the freedom of contract to determine the time and place of trial, as well as the identity of the judge. Unlike arbitration, however, privately judged trials may . . . be: (1) required to use the same rules of procedure and evidence used in ordinary litigation, (2) exposed to public view by court order, (3) adjudicated only by a former judge, and (4) subject to appeal in the same manner as other trial verdicts. In sum, private judging is essentially an ordinary bench trial except that the parties select, and pay for, the judge." Stephen J. Ware, *Alternative Dispute Resolution* § 2.54, at 113 (2001).

private land grant. See LAND GRANT.

private law. (18c) **1.** The body of law dealing with private persons and their property and relationships. Cf. PUBLIC LAW (1). **2.** See *special law* under LAW.

private letter ruling. See LETTER RULING.

private limited company. See COMPANY.

privately owned U.S. flag commercial vessel. See VESSEL.

private member's bill. See BILL (3).

private morality. See MORALITY (2).

private mortgage insurance. See *mortgage insurance* under INSURANCE.

private necessity. See NECESSITY (5).

private nonoperating foundation. See *private foundation* under FOUNDATION.

private nuisance. See NUISANCE.

private offering. See OFFERING.

private operating foundation. See FOUNDATION.

private-party rule. The doctrine that the exclusionary rule does not apply to searches and other conduct by persons not acting on behalf or at the direction of the government, esp. the police, as when a stepson searches his stepfather's personal effects to discover syringes and lethal doses of insulin after his mother has lapsed into a diabetic coma.

private person. See PERSON (1).

private placement. (1943) **1.** See *private adoption* under ADOPTION (1). **2.** *Securities.* See *private offering* under OFFERING.

private-placement adoption. See *private adoption* under ADOPTION (1).

private power. See POWER (3).

private prison. See PRISON.

private property. See PROPERTY.

private prosecution. See PROSECUTION (2).

private prosecutor. See PROSECUTOR (2).

private publication. See *limited publication* under PUBLICATION (2).

private reprimand. See REPRIMAND.

private right. See RIGHT.

private right of action. See RIGHT OF ACTION.

private right-of-way. See EASEMENT.

private river. See RIVER.

private sale. See SALE.

private school. See SCHOOL (1).

private seal. See SEAL.

private search. See SEARCH (1).

private secretary. See SECRETARY (3).

private sector. (1930) The part of the economy or an industry that is free from direct governmental control. Cf. PUBLIC SECTOR.

private servitude. See SERVITUDE (3).

private signature. See SIGNATURE.

private statute. See *special statute* under STATUTE.

private stream. See STREAM.

private treaty. See TREATY (3).

private trust. See TRUST (3).

private-use exception. (1964) *Patents.* An exception to the public-use statutory bar, allowing the inventor to use the invention for personal benefit for more than one year without abandoning patent rights under the statutory bars. — Also termed *prior-user right.*

private voluntary organization. See NONGOVERNMENTAL ORGANIZATION.

private war. See WAR (1).

private water. See WATER.

private way. See WAY.

private wharf. See WHARF.

private wrong. See WRONG.

private zoning. See ZONING.

privation (prɪ-vay-shən). (15c) **1.** The act of taking away or withdrawing. **2.** The condition of being deprived.

privatization (prɪ-və-tə-zay-shən), *n.* (1942) The act or process of converting a business or industry from governmental ownership or control to private enterprise. Cf. DENATIONALIZATION (2). — **privatize,** *vb.*

privatum (prɪ-vay-təm). [Latin] (18c) Private. • This term appeared in phrases such as *jus privatum* ("private law").

privies (**priv**-eez). See PRIVY.

privigna (prɪ-vig-nə), *n.* [Latin] *Roman & civil law.* A daughter of one's husband or wife by a previous marriage; a stepdaughter.

privignus (prɪ-vig-nəs). [Latin] *Roman & civil law.* A son of one's husband or wife by a previous marriage; a stepson.

privilege. (bef. 12c) **1.** A special legal right, exemption, or immunity granted to a person or class of persons; an exception to a duty. • A privilege grants someone the legal freedom to do or not to do a given act. It immunizes conduct that, under ordinary circumstances, would subject the actor to liability.

▸ **absolute privilege.** (18c) A privilege that immunizes an actor from suit, no matter how wrongful the action might be, and even though it is done with an improper motive. Cf. *qualified privilege.*

▸ **audit privilege.** See AUDIT PRIVILEGE.

▸ **conditional privilege.** See *qualified privilege.*

▸ **consular privilege.** See *consular immunity* under IMMUNITY (1).

▸ **courtroom privilege.** See *judicial privilege.*

▸ **defamation privilege.** See *litigation privilege.*

▸ **deliberative-process privilege.** (1977) **1.** The principle that a decision-maker's thoughts and how they led to a decision are not subject to revelation or scrutiny. • An exception to the rule may be allowed if a party can clearly show that the decision resulted from bias, bad faith, misconduct, or illegal or unlawful action. The privilege is meant to encourage open and independent discussion among those who develop government policy. *See U.S. v. Morgan*, 313 U.S. 409, 61 S.Ct. 999 (1941). — Also termed *mental-process privilege.* **2.** A privilege permitting the government to withhold documents relating to policy formulation to encourage open and independent discussion among those who develop government policy.

▸ **diplomatic privilege.** See DIPLOMATIC IMMUNITY.

▸ **fair-report privilege.** See FAIR-REPORT PRIVILEGE.

▸ **judicial privilege.** (1845) *Defamation.* **1.** The privilege protecting any statement made in the course of and with reference to a judicial proceeding by any judge, juror, party, witness, or advocate. **2.** See *litigation privilege.* — Also termed *courtroom privilege.*

▸ **judicial-proceedings privilege.** See *litigation privilege.*

▸ **legislative privilege.** (1941) *Defamation.* The privilege protecting (1) any statement made in a legislature by one of its members, and (2) any paper published as part of legislative business. — Also termed (in a parliamentary system) *parliamentary privilege.*

▸ **litigation privilege.** (1965) A privilege protecting the attorneys and parties in a lawsuit against tort claims based on certain acts done and statements made when related to the litigation. • The privilege is most often applied to defamation claims but may be extended to encompass other torts, such as invasion of privacy and disclosure of trade secrets. The facts of each case determine whether the privilege applies and whether it is qualified or absolute. — Also termed *judicial-proceedings privilege; judicial privilege; defamation privilege.*

▸ **mental-process privilege.** See *deliberative-process privilege* (1).

▸ **official privilege.** (1927) The privilege immunizing from a defamation lawsuit any statement made by one state officer to another in the course of official duty.

▸ **parliamentary privilege.** (17c) **1.** See *legislative privilege.* **2.** PRIVILEGE (5).

▸ **privilege from arrest.** (1840) An exemption from arrest, as that enjoyed by members of Congress during legislative sessions. U.S. Const. art. I, § 6, cl. 1.

▸ **qualified privilege.** (1865) A privilege that immunizes an actor from suit only when the privilege is properly exercised in the performance of a legal or moral duty. — Also termed *conditional privilege.* Cf. *absolute privilege.*

> "Qualified privilege . . . is an intermediate case between total absence of privilege and the presence of absolute privilege." R.F.V. Heuston, *Salmond on the Law of Torts* 165 (17th ed. 1977).

▸ **special privilege.** (17c) **1.** A privilege granted to a person or class of persons to the exclusion of others and in derogation of the common right. **2.** See *personal privilege* under PRIVILEGE (5).

▸ **testimonial privilege.** (1907) A right not to testify based on a claim of privilege; a privilege that overrides a witness's duty to disclose matters within the witness's knowledge, whether at trial or by deposition.

▸ **viatorial privilege** (vɪ-ə-**tor**-ee-əl). (1904) A privilege that overrides a person's duty to attend court in person and to testify.

▸ **work-product privilege.** See WORK-PRODUCT RULE.

2. An affirmative defense by which a defendant acknowledges at least part of the conduct complained of but asserts that the law authorized or sanctioned the defendant's conduct; esp., in tort law, a circumstance justifying or excusing an intentional tort. See JUSTIFICATION (2). Cf. IMMUNITY (2). **3.** An evidentiary rule that gives a witness the option to not disclose the fact asked for, even though it might be relevant; the right to prevent disclosure of certain information in court, esp. when the information was originally communicated in a professional or confidential relationship. • Assertion of an evidentiary privilege can be overcome by proof that an otherwise privileged communication was made in the presence of a third party to whom the privilege would not apply.

> "It remains to set forth specifically the meaning of 'privilege.' The term, as it will here be used, imports a defence from liability to an action. It is to be taken in a broad sense, broader than that in which it is commonly used. It is used as a convenient designation of all that class of defences whereby one has immunity or exemption from liability for conduct which but for the immunity would be tortious. In the broad sense privilege may be said to be a limited permission to inflict (otherwise wrongful) harm upon another, and will therefore include permission to do things not in point of fact harmful, such as violating a bare legal right." Melville M. Bigelow, *Elements of the Law of Torts* § 3, at 20 (6th ed. 1896).

▸ **accountant–client privilege.** (1956) The protection afforded to a client from an accountant's unauthorized disclosure of materials submitted to or prepared by the accountant. • The privilege is not widely recognized.

▸ **antimarital-facts privilege.** See *marital privilege* (2).

▸ **attorney–client privilege.** (1934) The client's right to refuse to disclose and to prevent any other person from disclosing confidential communications between the client and the attorney. — Also termed *lawyer–client privilege; client's privilege.*

> "There are a number of ways to organize the essential elements of the attorney-client privilege to provide for an orderly analysis. One of the most popular is Wigmore's schema: '(1) Where legal advice of any kind is sought (2) from a professional legal adviser in his capacity as such, (3) the communications relating to that purpose (4) made in confidence (5) by the client (6) are at his instance permanently protected (7) from disclosure by himself or by the legal adviser, (8) except the privilege be waived.' Though

this organization has its virtues, there is some question as to whether it completely states the modern privilege." 24 Charles Alan Wright & Kenneth W. Graham Jr., *Federal Practice and Procedure* § 5473, at 103–04 (1986) (quoting 8 John Henry Wigmore, *Evidence* § 2292, at 554 (John T. McNaughton rev., 1961)).

"At the present time it seems most realistic to portray the attorney–client privilege as supported in part by its traditional utilitarian justification, and in part by the integral role it is perceived to play in the adversary system itself. Our system of litigation casts the lawyer in the role of fighter for the party whom he represents. A strong tradition of loyalty attaches to the relationship of attorney and client, and this tradition would be outraged by routine examination of the lawyer as to the client's confidential disclosures regarding professional business. To the extent that the evidentiary privilege, then, is integrally related to an entire code of professional conduct, it is futile to envision drastic curtailment of the privilege without substantial modification of the underlying ethical system to which the privilege is merely ancillary." John W. Strong, *McCormick on Evidence* § 87, at 121–22 (4th ed. 1992).

▸ **bank-examination privilege.** (1990) The qualified privilege that protects a bank examiner's report from disclosure to preserve the confidentiality of internal decisions and protects the open communications between bank management and bank examiners. • This privilege — which applies to different agencies that oversee banks, such as the Federal Reserve and the Office of the Comptroller of the Currency — is based on the same grounds as the deliberative-process privilege. — Also termed *bank-examiner privilege*; *bank examiners' privilege.* Cf. *deliberative-process privilege.*

▸ **clergyman–penitent privilege.** See *priest–penitent privilege.*

▸ **client's privilege.** See *attorney–client privilege.*

▸ **doctor–patient privilege.** (1954) A patient's right to exclude from discovery and evidence in a legal proceeding any confidential communication between the patient and a physician for the purpose of diagnosis or treatment, unless the patient consents to the disclosure. — Also termed *patient–physician privilege*; *physician–patient privilege*; *physician–client privilege.*

▸ **editorial privilege.** See *journalist's privilege* (2).

▸ **evidentiary privilege.** (1929) A privilege that allows a specified person to refuse to provide evidence or to protect the evidence from being used or disclosed in a proceeding. • Examples include the privilege against self-incrimination and the attorney–client privilege.

▸ **executive privilege.** (1909) A privilege, based on the constitutional doctrine of separation of powers, that exempts the executive branch of the federal government from usual disclosure requirements when the matter to be disclosed involves national security or foreign policy; specif., the right of a president or other head of state to keep official records and papers secret. Cf. *executive immunity* under IMMUNITY (1).

▸ **hardship privilege.** See HARDSHIP PRIVILEGE.

▸ **husband–wife privilege.** See *marital privilege.*

▸ **informant's privilege.** (1962) The qualified privilege that a government can invoke to prevent disclosure of the identity and communications of its informants. • In exercising its power to formulate evidentiary rules for federal criminal cases, the U.S. Supreme Court has consistently declined to hold that the government must disclose the identity of informants in a preliminary hearing or in a criminal trial. *McCray v. Illinois*, 386 U.S. 300, 312, 87 S.Ct. 1056, 1063 (1967). A party can, however, usu. overcome the privilege by demonstrating that the need for the information outweighs the public interest in maintaining the privilege. — Also termed *informer's privilege.*

▸ **joint-defense privilege.** (1975) The rule that a defendant can assert the attorney–client privilege to protect a confidential communication made to a codefendant's lawyer if the communication was related to the defense of both defendants. — Also termed *common-interest doctrine*; *common-interest privilege*; *common-interest exception*; *pooled-information privilege.*

▸ **journalist's privilege.** (1970) **1.** A reporter's protection, under constitutional or statutory law, from being compelled to testify about confidential information or sources. — Also termed *reporter's privilege*; *newsman's privilege.* See SHIELD LAW (1). **2.** A publisher's protection against defamation lawsuits when the publication makes fair comment on the actions of public officials in matters of public concern. — Also termed *editorial privilege*; *common-interest privilege*; *common-interest exception.* See FAIR COMMENT. Cf. BURNING THE SOURCE.

▸ **lawyer–client privilege.** See *attorney–client privilege.*

▸ **manager's privilege.** An affirmative defense recognized in some states whereby a manager or agent who acts without malice to persuade the employer or principal to breach a contract when the manager or agent reasonably believes performance would be against the employer or principal's best interests.

▸ **marital privilege.** (1902) **1.** The privilege allowing a spouse not to testify, and to prevent another person from testifying, about confidential communications between the spouses during the marriage. — Also termed *marital-communications privilege.* **2.** The privilege allowing a spouse not to testify in a criminal case as an adverse witness against the other spouse, regardless of the subject matter of the testimony. — Also termed (in sense 2) *privilege against adverse spousal testimony*; *antimarital-facts privilege.* **3.** The privilege immunizing from a defamation lawsuit any statement made between husband and wife. — Also termed (in all senses) *spousal privilege*; *husband–wife privilege.*

▸ **medical privilege.** (1921) An exemption against the disclosure of medical records and other patient information in court.

▸ **national-security privilege.** See *state-secrets privilege.*

▸ **newsman's privilege.** See *journalist's privilege* (1).

▸ **patient–physician privilege.** See *doctor–patient privilege.*

▸ **peer-review privilege.** (1979) A privilege that protects from disclosure the proceedings and reports of a medical facility's peer-review committee, which reviews and oversees the patient care and medical services provided by the staff.

▸ **physician–client privilege.** See *doctor–patient privilege.*

▸ **political-vote privilege.** (1969) A privilege to protect from compulsory disclosure a vote cast in an election by secret ballot.

▸ **priest–penitent privilege.** (1958) The privilege barring a clergy member from testifying about a confessor's communications. — Also termed *clerical privilege*; *minister's privilege*; *clergyman–penitent privilege.*

▸ **privacy privilege.** (1967) A defendant's right not to disclose private information unless the plaintiff can show that (1) the information is directly relevant to the case, and (2) the plaintiff's need for the information outweighs the defendant's need for nondisclosure. • This privilege is recognized in California but in few other jurisdictions.

▸ **privilege against adverse spousal testimony.** See *marital privilege* (2).

▸ **privilege against self-incrimination.** (1891) *Criminal law.* **1.** RIGHT AGAINST SELF-INCRIMINATION. **2.** A criminal defendant's right not to be asked any questions by the judge or prosecution unless the defendant chooses to testify. — Also termed *right not to be questioned.*

> "According to the rule, neither the judge nor the prosecution is entitled at any stage to question the accused unless he chooses to give evidence. . . . This rule may be called the accused's right not to be questioned; in America it is termed the privilege against self-incrimination. The latter expression is more apt as the name for another rule, the privilege of any witness to refuse to answer an incriminating question; this is different from the rule under discussion, which, applying only to persons accused of crime, prevents the question from being asked. The person charged with crime has not merely the liberty to refuse to answer a question incriminating himself; he is freed even from the embarrassment of being asked the question." Glanville Williams, *The Proof of Guilt* 37–38 (3d ed. 1963).

▸ **psychotherapist–patient privilege.** (1968) A privilege that a person can invoke to prevent the disclosure of a confidential communication made in the course of diagnosis or treatment of a mental or emotional condition by or at the direction of a psychotherapist. • The privilege can be overcome under certain conditions, as when the examination is ordered by a court. — Also termed *psychotherapist–client privilege.*

▸ **reporter's privilege.** See *journalist's privilege* (1).

▸ **self-critical-analysis privilege.** (1982) A privilege protecting individuals and entities from divulging the results of candid assessments of their compliance with laws and regulations, to the extent that the assessments are internal, the results were intended from the outset to be confidential, and the information is of a type that would be curtailed if it were forced to be disclosed. • This privilege is founded on the public policy that it is beneficial to permit individuals and entities to confidentially evaluate their compliance with the law, so that they will monitor and improve their compliance with it. — Also termed *self-policing privilege*; *self-evaluation privilege.*

▸ **spousal privilege.** See *marital privilege.*

▸ **state-secrets privilege.** (1959) A privilege that the government may invoke against the discovery of a material that, if divulged, could compromise national security. — Also termed *national-security privilege.*

▸ **tax-return privilege.** (1980) A privilege to refuse to divulge the contents of a tax return or certain related documents. • The privilege is founded on the public policy of encouraging honest tax returns.

4. *Civil law.* A creditor's right, arising from the nature of the debt, to priority over the debtor's other creditors.

5. *Parliamentary law.* The status of a motion as outranking other business because of its relationship to the meeting's or a member's rights. — Also termed *parliamentary privilege.* See *question of privilege* under QUESTION (3).

▸ **general privilege.** A privilege that concerns the deliberative assembly as a body, rather than any particular member or members. — Also termed *privilege of the assembly*; *privilege of the house.* Cf. *personal privilege.*

▸ **parliamentary privilege.** (17c) **1.** A privilege under parliamentary law. **2.** See *legislative privilege* under PRIVILEGE (1).

▸ **personal privilege.** A privilege that concerns an individual member or members (e.g., a member's reputation or physical ability to hear the proceedings) rather than the deliberative assembly generally. — Also termed *special privilege.* See *procedural point* under POINT. Cf. *general privilege.*

▸ **privilege of the assembly.** See *general privilege.*

▸ **privilege of the floor.** (1854) *Parliamentary law.* (*usu. pl.*) The right of entering, passing through, and sitting on the floor during a meeting. See FLOOR (1).

> "The expression 'privileges of the floor,' sometimes used in legislative bodies or conventions, has nothing to do with *having the floor*, but means merely that a person is permitted to enter the portion of the hall floor otherwise restricted to members and necessary staff. It carries no right to speak or any other right of membership, except as may be determined by rules or action of the body." Henry M. Robert III et al., *Robert's Rules of Order Newly Revised* § 3, at 29 n. (11th ed. 2011).

▸ **privilege of the house.** See *general privilege.*

▸ **special privilege.** See *personal privilege.*

privileged, *adj.* (15c) **1.** Not subject to the usual rules or liabilities; esp., not subject to disclosure during the course of a lawsuit <a privileged document>. **2.** Enjoying or subject to a privilege. See *privileged motion* under MOTION (2).

privileged communication. See COMMUNICATION.

privileged copyhold. See COPYHOLD.

privileged debt. See DEBT.

privileged evidence. See EVIDENCE.

privileged motion. See MOTION (2).

privileged question. See QUESTION (3).

privileged subscription. See *rights offering* under OFFERING.

privileged villeinage. See VILLEINAGE.

privilege from arrest. See PRIVILEGE (1).

privilege of palace. (1895) The exemption of a dwelling that is used as a royal residence from the execution of legal process within its precincts. • The monarch does not have to be in residence at the time but must intend to retain the power to take up personal residence in the dwelling at will. Not all palaces are royal residences; England's Westminster Palace, for example, is occupied by the Parliament of the United Kingdom, not the Queen, who relinquished all control of the palace in 1965.

Privileges and Immunities Clause. (1911) *Constitutional law.* The constitutional provision (U.S. Const. art. IV, § 2, cl. 1) prohibiting a state from favoring its own citizens by discriminating against other states' citizens who come within its borders.

Privileges or Immunities Clause. (1918) *Constitutional law.* The constitutional provision (U.S. Const. amend. XIV, § 1) prohibiting state laws that abridge the privileges or immunities of U.S. citizens. • The clause was effectively nullified by the Supreme Court in the *Slaughter-House Cases*, 83 U.S. (16 Wall.) 36 (1873). Cf. DUE PROCESS CLAUSE; EQUAL PROTECTION CLAUSE.

privilege tax. See TAX.

privilegium (priv-ə-**lee**-jee-əm), *n.* [Latin] **1.** *Roman law.* A law passed against or in favor of a specific individual. **2.** *Roman law.* A special right, esp. one giving priority to a creditor. **3.** *Civil law.* Every right or favor that is granted by the law but is contrary to the usual rule.

privilegium clericale (priv-ə-**lee**-jee-əm kler-ə-**kay**-lee). [Law Latin] See BENEFIT OF CLERGY.

privity (**priv**-ə-tee). (16c) **1.** The connection or relationship between two parties, each having a legally recognized interest in the same subject matter (such as a transaction, proceeding, or piece of property); mutuality of interest <privity of contract>.

▸ **horizontal privity.** (1968) *Commercial law.* The legal relationship between a party and a nonparty who is related to the party (such as a buyer and a member of the buyer's family).

▸ **privity of blood.** (16c) **1.** Privity between an heir and an ancestor. **2.** Privity between coparceners.

▸ **privity of contract.** (17c) The relationship between the parties to a contract, allowing them to sue each other but preventing a third party from doing so. • The requirement of privity has been relaxed under modern laws and doctrines of implied warranty and strict liability, which allow a third-party beneficiary or other foreseeable user to sue the seller of a defective product.

> "To many students and practitioners of the common law *privity of contract* became a fetish. As such, it operated to deprive many a claimant of a remedy in cases where according to the *mores* of the time the claim was just. It has made many learned men believe that a *chose* in action *could not* be assigned. Even now, it is gravely asserted that a man cannot be made the debtor of another against his will. But the common law was gradually influenced by equity and by the law merchant, so that by assignment a debtor could become bound to pay a perfect stranger to himself, although until the legislature stepped in, the common-law courts characteristically made use of a fiction and pretended that they were not doing that which they really were doing." William R. Anson, *Principles of the Law of Contract* 335 (Arthur L. Corbin ed., 3d Am. ed. 1919).

> "It is an elementary principle of English law — known as the doctrine of 'Privity of Contract' — that contractual rights and duties only affect the parties to a contract, and this principle is the distinguishing feature between the law of contract and the law of property. True proprietary rights are 'binding on the world' in the lawyer's traditional phrase. Contractual rights, on the other hand, are only binding on, and enforceable by, the immediate parties to the contract. But this distinction, fundamental though it be, wears a little thin at times. On the one hand, there has been a constant tendency for contractual rights to be extended in their scope so as to affect more and more persons who cannot be regarded as parties to the transaction. On the other hand, few proprietary rights are literally 'binding on the world.'" P.S. Atiyah, *An Introduction to the Law of Contract* 265 (3d ed. 1981).

> "The doctrine of privity means that a person cannot acquire rights or be subject to liabilities *arising under* a contract to which he is not a party. It does not mean that a contract between A and B cannot affect the legal rights of C indirectly." G.H. Treitel, *The Law of Contract* 538 (8th ed. 1991).

▸ **privity of estate.** (17c) A mutual or successive relationship to the same right in property, as between grantor and grantee or landlord and tenant. — Also termed *privity of title; privity in estate.*

▸ **privity of possession.** (1818) Privity between parties in successive possession of real property. • The existence of this type of privity is often at issue in adverse-possession claims.

▸ **privity of title.** See *privity of estate.*

▸ **vertical privity.** (1968) **1.** *Commercial law.* The legal relationship between parties in a product's chain of distribution (such as a manufacturer and a seller). **2.** Privity between one who signs a contract containing a restrictive covenant and one who acquires the property burdened by it.

2. Joint knowledge or awareness of something private or secret, esp. as implying concurrence or consent <privity to a crime>.

privy (**priv**-ee), *n. pl.* (15c) A person having a legal interest of privity in any action, matter, or property; a person who is in privity with another. • Traditionally, there were six types of privies: (1) *privies in blood,* such as an heir and an ancestor; (2) *privies in representation,* such as an executor and a testator or an administrator and an intestate person; (3) *privies in estate,* such as grantor and grantee or lessor and lessee; (4) *privies in respect to a contract* — the parties to a contract; (5) *privies in respect of estate and contract,* such as a lessor and lessee where the lessee assigns an interest, but the contract between lessor and lessee continues because the lessor does not accept the assignee; and (6) *privies in law,* such as husband and wife. The term also appears in the context of litigation. In this sense, it includes someone who controls a lawsuit though not a party to it; someone whose interests are represented by a party to the lawsuit; and a successor in interest to anyone having a derivative claim. Pl. **privies.**

Privy Council. In the United Kingdom, the principal council of the sovereign, composed of the cabinet ministers and other persons chosen by royal appointment to serve as privy councilors. • The functions of the Privy Council are now mostly ceremonial. See JUDICIAL COMMITTEE OF THE PRIVY COUNCIL.

Privy Councillor. A member of the Privy Council. — Abbr. P.C.

privy purse. (16c) *English law.* The income set apart for the sovereign's personal use.

privy seal. (14c) **1.** A seal used in making out grants or letters patent before they are passed under the great seal. **2.** (*cap.*) LORD PRIVY SEAL.

privy signet. (15c) *Hist.* The signet or seal used by the sovereign in making out grants and private letters.

privy verdict. See VERDICT (1).

prize. (13c) **1.** Something of value awarded in recognition of a person's achievement. **2.** A vessel or cargo captured at sea or seized in port by the forces of a country at war, and therefore liable to being condemned or appropriated as enemy property.

prize court. See COURT.

prize fighting. (18c) Fighting for a reward or prize; esp., professional boxing.

"Prize fighting . . . was not looked upon with favor by the common law as was a friendly boxing match or wrestling match. On the other hand it was not punishable by the common law unless it was fought in a public place, or for some other reason constituted a breach of the peace." Rollin M. Perkins & Ronald N. Boyce, *Criminal Law* 480 (3d ed. 1982).

prize goods. See GOODS.

prize law. (18c) The system of laws applicable to the capture of prize at sea, dealing with such matters as the rights of captors and the distribution of the proceeds.

prize money. (17c) **1.** A dividend from the proceeds of a captured vessel, paid to the captors. **2.** Money offered as an award.

PRM. *abbr.* BUREAU OF POPULATION, REFUGEES, AND MIGRATION.

PRO. *abbr.* PEER-REVIEW ORGANIZATION.

pro (proh). [Latin] (15c) For.

proamita (proh-**am**-ə-tə). [Latin] (16c) *Roman & civil law.* A great-great aunt; the sister of one's great-grandfather.

proamita magna (proh-**am**-ə-tə **mag**-nə). [Latin] (17c) *Civil law.* A great-great-great-aunt.

proavia (proh-**ay**-vee-ə). [Latin] (16c) *Roman & civil law.* A great-grandmother.

proavunculus (proh-ə-**vəngk**-yə-ləs). [Latin] (16c) *Civil law.* A great-grandmother's brother.

proavus. (16c) *Civil law.* A great-grandfather.

probabilis causa (prə-**bay**-bə-lis **kaw**-zə). [Latin] (17c) Probable cause.

probabilis causa litigandi (prə-**bab**-ə-lis **kaw**-zə lit-i-**gan**-dɪ). [Law Latin] (17c) *Scots law.* A probable cause of action. • A person applying for legal aid has to show a reasonable basis for the proposed legal action.

probability, *n.* **1.** Something that is likely; what is likely. **2.** The degree to which something is likely to occur, often expressed mathematically; POSSIBILITY (1). **3.** The quality, state, or condition of being more likely to happen or to have happened than not; the character of a proposition or supposition that is more likely true than false. **4.** The amount of rational confidence with which a contingent event may be expected to materialize or become true.

probable, *adj.* Likely to exist, be true, or happen.

probable cause. (16c) **1.** *Criminal law.* A reasonable ground to suspect that a person has committed or is committing a crime or that a place contains specific items connected with a crime. • Under the Fourth Amendment, probable cause — which amounts to more than a bare suspicion but less than evidence that would justify a conviction — must be shown before an arrest warrant or search warrant may be issued. — Also termed *reasonable cause; sufficient cause; reasonable grounds; reasonable excuse.* See DUNAWAY HEARING. Cf. *reasonable suspicion* under SUSPICION.

"Probable cause may not be established simply by showing that the officer who made the challenged arrest or search subjectively believed he had grounds for his action. As emphasized in *Beck v. Ohio* [379 U.S. 89, 85 S.Ct. 223 (1964)]: 'If subjective good faith alone were the test, the protection of the Fourth Amendment would evaporate, and the people would be "secure in their persons, houses, papers, and effects" only in the discretion of the police.' The probable cause test, then, is an objective one; for there to be probable cause, the facts must be such as would warrant a belief by a reasonable man." Wayne R. LaFave & Jerold H. Israel, *Criminal Procedure* § 3.3, at 140 (2d ed. 1992).

2. *Torts.* A reasonable belief in the existence of facts on which a claim is based and in the legal validity of the claim itself. • In this sense, probable cause is usu. assessed as of the time when the claimant brings the claim (as by filing suit). **3.** A reasonable basis to support issuance of an administrative warrant based on either (1) specific evidence of an existing violation of administrative rules, or (2) evidence showing that a particular business meets the legislative or administrative standards permitting an inspection of the business premises.

probable-cause hearing. (1951) **1.** *Criminal procedure.* See PRELIMINARY HEARING. **2.** *Criminal procedure.* Any of several types of pretrial hearings to suppress evidence. See DUNAWAY HEARING; MAPP HEARING. **3.** *Family law.* See *shelter hearing* under HEARING.

probable consequence. See CONSEQUENCE.

probable-desistance test. (1974) *Criminal law.* A common-law test for the crime of attempt, focusing on whether the defendant has exhibited dangerous behavior indicating a likelihood of committing the crime. See ATTEMPT (2).

probable evidence. See *presumptive evidence* under EVIDENCE.

probandum (proh-**ban**-dəm), *n.* A fact to be proved. See *fact in issue* under FACT. Pl. **probanda.**

"[I]n judicial proceedings, the Probandum is always a known and definite thing, and thus it always furnishes a definite objective, towards which all evidentiary facts are supposed to point, and around which all evidence can be most usefully arranged. In the inquiries of natural science, the typical situation is that of a piece of evidence having multiple possibilities, with no fixed probandum. E.g., a chemist observes a peculiar and unusual reaction of hydrochloric acid on zinc; he asks himself what possible probandum this points to; there may be many; hence, he may perhaps prefer to classify from the point of view of the evidence, i.e. the reactions of the acid on zinc, iron, lead, etc. But the lawyer and the judge, *having always a known definite probandum before them,* find it more helpful to classify first from the point of view of the probandum. The probandum is like the magnet applied to a mass of iron filings; it immediately causes them all to align themselves in some position pointing to the probandum; and they can thus be readily sorted and classified." John Henry Wigmore, *The Science of Judicial Proof* § 27, at 51 (3d ed. 1937).

probata (proh-**bay**-tə). [Latin] *pl.* PROBATUM.

probate (**proh**-bayt), *n.* (15c) **1.** The judicial procedure by which a testamentary document is established to be a valid will; the proving of a will to the satisfaction of the court. • Unless set aside, the probate of a will is conclusive on the parties to the proceedings (and others who had notice of them) on all questions of testamentary capacity, the absence of fraud or undue influence, and due execution of the will. But probate does not preclude inquiry into the validity of the will's provisions or on their proper construction or legal effect. — Also termed *proof of will.*

▸ **antemortem probate.** (1884) Probate in which the living testator of a will petitions the court to determine the legal validity of the document submitted as the testator's will. • The court determines whether the document was properly executed in compliance with statutory formalities and was the product of the testator's free will, and whether the testator possessed testamentary capacity. If the court approves the submitted writing and the testator does not revoke it, the will is immediately established at the testator's death as the testator's final will. — Also termed *living probate.*

▸ **double probate.** A second grant of probate on one estate at the request of a joint executor who was not a party to the first grant.

▸ **independent probate.** See *informal probate.*

▸ **informal probate.** (1974) Probate designed to operate with minimal input and supervision of the probate court. • Most modern probate codes encourage this type of administration, with an independent personal representative. — Also termed *independent probate.* Cf. *independent executor* under EXECUTOR (2).

▸ **living probate.** See *antemortem probate.*

▸ **probate in common form.** (1824) Probate granted in the registry, without any formal procedure in court, on the executor's ex parte application. • The judgment is subject to being reopened by a party who has not been given notice.

▸ **probate in solemn form.** (1828) Probate granted in open court, as a final decree, when all interested parties have been given notice. • The judgment is final for all parties who have had notice of the proceeding, unless a later will is discovered.

▸ **small-estate probate.** (2004) An informal procedure for administering small estates, less structured than the normal process and usu. not requiring the assistance of an attorney.

2. Loosely, a personal representative's actions in handling a decedent's estate. **3.** Loosely, all the subjects over which probate courts have jurisdiction. **4.** *Archaic.* A nonresident plaintiff's proof of a debt by swearing before a notary public or other officer that the debt is correct, just, and due, and by having the notary attach a jurat.

probate, *vb.* (18c) **1.** To admit (a will) to proof. **2.** To administer (a decedent's estate). **3.** To grant probation to (a criminal); to reduce (a sentence) by means of probation.

probate asset. See *legal asset* under ASSET.

probate bond. See BOND (2).

probate code. (1931) A collection of statutes setting forth the law (substantive and procedural) of decedents' estates and trusts.

probate court. See COURT.

probate distribution. See DISTRIBUTION.

probate duty. See DUTY (4).

probate estate. (1930) A decedent's property subject to administration by a personal representative. • The probate estate comprises property owned by the decedent at the time of death and property acquired by the decedent's estate at or after the time of death. — Also termed *probate property.* See *decedent's estate* under ESTATE (3).

▸ **net probate estate.** (1949) The probate estate after the following deductions: (1) family allowances, (2) exempt property, (3) homestead allowances, (4) claims against the estate, and (5) taxes for which the estate is liable. — Also termed *net estate.* Cf. *adjusted gross estate* (1) under ESTATE (3).

probate fee. See FEE (1).

probate homestead. See HOMESTEAD (1).

probate in common form. See PROBATE.

probate in solemn form. See PROBATE.

probate judge. See JUDGE.

probate jurisdiction. See JURISDICTION.

probate law. (18c) The body of statutes, rules, cases, etc. governing all subjects over which a probate court has jurisdiction.

probate property. See PROBATE ESTATE.

probate register. See REGISTER.

probatio (prə-**bay**-shee-oh). [Latin] *Roman & civil law.* Proof.

▸ ***plena probatio.*** See *probatio plena.*

▸ ***probatio diabolica*** (prə-**bay**-shee-oh dɪ-ə-**bol**-i-kə). [Latin "devil's proof"] (1877) *Civil law.* The (usu. difficult) proof of ownership of an immovable thing by tracing its title back to the sovereign.

▸ ***probatio mortua*** (prə-**bay**-shee-oh **mor**-choo-ə). [Latin] (1875) Dead proof; proof by an inanimate object such as a deed or other instrument.

▸ ***probatio plena*** (prə-**bay**-shee-oh **plee**-nə). [Latin] *Civil law.* (1827) Full proof; proof by two witnesses or a public instrument. — Also termed *plena probatio.*

▸ ***probatio probata*** (prə-**bay**-shee-oh prə-**bay**-tə). [Law Latin] (17c) A proven proof; evidence that could not be contradicted.

▸ ***probatio prout de jure*** (proh-**bay**-shee-oh **proh**-ət dee [*or* di] **joor**-ee). [Law Latin] (18c) A proof according to any of the legal modes of proof applicable to the circumstance.

▸ ***probatio semi-plena*** (prə-**bay**-shee-oh sem-ɪ-**plee**-nə). [Latin] (1840) *Civil law.* Half-full proof; half-proof; proof by one witness or a private instrument.

▸ ***probatio viva*** (prə-**bay**-shee-oh **vɪ**-və). [Latin] (1854) Living proof; that is, proof by the mouth of a witness.

probation. (16c) **1.** A court-imposed criminal sentence that, subject to stated conditions, releases a convicted person into the community instead of sending the criminal to jail or prison, usu. on condition of routinely checking in with a probation officer over a specified period of time. Cf. PAROLE.

▸ **bench probation.** (1966) Probation in which the offender agrees to certain conditions or restrictions and reports only to the sentencing judge rather than a probation officer. — Also termed *bench parole; court probation.*

▸ **deferred-adjudication probation.** See *deferred judgment* under JUDGMENT (2).

▸ **shock probation.** (1972) Probation that is granted after a brief stay in jail or prison. • Shock probation is intended to awaken the defendant to the reality of confinement for failure to abide by the conditions of probation. This type of probation is discretionary with the sentencing judge and is usu. granted within 180 days of the original sentence. — Also termed *split sentence.* Cf. *shock incarceration* under INCARCERATION.

2. The period of time during which a sentence of probation is in effect. 3. A period of time during which an employer can see whether a new worker is suitable. 4. A period of time in which one must improve one's work or behave well to keep one's position. 5. The act of judicially proving a will. See PROBATE. — **probate,** *adj.*

probationary, *adj.* (17c) 1. Of, relating to, or involving probation or a probationer <probationary requests>. 2. Serving for a test or trial <a probationary period of employment>. 3. On probation <a probationary employee>.

probationary employee. See EMPLOYEE.

probation before judgment. See *deferred judgment* under JUDGMENT (2).

probationer. (1840) 1. A convicted criminal who is on probation. 2. Someone who is in a probationary period; a new hire, esp. in nursing or teaching, who is being tested for on-the-job suitability and competence.

probation officer. See OFFICER (1).

probation termination. (1970) The ending of a person's status as a probationer by (1) the routine expiration of the probationary period, (2) early termination by court order, or (3) probation revocation.

probation violation. (1932) *Criminal law.* A probationer's breaching a condition of the sentence, usu. including the noncompliance with a probation officer's conditions. — Abbr. VOP. — Also termed *violation of probation.*

probation-violation warrant. See *violation warrant* under WARRANT (1).

probation without judgment. See *deferred judgment* under JUDGMENT (2).

probatio plena. See PROBATIO.

probatio semi-plena. See PROBATIO.

probatio viva. See PROBATIO.

probative (**proh**-bə-tiv), *adj.* (17c) Tending to prove or disprove. • Courts can exclude relevant evidence if its probative value is substantially outweighed by the danger of unfair prejudice. Fed. R. Evid. 403. — **probativeness, probativity,** *n.*

probative evidence. See EVIDENCE.

probative fact. See FACT.

probative force. See PROBATIVE VALUE.

probative similiarity. See *substantial similarity* under SIMILARITY.

probative value. The degree to which one fact tends to make probable another posited fact. — Also termed *probative force.*

> "An essential requisite for the discovery of truth is the correct measurement of probative force. Now in this matter judicial action differs strikingly from the other departments of action and inquiry. In all other departments the measurement of probative force is left to the judgment of the individual in the individual case. In law, on the other hand, individual judgment is largely superseded by imperative rules for the measurement of probative force. The law gives to the judge a measure which he must use to the exclusion of his own discretion. Whether certain evidence is sufficient for proof is, in other departments than law, a question for the discretion of those with whom the decision rests; a matter to be determined not by rule but by natural reason and sound judgment. In law, however, there has been set up an external or objective measure of evidence and test of proof, and it is only where this measure and test does not apply that there is scope for individual judgment." John W. Salmond, *Essays in Jurisprudence and Legal History* 3–4 (1891).

probator (proh-**bay**-tər), *n.* (17c) *Hist.* An accused person who confesses to a crime but asserts that another also participated in the crime. • The probator had to undertake to prove the supposed accomplice's guilt.

probatory term. See *term probatory* (2) under TERM (5).

probatum (proh-**bay**-təm), *n.* [Latin] (16c) Something conclusively established or proved; proof. Cf. ALLEGATUM. Pl. ***probata.***

problem-oriented policing. (1986) A method that law-enforcement officers use to reduce crime by identifying and remedying the underlying causes of criminal incidents rather than merely seeking basic information (such as the identity of the perpetrator) about the crime being investigated. — Abbr. POP.

problem-solving, *n.* (1854) The activity or process of finding ways of doing things or arriving at solutions to difficult situations.

problem-solving court. See BOUTIQUE COURT; COURT.

pro bono (proh **boh**-noh), *adv.* & *adj.* [Latin *pro bono publico* "for the public good"] (1966) Uncompensated, esp. regarding free legal services performed for the indigent or for a public cause <took the case pro bono> <50 hours of pro bono work each year>. • The Model Rules of Professional Conduct ask that every lawyer aspire to rendering at least 50 hours of pro bono services a year. — **pro bono,** *n.*

> "The bar in this country has a long-standing tradition of service *pro bono publico* — legal services 'for the public good,' provided at no cost or a reduced fee. This concept encompasses a wide range of activities, including law reform efforts, participation in bar associations and civic organizations, and individual or group representation. Clients who receive such assistance also span a broad range including: poor people, nonprofit organizations, ideological or political causes, and friends, relatives, or employees of the lawyer." Deborah L. Rhode & Geoffrey C. Hazard, *Professional Responsibility* 162 (2002).

pro bono et malo (proh **boh**-noh et **mal**-oh). [Latin] (1805) For good and ill. See DE BONO ET MALO.

pro bono publico (proh **boh**-noh **pəb**-li-koh *or* **poo**-bli-koh). [Latin] (17c) *Hist.* For the public good. Cf. PRO PRIVATO COMMODO.

probus et legalis homo (**proh**-bəs et lə-**gay**-lis **hoh**-moh). [Law Latin] (18c) A good and lawful man. • This phrase referred to a juror who was legally competent to serve on a jury. Pl. ***probi et legales homines.***

procedendo (proh-sə-**den**-doh). [Latin] (15c) A higher court's order directing a lower court to determine and enter a judgment in a previously removed case. — Also termed *writ of procedendo.*

procedendo ad judicium. See DE PROCEDENDO AD JUDICIUM.

procedural arbitrability. See ARBITRABILITY.

procedural consolidation. See JOINT ADMINISTRATION.

procedural-default doctrine. (1980) The principle that a federal court lacks jurisdiction to review the merits of a habeas corpus petition if a state court has refused to review the complaint because the petitioner failed to follow reasonable state-court procedures.

procedural due process. See DUE PROCESS.

procedural error. See ERROR (2).

procedural law. (1896) The rules that prescribe the steps for having a right or duty judicially enforced, as opposed to the law that defines the specific rights or duties themselves. — Also termed *adjective law.* Cf. SUBSTANTIVE LAW.

procedural main motion. See *incidental main motion* under MOTION (2).

procedural motion. See MOTION (2).

procedural point. See POINT (2).

procedural presumption. See PRESUMPTION.

procedural right. See RIGHT.

procedural rule. See RULE OF PROCEDURE.

procedural ultra vires. See ULTRA VIRES.

procedural unconscionability. See UNCONSCIONABILITY.

procedure. (16c) **1.** A specific method or course of action. **2.** The judicial rule or manner for carrying on a civil lawsuit or criminal prosecution. — Also termed *rules of procedure.* See CIVIL PROCEDURE; CRIMINAL PROCEDURE.

proceeding. (16c) **1.** The regular and orderly progression of a lawsuit, including all acts and events between the time of commencement and the entry of judgment. **2.** Any procedural means for seeking redress from a tribunal or agency. **3.** An act or step that is part of a larger action. **4.** The business conducted by a court or other official body; a hearing. **5.** *Bankruptcy.* A particular dispute or matter arising within a pending case — as opposed to the case as a whole.

"'Proceeding' is a word much used to express the business done in courts. A proceeding in court is an act done by the authority or direction of the court, express or implied. It is more comprehensive than the word 'action,' but it may include in its general sense all the steps taken or measures adopted in the prosecution or defense of an action, including the pleadings and judgment. As applied to actions, the term 'proceeding' may include—(1) the institution of the action; (2) the appearance of the defendant; (3) all ancillary or provisional steps, such as arrest, attachment of property, garnishment, injunction, writ of *ne exeat*; (4) the pleadings; (5) the taking of testimony before trial; (6) all motions made in the action; (7) the trial; (8) the judgment; (9) the execution; (10) proceedings supplementary to execution, in code practice; (11) the taking of the appeal or writ of error; (12) the *remittitur*, or sending back of the record to the lower court from the appellate or reviewing court; (13) the enforcement of the judgment, or a new trial, as may be directed by the court of last resort." Edwin E. Bryant, *The Law of Pleading Under the Codes of Civil Procedure* 3–4 (2d ed. 1899).

▸ **adjudicatory proceeding.** See *adjudication hearing* under HEARING.

▸ **administrative proceeding.** See ADMINISTRATIVE PROCEEDING.

▸ **civil proceeding.** See CIVIL PROCEEDING.

▸ **collateral proceeding.** (18c) A proceeding brought to address an issue incidental to the principal proceeding.

▸ **competency proceeding.** (1925) A proceeding to assess a person's mental capacity. • A competency hearing may be held either in a criminal context to determine a defendant's competency to stand trial or as a civil proceeding to assess whether a person should be committed to a mental-health facility or should have a guardian appointed to manage the person's affairs.

▸ **contempt proceeding.** (1859) A judicial or quasi-judicial hearing conducted to determine whether a person has committed contempt.

▸ **core proceeding.** See CORE PROCEEDING.

▸ **criminal proceeding.** See CRIMINAL PROCEEDING.

▸ **ex parte proceeding** (eks **pahr**-tee). (18c) A proceeding in which not all parties are present or given the opportunity to be heard. — Also termed *ex parte hearing.*

▸ **in camera proceeding** (in **kam**-ə-rə). (1958) A proceeding held in a judge's chambers or other private place.

▸ **informal proceeding.** (18c) A trial conducted in a more relaxed manner than a typical court trial, such as an administrative hearing or a trial in small-claims court.

▸ **involuntary proceeding.** See *involuntary bankruptcy* under BANKRUPTCY.

▸ **judicial proceeding.** (16c) Any court proceeding; any proceeding initiated to procure an order or decree, whether in law or in equity.

▸ **legal proceeding.** (17c) Any proceeding authorized by law and instituted in a court or tribunal to acquire a right or to enforce a remedy.

▸ **noncore proceeding.** See RELATED PROCEEDING.

▸ **parallel proceeding.** (1857) A criminal, civil, or administrative proceeding that runs concurrently or simultaneously with another relating to the same core facts.

▸ **posttrial proceeding.** (1950) Action on a case that occurs after the trial is completed.

▸ **proceeding in rem.** (18c) A proceeding brought to affect all persons' interests in a thing that is subject to the power of a state.

▸ **proceeding quasi in rem.** (1831) A proceeding brought to affect particular persons' interests in a thing.

▸ **quasi-criminal proceeding.** (1844) *Procedure.* A civil proceeding that is conducted in conformity with the rules of a criminal proceeding because a penalty analogous to a criminal penalty may apply, as in some juvenile proceedings. • For example, juvenile delinquency is classified as a civil offense. But like a defendant in a criminal trial, an accused juvenile faces a potential loss of liberty. So criminal procedure rules apply.

▸ **related proceeding.** See RELATED PROCEEDING.

▸ **special proceeding.** (18c) **1.** A proceeding that can be commenced independently of a pending action and from which a final order may be appealed immediately. **2.** A proceeding involving statutory or civil remedies or rules rather than the rules or remedies ordinarily available under rules of procedure; a proceeding providing extraordinary relief.

▸ **summary proceeding.** (17c) A nonjury proceeding that settles a controversy or disposes of a case in a relatively prompt and simple manner. — Also termed *summary trial.* Cf. *plenary action* under ACTION (4).

"By summary proceedings are principally meant such as are directed by several acts of parliament for the conviction of offenders, and the infliction of penalties created by those acts of parliament. In these there is intervention of a jury, but the party accused is acquitted or condemned by the suffrage of such person only as the statute has appointed for his judge." John Wade, *The Cabinet Lawyer: A Popular Digest of the Laws of England* 47 (1847).

"Summary proceedings were such as were directed by Act of Parliament, there was no jury, and the person accused was acquitted or sentenced only by such person as statute had appointed for his judge. The common law was wholly a stranger to summary proceedings." A.H. Manchester, *Modern Legal History of England and Wales, 1750–1950* 160 (1980).

▸ **supplementary proceeding.** (17c) **1.** A proceeding held in connection with the enforcement of a judgment, for the purpose of identifying and locating the debtor's assets available to satisfy the judgment. **2.** A proceeding that in some way supplements another.

proceedings below. See STATEMENT OF THE CASE (1).

proceeds (**proh**-seedz), *n.* (13c) **1.** The value of land, goods, or investments when converted into money; the amount of money received from a sale <the proceeds are subject to attachment>. **2.** Something received upon selling, exchanging, collecting, or otherwise disposing of collateral. UCC § 9-102(a)(64). • Proceeds differ from other types of collateral because they constitute any collateral that has changed in form. For example, if a farmer borrows money and gives the creditor a security interest in the harvest, the harvested wheat is collateral. If the farmer then exchanges the harvest for a tractor, the tractor becomes the proceeds of the wheat. The term *proceeds* includes the account arising when the right to payment is earned under a contract right. (See CONTRACT RIGHT.) Money, checks, and the like are termed *cash proceeds*; all other proceeds are *noncash proceeds*.

▸ **net proceeds.** (18c) The amount received in a transaction minus the costs of the transaction (such as expenses and commissions). — Also termed *net balance*.

proceeds and avails. The cash-surrender value of a life-insurance policy, together with values built up since the policy's issue date and the benefits payable on maturity and at the death of the insured.

proceres (**pros**-ə-reez). [Latin] (18c) Nobles; lords. See DOMUS PROCERUM.

process, *n.* (14c) **1.** The proceedings in any action or prosecution <due process of law>. **2.** A summons or writ, esp. to appear or respond in court <service of process>. — Also termed *judicial process*; *legal process*.

"*Process* is so denominated because it *proceeds* or issues forth in order to bring the defendant into court, to answer the charge preferred against him, and signifies the writs or judicial means by which he is brought to answer." 1 Joseph Chitty, *A Practical Treatise on the Criminal Law* 338 (2d ed. 1826).

"The term 'process' is not limited to 'summons.' In its broadest sense it is equivalent to, or synonymous with, 'procedure,' or 'proceeding.' Sometimes the term is also broadly defined as the means whereby a court compels a compliance with its demands.

"'Process' and 'writ' or 'writs' are synonymous, in the sense that every writ is a process, and in a narrow sense of the term 'process' is limited to judicial writs in an action, or at least to writs or writings issued from or out of a court, under the seal thereof and returnable thereto; but it is not always necessary to construe the term so strictly as to limit it to a writ issued by a court in the exercise of its ordinary jurisdiction." 72 C.J.S. *Process* § 2, at 589 (1987).

▸ **alias process.** (18c) A process issued after an earlier process has failed for some reason. • Among the types of alias process are *alias execution*, *alias subpoena*, *alias summons*, and *alias writ*.

▸ **bailable process.** (18c) A process instructing an officer to take bail after arresting a defendant. • The defendant's discharge is required by law after the tender of suitable security.

▸ **civil process.** (17c) A process that issues in a civil lawsuit.

▸ **compulsory process.** (16c) A process, with a warrant to arrest or attach included, that compels a person to appear in court as a witness.

▸ **criminal process.** (16c) A process (such as an arrest warrant) that issues to compel a person to answer for a crime.

▸ **defective process.** (18c) Void or voidable process. See *void process*; *voidable process*.

▸ **final process.** (18c) A process issued at the conclusion of a judicial proceeding; esp., a writ of execution.

▸ **irregular process.** (18c) A process not issued in accordance with prescribed practice. • Whether the process is void or merely voidable depends on the type of irregularity. Cf. *regular process*.

▸ **legal process.** (17c) Process validly issued. — Also termed *lawful process*.

▸ **mesne process** (meen). (17c) **1.** A process issued between the commencement of a lawsuit and the final judgment or determination. **2.** The procedure by which a contumacious defendant is compelled to plead. — Also termed *writ of mesne process*; *writ of mesne*.

▸ **original process.** (17c) A process issued at the beginning of a judicial proceeding.

"Original process is any writ or notice by which a defendant is called upon to appear and answer the plaintiff's declaration. The commencement of the suit at common law was formerly by original writ. Judicial process was by summons, attachment, arrest and outlawry." Benjamin J. Shipman, *Handbook of Common-Law Pleading* § 3, at 17 (Henry Winthrop Ballantine ed., 3d ed. 1923).

▸ **regular process.** (17c) A process that issues lawfully according to prescribed practice. Cf. *irregular process*.

▸ **summary process.** (17c) **1.** An immediate process, issuing and taking effect without intermediate applications or delays. **2.** A legal procedure used to resolve a controversy more efficiently and expeditiously than ordinary methods. **3.** The legal documents achieving such a result. **4.** A procedure for repossessing real property from a tenant upon default. See *summary eviction* under EVICTION. **5.** SHOW-CAUSE PROCEEDING.

▸ **trust process.** In some states (particularly in New England), garnishment or foreign attachment.

▸ **voidable process.** (1823) A defective process with a curable defect.

▸ **void process.** (18c) Legal process that, in some material way, does not comply with the required form.

3. *Patents.* A method, operation, or series of actions intended to achieve some new and useful end or result by changing a material's chemical or physical characteristics. • Process is a statutory category of patentable invention. Cf. MACHINE; MANUFACTURE.

process, abuse of. See ABUSE OF PROCESS.

process agent. See AGENT.

process by foreign attachment. See FACTORIZING PROCESS.

process claim. See PATENT CLAIM.

processioning. (17c) The survey and inspection of land boundaries, performed esp. in the former English colonies along the southeastern seaboard, and analogous to the English *perambulation*.

process patent. See PATENT (3).

process server. (17c) A person authorized by law or by a court to formally deliver process to a defendant or respondent. See SERVICE (1).

processum continuando (prə-**ses**-əm kən-tin-yoo-**an**-doh). [Latin "for continuing process"] (17c) *Hist.* A writ for the continuation of process after the death of a justice authorized to review cases by a commission of oyer and terminer.

procès-verbal (proh-**say**-vair-**bahl**). [French "official record of oral proceedings"] (17c) *Civil & int'l law.* A detailed, authenticated written report of a proceeding, esp. of an international conference; PROTOCOL (3). • A *procès-verbal* may be cast in various forms, according to the style a country prefers.

prochein ami (**proh**-shen ə-**mee**). [Law French] See NEXT FRIEND.

pro-choice, *adj.* (1974) (Of a person or policy) favoring the belief that women should have the right to have an abortion.

proclaim, *vb.* (14c) To declare formally or officially.

proclamation. (14c) A formal public announcement made by the government.

proclamation by lord of manor. *Hist.* A proclamation (repeated three times) made by the lord of a manor requiring an heir or devisee of a deceased copyholder to pay a fine and be admitted to the estate, failing which the lord could seize the lands provisionally.

proclamation of exigents (**eks**-ə-jənts). (1911) *Hist.* Repeated proclamations by the sheriff of an imminent outlawing of a person in the county where the person lived. See EXIGENT.

proclamation of rebellion. (16c) *Hist.* A proclamation made by the sheriff, warning a person who failed to obey a Chancery subpoena or attachment that a commission of rebellion would issue if the person continued to resist the Chancery process. See COMMISSION OF REBELLION.

proclamation of recusants (**rek**-yə-zənts). *Hist.* A proclamation by which persons who willfully absented themselves from church could be convicted on nonappearance at the assizes.

proclamator (**prok**-lə-may-tər). (17c) *Hist.* An official at the English Court of Common Pleas responsible for making proclamations.

procompetitive, *adj.* (1949) Increasing, encouraging, or preserving competition. Cf. ANTICOMPETITIVE.

pro–con debate. See DEBATE.

pro–con divorce. See DIVORCE.

pro confesso (proh kən-**fes**-oh). [Latin] (16c) *Roman law.* As having confessed or admitted liability, as by failing to appear when required. • A defendant who failed to answer a bill in equity was often treated *pro confesso*.

pro consilio impendendo (proh kən-**sil**-ee-oh im-pen-**den**-doh). [Law Latin] (17c) For counsel to be given. • The phrase describes consideration in the form of a commitment to give legal advice in exchange for an annuity.

pro consilio impenso (proh kən-**sil**-ee-oh im-pen-**soh**). (17c) For counsel given.

proconsul (proh-**kon**-səl), *n.* [Latin] (14c) *Roman law.* **1.** An ex-consul whose consular powers were extended by the Senate or emperor after leaving office. **2.** The governor of certain senatorial provinces.

pro convicto. (17c) As convicted.

pro corpore regni (proh **kor**-pə-ree **reg**-nɪ). [Latin] (18c) In behalf of the body of the realm.

proctor. (14c) **1.** One appointed to manage the affairs of another. **2.** An advocate who represents clients in ecclesiastical courts; PROCURATOR (4). **3.** DIVORCE PROCTOR. **4.** An advocate who represents a party in the admiralty side of a district court. — Also termed (in sense 4) *proctor in admiralty.* **5.** Someone who monitors students taking a test to ensure that no cheating takes place.

proctorship. See PROCURATORIUM.

procuracy (**prok**-yə-rə-see). (15c) The document that grants power to an attorney-in-fact; a letter of agency.

procurare (prok-yə-**rair**-ee), *vb.* [Latin] To take care of another's affairs.

procuratio (prok-yə-**ray**-shee-oh). [Latin] Management of another's affairs; agency.

procuration (prok-yə-**ray**-shən). (15c) **1.** The act of appointing someone as an agent or attorney-in-fact.

> "In the common language of life, he, who, being competent, and *sui juris,* to do any act for his own benefit, or on his own account, employs another person to do it, is called the principal, constituent, or employer; and he, who is thus employed, is called the agent, attorney, proxy, or delegate of the principal, constituent, or employer. The relation, thus created, between the parties, is termed an agency. The power, thus delegated, is called in law an authority. And the act, when performed is often designated as an act of agency or procuration; the latter word being derived from the Roman law, in which *procuratio* signifies the same thing as agency, or the administration of the business of another." Joseph Story, *Commentaries on the Law of Agency* § 3, at 2-3 (Isaac R. Redfield ed., 7th ed. 1869).

2. The authority vested in a person so appointed; the function of an attorney-in-fact. **3.** PROCUREMENT.

procurationes ad resignandum in favorem (prok-yə-ray-shee-**oh**-neez ad rez-ig-**nan**-dəm in fə-**vor**-əm). [Law Latin] *Hist.* Procuratories of resignation in favor of the disponee of a vassal. • The phrase referred to the rule requiring a vassal's resignation before a superior had to receive the disponee of a vassal to the property. See RESIGNATION (3).

procuration fee. (1822) *English law.* A commission or brokerage allowed to a solicitor for obtaining a loan. — Also termed *procuration money.*

procurator (**prok**-yə-ray-tər), *n.* (13c) **1.** *Roman law.* A person informally appointed to represent another in a judicial proceeding. Cf. COGNITOR. **2.** *Roman law.* A government official, usu. subordinate in authority to a provincial governor; one of several imperial officers of the Roman Empire entrusted with the management of the financial affairs of the province and often having administrative powers in a province as agents of the emperor. **3.** *Hist. English law.* An agent, attorney, or servant. **4.** *Eccles. law.* An advocate of a religious house; a lawyer who represents a cleric or religious society in legal matters. — Also termed *proctor.* **5.** An agent or attorney-in-fact. **6.** *Scots law.* A solicitor who represents clients in the lower courts; formerly, any law agent.

procuratores ecclesiae parochialis (prok-yə-rə-**tor**-eez e-**klee**-z[h]ee-ee pə-roh-kee-**ay**-lis). [Latin] *Hist.* A churchwarden; a representative of a parish church.

procurator fiscal. (16c) *Scots law.* The representative of the Lord Advocate in inferior courts, responsible for investigating sudden deaths and crimes and for prosecuting in the sheriff or district court.

procurator in rem suam (prok-yə-**ray**-tər in rem **s[y]oo**-əm). [Latin] (17c) **1.** *Roman law.* An assignee of a right of action. • True agency did not exist in Roman law, so a principal whose agent had, for example, bought something on the principal's behalf would have to be made the agent's procurator to claim under that sale. **2.** *Scots law.* Procurator in his own affair. • This phrase refers to a situation in which a person acts under a power of attorney with reference to property that the person has acquired.

procuratorio nomine (prok-yə-rə-**tor**-ee-oh **nahm**-ə-nee). [Latin] (17c) *Hist.* In the name and character of a procurator. See PROCURATOR.

procuratorium (prok-yə-rə-**tor**-ee-əm), *n.* [Law Latin] *Hist.* The instrument by which a person appointed a procurator as the person's representative in litigation. — Also termed *proctorship; proxy.*

procurator litis (prok-yə-**ray**-tər **lI**-tis). [Latin] (1926) *Roman law.* Someone who represents another in a lawsuit. — Often shortened to *procurator.* Cf. DEFENSOR (1).

procurator negotiorum (prok-yə-**ray**-tər ni-goh-shee-**or**-əm). [Latin] *Civil law.* An attorney-in-fact; a manager of business affairs for another.

procurator provinciae (prok-yə-**ray**-tər prə-**vin**-shee-ee). [Latin] *Roman law.* See PROCURATOR (2).

procuratory (**prok**-yə-rə-tor-ee), *adj.* (15c) Of, relating to, or authorizing a procuration. See PROCURATION.

procuratory, *n.* (15c) **1.** *Civil law.* Authorization of one person to act for another. **2.** *Scots law.* A mandate or commission for one person to act for another; POWER OF ATTORNEY. See PROCURATOR.

procuratory of resignation. (17c) *Scots law.* A proceeding by which a vassal authorizes the return of a feu to his or her superior. • This is equivalent to the surrender of a copyhold under English law. See SURRENDER OF COPYHOLD.

procuratrix (prok-yə-**ray**-triks). [Latin] (16c) *Hist.* A female agent or attorney-in-fact.

procure, *vb.* (14c) **1.** To obtain (something), esp. by special effort or means. **2.** To achieve or bring about (a result). **3.** To obtain a sexual partner for another, esp. an unlawful partner such as a minor or a prostitute.

procurement (proh-**kyoor**-mənt), *n.* (14c) **1.** The act of getting or obtaining something or of bringing something about. — Also termed *procuration.* **2.** The act of persuading or inviting another, esp. a woman or child, to have illicit sexual intercourse. — **procure,** *vb.*

procurement contract. See CONTRACT.

procurement of breach of contract. See TORTIOUS INTERFERENCE WITH CONTRACTUAL RELATIONS.

procurer. (15c) Someone who induces or prevails on another to do something, esp. to engage in an illicit sexual act. See PIMP.

procuring agent. See AGENT.

procuring an abortion. See ABORTION (1).

procuring cause. See CAUSE (1).

procuring miscarriage. *Hist.* See ABORTION (1).

pro. def. *abbr.* PRO DEFENDENTE.

pro defectu emptorum (proh di-**fek**-t[y]oo emp-**tor**-əm). [Latin] For want of purchasers.

pro defectu exitus (proh di-**fek**-t[y]oo **eks**-ə-təs). [Latin] For, or in case of, default of issue.

pro defectu haeredis (proh di-**fek**-t[y]oo hə-**ree**-dis). [Latin] For want of an heir.

pro defectu justitiae (proh di-**fek**-t[y]oo jəs-**tish**-ee-ee). [Latin] For defect or want of justice.

pro defendente (proh def-ən-**den**-tee). [Latin] For the defendant. — Abbr. *pro. def.* Cf. PRO QUERENTE.

pro derelicto (proh der-ə-**lik**-toh). [Latin] As derelict or abandoned. • This refers to property subject to *usucapio.* See USUCAPIO.

prodigal (**prod**-ə-gəl), *n.* *Civil law.* A person whose affairs are managed by a curator because of the person's wasteful spending or other bad conduct. • In Roman law, the agnatic family of a prodigal (*prodigus*) or spendthrift could result in that person's being prohibited from engaging in certain legal transactions, and the person's estate being put in the charge of a curator. See *cura prodigi* under CURA.

pro dignitate regali (proh dig-nə-**tay**-tee ri-**gay**-lI). [Latin] In consideration of the royal dignity.

prodigus (**prod**-ə-gəs), *n.* & *adj.* [Latin "a spendthrift"] *Roman law.* See PRODIGAL.

prodition (prə-**dish**-ən). (15c) *Archaic.* Treason; treachery.

proditor (**prod**-i-tər), *n.* (15c) *Roman law.* **1.** A traitor. **2.** An informer.

proditorie (proh-di-**tor**-ee-ee), *adv.* [Latin] Treasonably. • This word formerly appeared in a treason indictment.

pro diviso (proh di-**vI**-zoh). [Latin] As divided; i.e., in severalty.

pro domino (proh **dom**-ə-noh). [Latin] As master or owner; in the character of a master.

pro donatione (proh də-**nay**-shee-oh-nee). [Latin] *Roman & civil law.* As a gift; as in case of gift. • This is a ground of *usucapio.* — Also written *pro donato.* See USUCAPIO.

pro dote (proh **doh**-tee). [Latin] *Civil law.* As a dowry; by title of dowry. • This is a ground of *usucapio.* See USUCAPIO.

produce (**proh**-doos), *n.* (17c) The product of natural growth, labor, or capital; esp., agricultural products.

produce (prə-**doos**), *vb.* (15c) **1.** To bring into existence; to create. **2.** To provide (a document, witness, etc.) in response to subpoena or discovery request. **3.** To yield (as revenue). **4.** To bring (oil, etc.) to the surface of the earth.

producent (prə-**d**[y]**oo**-sənt), *n.* (17c) *Hist. Eccles. law.* The party calling a witness.

producer. 1. See INSURANCE AGENT. **2.** See *insurance broker* under BROKER.

producer price index. (1918) An index of wholesale price changes, issued monthly by the U.S. Bureau of Labor Statistics. — Formerly also termed *wholesale price index.* Cf. CONSUMER PRICE INDEX.

producing cause. See *proximate cause* under CAUSE (1).

product. (1825) Something that is distributed commercially for use or consumption and that is usu. (1) tangible personal property, (2) the result of fabrication or processing, and (3) an item that has passed through a chain of commercial distribution before ultimate use or consumption. See ARTICLE OF MANUFACTURE; PRODUCTS LIABILITY.

▸ **dangerous product.** (1884) A product that is hazardous even when put to its intended use but accompanied by adequate warnings of the hazards. Cf. *unreasonably dangerous product.*

▸ **defective product.** (1903) A product that is unreasonably dangerous for a foreseeable use, as when it is not fit for its intended purpose, inadequate instructions are provided for its use, or it is inherently dangerous in its design or manufacture. — Also termed *defective manufacture.*

▸ **safe product.** (1897) A product that under intended and reasonably foreseeable conditions of use presents no risks or only minimal risks considered acceptable and consistent with a high level of protection for safety and health.

▸ **unreasonably dangerous product.** (1958) A product characterized by a hazard that an ordinary user could not contemplate because there is inadequate warning of the risk or the user is unaware of a hazard caused by the product's design or other defect. Cf. *dangerous product.*

product-by-process claim. See PATENT CLAIM.

product claim. See PATENT CLAIM.

product defect. See DEFECT.

product disparagement. See TRADE DISPARAGEMENT.

product-extension merger. See MERGER (8).

production. 1. The act or process of making or growing things, esp. those to be sold <the production of consumer goods>. **2.** The amount of goods that are made or grown; esp., the tangible result of industrial or other labor <annual production>. **3.** The creation of economic value; the making available of goods to satisfy human desires <the production and consumption of wealth>. **4.** The action of exhibiting or bringing forward a document or other piece of evidence <production of documents>. **5.** Collectively, the written documents or other things brought forward in support or defense of an action or prosecution <the defendant's production in this case>. **6.** A play, film, broadcast, etc. that is made for public viewing or consumption <a production of Coffee and Language Inc.>. **7.** *Mining.* The quantity or amount of natural resources actually extracted or mined <oil and gas production>. **8.** *Oil & gas.* The capability of being produced in paying quantities.

production burden. See BURDEN OF PRODUCTION.

production casing. See CASING.

production for commerce. (1938) The production of goods that an employer intends for interstate commerce. • This is one criterion by which an employer may be subject to the Fair Labor Standards Act.

production injunction. See INJUNCTION.

production of suit. (1830) *Common-law pleading.* The plaintiff's burden to produce evidence to confirm the allegations made in the declaration.

production payment. (1942) *Oil & gas.* A share of oil-and-gas production from property, free of the costs of production, ending when an agreed sum has been paid.

production request. See REQUEST FOR PRODUCTION.

productio sectae (prə-**dək**-shee-oh **sek**-tee). [Latin] See PRODUCTION OF SUIT.

product liability. See PRODUCTS LIABILITY.

product-line exception. (1979) An exception to the usual rule that a successor corporation is not liable for the acts of its predecessor, arising when the successor acquired all the predecessor's assets, held itself out as a continuation of the predecessor by producing the same product line under the same or a similar name, and benefited from the predecessor's goodwill.

product mark. See *product trademark* under TRADEMARK.

product market. See MARKET.

product recall. See RECALL (4).

product rule. A means of calculating the likelihood that a series of independent events will occur jointly, done by multiplying together the probability of each event.

products liability, *n.* (1925) **1.** A manufacturer's or seller's tort liability for any damages or injuries suffered by a buyer, user, or bystander as a result of a defective product. • Products liability can be based on a theory of negligence, strict liability, or breach of warranty. **2.** The legal theory by which liability is imposed on the manufacturer or seller of a defective product. **3.** The field of law dealing with this theory. — Also termed *product liability*; (specif.) *manufacturer's liability.* See LIABILITY; 402A ACTION. — **products-liability,** *adj.*

> "In contrast to product safety law, products liability law governs the private *litigation* of product accidents. Operating *ex post*, after a product accident has occurred, its rules define the legal responsibility of sellers and other commercial transferors of products for damages resulting from product defects and misrepresentations about a product's safety or performance capabilities." David G. Owen, *Products Liability Law* § 1.1, at 3 (2005).

▸ **strict products liability.** (1964) Products liability imposed on a commercial transferor who is legally responsible for the physical harms caused by a defect in the product that existed when the product was transferred, regardless of whether the defect was attributable to any negligence on the transferor's part. See *strict liability* under LIABILITY.

products-liability action. (1960) A lawsuit brought against a manufacturer, seller, or lessor of a product — regardless of the substantive legal theory or theories on which the lawsuit is brought — for personal injury, death, or property damage caused by the manufacture, construction, design, formulation, installation, preparation, or assembly of a product.

products-liability insurance. See INSURANCE.

products-liability loss. See LOSS.

product test. See DURHAM RULE.

product trademark. See TRADEMARK.

proem. See PROOEMIUM.

proembryo. See ZYGOTE.

proemium. See PROOEMIUM.

pro emptore (proh emp-**tor**-ee). [Latin] *Civil law.* As a purchaser; by the title of a purchaser. See USUCAPIO.

pro et durante. For and during.

pro facto (proh **fak**-toh). [Latin] For the fact; considered or held as fact.

pro falso clamore suo (proh **fal**-soh [*or* **fawl**-soh] klə-**mor**-ee **s[y]oo**-oh). [Latin "for his false claim"] A nominal amercement of a plaintiff for a false allegation, inserted in a judgment for the defendant.

profane, *adj.* (15c) (Of speech or conduct) irreverent to something held sacred.

profanity. (16c) Obscene, vulgar, or insulting language; BLASPHEMY. • Profanity is distinguished from mere vulgarity and obscenity by the additional element of irreverence toward or mistreatment of something sacred.

profectitium peculium (pro-fek-**tish**-ee-əm pə-*kyoo*-lee-əm). *Hist. Roman law.* Property that a father allowed a son in *patria potestas* to manage and use while the father retained ownership. — Also written *peculium profectitium.*

profectitius (proh-fek-**tish**-ee-əs). [Latin] That which descends from an ancestor.

profer (**proh**-fər). (14c) *Hist.* **1.** An offer or proffer. **2.** A return made by a sheriff of an account into the Exchequer.

proferens (proh-**fer**-enz). [Latin] (1928) The party that proposes a contract or a condition in a contract. Pl. ***proferentes*** (proh-fə-**ren**-teez).

profert (**proh**-fərt). (18c) *Common-law pleading.* A declaration on the record stating that a party produces in court the deed or other instrument relied on in the pleading.

▸ ***profert in curia*** (**proh**-fərt in **kyoor**-ee-ə). [Law Latin] (17c) He produces in court. • In common-law pleading, this phrase was used in a declaration asserting that the plaintiff was ready to produce, or had produced, the deed or other instrument on which the action was founded. — Formerly also termed *profert in curiam.*

profess, *vb.* (16c) To declare openly and freely; to confess.

professio juris (prə-**fes[h]**-ee-oh **joor**-is). [Latin] (1897) A recognition of the right of a contracting party to stipulate the law that will govern the contract <there may have been a period in which people might make any *professio juris* that they wanted>.

profession. (15c) **1.** A vocation requiring advanced education and training; esp., one of the three traditional learned professions — law, medicine, and the ministry.

> "Learned professions are characterized by the need of unusual learning, the existence of confidential relations, the adherence to a standard of ethics higher than that of the market place, and in a profession like that of medicine by intimate and delicate personal ministration. Traditionally, the learned professions were theology, law and medicine; but some other occupations have climbed, and still others may climb, to the professional plane." *Commonwealth v. Brown*, 20 N.E.2d 478, 481 (Mass. 1939).

2. Collectively, the members of such a vocation.

professional, *n.* (1846) Someone who belongs to a learned profession or whose occupation requires a high level of training and proficiency.

professional association. See ASSOCIATION.

professional corporation. See CORPORATION.

professional courtesy. See COURTESY (2).

professional goodwill. See *personal goodwill* under GOODWILL.

professionalism. (1856) The characteristics, ideas, and ideals of those who belong to a professional calling; specif., the practice of a learned art in a characteristically methodical, courteous, and ethical manner.

> "In the mid-1980s, the word 'professionalism' began to appear with some frequency in bar publications and to be heard increasingly at bar meetings large and small. The American Bar Association and some local bar groups formed committees on professionalism (or committees on the profession) to study the topic and write reports about it. . . . No one can say for sure how it came about that so many lawyers in so many bar associations decided, seemingly simultaneously, to spend so many hours at bar dinners debating what it means to be a professional and drafting codes of professionalism for others to put on their shelves. Your guess is as good as mine, but since I'm writing this, and you're not, I'll offer two thoughts: First, the advent of lawyer advertising, following the *Bates* decision protecting this activity in 1977, inspired (if that's the right word) many offensive marketing schemes, which, coupled with pervasive, if tamer, efforts at self-promotion, conveyed the impression that lawyers were absolutely *consumed* with the goal of making money. Professionalism might then be seen as an antidote to this apparent fixation. Second, as the number of lawyers in the nation dramatically increased relative to its nonlawyers population (from 1:625 in 1960 to less than half that by century's end), there was need to remind lawyers that they were members of an elite club, or if (alas) the club was no longer quite so elite, at least it behooved lawyers to behave as though it was. Whatever. Professionalism arrived and seems to have become a permanent theme in places where lawyers congregate." Stephen Gillers, *Regulation of Lawyers: Problems of Law and Ethics* 9–10 (7th ed. 2005).

professional negligence. See MALPRACTICE.

professional opinion. A source of law consisting of the informed thinking of those skilled in the law, including judicial obiter dicta, the prevailing views of the legal profession, professionally rendered legal opinions, and the thoughts of legal commentators.

professional relationship. See RELATIONSHIP.

professional responsibility. The heightened duty of those in a profession to behave ethically, according to an acknowledged code that applies to all members.

proffer (**prof**-ər), *vb.* (14c) To offer or tender (something, esp. evidence) for immediate acceptance. — **proffer,** *n.*

proffered evidence. See EVIDENCE.

proffer meeting. (1991) *Criminal procedure.* A conference at which prosecutors and police interview a criminal defendant to assess the value of the defendant's cooperation in related prosecutions. Cf. REVERSE PROFFER.

proficua (prə-**fik**-yoo-ə). [Law Latin] *Hist.* Profits; esp., the profits of an estate in land.

profile, *n.* (1989) *Criminal law.* A set of personal characteristics that alert police to carry out targeted reconnaissance procedures, such as stopping travelers whose behavior or other traits make them criminally suspect.

profiling. 1. See RACIAL PROFILING. **2.** See LINGUISTIC PROFILING.

profit, *n.* (13c) **1.** The excess of revenues over expenditures in a business transaction; GAIN (2). Cf. EARNINGS; INCOME.

▸ **accumulated profit.** (18c) Profit that has accrued but not yet been distributed; earned surplus. — Also termed *undivided profit.* See *retained earnings* under EARNINGS.

▸ **gross profit.** (18c) Total sales revenue less the cost of the goods sold, no adjustment being made for additional expenses and taxes. Cf. *net profit.*

▸ **lost profits.** See LOST PROFITS.

▸ **mesne profits.** (17c) The profits of an estate received by a tenant in wrongful possession between two dates. — Also termed (archaically) *medium tempus.* See ACTION FOR MESNE PROFITS.

▸ **net profit.** (17c) Total sales revenue less the cost of the goods sold and all additional expenses. — Also termed *net revenue.* Cf. *gross profit.*

▸ **operating profit.** (1905) Total sales revenue less all operating expenses, no adjustment being made for any nonoperating income and expenses, such as interest payments.

▸ **paper profit.** (1909) A profit that is anticipated but not yet realized. • Gains from stock holdings, for example, are paper profits until the stock is actually sold at a price higher than its original purchase price. — Also termed *unrealized profit.*

▸ **short-swing profits.** See SHORT-SWING PROFITS.

▸ **surplus profit.** (18c) *Corporations.* The excess of revenue over expenditures. • Some jurisdictions prohibit the declaration of a dividend from sources other than surplus profit.

▸ **undistributed profit.** See *retained earnings* under EARNINGS.

▸ **undivided profit.** See *accumulated profit.*

▸ **unrealized profit.** See *paper profit.*

2. A servitude that gives the right to pasture cattle, dig for minerals, or otherwise take away some part of the soil; PROFIT À PRENDRE. • A profit may be either appurtenant or in gross. See SERVITUDE (1).

▸ **profit appendant** (ə-pen-dənt). (17c) A profit annexed to land by operation of law; esp., a common of pasture. See *common appendant* under COMMON (1).

▸ **profit appurtenant** (ə-pərt-ən-ənt). (1807) A profit, whether several or in common, attached to land, for the benefit of certain other identified land, by the act of the parties (as by grant or by prescription). See *common appurtenant* under COMMON (1).

▸ **profit in gross** (in grohs). (1904) A profit exercisable by the owner independently of his or her ownership of land. See *common in gross* under COMMON (1).

> "[A] right to take fish from a canal without stint (i.e., without limit) can exist as a profit in gross, but not, as already seen, as a profit appurtenant. A profit in gross is an interest in land which will pass under the owner's will or intestacy or can be sold or dealt with in any of the usual ways." Robert E. Megarry & M.P. Thompson, *A Manual of the Law of Real Property* 377 (6th ed. 1993).

▸ ***profit pur cause de vicinage*** (pər **kawz** də **vis**-ə-nij). (1975) A profit arising when the holders of adjoining commons have allowed their cattle to stray on each other's lands. • A claim for this profit fails if one of the commoners fences off the common or has in the past driven off the other commoner's cattle.

profit-and-loss account. See ACCOUNT.

profit-and-loss statement. See INCOME STATEMENT.

profit à prendre (a **prawn**-drə *or* ah **prahn**-dər). [Law French "profit to take"] (*usu. pl.*) (17c) A right or privilege to go on another's land and take away something of value from its soil or from the products of its soil (as by mining, logging, or hunting). — Also termed *right of common.* Cf. EASEMENT. Pl. **profits à prendre.**

> "A profit à prendre has been described as 'a right to take something off another person's land.' This is too wide; the thing taken must be something taken out of the soil, i.e., it must be either the soil, the natural produce thereof, or the wild animals existing on it; and the thing taken must at the time of taking be susceptible of ownership. A right to 'hawk, hunt, fish, and fowl' may thus exist as a profit, for this gives the right to take creatures living on the soil which, when killed, are capable of being owned. But a right to take water from a spring or a pump, or the right to water cattle at a pond, may be an easement but cannot be a profit; for the water, when taken, was not owned by anyone nor was it part of the soil." Robert E. Megarry & M.P. Thompson, *A Manual of the Law of Real Property* 375–76 (6th ed. 1993).

profiteering, *n.* (1814) The taking advantage of unusual or exceptional circumstances to make excessive profits, as in the selling of scarce goods at inflated prices during war. — **profiteer,** *vb.*

profit insurance. See INSURANCE.

profitless, *adj.* (16c) **1.** Not making a profit despite being designed to do so. Cf. NONPROFIT. **2.** Not useful to do; providing no benefit to anyone.

profit-making, *adj.* (1856) Generating profits.

profit margin. (1868) **1.** The difference between the cost of something and the price for which it is sold. **2.** The ratio, expressed as a percentage, between this difference and the selling price. • For example, a widget costing a retailer $10 and selling for $15 has a profit margin of 33% ($5 difference divided by $15 selling price). — Often shortened to *margin.*

▸ **gross profit margin.** (1918) The ratio, as a percentage, of the total sales revenue less the cost of the goods sold, no adjustment being made for additional expenses and taxes, divided by the total sales revenue. — Also termed *gross margin.*

▸ **net profit margin.** (1926) The ratio, as a percentage, of the total sales revenue less the cost of the goods sold and all additional expenses, divided by the total sales revenue. — Also termed *net margin.*

profit-sharing, *n.* (1872) A system by which all the people who work for a company receive part of its profits.

profit-sharing plan. (1889) *Employment law.* An employee benefit plan that allows an employee to share in the company's profits. • ERISA governs the administration of many profit-sharing plans, which provide for discretionary employer contributions and provide a definite predetermination formula for allocating the contributions to the plan among the participants. Contributions are frequently allocated in proportion to each participant's compensation. — Abbr. PSP. See EMPLOYEE BENEFIT PLAN; EMPLOYEE RETIREMENT INCOME SECURITY ACT.

▸ **qualified profit-sharing plan.** (1948) A plan in which an employer's contributions are not taxed to the employee until distribution. • The employer is allowed to deduct the contributions. IRC (26 USCA) § 401(a). — Often shortened to *qualified plan*.

profits warning. (1955) *Corporations.* A company's announcement that its profits for a particular period will be less than earlier projected.

pro forma (proh **for**-mə), *adj.* [Latin "for form"] (16c) **1.** Made or done as a formality and not involving any actual choice or decision. **2.** (Of an invoice or financial statement) provided in advance to describe items, predict results, or secure approval.

pro forma amendment. See AMENDMENT (3).

pro forma earnings. See *operating earnings* under EARNINGS.

pro forma invoice. See INVOICE.

pro forma session. See SESSION (1).

pro foro externo (**proh for**-oh ek-**stər**-noh). [Latin] On behalf of a foreign forum.

progener (proh-**jee**-nər). [Latin] A grandson-in-law.

progeny (**proj**-ə-nee), *n. pl.* (14c) **1.** Children or descendants; offspring <only one of their progeny attended law school>. **2.** In a figurative sense, a line of precedents that follow a leading case <*Erie* and its progeny>.

prognosis (prog-**noh**-sis). (17c) **1.** The process of forecasting the probable outcome of a present medical condition (such as a disease). **2.** The forecast of such an outcome. Cf. DIAGNOSIS.

program. (18c) *Parliamentary law.* **1.** An agenda for a meeting or a convention, listing the order of business and possibly including educational or social events. See AGENDA; *business meeting* under MEETING. **2.** A speech or other presentation within a meeting offered for the assembly's information or for the members' education or entertainment, but not for their formal consideration or action as a deliberative assembly.

program committee. See COMMITTEE (1).

program trading. (1984) A form of computerized securities trading that usu. involves buying or selling large amounts of stocks while simultaneously selling or buying index futures in offsetting amounts.

pro gravitate admissi (proh grav-ə-**tay**-tee ad-**mis**-ɪ). [Latin] *Hist.* According to the gravity of the offense.

progressive, *adj.* (17c) **1.** Favoring new or modern ideas and methods, esp. in politics and education; specif., supporting political change and social improvement esp. through governmental action <progressive policies>. Cf. CONSERVATIVE (1); LIBERAL (2). **2.** Occurring or developing gradually over time <progressive increases>.

progressive encroachment. *Trademarks.* Unfair competition that begins when someone uses an infringing trademark in a market, then later significantly expands its business or redirects its marketing or manufacturing efforts under the infringing mark to compete more directly with the trademark's owner. • Under the doctrine of progressive encroachment, a plaintiff's delay in bringing suit may be excused until either the defendant's use of a mark becomes directly competitive or a likelihood of confusion arises. If established, progressive encroachment overcomes a laches defense.

progressive lawyering. See CAUSE LAWYERING.

progressive loss. See LOSS.

progressive tax. See TAX.

pro hac vice (proh hahk **vee**-chay *or* hak **vɪ**-see *also* hahk **vees**). [Latin] (17c) For this occasion or particular purpose. • The phrase usu. refers to a lawyer who has not been admitted to practice in a particular jurisdiction but who is admitted there temporarily for the purpose of conducting a particular case. — Abbr. *p.h.v.* See *admission pro hac vice* under ADMISSION (2). For *owner pro hac vice*, see *demise charter* under CHARTER (8).

prohibit, *vb.* (15c) **1.** To forbid by law. **2.** To prevent, preclude, or severely hinder.

prohibited and reserved trademarks. See TRADEMARK.

prohibited degree. See DEGREE.

prohibited substitution. See SUBSTITUTION.

prohibitio de vasto, directa parti (proh-hə-**bish**-ee-oh dee **vas**-toh, di-**rek**-tə **pahr**-tɪ). [Latin "prohibition of waste, directed to the party"] (17c) *Hist.* A writ issued during litigation to prohibit a tenant from committing waste.

prohibition. (15c) **1.** A law or order that forbids a certain action; PROSCRIPTION (1).

▸ **constitutional prohibition.** (18c) A prescription contained in a constitution, esp. one on the making of a particular type of statute (e.g., an ex post facto law) or on the performance of a specified type of act (e.g., an official's serving in incompatible capacities).

2. An extraordinary writ issued by an appellate court to prevent a lower court from exceeding its jurisdiction or to prevent a nonjudicial officer or entity from exercising a power. — Also termed (in sense 2) *writ of prohibition*; (in Scots law) *inhibition*. Cf. WRIT OF CONSULTATION.

> "Prohibition is a kind of common-law injunction to prevent an unlawful assumption of jurisdiction. . . . It is a common-law injunction against governmental usurpation, as where one is called coram non judice (before a judge unauthorized to take cognizance of the affair), to answer in a tribunal that has no legal cognizance of the cause. It arrests the proceedings of any tribunal, board, or person exercising judicial functions in a manner or by means not within its jurisdiction or discretion." Benjamin J. Shipman, *Handbook of Common-Law Pleading* § 341, at 542 (Henry Winthrop Ballantine ed., 3d ed. 1923).

> "The remedy by writ of prohibition is of ancient origin in our system of jurisprudence. It is an original remedial writ, as old as the common law itself. The writ is so ancient that forms of it are given in Glanville (Beames' Trans.) . . . , the first book of English law, written in the year 1189. The origin of the proceeding by prohibition was to secure the sovereign rights, and preserve the public quiet. It was an emanative of the great executive authority of the king, delegated to his courts, and particularly to the king's bench. It was one of his prerogative writs, necessary to perfect the administration of his justice and the control of subordinate functionaries and authorities. By the writ of prohibition he forbade what ought not to be done, in cases where the general authority was not denied, or not intended to be resumed." Forrest G. Ferris & Forrest G. Ferris Jr., *The Law of Extraordinary Legal Remedies* 414–15 (1926).

3. (*cap.*) The period from 1920 to 1933, when the manufacture, transport, and sale of alcoholic beverages in the United States was forbidden by the 18th Amendment to the Constitution. • The 18th Amendment was repealed by the 21st Amendment.

prohibitive statute. See STATUTE.

prohibitory injunction. See INJUNCTION.

prohibitory interdict. See INTERDICT (1).

prohibitus. See INTERDICTUM QUOD VI AUT CLAM.

pro illa vice (proh **il**-ə **vɪ**-see). [Latin] For that turn.

pro indefenso (proh in-də-**fen**-soh). [Latin] As undefended; as making no defense.

pro indiviso (proh in-də-**vɪ**-zoh), *adj.* [Latin "as undivided"] (Of property) owned or possessed by several persons at the same time, without partition.

pro interesse suo (proh in-tər-**es**-ee **s[y]oo**-oh). [Latin] According to his interest; to the extent of his interest. • A third party, for example, may be allowed to intervene *pro interesse suo.*

project financing. See FINANCING.

projectio (prə-**jek**-shee-oh). [Latin] Alluvion created by the sea. See ALLUVION.

projector. See PROMOTER.

projects. See HOUSING PROJECT.

projet (proh-**zhay**). [French] (1808) *Int'l law.* A draft of a proposed measure, statute, treaty, or convention.

pro laesione fidei (proh lee-zhee-**oh**-nee **fɪ**-dee-ɪ). [Latin] For breach of faith.

pro legato (proh lə-**gay**-toh). [Latin] As a legacy; by the title of a legacy, esp. as a ground of *usucapio.* See USUCAPIO.

proleptic lie. See LIE, *n.*

proles (**proh**-leez). [Latin] (17c) *Hist.* Legitimate offspring; esp., the issue of a lawful marriage.

proletariat (proh-lə-**tair**-ee-ət). (1847) The working class; specif., in Marxist doctrine, those without capital who sell their labor to survive.

proletarius (proh-lə-**tair**-ee-əs), *n.* [Latin] *Roman law.* One of the common people; a member of a lower class who owns little or no property.

prolicide (**proh**-lə-sɪd). (1826) **1.** The killing of offspring; esp., the crime of killing a child shortly before or after birth. **2.** Someone who kills a child shortly before or after birth. Cf. INFANTICIDE. — **prolicidal,** *adj.*

pro-life, *adj.* (1971) (Of a person or policy) favoring the belief that most or all abortions should be illegal. — Also termed *antichoice.*

prolixity (proh-**lik**-sə-tee). (14c) The unnecessary and superfluous recitation of facts and legal arguments in pleading or evidence.

prolixity rejection. See REJECTION.

pro loco et tempore (proh **loh**-koh et **tem**-pə-ree). [Latin] *Hist.* For the place and time.

prolocutor (proh-**lok**-yə-tər). (16c) **1.** *Eccles. law.* The president or chair of a convocation. **2.** *Hist.* The speaker of the British House of Lords. • This office now belongs to the Lord Chancellor. — Also termed (in sense 2) *forspeca.*

prolonged detention. See DETENTION (1).

pro majori cautela (proh mə-**jor**-ɪ kaw-**tee**-lə). [Latin] *Archaic.* For greater caution; by way of additional security. • This phrase usu. applies to an act done or to a clause put in an instrument as a precaution.

promatertera (proh-mə-**tər**-tər-ə). [Latin] *Roman & civil law.* A great-great-aunt; the sister of one's great-grandmother.

promatertera magna (proh-mə-**tər**-tər-ə **mag**-nə). [Latin] (17c) *Civil law.* A great-great-great-aunt.

promesse de porte forte (proh-**mes** də **port**[-ə] **fort**[-ə]). (2010) *Civil law.* A contract of security by which a person promises that a third party will render performance to the obligee. • The third person's consent to the transaction liberates the original promisor from the obligation. La. Civ. Code art. 1977 cmt. (b). Cf. SURETYSHIP.

promiscuous, *adj.* (16c) **1.** *Archaic.* Involving a wide range of different things; consisting of a heterogeneous mixture. **2.** Having many sexual partners; indulging in sexual relations with various people.

promise, *n.* (15c) **1.** The manifestation of an intention to act or refrain from acting in a specified manner, conveyed in such a way that another is justified in understanding that a commitment has been made; a person's assurance that the person will or will not do something. • A binding promise — one that the law will enforce — is the essence of a contract.

> "By common usage, a promise is an expression leading another person justifiably to expect certain conduct on the part of the promisor. Such an expression is a promise, whether enforceable at law or not. It is indeed an essential element in every contract. Society does not guarantee the fulfillment of all expectations so induced." William R. Anson, *Principles of the Law of Contract* 6 n.3 (Arthur L. Corbin ed., 3d Am. ed. 1919).

> "[*Promise*] means not only the physical manifestations of assurance by words or conduct, but also the moral duty to make good the assurance by performance. If by reason of other operative facts the promise is recognized as creating a legal duty, the promise is a contract." 1 Samuel Williston, *A Treatise on the Law of Contracts* § 1A, at 4 (Walter H.E. Jaeger ed., 3d ed. 1957).

> "It is well to make clear two points at the outset . . . . The first is that I do not believe that all promises are morally binding; accordingly, I use the term 'promise' without prejudging the question whether the promise creates an obligation. The second is that, where a promise does create an obligation, the reason for that may depend upon whether the promise was explicit or implied. There is thus, in my view, a fundamental distinction between explicit and implied promises, and when I use the word 'promise' without qualification, I normally mean an explicit promise." P.S. Atiyah, *Promises, Morals, and Law* 8 (1981).

2. The words in a promissory note expressing the maker's intention to pay a debt. • A mere written acknowledgment that a debt is due is insufficient to constitute a promise. — **promise,** *vb.*

▸ **absolute promise.** See *unconditional promise.*

▸ **aleatory promise** (**ay**-lee-ə-tor-ee). (1904) A promise conditional on the happening of a fortuitous or accidental event, or on an event that the parties believe is fortuitous or accidental.

▸ **alternative promise.** (17c) A contractual promise to do one of two or more things, any one of which qualifies as consideration.

> "A promise in the alternative may be made because each of the alternative performances is the object of desire to

the promisee. Or the promisee may desire one performance only, but the promisor may reserve an alternative which he may deem advantageous. In either type of case the promise is consideration if it cannot be kept without some action or forbearance which would be consideration if it alone were bargained for. But if the promisor has an unfettered choice of alternatives, and one alternative would not have been consideration if separately bargained for, the promise in the alternative is not consideration." Restatement (Second) of Contracts § 77 cmt. b (1981).

▸ **bare promise.** See *gratuitous promise.*

▸ **collateral promise.** (17c) A promise to guarantee another's debt, made primarily without benefit to the party making the promise. • Unlike an original promise, a collateral promise must be in writing to be enforceable. See MAIN-PURPOSE RULE.

▸ **conditional promise.** (16c) A promise that is conditioned on the occurrence of an event other than the lapse of time <she made a conditional promise to sell the gold on April 2 unless the price fell below $300 an ounce before that time>. • A conditional promise is not illusory as long as the condition is not entirely within the promisor's control.

▸ **corresponding promise.** (18c) A mutual promise calling for the performance of an act substantially similar to the act called for by the other mutual promise, both acts being in pursuit of a common purpose.

▸ **counterpromise.** See COUNTERPROMISE.

▸ **dependent promise.** (1829) A promise to be performed by a party only when another obligation has first been performed by another party. • A dependent promise is one type of conditional promise. See *conditional promise.*

▸ **discretionary promise.** A unilateral promise made without mutual agreement and subject to the promisor's decision about how to perform or whether to perform at all.

▸ **divisible promises.** (1891) Promises that are capable of being divided into independent parts.

▸ **false promise.** (16c) A promise made with no intention of carrying it out. Cf. *promissory fraud* under FRAUD.

▸ **fictitious promise.** See *implied promise.*

▸ **gratuitous promise.** (17c) A promise made in exchange for nothing; a promise not supported by consideration. • A gratuitous promise is usu. not legally enforceable. — Also termed *bare promise; naked promise.*

▸ **illegal promise.** (17c) A promise to do or permit something unlawful.

▸ **illusory promise.** (1841) A promise that appears on its face to be so insubstantial as to impose no obligation on the promisor; an expression cloaked in promissory terms but actually containing no commitment by the promisor. • An illusory promise typically, by its terms, makes performance optional with the promisor. For example, if a guarantor promises to make good on the principal debtor's obligation "as long as I think it's in my commercial interest," the promisor is not really bound.

"An apparent promise which, according to its terms, makes performance optional with the promisor no matter what may happen, or no matter what course of conduct in other respects he may pursue, is in fact no promise. Such an expression is often called an illusory promise." 1 Samuel Williston, *A Treatise on the Law of Contracts* § 1A, at 5 (Walter H.E. Jaeger ed., 3d ed. 1957).

▸ **implied promise.** (18c) A promise created by law to render a person liable on a contract so as to avoid fraud or unjust enrichment. — Also termed *fictitious promise.* See *promise implied in fact.*

"Under some circumstances the promise inferred is called an implied promise and in others it is referred to as a constructive promise. But whichever conclusion is reached, the result is the same. In other words an implied promise and a constructive promise are not treated differently. The theoretical difference between the two is that a promise implied from the conduct of the parties arises by construction of law, only when justice requires it under the circumstances." John D. Calamari & Joseph M. Perillo, *The Law of Contracts* § 4-12, at 234–35 (3d ed. 1987).

▸ **independent promise.** See *unconditional promise.*

▸ **joint-and-several promise.** (1809) A promise that is made by each of two or more persons and is enforceable against each person individually and all of them collectively.

▸ **joint promise.** (16c) A promise made together by two or more promisors.

"If several persons make a joint promise, each is liable to the promisee for the whole debt or liability, notwithstanding the fact that they are both liable. Neither is bound by himself, but each is bound to the full extent of the promise. If both are living and within the jurisdiction of the court, they should all be joined as defendants in an action on the contract. If one of them is sued alone, he is not bound to answer to the merits of the action without the others being sued with him. He may demur if the defect appears on the face of the pleading, or plead in abatement if it does not so appear. If the defect so appears, it is fatal, not only on demurrer, but on motion in arrest of judgment. If it does not so appear, the objection must be taken by plea in abatement; and, if the defendant pleads to the merits, he cannot object that others were jointly liable with him; for, when two are jointly bound in one bond or on one promise, though neither of them is bound by himself, yet neither of them can say that it is not his deed or promise." William L. Clark, *Handbook of the Law of Contracts* 476–77 (Archibald H. Throckmorton ed., 3d ed. 1914).

▸ **marriage promise.** (16c) *Family law.* A betrothal; an engagement to be married. — Also termed *agreement to marry; promise to marry; promise of marriage.* Cf. *promise in consideration of marriage.*

▸ **mutual promises.** (16c) Promises given simultaneously by two parties, each promise serving as consideration for the other. See *bilateral contract* under CONTRACT.

▸ **naked promise.** See *gratuitous promise.*

▸ **new promise.** A previously unenforceable promise that a promisor revives and agrees to fulfill, thereby making it enforceable, as when a debtor agrees to pay a creditor an amount discharged in the debtor's bankruptcy.

▸ **original promise.** A promise to guarantee the debt of another, made primarily for the benefit of the party making the promise. • An original promise need not be in writing to be enforceable. See MAIN-PURPOSE RULE.

▸ **promise implied in fact.** (1909) A promise existing by inference from the circumstances or actions of the parties. See *implied promise.*

▸ **promise in consideration of marriage.** (18c) A promise for which the actual performance of the marriage is the consideration, as when a man agrees to transfer property to a woman if she will marry him. • A promise to marry, however, is not considered a promise in consideration of marriage. Cf. *marriage promise.*

▸ **promise in restraint of trade.** (1887) A promise whose performance would limit competition in any business or restrict the promisor in the exercise of a gainful occupation. • Such a promise is usu. unenforceable.

▸ **remedial promise.** A seller's promise to repair or replace goods or to refund all or part of the price upon the happening of a specified event.

▸ **several promise.** (16c) A promise that a person makes separately from that of any other person and is enforceable only against the promiser.

▸ **unconditional promise.** (1802) A promise that either is unqualified or requires nothing but the lapse of time to make the promise presently enforceable. • A party who makes an unconditional promise must perform that promise even though the other party has not performed according to the bargain. — Also termed *independent promise*; *absolute promise.*

> "If a man undertake absolutely to perform his part of a contract, and do not make the performance of his promise conditional upon performance by the other party, a breach by the latter will entitle the former to bring an action for damages, but will not discharge him from the performance of his promise. When the promises of both parties are absolute and independent of each other, upon a breach of his promise by one party the other may sue him without averring that he has performed his own promise, and, of course, it is no defense to such an action for the defendant to plead that the plaintiff has failed to perform his part of the agreement." Robert Ralston, *The Principles of the Law Relating to the Discharge of Contracts* 38 (1886).

▸ **voidable promise.** (1839) A promise that one party may, under the law, declare void by reason of that party's incapacity or mistake, or by reason of the fraud, breach, or other fault of the other party.

promisee (prom-is-**ee**). (18c) One to whom a promise is made.

promise not to compete. See *covenant not to compete* under COVENANT (1).

promise of marriage. See *marriage promise* under PROMISE.

promise to marry. See *marriage promise* under PROMISE.

promisor (prom-is-**or**). (17c) Someone who makes a promise; esp., one who undertakes a contractual obligation.

promissor (**prom**-is-ər). [Latin] (17c) *Civil law.* **1.** A promisor; specif., a party who undertakes to do a thing in response to the interrogation of the other party (the *stipulator*). **2.** REUS PROMITTENDI.

promissory, *adj.* (15c) Containing or consisting of a promise <the agreement's promissory terms>.

promissory condition. See CONDITION (2).

promissory estoppel. See ESTOPPEL.

promissory fraud. See FRAUD.

promissory note. See NOTE (1).

promissory oath. See OATH.

promissory representation. See REPRESENTATION (1).

promissory restraint. (1936) An attempt in an otherwise effective conveyance or contract to discourage a later conveyance by imposing contractual liability on anyone who makes a later conveyance.

promissory warranty. See WARRANTY (3).

pro modo admissi (proh **moh**-doh ad-**mis**-I). [Latin] *Hist.* According to the measure of the offense.

promoter. (14c) **1.** Someone who encourages or incites. **2.** *Corporations.* A founder or organizer of a corporation or business venture; one who takes the entrepreneurial initiative in founding or organizing a business or enterprise. — Formerly also termed *projector.*

> "[A] person may be said to be a promoter of a corporation if before its organization, he directly or indirectly solicits subscriptions to its stock, or assumes to act in its behalf in the purchase of property, or in the securing of its charter, or otherwise assists in its organization. It must, however, be remembered that calling a person a 'promoter' does not of itself impose any responsibility upon him. The responsibility of the promoter depends upon what he does, not upon the name by which he is called." Manfred W. Ehrich, *The Law of Promoters* 15–16 (1916).

promoting prostitution. See PANDERING (1).

prompt, *vb.* (15c) To incite, esp. to immediate action.

prompt-arraignment statute. (1947) A legislative act requiring police to bring an arrested person before a court without unnecessary delay.

prompt complaint. See FRESH COMPLAINT.

prompt outcry. See FRESH COMPLAINT.

prompt-outcry rule. (1994) *Criminal procedure.* A hearsay-rule exception making a crime victim's nearly contemporaneous complaints admissible as evidence, esp. in sex-crimes cases.

prompt-suspension law. (1995) *Criminal law.* A statute requiring the court to suspend a driver's license at arraignment in a DWI or DUI case if certain conditions are met, such as a prior conviction or a specified blood alcohol level.

promulgare (proh-məl-**gair**-ee), *vb.* [Latin] *Roman law.* To promulgate; to make (a law) publicly known after its enactment.

promulgate (prə-**məl**-gayt *or* **prom**-əl-gayt), *vb.* (16c) **1.** To declare or announce publicly; to proclaim. **2.** To put (a law or decree) into force or effect. **3.** (Of an administrative agency) to carry out the formal process of rulemaking by publishing the proposed regulation, inviting public comments, and approving or rejecting the proposal. — **promulgation** (prom-əl-**gay**-shən *or* proh-məl-), *n.*

promulgation (prom-əl-**gay**-shən *or* proh-məl-). (16c) The official publication of a new law or regulation, by which it is put into effect.

promutuum (proh-**myoo**-choo-əm). [Latin "as if lent"] *Civil law.* A quasi-contract in which a person who received money or property in error agrees to return what was received to the person who paid it.

pronepos (proh-**nep**-ohs). [Latin] (16c) *Roman & civil law.* A great-grandson. Pl. ***pronepotes.***

proneptis (proh-**nep**-tis). [Latin] (16c) *Roman & civil law.* A great-granddaughter. Pl. ***proneptes.***

pro non adjecto (proh non ə-**jek**-toh). [Latin] *Hist.* As not added; as though it had not been added. • For example, a nonessential deed provision might be treated *pro non adjecto.*

pro non scripto (**proh** non **skrip**-toh). [Latin] As not written; as though it had not been written. • The phrase usu. referred to testamentary conditions that a court would disregard because the conditions were impossible, illegal, or meaningless.

pronotary (proh-**noh**-tə-ree), *n.* (16c) First notary.

pronounce, *vb.* (14c) To announce formally <pronounce judgment>.

pronunciation (prə-nən-see-**ay**-shən). (15c) *Archaic.* A sentence or decree.

pronurus (**proh**-nə-rəs). [Latin] (16c) *Roman & civil law.* The wife of a grandson or great-grandson. Pl. ***pronurus.***

prooemium (proh-**ee**-mee-əm), *n.* [Greek "foresong"] In classical rhetoric, a prefatory statement; a preface, prelude, or introduction. — Also written *proemium.* — Also termed *proem* (**proh**-əm).

> "Students were required to commit to memory passages dealing with general topics that recurred more or less frequently in all forensic oratory but especially in the *prooemium.* The purpose of the *prooemium* was to win the attention and good will of the audience. The speaker usually tried to achieve these ends by setting forth the situation in which he found himself. While no two situations are ever exactly alike, the number of elements that enter into them is after all limited. Accordingly, the rhetoricians were quick to seize upon these common elements and reduce them to formulas or commonplaces. Not only were the various topics that might be advantageously introduced into the *prooemium* set forth in the textbooks but collections of proems suitable for all sorts of cases and occasions were published." Robert J. Bonner, *Lawyers and Litigants in Ancient Athens* 151 (1927).

proof, *n.* (13c) **1.** The establishment or refutation of an alleged fact by evidence; the persuasive effect of evidence in the mind of a fact-finder. **2.** Evidence that determines the judgment of a court. **3.** An attested document that constitutes legal evidence.

▸ **affirmative proof.** (18c) Evidence establishing the fact in dispute by a preponderance of the evidence.

▸ **conditional proof.** (1931) A fact that amounts to proof as long as there is no other fact amounting to disproof. — Also termed *presumptive proof.*

▸ **double proof.** (1955) **1.** *Bankruptcy.* Proof of claims by two or more creditors against the same debt. • This violates the general rule that there can be only one claim with respect to a single debt. **2.** *Evidence.* Corroborating government evidence (usu. by two witnesses) required to sustain certain convictions.

▸ **full proof.** (16c) **1.** *Civil law.* Proof by two witnesses or by public instrument. **2.** Evidence that satisfies the minds of the jury of the truth of the fact in dispute beyond a reasonable doubt.

▸ **literal proof.** *Civil law.* Written evidence. Cf. *testimonial proof.*

▸ **negative proof.** (16c) Proof that establishes a fact by showing that its opposite is not or cannot be true. Cf. *positive proof.*

▸ **positive proof.** (17c) Direct or affirmative proof. Cf. *negative proof.*

▸ **preliminary proof.** (1802) *Insurance.* The first proof offered of a loss occurring under a policy, usu. sent in to the underwriters with a notification of the claim.

▸ **presumptive proof.** See *conditional proof.*

▸ **proof beyond a reasonable doubt.** (1834) *Criminal procedure.* Proof that precludes every reasonable hypothesis except that which it tends to support. • Formerly, this standard required evidence to "establish the truth of the fact to a reasonable and moral certainty" and "proof to a moral certainty as distinguished from an absolute certainty." *Moral certainty* is no longer a synonym for *proof beyond a reasonable doubt. See Victor v. Nebraska,* 511 U.S. 1, 8, 12, 114 S.Ct. 1239, 1244, 1246 (1994). See REASONABLE DOUBT.

▸ **testimonial proof.** (17c) *Civil law.* Proof by the evidence of witnesses, rather than proof by written instrument. Cf. *literal proof.*

4. *Scots law.* A bench trial.

proof, burden of. See BURDEN OF PROOF.

proof brief. See BRIEF (1).

proof of acknowledgment. (18c) An authorized officer's certification — based on a third party's testimony — that the signature of a person (who usu. does not appear before the notary) is genuine and was freely made. — Also termed *certificate of proof; certificate of acknowledgment.* See ACKNOWLEDGMENT (5).

proof of claim. (1812) *Bankruptcy.* A creditor's written statement that is submitted to show the basis and amount of the creditor's claim. — Abbr. POC. Pl. **proofs of claim.**

▸ **informal proof of claim.** (1930) A proof of claim stating a creditor's demand for payment and intent to hold the debtor's bankruptcy estate liable, but that does not comply with the Bankruptcy Code's form for proofs of claim. • A late-filed proof of claim may be given effect if the creditor had timely filed an informal proof of claim.

proof of debt. (18c) The establishment by a creditor of a debt in some prescribed manner (as by affidavit) as a first step in recovering the debt from an estate or property; PROOF OF CLAIM.

proof of loss. (18c) An insured's formal statement of loss required by an insurance company before it will determine whether the policy covers the loss.

proof of service. (18c) **1.** A document filed (as by a sheriff) in court as evidence that process has been successfully served on a party. — Also termed *return of service; return of process.* See SERVICE (1). **2.** CERTIFICATE OF SERVICE (1).

proof of will. See PROBATE (1).

pro omni alio onere (proh **om**-nɪ [*also* -nee] **ay**-lee-oh **on**-ər-ee). [Law Latin "for all other burden"] *Hist.* A portion of a charter clause restricting the vassal's duties to those explicitly named in the charter.

pro opere et labore (proh **op**-ə-ree et lə-**bor**-ee). [Latin] For work and labor.

propaganda. (1822) *Int'l law.* **1.** The systematic dissemination of doctrine, rumor, or selected information to promote or injure a particular doctrine, view, or cause. **2.** The ideas or information so disseminated. • The word *propaganda* originated as an abbreviated form of *Congregatio de propaganda fide,* a committee (of cardinals) for propagating the (Christian) faith.

▸ **defamatory propaganda.** (1936) Propaganda used to promote dissatisfaction among a country's citizens and undermine government authority. • Defamatory propaganda is common in wartime but is also used in peacetime as a means of incitement.

▸ **hostile propaganda.** (1909) Propaganda employed by a country to manipulate the people of another country to support or oppose their government. — Also termed *ideological aggression*. See *subversive propaganda*.

> "Ideological aggression . . . is the spreading of ideas intentionally and deliberately so as to manipulate by symbols controversial attitudes and positions. It is hostile propaganda indulged in by a state directly or vicariously to incite and influence the people of another state so as to maintain or alter the institutions and policies of that state. The campaign of hostile propaganda may emanate from within or without the territory of the victim state and can be carried on by any means of communications." Ann Van Wynen Thomas & A.J. Thomas, Jr., *The Concept of Aggression in International Law* 84 (1972).

▸ **subversive propaganda.** (1915) Propaganda calculated to incite a civil war or revolution. • When the instigator is another country, it is termed *hostile propaganda* or *ideological aggression*.

▸ **war-mongering propaganda.** (1935) Propaganda calculated to produce national support for a war and to encourage the government to declare or join in a war regardless of any legal constraints.

pro parte (proh **pahr**-tee). [Latin] *Hist.* Partly; in part.

pro parte legitimus, pro parte illegitimus (proh **pahr**-tee lə-**jit**-ə-məs, proh **pahr**-tee il-lə-**jit**-ə-məs). [Law Latin] *Hist.* Partly legitimate, partly illegitimate. • In Roman and civil law, an illegitimate child could be later legitimated through the marriage of the child's parents. But England did not fully recognize this legitimate status.

pro parte virili (proh **pahr**-tee və-**rɪ**-lɪ). [Latin "for the share per man"] *Hist.* In equal shares; for one's own proportion.

pro partibus liberandis (proh **pahr**-ti-bəs lib-ə-**ran**-dis). [Latin "to free the portions"] (17c) *Hist.* A writ for the partition of lands among coheirs.

propatruus (proh-**pay**-troo-əs *or* -**pa**-troo-əs). [Latin] (16c) *Roman & civil law.* A great-grandfather's brother.

propatruus magnus (proh-**pay**-troo-əs [*or* -**pa**-troo-əs] **mag**-nəs). [Latin] (17c) *Roman & civil law.* A great-great-great-uncle on the father's side.

propensity, *n.* (16c) A natural tendency to behave in a particular way; esp., the fact that a person is prone to a specific type of bad behavior.

pro per., *adv.* & *adj.* See PRO PERSONA; PROPRIA PERSONA.

pro per., *n.* See PRO SE.

proper, *adj.* **1.** Belonging to the natural or essential constitution of; peculiar; distinctive <proper Bavarian traditions>. **2.** Of, relating to, or involving the exact or particular part strictly so called <Dallas proper>. **3.** Appropriate, suitable, right, fit, or correct; according to the rules <a proper request>. **4.** Strictly pertinent or applicable; exact; correct <proper words in proper places>. **5.** Conforming to the best ethical or social usage; allowable, right, and becoming <using only proper means>. **6.** Thoroughly polite; mindful of what is socially correct <he is very formal and proper>.

proper care. See *reasonable care* under CARE (2).

proper conditional institute. See INSTITUTE (5).

proper evidence. See *admissible evidence* under EVIDENCE.

proper feud. See FEUD (1).

proper improbation. See IMPROBATION.

proper independent advice. See INDEPENDENT ADVICE.

proper law. *Conflict of laws.* The substantive law that, under the principles of conflict of laws, governs a transaction.

proper lookout, *n.* (1842) The duty of a vehicle operator to exercise caution to avoid collisions with pedestrians or other vehicles.

proper means. *Trade secrets.* Any method of discovering trade secrets that does not violate property-protection statutes or standards of commercial ethics. • Proper means include independent invention, reverse engineering, observing the product in public, and studying published literature. *See* Restatement (First) of Torts § 757 cmt. f (1939).

> "Trade secrets are protected . . . in a manner akin to private property, but only when they are disclosed or used through improper means. Trade secrets do not enjoy the absolute monopoly afforded patented processes, for example, and trade secrets will lose their character as private property when the owner divulges them or when they are discovered through proper means. . . . Thus, it is the employment of improper means to produce the trade secret, rather than mere copy or use, which is the basis of liability." *Chicago Lock Co. v. Fanberg*, 676 F.2d 400, 404 (9th Cir. 1982).

proper party. See PARTY (2).

pro persona (proh pər-**soh**-nə), *adv.* & *adj.* [Latin] For one's own person; on one's own behalf <a *pro persona* brief>. — Sometimes shortened to *pro per.* See PRO SE.

property. (14c) **1.** Collectively, the rights in a valued resource such as land, chattel, or an intangible. • It is common to describe property as a "bundle of rights." These rights include the right to possess and use, the right to exclude, and the right to transfer. — Also termed *bundle of rights*. **2.** Any external thing over which the rights of possession, use, and enjoyment are exercised <the airport is city property>.

> "'Property (from the Lat. *proprius*, meaning belonging to one; one's own) signifies, in a strict sense, one's exclusive right of ownership of a thing.' In their strict meanings, therefore, the right of ownership and property are synonymous, each term signifying a bundle or collection of rights. In a secondary meaning, however, the term 'property' is applied to every kind of valuable right and interest that can be made the subject of ownership, and in this sense, since it is the subject of ownership, land is called property. The term, therefore, includes both real and personal property, and it is often thus expressly defined in statutes. The word 'property,' however, may have different meanings, under different circumstances, according to the manner in which it is used." William L. Burdick, *Handbook of the Law of Real Property* 2–3 (1914) (citations omitted).

> "In its widest sense, property includes all a person's legal rights, of whatever description. A man's property is all that is *his in law*. This usage, however, is obsolete at the present day, though it is common enough in the older books. . . . In a second and narrower sense, property includes not all a person's rights, but only his proprietary as opposed to his personal rights. The former constitute his estate or property, while the latter constitute his status or personal condition. In this sense a man's land, chattels, shares, and the debts due to him are his property; but not his life or liberty or reputation. . . . In a third application, which is that adopted [here], the term includes not even all proprietary rights, but only those which are both proprietary and *in rem*. The law of property is the law of proprietary rights *in rem*, the law of proprietary rights *in personam* being distinguished from it as the law of obligations. According to this usage a freehold or leasehold estate in land, or a patent or copyright, is property; but a debt or the benefit

of a contract is not. . . . Finally, in the narrowest use of the term, it includes nothing more than corporeal property — that is to say, the right of ownership in a material object, or that object itself." John Salmond, *Jurisprudence* 423–24 (Glanville L. Williams ed., 10th ed. 1947).

▸ **abandoned property.** (1841) Property that the owner voluntarily surrenders, relinquishes, or disclaims. Cf. *lost property; mislaid property.*

▸ **absolute property.** (16c) Property that one has full and complete title to and control over.

▸ **adventitious property.** (18c) **1.** *Roman law.* Property coming to a son or daughter from anyone other than the paterfamilias. — Also termed *peculium adventitium.* **2.** *Hist.* Property coming to one from a stranger or collateral relative.

▸ **ancestral property.** (1838) Property, esp. immovable property, that the present owner has acquired from forebears, esp. when the owner's family has held the property for several generations at least.

▸ **appointive property.** (1932) A property interest that is subject to a power of appointment. See POWER OF APPOINTMENT.

▸ **common property.** (17c) **1.** Real property that is held by two or more persons with no right of survivorship. Cf. *joint property.* **2.** COMMON AREA.

▸ **community property.** See COMMUNITY PROPERTY.

▸ **complete property.** (18c) The entirety of the rights, privileges, powers, and immunities that it is legally possible for a person to have with regard to land or any other thing, apart from those that all other members of society have in the land or thing.

▸ **corporeal property.** (18c) **1.** The right of ownership in material things. **2.** Property that can be perceived, as opposed to incorporeal property. See *tangible property.*

▸ **distressed property.** (1927) Property that must be sold because of mortgage foreclosure or because it is part of an insolvent estate.

▸ **divisible property.** *Family law.* An asset that a court is statutorily permitted to divide between divorcing spouses. — Also termed *divisible asset.*

▸ **domestic-partnership property.** (1975) Property that would be marital property if the domestic partners were married to each other. See DOMESTIC PARTNERSHIP; DOMESTIC-PARTNERSHIP PERIOD.

▸ **dotal property.** (1811) *Civil law.* Separate property that the wife brings to the marriage to assist the husband with the marriage expenses. Cf. *extradotal property.*

▸ **exempt property.** See EXEMPT PROPERTY.

▸ **extradotal property** (ek-strə-**doh**-təl). (1826) *Civil law.* **1.** That portion of a wife's property over which she has complete control. **2.** All of a wife's effects that have not been settled on her as dowry; any property that a wife owns apart from her dowry. • In Louisiana, after January 1, 1980, all property acquired by the wife that is not community is neither dotal nor extradotal; it is simply her separate property, as has always been true of the husband. La. Civ. Code art. 2341. — Also termed *paraphernal property.* Cf. *dotal property.*

▸ **found property.** (1828) Property that appears to be lost or abandoned because the owner is unknown, and is recovered by another person. • The finder does not automatically become the property's new owner.

▸ **general property.** Property belonging to a general owner. See *general owner* under OWNER. Cf. *special property.*

▸ **income property.** (1883) Property that produces income, such as rental property.

▸ **incorporeal property.** (18c) **1.** An in rem proprietary right that is not classified as corporeal property. • Incorporeal property is traditionally broken down into two classes: (1) *jura in re aliena* (encumbrances), whether over material or immaterial things, examples being leases, mortgages, and servitudes; and (2) *jura in re propria* (full ownership) over immaterial things such as a patent, copyright, or trademark. **2.** A legal right in property having no physical existence. • Patent rights, for example, are incorporeal property. — Also termed *incorporeal chattel; incorporeal thing.*

▸ **intangible property.** (1843) Property that lacks a physical existence. • Examples include stock options and business goodwill. Cf. *tangible property.*

▸ **intellectual property.** See INTELLECTUAL PROPERTY.

▸ **joint property.** (16c) Real or personal property held by two or more persons with a right of survivorship. Cf. *common property.*

▸ **like-kind property.** See LIKE-KIND PROPERTY.

▸ **limited-market property.** See *special-purpose property.*

▸ **literary property.** See LITERARY PROPERTY.

▸ **lost property.** (1810) Property that the owner no longer possesses because of accident, negligence, or carelessness, and that cannot be located by an ordinary, diligent search. Cf. *abandoned property; mislaid property.*

▸ **marital property.** (1855) Property that is acquired during marriage and that is subject to distribution or division at the time of marital dissolution. • Generally, it is property acquired after the date of the marriage and before a spouse files for separation or divorce. The phrase *marital property* is used in equitable-distribution states and is roughly equivalent to *community property.* — Also termed *marital estate; matrimonial property.* See COMMUNITY PROPERTY; EQUITABLE DISTRIBUTION.

▸ **maternal property.** (18c) Property that comes from the mother of a party or some other ascendant of the maternal stock.

▸ **matrimonial property.** See *marital property.*

▸ **mislaid property.** (1915) Property that has been voluntarily relinquished by the owner with an intent to recover it later — but that cannot now be found. Cf. *abandoned property; lost property.*

"A distinction is drawn between lost property and mislaid property. An article is 'mislaid' if it is intentionally put in a certain place for a temporary purpose and then inadvertently left there when the owner goes away. A typical case is the package left on the patron's table in a bank lobby by a depositor who put the package there for a moment while he wrote a check and then departed without remembering to take it with him. There is always a 'clue' to the ownership of property which is obviously *mislaid* rather than *lost,* because of the strong probability that the owner will know where to return for his chattel when he realizes he has gone away without it." Rollin M. Perkins & Ronald N. Boyce, *Criminal Law* 310–11 (3d ed. 1982).

▸ **mixed property.** (18c) Property with characteristics of both real property and personal property — such as heirlooms and fixtures.

▸ **movable property.** See MOVABLE (1).

▸ **neutral property.** See NEUTRAL PROPERTY.

▸ **nonancestral property.** See *nonancestral estate* under ESTATE (1).

▸ **nonexempt property.** See NONEXEMPT ASSETS.

▸ **paraphernal property.** See *extradotal property.*

▸ **paternal property.** (17c) Property that comes from the father of a party or some other ascendant of the paternal stock.

▸ **personal property.** (18c) **1.** Any movable or intangible thing that is subject to ownership and not classified as real property. — Also termed *personalty; personal estate; movable estate;* (in plural) *things personal.* Cf. *real property.* **2.** *Tax.* Property not used in a taxpayer's trade or business or held for income production or collection.

▸ **private property.** (17c) Property — protected from public appropriation — over which the owner has exclusive and absolute rights.

▸ **public property.** (17c) State- or community-owned property not restricted to any one individual's use or possession.

▸ **qualified property.** (16c) A temporary or special interest in a thing (such as a right to possess it), subject to being totally extinguished by the occurrence of a specified contingency over which the qualified owner has no control.

▸ **qualified-terminable-interest property.** (1982) Property that passes by a QTIP trust from a deceased spouse to the surviving spouse and that (if the executor so elects) qualifies for the marital deduction on condition that the surviving spouse is entitled to receive all income in payments made at least annually for life and that no one has the power to appoint the property to anyone other than the surviving spouse. • The purpose of the marital deduction is to permit deferral of estate taxes until the death of the surviving spouse. But this property is included in the surviving spouse's estate at death, where it is subject to the federal estate tax. — Abbr. QTIP. See *QTIP trust* under TRUST (3).

▸ **quasi-community property.** See COMMUNITY PROPERTY.

▸ **real property.** (18c) Land and anything growing on, attached to, or erected on it, excluding anything that may be severed without injury to the land. • Real property can be either corporeal (soil and buildings) or incorporeal (easements). — Also termed *realty; real estate.* Cf. *personal property* (1).

"Real estate — or, to use the more formal term, real property — means primarily land, and everything which is naturally a part of the land, or is more or less permanently added to it. Trees, mineral deposits, gas and oil wells are all classed as real property so long as they remain a part of the land, but if the trees are cut down or the minerals extracted they cease to be real property and become personalty. Buildings and improvements of all kinds, which are permanent additions to the land upon which they stand, are a part of the real estate." William J. Grange, *Real Estate: A Practical Guide to Ownership, Transfer, Mortgaging, and Leasing of Real Property* 3 (1937).

"Historically, the line between real and personal property stems from the types of assets administered on death respectively, in the king's and in the church's courts. The king's courts, concerned with the preservation of the feudal structure, dealt with fees simple, fees tail and life estates. Estates for years, gradually evolving out of contracts made by feudally unimportant persons, clearly became interests in land but never fully attained the historical dignity of being 'real property.' The early economic unimportance of money, goods and things other than land permitted the church courts to take over the handling of all such assets on the death of the owner. When the development of trade and of capitalism caused assets of these types to assume great, and sometimes paramount, importance we found ourselves with the two important categories of property, namely 'real' and 'personal' property, each with its set of rules evolved from a different matrix. The pressure of modern society has been strongly for assimilation and the resultant elimination of this line, but this movement is far from complete attainment of its goal." 1 Richard R. Powell, *Powell on Real Property* § 5.04, at 5-7 to 5-8 (Patrick J. Rohan ed., rev. ed. 1998).

▸ **scheduled property.** (1841) *Insurance.* Property itemized on a list (usu. attached to an insurance policy) recording property values that provide the basis for insurance payments in the event of a loss under an insurance policy.

▸ **separate property.** See SEPARATE PROPERTY.

▸ **special-design property.** See *special-purpose property.*

▸ **special property.** Property that the holder has only a qualified, temporary, or limited interest in, such as (from a bailee's standpoint) bailed property. Cf. *general property.*

▸ **special-purpose property.** (1921) Property that has a unique design or layout, incorporates special construction materials, or has other features that limit the property's utility for purposes other than the one for which it was built. • Because of the property's specialized nature, the market for the property may be quite limited. — Also termed *limited-market property; special-design property.*

▸ **specialty property.** See SPECIALTY (3).

▸ **tangible personal property.** (1843) Corporeal personal property of any kind; personal property that can be seen, weighed, measured, felt, touched, or in any other way perceived by the senses, examples being furniture, cooking utensils, and books.

▸ **tangible property.** (1802) Property that has physical form and characteristics. Cf. *intangible property.*

▸ **terminable property.** (1859) Property (such as a leasehold) whose duration is not perpetual or indefinite but is limited in time or is liable to termination upon the occurrence of some specified event.

▸ **wasting property.** (1853) **1.** Property that is consumed in its normal use, such as a wasting asset, a leasehold interest, or a patent right. **2.** A right to or an interest in such property.

property, law of. See LAW OF PROPERTY.

property crimes. See CRIMES AGAINST PROPERTY.

property-damage insurance. See *property insurance* under INSURANCE.

property-disclosure statement. See DISCLOSURE STATEMENT.

property dividend. See *asset dividend* under DIVIDEND.

property division. See PROPERTY SETTLEMENT (1).

property insurance. See INSURANCE.

property interest. See INTEREST (2).

property of the debtor. (18c) *Bankruptcy.* Property that is owned or (in some instances) possessed by the debtor, including property that is exempted from the bankruptcy estate. 11 USCA § 541(b). — Also termed *debtor's property.*

property of the estate. (18c) *Bankruptcy.* The debtor's tangible and intangible property interests (including both legal and equitable interests) that fall under the bankruptcy court's jurisdiction because they were owned or held by the debtor when the bankruptcy petition was filed. 11 USCA § 541. — Also termed *estate's property.*

property *ratione privilegii* (ray-shee-**oh**-nee priv-i-**lee**-jee-ɪ). (1812) *Hist.* A common-law right, granted by a royal franchise, to take wild animals on another's land. • This principle made its way into American law. *See, e.g., Hanson v. Fergus Falls Nat'l Bank*, 65 N.W.2d 857, 862 (Minn. 1954). Cf. PROPERTY RATIONE SOLI.

> "Property Ratione privilegii is the right which, by a peculiar franchise anciently granted by the Crown in virtue of its prerogative, one man had of killing and taking animals Ferae naturae on the land of another; and in like manner the game, when killed or taken by virtue of the privilege, became the absolute property of the owner of the franchise, just as in the other case it becomes the absolute property of the owner of the soil." *Blades v. Higgs*, 11 Eng. Rep. 1474, 1479 (H.L. 1865).

property *ratione soli* (ray-shee-**oh**-nee **soh**-lɪ). (18c) The common-law right to take wild animals found on one's own land. Cf. PROPERTY RATIONE PRIVILEGII.

> "The exclusive common law right of a landowner to take game on his land, known as property ratione soli . . . has been recognized throughout the history of common law, with one exception: Following the Norman Conquest the King contended that he was lord paramount of the field, possessed of the right to the universal soil and of the exclusive right to take the game, but the irate landowners, vehemently objecting, quickly and decisively recaptured their rights and re-established the common law." *Alford v. Finch*, 155 So.2d 790, 792 (Fla. 1963).

property right. See RIGHT.

property room. A designated, secured repository used to store evidence related to criminal investigations or cases. — Also termed *evidence room; evidence locker.*

property settlement. (1882) **1.** A judgment in a divorce case determining the distribution of the marital property between the divorcing parties. • A property settlement includes a division of the marital debts as well as assets. — Also termed *property division; division of property.* **2.** A contract that divides up the assets of divorcing spouses and is incorporated into a divorce decree. — Also termed *integrated property settlement; property settlement agreement.* Cf. DIVORCE AGREEMENT. **3.** MARITAL AGREEMENT.

property settlement agreement. See PROPERTY SETTLEMENT (2).

property tax. See TAX.

property tort. See TORT.

property waste. See WASTE (1).

proper venue. 1. VENUE (1). **2.** VENUE (2).

prophylactic (proh-fə-**lak**-tik), *adj.* (16c) Designed or intended to prevent or stop something harmful or undesirable; preventive <a prophylactic rule>. — **prophylaxis** (proh-fə-**lak**-sis), **prophylactic,** *n.*

prophylactic cost. See COST (1).

prophylactic jury instruction. See *cautionary instruction* under JURY INSTRUCTION.

propinquity (prə-**ping**-kwə-tee). (15c) The quality, state, or condition of being near; specif., kindred or parentage <degrees of propinquity>.

propior sobrina (**proh**-pee-ər sə-**brɪ**-nə), *n.* [Latin] *Civil law.* The daughter of a great-uncle or great-aunt, paternal or maternal.

propior sobrino (**proh**-pee-ər sə-**brɪ**-noh), *n.* [Latin] *Civil law.* The son of a great-uncle or great-aunt, paternal or maternal.

propone (prə-**pohn**), *vb.* (14c) To put forward for consideration or adjudication <propone a will for probate>.

proponent, *n.* (16c) **1.** Someone who puts forward a legal instrument for consideration or acceptance; esp., one who offers a will for probate. — Also termed *propounder.* **2.** Someone who puts forward a proposal; one who argues in favor of something <a proponent of gun control>. **3.** *Parliamentary law.* A member who speaks in favor of a pending motion. Cf. OPPONENT (3).

proportionality. *Int'l law.* The principle that the use of force should be in proportion to the threat or grievance provoking the use of force.

proportionality review. (1976) *Criminal law.* A court's analysis of whether a sentence (esp. a death sentence) is appropriately calibrated to a certain crime, whereby the court compares the gravity of the offense and the severity of the punishment against the sentencing practices for similar crimes in other cases.

proportional quorum. See QUORUM.

proportional representation. (1870) **1.** An electoral system that allocates legislative seats to each political group in proportion to its actual voting strength in the electorate. **2.** See *proportional voting* under VOTING. • The term refers to two related but distinguishable concepts: proportional *outcome* (having members of a group elected in proportion to their numbers in the electorate) and proportional *involvement* (more precisely termed *proportional voting* and denoting the electoral system also known as *single transferable voting*). — Abbr. P.R.

proportional tax. See *flat tax* under TAX.

proportional voting. See VOTING.

proportionate-reduction clause. See LESSER-INTEREST CLAUSE.

proposal. (16c) **1.** Something offered for consideration or acceptance; a suggestion. **2.** The act of putting something forward for consideration.

proposed agenda. See AGENDA.

proposed regulation. See REGULATION (4).

proposition. 1. PROPOSAL (1). **2.** A point to be discussed or debated, usu. phrased as a complete sentence. **3.** See *main motion* under MOTION (2). **4.** A request to engage in sexual intercourse.

propositus (proh-**poz**-ə-təs). [Law Latin] (18c) *Civil law.* **1.** A person from whom descent is to be traced. **2.** The person whose rights or obligations are at issue.

3. Someone whose relations are sought to be ascertained by genealogical research. **4.** The first identified case of an inherited disease within a family. — Also termed *persona proposita*. Pl. **propposituses** or **propositi.**

pro possessore (proh pos-ə-**sor**-ee). [Latin] As a possessor; by title of a possessor; by virtue of possession alone.

pro posse suo (proh **pos**-ee **s[y]oo**-oh). [Latin] To the extent of one's power or ability.

propound (prə-**pownd**), *vb.* (16c) **1.** To offer for consideration or discussion. **2.** To make a proposal. **3.** To put forward (a will) as authentic.

propounder. An executor or administrator who offers a will or other testamentary document for admission to probate; PROPONENT.

propraetor (proh-**pree**-tər), *n.* (16c) *Roman law.* A magistrate who had served a one-year term as a praetor in Rome and who was then sent out to govern a province, esp. one with no army. Cf. PRAETOR. — **propraetorial** (proh-**pree**-tor-ee-əl), *adj.*

prop. reg. *abbr.* See *proposed regulation* under REGULATION (4).

propria persona (**proh**-pree-ə pər-**soh**-nə), *adj.* & *adv.* [Latin] (17c) In his own person; PRO SE. — Sometimes shortened to *pro per.* — Abbr. *p.p.*

proprietage (prə-**prɪ**-ə-tij), *n. Rare.* **1.** Property, abstractly considered. **2.** Collectively, property owners.

proprietary (prə-**prɪ**-ə-ter-ee), *adj.* (15c) **1.** Of, relating to, or involving a proprietor <the licensee's proprietary rights>. **2.** Of, relating to, or holding as property <the software designer sought to protect its proprietary data>. **3.** (Of a product) sold under a tradename.

proprietary act. See PROPRIETARY FUNCTION.

proprietary article. See ARTICLE.

proprietary capacity. See CAPACITY (2).

proprietary capital. See CAPITAL.

proprietary drug. See DRUG.

proprietary duty. See DUTY (2).

proprietary function. (1902) *Torts.* A municipality's conduct that is performed for the profit or benefit of the municipality, rather than for the benefit of the general public. • Generally, a municipality is not immune from tort liability for proprietary acts. But the distinction between proprietary acts and governmental functions has been abrogated by statute in many states. — Also termed *proprietary act.* Cf. GOVERNMENTAL FUNCTION.

proprietary government. See GOVERNMENT (3).

proprietary information. (1958) Information in which the owner has a protectable interest. See TRADE SECRET.

proprietary interest. See INTEREST (2).

proprietary lease. See LEASE.

proprietary license. See LICENSE.

proprietary name. See NAME.

proprietary power. See *power coupled with an interest* under POWER (3).

proprietary right. See RIGHT.

proprietary software. (1969) Software that cannot be used, redistributed, or modified without permission. • Proprietary software is usu. sold for profit, consists only of machine-readable code, and carries a limited license that restricts copying, modification, and redistribution. A user may usu. make a backup copy for personal use; but if the software is sold or given away, any backup copies must be passed on to the new user or destroyed. Cf. FREEWARE; SHAREWARE; SEMI-FREE SOFTWARE.

proprietary technology. (1965) *Intellectual property.* A body of knowledge or know-how that is owned or controlled by a person whose authorization is required before any other party may use that know-how or knowledge for commercial purposes. Cf. TRADE SECRET.

proprietary writ. See WRIT.

proprietas (prə-**prɪ**-ə-tas). [Latin] *Hist.* Ownership.

- ▸ ***proprietas nuda*** (prə-**prɪ**-ə-tas **n[y]oo**-də). (1965) Naked ownership; the mere title to property, without the usufruct.
- ▸ ***proprietas plena*** (prə-**prɪ**-ə-tas **plee**-nə). Full ownership, including both the title and the usufruct.

proprietate probanda (prə-prɪ-ə-**tay**-tee prə-**ban**-də). See DE PROPRIETATE PROBANDA.

proprietor, *n.* (16c) An owner, esp. one who runs a business. See SOLE PROPRIETORSHIP. — **proprietorship,** *n.*

proprietorial, *adj.* (18c) Behaving or feeling like the owner of something; manifesting consciousness of ownership.

propriety. (15c) *Hist.* Privately owned possessions; property.

propriis manibus (**proh**-pree-is **man**-ə-bəs). [Latin] *Hist.* By one's own hands.

proprio jure (**proh**-pree-oh **joor**-ee). [Latin] *Hist.* By one's own property right.

proprio nomine (**proh**-pree-oh **nahm**-ə-nee). [Latin] *Hist.* In one's own name.

proprio vigore (**proh**-pree-oh vi-**gor**-ee). [Latin] By its own strength.

proprium negotium (**proh**-pree-əm ni-**goh**-shee-əm). [Latin] (1873) *Hist.* One's own business.

pro privato commodo (proh prɪ-**vay**-toh **kom**-ə-doh). [Law Latin] *Hist.* For private benefit. • The phrase sometimes appeared in reference to a private road as distinguished from a public highway. Cf. PRO BONO PUBLICO.

propter (**prop**-tər). [Latin] For; on account of.

propter affectum (**prop**-tər ə-**fek**-təm). See *challenge propter affectum* under CHALLENGE (2).

propter commodum curiae (**prop**-tər **kom**-ə-dəm **kyoor**-ee-ee). [Law Latin] *Hist.* For the advantage or convenience of the court.

propter curam et culturam (**prop**-tər **kyoor**-əm et kəl-**t[y]oor**-əm). [Latin] *Hist.* For care and cultivation.

propter defectum (**prop**-tər də-**fek**-təm). See *challenge propter defectum* under CHALLENGE (2).

propter defectum sanguinis (**prop**-tər də-**fek**-təm **sang**-gwi-nis). [Latin] On account of failure of blood.

propter delectum personae (**prop**-tər də-**lek**-təm pər-**soh**-nee). [Law Latin] *Hist.* On account of the selection of persons. • For example, a person could not delegate the principal duties of an office when that person had been specifically chosen to perform those duties.

propter delictum (**prop**-tər də-**lik**-təm). See *challenge propter delictum* under CHALLENGE (2).

propter honoris respectum (**prop**-tər hə-**nor**-is ri-**spek**-təm). [Latin] On account of respect of honor or rank.

propter impotentiam (**prop**-tər im-pə-**ten**-shee-əm). [Latin] On account of helplessness. • This was formerly given as a ground for gaining a property interest in a wild animal, based on the animal's inability to escape (as where, for example, a young bird could not yet fly away).

propter ingratitudinem (**prop**-tər in-grat-ə-**t[y]oo**-də-nəm). [Latin] *Hist.* On account of ingratitude. • In some instances, a superior could revoke a gift based on the vassal's ingratitude, and a slaveowner could revoke the manumission of a slave.

propter majorem securitatem (**prop**-tər mə-**jor**-əm si-kyoor-ə-**tay**-təm). [Law Latin] *Hist.* For greater security.

propter negligentiam haeredis jus suum non prosequentis (**prop**-tər neg-li-**jen**-shee-əm hə-**ree**-dis jəs **s[y]oo**-əm non prahs-ə-**kwen**-tis). [Law Latin] *Hist.* On account of the negligence of the heir in not following up the heir's right. • If a vassal's heir failed, for a year and a day, to enter the estate, then the heir forfeited the right to the land.

propter privilegium (**prop**-tər priv-ə-**lee**-jee-əm). [Latin] On the account of privilege. • This phrase described a way of acquiring a qualified property interest in a wild animal, based on the claimant's exclusive right to hunt in a particular park or preserve.

propter quod fecerunt per alium (**prop**-tər kwod fi-**see**-rənt pər **ay**-lee-əm). [Law Latin] *Hist.* On account of what they have done by another. • The phrase usu. referred to an agent's actions.

propter rem ipsam non habitam (**prop**-tər rem **ip**-səm non **hab**-ə-təm). [Law Latin] *Hist.* On account of not having had possession of the thing itself. • The phrase appeared in reference to damages suffered by a party who failed to receive a thing for which he had contracted.

proquaestor (proh-**kwes**-tər *or* -**kwees**-), *n. Roman law.* A magistrate who had served as a quaestor in Rome and then had become associated with a provincial proconsul. See QUAESTOR.

pro quantitate haereditatis et temporis (proh kwon-ti-**tay**-tee hə-red-i-**tay**-tis et **tem**-pə-ris). [Law Latin] *Hist.* According to the extent of the succession.

pro quer. *abbr.* PRO QUERENTE.

pro querente (proh kwə-**ren**-tee). [Latin] For the plaintiff. • In old law reports, the plaintiff's advocate is designated *pro querente* and the opposing advocate *contra.* — Abbr. *pro quer.* Cf. PRO DEFENDENTE.

pro rata (proh **ray**-tə *or* **rah**-tə *or* **ra**-tə), *adv.* (16c) Proportionately; according to an exact rate, measure, or interest <the liability will be assessed pro rata between the defendants>. See RATABLE. — **pro rata,** *adj.*

pro rata clause. (1837) An insurance-policy provision — usu. contained in the "other insurance" section of the policy — that limits the insurer's liability to payment of the portion of the loss that the face amount of the policy bears to the total insurance available on the risk. — Also termed *pro rata distribution clause.* Cf. ESCAPE CLAUSE; EXCESS CLAUSE.

pro rata itineris (proh **ray**-tə ɪ-**tin**-ə-ris). [Latin] *Scots law.* For the proportion of the journey.

> "Where a ship, chartered to convey a cargo to a certain port . . . is prevented from completing the voyage . . . the master of the ship may transship the goods, and thus conveying them to their destination, earn his full freight. But if, when the ship has been prevented from proceeding on her voyage, the freighter himself transships the cargo, the master is entitled to freight *pro rata itineris,* for the proportion of the voyage which he has accomplished." John Trayner, *Trayner's Latin Maxims* 486 (4th ed. 1894).

prorate (**proh**-rayt *or* proh-**rayt**), *vb.* (1858) To divide or distribute proportionately; to assess ratably <prorate taxes between the buyer and the seller>. — **proration,** *n.*

pro rege, lege, et grege (proh **ree**-jee, **lee**-jee, et **gree**-jee). (18c) For the king, the law, and the people; for the ruler, the rule, and the ruled.

pro re nata (proh ree **nay**-tə). [Latin "in the light of what has arisen"] *Hist.* By reason of emergency; arising from exigent circumstances. • The phrase appeared, for example, in reference to a meeting called to address an emergency.

> "So far as may be, the state leaves the rule of right to be declared and constituted by the agreement of those concerned with it. So far as possible, it contents itself with executing the rules which its subjects have made for themselves. And in so doing it acts wisely. For, in the first place, the administration of justice is enabled in this manner to escape in a degree not otherwise attainable the disadvantages inherent in the recognition of rigid principles of law. Such principles we must have; but if they are established *pro re nata* by the parties themselves, they will possess a measure of adaptability to individual cases which is unattainable by the more general legislation of the state itself." John Salmond, *Jurisprudence* 352 (Glanville L. Williams ed., 10th ed. 1947).

prorogated jurisdiction. See JURISDICTION.

prorogatio de loco in locum (proh-roh-**gay**-shee-oh dee **loh**-koh in **loh**-kəm). [Law Latin] (18c) *Hist.* Prorogation (of jurisdiction) from one place to another.

prorogatio de tempore in tempus (proh-roh-**gay**-shee-oh dee **tem**-pə-ree in **tem**-pəs). [Law Latin] (18c) *Hist.* Prorogation (esp. of jurisdiction) from one time to another.

prorogatio fori (proh-roh-**gay**-shee-oh **for**-ɪ). [Latin] *Hist.* Prorogation of the forum. See PROROGATION.

prorogation (proh-rə-**gay**-shən). (14c) **1.** The act of putting off to another day; esp., the discontinuance of a legislative session until its next term. **2.** *Civil law.* The extension of a court's or judge's jurisdiction by consent of the parties to a case that it would otherwise be incompetent to hear. — **prorogative,** *adj.*

▸ **tacit prorogation.** (18c) *Civil law.* Consent to jurisdiction that arises when a party does not request recusal despite awareness that the judge is not qualified to try the case. Cf. *prorogated jurisdiction* under JURISDICTION.

prorogation clause. See FORUM-SELECTION CLAUSE.

prorogue (proh-**rohg** *or* prə-), *vb.* (15c) **1.** To postpone or defer. **2.** To discontinue a session of (a legislative assembly, esp. the British Parliament) without dissolution. **3.** To suspend or discontinue a legislative session.

proscribe, *vb.* (15c) **1.** To outlaw or prohibit; to forbid officially. **2.** *Roman & civil law.* To post or publish the name of (a person) as condemned to death, his or her property thereby being forfeited to the state.

proscription, *n.* (14c) **1.** The act of prohibiting something; specif., an instance of legally forbidding, outlawing, or interdicting. Cf. PRESCRIPTION (1). **2.** The quality, state, or condition of being prohibited. **3.** A prohibition or severe restriction. **4.** An act of condemning or rejecting from privilege or favor; a denunciation. **5.** *Roman law.* Outlawry; esp., a proclamation declaring that a person is an outlaw who may be lawfully killed by anyone and that the estate will be confiscated. — **proscriptive,** *adj.*

pro se (proh **say** *or* **see**), *adv.* & *adj.* [Latin] (1817) For oneself; on one's own behalf; without a lawyer <the defendant proceeded pro se> <a pro se defendant>. — Also termed *pro persona; in propria persona; propria persona; pro per.* See PROPRIA PERSONA.

pro se, *n.* (1857) One who represents oneself in a court proceeding without the assistance of a lawyer <the third case on the court's docket involving a pro se>. — Also termed *pro per; self-represented litigant;* (rarely) *pro se-er.*

prosecutable, *adj.* (18c) (Of a crime or person) subject to prosecution; capable of being prosecuted.

prosecute, *vb.* (15c) **1.** To commence and carry out (a legal action) <because the plaintiff failed to prosecute its contractual claims, the court dismissed the suit>. **2.** To institute and pursue a criminal action against (a person) <the notorious felon has been prosecuted in seven states>. **3.** To engage in; carry on <the company prosecuted its business for 12 years before going bankrupt>. — **prosecutory,** *adj.*

prosecuting attorney. See DISTRICT ATTORNEY.

prosecuting witness. See WITNESS.

prosecution. (16c) **1.** The commencement and carrying out of any action or scheme <the prosecution of a long, bloody war>. **2.** A criminal proceeding in which an accused person is tried <the conspiracy trial involved the prosecution of seven defendants>. — Also termed *criminal prosecution.*

▸ **deferred prosecution.** See DEFERRED PROSECUTION.

▸ **private prosecution.** (17c) *Hist.* A criminal prosecution initiated by a privately employed attorney or by a layperson or private organization, rather than a district attorney or other government-employed prosecutor. • Until the 19th century, victims often had the burden of directly prosecuting criminals who had harmed them. With the rise of public-prosecution services, the need for private prosecutions declined. Though uncommon, they are still sometimes permitted in England.

▸ **selective prosecution.** See SELECTIVE PROSECUTION.

▸ **sham prosecution.** (1903) A prosecution that seeks to circumvent a defendant's double-jeopardy protection by appearing to be prosecuted by another sovereignty, when it is in fact controlled by the sovereignty that already prosecuted the defendant for the same crime. • A sham prosecution is, in essence, a misuse of the dual-sovereignty doctrine. Under that doctrine, a defendant's protection against double jeopardy does not provide protection against a prosecution by a different sovereignty. For example, if the defendant was first tried in federal court and acquitted, that fact would not forbid the state authorities from prosecuting the defendant in state court. But a sham prosecution — for example, a later state-court prosecution that is completely dominated or manipulated by the federal authorities that already prosecuted the defendant, so that the state-court proceeding is merely a tool of the federal authorities — will not withstand a double-jeopardy challenge. See DUAL-SOVEREIGNTY DOCTRINE.

▸ **vertical prosecution.** See VERTICAL PROSECUTION.

▸ **vindictive prosecution.** (1834) A prosecution in which a person is singled out under a law or regulation because the person has exercised a constitutionally protected right. Cf. SELECTIVE ENFORCEMENT.

3. One or more government attorneys who initiate and maintain a criminal action against an accused defendant <the prosecution rests>. **4.** *Patents.* The process of applying for and pursuing a patent through the U.S. Patent and Trademark Office and negotiating with the patent examiner. — Also termed *patent-prosecution process.*

prosecution history. See FILE WRAPPER.

prosecution-history estoppel. See ESTOPPEL.

prosecution laches. See LACHES (1).

prosecution-laches doctrine. See CONTINUATION-APPLICATION LACHES DOCTRINE.

prosecutor, *n.* (16c) **1.** A legal officer who represents the state or federal government in criminal proceedings. See DISTRICT ATTORNEY; UNITED STATES ATTORNEY; ATTORNEY GENERAL. — Also termed *public prosecutor; state's attorney; public commissioner.*

▸ **public prosecutor. 1.** See PROSECUTOR (1). **2.** See DISTRICT ATTORNEY.

▸ **special prosecutor.** (1859) A lawyer appointed to investigate and, if justified, seek indictments in a particular case. See *independent counsel* under COUNSEL.

2. A private person who institutes and carries on a legal action, esp. a criminal action. — Also termed (in sense 2) *private prosecutor.* — **prosecutorial,** *adj.*

prosecutorial discretion. See DISCRETION (4).

prosecutorial immunity. See IMMUNITY (1).

prosecutorial misconduct. (1963) *Criminal law.* A prosecutor's improper or illegal act (or failure to act), esp. involving an attempt to avoid required disclosure or to persuade the jury to wrongly convict a defendant or assess an unjustified punishment. • If prosecutorial misconduct results in a mistrial, a later prosecution may be barred under the Double Jeopardy Clause.

prosecutorial vindictiveness. (1968) *Criminal law.* The act or an instance of intentionally charging a more serious crime or seeking a more severe penalty than is proper, esp. in retaliation for a defendant's lawful exercise of a constitutional right.

prosecutrix (pros-ə-**kyoo**-triks). (18c) *Archaic.* A female prosecutor; esp., a female complainant in a criminal case.

prosequi (**pros**-ə-kwɪ), *vb.* [Latin] To follow up or pursue; to sue or prosecute. Cf. NOLLE PROSEQUI.

prosequitur (prə-**sek**-wə-tər *or* proh-). [Latin] He follows or pursues; he prosecutes. Cf. NON PROSEQUITUR.

pro servitio burgali (proh sər-**vish**-ee-oh bər-**gay**-lɪ). [Law Latin] *Hist.* For burghal service. See BURGAGE-TENURE (2).

prosocer (**proh**-sə-sər). [Latin] (16c) *Civil law.* A father-in-law's father; a spouse's grandfather.

prosocerus (prə-**sos**-ə-rəs). [Latin] *Civil law.* A spouse's grandmother.

pro socio (proh **soh**-shee-oh). [Latin] As a partner. • This was the name of an action on behalf of a partner.

pro solido (proh **sol**-ə-doh). [Latin] For the whole; without division.

prospect (**prah**-spekt), *n.* (15c) **1.** A future probability based on present indications; a propitious indication. **2.** *Mining.* An indication or sample that suggests the presence of ore. **3.** A view, a survey, or an instance of panoramic observing. **4.** The direction one faces or outlook one has from a given location. **5.** Someone who may be persuaded to become a customer; a potential buyer, member, or subscriber.

prospectant evidence. See EVIDENCE.

prospective, *adj.* (18c) **1.** Effective or operative in the future <prospective application of the new statute>. Cf. RETROACTIVE. **2.** Anticipated or expected; likely to come about <prospective clients>.

prospective damages. See DAMAGES.

prospective heir. See HEIR.

prospective law. See *prospective statute* under STATUTE.

prospective nuisance. See *anticipatory nuisance* under NUISANCE.

prospective statute. See STATUTE.

prospective waiver. See WAIVER (1).

prospectivity. The quality, state, or condition of being concerned with or having reference to the future; esp., a statute's or legal ruling's effectiveness in the future. Cf. RETROACTIVITY.

▸ **selective prospectivity.** (1991) A court's decision to apply a new rule of law in the particular case in which the new rule is announced, but to apply the old rule in all other cases pending when the new rule is announced or cases in which the facts predate the new rule's announcement.

prospect theory. See INCENTIVE-TO-COMMERCIALIZE THEORY.

prospectus (prə-**spek**-təs). (18c) A printed document that describes the main features of an enterprise (often a corporation's business) and that is distributed to prospective buyers or investors; esp., a written description of a securities offering. • Under SEC regulations, a publicly traded corporation must provide a prospectus before offering to sell stock in the corporation. See REGISTRATION STATEMENT. Cf. TOMBSTONE. Pl. **prospectuses.**

▸ **newspaper prospectus.** (1936) A summary prospectus that the SEC allows to be disseminated through advertisements in newspapers, magazines, or other periodicals sent through the mails as second-class matter (though not distributed by the advertiser), when the securities involved are issued by a foreign national government with which the United States maintains diplomatic relations.

▸ **preliminary prospectus.** (1952) A prospectus for a stock issue that has been filed but not yet approved by the SEC. • The SEC requires such a prospectus to contain a notice — printed in distinctive red lettering — that the document is not complete or final. That notice, which is usu. stamped or printed in red ink, typically reads as follows: "The information here given is subject to completion or amendment. A registration statement relating to these securities has been filed with the Securities and Exchange Commission. These securities cannot be sold — and offers to buy cannot be accepted — until the registration statement becomes effective. This prospectus does not constitute an offer to buy. And these securities cannot be sold in any state where the offer, solicitation, or sale would be unlawful before registration or qualification under the securities laws of that state." — Also termed *red-herring prospectus*; *red herring*; *pathfinder document.*

prostitute, *n.* (16c) Someone who engages in sexual acts in exchange for money or anything else of value. — Also termed *sex worker.*

▸ **child prostitute.** See *prostituted child* under CHILD.

prostituted child. See CHILD.

prostitution, *n.* (16c) **1.** The act or practice of engaging in sexual activity for money or its equivalent; commercialized sex.

> "Prostitution is not itself a crime in England or Scotland, although certain activities of prostitutes and those who profit from prostitution are prohibited, such as soliciting in a public place, procuring, letting premises for the purpose of prostitution and so forth. On the other hand, prostitution was, at least at one time, prohibited in all American jurisdictions." Rollin M. Perkins & Ronald N. Boyce, *Criminal Law* 470 (3d ed. 1982).

▸ **child prostitution.** (1930) The act or practice of offering or using a minor for sex acts in exchange for money. See *prostituted child* under CHILD.

2. The act of debasing. — **prostitute,** *vb.* — **prostitute,** *n.*

pro tanto (proh **tan**-toh), *adv.* & *adj.* [Latin] (17c) To that extent; for so much; as far as it goes <the debt is pro tanto discharged> <a pro tanto payment>.

protected activity. (1918) Conduct that is permitted or encouraged by a statute or constitutional provision, and for which the actor may not be legally retaliated against. • For example, Title VII of the Civil Rights Act prohibits an employer from retaliating against an employee who opposes a discriminatory employment practice or helps in investigating an allegedly discriminatory employment practice. An employee who is retaliated against for engaging in one of those activities has a claim against the employer. 42 USCA § 2000e-3(a).

protected class. See CLASS (1).

protected person. See PERSON (1).

protecting power. (1826) *Int'l law.* A country responsible for protecting another country's citizens and interests during a conflict or a suspension of diplomatic ties between the citizens' country and a third party. • After a protecting power is accepted by both belligerents, it works to ensure the proper treatment of nationals who are in a belligerent's territory, esp. prisoners of war. If the parties cannot agree on a protecting power, the International Committee of the Red Cross is often appointed to this position.

protection, *n.* (14c) **1.** The act of protecting. **2.** PROTECTIONISM. **3.** COVERAGE (1). **4.** A document given by a notary public to sailors and other persons who travel abroad, certifying that the bearer is a U.S. citizen. — **protect,** *vb.*

▸ **witness protection. 1.** Protection given to a witness who has been threatened or may be intimidated against testifying. **2.** Protection provided before, during, and after trial, usu. by law-enforcement officers, to any person expected to testify. — Also termed *witness security.* See WITNESS-PROTECTION PROGRAM.

Protection and Advocacy for Individuals with Mental Illness Act. A 1986 federal statute that provides funding for the state-level establishment of independent organizations dedicated to monitoring and protecting the rights of mentally ill citizens. 42 USCA §§ 10801–10851. • Formerly titled the *Protection and Advocacy for Mentally Ill Individuals Act,* this statute was renamed in the Children's Health Act of 2000 (114 Stat. 1101). — Abbr. PAIMI Act.

Protection and Advocacy for Mentally Ill Individuals Act. See PROTECTION AND ADVOCACY FOR INDIVIDUALS WITH MENTAL ILLNESS ACT.

protection covenant. (1970) *Oil & gas.* The implied promise in an oil-and-gas lease that the lessee will protect the property against the loss of oil and gas by drainage from the producing reservoir by drilling one or more offsetting wells. • The covenant applies only if a reasonably prudent operator would drill the additional wells. — Also termed *covenant to protect against drainage.* See REASONABLY PRUDENT-OPERATOR STANDARD.

protectionism. (1844) The protection of domestic businesses and industries against foreign competition by imposing high tariffs and restricting imports. — **protectionist,** *adj.*

protection money. (18c) **1.** A bribe paid to an officer as an inducement not to interfere with the criminal activities of the briber. • Examples include payments to an officer in exchange for the officer's releasing an arrestee, removing records of traffic violations from a court's files, and refraining from making a proper arrest. **2.** Money extorted from a business owner by one who promises to "protect" the business premises, with the implied threat that if the owner does not pay, the person requesting the payment will harm the owner or damage the premises.

protection order. See RESTRAINING ORDER (1).

protective appeal. See APPEAL (2).

protective committee. (1899) A group of security holders or preferred stockholders appointed to protect the interests of their group when the corporation is liquidated or reorganized.

protective custody. See CUSTODY (1).

protective order. (1884) **1.** A court order prohibiting or restricting a party from engaging in conduct (esp. a legal procedure such as discovery) that unduly annoys or burdens the opposing party or a third-party witness. **2.** RESTRAINING ORDER (1).

▸ **blanket protective order.** (1962) A protective order that covers a broad subject or class. — Often shortened to *blanket order.* — Also termed *umbrella protective order.*

▸ **emergency protective order.** (1976) A temporary protective order granted on an expedited basis, usu. after an ex parte hearing (without notice to the other side), most commonly to provide injunctive relief from an abuser in a domestic-violence case; esp., a short-term restraining order that is issued at the request of a law-enforcement officer in response to a domestic-violence complaint from a victim who is in immediate danger. • A victim of domestic violence can obtain an EPO only through a law-enforcement officer. There is no notice requirement, but the abuser must be served with the order. The duration of an EPO varies from three to seven days, depending on state law. — Abbr. EPO. Cf. TEMPORARY RESTRAINING ORDER.

▸ **permanent protective order.** (1981) A protective order of indefinite duration granted after a hearing with notice to both sides; esp., a court order that prohibits an abuser from contacting or approaching the protected person for a long period, usu. years. Despite the name, permanent orders often have expiration dates set by state law. An order may also require the abuser to perform certain acts such as attending counseling or providing financial support for the protected person. — Abbr. PPO.

protective principle. *Int'l law.* The doctrine that a sovereign state has the power to assert jurisdiction over a person whose conduct outside its boundaries threatens its security or could interfere with the operation of its government functions.

protective search. See SEARCH (1).

protective sweep. (1973) A police officer's quick and limited search — conducted after the officer has lawfully entered a premises, esp. as incident to an arrest or to a warrantless entry to search — based on a reasonable belief drawn from specific and articulable facts that such a search is necessary to protect the officer or others from harm.

protective tariff. See TARIFF (2).

protective trust. See TRUST (3).

protector. (1833) **1.** An unrelated, disinterested overseer of a trust who possesses broader authority than a trustee. • Protectors are usu. appointed to manage offshore trusts, but the concept is slowly being applied to domestic trusts. Protectors often possess broad powers to act for the benefit of the trust, as by removing trustees and clarifying or modifying trust terms to promote the settlor's objectives. For these reasons, a protector is generally not a trustee or beneficiary of the trust. Cf. TRUSTEE. **2.** Someone who, having been named in an instrument creating a fee tail, has the responsibility of exercising discretion over whether the tenant in tail may bar the entail. — Also termed *protector of the settlement.*

> "The only additional restriction imposed upon the alienation of an estate tail is that the consent of the person who is called the Protector of the settlement is necessary to its being effectually barred. Alienation by tenant in tail without this consent binds his own issue, but not remaindermen or reversioners, and creates what is called a 'base fee.' The Protector of the settlement is usually the tenant for life in possession; but the settlor of the lands may appoint in his place any number of persons not exceeding three to be together Protector during the continuance of the estates preceding the estate tail." Kenelm E. Digby, *An Introduction to the History of the Law of Real Property* 255 (5th ed. 1897).

protectorate (prə-**tek**-tə-rət). (17c) **1.** *Int'l law.* The relationship between a weaker country and a stronger one when the weaker country has transferred the management of its more important international affairs to the stronger country. **2.** *Int'l law.* The weaker or dependent country within such a relationship.

> "**Protectorates.** The term 'protectorate' is applied to the relation established between a stronger and a weaker state,

by which the weaker is protected from foreign aggression and interference, but suffers in consequence some diminution of its rights of sovereignty and independence. This relation is established by treaty, by the terms of which the extent and character of the protectorate are determined. In most protectorates the foreign relations of the protected state, including the power to engage in war, are in great part regulated by the protector. In so far as other nations are concerned, however, the relations of the interested states forming the protectorate are regarded as strictly internal in character; 'the two constitute a single system, possessing and exercising all the powers which belong to civilized government, and not subject to the interference of any third state as to the distribution of those powers,' which is regulated by the interested states to the exclusion of all others." George B. Davis, *The Elements of International Law* 38 (4th ed. 1916).

3. (*usu. cap.*) The period in British history — from 1653 to 1659 — during which Oliver Cromwell and Richard Cromwell governed. **4.** The British government in the period from 1653 to 1659.

protégé. (18c) **1.** A person protected by or under the care or training of another person or an entity, esp. one who is established or influential. **2.** *Int'l law.* A country that is under the protection of another country. **3.** *Int'l law.* Someone who is a citizen of a protected country or otherwise recognized by treaty as a protected person.

pro tem. *abbr.* (18c) PRO TEMPORE.

pro tempore (proh **tem**-pə-ree), *adv.* & *adj.* [Latin] (15c) For the time being; appointed to occupy a position temporarily <a judge pro tempore>. — Abbr. pro tem.

protest, *n.* (15c) **1.** A formal statement or action expressing dissent or disapproval. • Under some circumstances, a protest is lodged to preserve a claim or right. **2.** A notary public's written statement that, upon presentment, a negotiable instrument was neither paid nor accepted. — Also termed *initial protest*; *noting protest.* Cf. NOTICE OF DISHONOR.

"Noting or initial protest is a memorandum made on [a dishonored] instrument, with the notary's initials, date, and the amount of noting charges, together with a statement of the cause of dishonor, such as 'no effects,' 'not advice,' or 'no account.' This is done to charge the memory of the notary, and should be done on the day of dishonor." Frederick M. Hinch, *John's American Notary and Commissioner of Deeds Manual* § 442, at 281 (3d ed. 1922).

3. A formal statement, usu. in writing, disputing a debt's legality or validity but agreeing to make payment while reserving the right to recover the amount at a later time. • The disputed debt is described as *under protest.* **4.** *Tax.* A taxpayer's statement to the collecting officer that payment is being made unwillingly because the taxpayer believes the tax to be invalid. **5.** *Int'l law.* A formal communication from one subject of international law to another objecting to conduct or a claim by the latter as violating international law. **6.** *Patents.* A proceeding in the U.S. Patent and Trademark Office to determine patentability of an invention after a third party has challenged it in a petition. • Unlike in a public use proceeding, the protestant has no right to participate in the proceeding beyond filing the petition and supporting documents. 37 CFR 1.291. Cf. PUBLIC-USE PROCEEDING. — **protest,** *vb.*

protestando (proh-tə-**stan**-doh). [Law Latin] Protesting. • This emphatic word was used in a protestation to allege or deny something in an oblique manner.

protestant. *Patents.* Someone who files a protest petition with the U.S. Patent and Trademark Office challenging the patentability of an invention. See PROTEST.

protestatio contraria facto (proh-tes-**tay**-shee-oh kən-**trair**-ee-ə **fak**-toh). [Law Latin] (17c) *Hist.* Protestation inconsistent with one's conduct while protesting.

protestation (prot-ə-**stay**-shən). (14c) **1.** *Common-law pleading.* A declaration by which a party makes an oblique allegation or denial of some fact, claiming that it does or does not exist or is or is not legally sufficient, while not directly affirming or denying the fact.

"The practice of protestation of facts not denied arose where the pleader, wishing to avail himself of the right to contest in a future action some traversable fact in the pending action, passes it by without traverse, but at the same time makes a declaration collateral or incidental to his main pleading, importing that the fact so passed over is untrue. The necessity for this arose from the rule that pleadings must not be double, and that every pleading is taken to admit such matters as it does not traverse. Such being its only purpose, it is wholly without effect in the action in which it occurs . . . ." Benjamin J. Shipman, *Handbook of Common-Law Pleading* § 207, at 358 (Henry Winthrop Ballantine ed., 3d ed. 1923).

2. *Scots law.* A defendant's act in a civil case to compel a pursuer (plaintiff) who has failed to take the necessary procedural steps either to proceed or to allow the action to fall.

protest certificate. (1889) A notarial certificate declaring (1) that a holder in due course has recruited the notary public to present a previously refused or dishonored negotiable instrument, (2) that the notary has presented the instrument to the person responsible for payment or acceptance (the *drawee*), (3) that the instrument was presented at a given time and place, and (4) that the drawee refused or dishonored the instrument. • In former practice, the notary would issue a protest certificate, which could then be presented to the drawee and any other liable parties as notice that the holder could seek damages for the dishonored negotiable instrument. — Also termed *notarial protest certificate.* See NOTICE OF DISHONOR.

protest fee. (1840) A fee charged by a bank or other financial institution when an item (such as a check) is presented but cannot be collected.

prothonotary (prə-**thon**-ə-ter-ee *or* proh-thə-**noh**-tə-ree), *n.* (15c) A chief clerk in certain courts of law. — Also termed *protonotary.* — **prothonotarial,** *adj.*

protocol. (15c) **1.** A summary of a document or treaty. **2.** A treaty amending and supplementing another treaty. **3.** The formal record of the proceedings of a conference or congress. — Also termed *procès-verbal.* **4.** The minutes of a meeting, usu. initialed by all participants after confirming accuracy. **5.** The rules of diplomatic etiquette; the practices that countries observe in the course of their contacts with one another.

protonotary. See PROTHONOTARY.

pro tribunali (proh trib-yə-**nay**-lɪ). [Latin] *Hist.* Before the court.

protutor (proh-**t[y]oo**-tər). (17c) *Civil law.* Someone who, though not legally appointed as a guardian, administers another's affairs.

prout de lege (**proh**-ət dee [*or* di] **lee**-jee). [Law Latin] According to law. • Proof *prout de lege* is proof by any legal means, as distinct from proof limited to writing. — Also termed *prout de jure* (**proh**-ət dee [*or* di] **joor**-ee).

> "A proof *prout de jure* is a proof by all the legal means of probation — viz.: writ, witnesses, and oath of party; although, in practice, the phrase is usually applied to a proof of facts and circumstances by parole, in contradistinction to a proof limited to writ or oath of party." William Bell, *Bell's Dictionary and Digest of the Law of Scotland* 871 (George Watson ed., 7th ed. 1890).

prout patet per recordum (**proh**-ət **pay**-tet pər ri-**kor**-dəm). [Latin] As appears by the record.

provable, *adj.* (15c) Capable of being proved.

prove, *vb.* (13c) To establish or make certain; to establish the truth of (a fact or hypothesis) by satisfactory evidence.

prover, *n.* (15c) **1.** Someone who or that which proves. **2.** *Hist.* APPROVER (1).

pro veritate accipitur (proh ver-i-**tay**-tee ak-**sip**-ə-tər). [Latin] *Hist.* Is held or received as the truth.

prove-up, *n.* The establishment of a prima facie claim. • A prove-up is necessary when a factual assertion is unopposed because even without opposition, the claim must be supported by evidence.

prove up, *vb.* (1832) To present or complete the proof of (something) <deciding not to put a doctor on the stand, the plaintiff attempted to prove up his damages with medical records only>.

provided, *conj.* (15c) **1.** On the condition or understanding (that) <we will sign the contract provided that you agree to the following conditions>. • For the Latin antecedent of this term, see DUMMODO. **2.** Except (that) <all permittees must be at least 18 years of age, provided that those with a bona fide hardship must be at least 15 years of age>. **3.** And <a railway car must be operated by a full crew if it extends for more than 15 continuous miles, provided that a full crew must consist of at least six railway workers>.

provident plea. See PLEA (1).

province, *n.* (14c) **1.** An administrative district into which a country has been divided. **2.** A sphere of activity of a profession such as medicine or law.

provincialis (prə-vin-shee-**ay**-lis). [Latin] Someone who has a domicile in a province.

provincial synod. See SYNOD.

proving the tenor. (17c) *Scots law.* An action to establish the terms of a deed or will that has been lost or destroyed.

provision. (15c) **1.** A clause in a statute, contract, or other legal instrument. **2.** A stipulation made beforehand. See PROVISO.

provisional, *adj.* (16c) **1.** Provided for the time being to supply a place to be occupied in the end by some more permanent arrangement; temporary or conditional <a provisional injunction>. **2.** Of, relating to, or involving an extraordinary proceeding to protect a litigant before final judgment.

provisional alimony. See *temporary alimony* under ALIMONY (1).

provisional application. See PATENT APPLICATION.

provisional attachment. See ATTACHMENT (1).

provisional court. See COURT.

provisional director. See DIRECTOR.

provisional driver's license. See DRIVER'S LICENSE.

provisional exit. (2004) *Criminal procedure.* A prisoner's temporary release from prison for a court appearance, hospital treatment, work detail, or other purpose requiring a release with the expectation of return.

provisional government. See GOVERNMENT (3).

provisional injunction. See *preliminary injunction* under INJUNCTION.

provisional license. See LICENSE.

provisional order. *English law.* An order by a governmental department authorizing some particular action by a local authority.

provisional partition. See PARTITION (2).

provisional patent application. See *provisional application* under PATENT APPLICATION.

provisional remedy. See REMEDY.

provisional right. (1975) *Patents.* The right to obtain a reasonable royalty for use of a patented invention or process by an infringer with actual notice during the period between the publication of a patent application and the time a patent is issued. • The right is only available if the invention as claimed in the issued patent is substantially identical to the invention as claimed in the published application. 35 USCA § 154.

provisional seizure. See ATTACHMENT (1).

provisione hominis (prə-vizh-ee-**oh**-nee **hom**-ə-nis), *adv.* [Law Latin] *Hist.* By an individual's appointment. • The phrase referred to heirs that a testator appoints, as distinguished from those who succeed by law.

provisione legis (prə-vizh-ee-**oh**-nee **lee**-jis), *adv.* [Law Latin] *Hist.* By provision of law.

> "Heirs who succeed according to the rules of law regulating succession, without the consent or appointment of their ancestor, are said to succeed *provisione legis*, and are known as heirs-at-law." John Trayner, *Trayner's Latin Maxims* 494 (4th ed. 1894).

provisione tenus (prə-vizh-ee-**oh**-nee **ten**-əs), *adv.* [Law Latin] *Hist.* To the extent of the provision.

provision of a fine. *Hist.* A proclamation made after the conveying of land by fine, read aloud in court 16 times — four times in the term when the fine was made, and four times in the three succeeding terms.

Provisions of Oxford. *Hist.* During the reign of Henry III, a constitution created by the Mad Parliament and forming the King's advisory council that met with a group of barons several times a year to handle the country's affairs and resolve grievances, esp. those resulting from the King's avoidance of his obligations under Magna Carta. • The Provisions were effective until the baron uprising in 1263 under Simon de Montfort.

proviso (prə-**vɪ**-zoh). (15c) **1.** A limitation, condition, or stipulation upon whose compliance a legal or formal document's validity or application may depend. **2.** In drafting, a provision that begins with the words *provided that* and supplies a condition, exception, or addition.

proviso canon. The doctrine that a proviso in a legal instrument conditions only the principal matter that it qualifies — almost always the matter immediately preceding.

provisor. (14c) **1.** *Hist.* A provider of care or sustenance. **2.** *Eccles. law.* A person nominated by the pope to be the next incumbent of a benefice that is vacant or about to become vacant.

provocation, *n.* (15c) **1.** The act of inciting another to do something, esp. to commit a crime. **2.** Something (such as words or actions) that affects a person's reason and self-control, esp. causing the person to commit a crime impulsively. — **provoke,** *vb.* — **provocative,** *adj.*

"Provocation is no ground for exempting one absolutely from criminal responsibility for his acts, but may be ground for mitigating the punishment.

"A person who commits a crime cannot escape liability altogether by showing that he was provoked; but the fact that a crime was committed under provocation may sometimes be ground for inflicting less severe punishment in cases of homicide and assault." William Lawrence Clark, *Handbook of Criminal Law* 42 (3d ed. 1915).

▸ **adequate provocation.** (1842) Something that would cause a reasonable person to act without self-control and lose any premeditated state of mind. • The usual form of adequate provocation is the heat of passion. Adequate provocation can reduce a criminal charge, as from murder to voluntary manslaughter. — Also termed *adequate cause; sudden provocation; indirect provocation; reasonable provocation.* See HEAT OF PASSION. Cf. SELF-DEFENSE; *partial excuse* under EXCUSE (2); EXTREME MENTAL OR EMOTIONAL DISTURBANCE.

▸ **direct provocation.** (18c) An act done or words said with the intent to provoke another to do something in response.

▸ **indirect provocation.** See *adequate provocation.*

▸ **reasonable provocation.** See *adequate provocation.*

provost. (bef. 12c) **1.** Someone appointed to superintend or preside over something; one who is appointed an official head. **2.** *Archaic.* The mayor or chief magistrate of a town. **3.** *Hist.* The steward, bailiff, or reeve of a manor or town. **4.** *Eccles. law.* The head of a cathedral or collegiate chapter. **5.** In education, a high administrative officer usu. in charge of strictly academic activities.

provost marshal. (16c) *Military law.* A staff officer who supervises a command's military police and advises the commander.

proxenete (prok-sə-**neet**). [Latin fr. Greek] (17c) *Roman & civil law.* **1.** Someone who negotiates or arranges the terms of a contract between parties; a broker. **2.** [Greek] Someone who negotiates marriages; a matchmaker. — Also termed *proxeneta.*

proximate (**prok**-sə-mit), *adj.* (17c) **1.** Immediately before or after. **2.** Very near or close in time or space. Cf. IMMEDIATE. — **proximateness,** *n.*

proximate cause. See CAUSE (1).

proximate consequence. See CONSEQUENCE.

proximate damages. See DAMAGES.

proximity. (15c) The quality, state, or condition of being near in time, place, order, or relation.

proximus pubertati (**prok**-sə-məs pyoo-bər-**tay**-tı). [Latin] (1802) *Roman law.* Near puberty — hence likely to know right from wrong.

proxy, *n.* (15c) **1.** Someone who is authorized to act as a substitute for another; esp., in corporate law, a person who is authorized to vote another's stock shares. Cf. *absentee voting* under VOTING. **2.** The grant of authority by which a person is so authorized. **3.** The document granting this authority. — Also termed (for sense 3 in Roman law) *procuratorium.*

▸ **irrevocable proxy.** (1837) A power to exercise voting rights associated with securities or a membership that the grantor may not countermand or terminate. • To create an irrevocable proxy that is legally effective requires compliance with law applicable to the entity that issued the securities. See *agency coupled with an interest* under AGENCY.

proxy contest. (1938) A struggle between two corporate factions to obtain the votes of uncommitted shareholders. • A proxy contest usu. occurs when a group of dissident shareholders mounts a battle against the corporation's managers. — Also termed *proxy fight.*

proxy directive. (1982) A document that appoints a surrogate decision-maker for the declarant's healthcare decisions. Cf. ADVANCE DIRECTIVE; INSTRUCTION DIRECTIVE; LIVING WILL.

proxy marriage. See MARRIAGE (3).

proxy solicitation. (1930) A request that a corporate shareholder authorize another person to cast the shareholder's vote at a corporate meeting.

proxy statement. (1939) An informational document that accompanies a proxy solicitation and explains a proposed action (such as a merger) by the corporation.

PRP. *abbr.* POTENTIALLY RESPONSIBLE PARTY.

PRS. *abbr.* Postrelease supervision.

PRT. *abbr.* See *personal-residence trust* under TRUST (3).

prudent, *adj.* (14c) Sensible and careful, esp. in trying to avoid unnecessary risks; circumspect or judicious in one's activities. — **prudence,** *n.*

prudential-standing doctrine. A judicial doctrine that even if a party has Article III standing, prudential rules should govern the determination whether a party should be granted standing to sue. • The most important rule of prudential standing is that a plaintiff who asserts an injury must come within the "zone of interest" arguably protected by the Constitution or a statute. A second rule is that a party may assert only his or her own rights and cannot raise the claims of a third party who is not before the court. A third rule is that a plaintiff cannot sue if the alleged injury is a generalized one widely shared with others.

prudent-investor rule. (1960) *Trusts.* The principle that a fiduciary must invest in only those securities or portfolios of securities that a reasonable person would buy. • The origin of the prudent-investor rule is *Harvard College v. Amory,* 26 Mass. 446 (1830). This case stressed two points for a trustee to consider when making investments: probable income and probable safety. The trustee must consider both when making investments. Originally termed the *prudent-man rule,* the Restatement (Third) of Trusts changed the term to *prudent-investor rule.* — Also termed *prudent-person rule.*

prudent lawyer. See LAWYER.

prudent-operator standard. See REASONABLY-PRUDENT-OPERATOR STANDARD.

prudent person. See REASONABLE PERSON.

prudent-person rule. See PRUDENT-INVESTOR RULE.

prurient (**pruur**-ee-ənt), *adj.* (17c) Characterized by, exhibiting, or arousing inappropriate, inordinate, or unusual sexual desire; having or showing too much interest in sex <films appealing to prurient interests>. See OBSCENITY. — **prurience,** *n.*

PRWO. *abbr.* Parole revoked, warrant ordered.

PRWORA. *abbr.* PERSONAL RESPONSIBILITY AND WORK OPPORTUNITY RECONCILIATION ACT.

p.s. *abbr.* (*usu. cap.*) (17c) **1.** Public statute. See PUBLIC LAW (2). **2.** Postscript.

psephology (sə-**fahl**-ə-jee). (1952) The study of how people vote in elections. — **psephological,** *adj.* — **psephologist,** *n.*

pseudo-foreign-corporation statute. (1976) A state law regulating foreign corporations that either derive a specified high percentage of their income from that state or have a high percentage of their stock owned by people living in that state.

pseudograph (**soo**-də-graf). (1814) A false writing; a forgery.

pseudo-guarantee treaty. See *guarantee treaty* under TREATY (1).

pseudonym (**sood**-ə-nim), *n.* (1817) A fictitious name or identity. Cf. ALIAS. — **pseudonymous** (soo-**don**-ə-məs), *adj.* — **pseudonymity** (sood-ə-**nim**-ə-tee), *n.*

pseudonymous work. See WORK (2).

pseudopresumption of law. See *presumption of law* under PRESUMPTION.

pseudo-stepparent adoption. See *second-parent adoption* under ADOPTION (1).

PSI. *abbr.* PRESENTENCE-INVESTIGATION REPORT.

PSIR. *abbr.* PRESENTENCE-INVESTIGATION REPORT.

PSP. *abbr.* **1.** PHANTOM STOCK PLAN. **2.** PROFIT-SHARING PLAN.

PSR. *abbr.* See PRESENTENCE-INVESTIGATION REPORT.

psychiatric (sɪ-kee-**at**-rik), *adj.* (1847) Of, relating to, or involving the study or treatment of mental, emotional, and behavioral disorders by medical doctors trained in the field of psychiatry.

psychiatric disorder. See MENTAL ILLNESS (1).

psychiatric examination. See *mental examination* under EXAMINATION.

psychological abuse. See *emotional abuse* under ABUSE.

psychological fact. See FACT.

psychological father. See *psychological parent* under PARENT.

psychological mother. See *psychological parent* under PARENT.

psychological parent. See PARENT (1).

psychological realism. See LEGAL REALISM.

psychopath. See SOCIOPATH.

psychosis (sɪ-**koh**-sis). (1847) A serious mental illness that can cause a person's character to change and to make the person unable to behave within the range of what is considered normal. — **psychotic,** *adj.*

psychotherapist–client privilege. See *psychotherapist-patient privilege* under PRIVILEGE (3).

psychotherapist–patient privilege. See PRIVILEGE (3).

PTA. *abbr.* PATENT-TERM ADJUSTMENT.

PTD. *abbr.* Pretrial diversion; a plan by which a judge allows a criminal defendant to go through some type of rehabilitation program as an alternative to a criminal prosecution.

PTE. *abbr.* PATENT-TERM EXTENSION.

PTI. See *previously taxed income* under INCOME.

PTO. *abbr.* Patent and Trademark Office. See UNITED STATES PATENT AND TRADEMARK OFFICE.

PTO Code of Professional Responsibility. Disciplinary rules and canons of ethics for practicing before the U.S. Patent and Trademark Office. • The Code is found at 37 CFR §§ 10.20-10.112. — Often shortened to PTO Code.

PTP. See *publicly traded partnership* under PARTNERSHIP.

PTSD. (1982) *abbr.* POST-TRAUMATIC STRESS DISORDER.

pubes (**pyoo**-beez), *n. pl.* [Latin] *Roman law.* A child who has reached puberty, whether or not having reached the age of majority. Cf. IMPUBES. Pl. ***puberes.***

puberty. (14c) **1.** The stage of physical development in which a person takes on secondary sexual characteristics, when it becomes possible to reproduce. • In females, the beginning of this stage is marked by the menarche. **2.** *Hist.* The earliest age at which one could presumptively consent and to legally enter into a binding marriage. • At English common law, children became marriageable at the onset of legal puberty (age 12 for girls and 14 for boys). At French civil law, a marriage was invalid if contracted before the end of legal puberty (age 15 for girls and 18 for boys). An underage spouse had the power to void the marriage. — Also termed (in English common law) *age of discretion.*

Pub. L. *abbr.* PUBLIC LAW (2).

public, *adj.* (14c) **1.** Of, relating to, or involving an entire community, state, or country. **2.** Open or available for all to use, share, or enjoy. **3.** (Of a company) having shares that are available on an open market.

public, *n.* (16c) **1.** The people of a country or community as a whole <a crime against the public>. **2.** A place open or visible to the public <in public>.

Public Access to Court Electronic Records. A computer system by which subscribers can obtain online information from the federal courts, including information from a court's docket sheet about the parties, filing, and orders in a specific case. — Abbr. PACER.

public accommodation. See ACCOMMODATION.

public account system. See STATE ACCOUNT SYSTEM.

public act. See PUBLIC LAW (2).

public action. See *civil action* under ACTION (4).

publica delicta (**pəb**-li-kə di-**lik**-tə). [Latin] (1856) *Roman law.* Public wrongs; crimes. See DELICT. Cf. PRIVATA DELICTA.

public administration. See ADMINISTRATION.

public administrator. See ADMINISTRATOR (2).

public advocate. (1850) An advocate with responsibility for representing the public or consumer interests in matters of public concern, such as utility rates or environmental quality.

public affairs. (16c) Politically relevant events and questions that have an effect on people generally.

public agency. See AGENCY (3).

public agent. See AGENT.

publican (**pəb**-li-kən). (12c) **1.** A person authorized by license to keep a public house for consumption of alcoholic beverages on or off the premises. **2.** PUBLICANUS.

publicanus (pəb-li-**kay**-nəs). [Latin] *Hist. Roman law.* A tax collector. • A *publicanus* was described as "a farmer of the public revenue," although the *publicanus* reaped only the money from that sown by the labor of others. — Often shortened to *publican.*

public appointment. See APPOINTMENT (1).

public assistance. Anything of value provided by or administered by a social-service department of government; government aid accorded to needy people, the elderly, or those who live in a disaster-stricken area.

publication, *n.* (14c) **1.** Generally, the act of declaring or announcing to the public. **2.** *Copyright.* The offering or distribution of copies of a work to the public. • At common law, publication marked the dividing line between state and federal protection, but the Copyright Act of 1976 superseded most of common-law copyright and thereby diminished the significance of publication. Under the Act, an original work is considered published only when it is first made publicly available without restriction.

> "The concept of publication was of immense importance under the 1909 Act. It became a legal word of art, denoting a process much more esoteric than is suggested by the lay definition of the term. That it thus evolved was due largely to the American dichotomy between common law and statutory copyright, wherein the act of publication constituted the dividing line between the two systems of protection [state and federal]." 1 Melville B. Nimmer & David Nimmer, *Nimmer on Copyright* § 4.01, at 4-3 (Supp. 1997).

▸ **divestitive publication.** (1902) *Archaic.* The public distribution of an author's work on a scale large enough to divest the author of any claim to state common-law copyright protection. • The Copyright Act of 1976 preempted most common-law copyright. — Sometimes (erroneously) written *divestive publication.*

▸ **general publication.** (17c) Distribution of an author's work to the public, as opposed to a selected group, whether or not restrictions are placed on the use of the work. • Before the Copyright Act of 1976, a general publication was generally held to divest common-law rights in a work. Rather, the author was deemed to have dedicated the work to the public. Cf. *limited publication.*

▸ **investitive publication.** (1902) *Archaic.* The public distribution of an author's work on a scale large enough to qualify for federal statutory copyright protection. • Since 1976 copyright has protected works since their creation, rather than their publication.

▸ **limited publication.** (18c) Distribution of copies of an author's work to a selected group for a limited purpose and with no permission to copy the work, at a time when copies are not available to the general public. • Before the Copyright Act of 1976 made publication irrelevant, courts distinguished between limited publication and general publication to decide whether federal copyright laws applied. Under that Act, a work published before January 1, 1978 without proper copyright notice entered the public domain unless the publication was limited. — Also termed *private publication.* Cf. *general publication.*

▸ **private publication.** See *limited publication.*

3. *Defamation.* The communication of defamatory words to someone other than the person defamed. • The communication may be in any form, verbal or nonverbal.

> "Publication means the act of making the defamatory statement known to any person or persons other than the plaintiff himself. It is not necessary that there should be any publication in the popular sense of making the statement public. A private and confidential communication to a single individual is sufficient. Nor need it be published in the sense of being written or printed; for we have seen that actions as well as words may be defamatory. A communication to the person defamed himself, however, is not a sufficient publication on which to found civil proceedings; though it is otherwise in the case of a criminal prosecution, because such a communication may provoke a breach of the peace. Nor does a communication between husband and wife amount to publication; domestic intercourse of this kind is exempt from the restrictions of the law of libel and slander. But a statement by the defendant to the wife or husband of the plaintiff is a ground of action." R.F.V. Heuston, *Salmond on the Law of Torts* 154 (17th ed. 1977).

> "The publication of a libel might be in the form of a book, pamphlet or newspaper, but nothing of that nature is required. A letter sent to a single individual is sufficient." Rollin M. Perkins & Ronald N. Boyce, *Criminal Law* 489 (3d ed. 1982).

4. *Wills & estates.* The formal declaration made by a testator when signing the will that it is the testator's will. • There is no requirement that the provisions of the will or the identities of the beneficiaries be revealed to the witnesses.

publication-quality drawings. (2004) *Patents.* Illustrations or drawings filed with a patent application and capable of being scanned.

publication right. (1998) *Copyright.* The right of an author or artist to decide when to reveal or display a creative work. • Publication is one of the moral rights of artists recognized in civil-law countries and much of Europe, but largely unavailable in the United States. — Also termed *right of disclosure.*

public attorney. See ATTORNEY (2).

public authority. See AUTHORITY (3).

public-authority defense. See DEFENSE (1).

public-authority justification. See JUSTIFICATION (2).

publica vindicta (**pəb**-li-kə vin-**dik**-tə). [Latin] (16c) *Hist.* The protection of the public interest.

public-benefit corporation. See *public corporation* (3) under CORPORATION.

public bill. See BILL (3).

public blockade. See BLOCKADE.

public boundary. See BOUNDARY (1).

public building. (16c) A building that is accessible to the public; esp., one owned by the government.

Public Buildings Service. A unit in the General Services Administration responsible for constructing federal buildings and managing federally owned and leased property through 11 regional offices. — Abbr. PBS.

public carrier. See *common carrier* under CARRIER (1).

public character. See PUBLIC FIGURE.

public-choice theory. The theory that legislation is a compromise among parties guided by their conflicting self-interests, not the product of representatives working for the good of the public as a whole.

public commissioner. See PROSECUTOR (1).

public contract. See CONTRACT.

Public Contracts Act. See WALSH–HEALEY ACT.

public controversy. See CONTROVERSY (2).

public-convenience-and-necessity standard. (1964) A common criterion used by a governmental body to assess whether a particular request or project should be granted or approved.

public corporation. See CORPORATION.

public debt. See DEBT.

public defender. (1827) A lawyer or staff of lawyers, usu. publicly appointed and paid, whose duty is to represent indigent criminal defendants. — Abbr. P.D. — Often shortened to *defender.* Cf. *duty solicitor* under SOLICITOR.

public delict. See DELICT (1).

public director. See DIRECTOR.

public disclosure of private facts. See DISCLOSURE (1).

public disturbance. See BREACH OF THE PEACE.

public document. See DOCUMENT (2).

public domain. (17c) **1.** Government-owned land. **2.** *Hist.* Government lands that are open to entry and settlement. • Today virtually all federal lands are off-limits to traditional entry and settlement. **3.** *Intellectual property.* The universe of inventions and creative works that are not protected by intellectual-property rights and are therefore available for anyone to use without charge. • When copyright, trademark, patent, or trade-secret rights are lost or expire, the intellectual property they had protected becomes part of the public domain and can be appropriated by anyone without liability for infringement.

> "[P]ublic domain is the status of an invention, creative work, commercial symbol, or any other creation that is not protected by any form of intellectual property. Public domain is the rule: intellectual property is the exception." 1 J. Thomas McCarthy, *McCarthy on Trademarks and Unfair Competition* § 1.01[2], at 1-3 (3d ed. 1996).

public-domain citation. See *publisher-neutral citation* under CITATION (3).

public-duty doctrine. (1976) *Torts.* The rule that a governmental entity (such as a state or municipality) cannot be held liable for an individual plaintiff's injury resulting from a governmental officer's or employee's breach of a duty owed to the general public rather than to the individual plaintiff. — Also termed *public-duty rule.* See SPECIAL-DUTY DOCTRINE.

public easement. See EASEMENT.

public employee. See CIVIL SERVANT.

public enemy. See ENEMY.

public entity. See ENTITY.

public-exchange offer. See OFFER (2).

public fact. See FACT.

public figure. (1871) Someone who has achieved fame or notoriety or who has voluntarily become involved in a public controversy. • A public figure (or public official) suing for defamation must prove that the defendant acted with actual malice. *New York Times Co. v. Sullivan,* 376 U.S. 254, 84 S.Ct. 710 (1964). — Also termed *public character.*

▸ **all-purpose public figure.** (1975) Someone who achieves such pervasive fame or notoriety that he or she becomes a public figure for all purposes and in all contexts. • For example, a person who occupies a position with great persuasive power and influence may become an all-purpose public figure whether or not the person actively seeks attention. *Gertz v. Robert Welch, Inc.,* 418 U.S. 323, 345, 94 S.Ct. 2997, 3009 (1974). — Also termed *general-purpose public figure.*

▸ **limited-purpose public figure.** (1979) Someone who, having become involved in a particular public issue, has achieved fame or notoriety only in relation to that particular issue.

public forum. (1935) *Constitutional law.* A public place where people traditionally gather to express ideas and exchange views. • To be constitutional, the government's regulation of a public forum must be narrowly tailored to serve a significant government interest and must usu. be limited to time-place-or-manner restrictions. — Also termed *open forum.* See TIME-PLACE-OR-MANNER RESTRICTION. Cf. NONPUBLIC FORUM.

> "[T]raditional public fora are open for expressive activity regardless of the government's intent. The objective characteristics of these properties require the government to accommodate private speakers. The government is free to open additional properties for expressive use by the general public or by a particular class of speakers, thereby creating designated public fora. Where the property is not a traditional public forum, the property is either a nonpublic forum or not a forum at all." *Arkansas Educ. Television Comm'n v. Forbes,* 523 U.S. 666, 678, 118 S.Ct. 1633, 1641 (1998).

▸ **designated public forum.** (1985) Public property that has not traditionally been open for public assembly and debate but that the government has opened for use by the public as a place for expressive activity, such as a public-university facility or a publicly owned theater. • Unlike a traditional public forum, the government does not have to retain the open character of a designated public forum. Also, the subject matter of the expression permitted in a designated public forum may be limited to accord with the character of the forum; reasonable, content-neutral time, place, and manner restrictions are generally permissible. But any prohibition based on the content of the expression must be narrowly drawn to effectuate a compelling state interest, as with a traditional public forum. — Also termed *limited public forum; nontraditional public forum.*

▸ **traditional public forum.** (1973) Public property that has by long tradition — as opposed to governmental designation — been used by the public for assembly and expression, such as a public street, public sidewalk, or public park. • To be constitutional, the government's content-neutral restrictions of the time, place, or manner of expression must be narrowly tailored to serve a significant government interest, and leave open ample alternative channels of communication. Any government regulation of expression that is based on the content of the expression must meet the much higher test of being necessary to serve a compelling state interest. — Also termed *quintessential public forum.*

public-function doctrine. See PUBLIC-FUNCTION TEST.

public-function rationale. See GOVERNMENTAL-FUNCTION THEORY.

public-function test. (1966) In a lawsuit brought under 42 USCA § 1983, the doctrine that a private person's actions constitute state action if the private person performs functions that are traditionally reserved to the state. — Also termed *public-function doctrine*; *public-function theory.* **public fund.** See FUND (1).

public grant. See PATENT (2).

public ground. See *public land* under LAND.

public health. See HEALTH.

Public Health Service. The combined offices and units of the U.S. Department of Health and Human Services responsible for promoting the physical and mental health of American citizens.

public hearing. See HEARING.

public highway. See HIGHWAY.

public house. (17c) **1.** *Archaic.* An inn. **2.** A tavern where alcoholic beverages may be bought and consumed on the premises. • The British term *pub* is an abbreviation of *public house.* — Also termed (in sense 2) *tippling house.*

public housing. See HOUSING.

public-housing authority. (1933) A governmental agency, usu. local, responsible for developing and administering subsidized housing and rental-assistance programs. • Public-housing authorities originated under the United States Housing Act of 1937.

publici juris (pəb-li-sɪ **joor**-is), *adj.* [Latin] Of public right; of importance to or available to the public <a city holds title to its streets as property *publici juris*> <words that are in general or common use and that are merely descriptive are *publici juris* and cannot be appropriated as a trademark>.

public improvement. See IMPROVEMENT.

public injury. See INJURY.

public insolvency. See *notorious insolvency* under INSOLVENCY.

public institution. See INSTITUTION (3).

public instrument. See PUBLIC WRITING.

public interest. (16c) **1.** The general welfare of a populace considered as warranting recognition and protection. **2.** Something in which the public as a whole has a stake; esp., an interest that justifies governmental regulation.

public-interest exception. (1957) The principle that an appellate court may consider and decide a moot case, even though such decisions are generally prohibited, if (1) the case involves a question of considerable public importance, (2) the question is likely to arise in the future, and (3) the question has evaded appellate review.

public-interest law. (1969) **1.** A statute that advances social justice or some other cause for the public good, such as environmental protection. **2.** Legal practice that advances social justice or other causes for the public good. • Although public-interest law primarily encompasses private not-for-profit work, the term is sometimes used to include the work of government agencies such as public-defender offices. Cf. CAUSE LAWYERING; *social justice* under JUSTICE (4).

public-interest lawyer. See LAWYER.

public international law. See INTERNATIONAL LAW.

public intoxication. See INTOXICATION.

public invitee. See INVITEE.

publicist. (18c) **1.** A public-relations specialist. **2.** An international-law scholar. • The term applies to scholars of both public and private international law.

publicity. 1. Public attention; notoriety. **2.** One or more efforts made to get public attention; public promotion; esp., PUBLIC RELATIONS (1).

Publicity Act. See FEDERAL CORRUPT PRACTICES ACT.

public-key encryption. See KEY ENCRYPTION.

public land. See LAND.

public law. (16c) **1.** The body of law dealing with the relations between private individuals and the government, and with the structure and operation of the government itself; constitutional law, criminal law, and administrative law taken together; JUS PUBLICUM (1). Cf. PRIVATE LAW (1). **2.** A statute affecting the general public — that is, the people of the whole state or of a particular portion of the state. • Federal public laws are first published in *Statutes at Large* and are eventually collected by subject in the U.S. Code. — Abbr. Pub. L.; P.L. — Also termed *public statute* (P.S.); *general statute*; (esp. BrE) *public act*; *general act.* Cf. *general law* (1) under LAW. **3.** Constitutional law. **4.** JUS PUBLICUM (2).

public-lending right. (1960) *Copyright.* In the United Kingdom and some other countries, the right of an author to a royalty for works that are lent out by a public library.

public-liability insurance. See *liability insurance* under INSURANCE.

publicly assisted housing. See *public housing* under HOUSING.

publicly held corporation. See *public corporation* (1) under CORPORATION.

publicly traded partnership. See PARTNERSHIP.

public market. See MARKET.

public-meeting law. See OPEN-MEETING LAW.

public minister. See MINISTER (3).

public morality. See MORALITY (2).

public necessity. See NECESSITY (5).

public notice. See NOTICE (3).

public nudity. See NUDITY.

public nuisance. See NUISANCE.

public offense. See OFFENSE (2).

public offer. See *offer to all the world* under OFFER (2).

public offering. See OFFERING.

public office. (15c) A position whose occupant has legal authority to exercise a government's sovereign powers for a fixed period.

> "[W]hen one takes upon himself the duties of a public office, he becomes not only responsible to the public for their faithful performance, but may be liable to individuals

for any injury resulting from his acts or omissions. In order to impress upon his mind the obligation he assumes, he is required, before entering upon his official duties, to promise, in the most solemn manner known to the law, that he will support the constitution of the United States, and the constitution of this state, and that he will faithfully discharge the duties of his office to the best of his ability. Having made this solemn promise, whether in the form of an oath or an affirmation, it is supposed to be binding upon his conscience; and every willful violation of his official duty whereby the public or individuals may be injured, partakes of the nature of a public offense." Sanford M. Green, *A Treatise on Townships, and the Powers and Duties of Township Officers* xix (2d ed. 1882).

"A public office is a franchise conferred by the Government of the State or Municipality, either by election or appointment, carrying with it the right and duty of exercising a public function. It differs from employment or agency in that the latter arises out of contract, in which the rights of the parties are definite and specific, and the duty and tenure of the employment are fixed." Arthur Adelbert Stearns, *The Law of Suretyship* § 145, at 237 (Wells M. Cook ed., 3d ed. 1922).

public official. See OFFICIAL (1).

public ownership. See OWNERSHIP.

public passage. A right held by the public to pass over a body of water, whether the underlying land is publicly or privately owned.

public-performance right. See PERFORMANCE RIGHTS.

public person. See PERSON (3).

public place. (15c) Any location that the local, state, or national government maintains for the use of the public, such as a highway, park, or public building.

public policy. (16c) **1.** The collective rules, principles, or approaches to problems that affect the commonwealth or (esp.) promote the general good; specif., principles and standards regarded by the legislature or by the courts as being of fundamental concern to the state and the whole of society <against public policy>. • Courts sometimes use the term to justify their decisions, as when declaring a contract void because it is "contrary to public policy." — Also termed *policy of the law.*

"The policy of the law, or public policy, is a phrase of common use in estimating the validity of contracts. Its history is obscure; it is most likely that agreements which tended to restrain trade or to promote litigation were the first to elicit the principle that the courts would look to the interests of the public in giving efficacy to contracts. Wagers, while they continued to be legal, were a frequent provocative of judicial ingenuity on this point, as is sufficiently shown by the case of *Gilbert v. Sykes* [16 East 150 (1812)] . . . : but it does not seem probable that the doctrine of public policy began in the endeavor to elude their binding force. Whatever may have been its origin, it was applied very frequently, and not always with the happiest results, during the latter part of the eighteenth and the commencement of the nineteenth century. Modern decisions, however, while maintaining the duty of the courts to consider the public advantage, have tended more and more to limit the sphere within which this duty may be exercised." William R. Anson, *Principles of the Law of Contract* 286 (Arthur L. Corbin ed., 3d Am. ed. 1919).

2. More narrowly, the principle that a person should not be allowed to do anything that would tend to injure the public at large.

public-policy limitation. (1961) *Tax.* A judicially developed principle that a person should not be allowed to deduct expenses related to an activity that is contrary to the public welfare. • This principle is reflected in the Internal Revenue Code's specific disallowance provisions (such as for kickbacks and bribes).

public pond. See GREAT POND.

public power. See POWER (3).

public–private partnership. A business and contractual relationship between a government agency and a private company to finance, construct, and operate public transportation networks, parks, convention centers, and similar projects intended to serve the public. • Use of a public–private partnership may enable earlier completion or make possible projects that would otherwise have been impossible.

public property. See PROPERTY.

public prosecutor. 1. See DISTRICT ATTORNEY. **2.** See PROSECUTOR (1).

public purpose. (18c) An action by or at the direction of a government for the benefit of the community as a whole.

"No court has ever formulated a definition of 'public purpose' which is at once both logically correct and adequate. It has been recognized by most courts that each case must be determined largely by its own specific circumstances. The result has been that the only feasible approach to the problem consists in indicating the factors invoked, and the general lines of reasoning employed, in dealing with it. The power to tax was conferred to enable government to finance the cost of performing its functions. The extent to which the requirement that taxes may be levied for public purposes only limits the taxing power cannot be rationally or reasonably determined without some theory as to what constitute the proper and permissible functions of government. It is not impossible, but highly improbable, that judicial theories on that matter will be uninfluenced by traditional conceptions based on both the practices of the governments of our constitutional system and the political theories generally accepted as implicit in that system. The result has been that the scope of permissible public purposes has gradually expanded as generally accepted political theories have assigned an increasing role to government in regulating the social and economic life of the people and in assuming service functions for the promotion of the general welfare. The influence of this factor cannot be precisely measured, but the long time trend of the decisions cannot be adequately understood if this factor is completely excluded." Henry Rottschaefer, *Handbook of American Constitutional Law* 631–32 (1939).

public record. See RECORD.

public-records doctrine. (1947) The principle, applicable in many states, that a third person acquiring or interested in real or immovable property may rely on the face of relevant public records and need not investigate further for unrecorded interests.

public-records exception. (1935) The exception to the hearsay rule for the contents of certain public records or the absence of a record where it would ordinarily be kept in public archives. Fed. R. Evid. 803(8)–(10).

public relations. (1898) **1.** The activity or business of creating or maintaining a company's goodwill or favorable public image. **2.** A company's existing goodwill or public image. — Abbr. PR.

public reprimand. See REPRIMAND.

public revenue. See REVENUE.

public right. See RIGHT.

public right-of-way. See RIGHT-OF-WAY.

public safety. (16c) The welfare and protection of the general public, usu. expressed as a governmental responsibility <Department of Public Safety>.

public-safety exception. (1937) *Criminal procedure.* An exception to the rules of evidence making a defendant's otherwise suppressible statement to police admissible when the police reasonably believe that there is an immediate need to protect the public by asking the defendant to make a statement related to the need without first giving the defendant a *Miranda* warning.

public sale. See SALE.

public school. See SCHOOL (1).

public seal. See SEAL.

public sector. (1934) The part of the economy or an industry that is owned and controlled by the government. Cf. PRIVATE SECTOR.

public security. See SECURITY (4).

public servant. (16c) Someone who works for the government; esp., one elected to a government post. See *public official* under OFFICIAL (1).

public service. (16c) **1.** A service provided or facilitated by the government for the general public's convenience and benefit. **2.** Government employment; work performed for or on behalf of the government. **3.** Broadly, any work that serves the public good, including government work and public-interest law.

public-service commission. See COMMISSION (3).

public-service corporation. See CORPORATION.

public-service homicide. See HOMICIDE.

public servitude. See SERVITUDE (3).

public session. See *open session* under SESSION (1).

public statute. **1.** See *general statute* under STATUTE. **2.** See PUBLIC LAW (2).

public stock. See STOCK.

public store. See STORE.

public tort. See TORT.

public transportation. (1851) The government-owned system of buses, trains, etc. that are available for everyone to use. — Also termed *public transport.*

public trial. See TRIAL.

public, true, and notorious. *Hist. Eccles. law.* The concluding words of each allegation in a court petition.

public trust. See *charitable trust* under TRUST (3).

public-trust doctrine. (1926) The principle that navigable waters are preserved for the public use, and that the state is responsible for protecting the public's right to the use.

publicum jus (**pəb**-li-kəm **jəs**). [Latin] See JUS PUBLICUM.

public use. See USE (1).

public-use bar. (1930) *Patents.* A statutory bar that prevents the granting of a patent for an invention that was publicly used or sold in the United States more than one year before the application date. 35 USCA § 102(b). • The doctrine can be invoked for any public use, any commercial use, any sale or offer of sale, or any private transfer made without a pledge of secrecy. Cf. PRIVATE-USE EXCEPTION. — Also termed *prior-use bar.*

public-use proceeding. (1894) *Patents.* An investigation into whether a patent is barred because the invention was publicly used or sold more than a year before the application was filed. • Rarely used, this procedure is instituted upon a petition by someone protesting the application. If the petition and supporting documents make out a prima facie case, the examiner will hold a hearing and issue a final decision, which is not reviewable. 37 CFR 1.292. — Abbr. PUP. Cf. PROTEST.

public utility. See UTILITY.

public utility district. See *municipal utility district* under DISTRICT.

Public Utility Holding Company Act. A 1935 federal statute enacted to protect investors and consumers from the economic disadvantages produced by the small number of holding companies that owned most of the country's utilities. • The Act also sought to protect the public from deceptive security advertising. Repealed in 2006, it was replaced by the Public Utility Holding Company Act of 2005 (42 USCA §§ 16451 et seq.), which gave the Federal Energy Regulatory Commission a limited role in allocating the costs of multistate electric-utility holding companies to individual operating subsidiaries. — Abbr. PUHCA.

public-values theory. The view that a court should decide text-based cases not by the original meaning of the governing text but by the court's understanding of current public values and practical considerations because the decision-making method should be "nautical" and dynamic, not "archaeological" and static. *See, e.g.,* Nicholas S. Zeppos, *The Use of Authority in Statutory Interpretation: An Empirical Analysis,* 70 Tex. L. Rev. 1073, 1081 (1992); T. Alexander Aleinikoff, *Updating Statutory Interpretation,* 87 Mich. L. Rev. 20, 21 (1988).

public verdict. See VERDICT (1).

public vessel. See VESSEL.

Public Vessels Act. A 1925 federal statute allowing claims against the United States for damages caused by one of its vessels. 46 USCA app. §§ 781–790. — Abbr. PVA.

public war. See WAR (1).

public water. See WATER.

public welfare. See WELFARE (1).

public-welfare offense. See OFFENSE (2).

public wharf. See WHARF.

public works. See WORKS.

public-works-and-ways system. (1917) *Criminal law.* The state's employment of its prisoners to construct or repair buildings, roads, or bridges, or to work on other public construction or maintenance projects.

public worship. See WORSHIP (1).

public writing. **1.** The written acts or records of a government (or its constituent units) that are not constitutionally or statutorily protected from disclosure. • Laws and judicial records, for example, are public writings. A private writing that becomes part of a public record may be a public writing in some circumstances. **2.** *Rare.* A document prepared by a notary public in the presence of the parties who sign it before witnesses. — Also termed (in both senses) *public instrument*; (in sense 2) *escritura publica.*

public wrong. See WRONG.

publish, *vb.* (14c) **1.** To distribute copies (of a work) to the public. **2.** To communicate (defamatory words) to someone other than the person defamed. See INTENT TO PUBLISH. **3.** To declare (a will) to be the true expression of one's testamentary intent. **4.** To make (evidence) available to a jury during trial. See PUBLICATION.

publisher-neutral citation. See CITATION (3).

PUC. *abbr.* Public Utilities Commission.

PUD. *abbr.* **1.** PLANNED-UNIT DEVELOPMENT. **2.** See *municipal utility district* under DISTRICT.

pudzeld. See WOOD-GELD.

pueblo (**pweb**-loh). [Spanish] (1808) A town or village, esp. in the southwestern United States.

puer (**pyoo**-ər), *n.* [Latin] *Roman law.* **1.** A child, esp. a boy. **2.** A male slave. Pl. ***pueri*** (**pyoor**-I).

puerility (pyoo-ə-**ril**-ə-tee *or* pyuu-**ril**-ə-tee). (16c) *Civil law.* A child's status between infancy and puberty.

pueritia (pyoo-ə-**rish**-ee-ə), *n.* [Latin] *Roman law.* Childhood, esp. up to the age of 17, the minimum age for pleading before a magistrate. Cf. AETAS INFANTIAE PROXIMA; AETAS PUBERTATI PROXIMA.

puffer. See BY-BIDDER.

puffing. (18c) **1.** The expression of an exaggerated opinion — as opposed to a factual misrepresentation — with the intent to sell a good or service. • Puffing involves expressing opinions, not asserting something as a fact. Although there is some leeway in puffing goods, a seller may not misrepresent them or say that they have attributes that they do not possess. — Also termed *puffery*; *sales puffery*; *dealer's talk*; *sales talk*.

> "'Dealer's puffing,' so long as it remains in the realm of opinion or belief, will not support a conviction of false pretenses however extravagant the statements." Rollin M. Perkins & Ronald N. Boyce, *Criminal Law* 369 (3d ed. 1982).

2. Fictitious or secret bidding at an auction by or on behalf of a seller; BY-BIDDING. — Also termed *puffing of a bid*.

Pugh clause. (1958) *Oil & gas.* A provision in an oil-and-gas lease modifying the effect of most lease-pooling clauses by severing pooled portions of the lease from unpooled portions of the lease. • Drilling or production on a pooled portion will not maintain the lease for the unpooled portions. The clause is named for Lawrence G. Pugh, an attorney from Cowley, Louisiana, who drafted the first version in 1947. In Texas it is termed a Freestone rider. See POOLING.

PUHCA. *abbr.* PUBLIC UTILITY HOLDING COMPANY ACT.

puis (pwis *or* pwee). [French] Afterward; since.

puis darrein continuance (**pwis dar**-ayn kən-**tin**-yoo-ənts). [Law French "since the last continuance"] See *plea puis darrein continuance* under PLEA (3).

puisne (**pyoo**-nee), *adj.* [Law French] (16c) Junior in rank; subordinate.

puisne judge. See JUDGE.

puisne mortgage. See *junior mortgage* under MORTGAGE.

Pullman **abstention.** See ABSTENTION.

pulsare (pəl-**sair**-ee), *vb.* [Latin] *Civil law.* To accuse or charge; to proceed against at law.

pulsator (pəl-**say**-tər). (18c) *Civil law.* A plaintiff or actor.

pumping unit. (1933) *Oil & gas.* Equipment used to pump oil to the surface when the pressure difference between the formation and the borehole is not strong enough to cause oil to rise to the surface. — Also termed *pumpjack*; *horsehead*.

pumpjack. See PUMPING UNIT.

punch list. A list of usu. minor jobs that will complete a project; esp., a roster of small but important jobs yet to be done on a construction site but necessary to be done before the construction can be considered completely finished. — Also termed *snagging list*.

punctuation canon. The interpretive doctrine that the punctuation in a legal instrument is a permissible indicator of meaning.

punctum temporis (**pəngk**-təm **tem**-pə-ris). [Latin] (17c) A point of time; an instant.

punies (**pyoo**-neez). (1986) *Slang.* Punitive damages. See *punitive damages* under DAMAGES.

punishable, *adj.* (15c) **1.** (Of a person) subject to a punishment <there is no dispute that Jackson remains punishable for these offenses>. **2.** (Of a crime or tort) giving rise to a specified punishment <a felony punishable by imprisonment for up to 20 years>. — **punishability,** *n.*

punishment, *n.* (15c) **1.** A sanction — such as a fine, penalty, confinement, or loss of property, right, or privilege — assessed against a person who has violated the law. See SENTENCE.

> "Punishment in all its forms is a loss of rights or advantages consequent on a breach of law. When it loses this quality it degenerates into an arbitrary act of violence that can produce nothing but bad social effects." Glanville Williams, *Criminal Law: The General Part* 575 (2d ed. 1961).

> "In the treatment of offenders there is a clear and unmistakable line of division between the function of the judge and that of the penologist. I should modify that: the law is clear only if it is first made clear in what sense the word 'treatment' is being used. For in this context the word can be used in two senses, one wide and the other narrow. Let me take the wide meaning first. The object of a sentence is to impose punishment. For 'punishment,' a word which to many connotes nothing but retribution, the softer word 'treatment' is now frequently substituted; this is the wider meaning. The substitution is made, I suppose, partly as a concession to the school which holds that crime is caused by mental sickness, but more justifiably as a reminder that there are other methods of dealing with criminal tendencies besides making the consequences of crime unpleasant." Patrick Devlin, *The Judge* 32–33 (1979).

▸ **capital punishment.** See CAPITAL PUNISHMENT.

▸ **collective punishment.** See COLLECTIVE PUNISHMENT.

▸ **corporal punishment.** (16c) Physical punishment; punishment that is inflicted on the body (including imprisonment).

> "Past forms of corporal punishment included branding, blinding, mutilation, amputation, and the use of the pillory and the stocks. It was also an element in such violent modes of execution as drowning, stoning, burning, hanging, and drawing and quartering . . . . In most parts of Europe and in the United States, such savage penalties were replaced by imprisonment during the late eighteenth and early nineteenth centuries, although capital punishment itself remained. Physical chastisement became less frequent until, in the twentieth century, corporal punishment was either eliminated as a legal penalty or restricted to beating with a birch rod, cane, whip, or other scourge. In ordinary usage the term now refers to such penal flagellation."

Gordon Hawkins, "Corporal Punishment," in 1 *Encyclopedia of Crime and Justice* 251, 251 (Sanford H. Kadish ed., 1983).

▸ **cruel and unusual punishment.** (17c) Punishment that is torturous, degrading, inhuman, grossly disproportionate to the crime in question, or otherwise shocking to the moral sense of the community. • Cruel and unusual punishment is prohibited by the Eighth Amendment.

"The Eighth Amendment prohibits cruel and unusual punishment, but leaves open the definition of what is 'cruel and unusual.' The Supreme Court has interpreted this prohibition flexibly, measuring punishments challenged as in violation of it against 'evolving standards of decency.' While it has refused, for example, to outlaw the death penalty as invariably cruel and unusual, it has applied that constitutional standard to prohibit states from imposing prison sentences upon those found 'guilty' of drug addiction. The court has generally indicated that it would apply the amendment to prohibit punishments it found barbaric or disproportionate to the crime punished." W. Allan Wilbur, "Cruel and Unusual Punishment," in *Congressional Quarterly's Guide to the U.S. Supreme Court* 575, 575 (Elder Witt ed., 1979).

▸ **cumulative punishment.** (1842) Punishment that increases in severity when a person is convicted of the same offense more than once.

▸ **deterrent punishment.** (1896) **1.** *Criminal law.* Punishment intended to deter the offender and others from committing crimes and to make an example of the offender so that like-minded people are warned of the consequences of crime. **2.** *Torts.* Punishment intended to deter a tortfeasor from repeating a behavior or failing to remove a hazard that led to an injury. • Punitive damages are usu. awarded as a deterrent punishment. — Also termed *exemplary punishment*

▸ **double punishment.** Two forms of punishment levied for the same wrongful act or for different offenses that arise from one act.

▸ **excessive punishment.** (17c) Punishment that is not justified by the gravity of the offense or the defendant's criminal record. See *excessive fine* (1) under FINE (5).

▸ **infamous punishment.** (16c) Punishment by imprisonment, usu. in a penitentiary. See *infamous crime* under CRIME.

▸ **nonjudicial punishment.** (1949) *Military law.* A procedure under which a commanding officer levies punishment against a minor offender who is subject to the Uniform Code of Military Justice. • In the Navy and Coast Guard, nonjudicial punishment is termed *captain's mast*; in the Marine Corps, it is termed *office hours*; and in the Army and Air Force, it is referred to as *Article 15.* Nonjudicial punishment is not a court-martial.

▸ **preventive punishment.** (1893) Punishment intended to prevent a repetition of wrongdoing by disabling the offender.

▸ **reformative punishment.** (1919) Punishment intended to change the character of the offender.

▸ **retributive punishment.** (1887) Punishment intended to satisfy the community's retaliatory sense of indignation that is provoked by injustice.

"The fact that it is natural to hate a criminal does not prove that retributive punishment is justified." Glanville Williams, *The Sanctity of Life and the Criminal Law* 60 (1957).

2. *Family law.* A negative disciplinary action administered to a minor child by a parent.

punitive, *adj.* (16c) Involving or inflicting punishment. — Also termed *punitory.*

punitive articles. (1950) Articles 77–134 of the Uniform Code of Military Justice. • These articles list the crimes in the military-justice system.

punitive damages. See DAMAGES.

punitive isolation. See *punitive segregation* under SEGREGATION (1).

punitive sanction. See SANCTION (2).

punitive segregation. See SEGREGATION (1).

punitive statute. See *penal statute* under STATUTE.

punitory. See PUNITIVE.

punitory damages. See *punitive damages* under DAMAGES.

PUP. *abbr.* PUBLIC-USE PROCEEDING.

pupil. (14c) *Scots & civil law.* Someone who has not reached or completed puberty. See MINORITY (1).

pupillarity (pyoo-pi-**lair**-ə-tee). (16c) *Scots & civil law.* The stage of a person's life that spans from infancy through puberty.

pupillary substitution (pyoo-pə-ler-ee). See SUBSTITUTION (5).

pupillus (pyoo-**pil**-əs), *n.* [Latin] *Roman law.* A child under the age of puberty and under the authority of a *sui juris* tutor. See TUTELA.

pur (pər *or* poor). [Law French] By; for.

pur autre vie (pər **oh**-trə [*or* **oh**-tər] **vee**). [Law French "for another's life"] (17c) For or during a period measured by another's life <a life estate *pur autre vie*>. — Also spelled *per autre vie.*

purchase, *n.* (15c) **1.** The act or an instance of buying. **2.** The acquisition of an interest in real or personal property by sale, discount, negotiation, mortgage, pledge, lien, issue, reissue, gift, or any other voluntary transaction. **3.** The acquisition of real property by one's own or another's act (as by will or gift) rather than by descent or inheritance. Cf. DESCENT (1). — **purchase,** *vb.*

▸ **bargain purchase.** See BARGAIN PURCHASE.

▸ **compulsory purchase.** *Rare.* See EMINENT DOMAIN.

purchase, words of. See WORDS OF PURCHASE.

purchase accounting method. See ACCOUNTING METHOD.

purchase agreement. (1909) A sales contract. Cf. REPURCHASE AGREEMENT.

▸ **blanket purchase agreement.** See BLANKET ORDER (3).

purchase money. (17c) The initial payment made on property secured by a mortgage.

purchase-money interest. See *purchase-money security interest* under SECURITY INTEREST.

purchase-money mortgage. See MORTGAGE.

purchase-money resulting trust. See TRUST (3).

purchase-money security interest. See SECURITY INTEREST.

purchase option. See *option to purchase real property* under OPTION (5).

purchase order. (1916) A document authorizing a seller to deliver goods with payment to be made later. — Abbr. P.O.

▸ **blanket purchase order.** See BLANKET ORDER (3).

purchase price. See PRICE.

purchaser. (14c) **1.** Someone who obtains property for money or other valuable consideration; a buyer.

▸ **affiliated purchaser.** (1958) *Securities.* Any of the following: (1) a person directly or indirectly acting in concert with a distribution participant in connection with the acquisition or distribution of the securities involved; (2) an affiliate who directly or indirectly controls the purchases of those securities by a distribution participant, or whose purchases are controlled by such a participant, or whose purchases are under common control with those of such a participant; (3) an affiliate, who is a broker or a dealer (except a broker-dealer whose business consists solely of effecting transactions in "exempted securities," as defined in the Exchange Act); (4) an affiliate (other than a broker-dealer) who regularly purchases securities through a broker-dealer, or otherwise, for its own account or for the account of others, or recommends or exercises investment discretion in the purchase or sale of securities (with certain specified exceptions). SEC Rule 10b-18(a)(2) (17 CFR § 240.10b-18(a)(2)).

▸ **bona fide purchaser.** (18c) **1.** Someone who buys something for value without notice of another's claim to the property and without actual or constructive notice of any defects in or infirmities, claims, or equities against the seller's title; one who has in good faith paid valuable consideration for property without notice of prior adverse claims. • Generally, a bona fide purchaser for value is not affected by the transferor's fraud against a third party and has a superior right to the transferred property as against the transferor's creditor to the extent of the consideration that the purchaser has paid. **2.** Under the UCC, one who purchases a security for value in good faith and without notice of any adverse claim and who takes delivery of the security in bearer form or in registered form, the security being issued or indorsed to the purchaser or in blank. — Abbr. BFP; BFPV — Also termed *bona fide purchaser for value; good-faith purchaser; purchaser in good faith; innocent purchaser; innocent purchaser for value.*

▸ **good-faith purchaser.** See *bona fide purchaser.*

▸ **innocent purchaser.** See *bona fide purchaser.*

▸ **innocent purchaser for value.** See *bona fide purchaser.*

▸ **purchaser for value.** (18c) A purchaser who pays consideration for the property bought.

> "The principle as to purchase for value . . . may be concisely stated as follows: A court of equity will not deprive a defendant of any right of property, whether legal or equitable, for which he has given value without notice of the plaintiff's equity, nor of any other common-law right acquired as an incident of his purchase. In all other cases the circumstance of innocent purchase is a fact of no legal significance." J.B. Ames, *Purchase for Value Without Notice,* 1 Harv. L. Rev. 1, 3 (1887).

▸ **purchaser in good faith.** See *bona fide purchaser.*

▸ **purchaser pendente lite.** (17c) Someone who buys an interest in something that is the subject of a pending lawsuit.

▸ **subsequent purchaser.** (18c) **1.** A later buyer of something. **2.** Someone who takes a security other than by original issue.

2. Someone who acquires real property by means other than descent, gift, or inheritance.

▸ **first purchaser.** (17c) An ancestor who first acquired an estate that still belongs to the family.

purchasing agent. See FACTOR (3).

purchasing power. (1824) **1.** The amount of money that a person or group has available to spend. **2.** The amount that a unit of money can buy.

pure, *adj.* **1.** Not mixed with anything else <pure silver>. **2.** Complete and total <pure speculation>. **3.** Containing nothing that is harmful; free from unhealthful contaminants <pure water supply>. **4.** Free from moral corruption; esp., sexually chaste. **5.** (Of a method, art, or study) pursued or done according to an accepted standard or pattern <pure comparative negligence>.

pure accident. See *unavoidable accident* under ACCIDENT.

pure annuity. See *nonrefund annuity* under ANNUITY.

pure-comparative-negligence doctrine. (1976) The principle that liability for negligence is apportioned in accordance with the percentage of fault that the fact-finder assigns to each party and that a plaintiff's percentage of fault reduces the amount of recoverable damages but does not bar recovery. See *comparative negligence* under NEGLIGENCE; APPORTIONMENT OF LIABILITY. Cf. 50-PERCENT RULE.

pure debt. See *pure obligation* under OBLIGATION.

pure democracy. See *direct democracy* under DEMOCRACY.

pure easement. See *easement appurtenant* under EASEMENT.

pure freezeout. See FREEZEOUT.

pure mark. See *technical trademark* under TRADEMARK.

pure obligation. See OBLIGATION.

pure plea. See PLEA (3).

pure race statute. See RACE STATUTE.

pure risk. See RISK.

pure speech. See SPEECH.

pure theory. (1927) The philosophy of Hans Kelsen, in which he contends that a legal system must be "pure" — that is, self-supporting and not dependent on extralegal values. • Kelsen's theory, set out in such works as *General Theory of Law and the State* (1945) and *The Pure Theory of Law* (1934), maintains that laws are norms handed down by the state. Laws are not defined in terms of history, ethics, sociology, or other external factors. Rather, a legal system is an interconnected system of norms, in which coercive techniques are used to secure compliance. The validity of each law, or legal norm, is traced to another legal norm. Ultimately, all laws must find their validity in the society's basic norm (*grundnorm*), which may be as simple as the concept that the constitution was validly enacted. See *basic norm* under NORM.

pure trademark. See *technical trademark* under TRADEMARK.

pure villeinage. See VILLEINAGE.

purgation (pər-**gay**-shən). (15c) *Hist.* The act of cleansing or exonerating oneself of a crime or accusation by an oath or ordeal.

▸ **canonical purgation.** (16c) Purgation by oath-helpers in an ecclesiastical court. See COMPURGATION.

▸ **vulgar purgation.** (16c) Purgation by fire, hot irons, battle, or cold water; purgation by means other than by oath-helpers. • Vulgar purgation was so called because it was not sanctioned by the church after 1215.

purgatory oath. See OATH.

purge, *vb.* (13c) To exonerate (oneself or another) of guilt <the judge purged the defendant of contempt>.

purlieu (**pər**-lyoo). **1.** An area near or surrounding a place; an outlying area. **2.** A piece of land that borders a forest, esp. one considered a part of the forest and therefore subject in part to forest laws.

> "A purlieu-man is he that hath free lands within the purlieu to the yearly value of forty shillings per annum. . . . A purlieu-man finding any wild beasts in his purlieu, may hunt them towards the forest, because he has a property in them *ratione soli,* and if he begins the course in his own lands, he may follow the chase through any man's grounds whatsoever; but if the beast return towards the forest, he must not forestall him with dogs or any manner of engine whatever. He may hunt and kill, provided he does it without forestalling." 12 Alexander Wood Renton & Max A. Robertson, *Encyclopaedia of the Laws of England* 147 (1908).

purpart (**pər**-pahrt). (15c) A share of an estate formerly held in common; a part in a division; an allotment from an estate to a coparcener. — Formerly also termed *purparty; perparts; pourparty.*

purparty (**pər**-pahr-tee). See PURPART.

purport (**pər**-port), *n.* (15c) **1.** The idea or meaning that is conveyed or expressed, esp. by a formal document. **2.** The general meaning of what someone says.

purport (pər-**port**), *vb.* (17c) To profess or claim, esp. falsely; to seem to be <the document purports to be a will, but it is neither signed nor dated>.

purported, *adj.* (1885) Reputed; rumored.

purpose. (13c) An objective, goal, or end; specif., the business activity that a corporation is chartered to engage in.

purpose approach. See MISCHIEF RULE.

purpose clause. (1919) In a statute or other legal instrument, a usu. prefatory or introductory clause that explains the background and reasons for its enactment or existence.

purposeful, *adj.* (1853) Done with a specific purpose in mind; deliberate.

purposeful-availment doctrine. The due-process rule that in order for a party to be subject to personal jurisdiction, that party must have availed itself of at least enough contact with the jurisdiction (i.e., minimum contacts) so as not to offend traditional notions of fair play and substantial justice. *International Shoe Co. v. Washington,* 326 U.S. 310, 66 S.Ct. 154 (1945). See AVAILMENT (1); MINIMUM CONTACTS.

purposely, *adv.* (15c) In such a manner that the actor engaged in prohibited conduct with the intention of causing the social harm that the law was designed to prevent. • Under the Model Penal Code, *purposely* denotes the mental state resulting in the highest level of criminal culpability. See CULPABILITY; MENS REA. Cf. KNOWINGLY.

> "A person acts purposely with respect to a material element of an offense when: (i) if the element involves the nature of his conduct or a result thereof, it is his conscious object to engage in conduct of that nature or to cause such a result; and (ii) if the element involves the attendant circumstances, he is aware of the existence of such circumstances or he believes or hopes that they exist." Model Penal Code § 2.02(2)(a).

purposive construction. See *purposive interpretation* under INTERPRETATION (1).

purposivism (**pər**-pəs-iv-izm). The doctrine that texts are to be interpreted to achieve the broad purposes that their drafters had in mind; specif., the idea that a judge-interpreter should seek an answer not only in the words of the text but also in its social, economic, and political objectives; (broadly) MISCHIEF RULE. See EQUITY-OF-THE-STATUTE RULE. Cf. FAIR READING; FORMALISM. — **purposivist,** *adj.* & *n.*

purpresture (pər-**pres**-chər). (14c) An encroachment on public rights and easements by appropriation to private use of that which belongs to the public. — Also spelled *pourpresture.* — Also termed *purprision.*

> "Purpresture or purprision was incurred by the vassal encroaching on the rights of the king or other superior as by encroaching on royal demesne lands, obstructing public highways or passages, diverting public streams from their courses, or erecting a building the king's burg or the king's street. The penalty was that all his lands held of the king were in the king's mercy and he had to restore what he had taken by encroachment though the king commonly imposed a fine; if he offended against a superior he forfeited the lands he held of that superior." 2 David M. Walker, *A Legal History of Scotland* 665 (1990).

purprise (pər-**prɪz**), *vb.* [Law French] (15c) *Hist.* To encroach on land illegally; to make a purpresture.

purse, *n.* (18c) A sum of money available to the winner of a contest or event; a prize.

purser. (15c) A person in charge of accounts and documents on a ship.

purse-snatching. (1880) The stealing of a handbag or other similar item by seizing or grabbing it from a victim's physical possession and then fleeing, often without harm or threat of harm to the victim. • Purse-snatching is usu. a type of larceny. But if the perpetrator uses great force to take the bag or injures or threatens to injure the victim, it may instead be classified as a robbery. Cf. LARCENY; ROBBERY.

pursuant to. (16c) **1.** In compliance with; in accordance with; under <she filed the motion pursuant to the court's order>. **2.** As authorized by; under <pursuant to Rule 56, the plaintiff moves for summary judgment>. **3.** In carrying out <pursuant to his responsibilities, he ensured that all lights had been turned out>. — Also termed *in pursuance of.*

pursue, *vb.* **1.** To follow persistently in order to seize or obtain; to chase or hunt <to pursue the deer>. **2.** To try persistently to gain or attain; to seek <to pursue a degree in biology>. **3.** To continue trying to find out about <to pursue the matter further>. **4.** To apply oneself or practice; to fix one's energies on <to pursue a career in politics>. **5.** To follow or proceed along with some particular end or object <the administration pursued a prudent strategy>. **6.** To prosecute or sue <to pursue for damages>.

7. To proceed with or according to <to pursue one's legal advice>. **8.** To continue to afflict <rheumatism pursued him till the end>.

pursuer. (15c) *Civil & Scots law.* A plaintiff.

pursuit. (14c) **1.** An occupation or pastime. **2.** The act of chasing to overtake or apprehend. See FRESH PURSUIT.

pursuit of happiness. (18c) The principle — announced in the Declaration of Independence — that a person should be allowed to pursue the person's desires (esp. in regard to an occupation) without unjustified interference by the government.

pur tant que (pər tant **kyoo** *or* poor **tahn** kə). [Law French] Forasmuch as; because; for the purpose of.

purus idiota (**pyoor**-əs id-ee-**oh**-tə). [Latin] (1807) An absolute or congenital idiot. See IDIOT.

purveyor. (14c) A person or business that supplies goods, services, or information, usu. for a profit. — **purvey,** *vb.*

purview (**pər**-vyoo). (15c) **1.** Scope; area of application. **2.** The main body of a statute; specif., the part of an act that follows the preamble, beginning with the words "Be it enacted" and usu. ending with a repealing clause.

> "The word 'purview' appears sometimes to be confined to so much of the body of the statute as would be left by omitting the exceptions, provisos, and savings clauses; and as the word is ambiguous, and not very useful at best, a wise course may be not to use it at all." William M. Lile et al., *Brief Making and the Use of Law Books* 336 (Roger W. Cooley & Charles Lesley Ames eds., 3d ed. 1914).

pusher. (1928) Someone who sells illicit drugs.

***Pushman* doctrine.** (1980) *Archaic.* The rule that transfer of an unpublished work transfers the common-law copyright to the work along with the work itself. • The name derives from *Pushman v. New York Graphic Soc'y, Inc.*, 39 N.E.2d (N.Y. 1942). The doctrine was rejected by § 202 of the Copyright Act of 1976, but it remains in effect for transfers completed before the provision's effective date of January 1, 1978.

> "[A]n outright sale of a material object, such as a book, canvas, or master tape of a musical work, does not transfer copyright. One possible exception to this rule is the *Pushman* doctrine under which an author or artist who has sold an unpublished work of art or a manuscript is presumed to have transferred his *common law* copyright, unless the copyright has been specifically reserved." Marshall A. Leaffer, *Understanding Copyright Law* 211 (3d ed. 1999).

put, *n.* See *put option* under OPTION (5).

putative (**pyoo**-tə-tiv), *adj.* (15c) Reputed; believed or supposed by most people.

putative damages. See DAMAGES.

putative father. See FATHER.

putative-father registry. (1979) *Family law.* An official roster in which an unwed father may claim possible paternity of a child for purposes of receiving notice of a prospective adoption of the child.

Putative Fathers Act. See UNIFORM PUTATIVE AND UNKNOWN FATHERS ACT.

putative marriage. See MARRIAGE (1).

putative matrimony. See *putative marriage* under MARRIAGE (1).

putative spouse. See SPOUSE.

putative-spouse doctrine. See *putative marriage* under MARRIAGE (1).

put bond. See BOND (3).

put in, *vb.* (15c) To place in due form before a court; to place among the records of a court.

put on notice. See CHARGED WITH NOTICE.

put option. See OPTION (5).

put out. See EVICT (1).

put price. See *strike price* under PRICE.

puttable (**puut**-ə-bəl), *adj.* (1979) (Of a security) capable of being required by the holder to be redeemed by the issuing company.

put the question. (17c) (Of the chair) to formally state a question in its final form for the purpose of taking a vote. Cf. STATE THE QUESTION.

putting in fear. (17c) The threatening of another person with violence to compel the person to hand over property. • These words are part of the common-law definition of robbery.

putting to the horn. *Scots law.* See HORNING.

put to the horn. (16c) *Scots law.* To declare (a person) an outlaw. — Also termed *be at the horn.*

put to the law. To subject to the rigors of judicial decision; esp., in historical times, to make (a person) go through an ordeal. See ORDEAL.

put-up job. (1838) An event or occurrence that seems real and spontaneous but in fact has been arranged in order to deceive someone.

PVA. *abbr.* PUBLIC VESSELS ACT.

PVFO. *abbr.* See *persistent violent felony offender* under OFFENDER.

PVPA. *abbr.* PLANT VARIETY PROTECTION ACT.

PVS. *abbr.* PERSISTENT VEGETATIVE STATE.

PWBA. *abbr.* PENSION AND WELFARE BENEFITS ADMINISTRATION.

pyramid distribution plan. See PYRAMID SCHEME.

pyramiding. (1895) A speculative method used to finance a large purchase of stock or a controlling interest by pledging an investment's unrealized profit. See LEVERAGE; MARGIN.

pyramiding inferences. See INFERENCE-STACKING.

pyramiding inferences, rule against. (1959) *Evidence.* A rule prohibiting a fact-finder from piling one inference on another to arrive at a conclusion. • Today this rule is followed in only a few jurisdictions. Cf. REASONABLE-INFERENCE RULE.

pyramid scheme. (1949) A dishonest and often illegal way of selling investments, whereby money from later investors is used to pay people in the system who have already invested; esp., a property-distribution scheme in which a participant pays for the chance to receive compensation for introducing new persons to the scheme, as well as for when those new persons themselves introduce participants. • Pyramid schemes are illegal in most states. — Also termed *endless-chain scheme; chain-referral scheme; multilevel-distribution program; pyramid distribution plan.* Cf. PONZI SCHEME; GIFTING CLUB.

pyramid selling. (1965) A hierarchical business scheme in which the main income of the higher-tiered participants derives from recruiting other people to invest or to sell products rather than from the recruiters' own investing or selling.

pyromaniac (pɪ-roh-**may**-nee-ak), *n.* (1845) Someone who suffers from a mental illness that manifests itself in the strong desire to start fires, esp. illegal ones; a person afflicted with the persistent impulse to start fires. — **pyromania,** *n.*

Q

Q. *abbr.* (16c) QUESTION (1). • This abbreviation is almost always used in deposition and trial transcripts to denote each question asked by the examining lawyer.

qadi (**kad**-ee), *n.* An Islamic judge. — Also spelled *cadi*; *kadi*; *kathi*; *qazi*.

Q-and-A. *abbr.* (1837) QUESTION-AND-ANSWER.

Q.B. *abbr.* (1864) QUEEN'S BENCH.

Q.B.D. *abbr.* (1876) QUEEN'S BENCH DIVISION.

Q.C. *abbr.* (1846) QUEEN'S COUNSEL.

qcf. *abbr.* QUARE CLAUSUM FREGIT.

QD. *abbr.* [Latin *quasi dicat*] (16c) As if he should say.

QDOT. *abbr.* See *qualified domestic trust* under TRUST (3).

QDRO (**kwah**-droh). *abbr.* QUALIFIED DOMESTIC-RELATIONS ORDER.

QE. *abbr.* QUALIFYING EVENT.

QED. *abbr.* [Latin *quod erat demonstrandum*] (17c) Which was to be demonstrated or proved.

QEF. *abbr.* [Latin *quod erat faciendum*] (1875) Which was to be done.

QEN. *abbr.* [Latin *quare executionem non*] Why execution should not be issued.

QMCSO. *abbr.* QUALIFIED MEDICAL CHILD- SUPPORT ORDER.

QPRT. *abbr.* See *qualified personal-residence trust* under TRUST (3).

qq.v. See Q.V.

QRI. *abbr.* See *qualified residence interest* under INTEREST (3).

Q.S. See *quarter session* under SESSION (1).

QSST. *abbr.* See *qualified S-corporation trust* under TRUST (3).

Q.T. *abbr.* QUI TAM ACTION.

QTIP (**kyoo**-tip). *abbr.* QUALIFIED-TERMINABLE-INTEREST PROPERTY.

QTIP trust. See TRUST (3).

qua (kway *or* kwah). [Latin] (17c) In the capacity of; as <the fiduciary, qua fiduciary, is not liable for fraud, but he may be liable as an individual>. • This term is used in formal writing to show that one is discussing the basic nature or job of someone or something.

quack. (17c) A charlatan who pretends to be skilled in medicine.

quackery. (17c) The pretensions or practices of one who falsely claims to have medical knowledge.

quacumque via data (kway-**kəm**-kwee **VI**-ə **day**-tə). [Latin] Whichever way given; whichever way you take it.

quadragesima (kwah-drə-**jes**-i-mə), *n.* [Latin "fortieth"] (16c) *Hist.* **1.** Lent — so called because it runs about 40 days. **2.** The first Sunday in Lent — so called because it is about the fortieth day before Easter.

quadragesimals (kwah-drə-**jes**-i-məlz), *n. pl.* [fr. Latin *quadragesima* "the fortieth"] (17c) *Hist.* Offerings made on Mid-Lent Sunday by daughter churches to the mother church.

quadriennium (kwah-dree-**en**-ee-əm), *n.* [Latin fr. *quatuor* "four" + *annus* "year"] (17c) **1.** *Roman law.* The four-year course of study required of law students before they were qualified to study the Code or collection of imperial constitutions. **2.** *Scots law.* See QUADRIENNIUM UTILE.

quadriennium utile (kwah-dree-**en**-ee-əm **yoo**-tə-lee). (17c) *Scots law.* A four-year period after the attainment of majority within which the young adult may seek to annul any contract made while the person was a minor. — Sometimes shortened to *quadriennium*.

quadripartite, *adj.* (15c) *Hist.* (Of an indenture, etc.) drawn, divided, or executed in four parts.

quadripartite, *n.* (15c) A book or treatise divided into four parts.

quadruplator (kwah-**droo**-plə-tor), *n.* [Latin] (17c) *Roman law.* An informer who, by law, could institute criminal proceedings and then receive a reward of a fourth part of the thing informed against, usu. relating to frauds on the *fiscus*. Pl. ***quadruplatores*** (kwah-drə-plə-**tor**-eez).

quadruplicatio (kwah-drə-pli-**kay**-shee-oh), *n.* [fr. Latin *quadruplicatus* "quadrupled"] **1.** *Roman law & civil law.* A defendant's pleading, following the *triplicatio* and similar to the *rebutter* at common law; the third defensive pleading. — Also termed *quadruplication*; (in old Scots law) *quadruply*. **2.** *Roman law.* A plaintiff's pleading, following the *triplicatio*, the *replicatio*, and the *exceptio*. Pl. ***quadruplicationes*** (kwah-drə-pli-kay-shee-**oh**-neez).

quae cadit in virum constantem (kwee **kay**-dit in **VI**-rəm kən-**stan**-təm). [Latin] *Hist.* That which would overcome a man of firmness and resolution.

quae cadunt in non causam (kwee **kay**-dənt in non **kaw**-zəm). [Law Latin] (17c) *Hist.* Those things that we lose on the cessation of the title by which we hold them.

quae est eadem (kwee est ee-**ay**-dəm). [Law Latin] (1831) *Hist.* Which is the same. • This phrase was used by a defendant in a trespass action to show that the trespass the defendant was justified in committing was the same as that alleged in the plaintiff's pleading; that is, the plaintiff gave the defendant permission to enter, and so the defendant entered the property. — Formerly also termed *que est le mesme*.

quae functionem recipiunt (kwee fungk-shee-**oh**-nəm ri-**sip**-ee-ənt). [Law Latin] *Hist.* Things whose value depends on the class of things to which they belong (e.g., money, corn, etc.). • The phrase appeared in reference to fungibles — that is, things that could be generically estimated by quantity or weight. Cf. QUAE NON RECIPIUNT FUNCTIONEM.

quae non mente sed manu tenentur (kwee non **men**-tee sed **man**-yoo tə-**nen**-tər). [Law Latin "things that are held not by the mind but by hand"] *Hist.* The natural parental duties arising from affection for one's child, as distinguished from purely legal obligations.

quae non recipiunt functionem (kwee non ri-**sip**-ee-ənt fungk-shee-**oh**-nəm). [Law Latin] *Hist.* They that do not supply the place of others. • The phrase appeared in reference to goods that are unique, specific, or irreplaceable. Cf. QUAE FUNCTIONEM RECIPIUNT.

quae perimunt causam (kwee **per**-ə-mənt **kaw**-zəm). [Latin] *Hist.* Pleas (such as peremptory defenses) that take away the basis of an action.

quae plura (kwee **ploor**-ə). [Law Latin "what more"] (17c) *Hist.* A writ ordering the escheator, when it appeared that not all of a decedent's property had been located, to inquire about any additional lands and tenements the decedent held at the time of death.

quaequidem (kwee-**kwid**-əm). [Law Latin "which indeed" or "accordingly"] *Hist.* The introductory words of a charter clause showing, among other things, the manner in which the grantor obtained title.

quaere (**kweer**-ee), *vb.* [Latin] (17c) Inquire; query; examine. • This term was often used in the syllabus of a reported case to show that a point was doubtful or open to question.

quaerens (**kweer**-enz), *n.* [Law Latin] *Hist.* Someone who complains; a plaintiff.

quaerens nihil capiat per billam (**kweer**-enz **nɪ**-hil **kap**-ee-ət pər **bil**-əm). [Law Latin] *Hist.* Let the plaintiff take nothing by his bill. • This was a form of judgment for the defendant.

quaerens non invenit plegium (**kweer**-enz non in-**vee**-nit **plee**-jee-əm). [Law Latin "the plaintiff did not find a pledge"] (17c) *Hist.* A sheriff's return to a writ requiring him to take security from the plaintiff for prosecution of the plaintiff's claim.

quaeritur (**kwee**-ri-tər *or* **kwer**-i-tər), *n.* [Latin] *Roman law.* It is questioned. • This term introduced a doubtful legal problem.

quae sapiunt delictum (kwee **say**-pee-ənt di-**lik**-təm). [Law Latin] (17c) *Hist.* Things that partake of the character of delict.

quae sequuntur personam (kwee si-**kwən**-tər pər-**soh**-nəm). [Latin] *Hist.* Things that follow the person. • The phrase usu. referred to movable property.

quae servando servari nequeunt (kwee sər-**van**-doh sər-**vair**-ɪ **nee**-kwee-ənt). [Latin] *Hist.* Things that cannot be preserved uninjured by keeping. • The phrase usu. referred to perishable goods.

quaesita. See QUAESTA.

quae solum Deum habent ultorem (kwee **soh**-ləm **dee**-əm **hay**-bənt əl-**tor**-əm). [Latin] *Hist.* Acts that have only God as avenger; crimes that can be punished only by God.

quaesta (**kwees**-tə), *n.* [Latin "demands"] Remissions of penance, authorized by the Pope to those who contributed a certain amount to the church. — Also termed *quesita*; *quaesita*.

quaestio (**kwes**-chee-oh *or* **kwees**-), *n.* [Latin fr. *quaerere* "to inquire"] *Roman law.* **1.** A special commission of the Senate appointed to hear criminal cases involving the public interest, sometimes with the power to try all cases of a given class arising within a specified period. — Also termed *quaestio extraordinaire.* **2.** QUAESTIO PERPETUA. **3.** An interrogation by inflicting torture. **4.** The torture so inflicted. Pl. ***quaestiones*** (kews-chee-**oh**-neez or kwees-).

quaestio extraordinaire. See QUAESTIO (1).

quaestionarius (kwes-chee-ə-**nair**-ee-əs). See QUAESTOR.

quaestio perpetua (kwes-chee-**oh**-neez pər-**pech**-oo-ee). [Latin "perpetual inquiry"] (1913) *Roman law.* A permanent commission to hear criminal cases; specif., a standing jury court created by statute to try and pass sentence on particular crimes. Pl. ***quaestiones perpetuae.***

> "Then in 149 the *lex Calpurnia* was passed, concerned not only with reparation but also punishment; it established a permanent court of senators as sworn jurors to deal with claims of provincial extortion. Thereafter, both the senatorial special commissions, and also the jurisdiction of the assemblies began in their turn to be superseded by the creation of *quaestiones perpetuae*, permanent jury courts, [which] provided, each for its own offence or range of offences a framework." O.F. Robinson, *The Criminal Law of Ancient Rome* 1–2 (1995).

quaestio vexata (**kwes**-chee-oh vek-**say**-tə). [Law Latin] See VEXED QUESTION.

quaestio voluntatis (**kwes**-chee-oh vol-ən-**tay**-tis). [Latin] *Hist.* A question of intention.

quaestor (**kwes**-tər *or* **kwees**-tər), *n.* [Latin] (14c) **1.** *Roman law.* A magistrate, subordinate to the consuls or provincial governors, who maintained and administered the public money, performing tasks such as making necessary payments, receiving revenues, keeping accurate accounts, registering debts and fines, supervising the accommodation of foreign ambassadors, and financing the burials and monuments of distinguished citizens. **2.** *Hist.* An agent of the Pope who carried *quaesita* from door to door. — Also termed *quaesitor*; *questionarius.* See QUAESTA. Pl. ***quaestores.*** — **quaestorial,** *adj.* — **quaestorship,** *n.*

> "The office of quaestor goes back at least to the beginning of the Republic. Each year two quaestors were nominated by the consuls, later elected by the comitia tributa, to assist the consuls in matters of finance. This continued to be their principal concern, but they enlarged their functions as their numbers increased." R.W. Lee, *The Elements of Roman Law* 15 (4th ed. 1956).

quaestores parricidii (kwes-**tor**-eez par-ə-**sɪ**-dee-ɪ), *n. pl.* [Latin "quaestors of parricide"] (16c) *Roman law.* Two officers of the early Republic who were deputized to search out and try all cases of parricide and other capital offenses. See LEX POMPEIA DE PARRICIDIIS.

quaestor sacri palatii (**kwes**-tər **say**-krɪ pə-**lay**-shee-ɪ). [Latin "quaestor of the sacred palace"] *Roman law.* An officer of the imperial court who acted as legal adviser to the emperor.

> "The *quaestor sacri palatii* was one of the highest civil functionaries in the later Empire, concerned with the preparation of enactments and legal decisions to be issued by the emperor. He was the principal legal adviser of the emperor and he was [often] chosen from among the persons with considerable legal training." Adolf Berger, *Encyclopedic Dictionary of Roman Law* 664 (1953).

quaestus (**kwes**-təs *or* **kwee**-stəs), *n.* [Latin] **1.** *Roman law.* Profit, esp. from a business. **2.** *Hist.* Acquisition; purchase. • This term refers to a purchased estate, as distinguished from *hereditas*, referring to an estate obtained by descent.

quae sunt in patrimonio nostro (kwee sənt in pa-trə-**moh**-nee-oh **nos**-troh). [Latin] (17c) *Hist.* Things that form part of our possession.

quae transeunt per commercium (kwee **tran**-see-ənt [*or* **tran**-zee] pər kə-**mər**-shee-əm). [Law Latin] (17c) *Hist.* Things that pass through commerce; things that are bought and sold.

quale jus (**kway**-lee *or* **kwah**-lee **jəs**). [Latin "what kind of right"] (16c) *Hist.* A writ ordering an escheator to inquire into the extent of a religious person's right to a judgment, before its execution, to make sure that the judgment was not collusively made to avoid the mortmain statute.

qualificate (kwah-li-fi-**kay**-tee). [Law Latin] *Hist.* Qualifiedly.

qualification. (16c) **1.** The possession of qualities or properties (such as fitness or capacity) inherently or legally necessary to make one eligible for a position or office, or to perform a public duty or function <voter qualification requires one to meet residency, age, and registration requirements>. **2.** A modification or limitation of terms or language; esp., a restriction of terms that would otherwise be interpreted broadly <the contract contained a qualification requiring the lessor's permission before exercising the right to sublet>. **3.** CHARACTERIZATION (1). — **qualify,** *vb.*

qualified, *adj.* (16c) **1.** Possessing the necessary qualifications; capable or competent <a qualified medical examiner>. **2.** Limited; restricted <qualified immunity>. — **qualify,** *vb.*

qualified acceptance. See *varying acceptance* under ACCEPTANCE (1).

qualified corporation. See *admitted corporation* under CORPORATION.

qualified disclaimer. See DISCLAIMER.

qualified domestic-relations order. (1984) A state-court order or judgment that relates to alimony, child support, or some other state domestic-relations matter and that (1) recognizes or provides for an alternate payee's right to receive all or part of any benefits due a participant under a pension, profit-sharing, or other retirement benefit plan, (2) otherwise satisfies § 414 of the Internal Revenue Code, and (3) is exempt from the ERISA rule prohibiting the assignment of plan benefits. • Among other things, the QDRO must set out certain facts, including the name and last-known mailing address of the plan participant and alternate payee, the amount or percentage of benefits going to the alternate payee, and the number of payments to which the plan applies. The benefits provided under a QDRO are treated as income to the actual recipient. IRC (26 USCA) § 414(p)(1)(A); 29 USCA § 1056(d)(3)(D)(i). — Abbr. QDRO.

qualified domestic trust. See TRUST (3).

qualified elector. See ELECTOR (2).

qualified endorsement. See *qualified indorsement* under INDORSEMENT.

qualified estate. See ESTATE (1).

qualified fee. 1. See *fee simple defeasible* under FEE SIMPLE. **2.** See *fee simple determinable* under FEE SIMPLE. **3.** See *base fee* under FEE (2).

qualified general denial. See DENIAL (3).

qualified immunity. See IMMUNITY (1).

qualified income trust. See *Miller trust* under TRUST (3).

qualified indorsement. See INDORSEMENT.

qualified institutional buyer. See BUYER.

qualified investor. See INVESTOR.

qualifiedly (**kwah**-lə-fıd-lee *or* -fı-əd-lee), *adv.* (16c) In a fit or qualified manner <qualifiedly privileged>.

qualifiedly privileged communication. See *conditionally privileged communication* under COMMUNICATION.

qualified martial law. See MARTIAL LAW (2).

qualified medical child-support order. (1993) A family-court order that enables a nonemployee custodial parent — without the employee parent's consent — to enroll the child, make claims, and receive payments as needed under the employee parent's group health plan, all at the employee parent's expense. • The group-health-plan administrator must find that the order meets the requirements of a QMCSO, which are established by § 609(a) of the Employee Retirement Income Security Act, 29 USCA § 1169(a). — Abbr. QMCSO.

qualified nuisance. See NUISANCE.

qualified opinion. An audit-report statement containing exceptions or qualifications to certain items in the accompanying financial statement.

qualified ownership. See OWNERSHIP.

qualified pension plan. See PENSION PLAN.

qualified personal-residence trust. See TRUST (3).

qualified plan. 1. See *qualified pension plan* under PENSION PLAN. **2.** See *qualified profit-sharing plan* under PROFIT-SHARING PLAN.

qualified privilege. See PRIVILEGE (1).

qualified profit-sharing plan. See PROFIT-SHARING PLAN.

qualified property. See PROPERTY.

qualified residence interest. See INTEREST (3).

qualified S-corporation trust. See TRUST (3).

qualified stock option. See STOCK OPTION.

qualified subchapter-S corporation trust. See *qualified S-corporation trust* under TRUST (3).

qualified-terminable-interest property. See PROPERTY.

qualified veto. See VETO.

qualified voter. 1. See *qualified elector* under ELECTOR (2). **2.** VOTER (2).

qualified witness. See WITNESS.

qualifying event. Any one of several specified occasions that, but for the continuation-of-coverage provisions under the Consolidated Omnibus Budget Reconciliation Act of 1985 (COBRA), would result in a loss of benefits to a covered employee under a qualified benefit plan. • These occasions include employment termination, a reduction in work hours, the employee's separation or divorce, the employee's death, and the employer's bankruptcy. IRC (26 USCA) § 4980B(f)(3). — Abbr. QE.

qualifying share. See SHARE (2).

qualitatively incidental private benefit. See PRIVATE BENEFIT.

quality. (13c) **1.** The particular character or properties of a person, thing, or act, often essential for a particular result <she has leadership quality> <greed is a negative quality>. **2.** The character or degree of excellence of a person or substance, esp. in comparison with others <the quality of work performed under the contract>.

quality of estate. (18c) **1.** The period when the right of enjoying an estate is conferred on the owner, whether at present or in the future. **2.** The manner in which the owner's right of enjoyment of an estate is to be exercised, whether solely, jointly, in common, or in coparcenary.

quality-of-products legislation. See LEMON LAW (2).

quamdiu (**kwam**-dee-yoo). [Latin] *Hist.* As long as; so long as. • This was a word of limitation formerly used in conveyances.

quamdiu bene se gesserint (**kwam**-dee-yoo **bee**-nee see **jes**-ər-int). [Law Latin] (17c) As long as they shall conduct themselves properly. • This term refers to the holding of an office, specif. the Act of Settlement, 1700, ch. 2, which provided that a judge's tenure was no longer at the king's pleasure, but could continue until death or improper conduct. This protected judges against arbitrary dismissal. The singular form is *quamdiu se bene gesserit* "as long as he behaves himself properly." — Also written *quamdiu se bene gesserint.* Cf. GOOD BEHAVIOR; DURANTE BENE PLACITO.

> "But at present, by the long and uniform usage of many ages, our kings have delegated their whole judicial power to the judges of their several courts . . . . And, in order to maintain both the dignity and independence of the judges in the superior courts, it is enacted by the statute 13 W. III. c.2 that their commissions shall be made (not as formerly, *durante bene placito,* but) *quamdiu bene se gesserint,* and their salaries ascertained and established; but that it may be lawful to remove them on the address of both houses of parliament." 1 William Blackstone, *Commentaries on the Laws of England* 267 (1765).

quamdiu se bene gesserint. [Latin] (17c) As long as they behave themselves properly. • The singular form is *quamdiu se bene gesserit* "as long as he behaves himself properly." The plural form appears in the Act of Settlement (1701) to protect judges against arbitrary dismissal. Cf. DUM SE BENE GESSERIT.

quamdiu sustinuit istam furiositatem (**kwam**-dee-yoo səs-**tin**-[y]oo-it **is**-təm fyoor-ee-ahs-ə-**tay**-təm). [Law Latin] *Hist.* How long he has labored under that insanity.

quamprimum (kwam-**prɪ**-məm). [Latin] *Hist.* As soon as possible.

quamvis non potuerit dare (**kwam**-vis non pah-tyoo-**air**-it [*or* pah-choo-] **dair**-ee). [Law Latin] *Hist.* Although he had not been able to give or administer it.

quando acciderent (**kwahn**-doh ak-si-**deer**-ənt). [Latin] (18c) A judgment entered against a decedent's personal representative, to be satisfied by the estate out of assets that the representative receives after judgment.

quandocunque (kwahn-doh-**kəng**-kwee). [Latin] *Hist.* At any time.

quandocunque decederit (kwahn-doh-**kəng**-kwee di-**see**-dər-it). [Latin] *Hist.* Whenever he died.

quango (**kwang**-goh). See QUASI-AUTONOMOUS NONGOVERNMENTAL ORGANIZATION. — Also spelled *qango.*

quanti minoris (**kwon**-tɪ mi-**nor**-is). [Latin "how much less"] (17c) *Civil law.* A lawsuit brought by a purchaser of an article to reduce the purchase price because of defects.

quantitatively incidental private benefit. See PRIVATE BENEFIT.

quantitative rule. (1919) An evidentiary rule requiring that a given type of evidence is insufficient unless accompanied by additional evidence before the case is closed. • Such a rule exists because of the known danger or weakness of certain types of evidence. — Also termed *synthetic rule.*

quantity, *n.* **1.** The amount of something measurable; the ascertainable number of countable things <a large quantity of drugs in his possession>. **2.** A large amount or number of something <the sheer quantity of photographs made sorting them laborious>.

quantity discount. See *volume discount* under DISCOUNT.

quantity surveyor. See SURVEYOR.

quantum (**kwon**-təm). [Latin "an amount"] (17c) The required, desired, or allowed amount; portion or share <a quantum of evidence>. Pl. **quanta** (**kwon**-tə).

quantum damnificatus (**kwon**-təm dam-nə-fi-**kay**-təs). [Latin "how much damnified"] (18c) *Hist.* The issue of damages submitted by a court of equity to the jury.

quantum et quale? (**kwon**-təm et **kway**-lee *or* **kwah**-lee). [Latin] (1840) *Roman & Scots law.* How much and of what kind?

> "It is not unusual for parties to a submission to agree that, in the event of no final decree-arbitral being pronounced, the proof taken in the course of the submission shall be received as legal probation *quantum et quale* (i.e., to the same extent and as of the same quality or effect) in any after-submission or process at law between the same parties regarding the same matter." John Trayner, *Trayner's Latin Maxims* 505 (4th ed. 1894).

quantum meruit (**kwon**-təm **mer**-oo-it). [Latin "as much as he has deserved"] (17c) **1.** The reasonable value of services; damages awarded in an amount considered reasonable to compensate a person who has rendered services in a quasi-contractual relationship. **2.** A claim or right of action for the reasonable value of services rendered. **3.** At common law, a count in an assumpsit action to recover payment for services rendered to another person. **4.** A claim for the market value of a party's performance under an implied-in-fact contract or an express contract that does not specify a price. **5.** A claim for the value of benefits provided without a contract, as when the plaintiff brings a claim for restitution and that value provides the measure of recovery. • The typical applications in restitution are to cases when the defendant asked for the benefits supplied, but when the claimant, for one reason or another, cannot recover on the basis of contract, express or implied. The term has long been ambiguous between senses 4 and 5, leading to confusing references in judicial opinions. *See* Restatement (Third) of Restitution and Unjust Enrichment § 49 cmt. f (2011). Cf. *implied-in-law contract* under CONTRACT.

quantum nunc valent (**kwon**-təm nəngk **vay**-lent). [Law Latin] (18c) *Hist.* How much they (the lands) are now worth. Cf. ANTIQUUS ET NOVUS EXTENTUS; QUANTUM VALUERUNT TEMPORE PACIS.

quantum ramifactus. [Latin] The amount of damages suffered.

quantum valebant (**kwon**-təm və-**lee**-bant *or* -bənt). [Latin "as much as they were worth"] (18c) **1.** The reasonable value of goods and materials. **2.** At common law, a count in an assumpsit action to recover payment for goods sold and delivered to another. • *Quantum valebant* — although less common than *quantum meruit* — is still used today as an equitable remedy to provide restitution for another's unjust enrichment.

quantum valuerunt tempore pacis (**kwon**-təm val-yoo-**air**-ənt **tem**-pə-ree **pay**-sis). [Law Latin] (1838) *Hist.* How much they (the lands) were worth in peacetime. Cf. ANTIQUUS ET NOVUS EXTENTUS; QUANTUM NUNC VALENT.

quarantina habenda. See DE QUARANTINA HABENDA.

quarantine. (17c) **1.** The isolation of a person or animal afflicted with a communicable disease or the prevention of such a person or animal from coming into a particular area, the purpose being to prevent the spread of disease. • Federal, state, and local authorities are required to cooperate in the enforcement of quarantine laws. 42 USCA § 243(a).

> "Power to make quarantine regulations is one of the most frequent powers conferred on boards of health. Such regulations constitute a proper exercise of the police power, provided they are not in conflict with federal regulations on the subject or that legislation by Congress is absent, and that they do not abridge rights protected by the Fourteenth Amendment." 39 Am. Jur. 2d *Health* § 59, at 529–30 (1999).

2. A place where a quarantine is in force. **3.** The period of time when a person or animal is isolated from others. **4.** *Hist.* A period of 40 days, esp. for the isolation and detention of ships containing persons or animals suspected of having or carrying a dangerous communicable disease, in order to prevent the spread of the disease.

> "QUARANTINE, a regulation by which all communication with individuals, ships, or goods, arriving from places infected with the plague, or other contagious disease, or supposed to be peculiarly liable to such infection, is interdicted for a certain definite period. The term is derived from the Italian *quaranta*, forty; it being generally supposed, that if no infectious disease break out within 40 days, or 6 weeks, no danger need be apprehended from the free admission of the individuals under quarantine. During this period, too, all the goods, clothes, &c. that might be supposed capable of retaining the infection, are subjected to a process of purification. This last operation, which is a most important part of the quarantine system, is performed either on board ship, or in establishments denominated *lazarettos*." 2 J.R. McCulloch, *A Dictionary, Practical, Theoretical, and Historical, of Commerce and Commercial Navigation* 959 (2d ed. 1834).

> "Quarantine . . . . The name is drawn from the fact that the period was formerly commonly 40 (Ital. *quaranta*) days. In 1423 Venice established a lazaretto or quarantine station on an island to check the growth of disease brought in by ships. In the sixteenth century quarantine became widespread and there developed the system of bills of health, certificates that the last port was free from disease; a clean bill entitled a ship to use the port without subjection to quarantine." David M. Walker, *The Oxford Companion to Law* 1022 (1980).

5. *Hist.* A widow's privilege to remain in her husband's house for 40 days after his death while her dower is being assigned. • This right was enforced by a writ *de quarantina habenda.* See DE QUARANTINA HABENDA. — Also spelled *quarentine*; *quarentene.* — **quarantine,** *vb.*

> "[I]t was provided by Magna Charta that the widow should give nothing for her dower, and that she should tarry in the chief house of her husband for forty days, (and which is called the widow's quarantine,) after the death of her husband, within which time her dower should be assigned her; and that, in the mean time, she should have reasonable estovers, or maintenance, out of the estate. The provision that the widow should pay nothing for the dower, was made with the generous intention of taking away the uncourtly and oppressive claim of the feudal lord, for a fine, upon allowing the widow to be endowed. This declaration of Magna Charta is, probably, the law in all the United States." 4 James Kent, *Commentaries on American Law* *61 (George Comstock ed., 11th ed. 1866).

quare (**kwair**-ee). [Latin] Why; for what reason; on what account. • This was used in various common-law writs, esp. writs in trespass.

quare clausum fregit (**kwair**-ee **klaw**-zəm **free**-jit). [Latin] (17c) Why he broke the close. — Abbr. *qu. cl. fr.*; *q.c.f.* See *trespass quare clausum fregit* under TRESPASS.

quare clausum querentis fregit. See *trespass quare clausum fregit* under TRESPASS.

quare ejecit infra terminum (**kwair**-ee i-**jee**-sit **in**-frə **tər**-mə-nəm), *n.* [Law Latin "why he ejected within the term"] (16c) *Hist.* A writ for a lessee who was prematurely ejected, when the ejector was not actually in possession but one claiming under the ejector was.

> "For this injury the law has provided him with two remedies . . . the writ of *ejectione firmae*; . . . and the writ of *quare ejecti infra terminum*; which lies not against the wrongdoer or ejector himself, but his feoffee or other person claiming under him. These are mixed actions, somewhat between real and personal; for therein are two things recovered, as well restitution of the term of years, as damages for the ouster or wrong." 3 William Blackstone, *Commentaries on the Laws of England* 199 (1768).

quare executionem non. [Latin] Why execution should not be issued. — Abbr. QEN.

quare impedit (**kwair**-ee **im**-pə-dit). [Latin "why he hinders"] (15c) *Hist. Eccles. law.* A writ or action to enforce a patron's right to present a person to fill a vacant benefice. — Also termed *writ of quare impedit.* See PRESENTATION (2); ADVOWSON.

> "The writ of *quare impedit* commands the disturbers, the bishop, the pseudo-patron, and his clerk, to permit the plaintiff to present a proper person (without specifying the particular clerk) to such a vacant church, which pertains to his patronage; and which the defendants, as he alleges, do obstruct: and unless they so do, then that they appear in court to shew the reason why they hinder him." 3 William Blackstone, *Commentaries on the Laws of England* 248 (1768).

quare incumbravit (**kwair**-ee in-kəm-**bray**-vit), *n.* [Law Latin "why he incumbered"] (16c) *Hist.* A writ or action to compel a bishop to explain why he encumbered the church when, within six months after the vacation of a benefice and after a *ne admittas* was received, the bishop conferred the benefice on his clerk while other clerks were contending for the right of presentation in a *quare impedit* action. • The writ was abolished by the Real Property Limitation Act of 1833, ch. 27.

quare intrusit (**kwair**-ee in-**troo**-sit), *n.* [Law Latin "why he thrust in"] (17c) *Hist.* A writ allowing a lord to recover the value of a marriage, when the lord offered a suitable marriage to a ward but the ward rejected it and married someone else. • It was abolished by the Tenures Abolition Act, 1660, ch. 24.

quare non permittit (**kwair**-ee non pər-**mit**-it), *n.* [Law Latin "why he does not permit"] (17c) *Hist.* A writ for one who has a right to present to a church, against the proprietor.

quarentena terrae (kwahr-en-**tee**-nə **ter**-ee), *n.* [Law Latin "a quantity of land"] (18c) *Hist.* A furlong.

quarentine. See QUARANTINE.

quare obstruxit (**kwair**-ee əb-**strək**-sit), *n.* [Law Latin "why he obstructed"] (17c) *Hist.* A writ for one who could not enjoy a privilege to pass through a neighbor's land because the neighbor had obstructed the path.

quarrel, *n.* (14c) **1.** An altercation or angry dispute; an exchange of recriminations, taunts, threats, or accusations between two persons. — **quarrel,** *vb.* **2.** *Archaic.* A complaint; a legal action.

> "Quarrels is derived from *querendo*, and extends not only to actions as well real as personal, but also to the causes of actions and suits: so that by the release of all quarrels, not only actions depending in suit, but causes of action and suit also are released; and quarrels, controversies and debates, are words of one sense, and of one and the same signification, Coke, lib. 8, fol. 153." *Termes de la Ley* 330 (1st Am. ed. 1812).

quarta divi Pii (**kwor**-tə **dɪ**-vɪ **pɪ**-ɪ). [Latin "quarter of the deified Pius"] *Roman law.* The quarter portion of a testator's estate required to be left to an adrogated child who had been unjustly emancipated or disinherited.

quarta Falcidiana (**kwor**-tə fal-**sid**-ee-ə). [Latin "Falcidian fourth"] See FALCIDIAN PORTION.

quarta Trebellianica (**kwor**-tə trə-bel-ee-**an**-ə-kə). [Latin "the quarter due under Trebellianus's *senatus consultum*"] *Hist.* The fourth portion that an heir could retain from a succession after transferring the succession as directed by the testator under a *fideicommissum.* — Also termed *quarta Trebelliana* (trə-bel-ee-**ay**-nə *or* -**an**-ə). Cf. FALCIDIAN PORTION.

quarter, *n.* (17c) **1.** In the law of war, the act of showing mercy to a defeated enemy by sparing lives and accepting a surrender <to give no quarter>. **2.** See *quarter section* under SECTION.

quarter day. See DAY.

quartering, *n.* (15c) *Hist.* **1.** The dividing of a criminal's body into quarters after execution, esp. as part of the punishment for a crime such as high treason. See HANGED, DRAWN, AND QUARTERED. **2.** The furnishing of living quarters to members of the military. • In the United States, a homeowner's consent is required before soldiers may be quartered in a private home during peacetime. During wartime, soldiers may be quartered in private homes only as prescribed by law. The Third Amendment generally protects U.S. citizens from being forced to use their homes to quarter soldiers. U.S. Const. amend. III. **3.** The dividing of a shield into four parts to show four different coats of arms. — **quarter,** *vb.*

quartering soldiers. The assigning of military personnel to a place for food and lodging, usu. in a barracks.

quarterly report. A financial report issued by a corporation (and by most mutual funds and investment managers) every three months.

quartermaster. 1. A military officer in charge of providing food, uniforms, and other necessities. **2.** A ship's officer in charge of signals and guiding the ship on the right course. **3.** TREASURER.

quarters, *n.* Housing that is provided esp. to soldiers or servants; permanent or temporary lodging given to a member of the armed services or to an entire military unit.

quarter seal. See SEAL.

quarter section. See SECTION.

quarter session. See SESSION (1).

Quarter Sessions Court. See COURT OF GENERAL QUARTER SESSIONS OF THE PEACE.

quarters of coverage. (1939) The number of quarterly payments made by a person into the social-security fund as a basis for determining the person's entitlement to benefits.

quarto die post (**kwor**-toh **dɪ**-ee **pohst**), *n.* [Law Latin "on the fourth day after"] (16c) The defendant's appearance day, being four days (inclusive) from the return of the writ.

quash (kwahsh), *vb.* (13c) **1.** To annul or make void; to terminate <quash an indictment> <quash proceedings>. **2.** To suppress or subdue; to crush <quash a rebellion>.

quashal (**kwahsh**-əl), *n.* (1805) The act of quashing something <quashal of the subpoena>.

quasi (**kway**-sɪ *or* **kway**-zɪ *also* **kwah**-zee). [Latin "as if"] (15c) Seemingly but not actually; in some sense or degree; resembling; nearly.

> "QUASI. A Latin word frequently used in the civil law, and often prefixed to English words. It is not a very definite word. It marks the resemblance, and supposes a little difference, between two objects, and in legal phraseology the term is used to indicate that one subject resembles another, with which it is compared, in certain characteristics, but that there are also intrinsic and material differences between them. It negatives the idea of identity, but implies a strong superficial analogy, and points out that the conceptions are sufficiently similar for one to be classed as the equal of the other." 74 C.J.S. *Quasi*, at 2 (1951).

quasi-admission. See ADMISSION (1).

quasi-affinity. See AFFINITY.

quasi-autonomous nongovernmental organization. (1980) A semipublic administrative body (esp. in the United Kingdom) having some members appointed and financed by, but not answerable to, the government, such as a tourist authority, a university-grants commission, a price-and-wage commission, a prison or parole board, or a medical-health advisory panel. • This term is more commonly written as an acronym, *quango* (**kwang**-goh), without capital letters.

quasi committee of the whole. See COMMITTEE (1).

quasi-community property. See COMMUNITY PROPERTY.

quasi-contract. See *implied-in-law contract* under CONTRACT.

quasi-corporation. See CORPORATION.

quasi-crime. See CRIME.

quasi-criminal proceeding. See PROCEEDING.

quasi-delict. See DELICT (1).

quasi-deposit. See DEPOSIT (5).

quasi-derelict. See DERELICT (1).

quasi-deviation. See DEVIATION.

quasi-domicile. See *commercial domicile* under DOMICILE.

quasi-dwelling-house. See DWELLING-HOUSE.

quasi-easement. See EASEMENT.

quasi-enclave. See ENCLAVE.

quasi-entail. See ENTAIL.

quasi-estoppel. See ESTOPPEL.

quasi ex contractu (**kway**-sɪ [*or* -zɪ] eks kən-**trak**-t[y]oo). [Latin] (17c) *Hist.* Arising as if from contract.

quasi ex delicto (**kway**-sɪ [*or* -zɪ] eks di-**lik**-toh). [Latin] (1806) *Hist.* Arising as if from delict. See DELICT.

quasi-fee. See FEE (2).

quasi feudum (**kway**-sɪ [*or* -zɪ] **fyoo**-dəm). [Law Latin "as if a (heritable) fee"] (17c) *Hist.* A heritable right, usu. in money.

quasi-governmental agency. See AGENCY (3).

quasi-guarantee treaty. See *guarantee treaty* under TREATY (1).

quasi-guardian. See GUARDIAN (1).

quasi-individual. See *private corporation* under CORPORATION.

quasi in rem. See IN REM.

quasi-in-rem jurisdiction. See JURISDICTION.

quasi-insurer. See INSURER.

quasi-judicial, *adj.* (1820) Of, relating to, or involving an executive or administrative official's adjudicative acts. • Quasi-judicial acts, which are valid if there is no abuse of discretion, often determine the fundamental rights of citizens. They are subject to review by courts.

> "Quasi-judicial is a term that is . . . not easily definable. In the United States, the phrase often covers judicial decisions taken by an administrative agency — the test is the nature of the tribunal rather than what it is doing. In England quasi-judicial belongs to the administrative category and is used to cover situations where the administrator is bound by the law to observe certain forms and possibly hold a public hearing but where he is a free agent in reaching the final decision. If the rules are broken, the determination may be set aside, but it is not sufficient to show that the administration is biased in favour of a certain policy, or that the evidence points to a different conclusion." George Whitecross Paton, *A Textbook of Jurisprudence* 336 (G.W. Paton & David P. Derham eds., 4th ed. 1972).

quasi-judicial act. (1840) **1.** A judicial act performed by an official who is not a judge. **2.** An act performed by a judge who is not acting entirely in a judicial capacity. See *judicial act* under ACT (2).

quasi-judicial duty. See DUTY (1).

quasi-judicial function. See FUNCTION.

quasi-judicial power. See POWER (3).

quasi-legislative, *adj.* (1934) (Of an act, function, etc.) not purely legislative in nature <the administrative agency's rulemaking, being partly adjudicative, is not entirely legislative — that is, it is quasi-legislative>.

quasi-legislative power. See POWER (3).

quasi-main motion. See *incidental main motion* under MOTION (2).

quasi-municipal corporation. See *quasi-corporation* under CORPORATION.

quasi-national domicile. See DOMICILE.

quasi-offense. 1. See OFFENSE (3). **2.** See *quasi-crime* under CRIME.

quasi-partner. See PARTNER.

quasi-personalty. See PERSONALTY.

quasi-possession. See *incorporeal possession* under POSSESSION.

quasi-posthumous child. See CHILD.

quasi-public corporation. See CORPORATION.

quasi-pupillary substitution. See SUBSTITUTION (5).

quasi-realty. See REALTY.

quasi-rent. (*often pl.*) (1890) *Law and economics.* Value over and above one's opportunity cost or next best alternative; the excess of an asset's value over its salvage value. • In the economic theory of marriage, a quasi-rent is a spouse's excess value of the marriage over the value of the next best option of not being in that specific marriage. The next best option may be separation, divorce, or divorce and remarriage, depending on the spouse's preferences and opportunities.

quasi-seisin. See SEISIN.

quasi-statute. See STATUTE.

quasi-suspect classification. See SUSPECT CLASSIFICATION.

quasi-tenant. See TENANT (1).

quasi-tort. See TORT.

quasi traditio (**kway**-sɪ [*or* -zɪ] trə-**dish**-ee-oh). [Latin "as if transfer"] (1848) *Roman law.* A party's acquisition of a servitude by using it with the informal permission or acquiescence of the owner.

> "According to the civil law again a servitude — that is, a limited right of user in respect of a thing not one's own, e.g. a usufruct or a right of way — could only be created by means of certain definite legal forms. The praetorian law, on the other hand, allowed a servitude to be created by a so-called quasi traditio servitutis; that is, it was satisfied if one party gave the other, without any form, permission to exercise the right of user in question." Rudolph Sohm, *The Institutes: A Textbook of the History and System of Roman Private Law* 82 (James Crawford Ledlie trans., 3d ed. 1907).

quasi-trustee. See TRUSTEE (1).

quasi-usufruct. See USUFRUCT.

quator tempora jejunii. See EMBER DAYS.

quatuor pedibus currit (**kwah**-too-or **ped**-ə-bəs **kər**-it). [Law Latin] It runs on four feet; it runs on all fours. • The term commonly described a precedent that was extremely close to a point being decided. See ON ALL FOURS.

quayage (**kee**-əj). (18c) A toll or fee charged for lading or unlading goods on a quay or wharf. — Also written *keyage.*

***Quayle* action.** (1965) *Patents.* An office action telling the patent applicant that the claims are allowable on the merits but that the form of the application still needs to be amended. *Ex parte Quayle*, 25 USPQ (BNA) 74, 1935 C.D. 11, 453 O.G. 213 (Comm'r Pat. 1935). • The applicant generally has two months to respond. A *Quayle* action ends the prosecution on the merits, and amendments that affect the merits will be treated in a manner similar to amendments after final rejection.

qu. cl. fr. *abbr.* QUARE CLAUSUM FREGIT.

queen. (bef. 12c) **1.** A woman who possesses, in her own right, the sovereignty and royal power in a monarchy. • Among the most famous English queens are Queen Mary I, Queen Elizabeth I, Queen Victoria, and Queen Elizabeth II. — Also termed *queen regnant.* **2.** The wife of a reigning king. • She has some royal prerogatives (such as having her own officers), but is in many ways legally no different from the rest of the king's subjects. — Also termed *queen consort.* **3.** A woman who rules in place of the actual sovereign (e.g., if the sovereign is a child). — Also termed *queen regent.* **4.** DOWAGER-QUEEN.

Queen Anne's Bounty. See FIRST FRUITS.

queen consort. See QUEEN (2).

queen dowager. See DOWAGER-QUEEN.

queen-for-a-day agreement. (1988) *Criminal procedure. Slang.* Contractual immunity, usu. granted in a letter to a suspect or defendant from a prosecutor, who agrees not to use any information provided against the informant, but reserving the right to use other evidence that may eventually derive from the informant's information.

queen mother. (16c) A queen who has children; esp., a dowager-queen whose child is the reigning monarch. See DOWAGER-QUEEN.

queen regent. See QUEEN (3).

queen regnant. See QUEEN (1).

Queen's Bench. *English law.* Historically, the highest common-law court in England, presided over by the reigning monarch. • The jurisdiction of this court now lies with the Queen's Bench Division of the High Court of Justice; when a king begins to reign, the name automatically changes to *King's Bench.* — Abbr. Q.B. — Also termed *Court of Queen's Bench.* Cf. KING'S BENCH.

Queen's Bench Division. *English law.* The English court, formerly known as the Queen's Bench or King's Bench, that presides over tort and contract actions, applications for judicial review, and some magistrate-court appeals. — Abbr. Q.B.D.

Queen's Counsel. (17c) *English law.* In the United Kingdom, Canada, and territories that have retained the rank, an elite, senior-level barrister or advocate. • Originally, a Queen's Counsel was appointed to serve as counsel to the reigning monarch. — Also termed *senior counsel.* — Abbr. Q.C. Cf. KING'S COUNSEL.

> "QCs do less paperwork than juniors (for example, they do not draw pleadings), though they do a lot of advisory work. One important factor explaining why the title of QC is so valuable is that when a solicitor is faced with a difficult point of law on which he wishes to obtain a specialist or more advanced opinion, he will often like to take the opinion of a QC, especially if the solicitor practices outside London and does not have a great deal of contact with the bar. To him, the title of QC is some assurance of standing and competence in the profession, and that is important, because one of the main reasons that often moves a solicitor (or indeed, a lay institution) to take counsel's opinion is that it may serve to insulate the solicitor (or institution) from liability for negligence. This insulation is not a matter of law, but a matter of what is reasonable: someone who relies on an opinion from a QC will normally be held to have acted reasonably, unless there are special circumstances suggesting for some reason that the opinion is unreliable." P.S. Atiyah & Robert S. Summers, *Form and Substance in Anglo-American Law* 361 (1987).

Queen's evidence. See EVIDENCE.

Queen's prison. *English law.* A prison established in 1842 in Southwark, to be used for debtors and criminals confined under authority of the superior courts at Westminster, the highest court of admiralty, and the bankruptcy laws. • It replaced the Queen's Bench Prison, Fleet Prison, and Marshalsea Prison but was closed in 1862.

Queen's proctor. (17c) *English law.* A solicitor who represents the Crown in domestic-relations, probate, and admiralty cases. • For example, in a suit for divorce or nullity of marriage, the Queen's proctor might intervene to prove collusion between the parties. — Also termed (when a king reigns) *King's proctor.*

que est le mesme (**kyoo** ay lə **mem**). [Law French] See QUAE EST EADEM.

quem nuptiae demonstrant (kwem **nəp**-shee-ee di-**mon**-strant). [Latin] *Roman & Scots law.* Whom the marriage indicates. • The phrase refers to the rebuttable presumption that a husband is the father of a child that his wife gives birth to. See *presumed father* and *putative father* under FATHER.

quem redditum reddit (**kwem red**-ə-təm **red**-it), *n.* [Law Latin "which return he made"] (17c) *Hist.* A writ for a grantee of a rent (not a rent service) to force the tenant to consent to the transfer.

querela (kwə-**ree**-lə), *n.* [Law Latin fr. Latin *queri* "to complain"] *Hist.* **1.** A complaint founding an action; the plaintiff's count or declaration. **2.** A cause of action. **3.** An action.

querela coram rege a concilio discutienda et terminanda (kwə-**ree**-lə **kor**-əm **ree**-jee ay kən-**sil**-ee-oh dis-kə-shee-**en**-də et tər-mə-**nan**-də), *n.* [Law Latin "a dispute to be discussed and resolved by the council in front of the king"] (17c) *Hist.* A writ ordering someone to appear before the king to answer to a trespass.

querela inofficiosi testamenti (kwə-**ree**-lə in-ə-fish-ee-**oh**-SI tes-tə-**men**-tI). [Latin "complaint of an undutiful will"] (1818) *Roman law.* An action allowing a descendant, ascendant, or sibling who was unjustly disinherited or passed over by a parent's will to have the will set aside as undutifully made.

> "By far the most important is due to the *querela inofficiosi testamenti.* By this procedure, though the forms had been complied with, near relatives with obvious claims (the classes of those entitled having been gradually widened) might attack the will as contrary to natural duty (*inofficiosum*) and get it set aside." W.W. Buckland, *A Manual of Roman Private Law* 199 (2d ed. 1939).

querens (**kweer**-enz), *n.* [Latin fr. *queri* "to complain"] *Hist.* A plaintiff; the complaining party.

query (**kweer**-ee), *n.* **1.** A question posed in order to elicit information or to verify whether something is accurate or correct. **2.** One or more search terms used in computer research.

questa (**kwes**-tə), *n.* [Law Latin] *Hist.* A quest; an inquest or inquiry upon the oaths of an impaneled jury.

question. (14c) **1.** A query directed to a witness. — Abbr. Q.

▸ **categorical question.** (18c) **1.** LEADING QUESTION. **2.** (*often pl.*) One of a series of questions, on a particular subject, arranged in systematic or consecutive order.

▸ **cross-question.** (17c) A question asked of a witness during cross-examination. — Abbr. XQ.

▸ **direct question.** (17c) A question asked of a witness during direct examination.

▸ **hypothetical question.** See HYPOTHETICAL QUESTION.

▸ **impertinent question.** (18c) A question that cannot properly be asked of a witness, esp. one that is insolent or rude.

▸ **irrelevant question.** (18c) A question that is not related to or has only a remote bearing on an issue.

▸ **leading question.** See LEADING QUESTION.

2. An issue in controversy; a matter to be determined.

▸ **certified question.** See CERTIFIED QUESTION.

▸ **federal question.** See FEDERAL QUESTION.

▸ **incidental question.** (17c) *Roman & civil law.* An issue related to the primary claim in a case.

▸ **judicial question.** See JUDICIAL QUESTION.

▸ **mixed question.** See MIXED QUESTION.

▸ **mixed question of law and fact.** See MIXED QUESTION OF LAW AND FACT.

▸ **nonjusticiable question.** See POLITICAL QUESTION.

▸ **political question.** See POLITICAL QUESTION.

▸ **question of fact.** See QUESTION OF FACT.

▸ **question of law.** See QUESTION OF LAW.

▸ **ultimate question.** See *ultimate issue* under ISSUE (1).

3. *Parliamentary law.* A motion that the chair has stated for a meeting's consideration in a form that the meeting can adopt or reject; a pending motion. • A question is technically only a "motion" until the chair states it for the meeting's consideration. But for most purposes, the parliamentary terms "motion" and "question" are interchangeable. See MOTION (2); PUT THE QUESTION; STATE THE QUESTION.

▸ **privileged question.** (1831) A privileged motion that that the chair has stated for a meeting's consideration. See *privileged motion* under MOTION (2). Cf. *question of privilege.*

▸ **question of consideration.** See OBJECTION (2).

▸ **question of information.** See *point of information* under POINT (2).

▸ **question of order.** See *point of order* under POINT (2).

▸ **question of privilege.** (1837) Any question that concerns the deliberative assembly's or a member's rights or privileges. See PRIVILEGE (5); RAISE A QUESTION OF PRIVILEGE. Cf. *privileged question.*

questionable, *adj.* (15c) **1.** Not likely to be true or correct; open to doubt or being called into question. **2.** Not likely to be good, honest, or useful; open to suspicion on ethical grounds.

question-and-answer. (17c) **1.** The portion of a deposition or trial transcript in which evidence is developed through a series of questions asked by the lawyer and answered by the witness. — Abbr. Q-and-A. **2.** The method for developing evidence during a deposition or at trial, requiring the witness to answer the examining lawyer's questions, without offering unsolicited information. **3.** The method of instruction used in many law-school classes, in which the professor asks questions of one or more students and then follows up each answer with another question. — Also termed *Socratic method.* See SOCRATIC METHOD.

questionarius. See QUAESTOR.

questioner. (15c) Someone who asks one or more questions, esp. a series of questions in a public discussion.

question of consideration. See OBJECTION (2).

question of fact. (17c) **1.** An issue that has not been predetermined and authoritatively answered by the law. • An example is whether a particular criminal defendant is guilty of an offense or whether a contractor has delayed unreasonably in constructing a building. **2.** An issue that does not involve what the law is on a given point. **3.** A disputed issue to be resolved by the jury in a jury trial or by the judge in a bench trial. — Also termed *fact question.* See FACT-FINDER. **4.** An issue capable of being answered by way of demonstration, as opposed to a question of unverifiable opinion. See *issue of fact* under ISSUE (1).

question of law. (17c) **1.** An issue to be decided by the judge, concerning the application or interpretation of the law <a jury cannot decide questions of law, which are reserved for the court>. See *legal issue* under ISSUE (1). **2.** A question that the law itself has authoritatively answered, so that the court may not answer it as a matter of discretion <the enforceability of an arbitration clause is a question of law>. **3.** An issue about what the law is on a particular point; an issue in which parties argue about, and the court must decide, what the true rule of law is <both parties appealed on the question of law>. See *issue of law* under ISSUE. (1). **4.** An issue that, although it may turn on a factual point, is reserved for the court and excluded from the jury; an issue that is exclusively within the province of the judge and not the jury <whether a contractual ambiguity exists is a question of law>. — Also termed *legal question; law question.*

question of privilege. See QUESTION (3).

questman. (15c) *Hist.* **1.** An instigator of a lawsuit or prosecution. **2.** Someone who was chosen to inquire into abuses, esp. those relating to weights and measures. **3.** A churchwarden; SIDESMAN. — Also termed *questmonger.*

questmonger. See QUESTMAN.

questus est nobis (kwes-təs est **noh**-bis), *n.* [Law Latin "hath complained to us"] (17c) *Hist.* By 1287, a writ against someone who continued a nuisance that existed before inheritance or purchase. • The former law provided recovery only against the party who had first caused the nuisance.

queue-jumping. (1947) The act or an instance of cutting in line — that is, getting something before other people who have been waiting longer.— Also termed *line-cutting.*

quia (**kwɪ**-ə *or* **kwee**-ə). [Latin] *Hist.* Because; whereas. • This term was used to point out the consideration in a conveyance.

quia alimenta liberis non debentur nisi in subsidium (**kwɪ**-ə *or* **kwee**-ə al-i-**men**-tə **lib**-ər-is non di-**ben**-tər **nɪ**-sɪ in səb-**sid**-ee-əm). [Law Latin] *Scots law.* Because aliment (alimony) is not due to children except in aid. • A parent was not required to support a child for whom another source, such as a separate estate, provided.

Quia Emptores (**kwɪ**-ə *or* **kwee**-ə emp-**tor**-eez). [Latin "since purchasers"] *Hist.* A 1290 English statute giving fee-simple tenants (other than those holding directly of the Crown) the power to alienate their land and bind the transferee to perform the same services for the lord as the transferor had been obliged to perform. • The statute tended to concentrate feudal lordships in the Crown by eliminating multiple layers of fealty. 18 Edw., ch. 1. — Also termed *Quia Emptores Terrarum.*

> "*Quia emptores* . . . was made in the interest of the great lords; but . . . it was accepted with satisfaction on all hands. It dealt a heavy blow to the consistency and elegance of the feudal theory, but made the conditions of land tenure far more simple. It was the first approximation

of feudal tenancy to the modern conception of full ownership." Frederick Pollock, *The Land Laws* 70 (3d ed. 1896).

"Edward I and his lords wished, for political reasons, to prevent the growth of subinfeudation, and in 1290 the Statute *Quia Emptores* was enacted. It took its name from the beginning of its preamble — 'Since purchasers . . . .'" L.B. Curzon, *English Legal History* 300 (2d ed. 1979).

quia erronice emanavit (**kwɪ**-ə i-**roh**-nə-see em-ə-**nay**-vit). [Law Latin] *Hist.* Because it issued erroneously.

quia ita lex scripta est (**kwɪ**-ə *or* **kwee**-ə ɪ-tə leks **skrip**-tə est). [Latin "because the law is so written"] *Hist.* Because that is the text of the statute.

quia succedunt in universum jus quod defunctus habuit (**kwɪ**-ə *or* **kwee**-ə sək-**see**-dənt in yoo-ni-**vər**-səm jəs kwod di-**fəngk**-təs **hab**-yoo-it). [Latin] *Roman & Scots law.* Because they succeed to every right that the decedent had. • The phrase appeared in reference to the position of heirs-at-law.

quia surrogatum sapit naturam surrogati (**kwɪ**-ə *or* **kwee**-ə sər-ə-**gay**-təm **say**-pit nə-**t[y]oor**-əm sər-ə-**gay**-tɪ). [Law Latin] *Hist.* Because the substitute partakes of the character of that for which it is substituted.

quia timet (**kwɪ**-ə **tɪ**-mət *or* **kwee**-ə **tim**-et). [Latin "because he fears"] (17c) A legal doctrine that allows a person to seek equitable relief from future probable harm to a specific right or interest.

"A second class of cases where equity courts act to prevent injury are known as 'quia timet' cases. The name comes from the two Latin words, once used when asking relief in this class of cases; the words mean, 'whereas he fears' that some injury will be inflicted in the future unless the court of equity assists him in advance, the plaintiff asks the assistance of the court to do this, that, or the other thing with respect to the defendant." Charles Herman Kinnane, *A First Book on Anglo-American Law* 648 (2d ed. 1952).

"Quia timet is the right to be protected against anticipated future injury that cannot be prevented by the present action. The doctrine of 'quia timet' permits equitable relief based on a concern over future probable injury to certain rights or interests, where anticipated future injury cannot be prevented by a present action at law, such as where there is a danger that a defense at law might be prejudiced or lost if not tried immediately." 27A Am. Jur. 2d *Equity* § 93, at 581 (1996).

***quia-timet* injunction.** See INJUNCTION.

quibble (**kwib**-əl), *n.* A small complaint or criticism about something unimportant. — **quibble,** *vb.*

quibus deficientibus (**kwib**-əs di-fish-ee-**en**-ti-bəs). [Latin] *Hist. Scots law.* Who failing. • In a disposition, this phrase appeared in reference to one or more who succeeded to an estate and then died. Cf. QUIBUS NON EXISTENTIBUS.

quibus non existentibus (**kwib**-əs non ek-si-**sten**-tə-bəs). [Latin] *Scots law.* Whom failing. • In a disposition, this phrase appeared in reference to one or more who never existed. Cf. QUIBUS DEFICIENTIBUS.

qui cedit foro (kwɪ **see**-dit **for**-oh). [Latin] (18c) *Hist.* Someone who stops payment; one who becomes bankrupt.

quick asset. See *quick asset* under ASSET.

quick-asset ratio. (1954) The ratio between an entity's current or liquid assets (such as cash and accounts receivable) and its current liabilities. — Also termed *quick ratio*; *acid-test ratio.*

quick condemnation. See CONDEMNATION (2).

quick dispatch. See DISPATCH (4).

quickening. (15c) The first motion felt in the womb by the mother of the fetus, usu. occurring near the middle of the pregnancy.

quick flip. See FLIP.

quickie divorce. See DIVORCE.

quickie plea. (1989) *Criminal law. Slang.* A criminal defendant's guilty plea entered quite soon after the charge in an effort to foreclose more serious charges by reason of the double-jeopardy bar.

quickie strike. See *wildcat strike* under STRIKE (1).

quick ratio. See QUICK-ASSET RATIO.

quick-take. See *quick condemnation* under CONDEMNATION (2).

quid actum est (kwid **ak**-təm est). [Latin] *Hist.* What has been done.

quidam (**kwɪ**-dəm), *n.* [Latin] (16c) *Hist.* Somebody. • This term has esp. been used in French law to designate a person whose name is unknown.

quid juratum est (kwid juu-**ray**-təm est). [Law Latin] *Hist.* What has been sworn. — Also termed *quid juravit.*

quid juravit. See QUID JURATUM EST.

quid juris? (kwid **joor**-is). [Latin] What is law? • This question was posed in difficult cases.

"Logically, of course, 'quid jus' always precedes 'quid juris'; for before one can determine what is lawful, he must first know what is law. Actually, however, the situation is reversed. There is widespread and thoroughgoing agreement as to particular questions of law — the 'quid juris'; the most complicated problems have been in part exhaustively investigated and treated. On the contrary, the higher we climb toward the general and fundamental, the darker and more thorny becomes the path. The summit of this ascent, the question 'quid jus?' is surrounded, so it would appear, by a heavy fog." Hans Reichel, "Del Vecchio's Legal Philosophy," in Giorgio Del Vecchio, *The Formal Bases of Law* 337, 340 (John Lisle trans., 1921).

quid jus? (kwid **jəs**). [Latin] What is law?

quid pro quo (**kwid** proh **kwoh**), *n.* [Latin "something for something"] (16c) An action or thing that is exchanged for another action or thing of more or less equal value; a substitute <the discount was given as a quid pro quo for the extra business>. See RECIPROCITY (2). Cf. CONSIDERATION.

quid pro quo harassment. See *quid pro quo sexual harassment* under SEXUAL HARASSMENT.

quid pro quo sexual harassment. See SEXUAL HARASSMENT.

quid valet nunc (kwid **vay**-let nəngk). [Latin] *Hist.* What it is now worth.

quiet, *vb.* (14c) **1.** To pacify or silence (a person, etc.). **2.** To make (a right, position, title, etc.) secure or unassailable by removing disturbing causes or disputes.

quieta non movere (kwɪ-**ee**-tə non moh-**veer**-ee). [Latin] Not to unsettle things that are established. See STARE DECISIS.

quietare (kwɪ-ə-**tair**-ee), *vb.* [Law Latin] *Hist.* To acquit, discharge, or hold harmless. • This term was used in conveyances.

quiet diplomacy. See *secret diplomacy* under DIPLOMACY (1).

quiete clamantia (kwɪ-**ee**-tee klə-**man**-shee-ə), *n.* [Law Latin] (17c) *Hist.* Quitclaim.

quiete clamare (kwɪ-**ee**-tee klə-**mair**-ee), *vb.* [Law Latin] *Hist.* To quitclaim or renounce all pretensions of right and title.

quiet enjoyment. See ENJOYMENT.

quiet-title action. See *action to quiet title* under ACTION (4).

quietus (kwɪ-**ee**-təs), *adj.* [Law Latin] (15c) **1.** Quit; acquitted; discharged, esp. from a debt or obligation, or from serving as an executor. • In England, this term was formerly used by the Clerk of the Pipe, in a discharge given to an accountant, usu. concluding with *abinde recessit quietus* ("hath gone quit thereof"), called *quietus est.* **2.** *Hist.* The removal of a judge from the bench.

quietus redditus (kwɪ-**ee**-təs **red**-ə-təs). [Law Latin] See QUIT RENT.

qui improvide (**kwɪ** im-**prov**-ə-dee). [Latin "who unforeseeably"] (18c) *Hist.* A supersedeas granted when a writ is erroneously sued out or wrongfully awarded.

qui justus esse debet (kwɪ **jəs**-təs **es**-ee **dee**-bet *or* **deb**-et). [Latin] *Hist.* Who is bound to be just.

Quinquaginta Decisiones. See FIFTY DECISIONS.

quinquepartite (kwin[g]-kwə-**pahr**-tɪt). [Latin "in five parts"] (17c) *Hist.* Consisting of five parts; divided into five parts.

quinquinnial prescription. See PRESCRIPTION.

quintal (**kwin**-təl). (15c) A weight of 100 pounds or 100 kilograms. — Also termed *kintal.*

quintessential public forum. See *traditional public forum* under PUBLIC FORUM.

quinto exactus (**kwin**-toh eg-**zak**-təs). [Latin "exacted the fifth time"] (16c) *Hist.* A sheriff's return made after a defendant had been called to five county courts but failed to appear. • The county coroners then ordered that the defendant be deprived of the benefits of the law.

> "And, if a *non est inventus* is returned upon all of them, a writ of *exigent* or *exigi facias* may be sued out, which requires the sheriff to cause the defendant to be proclaimed, required, or exacted, in five county courts successively, to render himself; and, if he does, then to take him, as in a *capias*: but if he does not appear, and is returned *quinto exactus*, he shall then be outlawed by the coroners of the county." 3 William Blackstone, *Commentaries on the Laws of England* 283 (1768).

Quiritarian (kwi-rə-**tair**-ee-ən), *adj.* (1838) *Roman law.* (In the context of ownership, with the full right available to citizens) legal as opposed to equitable; LEGAL (3). — Also termed *Quiritary.* Cf. BONITARIAN (1).

quis custodiet custodes ipsos. [Latin] Who is to guard the guardians themselves?

qui sibi vigilavit (kwɪ sib-ɪ vij-i-**lay**-vit). [Latin] *Hist.* Who has looked after his own interest.

quisling (**kwiz**-ling), *n.* [fr. Vidkun Quisling, 1887–1945, a Norwegian Nazi who betrayed Norway in 1940] (1940) A traitor; esp., someone who helps an invader take over his or her own country.

quit, *adj.* (13c) (Of a debt, obligation, or person) acquitted; free; discharged.

quit, *vb.* (15c) **1.** To cease (an act, etc.); to stop <he didn't quit stalking the victim until the police intervened>. **2.** To leave or surrender possession of (property) <the tenant received a notice to quit but had no intention of quitting the premises>.

qui tam action (**kee**-tam *or* **kwɪ** tam). [Latin *qui tam pro domino rege quam pro se ipso in hac parte sequitur* "who as well for the king as for himself sues in this matter"] (18c) An action brought under a statute that allows a private person to sue for a penalty, part of which the government or some specified public institution will receive. — Often shortened to *qui tam* (Q.T.). — Also termed *popular action.* See FALSE CLAIMS ACT.

quitclaim, *n.* (14c) **1.** A formal release of one's claim or right. **2.** See *quitclaim deed* under DEED.

quitclaim, *vb.* (14c) **1.** To relinquish or release (a claim or right). **2.** To convey all of one's interest in (property), to whatever extent one has an interest; to execute a quitclaim deed.

quitclaim deed. See DEED.

quit rent. (15c) *Hist.* A payment to a feudal lord by a freeholder or copyholder, so called because upon payment the tenant goes "quit and free" (discharged) of all other services. — Also spelled *quitrent.* — Also termed *quietus redditus.*

quittance. (13c) **1.** A release or discharge from a debt or obligation. **2.** The document serving as evidence of such a release. See ACQUITTANCE.

qui utuntur communi jure gentium (kwɪ yoo-**tən**-tər kə-**myoo**-nɪ **joor**-ee **jen**-shee-əm). [Law Latin] *Hist.* Who use the common law of nations; who conform to international law.

quoad (**kwoh**-ad). [Latin] As regards; with regard to <with a pledge, the debtor continues to possess *quoad* the world at large>.

quoad civilia (**kwoh**-ad sə-**vil**-ee-ə). [Latin] *Hist.* With regard to civil rights and benefits.

quoad creditorem (**kwoh**-ad kred-i-**tor**-əm). [Latin] *Hist.* With regard to the creditor.

quoad debitorem (**kwoh**-ad deb-i-**tor**-əm). [Latin] *Hist.* With regard to the debtor.

quoad defunctum (**kwoh**-ad di-**fəngkt**-əm). [Latin] So long as deceased.

quoad excessum (**kwoh**-ad ek-**ses**-əm). [Latin] (17c) *Hist.* With regard to the excess.

> "Where a husband makes a postnuptial provision in favour of his wife commensurate with his circumstances and natural duty, it is not subject to revocation by him as a donation. But if the provision be immoderate, it may be revoked *quoad excessum*, in so far as it is excessive." John Trayner, *Trayner's Latin Maxims* 525–26 (4th ed. 1894).

quoad fiscum (**kwoh**-ad **fis**-kəm). [Latin] *Hist.* With regard to the fisc; as regards the Crown's rights.

quoad hoc (**kwoh**-ad **hok**). [Latin] (17c) As to this; with respect to this; so far as this is concerned. • A prohibition *quoad hoc* is a prohibition of certain things among others, such as matters brought in an ecclesiastical court that should have been brought in a temporal court.

quoad jura (**kwoh**-ad **joor**-ə). [Latin] So far as the laws are concerned.

quoad maritum (**kwoh**-ad mə-**rɪ**-təm). [Latin] *Hist.* With regard to the husband.

quoad mobilia (**kwoh**-ad moh-**bil**-ee-ə). [Latin] *Hist.* With regard to movable property.

quoad non executa (**kwoh**-ad non ek-sə-**kyoo**-tə). [Law Latin] *Scots law.* With regard to the acts not done. • A second executor may be appointed *quoad non executa* upon the death of the first.

quoad potest (**kwoh**-ad **poh**-test). [Latin] *Hist.* Insofar as one is able.

quoad reliquum (**kwoh**-ad **rel**-ə-kwəm). [Latin] *Hist.* With regard to the remainder.

> "When a debtor, in an action brought against him by his creditor, pleads compensation to a certain extent of the debt sued for, *quoad* the sum due to him . . . the creditor's right of action falls; but *quoad reliquum*, after making deduction of the sum pled in compensation, the creditor's right of action remains." John Trayner, *Trayner's Latin Maxims* 526 (4th ed. 1894).

quoad sacra (**kwoh**-ad **say**-krə). [Latin] As to sacred things; for religious purposes. • This term often referred to property that was located so far from the parish to which it belonged that it was annexed *quoad sacra* to another parish, allowing the inhabitants to attend the closer parish's services. But the land continued to belong to the original parish for all civil purposes.

quoad ultra (**kwoh**-ad **əl**-trə). [Law Latin] *Hist.* With regard to the rest. • This reference was commonly used in pleading when a defendant admitted part of the plaintiff's claim and *quoad ultra* denied it.

quoad valet seipsum (**kwoh**-ad **vay**-let see-**ip**-səm). [Latin] *Hist.* With regard to its real value.

quoad valorem (**kwoh**-ad və-**lor**-əm). [Latin] *Hist.* With regard to the value.

quo animo (**kwoh an**-ə-moh), *adv.* [Latin] With what intention or motive. See ANIMUS.

quocumque modo velit, quocumque modo possit (kwoh-**kəm**-kwee **moh**-doh **vel**-it, kwoh-**kəm**-kwee **moh**-doh **pahs**-it). [Latin] In any way he wishes; in any way he can.

quodammodo jurisdictionis voluntariae (kwoh-**dam**-ə-doh joor-is-dik-shee-**oh**-nis vol-ən-**tair**-ee-ee). [Law Latin] *Hist.* Belonging in some measure to voluntary jurisdiction.

quod billa cassetur (kwod **bil**-ə kə-**see**-tər), *n.* [Latin "that the bill be quashed"] The common-law form of a judgment sustaining a plea in abatement that proceeds from a bill instead of an original writ. See CASSETUR BILLA.

quod clerici non eligantur in officio ballivi, etc. (kwod **kler**-ə-sɪ non el-ə-**gan**-tər in ə-**fish**-ee-oh bal-**lɪ**-vɪ), *n.* [Law Latin "that clerks are not chosen in the office of a bailiff, etc."] *Hist.* A writ exempting a clerk, who was to be appointed as a bailiff, beadle, reeve, or other officer, from serving in the office.

quod computet (kwod **kom**-pyə-tet). [Law Latin "that he account"] (17c) The first judgment in an action of account, requiring the defendant to give an accounting before auditors. — Also termed *judgment quod computet.*

> "In this action, if the plaintiff succeeds, there are two judgments: the first is, that the defendant do account (*quod computet*) before auditors appointed by the court; and, when such account is finished, then the second judgment is, that he do pay the plaintiff so much as he is found in arrear." 3 William Blackstone, *Commentaries on the Laws of England* 163 (1768).

quod cum (**kwod** kəm). [Law Latin] For that; whereas. • In common-law pleading, this phrase introduced explanations for the claims alleged, as in *assumpsit* actions.

quod ei deforceat (kwod **ee**-ɪ di-**for**-see-ət), *n.* [Law Latin "that he deforces him"] (17c) *Hist.* A writ allowed by St. Westm. 2, 13 Edw., ch. 4 for the owners of a particular estate (such as a life estate or fee tail) who had lost land unwittingly by default in a possessory action. • Up to that time, only owners in fee simple could recover property after such a default.

quod erat demonstrandum (kwod **er**-ət dem-ən-**stran**-dəm). See Q.E.D.

quod erat faciendum (kwod **er**-ət fay-shee-**en**-dəm). See Q.E.F.

quod fuit concessum (kwod **f[y]oo**-it kən-**ses**-əm). [Law Latin] Which was granted. • This phrase was used in old reports to indicate that an argument or point made by counsel was approved or allowed by the court.

quod jussu (kwod **jəs**-[y]oo). [Latin "which was done by order"] *Roman law.* See *actio quod jussu* under ACTIO.

quodlibet (**kwahd**-li-bet), *n.* (14c) **1.** A subtle or debatable point that is the subject of learned or scholastic disputation. **2.** By extension, a scholastic debate over trivialities. — **quodlibetic,** *adj.*

quod non fuit negatum (kwod non **f[y]oo**-it ni-**gay**-təm). [Law Latin] *Hist.* Which was not denied. • This phrase usu. signifies that an argument or proposal is not denied or controverted by the court.

quod nota (kwod **noh**-tə). [Latin] *Hist.* Which note; which mark. • This is a reporter's note directing attention to a point or rule.

quod partes replacitent (kwod **pahr**-teez ri-**plas**-i-tənt), *n.* [Law Latin "that the parties do replead"] (18c) *Hist.* The judgment ordering repleader when an issue is formed on so immaterial a point that the court does not know for whom to give a judgment. • The parties must then reconstruct their pleadings.

quod partitio fiat (kwod pahr-**tish**-ee-oh **fɪ**-ət). [Latin "that partition be made"] (18c) *Hist.* In a partition suit, a judgment granting the partition.

quod permittat (kwod pər-**mit**-it), *n.* [Latin "that he permit"] (16c) *Hist.* A writ to prevent an interference in the exercise of a right, such as a writ for the heir of someone disseised of a common of pasture against the heir of the disseisor.

> "The rights for which *quod permittat* evidently seemed appropriate were those which, like easements, avail specifically against the proprietary right of another." S.F.C. Milsom, *Studies in the History of the Common Law* 33 (1985).

quod permittat prosternere (kwod pər-**mit**-it proh-**stər**-nə-ree), *n.* [Law Latin "that he permit to abate"] (1803) *Hist.* A writ to abate a nuisance, similar in nature to a petition of right. • This writ was abolished by the Real Property Limitation Act of 1833.

> "This is a writ commanding the defendant to permit the plaintiff to abate, *quod permittat prosternere*, the nuisance complained of; and, unless he so permits, to summon him to appear in court, and shew cause why he will not. And this writ lies as well *for* the alienee of the party first injured, as *against* the alienee of the party first injuring; as hath been determined by all the judges. And the plaintiff shall have judgment herein to abate the nuisance, and to recover

damages against the defendant." 3 William Blackstone, *Commentaries on the Laws of England* 222 (1768).

quod recuperet (kwod ri-**k**[y]**oo**-pər-it), *n.* [Law Latin "that he do recover"] (17c) *Hist.* The ordinary judgment for a plaintiff in an action at law. • The judgment might be either final or interlocutory depending on whether damages had been ascertained at the time the judgment was rendered. — Also termed *judgment quod recuperet.*

quod si contingat (kwod **sɪ** kon-**ting**-at). [Law Latin] *Hist.* That if it happen. • These words were used to create a condition in a deed.

quod vide (kwod **vɪ**-dee *or* **vee**-day). See Q.V.

quod voluit non dixit (kwod **vol**-yoo-it non **dik**-sit). [Latin] *Hist.* That he did not say what he intended. • This phrase was sometimes used in an argument concerning the intention of a lawmaker or testator.

quo jure (kwoh **joor**-ee). [Law Latin "by what right"] *Hist.* A writ for someone holding land to which another claimed a common, to compel the latter to prove title. See COMMON (1).

quominus (**kwoh**-mə-nəs *or* kwoh-**mɪ**-nəs). [Latin *quo minus* "by which the less"] (16c) *Hist.* A 14th-century Exchequer writ alleging that the plaintiff had lent the defendant a sum of money and that the plaintiff was unable to repay a debt of similar amount to the Crown because of the debt to the defendant. • In effect, the plaintiff pleaded the fiction that he was a debtor of the king who could not repay that debt because of the defendant's failure to repay him. — Also termed *writ of quominus.*

> "[W]hat in the beginning had been permitted as a means of collecting the royal revenue came in the end to be nothing more or less than permitting any citizen to sue in the court of the king in order to collect a private debt. The old pretense that the matter concerned the royal revenue had to be kept up, and accordingly A had to allege that he was 'less able' to pay the king when his debtors would not pay him. But everyone, even the court itself, recognized this as a mere fiction, and that since the suit was in fact between A and B, B was not permitted to bring in other matters, such for example as a defense on the ground that A did not actually owe any taxes to the crown. This fiction came to be known as the 'quo minus' fiction, because these were the Latin words used in the litigation, which meant that A was 'less able' to pay the king." Charles Herman Kinnane, *A First Book on Anglo-American Law* 265–66 (2d ed. 1952).

quomodo constat (**kwoh**-mə-doh **kon**-stat). [Latin] *Hist.* As it appears (from the record, the pleadings, etc.).

quomodo desiit possidere (**kwoh**-mə-doh **des**-ee-it pos-ə-**dee**-ree). [Law Latin] *Scots law.* In what way he ceased to possess. • In an action to reclaim possession, the plaintiff was required to prove previous possession and *quomodo desiit possidere* (as by theft, etc.).

quondam (**kwon**-dəm), *adj.* Having been formerly; former <the quondam ruler>.

quondam, *n.* (16c) *Archaic.* Someone who once held an office or a position, esp. one who was involuntarily removed or deposed.

quorum, *n.* (17c) *Parliamentary law.* The smallest number of people who must be present at a meeting so that official decisions can be made; specif., the minimum number of members (a majority of all the members, unless otherwise specified in the governing documents) who must be present for a deliberative assembly to legally transact business. Pl. **quorums.**

▸ **constituency-based quorum.** See *interest-based quorum.*

▸ **disappearing quorum.** (1916) A quorum whose presence may be more presumptive than actual. See *presumption of a quorum* under PRESUMPTION.

▸ **interest-based quorum.** A quorum determined according to the presence or representation of various constituencies. — Also termed *constituency-based quorum.*

▸ **notice-based quorum.** A quorum determined according to how far in advance of the meeting its call was circulated. • Under a notice-based quorum, the later the call gets sent out, the larger the quorum grows.

▸ **proportional quorum.** A quorum calculated with reference to some defined or assumed set, usu. either the number of seats (including vacancies) or the number of sitting members (excluding vacancies).

▸ **registration-based quorum.** A quorum determined according to how many members have checked in at the meeting, either at some fixed time or throughout the time since the meeting began.

quorum bonorum (**kwor**-əm bə-**nor**-əm). [Latin] (18c) *Roman law.* A praetorian interdict by which a person was allowed to take possession of an estate. See BONORUM POSSESSIO CONTRA TABULAS.

quorum call. See CALL (1).

quorumless, *adj.* (1982) Lacking a quorum. — **quorumlessness,** *n.*

quorum nobis. See CORAM NOBIS.

quorum usus consistit in abusu (**kwor**-əm **yoo**-səs [*or* **yoo**-zəs] kən-**sis**-tit in ə-**byoo**-s[y]oo). [Law Latin] *Scots law.* The use of which consists in consuming them. • The phrase appeared in reference to fungibles.

quot. *Hist. Scots law.* Formerly, the 20th part of an estate's movables, calculated before the decedent's debts are paid, owed to the bishop of the diocese.

quota. (17c) **1.** A proportional share assigned to a person or group; an allotment <the university's admission standards included a quota for in-state residents>. **2.** An official limit on the number or amount of something that is allowed or required over a given period; a minimum or maximum number <Faldo met his sales quota for the month>.

▸ **export quota.** (1916) A restriction on the products that can be sold to foreign countries. • In the United States, export quotas can be established by the federal government for various purposes, including national defense, price support, and economic stability.

▸ **import quota.** (1931) A restriction on the volume of a certain product that can be brought into the country from a foreign country. • In the United States, the President may establish a quota on an item that poses a threat of serious injury to a domestic industry.

3. A particular number of votes that someone needs to be elected in a particular election.

quot articuli tot libelli (kwot ahr-**tik**-yə-lɪ taht li-**bel**-ɪ). [Law Latin] *Hist.* As many points of dispute as libels.

quotation. (17c) **1.** A statement or passage that is exactly reproduced, attributed, and cited. **2.** The amount stated as a stock's or commodity's current price.

▸ **market quotation.** (1847) The most current price at which a security or commodity trades.

3. A contractor's estimate for a given job. — Sometimes shortened to *quote.*

quot generationes tot gradus (kwot jen-ə-ray-shee-**oh**-neez taht **gray**-dəs). [Law Latin] *Hist.* As many generations as degrees (of relationship). • The phrase appeared in reference to degrees of relationship.

quotient verdict. See VERDICT (1).

quousque (kwoh-**əs**-kwee). [Latin] *Hist.* As long as; how long; until; how far. • This term was used in conveyances as a limitation.

quo vadis. [Latin] Where are you going?

quovis modo (**kwoh**-vis **moh**-doh). [Latin] In whatever manner.

quovis tempore (**kwoh**-vis **tem**-pə-ree). [Latin] *Hist.* At whatever time.

quo warranto (kwoh wə-**ran**-toh *also* kwoh **wahr**-ən-toh). [Law Latin "by what authority"] (15c) **1.** A common-law writ used to inquire into the authority by which a public office is held or a franchise is claimed. — Also termed *writ of quo warranto.* **2.** An action by which the state seeks to revoke a corporation's charter. • The Federal Rules of Civil Procedure are applicable to proceedings for quo warranto "to the extent that the practice in such proceedings is not set forth in statutes of the United States and has therefore conformed to the practice in civil actions." Fed. R. Civ. P. 81(a)(2).

"There are two modes of proceeding judicially to ascertain and enforce the forfeiture of a charter for default or abuse of power. The one is by scire facias; and that process is proper where there is a legal existing body, capable of acting, but who have abused their power. The other mode is by information in the nature of a *quo warranto*; which is in form a criminal, and in its nature a civil remedy; and that proceeding applies where there is a body corporate *de facto* only, but who take upon themselves to act, though, from some defect in their constitution, they cannot legally exercise their powers. Both these modes of proceeding are at the instance of and on behalf of the government. The state must be a party to the prosecution, for the judgment is that the parties be ousted, and the franchises seised into the hands of the government." 2 James Kent, *Commentaries on American Law* *313 (George Comstock ed., 11th ed. 1866).

"Quo warranto means 'by what warrant?' — or authority? — and was a proceeding to inquire whether authority existed to justify or authorize certain acts of a public character or interest. Originally the proceeding of quo warranto was a criminal one instituted by the crown, the purpose of which was to find out, in the course of a formal inquiry, whether or not persons or corporations were exercising a privilege or franchise illegally, or if persons who had no right to do so were occupying some public office. If it were found that the person or corporation was in fact illegally interfering with the prerogative power of the crown, or was in fact doing some other illegal act, it was ousted from the illegal practice or office. Accordingly, it can be seen at once that the proceeding on quo warranto was not one to be used by private parties in the conduct of ordinary litigation." Charles Herman Kinnane, *A First Book on Anglo-American Law* 662 (2d ed. 1952).

q.v. *abbr.* [Latin *quod vide*] (17c) Which see — used in non-*Bluebook* citations for cross-referencing. Pl. **qq.v.**

R

R. *abbr.* **1.** REX. **2.** REGINA. **3.** RANGE. **4.** *Trademarks.* When contained in a circle (and often superscripted), the symbol indicating that a trademark or servicemark is registered in the U.S. Patent and Trademark Office. See *registered trademark* under TRADEMARK; SERVICEMARK.

rabbicular trust. See TRUST.

rabbinical divorce. See DIVORCE.

rabbi trust. See TRUST.

RAC. *abbr.* See *refund-anticipation check* under CHECK.

race act. See RACE STATUTE.

race for the bottom. See RACE TO THE BOTTOM.

race-notice statute. (1968) A recording law providing that the person who records first, without notice of prior unrecorded claims, has priority. • About half the states have race-notice statutes. — Also termed *race-notice act*; *notice-race statute.* Cf. RACE STATUTE; NOTICE STATUTE.

race of diligence. (18c) *Bankruptcy.* A first-come, first-served disposition of assets.

race relations. (1878) The way in which people from different ethnicities, cultures, religions, etc. who are living in the same place interact with one another and feel about those who are different from themselves.

race statute. (1944) A recording act providing that the person who records first, regardless of notice, has priority. • Only Louisiana and North Carolina have race statutes. — Also termed *pure race statute*; *race act.* Cf. NOTICE STATUTE; RACE-NOTICE STATUTE.

race to the bottom. (1974) **1.** In socioeconomics, the competition between geopolitical units to make themselves more attractive to investors and businesses, coupled with adverse economic consequences such as deregulation that leads to irresponsibility. **2.** By extension, competition between businesses that results in risky business behaviors and destabilization of an industry. • An example is the use of subprime mortgages to attract more borrowers who paid higher origination fees but ultimately could not manage to repay the loans. — Also termed *race for the bottom.*

race to the courthouse. (1961) **1.** *Bankruptcy.* The competition among creditors to make claims on assets, usu. motivated by the advantages to be gained by those who act first in preference to other creditors. • Chapter 11 of the Bankruptcy Code, as well as various other provisions, is intended to prevent a race to the courthouse and instead to promote equality among creditors. **2.** *Civil procedure.* The competition between disputing parties, both of whom know that litigation is inevitable, to prepare and file a lawsuit in a favorable or convenient forum before the other side files in one that is less favorable or less convenient. • A race to the courthouse may result after one party informally accuses another of breach of contract or intellectual-property infringement. When informal negotiations break down, both want to resolve the matter quickly, usu. to avoid further business disruption. While the accuser races to sue for breach of contract or infringement, the accused seeks a declaratory judgment that no breach or infringement has occurred. See ANTICIPATORY FILING.

rachat (rah-**shah**), *n.* [French] **1.** Repurchase; redemption. **2.** Ransom.

racheter (rah-shə-**tay**), *vb.* [French] **1.** To repurchase or buy back. **2.** To ransom.

racial discrimination. See DISCRIMINATION (3).

racial gerrymandering. See GERRYMANDERING.

racial profiling. (1989) The law-enforcement practice of using race, national origin, or ethnicity as a salient basis for suspicion of criminal activity. • Originally, the term referred to the practice of stopping a disproportionate number of male African-American drivers on the assumption that they had a heightened likelihood of being involved in criminal activity. After the terrorist attacks of September 11, 2001, the term was frequently used in reference to searching and interrogating Middle Eastern men at airports. — Also termed *ethnic profiling*; *profiling.* Cf. LINGUISTIC PROFILING; DEPOLICING.

racism. (1903) **1.** The belief that some races are inherently superior to other races. **2.** Unfair treatment of people, often including violence against them, because they belong to a different race from one's own. — **racist,** *adj.* & *n.*

rack, *n.* (15c) *Hist.* An instrument of torture on which a person was slowly stretched, formerly used to interrogate someone charged with a crime.

racket, *n.* (1819) **1.** An organized criminal activity; esp., the extortion of money by threat or violence. **2.** A dishonest or fraudulent scheme, business, or activity.

racketeer, *n.* (1924) Someone who engages in racketeering; specif., someone who earns money from organized crime. — **racketeer,** *vb.*

Racketeer Influenced and Corrupt Organizations Act. A 1970 federal statute designed to attack organized criminal activity and preserve marketplace integrity by investigating, controlling, and prosecuting persons who participate or conspire to participate in racketeering. 18 USCA §§ 1961–1968. • The federal RICO statute applies only to activity involving interstate or foreign commerce. Many states have adopted similar statutes, sometimes called "little RICO" acts. The federal and most state RICO acts provide for enforcement not only by criminal prosecution but also by civil lawsuit, in which the plaintiff can sue for treble damages. — Abbr. RICO.

> "Before criminal or civil liability can attach under RICO, it must be shown that the two or more acts of racketeering alleged in the criminal indictment or civil complaint constitute a pattern of racketeering activity on the part of the culpable person. The statutory definition of pattern 'requires at least two' predicate acts occurring within ten years of each other, with one of them occurring after October 15, 1970. More broadly put, the pattern of racketeering activity is a scheme of unlawful conduct with a nexus to both the culpable person and the enterprise."

David R. McCormack, *Racketeering Influenced Corrupt Organizations* § 1.04, at 1-20 (1998).

racketeering, *n.* (1897) **1.** A system of organized crime traditionally involving the extortion of money from businesses by intimidation, violence, or other illegal methods. **2.** A pattern of illegal activity (such as bribery, extortion, fraud, and murder) carried out as part of an enterprise (such as a crime syndicate) that is owned or controlled by those engaged in the illegal activity. • The modern sense (sense 2) derives from the federal RICO statute, which greatly broadened the term's original sense to include such activities as mail fraud, securities fraud, and the collection of illegal gambling debts. *See* 18 USCA §§ 1951–1960.

rack rent, *n.* (17c) Rent equal to or nearly equal to the full annual value of the property; excessively or unreasonably high rent. — **rack-rent,** *vb.* — **rack-renter,** *n.*

radical lawyering. See CAUSE LAWYERING.

radical title. See *allodial title* under TITLE (2).

raffle, *n.* (18c) A form of lottery in which each participant buys one or more chances to win a prize.

rafter bid. See *fictitious bid* under BID (1).

RAI. *abbr.* RISK-ASSESSMENT INSTRUMENT.

raid, *n.* (1866) **1.** A sudden attack or invasion by law-enforcement officers, usu. to make an arrest or to search for evidence of a crime. **2.** An attempt by a business or union to lure employees or members from a competitor. **3.** An attempt by a group of speculators to cause a sudden fall in stock prices by concerted selling.

raider. See CORPORATE RAIDER.

railroad, *vb.* (1838) **1.** To transport by train. **2.** To send (a measure) hastily through a legislature so that there is little time for consideration and debate. **3.** To convict (a person) hastily, esp. by the use of false charges or insufficient evidence.

railroad-aid bond. See BOND (3).

railroad company. See *railroad corporation* under CORPORATION.

railroad corporation. See CORPORATION.

Railroad Retirement Board. A three-member federal board that administers the program providing retirement, unemployment, and sickness benefits to retired railroad employees and their families. • The Board was established by the Railroad Retirement Act of 1934. — Abbr. RRB.

Railway Labor Act. A 1926 federal law giving transportation employees the right to organize without management interference and establishing guidelines for the resolution of labor disputes in the transportation industry. • In 1934, the law was amended to include the airline industry and to establish the National Mediation Board. 45 USCA §§ 151–188. — Abbr. RLA. See NATIONAL MEDIATION BOARD.

rainmaker, *n.* (1971) A lawyer who generates a large amount of business for a law firm, usu. through wide contacts within the business community <the law firm fell on hard times when the rainmaker left and took his clients with him>. — **rainmaking,** *n.*

raise, *n.* See PAY RAISE.

raise, *vb.* (12c) **1.** To increase in amount or value <the industry raised prices>. **2.** To gather or collect <the charity raised funds>. **3.** To bring up for discussion or consideration; to introduce or put forward <the party raised the issue in its pleading>. **4.** To create or establish <the person's silence raised an inference of consent>. **5.** To increase the stated amount of (a negotiable instrument) by fraudulent alteration <the indorser raised the check>.

raise a question of privilege. (1842) To offer a question of privilege to be considered by the meeting or ruled on by the chair. See *question of privilege* under QUESTION (3).

raised check. See CHECK.

raised-eyebrow test. See RASCALITY TEST.

raised hand. See UPLIFTED HAND.

raising an instrument. The act of fraudulently altering a negotiable instrument, esp. a check, to increase the amount stated as payable. See *raised check* under CHECK.

***Rakas* rule.** (1980) *Criminal procedure.* The doctrine that a defendant charged with a possessory crime may invoke the exclusionary rule if the defendant's constitutional rights under the Fourth Amendment have been infringed. *Rakas v. Illinois,* 429 U.S. 128 (1978).

rake-off, *n.* (1887) A percentage or share of profits taken by or given to someone involved in the transaction; esp., an illegal bribe, payoff, or skimming of profits. — **rake off,** *vb.*

RAL. *abbr.* See *refund-anticipation loan* under LOAN.

rally, *n.* (1826) A sharp rise in price or trading (as of stocks) after a declining market.

RAM. See *reverse annuity mortgage* under MORTGAGE.

Rambo lawyer. See LAWYER.

ram raid, *n.* (1987) *Slang.* The smashing of a shop window or other commercial premises with a vehicle in order to break in and steal cash or goods. • The term is most common in the United Kingdom, Ireland, and Australia. — Also termed *crash-and-dash.* Cf. SMASH-AND-GRAB.

ram-raiding. (1990) The crime of driving a car through a storefront window in order to steal goods from the store. — **ram-raid,** *n.* & *vb.* — **ram-raider,** *n.*

Ramseyer rule. (1940) A rule of the U.S. House of Representatives requiring any committee reporting a bill that amends legislation in force to show in its report what wording the bill would strike from or insert into the current law. • The rule is named for Representative C. William Ramseyer (1875–1943) of Iowa, who proposed it. The analogous rule in the U.S. Senate is the Cordon rule. See CORDON RULE.

R and D. *abbr.* (1952) RESEARCH AND DEVELOPMENT.

R&R. *abbr.* (1952) **1.** Rest and relaxation. **2.** REPORT AND RECOMMENDATION.

range, *n.* (18c) *Land law.* In U.S. government surveys, a strip of public land running due north to south, consisting of a row of townships, at six-mile intervals. — Abbr. R.

ranger. (14c) **1.** *Hist. English law.* In England, an officer or keeper of a royal forest, appointed to patrol the forest, drive out stray animals, and prevent trespassing. **2.** An officer or warden who patrols and supervises the care and preservation of a public park or forest. **3.** One of a group of soldiers who patrol a given region; esp., in the U.S. military, a soldier specially trained for surprise raids and close combat. **4.** A member of a special state police force.

rank, *n.* (16c) **1.** A social or official position or standing, as in the armed forces <the rank of captain>. **2.** *Parliamentary law.* A motion's relative precedence. See PRECEDENCE (3).

▸ **diplomatic rank.** (18c) The professional and social position held by a person who is recognized as a diplomat with all the attached privileges and immunities.

▸ **military rank.** (17c) A member's rank within a branch of the armed forces.

rank and file. (18c) **1.** The enlisted soldiers of an armed force, as distinguished from the officers. **2.** The general membership of a union.

ranked-choice voting. See *preferential voting* under VOTING. — Abbr. RCV.

rank-order voting. See *preferential voting* under VOTING.

ransom, *n.* (13c) **1.** Money or other consideration demanded or paid for the release of a captured person or property. See KIDNAPPING. **2.** The release of a captured person or property in exchange for payment of a demanded price.

ransom, *vb.* (14c) **1.** To obtain the release of (a captive) by paying a demanded price. **2.** To release (a captive) upon receiving such a payment. **3.** To hold and demand payment for the release of (a captive).

ransom bill. (18c) *Int'l law.* A contract by which a vessel or other property captured at sea during wartime is ransomed in exchange for release and safe conduct to a friendly destination. — Also termed *ransom bond.*

ransom factor. (2003) *Slang.* The costliness of litigation considered as a disincentive to vindicate one's rights in court. • The term is used mostly in England.

RAP. *abbr.* RULE AGAINST PERPETUITIES.

rap, *n.* (1903) *Slang.* **1.** Legal responsibility for a criminal act <he took the rap for his accomplices>. **2.** A criminal charge <a murder rap>. **3.** A criminal conviction; esp., a prison sentence <a 20-year rap for counterfeiting>.

rape, *n.* (15c) **1.** At common law, unlawful sexual intercourse committed by a man with a woman not his wife through force and against her will. • The common-law crime of rape required at least a slight penetration of the penis into the vagina. Also at common law, a husband could not be convicted of raping his wife. — Formerly termed *rapture; ravishment.* **2.** Unlawful sexual activity (esp. intercourse) with a person (usu. a female) without consent and usu. by force or threat of injury. • Most modern state statutes have broadened the definition along these lines. Rape includes unlawful sexual intercourse without consent after the perpetrator has substantially impaired his victim by administering, without the victim's knowledge or consent, drugs or intoxicants for the purpose of preventing resistance. It also includes unlawful sexual intercourse with a person who is unconscious. Marital status is now usu. irrelevant, and sometimes so is the victim's gender. — Also termed (in some statutes) *unlawful sexual intercourse; sexual assault; criminal sexual conduct; sexual battery; sexual abuse;* (in Latin) *crimen raptus.* Cf. *sexual assault* under ASSAULT; *sexual battery* under BATTERY (1).

"[Another] offence, against the female part also of his majesty's subjects, but attended with greater aggravations than that of forcible marriage, is the crime of *rape, raptus mulierum,* or the carnal knowledge of a woman forcibly and against her will." 4 William Blackstone, *Commentaries on the Laws of England* 210 (1769).

"If force is to be declared an element of the crime [of rape] it becomes necessary to resort to the fiction of 'constructive force' to take care of those cases in which no force is needed beyond what is involved in the very act of intercourse itself. A better analysis is to recognize that the requirement of force is simply a means of demonstrating that the unlawful violation of the woman was without her consent and against her will. Therefore, evidence of serious force need not be shown in many cases. Hence the better view is that 'force' is not truly speaking an element of the crime itself, but if great force was not needed to accomplish the act the necessary *lack of consent* has been *disproved* in other than exceptional situations. The courts today frequently state the position that a woman's resistance need not be 'more than her age, strength, the surrounding facts, and all attending circumstances' make reasonable." Rollin M. Perkins & Ronald N. Boyce, *Criminal Law* 211–12 (3d ed. 1982).

▸ **acquaintance rape.** (1980) Rape committed by someone known to the victim, esp. by the victim's social companion. Cf. *date rape; relationship rape.*

▸ **command rape.** (2006) Coerced or forced sexual contact between a superior member and subordinate member of the armed forces.

▸ **corrective rape.** (2005) The use of rape against a person whose perceived sexual orientation or gender role is contrary to social norms in order to change the victim's sexuality or behavior. • This crime was first reported and the term coined in South Africa.

▸ **date rape.** (1975) Rape committed by a person who is escorting the victim on a social occasion. • The assaults in date-rape cases sometimes take place in contexts in which it might be reasonable to assume that consensual sexual activity might have occurred. Loosely, *date rape* also sometimes refers to what is more accurately called *acquaintance rape* or *relationship rape.*

"The new women's consciousness has focused attention also on 'date rape.' It forced recognition of an uncomfortable fact: most men who push unwanted sex on women are not psychopathic or brutal strangers: they are not strangers at all. Date-rape prosecutions were not common; but the problem was widely discussed on college campuses; and what was arguably an instance of date rape burst into national prominence in 1991, when a woman accused William Kennedy Smith, a nephew of the late John F. Kennedy, of rape. The couple met at a bar in Palm Beach, Florida, and went from there to the Kennedy estate, where they had sex — willingly, in Smith's account; violently, in hers. Millions saw the trial on television (the victim's face was reduced to an electronic blur). The six-person jury (four members were women) acquitted Smith, on December 11, 1991." Lawrence M. Friedman, *Crime and Punishment in American History* 433–34 (1993).

▸ **gang rape.** (1875) Rape committed by two or more people against the same victim in the same or sequential criminal episodes. • When large numbers of attackers are involved, it is also termed *mass rape.*

▸ **genocidal rape.** *Int'l law.* See *war rape.*

▸ **marital rape.** (1936) A husband's sexual intercourse with his wife by force or without her consent. • Marital rape was not a crime at common law, but under modern statutes the marital exemption no longer applies, and in most jurisdictions a husband can be prosecuted for raping his wife. — Also termed *spousal rape.*

▸ **mass rape. 1.** See *gang rape.* **2.** See *war rape.*

▸ **prior-relationship rape.** See *relationship rape.*

▸ **rape by means of fraud.** (1887) An instance of sexual intercourse that has been induced by fraud. • Authorities are divided on the question whether rape can occur when a woman is induced by fraudulent statements to have sexual intercourse. But the term *rape by means of fraud* is not uncommon in legal literature.

▸ **rape under age.** See *statutory rape.*

▸ **relationship rape.** (1999) Rape committed by someone with whom the victim has had a significant association, often (though not always) of a romantic nature. • This term encompasses all types of relationships, including family, friends, dates, cohabitants, and spouses, in which the victim has had more than brief or perfunctory interaction with the other person. Thus it does not extend to those with whom the victim has had only brief encounters or a nodding acquaintance. — Also termed *prior-relationship rape.* Cf. *date rape; acquaintance rape.*

▸ **spousal rape.** See *marital rape.*

▸ **statutory rape.** (1873) Unlawful sexual intercourse with a person under the age of consent (as defined by statute), regardless of whether it is against that person's will. • Generally, only an adult may be convicted of this crime. A person under the age of consent cannot be convicted. — Also termed *rape under age.* See *age of consent* under AGE.

> "Carnal knowledge of a child is frequently declared to be rape by statute and where this is true the offense is popularly known as 'statutory rape,' although not so designated in the statute." Rollin M. Perkins & Ronald N. Boyce, *Criminal Law* 198 (3d ed. 1982).

▸ **stranger rape.** (1973) Rape by someone unknown to the victim.

▸ **war rape.** (1949) *Int'l law.* The systematic use of rape as a physical and psychological weapon against civilians, esp. women and girls, by enemy soldiers during wartime. • War rape became a crime under Article 27 of the Fourth Geneva Convention in 1949. When many victims are involved or when many soldiers take turns raping the same victim over a period, it is also termed *mass rape.* In the context of ethnic cleansing, it is also termed *genocidal rape.*

3. *Archaic.* The act of seizing and carrying off a person (esp. a woman) by force; abduction. **4.** The act of plundering or despoiling a place. **5.** *Hist.* One of the six administrative districts into which Sussex, England was divided, being smaller than a shire and larger than a hundred.

rape, *vb.* (14c) **1.** To commit rape against; to force (someone) to have sex, esp. by using violence. **2.** *Archaic.* To seize and carry off by force; abduct. **3.** To plunder or despoil. — **rapist, raper,** *n.*

rape kit. (1975) *Criminal law.* An ensemble of instruments, vials, etc., to be used, typically in a specified order, for the systematic gathering of evidence relating to an alleged rape.

rape shield law. See SHIELD LAW (2).

rape shield statute. See SHIELD LAW (2).

rape under age. See *statutory rape* under RAPE (2).

rapina (rə-pɪ-nə). [Latin "robbery, pillage"] *Roman & civil law.* The forcible taking of another's movable property with the intent to appropriate it to one's own use.

> "Rapina is the taking away of a thing by violent means. It gives rise to the praetorian actio vi bonorum raptorum . . . ." Rudolph Sohm, *The Institutes: A Textbook of the History and System of Roman Private Law* 419 (James Crawford Ledlie trans., 3d ed. 1907).

rapine (**rap**-in). (15c) **1.** Forcible seizure and carrying off of another's property; pillage or plunder. **2.** *Archaic.* Rape.

rapport à succession (ra-**por** ah sook-ses-**syawn**), *n.* [French "return to succession"] *Civil law.* The restoration to an estate of property that an heir received in advance from the decedent, so that an even distribution may be made among all the heirs. Cf. HOTCHPOT (1).

rapporteur (ra-por-**tuur** *or* -**tər**), *n.* [French] (17c) An official who makes a report of committee proceedings for a larger body (esp. a legislature).

rapprochement (ra-prosh-**mahn**). [French] (18c) The establishment or restoration of cordial relations between two or more countries that were previously unfriendly. — Also spelled *rapprochment.*

rap sheet. (1960) *Slang.* A person's criminal record. — Also termed *criminal-history record.*

raptu haeredis (**rap**-t[y]oo hə-**ree**-dis), *n.* [Latin] (17c) *Hist.* A writ for taking away an heir held in socage. See SOCAGE.

rapture. (16c) *Archaic.* **1.** Forcible seizure and carrying off of another person (esp. a woman); abduction. **2.** RAPE (1).

raptu virginum (**rap**-t[y]oo **vər**-ji-nəm). See DE RAPTU VIRGINUM.

rapuit (**rap**-yoo-it). [Latin] *Hist.* Ravished. • The term was formerly used in indictments for rape. See RAVISHMENT.

RAR. *abbr.* REVENUE AGENT'S REPORT.

rascality test. (1994) A heightened standard that a business plaintiff (as opposed to a consumer plaintiff) must meet to show that an unfair or deceptive trade practice has occurred, the test being that a court should ask whether the defendant's conduct reached "a level of rascality that would raise an eyebrow of someone inured to the rough and tumble of the world of commerce." *Levings v. Forbes & Wallace, Inc.*, 396 N.E.2d 149, 153 (Mass. App. Ct. 1979). — Also termed *rascality standard; raised-eyebrow test.*

rasure (**ray**-zhər). (15c) **1.** The scraping or shaving of a document's surface to remove the writing from it; erasure. **2.** Obliteration. — **rase,** *vb.*

rat. *Slang.* **1.** STOOL PIGEON (1). **2.** SCAB.

ratable (**ray**-tə-bəl), *adj.* (16c) **1.** Proportionate <ratable distribution>. **2.** Capable of being estimated, appraised, or apportioned <because hundreds of angry fans ran onto the field at the same time, blame for the goalpost's destruction is not ratable>. **3.** Taxable <the government assessed the widow's ratable estate>. See PRO RATA. — **ratably,** *adv.*

ratchet theory. (1977) *Constitutional law.* The principle that Congress, in exercising its enforcement power under the 14th Amendment, can increase but not dilute the scope of 14th Amendment guarantees as previously defined by the Supreme Court. • The thought underlying the term is that the enabling clause works in only one direction, like a ratchet. The theory was stated by Justice Brennan in *Katzenbach v. Morgan*, 384 U.S. 641, 86 S.Ct. 1717 (1966), but was repudiated by the Supreme Court in *City of Boerne v. Flores*, 521 U.S. 507, 117 S.Ct.2157 (1997). — Also termed *one-way ratchet theory.*

rate, *n.* (15c) **1.** Proportional or relative value; the proportion by which quantity or value is adjusted <rate of inflation>. **2.** An amount paid or charged for a good or service <the rate for a business-class fare is $550>.

▸ **class rate.** (1897) A single rate applying to the transportation of several articles of the same general character.

▸ **confiscatory rate.** (1904) A utility rate set so low by the government that the utility company cannot realize a reasonable return on its investment.

▸ **freight rate.** (1865) A rate charged by a carrier for the transportation of cargo, usu. based on the weight, volume, or quantity of goods but sometimes also on the goods' value or the mileage.

▸ **joint rate.** (1889) A single rate charged by two or more carriers to cover a shipment of goods over a single route.

▸ **union rate.** (1895) The wage scale set by a union as a minimum wage to be paid and usu. expressed as an hourly rate or piecework rate.

3. INTEREST RATE <the rate on the loan increases by 2% after five years>. **4.** PREMIUM RATE. **5.** *English law.* A sum assessed or payable to the local government in the place where a ratepayer dwells or has property. See RATEPAYER. — **rate,** *vb.*

rate base. (1916) The investment amount or property value on which a company, esp. a public utility, is allowed to earn a particular rate of return.

rate-base value. See *net book cost* under COST (1).

rate of error. (1886) The probable size of the sampling error in an estimate.

rate of interest. See INTEREST RATE.

rate of return. (1830) **1.** The annual income from an investment, expressed as a percentage of the investment. — Abbr. ROR. See RETURN (5). **2.** A company's profit for a year, expressed as a percentage of the money that the company has spent during the year.

▸ **fair rate of return.** (1907) The amount of profit that a public utility is permitted to earn, as determined by a public utility commission.

▸ **internal rate of return.** (1935) *Accounting.* A discounted-cash-flow method of evaluating a long-term project, used to determine the actual return on an investment. — Abbr. IRR.

ratepayer. (18c) *English law.* Someone who pays local taxes; a person liable to pay rates. See RATE (5).

ratification, *n.* (15c) **1.** Adoption or enactment, esp. where the act is the last in a series of necessary steps or consents <The Ratification of the Conventions of nine States, shall be sufficient for the Establishment of this Constitution between the States so ratifying the Same>. • In this sense, ratification runs the gamut of a formal approval of a constitutional amendment to rank-and-file approval of a labor union's collective-bargaining agreement with management. See ADOPTION (5). Cf. SANCTION (1). **2.** Confirmation and acceptance of a previous act, thereby making the act valid from the moment it was done <the board of directors' ratification of the president's resolution>. • This sense includes action taken by the legislature to make binding a treaty negotiated by the executive. **3.** *Contracts.* A person's binding adoption of an act already completed but either not done in a way that originally produced a legal obligation or done by a third party having at the time no authority to act as the person's agent <an adult's ratification of a contract signed during childhood is necessary to make the contract enforceable>.

> "Ratification may take place by express words indicating an intention to confirm the contract. These words may consist of a new express promise, or such words as 'I do ratify and confirm.' A mere acknowledgment that the contract was in fact made and that it has not been performed is not sufficient as a ratification. It is sometimes said that a ratification is ineffective unless made with knowledge of the possession of a legal power to disaffirm, but the cases holding the contrary seem to have the better reason." William R. Anson, *Principles of the Law of Contract* 179–80 (Arthur L. Corbin ed., 3d Am. ed. 1919).

4. *Int'l law.* The final establishment of consent by the parties to a treaty to be bound by it, usu. including the exchange or deposit of instruments of ratification <the ratification of the nuclear-weapons treaty>. See INSTRUMENT OF RATIFICATION. **5.** *Agency.* The affirmance of someone's prior act, whereby the act is given the same effect as if it had been done by an agent acting with actual authority. • Ratification creates, after the fact of the person's action, the legal consequences of actual authority among an agent, the principal, and the third party. Cf. CONFIRMATION. — **ratify,** *vb.* — **ratifiable,** *adj.*

> "Ratification often serves the function of clarifying situations of ambiguous or uncertain authority. A principal's ratification confirms or validates an agent's right to have acted as the agent did. . . . If the principal ratifies the agent's act, it is not thereafter necessary to show that the agent acted with actual authority. Moreover, by replicating the effects of actual authority, the principal's ratification eliminates claims the principal would otherwise have against the agent for acting without actual authority." Restatement (Third) of Agency § 4.01 cmt. b (2006).

ratihabitio (rat-ə-hə-**bish**-ee-oh), *n.* [Latin fr. *ratum habere* "to hold ratified"] *Civil law.* Ratification or approval, esp. by a principal of an agent's transaction; confirmation. — Sometimes anglicized to *ratihabition.* Pl. ***ratihabitiones.***

rating. 1. *Marine insurance.* The determination of a vessel's quality, state, or condition as a factor of insurability. **2.** INSURANCE RATING.

ratio. See RATIO DECIDENDI.

ratiocination (rash-ee-os-ə-**nay**-shən), *n.* (16c) **1.** The process or an act of reasoning. **2.** A conclusion arrived at by reasoning. — **ratiocinative** (rash-ee-**os**-ə-nay-tiv), *adj.* — **ratiocinate** (rash-ee-**os**-ə-nayt), *vb.*

ratio decidendi (**ray**-shee-oh des-ə-**den**-dɪ), *n.* [Latin "the reason for deciding"] (18c) **1.** The principle or rule of law on which a court's decision is founded <many poorly written judicial opinions do not contain a clearly ascertainable *ratio decidendi*>. **2.** The rule of law on which a later court thinks that a previous court founded its decision; a general rule without which a case must have been decided otherwise <this opinion recognizes the Supreme Court's *ratio decidendi* in the school desegregation cases>. • In a classic essay on the subject, Arthur L. Goodhart said of *ratio decidendi*: "With the possible exception of the legal term 'malice,' it is the most misleading expression in English law, for the reason which the judge gives for his decision is never the . . . binding part of the precedent." A.L.G., "Determining the *Ratio*

Decidendi of a Case," in *Essays in Jurisprudence and the Common Law* 1, 2 (1931). — Often shortened to *ratio*. Pl. ***rationes decidendi*** (**ray**-shee-oh-neez des-ə-**den**-dɪ). Cf. OBITER DICTUM; HOLDING (1).

> "The phrase 'the *ratio decidendi* of a case' is slightly ambiguous. It may mean either (1) the rule that the judge who decided the case intended to lay down and apply to the facts, or (2) the rule that a later court concedes him to have had the power to lay down." Glanville Williams, *Learning the Law* 75 (11th ed. 1982).

> "There are . . . two steps involved in the ascertainment of the *ratio decidendi* . . . . First, it is necessary to determine all the facts of the case as seen by the judge; secondly, it is necessary to discover which of those facts were treated as material by the judge." Rupert Cross & J.W. Harris, *Precedent in English Law* 65–66 (4th ed. 1991).

ratio impertinens (**ray**-shee-oh im-**pər**-ti-nenz). [Latin] *Hist.* Out-of-place reasoning.

ratio juris. See RATIO LEGIS.

ratio legis (**ray**-shee-oh **lee**-jəs), *n.* [Latin] (17c) The reason or purpose for making a law <the Senator argued that the rapid spread of violent crime was a compelling *ratio legis* for the gun-control statute>. — Also termed *ratio juris*.

rationabile estoverium (rash-[ee]-ə-**nay**-bə-lee es-tə-**veer**-ee-əm), *n.* [Law Latin "reasonable necessaries"] (17c) *Hist.* Alimony.

rationabilibus divisis. See DE RATIONABILIBUS DIVISIS.

rationabili parte bonorum. See DE RATIONABILI PARTE BONORUM.

rational, *adj.* **1.** Endowed with the faculties of cognition traditionally thought to distinguish humans from the brutes <man as a rational being>. **2.** Based on logic rather than emotion; attained through clear thinking; not absurd, preposterous, foolish, or fanciful <a rational conclusion>. **3.** (Of a person) able to think clearly and sensibly; clear-headed and right-minded <Jones was rational at the time of the woman's death>.

rational-basis test. (1947) *Constitutional law.* The criterion for judicial analysis of a statute that does not implicate a fundamental right or a suspect or quasi-suspect classification under the Due Process or Equal Protection Clause, whereby the court will uphold a law if it bears a reasonable relationship to the attainment of a legitimate governmental objective. • Rational basis is the most deferential of the standards of review that courts use in due-process and equal-protection analysis. — Also termed *rational-purpose test*; *rational-relationship test*; *minimum scrutiny*; *minimal scrutiny.* Cf. STRICT SCRUTINY; INTERMEDIATE SCRUTINY.

rational-choice theory. (1979) The theory that behavioral choices, including the choice to engage in criminal activity, are based on purposeful decisions that the potential benefits outweigh the risks. — Sometimes shortened to *ratchoice* <our political-science department is strong in ratchoice theorists>. Cf. CONTROL THEORY; ROUTINE-ACTIVITIES THEORY; STRAIN THEORY.

rational doubt. See REASONABLE DOUBT.

rationale (rash-ə-**nal**), *n.* **1.** A statement of reasons; specif., a reasoned explanation or exposition of principles that underlie an art, science, procedure, opinion, etc. <the rationale for osteopathy>. **2.** The logical basis for a procedure, fact, position, etc.; a foundation <the rationale for removing the case to federal court>.

- ▸ **rationale ex ante.** Reasoning worked out beforehand based on information known earlier than some specific occurrence.
- ▸ **rationale ex post.** Reasoning worked out after some specific occurrence, often from information gained by hindsight.

rational interpretation. See *logical interpretation* under INTERPRETATION (1).

rationality. 1. The quality, state, or condition of being agreeable to or consonant with clear-headed, sensible thought <the rationality that underlies this argument>. **2.** The ability or tendency to view things from an emotionally detached and logically principled standpoint <she retained her rationality till the end of her life>. **3.** A reasonable view, practice, reason, or doctrine.

rationalization. 1. The act or process of regarding or treating something by relying on reason alone, independently of authority; esp., the interpretation of events, occurrences, behavior, texts, etc. in the manner of one who exalts reason as the sole arbiter. **2.** The act or process of rendering something conformable to reason; esp., an instance of making or showing something to be rational or reasonable, as by removing unreasonable elements. **3.** The act or process of ascribing one's acts, opinions, beliefs, etc. to causes that superficially seem reasonable and true but that are actually unconnected with reality, perhaps because of unconscious, discreditable, or disagreeable causes; esp., the invention of plausible but fake explanations for things that actually have other causes.

> "This practice of making ourselves appear, to ourselves and others, more rational than we are, has been termed 'rationalization.' Rationalization not only conceals the real foundations of our biased beliefs but also enables us to maintain, side by side as it were, beliefs which are inherently incompatible." Jerome Frank, *Law and the Modern Mind* 30 (1936).

4. The reorganization of an industry to minimize waste, standardize procedures, and maintain relatively stable prices. — **rationalize,** *vb.*

rational-purpose test. See RATIONAL-BASIS TEST.

rational-relationship test. See RATIONAL-BASIS TEST.

ratione (ray-shee-**oh**-nee *or* rash-ee-**oh**-nee). [Latin] By reason; on account.

- ▸ ***ratione bonorum*** (bə-**nor**-əm). By reason of property.
- ▸ ***ratione causae*** (**kaw**-zee). By reason of the nature of the case.
- ▸ ***ratione contractus*** (kən-**trak**-təs). By reason of the contract.

> "By entering into a contract, the contracting parties may . . . render themselves amenable to the jurisdiction of a judge to whose jurisdiction they would not have been amenable had the contract not been entered into. Thus, a foreigner, for the time being domiciled in Scotland, entering into a contract there with a Scotchman . . . renders himself amenable to the jurisdiction of the Scotch courts in any question arising out of the contract, for the parties . . . are presumed to have had the law and the courts of Scotland in view as the *forum* . . . and a jurisdiction thus founded is said to arise *ratione contractus*." John Trayner, *Trayner's Latin Maxims* 540 (4th ed. 1894).

- ▸ ***ratione delicti*** (di-**lik**-tɪ). On account of the delict.
- ▸ ***ratione domicilii*** (dom-ə-**sil**-ee-ɪ). By reason of domicile; on account of residence. • The phrase appeared in reference to the foundation of jurisdiction in many civil cases.

▸ ***ratione fori*** (**for**-I). [Latin] By reason of the forum.

▸ ***ratione habita*** (**hab**-i-tə). Regard being had (of particular factors or circumstances).

▸ ***ratione impotentiae*** (im-pə-**ten**-shee-ee). By reason of inability. • This was the basis for a property right in young wild animals that were unable to run or fly. See FERAE NATURAE.

▸ ***ratione incidentiae*** (in-si-**den**-shee-ee). By reason of the incident.

▸ ***ratione loci*** (**loh**-SI). By reason of place. • This was the basis for a property right in rabbits and hares.

▸ ***ratione materiae*** (mə-**teer**-ee-ee). By reason of the matter involved.

▸ ***ratione originis*** (ə-**rij**-ə-nis). By reason of one's origin.

▸ ***ratione personae*** (pər-**soh**-nee). By reason of the person concerned.

▸ ***ratione privilegii*** (priv-ə-**lee**-jee-I). By reason of privilege. • This was the basis for a property right in animals of warren. See WARREN.

▸ ***ratione rei sitae*** (**ree**-I **SI**-tee). By reason of the situation of a thing.

▸ ***ratione soli*** (**soh**-lI). By reason of the soil. • This was the basis for property rights over natural resources found on a landowner's property.

▸ ***ratione subjectae materiae*** (səb-**jek**-tee mə-**teer**-ee-ee). On account of the subject matter.

▸ ***ratione suspecti judicis*** (sə-**spek**-tI **joo**-di-sis). On account of the judge being suspected. • This referred to a judge's recusal in a case.

▸ ***ratione temporis*** (tem-**por**-is), *adv.* By reason of time or the times.

▸ ***ratione tenurae*** (**ten**-yə-ree). By reason of tenure.

rationes (ray-shee-**oh**-neez *or* rash-ee-**oh**-neez), *n.* [Latin "reasons"] *Hist.* The pleadings in a suit.

ratio pertinens. (1933) A pertinent reason (for a question).

ratio scientiae (**ray**-shee-oh SI-**en**-shee-ee). [Law Latin] (17c) *Hist.* The ground of knowledge; esp., the basis for a witness's testimony.

ratio scripta (**ray**-shee-oh **skrip**-tə). [Latin] (18c) *Roman law.* Written reason.

ratio verborum (**ray**-shee-oh vər-**bor**-əm). The rationale for the choice of words in a legal instrument.

rattening (**rat**-ning). (1828) *Hist.* The practice of taking away tools, destroying machinery, and the like in an attempt either to compel a worker to join a union or to enforce a company's compliance with union rules. • Rattening was formerly a common labor-union tactic in England, and it was a criminal offense.

ravishment, *n.* (15c) *Archaic.* **1.** Forcible seizure and carrying off of another person (esp. a woman); abduction. **2.** RAPE (1). • In this sense the term is widely considered inappropriate for modern usage, given its romantic connotations (in other contexts) of ecstasy and delight. In the Restatement (First) of Torts § 65a, the word was defined as including not just rape but any carnal intercourse of a criminal nature. See RAPUIT. — **ravish,** *vb.*

RBS. *abbr.* RURAL BUSINESS-COOPERATIVE SERVICE.

RCE. *abbr.* REQUEST FOR CONTINUED EXAMINATION.

RCFL. *abbr.* Regional computer forensic laboratory.

RCV. *abbr.* Ranked-choice voting. See *preferential voting* under VOTING.

RDA. *abbr.* RULES OF DECISION ACT.

RDAP. *abbr.* Residential drug-abuse program. See RESIDENTIAL DRUG-TREATMENT PROGRAM.

RDAT (**ahr**-dat). *abbr.* Residential drug-abuse treatment. — Also termed *residential drug-abuse-treatment program.* See RESIDENTIAL DRUG-TREATMENT PROGRAM.

rDNA. *abbr.* RECOMBINANT DNA TECHNOLOGY.

RDTP. *abbr.* RESIDENTIAL DRUG-TREATMENT PROGRAM.

re (ree *or* ray), *prep.* (18c) Regarding; in the matter of. • In the title of a case, it usu. signifies a legal proceeding regarding the disposition of real or personal property or a change in legal status. In American caselaw, the abbreviation commonly used is *in re* <In re Estate of Kirk>. In business correspondence, the term signals the subject matter <re: Board Meeting>. See IN RE.

REA. *abbr.* **1.** RURAL ELECTRIFICATION ADMINISTRATION. **2.** RETIREMENT EQUITY ACT OF 1984.

rea (**ree**-ə), *n.* [Latin] In civil and canon law, a defendant. Pl. ***reae.***

reacquired stock. See *treasury stock* under STOCK.

readback, *n.* (1958) A stenographer's or other person's oral recitation of a transcript, usu. one freshly made, for purposes of reorienting a line of questioning or for verifying or correcting the recordation of what has been said. — **read back,** *vb.*

reading. (16c) *Parliamentary law.* The recitation aloud of a bill or other main motion, sometimes by title only, usu. in a series of three such recitations necessary before a legislative body can pass a bill. See *reading clerk* under CLERK (7).

reading clerk. See CLERK (7).

read into, *vb.* See READ ON.

readjustment, *n.* (18c) Voluntary reorganization of a financially troubled corporation by the shareholders themselves, without a trustee's or a receiver's intervention. — **readjust,** *vb.*

read law, *vb.* (16c) **1.** To prepare for a legal career by working in a lawyer's office as a clerk while studying legal texts on one's own time. • Most American lawyers in the 18th and 19th centuries obtained their legal educations solely by reading law. Today, few American states allow applicants to take the bar exam without attending law school. **2.** To study law at a law school.

read on, *vb. Patents.* **1.** (Of a patent claim) to contain all the same features of (a prior-art reference). • If the patent claim reads on the prior art, the claim has been anticipated and the patent will be denied. See ANTICIPATED. **2.** (Of a patent claim) to describe an infringing product or process. • If all the patent claims read on the other product, that product infringes the patent.

ready-berth clause. (1937) *Admiralty.* A charterparty provision stipulating that laydays will begin to run as soon as the vessel arrives at the port where loading or discharge will take place, whether or not the ship is in berth. • Such a clause protects the shipowner from any delay in getting a berth. See LAYDAY.

ready, willing, and able. (1829) (Of a prospective buyer) legally and financially capable of consummating a purchase. — Often shortened to *willing and able*; *ready and able*.

> "'READY, WILLING, AND ABLE' — A phrase referring to a prospective buyer of property who is legally capable and financially able to consummate the deal. Traditionally, the broker earns a commission upon procuring a 'ready, willing, and able' buyer on the listing terms, regardless of whether the seller actually goes through with the sale. The 'ready and willing' means, generally, that the broker must in fact produce a buyer who indicates that he or she is prepared to accept the terms of the seller and is willing to enter into a contract for sale. The buyer is not 'ready and willing' when he or she enters into an option with the seller, but the buyer is 'ready and willing' when the option is exercised. The buyer is not 'ready and willing' when the offer is subject to any new conditions, such as making the closing date an unreasonably long period, for example, one year from the offer. . . . The 'able' requires that the buyer be financially able to comply with the terms of the sale in both initial cash payment and any necessary financing. The broker is not required to show that the purchaser has actual cash or assets to pay off the mortgage. But the broker is required to reveal the identity of the buyer if requested by the seller." John W. Reilly, *The Language of Real Estate* 326 (4th ed. 1993).

reaffirmation, *n.* (1857) **1.** Approval of something previously decided or agreed to; renewal <the Supreme Court's reaffirmation of this principle is long overdue>. **2.** *Bankruptcy.* An agreement between the debtor and a creditor by which the debtor promises to repay a prepetition debt that would otherwise be discharged at the conclusion of the bankruptcy <the debtor negotiated a reaffirmation so that he could keep the collateral>. • There are two main requirements for a reaffirmation to be enforceable: (1) the agreement must contain a clear and conspicuous provision stating that the debtor may rescind the reaffirmation agreement anytime before discharge or within 60 days after the agreement is filed with the court; and (2) for a debtor who is not represented by counsel, the court must determine that the reaffirmation is in the debtor's best interest and does not impose an undue hardship. 11 USCA § 524(c). — Also termed (in sense 2) *reaffirmation agreement*. — **reaffirm,** *vb.*

reaffirmation agreement. *Bankruptcy.* An debtor's agreement to continue paying a dischargeable debt after bankruptcy, usu. to keep collateral or mortgaged property that would otherwise be subject to repossession. See REAFFIRMATION (2).

reaffirmation hearing. (1979) *Bankruptcy.* A hearing at which the debtor and a creditor present a reaffirmation of a dischargeable debt for the court's approval. • The reaffirmation hearing is usu. held simultaneously with the discharge hearing. See DISCHARGE HEARING.

real, *adj.* (15c) **1.** Of, relating to, or involving things (such as lands and buildings) that are fixed or immovable <real property> <a real action>. **2.** *Civil law.* Of, relating to, or attached to a thing (whether movable or immovable) rather than a person <a real right>. **3.** Actual; genuine; true <real authority>. **4.** (Of money, income, etc.) measured in terms of purchasing power rather than nominal value; adjusted for inflation <real wages>.

real account. See ACCOUNT.

real action. See ACTION (4).

real asset. See ASSET.

real authority. See *actual authority* under AUTHORITY (1).

real burden. See BURDEN (4).

real chattel. See *chattel real* under CHATTEL.

real contract. See CONTRACT.

real covenant. See *covenant running with the land* under COVENANT (4).

real damages. See *actual damages* under DAMAGES.

real defense. See DEFENSE (4).

real earnings. See EARNINGS.

real estate. See *real property* under PROPERTY.

real-estate agent. See AGENT.

real-estate broker. **1.** See BROKER. **2.** See *buyer's broker* under BROKER.

real-estate investment trust. (1929) A company that invests in and manages a portfolio of real estate, with the majority of the trust's income distributed to its shareholders. • Such a trust may qualify for special income-tax treatment if it distributes 95% of its income to its shareholders. — Abbr. REIT. See *investment company* under COMPANY. Cf. REAL-ESTATE MORTGAGE TRUST.

▸ **umbrella-partnership real-estate investment trust.** (1993) A REIT that controls and holds most of its properties through an umbrella limited partnership, as a result of which the trust can acquire properties in exchange for the limited-partnership interests in the umbrella while triggering no immediate tax obligations for certain sellers. • This is a structure that many REITs now use. — Abbr. UPREIT.

real-estate-mortgage investment conduit. (1986) An entity that holds a fixed pool of mortgages or mortgage-backed securities (such as collateralized mortgage obligations), issues interests in itself to investors, and receives favorable tax treatment by passing its income through to those investors. • Real-estate-mortgage investment conduits were created by the Tax Reform Act of 1986. They can be organized as corporations, partnerships, or trusts. To qualify for tax-exempt status, the entity must meet two requirements: (1) almost all the entity's assets must be real-estate mortgages (though a few other cash-flow-maintaining assets are allowed); and (2) all interests in the entity must be classified as either regular interests (which entitle the holder to principal and interest income through debt or equity) or residual interests (which provide contingent income). — Abbr. REMIC.

real-estate mortgage trust. (1979) A real-estate investment trust that buys and sells the mortgages on real property rather than the real property itself. — Abbr. REMT. Cf. REAL-ESTATE INVESTMENT TRUST.

real estate owned. Property acquired by a lender, usu. through foreclosure, in satisfaction of a debt. — Abbr. REO.

Real Estate Settlement Procedures Act. A federal statute that requires lenders to provide home buyers with information about known or estimated settlement costs. 12 USCA §§ 2601–2617. — Abbr. RESPA. See REGULATION X.

real-estate syndicate. (1904) A group of investors who pool their money to buy and sell real property. • Most real-estate syndicates operate as limited partnerships or real-estate investment trusts.

real evidence. See EVIDENCE.

real forfeiture. See FORFEITURE.

realignment (ree-ə-**lɪn**-mənt), *n.* (1907) The process by which a court, usu. in determining diversity jurisdiction, identifies and rearranges the parties as plaintiffs and defendants according to their ultimate interests. — **realign,** *vb.*

real income. See INCOME.

realism. 1. LEGAL REALISM. **2.** A method of reasoning that determines a law's meaning by weighing the costs, benefits, probable consequences, and underlying values and purposes of the law, while also considering whether the interpretive result will be fair and just. — Also termed *policy analysis; practical reasoning.* See ANTIFORMALISM.

realization, *n.* (18c) **1.** Conversion of noncash assets into cash assets. **2.** *Tax.* An event or transaction, such as the sale or exchange of property, that substantially changes a taxpayer's economic position so that income tax may be imposed or a tax allowance granted. Cf. RECOGNITION (4). — **realize,** *vb.*

realized gain. See GAIN (3).

realized loss. See LOSS (2).

real law. The law of real property; real-estate law.

realm (relm), *n.* **1.** A country ruled by a king or queen. **2.** A general area of knowledge, activity, or thought.

real money. See MONEY.

real obligation. See OBLIGATION.

real party in interest. See PARTY (2).

real-party-in-interest rule. (1904) The principle that the person entitled by law to enforce a substantive right should be the one under whose name the action is prosecuted. Fed. R. Civ. P. 17(a).

real property. See PROPERTY.

real rate. See INTEREST RATE.

real right. See RIGHT.

real security. See SECURITY (4).

real servitude. See *servitude appurtenant* under SERVITUDE (3).

real statute. See STATUTE.

real subrogation. See SUBROGATION.

real suretyship. See SURETYSHIP.

real things. (18c) Property that is fixed and immovable, such as lands and buildings; real property. — Also termed *things real.* See *real property* under PROPERTY. Cf. *chattel real* under CHATTEL.

realtor (**reel**-tər). (1916) **1.** *(cap.) Servicemark.* A real-estate agent who is a member of the National Association of Realtors. **2.** Loosely, any real-estate agent or broker. See *real-estate agent* under AGENT.

real treaty. See TREATY (1).

realty. (17c) Land and anything growing on, attached to, or erected on it, that cannot be removed without injury to the land. — Also termed *real property.*

▸ **quasi-realty.** (1851) *Hist.* Things that the law treats as fixed to realty, but are themselves movable, such as title deeds.

realty trust. See *nominee trust* (2) under TRUST (3).

real union. *Int'l law.* A combination of two or more allied countries that share some state institutions as well as a common ruler.

real wages. See WAGE.

real warrandice. See WARRANDICE.

real wrong. See WRONG.

reapportionment, *n.* (1874) *Constitutional law.* Realignment of a legislative district's boundaries to reflect changes in population and ensure proportionate representation by elected officials. *See* U.S. Const. art. I, § 2, cl. 3. — Also termed *redistricting.* Cf. GERRYMANDERING. — **reapportion,** *vb.*

reargument, *n.* (18c) The presentation of additional arguments, which often suggest that a controlling legal principle has been overlooked, to a court (usu. an appellate court) that has already heard initial arguments. Cf. REHEARING. — **reargue,** *vb.*

rearrest. See ARREST (2).

reason, *n.* **1.** An expression or statement given by way of explanation or justification; whatever is supposed or affirmed to support a conclusion, inference, or plan of action <he proffered several reasons for the relief he requested>. **2.** A ground or cause that explains or accounts for something <weakened by reason of chronic illness>. **3.** The power of comprehending and inferring; collectively, the faculties that enable someone to think and draw conclusions; the normal exercise of rationality <reason itself distinguishes humans from brutes>. **4.** A sound mind; sanity <he lost his reason>. **5.** Correct thinking; the mature consensus of informed thought within a community <listen to reason>. **6.** A premise, esp. a minor premise — that is, a factual statement that implicates the principle used in a syllogism <What is the reason for that conclusion?>. See SYLLOGISM. **7.** A reasonable act; whatever is right or befitting <she ought within reason to be excused>.

reason, *vb.* **1.** To attempt to arrive at a conclusion through close examination, inference, and thought; to form a specific judgment about a situation after carefully considering the facts <the ability to reason>. **2.** To examine or deduce by means of close analysis and thought; to infer or conclude <to reason why it happened>. **3.** To persuade or dissuade by marshaling grounds for proving; to influence by argument <she reasoned with him for two hours>. **4.** To present or discuss (pros and cons); to debate <to reason the point with the judge>.

reasonable, *adj.* (14c) **1.** Fair, proper, or moderate under the circumstances; sensible <reasonable pay>. **2.** According to reason <your argument is reasonable but not convincing>. See PLAUSIBLE (1).

> "It is extremely difficult to state what lawyers mean when they speak of 'reasonableness.' In part the expression refers to ordinary ideas of natural law or natural justice, in part to logical thought, working upon the basis of the rules of law." John Salmond, *Jurisprudence* 183 n.(u) (Glanville L. Williams ed., 10th ed. 1947).

> "In one sense the word [*reasonable*] describes the proper use of the reasoning power, and in another it is no more than a word of assessment. Reasoning does not help much in fixing a reasonable or fair price or a reasonable or moderate length of time, or in estimating the size of a doubt. Lawyers say a reasonable doubt, meaning a substantial one; the Court of Appeal has frowned upon the

description of a reasonable doubt as one for which reasons could be given." Patrick Devlin, *The Judge* 134 (1979).

3. (Of a person) having the faculty of reason <a reasonable person would have looked both ways before crossing the street>. **4.** *Archaic.* Human <criminal homicide is traditionally called the unlawful killing of a "reasonable person">. — **reasonableness,** *n.*

reasonable accommodation. See ACCOMMODATION.

reasonable-apprehension test. (1977) *Patents.* A judicial analysis to decide whether there is a justiciable controversy between a patentee and an alleged infringer. • The test has two elements: (1) the patent owner must make an explicit threat or take other action that makes another person reasonably believe that an infringement suit is likely, and (2) the other person must be engaged in an activity that could constitute infringement or must be intentionally preparing to engage in possibly infringing activity. If either element is prospective or uncertain, the court will not consider the complaint.

reasonable attorney's fee. See under ATTORNEY'S FEE.

reasonable belief. See BELIEF.

reasonable care. See CARE (2).

reasonable cause. See PROBABLE CAUSE (1).

reasonable-consumer test. (1983) The prevailing test for determining whether advertisement is deceptive, determined by asking whether the reasonable consumer would believe that the claim is true. Cf. FOOL'S TEST.

reasonable-development covenant. (1964) *Oil & gas.* The implied promise in an oil-and-gas lease that once production is obtained the lessee will continue to develop the property as would a reasonably prudent operator, as opposed to merely holding the lease by the production already obtained. See FURTHER-EXPLORATION COVENANT.

reasonable deviation. See DEVIATION.

reasonable diligence. See DILIGENCE (2).

reasonable doubt. (18c) The doubt that prevents one from being firmly convinced of a defendant's guilt, or the belief that there is a real possibility that a defendant is not guilty. • "Beyond a reasonable doubt" is the standard used by a jury to determine whether a criminal defendant is guilty. *See* Model Penal Code § 1.12. In deciding whether guilt has been proved beyond a reasonable doubt, the jury must begin with the presumption that the defendant is innocent. — Also termed *rational doubt.* See MORAL CERTAINTY; BURDEN OF PERSUASION. Cf. *clear and convincing evidence* under EVIDENCE; PREPONDERANCE OF THE EVIDENCE.

> "Reasonable doubt . . . is a term often used, probably pretty well understood, but not easily defined. It is not a mere possible doubt; because every thing relating to human affairs, and depending on moral evidence, is open to some possible or imaginary doubt. It is that state of the case, which, after the entire comparison and consideration of all the evidence, leaves the minds of jurors in that condition that they cannot say they feel an abiding conviction, to a moral certainty, of the truth of the charge." *Commonwealth v. Webster,* 59 Mass. (5 Cush.) 295, 320 (1850).

> "The gravamen of Lord Goddard's objection to the formula of 'reasonable doubt' seems to have been the muddle occasionally created by an impromptu effort to explain to a jury the meaning of this phrase. A simple solution would be to refrain from explaining it, relying on the common sense of the jury. As Barton J. said in an Australian case, 'one embarks on a dangerous sea if he attempts to define with precision a term which is in ordinary use with reference to this subject-matter, and which is usually stated to a jury without embellishment as a well understood expression.' However, some modes of embellishment seem to be unobjectionable. There is probably no harm in telling the jury, as some judges do, that a reasonable doubt is one for which a sensible reason can be supplied." Glanville Williams, *Criminal Law: The General Part* 873 (2d ed. 1961).

reasonable excuse. See PROBABLE CAUSE.

reasonable-expectations doctrine. (1966) The principle that an ambiguous or inconspicuous term in a contract should be interpreted to favor the weaker party's objectively reasonable expectations from the contract, even though the explicit language of the terms may not support those expectations. • This principle is most often applied when interpreting insurance policies, consumer contracts, and other types of adhesion contracts. — Also written *reasonable-expectation doctrine.*

reasonable force. See FORCE.

reasonable grounds. See PROBABLE CAUSE (1).

reasonable-inference rule. (1945) An evidentiary principle providing that a jury, in deciding a case, may properly consider any reasonable inference drawn from the evidence presented at trial. Cf. PYRAMIDING INFERENCES, RULE AGAINST.

reasonable man. See REASONABLE PERSON.

reasonable medical probability. (1949) In proving the cause of an injury, a standard requiring a showing that the injury was more likely than not caused by a particular stimulus, based on the general consensus of recognized medical thought. — Also termed *reasonable medical certainty.*

reasonable notice. See NOTICE (3).

reasonable person. (1856) **1.** A hypothetical person used as a legal standard, esp. to determine whether someone acted with negligence; specif., a person who exercises the degree of attention, knowledge, intelligence, and judgment that society requires of its members for the protection of their own and of others' interests. • The reasonable person acts sensibly, does things without serious delay, and takes proper but not excessive precautions. *See* Restatement (Second) of Torts § 283(b). — Also termed *reasonable man; prudent person; ordinarily prudent person; reasonably prudent person; highly prudent person.* See *reasonable care* under CARE (2).

> "The reasonable man connotes a person whose notions and standards of behaviour and responsibility correspond with those generally obtained among ordinary people in our society at the present time, who seldom allows his emotions to overbear his reason and whose habits are moderate and whose disposition is equable. He is not necessarily the same as the average man — a term which implies an amalgamation of counter-balancing extremes." R.F.V. Heuston, *Salmond on the Law of Torts* 56 (17th ed. 1977).

2. *Archaic.* A human being.

> "In the antique phraseology which has been repeated since the time of Lord Coke the *actus reus* of murder (and therefore of any criminal homicide) was declared to be unlawfully killing a reasonable person who is in being and under the King's peace, the death following within a year and a day. In this sentence the word 'reasonable' does not mean 'sane,' but 'human.' In criminal law, a lunatic is a *persona* for all purposes of protection, even when not so treated for the assessment of liability." J.W. Cecil Turner, *Kenny's Outlines of Criminal Law* 102 (16th ed. 1952).

reasonable provocation. See *adequate provocation* under PROVOCATION.

reasonable royalty. See ROYALTY (1).

reasonable skill. See SKILL.

reasonable support. 1. See SUPPORT (1). **2.** See SUPPORT (2).

reasonable suspicion. See SUSPICION.

reasonable time. (1951) **1.** *Contracts.* The time needed to do what a contract requires to be done, based on subjective circumstances. • If the contracting parties do not fix a time for performance, the law will usu. presume a reasonable time. **2.** *Commercial law.* The time during which the UCC permits a party to accept an offer, inspect goods, substitute conforming goods for rejected goods, and the like.

reasonable use. See USE (1).

reasonable-use theory. (1933) *Property.* The principle that owners of riparian land may make reasonable use of their water if this use does not affect the water available to lower riparian owners.

reasonably believe. See BELIEVE.

reasonably-prudent-operator standard. (1976) *Oil & gas.* The test generally applied to determine a lessee's compliance with implied lease covenants by considering what a reasonable, competent operator in the oil-and-gas industry would do under the circumstances, acting in good faith and with economic motivation, and taking into account the lessor's interests as well as that of the operator. — Abbr. RPO standard. — Also termed *reasonable-prudent-operator standard*; *prudent-operator standard.*

reasonably prudent person. See REASONABLE PERSON.

reasonably suspect. See SUSPECT.

reasoned arbitration award. See ARBITRATION AWARD.

reasoning. (14c) **1.** The drawing of inferences or conclusions through a logical process. **2.** Ideas and opinions that are based on logical thinking.

▸ **abductive reasoning.** (1906) Reasoning based on using the best evidence available to make and test a hypothesis. • This form of reasoning is often used by jurors to make a decision based on the evidence presented to them.

▸ **deductive reasoning.** (1841) Reasoning that begins with a general statement or hypothesis and examines the possibilities before drawing a specific, logical conclusion. • Deductive reasoning can be expressed as a syllogism with a major premise ("All men are mortal"), a minor premise ("Socrates is a man"), and a conclusion ("Therefore, Socrates is mortal"). If the premises are true, the conclusion will be true. — Also termed *syllogistic reasoning.*

▸ **inductive reasoning.** (18c) Reasoning that begins with specific observations from which broad generalizations are drawn. • Even if the premises are true, the conclusion may be false. For example, "Tompkins is male. Tompkins is a judge. Therefore, all judges are male."

▸ **legal reasoning.** A mode of thought typical of lawyers and judges, who in their work seek to apply legal rules to specific fact patterns to arrive at enforceable decisions.

▸ **syllogistic reasoning.** See *deductive reasoning.*

reason of state. [fr. French *raison d'état*] The often unprincipled or unjust cause given by a ruler or government in explanation of a political action.

reasons for allowance. See RULE 109 STATEMENT.

reason to know. Information from which a person of ordinary intelligence — or of the superior intelligence that the person may have — would infer that the fact in question exists or that there is a substantial enough chance of its existence that, if the person exercises reasonable care, the person can assume the fact exists.

reassert, *vb.* (17c) **1.** To state (a fact, opinion, etc.) again, often more strongly or more clearly <she reasserted her position on family-law policy>. **2.** To make (one's authority, power, control, etc.) stronger after it has seemed weak <the President reasserted his authority over foreign affairs>. **3.** (*reflexive*) To return or become stronger after a period of being missing or weak <legal formalism reasserted itself after a period of quiescence>.

reassessment. See *reassessment* under ASSESSMENT (2).

reassurance. See REINSURANCE.

rebate, *n.* (15c) **1.** A return of part of a payment, serving as a discount or reduction. **2.** An amount of money that is paid back when someone has overpaid. — **rebate,** *vb.*

▸ **rent rebate.** (1910) Money that a person receives back, esp. from local government, to help pay rent.

rebellion. (14c) **1.** Open, organized, and armed resistance to an established government or ruler; esp., an organized attempt to change the government or leader of a country, usu. through violence. **2.** Open resistance or opposition to an authority or tradition. **3.** *Hist.* Disobedience of a legal command or summons. — **rebellious,** *adj.* — **rebel,** *n.*

rebuke, *n.* (15c) A sharp reproach or reprimand; reprobation.

rebuke, *vb.* (14c) To speak to (someone) severely about his or her misbehavior, misspeaking, etc.; to chide or criticize sharply.

rebus integris (**ree**-bəs **in**-tə-gris). [Latin] *Scots law.* (17c) Matters being complete; no performance having taken place. • For example, a contract could be rescinded if nothing had been done toward performance.

rebus ipsis et factis (**ree**-bəs **ip**-sis et **fak**-tis). [Latin] (1818) *Scots law.* By the facts and circumstances themselves. • A marital contract was sometimes inferred *rebus ipsis et factis.*

rebus sic stantibus (**ree**-bəs sik **stan**-ti-bəs). [Latin "matters so standing"] (16c) *Civil law & Int'l law.* The principle that all agreements are concluded with the implied condition that they are binding only as long as there are no major changes in the circumstances. See CLAUSA REBUS SIC STANTIBUS.

rebut, *vb.* (14c) To refute, oppose, or counteract (something) by evidence, argument, or contrary proof <rebut the opponent's expert testimony> <rebut a presumption of negligence>.

rebuttable (ri-**bət**-ə-bəl), *adj.* Capable of being proved false or untrue <rebuttable presumption>.

rebuttable presumption. See PRESUMPTION.

rebuttal, *n.* (1830) **1.** In-court contradiction of an adverse party's evidence. **2.** The time given to a party to present contradictory evidence or arguments; esp., the usu. short segment at the end of an oral argument designated for a movant, appellant, or petitioner to counter the other side's arguments. Cf. CASE-IN-CHIEF.

"Rebuttal is the hardest argument to make in any court. In the Supreme Court and in most courts of appeals, petitioner has to work hard to save any time at all for rebuttal. In the Supreme Court, rebuttal time comes directly out of the 30 minutes allotted to petitioner's side and, if the justices keep asking questions that use up petitioner's time, the case is submitted without rebuttal. Many courts of appeals permit counsel to reserve time for rebuttal, either through the clerk in advance of the argument or at the beginning of the argument itself. It is the rare court of appeals panel that does not permit counsel at least one minute of rebuttal, even when counsel's time has expired." David C. Frederick, *Supreme Court and Appellate Advocacy* § 7.3, at 178 (2003) (dealing only with oral rebuttals on appeal).

3. The arguments contained in a reply brief. See *reply brief* under BRIEF (1).

rebuttal evidence. See EVIDENCE.

rebuttal witness. See WITNESS.

rebutter. (16c) **1.** *Common-law pleading.* The defendant's answer to a plaintiff's surrejoinder; the pleading that followed the rejoinder and surrejoinder, and that might in turn be answered by the surrebutter. **2.** Someone who rebuts. **3.** An argument that rebuts.

rebutting evidence. See *rebuttal evidence* under EVIDENCE.

recall, *n.* (1902) **1.** Removal of a public official from office by popular vote. See *recall election* under ELECTION. **2.** A manufacturer's request to consumers for the return of defective products for repair or replacement. • A recall is often specifically termed a *food recall* or *product recall.* **3.** Revocation of a judgment for factual or legal reasons. **4.** A summoning for workers to return to their jobs after a layoff. — **recall,** *vb.*

recall election. See ELECTION (3).

recall exclusion. See *sistership exclusion* under EXCLUSION (3).

recall letter. See LETTER OF RECALL.

recall of mandate. (1884) The extraordinary action by an appellate court of withdrawing the order it issued to the trial court upon deciding an appeal, usu. after the deadline has passed for the losing party to seek a rehearing. • Because this action can interfere with trial-court proceedings on remand, and also because it clouds the waters that repose (the finality of a judgment) is meant to clear, courts are reluctant to use the power. But they will use it to correct clerical errors or to remedy a fraud on the court during the appeal. It has also been used when the original mandate would result in a grave injustice. See MANDATE (1).

recall referendum. See *recall election* under ELECTION.

recant (ri-**kant**), *vb.* (16c) **1.** To withdraw or renounce (prior statements or testimony) formally or publicly <the prosecution hoped the eyewitness wouldn't recant her corroborating testimony on the stand>. **2.** To withdraw or renounce prior statements or testimony formally or publicly <under grueling cross-examination, the witness recanted>. — **recantation,** *n.*

recapitalization, *n.* (1874) An adjustment or recasting of a corporation's capital structure — that is, its stocks, bonds, or other securities — through amendment of the articles of incorporation or merger with a parent or subsidiary. • An example of recapitalization is the elimination of unpaid preferred dividends and the creation of a new class of senior securities. Cf. REORGANIZATION (2). — **recapitalize,** *vb.*

▸ **leveraged recapitalization.** (1986) Recapitalization whereby the corporation substitutes debt for equity in the capital structure, usu. to make the corporation less attractive as a target for a hostile takeover. — Also termed *leveraging up.*

recaption. (17c) **1.** At common law, lawful seizure of another's property for a second time to secure the performance of a duty; a second distress. See DISTRESS. **2.** Peaceful retaking, without legal process, of one's own property that has been wrongfully taken.

recapture, *n.* (17c) **1.** The act or an instance of retaking or reacquiring; recovery. **2.** The lawful taking by the government of earnings or profits exceeding a specified amount; esp., the government's recovery of a tax benefit (such as a deduction or credit) by taxing income or property that no longer qualifies for the benefit. **3.** *Int'l law.* The retaking of a prize or booty so that the property is legally restored to its original owner. See POSTLIMINIUM (2). — **recapture,** *vb.*

"Upon recapture from pirates, the property is to be restored to the owner, on the allowance of a reasonable compensation to the retaker, in the nature of salvage; for it is a principle of the law of nations, that a capture by pirates does not, like a capture by an enemy in solemn war, change the title, or devest the original owner of his right to the property, and it does not require the doctrine of postliminy to restore it." 1 James Kent, *Commentaries on American Law* *107–08 (George Comstock ed., 11th ed. 1866).

recapture clause. (1920) **1.** A contract provision that limits prices or allows for the recovery of goods if market conditions greatly differ from what the contract anticipated. **2.** A commercial-lease provision that grants the landlord both a percentage of the tenant's profits above a fixed amount of rent and the right to terminate the lease — and thus recapture the property — if those profits are too low.

recapture rule. (1982) *Patents.* The doctrine that a patentee cannot regain, in a reissue patent, a claim that the patentee previously abandoned in order to gain allowance of the patent application. • The rule provides a defense in an infringement action by allowing the defendant to attack the validity of a reissue patent. An attempt to recapture a strategically abandoned claim cannot meet the statutory requirement that the error be made without deceptive intent. 35 USCA § 251.

recede, *vb.* (18c) (Of a house in a bicameral legislature) to withdraw from an amendment in which the other house has not concurred. See CONCUR (3).

"A vote to recede from amendments constitutes a final passage of the bill without the amendments from which the house has receded, since both houses have then agreed to the bill in its form prior to amendment." National Conference of State Legislatures, *Mason's Manual of Legislative Procedure* § 767, at 555 (2000).

receding market. See *bear market* under MARKET.

receipt, *n.* (14c) **1.** The act of receiving something, esp. by taking physical possession <my receipt of the document was delayed by two days>. **2.** A written acknowledgment that something has been received; esp., a piece of paper or an electronic notification that one has paid for something.

<keep the receipt for the gift>. — Also termed (in sense 2) *sales slip*.

▸ **accountable receipt.** (18c) A written acknowledgment of the receipt of money or goods to be accounted for by the receiver. • An account receipt differs from an ordinary receipt, which merely notes that the money has been paid.

▸ **debit receipt.** (1977) A written record showing that a customer owes money to a business. — Also termed *debit note*.

▸ **interim receipt.** (1904) The written acknowledgment of a premium paid on an insurance policy that is pending final approval.

▸ **warehouse receipt.** See WAREHOUSE RECEIPT.

3. (*usu. pl.*) Something received; INCOME <post the daily receipts in the ledger>.

receipt, *vb.* (18c) **1.** To acknowledge in writing the receipt of (something, esp. money) <the bill must be receipted>. **2.** To give a receipt for (something, esp. money) <the bookkeeper receipted the payments>.

receipt clause. (1826) In a conveyancing document, a clause that acts as a receipt for the consideration given. • This clause typically appears to avoid the necessity of a separate receipt.

receiptment (ri-**seet**-mənt). *Hist.* The willful harboring of a felon.

receiptor (ri-**see**-tər). (1814) Someone who receives from a sheriff another's property seized in garnishment and agrees to return the property upon demand or execution.

receivable, *adj.* (14c) **1.** Capable of being admitted or accepted <receivable evidence>. **2.** Awaiting receipt of payment <accounts receivable>. **3.** Subject to a call for payment <a note receivable>.

receivable, *n.* (14c) An amount owed, esp. by a business's customer. See *account receivable* under ACCOUNT.

▸ **unrealized receivable.** (1957) An amount earned but not yet received. • Unrealized receivables have no income-tax basis for cash-basis taxpayers.

receive, *vb.* **1.** To take (something offered, given, sent, etc.); to come into possession of or get from some outside source <to receive presents>. **2.** To give (someone) admittance; to admit to entrance <to receive visitors>. **3.** To accept with approval; to grant standing or recognition to <to receive ambassadors>. **4.** To gain knowledge of from some communication; to perceive mentally; to understand <to receive news>. **5.** To allow or undergo the imposition or impact of; to intercept or encounter the force of (a blow) <to receive three hard punches>. **6.** To take (goods) from a thief; to accept criminally <he received silver sets he knew to have been stolen>.

receiver. (18c) **1.** A disinterested person appointed by a court, or by a corporation or other person, for the protection or collection of property that is the subject of diverse claims (for example, because it belongs to a bankrupt or is otherwise being litigated). Cf. LIQUIDATOR.

> "An approved definition of a receiver is this: An indifferent person between the parties, appointed by the court to collect and receive the rents, issues, and profits of land, or the produce of real estate, or other things in question, pending the suit, which it does not seem reasonable to the court that either party should do, or where a party is incompetent to do so, as in the case of an infant." D.H. Chamberlain, *New-Fashioned Receiverships*, 10 Harv. L. Rev. 139, 139 (1896).

▸ **ancillary receiver.** (1882) Someone who is appointed as a receiver in a particular area to help a foreign receiver collect the assets of an insolvent corporation or other entity.

> "An ancillary receiver of a corporation or unincorporated association may be appointed (a) by a competent court of a state in which there are assets of the corporation or unincorporated association at the time of the commencement of the action for the appointment of such receiver, or (b) in the case of a corporation, by a competent court of the state of incorporation. . . . The purpose of such an ancillary receivership is to aid the foreign primary receivership in the collection and taking charge of assets of the estate being administered." 66 Am. Jur. 2d *Receivers* § 436, at 239 (1973).

▸ **general receiver.** See *principal receiver*.

▸ **judgment receiver.** (1873) A receiver who collects or diverts funds from a judgment debtor to the creditor. • A judgment receiver is usu. appointed when it is difficult to enforce a judgment in any other manner. — Also termed *receiver in aid of execution*.

▸ **local receiver.** (1845) *Conflict of laws.* A receiver appointed in the state where property is located or where an act is done.

▸ **principal receiver.** (1894) A receiver who is primarily responsible for the receivership estate. • A principal receiver may ordinarily (1) act outside the state of appointment, (2) sue in a foreign court, (3) exercise broad powers of assignment, and (4) handle all distributions. — Also termed *primary receiver*; *general receiver*; *original receiver*.

▸ **receiver in aid of execution.** See *judgment receiver*.

▸ **statutory receiver.** (1865) A receiver whose appointment is provided for in a statute.

2. *Criminal law.* A person who knows that a thing is stolen but accepts it, usu. for resale. — Also termed *receiver of stolen goods*. **3.** *Hist. English law.* An officer in the royal household who collected revenues and disbursed them in a lump sum to the treasurer, and who also acted as an attorney with the power to appear in any court in England. • The monarch and his or her consort each had a receiver, thus the full title was King's Receiver or Queen's Receiver.

receiver general. (15c) A public official in charge of a government's receipts and treasury. Pl. **receivers general.**

receiver's certificate. (1823) *Bankruptcy.* An instrument issued by a receiver as evidence that the holder is entitled to receive payment from funds controlled by the bankruptcy court.

receiver's deed. See DEED.

receivership. (15c) **1.** The quality, state, or condition of a business enterprise's, usu. a company's, being placed under the control of a receiver, often because of a lack of assets. **2.** The position or function of being a receiver appointed by a court or under a statute. **3.** A proceeding in which a court appoints a receiver.

▸ **ancillary receivership.** (1893) A receivership in which a further administrative proceeding is appointed in another state to help the principal receivership.

▸ **dry receivership.** (1891) A receivership in which there is no equity available to pay general creditors.

receivership estate. (1886) The totality of the interests that the receivers of an association in one or more states are appointed to protect.

receiving, *n.* See RECEIVING STOLEN PROPERTY.

receiving order. See ORDER (2).

receiving state. See STATE (1).

receiving stolen property. (1847) The criminal offense of acquiring or controlling property known to have been stolen by another person. • Some jurisdictions require the additional element of wrongful intent. In some jurisdictions it is a felony, but in others it is either a felony or a misdemeanor depending on the value of the property. *See* Model Penal Code §§ 223.1, 223.6. — Sometimes shortened to *receiving.* — Also termed *receiving stolen goods.* See FENCE (1).

recens insecutio (ree-senz in-sə-**kyoo**-shee-oh). [Latin "fresh pursuit"] (17c) *Hist.* Pursuit of a thief immediately after discovery of the theft. See FRESH PURSUIT.

receptator (ree-sep-**tay**-tor *or* -tər). [Latin fr. *receptare* "to harbor (a criminal or the proceeds of crime)"] (17c) *Scots law.* **1.** A harborer of a felon. **2.** A receiver of stolen property.

reception. (1931) The adoption in whole or in part of the law of one jurisdiction by another jurisdiction. • In the legal idiom, it is most common to speak of the reception of Roman law.

> "In many parts of Europe monarchs encouraged a 'reception' of Roman law at the expense of medieval customary systems. On the continent—in France, Holland, and Germany—the results of the reception of Roman law have tended to be permanent; the continental jurist in the twentieth century studies Roman law to grasp the jurisprudence underlying modern codes. And in the British Isles, the law of Scotland now contains so much borrowing from Roman law that there, too the road to legal practice leads through study of the corpus of Roman civil law compiled at Justinian's direction. But a reception of Roman law never occurred in England." Arthur R. Hogue, *Origins of the Common Law* 242 (1966).

receptitious (ree-sep-**tish**-əs), *adj.* (17c) *Roman law.* **1.** (Of a dowry) returnable by agreement to the donor upon the dissolution of the marriage. **2.** (Of property) retained by the wife and not included in the dowry.

receptus (ri-**sep**-təs). [Latin "(a person) having been received"] (16c) *Civil law.* An arbitrator. • The term takes its name from the idea that the arbitrator is "received" by the parties to settle their dispute.

recess (**ree**-ses), *n.* (17c) **1.** A brief break in judicial proceedings <the court granted a fifteen-minute recess so the attorney and plaintiff could confer>. Cf. CONTINUANCE (3). **2.** *Parliamentary law.* A motion that suspends but does not end a meeting, and that usu. provides for resumption of the meeting <the meeting had a 15-minute recess>. • The motion to recess, which merely suspends the meeting, differs from the motion to adjourn, which ends the meeting. Cf. ADJOURN. **3.** *Parliamentary law.* The interval between such a motion's adoption and the meeting's reconvening <election ballots were counted during the recess>. — **recess** (ri-**ses**), *vb.*

recess appointment. See APPOINTMENT.

recession. (1929) A period characterized by a sharp slowdown in economic activity, declining employment, and a decrease in investment and consumer spending. Cf. DEPRESSION (1). — **recessionary,** *adj.*

recessus maris (ri-**ses**-əs **mair**-əs). [Latin] (17c) A going back or retreat of the sea. See RELICTION.

recharacterization, *n.* A court's determination that an insider's loan to an entity in liquidation (such as a corporation or partnership) should be treated as a capital contribution, not as a loan, thereby entitling the insider to only part of the liquidation proceeds payable after all the business's debts have been discharged. • Factors influencing this determination include the amount of capital initially available, the ability of the entity to obtain loans from outside sources, how long the entity has existed, the treatment of the loan in the entity's business records, and past treatment of similar transactions made to that entity by an insider. — **recharacterize,** *vb.*

Recht (rekt). [German "right"] **1.** Law generally. **2.** A body of law. **3.** A right or claim.

Rechtsbesitz (**rekts**-be-zitz). See *possession of a right* under POSSESSION.

Rechtsphilosophie (**rekts**-fə-los-ə-fee). See *ethical jurisprudence* under JURISPRUDENCE.

recidivate (ri-**sid**-ə-vayt), *vb.* (1932) To return to a habit of criminal behavior; to relapse into crime.

recidivation. *Archaic.* See RECIDIVISM.

recidivism (ri-**sid**-ə-viz-əm), *n.* (1886) A tendency to relapse into a habit of criminal activity or behavior. — Also termed (archaically) *recidivation.* — **recidivous, recidivist,** *adj.*

recidivist (ri-**sid**-ə-vist), *n.* (1880) **1.** Someone who has been convicted of multiple criminal offenses, usu. similar in nature; a repeat offender <proponents of prison reform argue that prisons don't cure the recidivist>. **2.** A criminal who, having been punished for illegal activities, resumes those activities after the punishment has been completed <released last month, he's already a recidivist>. — Also termed *habitual offender*; *habitual criminal*; *repeater*; *career criminal*; *prior and persistent offender*; (slang) *old lag.* See LAG, *n.* (1).

reciprocal (ri-**sip**-rə-kəl), *adj.* (16c) **1.** Directed by each toward the other or others; MUTUAL <reciprocal trusts>. **2.** BILATERAL <a reciprocal contract>. **3.** Corresponding; equivalent <reciprocal discovery>. — **reciprocate,** *vb.*

reciprocal contract. See *bilateral contract* under CONTRACT.

reciprocal dealing. A business arrangement in which a buyer having greater economic power than a seller agrees to buy something from the seller only if the seller buys something in return. • Reciprocal dealing usu. violates antitrust laws. — Also termed *reciprocal-dealing arrangement.* Cf. TYING ARRANGEMENT.

reciprocal discovery. 1. See DISCOVERY. **2.** See *reverse Jencks material* under JENCKS MATERIAL.

reciprocal exchange. An association whose members exchange contracts and pay premiums through an attorney-in-fact for the purpose of insuring themselves and each other. • A reciprocal exchange can consist of individuals, partnerships, trustees, or corporations, but the exchange itself is unincorporated. — Also termed *interinsurance exchange; reciprocal insurance exchange; reciprocal interinsurance exchange.* See *reciprocal insurance* under INSURANCE; EXCHANGE (5).

reciprocal insurance. See INSURANCE.

reciprocal insurance exchange. See RECIPROCAL EXCHANGE.

reciprocal interinsurance exchange. See RECIPROCAL EXCHANGE.

reciprocal negative easement. See EASEMENT.

reciprocal trade agreement. (1904) An agreement between two countries providing for the exchange of goods between them at lower tariffs and better terms than exist between one of the countries and other countries.

reciprocal trust. See TRUST (3).

reciprocal will. See *mutual will* under WILL.

reciprocity (res-ə-**pros**-i-tee). (18c) **1.** Mutual or bilateral action <the Arthurs stopped receiving social invitations from friends because of their lack of reciprocity>. **2.** The mutual concession of advantages or privileges for purposes of commercial or diplomatic relations <Texas and Louisiana grant reciprocity to each other's citizens in qualifying for in-state tuition rates>. — Also termed *mutuality of benefits; quid pro quo; equivalence of advantages.* **3.** *Intellectual property.* The recognition by one country of a foreign national's intellectual-property rights only if and only to the extent that the other country would recognize those same rights for the first country's citizens. • Reciprocity is the most restrictive approach to international intellectual-property law rights. Cf. NATIONAL TREATMENT; UNIVERSALITY.

> "It has become common when introducing new categories of rights for them to be granted on the basis of reciprocity. The advantages of reciprocity are twofold. First, reciprocity benefits rights owners by providing incentives for non-conforming countries to change their laws. Secondly, it saves users in one country (A) from paying royalties for foreign authors from countries that do not pay royalties to the authors of country A." Lionel Bently & Brad Sherman, *Intellectual Property Law* 101 (2001).

recital. (16c) **1.** An account or description of some fact or thing <the recital of the events leading up to the accident>. **2.** A preliminary statement in a contract or deed explaining the reasons for entering into it or the background of the transaction, or showing the existence of particular facts <the recitals in the settlement agreement should describe the underlying dispute>. • Traditionally, each recital begins with the word *whereas.* — Also termed (in sense 2) *whereas clause.* See PREFATORY-MATERIALS CANON. — **recite,** *vb.*

> "The parties may wish to begin the agreement with a statement of their intentions. Often they do this through recitals, which were traditionally introduced by 'whereas,' but can simply state the background without this formality." Scott J. Burnham, *Contract Drafting Guidebook* § 8.4, at 158 (2d ed. 1992).

▸ **introductory recital.** (*usu. pl.*) (1838) A recital explaining how and why the existing state of affairs is to be altered.

▸ **narrative recital.** (*usu. pl.*) (1839) A recital dealing with matters such as how the buyer and the seller came together.

▸ **particular recital.** (16c) A recital that states a fact definitely.

recite, *vb.* See READ ON.

reckless, *adj.* (bef. 12c) Characterized by the creation of a substantial and unjustifiable risk of harm to others and by a conscious (and sometimes deliberate) disregard for or indifference to that risk; heedless; rash. • Reckless conduct is much more than mere negligence: it is a gross deviation from what a reasonable person would do. See RECKLESSNESS; RECKLESSLY. Cf. CARELESS.

> "Intention cannot exist without foresight, but foresight can exist without intention. For a man may foresee the possible or even probable consequences of his conduct and yet not desire them to occur; none the less if he persists on his course he knowingly runs the risk of bringing about the unwished result. To describe this state of mind the word 'reckless' is the most appropriate. The words 'rash' and 'rashness' have also been used to indicate this same attitude." J.W. Cecil Turner, *Kenny's Outlines of Criminal Law* 28 (16th ed. 1952).

reckless disregard. See DISREGARD.

reckless driving. (1902) The criminal offense of operating a motor vehicle in a manner that shows conscious indifference to the safety of others.

reckless endangerment. (1968) The criminal offense of putting another person at substantial risk of death or serious injury. • This is a statutory, not a common-law, offense. See ENDANGERMENT.

reckless homicide. See HOMICIDE.

reckless indifference. See *deliberate indifference* under INDIFFERENCE.

reckless knowledge. See KNOWLEDGE (1).

recklessly, *adv.* (bef. 12c) In such a manner that the actor knew that there was a substantial and unjustifiable risk that the social harm the law was designed to prevent would occur and ignored this risk when engaging in the prohibited conduct. • Under the Model Penal Code, *recklessly* denotes the minimum level of culpability required for criminal liability when the statute does not specify the required mental state. See RECKLESS; RECKLESSNESS. Cf. CULPABILITY; MENS REA; *criminal negligence* (2) under NEGLIGENCE.

> "A person acts recklessly with respect to a material element of an offense when he consciously disregards a substantial and unjustifiable risk that the material element exists or will result from his conduct. The risk must be of such a nature and degree that, considering the nature and purpose of the actor's conduct and the circumstances known to him, its disregard involves a gross deviation from the standard of conduct that a law-abiding person would observe in the actor's situation." Model Penal Code § 2.02(2)(c).

reckless negligence. See *gross negligence* under NEGLIGENCE.

recklessness, *n.* (bef. 12c) **1.** Conduct whereby the actor does not desire harmful consequence but nonetheless foresees the possibility and consciously takes the risk. • Recklessness involves a greater degree of fault than negligence but a lesser degree of fault than intentional wrongdoing. **2.** The state of mind in which a person does not care about the consequences of his or her actions. — Also termed *heedlessness.* Cf. WANTONNESS.

> "The ordinary meaning of the word [*recklessness*] is a high degree of carelessness. It is the doing of something which in fact involves a grave risk to others, whether the doer realises it or not. The test is therefore objective and not subjective." R.F.V. Heuston, *Salmond on the Law of Torts* 194 (17th ed. 1977).

> "An abiding difficulty in discussing the legal meaning of recklessness is that the term has been given several

different shades of meaning by the courts over the years. In the law of manslaughter, 'reckless' was long regarded as the most appropriate adjective to express the degree of negligence needed for a conviction: in this sense, it meant a high degree of carelessness. In the late 1950s the courts adopted a different meaning of recklessness in the context of *mens rea*, referring to D's actual awareness of the risk of the prohibited consequence occurring: we shall call this 'common-law recklessness.' Controversy was introduced into this area in the early 1980s, when the House of Lords purported to broaden the meaning of recklessness so as to include those who failed to give thought to an obvious risk that the consequence would occur . . . ." Andrew Ashworth, *Principles of Criminal Law* 154 (1991).

reclaim, *vb.* (14c) **1.** To get back (money that one has paid) <they were entitled to reclaim some tax>. **2.** To get back (something lost or taken away) <reclaimed the title she had lost the year before>. **3.** To make (a desert, wetland, or other unusable land) suitable for development or farming <land reclaimed for a new mall>. **4.** To obtain useful products from (waste material) <they reclaimed old bricks for paving streets>. Cf. IRRECLAIMABLE.

reclamation (rek-lə-**may**-shən), *n.* (1848) **1.** The act or an instance of improving the value of economically useless land by physically changing the land, such as irrigating a desert. **2.** *Commercial law.* A seller's limited right to retrieve goods delivered to a buyer when the buyer is insolvent. UCC § 2-702(2). See STOPPAGE IN TRANSITU. **3.** The act or an instance of obtaining valuable materials from waste materials. — **reclaim,** *vb.*

reclusion (ri-**kloo**-zhən). (18c) *Civil law.* Incarceration as punishment for a crime; esp., solitary confinement or confinement at hard labor in a penitentiary.

recognition, *n.* (16c) **1.** Confirmation that an act done by another person was authorized. See RATIFICATION. **2.** The formal admission that a person, entity, or thing has a particular status; esp., a country's act in formally acknowledging the existence of another country or national government. **3.** *Parliamentary law.* The chair's acknowledgment that a member is entitled to the floor <the chair recognizes the delegate from Minnesota>. See PRECEDENCE (4).

"When any member desires to speak or deliver any matter to the house, that person should rise and respectfully address the presiding officer. When the presiding officer recognizes the member by calling the member by name or by indicating recognition, that person is entitled to the floor and may address the body or present a matter of business, but may not yield the floor to any other member." National Conference of State Legislatures, *Mason's Manual of Legislative Procedure* § 91, at 76–77 (2000).

4. *Tax.* The act or an instance of accounting for a taxpayer's realized gain or loss for the purpose of income-tax reporting. Cf. NONRECOGNITION PROVISION; REALIZATION (2). **5.** An employer's acknowledgment that a union has the right to act as a bargaining agent for employees. **6.** *Int'l law.* Official action by a country acknowledging, expressly or by implication, *de jure* or *de facto*, the existence of a government or a country, or a situation such as a change of territorial sovereignty.

"There is no such thing as a uniform type of recognition or non-recognition. The terminology of official communications and declarations is not very consistent: there may be '*de iure* recognition,' '*de facto* recognition,' 'full diplomatic recognition,' 'formal recognition,' and so forth. The term 'recognition' may be absent, taking the form instead of agreement to establish diplomatic relations or a congratulatory message on independence day. The typical act of recognition has two legal functions. First, the determination of statehood, a question of law: such individual determination may have evidential value. Secondly, a condition of the establishment of formal relations, including diplomatic relations and the conclusion of bilateral treaties: it is this second function which has been described by some as 'constitutive,' but it is not a condition of statehood. Since states are not legally required to make a public declaration of recognition nor to undertake optional relations such as the exchange of ambassadors, the expression of state intent involved is political in the sense of being voluntary. But it may also be political in a more obvious sense. An absence of recognition may not rest on any legal basis at all, there being no attempt to pass on the question of statehood as such. Non-recognition may simply be part of a general policy of disapproval and boycott. Recognition may be part of a policy of aggression involving the creation of a puppet state: the legal consequences here stem from the breaches of international law involved." James Crawford, *Brownlie's Principles of Public International Law* 147 (8th ed., 2012).

▸ **de facto recognition.** *Int'l law.* Actual recognition that is not officially extended.

▸ **de jure recognition.** *Int'l law.* Official recognition

▸ **diplomatic recognition.** *Int'l law.* A country's unilateral acknowledgment of an act by or the status of another country or the government in control of that country.

7. RULE OF RECOGNITION. — **recognize,** *vb.*

recognition clause. *Real estate.* A clause providing that, when a tract of land has been subdivided for development, the ultimate buyers of individual lots are protected if the developer defaults on the mortgage. • Such a clause is typically found in a blanket mortgage or a contract for deed.

recognition picketing. See *organizational picketing* under PICKETING.

recognition strike. See STRIKE (1).

recognitor (ri-**kog**-nə-tər), *n.* (15c) **1.** *Hist.* A member of a jury impaneled on an assize or inquest. See RECOGNITION (1), (2). **2.** *Rare.* RECOGNIZOR.

recognizance (ri-**kog**-nə-zənts). (14c) **1.** A bond or obligation, made in court, by which a person promises to perform some act or observe some condition, such as to appear when called, to pay a debt, or to keep the peace; specif., an in-court acknowledgment of an obligation in a penal sum, conditioned on the performance or nonperformance of a particular act. • Most commonly, a recognizance takes the form of a bail bond that guarantees an unjailed criminal defendant's return for a court date <the defendant was released on his own recognizance>. See RELEASE ON RECOGNIZANCE.

"Recognizances are aptly described as 'contracts made with the Crown in its judicial capacity.' A recognizance is a writing acknowledged by the party to it before a judge or officer having authority for the purpose, and enrolled in a court of record. It usually takes the form of a promise, with penalties for the breach of it, to keep the peace, to be of good behavior, or to appear at the assizes." William R. Anson, *Principles of the Law of Contract* 80–81 (Arthur L. Corbin ed., 3d Am. ed. 1919).

"A recognizance is an acknowledgment of an obligation in court by the recognizor binding him to make a certain payment subject to the condition that on the performance of a specified act the obligation shall be discharged." 1 Samuel Williston, *A Treatise on the Law of Contracts* § 6, at 18 (Walter H.E. Jaeger ed., 3d ed. 1957).

▸ **personal recognizance.** (18c) The release of a defendant in a criminal case in which the court takes the defendant's word that he or she will appear for a scheduled matter or when told to appear. • This type of release dispenses with the necessity of the person's posting money or having a surety sign a bond with the court. **2.** See *bail bond* under BOND (2).

recognized gain. See GAIN (3).

recognized loss. See LOSS.

recognized market. See MARKET.

recognizee (ri-kog-nə-**zee**). (16c) A person in whose favor a recognizance is made; one to whom someone is bound by a recognizance.

recognizor (ri-kog-nə-**zor**). (16c) Someone who is obligated under a recognizance; one who is bound by a recognizance. — Also termed *recognitor.*

> "A recognizance is an acknowledgment upon record of a former debt, and he who so acknowledges such debt to be due is termed the recognizor, and he to whom or for whose benefit he makes such acknowledgment is termed the recognizee." John Indermaur, *Principles of the Common Law* 8 (Edmund H. Bennett ed., 1st Am. ed. 1878).

recollection, *n.* (17c) **1.** The action of recalling something to the mind, esp. through conscious effort. **2.** Something recalled to the mind. See PAST RECOLLECTION RECORDED; PRESENT RECOLLECTION REFRESHED. — **recollect,** *vb.*

▸ **hypnotically induced recollection.** See *hypnotically refreshed testimony* under TESTIMONY.

▸ **hypnotically refreshed recollection.** See *hypnotically refreshed testimony* under TESTIMONY.

recombinant (ri-**kom**-bə-nənt), *adj.* (1940) *Patents.* Of, relating to, or describing the introduction of DNA from one living organism into another.

recombinant DNA technology. (1975) *Patents.* The science of mutating organisms by splicing sections of one organism's DNA onto that of another. — Abbr. rDNA.

recommence, *vb.* (15c) To begin (something) again after stopping. — **recommencement,** *n.*

recommendation. (15c) **1.** A specific piece of advice about what to do, esp. when given officially. **2.** A suggestion that someone should choose a particular thing or person that one thinks particularly good or meritorious. — **recommend,** *vb.*

recommit. (17c) *Parliamentary law.* To refer (a motion) back to a committee that has considered it. • The motion is called "recommit" rather than "re-refer" for the sake of euphony. See REFER. Cf. *re-refer* under REFER. — **recommit,** *n.*

recompensable. See COMPENSABLE.

recompensation. (17c) *Scots law.* In an action for debt, a plaintiff's allegation that money owed to a defendant has already been paid and should not be considered as a setoff against an award to the plaintiff.

recompense (**rek**-əm-pents), *n.* (15c) Repayment, compensation, or retribution for something, esp. an injury or loss. — **recompense,** *vb.*

reconciliation (rek-ən-sil-ee-**ay**-shən), *n.* (14c) **1.** Restoration of harmony between persons or things that had been in conflict <a reconciliation between the plaintiff and the defendant is unlikely even if the lawsuit settles before trial>. **2.** *Family law.* Voluntary resumption, after a separation, of full marital relations between spouses <the court dismissed the divorce petition after the parties' reconciliation>. Cf. CONDONATION (2). **3.** *Accounting.* An adjustment of accounts so that they agree, esp. by allowing for outstanding items <reconciliation of the checking account and the bank statement>. — **reconcile** (**rek**-ən-sɪl), *vb.*

reconciliation agreement. (1877) *Family law.* A contract between spouses who have had marital difficulties but who now wish to save the marital relationship, usu. by specifying certain economic actions that might ameliorate pressures on the marriage. • This type of agreement serves a limited purpose. In fact, many states have statutes prohibiting enforcement of contracts for domestic services, so if the agreement governs anything other than economic behavior, it may be unenforceable.

reconciliation statement. (1912) An accounting or financial statement in which discrepancies are adjusted.

reconduction, *n.* (1833) **1.** *Civil law.* The renewal of a lease. — Also termed *relocation.* See TACIT RELOCATION. **2.** *Int'l law.* The forcible return of aliens (esp. illegal aliens, destitute or diseased aliens, or alien criminals who have served their punishment) to their country of origin. — Also termed (in sense 2) *renvoi.* — **reconduct,** *vb.*

reconnaissance. (18c) The military or spying activity of sending people or aircraft to find out about another's operations, esp. the activities of an enemy.

reconnoiter (ree-kə-**noy**-tər), *vb.* (18c) **1.** To try to ascertain the position and size of an enemy's army, as by flying planes over land where the enemy's soldiers are. **2.** To gather information about a rival, an area, etc. — Also spelled *reconnoitre.*

reconsider, *vb.* (16c) To discuss or take up (a matter) again <legislators voted to reconsider the bill>. • Under parliamentary law, a motion to reconsider sets aside a certain vote already taken and restores the motion on which the vote is being reconsidered to its status immediately before the vote occurred. Making a motion to reconsider suspends a vote already taken until the assembly decides whether to reconsider it. — **reconsideration,** *n.*

> "The motion to reconsider is a distinctively American motion (it was first made the subject of a rule in the U. S. House of Representatives in 1802).
>
> "This motion was unknown to the early British Parliament. When Parliament (the British Congress) passed an act, that act then stood as the judgment of the body until another law or supplementary act was afterward passed explaining or amending the previous act — a slow-moving and time-consuming process in the estimation of American lawmakers.
>
> "Consequently, the American love for celerity invented the motion to reconsider, and cleverly made it a mere procedural or restoratory motion. As a result, the motion to reconsider now makes possible immediate reconsideration of a question, even on the same day." George Demeter, *Demeter's Manual of Parliamentary Law and Procedure* 154 (1969).

▸ **reconsider and enter on the minutes.** (1964) *Parliamentary law.* To make a motion to reconsider for the purpose of suspending a vote already taken and bringing it back up at the next meeting. — Also termed *reconsider and enter; reconsider and have it entered on the minutes.*

reconsignment. (16c) A change in the terms of a consignment while the goods are in transit. See CONSIGNMENT.

reconstitute, *vb.* (1842) To form (an organization, group, etc.) again in a different way.

reconstruct, *vb.* (18c) **1.** To build (something) again after destruction, damage, or impairment <the mission is to reconstruct the aircraft>. **2.** To produce a complete depiction or copy of (an event) by collecting all kinds of data relating to it <the police tried to reconstruct their fatal date from beginning to end>.

reconstruction. (16c) **1.** The act or process of rebuilding, re-creating, or reorganizing something <an expert in accident reconstruction>. See ACCIDENT RECONSTRUCTION. **2.** *Patents.* A rebuilding of a broken, worn-out, or otherwise inoperative patented article in such a way that a new article is created, thus resulting in an infringement <the replacement of the machine's essential parts was an infringing reconstruction rather than a permissible repair>. Cf. REPAIR DOCTRINE. **3.** (*often cap.*) The work that is done to repair damage to a city, country, industry, etc., esp. after a war; esp., the process by which the Southern states that had seceded during the Civil War were readmitted into the Union during the years following the war (i.e., from 1865 to 1877) <the 13th, 14th, and 15th Amendments to the U.S. Constitution are a lasting legacy of Reconstruction>.

reconstruction hearing. (1972) A trial court's hearing, usu. at the direction of an appellate court, to fill in gaps in the trial court's record.

recontinuance. (16c) *Hist.* **1.** Resumption or renewal. **2.** The recovery of an incorporeal hereditament that had been wrongfully deprived.

reconvention. (15c) *Civil law.* The act or process of making a counterclaim. See COUNTERCLAIM.

reconventional demand. See DEMAND (1).

reconventione (ree-kən-ven-shee-**oh**-nee). [Law Latin] *Hist.* By reconvention. See RECONVENTION.

reconversion. The notional or imaginary process by which an earlier constructive conversion (a change of personal into real property or vice versa) is annulled and the converted property restored to its original character. See *equitable conversion* under CONVERSION (1).

reconveyance, *n.* (16c) The restoration or return of something (esp. an estate or title) to a former owner or holder. See *release deed* under DEED. — **reconvey,** *vb.*

recopyrighting. (2008) **1.** The act of obtaining a new copyright for a revised work whose original copyright has not expired. **2.** The act of obtaining a new domestic copyright for a work in the public domain because it is still protected by the copyright laws of a foreign jurisdiction. *See Golan v. Holder,* 132 S.Ct. 873 (2012).

record, *n.* (13c) **1.** A documentary account of past events, usu. designed to memorialize those events. **2.** Information that is inscribed on a tangible medium or that, having been stored in an electronic or other medium, is retrievable in perceivable form. UCC § 1-201(b)(31). **3.** MINUTES (2). **4.** The official report of the proceedings in a case, including the filed papers, a verbatim transcript of the trial or hearing (if any), and tangible exhibits. — Also termed (in some jurisdictions) *clerk's record;* (BrE) *bundle.* See DOCKET (1).

▸ **defective record.** (18c) **1.** A trial record that fails to conform to requirements of appellate rules. **2.** A flawed real-estate title resulting from a defect on the property's record in the registry of deeds.

▸ **official record.** (18c) A legally recognized original document, usu. prepared or recorded by someone with authority, that establishes a fact.

▸ **public record.** (16c) A record that a governmental unit is required by law to keep, such as land deeds kept at a county courthouse. • Public records are generally open to view by the public. Cf. *public document* under DOCUMENT (2).

▸ **reporter's record.** (1876) In some jurisdictions, a trial transcript. — Also termed *stenographer's record.*

▸ **silent record.** (1881) *Criminal procedure.* A record that fails to disclose that a defendant voluntarily and knowingly entered a plea, waived a right to counsel, or took any other action affecting his or her rights.

▸ **stenographer's record.** See *reporter's record.*

record, *vb.* To deposit (an original or authentic official copy of a document) with an authority <she recorded the deed in the county property office>.

recorda (ri-**kor**-də). *Hist. English law.* In England, records that contained the judgments and pleadings in actions tried before the barons of the Exchequer. Cf. ORIGINALIA.

record agent. See INSURANCE AGENT.

recordal. See RECORDATION.

recordare (ree-kor-**dair**-ee), *n.* [Law Latin] See RECORDARI.

recordari (ree-kor-**dair**-ɪ). (17c) A writ to bring up for review, as a substitute for an appeal, a judgment of a justice of the peace or other court not of record. • Writs of recordari are most common in North Carolina but are used infrequently in other states. — Also spelled *recordare.*

recordari facias loquelam (ree-kor-**dair**-ɪ **fay**-shee-əs lə-**kwee**-ləm), *n.* [Law Latin "you cause the plaint to be recorded"] (17c) *Hist. English law.* In England, a writ by which a suit or plaint in replevin could be removed from a county court to a superior court (esp. to one of the courts of Westminster Hall). — Abbr. *re. fa. lo.* See PLAINT (1).

recordation (rek-ər-**day**-shən), *n.* (1809) The act or process of recording an instrument, such as a deed or mortgage, in a public registry. • Recordation generally perfects a person's interest in the property against later purchasers (including later mortgagees), but the effect of recordation depends on the type of recording act in effect. — Also termed *recordal.*

recordatur (ri-**kor**-də-tuur). (17c) *Hist.* An order to record the verdict returned in a nisi prius case.

record date. See DATE.

recorded delivery. See *certified mail* under MAIL.

recorded recollection. See PAST RECOLLECTION RECORDED.

recorder. (15c) **1.** *Hist.* A magistrate with criminal jurisdiction in some British cities or boroughs. **2.** A municipal judge with the criminal jurisdiction of a magistrate or a police judge and sometimes also with limited civil jurisdiction. **3.** A municipal or county officer who keeps public records such as deeds, liens, and judgments.

▸ **court recorder.** (18c) A court official who records court activities using electronic recording equipment, usu. for the purpose of preparing a verbatim transcript. Cf. COURT REPORTER (1).

▸ **recorder of deeds.** See *register of deeds* under REGISTER (2).

4. SECRETARY (3).

recorder's court. See COURT.

recording act. (1802) A statute that establishes the requirements for recording a deed or other property interest and the standards for determining priorities between persons claiming interests in the same property (usu. real property). • Recording acts — the three main types of which are the *notice statute*, the *race statute*, and the *race-notice statute* — are designed to protect bona fide purchasers from earlier unrecorded interests. — Also termed *recording statute*. See NOTICE STATUTE; RACE STATUTE; RACE-NOTICE STATUTE.

recording agent. See INSURANCE AGENT.

recording officer. See SECRETARY (3).

recording secretary. See SECRETARY (3).

recording statute. See RECORDING ACT.

record notice. See NOTICE (3).

recordo et processu mittendis. See DE RECORDO ET PROCESSU MITTENDIS.

record of decision. (1982) *Environmental law.* A public document, generated under CERCLA, describing a federal agency's decision regarding an environmental problem, identifying the remedies considered and which one is best, stating whether practical means to minimize or prevent environmental harms caused by the chosen remedy have been adopted, and summarizing a plan for monitoring and enforcing any measures required to mitigate environmental harm. — Abbr. ROD.

record on appeal. (1829) The record of a trial-court proceeding as presented to the appellate court for review. — Abbr. ROA. — Also termed *appellate record*. See RECORD (4).

record owner. See OWNER.

record title. See TITLE (2).

recordum (ri-**kor**-dəm). [Law Latin] *Hist.* A record, esp. a judicial one.

recoupment (ri-**koop**-mənt), *n.* (17c) **1.** The getting back or regaining of something, esp. expenses. **2.** The withholding, for equitable reasons, of all or part of something that is due. See EQUITABLE RECOUPMENT (1), (2). **3.** Reduction of a plaintiff's damages because of a demand by the defendant arising out of the same transaction. See EQUITABLE RECOUPMENT (3). Cf. SETOFF (2). **4.** The right of a defendant to have the plaintiff's claim reduced or eliminated because of the plaintiff's breach of contract or duty in the same transaction. **5.** An affirmative defense alleging such a breach. **6.** *Archaic.* A counterclaim arising out of the same transaction or occurrence as the one on which the original action is based. • In modern practice, the recoupment has been replaced by the compulsory counterclaim. — **recoup,** *vb.*

recourse (**ree**-kors *or* ri-**kors**). (14c) **1.** The act of seeking help or advice. **2.** Enforcement of, or a method for enforcing, a right. **3.** The right of a holder of a negotiable instrument to demand payment from the drawer or indorser if the instrument is dishonored. See WITH RECOURSE; WITHOUT RECOURSE. **4.** The right to repayment of a loan from the borrower's personal assets, not just from the collateral that secured the loan.

recourse loan. See LOAN.

recourse note. See NOTE (1).

recover, *vb.* (14c) **1.** To get back or regain in full or in equivalence <the landlord recovered higher operating costs by raising rent>. **2.** To obtain (relief) by judgment or other legal process <the plaintiff recovered punitive damages in the lawsuit>. **3.** To obtain (a judgment) in one's favor <the plaintiff recovered a judgment against the defendant>. **4.** To obtain damages or other relief; to succeed in a lawsuit or other legal proceeding <the defendant argued that the plaintiff should not be allowed to recover for his own negligence>.

recoverable, *adj.* (14c) Capable of being recovered, esp. as a matter of law <court costs and attorney's fees are recoverable under the statute>. Cf. IRRECOVERABLE. — **recoverability,** *n.*

recovered-memory syndrome. See REPRESSED-MEMORY SYNDROME.

recoveree. (16c) *Hist.* The party against whom a judgment is obtained in a common recovery. See COMMON RECOVERY.

recoveror. (17c) *Hist.* The demandant who obtains a judgment in a common recovery. — Also spelled *recoverer.* See COMMON RECOVERY.

recovery. (15c) **1.** The regaining or restoration of something lost or taken away. **2.** The obtainment of a right to something (esp. damages) by a judgment or decree. **3.** COMMON RECOVERY. **4.** An amount awarded in or collected from a judgment or decree.

▸ **double recovery.** (1813) **1.** A judgment that erroneously awards damages twice for the same loss, based on two different theories of recovery. **2.** Recovery by a party of more than the maximum recoverable loss that the party has sustained.

recrimination (ri-krim-i-**nay**-shən), *n.* (16c) **1.** Blame or criticism of someone for something that has happened. **2.** *Family law. Archaic.* In a divorce suit, a countercharge that the complainant has been guilty of an offense constituting a ground for divorce. • When both parties to the marriage have committed marital misconduct that would be grounds for divorce, neither may obtain a fault divorce. Recriminations are now virtually obsolete because of the prevalence of no-fault divorce. See COMPARATIVE RECTITUDE. Cf. COLLUSION (2); CONNIVANCE (2); CONDONATION (2). **3.** *Criminal law.* An accused person's counteraccusation against the accuser. • The accusation may be for the same or a different offense. — **recriminatory,** *adj.*

recross-examination. (1869) A second cross-examination, after redirect examination. — Often shortened to *recross.* See CROSS-EXAMINATION.

recruit (ri-**kroot**), *n.* **1.** A new member of an organization, team, or group of people, esp. as the result of formally joining. **2.** Someone who has recently enlisted in the armed forces.

recta gubernatio (**rek**-tə g[y]oo-bər-**nay**-shee-oh), *n.* [Latin "right government"] A government in which the highest power, however strong and unified, is neither arbitrary nor irresponsible and is derived from a law that is superior to itself. — Also termed *legitima gubernatio.*

rectification (rek-tə-fi-**kay**-shən), *n.* (18c) **1.** A court's equitable correction of a contractual term that is misstated; the judicial alteration of a written contract to make it conform to the true intention of the parties when, in its original form, it did not reflect this intention. • As an equitable remedy, the court alters the terms as written so as to express the true intention of the parties. The court might do this when the rent is wrongly recorded in a lease or when the area of land is incorrectly cited in a deed. **2.** A court's slight modification of words of a statute as a means of carrying out what the court is convinced must have been the legislative intent. • For example, courts engage in rectification when they read *and* as *or* or *shall* as *may*, as they frequently must do because of unfastidious drafting. See REFORMATION. — **rectify,** *vb.*

rectification of boundaries. (1892) *Hist.* An action to determine or correct the boundaries between two adjoining pieces of land.

rectification of register. (1859) *Hist.* A process by which a person whose name was wrongly entered in or omitted from a record can compel the recorder to correct the error.

rectitudo (rek-tə-t[y]**oo**-doh). [Law Latin] A right or legal due; a tribute or payment.

recto de advocatione. See DE RECTO DE ADVOCATIONE.

recto de rationabili parte. See DE RECTO DE RATIONABILI PARTE.

recto patens. See DE RECTO PATENS.

rector (**rek**-tər). (14c) **1.** *Eccles. law.* The spiritual head and presiding officer of a parish. — Also termed *parson.* Cf. VICAR.

▸ **impropriate rector.** (18c) A lay rector as opposed to a clerical rector.

▸ **rector sinecure** (sɪ-nee-**kyoor**-ee). (1858) A rector who does not have the cure of souls.

2. *Roman law.* A governor or ruler.

▸ ***rector provinciae*** (prə-**vin**-shee-ee). (17c) A governor of a province.

rectum (**rek**-təm). [Latin] **1.** Right. **2.** A trial or accusation.

rectus (**rek**-təs). [Latin "right"] *Hist.* (Of a line of descent) straight; direct. Cf. OBLIQUUS.

rectus in curia (**rek**-təs in **kyoor**-ee-ə), *adj.* [Latin "right in the court"] (17c) *Hist.* Free from charge or offense; competent to appear in court and entitled to the benefit of law. See LEGALIS HOMO.

recuperatio (ri-k[y]oo-pə-**ray**-shee-oh), *n.* [Latin "recovery"] *Hist.* Judicial restitution of something that has been wrongfully taken or denied.

recuperator (ri-k[y]oo-pə-**ray**-tor), *n.* [Latin "assessor"] (17c) *Roman law.* **1.** A member of a mixed body of commissioners, appointed by a convention between two states for the purpose of adjusting any claims or disputes that might arise between the members of those states. **2.** One of a bank of judges, instead of a single *judex*, appointed to hear civil cases that had a public-interest element. Pl. ***recuperatores*** (ri-k[y]oo-pə-rə-**tor**-eez).

recurrent, *adj.* (17c) Occurring or appearing several times; happening repeatedly.

recurrent nuisance. See NUISANCE.

recusable (ri-**kyoo**-zə-bəl), *adj.* (1863) **1.** (Of an obligation) arising from a party's voluntary act and that can be avoided. Cf. IRRECUSABLE. **2.** (Of a judge) capable of being disqualified from sitting on a case. **3.** (Of a fact) providing a basis for disqualifying a judge from sitting on a case.

recusal (ri-**kyoo**-zəl), *n.* (1949) Removal of oneself as judge or policy-maker in a particular matter, esp. because of a conflict of interest. — Also termed *recusation; recusement.* Cf. DISQUALIFICATION (2).

recusant (**rek**-yə-zənt *or* ri-**kyoo**-zənt), *adj.* (16c) Refusing to submit to an authority or comply with a command <a recusant witness>.

recusant (**rek**-yə-zənt *or* ri-**kyoo**-zənt), *n.* (16c) **1.** *Eccles. law.* A person (esp. a Roman Catholic) who refuses to attend the services of the established Church of England. **2.** Someone who refuses to submit to an authority or comply with a command.

recusatio judicis (reh-kyoo-**zay**-shee-oh **joo**-dish-is), *n.* [Latin] (17c) *Eccles. law.* The procedure and grounds by which a judge may be challenged and removed from hearing a case. • The grounds for disqualification traditionally include great friendship or enmity with a party, close kinship to a party, acceptance of a bribe, previously giving counsel to a party, or demonstrated ignorance of the law. A panel of three arbiters, chosen by the challenging party and the judge, decides whether the party's complaint has merit.

recusation (rek-yə-**zay**-shən). (16c) **1.** *Civil law.* An objection, exception, or appeal; esp., an objection alleging a judge's prejudice or conflict of interest. **2.** RECUSAL.

recuse (ri-**kyooz**), *vb.* (16c) **1.** To remove (oneself) as a judge in a particular case because of a disqualification, such as prejudice or conflict of interest <the judge recused herself from the trial>. **2.** To challenge or object to (a judge, expert, etc.) as being disqualified to serve in a case because of prejudice or a conflict of interest <the defendant filed a motion to recuse the trial judge>. — **recusal,** *n.*

recusement. See RECUSAL.

redaction (ri-**dak**-shən), *n.* (18c) **1.** The careful editing of a document, esp. to remove confidential references or offensive material. **2.** A revised or edited document. — **redactional,** *adj.* — **redact,** *vb.*

red-circle wage. See WAGE.

red-cow case. See WHITEHORSE CASE.

reddendo (ri-**den**-doh). (17c) *Scots law.* **1.** A clause in a charter specifying a duty, rent, or service due from a vassal to a superior. **2.** The duty or service specified in this clause; feu duty.

reddendo singula singulis (ri-**den**-doh **sing**-gyə-lə **sing**-gyə-lis). [Latin "by rendering each to each"] (17c) Assigning or distributing separate things to separate persons, or separate words to separate subjects. • This was used as a rule of construction designed to give effect to the intention of the parties who drafted the instrument. — Often shortened to *reddendo singula.* — Also termed *referendo singula singulis.* See DISTRIBUTIVE-PHRASING CANON.

reddendum (ri-**den**-dəm). [Latin "that must be given back or yielded"] (17c) A clause in a deed by which the grantor reserves some new thing (esp. rent) out of what had been previously granted.

reddidit se (**red**-ə-dit **see**). [Latin "he has rendered himself"] (17c) *Hist.* Someone who has personally appeared in order to discharge bail.

reddition (ri-**dish**-ən). (16c) *Hist.* An acknowledgment in court that one is not the owner of certain property being demanded, and that it in fact belongs to the demandant.

redditus. See REDITUS.

redeemable, *adj.* (1821) Able to be exchanged for money or goods.

redeemable bond. See BOND (3).

redeemable ground rent. See *ground rent* (1) under RENT (1).

redeemable security. See SECURITY (4).

redeemable stock. See STOCK.

redelivery. (15c) An act or instance of giving back or returning something; restitution.

redelivery bond. See *replevin bond* under BOND (2).

redemise, *n.* (18c) An act or instance of conveying or transferring back (an estate) already demised. See DEMISE. — **redemise,** *vb.*

redemption, *n.* (16c) **1.** The act or an instance of reclaiming or regaining possession by paying a specific price. **2.** *Bankruptcy.* A debtor's right to repurchase property from a buyer who obtained the property at a forced sale initiated by a creditor. **3.** *Securities.* The reacquisition of a security by the issuer. • Redemption usu. refers to the repurchase of a bond before maturity, but it may also refer to the repurchase of stock and mutual-fund shares. — Also termed (in reference to stock) *stock redemption; stock repurchase; share repurchase; stock buyback; minimum-holding buyback.* **4.** *Property.* The payment of a defaulted mortgage debt by a borrower who does not want to lose the property. — Also termed *dismortgage.* See EQUITY OF REDEMPTION. — **redeemable, redemptive, redemptional** *adj.* — **redeem,** *vb.*

▸ **statutory redemption.** (1851) The statutory right of a defaulting mortgagor to recover property, within a specified period, after a foreclosure or tax sale, by paying the outstanding debt or charges. • The purpose is to protect against the sale of property at a price far less than its value. See REDEMPTION PERIOD.

▸ **tax redemption.** (1867) A taxpayer's recovery of property taken for nonpayment of taxes, accomplished by paying the delinquent taxes and any interest, costs, and penalties.

redemption agreement. See STOCK-REDEMPTION AGREEMENT.

redemptioner. (18c) Someone who redeems; esp., one who redeems real property under the equity of redemption or the right of redemption. See EQUITY OF REDEMPTION; STATUTORY RIGHT OF REDEMPTION.

redemption period. The statutory period during which a defaulting mortgagor may recover property after a foreclosure or tax sale by paying the outstanding debt or charges.

redemption price. See PRICE.

redemptio operis (ri-**demp**-shee-oh **op**-ə-ris), *n.* [Latin "redemption of work"] *Civil law.* A contract in which a worker agrees to perform labor or services for a specified price. Cf. *locatio operarum* under LOCATIO.

redemptor (ri-**demp**-tər), *n. Roman law.* A contractor. See CONDUCTOR (1).

redeundo (ree-dee-**ən**-doh). [Latin] Returning; in returning; while returning.

redevance (ruu-də-**vahns**). [French] *Hist.* Dues payable by a tenant to the lord, not necessarily in money.

redevelopment. (1908) *Real estate.* Rehabilitation of an urban-residential or commercial section that is subject to blight or in decline, esp. by erecting new buildings or renovating the old ones, often with public financing or tax-increment financing. — **redevelop,** *vb.*

red herring. (1884) **1.** An irrelevant legal or factual issue, usu. intended to distract or mislead <law students should avoid discussing the red herrings that professors raise in exams>. **2.** See *preliminary prospectus* under PROSPECTUS.

red-herring prospectus. See *preliminary prospectus* under PROSPECTUS.

redhibere (red-hi-**beer**-ee), *vb.* [Latin] *Civil law.* **1.** To return (a defective purchase) to the seller. **2.** (Of a seller) to take back (a defective purchase).

redhibition (red-[h]i-**bish**-ən), *n.* (17c) *Civil law.* The voidance of a sale as the result of an action brought on account of some defect in a thing sold, on grounds that the defect renders the thing either useless or so imperfect that the buyer would not have originally purchased it. La. Civ. Code art. 2531. See *actio redhibitoria* under ACTIO. — **redhibitory** (red-**hib**-ə-tor-ee), *adj.*

redhibitory action. See ACTION (4).

redhibitory defect. (1810) *Civil law.* A fault or imperfection in something sold, as a result of which the buyer may return the item and demand back the purchase price. La. Civ. Code art. 2520. — Also termed *redhibitory vice.*

redimere (ri-**dim**-ə-ree), *vb.* [Latin] **1.** To buy back; repurchase. **2.** To obtain the release of by payment; ransom.

redirect examination. (1865) A second direct examination, after cross-examination, the scope ordinarily being limited to matters covered during cross-examination. — Often shortened to *redirect.* — Also termed (in England) *reexamination.* See DIRECT EXAMINATION.

rediscount, *n.* (1836) **1.** The act or process of discounting a negotiable instrument that has already been discounted, as by a bank. **2.** (*usu. pl.*) A negotiable instrument that has been discounted a second time. See DISCOUNT. — **rediscount,** *vb.*

rediscount rate. See INTEREST RATE.

redisseisin (ree-dis-**see**-zin), *n.* (16c) **1.** A disseisin by one who has already dispossessed the same person of the same estate. **2.** A writ to recover an estate that has been dispossessed by redisseisin. — Also spelled *redisseizin.* See DISSEISIN. — **redisseise** (ree-dis-**seez**), *vb.*

redisseisina. See DE REDISSEISINA.

redistribution. (1825) The act or process of distributing something again or anew <redistribution of wealth>.

redistrict, *vb.* (1843) To organize into new districts, esp. legislative ones; reapportion.

redistricting. See REAPPORTIONMENT.

reditus (**red**-ə-təs), *n.* [Latin "return"] A revenue or return; esp., rent. — Also spelled *redditus.*

▸ ***reditus albi*** (**al**-bɪ). [Latin "white return"] (1811) Rent payable in silver or other money.

▸ ***reditus capitales*** (kap-ə-**tay**-leez). [Latin "capital return"] (1802) Chief rent paid by a freeholder to go quit of all other services. See QUIT RENT.

▸ ***reditus nigri*** (**nig**-rɪ). [Latin "black return"] (1803) Rent payable in goods or labor rather than in money.

▸ ***reditus quieti*** (kwɪ-**ee**-tɪ). [Latin "quiet return"] See QUIT RENT.

▸ ***reditus siccus*** (**sik**-əs). [Latin "dry return"] (17c) Rent seck. See *rent seck* under RENT (2).

red-light abatement laws. (1914) An ordinance or statute intended to eliminate and prohibit sex-oriented businesses, usu. on grounds that they are public nuisances. • Brothels were once typically identified by a red light displayed in a window or in the front yard.

redlining, *n.* (1973) **1.** Credit discrimination (usu. unlawful discrimination) by an institution that refuses to provide loans or insurance on properties in areas that are considered to be poor financial risks or to the people who live in those areas. **2.** The process, usu. automated, of creating, for an existing document, an interim version that shows, through strike-outs and other typographical features, all deletions and insertions made in the most recent revision. — **redline,** *vb.*

redraft, *n.* (17c) A second negotiable instrument offered by the drawer after the first instrument has been dishonored. — **redraft,** *vb.*

redress (ri-**dres** *or* **ree**-dres), *n.* (14c) **1.** Relief; remedy <money damages, as opposed to equitable relief, is the only redress available>. **2.** A means of seeking relief or remedy <if the statute of limitations has run, the plaintiff is without redress>. — **redressable,** *adj.* — **redress** (ri-**dres**), *vb.*

▸ **penal redress.** (1874) A form of penal liability requiring full compensation of the injured person as an instrument for punishing the offender; compensation paid to the injured person for the full value of the loss (an amount that may far exceed the wrongdoer's benefit). See RESTITUTION.

▸ **restitutionary redress.** (1970) Money paid to one who has been injured, the amount being the pecuniary value of the benefit to the wrongdoer. See RESTITUTION.

red tape. (18c) Collectively, the bureaucratic rules that must be followed before official action can be taken even if the rules are unnecessary and irrelevant; esp., time-consuming rules and regulations of an excessive bureaucracy. • The phrase originally referred to the red ribbons that lawyers and government officials once used to tie their papers together.

redubber. (16c) *Hist.* Someone who buys stolen cloth and redyes it or makes it into something so that the cloth is unrecognizable.

reductio ad absurdum (ri-**dək**-shee-oh *or* ri-**dək**-tee-oh ad ab-**sər**-dəm). [Latin "reduction to the absurd"] (18c) In logic, disproof of an argument by showing that it leads to a ridiculous conclusion.

reduction. *Civil law.* An action by which a donation (either inter vivos or causa mortis) in excess of the disposable portion of the decedent's estate is lowered in order to produce a quantity of property sufficient to fulfill a legitime. La. Civ. Code arts. 1503 & 1505. See LEGITIME.

reduction improbation. See IMPROBATION.

reduction in force. See LAYOFF.

reductionism (ri-**dək**-shən-iz-əm), *n.* (1925) The act, an instance, or the habit of trying to explain complicated ideas or systems in unduly simplistic ways; oversimplification. — **reductionist,** *adj.*

reduction to practice. (1847) *Patents.* The embodiment of the concept of an invention, either by physical construction and operation or by filing a patent application with a disclosure adequate to teach a person reasonably skilled in the art how to make and work the invention without undue experimentation. • The date of reduction to practice is critical in determining priority between inventors competing for a patent on the same invention. — Abbr. RTP. See INVENTION.

▸ **actual reduction to practice.** (1896) The empirical demonstration that an invention performs its intended purpose and is therefore complete for patent purposes; the use of an idea or invention — as by testing it — to establish that the idea or invention will perform its intended purpose. *Brunswick Corp. v. U.S.*, 34 Fed. Cl. 532, 584 (1995).

▸ **constructive reduction to practice.** (1895) The documented demonstration that an invention will perform its intended purpose, contained in a patent application that provides enough detail that a person skilled in the art could make and test the invention; the filing of a patent application for an invention or design. *Brunswick Corp. v. U. S.*, 34 Fed. Cl. 532, 584 (1995).

▸ **vicarious reduction to practice.** (2004) A doctrine that treats one party's actual reduction to practice of an invention as the opposing (usu. complaining) party's actual reduction to practice. • In a two-party interference, proof of derivation is usu. sufficient; showing an actual reduction to practice is unnecessary. The doctrine is more important in a three-party interference.

redundancy, *n.* **1.** A situation in which something is unnecessary because something else similar or the same is already present; esp., a word or phrase that is superfluous because its sense is already contained in the sentence or passage. **2.** *English law.* A situation in which an employee is laid off from work because the employer no longer needs the employee. Cf. DOWNSIZING. — **redundant,** *adj.*

redundancy pay. See SEVERANCE PAY.

reenactment canon. (1941) **1.** In statutory construction, the principle that when reenacting a law, the legislature implicitly adopts well-settled judicial or administrative interpretations of the law. — Also termed *reenactment rule.* **2.** Loosely, PRIOR-CONSTRUCTION CANON.

reentry, *n.* (15c) **1.** The act or an instance of retaking possession of land by someone who formerly held the land and who reserved the right to retake it when the new holder let it go. **2.** A landlord's resumption of possession of leased premises upon the tenant's default under the lease. See POWER OF TERMINATION. **3.** The return and reintegration, often through special programs, of formerly incarcerated persons into their home communities upon their release from prison. — **reenter,** *vb.*

reentry court. (2000) A court that has been established to facilitate a prisoner's reintegration into the community toward the end of the prison sentence.

reeve (reev). (bef. 12c) *Hist. English law.* **1.** A ministerial officer of high rank having local jurisdiction; the chief magistrate of a hundred. • The reeve executed process, kept the peace, and enforced the law by holding court within the hundred. **2.** A minor officer serving the Crown at the hundred level; a bailiff or deputy-sheriff. **3.** An overseer of a manor, parish, or the like. — Also spelled *reve.* — Also termed *greve.*

"All the freeholders, unless relieved by special exemption, 'owed suit' at the hundred-moot, and the reeve of the hundred presided over it. In Anglo-Saxon times, the reeve was an independent official, and the hundred-moot was not a preliminary stage to the shire-moot at all. . . . But after the Conquest the hundred assembly, now called a court as all the others were, lost its importance very quickly. Pleas of land were taken from it, and its criminal jurisdiction limited to one of holding suspects in temporary detention. The reeve of the hundred became the deputy of the sheriff, and the chief purpose of holding the hundred court was to enable the sheriff to hold his *tourn* and to permit a 'view of frankpledge,' i.e., an inspection of the person who ought to belong to the frankpledge system." Max Radin, *Handbook of Anglo-American Legal History* 174-75 (1936).

▸ **borough reeve.** (bef. 12c) *Hist. English law.* In England, the head of an unincorporated municipality.

▸ **landreeve.** See LANDREEVE.

▸ **shire-reeve.** (15c) *English law.* The reeve of a shire, or county. • The *shire-reeve* was a forerunner of the sheriff. — Also spelled *shire-reve.* — Also termed *shire-gerefa.* See SHIRE.

reexamination, *n.* (17c) **1.** REDIRECT EXAMINATION <the attorney focused on the defendant's alibi during reexamination>. **2.** *Patents.* A proceeding by the U.S. Patent and Trademark Office to determine whether prior art renders one or more claims of an already-issued patent invalid; specif., an administrative procedure by which a party can seek review of a patent on the basis of prior art by the PTO <the alleged infringer, hoping to avoid liability, sought reexamination of the patent to narrow its scope>. • A reexamination may be sought by anyone, even the patentee or an anonymous informant, at any time during the life of a patent. Only patents and publications may be considered as prior art. 35 USCA §§ 301–305. — **reexamine,** *vb.*

▸ **ex parte reexamination.** (1974) A reexamination procedure, created in the early 1980s, that allows a challenger to initiate a review by producing prior art and responding to a patentee's statements regarding the new prior art, but that excludes the challenger from further participation in the examination process. • Ex parte reexamination does not employ discovery mechanisms and witnesses are not examined. The challenger also has no right to participate in an appeal. *See* 35 USCA §§ 302–307. Cf. *inter partes reexamination.*

▸ **inter partes reexamination.** (1976) A reexamination procedure, created in 1999, that allows a challenger to initiate a review by producing prior art, to respond to a patentee's statements regarding the new prior art, to address the patentee's responses to any office actions, and to request a hearing. • Both parties must serve each other with documents filed in the proceeding, but there is no discovery and witnesses are not examined. Either party may appeal the PTO's final decision on patentability. Inter partes reexamination is available to patents that issue from original applications that were filed on or after November 29, 1999. *See* 35 USCA §§ 311–318. Cf. *ex parte reexamination.*

reexamination certificate. (1981) *Patents.* A certificate issued by the U.S. Patent and Trademark Office at the conclusion of a reexamination proceeding, confirming that a patent has been reexamined and the claims have been found to be patentable, confirming that claims determined to be unpatentable have been canceled, or incorporating into the patent any amended or new claims determined to be patentable. 35 USCA § 307.

reexchange, *n.* (15c) **1.** A second or new exchange. **2.** The process of recovering the expenses that resulted from the dishonor of a bill of exchange in a foreign country. **3.** The expenses themselves.

reexecution. (18c) The equitable remedy by which a lost or destroyed deed or other instrument is replaced. • Equity compels the party or parties to execute a new deed or instrument if a claimant properly proves a right under one that has been lost or destroyed.

reexport, *n.* (18c) **1.** The act of exporting again something imported. **2.** A good or commodity that is exported again. — **reexport,** *vb.*

reextent. (17c) *Hist.* A second extent made upon complaint that the earlier extent was improper. See EXTENT.

re. fa. lo. *abbr.* RECORDARI FACIAS LOQUELAM.

refare (ri-**fair**-ee), *vb.* [Latin] To bereave; rob; take away.

refection. (15c) *Civil law.* Repair or restoration, as of a building.

refer. (17c) *Parliamentary law.* To send (a motion) to a committee for its consideration or investigation, with a view to a report from the committee back to the referring body. — Also termed *commit.* Cf. RECOMMIT; DISCHARGE (9).

▸ **re-refer.** (1915) (Of the U.S. House of Representatives) to refer a bill to a different committee from the one it was originally referred to. Cf. RECOMMIT.

referee. (17c) **1.** A master appointed by a court to assist with certain proceedings. • In some jurisdictions, referees take testimony before reporting to the court. See MASTER (2). **2.** See *judicial officer* (3) under OFFICER. **3.** Someone who judges an article or research idea before it is published or money is provided for it. **4.** Someone who stays close to the action on a sporting ground to ensure that the rules of the sport are followed during play.

▸ **referee in bankruptcy.** (1898) A federal judicial officer who administers bankruptcy proceedings. • Abolished by the Bankruptcy Reform Act of 1978, these referees were replaced by bankruptcy judges. — Also termed *register in bankruptcy.* See *bankruptcy judge* under JUDGE.

referee's deed. See DEED.

reference, *n.* (16c) **1.** The act of sending or directing to another for information, service, consideration, or decision; esp., the act of sending a case to a master or referee for information or decision.

▸ **general reference.** (18c) A court's reference of a case to a referee, usu. with all parties' consent, to decide all issues of fact and law. • The referee's decision stands as the judgment of the court.

▸ **special reference.** (1831) A court's reference of a case to a referee for decisions on specific questions of fact. • The special referee makes findings and reports them to the trial judge, who treats them as advisory only and not as binding decisions.

2. An order sending a case to a master or referee for information or decision. **3.** Mention or citation of one document or source in another document or source. **4.** *Patents.* Information — such as that contained in a publication, another patent, or another patent application — that a patent examiner considers to be anticipatory prior art or proof of unpredictability in the art that forms a basis for one or more of an applicant's claims to be rejected. See CITATION (4). **5.** The act of consulting something for information <for future reference>. **6.** An already-known fact, idea, event, etc. that helps one understand or make a judgment about another situation <school experience as a frame of reference>. **7.** A book, article, essay, etc. from which information has been obtained <a lengthy list of references>. — **refer,** *vb.*

reference case. See CASE (1).

reference committee. See *resolutions committee* under COMMITTEE (1).

reference statute. See STATUTE.

referendarius (ref-ə-ren-**dair**-ee-əs), *n.* [Law Latin] **1.** *Roman law.* An officer who received petitions to the emperor and who delivered answers to the petitioners. **2.** See APOCRISARIUS.

referendo singula singulis. See REDDENDO SINGULA SINGULIS.

referendum. (1847) **1.** The process of referring a state legislative act, a state constitutional amendment, or an important public issue to the people for final approval by popular vote. **2.** A vote taken by this method. **3.** *Int'l law.* An ambassador's request for instructions on subject matter that the ambassador does not have sufficient power to address. Pl. **referendums, referenda.**

▸ **recall referendum.** See *recall election* under ELECTION.

referential legislation. See LEGISLATION (3).

referral. (1927) The act or an instance of sending or directing to another for information, service, consideration, or decision <referral of the client to an employment-law specialist> <referral of the question to the board of directors>.

referral fee. See FEE (1).

referral sales contract. (1966) A dual agreement consisting of an agreement by the consumer to purchase goods or services (usu. at an inflated price) and an agreement by the seller to compensate the consumer for each customer (or potential customer) referred to the seller. — Also termed *referral sales agreement.* Cf. PYRAMID SCHEME.

refinancing, *n.* (1902) An exchange of an old debt for a new debt, as by negotiating a different interest rate or term or by repaying the existing loan with money acquired from a new loan. — **refinance,** *vb.*

reflation. (1932) The purposeful increasing of the amount of money being used in a country as a stimulus to trade.

reformatio in peius (ref-ər-**may**-shee-oh in **pee**-əs). [Latin] *Hist.* A change for the worse.

reformation (ref-ər-**may**-shən), *n.* (1829) An equitable remedy by which a court will modify a written agreement to reflect the actual intent of the parties, usu. to correct fraud or mutual mistake in the writing, such as an incomplete property description in a deed. • In cases of mutual mistake, the actual intended agreement must usu. be established by clear and convincing evidence. In cases of fraud, there must be clear evidence of what the agreement would have been but for the fraud. See RECTIFICATION. — **reform,** *vb.*

> "The standard explanation of reformation is that the parties had an actual agreement, and that the writing does not reflect that agreement. . . . If the parties made a mistake about the premises of their agreement — a mistake about some fact in the world outside their word-processing machines — reformation is not a solution. The court cannot reform the contract because it cannot know what the parties would have agreed to but for the mistake." Douglas Laycock, *Modern American Remedies* 613 (4th ed. 2010).

reformation condition. See *conditional bequest* under BEQUEST.

reformative punishment. See PUNISHMENT (1).

reformatory, *n.* (1834) A penal institution in which young offenders, esp. minors, are disciplined and trained or educated. — Also termed *reform school.*

Reform Bill. *English law.* One of several statutes enacted to enlarge the number of voters in elections for members of the House of Commons and to remove inequalities in representation. • The first of these statutes, passed in 1832, disenfranchised many so-called rotten boroughs, gave increased representation to the large cities, and increased the number of the holders of the country and borough franchise. The second such statute, passed in 1867, promoted a more democratic representation, as did the Franchise Bill in 1884. — Also termed *Ballot Act.*

reformer. (15c) Someone who works to improve a social, political, or legal system.

reformist, *adj.* (18c) Desiring to change systems or situations, esp. in politics.

reform school. See REFORMATORY.

refoulement (ri-**fowl**-mənt). [French] (1925) Expulsion or return of a refugee from one state to another. Cf. NONREFOULEMENT.

refreshing memory. See PRESENT RECOLLECTION REFRESHED.

refreshing recollection. See PRESENT RECOLLECTION REFRESHED.

refugee. (17c) Someone who flees or is expelled from a place, esp. because of political or religious persecution or war, and seeks haven elsewhere; specif., one who flees to a foreign country to escape real or perceived danger. Cf. *displaced person* under PERSON (1); EVACUEE; STATELESS PERSON.

▸ **climate refugee.** (2007) Someone who has been displaced as a result of severe weather events or climate change, such as flooding or drought.

▸ **economic refugee.** Someone who migrates to another country solely for better job prospects and a higher standard of living. • Although the person may apply for asylum, the desire to escape poverty or low pay does not qualify someone as a refugee. — Also termed *economic migrant.*

refugeeism. (1848) The quality, state, or condition of being a refugee.

refund, *n.* (18c) **1.** The return of money to a person who overpaid, such as a taxpayer who overestimated tax liability or whose employer withheld too much tax from earnings. **2.** The money returned to a person who overpaid. **3.** The act of refinancing, esp. by replacing outstanding securities with a new issue of securities. — **refund,** *vb.*

refund annuity. See ANNUITY.

refund-anticipation check. See CHECK.

refund-anticipation loan. See LOAN.

refunding. See FUNDING (2).

refunding bond. See BOND (2).

re-funding bond. See BOND (3).

refusal. (15c) **1.** The denial or rejection of something offered or demanded <the lawyer's refusal to answer questions was based on the attorney–client privilege>. **2.** An opportunity to accept or reject something before it is offered to others; the right or privilege of having this opportunity <she promised her friend the first refusal on her house>. See RIGHT OF FIRST REFUSAL.

refusal hearing. See HEARING.

refusal to deal. *Antitrust.* **1.**A company's decision not to do business with another company. • A business has the right to refuse to deal only if it is not accompanied by an illegal restraint of trade. **2.** The unjust rejection of a proposal or the restriction of the quantity or quality of a necessary good or service in order to ensure that the rejecting party can carry out an illegal act or achieve an improper purpose.

refusal to pay. See VEXATIOUS DELAY.

refus de justice (ruu-**foo** də zhoos-**tees**). See DENIAL OF JUSTICE.

refusenik, *n.* (1981) *Slang.* Someone who steadfastly declines to take part in something or to obey a law.

refutantia (ref-yoo-**tan**-shee-ə), *n.* [Law Latin] *Hist.* An acquittance or an acknowledgment renouncing all future claims.

refutation. The act of disproving or overthrowing an argument, opinion, doctrine, or theory by effective disputation or countervailing proof; esp., an advocate's demonstration of the invalidity or falsity of an adversary's contention.

▸ **anticipatory refutation.** A preemptive refutation of a contention before an adversary has made it.

> "Anticipatory refutation is essential for five reasons. First, any judge who thinks of these objections even before your opponent raises them will believe that you've overlooked the obvious problems with your argument. Second, at least with respect to the obvious objections, responding only after your opponent raises them makes it seem as though you are reluctant, rather than eager, to confront them. Third, by systematically demolishing counterarguments, you turn the tables and put your opponent on the defensive. Fourth, you seize the chance to introduce the opposing argument in your own terms and thus to establish the context for later discussion. Finally, you seem more even-handed and trustworthy." Antonin Scalia & Bryan A. Garner, *Making Your Case: The Art of Persuading Judges* 16 (2008).

refute, *vb.* (16c) **1.** To prove (a statement) to be false. **2.** To prove (a person) to be wrong. Cf. REBUT.

Reg. *abbr.* (1904) **1.** REGULATION. **2.** REGISTER.

reg, *n.* (*usu. pl.*) (1904) *Slang.* REGULATION (3) <review not only the tax code but also the accompanying regs>.

regale episcoporum (ri-**gay**-lee ə-pis-kə-**por**-əm). *Eccles. law.* The temporal rights and privileges of a bishop.

regalem habens dignitatem (ri-**gay**-ləm **hay**-benz dig-ni-**tay**-təm). [Law Latin] *Hist.* Having royal dignity.

regalia (ri-**gay**-lee-ə). (16c) **1.** *Hist.* Rights and privileges held by the Crown under feudal law. • *Regalia* is a shortened form of *jura regalia.*

▸ ***regalia majora*** (mə-**jor**-ə). [Latin "greater rights"] (18c) The Crown's greater rights; the Crown's dignity, power, and royal prerogatives, as distinguished from the Crown's rights to revenues.

▸ ***regalia minora*** (mi-**nor**-ə). [Latin "lesser rights"] (17c) The Crown's lesser rights; the Crown's lesser prerogatives (such as the rights of revenue), as distinguished from its royal prerogatives.

2. *Hist.* Feudal rights usu. associated with royalty, but held by the nobility.

> "Counties palatine are so called *a palatio*; because the owners thereof, the earl of Chester, the bishop of Durham, and the duke of Lancaster, had in those counties *jura regalia*, as fully as the king hath in his palace . . . ." 1 William Blackstone, *Commentaries on the Laws of England* 113 (1765).

3. Emblems of royal authority, such as a crown or scepter, given to the monarch at coronation. **4.** Loosely, finery or special dress, esp. caps and gowns worn at academic ceremonies.

regard, *n.* (14c) **1.** Attention, care, or consideration <without regard for the consequences>. **2.** *Hist. English law.* In England, an official inspection of a forest to determine whether any trespasses have been committed. **3.** *Hist. English law.* The office or position of a person appointed to make such an inspection.

regardant (ri-**gahr**-dənt), *adj.* (15c) *Hist. English law.* Attached or annexed to a particular manor <a villein regardant>. See VILLEIN.

regarder. (16c) An official who inspects a forest to determine whether any trespasses have been committed. — Also termed *regarder of the forest.*

reg. brev. *abbr.* REGISTRUM BREVIUM.

rege inconsulto (**ree**-jee in-kən-**səl**-toh). [Latin] (17c) *Hist.* A writ issued by a sovereign directing one or more judges not to proceed, until advised to do so, in a case that might prejudice the Crown.

regency. (15c) **1.** The office or jurisdiction of a regent or body of regents. **2.** A government or authority by regents. **3.** The period during which a regent or body of regents governs.

regent. (15c) **1.** Someone who exercises the ruling power in a kingdom during the minority, absence, or other disability of the sovereign. **2.** A governor or ruler. **3.** A member of the governing board of an academic institution, esp. a state university. **4.** *Eccles. law.* A master or professor of a college.

Reg. FD. See REGULATION FAIR DISCLOSURE.

reg. gen. *abbr.* REGULA GENERALIS.

Regiam Majestatem (**ree**-jee-əm maj-ə-**stay**-təm). [Latin "the (books of the) Royal Majesty"] *Scots law.* An ancient collection of Scottish laws, so called from its opening words. • The four-book collection is generally believed to be genuine, although its origins are widely disputed. It was partly copied from Glanville's treatise *De Legibus et Consuetudinibus Angliae,* as appears from the works' similarities and the fact that the Glanville treatise opens with the words *Regiam potestatem.* It was at one time believed to have been compiled by David I, but this supposition is unfounded. Still others believed that Edward I was responsible for the compilation as part of his efforts to take over Scotland and assimilate the laws of that country and England, but modern scholars reject this view. It was probably compiled by an unknown cleric shortly before 1320.

regicide (**rej**-ə-sɪd). (16c) **1.** The killing or murder of a monarch. **2.** Someone who kills or murders a monarch, esp. to whom one is subject. — **regicidal,** *adj.*

regime (rə-**zheem** *or* ray-**zheem**). (18c) **1.** A particular system of rules, regulations, or government <the community-property regime>. **2.** A particular administration or government, esp. an authoritarian one. — Also spelled *régime.*

▸ **international regime.** (1876) A set of norms of behavior and rules and policies that cover international issues and that facilitate substantive or procedural arrangements among countries.

▸ **legal regime.** (1850) A set of rules, policies, and norms of behavior that cover any legal issue and that facilitate substantive or procedural arrangements for deciding that issue.

▸ ***régime dotal*** (ray-**zheem** doh-**tahl**). *Hist. Civil law.* The right and power of a husband to administer his wife's dotal property, the property being returned to the wife when the marriage is dissolved by death or divorce. See *dotal property* under PROPERTY.

▸ ***régime en communauté*** (ray-**zheem** on koh-moo-noh-**tay** *or* kom-yoo-). *Hist. Civil law.* The community of property between husband and wife arising automatically upon their marriage, unless excluded by marriage contract.

regina (ri-**jɪ**-nə). (*usu. cap.*) (bef. 12c) **1.** A queen. **2.** The official title of a queen. **3.** In a monarchy ruled by a queen, the prosecution side in criminal proceedings. — Abbr. R. Cf. REX.

regio assensu (**ree**-jee-oh ə-**sen**-s[y]oo). [Latin] (17c) *Eccles. law.* A writ by which a sovereign assents to the election of a bishop.

regional fund. See MUTUAL FUND.

regionalism. (1871) Loyalty to a particular part of a country, usu. combined with a desire to see it become more politically independent.

regional securities exchange. See SECURITIES EXCHANGE.

regional stock exchange. See *regional securities exchange* under SECURITIES EXCHANGE.

register, *n.* (16c) **1.** An official list of the names of people, companies, etc.; esp., a book containing such a list. **2.** A governmental officer who keeps official records <each county employs a register of deeds and wills>. Cf. REGISTRAR.

▸ **electoral register.** (1817) An official list of the voters who may participate in an election.

▸ **probate register.** (1887) Someone who serves as the clerk of a probate court and, in some jurisdictions, as a quasi-judicial officer in probating estates.

▸ **register of deeds.** (18c) A public official who records deeds, mortgages, and other instruments affecting real property. — Also termed *registrar of deeds; recorder of deeds.*

▸ **register of land office.** (18c) *Hist.* A federal officer appointed for each federal land district to take charge of the local records and to administer the sale, preemption, or other disposition of public lands within the district.

▸ **register of wills.** (18c) A public official who records probated wills, issues letters testamentary and letters of administration, and serves generally as clerk of the probate court. • The register of wills exists only in some states.

3. See *probate judge* under JUDGE. **4.** A book in which all docket entries are kept for the various cases pending in a court. — Also termed (in sense 3) *register of actions.* **5.** *Eccles. law.* A record book of significant events occurring in a parish, including marriages, births, christenings, and burials. • Registers became required in England around 1530. — Abbr. Reg.

register, *vb.* (14c) **1.** To enter in a public registry <register a new car>. **2.** To enroll formally <five voters registered yesterday>. **3.** To make a record of <counsel registered three objections>. **4.** (Of a lawyer, party, or witness) to check in with the clerk of court before a judicial proceeding <please register at the clerk's office before entering the courtroom>. **5.** To file (a new security issue) with the Securities and Exchange Commission or a similar state agency <the company hopes to register its securities before the end of the year>. — Also termed *enregister.*

registered agent. See AGENT.

registered bond. 1. (18c) A governmental or corporate obligation to pay money, represented by a single certificate delivered to the creditor. • The obligation is registered in the holder's name on the books of the debtor. See BOND (2). **2.** (1865) A bond that only the holder of record may redeem, enjoy benefits from, or transfer to another. See BOND (3). Cf. *bearer bond.*

registered broker. See BROKER.

registered check. See CHECK.

registered corporation. See CORPORATION.

registered dealer. See DEALER.

registered form. (1898) The condition of a security that specifies a person entitled either to the security itself or to rights it evidences, the transfer of the security being registrable on books maintained for that purpose by or on behalf of an issuer as stated on the certificate.

registered mail. See MAIL.

registered mark. See *registered trademark* under TRADEMARK.

registered offering. See OFFERING.

registered office. See OFFICE.

registered organization. An organization created under state or federal law, for which the state or federal government must maintain a public record showing that the organization has been duly organized. UCC § 9-102(a)(71).

registered patent agent. See *patent agent* under AGENT.

registered post. See *certified mail* under MAIL.

registered public offering. See *registered offering* under OFFERING.

registered representative. See REPRESENTATIVE (1).

registered security. See SECURITY (4).

registered stock. See *registered security* under SECURITY (4).

registered tonnage. See REGISTER TONNAGE.

registered trademark. See TRADEMARK.

registered voter. See VOTER.

register in bankruptcy. See *referee in bankruptcy* under REFEREE.

register number. (*usu. cap.*) (1972) *Criminal law.* A numerical designation assigned by the Federal Bureau of Prisons to an inmate (e.g., 24452-44), the two-character suffix indicating the court where the inmate was sentenced (44 denoting the Eastern District of Missouri).

register of actions. See REGISTER (3).

Register of Copyrights. The federal official who is in charge of the U.S. Copyright Office, which issues regulations and processes applications for copyright registration. — Also termed (erroneously) *Registrar of Copyrights.*

register of deeds. See REGISTER (2).

register of land office. See REGISTER (2).

register of ships. (1801) *Maritime law.* A record kept by a customs collector containing the names and owners of commercial vessels and other key information about the vessels. • When a ship logs in with customs, it receives a certificate of registry. Cf. REGISTRY (5).

Register of the Treasury. An officer of the U.S. Treasury whose duty is to keep accounts of receipts and expenditures of public money, to record public debts, to preserve adjusted accounts with vouchers and certificates, to record warrants drawn on the Treasury, to sign and issue government securities, and to supervise the registry of vessels under federal law. 31 USCA § 161.

register of wills. See REGISTER (2).

register's court. See COURT.

register tonnage. (18c) The volume of a vessel available for commercial use, officially measured and entered in a record for purposes of taxation. — Also termed *registered tonnage.*

registrant. (1890) Someone who registers; esp., one who registers something for the purpose of securing a right or privilege granted by law upon official registration.

registrar. (17c) Someone who keeps official records; esp., a school official who maintains academic and enrollment records. Cf. REGISTER (1).

registrarii liber (rej-ə-**strair**-ee-ɪ **lɪ**-bər). [Latin] *Hist.* The register's book in chancery, containing all decrees. — Abbr. *reg. lib.*

registrarius (rej-ə-**strair**-ee-əs). [Latin] *Hist.* A registrar or register; a notary.

Registrar of Copyrights. See REGISTER OF COPYRIGHTS.

registrar of deeds. See *register of deeds* under REGISTER (2).

registration, *n.* (16c) **1.** The act of recording or enrolling <the county clerk handles registration of voters>.

▸ **criminal registration.** (1893) The requirement in some communities that any felon who spends any time in the community must register his or her name with the police. • Since the late 1980s, many states have adopted strict registration laws for convicted sex offenders. See MEGAN'S LAW.

▸ **special registration.** Voter registration for a particular election only.

2. *Securities.* The complete process of preparing to sell a newly issued security to the public <the security is currently in registration>. — **register,** *vb.*

▸ **shelf registration.** (1959) Registration with the SEC of securities to be sold over time, the purpose being to avoid the delays and market uncertainties of individual registration.

> "It is generally contemplated that the entire allotment of securities covered by a registered offering will be made available for purchase on the effective date. This is not always the case, however. For example, insiders, promoters or underwriters might receive securities directly from the issuer with an intent to resell at a later date. . . . [I]t may be desirable to get a debt offering all ready to go by filing the applicable registration statement but then wait for a propitious moment to finalize it and offer the securities for sale. These and other delayed offerings have led to what is known as shelf registration. In a shelf registration the registration statement is filed but the securities are put on the shelf until the manner and date of the offering are determined." 1 Thomas Lee Hazen, *Treatise on the Law of Securities Regulation* § 3.8, at 175–76 (3d ed. 1995).

3. See REGISTRY (2).

registration and community-notification law. See MEGAN'S LAW.

registration-based quorum. See QUORUM.

registration number. See LICENSE-PLATE NUMBER.

registration rights. *Securities.* A securities owner's entitlement to have the securities registered for public sale or to participate in a public sale or resale of securities by the issuer or by another securities owner.

▸ **demand registration rights.** (1971) A securities holder's right to force the issuing company to register all or part of the securities so that the holder can resell them.

▸ **piggyback registration rights.** (1971) A securities holder's option to require the issuing company to include all or part of the holder's securities in a registration of other securities of the same class when a third party, such as a lender, requests the registration.

registration statement. (1933) A document containing detailed information required by the SEC for the public sale of corporate securities. • The statement includes the prospectus to be supplied to prospective buyers. See PROSPECTUS.

registration system. (1918) *Patents.* A patent system in which an invention is given patent protection when it is registered, without being subjected to official examination. • The United States operated under a registration system from 1790 until 1793. Cf. EXAMINATION SYSTEM.

registrum brevium (ri-**jis**-trəm **bree**-vee-əm). [Latin] (1816) *Hist.* The register of writs. — Abbr. *reg. brev.*

registrum judicale (ri-**jis**-trəm joo-di-**kay**-lee). [Latin] *Hist.* The register of judicial writs. — Abbr. *reg. jud.*

registrum originale (ri-**jis**-trəm ə-rij-ə-**nay**-lee). [Latin] *Hist.* The register of original writs. — Abbr. *reg. orig.*

registry. 1. A place where information used by an organization is kept, esp. the official records and lists; esp., the legal government building where one can get married and where births and deaths are officially recorded. — Also termed *registry office.* **2.** The place where a truck, ship, etc. is officially registered <the registry of that car>. — Also termed *registration.* **3.** See *probate judge* under JUDGE. **4.** REGISTER (2). **5.** *Maritime law.* The list or record of ships subject to a particular country's maritime regulations. • A ship is listed under the nationality of the flag it flies. See CERTIFICATE OF REGISTRY. Cf. REGISTER OF SHIPS; *enrollment of vessels* under ENROLLMENT.

registry office. See REGISTRY (1).

reg. jud. *abbr.* REGISTRUM JUDICALE.

reg. lib. *abbr.* REGISTRARII LIBER.

regnal (**reg**-nəl), *adj.* (17c) Of, relating to, or involving a monarch's reign <the regnal years of Henry II are 1154–1159>.

regnal year. (17c) A year of a monarch's reign, marked from the date or anniversary of the monarch's accession. • Before 1962, British statutes were cited by the regnal years in which they were enacted. Since 1962, British statutes have been cited by calendar year rather than regnal year. (A table of British regnal years is listed in Appendix F of this book.)

regnant (**reg**-nənt), *adj.* (17c) Exercising rule, authority, or influence; reigning <a queen regnant>.

reg. orig. *abbr.* REGISTRUM ORIGINALE.

reg. pl. *abbr.* REGULA PLACITANDI.

regrant, *n.* (17c) The act or an instance of granting something again; the renewal of a grant (as of property). — **regrant,** *vb.*

regrating, *n.* (15c) *Hist.* **1.** The purchase of market commodities (esp. necessary provisions) for the purpose of reselling them in or near the same market at a higher price. **2.** The resale of commodities so purchased. • In England, regrating was a criminal offense. — **regrater,** *n.*— **regrate,** *vb.*

> "Regrating is described by [5 & 6 Edw. 6, ch. 14] to be the buying of corn, or other dead victual, in any market, and selling them again in the same market, or within four miles of the place. For this also enhances the price of the provisions, as every successive seller must have a successive profit." 4 William Blackstone, *Commentaries on the Laws of England* 158 (1769).

regress, *n.* (14c) **1.** The act or an instance of going or coming back; return or reentry <free entry, egress, and regress>. **2.** The right or liberty of going back; reentry. Cf. EGRESS; INGRESS. **3.** *Hist.* The right to repayment or compensation; recourse. — **regress** (ri-**gres**), *vb.*

regressive tax. See TAX.

regula (**reg**-yə-lə). [Latin] (bef. 12c) A rule.

▸ ***regula generalis*** (**reg**-yə-lə jen-ə-**ray**-lis). [Latin] (18c) A general rule, esp. of a court. — Abbr. *reg. gen.*; r.g. Pl. ***regulae generales.***

▸ ***regula placitandi*** (**reg**-yə-lə plas-ə-**tan**-dɪ). [Latin] *Hist.* A rule of pleading. — Abbr. *reg. pl.*

▸ ***regula regulans*** (**reg**-yə-lə **reg**-yə-lanz). [Law Latin] (17c) *Hist.* The governing rule.

regula Catoniana (**reg**-yə-lə kay-toh-nee-**ay**-nə *or* kə-toh-). [Latin "rule attributed to Cato"] (1869) *Roman law.* The principle that the lapse of time does not cure something void at the outset. • This principle, named for the Roman legal scholar Cato, was ordinarily used to set aside a bequest when the testator did not have the capacity to make the bequest.— Also termed *Catoniana regula.*

regular army. See ARMY.

regular course of business. See COURSE OF BUSINESS.

regular election. See *general election* (1) under ELECTION (3).

regular income. See INCOME.

regularize. (18c) **1.** To make (a situation that has existed for some time) legal or official. **2.** To establish a routine pattern for (some activity); to routinize.

regular life policy. See *life policy* under INSURANCE POLICY.

regular meeting. See MEETING.

regular process. See PROCESS (2).

regular session. See SESSION (1).

regular term. See TERM (5).

regular use. See USE (1).

regulate, *vb.* (15c) **1.** To control (an activity or process) esp. through the implementation of rules. **2.** To make (a machine or one's body) work at a regular speed, temperature, etc.

regulation, *n.* (17c) **1.** Control over something by rule or restriction <the federal regulation of the airline industry>.

▸ **self-regulation.** The process by which an identifiable group of people, such as licensed lawyers, govern or direct their own activities by rules; specif., an organization's or industry's control, oversight, or direction of itself according to rules and standards that it establishes. • Self-regulation is often subject to the oversight of various governmental agencies, such as the Securities Exchange Commission and the Commodities Futures Trading Commission.

2. BYLAW (1) <the CEO referred to the corporate regulation>. **3.** An official rule or order, having legal force, usu. issued by an administrative agency <Treasury regulations explain and interpret the Internal Revenue Code>. — Abbr. (*usu. cap.*) reg. — Also termed (in sense 3) *agency regulation*; *subordinate legislation*; *delegated legislation.* See MERIT REGULATION.

▸ **police regulation.** (18c) An ordinance, rule, or code, enacted by a municipality or county, that applies to the residents of a particular region or district. *See Dist. of Columbia v. John R. Thompson Co.*, 346 U.S. 100, 113, 73 S.Ct. 1007, 1014 (1953).

4. *European law.* An ordinary piece of legislation that applies directly to the member states of the European

Union without the requirement of the individual member states' implementing legislation. — **regulatory, regulable,** *adj.*

▸ **proposed regulation.** A draft administrative regulation that is circulated among interested parties for comment. — Abbr. prop. reg.

Regulation A. An SEC regulation that exempts stock offerings of up to $5 million from certain registration requirements.

Regulation D. An SEC regulation that exempts certain stock offerings (such as those offered by private sale) from registration under the Securities Act of 1933.

Regulation Fair Disclosure. An October 2000 SEC rule requiring companies to disclose material information to all investors at the same time. • The regulation is intended to prevent some investors from receiving advance information about earnings, mergers and acquisitions, product discoveries, changes in auditors, and any other information that a reasonable investor would consider in making an investment decision. — Often shortened to *Regulation FD*; *Reg. FD.*

Regulation FD. See REGULATION FAIR DISCLOSURE.

Regulation J. A Federal Reserve Board regulation that governs the collection of checks by and the transfer of funds through member banks.

Regulation Q. A Federal Reserve Board regulation that sets interest-rate ceilings and regulates advertising of interest on savings accounts. • The Banking Act of 1933 is the basis of this regulation, which applies to all commercial banks.

Regulation T. A Federal Reserve Board regulation that limits the amount of credit that a securities broker or dealer may extend to a customer, and that sets initial margin requirements and payment rules for securities transactions. • The credit limit and margin rules usu. require the customer to provide between 40 and 60% of the purchase price.

Regulation U. A Federal Reserve Board regulation that limits the amount of credit that a bank may extend to a customer who buys or carries securities on margin.

Regulation X. A HUD regulation that implements the provisions of the Real Estate Settlement Procedures Act. See REAL ESTATE SETTLEMENT PROCEDURES ACT.

Regulation Z. A Consumer Financial Protection Bureau regulation that implements the provisions of the federal Truth in Lending Act for persons who extend consumer credit. • The Dodd–Frank Act transferred most rulemaking authority over the matters covered by Regulation Z from the Federal Reserve Board to the Consumer Financial Protection Bureau. See CONSUMER CREDIT PROTECTION ACT; TRUTH IN LENDING ACT.

regulatory agency. See AGENCY (3).

regulatory offense. See OFFENSE (1).

regulatory-out clause. See FERC-OUT CLAUSE.

regulatory scheme. See SCHEME (1).

regulatory search. See *administrative search* under SEARCH (1).

regulatory taking. See TAKING (2).

rehab. See DRUG REHABILITATION.

rehabere facias seisinam. See HABERE FACIAS SEISINAM.

rehabilitation, *n.* (1940) **1.** *Criminal law.* The process of seeking to improve a criminal's character and outlook so that he or she can function in society without committing other crimes <rehabilitation is a traditional theory of criminal punishment, along with deterrence and retribution>. Cf. DETERRENCE; RETRIBUTION (1). **2.** *Evidence.* The restoration of a witness's credibility after the witness has been impeached <the inconsistencies were explained away during the prosecution's rehabilitation of the witness>. **3.** *Bankruptcy.* The process of reorganizing a debtor's financial affairs — under Chapter 11, 12, or 13 of the Bankruptcy Code — so that the debtor may continue to exist as a financial entity, with creditors satisfying their claims from the debtor's future earnings <the corporation's rehabilitation was successful>. — Also termed *debtor rehabilitation.* Cf. LIQUIDATION (4). — **rehabilitative,** *adj.* — **rehabilitate,** *vb.*

▸ **drug rehabilitation.** See DRUG REHABILITATION.

rehabilitative alimony. See ALIMONY (1).

rehearing. (17c) A court's second or subsequent hearing of a case, a motion, or an appeal, usu. to consider an alleged error or omission in the court's judgment or opinion <the appellant, dissatisfied with the appellate court's ruling, filed a motion for rehearing>. — Abbr. reh'g. Cf. REARGUMENT.

reh'g. *abbr.* REHEARING.

rei (**ree**-ɪ). *pl.* REUS.

reif (reef). (bef. 12c) *Scots law.* Robbery.

reification (ree-ə-fi-**kay**-shən), *n.* (1846) **1.** Mental conversion of an abstract concept into a material thing.

> "Nowhere has the process of reification been more pronounced than in American legal theory. One of the most discouraging spectacles for the historian of legal thought is the unselfconscious process by which one generation's legal theories, developed out of the exigencies of particular political and moral struggles, quickly come to be portrayed as universal truths good for all time. This process of reification draws deep sustenance from a religious and unhistorical American culture." Morton J. Horwitz, *The Transformation of American Law: 1870–1960* 271 (1992).

2. *Civil procedure.* Identification of the disputed thing in a nonpersonal action and attribution of an in-state situs to it for jurisdictional purposes. **3.** *Commercial law.* Embodiment of a right to payment in a writing (such as a negotiable instrument) so that a transfer of the writing also transfers the right. — **reify** (**ree**-ə-fɪ *or* **ray**-), *vb.*

rei interitus (**ree**-ɪ in-**ter**-ə-təs). [Latin] (18c) *Hist.* The destruction of a thing.

rei interventus (**ree**-ɪ in-tər-**ven**-təs), *n.* [Latin "things intervening"] (18c) Actions or efforts by one party to a contract with the consent of the other party, so that the one party has made a partial performance and the other cannot repudiate without being in breach.

reimbursement, *n.* (16c) **1.** Repayment. **2.** Indemnification. — **reimburse,** *vb.*

reimbursement alimony. See ALIMONY (1).

reincarcerate, *vb.* To imprison again; to incarcerate for a subsequent time. — **reincarceration,** *n.*

reincarnated mortgage. See *zombie mortgage* under MORTGAGE.

re infecta (ree in-**fek**-tə). [Latin] (17c) *Hist.* The thing not having been done; the performance having failed.

reinscription, *n.* (1845) *Civil law.* A second or renewed recordation of a mortgage or other title document. — **reinscribe,** *vb.*

reinstate, *vb.* (17c) To place again in a former state or position; to restore <the judge reinstated the judgment that had been vacated>. — **reinstatement,** *n.*

reinsurance. (18c) Insurance of all or part of one insurer's risk by a second insurer, who accepts the risk in exchange for a percentage of the original premium. — Also termed *reassurance.*

> "The term 'reinsurance' has been used by courts, attorneys, and textwriters with so little discrimination that much confusion has arisen as to what that term actually connotes. Thus, it has so often been used in connection with transferred risks, assumed risks, consolidations and mergers, excess insurance, and in other connections that it now lacks a clean-cut field of operation. Reinsurance, to an insurance lawyer, means one thing only — the ceding by one insurance company to another of all or a portion of its risks for a stipulated portion of the premium, in which the liability of the reinsurer is solely to the reinsured, which is the ceding company, and in which contract the ceding company retains all contact with the original insured, and handles all matters prior to and subsequent to loss." 13A John Alan Appleman & Jean Appleman, *Insurance Law and Practice* § 7681, at 479–80 (1976).

> "The laying off of risk by means of reinsurance traditionally serves three basic purposes. First, reinsurance can increase the capacity of the insurer to accept risk. The insurer may be enabled to take on larger individual risks, or a large number of smaller risks, or a combination of both. . . . Secondly, reinsurance can promote financial stability by ameliorating the adverse consequences of an unexpected accumulation of losses or of single catastrophic losses, because these will, at least in part, be absorbed by reinsurers. Thirdly, reinsurance can strengthen the solvency of an insurer from the point of view of any regulations under which the insurer must operate which provide for a minimum 'solvency margin,' generally expressed as a ratio of net premium income over capital and free reserves." P.T. O'Neill & J.W. Woloniecki, *The Law of Reinsurance in England and Bermuda* 4 (1998).

▸ **excess reinsurance.** (1896) Reinsurance in which a reinsurer assumes liability only for an amount of insurance that exceeds a specified sum. See *excess insurance* under INSURANCE.

▸ **facultative reinsurance.** (1944) Reinsurance of an individual risk at the option (the "faculty") of the reinsurer.

▸ **flat reinsurance.** (1896) Reinsurance (esp. of marine insurance) that cannot be canceled or modified.

▸ **treaty reinsurance.** (1948) Reinsurance under a broad agreement of all risks in a given class as soon as they are insured by the direct insurer.

reinsurance treaty. (1914) A contract of reinsurance (usu. long-term) covering different classes or lines of business of the reinsured (such as professional liability, property, etc.) and obligating the reinsurer in advance to accept the cession of covered risks. • Rather than receive individual notice of each specific claim covered, the treaty reinsurer will generally receive periodic reports providing basic information on the losses paid. — Also termed *treaty of reinsurance.* See BORDEREAU. Cf. FACULTATIVE CERTIFICATE.

reinsured, *n.* (1840) An insurer that transfers all or part of a risk it underwrites to a reinsurer, usu. along with a percentage of the original premium. — Also termed *cedent; cedant.*

reinsurer. (18c) An insurer that assumes all or part of a risk underwritten by another insurer, usu. in exchange for a percentage of the original premium.

reinterpret, *vb.* (17c) To read, think about, show, or perform (a text, subject, play, etc.) in a new way <the Court reinterpreted the Fourteenth Amendment to invalidate all state laws relating to homosexual sodomy> <Jacobi reinterpreted Richard III to make him more sympathetic>.

reinvest, *vb.* (18c) To use (money that one has earned from investments) in order to buy additional investments.

reinvested dividend. See DIVIDEND.

reinvestment. (17c) **1.** The addition of interest earned on a monetary investment to the principal sum. **2.** A second, additional, or repeated investment; esp., the application of dividends or other distributions toward the purchase of additional shares (as of a stock or a mutual fund).

reissuable error. (1988) *Patents.* A type of nondeceptive mistake in a patent that may be corrected in a reissue patent. 35 USCA § 252.

reissuable note. See NOTE (1).

reissue. 1. An abstractor's certificate attesting to the correctness of an abstract. • A reissue is an important precaution when the abstract comprises an original abstract brought down to a certain date and then several later continuations or extensions. **2.** See *reissue patent* under PATENT (3).

reissue patent. See PATENT (3).

rei suae providus (**ree**-ɪ s[y]**oo**-ee prə-**vɪ**-dəs). [Latin] (17c) *Hist.* Careful of one's property.

> "Interdiction, whether voluntary or judicial, can only be recalled or removed by an interlocutor of Court, and it affords a good ground on which to apply for the removal of the restraint imposed by interdiction that the interdicted has become *rei suae providus.*" John Trayner, *Trayner's Latin Maxims* 546–47 (4th ed. 1894).

REIT (reet). *abbr.* (1961) REAL-ESTATE INVESTMENT TRUST.

reject, assume or. See ASSUME OR REJECT.

rejecting, *n.* A parent's or caregiver's pattern of refusing to acknowledge a child's worth or legitimate needs. Cf. ISOLATING; IGNORING.

rejection. (16c) **1.** A refusal to accept a contractual offer. **2.** A refusal to accept tendered goods as contractual performance. • Under the UCC, a buyer's rejection of nonconforming goods must be made within a reasonable time after tender or delivery, and notice of the rejection must be given to the seller. Cf. REPUDIATION (2); RESCISSION; REVOCATION (2). **3.** *Parliamentary law.* Failure of adoption or ratification. See LOST (3). **4.** *Patents.* A patent examiner's finding in an office action that a claim in an application is unpatentable. Cf. OBJECTION (4); RESTRICTION (4). — **reject,** *vb.*

▸ **aggregation rejection.** (1958) Rejection of a patent claim on the ground that it is a list of unrelated elements that, taken together, do not assert a claim.

▸ **alternativeness rejection.** (2004) Rejection of a patent claim on the ground that it seeks a broad monopoly on the invention as disclosed and on other unspecified variations. • For example, a claim using a phrase such as "and similar materials" would probably be too broad to be allowed.

▸ **duplicate-claiming rejection.** (2009) The nonart rejection of a patent claim because it is not substantially different from another claim.

▸ **exhausted-combination rejection.** See *old-combination rejection.*

▸ **failure-to-disclose-best-mode rejection.** (2004) Rejection of a patent application on the ground that the inventor has not disclosed the best way to use the invention. • To warrant rejection, the examiner must find deliberate concealment or a description so poorly drafted as to amount to concealment.

▸ **final rejection.** A patent examiner's finding, in a second or subsequent office action, that a claim in an application is unpatentable on the merits. • A final rejection is made in the final office action. Despite the misleading name, a final rejection need not end the prosecution. The rejection can be appealed, or the application can be reexamined or continued in another application. A rejection may also be appealed to the Board of Patent Appeals and Interferences. A decision of that Board may be reviewed by the U.S. District Court for the District of Columbia or appealed to the U.S. Court of Appeals for the Federal Circuit. 35 USCA §§ 141–145.

▸ **formal rejection.** Rejection of a patent claim because of an error in format rather than substance. • A formal rejection is actually an objection rather than a rejection, since it requires no substantive change in the claim. — Also termed *nonart rejection.*

▸ **functional rejection.** (1984) Rejection of a patent claim on the grounds that it broadly claims a function but does not disclose enough structure to account for achieving that function. Cf. FUNCTIONAL LIMITATION.

▸ **inaccuracy rejection.** (2009) Rejection of a patent claim on the ground that it is not consistent with the description.

▸ **incompleteness rejection.** (2000) Rejection of a patent application on the ground that an element of the device or a step in the process has been left out.

▸ **interference-estoppel rejection.** (1967) Rejection of a patent claim on the ground that the applicant failed to bring the claim into a previous interference contest where its priority could have been determined.

▸ **judicially-created-double-patenting rejection.** (2001) Rejection of a patent application on the ground that the invention is an obvious variation of another patented invention by the same inventor. — Also termed *obviousness-type double-patenting rejection.*

▸ **lack-of-antecedent-basis rejection.** (2001) Rejection of a patent application on the ground that a reference either in the specification or in the claim is missing.

▸ **lack-of-enablement rejection.** See *nonenablement rejection.*

▸ **lack-of-utility rejection.** (1962) Rejection of a patent claim on the ground that the invention is inoperative, frivolous, fraudulent, or against the public interest. • The classic examples are perpetual-motion machines (inoperative), cures for the common cold (frivolous because believed impossible, and also probably fraudulent), and gambling devices (formerly seen as against the public interest).

▸ **new-matter rejection.** (1960) Rejection of a patent claim on the ground that an amendment contains new matter.

▸ **nonart rejection.** See *formal rejection.*

▸ **nonenablement rejection.** (1974) Rejection of a patent application claim on the ground that its specification does not teach enough to enable a person skilled in the art to make and use the invention. — Also termed *lack-of-enablement rejection.*

▸ **obviousness-type double-patenting rejection.** See *judicially created double-patenting rejection.*

▸ **old-combination rejection.** (1953) Rejection of a patent claim on the ground that, despite the fact that one or more elements perform in a different way, all the elements perform the same function as a previously patented invention. • The improved element may be patentable, but the combination may not be. — Also termed *exhausted-combination rejection.*

▸ **prolixity rejection.** (2004) Rejection of a patent application on the ground that the language is so wordy and tedious that it tends more to hide than to disclose the invention.

▸ **rejection on issues of interference.** (2004) Rejection of a patent claim on the ground that the applicant has lost a final judgment of priority regarding the claim in an interference contest.

▸ **same-invention double patenting rejection.** See *statutory double patenting rejection.*

▸ **Section 101 rejection.** (1965) Rejection of a patent application on the ground that it is based on nonstatutory subject matter. 35 USCA § 101.

▸ **Section 102 rejection.** (1965) Rejection of a patent application for lack of novelty. 35 USCA § 102.

▸ **Section 103 rejection.** (1965) Rejection of a patent application for obviousness. 35 USCA § 103.

▸ **Section 112 rejection.** See *vague-and-indefinite rejection.*

▸ **shotgun rejection.** (1962) *Slang.* Denial of all or almost all claims in a patent application by the U.S. Patent and Trademark Office, esp. in the first office action.

▸ **statutory double patenting rejection.** (2002) Rejection of a patent application on the ground that the invention is the same subject matter as an already-patented invention by the same inventor. • This rejection is based on 35 USCA § 101. — Also termed *same-invention double patenting rejection.*

▸ **undue-breadth rejection.** (1962) Rejection of a patent claim on the ground that it seeks a patent monopoly on more than the invention. • For instance, a functional claim is too broad if it purports to include every other possible way of accomplishing that function. A claim on a chemical is more likely to be rejected for undue breadth than a claim on a machine, because future discoveries are less predictable.

▸ **undue-multiplicity-of-claims rejection.** (2004) Rejection of a patent application on the ground that it makes an unreasonable number of claims. See AGGREGATION OF CLAIMS.

▸ **vague-and-indefinite rejection.** (1966) Rejection of a patent claim on the ground that a person of ordinary skill in the art could not clearly understand it. • For example, terms used in more than one sense could make the meaning unclear. — Also termed *Section 112 rejection.*

rejoin, *vb.* (15c) **1.** *Archaic.* To answer, as the defendant to a plaintiff's replication. **2.** *Archaic.* To answer to a reply. **3.** To say as an answer or rejoinder. **4.** To reunite (two or more broken pieces, etc.) after separation. **5.** To go back to a group of people, organization, etc. that one was with before.

rejoinder, *n.* (15c) **1.** *Common-law pleading.* The defendant's answer to the plaintiff's reply (or replication). See PLEADING (quot.). **2.** Any answer to a reply. **3.** A retort; a sharp or rude reply.

> "REJOYNDER, in Law, signifies an Answer or Exception to a Replication; for first the Defendant puts in an Answer to the Plaintiff's Bill, which is something called, *An Exception*, the Plaintiff's Answer to that is called a *Rejoynder*, especially in Chancery. 'Tis by the Civilians called Duplicatio." John Harris, *Lexicon Technicum: Or, an Universal English Dictionary of Arts and Sciences* (1704) (s.v. *rejoynder*).

related, *adj.* **1.** Connected in some way; having relationship to or with something else <a closely related subject>. **2.** Connected by blood or marriage; allied by kinship, esp. by consanguinity <Are the two of you related?>. **3.** (Of plants, animals, languages, etc.) belonging to the same group <all the Indo-European languages are related>.

related good. (1935) *Trademarks.* A good that infringes a trademark because it appears to come from the same source as the marked good, despite not competing with the marked good. • For example, a cutting tool named "McKnife" might infringe the "McDonald's" trademark as a related good.

related proceeding. *Bankruptcy.* A proceeding that involves a claim that will affect the administration of the debtor's estate (such as a tort action between the debtor and a third party), but that does not arise under bankruptcy law and could be adjudicated in a state court. • A related proceeding must be adjudicated in federal district court unless the parties consent to bankruptcy-court jurisdiction or unless the district court refers the matter to the bankruptcy court or to state court. — Also termed *noncore proceeding.* Cf. CORE PROCEEDING (1).

related right. See NEIGHBORING RIGHT.

related-statutes canon. The doctrine that statutes *in pari materia* are to be interpreted together, as though they were one law. See IN PARI MATERIA (1).

relation. See RELATIVE.

relational contract theory. See ESSENTIAL CONTRACT THEORY.

relation back, *n.* (18c) **1.** The doctrine that an act done at a later time is, under certain circumstances, treated as though it occurred at an earlier time. • In federal civil procedure, an amended pleading may relate back, for purposes of the statute of limitations, to the time when the original pleading was filed. Fed. R. Civ. P. 15(c). **2.** A judicial application of that doctrine. — Also termed *doctrine of relation back.* Cf. NUNC PRO TUNC. — **relate back,** *vb.*

relationship. (18c) **1.** The way in which two people or two groups feel about each other and behave toward each other <the close relationship between the American and British peoples>. **2.** The way in which someone is related to a family member <the relationship between brother and sister>. **3.** A situation in which two people spend time together or live together and have romantic or sexual feelings for each other <they have been in a relationship for six months> **4.** The nature of the association between two or more people; esp., a legally recognized association that makes a difference in the participants' legal rights and duties of care.

▸ **attorney–client relationship.** (1930) The formal legal representation of a person by a lawyer. • An attorney–client relationship may be found, for disciplinary purposes, without any formal agreement.

▸ **confidential relationship.** (18c) **1.** See FIDUCIARY RELATIONSHIP. **2.** *Trade secrets.* A relationship in which one person has a duty to the other not to disclose proprietary information. • A confidential relationship can be expressly established, as by the terms of an employment contract. It can also be implied when one person knows or should know that the information is confidential, and the other person reasonably believes that the first person has consented to keep the information confidential. A confidential relationship might be implied, for instance, between two people negotiating the sale of a business.

▸ **doctor–patient relationship.** (1936) The association between a medical provider and one who is being diagnosed or treated. • The relationship imposes a duty on the doctor to ensure that the patient gives informed consent for treatment.

▸ **employer–employee relationship.** (1921) The association between a person employed to perform services in the affairs of another, who in turn has the right to control the person's physical conduct in the course of that service. • At common law, the relationship was termed "master-servant." That term is still used often, but "employer–employee" dominates in modern legal usage.

▸ **fiducial relationship.** See *trust relationship.*

▸ **fiduciary relationship.** See FIDUCIARY RELATIONSHIP.

▸ **marital relationship.** (1870) The relationship between spouses, including the legal rights and duties of each person.

▸ **master–servant relationship.** (1917) The association between one in authority and a subordinate, esp. between an employer and an employee. • At common law, this term also designated the husband–wife relationship for purposes of analyzing loss of consortium, but that usage is now obsolete. — Also termed *employer-employee relationship.* See MASTER AND SERVANT.

▸ **parent–child relationship.** (1921) The association between an adult and a minor in the adult's care, esp. an offspring or an adoptee. • The relationship imposes a high duty of care on the adult, including the duties to support, to rescue, to supervise and control, and to educate.

▸ **professional relationship.** (1853) An association that involves one person's reliance on the other person's specialized training. • Examples include one's relationship with a lawyer, doctor, insurer, banker, and the like.

▸ **special relationship.** A nonfiduciary relationship having an element of trust, arising esp. when one person trusts another to exercise a reasonable degree of care and the other knows or ought to know about the reliance. Cf. FIDUCIARY RELATIONSHIP.

▸ **trust relationship.** (1868) An association based on one person's reliance on the other person's specialized training. — Also termed *fiducial relationship.*

relationship rape. See RAPE (2).

relative, *n.* (14c) A person connected with another by blood or affinity; a person who is kin with another. — Also termed *relation; kinsman.* Cf. NEXT OF KIN (1).

▸ **blood relative.** (1863) Someone who shares an ancestor with another.

▸ **collateral relative.** (18c) A relative who is not in the direct line of descent, such as a cousin.

▸ **relative by affinity.** (1821) Someone who is related solely as the result of a marriage and not by blood or adoption. • A person is a relative by affinity (1) to any blood or adopted relative of his or her spouse, and (2) to any spouse of his or her blood and adopted relatives. Based on the theory that marriage makes two people one, the relatives of each spouse become the other spouse's relatives by affinity. See AFFINITY (2), (3). Cf. CONSANGUINITY.

▸ **relative of the half blood.** (1838) A collateral relative who shares one common ancestor. • A half brother, for example, is a relative of the half blood. See *half blood* under BLOOD.

relative confession. See CONFESSION (1).

relative-convenience doctrine. (2009) The principle that an injunction or other equitable relief may be denied if granting it would cause one party great inconvenience but denying it would cause the other party little or no inconvenience.

relative fact. See FACT.

relative nullity. See NULLITY.

relative power. See POWER (5).

relative-responsibility statute. (1949) A law requiring adult children to support or provide basic necessities for their indigent elderly parents.

relative right. See RIGHT.

relative simulated contract. See CONTRACT.

relator. (17c) **1.** The real party in interest in whose name a state or an attorney general brings a lawsuit. See EX REL. **2.** The applicant for a writ, esp. a writ of mandamus, prohibition, or quo warranto. **3.** Someone who furnishes information on which a civil or criminal case is based; an informer. **4.** A habeas corpus petitioner.

relatrix (ri-**lay**-triks). (1832) *Archaic.* A female relator.

relaxatio (ree-lak-**say**-shee-oh). [Law Latin] *Hist.* An instrument by which one relinquishes a right or claim to another; a release.

release, *n.* (14c) **1.** Liberation from an obligation, duty, or demand; the act of giving up a right or claim to the person against whom it could have been enforced <the employee asked for a release from the noncompete agreement>. — Also termed *discharge; surrender.* **2.** The relinquishment or concession of a right, title, or claim <Benson's effective release of the claim against Thompson's estate precluded his filing a lawsuit>. **3.** A written discharge, acquittance, or receipt; specif., a writing — either under seal or supported by sufficient consideration — stating that one or more of the worker's contractual or compensatory rights are discharged <Jones signed the release before accepting the cash from Hawkins>. • Beneficiaries of an estate are routinely required to sign a release discharging the estate from further liability before the executor or administrator distributes the property. **4.** A written authorization or permission for publication <the newspaper obtained a release from the witness before printing his picture on the front page>. **5.** The act of conveying an estate or right to another, or of legally disposing of it <the release of the easement on February 14>. **6.** A deed or document effecting a conveyance <the legal description in the release was defective>. See *deed of release* under DEED. **7.** The action of freeing or the fact of being freed from restraint or confinement <he became a model citizen after his release from prison>. **8.** A document giving formal discharge from custody <after the sheriff signed the release, the prisoner was free to go>. — **release,** *vb.*

▸ **conditional release.** (18c) **1.** A discharge from an obligation based on some condition, the failure of which defeats the release. **2.** An early discharge of a prison inmate, who is then subject to the rules and regulations of parole.

▸ **full and final release.** See *general release.*

▸ **general release.** (16c) **1.** A broad release of legal claims that is not limited to a particular claim or set of claims, such as those at issue in a pending or contemplated lawsuit, but instead covers any actual or potential claim by the releasing party against the released party based on any transaction or occurrence before the release. **2.** The document evidencing such a discharge. — Also termed *liability release; legal release; full and final release.*

▸ **legal release.** See *general release.*

▸ **liability release.** See *general release.*

▸ **limited release.** A release of legal claims that is limited by its terms to a particular claim or set of claims, usu. the claim or claims that are the subject of a civil action.

▸ **marginal release.** (1883) *Property.* An entry made in the margin of a property record by the recorder of deeds to show that a claim against the property has been satisfied.

▸ **mutual release.** (17c) A simultaneous exchange of releases of legal claims held by two or more parties against each other.

▸ **partial release.** (1837) A release of a portion of a creditor's claims against property; esp., a mortgagee's release of specified parcels covered by a blanket mortgage.

▸ ***Pierringer* release.** (1976) A release that allows a defendant in a negligence suit to settle with the plaintiff for a share of the damages and insulates the settling defendant against contribution claims by nonsettling defendants. • This type of release was first described in *Pierringer v. Hoger,* 124 N.W.2d 106, 110–11 (Wis. 1963). It is used in some jurisdictions that do not have contribution statutes. — Also spelled (incorrectly) *Perringer release.*

▸ **study release.** (1970) A program that allows a prisoner to be released for a few hours at a time to attend classes at a nearby college or technical institution. — Also termed *study furlough*.

▸ **supervised release.** (1929) *Criminal law.* **1.** A period of probation that is imposed in addition to a sentence of imprisonment rather than as a substitute for part or all of a sentence. **2.** Federal parole, which may be imposed in addition to a prison term.

▸ **unconditional release.** (1871) The final discharge of a prison inmate from custody.

9. *Environmental law.* The injection of contaminants or pollutants into the environment as a side effect of operations such as manufacturing, mining, or farming. **10.** See *release deed* under DEED. — Also termed *custody release*; *custodial release*.

release clause. *Real estate.* **1.** A blanket-mortgage provision that enables the mortgagor to obtain a release from the mortgage of a specific portion of the property upon paying a specific (usu. more than pro rata) portion of the loan. • Mortgagees commonly include a clause that disallows a partial release if the mortgagor is in default on any part of the mortgage. **2.** A purchase-agreement provision that allows a seller who has accepted an offer containing a contingency to continue to market the property and accept other offers. • If the seller accepts another buyer's offer, the original buyer typically has a specified time (such as 72 hours) to waive the contingency (such as the sale of the buyer's present house) or to release the seller from the agreement.

release deed. See DEED.

releasee. (17c) **1.** Someone who is released, either physically or by contractual discharge. **2.** One to whom an estate is released.

release of mortgage. (1872) A written document that discharges a mortgage upon full payment by the borrower and that is publicly recorded to show that the borrower has full equity in the property.

release on recognizance. (1913) The pretrial release of an arrested person who promises, usu. in writing but without supplying a surety or posting bond, to appear for trial at a later date. — Abbr. ROR. — Also termed *release on own recognizance*. See RECOGNIZANCE.

releaser. See RELEASOR.

release to uses. (1830) Conveyance of property, by deed of release, by one party to another for the benefit of the grantor or a third party. See *deed of release* under DEED; STATUTE OF USES; USE (4).

releasor. (17c) Someone who releases property or a claim to another. — Also spelled *releaser*.

relegatio (rel-ə-**gay**-shee-oh), *n.* [fr. Latin *relegare* "to send away"] *Roman law.* Temporary or permanent banishment of a condemned criminal from Rome and the criminal's native province, without loss of citizenship or forfeiture of all the criminal's property. Cf. DEPORTATIO.

> "Relegatio. The expulsion of a citizen ordered either by an administrative act of a magistrate or by judgment in a criminal trial. In the latter case the *relegatio* was sometimes combined with additional punishments, such as confiscation of the whole or of a part of the property of the condemned person, loss of Roman citizenship, confinement in a certain place. A milder form of *relegatio* was the exclusion of the wrongdoer from residence in a specified territory. Illicit return was punished with the death penalty." Adolf Berger, *Encyclopedic Dictionary of Roman Law* 673 (1953).

relegation, *n.* (16c) **1.** Banishment or exile, esp. a temporary one. **2.** Assignment or delegation. — **relegate,** *vb.*

relevance. (18c) The quality, state, or condition of being relevant; relation or pertinence to the issue at hand. — Also termed *relevancy*.

relevancy. See RELEVANCE.

relevant, *adj.* (16c) Logically connected and tending to prove or disprove a matter in issue; having appreciable probative value — that is, rationally tending to persuade people of the probability or possibility of some alleged fact. Cf. MATERIAL (2), (3).

> "The word 'relevant' means that any two facts to which it is applied are so related to each other that according to the common course of events one either taken by itself or in connection with other facts proves or renders probable the past, present, or future existence or non-existence of the other." James Fitzjames Stephen, *A Digest of the Law of Evidence* 2 (4th ed. 1881).

relevant art. See ART (3).

relevant conduct. *Criminal procedure.* In the law of criminal punishment, behavior that a judge may consider in imposing a sentence, including the defendant's acts or omissions, dismissed counts, acquitted counts, and other offenses that are part of the same course of behavior or common scheme or plan.

relevant evidence. See EVIDENCE.

relevant market. See MARKET.

relevatio. See RELIEF (1).

relevium. See RELIEF (1).

reliance, *n.* (17c) Dependence or trust by a person, esp. when combined with action based on that dependence or trust. — **rely,** *vb.*

▸ **detrimental reliance.** (1941) Reliance by one party on the acts or representations of another, causing a worsening of the first party's position. • Detrimental reliance may serve as a substitute for consideration and thus make a promise enforceable as a contract. See *promissory estoppel* under ESTOPPEL.

▸ **essential reliance.** (1936) *Contracts.* Reliance that causes a person to expect specified benefits and to perform as instructed by the contract.

▸ **incidental reliance.** (1936) *Contracts.* Reliance that motivates a person to act in ways that are not necessary to perform a contract but that follow from the contract.

reliance damages. See DAMAGES.

reliance interest. See INTEREST (2).

reliance-loss damages. See DAMAGES.

reliance materials. See EXPERT-RELIANCE MATERIALS.

relict (**rel**-ikt). (15c) *Archaic.* A surviving spouse; esp., a widow.

relicta verificatione (ri-**lik**-tə ver-ə-fi-kay-shee-**oh**-nee). [Latin "his pleading being abandoned"] (17c) *Hist.* A confession of judgment accompanied by a withdrawal of the plea. See COGNOVIT ACTIONEM.

reliction (ri-**lik**-shən). (17c) **1.** A process by which a river or stream shifts its location, causing the recession of water from its bank. **2.** The alteration of a boundary line because of the gradual removal of land by a river or stream. See ACCRETION (2); DERELICTION (2).

relief. (14c) **1.** A payment made by an heir of a feudal tenant to the feudal lord for the privilege of succeeding to the ancestor's tenancy. — Also termed *relevium*; *relevatio*.

> "A mesne lord could, upon the death of his tenant, accept the tenant's heir as tenant; but he was not required to do so. When he did accept his deceased tenant's heir as tenant, it was typically because the heir had paid the mesne lord a substantial sum (known as a *relief*) for the re-grant of the tenancy." Thomas F. Bergin & Paul G. Haskell, *Preface to Estates in Land and Future Interests* 8 (2d ed. 1984).

2. Aid or assistance given to those in need; esp., financial aid provided by the state.

▸ **disaster relief.** (1915) Aid given to state and local governments to relieve the damage and suffering resulting from disasters such as hurricanes, tornadoes, floods, earthquakes, volcanic eruptions, landslides, mudslides, drought, fire, and explosions.

▸ **poor relief.** See WELFARE (2).

3. The redress or benefit, esp. equitable in nature (such as an injunction or specific performance), that a party asks of a court. — Also termed *remedy*. Cf. REMEDY.

▸ **affirmative relief.** (1842) The relief sought by a defendant by raising a counterclaim or cross-claim that could have been maintained independently of the plaintiff's action.

▸ **alternative relief.** (1851) Judicial relief that is mutually exclusive with another form of judicial relief. • In pleading, a party may request alternative relief, as by asking for both specific performance and damages that would be averted by specific performance. Fed. R. Civ. P. 8(a). Cf. ELECTION OF REMEDIES.

▸ **coercive relief.** (1886) Judicial relief, either legal or equitable, in the form of a personal command to the defendant that is enforceable by physical restraint.

▸ **declaratory relief.** (1852) A unilateral request to a court to determine the legal status or ownership of a thing.

▸ **extraordinary relief.** (18c) Judicial relief that exceeds what is typically or customarily granted but is warranted by the unique or extreme circumstances of a situation. • The types of extraordinary relief most frequently sought are injunctions and extraordinary writs, esp. mandamus. See INJUNCTION; MANDAMUS; PROHIBITION (2). Cf. *extraordinary writ* under WRIT.

▸ **interim relief.** (1886) Relief that is granted on a preliminary basis before an order finally disposing of a request for relief.

▸ **therapeutic relief.** (1889) The relief, esp. in a settlement, that requires the defendant to take remedial measures as opposed to paying damages. • An example is a defendant-corporation (in an employment-discrimination suit) that agrees to undergo sensitivity training. — Often shortened to *therapeutics*.

religion. (13c) A system of faith and worship usu. involving belief in a supreme being and usu. containing a moral or ethical code; esp., such a system recognized and practiced by a particular church, sect, or denomination. • In construing the protections under the Establishment Clause and the Free Exercise Clause, courts have interpreted the term *religion* broadly to include a wide variety of theistic and nontheistic beliefs.

▸ **state religion.** (16c) A religion promoted, taught, or enforced by a government's acts to the exclusion of other religions. — Also termed *state church*; *official religion*; *established church*; *established religion*.

religion, freedom of. See FREEDOM OF RELIGION.

Religion Clause. *Constitutional law.* In the Bill of Rights, the provision stating that "Congress shall make no law respecting an establishment of religion or prohibiting the free exercise thereof." U.S. Const. amend. I. • Some writers use the plural form, "Religion Clauses," to mean both the Establishment Clause and the Free Exercise Clause, thus emphasizing the asserted common purpose of the two provisions.

religion discrimination. See *religious discrimination* under DISCRIMINATION (3).

religious-affinity fraud. See *affinity fraud* under FRAUD.

religious corporation. See CORPORATION.

religious discrimination. See DISCRIMINATION (3).

religious-exemption statute. See FAITH-HEALING EXEMPTION.

religious liberty. See LIBERTY.

religious minority. See MINORITY (3).

Religious Test Clause. (1925) *Constitutional law.* The clause of the U.S. Constitution that prohibits the use of a religious test as a qualification to serve in any office or public trust. U.S. Const. art. VI, par. 3, cl. 2. — Also termed *No Religious Test Clause*.

relinquishment, *n.* (15c) The abandonment of a right or thing. — **relinquish,** *vb.*

reliqua (**rel**-ə-kwə). [Latin] *Civil law.* The remainder of a debt after balancing or liquidating an account; money left unpaid.

relitigate, *vb.* (1826) To litigate (a case or matter) again or anew <relitigate the issue in federal court>. — **relitigation,** *n.*

relocatio (ree-loh-**kay**-shee-oh). [Latin] *Civil law.* The renewal of a lease; RECONDUCTION (1).

relocation. (16c) **1.** Removal and establishment of someone or something in a new place. **2.** *Mining law.* Appropriation of a new tract of land for a mining claim, as by an owner who wishes to change the boundaries of the original tract or by a stranger who wishes to claim an abandoned or forfeited tract. **3.** *Civil law.* RECONDUCTION (1).

RLA. *abbr.* RAILWAY LABOR ACT.

rem. See IN REM.

remainder. (15c) *Property.* **1.** A future interest arising in a third person — that is, someone other than the estate's creator, its initial holder, or the heirs of either — who is intended to take after the natural termination of the preceding estate. • For example, if a grant is "to A for life, and then to B," B's future interest is a remainder. If there is only one preceding estate and the remainder vests on that estate's expiration, the remainder is also termed *executed estate*. — Also termed *remainder estate*; *estate in remainder*. Cf. EXECUTORY INTEREST; REVERSION; POSSIBILITY OF REVERTER.

"Whether a remainder is vested or contingent depends upon the language employed. If the conditional element is incorporated into the description of, or the gift to the remainder-man, then the remainder is contingent; but if, after words giving a vested interest, a clause is added divesting it, the remainder is vested. Thus, on a devise to A. for life, remainder to his children, but if any child dies in the lifetime of A. his share to go to those who survive, the share of each child is vested, subject to be divested by his death. But on a devise to A. for life, remainder to such of his children as survive him, the remainder is contingent." John Chipman Gray, *The Rule Against Perpetuities* 66 (1886).

"Under the names of 'remainders' and 'executory limitations,' various classes of interests in land could be created in expectancy, either at the Common Law or under the Statute of Uses. The differences between the two classes were highly technical; and the learning involved in acquiring a knowledge of the rules of determining them [is] quite out of proportion to the value obtained." Edward Jenks, *The Book of English Law* 263 (P.B. Fairest ed., 6th ed. 1967).

▸ **accelerated remainder.** (1901) A remainder that has passed to the remainderman, as when the gift to the preceding beneficiary fails.

▸ **alternative remainder.** (1830) A remainder in which the disposition of property is to take effect only if another disposition does not take effect.

▸ **charitable remainder.** (1932) A remainder, usu. from a life estate, that is given to a charity; for example, "to Jane for life, and then to the American Red Cross."

▸ **contingent remainder.** (18c) A remainder that is either given to an unascertained person or made subject to a condition precedent. • An example is "to A for life, and then, if B has married before A dies, to B." — Also termed *executory remainder; remainder subject to a condition precedent.*

"Unlike a vested remainder, a contingent remainder is *either* subject to a condition precedent (in addition to the natural expiration of a prior estate), *or* owned by unascertainable persons, *or both.* But the contingent remainder, like the vested remainder, 'waits patiently' for possession. It is so created that it can become a present estate (if ever it does) immediately upon, and no sooner than, the natural expiration of particular estates that stand in front of it and were created simultaneously with it." Thomas F. Bergin & Paul G. Haskell, *Preface to Estates in Land and Future Interests* 73 (2d ed. 1984).

▸ **cross-remainder.** (18c) A future interest that results when particular estates are given to two or more persons in different parcels of land, or in the same land in undivided shares, and the remainders of all the estates are made to vest in the survivor or survivors. • Two examples of devises giving rise to cross-remainders are (1) "to A and B for life, with the remainder to the survivor and her heirs," and (2) "Blackacre to A and Whiteacre to B, with the remainder of A's estate to B on A's failure of issue, and the remainder of B's estate to A on B's failure of issue." • If no tenants or issue survive, the remainder vests in a third party (sometimes known as the *ulterior remainderman*). Each tenant in common has a reciprocal, or *cross*, remainder in the share of the others. This type of remainder could not be created by deed unless expressly stated. It could, however, be implied in a will.

"By a will also an estate may pass by mere implication, without any express words to direct its course. . . . So also, where a devise of black-acre to A and of white-acre to B in tail, and if they both die without issue, then to C in fee: here A and B have *cross remainders* by implication, and on the failure of either's issue, the other or his issue shall take the whole; and C's remainder over shall be postponed till the issue of both shall fail." 2 William Blackstone, *Commentaries on the Laws of England* 381 (1766).

▸ **defeasible remainder.** (18c) A vested remainder that will be destroyed if a condition subsequent occurs. • An example is "to A for life, and then to B, but if B ever sells liquor on the land, then to C." — Also termed *remainder subject to divestment.*

▸ **executed remainder.** See *vested remainder.*

▸ **executory remainder.** See *contingent remainder.*

▸ **indefeasible remainder.** (1898) A vested remainder that is not subject to a condition subsequent; specif., a remainder in which the remainderman is certain to acquire a present interest sometime in the future and will be entitled to retain the interest permanently. — Also termed *indefeasibly vested remainder; remainder indefeasibly vested.*

▸ **remainder subject to a condition precedent.** See *contingent remainder.*

▸ **remainder subject to divestment.** See *defeasible remainder.*

▸ **remainder subject to open.** (1838) A vested remainder that is given to a class of persons whose numbers may change over time and that is to be shared equally by each member of the class. • An example is "to A for life, and then equally to all of B's children." The class must have at least one member, but more can be added over time. — Also termed *remainder subject to partial divestment; remainder vested subject to open.*

▸ **vested remainder.** (18c) A remainder that is given to an ascertained person and that is not subject to a condition precedent. • An example is "to A for life, and then to B." — Also termed *executed remainder; present fixed right of future enjoyment.*

"The distinction between vested and contingent remainders is of fundamental importance, both in the old and in the modern law. A remainder is vested if two conditions are satisfied: (i) the person or persons entitled to it must be ascertained; and (ii) it must be ready to take effect in possession forthwith, and be prevented from doing so only by the existence of some prior interest or interests. If either condition is not satisfied, the remainder is contingent." Robert Megarry & H.W.R. Wade, *The Law of Real Property* 173-74 (4th ed. 1975).

▸ **vested remainder subject to complete defeasement.** See *vested remainder subject to total divestment.*

▸ **vested remainder subject to total divestment.** (1961) A remainder that is currently vested but will terminate if a specified event happens, whereupon the property will revert to the grantor. • For example, a grant that is effective as long as the property is used for a particular purpose will terminate if that use ever ends. — Also termed *vested remainder subject to complete defeasement.*

2. The property in a decedent's estate that is not otherwise specifically devised or bequeathed in a will. See *residuary estate* under ESTATE (3).

remainder bequest. See *residuary bequest* under BEQUEST.

remainderer. See REMAINDERMAN.

remainder estate. See REMAINDER (1).

remainder holder. See REMAINDERMAN.

remainder indefeasibly vested. See *indefeasible remainder* under REMAINDER.

remainder interest. (1815) The property that passes to a beneficiary after the expiration of an intervening income interest. • For example, if a grantor places real estate in trust with income to A for life and remainder to B upon A's death, then B has a remainder interest.

remainderman. (18c) Someone who holds or is entitled to receive a remainder. — Also termed *remainderer*; *remainderperson*; *remainder holder*; *remainor.*

▸ **ulterior remainderman.** (1830) A third party whose future interest in a property vests only if all the preceding reciprocal interests expire. See *cross-remainder* under REMAINDER.

remainder subject to partial divestment. See *remainder subject to open* under REMAINDER.

remainder vested subject to open. See *remainder subject to open* under REMAINDER.

remainor, *n.* See REMAINDERMAN.

remake rights. (1947) *Copyright.* The rights to produce one or more additional movies or screenplays based on what is substantially the same story as is contained in the original movie or screenplay for which the rights have been granted.

remancipate, *vb.* (17c) To mancipate (a thing or person) again.

remand (ri-**mand** *also* **ree**-mand), *n.* (18c) **1.** The act or an instance of sending something (such as a case, claim, or person) back for further action. **2.** An order remanding a case, claim, or person.

▸ **fourth-sentence remand.** (1990) In a claim for social-security benefits, a court's decision affirming, reversing, or modifying the decision of the Commissioner of Social Security. • This type of remand is called a fourth-sentence remand because it is based on the fourth sentence of 42 USCA § 405(g): "The court shall have power to enter, upon the pleadings and transcript of the record, a judgment affirming, modifying, or reversing the decision of the Commissioner of Social Security, with or without remanding the cause for a rehearing." *See Melkonyan v. Sullivan*, 501 U.S. 89, 111 S.Ct. 2157 (1991).

▸ **remand in custody.** (1917) The act of sending a criminal defendant from a court of law to prison to await trial.

▸ **remand on bail.** (1914) The act of allowing a criminal defendant to leave court and to go home for a time (upon payment of the required security) to await trial. See BAIL, *n.* (1).

▸ **sixth-sentence remand.** (1990) In a claim for social-security benefits, a court's decision that the claim should be reheard by the Commissioner of Social Security because new evidence is available, which was not available before, that might change the outcome of the proceeding. • This type of remand is called a sixth-sentence remand because it is based on the sixth sentence of 42 USCA § 405(g): "The court may, on motion of the Commissioner of Social Security made for good cause shown before the Commissioner files the Commissioner's answer, remand the case to the Commissioner of Social Security for further action by the Commissioner of Social Security, and it may at any time order additional evidence to be taken before the Commissioner of Social Security, but only upon a showing that there is new evidence which is material and that there is good cause for the failure to incorporate such evidence into the record in a prior proceeding . . . ." *See Melkonyan v. Sullivan*, 501 U.S. 89, 111 S.Ct. 2157 (1991).

remand (ri-**mand**), *vb.* (15c) **1.** To send (a case or claim) back to the court or tribunal from which it came for some further action <the appellate court reversed the trial court's opinion and remanded the case for new trial>. Cf. REMOVAL (2). **2.** To recommit (an accused person) to custody after a preliminary examination <the magistrate, after denying bail, remanded the defendant to custody>.

remand center. *English law.* (1937) A prisonlike place where people accused of crimes are kept while awaiting their trials.

remand home. *English law.* (1901) A prisonlike place where young people accused of crimes are kept while awaiting their trials.

remand in custody. See REMAND, *n.*

remand on bail. See REMAND, *n.*

remanentia (rem-ə-**nen**-shee-ə). [Law Latin] *Hist.* A remainder or perpetuity.

remanent pro defectu emptorum (**rem**-ə-nənt proh di-**fek**-t[y]oo emp-**tor**-əm). [Latin] (1822) *Hist.* Remains unsold for want of buyers. • This language was used in a return of a writ of execution when the sheriff could not sell the seized property.

remanet (**rem**-ə-net). (16c) **1.** A case or proceeding whose hearing has been postponed. **2.** A remainder or remnant.

remargining, *n.* (1905) *Securities.* The act or process of depositing additional cash or collateral with a broker when the equity in a margin account falls to an insufficient level. See *margin account* under ACCOUNT. — **remargin,** *vb.*

remarry, *vb.* (16c) To marry a second or later time, after a divorce or the death of one's spouse.

remediable, *adj.* (15c) Capable of being remedied, esp. by law <remediable wrongs>. — **remediability,** *n.*

remedial, *adj.* (17c) **1.** Affording or providing a remedy; providing the means of obtaining redress <a remedial action>. **2.** Intended to correct, remove, or lessen a wrong, fault, or defect <a remedial statute>. **3.** Of, relating to, or involving a means of enforcing an existing substantive right <a remedial right>.

remedial action. 1. *Environmental law.* An action intended to bring about or restore long-term environmental quality; esp., under CERCLA, a measure intended to permanently alleviate pollution when a hazardous substance has been released or might be released into the environment, so as to prevent or minimize any further release of hazardous substances and thereby minimize the risk to public health or to the environment. 42 USCA § 9601(24); 40 CFR § 300.6. — Also termed *remedy.* See CERCLA. Cf. REMOVAL ACTION. **2.** See *personal action* (1) under ACTION (4).

remedial enforcement. See *secondary right* under RIGHT.

remedial law. (17c) **1.** See *remedial statute* under STATUTE. **2.** A statute that corrects or modifies an existing law;

esp., a law providing a new or different remedy when the existing remedy, if any, is inadequate.

remedial liability. See LIABILITY.

remedial promise. See PROMISE.

remedial right. See RIGHT.

remedial statute. See STATUTE.

remedial trust. See *constructive trust* under TRUST (3).

remediation. (1986) *Environmental law.* The restoration of polluted land, water, or air to its former state, or as nearly so as is practical.

remedies, *n.* The field of law dealing with the means of enforcing rights and redressing wrongs.

remediis praetoriis (ri-**mee**-dee-is pri-**tor**-ee-is). [Latin] *Hist.* By praetorian remedies.

remedium extraordinarium (ri-**mee**-dee-əm ek-stror-di-**nair**-ee-əm *or* ek-strə-or-). [Latin] (17c) *Hist.* An extraordinary remedy.

remedy, *n.* (13c) **1.** The means of enforcing a right or preventing or redressing a wrong; legal or equitable relief. — Also termed *civil remedy.* **2.** REMEDIAL ACTION. **3.** A right by which an aggrieved party may seek relief without resort to a tribunal. Cf. RELIEF (3). — Also termed (in senses 1 & 2) *law of remedy.* — **remedy,** *vb.*

> "A remedy is anything a court can do for a litigant who has been wronged or is about to be wronged. The two most common remedies are judgments that plaintiffs are entitled to collect sums of money from defendants (damages) and orders to defendants to refrain from their wrongful conduct or to undo its consequences (injunctions). The court decides whether the litigant has been wronged under the substantive law that governs primary rights and duties; it conducts its inquiry in accordance with the procedural law. The law of remedies falls somewhere in between procedure and primary substantive rights. Remedies are substantive, but they are distinct from the rest of the substantive law, and sometimes their details blur into procedure. For long periods in our past, remedies were casually equated with procedure." Douglas Laycock, *Modern American Remedies* 1 (4th ed. 2010).

▸ **adequate remedy at law.** (18c) A legal remedy (such as an award of damages) that provides sufficient relief to the petitioning party, thus preventing the party from obtaining equitable relief. See IRREPARABLE INJURY RULE.

▸ **administrative remedy.** (1880) A nonjudicial remedy provided by an administrative agency. • Ordinarily, if an administrative remedy is available, it must be exhausted before a court will hear the case. See EXHAUSTION OF REMEDIES.

▸ **civil remedy.** See REMEDY (1).

▸ **concurrent remedy.** (18c) One of two or more legal or equitable actions available to redress a wrong.

▸ **cumulative remedy.** (18c) A remedy available to a party in addition to another remedy that still remains in force.

▸ **equitable remedy.** (18c) A remedy, usu. a nonmonetary one such as an injunction or specific performance, obtained when available legal remedies, usu. monetary damages, cannot adequately redress the injury. • Historically, an equitable remedy was available only from a court of equity. — Also termed *equitable relief; equitable damages.* See IRREPARABLE-INJURY RULE.

> "[T]here are certain species of equitable remedies which have become well established and familiarly known, and which are commonly designated by the term 'equitable remedies' wherever it is used. They may be separated into three classes: 1. Those which are entirely different from any kind of reliefs known and granted by the law. Of this class are the preventive remedy of Injunction, the restorative remedy of Mandatory Injunction, the remedies of Reformation, Specific Performance, and many others. 2. Those which the legal procedure recognizes, but does not *directly* confer, and the beneficial results of which it obtains in an indirect manner. A familiar example is the relief of Rescission or Cancellation. A court of equity entertains a suit for the express purpose of procuring a contract or conveyance to be canceled, and renders a decree conferring in terms that exact relief. A court of law entertains an action for the recovery of the possession of chattels, or, under some circumstances, for the recovery of land, or for the recovery of damages, and although nothing is said concerning it, either in the pleadings or in the judgment, a contract or a conveyance, as the case may be, is virtually rescinded; the recovery is based upon the fact of such rescission, and could not have been granted unless the rescission had taken place. Here the remedy of cancellation is not expressly asked for, nor granted by the court of law, but all its effects are indirectly obtained in the legal action. It is true, the equitable remedy is much broader in its scope, and more complete in its relief; for its effects are not confined to the particular action, but by removing the obnoxious instrument they extend to all future claims and actions based upon it. 3. Those which are substantially the same both in equity and at the law. Familiar examples of this class are the partition of land among co-owners, and the admeasurement of dower, in which the final relief granted by equity is the same as that obtained through the now almost obsolete legal actions; the process of accounting and determining the balance in favor of one or the other party; and even, under special circumstances, the award of pecuniary damages expresly." 1 John Norton Pomeroy, *A Treatise on Equity Jurisprudence* 123–25 (John Norton Pomeroy Jr., ed., 4th ed. 1918).

▸ **extrajudicial remedy.** (18c) A remedy not obtained from a court, such as repossession. — Also termed *self-help remedy.*

▸ **extraordinary remedy.** (16c) A remedy — such as a writ of mandamus or habeas corpus — not available to a party unless necessary to preserve a right that cannot be protected by a standard legal or equitable remedy. • Because there is no agreed list of extraordinary remedies, some standard remedies — such as preliminary and permanent injunctions — are sometimes described as extraordinary.

▸ **judicial remedy.** (18c) A remedy granted by a court.

▸ **legal remedy.** (17c) A remedy historically available in a court of law, as distinguished from a remedy historically available only in equity. • After the merger of law and equity, this distinction remained relevant in some ways, such as in determining the right to jury trial and the choice between alternate remedies.

▸ **provisional remedy.** (18c) A temporary remedy awarded before judgment and pending the action's disposition, such as a temporary restraining order, a preliminary injunction, a prejudgment receivership, or an attachment. • Such a remedy is intended to maintain the status quo by protecting a person's safety or preserving property.

▸ **remedy over.** (18c) A remedy that arises from a right of indemnification or subrogation. • For example, if a city is liable for injuries caused by a defect in a street, the city has a "remedy over" against the person whose act or negligence caused the defect.

▸ **self-help remedy.** See *extrajudicial remedy.*

▸ **specific remedy.** (18c) A remedy whereby the injured party is awarded the very performance that was contractually promised or whereby the injury threatened or caused by a tort is prevented or repaired. • A court awards a specific remedy by ordering a defaulting seller of goods to deliver the specified goods to the buyer (as opposed to paying damages).

▸ **speedy remedy.** (18c) A remedy that, under the circumstances, can be pursued expeditiously before the aggrieved party has incurred substantial detriment. • "Speedy remedy" is an informal expression with no fixed meaning — that is, what is considered speedy in one context may not be considered speedy in other contexts. For example, the Federal Tax Injunction Act requires a "plain, speedy, and efficient remedy" in state courts. But the Act does not require preliminary or injunctive relief — or even interest for delay.

> "'Speedy' is perforce a relative concept, and we must assess the 2-year delay against the usual time for similar litigation." *Rosewell v. LaSalle Nat'l Bank*, 450 U.S. 503, 518 (1981).

▸ **substitutional remedy.** (1987) A remedy intended to give the promisee something as a replacement for the promised performance or to give the plaintiff something in lieu of preventing or repairing an injury. • A court awards a substitutional remedy by ordering a defaulting seller of goods to pay the buyer damages (as opposed to delivering the promised goods). — Also termed *substitutionary remedy.*

> "With substitutionary remedies, plaintiff suffers harm and receives a sum of money. Specific remedies seek to avoid this exchange. They seek to prevent harm, or undo it, rather than let it happen and compensate for it. . . . [Money damages] are substitutionary both in the sense that the sum of money is substituted for plaintiff's original entitlement, and in the less obvious sense that the fact finder's valuation of the loss is substituted for plaintiff's valuation. Specific relief seeks to avoid both these substitutions, giving plaintiff the very thing he lost if that is what he wants." Douglas Laycock, *The Death of the Irreparable Injury Rule* 13 (1991).

remedy, mutuality of. See MUTUALITY OF REMEDY.

réméré (ray-may-**ray**), *n.* [French] The right of repurchase.

REMIC (**rem**-ik *or* **ree**-mik). *abbr.* REAL-ESTATE-MORTGAGE INVESTMENT CONDUIT.

remise (ri-**mɪz**), *vb.* (15c) To give up, surrender, or release (a right, interest, etc.) <the quitclaim deed provides that the grantor remises any rights in the property>.

remissio injuriae (ri-**mis**[**h**]-ee-oh in-**joor**-ee-ee). [Latin] (1830) *Hist.* Forgiveness of the offense.

remission. (13c) **1.** A cancellation or extinguishment of all or part of a financial obligation; a release of a debt or claim.

▸ **conventional remission.** (1913) *Civil law.* A remission expressly granted to a debtor by a creditor having capacity to alienate. La. Civ. Code art. 1840.

▸ **tacit remission.** (1840) *Civil law.* A remission arising by operation of law, as when a creditor surrenders an original title to the debtor. La. Civ. Code art. 1888.

2. A pardon granted for an offense. **3.** Relief from a forfeiture or penalty. **4.** A diminution or abatement of the symptoms of a disease.

remit, *vb.* (14c) **1.** To pardon or forgive <the wife could not remit her husband's infidelity>. **2.** To abate or slacken; to mitigate <the receipt of money damages remitted the embarrassment of being fired>. **3.** To refer (a matter for decision) to some authority, esp. to send back (a case) to a lower court <the appellate court remitted the case to the trial court for further factual determinations>. See REMAND. **4.** To send or put back to a previous condition or position <a landlord's breach of a lease does not justify the tenant's refusal to pay rent; instead, the tenant is remitted to the right to recover damages>. **5.** To transmit (as money) <upon receiving the demand letter, she promptly remitted the amount due>. — **remissible** (in senses 1–4), *adj.* — **remittable** (in sense 5), *adj.*

remittance. (18c) **1.** A sum of money sent to another as payment for goods or services. **2.** An instrument (such as a check) used for sending money. **3.** The action or process of sending money to another person or place.

remittance advice. See ADVICE.

remittee. (18c) One to whom payment is sent.

remitter. (16c) **1.** The principle by which a person having two titles to an estate, and entering on it by the later or more defective title, is deemed to hold the estate by the earlier or more valid title. **2.** The act of sending back a case to a lower court. **3.** Someone who sends payment to someone else. — Also spelled (in sense 3) *remittor.* **4.** Someone who purchases an instrument from its issuer if the instrument is payable to an identified person other than the purchaser. • For example, a customer might buy a cashier's check from a bank but direct that it be made payable to someone else. The customer's name may appear on the check as remitter to identify who bought it. *See* UCC § 3-103(a)(15).

remitting bank. See BANK.

remittit damna (ri-**mit**-it **dam**-nə). [Latin] (18c) *Hist.* An entry on the record by which a plaintiff declares that he or she remits part of the damages that have been awarded. — Also termed *remittitur damna*; *remittitur damnum.*

remittitur (ri-**mit**-i-tər). (18c) **1.** An order awarding a new trial, or a damages amount lower than that awarded by the jury, and requiring the plaintiff to choose between those alternatives <the defendant sought a remittitur of the $100 million judgment>. **2.** The process by which a court requires either that the case be retried, or that the damages awarded by the jury be reduced. Cf. ADDITUR.

remittitur damna. See REMITTIT DAMNA.

remittitur damnum. See REMITTIT DAMNA.

remittitur of record. (1848) The action of sending the transcript of a case back from an appellate court to a trial court; the notice for doing so.

remittor. See REMITTER (3).

remnants and surpluses. (1815) *Maritime law.* The proceeds remaining from the sale of a ship after claims for seamen's wages, bottomry bonds, salvage services, and supplies have been paid.

remonetization, *n.* (1874) The restoration of a precious metal (such as gold or silver) to its former use as legal tender. — **remonetize,** *vb.*

remonstrance (ri-**mon**-strənts), *n.* (16c) **1.** A presentation of reasons for opposition or grievance. **2.** A formal document stating reasons for opposition or grievance. **3.** A formal complaint or protest against governmental policy, actions, or officials. — **remonstrate** (ri-**mon**-strayt), *vb.*

remorse, *n.* A strong feeling of sincere regret and sadness over one's having behaved badly or done harm; intense, anguished self-reproach and compunction of conscience, esp. for a crime one has committed.

remortgage (ree-**mor**-gəj), *vb.* (17c) To borrow money by allowing a second mortgage to be placed on (one's house or other property) or by increasing one's current mortgage.

remote, *adj.* (15c) **1.** Far removed or separated in time, space, or relation. **2.** Slight. **3.** *Property.* Beyond the 21 years after some life in being by which a devise must vest. See RULE AGAINST PERPETUITIES.

remote cause. See CAUSE (1).

remote damages. See *speculative damages* (1) under DAMAGES.

remotely created consumer item. (2002) A check that is drawn on a consumer's account but is neither created by the payor bank nor signed by the drawer. • A remotely created consumer item might be created by a telemarketer from check information supplied by the consumer over the telephone or the Internet. *See* UCC § 3-103(a)(16).

remoteness of consequence. (1887) *Torts.* The lack of proximate causation with respect to an alleged act by a defendant. • Even if the plaintiff proves every other element for tortious liability, the defendant will not be liable if the harm suffered by the plaintiff is too far removed from the defendant's conduct. — Also termed *remoteness of damage.*

remote possibility. See POSSIBILITY.

remote vesting. (1849) Conditions or restrictions imposed by a grantor to delay or restrict future owners' ability to use, take, or transfer ownership of property. See RULE AGAINST PERPETUITIES.

remotis testibus (ri-**moh**-tis **tes**-ti-bəs). [Latin] (17c) *Hist.* The witnesses being absent.

removal, *n.* (16c) **1.** The transfer or moving of a person or thing from one location, position, or residence to another. **2.** The transfer of an action from state to federal court. • In removing a case to federal court, a litigant must timely file the removal papers and must show a valid basis for federal-court jurisdiction. 28 USCA § 1441. Cf. REMAND (1).

▸ **civil-rights removal.** (1964) Removal of a case from state to federal court because a person (1) has been denied or cannot enforce a civil right in the state court, (2) is being sued for performing an act under color of authority derived from a law providing for equal rights, or (3) is being sued for refusing to perform an act that would be inconsistent with equal rights.

3. The immediate termination of an officeholder's privilege to serve in that office, usu. after a vote. — **remove,** *vb.*

removal action. *Environmental law.* An action, esp. under CERCLA, intended to bring about the short-term abatement and cleanup of pollution (as by removing and disposing of toxic materials). See CERCLA. Cf. REMEDIAL ACTION.

removal bond. See BOND (2).

removal jurisdiction. See JURISDICTION.

rem pupilli salvam fore (rem pyoo-**pil**-ɪ **sal**-vəm **for**-ee). [Latin] (18c) *Roman law.* The guarantee required of a guardian that the estate of the person under puberty will be safe.

REMT. *abbr.* REAL-ESTATE MORTGAGE TRUST.

remuneration (ri-myoo-nə-**ray**-shən), *n.* (15c) **1.** Payment; compensation, esp. for a service that someone has performed. **2.** The act of paying or compensating. — **remunerative,** *adj.* — **remunerate,** *vb.*

remunerative donation. See DONATION (1).

remunerative sanction. See SANCTION (2).

remuneratory infraction. See *remunerative sanction* under SANCTION (2).

rencounter (ren-**kown**-tər). (16c) A hostile meeting or contest; a battle or combat. — Also spelled *rencontre* (ren-**kon**-tər).

render, *n.* (14c) *Hist.* **1.** A payment in money, goods, or services made by a feudal tenant to the landlord. **2.** A return conveyance made by the grantee to the grantor in a fine. See FINE (1).

render, *vb.* (14c) **1.** To transmit or deliver <render payment>. **2.** (Of a judge) to deliver formally <render a judgment>. **3.** (Of a jury) to agree on and report formally <render a verdict>. **4.** To pay as due <render an account>.

rendezvous, *n.* (16c) **1.** A place designated for meeting or assembly, esp. of troops or ships. **2.** The meeting or assembly itself.

rendition, *n.* (17c) **1.** The action of making, delivering, or giving out, such as a legal decision; esp., the filing of a court order with the clerk of court. • A court's written order is "rendered" upon filing. **2.** The return of a fugitive from one state to the state where the fugitive is accused or was convicted of a crime. — Also termed (in sense 2) *interstate rendition.* Cf. EXTRADITION. **3.** The transporting of a prisoner or fugitive from one jurisdiction to another that has rightfully requested custody.

▸ **erroneous rendition.** See EXTRAORDINARY RENDITION.

▸ **extraordinary rendition.** (1983) The transfer, without formal charges, trial, or court approval, of a person suspected of being a terrorist or supporter of a terrorist group to a foreign country for imprisonment and interrogation on behalf of the transferring country. • When an innocent person is subjected to extraordinary rendition, it is also termed *erroneous extradition.* When a transfer is made to a country notorious for human-rights violations, it may be colloquially termed *torture by proxy* or *torture flight.*

4. An interpretation or performance of a musical or dramatic piece. **5.** A translation.

rendition of judgment. (18c) The judge's oral or written ruling containing the judgment entered. Cf. ENTRY OF JUDGMENT.

rendition warrant. See WARRANT (1).

renege (ri-**nig** *or* ri-**neg**), *vb.* (16c) To fail to keep a promise or commitment; to back out of a deal.

renegotiable-rate mortgage. See MORTGAGE.

renegotiation, *n.* (1934) **1.** The act or process of negotiating again or on different terms; a second or further negotiation. **2.** The reexamination and adjustment of a government contract to eliminate or recover excess profits by the contractor. — **renegotiate,** *vb.*

renewable, *adj.* (1817) **1.** (Of an agreement or official document) capable of being made to continue for a further period of time after the current period ends. **2.** (Of an energy source) replacing itself naturally or else being so plentiful as to be easily replaced.

renewable term insurance. See INSURANCE.

renewal, *n.* (17c) **1.** The act of restoring or reestablishing. **2.** *Parliamentary law.* The introduction or consideration of a question that was already disposed of without being adopted. — Also termed *renewal of a motion.* **3.** The re-creation of a legal relationship or the replacement of an old contract with a new contract, as opposed to the mere extension of a previous relationship or contract. Cf. EXTENSION (1); REVIVAL (1). — **renew,** *vb.*

renewal note. See NOTE (1).

renewal of a motion. See RENEWAL (2).

Reno Rules. A 1993 set of ethical principles for federal prosecutors, formulated by Attorney General Janet Reno and published in the Code of Federal Regulations. • Because of a lack of statutory backing, the rules were not considered enforceable. In 1998, these rules and the Thornburgh memo were replaced by 28 USCA § 530B, which makes federal attorneys subject to the rules and codes of the states, and requires the Attorney General to ensure that the rules of the Department of Justice accord with § 530B. See THORNBURGH MEMORANDUM.

renounce, *vb.* (14c) **1.** To give up or abandon formally (a right or interest); to disclaim <renounce an inheritance>. **2.** To refuse to follow or obey; to decline to recognize or observe <renounce one's allegiance>.

renovare (ren-ə-**vair**-ee), *vb.* [Latin] *Hist.* To renew.

renovatio (ren-ə-**vay**-shee-oh). [Latin] *Hist.* A renewal (as of a lease).

rent, *n.* (13c) **1.** Consideration paid, usu. periodically, for the use or occupancy of property (esp. real property).

▸ **best rent.** See *open-market rent.*

▸ **ceiling rent.** (1944) The maximum rent that can be charged under a rent-control regulation.

▸ **crop rent.** (1904) The portion of a harvest given by a sharecropper to a landlord as rent. • Specific crop names, such as *grain rent* and *potato rent,* are commonly used.

▸ **double rent.** (16c) Twice the amount of rent agreed to; specif., a penalty of twice the amount of rent against a tenant who holds possession of the leased property after the date provided in the tenant's notice to quit. • The penalty was provided by the Distress for Rent Act, 1737, 11 Geo. 2., ch. 19, § 13.

▸ **dry rent.** (16c) **1.** Rent reserved without a distress clause allowing the rent to be collected by distress; rent that can be collected only by an ordinary legal action. — Formerly also termed *rent seck.* **2.** See *rent seck* under RENT (2).

▸ **economic rent.** See ECONOMIC RENT.

▸ **grain rent.** See *crop rent.*

▸ **ground rent.** (17c) **1.** Rent paid by a tenant under a long-term lease for the use of undeveloped land, usu. for the construction of a commercial building. — Also termed *redeemable ground rent.* See *ground lease* under LEASE. **2.** A heritable interest, in rental income from land, reserved by a grantor who conveys the land in fee simple. • This type of ground rent is found primarily in Maryland and Pennsylvania. — Also termed (in Scots law) *irredeemable ground rent; ground annual.*

▸ **guild rent.** (17c) *Hist.* Rent payable to the Crown by a guild. — Also spelled *gild-rent.*

▸ **irredeemable ground rent.** See *ground rent* (2).

▸ **land-rent,** *n.* (18c) Rent paid for the use of a farm.

▸ **net rent.** (18c) The rental price for property after payment of expenses, such as repairs, utilities, and taxes.

▸ **open-market rent.** (1919) The best rent that a willing landlord might receive from a willing tenant, assuming that (1) the property is on the open market with vacant possession, (2) standard marketing methods are used, (3) no extra incentives are added, and (4) the lease terms are within the standard range. — Also termed *best rent; market rent.*

▸ **rack-rent.** See RACK-RENT.

▸ **redeemable ground rent.** See *ground rent* (1).

2. *Hist.* A compensation or return made periodically by a tenant or occupant for the possession and use of lands or corporeal hereditaments; money, chattels, or services issuing usu. annually out of lands and tenements as payment for use.

▸ **peppercorn rent.** (17c) A nominal rent that is far below the market rate. • The rent may be a mere token payment. Historically in English law, some lease agreements called for a token annual rent payment of a single dried berry of black pepper. See PEPPERCORN.

▸ **quit rent.** See QUIT RENT.

▸ **rent charge.** See RENTCHARGE.

▸ **rent seck.** (15c) *Hist.* A rent reserved by deed but without any clause of distress. — Also spelled *rent-seck; rent-sec.* — Also termed *dry rent.* Pl. **rents seck.**

> "But rents-seck have long ceased to exist, because the inability of their owners to distrain was abolished by the Landlord and Tenant Act, 1730 (4 George II), which enacted that the owners of rents-seck, rents of assize and chief rents should have the same remedy by distress as existed in the case of rent reserved upon lease." G.C. Cheshire, *Modern Law of Real Property* 199 (3d ed. 1933).

> "At common law, the relationship of lord and tenant carried with it an automatic right of distress for any rent. If no such relationship existed, there was no common law right of distress, and consequently an express clause of distress was frequently inserted when reserving the rent. A rent supported by no right of distress was known as a rent seck (from the Latin *siccus*, dry, barren) . . .. Rent seck ceased to exist many years ago, for by the Landlord and Tenant Act 1730, the owners of rents seck were given the same rights of distress as a landlord has against his tenant under a lease, namely, a right to distrain as soon as the rent is in arrear." Robert E. Megarry & P.V. Baker, *A Manual of the Law of Real Property* 409 (4th ed. 1969).

▸ **rent service.** (14c) A rent with some corporeal service incident to it (as by fealty) and with a right of distress. — Also written *rent-service.*

> "[R]ent-service exists only where the relation of landlord and tenant is found, and in such a case rent derives its name from the fact that it was given as a substitute for

the services to which the land was originally liable." G.C. Cheshire, *Modern Law of Real Property* 198 (3d ed. 1933).

3. *Civil law.* A contract by which one party conveys to another party a tract of land or other immovable property, to be held by the other party as owner and in perpetuity, in exchange for payment of an annual sum of money or quantity of fruits. • Under Louisiana law, the rent is essentially redeemable even though stipulated to be perpetual. The seller may set the terms of the redemption, which must take place after a stipulated time (not to exceed 30 years) La. Civ. Code art. 2788. See FRUIT (2). — Also termed *rent of lands.* **4.** The difference between the actual return from a commodity or service and the cost of supplying it; the difference between revenue and opportunity cost. — **rent,** *vb.*

rent, *vb.* (16c) **1.** To pay for the use of another's property. **2.** *Hist. Slang.* EXTORT (2).

rentage. (17c) Rent or rental.

rent-a-judging. See PRIVATE JUDGING.

rental, *n.* (14c) **1.** The amount received as rent.

▸ **crescendo rental.** (1909) A rent payment that gradually increases at fixed periods during the lease term.

▸ **delay rental.** (1912) *Oil & gas.* A periodic payment made by an oil-and-gas lessee to postpone exploration during the primary lease term. See DRILLING-DELAY RENTAL CLAUSE; *"or" lease, "unless" lease* under LEASE; PAID-UP LEASE.

▸ **net rental.** (18c) The amount remaining after deducting all expenses from the gross rental income.

2. The income received from rent. **3.** A record of payments received from rent. — **rental,** *adj.*

Rental and Related Rights Directive. See DIRECTIVE ON RENTAL, LENDING AND CERTAIN NEIGHBORING RIGHTS.

Rental Directive. See DIRECTIVE ON RENTAL, LENDING AND CERTAIN NEIGHBORING RIGHTS.

rental division order. (1936) *Oil & gas.* A stipulation signed by those entitled to delay rentals, stating what interest each owns and how much rental each is to receive.

rental right. (1963) *Copyright.* The power of a copyright owner to control the use of copies of the work beyond the first sale, when that use involves offering the copy to the public for temporary use for a fee (as at a store renting DVDs and videotapes) or some other commercial advantage (as at a hotel offering the loan of DVDs or videotapes). • Rental rights are recognized among members of the European Commission and under TRIPs. The right also applies to the rental of computer software.

rentcharge. (14c) The right to receive an annual sum from the income of land, usu. in perpetuity, and to retake possession if the payments are in arrears. — Also spelled *rent-charge; rent charge.* — Also termed *fee-farm rent.*

> "Rent-charge is a rent with liberty to distrain. As when a man seised of land granteth by a deed poll, or by indenture, a yearly rent going out of the same land to another in fee or fee-tail, or for a term of life, etc. with clause of distress, or maketh a feoffment in fee by indenture, reserving to himself a certain yearly rent, with clause of distress." Henry Finch, *Law, or a Discourse Thereof* 155 (1759).

> "A rentcharge is an annual or periodic payment charged upon, and payable by the owner of, land. Unlike a rent service, in the case of a rentcharge there is no tenure or privity of estate between the parties. The owner of a rentcharge has no tenurial relationship with the land upon which it is charged. A rentcharge is a species of incorporeal property, but, unlike an easement, is incorporeal property in gross, being enjoyed by the owner personally and not in the capacity of proprietor of land." Peter Butt, *Land Law* 330 (2d ed. 1988).

▸ **ecclesiastical-tithe rentcharge.** (1936) *Hist. English law.* A rentcharge attached to a benefice or ecclesiastical corporation. • Under the Tithe Act 1925, a landowner liable for an ecclesiastical-tithe rentcharge could redeem the land and discharge the tithe obligation by making an annual sinking-fund payment to Queen Anne's Bounty. The tithe was due for 81.5 years if the rentcharge was attached to a corporation or 85 years if the rentcharge was attached to a benefice. The law was repealed in 1998. See QUEEN ANNE'S BOUNTY; BENEFICE.

rent control. (1931) A restriction imposed, usu. by municipal legislation, on the maximum rent that a landlord may charge for rental property, and often on a landlord's power of eviction.

rente (rawnt), *n.* [French "income, rent"] (1818) *French law.* **1.** Annual income or rent.

▸ ***rente foncière*** (fawn-**syair**) [French "ground rent"] (1818) A rent that is payable for the use of land and is perpetual.

▸ ***rente viagère*** (vee-ah-**zhair**). [French "life rent"] (1825) A rent charge or annuity that is payable for life; a life interest or annuity.

2. (*usu. pl.*) Interest paid annually by the French government on the public debt; a government stock, bond, or annuity.

rentee. (1855) *Rare.* A tenant.

renter's insurance. See INSURANCE.

rentier (rawn-**tyay**). [French] (17c) **1.** Someone who owns or holds *rentes.* See RENTE. **2.** A person or entity whose income is derived from investments, esp. any form of rent but also stocks or annuities.

rent of lands. See RENT (3).

rent rebate. See REBATE.

rent seck. See RENT (2).

rent-seeking, *n.* (1974) Economic behavior motivated by an incentive to overproduce goods that will yield a return greater than the cost of production. • The term is often used in the field of law and economics. See RENT (4).

rent service. See RENT (2).

rents, issues, and profits. (17c) The total income or profit arising from the ownership or possession of property.

rent strike. (1964) **1.** A concerted refusal by a group of tenants to pay rent until grievances with the landlord are heard or settled. **2.** The situation in which all or almost all the people living in a group of houses or apartments refuse to pay their rent in protest against something.

renunciation (ri-nən-see-**ay**-shən), *n.* (14c) **1.** The express or tacit abandonment of a right without transferring it to another. **2.** *Wills & estates.* The act of waiving a right under a will. • At one time, one *renounced* an inheritance by intestacy and *disclaimed* a gift by will. Today *disclaim* is common in both situations. — Also termed (in sense 2) *disclaimer.* See RIGHT OF ELECTION. Cf. DISCLAIMER. **3.** *Criminal law.* Complete and voluntary abandonment of criminal purpose — sometimes coupled with an attempt to thwart the activity's success — before a crime is committed. • Renunciation can be an affirmative defense to attempt, conspiracy, and the like. Model Penal Code § 5.01(4). — Also termed *withdrawal*; *abandonment*. **4.** See *anticipatory repudiation* under REPUDIATION. — **renunciative, renunciatory,** *adj.* — **renounce,** *vb.*

renvoi (ren-**voy**), *n.* [French "sending back"] (17c) **1.** The doctrine under which a court, in resorting to foreign law, also adopts the foreign law's conflict-of-laws principles, which may in turn refer the court back to the law of the forum. **2.** The problem arising when one state's rule on conflict of laws refers a case to the law of another state, and that second state's conflict-of-law rule refers the case either back to the law of the first state or to a third state. See CONFLICT OF LAWS. **3.** RECONDUCTION (2).

> "In England . . . irrespective of whether or not the doctrine of *renvoi* is part of English law, English courts in referring to a foreign domiciliary law will apply that law as the foreign court would apply it. If the foreign court uses a *renvoi*, the English court will follow it. If it does not, it will do likewise. To illustrate: X, a British subject, died domiciled de facto in France leaving a will of movables, the validity of which came before the English court. The court held that its validity must be determined by French law because English law applies the domicilary law, viz., French law. France refers to the national law of the testator, viz., English law, but accepts a *renvoi* back to the law of the domicil, viz., French law. Had the domicil been in Italy, English law would have been applied, because Italy recognizes the national law of the testator as authoritative, but does not accept *renvoi*." Arthur K. Kuhn, *Comparative Commentaries on Private International Law, or Conflict of Laws* 51–52 (1937).

REO. *abbr.* REAL ESTATE OWNED.

reo absente (ree-oh ab-**sten**-tee). [Latin] (17c) The defendant being absent; the absence of the defendant.

reopen. (Of a court) to review (an otherwise final and nonappealable judgment) for the purpose of possibly granting or modifying relief. • A court will reopen a judgment or case only in highly unusual circumstances. *See* Fed. R. Civ. P. 60.

reo praesente (**ree**-oh pri-**zen**-tee). [Latin] (1809) *Hist.* The defendant being present; the presence of the defendant.

reorganization, *n.* **1.** *Bankruptcy.* A financial restructuring of a corporation, esp. in the repayment of debts, under a plan created by a trustee and approved by a court. See CHAPTER 11.

▸ **haircut reorganization.** (2004) A restructuring that reduces the principal amount of indebtedness owed to creditors. • The more common usage is simply *haircut* <we took a haircut on that deal>. See HAIRCUT (3).

2. *Tax.* A restructuring of a corporation, as by a merger or recapitalization, in order to improve its tax treatment under the Internal Revenue Code. • The Code classifies the various types of reorganizations with different letters. IRC (26 USCA) § 368(a)(1). Cf. RECAPITALIZATION.

▸ **A reorganization.** A reorganization involving a merger or consolidation under a specific state statute.

▸ **B reorganization.** A reorganization in which one corporation exchanges its voting shares for another corporation's voting shares.

▸ **C reorganization.** A reorganization in which one corporation exchanges its voting shares for substantially all the assets of another corporation.

▸ **D reorganization.** A reorganization in which the corporation transfers some or all of its assets to another corporation that is controlled by the transferor or its shareholders, and then the stock of the transferee corporation is distributed.

▸ **E reorganization.** A reorganization involving a recapitalization.

▸ **F reorganization.** A reorganization involving a mere change in a corporation's identity, form, or place of organization.

▸ **G reorganization.** A reorganization involving a transfer of all or part of the corporation's assets to another corporation in a bankruptcy or similar proceeding.

reorganization bond. See *adjustment bond* under BOND (3).

reorganization plan. *Bankruptcy.* A plan of restructuring submitted by a corporation for approval by the court in a Chapter 11 case. See CHAPTER 11.

rep. *abbr.* (18c) **1.** REPORT. **2.** REPORTER. **3.** REPRESENTATIVE. **4.** REPUBLIC.

repair, *n.* **1.** The process of restoring something that has been subjected to decay, waste, injury, or partial destruction, dilapidation, etc.; an instance or a result of this process <the repair of a building> <hardly noticeable repairs>. **2.** The condition of something after being used or fixed; esp., the quality or state of being in good or sound condition <the house is out of repair>.

repair, *vb.* **1.** To restore to a sound or good condition after decay, waste, injury, partial destruction, dilapidation, etc.; to fix (something broken, split, or not working properly) <the repair the road>. **2.** To renew, revive, or rebuild after loss, expenditure, exhaustion, etc. <the body repairs its tissues>. **3.** To mend, remedy, heal, or make right again <to repair a broken relationship>. **4.** To make amends for (an injury, injustice, etc.); to indemnify someone for <to repair a loss>.

repair-and-replace provision. (1984) A contractual clause providing that a product's defect will be remedied by repairing or replacing the defective part or product.

repair doctrine. (1965) *Patents.* The rule that a licensee who is authorized to produce, use, or distribute a patented device also has the right to repair and replace unpatented components. — Also termed *permissible-repair doctrine.* Cf. RECONSTRUCTION.

reparable injury. See INJURY.

reparation (rep-ə-**ray**-shən). (14c) **1.** The act of making amends for a wrong. **2.** (*usu. pl.*) Compensation for an injury or wrong, esp. for wartime damages or breach of an international obligation. **3.** *Criminal law.* Recompense for out-of-pocket losses caused by an offense, but not including pain and suffering.

reparatione facienda. See DE REPARATIONE FACIENDA.

reparative injunction. See INJUNCTION.

reparole. (1916) A second release from prison on parole, served under the same sentence for which the parolee served the first term of parole.

repayable, *adj.* (16c) (Of a sum of money) required to be paid back, usu. by a specified time.

repeal, *n.* (16c) Abrogation of an existing law by express legislative act; RESCIND (3). — **repeal,** *vb.*

▸ **express repeal.** (17c) Repeal by specific declaration in a new statute or main motion.

▸ **implied repeal.** (18c) Repeal by irreconcilable conflict between an old law or main motion and a more recent law or motion. — Also termed *repeal by implication*.

"Repeals by implication are not favored. A statute will not be construed as repealing prior acts on the same subject (in the absence of express words to that effect) unless there is an irreconcilable repugnancy between them, or unless the new law is evidently intended to supersede all prior acts on the matter in hand and to comprise in itself the sole and complete system of legislation on that subject." Henry Campbell Black, *Handbook on the Construction and Interpretation of the Laws* § 107, at 351 (1911).

▸ **repeal by implication.** See *implied repeal*.

repealability canon. The doctrine that the legislature cannot derogate from its own authority or the authority of its successors. — Also termed *rule against irrepealable laws; rule against irrepealability; doctrine against irrepealability; anti-irrepealability canon; nonentrenchment doctrine*.

repealer. 1. A legislative act abrogating an earlier law. — Also termed *repealing act*. **2.** Someone who repeals.

▸ **desuetudinous repealer.** See DESUETUDE (2).

repealing clause. (17c) A statutory provision that repeals an earlier statute. — Also termed *repealer clause*.

repealing statute. See STATUTE.

repeal-of-repealer canon. The doctrine that the repeal or expiration of a repealing statute does not reinstate the original statute.

repeater. See RECIDIVIST.

repeat offender. See OFFENDER.

repetition. (15c) *Civil law.* A demand or action for restitution or repayment. See SOLUTIO INDEBITI.

repetitum namium (ri-**pet**-ə-təm **nay**-mee-əm). [Law Latin] *Hist.* A second, repeated, or reciprocal distress; WITHERNAM.

repetundae (rep-ə-**tən**-dee). [Latin "things or money claimed back"] *Roman law.* See RES REPETUNDAE.

replacement cost. See COST (1).

replacement-cost depreciation method. See DEPRECIATION METHOD.

replacement insurance. See INSURANCE.

replead, *vb.* (16c) **1.** To plead again or anew; to file a new pleading, esp. to correct a defect in an earlier pleading. **2.** To make a repleader.

repleader (ree-**plee**-dər). (17c) *Common-law pleading.* A court order or judgment — issued on the motion of a party who suffered an adverse judgment — requiring the parties to file new pleadings because of some defect in the original pleadings. — Also termed *judgment of repleader.* See MOTION FOR REPLEADER.

replegiare (ri-plee-jee-**air**-ee), *vb.* [Law Latin] *Hist.* To take back on pledge or surety; to replevy.

repleviable (ri-**plev**-ee-ə-bəl), *adj.* (16c) Capable of being replevied; recoverable by replevin <repleviable property>. — Also spelled *replevisable* (ri-**plev**-ə-sə-bəl). Cf. IRREPLEVIABLE.

"Property is said to be repleviable or replevisable when proceedings in replevin may be resorted to for the purpose of trying the right to such property." J.E. Cobbey, *A Practical Treatise on the Law of Replevin* 3 (2d ed. 1900).

replevin (ri-**plev**-in), *n.* [prob. fr. OF *plevir la fey* "to pledge one's word"] (17c) **1.** An action for the repossession of personal property wrongfully taken or detained by the defendant, whereby the plaintiff gives security for and holds the property until the court decides who owns it. — Also termed *claim and delivery*. **2.** A writ obtained from a court authorizing the retaking of personal property wrongfully taken or detained. — Also termed (in sense 2) *writ of replevin*. Cf. DETINUE; TROVER.

"Replevin consists in the redelivery of the goods taken to the owner; the name of one of the common-law actions, the distinguishing features of which are that it is brought to obtain possession of specific chattel property, and is prosecuted by the provisional seizure and delivery to the plaintiff of the thing in suit. Replevin is a personal action *ex delicto* brought to recover possession of goods unlawfully taken, the validity of which taking it is the regular mode of contesting." J.E. Cobbey, *A Practical Treatise on the Law of Replevin* 3 (2d ed. 1900).

"The action of replevin lies, where specific personal property has been wrongfully taken and is wrongfully detained, to recover possession of the property, together with damages for its detention. To support the action it is necessary: (a) That the property shall be personal. (b) That the plaintiff, at the time of suit, shall be entitled to the immediate possession. (c) That (at common law) the defendant shall have wrongfully taken the property (replevin in the cepit). But, by statute in most states, the action will now also lie where the property is wrongfully detained, though it was lawfully obtained in the first instance (replevin in the detinet). (d) That the property shall be wrongfully detained by the defendant at the time of suit." Benjamin J. Shipman, *Handbook of Common-Law Pleading* § 49, at 120 (Henry Winthrop Ballantine ed., 3d ed. 1923).

"In rare cases, the plaintiff might seek equitable relief to secure return of a chattel. More commonly, the claim for recovery of the chattel was pursued at common law under forms of action such as Detinue or Replevin. American statutes or court rules tracked the common law generally, referring to the recovery variously as replevin, detinue, claim-and-delivery, or sequestration. The statutes usually allowed the plaintiff to recover the disputed chattel before trial, though this is now subject to constitutional limits which have led to procedural revisions in many of the statutes." 1 Dan B. Dobbs, *Law of Remedies* § 5.17(1), at 917 (2d ed. 1993).

▸ **personal replevin.** (1844) At common law, an action to replevy a person out of prison or out of another's custody. • Personal replevin has been largely superseded by the writ of habeas corpus as a means of investigating the legality of an imprisonment. See HABEAS CORPUS.

▸ ***replevin in the cepit*** (**see**-pit). (18c) An action for the repossession of property that is both wrongfully taken and wrongfully detained. — Also termed *replevin in cepit*.

▸ **replevin in the detinet** (**det**-i-net). (18c) An action for the repossession of property that is rightfully taken but wrongfully detained. — Also termed *replevin in detinet*.

"In England the action in the progress of its development assumed three forms: *Cepit*, from the Latin *capio*, 'to take,' where the action was simply for the wrongful taking; and *detinet*, from *de* and *teneo*, 'to hold,' where the action was for a wrongful holding. If the goods were not taken on the writ by the officer, the action proceeded as *replevin in the detinet*, but if the goods were taken, the action was called *replevin in the detinuit*; the first meaning 'he detains,' the second 'he detained.' The action in the detinet has long fallen into disuse, and is never brought unless the distrainer has eloigned the goods so that they cannot be got at to make replevin." J.E. Cobbey, *A Practical Treatise on the Law of Replevin* 4 (2d ed. 1900).

▸ **replevin in the detinuit** (di-**tin**-yoo-it). An action for damages resulting from the wrongful taking and detention of goods that have since been returned to the owner. See DETINUIT. Cf. *replevin in the detinet*.

replevin, *vb.* (17c) *Archaic.* REPLEVY.

replevin bond. See BOND (2).

replevisable. See REPLEVIABLE.

replevisor (ri-**plev**-ə-sər). (1837) The plaintiff in a replevin action.

replevy (ri-**plev**-ee), *n.* (15c) *Archaic.* REPLEVIN.

replevy, *vb.* (16c) **1.** To recover possession of (goods) by a writ of replevin. **2.** To recover (goods) by replevin. **3.** *Archaic.* To bail (a prisoner).

replevy bond. See *replevin bond* under BOND (2).

repliant (ri-**plɪ**-ənt). (16c) A party who makes a replication (i.e., a common-law reply). — Also termed *replicant.*

replica, *n.* **1.** A duplicate of a work of art such as a painting or statue, esp. one executed by the original artist and regarded, equally with the true original, as an original <a replica of the famous Shakespeare bust by Carrier-Belleuse>. **2.** A reasonably exact duplicate that, when viewed, causes people to see substantially the same object as the original; a good copy, esp. of an artifact, building, or work of art <antique replicas>.

replicant. See REPLIANT.

replicare (rep-lə-**kair**-ee), *vb.* [Latin] *Hist.* To reply; to answer a defendant's plea.

replicatio (rep-li-**kay**-shee-oh), *n.* [Latin] *Roman law.* A plaintiff's rejection of what a defendant asserted in an *exceptio*; a counterexception. Cf. TRIPLICATIO; QUADRUPLICATIO. Pl. ***replicationes*** (rep-li-kay-shee-**oh**-neez).

replication (rep-lə-**kay**-shən). (15c) A plaintiff's or complainant's reply to a defendant's plea or answer; REPLY (2). See PLEADING (quot.).

"As the replication is in general governed by the plea, and most frequently denies it, the pleader has not often much difficulty in deciding what replication he should adopt. When the plea properly concludes to the *country*, the plaintiff cannot in general reply otherwise than by adding what is termed the *similiter*; but when the plea concludes with a verification, and the plaintiff does not *demur*, the replication may either, *first*, conclude the defendant by matter of *estoppel*; or, *secondly*, may *traverse* or *deny* the truth of the matter alleged in the plea either in whole or in part; or, *thirdly*, may *confess and avoid* the plea; in which case . . . the truth of the matter alleged in the plea must be admitted; or, *fourthly*, in the case of an evasive plea, may *new assign* the cause of action. And though at common law a replication cannot be double, or contain two or more answers to the same plea, and the Statute does not extend to replications, (except in the instance of a plea in bar to an avowry in replevin, which is in the nature of a replication,) yet the plaintiff in many cases has an *election* of different replications." 1 Joseph Chitty, *A Treatise on the Parties to Actions, the Forms of Actions, and on Pleading* 610 (John A. Dunlap & E.D. Ingraham eds., 6th annotated ed. fr. 5th London ed. 1833).

▸ **anticipatory replication.** (1884) *Equity pleading.* In an original bill, the denial of defensive matters that the defendant might assert. • A defendant who relies on the anticipated defense must traverse the anticipatory matter in addition to setting up the defense.

▸ **general replication.** (17c) *Equity pleading.* A replication consisting of a general denial of the defendant's plea or answer and an assertion of the truth and sufficiency of the bill.

▸ **replication *de injuria.*** (17c) *Common-law pleading.* A traverse occurring only in the replication whereby the plaintiff is permitted to traverse the whole substance of a plea consisting merely of legal excuse, when the matter does not involve a title or interest in land, authority of law, authority of fact derived from the opposing party, or any matter of record. — Also termed *replication de injuria sua propria, absque tali causa.*

▸ **replication *per fraudem.*** (18c) *Common-law pleading.* A replication asserting that the discharge pleaded by the defendant was obtained by fraud.

▸ **special replication.** (17c) *Equity pleading.* A replication that puts in issue a new fact to counter a new matter raised in the defendant's plea or answer.

reply, *n.* (18c) **1.** *Civil procedure.* In federal practice, the plaintiff's response to the defendant's counterclaim (or, by court order, to the defendant's or a third party's answer). Fed. R. Civ. P. 7(a). **2.** *Common-law pleading.* The plaintiff's response to the defendant's plea or answer. • The reply is the plaintiff's second pleading, and it is followed by the defendant's rejoinder. — Also termed (in sense 2) *replication.* See PLEADING (quot.). — **reply,** *vb.*

reply brief. See BRIEF (1).

reply-paid envelope. See POSTAGE-PAID ENVELOPE.

repo (**ree**-poh). (1956) **1.** REPOSSESSION. **2.** REPURCHASE AGREEMENT.

repo man. *Slang.* Someone whose job is to repossess cars when the payments for them have not been kept current. — Also termed *repossession agent.*

reproach, *n.* (15c) **1.** Criticism, blame, or disapproval. **2.** A remark expressing criticism, blame, or disapproval. **3.** The behavior giving rise to criticism, blame, or disapproval. — **reproach,** *vb.* — **reproachful,** *adj.*

reproductive-health clinic. 1. See FAMILY-PLANNING CLINIC. **2.** See ABORTION CLINIC.

report, *n.* (14c) **1.** A formal oral or written presentation of facts or a recommendation for action <according to the treasurer's report, there is $300 in the bank>.

▸ **committee report.** *Parliamentary law.* A report from a committee to a deliberative assembly on business referred to the committee or on a matter otherwise under its charge.

▸ **informational report.** (1897) *Parliamentary law.* A report without a recommendation for action.

▸ **insider report.** (1960) *Securities.* A monthly report that must be filed with the SEC when more than 10% of a company's stock is traded.

▸ **majority report.** (1833) *Parliamentary law.* A committee report, as distinguished from a minority report. See *committee report.* Cf. *minority report.*

▸ **minority report.** (1828) *Parliamentary law.* A report by a member or members who dissent from a committee report, setting forth their views, and sometimes proposing an alternative recommendation. • Some organizations require that a minority must reach a certain size (or obtain permission) before it can file a report.

A typical minimum is one-fourth of the committee's members, which guarantees that not more than one minority report will result.

▸ **officer's report.** *Parliamentary law.* A report from an officer to an organization or deliberative assembly on business relating to the officer's duties or on a matter otherwise under the officer's charge.

▸ **report with recommendation.** (1902) *Parliamentary law.* A report accompanied by a recommendation for action.

2. A written account of a court proceeding and judicial decision <the law clerk sent the court's report to counsel for both sides>. **3.** (*usu. pl.*) A published volume of judicial decisions by a particular court or group of courts <U.S. Reports>. • Generally, these decisions are first printed in temporary paperback volumes, and then printed in hardbound reporter volumes. Law reports may be either official (published by a government entity) or unofficial (published by a private publisher). Court citations frequently include the names of both the official and unofficial reports. — Also termed *reporter*; *law report*; *law reporter.* Cf. ADVANCE SHEETS.

▸ **case report.** (*usu. pl.*) An official or unofficial published collection of judicial opinions.

▸ **official report.** (*usu. pl.*) The governmentally approved set of reported cases within a given jurisdiction.

> "[I]t may justly be said that all reports are in a sense 'official,' or that to use the term 'official reports' as referring to any particular series of reports is a misnomer, for it is certainly misleading. The mere fact that each state authorizes or requires publication of reports of its Supreme Court decisions, and, to insure such publication, agrees to purchase a stated number of each volume of the reports, cannot be said to give such a series pre-eminence as an 'official' publication." William M. Lile et al., *Brief Making and the Use of Law Books* 33 (Roger W. Cooley & Charles Lesley Ames eds., 3d ed. 1914).

4. (*usu. pl.*) A collection of administrative decisions by one or more administrative agencies. **5.** MINUTES (2). — Abbr. rep. — **report,** *vb.*

report agenda. See *report calendar* under CALENDAR (4).

report and recommendation. (18c) A written statement of findings and a proposed course of action for consideration by another, esp. a superior.

report calendar. See CALENDAR (4).

reporter. (14c) **1.** A person responsible for making and publishing a report; esp., a lawyer-consultant who prepares drafts of official or semi-official writings such as court rules or Restatements <the reporter to the Advisory Committee on Bankruptcy Rules explained the various amendments>. **2.** REPORTER OF DECISIONS. **3.** REPORT (3) <Supreme Court Reporter>. — Abbr. rep.; rptr.

> "It may not come amiss to remark that the National Report System is usually spoken of as the 'Reporters,' and one of the component parts of that system is in like manner spoken of as a 'Reporter.' Wherever, in this or the succeeding chapters of this work, the word is used with a capital, it refers to one or more of the parts of the National Reporter System. When the word 'reporter' is used without capitalization, it refers to the person who reports or edits the cases in any series of reports to which reference is being made." William M. Lile et al., *Brief Making and the Use of Law Books* 37 (Roger W. Cooley & Charles Lesley Ames eds., 3d ed. 1914).

reporter of decisions. (1839) The person responsible for publishing a court's opinions. • The position began historically — in the years before systematic reporting of decisions was introduced — when lawyers attended the sessions of particular courts, were accredited to them by the judges, and reported the decisions of that court. Today, the reporter of decisions holds an administrative post as a court employee. The reporter often has duties that include verifying citations, correcting spelling and punctuation, and suggesting minor editorial improvements before judicial opinions are released or published. — Often shortened to *reporter.* — Also termed *court reporter.* See COURT REPORTER.

reporter's privilege. See *journalist's privilege* (1) under PRIVILEGE (3).

reporter's record. 1. See RECORD. **2.** See TRANSCRIPT.

reporter's syllabus. See HEADNOTE.

reporting company. See COMPANY.

report of proceedings. See TRANSCRIPT.

reports, *n.* See REPORT.

Reports, The. A series of 13 volumes of caselaw published in the 17th century by Sir Edward Coke.

report with recommendation. See REPORT (1).

repose (ri-**pohz**), *n.* (16c) **1.** Cessation of activity; temporary rest. **2.** A statutory period after which an action cannot be brought in court, even if it expires before the plaintiff suffers any injury. See STATUTE OF REPOSE.

repository (ri-**poz**-ə-tor-ee). (15c) **1.** A place or container in which something is deposited or stored, esp. in large quantities; a warehouse or storehouse. **2.** A website, book, or person that has a huge amount of information.

repossession, *n.* (15c) The act or an instance of retaking property; esp., a seller's retaking of goods sold on credit when the buyer has failed to pay for them. — Often shortened to *repo.* Cf. FORECLOSURE; RESCUE (3). — **repossess,** *vb.*

representation, *n.* (16c) **1.** A presentation of fact — either by words or by conduct — made to induce someone to act, esp. to enter into a contract; esp., the manifestation to another that a fact, including a state of mind, exists <the buyer relied on the seller's representation that the roof did not leak>. Cf. MISREPRESENTATION.

> "Representation . . . may introduce terms into a contract and affect performance: or it may induce a contract and so affect the intention of one of the parties, and the formation of the contract. . . . At common law, . . . if a representation did not afterwards become a substantive part of the contract, its untruth (save in certain excepted cases and apart always from fraud) was immaterial. But if it did, it might be one of two things: (1) it might be regarded by the parties as a vital term going to the root of the contract (when it is usually called a 'condition'); and in this case its untruth entitles the injured party to repudiate the whole contract; or (2) it might be a term in the nature only of an independent subsidiary promise (when it is usually called a 'warranty'), which is indeed a part of the contract, but does not go to the root of it; in this case its untruth only gives rise to an action *ex contractu* for damages, and does *not* entitle the injured party to repudiate the whole contract." William R. Anson, *Principles of the Law of Contract* 218, 222 (Arthur L. Corbin ed., 3d Am. ed. 1919).

▸ **affirmative representation.** (1842) A representation asserting the existence of certain facts about a given subject matter.

▸ **false representation.** See MISREPRESENTATION.

▸ **material representation.** (18c) A representation to which a reasonable person would attach importance in deciding his or her course of action in a transaction. • Material representation is a necessary element of an action for fraud.

▸ **mere representation.** (18c) A statement or assertion not intended to be legally binding. • A mere representation usu. does not become part of an agreement or result in liability.

▸ **promissory representation.** (1842) A representation about what one will do in the future; esp., a representation made by an insured about what will happen during the time of coverage, stated as a matter of expectation and amounting to an enforceable promise.

2. The act or an instance of standing for or acting on behalf of another, esp. by a lawyer on behalf of a client <Clarence Darrow's representation of John Scopes>.

▸ **concurrent representation.** (1947) The simultaneous representation of more than one person in the same matter; esp., a lawyer's representation of two or more clients with potentially conflicting interests. — Also termed *dual representation*; *joint representation*. See CONFLICT OF INTEREST (2).

▸ **dual representation.** See *concurrent representation*.

▸ **hybrid representation.** (1975) *Criminal law.* A lawyer who acts as cocounsel alongside a defendant. Cf. *standby counsel* under COUNSEL.

▸ **joint representation. 1.** See *concurrent representation*. **2.** Representation of one or more clients by more than one attorney.

▸ **stage representation.** The representation of a criminal defendant in only one phase of the prosecution, so that in the end the defendant will have been represented by various lawyers. • This practice, which sometimes occurs in public defenders' offices, has been criticized as resulting in lower-quality representation.

▸ **vertical representation.** See VERTICAL REPRESENTATION.

3. The fact of a litigant's having such a close alignment of interests with another person that the other is considered as having been present in the litigation <the named plaintiff provided adequate representation for the absent class members>.

▸ **adequate representation.** (1939) A close alignment of interests between actual parties and potential parties in a lawsuit, so that the interests of potential parties are sufficiently protected by the actual parties. • The concept of adequate representation is often used in procedural contexts. For example, if a case is to be certified as a class action, there must be adequate representation by the named plaintiffs of all the potential class members. Fed. R. Civ. P. 23(a)(4). And if a nonparty is to intervene in a lawsuit, there must not already be adequate representation of the nonparty by an existing party. Fed. R. Civ. P. 24(a)(2).

▸ **virtual representation.** (1934) A party's maintenance of an action on behalf of others with a similar interest, as a class representative does in a class action. See VIRTUAL-REPRESENTATION DOCTRINE.

4. The assumption by an heir of the rights of his or her predecessor <each child takes a share by representation>. See PER STIRPES. **5.** (*usu. pl.*) *Int'l law.* A friendly but firm statement of a perceived wrong. • This is the mildest form of complaint that one country can make to another. — Also termed *diplomatic representation*. — **represent,** *vb.*

> "Representations are in the nature of vigorous arguments employed in the hope of securing a modification of the action complained of without implying necessarily or expressly an intention ultimately to seek redress by more vigorous means." Ellery C. Stowell, *International Law: A Restatement of Principles in Conformity with Actual Practice* 427 (1931).

representation, estoppel by. See *estoppel by representation* under ESTOPPEL.

representational standing. See *associational standing* under STANDING.

representation election. See ELECTION (3).

representative, *n.* (17c) **1.** Someone who stands for or acts on behalf of another <the owner was the football team's representative at the labor negotiations>. See AGENT.

▸ **accredited representative.** (1846) A person with designated authority to act on behalf of another person, group, or organization, usu. by being granted that authority by law or by the rules of the group or organization <as an officer of the union, she was the accredited representative of the employees in the wage dispute>.

▸ **class representative.** (1942) Someone who sues on behalf of a group of plaintiffs in a class action. — Also termed *named plaintiff*. See CLASS ACTION.

▸ **independent personal representative.** See *personal representative*.

▸ **lawful representative.** (17c) **1.** A legal heir. **2.** An executor, administrator, or other legal representative. — Also termed *legal representative*. See *personal representative*.

▸ **legal-personal representative.** (18c) **1.** When used by a testator referring to personal property, an executor or administrator. **2.** When used by a testator referring to real property, one to whom the real estate passes immediately upon the testator's death. **3.** When used concerning the death of a mariner at sea, the public administrator, executor, or appointed administrator in the seaman's state of residence.

▸ **legal representative. 1.** See *lawful representative*. **2.** See *personal representative*.

▸ **personal representative.** (18c) Someone who manages the legal affairs of another because of incapacity or death, such as the executor of an estate. • Technically, an executor is a personal representative named in a will, while an administrator is a personal representative not named in a will. — Also termed *independent personal representative*; *legal representative*.

▸ **registered representative.** (1945) A person approved by the SEC and stock exchanges to sell securities to the public. — Formerly also termed *customer's man*; *customer's person*.

2. A member of a legislature, esp. of the lower house <one senator and one representative attended the rally>. — Abbr. rep.

representative action. (1911) **1.** CLASS ACTION. **2.** DERIVATIVE ACTION (1).

representative capacity. See CAPACITY (1).

representative democracy. See DEMOCRACY.

representative recall. See *recall election* under ELECTION.

representee. (1911) One to whom a representation is made.

> "First, where the representor can show that he was not negligent, he will not be liable under the 1967 Act; and secondly, where the representee wants to claim damages at the contractual rate, for loss of his bargain, it may be that the Misrepresentation Act will not suffice." P.S. Atiyah, *An Introduction to the Law of Contract* 165 (3d ed. 1981).

representor. (17c) Someone who makes a representation.

> "[I]t is arguable that even where a contracting party does not intend to guarantee the accuracy of what he says, the other party is at least entitled to assume that due care has been taken by the representor." P.S. Atiyah, *An Introduction to the Law of Contract* 309 (3d ed. 1981).

repressed-memory syndrome. (1993) A memory disorder characterized by an intermittent and extensive inability to recall important personal information, usu. following or concerning a traumatic or highly stressful occurrence, when the memory lapses cannot be dismissed as normal forgetfulness. • The theoretical basis for this syndrome was proposed by Sigmund Freud in 1895. The American Psychiatric Association has recognized the syndrome officially by the medical term *dissociative amnesia*. Although the APA has affirmed that some people suffering partial or total dissociative amnesia may later recover some or all of the memory of the traumatic or stressful event, the existence of the syndrome is controversial. Some studies indicate that "repressed" memories, at least in some patients, may be a product of suggestions made by mental-health therapists rather than of any actual experience. — Abbr. RMS. — Also termed *recovered-memory syndrome*; *dissociative amnesia*. Cf. FALSE-MEMORY SYNDROME.

repressive tax. See *sin tax* under TAX.

reprieve (ri-**preev**), *n.* (16c) **1.** A delay before something bad happens or resumes happening. **2.** Temporary postponement of the carrying out of a criminal sentence, esp. a death sentence; specif., an official order halting the execution of a prisoner on death row. Cf. COMMUTATION (2); PARDON. — **reprieve,** *vb.*

> "The term *reprieve* is derived from *reprendre*, to keep back, and signifies the withdrawing of the sentence for an interval of time, and operates in delay of execution." 1 Joseph Chitty, *A Practical Treatise on the Criminal Law* 757 (2d ed. 1826).

reprimand, *n.* (17c) In professional legal responsibility, a form of disciplinary action that is imposed after trial or formal charges and declares the lawyer's conduct to be improper but does not limit his or her right to practice law; a mild form of lawyer discipline that does not restrict the lawyer's ability to practice law. — **reprimand,** *vb.* — **reprimander,** *n.*

▸ **private reprimand.** An unpublished communication between a disciplinary agency and a wrongdoing attorney, admonishing the attorney about the improper conduct. • Sometimes a published reprimand that does not identify the lawyer by name is considered a private reprimand.

▸ **public reprimand.** A published notice, appearing usu. in a legal newspaper or bar journal, admonishing the attorney about improper conduct and describing the impropriety for the benefit of other members of the legal profession.

reprisal (ri-**prI**-zəl). (15c) **1.** (*often pl.*) *Int'l law.* The use of force, short of war, against another country to redress an injury caused by that country.

> "REPRIZALS, a right, according to the civil law and that of nations, which princes have to retake from their enemies such things as they unjustly detain from them, or other things equivalent thereto. — It is used also for a permission given by a prince sometimes to a subject, upon a full cognizance of the cause, authorizing him to retake, from the first person he meets with of the adverse party, as many effects as make an equivalent to what have been violently forced from him, and for which the opposite prince has refused to do him justice." 2 Jacques Savary des Brûlons, *The Universal Dictionary of Trade and Commerce* 580 (Malachy Postlethwayt, ed. and trans., 1755).

> "'Reprisals' is a word with a long history, and modern writers are not agreed on the meaning which should be given to it today. Literally and historically it denotes the seizing of property or persons by way of retaliation . . . . Reprisals when they are taken today are taken by a state, but some writers would still limit the word to acts of taking or withholding the property of a foreign state or its nationals, for example by an embargo, whilst others would abandon the historical associations and use it to denote any kind of coercive action not amounting to war whereby a state attempts to secure satisfaction from another for some wrong which the latter has committed against it." J.L. Brierly, *The Law of Nations* 321–22 (5th ed. 1955).

▸ **general reprisal.** (1894) A reprisal by which a country directs all its military officers and citizens to redress an injury caused by another country. • An example is a command to seize the property of the offending country wherever it is found.

▸ **negative reprisal.** (1933) A reprisal by which a country refuses to perform an obligation to another country, such as the fulfillment of a treaty.

▸ **positive reprisal.** (1933) A reprisal by which a country forcibly seizes another country's property or persons.

▸ **special reprisal.** (1933) A reprisal by which a country authorizes an aggrieved private citizen to redress an injury caused by another country. • An example is an authorization for a private citizen to seize a particular vessel of the offending country. See LETTERS OF MARQUE.

2. (*often pl.*) *Int'l law.* An act of forceful retaliation for injury or attack by another country; formerly, in war, the killing of prisoners in response to an enemy's war crimes (now unlawful). Cf. RETORSION. **3.** Any act or instance of retaliation, as by an employer against a complaining employee. — Also spelled (archaically) *reprizal.*

reprise (ri-**prIz**), *n.* (15c) An annual deduction, duty, or payment out of a manor or estate, such as an annuity.

reproach, *vb.* To censure with severity; to upbraid. — **reproach,** *n.* — **reproachable,** *adj.* — **reproachful,** *adj.*

reprobation (rep-rə-**bay**-shən). (15c) The act of raising an objection or exception, as to the competency of a witness or the sufficiency of evidence. — **reprobationary** (rep-rə-**bay**-shə-ner-ee), **reprobative** (**rep**-rə-bay-tiv), *adj.* — **reprobate** (**rep**-rə-bayt), *vb.*

reprobator (**rep**-rə-bay-tər). (17c) *Scots law. Hist.* A challenge to disqualify a witness or to invalidate the testimony of an objectionable witness. — Also termed *action of reprobator.*

reproduction right. (1905) *Copyright.* A copyright holder's exclusive right to make copies or phonorecords of the protected work. • Unauthorized copying constitutes infringement. — Also termed *right of reproduction.*

reproductive-health clinic. See ABORTION CLINIC.

reproductive rights. (1966) A person's constitutionally protected rights relating to the control of his or her procreative activities; specif., the cluster of civil liberties relating to pregnancy, abortion, and sterilization, esp. the personal bodily rights of a woman in her decision whether to become pregnant or bear a child. • The phrase includes the idea of being able to make reproductive decisions free from discrimination, coercion, or violence. Human-rights scholars increasingly consider many reproductive rights to be protected by international human-rights law.

reproof (ri-**proof**), *n.* (14c) **1.** The act of saying to a person that he or she has erred, the intention being to correct the error; authoritative censure for a fault. **2.** The disapproving words of someone who tells someone else about such an error or fault; the statements by which disapproval and blame are communicated.

reprovable (ri-**proov**-ə-bəl), *adj.* (14c) Worthy of reproof; blamable.

reproval, *n.* A censure or reprimand issued by a state high court or by the state bar; REPROOF. • This term is esp. common in California.

reprove (ri-**proov**), *vb.* (14c) **1.** To censure directly for some blameworthy fault or misbehavior; to engage in face-to-face blaming of (a person). **2.** To express disapproval of (an act).

republic, *n.* (16c) A system of government in which the people hold sovereign power and elect representatives who exercise that power. • It contrasts on the one hand with a pure democracy, in which the people or community as an organized whole wield the sovereign power of government, and on the other with the rule of one person (such as a king or dictator) or of an elite group (such as an oligarchy, aristocracy, or junta). — Abbr. rep. Cf. DEMOCRACY. — **republican,** *adj.*

> "A republic is a government which (a) derives all of its powers directly or indirectly from the great body of the people and (b) is administered by persons holding their office during pleasure, for a limited period, or during good behavior." Robert A. Dahl, *A Preface to Democratic Theory* 10 (1956).

Republican Form of Government Clause. See GUARANTEE CLAUSE (2).

republican government. See GOVERNMENT (3).

republicanism. (17c) **1.** The theory or principles of a government by elected representatives only, without a monarch. **2.** (*usu. cap.*) Collectively, the policies of the Republican Party. **3.** The quality, state, or condition of being republican or a Republican.

republication, *n.* (18c) **1.** The act or an instance of publishing again or anew. **2.** *Wills & estates.* Reestablishment of the validity of a previously revoked will by repeating the formalities of execution or by using a codicil. • The result is to make the old will effective from the date of republication. — Also termed *revalidation.* Cf. REVIVAL (2). **3.** *Defamation.* The act or an instance of repeating or spreading more widely a defamatory statement. — **republish,** *vb.*

repudiate, *vb.* (16c) **1.** To reject or renounce (a duty or obligation); esp., to indicate an intention not to perform (a contract). **2.** *Hist.* To divorce or disown (one's wife).

repudiatee (ri-pyoo-dee-ə-**tee**). (1936) A party to a contract that has been repudiated by the other party.

repudiation (ri-pyoo-dee-**ay**-shən), *n.* (16c) **1.** *Eccles. law. Rare.* A person's refusal to accept a benefice. **2.** *Contracts.* A contracting party's words or actions that indicate an intention not to perform the contract in the future; a threatened breach of contract. Cf. REJECTION (1), (2); RESCISSION; REVOCATION (2). — **repudiatory** (ri-**pyoo**-dee-ə-tor-ee), **repudiable** (r-**pyoo**-dee-ə-bəl), *adj.*

> "A repudiation is (a) a statement by the obligor to the obligee indicating that the obligor will commit a breach that would of itself give the obligee a claim for damages for total breach . . . , or (b) a voluntary affirmative act which renders the obligor unable or apparently unable to perform without such a breach." Restatement (Second) of Contracts § 250 (1979).

> "In order to constitute a repudiation, a party's language must be sufficiently positive to be reasonably interpreted to mean that the party will not or cannot perform. Mere expression of doubt as to his willingness or ability to perform is not enough to constitute a repudiation, although such an expression may give an obligee reasonable grounds to believe that the obligor will commit a serious breach and may ultimately result in a repudiation . . . . However, language that under a fair reading 'amounts to a statement of intention not to perform except on conditions which go beyond the contract' constitutes a repudiation." Restatement (Second) of Contracts § 250, cmt. b (1979).

▸ **anticipatory repudiation.** (1913) Repudiation of a contractual duty before the time for performance, giving the injured party an immediate right to damages for total breach, as well as discharging the injured party's remaining duties of performance. • This type of repudiation occurs when the promisor unequivocally disavows any intention to perform when the time for performance comes. Once the repudiation occurs, the nonrepudiating party has three options: (1) treat the repudiation as an immediate breach and sue for damages; (2) ignore the repudiation, urge the repudiator to perform, wait for the specified time of performance, and sue if the repudiating party does not perform; or (3) cancel the contract. — Also termed *renunciation.* See *anticipatory breach* under BREACH OF CONTRACT.

> The Restatement lists three actions that constitute anticipatory repudiation: "(a) a positive statement to the promisee or other person having a right under the contract, indicating that the promisor will not or cannot substantially perform his contractual duties; (b) transferring or contracting to transfer to a third person an interest in specific land, goods, or in any other thing essential for the substantial performance of his contractual duties; (c) any voluntary affirmative act which renders substantial performance of his contractual duties impossible, or apparently impossible." Restatement (Second) of Contracts § 318 (1979).

▸ **express repudiation.** Repudiation made by using clear, unequivocal words and actions.

▸ **implied repudiation.** Repudiation shown by acts indicating an unwillingness to perform as promised.

▸ **total repudiation.** (1859) An unconditional refusal by a party to perform the acts required by a contract. • This type of repudiation justifies the other party in refraining from performance.

repudiator (ri-**pyoo**-dee-ay-tər). (1825) Someone who repudiates; esp., a party who repudiates a contract.

repudiatory breach. See BREACH OF CONTRACT.

repudium (ri-**pyoo**-dee-əm), *n.* [Latin] *Roman law.* The revocation of betrothal or marriage by either the man or the woman. • After Augustus, it was necessary to send the other spouse a letter of repudiation in order to terminate the marriage. Cf. DIVORTIUM (1).

repugnancy (ri-pəg-nən-see). (1865) An inconsistency or contradiction between two or more parts of a legal instrument (such as a contract or statute).

repugnant (ri-pəg-nənt), *adj.* (14c) Inconsistent or irreconcilable with; contrary or contradictory to <the court's interpretation was repugnant to the express wording of the statute>.

repugnant verdict. See VERDICT (1).

repurchase, *n.* (16c) The act or an instance of buying something back or again; esp., a corporation's buying back of some or all of its stock at market price. See REDEMPTION; BUYBACK. — **repurchase,** *vb.*

repurchase agreement. (1891) A short-term loan agreement by which one party sells a security to another party but promises to buy back the security on a specified date at a specified price. — Often shortened to *repo.*

repurchase price. See *redemption price* under PRICE.

reputation, *n.* (1839) **1.** The esteem in which someone is held or the goodwill extended to or confidence reposed in that person by others, whether with respect to personal character, private or domestic life, professional and business qualifications, social dealings, conduct, status, or financial standing. • Evidence of reputation may be introduced as proof of character whenever character evidence is admissible. Fed. R. Evid. 405. — Also termed *personal reputation.* See *character evidence* under CHARACTER. **2.** The esteem in which a company is held by the public. — **reputational,** *adj.*

> "Reputations are ephemeral. If they are to be kept healthy and sound, they must be watered by good deeds and constant devotion. It is far easier to destroy a good reputation than to build one." Ferdinand F. Stone, *Handbook of Law Study* 157 (1952).

▸ **business reputation.** The public's evaluation of and regard for the quality of a company's goods or services.

▸ **market reputation.** See *business reputation.*

reputational evidence. See *reputation evidence* under EVIDENCE.

reputation evidence. See EVIDENCE.

reputed manor. See MANOR (1).

request, *n. Parliamentary law.* A motion by which a member invokes a right, seeks permission for the exercise of a privilege, or asks a question. Cf. MOTION (2); DEMAND, *n.* (2); INQUIRY (2); POINT (2).

▸ **request for information.** See *point of information* under POINT.

▸ **request for leave to modify a motion.** See *request for permission to modify a motion.*

▸ **request for leave to withdraw a motion.** See *request for permission to withdraw a motion.*

▸ **request for permission to modify a motion.** A motion by which the mover seeks an amendment to his or her own motion after the chair has stated the motion. • The mover controls a motion only until the chair states the question. After that, the motion belongs to the assembly and the mover cannot modify it without the assembly's permission. See *friendly amendment* under AMENDMENT (3). — Also termed *request for leave to modify a motion.*

▸ **request for permission to withdraw a motion.** A motion by the mover to end consideration of the motion without reaching a decision on its merits. See *request for permission to modify a motion.* — Also termed *request for leave to withdraw a motion.*

▸ **request to be excused from a duty.** A motion seeking relief from a duty that an officer or other member has been charged with.

▸ **request to read papers. 1.** A motion asking permission to read aloud from printed matter. • A member is usu. allowed to read short, pertinent extracts in debate, but formal permission is required if another member objects. **2.** A motion asking that the chair or secretary read aloud a document for the mover's or the assembly's information.

request for admission. (1939) *Civil procedure.* In pretrial discovery, a party's written factual statement served on another party who must admit, deny, or object to the substance of the statement. • Ordinarily, many requests for admission appear in one document. The admitted statements, along with any statements not denied or objected to, will be treated by the court as established and therefore do not have to be proved at trial. Fed. R. Civ. P. 36. — Abbr. RFA. — Also termed *request for admissions; request to admit; notice to admit.*

request for assurances. See DEMAND FOR ASSURANCES.

request for continued examination. (2002) *Patents.* A means of negating the final action on a patent so that the applicant can file amendments, new claims, etc. to show that the invention is patentable as of the original application date. • Unlike a continuation application, a request for continued examination keeps a patent alive as if no final decision had been made. It allows prosecution of claims that have been rejected in a final office action to continue. — Abbr. RCE. Cf. CONTINUATION.

request for instructions. (1942) *Procedure.* During trial, a party's written request that the court instruct the jury on the law as set forth in the request. *See* Fed. R. Civ. P. 51. — Abbr. RFI. — Also termed *request to charge.*

request for leave to modify a motion. See REQUEST.

request for leave to withdraw a motion. See REQUEST.

request for permission to modify a motion. See REQUEST.

request for permission to withdraw a motion. See REQUEST.

request for production. (1944) *Procedure.* In pretrial discovery, a party's written request that another party provide specified documents or other tangible things for inspection and copying. Fed. R. Civ. P. 34. — Abbr. RFP. — Also termed *document request; request for production of documents; notice to produce; demand for document inspection; request to produce or inspect documents.*

request for proposal. (1956) An invitation to prospective suppliers or contractors to submit proposals or bids to provide goods or services. • Unlike most invitations for bids, an RFP requires bidders to give more information than the proposed price. For instance, bidders may have to provide evidence of good financial condition, acceptable technical capability, stock availability, and customer satisfaction. — Abbr. RFP.

request for reconsideration. (1875) *Patents.* An applicant's submission of further arguments after a patent claim's rejection.

request for reexamination. (1971) *Patents.* A formal process of asking the Patent and Trademark Office to review an in-force patent's validity in light of prior-art references. • Anyone, including the patent owner or an infringer, may request a patent's reexamination.

request for relief. See PRAYER FOR RELIEF.

request for tenders. See INVITATION TO TENDER.

request to admit. See REQUEST FOR ADMISSION.

request to be excused from a duty. See REQUEST.

request to charge. See REQUEST FOR INSTRUCTIONS.

request to produce or inspect documents. See REQUEST FOR PRODUCTION.

request to read papers. See REQUEST.

required-records doctrine. (1945) The principle that the privilege against self-incrimination does not apply when one is being compelled to produce business records that are kept in accordance with government regulations and that involve public aspects. • Some courts have held that certain medical records and tax forms fall within this doctrine and are thus not protected by the privilege against self-incrimination.

required-request law. (1986) A law mandating that hospital personnel discuss with a deceased patient's relatives the possibility of an anatomical gift. • The Uniform Anatomical Gift Act (not in effect in some states) mandates a required-request law.

required reserve. See RESERVE (1).

requirement, *n.* **1.** Something that must be done because of a law or rule; something legally imposed, called for, or demanded; an imperative command <building requirements specified in the Americans with Disabilities Act>. **2.** Something that someone needs or asks for <the new telephone system meets all our requirements>. See *requirements contract* under CONTRACT. **3.** Something, such as good test results, that an employer, university, etc. sets as a necessary qualification; a requisite or essential condition <fulfilling the requirements for college admission>. **4.** The act of establishing something as a need or necessity; a demand <the requirement by management that no children under 10 be allowed at our workplace>.

requirement for division. See RESTRICTION (4).

requirement for restriction. See RESTRICTION (4).

requirements contract. See CONTRACT.

requirements testing. See ACCEPTANCE TESTING.

requisite (**rek**-wi-zit), *adj.* (15c) Required either by rule or by the nature of things; necessary.

requisite, *n.* (15c) That which cannot be dispensed with; a necessity either by rule or by the nature of things.

requisition (rek-wə-**zish**-ən), *n.* (15c) **1.** An authoritative, formal demand, usu. on the basis of some official right or authority <a state governor's requisition for another state's surrender of a fugitive>. **2.** A governmental seizure of property <the state's requisition of the shopping center during the weather emergency>. See TAKING (2). **3.** A list of requested supplies <they submitted the requisition to the quartermaster yesterday>. **4.** The quality, state, or condition of being demanded, called for, or pressed into service or use <they put leading political consultants in requisition for the campaign>. **5.** A formal demand that someone perform a duty, esp. when made through a notary <he sent a notarized requisition to his boss requesting statutorily authorized cost-of-living increases in his pay>. **6.** A formal demand made by one country or another for the surrender of a fugitive from justice; a formal request of extradition <the Mexican government pondered a requisition to the United States for the fugitive>. See EXTRADITION. **7.** A demand by a military invader that the local people of the invaded country provide supplies or labor <the invading army put up notices of requisition for all adult males to join in the rebuilding effort>. See REQUISITOR. **8.** *English law.* (*usu. pl.*) A series of inquiries or requests about land title made by the prospective buyer's attorney, the seller being called on to satisfy them <the conveyancer's requisitions were fully responded to by the seller>. **9.** *Scots law.* A formal demand for payment made by a creditor on his or her debtor <MacCormick sent McIntire a requisition for the £4,000 he had lent>. **10.** Broadly, a written call or invitation <a posted requisition for a town-hall meeting>. — **requisitory, requisitionary,** *adj.*

requisition, *vb.* (1837) **1.** To present a formal request to. **2.** To make an authoritative demand for (supplies, labor, buildings, etc.), esp. for military purposes. **3.** To take (supplies, labor, buildings, etc.) upon requisition.

requisitionist. (18c) Someone who makes a formal demand (as for the performance of an obligation or the return of a fugitive). — Also termed *requisitor.* See REQUISITION (1); REQUISITOR.

requisitor (ri-**kwiz**-ə-tor), *n.* (18c) **1.** Someone who makes an investigation on the authority of a requisition. See REQUISITION (7). **2.** REQUISITIONIST.

requisitorial, *n.* (18c) See REQUISITORY.

requisitory (ri-**kwiz**-ə-tor-ee), *n.* (1803) *French law.* A public prosecutor's demand for the punishment of a criminal defendant. — Also termed **requisitorial.**

requisitory letter. See LETTER OF REQUEST.

requisitum. [Neuter of Latin *reqisitus*] The solution to a problem; the answer to a difficult question under consideration.

requital (ri-**kwɪt**-əl), *n.* (16c) **1.** The act of repaying or making adequate return for good or ill. • In a positive sense, a requital is a reward or compensation. In a negative sense, it is a punishment or retaliation. **2.** That which repays what is due, whether for good or ill.

requite (ri-**kwɪt**), *vb.* (15c) **1.** To repay either good or evil to (a person); to compensate (someone) for good or evil. **2.** To repay (a benefit or injury); to reward, recompense, or avenge. See RETRIBUTOR.

rere-county (**reer**-kown-tee). (17c) *Hist.* A subsidiary English county court held by the sheriff on the day after the regular county court. — Also spelled *rere county*; *rier county.*

re-refer. See REFER.

res (rays *or* reez *or* rez), *n.* [Latin "thing"] (17c) **1.** An object, interest, or status, as opposed to a person <jurisdiction of the res — the real property in Colorado>. **2.** The subject matter of a trust; CORPUS (1) <the stock certificate is the res of the trust>. Pl. **res.**

res accessoria (rays ak-ses-**or**-ee-ə). [Latin] (1871) *Civil law.* An accessory thing; a thing that is related to a principal thing. Pl. ***res accessoriae.***

res adjudicata (rays ə-joo-di-**kay**-tə *or* -**kah**-tə). See RES JUDICATA.

resale, *n.* (17c) **1.** A retailer's selling of goods, previously purchased from a manufacturer or wholesaler, usu. to consumers or to someone else further down the chain of distribution. **2.** The act of selling goods or property — previously sold to a buyer who breached the sales contract — to someone else. UCC § 2-706. — **resell,** *vb.*

resale-price maintenance. (1914) A form of price-fixing in which a manufacturer forces or persuades several different retailers to sell the manufacturer's product at the same price, thus preventing competition. • Resale-price maintenance is not per se illegal under antitrust law, but it is illegal if it produces anticompetitive effects under the rule of reason. A manufacturer may suggest a retail price as long as it does not compel retailers to sell at that price. See RULE OF REASON; *vertical price-fixing* under PRICE-FIXING.

res alicuius (rays al-i-**kyoo**-əs). [Latin] *Hist.* Another person's thing.

res aliena (rays ay-lee-**ee**-nə *or* al-ee-). [Latin] (17c) *Archaic.* The property belonging to another.

res alienari prohibita (rays ay-**lee**-ə-**nair**-I proh-**hib**-i-tə). [Law Latin] *Hist.* A thing that cannot be alienated.

res aliena scienter legata (rays ay-lee-**ee**-nə [*or* al-ee-] SI-**en**-tər lə-**gay**-tə). [Latin] (1863) *Hist.* The property of another knowingly bequeathed — that is, property that a testator did not own but purported to bequeath by will.

res caduca (rays kə-**d[y]oo**-kə). [Latin] (18c) *Civil law.* A fallen thing; an escheat. Pl. ***res caducae.***

resceit (ri-**seet**). (16c) *Hist.* The admittance of an interested third party to plead in a case between two others; intervention.

rescind (ri-**sind**), *vb.* (17c) **1.** To abrogate or cancel (a contract) unilaterally or by agreement. **2.** To make void; to repeal or annul <rescind the legislation>. **3.** *Parliamentary law.* To void, repeal, or nullify a main motion adopted earlier. — Also termed *annulment; repeal.* — **rescindable,** *adj.*

▸ **rescind and expunge.** See EXPUNGE (2).

rescissio (ri-**sis[h]**-ee-oh). [Latin] *Civil law.* Annulment or voidance of a juridical act; rescission. Pl. ***rescissiones.***

rescission (ri-**sizh**-ən), *n.* (17c) **1.** A party's unilateral unmaking of a contract for a legally sufficient reason, such as the other party's material breach, or a judgment rescinding the contract; VOIDANCE. • Rescission is generally available as a remedy or defense for a nondefaulting party and is accompanied by restitution of any partial performance, thus restoring the parties to their precontractual positions. — Also termed *avoidance.* **2.** An agreement by contracting parties to discharge all remaining duties of performance and terminate the contract. — Often misspelled either *recision* or *recission.* — Also termed (in sense 2) *agreement of rescission; mutual rescission; abandonment.* Cf. REJECTION (2); REPUDIATION (2); REVOCATION (2). — **rescissory** (ri-**sis**-ə-ree *or* ri-**siz**-), *adj.*

"The [UCC] takes cognizance of the fact that the term 'rescission' is often used by lawyers, courts and businessmen in many different senses; for example, termination of a contract by virtue of an option to terminate in the agreement, cancellation for breach and avoidance on the grounds of infancy or fraud. In the interests of clarity of thought — as the consequences of each of these forms of discharge may vary — the Commercial Code carefully distinguishes three circumstances. 'Rescission' is utilized as a term of art to refer to a mutual agreement to discharge contractual duties. 'Termination' refers to the discharge of duties by the exercise of a power granted by the agreement. 'Cancellation' refers to the putting an end to the contract by reason of a breach by the other party. Section 2-720, however, takes into account that the parties do not necessarily use these terms in this way." John D. Calamari & Joseph M. Perillo, *The Law of Contracts* § 21-2, at 864–65 (3d ed. 1987).

▸ **equitable rescission.** (1889) Rescission that is decreed by a court of equity.

▸ **express rescission.** A straightforward, explicit agreement of the parties to a contract that it will no longer bind either of them. • The consideration for the promise of each party is the renunciation by the other of his rights under the contract.

▸ **legal rescission.** (1849) **1.** Rescission that is effected by the agreement of the parties. **2.** Rescission that is decreed by a court of law, as opposed to a court of equity.

rescissory action. See ACTION (4).

rescissory damages. See DAMAGES.

res communes (rays kə-**myoo**-neez), *n. pl.* [Latin "common things"] (18c) *Civil law.* Things common to all; things that cannot be owned or appropriated, such as light, air, and the sea. La. Civ. Code art. 449. — Also termed *res publicae.*

res controversa (rays kon-trə-**vər**-sə). [Latin] (16c) *Civil law.* A matter in controversy; a point in question. Pl. ***res controversae.***

res coronae (rays kə-**roh**-nee), *n. pl.* [Latin] *Hist.* Things of the Crown, such as ancient manors, homages of the king, and liberties.

res corporales (rays kor-pə-**ray**-leez), *n. pl.* [Latin] (18c) *Civil law.* Corporeal things; tangible things that are perceptible to the senses. La. Civ. Code art. 461. See *corporeal thing* under THING.

rescous (**res**-kəs). (14c) **1.** RESCUE (2). **2.** RESCUE (3).

rescript (**ree**-skript), *n.* (17c) **1.** A judge's written order to a court clerk explaining how to dispose of a case. **2.** An appellate court's written decision, usu. unsigned, that is sent down to the trial court. **3.** A Roman emperor's or a Pope's written answer to a legal inquiry or petition. Cf. PRECES. — Also termed (when the reply is to a private citizen) *annotation; subnotation; subscription; rescriptum;* (when the reply is to an official body) *epistle.* **4.** A duplicate or counterpart; a rewriting.

rescription, *n.* (16c) *Hist.* **1.** A written reply. **2.** A second or newly written copy of a document. **3.** A promissory note or warrant issued by a government.

rescriptum, *n.* (16c) RESCRIPT (3).

rescue, *n.* (14c) **1.** The act or an instance of saving or freeing someone from danger or captivity. **2.** The forcible and unlawful freeing of a person from arrest or imprisonment.

> "A *rescue* signifies a forcible setting at liberty, against law, of a person duly arrested. It is necessary, that the rescuer should have knowledge that the person whom he sets at liberty has been apprehended for a criminal offence, if he be in the custody of a private person; but if he be under the care of an officer, then he is to take notice of it at his peril." 1 Joseph Chitty, *A Practical Treatise on the Criminal Law* 62 (2d ed. 1826).

3. The forcible retaking by the owner of goods that have been lawfully distrained. — Also termed (in senses 2 & 3) *rescous*. Cf. REPOSSESSION. **4.** *Int'l law*. The retaking of a prize by persons captured with it, so that the property is legally restored to its original owner. See POSTLIMINIUM (3). — **rescue,** *vb.*

rescue clause. See SUE-AND-LABOR CLAUSE.

rescue doctrine. (1926) *Torts*. The principle that a tortfeasor who negligently endangered a person is liable for injuries to someone who reasonably attempted to rescue the person in danger. • The rationale for this doctrine is that an attempted rescue of someone in danger is always foreseeable. Thus, if the tortfeasor is negligent toward the rescuee, the tortfeasor is also negligent toward the rescuer. — Also termed *danger-invites-rescue doctrine*. Cf. EMERGENCY DOCTRINE (2); GOOD SAMARITAN DOCTRINE.

> "Danger invites rescue. The cry of distress is the summons to relief. The law does not ignore these reactions of the mind in tracing conduct to its consequences. It recognizes them as normal. It places their effects within the range of the natural and probable. The wrong that imperils life is a wrong to the imperiled victim; it is a wrong also to his rescuer . . . . The railroad company whose train approaches without signal is a wrongdoer toward the traveler surprised between the rails, but a wrongdoer also to the bystander who drags him from the path . . . . The emergency begets the man. The wrongdoer may not have foreseen the coming of a deliverer. He is accountable as if he had." *Wagner v. International Ry. Co.*, 133 N.E. 437, 437–38 (N.Y. 1921).

rescue syndrome. (1986) *Family law*. A situation in which a child in a custody battle expresses a preference for the parent perceived by the child to be the "weaker" of the two, in the belief that the parent needs the child. • This is a form of parent-alienation syndrome. One parent may overtly or subtly act increasingly dependent on the child, leading the child to believe that he or she is responsible for the parent's comfort, happiness, and protection. The child may also believe that one parent is actively harming the other and attempt to protect the "weaker" parent by choosing to stay with that parent, even if the child would actually prefer to live with the "stronger" parent. Cf. LOLLIPOP SYNDROME; PARENT-ALIENATION SYNDROME.

rescussu. See DE RESCUSSU.

res derelicta (rays der-ə-**lik**-tə). [Latin] (1839) A thing thrown away or forsaken by its owner; abandoned property.

res dominans (rays **dom**-ə-nanz). [Latin] (1864) The dominant property entitled to enjoy a servitude. See *dominant estate* under ESTATE.

research, *n.* **1.** Serious study of a subject with the purpose of acquiring more knowledge, discovering new facts, or testing new ideas. **2.** The activity of finding information that one needs to answer a question or solve a problem.

research and development. (1892) An effort (as by a company or business enterprise) to create or improve products or services, esp. by discovering new technology or advancing existing technology. — Abbr. R and D; R & D.

Research and Special Programs Administration. A unit in the U.S. Department of Transportation responsible for conducting research and engaging in special programs through several offices, including the Office of Hazardous Materials Safety, the Office of Pipeline Safety, the Transportation Systems Center, the Office of Emergency Transportation, the Office of Program Management and Administration, and the Office of Aviation Information Management. — Abbr. RSPA.

research attorney. See ATTORNEY.

research memorandum. See MEMORANDUM (2).

reseiser (ri-**see**-zər). (15c) *Hist*. The taking of lands by the monarch in a case in which a general livery or ouster le main was previously misused.

resemblance testimony. See TESTIMONY.

resentencing, *n.* (1878) The act or an instance of imposing a new or revised criminal sentence. — **resentence,** *vb.*

reservation. (15c) **1.** A keeping back or withholding. **2.** That which is kept back or withheld. **3.** The creation of a new right or interest (such as an easement), by and for the grantor, in real property being granted to another. Cf. EXCEPTION (3).

▸ **implied reservation.** (1867) An implied easement that reserves in a landowner an easement across a portion of sold land, such as a right-of-way over land lying between the seller's home and the only exit. • An implied reservation arises only if the seller could have expressly reserved an easement, but for some reason failed to do so. See *implied easement* under EASEMENT.

> "If the implied easement is in favor of the conveyee and is appurtenant to the tract conveyed, it is called an implied grant; if the implied easement is in favor of the conveyor and is appurtenant to the tract retained, it is called an implied reservation." Ralph E. Boyer et al., *The Law of Property* 311 (4th ed. 1991).

4. The right or interest so created in a grant. **5.** The deed clause in which such a right or interest is created. — Also termed *reserver*. **6.** The establishment of a limiting condition or qualification; esp., a country's formal declaration, upon signing or ratifying a treaty, that its willingness to become a party to the treaty is conditioned on the modification or amendment of one or more provisions of the treaty as applied in its relations with other parties to the treaty. **7.** An express notice that certain rights are not abandoned or waived, as in a copyrighted work. **8.** The setting apart of a designated part of a territory or tract of land for public uses or special appropriation. **9.** A part of a territory or tract of public land that is not open to settlers but is set apart for a special purpose; esp., a tract of land set aside for use by indigenous peoples. — Also termed (in sense 3) *reserve*; *reserved land*; *withdrawn land*.

reservation-of-rights letter. (1950) *Insurance*. A notice of an insurer's intention not to waive its contractual rights to contest coverage or to apply an exclusion that negates an insured's claim. — Abbr. ROR letter. — Also termed *reservation of rights*.

reservative (ri-**zərv**-ə-tiv), *adj.* (15c) Having the effect of creating an exception, as to a gift or grant; tending to keep back.

reserve, *n.* (17c) **1.** Something retained or stored for future use; esp., a fund of money set aside by a bank or an insurance company to cover future liabilities.

▸ **amortization reserve.** (1932) An account created for bookkeeping purposes to extinguish an obligation gradually over time.

▸ **bad-debt reserve.** (1925) A reserve to cover losses on uncollectible accounts receivable.

▸ **capital reserve.** (1874) An account on a company's balance sheet reserved for long-term capital-investment projects or other future expenses to be incurred; a corporate resource created from an organization's capital surplus, as when assets appreciate.

▸ **excess reserve.** (1907) The portion of a bank's reserve against deposits in excess of the amount of reserve required by law.

▸ **legal reserve.** (1862) The minimum amount of liquid assets that a bank or an insurance company must maintain by law to meet depositors' or claimants' demands.

▸ **loss reserve.** (1933) **1.** An insurance company's reserve that represents the estimated value of future payments, as for losses incurred but not yet reported. **2.** A bank's reserve set aside to cover possible losses, as from defaulting loans.

▸ **mean reserve.** (1902) In insurance, the average of the beginning reserve (after the premium has been paid for the policy year) and the ending reserve of the policy year.

▸ **policy reserve.** (1869) An insurance company's reserve that represents the difference between net premiums and expected claims for a given year. • This type of reserve is kept esp. by life-insurance companies.

▸ **required reserve.** (1913) The minimum amount of money, as required by the Federal Reserve Board, that a bank must hold in the form of vault cash and deposits with regional Federal Reserve Banks.

▸ **sinking-fund reserve.** (1916) A reserve used to pay long-term debt. See *sinking fund* under FUND (1).

▸ **unearned-premium reserve.** (1904) An insurance company's reserve that represents premiums that have been received in advance but not yet applied to policy coverage. • If a policyholder cancels coverage before the policy expires but has already paid a premium for the full policy period, the insurance company refunds the policyholder out of this reserve.

2. RESERVATION (3). **3.** See *net value* under VALUE (2). — **reserve,** *vb.*

reserve account. 1. See ESCROW (2). **2.** See *impound account* under ACCOUNT.

reserve bank. See *member bank* under BANK.

Reserve Board. See FEDERAL RESERVE BOARD OF GOVERNORS.

reserve calendar. See CALENDAR (2).

reserve clause. (1888) A clause in a professional athlete's contract restricting the athlete's right to change teams, even after the contract expires. • Reserve clauses are uncommon in modern professional sports. Cf. FREE AGENCY.

reserved easement. See EASEMENT.

reserved land. See RESERVATION (3).

reserved point of law. See POINT OF LAW.

reserved power. See POWER (3).

Reserved Power Clause. See TENTH AMENDMENT.

reserved surplus. See *appropriated surplus* (1) under SURPLUS.

reserve militia. See MILITIA.

reserve price. See PRICE.

reserver, *n.* (16c) **1.** Someone who or something that keeps back or withholds (reserves). **2.** A restrictive exception; RESERVATION (5). — Also written *reservor.*

reserve ratio. (1911) The Federal Reserve Board's measurement of a member bank's required reserves. See *required reserve* under RESERVE.

▸ **primary reserve ratio.** (1932) The ratio between a bank's required reserves (cash in vault plus deposits with Federal Reserve Banks) and its demand and time deposits.

▸ **secondary reserve ratio.** (1932) The ratio between a bank's government securities and its demand and time deposits.

reservor. See RESERVER.

reset, *n.* (15c) *Scots law.* **1.** The act or an instance of knowingly receiving stolen goods. **2.** *Archaic.* The harboring or sheltering of a criminal or outlaw. — **resetter,** *n.* — **reset,** *vb.*

resettlement, *n.* (17c) **1.** The settlement of one or more persons in a new or former place. See SETTLEMENT (6). **2.** The reopening of an order or decree for the purpose of correcting a mistake or adding something omitted. — **resettle,** *vb.*

res extincta (**rays** ek-**stingk**-tə). [Latin] *Hist.* Extinct thing.

res fit inempta (rays fit in-**emp**-tə). [Latin] *Hist.* The object is regarded as unbought. • This is the ancient way of saying, "The sale is off."

res fungibiles (rays fən-**jib**-ə-leez), *n. pl.* [Latin] (17c) *Civil law.* Fungible things; things that are commercially interchangeable.

res gestae (rays **jes**-tee *also* **jes**-tɪ), *n. pl.* [Latin "things done"] (17c) The events at issue, or other events contemporaneous with them. • In evidence law, words and statements about the res gestae are usu. admissible under a hearsay exception (such as present sense impression or excited utterance). Where the Federal Rules of Evidence or state rules fashioned after them are in effect, the use of *res gestae* is now out of place. *See* Fed. R. Evid. 803(1), (2). — Also termed *res gesta.*

> "[F]ew terms commonly employed in connection with the law of evidence are more notoriously ambiguous than the phrase *'res gestae.'* Only by the connection, and by no means always then, can it be known in which of its several distinct meanings the term is being used by a speaker or writer." 1 Charles Frederic Chamberlayne, *A Treatise on the Modern Law of Evidence* cxxi (1911).

> "The Latin expression 'res gestae' or 'res gesta,' literally 'things done' or 'thing transacted,' has long served as a catchword . . . . [T]he phrase has frequently served both to let in utterances which in strictness were not admissible and to exclude utterances which might well have been admitted. And frequently also its indefiniteness has served as a basis for rulings where it was easier for the judge to

invoke this imposing catchword than to think through the real question involved. The phrase is antiquated. By modern judges it is being gradually discarded. It is superfluous, and serves only to obscure the logic of the rules. It should be left to oblivion." John H. Wigmore, *A Students' Textbook of the Law of Evidence* 279 (1935).

"The res gestae embraces not only the actual facts of the transaction and the circumstances surrounding it, but the matters immediately antecedent to and having a direct causal connection with it, as well as acts immediately following it and so closely connected with it as to form in reality a part of the occurrence." *State v. Fouquette*, 221 P.2d 404, 416–17 (Nev. 1950).

res gestae witness. See WITNESS.

res habiles (rays **hab**-ə-leez), *n. pl.* [Latin] (1982) *Civil law.* Things that may be acquired by prescription.

resiance (**rez**-ee-ənts). (16c) *Archaic.* Residence; abode.

resiant (**rez**-ee-ənt), *adj.* (15c) *Archaic.* Continually dwelling or abiding in a place; resident.

resiant, *n.* (15c) *Archaic.* A resident.

residence. (14c) **1.** The act or fact of living in a given place for some time <a year's residence in New Jersey>. — Also termed *residency.* **2.** The place where one actually lives, as distinguished from a domicile <she made her residence in Oregon>. • *Residence* usu. just means bodily presence as an inhabitant in a given place; *domicile* usu. requires bodily presence plus an intention to make the place one's home. A person thus may have more than one residence at a time but only one domicile. Sometimes, though, the two terms are used synonymously. Cf. DOMICILE (2). **3.** A house or other fixed abode; a dwelling <a three-story residence>. **4.** The place where a corporation or other enterprise does business or is registered to do business <Pantheon Inc.'s principal residence is in Delaware>.

▸ **habitual residence.** (18c) **1.** *Family law.* A person's customary place of residence; esp., a child's customary place of residence before being removed to some other place. • The term, which appears as an undefined term in the Hague Convention, is used in determining the country having a presumed paramount interest in the child. **2.** *Copyright.* An established place, esp. a country, in which one lives for the long term, usu. without being a citizen of the place. • The Berne Convention makes habitual residence an alternative to legal domicile in a member country to qualify for copyright protection but leaves the exact definition of the term to member countries.

residency. (14c) **1.** A place of residence, esp. an official one <the diplomat's residency>. **2.** RESIDENCE (1) <one year's residency to be eligible for in-state tuition>.

resident, *adj.* (14c) **1.** Affiliated with or working for a particular person or company <resident agent>. **2.** Dwelling in a place other than one's home on a long-term basis <the hospital's resident patient>.

resident, *n.* (15c) **1.** Someone who lives in a particular place. **2.** Someone who has a home in a particular place. • In sense 2, a resident is not necessarily either a citizen or a domiciliary. Cf. CITIZEN (1); DOMICILIARY, *n.*

resident agent. See *registered agent* under AGENT.

resident alien. See ALIEN.

resident ambassador. See AMBASSADOR.

residential care. (1895) *Family law.* Foster-care placement involving residence in a group home or institution. • This type of foster care is most commonly used for adolescents who have been adjudged to be delinquents or status offenders.

residential cluster. (1918) *Land-use planning.* An area of land developed as a unit with group housing and open common space. Cf. PLANNED-UNIT DEVELOPMENT.

residential community treatment center. See HALFWAY HOUSE.

residential custody. See PHYSICAL CUSTODY (2).

residential drug-treatment program. (1970) An inpatient treatment regimen, often operated at a halfway house, to help substance-abusers curb their addictions and remain drug- and alcohol-free.

residential parent. See PARENT (1).

residential reentry center. (2004) A halfway house where prisoners are helped in their reintegration into society. — Abbr. RRC.

residential responsibility. (1986) Overnight responsibility for a child. *See Principles of the Law of Family Dissolution: Analysis and Recommendations* § 3.02 (2000). See CUSTODY (2); *dual-residential parent, residential parent* under PARENT (1).

▸ **primary residential responsibility.** (1986) Predominant overnight responsibility for a child.

residential time. See VISITATION (2).

residential treatment center. See HALFWAY HOUSE

residential treatment facility. See HALFWAY HOUSE

residua (ri-**zij**-oo-ə). *pl.* RESIDUUM.

residual, *adj.* (16c) Of, relating to, or constituting a residue; remaining; leftover <a residual claim> <a residual functional disability>.

residual, *n.* (1839) **1.** A leftover quantity; a remainder. **2.** (*often pl.*) A disability remaining after an illness, injury, or operation. **3.** (*usu. pl.*) A fee paid to a composer or performer for each repeated broadcast (esp. on television) of a film, program, or commercial.

residual estate. See *residuary estate* under ESTATE (3).

residual exception. See *catchall exception* under EXCEPTION (1).

residual value. See *salvage value* under VALUE (2).

residuary (ri-**zij**-oo-er-ee), *adj.* (18c) Of, relating to, or constituting a residue; residual <a residuary gift>.

residuary, *n.* **1.** See *residuary estate* under ESTATE (3). **2.** See *residuary legatee* under LEGATEE.

residuary bequest. See BEQUEST.

residuary clause. (18c) *Wills & estates.* A testamentary clause that disposes of any estate property remaining after the satisfaction of all other gifts. — Also termed *omnibus clause.*

residuary devise. See DEVISE.

residuary devisee. See DEVISEE.

residuary estate. See ESTATE (3).

residuary legacy. See LEGACY (1).

residuary legatee. See LEGATEE.

residue. (14c) **1.** Something that is left over after a part is removed or disposed of; a remainder. **2.** See *residuary estate* under ESTATE (3).

residuum (ri-**zij**-oo-əm). (17c) **1.** That which remains; a residue. **2.** See *residuary estate* under ESTATE (3). Pl. **residua** (ri-**zij**-oo-ə).

residuum rule. (1926) **1.** *Criminal procedure.* The doctrine that although hearsay is admissible at a probation or parole-violation hearing, some legal evidence (a "residuum") must be introduced to support a finding adverse to the defendant. **2.** *Administrative law.* The principle that an agency decision based partly on hearsay evidence will be upheld on judicial review only if the decision is founded on at least some competent evidence. • The residuum rule has generally been rejected by federal and state courts.

resign, *vb.* (14c) **1.** To formally announce one's decision to leave a job or an organization <to resign from the army>. **2.** To give up or give back (an office, trust, appointment, etc.) to those by whom it was given; to surrender <the officer resigned his commission>. **3.** To abandon the use or enjoyment of; to give up any claim to <the monk resigned his inheritance>.

resignation, *n.* (14c) **1.** The act or an instance of surrendering or relinquishing an office, right, or claim. **2.** A formal notification of relinquishing an office or position; an official announcement that one has decided to leave one's job or organization, often in the form of a written statement. **3.** *Hist.* The surrender to the lord of the vassal's interest in land. — **resign,** *vb.*

resile (ri-**zɪl**), *vb.* (16c) **1.** To retract (a statement, allegation, etc.). **2.** To draw back (from an agreement, contract, etc.). **3.** To return to one's original position.

res immobiles (rays i-**moh**-bə-leez), *n. pl.* [Latin] (18c) *Civil law.* Immovable things; chattels real. See IMMOBILIA.

res incorporales (rays in-kor-pə-**ray**-leez), *n. pl.* [Latin] (18c) *Civil law.* Incorporeal things; intangible things that are not perceptible to the senses. See *incorporeal thing* under THING.

res in privatorum patrimonio. See RES PRIVATAE.

res integra (rays **in**-tə-grə *also* in-**teg**-rə). [Latin "an entire thing"] See RES NOVA.

res inter alios. See RES INTER ALIOS ACTA.

res inter alios acta (rays **in**-tər **ay**-lee-ohs **ak**-tə). [Latin "a thing done between others"] (17c) **1.** *Contracts.* The common-law doctrine holding that a contract cannot unfavorably affect the rights of someone who is not a party to the contract. **2.** *Evidence.* The rule prohibiting the admission of collateral facts into evidence. — Often shortened to *res inter alios.*

> "Res Inter Alios; *facts not directly in issues, nor relevant thereto as above stated, are inadmissible.* — All facts not in issue themselves, and not connected with some fact in issue, or relevant thereto in some one of the above four ways, namely, either as forming part of the same transaction or subject matter; or as constituting a probable cause for it; or as the natural effect of it; or as necessary to explain or introduce it, are inadmissible in evidence for the purpose of forming the ground of an inference that such fact in issue or relevant fact probably did or did not exist, and are frequently designated, somewhat loosely, by the term, *res inter alios,* a phrase originally derived from the maxim *res inter alios, acta alteri nocere non debet,* but which is often used by the bench and bar in the sense of irrelevant. This principle, that courts are not at liberty to infer from one fact the probable existence or nonexistence of another fact merely because the two are similar, unless they can be first shown to be part of the same transaction, or to be connected together in some way by the chain of cause and effect, is one of the most distinguishing characteristics of the English law of evidence." William Reynolds, *The Theory of the Law of Evidence* § 12, at 14–15 (2d ed. 1890).

res in transitu (**rays** in **tran**-si-t[y]oo). [Latin] *Hist.* Thing in transit.

res ipsa loquitur (rays **ip**-sə **loh**-kwə-tər). [Latin "the thing speaks for itself"] (17c) *Torts.* The doctrine providing that, in some circumstances, the mere fact of an accident's occurrence raises an inference of negligence that establishes a prima facie case; specif., the doctrine whereby when something that has caused injury or damage is shown to be under the management of the party charged with negligence, and the accident is such that in the ordinary course of things it would not happen if those who have the management use proper care, the very occurrence of the accident affords reasonable evidence, in the absence of the explanation by the parties charged, that it arose from the want of proper care. • The principle does not normally apply unless (1) the occurrence resulting in injury was such as does not ordinarily happen if those in charge use due care; (2) the instrumentalities were under the management and control of the defendant; and (3) the defendant possessed superior knowledge or means of information about the cause of the occurrence. — Often shortened to *res ipsa.*

> "The phrase 'res ipsa loquitur' is a symbol for the rule that the fact of the occurrence of an injury, taken with the surrounding circumstances, may permit an inference or raise a presumption of negligence, or make out a plaintiff's prima facie case, and present a question of fact for defendant to meet with an explanation. It is merely a short way of saying that the circumstances attendant on the accident are of such a nature as to justify a jury, in light of common sense and past experience, in inferring that the accident was probably the result of the defendant's negligence, in the absence of explanation or other evidence which the jury believes." Stuart M. Speiser, *The Negligence Case: Res Ipsa Loquitur* § 1:2, at 5–6 (1972).

> "It is said that *res ipsa loquitur* does not apply if the cause of the harm is known. This is a dark saying. The application of the principle nearly always presupposes that some part of the causal process is known, but what is lacking is evidence of its connection with the defendant's act or omission. When the fact of control is used to justify the inference that defendant's negligence was responsible it must of course be shown that the thing in his control in fact caused the harm. In a sense, therefore, the cause of the harm must be known before the maxim can apply." H.L.A. Hart & Tony Honoré, *Causation in the Law* 419–20 (2d ed. 1985).

> "Res ipsa loquitur is an appropriate form of circumstantial evidence enabling the plaintiff in particular cases to establish the defendant's likely negligence. Hence the res ipsa loquitur doctrine, properly applied, does not entail any covert form of strict liability. . . . The doctrine implies that the court does not know, and cannot find out, what actually happened in the individual case. Instead, the finding of likely negligence is derived from knowledge of the causes of the type or category of accidents involved." Restatement (Third) of Torts § 15 cmt. a (Discussion Draft 1999).

res ipsa loquitur test (rays **ip**-sə **loh**-kwə-tər). (1962) A method for determining whether a defendant has gone beyond preparation and has actually committed an attempt, based on whether the defendant's act itself would have indicated to an observer what the defendant intended to do. — Also termed *equivocality test*. See ATTEMPT (2).

resisting arrest. (1851) The crime of obstructing or opposing a police officer who is making an arrest. — Also termed *resisting lawful arrest*.

resisting process. See OBSTRUCTION OF PROCESS.

resisting unlawful arrest. (1905) The act of opposing a police officer who is making an unlawful arrest. • Most jurisdictions have accepted the Model Penal Code position prohibiting the use of force to resist an unlawful arrest when the person arrested knows that a police officer is making the arrest. But some jurisdictions allow an arrestee to use nondeadly force to prevent the arrest. *See* Model Penal Code § 3.

res judicata (rays joo-di-**kay**-tə *or* -**kah**-tə). [Latin "a thing adjudicated"] (17c) **1.** An issue that has been definitively settled by judicial decision. **2.** An affirmative defense barring the same parties from litigating a second lawsuit on the same claim, or any other claim arising from the same transaction or series of transactions and that could have been — but was not — raised in the first suit. • The three essential elements are (1) an earlier decision on the issue, (2) a final judgment on the merits, and (3) the involvement of the same parties, or parties in privity with the original parties. Restatement (Second) of Judgments §§ 17, 24 (1982). — Also termed *former adjudication*; *res adjudicata*; *claim preclusion*; *doctrine of res judicata*. Cf. COLLATERAL ESTOPPEL.

> "'Res judicata' has been used in this section as a general term referring to all of the ways in which one judgment will have a binding effect on another. That usage is and doubtless will continue to be common, but it lumps under a single name two quite different effects of judgments. The first is the effect of foreclosing any litigation of matters that never have been litigated, because of the determination that they should have been advanced in an earlier suit. The second is the effect of foreclosing relitigation of matters that have once been litigated and decided. The first of these, preclusion of matters that were never litigated, has gone under the name, 'true res judicata,' or the names, 'merger' and 'bar.' The second doctrine, preclusion of matters that have once been decided, has usually been called 'collateral estoppel.' Professor Allan Vestal has long argued for the use of the names 'claim preclusion' and 'issue preclusion' for these two doctrines [Vestal, *Rationale of Preclusion*, 9 St. Louis U. L.J. 29 (1964)], and this usage is increasingly employed by the courts as it is by Restatement Second of Judgments." Charles Alan Wright, *The Law of Federal Courts* § 100A, at 722-23 (5th ed. 1994).

res litigiosae (rays li-tij-ee-**oh**-see), *n. pl.* [Latin] (1881) *Civil law.* Things that are in litigation; property or rights that are the subject of a pending action.

res mancipi (rays **man**-sə-pɪ). [Latin "things of mancipium"] (18c) *Roman law.* Property, specifically Italic land with its rustic servitudes and beasts of draft or burden, that can be transferred only by a formal ceremony of mancipation. — Also termed *mancipi res*; *things mancipi*. See MANCIPATION.

res merae facultatis (rays **meer**-ee fak-əl-**tay**-tis). [Law Latin] (18c) *Scots law.* A matter of mere power.

> "Res merae facultatis . . . . Such, for example, is the right which a proprietor has of building upon his own property, or which any one has of walking upon the seashore, or sailing upon the sea, or on any navigable river. It is a right which may or may not be exercised at the pleasure of him who holds it; and such rights are never lost by their non-exercise for any length of time, because it is of their essential character that they may be used or exercised at any time." John Trayner, *Trayner's Latin Maxims* 554 (4th ed. 1894).

res mobiles (rays **moh**-bə-leez), *n. pl.* [Latin] (1898) *Civil law.* Movable things; chattels personal.

res nec mancipi (rays nek **man**-sə-pɪ). [Latin "things not of mancipium"] (18c) *Roman law.* Property that can be transferred without a formal ceremony of mancipation. — Also termed *things nec mancipi*.

res non est integra (rays non est **in**-tə-grə). [Latin] (17c) *Hist.* The original position has changed; performance has taken place (in whole or in part).

res nova (rays **noh**-və). [Latin "new thing"] (18c) **1.** An undecided question of law. **2.** A case of first impression. — Also termed *res integra*. See *case of first impression* under CASE (1).

res nullius (rays nə-**lɪ**-əs). [Latin "thing of no one"] (16c) A thing that belongs to no one; an ownerless chattel.

> "Res nullius. Such as belonged to the first occupier. They are of two kinds. Such as never have belonged to anyone, and such as have ceased to belong to a former owner." John George Phillimore, *Private Law Among the Romans* 89 (1863).

resolution. (17c) **1.** *Parliamentary law.* A main motion that formally expresses the sense, will, or action of a deliberative assembly (esp. a legislative body). • A resolution is a highly formal kind of main motion, often containing a preamble, and one or more resolving clauses in the form, "*Resolved*, That . . . ."

- ▸ **concurrent resolution.** (17c) A resolution passed by one house and agreed to by the other. • It expresses the legislature's opinion on a subject but does not have the force of law.
- ▸ **joint resolution.** (17c) A legislative resolution passed by both houses. • It has the force of law and is subject to executive veto.
- ▸ **simple resolution.** (18c) A resolution passed by one house only. • It expresses the opinion or affects the internal affairs of the passing house, but it does not have the force of law.

2. Formal action by a corporate board of directors or other corporate body authorizing a particular act, transaction, or appointment. — Also termed *corporate resolution*.

- ▸ **general resolution.** A resolution whose acceptance or rejection depends on a simple majority of votes.
- ▸ **shareholder resolution.** (1912) A resolution by shareholders, usu. to ratify the actions of the board of directors.
- ▸ **special resolution.** A resolution whose acceptance depends on a specified percentage of votes in favor.

3. A document containing such an expression or authorization. **4.** A court's solemn judgment or decision. **5.** *Civil law.* The annulment of a contract.

resolutionist, *n.* (1818) Someone who makes or proposes a resolution.

resolutions committee. See COMMITTEE (1).

Resolution Trust Corporation. A federal agency established to act as a receiver for insolvent federal savings-and-loan associations and to transfer or liquidate those associations' assets. • The agency was created when the

Federal Savings and Loan Insurance Corporation was abolished in 1989. — Abbr. RTC. See FEDERAL SAVINGS AND LOAN INSURANCE CORPORATION.

resolutive condition. See *resolutory condition* under CONDITION (2).

resolutory (ri-**zahl**-yə-tor-ee), *adj.* (1818) Operating or serving to annul, dissolve, or terminate; having the effect of rescinding <a resolutory clause>.

resolutory condition. See CONDITION (2).

resolve, *vb.* (14c) **1.** To find an acceptable or even satisfactory way of dealing with (a problem or difficulty) <they resolved their conflicting claims>. **2.** To reduce to elementary principles or relations by intellectual analysis; to solve <he resolved the geometry problems>. **3.** To make intelligible; to explain in a way that minimizes the perplexities <the hieroglyphics were finally resolved by a clever puzzle expert>. **4.** To make a definite decision to (do something); to set one's mind to (a course of action) <she resolved never to marry again>. **5.** To make a formal decision, as by voting <the board members resolved to accept their colleague's resignation>. **6.** To render fixed in purpose; to cause to decide or determine <the defeat resolved him to try even harder>. **7.** To change in form of organization, as when a deliberative assembly might displace one mode of procedure for another (in a reflexive sense) <the standing committee resolved itself into a style committee of the whole>. **8.** To separate (something) into constituent parts; to take to pieces <the DNA samples were obtained and then resolved>. **9.** *Civil law.* To become void; to lapse <the gift resolved by ademption>. **10.** *Archaic.* To consult <she resolved with her lawyer about the problem>.

resolving clause. See CLAUSE.

resort, *n.* (15c) **1.** A place where people go for rest, recreation, or sport, esp. on vacation. **2.** That to which one looks for help; resource. **3.** The act of going to or making application; recourse. — **resort,** *vb.*

▸ **first resort.** That to which one looks for help early before recourse to other measures.

▸ **last resort.** That to which one looks for help late, after all other possible measures have failed.

resource, *n.* **1.** A useful or valuable quality or possession of a country, state, organization, or person <Texas's natural resources>. **2.** All the money, property, or skills that might need to be deployed in a given circumstance <he had no financial resources>. **3.** An educational or instructional item such as a book, film, or series of photographs used by a teacher or student to provide information <resources for learning>. **4.** A person's ability to deal with practical problems <a candidate with great resource and aplomb>.

RESPA (**res**-pə). *abbr.* REAL ESTATE SETTLEMENT PROCEDURES ACT.

res perit domino (**rays per**-it **dom**-i-noh). [Latin] *Hist.* Property lost to the owner.

res petita (**rays** pə-**ti**-tə). [Latin] *Hist.* A thing sued for.

respite (**res**-pit), *n.* (14c) **1.** A period of temporary delay; an extension of time. **2.** A temporary suspension of a death sentence; a reprieve. **3.** A delay granted to a jury or court for further consideration of a verdict or appeal. **4.** *Civil law.* An agreement between a debtor and several creditors for an extension of time to repay the various debts. La. Civ. Code art. 3084. — **respite,** *vb.*

▸ **forced respite.** (1811) A respite in which some of the creditors are compelled by a court to give the same extension of time that the other creditors have agreed to.

▸ **voluntary respite.** (1840) A respite in which all the creditors agree to the debtor's proposal for an extension of time.

respondeat ouster (ri-**spon**-dee-at **ow**-stər). [Law Latin "let him make further answer"] (17c) An interlocutory judgment or order that a party who made a dilatory plea that has been denied must now plead on the merits. — Also termed *judgment respondeat ouster.*

> "In case of felony, if the plea be held bad, the judgment is *respondeat ouster*; or rather, as the defendant generally pleads over to the felony, the jury are charged again, and that at the same time with the issue on the plea of autrefois acquit, to inquire of the second issue, and the trial proceeds as if no plea in bar had been pleaded." 1 Joseph Chitty, *A Practical Treatise on the Criminal Law* 461 (2d ed. 1826).

respondeat superior (ri-**spon**-dee-at soo-**peer**-ee-ər *or* sə-peer-ee-**or**). [Law Latin "let the superior make answer"] (17c) *Torts.* The doctrine holding an employer or principal liable for the employee's or agent's wrongful acts committed within the scope of the employment or agency. — Also termed *master–servant rule.* See SCOPE OF EMPLOYMENT.

> "Most courts have made little or no effort to explain the result, and have taken refuge in rather empty phrases, such as 'he who does a thing through another does it himself,' or the endlessly repeated formula of 'respondeat superior,' which in itself means nothing more than 'look to the man higher up.'" W. Page Keeton et al., *Prosser and Keeton on the Law of Torts* § 69, at 500 (5th ed. 1984).

***responde* book.** (17c) *Hist. Scots law.* The chancellery's record of all duties payable by heirs who obtained royal warrants for possession of the decedent's lands.

respondent. (16c) **1.** The party against whom an appeal is taken; APPELLEE. • In some appellate courts, the parties are designated as *petitioner* and *respondent.* In most appellate courts in the United States, the parties are designated as *appellant* and *appellee.* Often the designations depend on whether the appeal is taken by writ of certiorari (or writ of error) or by direct appeal. **2.** The party against whom a motion or petition is filed. Cf. PETITIONER. **3.** At common law, the defendant in an equity proceeding. **4.** *Civil law.* Someone who answers for another or acts as another's security.

respondent bank. See BANK.

respondentia (ree-spon-**den**-shee-ə *or* res-pon-). [Law Latin fr. Latin *respondere* "to answer"] (17c) A loan secured by the cargo on one's ship rather than the ship itself. Cf. BOTTOMRY.

respondentia bond. See BOND (2).

respondere non debet (ri-**spon**-də-ree non **deb**-ət). [Latin] (1809) *Common-law pleading.* The prayer of a plea in which the defendant insists that he or she does not have to answer — because of a privilege, for example.

responsalis (res-pon-**say**-lis). [Law Latin] **1.** *Hist.* Someone who appears and answers for another. **2.** *Eccles. law.* A proctor. **3.** See APOCRISARIUS.

responsa prudentium (ri-**spon**-sə proo-**den**-shee-əm). [Latin "the answers of the learned"] (17c) *Roman law.* The opinions and judgments of eminent lawyers or jurists on questions of law addressed to them. • The *responsa prudentium* originally constituted part of the early Roman civil law. Roman citizens seeking legal advice, as well as magistrates and judges, often referred legal questions to leading jurists so as to obtain their opinions (*responsa*). The *responsa* of some leading jurists were collected, much in the manner of caselaw digests, and many of them passed into Justinian's Digest. The phrase *responsa prudentium* gradually migrated to the common law, but today it is of primarily historical use. — Also spelled *responsa prudentum.*

> "[T]he *judex*, or as we would now call him, the referee, might have no technical knowledge of law whatever. Under such conditions the unlearned judicial magistrates naturally looked for light and leading to the jurisconsults who instructed them through their *responsa prudentium*, the technical name given to their opinions as experts, which were promptly recorded on tablets by their students or disciples." Hannis Taylor, *The Science of Jurisprudence* 90–91 (1908).

> "In [classical Latin] *responsa prudentium* is the usual form, but most of the legal sources . . . have *prudentum* following the example of Blackstone (1765)." *The Oxford English Dictionary* (2d ed. 1989).

response. 1. An argument or brief presented in answer to that of a movant, appellant, or petitioner. **2.** *Patents.* A patent applicant's answer to an office action, usu. countering the examiner's rejections and objections and often amending the claims.

responsibility, *n.* (18c) **1.** The quality, state, or condition of being answerable or accountable; LIABILITY (1). **2.** *Criminal law.* A person's mental fitness to answer in court for his or her actions. See COMPETENCY. **3.** *Criminal law.* Guilt. — Also termed (in senses 2 & 3) *criminal responsibility.* — **responsible,** *adj.*

> "[As for] the ambiguities of the word 'responsibility,' . . . it is, I think, still important to distinguish two of the very different things this difficult word may mean. To say that someone is legally responsible for something often means only that under legal rules he is liable to be made either to suffer or to pay compensation in certain eventualities. The expression 'he'll pay for it' covers both these things. In this the primary sense of the word, though a man is normally only responsible for his own actions or the harm he has done, he may be also responsible for the actions of other persons if legal rules so provide. Indeed in this sense a baby in arms or a totally insane person might be legally responsible — again, if the rules so provide; for the word simply means liable to be made to account or pay and we might call this sense of the word 'legal accountability.' But the new idea — the programme of eliminating responsibility — is not, as some have feared, meant to eliminate legal accountability: persons who break the law are not just to be left free. What is to be eliminated are enquiries as to whether a person who has done what the law forbids was responsible at the time he did it and responsible in this sense does not refer to the legal status of accountability. It means the capacity, so far as this is a matter of a man's mind or will, which normal people have to control their actions and conform to law. In this sense of responsibility a man's responsibility can be said to be 'impaired.'" H.L.A. Hart, "Changing Conceptions of Responsibility," in *Punishment and Responsibility* 186, 196–97 (1968).

> "Responsibility means answerability or accountability. It is used in the criminal law in the sense of 'criminal responsibility' and hence means answerability to the criminal law." Rollin M. Perkins & Ronald N. Boyce, *Criminal Law and Procedure: Cases and Materials* 399 (5th ed. 1977).

▸ **diminished responsibility.** See *diminished capacity* under CAPACITY (3).

4. That for which one is answerable or accountable; a trust, duty, or obligation. **5.** Ability to meet monetary or contractual obligations; esp., the ability to pay what is owed.

responsible bidder. (1833) Someone who bids on a contract, esp. for public works, who possesses the requisite skill, judgment, and integrity necessary to perform the contract requested, and who has the financial resources and abilities to carry the task to completion. — Often shortened to *bidder.*

responsible broker-dealer. See BROKER.

responsive, *adj.* (15c) Giving or constituting a response; answering <the witness's testimony is not responsive to the question>.

responsive action. (1933) *Patents.* A patent applicant's answer to an examiner rejections in an office action. • To be responsive, the answer must address all of the examiner's issues in detail, rather than merely submitting substitute claims.

responsive pleading. See PLEADING (1).

responsive verdict. See VERDICT (1).

res privatae (rays pri-**vay**-tee), *n. pl.* [Latin "private things"] (18c) *Roman & civil law.* Things that can be owned by individuals or by the state and its political subdivisions in their capacity as private citizens. La. Civ. Code art. 450. — Also termed *res in privatorum patrimonio.*

res publicae (rays **pəb**-li-see), *n. pl.* [Latin "public things"] (17c) **1.** *Roman & civil law.* Things that cannot be individually owned because they belong to the public, such as the sea, navigable waters, and highways. • Public things are owned by the state and its political subdivisions in their capacity as public persons. La. Civ. Code art. 449. **2.** RES COMMUNES.

res quotidianae (rays kwoh-tid-ee-**ay**-nee), *n. pl.* [Latin] *Civil law.* Everyday matters; familiar points or questions.

res religiosae (rays ri-lij-ee-**oh**-see), *n. pl.* [Latin] (1880) *Civil law.* Religious things; esp., burial places.

res repetundae (rays rep-ə-**tən**-dee). [Latin "things due to be repaid"] *Roman law.* **1.** Money or things that can be reclaimed by a person who was forced to give them to a public official. **2.** The illegal act of forcing someone to give money or things; extortion. — Sometimes (erroneously) shortened to *repetundae.* See CRIMEN REPETUNDARUM.

res sanctae (rays **sangk**-tee), *n. pl.* [Latin "sacred things"] (17c) *Roman law.* The walls of a city. • The Romans considered maintenance of city walls so important that damage to a city's walls was a capital offense.

res serviens (rays **sər**-vee-enz). [Latin] (1864) The servient property subject to a servitude. See *servient estate* under ESTATE (4).

res singulorum (rays sing-gyə-**lor**-əm). [Latin] (18c) *Hist.* The property of individuals.

res sua (rays s[y]oo-ə). [Latin] (1832) *Hist.* One's own property.

rest, *vb.* (1905) **1.** (Of a litigant) to voluntarily conclude presenting evidence in a trial <after the police officer's testimony, the prosecution rested>. **2.** (Of a litigant) to voluntarily conclude presenting evidence in (a trial) <the defense rested its case after presenting just two

witnesses>. • In sense 1, the verb is intransitive; in sense 2, it is transitive.

Restatement. One of several influential treatises published by the American Law Institute describing the law in a given area and guiding its development. • The Restatements use a distinctive format of black-letter rules, official comments, illustrations, and reporter's notes. Although the Restatements are frequently cited in cases and commentary, a Restatement provision is not binding on a court unless it has been officially adopted as the law by that jurisdiction's highest court. Restatements have been published in the following areas of law: Agency, Conflict of Laws, Contracts, Employment Law, Foreign Relations Law of the United States, Judgments, Law Governing Lawyers, Property, Restitution, Security, Suretyship and Guaranty, Torts, Trusts, and Unfair Competition. — Also termed *Restatement of the Law.*

> "We speak of the work which the organization should undertake as a restatement; its object should not only be to help make certain much that is now uncertain and to simplify unnecessary complexities, but also to promote those changes which will tend better to adapt the laws to the needs of life. The character of the restatement which we have in mind can be best described by saying that it should be at once analytical, critical and constructive." Committee on the Establishment of a Permanent Organization for the Improvement of the Law (Elihu Root, chairman), *Report Proposing the Establishment of an American Law Institute,* 1 ALI Proc. 14 (1923).

restater. (1955) An author or reporter of a Restatement.

restaur (res-**tor**). **1.** The recourse that insurers (esp. marine underwriters) have against each other according to the date of their insurance. **2.** The recourse that marine insurers have against a ship's master if a loss occurs through the master's fault or negligence. **3.** The recourse that one has against a guarantor or other person under a duty to indemnify. — Also spelled *restor.*

restitute, *vb.* (16c) **1.** To restore to a position or to a former state. **2.** To give (something) back; esp., to refund. **3.** To undergo restitution.

restitutio in genere (res-ti-**t[y]oo**-shee-oh in **jen**-ə-ree). [Latin] *Hist.* Restitution in kind.

restitutio in integrum (res-tə-**t[y]oo**-shee-oh in **in**-tə-grəm). [Latin] (17c) *Roman & civil law.* Restoration to the previous condition or the status quo. • In Roman law, a praetor could accomplish this by annulling a contract or transaction that was strictly legally valid but inequitable and by restoring the parties to their previous legal relationship. The phrase is still sometimes used in American law (esp. in Louisiana) when a court annuls a contract and orders restitution on equitable grounds.

> "*Restitutio in integrum.* This was the immediate interference of the magistrate to replace the suitor in a situation from which he had been inequitably and to his prejudice removed." John George Phillimore, *Private Law Among the Romans* 191 (1863).

restitution, *n.* (13c) **1.** A body of substantive law in which liability is based not on tort or contract but on the defendant's unjust enrichment. See UNJUST ENRICHMENT. **2.** The set of remedies associated with that body of law, in which the measure of recovery is usu. based not on the plaintiff's loss, but on the defendant's gain. Cf. COMPENSATION; DAMAGES. **3.** Return or restoration of some specific thing to its rightful owner or status. **4.** Compensation for loss; esp., full or partial compensation paid by a criminal to a victim, not awarded in a civil trial for tort, but ordered as part of a criminal sentence or as a condition of probation. — Also termed *criminal restitution.* **5.** *Archaic.* A judicial writ restoring to a successful appellant what had been lost by reason of the lower court's erroneous judgment. **6.** A judicial order for the restoration of stolen goods, or of their value, to the owner upon the thief's conviction. — **restitutionary,** *adj.*

> "The term 'restitution' appears in early decisions, but general recognition probably began with the publication of the *Restatement of Restitution* [in 1937]. The term is not wholly apt since it suggests restoration to the successful party of some benefit obtained from him. Usually this will be the case where relief is given, but by no means always. There are cases in which the successful party obtains restitution of something he did not have before, for example a benefit received by the defendant from a third person which justly should go to the plaintiff." 1 George E. Palmer, *The Law of Restitution* § 1.1, at 4 (1978).

> "'Restitution' is an ambiguous term, sometimes referring to the disgorging of something which has been taken and at times referring to compensation for injury done. Often, the result under either meaning of the term would be the same. If the plaintiff has been defrauded into paying $1,000 to the defendant, his loss and the defendant's gain coincide. Where they do not coincide, as where the plaintiff is out of pocket more than the defendant has gained and the defendant's conduct is tortious, the plaintiff will recover his loss in a quasi-contractual or equitable action for restitution. Unjust impoverishment as well as unjust enrichment is a ground for restitution. If the defendant is guilty of a nontortious misrepresentation, the measure of recovery is not rigid but, as in other cases of restitution, such factors as relative fault, the agreed upon risks, and the fairness of alternative risk allocations not agreed upon and not attributable to the fault of either party need to be weighed." John D. Calamari & Joseph M. Perillo, *The Law of Contracts* § 9-23, at 376 (3d ed. 1987).

restitutionary redress. See REDRESS.

restitution damages. See DAMAGES.

restitutione extracti ab ecclesia (res-tə-t[y]oo-shee-**oh**-nee ek-**strak**-tı ab e-**klee**-z[h]ee-ə). [Latin] (17c) *Eccles. law.* A writ restoring someone who had been suspected or accused of a felony to the church.

restitutione temporalium (res-tə-t[y]oo-shee-**oh**-nee tem-pə-**ray**-lee-əm). [Latin] (17c) *Eccles. law.* A writ directing the sheriff to restore the temporalities of a diocese to a bishop. See TEMPORALITY (2).

restitution interest. See INTEREST (2).

restitutory interdict. See INTERDICT (1).

restitutory right. See RIGHT.

restor. See RESTAUR.

restorative-justice sanction. See SANCTION (3).

restorative motion. See MOTION (2).

restoratory motion. See *restorative motion* under MOTION (2).

restraining order. (1876) **1.** A court order prohibiting family violence; esp., an order restricting a person from harassing, threatening, and sometimes merely contacting or approaching another specified person. • This type of order is issued most commonly in cases of domestic violence. A court may grant an ex parte restraining order in a family-violence case if it is necessary to (1) achieve the government's interest in protecting victims of family violence from further abuse, (2) ensure prompt action where there is an immediate threat of danger, and (3) provide governmental control by ensuring that judges grant such orders only where there is an immediate danger of such abuse. *Fuentes v. Shevin,* 407 U.S. 67, 92 S.Ct. 1983 (1972). — Also termed *protective order*; *order of protection*; *stay-away order.* See *ex parte motion* under MOTION (1). **2.** TEMPORARY RESTRAINING ORDER. **3.** A court order entered to prevent the dissipation or loss of property.

restraining power. See POWER (3).

restraining statute. See *disabling statute* under STATUTE.

restraint, *n.* (15c) **1.** Confinement, abridgment, or limitation <a restraint on the freedom of speech>. See PRIOR RESTRAINT. **2.** Prohibition of action; holding back <the victim's family exercised no restraint — they told the suspect exactly what they thought of him>. **3.** RESTRAINT OF TRADE. **4.** FORFEITURE RESTRAINT.

restraint of marriage. (16c) A condition or stipulation (esp. in a gift or bequest) that limits the beneficiary's free choice of marriage, as by directing against marriage with a particular class of persons or even attempting to restrict it to a union with one particular person. • Restraints of marriage are usu. void if they are general or unlimited in scope.

restraint of princes. (17c) *Archaic.* A restriction on the sailing of a vessel or the undertaking or completion of a voyage by reason of a blockade; an embargo. • The phrase still occasionally appears in marine-insurance contexts. — Also termed *restraint of princes and rulers*; *restraint of princes, rulers, and people.* See EMBARGO.

restraint of trade. (17c) **1.** A limitation on business dealings or professional or gainful occupations. **2.** *Antitrust.* An agreement between two or more businesses or a combination of businesses intended to eliminate competition, create a monopoly, artificially raise prices, or otherwise adversely affect the free market. • Restraints of trade are usu. illegal, but may be declared reasonable if they are in the best interests of both the parties and the public. — Often shortened to *restraint.* — Also termed *conspiracy in restraint of trade.* See PER SE RULE; RULE OF REASON.

▸ **horizontal restraint.** (1942) A restraint of trade imposed by agreement between competitors at the same level of distribution. • The restraint is horizontal not because it has horizontal effects, but because it is the product of a horizontal agreement. — Also termed *horizontal agreement*; *horizontal arrangement.*

▸ **unreasonable restraint of trade.** (1853) A restraint of trade that produces a significant anticompetitive effect and thus violates antitrust law.

▸ **vertical restraint.** (1930) A restraint of trade imposed by agreement between firms at different levels of distribution (as between manufacturer and retailer). — Also termed *vertical arrangement*

restraint on alienation. (18c) **1.** A restriction, usu. in a deed of conveyance, on a grantee's ability to sell or transfer real property; a provision that conveys an interest and that, even after the interest has become vested, prevents or discourages the owner from disposing of it at all or from disposing of it in particular ways or to particular persons. • Restraints on alienation are generally unenforceable as against public policy favoring the free alienability of land. — Also termed *unreasonable restraint on alienation.* **2.** A trust provision that prohibits or penalizes alienation of the trust corpus.

restricted driver's license. See *conditional driver's license* under DRIVER'S LICENSE.

restricted endorsement. See *conditional indorsement* under INDORSEMENT.

restricted indorsement. See *conditional indorsement* under INDORSEMENT.

restricted interpretation. See *restrictive interpretation* under INTERPRETATION (1).

restricted security. See SECURITY (4).

restricted stock. See *restricted security* under SECURITY (4).

restricted surplus. See SURPLUS.

restricted-use license. See DRIVER'S LICENSE.

restricted visitation. See *supervised visitation* under VISITATION.

restriction. (15c) **1.** Confinement within bounds or limits; a limitation or qualification. **2.** A limitation (esp. in a deed) placed on the use or enjoyment of property. See *restrictive covenant* under COVENANT (4).

> "A restriction may be defined as an agreement concerning the use of land by its owner which runs with the land in equity. Strictly speaking, restrictions did not exist till about 1840, for not till that time was the distinctive quality, that of running with the land, recognized. Long before this, however, covenants that to-day would be called restrictions had been enforced in equity; but the suits, being between the contracting parties, had raised only the ordinary questions of specific performance of contracts. When first suit was brought against a purchaser of the land from the covenantor, the question was still treated as one of specific performance. The inquiry was made whether the covenant ran with the land at law. If it ran, then the purchaser was subject to a legal obligation, which equity might specifically enforce. If not, then there was no obligation, either at law or in equity." Charles I. Giddings, *Restrictions Upon the Use of Land,* 5 Harv. L. Rev. 274, 274 (1892).

▸ **conservation restriction.** See *conservation easement* under EASEMENT.

3. *Military law.* A deprivation of liberty involving moral and legal, rather than physical, restraint. • A military restriction is imposed as punishment either by a commanding officer's nonjudicial punishment or by a summary, special, or general court-martial. Restriction is a lesser restraint because it permits the restricted person to perform full military duties. See *nonjudicial punishment* under PUNISHMENT.

▸ **restriction in lieu of arrest.** (1952) A restriction in which a person is ordered to stay within specific geographical limits, such as a base or a ship, and is permitted to perform full military duties.

4. *Patents.* A patent examiner's ruling that a patent application comprises two or more patentably distinct or independent inventions; the requirement that the applicant elect one invention to continue prosecuting under the original application by abandoning some of the original claims. • The applicant may defend the claims by traversing the requirement, abandon any nonelected invention, or continue prosecuting any nonelected invention under a separate divisional application. — Also termed *requirement for restriction*; *restriction requirement*; *division.* Cf. OBJECTION (4); REJECTION (4).

restriction application. See *divisional application* under PATENT APPLICATION.

restriction requirement. See RESTRICTION (4).

restrictive condition. See *negative condition* under CONDITION (2).

restrictive covenant. 1. See *covenant not to compete* under COVENANT (1). **2.** See COVENANT (4).

restrictive covenant in equity. See *restrictive covenant* (1) under COVENANT (4).

restrictive indorsement. See INDORSEMENT.

restrictive interpretation. See INTERPRETATION (1).

restrictive practice. (*usu. pl.*) **1.** An unreasonable rule that a labor union uses to limit the kind of work that members of other labor unions are allowed to do for a company. **2.** An unfair trade agreement between companies to limit competition.

restrictive principle of sovereign immunity. (1972) The doctrine by which a foreign country's immunity does not apply to claims arising from the country's private or commercial acts, but protects the country only from claims arising from its public functions. See COMMERCIAL-ACTIVITY EXCEPTION; JURE GESTIONIS; JURE IMPERII.

> "[T]he [Foreign Sovereign] Immunities Act codified the so-called 'restrictive' principle of sovereign immunity, as recognized in international law. Under this doctrine, the immunity of a foreign state in the courts of the United States is 'restricted' to claims involving the foreign state's public acts and does not extend to suits based on its commercial or private conduct." 14A Charles Alan Wright et al., *Federal Practice and Procedure* § 3662, at 161–62 (3d ed. 1998).

restrictive title. See TITLE (4).

restructuring, *n.* The act or practice of changing the way in which a government, business entity, or system is organized.

result, *n.* (17c) **1.** A consequence, effect, or conclusion. **2.** That which is achieved, brought about, or obtained, esp. by purposeful action; the answer to a problem, such as a legal problem resolved by a court. — Also termed (in senses 1 & 2) *resultant.* **3.** *Archaic.* A decision, resolution, or final determination of a deliberate or parliamentary body.

result (ri-zəlt), *vb.* (15c) **1.** To be a physical, logical, or legal consequence; to proceed as an outcome or conclusion <much good will result from this>. **2.** To terminate or end (followed by *in*) <this legislative bill will result in less liability for insureds>.

resultant, *n.* **1.** RESULT (1). **2.** RESULT (2).

resulting power. See POWER (3).

resulting trust. See TRUST (3).

resulting use. See USE (4).

resume consideration. See *take from the table* under TABLE.

resummons. (15c) A second or renewed summons to a party or witness already summoned. See SUMMONS.

resumption. (15c) **1.** The taking back of something (such as property previously given up or lost. **2.** The government's taking back of lands or other property, or of rights and privileges, wrongfully obtained. **3.** *English law.* The retaking by the Crown or other authority of lands or rights previously given to another, esp. as a result of false suggestion or other error. — **resume,** *vb.*

res universitatis (rays yoo-nə-vər-sə-**tay**-tis), *n. pl.* [Latin] (17c) *Roman law.* Things belonging to a community or corporate body and free to be used by all its members.

resurrender, *n.* (1816) *Hist.* The return of a copyhold estate to a mortgagor by the mortgagee after the debt has been repaid. See SURRENDER OF COPYHOLD.

retail, *n.* (14c) The sale of goods or commodities to ultimate consumers, as opposed to the sale for further distribution or processing. Cf. WHOLESALE. — **retail,** *adj.* — **retail,** *vb.*

retailer, *n.* (15c) A person or entity engaged in the business of selling personal property to the public or to consumers, as opposed to selling to those who intend to resell the items.

retail installment contract. See CONTRACT.

retail installment contract and security agreement. See *retail installment contract* under CONTRACT.

retail installment sale. See INSTALLMENT SALE.

retail price index. (1904) A list of certain goods and services to show how much their prices change month by month.

retail sales tax. See *sales tax* under TAX.

retain (ri-**tayn**), *vb.* (15c) **1.** To hold in possession or under control; to keep and not lose, part with, or dismiss. **2.** To hire; to engage for the provision of services (as by a lawyer, an accountant, an employee, etc.). **3.** To keep in one's mind or memory.

retainage (ri-**tayn**-ij). (1901) A percentage of what a landowner pays a contractor, withheld until the construction has been satisfactorily completed and all mechanic's liens are released or have expired. — Also termed *retained fund.*

retained earnings. See EARNINGS.

retained fund. See RETAINAGE.

retained income trust. See *grantor-retained income trust* under TRUST (3).

retainer, *n.* (18c) **1.** A client's authorization for a lawyer to act in a case <the attorney needed an express retainer before making a settlement offer>. **2.** A fee that a client pays to a lawyer simply to be available when the client needs legal help during a specified period or on a specified matter. **3.** A lump-sum fee paid by the client to engage a lawyer at the outset of a matter. — Also termed *engagement fee.* **4.** An advance payment of fees for work that the lawyer will perform in the future. — Also termed *retaining fee.* Cf. ATTORNEY'S FEE. **5.** A reduced amount of rent that one pays for a room, apartment, etc. when one is not there as consideration for having it available upon one's return. — **retain,** *vb.*

> "Over the years, attorneys have used the term 'retainer' in so many conflicting senses that it should be banished from the legal vocabulary. . . . If some primordial urge drives you to use the term 'retainer,' at least explain what you mean in terms that both you and the client will understand." Mortimer D. Schwartz & Richard C. Wydick, *Problems in Legal Ethics* 100, 101 (2d ed. 1988).

▸ **general retainer.** (18c) A retainer for a specific length of time rather than for a specific project.

▸ **special retainer.** (18c) A retainer for a specific case or project.

retaining fee. See RETAINER (4).

retaining lien. See LIEN.

retaliation (ri-tal-ee-**ay**-shən), *n.* (16c) The act of doing someone harm in return for actual or perceived injuries or wrongs; an instance of reprisal, requital, or revenge. See REVENGE. — **retaliate,** *vb.* — **retaliatory,** *adj.*

retaliatory discharge. See DISCHARGE (7).

retaliatory eviction. See EVICTION.

retaliatory law. (1820) A state law restraining another state's businesses — as by levying taxes — in response to similar restraints imposed by the second state on the first state's businesses.

retaliatory tariff. See TARIFF (2).

retallia (ri-**tal**-ee-ə). [Law Latin] *Hist.* The sale of goods or commodities in small quantities; retail.

retenementum (ri-ten-ə-**men**-təm). *Hist.* A withholding; restraint or detainment.

retenta possessione (ri-**ten**-tə pə-zes[h]-ee-**oh**-nee). [Latin] (17c) *Hist.* Possession being retained.

retention. (16c) *Scots law.* A possessor's right to keep a movable until the possessor's claim against the movable or its owner is satisfied; a lien.

▸ **general retention.** (1804) *Scots law.* A possessor's right to keep all property owned by a debtor as security for the debt.

▸ **special retention.** (1826) *Scots law.* A possessor's right to keep property owned by another until reimbursed for expenditures on the property for its repair or for its care and maintenance.

retention election. See ELECTION (3).

retention hearing. See HEARING.

retention judicial election. See *retention election* under ELECTION (3).

retention order. (1943) *Criminal procedure.* A court order requiring someone to be kept in custody who had earlier been committed to a psychiatric facility because of a not-guilty-by-reason-of-mental-disease finding.

retinue. (14c) A group of persons who are retained to follow and attend to a sovereign, noble, or other distinguished person.

retired stock. See *treasury stock* under STOCK.

retirement, *n.* (16c) **1.** Termination of one's own employment or career, esp. upon reaching a certain age or for health reasons; retirement may be voluntary or involuntary. **2.** Withdrawal from action or for privacy <Carol's retirement to her house by the lake>. **3.** Withdrawal from circulation; payment of a debt <retirement of a series of bonds>. See REDEMPTION. — **retire,** *vb.*

▸ **compulsory retirement.** (1842) Mandatory retirement based on a person's age, esp. as specified in a union contract, by corporate policy, or by statute.

retirement annuity. See ANNUITY.

Retirement Equity Act of 1984. A federal statute that requires private pension plans to comply with the court-ordered division of a pension between spouses and permits the plan administrator to pay all or part of a worker's pensions and survivor benefits directly to a former spouse if the plan has been served with a court order that meets the federal requirements for a qualified domestic-relations order. 29 USCA § 1056(d)(3). — Abbr. REA. See QUALIFIED DOMESTIC-RELATIONS ORDER.

retirement-income insurance. See INSURANCE.

retirement plan. See EMPLOYEE BENEFIT PLAN.

retorna brevium (ri-**tor**-nə **bree**-vee-əm). [Law Latin] (17c) *Hist.* The return of a writ. • This was the indorsement on a writ by a sheriff or other officer, reporting on the writ's execution.

retorno habendo. See DE RETORNO HABENDO.

retorsion (ri-**tor**-shən). (18c) *Int'l law.* An act of lawful retaliation in kind for another country's unfriendly or unfair act. • Examples of retorsion include suspending diplomatic relations, expelling foreign nationals, and restricting travel rights. — Also spelled *retortion.* Cf. REPRISAL (2). — **retorsive,** *adj.*

> "Retorsion (from *retorquere*, French, *retordre*, retort), or retaliation, is to apply the *lex talionis* to another nation, — treating it or its subjects in similar circumstances according to the rule which it has set. Thus, if a nation has failed in comity or politeness, if it has embarrassed intercourse by new taxes on commerce or the like, the same or an analogous course may be taken by the aggrieved power to bring it back to propriety and duty. The sphere of retorsion ought to be confined within the imperfect rights or moral claims of an opposite party. Rights ought not to be violated because another nation has violated them." Theodore D. Woolsey, *Introduction to the Study of International Law* 188 (5th ed. 1878).

retort (ri-**tort**), *vb.* (16c) To reply quickly, esp. with either anger or humor. — **retort,** *n.*

retraction, *n.* (14c) **1.** The act of taking or drawing back <retraction of anticipatory repudiation before breach of contract>. **2.** The act of recanting; specif., an official statement that something one said previously is not true <retraction of a defamatory remark>. **3.** *Wills & estates.* A withdrawal of a renunciation <because of her retraction, she took property under her uncle's will>. See RENUNCIATION (3). — Also termed (in senses 2 & 3) *retractation.* **4.** *Copyright.* The right of authors and artists to renounce their creative works and to forbid their sale or display. • Retraction is one of the moral rights of artists recognized in civil-law countries and much of Europe, but largely unavailable in the United States. — Also termed (in sense 4) *withdrawal.* — **retract,** *vb.*

retractus feudalis (ri-**trak**-təs fyoo-**day**-lis). [Law Latin "a recall of the fee"] (18c) *Scots law.* A superior's right to pay a debt of a vassal's lands in exchange for the return of the conveyance.

retraxit (ri-**trak**-sit). [Latin "he has withdrawn"] (16c) *Hist.* A plaintiff's voluntary withdrawal of a lawsuit in court so that the plaintiff forever forfeits the right of action. • In modern practice, retraxit is called *voluntary dismissal with prejudice.* A dismissal without prejudice does not operate as a retraxit. See *judgment of retraxit* under JUDGMENT (2).

retreat, *n.* (15c) **1.** A move away from a place or a person in order to escape from fighting or danger; esp., an army's movement away from the enemy after a defeat in battle. **2.** A change from previous beliefs or behavior because of unpopularity or other difficulty. **3.** A situation in which the value of stocks, bonds, etc. falls to a lower level. **4.** A private and safe place where one can go for peace and quiet. **5.** A period that one spends in contemplation and prayer, away from one's normal activities and duties.

retreat (ri-**treet**), *vb.* (15c) **1.** To withdraw from (a place, esp. one to which an advance has been made); to go back or backward; to move back or away to end or avoid contact <the suspect retreated from the police dog>. **2.** (Of the military) to withdraw, usu. in an orderly manner, from (an enemy or a threat); specif., to move away from (a place or an enemy) because of danger or of having been defeated <the army retreated>. **3.** Figuratively (as of an advocate), to recede from (a claim or controversy, esp. on a particular point in dispute); to change one's mind about (something) because of criticism or other difficulty <the advocate retreated from his former position>. **4.** To lose value <stock prices retreated>. — **retreat,** *n.*

retreat rule. (1935) *Criminal law.* The doctrine holding that the victim of an assault has a duty to withdraw instead of resorting to deadly force in self-defense, unless (1) the victim is at home or in his or her place of business (the so-called *castle doctrine*), or (2) the assailant is a person whom the victim is trying to arrest. • A minority of American jurisdictions have adopted this rule. — Also termed *rule of retreat; duty to retreat.* Cf. NO-RETREAT RULE.

> "The rationale for the retreat rule is not difficult to ascertain, at least in part. It rests upon the view that human life, even the life of an aggressor, is sufficiently important that it should be preserved when to do so requires only the sacrifice of the much less important interest in standing one's ground." George E. Dix, "Justification: Self-defense," in 3 *Encyclopedia of Crime and Justice* 946, 948–49 (Sanford H. Kadish ed., 1983).

retrial, *n.* (18c) A new trial of an action that has already been tried. See *trial de novo* under TRIAL. — **retry,** *vb.*

retribution, *n.* (14c) **1.** *Criminal law.* Punishment imposed for a serious offense; requital. Cf. DETERRENCE; REHABILITATION (1). **2.** Something justly deserved; repayment; reward. — **retributive,** *adj.* — **retribute,** *vb.*

retributive danger. See DANGER.

retributive punishment. See PUNISHMENT (1).

retributivism (ri-**trib**-yə-tə-viz-əm). (1966) A theory that justifies criminal punishment in terms of the ill-desert of the offender, regardless of whether deterrence or other good consequences would result. • Although more precise statements of the theory are notoriously controversial, retributivism is generally opposed to consequentialism: retributivism is said to be a "backward-looking" justification for punishment, whereas consequentialism is "forward-looking." Opponents of retributivism sometimes refer to it as "vindictive theory." See MIXED THEORY OF PUNISHMENT. Cf. CONSEQUENTIALISM (3); UTILITARIAN-DETERRENCE THEORY; *hedonistic utilitarianism* under UTILITARIANISM.

▸ **maximalist retributivism.** (1987) The classical form of retributivism, espoused by scholars such as Immanuel Kant, under which it is argued that society has a duty, not just a right, to punish a criminal who is guilty and culpable, that is, someone who has no justification or excuse for the illegal act.

▸ **minimalist retributivism.** (1987) The more contemporary form of retributivism, which maintains that no one should be punished in the absence of guilt and culpability (that is, unless punishment is deserved), and that a judge may absolve the offender from punishment, wholly or partially, when doing so would further societal goals such as rehabilitation or deterrence.

▸ **negative retributivism.** (1982) A theory that justifies punishment in terms of its good consequences but maintains that it is unjust to punish persons in the absence of their ill-desert or in excess of their ill-desert. • Believing that negative retributivism is more clearly classed as a subtype of consequentialist rather than retributivist justifications for punishment, many authorities prefer the term *side-constrained consequentialism.*

retributor (ri-**trib**-yo-tər), *n.* (17c) Someone who requites; esp., one who gives out rewards and punishments according to merit or demerit. See REQUITE.

retroact, *vb.* (18c) To have retrospective effect.

> "Where the statute is a special one, or is conceded to be expressly intended to *retroact*, there is nothing for the court but to decide whether the enactment is within the scope of legislative authority." William P. Wade, *A Treatise on the Operation and Construction of Retroactive Laws* 35 (1880).

retroactive, *adj.* (17c) (Of a statute, ruling, etc.) extending in scope or effect to matters that have occurred in the past. — Also termed *retrospective.* Cf. PROSPECTIVE (1). — **retroact,** *vb.*

retroactive law. (18c) A legislative act that looks backward or contemplates the past, affecting acts or facts that existed before the act came into effect. • A retroactive law is not unconstitutional unless it (1) is in the nature of an ex post facto law or a bill of attainder, (2) impairs the obligation of contracts, (3) divests vested rights, or (4) is constitutionally forbidden. — Also termed *retrospective law; retroactive statute; retrospective statute.* See PRESUMPTION AGAINST RETROACTIVITY.

> "There are numerous cases which hold that retrospective laws are not obnoxious to constitutional objection, while in others they have been held to be void. The different decisions have been based upon facts making the different rulings applicable. There is no doubt of the right of the legislature to make laws which reach back to and change or modify the effect of prior transactions, provided retrospective laws are not forbidden, *eo nomine*, by the State constitution, and provided further that no other objection exists than their retrospective character. But legislation of this description is exceedingly liable to abuse; and it is a sound rule of construction to give a statute a prospective operation only, unless its terms show a legislative intent that is should have retrospective effect. And some of the States have deemed it important to forbid such laws altogether by their constitutions." Thomas M. Cooley, *A Treatise on the Constitutional Limitations Which Rest upon the Legislative Power of the States of the American Union* 370 (1868).

retroactivity. The quality, state, or condition of having relation or reference to, or effect in, a prior time; specif., (of a statute, regulation, ruling, etc.) the quality of becoming effective at some time before the enactment, promulgation, imposition, or the like, and of having application to acts that occurred earlier. — Also termed *restrospectivity.* Cf. PROSPECTIVITY.

> "'Retroactivity' is a term often used by lawyers but rarely defined. On analysis it soon becomes apparent, moreover, that it is used to cover at least two distinct concepts. The first, which may be called 'true retroactivity,' consists in the application of a new rule of law to an act or transaction which was completed before the rule was promulgated. The second concept, which will be referred to as 'quasi-retroactivity,' occurs when a new rule of law is applied to an

act or transaction in the process of completion. . . . [T]he foundation of these concepts is the distinction between completed and pending transactions . . . ." T.C. Hartley, *The Foundations of European Community Law* 129 (1981).

retrocession. (17c) **1.** The act of ceding something back (such as a territory or jurisdiction). **2.** The return of a title or other interest in property to its former or rightful owner. **3.** The process of transferring all or part of a reinsured risk to another reinsurance company; reinsurance of reinsurance. • Subsequent retrocessions are referred to as *first retrocession, second retrocession*, and so on. **4.** The amount of risk that is so transferred. — **retrocede,** *vb.*

retrocessionaire. (1973) *Reinsurance.* A reinsurer of a reinsurer. See RETROCESSION.

retrocessional agreement. (1968) An agreement providing for reinsurance of reinsurance.

retrospectant evidence. See EVIDENCE.

retrospective, *adj.* See RETROACTIVE.

retrospective law. See RETROACTIVE LAW.

retrospective statute. See RETROACTIVE LAW.

retrospectivity. The quality, state, or condition of being concerned with or having reference to the past; RETROACTIVITY.

return, *n.* (15c) **1.** A court officer's bringing back of an instrument to the court that issued it; RETURN OF WRIT <a sheriff's return of citation>. **2.** A court officer's indorsement on an instrument brought back to the court, reporting what the officer did or found <a return of *nulla bona*>. See FALSE RETURN (1).

"The summons, where notice is given by summons, is served by the officer to whom it is addressed. The manner in which he must serve it is prescribed by law and differs in different cases, depending upon the nature of the case, upon whether the defendant is a natural or artificial person, and upon other circumstances. It is the officer's duty to follow the method prescribed and to make a correct statement thereof on the back of the summons. This is known as the officer's *return*. On or before the day upon which he is called upon in the face of the summons to return it into court, it is his duty to file it there. From the return on the summons may be ascertained the sufficiency of the service. The word 'return' is appropriately applied also to the delivery of the summons to the court. Until so delivered there is no return, although an endorsement of the manner of service may be made on the summons. This endorsement may be changed at any time before it is delivered to the court, but thereafter it can only be changed with the court's permission." Frank William Henicksman, "Practice," in 11 *American Law and Procedure* § 20, at 415, 431-32 (James Parker Hall ed., 1950).

3. TAX RETURN <file your return before April 15>. **4.** (*usu. pl.*) An official report of voting results <election returns>. **5.** Yield or profit <return on an investment>. See RATE OF RETURN. **6.** An appellate judge's statement summarizing proceedings in the appeal from a local-court judgment for which there was no transcript. — **return,** *vb.*

▸ **capital return.** (1901) *Tax.* Revenue that represents the repayment of cost or capital and thus is not taxable as income. — Also termed *return of capital.*

▸ **fair return on investment.** (1851) The usual or reasonable profit in a business, esp. a public utility.

▸ **net return.** (1823) The profit on an investment after deducting all investment expenses.

▸ **return of capital.** See *capital return.*

returnable, *adj.* (15c) **1.** Capable of being restored to a former condition. **2.** That must or may be returned; esp., (of goods) suitable for taking back for either exchange or reimbursement. **3.** (Of a writ) due and required to be brought back at a specified time and place by the responsible officer. — **returnability,** *n.*

return date. See *return day* under DAY.

return day. See DAY.

returnee. (1870) **1.** A refugee whom authorities have returned to the country of origin; one who has fled from the home country and then been sent back. **2.** A person who returns to his or her own country after living elsewhere.

return information. *Tax.* Confidential data relating to a person's potential liability for any tax, penalty, interest, fine, forfeiture, or other imposition or offense, obtained by the IRS or some other taxing authority from any source or through any means. • Under 26 USCA § 6103(b)(2), return information includes a taxpayer's identity; the nature, source, or amount of his or her income; payments; receipts; deductions; exemptions; credits; assets; liabilities; net worth; tax liability; tax withheld; deficiencies; overassessments; tax payments; and any other data regarding the determination of tax liability. *See Church of Scientology of Cal. v. IRS*, 484 U.S. 9, 11–12, 108 S.Ct. 271, 273 (1987). See TAX RETURN.

returning board. (1872) An official body or commission that canvasses election returns.

return of process. See PROOF OF SERVICE.

return of service. See PROOF OF SERVICE.

return of writ. (18c) The sheriff's bringing back a writ to the court that issued it, with a short written account (usu. on the back) of the manner in which the writ was executed. — Often shortened to *return.* See RETURN (1).

reunification. A reunion or reuniting; esp., the return of a child who has been removed from his or her parents because of abuse or neglect by one or both of them. • When a child has been removed from the home because of abuse or neglect, the state's primary goal is family reunification as long as this is in the best interests of the child. The state is required, in most instances, to provide the parent or parents with services that will enable them to provide adequately for their child upon his or her return. After the enactment of the Adoption and Safe Families Act in 1997, states became more concerned with limiting the time that children are in foster care and less concerned with lengthy reunification plans. — Also termed *family reunification.* See ADOPTION AND SAFE FAMILIES ACT; PERMANENCY PLAN; ADOPTION ASSISTANCE AND CHILD WELFARE ACT. — **reunify,** *vb.*

re-up, *vb.* (1906) **1.** To reenlist in one of the armed forces <the soldier re-upped the day after being discharged>. **2.** To sign an extension to a contract, esp. an employment agreement <the star athlete re-upped in a three-year deal worth $12 million>.

reus (**ree**-əs). [Latin] *Roman & civil law.* **1.** A defendant. Cf. ACTOR (3). **2.** A party to a suit, whether plaintiff or defendant. **3.** A party to a contract or transaction, esp. one assuming a debt or obligation. **4.** *Roman law.* In criminal law, an accused or convicted person. Pl. ***rei.*** Fem. ***rea,*** pl. ***reae.***

reus promittendi (**ree**-əs proh-mi-**ten**-dɪ). [Latin "party promising"] (18c) *Roman law.* The answerer in a Roman-law stipulation. — Also termed *promissor.* See STIPULATION (3).

reus stipulandi (**ree**-əs **stip**-yə-**lan**-dɪ). [Latin "party stipulating"] (18c) *Roman law.* The questioner in a Roman-law stipulation. — Also termed *stipulator.* See STIPULATION (3).

revalidation. See REPUBLICATION (2).

revaluation, *n.* An increase in the value of one currency in relation to another currency. Cf. DEVALUATION. — **revalue,** *vb.*

revaluation surplus. See SURPLUS.

rev'd. *abbr.* Reversed.

reve (reev). (bef. 12c) *Hist.* The bailiff of a franchise or manor. See REEVE.

reveland (**reev**-lənd), *n.* (bef. 12c) *Hist. English law.* Collectively, lands that, although recorded in the Domesday Book as thaneland, had reverted to the king and were not again granted, but instead remained in the charge of the reve or bailiff of the manor. See DOMESDAY BOOK. Cf. THANELAND.

revendication, *n.* (18c) **1.** The recovery or claiming back of something by a formal claim or demand. **2.** *Civil law.* An action to recover real rights in and possession of property that is wrongfully held by another. • This is analogous to the common-law replevin. See *petitory action* (2) under ACTION (4). — **revendicate,** *vb.*

revendicatory action. See *petitory action* under ACTION (4).

revenge, (ri-**venj**), *n.* (16c) **1.** Vindictive retaliation against a perceived or actual wrongdoer; the infliction of punishment for the purpose of getting even. **2.** The desire for vengeance; vindictiveness at its most spiteful. See RETALIATION. Cf. VENGEANCE. — **revenge,** *vb.*

revenue. (15c) **1.** Income from any and all sources; gross income or gross receipts. **2.** The total current income of a government, however derived; esp., taxes. **3.** The government department or branch of the civil service that collects taxes, esp. national taxes. **4.** A tax officer. — Also termed *revenuer.* **5.** A source of income. — Also termed *revenue stream.* **6.** The periodic yield or interest from investment.

▸ **general revenue.** (17c) The income stream from which a state or municipality pays its obligations unless a law calls for payment from a special fund. See *general fund* under FUND (1).

▸ **land revenue.** (17c) Revenue derived from lands owned by the Crown in the United Kingdom. • Since, over the years, crown lands have been largely granted to subjects, they are now transferred within very narrow limits. See *Crown land* under LAND.

▸ **marginal revenue.** (1932) The amount of revenue earned from the sale of one additional unit.

▸ **public revenue.** (16c) A government's income, usu. derived from taxes, levies, and fees.

revenue agent's report. (1924) A report indicating any adjustments made to a tax return as a result of an IRS audit. • After an audit, this report is mailed to the taxpayer along with a thirty-day letter. — Abbr. RAR. See THIRTY-DAY LETTER.

revenue bill. See BILL (3).

revenue bond. See BOND (3).

Revenue Procedure. An official statement by the IRS regarding the administration and procedures of the tax laws. — Abbr. Rev. Proc.

revenuer. See REVENUE (4).

Revenue Ruling. An official interpretation by the IRS of the proper application of the tax law to a specific transaction. • Revenue Rulings carry some authoritative weight and may be relied on by the taxpayer who requested the ruling. — Abbr. Rev. Rul.

revenue stamp. (1862) A stamp used as evidence that a tax has been paid.

revenue stream. See REVENUE (5).

revenue tariff. See TARIFF (2).

re, verbis, literis, consensu (ree, **vər**-bis, **lit**-ər-is, kən-**sen**-s[y]oo). [Latin] *Roman law.* By the performance (namely, handing over), by words, by writing, by consent. • The phrase appeared in reference to the four classes of Roman contract.

reversal, *n.* (15c) **1.** An annulling or setting aside; esp., an appellate court's overturning of a lower court's decision. **2.** *Securities.* A change in a security's near-term market-price trend.

reverse, *vb.* (15c) To overturn (a judgment or ruling), esp. on appeal. • Sometimes, the verb is used without a direct object <We reverse>. The equivalent expression in British English is *to allow the appeal.*

reverse acquisition. See BACK-DOOR LISTING.

reverse annuity mortgage. See MORTGAGE.

reverse *Batson* challenge. See CHALLENGE (1).

reverse bear hug. See BEAR HUG.

reverse bonus. See *reverse contingent fee* under CONTINGENT FEE.

reverse breakup fee. A fee paid by a prospective buyer to the target company for backing out of an agreed-to acquisition, usu. for failure to obtain financing or antitrust approval. • The amount is usu. a percentage of the acquisition price. The purpose is to compensate the target for the expenses of potential lawsuits or lost business, and to motivate the buyer to devote sufficient resources to obtain necessary financing and regulatory compliance.

reverse churning. See CHURNING.

reverse condemnation. See *inverse condemnation* under CONDEMNATION (2).

reverse confusion. See CONFUSION.

reverse-confusion doctrine. (1981) *Intellectual property.* The rule that it is unfair competition if the defendant's use of a title that is confusingly similar to the one used by the plaintiff leads the public to believe that the plaintiff's work is the same as the defendant's, or that it is derived from or associated in some manner with the defendant. • Under the conventional passing-off form of unfair competition, similarity of titles leads the public to believe that the defendant's work is the same as the plaintiff's work, or is in some manner derived from the plaintiff. But in reverse confusion, the unfair competition results from the confusion created about the origin of the plaintiff's work.

reverse consensus. (1993) *Intellectual property.* In a dispute-settlement procedure under TRIPs, an agreement between the parties that a dispute should not be submitted to a World Trade Organization panel for adjudication. • Before TRIPs, any party could delay formation of a WTO panel or adoption of its report by withholding consensus. Under TRIPs, each process is automatic unless all parties agree not to go forward.

reverse contingent fee. See CONTINGENT FEE.

reverse discovery. See *reverse Jencks material* under JENCKS MATERIAL.

reverse discrimination. See DISCRIMINATION (3).

reverse doctrine of equivalents. See DOCTRINE OF EQUIVALENTS.

reverse-engineering. (1957) *Intellectual property.* The process of discovering how an invention works by inspecting and studying it, esp. by taking it apart in order to learn how it works and how to copy it and improve it. • Reverse engineering is a proper means of discovering trade secrets, according to the Uniform Trade Secrets Act, and is a defense against a suit for misappropriation of trade secrets. But it is not a defense in a suit for patent infringement. — **reverse-engineer,** *vb.*

reverse *Erie* doctrine. (1955) **1.** The rule that a state court must apply federal law when state law is preempted by federal law or federal law prevails by an *Erie*-like balancing of the facts in situations not already regulated by Congress or the Constitution. **2.** *Maritime law.* The principle that a state court hearing an admiralty or maritime case must apply federal admiralty law even if that law conflicts with the law of the state. — Often shortened to *reverse Erie.* — Also termed *converse-Erie doctrine*; *inverse-Erie doctrine.* Cf. ERIE DOCTRINE.

reverse FOIA suit (**foy**-ə). (1974) A lawsuit by the owner of a trade secret or other information exempt from disclosure under a freedom-of-information act to prevent a governmental entity from making that information available to the public. See FREEDOM OF INFORMATION ACT.

reverse *Jencks*. See *reverse Jencks material* under JENCKS MATERIAL.

reverse *Jencks* material. See JENCKS MATERIAL.

reverse mortgage. See *reverse annuity mortgage* under MORTGAGE.

reverse palming off. See PASSING OFF.

reverse passing off. See PASSING OFF.

reverse proffer. (2003) A meeting at which prosecutors present to a criminal defendant and defense counsel the strength of the prosecution's case so that the defendant may consider a guilty plea as opposed to going to trial. Cf. PROFFER MEETING.

reverse spot zoning. See ZONING.

reverse sting. See STING.

reverse stock split. See STOCK SPLIT.

reverse subsidiary merger. See *reverse triangular merger* under MERGER (8).

reverse transfer statute. See TRANSFER STATUTE.

reverse triangular merger. See MERGER (8).

reversible error. See ERROR (2).

reversio (ri-**vər**-shee-oh). [Law Latin] *Hist.* The returning of land to the grantor.

reversion, *n.* (15c) **1.** The interest that is left after subtracting what the transferor has parted with from what the transferor originally had; specif., a future interest in land arising by operation of law whenever an estate owner grants to another a particular estate, such as a life estate or a term of years, but does not dispose of the entire interest. • A reversion occurs automatically upon termination of the prior estate, as when a life tenant dies. — Also termed *reversionary estate*; *estate in reversion*; *equitable reversion.* **2.** Loosely, REMAINDER. **3.** *Scots law.* The right of redemption of an estate that is security for a debt or judgment. **4.** A deferred annuity; esp., one that is to begin at some stated event, such as a designated death. Cf. POSSIBILITY OF REVERTER; REMAINDER. — **reversionary,** *adj.* — **revert,** *vb.*

▸ **automatic reversion.** (1943) The spontaneous revesting in a grantor of property that the grantor had earlier disposed of, as with a fee simple determinable. See *fee simple determinable* under FEE SIMPLE.

▸ **freehold reversion.** (18c) The termination of a lease and reversion of a property to freehold status.

▸ **leasehold reversion.** (18c) The termination of a sublease and consequent reversion of a leased property to the lessee.

reversionary estate. See REVERSION.

reversionary interest. See INTEREST (2).

reversionary lease. See LEASE.

reversioner. (17c) **1.** Someone who possesses the reversion to an estate; the grantor or heir in reversion. **2.** Broadly, one who has a lawful interest in land but not the present possession of it.

reversor. (1805) *Scots law.* A debtor who secures a debt by pledging property to a creditor and retaining a right of reversion.

reverter. See POSSIBILITY OF REVERTER.

reverter guarantee. (1978) *Real estate.* A mortgage clause protecting the mortgagee against a loss occasioned by the occurrence of a terminating event under a possibility of reverter. See POSSIBILITY OF REVERTER.

revest, *vb.* (16c) To clothe or vest again or anew, as with rank, authority, or ownership <revesting the former owner with title>.

rev'g. *abbr.* Reversing.

review, *n.* (15c) **1.** Consideration, inspection, or reexamination of a subject or thing. **2.** Plenary power to direct and instruct an agent or subordinate, including the right to remand, modify, or vacate any action by the agent or subordinate, or to act directly in place of the agent or subordinate <Subject to the Assembly's review, the Council enjoys the same powers of review and delegation as the Assembly.>. — **review,** *vb.*

▸ **administrative review.** (1928) **1.** Judicial review of an administrative proceeding. **2.** Review of an administrative proceeding within the agency itself.

▸ **appellate review.** (1837) Examination of a lower court's decision by a higher court, which can affirm, reverse, modify, or vacate the decision.

▸ **deferential review.** (1960) An appellate standard granting relief from a lower court's, esp. a trial court's, judgment only when earlier proceeding entailed an unreasonable application of clearly established law or a clearly unreasonable determination of the facts.

▸ **discretionary review.** (1914) The form of appellate review that is not a matter of right but that occurs only with the appellate court's permission. See CERTIORARI.

▸ **judicial review.** See JUDICIAL REVIEW.

▸ **review of costs.** (1974) The reexamination and retaxing of an erroneous bill of costs. See *bill of costs* under bill (2).

reviewable issue. See *appealable decision* under DECISION (1).

review hearing. See HEARING.

review of costs. See REVIEW.

revised statutes. See STATUTE.

revisio in jure (rə-viz-ee-oh in **joor**-ee). [Latin] *Hist.* Revision in law.

revision, *n.* (17c) **1.** A reexamination or careful review for correction or improvement. **2.** *Parliamentary law.* A general and thorough rewriting of a governing document, in which the entire document is open to amendment <bylaws revision>. **3.** *Military law.* The reconvening of a general or special court-martial to revise its action or to correct the record because of an improper or inconsistent action concerning the findings or the sentence. • A revision can occur only if it will not materially prejudice the accused. **4.** An altered version of a work.

revisionist, *n.* (1850) **1.** Someone who revises. **2.** Someone who favors revision of a statute, contract, text, creed, etc. **3.** Someone, esp. a judge or advocate, who favors the tacit revision of a legal text through judicial interpretation, so that the meaning changes even though the words remain the same. **4.** One who advocates a new interpretation of history based on new information or a posited better understanding of the facts. — **revisionist,** *adj.* — **revisionism,** *n.*

revival, *n.* (17c) **1.** Restoration to current use or operation; esp., the act of restoring the validity or legal force of an expired contract, an abandoned patent, or a dormant judgment. — Also termed (for a dormant judgment) *revival of judgment.* Cf. RENEWAL (3). **2.** *Wills & estates.* The reestablishment of the validity of a revoked will by revoking the will that invalidated the original will or in some other way manifesting the testator's intent to be bound by the earlier will. Cf. REPUBLICATION (2). **3.** *Patents.* Renewal of a patent prosecution that has been deemed abandoned because the applicant did not respond to an office action within the statutory period. • The applicant can petition for revival on the basis of unavoidable or unintentional delay. 37 CFR § 1.137. — **revive,** *vb.*

revival statute. See STATUTE.

revivor. (18c) A proceeding to revive an action ended because of either the death of one of the parties or some other circumstance.

***Revlon* duty.** (1987) *Delaware law.* The obligation of a company's board of directors, upon deciding to sell the company or when the sale of the company becomes inevitable, to act reasonably in seeking out and accepting a transaction that offers the best value to shareholders. • This duty was first applied in *Revlon v. MacAndrews & Forbes Holdings Inc.*, 506 A.2d 173, 181–82 (Del. 1986).

revocable (**rev**-ə-kə-bəl), *adj.* (15c) Capable of being canceled or withdrawn <a revocable transfer>.

revocable bailment. See *bailment at will* under BAILMENT (1).

revocable guaranty. See GUARANTY (1).

revocable letter of credit. See LETTER OF CREDIT.

revocable trust. See TRUST (3).

revocation (rev-ə-**kay**-shən), *n.* (15c) **1.** An annulment, cancellation, or reversal, usu. of an act or power. **2.** *Contracts.* Withdrawal of an offer by the offeror. Cf. REPUDIATION (2); RESCISSION; REJECTION (2). **3.** *Wills & estates.* Invalidation of a will by the testator, either by destroying the will or by executing a new one. • A will, or parts of a will, may be revoked by operation of law. For example, most states have a statute providing for the revocation, upon divorce, of all provisions relating to the testator's former spouse. — **revocatory** (**rev**-ə-kə-tor-ee), *adj.*

revocation hearing. See HEARING.

revocatory action (**rev**-ə-kə-tor-ee *or* ri-**vok**-ə-tor-ee). (1843) *Civil law.* An action brought by a creditor to annul a contract that has been entered into by the debtor and that will increase the debtor's insolvency. La. Civ. Code art. 2036.

revocatur (ree-voh-**kay**-tər). [Latin] *Hist.* It is recalled. • In former English practice, this was used as a notation on a judgment that was set aside because of a factual error (as opposed to being reversed because of legal error).

revoke (ri-**vohk**), *vb.* (14c) **1.** To annul or make void by taking back or recalling; to cancel, rescind, repeal, or reverse. **2.** *Archaic.* To recant.

revolt (ri-**vohlt**), *n.* (16c) **1.** An uprising against established authority; esp., a strong and often violent action by many people against their ruler or government; a rebellion <the military acted swiftly to quell the revolt>. **2.** *Criminal law.* MUTINY (1). **3.** A refusal to accept someone's authority or to obey rules or laws <the minority leader now faces a revolt among members of his own party>. **4.** An act by which protestors refuse to submit to certain conditions <production stopped because of the workers' revolt over changes in their pension plan>.

revolt (ri-**vohlt**), *vb.* (16c) **1.** (Of people) to take strong and often violent action against the government, usu. with the aim of weakening it. **2.** To commit mutiny. **3.** To refuse to accept someone's authority or to obey rules or laws <when the legislation was first proposed, party members revolted against the leadership>.

revolution, *n.* (16c) **1.** An overthrow of a government, usu. resulting in fundamental political change; a successful rebellion. **2.** A complete change in ways of thinking or methods of doing things. — **revolutionary,** *adj.* & *n.*

revolutionary war. See WAR (1).

revolutioneering, *n.* (1803) Someone's taking part in a revolution.

revolver loan. See LOAN.

revolving charge account. See *revolving credit* under CREDIT (4).

revolving credit. See CREDIT (4).

revolving door. Metaphorically, the repetitive changing of roles quickly and often. • The metaphor describes the practice of lawyers who leave government service to work for much higher pay at or on behalf of firms regulated by the agency they previously worked for. But it is also used in other contexts, as with the repeated arrest and release of the homeless; hospitalization and release of the mentally ill; and the shuffling of children through a series of foster homes.

revolving fund. See FUND (1).

revolving letter of credit. See LETTER OF CREDIT.

revolving loan. See LOAN.

revolving performance bond. See PERFORMANCE BOND.

Rev. Proc. *abbr.* REVENUE PROCEDURE.

Rev. Rul. *abbr.* REVENUE RULING.

Rev. Stat. *abbr.* See *revised statutes* under STATUTE.

reward, *n.* (14c) **1.** Something of value, usu. money, given in return for some service or achievement, such as recovering property or providing information that leads to the capture of a criminal. Cf. BOUNTY (1). **2.** SALVAGE (4). — **reward,** *vb.*

rewritten specification. See *substitute specification* under SPECIFICATION (3).

rex (reks). (*usu. cap.*) (bef. 12c) **1.** A king. **2.** The official title of a king. **3.** The prosecution side (as representatives of the king) in criminal proceedings in a monarchy. — Abbr. R. Cf. REGINA.

rezone, *vb.* (1951) To change the zoning boundaries or restrictions of (an area) <rezone the neighborhood>. See ZONING.

rezoning, *n.* (1918) A change made by a local government for the use or uses allowed for a piece of real property.

RFA. *abbr.* REQUEST FOR ADMISSION.

RFI. *abbr.* REQUEST FOR INSTRUCTIONS.

RFP. *abbr.* (1963) **1.** REQUEST FOR PRODUCTION. **2.** REQUEST FOR PROPOSAL.

r.g. *abbr.* REGULA GENERALIS.

rhadamanthine (rad-ə-**man**-thin), *adj.* (*often cap.*) (1840) (Of a judge) rigorous and inflexible; relentlessly strict <the judge's rhadamanthine interpretation of procedural requirements makes it essential to study the local rules before appearing in court>. — Also termed *rhadamantive.*

Rhadamanthus (rad-ə-**man**-thəs), *n.* [in Greek mythology, the son of Zeus and Europa who became a judge in Hades] (16c) An extremely rigorous judge; esp., a judicial martinet. — Also spelled *Rhadamanthos; Rhadamanthys.*

rhetoric. (14c) **1.** The art of speaking and writing to persuade or influence people; esp., the power of pleasing or persuading an audience <forensic rhetoric>. **2.** A textbook on the subject of effective discourse <Blair's and Campbell's rhetorics are among the best 18th-century books on the subject>. **3.** *Pejorative.* Affected and exaggerated display in the use of language; florid and spurious oratory <politicians need to move beyond the incessant posturing and rhetoric>. **4.** In the Jesuit educational system, the highest class in the literary course of a school, corresponding to the German gymnasium or English public school <he excels in rhetoric but has fallen behind in math>. — **rhetorical,** *adj.*

rhetorical question. (17c) A question that one poses as a way of making a statement, with no real expectation of an answer; a question used not to elicit an answer but instead for rhetorical effect (e.g., "Who does not admire the common-law system?").

Rhodian law (**roh**-dee-ən). (16c) As legend would have it, the earliest known system or code of maritime law, supposedly dating from 900 B.C. and adopted intact by the Romans. • Rhodian law was purportedly developed by the people of the island Rhodes, located in the Aegean Sea and now belonging to Greece. The ancient inhabitants of Rhodes are said to have controlled the seas because of their commercial prosperity and naval superiority. Despite the uncertainties about its history, Rhodian law has often been cited as a source of admiralty and maritime law.

> "A strong tradition says that a maritime code was promulgated by the Island of Rhodes, in the Eastern Mediterranean, at the height of its power; the ridiculously early date of 900 B.C. has even been assigned to this suppositious code — a date accepted uncritically by some legal scholars. But even the existence of such a code has been pretty well cast in doubt, and we know next to nothing of its contents, if it existed. It is interesting to note, however, that the root-principle of the highly distinctive maritime-law system of general average . . . is clearly stated in Justinian's Digest, and that the Rhodian Law is invoked as authority." Grant Gilmore & Charles L. Black Jr., *The Law of Admiralty* § 1-2, at 3–4 (2d ed. 1975).

RHS. *abbr.* RURAL HOUSING SERVICE.

ribbon-matching rule. See MIRROR-IMAGE RULE.

Richard Roe. (16c) A fictitious name for a male party to a legal proceeding, used because the party's true identity is unknown or because his real name is being withheld; esp., the second of two such parties. Cf. JOHN DOE.

***Richardson* error.** (2000) *Criminal law.* A jury's erroneous conviction that occurs when the jurors considering a continuing-criminal-enterprise case return a guilty verdict without first agreeing on which individual violations of the law were elements of the criminal enterprise. *Richardson v. U.S.*, 526 U.S. 813 (1999).

RICO (**ree**-koh). *abbr.* (1972) RACKETEER INFLUENCED AND CORRUPT ORGANIZATIONS ACT.

RICO person. (1983) Under the Racketeer Influenced and Corrupt Organizations Act, any individual or entity capable of holding a legal or beneficial interest in property and posing a continuous threat of engaging in the acts of racketeering.

ride-along DA. See *riding district attorney* under DISTRICT ATTORNEY.

rider. (17c) An attachment to some document, such as a legislative bill or an insurance policy, that amends or supplements the document. • A rider to a legislative bill often addresses subject matter unrelated to the main purpose of the bill. — Also termed *policy rider.*

riding DA. See DISTRICT ATTORNEY.

riding district attorney. See DISTRICT ATTORNEY.

rien culp (ryan kəlp). [Law French "not guilty"] *Hist.* A plea of not guilty.

rien dit (ryan dee). [Law French "says nothing"] *Hist.* A plea of *nihil dicit.* See NIHIL DICIT.

rien luy doit (**ryan** lwee **dwah**). [Law French "owes him nothing"] *Hist.* A plea of *nil debet.* See NIL DEBET.

riens en arrière (**ryan** aw-nah-ree-**air**). [Law French "nothing in arrear"] *Hist.* A plea in a debt action for arrearages of account.

riens passa per le fait (**ryan** pah-**sah** pair lə **fay**). [Law French "nothing passed by the deed"] *Hist.* A plea by which a party seeks to avoid the operation of a deed that has been enrolled or acknowledged in court.

riens per descent (**ryan** pair day-**sawn**). [Law French "nothing by descent"] (18c) *Hist.* The plea of an heir who is sued for the ancestor's debt and who received no land or assets from the ancestor.

rier county. See RERE-COUNTY.

RIF. *abbr.* (1966) Reduction in force. See LAYOFF.

rif, *vb.* (1994) *Slang.* To lay off (a worker). • The word derives from the acronym for *reduction in force.*

rigging the market. (1857) The practice of artificially inflating stock prices, by a series of bids, so that the demand for those stocks appears to be high and investors will therefore be enticed into buying the stocks. See MANIPULATION.

right, *n.* (bef. 12c) **1.** That which is proper under law, morality, or ethics <know right from wrong>. Cf. WRONG.

> "Right and wrong, in the legal sense, are that which the law of the State allows and forbids, and nothing else. To understand this is one of the first conditions of clear legal and political thinking, and it is Hobbes's great merit to have made this clear beyond the possibility of misunderstanding. No one who has grasped Hobbes's definition can ever be misled by verbal conceits about laws of the State which are contrary to natural right, or the law of nature, not being binding. All such language is mischievous, as confusing the moral and political grounds of positive law with its actual force. In practice we all know that the officers of the State cannot entertain complaints that the laws enacted by the supreme power in the State are in the complainant's opinion unjust. It would be impossible for government to be carried on if they did. Laws have to be obeyed, as between the State and the subject, not because they are reasonable, but because the State has so commanded. The laws may be, and in a wisely ordered State will be, the result of the fullest discussion which the nature of the case admits, and subsequent criticism may be allowed or even invited. But while the laws exist they have to be obeyed." Frederick Pollock, *An Introduction to the History of the Science of Politics* 61 (1906).

> "It has come to be well understood that there is no more ambiguous word in legal and juristic literature than the word 'right.' In its most general sense it means a reasonable expectation involved in life in civilized society. As a noun it has been used in the law books in [four] senses. (1) One meaning is interest, as in most discussions of natural rights. Here it may mean (*a*) an interest one holds ought to be recognize and secured. It is generally used in this sense in treatises on ethics. Or (*b*) it may mean the interest recognized, delimited with regard to other recognized interests and secured. (2) A second meaning is a recognized claim to acts or forbearances by another or by all others in order to make the interest effective, (*a*) legally, through application of the force of a politically organized society in order to secure it as the law has delimited it, or (*b*) morally, by the pressure of the moral sentiment of the community or of extra-legal agencies of social control. Analytical jurists have put this as a capacity of influencing others which is recognized or conferred in order to secure an interest. (3) A third use is to designate a capacity of creating, divesting, or altering rights in the second sense and so of creating or altering duties. Here the proper term is 'power.' (4) A fourth use is to designate certain conditions of general or special non-interference with natural faculties of action; certain conditions on which the law secures interests by leaving one to the free exercise of his natural faculties. These are better called liberties and privileges — liberties, general conditions of hands off as to certain situations; privileges, special conditions of hands off exempting certain persons or persons under certain situations from the rules which apply to persons generally or apply to all persons in ordinary situations." Roscoe Pound, *The Ideal Element in Law* 110–12 (1958) (mentioning five but reciting only four noun senses).

2. Something that is due to a person by just claim, legal guarantee, or moral principle <the right of liberty>. **3.** A power, privilege, or immunity secured to a person by law <the right to dispose of one's estate>. **4.** A legally enforceable claim that another will do or will not do a given act; a recognized and protected interest the violation of which is a wrong <a breach of duty that infringes one's right>. **5.** (*often pl.*) The interest, claim, or ownership that one has in tangible or intangible property <a debtor's rights in collateral> <publishing rights>. **6.** The privilege of corporate shareholders to purchase newly issued securities in amounts proportionate to their holdings. **7.** The negotiable certificate granting such a privilege to a corporate shareholder.

> "Right is a correlative to duty; where there is no duty there can be no right. But the converse is not necessarily true. There may be duties without rights. In order for a duty to create a right, it must be a duty *to act or forbear.* Thus, among those duties which have rights corresponding to them do not come the duties, if such there be, which call for an inward state of mind, as distinguished from external acts or forbearances. It is only to acts and forbearances that others have a right. It may be our duty to love our neighbor, but he has no right to our love." John Chipman Gray, *The Nature and Sources of the Law* 8–9 (2d ed. 1921).

> "[T]he word 'right' is one of the most deceptive of pitfalls; it is so easy to slip from a qualified meaning in the premise to an unqualified one in the conclusion. Most rights are qualified." *American Bank & Trust Co. v. Federal Reserve Bank of Atlanta,* 256 U.S. 350, 358, 41 S.Ct. 499, 500 (1921).

> "[I]n most European languages the term for law is identical with the term for right. The Latin *jus,* the German *Recht,* the Italian *diritto,* the Spanish *derecho,* the Slavonic *pravo* point both to the legal rule which binds a person and the legal right which every person claims as his own. Such coincidences cannot be treated as mere chance, or as a perversion of language likely to obscure the real meaning of words. On the contrary, they point to a profound connexion between the two ideas implied, and it is not difficult to see why expressions like *jus* and *Recht* face both ways: it may be said that on the one hand all private rights are derived from legal order, while, on the other hand, legal order is in a sense the aggregate of all the rights co-ordinated by it. We can hardly define a right better than by saying that it is the *range of action assigned to a particular will within the social order established by law.*" Paul Vinogradoff, *Common Sense in Law* 45 (H.G. Hanbury ed., 2d ed. 1946).

> "[In Hohfeldian terminology,] A is said to have a *right* that B shall do an act when, if B does not do the act, A can initiate legal proceedings that will result in coercing B. In such a situation B is said to have a *duty* to do the act. *Right* and *duty* are therefore correlatives, since in this sense there can never be a duty without a right." E. Allan Farnsworth, *Contracts* § 3.4, at 114. n.3 (3d ed. 1999).

▸ **absolute right.** (16c) **1.** A right that belongs to every human being, such as the right of personal liberty; a natural right. — Also termed *individual right.* See FUNDAMENTAL RIGHT (1). **2.** An unqualified right; specif., a right that cannot be denied or curtailed except under specific conditions <freedom of thought is an absolute right>. • For example, a plaintiff has an absolute right to voluntarily nonsuit a case before it is finally submitted;

after final submission, the court has discretion to grant or deny a voluntary nonsuit. Cf. *relative right.*

▸ **accessory right.** (1807) A supplementary right that has been added to the main right that is vested in the same owner. • For example, the right in a security is accessory to the right that is secured; a servitude is accessory to the ownership of the land for whose benefit the servitude exists. Cf. *principal right.*

▸ **accrued right.** (1842) A matured right; a right that is ripe for enforcement (as through litigation).

▸ **acquired right.** (17c) A right that a person does not naturally enjoy, but that is instead procured, such as the right to own property.

▸ **background right.** See *implied right.*

▸ **civil right.** See CIVIL RIGHT.

▸ **conditional right.** (17c) A right that depends on an uncertain event; a right that may or may not exist. • For example, parents have the conditional right to punish their child, the condition being that the punishment must be reasonable.

▸ **conjugal rights.** See CONJUGAL RIGHTS.

▸ **contingent right.** (18c) An entitlement that depends on the occurrence of some specified event — examples being an executory interest, a possibility coupled with an interest, and a right of entry.

▸ **contingent-value right.** (1990) An entitlement granted to the shareholders of an acquired company (or of a company undergoing major restructuring) whereby the shareholders are to receive an additional benefit if a specified event occurs. — Abbr. CVR.

▸ **contract right.** (1851) A right to payment under a contract not yet earned by performance and not evidenced by an instrument or chattel paper.

▸ **contractual right.** (1868) An entitlement arising out of a legally enforceable agreement, whether express, implied, or imposed by law or equity.

▸ **derogable right.** A right than can be limited or reduced in some circumstances.

▸ **enumerated right.** (1852) An express right embodied in writing, as in statutes and caselaw.

▸ **equitable right.** (17c) A right cognizable within a court of equity. • If a legal right and an equitable right conflict, the legal right ordinarily prevails over and destroys the equitable right even if the legal right arose after the equitable right. Breaches of equitable rights are remedied by means other than monetary damages, such as an injunction or specific performance. With the merger of law and equity in federal and most state courts, the procedural differences between legal and equitable rights have been largely abolished. Cf. *legal right* (1), (2).

▸ **exclusive right.** A right vested in one person, entity, or body to do something or be protected from something.

▸ **expectant right.** (1821) A right that is contingent on the occurrence of some future event; a contingent right.

▸ **first-generation rights.** (1981) The fundamental political rights of a people.

▸ **fundamental right.** See FUNDAMENTAL RIGHT.

▸ **group right.** (*usu. pl.*) (1900) A right possessed by a group as an entity rather than severally by the members; in a divided society, a distinctive power, privilege, or immunity secured to the collective people of a certain ethnicity, esp. as a matter of asserted public policy.

> "Group rights are part of the grammar of contemporary constitutional politics. In divided societies, in which ethnicity serves as the principal basis of political mobilization, ethnic groups — especially ethnic minorities — assert a range of group rights directly, or as the underlying root of a range of public policies. It is claimed that there are group rights to separate educational and social institutions, to federal subunits in which ethnic groups exclusively wield or dominate the exercise of political power, and to land and resources. Group rights are the basis for rules on internal migration and land ownership, for distinct systems of religious personal law, for official multilingualism, for executive power-sharing, and for a share of natural resource revenues. Moreover, the assertion of group rights is not just a political claim; it is also a legal claim directed at the very design of the constitutional order and its subsequent interpretation. Group rights serve two constitutional functions. They are shields and swords against majority rule, which protect ethnic minorities from being outvoted on policies that affect the interests that those rights protect. But equally importantly, the entrenchment of group rights reflects and projects a conception of the very nature of the constitutional order itself, in which the group which holds rights is constitutionally identified as a constituent element. Citizenship in the broader political community is mediated through membership in the group. Thus, group rights have both *regulative* and *constitutive* functions." Sujit Choudhry, "Group Rights in Comparative Constitutional Law: Culture, Economics, or Political Power?" in *The Oxford Handbook of Comparative Constitutional Law* 1099, 1100 (Michel Rosenfeld & András Sajó eds., 2012).

▸ **immediate right.** (17c) A right that may be exercised without delay.

▸ **imperfect right.** (17c) A right that is recognized by the law but is not enforceable. • Examples include time-barred claims and claims exceeding the local limits of a court's jurisdiction.

> "[T]here are certain rights, sometimes called imperfect rights, which the law recognizes but will not enforce directly. Thus a statute-barred debt cannot be recovered in a court of law, but for certain purposes the existence of the debt has legal significance. If the debtor pays the money, he cannot later sue to recover it as money paid without consideration; and the imperfect right has the faculty of becoming perfect if the debtor makes an acknowledgment of the debt from which there can be inferred a promise to pay." George Whitecross Paton, *A Textbook of Jurisprudence* 286 (G.W. Paton & David P. Derham eds., 4th ed. 1972).

▸ **implied right.** (18c) A right inferred from another legal right that is expressly stated in a statute or at common law. — Also termed *unenumerated right*; *penumbral right*; *background right.*

▸ **imprescriptible right.** (18c) A right that cannot be lost to prescription.

▸ **inalienable right.** (17c) A right that cannot be transferred or surrendered; esp., a natural right such as the right to own property. — Also termed *inherent right.*

▸ **incorporated right.** (*usu. pl.*) (1844) **1.** A right that is stated to be part of the text of a legal document, esp. a constitution. **2.** A right that exists only when attached to something else, such as a servitude in a deed.

▸ **incorporeal right.** (17c) A right to intangible, rather than tangible, property. • A right to a legal action (a *chose in action*) is an incorporeal right. See *chose in action* under CHOSE.

▸ **indigenous rights.** (1965) The human rights of an original, autochthonous people who dwelled in a land before outsiders invaded and colonized it.

▸ **individual right. 1.** See *absolute right.* **2.** See *personal right* (1).

▸ **inherent right.** See *inalienable right.*

▸ **legal right.** (17c) **1.** A right created or recognized by law. • The breach of a legal right is usu. remediable by monetary damages. **2.** A right historically recognized by common-law courts. Cf. *equitable right.* **3.** The capacity of asserting a legally recognized claim against one with a correlative duty to act.

▸ **minority right.** (*usu. pl.*) (1905) **1.** Collectively, the fundamental individual rights historically not guaranteed to a person who is of a particular minority race, class, ethnicity, religion, linguistic group, or sexual orientation. **2.** The collective rights of such people. — Also termed *rights of minorities.*

▸ **natural right.** (17c) A right that is conceived as part of natural law and that is therefore thought to exist independently of rights created by government or society, such as the right to life, liberty, and property. See NATURAL LAW.

▸ **negative right.** (17c) A right entitling a person to have another refrain from doing an act that might harm the person entitled. Cf. *positive right.*

▸ **nonderogable right.** A legal right that must be fully honored.

▸ **patent right.** (18c) A right secured by a patent.

▸ **penumbral right.** See *implied right.*

▸ **perfect right.** (16c) A right that is recognized by the law and is fully enforceable.

▸ **peripheral right.** (1962) A right that surrounds or springs from another right.

▸ **personal right.** (16c) **1.** A right that forms part of a person's legal status or personal condition, as opposed to the person's estate. — Also termed *individual right.* **2.** See *right in personam.*

▸ **political right.** (16c) The right to participate in the establishment or administration of government, such as the right to vote or the right to hold public office. — Also termed *political liberty.*

▸ **positive right.** (17c) A right entitling a person to have another do some act for the benefit of the person entitled. Cf. *negative right.*

▸ **precarious right.** (17c) A right enjoyed at the pleasure of another; a right that can be revoked at any time.

▸ **present fixed right of future enjoyment.** See *vested remainder* under REMAINDER.

▸ **primary right.** (17c) A right prescribed by the substantive law, such as a right not to be defamed or assaulted. • The enforcement of a primary right is termed *specific enforcement.*

▸ **principal right.** (17c) A right to which has been added a supplementary right in the same owner. Cf. *accessory right.*

▸ **private right.** (16c) A personal right, as opposed to a right of the public or the state. Cf. *public right.*

▸ **procedural right.** (1911) A right that derives from legal or administrative procedure; a right that helps in the protection or enforcement of a substantive right. Cf. *substantive right.*

▸ **property right.** (1853) A right to specific property, whether tangible or intangible.

▸ **proprietary right.** (17c) A right that is part of a person's estate, assets, or property, as opposed to a right arising from the person's legal status.

▸ **public right.** (16c) A right belonging to all citizens and usu. vested in and exercised by a public office or political entity. Cf. *private right.*

▸ **real right.** (17c) **1.** *Civil law.* A right that is connected with a thing rather than a person. • Real rights include ownership, use, habitation, usufruct, predial servitude, pledge, and real mortgage.

> "The term 'real rights' (*jura in re*) is an abstraction unknown to classical Roman law. The classical jurists were preoccupied with the availability of remedies rather than the existence of *substantive* rights, and did not have a generic term to include all 'rights' which civilian scholars of following generations classified as 'real.' The expression ('real rights') was first coined by medieval writers elaborating on the *Digest* in an effort to explain ancient procedural forms of action in terms of substantive rights." A.N. Yiannopoulos, *Real Rights in Louisiana and Comparative Law*, 23 La. L. Rev. 161, 163 (1963).

2. JUS IN RE. **3.** See RIGHT IN REM.

▸ **relative right.** (17c) A right that arises from and depends on someone else's right, as distinguished from an absolute right. Cf. *absolute right.*

▸ **remedial right.** (18c) The secondary right to have a remedy that arises when a primary right is broken. See *secondary right.*

▸ **restitutory right.** (1982) A right to restitution.

▸ **right in action.** See *chose in action* under CHOSE.

▸ **right in personam** (in pər-**soh**-nəm). (1832) An interest protected solely against specific individuals. — Also termed *personal right; jus in personam.* See IN PERSONAM.

▸ **right in rem** (in **rem**). (18c) A right, often negative, exercisable against the world at large. — Also termed *real right; jus in rem.* See IN REM.

> "A right *in rem* need not relate to a tangible *res.* Thus a right that one's reputation should not be unjustifiably attacked is today described as a right *in rem,* since it is a right that avails against persons generally. This shows how far the conception has developed from the Roman notion of *actio in rem,* for one who sues to protect his reputation is not asking for judgment for a specific *res.* It should also be noticed that on breach of a right *in rem,* a right *in personam* arises against the aggressor." George Whitecross Paton, *A Textbook of Jurisprudence* 300 (G.W. Paton & David P. Derham eds., 4th ed. 1972).

▸ **rights of minorities.** See *minority rights.*

▸ **secondary right.** (17c) A right prescribed by procedural law to enforce a substantive right, such as the right to damages for a breach of contract. • The enforcement of a secondary right is variously termed *secondary enforcement, remedial enforcement,* or *sanctional enforcement.* — Also termed *remedial right; sanctioning right.*

▸ **second-generation rights.** (1983) The social and economic rights of a people, including the right to be employed.

▸ **substantial right.** (18c) An essential right that potentially affects the outcome of a lawsuit and is capable of legal enforcement and protection, as distinguished from a mere technical or procedural right.

▸ **substantive right** (**səb**-stən-tiv). (18c) A right that can be protected or enforced by law; a right of substance rather than form. Cf. *procedural right.*

▸ **third-generation right.** (1979) (*usu. pl.*) The right of individuals to be part of whatever collective groups they identify with.

▸ **unenumerated right. 1.** A right retained by the people but not explicitly mentioned in the Bill of Rights. • The Ninth Amendment to the U.S. Constitution states: "The enumeration in the Constitution of certain rights shall not be construed to deny or disparage others retained by the people." This wording establishes the existence of unenumerated rights.

> "Without doubt, the Ninth Amendment and its problem of identifying unenumerated rights continue to bedevil interpreters, on and off the bench. Courts do continue to discover rights that have no textual existence and might be considered unenumerated, but for the judicial propensity to ignore the Ninth Amendment and make believe that some unspecified right under discussion derives from a right that is enumerated. Opponents of such rights howl their denunciation of judicial activism. Court-invented rights exceed in number the rights enumerated. Judges have composed rights great and small, including the *Miranda* rules, the right to engage in nude dancing with pasties and G-string, the right to engage in flag desecration, the right to secure an abortion, or the right against the invasion of an expectation of privacy." Leonard W. Levy, "Unenumerated Rights," in *Encyclopedia of the American Constitution* 557 (1st Supp., Leonard W. Levy ed., 1991).

2. See *implied right.*

▸ **vested right.** (18c) **1.** A right that so completely and definitely belongs to a person that it cannot be impaired or taken away without the person's consent. **2.** A right that the holder can transmit by deed to others, and has transmitted to his or her heirs, in the event of the holder's dying intestate.

right against self-incrimination. (1911) A criminal defendant's or a witness's constitutional right — under the Fifth Amendment, but waivable under certain conditions — guaranteeing that a person cannot be compelled by the government to testify if the testimony might result in the person's being criminally prosecuted. • Although this right is most often asserted during a criminal prosecution, a person can also "plead the Fifth" in a civil, legislative, administrative, or grand-jury proceeding. — Also termed *privilege against self-incrimination; right to remain silent.* See SELF-INCRIMINATION.

> "The right against self-incrimination, protected by the Fifth Amendment, is central to the accusatorial system of criminal justice: together with the presumption of innocence, the right against self-incrimination ensures that the state must bear the burden of prosecution. . . . The right against self-incrimination is personal. It may be claimed only by the person who himself might be at risk for testifying. It may not be claimed on behalf of another . . . ." Jethro K. Lieberman, *The Evolving Constitution* 481–82 (1992).

right-and-wrong test. See MCNAGHTEN RULES.

rightful, *adj.* (bef. 12c) **1.** (Of an action) equitable; fair <a rightful dispossession>. **2.** (Of a person) legitimately entitled to a position <a rightful heir>. **3.** (Of an office or piece of property) that one is entitled to <her rightful inheritance>.

right heir. See HEIR.

Right Honorable. See HONORABLE.

right in personam. See RIGHT.

right in re aliena. See JUS IN RE ALIENA.

right in rem. See RIGHT.

right in re propria. See JUS IN RE PROPRIA.

right not to be questioned. See *privilege against self-incrimination* under PRIVILEGE (3).

right of action. (16c) **1.** The right to bring a specific case to court. **2.** A right that can be enforced by legal action; a chose in action. Cf. CAUSE OF ACTION.

▸ **private right of action.** An individual's right to sue in a personal capacity to enforce a legal claim. See PRESUMPTION AGAINST IMPLIED RIGHT OF ACTION.

right of angary. See ANGARY.

right of appeal. (16c) The legal entitlement to request that an appellate court review a lower court's decision with the possibility of changing it. Pl. **rights of appeal.**

right of approach. (1843) *Int'l law.* The right of a warship on the high seas to draw near another vessel to determine its nationality.

right of assembly. (17c) The constitutional right — guaranteed by the First Amendment — of the people to gather peacefully for public expression of religion, politics, or grievances. — Also termed *freedom of assembly; right to assemble.* Cf. FREEDOM OF ASSOCIATION; *unlawful assembly* under ASSEMBLY (1).

right of audience. (18c) A right to appear and be heard in a given court. • The term is chiefly used in England to denote the right of a certain type of lawyer to appear in a certain type of court.

right of common. See PROFIT À PRENDRE.

right of confrontation. (1901) A criminal defendant's Sixth Amendment right to come face to face with witnesses at trial. — Also termed *confrontation right.*

right-of-conscience law. (1987) A statute allowing professionals and institutions in healthcare and related fields to refuse to provide services that they find morally objectionable, such as dispensing birth-control pills or performing abortions.

right of continuity. (1845) Constructive authority claimed over a larger territory than what is actually occupied.

right of contribution. See CONTRIBUTION (5).

right of disclosure. See PUBLICATION RIGHT.

right of discussion. *Scots law.* See BENEFIT OF DISCUSSION.

right of dissent and appraisal. See APPRAISAL REMEDY.

right of division. *Scots law.* See BENEFIT OF DIVISION.

right of election. *Wills & estates.* A surviving spouse's statutory right to choose either the gifts given by the deceased spouse in the will or a forced share or a share of the estate as defined in the probate statute. — Also termed *widow's election.* See ELECTION (2); *augmented estate* under ESTATE (3).

right of entry. (16c) **1.** The right of taking or resuming possession of land or other real property in a peaceable manner. **2.** POWER OF TERMINATION. **3.** The right to go into another's real property for a special purpose without committing trespass. • An example is a landlord's right to enter a tenant's property to make repairs. **4.** The right of an alien to go into a jurisdiction for a special purpose. • An example is an exchange student's right to enter another country to attend college.

right of entry for breach of condition. See POWER OF TERMINATION.

right of entry for condition broken. See POWER OF TERMINATION.

right of exoneration. See EQUITY OF EXONERATION.

right of family integrity. (1974) *Constitutional law.* A fundamental and substantive due-process right for a family unit to be free of unjustified state interference. • While not specifically mentioned in the U.S. Constitution, this right is said to emanate from it. The contours of the right are nebulous and incompletely defined, but it at least includes the right to bear children, to rear them, and to guide them according to the parents' beliefs, as well as the right of children to be raised by their parents free of unwarranted interference by state officials. The right restricts state action under the Fourteenth Amendment. Interference is not permitted in the absence of a compelling state interest and is reviewed under a strict-scrutiny standard. Most courts require a state to establish by clear and convincing evidence that interference in a familial relationship is justified. — Also termed *right to family integrity.* See PARENTAL-AUTONOMY DOCTRINE; PARENTAL-PRIVILEGE DOCTRINE. Cf. *freedom of intimate association* under FREEDOM OF ASSOCIATION.

right of first publication. See *common-law copyright* under COPYRIGHT.

right of first refusal. (1900) **1.** A potential buyer's contractual right to meet the terms of a third party's higher offer. • For example, if Beth has a right of first refusal on the purchase of Sam's house, and if Terry offers to buy the house for $300,000, then Beth can match this offer and prevent Terry from buying it. Cf. RIGHT OF PREEMPTION. **2.** *Family law.* The right of a parent to be offered the opportunity to have custody of a child other than during a usual visitation period before the other parent turns to a third-party caregiver. • The right may be exercised by either parent, and may exist in circumstances that are foreseeable (e.g., a business trip) or unforeseeable (e.g., an illness).

right of fishery. See FISHERY (1).

right of innocent passage. See INNOCENT PASSAGE.

right of occupancy. See INDIAN TITLE.

right of perpetual succession. The privilege that a corporation enjoys of continued and uninterrupted existence, even despite the death or resignation of any participants, for as long as the corporation has been granted its right to exist.

right of petition. See RIGHT TO PETITION.

right of possession. (16c) The right to hold, use, occupy, or otherwise enjoy a given property; esp., the right to enter real property and eject or evict a wrongful possessor.

right of preemption. (17c) A potential buyer's contractual right to have the first opportunity to buy, at a specified price, if the seller chooses to sell within the contracted period. • For example, if Beth has a right of preemption on Sam's house for five years at $100,000, Sam can either keep the house for five years (in which case Beth's right expires) or, if he wishes to sell during those five years, offer the house to Beth, who can either buy it for $100,000 or refuse to buy. If Beth refuses, Sam can sell to someone else. — Also termed *first option to buy.* Cf. RIGHT OF FIRST REFUSAL (1).

right of privacy. (1849) *Constitutional law.* **1.** The right to personal autonomy. • The U.S. Constitution does not explicitly provide for a right of privacy or for a general right of personal autonomy, but the Supreme Court has repeatedly ruled that a right of personal autonomy is implied in the "zones of privacy" created by specific constitutional guarantees. **2.** The right of a person and the person's property to be free from unwarranted public scrutiny or exposure. — Also termed *right to privacy.* See INVASION OF PRIVACY.

right of publicity. (1822) The right to control the use of one's own name, picture, or likeness and to prevent another from using it for commercial benefit without one's consent.

> "The right of publicity is a state-law created intellectual property right whose infringement is a commercial tort of unfair competition. It is a distinct legal category, not just a 'kind of' trademark, copyright, false advertising or right of privacy." 1 J. Thomas McCarthy, *The Rights of Publicity and Privacy* § 1:3, at 1-2 (2d ed. 2000).

right of redemption. 1. EQUITY OF REDEMPTION. **2.** STATUTORY RIGHT OF REDEMPTION.

right of reentry. See POWER OF TERMINATION.

right of relief. *Scots law.* See EQUITY OF SUBROGATION.

right of reproduction. See REPRODUCTION RIGHT.

right of rescission. See RIGHT TO RESCIND.

right of retainer. (17c) A trustee's power to withhold trust funds or property from distribution, exercisable when the beneficiary owes money to the trust.

right of retention. See RETENTION.

right of revolution. (1803) The inherent right of a people to cast out their rulers, change their polity, or effect radical reforms in their system of government or institutions, by force or general uprising, when the legal and constitutional methods of making such changes have proved inadequate or are so obstructed as to be unavailable.

right-of-right night. See DROIT DU SEIGNEUR.

right of search. (18c) *Int'l law.* The right to stop, visit, and examine vessels on the high seas to discover whether they or the goods they carry are liable to capture; esp., a belligerent state's right to stop any merchant vessel of a neutral state on the high seas and to search as reasonably necessary to determine whether the ship has become liable to capture under the international law of naval warfare. • This right carries with it no right to destroy without full examination, unless those on a given vessel actively resist. — Also termed *right of visit; right of visit and search; right of visitation; right of visitation and search.* See VISIT.

right of self-determination for peoples. *Int'l law.* (1918) The right of the postcolonial populations of the world's countries to be free to decide for themselves how they wish to be governed in a decolonized world. — Often shortened to *self-determination.*

right of subrogation. **1.** See SUBROGATION. **2.** See EQUITY OF SUBROGATION.

right of suit. (18c) A person's right to seek redress in a court.

right of support. (1839) *Property.* **1.** A landowner's right to have the land supported by adjacent land and by the underlying earth. **2.** A servitude giving the owner of a house the right to rest timber on the walls of a neighboring house.

right of survivorship. (16c) A joint tenant's right to succeed to the whole estate upon the death of the other joint tenant. — Also termed *jus accrescendi.* See SURVIVORSHIP; *joint tenancy* under TENANCY.

right of termination. (1867) A remedy involving the ending of contractual relations, accorded to a party to a contract when the other party breaches a duty that arises under the contract. • The right of termination is contrasted with a right to rescind, which arises when the other party breaches a duty that arises independently of the contract. — Also termed *right to terminate.*

right of transit passage. See TRANSIT PASSAGE.

right of visit. See RIGHT OF SEARCH.

right of visit and search. See RIGHT OF SEARCH.

right of visitation. (17c) **1.** VISITATION RIGHT. **2.** RIGHT OF SEARCH.

right of visitation and search. See RIGHT OF SEARCH.

right-of-way. (18c) **1.** The right to pass through property owned by another. • A right-of-way may be established by contract, by longstanding usage, or by public authority (as with a highway). Cf. EASEMENT. **2.** The right to build and operate a railway line or a highway on land belonging to another, or the land so used. **3.** The right to take precedence in traffic. **4.** The strip of land subject to a nonowner's right to pass through. — Also written *right of way.* Pl. **rights-of-way.**

▸ **private right-of-way.** See EASEMENT.

▸ **public right-of-way.** (1802) The right of passage held by the public in general to travel on roads, freeways, and other thoroughfares.

right of wharfing out. (1828) A right to the exclusive use of submerged lands, as by establishing a permanent structure or wharf on the land to dock oceangoing vessels.

rights arbitration. See *grievance arbitration* under ARBITRATION.

rights-consciousness. See CLAIMS-CONSCIOUSNESS.

rights issue. See *rights offering* under OFFERING.

rights-management information. (1995) *Intellectual property.* Information about an intellectual-property right, affixed to the subject matter when it is communicated to the public, esp. in electronic form, and identifying the right's owner, terms of use, indexing numbers or codes, or other identifying information. • The information facilitates contracting with the owner of the rights. In digital technology, laws may ban the removal or alteration of rights-management information as a form of intellectual-property protection. — Abbr. RMI.

rights of attribution. See ATTRIBUTION RIGHTS.

rights off. See EX RIGHTS.

rights offering. See OFFERING.

rights of man. (sometimes cap.) (18c) A declaration of fundamental human rights drafted during the French Revolution and embodied in all constitutions of the French Republic up to 1848. • This document was a forerunner to the Universal Declaration of Human Rights. See UNIVERSAL DECLARATION OF HUMAN RIGHTS.

rights of minorities. See *minority rights* under RIGHT.

rights on. See CUM RIGHTS.

rights revolution. **1.** In the United States, the expansion of civil rights, civil liberties, and the rights of criminal defendants in the 1960s and 1970s through national legislation and U.S. Supreme Court decisions. **2.** More generally, the expansion of human rights in the years following World War II, esp. through the United Nation Declaration of Human Rights and the Geneva Conventions.

right to assemble. See RIGHT OF ASSEMBLY.

right to assistance of counsel. See RIGHT TO COUNSEL.

right to bear arms. (17c) *Constitutional law.* The constitutional right of persons to own firearms. U.S. Const. amend II. See SECOND AMENDMENT.

right to be forgotten. See RIGHT TO OBLIVION.

right to choose. See FREEDOM OF CHOICE.

right-to-convey covenant. See *covenant of seisin* under COVENANT (4).

right to counsel. (1882) **1.** *Criminal law.* A criminal defendant's constitutional right, guaranteed by the Sixth Amendment, to representation by a court- appointed lawyer if the defendant cannot afford to hire one. • The Supreme Court has recognized a juvenile delinquent defendant's right to counsel. *In re Gault*, 387 U.S. 1, 87 S.Ct. 1428 (1967). — Also termed *benefit of counsel*; *right to assistance of counsel.* **2.** *Family law.* The right of a defendant in a suit for termination of parental rights to representation by a court-appointed lawyer if the defendant cannot afford to hire one. • Although some states appoint counsel for indigent defendants in a suit for termination of parental rights, the Supreme Court has held that the Constitution does not require that counsel be appointed for indigent defendants in all termination suits, but if a criminal charge may be made, the right to counsel may attach. *Lassiter v. Department of Soc. Servs.*, 452 U.S. 18, 101 S.Ct. 2153 (1981). — Also termed (in both senses) *access to counsel.* See ASSISTANCE OF COUNSEL.

right to die. (1893) The right of a terminally ill person to refuse life-sustaining treatment. — Also termed *right to refuse treatment.* See ADVANCE DIRECTIVE.

right to exclude. *Patents.* A patentee's right to prevent others from making, using, selling, or offering for sale the patentee's invention.

right to family integrity. See RIGHT OF FAMILY INTEGRITY.

right-to-know act. (1968) A federal or state statute requiring businesses (such as chemical manufacturers) that produce hazardous substances to disclose information about the substances both to the community where they are produced or stored and to employees who handle them. — Abbr. RTK act. — Also termed *right-to-know statute.*

right to oblivion. (2009) The theory that, to protect one's privacy, an individual should be entitled to delete all public information about himself or herself stored on the Internet. — Also termed *right to be forgotten.*

right to personal freedom. The notion that no one can be arrested or imprisoned except in accordance with due process of law. — Also termed *right to personal liberty.* See DUE PROCESS.

"The right to personal liberty as understood in England means in substance a person's right not to be subjected to imprisonment, arrest, or other physical coercion in any manner that does not admit of legal justification." A.V. Dicey, *Introduction to the Study of the Law of the Constitution* 207–08 (10th ed. 1959).

right to petition. (17c) The constitutional right — guaranteed by the First Amendment — of the people to make formal requests to the government, as by lobbying or writing letters to public officials. — Also termed *right of petition; freedom of petition.*

right to present a defense. (1833) *Criminal procedure.* A criminal defendant's constitutional entitlement to marshal and present evidence, to discover the existence of potential witnesses, to put them on the witness stand, to compel testimony over claims of privilege, and to have a trial presided over by a disinterested judge.

right to privacy. See RIGHT OF PRIVACY.

right to pursue happiness. See HAPPINESS, RIGHT TO PURSUE.

right to refuse treatment. See RIGHT TO DIE.

right to remain silent. See RIGHT AGAINST SELF-INCRIMINATION.

right to rescind. (18c) The remedy accorded to a party to a contract when the other party breaches a duty that arises independently of the contract. • The right to rescind is contrasted with a right of termination, which arises when the other party breaches a duty that arises under the contract. — Also termed *right of rescission.*

right-to-sue letter. (1971) *Employment law.* A letter issued by the EEOC to inform a person who filed a charge against an employer that the charge has been recorded and processed, and that the person has the right to file a lawsuit on the charge in state or federal court.

right to terminate. See RIGHT OF TERMINATION.

right to travel. (1838) A person's constitutional right — guaranteed by the Privileges and Immunities Clause — to travel freely between states.

right to vote. See SUFFRAGE (1).

right-to-work law. (1958) A state statute that prevents labor–management agreements requiring a person to join a union as a condition of employment. See *open shop* under SHOP. — Abbr. RTW law.

right-wrong test. See MCNAGHTEN RULES.

rigid constitution. See CONSTITUTION (3).

rigor juris (**rig**-ər **joor**-is). [Latin] (1870) Strictness of law. Cf. GRATIA CURIAE.

rigor mortis (**rig**-ər **mor**-tis). (1841) The temporary stiffening of a body's joints and muscles after death. • The onset of rigor mortis can vary from 15 minutes to several hours after death, depending on the body's condition and on atmospheric factors.

rimless-wheel conspiracy. See *wheel conspiracy* under CONSPIRACY.

ringing out. See RINGING UP.

ringing the changes. (18c) Fraud consisting in the offender's using a large bill to pay for a small purchase, waiting for the shopkeeper to put change on the counter, and then, by a series of maneuvers involving changes of mind — such as asking for some other article of little value or for smaller change for some of the money on the counter — creating a confused situation in which the offender picks up more the money than due.

ringing up. A method by which commodities dealers cooperate to discharge contracts for future delivery in advance by using offsets, cancellations, and price adjustments, thus saving the cost of actual delivery and change of possession. — Also termed *ringing out.*

riot, *n.* (14c) **1.** An assemblage of three or more persons in a public place taking concerted action in a turbulent and disorderly manner for a common purpose (regardless of the lawfulness of that purpose). **2.** An unlawful disturbance of the peace by an assemblage of usu. three or more persons acting with a common purpose in a violent or tumultuous manner that threatens or terrorizes the public or an institution. Cf. *unlawful assembly* under ASSEMBLY (1); CIVIL COMMOTION; ROUT; AFFRAY. — **riotous,** *adj.* — **riot,** *vb.*— **rioter,** *n.*

"A riot is defined as an unlawful assembly (i.e. an assembly come together in pursuance of an unlawful purpose), consisting of at least three persons, which has begun to create a breach of the peace. At Common Law it is an indictable misdemeanour, punishable by a fine and imprisonment. But the statutory form of it, introduced by the Riot Act of 1714, is better known. By that statute, passed to deal with Jacobite disturbances, it was provided that the members of a riotous assembly of twelve or more persons which does not disperse within an hour after the reading by a magistrate of the proclamation contained in the Act, become guilty of felony, which, at the time of the passing of the Act, was a capital offence, and is, even now, punishable with imprisonment for life." Edward Jenks, *The Book of English Law* 136 (P.B. Fairest ed., 6th ed. 1967).

"A riot is a tumultuous disturbance of the peace by three or more persons acting together (a) in the commission of a crime by open force, or (b) in the execution of some enterprise, lawful or unlawful, in such a violent, turbulent and unauthorized manner as to create likelihood of public terror and alarm. . . . When they come together for this purpose they are guilty of unlawful assembly. When they start on their way to carry out their common design they are guilty of *rout*. In the actual execution of their design they are guilty of *riot*." Rollin M. Perkins & Ronald N. Boyce, *Criminal Law* 483 (3d ed. 1982).

Riot Act. A 1714 English statute that made it a capital offense for 12 or more rioters to remain together for an hour after a magistrate has officially proclaimed that rioters must disperse. • This statute was not generally accepted in the United States and did not become a part of American common law. It did, however, become a permanent part of the English language in the slang phrase *reading the riot act* (meaning "to reprimand vigorously"), which originally referred to the official command for rioters to disperse.

riotous assembly. See ASSEMBLY (1).

ripae muniendae causa (rɪ-pee myoo-nee-**en**-dee **kaw**-zə). [Latin] *Hist.* For the purpose of strengthening a riverbank.

riparian (ri-**pair**-ee-ən *or* rɪ-), *adj.* (1841) Of, relating to, or located on the bank of a river or stream (or occasionally another body of water, such as a lake) <riparian land> <a riparian owner>. Cf. LITTORAL.

riparian erosion. See EROSION.

riparian habitat. See HABITAT.

riparian land. See LAND.

riparian proprietor. (1808) Someone who is in possession of riparian land or who owns an estate in it; a landowner whose property borders on a stream or river. See *riparian land* under LAND.

riparian right. (*often pl.*) (1860) The right of a landowner whose property borders on a body of water or watercourse. • Such a landowner traditionally has the right to make reasonable use of the water. — Also termed *water right.* See REASONABLE-USE THEORY.

riparian-rights doctrine. (1921) The rule that owners of land bordering on a waterway have equal rights to use the water passing through or by their property. Cf. PRIOR-APPROPRIATION DOCTRINE.

ripeness, *n.* **1.** The state of a dispute that has reached, but has not passed, the point when the facts have developed sufficiently to permit an intelligent and useful decision to be made. **2.** The requirement that this state must exist before a court will decide a controversy. See JUSTICIABILITY. Cf. MOOTNESS DOCTRINE; PREMATURITY (1). — **ripe,** *adj.* — **ripen,** *vb.*

ripper act. *Slang.* A statute that gives a government's chief executive broad powers to appoint and remove department heads or other subordinate officials.

ripper legislation. See LEGISLATION (3).

rise, *vb.* (15c) **1.** (Of a court) to adjourn finally at the end of a term. **2.** (Of spectators and participants in a courtroom) to stand when the judge enters or exits. **3.** (Of a court) to take a recess or temporary break, as at the end of a day. **4.** *Parliamentary law.* (Of a special committee that has exhausted its business) to dissolve and send a report to the referring body. • A committee's rising is equivalent to a deliberative assembly's adjourning sine die. — Also termed *rise and report.* Cf. *adjourn sine die* under ADJOURN.

rise and report. See RISE (4).

rising. *Criminal law.* A grand jury's issuance of a decision whether to prosecute or not to prosecute.

rising star. *Slang.* A company, institution, or borrower whose creditworthiness has significantly increased. Cf. FALLEN ANGEL.

rising vote. See VOTE (4).

rising vote of thanks. See *rising vote* under VOTE (4).

risk, *n.* (17c) **1.** The uncertainty of a result, happening, or loss; the chance of injury, damage, or loss; esp., the existence and extent of the possibility of harm <many feel that skydiving is not worth the risk>. See ASSUMPTION OF THE RISK. **2.** Liability for injury, damage, or loss if it occurs <the consumer-protection statute placed the risk on the manufacturer instead of the buyer>. **3.** *Insurance.* The chance or degree of probability of loss to the subject matter of an insurance policy <the insurer undertook the risk in exchange for a premium>. Cf. PERIL (2). **4.** *Insurance.* The amount that an insurer stands to lose <the underwriter took steps to reduce its total risk>. **5.** *Insurance.* A person or thing that an insurer considers a hazard; someone or something that might be covered by an insurance policy <she's a poor risk for health insurance>. **6.** *Insurance.* The type of loss covered by a policy; a hazard from a specified source <this homeowner's policy covers fire risks and flood risks>. — **risk,** *vb.*

▸ **absorbable risk.** (2004) A potential loss that a corporation believes that it can cover either with available capital or with self-insurance.

▸ **assigned risk.** (1946) Someone who is a poor risk for insurance but whom an insurance company is forced to insure because of state law. • For example, an accident-prone driver is an assigned risk in a state with a compulsory motor-vehicle-insurance statute.

▸ **classified risk.** (1982) In life- and health-insurance policies, the risk created by a policyholder's substandard health or other peril.

▸ **inherent risk.** (1912) **1.** A risk that is necessarily entailed in a given activity and involves dealing with a situation that carries a probability of loss unless action is taken to control or correct it. **2.** A fairly common risk that people normally bear whenever they decide to engage in a certain activity.

> "A risk is inherent in an activity if the ordinary participant would reasonably consent to the risk, and the risk cannot be tailored to satisfy the idiosyncratic needs of any particular participant like the plaintiff. For example, someone who knows nothing about baseball and is hit by a ball while sitting in the outfield bleachers is barred from recovery. The stadium cannot be designed with safety features tailored to each fan; safety decisions must be made by reference to the average or ordinary fan. The ordinary fan sitting directly behind home plate would want to be protected from foul balls, because the cost of the netting and the partially obstructed view are reasonable in light of the heightened risk. Other areas like the outfield bleachers have a much lower risk, and the ordinary fan would reasonably prefer an unobstructed view and an opportunity to catch a ball. Reasonable or objective consent can eliminate the tort duty, just like reasonable or objective consent can absolve a defendant of liability for an intentional tort. Anyone who participates in an activity assumes the risk in this primary sense, regardless of whether he or she actually consented to the risk." Mark A. Geistfeld, *Tort Law: The Essentials* 306–07 (2008).

▸ **material risk.** (18c) A risk about which information is important to a reasonable person making a decision whether to accept the risk.

▸ **noninsurable risk.** (1910) A risk for which insurance will not be written because the risk is too uncertain to be the subject of actuarial analysis.

▸ **pure risk.** (1874) A risk that can only result in a loss. • Insurance protects only against pure risks. Cf. *speculative risk.*

▸ **shifting risk.** (1892) The changing risk covered under an insurance policy insuring a stock of goods or similar property that varies in amount and composition in the course of trade.

▸ **speculative risk.** (1893) A risk that can result in either a loss or a gain. Cf. *pure risk.*

▸ **standard risk.** (1923) In life insurance, a person whose life expectancy is considered average.

▸ **substandard risk.** (1907) In life insurance, a person whose life expectancy is considered below the average, as by reason of heredity or life-shortening habits.

▸ **superstandard risk.** (1917) In life insurance, a person whose life expectancy is considered above the average, as by reason of heredity or good habits.

risk arbitrage. See ARBITRAGE.

risk assessment. (1957) **1.** *Family law.* A process for ascertaining the likelihood that a person, usu. a parent, will harm a child. • Before a child can be removed from his or her family by a governmental entity, a risk assessment should be performed to determine the likelihood of the child's being harmed in the future. **2.** The activity of identifying, estimating, and evaluating the probability of harm associated with an activity and determining an acceptable level of risk.

▸ **environmental risk assessment.** (1977) The activity of evaluating the interactions of humans, agents, and ecological resources to determine the probabilities and levels of harm that environmental contaminants would pose to human health and the ecosystem.

risk-assessment instrument. (1983) *Criminal law.* A written recommendation on the classification of a sex offender, usu. prepared by a board or panel established for the purpose of making such recommendations. — Abbr. RAI.

risk-averse, *adj.* (1961) (Of a person) uncomfortable with volatility or uncertainty; not willing to take risks; very cautious <a risk-averse investor>.

risk–benefit test. See RISK–UTILITY TEST.

risk capital. See CAPITAL.

risk–capital test. (1971) *Securities.* A test of whether a transaction constitutes the sale of a security (and is thus subject to securities laws) based on whether the seller is soliciting risk capital with which to develop a business venture. Cf. CAPITAL–RISK TEST.

risk distribution. (1912) The method by which a legal system allocates the risk of harm between the person who suffers it and the loss.

risk factor. (1907) **1.** Anything that increases the possibility of harm or any other undesirable result. **2.** *Insurance.* In life-insurance ratemaking, the estimated cost of present and future claims, based on a mortality table. • The risk factor is one element that a life insurer uses to calculate premium rates. See PREMIUM RATE. Cf. INTEREST FACTOR; MORTALITY FACTOR.

risk letter. *Criminal law.* An appellate defender's written communication to a criminal-defendant client explaining the risks of having the conviction reversed and remanded for retrial, such as the imposition of a higher sentence upon reconviction.

risk management. (1948) **1.** The procedures or systems used to minimize accidental losses, esp. to a business. **2.** The practice of managing investments to produce as much profit as possible while limiting the danger of loses.

Risk Management Agency. An agency in the U.S. Department of Agriculture responsible for administering the programs of the Federal Crop Insurance Corporation and for overseeing other programs relating to the risk management of crops and commodities. — Abbr. RMA.

risk of jury doubt. See BURDEN OF PERSUASION.

risk of loss. (18c) **1.** The danger or possibility of damage to, destruction of, or misplacement of goods or other property <commercial transportation always carries some risk of loss>. **2.** Responsibility for bearing the costs and expenses of such damage, destruction, or misplacement <the contract specifies who assumes the risk of loss>.

risk of nonpersuasion. See BURDEN OF PERSUASION.

risk-stops-here rule. See DOCTRINE OF SUPERIOR EQUITIES.

risk–utility test. (1982) A method of imposing product liability on a manufacturer if the evidence shows that a reasonable person would conclude that the benefits of a product's particular design versus the feasibility of an alternative safer design did not outweigh the dangers inherent in the original design. — Also termed *danger–utility test*; *risk–benefit test.* Cf. CONSUMER-CONTEMPLATION TEST.

RIT. *abbr.* Rochester Institute of Technology. See NATIONAL TECHNICAL INSTITUTE FOR THE DEAF.

river. (13c) A natural, flowing body of water that empties into another body of water, such as a lake, sea, or channel.

▸ **international river.** (1840) A river that flows through or between two or more countries.

▸ **national river.** (1860) A river wholly contained within a single country. • That country has exclusive territorial rights over the river.

▸ **private river.** (17c) A river to which a riparian owner may claim ownership of the riverbed because the river is unnavigable or navigable only by vessels with shallow drafts. • A navigable private river is not wholly owned by a private person and cannot be closed to public use; people may still make ordinary use of the river for transportation and navigation.

RL/C. See *revolving letter of credit* under LETTER OF CREDIT.

RMA. *abbr.* RISK MANAGEMENT AGENCY.

RMI. *abbr.* RIGHTS-MANAGEMENT INFORMATION.

RMS. *abbr.* REPRESSED-MEMORY SYNDROME.

ROA. *abbr.* RECORD ON APPEAL.

roadblock. (1913) **1.** A place where traffic is being stopped for any reason, as by law-enforcement officers. **2.** In military use, a barricade fitted with traps and mines to hold up an enemy at some point in the road, usu. where a mine will be triggered by the enemy's attempted passage. **3.** Something that impedes the progress of a plan.

road pricing. (1962) A system whereby drivers must pay to use certain roads at certain times as a way to alleviate traffic congestion.

road rage. (1988) A motorist's uncontrolled anger directed toward one or more other drivers, usu. as a result of the other drivers' perceived slowness or ineptitude, and often accompanied by aggressive behavior such as shouting and name-calling, or even violence.

roadside reduction. (2005) *Criminal procedure. Slang.* A police officer's discretionary lessening of the seriousness of a traffic violation, perhaps to no charge at all, because the motorist is cooperative or contrite.

roadstead. (14c) *Maritime law.* A convenient or safe place where vessels usu. anchor.

road tax. (18c) *English law.* A tax that a vehicle's owner must pay in order to drive it legally.

roadworthy, *adj.* (1818) (Of a vehicle) in a condition that is good enough and safe enough to drive; fit for use on streets, highways, etc.

robbery, *n.* (12c) The illegal taking of property from the person of another, or in the person's presence, by violence or intimidation; aggravated larceny. • Robbery is usu. a felony, but some jurisdictions classify some robberies as high misdemeanors. — Also termed (in Latin) *crimen roberiae.* See LARCENY; THEFT. Cf. BURGLARY. — **rob,** *vb.*

> "There are two kinds of robbery; from the *person,* and from the *house* . . .; the latter, *viz.* robbery from the house, belongeth to the titles *Larceny* and *Burglary.* . . . Robbery is a felony by the common law, committed by a violent assault upon the person of another, but putting him in fear, and taking from his person, his money or other goods, of any value whatsoever." Richard Burn, *The Justice of the Peace and Parish Officer* 612–13 (3d ed. 1756).

> "Robbery is larceny from the person by violence or intimidation. It is a felony both at common law and under modern statutes. Under some of the new penal codes robbery does not require an actual taking of property. If force or intimidation is used in the attempt to commit theft this is sufficient." Rollin M. Perkins & Ronald N. Boyce, *Criminal Law* 343 (3d ed. 1982).

▸ **aggravated robbery.** (1878) Robbery committed by a person who either carries a dangerous weapon — often called *armed robbery* — or inflicts bodily harm on someone during the robbery. • Some statutes also specify that a robbery is aggravated when the victim is a member of a protected class, such as children or the elderly.

▸ **armed robbery.** (1926) Robbery committed by a person carrying a dangerous weapon, regardless of whether the weapon is revealed or used. • Most states punish armed robbery as an aggravated form of robbery rather than as a separate crime.

▸ **conjoint robbery** (kən-**joynt**). (1902) A robbery committed by two or more persons.

▸ **highway robbery.** (18c) **1.** Robbery committed against a traveler on or near a public highway. **2.** Figuratively, a price or fee that is unreasonably high; excessive profit or advantage.

▸ **simple robbery.** (18c) Robbery that does not involve an aggravating factor or circumstance.

robe. (18c) **1.** The gown worn by a judge while presiding over court. • In the U.S., judges generally wear plain black gowns. In the U.K., judicial robes vary in color and adornment, depending on the judge's rank, the season, and the court, and are traditionally worn with white horsehair wigs. — Also termed *judicial robe.* **2.** (*often cap.*) The legal or judicial profession <eminent members of the robe>.

Robert's Rules. 1. A parliamentary manual titled *Robert's Rules of Order,* originally written in 1875–76 by Henry M. Robert (1837–1923). • The manual went through three editions under its original cover title *Robert's Rules of Order* — the formal title being *Pocket Manual of Rules of Order for Deliberative Assemblies* — and three more (beginning in 1915) under the title *Robert's Rules of Order Revised.* Since 1970 it has been titled *Robert's Rules of Order Newly Revised.* It is the best selling and most commonly adopted parliamentary manual in the United States. **2.** Any parliamentary manual that includes "Robert's Rules" in its title. • The copyright on the first several editions has expired, and many imitators have adapted those editions in varying degrees of faithfulness to the original. **3.** (*sing.*) RULE (3). See PARLIAMENTARY MANUAL.

Robinson–Patman Act. A federal statute (specif., an amendment to the Clayton Act) prohibiting price discrimination that hinders competition or tends to create a monopoly. 15 USCA § 13. — Abbr. RPA. See ANTITRUST LAW; CLAYTON ACT.

***Rochin* rule.** (1952) The now-rejected principle that unconstitutionally obtained evidence is admissible against the accused unless the evidence was obtained in a manner that shocks the conscience (such as pumping the stomach of a suspect to obtain illegal drugs that the suspect has swallowed, as occurred in the *Rochin v. California* case). • The Supreme Court handed down *Rochin* before the Fourth Amendment exclusionary rule applied to the states. *Rochin v. California,* 342 U.S. 165, 72 S.Ct. 205 (1952).

rocket docket. (1987) **1.** An accelerated dispute-resolution process. **2.** A court or judicial district known for its speedy disposition of cases. **3.** A similar administrative process, in which disputes must be decided within a specified time (such as 60 days). See FAST-TRACKING.

ROD. *abbr.* RECORD OF DECISION.

rod. (14c) *Property.* A unit of land measurement equal to 16.5 feet, or 25 links, or one-quarter of a chain. • This unit is sometimes found in old deeds. Historically, the measurement varied according to local usage, but was standardized by the 19th century. — Also termed *pole; perch; rood.* See LINK (2); CHAIN; PERCH (3); ROOD (1).

rogatio testium. (1826) The production of a witness who can testify to the making of a nuncupative will. • The witness must confirm that the testator declared or expressed that the words spoken were a will. See *nuncupative will* under WILL.

rogatory letter (rog-ə-tor-ee). See LETTER OF REQUEST.

rogue court. See COURT.

rogue jury. See JURY.

roll, *n.* (14c) **1.** A record of a court's or public office's proceedings. **2.** An official list of the persons and property subject to taxation. — Also termed (in sense 2) *tax roll; tax list; assessment roll.* Cf. TAXPAYERS' LISTS. **3.** *Parliamentary law.* The roster of those entitled to vote. — Also termed *roll of delegates; roll of members.*

roll call. See CALL (1).

roll-call vote. See VOTE (4).

rolled-up plea. See PLEA (3).

rolling stock. (1847) Movable property, such as locomotives and rail cars, owned by a railroad.

roll of delegates. See ROLL (3).

roll of members. See ROLL (3).

rollover, *n.* (1958) **1.** The extension or renewal of a short-term loan; the refinancing of a maturing loan or note. **2.** The transfer of funds (such as IRA funds) to a new investment of the same type, esp. so as to defer payment of taxes. — **roll over,** *vb.*

rollover mortgage. See *renegotiable-rate mortgage* under MORTGAGE.

Roman–Dutch law. (1820) A system of law in Holland from the mid-15th century to the early 19th century, based on a mixture of Germanic customary law and Roman law as interpreted in medieval and Renaissance lawbooks. • This law forms the basis of modern South African law, the law of several other countries in southern Africa, and the law of Sri Lanka.

"The 'Roman-Dutch' Law owes its name to its dual basis: it is the law resulting from the free incorporation of Roman materials into the ancient customary law of Holland, with modifications introduced by subsequent acts of legislation from time to time. It was this law which prevailed in the Dutch Republic through its short but brilliant life, during those two centuries when, in Motley's words, 'it threw a girdle of rich dependencies entirely round the globe, and attained so remarkable a height of commercial prosperity and political influence.' It was in this girdle of dependencies — especially the South African portion of it — that the Roman-Dutch Law found an abiding refuge when it was superseded [in 1811] in its birthplace." James Mackintosh, *Roman Law in Modern Practice* 88 (1934).

"The phrase 'Roman-Dutch Law' was invented by Simon van Leeuwen, who employed it as the sub-title of his work entitled *Paratitla Juris Novissimi,* published at Leyden in 1652. Subsequently his larger and better known treatise on the 'Roman-Dutch Law' was issued under that name in the year 1664.

"The system of law thus described is that which obtained in the province of Holland from the middle of the fifteenth to the early years of the nineteenth century. Its main principles were carried by the Dutch into their settlements in the East and West Indies; and when some of these, namely, the Cape of Good Hope, Ceylon, and part of Guiana, at the end of the eighteenth and the beginning of the nineteenth century, passed under the dominion of the Crown of Great Britain, the old law was retained as the common law of the territories which now became British colonies. With the expansion of the British Empire in South Africa, the sphere of the Roman-Dutch Law has extended its boundaries, until the whole of the area comprised within the Union of South Africa . . . has adopted this system as its common law. This is the more remarkable since in Holland itself and in the Dutch colonies of the present day the old law has been replaced by codes . . . ." R.W. Lee, *An Introduction to Roman-Dutch Law* 2 (4th ed. 1946).

Romanesque law. See CIVIL LAW (1).

romanette, *n.* (1999) One of a series of usu. parenthetical small Roman numerals formed with lowercase letters, such as (i), (ii), (iii), (iv), etc., commonly used in contracts, legislation, and regulations. • Many drafting experts recommend banishing Roman numerals from legal documents because they tend to cause dense paragraphs when not set out in tabulated style, they disturb alignment when they are set out in tabulated style, and modern lawyers are not well versed in counting with Roman numerals.

Romanist, *n.* (17c) Someone who is versed in or practices Roman law; a Roman-law specialist.

Roman law. (16c) The legal system of the ancient Romans, forming the basis of the modern civil law; CIVIL LAW (1).

"The Roman law is the body of rules that governed the social relations of many peoples in Europe, Asia, and Africa for some period between the earliest prehistoric times and 1453 A.D. This date should perhaps be extended to 1900 A.D., or even to the present time, and we might include America in the territory concerned. . . . Yet the essential fact is that no present-day community . . . consciously applies as binding upon its citizens the rules of Roman law in their unmodified form. That law is an historical fact. It would have only a tepid historical interest . . . if it were not for the circumstance that, before it became a purely historical fact, it was worked into the foundation and framework of what is called the civil law . . . ." Max Radin, *Handbook of Roman Law* 1 (1927).

"Roman law is not only the best-known, the most highly developed, and the most influential of all legal systems of the past; apart from English law, it is also the only one whose entire and unbroken history can be traced from early and primitive beginnings to a stage of elaborate perfection in the hands of skilled specialists." Hans Julius Wolff, *Roman Law: An Historical Introduction* 5 (1951).

Rome Act. *Copyright.* A 1928 revision of the Berne Convention adding the moral rights of attribution and integrity to the minimum standards of protection that member countries must recognize, creating a compulsory license of recorded performances for radio broadcasting, and specifying that the term of protection for joint works must be measured from the death of the last surviving coauthor. — Also termed *Rome Act of 1928; 1928 Rome Act.*

Rome Convention. See ROME CONVENTION ON RELATED RIGHTS.

Rome Convention on Related Rights. *Copyright.* A 1961 treaty setting minimum standards for neighboring rights of performers, producers, and broadcasters. • The United States is not a signatory. Neighboring rights were not protected under the Paris Convention or the Berne Convention. They are part of the copyright protection under the Agreement on Trade-Related Aspects of Intellectual Property (TRIPs). — Also termed *Convention for the Protection of Performers, Producers of Phonograms and Broadcasting Organizations.* — Often shortened to *Rome Convention.* See NEIGHBORING RIGHT.

rood, *n.* (bef. 12c) *Hist.* **1.** A unit of length (originally 5.5 yards but later 7 to 8 yards, depending on when and where it was used) for measuring lands, fences, walls, etc. **2.** A plot of land equal to a quarter of an acre. **3.** In timber and boards, 440 square feet. Cf. PERCH.

***Rooker–Feldman* doctrine.** (1986) The rule that a federal court cannot consider claims actually decided by a state court or claims inextricably intertwined with an earlier state-court judgment. *Rooker v. Fidelity Trust Co.*, 263 U.S. 413, 415–16, 44 S.Ct. 149, 150 (1923); *District of Columbia Ct. of App. v. Feldman*, 460 U.S. 462, 476, 103 S.Ct. 1303, 1311 (1983). • This doctrine precludes "a party losing in state court . . . from seeking what in substance would be appellate review of [a] state judgment in a United States district court, based on the losing party's claim that the state judgment itself violates the loser's federal rights." *Johnson v. De Grandy*, 512 U.S. 997, 1005–06, 114 S.Ct. 2647, 2654 (1994).

room and board. Lodging and food, usu. considered as included in someone's wages, school expenses, rent, or some other agreement. • With *full board,* the host provides all three daily meals; with *half board,* only morning and evening meals.

room doctrine. See DRUG-FACTORY PRESUMPTION.

root. (14c) *Civil law.* A descendant.

root of title. (1840) The recorded land transaction, usu. at least 40 years old, that is used to begin a title search. See CHAIN OF TITLE; TITLE SEARCH.

▸ **good root of title.** (1840) A root of title that contains a recognizable description of the property, shows all the legal and equitable ownership interests in the property, and does not contain anything that raises any doubts about the title's validity.

ROR. *abbr.* **1.** RELEASE ON RECOGNIZANCE. **2.** RATE OF RETURN.

ROR letter. *abbr.* RESERVATION-OF-RIGHTS LETTER.

Roth IRA. See INDIVIDUAL RETIREMENT ACCOUNT.

rotten borough. See BOROUGH (3).

rough justice. See JUSTICE (4).

round lot. See LOT (3).

round-up. See *dragnet arrest* under ARREST (2).

roup. (17c) *Scots law.* A sale by auction (usu. public).

roustabout. (1860) **1.** Someone who does work for which strength is needed, but not particularly skill, esp. in a port, an oilfield, or a circus. **2.** Someone having no permanent home or occupation.

rout (rowt), *n.* (15c) The offense that occurs when an unlawful assembly makes some move toward the accomplishment of its participants' common purpose. Cf. RIOT.

> "The word 'rout' comes from the same source as the word 'route.' It signifies that three or more who have gathered together in unlawful assembly are 'on their way.' It is not necessary for guilt of this offense that the design be actually carried out, nor that the journey be made in a tumultuous manner." Rollin M. Perkins & Ronald N. Boyce, *Criminal Law* 483 (3d ed. 1982).

routine-activities theory. (1985) The theory that criminal acts occur when (1) a person is motivated to commit the offense, (2) a vulnerable victim is available, and (3) there is insufficient protection to prevent the crime. Cf. CONTROL THEORY; RATIONAL-CHOICE THEORY; STRAIN THEORY.

roving bug. See BUG (3).

roving intercept. (1987) A surveillance technique for listening to a person's conversations while he or she is moving from place to place or using a mobile-communication device. See *roving surveillance* under SURVEILLANCE; *roving bug* under BUG (3); *roving wiretap* under WIRETAPPING.

roving surveillance. See SURVEILLANCE.

roving wiretap. See WIRETAPPING.

Royal Commission. (18c) An official group appointed by the U.K. government to make suggestions about a particular subject that may be in need of new laws.

royalism. (17c) **1.** Adherence to the cause of royalty. **2.** The principles underlying a particular monarchic dynasty. **3.** Collectively, the theories on which monarchies are based.

Royal Marriages Act. A 1772 English statute (12 Geo. 3, ch. 1) forbidding members of the royal family from marrying without the sovereign's permission, except on certain conditions.

> "Royal Marriages Act . . . . An Act occasioned by George III's fear of the effect on the dignity and honour of the royal family of members thereof contracting unsuitable marriages, two of his brothers having done so . . . . It provided that marriages of descendants of George II, other than the issue of princesses who marry into foreign families, should not be valid unless they had the consent of the King in Council, or, if the parties were aged over 25, they had given 12 months' notice to the Privy Council, unless during that time both Houses of Parliament expressly declare disapproval of the proposed marriage." David M. Walker, *The Oxford Companion to Law* 1091 (1980).

royalty. (1839) **1.** *Intellectual property.* A payment — in addition to or in place of an up-front payment — made to an author or inventor for each copy of a work or article sold under a copyright or patent. • Royalties are often paid per item made, used, or sold, or per time elapsed.

▸ **established royalty.** (1876) A royalty set at an agreed-on price. • In the absence of an established royalty, a court will determine a remedy for infringement based on what a reasonable royalty would have been.

▸ **reasonable royalty.** (1869) A royalty that a licensee would be willing to pay the holder of the thing's intellectual-property rights while still making a reasonable profit from its use. • The reasonable-royalty standard often serves as the measure of damages in a claim of patent, copyright, or trademark infringement, or for misappropriation of trade secrets. In deciding what royalty is reasonable in a trade-secrets suit, courts consider the unique circumstances of the case, as well as (1) how the use affected the parties' ability to compete; (2) the cost of past licenses; (3) the cost to develop the secret and its present value; (4) how the defendant intends to use the information; and (5) the availability of alternatives.

2. *Oil & gas.* A share of the product or profit from real property, reserved by the grantor of a mineral lease, in exchange for the lessee's right to mine or drill on the land. — Also termed (in sense 2) *override.*

▸ **haulage royalty.** (1924) A royalty paid to a landowner for moving coal via a subterranean passageway under the landowner's land from a mine located on an adjacent property. • The payment is calculated at a certain amount per ton of coal.

▸ **landowner's royalty.** (1922) A share of production or revenues provided for the lessor in the royalty clause of the oil-and-gas lease and paid at the well free of any costs of production. • Traditionally, except in California, the landowner's royalty has been ⅛ of gross production for oil and ⅛ of the proceeds received from the sale of gas. But today the size is often negotiated. — Also termed *leaseholder royalty.*

▸ **mineral royalty.** (1891) A right to a share of income from mineral production.

▸ **nonparticipating royalty.** (1933) A share of production — or of the revenue from production free its costs — carved out of the mineral interest. • A nonparticipating-royalty holder is entitled to the stated share of production or cash without regard to the terms of any lease. Nonparticipating royalties are often retained by mineral-interest owners who sell their rights.

▸ **overriding royalty.** (1921) A share of either production or revenue from production (free of the costs of production) carved out of a lessee's interest under an oil-and-gas lease. • Overriding-royalty interests are often used to compensate those who have helped structure a drilling venture. An overriding-royalty interest ends when the underlying lease terminates.

▸ **shut-in royalty.** (1946) A payment made by an oil-and-gas lessee to the lessor to keep the lease in force when a well capable of producing is not utilized because there is no market for the oil or gas. • Generally, without such a payment, the lease will terminate at the end of the primary term unless actual production has begun.

royalty interest. (1900) *Oil & gas.* A share of production — or the value or proceeds of production, free of the costs of production — when and if there is production. • A royalty interest is usu. expressed as a fraction (such as 1/6). A royalty-interest owner has no right to operate the property and therefore no right to lease the property or to share in bonuses or delay rentals. In some states a royalty owner has the right of ingress and egress to take the royalty production. Authorities are split over what costs are costs of production. Several different but related kinds of royalty interests are commonly encountered. See ROYALTY (2).

RPA. *abbr.* ROBINSON–PATMAN ACT.

RPO standard. *abbr.* REASONABLY-PRUDENT-OPERATOR STANDARD.

rptr. *abbr.* REPORTER.

RRB. *abbr.* RAILROAD RETIREMENT BOARD.

RRC. *abbr.* RESIDENTIAL REENTRY CENTER.

R.S. *abbr.* See *revised statutes* under STATUTE.

RSPA. *abbr.* RESEARCH AND SPECIAL PROGRAMS ADMINISTRATION.

RTC. *abbr.* RESOLUTION TRUST CORPORATION.

RTK. *abbr.* See RIGHT-TO-KNOW ACT.

RTM. *abbr.* See *reverse triangular merger* under MERGER (8).

RTP. *abbr.* REDUCTION TO PRACTICE.

RTW law. *abbr.* RIGHT-TO-WORK LAW.

RUAA. *abbr.* See UNIFORM ARBITRATION ACT.

rubber check. See *bad check* under CHECK.

rubber-stamp seal. See NOTARY SEAL.

rubric (**roo**-brik). [fr. Latin *rubrica* "red earth," from the practice of printing the exceptional parts of old manuscripts in red letters] (16c) **1.** The title of a statute or code <the rubric of the relevant statute is the Civil Rights Act of 1964>. **2.** A category or designation <assignment of rights falls under the rubric of contract law>. **3.** An introductory or explanatory note; a preface <a well-known scholar wrote the rubric to the book's fourth edition>. **4.** An established rule, custom, or law <what is the rubric in the Northern District of Texas regarding appearance at docket call?>. **5.** An authoritative rule, esp. for conducting a public worship service <the rubric dictates whether the congregation should stand or kneel>. — **rubrical,** *adj.*

RUL. *abbr.* See *restricted-use license* under DRIVER'S LICENSE.

rule, *n.* (13c) **1.** Generally, an established and authoritative standard or principle; a general norm mandating or guiding conduct or action in a given type of situation.

▸ **default rule.** A legal principle that fills a gap in a contract in the absence of an applicable express provision but remains subject to a contrary agreement. Cf. GAP-FILLER.

▸ **general rule.** (15c) A rule applicable to a class of cases or circumstances.

▸ **mandatory rule.** (1867) A legal rule that is not subject to a contrary agreement. • For example, the UCC obligation of good faith and fair dealing cannot be disclaimed.

▸ **peremptory rule.** (17c) A court order that must be obeyed without an opportunity to respond. • No objections may be lodged or arguments made.

▸ **special rule.** See SPECIAL RULE (1).

2. A regulation governing a court's or an agency's internal procedures; esp., the whole or any part of an agency statement of general or particular applicability and future effect, designed to implement, interpret, or prescribe law or policy or to describe the organization, approval, or practice requirements of the agency, including the approval or prescription for the future of rates, wages, corporate or financial structures, reorganizations of those structures, prices, facilities, appliances, services, allowance for any of the foregoing, valuation, costs, and accounting within the agency; or practices bearing on any of the foregoing. See COURT RULES.

▸ **procedural rule.** See RULE OF PROCEDURE.

3. *Parliamentary law.* A procedural rule (sense 1) for the orderly conduct of business in a deliberative assembly. — Also termed *rule of order (often pl.).*

▸ **Cordon rule.** See CORDON RULE.

▸ **joint rule.** A rule adopted by both houses of a bicameral legislature for the conduct of business or relations between them, such as when they meet in joint session, or for other matters in which they share an interest. See *joint session* under SESSION (1).

▸ **ordinary standing rule.** See *standing rule* (1).

▸ **Ramseyer rule.** See RAMSEYER RULE.

▸ **special rule. 1.** See SPECIAL RULE (2). **2.** See SPECIAL RULE (3).

▸ **standing rule.** (17c) **1.** A rule that relates to an organization's administration or operation rather than to its procedure in meetings. • For example, a rule about the time and place of regular meetings, or about a committee's jurisdiction, is a standing rule. — Also termed *ordinary standing rule.* **2.** A special rule of continuing force. • Many conventions and other deliberative assemblies collect both their administrative and procedural rules into a set titled "standing rules." See SPECIAL RULE (2).

4. A judicial order, decree, or direction; RULING (1).

▸ **rule nisi.** See *decree nisi* under DECREE.

▸ **rule to show cause.** (18c) An order that a party must do, or be allowed to do, a specified act, unless good cause is shown to the contrary.

rule, *vb.* (13c) **1.** To command or require; to exert control <the dictator ruled the country>. **2.** To decide a legal point; to make an official decision about a legal problem <the court ruled on the issue of admissibility>.

rule, the. An evidentiary and procedural rule by which all witnesses are excluded from the courtroom while another witness is testifying <invoking "the rule">. • The phrase "the rule" is used chiefly in the American South and Southwest, but it is a common practice to exclude witnesses before they testify.

Rule 1.53 application. See *continued-prosecution application* under PATENT APPLICATION.

Rule 10b-5. The SEC rule that prohibits deceptive or manipulative practices (such as material misrepresentations or omissions) in the buying or selling of securities. — Also termed *antifraud rule.*

Rule 11. *Civil procedure.* **1.** In federal practice, the procedural rule requiring the attorney of record or the party (if not represented by an attorney) to sign all pleadings, motions, and other papers filed with the court and — by this signing — to represent that the paper is filed in good faith after an inquiry that is reasonable under the circumstances. • This rule provides for the imposition of sanctions, upon a party's or the court's own motion, if an attorney or party violates the conditions stated in the rule. Fed. R. Civ. P. 11. **2.** In Texas practice, the procedural rule requiring agreements between attorneys or parties concerning a pending suit to be in writing, signed, and filed in the court's record or made on the record in open court. Tex. R. Civ. P. 11.

Rule 12(b)(6) motion. See MOTION (1).

Rule 29 motion. (1991) *Criminal procedure.* A posttrial defense motion for a judgment of acquittal.

Rule 35 motion. (1985) *Criminal procedure.* A government motion to reduce a criminal sentence based on cooperation.

Rule 109 statement. (1992) *Patents.* A statement by a patent examiner of the reasons for allowing a patent claim. • An examiner may file a Rule 109 statement at any time if it appears that the record does not adequately reflect the reasons for allowance. It should state how the claim differs from prior art and why that difference is nonobvious. PTO Reg. § 1.109; 37 CFR § 1.104(e). — Also termed *Reasons for Allowance.*

Rule 116 amendment. See *amendment after final action* under PATENT-APPLICATION AMENDMENT.

Rule 312 amendment. See *amendment after allowance* under PATENT-APPLICATION AMENDMENT.

rule absolute. See *decree absolute* under DECREE.

rule against accumulations. See ACCUMULATIONS, RULE AGAINST.

rule against inalienability. (1914) The principle that property must not be made nontransferable. — Also termed *rule against trusts of perpetual duration.* Cf. RULE AGAINST PERPETUITIES.

rule against irrepealability. See REPEALABILITY CANON.

rule against irrepealable laws. See REPEALABILITY CANON.

rule against perpetuities. (*sometimes cap.*) (18c) *Property.* The common-law rule prohibiting a grant of an estate unless the interest must vest, if at all, no later than 21 years (plus a period of gestation to cover a posthumous birth) after the death of some person alive when the interest was created. • The purpose of the rule was to limit the time that title to property could be suspended out of commerce because there was no owner who had title to the property and who could sell it or exercise other aspects of ownership. If the terms of the contract or gift exceeded the time limits of the rule, the gift or transaction was void. — Abbr. RAP. — Also termed *rule against remoteness.* See MEASURING LIFE. Cf. ACCUMULATIONS, RULE AGAINST.

> "The true form of the Rule against Perpetuities is believed to be this: — NO INTEREST SUBJECT TO A CONDITION PRECEDENT IS GOOD, UNLESS THE CONDITION MUST BE FULFILLED, IF AT ALL, WITHIN TWENTY-ONE YEARS AFTER SOME LIFE IN BEING AT THE CREATION OF THE INTEREST." John Chipman Gray, *The Rule Against Perpetuities* 144 (1886).

> "Another scholar who spent a substantial part of an academic lifetime attempting to bring order and add sense to the rule [against perpetuities], W. Barton Leach, described the rule as a 'technicality-ridden legal nightmare' and a 'dangerous instrumentality in the hands of most members of the bar.'" Thomas F. Bergin & Paul G. Haskell, *Preface to Estates in Land and Future Interests* 178 (2d ed. 1984) (quoting Leach, *Perpetuities Legislation, Massachusetts Style*, 67 Harv. L. Rev. 1349 (1954)).

> "The common law Rule Against Perpetuities (modified by statute in some states) provides that no interest is valid unless it must vest within 21 years after lives in being when the interest was created. The rule is something of a misnomer. It does not limit the duration of a condition in a bequest, but rather limits the testator's power to earmark gifts for remote descendants." Richard A. Posner, *Economic Analysis of Law* § 18.7, at 394 (2d ed. 1977).

rule against remoteness. See RULE AGAINST PERPETUITIES.

rule against trusts of perpetual duration. See RULE AGAINST INALIENABILITY.

rule against vitiation of a claim element. See ALL-ELEMENTS RULE.

rule day. See *return day* (3) under DAY.

rule in *Ex parte Campbell*. See PRIOR-CONSTRUCTION CANON.

rule in Heydon's case. See MISCHIEF RULE.

Rule in Queen Caroline's Case. (1952) The common-law principle that a witness who is impeached with a prior inconsistent statement on cross-examination must be given the opportunity to admit, explain, repudiate, or deny it before the statement is admissible into evidence. • In American law, Federal Rule of Evidence 613 embodies this principle, with some variations. The original rule is found in *Queen Caroline's Case*, (1820) 129 Eng. Rep. 976.

Rule in Shelley's Case. (18c) *Property.* The rule that if — in a single grant — a freehold estate is given to a person and a remainder is given to the person's heirs, the remainder belongs to the named person and not the heirs, so that the person is held to have a fee simple absolute. • The rule, which dates from the 14th century but draws its name from the famous 16th-century case, has been abolished in most states. *Wolfe v. Shelley*, 76 Eng. Rep. 206 (K.B. 1581).

> "[T]he rule in Shelley's Case, the Don Quixote of the law, which, like the last knight errant of chivalry, has long survived every cause that gave it birth and now wanders aimlessly through the reports, still vigorous, but equally useless and dangerous." *Stamper v. Stamper*, 28 S.E. 20, 22 (N.C. 1897).

Rule in Wild's Case. (1842) *Property.* The rule construing a grant to "A and A's children" as a fee tail if A's children do not exist at the effective date of the instrument, and as a joint tenancy if A's children do exist at the effective date. • The rule has been abolished along with the fee tail in most states.

ruleless, *adj.* (15c) **1.** Devoid of rules; lawless. **2.** (Of a region) having no government.

rulemaking, *n.* (1926) The process used by an administrative agency to formulate, amend, or repeal a rule or regulation. — Also termed *administrative rulemaking.* Cf. ADMINISTRATIVE ADJUDICATION; INFORMAL AGENCY ACTION. — **rulemaking,** *adj.*

▸ **formal rulemaking.** (1960) Agency rulemaking that, when required by statute or the agency's discretion, must be on the record after an opportunity for an agency hearing, and must comply with certain procedures, such as allowing the submission of evidence and the cross-examination of witnesses. Cf. *informal rulemaking.*

▸ **informal rulemaking.** (1968) Agency rulemaking in which the agency publishes a proposed regulation and receives public comments on the regulation, after which the regulation can take effect without the necessity of a formal hearing on the record. • Informal rulemaking is the most common procedure followed by an agency in issuing its substantive rules. — Also termed *notice-and-comment rulemaking.* See NOTICE-AND-COMMENT PERIOD. Cf. *formal rulemaking.*

rulemonger (**rool**-mong-ər), *n.* (1847) *Pejorative.* A monomaniacal adherent to rules and their strict application; a martinet in regulatory matters.

ruleness. The tendency of a prescription in a legal instrument, esp. a statute, to require (not merely allow) an implementing officer or other authorized person to apply a legal principle or directive to a particular case.

rule nisi. See *decree nisi* under DECREE.

rule of 72. (1966) A method for determining how many years it takes to double money invested at a compound interest rate. • For example, at a compound rate of 6%, it takes 12 years (72 divided by 6) for principal to double.

rule of 78. (1954) A method for computing the amount of interest that a borrower saves by paying off a loan early, when the interest payments are higher at the beginning of the loan period. • For example, to determine how much interest is saved by prepaying a 12-month loan after 6 months, divide the sum of the digits for the remaining six payments (21) by the sum of the digits for all twelve payments (78) and multiply that percentage by the total interest. — Also termed *rule of the sum of the digits.*

rule of capture. (1861) **1.** *Property.* The doctrine that if the donee of a general power of appointment manifests an intent to assume control of the property for all purposes and not just for the purpose of appointing it to someone, the donee captures the property and the property goes to the donee's estate. • One common way for the donee to show an intent to assume control for all purposes is to include provisions in his or her will blending the appointing property with the donee's own property. The doctrine applies in a minority of states. **2.** *Property.* The principle that wild animals belong to the person who captures them, regardless of whether they were originally on another person's land. **3.** *Water law.* The principle that a surface landowner can extract and appropriate all the groundwater beneath the land by drilling or pumping, even if doing so drains away groundwaters to the point of drying up springs and wells from which other landowners benefit. • This doctrine has been widely abolished or limited by legislation. **4.** *Oil & gas.* A fundamental principle of oil-and-gas law holding that there is no liability for drainage of oil and gas from under the lands of another so long as there has been no trespass and all relevant statutes and regulations have been observed. — Also termed *doctrine of capture; law of capture; capture doctrine.* Cf. AD COELUM DOCTRINE.

rule of completeness. See RULE OF OPTIONAL COMPLETENESS.

rule of construction. See *canon of construction* under CANON (1).

rule of court. (17c) A rule governing the practice or procedure in a given court <federal rules of court>. — Also termed *court rule.* See COURT RULES; LOCAL RULE.

rule of decision. (18c) A rule, statute, body of law, or prior decision that provides the basis for deciding or adjudicating a case.

rule of doubt. (1923) **1.** *Copyright.* The doctrine that unreadable or incomprehensible identifying material deposited with the U.S. Copyright Office may not be protected under copyright law because it cannot easily be examined to determine whether it qualifies. • This rule usu. applies to computer object code. • Unlike a Certificate of Registration, a filing under the rule of doubt is not prima facie evidence of a valid copyright. **2.** *Patents.* An abandoned judicial doctrine holding that when there is doubt whether an invention is patentable, the patent should be issued so that the inventor can test its validity in court.

rule of evidence. See EVIDENCE (4).

rule of four. (1949) The convention that for certiorari to be granted by the U.S. Supreme Court, four justices must vote in favor of the grant. See CERTIORARI.

rule of inconvenience. (1934) The principle of statutory interpretation holding that a court should not construe a statute in a way that will jeopardize an important public interest or produce a serious hardship for anyone, unless that interpretation is unavoidable. — Often shortened to *inconvenience.*

rule of interpretation. See *canon of construction* under CANON (1).

rule of justice. A jurisprudential principle that determines the sphere of individual liberty in the pursuit of individual welfare, so as to confine that liberty within limits that are consistent with the general welfare of humankind.

rule of law. (18c) **1.** A substantive legal principle <under the rule of law known as respondeat superior, the employer is answerable for all wrongs committed by an employee in the course of the employment>. **2.** The supremacy of regular as opposed to arbitrary power; the absence of any arbitrary power on the part of the government <citizens must respect the rule of law>. — Also termed *supremacy of law.* **3.** The doctrine that every person is subject to the ordinary law within the jurisdiction; the equal subordination of all citizens and classes to the ordinary law of the land <all persons within the United States are within the American rule of law>. **4.** The doctrine that general constitutional principles are the result of judicial decisions determining the rights of private individuals in the courts <under the rule of law, Supreme Court caselaw makes up the bulk of what we call "constitutional law">. **5.** Loosely, a legal ruling; a ruling on a point of law <the *ratio decidendi* of a case is any rule of law reached by the judge as a necessary step in the decision>.

> "Of all the dreams that drive men and women into the streets, from Buenos Aires to Budapest, the 'rule of law' is the most puzzling. We have a pretty good idea what we mean by 'free markets' and 'democratic elections.' But legality and the 'rule of law' are ideals that present themselves as opaque even to legal philosophers. Many American jurists treat the rule of law as though it were no more than governance by rules. Thus we find Justice Scalia arguing explicitly that the rule of law is no more than the law of rules. And philosophers, such as Friedrich Hayek and Joseph Raz, make the same assumption that the rule of law means that the government 'is bound by rules fixed and announced beforehand.' Playing by the rules is, in some dubious contexts, a great achievement, but once societies have minimized graft and arbitrary rule, the 'rule of law' seems to promise more than blindly playing the game. After

all, the rules of the game might be horribly unjust. There are in fact two versions of the rule of law, a modest version of adhering to the rules and a more lofty ideal that incorporates criteria of justice. We shuffle back and forth between them because we are unsure of the import of the term 'law' in the expression 'rule of law.'" George P. Fletcher, *Basic Concepts of Legal Thought* 11 (1996).

rule of lenity (len-ə-tee). (1958) The judicial doctrine holding that a court, in construing an ambiguous criminal statute that sets out multiple or inconsistent punishments, should resolve the ambiguity in favor of the more lenient punishment. — Also termed *lenity rule.* Cf. FAIR-WARNING CHALLENGE.

rule of marshaling assets. (18c) An equitable doctrine that requires a senior creditor, having two or more funds to satisfy its debt, to first dispose of the fund not available to a junior creditor. • It prevents the inequity that would result if the senior creditor could choose to satisfy its debt out of the only fund available to the junior creditor and thereby exclude the junior creditor from any satisfaction. — Also termed *marshaling doctrine; rule of marshaling securities; rule of marshaling remedies.*

rule of marshaling liens. See INVERSE-ORDER-OF-ALIENATION DOCTRINE.

rule of marshaling remedies. See RULE OF MARSHALING ASSETS.

rule of marshaling securities. See RULE OF MARSHALING ASSETS.

rule of necessity. A rule requiring a judge or other official to hear a case, despite bias or conflict of interest, when disqualification would result in the lack of any competent court or tribunal. — Often shortened to *necessity.*

rule of operation. *Patents.* A method of using a machine to produce its intended useful result. • A rule of operation and moving parts generally distinguish a machine from an article of manufacture.

rule of optional completeness. (1983) The evidentiary rule providing that when a party introduces part of a writing or an utterance at trial, the opposing party may require that the remainder of the passage be read to establish the full context. • The rule has limitations: first, no utterance can be received if it is irrelevant, and second, the remainder of the utterance must explain the first part. In many jurisdictions, the rule applies to conversations, to an opponent's admissions, to confessions, and to all other types of writings — even account books. But the Federal Rules of Evidence limit the rule to writings and recorded statements. Fed. R. Evid. 106. In most jurisdictions, including federal, the remainder is admissible unless its admission would be unfair or misleading. — Also termed *rule of completeness; doctrine of completeness; doctrine of optional completeness; completeness doctrine; optional-completeness rule; optional-completeness doctrine.*

rule of order. See RULE (3).

rule of prior exhaustion of domestic remedies. See EXHAUSTION-OF-LOCAL-REMEDIES RULE.

rule of prior exhaustion of local remedies. See EXHAUSTION-OF-LOCAL-REMEDIES RULE.

rule of procedure. A judicial rule or manner for carrying on a civil lawsuit or criminal prosecution. — Also termed *procedural rule.*

rule of rank. A doctrine of statutory construction holding that a statute dealing with things or persons of an inferior rank cannot by any general words be extended to things or persons of a superior rank. • Blackstone gives the example of a statute dealing with deans, prebendaries, parsons, vicars, *and others* having spiritual promotion. According to Blackstone, this statute is held not to extend to bishops, even though they have spiritual promotion, because deans are the highest persons named, and bishops are of a higher order. Cf. EJUSDEM GENERIS; EXPRESSIO UNIUS EST EXCLUSIO ALTERIUS; NOSCITUR A SOCIIS.

rule of reason. (1897) *Antitrust.* The judicial doctrine holding that a trade practice violates the Sherman Act only if the practice is an unreasonable restraint of trade, based on the totality of economic circumstances. See SHERMAN ANTITRUST ACT; RESTRAINT OF TRADE. Cf. PER SE RULE.

rule of recognition. (1959) In the legal theory of H.L.A. Hart, a legal system's fundamental rule, by which all other rules are identified and understood. • In *The Concept of Law* (1961), Hart contends that a society's legal system is centered on rules. There are primary rules of obligation, which prescribe how a person should act in society, and secondary rules, by which the primary rules are created, identified, changed, and understood. A "rule of recognition" is a secondary rule, and serves to instruct citizens on when a pronouncement or societal principle constitutes a rule of obligation. — Sometimes shortened to *recognition.* Cf. RULES OF CHANGE; *basic norm* under NORM.

"This rule [the rule of recognition] may amount to no more than specifying a list of primary rules carved on a public monument. Or it may actually be a complete set of rules . . . ." Martin P. Golding, *Philosophy of Law* 44 (1975).

rule of retreat. See RETREAT RULE.

rule of right. (18c) The source of a right; the rule that gives rise to a right.

"When the rule of right, which ought to direct the actions of the philosopher, as well as the ignorant, is a matter of controversy, not of fact, the people are slaves to the magistrates." Cesare Beccaria, *An Essay on Crimes and Punishments* 25 (rev. ed. 1793).

rule of thalweg. (1954) The doctrine that in navigable water separating states, the center of the main downstream navigation channel locates the boundary between the states that border on that water. See THALWEG.

rule of the destructibility of contingent remainders. See DESTRUCTIBILITY OF CONTINGENT REMAINDERS.

rule of the floating subtrahend. (1982) The common-law doctrine that a plaintiff whose damage was not caused entirely by the defendant must prove the amount of damage that is not attributable to the defendant (the subtrahend) or else recover nothing. • The reasoning behind the rule is that damage is an essential element of a tort claim, and the plaintiff has the burden of proof. If proved, the subtrahend is subtracted from the total damage to determine the plaintiff's recovery.

rule of the last antecedent. (1919) **1.** The doctrine that a pronoun, relative pronoun, or demonstrative adjective generally refers to the nearest reasonable antecedent. • Strictly speaking, "last antecedent" denotes a noun or noun phrase referred to by a pronoun or relative pronoun — since grammatically speaking, only pronouns are said to have antecedents. But in modern practice, and despite the misnomer, it is common to refer to the *rule of the last antecedent* when what is actually meant is the *nearest-reasonable-referent canon.* See NEAREST-REASONABLE-REFERENT CANON. **2.** An interpretive principle by which a court determines that qualifying words or phrases modify the words or phrases immediately preceding them and not words or phrases more remote, unless the extension is necessary from the context or the spirit of the entire writing. • For example, an application of this rule might mean that, in the phrase *Texas courts, New Mexico courts, and New York courts in the federal system,* the words *in the federal system* might be held to modify only *New York courts* and not *Texas courts* or *New Mexico courts.* — Also termed *doctrine of the last antecedent; doctrine of the last preceding antecedent; last-antecedent canon.* Cf. SERIES-QUALIFIER CANON.

rule of the shorter term. (1968) *Copyright.* A provision of the Universal Copyright Convention stating that no member country is required to extend a longer term of protection than the work receives in the country where it is first published. — Also termed *shorter-term rule.*

rule of the sum of the digits. See RULE OF 78.

rule of thumb. (17c) A roughly practical measure that is neither precise nor invariable. • There is an urban legend, dating from the 1970s, to the effect that the phrase is offensive because it originally denoted the width of a rod with which English law allowed husbands to beat their wives. If that were historically accurate, of course, the phrase would be repugnant in the extreme. The best account of the debunking of the legend is to be found in James E. Clapp et al., *Lawtalk: The Unknown Stories Behind Familiar Legal Expressions* 219–25 (2011).

rule of universal inheritance. See UNIVERSAL-INHERITANCE RULE.

rules committee. See COMMITTEE (1).

rules of change. (1961) In the legal theory of H.L.A. Hart, the fundamental rules by which a legal system's other rules are altered. • In Hart's theory, a legal system's primary rules are subject to identification and change by secondary rules. Among those rules are "rules of change," which prescribe how laws are altered or repealed. Cf. RULE OF RECOGNITION.

rules of court. See COURT RULES.

Rules of Decision Act. A federal statute (28 USCA § 1652) providing that a federal court, when exercising diversity jurisdiction, must apply the substantive law of the state in which the court sits. — Abbr. RDA. See *diversity jurisdiction* under JURISDICTION.

rules of evidence. See EVIDENCE (4); FEDERAL RULES OF EVIDENCE.

rules of navigation. (16c) *Maritime law.* The principles and regulations that govern the steering and sailing of vessels to avoid collisions. • Examples include the International Rules governing conduct on the high seas and the Inland Rules governing navigation on the inland waters of the United States and U.S. vessels on the Canadian waters of the Great Lakes. 33 USCA §§ 1602–1608, 2001–2073.

rules of order. See RULE (3).

rules of procedure. See PROCEDURE (2).

Rule 30(b)(6) deposition. See *30(b)(6) deposition* under DEPOSITION (2).

rule to show cause. **1.** See SHOW-CAUSE PROCEEDING. **2.** See *show-cause order* under ORDER (2). **3.** See RULE (4).

ruling, *n.* (16c) **1.** Government; the act of one who governs or rules. See RULE (4). **2.** The outcome of a court's decision either on some point of law or on the case as a whole. — Also termed *legal ruling.* Cf. JUDGMENT (2); OPINION (1).

> "A distinction is sometimes made between rules and rulings. Whether or not a formal distinction is declared, in common usage 'legal ruling' (or simply 'ruling') is a term ordinarily used to signify the outcome of applying a legal test when that outcome is one of relatively narrow impact. The immediate effect is to decide an issue in a single case. This meaning contrasts, for example, with the usual meaning of 'legal rule' (or simply 'rule'). The term 'rule' ordinarily refers to a legal proposition of general application. A 'ruling' may have force as precedent, but ordinarily it has that force because the conclusion it expresses (for example, 'objection sustained') explicitly depends upon and implicitly reiterates a 'rule' — a legal proposition of more general application . . . ." Robert E. Keeton, *Judging* 67–68 (1990).

3. *Parliamentary law.* The chair's decision on a point of order. — **rule,** *vb.*

ruling case. See LEADING CASE (3).

ruling letter. See DETERMINATION LETTER.

RULPA. *abbr.* Revised Uniform Limited Partnership Act. See UNIFORM LIMITED PARTNERSHIP ACT.

run, *vb.* (bef. 12c) **1.** To expire after a prescribed period <the statute of limitations had run, so the plaintiff's lawsuit was barred>. **2.** To accompany a conveyance or assignment of (land) <the covenant runs with the land>. **3.** To apply <the injunction runs against only one of the parties in the dispute>.

runaway. (16c) **1.** Someone who is fleeing or has escaped from custody, captivity, restraint, or control; esp., a minor who has voluntarily left home without permission and with no intent to return. Cf. THROWAWAY. **2.** An animal or thing that is out of control or has escaped from confinement. — **run away,** *vb.*

runaway grand jury. See GRAND JURY.

runner. (18c) **1.** A law-office employee who delivers papers between offices and files papers in court. **2.** Someone who solicits personal-injury cases for a lawyer. — Also termed *capper.* **3.** A smuggler. **4.** *BrE. Slang.* An escape; flight (from something); a voluntary disappearance.

running account. See ACCOUNT.

running description. See METES AND BOUNDS.

running-down clause. (1896) *Marine insurance.* A provision for the hull insurer's paying a proportion of the damages sustained by the other vessel in a collision.

running objection. See *continuing objection* under OBJECTION.

running policy. See *floating policy* under INSURANCE POLICY.

running with the land. *Property law.* See *covenant running with the land* under COVENANT (4).

runoff, *n.* **1.** A second election or competition that is arranged when there is no clear winner of the first one. **2.** Rain or other liquid that flows off the land into rivers.

runoff election. See ELECTION (3).

rural, *adj.* **1.** Of, relating to, or involving the country or countryside, as opposed to a city or town; characteristic of, suited to, or living in a rustic setting. Cf. URBAN (1). **2.** Of, relating to, or involving country people, farmers, etc. **3.** *Civil law.* Of, relating to, or involving a tenement in land adapted to and used for agricultural or pastoral purposes. Cf. URBAN (2).

Rural Business-Cooperative Service. An agency in the U.S. Department of Agriculture responsible for making loans and grants to public agencies and private parties to develop rural businesses. — Abbr. RBS.

Rural Electrification Administration. A former agency in the U.S. Department of Agriculture responsible for making or guaranteeing loans to rural electric and telephone utilities. • Its duties were transferred to the Rural Utilities Service in 1994. — Abbr. REA. See RURAL UTILITIES SERVICE.

Rural Housing Service. An agency in the U.S. Department of Agriculture responsible for making or guaranteeing loans for rural housing. — Abbr. RHS.

rural servitude. See SERVITUDE (3).

Rural Utilities Service. An agency in the U.S. Department of Agriculture responsible for making or guaranteeing loans to rural electric and telecommunication utilities. • The agency is the successor to the Rural Electrification Administration. — Abbr. RUS.

RUS. *abbr.* **1.** RURAL UTILITIES SERVICE. **2.** Release under supervision.

rustica et urbana (**rəs**-ti-kə et ər-**bay**-nə). [Latin] *Hist.* Rural and urban. • The phrase appeared in reference to servitudes. See SERVITUS.

rustic servitude. See *rural servitude* under SERVITUDE (3).

rusticum forum (**rəs**-ti-kəm **for**-əm). (1908) Any nonjudicial body (such as an arbitral panel or workers'-compensation review board) that has authority to make a binding decision. — Also termed *poor man's court.*

rusticum judicium (**rəs**-ti-kəm joo-**dish**-ee-əm). (1836) **1.** The division of liability so that one party (usu. a defendant) must pay only part (usu. half) of another party's (usu. the plaintiff's) loss. • *Rusticum judicium* originated in 17th century maritime law as a means of efficiently resolving collision cases in which both ships were at fault. In maritime law, damages were equally divided. — Also termed *rusticum jus.* Cf. *comparative negligence* under NEGLIGENCE. **2.** *Rare.* Rough justice; a rustic tribunal. • This is a literal translation of the term, used colloquially rather than accurately. — Sometimes misspelled *rusticum judicum.*

rusticum jus (**rəs**-ti-kəm jəs). *Maritime law.* See RUSTICUM JUDICIUM (1).

S

s. *abbr.* **1.** STATUTE. **2.** SECTION (1). **3.** (*usu. cap.*) SENATE.

S-1. An SEC form that a company usu. must file before listing and trading its securities on a national exchange. • Used primarily by first-time issuers of securities, this form is the basic, full-length registration statement that requires a great deal of information about the issuer and the securities being sold. The SEC has also adopted modified forms for smaller enterprises, such as Forms SB-1 and SB-2. — Also termed *Form S-1*.

SAA. *abbr.* SAFETY APPLIANCE ACT.

sabbath (**sab**-əth), *n.* (*usu. cap.*) The day of the week kept by a particular religious group for rest and worship, and esp. (in some belief systems) for cessation of all labor. • In general terms, the Muslim sabbath is Friday, the Jewish sabbath Saturday, and the Christian sabbath Sunday. — Also termed (for Quakers) *First-day*; (for Christians) *Lord's day*.

Sabbath-breaking. (17c) The violation of laws or rules on observing the Sabbath; esp., the violation of a blue law.

Sabbath law. See BLUE LAW.

sabotage (**sab**-ə-tahzh), *n.* (1910) **1.** Deliberate damage done to equipment, vehicles, etc. in order to prevent an enemy or adversary from using them; specif., the destruction, damage, or knowingly defective production of materials, premises, or utilities used for national defense or for war. 18 USCA §§ 2151 et seq. **2.** The willful and malicious destruction of an employer's property or interference with an employer's normal operations, esp. during a labor dispute. — **sabotage,** *vb.*

saboteur (sab-ə-**tər**), *n.* (1921) Someone who commits sabotage; specif., someone who deliberately damages, destroys, or spoils someone else's property or activities in order to prevent an enemy or adversary from deriving benefit from them.

sac, *n.* See SOC.

sacer (**sas**-ər), *adj.* [Latin "sacred; forfeited to a god"] *Roman law.* (Of an outlaw or a wrongdoer) punished by being placed outside the law's protection. See CONSECRATIO CAPITIS; OUTLAWRY.

sachbaro. See SAGIBARO.

Sache (**zahk**-ə). [German] A thing; an article or matter. See THING.

sacramental action. See SACRAMENTO.

sacramentalis (sak-rə-men-**tay**-leez), *n. pl.* [Law Latin fr. Latin *sacramentum* "an oath-taker"] *Hist.* A compurgator; one who takes an oath swearing to a defendant's innocence. Pl. ***sacramentales.***

sacramento (sak-rə-**men**-toh), *n.* [Latin "by oath"] *Roman law.* A legal action in the earliest form of civil procedure in which, at its commencement, each of the contending parties deposited or gave security for a certain sum (called the *sacramentum*), which the loser forfeited to the public. — Also termed *legis actio sacramento*; *actio sacramenti*; *sacramental action.* See LEGIS ACTIO.

> "The characteristic feature of the *legis actio sacramento* (or *actio sacramenti*) as described by Gaius, and that from which it derived its name, was that the parties, after a somewhat dramatic performance before the consul or praetor, each challenged the other to stake a certain sum, whose amount was fixed by statute, and which was to abide the issue of the inquiry by the court or judge to whom the cause was eventually remitted. This stake Gaius refers to indifferently as *sacramentum, summa sacramenti,* and *poena sacramenti.* The formal question the court had to determine was, — whose stake had been justified, whose had not (*cujus sacramentum justum, cujus injustum*); the first was returned to the staker, the second forfeited originally to sacred and afterwards to public uses. But the decision on this formal question necessarily involved a judgment on the matter actually in dispute." James Muirhead, *Historical Introduction to the Private Law of Rome* 177–78 (Henry Goudy ed., 2d ed. 1899).

sacramentum (sak-rə-**men**-təm), *n.* [Latin "an oath"] *Roman law.* **1.** SACRAMENTO. **2.** An oath of allegiance given by a soldier upon enlistment.

sacramentum decisionis (sak-rə-**men**-təm di-sizh-ee-**oh**-nis). [Latin "the oath of decision"] (1823) *Civil law.* The offer by one party to accept the opposing party's oath as decisive of the issues involved in a lawsuit. Pl. ***sacramenta decisionis.***

> "The defendant or person accused was . . . to make oath of his own innocence, and to produce a certain number of compurgators, who swore they believed his oath. Somewhat similar also to this is the *sacramentum decisionis*, or the voluntary and decisive oath of the civil law; where one of the parties to the suit, not being able to prove his charge, offers to refer the decision of the cause to the oath of his adversary: which the adversary was bound to accept, or tender the same proposal back again; otherwise the whole was taken as confessed by him." 3 William Blackstone, *Commentaries on the Laws of England* 342 (1768).

sacramentum fidelitatis (sak-rə-**men**-təm fi-del-ə-**tay**-tis). [Law Latin] (17c) *Hist.* The oath of fidelity, given by a vassal to a lord.

sacrilege (**sak**-rə-lij). (13c) **1.** The act or an instance of desecrating or profaning a sacred thing. **2.** *Hist.* Larceny of sacred objects, as from a church; esp., the breaking into a church with intent to commit a felony, or breaking out after committing a felony; burglary of a church. **3.** *Hist.* The selling to a layman of property given for religious purposes. — **sacrilegious,** *adj.*

sacrilegium (sak-rə-**lee**-jee-əm), *n.* [Latin fr. *sacer* "sacred" + *legere* "to steal"] *Roman law.* **1.** The theft of a sacred thing, usu. a capital offense. See CAPITALIS. **2.** Violation of an imperial law.

> "In the later Empire the conception of *sacrilegium* was somewhat distorted and those 'who through ignorance or negligence confound, violate and offend the sanctity of a divine law' . . . were considered guilty of *sacrilegium*. 'Divine' is here used in the sense of imperial, issued by the emperor . . . . Thus *sacrilegium* and *sacrilegus* became rather general terms applied to the neglect or violation of imperial orders or enactments." Adolf Berger, *Encyclopedic Dictionary of Roman Law* 689 (1953).

sacrilegus (sə-**kril**-ə-gəs), *adj.* & *n.* [Latin "sacrilegious"] *Roman law.* (A person) guilty of *sacrilegium.* See SACRILEGIUM.

sacristan (**sak**-ri-stən). [Latin] (15c) *Hist.* A caretaker of a church; a sexton of a church.

sacristy (**sak**-ri-stee). See VESTRY (1).

sadaq. See MAHR.

saemend (**see**-mənd). [Old English] *Hist.* An arbitrator; an umpire.

SAET. *abbr.* SUBSTANCE-ABUSE EVALUATION AND TREATMENT.

saevitia (si-**vish**-ee-ə). [Latin fr. *saevus* "cruel"] *Hist.* Cruelty in a marriage, as a result of which cohabitation is dangerous enough to justify a decree of separation.

SAFE. *abbr.* Sexual-assault forensic examiner.

safe, *adj.* (14c) **1.** Not exposed to danger; not causing danger <driving at a safe limit of speed>. **2.** Unlikely to be overturned or proved wrong.

safe-berth clause. (1950) *Maritime law.* A provision in a voyage or time charterparty obligating the charterer to choose a berth for loading and unloading the chartered ship where the ship will be safe from damage. • The ship's master can refuse to enter the berth without breaching the charter. But if the master reasonably enters the berth and the ship is damaged, the charterer is liable. Cf. SAFE-PORT CLAUSE.

safe blower. (1867) Someone who uses explosives to open a safe, esp. for the purpose of stealing the contents. Cf. SAFE CRACKER.

safe breaker. See SAFE CRACKER.

safe conduct. (14c) *Int'l law.* **1.** A privilege granted by a belligerent allowing an enemy, a neutral, or some other person to travel within or through a designated area for a specified purpose. **2.** A document conveying this privilege. — Sometimes written *safe-conduct.* — Also termed *safe passage*; *safeguard*; *passport.*

> "Passports and safeguards, or safe conducts, are letters of protection, with or without an escort, by which the person of an enemy is rendered inviolable. These may be given in order to carry on the peculiar commerce of war, or for reasons which have no relation to it, which terminate in the person himself." Theodore D. Woolsey, *Introduction to the Study of International Law* § 155, at 265 (5th ed. 1878).

> "Safe-conduct . . . . The grantee is inviolable so long as he complies with the conditions imposed on him or necessitated by the circumstances of the case. Unless stated, a safe-conduct does not cover goods or luggage. They may be given also for ships and for goods. To be effective under international law the grant must have been arranged between belligerents." David M. Walker, *The Oxford Companion to Law* 1098 (1980).

safe cracker. (1873) Someone who breaks into a safe, esp. for the purpose of stealing the contents. — Also termed *safe breaker.* Cf. SAFE BLOWER.

safe-deposit box. (1874) A lockbox stored in a bank's vault to secure a customer's valuables. • It usu. takes two keys (one held by the bank and one held by the customer) to open the box. — Often shortened to *deposit box.* — Also termed *safety-deposit box.*

safe-deposit company. See DEPOSITARY (1).

safeguard. See SAFE CONDUCT.

safeguarding. The ensuring of a person's or thing's security, esp. from loss or theft; SAFEKEEPING (1).

safe harbor. (1960) **1.** An area or means of protection. **2.** A provision (as in a statute or regulation) that affords protection from liability or penalty. • SEC regulations, for example, provide a safe harbor for an issuer's business forecasts that are made in good faith. — Also termed *safe-harbor clause*; *safe-harbor provision.*

safe-haven law. (1985) *Family law.* A statute that protects a parent who abandons a baby at a designated place such as a hospital, a physician's office, or a fire station, where it can receive emergency medical assistance as needed. • The law typically stipulates that a parent who leaves a baby at such a place will not be publicly identified or prosecuted. Such laws have been enacted in many states in response to a perceived increase in incidents of child abandonment. — Also termed *Baby Moses law.*

safe house. (1928) A residence where people live under protection, usu. in anonymity. • Safe houses are operated for a range of purposes, both legal and illegal. Shelters for abused spouses and runaway children are safe houses. Law-enforcement agencies keep safe houses for undercover operations and to protect witnesses who have been threatened. Lawbreakers use them to shield criminal activity such as drug manufacturing.

safekeeping. (15c) **1.** The act of protecting something in one's custody; secure guardianship. — Also termed *safeguarding.* **2.** Under the Securities Investors Protection Act, the holding of a security on behalf of the investor or broker that has paid for it. 15 USCA § 78lll(2).

safe passage. See SAFE CONDUCT.

safe-pledge. See PLEDGE (5).

safe-port clause. (1951) *Maritime law.* A provision in a voyage or time charterparty obligating the charterer to choose a port where the ship will be safe from damage. • The ship's master can refuse to enter the port without breaching the charter. But if the master reasonably enters the port and the ship is damaged, the charterer is liable. Cf. SAFE-BERTH CLAUSE.

safe product. See PRODUCT.

safe-storage statute. (1999) A law that prohibits persons from leaving firearms unattended in places where children may gain access to them. — Also termed *child-access prevention statute.*

Safety Appliance Act. A federal law regulating the safety of equipment used by railroads in interstate commerce. 49 USCA §§ 20301 et seq. — Abbr. SAA.

safety-deposit box. See SAFE-DEPOSIT BOX.

safety engineering. (1911) The inspection and study of potentially dangerous conditions, usu. in an industrial environment, so that precautionary measures can be taken.

safety hearing. *Criminal law.* An administrative hearing held by a department of motor vehicles to decide whether a motorist's license should be suspended, as when a motorist has refused a chemical test or has caused a fatality. See *refusal hearing, fatality hearing* under HEARING.

safety net. (1877) **1.** A meshed fabric designed to catch and cushion something or someone that might fall, esp. from a dangerous height. **2.** A system or arrangement that exists to help anyone who has serious problems or gets into a difficult predicament.— Also termed *social safety net.* **3.** A guarantee designed to protect someone against an adverse contingency.

safety officer. See OFFICER (1).

safe workplace. (1910) A place of employment in which all dangers that should reasonably be removed have been removed; a place of employment that is reasonably safe given the nature of the work performed. See OCCUPATIONAL SAFETY AND HEALTH ADMINISTRATION.

sagibaro (**sag**-ə-bar-oh), *n.* [Old English] (17c) *Hist.* A determiner of disputes; a judge. — Also termed *sachbaro* (**sak**-bar-oh).

said, *adj.* (13c) Aforesaid; above-mentioned. • The adjective *said* is obsolescent in legal drafting, its last bastion being patent claims. But even in that context the word is giving way to the ordinary word *the,* which if properly used is equally precise. See AFORESAID.

> "The word 'said' is used by many practitioners rather than 'the' to refer back to previously recited elements, sometimes to a previously cited anything. This practice is unobjectionable, although perhaps overly legalistic. If 'saids' or 'thes' are used, one should be consistent in the usage and not alternate between those words in repetitions of the same element or among different elements." Robert C. Faber, *Landis on Mechanics of Patent Claim Drafting* § 23, at 50 (3d ed. 1990).

sailor. See SEAMAN.

sailor's will. See *soldier's will* under WILL.

Saint Lawrence Seaway Development Corporation. A wholly-owned corporation in the U.S. Department of Transportation responsible for developing, operating, and maintaining a part of the St. Lawrence Seaway from Montreal to Lake Erie. • It charges tolls at rates negotiated with the St. Lawrence Seaway Authority of Canada. — Abbr. SLSDC.

sake and soke (sayk / sohk). (16c) *Hist.* A lord's right to hold court and compel attendance. — Also spelled *sak and soc* (sak / sok). See SOC.

salable (**say**-lə-bəl *or* **sayl**-ə-bəl), *adj.* (16c) Fit for sale in the usual course of trade at the usual selling price; MERCHANTABLE. — **salability** (say-lə-**bil**-ə-tee *or* sayl-ə-**bil**-ə-tee), *n.*

salable value. See *fair market value* under VALUE (2).

salarium (sə-**lair**-ee-əm), *n.* [Latin "salt money"] **1.** *Roman law.* An allowance, esp. for living expenses, given to persons in noble professions (such as teachers or doctors) who were not allowed to sue for fees. **2.** *Roman law.* Wages for persons engaged in military service on an emergency basis. • The regular soldier's pay is a *stipendium.* **3.** *Hist.* The rent or profits of a hall or house.

salary. (13c) An agreed compensation for services — esp. professional or semiprofessional services — usu. paid at regular intervals on a yearly basis, as distinguished from an hourly basis. • Salaried positions are usu. exempt from the requirements of the Fair Labor Standards Act (on overtime and the like) but are subject to state regulation. Cf. WAGE, *n.*

▸ **accrued salary.** (1893) A salary that has been earned but not yet paid.

sale, *n.* (bef. 12c) **1.** The transfer of property or title for a price. *See* UCC § 2-106(1). **2.** The agreement by which such a transfer takes place. • The four elements are (1) parties competent to contract, (2) mutual assent, (3) a thing capable of being transferred, and (4) a price in money paid or promised.

> "A sale is a transfer of the absolute title to property for a certain agreed price. It is a contract between two parties, one of whom acquires thereby a property in the thing sold, and the other parts with it for a valuable consideration. If the property in any commodity be voluntarily transferred without a valuable consideration, it is a gift; if one article be exchanged for another, it is a barter; but a sale takes place only, when there is a transfer of the title to property, for a price." William W. Story, *A Treatise on the Law of Sales of Personal Property* § 1, at 1 (1853).

▸ **absolute sale.** (17c) A sale in which possession and title to the property pass to the buyer immediately upon the completion of the bargain. Cf. *conditional sale.*

▸ **approval sale.** See *sale on approval.*

▸ **auction sale.** See AUCTION.

▸ **average gross sales.** (1927) The amount of total sales divided by the number of sales transactions in a specific period.

▸ **bargain sale.** See BARGAIN SALE.

▸ **bona fide sale.** (18c) A sale made by a seller in good faith, for valuable consideration, and without notice of a defect in title or any other reason not to hold the sale.

▸ **bootstrap sale.** (1960) **1.** A sale in which the purchase price is financed by earnings and profits of the thing sold; esp., a leveraged buyout. See BUYOUT. **2.** A seller's tax-saving conversion of a business's ordinary income into a capital gain from the sale of corporate stock.

▸ **bulk sale.** See BULK SALE.

▸ **cash-against-documents sale.** See *documentary sale.*

▸ **cash sale.** (1823) **1.** A sale in which cash payment is concurrent with the receipt of the property sold. **2.** A securities transaction on the stock-exchange floor requiring cash payment and same-day delivery.

▸ **compulsory sale.** (18c) The forced sale of real property in accordance with either an eminent-domain order or an order for a judicial sale arising from nonpayment of taxes.

▸ **conditional sale.** (18c) **1.** A sale in which the buyer gains immediate possession but the seller retains title until the buyer performs a condition, esp. payment of the full purchase price. See *retail installment contract* under CONTRACT. **2.** A sale accompanied by an agreement to resell on specified terms. Cf. *absolute sale.*

▸ **consignment sale.** (1930) A sale of an owner's property (such as clothing or furniture) by a third party entrusted to make the sale. UCC § 9-102(a)(20). See CONSIGNMENT.

▸ **consumer-credit sale.** (1966) A sale in which the seller extends credit to the consumer. • A consumer-credit sale includes a lease in which the lessee's rental payments equal or exceed the retail value of the item rented.

▸ **consumer sale.** (1941) A retail transaction in which something is sold in the normal course of a seller's business and is bought for private use and not in the normal course of the buyer's business.

▸ **convoyed sale.** *Patents.* The sale of unpatented collateral products that are functionally or economically related to the sale of an infringing product. • The sale of such products may be considered in awarding patent damages in certain cases.

▸ **credit sale.** (1822) A sale of goods to a buyer who is allowed to pay for the goods at a later time.

▸ **distress sale.** (1883) **1.** A form of liquidation in which the seller receives less for the goods than what would be received under normal sales conditions; esp., a going-out-of-business sale. **2.** A foreclosure or tax sale.

▸ **dock sale.** (1949) A sale in which a purchaser takes possession of the product at the seller's shipping dock, esp. for transportation outside the state.

▸ **documentary sale.** (1936) A sale in which the buyer pays upon the seller's tender of documents of title covering the goods, plus a sight draft requiring the buyer to pay "at sight." • This type of sale typically occurs before delivery of the goods, which might be en route when the buyer pays. — Also termed *cash-against-documents sale.*

▸ **exclusive sale.** (18c) A sale made by a broker under an exclusive-agency listing. See *exclusive-agency listing* under LISTING.

▸ **execution sale.** (1843) A forced sale of a debtor's property by a government official carrying out a writ of execution. — Also termed *forced sale; judgment sale; sheriff's sale.* See EXECUTION.

▸ **executory sale.** (1839) A sale agreed on in principle but with a few minor details remaining.

▸ **fair sale.** (16c) A foreclosure sale or other judicial sale conducted with fairness toward the rights and interests of the affected parties.

▸ **fire sale.** (1891) **1.** A sale of merchandise at reduced prices because of fire or water damage. **2.** Any sale at greatly reduced prices, esp. because of an emergency. • Fire sales are often regulated to protect the public from deceptive sales practices.

▸ **forced sale.** (18c) **1.** See *execution sale.* **2.** A hurried sale by a debtor because of financial hardship or a creditor's action. Cf. *voluntary sale.*

▸ **foreclosure sale.** (1855) The sale of mortgaged property, authorized by a court decree or a power-of-sale clause, to satisfy the debt. See FORECLOSURE.

▸ **fraudulent sale.** (18c) A sale made to defraud the seller's creditors by converting into cash property that should be used to satisfy the creditors' claims.

▸ **gross sales.** (16c) Total sales (esp. in retail) before deductions for returns and allowances. — Also termed *sales in gross.*

▸ **installment sale.** See INSTALLMENT SALE.

▸ **isolated sale.** (1855) An infrequent or one-time sale that does not carry an implied warranty of merchantability because the seller is not a merchant with respect to goods of that kind. UCC § 2-314(1).

▸ **judgment sale.** See *execution sale.*

▸ **judicial sale.** (18c) A sale conducted under the authority of a judgment or court order, such as an execution sale. — Also termed *sheriff's sale.*

▸ **lumping sale.** (1803) A court-ordered sale in which several distinct pieces of property are sold together for a single sum.

▸ **memorandum sale.** (1966) A conditional sale in which the buyer takes possession but does not accept title until approving the property.

▸ **net sale.** (18c) The amount of money remaining from a sale, after deducting returns, allowances, rebates, discounts, and other expenses.

▸ **perfect sale.** See EMPTIO PERFECTA.

▸ **present sale.** Under the UCC, a sale accomplished by the making of a contract. UCC § 2-106(1).

▸ **private sale.** (18c) An unadvertised sale negotiated and concluded directly between the buyer and seller, not through an agent.

▸ **public sale.** (16c) **1.** A sale made after public notice, such as an auction or sheriff's sale; specif., a sale to which the public has been invited by advertisement to appear and bid at auction for the items to be sold. **2.** *Patents.* An actual exchange for value or an offer through some medium (e.g., a sales brochure) of an article, product, or process to a member of the general public.

▸ **retail installment sale.** See INSTALLMENT SALE.

▸ **sale against the box.** See *short sale against the box.*

▸ **sale and leaseback.** See LEASEBACK.

▸ **sale and return.** See *sale or return.*

▸ **sale as is.** A sale in which the buyer accepts the property in its existing condition unless the seller has misrepresented its quality. — Also termed *sale with all faults.*

▸ **sale by sample.** (18c) A sale in which the parties understand that the goods exhibited constitute the standard with which the goods not exhibited correspond and to which all deliveries should conform. • Any sample that is made part of the basis of the bargain creates an express warranty that the whole of the goods will conform to the sample or model. *See* UCC § 2-313(1)(c). — Also termed *sample sale.*

▸ **sale in gross.** (17c) **1.** A sale of a tract of land made with no guarantee about the exact amount or size of the land being sold. **2.** (*pl.*) See *gross sales.*

▸ **sale-leaseback.** See LEASEBACK.

▸ **sale on approval.** (1847) A sale in which completion hinges on the buyer's satisfaction, regardless of whether the goods conform to the contract. • Title and risk of loss remain with the seller until the buyer approves. UCC § 2-326(1)(a). — Also termed *approval sale.*

▸ **sale on credit.** (18c) A sale accompanied by delivery of possession, but with payment deferred to a later date.

▸ **sale or return.** A sale in which the buyer may return the goods to the seller, regardless of whether they conform to the contract, if the goods were delivered primarily for resale. • This transaction is a type of consignment in which the seller (usu. a distributor) sells goods to the buyer (often a retailer), who then tries to resell the goods, but a buyer who cannot resell is allowed to return them to the seller. Title and risk of loss are with the buyer until the goods are returned. UCC § 2-326(1)(b). — Also termed *sale and return.* Cf. SALES GUARANTEED.

▸ **sale per aversionem** (pər ə-vər-zhee-**oh**-nəm). (1826) *Civil law.* A conveyance of all immovable property that falls within the boundaries stated in a purchase agreement, as opposed to a specified amount of acreage. • The sales price will not be modified because of a surplus or shortage in the amount of property that is exchanged, because the boundary description is the binding definition of the property conveyed. La. Civ. Code art. 2495.

▸ **sale positive.** (1873) A sale with no reserve price.

▸ **sale short.** See *short sale.*

▸ **sales in gross.** See *gross sales.*

▸ **sale with all faults.** See *sale as is.*

▸ **sale with right of redemption.** (1836) A sale in which the seller reserves the right to retake the goods by refunding the purchase price.

▸ **sample sale.** See *sale by sample.*

▸ **sheriff's sale.** **1.** See *execution sale.* **2.** See *judicial sale.*

▸ **short sale.** (1870) *Securities.* A sale of a security that the seller does not own or has not contracted for at the time of sale, and that the seller must borrow to make delivery. • Such a sale is usu. made when the seller expects the security's price to drop. If the price does drop, the seller can make a profit on the difference between the price of the shares sold and the lower price of the shares bought to pay back the borrowed shares. — Also termed *sale short.*

▸ **short sale against the box.** (1934) *Securities.* A short sale of a security by a seller who owns enough shares of the security to cover the sale but borrows shares anyway because the seller wants to keep ownership a secret or because the owned shares are not easily accessible. • Delivery may be made with either the owned or the borrowed shares, so it is less risky than an ordinary short sale. The phrase *against the box* refers to the owned shares that are in safekeeping; formerly, the "box" was a container used to store stock certificates. — Often shortened to *sale against the box.*

▸ **similar sales.** *Eminent domain.* Sales of like property in the same locality and time frame, admissible in a condemnation action to determine the market value of the particular property at issue.

▸ **simulated sale.** (1817) A sale in which no price or other consideration is paid or intended to be paid, and in which there is no intent to actually transfer ownership. • Simulated sales are usu. done in an attempt to put property beyond the reach of creditors. — Also termed *simulated transaction.*

▸ **tax sale.** (1818) A sale of property because of nonpayment of taxes. See *tax deed* under DEED.

▸ **voluntary sale.** (17c) A sale made freely with the seller's consent. Cf. *forced sale.*

▸ **wash sale.** (1848) *Securities.* A sale of securities made at about the same time as a purchase of the same securities (such as within 30 days), resulting in no change in beneficial ownership. • A loss from a wash sale is usu. not tax-deductible. And securities laws prohibit a wash sale made to create the false appearance of market activity. — Also termed *wash transaction.*

sale against the box. See *short sale against the box* under SALE.

sale and exchange. See SALE OR EXCHANGE.

sale and leaseback. See LEASEBACK.

sale and return. See *sale or return* under SALE.

sale as is. See SALE.

sale by sample. See SALE.

sale in gross. See SALE.

sale-leaseback. See LEASEBACK.

sale note. See NOTE (1).

sale-of-business doctrine. (1981) The outmoded rule holding that the transfer of stock incident to the sale of a business does not constitute a transfer of securities. • This doctrine was rejected by the U.S. Supreme Court in *Landreth Timber Co. v. Landreth*, 471 U.S. 681, 105 S.Ct. 2297 (1985), and its companion case, *Gould v. Ruefenacht*, 471 U.S. 701, 105 S.Ct. 2308 (1985).

sale of land. (16c) A transfer of title to real estate from one person to another by a contract of sale. • A transfer of real estate is often referred to as a conveyance rather than a sale.

sale on approval. See SALE.

sale on credit. See SALE.

sale or exchange. (1905) **1.** *Tax.* A voluntary transfer of property for value (as distinguished from a gift) resulting in a gain or loss recognized for federal tax purposes. **2.** A transfer of property; esp., a situation in which proceeds of a sale are to be vested in another estate of the same character and use. — Also termed (in both senses) *sale and exchange.*

sale or return. See SALE.

sale per aversionem. See SALE.

sale positive. See SALE.

sales agreement. (1920) A contract in which ownership of property is transferred from a seller to a buyer for a fixed sum at a fixed date. UCC § 2-106(1).

sales-assessment-ratio study. (1955) A method for calculating the assessment level for taxable property in a jurisdiction by comparing the assessed value and the actual sales price of a statistically reliable sample of nearby property to determine the percentage by which the assessed values differ from the sales prices.

sales bill. See *sales draft* under DRAFT (1).

sales bill of exchange. See *sales draft* under DRAFT (1).

sales draft. See DRAFT (1).

sales finance company. See FINANCE COMPANY.

sales guaranteed. *Hist.* As used in a sale-of-goods contract, the seller's promise to accept the purchaser's return of unsold or unsalable goods and to grant the purchaser a proportional credit or refund. • Under the UCC, the modern equivalent is *sale or return.* Cf. *sale or return* under SALE.

sale short. See *short sale* under SALE.

sales in gross. See *gross sales* under SALE.

sales invoice. See INVOICE.

sales journal. (1892) A book used to record sales of merchandise on account.

sales load. See LOAD.

sales mix. (1951) The relative combination of individual-product sales to total sales.

sales price. See PRICE.

sales puffery. See PUFFING (1).

sales slip, *n.* A small piece of paper that a customer is given upon buying and paying for something; RECEIPT (2).

sales talk. See PUFFING (1).

sales tax. See TAX.

sale with all faults. See *sale as is* under SALE.

sale with right of redemption. See SALE.

Salic law (**sal**-ik *or* **say**-lik). (16c) An influential early medieval Frankish code of law that originated with the Salian Franks and that deals with a variety of civil property and family issues but is primarily a penal code listing the punishments for various crimes. • Salic law is the principal compilation of the early Germanic laws known collectively as *leges barbarorum* ("laws of the barbarians"). Salic law also designated a rule barring females from the line of succession to the throne, as a result of which references to *Salic law* have sometimes referred only to the code provision excluding women from inheriting certain lands (which probably existed only because military duties were connected with the inheritance). In the late 19th century, Oliver Wendell Holmes revived scholarly interest in Salic law by referring to it throughout *The Common Law* (1881). — Also termed *Salique law*; *law Salique* (sə-**leek** *or* **sal**-ik); *lex Salica* (leks **sal**-ə-kə); *Carolingian law.*

salic marriage. See *morganatic marriage* under MARRIAGE (1).

salting, *n. Labor law.* A union tactic whereby a paid union employee goes to work for a targeted nonunion employer with the intention of organizing the workforce. • The union agent (known as a *salt*) is considered an employee of the nonunion company and is protected by the National Labor Relations Act.

salus (**sal**-əs), *n.* [Latin] (13c) Health; prosperity; safety.

salva gardia. See DE SALVA GARDIA.

salvage (**sal**-vij), *n.* (17c) **1.** The rescue of imperiled property; esp., the act of saving a ship from loss, as in a storm, a fire, or a pirate attack.

▸ **civil salvage.** (1815) The rescue of maritime property in a situation unconnected with a war.

▸ **military salvage.** (1801) The rescue of maritime property from the enemy in time of war.

2. The property saved or remaining after a fire or other loss, sometimes retained by an insurance company that has compensated the owner for the loss. **3.** Property that is no longer useful but has scrap value. **4.** Compensation allowed to a person who, having no duty to do so, helps save a ship or its cargo; reward for saving a ship, the lives of crew members, or cargo, esp. from fire or capture, despite having no duty to do so. • Salvage in this sense is payable by the shipowner or cargo owner to the salvor. — Also termed (in sense 3) *salvage award*; *reward.* — **salvage,** *vb.*

> "Salvage is a reward payable either by the shipowner or by the owners of goods carried in the ship to persons who save the ship or cargo from shipwreck, capture or other loss. The right to salvage is an ancient rule of maritime law and is not based on contractual rights. The actual amount payable is, as a rule, assessed by the Court. Sometimes an express agreement, fixing an amount, is made before the assistance is rendered, but this is not a question of salvage in the strict sense, which always implies service by persons who are under no obligation to render it." 2 E.W. Chance, *Principles of Mercantile Law* 98 (P.W. French ed., 10th ed. 1951).

> "With reference to aid rendered to distressed property on navigable waters the word 'salvage' is often used indifferently to describe the salvage operation and the salvage operation and the salvage award — the latter being the compensation granted for the services rendered." Martin J. Norris, *The Law of Salvage* § 2, at 2 (1958).

> "A salvage award, or reward, is the compensation allowed to the volunteer whose services on navigable waters have aided distressed property in whole or in part. The award is not regarded merely as pay on the principle of quantum meruit or as remuneration pro opera et labore, but as a reward to persons participating and the owners of salving property, voluntarily rendering their services and to encourage others to similarly undertake the saving of life and property. That part of the award constituting more than quantum meruit has, on occasions, been referred to as a 'bounty,' 'gratuity,' and 'bonus.'" Martin J. Norris, *The Law of Salvage* § 3, at 3–4 (1958).

salvage award. See SALVAGE (4).

salvage charges. (18c) *Insurance.* Costs necessarily incurred in salvage.

salvage corps. (1883) A body of men and women who work with a fire department, sometimes with the support of insurance companies, to save property during or after a fire.

salvagee (sal-və-**jee**), *n.* (1941) *Maritime law.* A person in whose favor salvage has been accomplished; a person on whose behalf a salvor works.

salvage loss. See LOSS.

salvager. See SALVOR.

salvage service. (1804) The aid or rescue given, either voluntarily or by contract, to a vessel in need of assistance because of present or apprehended danger. • Although salvage may involve towing, it is distinguished from *towing service*, which is rendered merely to expedite a voyage, not to respond to dangerous circumstances. Under federal law, there is a two-year statute of limitations to sue for remuneration for salvage services performed. *See* 46 USCA § 80107(c).

salvage value. See VALUE (2).

salvam fecit totius pignoris causam (**sal**-vəm **fee**-sit **toh**-shee-əs **pig**-nə-ris **kaw**-zəm). [Law Latin] *Scots law.* He furnished the means of saving the whole pledge. • A bottomry creditor posting the last bond obtained preference over the remaining bottomry creditors because the later loan preserved the property for the earlier creditors. See *bottomry bond* under BOND (2).

salva substantia (**sal**-və səb-**stan**-shee-ə). [Latin] (17c) *Roman & civil law.* The substance (of the property) being preserved; the substance remaining intact. — Also termed *salva rei substantia.*

> "A right of liferent, therefore, cannot be constituted in a subject which necessarily perishes in the use; it must be a subject which can be used *salva substantia*." John Trayner, *Trayner's Latin Maxims* 563 (4th ed. 1894).

salvo (**sal**-voh). [Latin fr. *salvus* "safe"] *Hist.* **1.** Saving; excepting. • This term was used in deeds. **2.** A saving clause; a proviso.

salvo beneficio competentiae (**sal**-voh ben-ə-**fish**-ee-oh kom-pə-**ten**-shee-ee). [Latin] (1837) *Hist.* Saving the benefit of being held liable only to the extent that one's means permit. See BENEFICIUM COMPETENTIAE.

salvo conductu. See DE SALVO CONDUCTU.

salvo jure (**sal**-voh **joor**-ee). [Latin "the rule being safe"] (17c) Without prejudice to; the right being preserved.

salvor (**sal**-vər), *n.* [Law Latin] (17c) **1.** Someone who saves; esp., one who saves a vessel or its cargo from danger or loss. See SALVAGE (1). **2.** Someone who rescues a person from drowning. **3.** A vessel used in salvage. — Also spelled *salver.* — Also termed *salvager.*

> "A 'salvor' is a person who, without any particular relation to a ship in distress, proffers useful service, and gives it as a volunteer adventurer, without any pre-existing covenant that connected him with the duty of employing himself for the preservation of the ship. To be a salvor, one must have the intention and capacity to save the distressed property involved, but need not have an intent to acquire it." 68 Am. Jur. 2d *Salvage* § 2, at 270 (1993).

salvus plegius (**sal**-vəs **plee**-jee-əs). [Law Latin] (17c) *Hist.* A safe pledge; a satisfactory pledge. See PLEDGE. — Also termed *certus plegius.*

SAM. *abbr.* See *shared-appreciation mortgage* under MORTGAGE.

same, *adj.* Identical or equal; resembling in every relevant respect.

same, *pron.* (14c) The very thing just mentioned or described; it or them <two days after receiving the goods, Mr. Siviglio returned same>.

same-actor inference. (1995) *Employment law.* The doctrine that when an employee is hired and fired by the same person, esp. when the termination occurs a reasonably short time after the hiring, the termination will be presumed not to be based on a discriminatory reason. • Proximity between the hiring and firing is not an essential element of the same-actor inference if the employee's protected class has not changed.

same-conduct test. (1951) *Criminal law.* A test for determining whether a later charge arising out of a single incident is barred by the Double Jeopardy Clause; specif., an analysis of whether the later charge requires the state to prove the same conduct that it was required to prove in a previous trial against the same defendant. • The Supreme Court abandoned the *Blockburger* test and adopted the same-conduct test in 1990 (*Grady v. Corbin*, 495 U.S. 508, 110 S.Ct. 2084), but overruled that decision and revived *Blockburger* three years later (*U.S. v. Dixon*, 509 U.S. 688, 113 S.Ct. 2849 (1993)). Cf. BLOCKBURGER TEST; SAME-TRANSACTION TEST.

same-elements test. 1. See BLOCKBURGER TEST. **2.** See LEGAL-ELEMENTS TEST.

same-evidence test. See BLOCKBURGER TEST.

same invention. *Patents.* **1.** A second invention claiming the identical subject matter as a previous invention. **2.** Within a reissue statute, the invention described in the original patent.

same-invention double patenting. See *statutory double patenting* under DOUBLE PATENTING.

same-invention double patenting rejection. See *statutory double patenting rejection* under REJECTION.

same offense. See OFFENSE (2).

same-sex harassment. See *same-sex sexual harassment* under SEXUAL HARASSMENT.

same-sex marriage. See MARRIAGE (1).

same-sex sexual harassment. See SEXUAL HARASSMENT.

same-transaction test. (1888) *Criminal law.* A double-jeopardy test, never adopted, that would require the government to bring all charges arising out of a single incident against a defendant in one prosecution. • Beginning in 1959, Justice Brennan advocated for the same-transaction test. *See Abbate v. U.S.*, 359 U.S. 187, 79 S.Ct. 666 (1959); *Harris v. Okla.*, 433 U.S. 682, 97 S.Ct. 2912 (1977). While Justice Brennan's argument has been adopted in several states, the Supreme Court of the United States has consistently rejected it. *See, e.g., U.S. v. Dixon*, 509 U.S. 688, 113 S.Ct. 2849 (1993). Cf. BLOCKBURGER TEST; SAME-CONDUCT TEST.

same-wrongdoer rule. (1991) *Commercial law.* A rule that places the risk of loss on a bank customer for later forgeries by the same wrongdoer if the customer has not notified the bank of the initial forgery within 30 days of receiving the bank statement showing the transaction. *See* UCC § 4-406(d)(2). — Also termed *same-wrongdoer defense.*

sample sale. See *sale by sample* under SALE.

sampling, *n.* (1986) *Copyright.* The process of taking a small portion of a sound recording and digitally manipulating it as part of a new recording. • Sampling may infringe the copyright of the sample's source, esp. the musical-works and sound-recording copyrights. — Also termed *digital sampling.*

sanae mentis (**san**-ee **men**-tis). [Law Latin] *Hist.* Of sound mind; of sane mind.

sancire (san-**SI**-ree), *vb.* [Latin] *Roman law.* To enact; confirm; prescribe.

sanctio (**sangk**-shee-oh), *n.* [Latin fr. *sancio* "to ordain, confirm, or forbid under penalty"] *Roman law.* A particular clause in a statute imposing a penalty on any violation of that statute. Pl. ***sanctiones*** (sangk-shee-**oh**-neez).

> "Sanctio (legis). A clause in a statute which strengthens its efficacity by fixing a penalty for its violation, by forbidding its derogation through a later enactment, or by releasing from responsibility any one who by acting in accordance with the statute violated another law. The purpose of the sanction clause was to settle the relation between the new statute and former and future legislation. Thus the *sanctio* could also state that a previous statute remained fully or partially in force without being changed by the new one." Adolf Berger, *Encyclopedic Dictionary of Roman Law* 689 (1953).

sanction (**sangk**-shən), *n.* (15c) **1.** Official approval or authorization; solemn and final confirmation <the committee gave sanction to the proposal>. Cf. RATIFICATION (1). **2.** A provision that gives force to a legal imperative by either rewarding obedience or punishing disobedience.

▸ **punitive sanction.** (1878) A penalty for some legal infraction.

▸ **remunerative sanction.** (2011) A reward for obedience to a legal requirement. — Also termed *remuneratory infraction.*

3. A penalty or coercive measure that results from failure to comply with a law, rule, or order <a sanction for discovery abuse>. • This negative sense represents a narrowing of sense 2. The pejorative became much more common because the law tends to punish much more than it rewards. So sense 3 now is far more usual than sense 2. Essentially, sense 3 is a shortened version of *punitive sanction.* Cf. DISCIPLINE (1).

"Without adequate sanctions the procedure for discovery would often be ineffectual. Under Rule 37 [of the Federal Rules of Civil Procedure], . . . any party or person who seeks to evade or thwart full and candid discovery incurs the risk of serious consequences, which may involve imprisonment for contempt of court, an order that designated facts be taken to be established, an order refusing the delinquent party the right to support or oppose designated claims or defenses, striking out pleadings or parts of pleadings, rendering judgment by default, dismissal of the action or a claim therein, or assessment of expenses and attorney's fees. Sanctions are intended to prompt a party to respond." 8A Charles Alan Wright et al., Federal Practice and Procedure § 2281, at 595–95 (2d ed. 1994).

▸ **criminal sanction.** (1872) A sanction attached to a criminal conviction, such as a fine or restitution. — Also termed *penal sanction*.

"A criminal sanction . . . is a legally authorized post-conviction deprivation suffered by a human being through governmental action. By using the words 'post-conviction' in that definition, criminal sanctions are thus limited to those imposed upon defendants in criminal proceedings who, by reason or in consequence of a judgment entered upon a verdict of guilty found by a jury, or judge sitting without a jury (the latter having been legally waived), or upon a plea of guilty, or a plea of nolo contendere, stand convicted." *A Treatise on the Law of Crimes* § 2.00, at 66 (Marian Quinn Barnes ed., 7th ed. 1967).

▸ **death-penalty sanction.** (1991) *Civil procedure.* A court's order dismissing the suit or entering a default judgment in favor of the plaintiff because of extreme discovery abuses by a party or because of a party's action or inaction that shows an unwillingness to participate in the case. • Such a sanction is rarely ordered, and is usu. preceded by orders of lesser sanctions that have not been complied with or that have not remedied the problem. — Often shortened to *death penalty*.

▸ **discovery sanction.** (1956) A penalty levied by a court against a party or attorney who abuses the discovery process or inexcusably fails to comply with another party's discovery requests or the court's discovery orders.

▸ **restorative-justice sanction.** (1848) An alternative delinquency sanction focused on repairing the harm done, meeting the victim's needs, and holding the offender responsible for his or her actions. • Restorative-justice sanctions use a balanced approach, producing the least restrictive disposition while stressing the offender's accountability and providing relief to the victim. The offender may be ordered to make restitution, to perform community service, or to make amends in some other way that the court orders.

▸ **shame sanction.** (1991) A criminal sanction designed to stigmatize or disgrace a convicted offender, and often to alert the public about the offender's conviction. • A shame sanction usu. publicly associates the offender with the crime that he or she committed. An example is being required to post a sign in one's yard stating, "Convicted Child Molester Lives Here." — Also termed *shame sentence*; *shaming sanction*; *shaming sentence*; *scarlet-letter punishment*; *scarlet-letter sentence*.

4. *Int'l law.* An economic or military coercive measure taken by one or more countries toward another to force it to comply with international law <U.N. sanctions against a renegade nation>.

sanction, *vb.* (18c) **1.** To approve, authorize, or support <the court will sanction the trust disposition if it is not against public policy>. **2.** To penalize by imposing a sanction <the court sanctioned the attorney for violating the gag order>.

sanctionable, *adj.* (18c) **1.** (Of conduct or action) meriting punishment by sanction; likely to be punished by sanction. **2.** Worthy of approbation or approval.

sanctional enforcement. See *secondary right* under RIGHT.

sanctioning right. See *secondary right* under RIGHT.

sanctions tort. A means of recovery for another party's discovery abuse, whereby the judge orders the abusive party to pay a fine to the injured party for the discovery violation. • This is not a tort in the traditional sense, but rather a form of punishment that results in monetary gain for the injured party.

sanctity of contract. (1831) The principle that the parties to a contract, having duly entered into it, must honor their obligations under it.

"[Sanctity of contract] is merely another facet of freedom of contract, but the two concepts cover, to some extent, different grounds. The sanctity of contractual obligations is merely an expression of the principle that once a contract is freely and voluntarily entered into, it should be held sacred, and should be enforced by the Courts if it is broken. No doubt this very sanctity was an outcome of freedom of contract, for the reason why contracts were held sacred was the fact that the parties entered into them of their own choice and volition, and settled the terms by mutual agreement." P.S. Atiyah, *An Introduction to the Law of Contract* 12 (3d ed. 1981).

sanctuary. (14c) **1.** A safe place, esp. where legal process cannot be executed; asylum.

"Every consecrated church was a sanctuary. If a malefactor took refuge therein, he could not be extracted; but it was the duty of the four neighbouring vills to beset the holy place, prevent his escape and send for a coroner. . . . [A]fter he had enjoyed the right of asylum for forty days, he was to be starved into submission; but the clergy resented this interference with the peace of Holy Church." 2 Frederick Pollock & Frederic W. Maitland, *History of English Law Before the Time of Edward I* 590–91 (2d ed. 1899).

"In medieval England, as elsewhere in Europe, there were a number of ecclesiastical places where the king's writ did not run. The underlying theory was that consecrated places should not be profaned by the use of force, but the result in practice was that thieves and murderers could take refuge and thereby gain immunity even against the operation of criminal justice. This was the privilege called 'sanctuary.' In the case of parochial churches, the sanctuary lasted for forty days only. Before the expiration of this period, the fugitive had to choose whether to stand trial or 'abjure' the realm . . . . This was only permitted if he made a written confession to the coroner, which resulted in the forfeiture of his property as on conviction; his life only was spared . . . ." J.H. Baker, *An Introduction to English Legal History* 585 (3d ed. 1990).

2. A holy area of a religious building; esp., the area in a church or temple where the main altar or tabernacle is located.

sandbagging, *n.* **1.** The act or practice of a trial lawyer's remaining cagily silent when a possible error occurs at trial, with the hope of preserving an issue for appeal if the court does not correct the problem. • Such a tactic does not usu. preserve the issue for appeal because objections must be promptly made to alert the trial judge of the possible error. **2.** *Corporations.* An antitakeover tactic wherein the target company delays a hostile bidder's final offer by agreeing to negotiate then prolonging bad-faith negotiations as long as possible in hopes that a more favorable company will initiate a takeover. — **sandbag,** *vb.*

S & L. *abbr.* (1951) SAVINGS-AND-LOAN ASSOCIATION.

sandpapering, *n.* A lawyer's general preparation of a witness before a deposition or trial. Cf. HORSESHEDDING.

S&T. *abbr.* SCIENCE AND TECHNOLOGY DIRECTORATE.

sandwich lease. See LEASE.

SANE. *abbr.* Sexual-assault nurse examiner.

sane, *adj.* (17c) Having a relatively sound and healthy mind; capable of reason and of distinguishing right from wrong. • In criminal proceedings, the term is used to describe whether a defendant is mentally competent to stand trial.

sane automatism. See AUTOMATISM.

sane memory. See CAPACITY (3).

sanguis (sang-gwis), *n.* [Latin "blood"] **1.** *Roman law.* Blood relationship. **2.** *Hist.* Consanguinity. **3.** *Hist.* The right of a chief lord to judge cases involving bloodshed.

sanitary code. (1861) A set of ordinances regulating the food and healthcare industries.

sanity. (15c) The quality, state, or condition of having a relatively sound and healthy mind and of being legally responsible for one's actions. Cf. INSANITY.

sanity hearing. (1925) **1.** An inquiry into the mental competency of a person to stand trial. See COMPETENCY. **2.** A proceeding to determine whether a person should be institutionalized.

sans ce que (sanz **see** kə *or* **sawn** sə **kə**). [Law French "without what"] See ABSQUE HOC.

sans frais (sawn **fray**). [Law French] Without expense.

sans impeachment de wast (sanz im-**peech**-mənt də **wayst**). [Law French] *Hist.* Without impeachment of waste.

sans jour (saw*n* **zhoor** *or* sanz **joor**). [Law French] *Hist.* Without day; SINE DIE. See ALLER SANS JOUR.

sans recours (saw*n* rə-**koor** *or* sanz ri-**kuur**). See WITHOUT RECOURSE.

Santa Claus dad. See *Disneyland parent* under PARENT.

sap, *n.* (1899) **1.** A club, a blackjack, a hose containing rocks in the middle, or any other object generally used as a bludgeon. **2.** *Slang.* A gullible person; a dupe.

sapiens naturam delicti (**say**-pee-enz nə-**t**[y]**oor**-əm di-**lik**-tI). [Law Latin] *Hist.* Partaking of the character or nature of a delict.

SAPJ. See *senior administrative patent judge* under JUDGE.

SAR. *abbr.* **1.** STOCK-APPRECIATION RIGHT. **2.** SUSPICIOUS-ACTIVITY REPORT.

Sarbanes–Oxley Act. A 2002 federal statute that mandates strict internal controls and regulations for corporate accounting and management practices and prescribes strict penalties for violations. • The Act was proposed in response to accounting scandals, such as Enron and WorldCom, in the early 2000s. — Abbr. *SOA*; *SOX*.

Sarbanes-Oxley Act claim. (2004) An employee's claim that his or her employment was terminated as retaliation for whistleblowing. — Abbr. *SOX Act claim.* — Often shortened to *Sarbanes-Oxley claim.*

SARE. *abbr.* SINGLE-ASSET REAL ESTATE.

sasine. See SEISIN.

satellite litigation. (1983) **1.** One or more lawsuits related to a major piece of litigation that is being conducted in another court <the satellite litigation in state court prevented the federal judge from ruling on the issue>. **2.** Peripheral skirmishes involved in the prosecution of a lawsuit <the plaintiffs called the sanctions "satellite litigation," drummed up by the defendants to deflect attention from the main issues in the case>.

satellite state. See *client state* under STATE (1).

satisdare (sat-is-**dair**-ee), *vb.* [Latin fr. *satis* "sufficient" + *dare* "to give"] *Roman law.* To give a guarantee to; esp., to give security in the form of *satisdatio.* See SATISDATIO.

satisdatio (sat-is-**day**-shee-oh), *n.* [Latin fr. *satisdare*] *Roman law.* Security given by a person, such as a debtor, through a surety. Pl. ***satisdationes*** (sat-is-day-shee-**oh**-neez).

satisdation (sat-is-**day**-shən), *n.* (17c) *Civil law.* **1.** The giving of security. **2.** SECURITY (1).

satisfaction, *n.* (14c) **1.** The giving of something with the intention, express or implied, that it is to extinguish some existing legal or moral obligation. • Satisfaction differs from performance because it is always something given as a substitute for or equivalent of something else, while performance is the identical thing promised to be done. — Also termed *satisfaction of debt.* **2.** The fulfillment of an obligation; esp., the payment in full of a debt. See ACCORD AND SATISFACTION. — **satisfy,** *vb.*

> "Satisfaction closely resembles performance. Both depend upon presumed intention to carry out an obligation, but in satisfaction the thing done is something different from the thing agreed to be done, whereas in performance the *identical* act which the party contracted to do is considered to have been done. The cases on satisfaction are usually grouped under four heads, namely, (i) satisfaction of debts by legacies; (ii) satisfaction of legacies by legacies; (iii) satisfaction (or ademption) of legacies by portions; and (iv) satisfaction of portion-debts by legacies, or by portions. Strictly, however, only the first and last of these heads are really cases of satisfaction; for satisfaction presupposes an obligation, which, of course, does not exist in the case of a legacy in the will of a living person." R.E. Megarry, *Snell's Principles of Equity* 226–27 (23d ed. 1947).

3. SATISFACTION PIECE. **4.** *Wills & estates.* The payment by a testator, during the testator's lifetime, of a legacy provided for in a will; ADVANCEMENT (1). Cf. ADEMPTION. **5.** *Wills & estates.* A testamentary gift intended to satisfy a debt owed by the testator to a creditor. **6.** *Int'l law.* In the law of state responsibility, a form of nonpecuniary reparation intended to repair immaterial damages, as opposed to material ones, caused by an internationally wrongful act.

> "It is well established that immaterial damages caused to a State may be repaired by symbolic forms of satisfaction. They mostly correspond to the offences against the 'honour' of a State. In such cases, the most common forms of satisfaction are formal apologies, made in written form or orally, by high ranking officials or the head of State." Cristina Hoss, "Satisfaction," in 9 *The Max Planck Encyclopedia of Public International Law* 25, 27 (Rüdiger Wolfrum ed., 2012).

7. See *release deed* under DEED.

satisfaction clause. See CLAUSE.

satisfaction contract. See CONTRACT.

satisfaction of debt. See SATISFACTION (1).

satisfaction of judgment. (17c) **1.** The complete discharge of obligations under a judgment. **2.** The document filed and entered on the record indicating that a judgment has been paid.

> "Generally, a satisfaction of a judgment is the final act and end of a proceeding. Satisfaction implies or manifests an expression of finality as to all questions of liability and damages involved in the litigation. Once satisfaction occurs, further alteration or amendment of a final judgment generally is barred. Satisfaction of a judgment, when entered of record by the act of the parties, is prima facie evidence that the creditor has received payment of the amount of the judgment or its equivalent, and operates as an extinguishment of the judgment debt." 47 Am. Jur. 2d *Judgments* § 1006, at 443 (1995).

satisfaction of lien. (1833) **1.** The fulfillment of all obligations made the subject of a lien. **2.** The document signed by the lienholder releasing the property subject to a lien.

satisfaction of mortgage. (18c) **1.** The complete payment of a mortgage. **2.** A discharge signed by the mortgagee or mortgage holder indicating that the property subject to the mortgage is released or that the mortgage debt has been paid and the mortgage conditions have been fully satisfied.

satisfaction of record. (1840) The entry on the record of a judgment or mortgage that it has been fully paid or satisfied.

satisfaction piece. (1831) A written statement that one party (esp. a debtor) has discharged its obligation to another party, who accepts the discharge; esp., the formal acknowledgment given by a judgment creditor or a mortgagee that the debt has been paid and authorizing the entry of the satisfaction on the record. — Also termed *certificate of discharge*; *satisfaction*.

satisfactory evidence. See EVIDENCE.

satisfactory proof. See *satisfactory evidence* under EVIDENCE.

satisfied term. See TERM (4).

SATP. *abbr.* Sex-abuse treatment program.

Saturday-night special. (1959) **1.** A handgun that is easily obtained and concealed; esp., a low-quality, inexpensive handgun. **2.** *Corporations.* A surprise tender offer typically held open for a limited offering period (such as one week) to maximize pressure on a shareholder to accept. • These tender offers are now effectively prohibited by section 14(e) of the Williams Act. 15 USCA § 78n(e).

saunkefin (sawn-kə-**fan**). [fr. Law French *sang quifin*] (17c) *Hist.* End of blood; the failure of a line of succession.

SAUSA. *abbr.* Special Assistant to the United States Attorney. See UNITED STATES ATTORNEY.

sauvagine (soh-və-**zheen**). [Law French] *Hist.* **1.** Wild animal. **2.** Wild nature of an animal.

save, *vb.* (13c) **1.** To preserve from danger or loss <save a ship in distress>. **2.** To lay up; to hoard <save money>. **3.** To toll or suspend (the operation, running, etc.) of something <save a statute of limitations>. **4.** To except, reserve, or exempt (a right, etc.) <to save vested rights>. **5.** To lessen or avoid (a cost, resource, etc.) <save labor>.

save harmless. See HOLD HARMLESS.

save-harmless agreement. See HOLD-HARMLESS AGREEMENT.

save-harmless clause. See INDEMNITY CLAUSE.

saver default (say-vər di-**fawlt**). [Law French] (17c) *Hist.* To excuse a default. — Also spelled *saver de fault*; *saver defaut*.

> "Saver default is the same as to excuse a default. And this is properly when a man having made default in court, comes afterwards, and alleges a good cause why he did it, as imprisonment at the same time, or the like." *Termes de la Ley* 352 (1st Am. ed. 1812).

saving, *n.* (15c) An exception; a reservation.

saving clause. (17c) **1.** A statutory provision exempting from coverage something that would otherwise be included. • A saving clause is generally used in a repealing act to preserve rights and claims that would otherwise be lost. **2.** SAVING-TO-SUITORS CLAUSE. **3.** SEVERABILITY CLAUSE. — Also termed *savings clause*.

savings account. See ACCOUNT.

savings-account trust. See *Totten trust* under TRUST (3).

savings-and-loan association. (1884) A financial institution, often organized and chartered like a bank, that specializes in making home-mortgage loans but also usu. maintains checking accounts and provides other banking services. — Often shortened to S & L. — Also termed *savings-and-loan bank*; *loan association*; *thrift institution*; *thrift*. Cf. BUILDING-AND-LOAN ASSOCIATION.

> "The American savings and loan (S & L) industry began in 1831 as a way to help people of modest means to become homeowners. Modeled on the British building society movement, early S & Ls (originally called 'building and loans' or 'thrifts') required members to subscribe to shares in the institution, which they agreed to pay in regular monthly installments. As these payments accumulated, the thrift would lend the money back to the members so they could purchase homes. Since the loan amount equaled the par value of the subscribed shares, these loans were actually advances on the unpaid shares. As a result, to repay the loans members simply continued to make their regular monthly share payments, along with interest on the loan." David L. Mason, "Savings and Loan Associations," in 2 *The Oxford Companion to American Politics* 302, 302 (David Coates ed., 2012).

savings-and-loan bank. See BANK.

savings bank. See BANK.

savings-bank trust. See *Totten trust* under TRUST (3).

savings bond. See BOND (3).

savings clause. See SAVING CLAUSE.

savings note. See NOTE (1).

saving-to-suitors clause. (1920) *Maritime law.* In the federal statutory provision granting admiralty and maritime jurisdiction to the federal courts, a clause that preserves the option to file suit in a nonadmiralty court. 28 USCA § 1333(1). • The nonadmiralty court is typically either a state court or a law-side federal court. Under the reverse-*Erie* doctrine, the nonadmiralty court is required to apply the same law that the admiralty court would have used. — Also termed *saving clause*.

savor, *vb.* (16c) To partake of the character of or bear affinity to (something). • In traditional legal idiom, an interest arising from land is said to "savor of the realty." — Also spelled *savour*.

S.B. See *senate bill* under BILL (3).

SBA. *abbr.* (1953) SMALL BUSINESS ADMINISTRATION.

SBC. *abbr.* SMALL-BUSINESS CONCERN.

SBI. *abbr.* See *serious bodily injury* under INJURY.

SBIC. *abbr.* SMALL- BUSINESS INVESTMENT COMPANY.

SBP. *abbr.* STOCK BONUS PLAN.

SBS. *abbr.* (1984) SHAKEN-BABY SYNDROME.

sc. *abbr.* SCILICET.

S.C. *abbr.* **1.** SUPREME COURT. **2.** Same case. • In former practice, when put between two citations, the abbreviation indicated that the same case was reported in both places. **3.** SENATUS CONSULTUM.

scab. (18c) Someone who works under conditions contrary to a union contract; esp., a worker who crosses a union picket line to replace a union worker during a strike. — Also termed *strikebreaker*; (BrE) *black-leg labor*; *knob-stick*; *rat*.

scabini (skə-**bɪ**-nɪ). [Law Latin] (16c) *Hist.* Judges or the judge's assessors in the court held by the count; magistrates. • The term was found in a charter from the wardens of Lynn in Norfolk, during the reign of Henry VIII. But even earlier than that, the title was used in Charlemagne's empire (the French equivalent being *édevins*) and later Germanized as *Schöffen*.

scalam (**skay**-ləm), *n.* [Latin] *Hist.* Scale. • *Ad scalam* was the method of paying money to the Exchequer, in which sixpence was added to each twenty shillings to compensate for a deficiency in weight, although no scales were actually used.

scale, *n.* (15c) **1.** A progression of degrees; esp., a range of wage rates. **2.** A wage according to a range of rates. **3.** An instrument for weighing. **4.** *Hist.* In the practice of the English Supreme Court of Judicature, the fee charged by a solicitor for a particular type of case. • Unless the court ordered otherwise, the *lower scale* applied to all causes and matters assigned by the Judicature Acts to the King's Bench, or the Probate, Divorce, and Admiralty divisions; to all actions for debt, contract, or tort; and to almost all causes and matters assigned by the acts to the Chancery division and in which the amount in controversy was less than £1,000. The *higher scale* applied in all other cases, and in actions falling under one of the lower-scale classes if the principal relief sought was injunctive.

scale order. See ORDER (8).

scales of justice. A weighing device with two trays suspended in equal balance, held by the personified version of Justice for assessing the figurative weight of two sides in a dispute. — Sometimes capitalized *scales of Justice*.

> "The scales, the traditional symbol of justice, are the mechanical representation of the play of psychic forces which make the judicial process function. The competing lawyers must enter the picture, presenting their contrasting arguments so that the judge, after a few oscillations, may settle on the truth.
>
> "The further the opposing weights radiate from the center (or the point of impartiality) the more sensitive must be the mechanism, the more exact the measurement. As each lawyer presents the most favorable case possible for his client, between them they create the equilibrium which the judge is seeking. He who would blame the lawyers for their partiality should also blame the weights on the scales." Piero Calamandrei, *Eulogy of Judges* 38 (John Clarke Adams & C. Abbott Phillips Jr. trans., 1942).

scale tolerance. (1926) The nominal variation of the mass or weight of the same goods on different scales.

scaling law. (1882) *Hist.* A statute establishing a process for adjusting value differences between depreciated paper money and specie. • Statutes of this type were necessary when paper depreciated after both the American Revolution and the Civil War.

scalp act. (1894) **1.** Any one of several state statutes providing for a state bounty (as calculated on a per-scalp basis) for the destruction of specified animals regarded as pestiferous. • Many 19th-century scalp acts resulted in the killing of tens of thousands of hawks and owls. **2.** *Hist.* Any one of several colonial (or, later, state) statutes providing for a bounty to be paid for Indian scalps during 17th- to 19th-century hostilities with American Indians. • The earliest such statute was enacted in Massachusetts (1694), and by 1717 all the New England colonies had scalp acts in place. With the spread of the frontier in the 19th century, many states and territories enacted such statutes.

scalper. (1869) **1.** Someone who engages in the violent or warlike act of scalping. See SCALPING (1). **2.** A seller who buys something (esp. a ticket) at face value (or less) and then tries to resell it for a higher price. — Also termed *ticket speculator.* **3.** An investment adviser who buys a security before recommending it to clients. **4.** A market-maker who puts an excessive markup or markdown on a transaction.

scalping, *n.* (1882) **1.** The practice or an instance of tearing or removing the skin and hair from the top of a skull, esp. that of a slain or captured enemy, for a war-trophy or for the payment of a statutory or private bounty. **2.** The practice of selling something (esp. a ticket) at a price above face value once it becomes scarce (usu. just before a high-demand event begins). **3.** The purchase of a security by an investment adviser before the adviser recommends that a customer buy the same security. • This practice is usu. considered unethical because the customer's purchase will increase the security's price, thus enabling the investment adviser to sell at a profit. **4.** The illegally excessive markup or markdown on a transaction by a market-maker. **5.** Any trading strategy that attempts to profit from small price changes. — **scalp,** *vb.*

scandal. (13c) **1.** Disgraceful, shameful, or degrading acts or conduct. **2.** Defamatory reports or rumors; esp., slander. See SCANDALOUS MATTER.

> "Scandal consists in the allegation of anything which is unbecoming the dignity of the court to hear, or is contrary to decency or good manners, or which charges some person with a crime not necessary to be shown in the cause, to which may be added that any unnecessary allegation, bearing cruelly upon the moral character of an individual, is also scandalous. The matter alleged, however, must be not only offensive, but also *irrelevant* to the cause, for however offensive it be, if it be pertinent and material to the cause the party has a right to plead it. It may often be necessary to charge false representations, fraud and immorality, and the pleading will not be open to the objection of scandal, if the facts justify the charge." Eugene A. Jones, *Manual of Equity Pleading and Practice* 50–51 (1916).

scandalous matter. (17c) *Civil procedure.* Information that is improper in a court paper because it is both grossly disgraceful (or defamatory) and irrelevant to an action or defense. • Upon a party's motion or on its own, a federal court can order a scandalous matter struck from a pleading. Fed. R. Civ. P. 12(f). Cf. IMPERTINENT MATTER.

scandalous subject matter. (1982) *Trademarks.* A word, phrase, symbol, or graphic depiction that the U.S. Patent and Trademark Office may refuse to register because it is shockingly offensive to social mores. • Although the

Lanham Act uses the phrase "immoral, deceptive, or scandalous subject matter," courts have not distinguished "scandalous" from "immoral."

scandalum magnatum **(skan**-də-ləm mag-**nay**-təm). [Law Latin "scandal of magnates"] (16c) *Hist.* Actionable slander of powerful people; specif., defamatory comments regarding persons of high rank, such as peers, judges, or state officials.

> "Words spoken in derogation of a peer or judge, or other great officer of the realm, are usually called *Scandalum Magnatum*; and though they be such as would not be actionable when spoken of a private person, yet when applied to persons of high rank and dignity, they constitute a more heinous injury, which is redressed by an action on the case founded on many ancient statutes, as well as on behalf of the crown, to inflict the punishment of imprisonment of the slanderer, as on the behalf of the party to recover damages for the injury sustained." Thomas Starkie, *A Treatise on the Law of Slander, Libel, Scandalum Magnatum, and False Rumours* 155 (Edward D. Ingraham ed., 1st Am. ed. 1826).

scarlet-letter punishment. See *shame sanction* under SANCTION.

scarlet-letter sentence. See *shame sanction* under SANCTION.

scatter-point analysis. (1993) A method for studying the effect that minority-population changes have on voting patterns, involving a plotting of the percentage of votes that candidates receive to determine whether voting percentages increase or decrease as the percentages of voters of a particular race increase or decrease.

scènes à faire **(sen** ah **fair).** [French "scenes for action"] (1945) *Copyright.* Standard or general themes that are common to a wide variety of works and are therefore not copyrightable. • Examples of *scènes à faire* are obvious plot elements and character types.

schedule, *n.* (15c) A written list or inventory; esp., a statement that is attached to a document and that gives a detailed showing of the matters referred to in the document <Schedule B to the title policy lists the encumbrances on the property>. — **schedule,** *vb.* — **scheduled,** *adj.*

scheduled injury. See INJURY.

scheduled property. See PROPERTY.

scheduling order. See ORDER (2).

scheme. (16c) **1.** A systemic plan; a connected or orderly arrangement, esp. of related concepts <legislative scheme>. **2.** An artful plot or plan, usu. to deceive others <a scheme to defraud creditors>.

▸ **legislative scheme.** (18c) A scheme created by a legislature.

▸ **regulatory scheme.** (1921) A scheme composed of regulations promulgated by an authoritative body.

scheme of arrangement. (1884) *English law.* A court-approved reorganization of a company's capital structure or debts. • The company seeking to reorganize is usu. in financial trouble but may not yet be insolvent.

▸ **creditors' scheme of arrangement.** (1990) A reorganization plan in which creditors agree to defer demands for payment, in hopes of eventually receiving more than they would if the company were immediately liquidated.

▸ **members' scheme of arrangement.** (1998) A reorganization plan voted on and approved by the company's shareholders. • This type of scheme may be used to prepare for a merger. — Also termed *shareholders' scheme of arrangement.*

▸ **shareholders' scheme of arrangement.** See *members' scheme of arrangement.*

schism (siz-əm *or* **skiz**-əm). (14c) **1.** A breach or rupture; a division, esp. among members of a group, as of a union, typically caused by discord. **2.** A separation of beliefs and doctrines by persons of the same organized religion, religious denomination, or sect.

> "It has been held that the civil courts are not concerned with mere schisms stemming from disputations over matters of religious doctrine, not only because such questions are essentially ecclesiastical rather than judicial, but also because of the separation between the church and the state . . . . However, it has also been held that the situation is different in the case of self-governing congressional churches, for here the courts do not hesitate to assume jurisdiction when a schism affects property rights, for in this form . . . each local congregation is independent and autonomous and there is no recourse within the denomination." 66 Am. Jur. 2d *Religious Societies* § 51, at 804 (1973).

school, *n.* (bef. 12c) **1.** An institution of learning and education, esp. for children.

> "Although the word 'school' in its broad sense includes all schools or institutions, whether of high or low degree, the word 'school' frequently has been defined in constitutions and statutes as referring only to the public common schools generally established throughout the United States . . . . When used in a statute or other contract, 'school' usually does not include universities, business colleges, or other institutions of higher education unless the intent to include such institutions is clearly indicated." 68 Am. Jur. 2d *Schools* § 1, at 355 (1993).

▸ **common school.** See *public school.*

▸ **district school.** (18c) A public school contained in and maintained by a school district. See SCHOOL DISTRICT.

▸ **private school.** (16c) A school maintained by private individuals, religious organizations, or corporations, funded, at least in part, by fees or tuition, and open only to pupils selected and admitted based on religious affiliations or other particular qualifications.

▸ **public school.** (16c) An elementary, middle, or high school established under state law, regulated by the local state authorities in the various political subdivisions, funded and maintained by public taxation, and open and free to all children of the particular district where the school is located. — Also termed *common school.*

2. The collective body of students under instruction in an institution of learning. **3.** A group of people adhering to the same philosophy or system of beliefs.

school board. (1833) An administrative body, made up of a number of directors or trustees, responsible for overseeing public schools within a city, county, or district. Cf. BOARD OF EDUCATION.

school bond. See BOND (3).

school district. (18c) An area within a particular state demarcated for the governance of all the public schools within that area; specif., a political subdivision of a state, created by the legislature and invested with local powers of self-government, to build, maintain, fund, and support the public schools within its territory and to otherwise help the state administer its educational responsibilities.

▸ **consolidated school district.** (1918) A public-school district in which two or more existing schools have consolidated into a single district.

school land. See LAND.

school voucher. See *tuition voucher* under VOUCHER.

Schumer box. (1988) In a credit-card agreement, a table that summarizes all the costs for which the cardholder is liable, so that the cardholder can more easily compare credit-card agreements. • The term derives from the name of Senator Charles Schumer, who proposed the disclosure requirements. The box must contain the information listed in 15 USCA §§ 1637(c)(1)(A)–(B). — Also termed *Schumer's box.*

Science and Technology Directorate. The primary division of the Department of Homeland Security responsible for coordinating research and development, including preparing for and responding to terrorist threats involving weapons of mass destruction. • The Directorate also works with the Chemical, Biological, Radiological, and Nuclear Countermeasures Program and the Environmental Measurements Lab in the Department of Energy, the National BW (biological warfare) Defense Analysis Center in the Department of Defense, and the Plum Island Animal Disease Center — Abbr. S&T.

science of legislation. See LAW REFORM.

sciendum est (sI-**en**-dəm **est**). [Latin] *Roman law.* It is to be known or understood. • This phrase often introduced a particular topic or explanation.

sciens et prudens (**sI**-enz et **proo**-denz). [Latin] *Hist.* In full knowledge and understanding.

scienter (sI-**en**-tər *or* see-), *n.* [Latin "knowingly"] (1824) **1.** A degree of knowledge that makes a person legally responsible for the consequences of his or her act or omission; the fact of an act's having been done knowingly, esp. as a ground for civil damages or criminal punishment. See KNOWLEDGE; MENS REA. **2.** A mental state consisting in an intent to deceive, manipulate, or defraud. • In this sense, the term is used most often in the context of securities fraud. The Supreme Court has held that to establish a claim for damages under Rule 10b-5, a plaintiff must prove that the defendant acted with scienter. *Ernst & Ernst v. Hochfelder,* 425 U.S. 185, 96 S.Ct. 1375 (1976). **3.** The clause in an indictment or other pleading charging a defendant with knowledge that gives rise to criminal or civil liability for an act.

scienter action. (1937) A lawsuit in which the plaintiff must prove that the defendant acted knowingly or knew of the danger — e.g., at common law an action for damage caused by a domestic animal. See SCIENTER.

scientific creationism. See CREATIONISM.

scientific evidence. See EVIDENCE.

scientific knowledge. See KNOWLEDGE (1).

scientific method. (1854) The process of generating hypotheses and testing them through experimentation, publication, and replication. • Evidence that purports to be scientific is "ground[ed] in the methods and procedures of science." *Daubert v. Merrell Dow Pharm.,* 509 U.S. 579, 590 (1993). A great deal of debate has surrounded the question whether there is only one type of "scientific method," and precisely how the phrase should be defined. Generally, scientists agree that "[k]nowledge is produced through a series of steps during which data are accumulated methodically, strengths and weaknesses of information are assessed, and knowledge about causal relationships are inferred. . . . Hypotheses are developed, are measured against data, and either supported or refuted. Scientists continually observe, test, and modify the body of knowledge. Rather than claiming absolute truth, science approaches truth either through breakthrough discoveries or incrementally, by testing theories repeatedly." National Academy of Sciences, *Strengthening Forensic Science in the United States: A Path Forward* 112 (2009). Good scientific practice remains open to new ideas, including criticism and refutation. *Id.* at 113. See FALSIFIABILITY.

sci. fa. *abbr.* SCIRE FACIAS.

scil. *abbr.* SCILICET.

scilicet (**sil**-ə-set *or* -sit). [fr. Latin *scire licet* "that you may know"] (14c) That is to say; namely; VIDELICET. • Like *videlicet,* this word is used in pleadings and other instruments to introduce a more particular statement of matters previously mentioned in general terms. It has never been quite as common, however, as *videlicet.* — Abbr. sc.; scil.; (erroneously) ss.

SCIN. *abbr.* See *self-canceling installment note* under NOTE (1).

scintilla (sin-**til**-ə). (13c) A spark or trace <the standard is that there must be more than a scintilla of evidence>. Pl. **scintillas** (sin-**til**-əz).

scintilla juris (sin-**til**-ə **joor**-is). [Law Latin "a spark of right"] (17c) *Hist.* A fragment of law or right. • This refers to a figurative expression in the law of uses providing a trace of seisin rights to remain in the feoffees sufficient to allow contingent uses to be executed under the Statute of Uses. It was abolished in the Law of Property Amendment Act of 1860. See STATUTE OF USES.

scintilla-of-evidence rule. (1896) A common-law doctrine holding that if even the slightest amount of relevant evidence exists on an issue, then a motion for summary judgment or for directed verdict should not be granted and the issue must go to the jury. • Federal courts do not follow this rule, but some states apply it. — Also termed *scintilla rule.*

scire facias (**sI**-ree **fay**-shee-əs). [Law Latin "you are to make known, show cause"] (15c) A writ requiring the person against whom it is issued to appear and show cause why some matter of record should not be enforced, annulled, or vacated, or why a dormant judgment against that person should not be revived; esp., a writ commanding the party against whom it is issued to show cause why the movant, plaintiff, or petitioner should not have the advantage of or execution on a judicial record, such as a judgment or recognizance, or why a nonjudicial record, such as letters patent for land or an invention, should not be nullified. — Abbr. *sci. fa.*

▸ **amicable scire facias to revive a judgment.** (1828) A written agreement in which a person against whom a revival of an action is sought agrees to the entry of an adverse judgment.

▸ ***scire facias ad audiendum errores*** (**sI**-ree **fay**-shee-əs ad aw-dee-**en**-dəm e-**ror**-eez). [Law Latin "that you cause to know to hear errors"] (17c) *Hist.* A common-law writ allowing a party who had assigned error to compel the opposing party to plead. • It was abolished in 1875.

▸ ***scire facias ad disprobandum debitum*** (sɪ-ree **fay**-shee-əs ad dis-proh-**ban**-dəm **deb**-ə-təm). [Law Latin "that you cause to know to disprove the debt"] (18c) *Hist.* A writ allowing a defendant in a foreign attachment against the plaintiff to disprove or avoid the debt recovered by the plaintiff, within a year and a day from the time of payment.

▸ ***scire facias ad rehabendam terram*** (sɪ-ree **fay**-shee-əs ad re-hə-**ben**-dəm **ter**-əm), *n.* [Law Latin "that you cause to know to recover the land"] (1815) *Hist.* A writ allowing a judgment debtor to recover lands taken in execution after the debtor has satisfied the judgment.

▸ ***scire facias quare restitutionem non*** (sɪ-ree **fay**-shee-əs **kwair**-ee res-tə-t[y]oo-shee-**oh**-nəm non), *n.* [Law Latin "that you cause to know why (there is not) restitution"] (1825) *Hist.* A writ for restitution after an execution on a judgment is levied but not paid and the judgment is later reversed on appeal.

▸ ***scire facias sur* mortgage** (sɪ-ree **fay**-shee-əs sər **mor**-gij), *n.* [Law Latin "that you cause to know on mortgage"] (1837) *Hist.* A writ ordering a defaulting mortgagor to show cause why the mortgage should not be foreclosed and the property sold in execution.

▸ ***scire facias sur* municipal claim** (sɪ-ree **fay**-shee-əs sər myoo-**nis**-ə-pəl **klaym**), *n.* [Law Latin "that you cause to know on municipal claim"] (1876) *Hist.* A writ compelling the payment of a municipal claim out of the property to which a municipal lien is attached.

scire facias ad audiendum errores. See SCIRE FACIAS.

scire facias ad disprobandum debitum. See SCIRE FACIAS.

scire facias ad rehabendam terram. See SCIRE FACIAS.

scire facias quare restitutionem non. See SCIRE FACIAS.

***scire facias sur* morgage.** See SCIRE FACIAS.

***scire facias sur* municipal claim.** See SCIRE FACIAS.

scire feci (sɪ-ree **fee**-sɪ). [Latin "I have caused to know"] (17c) *Hist.* The sheriff's return to a writ of scire facias, indicating that notice was given to the parties against whom the writ was issued.

***scire fieri* inquiry** (sɪ-ree **fɪ**-ə-rɪ), *n.* [Law Latin] (18c) *Hist.* A writ to ascertain the location of a testator's property from an executor, when the sheriff returned nulla bona to a writ of execution *fieri facias de bonis testatoris.* See FIERI FACIAS.

scite (sɪt). [fr. Latin *situs*] (17c) *Archaic.* **1.** A location; a site. **2.** The site of a capital messuage. **3.** A municipal ordinance. — Also termed *site.*

SCO. *abbr.* See *show-cause order* under ORDER (2).

scoff, *n. Criminal law. Slang.* A notice or directive sent to someone who has failed to respond to a traffic-violation charge or to pay a traffic fine, usu. admonishing the recipient that a further failure to respond will result in a suspension of his or her driver's license.

scofflaw (**skof**-law). (1924) **1.** Someone who treats the law with contempt; esp., one who avoids various laws that are not easily enforced <some scofflaws carry mannequins in their cars in order to drive in the carpool lane>. **2.** *Hist.* Someone who consumes illegally made or obtained alcoholic beverages. • This was the original meaning. In fact, the word originated during the Prohibition era in the 1920s as the winning entry in a contest seeking a new word for "a lawless drinker of illegally made or illegally obtained liquor."

scold, *n.* (12c) *Hist.* Someone who regularly breaks the peace by scolding people, increasing discord, and generally being a public nuisance to the neighborhood. • This behavior was formerly punishable in various ways, including having an iron bridle fitted to the person's mouth. — Also termed *common scold*; *objurgatrix.* See BRANKS.

scolding bridle. See BRANKS.

scope note. (1903) In a digest, a précis appearing after a title and showing concisely what subject matter is included and what is excluded.

> "In the Century and Decennial Digests, though not in the various digests of the Key-Number Series, there is printed immediately following each topic title a couple of paragraphs which are called the Scope-Note. The first paragraph of this scope-note shows very briefly the character of the subject-matter included under the title. The second paragraph shows the 'Exclusions' — i.e., what related matter has been excluded in order to conform to the plan of the Digest — and directs the reader to the proper title under which such related matter may be found. Consequently a little study of the scope-note will ofttimes repay the searcher for a few moments' time consumed in so doing." William M. Lile et al., *Brief Making and the Use of Law Books* 116 (Roger W. Cooley & Charles Lesley Ames eds., 3d ed. 1914).

scope of a patent. (1866) *Patents.* The limits of a patent's protection, as defined by the allowed claims.

scope of authority. (1805) *Agency.* The range of reasonable power that an agent has been delegated or might foreseeably be delegated in carrying out the principal's business. See SCOPE OF EMPLOYMENT; RESPONDEAT SUPERIOR.

scope of business. (1841) The range of activities that are reasonably necessary to operate a commercial venture successfully, as determined by the nature of the venture and the activities of others engaged in the same occupation in the same area.

scope of discovery. (1902) The limits within which a court allows litigants to employ devices, such as asking one another to produce materials and taking depositions from witnesses, to learn or find information relevant to the litigation. — Also termed *discovery scope.* See DISCOVERY.

scope of employment. (1836) The range of reasonable and foreseeable activities that an employee engages in while carrying out the employer's business; the field of action in which a servant is authorized to act in the master–servant relationship. • An employer is not vicariously liable for torts committed by an employee acting outside the scope of employment. An employer that is culpable in some way may be subject to direct liability. See RESPONDEAT SUPERIOR. Cf. COURSE OF EMPLOYMENT; ZONE OF EMPLOYMENT.

scope-of-work clause. (1965) A contractual provision that details what work is to be performed under the contract.

scorched-earth, *adj.* (1937) **1.** Of, relating to, or involving a military policy of deliberate, massive destruction within a given geographic area, including all kinds of property, improvements, and other resources, so that the enemy cannot benefit by using them. **2.** Aiming at victory or supremacy whatever the cost; ruthless. — Also termed *scorched-earth tactic.*

scorched-earth defense. *Corporations.* An antitakeover tactic by which a target corporation sells its most valuable assets or divisions in order to reduce its value after acquisition and thus try to defeat a hostile bidder's tender offer. Cf. CROWN-JEWEL DEFENSE; PAC-MAN DEFENSE.

S corporation. See CORPORATION.

scot. (12c) *Hist.* A payment; esp., a customary tax.

▸ **soul scot.** (bef. 12c) *Hist. Eccles. law.* See MORTUARY. — Also written *soul shot.*

scotal (**skot**-əl). (12c) *Hist.* An extortionary practice by which forest officers forced people to patronize the officers' alehouses, often in exchange for the officers' ignoring forest offenses. • This practice was prohibited in 1217 by the Charter of the Forest, ch. 7. — Also spelled *scotale* (**skot**-ayl).

scot and lot. (16c) *Hist.* **1.** The customary payment of a share of taxes based on one's ability. **2.** A municipal tax on the right to vote.

Scotch marriage. See MARRIAGE (1).

Scotch verdict. See NOT PROVEN.

scottare (skə-**tair**-ee), *vb.* [Law Latin] *Hist.* To pay a tax.

SCOTUS. *abbr.* (1879) SUPREME COURT OF THE UNITED STATES.

SCPA. *abbr.* SEMICONDUCTOR CHIP PROTECTION ACT.

SCRAM. *abbr.* Secure continuous remote alcohol monitoring.

scrambling possession. See POSSESSION.

scrap value. See *salvage value* under VALUE (2).

scratch-and-dent loan. See LOAN.

scratching the ticket. A party member's rejection of a candidate on a regular party ticket by canceling the candidate's name or by voting for one or more nominees of the opposing political party.

scrawl. See SCROLL (3).

screening committee. 1. See *nominating committee* under COMMITTEE (1). **2.** See *resolutions committee* under COMMITTEE (1).

screening grand jury. See GRAND JURY.

screening mechanism. See ETHICAL WALL.

screen-scraping, *n.* (1995) *Intellectual property.* The practice of extracting data directly from one website and displaying it on another website. • The source website's database is not used — only the display. Screen-scraping may infringe the extracted website-owner's copyright in the contents. — **screen-scrape,** *vb.*

scriba (**skrɪ**-bə), *n.* [Latin] *Roman law.* A court or office clerk; a scribe; a secretary. • In England, the *scriba regis* was the king's secretary. Cf. NOTARIUS.

scribe. See SECRETARY (3).

scribere est agere (**skrɪ**-bə-ree est **aj**-ə-ree). [Latin] (17c) *Hist.* To write is to act.

> "But now it seems clearly to be agreed, that, by the common law and the statute of Edward III, words spoken amount only to a high misdemeanor, and no treason. For they may be spoken in heat, without any intention .... If the words be set down in writing, it argues more deliberate intention; and it has been held that writing is an overt act of treason; for *scribere est agere*. But even in this case the bare words are not the treason, but the deliberate act of writing them." 4 William Blackstone, *Commentaries on the Laws of England* 80 (1769).

Scribes. See AMERICAN SOCIETY OF WRITERS ON LEGAL SUBJECTS.

scrip. (18c) **1.** A document that entitles the holder to receive something of value. See LAND SCRIP. **2.** Money, esp. paper money, that is issued for temporary use as a substitute for legal tender. • It constitutes a form of credit.

▸ **Internet scrip.** (1998) **1.** Value that may be exchanged over the Internet but may not be exchanged for money. • Internet scrip is analogous to coupons or bonus points that can be exchanged by a consumer for goods or services but that have no cash value. **2.** See *e-money* under MONEY. — Also termed *online scrip.*

▸ **on-line scrip.** See *Internet scrip.*

scrip dividend. See DIVIDEND.

scrip issue. See BONUS ISSUE.

script (14c), *n.* **1.** An original or principal writing. **2.** Handwriting.

scripto (**skrip**-toh). [Latin] *Hist.* By writing.

scripto vel juramento (**skrip**-toh vel joor-ə-**men**-toh). [Law Latin] *Hist.* By writ or oath. • The phrase appeared in reference to the mode of proof required in certain cases.

scriptum indentatum (**skrip**-təm in-den-**tay**-təm). [Law Latin "indented writing"] (17c) *Hist.* An indenture.

scrivarius. *Law Latin.* A notary public.

scrivener (**skriv**-[ə]-nər). (14c) A writer; esp., a professional drafter of contracts or other documents.

▸ **money scrivener.** See MONEY SCRIVENER.

scrivener's error. See *clerical error* under ERROR (2).

scrivener's exception. (1978) The rule that the attorney–client privilege does not apply when the attorney is retained solely to perform a ministerial task for the client, such as preparing a statutory-form deed.

scroll, *n.* (15c) **1.** A roll of paper, esp. one containing a writing; a list. **2.** A draft or outline to be completed at a later time. **3.** A written mark; esp., a character affixed to a signature in place of a seal. — Also termed (in sense 3) *scrawl.*

Scroops's Inn. See SERJEANT'S INN.

scruet-roll (**skroo**-ət-**rohl**). (17c) *Hist.* The record of bail accepted in a habeas corpus case.

scrutator (skroo-**tay**-tər), *n.* [Latin fr. *scrutari* "to search"] **1.** *Hist.* A bailiff or officer who enforces the king's water rights, as by supervising wreckage, flotsam, and jetsam; a customs officer. **2.** *Archaic.* A close examiner or inquirer.

S.Ct. *abbr.* **1.** SUPREME COURT. **2.** Supreme Court Reporter.

scurrility. 1. One or more slanderous, abusive, or off-color remarks; vulgar, indecent, or abusive language. **2.** The quality of whatever is scandalous, abusive, or indecent. — **scurrilous,** *adj.*

scutage (**skyoo**-tij), *n.* [fr. Latin *scutum* "a shield"] (15c) *Hist.* **1.** A monetary payment levied by the king on barons as a substitute for some or all of the knights to be supplied to the king by each baron. • This payment seems to date from the 12th century, Henry II (1154–1189) having levied five scutages in the first 11 years of his reign. **2.** A fee paid by a tenant-in-chief by knight-service in lieu of serving in a war. **3.** A tax on a knight's estate to help furnish the army. — Also termed *escuage*; *shield-money*.

> "Scutage . . . . Shield-money, in mediaeval feudal law, a payment in lieu of military service, paid by a tenant-in-chief in respect of the service of knights which he owed to the Crown. His personal obligation to serve could not be discharged by scutage but only by fine. Payment of scutage, though known in France and Germany, was most highly developed in England where it became a general tax on knights' estates at rates which by the thirteenth century were standardized. King John demanded frequent and heavy scutages and Magna Carta forbade the levying of scutage without the consent of a general council. Scutage was divided between the King and the tenants-in-chief who gave personal service in the campaign. It became obsolete by the fourteenth century." David M. Walker, *The Oxford Companion to Law* 1121 (1980).

scutagio habendo. See DE SCUTAGIO HABENDO.

scyra (**shy**-rə), *n.* [Law Latin "shire"] *Hist.* **1.** A county; shire. **2.** A county's inhabitants.

S.D. *abbr.* Southern District, in reference to U.S. judicial districts.

s/d b/l. *abbr.* Sight draft with bill of lading attached. See *sight draft* under DRAFT (1).

SDP. *abbr.* Sexually dangerous person.

S.E. *abbr.* SOUTH EASTERN REPORTER.

sea. (bef. 12c) **1.** The ocean <on the sea>. **2.** A large landlocked part of the ocean; a large body of salt water smaller than a regular ocean <the Mediterranean Sea>. **3.** The ocean swell <a rough sea>. **4.** An extremely large or extended quantity <a sea of documents>.

- ▸ **free seas.** See *high seas.*
- ▸ **high seas.** (13c) *Int'l law.* The ocean waters beyond the jurisdiction of any country. • Under traditional international law, the high seas began 3 miles from the coastline. Under the 1982 U.N. Convention on the Law of the Sea, which is generally accepted as international law today, the high seas begin 200 nautical miles from the coastline, outside any country's exclusive economic zone. — Also termed *free seas*; *open seas*; *main seas.*
- ▸ **main sea.** (16c) *Archaic.* The open ocean; high seas.
- ▸ **navigable sea.** See NAVIGABLE SEA.
- ▸ **open seas.** See *high seas.*
- ▸ **territorial sea.** (18c) *Int'l law.* The ocean waters over which a coastal country has sovereignty, extending seaward up to 12 nautical miles from the coastline. Cf. *territorial waters* under WATERS.

seabed. (1838) The sea floor; the ground underlying the ocean, over which countries may assert sovereignty, esp. if underlying their territorial waters.

sea brief. See SEA LETTER.

sea carriage. See CARRIAGE BY SEA.

sea-customs zone. See CUSTOMS ZONE.

seagoing vessel. See VESSEL.

seal, *n.* (13c) **1.** A fastening that must be broken before access can be obtained; esp., a device or substance that joins two things, usu. making the seam impervious. — Also termed *common-law seal.* **2.** A piece of wax, a wafer, or some other substance affixed to the paper or other material on which a promise, release, or conveyance is written, together with a recital or expression of intention by which the promisor, releasor, or grantor manifests that a piece of wax, wafer, or other substance is a seal. • The purpose of a seal is to secure or prove authenticity. **3.** A design embossed or stamped on paper to authenticate, confirm, or attest; an impression or sign that has legal consequence when applied to an instrument.

> "[W]hen seals came into use they obviously made the evidence of the charter better, in so far as the seal was more difficult to forge than a stroke of the pen. Seals acquired such importance, that, for a time, a man was bound by his seal, although it was affixed without his consent. At least a seal came to be required, in order that a charter should have its ancient effect. A covenant or contract under seal was no longer a promise well proved; it was a promise of a distinct nature, for which a distinct form of action came to be provided. . . . The man who had set hand to a charter, from being bound because he had consented to be, and because there was a writing to prove it, was now held by force of the seal and by deed alone as distinguished from all other writings. And to maintain the integrity of an inadequate theory, a seal was said to input a consideration." Oliver Wendell Holmes, *The Common Law* 272–73 (1881).

> "The use of the seal in England seems to have begun after the Norman Conquest, spreading from royalty and a few of the nobility to those of lesser rank. Originally a seal often consisted of wax bearing the imprint of an individualized signet ring, and in the seventeenth century Lord Coke said that wax without impression was not a seal. But in the United States the courts have not required either wax or impression. Impressions directly on the paper were recognized early and are still common for notarial and corporate seals, and gummed wafers have been widely used. In the absence of statute decisions have divided on the effectiveness of the written or printed word 'seal,' the printed initials 'L.S.' (locus sigilli, meaning place of the seal), a scrawl made with a pen (often called a 'scroll') and a recital of sealing. Most states in which the seal is still recognized now have statutes giving effect to one or more such devices." Restatement (Second) of Contracts § 96 cmt. a (1979).

> "The time-honoured form of seal was a blob of wax at the foot of the document, bearing an imprint of some kind, often a crest or motto. The use of wax was not, however, necessary for a seal, and any mark or impression on the paper was sufficient as long as it was made with the intention of affixing a seal. Recent English cases have been willing to find the necessary intention in circumstances where courts in the past would almost certainly have declined; so much so that it may now be the common law that a document purporting to be executed as a deed but lacking actual sealing will be regarded as sealed as long as it contains a printed or written indication of where the mark or impression constituting the seal should be placed if it were to be affixed." Peter Butt, *Land Law* 481–82 (2d ed. 1988).

- ▸ **corporate seal.** (18c) A seal adopted by a corporation for executing and authenticating its corporate and legal instruments. — Also termed *corporation seal.*
- ▸ **great seal.** (15c) **1.** The official seal of the United States, of which the Secretary of State is the custodian, used to authenticate certain documents issued by the federal government. — Also termed *seal of the United States.* **2.** The official seal of a particular state. — Also termed *seal of the state*; *state seal.* **3.** The official seal of Great Britain, of which the Lord Chancellor is the custodian.
- ▸ **notary seal.** See NOTARY SEAL.
- ▸ **private seal.** (16c) A corporate or individual seal, as distinguished from a public seal.
- ▸ **public seal.** (16c) A seal used to certify documents belonging to a public authority or government bureau.

▸ **quarter seal.** (15c) A seal (originally a quarter section of the great seal) maintained in the Scotch chancery to be used on particular grants from the Crown. See *great seal* (3).

▸ **seal of the state.** See *great seal* (2).

▸ **seal of the United States.** See *great seal* (1).

▸ **state seal.** See *great seal* (2).

▸ **wafer seal.** (17c) A plastic or paper disk, usu. red or gold, affixed to a legal document as a substitute for a wax seal. • Wafers are more common in the United Kingdom than in the U.S. — Sometimes shortened to *wafer.*

seal, *vb.* (14c) **1.** To fasten up or enclose securely with or as if with a seal <to seal a letter> <to seal a door>. **2.** To prevent access to (a document, record, etc.), esp. by court order <to seal the record of the proceedings>. **3.** Figuratively, to close up tightly or keep secret <to seal one's thoughts and feelings>. **4.** To affix a seal to in attestation of authenticity <to seal a deed>. **5.** To signify agreement to as if by attaching one's seal <they sealed the deal>. **6.** To establish or settle beyond question; to confirm <to seal his fate>. **7.** *Archaic.* To designate irrevocably <King Mongkut sealed the girl for his own>. **8.** *Eccles. law.* To sign with the cross <the priest sealed them as husband and wife>. **9.** *Eccles. law.* To baptize <the baby was sealed on March 26>.

sea lane. (1878) *Int'l & maritime law.* A designated course or regularly used route for oceangoing ships, esp. in restricted waters such as harbors and straits. • Although sea lanes have obvious safety advantages, they were long resisted by sea captains, who saw them as a threat to their freedom to navigate.

sea law. See MARITIME LAW.

sealed and delivered. See SIGNED, SEALED, AND DELIVERED.

sealed bid. See BID (2).

sealed-container rule. (1961) *Products liability.* The principle that a seller is not liable for a defective product if the seller receives the product from the manufacturer and sells it without knowing of the defect or having a reasonable opportunity to inspect the product.

sealed contract. See *contract under seal* under CONTRACT.

sealed document. See *sealed instrument* under INSTRUMENT (2).

sealed indictment. See INDICTMENT.

sealed instrument. See INSTRUMENT (2).

sealed-record statute. See CONFIDENTIALITY STATUTE.

sealed testament. See *mystic will* under WILL.

sealed verdict. See VERDICT (1).

sealed will. See *mystic will* under WILL.

sealer, *n.* (14c) **1.** An official inspector of weights and measures who stamps as correct those that are formed to be so. **2.** Someone whose job is to affix official seals to legal instruments and other documents.

sea letter. (17c) *Hist.* A manifest issued during a war by authorities of a port where a neutral vessel is fitted, certifying the vessel's nationality, specifying the nature of and destination of the vessel's cargo, and allowing the vessel to sail under the neutral flag of its owner. • The last sea letter was issued at the Port of New York in 1806, and the use of sea letters was discontinued by proclamation of President James Madison. — Also spelled *sea-letter.* — Also termed *sea brief; sea pass; passport.*

> "Our laws require masters of vessels, on entering a port for traffic, to lodge with the consul their registers, sea-letters, and passports . . . ." Theodore D. Woolsey, *Introduction to the Study of International Law* 161–62 (5th ed. 1878).

sealing of records. (1953) The act or practice of officially preventing access to particular (esp. juvenile-criminal) records, in the absence of a court order. Cf. EXPUNGEMENT OF RECORD.

seal of cause. (17c) *Scots law.* The seal of a burgh court, by which a royal burgh could, consistently with its charter powers, create a subordinate corporation by charter. • The seal of cause was most commonly used to create charitable corporations and craft guilds.

seal of the state. See *great seal* (2) under SEAL.

seal of the United States. See *great seal* (1) under SEAL.

seaman. (bef. 12c) *Maritime law.* Under the Jones Act and the Longshore and Harbor Workers' Compensation Act, a person who is attached to a navigating vessel as an employee below the rank of officer and contributes to the function of the vessel or the accomplishment of its mission. • Seamen's injuries are covered under the Jones Act and the general maritime law. — Also termed *crew member; mariner; sailor; member of a crew.* See JONES ACT. Cf. STEVEDORE.

> "The Jones Act plaintiff must be a 'seaman' who is injured (or killed) 'in the course of his employment.' The 'course of . . . employment' requirement at least excluded passengers, guests, trespassers, pirates (unless of course the pirate was suing his own employer) and so on. Who else might be excluded (or included) was, as a matter of initial construction, impossible to say. After a half-century of litigation the answer to the riddle is not apparent. The Supreme Court has alternated between giving the term 'seaman' an exceedingly broad construction and giving it a much narrower one. Consequently defendants have been encouraged to argue, in all but the most obvious cases, that plaintiff is not a Jones Act seaman and that the action must be dismissed. Thus there has always been, there continues to be, and presumably there will go on being a substantial volume of depressing litigation of this type." Grant Gilmore & Charles L. Black Jr., *The Law of Admiralty* § 6-21, at 328 (2d ed. 1975).

▸ **able-bodied seaman.** (18c) An experienced seaman who is qualified for all seaman's duties and certified by an inspecting authority. — Abbr. AB; ABS. — Also termed *able seaman; bluewater seaman.*

▸ **merchant seaman.** (1824) A sailor employed by a private vessel, as distinguished from one employed in public or military service; a member of the merchant marine. See MERCHANT MARINE.

▸ **ordinary seaman.** (18c) A seaman who has some experience but not enough to be classified as an able-bodied seaman. — Abbr. OS; OD.

seaman's will. See *soldier's will* under WILL.

sea pass. See SEA LETTER.

sea power. (17c) **1.** Naval strength; the size and relative might of a country's navy. **2.** A country with a powerful navy.

search, *n.* (14c) **1.** *Criminal procedure.* An examination of a person's body, property, or other area that the person would reasonably be expected to consider as private, conducted by a law-enforcement officer for the purpose of finding evidence of a crime. • Because the Fourth Amendment prohibits unreasonable searches (as well as seizures), a search cannot ordinarily be conducted without probable cause.

"It must be recognized that whenever a police officer accosts an individual and restrains his freedom to walk away, he has 'seized' that person. And it is nothing less than sheer torture of the English language to suggest that a careful exploration of the outer surfaces of a person's clothing all over his or her body in an attempt to find weapons is not a 'search.'" *Terry v. Ohio*, 392 U.S. 1, 16, 88 S.Ct. 1868, 1877 (1968).

▸ **administrative search.** (1960) *Administrative law.* The inspection of a facility by one or more officials of an agency with jurisdiction over the facility's fire, health, or safety standards. • The administrative search is an exception to the rule that searches require a warrant based on probable cause. Because an administrative search is not related to a criminal investigation, no warrant is usu. required. — Also termed *regulatory search*; *inspection search*.

▸ **border search.** (1922) **1.** A search conducted at the border of a country, esp. at a checkpoint, to exclude illegal aliens and contraband.

"[W]arrantless searches and seizures conducted at national boundaries are permitted under the general authority of the United States to ensure the integrity of its borders. As the Supreme Court stated in *Carroll v. United States*, such activity ensures 'national self-protection reasonably requiring one entering the country to identify himself as entitled to come in, and his belongings as effects which may be lawfully brought in.' [267 U.S. 132, 154, 45 S.Ct. 280, 285 (1925).] Thus, the right to remain silent and protect one's personal belongings from government intrusion, normally afforded constitutional protection, are surrendered at the border." Charles H. Whitebread, *Criminal Procedure* § 12.02, at 227 (1980).

2. Loosely, a search conducted near the border of a country. • Generally, searches near the U.S. border are treated no differently from those conducted elsewhere in the country.

▸ **checkpoint search.** (1973) **1.** A search anywhere on a military installation. **2.** A search in which police officers set up roadblocks and stop motorists to ascertain whether the drivers are intoxicated.

▸ ***Chimel* search.** See *protective search*.

▸ **consent search.** (1965) A search conducted after a person with the authority to do so voluntarily waives Fourth Amendment rights. • The government has the burden to show that the consent was given freely — not under duress. *Bumper v. North Carolina*, 391 U.S. 543, 548–49, 88 S.Ct. 1788, 1792 (1968). — Also termed *consensual search*; *permissive search*.

▸ **constructive search.** (1946) A subpoena of a corporation's records.

"[I]t is settled that the so-called 'constructive search' involved in an administrative subpoena of corporate books or records constitutes a 'search' or 'seizure' within the meaning of the Fourth Amendment." 68 Am. Jur. 2d *Searches and Seizures* § 44, at 674 (1993).

▸ **digital body-cavity search.** See *manual body-cavity search*.

▸ **emergency search.** (1971) A warrantless search conducted by a police officer who has probable cause and reasonably believes that, because of a need to protect life or property, there is not enough time to obtain a warrant. See EMERGENCY DOCTRINE (3).

▸ **exigent search** (**eks**-ə-jənt). (1974) A warrantless search carried out under exigent circumstances, such as an imminent danger to human life or a risk of the destruction of evidence. See *exigent circumstances* under CIRCUMSTANCE.

▸ **illegal search.** See *unreasonable search*.

▸ **inspection search.** See *administrative search*.

▸ **inventory search.** (1966) A complete search of an arrestee's person before the arrestee is booked into jail. • All possessions found are typically held in police custody.

▸ **investigative search.** (1964) A search, esp. a police search, of the contents of a place, vehicle, bag, or the like for the purpose of cataloguing the items, eliminating dangerous items, and protecting the custodian from theft claims.

▸ **manual body-cavity search.** (1982) A strip search in which the police engage in some touching or probing of a person's orifices. — Also termed *digital body-cavity search*. Cf. *visual body-cavity search*.

▸ **no-knock search.** (1970) A search of property by the police without knocking and announcing their presence and purpose before entry. • A no-knock search warrant may be issued under limited circumstances, as when a prior announcement would probably lead to the destruction of the objects searched for, or would endanger the safety of the police or another person. Such a search is usu. effected by knocking down (not on) a door. See *no-knock search warrant* under SEARCH WARRANT.

▸ **permissive search.** See *consent search*.

▸ **pretextual search.** (1968) A police search of a person or vehicle for fabricated reasons that are calculated to forestall or preclude constitutional objections. — Also termed *pretext search*.

▸ **private search.** A search conducted by a private person rather than by a law-enforcement officer. • Items found during a private search are generally admissible in evidence if the person conducting the search was not acting at the direction of a law-enforcement officer.

▸ **protective search.** (1967) **1.** A search of a detained suspect and the area within the suspect's immediate control, conducted to protect the arresting officer's safety (as from a concealed weapon) and often to preserve evidence. • Typically broader than a search incident to arrest, a protective search can be conducted without a warrant. *Chimel v. California*, 395 U.S. 752, 89 S.Ct. 2034 (1969). — Also termed *Chimel search* (shə-**mel**). Cf. *search incident to arrest*. **2.** Broadly, any search conducted to secure an area.

▸ **regulatory search.** See *administrative search*.

▸ **search incident to arrest.** (1930) A warrantless search of a suspect's person and immediate vicinity, no warrant being required because of the need to keep officers safe and to preserve evidence. • Although protective in nature, a search incident to arrest is typically narrower than a protective search (in sense 2), confined to an area within reach of the arrested person and perhaps companions. Cf. *protective search*.

▸ **sector search.** See *zone search*.

▸ **shakedown search.** (1952) A usu. unannounced and warrantless search for illicit or contraband material (such as weapons or drugs) in a prisoner's cell <no weapons were found during the shakedown>. — Often shortened to *shakedown*.

▸ **strip search.** (1955) A search of a suspect whose clothes have been removed, the purpose usu. being to find any contraband the person might be hiding.

▸ **unreasonable search.** (18c) A search conducted without probable cause or other considerations that would make it legally permissible. — Also termed *illegal search*.

▸ **visual body-cavity search.** (1980) A strip search in which, without touching, a law-enforcement officer closely inspects a person's orifices. — Also termed *visual body-cavity inspection*. Cf. *manual body-cavity search*.

▸ **voluntary search.** (1936) A search in which no duress or coercion has been applied to obtain the defendant's consent. See *consent search*.

▸ **warranted search.** (1968) A search conducted under authority of a search warrant.

▸ **warrantless search.** (1950) A search conducted without obtaining a warrant. • Warrantless searches are permissible under exigent circumstances or when conducted incident to an arrest. See *exigent circumstances* under CIRCUMSTANCE; *protective search*.

▸ **zone search.** A search of a crime scene (such as the scene of a fire or explosion) by dividing it up into specific sectors. — Also termed *sector search*.

2. An examination of public documents or records for information; esp., TITLE SEARCH. **3.** *Int'l law*. The wartime process of boarding and examining the contents of a merchant vessel for contraband. • A number of treaties regulate the manner in which the search must be conducted. See RIGHT OF SEARCH.

search-and-rescue dog. See *search dog* under DOG (1).

search-and-seizure warrant. See SEARCH WARRANT.

search book. (1912) A lawbook that contains no statements of the law but instead consists of lists or tables of cases, statutes, and the like, used simply to help a researcher find the law. • Most indexes, other than index-digests, are search books.

search committee. See COMMITTEE (1).

search dog. See DOG (1).

searcher, *n*. (14c) **1.** Anyone who searches. **2.** A customs officer charged with searching passengers, suitcases, trunks, etc., for concealed dutiable goods. **3.** A person employed by a transportation company to search for lost goods. **4.** One whose business is to search public records for information on land titles, encumbrances, and the like. **5.** A police or prison official who searches arrestees and prisoners. **6.** *Hist. Scots law*. An officer responsible for arresting loiterers and disorderly persons during church services. **7.** *Hist. English law*. A person appointed to hold inquests.

search incident to arrest. See SEARCH (1).

search of patentability. See PATENTABILITY SEARCH.

search order. (1969) A court order directing a probation officer to search a probationer or the probationer's residence upon reasonable suspicion that a condition of probation has been violated.

search party. (1884) A group of people organized to look for someone or something that is missing or lost.

search report. *Patents*. A list of prior-art documents cited by the patent examiner during the patent application's preliminary examination.

search warrant. (18c) *Criminal law*. A judge's written order authorizing a law-enforcement officer to conduct a search of a specified place and to seize evidence. *See* Fed. R. Crim. P. 41. — Also termed *search-and-seizure warrant*. See WARRANT (1).

▸ **all-persons-present search warrant.** (1989) A search warrant that allows the police to search everyone present at a location identified in the warrant.

▸ **anticipatory search warrant.** (1973) A conditional search warrant that becomes effective only if and when some event occurs that itself creates the probable cause that permits the search. • For example, an anticipatory search warrant might take effect upon the mail delivery and acceptance of a package that tests positive for contraband.

▸ **blanket search warrant.** (1921) **1.** A single search warrant that authorizes the search of more than one area. **2.** An unconstitutional warrant that authorizes the seizure of everything found at a given location, without specifying which items may be seized. See *general warrant* (2) under WARRANT (1).

▸ **covert-entry search warrant.** (2004) A warrant authorizing law-enforcement officers to clandestinely enter private premises in the absence of the owner or occupant without prior notice, and to search the premises and collect intangible evidence, esp. photographs and eyewitness information. • Although previously used in federal criminal investigations, these types of warrants were first given express statutory authority by the USA Patriot Act. 18 USCA § 3103a. Information gathered while executing a sneak-and-peek warrant can later be used to support a search warrant under which physical evidence can be seized. — Also termed *sneak-and-peek search warrant*; *surreptitious-entry search warrant*.

▸ **general search warrant.** (18c) *Hist*. A search warrant that specifies neither the place to be searched nor a particular person to be apprehended, giving the holder almost limitless discretion. • General warrants violate the Fourth Amendment.

▸ **no-knock search warrant.** (1972) A search warrant that authorizes the police to enter premises without knocking and announcing their presence and purpose before entry because a prior announcement would lead to the destruction of the objects searched for or would endanger the safety of the police or another person. See *no-knock search* under SEARCH (1). Cf. KNOCK-AND-ANNOUNCE RULE .

▸ **sneak-and-peek search warrant.** (1993) See *covert-entry search warrant*.

▸ **surreptitious-entry search warrant.** See *covert-entry search warrant*.

▸ **video-surveillance warrant.** (1985) A search warrant permitting police to use video cameras or similar devices, with or without recording what is viewed.

search-warrant affidavit. See AFFIDAVIT.

sea reeve (see reev). (1855) *Hist.* An officer appointed to watch the shore and enforce a lord's maritime rights, including the right to wreckage.

sea rover. (16c) **1.** Someone who roves the sea for plunder; a pirate. **2.** A pirate vessel.

***Sears–Compco* doctrine.** (1966) The principle that Congress, by passing copyright, trademark, and patent laws, has preempted some state-law protection of information that is not protected by those statutes. *Sears, Roebuck & Co. v. Stiffel Co.*, 376 U.S. 225, 84 S.Ct. 784 (1964); *Compco Corp. v. Day-Brite Lighting, Inc.*, 376 U.S. 234, 84 S.Ct. 779 (1964). • The doctrine reflects a congressional policy decision that public access to information outweighs private economic incentives to collect and disseminate it. It limits how far states may protect against misappropriation.

seasonable, *adj.* (15c) Within the time agreed on; within a reasonable time <seasonable performance of the contract>.

seasonal agricultural worker. See *migrant worker* under WORKER (1).

seasonal employee. See EMPLOYEE.

seasonal employment. See EMPLOYMENT.

seat, *n.* (16c) **1.** Membership and privileges in an organization; esp., membership on a securities or commodities exchange <her seat at the exchange dates back to 1998>. **2.** The center of some activity <the seat of government>.

▸ **arbitral seat.** (1981) The legal or juridical home of an arbitration. • An arbitration award is "made" at the arbitral seat. — Also termed *place of arbitration*; *arbitral situs.*

> "The juridical function of the seat is to affiliate the arbitration with a particular legal system and its arbitration law and to indicate where, in a technical sense, any resulting award is considered made. The designation of an arbitral seat does not establish the place at which designated physical activities necessarily occur, but rather has several juridical consequences. The arbitration law of the seat ordinarily governs the arbitral proceedings, and customarily only the courts of the seat are empowered to set aside awards rendered there. . . . A place becomes the arbitral seat by virtue of having been designated as the seat by the parties or by an arbitral institution or a court on their behalf." Restatement (Third) of the U.S. Law of International Commercial Arbitration § 1-1 cmt. aa (Tent. Draft No. 2, May 22, 2012).

seated land. See LAND.

seat of government. (16c) The country's capital, a state capital, a county seat, or other location where the principal offices of the national, state, and local governments are located.

seaward. See CUSTOS MARIS.

seaworthy, *adj.* (1807) (Of a vessel) properly equipped and sufficiently strong and tight to resist the perils reasonably incident to the voyage for which the vessel is insured. • An implied condition of marine-insurance policies, unless otherwise stated, is that the vessel will be seaworthy. — **seaworthiness,** *n.*

seaworthy vessel. See VESSEL.

sec. *abbr.* (1934) **1.** (all cap.) SECURITIES AND EXCHANGE COMMISSION. **2.** Section. See SECTION (1).

secede, *vb.* (18c) To withdraw from an organization; esp., (of a country or state) to stop being part of another country by becoming independent.

secession. (17c) The process or act of withdrawing, esp. from a religious or political association; specif., a country or state's official ceasing to be part of another country by becoming independent <a secession from the established church> <the secession of 11 states at the time of the Civil War>.

secessionist, *n.* (1860) Someone who advocates secession, esp. of his or her own country or state from another country.

seck (sek), *adj.* (15c) *Hist.* **1.** Lacking the right or remedy of distress. **2.** Lacking profits, usu. because of a reversion without rent or other service. See RENT SECK.

second, *n.* (17c) *Parliamentary law.* **1.** A statement by a member other than a motion's maker that the member also wants the assembly to consider the motion <Is there a second to the motion?>. **2.** *Criminal law.* Someone who directs, assists, or supports another engaged in a duel. See DUEL (2). — **second,** *vb.*

Second Amendment. The constitutional amendment, ratified with the Bill of Rights in 1791, guaranteeing the right to keep and bear arms as necessary for securing freedom through a well-regulated militia. See RIGHT TO BEAR ARMS.

secondary, *adj.* (14c) (Of a position, status, use, etc.) subordinate or subsequent.

secondary, *n.* (17c) *Hist.* An officer of the courts of the King's Bench and common pleas, so called because he was next to the chief officer. • By the Superior Courts (Officers) Act (1837), the secondary office was abolished. St. 7 Will. 4; 1 Vict., ch. 30.

secondary abuse. See ABUSE.

secondary activity. (1942) *Labor law.* A union's picketing or boycotting of a secondary or neutral party, with the goal of placing economic pressure on that party so that it will stop doing business with the employer that is the primary subject of the labor dispute. • Secondary activities are forbidden by the Labor–Management Relations Act. 29 USCA § 158(b)(4). See *secondary boycott* under BOYCOTT; *secondary picketing* under PICKETING. Cf. PRIMARY ACTIVITY.

secondary affinity. See AFFINITY.

secondary amendment. See AMENDMENT (3).

secondary assumption of risk. See ASSUMPTION OF THE RISK.

secondary authority. See AUTHORITY (4).

secondary beneficiary. See *contingent beneficiary* (2) under BENEFICIARY.

secondary boycott. See BOYCOTT.

secondary consideration. See SECONDARY FACTOR.

secondary conveyance. See CONVEYANCE (1).

secondary creditor. See CREDITOR.

secondary devise. See *alternative devise* under DEVISE.

secondary distribution. See DISTRIBUTION.

secondary easement. See EASEMENT.

secondary-effects test. (1988) A judicial standard for assessing whether a regulation affecting free-speech interests is actually intended to diminish or eliminate an indirect harm flowing from the regulated expression. • Courts frequently apply the test in litigation relating to adult entertainment and gambling establishments. Its purpose is to distinguish content-specific regulation from content-neutral regulation. A regulation that is facially content-specific may be treated as content-neutral if its purpose is to diminish or eliminate a secondary effect of the speech, such as a zoning regulation for adult theaters when it is intended to limit crime. The test was first enunciated in *City of Renton v. Playtime Theatres, Inc.*, 475 U.S. 41, 106 S.Ct. 925 (1986).

secondary enforcement. See *secondary right* under RIGHT.

secondary evidence. See EVIDENCE.

secondary factor. (*usu. pl.*) *Patents.* Objective evidence that courts consider in determining a patent claim's nonobviousness. • Secondary factors include "commercial success, long-felt but unsolved need, failure of others, and unexpected results." *Graham v. John Deere Co.*, 383 U.S. 1, 17–18 (1966). — Also termed *secondary consideration.*

secondary insured. See *additional insured* under INSURED.

secondary insurer. See *excess insurer* under INSURER.

secondary invention. (1885) *Patents.* An invention that uses or incorporates established elements or combinations to achieve a new and useful result.

secondary lender. (1977) A wholesale mortgage buyer who purchases first mortgages from banks and savings-and-loan associations, enabling them to restock their money supply and loan more money.

secondary liability. See LIABILITY.

secondary-line competition. See *vertical competition* under COMPETITION.

secondary-line injury. (1954) *Antitrust.* Under the price-discrimination provisions of the Robinson-Patman Act, the act of hindering or seeking to hinder competition among a seller's customers by selling substantially the same products at favorable prices to one customer, or a select group of customers, to the detriment of others. 15 USCA § 13(a). • A secondary-line injury, which refers to competition among the seller's customers, is distinguishable from a primary-line injury, which refers to the anticompetitive effects that predatory pricing has on the direct competitors of the seller. Cf. PRIMARY-LINE INJURY.

secondary market. See MARKET.

secondary meaning. *Intellectual property.* A special sense that a trademark or tradename for a business, goods, or services has acquired even though the trademark or tradename was originally merely descriptive and therefore not protectable. • The term does not refer to a subordinate or rare meaning, but rather to a later meaning that has been added to the original one borne by the mark or name and that has now become in the market its usual and primary meaning. — Also termed *special meaning*; *trade meaning.*

> "Secondary meaning is *association*, nothing more. It exists only in the minds of those of the public who have seen or known or have heard of a brand of goods by some name or sign and have associated the two in their minds." Harry D. Nims, *The Law of Unfair Competition and Trade-Marks* 105 (1929).

secondary mortgage market. See MORTGAGE MARKET.

secondary motion. See MOTION (2).

secondary obligation. See OBLIGATION.

secondary offering. See OFFERING.

secondary party. *Commercial law.* **1.** A party not primarily liable under an instrument, such as a guarantor. **2.** The drawer or indorser of a negotiable instrument.

secondary picketing. See PICKETING.

secondary register. See SUPPLEMENTAL REGISTER.

secondary reserve ratio. See RESERVE RATIO.

secondary right. See RIGHT.

secondary source. **1.** A book, article, essay, etc. that analyzes something such as a legal doctrine or a historical event in such a way that it can be used to support an argument. **2.** See *secondary authority* under AUTHORITY (4).

secondary strike. See STRIKE (1).

secondary term. (1940) *Oil & gas.* The term of an oil-and-gas lease after production has been established, typically lasting "as long thereafter as oil and gas is produced from the premises." See HABENDUM CLAUSE. Cf. PRIMARY TERM.

secondary trading. See TRADING.

secondary use. See *shifting use* under USE (4).

second chair, *n.* (1968) A lawyer who helps the lead attorney in court, usu. by examining some of the witnesses, arguing some of the points of law, and handling parts of the voir dire, opening statement, and closing argument <the young associate was second chair for the fraud case>. Cf. FIRST CHAIR. — **second-chair,** *vb.*

second-collision doctrine. See CRASHWORTHINESS DOCTRINE.

second cousin. See COUSIN.

second-degree amendment. See *secondary amendment* under AMENDMENT (3).

second-degree manslaughter. See *involuntary manslaughter* under MANSLAUGHTER.

second-degree murder. See MURDER.

second-degree principal. See *principal in the second degree* under PRINCIPAL (2).

second deliverance. See DELIVERANCE (4).

second delivery. See DELIVERY.

second distress. See DISTRESS (2).

second-generation rights. See RIGHT.

secondhand evidence. See HEARSAY.

second-impact doctrine. See CRASHWORTHINESS DOCTRINE.

second lien. See LIEN.

second-look doctrine. (1962) **1.** WAIT-AND-SEE PRINCIPLE. **2.** An approach that courts use to monitor the continuing effectiveness or validity of an earlier order. • For example, a family court may reconsider a waiver of alimony, and a federal court may reconsider a statute that Congress has passed a second time after the first law was struck down as unconstitutional.

secondment (si-**kond**-mənt), *n.* (1897) A period of time that a worker spends away from his or her usual job, usu. either doing another job or studying.

second mortgage. See MORTGAGE.

second offense. See OFFENSE (2).

second-parent adoption. See ADOPTION (1).

second-permittee doctrine. (1994) *Insurance.* The principle that, when a third person is allowed to use an insured's car by permission granted by someone else to whom the insured gave permission to use the car, the third person's use of the car will be a permissive use, under the insured's automobile-liability-insurance policy, as long as that use falls within the scope of the permission originally given by the insured.

seconds, *n.* (17c) *Commercial law.* Goods that are defective or nonconforming because they do not meet a recognized standard.

second season. *Criminal law. Slang.* The period after a criminal defendant has exhausted state-court appeals and has begun habeas corpus proceedings in federal court.

second-step freezeout. See FREEZEOUT.

second surcharge. See SURCHARGE.

second-tier patent. See UTILITY MODEL.

second user. See JUNIOR USER.

secrecy. (15c) The quality, state, or condition of being concealed, esp. from those who would be affected by the concealment; hidden.

secret, *n.* (14c) **1.** Something that is kept from the knowledge of others or shared only with those concerned; something that is studiously concealed. See STATE SECRET; TRADE SECRET. **2.** Information that cannot be disclosed without a breach of trust; specif., information that is acquired in the attorney–client relationship and that either (1) the client has requested be kept private or (2) the attorney believes would be embarrassing or likely to be detrimental to the client if disclosed. • Under the ABA Code of Professional Responsibility, a lawyer usu. cannot reveal a client's secret unless the client consents after full disclosure. DR 4-101. Cf. CONFIDENCE (3).

secret agent. (18c) Someone whose job is to discover and report on the military and political secrets of other countries.

secretarius (sek-rə-**tair**-ee-əs), *n.* [Law Latin] See APOCRISARIUS.

secretary. (15c) **1.** An administrative assistant. **2.** A corporate officer in charge of official correspondence, minutes of board meetings, and records of stock ownership and transfer. — Also termed *clerk of the corporation.* **3.** *Parliamentary law.* An officer charged with recording a deliberative assembly's proceedings. — Also termed *clerk*; *recorder*; *recording secretary*; *recording officer*; *scribe*.

▸ **corporate secretary.** See CORPORATE SECRETARY.

▸ **corresponding secretary.** (18c) An officer in charge of an organization's correspondence, usu. including notices to members.

▸ **financial secretary.** (1836) **1.** An officer in charge of billing, collecting, and accounting for dues from the members. **2.** TREASURER.

▸ **private secretary.** (17c) One whose job it is to attend to correspondence, keep records, or transact other business for an individual, esp. an official.

4. An executive officer who manages and superintends a particular department of government of which he or she is the chief <Secretary of State>.

Secretary General. The chief administrative officer of the United Nations, nominated by the Security Council and elected by the General Assembly.

Secretary of Agriculture. The member of the President's cabinet who heads the U.S. Department of Agriculture.

Secretary of Commerce. The member of the President's cabinet who heads the U.S. Department of Commerce.

Secretary of Defense. The member of the President's cabinet who heads the U.S. Department of Defense.

Secretary of Education. The member of the President's cabinet who heads the U.S. Department of Education.

secretary of embassy. (18c) A diplomatic officer appointed as secretary or assistant, usu. to an ambassador or minister plenipotentiary.

Secretary of Energy. The member of the President's cabinet who heads the U.S. Department of Energy.

Secretary of Health and Human Services. The member of the President's cabinet who heads the U.S. Department of Health and Human Services.

Secretary of Homeland Security. The member of the President's cabinet who heads the U.S. Department of Homeland Security.

Secretary of Housing and Urban Development. The member of the President's cabinet who heads the U.S. Department of Housing and Urban Development.

Secretary of Labor. The member of the President's cabinet who heads the U.S. Department of Labor.

secretary of legation. (18c) An officer employed to attend a foreign mission and perform certain clerical duties.

Secretary of State. (18c) **1.** The member of the President's cabinet who heads the U.S. Department of State. • The Secretary is the first-ranking member of the cabinet and is also a member of the National Security Council. He or she is fourth in line of succession to the presidency after the Vice President, the Speaker of the House, and the President pro tempore of the Senate. **2.** A state government official who is responsible for the licensing and incorporation of businesses, the administration of elections, and other formal duties. • The secretary of state is elected in some states and appointed in others.

Secretary of the Interior. The member of the President's cabinet who heads the U.S. Department of the Interior.

Secretary of the Treasury. The member of the President's cabinet who heads the U.S. Department of the Treasury.

Secretary of Transportation. The member of the President's cabinet who heads the U.S. Department of Transportation.

Secretary of Veterans Affairs. The member of the President's cabinet who heads the U.S. Department of Veterans Affairs.

secret ballot. See BALLOT (2).

secret detainee. See DETAINEE.

secret detention. See DETENTION (1).

secret diplomacy. See DIPLOMACY (1).

secrete (si-**kreet**), *vb.* (17c) To remove or keep from observation, or from the knowledge of others; specif., to conceal or secretly transfer (property, etc.), esp. to hinder or prevent officials or creditors from finding it. — **secretion,** *n.*

secret equity. See *latent equity* under EQUITY (5).

secret evidence. See EVIDENCE.

secretion of assets. (1843) The hiding of property, usu. for the purpose of defrauding an adversary in litigation or a creditor.

secret lien. See LIEN.

secret mission. See *covert mission* under MISSION.

secret partner. See PARTNER.

secret police. (1823) In some countries, a government-controlled law-enforcement unit that surreptitiously tries to thwart or suppress the government's political enemies.

Secret Service. 1. UNITED STATES SECRET SERVICE. **2.** A U.K. government organization that both protects the country's military and political secrets and assets, as well as trying to obtain secrets about other countries.

secret session. See *executive session* under SESSION (1).

secret testament. See *mystic will* under WILL.

secret trust. See TRUST (3).

secret will. See *mystic will* under WILL.

secta (**sek**-tə), *n.* [Latin "suit"] **1.** *Roman law.* A group of followers, as of a particular religion or school of philosophy, law, etc.; a religious sect. **2.** *Hist.* People whom a plaintiff must bring to court to support the plaintiff's case. **3.** *Hist.* A lawsuit.

secta ad molendinum. See DE SECTA AD MOLENDINUM.

secta curiae (**sek**-tə **kyoor**-ee-ee). [Latin "suit of court"] (17c) *Hist.* Attendance at court, esp. by feudal tenants, who are obligated to attend the lord's court as jurors or parties.

secta facienda per illam quae habet eniciam partem (**sek**-tə fay-shee-**en**-də pər **il**-əm kwee **hay**-bət i-**nish**-ee-əm **pahr**-təm), *n.* [Law Latin "suit to be performed by her who has the eldest part"] (17c) *Hist.* A writ ordering the eldest heir or coparcener to perform suit and services for all the coheirs or coparceners.

secta regalis (**sek**-tə ri-**gay**-lis). [Latin "king's suit"] (17c) *Hist.* An obligation to attend the sheriff's court twice a year, so called because it had the same functions and jurisdiction as the king's court.

sectarian, *adj.* (17c) **1.** Of, relating to, or involving a particular religious sect; esp., supporting a particular religious group and its beliefs <sectarian college>. **2.** (Of violence, murder, etc.) related to the strong feelings of people who belong to different religious groups <sectarian clashes>. **3.** Limited in scope; parochial.

sectatoris (sek-tə-**tor**-is), *n.* [Latin] *Roman law.* A supporter of a candidate for office, who accompanied a candidate during a campaign, primarily to impress voters. Pl. ***sectatores.***

secta unica tantum facienda pro pluribus haereditatibus (**sek**-tə **yoo**-nə-kə **tan**-təm fay-shee-**en**- də proh **ploor**-ə-bəs hə-red-ə-**tay**-tə-bəs), *n.* [Law Latin "one suit alone to be performed for several inheritances"] (17c) *Hist.* A writ exempting the eldest heir, distrained by a lord to perform several services for the coheirs, from performing all services but one.

section. (16c) **1.** A distinct part or division of a writing, esp. a legal instrument. — Abbr. §; sec.; s. **2.** *Real estate.* A piece of land containing 640 acres, or one square mile. • Traditionally, public lands in the United States were divided into 640-acre squares, each one called a "section." — Also termed *section of land.*

▸ **half section.** (1809) A piece of land containing 320 acres, laid off either by a north-and-south or by an east-and-west line; half a section of land.

▸ **quarter section.** (1809) A piece of land containing 160 acres, laid off by a north-south or east-west line; one quarter of a section of land, formerly the amount usu. granted to a homesteader. — Often shortened to *quarter.*

Section 8 affidavit. See DECLARATION OF USE.

Section 8 and 15 affidavit. See COMBINED § 8 AND § 15 AFFIDAVIT.

Section 8 and 15 declaration. See COMBINED § 8 AND § 15 AFFIDAVIT.

Section 8 declaration. See DECLARATION OF USE.

section 8(f) agreement. (1973) *Labor law.* A labor contract that is negotiated between an employer in the construction business and a union that cannot demonstrate that it represents a majority of the employees at the time the contract is executed. 29 USCA § 158(f). • This is an exception to the general rule that an employer need only negotiate with a union that can demonstrate majority status. It was enacted in part because of the nature of the construction industry, in which the employers may have several different jobs in different parts of the country, the jobs are typically completed in a relatively short time, and the workforce is often transient. Since the workforce often does not have sufficient ties to a particular employer to petition for a certification election, section 8(f) agreements provide a certain level of protection in recognition of that fact. But section 8(f) agreements are not equivalent to collective-bargaining agreements. For example, the employer can legally repudiate the agreement at any time, and the employees may not legally picket to enforce the agreement. The main protection such an agreement provides is a monetary obligation, which can be enforced, if necessary, in federal court. And if the union achieves majority status, the section 8(f) agreement will essentially become a fully enforceable collective-bargaining agreement.

Section 15 affidavit. See DECLARATION OF INCONTESTABILITY.

Section 15 declaration. See DECLARATION OF INCONTESTABILITY.

Section 43(a) action. (1980) *Trademarks.* A private cause of action codified in the Lanham Trademark Act and covering a broad spectrum of deceptive trade practices, including passing off, false advertising, trade-dress infringement, trademark dilution, and cyberpiracy. 15 USCA § 1125(a).

Section 101 rejection. See REJECTION.

Section 102 rejection. See REJECTION.

Section 103 rejection. See REJECTION.

Section 112 rejection. See *vague-and-indefinite rejection* under REJECTION.

Section 337 investigation. *Intellectual property.* An in rem proceeding conducted by the U.S. International Trade Commission to determine whether products imported into the United States infringe intellectual-property rights or otherwise constitute unfair competition under federal law. 19 USCA § 337. • If the Commission determines that imported products infringe or violate another's intellectual-property rights, it may issue an exclusion order barring their importation. See EXCLUSION ORDER (3).

section of land. See SECTION (2).

sectis non faciendis (**sek**-tis non fay-shee-**en**-dis). See DE SECTIS NON FACIENDIS.

sector (sek-**tor**), *n.* [Latin] *Roman law.* A successful bidder at a public auction. Pl. ***sectores.***

sector search. See *zone search* under SEARCH (1).

secular, *adj.* (13c) Worldly, as distinguished from spiritual <secular business>.

secular clergy. (16c) **1.** Clergy who have no particular religious affiliation or do not belong to a particular religious denomination. **2.** Clergy who live in their parishes and minister there, as contrasted with regular clergy who live in monasteries.

secular trust. See TRUST (3).

secundem legem. (si-**ken**-dem **lee**-jəm. [Latin] (18c) According to law.

secundo (si-**kən**-doh), *adv.* [Latin] Secondly; in the second (place, year, etc.).

secundogeniture (si-kən-doh-**jen**-i-chər), *n.* (1855) **1.** The quality, state, or condition of being a second-born child, esp. a second-born son. **2.** A right or custom by which inheritance belongs to the second-born son. **3.** An estate or possession so inherited. Cf. PRIMOGENITURE.

secundum (si-**kən**-dəm), *adj.* [Latin] *Roman law.* According to; in favor of, as in *secundum actorem* ("in favor of the plaintiff").

secundum aequum et bonum (si-**kən**-dəm **ee**-kwəm et **boh**-nəm). [Latin] *Hist.* According to what is just and good.

secundum allegata et probata (si-**kən**-dəm al-ə-**gay**-tə et prə-**bay**-tə). [Latin] *Hist.* According to what is alleged and proved.

secundum artem (si-**kən**-dəm **ahr**-təm). [Latin] *Hist.* According to the art or trade.

secundum bonos mores (si-**kən**-dəm **boh**-nohs **mor**-eez). [Latin] *Hist.* According to good usages; customary.

secundum bonum et aequum (sə-**kən**-dəm **boh**-nəm et **ee**-kwəm). [Latin] *Hist.* According to that which is good and equitable.

secundum chartam conficiendam (sə-**kən**-dəm **kahr**-təm kən-fish-ee-**en**-dəm). [Law Latin] *Hist.* According to a charter to be granted. Cf. SECUNDUM TENOREM CHARTAE CONFECTAE.

secundum consuetudinem manerii (si-**kən**-dəm kon-swə-**t[y]oo**-də-nəm mə-**neer**-ee-ɪ). [Law Latin] *Hist.* According to the custom of the manor.

secundum formam chartae (si-**kən**-dəm **for**-məm **kahr**-tee). [Law Latin] *Hist.* According to the form of the charter.

secundum formam doni (si-**kən**-dəm **for**-məm **doh**-nɪ). [Latin] *Hist.* According to the form of the gift or grant.

secundum formam statuti (si-**kən**-dəm **for**-məm stə-**t[y]oo**-tɪ). [Law Latin] *Hist.* According to the form of the statute.

secundum legem communem (si-**kən**-dəm **lee**-jəm kə-**myoo**-nəm). [Law Latin] *Hist.* According to the common law.

secundum legem domicilii, vel loci contractus (sə-**kən**-dəm **lee**-jəm dom-ə-**sil**-ee-ɪ, vel **loh**-sɪ kən-**trak**-təs). [Law Latin] *Hist.* According to the law of the domicile or of the place where the contract was entered into. See *lex loci contractus* under LEX LOCI.

secundum materiam subjectam (sə-**kən**-dəm mə-**teer**-ee-əm səb-**jek**-təm). [Latin] *Hist.* According to the subject matter.

secundum naturam. [Latin] According to nature.

secundum normam legis (si-**kən**-dəm **nor**-məm **lee**-jis). [Latin] *Hist.* According to the rule of law; by rule of law.

secundum regulam (si-**kən**-dəm **reg**-yə-ləm). [Latin] *Hist.* According to the rule; by rule.

secundum subjectam materiam (si-**kən**-dəm səb-**jek**-təm mə-**teer**-ee-əm). [Law Latin] *Hist.* According to the subject matter.

secundum tenorem chartae confectae (sə-**kən**-dəm tə-**nor**-əm **kahr**-tee kən-**fek**-tee). [Latin] *Hist.* According to the tenor of the charter already granted. Cf. SECUNDUM CHARTAM CONFICIENDAM.

secundum vires hereditatis (sə-**kən**-dəm **vɪ**-reez hə-red-i-**tay**-tis). [Law Latin] *Hist.* According to the extent of the inheritance.

secundum vires inventarii (sə-**kən**-dəm **vɪ**-reez in-ven-**tair**-ee-ɪ). [Law Latin] *Hist.* According to the extent of the inventory.

secured, *adj.* (1875) **1.** (Of a debt or obligation) supported or backed by security or collateral. **2.** (Of a creditor) protected by a pledge, mortgage, or other encumbrance of property that helps ensure financial soundness and confidence. See SECURITY (1).

secured bond. See BOND (3).

secured claim. See CLAIM (5).

secured creditor. See CREDITOR.

secured debt. See DEBT.

secured loan. See LOAN.

secured note. See NOTE (1).

secured party. See *secured creditor* under CREDITOR.

secured transaction. (1936) A business arrangement by which a buyer or borrower gives collateral to the seller or lender to guarantee payment of an obligation. • Article 9 of the UCC deals with secured transactions. See SECURITY AGREEMENT.

securing order. A court order setting forth the conditions of release for an incarcerated defendant.

securitas (si-**kyoor**-i-tas), *n.* [Latin] **1.** *Roman law.* Security; freedom from liability after performance. **2.** *Civil law.* A release.

securitatem inveniendi (si-kyoor-i-**tay**-təm in-vee-nee-**en**-dɪ), *n.* [Law Latin] (17c) *Hist.* A writ from the Crown requiring subjects to find security to ensure that they would not leave the kingdom without the Crown's permission. • It was replaced by *ne exeat regno.* See NE EXEAT.

securitate pacis (si-kyoor-i-**tay**-tee **pay**-sis), *n.* [Law Latin "of security of the peace"] (17c) *Hist.* A writ for someone fearing bodily harm from another, as when the person has been threatened with violence. — Also termed *securitatis pacis; writ of threats.*

securities act. (1933) A federal or state law protecting the public by regulating the registration, offering, and trading of securities. See SECURITIES ACT OF 1933; SECURITIES EXCHANGE ACT OF 1934; BLUE-SKY LAW.

Securities Act of 1933. The federal law regulating the registration and initial public offering of securities, with an emphasis on full public disclosure of financial and other information. 15 USCA §§ 77a–77aa. — Also termed *Securities Act; 1933 Act.*

securities analyst. (1933) A person, usu. an employee of a bank, brokerage, or mutual fund, who studies a company and reports on the company's securities, financial condition, and prospects.

Securities and Exchange Commission. The five-member federal agency that regulates the issuance and trading of securities to protect investors against fraudulent or unfair practices. • The Commission was established by the Securities Exchange Act of 1934. — Abbr. SEC.

Securities and Investment Board. See FINANCIAL SERVICES AGENCY. — Abbr. SIB.

securities broker. See BROKER.

securities exchange. (1909) **1.** A marketplace or facility for the organized purchase and sale of securities, esp. stocks. **2.** A group of people who organize themselves to create such a marketplace; EXCHANGE (5). — Often shortened to *exchange.* — Also termed *stock exchange.*

▸ **regional securities exchange.** (1964) A securities exchange that focuses on stocks and bonds of local interest, such as the Boston, Philadelphia, and Midwest stock exchanges. — Also termed *regional stock exchange.*

Securities Exchange Act of 1934. The federal law regulating the public trading of securities. • This law provides for periodic disclosures by issuers of securities and for the registration and supervision of securities exchanges and brokers, and regulates proxy solicitations. The Act also established the SEC. 15 USCA §§ 78a et seq. — Also termed *Exchange Act; 1934 Act.*

Securities Investor Protection Act. A 1970 federal law establishing the Securities Investor Protection Corporation that, although not a governmental agency, is designed to protect investors whose brokers and dealers are in financial trouble. — Abbr. SIPA. 15 USCA §§ 78aaa et seq.

Securities Investor Protection Corporation. A federally chartered corporation established under the Securities Investor Protection Act to protect investors and help brokers in financial trouble. — Abbr. SIPC. See SECURITIES INVESTOR PROTECTION ACT.

securities-offering distribution. See DISTRIBUTION.

securities option. See STOCK OPTION.

securitizable, *adj.* (1986) **1.** Of, relating to, or constituting the class of obligations that a creditor (originator) may package and sell to others for corporate purposes. **2.** (Of an asset) capable of being rapidly converted to cash, as with commercial-loan receivables and trade accounts receivable.

securitize, *vb.* (1981) To convert (assets) into negotiable securities for resale in the financial market, allowing the issuing financial institution to remove assets from its books, and thereby improve its capital ratio and liquidity, and to make new loans with the security proceeds if it so chooses. — **securitized,** *adj.* — **securitization,** *n.*

security, *n.* (15c) **1.** Collateral given or pledged to guarantee the fulfillment of an obligation; esp., the assurance that a creditor will be repaid (usu. with interest) any money or credit extended to a debtor. See SATISDATION (1).

▸ **chattel security.** (1840) A security consisting of personal property. See CHATTEL.

2. Someone who is bound by some type of guaranty; SURETY. **3.** The quality, state, or condition of being secure, esp. from danger or attack. **4.** An instrument that evidences the holder's ownership rights in a firm (e.g., a stock), the holder's creditor relationship with a firm or government (e.g., a bond), or the holder's other rights (e.g., an option). • A security indicates an interest based on an investment in a common enterprise rather than direct participation in the enterprise. Under an important statutory definition, a security is any interest or instrument relating to finances, including a note, stock, treasury stock, bond, debenture, evidence of indebtedness, certificate of interest or participation in a profit-sharing agreement, collateral trust certificate, preorganization certificate or subscription, transferable share, investment contract, voting trust certificate, certificate of deposit for a security, fractional undivided interest in oil, gas, or other mineral rights, or certificate of interest or participation in, temporary or interim certificate for, receipt for, guarantee of, or warrant or right to subscribe to or purchase any of these things. A security also includes any put, call, straddle, option, or privilege on any security, certificate of deposit, group or index of securities, or any such device entered into on a national securities exchange, relating to foreign currency. 15 USCA § 77b(1). — Also termed (in sense 4) *evidence of indebtedness; evidence of debt.* Cf. SHARE, *n.* (2); STOCK (4).

> "What do the following have in common: scotch whisky, self-improvement courses, cosmetics, earthworms, beavers, muskrats, rabbits, chinchillas, fishing boats, vacuum cleaners, cemetery lots, cattle embryos, master recording contracts, animal feeding programs, pooled litigation funds, and fruit trees? The answer is that they have all been held to be securities within the meaning of federal or state securities statutes. The vast range of such unconventional investments that have fallen within the ambit of the securities laws' coverage is due to the broad statutory definition of a 'security' . . . ." 1 Thomas Lee Hazen, *Treatise on the Law of Securities Regulation* § 1.5, at 28–29 (3d ed. 1995).

▸ **adjustment security.** (2004) A stock or bond that is issued during a corporate reorganization. • The security holders' relative interests are readjusted during this process.

▸ **assessable security.** (1974) A security on which a charge or assessment covering the obligations of the issuing company is made. • Bank and insurance-company stock may be assessable.

▸ **asset-backed security.** (1982) A debt security (such as a bond) that is secured by assets that have been pooled and secured by the assets from the pool. — Abbr. ABS.

▸ **bearer security.** (1910) An unregistered security payable to the holder. Cf. *bearer bond* under BOND (3).

▸ **callable security.** See *redeemable security.*

▸ **certificated security.** (1975) A security that is a recognized investment vehicle, belongs to or is divisible into a class or series of shares, and is represented on an instrument payable to the bearer or a named person. *See* UCC § 8-102(a)(4).

▸ **collateral security.** (17c) **1.** A security, subordinate to and given in addition to a primary security, that is intended to guarantee the validity or convertibility of the primary security. **2.** COLLATERAL (2).

"'Collateral security' is a separate obligation, as the negotiable bill of exchange or promissory note of a third person, or document of title, or other representative of value, indorsed where necessary, and delivered by a debtor to his creditor, to secure the payment of his own obligation, represented by an independent instrument. Such collateral security stands by the side of the principal promise as an additional or cumulative means for securing the payment of the debt. The transfer, however, of the debtor's own negotiable promissory notes as collateral security for the payment of other notes made by him, does not come within any definition of collateral security; nor where the proposed collateral security is a negotiable promissory note of a person already liable on a bill of exchange, the payment of which is to be secured." William Colebrooke, *A Treatise on the Law of Collateral Securities* 2-3 (1883).

"The term 'collateral security' or 'collateral' means a pledge of incorporeal property assigned or transferred and delivered by a debtor or some one for him to a creditor as security for the payment of a debt or the fulfilment of an obligation. It stands by the side of the principal obligation as an additional means to secure the payment of the debt or fulfilment of the obligation." Leonard A. Jones, *A Treatise on the Law of Collateral Securities and Pledges* 2 (Edward M. White ed., 3d ed. 1912).

"The term 'collateral security' has come into quite frequent use of late to designate pledges of incorporeal personalty, and, when so used, it distinguishes in general the business of the banker from that of the pawnbroker. As thus used, the term is convenient and unobjectionable. Unfortunately, however, it is loosely applied to mortgages either of realty or personalty, and is often improperly used in still other senses." Armistead M. Dobie, *Handbook on the Law of Bailments and Carriers* 179 (1914).

▸ **consolidated security.** (*usu. pl.*) (1934) A security issued in large enough numbers to provide the funds to retire two or more outstanding issues of debt securities.

▸ **conversion security.** (1950) The security into which a convertible security may be converted, usu. common stock.

▸ **convertible security.** (1818) A security (usu. a bond or preferred stock) that may be exchanged by the owner for another security, esp. common stock from the same company, and usu. at a fixed price on a specified date. — Also termed (specif.) *convertible debt*; *convertible stock.*

▸ **coupon security.** (1972) A security with detachable interest coupons that the holder must present for payment as they mature. • Coupon securities are usu. in denominations of $1,000, and they are negotiable.

▸ **covered security.** (1968) A security that under federal law is exempt from state restrictions and regulation. • Because state laws set different requirements for individual companies to register, file, and comply with state regulations, the National Securities Market Improvement Act of 1996 created a uniform set of rules to standardize security regulations and filings nationwide. Most stocks traded in the U.S. are covered securities. — Also termed *federal covered security.*

▸ **debt security.** (1846) A security representing funds borrowed by the corporation from the holder of the debt obligation; esp., a bond, note, or debenture. • Generally, a debt security is any security that is not an equity security. See BOND (3).

▸ **dematerialized security.** See *uncertificated security.*

▸ **derivative security.** See DERIVATIVE (2).

▸ **divisional security.** (1880) A special type of security issued to finance a particular project.

▸ **equity security.** (1883) A security representing an ownership interest in a corporation (such as a share of stock) rather than a debt interest (such as a bond); any stock or similar security, or any security that is convertible into stock or similar security or carrying a warrant or right to subscribe to or purchase stock or a similar security, and any such warrant or right.

▸ **exempt security.** (1934) A security that need not be registered under the provisions of the Securities Act of 1933 and is exempt from the margin requirements of the Securities Exchange Act of 1934.

▸ **federal covered security.** See *covered security.*

▸ **first security.** See *first lien* under LIEN.

▸ **fixed-income security.** (1939) A security that pays a fixed rate of return, such as a bond with a fixed interest rate or a preferred stock with a fixed dividend.

▸ **fixed security.** A security representing a lien on a specified item or items.

▸ **government security.** (18c) A security issued by a government, a government agency, or a government corporation; esp., a security (such as a Treasury bill) issued by a U.S. government agency, with the implied backing of Congress. — Also termed *government-agency security*; *agency security*; *government bond.*

▸ **heritable security.** (1820) *Scots law.* A debt instrument secured by a charge on heritable property. — Also termed *inheritable security.* See *heritable bond* under BOND (2).

▸ **high-grade security.** (1930) A security issued by a company of sound financial condition and having the ability to maintain good earnings (e.g., a utility company security).

▸ **high-yield security.** See *high-yield bond* under BOND (3).

▸ **hybrid security.** (1936) A security with features of both a debt instrument (such as a bond) and an equity interest (such as a share of stock). • An example of a hybrid security is a convertible bond, which can be exchanged for shares in the issuing corporation and is subject to stock-price fluctuations.

▸ **investment security.** (1894) An instrument issued in bearer or registered form as a type commonly recognized as a medium for investment and evidencing a share or other interest in the property or enterprise of the issuer.

▸ **junior security.** (1885) A security that is subordinate to a senior security. • Junior securities have a lower priority in claims on assets and income.

▸ **landed security.** (18c) A mortgage or other encumbrance affecting land.

▸ **letter security.** See *restricted security.*

▸ **listed security.** (1910) A security accepted for trading on a securities exchange. • The issuing company must have met the SEC's registration requirements and complied with the rules of the particular exchange. — Also termed *listed stock.* See DELISTING.

▸ **long-term security.** (1912) **1.** A new securities issue with an initial maturity of ten years or more. **2.** On a balance sheet, a security with a remaining maturity of one year or more.

▸ **low-grade security.** (1949) A security with low investment quality. • Low-grade securities usu. offer higher yields to attract capital. See *high-yield bond* under BOND (3).

▸ **marginable security.** (1974) A security that can be bought on margin. — Also termed *margin stock.* See MARGIN.

▸ **margined security.** (1973) A security that is bought on margin and that serves as collateral in a margin account. See MARGIN.

▸ **marketable security.** (1835) A security that the holder can readily sell on a stock exchange or an over-the-counter market.

▸ **mortgage-backed security.** (1968) A security (esp. a pass-through security) backed by mortgages. • The cash flow from these securities depends on principal and interest payments from the pool of mortgages. See *stripped mortgage-backed security.*

▸ **municipal security.** See *municipal bond* under BOND (3).

▸ **noncallable security.** (1979) A security that cannot be redeemed, or bought back, at the issuer's option. — Also termed (specif.) *noncallable bond.*

▸ **nonmarketable security.** (1934) **1.** A security that cannot be sold on the market and can be redeemed only by the holder. **2.** A security that is not of investment quality.

▸ **outstanding security.** (1831) A security that is held by an investor and has not been redeemed by the issuing corporation.

▸ **pass-through security.** (1970) A security that passes through payments from debtors to investors. • Pass-through securities are usu. assembled and sold in packages to investors by private lenders who deduct a service fee before passing the principal and interest payments through to the investors.

▸ **personal security.** (18c) **1.** An obligation for the repayment of a debt, evidenced by a pledge or note binding a natural person, as distinguished from property. **2.** A person's legal right to enjoy life, health, and reputation.

▸ **public security.** A negotiable or transferable security that is evidence of government debt.

▸ **real security.** The security of mortgages or other liens or encumbrances on land. See COLLATERAL (2).

▸ **redeemable security.** (1830) Any security, other than a short-term note, that, when presented to the issuer, entitles the holder to receive a share of the issuer's assets or the cash equivalent. — Also termed *callable security.*

▸ **registered security.** (1834) **1.** A security whose owner is recorded in the issuer's books. • The issuer keeps a record of the current owners for purposes of sending dividends, interest payments, proxies, and the like. **2.** A security that is to be offered for sale and for which a registration statement has been submitted. — Also termed (specif.) *registered stock.*

▸ **restricted security.** (1939) A security that is not registered with the SEC and therefore may not be sold publicly unless specified conditions are met. • A restricted security is usu. acquired in a nonpublic transaction in which the buyer gives the seller a letter stating the buyer's intent to hold the stock as an investment rather than resell it. — Also termed *restricted stock; letter security; letter stock; unregistered security.*

▸ **senior security.** (1893) A security of a class having priority over another class as to the distribution of assets or the payment of dividends. 15 USCA § 77r(d)(4).

▸ **shelf security.** (1963) A security that is set aside for shelf registration.

▸ **short-term security.** (1926) A bond or note that matures and is payable within a brief period (often one year).

▸ **speculative security.** (1832) A security that, as an investment, involves a risk of loss greater than would usu. be involved; esp., a security whose value depends on proposed or promised future promotion or development, rather than on present tangible assets or conditions.

▸ **stripped mortgage-backed security.** (1986) A derivative security providing distributions to classes that receive different proportions of either the principal or interest payments from a pool of mortgage-backed securities. — Abbr. SMBS. See *mortgage-backed security.*

▸ **structured security.** (*usu. pl.*) (1987) **1.** A security whose cash-flow characteristics depend on one or more indexes, or that has an embedded forward or option. **2.** A security for which an investor's investment return and the issuer's payment obligations are contingent on, or highly sensitive to, changes in the value of the underlying assets, indexes, interest rates, or cash flows. SEC Rule 434(h) (17 CFR § 230.434(h)).

▸ **treasury security.** See *treasury stock* under STOCK.

▸ **uncertificated security.** (1976) A share or other interest in property or an enterprise, or an obligation of the issuer that is not represented by an instrument but is registered on the issuer's books. UCC § 8-102(a)(18). • This term was called *uncertified security* in earlier versions of the UCC. — Also termed (BrE) *dematerialized security.*

▸ **unlisted security.** (1932) An over-the-counter security that is not registered with a stock exchange. — Also termed *unlisted stock.*

▸ **unregistered security.** See *restricted security.*

▸ **voting security.** See *voting stock* under STOCK.

▸ **when-issued security.** (1945) A security that can be traded even though it has not yet been issued. • Any transaction that takes place does not become final until the security is issued.

▸ **worthless security.** (1852) A security that has lost its value, for which a loss (usu. capital) is allowed for tax purposes. IRC (26 USCA) § 165.

▸ **zero-coupon security.** (1981) A security (esp. a bond) that is issued at a large discount but pays no interest. • The face value of the bond is payable at maturity.

security agreement. (1909) An agreement that creates or provides for an interest in specified real or personal property to guarantee the performance of an obligation. • It must provide for a security interest, describe the collateral, and be signed by the debtor. The agreement may include other important covenants and warranties.

security clearance. (1963) Official permission for someone to enter a place or building, or to view secret documents and the like, typically after a rigorous background check.

Security Council. A principal organ of the United Nations, consisting of five permanent members (China, France, Russia, the United Kingdom, and the United States) and ten additional members elected at stated intervals, charged with the responsibility of maintaining international peace and security, and esp. of preventing or halting wars by diplomatic, economic, or military action. • The nonpermanent members are elected from each of the world's major regions, based on a distribution formula.

security deposit. See DEPOSIT (3).

security for costs. (17c) Money, property, or a bond given to a court by a plaintiff or an appellant to secure the payment of court costs if that party loses.

security grade. See SECURITY RATING.

security grading. See SECURITY RATING.

security interest. (1951) A property interest created by agreement or by operation of law to secure performance of an obligation, esp. repayment of a debt; specif., an interest in personal property or fixtures securing payment or performance of an obligation. • Although the UCC limits the creation of a security interest to personal property, the Bankruptcy Code defines the term to mean "a lien created by an agreement." 11 USCA § 101(51).

▸ **first security interest.** See *first lien* under LIEN.

▸ **perfected security interest.** (1955) A security interest that complies with the statutory requirements for achieving priority over a trustee in bankruptcy and unperfected interests. • A perfected interest may also have priority over another interest that was perfected later in time. See PERFECT.

▸ **purchase-money security interest.** (1957) A security interest that is created when a buyer uses the lender's money to make the purchase and immediately gives the lender security by using the purchased property as collateral (UCC § 9-103); a security interest that is either (1) taken or retained by the seller of the collateral to secure all or part of its price or (2) taken by a person who by making advances or incurring an obligation gives value to enable the debtor to acquire rights in or the use of collateral if that value is in fact so used. • If a buyer's purchase of a boat, for example, is financed by a bank that loans the amount of the purchase price, the bank's security interest in the boat that secures the loan is a purchase-money security interest. — Abbr. PMSI. — Also termed *purchase-money interest.*

▸ **unperfected security interest.** (1957) A security interest held by a creditor who has not established priority over any other creditor. • The only priority is over the debtor.

security police. (1915) **1.** Police whose mission is counterespionage. **2.** The military police of an air force. — Also termed (in sense 2) *air police.*

security rating. (1938) **1.** The system for grading or classifying a security by financial strength, stability, or risk. • Firms such as *Standard and Poor's* and *Moody's* grade securities. **2.** The classification that a given security is assigned to under this system. — Also termed *security grade; security grading; security rate.*

security risk. (1948) **1.** A situation that could endanger people. **2.** Someone within an organization, esp. government, who cannot be trusted with important secrets because he or she might divulge them to an enemy.

security service. (1918) A government organization whose mission is to protect a country's secrets and assets from enemy countries and to protect the government against any attempt to diminish its power.

secus (**see**-kəs). [Latin] Otherwise; to the contrary.

sedato animo (si-**day**-toh **an**-ə-moh). [Latin] With stated or settled purpose.

se defendendo (**see** def-en-**den**-doh), *adv.* [Law Latin] In self-defense; in defending oneself <homicide *se defendendo*>.

> "Homicide *se defendendo* is of two kinds. (1) Such, as tho it excuseth from death, yet it excuseth not the forfeiture of goods, . . . (2) Such as wholly acquits from all kinds of forfeiture." 1 Hale P.C. 478.

sedentary work. See WORK (1).

sedente curia (si-**den**-tee **kyoor**-ee-ə). [Latin] (18c) The court sitting; during the court sitting.

sede plena (**see**-dee **plee**-nə). [Latin] (1824) *Hist.* The see being filled. • This term indicated that a bishop's see was not vacant.

sederunt. See ACT OF SEDERUNT.

sedes (**see**-deez), *n.* [Latin "a seat"] **1.** *Roman law.* A private residence. **2.** *Roman law.* Judicial office; the bench. **3.** *Hist.* A see; a bishop's dignity.

sede vacante (**see**-dee və-**kan**-tee). [Law Latin] (17c) *Hist.* The benefice being vacant.

sedge flat. (1811) A tract of land below the high-water mark.

sedition, *n.* (14c) **1.** An agreement, communication, or other preliminary activity aimed at inciting treason or some lesser commotion against public authority. **2.** Advocacy aimed at inciting or producing — and likely to incite or produce — imminent lawless action. • At common law, sedition included defaming a member of the royal family or the government. The difference between *sedition* and *treason* is that the former is committed by preliminary steps, while the latter entails some overt act for carrying out the plan. But if the plan is merely for some small commotion, even accomplishing the plan does not amount to treason. Cf. TREASON. — **seditious,** *adj.*

> "*Sedition* — This, perhaps the very vaguest of all offences known to the Criminal Law, is defined as the speaking or writing of words calculated to excite disaffection against the Constitution as by law established, to procure the alteration of it by other than lawful means, or to incite any person to commit a crime to the disturbance of the peace, or to raise discontent or disaffection, or to promote ill-feeling between different classes of the community. A charge of sedition is, historically, one of the chief means by which Government, especially at the end of the eighteenth and the beginning of the nineteenth century, strove to put down hostile critics. It is evident that the vagueness of the charge is a danger to the liberty of the subject, especially if the Courts of Justice can be induced to take a view favourable to the Government." Edward Jenks, *The Book of English Law* 136 (P.B. Fairest ed., 6th ed. 1967).

Sedition Act. *Hist.* A 1798 federal statute that prohibited the malicious publication of defamatory material about the government, Congress, or the President. • The act expired in 1801.

seditious conspiracy. See CONSPIRACY.

seditious libel. See LIBEL (2).

seditious speech. See SPEECH.

sed non allocatur (sed non al-ə-**kay**-tər). [Law Latin] (18c) *Hist.* But it is not allowed or upheld. • This phrase was formerly used to indicate the court's disagreement with the arguments of counsel.

sed per curiam (sed pər **kyoor**-ee-əm). [Latin] (18c) But by the court. • This phrase is used to introduce (1) a statement made by the court disagreeing with counsel's arguments; or (2) the opinion of the whole court when different from the opinion of the single judge immediately before quoted.

sed quaere (sed **kweer**-ee). [Latin] (18c) But inquire; examine this further. • This remark indicates that the correctness of a particular statement is challenged.

seduction. (16c) *Archaic.* The offense that occurs when a man entices a woman of previously chaste character to have unlawful intercourse with him by means of persuasion, solicitation, promises, or bribes, or other means not involving force. • Many states have abolished this offense for persons over the age of legal consent. Traditionally, the parent of a young woman had an action to recover damages for the loss of her services. But in measuring damages, the jury could consider not just the loss of services but also the distress and anxiety that the parent had suffered in being deprived of her comfort and companionship. Though seduction was not a crime at common law, many American states made it a statutory crime until the late 20th century. — **seduce,** *vb.* — **seducer,** *n.*

sed vide (sed **VI**-dee). [Latin] (18c) But see. • This remark, followed by a citation, directs the reader's attention to an authority or a statement that conflicts with or contradicts the statement or principle just given. — Also termed *but see.*

see, *n.* (15c) The area or district of a bishop's jurisdiction <the see of Canterbury>.

seed money. (1966) Start-up money for a business venture; the money one has available to start a new business. — Also termed *front money; front-end money; seed capital.*

seeing-eye dog. See *service dog* under DOG (1).

seeming danger. See DANGER.

segregate, *vb.* (16c) **1.** To separate or make distinct from others or from a general aggregate; to isolate. **2.** To cause or require separation from others. **3.** To separate (a group of people) from others, esp. on grounds of race, sex, or religion; to practice or enforce a policy of segregation.

segregated, *adj.* (1948) **1.** Separated or set apart from others of the same or a similar kind or class <a segregated separate-property bank account>. **2.** (Of a school or other institution) accessible or available only to members of certain races, religion, etc. <segregated colleges>. **3.** (Of a system or institution) divided in facilities or administered independently for members of different groups or races <segregated restrooms>. **4.** Practicing or maintaining segregation, esp. of races <segregated states>.

segregation, *n.* (16c) **1.** The act or process of separating one thing or group from another; the quality or state of being separated.

- ▸ **punitive segregation.** (1958) The act of removing a prisoner from the prison population for placement in separate or solitary confinement, usu. for disciplinary reasons. — Also termed *punitive isolation.*

2. The unconstitutional policy of separating people on the basis of color, nationality, religion, or the like. Cf. DESEGREGATION. — **segregative,** *adj.*

- ▸ **de facto segregation.** (1958) Segregation that occurs without state authority, usu. on the basis of socioeconomic factors.
- ▸ **de jure segregation.** (1963) Segregation that is permitted by law.

segregationist. (1955) Someone who favors or practices segregation, esp. of the races.

seigneurial justice. See JUSTICE SEIGNEURIALE.

seignior (**seen**-yər), *n.* [Law French] (14c) *Hist.* An owner of something; a lord of a fee or manor. — Also spelled *seigneur* (seen- *or* sayn-**yər**); *seignor.* See SEIGNIORY.

- ▸ **seignior in gross** (**seen**-yər in **grohs**), *n.* [Law French] A lord having no manor but enjoying the other rights of lordship.

seigniorage (**seen**-yər-ij), *n.* [Law French] (15c) **1.** *Hist.* The tenure existing between lord and vassal. **2.** *Hist.* A prerogative of the Crown; specif., the charge made by the government for coining bullion into money; mintage. See BRASSAGE. **3.** The difference between the cost of bullion purchased by a government for coining and the nominal or face value of the coins that have been minted. **4.** *Archaic.* A royalty, as on a patent or copyright, or on mineral rights. • Most often, *seigniorage* in this sense denotes an overlord's royalty on the output of certain minerals on his lands.

seignioress (**seen**-yər-es *or* -is), *n.* [Law French] (17c) *Hist.* A female superior; a lady.

seigniory (**seen**-yər-ee), *n.* [Law French] (13c) *Hist.* **1.** The rights and powers of a lord; esp., a grantor's retained right to have the grantee perform services in exchange for the transfer of land. **2.** A lord's dominions; a feudal or manor lordship; esp., land held subject to such a retained right in the grantor. — Also spelled *seignory.*

seigniory in gross (**seen**-yər-ee in **grohs**). See *reputed manor* under MANOR.

seignor in gross. See SEIGNIOR.

seignory. See SEIGNIORY.

seise (seez), *vb.* (13c) To invest with seisin or establish as a holder in fee simple; to put in possession <he became seised of half a section of farmland near Amarillo>.

seised to uses. See STANDING SEISED TO USES.

seisin (**see**-zin), *n.* (14c) **1.** *Hist.* Completion of the ceremony of feudal investiture, by which the tenant was admitted into freehold. **2.** Possession of a freehold estate in land; ownership. **3.** *Louisiana law.* The right that the law accords universal successors to own and possess a person's estate directly and immediately upon that person's death. La. Civ. Code arts. 935 et seq. — Also spelled *seizin.* — Also termed *vesture; seisina;* (in Scots law) *sasine.*

> "Originally, seisin meant simply possession and the word was applicable to both land and chattels. Prior to the fourteenth century it was proper to speak of a man as being seised of land or seised of a horse. Gradually, seisin and possession became distinct concepts. A man could be said to be in possession of chattels, or of lands wherein he had an estate for years, but he could not be said to be seised of them. Seisin came finally to mean, in relation to land, possession under claim of a freehold estate therein. The tenant for years had possession but not seisin; seisin was in the reversioner who had the fee. And although the word 'seisin' appears in modern statutes with a fair degree of frequency, it is usually treated as synonymous with ownership." Cornelius J. Moynihan, *Introduction to the Law of Real Property* 98–99 (2d ed. 1988).

> "It is difficult to define seisin satisfactorily. It has nothing to do with 'seizing,' with its implication of violence. To medieval lawyers it suggested the very opposite: peace and quiet. A man who was put in seisin of land was 'set' there and continued to 'sit' there. Seisin thus denotes quiet possession of land, but quiet possession of a particular kind. . . . Although it seems impossible to frame a satisfactory definition . . . , to call it 'that feudal possession of land which only the owner of a freehold estate in freehold land could have' is to express the most important elements." Robert E. Megarry & M.P. Thompson, *A Manual of the Law of Real Property* 27–28 (6th ed. 1993).

▸ **actual seisin.** See *seisin in deed.*

▸ **constructive seisin.** See *seisin in law.*

▸ **covenant of seisin.** See COVENANT (4).

▸ **customary seisin.** See *quasi-seisin.*

▸ **equitable seisin.** (18c) **1.** Possession or enjoyment of a property interest or right enforceable in equity. **2.** See *seisin in law.*

▸ **fictitious seisin.** See *seisin in law.*

▸ **legal seisin.** See *seisin in law.*

▸ **livery of seisin.** See LIVERY OF SEISIN.

▸ **primer seisin** (**prim**-ər *or* **prɪ**-mər **see**-zin). (15c) *Hist.* A right of the Crown to receive, from the heir of a tenant who died in possession of a knight's fee, one year's profits of the inherited estate (or half a year's profits if the estate was in reversion); FIRST FRUITS (1).

▸ **quasi-seisin.** (1814) A copyholder's possession of lands, the freehold possession being in the lord. — Also termed *customary seisin.*

▸ **seisin in deed.** (17c) Actual possession of a freehold estate in land, by oneself or by one's tenant or agent, as distinguished from legal possession. — Also termed *seisin in fact; actual seisin.*

▸ **seisin in fact.** See *seisin in deed.*

▸ **seisin in law.** (17c) The right to immediate possession of a freehold estate in land, as when an heir inherits land but has not yet entered it. — Also termed *legal seisin; constructive seisin; equitable seisin; fictitious seisin.*

> "Seisin in law is, when something is done, which the law accounteth a *seisin;* as an inrollment." 2 Ephraim Chambers, *Cyclopedia: Or, an Universal Dictionary of Arts and Sciences* (1743), s.v. SEISIN IN FACT.

seisina (**see**-zin-ə), *n.* [Law Latin] *Hist.* Seisin.

seisina habenda (**see**-zin-ə hə-**ben**-də). See DE SEISINA HABENDA.

seisin in fact. See *seisin in deed* under SEISIN.

seisin in law. See SEISIN.

seisor (**see**-zər), *n.* (16c) Someone who takes possession of a freehold.

seize, *vb.* (13c) **1.** To forcibly take possession (of a person or property). **2.** To place (someone) in possession. **3.** To be in possession (of property). **4.** To be informed of or aware of (something). See SEISIN; SEIZURE.

seizin. See SEISIN.

seizure, *n.* (15c) The act or an instance of taking possession of a person or property by legal right or process; esp., in constitutional law, a confiscation or arrest that may interfere with a person's reasonable expectation of privacy.

▸ **constructive seizure.** (1830) A manifest intent to seize and take possession of another person's property, usu. either by lawfully acquiring actual custody and control of the property or by posting notice of the property's pending foreclosure.

seizure warrant. See WARRANT (1).

select committee. See *special committee* under COMMITTEE (1).

select council. See COUNCIL (1).

selecti judices (si-**lek**-tɪ **joo**-di-seez). [Latin] (16c) *Roman law.* Jurors on the official panel prepared by the praetor, who for a specific trial were drawn by lot subject to challenge and sworn to office in a similar manner to modern juries.

selective disclosure. (1963) The act of divulging part of a privileged communication, or one of several privileged communications, usu. because the divulged portion is helpful to the party giving the information, while harmful portions of the communication are withheld. • Such a disclosure can result in a limited waiver of the privilege for all communications on the same subject matter as the divulged portion.

selective-draft law. (1917) A statute empowering the federal government to conscript citizens for military duty. • The constitutionality of the first selective-draft law was challenged and upheld in the Selective-Draft-Law Cases. *See Arver v. U.S.,* 245 U.S. 366, 38 S.Ct. 159 (1918).

selective enforcement. (1958) The practice of law-enforcement officers who use wide or even unfettered discretion about when and where to carry out certain laws; esp., the practice of singling a person out for prosecution or punishment under a statute or regulation because the person is a member of a protected group or because the person has exercised or is planning to exercise a constitutionally protected right. — Also termed *selective prosecution.* Cf. *vindictive prosecution* under PROSECUTION (2).

"The chief of police of a New England town once declared to the press that he believed in a strict curfew law, 'selectively enforced.' 'Selective enforcement' in this case means that the policeman decides for himself who ought to be sent home from the street; legislative candour would suggest that if this is the intention it ought to be expressed in the law itself, instead of being concealed behind words that are 'strict' and categorical." Lon L. Fuller, *Anatomy of the Law* 42 (1968).

selective incorporation. See INCORPORATION (2).

selective prosecution. (1967) **1.** SELECTIVE ENFORCEMENT. **2.** The practice or an instance of a criminal prosecution brought at the discretion of a prosecutor rather than one brought as a matter of course in the normal functioning of the prosecuting authority's office. • Selective prosecution violates the Equal Protection Clause of the Fourteenth Amendment if a defendant is singled out for prosecution when others similarly situated have not been prosecuted and the prosecutor's reasons for doing so are impermissible.

selective prospectivity. See PROSPECTIVITY.

Selective Service System. The federal agency that registers all persons 18–26 who are eligible for military service military service and provides personnel to the Armed Forces during emergencies. • It was established in 1940 as a part of the War Manpower Commission and became independent in 1943. — Abbr. SSS.

selective waiver. See WAIVER (2).

selectman. (17c) A municipal officer elected annually in some New England towns to transact business and perform some executive functions.

self-applying, *adj.* (1894) (Of a statute, ordinance, etc.) requiring no more for interpretation than a familiarity with the ordinary meanings of words.

self-authenticating will. See *self-proved will* under WILL.

self-authentication. See AUTHENTICATION.

self-canceling installment note. See NOTE (1).

self-certification. (1951) The signing of a form or note to verify that one has done something or to explain why one has not done something.

self-crimination. See SELF-INCRIMINATION.

self-critical-analysis privilege. See PRIVILEGE (3).

self-dealing, *n.* (1940) Participation in a transaction that benefits oneself instead of another who is owed a fiduciary duty. • For example, a corporate director might engage in self-dealing by participating in a competing business to the corporation's detriment. Cf. FAIR DEALING (1), (2). — **self-deal,** *vb.*

self-declared trust. See TRUST (3).

self-defense, *n.* (1651) **1.** The use of force to protect oneself, one's family, or one's property from a real or threatened attack. • Generally, a person is justified in using a reasonable amount of force in self-defense if he or she reasonably believes that the danger of bodily harm is imminent and that force is necessary to avoid this danger. — Also termed *defense of self.* Cf. *adequate provocation* under PROVOCATION.

"The law of self-defence, as it is applied by the courts, turns on two requirements: the force must have been necessary, and it must have been reasonable." Andrew Ashworth, *Principles of Criminal Law* 114 (1991).

▸ **anticipatory self-defense.** (1946) See *preemptive self-defense.*

▸ **imperfect self-defense.** (1882) *Criminal law.* A good-faith but ultimately mistaken belief, acted on by a criminal defendant, that self-defense is necessary to repel an attack. • In some jurisdictions, such a self-defender will be charged with a lesser offense than the one committed.

▸ **perfect self-defense.** (1883) The use of force by one who accurately appraises the necessity and the amount of force to repel an attack.

▸ **preemptive self-defense.** (1969) An act of aggression by one person or country to prevent another person or country from pursuing a particular course of action that is not yet directly threatening but that, if permitted to continue, could result at some future point in an act of aggression against the preemptive actor. • In domestic-relations law, the phrase refers to the use of force to prevent another person from taking possibly lethal action against oneself. It is disfavored in the law. — Also termed *anticipatory self-defense* (ASD); *preventive self-defense.*

▸ **preventive self-defense.** See *preemptive self-defense.*

2. *Int'l law.* The right of a state to defend itself against a real or threatened attack. *See* United Nations Charter, art. 51 (59 Stat. 1031). — Also spelled (esp. BrE) *self-defence.* — **self-defender,** *n.*

"Self-defence, properly understood, is a legal right, and as with other legal rights the question whether a specific state of facts warrants its exercise is a legal question. It is not a question on which a state is entitled, in any special sense, to be a judge in its own cause." J.L. Brierly, *The Law of Nations* 319 (5th ed. 1955).

self-destruct clause. A provision in a trust for a condition that will automatically terminate the trust. • Discretionary trusts, esp. supplemental-needs trusts, often include a self-destruct provision. For example, a trust to provide for the needs of a disabled person may terminate if the beneficiary becomes ineligible for a government-benefits program such as Medicaid.

self-destruction. See SUICIDE (1).

self-determination. *Int'l law.* The right of each culturally homogeneous country to constitute an independent state. See RIGHT OF SELF-DETERMINATION FOR PEOPLES.

"The political origins of the modern concept of self-determination can be traced back to the Declaration of Independence of the United States of America of 4 July 1776, which proclaimed that governments derived 'their just powers from the consent of the governed' and that 'whenever any Form of Government becomes destructive to these ends, it is the Right of the People to alter or to abolish it.' The principle of self-determination was further shaped by the leaders of the French Revolution, whose doctrine of popular sovereignty, at least initially, required renunciation of all wars of conquest and contemplated annexations of territory to France only after plebiscites." Daniel Thürer & Thomas Burri, "Self-Determination," in 9 *The Max Planck Encyclopedia of Public International Law* 113, 114 (Rüdiger Wolfrum ed., 2012).

self-determination contract. See CONTRACT.

self-determination election. See GLOBE ELECTION.

self-disserving declaration. *Hist.* See *declaration against interest* under DECLARATION (6).

self-employed retirement plan. See KEOGH PLAN.

self-employment tax. See TAX.

self-evaluation privilege. See *self-critical-analysis privilege* under PRIVILEGE (3).

self-executing, *adj.* (1857) (Of an instrument) effective immediately without the need of any type of implementing action <the wills had self-executing affidavits attached>. • Legal instruments may be self-executing according to various standards. For example, treaties are self-executing under the Supremacy Clause of the U.S. Constitution (art. VI, § 2) if textually capable of judicial enforcement and intended to be enforced in that manner.

self-executing order. See ORDER (2).

self-governing, *adj.* (1845) (Of a country, organization, or person) controlled from within and not by some outside power or influence; autonomous.

self-government. (18c) **1.** Government controlled and directed by locals and not by outsiders. **2.** Control of one's own affairs; independence. **3.** Restraint exercised over one's own actions or impulses; self-control.

self-harm. (17c) Physical harm that one deliberately does to one's own body, as by cutting oneself with a knife.

self-help, *n.* (1831) An attempt to redress a perceived wrong by one's own action rather than through the normal legal process. • The UCC and other statutes provide for particular self-help remedies (such as repossession) if the remedy can be executed without breaching the peace. UCC § 9-609. — Also termed *self-redress; extrajudicial enforcement.* Cf. *claim-of-right defense* under DEFENSE (1).

> "Notice to the debtor is generally not required prior to self-help repossession of collateral by the creditor upon default, although the provision for self-help repossession has been held to violate due process requirements in some instances, and states under the Uniform Consumer Credit Code require particular notice requirements. Furthermore, while the UCC generally does not require notice to the debtor upon self-help repossession of the collateral upon the debtor's default, the agreement between the parties may require such notice prior to repossession." 68A Am. Jur. 2d *Secured Transactions* § 608, at 466 (1993).

self-help defense. See *claim-of-right defense* under DEFENSE (1).

self-help remedy. See *extrajudicial remedy* under REMEDY.

self-incriminating, *adj.* (1925) Tending to put the blame or criminal responsibility on oneself; inculpatory to oneself.

self-incrimination. (1853) The act of indicating one's own involvement in a crime or exposing oneself to prosecution, esp. by making a statement. — Also termed *self-crimination; self-inculpation.* See RIGHT AGAINST SELF-INCRIMINATION.

Self-Incrimination Clause. (1925) *Constitutional law.* The clause of the Fifth Amendment to the U.S. Constitution barring the government from compelling criminal defendants to testify against themselves.

self-inculpation. See SELF-INCRIMINATION.

self-induced frustration. See FRUSTRATION (1).

self-induced intoxication. See *voluntary intoxication* under INTOXICATION.

self-inflicted, *adj.* (18c) (Of wounds, pains, problems, illnesses, etc.) caused by oneself <self-inflicted gunshot wound>.

self-insurance. See INSURANCE.

self-insured retention. (1963) *Insurance.* The amount of an otherwise-covered loss that is not covered by an insurance policy and that usu. must be paid before the insurer will pay benefits <the defendant had a $1 million CGL policy to cover the loss, but had to pay a self-insured retention of $100,000, which it had agreed to so that the policy premium would be lower>. — Abbr. SIR. Cf. DEDUCTIBLE, *n.*

self-killing. See SUICIDE (1).

self-liquidating mortgage. See *amortized mortgage* under MORTGAGE.

self-murder. See SUICIDE (1).

self-policing privilege. See *self-critical-analysis privilege* under PRIVILEGE (3).

self-preservation. *Int'l law.* **1.** The right of a state to engage in unilateral action in response to a compelling need to allow the state to endure in one form or another. • Although self-preservation is often equated with military action, it need not entail a use of military force. **2.** The unilateral action itself.

> "In its narrowest form, the term 'self-preservation' has been used as a synonym for the concept of necessity . . . . In this incarnation, self-preservation constitutes a unilateral action taken in response to a situation of 'grave and imminent peril' affecting the 'essential interests' of the responding State . . . . This allows for States to preclude the wrongfulness of obligations owed to other States in extreme circumstances. Historically, this potentially allowed for the use of military force against States that were not themselves necessarily in breach of international law, to secure the interests of the invoking State. More commonly, self-preservation has been employed in a broader sense: this is an interpretation that includes the concept of necessity, but is not limited to it. Therefore, self-preservation is perhaps best understood as an 'umbrella' term. It should be seen as a label that encompasses a range of concepts that all possess a good deal more specificity under contemporary international law than self-preservation does itself. Traditionally, then, self-preservation has encompassed the following legal concepts: self-defence, counter-measures (either in the form of reprisals or self-help) and necessity." James A. Green, "Self-Preservation," in 9 *The Max Planck Encyclopedia of Public International Law* 128, 129 (Rüdiger Wolfrum ed., 2012).

self-proved will. See WILL.

self-proving affidavit. See AFFIDAVIT.

self-redress. See SELF-HELP.

self-regulating, *adj.* (1837) (Of a system, industry, organization, etc.) exercising self-government and internal enforcement, as opposed to having an external organization with powers of oversight. — Also termed *self-regulatory.*

self-regulation. See REGULATION (1).

self-regulatory organization. (1964) A nongovernmental organization that is statutorily empowered to regulate its members by adopting and enforcing rules of conduct, esp. those governing fair, ethical, and efficient practices. — Abbr. SRO.

self-represented litigant. See PRO SE.

self-restraint. (18c) The ability to stop oneself from doing or saying something, despite wanting to, because doing it or saying it may be unwise.

self-serving declaration. See DECLARATION (6).

self-settled trust. See TRUST (3).

self-slaughter. See SUICIDE (1).

self-stultification. (1862) The act or an instance of testifying about one's own deficiencies. See STULTIFY.

sell, *vb.* (bef. 12c) To transfer (property) by sale.

seller. (13c) **1.** Someone who sells or contracts to sell goods; a vendor. UCC § 2-103(1)(d). **2.** Generally, a person who sells anything; the transferor of property in a contract of sale.

seller's market. See MARKET.

seller's option. See OPTION (5).

***Sell* hearing.** See HEARING.

selling agent. 1. See AGENT. **2.** See FACTOR (3).

selling price. See *sales price* under PRICE.

sell-off, *n.* (1937) A period when heavy pressure to sell causes falling stock-market prices.

sell order. See ORDER (8).

semantics, *n.* (1893) **1.** The study of the meanings of words and phrases as signs and symbols, esp. when viewed historically and psychologically. — Also termed *semasiology.* Cf. SEMIOTICS. **2.** The meaning or meanings of a word, phrase, sign, or set of signs, esp. as regards connotation. **3.** The language used to achieve a desired effect on an audience, esp. through persuasion, advertising, or propaganda. — **semantic,** *adj.*

semasiology. See SEMANTICS (1).

semble (**sem**-bəl). [Law French] (1817) It seems; it would appear <semble that the parties' intention was to create a binding agreement>. • This term is used chiefly to indicate an obiter dictum in a court opinion or to introduce an uncertain thought or interpretation. — Abbr. sem.; semb.

semester, *n.* One of the two periods that a high-school or college year is divided into, esp. at American institutions. Cf. TRIMESTER (2).

semestria (si-**mes**-tree-ə), *n.* [Latin "half-yearly matters"] *Roman law.* The collected decisions of Roman emperors, issued every six months.

Semiconductor Chip Protection Act. *Intellectual property.* A 1984 statute protecting manufacturers against the unauthorized copying or use of semiconductor chips and the mask works used to manufacture them. • Semiconductor chips do not qualify for patent protection since technological advancements are small and usu. obvious. Mask works are multi-layered, three-dimensional templates used to produce semiconductor chips. Mask-work design is more functional than expressive and so traditional copyright protection was inapplicable until 1984. The Act provides copyright protection to the mask works for a period of ten years. 17 USCA §§ 901–914. — Abbr. SCPA.

semi-free software. (1996) Software that does not include source code but comes with permission for individuals to use, copy, modify, and distribute the software for nonprofit purposes. Cf. FREEWARE; PROPRIETARY SOFTWARE; SHAREWARE.

semi-matrimonium (**sem**-I ma-trə-**moh**-nee-əm), *n.* [Latin] A half-marriage.

seminary. (16c) **1.** An educational institution such as a college, academy, or other school; esp., one that trains students for the clergy. **2.** The building in which the institution performs its functions.

seminaufragium (sem-I-naw-**fray**-jee-əm), *n.* [Latin] (1884) *Hist.* A half-shipwreck, as when goods are cast overboard in a storm or when a damaged ship's repair costs are more than the ship's worth.

semiotics, *n.* (1880) **1.** The way in which people communicate through signs and images. **2.** The study of signs and images, esp. as they relate to language. Cf. SEMANTICS (1). — **semiotic,** *adj.* — **semiotician, semiologist,** *n.*

semiplena probatio (sem-I-**plee**-nə proh-**bay**-shee-oh), *n.* [Latin] (17c) Half-proof.

> "In actions of filiation, a pursuer was formerly entitled, on adducing a *semiplena probatio*, to her oath in supplement to prove that the defender was the father of her child. A *semiplena probatio* was such a proof as induced, not merely a suspicion, but a reasonable belief that the pursuer's case was well-founded, and consisted generally of a proof of opportunity for connection, acts of familiarity on the part of the defender towards the pursuer, &c . . . ." John Trayner, *Trayner's Latin Maxims* 569 (4th ed. 1894).

semiretired, *adj.* (1974) (Of a person) still working, but at reduced hours, usu. because of advancing age or ill health. — **semiretirement,** *n.*

semi-secret trust. See TRUST (3).

semi-skilled work. See WORK (1).

semper (**sem**-pər). [Latin] Always. • This term introduces several Latin maxims, such as *semper in dubiis benigniora praeferenda sunt* ("in doubtful cases, the more favorable constructions are always to be preferred").

semper eadem (**sem**-pər **ay**-ə-dəm). [Latin] Always the same.

semper paratus. (17c) A defendant's pleading that he or she has always been ready to perform as the plaintiff demanded.

semper ubique et ab omnibus (**sem**-pər yoo-**bi**-kwee [*or* yoo-**bee**-kway] et ab **om**-ni-bəs). [Latin] Always everywhere and by everyone.

senage (**see**-nij). [French] (14c) Money paid for synodals; tribute-money. See SYNODAL.

senate. (13c) **1.** The upper chamber of a bicameral legislature. **2.** (*cap.*) The upper house of the U.S. Congress, composed of 100 members — two from each state — who are elected to six-year terms. — Abbr. S.

senate bill. See BILL (3).

Senate Judiciary Committee. A U.S. Senate standing committee created in 1816 to be responsible for a vast array of constitutional and legislative issues, including conducting hearings on federal judicial nominees. — Also termed (more formally) *United States Senate Committee on the Judiciary.*

senator. (13c) **1.** A member of a senate. **2.** *Hist. English law.* A king's councilor. **3.** *Hist. English law.* Before the Norman Conquest, one of a class of chieftains or rulers who was responsible for local or regional government.

senatores (sen-ə-**tor**-eez), *n. pl.* [Latin] *Roman law.* **1.** Members of the Roman senate. **2.** Members of municipal councils.

senatorial courtesy. (1884) **1.** The tradition that the President should take care in filling a high-level federal post (such as a judgeship) with a person agreeable to the senators from the nominee's home state, lest the senators defeat confirmation.

"The risk of a deadlock is minimized by [the President's] consulting informally with the Senators from the State in which the office lies, if they are members of his own political party. Actually this amounts in most instances to his taking the advice of these two Senators as to a selection. A nomination approved by them is practically certain of final confirmation by the Senate as a whole. The arrangement is a 'log-rolling' one, which has been dignified by the name of 'Senatorial courtesy.' 'If you will help me to get the appointments I want in my State, I will help you get the appointments you want in your State.'" Herbert W. Horwill, *The Usages of the American Constitution* 129 (1925).

2. Loosely, civility among senators <a decline of senatorial courtesy>.

Senator of the College of Justice. *Scots law.* See LORD OF SESSION.

senatus (si-**nay**-təs), *n.* [Latin] *Roman law.* **1.** The Roman senate. **2.** The meeting place for the Roman senate.

senatus consulto (si-**nay**-təs kən-**səl**-toh). [Latin] *Roman law.* By the decree of the Senate.

senatus consultum (si-**nay**-təs kən-**səl**-təm). [Latin] (16c) *Roman law.* In the Republic, a resolution of the Roman Senate, which did not have the force of law (though usu. followed). • In the first century A.D., these resolutions replaced the legislation of the *comitia*, but by the end of the second century, they were merely the Senate's official expression of the imperial will. The senate often adopted the text of a speech (*oratio*) by the emperor. — Sometimes written *senatusconsultum.* — Also termed *senatus consult.* — Abbr. S.C. Pl. ***senatus consulta.***

"*Senatus consulta.* — In the regal and republican periods the Senate enjoyed no legislative power. It was an advisory body, nominated by the King, and at first purely patrician. Later it . . . included patricians and plebeians . . . its chief duty still being to tender advice to the magistrates . . . . The theory still was, till the time of Hadrian, that *senatus consulta* were directions to the magistrates, who were now in fact, if not in name, bound to give effect to them, till by a process of gradual usurpation *senatus consulta* came to be direct legislation." R.W. Leage, *Roman Private Law* 12–13 (C.H. Ziegler ed., 2d ed. 1930).

senatus consultum Macedonianum (si-**nay**-təs kən-**səl**-təm mas-ə-doh-nee-**ay**- nəm). [Latin "Macedo's Resolution"] *Roman law.* A senate decree under Vespasian to protect fathers from children in their power who had borrowed excessive sums in expectation of their father's death, by making actions to recover such loans unlawful. — Also termed *Macedonian Decree.*

"In the principate of Vespasian, 69-79 A.D., a *senatus consultum* was passed which forbade loans to a *filius-familias.* It was called the *senatus consultum — Macedonianum,* after one Macedo, a usurer who had made such a loan and thereby instigated a hard-pressed debtor to kill his father in order to enter into his inheritance. To prevent tragic possibilities like these, the *senatus consultum* declared that no action would lie to recover money lent to a *filius-familias.*" Max Radin, *Handbook of Roman Law* 188–89 (1927).

"The *senatus consultum Macedonianum* reads as follows: 'Whereas Macedo's borrowings gave him an added incentive to commit a crime to which he was naturally predisposed and whereas those who lend money on terms which are dubious, to say the least, often provide evil men with the means of wrongdoing, it has been decided, in order to teach pernicious moneylenders that a son's debt cannot be made good by waiting for his father's death, that a person who has lent money to a son-in-power is to have no claim or action even after the death of the person in whose power he was.'" *Digest of Justinian* 14.6.1 (Ulpian, Ad Sabinum 49).

senatus consultum ultimum necessitatis (si-**nay**-təs kən-**səl**-təm **əl**-tə-mee nə-ses-i-**tay**-tis). [Latin] (1934) *Roman law.* A decree of the senate of the last necessity. • This decree usu. preceded the nomination of a leader with absolute power in a time of emergency. — Also termed *senatus consultum ultimae necessitatis.*

senatus consultum Velleianum (si-**nay**-təs kən-**səl**-təm vel-ee-**ay**-nəm). [Latin "Velleian Decree"] *Roman law.* A senate decree, probably of A.D. 46, to protect women from making unconscionable guarantees, suretyship undertakings, or debt assumptions for their husbands and for others generally, by making actions to enforce such undertakings unlawful.

senatus decreta (si-**nay**-təs di-**kree**-tə). [Latin] (18c) *Roman law.* The senate's decisions.

send, *vb.* (bef. 12c) **1.** To cause or direct to go or pass; to authorize to go and act <to send a messenger>. **2.** To cause to be moved or conveyed from a present location to another place; esp., to deposit (a writing or notice) in the mail or deliver for transmission by any other usual means of communication with postage or cost of transmission provided for and properly addressed <to send a message>. **3.** To throw, cast, hurl, or impel by force <to send an arrow over the barricade>.

sending state. See STATE (1).

senescallus (sen-əs-**kal**-əs), *n.* [Law Latin] See SENESCHAL.

seneschal (**sen**-ə-shəl), *n.* [Law French] (14c) *Hist.* **1.** A French title of office, equivalent to a steward in England. • A seneschal was originally a duke's lieutenant or a lieutenant to other dignities of the kingdom. **2.** The steward of a manor. **3.** *Hist.* An administrative or judicial officer, such as the governor of a city or province. — Also termed *senescallus.*

senile dementia. See SENILITY.

senility. (18c) Mental feebleness or impairment caused by old age. • A senile person (in the legal, as opposed to the popular, sense) is incompetent to enter into a binding contract or to execute a will. — Also termed *senile dementia* (**see**-nıl di-**men**-shee-ə). — **senile,** *adj.*

senior, *adj.* (14c) **1.** (Of a debt, etc.) first; preferred, as over junior obligations. **2.** (Of a person) older than someone else. **3.** (Of a person) higher in rank or service. **4.** (Of a man) elder, as distinguished from the man's son who has the same name.

senior administrative patent judge. See JUDGE.

senior counsel. 1. See *lead counsel* under COUNSEL. **2.** KING'S COUNSEL; QUEEN'S COUNSEL.

senior debt. See DEBT.

senior interest. See INTEREST (2).

seniority. (15c) **1.** The status of being older or more senior. **2.** The preferential status, privileges, or rights given to an employee based on the employee's length of service with an employer. • Employees with seniority may receive additional or enhanced benefit packages and obtain competitive advantages over fellow employees in layoff and promotional decisions.

▸ **benefit seniority.** (1967) The status used to determine an employee's level of benefits, such as pension benefits or vacation time, measured by length of the employee's service. *See Franks v. Bowman Transp. Co.*, 424 U.S. 747, 766, 96 S.Ct. 1251, 1265 (1976).

▸ **competitive seniority.** (1969) The status used to determine an employee's level of benefits, such as pension benefits, vacation time, or promotions or nondemotions, measured by the quality of the employee's service and performance. *See Franks v. Bowman Transp. Co.*, 424 U.S. 747, 766-67, 96 S.Ct. 1251, 1265-66 (1976).

seniority system. (1850) *Employment law.* Any arrangement that recognizes length of service in making decisions about job layoffs and promotions or other advancements.

senior judge. See JUDGE.

senior lien. See LIEN.

senior mortgage. See MORTGAGE.

senior partner. See PARTNER.

senior party. (1897) *Intellectual property.* In an interference proceeding, the first person to file an application for a property's legal protection, e.g., an invention patent or a trademark registration. • In the United States, merely being the first to file does not entitle the party to the protection. The proceeding's administrator also takes other factors into account. For instance, in a patent-interference proceeding the invention's conception date and the inventor's diligence in reducing the invention to practice are relevant factors. Priority in the filing date is prima facie evidence that the senior party is the first inventor, so the challenger has the burden of proof. Cf. JUNIOR PARTY.

senior security. See SECURITY (4).

senior status. (1970) The employment condition of a semiretired judge who continues to perform certain judicial duties that the judge is willing and able to undertake.

senior user. (1939) *Trademarks.* The first person to use a mark. • That person is usu. found to be the mark's owner. — Also termed *first user.* Cf. JUNIOR USER.

senseless, *adj.* (16c) **1.** Occurring or done for no good reason or rational purpose; contrary to reason and good sense <a senseless waste of life>. **2.** Bereft of bodily feeling; unconscious or insentient <beaten senseless>.

sensible, *adj.* (14c) **1.** (Of a person) reasonable, practical, and showing good judgment; possessed of sound sense and rationality <a sensible seller>. **2.** (Of a product, approach, or other thing) suitable for a particular purpose, and designed for practicality rather than fashionable appearance <a sensible plan>. **3.** Perceptible through the senses; appreciable <visible and sensible things>. **4.** Capable of being acted on through the feelings or emotions <sensible to embarrassment>. **5.** Fully aware; cognizant <sensible of one's own cognition>. **6.** Sensitive to minute changes <sensible of variations in temperature>.

sensitive information. Information that could bring harm if not kept secret, such as trade secrets and scandalous personal information.

sensitivity training. (1956) One or more instructional sessions for management and employees, designed to counteract the callous treatment of others, esp. women and minorities, in the workplace.

sensus (**sen**-səs). [Latin] *Hist.* Sense; meaning; signification. • The word appears in its inflected form in phrases such as *malo sensu* ("an evil sense"), *mitiori sensu* ("in a milder sense"), and *sensu honesto* ("in an honest sense").

sensu stricto (**sen**[t]-soo **strik**-too), *adv.* [Latin] In the strict sense of the words; strictly speaking.

sentence, *n.* (14c) *Criminal law.* The judgment that a court formally pronounces after finding a criminal defendant guilty; the punishment imposed on a criminal wrongdoer <a sentence of 20 years in prison>. *See* Fed. R. Crim. P. 32. — Also termed *judgment of conviction.* — **sentence,** *vb.*

▸ **accumulative sentences.** See *consecutive sentences.*

▸ **aggregate sentence.** (1879) The total sentence imposed for multiple convictions, reflecting appropriate calculations for consecutive as opposed to cumulative periods, reductions for time already served, and statutory limitations.

▸ **alternative sentence.** (1841) A sentence other than imprisonment. • Examples include community service and victim restitution. — Also termed *creative sentence.*

▸ **back-to-back sentences.** See *consecutive sentences.*

▸ **blended sentence.** (1996) In a juvenile-delinquency disposition, a sanction that combines delinquency sanctions and criminal punishment.

▸ **concurrent sentences.** (1905) Two or more sentences of jail time to be served simultaneously. • For example, if a convicted criminal receives concurrent sentences of 5 years and 15 years, the total amount of jail time is 15 years.

▸ **conditional sentence.** (1843) A sentence of confinement if the convicted criminal fails to perform the conditions of probation.

▸ **consecutive sentences.** (1844) Two or more sentences of jail time to be served in sequence. • For example, if a convicted criminal receives consecutive sentences of 20 years and 5 years, the total amount of jail time is 25 years. — Also termed *cumulative sentences; back-to-back sentences; accumulative sentences.*

▸ **consolidated sentence.** See *general sentence.*

▸ **creative sentence.** See *alternative sentence.*

▸ **custodial sentence.** See PRISON SENTENCE.

▸ **death sentence.** (1811) A sentence that imposes the death penalty. See Model Penal Code § 210.6. — Also termed *judgment of blood.* See DEATH PENALTY.

▸ **deferred sentence.** (1915) A sentence that will not be carried out if the convicted criminal meets certain requirements, such as complying with conditions of probation.

▸ **definite sentence.** (16c) **1.** See *determinate sentence* (1). **2.** A fixed jail term of relatively short duration, usu. one year or less, often with the possibility of an early release for good behavior.

▸ **delayed sentence.** (1906) A sentence that is not imposed immediately after conviction, thereby allowing the convicted criminal to satisfy the court (usu. by complying with certain restrictions or conditions during the delay period) that probation is preferable to a prison sentence.

▸ **determinate sentence.** (1885) **1.** A jail term of a specified duration. **2.** A jail term of a relatively long duration, usu. more than a year, often after a conviction of a serious crime such as a violent felony or drug felony. — Also termed *definite sentence; definitive sentence; fixed sentence; flat sentence; straight sentence.*

▸ **enhanced sentence.** (1927) A punishment more severe than usual, imposed typically because of the presence of aggravating circumstances.

▸ **excessive sentence.** (1879) A sentence that gives more punishment than is allowed by law.

▸ **fixed sentence. 1.** See *determinate sentence.* **2.** See *mandatory sentence.*

▸ **flat sentence.** See *determinate sentence.*

▸ **general sentence.** (1891) An undivided, aggregate sentence in a multicount case; a sentence that does not specify the punishment imposed for each count. • General sentences are prohibited. — Also termed *consolidated sentence.*

▸ **indeterminate sentence.** (1885) **1.** A sentence of an unspecified duration, such as one for jail time of 10 to 20 years. **2.** A maximum jail term that the parole board can reduce, through statutory authorization, after the inmate has served the minimum time required by law. — Also termed *indefinite sentence.* See INDETERMINATE SENTENCING.

▸ **intermittent sentence.** (1964) A sentence consisting of periods of jail time interrupted by periods of freedom. — Also termed (when served on weekends) *weekend sentence.*

▸ **life sentence.** (1878) A sentence that imprisons the convicted criminal for life — though in some jurisdictions the prisoner may become eligible for release on good behavior, rehabilitation, or the like.

▸ **mandatory sentence.** (1926) A sentence set by law with no discretion for the judge to individualize punishment. — Also termed *mandatory penalty; mandatory punishment; fixed sentence.*

▸ **manifestly excessive sentence.** (1939) A sentence that is plainly heavier than is typical for similar offenses and is unsupported by the evidence or law.

▸ **maximum sentence.** (1898) The highest level of punishment provided by law for a particular crime.

▸ **minimum sentence.** (1891) The least amount of time that a convicted criminal must serve in prison before becoming eligible for parole.

▸ **multiple sentences.** (1938) Concurrent or consecutive sentences, if a convicted criminal is found guilty of more than one offense.

▸ **nominal sentence.** (1852) A criminal sentence in name only; an exceedingly light sentence.

▸ **noncustodial sentence.** (1971) A criminal sentence (such as probation) not requiring jail time.

▸ **presumptive sentence.** (1978) An average sentence for a particular crime (esp. provided under sentencing guidelines) that can be raised or lowered based on the presence of mitigating or aggravating circumstances.

▸ **prior sentence.** (1863) A sentence previously imposed on a criminal defendant for a different offense, whether by a guilty verdict, a guilty plea, or a nolo contendere.

▸ **revocable sentence.** (1972) A probationary sentence, conditional sentence, or intermittent sentence that is subject to being withdrawn upon the violation of a condition.

▸ **split sentence.** (1927) A sentence in which part of the time is served in confinement — to expose the offender to the unpleasantness of prison — and the rest on probation. See *shock probation* under PROBATION.

▸ **straight sentence.** See *determinate sentence.*

▸ **suspended sentence.** (1919) A sentence postponed so that the convicted criminal is not required to serve time unless he or she commits another crime or violates some other court-imposed condition. • A suspended sentence, in effect, is a form of probation. — Also termed *withheld sentence.*

▸ **weekend sentence.** See *intermittent sentence.*

sentence bargain. See PLEA BARGAIN.

sentence cap. (1987) **1.** *Military law.* A pretrial plea agreement in a court-martial proceeding by which a ceiling is placed on the maximum penalty that can be imposed. **2.** See CAP PLEA.

sentenced to time served. (1959) A sentencing disposition whereby a criminal defendant is sentenced to the same jail time that the defendant is credited with serving while in custody awaiting trial. • The sentence results in the defendant's release from custody. Cf. BALANCE OF SENTENCE SUSPENDED.

sentence enhancement. (1971) The increase of a criminal defendant's punishment based usu. on a prior conviction.

sentence entrapment. See *sentencing entrapment* under ENTRAPMENT.

sentence-factor manipulation. See *sentencing entrapment* under ENTRAPMENT.

sentence-package rule. (1996) *Criminal procedure.* The principle that a defendant can be resentenced on an aggregate sentence — that is, one arising from a conviction on multiple counts in an indictment — when the defendant successfully challenges part of the conviction, as by successfully challenging some but not all of the counts.

sentencing. (1933) The judicial determination of the penalty for a crime.

▸ **determinate sentencing.** See *mandatory sentencing.*

▸ **discretionary sentencing.** See *indeterminate sentencing.*

▸ **fixed sentencing.** See *mandatory sentencing.*

▸ **indeterminate sentencing.** (1941) Sentencing that is left up to the court, with few or very flexible guidelines. — Also termed *discretionary sentencing.*

▸ **mandatory sentencing.** (1950) A statutorily specified penalty that automatically follows a conviction for the offense, often with a minimum mandatory term. — Also termed *determinate sentencing; fixed sentencing.*

▸ **presumptive sentencing.** (1976) A statutory scheme that prescribes a sentence or range of sentences for an offense but allows the court some flexibility in atypical cases.

sentencing council. (1973) A panel of three or more judges who confer to determine a criminal sentence. • Sentencing by a council occurs less frequently than sentencing by a single trial judge.

sentencing entrapment. See ENTRAPMENT.

sentencing guidelines. (1970) A set of standards for determining the punishment that a convicted criminal should receive, based on the nature of the crime and the offender's criminal history. • The federal government and several states have adopted sentencing guidelines in an effort to make judicial sentencing more consistent. — Often shortened to *guidelines.*

sentencing hearing. See PRESENTENCE HEARING.

sentencing phase. See PENALTY PHASE.

Sentencing Reform Act of 1984. A federal statute enacted to bring greater uniformity to punishments assessed for federal crimes by creating a committee of federal judges and other officials (the United States Sentencing Commission) responsible for producing sentencing guidelines to be used by the federal courts. 28 USCA § 994(a)(1). — Abbr. SRA.

Sentencing Table. A reference guide used by federal courts to calculate the appropriate punishment under the sentencing guidelines by taking into account the gravity of the offense and the convicted person's criminal history.

sententia (sen-**ten**-shee-ə), *n.* [Latin] *Roman & civil law.* **1.** Sense; meaning. **2.** An opinion, esp. a legal opinion. **3.** A judicial decision.

sententia voluntatis (sen-**ten**-shee-ə vol-ən-**tay**-tis). [Law Latin] (1856) *Hist.* The determination of the will.

SEP. *abbr.* See *simplified employee pension plan* under EMPLOYEE BENEFIT PLAN.

separability. The capability of a thing's being divided or severed from another. • In the law of copyright, separability is an element of various judicial tests used to determine whether a design in a functional article is a copyrightable work of applied art, or an uncopyrightable industrial design, the test being based on whether the beholder separates the work's artistic appearance from its useful function. Some courts use a strict physical separability test, but most look at whether the work's two roles are conceptually separate. In the law of arbitration, separability is a doctrine under which an arbitration clause in a main contract is treated as a distinct agreement from the main contract, so that challenges to the enforceability of the main contract do not affect the enforceability of the arbitration clause. — Also termed *severability.*

> "[W]hat is the proper name for the doctrine? The Supreme Court in *Prima Paint* described arbitration clauses as 'separable,' while the Court in *Buckeye* called the doctrine 'severability' rather than 'separability.' The more common terminology in academic writings is 'separability'; courts seem to prefer 'severability.' My view is that 'separability' is the better label. The usual context in which courts analyze whether a contract provision is 'severable' from the contract is when the provision is unenforceable, and the courts are trying to determine whether the illegality of that provision invalidates the rest of the contract. If sufficiently distinct, the illegal provision is severed from the contract while the rest of the contract remains enforceable. With separability, it is the main contract that is challenged as unenforceable, not the arbitration clause, and the issue is whether the unenforceability of the main contract infects the arbitration clause, not the other way around. Moreover, the timing is different. Separability often comes into play before any determination of unenforceability is made — in deciding who is going to make that determination. For both of these reasons, it makes sense to use a different label — separability rather than severability." Christopher R. Drahozal, Buckeye Check Cashing *and the Separability Doctrine,* 1 Y.B. Arb. & Med. 55, 57 (2009).

separability clause. See SEVERABILITY CLAUSE.

separability thesis. (1977) In legal philosophy, the positivist view that law and morality are conceptually distinct.

separable, *adj.* (14c) Capable of being separated or divided <a separable controversy>.

separable controversy. See CONTROVERSY (2).

separaliter (sep-ə-**ray**-lə-tər). [Latin] *Hist.* Separately. • This term was formerly used in an indictment to emphasize that multiple defendants were being charged with separate offenses, when it appeared from the general language of the indictment that the defendants were jointly charged.

separate, *adj.* (15c) (Of liability, cause of action, etc.) individual; distinct; particular; disconnected.

separate action. See ACTION (4).

separate and apart. See LIVING SEPARATE AND APART.

separate-but-equal doctrine. (1950) The now-defunct doctrine that African-Americans could be segregated if they were provided with equal opportunities and facilities in education, public transportation, and jobs. • This rule was established in *Plessy v. Ferguson,* 163 U.S. 537, 16 S.Ct. 1138 (1896), and overturned in *Brown v. Board of Education,* 347 U.S. 483, 74 S.Ct. 686 (1954).

separate caucus. See CAUCUS.

separate count. See COUNT (2).

separate covenant. See *several covenant* under COVENANT (1).

separate demise. See DEMISE.

separate estate. See ESTATE (1).

separate examination. (18c) **1.** The private interrogation of a witness, apart from the other witnesses in the same case. **2.** The interrogation of a wife outside the presence of her husband by a court clerk or notary for the purpose of acknowledging a deed or other instrument. • This was done to ensure that the wife signed without being coerced to do so by her husband.

separate goodwill. See *personal goodwill* under GOODWILL.

separate maintenance. See MAINTENANCE (5).

separate offense. See OFFENSE (2).

separate property. (18c) **1.** Property that a spouse owned before marriage or acquired during marriage by inheritance or by gift from a third party, and in some states property acquired during marriage but after the spouses have entered into a separation agreement and have begun living apart or after one spouse has commenced a divorce action. — Also termed *individual property.* Cf. COMMUNITY PROPERTY; *marital property* under PROPERTY. **2.** In some common-law states, property titled to one spouse or acquired by one spouse individually during marriage. **3.** Property acquired during the marriage in exchange for separate property (in sense 1 or sense 2).

separate-property state. See COMMON-LAW STATE (2).

separate return. See TAX RETURN.

separate-sovereigns rule. (1995) *Criminal procedure.* The principle that a person may be tried twice for the same offense — despite the Double Jeopardy Clause — if the prosecutions are conducted by separate sovereigns, as by the federal government and a state government or by two different states. See DOUBLE JEOPARDY. Cf. PETITE POLICY.

separate-spheres doctrine. (1981) *Hist. Family law.* The common-law doctrine that wives were limited to control of the home — the personal or domestic sphere — and that husbands had control of the public sphere. • Under this-early-19th century doctrine, the wife was to tend to the home and family and the husband was to be the breadwinner. — Also termed *doctrine of separate spheres.*

separate support. See *separate maintenance* under MAINTENANCE (5).

separate trading of registered interest and principal of securities. (1985) A treasury security by which the owner receives either principal or interest, but usu. not both. — Abbr. STRIP.

separate trial. See TRIAL.

separatim (sep-ə-**ray**-tim). [Latin] *Hist.* Severally. • This term referred to the formation of several covenants in a deed.

separatio (sep-ə-**ray**-shee-oh), *n.* See FRUCTUS (1).

separatio bonorum. See BENEFICIUM SEPARATIONIS.

separation. (17c) **1.** An arrangement whereby a husband and wife live apart from each other while remaining married, either by mutual consent (often in a written agreement) or by judicial decree; the act of carrying out such an arrangement. — Also termed *separation from bed and board.* See *divorce a mensa et thoro* under DIVORCE. **2.** The status of a husband and wife having begun such an arrangement, or the judgment or contract that brought about the arrangement. — Also termed (in both senses) *legal separation; judicial separation.* **3.** Cessation of a contractual relationship, esp. in an employment situation. — **separate,** *vb.*

separation agreement. (1886) **1.** An agreement between spouses in the process of a divorce or legal separation concerning alimony, maintenance, property division, child custody and support, and the like. — Also termed *separation order* (if approved or sanctioned judicially). See *temporary order* under ORDER. **2.** DIVORCE AGREEMENT.

separation a mensa et thoro. See *divorce a mensa et thoro* under DIVORCE.

separation from bed and board. (16c) **1.** SEPARATION (1). **2.** See *divorce a mensa et thoro* under DIVORCE.

separation of patrimony. (1838) *Civil law.* The act of providing creditors of a succession the right to collect against the class of estate property from which the creditors should be paid, by separating certain succession property from property rights belonging to the heirs.

separation of powers. (1896) **1.** The division of governmental authority into three branches of government — legislative, executive, and judicial — each with specified duties on which neither of the other branches can encroach. • The first tentative formulation of the proposition that this is the most desirable form of government appeared in John Locke's *Two Treatises of Government* (1689) and was later elaborated more fully in Montesquieu's *Spirit of Laws* (1748). Cf. DIVISION OF POWERS. **2.** The doctrine that such a division of governmental authority is the most desirable form of government because it establishes checks and balances designed to protect the people against tyranny.

> "The doctrine of the separation of powers was adopted by the convention of 1787 not to promote efficiency but to preclude the exercise of arbitrary power. The purpose was not to avoid friction, but, by means of the inevitable friction incident to the distribution of the governmental powers among three departments, to save the people from autocracy." *Myers v. U.S.*, 272 U.S. 50, 293, 47 S.Ct. 21, 85 (1926) (Brandeis, J., dissenting).

> "Although in political theory much has been made of the vital importance of the separation of powers, it is extraordinarily difficult to define precisely each particular power. In an ideal state we might imagine a legislature which had supreme and exclusive power to lay down general rules for the future without reference to particular cases; courts whose sole function was to make binding orders to settle disputes between individuals which were brought before them by applying these rules to the facts which were found to exist; an administrative body which carried on the business of government by issuing particular orders or making decisions of policy within the narrow confines of rules of law that it could not change. The legislature makes, the executive executes, and the judiciary construes the law." George Whitecross Paton, *A Textbook of Jurisprudence* 330 (G.W. Paton & David P. Derham eds., 4th ed. 1972).

> "Separation of powers means something quite different in the European context from what it has come to mean in the United States. . . . Separation of powers to an American evokes the familiar system of checks and balances among the three coordinate branches of government — legislative, executive, and judiciary — each with its independent constitutional basis. To a European, it is a more rigid doctrine and inseparable from the notion of legislative supremacy." Mary Ann Glendon et al., *Comparative Legal Traditions* 67 (2d ed. 1994).

separation of witnesses. (1819) The exclusion of witnesses (other than the plaintiff and defendant) from the courtroom to prevent them from hearing the testimony of others.

separation order. 1. See SEPARATION AGREEMENT. **2.** See ORDER (2). **3.** A court order directing a cooperative prisoner who is actively helping the prosecution to be kept separate from the rest of the jail population, esp. his or her codefendants.

separation pay. See SEVERANCE PAY.

separatio tori (sep-ə-**ray**-shee-oh **tor**-I). [Law Latin] (1838) *Hist.* A separation of the marriage bed. See A MENSA ET THORO.

separator, *n. Oil & gas.* Equipment used at a well site to separate oil, water, and gas produced in solution with oil. • Basic separators simply heat oil to speed the natural separation process. More complex separators may use chemicals.

separatum tenementum (sep-ə-**ray**-təm ten-ə-**men**-təm). [Law Latin] (17c) *Hist.* A separate tenement.

SEP-IRA. See *simplified employee pension plan* under EMPLOYEE BENEFIT PLAN.

sequatur sub suo periculo (si-**kway**-tər səb **s[y]oo**-oh pə-**rik**-[y]ə-loh), *n.* [Law Latin "let him follow at his peril"] (17c) *Hist.* A writ available when a sheriff returned nihil to several summonses; specif., a writ issued after the sheriff returned nihil to a warrant *ad warrantizandum* and following an *alias* and a *pluries* writ. See SICUT ALIAS.

sequela (si-**kwee**-lə), *n.* [Latin "that which follows"] *Hist.* Suit; process, as in *sequela curiae* ("a suit of court") and *sequela causae* ("the process of a cause"). Pl. ***sequelae*** (si-**kwee**-lee).

sequela villanorum (si-**kwee**-lə vil-ə-**nor**-əm). [Law Latin] (18c) *Hist.* The family and appurtenances to a villein's goods, which were at the lord's disposal.

sequence listing. (2006) *Patents.* A description of the nucleotide or amino-acid chain in a biotechnological invention.

sequential instruction. See *acquit-first instruction* under JURY INSTRUCTION.

sequential journal. See JOURNAL OF NOTARIAL ACTS.

sequential lineup. See LINEUP.

sequential marriage. See BIGAMY (2).

sequential photo array. See PHOTO ARRAY.

sequester (si-**kwes**-tər), *n.* (14c) **1.** An across-the-board cut in government spending. **2.** A person with whom litigants deposit property being contested until the case has concluded; SEQUESTRATOR (2).

sequester, *vb.* (15c) **1.** To separate or isolate from other people or things; to remove or seclude. **2.** To segregate or isolate (a jury or witness) during trial. **3.** To separate (property) from an owner or claimant for a time; esp., to take into judicial custody until a controversy has been decided or a claim satisfied. **4.** *Civil law.* To deposit (a thing) into the hands of a neutral third party pending the determination of its ownership. **5.** To take possession of for a time, as by court order, until creditors' claims have been duly settled. — Also termed (esp. in sense 4) *sequestrate.* **6.** To seize (property) by a writ of sequestration; specif., to seize (a defendant's property) by judicial order until the claims in a lawsuit have been resolved. **7.** (Of a government) to confiscate or appropriate property for the state's use, esp. enemy assets during time of war. **8.** To disclaim or renounce (property), as a surviving spouse might do in the settlement of the deceased spouse's estate. **9.** *Hist.* To remove from office or membership, as by excommunication. **10.** To engage in across-the-board government cuts in spending. See EXCOMMUNICATION. — Also (erroneously) termed *sequestrate.*

sequestered account. See ACCOUNT.

sequesterer. See SEQUESTRATOR.

sequestrable (si-**kwes**-trə-bəl), *adj.* (17c) Liable to sequestration; legally forfeitable.

sequestrari facias (see-kwes-**trair**-ɪ **fay**-shee-əs), *n.* [Law Latin "you are to cause to be sequestered"] (1808) *Hist. Eccles. law.* A process to enforce a judgment against a clergyman in a benefice, by which the bishop was ordered to sequester a church's rents, tithes, or other profits until the debt was paid.

sequestrate, *vb.* See SEQUESTER (esp. sense 4).

sequestratio (see-kwes-**tray**-shee-oh), *n.* [Latin] *Roman law.* The depositing of an object in dispute with a holder, the sequester, either voluntarily or by court order. Pl. ***sequestrationes*** (see-kwes-tray-shee-**oh**-neez).

sequestration (see-kwes-**tray**-shən), *n.* (16c) **1.** The act or process of separating, isolating, or secluding one or more people or things from others. **2.** The quality, state, or condition of being separated, isolated, or secluded; esp., retirement or withdrawal from society. **3.** Custodial isolation of a trial jury to prevent tampering and exposure to publicity, or of witnesses to prevent them from hearing the testimony of others. — Also termed (in sense 2) *jury sequestration.* **4.** The separation of a thing in controversy from the possession of those who claim it; esp., the removal of property from its possessor pending the outcome of a dispute in which two or more parties contend for it. **5.** *Civil law.* The deposit of property with a neutral third party, either by agreement or by judicial order, by one or both parties while the property is being subjected to adverse claims, until the question of ownership is decided. Cf. ATTACHMENT (1); GARNISHMENT.

▸ **conventional sequestration.** (1919) The parties' voluntary deposit of the property at issue in a lawsuit.

▸ **judicial sequestration.** (17c) The court-ordered deposit of the property at issue in a lawsuit.

6. *Eccles. law.* The taking possession and management of a vacant benefice pending the naming of a new incumbent; esp., the gathering together of the fruits of a vacant benefice for the use of the next incumbent. **7.** *Eccles. law.* A form of execution against a beneficed clergyman who has fallen into arrears, the writ being issued by the bishop of the diocese so that the rents or profits of the benefice will be paid over to creditors until the debts are paid. **8.** *Wills & estates.* The setting apart of a decedent's personal property when no one has been willing to act as a personal representative for the estate; the isolating of a decedent's goods and chattels when no one has been able and willing to take out an administration of the estate. **9.** A judicial writ commanding the sheriff or other officer to seize the goods of a person named in the writ. • Historically, a sequestration in this sense was a chancery writ directed to commissioners commanding them to seize the goods of the person against whom it was directed. It might be issued against a defendant who was in contempt by reason of neglect or refusal to appear or answer in court, or who disobeyed a judicial decree. **10.** *Scots law.* The court-ordered seizure of a bankrupt's estate for the benefit of creditors. **11.** *Int'l law.* The seizure by a belligerent power of enemy assets; esp., the seizure by a belligerent state of debts due by its citizens to the enemy. **12.** *Wills & estates.* The process by which a renounced interest is subjected to judicial management and is distributed as the testator would have wished if he or she had known about the renunciation. **13.** The removal of a person from office or membership, as by excommunication. **14.** The freezing of a government agency's funds. See SEQUESTER, *vb.* (10).

sequestration for rent. (1820) *Scots law.* A landlord's remedy to recover up to one year's unpaid rent by seizing and selling, under court order, the tenant's personal property. Cf. DISTRESS (2).

sequestrator (see-kwes-tray-tər). (15c) **1.** An officer appointed to execute a writ of sequestration.

> "[A] sequestrator was an officer of the Court of Chancery acting under the order of that court in seizing property. The law courts appear, however, to have held that the holder of the property could resist seizure by the officer of the Court of Chancery, and indeed kill that officer if necessary to prevent the seizure. And if he killed the officer, he would not be held guilty of murder because the Court of Chancery was an illegal tribunal or its decrees were illegal, and could not justify an officer in seizing the property mentioned in the order." Charles Herman Kinnane, *A First Book on Anglo-American Law* 306 (2d ed. 1952).

2. Someone who holds property in sequestration. — Also termed *sequesterer.*

sequestro habendo (si-**kwes**-troh hə-**ben**-doh), *n.* [Law Latin] (17c) *Hist. Eccles. law.* A writ from the sovereign to the bishop ordering the discharge of the sequestration of a benefice's profits.

serendipity doctrine. (1989) *Criminal procedure.* The principle that all evidence discovered during a lawful search is eligible to be admitted into evidence at trial.

serf. (15c) *Hist.* A person in a condition of feudal servitude, bound to labor at the will of a lord; a villein. • Serfs differed from slaves in that they were bound to the native soil rather than being the absolute property of a master.

> "As the categories became indistinct, the more abject varieties of slavery disappeared and in the twelfth century the word 'villein' became the general term for unfree peasants. 'Serf' did not become a legal term of art, and in so far as it remained in use it did not connote a status lower than that of villein. The merger was to the detriment of the *villani*, but it ensured that full slavery was not received as part of the common law." J.H. Baker, *An Introduction to English Legal History* 532 (3d ed. 1990).

sergeant. (13c) **1.** *Hist.* Someone who is not a knight but holds lands by tenure of military service. **2.** *Hist.* A municipal officer performing duties for the Crown. **3.** *Hist.* A bailiff. **4.** SERGEANT-AT-ARMS. **5.** A noncommissioned officer in the armed forces ranking a grade above a corporal. **6.** An officer in the police force ranking below a captain or lieutenant. — Also spelled *serjeant.*

sergeant-at-arms. (14c) **1.** *Hist.* An armed officer attending a sovereign. **2.** An officer the Crown assigns to attend a session of Parliament. **3.** A legislative officer charged with maintaining order and serving notices and process on behalf of the legislative body and its committees. **4.** *Parliamentary law.* An officer charged with helping keep order in a meeting under the chair's direction. — Also spelled (in senses 1, 2 & 4) *serjeant-at-arms.* — Also termed (in sense 4) *warden*; *warrant officer.*

sergeantry. See SERJEANTY.

Sergeant Schultz defense. (1995) *Slang.* An assertion by a criminal or civil defendant who claims that he or she was not an active participant in an alleged scheme or conspiracy, and that he or she knew nothing, saw nothing, and heard nothing. • This defense is named after a character from the television series *Hogan's Heroes*, in which Sergeant Schultz, a German guard in charge of prisoners of war during World War II, would avoid responsibility for the prisoners' schemes by proclaiming that he saw nothing and knew nothing. Cf. NUREMBERG DEFENSE (1).

sergeanty. See SERJEANTY.

serial bond. See BOND (3).

serial consideration. See *consideration seriatim* under CONSIDERATION (2).

serial monogamy. See MONOGAMY.

serial murder. See MURDER.

serial note. See *installment note* under NOTE (1).

serial number. (1851) **1.** A number assigned to a specific thing, esp. a product, to identify it from other things of the same kind. • While serial numbers are usually assigned in numerical order, they may also be random. **2.** *Patents & Trademarks.* An identifying number assigned to a completed patent or trademark application. • The serial number is assigned when the application is received or completed. See APPLICATION NUMBER.

serial polygamy. See POLYGAMY (2).

serial right. (1897) The right of publication; esp., a right reserved in a publishing contract giving the author or publisher the right to publish the manuscript in installments (as in a magazine) before or after the publication of the book.

serial violation. (1989) *Civil-rights law.* The practice by an employer of committing a series of discriminatory acts against an employee, all of which arise out of the same discriminatory intent or animus. • Such a series of discriminatory acts will usu. be considered a continuing violation. For a claim on the violation to be timely, at least one of the discriminatory acts must have taken place within the time permitted to assert the claim (e.g., 300 days for a Title VII claim). Cf. SYSTEMATIC VIOLATION.

seriatim (seer-ee-**ay**-tim), *adj.* (1871) Occurring in a series.

seriatim, *adv.* [Latin] (17c) One after another; in a series; successively <the court disposed of the issues seriatim>. — Also termed *seriately* (**seer**-ee-ət-lee). See *consideration seriatim* under CONSIDERATION (2).

seriatim opinions. See OPINION (1).

series bonds. See BOND (3).

series code. (1994) *Patents & Trademarks.* A numerical designation assigned to any of a group of applications for patent or trademark registration filed in the U.S. Patent and Trademark Office. • The series code is part of an application number and is followed by a slash. For example, if the application number is 09/445,323, then 09 is the series code, and the application is the 445,323rd application in that batch. For ordinary patent applications, series codes are assigned for a group of applications filed during a particular period. Nonprovisional patent applications are assigned series codes from 01 to 10, depending on the period during which the application was filed. The series code for design applications is 29, for provisional applications 60, for ex parte reexamination proceedings 90, and for *inter partes* reexamination proceedings 95. For trademark applications, the series code usu. begins with numbers between 70 and 75. — Also termed *batch number.*

series-qualifier canon. The presumption that when there is a straightforward, parallel construction that involves all nouns or verbs in a series, a prepositive or postpositive modifier normally applies to the entire series. — Also termed *prepositive/postpositive-qualifier canon*; *prepositive/postpositive-modifier canon.*

series rerum judicatarum (**seer**-ə-eez *or* **seer**-eez **reer**-əm joo-di-kə-**tor**-əm). [Law Latin] (18c) *Scots law.* A succession of decisions deciding a particular principle, as a result of which a precedent has been established.

serious, *adj.* (15c) **1.** (Of conduct, opinions, etc.) weighty; important <serious violation of rules>. **2.** (Of an injury, illness, accident, etc.) dangerous; potentially resulting in death or other severe consequences <serious bodily harm>.

serious and willful misconduct. (1910) *Workers' compensation.* An intentional act performed with the knowledge that it is likely to result in serious injury or with a wanton and reckless disregard of its probable consequences.

serious bodily harm. See *serious bodily injury* under INJURY.

serious bodily injury. See INJURY.

serious crime. 1. See *serious offense* under OFFENSE (2). **2.** See FELONY (1).

serious felony. See FELONY (1).

serious health condition. (1987) Under the Family and Medical Leave Act, an illness, injury, or physical or mental state that involves in-patient care or continuing treatment by a healthcare provider for several days. • Excluded from the definition are cosmetic treatments and minor illnesses that are not accompanied by medical complications.

serious illness. (1838) *Insurance.* A disorder that permanently or materially impairs, or is likely to permanently or materially impair, the health of the insured or an insurance applicant.

seriously harmful behavior. See HARMFUL BEHAVIOR.

serious misdemeanor. See MISDEMEANOR (1).

serious offense. 1. See OFFENSE (2). **2.** See *serious crime* under CRIME.

seritium. See SERVICE (6).

serjeant. 1. See SERGEANT. **2.** See SERJEANT-AT-LAW.

serjeant-at-arms. See SERGEANT-AT-ARMS.

serjeant-at-law. (15c) *Hist. English law.* A barrister of superior grade; one who had achieved the highest degree of the legal profession, having (until 1846) the exclusive privilege of practicing in the Court of Common Pleas. • Every judge of the common-law courts was required to be a serjeant-at-law until the Judicature Act of 1873. The rank was gradually superseded by that of Queen's Counsel. — Often shortened to *serjeant.* — Also spelled *sergeant-at-law.* — Also termed *serjeant at the law; serjeant of the law; serjeant of the coif; serviens narrator.*

▸ **premier serjeant.** (18c) The serjeant given the primary right of preaudience by royal letters patent. — Also termed *prime serjeant.* See PREAUDIENCE.

Serjeants' Inn. *Hist.* A building on Chancery Lane, London, that housed the Order of Serjeants-at-Law. • The building was sold and demolished in 1877. Until 1416, the Inn was called *Faryndon's Inn* or *Faryndon Inn,* after Robert Faryndon, who held the lease. Two other inns in the 15th and 16th centuries were also called Serjeants' Inn, one in Holborn (sometimes called *Scroops's Inn*) and one in Fleet Street.

serjeanty (**sahr**-jən-tee). (15c) *Hist.* A feudal lay tenure requiring some form of personal service to the king. • The required service was not necessarily military. Many household officers of the Crown, even those as humble as bakers and cooks, held lands in serjeanty. — Also spelled *sergeanty; sergeantry.*

▸ **grand serjeanty.** (15c) *Hist.* Serjeanty requiring the tenant to perform a service relating to the country's defense. • The required service could be as great as fielding an army or as small as providing a fully equipped knight. Sometimes the service was ceremonial or honorary, such as carrying the king's banner or serving as an officer at the coronation.

▸ **petit serjeanty** (**pet**-ee). (16c) *Hist.* Serjeanty requiring only a minor service of small value, usu. with military symbolism. • Examples include presenting an arrow or an unstrung bow to the king.

serment (**sər**-mənt). (14c) *Hist.* An oath.

sermon. (12c) **1.** A religious discourse usu. delivered orally by a member of the clergy as part of a worship service and often taken from a scriptural passage. — Also termed *homily.* **2.** A speech conveying religious instruction; catechism. **3.** A speech of reproof, esp. regarding conduct or duty. *See Fowler v. Rhode Island,* 345 U.S. 67, 70, 73 S.Ct. 526, 527 (1953).

serological test (seer-ə-**loj**-ə-kəl). (1931) A blood examination to detect the presence of antibodies and antigens, as well as other characteristics, esp. as indicators of disease. • Many states require serological tests to determine the presence of venereal disease in a couple applying for a marriage license. See BLOOD TEST.

serpentine vote. See VOTE (4).

***Serrano* plea.** See ALFORD PLEA.

serva aliena. See SERVUS.

servage (**sər**-vij). (13c) *Hist.* A feudal service that a serf was required to perform for the lord or else pay the equivalent value in kind or money.

servant. (13c) Someone who is employed by another to do work under the control and direction of the employer. • A servant, such as a full-time employee, provides personal services that are integral to an employer's business, so a servant must submit to the employer's control of the servant's time and behavior. See EMPLOYEE. Cf. MASTER (1).

> "A servant, strictly speaking, is a person who, by contract or operation of law, is for a limited period subject to the authority or control of another person in a particular trade, business or occupation . . . . The word *servant,* in our legal *nomenclature,* has a broad significance, and embraces all persons of whatever rank or position who are in the employ, and subject to the direction or control of another in any department of labor or business. Indeed it may, in most cases, be said to be synonymous with employee." H.G. Wood, *A Treatise on the Law of Master and Servant* § 1, at 2 (2d ed. 1886).

▸ **assigned servant.** (1991) *Hist.* In early colonial times, an unpaid servant, usu. a deported convict, sentenced to labor on an estate, esp. in America or Australia. — Also termed *assignee.* See ASSIGNMENT SYSTEM.

▸ **civil servant.** See CIVIL SERVANT.

▸ **fellow servant.** See FELLOW SERVANT.

▸ **indentured servant.** (18c) *Hist.* A servant who contracted to work without wages for a fixed period in exchange for some benefit, such as learning a trade or cancellation of a debt or paid passage to another country, and the promise of freedom when the contract period expired. • Indentured servitude could be voluntary or involuntary. A contract usu. lasted from four to ten years, but the servant could terminate the contract sooner by paying for the unexpired time. Convicts transported to the colonies were often required to serve as indentured servants as part of their sentences.

▸ **servant of servants.** (15c) *Hist.* A person degraded to extreme servitude.

servantry, *n.* (1860) Servants collectively.

serve, *vb.* (15c) **1.** To make legal delivery of (a notice or process) <a copy of the pleading was served on all interested parties>. **2.** To present (a person) with a notice or process as required by law <the defendant was served with process>.

service, *n.* (15c) **1.** The status or condition of a servant, esp. a domestic servant <in service at Blenheim Palace>. **2.** Labor performed in the interest or under the direction of others; specif., the performance of some useful act or series of acts for the benefit of another, usu. for a fee <goods and services>. • In this sense, *service* denotes an intangible commodity in the form of human effort, such as labor, skill, or advice. See PERSONAL SERVICE (2).

▸ **gratuitous service.** (18c) Service provided with no expectation of compensation.

3. The official work or duty that one is required to perform. **4.** Any institution or organization instituted for the accomplishment of such a duty <military service>. See CIVIL SERVICE. **5.** A person or agency that accomplishes some constantly recurring work or fills some perpetual demand <cleaning service>. See SALVAGE SERVICE. **6.** *Hist.* Whatever service a feudal tenant was bound to render to his lord for the use and occupancy of the land; any render made for the enjoyment of land; SERVITIUM. — Also termed *feudal service.*

▸ **base service.** (18c) *Hist.* Agricultural work performed by a villein tenant in exchange for the lord's permission to hold the land. Cf. *knight-service.*

▸ **free service.** (16c) *Hist.* Such renders toward the lord as were befitting a soldier or freeman, such as serving under his lord in war.

▸ **knight-service.** (15c) *Hist.* A type of lay tenure in which a knight held land of another person or the Crown in exchange for a pledge of military service. — Also termed *knight's service*; (Scots law) *ward holding.* Cf. *base service*; VILLEINAGE.

"By far the greater part of England is held of the king by knight's service (*per servitium militare*): it is comparatively rare for the king's tenants in chief to hold by any of the other tenures. In order to understand this tenure we must form the conception of a unit of military service. That unit seems to be the service of one knight or fully armed horseman (*servitium unius militis*) to be done to the king in his army for forty days in the year, if it be called for." 1 Frederick Pollock & Frederic W. Maitland, *The History of English Law Before the Time of Edward I* 254 (2d ed. 1898).

7. The formal delivery of a writ, summons, or other legal process, pleading, or notice to a litigant or other party interested in litigation; the legal communication of a judicial process <service by mail>.

▸ **actual service.** See PERSONAL SERVICE (1).

▸ **constructive service.** (1808) **1.** See *substituted service.* **2.** Service accomplished by a method or circumstance that does not give actual notice.

▸ **nail-and-mail service.** (1968) Service of process that is made by affixing a summons to the door of the recipient's business, dwelling, or usual place of abode in addition to mailing the summons to the recipient and filing proof of service with the court. • This type of service may typically be used only after attempting personal service with due diligence.

▸ **personal service.** See PERSONAL SERVICE (1).

▸ **service by publication.** (1826) The service of process on an absent or nonresident defendant by publishing a notice in a newspaper or other public medium.

▸ **sewer service.** (1953) *Slang.* The fraudulent service of process on a debtor by a creditor seeking to obtain a default judgment.

▸ **substituted service.** (1840) Any method of service allowed by law in place of personal service, such as service by mail. — Also termed *constructive service.*

service, *vb.* (1927) To provide service for; specif., to make interest payments on (a debt) <service the deficit>.

service by publication. See SERVICE (7).

service charge. (1929) **1.** A charge assessed for performing a service, such as the charge assessed by a restaurant for waiters or by a bank against the expenses of maintaining or servicing a customer's checking account. **2.** The sum of (1) all charges payable by the buyer and imposed by the seller as an incident to the extension of credit and (2) charges incurred for investigating the collateral or creditworthiness of the buyer or for commissions for obtaining the credit. UCCC § 2.109. — Also termed (in sense 2) *credit service charge.* **3.** An amount of money paid to the owner of an apartment building for amenities such as cleaning the common areas.

service contract. See CONTRACT.

service dog. See DOG (1).

service establishment. (1938) Under the Fair Labor Standards Act, an establishment that, although having the characteristics of a retail store, primarily furnishes services to the public, such as a barber shop, laundry, or automobile-repair shop.

service life. (1921) The period of an asset's expected usefulness. • It may or may not coincide with the asset's depreciable life for income-tax purposes.

servicemark. (1945) *Trademarks.* A name, phrase, or other device used to identify and distinguish the services of a certain provider. • Servicemarks identify and afford protection to intangible things such as services, as distinguished from the protection already provided for marks affixed to tangible things such as goods and products. — Often shortened to *mark.* — Also spelled *service mark*; *service-mark.* Cf. TRADEMARK (1); *registered trademark* under TRADEMARK.

servicemark application. See TRADEMARK APPLICATION.

service-occupation tax. See TAX.

service of process. See SERVICE (1).

serviens narrator (sər-vee-enz nə-**ray**-tər). See SERJEANT-AT-LAW.

servient (sər-vee-ənt), *adj.* (17c) (Of an estate) subject to a servitude or easement. See *servient estate* under ESTATE (4).

servient estate. See ESTATE (4).

servient praedium. See *praedium serviens* under PRAEDIUM.

servient property. See *servient estate* under ESTATE (4).

servient tenant. See TENANT (1).

servient tenement. See *servient estate* under ESTATE (4).

servile, *adj.* (14c) **1.** Of, relating to, or involving slaves or servants <a servile insurrection>. **2.** Belonging to a subjugated class <servile laborers>. **3.** (Of work, tasks, etc.) appropriate to slaves or servants; menial <servile jobs>. **4.** Unconsciously controlled in one's conduct or life <servile to praise>. **5.** *Eccles. law.* (Of work) performed with the hands and therefore forbidden to be done on the Sabbath and holidays; manual <servile tasks>. **6.** *Hist.* Of or relating to a land tenure subject to conditions distinguished from those of freehold, such as labor instead of rent <servile tenures>. **7.** Submissive in a low, abject way; meanly subservient <his servile, sycophantic manner>.

servitia solita et consueta (sər-**vish**-ee-ə **sol**-ə-tə kən-**swee**-tə). [Law Latin "services used and wont"] (1812) *Scots law.* A common return required by certain charters, usu. implying military service, from a vassal to a lord.

servitii praestatio (sər-**vish**-ee-ɪ pri-**stay**-shee-oh). [Law Latin] *Hist.* The performance of services.

servitiis acquietandis (sər-**vish**-ee-is ə-kwɪ-ə-**tan**-dis), *n.* [Law Latin "for being quit of service"] (17c) *Hist.* A writ exempting a person from performing certain services, either because they are not due or because they are due someone other than the distrainor.

servitium (sər-**vish**-ee-əm), *n.* [Latin "service"] *Hist.* The duty of service; esp., a tenant's duties of performance and obedience to the lord.

servitium feodale et praediale (sər-**vish**-ee-əm fee-ə-**day**-lee [*or* fyoo-**day**-lee] et pree-dee-**ay**-lee), *n.* [Law Latin] *Hist.* A personal service due only by reason of lands held in fee.

servitium forinsecum (sər-**vish**-ee-əm fə-**rin**-si-kəm), *n.* [Law Latin] (17c) *Hist.* A service due the king rather than a lord.

servitium intrinsecum (sər-**vish**-ee-əm in-**trin**-si-kəm), *n.* [Law Latin] *Hist.* The ordinary service due from a tenant to the chief lord.

servitium liberum (sər-**vish**-ee-əm **lib**-ər-əm), *n.* [Law Latin] (17c) *Hist.* The service by a free tenant (not a vassal) to the lord, as by attending the lord's court or accompanying the lord into military service. — Also termed *liberum servitium; servitium liberum armorum.*

servitium regale (sər-**vish**-ee-əm ri-**gay**-lee). [Latin "royal service"] (17c) *Hist.* The right of a lord of a royal manor to settle disputes, to assess fees and fines, to mint money, and the like.

servitium scuti (sər-**vish**-ee-əm **sk[y]oo**-tɪ). [Latin "service of the shield"] (17c) *Hist.* Knight-service.

servitium socae (sər-**vish**-ee-əm **soh**-see). [Latin "service of the plow"] (17c) *Hist.* Socage.

servitor (**sərv**-i-tər), *n.* (14c) **1.** *Hist.* A messenger of the marshal of the Court of King's Bench whose job was to serve writs of summons. **2.** A follower, attendant, or servant of any kind. **3.** *Hist.* One in military service; a soldier. **4.** A male servant. — **servitorial,** *adj.* — **servitorship,** *n.*

servitor of bills (**sər**-vi-tər). (16c) *Hist.* A messenger of the marshal of the King's Bench, sent out to summon people to court. — Also termed *tip-stave.*

servitude. (16c) **1.** An encumbrance consisting in a right to the limited use of a piece of land or other immovable property without the possession of it; a charge or burden on an estate for another's benefit <the easement by necessity is an equitable servitude>. • Servitudes include easements, irrevocable licenses, profits, and real covenants. See EASEMENT; LICENSE; PROFIT (2); *covenant running with the land* under COVENANT (4). **2.** *Roman & civil law.* The right exercised by a dominant tenement over a servient tenement, either adjoining or neighboring. • This right was perpetual except for personal servitudes; the land, rather than its owner, enjoyed the right. Although a servitude could not be possessed because it was incorporeal, it could be protected by interdict. Generally, a servitude had to be exercised *civiliter,* with as little inconvenience as possible. There was never a closed list of what constituted a servitude; for example, Justinian classed personal rights *in re aliena* as personal servitude. See SERVITUS (2).

▸ **acquired servitude.** (1971) A servitude requiring a special mode of acquisition before it comes into existence.

▸ **additional servitude.** (18c) A servitude imposed on land taken under an eminent-domain proceeding for a different type of servitude, as when a highway is constructed on land condemned for a public sidewalk. • A landowner whose land is burdened by an additional servitude is entitled to further compensation.

▸ **affirmative servitude.** *Civil law.* See *positive servitude.*

▸ **apparent servitude.** (1834) *Civil law.* A servitude appurtenant that is manifested by exterior signs or constructions, such as a roadway. Cf. *nonapparent servitude.*

▸ **conservation servitude.** See *conservation easement* under EASEMENT.

▸ **continuous servitude.** *Louisiana law.* See *continuous easement* under EASEMENT. La. Civ. Code art. 646.

▸ **conventional servitude.** (18c) *Civil law.* A servitude established by agreement or through acquisitive prescription.

▸ **discontinuous servitude.** See *discontinuous easement* under EASEMENT.

▸ **equitable servitude.** See *restrictive covenant* (1) under COVENANT (4).

▸ **landed servitude.** See *servitude appurtenant.*

▸ **legal servitude.** (18c) *Civil law.* A limitation that the law imposes on the use of an estate for the benefit of the general public or of a particular person or persons. • Examples of legal servitudes are restrictions on certain uses of the shores of navigable rivers, and the obligation of a landowner to provide a passage to an enclosed estate.

▸ **mineral servitude.** (1931) *Louisiana law.* A servitude granting the right to enter another's property to explore for and extract minerals; specif., under the Louisiana Mineral Code, a charge on land in favor of a person or another tract of land, creating a limited right to use the land to explore for and produce minerals. • The servitude is generally equivalent to the severed mineral interest in a common-law state.

▸ **natural servitude.** (18c) **1.** A servitude naturally appurtenant to land, requiring no special mode of acquisition. • An example is the right of land, unencumbered by buildings, to the support of the adjoining land. **2.** *Civil law.* A servitude imposed by law because of the natural situation of the estates. • An example of a natural servitude is a lower estate that is bound to receive waters flowing naturally from a higher estate.

▸ **navigation servitude.** (1943) An easement allowing the federal government to regulate commerce on navigable water without having to pay compensation for interfering with private ownership rights. See NAVIGABLE WATER.

3. An easement, based on the state police power or public-trust doctrine, that allows a state to regulate commerce on navigable water and provide limited compensation for interference with private ownership rights. • A state servitude is inferior to the federal servitude.

▸ **negative servitude.** (17c) *Civil law.* A servitude appurtenant allowing a dominant landowner to prohibit the servient landowner from exercising a right. • For example, a negative servitude, such as *jus ne luminibus officiatur,* prevents a landowner from building in a way that blocks light from reaching another person's house.

▸ **nonapparent servitude.** (1837) *Civil law.* A servitude appurtenant that is not obvious because there are no exterior signs of its existence. • An example is a prohibition against building above a certain height. Cf. *apparent servitude.*

▸ **personal servitude.** (17c) **1.** A servitude granting a specific person certain rights in property. **2.** A specific person's right over the property of another, regardless of who the owner might be. • A personal servitude lasts for the person's lifetime and is not transferable. **3.** *Louisiana law.* A servitude that benefits a person or an immovable. La. Civ. Code art. 534.

▸ **positive servitude.** (17c) *Civil law.* A real servitude allowing a person to lawfully do something on the servient landowner's property, such as entering the property. — Also termed *affirmative servitude.*

▸ **predial servitude.** See *servitude appurtenant.*

▸ **private servitude.** (1922) A servitude vested in a particular person. • Examples include a landowner's personal right-of-way over an adjoining piece of land or a right granted to one person to fish in another's lake.

▸ **public servitude.** (1805) A servitude vested in the public at large or in some class of indeterminate individuals. • Examples include the right of the public to use a highway over privately owned land and the right to navigate a river the bed of which is privately owned.

▸ **real servitude.** See *servitude appurtenant.*

▸ **rural servitude.** (18c) *Roman law.* A servitude chiefly affecting agricultural land or land in the country. • The four oldest types, *iter, actus, via,* and *aqueductus* were all *res mancipi* despite being incorporeal. Most rural servitudes were easements, but some were profits. — Also termed *rustic servitude; praedium rusticum; jus rusticorum praediorum.*

▸ **servitude appurtenant.** (1893) A servitude that is not merely an encumbrance of one piece of land but is accessory to another piece; the right of using one piece of land for the benefit of another, such as the right of support for a building. — Also termed *real servitude; predial* (or *praedial*) *servitude; landed servitude.* La. Civ. Code art. 646.

▸ **servitude in gross.** (1884) A servitude that is not accessory to any dominant estate for whose benefit it exists but is merely an encumbrance on a given piece of land.

▸ **servitude of drip.** (1828) *Louisiana law.* A servitude appurtenant that binds the servient estate's owner to maintain a roof so that rainwater does not drip or drain onto the dominant estate. La. Civ. Code art. 664. — Also termed *servitude of drip and drain.*

▸ **servitude of passage.** (1837) *Civil law.* The dominant estate owner's right of easement through the servient estate.

▸ **servitude of view.** (1847) *Louisiana law.* The dominant estate owner's right to enjoy a view through the servient estate and to prevent its obstruction. La. Civ. Code art. 701.

▸ **urban servitude.** (1831) **1.** A servitude appertaining to the building and construction of houses in a city, such as the right to light and air. **2.** *Roman law.* A servitude that primarily affects buildings or urban land. • With the exception of *oneris ferendi,* urban servitudes were passive. They could be affected by planning legislation. — Also termed (in sense 2) *praedium urbanum; jus urbanorum praediorum.*

4. The condition of being a servant or slave; SLAVERY (1), (2) <under the 15th Amendment, an American citizen's right to vote cannot be denied on account of race, color, or previous condition of servitude>. **5.** The condition of a prisoner who has been sentenced to forced labor <penal servitude>.

▸ **involuntary servitude.** (18c) The condition of one forced to labor — for pay or not — for another by coercion or imprisonment.

servitude of drip and drain. See *servitude of drip* under SERVITUDE (3).

servitude of passage. See SERVITUDE (3).

servitus (**sər**-vi-təs), *n.* [Latin fr. *servire* "to serve"] *Roman law.* **1.** Slavery; bondage. **2.** A servitude, usu. one appurtenant as opposed to a personal servitude such as usufruct; an easement. See *rural servitude* and *urban servitude* under SERVITUDE (3). Pl. ***servitutes.***

> "In a word, *servitus* or easement gives to the entitled party, a power or liberty of applying the subject to exactly determined purposes. Property or dominion gives to the entitled party, the power or liberty of applying it to *all* purposes, *save* such purposes as are not consistent with his relative or absolute duties." 2 John Austin, *Lectures on Jurisprudence* 795 (Robert Campbell ed., 5th ed. 1885).

▸ ***servitus actus*** (**ak**-təs). [Latin "the servitude of driving cattle"] *Roman law.* A type of right-of-way; a rural servitude entitling one to walk, ride, or drive animals over another's property.

▸ ***servitus altius non tollendi*** (**al**-shee-əs non tə-**len**-dı). [Latin "the servitude of not building higher"] (1875) *Roman law.* An urban servitude allowing a person to prevent a neighbor from building a taller house.

▸ ***servitus aquae ducendae*** (**ak**-wee d[y]oo-**sen**-dee). [Latin "the servitude of leading water"] *Roman law.* A rural servitude allowing one to bring water to property through another's land, as by a canal. — Also termed *aquaeductus.*

▸ ***servitus aquae educendae*** (**ak**-wee ee-d[y]oo-**sen**-dee). [Latin "the servitude of leading off water"] *Roman law.* An urban servitude entitling a person to discharge water onto another's land.

▸ ***servitus aquae hauriendae*** (haw-ree-**en**-dee). [Latin "the servitude of drawing water"] *Roman law.* See AQUAEHAUSTUS.

▸ ***servitus aquaehaustus*** (**ak**-wee-**haws**-təs). [Latin "the servitude of drawing water"] *Roman law.* See AQUAEHAUSTUS.

▸ ***servitus fluminis*** (**floo**-mə-nəs). [Latin "the servitude of a stream of rainwater"] *Roman law.* An urban servitude consisting in the right to divert rainwater as opposed to drip (*stillicidium*) onto another's land.

▸ ***servitus fumi immittendi*** (**fyoo**-mI im-ə-**ten**-dI). [Latin "the servitude of discharging smoke"] *Roman law.* An urban servitude allowing a person's chimney smoke to be directed over a neighbor's property.

▸ ***servitus itineris*** (I-**tin**-ər-is). [Latin "the servitude of way"] See ITER.

▸ ***servitus luminum*** (**loo**-mə-nəm). [Latin "the servitude of lights"] (1888) *Roman law.* An urban servitude entitling one to receive light from a neighbor's land, as by building windows in a common wall to light a room.

▸ ***servitus ne luminibus officiatur*** (nee loo-**min**-ə-bəs ə-fish-ee-**ay**-tər). [Latin "the servitude not to hinder light"] (1869) *Roman law.* An urban servitude preventing someone's light from being obstructed by a neighbor's building.

▸ ***servitus ne prospectui officiatur*** (nee prə-**spek**-too-I ə-fish-ee-**ay**-tər). [Latin "the servitude not to intercept one's prospect"] *Roman law.* An urban servitude entitling someone to an unobstructed view.

▸ ***servitus oneris ferendi*** (**on**-ə-ris fə-**ren**-dI). [Latin "the servitude of bearing weight"] (1839) *Roman law.* The urban servitude allowing a person's building to rest on a neighbor's building, wall, or pillar. See ONERIS FERENDI; JUS ONERIS FERENDI.

▸ ***servitus pascendi*** (pa-**sen**-dI). [Latin "the servitude of pasturing"] (1827) *Roman law.* A rural servitude allowing one to pasture cattle on another's land. — Also termed *jus pascendi.*

▸ ***servitus pecoris ad aquam adpulsum*** (**pek**-ə-ris ad **ak**-wəm ad-**pəl**-səm). [Latin "the servitude to drive cattle to water"] *Roman law.* A rural servitude allowing one to drive cattle to water across another's land.

▸ ***servitus praedii rustici*** (**pree**-dee-I **rəs**-ti-sI). [Latin "the servitude of a country estate"] *Roman law.* A rural servitude; a servitude attached to land, as in *servitus pecoris ad aquam adpulsus.* Cf. *rural servitude* under SERVITUDE (3).

▸ ***servitus praedii urbani*** (**pree**-dee-I ər-**bay**-nI). [Latin "the servitude of an urban estate"] *Roman law.* An urban servitude; a servitude attached to a building, as in *servitus oneris ferendi.* See *urban servitude* under SERVITUDE (3).

▸ ***servitus praediorum*** (pree-dee-**or**-əm). [Latin "praedial servitude"] (17c) *Roman law.* A burden on one estate for the benefit of another. See *servitude appurtenant* under SERVITUDE (3).

▸ ***servitus projiciendi*** (prə-jish-ee-**en**-dI). [Latin "the servitude of projecting"] (1870) *Roman law.* An urban servitude allowing a projection from one's building into the open space over a neighbor's property.

▸ ***servitus stillicidii*** (stil-ə-**sid**-ee-I). [Latin "the servitude of drip"] (1838) *Roman law.* An urban servitude allowing water to drip from one's house onto a neighbor's house or ground. Cf. AQUAE IMMITTENDAE; DRIP RIGHTS.

▸ ***servitus tigni immittendi*** (**tig**-nI im-ə-**ten**-dI). [Latin "the servitude of letting in a beam"] (1839) *Roman law.* An urban servitude allowing one to insert beams into a neighbor's wall.

▸ ***servitus viae*** (**vI**-ee). [Latin "the servitude of road way"] *Roman law.* A rural servitude allowing a right-of-way over another's land. See VIA (2).

servus (**sər**-vəs), *n.* [Latin] **1.** *Roman law.* A slave; a human being who was property, and could be bought, sold, pledged, and testated. • A Roman slave who was formally freed became a Roman citizen. Cf. INGENUUS; LATINI JUNIANI; LIBERTINII. **2.** *Hist.* A bondman; a servant.

sess, *n.* See CESS.

sessio (**sesh**-ee-oh), *n.* [Latin "a sitting"] *Hist.* A session; a sitting, as in *sessio parliamenti* ("the sitting of Parliament").

session. (15c) **1.** *Parliamentary law.* A meeting or series of related meetings throughout which a court, legislature, or other deliberative assembly conducts business in a continuing sequence <the court's spring session>. • The terms *meeting* and *session* have opposite but sometimes interchangeable meanings. An organization's annual convention may consist of several consecutive meetings that it calls *sessions,* such as a morning session and an afternoon session, or a Friday session and a Saturday session, which are technically meetings rather than sessions. Likewise, the organization may call its convention an *annual meeting,* which technically comprises several meetings that constitute a single session. — Also termed (for a court) *sitting.* See TERM (5). Cf. MEETING.

> "Parliament have three modes of separation, to wit, by adjournment, by prorogation, or dissolution by the king, or by the efflux of the term for which they were elected. Prorogation or dissolution constitutes there what is called a session, provided some act has passed. In this case all matters depending before them are discontinued, and at their next meeting are to be taken up de novo, if taken up at all. Adjournment, which is by themselves, is no more than a continuance of the session from one day to another, or for a fortnight, a month, &c. ad libitum. All matters depending remain in statu quo, and when they meet again, be the term ever so distant, are resumed without any fresh commencement, at the point at which they were left. Their whole session is considered in law but as one day, and has relation to the first day thereof." Thomas Jefferson, *A Manual of Parliamentary Practice* 127–28 (1801) (citations omitted).

▸ **biennial session.** (1854) A legislative session held every two years. • Most state legislatures have biennial sessions, usu. held in odd-numbered years.

▸ **borough session.** (*usu. pl.*) (1835) A criminal-court session of limited jurisdiction held before a municipal recorder. Cf. BOROUGH COURT; RECORDER (1).

▸ **closed session.** (1956) **1.** See *executive session.* **2.** A session to which parties not directly involved are not admitted. **3.** *Military law.* A period during a court-martial when the members (or the judge, if trial is before a military judge) deliberate alone. — Also termed *closed court.*

▸ **executive session.** (18c) A meeting, usu. held in secret, that only the members and invited nonmembers may attend. • The term originated in the United States Senate, which until 1929 sat behind closed doors when it advised the President about executive business such as appointments and treaties. — Also termed *closed session*; *secret session*.

"All open meeting statutes expressly authorize the use of executive sessions, typically specifying the particular circumstances in which executive sessions are permitted. When the specific circumstances are specified, generally no other exceptions are permitted . . . . Use of the executive session to discuss matters not properly hidden from the public is a clear violation of the open meeting law. . . . Many States expressly or implicitly forbid use of the executive session as a subterfuge to defeat the purposes of the open meeting law." 2 Ann Taylor Schwing, *Open Meeting Laws* § 7.1, at 612–15 (3d ed. 2011).

▸ **extraordinary session.** See *special session*.

▸ **extra session.** See *special session*.

▸ **general session.** (*usu. pl.*) (15c) *Hist. English law.* A session of court held by two or more justices, one of whom is of the quorum, for criminal trials.

▸ **joint session.** (1853) The combined meeting of two legislative bodies (such as the House of Representatives and the Senate) to pursue a common agenda.

"When the two houses meet in a joint session, they, in effect, merge into one house where the quorum is a majority of the members of both houses, where the votes of members of each house have equal weight, and where special rules can be adopted to govern joint sessions or they can be governed by the parliamentary common law." National Conference of State Legislatures, *Mason's Manual of Legislative Procedure* § 782, at 573 (2000).

▸ **lame-duck session.** (1924) A post-election legislative session in which some of the participants are voting during their last days as elected officials. See LAME DUCK.

▸ **open session.** (1810) **1.** A session that is fully accessible to the general public. — Also termed *public session*. **2.** *Military law.* The period during a court-martial in which all participants are in the courtroom. • Generally, the public may attend a court-martial's open session.

▸ **petty session.** (*usu. pl.*) (16c) *Hist. English law.* A court with jurisdiction over minor misdemeanors, presided over by a justice of the peace acing summarily (without a jury).

▸ **plenary session.** (1936) A meeting of all the members of a deliberative assembly, not just a committee.

▸ **pro forma session.** (1928) A legislative session held not to conduct business but only to satisfy a constitutional provision that neither house may adjourn for longer than a certain time (usu. three days) without the other house's consent.

▸ **public session.** See *open session* (1).

▸ **quarter session.** (*usu. pl.*) (16c) **1.** *English law.* A meeting held four times a year by a county's justices of the peace to transact business, including trying certain criminal and civil matters as specified by statute. • The quarter sessions were abolished in 1971 and replaced by the Crown Court system. **2.** *Scots law.* A meeting formerly held four times a year by the justices to review criminal sentences. — Abbr. Q.S.

▸ **regular session.** (18c) A session that takes place at fixed intervals or specified times.

▸ **secret session.** See *executive session*.

▸ **special session.** (17c) **1.** A legislative session, usu. called by the executive, that meets outside its regular term to consider a specific issue or to reduce backlog. — Also termed *extra session*; *extraordinary session*. **2.** (*usu. pl.*) *Hist. English law.* A session of court held by two or more justices for the exercise of some special authority, such as the administration of the licensing laws.

2. The period within any given day during which a deliberative body is assembled and performing its duties <court is in session>. **3.** A trading day in a stock market.

▸ **triple witching session.** (1986) A stock-market session on the third Friday in March, June, September, and December during which stock options, index options and futures contracts all expire. • Stock-market volatility and share volume are often high on these days

sessional, *adj.* (18c) Of, relating to, or involving a session or sessions.

sessional order. See ORDER (2).

sessioner, *n.* (16c) **1.** *Scots law.* A member of the Court of Sessions. **2.** *Hist. Scots law.* An ecclesiastical member of a consistory court or episcopal session during the reign of Charles II. See CONSISTORY COURT.

session laws. (18c) **1.** The body of statutes enacted by a legislature during a particular annual, biennial, or special session. **2.** The softbound booklets containing these statutes. — Also termed *acts of assembly*; *blue books*; *sheet acts*.

sessions. See COURT OF GENERAL QUARTER SESSIONS OF THE PEACE.

SET. *abbr.* See *self-employment tax* under TAX.

set-aside, *n.* (1943) **1.** Something (such as a percentage of funds) that is reserved or put aside for a specific purpose. **2.** An arrangement in which a local government helps small businesses develop by making financial assistance available to them. **3.** An affirmative-action program requiring a percentage of opportunities for jobs, promotions, funding, etc. to be reserved for members of an underrepresented group. **4.** An arrangement in which a government pays farmers to leave some space of their fields unplanted so as to avoid an overabundance of crops and to keep prices relatively high.

set aside, *vb.* (18c) (Of a court) to annul or vacate (a judgment, order, etc.) <the judge refused to set aside the default judgment>.

setback, *n.* (1916) *Real estate.* The minimum amount of space required between a lot line and a building line <a 12-foot setback>. • Typically contained in zoning ordinances or deed restrictions, setbacks are designed to ensure that enough light and ventilation reach the property and to keep buildings from being erected too close to property lines. See BUSINESS LINE.

setback requirement. See BUILDING LINE.

set down, *vb.* (18c) To schedule (a case) for trial or hearing, usu. by making a docket entry.

se te fecerit securum (see tee **fes**-ər-it si-**kyoor**-əm). [Latin] See SI FECERIT TE SECURUM.

set forth. See SET OUT.

seti (set-ee). *Mining law.* A lease.

set of exchange. (18c) *Commercial law.* A single bill of lading drawn in a set of parts, each of which is valid only if the goods have not been delivered against any other part. • Bills may be drawn in duplicate or triplicate, the first part being "first of exchange," the second part being "second of exchange," and so on. When one part has been paid, the other parts become void.

setoff, *n.* (18c) **1.** A defendant's counterdemand against the plaintiff, arising out of a transaction independent of the plaintiff's claim.

> "Set off is a mode of defence by which the defendant acknowledges the justice of the plaintiff's demand, but sets up a demand of his own against the plaintiff, to counterbalance it either in whole or in part." Oliver L. Barbour, *A Treatise on the Law of Set Off* 3 (1841).

> "Set-off is defined to be a counter-demand, generally of a liquidated debt *growing out of an independent transaction* for which an action might be maintained by the defendant against the plaintiff." Eugene A. Jones, *Manual of Equity Pleading and Practice* 65 n.42 (1916).

2. A debtor's right to reduce the amount of a debt by any sum the creditor owes the debtor; the counterbalancing sum owed by the creditor. — Also written *set-off.* — Also termed (in civil law) *compensation; stoppage.* See COUNTERCLAIM; OFFSET. Cf. RECOUPMENT (3). **3.** OFFSET; esp., the balancing of mutual liabilities with respect to a pledge relationship. — **set off,** *vb.*

> "Set-off signifies the subtraction or taking away of one demand from another opposite or cross demand, so as to distinguish the smaller demand and reduce the greater by the amount of the less; or, if the opposite demands are equal, to extinguish both. It was also, formerly, sometimes called stoppage, because the amount to be set-off was *stopped* or deducted from the cross demand." Thomas W. Waterman, *A Treatise on the Law of Set-Off, Recoupment, and Counter Claim* § 1, at 1 (2d ed. 1872).

> "Before considering the counter-claim, a brief reference to 'the set-off' as known in former practice is necessary. By the common law, the setting off of one demand against another in the same action was unknown. If A had a cause of action in debt against B, and B had another cause of action in debt in equal amount against A, each must bring his action. One could not be set off against the other. This was changed by statute in England in 1729, by a provision which, somewhat enlarged and modified, has been generally adopted in this country." Edwin E. Bryant, *The Law of Pleading Under the Codes of Civil Procedure* 250–51 (2d ed. 1899).

▸ **equitable setoff.** (18c) A setoff that a court may allow based on principles of fairness.

▸ **legal setoff.** (18c) A setoff that meets statutory requirements.

set out, *vb.* (16c) To recite, explain, narrate, or incorporate (facts or circumstances) <set out the terms of the contract>. — Also termed *set forth.*

set over, *vb.* (16c) To transfer or convey (property) <to set over the land to the purchaser>.

setter, *n.* (15c) *Scots law.* A lessor. See LESSOR.

setting, *n.* The date and time established by a court for a trial or hearing <the plaintiff sought a continuance of the imminent setting>.

▸ **special setting.** (1916) A preferential setting on a court's calendar, usu. reserved for older cases or cases given priority by law, made either on a party's motion or on the court's own motion. • For example, some jurisdictions authorize a special setting for cases involving a party over the age of 70. — Also termed *special trial setting; trial-setting preference.*

settle, *vb.* (bef. 12c) **1.** To place on a permanent orderly basis by regulation <to settle the government>. **2.** To end or resolve (an argument or disagreement, etc.); to bring to a conclusion (what has been disputed or uncertain) <they settled their dispute>. **3.** To adjust differences; to come to a good understanding <settle with an opponent>. **4.** To decide on (a course of action); to resolve what one is going to do, esp. so that one can make definite arrangements <they settled on going to Portland>. **5.** To put in order; esp., to deal with all the details of a business or of someone's money or property so that nothing remains to be done <she settled her late husband's affairs>. **6.** To determine the precise form or language of <to settle the pleadings>. **7.** To secure to someone by a fixed arrangement; to make over as a right or property by legal act <settled Blackacre on Jones in fee simple absolute>. **8.** To set or appoint a time <to settle a day for hearing>. **9.** To ascertain (a balance due, an amount owed, etc.) <to settle the amount due on the unclear account>. **10.** To pay (money that is owed); to liquidate (a debt) <she settled her accounts>. **11.** To go to a place to live permanently or for a long time, sometimes when no people have lived there before; to fix one's home or abode <the Germans settled in Umbarger in 1895>. **12.** To plant or furnish with inhabitants; to colonize <the English settled Bermuda>. **13.** To put oneself or someone else into a comfortable position <the lawyer settled his client into an oversized chair>. **14.** To become or to make someone quiet or calm; to free from agitation or disturbance <the children had settled themselves>. **15.** To sink gradually; to subside <the land settled after the cellar was dug>.

settled estate. See ESTATE (1).

settled insanity. See DELIRIUM TREMENS.

settled land. See LAND.

settlement, *n.* (17c) **1.** The conveyance of property — or of interests in property — to provide for one or more beneficiaries, usu. members of the settlor's family, in a way that differs from what the beneficiaries would receive as heirs under the statutes of descent and distribution <in marriage settlements, historically, the wife waived her right to claim dower or to succeed to her husband's property>.

▸ **family settlement.** (18c) *English law.* An arrangement for retaining an estate within the family, as far as the law will allow, by means of devising it to the eldest son, with portions for the younger children, and annuities by means of jointure to the widows of the various tenants for life.

▸ **strict settlement.** (17c) *Hist.* A property settlement that aimed to keep the estate within the family by creating successive interests in tail and shielding remainders from destruction by the interposition of a trust. Cf. *trader's settlement.*

▸ **trader's settlement.** (1889) *Hist.* A property settlement in which the land is put into a trust for sale, the proceeds to be either paid out to beneficiaries over time or divided among the settlor's heirs. Cf. *strict settlement.*

▸ **voluntary settlement.** (17c) A property settlement made without valuable consideration — other than psychological or emotional consideration such as love and affection — from the beneficiary.

2. An agreement ending a dispute or lawsuit <the parties reached a settlement the day before trial>.— Also termed *settlement agreement.*

▸ **derivative settlement.** (18c) **1.** The negotiated outcome of a derivative action. See DERIVATIVE ACTION. **2.** A person's legal-residence status that is acquired though another person, as with a child through one or both parents.

▸ **final settlement.** (17c) A court order discharging an executor's duties after an estate's execution.

▸ **full settlement.** (17c) A settlement and release of all pending claims between the parties.

▸ **judicial settlement.** The settlement of a civil case with the help of a judge who is not assigned to adjudicate the dispute. • Parties sometimes find this procedure advantageous because it capitalizes on judicial experience in evaluating a claim's settlement value.

▸ **mediated settlement agreement.** (1982) A settlement agreement arrived at through mediation. — Abbr. MSA.

▸ **nuisance settlement.** (1935) A settlement in which the defendant pays the plaintiff purely for economic reasons — as opposed to any notion of responsibility — because without the settlement the defendant would spend more money in legal fees and expenses caused by protracted litigation than in paying the settlement amount. • The money paid in such a settlement is often termed *nuisance money.*

▸ **out-of-court settlement.** (1930) The settlement and termination of a pending suit, arrived at without the court's participation.

▸ **settlement offer.** See SETTLEMENT OFFER.

▸ **structured settlement.** (1978) A settlement in which the defendant agrees to pay periodic sums to the plaintiff for a specified time.

> "Especially in personal injury and product liability cases, structured settlements — i.e., those which provide for an initial cash payment followed by deferred payments in future years, normally on some annuity basis — are becoming more frequent. . . . Such a structured settlement may have advantages over a lump-sum cash payment. Deferred payments or arranged settlements may serve particular purposes that a cash settlement could not reach, and there will be instances when a structured settlement will be in lieu of an all-cash settlement that would not be acceptable to one party or the other." Alba Conte, *Attorney Fee Awards* § 2.31, at 101 (1993).

3. Payment, satisfaction, or final adjustment; esp., an adjustment with regard to accounts <settlement of accounts> <the seller shipped the goods after confirming the buyer's settlement of the account>.

▸ **viatical settlement** (vɪ-**at**-ə-kəl). [fr. Latin *viaticus* "relating to a road or journey"] (1991) A transaction in which a terminally or chronically ill person sells the benefits of a life-insurance policy to a third party in return for a lump-sum cash payment equal to a percentage of the policy's face value. • Viatical settlements are common with AIDS patients, many of whom sell their policies at a 20% to 40% discount, depending on life expectancy. When the insured (called the "viator") dies, the investor receives the insurance benefit. — Also termed *life settlement.*

4. A fixed time or period for settling accounts or concluding a transaction; CLOSING <the settlement on their new house will be Friday at noon>. **5.** *Wills & estates.* The complete execution of an estate by the executor <the settlement of the estate was long and complex>. **6.** The establishment of a legal residence. • This sense was frequently used in poor-relief contexts. Cf. (in sense 6) STATUS OF IRREMOVABILITY. **7.** A regular or settled place of living; one's dwelling-place or residence. **8.** An area of a country newly occupied by those intending to live and work there; a colonized region.

settlement account. See *concentration account* under ACCOUNT.

settlement agent. 1. See AGENT. **2.** See *settlement attorney* under ATTORNEY.

settlement agreement. See SETTLEMENT (2).

settlement attorney. See ATTORNEY.

settlement class. See CLASS (4).

settlement counsel. See COUNSEL.

settlement credit. (1979) *Civil procedure.* A court's reduction of the amount of a jury verdict — or the effect of the verdict on nonsettling defendants — to account for settlement funds the plaintiff has received from former defendants or from other responsible parties.

settlement date. See DATE.

settlement day. See *settlement date* under DATE.

settlement-first method. (1996) A means by which to apply a settlement credit to a jury verdict, by first reducing the amount of the verdict by subtracting the amount of all settlements the plaintiff has received on the claim, then reducing the remainder by the percentage of the plaintiff's comparative fault. See SETTLEMENT CREDIT. Cf. FAULT-FIRST METHOD.

settlement offer. (1978) An offer by one party to settle a dispute amicably (usu. by paying money) to avoid or end a lawsuit or other legal action. • A settlement offer is usu. not admissible at trial as evidence of the offering party's liability but may be admissible for other purposes. — Also termed *offer in compromise*; *offer of compromise*; *offer of settlement.*

Settlement of the Crown. See ACT OF SETTLEMENT.

settlement option. See OPTION (5).

settlement right. (18c) *Hist.* A government-issued certificate granting land to a settler.

settlement sheet. See CLOSING STATEMENT (2).

settlement statement. See CLOSING STATEMENT (2).

settlement value. See VALUE (2).

settler. (17c) **1.** Someone who occupies property with the intent to establish a residence; esp., someone who goes to live in a country or area where few similar people have lived before and where no established communities are nearby. • The term is usu. applied to an early resident of a country or region. **2.** SETTLOR.

settle up, *vb.* (1884) To collect, pay, and turn over debts and property (e.g., of a decedent, bankrupt, or insolvent business).

settlor (**set**-lər). (18c) **1.** Someone who makes a settlement of property; esp., one who sets up a trust. — Also termed *creator*; *donor*; *trustor*; *grantor*; *founder.* **2.** A party to an instrument. — Also spelled (in both senses) *settler.*

set up, *vb.* To raise (a defense) <the defendant set up the insanity defense on the murder charge>.

Seventeenth Amendment. The constitutional amendment, ratified in 1913, transferring the power to elect U.S. senators from the state legislatures to the states' voters.

Seventh Amendment. The constitutional amendment, ratified with the Bill of Rights in 1791, guaranteeing the right to a jury trial in federal civil cases that are traditionally considered to be suits at common law and that have an amount in controversy exceeding $20.

72 COLREGS. See INTERNATIONAL RULES OF THE ROAD.

seven-years'-absence rule. (1920) The principle that a person who has been missing without explanation for at least seven years is legally presumed dead. Cf. ENOCH ARDEN LAW.

> "[I]n the United States, it is quite generally held or provided by statute that a presumption of death arises from the continued and unexplained absence of a person from his home or place of residence without any intelligence from or concerning him for the period of 7 years. The presumption has been regarded as a procedural expedient and a rule of evidence." 22A Am. Jur. 2d *Death* § 551, at 527 (1988).

severability. 1. See BLUE-PENCIL TEST. **2.** See SEPARABILITY.

severability clause. (1935) A provision that keeps the remaining provisions of a contract or statute in force if any portion of that contract or statute is judicially declared void, unenforceable, or unconstitutional. — Also termed *saving clause*; *separability clause*. See *severable contract* under CONTRACT; *severable statute* under STATUTE.

severable contract. See CONTRACT.

severable statute. See STATUTE.

several, *adj.* (15c) **1.** (Of a person, place, or thing) more than one or two but not a lot <several witnesses>. **2.** (Of liability, etc.) separate; particular; distinct, but not necessarily independent <a several obligation>. **3.** (Of things, etc.) different; various <several settlement options>.

several action. See *separate action* under ACTION (4).

several contract. See *severable contract* under CONTRACT.

several count. See COUNT (2).

several covenant. See COVENANT (1).

several demise. See DEMISE.

several fishery. See FISHERY (1).

several inheritance. See INHERITANCE.

several judgment. See JUDGMENT (2).

several liability. See LIABILITY.

severally, *adj.* (14c) Distinctly; separately <severally liable>.

several obligation. See OBLIGATION.

several promise. See PROMISE.

several-remedies rule. (1975) A procedural rule that tolls a statute of limitations for a plaintiff who has several available forums (such as a workers'-compensation proceeding and the court system) and who timely files in one forum and later proceeds in another forum, as long as the defendant's right and claims are not affected.

several tail. See TAIL.

several tenancy. See TENANCY.

severalty (sev-[ə]-rəl-tee). (15c) **1.** The quality, state, or condition of being separate or distinct <the individual landowners held the land in severalty, not as joint tenants>. **2.** The holding of land in one's own right, with no other person or community or tribe connected with the holder in point of interest while the estate continues; a sole tenancy. • The phrase *in severalty* means "in exclusive ownership" or "in one's own right," and it is used in reference to an estate or part of an estate that has been partitioned.

severance, *n.* (15c) **1.** The act of cutting off or severing; the quality, state, or condition of being cut off or severed; PARTITION (2). **2.** *Civil procedure.* The separation, by the court, of multiple parties' claims either to permit separate actions on each claim or to allow certain interlocutory orders to become final. — Also termed *severance of actions*; *severance of claims*. See *bifurcated trial* under TRIAL. Cf. CONSOLIDATION (3). **3.** *Criminal procedure.* The separation of criminal charges or criminal defendants for trial, as when codefendants have conflicting defenses so that prejudice might result to one or more of them.

▸ **partial severance.** The severance of some but not all counts or claims. — Also termed *limited severance*.

4. The termination of a joint tenancy, usu. by converting it into a tenancy in common. **5.** The removal of anything (such as crops or minerals) attached or affixed to real property, making it personal property rather than a part of the land. • Mineral rights are frequently severed from surface rights on property that may contain oil and gas or other minerals. **6.** See SEVERANCE PAY. — **sever,** *vb.* — **severable,** *adj.*

severance damages. See DAMAGES.

severance of actions. See SEVERANCE (2).

severance of claims. See SEVERANCE (2).

severance of estates. (1864) The termination of an estate in joint tenancy by the act of a joint tenant or by operation of law. See *joint tenancy* under TENANCY.

severance pay. (1939) Money (apart from back wages or salary) that an employer pays to a dismissed employee. • The payment may be made in exchange for a release of any claims that the employee might have against the employer. — Sometimes shortened to *severance*. — Also termed *separation pay*; *dismissal compensation*; (BrE) *redundancy pay*.

severance tax. See TAX.

severe impairment. See IMPAIRMENT.

seward. See CUSTOS MARIS.

sewer service. See SERVICE (7).

sex. (14c) **1.** The sum of the peculiarities of structure and function that distinguish a male from a female organism; gender. **2.** Sexual intercourse. **3.** SEXUAL RELATIONS (2).

sex abuse. See *sexual abuse* under ABUSE.

sex act. 1. See SEXUAL RELATIONS (2). **2.** COMMERCIAL SEX ACT.

sex bias. The unfair treatment of people on grounds that they are either male or female.

sex change. See SEX REASSIGNMENT.

sex discrimination. See DISCRIMINATION (3).

sex industry. The business and activities related to pornography and prostitution.

sex-offender registry. (1987) A publicly available list of the names and addresses of sex offenders who have been released from prison. • The registries were started by state statutes known as "Megan's laws." The lists are often posted on the Internet, and some states require publication of the offender's photograph, name, and address in local newspapers. See MEGAN'S LAW.

sex reassignment. (1965) Medical treatment intended to effect a sex change; surgery and hormonal treatments designed to alter a person's gender. — Also termed *sex change.*

sexting. (2005) The creation, possession, or distribution of sexually explicit images via cellphones. • The term is a portmanteau of *sex* and *texting.*

sex trafficking. (1982) The act or practice of recruiting, harboring, transporting, providing, or procuring a person, or inducing a person by fraud, force, or coercion, to perform a sex act for pay. • Under the Trafficking Victims Protection Act, victims of severe forms of sex trafficking are those who are induced or are less than 18 years old, or both. Sex trafficking is a type of human trafficking. See HUMAN TRAFFICKING.

sex trafficking of minors. See COMMERCIAL SEXUAL EXPLOITATION OF A MINOR.

sexual abuse. 1. See ABUSE. **2.** See RAPE (2).

sexual activity. (1895) See SEXUAL RELATIONS.

sexual assault. 1. See ASSAULT. **2.** See RAPE (2).

sexual assault by contact. See *sexual assault* (2) under ASSAULT.

sexual battery. 1. See BATTERY (1). **2.** See RAPE (2).

sexual exploitation. (1935) The use of a person, esp. a child, in prostitution, pornography, or other sexually manipulative activity. — Sometimes shortened to *exploitation.*

sexual harassment. (1973) A type of employment discrimination consisting in verbal or physical abuse of a sexual nature, including lewd remarks, salacious looks, and unwelcome touching. See HARASSMENT.

▸ **hostile-environment sexual harassment.** (1986) Sexual harassment in which a work environment is created where an employee is subject to unwelcome verbal or physical sexual behavior that is either severe or pervasive. • This type of harassment might occur, for example, if a group of coworkers repeatedly e-mailed pornographic pictures to a colleague who found the pictures offensive. — Also termed *hostile-work-environment harassment.*

▸ **quid pro quo sexual harassment.** (1982) Sexual harassment in which an employment decision is based on the satisfaction of a sexual demand. • This type of harassment might occur, for example, if a boss fired or demoted an employee who refused to go on a date with the boss. — Also termed *quid pro quo harassment.*

▸ **same-sex sexual harassment.** (1981) Sexual harassment by a supervisor of an employee of the same sex. — Also termed *same-sex harassment.*

sexual intercourse. See INTERCOURSE (2).

sexually-abused-child syndrome. (1983) A medically recognized mental disorder that causes a person to behave in highly sexualized ways, usu. as a result of incest, molestation, or other sexual acts during childhood. • Other symptoms frequently described are age-inappropriate sexual knowledge, difficulty trusting others, withdrawal, anxiety, depression, guilt, and shame.

sexually dangerous, *adj.* (1948) (Of a person) having serious difficulty in refraining from sexually violent conduct or child molestation. • Under federal law, the government may detain a mentally ill, sexually dangerous federal prisoner beyond the release date only if it first establishes, by clear and convincing evidence, that the prisoner "(1) has previously 'engaged or attempted to engage in sexually violent conduct or child molestation,' (2) currently 'suffers from a serious mental illness, abnormality, or disorder,' and (3) 'as a result of that mental illness, abnormality, or disorder is 'sexually dangerous' to others,' in that 'he would have serious difficulty in refraining from sexually violent conduct or child molestation if released.'" *U.S. v. Comstock,* 130 S.Ct. 1949, 1954 (2010) (quoting 18 USCA § 4247(a)(5)). See SEXUAL PREDATOR.

sexually dangerous person. See SEXUAL PREDATOR.

sexually transmitted disease. (1962) A disease transmitted only or chiefly by engaging in sexual acts with an infected person. • Common examples are syphilis, gonorrhea, and HIV. — Abbr. STD. — Also termed *venereal disease.*

sexually violent predator. See SEXUAL PREDATOR; SEXUALLY DANGEROUS.

sexual offense. See OFFENSE (2).

sexual orientation. (1931) A person's predisposition or inclination toward sexual activity or behavior with other males or females; heterosexuality, homosexuality, or bisexuality.

sexual-orientation discrimination. See DISCRIMINATION (3).

sexual predator. (1960) Someone who has committed many violent sexual acts or who has a propensity for committing violent sexual acts. — Also termed *predator*; *sexually dangerous person*; *sexually violent predator.* See SEXUALLY DANGEROUS.

sexual relations. (1909) **1.** Sexual intercourse; SEX (2). — Also termed *carnalis copula.* **2.** Physical sexual activity that does not necessarily culminate in intercourse. • Sexual relations usu. involve the touching of another's breast, vagina, penis, or anus. Both persons (the toucher and the person touched) are said to engage in sexual relations. — Also termed *sexual activity*; *sex act.*

sex worker. See PROSTITUTE.

SF. *abbr.* See *sinking fund* under FUND (1).

S/F. *abbr.* STATUTE OF FRAUDS.

SG. *abbr.* **1.** SOLICITOR GENERAL. **2.** SURGEON GENERAL.

shack. (17c) *Hist.* The straying and escaping of cattle out of their owner's land into other unenclosed land; an intercommoning of cattle.

shadow counsel. See *standby counsel* under COUNSEL.

shadow easement. See EASEMENT.

shadow economy. (1958) Collectively, the unregistered economic activities that contribute to a country's gross national product. • A shadow economy may involve the legal and illegal production of goods and services, including gambling, prostitution, and drug-dealing, as well as barter transactions and unreported incomes. — Also termed *black economy*; *black market*; *underground economy.*

shadow jury. See JURY.

shadow stock plan. See PHANTOM STOCK PLAN.

shakedown. (1902) **1.** An extortion of money using threats of violence or, in the case of a police officer, threats of arrest <an organized-crime shakedown>. **2.** An all-but-frivolous civil lawsuit or threat of litigation intended to coerce a settlement from a defendant who has done no wrong <Duboef sued Renrag in what insiders saw as a brazen shakedown>. **3.** See *shakedown search* under SEARCH (1). **4.** A period when people become accustomed to a new arrangement <how the reorganized companies fared during the shakedown>. **5.** A period when prices are falling in a financial market <prices finally stabilized after the shakedown>.

shakedown search. See SEARCH (1).

shaken-baby syndrome. (1987) The medical condition of a child who has suffered forceful shaking, with resulting brain injury. • The syndrome was first identified in the early 1970s. Common injuries include retinal hemorrhage and subdural and subarachnoid hemorrhage, with minimal or no signs of external cranial trauma. Many victims suffer blindness or death. — Abbr. SBS.

shakeout, *n.* (1939) An elimination of weak or nonproductive businesses in an industry, esp. during a period of intense competition or declining prices.

shall, *vb.* (bef. 12c) **1.** Has a duty to; more broadly, is required to <the requester shall send notice> <notice shall be sent>. • This is the mandatory sense that drafters typically intend and that courts typically uphold. **2.** Should (as often interpreted by courts) <all claimants shall request mediation>. **3.** May <no person shall enter the building without first signing the roster>. • When a negative word such as *not* or *no* precedes *shall* (as in the example in angle brackets), the word *shall* often means *may.* What is being negated is permission, not a requirement. **4.** Will (as a future-tense verb) <the corporation shall then have a period of 30 days to object>. **5.** Is entitled to <the secretary shall be reimbursed for all expenses>. • Only sense 1 is acceptable under strict standards of drafting.

sham, *n.* (17c) **1.** A false pretense or fraudulent show; an imposture. **2.** Something that is not what it seems; a counterfeit. **3.** Someone who pretends to be something that he or she is not; a faker. — **sham,** *vb.* — **sham,** *adj.*

sham action. See ACTION (4).

sham affidavit. See AFFIDAVIT.

sham bidder. See BY-BIDDER.

sham consideration. See CONSIDERATION (1).

sham defense. See DEFENSE (1).

shame sanction. See SANCTION (3).

shame sentence. See *shame sanction* under SANCTION.

sham exception. (1969) An exception to the *Noerr–Pennington* doctrine whereby a company that petitions the government will not receive First Amendment protection or an exemption from the antitrust laws if its intent in petitioning the government for favorable government action or treatment is really an effort to harm its competitors. See NOERR–PENNINGTON DOCTRINE; *sham action* under ACTION (4).

shaming sentence. See *shame sanction* under SANCTION.

sham lawsuit. See *sham action* under ACTION (4).

sham litigation. See *sham action* under ACTION (4).

sham marriage. See MARRIAGE (1).

sham petitioning. See *sham action* under ACTION (4).

sham plea. See *sham pleading* under PLEADING (1).

sham pleading. See PLEADING (1).

sham prosecution. See PROSECUTION (2).

sham suit. See *sham action* under ACTION (4).

sham transaction. (1937) An agreement or exchange that has no independent economic benefit or business purpose and is entered into solely to create a tax advantage (such as a deduction for a business loss). • The Internal Revenue Service is entitled to ignore the purported tax benefits of a sham transaction.

sham will. See *bogus will* under WILL.

shanghaiing (shang-**hI**-ing). (1872) The act or an instance of coercing or inducing someone to do something by fraudulent or other wrongful means; specif., the practice of drugging, tricking, intoxicating, or otherwise illegally inducing a person to work aboard a vessel, usu. to secure advance money or a premium. — Also termed *shanghaiing sailors.* 18 USCA § 2194.

shank, *n.* (1953) A pointed or sharp-edged weapon, usu. a dagger or knife, that is usu. either homemade or made by a prisoner. • Shanks are most often metal but can also be made of plastic and other inflexible materials.

shank, *vb.* (1949) To stab, slash, or cut with a knife-like weapon.

share, *n.* (14c) **1.** An allotted portion owned by, contributed by, or due to someone; a single portion distributed among several <each partner's share of the profits>.

▸ **intestate share.** (18c) The share that the renouncer of a will would take in the decedent's assets if the decedent had left no will affecting in any way the distribution of assets.

2. One of the definite number of equal parts into which the capital stock of a corporation or joint-stock company is divided <the broker advised his customer to sell the stock shares when the price reaches $29>. • A share represents an equity or ownership interest in the corporation or joint-stock company. Cf. STOCK (4); SECURITY (4).

▸ **American share.** *Securities.* A share of stock in a foreign corporation issued directly to U.S. investors through a transfer agent.

▸ **fractional share.** An unmarketable share that is less than one full share. • Fractional shares usu. result from stock splits and dividend-reinvestment plans. See STOCK SPLIT; DIVIDEND-REINVESTMENT PLAN.

▸ **fully paid share.** (1873) A share issued to a stockholder after the price of the share is met.

▸ **golden share.** (1982) A share that controls more than half of a corporation's voting rights and gives the shareholder veto power over changes to the company's charter.

▸ **preference share.** See *preferred stock* under STOCK.

▸ **preferred share.** See *preferred stock* under STOCK.

▸ **qualifying share.** (1875) A share of common stock purchased by someone in order to become a director of a corporation that requires its directors to be shareholders.

3. An equitable part of nothing enjoyed or suffered in common.

share, *vb.* (16c) **1.** To divide (something) into portions. **2.** To enjoy or partake of (a power, right, etc.).

share account. See *share-draft account* under ACCOUNT.

share acquisition. (1931) The acquisition of a corporation by purchasing all or most of its outstanding shares directly from the shareholders; TAKEOVER. — Also termed *share-acquisition transaction*; *stock acquisition*; *stock-acquisition transaction.* Cf. ASSET ACQUISITION.

share and share alike. (1841) To divide (assets, etc.) in equal shares or proportions; to engage in per capita division. See PER CAPITA.

share certificate. See STOCK CERTIFICATE.

sharecropping. (1945) An agricultural arrangement in which a landowner leases land to a tenant who, in turn, gives the landlord a portion of the crop as rent. • The landlord usu. provides the seed, fertilizer, and equipment. — **sharecropper,** *n.*

shared-appreciation mortgage. See MORTGAGE.

shared custody. See *joint custody* under CUSTODY (2).

shared-equity mortgage. See MORTGAGE.

shared parenting. See PARENTING.

share draft. See DRAFT (1).

share-draft account. See ACCOUNT.

shared residency. See *joint physical custody* under CUSTODY.

shareholder. (1832) Someone who owns or holds a share or shares in a company, esp. a corporation. — Also termed *shareowner*; (in a corporation) *stockholder.*

▸ **controlling shareholder.** (1894) A shareholder who can influence the corporation's activities because the shareholder either owns a majority of outstanding shares or owns a smaller percentage but a significant number of the remaining shares are widely distributed among many others.

▸ **dissenting shareholder.** A shareholder who opposes a corporate action and usu. demands that the corporation buy back the shareholder's stock

▸ **dummy shareholder.** (1902) A shareholder who owns stock in name only for the benefit of the true owner, whose identity is usu. concealed.

▸ **interested shareholder.** (1920) Someone who owns enough of a corporation's stock to affect corporate decision-making, usu. at least 15–20% of the corporation's outstanding stock. — Also termed *interested stockholder.*

▸ **majority shareholder.** (1887) A shareholder who owns or controls more than half the corporation's stock.

▸ **minority shareholder.** (1870) A shareholder who owns less than half the total shares outstanding and thus cannot control the corporation's management or singlehandedly elect directors.

▸ **shareholder of record.** See STOCKHOLDER OF RECORD.

shareholder-control agreement. See POOLING AGREEMENT.

shareholder derivative suit. See DERIVATIVE ACTION (1).

shareholder oppression. See OPPRESSION (4).

shareholder proposal. (1951) A proposal by one or more corporate stockholders to change company policy or procedure. • Ordinarily, the corporation informs all stockholders about the proposal before the next shareholder meeting.

shareholder resolution. See RESOLUTION (2).

shareholders' equity. See OWNERS' EQUITY.

shareholder's liability. See LIABILITY.

shareholders' scheme of arrangement. See SCHEME OF ARRANGEMENT.

shareholder voting agreement. See POOLING AGREEMENT.

share index. An official or public list of stock prices.

share option. See STOCK OPTION.

share-out, *n.* **1.** The division of money or property between two or more people. **2.** The amount of money or property that each person receives in such a division.

shareowner. See SHAREHOLDER.

share repurchase. See REDEMPTION (3).

shares outstanding. See *outstanding stock* under STOCK.

share split. See STOCK SPLIT.

shareware. (1983) **1.** Free or very inexpensive software that has limited features or that one can use for a short period while deciding whether to buy it. **2.** Software that can be redistributed but not modified and requires all users to pay a license fee. • The license fee applies to both originals and distributed copies. Cf. FREEWARE; PROPRIETARY SOFTWARE; SEMI-FREE SOFTWARE.

share-warrant to bearer. (1927) A warrant providing that the bearer is entitled to a certain number of fully paid stock shares. • Delivery of the warrant operates as a transfer of the shares of stock.

Sharia (shə-ree-ə). (1855) *Islamic law.* The body of Islamic religious law applicable to police, banking, business, contracts, and social issues. • Sharia is a system of laws, rather than a codification of laws, based on the Koran and other Islamic sources.

shark repellent. (1977) **1.** TAKEOVER DEFENSE. **2.** More specifically, a charter or bylaw provision designed to impede hostile bids to acquire a controlling interest in a corporation.

sharp, *adj.* (1886) (Of a clause in a mortgage, deed, etc.) empowering the creditor to take immediate and summary action upon the debtor's default. See DROP-DEAD PROVISION.

sharp practice. (1836) Unethical action and trickery, esp. by a lawyer. — Also termed (archaically) *unhandsome dealing.* — **sharp practitioner,** *n.*

shave, *vb.* (1832) **1.** To purchase (a negotiable instrument) at a greater than usual discount rate. **2.** To reduce or deduct from (a price).

sheer, *n.* (17c) *Maritime law.* A vessel's sudden deviation from its line of course; a swerve.

sheet acts. See SESSION LAWS.

shelf company. See COMPANY.

shelf corporation. See *shelf company* under COMPANY.

shelf issue. See ISSUE (2).

shelf registration. See REGISTRATION (2).

shelf security. See SECURITY (4).

shell company. See *shell corporation* under CORPORATION.

shell corporation. See CORPORATION.

Shelley's Case, Rule in. See RULE IN SHELLEY'S CASE.

shell game. (1890) A sleight-of-hand game that uses three cups or thimble-like objects, one of which has a pea, ball, or other small object underneath. • This is a game of chance in which one player bets that he or she can remember under which cup the object is. The cups are moved around so quickly that the player finds it difficult to remember where the object is. When played casually on public streets, the shell game is usu. a swindle because the operator palms the object rather than leaving it under a cup, so the player has no chance of winning. — Also termed *thimblerig*; *thimbles and balls*. See GAME OF CHANCE.

shelter, *n.* (16c) **1.** A place of refuge providing safety from danger, attack, or observation.

▸ **homeless shelter.** (1931) A privately or publicly operated residential facility providing overnight accommodation free of charge to homeless people. • Most homeless shelters accept occupants on a first-come-first-served basis and are open only from early evening to early morning. Those that serve homeless families may remain open throughout the day to women and children. Some shelters offer occupants help such as advice on finding and applying for public assistance, employment, and medical care.

▸ **women's shelter.** (1932) A privately or publicly operated residential facility providing women (and their children) who are victims of domestic violence with temporary lodging, food, and other services such as employment assistance, counseling, and medical care. — Also termed *family shelter*.

▸ **youth shelter.** (1931) **1.** A privately or publicly operated residential facility offering young runaway or throwaway children and homeless young people a safe place to stay, usu. for a short time. • The residents enter the shelter voluntarily and can leave anytime they wish. Some shelters offer long-term transitional training so that young people can leave street life and eventually lead independent, productive lives. **2.** An alternative type of juvenile-detention center that is less physically restrictive than a jail or boot camp. • Delinquent juveniles are usu. brought to these shelters by police or ordered to reside there by a court. Residents attend school or work in the daytime and may be permitted weekend visits at their family homes.

2. See TAX SHELTER <the shelter saved the taxpayer over $2,000 in taxes>. — **shelter,** *vb.*

shelter-care hearing. See *shelter hearing* under HEARING.

shelter doctrine. (1955) **1.** *Commercial law.* The principle that a person to whom a holder in due course has transferred commercial paper, as well as any later transferee, will succeed to the rights of the holder in due course. • As a result, transferees of holders in due course are generally not subject to defenses against the payment of an instrument. This doctrine ensures the free transferability of commercial paper. Its name derives from the idea that the transferees "take shelter" in the rights of the holder in due course. **2.** SHELTER RULE.

shelter hearing. See HEARING.

shelter rule. (1951) **1.** *Property.* The doctrine that a person who takes land from a bona fide purchaser protected by a recording statute acquires the same rights as those enjoyed by the grantor. • The rule helps to establish priority of rights under recording statutes. **2.** SHELTER DOCTRINE.

shelving. *Patents.* The failure to begin or the stopping of commercial use of a patent during a specified period, usu. the term of the license. • A licensor may place an anti-shelving provision in a license to ensure the licensed product's manufacture and sale. The term usu. applies to patented inventions, but licenses for trademarked products may also address shelving.

shelving clause. See ANTISHELVING CLAUSE.

shepardize, *vb.* (1928) **1.** (*often cap.*) To determine the subsequent history and treatment of (a case) by using a printed or computerized version of *Shepard's Citators*. **2.** Loosely, to check the precedential value of (a case) by the same or similar means. See KEYCITE. — **shepardization, shepardizing,** *n.*

sheriff. [Middle English *shire reeve* from Anglo-Saxon *scirgerefa*] (bef. 12c) **1.** A county's chief peace officer, usu. elected, who in most jurisdictions acts as custodian of the county jail, executes civil and criminal process, and carries out judicial mandates within the county.

▸ **deputy sheriff.** (17c) An officer who, acting under the direction of a sheriff, may perform most of the duties of the sheriff's office. • Although *undersheriff* is broadly synonymous with *deputy sheriff*, writers have sometimes distinguished between the two, suggesting that a deputy is appointed for a special occasion or purpose, while an undersheriff is permanent. — Also termed *undersheriff*; *general deputy*; *vice-sheriff*.

2. *Scots law.* The chief judge at the county level, with limited criminal and unlimited civil jurisdiction. • A sheriff may not hear cases of murder or of some minor offenses. In medieval times, the sheriff was the king's representative in the shires, having military, administrative, and judicial functions. The office was hereditary until the Heritable Jurisdictions Act of 1746. **3.** The representative of the king or queen in a county of England or Wales, having mostly ceremonial duties. — Also termed (in sense 3) *high sheriff*; *vice-comes*.

sheriffalty. See SHRIEVALTY.

sheriff clerk. (14c) *Scots law.* The clerk of a sheriff's court.

sheriff court. See *sheriff's court* under COURT.

sheriff-depute. (15c) *Hist. Scots law.* The qualified judge of a district or county, acting for the titular, unqualified sheriff.

sheriffdom, *n.* (14c) The territory or district under a sheriff's jurisdiction.

sheriff principal. (16c) *Scots law.* The chief judge of a sheriffdom comprising one or more counties.

sheriff's court. See COURT.

sheriff's deed. See DEED.

sheriff's jury. See JURY.

sheriff's rotation. See SHERIFF'S TOWN.

sheriff's sale. See SALE.

sheriff's town. (18c) *Hist. English law.* The great court-leet of the county held twice yearly by the sheriff. See COURT-LEET. — Also termed *sheriff's rotation.*

Sherman Act. 1. An 1890 federal statute directing the Secretary of the Treasury to purchase at market rates 4.5 million ounces of fine silver bullion each month, as much as might be available, but not to exceed $1 for 371.25 grains. • The statute was repealed in 1893. **2.** SHERMAN ANTITRUST ACT.

Sherman Antitrust Act. An 1890 federal statute that prohibits direct or indirect interference with the freely competitive interstate production and distribution of goods. • This Act was amended by the Clayton Act in 1914. 15 USCA §§ 1–7. — Often shortened to *Sherman Act.* — Also termed *Antitrust Law.*

***Sherman–Sorrells* doctrine.** (1998) The principle that a defendant may claim as an affirmative defense that he or she was not disposed to commit the offense until a public official (often an undercover police officer) encouraged the defendant to do so. • This entrapment defense, which is recognized in the federal system and a majority of states, was developed in *Sherman v. U.S.*, 356 U.S. 369, 78 S.Ct. 819 (1958), and *Sorrells v. U.S.*, 287 U.S. 435, 53 S.Ct. 210 (1932). — Also termed *subjective method.* See ENTRAPMENT. Cf. HYPOTHETICAL-PERSON DEFENSE.

shield law. (1971) **1.** A statute that affords journalists the privilege not to reveal confidential sources. See *journalist's privilege* under PRIVILEGE (3).

> "More than half of the states have 'shield laws' creating 'reporters' privileges' that are sometimes broader than the First Amendment version of that privilege." David A. Anderson, *Freedom of the Press*, 80 Texas L. Rev. 429, 432 (2002).

2. A statute that restricts or prohibits the use, in rape or sexual-assault cases, of evidence about the victim's past sexual conduct. — Also termed (in sense 2) *rape shield law; rape shield statute.*

> "The 'rape shield law.' At common law the character of the woman as to chastity or unchastity was held to be admissible in evidence on the theory that it had probative value in determining whether she did or did not consent. Defense counsel, in unrestrained zeal for an acquittal, took advantage of this to the point that it often seemed as if it was the victim of the rape, rather than the perpetrator, who was on trial. . . . A typical 'rape shield statute' does not prevent the introduction of any relevant and otherwise admissible evidence, but requires that the relevancy of any evidence of the previous sexual conduct of the complaining witness must be determined in a pretrial hearing before the judge in camera." Rollin M. Perkins & Ronald N. Boyce, *Criminal Law* 206 (3d ed. 1982).

shield-money. See SCUTAGE (3).

shifting, *adj.* (1874) (Of a position, place, etc.) changing or passing from one to another <a shifting estate>.

shifting clause. (1813) At common law, a clause under the Statute of Uses prescribing a substituted mode of devolution in the settlement of an estate. See STATUTE OF USES.

shifting executory interest. See EXECUTORY INTEREST.

shifting ground. *Patents.* The broadening of a patent application in an amendment by claiming a feature of the invention that was disclosed but not claimed in the original application.

shifting inheritance. See INHERITANCE.

shifting risk. See RISK.

shifting stock of merchandise. (1853) Merchandise inventory subject to change by purchases and sales in the course of trade.

shifting the burden of proof. (1805) In litigation, the transference of the duty to prove a fact from one party to the other; the passing of the duty to produce evidence in a case from one side to another as the case progresses, when one side has made a prima facie showing on a point of evidence, requiring the other side to rebut it by contradictory evidence. See BURDEN OF PROOF.

shifting trust. See TRUST (3).

shifting use. See USE (4).

shill. (1916) **1.** Someone who poses as an innocent bystander at a confidence game but actually serves as a decoy for the perpetrators of the scheme. **2.** BY-BIDDER. — **shill,** *vb.*

shilling, *n.* (bef. 12c) **1.** The practice of fraudulently bidding on items at an auction solely to drive up the price. • The seller might collude with another person to bid or might act alone and anonymously. Cf. BIDDING UP; BY-BIDDING. **2.** *Hist.* An English coin equal to 12 pence or 1/20th of a pound. • Shillings were revalued as five pence and phased out when decimalization was adopted in the early 1970s. The modern five-pence coin, like its predecessor equal to 1/20th of a pound, is sometimes nostalgically referred to as a shilling.

shingle. (1847) A small, usu. dignified sign that marks the office door of a lawyer or other professional.

shingle theory. (1846) *Securities.* The notion that a broker-dealer must be held to a high standard of conduct because by engaging in the securities business ("hanging out a shingle"), the broker-dealer implicitly represents to the world that the conduct of all its employees will be fair and meet professional norms.

> "[I]n judging the appropriate standard of care that attaches to a broker-dealer in recommending securities to his or her customers and in dealing with the customers' accounts generally, the Commission has relied upon the 'shingle theory.' The shingle theory is but an extension of the common law doctrine of 'holding out.' When brokers hold themselves out as experts either in investments in general or in the securities of a particular issuer, they will be held to a higher standard of care in making recommendations." 2 Thomas Lee Hazen, *Treatise on the Law of Securities Regulation* § 10.6, at 93 (3d ed. 1995).

shin plaster. (1824) *Hist. Slang.* **1.** A bank note that has greatly depreciated in value; esp., the paper money of the Republic of Texas in relation to the U.S. dollar. **2.** Paper money in denominations less than one dollar. See *fractional currency* under CURRENCY.

ship, *n.* (bef. 12c) A type of vessel used or intended to be used in navigation. See VESSEL.

▸ **chartered ship.** (18c) **1.** A ship specially hired to transport the goods of only one person or company. **2.** A ship on which a shipper has chartered space for a cargo.

▸ **free ship.** (17c) The ship of a neutral country, which in wartime is traditionally free of capture even if it happens to be carrying enemy's goods.

▸ **general ship.** A ship that is set for a particular voyage to carry the goods of any persons willing to ship goods on it for that voyage.

ship, *vb.* (15c) To send (goods, documents, etc.) from one place to another, esp. by delivery to a carrier for transportation.

ship broker. (1816) *Maritime law.* **1.** The business agent of a shipowner or charterer; an intermediary between an owner or charterer and a shipper. **2.** Someone who negotiates the purchase and sale of a ship.

ship channel. (18c) *Maritime law.* The part of a navigable body of water where the water is deep enough for large vessels to travel safely.

shipmaster. See MASTER OF A SHIP.

shipment. (18c) **1.** The transportation of goods by sea, road, or air; esp., the delivery of goods to a carrier and subsequent issuance of a bill of lading. **2.** A load of goods so shipped; an order of goods.

shipment contract. See CONTRACT.

Ship Mortgage Act. A federal law regulating mortgages on ships registered as U.S. vessels by, among other things, providing for enforcement of maritime liens in favor of those who furnish supplies or maintenance to the vessels. 46 USCA §§ 30101, 31301–31343.

shipowner. Someone who has legal title to one or more ships.

shipowner-negligence doctrine. The principle that a shipowner is liable for an assault on a crew member if the crew member was assaulted by a superior, during an activity undertaken for the benefit of the ship's business, and if the ship's officers could reasonably have foreseen the assault.

shipper. (18c) **1.** Someone who ships goods to another. **2.** Someone who contracts with a carrier for the transportation of cargo. • As a legal term of art, the shipper may not be the person who owns the cargo, but an agent or an independent contractor. Cf. CARRIER (1).

shipping articles. (1840) *Maritime law.* A document (provided by a master of a vessel to the mariners) detailing voyage information, such as the voyage term, the number of crew, and the wage rates. 46 USCA § 10302.

shipping commissioner. (1865) An officer, appointed by the secretary of the treasury, who is posted at a port of entry, and vested with general supervisory authority over seamen's contracts and welfare. • In 1993, the term was changed to "master or individual in charge." See Pub. L. 103-206 § 403.

shipping document. (1843) Any paper that covers a shipment in trade, such as a bill of lading or letter of credit.

shipping lane. An officially approved path of travel that ships must follow.

shipping law. See LAW OF SHIPPING.

shipping order. (1844) A copy of the shipper's instructions to a carrier regarding the disposition of goods to be transported.

ship's husband. (18c) *Maritime law.* A person appointed to act as general agent of all the coowners of a ship, as by contracting for all necessary services, equipment, and supplies. Cf. EXERCITOR.

ship's papers. (1853) *Maritime law.* The papers that a vessel is required to carry to provide the primary evidence of the ship's national character, ownership, nature and destination of cargo, and compliance with navigation laws. •These papers includes certificates of health, charter-party, muster-rolls, licenses, and bills of lading.

shipwreck. (bef. 12c) *Maritime law.* **1.** A ship's wreckage. **2.** The injury or destruction of a vessel because of circumstances beyond the owner's control, rendering the vessel incapable of carrying out its mission.

> "There are two kinds of shipwreck: (1.) When the vessel sinks or is dashed to pieces. (2.) When she is stranded, which is, when she grounds and fills with water. The latter may terminate in shipwreck, or may not, and it depends on circumstances whether it will or will not justify an abandonment." 4 James Kent, *Commentaries on American Law* *323 n.(b) (George Comstock ed., 11th ed. 1866).

shire. (bef. 12c) A county in the United Kingdom (esp. England), originally made up of many hundreds but later consisting of larger divisions set off by metes and bounds.

shire-gerefa. See *shire-reeve* under REEVE.

shire-reeve. See REEVE.

***Shively* presumption** (shɪv-lee). (1979) The doctrine that any prestatehood grant of public property does not include tidelands unless the grant specifically indicates otherwise. *Shively v. Bowlby*, 152 U.S. 1, 14 S.Ct. 548 (1894); *U.S. v. Holt State Bank*, 270 U.S. 49, 46 S.Ct. 197 (1925). See EQUAL-FOOTING DOCTRINE.

shock, *n.* (17c) A profound and sudden disturbance of the physical or mental senses; a sudden and violent physical or mental impression depressing the body's vital forces, as by a sudden injury or medical procedure.

▸ **mental shock.** (18c) Shock caused by agitation of the mental senses and resulting in extreme grief or joy, as by witnessing the horrific death of a family member or winning the lottery. Cf. *emotional distress* under DISTRESS (4).

▸ **physical shock.** (18c) Shock caused by agitation of the physical senses, as from a sudden violent blow, impact, collision, or concussion.

shock-and-awe, *n.* The rapid use of massive military force to quell any resistance and eliminate the will to fight back.

shock incarceration. See INCARCERATION.

shock probation. See PROBATION (1).

shock the conscience. (18c) To cause intense ethical or humanitarian discomfort. • This phrase is used as an equitable standard for gauging whether (1) state action amounts to a violation of a person's substantive-due-process rights, (2) a jury's award is excessive, (3) a fine, jail term, or other penalty is disproportionate to the crime, or (4) a contract is unconscionable. See CONSCIENCE OF THE COURT (2).

shop, *n.* (13c) A business establishment or place of employment; a factory, office, or other place of business.

▸ **agency shop.** (1951) A shop in which a union acts as an agent for the employees, regardless of their union membership. • Nonunion members must pay union dues because it is presumed that any collective bargaining will benefit nonunion as well as union members.

▸ **closed nonunion shop.** (1915) A shop in which the employer restricts employment to workers who are unaffiliated with any labor union.

▸ **closed shop.** (1903) A shop in which the employer, by agreement with a union, employs only union members in good standing. • Closed shops were made illegal under the federal Labor-Management Relations Act. — Also termed *closed union shop.* See PREHIRE AGREEMENT. Cf. *closed union* under UNION.

▸ **open closed shop.** (1920) A shop in which the employer hires nonunion workers on the understanding that they will become union members within a specified period. — Also termed *open shop.*

▸ **open shop.** (1885) **1.** A shop in which the employer hires workers without regard to union affiliation. See RIGHT-TO-WORK LAW. Cf. *open union* under UNION. **2.** See *open closed shop.*

▸ **preferential nonunion shop.** (1930) A shop in which nonunion members are given preference over main members in employment matters.

▸ **preferential shop.** See *preferential union shop.*

▸ **preferential union shop.** (1911) A shop in which union members are given preference over nonunion members in employment matters. — Also termed *preferential shop.*

▸ **union shop.** (1888) A shop in which the employer may hire nonunion employees on the condition that they join a union within a specified time (usu. at least 30 days).

shop-book rule. (1898) *Evidence.* An exception to the hearsay rule permitting the admission into evidence of original bookkeeping records if the books' entries were made in the ordinary course of business and the books are authenticated by somebody who maintains them.

shop books. (17c) Records of original entry maintained in the usual course of business by a shopkeeper, trader, or other businessperson. — Also termed *books of account; account books.*

shop committee. (1891) A union committee that resolves employee complaints within a union shop. See *union shop* under SHOP.

shopkeeper's privilege. (1973) A privilege permitting a shopkeeper to detain a person to investigate the ownership of property if the shopkeeper reasonably believes that the person has stolen or is attempting to steal store merchandise, as long as the detention takes place in a reasonable manner and for a reasonable time.

shoplifting, *n.* (17c) Theft of merchandise from a store or business; specif., larceny of goods from a store or other commercial establishment by willfully taking and concealing the merchandise with the intention of converting the goods to one's personal use without paying the purchase price. See LARCENY. — **shoplift,** *vb.*

> "Shoplifting is a form of larceny . . . . As a practical matter, however, the difficulty of proving the wrongful taking and the felonious intent requisites for a conviction under the general larceny statutes, together with the risk of retributory civil action against the shopkeeper consequent to acquittal of an accused shoplifter, have caused shoplifting to be established as a specific statutory crime in many jurisdictions." 50 Am. Jur. 2d *Larceny* § 71, at 79–80 (1995).

shop right. (1879) *Patents.* An employer's right to an irrevocable, nonassignable, nonexclusive, royalty-free license in an employee's invention, if the employee conceived and developed the invention during the course of employment and used company funds and materials. • The term derives from the idea that the right belongs to the shop, not to the employee. Employment contracts frequently contain patent-assignment clauses, but the employer is entitled to the license even if the employee retains the patent. If the employee or consultant was hired to invent, then the employer owns the resulting inventions. If an employee develops an invention independently, the employee is its sole owner. But if an employees uses the employer's resources to make the invention, courts use the shop-right doctrine to order the employee to compensate the employer.

shop steward. See STEWARD (2).

shore. (14c) **1.** Land lying between the lines of high- and low-water mark; lands bordering on the shores of navigable waters below the line of ordinary high water. **2.** Land adjacent to a body of water regardless of whether it is below or above the ordinary high- or low-water mark. — Also termed *shore land.*

short, *adj.* (1949) **1.** Not holding at the time of sale the security or commodity that is being sold in anticipation of a fall in price <the trader was short at the market's close>. **2.** Of, relating to, or involving a sale of securities or commodities not in the seller's possession at the time of sale <a short position>. See *short sale* under SALE. Cf. LONG.

short, *adv.* (1852) By a short sale <sold the stock short>. See *short sale* under SALE.

short, *vb.* (1959) To sell (a security or commodity) by a short sale <shorted 1,000 shares of Pantheon stock>. See *short sale* under SALE.

shortage. A situation in which there is not enough of something that people want or need; a deficit.

short cause. See CAUSE (3).

short-cause calendar. See CALENDAR (2).

short-cause trial. See *short cause* under CAUSE (3).

shortchange, *vb.* **1.** To give less than the right amount of change to; to return to (a customer) too little money when more than enough has been paid. **2.** To give (someone) less than is due; esp., to treat unfairly by not according what is deserved or hoped for.

shortened statutory period. (1992) *Patents.* An amount of time less than 6 months, but not less than 30 days, given in certain circumstances to a patent applicant to respond to an office action. • The period for most responses can be extended up to the statutory period of 6 months. MPEP 710.02.

shorter-term rule. See RULE OF THE SHORTER TERM.

shortfall. (1895) **1.** The difference between the amount one has and the amount one needs or expects. **2.** A failure to meet expectations or needs.

short-form agreement. (1961) *Labor law.* A contract usu. entered into by a small independent contractor whereby the contractor agrees to be bound by a collective-bargaining agreement negotiated between a union and a multi-employer bargaining unit.

short-form bill of lading. See BILL OF LADING.

short-form complaint. See COMPLAINT.

short-form merger. See MERGER (8).

short interest. *Securities.* In a short sale, the number of shares that have not been purchased for return to lenders. See *short sale* under SALE.

short lease. See LEASE.

short list. 1. A greatly abridged list of items or individuals. **2.** A brief list of the most suitable people for a nomination or prize, selected from a much longer list of those considered. — **short-list,** *vb.*

short notice. See NOTICE (3).

short position. (1931) The position of an investor who borrowed stock to make a short sale but has not yet purchased the stock to repay the lender. See *short sale* under SALE.

short sale. See SALE.

short sale against the box. See SALE.

short-shipped, *adj.* (1891) *Commercial law.* Partially filled; containing fewer units than requested or paid for.

short summons. See SUMMONS.

short-swing profits. (1945) Profits made by a corporate insider on the purchase and sale (or sale and purchase) of company stock within a six-month period. • These profits are subject to being returned to the company.

short-term alimony. See *rehabilitative alimony* under ALIMONY (1).

short-term capital gain. See CAPITAL GAIN.

short-term debt. 1. See DEBT. **2.** See *current liability* under LIABILITY.

short-term loan. See LOAN.

short-term security. See SECURITY (4).

short-term trading. See TRADING.

short-term trust. See *Clifford trust* under TRUST (3).

short title. See TITLE (3).

short ton. See TON.

shotgun instruction. See ALLEN CHARGE.

shotgun pleading. See PLEADING (1).

shotgun rejection. See REJECTION.

show, *vb.* (12c) To make (facts, etc.) apparent or clear by evidence; to prove.

show cause. (16c) To produce a satisfactory explanation or excuse, usu. in connection with a motion or application to a court.

show-cause motion. See MOTION (1).

show-cause order. See ORDER (2).

show-cause proceeding. (1922) A usu. expedited proceeding on a show-cause order. — Also termed *rule to show cause; summary process; summary procedure; expedited proceeding.*

show-cause rule. See *show-cause order* under ORDER (2).

shower (shoh-ər), *n.* (1838) A person commissioned by a court to take jurors to a place so that they may observe it as they consider a case on which they are sitting. See VIEW (3).

showing, *n.* (1857) The act or an instance of establishing through evidence and argument; proof <a prima facie showing>.

showing agent. See AGENT.

show of hands. See *vote by show of hands* under VOTE (4).

show-stopper. *Corporations.* An antitakeover tactic by which the target company seeks an injunction barring the takeover offer, usu. because the proposed merger violates antitrust laws.

show trial. (1937) A trial, usu. in a nondemocratic country, that is staged primarily for propagandistic purposes, with the outcome predetermined.

showup, *n.* (1924) A police procedure in which a suspect is shown singly to a witness for identification, rather than as part of a lineup. • In a showup, a witness is brought to the scene and asked whether a detained or arrested suspect is the perpetrator. *See* R.C.L. Lindsay et al., *Simultaneous Lineups, Sequential Lineups, and Showups: Eyewitness Identification Decisions of Adults and Children*, 21 Law & Hum. Behav. 391, 393 (1997). The U.S. Supreme Court has held that "[t]he admission of evidence of a showup without more does not violate due process." *Neil v. Biggers*, 409 U.S. 188, 198 (1972). Cf. LINEUP.

shrievalty (shreev-əl-tee or shrɪv-əl-tee), *n.* (16c) The office, term or jurisdiction of a sheriff. — Also spelled *shrivalty.* — Also termed *sheriffalty.*

shrieve (shreev or shrɪv), *n.* (16c) *Archaic.* A sheriff.

shrinkage. (1961) The reduction in inventory caused by theft, breakage, or waste.

shrinkwrap agreement. See *shrinkwrap license* under LICENSE.

shrinkwrap license. See LICENSE.

shrivalty. See SHRIEVALTY.

SHU. *abbr.* SPECIAL HOUSING UNIT.

shutdown. (1884) A cessation of work production, esp. in a factory.

shut-in royalty. See ROYALTY (2).

shut-in royalty clause. (1955) *Oil & gas.* A provision in an oil-and-gas lease allowing the lessee to maintain the lease while there is no production from the property because wells capable of production are shut in. • The lessee pays the lessor a shut-in royalty in lieu of production.

shuttle diplomacy. See DIPLOMACY (1).

shyster (shɪs-tər). (1843) A person (esp. a lawyer) whose business affairs are unscrupulous, deceitful, or unethical; a lawyer without professional honor.

si actio (sɪ **ak**-shee-oh), *n.* [Latin] (17c) *Hist.* The closing statement in a defendant's plea demanding judgment.

si aliquid sapit (sɪ **al**-i-kwid **say**-pit). [Law Latin] *Hist.* If he knows anything.

si antecedit ictum licet non congressum (sɪ an-ti-**see**-dit **ik**-təm **lɪ**-set non kən-**gres**-əm). [Law Latin] *Hist.* If it precedes the blow, although not actually connected with it. • The phrase appeared in reference to the malice sufficient to warrant a capital murder conviction.

SIB. *abbr.* **1.** Securities and Investment Board. See FINANCIAL SERVICES AGENCY. **2.** See *survivor-income benefit plan* under EMPLOYEE BENEFIT PLAN.

sibi imputet (**sib**-ɪ **im**-pyə-tet). [Latin] (17c) *Hist.* Let it be imputed to himself.

sibi invigilare (**sib**-ɪ in-vij-ə-**lair**-ee). [Latin] *Hist.* To watch for themselves.

sibling. (bef. 12c) A brother or sister.

sibship. (1908) **1.** The quality, state, or condition of being a blood relative, esp. a sibling. See DEGREE (6); CONSANGUINITY.

> "[T]he ancient Germans knew yet another calculus of kinship, which was bound up with their law of inheritance. Within the household composed of a father and children there was no degree; this household was regarded for this purpose as a unit, and only when, in default of children, the inheritance fell to remoter kinsmen, was there any need to count the grades of 'sibship.' Thus first cousins are in the first degree of sibship; second cousins in the second." 2 Frederick Pollock & Frederic W. Maitland, *History of English Law Before the Time of Edward I* 386 (2d ed. 1899).

2. A group of blood relatives; kindred.

sic (sik). [Latin "so, thus"] (1859) Spelled or used as written. • *Sic,* invariably bracketed and usu. set in italics, is used to indicate that a preceding word or phrase in a quoted passage is reproduced as it appeared in the original document <"that case peeked [*sic*] the young lawyer's interest">.

sick leave. See LEAVE.

sickness. 1. The quality, state, or condition of suffering from a disease, esp. a disease that interferes with one's vocation and avocations; ILLNESS (1) <his sickness continues>. **2.** Any disease of the body or mind, esp. one that deprives the body temporarily of the power to fulfill its usual functions; any morbid condition of the body hindering or preventing organs from serving their normal functions <the falling sickness>. **3.** Nausea; the feeling that one is about to vomit, or the act of vomiting <travel sickness>. **4.** Any disordered or weakened state of body or mind <sickness of the spirit>. **5.** Figuratively, disgust or weariness <his employer's actions caused a kind of sickness within him>. Cf. AILMENT.

sickness and accident insurance. See *health insurance* under INSURANCE.

sickness benefit. Money paid by the government to someone who is too ill to work.

sickout, *n.* A labor strike in which all or most of the workers at a company say they are sick and stay home on the same day.

sick pay. Salary or wages paid by an employer to a worker who is temporarily too ill to work.

si constet de persona (sɪ **kon**-stet dee pər-**soh**-nə). [Latin] If it is certain who is the person meant.

si contingat (sɪ kon-**ting**-at). [Law Latin] If it happens. • This term was formerly used to describe conditions in a conveyance.

sicut alias (**sɪ**-kət **ay**-lee-əs), *n.* [Latin "as at another time"] (16c) *Hist.* A second writ issued when the first one was not executed.

> "But where a defendant absconds, and the plaintiff would proceed to an outlawry against him, an original writ must then be sued out regularly, and after that a *capias*. And if the sheriff cannot find the defendant upon the first writ . . . there issues out an *alias* writ, and after that a *pluries*, to the same effect as the former: only after these words 'we command you,' this clause is inserted, 'as we have *formerly*,' or, 'as we have *often* commanded you;' '*sicut* alias' . . . ." 3 William Blackstone, *Commentaries on the Laws of England* 283 (1768).

sicut me Deus adjuvet (**sik**-ət mee **dee**-əs **aj**-ə-vet). [Latin] So help me God.

side, *n.* (13c) **1.** The position of a person or group opposing another <the law is on our side>. **2.** Either of two parties in a transaction or dispute <each side put on a strong case>. **3.** *Archaic.* The field of a court's jurisdiction <equity side> <law side>. **4.** *Property.* In a description of more or less rectangularly shaped land, either of the two long boundary lines.

side agreement. See AGREEMENT.

sidebar. (1856) **1.** A position at the side of a judge's bench where counsel can confer with the judge beyond the jury's earshot <the judge called the attorneys to sidebar>. **2.** SIDEBAR CONFERENCE <during the sidebar, the prosecutor accused the defense attorney of misconduct>. **3.** A short, secondary article within or accompanying a main story in a publication <the sidebar contained information on related topics>. **4.** SIDEBAR COMMENT.

sidebar comment. (1922) An unnecessary, often argumentative remark made by an attorney or witness, esp. during a trial or deposition <the witness paused after testifying, then added a sidebar>. — Often shortened to *sidebar.* — Also termed *sidebar remark.*

sidebar conference. (1925) **1.** A discussion among the judge and counsel, usu. over an evidentiary objection, outside the jury's hearing. — Also termed *bench conference.* **2.** A discussion, esp. during voir dire, between the judge and a juror or prospective juror. — Often shortened to *sidebar.*

sidebar remark. See SIDEBAR COMMENT.

sidebar rule. (1811) *Hist. English law.* An order or rule allowed by the court without formal application, such as an order to plead within a particular time. • Formerly, the rules or orders were made on the motion of the attorneys at the sidebar in court.

side-constrained consequentialism. See *negative retributivism* under RETRIBUTIVISM.

side judge. See JUDGE.

side lines. (18c) **1.** The margins of something, such as property. **2.** A different type of business or goods than one principally engages in or sells. **3.** *Mining law.* The boundary lines of a mining claim not crossing the vein running on each side of it. — Also written *sidelines.* Cf. END LINES.

sidenote. See MARGINAL NOTE.

si deprehendatur (sɪ dep-ri-hen-**day**-tər). [Latin] *Hist.* If captured.

side reports. (1943) **1.** Unofficial volumes of case reports. **2.** Collections of cases omitted from the official reports.

sidesman. (17c) *Eccles. law.* A church officer who originally reported to the bishop on clerical and congregational misdeeds, including heretical acts, and later became a standing officer whose duties gradually devolved by custom on the churchwarden. — Also termed *synodsman; questman.*

si deventum sit ad actum maleficio proximum (sɪ di-**ven**-təm sit ad **ak**-təm mal-ə-**fish**-ee-oh **prok**-sə-məm). [Law Latin] *Hist.* If it approaches an act bordering on crime. • The phrase described the determination of a criminal attempt.

sidewalk counseling. (1983) A form of abortion protesting in which activists gather outside an abortion clinic to display signs, pass out pamphlets, show movies, or speak directly to women in an attempt either to dissuade the women from going inside to have an abortion or to change the women's position on abortion in general. • Some states place limits on how close the participants may be to the building.

siege (seej). **1.** The stationing or sitting down of an attacking force in a strong encampment surrounding an area, esp. a fortification, for the purpose of capturing it by continuous offensive operations; the act or process of besieging.

> "**Siege** (Fr. *siege*, 'a seat, a sitting down'). Is the sitting of an army before a hostile town or fortress with the intention of capturing it. With certain elements, the success of a siege is beyond doubt; the result being merely a question of time. These elements are: First, the force of the besiegers shall be sufficient to overcome the besieged in actual combat, man to man. If this be not the case, the besieged, by a sortie, might destroy the opposing works and drive away the besiegers. The second element is, that the place must be thoroughly invested, so that no provisions, reinforcements, or other aliment of war can enter. The third element is, that the besiegers be undisturbed from without. For this it is essential that there shall not be a hostile army in the neighborhood; or if there be, that the operations of the besiegers be protected by a covering army able to cope with the enemy's force in the field. The ancients executed gigantic works to produce these effects." Thomas Wilhelm, *A Military Dictionary and Gazetteer* 530 (rev. ed. 1881).

2. By extension, any continued attempt to gain possession.

Sierra Club. An American environmental organization that seeks to protect forests, mountains, rivers, and wildlife through lawsuits and educational programs. • Founded in San Francisco in 1892, its mission is to promote and preserve the earth's ecosystems by all lawful means.

***Sierra–Mobile* doctrine.** See MOBILE–SIERRA DOCTRINE.

si fecerit te securum (SI **fes**-ər-it tee si-**kyoor**-əm). [Law Latin] *Hist.* If he has made you secure. • These were the initial words of a writ ordering the sheriff, upon receipt of security from the plaintiff, to compel the defendant's appearance in court. — Also spelled (erroneously) *se te fecerit securum.*

SIG. *abbr.* Special-interest group. See INTEREST GROUP.

sight. (1810) A drawee's acceptance of a draft <payable after sight>. • The term *after sight* means "after acceptance."

sight bill. See *bill payable at sight* under BILL (6).

sight draft. See DRAFT (1).

sight strike. See STRIKE (2).

sigil (**sij**-əl), *n.* (17c) A seal or an abbreviated signature used as a seal; esp., a seal formerly used by civil-law notaries.

sigillum (si-**jil**-əm), *n.* [Latin] (1927) A seal, esp. one impressed on wax.

sigla (**sig**-lə), *n. pl.* [Latin] (18c) Abbreviations and signs used in writing, esp. by the Glossators.

sign, *vb.* (15c) **1.** To identify (a record) by means of a signature, mark, or other symbol with the intent to authenticate it as an act or agreement of the person identifying it <both parties signed the contract>. **2.** To agree with or join <the commissioner signed on for a four-year term>.

signal. (1949) **1.** A means of communication, esp. between vessels at sea or between a vessel and the shore. • The international code of signals assigns arbitrary meanings to different arrangements of flags or light displays. **2.** In the citation of legal authority, an abbreviation or notation supplied to indicate some basic fact about the authority. • For example, according to the *Bluebook*, the signal *See* means that the cited authority plainly supports the proposition, while *Cf.* means that the cited authority supports a proposition analogous to (but in some way different from) the main proposition. For these and other signals, see *The Bluebook: A Uniform System of Citation* § 1.2, at 22–24 (17th ed. 2000). — Also termed (in sense 2) *citation signal.*

signatorius anulus (sig-nə-**tor**-ee-əs **an**-yə-ləs). [Latin] (16c) *Roman law.* A signet ring.

signatory (**sig**-nə-tor-ee), *n.* (1866) A person or entity that signs a document, personally or through an agent, and thereby becomes a party to an agreement <eight countries are signatories to the treaty>. — **signatory,** *adj.*

signatory authority. (1953) **1.** License to make a decision, esp. to withdraw money from an account or to transfer a negotiable instrument. **2.** *Patents.* In the U.S. Patent and Trademark Office, the power of an examiner to approve an office action.

signature. (16c) **1.** A person's name or mark written by that person or at the person's direction; esp., one's handwritten name as one ordinarily writes it, as at the end of a letter or a check, to show that one has written it. — Also termed *sign manual.* **2.** *Commercial law.* Any name, mark, or writing used with the intention of authenticating a document. UCC §§ 1-201(b)(37), 3-401(b). — Also termed *legal signature.* **3.** The act of signing something; the handwriting of one's name in one's usual fashion.

> "The signature to a memorandum may be any symbol made or adopted with an intention, actual or apparent, to authenticate the writing as that of the signer." Restatement (Second) of Contracts § 134 (1979).

▸ **cosignature.** The signature of another person, usu. one who promises to assume the principal signer's obligations if that signer defaults. See COSIGN.

▸ **digital signature.** (1978) A secure, digital code attached to an electronically transmitted message that uniquely identifies and authenticates the sender. • A digital signature consists of a "hashed" number combined with a number assigned to a document (a private-encryption key). Generating a signature requires the use of private- and public-key-encryption software, and is often activated by a simple command or act, such as clicking on a "place order" icon on a retailer's website. Digital signatures are esp. important for electronic commerce and are a key component of many electronic message-authentication schemes. Several states have passed legislation recognizing the legality of digital signatures. See E-COMMERCE; KEY ENCRYPTION.

▸ **electronic signature.** (1957) An electronic symbol, sound, or process that is either attached to or logically associated with a document (such as a contract or other record) and executed or adopted by a person with the intent to sign the document. • Types of electronic signatures include a typed name at the end of an email, a digital image of a handwritten signature, and the click of an "I accept" button on an e-commerce site. The term *electronic signature* does not suggest or require the use of encryption, authentication, or identification measures. A document's integrity (unaltered content), authenticity (sender's identity), and confidentiality (of the signer's identity or document's contents) are not ensured merely because an electronic signature is provided for.

▸ **facsimile signature.** (1892) **1.** A signature that has been prepared and reproduced by mechanical or photographic means. **2.** A signature on a document that has been transmitted by a facsimile machine. See FAX.

▸ **private signature.** (18c) *Civil law.* A signature made on a document (such as a will) that has not been witnessed or notarized.

▸ **unauthorized signature.** (1859) A signature made without actual, implied, or apparent authority. • It includes a forgery. UCC § 1-201(b)(41).

signature card. (1902) A financial-institution record consisting of a customer's signature and other information that assists the institution in monitoring financial transactions, as by comparing the signature on the record with signatures on checks, withdrawal slips, and other documents.

signature crime. See CRIME.

signature evidence. See EVIDENCE.

signature loan. See LOAN.

signature offense. See *signature crime* under CRIME.

signed, sealed, and delivered. (17c) In a certificate of acknowledgment, a statement that the instrument was executed by the person acknowledging it. — Often shortened to *sealed and delivered.*

signed writing. See WRITING.

signet. (14c) **1.** *Civil law.* An elaborate hand-drawn symbol (usu. incorporating a cross and the notary's initials) formerly placed at the base of notarial instruments, later replaced by a seal. **2.** *Scots law.* A seal used to authenticate summonses in civil matters before the Court of Session. • Originally, this was the monarch's personal seal. Cf. WRITER TO THE SIGNET.

significant, *adj.* (16c) **1.** Embodying or bearing some meaning; having or expressing a sense. **2.** Standing as a subtle sign of something; expressive of some hidden or obscure meaning. **3.** Of special importance; momentous, as distinguished from insignificant.

significant-connection jurisdiction. See JURISDICTION.

significant-connection/substantial-evidence jurisdiction. See *significant-connection jurisdiction* under JURISDICTION.

significant-relationship theory. See CENTER-OF-GRAVITY DOCTRINE.

significavit (sig-ni-fi-**kay**-vit), *n.* [Latin "he has signified"] (15c) *Eccles. law.* **1.** A bishop's certificate that a person has been in a state of excommunication for more than 40 days. **2.** A notice to the Crown in chancery, based on the bishop's certificate, whereby a writ *de contumace capiendo* (or, earlier, a writ *de excommunicato capiendo*) would issue for the disobedient person's arrest and imprisonment. See DE CONTUMACE CAPIENDO.

sign manual. (15c) **1.** See SIGNATURE (1). **2.** A symbol or emblem, such as a trademark, representing words or an idea.

signum (**sig**-nəm), *n.* [Latin] (17c) *Roman law.* **1.** A sign; a seal.

> "Signum. (On written documents.) A seal (a stamp) put on to close a document in order to make its contents inaccessible to unauthorized persons and protect against forgery, or at the end of it after the written text. In the latter case the seal (without or with a signature) indicated that the sealer recognized the written declaration as his . . . . *Signum* is also the seal of a witness who was present at the making of a document." Adolf Berger, *Encyclopedic Dictionary of Roman Law* 707 (1953).

2. An indication of something seen or otherwise perceived by the senses, such as a bloodstain on a murder suspect. Pl. ***signa.***

si institutus sine liberis decesserit (sɪ in-sti-**t[y]oo**-təs sɪ-nee **lib**-ər-is di-**ses**-ər-it). [Latin] *Hist.* If the instituted heir should die without issue. See SUBSTITUTION.

si ita est (sɪ **ɪ**-tə est). [Latin] If it be so. • This phrase was formerly used in a mandamus writ to order a judge to affix a seal to a bill of exceptions, if the facts were accurately stated.

silence, *n.* (13c) **1.** A restraint from speaking. • In criminal law, silence includes an arrestee's statements expressing the desire not to speak and requesting an attorney. **2.** A failure to reveal something required by law to be revealed. See *estoppel by silence* under ESTOPPEL. — **silent,** *adj.*

silent confirmation. See CONFIRMATION (6).

silentiary (sɪ-len-shee-**air**-ee), *n.* (17c) **1.** *Roman law.* An official who maintains order in the imperial palace and on the imperial council; a chamberlain. **2.** *Hist.* An officer who is sworn to silence about state secrets; esp., a privy councillor so sworn. **3.** *Hist.* A court usher who maintains order and esp. silence in the court. — Also termed *silentiarius.*

silent indictment. See SEALED INDICTMENT.

silent misrepresentation. See *passive misrepresentation* (1) under MISREPRESENTATION.

silent partner. See PARTNER.

silent record. See RECORD.

silent-witness theory. (1973) *Evidence.* A method of authenticating and admitting evidence (such as a photograph), without the need for a witness to verify its authenticity, upon a sufficient showing of the reliability of the process of producing the evidence, including proof that the evidence has not been altered.

silk gown. (1836) **1.** The professional robe worn by a Queen's Counsel. **2.** Someone who is a Queen's Counsel. — Often shortened (in sense 2) to *silk.* Cf. STUFF GOWN.

silver certificate. (1878) *Hist.* A banknote issued by the United States Treasury from 1878 to 1963 and redeemable in silver. • The notes represented that a certain amount of silver was on deposit with the government and would be paid to the bearer on demand. Originally, these notes were not legal tender and could be used only to pay taxes and other public obligations. In 1967, Congress abolished redemption in silver after June 1968. Silver certificates now have the same status as Federal Reserve notes, which are not redeemable for precious metal. Cf. FEDERAL RESERVE NOTE; GOLD CERTIFICATE.

silver parachute. See TIN PARACHUTE.

silver-platter doctrine. (1958) *Criminal procedure.* The principle that a federal court could admit evidence obtained illegally by a state police officer as long as a federal officer did not participate in or request the search.

• The Supreme Court rejected this doctrine in *Elkins v. U.S.*, 364 U.S. 206, 80 S.Ct. 1437 (1960).

si malitia suppleat aetatem (sɪ mə-**lish**-ee-ə **səp**-lee-at ee-**tay**-təm). [Latin] *Hist.* If malice should supply the want of age.

similar happenings. *Evidence.* Events that occur at a time different from the time in dispute and are therefore usu. inadmissible except to the extent that they provide relevant information on issues that would be fairly constant, such as the control of and conditions on land on the day in question.

similarity. *Intellectual property.* The resemblance of one trademark or copyrighted work to another. • How closely a trademark must resemble another to amount to infringement depends on the nature of the product and how much care the typical buyer would be expected to take in making the selection in that particular market. It is a question of overall impression rather than an element-by-element comparison of the two marks. — Also termed *imitation*; *colorable imitation*. Cf. *substantial similarity*.

> "It is the buyer who uses ordinary caution in making his purchase, who is buying with the care usually exercised in such transactions, who must be deceived by this similarity. He who buys a box of candy does not use as much care as he who buys a watch. He who buys a handkerchief does not usually examine the goods offered him as carefully as he who buys a suit of clothes." Harry D. Nims, *The Law of Unfair Competition and Trade-Marks* 836 (1929).

▸ **comprehensive nonliteral similarity.** (1970) *Copyright.* Similarity evidenced by the copying of the protected work's general ideas or structure (such as a movie's plot) without using the precise words or phrases of the work. — Also termed *pattern similarity*.

▸ **fragmented literal similarity.** (1970) *Copyright.* Similarity evidenced by the copying of verbatim portions of the protected work.

▸ **substantial similarity.** *Copyright.* A strong resemblance between a copyrighted work and an alleged infringement, thereby creating an inference of unauthorized copying. • The standard for substantial similarity is whether an ordinary person would conclude that the alleged infringement has appropriated nontrivial amounts of the copyrighted work's expressions. — Also termed *probative similarity*. See *derivative work* under WORK (2).

similar sales. See SALE.

similiter (si-**mil**-i-tər). [Latin "similarly"] *Common-law pleading.* A party's written acceptance of an opponent's issue or argument; a set form of words by which a party accepts or joins in an issue of fact tendered by the other side. See *joinder of issue* (2) under JOINDER.

si minor se majorem dixerit (sɪ **mɪ**-nər see mə-**jor**-əm **dik**-sər-it). [Latin] *Hist.* If the minor has said that he is major. • The phrase refers to a defense that might be raised in a suit for a minor's claim for restitution for minority.

***Simmons* rule.** (1968) *Criminal procedure.* The doctrine that a criminal defendant's testimony at a suppression hearing cannot be used in the prosecution's case-in-chief at trial, on the principle that a defendant cannot be made to trade one constitutional right for another. *Simmons v. U.S.*, 390 U.S. 397 (1968). • Nevertheless, a criminal defendant who testifies at trial may be cross-examined with testimony from the suppression hearing.

simony (**sim**-ə-nee *or* **sɪ**-mə-nee), *n.* [fr. Latin *simonia* "payment for things spiritual," fr. the proper name *Simon Magus* (see below)] (13c) *Hist. Eccles. law.* The unlawful practice of giving or receiving money or gifts in exchange for spiritual promotion; esp., the unlawful buying or selling of a benefice or the right to present clergy to a vacant benefice. Cf. BARRATRY (4).

> "By *simony*, the right of presentation to a living is forfeited, and vested *pro hac vice* in the crown. Simony is the corrupt presentation of any one to an ecclesiastical benefice for money, gift, or reward. It is so called from the resemblance it is said to bear to the sin of Simon Magus, though the purchasing of holy orders seems to approach nearer to his offence. It was by the canon law a very grievous crime: and is so much the more odious, because, as sir Edward Coke observes, it is ever accompanied with perjury; for the presentee is sworn to have committed no simony." 2 William Blackstone, *Commentaries on the Laws of England* 278 (1766).

> "Simony is an offence which consists in the buying and selling of holy orders, and any bond or contract involving simony is illegal and void." John Indermaur, *Principles of the Common Law* 195 (Edmund H. Bennett ed., 1st Am. ed. 1878).

simple, *adj.* (16c) **1.** (Of a crime) not accompanied by aggravating circumstances. Cf. AGGRAVATED (1). **2.** (Of an estate or fee) heritable by the owner's heirs with no conditions concerning tail. **3.** (Of a contract) not made under seal.

simple agreement. See AGREEMENT.

simple assault. 1. See ASSAULT (1). **2.** See ASSAULT (2).

simple average. See *particular average* under AVERAGE (3).

simple battery. See BATTERY (1).

simple blockade. See BLOCKADE.

simple bond. See BOND (2).

simple contract. 1. See *informal contract* (1) under CONTRACT. **2.** See *parol contract* (2) under CONTRACT.

simple-contract debt. See DEBT.

simple interest. See INTEREST (3).

simple kidnapping. See KIDNAPPING.

simple larceny. See LARCENY.

simple listing. See *open listing* under LISTING (1).

simple majority. See MAJORITY.

simple mortgage clause. See *open mortgage clause* under MORTGAGE CLAUSE.

simple negligence. See *inadvertent negligence* under NEGLIGENCE.

simple obligation. See OBLIGATION.

SIMPLE plan. See EMPLOYEE BENEFIT PLAN.

simple possession. See POSSESSION.

simple reduction. (18c) *Scots law.* A court's temporary ruling that a document is of no effect until it is produced in court.

simple resolution. See RESOLUTION (1).

simple robbery. See ROBBERY.

simple state. See *unitary state* under STATE (1).

simple-tool rule. (1908) The principle that an employer has no duty to warn its employees of dangers that are obvious to everyone involved, and has no duty to inspect a tool that is within the exclusive control of an employee when that employee is fully acquainted with the tool's condition.

simple trespass. See TRESPASS.

simple trust. 1. See *mandatory trust* under TRUST (3). **2.** See *passive trust* under TRUST (3).

simple ultra vires. See *narrow ultra vires* under ULTRA VIRES.

simplex (**sim**-pleks), *adj.* [Latin] (16c) Simple; pure; unconditional.

simplex dictum. See DICTUM.

simplex passagium (**sim**-pleks pə-**say**-jee-əm). [Law Latin] *Hist.* Simple passage (to the holy land alone). • This type of pilgrimage served as an excuse for absence from court during the Crusades. — Also termed *simplex peregrinatio.* Cf. IN GENERALI PASSAGIO.

simpliciter (sim-**plis**-i-tər), *adv.* [Latin] (16c) **1.** In a simple or summary manner; simply. **2.** Absolutely; unconditionally; per se.

simplified employee pension plan. See EMPLOYEE BENEFIT PLAN.

simplified traffic information. (1963) *Criminal law. Jargon.* A traffic ticket.

simplify, *vb.* To make clear and straightforward through lucid explanation; to purge of needless complexity.

> "Your brief should march, not meander. It should run like a greyhound, not waddle like a duck. Irrelevancies should be carefully eliminated. Sometimes an irrelevancy may have in your opinion a helpful emotional effect upon a certain judge or upon more than one. But generally, as in oral argument, your purpose is to simplify, simplify, simplify." Ben W. Palmer, *Courtroom Strategies* 197–98 (1959).

simplum (**sim**-pləm), *n.* [Latin] *Roman law.* The single value of something. Cf. DUPLUM.

simulated contract. See CONTRACT.

simulated fact. See FACT.

simulated judgment. See JUDGMENT (2).

simulated sale. See SALE.

simulated transaction. See *simulated sale* under SALE.

simulatio latens (sim-yə-**lay**-shee-oh **lay**-tenz). [Latin "hidden pretence"] (1823) *Hist.* Feigned enhancement of illness, as when symptoms are present but not nearly as severe as is pretended.

simulation. (14c) **1.** An assumption of an appearance that is feigned, false, or deceptive. **2.** *Civil law.* A feigned, pretended act, usu. to mislead or deceive. **3.** See *simulated contract* under CONTRACT.

simul cum (**sɪ**-məl kəm). [Latin] Together with. • This phrase was formerly used in an indictment or other instrument to indicate that a defendant had committed an injury jointly with others unknown.

simul et semel (**sɪ**-məl et **sem**-əl). [Latin] Together at one time.

simultaneous death. See DEATH.

simultaneous-death act. See UNIFORM SIMULTANEOUS DEATH ACT.

simultaneous-death clause. (1953) A testamentary provision mandating that if the testator and beneficiary die in a common disaster, or the order of their deaths is otherwise unascertainable, the testator is presumed to have survived the beneficiary. • If the beneficiary is the testator's spouse, an express exception is often made so that the spouse with the smaller estate is presumed to have survived. See *simultaneous death* under DEATH. Cf. SURVIVAL CLAUSE.

simultaneous identification procedure. See *conventional lineup* under LINEUP.

simultaneous lineup. See LINEUP.

simultaneous polygamy. See POLYGAMY (1).

sine (**sɪ**-nee or **sin**-ay), *prep.* [Latin] Without.

sine animo remanendi (**sɪ**-nee **an**-ə-moh rem-ə-**nen**-dɪ). [Law Latin] *Hist.* Without the intention of remaining.

sine animo revertendi (**sɪ**-nee **an**-ə-moh ree-vər-**ten**-dɪ). [Latin] Without the intention of returning. See *animus revertendi* under ANIMUS.

sine assensu capituli (**sɪ**-nee ə-**sen**-s[y]oo kə-**pich**-[y]ə-lɪ), *n.* [Law Latin "without the consent of the chapter"] (16c) *Hist.* A writ for a successor to recover land that the former bishop, abbot, or prior had alienated without the chapter's permission.

sine consideratione curiae (**sɪ**-nee kən-sid-ə-ray-shee-**oh**-nee **kyoor**-ee-ɪ). [Law Latin] Without the judgment of the court.

sine cura et cultura (**sɪ**-nee **kyoor**-ə et kəl-**t[y]oor**-ə). [Latin] *Hist.* Without care and culture. • Natural fruits fitting this description automatically passed to the purchaser of property. But industrial fruits that had to be cultivated required a special conveyance.

sinecure (**sɪ**-nə-kyoor *or* **sin**-ə-kyoor). [fr. Latin *sine cura* "without duties"] (17c) *Hist.* A post without any duties attached; an office for which the holder receives a salary but has no responsibilities. — **sinecural** (**sɪ**-nə-kyoor-əl *or* sɪ-nə-**kyoor**-əl), *adj.*

sine damno. See INJURIA ABSQUE DAMNO.

sine decreto (**sɪ**-nee di-**kree**-toh). [Latin] Without a judge's authority.

sine die (**sɪ**-nee **dɪ**-ee *or* **dɪ**- *or* **sin**-ay **dee**-ay). [Latin "without day"] (17c) With no day being assigned (as for resumption of a meeting or hearing). See *adjourn sine die* under ADJOURN; GO HENCE WITHOUT DAY.

sine fraude (**sɪ**-nee **fraw**-dee). [Latin] *Hist.* Without fraud.

sine hoc quod (**sɪ**-nee hok **kwod**). [Law Latin] Without this, that. See ABSQUE HOC.

sine mora (**sɪ**-nee **mor**-ə). [Latin] Without delay.

sine numero (**sɪ**-nee **n[y]oo**-mər-oh). [Law Latin "without number"] Countless; without limit.

sine pacto (**sɪ**-nee **pak**-toh). [Latin] *Hist.* Without an agreement.

sine prole (**sɪ**-nee **proh**-lee). [Latin] Without issue. • This phrase was used primarily in genealogical tables. — Abbr. s.p. See DECESSIT SINE PROLE.

sine qua non (**sɪ**-nee kway **non** *or* **sin**-ay kwah **nohn**), *n.* [Latin "without which not"] (17c) An indispensable condition or thing; something on which something else necessarily depends. — Also termed *conditio sine qua non.*

sine quibus funus honeste duci non potest (**sɪ**-nee **kwib**-əs **fyoo**-nəs [h]ə-**nes**-tee **d[y]oo**-sɪ non **poh**-test). [Latin] *Scots law.* Without which the funeral cannot be decently conducted. • The phrase appeared in reference to funeral expenses that could be deducted against the decedent's estate.

sine vi aut dolo (SI-nee VI awt **doh**-loh). [Latin] *Hist.* Without force or fraud.

single, *adj.* (14c) **1.** Unmarried <single tax status>. **2.** Consisting of one alone; individual <single condition> <single beneficiary>.

single-act statute. See LONG-ARM STATUTE.

single adultery. See ADULTERY.

single-asset real estate. (1976) *Bankruptcy.* A single piece of real property (apart from residential property with fewer than four residential units) that a debtor operates for business purposes, that provides the debtor with substantially all his or her gross income, and that carries aggregate, liquidated, noncontingent secured debts of $4 million or less. 11 USCA § 101(51B). — Abbr. SARE.

single bill. See *bill single* under BILL (7).

single bond. See *bill obligatory* under BILL (7).

single carriageway. See CARRIAGEWAY.

single combat. See DUEL (2).

single condition. See CONDITION (2).

single-controversy doctrine. See ENTIRE-CONTROVERSY DOCTRINE.

single-country fund. See MUTUAL FUND.

single creditor. See CREDITOR.

single-criminal-intent doctrine. See SINGLE-LARCENY DOCTRINE.

single-date-of-removal doctrine. (2009) *Civil procedure.* The principle that the deadline for removing a case from state court to federal court is 30 days from the day that any defendant receives a copy of the state-court pleading on which the removal is based. • If a later-served defendant seeks to remove a case to federal court more than 30 days after the day any other defendant received the pleading, the removal is untimely even if effectuated within 30 days after the removing defendant received the pleading. One theory underlying this doctrine is that all defendants must consent to remove a case to federal court, and a defendant who has waited longer than 30 days to remove does not have the capacity to consent to removal. 28 USCA § 1446(b). See NOTICE OF REMOVAL.

single demise. See DEMISE.

single-element means claim. See *single-means claim* under PATENT CLAIM.

single-employer doctrine. (1962) The rule that related companies, such as a parent company and its affiliates, may be treated as one employer for purposes of employment-discrimination laws. — Also termed *single-employer rule.*

single-entry bookkeeping. See BOOKKEEPING.

single-filing rule. (1982) *Civil-rights law.* The principle that an administrative charge filed by one plaintiff in a civil-rights suit (esp. a Title VII suit) will satisfy the administrative-filing requirements for all coplaintiffs who are making claims for the same act of discrimination. • But this rule will not usu. protect a coplaintiff's claims if the coplaintiff also filed an administrative charge, against the same employer, in which different discriminatory acts were complained of, because the administrative agency (usu. the EEOC) and the employer are entitled to rely on the allegations someone makes in an administrative charge.

single-impulse plan. See SINGLE-LARCENY DOCTRINE.

single-juror direction. See *single-juror instruction* under JURY INSTRUCTION.

single-juror instruction. See JURY INSTRUCTION.

single-larceny doctrine. (1969) *Criminal law.* The principle that the taking of different items of property belonging to either the same or different owners at the same time and place constitutes one act of larceny if the theft is part of one larcenous plan, as when it involves essentially one continuous act or if control over the property is exercised simultaneously. • The thief's intent determines the number of occurrences. — Also termed *single-impulse plan; single-larceny rule; single-criminal-intent doctrine.*

single-means claim. See PATENT CLAIM.

single-name paper. (1893) A negotiable instrument signed by only one maker and not backed by a surety.

single obligation. See OBLIGATION.

single ordeal. See ORDEAL.

single original. (1815) An instrument executed singly, not in duplicate.

single-paragraph form. (1983) *Patents.* A style of writing patent claims that uses a colon after the introductory phrase and a semicolon between each element. Cf. COLON-SEMICOLON FORM; OUTLINE FORM; SUBPARAGRAPH FORM.

single-premium deferred annuity. See ANNUITY.

single-premium insurance. See *single-premium life insurance* under LIFE INSURANCE.

single-premium life insurance. See LIFE INSURANCE.

single-publication rule. (1947) The doctrine that a plaintiff in a libel suit against a publisher has only one claim for each mass publication, not a claim for every book or issue in that run.

single-purpose project. (1951) A facility that is designed, built, and used for one reason only, such as to generate electricity. • This term most often refers to large, complex, expensive projects such as power plants, chemical-processing plants, mines, and toll roads. Projects of this type are often funded through project financing, in which a special-purpose entity is established to perform no function other than to develop, own, and operate the facility, the idea being to limit the number of the entity's creditors and thus provide protection for the project's lenders. See *project financing* under FINANCING; SPECIAL-PURPOSE ENTITY; BANKRUPTCY-REMOTE ENTITY.

single-recovery rule. See ONE-SATISFACTION RULE.

single-registration rule. (1990) *Copyright.* The U.S. Copyright Office doctrine that permits only one registration for each original work. • Exceptions to the rule are routinely made for unpublished works that are later published. Generally, revised works cannot be registered a second time if the revisions are not substantial, but the creator may be allowed to file a supplemental registration.

single-source requirement. (1975) Under the common-law tort of false advertising, the necessity to show that the plaintiff is the only supplier of the genuine goods in question and that buyers would have bought the plaintiff's goods if the true nature of the defendant's goods had been known. *Ely-Norris Safe Co. v. Mosler Safe Co.*, 7 F.2d 603 (2d Cir. 1925). • This is a narrow exception to the common-law rule that the tort of false advertising applies only in instances of passing off, trade defamation, or trade disparagement.

singles' penalty. See MARRIAGE BONUS.

single transferable vote. See VOTE (1).

singular, *adj.* (14c) **1.** Individual; each <all and singular>. **2.** *Civil law.* Of, relating to, or involving separate interests in property, rather than the estate as a whole <singular succession>.

singular successor. See SUCCESSOR.

singular title. See TITLE (2).

singuli in solidum (**sing**-gyə-lɪ in **sol**-ə-dəm). [Latin] *Hist.* Each for the whole.

> "Where there are several co-obligants in one obligation, each bound in full performance, they are said to be liable *singuli in solidum*; and where each is liable only for his own proportion of the debt, they are said to be liable *pro rata*." John Trayner, *Trayner's Latin Maxims* 580 (4th ed. 1894).

sinking fund. See FUND (1).

sinking-fund bond. See BOND (3).

sinking-fund debenture. See DEBENTURE (3).

sinking-fund depreciation method. See DEPRECIATION METHOD.

sinking-fund reserve. See RESERVE (1).

sinking-fund tax. See TAX.

si non jure seminis, saltem jure soli (sɪ non **joor**-ee **sem**-i-nis, **sal**-tem **joor**-ee **soh**-lɪ). [Law Latin] *Hist.* If not by right of seed, at least by right of soil.

si non omnes (sɪ non **om**-neez). [Latin "if not all"] (17c) *Hist.* A writ allowing two or more judges to proceed in a case if the whole commission cannot be present on the assigned day.

sin tax. See TAX.

SIPA (**see**-pə). *abbr.* SECURITIES INVESTOR PROTECTION ACT.

si parcere ei sine suo periculo non potest (sɪ **pahr**-sər-ee **ee**-ɪ **sɪ**-nee s[y]**oo**-oh pə-**rik**-yə-loh non **poh**-test). [Latin] *Roman law.* If he could not spare him except at his own peril. • This phrase defined the circumstances in which a defendant could plead self-defense.

si paret (sɪ **par**-et). [Latin] If it appears. • In Roman law, this phrase was part of the praetor's formula by which judges were appointed and told how they were to decide.

SIPC. *abbr.* SECURITIES INVESTOR PROTECTION CORPORATION.

si petatur tantum (sɪ pi-**tay**-tər **tan**-təm). [Law Latin] *Hist.* If asked only.

> "In blench holdings, where the return for the lands is generally elusory, that return is for the most part due and payable *si petatur tantum*; and this clause, by universal practice, has been interpreted to mean, if asked only within the year (*si petatur intra annum*). If the duty is not demanded within the year, the vassal is not liable for it." John Trayner, *Trayner's Latin Maxims* 575 (4th ed. 1894).

si prius (sɪ **prɪ**-əs). [Law Latin] If before. • This phrase is used in a writ summoning a jury.

si quis (sɪ **kwis**). [Latin] *Roman law.* If any one. • This term was used in praetorian edicts. In England, it was also mentioned in notices posted in parish churches requesting anyone who knows of just cause why a candidate for holy orders should not be ordained to inform the bishop.

SIR. *abbr.* **1.** SELF-INSURED RETENTION. **2.** STATUTORY INVENTION REGISTRATION.

si recognoscat (sɪ rek-əg-**nos**-kat). [Latin "if he acknowledges"] (17c) *Hist.* A writ allowing a creditor to obtain money counted — that is, a specific sum that the debtor had acknowledged in county court to be owed.

si sine liberis decesserit (sɪ **sɪ**-nee **lib**-ər-**is** di-**ses**-ər-it). [Latin] *Hist.* If he shall have died without children.

si sit admodum grave (sɪ sit ad-**moh**-dəm **gray**-vee). [Latin] *Hist.* If it be very heinous.

si sit incompos mentis, fatuus, et naturaliter idiota (sɪ sit in-**kom**-pəs **men**-tis, **fach**-oo-əs et nach-ə-**ray**-li-tər id-ee-**oh**-tə). [Law Latin] *Scots law.* If he is of unsound mind, fatuous, and naturally an idiot. • The phrase appeared in reference to an inquiry that was posed to a jury required to make an idiocy determination.

si sit legitimae aetatis (sɪ sit lə-**jit**-ə-mee ee-**tay**-tis). [Latin] *Hist.* If he (or she) is of lawful age.

SIST. *abbr.* Strict and intensive supervision and treatment.

sist (sist), *n.* (17c) *Scots law.* An order staying or suspending legal proceedings. — Also termed *supersedere.*

sist, *vb.* (17c) *Scots law.* **1.** To bring into court; to summon. **2.** To stay (a judicial proceeding, etc.), esp. by court order. **3.** To intervene in legal proceedings as an interested third party, e.g., a trustee.

sister. (bef. 12c) A female who has one parent or both parents in common with another person.

- ▸ **consanguine sister** (kon-**sang**-gwin *or* kən-**san**-gwin). (1812) *Civil law.* A sister who has the same father, but a different mother.
- ▸ **half sister.** (13c) A sister who has the same father or the same mother, but not both.
- ▸ **sister-german.** (14c) A full sister; the daughter of both of one's parents. See SISTER.
- ▸ **stepsister.** (15c) The daughter of one's stepparent.
- ▸ **uterine sister** (**yoo**-tər-in). (17c) *Civil law.* A sister who has the same mother, but a different father.

sister corporation. See CORPORATION.

sister-german. See SISTER.

sisterhood. See GIFTING CLUB.

sister-in-law. (15c) The sister of one's spouse or the wife of one's brother. • The wife of one's spouse's brother is also sometimes considered a sister-in-law. Pl. **sisters-in-law.**

sistership exclusion. See EXCLUSION (3).

sistren, *n.* (1884) Sisters, esp. those considered spiritual kin (such as female colleagues on a court). Cf. BRETHREN.

sit, *vb.* (14c) **1.** (Of a judge) to occupy a judicial seat <Judge Wilson sits on the trial court for the Eastern District of Arkansas>. **2.** (Of a judge) to hold court or perform official functions <is the judge sitting this week?>. **3.** (Of a court or legislative body) to hold proceedings <the U.S. Supreme Court sits from October to June>.

sit-and-squirm test. (1976) An adjudicator's personal observations of a purportedly disabled person's physical condition for manifestations of pain, disability, or other factors, and the use of those observations in making a decision. • The doctrine is adhered to only in some federal circuits and has been expressly rejected in others. Generally, an administrative-law judge may observe a claimant's demeanor in evaluating the credibility of the complaint. Yet it is error for the judge to base a judgment solely on personal observation and not on the record as a whole. The term was coined by the plaintiff in *Tyler v. Weinberger*, 409 F.Supp. 776, 789 (D. Va. 1976).

sit-down strike. See STRIKE (1).

site. (14c) **1.** A place or location; esp., a piece of property set aside for a specific use. **2.** SCITE.

site assessment. See *transactional audit* under AUDIT.

site license. See LICENSE.

site plan. (1937) An illustrated proposal for the development or use of a particular piece of real property. • The illustration is usu. a map or sketch of how the property will appear if the proposal is accepted. Some zoning ordinances require a developer to present a site plan to the city council and to receive council approval before certain projects may be completed.

sit-in, *n.* (1937) An organized, passive demonstration in which participants usu. sit (or lie) down and refuse to leave a place as a means of protesting against policies or activities. • Sit-ins originated as a communal act of protesting racial segregation. People who were discriminated against would sit in places that were prohibited to them and refuse to leave. Later the term came to refer to any group protest, as with anti–Vietnam War protests and some labor strikes. Cf. *sit-down strike* under STRIKE (1).

sitio ganado mayor (sit-yoh gah-**nah**-doh mɪ-**yor**). (1874) *Spanish & Mexican law.* A square unit of land with each side measuring 5,000 varas (about 4,583 yards). • This term is found in old land grants in states that were formerly Spanish provinces or governed by Mexico. See VARA.

sitting, *n.* (14c) A court session; esp., a session of an appellate court. See SESSION (1).

▸ **en banc sitting.** (1944) A court session in which all the judges (or a quorum) participate. See EN BANC.

▸ **in camera sitting.** (1976) A court session conducted by a judge in chambers or elsewhere outside the courtroom. See IN CAMERA.

sitting member. Someone who is currently serving in a legislature, esp. a parliament.

situation. (15c) **1.** Condition; position in reference to circumstances <dangerous situation>. **2.** The place where someone or something is occupied; a location <situation near the border>.

situational ethics. A philosophy based on flexibility of ethical decisions to fit different contexts and circumstances rather than rigid dogma. See ETHICS.

situational offender. See OFFENDER.

situation of danger. See DANGEROUS SITUATION.

situation room. See INCIDENT ROOM.

situs (sɪ-təs). [Latin] (1834) The location or position (of something) for legal purposes, as in *lex situs*, the law of the place where the thing in issue is situated. See LOCUS.

▸ **arbitral situs.** See *arbitral seat* under SEAT.

▸ **tax situs.** See TAX SITUS.

si vidua manserit et non nupserit (sɪ **vij**-yoo-ə **man**-sər-it et non **nəp**-sər-it). [Law Latin] *Hist.* If she should remain a widow and not marry. • This requirement was a common condition in a widow's provision.

Six Clerks. *Hist.* A collective name for the clerks of the English Court of Chancery who filed pleadings and other papers. • The office was abolished in 1842, and its duties transferred to the Clerk of Enrollments in Chancery and to the Clerks of Records and Writs.

six pack. *Criminal law. Slang.* A series of six photographs of individuals that police use to identify a suspect. See ARRAY. Cf. PHOTO ARRAY.

678 trust. See *nongrantor-owner trust* under TRUST (3).

Sixteenth Amendment. The constitutional amendment, ratified in 1913, allowing Congress to tax income.

Sixth Amendment. The constitutional amendment, ratified with the Bill of Rights in 1791, guaranteeing in criminal cases the right to a speedy and public trial by jury, the right to be informed of the nature of the accusation, the right to confront witnesses, the right to counsel, and the right to compulsory process for obtaining favorable witnesses.

sixth-sentence remand. See REMAND.

sixty clerks. See SWORN CLERKS IN CHANCERY.

sixty-day notice. (1947) *Labor law.* Under the Taft-Hartley Act, the 60-day advance notice required for either party to a collective-bargaining agreement to reopen or terminate the contract. • During this period, strikes and lockouts are prohibited. 29 USCA § 158(d)(1).

S.J.D. See DOCTOR OF JURIDICAL SCIENCE.

SJI. See STATE JUSTICE INSTITUTE.

SJT. *abbr.* See *summary jury trial* under TRIAL.

skeletal legislation. See LEGISLATION (3).

skeleton bill. See BILL (7).

skeleton bill of exceptions. See BILL (2).

skeleton legislation. See *skeletal legislation* under LEGISLATION (3).

skeptical realism. See LEGAL REALISM.

skill. (13c) Special ability and proficiency; esp., the practical and familiar knowledge of the principles and processes of an art, science, or trade, combined with the ability to apply them appropriately, with readiness and dexterity. • Skill is generally considered more than mere competence. It is a special competence that is not a part of the reasonable person's ordinary equipment, but that results from aptitude cultivated through special training and experience.

▸ **ordinary skill.** (16c) The skill of a typical person who performs a given task or job.

▸ **reasonable skill.** (16c) The skill ordinarily possessed and used by persons engaged in a particular business.

skilled artisan. See ARTISAN.

skilled witness. See *expert witness* under WITNESS.

skilled work. See WORK (1).

skip bail. See JUMP BAIL.

skip person. (1988) *Tax.* A beneficiary who is more than one generation removed from the transferor and to whom assets are conveyed in a generation-skipping transfer. IRC (26 USCA) § 2613(a). See GENERATION-SKIPPING TRANSFER.

skippeson. See ESKIPPESON.

skiptracing agency. (1984) A service that locates persons (such as delinquent debtors, missing heirs, witnesses, stockholders, bondholders, etc.) or missing assets (such as bank accounts).

skunk-throwing. *Criminal law. Slang.* Incurable prosecutorial misconduct. • The term derives from Judge Walter Gewin's memorable epigram: "If you throw a skunk in a jury box, you can't instruct the jury not to smell it." *Dunn v. U.S.*, 307 F.2d 883, 886 (5th Cir. 1962).

skyjack, *vb.* (1961) *Slang.* To hijack an aircraft. See HIJACK (1). — **skyjacking,** *n.*

sky marshal. A specially trained law-enforcement officer who carries a gun and whose job is to travel on passenger planes and protect them from skyjackings and terrorist attacks.

S.L. *abbr.* **1.** Session law. See SESSION LAWS. **2.** Statute law.

slack tax. See *pickup tax* under TAX.

slamming. (1987) The practice by which a long-distance telephone company wrongfully appropriates a customer's service from another company, usu. through an unauthorized transfer or by way of a transfer authorization that is disguised as something else, such as a form to sign up for a free vacation.

slander, *n.* (13c) **1.** A defamatory assertion expressed in a transitory form, esp. speech; esp., false and defamatory words that are said in reference to another, such as those charging criminal conduct, imputing a horrible or loathsome disease, alleging malfeasance or incompetence in reference to the person's professional responsibilities, or otherwise causing special damage to the person's reputation. • Damages for slander — unlike those for libel — are not presumed and thus must be proved by the plaintiff (unless the defamation is slander per se). **2.** The act of making such a statement. — Also termed *oral defamation.* See DEFAMATION. Cf. LIBEL (1), (2). — **slander,** *vb.* — **slanderous,** *adj.*

> "Although [in English law] libel and slander are for the most part governed by the same principles, there are two important differences: (1) Libel is not merely an actionable tort, but also a criminal offence, whereas slander is a civil injury only. (2) Libel is in all cases actionable *per se*; but slander is, save in special cases, actionable only on proof of actual damage. This distinction has been severely criticised as productive of great injustice." R.F.V. Heuston, *Salmond on the Law of Torts* 139 (17th ed. 1977).

▸ **slander per quod.** (18c) Slander that does not qualify as slander per se, thus forcing the plaintiff to prove special damages.

▸ **slander per se.** (1841) Slander for which special damages need not be proved because it imputes to the plaintiff any one of the following: (1) a crime involving moral turpitude, (2) a loathsome disease (such as a sexually transmitted disease), (3) conduct that would adversely affect one's business or profession, or (4) unchastity (esp. of a woman).

▸ **trade slander.** (1923) Trade defamation that is spoken but not recorded. See *trade defamation* under DEFAMATION. Cf. *trade libel* under LIBEL.

slanderer, *n.* (13c) Someone who commits slander; esp., one who habitually slanders.

slander of goods. See DISPARAGEMENT (3).

slander of title. (18c) A false statement, made orally or in writing, that casts doubt on another person's ownership of property and thereby causing damage or loss. — Also termed *jactitation of title.* See DISPARAGEMENT (3).

slander per quod. See SLANDER.

slander per se. See SLANDER.

SLAPP (slap). *abbr.* (1989) A strategic lawsuit against public participation — that is, a suit brought by a developer, corporate executive, or elected official to stifle those who protest against some type of high-dollar initiative or who take an adverse position on a public-interest issue (often involving the environment). — Also termed *SLAPP suit.*

slate. (1842) A list of candidates, esp. for political office or a corporation's board of directors, that usu. includes as many candidates for election as there are representatives being elected.

slave. *Roman law.* See SERVUS (1).

slave labor. 1. Work done by slaves. **2.** By extension, work for which one is paid an unfairly small amount of money. **3.** A workforce made up of slaves.

slaver. 1. A slave-trader; one who enslaves. **2.** An owner of one or more slaves.

slavery. (16c) **1.** A situation in which one person has absolute power over the life, fortune, and liberty of another. **2.** The practice of keeping individuals in such a state of bondage or servitude. • Slavery was outlawed by the 13th Amendment to the U.S. Constitution.

> "Slavery was a big problem for the Constitution makers. Those who profited by it insisted on protecting it; those who loathed it dreaded even more the prospect that to insist on abolition would mean that the Constitution would die aborning. So the Framers reached a compromise, of sorts. The words 'slave' and 'slavery' would never be mentioned, but the Constitution would safeguard the 'peculiar institution' from the abolitionists." Jethro K. Lieberman, *The Evolving Constitution* 493 (1992).

> "Although the substance of slavery has varied from place to place, and over time, systems of slavery include most, or all, of the following conditions: (1) slaves are property, and can be sold, traded, given away, bequeathed, inherited, or exchanged for other things of value; (2) the status of a slave is inheritable, usually through the mother; (3) formal legal structures or informal agreements regulate the capture and return of fugitives [*sic*] slaves; (4) slaves have limited (or no) legal rights or protections; (5) slaves may be punished by slave owners (or their agents) with minimal or no legal limitations; (6) masters may treat, or mistreat, slaves as they wish, although some societies required that masters treat slaves 'humanely' and some societies banned murder and extreme or barbaric forms of punishment and torture; (7) masters have unlimited rights to sexual activity with their slaves; (8) slaves have very limited or no appeal

to formal legal institutions; (9) slaves are not allowed to give testimony against their masters or (usually) other free people, and in general their testimony is not given the same weight as a free person's; (10) the mobility of slaves is limited by owners and often by the State; (11) owners are able to makes [*sic*] slaves into free persons through a formal legal process (manumission), but often these freed persons are not given full legal rights; (12) slave ownership is supported by laws, regulations, courts, and legislatures, including provisions for special courts and punishments for slaves, provisions for the capture and return of fugitive slaves, and provisions and rules for regulating the sale of slaves. All of these aspects of slavery have been part of the development of the international law regulating slavery." Seymour Drescher & Paul Finkelman, "Slavery," in *The Oxford Handbook of the History of International Law* 890, 890–91 (Bardo Fassbender & Anne Peters eds., 2012).

slavery, badge of. See BADGE OF SLAVERY.

slave wage. See WAGE.

slay, *vb.* (bef. 12c) To kill (a person), esp. in battle.

slayer's rule. (1986) *Criminal law.* The doctrine that a killer or killer's estate cannot profit from his victim's death, as by inheritance or descent. • Originally adopted by a minority of American jurisdictions as a judge-made rule, it has now been statutorily prescribed in all American jurisdictions. — Also termed *slayer rule.*

slayer statute. (1950) *Slang.* A statute that prohibits a person's killer from taking any part of the decedent's estate through will or intestacy. • The Uniform Probate Code and nearly all jurisdictions have a slayer-statute provision.

SL/C. See *standby letter of credit* under LETTER OF CREDIT.

SLC. *abbr.* **1.** SPECIAL LITIGATION COMMITTEE. **2.** See *standby letter of credit* under LETTER OF CREDIT.

sleeper. A security that has strong market potential but is underpriced and lacks investor interest.

sleeping on rights. See LACHES (1).

sleeping partner. See *secret partner* under PARTNER.

sleepwalking defense. See AUTOMATISM.

sliding scale. (1842) A pricing method in which prices are determined by a person's ability to pay.

slight care. See CARE (2).

slight diligence. See DILIGENCE (2).

slight evidence. See EVIDENCE.

slight-evidence rule. (1936) **1.** The doctrine that if evidence establishes the existence of a conspiracy between at least two other people, the prosecution need only offer slight evidence of a defendant's knowing participation or intentional involvement in the conspiracy to secure a conviction. • This rule was first announced in *Tomplain v. U.S.,* 42 F.2d 202, 203 (5th Cir. 1930). In the decades after *Tomplain,* other circuits adopted the rule, but not until the 1970s did the rule become widespread. Since then, the rule has been widely criticized and, in most circuits, abolished. *See, e.g., U.S. v. Durrive,* 902 F.2d 1379, 1380 n.* (7th Cir. 1990). But its vitality remains undiminished in some jurisdictions. **2.** The doctrine that only slight evidence of a defendant's participation in a conspiracy need be offered in order to admit a coconspirator's out-of-court statement under the coconspirator exception to the hearsay rule. *See* Fed. R. Evid. 801(d)(2)(E).

slight negligence. See NEGLIGENCE.

slip-and-fall case. (1952) **1.** A lawsuit brought for injuries sustained in slipping and falling, usu. on the defendant's property. **2.** Loosely, any minor case in tort.

slip decision. See *slip opinion* under OPINION (1).

slip law. (1922) An individual pamphlet in which a single enactment is printed immediately after its passage but before its inclusion in the general laws (such as the session laws or the *U.S. Statutes at Large*). — Also termed *slip-law print.*

slip opinion. See OPINION (1).

slippery slope. (1951) A limited step that if taken now, in the view of one who warns against it, will inevitably lead to further, objectionable steps later. • The slippery-slope argument is commonly invoked in constitutional settings: allowing a small encroachment on liberty, it may be admonished, will lead to greater encroachments in the future, perhaps because it will be too hard to draw principled distinctions between the smaller one made now and the larger one proposed later. — Also termed *entering wedge; thin end of the wedge.* Cf. WEDGE PRINCIPLE; PARADE OF HORRIBLES.

"Though the metaphor of the slippery slope suggests that there's one fundamental mechanism through which the slippage happens, there are actually many different ways that decision A can make decision B more likely. Many of these ways have little to do with the mechanisms that people often think of when they hear the phrase 'slippery slope': development by analogy, by changes in people's moral and empirical attitudes, or by 'desensitization' of people to earlier decisions." Eugene Volokh, *Mechanisms of the Slippery Slope,* 116 Harv. L. Rev. 1026, 1033 (2003).

"Slippery slopes are familiar to anyone who has spent more than ten minutes arguing about anything. You suggest that people should have to register their handguns; I reply that it's a slippery slope: next thing you know, everyone's handguns will be confiscated. Someone says they favor gay marriage, and back comes the argument that it will put us on a slippery slope toward legalized polygamy. Or perhaps you favor assisted suicide, or a ban on hateful speech, and in either case your antagonist describes a 'parade of horribles' that could follow — mercy killings, or a ban on other kinds of speech. You are warned that after the first decision the camel's nose will be under the tent, or that the decision will serve as an entering wedge for a worse one, but the slippery slope will do fine as a placeholder for all those metaphors. The general structure of it is always the same. The decision at hand — 'decision one,' let us say — is acceptable (or so we may assume), but it might lead to a second decision later that sounds scarier: confiscating everyone's guns, making polygamy legal, and so forth. But of course the people who want decision one say that it by no means must lead to decision two, and they dismiss the concern about slippery slopes as a cliché." Ward Farnsworth & Eugene Volokh, "Slippery Slopes," in Farnsworth, *The Legal Analyst: A Toolkit for Thinking About the Law,* 172, 172 (2007).

slippery-slope principle. See WEDGE PRINCIPLE.

slipsheet. See *slip opinion* under OPINION (1).

slot charter. See CHARTER (8).

slot charterparty. See *slot charter* under CHARTER (8).

slough. (bef. 12c) **1.** (sloo) An arm of a river, separate from the main channel. **2.** (slow) A bog; a place filled with deep mud.

slowdown. (1937) An organized effort by workers to decrease production to pressure the employer to take some desired action.

slowdown strike. See STRIKE (1).

SLSDC. *abbr.* SAINT LAWRENCE SEAWAY DEVELOPMENT CORPORATION.

slum, *n.* (1825) **1.** An urban area where very poor people live in substandard conditions characterized by filth, squalor, and frequent violence. **2.** A house or apartment located in such a place.

slumlord, *n.* (1953) **1.** A real-property owner who rents substandard housing units in a crowded, economically depressed area and allows the units to fall into further disrepair, esp. while charging unfairly high rents. **2.** Loosely, the owner of any run-down rental property. — Also termed (BrE) *slum landlord.*

slump, *n.* (1888) A temporary downturn in the economy and particularly in the stock market, characterized by falling market prices.

slush fund. (1874) Money that is set aside for undesignated purposes, often corrupt ones, and that is not subject to financial procedures designed to ensure accountability.

SM. *abbr.* SERVICEMARK.

Small Business Administration. A federal agency that helps small businesses by assuring them a fair share of government contracts, guaranteeing their loans or lending them money directly, and providing disaster relief. • The agency was established by the Small Business Act of 1953. — Abbr. SBA.

small-business case. *Bankruptcy.* A special type of Chapter 11 case without a creditors' committee but with more than usual oversight by the U.S. trustee. • Bankruptcy Code provisions are designed to reduce the time a small-business debtor is in bankruptcy.

small-business concern. A business qualifying for an exemption from freight undercharges because it is independently owned and operated and is not dominant in its field of operation, with limited numbers of employees and business volume. 15 USCA § 632. — Abbr. SBC. — Often shortened to *small business.*

small-business corporation. See CORPORATION.

Small Business Investment Act. A 1958 federal statute under which investment companies may be formed and licensed to supply long-term equity capital to small businesses. • The statute is implemented by the Small Business Administration. 15 USCA §§ 661 et seq.

small-business investment company. (1958) A corporation created under state law to provide long-term equity capital to small businesses, as provided under the Small Business Investment Act and regulated by the Small Business Administration. 15 USCA §§ 661 et seq. — Abbr. SBIC.

small claim. A claim for damages at or below a specified monetary amount. See *small-claims court* under COURT.

small-claims court. See COURT.

small-debts court. See *small-claims court* under COURT.

small entity. (1988) *Patents.* An independent inventor, a nonprofit organization, or a company with 500 or fewer employees. • A small entity is usu. charged a lower fee for patent applications and related expenses as long as the patent rights are not assigned or licensed to a large entity (a for-profit organization with more than 500 employees). 37 CFR § 1.27.

small-estate probate. See PROBATE (1).

smallholder. Someone who farms on a piece of land that is significantly smaller than an ordinary farm.

smallholding, *n.* A very small farm.

small invention. See UTILITY MODEL.

small-loan act. (1914) A state law fixing the maximum legal interest rate and other terms on small, short-term loans by banks and finance companies.

small-loan company. See *consumer finance company* under FINANCE COMPANY.

smart card. See STORED-VALUE CARD.

smart money. See MONEY.

smash-and-grab. (1927) *Slang.* The act of breaking a window or other glass barrier in order to seize goods beyond it before fleeing. • In a smash-and-grab, the criminal usu. breaks a shop window or a glass display case with a handheld tool and seizes whatever merchandise is nearest. Cf. RAM RAID.

SMBS. *abbr.* See *stripped mortgage-backed security* under SECURITY (4).

smear campaign. The deliberate telling and repetition of untrue or distorted stories about a person in order to make others lose respect for that person.

Smith Act. A 1948 federal antisedition statute that criminalizes advocating the forcible or violent overthrow of the government. 18 USCA § 2385.

> "The Smith Act is aimed at the advocacy and teaching of concrete action for the forcible overthrow of the government, and not at advocacy of principles divorced from action. The essential distinction is that those to whom the advocacy is addressed must be urged to do something, now or in the future, rather than merely to believe in something." 70 Am. Jur. 2d *Sedition, Etc.* § 63, at 59 (1987).

Smithsonian Institution. An independent trust of the United States responsible for conducting scientific and scholarly research; publishing its results; maintaining over 140 million artifacts, works of art, and scientific specimens for study, display, and circulation throughout the country; and engaging in educational programming and international cooperative research. • It was created in 1846 to give effect to the terms of the will of a British scientist, James Smithson, who left his entire estate to the United States.

smoke bomb. See BOMB.

smoking gun. (1974) A piece of physical or documentary evidence that conclusively impeaches an adversary on an outcome-determinative issue or destroys the adversary's credibility.

Smoot–Hawley Tariff Act. *Hist.* A 1930 protectionist statute that raised tariff rates on most articles imported into the U.S., and provoked U.S. trading partners to institute comparable tariff increases. • This act is often cited as a factor in precipitating and spreading the Great Depression. The Act was named for the legislators who sponsored it, Senator Reed Smoot of Utah and Representative Willis C. Hawley of Oregon. It is sometimes called the *Grundy Tariff* for Joseph Grundy, who was president of the Pennsylvania Manufacturers Association and the chief lobbyist supporting the Act. — Also termed *Tariff Act of 1930.*

smuggled person. See PERSON (1).

smuggling, *n.* (17c) The crime of importing or exporting illegal articles or articles on which duties have not been paid. See CONTRABAND. Cf. PEOPLE-SMUGGLING; TRAFFICKING. — **smuggle,** *vb.*

▸ **alimentary-canal smuggling.** (1984) Smuggling carried out by swallowing packets, usu. balloons, filled with contraband, which stays in the smuggler's stomach or intestines during the crossing of a border.

smurf, *n.* (1985) *Slang.* **1.** Someone who participates in a money-laundering operation by making transactions of less than $10,000 (the amount that triggers federal reporting requirements) at each of many banks. • The name derives from a cartoon character of the 1980s. See ANTISTRUCTURING STATUTE. **2.** CURRENCY-TRANSACTION REPORT.

snagging list. See PUNCH LIST.

snakehead. (1965) *Slang.* **1.** A professional smuggler who is paid to bring illegal immigrants, esp. from China, into other countries. See PEOPLE-SMUGGLING. **2.** A person involved in human trafficking, esp. of victims from China. See *human trafficking* under TRAFFICKING.

SNAP. *abbr.* SUPPLEMENTAL NUTRITION ASSISTANCE PROGRAM.

sneak-and-peek search warrant. See *covert-entry search warrant* under SEARCH WARRANT.

sniffer dog. See *detection dog* under DOG (1).

sniffing dog. See *detection dog* under DOG (1).

snowmobiling while intoxicated. (1994) *Criminal law.* The criminal offense of operating a snowmobile with a blood alcohol content above a specified amount (often .08%). — Abbr. SWI.

SNS. *abbr.* STRATEGIC NATIONAL STOCKPILE.

SNT. *abbr.* See *supplemental-needs trust* under TRUST (3).

So. *abbr.* SOUTHERN REPORTER.

SOA. *abbr.* SARBANES–OXLEY ACT.

sober, *adj.* (14c) **1.** (Of a person) not under the influence of drugs or alcohol. **2.** (Of a person) regularly abstinent or moderate in the use of intoxicating liquors. **3.** (Of a situation, person, etc.) serious; grave. **4.** (Of facts, arguments, etc.) basic; unexaggerated. **5.** (Of a person) rational; having self-control.

sober house. See SOBER-LIVING RESIDENCE.

sober-living residence. (1992) A transitional form of group housing for people recovering from alcoholism or drug abuse. • The residents typically receive counseling about how to function without mind-altering substances. — Sometimes shortened to *sober living.* — Also termed *sober-living housing; sober house.*

sobrante. (1855) Surplus. • This term is sometimes found in old land grants in states that were formerly governed by Mexico.

sobrestadia. See ESTADIA.

sobriety checkpoint. (1984) A part of a roadway where police officers maintain a roadblock to stop vehicles to test drivers for intoxication or the use of illegal drugs.

sobriety test. (1931) A method of determining whether a person is intoxicated. • Common sobriety tests are coordination tests and the use of mechanical devices to measure the blood alcohol content of a person's breath sample. See BREATHALYZER; HORIZONTAL-GAZE NYSTAGMUS TEST.

▸ **field sobriety test.** (1956) A motor-skills test or tasks that a police officer may ask a driver to perform to determine whether his or her ability to drive is impaired. • The tests assess balance, coordination, and the driver's ability to divide his or her attention between two tasks. The three most common types of tests are the walk-and-turn, the one-leg stand, and the horizontal-gaze nystagmus. — Abbr. FST. Cf. *preliminary breath test* under BREATH TEST.

sobrini (sə-**brɪ**-nɪ), *n. pl.* [Latin] *Roman law.* Children of first cousins; second cousins.

soc (sohk *or* **sok),** *n.* [Law Latin] (13c) *Hist.* **1.** A liberty of exercising private jurisdiction; specif., the privilege granted to a seigniory of holding a tenant's court. **2.** The territory subject to such private jurisdiction. — Also spelled *soke; soca; sac.*

▸ **fold soc.** See FALDAGE (1).

soca (soh-kə *or* **sok-**ə), *n.* See SOC.

socage (sok-ij). (14c) *Hist.* A type of lay tenure in which a tenant held lands in exchange for providing the lord husbandry-related (rather than military) service. • Socage, the great residuary tenure, was any free tenure that did not fall within the definition of knight-service, serjeanty, or frankalmoin. Cf. *knight-service* under SERVICE (6); VILLEINAGE.

> "If they [the peasant's duties] were fixed — for instance, helping the lord with sowing or reaping at specified times — the tenure was usually called *socage.* This was originally the tenure of *socmen;* but it became . . . a generic term for all free services other than knight-service, serjeanty, or spiritual service." J.H. Baker, *An Introduction to English Legal History* 260 (3d ed. 1990).

▸ **free socage.** (16c) Socage in which the services were both certain and honorable. • By the statute 12 Car. 2, ch. 24 (1660), all the tenures by knight-service were, with minor exceptions, converted into free socage. — Also termed *free and common socage; liberum socagium.*

> "Tenure in free socage (which still subsists under the modern denomination of freehold) denotes, in its most general and extensive signification, a tenure by any certain and determinate but non-military service, as to pay a fixed money rent, or to plough the lord's land for a fixed number of days in the year. In this sense it is constantly opposed, by our ancient legal writers, to tenure by knight's service, where the service, though esteemed more honourable, was more onerous. Not being held by military service, socage tenure lacked one of the elements of a fief, but the spirit of feudalism was all-embracing and affected every tenure and every institution. Thus we find that tenure in socage, like that by knight-service, was created by words of pure donation accompanied by livery of seisin, and was liable to the obligation of fealty invariably, sometimes of homage; and was in like manner subject, but in a modified form, to many of the incidents of tenure by knight's service. Though considered less honourable than the latter, socage was practically much more beneficial, especially in its freedom from the grievous burdens of scutage, feudal wardship and marriage." Thomas Pitt Taswell-Langmead, *English Constitutional History: From the Teutonic Conquest to the Present Time* 39 (Theodore F.T. Plucknett ed., 11th ed. 1960).

▸ **villein socage (vil-**ən). (18c) Socage in which the services, though certain, were of a baser nature than those provided under free socage.

socager (sok-ij-ər). (17c) A tenant by socage; SOCMAN.

socer (**soh**-sər), *n.* [Latin] (16c) *Roman law.* A father-in-law.

social contract. (1837) The express or implied agreement between citizens and their government whereby individuals agree to surrender certain freedoms in exchange for mutual protection; an agreement forming the foundation of a political society. • The term is primarily associated with political philosophers, such as Thomas Hobbes, John Locke, and esp. Jean Jacques Rousseau, though it can be traced back to the Greek Sophists.

> "Of all theories of the origin of the state, . . . that of the social contract is the most famous. The theory appears in two principal forms — that propounded by Locke, and modified by Rousseau, and that developed by Hobbes from certain propositions advanced in 1594 by Richard Hooker in *The Laws of Ecclesiastical Polity*. In the view of Hobbes, before the evolution of political society, men recognise no law but that of the strongest, and consequently live in a state of perpetual fear. To remedy this some common authority is established." G.W. Keeton, *The Elementary Principles of Jurisprudence* 33 (2d ed. 1949).

social cost. See COST (1).

social democracy. See DEMOCRACY.

social engineering. The practice of changing laws, and esp. of changing interpretations of fundamental law, to change society in accordance with political ideals.

social-fact thesis. (1978) In legal philosophy, the positivist view that law is a social phenomenon dependent on human choices and practices, such as a lawmaker's having issued a certain command or legal officials' having accepted certain standards of legal validity for determining the outcome of legal disputes.

social-framework evidence. See EVIDENCE.

social guest. See GUEST.

social harm. See HARM.

social heredity. Collectively, the habits, knowledge, expedients, institutions, and all the aspects of culture handed down from one generation to another through education, learning, and unconscious conditioning.

> "[T]he process of social heredity differs from that of biological inheritance not only in degree but in kind. From time to time it has been suggested that culture, or certain culture traits, are transmitted in the germ plasm. This is a view which has been put forward in recent years by Bateson, Gates and Conklin among others, but the evidence to support it is completely lacking. All the evidence we possess points in fact towards the conclusion that what is termed social heredity is transmitted essentially by the processes of teaching, learning and unconscious conditioning. The evidence for this view is overwhelming and has been collected with great industry by Biffault. A simple imaginary example of McDougall will illustrate the point. He suggests that if by a magical operation all the babies born to English parents were at once exchanged for infants born to French parents, so that the latter country had been secretly peopled by pure Englishmen, and England by Frenchmen, the exchange would produce practically no effect. 'Faith comes by hearing.' A man, as Biffault concludes, will be a Buddhist in China and a Quaker in Pennsylvania, by virtue of traditional, and not of racial, heredity. He will, on principle, be a polygamist in Persia, a monogamist in modern Europe. In the Congo he will 'think cannibal thoughts.' It is more accurate, in fact, to borrow an expression of Wallas, to say that we have become biologically parasitic upon our social heritage." Huntington Cairns, *The Theory of Legal Science* 45–46 (1941).

social insurance. See INSURANCE.

socialism. (1833) A political, economic, and philosophical system that promotes government or community ownership of capital, property, and industry to equalize citizens' income, opportunities, and outcomes. Cf. CAPITALISM. — **socialist,** *n.*

▸ **state socialism.** (1851) A type of socialism that uses state-directed means, such as a progressive tax or compulsory insurance, for the benefit of all citizens.

socialization. 1. The process of making something operate in accordance with socialist principles <the socialization of healthcare>. **2.** The process by which people, esp. children of an impressionable age, are made to behave in a way that is regarded as proper in their society <the acquisition of language is an important step in children's socialization>. — **socialize,** *vb.*

social justice. See JUSTICE (4).

social restriction. (18c) **1.** The curtailment of individuals' liberties ostensibly for the general benefit. **2.** A governmental measure that has this effect.

social safety net. See SAFETY NET (2).

social science. 1. The study of people in society; specif., a branch of knowledge dealing with a particular phase or aspect of human society. **2.** One of several subjects relating to the study of people in society, examples being history, politics, sociology, sociolinguistics, and anthropology.

social security. 1. The doctrine or belief that the government should provide a minimum level of economic security and social welfare for citizens and their families. **2.** Government money that is paid to people who are out of work, ill, or old; specif., money that is paid out as part of a social-security program.

Social Security Act. A 1935 federal statute enacted in response to the Great Depression, creating a system of benefits, including old-age and survivors' benefits, and establishing the Social Security Administration. 42 USCA §§ 401–433.

Social Security Administration. A federal agency in the executive branch responsible for administering the country's retirement program and its survivors- and disability-insurance program. • The agency was established under the Social Security Act of 1935 and became independent in 1995. — Abbr. SSA.

Social Security Disability Insurance. (1960) A benefit for adults with disabilities, paid by the Social Security Administration to wage-earners who have accumulated enough quarters of coverage and then become disabled. • Benefits are also available to disabled adult children and to disabled widows and widowers of qualified wage-earners. — Abbr. SSDI.

social service. 1. A service that helps society work better; esp., organized philanthropic assistance for those most in need. — Also termed *social welfare*. **2.** In some governmental systems, a public department that helps people with family problems, money problems, medical problems, etc. **3.** The services provided by such a department.

social-service state. See STATE (1).

social study. See HOME-STUDY REPORT.

social value. See VALUE (1).

social welfare. See SOCIAL SERVICE (1).

social work. Any activity undertaken by government or by a private organization to improve the conditions of economically, physically, mentally, or socially disadvantaged people, esp. through treatment, education, and material aid. — **social worker,** *n.*

socida (sə-**sɪ**-də), *n.* [Latin] *Civil law.* A contract of bailment by which the bailee assumes the risk of loss; specif., a bailment by which a person delivers animals to another for a fee, on the condition that if any animals perish, the bailee will be liable for the loss.

societas (sə-**sɪ**-ə-tas), *n.* [Latin] *Roman law.* A partnership between two or more people agreeing to share profits and losses; a partnership contract.

> "*Societas* in its widest acceptation denotes two or more persons who unite or combine for the prosecution of a common object; in its more restricted sense it denotes a mercantile partnership . . . , the individual members being termed *Socii.*" William Ramsay, *A Manual of Roman Antiquities* 316 (Rodolfo Lanciani ed., 15th ed. 1894).

societas leonina (sə-**sɪ**-ə-tas lee-ə-**nɪ**-nə). [Latin "partnership with a lion"] (18c) *Roman law.* An illegal partnership in which a partner shares in only the losses, not the profits; a partnership in which one person takes the lion's share. — Also termed *leonina societas.*

> "But an arrangement by which one party should have *all* the gain was not recognized as binding; it was considered as contrary to the nature and purposes of the *societas,* the aim of which was gain for all the parties concerned. Such an arrangement the lawyers called *societas leonina,* a partnership like that which the lion in the fable imposed upon the cow, the sheep, and the she-goat, his associates in the chase." James Hadley, *Introduction to Roman Law* 231–32 (1881).

societas navalis (sə-**sɪ**-ə-tas nə-**vay**-lis), *n.* [Latin] *Hist.* A naval partnership; an assembly of vessels for mutual protection. — Also termed *admiralitas.*

societas universorum bonorum (sə-**sɪ**-ə-tas yoo-ni-vər-**sor**-əm bə-**nor**-əm), *n.* (1846) *Hist.* An entire partnership, including all the individual partners' property.

société (soh-see-ay-**tay**), *n.* [French] *French law.* A partnership.

▸ ***société anonyme*** (soh-see-ay-**tay** an-aw-**neem**), *n.* [French] (1845) *French law.* An incorporated joint-stock company.

▸ ***société d'acquêts*** (soh-see-ay-**tay** dah-**kay**), *n.* [French] *French law.* A written agreement between husband and wife designating community property to be only that property acquired during marriage.

▸ ***société en commandite*** (soh-see-ay-**tay** aw*n* koh-maw*n*-**deet**), *n.* [French] (1845) *French law.* A limited partnership.

▸ ***société en nom collectif*** (soh-see-ay-**tay** aw*n* naw*n* koh-lek-**teef**), *n.* [French] (1845) *French law.* A partnership in which all members are jointly and severally liable for the partnership debts; an ordinary partnership.

▸ ***société en participation*** (soh-see-ay-**tay** aw*n* pahr-tee-see-pah-**syawn**), *n.* [French] (1976) *French law.* A joint venture.

▸ ***société par actions*** (soh-see-ay-**tay** pahr ak-**syawn**), *n.* [French] (1995) *French law.* A joint-stock company.

society. (16c) **1.** A community of people, as of a country, state, or locality, with common cultures, traditions, and interests.

▸ **civil society.** (16c) The political body of a state or country; the body politic.

2. An association or company of persons (usu. unincorporated) united by mutual consent, to deliberate, determine, and act jointly for a common purpose; ORGANIZATION (1). **3.** The general love, affection, and companionship that family members share with one another.

sociolegal (**soh**-see-oh **lee**-gəl), *adj.* Of, relating to, or involving the field of study known as law and society.

sociological jurisprudence. See JURISPRUDENCE.

sociology of law. See *sociological jurisprudence* under JURISPRUDENCE.

sociopath (**soh**-see-ə-path), *n.* (1885) **1.** A person with a mental disorder characterized by an extremely antisocial personality that often leads to aggressive, perverted, or criminal behavior. • The formal psychiatric term for the mental illness from which a sociopath suffers is *antisocial personality disorder.* — Also termed *antisocial* (n.); (archaic) *psychopath.* **2.** Loosely, a person who is mentally ill or unstable. — **sociopathy,** *n.* — **sociopathic,** *adj.*

> "[T]he terms *psychopath* and *sociopath* . . . compete for clinical currency in describing individuals who flagrantly and pervasively violate the rights of others. Antisocial personality disorder is currently the official term used in *DSM-IV* (APA, 1994). However, the terms *psychopath* and *sociopath* are often bantered about to describe the people who commit heinous crimes. A writer's choice of one term versus the other is often arbitrary or a matter of preference rather than based on concrete scientific differentiations." Theodore Millon, *Personality Disorders in Modern Life* 153 (2d ed. 2004).

> "The essential feature of antisocial personality disorder is a pervasive pattern of disregard for, and violation of, the rights of others that begins in childhood or early adolescence and continues into adulthood. This pattern has also been referred to as *psychopathy, sociopathy,* or *dyssocial personality disorder.* Because deceit and manipulation are central features of antisocial personality disorder, it may be especially helpful to integrate information acquired from systematic clinical assessment with information collected from collateral sources.
>
> "For this diagnosis to be given, the individual must be at least age 18 years (Criterion B) and must have had a history of some symptoms of conduct disorder before age 15 years (Criterion C). Conduct disorder involves a repetitive and persistent pattern of behavior in which the basic rights of others or major age-appropriate societal norms or rules are violated. The specific behaviors characteristic of conduct disorder fall into one of four categories: aggression to people and animals, destruction of property, deceitfulness or theft, or serious violation of rules." American Psychiatric Association, *Diagnostic and Statistical Manual of Mental Disorders* 659 (5th ed. 2013).

socius (**soh**-shee-əs), *n.* [Latin] (15c) *Roman law.* **1.** A partner. **2.** An accomplice; an accessory. **3.** A political ally. Pl. ***socii*** (**soh**-shee-ɪ).

socius criminis (**soh**-shee-əs **krim**-ə-nis). (16c) An associate in crime; an accomplice.

sockman. See SOCMAN.

socman (**sok**-mən). (16c) *Hist.* Someone who holds land by socage tenure. — Also spelled *sokeman; sockman.* — Also termed *socager; gainor.* See SOCAGE.

socmanry (**sok**-mən-ree). (1818) *Hist.* **1.** Free tenure by socage. **2.** Land and tenements held only by simple services; land enfranchised by the sovereign from ancient demesne. • The tenants were socmen. **3.** The quality, state, or condition of being a socman.

socna (**sok**-nə). (17c) *Hist.* A privilege; a liberty; a franchise.

Socratic method. (18c) A technique of philosophical discussion — and of law-school instruction — by which the questioner (a law professor) questions one or more followers (the law students), building on each answer with another question, esp. an analogy incorporating the answer. • This method takes its name from the Greek philosopher Socrates, who lived in Athens from about 469–399 B.C. His method is a traditional one in law schools, primarily because it forces law students to think through issues rationally and deductively — a skill required in the practice of law. Most law professors who employ this method call on students randomly, an approach designed to teach students to think quickly, without stage fright. — Also termed *question-and-answer method*. See QUESTION-AND-ANSWER (3). Cf. CASEBOOK METHOD; HORNBOOK METHOD.

> "[Socrates] himself did not profess to be capable of teaching anything, except consciousness of ignorance .... He called his method of discussion (the *Socratic method*) *obstetrics* . . . because it was an art of inducing his interlocutors to develop their own ideas under a catechetical system." 5 *The Century Dictionary and Cyclopedia* 5746 (rev. ed. 1914).

socrus **(sok-rəs),** *n.* [Latin] (16c) *Roman law.* A mother-in-law.

SOCTP. *abbr.* Sex-offender counseling and treatment program.

SODDI defense (sahd-ee). (1985) *Slang.* The some-other-dude-did-it defense; a claim that somebody else committed a crime, usu. made by a criminal defendant who cannot identify the third party.

sodomy (sod-ə-mee), *n.* (13c) **1.** Oral or anal copulation between humans, esp. those of the same sex. **2.** Oral or anal copulation between a human and an animal; bestiality. — Also termed *buggery*; *crime against nature*; *abominable and detestable crime against nature*; *unnatural offense*; *unspeakable crime*; (archaically) *sodomitry*; (in Latin) *crimen innominatum*. Cf. PEDERASTY. — **sodomize,** *vb.* — **sodomitic,** *adj.* — **sodomist, sodomite,** *n.*

> "Sodomitry is a carnal copulation against nature; to wit, of man or woman in the same sex, or of either of them with beasts." Henry Finch, *Law, or a Discourse Thereof* 219 (1759).

> "Sodomy was not a crime under the common law of England but was an ecclesiastical offense only. It was made a felony by an English statute so early that it is a common-law felony in this country, and statutes expressly making it a felony were widely adopted. 'Sodomy' is a generic term including both 'bestiality' and 'buggery.'" Rollin M. Perkins & Ronald N. Boyce, *Criminal Law* 465 (3d ed. 1982).

▸ **aggravated sodomy.** (1965) Criminal sodomy that involves force or results in serious bodily injury to the victim in addition to mental injury and emotional distress. • Some laws provide that sodomy involving a minor is automatically aggravated sodomy.

SOF. *abbr.* STATUTE OF FRAUDS.

SOFA. *abbr.* STATEMENT OF FINANCIAL AFFAIRS.

soft, *adj.* **1.** (Of a market) having prices that are declining. **2.** (Of a currency) having an excess supply and therefore tending to decline in value in relation to other currencies.

soft commodity. See COMMODITY.

soft currency. See CURRENCY.

soft dollars. 1. *Securities.* The credits that brokers give their clients in return for the clients' stock-trading business. **2.** The portion of an equity investment that is tax-deductible in the first year. Cf. HARD DOLLARS.

soft goods. See GOODS.

soft intellectual property. See INTELLECTUAL PROPERTY.

soft law. (1946) **1.** Collectively, rules that are neither strictly binding nor completely lacking in legal significance. **2.** *Int'l law.* Guidelines, policy declarations, or codes of conduct that set standards of conduct but are not legally binding.

soft legal positivism. See *inclusive legal positivism* under LEGAL POSITIVISM.

soft market. See MARKET.

soft money. See MONEY.

soft positivism. See INCORPORATIONISM.

soft sell. (1955) A low-key sales practice characterized by sincerity and professionalism. Cf. HARD SELL.

software. 1. The sequence of instructions by which a computer accepts and translates input symbols, executes actions, and outputs symbols such as numbers, characters in an e-mail message, pictures in a text message, the music played on a mobile device, or GPS coordinates. **2.** More broadly, anything that can be stored electronically. Cf. HARDWARE.

> "Computer software is a set of instructions that runs on a computer. It does not consist solely of programming language. Rather, from a technical perspective, software is defined as a program and all of the associated information and materials needed to support its installation, operation, repair, and enhancement. It also includes written programs, procedures, rules, and associated documentation pertaining to the operation of a computer system, which are stored on digital medium. Indeed, because computer software instructs a computer how to perform actions, in the broadest sense, it includes everything that is not hardware. Put another way, computers are, in effect, incomplete machines when manufactured and acquire functionality only after being coupled with software." Daniel B. Garrie & Francis M. Allegra, *Plugged In: Guidebook to Software and the Law* § 2.1, at 45–46 (2013).

software-based invention. See INVENTION.

software beta-test agreement. See BETA-TEST AGREEMENT.

Software Directive. See DIRECTIVE ON THE LEGAL PROTECTION OF COMPUTER PROGRAMS.

Software Patent Institute. A Kansas-based nonprofit institute that collects and organizes nonpatented prior-art software references in a database for patent researchers.

so help me God. (16c) The final words of the common oath. • The phrase is a translation, with a change to first person, of the Latin phrase *ita te Deus adjuvet* "so help you God." See ITA TE DEUS ADJUVET.

soil bank. (1955) A federal agricultural program in which farmers are paid to not grow crops or to grow noncommercial vegetation, to preserve the quality of the soil and stabilize commodity prices by avoiding surpluses. See LAND BANK (2).

Soil Conservation Service. See NATURAL RESOURCES CONSERVATION SERVICE.

soit **(swah).** [Law French] Be; let it be. • This term was used in English-law phrases, esp. to indicate the will of the sovereign in a formal communication with Parliament.

soit baile aux commons (swah **bayl** oh **kom**-ənz). [Law French] Let it be delivered to the commons. • This is an indorsement on a bill sent to the House of Commons.

soit baile aux seigneurs (swah **bayl** oh sen-**yərz**). [Law French] Let it be delivered to the lords. • This is an indorsement on a bill sent to the House of Lords.

soit droit fait al partie (swah **droyt** [*or* **drwah**] **fayt** [*or* **fay**] ahl pahr-**tee**). [Law French] *Hist.* Let right be done to the party. • This phrase is written on a petition of right and subscribed by the Crown.

soit fait comme il est desire (swah **fay**[**t**] **kawm** eel ay day-zeer-**ay**). [Law French] Let it be as it is desired. • This is the phrase indicating royal assent to a private act of Parliament.

sojourn (**soh**-jərn), *n.* (14c) A temporary stay by someone who is not just passing through a place but is also not a permanent resident <she set up a three-month sojourn in France>. — **sojourn** (**soh**-jərn *or* soh-**jərn**), *vb.* — **sojourner** (**soh**-jər-nər *or* soh-**jər**-nər), *n.*

soke. See SOC.

sokeman. See SOCMAN.

soke-reeve (**sohk**-reev). (13c) *Hist.* The lord's rent-collector in the soc.

solar (soh-**lahr**). (1817) *Hist. Spanish & Mexican law.* A residential lot; a small, privately owned tract of land. • This term is sometimes found (esp. in the plural form *solares*) in old land grants in states that were formerly Spanish provinces or governed by Mexico.

solar day. See DAY.

solar easement. See EASEMENT.

solarium (sə-**lair**-ee-əm), *n.* [Latin fr. *solum* "soil"] *Roman law.* Rent paid for building on public land; ground rent.

solar month. See MONTH (4).

sola superviventia (**soh**-lə soo-pər-vI-**ven**-shee-ə). [Law Latin] *Hist.* By mere survivance.

solatium (sə-**lay**-shee-əm), *n.* [Latin "solace"] (1817) *Scots law.* Compensation; esp., damages allowed for hurt feelings or grief, as distinguished from damages for physical injury.

Soldiers' and Sailors' Civil Relief Act. A 1940 federal statute that protects the civil rights of those in military service, as by modifying their civil liability, placing limits on interest rates charged against their obligations, and prescribing specific procedures for claims made against them. 50 USCA app. §§ 501 et seq. — Abbr. SSCRA.

soldier's and sailor's will. See *soldier's will* under WILL.

soldier's will. See WILL.

sold note. 1. See NOTE (1). **2.** See CONFIRMATION SLIP.

sole-actor doctrine. (1923) *Agency.* The rule charging a principal with knowledge of the agent's actions, even if the agent acted fraudulently.

sole and separate use. See *entire use* under USE (4).

sole and unconditional owner. See OWNER.

sole arbitrator. See ARBITRATOR.

sole cause. See CAUSE (1).

sole corporation. See CORPORATION.

sole custody. See CUSTODY (2).

sole discretion. See DISCRETION (2).

solemn admission. See *judicial admission* under ADMISSION (1).

solemnitas attachiamentorum (sə-**lem**-ni-tas ə-tach-ee-ə-men-**tor**-əm). [Law Latin] (1848) *Hist.* The formality required in issuing attachments of property.

solemnity (sə-**lem**-nə-tee). (14c) **1.** A formality (such as a ceremony) required by law to validate an agreement or action <solemnity of marriage>. **2.** The state of seriousness or solemn respectfulness or observance <solemnity of contract>.

solemnity of contract. (1812) The concept that two people may enter into any contract they wish and that the resulting contract is enforceable if formalities are observed and no defenses exist.

solemnization. (15c) The performance of a formal ceremony (such as a marriage ceremony) before witnesses, as distinguished from a clandestine ceremony.

solemnize (**sol**-əm-nIz), *vb.* (14c) To enter into (a marriage, contract, etc.) by a formal act, usu. before witnesses.

solemn oath. See *corporal oath* under OATH.

solemn occasion. In some states, the serious and unusual circumstance in which the supreme court is constitutionally permitted to render advisory opinions to the remaining branches of government, as when the legislature doubts the legality of proposed legislation and a determination must be made to allow the legislature to exercise its functions. • Some factors that have been considered in determining whether a solemn occasion exists include whether an important question of law is presented, whether the question is urgent, whether the matter is ripe for an opinion, and whether the court has enough time to consider the question.

solemn war. See WAR (1).

sole practitioner. (1946) A lawyer who practices law without any partners or associates. — Often shortened to *solo.* — Also termed *solo practitioner.*

sole proprietorship. (1860) **1.** A business in which one person owns all the assets, owes all the liabilities, and operates in his or her personal capacity. **2.** Ownership of such a business. — Also termed *individual proprietorship.*

sole selling agency. See *exclusive agency* under AGENCY (1).

sole-source rule. (2009) In a false-advertising action at common law, the principle that a plaintiff may not recover unless it can demonstrate that it has a monopoly in the sale of goods possessing the advertised trait, because only then is it clear that the plaintiff would be harmed by the defendant's advertising.

sole use. See *entire use* under USE (4).

solicitation, *n.* (16c) **1.** The act or an instance of requesting or seeking to obtain something; a request or petition <a solicitation for volunteers to handle at least one pro bono case per year>. **2.** The criminal offense of urging, advising, commanding, or otherwise inciting another to commit a crime <convicted of solicitation of murder>. • Solicitation is an inchoate offense distinct from the solicited crime. Under the Model Penal Code, a defendant is guilty of solicitation even if the command or urging was not actually communicated to the solicited person, as long as it was designed to be communicated. Model Penal Code

§ 5.02(2). — Also termed *criminal solicitation*; *incitement*. Cf. ATTEMPT (2). **3.** An offer to pay or accept money in exchange for sex <the prostitute was charged with solicitation>. — Also termed *soliciting*. Cf. PATRONIZING A PROSTITUTE. **4.** An attempt or effort to gain business <the attorney's solicitations took the form of radio and television ads>. • The Model Rules of Professional Conduct place certain prohibitions on lawyers' direct solicitation of potential clients. **5.** *Securities*. A request for a proxy; a request to execute, not execute, or revoke a proxy; the furnishing of a form of proxy; or any other communication to security holders under circumstances reasonably calculated to result in the procurement, withholding, or revocation of a proxy. — **solicit,** *vb.*

solicitation for bids. See INVITATION TO NEGOTIATE.

solicitation of a bribe. (1823) The crime of asking or enticing another to commit bribery. 18 USCA § 201. See BRIBERY.

solicitation of chastity. (17c) *Hist.* The act of trying to persuade another person to engage in unlawful sexual intercourse.

solicitee. (1887) Someone who is solicited. See SOLICITATION.

soliciting, *n.* See SOLICITATION (3).

soliciting agent. See AGENT.

solicitor. (15c) **1.** Someone who seeks business or contributions from others; an advertiser or promoter. **2.** Someone who conducts matters on another's behalf; an agent or representative. **3.** The chief law officer of a governmental body or a municipality. **4.** In the United Kingdom, a lawyer who consults with clients and prepares legal documents but is not generally heard in High Court or (in Scotland) Court of Session unless specially licensed. Cf. BARRISTER. **5.** See *special agent* under INSURANCE AGENT. **6.** A prosecutor (in some jurisdictions, such as South Carolina).

▸ **duty solicitor.** A solicitor in private practice who can be called to a police station or to a magistrate's court to represent pro bono a person suspected of or charged with a crime when the person cannot afford to hire a solicitor. — Also termed (in Canada) *duty counsel*. Cf. PUBLIC DEFENDER.

solicitor general. (*usu. cap.*) (17c) The second-highest-ranking legal officer in a government (after the attorney general); esp., the chief courtroom lawyer for the executive branch. • On the use of *General* as a title in reference to the solicitor general, see ATTORNEY GENERAL. — Abbr. SG. Pl. **solicitors general.**

> "By [federal] law, only the Solicitor General or his designee can conduct and argue before the Supreme Court cases 'in which the United States is interested.' Thus, if a trial court appoints a special, independent prosecutor in order to prosecute a criminal contempt of court, that court-appointed special prosecutor cannot represent the United States in seeking Supreme Court review of any lower court decision unless the Solicitor General authorizes the filing of such a petition. . . . Although the Solicitor General serves at the pleasure of the President, by tradition the Solicitor General also acts with independence. Thus, if the Solicitor General does not believe in the legal validity of the arguments that the government wants presented, he will refuse to sign the brief. In close cases the Solicitor General will sign the brief but tag on a disclaimer that has become known as 'tying a tin can.' The disclaimer would state, for example, 'The foregoing is presented as the position of the Internal Revenue Service.' The justices would then know that the Solicitor General, although not withholding a legal argument, was not personally sponsoring or adopting the particular legal position." Ronald D. Rotunda & John E. Nowak, *Treatise on Constitutional Law* § 2.2, at 86–88 (3d ed. 1999).

solicitor's hypothec. See HYPOTHEC.

solidarity. (1875) **1.** The quality, state, or condition of being jointly and severally liable (as for a debt); the relationship between parties to an obligation by several debtors, any one of whom is liable for the whole. **2.** The joint right of several creditors, any one of whom may collect the debt, thereby acquitting all the others. See *solidary obligation* under OBLIGATION. Cf. CORREALITY. — **solidarily,** *adv.*

solidary (**sol**-ə-der-ee), *adj.* (1818) (Of a liability or obligation) joint and several. See JOINT AND SEVERAL.

> "It is a single debt of £100 owing by each of them, in such fashion that each of them may be compelled to pay the whole of it, but that when it is once paid by either of them, both are discharged from it. Obligations of this description may be called solidary, since in the language of Roman law, each of the debtors is bound *in solidum* instead of *pro parte*; that is to say, for the whole, and not for a proportionate part. A solidary obligation, therefore, may be defined as one in which two or more debtors owe the same thing to the same creditor." John Salmond, *Jurisprudence* 462–63 (Glanville L. Williams ed., 10th ed. 1947).

> "The concept of solidary obligations refers to a situation where several debtors are bound to render one and the same performance to a creditor with the effect that the creditor can claim it from any one of them until full performance has been received. Performance by one of the debtors will discharge the others. All European legal systems have an institution that exhibits these features. While English law speaks of joint (and several) liability, the majority of the continental legal systems use the term 'solidarity' . . . . Some countries even have two forms of this institution (eg *solidarité* and *obligation in solidum* under French law; or 'joint liability' and 'joint and several liability' under English law). The rules on solidarity determine when solidary obligations arise and regulate both the external relationship between the creditor and the debtors and the internal relationship between the debtors themselves. The basic structures of these rules demonstrate remarkable similarities due to a common historical tradition: rules about different kinds of solidary obligations can be found as early as in the Roman sources. They were developed into a unitary institution of solidarity under the *ius commune*, which in turn greatly influenced the various national legal codes. Even the English law of joint and several obligations does not fundamentally differ from the continental European rules." Sonja Meier, "Solidary Obligations," in 2 *The Max Planck Encyclopedia of European Private Law* 1573, 1573 (Jürgen Basedow et al. eds., 2012).

solidary liability. See LIABILITY.

solidary obligation. See OBLIGATION.

solidum (**sol**-ə-dəm), *n.* [Latin] **1.** *Roman law.* A whole; an undivided thing. See SOLIDARY. **2.** *Scots law.* A complete sum.

solid waste. See WASTE (2).

solinum (sə-**lı**-nəm), *n.* [Law Latin] *Hist.* **1.** Slightly less than two and a half plowlands. **2.** A single plowland.

solitary confinement. (17c) Separate confinement that gives a prisoner extremely limited access to other people; esp., the complete isolation of a prisoner.

sollertia (sə-**lər**-shee-ə). [Latin] *Hist.* Shrewdness; resourcefulness; cleverness.

solo, *n.* See SOLE PRACTITIONER.

solo animo (**soh**-loh **an**-ə-moh). [Latin] *Hist.* By mere intention.

Solomon Amendment. A federal law authorizing the Secretary of Defense to withhold federal funding from schools that do not allow military recruiters on their campuses or deny access equal to that enjoyed by other types of recruiters. • The amendment is named for Representative Gerald B.H. Solomon of New York. 10 USCA § 983.

Solomonic, *adj.* **1.** Of, relating to, or involving Solomon, king of Israel (ca. 970–931 B.C.). **2.** Characterized by wisdom, esp. in making difficult decisions; sagacious; sage. See JUDGMENT OF SOLOMON; SPLIT THE BABY.

solo practitioner. See SOLE PRACTITIONER.

solum italicum (**soh**-ləm ɪ-**tal**-ə-kəm). [Latin "Italian land"] (1864) *Roman law.* Land in Italy (an extension of the old *ager Romanus*) needing, for full ownership to pass, to be transferred by formal methods, such as *mancipatio* or *cession in jure.* Cf. SOLUM PROVINCIALE.

solum provinciale (**soh**-ləm prə-vin-shee-**ay**-lee). [Latin "provincial land"] (1869) *Roman law.* Provincial land ultimately held by the Emperor or state, with private holders having only, in theory, a possessory title without the right to transfer the property by formal methods, as distinguished from *solum italicum.* • Justinian abolished all distinctions between the two, allowing all land to be conveyed by *traditio.* Cf. SOLUM ITALICUM.

> "Ownership of provincial land. The *dominium* of this was in Caesar or the *populus* according as it was an imperial or a senatorial province . . . . The holders were practically owners, but as they were not *domini* formal methods of transfer were not applicable. The holdings were however transferable informally . . . . The case disappeared when Justinian abolished the distinction between Italic and provincial land. Not all land in the provinces was *solum provinciale*: many provincial communities were given *ius italicum*, the chief result being that the land was in the *dominium* of the holder and not of the State, so that it could be transferred and claimed at law by civil law methods." W.W. Buckland, *A Text-book of Roman Law from Augustus to Justinian* 190 (Peter Stein ed., 3d ed. 1963).

solus (**soh**-ləs), *adj. Latin.* Alone.

solus cum sola in loco suspecto (**soh**-ləs kəm **soh**-lə in **loh**-koh sə-**spek**-toh). [Law Latin] (1843) *Hist.* A man alone with a woman in a suspicious place.

solutio (sə-**loo**-shee-oh), *n.* [Latin "payment"] *Roman law.* Performance of an obligation; satisfaction. Pl. ***solutiones*** (sə-loo-shee-**oh**-neez).

solutio indebiti (sə-**loo**-shee-oh in-**deb**-ə-tɪ). [Latin "payment of what is not owing"] (18c) *Roman law.* Payment of a nonexistent debt. • If the payment was made in error, the recipient had a duty to give back the money.

solutio obligationis (sə-**loo**-shee-oh ob-li-gay-shee-**oh**-nis). (1879) *Roman law.* The unfastening of a legal bond, so that a party previously bound need not perform any longer. Cf. VINCULUM JURIS.

solutus (sə-**loo**-təs), *adj.* [Latin fr. *solvere* "to loose"] **1.** *Roman law.* Set free; released from obligation or confinement. **2.** *Scots law.* Purged, esp. in reference to counsel.

solvabilité (sawl-vah-beel-ee-**tay**), *n.* [French] *French law.* Solvency.

solve et repete (**sol**-vee et **rep**-ə-tee). [Latin] *Hist.* Pay and seek again.

solvency, *n.* (18c) The ability to pay debts as they come due. Cf. INSOLVENCY. — **solvent,** *adj.*

solvendi causa (sol-**ven**-dɪ **kaw**-zə). [Latin] *Hist.* For the sake of discharging.

solvendo esse (sol-**ven**-doh **es**-ee). [Latin] *Hist.* To be solvent; to be able to pay an obligation.

solvendum in futuro (sol-**ven**-dəm in f[y]oo-**t[y]oor**-oh). [Latin "to be paid in the future"] (1810) *Hist.* (Of a debt) due now but payable in the future.

solvent, *adj.* Having enough money to pay one's debts; capable of paying all legal debts.

solvent abuse. The act of breathing in of gases from glues or similar substances in order to become stupefied or intoxicated, esp. when the perpetrator has become dependent on this act as a habit.

solvent debtor. See DEBTOR.

solvere (**sol**-və-ree), *vb.* [Latin "to unbind"] *Roman law.* To pay (a debt); to release (a person) from an obligation.

solvere poenas (səl-**veer**-ee **pee**-nəs). [Latin] *Hist.* To pay the penalty.

solvit (**sol**-vit). [Latin] He paid; paid.

solvit ad diem (**sol**-vit ad **dɪ**-əm). [Law Latin "he paid on the day"] (17c) *Hist.* In a debt action, a plea that the defendant paid the debt on the due date.

solvit ante diem (**sol**-vit **an**-tee **dɪ**-əm). [Law Latin "he paid before the day"] (18c) *Hist.* In a debt action, a plea that the defendant paid the money before the due date.

solvit post diem (**sol**-vit pohst **dɪ**-əm). [Law Latin "he paid after the day"] (18c) *Hist.* In a debt action on a bond, a plea that the defendant paid the debt after the due date but before commencement of the lawsuit.

somnambulism (sahm-**nam**-byə-liz-əm). (18c) Sleepwalking. • Generally, a person will not be held criminally responsible for an act performed while in this state. See AUTOMATISM.

somnolentia (sahm-nə-**len**-shee-ə). (1879) **1.** The state of drowsiness. **2.** A condition of incomplete sleep resembling drunkenness, during which part of the faculties are abnormally excited while the others are dormant; the combined condition of sleeping and wakefulness producing a temporary state of involuntary intoxication. • To the extent that it destroys moral agency, somnolentia may be a defense to a criminal charge.

son. (bef. 12c) **1.** A person's male child, whether natural or adopted; a male of whom one is the parent. **2.** An immediate male descendant. **3.** *Slang.* Any young male person.

son assault demesne (sohn ə-**sawlt** di-**mayn**). [French "his own assault"] (17c) The plea of self-defense in a tort action, by which the defendant alleges that the plaintiff originally engaged in an assault and that the defendant used only the force necessary to repel the plaintiff's assault and to protect person and property. See SELF-DEFENSE (1).

Sonderrecht. [German] Privilege.

son-in-law. (14c) The husband of one's daughter.

Sonny Bono Copyright Term Extension Act. *Copyright.* A federal law extending the copyright term by 20 years for all works published in the United States after January 1, 1978, and settling the copyright term for works created before 1978 as 95 years from the original copyright date. • Before the extension, the copyright term was the life of the author plus 50 years. Pub. L. 105-298, 112 Stat. 2827.

The statute was named in honor of congressman Sonny Bono, who had previously suggested similar legislation but died nine months before this Act was ultimately passed. — Abbr. CTEA. — Also termed *Copyright Term Extension Act*; *Sonny Bono Act*; (derisively) *Mickey Mouse Protection Act*.

Son of Sam law. (1981) A state statute that prohibits a convicted criminal from profiting by selling his or her story rights to a publisher or filmmaker. • State law usu. authorizes prosecutors to seize royalties from a convicted criminal and to place the money in an escrow account for the crime victim's benefit. This type of law was first enacted in New York in 1977, in response to the lucrative book deals that publishers offered David Berkowitz, the serial killer who called himself "Son of Sam." In 1992, the U.S. Supreme Court declared New York's Son-of-Sam law unconstitutional as a content-based speech regulation, prompting many states to amend their laws in an attempt to avoid constitutionality problems. *Simon & Schuster, Inc. v. New York State Crime Victims Bd.*, 502 U.S. 105, 112 S.Ct. 501 (1992).

sonticus (**sahn**-ti-kəs), *n.* [Latin] *Roman law.* Serious; more than trivial. • The term was used in the Twelve Tables to refer to a serious illness (*morbus sonticus*) that gave a defendant a valid reason not to appear in court.

***Sony* doctrine.** See COMMERCIALLY SIGNIFICANT NONINFRINGING USE.

so-ordered subpoena. See SUBPOENA.

sophisticated investor. See INVESTOR.

sophistry (**sof**-i-stree), *n.* (14c) **1.** The use of plausible but fallacious arguments; ingenious argumentative trickery; CASUISTRY (2). **2.** The habit or practice of using plausible but fallacious arguments; habitual, esp. professional, speciousness.

soror (**sor**-or), *n.* [Latin] *Roman law.* A sister.

sororicide (sə-**ror**-ə-sɪd). (17c) **1.** The act of killing one's own sister. **2.** Someone who kills his or her sister. Cf. FRATRICIDE. — **sororicidal,** *adj.*

sorority (sə-**ror**-i-tee). [Latin *sororitas* "sisterhood"] **1.** The quality, state, or condition of being sisters, or of being a sister; sisterliness. **2.** A body of women associated for some common interest <a charitable sorority>. **3.** Women of the same class, profession, occupation, or taste <the judicial sorority or troika on the Supreme Court>. Cf. FRATERNITY.

sors (sors), *n.* [Latin] **1.** *Roman law.* A lot; a chance. **2.** *Scots law.* A partnership's capital. **3.** *Hist.* Principal, as distinguished from interest. **4.** *Hist.* Something recovered in an action, as distinguished from mere costs.

sortitio (sor-**tish**-ee-oh), *n.* [Latin fr. *sortiri* "to cast lots"] *Roman law.* The drawing of lots, used, for example, in selecting judges for a criminal trial. — Also termed (in English) *sortition*; *sortilege.*

SOT. *abbr.* See *service-occupation tax* under TAX.

SOTP. *abbr.* Sex-offender treatment program.

soul scot. See MORTUARY (3).

soul shot. See MORTUARY (3).

sound, *adj.* (12c) **1.** (Of health, mind, etc.) good; whole; free from disease or disorder. **2.** (Of property) good; marketable. **3.** (Of discretion) exercised equitably under the circumstances. — **soundness,** *n.*

sound, *vb.* (18c) **1.** To be actionable (in) <her claims for physical injury sound in tort, not in contract>. **2.** To be recoverable (in) <his tort action sounds in damages, not in equitable relief>.

sound disposing mind. See *testamentary capacity* under CAPACITY (3)

sound health. *Insurance.* **1.** A policy applicant's good mental and physical condition; a state of health characterized by a lack of grave impairment or disease, or of any ailment that seriously affects the applicant's health. **2.** GOOD HEALTH.

sound judgment. See *good judgment* under JUDGMENT (1).

sound mind. (16c) **1.** MIND (2). **2.** See *testamentary capacity* under CAPACITY (3). — Also termed *sound disposing mind.* Cf. NON COMPOS MENTIS.

Sound Recording Amendment of 1972. A Copyright Act of 1909 amendment that established copyright protection for sound recordings.

source, *n.* (14c) The originator or primary agent of an act, circumstance, or result <she was the source of the information> <the side business was the source of income>.

source code. (1965) *Copyright.* The nonmachine language used by a computer programmer to create a program. • If it is not included with the software sold to the public, source code is protected by trade secret laws as well as copyright and patent laws. Source code may be deposited with the U.S. Copyright Office but, because of the need to protect a trade secret, and because a skilled programmer could figure out how to duplicate the source code's functions without necessarily copying it, strategic parts may be blacked out. Cf. OBJECT CODE.

source of law. (1892) Something (such as a constitution, treaty, statute, or custom) that provides authority for legislation and for judicial decisions; a point of origin for law or legal analysis. — Also termed *fons juris.*

> "The term 'sources of law' is ordinarily used in a much narrower sense than will be attributed to it here. In the literature of jurisprudence the problem of 'sources' relates to the question: Where does the judge obtain the rules by which to decide cases? In this sense, among the sources of law will be commonly listed: statutes, judicial precedents, custom, the opinion of experts, morality, and equity. In the usual discussions these various sources of law are analyzed and some attempt is made to state the conditions under which each can appropriately be drawn upon in the decision of legal controversies. Curiously, when a legislature is enacting law we do not talk about the 'sources' from which it derives its decision as to what the law shall be, though an analysis in these terms might be more enlightening than one directed toward the more restricted function performed by judges. Our concern here will be with 'sources' in a much broader sense than is usual in the literature of jurisprudence. Our interest is not so much in sources of laws, as in sources of law. From whence does the law generally draw not only its content but its force in men's lives?" Lon L. Fuller, *Anatomy of the Law* 69 (1968).

> "In the context of legal research, the term 'sources of law' can refer to three different concepts which should be distinguished. One, sources of law can refer to the origins of legal concepts and ideas. . . . Two, sources of law can refer to governmental institutions that formulate legal rules. . . . Three, sources of law can refer to the published manifestations of the law. The books, computer databases, microforms, optical disks, and other media that contain legal information are all sources of law." J. Myron Jacobstein &

Roy M. Mersky, *Fundamentals of Legal Research* 1-2 (5th ed. 1990).

South Eastern Reporter. A set of regional lawbooks, part of the West Group's National Reporter System, containing every published appellate decision from Georgia, North Carolina, South Carolina, Virginia, and West Virginia, from 1887 to date. • The first series ran from 1886 to 1939. The second series is the current one. — Abbr. S.E.; S.E.2d.

Southern Common Market. See MERCOSUR.

Southern Reporter. A set of regional lawbooks, part of the West Group's National Reporter System, containing every published appellate decision from Alabama, Florida, Louisiana, and Mississippi, from 1887 to date. • The first series ran from 1886 to 1941. The second series ran from 1941 to 2009. The third series is the current one. — Abbr. So.; So.2d; So.3d.

South Western Reporter. A set of regional lawbooks, part of the West Group's National Reporter System, containing every published appellate decision from Arkansas, Kentucky, Missouri, Tennessee, and Texas, from 1886 to date. • The first series ran from 1886 to 1928. The second series ran from 1928 to 1999. The third series is the current one. — Abbr. S.W.; S.W.2d; S.W.3d.

sovereign, *adj.* (17c) (Of a state) characteristic of or endowed with supreme authority <sovereign nation> <sovereign immunity>.

sovereign, *n.* (13c) **1.** A person, body, or state vested with independent and supreme authority. **2.** The ruler of an independent state. — Also spelled *sovran.* See SOVEREIGNTY.

sovereign equality. (1894) *Int'l law.* The principle that countries have the right to enjoy territorial integrity and political independence, free from intervention by other countries,. • The United Nations "is based on the principle of the sovereign equality of all its Members." UN Charter art. 2, ¶ 1.

sovereign immunity. See IMMUNITY (1).

sovereign people. (17c) The political body consisting of the collective number of citizens and qualified electors who possess the powers of sovereignty and exercise them through their chosen representatives.

sovereign political power. See POLITICAL POWER.

sovereign power. (15c) **1.** The power to make and enforce laws. **2.** See *sovereign political power* under POLITICAL POWER.

sovereign right. (16c) A unique right possessed by a state or its agencies that enables it to carry out its official functions for the public benefit, as distinguished from certain proprietary rights that it may possess like any other private person.

sovereign state. (17c) **1.** A state that possesses an independent existence, being complete in itself, without being merely part of a larger whole to whose government it is subject. **2.** A political community whose members are bound together by the tie of common subjection to some central authority, whose commands those members must obey. — Also termed *independent state.* Cf. *client state, nonsovereign state* under STATE (1).

"The essence of statehood is sovereignty, the principle that each nation answers only to its own domestic order and is not accountable to a larger international community, save only to the extent it has consented to do so. Sovereign states are thus conceived as hermetically sealed units, atoms that spin around an international orbit, sometimes colliding, sometimes cooperating, but always separate and apart." David J. Bederman, *International Law Frameworks* 50 (2001).

▸ **part-sovereign state.** (1895) A political community in which part of the powers of external sovereignty are exercised by the home government, and part are vested in or controlled by some other political body or bodies. • Such a state is not fully independent because by the conditions of its existence it is not allowed full freedom of action in external affairs.

sovereignty (sahv-[ə-]rin-tee). (14c) **1.** Supreme dominion, authority, or rule.

"The principle of legal sovereignty is an abstraction from a number of relevant rules: (1) Without its consent, a subject of international law is bound by applicable rules of universal or general international customary law and general principles of law recognised by civilised nations. (2) Additional international obligations may be imposed on any subject of international law only with its consent. (3) Unless the territorial jurisdiction of a State is excluded or limited by rules of international law, its exercise is exclusively the concern of the State in question. (4) Subjects of international law may *claim* potential jurisdiction over persons or things outside the territorial jurisdiction. In the absence of permissive rules to the contrary, however, they may actually *exercise* such jurisdiction in concrete instances only within their territories. (5) Unless authorised by permissive rules to the contrary, intervention by subjects of international law in one another's sphere of exclusive domestic jurisdiction constitutes a breach of international law." Georg Schwarzenberger, *A Manual of International Law* 65 (5th ed. 1967).

"For the practical purposes of an international lawyer, sovereignty is not a metaphysical concept, nor is it part of the essence of statehood; it is merely a term which designates an aggregate of particular and very extensive claims that states habitually make for themselves in their relations with other states. To the extent that sovereignty has come to imply that there is something inherent in the nature of states that makes it impossible for them to be subjected to law, it is a false doctrine which the facts of international relations do not support. But to the extent that it reminds us that the challenge of subjection of states to law is an aim as yet only very imperfectly realized, it is a doctrine which we cannot afford to disregard." Andrew Clapham, *Brierly's Law of Nations: An Introduction to the Role of International Law in International Relations* 46 (7th ed. 2012).

"In origins and evolution, sovereignty is definitely a Western concept, and it was not shared by other regions until the twentieth century. (Certain non-Western parallels do exist, however.) In contemporary discussion, the concept of sovereignty is accepted as an indispensable term in both academic and diplomatic discussions of political life throughout the world. Its importance is confirmed in Marxist, realist, and liberal political discourse, but the range of usage varies widely, reflecting differences in ideology and political priorities. The very centrality of sovereignty ensures its contested character. In each setting, meanings are attributed to sovereignty that accord with the interpreter's project. There is little neutral ground when it comes to sovereignty." Richard Falk, "Sovereignty," in 2 *The Oxford Companion to Comparative Politics* 398, 398 (Joel Krieger ed., 2013).

▸ **external sovereignty.** (18c) The power of dealing on a country's behalf with other national governments.

▸ **internal sovereignty.** (18c) The power enjoyed by a governmental entity of a sovereign state, including affairs within its own territory and powers related to the exercise of external sovereignty.

▸ **popular sovereignty.** (17c) A system of government in which policy choices reflect the preferences of the majority of citizens.

> "Popular sovereignty, at bottom, is an identification, contrary to fact, of the government and the people. Now 'We the people' do not govern ourselves; we have established a government to do it, and it does it. If the people really governed, it would, of course, be both absurd and impossible to try to limit governmental action by any law. The notion that our government *is* the people, therefore naturally leads to the conclusion that the government has no limits. The logic is sound, the premise is utterly untrue. This unwarranted belief, necessarily destructive of all constitutionalism and of all bills of rights, has been fostered by a strange unhistorical conception of 'sovereignty.' We are only able to accept 'popular' sovereignty, because of our peculiar notions of what sovereignty itself is. Blind followers of the blind have persuaded us — mostly lawyers who have taken Blackstone literally and uncritically — that sovereignty is might, not right, and that this might could not conceivably be the might of any true sovereign if it had any legal limits whatsoever. These men have hopelessly confused authority with power, and apparently have been entirely oblivious of the fact that their conception of political supremacy, fathered by Hobbes and nurtured by John Austin, is completely subversive of the constitutional system under which we all live and to which they themselves have usually paid the most extravagant lip service." C.H. McIlwain, *Constitutionalism & the Changing World* 291–92 (1939).

▸ **state sovereignty.** See STATE SOVEREIGNTY.

2. The supreme political authority of an independent state. **3.** The state itself.

> "It is well to [distinguish] the senses in which the word Sovereignty is used. In the ordinary popular sense it means Supremacy, the right to demand obedience. Although the idea of actual power is not absent, the prominent idea is that of some sort of title to exercise control. An ordinary layman would call that person (or body of persons) Sovereign in a State who is obeyed because he is acknowledged to stand at the top, whose will must be expected to prevail, who can get his own way, and make others go his, because such is the practice of the country. Etymologically the word of course means merely superiority, and familiar usage applies it in monarchies to the monarch, because he stands first in the State, be his real power great or small." James Bryce, *Studies in History and Jurisprudence* 504–05 (1901).

sovereign wealth fund. See FUND.

sovran. See SOVEREIGN.

SOW. *abbr.* STATEMENT OF WORK.

SOX. *abbr.* SARBANES–OXLEY ACT.

SOX Act claim. See SARBANES–OXLEY ACT CLAIM.

s.p. *abbr.* **1.** SINE PROLE. **2.** Same principle; same point. • This notation, when inserted between two citations, indicates that the second involves the same principles as the first.

space arbitrage. See ARBITRAGE.

space charter. See CHARTER (8).

space charterparty. See *space charter* under CHARTER (8).

spacial jurisdiction. See JURISDICTION.

spado (**spay**-doh), *n.* [Latin] (15c) *Roman law.* **1.** A eunuch. **2.** Someone who is incapable of sexual intercourse by reason of impotence. Pl. ***spadones*** (spə-**doh**-neez).

spam. (1994) Unsolicited commercial e-mail.

spanking, *n.* The act of hitting a child on or near the buttocks with the hand, a belt, a hairbrush, or the like, usu. as means of corporal punishment. See *corporal punishment* under PUNISHMENT.

sparsim (**spahr**-sim). [Latin] (16c) *Hist.* Scattered; here and there. • This term was used in several situations — for example, when an action to recover for waste not only when the injury was complete, but also when the injury was partial or scattered.

> "And if waste be done *sparsim*, or here and there, all over a wood, the whole wood shall be recovered; or if in several rooms of a house, the whole house shall be forfeited; because it is impracticable for the reversioner to enjoy only the identical places wasted, when lying interspersed with the other. But if waste be done only in one end of a wood (or perhaps in one room of a house) if that can be conveniently separated from the rest, that part only is the *locus vastatus*, or thing wasted, and that only shall be forfeited to the reversioner." 2 William Blackstone, *Commentaries on the Laws of England* 283–84 (1766).

spatae placitum (**spay**-tee **plas**-ə-təm), *n.* [Latin "the plea of the sword] *Hist.* During the reign of Henry II, a court providing swift justice in military matters.

SPD. *abbr.* SUMMARY PLAN DESCRIPTION.

SPDA. *abbr.* See *single-premium deferred annuity* under ANNUITY.

SPE. *abbr.* SPECIAL-PURPOSE ENTITY.

speakeasy. In the 1920s and 1930s, an American place where, despite Prohibition, alcohol could be purchased.

speaker. (14c) **1.** Someone who speaks or makes a speech <the slander claim was viable only against the speaker>. **2.** The presiding officer of a large deliberative assembly, esp. a legislature's more numerous house, such as the House of Representatives <Speaker of the House>. See CHAIR (1).

speaking a vessel. (18c) *Maritime law.* A pilot's offer of services.

speaking demurrer. See DEMURRER.

speaking motion. See MOTION (1).

speaking objection. See OBJECTION.

speaking statute. See STATUTE.

spear phishing. See PHISHING.

spec. *abbr.* (1856) SPECIFICATION.

special, *adj.* (13c) **1.** Of, relating to, or designating a species, kind, or individual thing. **2.** (Of a statute, rule, etc.) designed for a particular purpose. **3.** (Of powers, etc.) unusual; extraordinary.

special acceptance. See ACCEPTANCE (3).

special act. See *special law* under LAW.

special administration. See ADMINISTRATION.

special administrator. See ADMINISTRATOR (2).

special advocate. See *guardian ad litem* under GUARDIAN (1).

special agency. See AGENCY (1).

special agent. See AGENT.

special agreement. See *ad hoc compromis* under COMPROMIS (1).

special allocatur. See ALLOCATUR.

special allowance. See ALLOWANCE (4).

special appearance. See APPEARANCE.

special assessment. See ASSESSMENT (2).

special-assessment bond. See *special-tax bond* under BOND (3).

Special Assistant to the United States Attorney. See UNITED STATES ATTORNEY.

special assumpsit. See ASSUMPSIT.

special attorney. See *special counsel* under COUNSEL.

special authority. See AUTHORITY (1).

special bail. See *bail to the action* under BAIL (4).

special bailiff. See BAILIFF (2).

special benefit. See BENEFIT (2).

special calendar. See CALENDAR (2).

special case. See *case reserved* (1) under CASE (1).

special charge. **1.** See CHARGE (7). **2.** See *special instruction* under JURY INSTRUCTION.

special charter. See CHARTER (3).

special circumstances. See *exigent circumstances* under CIRCUMSTANCE.

special-circumstances rule. See SPECIAL-FACTS RULE.

special committee. See COMMITTEE (1).

special concurrence. See CONCURRENCE (2).

special consortium. See CONSORTIUM (1).

special constable. See CONSTABLE.

special contract. See CONTRACT.

special-contract debt. See DEBT.

special counsel. See COUNSEL.

special count. See COUNT (2).

special court-martial. See COURT-MARTIAL (2).

special covenant against encumbrances. See COVENANT (4).

special custom. See *local custom* under CUSTOM (1).

special damages. See DAMAGES.

special demurrer. See DEMURRER.

special deposit. See DEPOSIT (2).

special deputy. See DEPUTY.

special-design property. See *special-purpose property* under PROPERTY.

special deterrence. See *specific deterrence* under DETERRENCE.

special diligence. See DILIGENCE (2).

special direction. See *special instruction* under JURY INSTRUCTION.

special district. See DISTRICT.

special dividend. See *extraordinary dividend* under DIVIDEND.

special-duty doctrine. (1980) *Torts.* The rule that a governmental entity (such as a state or municipality) can be held liable for an individual plaintiff's injury when the entity owed a duty to the plaintiff but not to the general public. • This is an exception to the public-duty doctrine. The special-duty doctrine applies only when the plaintiff has reasonably relied on the governmental entity's assumption of the duty. — Also termed *special-duty exception.* See PUBLIC-DUTY DOCTRINE.

special-duty exception. (1973) **1.** SPECIAL-DUTY DOCTRINE. **2.** SPECIAL-ERRAND DOCTRINE.

special election. See ELECTION (3).

special employee. See *borrowed employee* under EMPLOYEE.

special employer. See EMPLOYER.

special endorsement. See *special indorsement* under INDORSEMENT.

special-errand doctrine. (1938) The principle that workers' compensation covers an employee's injuries occurring while the employee is on a journey or special duty for the employer away from the workplace. • This is an exception to the general rule that an employee is not covered for injuries occurring away from work. — Also termed *special-duty exception*; *special-mission exception.* See GOING-AND-COMING RULE. Cf. SPECIAL-HAZARD RULE.

special exception. **1.** A party's objection to the form rather than the substance of an opponent's claim, such as an objection for vagueness or ambiguity. See DEMURRER. Cf. *general exception* (1) under EXCEPTION (1). **2.** An allowance in a zoning ordinance for special uses that are considered essential and are not fundamentally incompatible with the original zoning regulations. — Also termed (in sense 2) *conditional use*; *special use.* Cf. VARIANCE (2).

special execution. See EXECUTION (4).

special executor. See EXECUTOR (2).

special-facts rule. (1937) *Corporations.* The principle that a director or officer has a fiduciary duty to disclose material inside information to a shareholder when engaging in a stock transaction under special circumstances, as when the shareholder lacks business acumen, the shares are closely held with no readily ascertainable market value, or the director or officer instigated the transaction. • This is an exception to the "majority rule." — Also termed *special-circumstances rule.* Cf. MAJORITY RULE (3).

special finding. See FINDING OF FACT.

special forces. Soldiers who have been specifically trained to fight against guerrilla and terrorist groups.

special-form drawing. See DRAWING.

special franchise. See FRANCHISE (2).

special grand jury. See GRAND JURY.

special guaranty. See GUARANTY (1).

special guardian. See GUARDIAN (1).

special-hazard rule. (1970) The principle that workers' compensation covers an employee for injuries received while traveling to or from work if the route used contains unique risks or hazards and is not ordinarily used by the public except in dealing with the employer. • This is an exception to the general rule that an employee is not covered for injuries occurring during the employee's commute. See GOING-AND-COMING RULE. Cf. SPECIAL-ERRAND DOCTRINE.

special housing unit. (1970) *Criminal law.* A segregated block of cells or holding facility used to house inmates who have been separated from the general prison population, usu. for disciplinary purposes but sometimes for safety reasons. • Inmates in special housing units typically have fewer privileges than other inmates. — Abbr. SHU.

special imparlance. See IMPARLANCE.

special indorsement. See INDORSEMENT.

special injunction. See INJUNCTION.

special instruction. See JURY INSTRUCTION.

special-interest group. See INTEREST GROUP.

special interrogatory. See INTERROGATORY.

special issue. 1. See ISSUE (1). **2.** See *special interrogatory* under INTERROGATORY.

specialist. 1. A lawyer who has been board-certified in a specific field of law. See BOARD OF LEGAL SPECIALIZATION. **2.** *Securities.* A securities-exchange member who makes a market in one or more listed securities. • The exchange assigns securities to various specialists and expects them to maintain a fair and orderly market as provided by SEC standards.

special judge. See JUDGE.

special jurisdiction. See *limited jurisdiction* under JURISDICTION.

special jury. See JURY.

special law. See LAW.

special legacy. See *specific legacy* under LEGACY (1).

special letter of credit. See LETTER OF CREDIT.

special lien. See *particular lien* under LIEN.

special limitation. See LIMITATION (4).

special litigation committee. (1977) *Corporations.* A committee of independent corporate directors assigned to investigate the merits of a shareholder derivative suit and, if appropriate, to recommend maintaining or dismissing the suit. — Abbr. SLC. — Also termed *independent investigation committee*; *authorized committee.* See DERIVATIVE ACTION.

specially accredited agent. See AGENT.

special malice. See *particular malice* under MALICE.

special master. (18c) **1.** MASTER. **2.** See *judicial officer* (3) under OFFICER.

special master's deed. See DEED.

special master's in chancery deed. See *special master's deed* under DEED.

special matter. See MATTER.

special meaning. See SECONDARY MEANING.

special meeting. See MEETING.

special message. See MESSAGE.

special-mission exception. See SPECIAL-ERRAND DOCTRINE.

special mortgage. See MORTGAGE.

special motion. See MOTION (1).

special-needs analysis. (1989) *Criminal procedure.* A balancing test used by the Supreme Court to determine whether certain searches (such as administrative, civil-based, or public-safety searches) impose unreasonably on individual rights.

special-needs child. See CHILD.

special-needs trust. See *supplemental-needs trust* under TRUST (3).

special *non est factum*. See NON EST FACTUM.

special occupant. See OCCUPANT.

special offering. See OFFERING.

special order. See ORDER (4).

special-order agenda. See *special-order calendar* under CALENDAR (4).

special-order calendar. See CALENDAR (4).

special order of conditions. (2007) *Criminal procedure.* An order issued after an insanity plea, requiring the defendant to stay away from the victim and all witnesses. • Such an order is in the nature of an order of protection. See ORDER OF PROTECTION.

special owner. See OWNER.

special partner. See *limited partner* under PARTNER.

special partnership. See PARTNERSHIP.

special permit. See SPECIAL-USE PERMIT.

special-permit zoning. See *conditional zoning* under ZONING.

special plea. See PLEA (3).

special pleader. See PLEADER.

special pleading. (17c) **1.** The common-law system of pleading that required the parties to exchange a series of court papers (such as replications, rebutters, and surrebutters) setting out their contentions in accordance with hypertechnical rules before a case could be tried. • Often, therefore, cases were decided on points of pleading and not on the merits. **2.** The art of drafting pleadings under this system. **3.** An instance of drafting such a pleading. **4.** A responsive pleading that does more than merely deny allegations, as by introducing new matter to justify an otherwise blameworthy act. **5.** An argument that is unfairly slanted toward the speaker's viewpoint because it omits unfavorable facts or authorities and develops only favorable ones.

special plea in bar. See PLEA IN BAR.

special plea in error. At common law, a plea alleging some extraneous matter as a ground for defeating a writ of error (such as a release or expiration of the time within which error can be brought), to which the plaintiff in error must reply or demur. — Often shortened to *plea in error.*

special power. 1. See POWER (3). **2.** See *limited power of appointment* under POWER OF APPOINTMENT.

special power of appointment. See *limited power of appointment* under POWER OF APPOINTMENT.

special power of attorney. See POWER OF ATTORNEY.

special prayer. See PRAYER FOR RELIEF.

special privilege. 1. See PRIVILEGE (1). **2.** See *personal privilege* under PRIVILEGE (5).

special proceeding. See PROCEEDING.

special property. See PROPERTY.

special prosecutor. See PROSECUTOR (1).

special-purpose entity. (1970) A business established to perform no function other than to develop, own, and operate a large, complex project (usu. called a *single-purpose project*), esp. so as to limit the number of creditors claiming against the project. • A special-purpose entity provides additional protection for project lenders, which are usu. paid only out of the money generated by the entity's business, because there will be fewer competing claims for that money and because the entity will be less likely to be forced into bankruptcy. A special-purpose entity will sometimes issue securities instead of just receiving a direct loan. — Abbr. SPE. — Also termed *special-purpose vehicle* (SPV). See BANKRUPTCY-REMOTE ENTITY; SINGLE-PURPOSE PROJECT; *project financing* under FINANCING.

special-purpose property. See PROPERTY.

special-purpose vehicle. See SPECIAL-PURPOSE ENTITY.

special reference. See REFERENCE (1).

special registration. See REGISTRATION (1).

special relationship. See RELATIONSHIP.

special-relationship doctrine. (1981) The theory that if a state has assumed control over an individual sufficient to trigger an affirmative duty to protect that individual (as in an involuntary hospitalization or custody), then the state may be liable for the harm inflicted on the individual by a third party. • This is an exception to the general principle prohibiting members of the public from suing state employees for failing to protect them from third parties. — Also termed *special-relationship exception.* Cf. DANGER-CREATION DOCTRINE.

special relief. *Copyright.* A variance from a formal requirement for copyright registration or deposit granted by the U.S. Copyright Office when an applicant shows a good reason for the variance.

special replication. See REPLICATION.

special reprisal. See REPRISAL (1).

special resolution. See RESOLUTION (2).

special retainer. See RETAINER.

special retention. See RETENTION.

special rule. (16c) **1.** A rule applicable to a particular case or circumstance only. See RULE (1). **2.** A deliberative assembly's rule that supplements or supersedes its parliamentary authority. See PARLIAMENTARY AUTHORITY. **3.** A rule that applies only to a particular matter, such as a specific bill. In senses 2 & 3, see RULE (2), (3).

specials. See *special damages* under DAMAGES.

special-sensitivity rule. See EGGSHELL-SKULL RULE.

special session. See SESSION (1).

special setting. See SETTING.

special-skill enhancement. (1989) *Criminal law.* A ground for increasing a sentence under the federal sentencing guidelines because the defendant has a pronounced talent for crime.

special statute. See STATUTE.

special stock. See STOCK.

Special Supplemental Nutrition Program for Women, Infants, and Children. A federal assistance program that works to improve the health of low-income women, infants, and children up to age five who are at nutritional risk, by providing nutritious supplemental foods, education and counseling on healthful nutrition, and referrals to healthcare and other social services. — Abbr. WIC. — Also termed *WIC Program.*

special tail. See *tail special* under TAIL.

special tax. See TAX.

special-tax bond. See BOND (3).

special term. See TERM (5).

Special 301. *Intellectual property.* A provision of the Omnibus Trade and Competitiveness Act of 1988 directing the U.S. Trade Representative to report annually on countries that do not provide adequate and effective protection against the pirating of goods protected by U.S. intellectual-property rights. • Countries that fail the annual audit are put on a watch list and may face trade sanctions. 19 USCA §§ 2411 et seq.

special traverse. See TRAVERSE.

special trial setting. See *special setting* under SETTING.

special truce. See TRUCE.

special trust. See *active trust* under TRUST (3).

specialty. (15c) **1.** See *contract under seal* under CONTRACT. **2.** DOCTRINE OF SPECIALTY. **3.** *Eminent domain.* Unique property (such as a church or cemetery) that is essentially not marketable, so that its value for condemnation purposes is determined by measuring the property's reproduction cost less any depreciation. — Also termed (in sense 3) *specialty property.*

specialty bar. See *specialty bar association* under BAR ASSOCIATION.

specialty bar association. See BAR ASSOCIATION.

specialty contract. See *contract under seal* under CONTRACT.

specialty creditor. See CREDITOR.

specialty debt. See *special-contract debt* under DEBT.

specialty doctrine. See DOCTRINE OF SPECIALTY.

specialty property. See SPECIALTY (3).

special use. See SPECIAL EXCEPTION (2).

special-use account. See *concentration account* under ACCOUNT.

special-use permit. (1949) A zoning board's authorization to use property in a way that is identified as a special exception in a zoning ordinance. • Unlike a variance, which is an authorized violation of a zoning ordinance, a special-use permit is a permitted exception. — Abbr. SUP. — Also termed *conditional-use permit; special permit.* See SPECIAL EXCEPTION (2). Cf. VARIANCE (2).

special-use valuation. See VALUATION.

special-use zoning. See *conditional zoning* under ZONING.

special venire. See VENIRE (1).

special verdict. See VERDICT (1).

special warranty. See WARRANTY (1).

special warranty deed. See DEED.

specie (**spee**-shee). See IN SPECIE.

species (**spee**-sheez). (17c) **1.** A taxonomic class of organisms uniquely distinguished from other classes by shared characteristics and usu. by an inability to interbreed with members of other classes.

▸ **alien species.** A nonnative species of plant or animal that is accidentally or intentionally introduced to a place by human activity. — Also termed *exotic species; introduced species; nonnative species.*

▸ **candidate species.** (1981) *Environmental law.* Plants and animals identified by the Fish and Wildlife Service or National Marine Fisheries Service as potentially endangered or threatened but not of high enough priority to develop a proposed listing regulation under the Endangered Species Act. • Candidate species are not protected by federal law. — Also termed *listed species.*

▸ **endangered species.** (1899) A species in danger of becoming extinct; esp., under federal law, a species that is in danger of extinction throughout all or a significant part of its range. • Federal law excludes from the definition a species of the class Insecta if the Environmental Protection Agency determines that it constitutes a pest whose protection would present a significant risk to the human population. 50 CFR § 81.

▸ **exotic species.** (1841) See *alien species.*

▸ **focal species.** (1970) **1.** A single species of plant or animal whose distribution and abundance in an area can be used to infer data about the conservation needs of other species. **2.** The set of target species used to develop plans for managing and conserving environments, habitats, and landscapes.

▸ **introduced species.** See *alien species.*

▸ **invasive species.** (1928) **1.** An alien species that adversely affects the environment by escaping control, spreading into habitats or regions where it was not meant to be introduced, and adversely affected them environmentally or economically, such as by crowding out or otherwise harming indigenous species. **2.** A species, native or alien, that overruns a habitat or region because there are few, if any, natural population controls to keep it in check and causes environmental and economic harm. — Also termed (in both senses) *invasive exotics; exotics.*

▸ **listed species.** See *candidate species.*

▸ **nonnative species.** See *alien species.*

▸ **threatened species.** (1891) A species that, within the foreseeable future, is likely to become an endangered species throughout all or a significant part of its range. 16 USCA § 1532(20).

2. A specific class or kind of thing within a larger, general class. • For example, *tort* refers to a general class or genus. *Slander* refers to a specific kind of tort. Cf. GENUS. **3.** *Patents.* An element, usu. one of several mutually exclusive alternatives, that may be used in an invention to achieve a desired result <magnetic metals, including iron and steel>. • Species may be structures, steps, parts, compounds, and so on.

▸ **ultimate species.** (1883) A species that has been fully and narrowly defined. • For example, a species may be defined generally as "magnetic metals, including iron and steel," or particularly, such as "sodium chloride."

species claim. See PATENT CLAIM.

species facti (**spee**-shee-eez *or* **spee**-sheez **fak**-tɪ). [Latin] (18c) *Scots law.* The particular character of the thing done. • The phrase appeared in reference to the specific criminal act or civil wrong alleged.

specific, *adj.* (17c) **1.** Of, relating to, or designating a particular or defined thing; explicit <specific duties>. **2.** Of, relating to, or involving a particular named thing <specific item>. **3.** Conformable to special requirements <specific performance>. — **specificity** (spes-ə-**fis**-i-tee), *n.* — **specifically,** *adv.*

specific appropriation. See APPROPRIATION (3).

specificatio (spes-ə-fi-**kay**-shee-oh), *n.* [Latin fr. *species* "form" + *facere* "to make"] *Roman & civil law.* **1.** A giving of form to materials; the process of making something new from existing property. **2.** A mode of acquisition by which a person makes something new from existing material (for example, wine from grapes or a ship from timber). See ACCESSION (4). Pl. ***specificationes.***

> "*Specificatio.* This may be described as acquisition of a new thing by making it, out of materials wholly or partly belonging to another person. We shall deal only with the case in which the materials are wholly another's. There was in classical law a conflict of opinion on this topic . . . . Justinian tells us that there had been a *media sententia* according to which it belonged to the maker if (i) it was irreducible to its former state, and (ii) it really was a *nova species*, where *species* means thing. And this view he adopts as law." W.W. Buckland, *A Manual of Roman Private Law* 143 (2d ed. 1939).

specification. (17c) **1.** The act of making a detailed statement, esp. of the measurements, quality, materials, or other items to be provided under a contract. **2.** The statement so made. **3.** *Patents.* The part of a patent application describing how an invention is made and used, the best mode of operation of the claimed invention, and the inventor's claims. • The specification must be clear and complete enough to enable a person of ordinary skill in the art to make and use the invention. It must also disclose the best mode of working the invention. The term may also refer to the description as separate from the claims. — Abbr. spec. Cf. PATENT CLAIM.

> "The specification and claims of a patent, particularly if the invention be at all complicated, constitute one of the most difficult legal instruments to draw with accuracy; and, in view of the fact that valuable inventions are often placed in the hands of inexperienced persons to prepare such specifications and claims, it is no matter of surprise that the latter frequently fail to describe with requisite certainty the exact invention of the patentee, and err either in claiming that which the patentee had not in fact invented, or in omitting some element which was a valuable or essential part of his actual invention." *Topliff v. Topliff*, 145 U.S. 156, 170, 12 S.Ct. 825, 831 (1892).

▸ **substitute specification.** (1895) A patent specification that is rewritten (1) to include amendments made to the specification after filing; (2) to replace an illegible or unreadable original; or (3) to prepare the papers for printing. • A substitute specification must be accompanied by a statement that it contains no new matter, and by a copy showing what has been added and deleted since the original specification. Substitute specifications are allowed under 37 CFR 1.125. — Also termed *rewritten specification.*

4. A statement of charges against one who is accused of an offense, esp. a military offense.

> "A *charge* sets forth an *offense* — that is, a particular kind of act or conduct that entail liability to penalty under the governing rules — of which the accused is alleged to be guilty. A *specification* states *what the accused is alleged to have done* which, if true, constitutes an instance of the offense indicated in the charge. An accused officer or member must be found guilty of a *charge* before a penalty can be imposed." Henry M. Robert III et al., *Robert's Rules of Order Newly Revised* § 63, at 662 (11th ed. 2011).

5. The acquisition of title to materials belonging to another person by converting those materials into a new and different form, as by changing grapes into wine, lumber into shelving, or corn into liquor. • The effect is that the original owner of the materials loses the property rights in them and is left with a right of action for their original value. — Abbr. spec.

specific bequest. See BEQUEST.

specific denial. See DENIAL (3).

specific deposit. See DEPOSIT (2).

specific deterrence. See DETERRENCE.

specific devise. See DEVISE.

specific duty. See DUTY (4).

specific enforcement. See *primary right* under RIGHT.

specific example. See EXAMPLE.

specific guaranty. See GUARANTY (1).

specific intent. See INTENT (1).

specific-intent defense. (1976) *Criminal law.* A defendant's claim that he or she did not have the capacity (often supposedly because of intoxication or mental illness) to form the intent necessary for committing the crime alleged.

specific jurisdiction. See JURISDICTION.

specific legacy. See LEGACY (1).

specific legatee. See LEGATEE.

specific lien. See LIEN.

specific main motion. See *incidental main motion* under MOTION (2).

specific objection. See OBJECTION (1).

specific performance. (18c) The rendering, as nearly as practicable, of a promised performance through a judgment or decree; specif., a court-ordered remedy that requires precise fulfillment of a legal or contractual obligation when monetary damages are inappropriate or inadequate, as when the sale of real estate or a rare article is involved. • Specific performance is an equitable remedy that lies within the court's discretion to award whenever the common-law remedy is insufficient, either because damages would be inadequate or because the damages could not possibly be established. — Also termed *specific relief; performance in specie.*

> "The rationale of specific performance is that the common law remedy of damages was often inadequate. It would in effect compel a promisee to sell his right to performance for a pecuniary consideration. Now there are many cases into which the personal element enters to such an extent that no amount of damages can really compensate a disappointed promisee, who wants performance and only performance. To give him an unwanted cheque is a condonation of iniquity. For instance, A., after waiting for years for the opportunity of getting the old family mansion of Dale into his hands again, at length has prevailed on B., its owner, to agree to sell it to him. Clearly no amount of money will assuage his disappointment if the cup is dashed at the last moment from his lips. The object of the equitable remedy is to put A. into the same position, by personal compulsion of B., as he would already have been in if B. had performed voluntarily what now he is being compelled to do." Harold Greville Hanbury, *Modern Equity: The Principles of Equity* 445–46 (3d ed. 1943).

> "In essence, the remedy of specific performance enforces the execution of a contract according to its terms, and it may therefore be contrasted with the remedy of damages, which is compensation for non-execution. In specific performance, execution of the contract is enforced by the power of the Court to treat disobedience of its decree as contempt, for which the offender may be imprisoned until he is prepared to comply with the decree. Actually, . . . it is not strictly accurate to say that the Court enforces execution of the contract according to its terms, for the Court will not usually intervene until default upon the contract has occurred, so that enforcement by the Court is later in time than performance carried out by the person bound, without the intervention of the Court." G.W. Keeton, *An Introduction to Equity* 304 (5th ed. 1961).

specific personal jurisdiction. See JURISDICTION.

specific policy. See *basic-form policy* under INSURANCE POLICY.

specific-purpose rule. (1976) *Insurance.* The principle that a nonowner driver of a vehicle is treated as an omnibus insured under the vehicle owner's liability coverage only if the driver's actual use of the vehicle at the time of the accident is the exact use that the owner contemplated when granting permission or consent to the nonowner driver. • The time at which the bailment of the vehicle was to expire must not have passed, the place where the vehicle was being used must be as specified or contemplated by the insured, and the use of the vehicle must comport with the type of use that the insured had in mind when the bailment was created. Otherwise, the permittee's use of the vehicle will be regarded as a conversion. — Also termed *conversion rule; strict rule.*

specific relief. See SPECIFIC PERFORMANCE.

specific remedy. See REMEDY.

specific-subordination agreement. See SUBORDINATION AGREEMENT.

specific tax. See TAX.

specific traverse. See *common traverse* under TRAVERSE.

specimen. (17c) An actual sample of something; esp., an example of a trademark as it is used in commerce. • In the field of trademarks, a specimen typically consists of a label, a container, a display, or a photograph of the mark used for selling or advertising the goods or services.

specious, *adj.* (17c) Falsely appearing to be true, accurate, or just <specious argument>.

spectrograph. (1884) An electromagnetic machine that analyzes sound, esp. a human voice, by separating and mapping it into elements of frequency, time lapse, and intensity (represented by a series of horizontal and vertical bar lines) to produce a final voiceprint. See VOICEPRINT.

speculation, *n.* (14c) **1.** The buying or selling of something with the expectation of profiting from price fluctuations <he engaged in speculation in the stock market>. **2.** The act or practice of theorizing about matters over which there is no certain knowledge <the public's speculation about the assassination of John F. Kennedy>. — **speculate,** *vb.* — **speculative,** *adj.*

speculative damages. See DAMAGES.

speculative risk. See RISK.

speculative security. See SECURITY (4).

speculator. (18c) A knowledgeable, aggressive investor who trades securities to profit from fluctuating market prices.

speech. (bef. 12c) **1.** The expression or communication of thoughts or opinions in spoken words; something spoken or uttered. See FREEDOM OF SPEECH.

▸ **commercial speech.** (1963) Communication (such as advertising and marketing) that involves only the commercial interests of the speaker and the audience, and is therefore afforded lesser First Amendment protection than social, political, or religious speech. Cf. *pure speech*.

▸ **core political speech.** (1983) *Civil rights.* Conduct or words that are directly intended to rally public support for a particular issue, position, or candidate; expressions, proposals, or interactive communication concerning political change. *See Meyer v. Grant*, 486 U.S. 414, 421, 108 S.Ct. 1886, 1891–92 (1988).

"Our First Amendment decisions have created a rough hierarchy in the constitutional protection of speech. Core political speech occupies the highest, most protected position; commercial speech and nonobscene, sexually explicit speech are regarded as a sort of second-class expression; obscenity and fighting words receive the least protection of all." *R.A.V. v. City of St. Paul*, 505 U.S. 377, 422, 112 S.Ct. 2538, 2564 (1992) (Stevens, J., concurring in the judgment).

▸ **corporate speech.** (1959) Speech deriving from a corporation and protected under the First Amendment. • It does not lose protected status simply because of its corporate source.

▸ **hate speech.** (1988) Speech that carries no meaning other than the expression of hatred for some group, such as a particular race, esp. in circumstances in which the communication is likely to provoke violence. Cf. *hate crime* under CRIME; *group libel* under LIBEL.

▸ **incendiary speech.** (1886) Speech that is intended to excite passion, esp. anger or hatred, or to incite violence. See *hate speech*.

▸ **pure speech.** (1943) Words or conduct limited in form to what is necessary to convey the idea. • This type of speech is given the greatest constitutional protection. Cf. *commercial speech*; *symbolic speech*.

▸ **seditious speech.** (1920) Speech advocating the violent overthrow of government. See SEDITION.

▸ **speech-plus.** See *symbolic speech*.

▸ **symbolic speech.** (1966) Conduct that expresses opinions or thoughts, such as a hunger strike or the wearing of a black armband. • Symbolic speech does not enjoy the same constitutional protection that pure speech does. — Also termed *speech-plus*. Cf. *pure speech*.

2. *English law.* An opinion delivered by a Law Lord; JUDGMENT (3). 3. *Parliamentary law.* The unit of debate; specif., one statement, usu. subject to a time limit, on one question by one member. • When finished, the speaker must relinquish the floor and ordinarily cannot yield it to another member.

Speech Clause. *Constitutional law.* **1.** The First Amendment provision that "Congress shall make no law . . . abridging the freedom of speech." U.S. Const. amend I. — Also termed *Freedom of Speech Clause*. **2.** SPEECH OR DEBATE CLAUSE.

Speech or Debate Clause. (1965) *Constitutional law.* The clause of the U.S. Constitution giving members of Congress immunity for statements made during debate in either the House or the Senate. • This immunity is extended to other areas where it is necessary to prevent impairment of deliberations and other legitimate legislative activities, such as subpoenaing bank records for an investigation. U.S. Const. art. I, § 6., cl. 1. — Also termed *Speech and Debate Clause*; *Speech Clause*. See *congressional immunity* under IMMUNITY (1).

speech-plus. See *symbolic speech* under SPEECH (1).

speedy execution. See EXECUTION (4).

speedy remedy. See REMEDY.

speedy trial. (18c) *Criminal procedure.* A trial that the prosecution, with reasonable diligence, begins promptly and conducts expeditiously. • The Sixth Amendment secures the right to a speedy trial. In deciding whether an accused has been deprived of that right, courts generally consider the length of and reason for the delay, and the prejudice to the accused.

Speedy Trial Act of 1974. A federal statute establishing time limits for carrying out the major events (such as information, indictment, arraignment, and trial commencement) in the prosecution of federal criminal cases. 18 USCA §§ 3161–3174. — Abbr. STA.

spending bill. See *appropriations bill* under BILL (3).

spending power. See POWER (3).

spendthrift, *n.* (16c) Someone who spends lavishly and wastefully; a profligate. — **spendthrift,** *adj.*

spendthrift trust. See TRUST (3).

spent bill of lading. See BILL OF LADING.

spe numerandae pecuniae (spee n[y]oo-mə-**ran**-dee pi-**kyoo**-nee-ee). [Law Latin] (1894) *Scots law.* In the hope of the money being paid.

"So, also, where one delivers a conveyance, which acknowledges receipt of the consideration price, and discharges the disponee, this does not exclude his action for the price, if the disponee, on receiving delivery, refuses payment; the disponee is still liable *ex dolo*, the deed having been delivered *spe numerandae pecuniae*." John Trayner, *Trayner's Latin Maxims* 582 (4th ed. 1894).

sperate (**speer**-ət), *adj.* (16c) *Archaic.* (Of a debt) recoverable; not hopeless. • In determining whether a debt could be collected, consideration was formerly given to whether the debt was *desperate* or *sperate*.

spes accrescendi (**speez** ak-rə-**sen**-dɪ). [Latin "hope of accrual"] (1827) Hope of acquiring an extra share of a legacy or inheritance by survival.

spes obligationis (**speez** ob-li-gay-shee-**oh**-nis). [Latin] (1828) *Hist.* The hope of an obligation yet to emerge.

spes recuperandi (**speez** ri-k[y]oo-pə-**ran**-dɪ). [Latin "hope of recovery"] (18c) Hope of recovering a prize, as from a captured vessel.

spes successionis (**speez** sək-sesh-ee-**oh**-nis). [Latin "hope of succession"] (17c) Hope of succeeding to a right; a hope of succession to a fund or subject, to which one has a prospect of succeeding but no vested right.

"A mere *spes successionis* must be distinguished from a contingent right. If Matilda has nursed her invalid friend for thirty years, she may have every hope of succeeding to the property, but she has no right." George Whitecross Paton, *A Textbook of Jurisprudence* 306 (G.W. Paton & David P. Derham eds., 4th ed. 1972).

spes successionis in destinatione (**speez** sək-ses[h]-ee-**oh**-nis in des-ti-nay-shee-**oh**-nee). [Law Latin] (1887) *Hist.* A hope of succeeding under a destination (that is, an appointment by will).

spes successionis in obligatione (**speez** sək-ses[h]-ee-**oh**-nis in ob-li-gay-shee-**oh**-nee). [Law Latin] (1830) *Hist.* A hope of succeeding to a right under an existing obligation.

***Spielberg* doctrine.** (1963) *Labor law.* The policy of the National Labor Relations Board to defer to an arbitrator's decision regarding a contract dispute if (1) the decision is not repugnant to the NLRB, (2) the arbitration proceedings provided a hearing as fair as would have been provided before the NLRB, and (3) the contract requires binding arbitration. *Spielberg Mfg. Co.*, 112 NLRB Dec. (CCH) 86 (1955). Cf. COLLYER DOCTRINE.

***Spies* evasion.** (1995) *Criminal law.* The failure to file a tax return, coupled with an affirmative act of tax evasion. • Affirmative acts of tax evasion include falsely stating that no income was earned during the tax period, keeping double sets of accounting records, making false or altered entries, making false invoices, destroying records, concealing sources of income, and any other conduct likely to conceal income. *Spies v. U.S.*, 317 U.S. 492 (1943).

spigurnel (spig-ər-**nel**), *n.* (17c) *Hist.* An early officer of the Chancery, equivalent to the Sealer of the king's writs in later times.

spiking, *n.* **1.** The unlawful addition of a foreign substance to something that will be consumed without the consumer's knowledge or consent. **2.** The act of adding a foreign substance to a consumable. — **spike,** vb.

- ▸ **drink-spiking. 1.** The addition of an alcoholic-beverage to another beverage. **2.** The addition of a drug to a beverage for an unlawful purpose, esp. rape.
- ▸ **food-spiking.** The unlawful addition of an intoxicating or other foreign substance to food.

spillover. See EXTERNALITY.

spillover effect. *Criminal law.* An example of reification of the spillover theory; the prejudicial effect on a codefendant of being tried jointly with another defendant to whom the jurors react negatively.

spillover theory. (1985) The principle that a severance must be granted only when a defendant can show that a trial with a codefendant would substantially prejudice the defendant's case, as when the jury might wrongly use evidence relating to one defendant against the other. See BRUTON ERROR.

> "The spillover theory involves the question of whether a jury's unfavorable impression of a defendant against whom the evidence is properly admitted will influence the way the jurors view a codefendant . . . . The test . . . is whether the jury can keep separate the evidence that is relevant to each defendant and render a fair and impartial verdict." 22A C.J.S. *Criminal Law* § 571, at 190–91 (1989).

spinning. *Securities.* The giving of shares or preferred opportunities to buy shares in an initial public offering to key investment-banking clients in order to solicit or retain profitable business in the future.

spin-off, *n.* (1951) **1.** A corporate divestiture in which a division of a corporation becomes an independent company and stock of the new company is distributed to the corporation's shareholders. **2.** The company created by this divestiture. — Also written *spinoff.* Cf. SPLIT-OFF; SPLIT-UP.

spirit. The putative fundamental intention of the creator or creators of a legal instrument, whether it is a statute, a regulation, a contract, a will, or some other document having a legal effect; esp., the general drift of a statute, as opposed to its literal content. — Also termed *spirit of the law.* Cf. LETTER OF THE LAW.

spirit-over-letter concept. The notion that the "spirit" of a legal text should prevail over its letter.

spiritual, *adj.* (14c) Of, relating to, or involving ecclesiastical rather than secular matters <spiritual corporation>. Cf. TEMPORAL (1).

spiritual corporation. See CORPORATION.

spiritual court. See *ecclesiastical court* under COURT.

spiritual lord. (14c) An archbishop or bishop having a seat in the House of Lords.

spiritual tenure. See TENURE.

spiritual-treatment exemption. See FAITH-HEALING EXEMPTION.

spirituous (**speer**-i-choo-wəs or [-tyoo-]), *adj.* (17c) Containing a significant percentage of alcohol, often a statutorily specified amount (such as 21% alcohol by volume). See ALCOHOL; LIQUOR.

spital (**spit**-əl). (13c) *Archaic.* A hospital. — Also termed *spittle.*

spite fence. (1901) A fence erected solely to annoy a neighbor, as by blocking the neighbor's view or preventing the neighbor from acquiring an easement of light <the court temporarily enjoined the completion of the 25-foot spite fence>. Cf. LAWFUL FENCE.

spittle. See SPITAL.

splinter group. A group of people who have separated from a political or religious organization because they have different ideas; a faction that has broken away from a parent body.

split, *vb.* (1927) **1.** To divide (a cause of action) into segments or parts. **2.** To issue two or more shares for each old share without changing the shareholder's proportional ownership interest. See STOCK SPLIT; SPLIT-INTEREST PURCHASE OF PROPERTY.

split custody. See CUSTODY (2).

split-dollar life insurance. See LIFE INSURANCE.

split fund. See *dual fund* under MUTUAL FUND.

split-funded plan. See EMPLOYEE BENEFIT PLAN.

split gift. See GIFT.

split income. See INCOME.

split-interest purchase of property. (1995) An arrangement between two parties to purchase an asset whereby one party (often a parent) purchases a life estate and the other party (often a child or grandchild of the life tenant) purchases a remainder interest. • Each party to a split pays the actuarial value of the interest purchased. — Often shortened to *split.* — Also termed *joint-interest purchase.*

split-interest trust. See *charitable-remainder trust* under TRUST (3).

split-level statute. See STATUTE.

split-off, *n.* **1.** The creation of a new corporation by an existing corporation that gives its shareholders stock in the new corporation in return for their stock in the original corporation. **2.** The corporation created by this process. — Also written *splitoff.* Cf. SPIN-OFF; SPLIT-UP.

split order. See ORDER (8).

split sentence. See SENTENCE.

split the baby. [fr. the biblical story of King Solomon, 1 Kings 3:16–28] (1940) To moderate the relief granted to a complainant so that the defendant and the complainant alike might claim both a partial victory and a partial defeat, neither one being too upset (or so the decision-maker supposes) by a lopsided result. • The origin of the metaphor is inapposite to the modern meaning, since Solomon only threatened to have a baby sliced in half, each woman contending to be its mother to take half the child. When one of the two women pleaded for the child's life, Solomon knew that he had identified the real mother. — Also termed *cut the baby in half.* See JUDGMENT OF SOLOMON.

split ticket. In an election, a ballot in which a voter has voted for some candidates from one party and some from the other. Cf. STRAIGHT TICKET.

splitting a cause of action. (1850) Separating parts of a demand and pursuing it piecemeal; presenting only a part of a claim in one lawsuit, leaving the rest for a second suit. • This practice has long been considered procedurally impermissible.

split-up, *n.* (1928) The division of a corporation into two or more new corporations. • The shareholders in the original corporation typically receive shares in the new corporations, and the original corporation goes out of business. — Also written *splitup.* Cf. SPIN-OFF; SPLIT-OFF.

split verdict. See VERDICT (1).

spoiled ballot. See BALLOT (2).

spoils of war. See BOOTY (1).

spoils system. (1839) The practice of awarding government jobs to supporters and friends of the victorious political party. Cf. MERIT SYSTEM.

> "SPOILS SYSTEM, The. This phrase designates a theory of politics and a use of official authority — more especially that of appointment and removal — according to which the merits of candidates and the general welfare are subordinated to the selfish interests of individuals, factions, or parties. The range of this subordination is very great. It extends all the way from the case of a party which, honestly holding none but its followers to be fit for a clerkship, selects the best of them, but bars the gates of office against all others, down to the faction leaders, who, excluding all but their own henchmen, corruptly make promotions for money, and promise places for votes; all the way from the great officer who, hardly conscious of wrong, accepts for the party the offerings of his subordinates, down to the official robber who mercilessly demands the places or the money of those serving under him; all the way from the head of a bureau or a department who requests more clerks, that they may work for his party, or serve as waiters or coachmen in his own family, down to the legislators who vote appropriations in aid of their re-election, and city aldermen who bribe electors by corrupt contracts, and conciliate thieves, gamblers, and grog-shop keepers by winking at their offenses." Dorman B. Eaton, "The Spoils System," in 3 *Cyclopaedia of Political Science, Political Economy, and of the Political History of the United States* 782–83 (John J. Lalor ed., 1893).

spoliation (spoh-lee-**ay**-shən), *n.* (18c) **1.** The intentional destruction, mutilation, alteration, or concealment of evidence, usu. a document. • If proved, spoliation may be used to establish that the evidence was unfavorable to the party responsible. — Also termed *spoliation of evidence.* **2.** The seizure of personal or real property by violent means; the act of pillaging. **3.** The taking of a benefit properly belonging to another. **4.** *Eccles. law.* The wrongful deprivation of a cleric of his benefice. — **spoliate** (**spoh**-lee-ayt), *vb.* — **spoliator** (**spoh**-lee-ay-tər), *n.*

spolium (**spoh**-lee-əm), *n.* [Latin "booty"] *Roman law.* Something taken from an enemy in war or plundered from a fellow-citizen. • The plural *spolia* was more common than the singular.

Spondesne? Spondeo (**spon**-deez **spon**-dee-oh). [Latin] *Roman law.* Do you agree to undertake? I undertake. • This was the special phrase, available only to citizens, that created a *sponsio.* See SPONSIO; STIPULATIO.

spondet peritiam artis (**spon**-det pə-**rish**-ee-əm **ahr**-tis). [Latin "he guarantees his professional skill"] *Hist.* He promised to use the skill of his art. • This phrase is used in construction contracts to indicate an implied agreement to perform in a workmanlike manner.

sponge tax. See *pickup tax* under TAX.

sponsalia (spon-**say**-lee-ə), *n.* [Latin] (16c) *Hist.* **1.** A betrothal; an engagement to marry.

> "Marriage is preceded by a formal betrothal (*sponsalia*). For this preliminary verbal contract consent only of the parties and of their *patresfamilias* (if they are under power) is necessary, but they must not be under the age of seven." T. Whitcombe Greene, *Outlines of Roman Law* 45 (3d ed. 1875).

2. An engagement gift. — Also termed *stipulatio sponsalitia.*

sponsalia per verba de futuro (spon-**say**-lee-ə pər **vər**-bə dee f[y]oo-**t[y]oor**-oh). [Latin "espousals by words about the future"] (1832) *Hist.* A promise to marry in the future.

> "[A] promise to marry in the future (*sponsalia per verba de futuro*) gave rise only to an executory contract of marriage. The regular way of executing the contract was to solemnise the marriage, using present words. But the Canon law acknowledged that it could also be turned into the indissoluble bond of present matrimony by physical consummation . . . . Thus, in the absence of carnal copulation, the validity of a marriage had come to depend on whether the contract was by words *de praesenti* or *de futuro* . . . . It is hardly surprising that it gave rise to so much wrangling and fraud, and that the commonest species of matrimonial suit in the medieval consistory courts was to interpret and enforce 'espousals.'" J.H. Baker, *An Introduction to English Legal History* 546 (3d ed. 1990).

sponsalia per verba de praesenti (spon-**say**-lee-ə pər **vər**-bə dee pri-**zen**-tɪ *or* pree-). (1841) *Eccles. law.* A type of informal marriage that occurred when the parties made an informal agreement to have each other as husband and wife. • This type of informal marriage was based on nothing more than the present consent to be married but was entirely valid and would take precedence over a later formal ceremonial marriage that either of the parties attempted to contract with someone else. Cf. *common-law marriage* under MARRIAGE (1).

sponsio (**spon**-shee-oh), *n.* [Latin] *Roman law.* An undertaking, available only to citizens, in the form of an answer to a question using a solemn form of words with religious overtones. • This was the original form of stipulation. See STIPULATIO.

▸ ***sponsio judicialis*** (**spon**-shee-oh joo-dish-ee-**ay**-lis). [Latin] (1823) *Roman law.* A formal promise that the judge is entitled to acquire by virtue of his office. Pl. ***sponsiones judiciales.***

▸ ***sponsio ludicra*** (**spon**-shee-oh **loo**-di-krə). [Latin "a laughable promise"] (1825) **1.** *Civil law.* An informal or illicit understanding that is not enforceable. **2.** *Scots law.* An obligation that a court will not enforce because it does not concern a worthy subject; e.g., a gambling agreement. Pl. ***sponsiones ludicrae.***

sponsion (**spon**-shən), *n.* [fr. Latin *spondere* "to engage"] (17c) **1.** The formal pledge by which a person becomes a surety. **2.** *Int'l law.* An ultra vires promise of an official agent (such as a general in wartime), requiring later ratification by the principal. **3.** *Roman law.* A form of guarantee accessory to an oral contract. • Only Roman citizens could make this type of guarantee. See ADPROMISSION (1). — **sponsional** (**spon**-shən-əl), *adj.*

sponsor. (17c) **1.** Someone who acts as a surety for another. **2.** A legislator who proposes a bill. **3.** *Civil law.* Someone who voluntarily intervenes for another without being requested to do so. **4.** GODPARENT.

spontaneous abortion. See MISCARRIAGE (1).

spontaneous crime. See CRIME.

spontaneous declaration. (1840) *Evidence.* A statement that is made without time to reflect or fabricate and is related to the circumstances of the perceived occurrence. — Also termed *spontaneous statement*; *spontaneous exclamation*; *spontaneous utterance.* See EXCITED UTTERANCE; PRESENT SENSE IMPRESSION.

spontaneous offense. See *spontaneous crime* under CRIME.

spontaneous statement. See STATEMENT.

sponte (**spon**-tee). [Latin] *Hist.* Spontaneously; voluntarily. See SUA SPONTE.

sponte oblata (**spon**-tee ə-**blay**-tə). [Latin "freely offered"] (17c) *Hist.* A gift to the Crown.

sponte sua. See SUA SPONTE.

spoofing. (1972) Any act of creating and using false identification information to gain unauthorized access to an electronic system.

▸ **e-mail spoofing.** (1996) The falsification of an e-mail sender's address and other parts of the e-mail header to make it appear that the e-mail originated from a different person or source. • An e-mail spoof is not necessarily intended to elicit a reply. Cf. PHISHING.

▸ **IP spoofing.** (1995) The falsification of information that identifies the origin of an electronic data transmission, usu. to evade attempts to block the transmissions. • *IP* stands for Internet protocol, which includes numerical codes to identify a transmission's source and destination. IP spoofing is most often used in denial-of-service attacks. See DENIAL-OF-SERVICE ATTACK.

▸ **website spoofing.** (1997) The creation of a website that has a design similar to another website, and often a similar URL, in order to mislead visitors about who created the website and to perpetrate a hoax or fraud.

sports franchise. See FRANCHISE (4).

sportula (**spor**-chə-lə), *n.* [Latin] (17c) *Roman law.* **1.** A present; a donation, as to the poor. **2.** A fee paid to certain officials for performing judicial duties. — Also termed *sportella.*

spot, *adj.* (1881) Made, paid, or delivered immediately <a spot sale> <spot commodities>.

spot chartering. (1968) The practice or an instance of entering into charterparties, esp. voyage or time charterparties, on the basis of a shipper's immediate need to ship cargo at an offered rate and the shipper's immediate availability.

spot market. See MARKET.

spot price. See PRICE.

spot zoning. See ZONING.

spousal abandonment. See ABANDONMENT (4).

spousal abuse. See ABUSE.

spousal allowance. See ALLOWANCE (1).

spousal consortium. See CONSORTIUM.

spousal-impoverishment provision. (1988) A section of the Medicare Catastrophic Coverage Act allowing the stay-at-home spouse of a person residing in a nursing home to retain certain assets and some joint income, and to earn income without jeopardizing the institutionalized spouse's eligibility for Medicaid. • Before the provision was enacted in 1988, almost all of a couple's joint assets and the noninstitutionalized spouse's income had to go toward the cost of the nursing-home resident's care before Medicaid provided any support. 42 USCA § 1396r-5.

spousal labor. (1963) *Family law.* Work by either spouse during the marriage. • This term is typically used in community-property states.

spousal privilege. See *marital privilege* under PRIVILEGE (3).

spousal rape. See *marital rape* under RAPE (2).

spousals. (14c) *Hist.* Mutual promises to marry.

spousal support. See ALIMONY (1).

spousal-unity doctrine. (1995) *Hist.* **1.** *Family law.* The common-law rule that a husband and wife were a legal unity. • Under the spousal-unity doctrine, the husband had all rights to the possession, management, control, and alienation of property. The wife had no interests in property. — Also termed *doctrine of spousal unity.* Cf. LEGAL-UNITIES DOCTRINE. See MARRIED WOMEN'S PROPERTY ACTS. **2.** *Tax.* The rule that a person and that person's spouse are treated as one. • This rule has been repealed. — Also termed *spousal-unity rule.*

spouse. (12c) One's husband or wife by lawful marriage; a married person.

▸ **innocent spouse.** (1924) *Tax.* A spouse who may be relieved of liability for taxes on income that the other spouse did not include on a joint tax return. • The innocent spouse must prove that the other spouse omitted the income, that the innocent spouse did not know and had no reason to know of the omission, and that it would be unfair under the circumstances to hold the innocent spouse liable.

▸ **putative spouse.** (1842) *Family law.* A spouse who believes in good faith that his or her invalid marriage is legally valid. See *putative marriage* under MARRIAGE (1).

▸ **surviving spouse.** (18c) A spouse who outlives the other spouse.

spouse-breach. See ADULTERY.

spray trust. See *sprinkle trust* under TRUST (3).

spread, *n.* (1879) **1.** *Banking.* The difference between the interest rate that a financial institution must pay to attract deposits and the rate at which money can be loaned. **2.** *Securities.* The difference between the highest price a buyer will pay for a security (the *bid price*) and the lowest price at which a seller will sell a security (the *asked price*). **3.** *Securities.* The simultaneous buying and selling of one or more options or futures contracts on the same security in order to profit from the price difference. **4.** In investment banking, the difference between the price the underwriter pays the issuer of the security and the price the public paid in the initial offering. • The spread compensates the underwriter for its services; it comprises the manager's fee, the underwriter's discount, and the selling-group concession or discount. — Also termed (in sense 4) *gross spread*; *underwriting spread.*

spread eagle. See STRADDLE.

spreadsheet. (1982) **1.** A multicolumn worksheet used esp. by accountants and auditors to summarize and analyze financial transactions. **2.** A computer-generated ledger that can show and manipulate information.

spread upon the minutes. (1876) *Parliamentary law.* To incorporate into the minutes a statement expressing a sentiment, such as a memorial celebrating a deceased member's life.

spreta auctoritate judicis (**spree**-tə awk-tor-ə-**tay**-tee **joo**-di-sis). [Law Latin] *Hist.* The authority of the judge being disregarded.

spreta inhibitione (**spree**-tə in-hi-bish-ee-**oh**-nee). [Law Latin] *Hist.* In contempt of an inhibition.

spring gun. A gun whose trigger is connected to a wire or cord that will cause the gun to fire at any person who comes in contact with the wire.

springing durable power of attorney. See *springing power of attorney* under POWER OF ATTORNEY.

springing executory interest. See EXECUTORY INTEREST.

springing power of attorney. See POWER OF ATTORNEY.

springing use. See USE (4).

spring tide. See TIDE.

sprinkle power. (1966) In a sprinkle trust, the trustee's discretion about when and how much of the trust principal and income are to be distributed to the beneficiaries. See *sprinkle trust* under TRUST (3).

sprinkle trust. See TRUST (3).

sprint report. (1984) A telephone operator's brief paraphrased account of a 911 call, summarized in a printout.

spuilzie (**spuul**-yee), *n.* (16c) *Scots law.* **1.** The wrongful taking of corporeal movable property from another's possession. • This is the Scottish equivalent of common-law conversion. **2.** An action to recover wrongfully taken movables, and often for either profits made with them while in the taker's possession or reparations for unjust dispossession. — Also spelled *spulzie*; *spulyie.* — **spuilzied,** *adj.*

spurious (**spyoor**-ee-əs), *adj.* (16c) **1.** Deceptively suggesting an erroneous origin; fake <spurious trademarks>. **2.** Of doubtful or low quality <spurious goods that fell apart>. **3.** *Archaic.* Of illegitimate birth <spurious offspring>.

spurious bank bill. See *spurious banknote* under BANKNOTE.

spurious banknote. See BANKNOTE.

spurious class action. See CLASS ACTION.

spurious interpretation. See INTERPRETATION (1).

spurius (**spyuur**-ee-əs), *n.* [Latin] *Roman law.* A bastard; the offspring of unlawful intercourse. See NOTHUS. Pl. ***spurii*** (**spyuur**-ee-I).

SPV. *abbr.* Special-purpose vehicle. See SPECIAL-PURPOSE ENTITY.

spy. (14c) Someone who secretly observes and collects secret information or intelligence about what another government or company is doing or plans to do; one who commits espionage. See ESPIONAGE.

squalor carceris (**skway**-lor **kahr**-sər-is). [Law Latin] (17c) *Scots law.* The strictness of imprisonment.

> "This term means merely the strictness of imprisonment which a creditor is entitled to enforce, with the view of compelling the debtor to pay the debt, or disclose any funds which he may have concealed. It does not imply (as it did with the ancient churchmen, from whom the term is derived) anything loathsome or unhealthy in the imprisonment in Scotland, which is indeed less close than in England. *Squalor carceris* is not necessary in imprisonment on *meditatio fugae* warrant, security being all that is required in such cases." William Bell, *Bell's Dictionary and Digest of the Law of Scotland* 1032 (George Watson ed., 7th ed. 1890).

squalor morbi (**skway**-lor **mor**-bI). [Law Latin] (17c) *Hist.* The dregs of disease.

square, *n.* (17c) **1.** A certain portion of land within a city limit. — Also termed *block.* **2.** A space set apart for public use. **3.** In a government survey, an area measuring 24 by 24 miles.

squatter. (18c) **1.** Someone who settles on property without any legal claim or title. **2.** Someone who settles on public land under a government regulation allowing the person to acquire title upon fulfilling specified conditions.

squatter's rights. (1855) The right to acquire title to real property by adverse possession, or by preemption of public lands. See ADVERSE POSSESSION.

squeeze-out, *n.* An action taken in an attempt to eliminate or reduce a minority interest in a corporation. Cf. FREEZEOUT.

***Squires* claim.** See PATENT CLAIM.

***Squires* doctrine.** (2004) *Patents.* A rule of the U.S. Patent and Trademark Office that a utility-patent claim may incorporate drawings or tables by reference, but only when there is no practical way to express the information in words, and when referring to the artwork is a concise way to communicate the information. • The namesake case involved a numerical font designed to be readable in the dim red light inside a submarine. It is allowed only when necessary, and is not available just for the convenience of an applicant. *Ex parte Squires*, 133 USPQ (BNA) 598 (Bd. App. 1961).

SRA. *abbr.* SENTENCING REFORM ACT OF 1984.

SRO. *abbr.* SELF-REGULATORY ORGANIZATION.

SRP. *abbr.* See *suggested retail price* under PRICE.

ss. *abbr.* **1.** Sections. **2.** *Subscripsi* (i.e., signed below). **3.** Sans (i.e., without). **4.** (Erroneously) scilicet.

> "Many possible etymologies have been suggested for this mysterious abbreviation. One is that it signifies *scilicet* (= namely, to wit), which is usually abbreviated *sc.* or *scil.*

Another is that *ss.* represents '[t]he two gold letters at the ends of the chain of office or "collar" worn by the Lord Chief Justice of the King's Bench . . . .' Max Radin, *Law Dictionary* 327 (1955). Mellinkoff suggests that the precise etymology is unknown: 'Lawyers have been using *ss* for nine hundred years and still are not sure what it means.' David Mellinkoff, *The Language of the Law* 296 (1963). In fact, though, it is a flourish deriving from the Year Books — an equivalent of the paragraph mark: '¶.' Hence Lord Hardwicke's statement that *ss.* is nothing more than a division mark. See *Jodderrell v. Cowell*, 95 Eng. Rep. 222, 222 (K.B. 1737) . . . . An early formbook writer incorporated it into his forms, and ever since it has been mindlessly perpetuated by one generation after another." Bryan A. Garner, *Garner's Dictionary of Legal Usage* 839 (3d ed. 2011).

SSA. *abbr.* SOCIAL SECURITY ADMINISTRATION.

SSCRA. *abbr.* SOLDIERS' AND SAILORS' CIVIL RELIEF ACT.

SSDI. *abbr.* SOCIAL SECURITY DISABILITY INSURANCE.

SSI. *abbr.* SUPPLEMENTAL SECURITY INCOME.

SSM. *abbr.* Sua sponte motion.

SSO. *abbr.* STANDARD-SETTING ORGANIZATION.

SSS. *abbr.* SELECTIVE SERVICE SYSTEM.

STA. *abbr.* SPEEDY TRIAL ACT OF 1974.

stabilize, *vb.* (1861) **1.** To make firm or steadfast <to stabilize the ship>. **2.** To maintain a particular level or amount <stabilize prices>.

stable stand. (16c) *Hist.* In forest law, a person found standing in a forest either with a bow bent, ready to shoot a deer, or close to a tree with greyhounds on a leash and ready to slip, being presumptive evidence of an intent to steal the Crown's deer.

stacking. (1982) **1.** *Insurance.* The process of obtaining benefits from a second policy on the same claim when recovery from the first policy alone would be inadequate.

▸ **judicial stacking.** (1983) The principle that a court can construe insurance policies to permit stacking, under certain circumstances, when the policies do not specifically allow stacking but public policy is best served by permitting it.

▸ **policy stacking.** Stacking that is permitted by the express terms of an insurance policy.

2. A gerrymandering technique in which a large political or racial group is combined in the same district with a larger opposition group. Cf. CRACKING; PACKING.

staff attorney. 1. See ATTORNEY. **2.** See CLERK (5).

staff director. See EXECUTIVE DIRECTOR.

staff judge advocate. See JUDGE ADVOCATE.

staff officer. See OFFICER (1).

stage representation. See *stage representation* under REPRESENTATION (2).

stagflation (stag-**flay**-shən), *n.* (1965) A period of slow economic growth or recession characterized by high inflation, stagnant consumer demand, and high unemployment. — **stagflationary,** *adj.*

staggered board of directors. See BOARD OF DIRECTORS.

stagiarius (stay-jee-**air**-ee-əs), *n.* [Latin] *Hist.* **1.** *Eccles. law.* A resident canon; an ecclesiastic bound to keep terms of residence. **2.** A stagiary; a law student keeping terms before admission to the bar.

stake, *n.* (bef. 12c) **1.** Something (such as property) deposited by two or more parties with a third party pending the resolution of a dispute; the subject matter of an interpleader. **2.** An interest or share in a business venture. **3.** Something (esp. money) bet in a wager, game, or contest. **4.** A boundary marker used in land surveys.

stakeholder. (18c) **1.** A disinterested third party who holds money or property, the right to which is disputed between two or more other parties. See INTERPLEADER. **2.** Someone who has an interest or concern in a business or enterprise, though not necessarily as an owner. **3.** A person who has an interest or concern (not necessarily financial) in the success or failure of an organization, system, plan, or strategy, or who is affected by a course of action. **4.** Someone who holds the money or valuables bet by others in a wager.

stale check. See CHECK.

stale claim. See CLAIM (3).

stale-dated check. See *stale check* under CHECK.

stale demand. 1. See DEMAND (1). **2.** See *stale claim* under CLAIM (3).

staleness rule. (1980) *Criminal law.* The doctrine that an application for a search warrant is bad if too much time has passed since probable cause was known to have existed.

Stalingrad defense. See DEFENSE (2).

stalking. (bef. 12c) **1.** The act or an instance of following another by stealth. **2.** The offense of following or loitering near another, often surreptitiously, to annoy or harass that person or to commit a further crime such as assault or battery. • Some statutory definitions include an element that the person being stalked must reasonably feel harassed, alarmed, or distressed about personal safety or the safety of one or more persons for whom that person is responsible. And some definitions include acts such as telephoning another and remaining silent during the call. Cf. CYBERSTALKING. — **stalker,** *n.*

stalking-horse theory. (2002) *Criminal procedure.* The notion that a probation officer's search of a probationer or his home is inappropriate if the officer was acting at the behest of police who were trying to evade the probable-cause requirement.

stallage (**stawl**-ij), *n.* (14c) *Hist.* **1.** The right to erect stalls in public markets. **2.** The cost for that right.

stamp, *n.* (15c) An official mark or seal placed on a document, esp. to indicate that a required tax (such as duty or excise tax) has been paid.

stamp acts. (18c) English statutes requiring and regulating stamps on deeds, contracts, legal papers, bills, or other documents.

stamp duty. (18c) *Hist.* A tax raised by requiring stamps sold by the government to be affixed to designated documents, thus forming part of the perpetual revenue. See *stamp tax* under TAX.

"A fifth branch of the perpetual revenue consists in the stamp duties, which are a tax imposed upon all parchment and paper whereon any legal proceedings, or private instruments of almost any nature whatsoever, are written; and also upon licenses . . . and pamphlets containing less than six sheets of paper. These imposts are very various, according to the nature of the thing stamped, rising gradually from a penny to ten pounds." 1 William Blackstone, *Commentaries on the Laws of England* 312–13 (1765).

stamp tax. See TAX.

stand. See WITNESS STAND.

stand adjourned. (17c) (Of a meeting or proceeding) to be in a state of adjournment <this court stands adjourned until 10:00 a.m. tomorrow>. • This status is usu. announced by a judge or other presiding officer concerning the business scheduled to continue at a later time. — Often shortened to *adjourned.*

standard, *n.* (15c) **1.** A model accepted as correct by custom, consent, or authority <what is the standard in the ant-farm industry?>. **2.** A criterion for measuring acceptability, quality, or accuracy <the attorney was making a nice living — even by New York standards>. — **standard,** *adj.*

▸ **objective standard.** (1915) A legal standard that is based on conduct and perceptions external to a particular person. • In tort law, for example, the reasonable-person standard is considered an objective standard because it does not require a determination of what the defendant was thinking.

"The objective theory of negligence, which is orthodox in the leading systems of law, requires people to display the same competence as a hypothetical model person. To bring in a model person is to translate a normative standard into a hypothetical descriptive standard. The model is variously depicted in different legal cultures. He or she is seen as a diligent father, a reasonable man/woman, an abstract type, or a careful and conscientious member of the class in question. The class may, according to the case, be that of doctor, driver, company director, air pilot, pedestrian etc. The classification depends on the type of person expected to undertake the task performance of which goes wrong (operating, driving, running a business, crossing the street), and to display care or skill in doing so. The objective standard has, on the orthodox view, to be met both in avoiding harm to others and in protecting oneself. Failure to meet it may either make the injurer liable to pay damages as defendant or may bar the inured, in whole or in part, from recovering damages as plaintiff." Tony Honoré, *Responsibility and Fault* 17 (1999).

▸ **subjective standard.** (1915) A legal standard that is peculiar to a particular person and based on the person's individual views and experiences. • In criminal law, for example, a subjective standard applies to determine premeditation because it depends on the defendant's mental state.

Standard & Poor's. An investment-analysis and -advisory service. • Standard & Poor's rates the financial strength of businesses from AAA (strongest) to AA, A, BBB, and so on to CCC. Most grades may also be modified with a plus- or minus-sign according to the business's relative strength among similar companies. A rating of R means that the company is the subject of some regulatory action.

standard characteristics. See STANDARD DESCRIPTIVE CHARACTERISTICS.

standard deduction. See DEDUCTION (2).

standard descriptive characteristics. (2004) *Parliamentary law.* The basic rules that apply to and define a motion. • The characteristics include when the motion is in order; its rank — that is, what it takes precedence over, and what yields to it; whether making it may interrupt a speaker; whether it needs a second; whether it is debatable; whether it is amendable; what vote its adoption takes; and whether it can be reconsidered. — Also termed *standard characteristics.*

standard direction. See *standard instruction* under JURY INSTRUCTION

standard-form contract. See CONTRACT.

standard instruction. See JURY INSTRUCTION.

standardized contract. See *standard-form contract* under CONTRACT.

standard mortgage clause. See MORTGAGE CLAUSE.

standard of care. (1890) *Torts.* In the law of negligence, the degree of care that a reasonable person should exercise. See CARE (2).

standard of need. In public-assistance law, the total subsistence resources required by an individual or family unit as determined by a state and, when unsatisfied by available resources, entitles the individual or family unit to public assistance.

standard of proof. (1857) The degree or level of proof demanded in a specific case, such as "beyond a reasonable doubt" or "by a preponderance of the evidence"; a rule about the quality of the evidence that a party must bring forward to prevail. — Also termed *degree of proof.* See BURDEN OF PERSUASION. Cf. BURDEN OF PROOF.

standard of review. (1928) The criterion by which an appellate court exercising appellate jurisdiction measures the constitutionality of a statute or the propriety of an order, finding, or judgment entered by a lower court.

standard policy. See INSURANCE POLICY.

standard risk. See RISK.

standards body. See STANDARD-SETTING ORGANIZATION.

standard-setting organization. (1948) A body that sets, describes, or documents uniform operating, technological, or other norms for participants in a particular field or industry. — Abbr. SSO. — Also termed *standards body.*

Standards for Imposing Lawyer Sanctions. The ABA's 1986 supplement to the Standards for Lawyer Discipline, prescribing a range of sanctions and guidelines for applying them. • Sanctions range from reprimands to disbarment.

Standards for Lawyer Discipline. A set of model rules, created by the ABA in 1979, establishing procedures for disciplining lawyers who violate ethics rules or commit crimes. • The rules stress that the process is an inquiry to determine an attorney's fitness to practice, not to determine a punishment.

stand at ease. (1958) *Parliamentary law.* To take an informal pause during a meeting without taking a recess, at the instance of the chair.

standby charge. (1930) A property levy, often based on acreage, imposed on the mere availability of a service, whether or not the service is actually used.

standby commitment. (1964) An arrangement between an underwriter and an issuer of securities whereby the underwriter agrees, for a fee, to buy any unsold shares remaining after the public offering. — Also termed *standby underwriting agreement.*

standby counsel. See COUNSEL.

standby guardian. See GUARDIAN (1).

standby guardianship. See GUARDIANSHIP.

standby letter of credit. See LETTER OF CREDIT.

standby trust. See TRUST (3).

standby underwriting. See UNDERWRITING.

standby underwriting agreement. See STANDBY COMMITMENT.

standing, *n.* (1924) A party's right to make a legal claim or seek judicial enforcement of a duty or right. • To have standing in federal court, a plaintiff must show (1) that the challenged conduct has caused the plaintiff actual injury, and (2) that the interest sought to be protected is within the zone of interests meant to be regulated by the statutory or constitutional guarantee in question. — Also termed *standing to sue.* Cf. JUSTICIABILITY.

> "Have the appellants alleged such a personal stake in the outcome of the controversy as to assure that concrete adverseness which sharpens the presentation of issues upon which the court so largely depends for illumination of difficult constitutional questions? This is the gist of the question of standing." *Baker v. Carr,* 369 U.S. 186, 204, 82 S.Ct. 691, 703 (1962).

> "The word *standing* is rather recent in the basic judicial vocabulary and does not appear to have been commonly used until the middle of our own century. No authority that I have found introduces the term with proper explanations and apologies and announces that henceforth *standing* should be used to describe who may be heard by a judge. Nor was there any sudden adoption by tacit consent. The word appears here and there, spreading very gradually with no discernible pattern. Judges and lawyers found themselves using the term and did not ask why they did so or where it came from." Joseph Vining, *Legal Identity* 55 (1978).

▸ **associational standing.** (1971) *Constitutional law.* The legal status of an organization suing or defending in a representative capacity and having at least one member who has standing in his or her own right, so that the association may present the claim or type of claim pleaded. — Also termed *organizational standing; representational standing.*

> "A party to a lawsuit acquires associational standing by showing that '(1) its members would otherwise have standing to sue in their own right; (2) the interests it seeks to protect are germane to the organization's purpose; and (3) neither the claims asserted nor the relief requested requires the participation of the individual members in the lawsuit.'" *Hunt v. Washington State Apple Adver. Comm'n,* 432 U.S. 333, 343, 97 S.Ct. 2434, 2441 (1977) (quoting the district court).

▸ **representational standing.** See *associational standing.*

▸ **third-party standing.** (1968) Standing held by someone claiming to protect the rights of others. • For example, in most jurisdictions, only a parent has standing to bring a suit for custody or visitation; in some, however, a third party — for instance, a grandparent or a person with whom the child has substantial contacts — may have standing to bring an action for custody or visitation. See GRANDPARENT RIGHTS.

standing aside a juror. (1875) The prosecution practice of provisionally placing a juror aside until the panel is exhausted, without providing a reason, instead of challenging the juror or showing cause. • The practice originally developed as a method of avoiding the Challenge of Jurors Act (1305), which prohibited the Crown from challenging a juror without showing cause. A similar practice was formerly used in Pennsylvania.

standing by. (14c) **1.** The awaiting of an opportunity to respond, as with assistance. **2.** Silence or inaction when there is a duty to speak or act; esp., the tacit possession of knowledge under circumstances requiring the possessor to reveal the knowledge. See *estoppel by silence* under ESTOPPEL.

standing committee. See COMMITTEE (1).

Standing Committee on Rules of Practice and Procedure. A group of judges, lawyers, and legal scholars appointed by the Chief Justice of the United States to advise the Judicial Conference of the United States on possible amendments to the procedural rules in the various federal courts and on other issues relating to the operation of the federal courts. 28 USCA § 331.

> "[Under 28 USCA § 331], the Judicial Conference of the United States has created a Standing Committee on Rules of Practice and Procedure and has authorized the appointment from time to time of various advisory committees. These committees make recommendations regarding amendments of the rules to the Judicial Conference, which in turn transmits those recommendations it approves to the Supreme Court. Under this new plan, as under the machinery in effect from 1934 to 1956, the Court retains the ultimate responsibility for the adoption of amendments to the rules." 4 Charles Alan Wright & Arthur R. Miller, *Federal Practice and Procedure* § 1007, at 35 (2d ed. 1987).

standing crops. See CROPS.

standing division. See *standing vote* under VOTE (4).

standing master. See MASTER.

standing mortgage. See *interest-only mortgage* under MORTGAGE.

standing mute. See MUTE (2).

standing objection. See OBJECTION (1).

standing offer. See OFFER (2).

standing order. 1. See ORDER (2). **2.** See *split order* under ORDER (8).

standing rule. See RULE (3).

standing seised to uses. (1828) The holding of title for the benefit or use of another, such as a relative in consideration of blood or marriage. • A covenant to stand seised to uses is a type of conveyance that depends on the Statute of Uses for its effect. — Often shortened to *seised to uses.* See STATUTE OF USES.

standing to sue. See STANDING.

standing vote. See VOTE (4).

stand mute. (16c) **1.** *Criminal law.* (Of a defendant) to refuse to enter a plea to a criminal charge; esp., to remain silent when required to answer and plead. See MUTE (2). • Standing mute is treated as a plea of not guilty. See PEINE FORTE ET DURE.

> "A candid historian cannot pretend that our criminal law and procedure has been at all times humane. Torture was, except in one particular, the monopoly of the Court of Star Chamber, but one form of torture was well known at common law. It arose out of the rule that a prisoner could not be tried by a jury without his consent. If, therefore, an accused person would not plead, but elected to 'stand mute,' the trial could not proceed. But the law would not suffer itself to be thus baffled without a terrible struggle. A statute of 1275 authorized the use of the 'peine forte et dure' to extort consent. This consisted in pressing the accused beneath heavy weights until he consented or died. The reason why persons would chose to suffer these appalling agonies rather than plead was that thus they would avoid the forfeiture of property which would, until its

abolition in 1870, follow a conviction for treason or felony. In 1772 the barbarity that had so long disfigured the law was ended by an enactment that standing mute in cases of felony should be equivalent to a conviction. In 1827 the law was again altered, and it was provided that, if the prisoner, in any criminal case, stands mute, a plea of not guilty shall be entered, and the trial shall proceed as if he had thus pleaded." Harold Greville Hanbury, *English Courts of Law* 121–22 (1944).

2. (Of any party) to raise no objections; esp., to refrain from answering or responding to a motion, so that the court must decide the matter solely on the movant's arguments.

standstill agreement. (1934) Any agreement to refrain from taking further action; esp., an agreement by which a party agrees to refrain from further attempts to take over a corporation (as by making no tender offer) for a specified period, or by which financial institutions agree not to call bonds or loans when due.

stand trial. (17c) To submit to a legal proceeding, esp. a criminal prosecution.

stand-your-ground law. (2006) A statute providing that a potential victim of a crime need not retreat before responding with force in self-defense to a threat, even if flight is possible. • The stand-your-ground law immunizes the actor against civil suits and criminal charges when force was used justifiably in self-defense.

Stanley Commission. An American Bar Association task force created to study professionalism within the legal profession. • Formed in 1985 on the recommendation of Chief Justice Warren Burger, the commission issued its report, *"In the Spirit of Public Service": A Blueprint for the Rekindling of Lawyer Professionalism*, the following year. The commission was named for its chair, former ABA president Justin Stanley.

stante matrimonio (**stan**-tee ma-trə-**moh**-nee-oh). [Latin] *Hist.* The marriage remaining undissolved.

staple (**stay**-pəl). (14c) **1.** A key commodity such as wool, leather, tin, lead, butter, or cheese (collectively termed *the staple*). **2.** *Hist.* A town appointed by the Crown as an exclusive market for staple products. See STATUTE STAPLE. **3.** *Patents.* An unpatented thing or material that is a component of a patented product or is used in a patented process, but also has other practical uses. • Patentees may not gain control of the market for staples through tying agreements. Cf. NONSTAPLE.

Star Chamber. (14c) **1.** *Hist.* An English court having broad civil and criminal jurisdiction at the king's discretion and noted for its secretive, arbitrary, and oppressive procedures, including compulsory self-incrimination, inquisitorial investigation, and the absence of juries. • The Star Chamber was abolished in 1641 because of its abuses of power. — Also termed *Court of Star Chamber*; *Camera Stellata.*

"The Star-Chamber is said to have been in early times one of the apartments of the king's palace at Westminster which was used for the despatch of public business. The Painted Chamber, the White Chamber, and the Chambre Markolph were occupied by the triers and receivers of petitions, and the king's council held its sittings in the Camera Stellate, or Chambre des Estoylles, which was so called probably from some remarkable feature in its architecture or embellishment. Whatever may be the etymology of the term, there can be little doubt that the court of Star-Chamber derived its name for the place in which it was holden. 'The lords sitting in the Star-Chamber' is used as a well-known phrase in records of the time of Edward III, and the name became permanently attached to the jurisdiction, and continued long after the local situation of the court was changed." 4 *The Standard Library Cyclopaedia of Political, Constitutional, Statistical and Forensic Knowledge* 746 (1853).

2. (*usu. lowercase*) Any secretive, arbitrary, or oppressive tribunal or proceeding; less negatively, any group of people who meet secretly to make important decisions.

stare decisis (**stahr**-ee di-**SI**-sis *or* **stair**-ee), *n.* [Latin "to stand by things decided"] (18c) The doctrine of precedent, under which a court must follow earlier judicial decisions when the same points arise again in litigation. — Also termed *traditional stare decisis*; *institutional stare decisis.* See PRECEDENT; NON QUIETA MOVERE. Cf. RES JUDICATA; LAW OF THE CASE; (in civil law) *jurisprudence constante* under JURISPRUDENCE.

"The rule of adherence to judicial precedents finds its expression in the doctrine of stare decisis. This doctrine is simply that, when a point or principle of law has been once officially decided or settled by the ruling of a competent court in a case in which it is directly and necessarily involved, it will no longer be considered as open to examination or to a new ruling by the same tribunal, or by those which are bound to follow its adjudications, unless it be for urgent reasons and in exceptional cases." William M. Lile et al., *Brief Making and the Use of Law Books* 321 (Roger W. Cooley & Charles Lesley Ames eds., 3d ed. 1914).

"The general orthodox interpretation of *stare decisis* . . . is *stare rationibus decidendis* ('keep to the *rationes decidendi* of past cases'), but a narrower and more literal interpretation is sometimes employed. To appreciate this narrower interpretation it is necessary to refer . . . to Lord Halsbury's assertion that a case is only authority for what it actually decides. We saw that situations can arise in which all that is binding is the decision. According to Lord Reid, such a situation arises when the *ratio decidendi* of a previous case is obscure, out of accord with authority or established principle, or too broadly expressed." Rupert Cross & J.W. Harris, *Precedent in English Law* 100–01 (4th ed. 1991).

▸ **horizontal stare decisis.** (1977) The doctrine that a court, esp. an appellate court, must adhere to its own prior decisions, unless it finds compelling reasons to overrule itself.

▸ **local stare decisis.** (1956) The adherence of a group of judges making up a current court (as of a regional court of appeals or a subregional trial bench) to the previous exercises of judicial discretion within the group, so as to lead to greater consistency in judgments or voting patterns.

▸ **personal stare decisis.** (1963) The adherence of a judge to his or her own previous exercises of judicial discretion, so as to lead to a consistency in judgments or voting patterns.

▸ **super stare decisis.** (1992) The theory that courts must follow earlier court decisions without considering whether those decisions were correct. • Critics argue that strict adherence to old decisions can result in grave injustices and cite as an example the repudiation of *Plessy v. Ferguson*, 163 U.S. 537, 16 S.Ct. 1138 (1896) by *Brown v. Board of Education*, 347 U.S. 483, 74 S.Ct. 686 (1954).

▸ **vertical stare decisis.** (1977) The doctrine that a court must strictly follow the decisions handed down by higher courts within the same jurisdiction.

stare decisis et non quieta movere (**stair**-ee di-**SI**-sis et non kwɪ-**ee**-tə moh-**veer**-ee). [Latin] To stand by things decided, and not to disturb settled points. See STARE DECISIS.

stare enim religioni debet (**stair**-ee **ee**-nim ri-lij-ee-**oh**-nee **dee**-bet *or* **deb**-et). [Latin] *Hist.* For one ought to abide by one's solemn obligation.

stare in judicio (**stair**-ee in joo-**dish**-ee-oh). [Latin] *Hist.* To appear before a tribunal as either a plaintiff or a defendant.

star paging, *n.* (1873) **1.** A method of keying the pages of a book to the pagination of an earlier edition of the book, esp. a legal source, by displaying asterisked numbers at the places in the text where page breaks occur in the earlier edition. • This method creates a uniform way of citing passages with consistent numbering. Many editions of Blackstone's *Commentaries on the Laws of England* (1765) contain star paging. **2.** By extension, the method of displaying on a computer screen the page breaks that occur in printed documents such as law reports and law reviews. — Also termed *star pagination.* — **star page,** *n.*

starr (stahr), *n.* [fr. Latin *starrum* fr. Hebrew *sh'tar* "a writing"] (17c) *Hist.* A Jewish contract (esp. for release of an obligation) that Richard I declared to be invalid unless it was placed in a lawful repository, the largest being in the king's Exchequer at Westminster. — Also termed *starra.*

> "It is well known that, before the banishment of the Jews under Edward I, their contracts and obligations were denominated in our ancient records *starra* or *starrs,* from a corruption of the Hebrew word, *shetàr,* a covenant. . . . These starrs, by an ordinance of Richard the first . . . were commanded to be enrolled and deposited in chests under three keys in certain places; one, and the most considerable, of which was in the king's exchequer at Westminster . . . . [T]he room at the exchequer, where the chests containing these starrs were kept, was probably called the *starr-chamber,* and, when the Jews were expelled from the kingdom, was applied to the use of the king's council, when sitting in their judicial capacity." 4 William Blackstone, *Commentaries on the Laws of England* 263 n.a (1769).

stash, *vb.* (18c) To hide or conceal (money or property).

stat. *abbr.* STATUTE.

state, *n.* (16c) **1.** The political system of a body of people who are politically organized; the system of rules by which jurisdiction and authority are exercised over such a body of people <separation of church and state>. — Also termed *political society.* Cf. NATION.

> "A STATE is a community of persons living within certain limits of territory, under a permanent organization which aims to secure the prevalence of justice by self-imposed law. The organ of the state by which its relations with other states are managed is the government." Theodore D. Woolsey, *Introduction to the Study of International Law* § 36, at 34 (5th ed. 1878).

> "A state or political society is an association of human beings established for the attainment of certain ends by certain means. It is the most important of all the various kinds of society in which men unite, being indeed the necessary basis and condition of peace, order, and civilisation. What then is the difference between this and other forms of association? In what does the state differ from such other societies as a church, a university, a joint-stock company, or a trade union? The difference is clearly one of *function.* The state must be defined by reference to such of its activities and purposes as are essential and characteristic." John Salmond, *Jurisprudence* 129 (Glanville L. Williams ed., 10th ed. 1947).

> "A state is an *institution,* that is to say, it is a system of relations which men establish among themselves as a means of securing certain objects, of which the most fundamental is a system of order within which their activities can be carried on. Modern states are territorial; their governments exercise control over persons and things within their frontiers, and today the whole of the habitable world is divided between about seventy of these territorial states. A state should not be confused with the whole community of persons living on its territory; it is only one among a multitude of other institutions, such as churches and corporations, which a community establishes for securing different objects, though obviously it is one of tremendous importance; none the less it is not, except in the ideology of totalitarianism, an all-embracing institution, not something from which, or within which, all other institutions and associations have their being; many institutions, e.g. the Roman Catholic Church, and many associations, e.g. federations of employers and of workers, transcend the boundaries of any single state." J.L. Brierly, *The Law of Nations* 118 (5th ed. 1955).

▸ **client state.** (1918) A country that is obliged in some degree to cede some of the control of its external relations to some foreign power or powers. — Also termed *satellite state.* Cf. SOVEREIGN STATE.

▸ **coastal state.** (1910) A country that borders on an ocean or sea.

▸ **code state.** See CODE STATE.

▸ **composite state.** (1832) A state that comprises an aggregate or group of constituent states.

▸ **dependent state.** See *nonsovereign state.*

▸ **failed state.** A state that does not or cannot meet or maintain some of the basic social, economic, or political conditions and responsibilities of a sovereign government. • Some attributes of a failed state include the loss of physical control of its territory, an inability to provide reasonable public services, and the erosion of legitimate authority.

▸ **federal state.** (18c) A composite state in which the sovereignty of the entire state is divided between the central or federal government and the local governments of the several constituent states; a union of states in which the control of the external relations of all the member states has been surrendered to a central government so that the only state that exists for international purposes is the one formed by the union. Cf. *confederation of states* under CONFEDERATION.

▸ **free state.** (16c) A political community organized independently of all others.

▸ **imperial state.** (16c) *Archaic.* A composite state in which a common or central government possesses in itself the entire sovereignty, so that the constituent states possess no portion of this sovereignty.

▸ **littoral state.** (1858) A state that has a coast.

▸ **microstate.** An entity that consists of a small territory and a small population and that is recognized as a state for international-law purposes. — Also written *micro state.*

> "A number of entities of diminutive population and territory are widely or universally accepted as States for purposes of international law. The term micro State is sometimes used by legal writers; some very small States even refer to themselves as micro States. But micro State is not generally regarded as a legal term of art. There is as such no authoritative legal definition of micro State. Nor is there a precise definition in international relations. The class that the term denotes is best identified by reference to some of the States which have been called micro States, and to others which, though small relative to most States, are usually not so termed. Four European States with

origins in the early modern period are typically referred to as micro States: Andorra, Liechtenstein, Monaco, and San Marino. The Vatican City, territorial base of the Holy See, is also sometimes referred to as a micro State. These may be identified as the core cases. Luxembourg and Malta, though the smallest States to accede so far to the European Union ('EU'), generally are not placed in the same category. The former, with 2500 km² of territory and nearly half a million inhabitants, would be a giant amongst the confirmed examples. The latter, though an island with less territory than Andorra, arguably must be excluded on grounds of population. Malta has approximately 400,000 inhabitants; Iceland and Andorra—the States in Europe next on the scale from largest to smallest population—have 301,000 and 71,000 respectively. Iceland, with over 100,000 km² of territory, is most certainly not a micro State. Nor is Singapore, with 692 km² and 4.5 million inhabitants, though it might be called a 'city State.'" Thomas D. Grant, "Micro States," in 7 *The Max Planck Encyclopedia of Public International Law* 133, 134 (Rüdiger Wolfrum ed., 2012).

▸ **nonsovereign state.** (1896) A state that is a constituent part of a greater state that includes both it and one or more others, and to whose government it is subject; a state that is not complete and self-existent. • Among other things, a nonsovereign state has no power to engage in foreign relations. — Also termed *dependent state.* Cf. SOVEREIGN STATE.

▸ **part-sovereign state.** See SOVEREIGN STATE.

▸ **police state.** (1851) A state in which the political, economic, and social life of its citizens is subject to repressive governmental control and arbitrary uses of power by the ruling elite, which uses the police as the instrument of control; a totalitarian state.

▸ **receiving state.** (17c) The country to which a diplomatic agent or consul is sent by the country represented by that agent. Cf. *sending state.*

▸ **satellite state.** See *client state.*

▸ **sending state.** (1920) The country from which a diplomatic agent or consul is sent abroad. Cf. *receiving state.*

▸ **simple state.** See *unitary state.*

▸ **social-service state.** (1931) A state that uses its power to create laws and regulations to provide for the welfare of its citizens.

▸ **sovereign state.** See SOVEREIGN STATE.

▸ **unitary state.** (1853) A state that is not made up of territorial divisions that are states themselves. — Also termed (archaically) *simple state.*

2. An institution of self-government within a larger political entity; esp., one of the constituent parts of a country having a federal government <the 50 states>. **3.** (*often cap.*) The people of a state, collectively considered as the party wronged by a criminal deed; esp., the prosecution as the representative of the people <the State rests its case>.

state account system. (1889) *Criminal law.* A prison disciplinary system in which prison industries are run either by a proprietor or by the state itself, the prisoners furnishing the labor; specif., a convict-labor system in which prisoners work in factories or prison facilities with state-supplied raw materials and the government sells the products in the open market. — Also termed *public account system.* Cf. STATE-USE SYSTEM.

state action. (1893) Anything done by a government; esp., in constitutional law, an intrusion on a person's rights (esp. civil rights) either by a governmental entity or by a private requirement that can be enforced only by governmental action (such as a racially restrictive covenant, which requires judicial action for enforcement).

state-action doctrine. *Antitrust.* The principle that the antitrust laws do not prohibit a state's anticompetitive acts, or official acts directed by a state. *Parker v. Brown*, 317 U.S. 341, 63 S.Ct. 307 (1943). — Also termed *Parker doctrine.* See MIDCAL TEST.

state agency. See AGENCY (3).

state-all-facts interrogatory. See *identification interrogatory* under INTERROGATORY.

state appeal. See APPEAL (2).

state auditor. See AUDITOR.

state bank. See BANK.

state bar. See *state bar association* under BAR ASSOCIATION.

state bar association. See BAR ASSOCIATION.

state benefit. See WELFARE (2).

state body. See *state agency* under AGENCY (3).

state bond. See BOND (3).

state capitalism. See CAPITALISM.

state-compulsion test. (1978) *Civil-rights law.* The rule that a state is responsible for discrimination that a private party commits while acting under the requirements of state law, as when a restaurant owner is required by state law to refuse service to minorities. *Adickes v. S.H. Kress & Co.*, 398 U.S. 144, 90 S.Ct. 1598 (1970). See SYMBIOTIC-RELATIONSHIP TEST; NEXUS TEST.

state constitution. See CONSTITUTION (3).

state court. See COURT.

statecraft. (17c) Governmental management; the art of conducting political affairs.

state criminal. See CRIMINAL.

stated, *adj.* (17c) **1.** Fixed; determined; settled <at the stated time> <settlement for a stated amount>. **2.** Expressed; declared <stated facts>.

stated account. See *account stated* under ACCOUNT.

stated capital. See CAPITAL.

stated case. See *case stated* under CASE (1).

State Department. See DEPARTMENT OF STATE.

stated-income loan. See LOAN.

stated interest rate. See *nominal rate* under INTEREST RATE.

stated meeting. See *regular meeting* under MEETING.

stated rate. See *nominal rate* under INTEREST RATE.

stated term. See *general term* under TERM (5).

stated value. See PAR VALUE.

state government. See GOVERNMENT (3).

statehood. 1. The condition of being a state, esp. one of the states in the United States. **2.** *Int'l law.* The condition of being a recognized country under international law. • In sense 2, the classic indicia of statehood are (1) a permanent population, (2) a defined territory, (3) a government, and (4) the capacity to enter into relations with other states.

statehouse. (*often cap.*) (18c) A state capitol; specif., the building in which a state legislature holds its sessions, many if not most of its members usu. having their offices there as well. — Also written *state house*.

state interest. See GOVERNMENTAL INTEREST.

state jurisdiction. See JURISDICTION.

State Justice Institute. A nonprofit federal corporation charged with improving judicial administration in state courts. • It was created by the State Justice Institute Act of 1984. 42 USCA §§ 10701–10713. — Abbr. SJI.

state law. (18c) A body of law in a particular state consisting of the state's constitution, statutes, regulations, and common law. Cf. FEDERAL LAW.

stateless person. (1930) *Int'l law.* A natural person who is not considered a national by any country. • The Convention Relating to Status of Stateless Persons (1954) provides these people with certain protections in signatory countries and obliges them to abide by the laws of the country where they reside. The Convention on the Reduction of Stateless Persons (1961) reduced the number of people classifiable as stateless persons. Cf. REFUGEE.

state line. (18c) The surveyed boundary line of a state; a boundary between states.

statement. (18c) **1.** *Evidence.* A verbal assertion or nonverbal conduct intended as an assertion. **2.** A formal and exact presentation of facts. — Also termed (for plaintiff) *statement of cause of action.* **3.** *Criminal procedure.* An account of a person's knowledge of a crime, taken by the police during their investigation of the offense. Cf. CONFESSION. **4.** STATEMENT OF THE CASE (2).

▸ **consonant statement.** (1889) A witness's previous declaration, testified to by a person to whom the declaration was made and allowed into evidence only after the witness's testimony has been impeached. • This type of evidence would, but for the impeachment of the witness, be inadmissible hearsay. Cf. *prior consistent statement.*

▸ **false statement.** (18c) **1.** An untrue statement knowingly made with the intent to mislead. See PERJURY. **2.** Any one of three distinct federal offenses: (1) falsifying or concealing a material fact by trick, scheme, or device; (2) making a false, fictitious, or fraudulent representation; and (3) making or using a false document or writing. 18 USCA § 1001.

▸ **financial statement.** See FINANCIAL STATEMENT.

▸ **incriminating statement.** (1896) A statement that tends to establish the guilt of someone, esp. the person making it.

▸ **prior consistent statement.** (1883) A witness's earlier statement that is consistent with the witness's testimony at trial. • A prior consistent statement is not hearsay if it is offered to rebut a charge that the testimony was improperly influenced or fabricated. Fed. R. Evid. 801(d)(1)(B). Cf. *consonant statement.*

▸ **prior inconsistent statement.** (1885) A witness's earlier statement that conflicts with the witness's testimony at trial. • In federal practice, extrinsic evidence of an unsworn prior inconsistent statement is admissible — if the witness is given an opportunity to explain or deny the statement — for impeachment purposes only. Fed. R. Evid. 613(b). Sworn statements may be admitted for all purposes. Fed. R. Evid. 801(d)(1)(A).

▸ **spontaneous statement.** (1850) A statement that was elicited, induced, provoked, or even encouraged.

▸ **sworn statement.** (1831) **1.** A statement given under oath; an affidavit. Cf. AFFIDAVIT; DECLARATION (8). **2.** A contractor-builder's listing of suppliers and subcontractors, and their respective bids, required by a lending institution for interim financing.

▸ **voluntary statement.** (1817) A statement made without the influence of duress, coercion, or inducement.

▸ **witness statement.** See WITNESS STATEMENT.

Statement and Account Clause. (1975) *Constitutional law.* The clause of the U.S. Constitution requiring the regular publication of the receipts and expenditures of the federal government. U.S. Const. art. I, § 9, cl. 7. Cf. APPROPRIATIONS CLAUSE.

statement against interest. (1867) **1.** See *admission against interest* under ADMISSION (1). **2.** See *declaration against interest* under DECLARATION (6).

statement of account. (1834) **1.** A report issued periodically (usu. monthly) by a bank to a customer, providing certain information on the customer's account, including the checks drawn and cleared, deposits made, charges debited, and the account balance. — Also termed *bank statement.* See ACCOUNT (4). **2.** A report issued periodically (usu. monthly) by a creditor to a customer, providing certain information on the customer's account, including the amounts billed, credits given, and the balance due. — Also termed *account statement.*

statement of affairs. (18c) **1.** STATEMENT OF FINANCIAL AFFAIRS. **2.** A balance sheet showing immediate liquidation values (rather than historical costs), usu. prepared when insolvency or bankruptcy is imminent.

statement of cause of action. See STATEMENT (2).

statement of claim. (1811) **1.** COMPLAINT (1). **2.** *English law.* A plaintiff's initial pleading in a civil case; DECLARATION (7).

statement of condition. See BALANCE SHEET.

statement of confession. See CONFESSION OF JUDGMENT.

statement of defense. (1876) The assertions by a defendant; esp., in England, the defendant's answer to the plaintiff's statement of claim.

statement of fact. (18c) A declaration that asserts or implies the existence or nonexistence of a fact. • The term includes not just a particular statement that a particular fact exists or has existed, but also an assertion that, although perhaps expressed as an opinion, implies the existence of some fact or facts that have led the assertor to hold the opinion in question. See *affirmative testimony* under TESTIMONY.

statement of facts. (18c) A party's written presentation of the facts leading up to or surrounding a legal dispute, usu. recited toward the beginning of a brief. Cf. STATEMENT OF THE CASE.

> "The statement of facts is another of those critical parts of the brief . . . . Two principles are at war in drafting the statement of facts. First, judges want and some circuit rules require a nonargumentative, 'fair summary without argument or comment.' Conversely, you want a statement of facts that persuades the judges to rule for you as soon as they finish reading it. Satisfying both ends requires some balancing." David G. Knibb, *Federal Court of Appeals Manual* § 31.7, at 549 (4th ed. 2000).

▸ **agreed statement of facts.** (1801) A narrative statement of facts that is stipulated to be correct by the parties and is submitted to a tribunal for a ruling. • When the narrative statement is filed on appeal instead of a report of the trial proceedings, it is called an *agreed statement on appeal.*

statement of financial affairs. (1906) *Bankruptcy.* A document that an individual or corporate debtor must file to answer questions about the debtor's past and present financial status, including any lawsuits, administrative proceedings, transfers of property, and other transactions that are relevant to the bankruptcy and occurred within a specified period of time. — Abbr. SOFA. — Also termed *statement of affairs.*

statement of financial condition. See BALANCE SHEET.

statement of financial performance. See BALANCE SHEET.

statement of financial position. See BALANCE SHEET.

statement of income. See INCOME STATEMENT.

statement of intention. *Bankruptcy.* A preliminary statement filed by an individual debtor in a Chapter 7 case, in which the debtor details, among other things, whether property of the bankruptcy estate securing any debt will be retained or surrendered and whether the property is claimed as exempt. • The statement must be filed on or before the date of the first creditors' meeting or within 30 days after the bankruptcy petition is filed, whichever is earlier. 11 USCA § 521 (a)(2).

statement of particulars. See BILL OF PARTICULARS.

statement of principle. In legislative drafting, a sentence or paragraph that explains the legislature's purpose, guiding philosophy, or motivation in passing a statute. • Although a statement of principle often resembles a preamble (usu. both do not appear in a single statute), it differs in that it typically appears in a numbered section of the statute. — Also termed *statement of purpose.*

statement of prior-art references. See *information-disclosure statement* under DISCLOSURE STATEMENT.

statement of purpose. See STATEMENT OF PRINCIPLE.

statement of readiness. (1957) A prosecutor's pronouncement, usu. in writing, of the ability and willingness to prosecute on the date set for trial, sent to the court usu. in compliance with a speedy-trial requirement. — Also termed *certificate of readiness.*

statement of record. A detailed statement required of certain property developers and agents by the Interstate Land Sales Full Disclosure Act, to be filed with the U.S. Department of Housing and Urban Development, before any lot sales or leases involving interstate commerce or the use of the mail will be allowed. 15 USCA §§ 1701–1720.

statement of the case. 1. In an appellate brief, a short review of what has happened procedurally in the lawsuit and how it reached the present court. • The statement introduces the reviewing court to the case by reciting the facts, procedures, decisions of the court or courts below as they are relevant to the appeal, and the reasons for those decisions. — Also termed *proceedings below.* **2.** In the briefs filed in some courts, including the Supreme Court of the United States, the statement of facts blended continuously into the procedural history of the lawsuit. — Often shortened to *statement.* Cf. STATEMENT OF FACTS. **3.** In a judicial opinion, a similar account given by either the court or the reporter of decisions.

> "The statement of the case, furnished either by the reporter or by the court, usually precedes the opinion, but is sometimes, in whole or in part, embodied in it. For example, in *Tinn v. Hoffman & Co.*, 29 Law T. R. (N.S.) 271; 1 Williston's Cases on Contracts (2 ed.) 120; Corbin's Cases on Contracts, 155, the facts are set forth at length preceding the opinion; in *Stanton v. Dennis*, 64 Wash. 85, Corbin's Cases, 11, and in *Wheat v. Cross*, 31 Md. 99, Williston's Cases 131, they are stated by the court at the opening of the opinion; and in *Lewis v. Browning*, 130 Mass. 173, as printed in Corbin's Cases, 42, they are given in the last paragraph of the opinion. Besides showing the facts upon which the controversy turns, the statement of the case should set out the manner in which the points in dispute were brought to the attention of the trial court, whether, for example, on an objection to the introduction of evidence, on a demurrer, or on a motion. If the report is of a review of the trial court's decision, the statement should also make clear the proceedings in the trial court so far as pertinent to the questions to be reviewed, the manner in which the case is brought to the reviewing court, and the grounds on which a reversal is sought." Edmund M. Morgan, *Introduction to the Study of Law* 105–06 (1926).

statement of use. See *amendment to allege use* under TRADEMARK-APPLICATION AMENDMENT.

statement of utility. (1873) *Patents.* The portion of a patent-application disclosure statement that explains how the invention is useful.

statement of work. (1850) A contractual provision or exhibit that defines what one party (e.g., the seller) is going to do for the other (e.g., the buyer). • The statement of work often covers such terms as (1) inspection and acceptance, (2) quality-assurance requirements, (3) packing and marking, (4) data requirements, and (5) training. There are generally two types of specifications in a statement of work: a performance specification establishing the minimum requirements for items to be supplied, and a design specification establishing the methods to be used in meeting those minimum requirements. — Abbr. SOW. — Also termed *statement-of-work clause.*

statement under belief of impending death. See *dying declaration* under DECLARATION (6).

statemonger. (17c) *Pejorative slang.* A politician; esp., a political dilettante. — Also termed *statesmonger.*

state of art. See STATE OF THE ART.

state of emergency. A situation that is so unusually difficult or dangerous that a government gives itself special powers to deal with it, often involving limitation on people's freedom.

state officer. See OFFICER (1).

state of mind. (17c) **1.** The condition or capacity of a person's mind; MENS REA. **2.** Loosely, a person's reasons or motives for committing an act, esp. a criminal act.

state-of-mind defense. See DEFENSE (1).

state-of-mind exception. (1949) *Evidence.* The principle that an out-of-court declaration of an existing motive is admissible, even when the declarant cannot testify in person. • This principle is an exception to the general rule that hearsay is inadmissible.

state of nature. (16c) The lack of a politically organized society. • The term is a hypothetical construct for the period in human history predating any type of political society.

> "[W]e may make use of the contrast, familiar to the philosophy of the seventeenth and eighteenth centuries, between the civil state and the state of nature. This state of nature is now commonly rejected as one of the fictions which flourished in the era of the social contract, but such treatment is needlessly severe. The term certainly became associated with much false or exaggerated doctrine touching the golden age, on the one hand, and the *bellum omnium contra omnes* of Hobbes, on the other, but in itself it nevertheless affords a convenient mode for the expression of an undoubted truth. As long as there have been men, there has probably been some form of human society. The state of nature, therefore, is not the absence of society, but the absence of a society so organised on the basis of physical force as to constitute a state. Though human society is coeval with mankind, the rise of political society, properly so called, is an event in human history." John Salmond, *Jurisprudence* 103–04 (Glanville L. Williams ed., 10th ed. 1947).

state of the art. (1910) *Products liability.* The level of pertinent scientific and technical knowledge existing at the time of a product's manufacture, and the best technology reasonably available at the time the product was sold. — Also termed *state of art.* — **state-of-the-art,** *adj.*

> "While the statutes in effect in some jurisdictions speak in terms of a state of the art defense, statutes in other jurisdictions provide that state of the art evidence is admissible or may be considered by the trier of fact by statute, and that in determining whether a product was in a defective condition or unreasonably dangerous at the time it left the control of the manufacturer or seller, consideration is given to the state of scientific and technical knowledge available to the manufacturer or seller at the time the product was placed on the market, and to the customary designs, methods, standards, and techniques of manufacturing, inspecting, and testing used by other manufacturers or sellers of similar products." 63A Am. Jur. 2d *Products Liability* § 1319, at 472 (2008).

state of the case. (16c) The posture of litigation as it develops, as in discovery, at trial, or on appeal.

State of the Union. 1. See *Presidential message* under MESSAGE. **2.** One of the states in the United States.

> "The word 'State' in the Constitution refers to a State of the Union. For while the Constitution was made, 'ordained and established by the people of the United States for themselves,' it was made for the people of the United States in States. Thus it follows that over a domain not constituting a State, that is, over a domain consisting of a ceded district, or a territory, or an outlying possession, Congress has sole jurisdiction. Only the United States and the several States possess sovereignty." Francis Newton Thorpe, *The Essentials of American Constitutional Law* 47 (1917) (citations omitted).

state of war. (16c) A situation in which war has been declared or armed conflict is in progress. See WAR (1).

state paper. (17c) **1.** A document prepared by or relating to a state or national government and affecting the administration of that government in its political or international relations. **2.** A newspaper officially designated for the publication of public statutes, resolutions, notices, and advertisements.

State Paper Office. (18c) *Hist.* An office established in London in 1578, headed by the Clerk of the Papers, to maintain custody of state documents.

state park. A park owned and managed by one of the U.S. states, usu. a large park in an area of natural beauty <Palo Duro State Park, in the second-largest U.S. canyon, is well known for its summer musical>.

state police. (1843) The department or agency of a state government empowered to maintain order, as by investigating and preventing crimes, and making arrests.

state police power. (1849) The power of a state to enforce laws for the health, welfare, morals, and safety of its citizens, if enacted so that the means are reasonably calculated to protect those legitimate state interests.

state prison. See PRISON.

state prisoner. See PRISONER (3).

state religion. See *state religion* under RELIGION.

state's attorney. 1. See DISTRICT ATTORNEY. **2.** See PROSECUTOR (1).

state seal. See *great seal* (2) under SEAL.

state secret. (1822) A governmental matter that would be a threat to the national defense or diplomatic interests of the United States if revealed; information possessed by the government and of a military or diplomatic nature, the disclosure of which would be contrary to the public interest. • State secrets are privileged from disclosure by a witness in an ordinary judicial proceeding. — Also termed *governmental secret; government secret.* See *executive privilege* & *state-secrets privilege* under PRIVILEGE (3).

state-secrets privilege. See PRIVILEGE (3).

state's evidence. See EVIDENCE.

state's evidence, turn. See TURN STATE'S EVIDENCE.

statesman. (16c) **1.** One skilled in the art of government; a sage and efficacious politician.

▸ **elder statesman.** (1921) **1.** Someone old and respected, esp. a venerable politician whose advice people rely on because it is based on broad experience and wise judgment. **2.** Loosely, any old politician.

2. *English law.* A small landowner.

statesmonger. See STATEMONGER.

state socialism. See SOCIALISM.

state sovereignty. (18c) The right of a state to self-government; the supreme authority exercised by each state.

state-sponsored terrorism. See TERRORISM.

state's prison. See *state prison* under PRISON.

states' rights. (1839) Under the Tenth Amendment, rights neither conferred on the federal government nor forbidden to the states. — Also termed *state rights.*

State Street Bank. *Patents.* A landmark 1998 decision in the Federal Circuit that made it easier to get patents on computer software, and also rejected the long-accepted notion that business methods are per se unpatentable. • The court struck down *per se* rules against patenting mathematical algorithms (the soul of software), focusing instead on whether the ultimate result was useful, concrete, and tangible in practice. *State Street Bank & Trust C. v. Signature Fin. Group, Inc.*, 149 F.3d 1368 (Fed. Cir. 1998).

state's ward. See *ward of the state* under WARD.

state tax. See TAX.

state terrorism. See TERRORISM.

state the question. (17c) *Parliamentary procedure.* (Of the chair) to formally state a motion as in order and ready for consideration. Cf. PUT THE QUESTION.

state trial. See TRIAL.

state trooper. A law-enforcement officer whose police force is controlled by one of the U.S. state governments. • The jurisdiction of such an officer is statewide.

state-use system. (1911) *Criminal law.* The state's employment of its prisoners to produce goods for only the state's use, not for introduction into the public market. • Many states require their agencies to purchase inmate-produced goods if available. See PUBLIC-WORKS-AND-WAYS SYSTEM. Cf. STATE ACCOUNT SYSTEM.

stateway, *n.* (1932) A governmental policy or law. • This term is formed on the analogy of *folkway.*

statim (**stay**-tim). [Latin] *Hist.* Immediately; at the earliest possible time when an act might lawfully be completed.

station. (17c) **1.** Social position or status. See STATUS. **2.** A place where military duties are performed or military goods are stored. **3.** A headquarters, as of a police department. **4.** A place where both freight and passengers are received for transport or delivered after transport. **5.** *Civil law.* A place where ships may safely travel.

Stationers' Company. *Hist.* An association of stationers and their successors, formed in London in 1403 and granted a royal charter in 1557, entrusted by order of the Privy Council with censorship of the press. • This company was the holder of the first rights we associate today with copyright.

Stationers' Hall. *Hist.* The hall of the Stationers' Company, established in London in 1553, at which every person claiming a copyright was required to register as a condition precedent to filing an infringement action.

> "'Entered at Stationers' Hall' on the title page of books was a form of warning to pirates that the owner of the copyright could and might sue. This requirement disappeared with the Copyright Act, 1911." David M. Walker, *The Oxford Companion to Law* 1182 (1980).

Stationery Office. *Hist. English law.* A government office established in 1786 as a department of the treasury, to supply government offices (including Parliament) with stationery and books, and to print and publish government papers. — Also termed *Her Majesty's Stationery Office.*

stationhouse. (1836) **1.** A police station or precinct. **2.** The lockup at a police precinct.

stationhouse bail. See *cash bail* under BAIL (1).

station-in-life test. (1944) *Family law.* An analysis performed by a court to determine the amount of money reasonably needed to maintain a particular person's accustomed lifestyle. • The elements were first set forth in *Canfield vs. Security-First Nat'l Bank,* 87 P.2d 830, 840 (Cal. 1939). The court takes into account the person's station in society and the costs of the person's support in that station, including housing and related expenses, medical care, further education, and other reasonably necessary expenses, but not including luxuries or extravagant expenditures. See NECESSARIES (1), (2).

statist (**stay**-tist). (16c) **1.** *Archaic.* A statesman; a politician. **2.** A statistician.

statistical-decision theory. (1966) A method for determining whether a panel of potential jurors was selected from a fair cross section of the community, by calculating the probabilities of selecting a certain number of jurors from a particular group to analyze whether it is statistically probable that the jury pool was selected by mere chance. • This method has been criticized because a pool of potential jurors is not ordinarily selected by mere chance; potential jurors are disqualified for many legitimate reasons. See FAIR-CROSS-SECTION REQUIREMENT; ABSOLUTE DISPARITY; COMPARATIVE DISPARITY; DUREN TEST.

statuliber (stach-ə-**lɪ**-bər), *n.* [Latin] *Roman law.* A person whose freedom under a will is made conditional or postponed; a person who will be free at a particular time or when certain conditions are met. — Also written *statu liber* (**stay**-t[y]oo **lɪ**-bər).

> "The *statuliber* is one who has freedom arranged to take effect on completion of a period or fulfillment of a condition. Men become *statuliberi* as a result of an express condition, or by the very nature of the case. The meaning of 'express condition' presents no problem. The status arises from the very nature of the case when men are manumitted for the purpose of defrauding a creditor; for so long as it is uncertain whether the creditor will use his right, the men remain *statuliberi,* since fraud is taken in the *lex Aelia Sentia* to involve actual damage." *Digest of Justinian* 40.7.1 (Paul, ad Sabinum 5).

status. (17c) **1.** A person's legal condition, whether personal or proprietary; the sum total of a person's legal rights, duties, liabilities, and other legal relations, or any particular group of them separately considered <the status of a landowner>. **2.** A person's legal condition regarding personal rights but excluding proprietary relations <the status of a father> <the status of a wife>. **3.** A person's capacities and incapacities, as opposed to other elements of personal status <the status of minors>. **4.** A person's legal condition insofar as it is imposed by the law without the person's consent, as opposed to a condition that the person has acquired by agreement <the status of a slave>. • For an insightful discussion of these four senses, see C.K. Allen, "Status and Capacity," in *Legal Duties and Other Essays in Jurisprudence* 28–70 (1931).

> "By the status (or standing) of a person is meant the position that he holds with reference to the rights which are recognized and maintained by the law — in other words, his capacity for the exercise and enjoyment of legal rights." James Hadley, *Introduction to Roman Law* 106 (1881).

> "The word 'status' itself originally signified nothing more than the position of a person before the law. Therefore, every person (except slaves, who were not regarded as persons, for legal purposes) had a *status.* But, as a result of the modern tendency towards legal equality formerly noticed, differences of *status* became less and less frequent, and the importance of the subject has greatly diminished, with the result that the term *status* is now used, at any rate in English Law, in connection only with those comparatively few classes of persons in the community who, by reason of their conspicuous differences from normal persons, and the fact that by no decision of their own can they get rid of these differences, require separate consideration in an account of the law. But professional or even political differences do not amount to *status;* thus peers, physicians, clergymen of the established Church, and many other classes of persons, are not regarded as the subjects of *status,* because the legal differences which distinguish them from other persons, though substantial, are not enough to make them legally abnormal. And landowners, merchants, manufacturers, and wage-earners are not subjects of the Law of Status, though the last-named are, as the result of recent legislation, tending to approach that position." Edward Jenks, *The Book of English Law* 109 (P.B. Fairest ed., 6th ed. 1967).

status, law of. See LAW OF STATUS.

STAT-USA. A unit in the U.S. Department of Commerce responsible for disseminating economics and trade information compiled by other federal agencies to businesses and individuals through subscription services and federal depository libraries. • STAT-USA is an agency within the Department's Economics and Statistics Administration.

status-based fiduciary relationship. See FIDUCIARY RELATIONSHIP.

status crime. See CRIME.

status de manerio (stay-təs dee mə-**neer**-ee-oh). [Law Latin "the state of a manor"] (18c) *Hist.* The assembly of tenants to attend the lord's court.

status libertatis (**stay**-tis lib-ər-**tay**-tis). [Latin] *Hist.* A state of freedom.

status offender. See OFFENDER.

status offense. See OFFENSE (2).

status-offense jurisdiction. See JURISDICTION.

status of irremovability. (1855) *Hist.* A pauper's right not to be removed from a parish after residing there for one year. Cf. SETTLEMENT (6).

status quo (**stay**-təs *or* **stat**-əs **kwoh**). [Latin "state in which"] (1807) The situation that currently exists.

status quo ante (**stay**-təs **kwoh an**-tee). [Latin "state in which previously"] (1877) The situation that existed before something else (being discussed) occurred.

statutable (**stach**-ə-tə-bəl), *adj.* (17c) **1.** Prescribed or authorized by statute. **2.** Conforming to the legislative requirements for quality, size, amount, or the like. **3.** (Of an offense) punishable by law. See STATUTORY.

statute. (14c) A law passed by a legislative body; specif., legislation enacted by any lawmaking body, such as a legislature, administrative board, or municipal court. • The term *act* or *legislation* is interchangeable as a synonym. For each of the subentries listed below, *act* or *legislation* is sometimes substituted for *statute.* — Abbr. s.; stat.

> "**Statutes.** Acts of parliament. The *lex scripta*, or, for the most part, gradual encroachments upon the liberty of the subject." Charles Pigott, *A Political Dictionary* 159 (1798).

> "[W]e are not justified in limiting the statutory law to those rules only which are promulgated by what we commonly call 'legislatures.' Any positive enactment to which the state gives the force of a law is a 'statute,' whether it has gone through the usual stages of legislative proceedings, or has been adopted in other modes of expressing the will of the people or other sovereign power of the state. In an absolute monarchy, an edict of the ruling sovereign is statutory law. Constitutions, being direct legislation by the people, must be included in the statutory law, and indeed they are examples of the highest form that the statute law can assume. Generally speaking, treaties also are statutory law, because in this country, under the provisions of the United States Constitution, treaties have not the force of law until so declared by the representatives of the people." William M. Lile et al., *Brief Making and the Use of Law Books* 8 (Roger W. Cooley & Charles Lesley Ames eds., 3d ed. 1914).

▸ **affirmative statute.** (16c) A law expressed in positive terms to require that something be done; one that directs the doing of an act. Cf. *negative statute.*

▸ **always-speaking statute.** See *speaking statute.*

▸ **amending statute.** (1843) A law that alters the operation of an earlier law, often by inserting or deleting words or provisions of the original text. — Also termed *amending act.*

▸ **antideficiency statute.** See *antideficiency legislation* under LEGISLATION (3).

▸ **beneficial statute.** See *remedial statute.*

▸ **blocking statute.** (1923) A statute prohibiting a party to request, seek, or disclose economic, commercial, industrial, financial, or technical documents or information that might lead to evidence for foreign judicial or administrative proceedings. • Blocking statutes are subject to treaties, international agreements, and applicable laws and regulations. *See Société Nationale Industrielle Aérospatiale v. S.D. Iowa*, 482 U.S. 522, 526 n.6, 107 S.Ct. 2542, 2546 n.6 (1987).

▸ **codifying statute.** (1908) A law that purports to be exhaustive in restating the whole of the law on a particular topic, including prior caselaw as well as legislative provisions. • Courts generally presume that a codifying statute supersedes prior caselaw. Cf. *consolidating statute.*

▸ **compiled statutes.** (1841) Laws that have been arranged by subject but have not been substantively changed; COMPILATION (2). Cf. *revised statutes.*

> "The term 'compiled statutes' is properly applied to a methodical arrangement, without revision or reenactment, of the existing statutes of a State, all the statutes on a given subject being collected in one place. The work is usually performed by private persons; and the former statutes, as they were before the compilation, remain the authority." Frank Hall Childs, *Where and How to Find the Law* 12 (1922).

▸ **consolidating statute.** (1886) A law that collects the legislative provisions on a particular subject and embodies them in a single statute, often with minor amendments and drafting improvements. • Courts generally presume that a consolidating statute leaves prior caselaw intact. — Also termed *consolidating act.* Cf. *codifying statute.*

> "A distinction of greater importance in this field is that between consolidating and codifying statutes. A consolidating statute is one which collects the statutory provisions relating to a particular topic, and embodies them in a single Act of Parliament, making only minor amendments and improvements. A codifying statute is one which purports to state exhaustively the whole of the law on a particular subject (the common law as well as previous statutory provisions). . . . The importance of the distinction lies in the courts' treatment of the previous case law, the existence of special procedural provisions with regard to consolidating statutes and the existence of a presumption that they do not change the law." Rupert Cross, *Statutory Interpretation* 5 (1976).

▸ **construction statute.** A legislative directive included in a statute, intended to guide or direct a court's interpretation of the statute. • A construction act can, for example, be a simple statement such as "The word 'week' means seven consecutive days" or a broader directive such as "Words and phrases are to be read in context and construed according to the rules of grammar and common usage. Words and phrases that have acquired a technical or particular meaning, whether by legislative definition or otherwise, are to be construed accordingly." Cf. INTERPRETATION CLAUSE.

▸ **criminal statute.** (18c) See *penal statute.*

▸ **curative statute.** (1843) **1.** An act that corrects an error in a statute's original enactment, usu. an error that interferes with interpreting or applying the statute. Cf. *validating statute.* **2.** See *remedial statute.* — Also termed *curative law.*

▸ **declaratory statute.** (17c) A law enacted to clarify prior law by reconciling conflicting judicial decisions or by explaining the meaning of a prior statute. — Also termed *expository statute*.

▸ **directory statute.** (1834) A law that indicates only what should be done, with no provision for enforcement. Cf. *mandatory statute*; *permissive statute*.

▸ **disabling statute.** (18c) A law that limits or curbs certain rights.

▸ **enabling statute.** (18c) A law that permits what was previously prohibited or that creates new powers; esp., a congressional statute conferring powers on an executive agency to carry out various delegated tasks.

▸ **expository statute.** See *declaratory statute*.

▸ **general statute.** (16c) A law relating to an entire community or all persons generally. — Also termed *public statute*. See PUBLIC LAW (2).

▸ **imperfect statute.** (1847) A law that prohibits, but does not render void, an objectionable transaction. • Such a statute provides a penalty for disobedience without depriving the violative transaction of its legal effect.

▸ **interpretation statute.** See INTERPRETATION ACT.

▸ **local statute. 1.** See LOCAL LAW (1). **2.** See LOCAL LAW (2).

▸ **mandatory statute.** (18c) A law that requires a course of action as opposed to merely permitting it. Cf. *directory statute*; *permissive statute*.

▸ **model statute.** See *uniform statute*.

▸ **negative statute.** (16c) A law prohibiting something; a law expressed in negative terms. Cf. *affirmative statute*.

"An old division of statutes is into affirmative and negative; the former being such as are in affirmative, the later in negative, words. A provision, for example, that it *shall be lawful* for a tenant in fee-simple to make a lease for twenty-one years, or that such lease *shall be good*, is affirmative; one that it *shall not be lawful* to make a lease for above twenty-one years, or that a lease for more *shall not be good*, is negative. A negative statute, being in its terms a negation, or denial, of the prior law, repeals it; and obviously this repeal is express." Joel Prentiss Bishop, *Commentaries on the Written Laws and their Interpretation* § 153, at 139 (1882).

▸ **nonclaim statute.** (18c) **1.** STATUTE OF LIMITATIONS. **2.** A law that sets a time limit for creditors to bring claims against a decedent's estate. • Unlike a statute of limitations, a nonclaim statute is usu. not subject to tolling and is not waivable. — Also termed (in sense 2) *statute of repose*.

▸ **organic statute.** (1856) A law that establishes an administrative agency or local government. — Also termed *organic act*. Cf. ORGANIC LAW.

▸ **penal statute.** (16c) A statute by which punishments are imposed for transgressions of the law, civil as well as criminal; esp., a statute that defines a crime and prescribes its corresponding fine, penalty, or punishment. — Also termed *penal law*; *punitive statute*; *criminal statute*. See PENAL CODE.

"It is a familiar and well-settled rule that penal statutes are to be construed strictly, and not extended by implications, intendments, analogies, or equitable considerations. Thus, an offense cannot be created or inferred by vague implications. And a court cannot create a penalty by construction, but must avoid it by construction unless it is brought within the letter and the necessary meaning of the act creating it." Henry Campbell Black, *Handbook on the Construction and Interpretation of the Laws* 287 (1896).

▸ **permanent statute.** See *perpetual statute*.

▸ **permissive statute.** (1833) A statute that allows certain acts but does not command them. • A permissive statute creates a license or privilege, or allows discretion in performing an act. Cf. *directory statute*; *mandatory statute*.

▸ **perpetual statute.** (16c) A law containing no provision for repeal, abrogation, or expiration. — Also termed *permanent statute*. Cf. *temporary statute* (1).

▸ **personal statute.** (1813) *Civil law*. A law that primarily affects a person's condition or status (such as a statute relating to capacity or majority) and affects property only incidentally.

▸ **preceptive statute.** (1851) A statute expressing a direct command that is prescriptive, general, definite, and fairly complete. • In form, a preceptive statute is similar to a rule.

▸ **private statute.** See *special statute*.

▸ **prohibitive statute.** (1841) A statute that forbids certain acts. • An example of a noncriminal prohibitive statute is one forbidding the execution of a mentally retarded criminal because a person who lacks mental capacity cannot understand the reason for the punishment.

▸ **prospective statute.** (1831) A law that applies to future events.

▸ **public statute.** See PUBLIC LAW (2).

▸ **punitive statute.** See *penal statute*.

▸ **quasi-statute.** (1848) An executive or administrative order, or a regulation promulgated by a governmental agency, that has the binding effect of legislation.

"Quasi-Statutes. Executive and administrative orders by the government as well as military regulations, while not called statutes, not originating as statutes usually do, are, nevertheless, in force and effect, laws. Copies of general orders and proclamations are issued to the public press for publication, but military regulations may for public reasons be kept private." Jesse Franklin Brumbaugh, *Legal Reasoning and Briefing* 223 (1917).

▸ **real statute.** (18c) *Civil law*. A law primarily affecting the operation, status, and condition of property, and addressing persons only incidentally.

▸ **recording statute.** See RECORDING ACT.

▸ **reference statute.** (1934) A law that incorporates and adopts by reference provisions of other laws.

▸ **remedial statute.** (18c) **1.** Any statute other than a private bill; a law providing a means to enforce rights or redress injuries. • William Blackstone defined the term as follows: "Remedial statutes are those which are made to supply such defects, and abridge such superfluities, in the common law, as arise either from the general imperfection of all human laws, from change of time and circumstances, from the mistakes and unadvised determinations of unlearned judges, or from any other cause whatsoever." 1 William Blackstone, *Commentaries on the Laws of England* 86 (4th ed. 1770). **2.** A statute enacted to correct one or more defects, mistakes, or omissions. — Also termed *beneficial statute*; *curative statute*; *remedial law*.

▸ **repealing statute.** (17c) A statute that revokes, and sometimes replaces, an earlier statute. • A repealing statute may work expressly or by implication.

▸ **restraining statute.** See *disabling statute.*

▸ **retroactive statute.** See RETROACTIVE LAW.

▸ **retrospective statute.** See RETROACTIVE LAW.

▸ **revised statutes.** (18c) Laws that have been collected, arranged, and reenacted as a whole by a legislative body. — Abbr. Rev. Stat.; R.S. See CODE (1). Cf. *compiled statutes.*

▸ **revival statute.** (1899) A law that provides for the renewal of actions, of wills, and of the legal effect of documents. • A revival statute cannot resurrect a time-barred criminal prosecution. *Stogner v. California*, 539 U.S. 607, 123 S.Ct. 2446 (2003).

▸ **severable statute.** (1930) A law that remains operative in its remaining provisions even if a portion of the law is declared unconstitutional.

▸ **single-act statute.** See LONG-ARM STATUTE.

▸ **speaking statute.** (2000) A statute to be interpreted in light of the understanding of its terms prevailing at the time of interpretation. — Also termed *always-speaking statute.*

▸ **special statute.** (17c) A law that applies only to specific individuals, as opposed to everyone. — Also termed *private statute.*

> "It is ancient wisdom, tracing back at least as far as the Roman taboo against the *privilegium*, that laws ought to be *general*, they ought to be addressed, not to particular persons, but to persons generally or to classes of persons (say, 'all householders'). Accordingly, a number of American states have inserted in their constitutions prohibitions against 'private or special' statutes. These have given rise to endless difficulties." Lon L. Fuller, *Anatomy of the Law* 102–03 (1968).

> "Differences of definition threaten unity of understanding, and in part these exist because of the lack of proper words. For instance, Blackstone defines a 'general or public act' as 'a universal rule that regards the whole country;' and says that 'special or private acts are rather exceptions than rules, being those which only operate upon particular persons and private concerns.' Note that he seems to treat 'general' and 'public' as synonymous; 'special' and 'private' as synonymous. Yet in each case usage frequently discriminates. Since his time the tendency in England has been to drop 'general' and 'special' in the description of laws, with the result that the word 'private' is applied to many bills not private at all, in the ordinary acceptance of the word. May showed the inaccuracy of the term when he defined a private bill as one that is for the particular interest or benefit of some person or persons, whether an individual or a number of individuals, a public company or corporation, a parish, city, county, or other locality having not a legal but a popular name only. This was an improvement on Blackstone, yet is open to criticism because it does not reach exceptions to general rules that are distinctly not to the interest or benefit of all the persons concerned, but quite the contrary. . . . With us [in BrE] the confusion of terms has taken a different direction. We have used 'private' and 'special' indiscriminately, with 'local' as a sort of explanatory sub-title. Were it possible to ordain the use of language (which it is not), a benevolent despot might well try to secure that general-special (or general-local) be determined by territorial extent; public-private, by subject matter. Lacking acceptance of such a classification, Americans may go on thinking that their use of 'special' is better than the English 'private' to cover everything not 'general;' and may justify their tendency to use 'public' for laws applying indiscriminately to all members of a community." Robert Luce, *Legislative Problems* 532–34 (1971).

▸ **split-level statute.** (1980) A law that includes officially promulgated explanatory materials in addition to its substantive provisions, so that courts are left with two levels of documents to construe.

▸ **statute of descent and distribution.** See STATUTE OF DISTRIBUTION.

▸ **statute of distribution.** See STATUTE OF DISTRIBUTION.

▸ **statute of frauds.** See STATUTE OF FRAUDS.

▸ **statute of limitations.** See STATUTE OF LIMITATIONS.

▸ **statute of repose.** See STATUTE OF REPOSE.

▸ **temporary statute.** (17c) **1.** A law that specifically provides that it is to remain in effect for a fixed, limited period. Cf. *perpetual statute.* **2.** A law (such as an appropriation statute) that, by its nature, has only a single and temporary operation.

▸ **uniform statute.** A law drafted in hopes that it will be widely adopted; UNIFORM LAW. — Also termed *model statute; uniform act.* Cf. MODEL ACT.

▸ **validating statute.** (1882) A law whose purpose is either to remove errors from an existing statute or to add provisions to conform it to constitutional requirements. — Also termed *validation statute.* Cf. *curative statute.*

statute book. (16c) A bound collection of statutes, usu. as part of a larger set of books containing a complete body of statutory law, such as the United States Code Annotated.

Statute De Donis Conditionalibus. See DE DONIS CONDITIONALIBUS.

statute fair. (18c) *Hist.* A fair during which the fixed labor rates were announced and laborers of both sexes offered themselves for hire. — Also termed *mop fair.*

statute law. See STATUTORY LAW.

statute-making. See LEGISLATION (1).

statute merchant. (15c) *Hist.* **1.** (*cap.*) One of two 13th-century statutes establishing procedures to better secure and recover debts by, among other things, providing for a commercial bond that, if not timely paid, resulted in swift execution on the debtor's lands, goods, and body. 13 Edw. I, ch. 6 (1283); 15 Edw. I, ch. 6 (1285). • These statutes were repealed in 1863. — Also termed *pocket judgment.* **2.** The commercial bond so established. Cf. STATUTE STAPLE.

> "It is not a little remarkable that our common law knew no process whereby a man could pledge his body or liberty for payment of a debt . . . . Under Edward I, the tide turned. In the interest of commerce a new form of security, the so-called 'statute merchant,' was invented, which gave the creditor power to demand the seizure and imprisonment of his debtor's body." 2 Frederick Pollock & Frederic W. Maitland, *The History of English Law Before the Time of Edward I* 596–97 (2d ed. 1899).

statute mile. See MILE (1).

Statute of Accumulations. *Hist.* A statute forbidding the accumulation, beyond a certain period, of property settled by deed or will. 39 & 40 Geo. 3, ch. 98 (1800).

Statute of Allegiance de Facto. *Hist.* A statute requiring subjects to give allegiance to the actual (de facto) king, and protecting them in so doing. 11 Hen. 7, ch. 1.

Statute of Amendments and Jeofails (**jef**-aylz). *Hist.* One of several 15th- and 16th-century statutes allowing a party who acknowledges a pleading error to correct it. 1 Hen. 5, ch. 5 (1413); 32 Hen. 8, ch. 30 (1540); 37 Hen. 8, ch. 6 (1545). See JEOFAIL.

Statute of Anne. *Hist. English law.* **1.** The Copyright Act of 1709, which first granted copyright protection to book authors. 8 Anne, ch. 19 (1709). **2.** The statute that modernized the English bankruptcy system and first introduced the discharge of the debtor's existing debts. 4 Anne, ch. 17 (1705).

statute of bread and ale. See ASSISA PANIS ET CEREVISIAE.

statute of descent and distribution. See STATUTE OF DISTRIBUTION.

statute of distribution. (18c) A state law regulating the distribution of an estate among an intestate's heirs and relatives. • Historically, the statute specified separate, and often different, patterns for distributing an intestate's real property and personal property. Generally, land descended to the heirs and personalty descended to the next of kin. — Also termed *statute of descent and distribution.*

Statute of Elizabeth. *Hist. English law.* A 1571 penal statute that contained provisions against conveyances made to defraud creditors. 13 Eliz., ch. 5. • The fundamental provisions of this statute formed the basis for modern laws against fraudulent conveyances. — Also termed *Act of Elizabeth.*

> "The law of fraudulent conveyances is not new. The creditor's right of realization was approached, for the most part, by common law paths. And the common law mind naturally required a statute in aid of any one who would say that a conveyance was not a conveyance simply because it brought harm to others. As we shall see, it was not left to equity to play its part. Like bankruptcy, this idea of the fraudulent conveyance at large traces back to a statute of the period of Elizabeth. Like bankruptcy, too, the Elizabethan statute was not the prototype. There was a bankruptcy law of the time of Henry VIII; and there were statutes of fraudulent conveyances in earlier reigns. But our mode of thinking has always travelled, in both branches of law, bankruptcy and fraudulent conveyances, to two acts of the reign of Elizabeth, passed in the same session of Parliament. It is probable, as the writer thinks, that this is due to the restatement of the law which was made by Coke. He took care to devote, in his Reports (really case notes of the sort with which modern Law Reviews have made us familiar), one reading to the statute of bankruptcy and two to the statute of fraudulent conveyances. Later, no one cared to go back further. The law of fraudulent conveyances then, from a practical standpoint, may be ascribed to the Act of Elizabeth. In truth it dates from Coke." Garrard Glenn, *The Law of Fraudulent Conveyances* 7–8 (1931).

statute of frauds. (18c) **1.** *(cap.) Hist.* A 1677 English statute that declared certain contracts judicially unenforceable (but not void) if they were not committed to writing and signed by the party to be charged. • The statute was entitled "An Act for the Prevention of Frauds and Perjuries" (29 Car. 2, ch. 3). — Also termed *Statute of Frauds and Perjuries.*

> "The best known, and until recently, most important, Act prescribing written formalities for certain contracts only required that those contracts should be evidenced in writing, or to put it another way, that the contract would be unenforceable in a Court (but not void) in the absence of writing. This was the Statute of Frauds 1677, sections 4 and 17 of which required written evidence of a somewhat curious list of contracts. Today, all that is left of these provisions is that part of section 4, which requires contracts of guarantee to be evidenced in writing, and section 40 of the Law of Property Act 1925 (replacing another part of section 4), which deals with contracts of sale of an interest in land." P.S. Atiyah, *An Introduction to the Law of Contract* 141 (3d ed. 1981).

2. A statute (based on the English Statute of Frauds) designed to prevent fraud and perjury by requiring certain contracts to be in writing and signed by the party to be charged. • Statutes of frauds traditionally apply to the following types of contracts: (1) a contract for the sale or transfer of an interest in land, (2) a contract that cannot be performed within one year of its making, (3) a contract for the sale of goods valued at $500 or more, (4) a contract of an executor or administrator to answer for a decedent's debt, (5) a contract to guarantee the debt or duty of another, and (6) a contract made in consideration of marriage. UCC § 2-201. — Abbr. S/F; SOF.

> "[T]he primary theory of statutes of frauds, past and present, is that they are means to the end of preventing successful courtroom perjury. The means to this end is simply the requirement of a writing signed by the party to be charged. . . . [B]ut the statute of frauds writing requirement is . . . so far from any kind of guarantee against successful perjury that it is inappropriate even to call it a means to fraud prevention at all." 1 James J. White & Robert S. Summers, *Uniform Commercial Code* § 2-8, at 82 (4th ed. 1995).

Statute of Frauds Amendment Act 1828. See TENTERDEN'S ACT.

Statute of Frauds and Perjuries. See STATUTE OF FRAUDS (1).

Statute of Gloucester (**glos**-tər). *Hist. English law.* A 1278 statute providing for certain writs and for the award of costs in lawsuits. 6 Edw., ch. 1.

> "The statute of Gloucester (1278) provided a writ of waste against tenants for life, years, or a woman holding by right of dower. Those convicted of waste were punished by forfeiture of the thing wasted and triple damages. To come within the statute the waste must have been caused by the voluntary act of the tenant—the fact that it had been caused accidentally or by *vis major* was a good defense. How far tenants were liable for merely permissive waste, i.e. for doing nothing, with the result that the premises decayed, was not settled till a later period." W.S. Holdsworth, *An Historical Introduction to the Land Law* 61 (1927).

statute of jeofails (**jef**-aylz). (16c) A law permitting a litigant to acknowledge an error in a pleading and correct or amend the pleading without risking dismissal of the claim. See JEOFAIL.

statute of limitations. (18c) **1.** A law that bars claims after a specified period; specif., a statute establishing a time limit for suing in a civil case, based on the date when the claim accrued (as when the injury occurred or was discovered). • The purpose of such a statute is to require diligent prosecution of known claims, thereby providing finality and predictability in legal affairs and ensuring that claims will be resolved while evidence is reasonably available and fresh. — Also termed *nonclaim statute*; *limitations period.*

> "Statutes of limitations, like the equitable doctrine of laches, in their conclusive effects are designed to promote justice by preventing surprises through the revival of claims that have been allowed to slumber until evidence has been lost, memories have faded, and witnesses have disappeared." *Order of R.R. Telegraphers v. Railway Express Agency*, 321 U.S. 342, 348–49, 64 S.Ct. 582, 586 (1944).

2. A statute establishing a time limit for prosecuting a crime, based on the date when the offense occurred. — Abbr. S/L; SOL. Cf. STATUTE OF REPOSE.

> "The purpose of a statute of limitations is to limit exposure to criminal prosecution to a certain fixed period of time following the occurrence of those acts the legislature had decided to punish by criminal sanctions. Such a limitation

is designed to protect individuals from having to defend themselves against charges when the basic facts have become obscured by the passage of time and to minimize the danger of official punishment because of acts in the far-distant past. Such a time limit may also have the salutary effect of encouraging law enforcement officials promptly to investigate suspected criminal activity." *Toussie v. U.S.*, 397 U.S. 112, 90 S.Ct. 858 (1970).

Statute of Monopolies. *Hist.* A 1624 act of the English Parliament banning the Crown's practice of granting monopolies with the single exception of letters patent, which gave an inventor the exclusive right to make and use the invention for 14 years. 21 Jac. 1, ch. 3.

statute of mortmain. See MORTMAIN STATUTE.

statute of repose. (18c) **1.** A statute barring any suit that is brought after a specified time since the defendant acted (such as by designing or manufacturing a product), even if this period ends before the plaintiff has suffered a resulting injury. Cf. STATUTE OF LIMITATIONS.

"A statute of repose . . . limits the time within which an action may be brought and is not related to the accrual of any cause of action; the injury need not have occurred, much less have been discovered. Unlike an ordinary statute of limitations which begins running upon accrual of the claim, the period contained in a statute of repose begins when a specific event occurs, regardless of whether a cause of action has accrued or whether any injury has resulted." 54 C.J.S. *Limitations of Actions* § 4, at 20–21 (1987).

2. See *nonclaim statute* under STATUTE.

Statute of the International Court of Justice. The 1945 legislation that organized the composition and function of the International Court of Justice. • The statute is annexed to the Charter of the United Nations and is treated as an integral part of it. It may be amended only in the same way as the Charter: by a two-thirds vote in the General Assembly and ratification of twothirds of the states. See INTERNATIONAL COURT OF JUSTICE; CHARTER OF THE UNITED NATIONS 1945.

Statute of Uses. *Hist.* An English statute of 1535 that converted the equitable title held by a cestui que use (i.e., a beneficiary) to a legal one in order to make the cestui que use liable for feudal dues, as only a legal owner (the *feoffee to uses*) could be. 27 Hen. 8, ch. 10. • This statute was the culmination of a series of enactments designed by the Tudors to stop the practice of creating uses in land that deprived feudal lords of the valuable incidents of feudal tenure. The statute discouraged the granting of property subject to another's use by deeming the person who enjoys the use to have legal title with the right of absolute ownership and possession. So after the statute was enacted, if A conveyed land to B subject to the use of C, then C became the legal owner of the land in fee simple. Ultimately, the statute was circumvented by the courts' recognition of the use of equitable trusts in land-conveyancing. See CESTUI QUE USE; GRANT TO USES; USE (4). Cf. DOCTRINE OF USES.

"The Statute of 27 H.8. hath advanced Uses, and hath established Surety for him that hath the Use against the Feoffees: for before the Statute the Feoffees were Owners of the Land, but now it is destroyed, and the *cestuy que use* is the Owner of the same: before the Possession ruled the Use, but since the Use governeth the Possession." William Noy, *A Treatise of the Principal Grounds and Maxims of the Laws of This Nation* 73 (4th ed. 1677; repr. C. Sims ed., 1870).

Statute of Westminster the First. See WESTMINSTER THE FIRST, STATUTE OF.

statute of wills. (17c) **1.** (*cap.*) A 1540 English statute establishing the right of a person to devise real property by will. — Also termed *Wills Act.* **2.** A state statute, usu. derived from the English statute, providing for testamentary disposition and if certain requirements for valid execution in that jurisdiction are met.

Statute of Winchester. See WINCHESTER, STATUTE OF.

Statute of York. See YORK, STATUTE OF.

statute roll. (16c) *Hist.* A roll on which a statute was formally entered after receiving the royal assent.

Statutes at Large. An official compilation of the acts and resolutions that become law from each session of Congress, printed in chronological order.

statute staple. (15c) *Hist.* **1.** A 1353 statute establishing procedures for settling disputes among merchants who traded in staple towns. • The statute helped merchants receive swift judgments for debt. Cf. STATUTE MERCHANT. **2.** A bond for commercial debt. • A statute staple gave the lender a possessory right in the land of a debtor who failed to repay a loan. See STAPLE.

"A popular form of security after 1285 . . . was the . . . 'statute staple' — whereby the borrower could by means of a registered contract charge his land and goods without giving up possession; if he failed to pay, the lender became a tenant of the land until satisfied . . . . The borrower under a statute or recognizance remained in possession of his land, and it later became a common practice under the common-law forms of mortgage likewise to allow the mortgagor to remain in possession as a tenant at will or at sufferance of the mortgagee." J.H. Baker, *An Introduction to English Legal History* 354 (3d ed. 1990).

statuti (stə-**t**[**y**]**oo**-tɪ), *n. pl.* [Latin] *Roman law.* Licensed officials, esp. advocates, whose names are inscribed in registers of matriculation, forming part of the college of advocates. Cf. SUPERNUMERARII.

statuto mercatorio. See DE STATUTO MERCATORIO.

statutorification (stach-ə-tor-i-fi-**kay**-shən), *n.* (1982) The excessive reliance on legislation to cure society's ills. • This neologism first appeared in a work by Guido Calabresi: *A Common Law for the Age of Statutes* (1982). — **statutorify**, *vb.*

statutory (**stach**-ə-tor-ee), *adj.* (18c) **1.** Of, relating to, or involving legislation <statutory interpretation>. **2.** Legislatively created <the law of patents is purely statutory>. **3.** Conformable to a statute <a statutory act>.

statutory action. See ACTION (4).

statutory agent. See AGENT.

statutory arson. See ARSON (2).

statutory bar. *Patents.* A patent law provision that denies patent protection to inventors who wait too long to apply. • This "loss of right" may occur when an inventor publishes an article about the work, sells it, offers it for sale, or makes public use of the invention. The inventor has one year after the disclosure to apply for a patent. See BAR (7). Cf. GRACE PERIOD (2).

statutory bond. (1802) A bond that literally or substantially meets the requirements of a statute. See BOND (2), (3).

statutory burglary. See BURGLARY (2).

statutory construction. (1813) **1.** The act or process of interpreting a statute. **2.** Collectively, the principles developed by courts for interpreting statutes. — Also termed *statutory interpretation.* See CONSTRUCTION (2).

"[T]here is not, and probably never can be, anything meriting the description of a coherent body of case-law on statutory interpretation as a whole as distinct from the interpretation of a particular statute." Rupert Cross, *Statutory Interpretation* 39 (1976).

statutory contract. See CONTRACT.

statutory crime. See CRIME.

statutory damages. See DAMAGES.

statutory dedication. See DEDICATION.

statutory deed. See DEED.

statutory disclaimer. See DISCLAIMER.

statutory double patenting. See DOUBLE PATENTING.

statutory double-patenting rejection. See REJECTION.

statutory employee. See EMPLOYEE.

statutory employer. See EMPLOYER.

statutory exception. See EXCEPTION (2).

statutory exclusion. *Criminal procedure.* The removal, by law, of certain crimes from juvenile-court jurisdiction. • Many states now remove certain particularly serious crimes committed by older juveniles from the jurisdiction of the juvenile courts. In this kind of case, the juvenile court never has jurisdiction, so a transfer hearing is not required or necessary. — Also termed *legislative exclusion.* Cf. MANDATORY WAIVER.

statutory exposition. (1854) A statute's special interpretation of the ambiguous terms of a previous statute <the statute contained a statutory exposition of the former act>.

statutory extortion. See EXTORTION.

statutory forced share. See ELECTIVE SHARE.

statutory foreclosure. See *power-of-sale foreclosure* under FORECLOSURE.

statutory guardian. See GUARDIAN (1).

statutory history. The enacted lineage of a statute, including prior laws, amendments, codifications, and repeals. Cf. LEGISLATIVE HISTORY.

statutory homestead. See *constitutional homestead* under HOMESTEAD (1).

statutory indemnity. See INDEMNITY.

statutory insolvency. See BANKRUPTCY (4).

statutory instrument. (1946) A British administrative regulation or order; an order or regulation issued by an authority empowered by statute to do so, usu. to give detailed effect to the statute.

statutory interpretation. See STATUTORY CONSTRUCTION.

statutory invention registration. (1984) *Patents.* An official procedure for placing an invention in the public domain by publishing the patent abstract (which is included with the invention's original application) in the U.S. Patent and Trademark Office's Official Gazette, thus making the abstract a prior-art reference as of the application's filing date. • The process results in abandonment of the patent application. If an alternative form of disclosure is used, the prior-art reference's effective date is the date of publication. 35 USCA § 157. — Abbr. SIR. See DEFENSIVE DISCLOSURE.

statutory law. (17c) The body of law derived from statutes rather than from constitutions or judicial decisions. — Also termed *statute law*; *legislative law*; *ordinary law.* Cf. COMMON LAW (1); CONSTITUTIONAL LAW.

statutory liability. See LIABILITY.

statutory lien. See LIEN.

statutory merger. See MERGER (8).

statutory obligation. See OBLIGATION.

statutory offense. See *statutory crime* under CRIME.

statutory omnibus clause. See OMNIBUS CLAUSE (1).

statutory partition. See PARTITION (2).

statutory partnership association. See PARTNERSHIP ASSOCIATION.

statutory penalty. See PENALTY (1).

statutory period. (18c) **1.** A time limit specified in a statute; esp., the period prescribed in the relevant statute of limitations. • This period includes, in addition to a fixed number of years, whatever time local law allows because of infancy, insanity, coverture, and other like circumstances. **2.** *Patents.* The time available to a patent applicant to answer an examiner's office action. • Since the six-month period is set by statute, it cannot be extended but it can be shortened to as few as 30 days. 35 USCA § 133. Cf. SHORTENED STATUTORY PERIOD.

statutory presumption. See PRESUMPTION.

statutory rape. See RAPE (2).

statutory rate. See MECHANICAL ROYALTY.

statutory receiver. See RECEIVER (1).

statutory redemption. See REDEMPTION.

statutory release. (1846) **1.** *Hist.* A method of conveyance superseding the compound assurance by lease and release, created by the Conveyance by Release Without Lease Act of 1841 (St. 4 & 5 Vict., ch. 21). **2.** *Canadian law.* The right of certain prison inmates to be released after serving two-thirds of their sentences, in accordance with the Corrections and Conditional Release Act of 1992.

statutory right of redemption. (1857) **1.** The right of a mortgagor in default to recover property after a foreclosure sale by paying the principal, interest, and other costs that are owed, together with any other measure required to cure the default. • This statutory right exists in many states but is not uniform. See EQUITY OF REDEMPTION; REDEMPTION (4). **2.** A debtor's statutory right to reclaim property seized by a creditor either by paying to the creditor the entire debt plus any expenses incurred by the creditor or by reimbursing the buyer of the property for the purchase price. — Also termed *right to redeem.*

statutory share. See ELECTIVE SHARE.

statutory staple. *Hist.* A writ to seize the lands, goods, and person of a debtor for forfeiting a statute staple. See STATUTE STAPLE.

statutory subject matter. See PATENTABLE SUBJECT MATTER.

statutory successor. See SUCCESSOR.

statutory tenant. See TENANT (1).

statuto stapulae. See DE STATUTO STAPULAE.

statutum (stə-t[y]oo-təm), *adj.* Established; determined.

statutum, *n.* **1.** *Hist.* An act of Parliament, esp. one that has been approved by the monarch. Cf. ACTUS (2). **2.** *Roman law.* An ordinance; esp., an imperial law.

Statutum de Nova Custuma (stə-**t**[y]**oo**-təm dee **noh**-və **kəs**-chə-mə *or* kəs-tyə-mə). See CARTA MERCATORIA.

stay, *n.* (16c) **1.** The postponement or halting of a proceeding, judgment, or the like. **2.** An order to suspend all or part of a judicial proceeding or a judgment resulting from that proceeding. — Also termed *stay of execution; suspension of judgment.* — **stay,** *vb.* — **stayable,** *adj.*

▸ **automatic stay.** (1922) *Bankruptcy.* A bar to all judicial and extrajudicial collection efforts against the debtor or the debtor's property, subject to specific statutory exceptions. 11 USCA §§ 362(a)–(b). • The policy behind the automatic stay, which is effective upon the filing of the bankruptcy petition, is that all actions against the debtor should be halted pending the determination of creditors' rights and the orderly administration of the debtor's assets free from creditor interference. — Also termed *automatic suspension.*

stay-away order. (1983) **1.** In a domestic-violence case, an order forbidding the defendant to contact the victim. • A stay-away order usu. prohibits the defendant from coming within a certain number of feet of the victim's home, school, work, or other specific place. Stay-away orders are most often issued in criminal cases. **2.** RESTRAINING ORDER (1). **3.** In a juvenile-delinquency case, an order prohibiting a youthful offender from frequenting the scene of the offense or from being in the company of certain persons. — Also termed *no-contact order; stay-away order of protection.*

stay of execution. See STAY.

stay of mandate. (1881) **1.** The suspension of a lower court's order of execution, imposed by a higher court. See MANDATE (1). **2.** An appellate court's suspension of its own judgment pending reconsideration or further appeal.

stayor. (1842) *Rare. Tennessee law.* A surety for a judgment.

stay-put rule. (1980) *School law.* The principle that a child must remain in his or her current educational placement while an administrative claim under the Individuals with Disabilities Education Act (usu. for an alternative placement or for mainstreaming) is pending. 20 USCA § 1415(j).

STB. *abbr.* SURFACE TRANSPORTATION BOARD.

STD. *abbr.* (1974) SEXUALLY TRANSMITTED DISEASE.

steady course. (17c) *Maritime law.* A ship's path that can be readily ascertained either because the ship is on a straight heading or because the ship's future positions are easy to plot based on the ship's current position and movements.

steal, *vb.* (bef. 12c) **1.** To take (personal property) illegally with the intent to keep it unlawfully. **2.** To take (something) by larceny, embezzlement, or false pretenses.

stealing by finding. See *larceny by finding* under LARCENY.

stealth. (14c) **1.** *Hist.* Theft; an act or instance of stealing. • Etymologically, this term is the noun corresponding to the verb *steal.*

> "Stealth is the wrongful taking of goods without pretence of title: and therefore altereth not the property, as a trespass doth, so as upon an appeal the party shall re-have them." Henry Finch, *Law, or a Discourse Thereof* 210 (1759).

2. Surreptitiousness; furtive slyness.

stealth juror. See JUROR.

steering committee. 1. A special subgroup of legislators who determine the order in which business will be considered by the full legislature. **2.** Any select group that guides or direct a particular activity.

steganography (steg-ə-**nog**-rə-fee), *n.* (16c) A cryptographic method that digitally embeds or encodes one item of information within another. • Because digitized audio or visual files usu. have unused data areas, indelible (and nearly undetectable) information can be added without altering the file's quality. Copyright or trademark tags can be hidden in every fragment of a digital work, making disassociation almost impossible. — Also termed *digital fingerprinting; digital watermarking.*

stellionatus (stel-ee-ə-**nay**-təs *or* stel-yə-). [Latin "underhand dealing"] (17c) *Roman & Scots law.* Conduct that is fraudulent but does not fall within a specific class of offenses. • This term applies primarily to fraudulent practices in the sale or hypothecation of land. — Also termed (in Scots law) *stellionate.* Cf. COZENING.

> "STELLIONATE . . . is a term applied, in the law of Scotland, either to any crime which, though indictable, goes under no general denomination, and is punishable arbitrarily, or to any civil delinquency of which fraud is an ingredient. Those, e.g., who grant double conveyances of the same subject, are guilty of this crime . . . and are punishable arbitrarily in their persons and goods, besides becoming infamous." William Bell, *Bell's Dictionary and Digest of the Law of Scotland* 940 (George Watson ed., 1882).

> "Though *pignus* and hypothec are almost different names for the same thing, there were differences. Hypothec was used mainly for land, which cannot be removed. A thing could be pledged only to one, but successive hypothecs might be created over a thing. There was no fraud in this but it was the offence of *stellionatus* to give a hypothec without declaring existing hypothecs." W.W. Buckland, *A Manual of Roman Private Law* 355 (2d ed. 1939).

stenographer's record. See *reporter's record* under RECORD.

stent, *n.* (14c) *Scots law.* A property assessment made for taxation purposes.

stent, *vb.* (15c) *Scots law.* To assess or charge (a person or community) for taxation purposes.

stepbrother. See BROTHER.

stepchild. See CHILD.

STEP court. *abbr.* Supervised-treatment and education-program court.

stepfather. See FATHER.

step-in-the-dark rule. (1955) *Torts.* The contributory-negligence rule that a person who enters a totally unfamiliar area in the darkness has a duty, in the absence of unusual stress, to refrain from proceeding until first ascertaining whether any dangerous obstacles exist. See *contributory negligence* under NEGLIGENCE.

stepmother. See MOTHER.

stepparent. See PARENT (1).

stepparent adoption. See ADOPTION (1).

stepped-up basis. See BASIS.

stepped-up visitation. See VISITATION.

step-rate-premium insurance. See INSURANCE.

stepsister. See SISTER.

step-transaction doctrine. (1951) A method used by the Internal Revenue Service to determine tax liability by viewing the transaction as a whole and disregarding one or more nonsubstantive, intervening transactions taken to achieve the final result. — Also termed *step-transaction approach*.

sterilization. (1905) **1.** The act of making (a person or other living thing) permanently unable to reproduce. **2.** The act of depriving (a person or other living thing) of reproductive organs; esp., castration. — Also termed (in both senses) *asexualization*.

sterling, *adj.* (14c) **1.** Of or conforming to a standard of national value, esp. of English money or metal <a pound sterling>. **2.** (Of an opinion, value, etc.) valuable; authoritative <a sterling report>.

stet (stet), *n.* [Latin "let it stand"] (18c) **1.** An order staying legal proceedings, as when a prosecutor determines not to proceed on an indictment and places the case on a stet docket. • The term is used chiefly in Maryland. **2.** An instruction to leave a text as it stands.

stet processus (stet prə-**ses**-əs), *n.* [Law Latin "let the process stand"] (1813) *Hist.* **1.** A record entry, similar to a nolle prosequi, by which the parties agree to stay further proceedings. **2.** The agreement between the parties to stay those proceedings. • This was typically used by a plaintiff to suspend an action rather than suffer a nonsuit.

stevedore (**stee**-və-dor). (18c) *Maritime law.* A person or company that hires longshore and harbor workers to load and unload ships. Cf. SEAMAN; LONGSHOREMAN.

steward. (bef. 12c) **1.** A person appointed to manage the affairs of another. **2.** A union official who represents union employees and who oversees the performance of union contracts. — Also termed (in sense 2) *union steward; shop steward*.

▸ **steward of all England.** (15c) *Hist.* An officer vested with various powers, including the power to preside over the trial of peers.

▸ **steward of a manor.** (16c) *Hist.* An officer who handles the business matters of a manor, including keeping the court rolls and granting admittance to copyhold lands.

Steward of Chiltern Hundreds (**chil**-tərn). *English law.* Formerly, a royal officer charged with protecting residents from robbers and thieves who hid in the hundreds' wooded areas. • Today, a member of Parliament can accept this royal appointment as a step toward resigning, which is generally forbidden by statute. By law, for a member to accept this and certain other Crown appointments is to forfeit his or her seat. A resignation from the office of Steward completes the resignation process.

STI. *abbr.* Simplified traffic information.

stickering. *Securities.* The updating of a prospectus by affixing stickers that contain the new or revised information. • Stickering avoids the expense of reprinting an entire prospectus.

stickler. (16c) *Hist.* An arbitrator.

stickup. (1904) An armed robbery in which the victim is threatened by the use of weapons. — Also termed *holdup*. See *armed robbery* under ROBBERY.

stiffening note. (1854) *Maritime law.* A permit, issued by a customs collector to the ship's master, that authorizes the receipt and loading of heavy goods necessary to ballast a vessel before the inward-bound cargo has been completely unloaded. Cf. JERK NOTE.

stifling of a prosecution. (1866) An illegal agreement, in exchange for money or other benefit, to abstain from prosecuting a person.

stigma damages. See DAMAGES.

stigma-plus doctrine. (1979) The principle that defamation by a government official is not actionable as a civil-rights violation unless the victim suffers not only embarrassment but also the loss of a property interest (such as continued employment in a government job).

still, *n.* (16c) An instrument or apparatus used for making distilled liquor or alcohol.

stillborn child. See CHILD.

stillicidium (stil-ə-**sid**-ee-əm), *n.* [Latin fr. *stilla* "a drop" + *cadere* "to fall"] (18c) *Roman law.* **1.** Eavesdropping. **2.** See AQUAE IMMITTENDAE. **3.** See *servitus stillicidii* under SERVITUS.

stilus curiae (**stɪ**-ləs **kyoor**-ee-ee). [Law Latin] (17c) *Hist.* The form of court.

sting. (1976) An undercover operation in which law-enforcement agents pose as criminals to catch actual criminals engaging in illegal acts.

▸ **reverse sting.** (1982) An undercover operation in which the government agent or informant sells, rather than buys, contraband.

stink bomb. See BOMB.

stint. (15c) **1.** *English law.* Limitation; restriction <a right to take fish from a canal without stint can exist as a profit in gross>.

> "All these species, of pasturable common, may be and usually are limited as to number and time; but there are also commons without stint, and which last all the year." 2 William Blackstone, *Commentaries on the Laws of England* 34 (1766).

2. A specific quantity of work; the time spent performing a specific activity <he has done his stint>.

stipend (**stɪ**-pend *or* -pənd). (15c) **1.** A salary or other regular, periodic payment. **2.** A tribute to support the clergy, usu. consisting of payments in money or grain.

stipendiary, See *stipendiary magistrate* under MAGISTRATE.

stipendiary estate (stɪ-**pen**-dee-er-ee). See ESTATE (1).

stipendiary magistrate. See MAGISTRATE.

stipendium (stɪ-**pen**-dee-əm), *n.* [Latin] *Roman law.* A soldier's regular pay. Cf. SALARIUM.

stipes (**stɪ**-peez), *n.* [Latin "a trunk"] *Hist.* Family stock; a source of descent or title. Pl. ***stipites*** (**stip**-ə-teez).

stipital (**stip**-i-təl), *adj.* See STIRPITAL.

stipulated authority. See *express authority* under AUTHORITY (1).

stipulated bench trial. See BENCH TRIAL.

stipulated damages. See *liquidated damages* under DAMAGES.

stipulated judgment. See *agreed judgment* under JUDGMENT (2).

stipulatio (stip-yə-**lay**-shee-oh), *n.* [Latin] *Roman law.* An oral contract requiring a formal question and reply, binding the replier to do what was asked. • It is essential that both parties speak, and that the reply directly conforms to the question asked and is made with the intent to enter into a contractual obligation. No consideration is required. See *actio ex stipulatu* under ACTIO. Pl. ***stipulationes*** (stip-yə-lay-shee-**oh**-neez).

> "[I]t must be remembered that the law-forms used by the Romans had their origin in times when writing was neither easy nor common. It is not surprising, therefore, that among them a form of spoken words, a verbal contract, should hold the place which among us is occupied by written notes. This form . . . *stipulatio* — was of a very simple character, consisting only of a question asked by one party, and an answer returned by the other . . . . Such forms as *Spondesne mihi decem aureos dare* (do you engage to give me ten aurei, or gold-pieces): answer, *Spondeo* (I engage) . . . ." James Hadley, *Introduction to Roman Law* 210 (1881).

> "The oldest Roman contract was the *stipulatio*, an oral promise made by an answer to an immediately preceding question, with the promisor using the same verb. The contract was unilateral. Only one party, the promisor, was legally liable, and he was bound strictly by the words used." Alan Watson, *Ancient Law and Modern Understanding* 96 (1998).

stipulatio aquiliana (stip-yə-**lay**-shee-oh ə-kwil-ee-**ay**-nə). [Latin] (17c) *Roman law.* A type of *stipulatio* used to collect and discharge all the liabilities owed on various grounds by a single contract.

> "[S]*tipulatio Aquiliana*, a device credited to Aquilius Gallus, of Cicero's time. Where two persons with complex relations between them desired to square or simplify their accounts they could work out the items and arrive at the balance . . . . This balance being paid or otherwise arranged, each party would then make with the other this *stipulatio*, which was a comprehensive formula . . . . This would novate all the claims and turn them into a single promise, for an *incertum*. These mutual stipulations might then be released by *acceptilatio*." W.W. Buckland, *A Manual of Roman Private Law* 348 (2d ed. 1939).

stipulatio juris (stip-yə-**lay**-shee-oh **joor**-is). [Latin "stipulatio as to the law"] (1951) The parties' agreement on a question of law or its applicability. • The court is not bound to accept the stipulation if it is erroneous. But the parties are allowed to stipulate the law to be applied to a dispute.

stipulation (stip-yə-**lay**-shən), *n.* (18c) **1.** A material condition or requirement in an agreement; esp., a factual representation that is incorporated into a contract as a term <breach of the stipulation regarding payment of taxes>. • Such a contractual term often appears in a section of the contract called "Representations and Warranties." **2.** A voluntary agreement between opposing parties concerning some relevant point; esp., an agreement relating to a proceeding, made by attorneys representing adverse parties to the proceeding <the plaintiff and defendant entered into a stipulation on the issue of liability>. • A stipulation relating to a pending judicial proceeding, made by a party to the proceeding or the party's attorney, is binding without consideration.

> "Breach of a stipulation should not be confused with *misrepresentation*, which is a false statement made before or at the time the contract is made, and which induces the contract; only if it is incorporated into the contract does it become a stipulation or term, the breach of which will entitle the injured party to pursue the usual remedies which are available where there has been a breach of a warranty or of a condition." 1 E.W. Chance, *Principles of Mercantile Law* 239 (P.W. French ed., 13th ed. 1950).

> "Stipulations with respect to matters of form and procedure serve the convenience of the parties to litigation and often serve to simplify and expedite the proceeding. In some cases they are supported by the policy of favoring compromise in order to reduce the volume of litigation. Hence they are favored by the courts and enforced without regard to consideration." Restatement (Second) of Contracts § 94 cmt. a (1979).

3. *Roman law.* A formal contract by which a promisor (and only the promisor) became bound by oral question and answer. • By the third century A.D., stipulations were always evidenced in writing. See REUS PROMITTENDI; REUS STIPULANDI. — **stipulate** (**stip**-yə-layt), *vb.* — **stipulative** (**stip**-yə-lə-tiv), *adj.*

> "A stipulation consisted in a question and answer, the question being put by the person who was to acquire a right, the answer being given orally by the person who undertook the obligation. The matter of the agreement being stated, the binding words were usually simple; those used by (and peculiar to) Romans being *Spondesne?* or *spondes? Spondeo.* A stipulation made with a foreigner in these terms was invalid. The questioner was called *stipulator*, sometimes *reus stipulandi* ('[stipulating party]'), the answerer usually *promissor* (or *reus promittendi* [the promising party]) . . . ." 2 Henry John Roby, *Roman Private Law in the Times of Cicero and of the Antonines* 12 (1902).

stipulation in lieu of motions. (1988) An agreement between opposing counsel, usu. in a criminal case, about what pretrial discovery will take place and about what suppression hearings will be held.

stipulation pour autrui (**poor** oh-troo-**ee**). [French "for other persons"] (1826) *Civil law.* A contractual provision that benefits a third party and gives the third party a cause of action against the promisor for specific performance. La. Civ. Code art. 1978. See *third-party beneficiary* under BENEFICIARY.

stipulatio sponsalitia (stip-yə-**lay**-shee-oh spon-sə-**lish**-ee-ə). [Latin] (1827) *Roman law.* In early law a solemn promise by a father (paterfamilias) that his child would marry someone else's child. • In some cases, there was a penalty if the marriage did not occur. In classical and later Roman law, in which free marriage was the rule, such a promise was unenforceable because it was regarded as immoral (*contra bonos mores*).

stipulative definition. See DEFINITION.

stipulator. (17c) **1.** Someone who makes a stipulation. **2.** *Civil law.* The promisee in a stipulation pour autrui, accepting the promise of a benefit to a third party; obligee. See REUS STIPULANDI.

stirpal (**stər**-pəl), *adj.* See STIRPITAL.

stirpes (**stər**-peez). (*pl.*) See STIRPS.

stirpital (**stər**-pə-təl), *adj.* (1886) Of, relating to, or involving per stirpes distribution. See PER STIRPES. — Also termed *stipital*; *stirpal*.

stirps (stərps), *n.* [Latin "stock"] (17c) A branch of a family; a line of descent. Pl. **stirpes** (**stər**-peez). See PER STIRPES.

stock, *n.* (14c) **1.** The original progenitor of a family; a person from whom a family is descended; BRANCH (2) <George Harper, Sr. was the stock of the Harper line>. **2.** A merchant's goods that are kept for sale or trade <the car dealer put last year's models on sale to reduce its stock>. **3.** The capital or principal fund raised by a corporation through subscribers' contributions or the sale of shares <Acme's stock is worth far more today than it was 20 years ago>. **4.** A proportional part of a corporation's capital represented by the number of equal units (or shares) owned, and granting the holder the right to participate in the company's general management and to share in its net profits or earnings <Julia sold her stock in

Pantheon Corporation>. See SHARE, *n.* (2). Cf. SECURITY (4).

▸ **adjustable-rate preferred stock.** (1983) Preferred stock whose dividend is periodically changed according to changes in a benchmark interest rate, such as that of Treasury bills. — Abbr. ARPS.

▸ **assented stock.** (1890) Stock that an owner deposits with a third person according to an agreement by which the owner voluntarily accepts a change in the corporation's securities.

▸ **assessable stock.** (1887) Stock that is subject to resale by the issuer if the holder fails to pay any assessment levied on it.

▸ **authorized stock.** See *capital stock* (1).

▸ **bailout stock.** (1956) Nontaxable preferred stock issued to stockholders as a dividend. • Bailout stock is issued to gain favorable tax rates by distributing corporate earnings at capital gains rates rather than by distributing dividends at ordinary income rates. This practice is now prohibited by the Internal Revenue Code. IRC (26 USCA) § 306.

▸ **barometer stock.** (1921) A stock whose price fluctuates according to market conditions; an individual stock considered to be indicative of the strength of the market in general. — Also termed *bellwether stock.*

▸ **bearer stock.** (1922) *Rare.* Stock that has no recorded ownership information so the physical bearer of the stock certificate is presumed to be the owner,

▸ **blank stock.** (1930) *Securities.* Stock with voting powers and rights set by the issuer's board of directors after the stock has been sold.

▸ **blue-chip stock.** See BLUE CHIP.

▸ **bonus stock.** (1891) A stock share that is issued for no consideration, as an enticement to buy some other type or class of security. • It is considered a type of watered stock. — Also termed *bonus share.*

▸ **book-value stock.** (1975) Stock offered to executives at a book-value price, rather than at its market value. • The stock is offered with the understanding that when its book value has risen, the company will buy back the stock at the increased price or will make payments in stock equal to the increased price.

▸ **callable preferred stock.** (1936) Preferred stock that may be repurchased by the issuing corporation at a prestated price, usu. at or slightly above par value.

▸ **capital stock.** (16c) **1.** The total number of shares of stock that a corporation may issue under its charter or articles of incorporation, including both common stock and preferred stock. • A corporation may increase the amount of capital stock if the shareholders approve an amendment to its charter or articles of incorporation. — Also termed *authorized stock; authorized capital stock; authorized stock issue; authorized shares.* **2.** The total par value or stated value of this stock; CAPITALIZATION (4). **3.** See *common stock.*

▸ **cheap stock.** Stock or stock options issued to the issuer's directors, employees, consultants, promoters, and the like at a price lower than the public-offering price up to 12 months before the offering.

▸ **common stock.** (1888) A class of stock entitling the holder to vote on corporate matters, to receive dividends after other claims and dividends have been paid (esp. to preferred shareholders), and to share in assets upon liquidation. • Common stock is often called *capital stock* if it is the corporation's only class of stock outstanding. — Also termed *ordinary shares.* Cf. *preferred stock.*

▸ **convertible stock.** See *convertible security* under SECURITY (4).

▸ **corporate stock.** (1819) An equity security issued by a corporation.

▸ **cumulative preferred stock.** (1903) Preferred stock that must receive dividends in full before common shareholders may receive any dividend. • If the corporation omits a dividend in a particular year or period, it is carried over to the next year or period and must be paid before the common shareholders receive any payment. — Also termed *cumulative stock; cumulative preference share.*

▸ **deferred stock.** (18c) Stock whose holders are entitled to dividends only after the corporation has met some other specified obligation, such as the discharge of a liability or the payment of a dividend to preferred shareholders.

▸ **discount stock.** (1919) A stock share issued for less than par value. • Discount stock is considered a type of watered stock, the issuance of which may impose liability on the recipient for the difference between the par value and the cash amount paid. — Also termed *discount share.*

▸ **donated stock.** (1909) Stock donated to a charity or given to a corporation by its own stockholders, esp. for resale.

▸ **equity stock.** (1934) Stock of any class having unlimited dividend rights, regardless of whether the stock is preferred.

▸ **floating stock.** (1852) Stock that is offered for sale on the open market and that has not yet been purchased; the number of outstanding shares available for trading.

▸ **full-paid stock.** (1866) Stock on which no further payments can be demanded by the issuing company. — Also termed *paid-up stock.*

▸ **glamour stock.** See *growth stock* (2).

▸ **growth stock.** (1957) **1.** Stock issued by a growth company. • Because a growth company usu. reinvests a large share of its income back into the company, growth stock pays relatively low dividends, though its price usu. has a relatively high appreciation in market value over time. **2.** Stock that has produced or is expected to produce above-average returns and usu. receives small or no dividends. — Also termed *glamour stock.*

▸ **guaranteed stock.** (1850) Preferred stock on which a dividend is guaranteed by someone (usu. a parent corporation) other than the issuer.

▸ **guarantee stock.** (1839) A fixed, nonwithdrawal investment in a building-and-loan association. • This type of stock guarantees to all other investors in the association a fixed dividend or interest rate. See BUILDING-AND-LOAN ASSOCIATION.

▸ **guaranty stock.** (1854) A savings-and-loan association's stock yielding dividends to the holders after dividends have been paid to the depositors.

▸ **half-stock,** *n.* Stock with 50% of the normal par value.

▸ **hot stock.** See *hot issue* under ISSUE (2).

▸ **inactive stock.** (1934) A low-volume stock.

▸ **income stock.** (1958) A stock with a history of high yields or dividend payments (e.g., public utilities and well-established corporations).

▸ **inscribed stock.** (1874) Stock for which the owner's name is recorded, and only the recorded owner is entitled to ownership rights. • Formerly, the owner's name was inscribed on a certificate, but now ownership records are usu. electronic.

▸ **issued stock.** Capital stock that has been authorized and sold to subscribers, but may be reacquired, such as treasury stock.

▸ **joint stock.** Capital invested in an unincorporated business and divided into shares proportionate to the size of each investment.

▸ **letter stock.** See *restricted security* under SECURITY (4).

▸ **listed stock.** See *listed security* under SECURITY (4).

▸ **margin stock.** See *marginable security* under SECURITY (4).

▸ **nonassessable stock.** (1887) Stock owned by a holder whose potential liability is limited to the amount paid for the stock and who cannot be charged additional funds to pay the issuer's debts. • Stock issued in the United States is usu. nonassessable.

▸ **noncumulative preferred stock.** (1892) Preferred stock that does not have to be paid dividends that are in arrears. • Once a periodic dividend is omitted, it will not be paid. — Also termed *noncumulative stock.*

▸ **nonparticipating preferred stock.** (1926) Preferred stock that does not give the shareholder the right to additional earnings — usu. surplus common-stock dividends — beyond those stated in the preferred contract.

▸ **nonvoting stock.** (1912) Stock that has no voting rights under most situations.

▸ **no-par stock.** (1920) Stock issued without a specific value assigned to it. • For accounting purposes, it is given a legal or stated value that has little or no connection to the stock's actual value. — Sometimes shortened to *no par.* — Also termed *no-par-value stock.*

▸ **outstanding stock.** (1847) Stock that is held by investors and has not been redeemed by the issuing corporation. — Also termed *outstanding capital stock*; *shares outstanding.*

▸ **paid-up stock.** See *full-paid stock.*

▸ **participating preferred stock.** (1926) Preferred stock whose holder is entitled to receive stated dividends and to share with the common shareholders in any additional distributions of earnings.

▸ **participation stock.** (1927) Stock permitting the holder to participate in profits and surplus.

▸ **par-value stock.** (1856) Stock originally issued for a fixed value derived by dividing the total value of capital stock by the number of shares to be issued. • The par value does not bear a necessary relation to the actual stock value because surplus plays a role in the valuation.

▸ **penny stock.** (1921) An equity security that is not traded in established markets, represents no tangible assets, or has average revenues less than required for trading on an exchange. • Typically, a penny stock is highly speculative and can be purchased for less than $5 a share.

▸ **performance stock.** See *glamour stock.*

▸ **phantom stock.** (1959) Imaginary stock that is credited to a corporate executive account as part of the executive's compensation package. See PHANTOM STOCK PLAN.

▸ **preferred stock.** (1848) A class of stock giving its holder a preferential claim to dividends and to corporate assets upon liquidation but that usu. carries no voting rights. — Also termed *preference shares; preferred shares.* Cf. *common stock.*

▸ **premium stock.** (1858) Stock that carries a premium for trading, as in the case of short-selling.

▸ **prior preferred stock.** (1938) Preferred stock that has preference over another class of preferred stock from the same issuer. • The preference usu. relates to dividend payments or claims on assets.

▸ **public stock.** **1.** See *public security* under SECURITY (4). **2.** Stock of a publicly traded corporation.

▸ **reacquired stock.** See *treasury stock.*

▸ **redeemable stock.** (1889) Preferred stock that can be called by the issuing corporation and retired.

▸ **registered stock.** See *registered security* under SECURITY (4).

▸ **restricted stock.** See *restricted security* under SECURITY (4).

▸ **retired stock.** See *treasury stock.*

▸ **special stock.** *Hist.* Corporate stock that guarantees investors an annual dividend and gives them creditor status to the extent that dividends have become payable. • In contrast, preferred-stock holders' claims for dividends payable are secondary to creditors' claims. Special stock was statutorily authorized only in Massachusetts.

▸ **subscribed stock.** (1826) A stockholder's equity account showing the capital that will be contributed when the subscription price is collected. See SUBSCRIPTION (2).

▸ **tainted stock.** Stock owned or transferred by a person disqualified from serving as a plaintiff in a derivative action. • A good-faith transferee is also disqualified from filing a derivative action.

▸ **treasury stock.** (1891) Stock issued by a company but then reacquired and either canceled or held. • Some states have eliminated this classification and treat such stock as if it is authorized but unissued. — Also termed *treasury security; treasury share; reacquired stock; retired stock.*

▸ **unissued stock.** (1879) Stock that is authorized by the corporate charter but not yet distributed.

▸ **unlisted stock.** See *unlisted security* under SECURITY (4).

▸ **volatile stock.** (1873) Stock subject to wide and rapid fluctuations in price. — Also termed *yo-yo stock.*

▸ **voting stock.** (1894) Stock that entitles the holder to vote in the corporation's election of directors and on other matters that are put to a vote. — Also termed *voting security.*

▸ **watered stock.** (1869) Stock issued for less than par value.

▸ **whisper stock.** (1986) The stock of a company that is rumored to be the target of a takeover attempt.

▸ **yo-yo stock.** See *volatile stock.*

stock acquisition. See SHARE ACQUISITION.

stock-appreciation right. (*usu. pl.*) (1974) A right, typically granted in tandem with a stock option, to be paid the option value (usu. in cash) when exercised along with the simultaneous cancellation of the option. — Abbr. SAR.

stock association. See *joint-stock company* under COMPANY.

stock attribution. See ATTRIBUTION (3).

stock bailout. A stock redemption in the form of a preferred stock dividend.

stock/bond power. See STOCK POWER.

stock bonus plan. (1933) A special type of profit-sharing plan in which the distribution of benefits consists of the employer-company's own stock. — Abbr. SBP.

stockbroker. (18c) Someone who buys or sells stocks and bonds as an agent for others. — Also termed *account executive; account representative.*

▸ **street stockbroker.** A stockbroker who, not being a member of a stock exchange, carries out the orders of others by transactions in the streets, or by going from office to office. — Often shortened to *street broker* or *curbstone broker.* — Also termed *curbstone stockbroker.*

stock buyback. See REDEMPTION (3).

stock certificate. (1863) An instrument evidencing ownership of shares of stock; specif., an official document showing that one owns shares in a company. — Also termed *certificate of stock; share certificate.*

▸ **face-amount certificate.** (1940) **1.** A certificate, investment contract, or other security representing an obligation by its issuer to pay a stated or determinable sum, at a fixed or determinable date or dates more than 24 months after the date of issuance, in consideration of the payment of periodic installments of a stated or determinable amount. — Also termed *face-amount certificate of the installment type.* **2.** A security representing a similar obligation on the part of the issuer of a face-amount certificate, the consideration for which is the payment of a single lump sum. *See* 15 USCA § 80a-2(a)(15). — Also termed *fully paid face-amount certificate.*

▸ **periodic-payment-plan certificate.** (1955) A certificate, investment contract, or other security providing for a series of periodic payments by the holder and representing an undivided interest in certain specified securities or in a unit or fund of securities purchased wholly or partly with the proceeds of those payments. • The term also includes any security whose issuer is also issuing the certificates described above and whose holder has substantially the same rights and privileges as those holders have upon completing the periodic payments for which the securities provide. *See* 15 USCA § 80a-2(a)(27).

stock clearing. (1895) The actual exchange of money and stock between buyer and seller, typically performed by a clearing corporation.

stock clearing corporation. (1924) A New York Stock Exchange subsidiary that is a central agency for securities deliveries and payments between member firms.

stock control. (1943) A system of inventory management by which a business maintains perpetual records of its inventory.

stock corporation. See CORPORATION.

stock dividend. See DIVIDEND.

stock exchange. See SECURITIES EXCHANGE.

stock-for-assets exchange. (1959) *Mergers & acquisitions.* A merger in which one corporation agrees to dissolve and transfers all or most of its assets to another corporation, which then distributes shares of its own stock to the dissolving corporation's shareholders.

stock-for-stock exchange. See *stock swap* under SWAP.

stockholder. See SHAREHOLDER.

stockholder derivative suit. See DERIVATIVE ACTION (1).

stockholder of record. (1886) The person who is listed in the issuer's books as the owner of stock on the record date. — Also termed *shareholder of record; holder of record; owner of record; record owner.* See *record date* under DATE.

stockholders' equity. See OWNERS' EQUITY.

stockholder's liability. See *shareholder's liability* under LIABILITY.

stock index. An official public list of stock prices.

stock insurance company. See INSURANCE COMPANY.

stock in trade. (18c) **1.** The inventory carried by a retail business for sale in the ordinary course of business. **2.** The tools and equipment owned and used by a person engaged in a trade. **3.** The equipment and other items needed to run a business.

stock issue. See ISSUE (2).

stock-jobber. See JOBBER (2).

stockjobbing, *n.* (17c) The business of dealing in stocks or shares; esp., the buying and selling of stocks and bonds by jobbers who operate on their own account. — Also termed *stockjobbery.*

stock-law district. See DISTRICT.

stock life-insurance company. See INSURANCE COMPANY.

stock manipulation. See MANIPULATION.

stock market. 1. See MARKET (5). **2.** See MARKET (6).

stock merger. See MERGER (8).

stock note. See NOTE (1).

stock option. (1888) **1.** An option to buy or sell a specific quantity of stock at a designated price for a specified period regardless of shifts in market value during the period. **2.** An option that allows a corporate employee to buy shares of corporate stock at a fixed price or within a fixed period. • Such an option is usu. granted as a form of compensation and can qualify for special tax treatment under the Internal Revenue Code. — Also termed *share option; securities option;* (in sense 2) *employee stock option; incentive stock option* (ISO).

▸ **nonqualified stock option.** (1961) A stock-option plan that does not receive capital-gains tax treatment, thus allowing a person to buy stock for a period (often ten years) at or below the market price. — Abbr. NQSO.

▸ **qualified stock option.** (1957) A now-rare stock-option plan that allows a person to buy stock for a period (often five years) at the market price, the stock being subject to capital-gains tax treatment.

stock-option contract. See CONTRACT.

stock-parking, *n.* See PARKING (2).

stock power. A power of attorney permitting a person, other than the owner, to transfer ownership of a security to a third party. — Also termed *stock/bond power.*

stock-purchase plan. (1927) An arrangement by which an employer corporation allows employees to purchase shares of the corporation's stock.

stock redemption. See REDEMPTION (3).

stock-redemption agreement. (1953) An agreement between a corporation's individual owners and the corporation itself, whereby the corporation agrees to purchase (i.e., redeem) the stock of a withdrawing or deceased owner. — Often shortened to *redemption agreement.* — Also termed *stock-retirement agreement.*

stock repurchase. See REDEMPTION (3).

stock-repurchase plan. (1960) A program by which a corporation buys back its own shares in the open market, usu. when the corporation believes the shares are undervalued.

stock-retirement agreement. See STOCK-REDEMPTION AGREEMENT.

stock right. See SUBSCRIPTION RIGHT.

stocks, *n.* (14c) A punishment device consisting of two boards that together form holes for trapping an offender's feet and hands. — Formerly also termed *cippi.* Cf. BILBOES (1); PILLORY.

stock sale. *Mergers & acquisitions.* A takeover in which the acquiring corporation buys stock directly from the target corporation's shareholders until it controls all or a majority of the target's stock.

stock split. (1955) The issuance of two or more new shares in exchange for each old share without changing the proportional ownership interests of each shareholder; specif., readjustment of a corporation's financial plan whereby each existing share of stock is split into a specified number of new shares as determined by corporate management. • For example, a 3-for-1 split would give an owner of 100 shares a total of 300 shares, or 3 shares for each share previously owned. A stock split lowers the price per share and thus makes the stock more attractive to potential investors. — Also termed *share split; stock split-up.*

▸ **reverse stock split.** (1957) A reduction in the number of a corporation's shares by calling in all outstanding shares and reissuing fewer shares having greater value.

stock subscription. See SUBSCRIPTION (2).

stock swap. See SWAP.

stock-transfer agent. See *transfer agent* under AGENT.

stock-transfer tax. See TAX.

stock warrant. See WARRANT (4).

stolen goods. See GOODS.

stolen property. (18c) Goods acquired by larceny, robbery, or theft.

stonewall, *vb.* (1974) To persistently refuse to cooperate in an investigation; esp., to refuse to testify or to hand over requested material until every available legal challenge has been exhausted. — **stonewalling,** *n.*

stool pigeon. (1836) *Slang.* **1.** An informant, esp. a police informant. **2.** Someone who acts as a decoy, esp. on behalf of a gambler or swindler, or for the police to help make an arrest. — Also termed (in sense 1) *rat;* (in sense 2) *capper.*

stop, *n.* (16c) Under the Fourth Amendment, a temporary restraint that prevents a person from walking or driving away.

▸ **pretextual stop.** (1973) A police stop of a person or vehicle for fabricated reasons that are calculated to forestall or preclude constitutional objections. — Also termed *pretext stop.*

stop-and-frisk, *n.* (1963) *Criminal law.* A police officer's brief detention, questioning, and search of a person for a concealed weapon when the officer reasonably suspects that the person has committed or is about to commit a crime. • The stop-and-frisk, which can be conducted without a warrant or probable cause, was held constitutional by the Supreme Court in *Terry v. Ohio,* 392 U.S. 1, 88 S.Ct. 1868 (1968). — Also termed *investigatory stop; investigatory detention; Terry stop; Terry search; field stop.* See *reasonable suspicion* under SUSPICION.

stop-and-frisk database law. (2010) *Criminal procedure.* A statute that bars police from keeping records on people who have been stopped, questioned, or frisked by police.

stopgap tax. See TAX.

stopgap zoning. See *interim zoning* under ZONING.

stop-limit order. See *stop order* under ORDER (8).

stop-list. (1921) *Antitrust.* An illegal means by which manufacturers sometimes attempt to enforce price maintenance, by having suppliers agree among themselves not to supply any party who competes actively and breaks anticompetitive price "rules."

stop-loss insurance. See INSURANCE.

stop-loss order. See *stop order* under ORDER (8).

stop-notice statute. (1963) A law providing an alternative to a mechanic's lien by allowing a contractor, supplier, or worker to make a claim against the construction lender and, in some instances, the owner for a portion of the undisbursed construction-loan proceeds. See *mechanic's lien* under LIEN.

stop order. (1875) **1.** See ORDER (8). **2.** An SEC order that suspends a registration statement containing false, incomplete, or misleading information. **3.** A bank customer's order instructing the bank not to honor one of the customer's checks. — Also termed (in sense 3) *stop-payment order.*

stoppage, *n.* (15c) **1.** An obstruction or hindrance to the performance of some act <stoppage of goods or persons in transit for inspection>. **2.** *Civil law.* SETOFF <stoppage in pay for money owed>.

stoppage *in transitu* (in **tran**-si-t[y]oo *or* **tranz**-i-t[y]oo). (18c) The right of a seller of goods to regain possession of those goods from a common carrier under certain circumstances, even though the seller has already parted with them under a contract for sale. • This right traditionally applies when goods are consigned wholly or partly on credit from one person to another, and the consignee becomes bankrupt or insolvent before the goods arrive — in which event the consignor may direct the carrier to deliver the goods to someone other than the consignee (who can no longer pay for them). — Also termed *stoppage in transit*. See RECLAMATION (2).

stop-payment order. See STOP ORDER (3).

storage. 1. The act of putting something away for future use; esp., the keeping or placing of articles in a place of safekeeping, such as a warehouse or depository <the storage of literary archives>. **2.** The quality, state, or condition of having been put away for future use <books in storage>. **3.** Space for keeping goods safe for future use or consumption; esp., a storehouse <5,000 square feet in storage>. **4.** The price or amount charged for keeping goods safe for future use or consumption <$650 per month in storage>. **5.** The means by which information is kept in digital form <data storage>.

store, *n.* (13c) **1.** A place where goods are deposited for purchase or sale. **2.** (*usu. pl.*) A supply of articles provided for the subsistence and accommodation of a ship's crew and passengers. **3.** A place where goods or supplies are stored for future use; a warehouse.

▸ **public store.** A government warehouse administratively maintained, as for the storage of imported goods or military supplies.

store, *vb.* (13c) To keep (goods, etc.) in safekeeping for future delivery in an unchanged condition.

stored-value card. (1989) A device that provides access to a specified amount of funds for making payments to others, is the only means of routine access to the funds, and does not have an associated account in the name of the holder. • Typically, a consumer pays a bank or merchant money in exchange for a stored-value card; the consumer uses the card rather than paper currency to purchase goods and services. — Abbr. SVC. — Also termed *smart card*; *prepaid card*; *value-added card*.

store-receiver exemption. See AIKEN EXEMPTION.

stouthrief. (15c) *Scots law.* Robbery that takes place in or near one's dwelling, but is not coupled with housebreaking.

stowage (**stoh**-ij). (14c) *Maritime law.* **1.** The storing, packing, or arranging of cargo on a vessel to protect the goods from friction, bruising, or water damage during a voyage. • The bill of lading will often prescribe the method of stowage to be used. **2.** The place (such as a ship's hull) where goods are stored. **3.** The goods so stored. **4.** A fee paid for the storage of goods; a storage fee.

stowaway. (1850) Someone who hides on board an outgoing or incoming vessel or aircraft to obtain free passage. 18 USCA § 2199.

STR. *abbr.* SUSPICIOUS-TRANSACTION REPORT.

straddle, *n.* (1883) In securities and commodities trading, a situation in which an investor holds contracts to buy and to sell the same security or commodity, thus ensuring a loss on one of the contracts. • The aim of this strategy is to defer gains and use losses to offset other taxable income. — Also termed *spread eagle*; *combination*. — **straddle,** *vb.*

straight annuity. See ANNUITY.

straight bankruptcy. See CHAPTER 7 (2).

straight bill of lading. See BILL OF LADING.

straight deductible. See DEDUCTIBLE.

straight letter of credit. See LETTER OF CREDIT.

straight life annuity. See *nonrefund annuity* under ANNUITY.

straight life insurance. See *whole life insurance* under LIFE INSURANCE.

straight-line depreciation method. See DEPRECIATION METHOD.

straight-line interest. See *simple interest* under INTEREST (3).

straight mortgage. See MORTGAGE.

straight sentence. See *determinate sentence* under SENTENCE.

straight-term mortgage. See *interest-only mortgage* under MORTGAGE.

straight ticket. In an election, a ballot in which a voter has voted for all the candidates from one particular political party. Cf. SPLIT TICKET.

straight up. See S.U.

straight voting. See *noncumulative voting* under VOTING.

strain theory. (18c) The theory that people commit crimes to alleviate stress created by the disjunction between their station in life and the station to which society has conditioned them to aspire. Cf. CONTROL THEORY; RATIONAL-CHOICE THEORY; ROUTINE-ACTIVITIES THEORY.

stramineus homo (strə-**min**-ee-əs **hoh**-moh). [Latin "man of straw"] See STRAW MAN.

strand, *n.* (bef. 12c) A shore or bank of an ocean, lake, river, or stream.

stranding, *n.* (1810) *Maritime law.* A ship's drifting, driving, or running aground on a strand. • The type of stranding that occurs determines the method of apportioning the liability for any resulting losses.

▸ **accidental stranding.** (1818) Stranding caused by natural forces, such as wind and waves. — Also termed *involuntary stranding.* See *general average* and *particular average* under AVERAGE.

> "Damage to a vessel from involuntary stranding or wreck, and the cost of repairs, are particular average only. Where, however, the ship and cargo are exposed to a common peril by the accidental stranding, the expenses of unloading and taking care of the cargo, rescuing the vessel, reloading the cargo, and other expenses other than repairs requisite to enable the vessel to proceed on the voyage, are brought into general average, provided the vessel and cargo were saved by the same series of measures during the continuance of the common peril which created the joint necessity for the expenses." 70 Am. Jur. 2d *Shipping* § 961, at 1069 (1987).

▸ **voluntary stranding.** (1810) Stranding to avoid a more dangerous fate or for fraudulent purposes.

> "The loss occurring when a ship is voluntarily run ashore to avoid capture, foundering, or shipwreck is to be made good by general average contribution, if the ship is afterwards recovered so as to be able to perform its voyage, as such a claim is clearly within the rule that whatever is sacrificed for the common benefit of the associated interests shall be made good by all the interests exposed to the common peril which were saved from the common danger by the sacrifice . . . . A vessel cannot, however, claim contribution

founded on even a voluntary stranding made necessary by . . . unseaworthiness or the negligence of those in charge, except in pursuance of a valid agreement to that effect." 70 Am. Jur. 2d *Shipping* § 961, at 1069 (1987).

stranger. (14c) **1.** Someone who is not party to a given transaction; esp., someone other than a party or the party's employee, agent, tenant, or immediate family member. **2.** One not standing toward another in some relation implied in the context; esp., one who is not in privity. **3.** Someone who voluntarily pays another person's debt even though the payor cannot be held liable for the debt and the payor's property is not affected by the creditor's rights. • Subrogation does not apply to a stranger if the debtor did not agree to or assign subrogation rights.

stranger in blood. (17c) **1.** One not related by blood, such as a relative by affinity. **2.** Any person not within the consideration of natural love and affection arising from a relationship.

stranger rape. See RAPE (2).

stranger test. An analysis for determining whether a business deal between a lawyer and a client is fair by considering whether a reasonable lawyer would advise the client to enter into the same transaction with a stranger.

stratagem. (15c) A trick or deception to obtain an advantage, esp. in a military conflict.

strategic alliance. (1983) A coalition formed by two or more persons in the same or complementary businesses to gain long-term financial, operational, or marketing advantages without jeopardizing competitive independence <through their strategic alliance, the manufacturer and distributor of a co-developed product shared development costs>. Cf. ALLIANCE (1); JOINT VENTURE; PARTNERSHIP.

Strategic National Stockpile. A national repository of medicines and healthcare supplies maintained jointly by the U.S. Department of Homeland Security and the U.S. Department of Health and Human Services to respond to public-health emergencies. • Created as the National Pharmaceutical Stockpile in 1999, the agency caches antibiotics, chemical antidotes, antitoxins, life-support medications, IV administration, airway maintenance supplies, and medical supplies. — Abbr. SNS.

stratocracy (strə-**tok**-rə-see). (17c) A military government.

strator (**stray**-tər). *Hist.* A surveyor of the highways.

straw bail. See *bail common* under BAIL (4).

straw bond. See BOND (2).

straw man. (1896) **1.** A fictitious person, esp. one that is weak or flawed. **2.** A tenuous and exaggerated counterargument that an advocate makes for the sole purpose of disproving it. — Also termed *straw-man argument.* **3.** A third party used in some transactions as a temporary transferee to allow the principal parties to accomplish something that is otherwise impermissible. Cf. DUMMY, *n.* **4.** A person hired to post a worthless bail bond for the release of an accused. — Also termed *stramineus homo.*

straw-man scam. (2009) *Criminal law.* A scheme in which an innocent third person is hired to receive fraudulently obtained money and wire it to a location outside the country.

straw poll. (1932) A nonbinding vote, taken as a way of informally gauging support or opposition but usu. without a formal motion or debate; esp., an informal test of several people's opinions to see what the general feeling about something is.

straw purchase. (1978) Someone's buying of a firearm for another who is prohibited to make such a purchase because of a prior conviction, an order of protection, or some similar judicially imposed proscription.

stray remarks. *Employment law.* Statements to or about an employee by a coworker or supervisor, concerning the employee's race, sex, age, national origin, or other status, that are either objectively or subjectively offensive, but that do not represent harassment or discrimination by the employer because of (1) their sporadic, unsystematic, and unofficial nature, (2) the circumstances in which they were made, or (3) their not showing any intention to hamper the employee's continued employment. — Also termed *stray comments.*

stream. (bef. 12c) Anything liquid that flows in a line or course; esp., a current of water consisting of a bed, bank, and watercourse, usu. emptying into other bodies of water but not losing its character even if it breaks up or disappears.

▸ **private stream.** (18c) A watercourse, the bed, channel, or waters of which are exclusively owned by private parties.

stream-of-commerce theory. (1942) **1.** The principle that a state may exercise personal jurisdiction over a defendant if the defendant places a product in the general marketplace and the product causes injury or damage in the forum state, as long as the defendant also takes other acts to establish some connection with the forum state, as by advertising there or by hiring someone to serve as a sales agent there. *Asahi Metal Indus. Co., Ltd. v. Superior Court of Cal.*, 480 U.S. 102, 107 S.Ct. 1026 (1987). **2.** The principle that a person who participates in placing a defective product in the general marketplace is strictly liable for harm caused by the product. Restatement (Second) of Torts § 402A (1979).

street. (bef. 12c) A road or public thoroughfare used for travel in an urban area, including the pavement, shoulders, gutters, curbs, and other areas within the street lines.

"Strictly speaking, a 'street' is a public thoroughfare in an urban community such as a city, town, or village, and the term is not ordinarily applicable to roads and highways outside of municipalities. Although a street, in common parlance, is equivalent to a highway, it is usually specifically denominated by its own proper appellation. . . . Whether a particular highway is to be regarded as a 'street' within the meaning of that term as used in a statute must, of course, be resolved by construction." 39 Am. Jur. 2d *Highways, Streets, and Bridges* § 8, at 588–89 (1999).

▸ **paper street.** (1874) A thoroughfare that appears on plats, subdivision maps, and other publicly filed documents, but that has not been completed or opened for public use.

street crime. See CRIME.

street gang. See GANG.

street name. A brokerage firm's name in which securities owned by another are registered. • A security is held by a broker in street name (at the customer's request) to simplify trading because no signature on the stock certificate is required. A street name may also be used for securities purchased on margin. The word "street" in this term is a reference to Wall Street.

street-name security. See *nominee account* under ACCOUNT.

street offense. See *street crime* under CRIME.

street stockbroker. See STOCKBROKER.

street sweep. *Mergers & acquisitions. Slang.* A bidder's cancellation of a tender offer followed by the open-market purchase of large blocks of stock in the target corporation.

street time. (1963) *Criminal law.* The period between a person's release from prison on parole and a court's revocation of that parole.

street value. See VALUE.

Streisand effect. (2006) The increase in unwanted attention produced by a lawsuit filed for the purpose of protecting the plaintiff's privacy. • The term derives from Barbra Streisand, the singer and actress, who tried to stop the publication of aerial photos of her home and instead drew more public interest to her private life.

strepitus judicialis (**strep**-ə-təs joo-dish-ee-**ay**-lis), *n.* [Law Latin] *Hist.* Disruptive behavior in court.

***Strickland* standard.** (1984) *Criminal law.* The minimum standard of lawyer competence in the representation of a criminal defendant, two conditions being necessary for a defendant later to show that the lawyer's representation was constitutionally substandard: (1) the lawyer's performance must have been outside the broad range of professionally acceptable assistance (the performance prong), and (2) there must be a reasonable probability that, but for the attorney's unprofessional errors, the result of the proceeding would have been different (the prejudice prong). *See Strickland v. Washington*, 466 U.S. 668 (1984).

strict, *adj.* (15c) **1.** Narrow; restricted <strict construction>. **2.** Rigid; exacting <strict statutory terms>. **3.** Severe <strict punishment>. **4.** Absolute; requiring no showing of fault <strict liability>.

strict-compliance rule. *Wills & estates.* The doctrine that a writing cannot be admitted to probate as the testator's will if there is any defect, no matter how trivial, unintentional, or unimportant, in complying with the statutorily prescribed formalities of execution. Cf. HARMLESS-ERROR RULE.

strict construction. See *strict interpretation* under INTERPRETATION (1).

strict constructionism. See CONSTRUCTIONISM.

strict constructionist. See CONSTRUCTIONIST.

strict foreclosure. See FORECLOSURE.

stricti juris (**strik**-tɪ **joor**-is). [Latin] **1.** Of strict right of law; according to the exact law, without extension or enhancement in interpretation. • This term was often applied to servitudes because they are a restriction on the free exercise of property rights. **2.** *Roman law.* (Of a contract) required to be interpreted strictly on its terms, regardless of circumstances. See BONA FIDES (2).

strict interpretation. See INTERPRETATION (1).

strictissimi juris (strik-**tis**-ə-mɪ **joor**-is). [Latin] Of the strictest right or law; to be interpreted in the strictest manner. • This term was usu. applied to certain statutes, esp. those imposing penalties or restraining natural liberties.

strict liability. See LIABILITY.

strict-liability crime. See CRIME.

strict-liability offense. **1.** See OFFENSE (2). **2.** See *strict-liability crime* under CRIME.

stricto jure (**strik**-toh **joor**-ee). [Latin] In strict law.

strict products liability. See PRODUCTS LIABILITY.

strict rule. See SPECIFIC-PURPOSE RULE.

strict scrutiny. (1941) *Constitutional law.* In due-process analysis, the standard applied to suspect classifications (such as race) in equal-protection analysis and to fundamental rights (such as voting rights). • Under strict scrutiny, the state must establish that it has a compelling interest that justifies and necessitates the law in question. See COMPELLING-STATE-INTEREST TEST; SUSPECT CLASSIFICATION; FUNDAMENTAL RIGHT. Cf. INTERMEDIATE SCRUTINY; RATIONAL-BASIS TEST.

strict settlement. See SETTLEMENT (1).

strict test. *Evidence.* The principle that disclosure of a privileged document, even when inadvertent, results in a waiver of the attorney–client privilege regarding the document, unless all possible precautions were taken to protect the document from disclosure. Cf. LENIENT TEST; HYDRAFLOW TEST.

strictum jus (**strik**-təm **jəs**). See JUS STRICTUM.

strict underwriting. See *standby underwriting* under UNDERWRITING.

strike, *n.* (1810) **1.** An organized cessation or slowdown of work by employees to compel the employer to meet the employees' demands; a concerted refusal by employees to work for their employer, or to work at their customary rate of speed, until the employer grants the concessions that they seek. — Also termed *walkout.* Cf. LOCKOUT; BOYCOTT; PICKETING.

▸ **ca'canny strike.** See *slowdown strike.*

▸ **economic strike.** (1901) A strike resulting from an economic dispute with the employer (such as a wage dispute); a dispute for reasons other than unfair labor practices. • An employer can permanently replace an economic striker but cannot prevent the worker from coming back to an unreplaced position simply because the worker was on strike.

▸ **general strike.** (1810) A strike organized to affect an entire industry.

▸ **hunger strike.** See HUNGER STRIKE.

▸ **illegal strike.** (1907) **1.** A strike using unlawful procedures. **2.** A strike to obtain unlawful objectives, as in a strike to force an employer to stop doing business with a particular company.

▸ **jurisdictional strike.** (1918) A strike resulting from a dispute between members of different unions over work assignments.

▸ **organizational strike.** See *recognition strike.*

▸ **outlaw strike.** See *wildcat strike.*

▸ **quickie strike.** See *wildcat strike.*

▸ **recognition strike.** (1950) A strike by workers seeking to force their employer to acknowledge the union as their collective-bargaining agent. • After the National Labor Relations Act was enacted in 1935, recognition strikes became unnecessary. Under the Act, the employer is required to recognize an NLRB-certified union for bargaining purposes. — Also termed *organizational strike.*

▸ **rent strike.** See RENT STRIKE.

▸ **secondary strike.** (1907) A strike against an employer because that employer has business dealings with another employer directly involved in a dispute with the union. See *secondary boycott* under BOYCOTT; *secondary picketing* under PICKETING.

▸ **sit-down strike.** (1936) A strike in which employees occupy the workplace but do not work. See SIT-IN.

▸ **slowdown strike.** (1939) A strike in which the workers remain on the job but work at a slower pace to reduce their output. — Also termed *ca'canny strike.*

▸ **sympathy strike.** (1905) A strike by union members who have no grievance against their own employer but who want to show support for another union involved in a labor dispute.

▸ **whipsaw strike.** (1957) A strike against some but not all members of a multiemployer association, called for the purpose of pressuring all the employees to negotiate a labor contract. • Employers whose workers are not on strike have the right to lock out employees to exert counterpressure on the union.

▸ **wildcat strike.** (1937) A strike not authorized by a union or by a collective-bargaining agreement. — Also termed *outlaw strike*; *quickie strike.*

2. The removal of a prospective juror from the jury panel <a peremptory strike>. See CHALLENGE (2).

▸ **sight strike.** (1992) The elimination of a veniremember based solely on appearance. See *peremptory challenge* under CHALLENGE (2).

3. A failure or disadvantage, as by a criminal conviction <a strike on one's record>. **4.** *Parliamentary law.* A form of the motion to amend by deleting one or more words. See *amendment by striking out* under AMENDMENT (3).

strike, *vb.* (14c) **1.** (Of an employee or union) to engage in a strike <the flight attendants struck to protest the reduction in benefits>. **2.** To remove (a prospective juror) from a jury panel by a peremptory challenge or a challenge for cause <the prosecution struck the panelist who indicated an opposition to the death penalty>. See *peremptory challenge* under CHALLENGE (2). **3.** To expunge, as from a record <motion to strike the prejudicial evidence>. **4.** *Parliamentary law.* To amend by deleting one or more words. See *amendment by striking out* under AMENDMENT (3). — Also termed (in sense 4) *strike out.*

strikebreaker. See SCAB.

strike down. (1894) To invalidate (a statute); to declare void.

strike-down method. (2001) *Civil procedure & criminal procedure.* A jury-selection technique whereby once the for-cause challenges have been exercised, the court adds up the total number of jurors and alternates who will serve, plus the total number of peremptory challenges that might be exercised by the two sides, and then selects that many prospective jurors, so that once the peremptory challenges have been exercised, the jurors remaining are impaneled. — Also termed *struck method.*

strike fund. (1906) A union fund that provides benefits to its members who are on strike, esp. for subsistence while the members are not receiving wages.

strike off. 1. (Of a court) to order (a case) removed from the docket. **2.** (Of an auctioneer or sheriff) to announce, usu. by the falling of the hammer, that an item of personal or real property has been sold. **3.** DISBAR.

strike out, *n.* See STRIKE (1).

strike out, *vb.* **1.** To remove or expunge (part of a text) from the rest <the parties struck out the language beginning with "including" and ending with "other claims">. **2.** To embark on a new enterprise, usu. on one's own <she struck out on her own and became a sole practitioner>.

strike price. See PRICE.

strike suit. See SUIT.

strike zone. *Slang.* The period in jury selection in which veniremembers are subject to being struck by peremptory challenge before the jury is seated. • If a court requires 12 jurors and allows each side 10 peremptory strikes, the strike zone would be the first 32 veniremembers.

striking a jury. (1859) The selecting of a jury out of all the candidates available to serve on the jury; esp., the selecting of a special jury. See *struck jury, special jury* under JURY.

striking off the roll. See DISBARMENT.

striking price. See *strike price* under PRICE.

string of title. See CHAIN OF TITLE (1).

strip, *n.* (16c) **1.** The act of separating and selling a bond's coupons and corpus separately. **2.** The act of a tenant who, holding less than the entire fee in land, spoils or unlawfully takes something from the land.

STRIP (strip). *abbr.* SEPARATE TRADING OF REGISTERED INTEREST AND PRINCIPAL OF SECURITIES.

stripped mortgage-backed security. See SECURITY (4).

stripper well. See WELL.

strip search. See SEARCH (1).

strong-arm clause. See CLAUSE.

strongly corroborated. (18c) (Of testimony) supported from independent facts and circumstances that are powerful, satisfactory, and clear to the court and jury.

strong mark. See *strong trademark* under TRADEMARK.

strong market. See *bull market* under MARKET.

strong trademark. See TRADEMARK.

struck-box method. *Criminal procedure. Slang.* A jury-selection process in which the prosecution and defense examine all the veniremembers and exercise challenges for cause until the venire has at least the total number of prospective jurors potentially needed — twelve, plus the aggregate number of peremptories allowed to both sides — before peremptory challenges are exercised. — Also termed *struck-box system.* Cf. FULL-BOX METHOD.

struck jury. See JURY.

struck method. See STRIKE-DOWN METHOD.

struck off. 1. Removed from an active docket, usu. because of a want of prosecution or jurisdiction. **2.** *BrE.* Removed from the register of qualified persons and, in the case of a professional, forbidden to practice.

structural alteration. See ALTERATION (1).

structural error. See ERROR (2).

structuralism, *n.* A method of studying society, language, literature, etc. by examining the relationships of the different parts or ideas in order to arrive at a meaningful analysis. — **structuralist,** *adj.* & *n.*

structural takeover defense. See TAKEOVER DEFENSE.

structural unemployment. See UNEMPLOYMENT (1).

structure, *n.* (15c) **1.** Any construction, production, or piece of work artificially built up or composed of parts purposefully joined together <a building is a structure>. **2.** The organization of elements or parts <the corporate structure>. **3.** A method of constructing parts <the loan's payment structure was a financial burden>.

structure, *vb.* To arrange (a transaction) so as to avoid reporting the receipt of cash or a cash equivalent on IRS Form 8300. *See* 21 USCA § 6050I(f); 31 USCA § 5234. Cf. SUSPICIOUS-ACTIVITY REPORT. — **structuring,** *n.*

structured security. See SECURITY (4).

structured settlement. See SETTLEMENT (2).

student-benefit theory. (1967) A principle that allows state funds to be provided to private-school pupils if the allotment can be justified as benefiting the child. • Under this theory, the Supreme Court upheld a Louisiana statute that allowed the purchase of textbooks for all children throughout the state, even those in private schools. *Cochran v. Louisiana State Bd. of Educ.*, 281 U.S. 370, 50 S.Ct. 335 (1930). — Also termed *child-benefit theory.*

student visa. See VISA.

study furlough. See *study release* under RELEASE.

study release. See RELEASE (8).

stuff gown. (1867) **1.** The professional robe worn by barristers of the outer bar who have not been appointed Queen's Counsel. **2.** A junior barrister. Cf. SILK GOWN.

stultify, *vb.* (18c) **1.** To make (something or someone) appear stupid or foolish <he stultified opposing counsel's argument>. **2.** To testify about one's own lack of mental capacity. **3.** To contradict oneself, as by denying what one has already alleged.

stultiloquium (stəl-ti-**loh**-kwee-əm). [fr. Latin *stultus* "foolish" + *loqui* "to speak"] *Hist.* A frivolous pleading punishable by fine. • This may have been the origin of the beaupleader. See BEAUPLEADER.

stumpage (**stəmp**-ij). (1835) **1.** The timber standing on land. **2.** The value of the standing timber. **3.** A license to cut the timber. **4.** The fee paid for the right to cut the timber.

stun grenade. See FLASH-BANG DIVERSIONARY DEVICE.

stuprum (**st**[y]**oo**-prəm), *n.* [Latin] *Roman & civil law.* Disgrace by unchastity; a man's illegal sexual intercourse with a woman, usu. a virgin or widow, or with a male (pederasty). Pl. ***stupra.***

> "The law refers to *stuprum* and adultery indiscriminately and with rather a misuse of terms. But properly speaking adultery is committed with a married woman, the name being derived from children conceived by another (*alter*); *stuprum*, however, is committed against a virgin or a widow; the Greeks call it corruption." *Digest of Justinian* 48.5.6.1 (Papinian, De Adulteriis 1).

> "In general terms, *stuprum* could refer to any sort of sexual immorality, including adultery. Once the Augustan *lex Julia* constituted adultery as a separate criminal offence, *stuprum* took on in addition a more restricted meaning. Though the law sometimes used the words interchangeably (adultery being one kind of unlawful intercourse), 'adultery,' we are told, should be used specifically of relations with a married woman, and *stuprum* of those with unmarried or widowed women (or indeed with boys). Sexual relations with marriageable women were not to be encouraged, since they undermined that marriage and production of legitimate children on which the continuance of the *familia* depended." Jane F. Gardner, *Women in Roman Law & Society* 121 (1986).

STV. See *single transferable vote* under VOTE (1).

style, *n.* (15c) **1.** A case name or designation <the style of the opinion is *Connor v. Gray*>. — Also termed *title.* Cf. CAPTION (1). **2.** *Scots law.* A form of writ or deed used in conveyancing. • A book of styles is essentially a formbook; a typical Scottish example is John Hendry's *Styles of Deeds and Instruments* (2d ed. 1862).

stylized drawing. See *special-form drawing* under DRAWING.

s.u. *abbr.* Straight up. • When a prosecutor writes this on a defendant's file, it usu. means that the prosecutor plans to try the case — that is, not enter into a plea bargain.

suable, *adj.* (17c) **1.** Capable of being sued <a suable party>. **2.** Capable of being enforced <a suable contract>. — **suability,** *n.*

sua potestas (**s**[y]**oo**-ə pə-**tes**-təs *or* -tas). [Latin] *Hist.* The natural power that one has over oneself.

suapte natura (s[y]oo-**ap**-tee nə-**t**[y]**oor**-ə). [Latin] In its own nature — as in *suapte natura sterilia* ("barren of its own nature").

sua sponte (**s**[y]**oo**-ə **spon**-tee). [Latin "of one's own accord; voluntarily"] Without prompting or suggestion; on its own motion <the court took notice sua sponte that it lacked jurisdiction over the case>. • A multimember court may use the form *nostra sponte* [Latin "of our own accord"] to distinguish its collective action from that of a single judge. — Also termed *sponte sua.*

sub (səb). [Latin] (1818) Under; upon.

sub. See *subsidiary corporation* under CORPORATION.

subagent. See AGENT.

subaltern (səb-**awl**-tərn), *n.* (17c) An inferior or subordinate officer.

subassignee. See ASSIGNEE.

sub ballivus (səb bə-**lɪ**-vəs), *n.* [Law Latin] *Hist.* An undersheriff; a sheriff's deputy. See BAILIWICK.

subchapter-C corporation. See *C corporation* under CORPORATION.

subchapter-S corporation. See *S corporation* under CORPORATION.

sub colore juris (səb kə-**lor**-ee **joor**-is). [Latin] Under color of right; under an appearance of right.

sub colore officii (səb kə-**lor**-ee ə-**fish**-ee-ɪ). [Law Latin] *Hist.* Under color of office.

subcombination claim. See PATENT CLAIM.

subcommittee. See COMMITTEE (1).

sub conditione (səb kən-dish-ee-**oh**-nee). [Law Latin] Under condition. • This term creates a condition in a deed.

subcontract. See CONTRACT.

subcontractor. (1834) Someone who is awarded a portion of an existing contract by a contractor, esp. a general contractor. • For example, a contractor who builds houses typically retains subcontractors to perform specialty work such as installing plumbing, laying carpet, making cabinetry, and landscaping — each subcontractor is paid a somewhat lesser sum than the contractor receives for the work.

sub cura mariti (səb **kyoor**-ə mə-**rI**-tI). [Law Latin] *Hist.* Under the care of one's husband.

sub cura uxoris (səb **kyoor**-ə ək-**sor**-is). [Law Latin] *Hist.* Under the care of one's wife.

sub curia (səb **kyoor**-ee-ə). [Latin] Under law.

sub disjunctione (səb dis-jəngk-shee-**oh**-nee). [Latin] In the alternative.

subditus (**səb**-də-təs). [Latin] *Hist.* Someone under another's power; a vassal.

subdivision, *n.* (15c) **1.** The division of a thing into smaller parts. **2.** A parcel of land in a larger development. — **subdivide,** *vb.*

▸ **illegal subdivision.** (1952) The division of a tract of land into smaller parcels in violation of local subdivision regulations, as when a developer begins laying out streets, installing sewer and utility lines, and constructing houses without the local planning commission's authorization.

▸ **legal subdivision.** (1820) The governmentally approved division of a tract of land into smaller parcels using ordinary and legally recognized methods for surveying and platting land and publicly recording the results.

subdivision exaction. (1964) A charge that a community imposes on a subdivider as a condition for permitting recordation of the subdivision map and sale of the subdivided parcels.

subdivision map. (1887) A map that shows how a parcel of land is to be divided into smaller lots, and generally showing the layout and utilities.

sub domino (səb **dom**-ə-noh). [Law Latin] *Hist.* Under a lord.

subfeudum (səb-**fyoo**-dəm). [Law Latin] *Hist.* A subfee.

subinfeudate (səb-in-**fyoo**-dayt), *vb.* (17c) *Hist.* (Of a subvassal) to grant land to another, who then holds the land as the grantor's vassal rather than as the vassal of the grantor's superior. — Also termed *subinfeud* (səb-in-**fyood**).

> "[A] more common method of obtaining the annual quota of knights was to *subinfeudate* portions of the baronial lands to individual knights in exchange for their obligations to spend a fixed portion of time annually in the king's or baron's service. A knight who so received a portion of a baron's land would hold *of* his baron in much the same way as the baron held *of* the king." Thomas F. Bergin & Paul G. Haskell, *Preface to Estates in Land and Future Interests* 4 (2d ed. 1984).

subinfeudation (səb-in-fyoo-**day**-shən), *n.* (18c) *Hist.* The system under which the tenants in a feudal system granted smaller estates to their tenants, who in turn did the same from their pieces of land. • As this system proceeded down the social scale, the lords were deprived of their feudal profits, as a result of which the system was suppressed by the statute *Quia Emptores* in 1290. Instead of subinfeudation, alienation in the modern sense was introduced. Cf. INFEUDATION; SUPERINFEUDATION.

> "The first step taken in mitigation of the rigors of the law of feuds, and in favor of voluntary alienations, was the countenance given to the practice of subinfeudations. They were calculated to elude the restraint upon alienation, and consisted in carving out portions of the fief to be held of the vassal by the same tenure with which he held of the chief lord of the fee. The alienation prohibited by the feudal law, all over Europe, was the substitution of a new feudatory in the place of the old one; but subinfeudation was a feoffment by the tenant to hold of himself. The purchaser became his vassal, and the vendor still continued liable to the chief lord for all the feudal obligations. Subinfeudations were encouraged by the subordinate feudatories, because they contributed to their own power and independence; but they were found to be injurious to the fruits of tenure, such as reliefs, marriages and wardships, belonging to the paramount lords." 4 James Kent, *Commentaries on American Law* *443–44 (George Comstock ed., 11th ed. 1866).

subinfeudatory (səb-in-**fyoo**-də-tor-ee), *n.* (1812) A tenant holding lands by subinfeudation.

subjacent (səb-**jay**-sənt), *adj.* (16c) Located underneath or below <the land's subjacent support>.

subjacent support. See SUPPORT (4).

subject (**səb**-jəkt), *adj.* (14c) **1.** *Int'l law.* Under the power of dominion of another; specif., owing allegiance to a particular sovereign or state <subject peoples>. **2.** Exposed, liable, or prone <a climate subject to extreme temperatures>. **3.** Dependent on or exposed to (some contingency); esp., being under discretionary authority <funding is subject to the board's approval>. **4.** Referred to above; having relevance to the current discussion <the subject property was then sold to Smith>.

subject, *n.* (14c) **1.** Someone who owes allegiance to a sovereign, esp. a monarch, and is governed by that sovereign's laws; one who is under the governing power of another <the monarchy's subjects>.

> "Speaking generally, we may say that the terms subject and citizen are synonymous. Subjects and citizens are alike those whose relation to the state is personal and not merely territorial, permanent and not merely temporary. This equivalent, however, is not absolute. For in the first place, the term subject is commonly limited to monarchical forms of government, while the term citizen is more specially applicable in the case of republics. A British subject becomes by naturalisation a citizen of the United States of America or of France. In the second place, the term citizen brings into prominence the rights and privileges of the status, rather than its correlative obligations, while the reverse is the case with the term subject. Finally it is to be noticed that the term subject is capable of a different and wider application, in which it includes all members of the body politic, whether they are citizens (i.e., subjects *stricto sensu*) or resident aliens. All such persons are subjects, all being subject to the power of the state and to its jurisdiction, and as owing to it, at least temporarily, fidelity and obedience." John Salmond, *Jurisprudence* 133 (Glanville L. Williams ed., 10th ed. 1947).

▸ **liege subject.** See *natural-born subject.*

▸ **natural-born subject.** (17c) A person born within the dominion of a monarchy, esp. England. — Also termed *liege subject.* Cf. NATIONAL, *n.*

2. The matter of concern over which something is created; something about which thought or the constructive faculty is employed <the subject of the statute>. — Also termed (in sense 2) *subject matter.*

subject (səb-**jekt**), *vb.* **1.** To cause to undergo some action, agent, or operation <to subject someone to a test>. **2.** To expose to the operation of some law or agency; to render liable to be affected <that behavior may well subject her to prosecution>. **3.** To place before consideration, judgment, and disposition <I now subject my proposal to the committee's scrutiny>. **4.** To cause to become subordinate or subservient; esp., to exercise dominion over (a group of people, a country, etc.), and to do so strictly; to subjugate <the Africans were cruelly subjected to early European immigrants in America>. **5.** To predispose; to make liable <gullibility subjects a person to fraud>.

subjection. (14c) **1.** The act of subjecting someone to something <their subjection to torture was unconscionable>. **2.** The condition of a subject in a monarchy; the obligations surrounding such a person <a subject, wherever residing, owes fidelity and obedience to the Crown, while an alien may be released at will from all such ties of subjection>. **3.** The condition of being subject, exposed, or liable; liability <the defendants' subjection to the plaintiffs became clear shortly after the trial began>. — Also termed (in sense 3) *liability*; *susceptibility*.

subjective, *adj.* (18c) **1.** Based on an individual's perceptions, feelings, or intentions, as opposed to externally verifiable phenomena <the subjective theory of contract — that the parties must have an actual meeting of the minds — is not favored by most courts>. **2.** Personal; individual <subjective judgments about popular music>. Cf. OBJECTIVE.

subjective ethics. See MORAL RELATIVISM.

subjective impossibility. See IMPOSSIBILITY.

subjective meaning. See MEANING.

subjective method. See SHERMAN–SORRELLS DOCTRINE.

subjective novation. See NOVATION.

subjective standard. See STANDARD.

subjective theory of contract. (1928) The doctrine (now largely outmoded) that a contract is an agreement in which the parties have a subjective meeting of the minds. — Often shortened to *subjective theory*. See MEETING OF THE MINDS. Cf. OBJECTIVE THEORY OF CONTRACT.

subject matter. (16c) **1.** The issue presented for consideration; the thing in which a right or duty has been asserted; the thing in dispute. **2.** PATENTABLE SUBJECT MATTER. — Sometimes written (as a noun) *subject-matter*. See SUBJECT (2); CORPUS (1). — **subject-matter,** *adj.*

subject-matter jurisdiction. See JURISDICTION.

subject-matter-neutral. See NEUTRAL.

subject-matter test. (1974) A method of determining whether an employee's communication with a corporation's lawyer was made at the direction of the employee's supervisors and in the course and scope of the employee's employment, so as to be protected under the attorney–client privilege, despite the fact that the employee is not a member of the corporation's control group. *Harper & Row Pubs., Inc. v. Decker*, 423 F.2d 487 (7th Cir. 1970), *aff'd per curiam by equally divided Court*, 400 U.S. 348, 91 S.Ct. 479 (1971). — Also termed *Decker test*. Cf. CONTROL-GROUP TEST.

subject-matter waiver. See WAIVER (1).

subject of an action. (18c) The right or property at issue in a lawsuit; the basis of a legal claim. Cf. *object of an action* under OBJECT, *n.* (2).

subject of a right. (1876) **1.** The owner of a right; the person in whom a legal right is vested. **2.** OBJECT OF A RIGHT.

subject to liability, *adj.* (1835) (Of a person) susceptible to a lawsuit that would result in an adverse judgment; specif., having engaged in conduct that would make the actor liable for another's injury because the actor's conduct is the legal cause of the injury, the injured party having no disability for bringing the lawsuit.

subject to open. (1906) Denoting the future interest of a class of people when this class is subject to a possible increase or decrease in number.

sub judice (səb **joo**-di-see *also* suub **yoo**-di-kay), *adv.* [Latin "under a judge"] (17c) Before the court or judge for determination; at bar <in the case sub judice, there have been no out-of-court settlements>. • Legal writers sometimes use *case sub judice* where *the present case* would be more comprehensible.

subjugation. See DEBELLATIO.

sublease, *n.* (18c) A lease by a lessee to a third party, transferring the right to possession to some or all of the leased property for a term shorter than that of the lessee, who retains a right of reversion. • For example, if A leases to B for a term of five years, and one year later B transfers his right to possession to C for two years, C holds a sublease. Under the majority test used in the U.S., the so-called objective standard, if the lessee transfers his right to possession for *all* of his term, this is an assignment, not a sublease; but if the lessee transfers his right to possession for only *part* of his term, this is a sublease, even if the lessee reserves the right to possession for only the last minute. — Also termed *subtenancy*; *derivative lease*; (esp. in England) *underlease*. Cf. ASSIGNMENT. — **sublease, sublet,** *vb.*

sublegacy. See LEGACY (2).

sublessee. (17c) A third party who receives the right to possession of leased property by a contract with a current tenant. — Also termed *subtenant*; (esp. in England) *undertenant*.

sublessor. (1813) A lessee who transfers the right to possession of leased property to a third person by a sublease. — Also termed (esp. in England) *underlessor*.

sublicense. (1880) A license or contract granting to a third party a portion or all of the rights granted to the licensee under an original license.

submarine patent. See PATENT (3).

submission, *n.* (14c) **1.** A yielding, or readiness to yield, to the authority or will of another <his resistance ended in an about-face: complete submission>. **2.** A contract in which the parties agree to refer their dispute to a third party for resolution <in their submission to arbitration, they referred to the rules of the American Arbitration Association>. — Also termed *submission agreement*. **3.** An advocate's argument <neither the written nor the oral submissions were particularly helpful>. — **submit,** *vb.*

> "Written submissions are intended as documents to persuade. The context in which they are created are numerous and not confined to court or tribunal hearings. Letters of demand and applications to government or other

regulatory authorities can be seen as forms of written submissions. In their most basic form written submissions are written contentions for a position. The person or body to whom they are addressed may have forms, procedures or guidelines about how submissions should be prepared and presented and these will create the structured context and constraints which the written submissions must follow." G.T. Pagone, "Written Advocacy: Writing with Effect and Persuasion," in *Essays in Advocacy* 119, 127 (Tom Gray et al. eds., 2012).

submission agreement. 1. See ARBITRATION AGREEMENT. **2.** See SUBMISSION (2).

submission bond. See BOND (2).

submission date. See DATE.

submission of controversy. (1878) **1.** The completion of the series of acts by which the parties to a particular dispute place any matter of real controversy existing between them before a court with jurisdiction for a final determination. **2.** A statutory action in which the parties submit their dispute to a court that has jurisdiction, agree on and sign a statement of facts, swear that the controversy is real, and swear that the suit is brought in good faith.

submission to a finding. (1982) The admission to facts sufficient to warrant a finding of guilt. — Also termed *admission to sufficient facts.*

submission to the jury. (1818) The process by which a judge gives a case to the jury for its consideration and verdict, usu. after all evidence has been presented, arguments have been completed, and jury instructions have been given.

submit, *vb.* To end the presentation of further evidence in (a case) and tender a legal position for decision <case submitted, Your Honor>.

sub modo (səb **moh**-doh). [Latin] (16c) Subject to a modification or qualification; on condition that <the riparian landowner enjoys the property *sub modo*, i.e., subject to the right of the public to reserve enough space for levees, public roads, and the like>. See MODUS.

submortgage. See MORTGAGE.

sub nomine (səb **nom**-ə-nee). [Latin] (1861) Under the name of. • This phrase, typically in abbreviated form, is often used in a case citation to indicate that there has been a name change from one stage of the case to another, as in *Guernsey Memorial Hosp. v. Secretary of Health and Human Servs.*, 996 F.2d 830 (6th Cir. 1993), *rev'd sub nom. Shalala v. Guernsey Memorial Hosp.*, 514 U.S. 87, 115 S.Ct. 1232 (1995). — Abbr. *sub nom.*

subnotation. (1839) See RESCRIPT (3).

subordinate (sə-**bor**-də-nit), *adj.* (15c) **1.** Placed in or belonging to a lower rank, class, or position <a subordinate lien>. **2.** Subject to another's authority or control <a subordinate lawyer>.

subordinate (sə-**bor**-də-nayt), *vb.* (17c) To place in a lower rank, class, or position; to assign a lower priority to <subordinate the debt to a different class of claims>.

subordinate agent. See AGENT.

subordinated bond. See *junior bond* under BOND (3).

subordinate debenture. See DEBENTURE (3).

subordinate debt. See DEBT.

subordinate legislation. See LEGISLATION (3).

subordinate officer. See OFFICER (1).

subordinate political power. See POLITICAL POWER.

subordinating/superordinating-language canon. The doctrine that in a legal instrument, subordinating language (signaled by *subject to*) or superordinating language (signaled by *notwithstanding* or *despite*) merely shows which provision prevails in the event of a clash — but does not necessarily denote a clash of provisions.

subordination, *n.* (17c) **1.** The act or an instance of moving something (such as a right or claim) to a lower rank, class, or position <subordination of a first lien to a second lien>. **2.** *Parliamentary law.* The status and relation of a lower-ranking governing document to a higher-ranking one. • A higher-ranking document supersedes and controls a subordinate document if there is any inconsistency between them. See *governing document* under DOCUMENT (2). — **subordinate,** *adj.*

▸ **equitable subordination.** (1941) A court's act of lowering a claim's priority for purposes of equity, esp. when the claimant engaged in unfair conduct toward junior claimants. • Both secured and unsecured claims may be equitably subordinated.

▸ **subordination clause.** (1907) **1.** In a legal instrument, a clause that explicitly acknowledges the one party's claim of interest is inferior to that of another party. **2.** A covenant in a junior mortgage enabling the first lien to keep its priority in case of renewal or refinancing. **3.** In a legal instrument, a clause that explicitly subjects its provisions to those in a higher-ranking document.

subordination agreement. (1908) An agreement by which one who holds an otherwise senior interest agrees to subordinate that interest to a normally lesser interest, usu. when a seller agrees to subordinate a purchase-money mortgage so that the buyer can obtain a first-mortgage loan to improve the property.

▸ **debt-subordination agreement.** A contract under which a junior creditor must wait for payment until all the debtor's existing senior creditors are paid. — Also termed *debt subordination.*

▸ **general-subordination agreement.** A contract binding a junior creditor to subordinate its claim to those of every other creditor, existing and future.

▸ **specific-subordination agreement.** A contract under which a junior creditor agrees to subordinate a claim only to another particular obligation of the debtor.

suborn (sə-**born**), *vb.* [Latin *subonare*, from *sub* "secretly + *ornare* "to furnish; equip"] (16c) **1.** To induce (a person) to commit an unlawful or wrongful act, esp. in a secret or underhanded manner. **2.** To induce (a person) to commit perjury; specif., to persuade (someone) to lie under oath, esp. in court, usu. by paying money. **3.** To obtain (perjured testimony) from another. — **subornation** (səb-or-**nay**-shən), *n.* — **suborner** (sə-**bor**-nər), *n.*

subornation of perjury. (16c) The crime of persuading another to commit perjury; the act of procuring a witness to testify falsely. — Sometimes shortened to *subornation.*

subparagraph form. (1960) A style of legal drafting that uses indented subparagraphs for enumerated items; esp., a style of drafting patent claims in this form so as to distinguish clearly between each of the claimed elements. — Also termed *tabular form.* Cf. COLON-SEMICOLON FORM; OUTLINE FORM; SINGLE-PARAGRAPH FORM.

subpartnership. See PARTNERSHIP.

sub pede sigilli (səb **pee**-dee si-**jil**-ɪ). [Latin] Under the foot of the seal.

subpena. See SUBPOENA.

subpermittee. See PERMITTEE.

subpoena (sə-**pee**-nə), *n.* [Latin "under penalty"] (15c) A writ or order commanding a person to appear before a court or other tribunal, subject to a penalty for failing to comply. — Also spelled *subpena*. Pl. **subpoenas.**

▸ **accommodation subpoena.** See *friendly subpoena*.

▸ **administrative subpoena.** (1925) A subpoena issued by an administrative agency to compel an individual to provide information to the agency. • The subpoena may take the form of a *subpoena ad testificandum* or a *subpoena duces tecum*.

▸ **alias subpoena** (**ay**-lee-əs sə-**pee**-nə). (18c) A second subpoena issued after an initial subpoena has failed.

▸ **deposition subpoena.** (1941) **1.** A subpoena issued to summon a person to make a sworn statement in a time and place other than a trial. **2.** In some jurisdictions, a subpoena duces tecum.

▸ **friendly subpoena.** (1997) A subpoena issued to a person or entity that is willing to testify or produce documents, but only if legally required to do so. • The subpoena may protect the information provider from retaliation from others because the provider is required to comply. — Also termed *accommodation subpoena*.

▸ **so-ordered subpoena.** (1982) A subpoena *duces tecum* issued not by an attorney, but by a judge, with particular directions and concluding, "So ordered."

▸ **subpoena ad testificandum** (sə-**pee**-nə ad tes-tə-fi-**kan**-dəm). [Law Latin] (1807) A subpoena ordering a witness to appear and give testimony.

▸ **subpoena duces tecum** (sə-**pee**-nə **d**[y]**oo**-seez **tee**-kəm *also* **doo**-səz **tay**-kəm). [Law Latin] (18c) A subpoena ordering the witness to appear in court and to bring specified documents, records, or things. — Also termed *deposition subpoena duces tecum*.

subpoena, *vb.* (17c) **1.** To serve with a subpoena to appear before a court or other tribunal <subpoena the material witnesses>. **2.** To order the production of (documents or other things) by subpoena duces tecum <subpoena the corporate records>. — Also spelled *subpena*.

subpoena ad respondendum. *Hist.* In chancery practice, a mandatory writ or process directed to and requiring one or more persons to appear at a designated time and place to answer the matters charged.

> "The *subpoena ad respondendum* was the only original process of the court of Chancery and the means whereby defendants were summoned to appear and make their answers. The *subpoena* derived its name from the penalty of £100 mentioned in it, although this could not be enforced even if the defendant or his attorney did not appear by the return of the writ. The defendant was required to appear personally in Chancery by a certain day. He could be unaware of the nature of the complaint until he made his appearance, for the writ gave him no information and there was no reason why the person who served it should oblige him with the details. A natural consequence of this can be seen in the constant tide of complaints that people were being called up from all parts of the country to answer what might well be frivolous or vexatious bills. Yet the basic simplicity of the writ was its greatest strength, and it was representative of the general theory which had come to surround the jurisdiction of the Lord Chancellor. The purpose of a writ at law was to give the judge jurisdiction. However, a general delegation of an express or implicit nature was assumed to have been made from the King to the Chancellor. It was unnecessary to accord him jurisdiction in each individual case, and hence the *subpoena* did not specify the nature of the complaint. The jurisdiction of the Chancellor, like the issue of a *subpoena* was a matter of grace." W.J. Jones, *The Elizabethan Court of Chancery* 177–78 (1967).

subpoenal (sə-**pee**-nəl), *adj.* (1969) Required or done under penalty, esp. in compliance with a subpoena.

sub potestate (səb poh-tes-**tay**-tee). [Latin] Under the power of another, as with a child or other person not *sui juris*. Cf. SUI JURIS.

sub potestate parentis (səb poh-tes-**tay**-tee pə-**ren**-tis). [Latin] *Hist.* Under the authority of a parent.

sub potestate viri. *Hist.* (Of a wife) under the protection of a husband.

subprime, *adj.* (Of a loan) involving an amount of money that a borrower may not be able to pay back, usu. at a high rate of interest.

subprime debt. See DEBT.

subprime loan. See LOAN.

subpurchaser. A buyer who buys from a buyer; a secondhand buyer.

subreptio (səb-**rep**-shee-oh), *n.* [Latin "surreptitious removal"] *Roman law.* **1.** Theft. **2.** The obtaining of a grant from the emperor under false pretenses. — Also termed (in French law) *subreption*. Pl. ***subreptiones*** (səb-rep-shee-**oh**-neez).

subreptione vel obreptione (səb-rep-shee-**oh**-nee vel ob-rep-shee-**oh**-nee), *adv.* [Latin] *Hist.* By deceit or surprise; by concealing the truth or affirming a falsehood.

subrogate (**səb**-rə-gayt), *vb.* (15c) To substitute (a person) for another regarding a legal right or claim.

subrogation (səb-rə-**gay**-shən), *n.* (15c) **1.** The substitution of one party for another whose debt the party pays, entitling the paying party to rights, remedies, or securities that would otherwise belong to the debtor. • For example, a surety who has paid a debt is, by subrogation, entitled to any security for the debt held by the creditor and the benefit of any judgment the creditor has against the debtor, and may proceed against the debtor as the creditor would. Subrogation most commonly arises in relation to insurance policies. **2.** The equitable remedy by which such a substitution takes place. **3.** The principle under which an insurer that has paid a loss under an insurance policy is entitled to all the rights and remedies belonging to the insured against a third party with respect to any loss covered by the policy. See EQUITY OF SUBROGATION; ANTISUBROGATION RULE.

> "Subrogation is equitable assignment. The right comes into existence when the surety becomes obligated, and this is important as affecting priorities; but such right of subrogation does not become a cause of action until the debt is fully paid. Subrogation entitles the surety to use any remedy against the principal which the creditor could have used, and in general to enjoy the benefit of any advantage that the creditor had, such as a mortgage, lien, power to confess judgment, to follow trust funds, to proceed against a third person who has promised either the principal or the creditor to pay the debt." Laurence P. Simpson, *Handbook on the Law of Suretyship* 205 (1950).

"Subrogation simply means substitution of one person for another; that is, one person is allowed to stand in the shoes of another and assert that person's rights against the defendant. Factually, the case arises because, for some justifiable reason, the subrogation plaintiff has paid a debt owed by the defendant." 1 Dan B. Dobbs, *Law of Remedies* § 4.3(4), at 604 (2d ed. 1993).

▸ **conventional subrogation.** (1818) Subrogation that arises by contract.

▸ **equitable subrogation.** (1829) Subrogation that arises by operation of law or by implication in equity to prevent fraud or injustice. • Equitable subrogation usu. arises when (1) the paying party has a liability, claim, or fiduciary relationship with the debtor, (2) the party pays to fulfill a legal duty or because of public policy, (3) the paying party is a secondary debtor, (4) the paying party is a surety, or (5) the party pays to protect its own rights or property. The synonymous phrase *legal subrogation* is sometimes used not to suggest an origin in law rather than equity (subrogation of this type may arise from either source), but to distinguish subrogation imposed by a court from subrogation arising by contract (see *conventional subrogation*). — Also termed *legal subrogation*.

▸ **legal subrogation.** See *equitable subrogation*.

▸ **real subrogation.** (1862) *Civil law.* The substitution of one thing for another.

subrogation clause. (1872) **1.** *Insurance.* A provision in a property- or liability-insurance policy whereby the insurer acquires certain rights upon paying a claim for a loss under the policy. • These rights include (1) taking legal action on behalf of the insured to recover the amount of the loss from the party who caused the loss, and (2) receiving a full or proportionate amount of the benefits (such as disability compensation) paid to the insured under a statutory plan. **2.** *Oil & gas.* A provision in an oil-and-gas lease permitting the lessee to pay taxes, mortgages, or other encumbrances on the leased property and to recover those payments out of future proceeds under the lease.

subrogative (**səb**-rə-gay-tiv), *adj.* (17c) Of, relating to, or involving subrogation <subrogative rights>. — Also termed *subrogatory*; *subrogational*.

subrogee (səb-rə-**jee**). (1851) Someone who is substituted for another in having a right, duty, or claim; esp., the person or entity that assumes the right to attempt to collect on another's claim against a third party by paying the other's claim-related debts or expenses. • An insurance company frequently becomes a subrogee after paying a policy claim, as a result of which it is then in a position to sue a tortfeasor who injured the insured or otherwise caused harm.

subrogor (səb-rə-**gor**). (1882) Someone who allows another to be substituted for oneself as creditor, with a transfer of rights and duties; esp., one who transfers a legal right to collect a claim to another in return for payment of the transferor's claim-related debts or expenses.

sub rosa (səb **roh**-zə), *adj.* [Latin "under the rose"] (1824) *Hist.* Confidential; secret; not for publication.

sub salvo et securo conductu (səb **sal**-voh et si-**kyoor**-oh kən-**dək**-t[y]oo). [Law Latin] *Hist.* Under safe and secure conduct. • This phrase was used in writs of habeas corpus.

subscribe, *vb.* **1.** To write (one's name) underneath; to put (one's signature) on a document <she subscribed a false name>. **2.** To sign one's name to a letter or other document in acknowledgment of being its writer or creator <he subscribed after the complimentary close>. **3.** To give consent to by signing with one's own hand; to bind oneself to the terms of <to subscribe the contract>. **4.** To attest by signature <two witnesses subscribed the will>. **5.** To sanction or adhere to <all states subscribe to some form of drug control>. **6.** To promise to give or contribute <each attendee subscribed $500>. **7.** To agree to take and pay for something, esp. something regularly delivered; esp., to pay money, usu. annually, to receive a weekly or monthly service, such as a newspaper or magazine <to subscribe to a newsweekly>. **8.** To publish by subscription <Lindley Murray's American publishers subscribed a new edition of his *Grammar*>. **9.** To pledge oneself, esp. by writing, to paying a given sum of money <the couple subscribed to donate $5,000>. **10.** To agree to buy or pay for (shares, stock, etc.) <each executive may subscribe for up to 5,000 shares>. **11.** To be in favor; to adhere <I subscribe to that view>.

subscribed capital. See CAPITAL.

subscribed-share capital. See *subscribed capital* under CAPITAL.

subscribed stock. See STOCK.

subscribing witness. See WITNESS.

subscriptio (səb-**skrip**-shee-oh), *n.* [Latin] *Roman law.* **1.** A signature, esp. a name written under or at the bottom of a document to authenticate it; an imperial rescript. **2.** A signature to a will, required in certain cases in addition to the seals of witnesses. Pl. ***subscriptiones*** (səb-skrip-shee-**oh**-neez).

subscription, *n.* (15c) **1.** The act of signing one's name on a document; the signature so affixed. **2.** *Securities.* A written contract to purchase newly issued shares of stock or bonds. — Also termed (in connection with stock) *stock subscription*. **3.** An oral or a written agreement to contribute a sum of money or property, gratuitously or with consideration, to a specific person or for a specific purpose. — Also termed *subscription contract*; *contract of subscription*. **4.** RESCRIPT (3). — **subscribe,** *vb.* — **subscriber,** *n.*

subscription contract. See SUBSCRIPTION (3).

subscription list. (18c) An enumeration of subscribers to an agreement, periodical, or service.

subscription price. (17c) The fixed price at which investors can buy shares in a new stock offering before the shares are offered to the public.

subscription privilege. See PREEMPTIVE RIGHT.

subscription right. (1870) A certificate evidencing a shareholder's right (known as a *preemptive right*) to purchase newly issued stock before the stock is offered to the public. • Subscription rights have a market value and are actively traded because they allow the holder to purchase stock at favorable prices. — Also termed *stock right*. See PREEMPTIVE RIGHT.

subscription warrant. See WARRANT (4).

subscriptor (səb-**skrip**-tor *or* -tər), *n.* [Latin] (16c) *Roman law.* **1.** Someone who made or signed a written accusation of crime against a particular person. **2.** The witness to a will. Pl. ***subscriptores***.

subsellia (səb-**sel**-ee-ə), *n.* [Latin fr. *sub* "under" + *sella* "seat"] (17c) *Roman law.* Lower seats in a court, usu. occupied by the parties or their witnesses, as distinguished from the seat of the tribunal.

subsequent, *adj.* (15c) (Of an action, event, etc.) occurring later; coming after something else.

subsequent-act evidence. See EVIDENCE.

subsequent-advance rule. (1974) *Bankruptcy.* The principle that a preferential transfer by the debtor will not be avoided or rescinded by the debtor's bankruptcy trustee if (1) the creditor extended new value to the debtor after receiving the preferential transfer, (2) the new value is unsecured, and (3) the new value remains unpaid after its transfer. 11 USCA § 547(c)(4).

subsequent creditor. See CREDITOR.

subsequente copula (səb-si-**kwen**-tee **kop**-yə-lə). [Law Latin] *Hist.* Carnal intercourse having followed.

subsequent legislative history. See LEGISLATIVE HISTORY.

subsequent negligence. See NEGLIGENCE.

subsequent-negligence doctrine. See LAST-CLEAR-CHANCE DOCTRINE.

subsequent purchaser. See PURCHASER (1).

subsequent remedial measure. (*usu. pl.*) (1956) *Evidence.* An action taken after an event, which, if taken before the event, would have reduced the likelihood of the event's occurrence. • Evidence of subsequent remedial measures, such as repairs made after an accident or the installation of safety equipment, is not admissible to prove negligence, but it may be admitted to prove ownership, control, feasibility, or the like. Fed. R. Evid. 407.

subservant. See *subagent* under AGENT.

subsidence (səb-**sɪd**-ən[t]s), *n.* (17c) Any downward movement of the soil from its natural position; esp., a sinking of soil.

subsidiarie (səb-sid-ee-**air**-ee-ee). [Law Latin] *Scots law.* Subsidiarily.

subsidiarity (səb-sid-ee-**air**-i-tee) (1930) **1.** The quality, state, or condition of being subsidiary. • This sense is derived from the German *subsidiarität* as used by Pope Pius XI in a 1931 speech. In legal contexts, this sense is the more common. **2.** The principle that a central authority's function should be subsidiary, performing only tasks that cannot be performed effectively at a more immediate or local level; the doctrine that the power to make chiefly local decisions should vest with local authorities, not with a dominant central organization. • The term appears most commonly in discussion of the European Union's granting power to its member countries.

subsidiary (səb-**sid**-ee-er-ee), *adj.* (17c) Subordinate; under another's control. See *subsidiary corporation* under CORPORATION.

subsidiary, *n.* See *subsidiary corporation* under CORPORATION.

subsidiary corporation. See CORPORATION.

subsidiary fact. See *minor fact* under FACT.

subsidiary merger. See *triangular merger* under MERGER.

subsidiary motion. See MOTION (2).

subsidize, *vb.* **1.** To aid or promote (an undertaking) through financial support. **2.** To grant a regular allowance or monetary assistance to.

subsidy (**səb**-sə-dee), *n.* (14c) **1.** A grant, usu. made by the government, to any enterprise whose promotion is considered to be in the public interest. • Although governments sometimes make direct payments (such as cash grants), subsidies are usu. indirect. They may take the form of research-and-development support, tax breaks, provision of raw materials at below-market prices, or low-interest loans or low-interest export credits guaranteed by a government agency. — Also termed *grant.* **2.** A specific financial contribution by a foreign government or public entity conferring a benefit on exporters to the United States. • Such a subsidy is countervailable under 19 USCA §§ 1671, 1677.

▸ **countervailable subsidy** (kown-tər-**vayl**-ə-bəl). (1980) A foreign government's subsidy on the manufacture of goods exported to another country, giving rise to the importing country's entitlement to impose a countervailing duty on the goods if their import caused or threatens to cause material injury to domestic industry. See *countervailing duty* under DUTY (4).

3. *Int'l law.* Financial assistance given by one country to another to preserve the receiving country's neutrality or to support it in a war, even if the donor country does not directly participate.

sub sigillo (səb si-**jil**-oh). [Latin "under the seal (of confession)"] (17c) *Hist.* In the strictest confidence.

sub silentio (səb si-**len**-shee-oh). [Latin] (17c) Under silence; without notice being taken; without being expressly mentioned (such as precedent *sub silentio*).

subsistence. (17c) Support; means of support. See NECESSARIES.

sub specie legis ferendae (səb **spee**-shee-ee [*or* **spee**-shee] **lee**-jis fə-**ren**-dee). [Latin] Under pretense of what is to be proposed as law.

sub spe reconciliationis (səb **spee** rek-ən-sil-ee-ay-shee-**oh**-nis). [Latin] *Hist.* Under the hope of reconcilement.

substance. (14c) **1.** The essence of something; the essential quality of something, as opposed to its mere form <matter of substance>. **2.** Any matter, esp. an addictive drug <illegal substance> <abuse of a substance>.

substance-abuse evaluation and treatment. (1983) A drug offender's court-ordered participation in a drug rehabilitation program. • This type of treatment is esp. common in DUI cases. — Abbr. SAET.

substandard risk. See RISK.

substantial, *adj.* **1.** Of, relating to, or involving substance; material <substantial change in circumstances>. **2.** Real and not imaginary; having actual, not fictitious, existence <a substantial case on the merits>. **3.** Important, essential, and material; of real worth and importance <a substantial right>. **4.** Strong, solid, and firm <a substantial piece of Victorian furniture>. **5.** At least moderately wealthy; possessed of sufficient financial means <a substantial supporter>. **6.** Considerable in amount or value; large in volume or number <substantial support and care>. **7.** Having permanence or near-permanence; long-lasting <the substantial presence of English-language books in libraries worldwide>. **8.** Containing the essence of a thing;

conveying the right idea even if not the exact details <a substantial portrait of the leader, even if some matters were slighted>. **9.** Nourishing; affording sufficient nutriment <a substantial meal>.

substantial-capacity test. (1968) *Criminal law.* The Model Penal Code's test for the insanity defense, stating that a person is not criminally responsible for an act if, as a result of a mental disease or defect, the person lacks substantial capacity either to appreciate the criminality of the conduct or to conform the conduct to the law. • This test combines elements of both the *McNaghten* rules and the irresistible-impulse test by allowing consideration of both volitional and cognitive weaknesses. This test was formerly used by the federal courts and many states, but since 1984 many jurisdictions (including the federal courts) — in response to the acquittal by reason of insanity of would-be presidential assassin John Hinckley — have narrowed the insanity defense and adopted a new test resembling the *McNaghten* rules, although portions of the substantial-capacity test continue to be used. Model Penal Code § 4.01. — Also termed *Model Penal Code test; MPC test; American Law Institute test; ALI test.* See INSANITY DEFENSE.

substantial-cause test. (1929) *Torts.* The principle that causation exists when the defendant's conduct is an important or significant contributor to the plaintiff's injuries. — Also termed *substantial-factor test.* Cf. BUT-FOR TEST.

substantial-certainty test. *Copyright.* The test for deciding whether a second work was copied from the first. • The question is whether a reasonable observer would conclude with substantial certainty that the second work is a copy.

substantial change in circumstances. See CHANGE IN CIRCUMSTANCES.

substantial-compliance rule. See SUBSTANTIAL-PERFORMANCE DOCTRINE.

substantial-continuity doctrine. (1987) A principle for holding a successor corporation liable for the acts of its predecessor corporation, if the successor maintains the same business as the predecessor, with the same employees, doing the same jobs, for the same supervisors, under the same working conditions, and using the same production processes to produce the same products for the same customers. — Also termed *continuity-of-enterprise doctrine.* Cf. MERE-CONTINUATION DOCTRINE.

substantial damages. See DAMAGES.

substantial equivalent. *Patents.* A device or process that falls outside a patent claim's literal scope but performs the same function in substantially the same way. — Also termed *substantial equivalent of a patented device.* See **tripartite test.**

substantial error. See ERROR (2).

substantial evidence. See EVIDENCE.

substantial-evidence jurisdiction. See *significant-connection jurisdiction* under JURISDICTION.

substantial-evidence rule. (1938) The principle that a reviewing court should uphold an administrative body's ruling if it is supported by evidence on which the administrative body could reasonably base its decision.

substantial-factor test. (1929) See SUBSTANTIAL-CAUSE TEST.

substantial justice. See JUSTICE (4).

substantially justified. (Of conduct, a position, etc.) having a reasonable basis in law and in fact. • Under the Equal Access to Justice Act, a prevailing party in a lawsuit against the government will be unable to recover its attorney's fees if the government's position is substantially justified.

substantial new question of patentability. (1975) *Patents.* A significant, freshly arisen issue relating to the validity of a patent, triggering the statutory threshold required for the Director of the U.S. Patent and Trademark Office to order that a patent's validity be reexamined. • An examination cannot be reopened solely on issues of prior art and issues that came up during the original examination. The Director's determination is final and not appealable. 35 USCA §§ 303–04.

substantial noninfringing use. See COMMERCIALLY SIGNIFICANT NONINFRINGING USE.

substantial performance. See PERFORMANCE (1).

substantial-performance doctrine. (1936) The rule that if a good-faith attempt to perform does not precisely meet the terms of an agreement or statutory requirements, the performance will still be considered complete if the essential purpose is accomplished, subject to a claim for damages for the shortfall. • Under the Uniform Probate Code, a will that is otherwise void because some formality has not been followed may still be valid under the substantial-performance doctrine. But this rule is not widely followed. — Also termed *substantial-compliance rule.* Cf. PERFECT-TENDER RULE.

> "There has arisen in the United States an indefinite doctrine sometimes referred to as that of substantial performance. It is a doctrine that deals not with performance of a duty as a discharge thereof but with performance by the plaintiff as a condition precedent to the active duty of performance by the defendant. Where a defendant is sued for nonperformance he cannot avoid paying damages by showing that he substantially performed or came near performing or gave something equally good; but he can always successfully defend if in fact some condition precedent to his own duty has not been fulfilled by the plaintiff." William R. Anson, *Principles of the Law of Contract* 422 (Arthur L. Corbin ed., 3d Am. ed. 1919).

substantial possession. See *pedis possessio* under POSSESSIO.

substantial right. See RIGHT.

substantial similarity. See SIMILARITY.

substantial-step test. (1980) *Criminal law.* The Model Penal Code's test for determining whether a person is guilty of attempt, based on the extent of the defendant's preparation for the crime, the criminal intent shown, and any statements personally made that bear on the defendant's actions. Model Penal Code § 5.01(1)(c). See ATTEMPT.

substantiate, *vb.* (17c) To establish the existence or truth of (a fact, etc.), esp. by competent evidence; to verify.

substantive arbitrability. See ARBITRABILITY.

substantive canon. See CANON (1).

substantive consolidation. See CONSOLIDATION (4).

substantive crime. See *substantive offense* under OFFENSE (2).

substantive due process. See DUE PROCESS.

substantive error. See *substantial error* under ERROR (2).

substantive evidence. See EVIDENCE.

substantive examination. (1963) *Patents.* A patent examiner's in-depth study of a patent application to determine whether a patent should be granted.

substantive felony. See *substantive offense* under OFFENSE (2).

substantive law (**səb**-stən-tiv). (18c) The part of the law that creates, defines, and regulates the rights, duties, and powers of parties. Cf. PROCEDURAL LAW.

> "So far as the administration of justice is concerned with the application of remedies to violated rights, we may say that the substantive law defines the remedy and the right, while the law of procedure defines the modes and conditions of the application of the one to the other." John Salmond, *Jurisprudence* 476 (Glanville L. Williams ed., 10th ed. 1947).

substantive main motion. See *original main motion* under MOTION (2).

substantive motion. See *original main motion* under MOTION (2).

substantive offense. 1. See OFFENSE (2). **2.** See *substantive crime* under CRIME.

substantive right. See RIGHT.

substantive rule. See LEGISLATIVE RULE.

substantive unconscionability. See UNCONSCIONABILITY.

substantivistic, *adj.* (1987) Of, relating to, or involving a substantive rule applied beyond its appropriate scope or range. *See* P.S. Atiyah & R.S. Summers, *Form and Substance in Anglo-American Law* 30 (1987).

substitute, *n.* (14c) **1.** Someone who stands in another's place <a substitute for a party>. See SUBSTITUTION OF PARTIES; SUBROGATION. **2.** *Civil law.* A person named in a will as heir to an estate after the estate has been held and then passed on by another specified person (called the *institute*); a person taking under a destination after one or more persons have previously taken. • For example, in "to B, whom failing, to C," if B takes and does not nullify the destination, C succeeds as substitute. See INSTITUTE (5). **3.** *Parliamentary law.* A form of the motion to amend by replacing one or more words with others. See *amendment by substituting* under AMENDMENT (3). **4.** *Scots law.* A deputy. — **substitute,** *vb.*

substitute amendment. See AMENDMENT (3).

substitute application. See PATENT APPLICATION.

substitute check. See CHECK.

substituted agreement. See NOVATION.

substituted basis. See BASIS.

substituted complaint. See *amended complaint* under COMPLAINT.

substituted contract. See CONTRACT.

substituted executor. See EXECUTOR (2).

substituted-judgment doctrine. (1967) A principle that allows a surrogate decision-maker to attempt to establish, with as much accuracy as possible, what healthcare decision an incompetent patient would make if he or she were competent to do so. • The standard of proof is by clear and convincing evidence. Generally, the doctrine is used for a person who was once competent but no longer is. — Also termed *doctrine of substituted judgment.* Cf. FAITH-HEALING EXEMPTION; *medical neglect* under NEGLECT.

substitute drawing. See DRAWING.

substituted service. See SERVICE (7).

substitute gift. See GIFT.

substitute heir. See HEIR.

substitute information in lieu of indictment. See INFORMATION.

substitute obligation. See OBLIGATION.

substitute specification. See SPECIFICATION (3).

substitutio heredis (səb-stə-**t[y]oo**-shee-oh hə-**ree**-dis). [Latin] *Roman law.* **1.** See SUBSTITUTION (3). **2.** See SUBSTITUTION (4).

substitution. (14c) **1.** A designation of a person or thing to take the place of another person or thing. **2.** The process by which one person or thing takes the place of another person or thing. **3.** *Parliamentary law.* An amendment by replacing one or more words with others. See *amendment by substituting* under AMENDMENT (3). **4.** *Roman law.* The nomination of a person to take the place of a previously named heir who has refused or failed to accept an inheritance. — Also termed *common substitution; vulgar substitution.* **5.** *Roman law.* The nomination of a person to take the place of, or to succeed, a descendant who is under the age of puberty and in the *potestas* of the testator, if the descendant has died before reaching puberty. • This type of substitution was known as a *pupillary substitution.* If a descendant of any age failed to take by reason of lunacy, the substitution was known as an *exemplary substitution* or *quasi-pupillary substitution.* **6.** *Roman law.* A testator's designation of a person to whom the property was to be given by the person named as heir, or by the heir of that person. See FIDEICOMMISSUM. **7.** *Civil law.* The designation of a person to succeed another as beneficiary of an estate, usu. involving a fideicommissum. — Also termed (in senses 6 & 7) *fideicommissary substitution.*

▸ **prohibited substitution.** (1838) *Louisiana law.* The designation of a person who is not a trustee to take full ownership of property and deliver it to another designated person at death. • The first donee is called the *institute,* the second the *substitute.* See INSTITUTE (5); SUBSTITUTE (2).

substitutional, *adj.* (14c) Capable of taking or supplying the position of another <substitutional executor> <substitutional issue>. — Also termed *substitutionary.*

substitutional gift. See *substitute gift* under GIFT.

substitutional legacy. See LEGACY (1).

substitutional remedy. See REMEDY.

substitutionary. See SUBSTITUTIONAL.

substitutionary evidence. See *secondary evidence* under EVIDENCE.

substitutionary remedy. See REMEDY.

substitution-of-judgment doctrine. (1963) **1.** *Administrative law.* The standard for reviewing an agency's decision, by which a court uses its own independent judgment in interpreting laws and administrative regulations — rather than deferring to the agency — when the agency's interpretation is not instructive or the regulations do not involve matters requiring the agency's expertise. **2.** *Wills & estates.* The principle that a guardian, conservator, or committee of an incompetent person may make gifts out of that person's estate.

substitution of parties. (1833) The replacement of one litigant by another because of the first litigant's death, incompetency, transfer of interest, or, when the litigant is a public official, separation from office.

substraction (səb-**strak**-shən), *n.* (1814) The secret misappropriation of property, esp. from a decedent's estate.

subsume (səb-**s[y]oom**), *vb.* (1825) To judge as a particular instance governed by a general principle; to bring (a case) under a broad rule. — **subsumption** (səb-**səmp**-shən), *n.*

sub suo periculo (səb **s[y]oo**-oh pə-**rik**-[y]ə-loh). [Law Latin] *Hist.* At his own risk.

subsurety (səb-**shuur**[-ə]-tee). (1916) A person whose undertaking is given as additional security, usu. conditioned not only on nonperformance by the principal but also on nonperformance by an earlier promisor as well; a surety with the lesser liability in a subsuretyship.

subsuretyship (səb-**shuur**[-ə]-tee-ship). (1967) The relation between two (or more) sureties, in which a principal surety bears the burden of the whole performance that is due from both sureties; a relationship in which one surety acts as a surety for another.

subsurface interest. (1942) **1.** A landowner's right to the minerals and water below the property. **2.** A similar right held by another through grant by, or purchase from, a landowner. Cf. SURFACE INTEREST; MINERAL INTEREST.

subtenancy. See SUBLEASE.

subtenant. See SUBLESSEE.

subterfuge (**səb**-tər-fyooj). (16c) **1.** A clever plan or idea used to escape, avoid, or conceal something; an artifice employed to evade censure or punishment <a subterfuge to avoid liability under a statute>. **2.** The use of a secret trick or an ingeniously dishonest way of doing something <he evaded answering by subterfuge>.

subterfuge arrest. See ARREST (2).

subterranean water. See WATER.

subtraction. (15c) **1.** The process of deducting one number from another number to determine the difference. **2.** *Hist.* The act of neglecting a duty or service that one party owes to another, esp. one that arises out of land tenure.

> "Subtraction, which is the fifth species of injuries affecting a man's real property, happens, when any person who owes any suit, duty, custom, or service to another, withdraws or neglects to perform it. It differs from a disseisin, in that *this* is committed without any denial of the right, consisting merely in non-performance; *that* strikes at the very title of the party injured, and amounts to an ouster or actual dispossession. Subtraction however, being clearly an injury, is remediable by due course of law: but the remedy differs according to the nature of the services; whether they be due by virtue of any tenure, or by custom only." 3 William Blackstone, *Commentaries on the Laws of England* 230 (1768).

subtraction of conjugal rights. (18c) *Hist.* The act of a husband and wife unlawfully living apart.

subtrahend (**səb**-trə-hend). (17c) In a mathematical equation, the amount subtracted from another number (the minuend) to arrive at a remainder or balance. • The term is used in law in a variety of accounting contexts. Cf. MINUEND.

suburbani (səb-ər-**bay**-nɪ), *n.* [Latin] *Roman law.* **1.** Husbandmen. **2.** Large country estates just outside Rome.

subvention (səb-**ven**-shən). (16c) **1.** A grant of financial aid or assistance; a subsidy. **2.** A gift of money, esp. from a government, for a particular use.

subversion. (14c) The process of overthrowing, destroying, or corrupting <subversion of legal principles> <subversion of the government>.

> "Subversion can succeed where diplomacy has failed. Subversion exceeds the bounds of diplomacy in that it employs methods which diplomacy abhors; it does not wince at assassination, riot, pillage, and arson, if it believes these to be useful in the attainment of its ends. Subversion is a form of war. It may include the use of propaganda . . . to sway the thinking and action of influential social groups, especially attempting to discredit the leadership of the target area, labeling it as the 'tool' of . . . any convenient target for emotional hatred. By inflaming passion, the purveyors of violent propaganda can stir up peaceful citizens so that in minutes they are transformed into a terrifying mob. The art of subversion has developed the technique of the manipulation of mobs to a high degree." T. Wyckoff, *War by Subversion*, 59 South Atlantic Q. 36 (1960).

> "Prior to World War II, subversive activities were thought to cover cases where states attempted to achieve certain political ends of fomenting civil strife in another state or by supporting rebellion against the legally established government of another state by giving to the rebels supplies of personnel, training facilities, war materials, or munitions and by engaging in hostile propaganda against the victim state and its government. . . . By the beginning of World War II, the concept of subversion had been expanded to include the attempt of one state to weaken or overthrow the government of another by means of infiltration of its governmental apparatus with conspirators who strongly opposed the domestic policy of their own government and willingly served as clandestine instruments in the conduct of an alien state's foreign policy. But with increased militancy of modern ideologies, . . . subversive activities are no longer seen in many quarters as advancing the foreign policy of a nation or nations, but rather are thought to advance universal human values, i.e., the specific ideological theory adhered to.
>
> "Today, the term *subversion* designates all illegal activities, whether direct or indirect, overt or covert, conducted under the auspices of a state and designed to overthrow the established government or vitally disrupt the public order of another state. Subversion combines psychological, political, social, and economic actions, as well as active military or paramilitary operations, and it is generally a sustained, long-run, intermeshed, and coordinated process. Consequently, it is usually impossible to place acts of subversion into neat little categorical definitions. Subversion, being a technique of opportunity, is successful mainly in areas where social and political revolution is at least incipient." Ann Van Wynen Thomas & A.J. Thomas Jr., *The Concept of Aggression in International Law* 72–73, 80–81 (1972).

Subversive Activities Control Act of 1950. See MCCARRAN ACT.

subversive activity. (1939) A pattern of acts designed to overthrow a government by force or other illegal means.

subversive propaganda. See PROPAGANDA.

success fee. See FEE (1).

successful party. See *prevailing party* under PARTY (2).

successio (sək-**sesh**-ee-oh), *n.* [Latin] *Roman law.* A succession to something, as to an estate by will or by the laws of intestacy.

successio ab intestato. See *intestate succession* under SUCCESSION (2).

successio in universum jus (sək-**ses[h]**-ee-oh in yoo-ni-**vər**-səm **jəs**). [Latin "succession to universal right"] (1927) *Roman law.* The succession on death to the entirety of a deceased person's assets and liabilities. See *hereditas jacens* under HEREDITAS.

succession, *n.* (14c) **1.** The act or right of legally or officially taking over a predecessor's office, rank, or duties. **2.** The acquisition of rights or property by inheritance under the laws of descent and distribution; DESCENT (1). — **succeed,** *vb.*

▸ **hereditary succession.** See *intestate succession.*

▸ **intestate succession.** (18c) **1.** The method used to distribute property owned by a person who dies without a valid will. **2.** Succession by the common law of descent. — Also termed *hereditary succession*; *descent and distribution*; *successio ab intestato.* See DESCENT (1). Cf. *testate succession.*

▸ **irregular succession.** (17c) Succession by special laws favoring certain persons or the state, rather than heirs (such as testamentary heirs) under the ordinary laws of descent.

▸ **legal succession.** (18c) The succession established by law, usu. in favor of the nearest relation of a deceased person.

▸ **lucrative succession.** *Scots law.* See PRAECEPTIO HAEREDITATIS.

▸ **natural succession.** (18c) Succession between natural persons, as in descent on the death of an ancestor.

▸ **testamentary succession.** (17c) *Civil law.* Succession resulting from the designation of an heir in a testament executed in the legally required form.

▸ **testate succession.** (18c) The passing of rights or property by will. Cf. *intestate succession.*

▸ **universal succession.** (16c) Succession to an entire estate of another at death. • This type of succession carries with it the predecessor's liabilities as well as assets. Originally developed by Roman law and later continued by civil law, this concept has now been widely adopted as an option endorsed and authorized by the Uniform Probate Code. La. Civ. Code art. 3506(28).

▸ **vacant succession.** (18c) *Civil law.* **1.** A succession that fails either because there are no known heirs or because the heirs have renounced the estate. **2.** An estate that has suffered such a failure. See ESCHEAT.

3. The right by which one group, in replacing another group, acquires all the goods, movables, and other chattels of a corporation. **4.** The continuation of a corporation's legal status despite changes in ownership or management. — Also termed *artificial succession.*

▸ **perpetual succession.** The continuous succession of a corporation — despite changes in shareholders and officers — for as long as the corporation legally exists.

> "As a general rule, the words 'perpetual succession,' as used in charters, often in connection with a further provision limiting the period of corporate existence to a certain number of years, mean nothing more than that the corporation shall have continuous and uninterrupted succession so long as it shall continue to exist as a corporation, and are not intended to define its duration." 18 Am. Jur. 2d *Corporations* § 69, at 883 (1985).

successional, *adj.* (14c) Of, relating to, or involving acquiring rights or property by inheritance under the laws of descent and distribution.

succession duty. See DUTY (4).

succession tax. See *inheritance tax* (1) under TAX.

successio praedilecta (sək-**ses**[**h**]-ee-oh pree-di-**lek**-tə). [Law Latin] *Hist.* A preferred succession; a succession that the testator prefers.

successive, *adj.* (15c) **1.** *Archaic.* (Of an estate) hereditary. **2.** (Of persons, things, appointments, etc.) following in order; consecutive.

successive polygamy. See POLYGAMY (2).

successive surety. See SURETY (1).

successive tortfeasors. See TORTFEASOR.

successive-writ doctrine. (1987) *Criminal procedure.* The principle that a second or supplemental petition for a writ of habeas corpus may not raise claims that were heard and decided on the merits in a previous petition. Cf. ABUSE-OF-THE-WRIT DOCTRINE.

successor. (14c) **1.** Someone who succeeds to the office, rights, responsibilities, or place of another; one who replaces or follows a predecessor. **2.** A corporation that, through amalgamation, consolidation, or other assumption of interests, is vested with the rights and duties of an earlier corporation.

▸ **particular successor.** (18c) *Civil law.* Someone who succeeds to rights and obligations that pertain only to the property conveyed.

▸ **singular successor.** (17c) Someone who succeeds to a former owner's rights in a single piece of property.

▸ **statutory successor.** (1881) Someone who succeeds to the assets of a corporation upon its dissolution; specif., the person to whom all corporate assets pass upon a corporation's dissolution according to the statute of the state of incorporation applicable at the time of the dissolution. *See* Restatement (Second) of Conflict of Laws § 388 cmt. a (1971).

▸ **universal successor.** (17c) **1.** Someone who succeeds to all the rights and powers of a former owner, as with an intestate estate or an estate in bankruptcy. **2.** *Louisiana law.* An heir or legatee who succeeds in the entire estate of the deceased or a specified portion of it, rather than by particular title as legatee of a specific thing. • A universal successor succeeds in all of the decedent's rights and charges, whereas the particular legatee succeeds only to the rights and charges relating to the bequeathed thing. La. Civ. Code art. 3506(28).

successor agent. See AGENT.

successor fiduciary. See FIDUCIARY.

successor guardian. See GUARDIAN (1).

successor in interest. (1832) Someone who follows another in ownership or control of property. • A successor in interest retains the same rights as the original owner, with no change in substance.

successor titulo lucrativo post contractum debitum (sək-**ses**-or [*or* -ər] **tich**-ə-loh loo-krə-**tɪ**-voh pohst kən-**trak**-təm **deb**-i-təm). [Law Latin] (17c) *Hist.* A successor under a lucrative title after debt has been contracted. • Such a successor is liable to pay all debts contracted by the grantor.

successor trustee. See TRUSTEE (1).

sucesión legítima (soo-se-**syon** lay-**hee**-tee-mah). (1906) *Spanish law.* The process of regular inheritance, the rules of which may not be altered by will. *See Ortiz De Rodriguez v. Vivoni*, 201 U.S. 371, 376–77, 26 S.Ct. 475, 476 (1906).

such, *adj.* (bef. 12c) **1.** Of this or that kind <she collects a variety of such things>. **2.** That or those; having just been mentioned <a newly discovered Fabergé egg will be on auction next week; such egg is expected to sell for more than $500,000>.

sudden-and-accidental pollution exclusion. See *pollution exclusion* under EXCLUSION (3).

sudden-death jurisdiction. (2004) *Wills & estates.* A jurisdiction in which a will once revoked cannot be revived, and instead must be reexecuted. See REVIVAL (2).

sudden-emergency doctrine. See EMERGENCY DOCTRINE (1).

sudden heat. See HEAT OF PASSION.

sudden heat and passion. See HEAT OF PASSION.

sudden heat of passion. See HEAT OF PASSION.

sudden-onset rule. (1981) The principle that medical testimony is unnecessary to prove causation of the obvious symptoms of an injury that immediately follows a known traumatic incident.

sudden passion. See HEAT OF PASSION.

sudden-peril doctrine. See EMERGENCY DOCTRINE (1).

sudden-peril rule. See EMERGENCY DOCTRINE (1).

sudden provocation. See *adequate provocation* under PROVOCATION.

sue, *vb.* (13c) To institute a lawsuit against (another party).

sue-and-labor clause. (1866) *Marine insurance.* A provision in property- and marine-insurance policies requiring the insured to protect damaged property against further loss. • The clause generally requires the insured to "sue and labor" to protect the insured party's interests. — Also termed *rescue clause.*

> "Some insurance today is written against 'all risks' . . . . Besides the perils clause . . . recovery under the policy can be had on the entirely separate 'sue and labor' clause . . . . Under this clause, the underwriter may become liable for certain charges incurred by the assured in caring for the insured property, whether or not there is any actual loss or damage. Where sue-and-labor charges are incurred and loss also occurs, the underwriter may become liable for more than the policy amount, which limits only a claim for loss of or damage to the goods or vessel." Grant Gilmore & Charles L. Black Jr., *The Law of Admiralty* § 2-10, at 75 (2d ed. 1975).

sue facts. (1980) Facts that determine whether a party should bring a lawsuit; esp., facts determining whether a shareholder-derivative action should be instituted under state law.

sue out, *vb.* (15c) **1.** To apply to a court for the issuance of (a court order or writ). **2.** To serve (a complaint) on a defendant.

suerte (**swer**-tə). *Spanish law.* **1.** Chance; destiny; fate. **2.** A small plot of land. **3.** Land within a municipality's boundaries, reserved for cultivating or planting because of its proximity to water. • This term appears in the caselaw of states that were formerly Spanish or Mexican possessions.

suffer, *vb.* (14c) **1.** To experience or sustain physical or emotional pain, distress, or injury <suffer grievously><suffer damages>. **2.** To allow or permit (an act, etc.) <to suffer a default>.

sufferance (**səf**-ər-ənts *or* **səf**-rənts). (14c) **1.** Toleration; passive consent. **2.** The state of one who holds land without the owner's permission. See *tenancy at sufferance* under TENANCY. **3.** A license implied from the omission to enforce a right.

sufferance wharf. (1848) *Hist. English law.* A wharf designated by the Commissioner of the Customs to receive goods before any duties must be paid.

sufferentia pacis (səf-ə-**ren**-shee-ə **pay**-sis), *n.* [Latin] A grant of peace; a truce; an armistice.

suffering a recovery. (17c) *Hist.* A conveyor's act of allowing, for the purposes of a conveyance, a fictitious action to be brought by the conveyee and a judgment to be recovered for the land in question.

sufficiency of disclosure. See ADEQUACY OF DISCLOSURE.

sufficiency-of-evidence test. (1972) *Criminal procedure.* **1.** The guideline for a grand jury considering whether to indict a suspect: if all the evidence presented were uncontradicted and unexplained, it would warrant a conviction by the fact-trier. **2.** A standard for reviewing a criminal conviction on appeal, based on whether enough evidence exists to justify the fact-trier's finding of guilt beyond a reasonable doubt. — Also termed *sufficiency-of-the-evidence test.*

sufficient, *adj.* (14c) Adequate; of such quality, number, force, or value as is necessary for a given purpose <sufficient consideration> <sufficient evidence>.

sufficient cause. 1. See *good cause* under CAUSE (2). **2.** PROBABLE CAUSE.

sufficient consideration. See CONSIDERATION (1).

sufficient evidence. See *satisfactory evidence* under EVIDENCE.

suffocate, *vb.* **1.** To die from the inability to breathe. **2.** To kill (someone) by preventing the person from breathing, as by choking; to obstruct the respirations of. **3.** To prevent (a relationship, plan, business, etc.) from developing well or becoming successful; to stifle. — **suffocation,** *n.*

suffragan (**səf**-rə-gən *or* -jən). (14c) A titular bishop ordained to assist a bishop of the diocese in the church business; a deputy or assistant bishop. • Suffragans were originally appointed only to replace absent bishops and were called *chorepiscopi* ("bishops of the county"), as distinguished from the regular bishops of the city or see.

suffrage (**səf**-rij). (14c) **1.** The right or privilege of casting a vote at a public election. — Also termed *right to vote.*

> "In the United States suffrage is a privilege, franchise or trust conferred by the people upon such persons as it deems fittest to represent it in the choice of magistrates or in the performance of political duties which it would be inexpedient or inconvenient for the people to perform in a body. The person upon whom the franchise is conferred is called an elector or voter. No community extends suffrage to all persons, but places such restrictions upon it as may best subserve the ends of government." George W. McCrary, *A Treatise on the American Law of Elections* § 1, at 2 (Henry L. McCune ed., 4th ed. 1897).

▸ **women's suffrage.** The right of women to vote. • In the United States, the right is guaranteed by the 19th

Amendment to the Constitution. — Also termed *female suffrage*; *female franchise*.

2. A vote; the act of voting.

suffragette, *n. Archaic.* A woman who advocated for the right of women to vote in public elections, esp. as a member of a group in the United States or the U.K. during the early 20th century.

suffragium (sə-**fray**-jee-əm), *n.* [Latin "voting tablet"] *Roman law.* **1.** A vote; the right to vote. **2.** A recommendation of someone for a special privilege or office.

suggested retail price. See PRICE.

suggestibility, *n.* (1890) The readiness with which a person accepts another's suggestion. — **suggestible,** *adj.*

suggestio falsi (səg-**jes**-tee-oh **fal**-SI *or* **fawl**-SI). [Latin] (18c) A false representation or misleading suggestion. Cf. SUPPRESSIO VERI.

suggestion, *n.* (14c) **1.** An indirect presentation of an idea <the client agreed with counsel's suggestion to reword the warranty>. **2.** *Procedure.* A statement of some fact or circumstance that will materially affect the further proceedings in the case <suggestion for rehearing en banc>.

▸ **suggestion of bankruptcy.** (1869) A pleading by which a party notifies the court that the party has filed for bankruptcy and that, because of the automatic stay provided by the bankruptcy laws, the court cannot take further action in the case.

▸ **suggestion of death.** (18c) A pleading filed by a party, or the party's representatives, by which the court is notified that a party to a suit has died.

▸ **suggestion of error.** (1811) An objection made by a party to a suit, indicating that the court has committed an error or that the party wants a rehearing of a particular issue.

▸ **suggestion on the record.** (18c) A formal written or oral statement informing the court of an important fact that may require a stay of proceedings or affect the court's decision. • Suggestions on the record include suggestion of bankruptcy, suggestion of death, and suggestion of error.

3. *Archaic. Wills & estates.* UNDUE INFLUENCE. — **suggest** (for senses 1 & 2), *vb.*

suggestive interrogation. See LEADING QUESTION.

suggestive mark. See *suggestive trademark* under TRADEMARK.

suggestive name. See *suggestive trademark* under TRADEMARK.

suggestive question. See LEADING QUESTION.

suggestive trademark. See TRADEMARK.

sui. See SUI HEREDES.

suicide, *n.* (17c) **1.** The act of taking one's own life. — Also termed *self-killing*; *self-destruction*; *self-slaughter*; *self-murder*; *felony-de-se*; *death by one's own hand.*

▸ **assisted suicide.** (1976) The intentional act of providing a person with the medical means or the medical knowledge to commit suicide. — Also termed *assisted self-determination*; (when a doctor provides the means) *physician-assisted suicide.* Cf. EUTHANASIA.

▸ **attempted suicide.** (1880) An unsuccessful suicidal act.

▸ **physician-assisted suicide.** See *assisted suicide.*

▸ **police-assisted suicide.** See *suicide-by-cop.*

▸ **suicide-by-cop.** (1988) *Slang.* A form of suicide in which the suicidal person intentionally engages in life-threatening behavior to induce a police officer to shoot the person. • Frequently, the decedent attacks the officer or otherwise threatens the officer's life, but occasionally a third person's life is at risk. A suicide-by-cop is distinguished from other police shootings by three elements. The person must (1) evince an intent to die; (2) consciously understand the finality of the act; and (3) confront a law enforcement official with behavior so extreme that it compels that officer to act with deadly force. — Also termed *police-assisted suicide*; *victim-precipitated homicide.*

2. Someone who has taken his or her own life. — Also termed *felo-de-se*; *felon-de-se*; *felon of oneself.* — **suicidal,** *adj.*

suicide bomber. Someone who hides a bomb on his or her person, usu. under clothing, and explodes it in a public place, thereby killing usu. others as well as himself or herself, most often for political reasons.

suicide-by-cop. See SUICIDE (1).

suicide clause. (1870) *Insurance.* A life-insurance-policy provision either excluding suicide as a covered risk or limiting the insurer's liability in the event of a suicide to the total premiums paid.

suicide letter of credit. See *clean letter of credit* under LETTER OF CREDIT.

suicide pact. An agreement between two or more people to kill themselves, usu. simultaneously.

sui generis (s[y]**oo**-I *or* **soo**-ee **jen**-ə-ris). [Latin "of its own kind"] (18c) Of its own kind or class; unique or peculiar. • The term is used in intellectual-property law to describe a regime designed to protect rights that fall outside the traditional patent, trademark, copyright, and trade-secret doctrines. For example, a database may not be protected by copyright law if its content is not original, but it could be protected by a sui generis statute designed for that purpose.

sui heredes (s[y]**oo**-I hə-**ree**-deez). [Latin "one's own heirs"] (16c) *Roman law.* A person's direct descendants who were unemancipated, and who would be heirs on intestacy.— Also spelled *sui haeredes.* — Often shortened to *sui.* See *suus heres* under HERES.

> "If a man died without a will, his property went to his *sui heredes* (own heirs, direct heirs), that is, to the persons who were previously under his *potestas*, but were released from it by his death. If he had adopted as son a person not connected with him by birth, that person was included among the *sui heredes*; on the other hand, a son by birth whom he had emancipated was . . . excluded from the *sui heredes* . . . ." James Hadley, *Introduction to Roman Law* 134 (1881).

sui juris (s[y]**oo**-I *or* **soo**-ee **joor**-is). [Latin "of one's own right; independent"] (17c) **1.** Of full age and capacity. **2.** Possessing full social and civil rights. **3.** *Roman law.* Of, relating to, or involving anyone of any age, male or female, not in the *postestas* of another, and therefore capable of owning property and enjoying private law rights. • As a status, it was not relevant to public law.

sui potens (s[y]oo-I **poh**-tenz). [Latin] (1906) *Hist.* Able to do something, as in to enter a contract.

suit. (14c) Any proceeding by a party or parties against another in a court of law; CASE (1). — Also termed *lawsuit*; *suit at law*. See ACTION (4).

"All these nouns [*suit, lawsuit, action, case,* and *cause*] denote proceedings instituted for the purpose of enforcing a right or otherwise seeking justice. Although they are all in frequent use as synonyms for a court proceeding, their etymological development has lent them shades of meaning that they still faintly bear. *Suit* stresses the sense of campaign — originally a lover's persistent efforts to win love as a suitor but now a complainant's attempt to redress a wrong, enforce a right, or compel application of a rule. *Suit* is historically most closely associated with proceedings in equity <suit in equity>. In the legal sense, *suit* refers to an ongoing dispute at any stage, from the initial filing to the ultimate resolution. *Lawsuit* more clearly implies courtroom proceedings before a judge, as opposed to a dispute before some other type of tribunal. *Action* is close to *suit* and *lawsuit* <action on the case>, but historically *action* was closely tied to legal as opposed to equitable proceedings. Because *action* denotes a mode of proceeding in court not just to enforce a private right or to redress or prevent a private wrong, but also to punish a public offense, it is possible to speak of criminal actions. When the jurisdictional distinction between law and equity existed, an *action* ended at judgment, but a *suit* in equity ended after judgment and execution. Today, since virtually all jurisdictions have merged the administration of law and equity, the terms *action* and *suit* are interchangeable. . . . *Case* can apply either to the entire proceedings <the case has been pending for 19 months> or to the merits of the action from either side's point of view <the plaintiff has a good case> <the defendant has a good case>. *Cause*, a legalism, emphasizes the merits of the action from the plaintiff's point of view, especially with the connotation of seeking justice <the ex-employee's cause for wrongful discharge>. . . . Although *cause* and *action* are nearly synonymous, the legal idioms in which the phrases are used differ. So an *action* or *suit* is said to be 'commenced,' but a *cause* is not. Similarly, a *cause* but not an *action* is said to be 'tried.' The distinction between the words is subtle: broadly, *action* connotes legal procedure and *cause* denotes the merits of the dispute (again, from the plaintiff 's vantage). The first edition of *Black's Law Dictionary* noted the differentiation between *case* and *cause*, although if it does exist at all it is little heeded: '*case* is of a more limited signification, importing a collection of facts, with the conclusion of law thereon,' whereas '*cause* imports a judicial proceeding entire, and is nearly synonymous with *lis* in Latin, or *suit* in English.'" Bryan A. Garner, *Garner's Dictionary of Legal Usage* 862–63 (3d ed. 2011) (citations omitted).

▸ **ancillary suit** (**an**-sə-ler-ee). (1845) An action, either at law or in equity, that grows out of and is auxiliary to another suit and is filed to aid the primary suit, to enforce a prior judgment, or to impeach a prior decree. — Also termed *ancillary bill; ancillary proceeding; ancillary process.*

▸ **blackmail suit.** (1892) A suit filed by a party having no genuine claim but hoping to extract a favorable settlement from a defendant who would rather avoid the expense and inconvenience of litigation.

▸ **class suit.** See CLASS ACTION.

▸ **derivative suit.** See DERIVATIVE ACTION (1).

▸ **frivolous suit.** (1837) A lawsuit having no legal basis, often filed to harass or extort money from the defendant.

▸ **interest suit.** (1862) *Rare. Wills & estates.* A lawsuit to determine which persons have a valid interest in an estate. See INTEREST (2).

▸ **official-capacity suit.** (1978) A lawsuit that is nominally against one or more individual state employees but that has as the real party in interest the state or a local government. Cf. *personal-capacity suit.*

▸ **personal-capacity suit.** (1985) An action to impose personal, individual liability on a government officer. Cf. *official-capacity suit.*

▸ **petitory suit.** See *petitory action* under ACTION (4).

▸ **plenary suit** (**plee**-nə-ree *or* **plen**-ə-ree). (1817) An action that proceeds on formal pleadings under rules of procedure. Cf. *summary proceeding* under PROCEEDING.

▸ **sham suit.** See *sham action* under ACTION (4).

▸ **strike suit.** (1902) A suit (esp. a derivative action), often based on no valid claim, brought either for nuisance value or as leverage to obtain a favorable or inflated settlement.

▸ **suit at law.** (16c) A suit conducted according to the common law or equity, as distinguished from statutory provisions. • Under the current rules of practice in federal and most state courts, the term *civil action* embraces an action both at law and in equity. Fed. R. Civ. P. 2. See *action at law* under ACTION (4).

▸ **suit in equity.** (17c) A civil suit stating an equitable claim and asking for an exclusively equitable remedy. — Also termed *action in equity.*

▸ **suit of a civil nature.** (18c) A civil action. See *civil action* under ACTION (4).

suitable, *adj.* (16c) (Of goods, etc.) fit and appropriate for their intended purpose.

suitas (s[y]oo-ə-tas), *n.* [Law Latin] The status of a proper heir.

suit for exoneration. (1928) A suit in equity brought by a surety to compel the debtor to pay the creditor. • If the debtor has acted fraudulently and is insolvent, a suit for exoneration may include further remedies to ensure that the debtor's assets are applied equitably to the debtor's outstanding obligations. — Also termed *suit to compel payment.*

suit money. (1846) Attorney's fees and court costs allowed or awarded by a court; esp., in some jurisdictions, a husband's payment to his wife to cover her reasonable attorney's fees in a divorce action.

suitor. (16c) **1.** A party that brings a lawsuit; a plaintiff or petitioner. **2.** An individual or company that seeks to take over another company.

Suitors' Deposit Account. (1873) *English law.* An account consisting of suitors' fees paid in the Court of Chancery that, by the Chancery Act of 1872, were to be invested in government securities bearing interest at 2% per annum on behalf of the investing suitor, unless the suitor directed otherwise.

Suitors' Fee Fund. (1833) *Hist.* A fund consisting largely of fees generated by the Court of Chancery out of which the court officers' salaries and expenses were paid. • In 1869 the fund was transferred to the Commissioners for the Reduction of the National Debt.

suit papers. See COURT PAPERS.

suit *pro laesione fidei* (proh lee-zhee-**oh**-nee **fI**-dee-I), *n.* [Latin "for injury to faith"] *Hist. Eccles. law.* A suit in ecclesiastical court for spiritual offenses against conscience, nonpayment of debts, or a breach of contract, esp. an oral contract made by oath.

Suits in Admiralty Act. A 1920 federal law giving injured parties the right to sue the government in admiralty. 46 USCA app. §§ 741–752.

suit to compel payment. See SUIT FOR EXONERATION.

sum. (13c) **1.** A quantity of money. **2.** *English law.* A legal summary or abstract; a compendium; a collection. • Several treatises are called *sums.*

▸ **fixed sum.** An amount of money specified by agreement.

▸ **liquidated sum.** See LIQUIDATED AMOUNT.

▸ **lump sum.** (1867) A single payment made once, usu. at a particular time, as opposed to a series of smaller payments. Cf. INSTALLMENT.

sum and substance. A paraphrased summary or précis of a defendant's statement made to police; the gist of a police interview.

sum certain. (16c) **1.** Any amount that is fixed, settled, or exact. **2.** *Commercial law.* In a negotiable instrument, a sum that is agreed on in the instrument or a sum that can be ascertained from the document.

summa injuria (**səm**-ə in-**joor**-ee-ə). [Latin] (16c) The greatest injury or injustice.

summa necessitate (**səm**-ə ni-ses-ə-**tay**-tee). [Latin] *Hist.* In extreme necessity. See NECESSITY.

summa potestas (**səm**-ə pə-**tes**-təs), *n.* [Latin "sum or totality of power"] (16c) The final authority or power in government.

summary, *adj.* (15c) **1.** Short; concise <a summary account of the events on March 6>. **2.** Without the usual formalities; esp., without a jury <a summary trial>. **3.** Immediate; done without delay <the new weapon was put to summary use by the military>. — **summarily** (**səm**-ər-ə-lee *or* sə-**mair**-ə-lee), *adv.*

summary, *n.* (16c) **1.** An abridgment or brief. **2.** A short application to a court without the formality of a full proceeding.

summary adjudication. See *partial summary judgment* under SUMMARY JUDGMENT.

summary conviction. See CONVICTION (2).

summary court-martial. See COURT-MARTIAL (2).

summary disposition. See SUMMARY JUDGMENT.

summary eviction. See EVICTION.

summary judgment. (18c) A judgment granted on a claim or defense about which there is no genuine issue of material fact and on which the movant is entitled to prevail as a matter of law. • The court considers the contents of the pleadings, the motions, and additional evidence adduced by the parties to determine whether there is a genuine issue of material fact rather than one of law. This procedural device allows the speedy disposition of a controversy without the need for trial. Fed. R. Civ. P. 56. — Also termed *summary disposition; judgment on the pleadings.* See JUDGMENT (2).

▸ **partial summary judgment.** (1924) A summary judgment that is limited to certain issues in a case and that disposes of only a portion of the whole case. — Also termed *summary adjudication.*

summary-judgment motion. See MOTION FOR SUMMARY JUDGMENT.

summary jurisdiction. See JURISDICTION.

summary jury trial. See TRIAL.

summary of argument. See SUMMARY OF THE ARGUMENT.

Summary of Commentary on Current Economic Conditions by Federal Reserve District. See BEIGE BOOK.

summary offense. 1. See OFFENSE (2). **2.** See MISDEMEANOR (1).

summary of the argument. The part of a brief, esp. an appellate brief, in which the advocate condenses the argument to a précis or synopsis, directing the court to the heart of the argument on each point. • A summary typically runs from one to four pages. — Also termed *summary of argument.*

> "A summary of the argument, suitably paragraphed. The summary should be a clear and concise condensation of the argument made in the body of the brief; mere repetition of the headings under which the argument is arranged is not sufficient." Sup. Ct. R. 24.1(h).

summary of the invention. (1859) *Patents.* In a U.S. patent application, the section that describes the nature, operation, and purpose of the invention in enough detail that the examiner and anyone searching the patent literature for prior art can understand the unique character of the invention.

summary plan description. (1974) Under the Employee Retirement Security Act (ERISA), an outline of an employee benefit plan, containing such information as the identity of the plan administrator, the requirements for eligibility and participation in the plan, circumstances that may result in disqualification or denial of benefits, and the identity of any insurers responsible for financing or administering the plan. • A summary plan description must generally be furnished to all employee-benefit-plan participants and beneficiaries. 29 USCA § 1022. — Abbr. SPD.

summary procedure. See SHOW-CAUSE PROCEEDING.

summary proceeding. See PROCEEDING.

summary process. See PROCESS (2).

summary-reversal motion. (1968) *Criminal procedure.* A criminal appellate lawyer's motion to dismiss a judgment of conviction outright on grounds of the unavailability of any transcript of the proceeding below.

summary trial. See *summary proceeding* under PROCEEDING.

summation. See CLOSING ARGUMENT.

summer associate. See CLERK (4).

summer clerk. See CLERK (4).

summing up. (18c) **1.** CLOSING ARGUMENT. **2.** *English law.* A judge's review of the key points of evidence presented in a case and instructions to the jury on the law it is to apply to the evidence. • The judge's summing up follows the advocates' closing speeches. — **sum up,** *vb.*

summo jure (**səm**-oh **joor**-ee). [Latin] *Hist.* In the highest right.

summon, *vb.* (13c) To command (a person) by service of a summons to appear in court. — Also termed *summons.*

summoneas (sə-**moh**-nee-əs), *n.* [Law Latin "you are to summon"] (16c) *Hist.* A writ ordering a party to appear in court.

summoner. (14c) *Hist.* A petty officer charged with summoning parties to appear in court. See NUNTIUS.

> "But process, as we are now to consider it, is the method taken by the law to compel a compliance with the original writ, of which the primary step is by giving the party notice to obey it. This notice is given . . . by *summons;* which is a warning to appear in court . . . given to the defendant by two of the sheriff's messengers called *summoners,* either in person or left at his house or land." 3 William Blackstone, *Commentaries on the Laws of England* 279 (1768).

summonitio (səm-ə-**nish**-ee-oh), *n.* [Law Latin fr. Latin *summonere* "to summon"] *Hist.* A summons.

summonitores scaccarii (səm-ən-ə-**tor**-eez skə-**kair**-ee-ɪ). [Law Latin] *Hist.* Exchequer officers who assisted in revenue collections by summoning defaulters to court.

summons, *n.* (13c) **1.** A writ or process commencing the plaintiff's action and requiring the defendant to appear and answer. **2.** A notice requiring a person to appear in court as a juror or witness. **3.** *Hist.* A writ directing a sheriff to summon a defendant to appear in court. **4.** *English law.* The application to a common-law judge on which an order is made. Pl. **summonses.**

▸ **adjourned summons.** (1855) *English law.* **1.** A judicial summons that is postponed to another day. **2.** A High Court summons that, having initially been heard before a master, has been postponed for further hearing before a judge.

▸ **alias summons.** (17c) A second summons issued after the original summons has failed for some reason.

▸ **default summons.** A summons issued to begin proceedings in a county court when the only relief sought is a summary recovery for a debt or liquidated demand.

▸ **John Doe summons.** (1918) **1.** A summons to a person whose name is unknown at the time of service. **2.** *Tax.* A summons from the Internal Revenue Service to a third party to provide information on an unnamed, unknown taxpayer with potential tax liability. — Also termed *third-party record-custodian summons.*

▸ **judgment summons.** (1848) A process used by a judgment creditor to start an action against a judgment debtor to enforce the judgment.

▸ **short summons.** (17c) A summons having a response time less than that of an ordinary summons, usu. served on a fraudulent or nonresident debtor.

▸ **third-party record-custodian summons.** See *John Doe summons.*

summons, *vb.* (17c) **1.** SUMMON. **2.** To request (information) by summons.

> "The horrible expression 'summonsed for an offence' (turning the noun 'summons' into a verb) has now become accepted usage, but 'summoned' remains not only allowable but preferable." Glanville Williams, *Learning the Law* 15 n.28 (11th ed. 1982).

▸ **uniform summons.** (1900) A standard-form summons used for minor infractions, typically satisfying all the requirements of an information.

summum bonum (**səm**-əm **boh**-nəm *also* **suum**-uum **baw**-nuum). [Latin] (16c) The greatest good.

summum cancellarius. See ARCHICAPELLANUS.

summum imperium (səm-əm im-**peer**-ee-əm). [Latin] *Hist.* The highest authority.

summum jus (**səm**-əm **jəs**). [Latin] (16c) The highest law.

sumner (**səm**-nər), *n.* (14c) *Hist.* A summoning officer, esp. in an ecclesiastical court. See SUMMONER.

sum-of-the-years'-digits depreciation method. See DEPRECIATION METHOD.

sum payable. (17c) An amount due; esp., the amount for which the maker of a negotiable instrument becomes liable and must tender in full satisfaction of the debt.

sumptuary law (**səmp**-choo-er-ee). (16c) **1.** A statute, ordinance, or regulation that limits the expenditures that people can make for personal gratification or ostentatious display. **2.** More broadly, any law whose purpose is to regulate conduct thought to be immoral, such as prostitution, gambling, or drug abuse.

Sunday-closing law. See BLUE LAW.

Sunday law. See BLUE LAW.

sundries (**sən**-dreez). (18c) Miscellaneous items that may be considered together, without being separately specified or identified.

sundry (**sən**-dree), *adj.* (bef. 12c) Separate; diverse; various.

sunk cost. See COST (1).

sunna. See FEMALE GENITAL MUTILATION.

sunset law. (1976) A statute under which a governmental agency or program automatically terminates at the end of a fixed period unless it is formally renewed.

sunset legislation. See SUNSET LAW.

sunshine committee. (2000) An official or quasi-official committee whose proceedings and work are open to public access.

sunshine law. See OPEN-MEETING LAW.

suo nomine (**s[y]oo**-oh **nom**-ə-nee). [Latin] In one's own name.

suo periculo. See SUB SUO PERICULO.

SUP. *abbr.* SPECIAL-USE PERMIT.

sup. ct. *abbr.* SUPREME COURT.

super (**s[y]oo**-pər). [Latin] Above; over; higher.

super aliquam partem fundi (**s[y]oo**-pər **al**-i-kwam **pahr**-tem **fən**-dɪ). [Law Latin] *Hist.* On any part of the land.

super altum mare (s[y]oo-pər **al**-təm **mair**-ee *or* **mahr**-ee). [Latin] On the high sea.

super attentatis aut innovatis lite dependente (**s[y]oo**-pər a-ten-**tay**-tis awt in-ə-**vay**-tis **lɪ**-tee dee-pen-**den**-tee). [Law Latin] *Hist.* Concerning those things allegedly due during the pendency of the case.

supercargo. (17c) *Maritime law.* A person specially employed and authorized by a cargo owner to sell cargo that has been shipped and to purchase returning cargo, at the best possible prices; the commercial or foreign agent of a merchant.

> "Supercargoes are persons employed by commercial companies or by private merchants to take charge of the cargoes they export to foreign countries, to sell them there to the best advantage, and to purchase proper commodities to relade the ships on their return home. They usually go out with the ships on board of which the goods are embarked,

"... and return home with them, and in this they differ from factors who live abroad .... The supercargo is the agent of the owners, and disposes of the cargo and makes purchases under their general instructions on his own responsibility." 70 Am. Jur. 2d *Shipping* § 886, at 1025 (1987).

superductio (s[y]oo-pər-**dək**-shee-oh), *n.* [Latin] *Roman law.* The obliteration of part of a will or other document by writing over something erased within it. Pl. ***superductiones*** (s[y]oo-pər-dək-shee-**oh**-neez).

super eisdem deductis (**s[y]oo**-pər ee-**is**-dəm di-**dək**-tis). [Law Latin] *Hist.* On the same grounds.

superfeudation. See SUPERINFEUDATION.

superficiarius (s[y]oo-pər-fish-ee-**air**-ee-əs), *n.* [Latin] (16c) *Roman law.* Someone who had a hereditary and alienable right to a building on municipal or other public land, subject to the payment of an annual rent. • In classical law this right was extended to private land. Cf. EMPHYTEUSIS.

superficies (s[y]oo-pər-**fish**-ee-eez *or* -**fish**-eez), *n.* [Latin "surface"] (18c) *Roman & civil law.* **1.** The surface of the ground. **2.** An improvement that stands on the surface of the ground, such as a building, other construction, trees, plants, or crops. **3.** The right of a *superficiarius.* See SUPERFICIARIUS.

"[T]he tenant erecting [a building], 'superficiarius,' had a peculiar right called 'superficies': it was that of acting as the owner of the building on payment of a yearly ground rent." John George Phillimore, *Private Law Among the Romans* 148 (1863).

Superfund. (1977) **1.** The program that funds and administers the cleanup of hazardous-waste sites through a trust fund (financed by taxes on petroleum and chemicals and a tax on certain corporations) created to pay for cleanup pending reimbursement from the liable parties. **2.** The popular name for the act that established this program — the Comprehensive Environmental Response, Compensation, and Liability Act of 1980 (CERCLA). See CERCLA.

superinfeudation. *Hist.* The granting of one or more feuds out of a feudal estate. — Also termed *superfeudation.* Cf. INFEUDATION; SUBINFEUDATION.

"Whatever may be the proper view of its origin and legal nature, the best mode of vividly picturing to ourselves the feudal organisation is to begin with the basis, to consider the relation of the tenant to the patch of soil which created and limited his services — and then to mount up, through narrowing circles of super-feudation, till we approximate to the apex of the system." Henry S. Maine, *Ancient Law* 88 (17th ed. 1901).

superinjunction. See INJUNCTION.

superinstitution. (17c) *Eccles. law.* The investiture of one person in an office that already has an incumbent, as when two individuals claim a benefice by adverse titles.

superintendent. (16c) A person with the power to direct activities; a manager.

superintending control. See CONTROL.

superior, *adj.* (14c) (Of a rank, office, power, etc.) higher; elevated; possessing greater power or authority; entitled to exert authority or command over another <superior estate> <superior force> <superior agent>. — **superior,** *n.*

superior agent. See AGENT.

superior commissioned officer. See OFFICER (2).

superior court. See COURT.

superior fellow servant. See FELLOW SERVANT.

superior force. **1.** FORCE MAJEURE. **2.** ACT OF GOD. **3.** VIS MAJOR.

superior knowledge. See KNOWLEDGE (1).

superior-knowledge rule. (1953) The doctrine that when a property owner knows or should know that a hazardous condition exists on the property, and the condition is not obvious to a person exercising reasonable care, the owner must make the premises reasonably safe or else warn others of the hazardous condition. • An exception to the rule is sometimes allowed for obvious dangers or dangers of which the invitee is aware. Restatement (Second) of Torts § 343A. But the exception is neither automatic nor absolute. See *id.* § 343A(1) & cmt. f. — Also termed *equal-or-superior-knowledge rule.* Cf. EQUAL-KNOWLEDGE RULE.

superior orders. See NUREMBERG DEFENSE (1).

superior-orders defense. See NUREMBERG DEFENSE (1).

superior servant. See *superior fellow servant* under FELLOW SERVANT.

superior-servant doctrine. See FELLOW-SERVANT RULE.

superjurare (s[y]oo-pər-juu-**rair**-ee). [Latin "to overswear"] *Hist.* To swear too strenuously. • This describes the situation in which an obviously guilty criminal attempted to avoid conviction by producing oaths of several parties but was convicted by an overwhelming number of witnesses.

super jure naturae alendi liberos (**s[y]oo**-pər **joor**-ee nə-**tyoor**-ee ə-**len**-dɪ **lib**-ər-ohs). [Law Latin] *Hist.* On the ground of natural law, obligating persons to support their children.

superlien. (1984) A government's lien that is imposed on a property whose condition violates environmental and public-health and public-safety rules and that has priority over all other liens, so that the government can recover public funds spent on cleanup operations. • A statutory lien is superior to all existing liens and all later-filed liens on the same property. Superliens are sometimes granted to a state's environmental-protection agency. Several states — including Arkansas, Connecticut, Massachusetts, New Hampshire, New Jersey, and Tennessee — have enacted statutes creating superliens on property owned by a party responsible for environmental cleanup. See LIEN.

supermajority. See MAJORITY.

supermajority provision. (1970) A clause in a corporation's articles of incorporation requiring more than a simple majority of shareholders to vote in favor of a merger or substantial sale of assets.

supermax prison. See PRISON.

supernumerarii (s[y]oo-pər-n[y]oo-mə-**rair**-ee-ɪ), *n.* [Latin "persons above the number"] *Roman law.* Officials beyond the permitted number; esp., advocates who were unregistered and not attached to a particular bar. Cf. STATUTI.

supernumerary witness. See WITNESS.

superoneratio (s[y]oo-pər-on-ə-**ray**-shee-oh). [Law Latin] *Hist.* **1.** The act or practice of surcharging a common. **2.** The placement of more cattle on a common than is allowed; overstocking.

superoneratione pasturae. See DE SUPERONERATIONE PASTURAE.

superplusagium (s[y]oo-pər-plə-**say**-jee-əm), *n.* [Law Latin] *Hist.* A surplus; a remainder.

super praerogativa regis (s[y]**oo**-pər pri-rog-ə-**tɪ**-və **ree**-jis), *n.* [Law Latin] (17c) *Hist.* A writ against the king's tenant's widow for marrying without royal permission.

superprecedent. See PRECEDENT (2).

superpriority. (1942) *Bankruptcy.* The special priority status granted by the court to a creditor for extending credit to a debtor or trustee that cannot obtain unsecured credit from a willing lender. • This priority may be either an administrative claim outranking other administrative claims or, if certain statutory requirements are met, a security interest in property. 11 USCA § 364(c)(1).

supersede, *vb.* (17c) **1.** To annul, make void, or repeal by taking the place of <the 1996 statute supersedes the 1989 act>. **2.** To invoke or make applicable the right of supersedeas against (an award of damages) <what is the amount of the bond necessary to supersede the judgment against her?>. — **supersession** (in sense 1), *n.*

supersedeas (soo-pər-**seed**-ee-əs), *n.* [Latin "you shall desist"] (14c) **1.** A writ or bond that suspends a judgment creditor's power to levy execution, usu. pending appeal. — Also termed *writ of supersedeas.* **2.** See *supersedeas bond* under BOND (2). Pl. **supersedeases** (soo-pər-**see**-dee-əs-iz).

supersedeas bond. See BOND (2).

supersedere (s[y]oo-pər-sə-**deer**-ee). [Law Latin] *Hist.* (17c) SIST.

> "When creditors voluntarily agree to supersede or sist diligence against their debtor for a certain period, such an agreement is called a *supersedere*; and the same name is given to any judicial act by which creditors are restrained from doing diligence. A creditor who commits a breach of the *supersedere*, whether it be voluntary or judicial, is liable to the debtor in damages." John Trayner, *Trayner's Latin Maxims* 591 (4th ed. 1894).

superseding cause. See CAUSE (1).

superseding indictment. See INDICTMENT.

superseding information. See INFORMATION.

Super Speculam. A 1219 papal bull by which Pope Honorius III extended to beneficed clerks the prohibition for regular clergy to leave their cloisters to hear lectures on law and physic. See BENEFICED.

superstandard risk. See RISK.

super stare decisis. See STARE DECISIS.

super statuto (s[y]**oo**-pər stə-**t**[y]**oo**-toh), *n.* [Law Latin] (18c) *Hist.* A writ against tenants-in-chief who transferred their land without the king's permission in violation of the Statute of Westminster II, chs. 12 & 13.

super statuto de articulis cleri (s[y]**oo**-pər stə-**t**[y]**oo**-toh dee ahr-**tik**-yə-lis **kleer**-ɪ), *n.* [Law Latin] (18c) *Hist.* A writ against a sheriff who unlawfully distrains goods.

super statuto facto pour seneschal et marshal de roy (s[y]**oo**-pər stə-**t**[y]**oo**-toh **fak**-toh poor sen-ə-**shahl** ay mahr-[ə-]**shahl** də **roy**), *n.* [Law Latin] (18c) *Hist.* A writ to restrain the court of the Marshalsea from interfering in matters outside its jurisdiction.

super statuto versus servantes et laboratores (s[y]**oo**-pər stə-**t**[y]**oo**-toh **vər**-səs sər-**van**-teez et lab-ər-ə-**tor**-eez), *n.* [Law Latin] (18c) *Hist.* **1.** A writ against someone who employs laborers who unlawfully left former employments. **2.** A writ against a person who refused to work at the required wage.

superstitious use. See USE (1).

supervening cause. See *intervening cause* under CAUSE (1).

supervening impossibility. See IMPOSSIBILITY.

supervening negligence. See *subsequent negligence* under NEGLIGENCE.

supervening-negligence doctrine. See LAST-CLEAR-CHANCE DOCTRINE.

supervised release. See RELEASE (8).

supervised visitation. See VISITATION.

supervision, *n.* (15c) The series of acts involved in managing, directing, or overseeing persons or projects. — **supervise,** *vb.* — **supervisory** (soo-pər-**vɪ**-zə-ree), *adj.*

supervision order. See ORDER (2).

supervisor, *n.* (15c) **1.** One having authority over others; a manager or overseer. • Under the National Labor Relations Act, a supervisor is any individual having authority to hire, transfer, suspend, lay off, recall, promote, discharge, discipline, and handle grievances of other employees, by exercising independent judgment. **2.** The chief administrative officer of a town or county. — **supervisorial** (soo-pər-vɪ-**zor**-ee-əl), *adj.*

supervisory authority. *Military law.* An officer who, exercising general court-martial jurisdiction, reviews summary and special court-martial trial records after the convening authority has reviewed them.

supervisory control. The control exercised by a higher court over a lower court, as by prohibiting the lower court from acting extrajurisdictionally and by reversing its extrajurisdictional acts. See MANDAMUS.

supine negligence. See *advertent negligence* under NEGLIGENCE.

supplanting limitation. See LIMITATION (4).

supplemental, *adj.* (17c) Supplying something additional; adding what is lacking <supplemental rules>.

supplemental affidavit. See AFFIDAVIT.

supplemental agreement. See *side agreement* under AGREEMENT.

supplemental bill. See BILL (2).

supplemental bill in the nature of a bill of review. See *bill in the nature of a bill of review* under BILL (2).

supplemental brief. See BRIEF (1).

supplemental claim. See CLAIM (4).

supplemental complaint. See COMPLAINT.

supplemental declaration. *Patents.* A sworn document, filed after the U.S. Patent and Trademark Office allows a patent's issuance. See SUPPLEMENTAL OATH.

supplemental disclosure. See DISCLOSURE (1).

supplemental grant of probate. See *cessate grant* under GRANT (4).

supplemental jurisdiction. See JURISDICTION.

supplemental-needs trust. See TRUST (3).

Supplemental Nutrition Assistance Program. A government program run by the Food and Nutrition Service to give benefits for the purchase of healthful food to low-income individuals and families who meet certain tests based on factors such as income, resources, and employment. — Abbr. SNAP. — Formerly termed *Food Stamp Program.* See FOOD AND NUTRITION SERVICE.

supplemental pleading. See PLEADING (1).

supplemental register. (1940) *Trademarks.* A roll of trademarks that are ineligible for listing on the Principal Register because they are not distinctive. • Marks on the supplemental register are not protected by trademark law, except to the extent that the listing may bar the registration of a similar mark. The listing may be required, however, for the mark to be registered in other countries. 15 USCA § 1091. Cf. PRINCIPAL REGISTER. — Also termed *secondary register.*

Supplemental Rules for Certain Maritime and Admiralty Claims. A supplement to the Federal Rules of Civil Procedure, setting out procedures for suits in admiralty and maritime law.

Supplemental Security Income. A welfare or needs-based program providing monthly income to the aged, blind, or disabled. • It is authorized by the Social Security Act. — Abbr. SSI.

supplemental surety. See SURETY (1).

supplementary disclosure. See *supplemental disclosure* under DISCLOSURE (1).

supplementary proceeding. See PROCEEDING.

supplementary term. See TERM (2).

supplendo vices (sə-**plen**-doh VI-seez). [Law Latin] *Hist.* By supplying the place.

suppletory oath (**səp**-lə-tor-ee). See OATH.

suppliant (**səp**-lee-ənt). (15c) Someone who humbly requests something; specif., the actor in a petition of right. — Also termed *supplicant.*

supplicatio (səp-li-**kay**-shee-oh), *n.* [Latin] *Roman law.* **1.** A petition to the emperor requesting him to decide a case, not already before a court, in first instance or, sometimes, to reopen a case in which no appeal is normally allowed. Pl. ***supplicationes*** (səp-li-kay-shee-**oh**-neez).

> "Another mode was *supplicatio,* petition to the Emperor by a private person, not allowed when the question was already before a court or had been decided and not properly appealed. It was mainly used to bring matters before the Emperor or his delegate, in first instance, where for any reason it was unlikely that justice would be done, e.g. where the claimant was humble and the opponent a '*potentior,*' or where the claimant was of too high rank to go before the ordinary court, or the decision was of an unappealable magistrate." W.W. Buckland, *Elementary Principles of the Roman Private Law* 671 (1912).

2. A petition for a pardon on a first offense. **3.** *Hist.* A pleading similar to a rejoinder. — Also termed *supplication.*

supplicavit (səp-li-**kay**-vit). [Latin "he has begged"] (15c) *Hist.* A writ issued by the King's Bench or Chancery for taking sureties of the peace, obligating a person to be on good behavior for a specified period. • It is commonly directed to the justices of the peace who are hesitant to intervene in their judicial capacities. See *surety of the peace* under SURETY (1).

> "Any justices of the peace, by virtue of their commission, or those who are *ex officio* conservators of the peace . . . may demand such security according to their own discretion: or it may be granted at the request of any subject, upon due cause shewn . . . . Or, if the justice is averse to act, it may be granted by a mandatory writ, called a *supplicavit,* issuing out of the court of king's bench or chancery; which will compel the justice to act, as a ministerial and not as a judicial officer . . . ." 4 William Blackstone, *Commentaries on the Laws of England* 250 (1769).

supplicium (sə-**plish**-ee-əm), *n.* [Latin "atonement"] *Roman law.* A punishment. • *Ultimum supplicium* is the death penalty.

supplier, *n.* (14c) **1.** A person or business engaged, directly or indirectly, in making a product available to consumers.

> "The supplier may be the seller, the manufacturer, or anyone else in the chain who makes the product available to the consumer." 1 Julian B. McDonnell & Elizabeth J. Coleman, *Commercial and Consumer Warranties* ¶ 6.06[2], at 6-33 (1991).

2. Someone who gives possession of a chattel for another's use or allows someone else to use or occupy it while it is in the person's possession or control.

supplies, *n.* (16c) **1.** Means of provision or relief; stores available for distribution. **2.** In parliamentary proceedings, the annual grant voted on by the House of Commons for maintaining the Crown and various public services.

supply, *n.* (18c) The amount of goods produced or available at a given price.

▸ **aggregate supply.** The total amount of goods and services generated in an economy during a specific period.

supply contract. See CONTRACT.

supply curve. (1889) A line on a price-output graph showing the relationship between a good's price and the quantity supplied at a given time.

supply-side economics. The theory that if the government minimizes taxes, as by reducing them if they are substantial, people will be encouraged to earn more, save more, and invest more, thereby expanding economic activity and the entire national taxable income.

support, *n.* (14c) **1.** Sustenance or maintenance; esp., articles such as food and clothing that allow one to live in the degree of comfort to which one is accustomed. See MAINTENANCE; NECESSARIES.

> "Generally speaking, the words 'support' and 'maintenance' are used synonymously to refer to food, clothing and other conveniences, and shelter, including, in some cases, medicines, medical care, nursing care, funeral services, education, and reasonable personal care, and the courtesies and kindness usually obtaining between individuals that have the same ties of blood in families of similar station as the contracting parties." 73 Am.Jur.2d *Support of Persons* § 1, at 880–81 (2d ed. 1974).

2. One or more monetary payments to a current or former family member for the purpose of helping the recipient maintain an acceptable standard of living. — Also termed (in both senses) *reasonable support.* See ALIMONY. Cf. NONSUPPORT; MAINTENANCE (5).

▸ **child support.** See CHILD SUPPORT.

▸ **family support.** See FAMILY SUPPORT.

▸ **spousal support.** See ALIMONY (1).

3. Basis or foundation. **4.** The bracing of land so that it does not cave in because of another landowner's actions. — **support,** *vb.*

▸ **lateral support.** (1839) Support by the land that lies next to the land under consideration. — Also termed *easement of natural support.*

▸ **subjacent support.** (1856) Support by the earth that lies underneath the land under consideration.

support agreement. (2004) *Oil & gas.* A contract between people or entities in the oil-and-gas industry to promote exploratory operations. • Generally, one party agrees to contribute money or property to another if the other will drill a well on leases that it holds and provide the contributing party with information from tests conducted. For the contributing party, a support agreement is a purchase of geological or technological information. For the party receiving the support, the contribution lessens the cost or the risk of drilling operations. — Also termed *contribution agreement.* See DRY-HOLE AGREEMENT; BOTTOM-HOLE AGREEMENT; ACREAGE-CONTRIBUTION AGREEMENT.

support deed. See DEED.

supporting deposition. See DEPOSITION (2).

support obligation. (1938) A secondary obligation or letter-of-credit right that supports the payment or performance of an account, chattel paper, general intangible, document, healthcare-insurance receivable, instrument, or investment property. UCC § 9-102(a)(78).

support order. (1948) A court decree requiring a party (esp. one in a divorce or paternity proceeding) to make payments to maintain a child or spouse, including medical, dental, and educational expenses. — Also termed *maintenance order.*

▸ **foreign support order.** (1948) An out-of-state support order.

support price. See PRICE.

support trust. See TRUST (3).

supposition (səp-ə-**zish**-ən), *n.* (15c) An assumption that something is true, without proof of its veracity; the act of supposing. — **suppose,** *vb.* — **supposable,** *adj.*

suppress, *vb.* (14c) To put a stop to, put down, or prohibit; to prevent (something) from being seen, heard, known, or discussed <the defendant tried to suppress the incriminating evidence>. — **suppression,** *n.* — **suppressible, suppressive,** *adj.*

suppression hearing. See HEARING.

suppression motion. See MOTION TO SUPPRESS.

suppression of evidence. (18c) **1.** A trial judge's ruling that evidence offered by a party should be excluded because it was illegally acquired. **2.** The destruction of evidence or the refusal to give evidence at a criminal proceeding. • This is usu. considered a crime. See OBSTRUCTION OF JUSTICE. **3.** The prosecution's withholding from the defense of evidence that is favorable to the defendant.

suppressio veri (sə-**pres**[**h**]-ee-oh **veer**-ɪ). [Latin] (17c) Suppression of the truth; an indirect lie, whether by words, conduct, or artifice; a type of fraud. Cf. SUGGESTIO FALSI.

supra (s[y]oo-prə). [Latin "above"] (15c) Earlier in this text; used as a citational signal to refer to a previously cited authority. Cf. INFRA.

supra citatum (s[y]**oo**-prə sɪ-**tay**-təm). [Law Latin] (17c) *Hist.* Above cited. — Abbr. *sup. cit.*

supralegal, *adj.* (17c) Above or beyond the law <a supralegal sovereign>.

supranational, *adj.* (1846) **1.** Free from the political limitations of countries; transcending national boundaries. **2.** Involving more than one country.

supra protest. (18c) (Of a debt) under protest. See PROTEST (3).

supra riparian (**soo**-prə ri-**pair**-ee-ən *or* rɪ-). (1857) Upper riparian; higher up the stream. • This phrase describes the estate, rights, and duties of a riparian owner whose land is situated nearer the source of a stream than the land it is compared to.

supremacy. (16c) The position of having the superior or greatest power or authority.

Supremacy Clause. (1940) *Constitutional law.* The clause in Article VI of the U.S. Constitution declaring that the Constitution, all laws made in furtherance of the Constitution, and all treaties made under the authority of the United States are the "supreme law of the land" and enjoy legal superiority over any conflicting provision of a state constitution or law. See PREEMPTION.

supremacy of law. See RULE OF LAW (2).

supremacy-of-text principle. The textualist doctrine that the words of a governing legal instrument are of paramount concern, and what they convey, in their context, is what the text means.

supreme, *adj.* (16c) (Of a court, power, right, etc.) highest; superior to all others.

Supreme Civil Court in Scotland. See COURT OF SESSION (1).

supreme court. (17c) **1.** (*cap.*) SUPREME COURT OF THE UNITED STATES. **2.** An appellate court existing in most states, usu. as the court of last resort. **3.** In New York, a court of general jurisdiction with trial and appellate divisions. • The Court of Appeals is the court of last resort in New York. **4.** SUPREME COURT OF JUDICATURE. — Abbr. S.C.; S.Ct.; Sup. Ct.

Supreme Court of Appeals. The highest court in West Virginia.

Supreme Court of Errors. *Hist.* The court of last resort in Connecticut. • The court is now called the *Supreme Court.*

Supreme Court of Judicature. *English law.* The highest court in England and Wales, consisting of the High Court of Justice, the Court of Appeal, and the Crown Court. • The Supreme Court was created under the Judicature Act of 1873 that consolidated the existing superior courts, including the High Court of Chancery, the court of Queen's Bench, the court of Exchequer, the High Court of Admiralty, the court of Probate, and the London court of Bankruptcy. — Sometimes shortened to *Supreme Court.*

Supreme Court of the United Kingdom. *English law.* The highest appellate court in all civil and criminal cases from England, Wales, Northern Ireland, and Scotland — except that in Scotland the High Court of Justiciary is the court of final resort in criminal matters. • First convened in 2009, the Supreme Court of the United Kingdom is the successor to the appellate committee of the House of Lords.

Supreme Court of the United States. The court of last resort in the federal system, whose members are appointed by the President and approved by the Senate. • The Court was established in 1789 by Article III of the U.S. Constitution, which vests the Court with the "judicial power of the United States." — Abbr. SCOTUS. — Often shortened to *Supreme Court.* — Also termed *United States Supreme Court.*

> "Among the uncontroversial features of the new federal government created by the Constitution had been a Supreme Court. In the period between independence and the calling of the Philadelphia convention nothing like a federal judiciary had existed, although it was widely recognized that the state courts were not capable of dealing adequately with certain issues, notably admiralty, maritime, and prize disputes and boundary disputes between states. The framers of the Constitution were determined that one of the distinguishing features of the federal Union they created would be a court which would entertain and help to resolve those issues. What they very likely did not contemplate was that fifty years after the Philadelphia convention the Supreme Court of the United States would have intervened in nearly every contentious issue in American political life." 1 G. Edward White, *Law in American History: From the Colonial Years Through the Civil War* 193 (2012).

Supreme Judicial Court. See COURT.

supreme law of the land. (18c) **1.** The U.S. Constitution. **2.** Acts of Congress made in accordance with the U.S. Constitution. **3.** U.S. treaties. See SUPREMACY CLAUSE.

supreme legislation. See LEGISLATION (3).

supreme power. See *sovereign political power* under POLITICAL POWER.

sur (sər). [Law French] *Hist.* Upon. • This term appears in various phrases, such as *sur cognizance de droit* ("upon acknowledgment of right").

surcharge, *n.* (16c) **1.** An additional tax, charge, or cost, usu. one that is excessive. **2.** An additional load or burden. **3.** A second or further mortgage. **4.** The omission of a proper credit on an account. **5.** The amount that a court may charge a fiduciary that has breached its duty. **6.** An overprint on a stamp, esp. one that changes its face value. **7.** The overstocking of an area with animals. — **surcharge,** *vb.*

surcharge, *vb.* (15c) **1.** To impose an additional (usu. excessive) tax, charge, or cost. **2.** To impose an additional load or burden. **3.** (Of a court) to impose a fine on a fiduciary for breach of duty. **4.** To overstock (an area) with animals.

▸ **second surcharge.** (18c) To overstock (a common) a second time for which a writ of second surcharge was issued.

▸ **surcharge and falsify.** (18c) To scrutinize particular items in an account to show items that were not credited as required (to surcharge) and to prove that certain items were wrongly inserted (to falsify). • The courts of chancery usu. granted plaintiffs the opportunity to surcharge and falsify accounts that the defendant alleged to be settled.

sur cui ante divortium (sər kɪ [*or* kwɪ *or* kwee] **an**-tee də-**vor**-shee-əm). See CUI ANTE DIVORTIUM.

sur cui in vita (sər kɪ [*or* kwɪ *or* kwee] in **vɪ**-tə). See CUI IN VITA.

sur disclaimer. (16c) *Hist.* A writ brought by a lord against a tenant who has disclaimed tenure, to recover the land.

surdus (**sər**-dəs), *n.* [Latin] *Roman law.* A deaf person. • A wholly deaf and mute person could not lawfully make a will before the time of Justinian, who modified the law.

surety (**shuur**[-ə]-tee). (14c) **1.** Someone who is primarily liable for paying another's debt or performing another's obligation; specif., a person who becomes a joint obligor, the terms of the undertaking being identical with the other obligor's, and the circumstances under which the joint obligation is assumed being such that, if the joint obligor becomes required to pay anything, he or she will be entitled to complete reimbursement. • Although a surety is similar to an insurer, one important difference is that a surety often receives no compensation for assuming liability. A surety differs from a guarantor, who is liable to the creditor only if the debtor does not meet the duties owed to the creditor; the surety is directly liable. Cf. GUARANTOR.

> "The words surety and guarantor are often used indiscriminately as synonymous terms; but while a surety and a guarantor have this in common, that they are both bound for another person, yet there are points of difference between them which should be carefully noted. A surety is usually bound with his principal by the same instrument, executed at the same time and on the same consideration. He is an original promisor and debtor from the beginning, and is held ordinarily to know every default of this principal. Usually the surety will not be discharged, either by the mere indulgence of the creditor to the principal, or by want of notice of the default of the principal, no matter how much he may be injured thereby. On the other hand, the contract of the guarantor is his own separate undertaking, in which the principal does not join. It is usually entered into before or after that of the principal, and is often founded on a separate consideration from that supporting the contract of the principal." 1 George W. Brandt, *The Law of Suretyship and Guaranty* § 2, at 9 (3d ed. 1905).

> "A surety, in the broad sense, is one who is liable for the debt or obligation of another, whether primarily or secondarily, conditionally or unconditionally. In other words, the term surety includes anyone who is bound on an obligation which, as between himself and another person who is bound to the obligee for the same performance, the latter obligor should discharge. In this sense, suretyship includes all accessorial obligations. By such terminology, guarantors and indorsers are kinds of sureties. . . . A surety, in the narrow sense, is one who is liable in form primarily on the debt or obligation of another. His obligation is accessorial to that of the principal debtor, but it is direct and not conditioned on the principal debtor's default. In this sense, suretyship differs from guaranty and indorsement, which are conditional, secondary obligations. . . . The word surety is in the majority of American decisions used in the narrower sense to indicate a primary obligation to pay another's debt, to distinguish it from the secondary obligation of a guarantor. This terminology has the advantage of indicating by the use of the one word 'surety' an obligation which is at once one to pay another's debt, but which at the same time is not conditioned upon another's default." Laurence P. Simpson, *Handbook on the Law of Suretyship* 6, 8–9 (1950).

▸ **accommodation surety.** See *voluntary surety.*

▸ **compensated surety.** (1902) A surety who is paid for becoming obliged to the creditor; esp., one that engages in the business of executing suretyship contracts in exchange for premiums, which are determined by an actuarial computation of risks. • A bonding company is a typical example of a compensated surety. — Also termed *commercial surety.*

▸ **cosurety.** See COSURETY.

▸ **gratuitous surety.** (1900) A surety who is not compensated for becoming obliged to the creditor. • Perhaps the most common example is the parent who signs as a surety for a child.

▸ **guarantor surety.** See GUARANTOR.

▸ **subsurety.** See SUBSURETY.

▸ **successive surety.** (1829) A surety whose obligee is also the principal for whom another set of sureties is liable.

> "The term successive sureties indicates the relations that exist where the obligee of one set of sureties is the principal for whom another set of sureties is liable. . . . The relation of successive sureties exists where the obligee of one or more sureties is also the principal for whom another set of sureties is liable. For example, A and B are sureties on a sheriff's official bond. The sheriff appoints a deputy and C and D sign his bond to the sheriff as sureties. If the sheriff's sureties are required to pay for the deputy's default, they are entitled to reimbursement either from the sheriff, their principal, or from those who are liable to the sheriff, namely, the deputy sheriff or his sureties." Herschel W. Arant, *Handbook of the Law of Suretyship and Guaranty* 13 (1931).

▸ **supplemental surety.** (1817) Someone who has given a promise of a security to an obligee, in addition to the promises of the principal and one or more sureties.

> "The term supplemental surety is used to designate a person who has given his promise as security to an obligee, in addition to those of the principal and one or more sureties. The sureties who are bound in the first instance with the principal are usually sureties in the restricted sense, since their promise is usually in the same terms as that of the principal, and the supplemental surety, strictly speaking, is generally a guarantor, his undertaking usually being expressly conditioned on nonperformance by the principal and the other sureties. One may, however, though he is a surety in the restricted sense, still be a supplemental surety, if it is understood between himself and the other obligors that he may require full reimbursement in case he is required to pay. As to the supplemental surety, each of the other obligors is a principal, and each owes a duty to reimburse him, if he is required to pay. In the absence of an agreement to the contrary, each indorser of a bill or note is a supplemental surety for each prior party." Herschel W. Arant, *Handbook of the Law of Suretyship and Guaranty* 12–13 (1931).

▸ **surety of the peace.** (16c) *Hist.* A surety responsible for ensuring that a person will not commit a future offense. • It is required of one against whom there are probable grounds to suspect future misbehavior. — Also termed *surety for the peace*; *surety for the good behavior.* See SUPPLICAVIT.

> "Surety for the good behaviour resembles in so many instances surety for the peace, both as to the manner in which it is to be taken, superseded, and discharged, that it will not require a particular consideration . . . . [A] man may be bound to his good behaviour for causes of scandal *against good morals*, as well as *against the peace*; as for haunting bawdy houses with women of bad fame, or for keeping such women in his house. Thus, also, night-walkers; eaves-droppers; such as keep suspicious company or are reported to be pilferers or robbers; such as sleep in the day and walk in the night, common drunkards; whoremasters; the putative fathers of bastards; cheats; idle vagabonds; and other persons whose misbehaviour may reasonably bring them within the general words of the statute, as persons not of good fame; an expression it must be owned of so great a latitude, as leaves much to be determined by the discretion of the magistrate himself. But if he commits a man for want of sureties, he must express the cause thereof with convenient certainty; and take care that such case be a good one." William Waller Hening, *The Virginia Justice* 685 (4th ed. 1825).

▸ **voluntary surety.** (17c) A surety who receives no consideration for the promise to act as a surety. — Also termed *accommodation surety.*

2. A formal assurance; esp., a pledge, bond, guarantee, or security given for the fulfillment of an undertaking.

surety and fidelity insurance. See *fidelity insurance* under INSURANCE.

surety bond. See PERFORMANCE BOND.

surety company. See COMPANY.

surety insurance. See *guaranty insurance* under INSURANCE.

surety of the peace. See SURETY (1).

suretyship. (16c) **1.** The legal relation that arises when one party assumes liability for a debt, default, or other failing of a second party. • The liability of both parties begins simultaneously. In other words, under a contract of suretyship, a surety becomes a party to the principal obligation. Cf. GUARANTY (1).

> "[C]ourts and writers do not always use either term, surety or guarantor, in the same sense. Indeed, instances are not hard to find where inconsistent meanings have been attributed to these terms in a single opinion. It is fortunate, in view of this, that it is generally unnecessary to distinguish between suretyship and guaranty." Herschel W. Arant, *Handbook of the Law of Suretyship and Guaranty* 14–15 (1931).

2. The lending of credit to aid a principal who does not have sufficient credit. • The purpose is to guard against loss if the principal debtor were to default. **3.** The position or status of a surety.

▸ **involuntary suretyship.** (1903) A suretyship that arises incidentally, when the chief object of the contract is to accomplish some other purpose.

▸ **personal suretyship.** (1868) A suretyship in which the surety is answerable in damages.

▸ **real suretyship.** (1846) A suretyship in which specified property can be taken, but the surety is not answerable in damages.

▸ **suretyship by operation of law.** (1903) A suretyship that the law creates when a third party promises a debtor to assume and pay the debt that the debtor owes to a creditor.

▸ **voluntary suretyship.** (17c) A suretyship in which the chief object of the contract is to make one party a surety.

surface. (16c) **1.** The top layer of something, esp. of land. **2.** *Mining law.* An entire portion of land, including mineral deposits, except those specifically reserved. • The meaning of the term varies, esp. when used in legal instruments, depending on the language used, the intention of the parties, the business involved, and the nature and circumstances of the transaction. **3.** *Mining law.* The part of the geologic section lying over the minerals in question.

surface casing. See CASING.

surface-damage clause. (1952) *Oil & gas.* A lease provision requiring the lessee to pay the lessor or the surface-interest owner for all or for a specified kind or degree of damage to the surface that results from oil-and-gas operations. — Also termed *location-damage clause*; *damages clause.*

surface interest. (1878) *Oil & gas.* Every right in real property other than the mineral interest. • The surface-interest owner has the right to the surface subject to the right of the mineral-interest owner to use the surface. The surface-interest owner is entitled to all whatever nonmineral substances are found in or under the soil. — Also termed *surface right*. Cf. MINERAL INTEREST; SUBSURFACE INTEREST.

surface issue. See ISSUE (1).

surface right. See SURFACE INTEREST.

Surface Transportation Board. A unit in the U.S. Department of Transportation responsible for the economic regulation of interstate surface transportation, primarily railroads. • Its jurisdiction includes railroad-rate and -service issues, railroad-company mergers and related labor matters; certain truck and ocean shipping rates; certain intercity bus-company structures; and certain pipeline matters not regulated by the Federal Energy Regulatory Commission. — Abbr. STB.

surface water. See WATER.

Surgeon General. (18c) **1.** The chief medical officer of the U.S. Public Health Service or of a state public-health agency. **2.** The chief officer of the medical departments in the armed forces. — Abbr. SG.

surmise (sər-**mɪz**), *n.* (18c) **1.** An idea based on weak evidence; conjecture. **2.** *Hist.* A suggestion, esp. to a court. **3.** *Hist. Eccles. law.* An allegation in the complaint. • A collateral surmise is a surmise of a fact not contained in the libel. See LIBEL (3).

surname. See NAME.

surplice fees (**sər**-plis **feez**). (18c) *Eccles. law.* Fees paid to clergy for performing occasional duties, such as marriages, funerals, and baptisms.

surplus. (14c) **1.** An amount of something that is more than what is required or used; the residue or excess. **2.** The excess of receipts over disbursements. **3.** Funds that remain after a partnership has been dissolved and all its debts paid. **4.** The amount of money that a country has left after all its bills have been paid. **5.** A corporation's net worth, beyond the par value of capital stock. — Also termed *overplus.*

▸ **accumulated surplus.** (18c) Earnings in excess of a corporation's capital and liabilities.

▸ **acquired surplus.** The surplus gained by the purchase of another business.

▸ **actuarial surplus.** See ACTUARIAL SURPLUS.

▸ **appreciation surplus.** See *revaluation surplus.*

▸ **appropriated surplus. 1.** The portion of surplus earmarked for a specific purpose. — Also termed *reserved surplus.* **2.** See *appropriated retained earnings* under EARNINGS.

▸ **capital surplus. 1.** All surplus (such as paid-in surplus or donated surplus) not arising from the accumulation of profits; a company's surplus other than earned surplus, usu. created by financial reorganization or gifts. **2.** See *paid-in surplus.*

▸ **donated surplus.** (1919) **1.** Assets (such as stock) contributed to a corporation. **2.** The increase in the shareholders' equity account resulting from such a contribution.

▸ **earned surplus.** See *retained earnings* under EARNINGS.

▸ **initial surplus.** (1887) The surplus that appears on the financial statement at the beginning of an accounting period, but that does not reflect the operations for the statement's period.

▸ **paid-in surplus.** (1910) The surplus gained by the sale, exchange, or issuance of capital stock at a price above par value. — Also termed *capital surplus; premium on capital stock.*

▸ **reserved surplus.** See *appropriated surplus* (1).

▸ **restricted surplus.** (1953) A surplus with a limited or restricted use; esp., the portion of retained earnings that cannot be distributed as dividends. • The restriction is usu. due to preferred dividends in arrears, a covenant in a loan agreement, or some decision of the board of directors. See *retained earnings* under EARNINGS.

▸ **revaluation surplus.** (1911) Surplus that is gained when assets are reappraised at a higher value. — Also termed *appreciation surplus.*

▸ **trade surplus.** (1919) The excess of merchandise exports over merchandise imports during a specific period. Cf. *trade deficit* under DEFICIT (1).

▸ **unearned surplus.** (1911) *Corporations.* The total of amounts assigned to shares in excess of stated capital, surplus arising from a revaluation of assets above cost, and contributions other than for shares, whether from shareholders or others.

surplusage (**sər**-pləs-ij). (15c) **1.** Redundant words in a statute or legal instrument; language that does not add meaning <the court must give effect to every word, reading nothing as mere surplusage>. **2.** Extraneous matter in a pleading <allegations that are irrelevant to the case will be treated as surplusage>.

> "Surplusage is to be avoided. The perfection of pleading is to combine the requisite certainty and precision with the greatest possible brevity of statement. 'Surplusage' . . . includes matter of any description which is unnecessary to the maintenance of the action or defense. The rule requires the omission of such matter in two instances: (1) Where the matter is wholly foreign and irrelevant to the merits of the case. (2) When, though not wholly foreign, such matter need not be stated." Benjamin J. Shipman, *Handbook of Common-Law Pleading* § 316, at 514 (Henry Winthrop Ballantine ed., 3d ed. 1923).

surplusage canon. The doctrine that, if possible, every word and every provision in a legal instrument is to be given effect. — Also termed *presumption against surplusage; presumption against superfluities.*

> "The surplusage canon holds that it is no more the court's function to revise by subtraction than by addition. A provision that seems to the court unjust or unfortunate (creating the so-called *casus male inclusus*) must nonetheless be given effect." Antonin Scalia & Bryan A. Garner, *Reading Law: The Interpretation of Legal Texts* 174 (2012).

surplus earnings. See EARNINGS.

surplus-lines insurance. See INSURANCE.

surplus profit. See PROFIT (1).

surplus revenue. See *appropriated retained earnings* under EARNINGS.

surplus value. See VALUE.

surplus water. See WATER.

surprise. (15c) An occurrence for which there is no adequate warning or that affects someone in an unexpected way. • In a trial, the procedural rules are designed to limit surprise — or trial by ambush — as much as possible. For example, the parties in a civil case are permitted to conduct discovery, to determine the essential facts of the case and the identities of possible witnesses, and to inspect relevant documents. At trial, if a party calls a witness who has not been previously identified, the witness's testimony may be excluded if it would unfairly surprise and prejudice the other party. And if a party has diligently prepared the case and is nevertheless taken by surprise on a material point at trial, that fact can sometimes be grounds for a new trial or for relief from the judgment under Rules 59 and 60 of the Federal Rules of Civil Procedure.

▸ **unfair surprise.** See UNFAIR SURPRISE.

surprise witness. See WITNESS.

surrebuttal (sər-ri-**bət**-əl). (1853) The response to the opposing party's rebuttal in a trial or other proceeding; a rebuttal to a rebuttal <called two extra witnesses in surrebuttal>. — **surrebut,** *vb.*

surrebutter (sər-ri-**bət**-ər). *Common-law pleading.* (17c) The plaintiff's answer of fact to the defendant's rebutter.

surrejoinder (sər-ri-**joyn**-dər). *Common-law pleading.* (16c) The plaintiff's answer to the defendant's rejoinder. See REPLICATION; PLEADING (quot.). — **surrejoin,** *vb.*

> "Where the common-law system of pleading is in force, the pleadings do not terminate with the plaintiff's replication. The defendant may interpose a rejoinder to the replication, and the plaintiff a surrejoinder to the defendant's rejoinder. Then follows the rebutter, which in turn may be met by a surrebutter." 61A Am. Jur. 2d *Pleading* § 193, at 192 (1981).

surrender, *n.* (15c) **1.** The act of yielding to another's power or control.

▸ **voluntary surrender.** (17c) *Criminal law.* A defendant's surrender to law-enforcement officers without the need for their pursuing the defendant in any further way.

2. The giving up of a right or claim; RELEASE (1). **3.** The return of an estate to the person who has a reversion or remainder, so as to merge the estate into a larger estate. Cf. MERGER (4).

> "Merger bears a very near resemblance, in circumstances and effect, to a surrender; but the analogy does not hold in all cases, though there is not any case in which merger will take place, unless the right of making and surrender resided in the parties between whom the merger takes place. To a surrender, it is requisite that the tenant of the particular estate should *relinquish* his estate in favor of the tenant of the next vested estate, in remainder or reversion. But merger is confined to the cases in which the tenant of the estate in reversion or remainder *grants* that estate to the tenant of the particular estate, or in which the particular tenant grants his estate to him in reversion or remainder. Surrender is the act of the party, and merger is the act of the law." 4 James Kent, *Commentaries on American Law* *100 (George Comstock ed., 11th ed. 1866).

4. *Commercial law.* The delivery of an instrument so that the delivery releases the deliverer from all liability. **5.** A tenant's relinquishment of possession before the lease has expired, allowing the landlord to take possession and treat the lease as terminated. — Also termed (in sense 5) *surrender of term.* — **surrender,** *vb.*

▸ **express surrender.** (17c) The relinquishment of leased property occurring when the tenant signs a written agreement to terminate the lease early.

▸ **implied surrender.** (18c) Surrender shown by the actions of both the tenant and the landlord, as when the tenant vacates the property and the landlord reoccupies it.

surrender by bail. (18c) A surety's delivery of a prisoner, who had been released on bail, into custody.

surrender by operation of law. (1836) An act that is an equivalent to an agreement by a tenant to abandon property and the landlord to resume possession, as when the parties perform an act so inconsistent with the landlord–tenant relationship that surrender is presumed, or when a tenant performs some act that would not be valid if the estate continued to exist.

surrender clause. (1900) *Oil & gas.* A provision commonly found in oil-and-gas leases authorizing a lessee to release its rights to all or any portion of the leased property at any time and to be relieved of further obligations on the acreage surrendered.

surrenderee. (17c) One to whom a surrender is made. See SURRENDER.

surrenderer. See SURRENDEROR.

surrender of a criminal. (18c) An officer's delivery of a prisoner to the authorities in the appropriate jurisdiction. See EXTRADITION; RENDITION.

surrender of a preference. (1900) *Bankruptcy.* The yielding of a voidable conveyance, transfer, assignment, or encumbrance by a creditor to the trustee as a condition of allowing the creditor's claim.

surrender of charter. (1836) *Corporations.* The dissolution of a corporation by a formal yielding of its charter to the state under which it was created and the subsequent acceptance of that charter by the state.

> "The surrender of a charter can be made only by some formal, solemn act of the corporation, and will be of no avail until accepted by the government. There must be the same agreement of the parties to dissolve that there was to form the compact. It is the acceptance which gives efficacy to the surrender. Consent of the state is sometimes given by general statute." 19 Am. Jur. 2d *Corporations* § 2738, at 546 (1986).

surrender of copyhold. (17c) *Hist.* The transfer by a tenant of a copyhold estate by yielding it to the lord in trust for the transferee according to the terms in the surrender. • In normal practice, the tenant went to the steward of the manor and delivered a rod, a glove, or other customary symbol, thereby conveying to the lord (through the steward) all interest and title to the estate, in trust, to be then granted by the lord to the transferee. See COPYHOLD.

surrender of term. See SURRENDER (5).

surrenderor. (17c) Someone who surrenders; esp., one who yields up a copyhold estate for conveyance. — Also spelled *surrenderer.* See COPYHOLD.

surrender to uses of will. (1821) *Hist.* A required yielding of a copyhold interest passed by will to the will's uses. • The requirement was abolished by St. 55 Geo. 3, ch. 192.

surrender value. See *cash surrender value* under VALUE (2).

surreply. (17c) A movant's second supplemental response to another party's opposition to a motion, usu. in answer to a surresponse. • In most jurisdictions, a party must seek leave of court before filing a surreply. — Sometimes written *sur-reply.* Cf. SURRESPONSE.

surreptitious (sər-əp-**tish**-əs), *adj.* (15c) (Of conduct) unauthorized and clandestine; done by stealth and without legitimate authority <surreptitious interception of electronic communications is prohibited under wiretapping laws>.

surreptitious-entry search warrant. See *covert-entry search warrant* under SEARCH WARRANT.

surreptitious-entry warrant. See WARRANT (1).

surresponse. A second response by someone who opposes a motion. • A surresponse (rarely allowed) comes in answer to the movant's reply. Cf. SURREPLY.

surrogacy. (1811) **1.** The act of performing some function in the place of someone else. **2.** The process of carrying and delivering a child for another person.

▸ **gestational surrogacy.** (1986) A pregnancy in which one woman (the genetic mother) provides the egg, which is fertilized, and another woman (the surrogate mother) carries the fetus and gives birth to the child.

▸ **traditional surrogacy.** (1988) A pregnancy in which a woman provides her own egg, which is fertilized by artificial insemination, and carries the fetus and gives birth to a child for another person.

surrogacy contract. See SURROGATE-PARENTING AGREEMENT.

surrogate (sər-ə-git), *n.* (17c) **1.** A substitute; esp., a person appointed to act in the place of another <in his absence, Sam's wife acted as a surrogate>. See SURROGACY; *surrogate mother* under MOTHER. **2.** A probate judge <the surrogate held that the will was valid>. See *probate judge* under JUDGE. **3.** Someone who acts in place of another. — **surrogate,** *adj.* — **surrogacy** (sər-ə-gə-see), **surrogateship,** *n.*

surrogate carrier. See *surrogate mother* (1) under MOTHER.

surrogate court. See *probate court* under COURT.

surrogate mother. See MOTHER.

surrogate parent. 1. See PARENT (1). **2.** See *surrogate mother* under MOTHER.

surrogate-parenting agreement. (1985) A contract between a woman and typically an infertile couple under which the woman provides her uterus to carry an embryo throughout pregnancy; esp., an agreement between a person (the intentional parent) and a woman (the surrogate mother) providing that the surrogate mother will (1) bear a child for the intentional parent, and (2) relinquish any and all rights to the child. • If the surrogate mother is married, her husband must also consent to the terms of the surrogacy contract. The agreement usu. provides that the woman will relinquish to the couple any parental rights she may have upon the birth of the child. Complex issues arise concerning who is the parent of the resulting child: the genetic donor of egg or sperm, a spouse of either donor, the surrogate, or the person intending to care for the resulting child? American jurisdictions are split on the interpretation and enforceability of these contracts. — Also termed *surrogacy contract.* See *surrogate mother* under MOTHER; *intended child* under CHILD; *intentional parent* under PARENT.

surrogate's court. See *probate court* under COURT.

surrounding circumstances. (1828) The facts underlying an act, injury, or transaction — usu. one at issue in a legal proceeding.

sursise (sər-SIZ). [Law French] *Hist.* Neglect; omission.

sursum reddere (**sər**-səm **red**-ər-ee), *vb.* [Law Latin] (17c) *Hist.* In conveyancing, to render up or surrender (property rights, etc.).

sursum redditio (**sər**-səm rə-**dish**-ee-oh). [Law Latin] (17c) *Hist.* In conveyancing, a surrender of an estate by mutual agreement.

surtax. See TAX.

surtax exemption. (18c) **1.** An exclusion of an item from a surtax. **2.** An item or an amount not subject to a surtax. See *surtax* under TAX.

surveillance (sər-**vay**-lənts), *n.* (1802) Close observation or listening of a person or place in the hope of gathering evidence. — **surveil** (sər-**vayl**), *vb.*

▸ **roving surveillance.** (1987) The interception of conversations in moving vehicles or places that cannot be practically specified because the person under surveillance does not remain in one place or uses a communications device associated with one service provider. See *roving bug* under BUG (3); *roving wiretap* under WIRETAPPING.

survey, *n.* (16c) **1.** A general consideration of something; appraisal <a survey of the situation>. **2.** The measuring of a tract of land and its boundaries and contents; a map indicating the results of such measurements <the lender requires a survey of the property before it will issue a loan>.

▸ **government survey.** (1812) A survey made by a governmental entity of tracts of land (as of townships and sections and quarter-sections of land). — Also termed (when conducted by the federal government) *congressional survey.*

▸ **inclusive survey.** (1803) A survey that includes within the described boundaries land that is owned or claimed by others and excluded from the survey's computed area.

▸ **topographical survey.** (18c) A survey that determines a property's elevation above sea level.

3. A governmental department that carries out such measurements <please obtain the boundaries from survey>. **4.** A poll or questionnaire, esp. one examining popular opinion <the radio station took a survey of the concert audience>. **5.** *Maritime law.* A written assessment of the current condition of a vessel or cargo. — Also termed (in sense 5) *survey of a vessel.* — **survey,** *vb.*

survey of a vessel. See SURVEY (5).

surveyor (sər-**vay**-ər), *n.* (15c) Someone who surveys land and buildings. — Also termed *land-measurer.* — **surveyorship,** *n.*

▸ **quantity surveyor.** (1872) Someone whose job is to figure out the amount and kinds of material required to build something properly, how long it will take, and how much it will cost.

surveyor of the port. (18c) *Hist.* A U.S. customs revenue officer appointed for each principal port of entry to oversee the inspection and valuation of imports. • The office was abolished in 1953.

survival action. (1938) A lawsuit brought on behalf of a decedent's estate for injuries or damages incurred by the decedent immediately before dying. • A survival action derives from the claim that a decedent would have had — such as for pain and suffering — if he or she had survived. In contrast is a claim that the beneficiaries may have in a wrongful-death action, such as for loss of consortium or loss of support from the decedent. Cf. WRONGFUL-DEATH ACTION.

survival clause. (1910) *Wills & estates.* A testamentary provision conditioning a bequest on a beneficiary's living for a specified period, often 60 days, after the testator's death. • If the beneficiary dies within the stated period, the testamentary gift usu. accrues to the residuary estate. — Also termed *survivorship clause.* Cf. SIMULTANEOUS-DEATH CLAUSE.

survival statute. (1892) A law that modifies the common law by allowing certain actions to continue in favor of a personal representative after the death of the party who could have originally brought the action; esp., a law that provides for the estate's recovery of damages incurred by the decedent immediately before death. Cf. DEATH STATUTE.

survivance. (17c) The right of succession (as to an office or to an estate) of a survivor named before the death of the incumbent or the holder.

surviving, *adj.* (16c) Remaining alive; living beyond the happening of an event so as to entitle one to a distribution of property or income <surviving spouse>. See SURVIVAL ACTION.

surviving corporation. See CORPORATION.

surviving partner. See PARTNER.

surviving spouse. See SPOUSE.

survivor. (15c) **1.** Someone who outlives another. **2.** A trustee who administers a trust after the cotrustee has been removed, has refused to act, or has died.

survivor-income benefit plan. See EMPLOYEE BENEFIT PLAN.

survivorship. (17c) **1.** The quality, state, or condition of being the one person out of two or more who remains alive after the others die. **2.** The right of a surviving party having a joint interest with others in an estate to take the whole. See RIGHT OF SURVIVORSHIP.

> "[T]he grand incident of joint estates is the doctrine of *survivorship*, 'by which, when two or more persons are seized of a joint estate, for their own lives, or *pur auter vie*, or are jointly possessed of any chattel interest, the entire tenancy upon the decease of any of them remains to the survivors, and at length to the last survivor; and he shall be entitled to the whole estate, whatever it may be.' This right of survivorship arises when one of the tenants suffers a civil, as well as when he undergoes a physical death." A.C. Freeman, *Cotenancy and Partition* 66 (2d ed. 1886) (quoting 2 William Blackstone, *Commentaries on the Laws of England* 183–84 (16th ed. 1825)).

survivorship annuity. See ANNUITY.

survivorship clause. See SURVIVAL CLAUSE.

survivorship policy. See INSURANCE POLICY.

susceptibility. See SUBJECTION (3).

suspect, *n.* (14c) A person believed to have committed a crime or offense; someone thought to be guilty of malfeasance.

▸ **suspect at large.** (1949) A suspect who is not in custody and is being sought by law-enforcement officers.

suspect, *vb.* (15c) **1.** To consider (something) to be probable. **2.** To consider (something) possible. **3.** To consider (a person) as having probably committed wrongdoing, but without certain truth.

▸ **reasonably suspect.** (17c) **1.** To consider (something) to be probable under circumstances in which a reasonable person would be led to that conclusion. **2.** To consider (someone) as having probably committed wrongdoing under circumstances in which a reasonable person would be led to that conclusion.

suspect class. (1952) A group identified or defined in a suspect classification.

suspect classification. (1949) *Constitutional law.* A statutory classification based on race, national origin, or alienage, and thereby subject to strict scrutiny under equal-protection analysis. • Examples of laws creating suspect classifications are those permitting only U.S. citizens to receive welfare benefits and setting quotas for the government's hiring of minority contractors. See STRICT SCRUTINY. Cf. FUNDAMENTAL RIGHT.

▸ **quasi-suspect classification.** (1972) A statutory classification based on gender or legitimacy, and therefore subject to intermediate scrutiny under equal-protection analysis. • Examples of laws creating a quasi-suspect classification are those permitting alimony for women only and providing for an all-male draft. See INTERMEDIATE SCRUTINY.

suspect evidence. See EVIDENCE.

suspend, *vb.* (14c) **1.** To interrupt; postpone; defer <the fire alarm suspended the prosecutor's opening statement>. **2.** To temporarily keep (a person) from performing a function, occupying an office, holding a job, or exercising a right or privilege <the attorney's law license was suspended for violating the Model Rules of Professional Conduct>.

▸ **suspend payments.** (Of a bank) to cease or refuse to pay money in the ordinary course of business, as because of a closure by supervisory authorities or of the appointment of a public officer to take over the business.

▸ **suspend the rules.** (1832) *Parliamentary law.* To pass a motion that overrides an agenda or other procedural rule, for a limited time and purpose, so that the deliberative assembly may take some otherwise obstructed action.

> "When a body wishes to do something that cannot be done without violating its own rules, but yet that is not in conflict with the constitution or with any controlling statutory provision, it 'suspends the rules that interfere with' the proposed action. Suspension differs from amendment because it is limited in scope and in time. The object of the suspension must be specified, and nothing falling outside the stated limits of the motion to suspend the rules can be done under the suspension." National Conference of State Legislatures, *Mason's Manual of Legislative Procedure* § 279, at 211 (2000).

suspendatur per collum (səs-pen-**day**-tər pər **kahl**-əm). [Law French] *Hist.* Let him be hanged by the neck. • This phrase was written by a judge in the margin of the sheriff's calendar, opposite the name of a prisoner who had been sentenced to death. — Abbr. *sus. per coll.*

> "And now the usage is, for the judge to sign the calendar, or list of all the prisoners' names, with their separate judgments in the margin, which is left with the sheriff. As, for capital felony, it is written opposite to the prisoner's name, 'hanged by the neck;' formerly, in the days of Latin and abbreviation, '*sus. per coll.*' for '*suspendatur per collum.*' And this is the only warrant that the sheriff has for so material an act as taking away life of another." 4 William Blackstone, *Commentaries on the Laws of England* 396 (1769).

suspended sentence. See SENTENCE.

suspended trading. See TRADING HALT.

suspense. (15c) The quality, state, or condition of being suspended; temporary cessation <a suspense of judgment>.

suspense account. 1. See ACCOUNT. **2.** See *concentration account* under ACCOUNT.

suspense reserve. See *appropriated retained earnings* under EARNINGS.

suspension. (15c) **1.** The act of temporarily delaying, interrupting, or terminating something <suspension of business operations> <suspension of a statute>. **2.** The state of such delay, interruption, or termination <corporate transfers were not allowed because of the suspension of business>. **3.** The temporary deprivation of a person's powers or privileges, esp. of office or profession; esp., a fairly stringent level of lawyer discipline that prohibits the lawyer from practicing law for a specified period, usu. from several months to several years <suspension of the bar license>. • Suspension may entail requiring the lawyer to pass a legal-ethics bar examination, or to take one or more ethics courses as continuing legal education, before being readmitted to active practice. **4.** The temporary withdrawal from employment, as distinguished from permanent severance <suspension from teaching without pay>. **5.** *Eccles. law.* An ecclesiastical censure that can be temporary or permanent, and partial or complete. See DEPRIVATION. **6.** *Scots law.* The process of staying a judgment pending an appeal to the Supreme Court.

suspension of arms. See TRUCE.

suspension of judgment. See STAY.

suspension of trading. (1914) The temporary cessation of all trading of a particular stock on a stock exchange because of some abnormal market condition.

suspensive appeal. See APPEAL (2).

suspensive condition. See CONDITION (2).

suspensive veto. See *suspensory veto* under VETO.

suspensory veto. See VETO.

sus. per coll. *abbr.* SUSPENDATUR PER COLLUM.

suspicion. (14c) The apprehension or imagination of the existence of something wrong based only on inconclusive or slight evidence, or possibly even no evidence.

▸ **reasonable suspicion.** (18c) A particularized and objective basis, supported by specific and articulable facts, for suspecting a person of criminal activity. • A police officer must have a reasonable suspicion to stop a person in a public place. See STOP-AND-FRISK. Cf. PROBABLE CAUSE.

suspicious-activity report. (1996) A form that, as of 1996, a financial institution must complete and submit to federal regulatory authorities if it suspects that a federal crime has occurred in the course of a monetary transaction. • This form superseded two earlier forms, the criminal-referral form and the suspicious-transaction report. — Abbr. SAR. Cf. STRUCTURE.

suspicious character. (18c) In some states, a person who is strongly suspected or known to be a habitual criminal and therefore may be arrested or required to give security for good behavior.

suspicious-transaction report. (1993) A checkbox on IRS Form 4789 formerly (1990–1995) requiring banks and other financial institutions to report transactions that might be relevant to a violation of the Bank Secrecy Act or its regulations or that might suggest money-laundering or tax evasion. • This checkbox, like the criminal-referral form, has since been superseded by the suspicious-activity report. — Abbr. STR.

sustain, *vb.* (13c) **1.** To support or maintain, esp. over a long period <enough oxygen to sustain life>. **2.** To nourish and encourage; lend strength to <she helped sustain the criminal enterprise>. **3.** To undergo; suffer <Charles sustained third-degree burns>. **4.** (Of a court) to uphold or rule in favor of <objection sustained>. **5.** To substantiate or corroborate <several witnesses sustained Ms. Sipes's allegation>. **6.** To persist in making (an effort) over a long period <he sustained his vow of silence for the last 16 years of his life>. — **sustainment, sustentation,** *n.* — **sustainable,** *adj.*

sustainable development. (1975) *Int'l law.* The use of natural resources in a manner that can be maintained and supported over time, taking into account the needs of future generations.

> "Throughout the ages, mankind has, for economic and other reasons, constantly interfered with nature. In the past, this was often done without consideration of the effects upon the environment. Owing to new scientific insights and to a growing awareness of the risks for mankind — for present and future generations — of pursuit of such interventions at an unconsidered and unabated pace, new norms and standards have been developed. . . . Such new norms have to be taken into consideration, and such new standards given proper weight, not only when States contemplate new activities but also when continuing with activities begun in the past. The need to reconcile economic development with protection of the environment is aptly expressed in the concept of sustainable development." *Case Concerning the Gabcikovo-Nagymaros Project*, 1997 I.C.J. 7, 157–58.

suthdure (suuth-**door**). *Hist. Eccles. law.* The south door of a church, where purgations and other acts were performed and complaints were heard and resolved.

suum cuique tribuere (s[y]oo-əm **k[w]ɪ**-kwee tri-**byoo**-ər-ee), *vb.* [Latin] *Roman law.* To render to every person his due. • This was one of the three general precepts in which Justinian expressed the requirements of the law. Cf. ALTERUM NON LAEDERE; HONESTE VIVERE.

suus heres. See HERES.

suus judex (s[y]oo-əs **joo**-deks). [Law Latin] *Hist.* A proper judge in a cause.

suzerain (**soo**-zə-rin *or* -rayn), *n.* [Law French] (1807) **1.** *Hist.* A Crown tenant; a tenant *in capite* holding an estate immediately of the Crown. **2.** *Int'l law.* A country that exercises control over another country's foreign relations. — Also spelled *suzereign.*

suzerainty (**soo**-zə-rin-tee *or* -rayn-tee). (1823) **1.** *Hist.* The power of a feudal overlord to whom fealty is due. See FEALTY. **2.** *Int'l law.* The dominion of a country that controls the foreign relations of another country but allows it autonomy in its domestic affairs.

> "At the present time there appears to be no instance of a relation between states which is described as a suzerainty. The term was applied to the relation between Great Britain and the South African Republic, and also to that between Turkey and Bulgaria from 1878 to 1909, but it seems likely to disappear from diplomatic terminology." J.L. Brierly, *The Law of Nations* 128 (5th ed. 1955).

suzereign. See SUZERAIN.

SVC. *abbr.* STORED-VALUE CARD.

SVPA. *abbr.* Any one of several sexually violent predator acts (statutes).

S.W. *abbr.* SOUTH WESTERN REPORTER.

swamp and overflowed land. See LAND.

swap, *n.* (1956) *Commercial law.* **1.** An exchange of one security for another. **2.** A financial transaction between two parties, usu. involving an intermediary or dealer, in which payments or rates are exchanged over a specified period and according to specified conditions.

▸ **currency swap.** (1963) An agreement to swap specified payment obligations denominated in one currency for specified payment obligations denominated in a different currency.

▸ **stock swap.** (1956) In a corporate reorganization, an exchange of one corporation's stock for another corporation's stock. — Also termed *stock-for-stock exchange.*

swarf money. (17c) *Hist.* A payment made in lieu of the service of maintaining a lord's castle.

swatting, *n. Slang.* The act of falsely telephoning a report of a serious crime or emergency in progress in order to provoke a response from a law-enforcement agency, esp. the dispatch of a SWAT (Special Weapons and Tactics) team. • Swatting schemes are often elaborate, involving the use of electronic tools to mask the caller's true identity and location, such as voice-changing devices, fake caller-IDs, and the like. — **swatter,** *n.*

swear, *vb.* (bef. 12c) **1.** To administer an oath to (a person). **2.** To take an oath. **3.** To use obscene or profane language.

swearability, *n.* (1986) The ability to understand the nature of an oath and to testify under oath.

swearability hearing. (1992) A proceeding to determine the capacity of a witness, esp. a child witness, to understand the nature of an oath and to testify under oath.

swearing behind. (1972) *Patents.* A patent applicant's showing that an invention was conceived of or reduced to practice before the effective date of a prior-art reference cited by a patent examiner as grounds for rejecting an application. 37 CFR § 1.131. — Also termed *swearing behind the reference.* See ANTEDATING OF A PRIOR-ART REFERENCE. — **swear behind,** *vb.*

swearing behind a prior-art reference. See ANTEDATING OF A PRIOR-ART REFERENCE.

swearing contest. See SWEARING MATCH.

swearing-in, *n.* (1900) The administration of an oath to a person who is taking office or testifying in a legal proceeding. See OATH.

swearing match. (1907) A dispute in which determining a vital fact involves the credibility choice between one witness's word and another's — the two being irreconcilably in conflict and there being no other evidence. • In such a dispute, the fact-finder is generally thought to believe the more reputable witness, such as a police officer over a convicted drug-dealer. — Also termed *swearing contest; oath against an oath.*

swearing the peace. (17c) *Hist.* The giving of proof to a magistrate that one fears for one's own safety, so that the magistrate will order the troublemaker to keep the peace by issuing a supplicavit. See SUPPLICAVIT.

swear out, *vb.* (1850) To obtain the issue of (an arrest warrant) by making a charge under oath <Franklin swore out a complaint against Sutton>.

sweat equity. (1966) Financial equity created in property by the owner's labor in improving the property <the lender required the homeowner to put 300 hours of sweat equity into the property>.

sweating. (1824) *Criminal procedure.* The illegal interrogation of a prisoner by use of threats or similar means to extort information.

sweat-of-the-brow doctrine. (1982) *Copyright.* The now-discarded principle that copyrights can protect the labor and expense that went into a work, rather than the work's originality. • The Supreme Court rejected the sweat-of-the-brow doctrine in *Feist Pubs., Inc. v. Rural Tel. Servs. Co.*, 499 U.S. 340, 111 S.Ct. 1282 (1991). Cf. SWEATWORK.

sweatshop. (1890) *Slang.* A business where the employees are overworked and underpaid in extreme conditions; esp., in lawyer parlance, a law firm that requires associates to work so hard that they barely (if at all) maintain a family or social life — though the firm may, in return, pay higher salaries.

sweatwork. *Slang.* A compilation, esp. a searchable computer database, that does not qualify for U.S. copyright protection because the underlying facts are not copyrightable and the compilation is not a nontrivial arrangement. • New forms of intellectual-property laws are aimed at protecting the "sweat-of-the-brow" investment that goes into compiling databases. Cf. SWEAT-OF-THE-BROW DOCTRINE.

sweep account. See *concentration account* under ACCOUNT.

sweeping, *adj.* (18c) **1.** Comprehensive in scope <a sweeping objection><sweeping legislation>. **2.** Overwhelming <sweeping voter turnout>.

Sweeping Clause. See NECESSARY AND PROPER CLAUSE.

sweepstakes. (18c) **1.** A race (esp. a horse race) in which the winner's prize is the sum of the stakes contributed by the various competitors. **2.** A contest, often for promotional purposes, that awards prizes based on the random selection of entries. • State and federal laws prohibit conducting a sweepstakes as a scheme to obtain money or property through the mail by false representations. 39 USCA § 3005.

sweetener. 1. An inducement offered to a brokerage firm to enter into an underwriting arrangement with an issuer. **2.** A special stock feature (such as convertibility) that enhances the stock's marketability.

sweetheart deal. (1959) A collusive agreement; esp., a collective-bargaining agreement made as a result of collusion between an employer and a union representative, usu. allowing the employer to pay lower wages in exchange for payoffs to the union representative.

swein (swayn). (17c) *Hist.* A forest freeholder. — Also spelled *swain.*

sweinmote (**swayn**-moht). (12c) *Hist.* A forest court held three times a year, before verderors as judges and freeholders of the forest as jurors, to try forest offenses. — Also spelled *swainmote; swanimote; swainemote; swaingemote.*

"The court of *sweinmote* is to be holden before the verderors, as judges, by the steward of the sweinmote thrice in every year . . . . The principal jurisdiction of this court is, first, to enquire into the oppressions and grievances committed by the officers of the forest . . . and, secondly, to receive and try presentments certified from the court of attachments against offences in vert and venison." 3 William Blackstone, *Commentaries on the Laws of England* 72 (1768).

swell, *n.* (17c) **1.** An expansion in the bulk of something <a swell resulting from defective canning procedures>. **2.** A gradual rise of something <a swell of damages>. **3.** A large, unbroken wave; the collective waves, particularly following a storm <a rough swell caused the shipwreck>.

SWI. *abbr.* SNOWMOBILING WHILE INTOXICATED.

swift witness. See *zealous witness* under WITNESS.

swindle, *vb.* (18c) To cheat (a person) out of property <Johnson swindled Norton out of his entire savings> <Johnson swindled Norton's entire savings out of him>. — **swindle,** *n.* — **swindling,** *n.*

swindler. (18c) Someone who willfully defrauds or cheats another.

swinging-door chad. See CHAD.

swing loan. See *bridge loan* under LOAN.

swing vote. (1962) The vote that determines an issue when all other voting parties, such as appellate judges, are evenly split.

swipe, *vb.* (1825) **1.** To strike or try to strike with a swinging blow <the cat swiped its claws across my hand>. **2.** To steal <the thief swiped the ring out of the display case>. **3.** To pass a card with a magnetic stripe through a machine that reads the stripe <I swiped my credit card through the pay phone's reader and made my call>. — Sometimes termed (in sense 3) *wipe.*

Swiss sandwich. See DOUBLE IRISH.

switching. (1932) In mutual funds, the practice of selling shares in one fund to buy shares in another.

swoling (**swuul**-ing). (bef. 12c) *Hist.* The quantity of land that can be plowed in a year; a hide of land. — Also spelled *suling* (**suul**-ing); *sulung* (**suu**-luung). — Also termed *swoling of land.*

sworn brothers. (14c) *Hist.* Persons who, by mutual oaths, swear to share in each other's fortunes.

sworn clerks in chancery. (18c) *Hist.* Certain officers in the Court of Chancery who assist the six principal clerks by performing clerical tasks, including keeping records and making copies of pleadings. • The offices were abolished in 1842 by the Court of Chancery Act. St. 5 & 6 Vict., ch. 103. — Also termed *sixty clerks.*

sworn statement. See STATEMENT.

SYD. *abbr.* Sum of the years' digits. See *sum-of-the-years'-digits depreciation method* under DEPRECIATION METHOD.

SYD method. See *sum-of-the-year's-digits depreciation method* under DEPRECIATION METHOD.

syllabus (**sil**-ə-bəs). (17c) **1.** An abstract or outline of a topic or course of study. **2.** A case summary appearing before the printed judicial opinion in a law report, briefly reciting the facts and the holding of the case. • The syllabus is ordinarily not part of the court's official opinion. — Sometimes termed *headnote.* Cf. HEADNOTE. Pl. **syllabuses, syllabi** (**sil**-ə-bɪ).

syllogism (**sil**-ə-jiz-əm), *n.* **1.** A three-part statement of a formal argument consisting of a major premise (an established rule), a minor premise (a factual statement showing the applicability or inapplicability of the rule to the present circumstance), and a conclusion (the application of the rule to the present circumstance). • Hence: *Every virtue is praiseworthy. Kindness is a virtue. Therefore kindness is a virtue.* The two premises are related by a middle term (in that example *virtue*) that disappears in the conclusion. The truth of a syllogism depends on the truth of its premises. Cf. ENTHYMEME. **2.** See *deductive reasoning* under REASONING. — **syllogistic,** *adj.* — **syllogize,** *vb.*

"Logical reasoning is a scientific method based upon a simple formula called the syllogism. The syllogism consists of a major premise, a minor premise, and a conclusion. The major premise sets forth a proposition, the minor premise states a fact related to the proposition, and the conclusion automatically follows. For example: All men are wise; Adam is a man; Adam is wise. If this process of reasoning is used, the conclusion is inescapable. Its value, however, is dependent upon the truth of the premises." William Zelermyer, *Legal Reasoning* 4 (1960).

"Formalist arguments . . . conform to the structure of a syllogism of deductive logic: the rule of law is the major premise, the facts of the case are the minor premise, and the legal result is the conclusion." Wilson Huhn, *The Stages of Legal Reasoning: Formalism, Analogy, and Realism,* 48 Vill. L. Rev. 305, 309 (2003).

syllogistic reasoning. See *deductive reasoning* under REASONING.

symbiotic-relationship test. (1973) The standard by which a private person may be considered a state actor — and may be liable for violating someone's constitutional rights — if the relationship between the private person and the government is so close that they can fairly be said to be acting jointly. • Private acts by a private person do not generally create liability for violating someone's constitutional rights. But if a private person violates someone's constitutional rights while engaging in state action, the private person, and possibly the government, can be held liable. State action may be shown by proving that the private person and the state have a mutually dependent (symbiotic) relationship. For example, a restaurant in a public parking garage was held to have engaged in discriminatory state action by refusing to serve African-Americans. *Burton v. Wilmington Parking Authority,* 365 U.S. 715, 81 S.Ct. 856 (1961). There, the Court found a symbiotic relationship because the restaurant relied on the garage for its existence and significantly contributed to the municipal parking authority's ability to maintain the garage. But the symbiotic-relationship test is strictly construed. For example, the fact that an entity receives financial support from — or is heavily regulated by — the government is probably insufficient to show a symbiotic relationship. Thus, although a state had granted a partial monopoly to a public utility, the Court refused to find a symbiotic relationship between them. *Jackson v. Metropolitan Edison Co.,* 419 U.S. 345, 95 S.Ct. 449 (1974). See JOINT PARTICIPATION. Cf. STATE-COMPULSION TEST; NEXUS TEST.

symbol, *n.* **1.** A picture or shape that signifies a particular idea or represents a particular organization. **2.** A letter, number, or sign that represents a sound, an amount, a chemical substance, or the like. **3.** Someone or something that represents a particular quality or idea. — **symbolize,** *vb.*

symbolaeography (sim-bə-lee-**og**-rə-fee). (16c) The art of drafting legal instruments.

symbolic, *adj.* (Of a signature) consisting of a symbol or mark. Cf. ONOMASTIC (2); HOLOGRAPH.

symbolic delivery. See DELIVERY.

symbolic speech. See SPEECH.

symbolum animae (**sim**-bə-ləm **an**-ə-mee). [Latin] (17c) *Hist.* A mortuary. See MORTUARY (2).

sympathy strike. See STRIKE (1).

synallagmatic contract. See CONTRACT.

synchronization license. See LICENSE.

syndic (**sin**-dik), *n.* [French "governmental representative"] (17c) **1.** An agent (esp. of a government or corporation) appointed to transact business for others. **2.** *Civil law.* A bankruptcy trustee.

syndicalism (**sin**-di-kə-liz-əm), *n.* (1907) A direct plan or practice implemented by trade-union workers seeking to control the means of production and distribution, esp. by using a general strike. — **syndicalist,** *n.*

▸ **criminal syndicalism.** (1917) Any doctrine that advocates or teaches the use of illegal methods to change industrial or political control.

syndicate (**sin**-di-kit), *n.* (17c) A group organized for a common purpose; esp., an association formed to promote a common interest, carry out a particular business transaction, or (in a negative sense) organize criminal enterprises. — Also termed (in negative sense) *criminal syndicate.* See ORGANIZED CRIME. — **syndicate** (**sin**-di-kayt), *vb.* — **syndication** (sin-di-**kay**-shən), *n.* — **syndicator** (**sin**-di-kay-tər), *n.*

▸ **buying syndicate.** (1884) A group of investment bankers who share the risk in underwriting a securities issue.

syndicate book. (1985) *Securities.* A list of investors who have expressed an interest in purchasing shares in a forthcoming public offering. • The lead managing underwriter of the offering compiles and maintains the list during the offering.

syndicating. (1886) **1.** The act or process of forming a syndicate. **2.** The gathering of materials for newspaper publication from various writers and distribution of the materials at regular intervals to newspapers throughout the country for publication on the same day.

syndicus (**sin**-di-kəs), *n.* [Latin "advocate" fr. Greek *syn-* "with" + dike "lawsuit"] *Roman law.* One chosen (by a corporate body such as a municipality, college, etc.) to represent it at law. See SYNDIC.

synergism (**sin**-ər-jiz-əm), *n.* (1940) *Patents.* **1.** A combination of known elements or functions that create a result greater than the sum of the individual elements or functions. • Demonstrating that synergism exists is sometimes useful in proving nonobviousness. The U.S. Supreme Court held that synergism was a requirement for a combination patent in *Great Atl. & Pac. Tea Co. v. Supermarket Equip. Corp.*, 340 U.S. 147 (1950). But that holding was overturned by the Patent Act of 1952. 35 USCA § 103. **2.** A patentable device that produces a new or different function or an unusual or surprising consequence. — Also termed *synergy; synergistic result.* — **synergistic** (sin-ər-**jis**-tik), **synergetic** (sin-ər-**jet**-ik), *adj.*

syngraph (**sin**-graf). (17c) A written contract or bond signed by all the parties.

synod (**sin**-əd). (14c) *Eccles. law.* An ecclesiastical council lawfully assembled to determine church matters; esp., a meeting of several adjoining presbyteries in the Presbyterian church.

▸ **diocesan synod** (dy-**os**-ə-sən). (17c) A synod composed of clergy from one diocese.

▸ **general synod.** (15c) A synod composed of bishops from all. — Also termed *universal synod.*

▸ **national synod.** (16c) A synod composed of clergy from a single country.

▸ **provincial synod.** (16c) A synod composed of clergy from a single province. — Also termed *convocation.*

synodal (**sin**-ə-dəl), *n.* (15c) **1.** A collection of ordinances of diocesan synods. **2.** A tribute of money given by clergy to a bishop at the Easter visitation.

synodales testes (sin-ə-**day**-leez **tes**-teez), *n.* [Law Latin "synods-men"] (18c) *Hist.* Persons who gave evidence at synods (or later at visitations), informing them of misconduct by clergy or laity.

synodsman. See SIDESMAN.

synopsis (si-**nop**-sis), *n.* (17c) A brief or partial survey; a summary or outline; HEADNOTE. — **synopsize** (si-**nop**-SIZ), *vb.*

synthetic lease. See LEASE.

synthetic rule. See QUANTITATIVE RULE.

systematic discrimination. See *systemic discrimination* under DISCRIMINATION (3).

systematic jurisprudence. See *expository jurisprudence* under JURISPRUDENCE.

systematic violation. (1980) *Civil-rights law.* An employer's policy or procedure that discriminates against an employee. • Such a policy or procedure will usu. be considered a continuing violation. So an employee's claim of unlawful discrimination will not be barred as untimely as long as some discriminatory effect of the policy or procedure occurs within the limitations period (e.g., 300 days for a Title VII claim). Cf. SERIAL VIOLATION.

systemic discrimination. See DISCRIMINATION (3).

T

T. 1. *Hist.* A letter branded on the base of the thumb of a person who claimed the benefit of clergy to prevent the person from claiming it again. • This practice was formally abolished by the Criminal Statutes (England) Repeal Act of 1827. Cf. F (2). **2.** *Hist.* In Pennsylvania, a letter sewn onto the left sleeve of a convicted thief. • This letter — required by a 1698 statute — had to be at least four inches high and of a different color from the rest of the garment. **3.** A trillion, esp. in reference to a sum of money.

TAB. *abbr.* TAX-ANTICIPATION BILL.

table, *n.* (bef. 12c) **1.** A synopsized representation, esp. in columnar form, of the particulars of a subject, usu. to present diverse items in a way that can be more easily understood. • Examples include actuarial tables, genealogical tables (which show the names and relationships of all the persons constituting a family), and interest tables. **2.** A formulation of laws inscribed on tablets, such as the Twelve Tables of Roman law. See TWELVE TABLES. **3.** *Parliamentary law.* The secretary's desk.

table, *vb.* (1849) **1.** *Parliamentary law.* (Of a deliberative assembly) to set aside the pending business until the assembly votes to resume its consideration. • A matter that has been tabled may be brought up again by a vote of the assembly. — Also termed *lay on the table*; *postpone temporarily.* See LAY ON THE TABLE (1). Cf. TAKE FROM THE TABLE.

> "The early name of the motion to postpone temporarily was '*lay on the table.*' (In American usage the phrase has been shortened, and the motion is now generally referred to as the motion '*to table.*') The term grew out of the legislative custom of literally laying a bill awaiting further consideration on the clerk's table.
>
> "The reference to 'laying the motion on the table' or 'tabling' is still widely used, but the more precise term, 'postpone temporarily,' is preferred when that is its purpose, because the term is self-explanatory.
>
> "Sometimes, however, the purpose of the motion is *not* merely to postpone temporarily, but to set the motion aside indefinitely — in effect, to 'kill' it . . . ." Alice Sturgis, *The Standard Code of Parliamentary Procedure* 70 (4th ed. 2001).

2. *English law.* To put forward (a bill, proposal, resolution, etc.) for consideration and discussion by a legislative or deliberative assembly.

tableau of distribution. (1814) *Civil law.* A list of creditors of an estate, stating what each is entitled to. See *judgment homologating the tableau* under JUDGMENT (2).

tableaux vivant. (1821) *Copyright.* A performance by actors dressed as characters in a painting and acting out the event portrayed in the painting.

table of authorities. See INDEX OF AUTHORITIES.

table of cases. (18c) **1.** An alphabetical list of the cases cited in a brief or lawbook, usu. prefixed or appended to it, with one or more page numbers or section numbers showing where in the text each case is cited. **2.** INDEX OF AUTHORITIES.

Tablets of Amalfi. See AMALPHITAN CODE.

tabula in naufragio. [Latin "the last plank from the shipwreck"] (18c) Something added to a lawsuit, often on appeal, as a last-ditch argument or as an afterthought.

tabula rasa (**tab**-yə-lə **rah**-sə *or* -zə). [Latin "scraped tablet"] (16c) A blank tablet ready for writing; a clean slate. Pl. ***tabulae rasae*** (**tab**-yə-lee-**rahs**-ɪ).

tabular form. See SUBPARAGRAPH FORM.

tabulis exhibendis. See DE TABULIS EXHIBENDIS.

TAC. *abbr.* TIME-ALLOWANCE COMMITTEE.

T-account. (1936) An accounting form shaped like the letter *T*, with the account's name above the horizontal line, debits listed to the left of the vertical line, and credits to the right.

tacere per quadriennium utile (tə-**seer**-ee pər kwod-ree-**en**-ee-əm **yoo**-tə-lee). [Law Latin] *Hist.* To be silent throughout the four years after majority. • A person is estopped from challenging a deed made when that person was a minor if the right is not exercised within the four years after the person reaches the age of majority.

tacit (**tas**-it), *adj.* (17c) **1.** Implied but not actually expressed; implied by silence or silent acquiescence <a tacit understanding> <a tacit admission>. **2.** *Civil law.* Arising by operation of law; constructive <a tacit mortgage> <tacit relocation>. La. Civ. Code art. 3506(30). — **tacitly,** *adv.*

tacit acceptance. (1816) *Civil law.* **1.** An acceptance of an offer indicated by circumstances or operation of law rather than express words. La. Civ. Code art. 1927. **2.** An acceptance of an inheritance, indicated by the heir's doing some act that shows an intent to accept it and that the heir would have no right to do except in that capacity.

tacit admission. See *implied admission* under ADMISSION (1).

tacit-admission doctrine. (1966) The principle that silence in the face of accusatory remarks implies an admission of the accusation. • A major exception to this principle is that a criminal defendant's silence while in custody does not constitute an adoptive admission, regardless of what the interrogators say to the defendant. See *implied admission* under ADMISSION (1).

tacit collusion. See CONSCIOUS PARALLELISM.

tacit contract. See CONTRACT.

tacit dedication. See DEDICATION.

tacit hypothecation. See HYPOTHECATION.

tacit law. See LAW.

tacit mortgage. 1. See *legal mortgage* under MORTGAGE. **2.** See *tacit hypothecation* under HYPOTHECATION.

tacit prorogation. See PROROGATION.

tacit relocation. (17c) The implied or constructive renewal of a lease, usu. on a year-to-year basis, when the landlord and tenant have failed to indicate their intention to have the lease terminated at the end of the original term.

tacit-relocation doctrine. (1999) The principle that a lease is presumed to continue (usu. for a one-year period) beyond its expiration date if the parties do not expressly agree that it should terminate at the stipulated date.

tacit remission. See REMISSION (1).

tack, *n.* (15c) *Scots law.* A deed creating a lease of land or other immovable property for an annual rent payable in money, services, or fruits produced on the land. • The lessee may be referred to as a *tacksman* or *tackswoman.* — **tack,** *vb.*

tack, *vb.* (18c) **1.** To add (one's own period of land possession) to a prior possessor's period to establish continuous adverse possession for the statutory period. **2.** To annex (a junior lien) to a first lien to acquire priority over an intermediate lien.

> "It is the established doctrine in the English law, that if there be three mortgages in succession, and all duly registered, or a mortgage, and then a judgment, and then a second mortgage upon the estate, the junior mortgagee may purchase in the first mortgage, and tack it to his mortgage, and by that contrivance 'squeeze out' the middle mortgage and gain preference over it. The same rule would apply if the first as well as the second incumbrance was a judgment; but the incumbrancer who tacks must always be a mortgagee, for he stands in the light of a bonâ fide purchaser, parting with his money upon the security of the mortgage." 4 James Kent, *Commentaries on American Law* *176 (George Comstock ed., 11th ed. 1866).

3. *Scots law.* To lease land or other immovable property for an annual rent payable in money, services, or fruits produced on the land.

tacking. (18c) **1.** The joining of consecutive periods of possession by different persons to treat the periods as one continuous period; esp., the adding of one's own period of land possession to that of a prior possessor to establish continuous adverse possession for the statutory period. See ADVERSE POSSESSION. **2.** The joining of a junior lien with the first lien in order to acquire priority over an intermediate lien.

tactic, *n.* **1.** An adroit or artful maneuver, esp. against an adversary. **2.** A method of employing or redirecting force in combat. **3.** (*pl.*) The study of military and naval maneuvers, esp. during hostilities; specif., the art of handling troops in proximity of the enemy or applying practiced movements on the battlefield.

Taft–Hartley Act. See LABOR–MANAGEMENT RELATIONS ACT.

Taft–Hartley fund. See *joint-welfare fund* under FUND (1).

tail, *n.* (14c) The limitation of an estate so that it can be inherited only by the fee owner's issue or class of issue. See FEE TAIL; ENTAIL. — Also termed (in Scots law) *tailzie* (**tay**-lee).

▸ **several tail.** (17c) A tail that designates two separate heirs or classes of heirs who are eligible to inherit.

▸ **tail female.** (18c) A limitation to female heirs.

▸ **tail general.** (15c) **1.** A tail limited to the issue of a particular person, but not to that of a particular couple. — Also termed *general tail.* **2.** See *tail male.*

▸ **tail male.** (17c) A limitation to male heirs. — Also termed *tail general.*

▸ **tail special.** (15c) A tail limited to specified heirs of the donee's body. — Also termed *special tail.*

> "Estates-tail are either *general,* or *special* . . . . Tenant in tail-special is where the gift is restrained to certain heirs . . . and does not go to all of them in general. And this may happen in several ways. I shall instance in only one: as where lands and tenements are given to a man and the *heirs of his body, on Mary his now wife to be begotten;* here no issue can inherit, but such special issue as is engendered, between them two; not such as the husband may have by another wife: and therefore it is called special tail." 2 William Blackstone, *Commentaries on the Laws of England* 113–14 (1766).

tail coverage. (1975) *Insurance.* An extension of a claims-made professional-liability policy to protect against claims and lawsuits filed after the end of the policy period but based on negligent acts that occurred during the policy period. — Also termed *extended-reporting-period endorsement.* Cf. PRIOR-ACTS COVERAGE.

tailzie (**tay**-lee), *n. Scots law.* **1.** See ENTAIL. **2.** See TAIL.

tainland. See THANELAND.

taint, *n.* (16c) **1.** A conviction of felony. **2.** A person so convicted. See ATTAINDER.

taint, *vb.* (14c) **1.** To imbue with a noxious quality or principle. **2.** To contaminate or corrupt. **3.** To tinge or affect for the worse. • Originally, to taint was to affect only slightly; today, however, to taint is normally to affect seriously for the worse. — **taint,** *n.*

tainted evidence. See EVIDENCE.

tainted stock. See STOCK.

taint hearing. (1967) *Criminal procedure.* A pretrial evidentiary proceeding to determine whether, esp. in child-sexual-abuse cases, a child complainant's statements are reliable and to ensure that the statements were not elicited by a prejudicially suggestive interview regimen.

take, *vb.* (bef. 12c) **1.** To obtain possession or control, whether legally or illegally <it's a felony to take that property without the owner's consent>. **2.** To seize with authority; to confiscate or apprehend <take the suspect into custody>. **3.** To acquire (property) for public use by eminent domain; (of a governmental entity) to seize or condemn property <the state took the land under its eminent-domain powers>. **4.** To acquire possession by virtue of a grant of title, the use of eminent domain, or other legal means; esp., to receive property by will or intestate succession <the probate code indicates the proportions according to which each heir will take>. See TAKING. **5.** To claim one's rights under <she took the Fifth Amendment>.

take a default judgment. (1882) To reduce to final judgment a defendant's failure to timely answer a lawsuit. • The process usu. involves informing the court of the defendant's failure to answer, proving damages, and submitting a proposed judgment for the judge to sign. See DEFAULT JUDGMENT.

take a deposition. (18c) To obtain the testimony of a witness by deposition. See DEPOSITION (1).

take away, *vb. Hist.* To entice or persuade (esp. a female under the age of 18) to leave her family for marriage, prostitution, or illicit sex. See ABDUCTION (2).

take back, *vb.* (18c) To revoke; to retract.

take by stealth. (16c) To steal (personal property); to pilfer or filch.

take care of. (16c) **1.** To support or look after (a person). **2.** To pay (a debt). **3.** To attend to (some matter).

take delivery. (1829) To receive something purchased or ordered; esp., to receive a commodity under a futures contract or spot-market contract, or to receive securities recently purchased.

take effect, *vb.* (14c) **1.** To become operative or executed. **2.** To be in force; to go into operation.

take from the table. (1837) *Parliamentary law.* To resume consideration of (business previously tabled). — Also termed *resume consideration.*

take-home pay. (1943) Gross wages or salary reduced by deductions such as income taxes, social-security taxes, voluntary contributions, and union dues; the net amount of a paycheck.

take-it-or-leave-it contract. See *adhesion contract* under CONTRACT.

take-nothing judgment. See JUDGMENT (2).

take-or-pay contract. See CONTRACT.

takeover. (1958) The acquisition of ownership or control of a corporation. • A takeover is typically accomplished by a purchase of shares or assets, a tender offer, or a merger.

▸ **friendly takeover.** (1971) A takeover that is approved by the target corporation.

▸ **hostile takeover.** (1969) A takeover that is resisted by the target corporation. — Also termed *unfriendly takeover.*

▸ **unfriendly takeover.** See *hostile takeover.*

takeover agreement. See AGREEMENT.

takeover bid. (1962) An attempt by outsiders to wrest control from the incumbent management of a target corporation. — Also termed *tender offer.* See TENDER OFFER.

takeover defense. (1973) A measure taken by a corporation to discourage hostile takeover attempts. — Often shortened to *defense.* — Also termed *shark repellent.*

▸ **structural takeover defense.** (1990) A legal mechanism adopted by a corporation to thwart any future takeover bid without having any financial or operational effect on the target corporation.

▸ **transactional takeover defense.** (2004) A financial or operational transaction designed to make a present or future takeover bid more difficult by raising a company's share price, paying off the bidder, or reducing a bidder's profit. • Examples include issuing new shares of stock, acquiring expensive assets, and adopting a poison-pill defense. See POISON PILL; PORCUPINE PROVISION.

takeover offer. See TENDER OFFER.

taker, *n.* (18c) Someone who acquires; esp., one who receives property by will, by power of appointment, or by intestate succession.

▸ **first taker.** (18c) Someone who receives an estate that is subject to a remainder or executory devise.

▸ **presumptive taker.** (1836) Someone who would take under the applicable provisions if the takers were to be finally ascertained at the present moment.

▸ **taker in default.** (1911) Someone who will receive property not effectively appointed; esp., a person designated by a donor to receive property under a power of appointment if the donee fails to exercise that power.

take the Fifth. (1940) To assert one's right against self-incrimination under the Fifth Amendment by refusing to testify under oath on the ground that answering might provide evidence against the witness in a future criminal prosecution. • A common but loose variant of the phrase is *plead the Fifth*; invoking the right is not a plea. See RIGHT AGAINST SELF-INCRIMINATION.

take the witness. (1830) You may now question the witness. • This phrase is a lawyer's courtroom announcement that ends one side's questioning and prompts the other side to begin its questioning. Synonymous phrases are *your witness* and *pass the witness.*

take up, *vb.* (1832) **1.** To pay or discharge (a note). **2.** To retire (a negotiable instrument); to discharge one's liability on (a negotiable instrument), esp. the liability of an indorser or acceptor. **3.** To purchase (a note).

taking, *n.* (14c) **1.** *Criminal & tort law.* The act of seizing an article, with or without removing it, but with an implicit transfer of possession or control.

▸ **constructive taking.** (1843) An act that does not equal an actual appropriation of an article but that does show an intention to convert it, as when a person entrusted with the possession of goods starts using them contrary to the owner's instructions.

▸ **original taking.** The acquisition of possession of an article that has had no prior possessor, as with the catching of a wild beast.

2. *Constitutional law.* The government's actual or effective acquisition of private property either by ousting the owner or by destroying the property or severely impairing its utility. • There is a taking of property when government action directly interferes with or substantially disturbs the owner's use and enjoyment of the property. — Also termed *constitutional taking.* See CONDEMNATION (2); EMINENT DOMAIN.

▸ **actual taking.** See *physical taking.*

▸ **de facto taking** (di **fak**-toh). (1921) **1.** Interference with the use or value or marketability of land in anticipation of condemnation, depriving the owner of reasonable use and thereby triggering the obligation to pay just compensation. **2.** A taking in which an entity clothed with eminent-domain power substantially interferes with an owner's use, possession, or enjoyment of property.

▸ **permanent taking.** A government's taking of property with no intention to return it. • The property owner is entitled to just compensation.

▸ **physical taking.** A physical appropriation of an owner's property by an entity clothed with eminent-domain authority. — Also termed *actual taking.*

▸ **regulatory taking.** (1959) A taking of property under the Fifth Amendment by way of regulation that seriously restricts a property owner's rights. *See Pa. Coal Co. v. Mahon*, 260 U.S. 393, 413, 415 (1922) ("if regulation goes too far it will be recognized as a taking").

▸ **temporary taking.** A government's taking of property for a finite time. • The property owner may be entitled to compensation and damages for any harm done to the property.

taking a case from the jury. See *directed verdict* under VERDICT (1).

Takings Clause. (1955) The Fifth Amendment provision that prohibits the government from taking private property for public use without fairly compensating the owner. — Also termed *Just Compensation Clause.* See EMINENT DOMAIN.

taking the Fifth. See TAKE THE FIFTH.

tales (**tay**-leez *or* taylz). [Latin, pl. of *talis* "such," in the phrase *tales de circumstantibus* "such of the bystanders"] (15c) **1.** A supply of additional jurors, usu. drawn from the bystanders at the courthouse, summoned to fill a panel that has become deficient in number because of juror challenges or exemptions. **2.** A writ or order summoning these jurors. — Also termed *pray tales.*

tales-juror. See TALESMAN.

talesman (**taylz**-mən *or* **tay**-leez-mən). (17c) *Archaic.* **1.** A person selected from among the bystanders in court to serve as a juror when the original jury panel has become deficient in number. **2.** VENIREMEMBER. — Also termed *tales-juror.*

talisman (**tal**-is-mən), *n.* (17c) A charm, amulet, or other physical thing thought by some people to be capable of working wonders <private property is not some sacred talisman that can never be touched by the state — it can be taken for public use as long as the owner is justly compensated>. — **talismanic** (tal-is-**man**-ik), *adj.*

talis qualis (**tay**-lis **kway**-lis). [Latin] *Hist.* Such as it is. • A purchaser who accepts title as it stands at the time of sale takes the title *talis qualis.*

tallage. (13c) **1.** *Hist.* An arbitrary tax levied by the monarch on towns and lands belonging to the crown. • Royal tallages were abolished in the 14th century when Parliament gained the power to approve or disapprove the monarch's direct-taxation schemes. **2.** *Hist.* A levy demanded by a feudal lord from tenants in lieu of the tenants' provision of goods and services. • The timing and amount of the levy varied according to local custom, type of tenure, and caprice. Cf. AUXILIUM. **3.** TOLLAGE.

> "TALLAGE, TALLAGIUM, a certain rate, according to which barons and knights were anciently taxed by the king towards the expences of the state, and inferior tenants by their lords, on certain occasions. This latter *Tallage* of the customary tenants was sometimes fixed and certain, and sometimes at the pleasure of the lord; and was also sometimes compounded for. Tallages were anciently called Cuttings; which name is still retained in *Ireland*, though in a different signification. *Tallage*, says Sir Ed. Coke, is a general name including all taxes." 2 Ephraim Chambers, *Cyclopaedia: Or, an Universal Dictionary of Arts and Sciences* (5th ed. 1743) (s.v. *tallage*) (internal cross-references omitted).

tally. (15c) **1.** *Hist.* A stick cut into two parts and marked with notches to show what was due between a debtor and creditor.

> "A thousand pounds was marked by cutting out the thickness of the palm of the hand, a hundred by the breadth of the thumb, a score by the breadth of the little finger, one pound by that of a swelling barley-corn . . . . The terminology has left a permanent imprint on our language. If you lent money to the Bank of England, tallies were cut for the amount: the Bank kept the foil and you received the stock; you thus held 'Bank Stock' of the amount recorded upon it. When the form of cheque was adopted, it was not indeed called a foil, but the part retained by the payer is still the counterfoil; and the word 'cheque' itself goes back ultimately to the same root as 'exchequer.'" Reginald L. Poole, *The Exchequer in the Twelfth Century* 86–93 (1912).

> "The tally, used as a receipt for money or chattels, was a narrow wooden stick with notches of varying dimensions to represent the amount received. After the notches had been cut, the stick was split lengthwise into two unequal pieces. The longer, which contained a stump or handle and was called the 'stock,' was given to the person making the payment, and the shorter, a flat strip called the 'foil,' to the other party. If the sum involved was disputed, the two pieces could be fitted one to the other to see if they would 'tally.'" C.H.S. Fifoot, *History and Sources of the Common Law: Tort and Contract* 223 (1949).

> "From early times tallies were used in the Exchequer and this lasted until 1826. The burning of a large quantity of old tallies led to the burning down of the old Houses of Parliament." David M. Walker, *The Oxford Companion to Law* 1207 (1980).

2. Anything used to record an account. **3.** An account; a score.

Talmud (**tahl**-muud *or* **tal**-məd), *n.* A work embodying the civil and canonical law of the Jewish people. — **Talmudic** (tahl-**moo**-dik *or* tal-), *adj.*

talweg. See THALWEG.

TAM. *abbr.* TECHNICAL ADVICE MEMORANDUM.

tame, *adj.* (bef. 12c) (Of an animal) domesticated; accustomed to humans. See *domestic animal* under ANIMAL.

tam facti quam animi (tam **fak**-tı kwam **an**-ə-mı). [Latin] *Hist.* In deed as well as in intention.

tamper, *vb.* (16c) **1.** To meddle so as to alter (a thing); esp., to make changes that are illegal, corrupting, or perverting. **2.** To interfere improperly; to meddle.

tampering, *n.* (17c) **1.** The act of altering a thing; esp., the act of illegally altering a document or product, such as written evidence or a consumer good. *See* Model Penal Code §§ 224.4, 241.8; 18 USCA § 1365. **2.** The act or an instance of engaging in improper or underhanded dealings, esp. in an attempt to influence. • Tampering with a witness or jury is a criminal offense. See WITNESS-TAMPERING; OBSTRUCTION OF JUSTICE; EMBRACERY.

TAN. See *tax-anticipation note* under NOTE (1).

TANF. *abbr.* TEMPORARY ASSISTANCE TO NEEDY FAMILIES.

tangible, *adj.* (16c) **1.** Having or possessing physical form; CORPOREAL. **2.** Capable of being touched and seen; perceptible to the touch; capable of being possessed or realized. **3.** Capable of being understood by the mind.

tangible asset. See ASSET.

tangible chattel paper. See CHATTEL PAPER.

tangible cost. See COST (1).

tangible damages. See *actual damages* under DAMAGES.

tangible evidence. See EVIDENCE.

tangible medium of expression. (1958) *Copyright.* Any material form in which a work can be expressed and communicated, either directly or through a machine. • A requirement for copyright is that the work be fixed in a tangible medium of expression.

tangible personal property. See PROPERTY.

tangible-personal-property memorandum. (1996) A handwritten or signed document that lists items of tangible personal property (such as jewelry, artwork, or furniture) and the persons who should receive the property upon the owner's death. • This memorandum is a separate document from the property owner's will, and if referred to by the will, it is a valid testamentary disposition. Unif. Probate Code § 2-513. — Abbr. TPPM.

tangible property. See PROPERTY.

tangible thing. See *corporeal thing* under THING.

tangible worth. See WORTH (3).

tanker. (1900) A vehicle or vessel used primarily for transporting bulk liquid cargoes, such as molasses, milk, and liquid petroleum products.

Tanner scale. (1978) A method of measuring the physical development of an individual to assess sexual development during puberty so as to determine whether the person should be classified physically as a child, an adolescent, or an adult. • The scale is based on physical measurements and development of external primary and secondary sex characteristics. It was created by Dr. James Tanner (1920–2010), a British pediatrician. — Also termed *Tanner stages.*

tanquam bonus vir (**tan**-kwam **boh**-nəs veer). [Law Latin] *Scots law.* As an honest or honorable man. • A tenant was required to run his farm *tanquam bonus vir.* — Also spelled *tamquam bonus vir.*

tanquam dominus (**tan**-kwam **dom**-ə-nəs). [Law Latin] *Hist.* As owner.

tanquam in libello (**tan**-kwam in lə-**bel**-oh). [Law Latin] *Hist.* As if alleged in the libel.

tanquam interim dominus (**tan**-kwam **in**-tər-im **dom**-ə-nəs). [Law Latin] *Hist.* As the temporary owner.

tanquam jure devoluto (**tan**-kwam **joor**-ee dee-və-**loo**-toh). [Law Latin] *Hist.* As if the right had devolved. See JUS DEVOLUTUM.

tanquam optimum maximum (**tan**-kwam **op**-tə-məm **mak**-sə-məm). [Law Latin] *Hist.* At its best and fullest. • The phrase was often used in the conveyance of an estate.

tanquam quilibet (**tan**-kwam **kwɪ**-lə-bet). [Law Latin] *Hist.* Like any other person. • The phrase usu. referred to certain transactions of the sovereign.

tantum et tale (**tan**-təm et **tay**-lee). [Latin] *Hist.* So much and of such a kind.

> "When a purchaser accepts a subject from the seller *tantum et tale* as it stands in the person of the latter, he accepts it with all its advantages and all its faults; he comes precisely into the right and place of the seller: if the subject or the right sold turns out to be more valuable than was thought, the purchaser has the advantage; if otherwise, he bears the loss." John Trayner, *Trayner's Latin Maxims* 595 (4th ed. 1894).

tapper, *n.* (1930) **1.** Someone who approaches another for money; a beggar. **2.** By extension, a thief.

tapping, *n.* See WIRETAPPING.

TAR. *abbr.* Transit authority regulation.

***Tarasoff* letter.** (1992) A communication, usu. in writing, from a psychotherapist or psychiatrist warning the recipient that a patient has threatened to commit a violent act against that person. • The communication satisfies the duty to warn third parties when the therapist knows that the patient poses a threat of serious harm to others and believes that the threat is real. The basis for and creation of the duty arose in *Tarasoff v. Regents of University of California*, 17 Cal. 3d 425 (1976).

tarde venit. (16c) A return of a writ that was delivered to the sheriff too late to be executed before the return day. See *return day* under DAY.

tare (tair), *n.* (15c) **1.** A deficiency in the weight or quantity of merchandise resulting from including its container's weight in the total. **2.** An allowance or abatement of a certain weight or quantity that a seller makes to the buyer because of the container's weight. Cf. TRET.

target benefit plan. See EMPLOYEE BENEFIT PLAN.

target corporation. See CORPORATION.

target defendant. See DEFENDANT.

target letter. (1980) A prosecutor's letter to a potential defendant stating that a criminal investigation is underway and suggesting that the recipient consult counsel.

target offense. See *object offense* under OFFENSE (2).

target price. See PRICE.

target witness. See WITNESS.

tariff, *n.* (16c) **1.** A schedule or system of duties imposed by a government on imported or exported goods. • In the United States, tariffs are imposed on imported goods only. — Also termed *tariff schedule*; *tariff system.* **2.** A duty imposed on imported or exported goods under such a schedule or system. See DUTY (4).

▸ **ad valorem tariff.** (1856) A tariff set as a percentage of the imported goods' value. • This is the primary method used to calculate customs duties.

▸ **antidumping tariff.** (1919) A tariff equaling the difference between the price at which the product is sold in the exporting country and the price at which the importer will sell the product in the importing country. • These tariffs are designed to prevent foreign businesses from artificially lowering their prices and gaining unfair advantages outside their home market. — Also termed *antidumping duty.* See ANTIDUMPING LAW.

▸ **autonomous tariff.** (1887) A tariff set by legislation rather than by commercial treaty.

▸ **common external tariff.** (1941) A tariff rate that members of a customs union, common market, or economic union uniformly apply to imports from nonmember countries. — Abbr. CXT. — Also termed *tariff exterior commun.*

▸ **discriminatory tariff.** (1900) A tariff containing duties that are applied unequally to different countries or manufacturers.

▸ **preferential tariff.** (1879) A tariff that favors the products of one country over those of another. Cf. MOST-FAVORED-NATION CLAUSE.

▸ **protective tariff.** (1833) A tariff designed primarily to give domestic manufacturers economic protection against price competition from abroad, rather than to generate revenue.

▸ **retaliatory tariff.** (1833) A tariff imposed to pressure another country into removing its own tariffs or making trade concessions.

▸ **revenue tariff.** (1827) A tariff enacted solely or primarily to raise revenue.

▸ **tariff exterior commun.** [French] See *common external tariff.* — Abbr. TEC.

3. A fee that a public utility or telecommunications company may assess for its services. • The tariffs that a provider may charge are limited by statute. **4.** A schedule listing the rates charged for services provided by a public utility, the U.S. Postal Service, or a business (esp. one that must by law file its rates with a public agency). **5.** A scale of sentences and damages for crimes and injuries, arranged by severity. — **tariff,** *vb.*

▸ **joint tariff.** (1854) A rate schedule established by two or more carriers covering shipments between places requiring the use of facilities owned by those carriers.

Tariff Act of 1930. See SMOOT–HAWLEY TARIFF ACT.

tariff schedule. See TARIFF (2).

tariff system. See TARIFF (2).

tarnishment. (1953) *Trademarks.* A form of dilution that occurs when a trademark's unauthorized use degrades the mark and diminishes its distinctive quality. Cf. BLURRING.

TASC. *abbr.* Treatment alternatives to street crime.

task order. See *task-order contract* under CONTRACT.

task-order contract. See CONTRACT.

tax, *n.* (14c) A charge, usu. monetary, imposed by the government on persons, entities, transactions, or property to yield public revenue. • Most broadly, the term embraces all governmental impositions on the person, property, privileges, occupations, and enjoyment of the people, and includes duties, imposts, and excises. Although a tax is often thought of as being pecuniary in nature, it is not necessarily payable in money. — **tax,** *vb.*

> "Taxes are the enforced proportional contributions from persons and property, levied by the state by virtue of its sovereignty for the support of government and for all public needs. This definition of taxes, often referred to as 'Cooley's definition,' has been quoted and indorsed, or approved, expressly or otherwise, by many different courts. While this definition of taxes characterizes them as 'contributions,' other definitions refer to them as 'imposts,' 'duty or impost,' 'charges,' 'burdens,' or 'exactions'; but these variations in phraseology are of no practical importance." 1 Thomas M. Cooley, *The Law of Taxation* § 1, at 61–63 (Clark A. Nichols ed., 4th ed. 1924).

▸ **accrued tax.** (1872) A tax that has been incurred but not yet paid or payable.

▸ **accumulated-earnings tax.** (1957) A penalty tax imposed on a corporation that has retained its earnings in an effort to avoid the income-tax liability arising once the earnings are distributed to shareholders as dividends. — Also termed *undistributed-earnings tax.*

▸ **additional tax.** See *stopgap tax.*

▸ **admission tax.** (1924) A tax imposed as part of the price of being admitted to a particular event.

▸ **ad valorem tax.** (1810) A tax imposed proportionally on the value of something (esp. real property), rather than on its quantity or some other measure.

> "[A]n ad valorem tax is a tax of a fixed proportion of the value of the property with respect to which the tax is assessed, and requires the intervention of assessors or appraisers to estimate the value of such property before the amount due from each taxpayer can be determined." 71 Am. Jur. 2d *State and Local Taxation* § 20, at 355 (1973).

▸ **alternative minimum tax.** (1972) A tax, often a flat rate, potentially imposed on corporations and higher-income individuals to ensure that those taxpayers do not avoid too much (or all) income-tax liability by legitimately using exclusions, deductions, and credits. — Abbr. AMT. — Also termed *minimum tax.*

▸ **amusement tax.** (1918) A tax on a ticket to a concert, sporting event, or the like. • The tax is usu. expressed as a percentage of the ticket price.

▸ **back tax.** (*often pl.*) (18c) A tax that, though assessed for a previous year or years, remains due and unpaid.

▸ **betterment tax.** See BETTERMENT TAX.

▸ **capital-gains tax.** (1930) A tax on income derived from the sale of a capital asset. • The federal income tax on capital gains typically has a more favorable tax rate — for example, 20% for an individual and 34% for a corporation — than the otherwise applicable tax rate on ordinary income. See CAPITAL GAIN.

▸ **capital-stock tax.** (1876) **1.** A tax on capital stock in the hands of a stockholder. **2.** A state tax for conducting business in the corporate form, usu. imposed on out-of-state corporations for the privilege of doing business in the state. • The tax is usu. assessed as a percentage of the par or assigned value of a corporation's capital stock.

▸ **capitation tax.** See *poll tax.*

▸ **child's income tax.** See *kiddie tax.*

▸ **classified tax.** (1874) A tax system in which different rates are assessed against different types of taxed property.

▸ **collateral-inheritance tax.** (1829) A tax levied on the transfer of property by will or intestate succession to a person other than the spouse, a parent, or a descendant of the decedent. Cf. *legacy tax.*

▸ **commutation tax.** (18c) **1.** A combination of two or more taxes that is or can be substituted for something else that could be imposed, such as a demand for other taxes or the performance of personal services. • For example, an excise or franchise tax may be combined with a local tax in lieu of all other taxes related to the subject matter. **2.** *Hist.* A tax imposed on shipowners, requiring them to post a bond or remit a payment per foreign passenger. • In the 19th-century, the tax was used to discourage immigration and to raise revenue to defray the costs of supporting indigent immigrants who had remained in the U.S. **3.** *Hist.* A 1784 tax intended to reduce tea-smuggling and increase tax revenue by cutting the tax on tea and raising the tax on windows. • To avoid payment of the tax, many people boarded up their windows.

▸ **consumption tax.** (17c) A tax imposed on sale of goods or services to be consumed.

▸ **death tax. 1.** See *estate tax.* **2.** See *inheritance tax.*

▸ **delinquent tax.** (1820) A tax not paid when due.

▸ **direct tax.** (18c) A tax that is imposed on property, as distinguished from a tax on a right or privilege. • A direct tax is presumed to be borne by the person on whom it is assessed, and not "passed on" to some other person. Ad valorem and property taxes are direct taxes.

▸ **documentary-stamp transfer tax.** See *stamp tax.*

▸ **erroneous tax.** (1869) **1.** A tax levied without statutory authority. **2.** A tax on property not subject to taxation. **3.** A tax levied by an officer who lacks authority to levy the tax. — Also termed *illegal tax.*

▸ **estate tax.** (1928) A tax imposed on the transfer of property by will or by intestate succession. — Also termed *death tax*; *death duty.* Cf. *inheritance tax.*

▸ **estimated tax.** (1926) A tax paid quarterly by a taxpayer not subject to withholding (such as a self-employed person) based on either the previous year's tax liability or an estimate of the current year's tax liability.

▸ **excess-profits tax.** (1918) A tax levied on profits that are beyond a business's normal profits. • This type of tax is usu. imposed only in times of national emergency (such as war) to discourage profiteering.

▸ **excise lieu property tax.** (1937) A tax on the gross premiums received and collected by designated classes of insurance companies.

▸ **excise tax.** See EXCISE.

▸ **export tax.** (1841) A tax levied on merchandise and goods shipped or to be shipped out of a country.

▸ **flat tax.** (1952) A tax whose rate remains fixed regardless of the amount of the tax base. • Most sales taxes are flat taxes. — Also termed *proportional tax.* Cf. *progressive tax*; *regressive tax.*

▸ **floor tax.** (1921) A tax imposed on distilled spirits stored in a warehouse.

▸ **franchise tax.** (1866) A tax imposed on the privilege of carrying on a business (esp. as a corporation), usu. measured by the business's income. See FRANCHISE.

▸ **general tax.** (16c) **1.** A tax that returns no special benefit to the taxpayer other than the support of governmental programs that benefit all. **2.** A property tax or an ad valorem tax that is imposed for no special purpose except to produce public revenue. Cf. *special assessment* under ASSESSMENT.

▸ **generation-skipping tax.** (1977) A tax on a property transfer that skips a generation. • The tax limits the use of generation-skipping techniques as a means of avoiding estate taxes. — Abbr. GST.

▸ **generation-skipping transfer tax.** (1984) A gift or estate tax imposed on a generation-skipping transfer or a generation-skipping trust. IRC (26 USCA) §§ 2601–2663. — Abbr. GSTT. — Sometimes shortened to *generation-skipping tax*; *transfer tax.* See DIRECT SKIP; GENERATION-SKIPPING TRANSFER; *generation-skipping trust* under TRUST (3); TAXABLE DISTRIBUTION.

▸ **gift tax.** (1925) A tax imposed when property is voluntarily and gratuitously transferred. • Under federal law, the gift tax is imposed on the donor, but some states tax the donee.

▸ **graduated tax.** (1830) **1.** A tax employing a rate schedule with higher marginal rates for larger taxable bases (income, property, transfer, etc.) **2.** See *progressive tax.*

▸ **gross-income tax.** (1916) A tax on gross income, possibly after the deduction for costs of goods sold, rather than on net profits; an income tax without allowance for expenses or deductions. — Abbr. GIT. See *gross income* under INCOME.

▸ **gross-receipts tax.** (1873) A tax on a business's gross receipts, without a deduction for costs of goods sold, or allowance for expenses or deductions. — Abbr. GRT. See GROSS RECEIPTS.

▸ **head tax.** (1862) **1.** See *poll tax.* **2.** HEAD MONEY (3).

▸ **hidden tax.** (1935) A tax that is paid, often unknowingly, by someone other than the person or entity on whom it is levied; esp., a tax imposed on a manufacturer or seller (such as a gasoline producer) who passes it on to consumers in the form of higher sales prices.

▸ **highway tax.** (18c) A tax raised to pay for the construction, repair, and maintenance of highways.

▸ **holding-company tax.** (1935) A federal tax imposed on undistributed personal-holding-company income after allowing deductions for such things as dividends paid. IRC (26 USCA) § 545. — Also termed *personal-holding-company tax.*

▸ **household-employment tax.** See *nanny tax.*

▸ **illegal tax.** (17c) **1.** A tax that violates the law, esp. the constitution. • For an example, see *poll tax.* **2.** See *erroneous tax.*

▸ **income tax.** (18c) A tax on an individual's or entity's net income. • The federal income tax — set forth in the Internal Revenue Code — is the federal government's primary source of revenue, and most states also have income taxes. Cf. *property tax*; EXCISE.

> "An income tax is distinguished from other forms of taxation in this respect, that it is not levied upon property, nor upon the operations of trade and business or the subjects employed therein, nor upon the practice of a profession or the pursuit of a trade or calling, but upon the acquisitions of the taxpayer arising from one or more of these sources or from all combined, annually or at other state intervals, and generally, but not necessarily, only upon the excess of such acquisitions over a certain minimum sum. It is not a tax upon accumulated wealth, but upon its periodical accretions. It is not a tax upon personal exertion for gain, whether combined with the employment of capital or not, but upon the fruits thereof. An income tax is in effect a tax upon earnings, taking that term in its broadest sense, and irrespective of the question whether the person whose income is taxed has actively earned it or has merely profited by loaning his capital for active employment by another." Henry Campbell Black, *A Treatise on the Law of Income Taxation under Federal and State Laws* § 1, at 1 (1913).

▸ **indirect tax.** (18c) **1.** A tax on a right or privilege, such as an occupation tax or franchise tax. • An indirect tax is often presumed to be partly or wholly passed on from the nominal taxpayer to another person. **2.** A tax that is added to the cost of goods or services.

▸ **inheritance tax.** (18c) **1.** A tax imposed on a person who inherits property from another (unlike an estate tax, which is imposed on the decedent's estate). • There is no federal inheritance tax, but some states have an inheritance tax (though it is creditable or deductible under the federal estate tax). — Also termed *succession tax*; *death tax.* Cf. *estate tax.* **2.** Loosely, an estate tax.

▸ **in lieu tax.** (1930) A tax imposed as a substitute for another.

▸ **intangible tax.** (1917) A state tax imposed on the privilege of owning, transferring, devising, or otherwise dealing with intangible property.

▸ **interest-equalization tax.** (1963) A tax imposed on a U.S. citizen's acquisition of stock issued by a foreign issuer or a debt obligation of a foreign obligor, but only if the obligation did not mature within a year. • This tax was repealed in the mid-1970s. IRC (26 USCA) § 4911. — Abbr. IET.

▸ **kiddie tax.** (18c) *Slang.* A federal tax imposed on a child's unearned income (above an exempt amount) at the parents' tax rate if the parents' rate is higher and if the child is under 18 years old. — Also termed *child's income tax.*

▸ **land tax.** See *property tax.*

▸ **legacy tax.** (18c) A tax on a legacy, often with the provision that the rate increases as the relationship of the legatee becomes more remote from the testator. • In English law, this tax was known as a *legacy duty*; it was abolished in 1949. Cf. *collateral-inheritance tax.*

▸ **luxury tax.** (1925) An excise tax imposed on high-priced items that are not deemed necessities (such as cars costing more than a specified amount). Cf. *sin tax.*

▸ **minimum tax.** See *alternative minimum tax.*

▸ **nanny tax.** (1993) *Slang.* A federal social-security tax imposed on the employer of a domestic employee if the employer pays that employee more than a specified amount in total wages in a year. • The term, which is not a technical legal phrase, was popularized in the mid-1990s, when several of President Clinton's nominees were found not to have paid the social-security tax for their nannies. — Also termed *household-employment tax.*

▸ **occupation tax.** (1879) An excise tax imposed for the privilege of carrying on a business, trade, or profession. • For example, many states require lawyers to pay an occupation tax. — Also termed *occupational tax.*

▸ **payroll tax.** (1936) **1.** A tax payable by an employer based on its payroll (such as a social-security tax or an unemployment tax). **2.** A tax collected by an employer from its employees' gross pay (such as an income tax or a social-security tax). See *withholding tax.*

▸ **per capita tax.** See *poll tax.*

▸ **personal-holding-company tax.** See *holding-company tax.*

▸ **personal-property tax.** (1863) A tax on personal property (such as jewelry or household furniture) levied by a state or local government.

▸ **pickup tax.** (1955) *Slang.* A state death tax levied in an amount equal to the federal death-tax credit. — Also termed *sponge tax*; *slack tax.*

▸ **poll tax.** (17c) A fixed tax levied on each person within a jurisdiction. • The 24th Amendment prohibits the federal and state governments from imposing poll taxes as a condition for voting. — Also termed *per capita tax*; *capitation tax*; *capitation*; *head tax.*

▸ **premium tax.** (1871) A state tax paid by an insurer on premiums paid by the insured.

▸ **privilege tax.** (1845) A tax on the privilege of carrying on a business or occupation for which a license or franchise is required.

▸ **progressive tax.** (1886) **1.** A tax structured so that the effective tax rate increases more than proportionately as the tax base increases, or so that an exemption remains flat or diminishes. • With this type of tax, the percentage of income paid in taxes increases as the taxpayer's income increases. Most income taxes are progressive, so that higher incomes are taxed at a higher rate. But a tax can be progressive without using graduated rates. — Also termed *graduated tax.* Cf. *regressive tax*; *flat tax.* **2.** See *graduated tax.*

▸ **property tax.** (1808) A tax levied on the owner of property (esp. real property), usu. based on the property's value. • Local governments often impose property taxes to finance school districts, municipal projects, and the like. — Also termed (specif.) *land tax.* Cf. *income tax*; EXCISE.

▸ **proportional tax.** See *flat tax.*

▸ **regressive tax.** (1893) A tax structured so that the effective tax rate decreases as the tax base increases. • With this type of tax, the percentage of income paid in taxes decreases as the taxpayer's income increases. A flat tax (such as the typical sales tax) is usu. considered regressive — despite its constant rate — because it is more burdensome for low-income taxpayers than high-income taxpayers. A growing exemption also produces a regressive tax effect. Cf. *progressive tax*; *flat tax.*

▸ **repressive tax.** See *sin tax.*

▸ **road tax.** See ROAD TAX.

▸ **sales tax.** (1921) A tax imposed on the sale of goods and services, usu. measured as a percentage of their price. — Also termed *retail sales tax.* See *flat tax.*

> "While the term 'sales tax' encompasses a large variety of levies, the term often refers to the 'retail sales tax,' where the tax is separately stated and collected on a transaction-by-transaction basis from the consumer; although the economic burden of the sales tax falls upon the consumer, the seller has the statutory duty to collect the tax for the taxing jurisdiction." 68 Am. Jur. 2d *Sales and Use Tax* § 1, at 11 (1993).

▸ **self-employment tax.** (1947) The Social-Security and Medicare tax imposed on the net earnings of a self-employed person. — Abbr. SET.

▸ **service-occupation tax.** (1961) A tax imposed on persons who sell services, usu. computed as a percentage of net cost of the tangible personal property (e.g., materials and goods) transferred as an incident to the sale. — Abbr. SOT.

▸ **severance tax.** (1922) A tax imposed on the value of oil, gas, timber, or other natural resources extracted from the earth.

▸ **sinking-fund tax.** (1859) A tax to be applied to the repayment of a public loan.

▸ **sin tax.** (1971) An excise tax imposed on goods or activities that are considered harmful or immoral (such as cigarettes, liquor, or gambling). — Also termed *repressive tax.* Cf. *luxury tax.*

▸ **slack tax.** See *pickup tax.*

▸ **special tax.** (18c) **1.** A tax levied for a unique purpose. **2.** A tax (such as an inheritance tax) that is levied in addition to a general tax.

▸ **specific tax.** (18c) A tax imposed as a fixed sum on each article or item of property of a given class or kind without regard to its value.

▸ **sponge tax.** See *pickup tax.*

▸ **stamp tax.** (18c) A tax imposed by requiring the purchase of a revenue stamp that must be affixed to a legal document (such as a deed or note) before the document can be recorded. — Also termed *documentary-stamp transfer tax.*

▸ **state tax.** (18c) **1.** A tax — usu. in the form of a sales or income tax — earmarked for state, rather than federal or municipal, purposes. **2.** A tax levied under a state law.

▸ **stock-transfer tax.** (1906) A tax levied by the federal government and by some states on the transfer or sale of shares of stock. — Often shortened to *transfer tax.*

"Some state statutes impose special taxes, usually in the form of a stamp tax, upon sales and agreements for sale and other transfers of stock in corporations. Such a tax is in the nature of an excise tax on the transfer. Taxes on the issuance and transfer of corporate stock, commonly known as 'stock transfer taxes' and payable by means of stamps, are constitutional, as within the power of state governments." 71 Am. Jur. 2d *State and Local Taxation* § 643, at 896 (1973).

▸ **stopgap tax.** (1957) A tax, usu. temporary, levied during the term of a budget to cover an unexpected deficit. — Also termed *additional tax.*

▸ **succession tax.** See *inheritance tax* (1).

▸ **surtax.** (1881) An additional tax imposed on something being taxed or on the primary tax itself.

▸ **tonnage tax.** See *tonnage duty* under DUTY (4).

▸ **transfer tax.** (1890) **1.** A tax imposed on the transfer of property, esp. by will, inheritance, or gift. **2.** See *stock-transfer tax.* **3.** See *generation-skipping transfer tax.*

▸ **undistributed-earnings tax.** See *accumulated-earnings tax.*

▸ **unemployment tax.** (1937) A tax imposed on an employer by state or federal law to cover the cost of unemployment insurance. • The Federal Unemployment Tax Act (FUTA) provides for a tax based on a percentage of employee earnings but allows a credit for amounts paid in state unemployment taxes.

▸ **unified transfer tax.** (1948) The federal transfer tax imposed equally on property transferred during life or at death. • Until 1977, gift-tax rates were lower than estate taxes. — Also termed *unified estate-and-gift tax.*

▸ **unitary tax.** A tax of income earned locally by a business that transacts business through an affiliated company outside the state or country. See UNITARY BUSINESS.

▸ **unrelated-business-income tax.** (1962) A tax levied on a not-for-profit organization's taxable income, such as advertising revenue from a publication. — Abbr. UBIT.

▸ **use tax.** (1910) A tax imposed on the use of certain goods that are bought outside the taxing authority's jurisdiction. • Use taxes are designed to discourage the purchase of products that are not subject to the sales tax.

▸ **value-added tax.** (1935) A tax assessed at each step in the production of a commodity, based on the value added at each step by the difference between the commodity's production cost and its selling price. • A value-added tax — which is levied in several European countries — effectively acts as a sales tax on the ultimate consumer. — Abbr. VAT.

▸ **windfall-profits tax.** (1973) A tax imposed on a business or industry as a result of a sudden increase in profits. • An example is the tax imposed on oil companies in 1980 for profits resulting from the Arab oil embargo of the 1970s.

▸ **window tax.** (18c) *Hist. English law.* A tax imposed on a house containing a certain number of windows (usu. more than six). • It was established under the Taxation Act of 1695 and replaced with a tax on inhabited houses established under the House Tax of 1851. See HOUSE-DUTY.

▸ **withholding tax.** (1927) A portion of income tax that is subtracted from salary, wages, dividends, or other income before the earner receives payment. • The most common example is the income tax and social-security tax withheld by an employer from an employee's pay.

taxable, *adj.* (16c) **1.** Subject to taxation <interest earned on a checking account is taxable income>. **2.** (Of legal costs or fees) assessable <expert-witness fees are not taxable court costs>.

taxable cost. See COST (3).

taxable distribution. (1927) A generation-skipping transfer from a trust to the beneficiary (i.e., the skip person) that is neither a direct skip nor a taxable termination. See GENERATION-SKIPPING TRANSFER; *generation-skipping transfer tax* under TAX; *generation-skipping trust* under TRUST (3); SKIP PERSON.

taxable estate. See ESTATE (3).

taxable gift. See GIFT.

taxable income. See INCOME.

taxable termination. (1988) A taxable event that occurs when (1) an interest in a generation-skipping trust property terminates (as on the death of a skip person's parent who possessed the interest), (2) no interest in the trust is held by a nonskip person, and (3) a distribution may be made to a skip person. • Before the creation of taxable terminations in 1976, a taxpayer could create a trust that paid income to a child for life, then to that child's child for life, and so on without incurring an estate or gift tax liability at the death of each generation's beneficiary. See GENERATION-SKIPPING TRANSFER; *generation-skipping transfer tax* under TAX; *generation-skipping trust* under TRUST (3); SKIP PERSON.

taxable year. See *tax year* under YEAR.

tax accounting. The accounting rules and methods used in determining a taxpayer's liability.

tax-anticipation bill. (1953) A short-term obligation issued by the U.S. Treasury to meet the cash-flow needs of the government. • Corporations can tender these bills at par value to make quarterly tax payments. — Abbr. TAB.

tax-anticipation note. See NOTE (1).

tax-anticipation warrant. See WARRANT (2).

tax-apportionment clause. (1949) A testamentary provision directing how inheritance and estate taxes should be paid.

tax assessment. See ASSESSMENT (3).

tax assessor. See ASSESSOR (1).

taxation. (14c) **1.** The imposition or assessment of a tax; the means by which the state obtains the revenue required for its activities.

▸ **double taxation.** (18c) **1.** The imposition of two taxes on the same property during the same period and for the same taxing purpose. **2.** The imposition of two taxes on one corporate profit; esp., the structure of taxation employed by Subchapter C of the Internal Revenue Code, under which corporate profits are taxed twice, once to the corporation when earned and once to the shareholders when the earnings are distributed as dividends. **3.** *Int'l law.* The imposition of comparable taxes in two or more states on the same taxpayer for the same subject matter or identical goods. — Also termed *duplicate taxation.*

▸ **duplicate taxation.** See *double taxation.*

▸ **equal and uniform taxation.** (1846) A tax system in which no person or class of persons in the taxing district — whether it be a state, city, or county — is taxed at a different rate from others in the same district on the same value or thing.

▸ **pass-through taxation.** (1998) The taxation of an entity's owners for the entity's income without taxing the entity itself. • Partnerships and S corporations are taxed under this method. So are limited liability companies and limited liability partnerships unless they elect to be taxed as corporations by "checking the box" on their income tax returns. The election is made on Form 8832 (Entity Classification Election). *See* Treas. Reg. § 301.7701-(3)(b)(1). — Also termed *conduit taxation.*

2. TAXATION OF COSTS.

taxation of costs. The process of fixing the amount of litigation-related expenses that a prevailing party is entitled to be awarded. — Sometimes shortened to *taxation.*

tax audit. See AUDIT.

tax avoidance. (1927) The act of taking advantage of legally available tax-planning opportunities in order to minimize one's tax liability. Cf. TAX EVASION.

tax base. (1918) **1.** The total property, income, or wealth subject to taxation in a given jurisdiction. **2.** The aggregate value of the property being taxed by a particular tax. Cf. BASIS (2).

tax basis. See BASIS (2).

tax-benefit doctrine. See TAX-BENEFIT RULE.

tax-benefit rule. (1942) The principle that if a taxpayer recovers a loss or expense that was deducted in a previous year, the recovery must be included in the current year's gross income to the extent that it was previously deducted. — Also termed *tax-benefit doctrine.*

tax bracket. (1923) A particular range of income levels on which a given rate of tax is paid; specif., a categorized level of income subject to a particular tax rate under federal or state law <28% tax bracket>.

tax certificate. (1832) An instrument issued to the buyer of property at a tax sale, certifying the sale and entitling the buyer to a tax deed and possession of the property upon the expiration of the redemption period. • If the property is redeemed, the tax certificate is voided. See REDEMPTION PERIOD; *tax sale* under SALE. Cf. *tax deed* under DEED.

tax collector. A government employee whose job is to make sure that people and businesses pay their taxes.

tax court. (1841) **1.** TAX COURT, U.S. **2.** In some states, a court that hears appeals in nonfederal tax cases and can modify or change any valuation, assessment, classification, tax, or final order that is appealed.

Tax Court, U.S. A federal court that hears appeals by taxpayers from adverse IRS decisions about tax deficiencies. • The Tax Court was created in 1942, replacing the Board of Tax Appeals. — Abbr. T.C.

tax credit. (1946) An amount subtracted directly from one's total tax liability, dollar for dollar, as opposed to a deduction from gross income. — Often shortened to *credit.* Cf. DEDUCTION (2).

▸ **child- and dependent-care tax credit.** (2001) A tax credit available to a person who is employed full-time and who maintains a household for a dependent child or a disabled spouse or dependent.

▸ **earned-income tax credit.** (1927) A refundable federal tax credit on the earned income of a low-income worker with dependent children; a tax credit that reduces income taxes on a dollar-for-dollar basis when a taxpayer's income from work is below a prescribed threshold. • The credit is paid to the taxpayer even if it exceeds the total tax liability. See IRC (26 USCA) § 32. — Abbr. EIC; EITC. — Also termed *earned-income credit.*

▸ **foreign tax credit.** (1928) A tax credit against U.S. income taxes for a taxpayer who earns income overseas and has paid foreign taxes on that income. See FOREIGN-EARNED-INCOME EXCLUSION.

> "Since direct foreign investments and business operations of United States persons often attract foreign income taxes along with the baseline U.S. tax, the specter of double taxation is bound to haunt the pursuit of foreign income. The principal accommodation of the U.S. tax system to the possibility of source-based taxation by other countries is the foreign tax credit. From a simple idea — a dollar-for-dollar reduction of U.S. tax for income taxes paid to foreign countries — the foreign tax credit has evolved into an elaborate statutory structure capable of engulfing an entire professional career." Joseph Isenbergh, *International Taxation* 14 (2000).

▸ **investment tax credit.** (1965) A tax credit intended to stimulate business investment in capital goods by allowing a percentage of the purchase price as a credit against the taxpayer's income taxes. • The Tax Reform Act of 1986 generally repealed this credit retroactively for most property placed in service after January 1, 1986. — Abbr. ITC.

▸ **unified credit.** See *unified estate-and-gift tax credit.*

▸ **unified estate-and-gift tax credit.** (1988) A tax credit applied against the federal unified transfer tax. IRC (26 USCA) § 2001(c)(2). — Often shortened to *unified credit.* — Also termed *applicable exclusion credit.*

tax-deductible, *adj.* Allowed to be subtracted from one's total income before it is taxed.

tax deduction. See DEDUCTION (2).

tax deed. See DEED.

tax-deferred, *adj.* (1948) Not taxable until a future date or event <a tax-deferred retirement plan>.

tax-deferred account. See ACCOUNT.

tax-deferred annuity. See *403(b) plan* under EMPLOYEE BENEFIT PLAN.

tax deficiency. See DEFICIENCY (2).

tax-deficiency notice. See NINETY-DAY LETTER.

tax denier. See TAX PROTESTER.

tax evasion. (1922) The willful attempt to defeat or circumvent the tax law in order to illegally reduce one's tax liability. • Tax evasion is punishable by both civil and criminal penalties. — Also termed *tax fraud.* Cf. TAX AVOIDANCE.

tax-exempt, *adj.* (1923) **1.** By law not subject to taxation <a tax-exempt charity>. **2.** Bearing interest that is free from income tax <tax-exempt municipal bonds>. — Also termed *tax-free.*

tax-exempt bond. See BOND (3).

tax exile. **1.** Someone who lives in a foreign country to avoid the high taxes of his or her home country. **2.** The state or condition of one who lives abroad for this reason.

tax ferret. (1888) A private person engaged in the business of searching for taxable property that has somehow not been taxed.

tax foreclosure. See FORECLOSURE.

tax fraud. See TAX EVASION.

tax-free, *adj.* See TAX-EXEMPT.

tax-free exchange. (1927) A transfer of property for which the tax law specifically defers (or possibly exempts) income-tax consequences. • For example, a transfer of property to a controlled corporation under IRC (26 USCA) § 351(a) and a like-kind exchange under IRC (26 USCA) § 1031(a). — Also termed *1031 exchange.* Cf. 1031 EXCHANGE.

tax haven. (18c) A jurisdiction, esp. a country, that imposes little or no tax on the profits from transactions carried on there or on persons resident there.

> "Among the reasons for this complexity [in international taxation] is the elusive nature of tax havens. A tax haven is not always immediately obvious. What makes a particular environment a tax haven is not invariably a low rate of tax, but relations with other tax regimes that permit the ultimate deflection of income to a low-tax environment with which the income may have little indigenous connection." Joseph Isenbergh, *International Taxation* 16 (2000).

tax home. (18c) A taxpayer's principal business location, post, or station. • Travel expenses are tax-deductible only if the taxpayer is traveling away from home.

tax-identification number. (1968) A nine-digit tracking number assigned by the Internal Revenue Service to the tax accounts of businesses and also to entities or individuals who are required to file business tax returns. — Abbr. TIN. — Often shortened to *tax i.d.* — Also termed *employer-identification number* (EIN); *federal-employer-identification number* (FEIN).

tax incentive. (18c) A governmental enticement, through a tax benefit, to engage in a particular activity, such as the contribution of money or property to a qualified charity.

tax-increment financing. (1974) A technique used by a municipality to finance commercial developments usu. involving issuing bonds to finance land acquisition and other up-front costs, and then using the additional property taxes generated from the new development to service the debt. — Abbr. TIF.

taxing district. See DISTRICT.

taxing power. See POWER (3).

tax injunction act. (1947) A federal law prohibiting a federal court from interfering with the assessment or collection of any state tax where the state affords a plain, speedy, and efficient remedy in its own courts. 28 USCA § 1341. — Abbr. TIA.

tax inspector. (1959) A government official who calculates what tax each person or company should pay. — Also termed *inspector of taxes.*

tax law. (18c) **1.** INTERNAL REVENUE CODE. **2.** The statutory, regulatory, constitutional, and common-law rules that constitute the law applicable to taxation. **3.** The area of legal study dealing with taxation.

tax lease. See LEASE.

tax levy. See LEVY (1).

tax liability. (1932) The amount that a taxpayer legally owes after calculating the applicable tax; the amount of unpaid taxes.

tax lien. See LIEN.

tax list. (1898) An official schedule listing the taxable items within a jurisdiction; ROLL (2).

tax loophole. See LOOPHOLE.

tax-loss carryback. See CARRYBACK.

tax-loss carryforward. See CARRYOVER.

tax-loss carryover. See CARRYOVER.

tax negligence. See NEGLIGENCE.

tax-option corporation. See *S corporation* under CORPORATION.

taxpayer. (1816) Someone who pays or is subject to a tax. Cf. TAX PROTESTER.

taxpayers' bill of rights. (1988) Federal legislation granting taxpayers specific rights when dealing with the Internal Revenue Service, such as the right to have representation and the right to receive written notice of a levy 30 days before enforcement.

taxpayers' lists. Written exhibits required of taxpayers in some taxing districts, listing all property owned by them and subject to taxation, used as a basis for assessment and valuation. Cf. ROLL (2).

taxpayer-standing doctrine. (1977) *Constitutional law.* The principle that a taxpayer has no standing to sue the government for allegedly misspending the public's tax money unless the taxpayer can demonstrate a personal stake and show some direct injury.

tax-preference items. (1971) Certain items that, even though lawfully deducted in arriving at taxable income for regular tax purposes, must be considered in calculating a taxpayer's alternative minimum tax. See *alternative minimum tax* under TAX.

tax protest. (1929) A taxpayer's formal, usu. written, statement that he or she does not acknowledge a legal or just basis for the tax or a duty to pay it. • The purpose of the protest is to make clear that any payment is made "under protest" and to avoid waiving the right to recover the money paid if the tax is later invalidated.

tax protester. (1941) **1.** Someone who files a tax protest. **2.** Someone who opposes tax laws and seeks or employs ways, often illegal, to avoid the laws' effects; esp., a person who refuses to pay a tax on grounds that the government has no authority to levy the tax. — Sometimes spelled *tax protestor.* — Also termed *tax denier.* Cf. TAXPAYER.

▸ **illegal tax protester.** (1981) *Hist.* The name once used by the IRS to designate a person believed to have used illegal means to avoid or reduce tax liability. • In the Internal Revenue Service Restructuring and Reform Act of 1998, Congress forbade the IRS to continue using the label. Today the term *nonfiler* is typically used instead.

tax-protest scheme. (1983) A plan designed to avoid or express dissatisfaction with tax laws, usu. by unlawful means. • The most common schemes involve illegally evading or reducing tax liabilities, or interfering with the administration of the tax laws.

tax rate. (1876) A mathematical figure for calculating a tax, usu. expressed as a percentage.

▸ **average tax rate.** (1895) A taxpayer's tax liability divided by the amount of taxable income. — Abbr. ATR. — Also termed *effective tax rate.*

▸ **effective marginal tax rate.** The percentage of each extra unit of income that covers taxes and any reductions in tax credits and welfare payments.

▸ **effective tax rate.** See *average tax rate.*

▸ **marginal tax rate.** (1939) In a tax scheme, the rate applicable to the last dollar of income earned by the taxpayer. • This concept is useful in calculating the tax effect of receiving additional income or claiming additional deductions. — Abbr. MTR. See TAX BRACKET.

tax-rate schedule. (1951) A schedule used to determine the tax on a given level of taxable income and based on a taxpayer's status (for example, married filing a joint income-tax return). — Also termed *tax table.*

tax rebate. See TAX REFUND.

tax redemption. See REDEMPTION.

tax refund. (1906) Money that a taxpayer overpaid and is thus returned by the taxing authority. — Also termed *tax rebate.*

tax relief. A tax exemption or reduction on part of what one earns, esp. when the exemption is granted because of the purpose to which one puts the money.

tax return. (1870) An income-tax form on which a person or entity reports income, deductions, and exemptions, and on which tax liability is calculated. — Often shortened to *return.* — Also termed *income-tax return.*

▸ **amended return.** (1861) A return filed after the original return, usu. to correct an error in the original.

▸ **consolidated return.** A return that reflects combined financial information for a group of affiliated corporations.

▸ **false return.** See FALSE RETURN (2).

▸ **information return.** (1920) A return, such as a W-2, filed by an entity to report some economic information related to, but other than, tax liability.

▸ **joint return.** (1930) A return filed together by spouses. • A joint return can be filed even if only one spouse had income, but each spouse is usu. individually liable for the tax payment.

▸ **separate return.** (1913) A return filed by each spouse separately, showing income and liability. • Unlike with a joint return, each spouse is individually liable only for taxes due on the separate return.

tax-return privilege. See PRIVILEGE (3).

tax roll. See ROLL (2).

tax sale. See SALE.

tax shelter, *n.* (1952) A financial operation or investment (such as a partnership or real-estate investment trust) that is created primarily for the purpose of reducing or deferring income-tax payments. • The Tax Reform Act of 1986 — by restricting the deductibility of passive losses — sharply limited the effectiveness of tax shelters. — Often shortened to *shelter.* — **tax-sheltered,** *adj.*

tax-sheltered annuity. See *403(b) plan* under EMPLOYEE BENEFIT PLAN.

tax situs (sɪ-təs). (1888) A state or other jurisdiction that has a substantial connection with assets that are subject to taxation.

tax-straddle rule. (1985) A rule preventing undue deferral of tax on income or conversion of ordinary income or short-term capital gain into long-term capital gain by disallowing the premature deduction of a loss on sale or disposition of one leg of a straddle position while retaining the other, offsetting leg or position. • For example, in a straddle position a promise to sell may be offset by a promise to buy, such as in a futures contract. This practice has been greatly restricted by the requirement that gains and losses on commodities transactions must be reported based on their value at year end. IRC (26 USCA) § 165(c)(2). See STRADDLE.

tax table. See TAX-RATE SCHEDULE.

tax title. See TITLE (2).

tax warrant. See WARRANT (1).

tax write-off. (1955) A deduction of depreciation, loss, or expense from taxable income.

tax year. See YEAR.

TBC. *abbr.* Trial before the court. See *bench trial* under TRIAL.

T-bill. *abbr.* (1982) TREASURY BILL.

T-bond. *abbr.* (1974) TREASURY BOND.

T.C. *abbr.* TAX COURT, U.S.

T.C.M. See T.C. MEMO.

T.C. memo. *abbr.* A memorandum decision of the U.S. Tax Court. — Also abbreviated T.C.M.

TCPA. *abbr.* TELEPHONE CONSUMER PROTECTION ACT.

TDA. *abbr.* UNITED STATES TRADE AND DEVELOPMENT AGENCY.

teach, *vb. Patents.* **1.** (Of a patent specification) to instruct (a person of ordinary skill in the art how to make and use an invention). **2.** (Of a prior-art reference) to anticipate (the invention being examined) by discussing, describing, or analyzing the invention's essential elements or technology. • In this sense, prior art that discourages an inventor from pursuing an invention "teaches away from" that invention. A teaching raises a statutory bar to an invention's patentability.

***Teague* doctrine.** (1989) The principle that in post-conviction habeas corpus proceedings, a petitioner cannot (1) seek to enforce a new rule of law that was announced after the conviction became final, (2) try to create a new rule, or (3) seek to apply a settled precedent in a novel way that would create a new rule. • There are two exceptions to the doctrine. A petitioner may seek to enforce rules prohibiting punishment for private, primarily individual conduct that the criminal-law-making authority lacks power to proscribe, and rules that are implicit in the concept of ordered liberty. The doctrine was announced in *Teague v. Lane*, 489 U.S. 288 (1989). — Also termed *Teague retroactivity doctrine.*

teamwork. (1828) Work done by a team; esp., work by a team of animals as a substantial part of one's business, such as farming, express carrying, freight hauling, or transporting material. • In some jurisdictions, animals (such as horses) that work in teams are exempt from execution on a civil judgment.

tear-me-open license. See *shrinkwrap license* under LICENSE.

TEAS. *abbr.* TRADEMARK ELECTRONIC APPLICATION SYSTEM.

TEC. *abbr.* Tariff exterior commun. See *common external tariff* under TARIFF (2).

TECA (tee-kə). *abbr.* TEMPORARY EMERGENCY COURT OF APPEALS.

technical adjustment. A brief change in the general upward or downward trend of stock-market prices, such as a short rally during a bear market.

Technical Advice Memorandum. (1967) A publication issued by the national office of the IRS, usu. at a taxpayer's request, to explain some complex or novel tax-law issue. — Abbr. TAM.

technical conversion. See CONVERSION (2).

technical error. See *harmless error* under ERROR (2).

technical estoppel. See ESTOPPEL.

technical mark. See *technical trademark* under TRADEMARK.

technical-meaning exception. The doctrine that a word or phrase in a legal instrument is not to be understood in its ordinary, everyday meaning when that word or phrase has acquired a specialized or peculiar meaning in a given context and appears in that context. See ORDINARY-MEANING CANON.

technical mortgage. See MORTGAGE.

technical trademark. See TRADEMARK.

technical trust. See *passive trust* under TRUST (3).

technology, *n.* **1.** Modern equipment, machines, and methods based on contemporary knowledge of science and computers. **2.** The practical, esp. industrial use of scientific and mathematical discoveries.

Technology Administration. A unit in the U.S. Department of Commerce responsible for working with industry on ways to use technology to stimulate economic growth. • The agency also carries out technology programs and disseminates information about technology. It has three offices: the Office of Technology Policy (OTP), the National Institute of Standards and Technology (NIST), and the National Technical Information Service (NTIS). It was established in 1988. 15 USCA § 3704.

technology transfer. (1963) **1.** The sale or licensing of intellectual property. **2.** The field involving the sale and licensing of intellectual property. • Many major universities have an office of technology transfer to control the university's intellectual property and generate income from it.

teen court. See COURT.

teind (teend). (*usu. pl.*) (13c) *Scots law.* A tithe. **teind,** *vb.* — **teindable,** *adj.*

▸ **free teind.** A teind that has not yet been appropriated as a stipend to be paid to a parish minister. — Also termed *unexhausted teind.*

Teind Court. *Scots law.* A court that adjudicates questions relating to teinds, esp. increases in the stipends of parish ministers. • It includes one of the judges of the Court of Session, sitting as Commissioner of Teinds. — Also termed *Court of Teinds.*

telecommuting. See TELEWORK.

teleconference. See *telephone meeting* under MEETING.

telecopier. See FAX (2).

telegram. (1852) A message or other communication sent esp. by telegraph, but also including one sent by radio, teletype, cable, or other mechanical method of transmission. — Also termed *telegraph.* — **telegrammic,** *adj.*

telegraph. (18c) **1.** An apparatus or device for sending messages or signals over a distance, esp. one having electricity as the agent of the transmission. **2.** A mechanical or electrical device for signaling from one part of a ship to another, as from the engine room to the bridge. **3.** TELEGRAM.

telemeeting. See *telephone meeting* under MEETING.

teleological interpretation. See INTERPRETATION (1).

teleology (tel-ee-**ahl**-ə-jee), *n.* **1.** The fact or quality of being directed toward some known purpose or end. **2.** The use of design, purpose, or utility as an explanation of some phenomenon. **3.** The doctrine or belief that ends or purposes are inherent in nature; the belief that everything has a special purpose or use. — **teleological,** *adj.* — **teleologist,** *n.*

telephone appearance. See APPEARANCE.

Telephone Consumer Protection Act. *Telecommunications.* A 1991 federal statute that regulates telemarketing and the use of automated telephone equipment. 47 USCA § 227. — Abbr. TCPA.

telephonic appearance. See *telephone appearance* under APPEARANCE.

telephonic meeting. See *telephone meeting* under MEETING.

telescam. (1989) A fraud committed by using telemarketing to induce the victim to disclose sensitive personal information or send money to the perpetrator. Cf. BOILER-ROOM TRANSACTION; PHISHING.

telework, *n.* The use of electronic and other tools and devices, such as home computers, telephones, fax machines, etc., to enable a person to work at a place outside the office while maintaining contact with a central office, coworkers, clients, and customers. — Also termed *telecommuting.*

teller. (15c) **1.** A bank clerk who deals directly with customers by receiving and paying out money. **2.** *Parliamentary law.* A member of a tellers committee; esp., a vote-counter at an election. See *tellers committee* under COMMITTEE (1); CANVASSER.

Teller in Parliament. One of the members of the British House of Commons — two from government and two from the opposition — appointed by the Speaker to count votes.

teller's check. See CHECK.

tellers committee. See COMMITTEE (1).

teller vote. See *lobby vote* under VOTE (4).

temerarium perjurium super assisam (tem-ə-**rair**-ee-əm pər-**joor**-ee-əm s[y]**oo**-pər ə-**SI**-zəm). [Law Latin] *Hist.* Rash perjury on an assize. • The phrase described a perverse verdict returned by a jury.

temerary, *adj.* Reprehensibly heedless or careless; culpably negligent.

temere jurantes super assisam (**tem**-ə-ree joor-**an**-teez **s[y]oo**-pər ə-**SI**-zəm). [Law Latin] (16c) *Hist.* Persons swearing rashly on an assize. See TEMERARIUM PERJURIUM SUPER ASSISAM.

temere litigare (**tem**-ə-ree lit-ə-**gair**-ee), *vb.* [Latin] *Hist.* To litigate rashly.

temperament. 1. Someone's constitution or frame of mind; the character of mind or of mental reactions characteristic of a person. **2.** The sum total of inherited biological influences on personality, showing continuity across a person's life span.

temperance. (14c) **1.** Habitual moderation regarding the indulgence of the natural appetites and passions; restrained or moderate indulgence (esp. of alcoholic beverages). **2.** Abstinence.

temperate damages. See DAMAGES.

tempestive (tem-**pes**-tiv) *adj.* (17c) *Scots law.* Of, relating to, or involving the proper time; timely; timeous.

templar. (16c) A barrister who has chambers in the Temple of the Inns of Court. • The Middle and Inner Temples are so named because they are housed in buildings on land that once belonged to the Knights Templars.

temporal, *adj.* (14c) **1.** Of, relating to, or involving the affairs of the world and of human life, as opposed to spiritual matters; earthly <temporal harm>. Cf. SPIRITUAL. **2.** Of, relating to, or involving time, as opposed to eternity; relating to the lapse of or a span of time <temporal limitations>.

temporality. (14c) **1.** Civil or political power, as distinguished from ecclesiastical power. **2.** (*usu. pl.*) The secular properties or revenues of an ecclesiastic.

temporal jurisdiction. See JURISDICTION.

temporal lord. See LORD.

temporal loss. See LOSS.

temporal power. See POWER.

temporary, *adj.* (16c) Lasting for a time only; existing or continuing for a limited (usu. short) time; transitory.

temporary administration. See ADMINISTRATION.

temporary alimony. See ALIMONY (1).

temporary allegiance. See ALLEGIANCE (1).

Temporary Assistance to Needy Families. A combined state and federal program that provides limited financial assistance to families in need. 42 USCA §§ 601–603a. • This program replaced Aid to Families with Dependent Children. TANF differs from AFDC because families are limited to no more than five years of assistance, and states have more control over eligibility requirements. — Abbr. TANF.

temporary-cessation-of-production doctrine. (1960) *Oil & gas.* The rule that an oil-and-gas lease term "for so long thereafter as oil and gas are produced" will not terminate once production is attained unless the cessation of production is for an unreasonable length of time. See CESSATION-OF-PRODUCTION CLAUSE.

temporary committee. See *special committee* under COMMITTEE (1).

temporary damages. See DAMAGES.

temporary detention. See *pretrial detention* under DETENTION (1).

temporary disability. See DISABILITY (2).

Temporary Emergency Court of Appeals. *Hist.* A special U.S. court created in 1971 with exclusive jurisdiction over appeals from federal district courts in cases arising under the wage-and-price-control program of the Economic Stabilization Act of 1970. • The court consisted of nine district and circuit judges appointed by the Chief Justice. This court was abolished in 1992. — Abbr. TECA. Cf. EMERGENCY COURT OF APPEALS.

temporary employment. See EMPLOYMENT.

temporary exclusion order. See EXCLUSION ORDER (3).

temporary executor. See *acting executor* under EXECUTOR (2).

temporary fiduciary. See FIDUCIARY.

temporary frustration. See FRUSTRATION (1).

temporary injunction. See *preliminary injunction* under INJUNCTION.

temporary injury. See INJURY.

temporary innocent possession. See POSSESSION.

temporary insanity. See INSANITY.

temporary insider. See INSIDER (1).

temporary judge. See *visiting judge* under JUDGE.

temporary marriage. See MARRIAGE (1).

temporary nuisance. See NUISANCE.

temporary order. See ORDER (2).

temporary perfection. See PERFECTION.

temporary restraining order. (1861) **1.** A court order preserving the status quo until a litigant's application for a preliminary or permanent injunction can be heard. • A temporary restraining order may sometimes be granted without notifying the opposing party in advance. Cf. *emergency protective order* under PROTECTIVE ORDER. **2.** See *ex parte injunction* under INJUNCTION. — Often shortened to *restraining order.* — Abbr. TRO.

temporary statute. See STATUTE.

temporary taking. See TAKING (2).

temporary total disability. See DISABILITY (2).

temporary ward. See WARD.

temporary wife. See WIFE.

tempus (**tem**-pəs), *n.* [Latin] *Hist.* Time; a specified duration.

▸ ***tempus continuum*** (**tem**-pəs kən-**tin**-yoo-əm), *n.* [Latin] (17c) *Hist.* Time continuing without interruption; a continuous period.

▸ ***tempus deliberandi*** (**tem**-pəs di-lib-ə-**ran**-dɪ), *n.* [Latin] (1824) *Hist.* The period allowed for deliberation; esp., the time during which an heir could consider whether to accept or reject an inheritance. Cf. JUS DELIBERANDI.

▸ *tempus lugendi* (**tem**-pəs loo-**gen**-DI). *n.* See LUCTUS.

▸ *tempus semestre* (**tem**-pəs si-**mes**-trə), *n.* [Latin] (17c) A period of 182 days (half a year).

▸ *tempus utile* (**tem**-pəs **yoo**-tə-lee), *n.* [Latin "useful time"] (17c) *Hist.* Time that one can use to exercise his or her legal rights; the period within which an action or proceeding must be brought. • This is the period before prescription or limitation cuts off a right.

tenancy. (16c) **1.** The possession or occupancy of land under a lease; a leasehold interest in real estate. **2.** The period of such possession or occupancy. See ESTATE (1). **3.** The possession of real or personal property by right or title, esp. under a conveying instrument such as a deed or will.

▸ **at-will tenancy.** See *tenancy at will.*

▸ **common tenancy.** See *tenancy in common.*

▸ **cotenancy.** (1875) A tenancy with two or more coowners who have unity of possession. • Examples are a joint tenancy and tenancy in common.

▸ **entire tenancy.** (17c) A tenancy possessed by one person, as opposed to a joint or common tenancy. See *estate by entirety* under ESTATE (1).

▸ **general tenancy.** (18c) A tenancy that is not of fixed duration under the parties' agreement.

▸ **holdover tenancy.** See *tenancy at sufferance.*

▸ **joint tenancy.** (17c) A tenancy with two or more coowners who are not spouses on the date of acquisition and have identical interests in a property with the same right of possession. • A joint tenancy differs from a tenancy in common because each joint tenant has a right of survivorship to the other's share (in some states, this right must be clearly expressed in the conveyance — otherwise, the tenancy will be presumed to be a tenancy in common). See RIGHT OF SURVIVORSHIP; SEVERANCE OF ESTATES. Cf. *tenancy in common.*

"As joint-tenancy was a favorite of the common law, no special words or limitations were necessary to call it into being. On the other hand, words or circumstances of negation were indispensable to avoid it. Whenever it was shown that property had vested in two or more persons, by the same joint purchase, there arose at once, both in law and in equity, the presumption that it vested as an estate in joint-tenancy. This presumption is liable to be overthrown in equity by proof of circumstances from which the Court may infer that the parties intended a several rather than a joint estate." A.C. Freeman, *Cotenancy and Partition* 71 (2d ed. 1886).

"The rules for creation of a joint tenancy are these: The joint tenants must get their interests at the same time. They must become entitled to possession at the same time. The interests must be physically undivided interests, and each undivided interest must be an equal fraction of the whole — e.g., a one-third undivided interest to each of three joint tenants. The joint tenants must get their interests by the same instrument — e.g., the same deed or will. The joint tenants must get the same kinds of estates — e.g., in fee simple, for life, and so on." Thomas F. Bergin & Paul G. Haskell, *Preface to Estates in Land and Future Interests* 55 (2d ed. 1984).

▸ **life tenancy.** See *life estate* under ESTATE (1).

▸ **periodic tenancy.** (1891) A tenancy that automatically continues for successive periods — usu. month to month or year to year — unless terminated at the end of a period by notice. • A typical example is a month-to-month apartment lease. This type of tenancy originated through court rulings that, when the lessor received a periodic rent, the lease could not be terminated without reasonable notice. — Also termed *tenancy from period to period; periodic estate; estate from period to period;* (more specif.) *month-to-month tenancy* (or *estate*); *year-to-year tenancy* (or *estate*); *week-to-week tenancy* (or *estate*).

▸ **several tenancy.** (17c) A tenancy that is separate and not held jointly with another person.

▸ **tenancy at sufferance.** (18c) A tenancy arising when a person who has been in lawful possession of property wrongfully remains as a holdover after his or her interest has expired. • A tenancy at sufferance takes the form of either a tenancy at will or a periodic tenancy. — Also termed *holdover tenancy; estate at sufferance.* See HOLDING OVER (1).

"A tenancy at sufferance arises where a tenant, having entered upon land under a valid tenancy, holds over without the landlord's assent or dissent. Such a tenant differs from a trespasser in that his original entry was lawful, and from a tenant at will in that his tenancy exists without the landlord's assent. No rent, as such, is payable, but the tenant is liable to pay compensation for his use and occupation of the land. The tenancy may be determined [i.e., terminated] at any time, and may be converted into a yearly or other periodic tenancy in the usual way, e.g., if rent is paid and accepted with reference to a year in circumstances where the parties intended there to be a tenancy." Robert E. Megarry & M.P. Thompson, *A Manual of the Law of Real Property* 319 (6th ed. 1993).

▸ **tenancy attendant on the inheritance.** (1999) A tenancy for a term that is vested in a trustee in trust for the owner of the inheritance. • The tenancy is a form of personal property to the trustee. — Also termed *tenancy attendant on an inheritance; term attendant on the inheritance.*

▸ **tenancy at will.** (17c) A tenancy in which the tenant holds possession with the landlord's consent but without fixed terms (as for duration or rent); specif., a tenancy that is terminable at the will of either the transferor or the transferee and that has no designated period of duration. • Such a tenancy may be terminated by either party upon fair notice. — Also termed *at-will tenancy; estate at will.*

▸ **tenancy by the curtesy.** See CURTESY.

▸ **tenancy by the entirety** (en-**tI**-ər-tee). See *estate by entirety* under ESTATE (1).

"Tenancy by the entireties is a form of joint tenancy. It resembles joint tenancy in that upon the death of either husband or wife the survivor automatically acquires title to the share of the deceased spouse. Like a joint tenancy, also, it is necessary for the creation of a tenancy by the entireties that the husband and wife acquire title by the same deed or will." Robert Kratovil, *Real Estate Law* 198 (6th ed. 1974).

"Where [tenancy by the entirety] is recognized, it may exist only between a husband and a wife. It resembles, in most respects, the joint tenancy. The only major difference is that a tenant by the entirety may not destroy the other spouse's right of survivorship by transferring his or her interest to another. Whether a tenant by the entirety may transfer *any* interest to a third party — for example, the right of present possession or the contingent right of survivorship — is a matter on which the states differ. Most take the view that no interest may be transferred. The husband and wife may, of course, together convey their estate to a third person. If they *both* wish to convert their tenancy into a tenancy in common or a joint tenancy, they may do so. Upon the death of a tenant by the entirety, no interest passes, in theory, to the surviving spouse. As was true of the joint tenancy, the survivor's ownership is thought simply to expand to absorb the relinquished ownership of the decedent." Thomas F. Bergin & Paul G. Haskell, *Preface to Estates in Land and Future Interests* 55 (2d ed. 1984).

"A tenancy by the entireties could exist in any estate, whether in fee, for life, for years or otherwise. The nature of the tenancy was virtually that of an unseverable joint tenancy; neither husband nor wife could dispose of any interest in the land without the concurrence of the other, nor could one of them cause a forfeiture of the land. The unity of husband and wife was regarded as so complete that they were said to be seised '*per tout et non per mie*,' the survivor being entitled to the whole of the land by force of the original limitation, discharged of the other's right to participate, and not, as in the case of joint tenancy, by virtue of survivorship on the death of the other tenant. Unlike joint tenants, neither tenant was regarded as having any potential share in the land; 'between husband and wife there are no moieties.'" Robert E. Megarry & P.V. Baker, *A Manual of the Law of Real Property* 232–33 (4th ed. 1969) (quoting *Marquis of Winchester's Case*, 3 Co. Rep. 1a, 5a (1583)).

▸ **tenancy by the rod.** See COPYHOLD.

▸ **tenancy by the verge.** See COPYHOLD.

▸ **tenancy for a term.** (17c) A tenancy whose duration is known in years, weeks, or days from the moment of its creation. — Also termed *tenancy for a period*; *tenancy for years*; *term for years*; *term of years*; *estate for a term*; *estate for years*; *lease for years.*

▸ **tenancy from period to period.** See *periodic tenancy.*

▸ **tenancy in common.** (17c) A tenancy by two or more persons, in equal or unequal undivided shares, each person having an equal right to possess the whole property but no right of survivorship. — Also termed *common tenancy*; *estate in common.* Cf. *joint tenancy.*

"If there be a doubt whether an estate was, at its creation, a joint-tenancy or a tenancy in common; or if, conceding the estate to have been a joint-tenancy at its creation, there be a doubt whether there has not been a subsequent severance of the jointure — in all such cases equity will resolve the doubt in favor of tenancy in common." A.C. Freeman, *Cotenancy and Partition* 67 (2d ed. 1886).

"The central characteristic of a tenancy in common is simply that each tenant is deemed to own by himself, with most of the attributes of independent ownership, a physically undivided part of the entire parcel." Thomas F. Bergin & Paul G. Haskell, *Preface to Estates in Land and Future Interests* 54 (2d ed. 1984).

▸ **tenancy in coparcenary.** See COPARCENARY.

▸ **tenancy in fee.** See FEE SIMPLE.

▸ **tenancy in gross.** (1860) A tenancy for a term that is outstanding — that is, one that is unattached to or disconnected from the estate or inheritance, such as one that is in the hands of some third party having no interest in the inheritance.

▸ **tenancy in tail.** See FEE TAIL.

▸ **tenancy par la verge.** See COPYHOLD.

▸ **year-to-year tenancy.** See *periodic tenancy.*

tenancy agreement. See LEASE.

tenant, *n.* (14c) **1.** Someone who holds or possesses lands or tenements by any kind of right or title. See TENANCY.

▸ **copyhold tenant.** See *customary tenant.*

▸ **customary tenant.** (16c) A tenant holding by the custom of the manor. • Over time, customary tenants became known as *copyhold tenants.* See COPYHOLD.

"The lord has a court; in that court the tenant in villeinage, even though he be personally unfree, appears as no mere tenant at will, but as holding permanently, often heritably, on fairly definite terms. He is a customary tenant, *customarius, consuetudinarius*; he holds according to the custom of the manor. . . . Then gradually . . . [d]ealings with villein tenements are set forth upon the rolls of the lord's court; the villein tenement is conceived to be holden 'by roll of court,' or even 'by copy of court roll,' and the mode of conveyance serves to mark off the most beneficial of villeinholds from the most onerous of freeholds . . . . In Henry III's time this process which secured for the tenant in villeinage a written, a registered title, and gave him the name of 'copyholder,' was but beginning . . . ." 2 Frederick Pollock & Frederic W. Maitland, *The History of English Law Before the Time of Edward I* 361, 375 (2d ed. 1899).

▸ **dominant tenant.** (1808) The person who holds a dominant estate and therefore benefits from an easement. Cf. *servient tenant.*

▸ **holdover tenant.** (1880) Someone who remains in possession of real property after a previous tenancy (esp. one under a lease) expires, thus giving rise to a tenancy at sufferance. — Sometimes shortened to *holdover.* See *tenancy at sufferance* under TENANCY.

▸ **hypothetical tenant.** See HYPOTHETICAL TENANT.

▸ **illusory tenant.** (1984) **1.** A fictitious person who, as the landlord's alter ego, subleases an apartment to permit the landlord to circumvent rent-law regulations. **2.** A tenant whose business is to sublease rent-controlled apartments.

▸ **joint tenant.** See *joint tenancy* under TENANCY.

▸ **life tenant.** See LIFE TENANT.

▸ **particular tenant.** A tenant of a limited estate taken out of a fee. See *particular estate* under ESTATE (1).

▸ **prime tenant.** (1942) A commercial or professional tenant with an established reputation that leases substantial, and usu. the most preferred, space in a commercial development. • A prime tenant is important in securing construction financing and in attracting other desirable tenants.

▸ **quasi-tenant.** (18c) A sublessee that the new tenant or reversioner allows to hold over.

▸ **servient tenant.** (1827) The person who holds a servient estate and is therefore burdened by an easement. Cf. *dominant tenant.*

▸ **statutory tenant.** (1881) Someone who is legally entitled to remain on property after the tenancy expires.

▸ **tenant at sufferance.** (17c) A tenant who has been in lawful possession of property and wrongfully remains as a holdover after the tenant's interest has expired. • The tenant may become either a tenant at will or a periodic tenant. — Also termed *permissive tenant.* See *tenancy at will*; *periodic tenancy.*

"**Of Estates at Sufferance.** — A tenant at sufferance is one that comes into the possession of land by lawful title, but holdeth over by wrong, after the determination of his interest. He has only a naked possession, and no estate which he can transfer or transmit, or which is capable of enlargement by release; for he stands in no privity to his landlord, nor is he entitled to notice to quit; and, independent of statute, he is not liable to pay any rent. He holds by the laches of the landlord, who may enter, and put an end to the tenancy when he pleases; but before entry he cannot maintain an action of trespass against the tenant by sufferance." 4 James Kent, *Commentaries on American Law* § 3, at 117 (Charles M. Barnes ed., 13th ed. 1884).

▸ **tenant by elegit.** See ELEGIT.

▸ **tenant by the curtesy.** (15c) A life tenant who receives the estate from his deceased wife by whom he has had legitimate children. • The children hold the remainder interest. See CURTESY.

▸ **tenant by the verge.** See COPYHOLDER.

▸ **tenant for a term.** (18c) A tenant whose tenancy is for a defined number of years, months, weeks, or days, set when the tenancy is created. — Also termed *tenant for a period.*

▸ **tenant for life.** See LIFE TENANT.

▸ **tenant in chief.** (17c) *Hist.* Someone who held land directly of the king. — Also termed *tenant in capite.* See IN CAPITE.

▸ **tenant in common.** (16c) One of two or more tenants who hold the same land by unity of possession but by separate and distinct titles, with each person having an equal right to possess the whole property but no right of survivorship. See *tenancy in common* under TENANCY.

▸ **tenant in demesne** (di-**mayn** *or* di-**meen**). (17c) A feudal tenant who holds land of, and owes services to, a tenant in service. Cf. *tenant in service.*

▸ **tenant in dower.** (15c) A life tenant who is entitled to hold and use one-third of all the real property owned by her deceased husband. See DOWER.

▸ **tenant in fee.** (16c) The owner of land held in fee. — Also termed *tenant in fee simple.*

> "A tenant in fee simple is [one who owns] lands, tenements, or hereditaments, to hold to him and his heirs forever; generally, absolutely, and simply, without mentioning what heirs, but referring that to his own pleasure, or to the disposition of the law. An estate in fee simple is an estate of inheritance without condition, belonging to the owner, and alienable by him or transmissible to his heirs absolutely and simply; it is an estate or interest in land of one holding absolute and exclusive control and dominion over it, no matter how acquired." 31 C.J.S. *Estates* § 11, at 27 (1996).

▸ **tenant in service.** (17c) A feudal tenant who grants an estate to another (a *tenant in demesne*) and is therefore entitled to services from the latter. Cf. *tenant in demesne.*

▸ **undertenant.** See SUBLESSEE.

▸ **week-to-week tenancy.** See *periodic tenancy.*

2. Someone who pays rent for the temporary use and occupation of another's land under a lease or similar arrangement. See LESSEE. **3.** *Archaic.* The defendant in a real action (the plaintiff being called a *demandant*). See *real action* under ACTION (4).

tenantable repair. (17c) A repair that will render premises fit for present habitation. See HABITABILITY.

tenantlike, *adj.* (1812) In accordance with the rights and obligations of a tenant, as in matters of repairs, waste, etc.

tenant paravail. (17c) *Archaic.* A tenant's tenant; a sublessor.

tenant par la verge. See COPYHOLDER.

tenant-right. (16c) *English law.* A tenant's right, upon termination of the tenancy, to payment for unexhausted improvements made on the holding. • This right is governed by the Agricultural Holdings Act of 1986.

tenantry. (17c) A body or group of tenants.

tenant's fixture. See FIXTURE.

tend, *vb.* (14c) **1.** To be disposed toward (something). **2.** To serve, contribute, or conduce in some degree or way; to have a more or less direct bearing or effect. **3.** To be directed or have a tendency to (an end, object, or purpose).

ten-day rule. The doctrine that one who sells goods on credit and then learns that the buyer is insolvent has ten days after the buyer receives the goods to demand their return. • The seller has even longer to demand return if the buyer has made a written representation of solvency to the seller within three months before delivery.

tender, *n.* (16c) **1.** A valid and sufficient offer of performance; specif., an unconditional offer of money or performance to satisfy a debt or obligation <a tender of delivery>. • The tender may save the tendering party from a penalty for nonpayment or nonperformance or may, if the other party unjustifiably refuses the tender, place the other party in default. Cf. OFFER OF PERFORMANCE; CONSIGNATION.

▸ **tender of delivery.** (1821) A seller's putting and holding conforming goods at the buyer's disposition and giving the buyer any notification reasonably necessary to take delivery. • The manner, time, and place for tender are determined by the agreement and by Article 2 of the Uniform Commercial Code.

▸ **tender of performance.** (18c) An obligor's demonstration of readiness, willingness, and ability to perform the obligation; esp., a buyer's demonstration of readiness, willingness, and ability to pay the purchase money, or a seller's offer to deliver merchantable title.• An offer to perform is usu. necessary to hold the defaulting party to a contract liable for breach.

2. Something unconditionally offered to satisfy a debt or obligation. **3.** *Contracts.* Attempted performance that is frustrated by the act of the party for whose benefit it is to take place. • The performance may take the form of either a tender of goods or services, or a tender of payment. Although this sense is quite similar to sense 1, it differs in making the other party's refusal part of the definition itself.

▸ **extrajudicial tender.** (1865) *Civil law.* An out-of-court tender and delivery.

▸ **judicial tender.** (1836) *Civil law.* A tender with actual delivery of money to a party while in court. • The object is to avoid further expense. If the pursuer is awarded no higher sum than that tendered, the pursuer is then found liable for the defender's expenses from the date of the tender. — Also termed *tender in open court.*

▸ **perfect tender.** (18c) A seller's tender that meets the contractual terms entered into with the buyer concerning the quality and specifications of the goods sold. See PERFECT-TENDER RULE.

▸ **tender in open court.** See *judicial tender.*

4. An offer or bid put forward for acceptance <a tender for the construction contract>. **5.** Something that serves as a means of payment, such as coin, banknotes, or other circulating medium; money <legal tender>. — **tender,** *vb.*

tender, plea of. See PLEA OF TENDER.

tender in open court. See *judicial tender* under TENDER (3).

tender offer. (1964) A public offer to buy a minimum number of shares directly from a corporation's shareholders at a fixed price, usu. at a substantial premium over the market price, in an effort to take control of the corporation. — Also termed *takeover offer*; *takeover bid*. Cf. *public-exchange offer* under OFFER.

"Cash tender offers are a species of corporate control transaction. One firm solicits 'tenders' of another's stock. The offer runs to the shareholders, not the managers. If the bidder obtains enough stock, it takes control through one of the standard devices: it uses the shares to vote out the existing board and install its own, or it merges the acquired firm into itself or a subsidiary. Because the tender offer is a voluntary transaction between the bidder and the target's investors, it has a built-in market test. Investors won't tender unless the offer is higher than the one prevailing in the market (which reflects the price of potentially competitive bids); bidders won't make such offers unless they believe they can use the target's assets well enough to make the premium payment profitable, which implies increased productivity." Frank H. Easterbrook & Daniel R. Fischel, *The Economic Structure of Corporate Law* 162 (1991).

"Broadly speaking, a direct solicitation of a corporation's stockholders to sell their shares to an acquirer is known as a tender offer (because the acquirer is asking the existing stockholders to tender their shares for sale)." Franklin A. Gevurtz, *Corporation Law* § 7.3, at 673 (2000).

▸ **cash tender offer.** (1966) A tender offer in which the bidder offers to pay cash for the target's shares, as opposed to offering other corporate shares in exchange. • Most tender offers involve cash.

▸ **creeping tender offer.** See *creeping acquisition* under ACQUISITION.

tender of issue. (1811) *Common-law pleading.* A form attached to a traverse, by which the traversing party refers the issue to the proper mode of trial.

"[I]t is the object of all pleadings to bring the parties, in the course of their mutual altercations, to an issue that is a single entire point, affirmed on the one side and denied on the other; and it is to effect this object that the above rule was established. There can be no arrival at this point until one or the other of the parties, by the conclusion of his pleading, offers an issue for the acceptance of his opponent, and this offer is called the 'tender of issue.'" Benjamin J. Shipman, *Handbook of Common-Law Pleading* § 254, at 446 (Henry Winthrop Ballantine ed., 3d ed. 1923).

tender-years doctrine. (1954) *Family law.* The doctrine holding that custody of very young children (usu. five years of age and younger) should generally be awarded to the mother in a divorce unless she is found to be unfit. • This doctrine has been rejected in most states and replaced by a presumption of joint custody. See MATERNAL-PREFERENCE DOCTRINE; PRIMARY-CAREGIVER DOCTRINE.

tender-years hearsay exception. See HEARSAY EXCEPTION.

tenement. (14c) **1.** Property (esp. land) held by freehold; an estate or holding of land.

▸ **dominant tenement.** See *dominant estate* under ESTATE (4).

▸ **servient tenement** (sər-vee-ənt). See *servient estate* under ESTATE (4).

2. A house or other building used as a residence. **3.** An apartment. **4.** TENEMENT HOUSE.

tenement house. (1858) A low-rent apartment building, usu. in poor condition and often meeting only minimal safety and sanitary conditions. — Sometimes shortened to *tenement.*

tenendas (tə-**nen**-das), *n.* [Law Latin "to be held"] (17c) *Hist.* The charter clause stating the nature of the tenure, so called because of the first word of the clause.

tenendum (tə-**nen**-dəm). [Latin "to be held"] (17c) A clause in a deed designating the kind of tenure by which the things granted are to be held. — Also termed *tenendum clause*; (in Scots law) *tenendas*. See HABENDUM ET TENENDUM. Cf. HABENDUM CLAUSE (1).

10-K. A financial report filed annually with the SEC by a registered corporation. • The report typically includes an audited financial statement, a description of the corporation's business and financial condition, and summaries of other financial data. — Also termed *Form 10-K*. Cf. 8-K; 10-Q.

Tennessee Valley Authority. A government-owned corporation, created in 1933, that conducts a unified program of resource development to advance economic growth in the Tennessee Valley region. • The Authority's activities include flood control, navigation development, electric-power production, fertilizer development, recreation improvement, and forestry-and-wildlife development. Though its power program is financially self-supporting, the Authority's other programs are financed primarily by congressional appropriations. — Abbr. TVA.

tenor, *n.* (14c) **1.** An exact copy of an instrument. **2.** The exact words of a legal document, esp. as cited in a pleading. **3.** The meaning of a legal document.

ten-percent bond. See BOND (2).

10-Q. An unaudited financial report filed quarterly with the SEC by a registered corporation. • The 10-Q is less detailed than the 10-K. — Also termed *Form 10-Q*. Cf. 10-K.

tentative agenda. See *proposed agenda* under AGENDA.

tentative trust. See *Totten trust* under TRUST (3).

Tenterden's Act. *English law.* An 1828 statute that amended the Statute of Frauds (1677) by preventing parties from circumventing the promise-must-be-in-writing requirement by suing instead for the tort of deceit. — Also termed *Lord Tenterden's Act*; *Statute of Frauds Amendment Act 1828*.

tenth. See TITHE.

Tenth Amendment. The constitutional amendment, ratified as part of the Bill of Rights in 1791, providing that any powers not constitutionally delegated to the federal government, nor prohibited to the states, are reserved for the states or the people. — Also termed *Reserved Power Clause*.

1031 exchange (ten-thər-tee-**wən**). (1972) **1.** An exchange of like-kind property that is exempt from income-tax consequences under IRC (26 USCA) § 1031. Cf. TAX-FREE EXCHANGE. **2.** TAX-FREE EXCHANGE.

tenure (**ten**-yər), *n.* (15c) **1.** A right, term, or mode of holding lands or tenements in subordination to a superior. • In feudal times, real property was held predominantly as part of a tenure system. — Also termed *feudal tenure*. **2.** A particular feudal mode of holding lands, such as socage, gavelkind, villeinage, and frankalmoign.

"Most of the feudal incidents and consequences of socage tenure were expressly abolished in New York by the act of

1787; and they were [later] wholly and entirely annihilated by the New York Revised Statutes . . . . They were also abolished by statute in Connecticut, 1793; and they have never existed, or they have ceased to exist, in all essential respects, in every other state. The only feudal fictions and services to be retained in any part of the United States consist of the feudal principle, that the lands are held of some superior or lord, to whom the obligation of fealty, and to pay a determinate rent, are due. . . . The lord paramount of all socage land was none other than the people of the state, and to them, and them only, the duty of fealty was to be rendered . . . ." 3 James Kent, *Commentaries on American Law* *509–10 (George Comstock ed., 11th ed. 1866).

▸ **base tenure.** (15c) *Hist.* The holding of property in villeinage rather than by military service or free service. See VILLEINAGE.

▸ **copyhold tenure.** See COPYHOLD.

▸ **ecclesiastical tenure.** See *tenure by divine service.*

▸ **free tenure.** (16c) *Feudal law.* The relationship between a landowner and a tenant who was a free man under a duty to render services or pay money for the use of the land granted as a tenancy in freehold. See *military tenure*; *tenure by divine service*; SOCAGE. Cf. *unfree tenure.*

▸ **lay tenure.** (18c) *Hist.* Any tenure not held through religious service, such as a base tenure or a freehold tenure. • The three historical types of lay tenures are *knight-service, socage,* and *serjeanty.* See *knight-service* under SERVICE (6); SOCAGE; SERJEANTY. Cf. *tenure by divine service.*

▸ **military tenure.** (17c) A tenure that bears some relation to military service, such as knight-service, grand serjeanty, and cornage. — Also termed *tenure in chivalry.*

▸ **spiritual tenure.** (17c) A tenure that bears some relation to religious exercises, such as frankalmoign and tenure by divine service.

▸ ***tenure ad furcam et flagellum*** (ad **fər**-kəm et flə-**jel**-əm). [Latin] *Hist.* Tenure by gallows and whip. • This was the meanest of the servile tenures — the bondman was at the disposal of the lord for life and limb.

▸ **tenure by divine service.** (16c) *Hist.* A tenure obligating the tenant to perform an expressly defined divine service, such as singing a certain number of masses or distributing a fixed sum of alms. — Also termed *ecclesiastical tenure.* Cf. *lay tenure.*

▸ **tenure in chivalry.** See *military tenure.*

▸ **unfree tenure.** *Hist.* A tenure held by anyone other than a freeman. Cf. *free tenure.*

"The greater part of the land was . . . actually cultivated by men who held by unfree tenure. The technical distinction between free and unfree tenure was that the common-law courts protected free tenure, but did not protect unfree tenure, or, in other words, the ancient actions, both proprietory and possessory, were available only for 'freeholders.' The social distinction, speaking broadly, was that, as a rule, unfree tenants comprised the humblest classes, and were known as villeins." William L. Burdick, *Handbook of the Law of Real Property* 48–49 (1914).

▸ **villein tenure.** See VILLEINAGE.

3. A status afforded to a teacher or professor as a protection against summary dismissal without sufficient cause. • This status has long been considered a cornerstone of academic freedom. **4.** More generally, the legal protection of a long-term relationship, such as employment. — **tenurial** (ten-**yuur**-ee-əl), *adj.*

tenure ad furcam et flagellum. See TENURE (2).

tenure by divine service. See TENURE (2).

tenured faculty. (1953) The members of a school's teaching staff who hold their positions for life or until retirement, and who may not be discharged except for cause.

tenure in capite. See IN CAPITE.

tenure in chivalry. See *military tenure* under TENURE (2).

tepid bench. See *lukewarm bench* under BENCH.

teratogen (tə-**rat**-ə-jən), *n.* (1959) An agent, usu. a chemical, that causes injury to a fetus or causes any of various birth defects <alcohol is a teratogen to the developing brain of a fetus>. — **teratogenic** (tə-rat-ə-**jen**-ik), *adj.*

terce. (15c) *Hist. Scots law.* A widow's interest in one-third of her husband's real property, if she has not accepted some other special provision. • The couple must have been married at least a year and a day or else have produced a living child together. See DOWER.

terce land. (16c) *Hist. Scots law.* Income-producing real property in which a widow has a pecuniary interest because it was owned by her husband.

tercer. (16c) *Hist. Scots law.* A widow who has an interest in one-third of her husband's real property. — Also spelled *tiercear.*

tergiversatio (tər-jiv-ər-**say**-shee-oh), *n.* [Latin "being reluctant, hanging back"] *Roman law.* A delay tactic, esp. an accuser's failure to pursue a criminal charge, perhaps by not appearing at the trial. • To withdraw an accusation, it was necessary to obtain the court's permission for an annulment (*abolitio*). In A.D. 61, a law was passed by which anyone convicted of *tergiversatio* was subject to a fine. See CALUMNIA. Cf. PRAEVARICATIO. Pl. ***tergiversationes*** (tər-jiv-ər-say-shee-**oh**-neez).

tergiversation. **1.** The failure to give a straight answer; verbal evasion. **2.** Abandonment of a claim, a stand, or a belief; specif., the relinquishment of a position formerly taken or advocated. — **tergiversate,** *vb.*

term, *n.* (14c) **1.** A word or phrase; esp., an expression that has a fixed meaning in some field <term of art>. **2.** A contractual stipulation <the delivery term provided for shipment within 30 days>. See CONDITION (3).

▸ **collateral term.** See *supplementary term.*

▸ **essential term.** See *fundamental term.*

▸ **fundamental term.** (1873) **1.** A contractual provision that must be included for a contract to exist; a contractual provision that specifies an essential purpose of the contract, so that a breach of the provision through inadequate performance makes the performance not only defective but essentially different from what had been promised. **2.** A contractual provision that must be included in the contract to satisfy the statute of frauds. — Also termed *essential term*; *vital term.*

▸ **implied term.** (18c) A provision not expressly agreed to by the parties but instead read into the contract by a court as being implicit. • An implied term should not, in theory, contradict the contract's express terms.

▸ **material term.** (1839) A contractual provision dealing with a significant issue such as subject matter, price, payment, quantity, quality, duration, or the work to be done.

▸ **nonessential term.** See *nonfundamental term.*

▸ **nonfundamental term.** (1969) Any contractual provision that is not regarded as a fundamental term. — Also termed *nonessential term; nonvital term.*

▸ **parol term.** See *supplementary term.*

▸ **supplementary term.** (1900) A contractual term, esp. an oral one, additional to those set forth in a written contract. — Also termed *collateral term; parol term.*

"If the parties to a contract have not put all its terms in writing, parol evidence of the supplementary terms is admissible, not to vary, but to complete, the written contract. Thus, where a written contract for the sale of goods mentions the price, but is silent as to the terms of payment, the terms may be shown by parol evidence. And a subsequent agreement changing the terms of a written contract may be shown by parol evidence." William L. Clark, *Handbook of the Law of Contracts* 492 (Archibald H. Throckmorton ed., 3d ed. 1914).

▸ **vital term.** See *fundamental term.*

3. (*pl.*) Provisions that define an agreement's scope; conditions or stipulations <terms of sale>. **4.** A fixed period of time; esp., the period for which an estate is granted <term of years>.

▸ **attendant term.** (1983) A long period (such as 1,000 years) specified as the duration of a mortgage, created to protect the mortgagor's heirs' interest in the land by not taking back title to the land once it is paid for, but rather by assigning title to a trustee who holds the title in trust for the mortgagor and the mortgagor's heirs. • This arrangement gives the heirs another title to the property in case the interest they inherited proves somehow defective. These types of terms have been largely abolished. See *tenancy attendant on the inheritance* under TENANCY.

"The advantage derived from attendant terms is the security which they afford to purchasers and mortgagees. If the *bona fide* purchaser or mortgagee should happen to take a defective conveyance or mortgage, by which he acquires a mere equitable title, he may, by taking an assignment of an outstanding term to a trustee for himself, cure the defect, so far as to entitle himself to the legal estate during the term, in preference to any creditor, of whose incumbrance he had not notice, at or before the time of completing his contract for the purchase or mortgage. He may use this term to protect his possessions, or to recover it when lost. This protection extends generally as against all estates and incumbrances created intermediately between the raising of the term and the time of the purchase or mortgage; and the outstanding term, so assigned to a trustee for the purchaser or mortgagee, will prevail over the intermediate legal title to the inheritance." 4 James Kent, *Commentaries on American Law* *87 (George Comstock ed., 11th ed. 1866).

▸ **primary term.** See PRIMARY TERM.

▸ **satisfied term.** (18c) A term of years in land that has satisfied the purpose for which it was created before the term's expiration.

▸ **secondary term.** See SECONDARY TERM.

▸ **term for deliberating.** (1843) The time given a beneficiary to decide whether to accept or reject an inheritance or other succession.

▸ **term in gross.** (1852) A term that is unattached to an estate or inheritance. See *tenancy in gross* under TENANCY.

▸ **term of years.** (16c) **1.** A fixed period covering a precise number of years. — Also termed *tenancy for a term.* **2.** *English law.* A fixed period covering less than a year, or a specified number of years and a fraction of a year. • This sense applies under a seminal English statute — the Law of Property Act of 1925.

"In effect, 'term of years' seems to mean a term for any period having a fixed and certain duration as a minimum. Thus, in addition to a tenancy for a specified number of years (e.g., 'to X for ninety-nine years'), such tenancies as a yearly tenancy or a weekly tenancy are 'terms of years' within the definition, for there is a minimum duration of a year or a week respectively. But a lease 'for the life of X' cannot exist as a legal estate, and the same, perhaps, applies to tenancies at will or at sufferance (if they are estates at all) for their duration is wholly uncertain." Robert E. Megarry & M.P. Thompson, *A Manual of the Law of Real Property* 74 (6th ed. 1993).

▸ **unexpired term.** (18c) The remainder of a period prescribed by law or by agreement.

5. The period or session during which a court conducts judicial business <the most recent term was busy indeed>. — Also termed (in sense 5) *term of court.* See SESSION.

▸ **additional term.** A distinct, added term to a previous term.

▸ **adjourned term.** (18c) A continuance of a previous or regular term but not a separate term; the same term prolonged.

▸ **appearance term.** (18c) The regular judicial term in which a party is required to appear, usu. the first one after legal service has been made.

▸ **civil term.** The period during which a civil court hears cases.

▸ **criminal term.** (1839) A term of court during which indictments are found and returned, and criminal trials are held.

▸ **equity term.** (1836) The period during which a court tries only equity cases.

▸ **general term.** A regular term of court — that is, the period during which a court ordinarily sits. — Also termed *stated term.*

▸ **regular term.** (1820) A term of court begun at the time appointed by law and continued, in the court's discretion, until the court lawfully adjourns.

▸ **special term.** (1803) A term of court scheduled outside the general term, usu. for conducting extraordinary business.

▸ **stated term.** See *general term.*

▸ **term probatory.** (16c) *Eccles. law.* **1.** The period given to the promoter of an ecclesiastical suit to produce witnesses and prove the case. **2.** *Hist.* The time assigned for taking testimony. — Sometimes termed (in sense 2) *probatory term.*

▸ **term to conclude.** (18c) *Eccles. law.* A deadline imposed by the judge for all parties to renounce any further exhibits and allegations.

▸ **term to propound all things.** (18c) *Eccles. law.* A deadline imposed by the judge for the parties to exhibit all evidence supporting their positions.

6. *Hist. English law.* One of the four periods in a year during which the courts are in session to conduct judicial business. • Terms came into use in the 13th century, and their dates varied. The four terms — Hilary, Easter, Trinity, and Michaelmas — were abolished by the Judicature Acts of 1873–1875, and the legal year was divided into sittings and vacations. Terms are still maintained by the Inns of Court to determine various time periods and dates, such as a call to the bar or observance of a Grand Day.

term annuity. See *annuity certain* under ANNUITY.

term attendant on the inheritance. See *tenancy attendant on the inheritance* under TENANCY.

term bond. See BOND (3).

term clause. See HABENDUM CLAUSE.

term day. See *quarter day* under DAY.

term deposit. See *time deposit* under DEPOSIT (2).

term fee. (1828) *English law.* A sum that a solicitor may charge a client, and that the client (if successful) may recover from the losing party, payable for each term in which any proceedings following the summons take place.

term for deliberating. See TERM (4).

term for years. See *tenancy for a term* under TENANCY.

terminable interest. See INTEREST (2).

terminable property. See PROPERTY.

terminal disclaimer. See DISCLAIMER.

terminal value. (1882) **1.** MATURITY VALUE. **2.** See *salvage value* under VALUE (2).

terminate, *vb.* (17c) **1.** To put an end to; to bring to an end. **2.** To end; to conclude.

termination, *n.* (15c) **1.** The act of ending something; EXTINGUISHMENT <termination of the partnership by winding up its affairs>.

▸ **termination of conditional contract.** (1985) The act of putting an end to all unperformed portions of a conditional contract.

▸ **termination of employment.** (1843) The complete severance of an employer–employee relationship.

2. The end of something in time or existence; conclusion or discontinuance <the insurance policy's termination left the doctor without liability coverage>. **3.** A medical operation to end the life of a fetus before birth; abortion. • In sense 3, *termination* is merely a euphemism. — **terminate,** *vb.* — **terminable,** *adj.*

termination clause. See CANCELLATION CLAUSE.

termination fee. (1938) A fee paid if a party voluntarily backs out of a deal to sell or purchase a business or a business's assets. • Termination fees are usu. negotiated and agreed on as part of corporate merger or acquisition negotiations. The fee is designed to protect the prospective buyer and to deter the target corporation from entertaining bids from other parties. — Also termed *breakup fee.*

termination-for-convenience clause. (1944) A contractual provision allowing the government to terminate all or a portion of a contract when it chooses. • Among the governmental contracts that often include a termination-for-convenience clause are service contracts, research-and-development contracts, and fixed-price contracts. *See* 48 CFR § 52.249-1, -2.

termination hearing. See *termination-of-parental-rights hearing* under HEARING.

termination of parental rights. (1939) *Family law.* The legal severing of a parent's rights, privileges, and responsibilities regarding his or her child. • Termination of a parent's rights frees the child to be adopted by someone else. — Abbr. TPR. See *termination-of-parental-rights hearing* under HEARING; PARENTAL RIGHTS.

termination-of-parental-rights hearing. See HEARING.

termination proceeding. (1939) An administrative action to end a person's or entity's status or relationship. • For example, the International Banking Act authorizes the International Banking Board to institute a termination proceeding when a foreign bank or its U.S. agency or branch is convicted of money-laundering. 12 USCA § 3105(e).

terminer. See OYER AND TERMINER.

term in gross. See TERM (4).

termini habiles (**tər**-mi-nɪ **hab**-ə-leez), *n.* [Law Latin] *Hist.* (18c) Sufficient grounds. • The phrase usu. referred to the facts necessary to establish a prescriptive right.

termini sanctorum (**tər**-mi-nɪ sangk-**tor**-əm), *n.* [Law Latin] *Hist.* The limits of a sanctuary. See SANCTUARY (1).

term interest. *Oil & gas.* A mineral interest or royalty interest that is not perpetual. • A term interest may be for a fixed term (e.g., for 25 years) or defeasible (e.g., for 25 years and so long thereafter as there is production from the premises).

terminus ad quem (**tər**-mi-nəs ad kwem). [Law Latin] (16c) *Hist.* The point to which. • The phrase appeared in reference to the point before which some action must be taken.

terminus a quo (**tər**-mi-nəs ay kwoh). [Law Latin] (16c) *Hist.* The point from which. • The phrase appeared in reference to the point from which something is calculated, or the earliest time at which some action is possible.

term life insurance. See LIFE INSURANCE.

term loan. See LOAN.

term of art. (17c) **1.** A word or phrase having a specific, precise meaning in a given specialty, apart from its general meaning in ordinary contexts. • Examples in law include *and his heirs* and *res ipsa loquitur.* **2.** Loosely, a jargonistic word or phrase. — Also termed *word of art.*

> "As for *Terms of Art,* which are above the Reach of the common People, the Rule is, That *they be taken according to the Definition of the Learned in each Art.*" Samuel Pufendorf, *Of the Law of Nature and Nations* 536 (Basil Kennett trans., 4th ed. 1719).

term-of-art canon. (1994) In statutory construction, the principle that if a term has acquired a technical or specialized meaning in a particular context, the term should be presumed to have that meaning if used in that context.

term of court. See TERM (5).

term of office. (16c) The period during which an elected officer or appointee may hold office, perform its functions, and enjoy its privileges and emoluments.

term of years. 1. See TERM (4). **2.** See *tenancy for a term* under TENANCY.

termor (**tər**-mər). (14c) Someone who holds lands or tenements for a term of years or for life.

term paper. See TERM SHEET (1).

term policy. See INSURANCE POLICY.

term probatory. See TERM (5).

terms. See YEAR BOOKS.

term sheet. *Securities.* **1.** A document setting forth all information that is material to investors about the offering but is not disclosed in the accompanying prospectus or the confirmation. — Also termed *term paper.* **2.** LETTER OF INTENT.

▸ **abbreviated term sheet.** (1995) A term sheet that includes (1) the description of the securities as required by Item 202 of SEC Regulation S-K, or a good summary of that information; and (2) all material changes to the issuer's affairs required to be disclosed on SEC Form S-3 or F-3, as applicable.

termtime. (15c) The time of the year when a court is in session.

term to conclude. See TERM (5).

term to propound all things. See TERM (5).

terra, *n.* [Latin] Land.

terra nullius (**ter**-ə **nəl**-ee-əs), *n.* [Latin "the land of no one"] (1885) A territory not belonging to any particular country.

terre-tenant (**tair** ten-ənt). (15c) **1.** Someone who has actual possession of land; the occupant of land. **2.** Someone who has an interest in a judgment debtor's land after the judgment creditor's lien has attached to the land (such as a subsequent purchaser). — Also spelled *tertenant* (**tər**-ten-ənt). — Also termed *land-tenant.*

territorial, *adj.* (17c) Having to do with a particular geographical area.

territorial court. See COURT.

territorialism. (1977) The traditional approach to choice of law, whereby the place of injury or of contract formation determines which state's law will be applied in a case. See CHOICE OF LAW. — **territorialist,** *adj.* & *n.*

territoriality. *Int'l law.* The principle that a country has the right of sovereignty within its borders.

> "Three maxims formulated by the seventeenth-century Dutch scholar Ulrich Huber undergird the modern concept of territoriality: (1) a state's laws have force only within the state's boundaries; (2) anyone found within the state's boundaries is subject to the state's authority; and (3) comity will discipline sovereign exercises of authority so that the territorial effect of each state's laws is respected." Paul Goldstein, *International Copyright: Principles, Law, and Practice* 64 (2001).

territorial jurisdiction. See JURISDICTION.

territorial law. The law that applies to all persons within a given territory regardless of their citizenship or nationality. Cf. PERSONAL LAW.

> "[T]he expression 'territorial law' . . . is not confined to the positive rules that regulate acts and events occurring within the jurisdiction, but includes also rules for the choice of law. English rules for the choice of law are part of the law of England and when a court, for instance, tests the substantial validity of a contract made by two foreigners in Paris by reference to French law, it applies a rule imposed by the English sovereign and it may accurately be described as putting into force part of the territorial law of England." G.C. Cheshire, *Private International Law* 32 (6th ed. 1961).

territorial property. (17c) Land and water over which a state has jurisdiction and control, whether the legal title is held by the state or by a private individual or entity. • Lakes and waters wholly within a state are generally its property, as is the marginal sea within the three-mile limit, but bays and gulfs are not always recognized as state property.

territorial sea. See SEA.

territorial waters. See WATERS.

territory, *n.* (14c) **1.** A geographical area included within a particular government's jurisdiction; the portion of the earth's surface that is in a state's exclusive possession and control. Cf. DEPENDENCY; INSULAR AREA.

▸ **non-self-governing territory.** (1941) *Int'l law.* A territory that is governed by another country. • These types of territories are rarely allowed representation in the governing country's legislature.

▸ **occupied territory.** (18c) Territory that is under the effective control and authority of a belligerent armed force. • The term does not normally apply to a territory whose civil authority has an agreement, express or implied, for an outside entity's administration of territorial affairs.

▸ **trust territory.** (1945) *Int'l law.* A territory to which the United Nations' international trusteeship system formerly applied; a territory once administered by the United Nations or a member state for the political, economic, educational, and social advancement of its inhabitants. • All territories that were subject to this system either became independent countries or opted to become part of another country.

2. A part of the United States not included within any state but organized with a separate legislature (such as Guam and the U.S. Virgin Islands). Cf. COMMONWEALTH (2); DEPENDENCY. — **territorial,** *adj.*

> "The United States has had territories from its inception. The Northwest Territory, along with the thirteen original states, was a part of the nation when the constitution was ratified. The original U.S. constitution expressly granted Congress the power to govern territories. Before the Civil War all of the territories were on the North American continent and contiguous with the states or the other territories. After the Civil War with the purchase of Alaska in 1867 (called 'Seward's Folly' or 'Seward's Icebox' by detractors) came the United States' first acquisition of non-contiguous territory. Alaska did, however, have certain basics in common with earlier U.S. territories. Alaska was on the North American continent and sparsely populated. . . . In the latter part of the 19th century, the U.S. became interested in various islands around the world." Stanley K. Laughlin Jr., *The Law of United States Territories and Affiliated Jurisdictions* § 3.1, at 25–26 (1995).

territory of a judge. (18c) The territorial jurisdiction of a particular court. See JURISDICTION (3).

terror, *n.* **1.** Extreme fear. **2.** One or more violent acts that cause extreme fear.

terrorem clause. See NO-CONTEST CLAUSE.

terrorism, *n.* (18c) The use or threat of violence to intimidate or cause panic, esp. as a means of achieving a political end. *See* 18 USCA § 2331. See also *terroristic threat* under THREAT; *terrorism insurance* under INSURANCE. — **terrorist,** *adj.* & *n.*

> "Terrorism as a tactic has a very long history and generally refers to the intentional use of terror-induced fear by an individual or group to amplify the effects of a strategic act

of violence. It has often been associated with actors who are at a distinct military or tactical disadvantage against a larger threat or enemy, and who have a limited capacity to strike back on an equal or sustained basis; hence, the perceived need to use a strategy that would enhance an otherwise limited capacity. Nevertheless, it is also possible for dominant actors, including states, to utilize terror-based tactics, sometimes due to a perceived lack of more creative strategic options, and sometimes due to a sense of impunity and superiority. Regardless of the actors or their motivation, at least in contemporary practice, terrorism is always and everywhere in violation of international law." Darren C. Zook, "Terrorism," in 4 *The Oxford International Encyclopedia of Peace* 145, 145 (Nigel J. Young ed., 2010).

▸ **agriterrorism.** Terrorism focused on disrupting or destroying a country's food supply by attacking agricultural industries with plant or animal pathogens. — Also spelled *agroterrorism.*

▸ **bioterrorism.** (1987) Terrorism involving the intentional release of harmful biological agents, such as bacteria or viruses, into the air, food, or water supply, esp. of humans. — Also termed *biological terrorism.*

▸ **cyberterrorism.** (1994) Terrorism committed by using a computer to make unlawful attacks and threats of attack against computers, networks, and electronically stored information, and actually causing the target to fear or experience harm.

▸ **domestic terrorism.** (1858) **1.** Terrorism that occurs primarily within the territorial jurisdiction of the United States. 18 USCA § 2331(5). **2.** Terrorism that is carried out against one's own government or fellow citizens.

"Domestic terrorism consists of acts of violence perpetrated by an individual or a group against others within the United States, with the purpose of frightening portions of a population or making a political statement. Means of attack can range from shootings to arson, bombings, kidnappings, and sabotage. Usually these acts are extralegal — not officially sanctioned by the state or local governments — although there have been exceptions in the case of white-supremacist violence. Acts of domestic terror have occurred in the United States since the seventeenth century." Catherine McNicol Stock & Laura Koroski, "Terrorism, Domestic," in 2 *The Oxford Encyclopedia of American Social History* 419, 419 (Lynn Dumenil ed., 2012).

▸ **ecoterrorism.** (1980) Terrorism related to environmental issues or animal rights; esp., someone's effort to disrupt a company or other entity whose practices are seen to harm the environment or threaten animal welfare. — Also termed *enviroterrorism*; *ecological terrorism*; *environmental terrorism*; *ecosabotage*; *ecovandalism.*

▸ **international terrorism.** (1926) Terrorism that occurs primarily outside the territorial jurisdiction of the United States, or that transcends national boundaries by the means in which it is carried out, the people it is intended to intimidate, or the place where the perpetrators operate or seek asylum. 18 USCA § 2331(1). Cf. *state-sponsored terrorism.*

▸ **paper terrorism.** (1995) The fraudulent use of Uniform Commercial Code filings to harass public officials and government employees by attaching liens to their private property.

▸ **state-sponsored terrorism.** (1973) **1.** International terrorism supported by a sovereign government to pursue strategic and political objectives. **2.** See *state terrorism* (1). Cf. *international terrorism.*

▸ **state terrorism.** (1971) **1.** Terrorism practiced by a sovereign government, esp. against its own people. • Under international legal principles of sovereignty, a government's conduct that has effects only within its borders is generally not subject to interference from other countries. **2.** See *state-sponsored terrorism* (1).

terrorism insurance. See INSURANCE.

terrorist. Someone who uses violence such as bombing, shooting, or kidnapping in an attempt to intimidate or cause panic, esp. as a means of achieving a political end.

terroristic threat. See THREAT (1).

terrorizing, *n. Family law.* A parent's or caregiver's act of orally assaulting, bullying, or frightening a child, or causing the child to believe that the world is a hostile place.

***Terry* search.** See STOP-AND-FRISK.

***Terry* stop.** See STOP-AND-FRISK.

tertenant. See TERRE-TENANT.

tertia (**tər**-shee-ə), *n. Hist.* A third. • A widow's terce was usu. referred to as *tertia rationabilis* ("a reasonable third").

tertium quid (**tər**-shee-əm kwid). [Latin] (18c) *Scots law.* A third thing that has qualities distinct from the prior two components.

"Thus where, by the confusion of liquids or commixture of solids, the subject produced is of a character different from that of either of its component parts, it is called a *tertium quid.*" John Trayner, *Trayner's Latin Maxims* 598 (4th ed. 1894).

tertius gaudens (**tər**-shee-əs **gaw**-denz). [Latin "a rejoicing third"] (1892) A third party who profits when two others dispute.

test, *n.* **1.** A set of questions, exercises, or practical activities that measure either what someone knows or what someone or something is like or can do. **2.** A medical examination on part of one's body, usu. administered for diagnostic reasons. **3.** A procedure designed to discover whether equipment or a product works correctly, or else to discover more about it. **4.** A difficult situation in which a person's or thing's qualities are revealed.

testable, *adj.* (17c) **1.** Capable of being tested <a testable hypothesis>. **2.** Capable of being transferred by will <today virtually all property is considered testable>. **3.** Capable of making a will <an 18-year-old person is testable in this state>. **4.** Legally qualified to testify as a witness or give evidence <the witness is testable about the statement>.

Test Act. *Hist.* An English statute that required a person who occupied a public office or position of trust to be a member of the Church of England, to swear the Oath of Supremacy, and to sign a declaration against transubstantiation. 25 Car. 2, ch. 2 (1673). • The Act was repealed in 1828.

test action. See *test case* (2) under CASE (1).

testacy. (1864) The quality, state, or condition of a person having died with a valid will. Cf. INTESTACY.

testament (**tes**-tə-mənt). (14c) **1.** Traditionally, a will disposing of personal property. Cf. DEVISE (4). **2.** WILL (2).

▸ **closed testament.** See *mystic will* under WILL.

▸ **inofficious testament.** (17c) *Civil law.* A will that does not dispose of property to the testator's natural heirs; esp., a will that deprives the heirs of a portion of the estate to which they are entitled by law. — Also termed *inofficious will; unofficious will.* See *forced heir* under HEIR.

▸ **military testament.** See *soldier's will* under WILL.

▸ **mutual testament.** See *mutual will* under WILL.

▸ **mystic testament.** See *mystic will* under WILL.

▸ **officious testament.** (1802) *Civil law.* A will that disposes of property to the testator's family; a will that reserves the legitime for the testator's children and other natural heirs. — Also termed *officious will.* See LEGITIME.

▸ **sealed testament.** See *mystic will* under WILL.

▸ **secret testament.** See *mystic will* under WILL.

testamentary (tes-tə-**men**-tə-ree *or* -tree), *adj.* (14c) **1.** Of, relating to, or involving a will or testament <testamentary intent>. **2.** Provided for or appointed by a will <testamentary guardian>. **3.** Created by a will <testamentary gift>.

testamentary capacity. See CAPACITY (3).

testamentary class. See CLASS (3).

testamentary condition. See CONDITION (2).

testamentary disposition. See DISPOSITION (1).

testamentary executor. See EXECUTOR (2).

testamentary gift. See GIFT.

testamentary guardian. See GUARDIAN (1).

testamentary heir. See HEIR.

testamentary instrument. See WILL.

testamentary intent. See INTENT (1).

testamentary power of appointment. See POWER OF APPOINTMENT.

testamentary succession. See SUCCESSION (2).

testamentary transfer. See TRANSFER.

testamentary trust. See TRUST (3).

testamentary trustee. See TRUSTEE (1).

testamenti factio (tes-tə-**men**-tɪ **fak**-shee-oh). [Latin "right to make a testament"] (1807) *Roman law.* **1.** Broadly, the capacity to take part in a will, as testator, heir, or witness. **2.** The capacity to make a will, open to any citizen, male or female, *sui juris*, and over puberty. • This term is sometimes known as "active" *testamenti factio* or *testamenti factio activa*, though the latter phrase was not known to the Roman law. **3.** The capacity to receive property by will. • Junian Latini and peregrini did not have this capacity. It is also known as "passive" *testamenti factio* or *testamenti factio passiva*, though the latter phrase was (like *testamenti factio activa*) unknown to the Roman law. **4.** The capacity to witness a will. • Women did not have this capacity. — Also termed *factio testamenti.*

> "Under the civil law, this was a power . . . vested only in the Roman citizen . . . . The *testamenti factio* was necessary to any participation whatever in a testament. Without it, no one could make a will, or take a legacy, or even be a witness to the execution of a will . . . . In Scotch law, this phrase can only signify the power of making a will, as any one may be a beneficiary under another's settlement." John Trayner, *Trayner's Latin Maxims* 216–17 (4th ed. 1894).

testamentum (tes-tə-**men**-təm), *n.* [Latin] *Roman law.* A will. • In early and classical law, the mancipatory will was standard. It was still used in the Later Empire but the in A.D. 446, the holographic will was accepted in the Western Empire. A will could also be made by registration on the court *acta.* See *holographic will, mancipatory will* under WILL.

▸ ***testamentum calatis comitiis*** (kə-**lay**-tis kə-**mish**-ee-is). [Latin "will made before the *comitia curiata*"] (1815) *Roman law.* In early Rome, a will made before the *comitia curiata*, having an effect comparable to adrogation. • The *comitia curiata* was known as the *comitia calata* when it met twice a year for the purpose of making wills. See *comitia curiata* under COMITIA.

▸ ***testamentum holografum*** (tes-tə-**men**-təm hol-ə-**graf**-əm). [Latin] See *holographic will* under WILL.

▸ ***testamentum in procinctu*** (in prə-**singk**-t[y]oo). [Latin "will made before the army"] (1826) *Roman law.* A will made by a soldier before a fellow soldiers while preparing for battle.

▸ ***testamentum militum*** (tes-tə-**men**-təm **mil**-ə-təm). [Latin] See *soldier's will* under WILL.

▸ ***testamentum tripertitum*** (trɪ-pər-**tɪ**-təm). [Latin "tripartite will"] (1875) *Roman law.* A will made without interruption, with seven witnesses to seal it, and signed by the testator. • This form of will was valid in Justinian's law. It was called "tripartite" because the authority for various parts of it derived from three sources: the civil law (requiring that the will be made at one and the same time before witnesses); the praetor's edict (requiring that there be seven witnesses and that they must seal it); and imperial constitutions (requiring that the testator must sign at the end).

testate (**tes**-tayt), *adj.* (15c) Having left a will at death <she died testate>. Cf. INTESTATE, *adj.*

testate, *n.* See TESTATOR.

testate succession. See SUCCESSION (2).

testatio mentis (tes-**tay**-shee-oh **men**-tis), *n.* [Latin] (17c) *Hist.* An expression of a testator's mind; a testament.

testation (te-**stay**-shən). (17c) **1.** The disposal of property by will; the power to dispose of property by will. **2.** *Archaic.* Attestation; a witnessing.

testator (**tes**-tay-tər *also* te-**stay**-tər). (14c) Someone who has made a will; esp., a person who dies leaving a will. • Because this term is usu. interpreted as applying to both sexes, *testatrix* has become archaic. — Also termed *testate.* Cf. INTESTATE, *n.*

testator's-family maintenance. See MAINTENANCE (7).

testatrix (te-**stay**-triks *or* **tes**-tə-triks). (16c) *Archaic.* A female testator. • In modern usage, a person who leaves a will is called a testator, regardless of sex. Pl. **testatrixes, testatrices.**

testatum (tes-**tay**-təm). [Latin "attested"] (17c) **1.** A writ issued in a county where a defendant or a defendant's property is located when venue lies in another county. • This writ, when issued after a ground writ, allowed the seizure of the defendant or the defendant's property in another county. — Also termed *writ of testatum fieri facias; writ fi. fa.*; *testatum bill; testatum writ; latitat* (**lat**-ə-tat). Cf. *ground writ* under WRIT.

"But if the defendant had removed into another county, the next process the plaintiff might sue out against him was a *testatum bill*, directed to the sheriff thereof, which soon gained the name of a *latitat*, from that word being within it." 1 George Crompton, *Practice Common-Placed: Rules and Cases of Practice in the Courts of King's Bench and Common Pleas* xxxv (3d ed. 1787).

2. The operative part of a deed by which the seller acknowledges the amount and receipt of the purchase money, whether or not the buyer has actually paid any money to the seller. — Also termed *witnessing part*.

testatum clause. See TESTIMONIUM CLAUSE.

testatus (tes-**tay**-təs), *n.* [Latin] *Civil law.* See TESTATOR.

test case. See CASE (1).

teste (**tes**-tee). [Latin *teste meipso* "I myself being a witness"] (15c) **1.** In drafting, the clause that states the name of a witness and evidences the act of witnessing. — Also termed *teste of process*; *teste of writ*. **2.** The final clause in a royal writ naming the person who authorizes the affixing of the king's seal. • The clause generally contains the place and date of the sealing. When the monarch authenticates the sealing, the clause begins with the phase *teste meipso* ("by my own witness"). Otherwise, the authenticator states his or her name and office.

teste meipso. See TESTE (2).

testifier. (17c) Someone who testifies; WITNESS. — Also termed (archaically) *testificator* (**tes**-tə-fi-kay-tər).

testify, *vb.* (14c) **1.** To give evidence as a witness <she testified that the Ford Bronco was at the defendant's home at the critical time>. **2.** (Of a person or thing) to bear witness <the incomplete log entries testified to his sloppiness>.

testifying expert. See EXPERT.

testilying. [portmanteau word fr. *testify* + *lie*] (1994) *Slang.* The act of lying under oath by a public official, usu. a police officer, to advance or strengthen a case against a defendant or to cover up improprieties by the police officer or a public department.

testimonial evidence. 1. See TESTIMONY. **2.** See EVIDENCE.

testimonial immunity. See IMMUNITY (3).

testimonial incapacity. See INCAPACITY.

testimonial privilege. See PRIVILEGE (1).

testimonial proof. See PROOF.

testimonium clause. (1823) A provision at the end of an instrument (esp. a will) reciting the date when the instrument was signed, by whom it was signed, and in what capacity. • This clause traditionally begins with the phrase "In witness whereof." — Also termed *testatum clause*; *witness clause*. Cf. ATTESTATION CLAUSE.

testimony, *n.* (14c) Evidence that a competent witness under oath or affirmation gives at trial or in an affidavit or deposition. — Also termed *testimonial evidence*; *personal evidence*. — **testimonial,** *adj.*

▸ **affirmative testimony.** (1806) Testimony about whether something occurred or did not occur, based on what the witness saw or heard at the time and place in question. — Also termed *positive testimony*; (formerly) *statement of fact*. See *direct evidence* under EVIDENCE.

▸ **cumulative testimony.** (1818) Identical or similar testimony by more than one witness, and usu. by several, offered by a party usu. to impress the jury with the apparent weight of proof on that party's side. • The trial court typically limits cumulative testimony.

▸ **dropsy testimony.** (1970) *Slang.* A police officer's false testimony that a fleeing suspect dropped an illegal substance that was then confiscated by the police and used as probable cause for arresting the suspect. • Dropsy testimony is sometimes given when an arrest has been made without probable cause, as when illegal substances have been found through an improper search.

"Before [*Mapp v. Ohio*, 367 U.S. 643 (1961)], the policeman typically testified that he had stopped the defendant for little or no reason, searched him, and found narcotics on his person. This had the ring of truth. It was an illegal search (not based upon 'probable cause'), but the evidence was admissible because *Mapp* had not yet been decided. Since it made no difference, the policeman testified truthfully. After, the decision in *Mapp* it made a great deal of difference. [¶] For the first few months, New York policemen continued to tell the truth about the circumstances of their searches, with the result that evidence was suppressed. Then the police made the great discovery that if the defendant drops the narcotics on the ground, after which the policeman arrests him, then the search is reasonable and the evidence is admissible. Spend a few hours in the New York City Criminal Court nowadays and you will hear case after case in which a policeman testifies that the defendant dropped the narcotics on the ground whereupon the policeman arrested him. [¶] Usually the very language of the testimony is identical from one case to another. This is now known among defense lawyers and prosecutors as 'dropsy' testimony. The judge has no reason to disbelieve it in any particular case, and of course the judge must decide each case on its own evidence, without regard to the testimony in other cases. Surely, though, not in every case was the defendant unlucky enough to drop his narcotics." Irving Younger, "The Perjury Routine," *The Nation*, May 3, 1967, at 596–97.

▸ **expert testimony.** See *expert evidence* under EVIDENCE.

▸ **false testimony.** (16c) Testimony that is not true. • This term is broader than *perjury*, which has a state-of-mind element. Unlike perjury, false testimony does not denote a crime. — Also termed *false evidence*.

▸ **former testimony.** (18c) Testimony given in the same action or an earlier one, or given in a deposition in the same action or a different one. • Former testimony may be admissible as an exception to the hearsay rule if the witness is unavailable when the trial is held. *See* Fed. R. Evid. 804(b)(1).

▸ **hypnotically refreshed testimony.** (1979) Testimony given by a witness who has undergone hypnosis, which purportedly renewed or restored the witness's memory. — Also termed *hypnotically induced testimony*; *hypnotically refreshed recollection* (or *evidence*); *hypnotically induced recollection*.

▸ **interpreted testimony.** Testimony translated because the witness cannot communicate in the language of the tribunal.

▸ **lay opinion testimony.** (1942) Evidence given by a witness who is not qualified as an expert but who testifies to opinions or inferences. • In federal court, the admissibility of this testimony is limited to opinions or inferences that are rationally based on the witness's perception and that will be helpful to a clear understanding of the witness's testimony or the determination of a fact in issue. Fed. R. Evid. 701.

▸ **mediate testimony.** See *secondary evidence* under EVIDENCE.

▸ **negative testimony.** See *negative evidence* under EVIDENCE.

▸ **nonverbal testimony.** (1922) A photograph, drawing, map, chart, or other depiction used to aid a witness in testifying. • The witness need not have made it, but it must accurately represent something that the witness saw. See *demonstrative evidence* under EVIDENCE.

▸ **opinion testimony.** (1925) Testimony based on one's belief or idea rather than on direct knowledge of the facts at issue. • Opinion testimony from either a lay witness or an expert witness may be allowed in evidence under certain conditions. See *opinion evidence* under EVIDENCE.

▸ **positive testimony.** See *affirmative testimony.*

▸ **resemblance testimony.** (1958) *Criminal law.* Testimony about the looks, clothing, and other characteristics of the perpetrator of a crime.

▸ ***testimony de bene esse*** (dee **bee**-nee **es**-ee *also* day **ben**-ay **es**-ay). (1805) Testimony taken because it is in danger of being lost before it can be given at a trial or hearing, usu. because of the impending death or departure of the witness. • Such testimony is taken in aid of a pending case, while testimony taken under a bill to perpetuate testimony is taken in anticipation of future litigation. See *deposition de bene esse* under DEPOSITION (2).

▸ **written testimony.** (17c) **1.** Testimony given out of court by deposition or affidavit. • The recorded writing, signed by the witness, is considered testimony. **2.** In some administrative agencies and courts, direct narrative testimony that is reduced to writing, to which the witness swears at a hearing or trial before cross-examination takes place in the traditional way.

testing clause. (18c) *Scots law.* The clause at the end of a formal written instrument or deed by which it is authenticated according to the forms of law. • Traditionally, the clause states the name and address of the writer, the number of pages in the instrument, any alterations or erasures, the names and addresses of the witnesses, the name and address of the person who penned the instrument, and the date and place of signing.

testis. [Latin] (15c) *Hist.* A witness. Pl. **testes.**

test oath. See *oath of allegiance* under OATH.

test paper. (1847) A writing that has been proved genuine and submitted to a jury as a standard by which to determine the authenticity of other writings. • The court decides the test paper's authenticity as a matter of law before it is used by the jury. Direct evidence, such as a witness to the writing's creation or an admission by the party, is preferred, but strong circumstantial evidence is usu. acceptable. In Pennsylvania, a paper or instrument shown to the jury as evidence is still called a *test paper* (sometimes written *test-paper*).

tetrarchy (**tet**-trahr-kee), *n.* **1.** The quality, state, or condition of being ruled by four powers. **2.** Collectively, four ruling powers.

> "Among the great number of states participating in the Congress, Austria, England, Prussia, and Russia — the 'tetrarchy' — were dominant. They were the Great Powers: a political rather than a legal term, which was extended to France in 1818 when she was admitted to the dominant group, thus turning it from a 'tetrarchy' into a 'pentarchy' (a development which in more than one respect brings to mind analogous events of 1945). Earlier, in the Treaty of Chaumont (March 1, 1814), Austria, England, Prussia, and Russia, in forming an alliance against Napoleon, had undertaken to use their means *dans un parfait concert.* As a result, the term 'European Concert' was, in common parlance, now transferred to the tetrarchy or pentarchy itself; and, inasmuch as the Great Powers pretended to act in the Common European interest, the term came also to refer to the general cooperation, based on international law, of the European nations." Arthur Nussbaum, *A Concise History of the Law of Nations* 187 (rev. ed. 1961).

3. The district, office, or jurisdiction of one who governs one-fourth of a region.

Texas ballot. See BALLOT (4).

textbook digest. (1922) A legal text whose aim is to set forth the law of a subject in condensed form, with little or no criticism or discussion of the authorities cited, and no serious attempt to explain or reconcile apparently conflicting decisions.

textual canon. See CANON (1).

textual citation. See CITATION (4).

textual-integrity canon. See WHOLE-TEXT CANON.

textual interpretation. See TEXTUALISM.

textualism. The doctrine that the words of a governing text are of paramount concern and that what they fairly convey in their context is what the text means. — Also termed *verbal-meaning theory*; *textual interpretation.* See *strict constructionism* under CONSTRUCTIONISM. — **textualist,** *adj.* & *n.*

TFRP. *abbr.* TRUST-FUND-RECOVERY PENALTY.

thalweg (**tahl**-vayk *or* -veg). (1831) **1.** A line following the lowest part of a (usu. submerged) valley. **2.** The middle of the primary navigable channel of a waterway, constituting the boundary between states. See RULE OF THALWEG. — Also spelled *talweg.* — Also termed *midway.*

▸ **live thalweg.** (1955) The part of a river channel that is most followed, usu. at the middle of the principal channel. *Louisiana v. Mississippi,* 466 U.S. 96, 104 S.Ct. 1645 (1984).

thaneland (**thayn**-lənd), *n.* (17c) *Hist. English law.* Land granted to a thane (a freeman, who, as a significant landowner in medieval times, had a special appointment in the king's hall and was bound to render services in war). —Also termed *tainland.* Cf. REVELAND.

Thayer presumption. (1958) A presumption that allows the party against whom the presumption operates to come forward with evidence to rebut the presumption, but that does not shift the burden of proof to that party. *See* James B. Thayer, *A Preliminary Treatise on Evidence* 31–44 (1898). • Most presumptions that arise in civil trials in federal court are interpreted in this way. Fed. R. Evid. 301. Cf. MORGAN PRESUMPTION.

The Federalist. See FEDERALIST PAPERS.

theft, *n.* (bef. 12c) **1.** The wrongful taking and removing of another's personal property with the intent of depriving the true owner of it; larceny. **2.** Broadly, any act or instance of stealing, including larceny, burglary, embezzlement, and false pretenses. • Many modern penal codes have consolidated such property offenses under the name "theft." — Also termed (in Latin) *crimen furti.* See LARCENY. Cf. ROBBERY.

> "[T]he distinctions between larceny, embezzlement and false pretenses serve no useful purpose in the criminal

law but are useless handicaps from the standpoint of the administration of criminal justice. One solution has been to combine all three in one section of the code under the name of 'larceny.' This has one disadvantage, however, because it frequently becomes necessary to add a modifier to make clear whether the reference is to common-law larceny or to statutory larceny. To avoid this difficulty some states have employed another word to designate a statutory offense made up of a combination of larceny, embezzlement, and false pretenses. And the word used for this purpose is 'theft.' 'Theft' is not the name of any common-law offense. At times it has been employed as a synonym of 'larceny,' but for the most part has been regarded as broader in its general scope. Under such a statute it is not necessary for the indictment charging theft to specify whether the offense is larceny, embezzlement or false pretenses." Rollin M. Perkins & Ronald N. Boyce, *Criminal Law* 389–90 (3d ed. 1982).

▸ **cybertheft.** See CYBERTHEFT.

▸ **identity theft.** See IDENTITY THEFT.

▸ **petty theft.** (16c) A theft of a small quantity of cash or of low-value goods or services. • This offense is usu. a misdemeanor.

▸ **theft by deception.** (1930) The use of trickery to obtain another's property, esp. by (1) creating or reinforcing a false impression (as about value), (2) preventing one from obtaining information that would affect one's judgment about a transaction, or (3) failing to disclose, in a property transfer, a known lien or other legal impediment. Model Penal Code § 223.

▸ **theft by extortion.** (1969) Larceny in which the perpetrator obtains property by threatening to (1) inflict bodily harm on anyone or commit any other criminal offense, (2) accuse anyone of a criminal offense, (3) expose any secret tending to subject any person to hatred, contempt, or ridicule, or impair one's credit or business reputation, (4) take or withhold action as an official, or cause an official to take or withhold action, (5) bring about or continue a strike, boycott, or other collective unofficial action, if the property is not demanded or received for the benefit of the group in whose interest the actor purports to act, (6) testify or provide information or withhold testimony or information with respect to another's legal claim or defense, or (7) inflict any other harm that would not benefit the actor. Model Penal Code § 223.4. — Also termed *larceny by extortion.* See EXTORTION.

▸ **theft by false pretext.** (1888) The use of a false pretext to obtain another's property.

▸ **theft by finding.** See *larceny by finding* under LARCENY.

▸ **theft of property lost, mislaid, or delivered by mistake.** (1973) Larceny in which one obtains control of property the person knows to be lost, mislaid, or delivered by mistake (esp. in the amount of property or identity of recipient) and fails to take reasonable measures to restore the property to the rightful owner. Model Penal Code § 223.5. — Also termed *larceny of property lost, mislaid, or delivered by mistake.*

▸ **theft of services.** (1946) The act of obtaining services from another by deception, threat, coercion, stealth, mechanical tampering, or using a false token or device. See Model Penal Code § 223.7.

theftbote. (**theft**-boht) See BOTE (3).

theftuous (**thef**-choo-əs), *adj.* (14c) **1.** (Of an act) characterized by theft. **2.** (Of a person) given to stealing. — Also spelled *theftous.*

thence, *adv.* (13c) **1.** From that place; from that time. • In surveying, and in describing land by courses and distances, this word, preceding each course given, implies that the following course is continuous with the one before it <south 240 feet to an iron post, thence west 59 feet>. **2.** On that account; therefore.

thence down the river. (16c) With the meanders of a river. • This phrase appears in the field notes of patent surveyors, indicating that the survey follows a meandering river unless evidence shows that the meander line as written was where the surveyor in fact ran it. Meander lines show the general course of the river and are used in estimating acreage, but are not necessarily boundary lines. See MEANDER LINE.

theocracy (thee-**ok**-rə-see). (17c) **1.** Government of a state by those who are believed to be or represent that they are acting under the immediate direction of God or some other divinity. **2.** A state in which power is exercised by ecclesiastics.

Theodosian Code (thee-ə-**doh**-shən). *Roman law.* A compilation of imperial enactments prepared at the direction of the emperor Theodosius II and published in A.D. 438. • The Theodosian Code replaced all other imperial legislation from the time of Constantine I (A.D. 306–337), and remained the basis of Roman law until it was superseded by the first Justinian Code in A.D. 529. — Also termed (in Latin) *Codex Theodosianus* (**koh**-deks thee-ə-doh-shee-**ay**-nəs); *Code of Theodosius.*

"As a literary work the Theodosian Code has a dismal reputation . . . . Some quaestors possessed an elegant, powerful, or agreeably ornate style. . . . Against these may be set others with literary pretensions whose prose is ponderous or marred by excessive alliteration, assonance, pleonasm, or fondness for technical terms, or whose compositions are in other ways inept." Tony Honoré, *Law in the Crisis of Empire 379–455 AD* 21 (1998).

theolonio. See DE THEOLONIO.

theory-of-defense instruction. See JURY INSTRUCTION.

theory of law. 1. See *general jurisprudence* under JURISPRUDENCE. **2.** LEGAL THEORY (2).

theory-of-pleading doctrine. (1956) The principle — now outmoded — that one must prove a case exactly as pleaded. • Various modern codes and rules of civil procedure have abolished this strict pleading-and-proof requirement. For example, Fed. R. Civ. P. 15 allows amendment of pleadings to conform to the evidence.

theory of the case. 1. See CAUSE OF ACTION. **2.** See CASE THEORY.

therapeutic abortion. See *medically necessary abortion* under ABORTION.

therapeutic jurisprudence. See JURISPRUDENCE.

therapeutic relief. See RELIEF (3).

therapeutics. See *therapeutic relief* under RELIEF (3).

thereabouts, *adv.* (bef. 12c) Near that time or place <Schreuer was seen in Rudolf Place or thereabouts>. — Also termed *thereabout.*

thereafter, *adv.* (bef. 12c) Afterward; later <Skurry was thereafter arrested>.

thereat, *adv.* (bef. 12c) **1.** At that place or time; there. **2.** Because of that; at that occurrence or event.

thereby, *adv.* (bef. 12c) By that means; in that way <Blofeld stepped into the embassy and thereby found protection>.

therefor, *adv.* (bef. 12c) For it or them; for that thing or action; for those things or actions <she lied to Congress but was never punished therefor>.

therefore, *adv.* (14c) **1.** For that reason; on that ground or those grounds <a quorum was not present; therefore, no vote was taken>. **2.** To that end <she wanted to become a tax lawyer, and she therefore applied for the university's renowned LL.M. program in taxation>. — Also termed *thereupon.*

therefrom, *adv.* (13c) From that, it, or them <Hofer had several financial obligations to Ricks, who refused to release Hofer therefrom>.

therein, *adv.* (bef. 12c) **1.** In that place or time <the Dallas/Fort Worth metroplex has a population of about 3 million, and some 20,000 lawyers practice therein>. **2.** Inside or within that thing; inside or within those things <there were 3 school buses with 108 children therein>. **3.** In that regard, circumstance, or particular <therein lies the problem>.

thereinafter, *adv.* (1818) Later in that thing (such as a speech or document) <the book's first reference was innocuous, but the five references thereinafter were libelous per se>.

thereof, *adv.* (bef. 12c) Of that, it, or them <although the disease is spreading rapidly, the cause thereof is unknown>.

thereon, *adv.* (bef. 12c) On that or them <Michaels found the online reports of the cases and relied thereon instead of checking the printed books>. — Also termed *thereupon.*

thereto, *adv.* (bef. 12c) To that place, thing, issue, or the like <the jury awarded $750,000 in actual damages, and it added thereto another $250,000 in punitive damages>. — Also termed *thereunto.*

theretofore, *adv.* (14c) Until that time; before that time <theretofore, the highest award in such a case has been $450,000>.

thereunder, *adv.* (bef. 12c) Under that or them <on the top shelf were three books, and situated thereunder was the missing banknote> <section 1988 was the relevant fee statute, and the plaintiffs were undeniably proceeding thereunder>.

thereunto, *adv.* See THERETO.

thereupon, *adv.* (13c) **1.** Immediately; without delay; promptly <the writ of execution issued from the court, and the sheriff thereupon sought to find the judgment debtor>. **2.** THEREON. **3.** THEREFORE.

thesauri inventio (thi-**sawr**-ɪ in-**ven**-shee-oh). [Latin "discovery of treasure"] *Roman law.* The principle according to which the finder of treasure acquires full or partial ownership of it.

thesaurus (thi-**sawr**-əs), *n.* [Latin] (1823) *Roman law.* **1.** Treasure; specif., valuables that have been hidden for so long that the owner's identity can no longer be established. **2.** A storehouse. **3.** A book listing synonyms and other closely allied words. Pl. **thesauri, thesauruses.**

the three estates. See ESTATES OF THE REALM.

***Thibodaux* abstention** (tib-ə-doh). See ABSTENTION.

thief. (bef. 12c) Someone who steals, esp. without force or violence; one who commits theft or larceny. See THEFT.

▸ **common thief.** (16c) A thief who has been convicted of theft or larceny more than once. — Also termed *common and notorious thief.*

▸ **manifest thief.** See FUR MANIFESTUS.

thieve, *vb.* (bef. 12c) To steal; to commit theft or larceny. See THEFT.

thievery. (16c) The act or practice of stealing.

thimblerig. See SHELL GAME.

thimbles and balls. See SHELL GAME.

thin capitalization. See CAPITALIZATION.

thin corporation. See CORPORATION.

thin end of the wedge. See SLIPPERY SLOPE.

thing. (bef. 12c) **1.** The subject matter of a right, whether it is a material object or not; any subject matter of ownership within the sphere of proprietary or valuable rights. • Things are divided into three categories: (1) things real or immovable, such as land, tenements, and hereditaments, (2) things personal or movable, such as goods and chattels, and (3) things having both real and personal characteristics, such as a title deed and a tenancy for a term. The civil law divided things into corporeal (*tangi possunt*) and incorporeal (*tangi non possunt*). La. Civ. Code art. 461.

▸ **accessory thing.** (16c) A thing that stands in a dependency relationship with another thing (the principal thing). • An accessory thing ordinarily serves the economic or other purpose of the principal thing and shares its legal fate in case of transfer or encumbrance.

▸ **corporeal thing.** (17c) The subject matter of corporeal ownership; a material object. — Also termed *res corporales; tangible thing.*

▸ **immovable thing.** See IMMOVABLE.

▸ **incorporeal thing.** (17c) The subject matter of incorporeal ownership; any proprietary right apart from the right of full dominion over a material object. — Also termed *res incorporale; intangible thing.*

▸ **movable thing.** See MOVABLE (1).

▸ **real things.** See REAL THINGS.

▸ **thing in action.** See *chose in action* under CHOSE.

▸ **thing in possession.** See *chose in possession* under CHOSE.

2. Anything that is owned by someone as part of that person's estate or property. — Also termed *res; chose.*

thing in action. See *chose in action* under CHOSE.

thing in possession. See *chose in possession* under CHOSE.

things mancipi. See RES MANCIPI.

things nec mancipi. See RES NEC MANCIPI.

things personal. See *personal property* (1) under PROPERTY.

things real. See REAL THINGS.

thin market. See MARKET.

thin-skull rule. See EGGSHELL-SKULL RULE.

Third Amendment. The constitutional amendment, ratified as part of the Bill of Rights in 1791, prohibiting the quartering of soldiers in private homes except during wartime.

third cousin. See COUSIN.

third degree, *n.* (1900) The process of extracting a confession or information from a suspect or prisoner by prolonged questioning, the use of threats, or physical torture <the police gave the suspect the third degree>.

third-degree instruction. See ALLEN CHARGE.

third-degree murder. See MURDER.

third estate. (1922) *Property.* A landowner's right to have the land supported below the surface against subsidence when it is undermined by tunnels, such as those made for mining operations. • The phrase appears most frequently in Pennsylvania, where the common law traditionally recognizes three estates in land: the surface (first or surface estate), the minerals (second or mineral estate), and an estate in the support of the surface (the third estate). The third estate originated with the common-law duty of miners to support the surface estate.

third-generation rights. See RIGHT.

third opposition. (1815) *Civil law.* A species of intervention, usu. in a real-property case, in which the third party asserts a claim of ownership or other real right to seized property, and the claim does not depend on the outcome of the original suit between the plaintiff and the defendant. La. Code Civ. Proc. art. 1092. *See, e.g., Atkins v. Smith*, 15 So. 2d 855 (La. 1943). See INTERVENTION (1).

third party, *n.* (1818) Someone who is not a party to a lawsuit, agreement, or other transaction but who is usu. somehow implicated in it; someone other than the principal parties. — Also termed *outside party*; *third person.* See PARTY. — **third-party,** *adj.*

third-party, *vb.* (1965) To bring (a person or entity) into litigation as a third-party defendant <seeking indemnity, the defendant third-partied the surety>.

third-party action. See ACTION (4).

third-party beneficiary. See BENEFICIARY.

third-party-beneficiary contract. See CONTRACT.

third-party business-buyout agreement. See AGREEMENT.

third-party check. (1904) A check that the payee indorses to another party — for example, a customer check that the payee indorses to a supplier. • A person who takes a third-party check in good faith and without notice of a security interest can be a holder in due course.

third-party complaint. See COMPLAINT.

third-party consent. (1942) A person's agreement to official action (such as a search of premises) that affects another person's rights or interests. • To be effective for a search, third-party consent must be based on the consenting person's common authority over the place to be searched or the items to be inspected. See COMMON-AUTHORITY RULE.

third-party defendant. (1927) A party brought into a lawsuit by the original defendant.

third-party doctrine. The principle that one has no reasonable expectation of privacy in information that one has voluntarily disclosed to one or more third parties.

third-party equity lease. See *leveraged lease* under LEASE.

third-party guilt. See GUILT.

third-party insurance. See *liability insurance* under INSURANCE.

third-party logistical service provider. See FREIGHT FORWARDER. — Abbr. TPL.

third-party plaintiff. (1857) A defendant who files a pleading in an effort to bring a third party into the lawsuit. See *third-party complaint* under COMPLAINT.

third-party practice. See IMPLEADER.

third-party record-custodian summons. See *John Doe summons* under SUMMONS.

third-party standing. See STANDING.

third-party volunteer. See VOLUNTEER.

third person. See THIRD PARTY.

third possessor. (18c) *Civil law.* Someone who acquires mortgaged property but is not personally bound by the obligation secured by the mortgage.

Third World. (1958) *Int'l law.* **1.** DEVELOPING COUNTRY. **2.** The group of countries (esp. in Africa and Asia) not aligned with major powers, whether Western democracies (i.e., the *First* — or *Free* — *World*) or countries that were formerly part of the Soviet bloc (i.e., the *Second World*). • Although Third World countries are often underdeveloped, the term *Third World* may denote only their political rather than their economic status.

Third World country. See DEVELOPING COUNTRY.

Thirteenth Amendment. The constitutional amendment, ratified in 1865, that abolished slavery and involuntary servitude.

> "The thirteenth amendment is fairly unique in two respects. First, it contains an absolute bar to the existence of slavery or involuntary servitude; there is no requirement of 'state action.' Thus it is applicable to individuals as well as states . . . . Secondly, like the fourteenth and fifteenth amendments, it contains an enforcement clause, enabling Congress to pass all necessary legislation." John E. Nowak & Ronald D. Rotunda, *Constitutional Law* § 15.6, at 918 (4th ed. 1991).

30(b)(6) deposition. See DEPOSITION (2).

thirty-day letter. (1929) *Tax.* A letter that accompanies a revenue agent's report issued as a result of an Internal Revenue Service audit or the rejection of a taxpayer's claim for refund and that outlines the taxpayer's appeal procedure before the Internal Revenue Service. • If the taxpayer does not request any such procedure within the 30-day period, the IRS will issue a statutory notice of deficiency. Cf. NINETY-DAY LETTER.

Thornburgh memorandum. (1989) A 1989 memo by Attorney General Richard Thornburgh declaring that federal prosecutors were not bound by state ethics rules and that any compliance was voluntary. • The memo was not legally binding. In 1993, the Justice Department replaced the Thornburgh memorandum with the Reno Rules. See RENO RULES.

threat, *n.* (bef. 12c) **1.** A communicated intent to inflict harm or loss on another or on another's property, esp. one that might diminish a person's freedom to act voluntarily or with lawful consent; a declaration, express or implied, of an intent to inflict loss or pain on another <a kidnapper's threats of violence>. — **threatener,** *n.*

▸ **terroristic threat.** (1959) A threat to commit any crime of violence with the purpose of (1) terrorizing another, (2) causing the evacuation of a building, place of assembly, or facility of public transportation, (3) causing serious public inconvenience, or (4) recklessly disregarding the risk of causing such terror or inconvenience. Model Penal Code § 211. — Also termed *terrorist threat.* See TERRORISM.

2. An indication of an approaching menace; the suggestion of an impending detriment <the threat of bankruptcy>. **3.** A person or thing that might well cause harm <Mrs. Harrington testified that she had never viewed her husband as a threat>. — **threaten,** *vb.* — **threatening,** *adj.*

threatened species. See SPECIES (1).

threat of continuing harm. See CONTINUING THREAT OF HARM.

threat of continuing injury. See CONTINUING THREAT OF HARM.

three estates, the. See ESTATES OF THE REALM (1).

threefold ordeal. See *triple ordeal* under ORDEAL.

three-hat judge. See JUDGE.

341 meeting. See *creditors' meeting* under MEETING.

312 amendment. See *amendment after allowance* under PATENT-APPLICATION AMENDMENT.

three-judge court. See COURT.

three-mile limit. (1869) The distance of one marine league or three miles offshore, usu. recognized as the limit of territorial jurisdiction.

three-of-five test. *Tax.* A rebuttable IRS presumption that a business venture that fails to make a profit in three out of five consecutive years of operation is a hobby and not a business, thereby invalidating business deductions.

three-step test. *Copyright.* An analysis of an infringement defense under TRIPs and the Berne Convention, looking at whether the defendant's use of a protected work (1) is inherently limited to special cases, (2) did not conflict with the owner's normal exploitation of the work, and (3) did not unreasonably prejudice the legitimate interests of the owner. • The test is analogous to the analysis under the fair-use doctrine in U.S. law.

three-strikes law. (1984) *Slang.* A statute prescribing an enhanced sentence, esp. life imprisonment, for a repeat offender's third felony conviction. • About half the states have enacted a statute of this kind. — Also termed *three-strikes-and-you're-out law.*

three wicked sisters of the common law, the. (1941) *Slang. Hist.* The common-law defenses, specifically contributory negligence, the fellow-servant rule, and assumption of risk, used by employers to avoid liability for on-the-job injuries suffered by workers. • The defenses often succeeded in 19th-century courts, denying recovery to workers injured on the job. — Also termed *unholy trinity.* See WORKERS' COMPENSATION.

> "These three common law defenses, contributory negligence, fellow servant rule, and assumption of the risk, became known as the 'three wicked sisters,' because of their preclusive effect on the ability of injured workers to recover. . . . By precluding application of the traditional respondeat superior concept for acts of fellow servants and by presuming that workers assumed the risks associated with their employment, courts made it extremely difficult for employees to recover from their employers for the increasing number of work-related injuries. . . . By the late 1800s, courts began to recognize the harsh results generated by rote application of the fellow servant, assumption of the risk, and contributory negligence doctrines." Mark A. Rothstein et al., *Employment Law* § 7.2, at 404 (1994).

threshold. *Parliamentary law.* The number or proportion of votes needed for election.

threshold confession. See CONFESSION (1).

thrift institution. See SAVINGS-AND-LOAN ASSOCIATION.

through bill of lading. See BILL OF LADING.

through lot. A lot that abuts a street at each end.

throughput, *n.* The quantity of work, goods, or people that are dealt with in a particular period.

through rate. (1858) The total shipping cost when two or more carriers are involved. • The carriers agree in advance on a through rate, which is typically lower than the sum of the separate rates.

throwaway, *n. Slang.* **1.** An unemancipated minor whose parent or caregiver has forced him or her to leave home. **2.** A runaway whose parent or caregiver refuses to allow him or her to return home. Cf. RUNAWAY (1).

throwback rule. (1972) *Tax.* **1.** In the taxation of trusts, a rule requiring that an amount distributed in any tax year that exceeds the year's distributable net income must be treated as if it had been distributed in the preceding year. • The beneficiary is taxed in the current year although the computation is made as if the excess had been distributed in the previous year. If the trust did not have undistributed accumulated income in the preceding year, the amount of the throwback is tested against each of the preceding years. IRC (26 USCA) §§ 665–668. **2.** A taxation rule requiring a sale that would otherwise be exempt from state income tax (because the state to which the sale would be assigned for apportionment purposes does not have an income tax, even though the seller's state does) to be attributed to the seller's state and thus subjected to a state-level tax. • This rule applies only if the seller's state has adopted a throwback rule.

throw out, *vb.* (1817) To dismiss (a claim or lawsuit).

thrust-upon conflict. See CONFLICT OF INTEREST.

thumbprint. See FINGERPRINT.

TIA. *abbr.* TAX INJUNCTION ACT.

ticket, *n.* (17c) **1.** A certificate indicating that the person to whom it is issued, or the holder, is entitled to some right or privilege <she bought a bus ticket for Miami>.

> "A ticket is a formal document, valid and interpretable by some well-known business custom, requiring the party issuing it to do something, or to give something, not money, to the bearer at or within a certain time. It secures a future right to the bearer; thus differing from a receipt or voucher, which merely proves a right already secured." Joseph H. Beale Jr., *Tickets,* 1 Harv. L. Rev. 17, 17 (1887).

2. CITATION (2) <he got a speeding ticket last week>. **3.** BALLOT (2) <they all voted a straight-party ticket>.

ticket of leave. (18c) *Archaic.* The English equivalent of parole.

ticket-of-leave man. (1837) A convict who has obtained a ticket of leave.

ticket speculator. (1885) Someone who buys tickets and then resells them for more than their face value; in slang, a scalper. See SCALPER (2).

ticking fee. A payment made by a prospective buyer to the seller from the initial agreement until closing occurs to mitigate risk that the seller bears during that interval. • The fee can take several forms, including daily payments, a single payment at a certain time, or payments in increasing amounts over time.

tidal, *adj.* (1808) Affected by or having tides. • For a river to be "tidal" at a given spot, the water need not necessarily be salt, but the spot must be one where the tide, in the ordinary and regular course of things, flows and reflows.

tide. (15c) The rising and falling of seawater that is produced by the attraction of the sun and moon, uninfluenced by special winds, seasons, or other circumstances that create meteorological and atmospheric meteorological tides; the ebb and flow of the sea. • Tides are used to measure a shore's upland boundary. — Also termed *predicted tide*; *astronomical tide.*

▸ **lower low tide.** (1930) The lowest point of the daily tide.

▸ **mean high tide.** (1856) The average of all high tides, esp. over a period of 18.6 years. — Also termed *ordinary high tide.*

▸ **mean lower low tide.** (1932) The average of lower low tides over a fixed period.

▸ **mean low tide.** (1856) The average of all low tides — both low and lower low — over a fixed period.

▸ **neap tide** (neep). (16c) A tide, either high tide or low tide, that is lower than average because it occurs during the first or last quarter of the moon, when the sun's attraction partly counteracts the moon's.

▸ **ordinary high tide.** See *mean high tide.*

▸ **spring tide.** (16c) A tide, either high tide or low tide, that is higher than average because it occurs during the new moon and full moon.

tideland. (18c) Land between the lines of the ordinary high and low tides, covered and uncovered successively by the ebb and flow of those tides; land covered and uncovered by the ordinary tides.

tidesman. (17c) *English law.* A customhouse officer appointed to watch or attend ships until the customs are paid. • A tidesman boards a ship at its arrival in the mouth of the Thames and comes up with the tide. See CUSTOMHOUSE.

tidewater. (18c) Water that falls and rises with the ebb and flow of the tide. • The term is not usu. applied to the open sea, but to coves, bays, and rivers.

tideway. (18c) Land between high- and low-water marks.

tie, *n.* (17c) **1.** An equal number of votes for two candidates in an election. **2.** An equal number of votes cast for and against a particular measure by a legislative or deliberative body. • In the U.S. Senate, the Vice President has the deciding vote in the event of a tie. U.S. Const. art. I, § 3. See *tie vote* under VOTE (3). **3.** *Property.* (In a deed or a surveyor's field notes) a reference to a monument that runs alongside or marks an end of a boundary line. • For example, the call "thence east 100 feet along the centerline of Main Street" contains a tie to the centerline of Main Street. See CALL (5) & (6).

tiebreaking vote. See *casting vote* under VOTE (1).

tied product. See TYING ARRANGEMENT (1).

tied service. See TYING ARRANGEMENT (1).

tie-in arrangement. See TYING ARRANGEMENT.

tiempo inhabil. (1826) *Hist. Louisiana law.* The time at which a person becomes insolvent.

tiercear. See TERCER.

tiered partnership. See PARTNERSHIP.

tie vote. See VOTE (3).

TIF. *abbr.* TAX-INCREMENT FINANCING.

tight, *adj. Slang.* (Of a note, bond, mortgage, lease, etc.) characterized by summary and stringent clauses providing the creditor's remedies in case of default.

TILA. *abbr.* TRUTH IN LENDING ACT.

tillage (**til**-ij), *n.* (15c) A place tilled or cultivated; land under cultivation as opposed to land lying fallow or in pasture.

till-tapping. (1893) *Slang.* Theft of money from a cash register.

timber easement. See EASEMENT.

timber lease. See LEASE.

timber rights. See *timber easement* under EASEMENT.

time. (bef. 12c) **1.** A measure of duration; that which is measured in minutes, hours, days, and years using clocks. **2.** A point in or period of duration at or during which something happens or is alleged to have occurred. **3.** *Slang.* A convicted criminal's period of incarceration.

▸ **dead time.** (1909) Time that does not count for a particular purpose, such as time not included in calculating an employee's wages or time not credited toward a prisoner's sentence. • The time during which a prisoner has escaped, for example, is not credited toward the prisoner's sentence. — Often written *deadtime.* — Also termed *nonrun time.*

▸ **earned time.** *Criminal law.* A credit toward a sentence reduction awarded to a prisoner who takes part in activities designed to lessen the chances that the prisoner will commit a crime after release from prison. • Earned time, which is usu. awarded for taking educational or vocational courses, working, or participating in certain other productive activities, is distinct from good time, which is awarded simply for refraining from misconduct. Cf. *good time.*

▸ **excludable time.** (1977) In the calculation of a statutory deadline under a speedy-trial statute, any relevant days that for some reason are not counted against the prosecution.

▸ **flat time.** (1943) *Criminal law.* A prison term that is to be served without the benefit of time-reduction allowances for good behavior and the like.

▸ **good time.** (1886) *Criminal law.* The credit awarded to a prisoner for good conduct, which can reduce the duration of the prisoner's sentence. Cf. GOOD BEHAVIOR; *earned time.*

▸ **jail-credit time.** See JAIL CREDIT.

▸ **nonrun time.** See *dead time.*

▸ **street time.** *Criminal law.* The time that a convicted person spends on parole or on other conditional release. • If the person's parole is revoked, this time may or may not be credited toward the person's sentence, depending on the jurisdiction and the particular conditions of that person's parole. See *dead time*.

▸ **time served.** (1832) *Criminal law.* **1.** The time that a person has actually spent in jail or prison. **2.** The presentence time that a defendant spent incarcerated, usu. credited toward the sentence imposed.

time agreement. 1. A pact made by the party leaders in the U.S. Senate to limit the time allowed for debate on a bill or amendment. **2.** See UNANIMOUS-CONSENT AGREEMENT.

time-allowance committee. (1972) In some states, a panel that makes recommendation about good-behavior allowances for prison inmates who might be eligible for early parole or early release. — Abbr. TAC.

time and a half. A rate of pay 1.5 times the normal wage or salary, as for overtime or holiday work.

time arbitrage. See ARBITRAGE.

time-bar, *n.* (1881) A bar to a legal claim arising from the lapse of a defined length of time, esp. one contained in a statute of limitations. — **time-barred,** *adj.*

time-bargain. See FUTURES CONTRACT.

time bill. See *time draft* under DRAFT (1).

time bomb. See BOMB.

time certain. 1. A definite, specific date and time. Cf. DATE CERTAIN. **2.** *Parliamentary law.* A specified time or condition for which a matter's consideration is scheduled or to which its consideration is postponed. See *postpone definitely* under POSTPONE (3); *special order* under ORDER (4).

time charter. See CHARTER (8).

time charterparty. See *time charter* under CHARTER (8).

time check. See TIMESHEET.

time deposit. See DEPOSIT (2).

time draft. See DRAFT (1).

time immemorial. (17c) **1.** A point in time so far back that no living person has knowledge or proof contradicting the right or custom alleged to have existed since then. • At common law, that time was fixed as the year 1189, the year that Henry II of England died. In Latin, the idea was fixed in the phrase *a tempore cujus contrarii memoria non existet*, meaning "from a time when there is no memory to the contrary." — Also termed *time out of memory*; *time out of mind*; *time of memory*. **2.** A point in time beyond which legal memory cannot go. See LEGAL MEMORY. **3.** A very long time.

time insurance. See INSURANCE.

time is of the essence. See OF THE ESSENCE.

time-is-of-the-essence clause. (1926) *Contracts.* A contractual provision making timely performance a condition.

timekeeper, *n.* (17c) **1.** A worker, usu. a professional, whose time is billed to clients by hours and increments of hours expended. **2.** A clerk who records the time worked by employees. **3.** Someone who officially records the times taken to do things, as at sporting events. **4.** An employer who is good or bad about arriving at work on time and leaving at the appropriate time. **5.** A timepiece.

timekeeping. The tracking of the passage of time; esp., the activity of a lawyer's or other professional's recording the hours or portions of hours expended on behalf of a client in a given matter.

time letter of credit. See LETTER OF CREDIT.

time loan. See *term loan* under LOAN.

time note. See NOTE (1).

time of memory. *Archaic.* See TIME IMMEMORIAL (1).

time option. See OPTION (2).

time order. See ORDER (8).

time out of memory. See TIME IMMEMORIAL.

time out of mind. See TIME IMMEMORIAL.

time-place-or-manner restriction. (1974) *Constitutional law.* A government's limitation on when, where, or how a public speech or assembly may occur, but not on the content of that speech or assembly. • As long as such restrictions are narrowly tailored to achieve a legitimate governmental interest, they do not violate the First Amendment. — Abbr. TPM restriction. — Also written *time, place, or manner restriction*. — Also termed *time-place-and-manner restriction*. See PUBLIC FORUM.

time policy. See INSURANCE POLICY.

time-price differential. (1938) **1.** A figure representing the difference between the current cash price of an item and the total cost of purchasing it on credit. **2.** The difference between a seller's price for immediate cash payment and a different price when payment is made later or in installments.

time-price doctrine. (1950) The rule that if a debt arises out of a purchase and sale, the usury laws do not apply. • If a higher price is charged for a deferred payment than for an immediate payment, the difference between the time price and the cash price is deemed compensation to the seller for the risk that the buyer will default and for the interest that the seller could have earned on an immediate payment. Because the buyer can usu. choose to postpone a purchase and save up the cash price, the buyer does not have the same status as a needy borrower who must deal with a potentially predatory lender.

time served. See TIME.

timeshare contract. (1981) A legal transaction whereby one party grants to another party the right, over a substantial period, to use property (such as a holiday home) on a regularly recurring basis. • The principle underlying timeshare contracts is the optimization and distribution of costs by proportionate use of the property. — Also termed *timeshare agreement*.

timesharing, *n.* (1976) **1.** Joint ownership or rental of property (such as a vacation condominium) by several persons who take turns occupying the property. — Also termed *timeshare*. **2.** A situation in which one computer is being used simultaneously by many people at separate terminals. — Usu. spelled (in sense 2) *time-sharing*. — **timeshare,** *vb.*

timesheet. (1970) **1.** An employee's record of time spent on the job. **2.** An attorney's daily record of billable and nonbillable hours, used to generate clients' bills. — Also termed (formerly) *time check*. See BILLABLE HOUR.

time-shifting. (1977) The practice of recording a broadcast for viewing at a later time. • Time-shifting was found to be a noninfringing fair use of videotape recorders in *Sony Corp. v. Universal Studios, Inc.*, 464 U.S. 417, 104 S.Ct. 774 (1984).

Times, Places, and Manner Clause. See ELECTIONS CLAUSE.

time unity. See *unity of time* under UNITY.

time value. The price associated with the length of time that an investor must wait until an investment matures or the related income is earned. Cf. YIELD TO MATURITY.

timocracy (tɪ-**mok**-rə-see). (15c) **1.** An aristocracy of property; government by propertied, relatively rich people. **2.** A government in which the rulers' primary motive is the love of honor.

TIN. *abbr.* TAX-IDENTIFICATION NUMBER.

tin parachute. (1987) An employment-contract provision that grants a corporate employee (esp. one below the executive level) severance benefits in the event of a takeover. • These benefits are typically less lucrative than those provided under a golden parachute. — Also termed *silver parachute.* Cf. GOLDEN PARACHUTE.

tip, *n.* (18c) **1.** A piece of special information; esp., in securities law, advance or inside information passed from one person to another. See INSIDE INFORMATION; INSIDER TRADING. **2.** A gratuity for service given. • Tip income is taxable. IRC (26 USCA) § 61(a).

tippee. (1961) *Securities.* Someone who acquires material nonpublic information from someone in a fiduciary relationship with the company to which that information pertains.

tipper. *Securities.* Someone who is in a fiduciary relationship with a company that the person possesses material inside information about, and who selectively discloses that information for trading or other personal purposes <the tippee traded 5,000 shares after her conversation with the tipper>.

tippling house. See PUBLIC HOUSE.

TIPS. *abbr.* See *TIPS bond* under TREASURY BOND.

TIPS bond. See TREASURY BOND.

tip sheet. (1945) A newspaper or website that gives information and advice about what shares should be bought and sold.

tipstaff. (16c) A court crier. • The name derives from the crier's former practice of holding a staff tipped with silver as a badge of office. See CRIER. Pl. **tipstaves, tipstaffs.**

tip-stave. See SERVITOR OF BILLS.

TIS. *abbr.* Taken in satisfaction.

tithe (tɪth), *n.* (12c) **1.** A tenth of one's income, esp. in reference to a religious or charitable gift or obligation. **2.** *Hist.* A small tax or assessment, esp. in the amount of one-tenth. — Also termed *tenth.* — **tithe,** *vb.* — **tithable,** *adj.*

> "A tithe was the right of a rector to a tenth part of the produce of all the land in his parish. In some cases a rector was an individual, while in others the rectory was vested in a monastery, which appointed a vicar to perform the necessary ecclesiastical duties 'vicariously' for the monastery. On the dissolution of the monasteries in the reign of Henry VIII many rectories passed into the royal hands and were granted to laymen; the result was that the right to tithes in many cases passed into lay hands. Like advowsons, tithes were deemed to be land in which the various estates could exist." Robert E. Megarry & P.V. Baker, *A Manual of the Law of Real Property* 415 (4th ed. 1969).

> "As it had evolved by the sixteenth century, the canon law held that every person owed to his parish church a full tenth of the yearly increase of his crops and his flocks. This was the praedial tithe. He also owed a tenth of the income of his industry, as for instance that earned from weaving, calculated after deducting legitimate expenses. This was the personal tithe. There was also a 'mixed' tithe, covering income that partook of both kinds, such as that derived from making cheese from the milk of cows. A distinction was also drawn between the lesser and the greater tithes, a distinction that normally determined which tithes would go to the rector, which to the vicar, of each parish. In practice, there was room for disagreement about the class into which particular tithes should be put, and there was considerable local variation in their incidence and destination, so that academic definitions sometimes served merely as starting points." R.H. Helmholz, *Roman Canon Law in Reformation England* 90 (1990).

▸ **great tithe.** (*usu. pl.*) (17c) A tithe paid in kind and therefore considered more valuable than other tithes. • The great tithes often consisted of corn, peas, beans, hay, and wood.

▸ **mixed tithes.** (16c) A tithe consisting of a natural product, such as milk or wool, obtained or cultivated by human effort.

> "A second species of incorporeal hereditaments is that of tithes . . . the first species being usually called *predial*, as of corn, grass, hops, and wood; the second *mixed*, as of wool, milk, pigs, etc., consisting of natural products, but nurtured and preserved in part by the care of man; and of these the tenth must be paid in gross: the third *personal*, as of manual occupations, trades, fisheries, and the like; and of these only the tenth part of the clear gains and profits is due." 2 William Blackstone, *Commentaries on the Laws of England* 24 (1766).

▸ **personal tithe.** (16c) A tithe of profits from manual occupations or trades.

▸ **predial tithe.** (16c) A tithe of crops (such as corn). — Also spelled *praedial tithe.*

▸ **vicarial tithe** (vɪ-**kair**-ee-əl). (18c) A small tithe payable to a vicar.

tithe of agistment (ə-**jist**-mənt). (16c) *Hist.* A church-levied charge on grazing land. • The tithe was paid by the occupier of the land rather than the person whose cattle grazed on the land. See AGISTMENT.

tithing. See DECENARY.

Titius heres esto (**tish**-ee-əs **heer**-eez **es**-toh). [Latin] *Roman law.* Let Titius be my heir. • The phrase was the testamentary form for appointing an heir. Titius was a fictitious name often used by way of example in legal writing, esp. in forms.

title. (15c) **1.** The union of all elements (as ownership, possession, and custody) constituting the legal right to control and dispose of property; the legal link between a person who owns property and the property itself <no one has title to that land>. Cf. OWNERSHIP; POSSESSION. **2.** Legal evidence of a person's ownership rights in property; an instrument (such as a deed) that constitutes such evidence <record your title with the county clerk>.

> "Though employed in various ways, [*title*] is generally used to describe either the manner in which a right to real property is acquired, or the right itself. In the first sense, it refers to the conditions necessary to acquire a valid claim to land; in the second, it refers to the legal consequences of such conditions. These two senses are not only interrelated, but inseparable: given the requisite conditions, the legal consequences or rights follow as of course; given the rights, conditions necessary for the creation of those rights must have been satisfied. Thus, when the word 'title' is used in one sense, the other sense is necessarily implied." Kent McNeil, *Common Law Aboriginal Title* 10 (1989).

▸ **aboriginal title.** (18c) **1.** Land ownership, or a claim of land ownership, by an indigenous people in a place that has been colonized. — Also termed *native title*. **2.** INDIAN TITLE.

▸ **absolute title.** (17c) An exclusive title to land; a title that excludes all others not compatible with it. See *fee simple absolute* under FEE SIMPLE.

▸ **adverse title.** (18c) A title acquired by adverse possession. See ADVERSE POSSESSION.

▸ **after-acquired title.** (1810) Title held by a person who bought property from a seller who acquired title only after purporting to sell the property to the buyer. See AFTER-ACQUIRED-TITLE DOCTRINE. Cf. *title by estoppel*.

▸ **allodial title.** Real-property ownership without a duty of service to, control by, or acknowledgment of any superior landlord. — Also termed *radical title*.

▸ **apparent title.** See COLOR OF TITLE.

▸ **bad title. 1.** See *defective title*. **2.** See *unmarketable title*.

▸ **clear title.** (17c) **1.** A title free from any encumbrances, burdens, or other limitations. **2.** See *marketable title*. — Also termed *good title*.

▸ **defeasible title.** (17c) A title voidable on the occurrence of a contingency, but not void on its face.

▸ **defective title.** (17c) A title that cannot legally convey the property to which it applies, usu. because of some conflicting claim to that property. — Also termed *bad title*.

▸ **derivative title.** (17c) **1.** A title that results when an already existing right is transferred to a new owner. **2.** The general principle that a transferee of property acquires only the rights held by the transferor and no more.

▸ **dormant title.** (17c) A title in real property held in abeyance.

▸ **doubtful title.** (17c) A title that exposes the party holding it to the risk of litigation with an adverse claimant. See *unmarketable title*.

> "Doubtful titles are those which turn upon some question of law or fact which the court considers so doubtful that the purchaser will not be compelled to accept the title and incur the risk of a lawsuit by adverse claimants." Chapman W. Maupin, *Marketable Title to Real Estate* 2 (2d ed. 1907).

▸ **equitable title.** (17c) A title that indicates a beneficial interest in property and that gives the holder the right to acquire formal legal title. • Before the Statute of Uses (1536), an equitable title was enforceable only in a court of chancery, not of law. Cf. *legal title*.

▸ **good title.** (16c) **1.** A title that is legally valid or effective. **2.** See *clear title* (1). **3.** See *marketable title*.

> "A good title consists in the rightful ownership of the property and in the rightful possession thereof, together with the appropriate legal evidence of rightful ownership. The rightful owner of an estate may be in the rightful possession thereof, but unless he is supplied with the documentary evidence of title, where he holds by purchase, or can prove his right by the testimony of witnesses or other instruments of evidence, where he holds as heir, that is, by descent, his title cannot be said to be good. Sir William Blackstone declares that a perfect title consists in the union of the possession, the right of the possession and the right of property in one and the same person. This is true in a general sense, but the definition scarcely embraces all the elements of a good title, as that term is employed between vendor and purchaser. A purchaser in possession who has paid the whole purchase money, but who has not received a conveyance, may be said to have the possession, the right of possession and the right of property, but not having received a deed, the indispensable evidence of legal title in such a case, his title cannot be said to be good." Chapman W. Maupin, *Marketable Title to Real Estate* 1–2 (2d ed. 1907).

▸ **imperfect title.** (18c) A title that requires a further exercise of the granting power to pass land in fee, or that does not convey full and absolute dominion.

▸ **Indian title.** See INDIAN TITLE.

▸ **just title.** *Civil law.* In a case of prescription, a title that the possessor received from someone whom the possessor honestly believed to be the real owner, the title having been intended to transfer ownership of the property. La. Civ. Code art. 3483. — Also termed *justus titulus*.

▸ **legal title.** (17c) A title that evidences apparent ownership but does not necessarily signify full and complete title or a beneficial interest. • Before the Statute of Uses (1536), a legal title was enforceable only in a court of law, not chancery. Cf. *equitable title*.

▸ **lucrative title.** (17c) *Civil law.* A title acquired without giving anything in exchange for the property; title by which a person acquires anything that comes as a clear gain, as by gift, descent, or devise. • Because lucrative title is usu. acquired by gift or inheritance, it is treated as the separate property of a married person. Cf. *onerous title*.

▸ **marketable title.** (18c) A title that a reasonable buyer would accept because it appears to lack any defect and to cover the entire property that the seller has purported to sell; a title that enables a purchaser to hold property in peace during the period of ownership and to have it accepted by a later purchaser who employs the same standards of acceptability. — Also termed *good title*; *merchantable title*; *clear title*.

> "One definition of a marketable title which has been put forward repeatedly is one free from all reasonable doubt. Stated another way, a marketable title is one which does *not* contain any manner of defect or outstanding interest or claim which may conceivably operate to defeat or impair the interest which is bargained for and is intended to be conveyed. This negative concept of marketability has become an implied invitation for courts to declare titles unmarketable if an examiner has entertained any doubt whatever with respect to them. The digests attest the painful truth that claims of a bygone era cling like barnacles to land titles and encumber them long after they should have been scraped clean. . . . We need to replace this negative approach by a positive one which will make the marketability of titles depend solely upon their state during some recent interval of time rather than upon their entire history." Paul E. Basye, *Clearing Land Titles* § 371, at 539 (1953).

▸ **native title.** See *aboriginal title* (1).

▸ **nonmerchantable title.** See *unmarketable title*.

▸ **onerous title** (**on**-ər-əs). (17c) **1.** *Civil law.* A title acquired by giving valuable consideration for the property, as by paying money or performing services. **2.** A title to property that is acquired during marriage through a spouse's skill or labor and is therefore treated as community property. Cf. *lucrative title*.

▸ **original title.** A title that creates a right for the first time.

> "The catching of fish is an original title of the right of ownership, whereas the purchase of them is a derivative title. The right acquired by the fisherman is newly created; it

did not formerly exist in any one." John Salmond, *Jurisprudence* 345 (Glanville L. Williams ed., 10th ed. 1947).

▸ **paper title.** See *record title.*

▸ **paramount title.** (18c) **1.** *Archaic.* A title that is the source of the current title; original title. **2.** A title that is superior to another title or claim on the same property.

▸ **particular title.** *Civil law.* A title acquired from an ancestor by purchase, gift, or inheritance before or after the ancestor's death.

▸ **perfect title.** (16c) **1.** FEE SIMPLE. **2.** A grant of land that requires no further act from the legal authority to constitute an absolute title to the land. **3.** A title that does not disclose a patent defect that may require a lawsuit to defend it. **4.** A title that is good both at law and in equity. **5.** A title that is good and valid beyond all reasonable doubt.

▸ **presumptive title.** (17c) A title of the lowest order, arising out of the mere occupation or simple possession of property without any apparent right, or any pretense of right, to hold and continue that possession.

▸ **radical title.** See *allodial title.*

▸ **record title.** (18c) A title as it appears in the public records after the deed is properly recorded. — Also termed *title of record*; *paper title.*

▸ **singular title.** (17c) The title by which one acquires property as a singular successor.

▸ **tax title.** (1831) A title to land purchased at a tax sale.

▸ **title by descent.** (17c) A title that one acquires by law as an heir of the deceased owner.

▸ **title by devise.** (1819) A title created by will.

▸ **title by estoppel.** (17c) Title acquired from a person who did not have title at the time of a purported conveyance with a warranty but later acquired the title, which then inures to the benefit of the grantee. Cf. *after-acquired title.*

▸ **title by prescription.** (17c) A title acquired by prescription. See PRESCRIPTION (5).

▸ **title defective in form.** (1836) A title for which some defect appears on the face of the deed, as opposed to a defect that arises from circumstances or extrinsic evidence. • Title defective in form cannot be the basis of prescription. See PRESCRIPTION (5).

▸ **title of entry.** (16c) The right to enter onto lands.

▸ **title of record.** See *record title.*

▸ **universal title.** (17c) A title acquired by a conveyance causa mortis of a stated portion of all the conveyor's property interests so that on the conveyor's death the recipient stands as a universal successor.

▸ **unmarketable title.** (18c) A title that a reasonable buyer would refuse to accept because of possible conflicting interests in or litigation over the property. — Also termed *bad title*; *unmerchantable title*; *nonmerchantable title.*

▸ **voidable title.** (17c) A valid title that may be annulled by a person with an earlier claim to the property, usu. because title was fraudulently transferred.

▸ **wild title.** A title that is false or questionable validity.

▸ **zombie title.** (2013) *Slang.* Title to a property that is the subject of an incomplete and usu. long-stalled foreclosure process, leaving legal title and all ownership responsibilities for the property, including maintenance and taxes, on the delinquent debtor, even if the debtor vacates the property in anticipation of eviction. • An entity that gives notice of foreclosure need not proceed to foreclose promptly and regain ownership of the property, preferring to leave the debtor legally liable for the property's expenses whether or not the debtor enjoys its ownership.

3. The heading of a statute or other legal document <the title of the contract was "Confidentiality Agreement">.

▸ **general title.** A statute's name that broadly and comprehensively identifies the subject matter addressed by the legislature. Cf. *restrictive title.*

▸ **long title.** The full, formal title of a statute, usu. containing a brief statement of legislative purpose.

"The first Acts of Parliament did not have titles. The first time that an Act of Parliament was given a title was about 1495. Even when the long title came to be added to each Act of Parliament as a matter of course, as it did from about 1513, the long title was not regarded as part of the Act of Parliament itself. Today, however, the position is different: the long title is part of the Act of Parliament." D.J. Gifford & John Salter, *How to Understand an Act of Parliament* 19 (1996).

"Because Parliament's clerks, rather than Parliament, provided the titles of acts, the traditional rule has been that the title could not be used for interpretive purposes. . . . This is no longer the practice in most English-speaking jurisdictions, for the long title, and often a short title as well, are part of the legislative bill from the very beginning. In the United States, most state constitutions require the legislative enactment to have a title that gives accurate notice of the contents of the law." William N. Eskridge Jr., Philip P. Frickey & Elizabeth Garett, *Cases and Materials on Legislation* 831 (2001).

▸ **short title.** The abbreviated title of a statute by which it is popularly known; a statutory nickname.

▸ **title of an invention.** *Patents.* A short, specific description of an invention on the first page of a patent or patent application.

4. A subdivision of a statute or code <Title IX>.

▸ **restrictive title.** A statute's name that narrowly identifies the particular subject matter addressed by the legislature. Cf. *general title.*

5. The name by which a court case or other legal proceeding is distinguished from others; STYLE (1). **6.** An appellation of office, dignity, or distinction <after the election, he bore the title of mayor for the next four years>.

title, abstract of. See ABSTRACT OF TITLE.

title, action to quiet. See *action to quiet title* under ACTION (4).

title, chain of. See CHAIN OF TITLE.

title, cloud on. See CLOUD ON TITLE.

title, color of. See COLOR OF TITLE.

title, covenant for. See *covenant for title* under COVENANT (4).

title, document of. See DOCUMENT OF TITLE.

title, indicia of. See INDICIA OF TITLE.

title, muniment of. See MUNIMENT OF TITLE.

title, root of. See ROOT OF TITLE.

title, warranty of. See *warranty of title* under WARRANTY (2).

title abstraction. See ABSTRACT OF TITLE.

title-and-headings canon. The doctrine that the title and headings of legal instruments, esp. statutes, are permissible indicators of meaning. — Also termed (more narrowly) *headings canon.*

title clause. A legislative provision setting forth the official name of a statute, and sometimes also a shortened or informal version of its name.

> "Statutes, for the most part, follow traditional lines of form and structure. . . . There is usually a *title clause* describing more or less accurately the content of the enactment; this clause is made mandatory by constitutional provisions of many of the states." Burke Shartel, *Our Legal System and How It Operates* § 4-19, at 290 (rev. ed. 1971).

title clearance. (1916) The removal of impediments to the marketability of land, esp. through title examinations.

title company. See COMPANY.

title covenant. See *covenant for title* under COVENANT (4).

title deed. See DEED.

title division. *Archaic.* A common-law system for dividing property acquired during marriage upon the dissolution of the marriage, the divisions being based on who holds legal title to the property. • Under title division, when a marriage ends in divorce, property purchased during the marriage is awarded to the person who holds title to the property. Cf. COMMUNITY PROPERTY; EQUITABLE DISTRIBUTION.

Title VIII of the Civil Rights Act of 1968. See FAIR HOUSING ACT.

title examination. See ABSTRACT OF TITLE.

title-guaranty company. See *title company* under COMPANY.

title insurance. See INSURANCE.

title jurisdiction. See TITLE THEORY.

title loan. See LOAN.

title member. See *name partner* under PARTNER.

Title IX of the Educational Amendments of 1972. A federal statute generally prohibiting sex discrimination and harassment by educational facilities that receive federal funds. • This term is often referred to simply as Title IX. 20 USCA §§ 1681 et seq.

title-object clause. See CLAUSE.

title of an invention. See TITLE (3).

title of entry. See TITLE (2).

title of record. See *record title* under TITLE (2).

title of right. (1917) A court-issued decree creating, transferring, or extinguishing rights. • Examples include a decree of divorce or judicial separation, an adjudication of bankruptcy, a discharge in bankruptcy, a decree of foreclosure against a mortgagor, an order appointing or removing a trustee, and a grant of letters of administration. In all the examples listed, the judgment operates not as a remedy but as a title of right.

title opinion. See OPINION (2).

title registration. (1971) A system of registering title to land with a public registry, such as a county clerk's office. See TORRENS SYSTEM.

title retention. (1936) A form of lien, in the nature of a chattel mortgage, to secure payment of a loan given to purchase the secured item.

title search. (1965) An examination of the public records to determine whether any defects or encumbrances exist in a given property's chain of title. • A title search is typically conducted by a title company or a real-estate lawyer at a prospective buyer's or mortgagee's request.

Title VII of the Civil Rights Act of 1964. A federal statute that prohibits employment discrimination and harassment on the basis of race, sex, pregnancy, religion, and national origin, as well as prohibiting retaliation against an employee who opposes illegal harassment or discrimination in the workplace. • This term is often referred to simply as Title VII. 42 USCA §§ 2000e et seq.

title standards. (1938) Criteria by which a real-estate title can be evaluated to determine whether it is defective or marketable. • Many states, through associations of conveyancers and real-estate attorneys, still adhere to title standards.

title state. See TITLE THEORY.

title theory. (1907) *Property law.* The idea that a mortgage transfers legal title of the property to the mortgagee, who retains it until the mortgage has been satisfied or foreclosed. • Only a few American states — known as *title states, title jurisdictions,* or *title-theory jurisdictions* — have adopted this theory. Cf. LIEN THEORY.

title transaction. (1939) A transaction that affects title to an interest in land.

title unity. See *unity of title* under UNITY.

titulo lucrativo, qui titulus est post contractum debitum (**tich**-ə-loh loo-krə-**tɪ**-voh, kwɪ **tich**-ə-ləs est pohst kən-**trak**-təm **deb**-i-təm). [Law Latin] *Hist.* By a lucrative title, which occurs after the contracting of debt.

titulo singulari (**tich**-ə-loh sing-gyə-**lair**-ɪ). [Law Latin] *Hist.* By a singular title. • Those acquiring property by means other than succession held the property under a *titulus singularis.*

titulo universali (**tich**-ə-loh yoo-ni-vər-**say**-lɪ). [Law Latin] *Hist.* By a universal title. • An heir succeeding to an ancestor's estate held title *titulo universali.*

titulus transferendi (**tich**-ə-ləs trans-fər-**en**-dɪ). [Law Latin] *Hist.* The legal title for transferring. — Also spelled *titulus transferrendi.* Cf. MODUS TRANSFERENDI.

TM. *abbr.* TRADEMARK. • Typically used as a superscript after a mark (™), it signals only that someone claims ownership of the mark; it does not mean that the mark is registered.

TMEP. *abbr.* TRADEMARK MANUAL OF EXAMINING PROCEDURE.

T-note. *abbr.* (1983) TREASURY NOTE.

tocher. (15c) *Scots law.* Dowry.

TOD motion. See MOTION FOR DIRECTED VERDICT.

TOD registration. *abbr.* TRANSFER-ON-DEATH REGISTRATION.

to-have-and-to-hold clause. See HABENDUM CLAUSE (1).

token, *n.* (bef. 12c) **1.** A sign or mark; a tangible evidence of the existence of a fact. **2.** A sign or indication of an intention to do something, as when a buyer places a small order with a vendor to show good faith with a view toward later placing a larger order. **3.** A coin or other legal tender. • Although *token* most commonly refers to a piece of metal, the term may also denote a bill or other medium of exchange.

▸ **false token.** (16c) A counterfeit coin, bill, or the like.

token use. *Trademarks.* The use of a trademark for the specific purpose of obtaining trademark rights without a bona fide use in the ordinary course of business. • Token use of a mark may be insufficient to establish trademark rights under federal law.

tolerance, *n.* **1.** TOLERATION (1). **2.** TOLERATION (2). **3.** The degree to which someone or something can be subjected to difficulty, high stress, pain, etc. without being harmed or damaged.

tolerance zone. (1924) An area of a town or city where prostitutes are either allowed to work without fear of arrest or prosecution or officially allowed to work legally.

toleration, *n.* (16c) **1.** The act or practice of permitting or enduring something not wholly approved of; the act or practice of allowing something in a way that does not hinder. **2.** The allowance of opinions and beliefs, esp. religious ones, that differ from prevailing norms. **3.** *Archaic.* Legal permission or authorization; LICENSE (1). — **tolerate,** *vb.*

toll, *n.* (bef. 12c) **1.** A tax or due paid for the use of something; esp., the consideration paid either to use a public road, highway, or bridge, or to maintain a booth for the sale of goods at a fair or market. **2.** A right to collect such a tax or due. **3.** The privilege of being free from such a tax or due. **4.** A charge for a long-distance telephone call.

toll, *vb.* (15c) **1.** To annul or take away <toll a right of entry>. **2.** (Of a time period, esp. a statutory one) to stop the running of; to abate <toll the limitations period>. See EQUITABLE TOLLING. **3.** *Hist.* To raise or collect a tax or due for the use of something.

tollage (**toh**-lij). (16c) **1.** Payment of a toll. **2.** Money charged or paid as a toll. **3.** The liberty or franchise of charging a toll.

tolling agreement. (1934) An agreement between a potential plaintiff and a potential defendant by which the defendant agrees to extend the statutory limitations period on the plaintiff's claim, usu. so that both parties will have more time to resolve their dispute without litigation.

tolling statute. (1899) A law that interrupts the running of a statute of limitations in certain situations, as when the defendant cannot be served with process in the forum jurisdiction.

toll manufacturing. (1977) An arrangement under which a customer provides the materials for a manufacturing process and receives the finished goods from the manufacturer. • The same party owns both the input and the output of the manufacturing process. This is a specialized form of contract manufacturing. — Also termed *toll processing.* Cf. CONTRACT MANUFACTURING.

tolt (tohlt). (17c) *Hist.* A writ for removing a case pending in a court baron to a county court. — Also termed *writ of tolt.* See COURT BARON; *county court* under COURT.

> "Where the disputed interest in the land was not a fee held of the king in chief but a fee held of a 'mesne lord' the writ was directed to him bidding him do full right between the parties in the matter of the land in question under pain of the case being removed from his court to the sheriff's court if he failed to do justice. This removal was effected (if necessary) by the process known as 'tolt' under which a sheriff on a complaint to him in his county court of a failure of the lord to do justice ordered his bailiff to attend the lord's court and take away the plaint into the county court." Geoffrey Radcliffe & Geoffrey Cross, *The English Legal System* 38 (G.J. Hand & D.J. Bentley eds., 6th ed. 1977).

tombstone. (1968) *Securities.* An advertisement (esp. in a newspaper) for a public securities offering, describing the security and identifying the sellers. • The term gets its name from the ad's traditional black border and plain print. — Also termed *tombstone advertisement; tombstone ad.* Cf. PROSPECTUS.

ton. (15c) A measure of weight fixed at either 2,000 pounds avoirdupois or 20 hundredweights, each hundredweight being 112 pounds avoirdupois.

▸ **long ton.** (1829) Twenty long hundredweight (2,240 pounds), or 1.016 metric tons.

▸ **short ton.** (1881) Twenty short hundredweight (2,000 pounds), or 0.907 metric tons.

ton mile. (1900) In transportation, a measure equal to the transportation of one ton of freight one mile.

tonnage (**tən**-ij). (15c) **1.** The capacity of a vessel for carrying freight or other loads, calculated in tons. — Also termed *net tonnage.* **2.** The total shipping capacity of a country or port. **3.** See *tonnage duty* under DUTY (4). **4.** The total number of tons what something weighs.

tonnage contract. See CONTRACT OF AFFREIGHTMENT.

tonnage duty. See DUTY (4).

tonnage-rent. (1840) A rent reserved by a mining lease or similar transaction, consisting of a royalty on every ton of minerals extracted from the mine.

tonnage tax. See *tonnage duty* under DUTY (4).

tonsure. (14c) *Hist.* The shaving of a person's (usu. a cleric's) head. • Serjeants-at-law supposedly wore coifs to conceal their shaved heads.

tontine (**ton**-teen *or* ton-**teen**), *n.* (18c) **1.** A financial arrangement in which a group of participants share in the arrangement's advantages until all but one has died or defaulted, at which time the whole goes to that survivor. **2.** A financial arrangement in which an entire sum goes to the contributing participants still alive and not in default at the end of a specified period.

tontine policy. See INSURANCE POLICY.

tools-of-the-trade evidence. (1992) *Criminal law.* Physical evidence consisting of impediments of a criminal or of a criminal enterprise, such as guns and ammunition in a drug-dealing case.

TOP. *abbr.* Temporary order of protection. See ORDER OF PROTECTION.

top-down reasoning. (1983) Rational thought that begins with general principles or rules and applies them to particular instances to be decided or judged; DEDUCTION (4). Cf. BOTTOM-UP REASONING.

top-hat pension plan. See PENSION PLAN.

top lease. See LEASE.

top-level domain name. See DOMAIN NAME.

top management. See MANAGEMENT (1).

topographical survey. See SURVEY (2).

topside brief. See BRIEF (1).

torpedo doctrine. See ATTRACTIVE-NUISANCE DOCTRINE.

Torrens system (**tor**-ənz *or* **tahr**-ənz). (1863) A system for establishing title to real estate in which a claimant first acquires an abstract of title and then applies to a court for the issuance of a title certificate, which serves as conclusive evidence of ownership. • This system — named after Sir Robert Torrens, a 19th-century reformer of Australian land laws — has been adopted in the United States by several counties with large metropolitan areas. — Also termed *Torrens title system*. See CAVEAT (3).

"In 1840, Robert Torrens moved from England to South Australia, where he assumed the post of Collector of Customs. While in that post, he developed a new system of conveyancing based on title certificates and enacted in the Real Property Act 1862. In the U.S., the *Torrens system* is one of four types of evidence of title to real estate (the other three being *abstract and opinion, certificate of title*, and *title insurance*). A few counties with large metropolitan areas — e.g., Boston, Chicago, Minneapolis, and New York City — have adopted the *Torrens system*. Under this system, one who wants to establish title first acquires an abstract of title and then applies to a court for issuance of a certificate. This proceeding amounts to a lawsuit against all claimants to the land. Once the certificate is issued, it is conclusive evidence of ownership." Bryan A. Garner, *Garner's Dictionary of Legal Usage* 898 (3d ed. 2011).

tort (tort). (16c) **1.** A civil wrong, other than breach of contract, for which a remedy may be obtained, usu. in the form of damages; a breach of a duty that the law imposes on persons who stand in a particular relation to one another • Tortious conduct is typically one of four types: (1) a culpable or intentional act resulting in harm; (2) an act involving culpable and unlawful conduct causing unintentional harm; (3) a culpable act of inadvertence involving an unreasonable risk of harm; and (4) a nonculpable act resulting in accidental harm for which, because of the hazards involved, the law imposes strict or absolute liability despite the absence of fault. **2.** (*pl.*) The branch of law dealing with such wrongs.

"To ask concerning any occurrence 'Is this a crime or is it a tort?' is — to borrow Sir James Stephen's apt illustration — no wiser than it would be to ask concerning a man 'Is he a father or a son?' For he may well be both." J.W. Cecil Turner, *Kenny's Outlines of Criminal Law* 543 (16th ed. 1952).

"We may . . . define a tort as a civil wrong for which the remedy is a common-law action for unliquidated damages, and which is not exclusively the breach of a contract or the breach of a trust or other merely equitable obligation." R.F.V. Heuston, *Salmond on the Law of Torts* 13 (17th ed. 1977).

"It might be possible to define a tort by enumerating the things that it is not. It is not crime, it is not breach of contract, it is not necessarily concerned with property rights or problems of government, but is the occupant of a large residuary field remaining if these are taken out of the law. But this again is illusory, and the conception of a sort of legal garbage-can to hold what can be put nowhere else is of no help. In the first place, tort is a field which pervades the entire law, and is so interlocked at every point with property, contract and other accepted classifications that, as the student of law soon discovers, the categories are quite arbitrary. In the second, there is a central theme, or basis or idea, running through the cases of what are called torts, which, although difficult to put into words, does distinguish them in greater or less degree from other types of cases." W. Page Keeton et al., *Prosser and Keeton on the Law of Torts* § 1, at 2-3 (5th ed. 1984).

▸ **business tort.** (1935) A tort that impairs some aspect of an economic interest or business relationship, causing economic loss rather than property damage or bodily harm. • Business torts include tortious interference with contractual relations, tortious interference with prospective advantage, unfair business practices, misappropriation of trade secrets, and product disparagement. — Also termed *economic tort*.

▸ **constitutional tort.** (1966) A violation of one's constitutional rights by a government officer, redressable by a civil action filed directly against the officer. • A constitutional tort committed under color of state law (such as a civil-rights violation) is actionable under 42 USCA § 1983. — Sometimes (informally) shortened to *contort*.

▸ **dignitary tort** (**dig**-nə-tair-ee). (1996) A tort involving injury to one's reputation or honor. • In the few jurisdictions in which courts use the phrase *dignitary tort* (such as Maine), defamation is commonly cited as an example. — Also (erroneously) termed *dignatory tort*.

▸ **economic tort.** See *business tort*.

▸ **environmental tort.** (1970) A tort involving exposure to disagreeable or harmful environmental conditions or harm to and degradation of an environment (e.g., the pouring of acid on golf greens). • An environmental tort is usu. harmful to land rather than people, though people may find it unpleasant (e.g., odors from a landfill). By contrast, toxic torts involve exposure to harmful substances that cause personal physical injury or disease. Cf. *toxic tort*.

▸ **government tort.** (1945) A tort committed by the government through an employee, agent, or instrumentality under its control. • The tort may or may not be actionable, depending on whether the government is entitled to sovereign immunity. A tort action against the U.S. government is regulated by the Federal Tort Claims Act, while a state action is governed by the state's tort claims act. See FEDERAL TORT CLAIMS ACT; *sovereign immunity* under IMMUNITY (1).

▸ **intentional tort.** (1860) A tort committed by someone acting with general or specific intent. • Examples include battery, false imprisonment, and trespass to land. — Also termed *willful tort*. Cf. NEGLIGENCE.

▸ **marital tort.** (1951) A tort by one spouse against the other. • Since most jurisdictions have abolished interspousal tort immunity, courts have had to decide which tort claims to recognize between married persons. Among those that some, but not all, courts have chosen to recognize are assault and battery, including claims for infliction of sexually transmitted disease, and intentional and negligent infliction of emotional distress. — Also termed *domestic tort*. Cf. *husband–wife immunity* under IMMUNITY (2).

▸ **maritime tort.** (1812) Any tort within the admiralty jurisdiction.

▸ **mass tort.** (1940) A civil wrong that injures many people. • Examples include toxic emissions from a factory, the crash of a commercial airliner, and contamination from an industrial-waste-disposal site. Cf. *toxic tort*.

▸ **negligent tort.** (1865) A tort committed by failure to observe the standard of care required by law under the circumstances. See NEGLIGENCE.

▸ **personal tort.** (17c) A tort involving or consisting in an injury to one's person, reputation, or feelings, as distinguished from an injury or damage to real or personal property.

▸ **preconception tort.** (1977) A tort that is committed before the victim has been conceived.

▸ **prenatal tort.** (1960) **1.** A tort committed against a fetus. • If born alive, a child can sue for injuries resulting from tortious conduct predating the child's birth. **2.** Loosely, any of several torts relating to reproduction, such as those giving rise to wrongful-birth actions, wrongful-life actions, and wrongful-pregnancy actions.

▸ **prima facie tort** (**prɪ**-mə **fay**-shee-ee *or* -shee *or* -shə). (1938) An unjustified, intentional infliction of harm on another person, resulting in damages, by one or more acts that would otherwise be lawful. • Some jurisdictions have established this tort to provide a remedy for malicious deeds — esp. in business and trade contexts — that are not actionable under traditional tort law.

▸ **property tort.** (1898) A tort involving damage to property.

▸ **public tort.** (1949) A minor breach of the law (such as a parking violation) that, although it carries a criminal punishment, is considered a civil offense rather than a criminal one because it is merely a prohibited act (*malum prohibitum*) and not inherently reprehensible conduct (*malum in se*). — Also termed *civil offense*. Cf. *civil wrong* under WRONG; *public delict* under DELICT.

▸ **quasi-tort.** (1809) A wrong for which a nonperpetrator is held responsible; a tort for which one who did not directly commit it can nonetheless be found liable, as when an employer is held liable for a tort committed by an employee. — Also spelled *quasi tort*. See *vicarious liability* under LIABILITY; RESPONDEAT SUPERIOR.

▸ **sanctions tort.** See SANCTIONS TORT.

▸ **toxic tort.** (1979) A civil wrong arising from exposure to a toxic substance, such as asbestos, radiation, or hazardous waste. • A toxic tort can be remedied by a civil lawsuit (usu. a class action) or by administrative action. Cf. *mass tort*; *environmental tort*.

▸ **willful tort.** See *intentional tort*.

tort-claims act. A federal or state statute that, under stated circumstances, waives sovereign immunity and allows lawsuits by people who claim they have been injured by the government or its agents and employees. • These laws typically require the prospective plaintiff to file a claim before starting litigation, giving the government an opportunity to engage in discovery and, sometimes, settle. Although often called tort-claims acts, these laws often apply to contract claims as well.

tort damages. See DAMAGES.

tortfeasor (**tort**-fee-zər). (17c) Someone who commits a tort; a wrongdoer.

▸ **concurrent tortfeasors.** (1921) Two or more tortfeasors whose simultaneous actions cause injury to a third party. • Such tortfeasors are jointly and severally liable.

▸ **consecutive tortfeasors.** (1955) Two or more tortfeasors whose actions, while occurring at different times, combine to cause a single injury to a third party. • Such tortfeasors are jointly and severally liable.

▸ **joint tortfeasors.** (1822) Two or more tortfeasors who contributed to the claimant's injury and who may be joined as defendants in the same lawsuit. See *joint and several liability* under LIABILITY.

▸ **successive tortfeasors.** (1954) Two or more tortfeasors whose negligence occurs at different times and causes different injuries to the same third party.

tortious (**tor**-shəs), *adj.* (16c) **1.** Constituting a tort; wrongful <tortious conduct>. **2.** In the nature of a tort <tortious cause of action>.

tortious act. See ACT (2).

tortious battery. See BATTERY (2).

tortious conduct. See CONDUCT.

tortious denial of benefits. See *tortious denial of benefits* under DENIAL (4).

tortious interference with a business advantage. See TORTIOUS INTERFERENCE WITH PROSPECTIVE ADVANTAGE.

tortious interference with contractual relations. (1954) A third party's intentional inducement of a contracting party to break a contract, causing damage to the relationship between the contracting parties. — Also termed *unlawful interference with contractual relations*; *interference with a contractual relationship*; *interference with contract*; *inducement of breach of contract*; *procurement of breach of contract*.

tortious interference with economic relations. See TORTIOUS INTERFERENCE WITH PROSPECTIVE ADVANTAGE.

tortious interference with prospective advantage. (1973) An intentional, damaging intrusion on another's potential business relationship, such as the opportunity of obtaining customers or employment. — Also termed *intentional interference with prospective economic advantage*; *interference with a business relationship*; *tortious interference with a business advantage*; *tortious interference with economic relations*.

tortious liability. See LIABILITY.

tort-of-another doctrine. (1986) *Torts.* In some states, a statutory rule that authorizes a court to award litigation-related expenses, including attorney's fees, to a prevailing party forced to bring or defend a lawsuit against a third party for a tort committed by someone else who refused, after notice, to bring or defend the lawsuit. • The tort-of-another doctrine is an exception to the general American rule about attorney's fees. See AMERICAN RULE (1).

tort reform. (1974) A movement to reduce the amount of tort litigation, usu. involving legislation that restricts tort remedies or that caps damages awards (esp. for punitive damages). • Advocates of tort reform argue that it lowers insurance and healthcare costs and prevents windfalls, while opponents contend that it denies plaintiffs the recovery they deserve for their injuries.

torture, *n.* (16c) The infliction of intense pain to the body or mind to punish, to extract a confession or information, or to obtain sadistic pleasure. — Also termed *extraordinary interrogation technique*. — **torture,** *vb.*

"Every thing . . . openly and visibly tending to a man's destruction, either as to life, limb, or the capacity of sustaining life, is hereby directly forbid: So that, *torture*, as it indangers life and limbs, and may prevent a man from earning his livelihood, is, on all these three accounts, unlawful, though common among all other nations of Europe, who have borrowed it from the old Roman law with respect to slaves; a plain indication, in what light the introducers of it looked on their subjects. It cannot be said that this hath never been violated in England in arbitrary times; (as what nation is there, whose fundamental laws have not been, on occasions, violated?) yet, in five hundred years, I do not believe the English history can afford ten instances." Francis Stoughton Sullivan, *An Historical Treatise on the Feudal Law, and the Constitution and Laws of England* 409 (1772).

"By *torture* I mean the infliction of physically founded suffering or the threat immediately to inflict it, where such infliction or threat is intended to elicit, or such infliction is incidental to means adopted to elicit, matter of intelligence or forensic proof and the motive is one of military, civil, or ecclesiastical interest." James Heath, *Torture and English Law* 3 (1982).

torture by proxy. See *extraordinary rendition* under RENDITION.

torture flight. See *extraordinary rendition* under RENDITION.

total, *adj.* (14c) **1.** Whole; not divided; full; complete. **2.** Utter; absolute.

total assignment. See ASSIGNMENT (2).

total breach. See BREACH OF CONTRACT.

total disability. See DISABILITY (2).

total-disability insurance. See *general-disability insurance* under INSURANCE.

total eviction. See EVICTION.

total failure of consideration. See FAILURE OF CONSIDERATION.

total incorporation. See INCORPORATION (2).

totality-of-the-circumstances test. (1959) *Criminal procedure.* A standard for determining whether hearsay (such as an informant's tip) is sufficiently reliable to establish probable cause for an arrest or search warrant. • Under this test — which replaced *Aguilar–Spinelli*'s two-pronged approach — the reliability of the hearsay is weighed by focusing on the entire situation as described in the probable-cause affidavit, and not on any one specific factor. *Illinois v. Gates*, 462 U.S. 213, 103 S.Ct. 2317 (1983). Cf. AGUILAR–SPINELLI TEST.

total loss. See LOSS.

total-offset rule. (1980) *Torts.* A theory of damages holding that the eroding effect of inflation offsets the accrual of interest on an award and makes it unnecessary to discount future damages to their present value.

total repudiation. See REPUDIATION.

tota materia perspecta. See TOTA RE PERSPECTA.

tota re perspecta (**toh**-tə ree pər-**spek**-tə). [Latin] (1842) *Hist.* The whole matter being taken into account or considered. — Also termed *tota materia perspecta.*

totidem verbis. [Latin] In so many words.

toties quoties (**toh**-shee-eez **kwoh**-shee-eez *or* **toh**-sheez **kwoh**-sheez). [Latin] *Hist.* As often as.

toto caelo (**toh**-toh **see**-loh), *adv.* [Latin "by the whole extent of the heavens"] As far as possible; diametrically <the parties differ with each other *toto caelo*>.

toto genere (**toh**-toh **jen**-ə-ree). [Latin] *Hist.* In their whole character; entirely.

Totten trust. See TRUST (3).

touch, *vb.* (16c) *Marine insurance.* To stop at a port, usu. for a brief period.

touch and stay. (17c) *Marine insurance.* A right, granted by an insurer to an insured vessel, to stop and remain at certain designated points in the course of the voyage. • A vessel that has the power to touch and stay at a place must confine itself strictly to the terms of the permission given, and any deviation during a stay — for example, by shipping or landing goods — will discharge the underwriters, unless the vessel has permission to trade as well as to touch and stay.

***Touhy* regulations.** (1989) The rules governing procedures for document production by federal agencies for purposes of litigation. 28 CFR 16.21 et seq. • The term comes from *United States ex rel. Touhy v. Ragen*, 340 U.S. 462, 71 S.Ct. 416 (1951). In that case, an FBI agent refused to produce certain records under a subpoena duces tecum because a departmental regulation expressly stated that the Attorney General was the only person with authority to produce the documents. The United States Supreme Court upheld the regulation's validity.

tout court (too **koor**), *adv.* [French "simply, without qualification"] (18c) Very briefly; without explanation.

tout ensemble (toot on-**son**-blə), *n.* [French "all together"] The overall visual effect of a design; general effect. • The phrase denotes a way of comparing two designs, by looking at the total impact rather than comparing individual design elements. That is the technique used in determining whether a design infringes someone's trade-dress rights, or if a design-patent application shows a novel and nonobvious change from existing designs. Although the phrase is adverbial in French, it is typically used as a noun in English. See ANTIDISSECTION RULE.

touting, *n.* (18c) The solicitation of business by highly recommending a security or product, esp. when the recommendation's basis is largely puffery.

tout temps prist et encore prist. [Law French] *Common-law pleading.* The clause in a plea of tender stating that the pleader is and always has been ready to pay. See PLEA OF TENDER.

towage (**toh**-ij), *n.* (14c) **1.** The act or service of towing ships and vessels, usu. by means of a small vessel called a *tug.* **2.** The charge for such a service.

toward, *adj.* (bef. 12c) **1.** In the direction of; on a course or line leading to (some place or something). **2.** Coming soon; not long before.

to wit (too **wit**), *adv.* (14c) *Archaic.* That is to say; namely <the district attorney amended the complaint to include embezzlement, to wit, "stealing money that the company had entrusted to the accused">. — Sometimes spelled *to-wit; towit.*

town. (bef. 12c) **1.** A center of population that is larger and more fully developed than a village, but that (traditionally speaking) is not incorporated as a city. **2.** The territory within which this population lives. **3.** Collectively, the people who live within this territory. — Also termed *township.* Cf. CITY.

> "A town is a precinct anciently containing ten families, whereupon in some countries they are called tithings, within one of which tithings every man must be dwelling, and find sureties for his good behaviour, else he that taketh him into his house is to be amerced in the leet." Henry Finch, *Law, or a Discourse Thereof* 80 (1759).

town-bonding act. (1872) A law authorizing a town, county, or other municipal corporation to issue its corporate bonds for the purpose of aiding in construction, often of railroads. — Also termed *town-bonding law.*

town clerk. See CLERK (1).

town collector. (18c) A town officer charged with collecting the taxes assessed by a town.

town commissioner. See COMMISSIONER.

town council. See CITY COUNCIL.

town crier. (17c) *Hist.* A town officer responsible for making proclamations related to town business, usu. by walking the streets and shouting news, alerts, warning, etc. — Often shortened to *crier.*

town hall. (15c) **1.** A building that houses the offices of a town's government. **2.** An informal public meeting where participants voice their opinions and pose questions to elected officials, political candidates, or others involved in issues important to the community. — Also termed (in sense 2) *town-hall meeting; town meeting.* Cf. CITY HALL.

townhouse. (1965) A dwelling unit having usu. two or three stories and often connected to a similar structure by a common wall and (particularly in a planned-unit development) sharing and owning in common the surrounding grounds. — Also termed *townhome.*

town meeting. (17c) **1.** A legal meeting of a town's qualified voters for the administration of local government or the enactment of legislation. • Town meetings of this type are common in some New England states. **2.** More generally, any assembly of a town's citizens for the purpose of discussing political, economic, or social issues. **3.** Modernly, a televised event in which one or more politicians meet and talk with representative citizens about current issues.

town officer. See *municipal officer* under OFFICER (1).

town order. (18c) An official written direction by the auditing officers of a town, directing the treasurer to pay a sum of money. — Also termed *town warrant.*

town purpose. (1827) A municipal project or expenditure that concerns the welfare and advantage of the town as a whole.

township. (17c) **1.** In a government survey, a square tract six miles on each side, containing thirty-six square miles of land. **2.** In some states, a civil and political subdivision of a county having some local government. **3.** TOWN (1). **4.** TOWN (2). **5.** TOWN (3). — Abbr. tp.

township trustee. See TRUSTEE (1).

townsite. (1821) A portion of the public domain segregated by proper authority and procedure as the site for a town.

town treasurer. (17c) An officer responsible for maintaining and disbursing town funds.

town warrant. See TOWN ORDER.

toxic, *adj.* (17c) Having the character or producing the effects of a poison; produced by or resulting from a poison; poisonous. — Also termed *toxical.* Cf. NONTOXIC.

toxicant (**tok**-si-kənt), *n.* (1879) A poison; a toxic agent; any substance capable of producing toxication or poisoning.

toxic asset. See *troubled asset* under ASSET.

toxicate, *vb.* (17c) *Archaic.* To poison. See INTOXICATION.

toxic convert. See DEATH-SPIRAL DEAL.

toxicology (tok-si-**kol**-ə-jee). (18c) The branch of medicine that concerns poisons, their effects, their recognition, their antidotes, and generally the diagnosis and therapeutics of poisoning; the science of poisons. — **toxicological** (tok-si-kə-**loj**-i-kəl), *adj.*

toxic tort. See TORT.

toxic waste. See WASTE (2).

toxin, *n.* (1886) **1.** Broadly, any poison or toxicant. **2.** As used in pathology and medical jurisprudence, any diffusible alkaloidal substance — such as the ptomaines, abrin, brucin, or serpent venoms — and esp. the poisonous products of disease-producing bacteria.

tp. *abbr.* TOWNSHIP.

TPL. *abbr.* Third-party logistical service provider. See FREIGHT FORWARDER.

TPM restriction. *abbr.* TIME-PLACE-OR-MANNER RESTRICTION.

TPO. *abbr.* Time and place of occurrence.

TPPM. *abbr.* TANGIBLE-PERSONAL-PROPERTY MEMORANDUM.

TPR. *abbr.* TERMINATION OF PARENTAL RIGHTS.

TPR hearing. *abbr.* See *termination-of-parental-rights hearing* under HEARING.

trace, *n.* **1.** A small or slight indication that someone or something was present at a place or existed. **2.** An extremely small amount of a substance, quality, emotion, etc. that is difficult to see or notice. **3.** An electronic search to find out where a telephone call originated. **4.** The mark or pattern made on a computer screen or paper by a machine that records electronic signals.

tracer, *n.* A bullet that, when shot, leaves a line of smoke or flame behind it.

traces, *n.* See *retrospectant evidence* under EVIDENCE.

tracing, *n.* (16c) **1.** The process of tracking property's ownership or characteristics from the time of its origin to the present <tracing the vehicle's history>. • Parties in a divorce will be expected to trace the origins of property in existence at the time of marital dissolution in order to characterize each asset as separate or marital property (or as community property in some states). — Also termed *tracing of funds; tracing of property.* Cf. COMMINGLE. **2.** The act of discovering and following a person's actions or movements <tracing the robber's steps>.

tracking dog. See DOG (1).

tract. (14c) A specified parcel of land <a 40-acre tract>.

tract index. See INDEX (1).

tractus futuri temporis (**trak**-təs fyoo-**t**[y]**oor**-ɪ **tem**-pə-ris). [Latin] (1805) *Hist.* A tract of future time.

trade, *n.* (14c) **1.** The business of buying and selling or bartering goods or services; COMMERCE.

▸ **fair trade.** See FAIR TRADE.

▸ **illegal trade.** Traffic or commerce carried on in violation of federal, state, or local law.

▸ **inland trade.** (17c) Trade wholly carried on within a country, as distinguished from foreign commerce.

▸ **precarious trade.** *Int'l law.* Trade by a neutral country between two belligerent powers, allowed to exist at the latter's sufferance.

▸ **unfair trade.** See UNFAIR TRADE.

2. A transaction or swap. **3.** A business or industry occupation; a craft or profession. — **trade,** *vb.*

trade acceptance. See ACCEPTANCE (4).

trade agreement. (1898) **1.** An agreement — such as the North American Free Trade Agreement — between two or more countries concerning the buying and selling of each country's goods. **2.** COLLECTIVE-BARGAINING AGREEMENT.

trade and commerce. (16c) Every business occupation carried on for subsistence or profit and involving the elements of bargain and sale, barter, exchange, or traffic.

Trade and Development Program. See UNITED STATES TRADE AND DEVELOPMENT AGENCY.

trade association. See ASSOCIATION.

trade balance. See BALANCE OF TRADE.

trade council. (1876) A central labor union; the central organization of a local trade union. — Also termed *trades council.* See UNION.

trade defamation. See DEFAMATION.

trade deficit. See DEFICIT (1).

trade discount. See DISCOUNT.

trade disparagement. (1930) The common-law tort of belittling someone's business, goods, or services with a remark that is false or misleading but not necessarily defamatory. • To succeed at the action, a plaintiff must prove that (1) the defendant made the disparaging remark; (2) the defendant either intended to injure the business, knew the statement was false, or recklessly disregarded whether it was true; and (3) the statement resulted in special damages to the plaintiff, usu. by passing off. — Also termed *commercial disparagement*; *product disparagement*; *injurious falsehood.* Cf. *trade defamation* under DEFAMATION.

trade dispute. (1875) **1.** *Int'l law.* A dispute between two or more countries arising from tariff rates or other matters related to international commerce. **2.** *Labor law.* A dispute between an employer and employees over pay, working conditions, or other employment-related matters. • An employee who leaves during a trade dispute is not entitled to benefits under the Unemployment Insurance Act.

trade dollar. (1878) *Hist.* A United States dollar coin, made of silver, issued from 1873 to 1878 for use in foreign trade, esp. in eastern Asia. • A trade dollar was legal tender within the U.S. until 1876 when the coin's silver content fell to less than one dollar. From 1878 to 1885, trade dollars were minted only in proof sets, then discontinued.

trade draft. See DRAFT (1).

trade dress. (1899) *Trademarks.* The overall appearance and image in the marketplace of a product or a commercial enterprise. • For a product, trade dress typically comprises packaging and labeling. For an enterprise, it typically comprises design and decor. If a trade dress is distinctive and nonfunctional, it may be protected under trademark law. — Also termed *get-up*; *look and feel.*

> "The 'trade dress' of a product is essentially its total image and overall appearance. It 'involves the total image of a product and may include features such as size, shape, color or color combinations, texture, graphics, or even particular sales techniques.'" *Two Pesos, Inc. v. Taco Cabana, Inc.*, 505 U.S. 763, 765 n.1, 112 S.Ct. 2755, 2755 n.1 (1992).

trade embargo. See EMBARGO (3).

trade fixture. See FIXTURE.

trade gap. See *trade deficit* under DEFICIT (1).

trade guild. See GUILD (1).

trade-in, *n.* (1917) **1.** A consumer product (such as a car, refrigerator, or cellphone) given as payment, or more usu. partial payment, for a purchase usu. of a similar product. **2.** The method of purchase that uses such a payment. — Also termed (BrE) *part exchange.*

tradeland. A fee property donated to a nonprofit with the expectation that the nonprofit will sell the property and use the funds to further its work. • The donor may qualify for a tax deduction. These properties may or may not have significant characteristics suitable to the nonprofit's substantive mission, but the proceeds of sale benefit that mission.

trade libel. See LIBEL (2).

trademark, *n.* (1838) **1.** A word, phrase, logo, or other sensory symbol used by a manufacturer or seller to distinguish its products or services from those of others. • The main purpose of a trademark is to designate the source of goods or services. In effect, the trademark is the commercial substitute for one's signature. To receive federal protection, a trademark must be (1) distinctive rather than merely descriptive or generic; (2) affixed to a product that is actually sold in the marketplace; and (3) registered with the U.S. Patent and Trademark Office. In its broadest sense, the term *trademark* includes a servicemark. Unregistered trademarks are protected under common-law only, and distinguished with the mark "TM." — Often shortened to *mark.* **2.** The body of law dealing with how businesses distinctively identify their products. — Abbr. TM. See LANHAM ACT; MERCHANT'S MARK. Cf. SERVICEMARK; *registered trademark*; BRAND; TRADENAME.

> "The protection of trade-marks is the law's recognition of the psychological function of symbols. If it is true that we live by symbols, it is no less true that we purchase goods by them. A trade-mark is a merchandising short-cut which induces a purchaser to select what he wants, or what he has been led to believe he wants. The owner of a mark exploits this human propensity by making every effort to impregnate the atmosphere of the market with the drawing power of a congenial symbol. Whatever the means employed, the aim is the same — to convey through the mark, in the minds of potential customers, the desirability of the commodity upon which it appears. Once this is attained, the trade-mark owner has something of value. If another poaches upon the commercial magnetism of the symbol he has created, the owner can obtain legal redress." *Mishawaka Rubber & Woolen Mfg. Co. v. S.S. Kresge Co.*, 316 U.S. 203, 205, 62 S.Ct. 1022, 1024 (1942).

> "A trademark functions on three different levels: as an indication of origin or ownership, as a guarantee of constancy of the quality or other characteristics of a product or service, and as a medium of advertisement. Thus, a trademark guarantees, identifies, and sells the product or service to which it refers. These three facets of a trademark — of differing

importance at different times, in different lines of business and for different products or services — are somewhat correlative. The classical function, that of identification, has been primarily responsible for molding the development of trademark law. The significance of the guarantee function has been somewhat exaggerated, while the implications of the advertisement function still await full recognition in the law." 3 Rudolf Callmann, *The Law of Unfair Competition, Trademarks and Monopolies* § 17.01, at 2 (4th ed. 1998).

"Trademarks may consist of virtually any form of sign, including letters and words, designs, colors, shapes, sounds, and scents. A trademark allows its holder to prevent others from using an identical or confusingly similar sign to identify its goods or services in commerce. Trademark rights may last as long as the right holder continues to use the mark in commerce. In civil-law jurisdictions, trademark rights are typically based on registration. In common-law jurisdictions, trademark rights may be based either on registration or on use in commerce." Frederick M. Abbott, Thomas Cottier & Francis Gurry, *International Intellectual Property in an Integrated World Economy* 8 (2007).

▸ **abandoned trademark.** (1890) A mark whose owner has discontinued using it and has no intent to resume using it in the ordinary course of trade, or has allowed it to become a generic term or otherwise to lose its distinctive significance. • Under § 45 of the Lanham Act, nonuse of a mark for three consecutive years is prima facie evidence of abandonment. The owner of an abandoned mark has no trademark rights to exclude others from using it. — Also termed *abandoned mark.*

▸ **arbitrary trademark.** (1877) A trademark containing common words that do not describe or suggest any characteristic of the product to which the trademark is assigned. • Because arbitrary marks are neither descriptive nor suggestive of the goods or services in connection with which they are used, they are inherently distinctive, require no proof of secondary meaning, and are entitled to strong legal protection. A name that would be generic if used with one product may be arbitrary if used with another. For example, "Bicycle" may be registered to identify playing cards, but it could not be protected as a mark to identify bicycles. — Also termed *arbitrary mark*; *arbitrary name.*

▸ **certification trademark.** (1937) A word, symbol, or device used on goods or services to certify the place of origin, material, mode of manufacture, quality, or other characteristic. *See* 15 USCA § 1127. — Also termed *certification mark.* Cf. *collective trademark.*

▸ **coined trademark.** See *fanciful trademark.*

▸ **collective trademark.** (1941) A trademark or servicemark used by an association, union, or other group either to identify the group's products or services or to signify membership in the group. • Collective marks — such as "Realtor" or "American Peanut Farmers" — can be federally registered under the Lanham Act. — Also termed *collective mark.* Cf. *certification trademark.*

▸ **Community trademark.** (1961) A trademark registered with the European Union Trademark Office and recognized in all EU countries. — Also termed *Community mark.*

▸ **composite trademark.** (kəm-**poz**-it mahrk). (1920) A trademark or servicemark made up of several words that form a distinctive whole, even if the individual words are ordinary. • Advertising slogans are often protectable as composite marks. A trademark registrant can establish ownership in the whole mark, but must disclaim ownership in any unregistrable parts. — Also termed *composite mark*; *hybrid mark*; *hybrid trademark.*

▸ **counterfeit trademark.** (1862) A spurious mark that is identical to, or substantially indistinguishable from, a registered trademark. 15 USCA § 1116(d)(1)(B). — Also termed *counterfeit mark.*

▸ **descriptive trademark.** (1917) A trademark that is a meaningful word in common usage or that merely describes or suggests a product. • This type of trademark is entitled to protection only if it has acquired distinctiveness over time. — Also termed *descriptive mark*; *weak mark*; *weak trademark.* See SECONDARY MEANING.

▸ **disparaging trademark.** (1976) A trademark that tends to bring a person or class of people into contempt or disrepute. • Section 2(a) of the Lanham Act prohibits the registration of disparaging marks. *See* 15 USCA § 1052(a). — Also termed *disparaging mark.* See *prohibited and reserved trademark.*

▸ **distinctive trademark.** (1860) A very strong trademark, one that consumers immediately and consistently associate with specific goods and services. • Distinctive trademarks are usu. fanciful, arbitrary, or suggestive, but descriptive trademarks and common names can become distinctive if they become so well known as to acquire a secondary meaning. — Also termed *distinctive mark.*

▸ **evocative trademark.** See *suggestive trademark.*

▸ **famous trademark.** (1907) A trademark that not only is distinctive but also has been used and heavily advertised or widely accepted in the channels of trade over a long time, and is so well known that consumers immediately associate it with one specific product or service. • Only famous marks are protected from dilution. Eight nonexclusive statutory factors are often used in determining whether a particular mark is famous. *See* 15 USCA §§ 1125 (c)(1)(A)–(H). — Also termed *famous mark.*

▸ **fanciful trademark.** (1904) A trademark consisting of a made-up or coined word; a distinctive trademark or tradename having no independent meaning. • This type of mark is considered inherently distinctive and thus protected at common law, and is eligible for trademark registration from the time of its first use. — Also termed *fanciful mark*; *fanciful term*; *coined trademark*; *coined mark*; *coined term.*

▸ **geographically descriptive trademark.** (1981) A trademark that uses a geographic name to indicate where the goods are grown or manufactured (e.g., "Champagne"). • This type of mark is protected at common law, and can be registered only on proof that it has acquired distinctiveness over time. — Also termed *geographically descriptive mark.* See GEOGRAPHIC INDICATOR; SECONDARY MEANING.

▸ **house trademark.** (1942) A trademark that identifies a company, a division of a company, or a company's product line as the source of a product or service. • A house mark and a product mark often appear together on a label. — Also termed *house mark.* Cf. *product trademark.*

▸ **hybrid trademark.** See *composite trademark.*

▸ **product trademark.** (1950) A trademark that identifies a single good or service, rather than the producing company, a division of a company, or a product line. • A product mark and a house mark often appear together on a label. — Also termed *product mark*. Cf. *house trademark*.

▸ **prohibited and reserved trademark.** (2004) A mark that is not protected under the Lanham Act because it either falls into an expressly excluded category or else is similar to a mark granted by statute to another. 15 USCA § 1052. — Also termed *prohibited and reserved mark*.

▸ **pure trademark.** See *technical trademark*.

▸ **registered trademark.** (1865) A trademark that has been filed and recorded with the Patent and Trademark Office. • A federally registered trademark is usu. marked by the symbol "®" or a phrase such as "Registered U.S. Patent & Trademark Office" so that the trademark owner can potentially collect treble damages or the defendant's profits for an infringement. If the symbol is not used, the owner can collect these damages or profits only by proving that the defendant actually knew that the mark was registered. — Also termed *registered mark*. Cf. SERVICEMARK.

▸ **strong trademark.** (1946) An inherently distinctive trademark that is used — usu. by the owner only — in a fictitious, arbitrary, and fanciful manner, and is therefore given greater protection than a weak mark under the trademark laws. — Also termed *strong mark*.

▸ **suggestive trademark.** (1894) A trademark that suggests rather than describes the particular characteristics of a product, thus requiring a consumer to use imagination to draw a conclusion about the nature of the product. • A suggestive trademark is entitled to protection without proof of secondary meaning. — Also termed *evocative mark*; *suggestive mark*; *suggestive name*. See SECONDARY MEANING.

▸ **technical trademark.** (1868) A mark that satisfies all the elements of a common-law trademark. • The essential elements of a technical trademark are as follows: (1) its use to designate a commercial source would not interfere with anyone else's right to use the mark; (2) it must primarily identify the source, rather than the product's category or grade of quality; (3) it must be attached to the product, label, or collateral materials rather than merely used in advertising; and (4) its use must not undermine some public policy, as by being scandalous or deceptive. — Also termed *pure trademark*; *technical mark*; *true trademark*.

▸ **true trademark.** See *technical trademark*.

▸ **weak trademark.** See *descriptive trademark*.

Trademark Act of 1946. See LANHAM ACT.

trademark application. (1890) A mark owner's written request, filed with the U.S. Patent and Trademark Office, for federal registration of a mark, accompanied by a sample of the mark to be protected and the filing fee. • The application may describe either an existing mark that is in use or a proposed mark. — Also termed *servicemark application*.

▸ **combined application.** (1966) An application to register a mark to be used in more than one class of goods or services. • A combined application is given a single serial number, but it is examined as if it were a set of distinct single applications. Separate filing fees must be paid for each class. — Also termed *multiple-class application*.

▸ **intent-to-use application.** (1963) An application filed with the U.S. Patent and Trademark Office to protect a trademark or servicemark that is not currently in commercial use but whose owner has a bona fide intent to use the mark commercially in the foreseeable future. • Trademark rights have traditionally been restricted to marks actually used in trade, but a 1988 amendment to the Lanham Act permitted applications to be filed before actual use begins if the mark otherwise qualifies for the Principal Register. 15 USCA § 1051(b). See PRINCIPAL REGISTER.

▸ **multiple-class application.** See *combined application*.

trademark-application amendment. (2004) A proposed modification to a registered trademark or to an application for trademark registration.

▸ **amendment of registration.** (1960) *Trademarks.* Amendment of an existing trademark registration to make minor changes in the design of a mark to reflect how the mark is actually used. • The U.S. Patent and Trademark Office permits an amendment of registration only if it does not materially alter the character of the mark. The PTO amends a registration by attaching to the printed registration a printed certificate showing the amendment. — Also termed *amendment of mark in registration*.

▸ **amendment to allege use.** (1989) *Trademarks.* A supplement to a trademark applicant's intent-to-use application filed to inform the U.S. Patent and Trademark Office that a trademark is actually in use in interstate commerce. • The form is titled "Allegation of Use for Intent to Use Application." — Abbr. AAU. — Also termed *statement of use*; *allegation of use*. See DECLARATION OF USE.

▸ **amendment to different register.** (2004) *Trademarks.* An amendment to an application for registration on the Principal Register, requesting that the mark instead be placed on the supplemental register.

trademark bullying. (2006) The attempted enforcement of an unreasonable interpretation of trademark rights, usu. through intimidation tactics.

trademark class. Any one of 42 international trademark-protection categories, each comprising similar goods or services. • There are 34 goods classes and 8 services classes. A trademark is protected in each class that is relevant to the product's or service's business area.

Trademark Cyberpiracy Prevention Act. See ANTICYBERSQUATTING CONSUMER PROTECTION ACT.

Trademark Electronic Application System. A method of applying to the U.S. Patent and Trademark Office for a trademark over the Internet. • The system is available at http://www.uspto.gov/teas/index.html. — Abbr. TEAS.

trademark infringement. See INFRINGEMENT.

Trademark Law Treaty. A 1994 treaty that reduces barriers to applying for and registering trademarks internationally, and establishes a model international-trademark-registration form acceptable by all signatory countries. • The United States is a party to the treaty.

Trademark Manual of Examining Procedure. *Trademarks.* The U.S. Patent and Trademark Office book containing guidelines and procedures for trademark examiners. — Abbr. TMEP.

Trademark Office. See UNITED STATES PATENT AND TRADEMARK OFFICE.

trademark-registration notice. (1930) A notice that a mark is protected by registration with the U.S. Patent and Trademark Office, shown by placing a symbol next to the mark. • In the U.S., the R-within-a-circle symbol (®) is common but the legend "Reg. U.S. Pat. Off." is acceptable. Only federally registered marks may use this notice.

Trademark Trial and Appeal Board. An administrative body that hears and decides disputes involving trademark ownership, conflicts between marks, and registrability of marks. — Abbr. TTAB.

> "No judicial body has administered our trademark laws with more regularity than the Trademark Trial and Appeal Board . . . , the administrative tribunal of the U.S. Patent and Trademark Office that decides trademark proceedings. Established by Congress in 1958, the Board has seen its caseload increase dramatically over time, reflecting the growing importance of trademarks in our competitive marketplace." 1 Jeffery A. Handelman, *Guide to TTAB Practice* § 1.01, at 1-3 (2008).

trademark warehousing. The practice of making intermittent or token uses of a mark without any intent to commercially use the mark for the purpose of securing or preserving the lapse of trademark rights.

trade meaning. See SECONDARY MEANING.

tradename. (1861) *Intellectual property.* **1.** A name, style, or symbol used to distinguish a company, partnership, or business (as opposed to a product or service); the name under which a business operates. • A tradename is a means of identifying a business — or its products or services — to establish goodwill. It symbolizes the business's reputation. Cf. BRAND; D/B/A; TRADEMARK. **2.** A trademark that was not originally susceptible to exclusive appropriation but has acquired a secondary meaning. — Also termed *brand name*; *commercial name.*

trade name. See *business name* under NAME.

trade or business. *Tax.* Any business or professional activity conducted by a taxpayer with the objective of earning a profit. • If the taxpayer can show that the primary purpose and intention is to make a profit, the taxpayer may deduct certain expenses as trade-or-business expenses under the Internal Revenue Code.

trade practice. A customary way of doing business; esp., a method of using specifications for size, thickness, shape, or quality adopted within a given industry.

trade price. See PRICE.

trader. (16c) **1.** A merchant; a retailer; one who buys goods to sell them at a profit. **2.** Someone who sells goods substantially in the form in which they are bought; one who has not converted them into another form of property by skill and labor. **3.** Someone who, as a member of a stock exchange, buys and sells securities on the exchange floor either for brokers or on his or her own account. **4.** Someone who buys and sells commodities and commodity futures for others or for his or her own account in anticipation of a speculative profit.

Trade-Related Aspects of Intellectual Property Rights. See TRIPS.

trader's settlement. See SETTLEMENT (1).

trades council. See TRADE COUNCIL.

trade secret. (1862) **1.** A formula, process, device, or other business information that is kept confidential to maintain an advantage over competitors; information — including a formula, pattern, compilation, program, device, method, technique, or process — that (1) derives independent economic value, actual or potential, from not being generally known or readily ascertainable by others who can obtain economic value from its disclosure or use, and (2) is the subject of reasonable efforts, under the circumstances, to maintain its secrecy. • This definition states the majority view, which is found in the Uniform Trade Secrets Act. **2.** Information that (1) is not generally known or ascertainable, (2) provides a competitive advantage, (3) has been developed at the plaintiff's expense and is used continuously in the plaintiff's business, and (4) is the subject of the plaintiff's intent to keep it confidential. • This definition states the minority view, which is found in the Restatement of Torts § 757 cmt. b (1939). — Also termed *undisclosed information.*

> "So long as the owner of a secret keeps it a secret he has a monopoly. While equity affords protection to trade secrets against betrayal by those under contract or in confidential relations with the owners of the secret, there is no difference between contracts as to trade secrets and contracts as to any other personal property, as far as restraint of trade is concerned." Harry D. Nims, *The Law of Unfair Competition and Trade-Marks* 406 (1929).

> "The concept of protecting trade secrets is related to the principles of trademark and patent law. The scope of trade secret protection, however, goes well beyond that of patent law. Unlike patent law, protection under trade secret law is not tied to the information's novelty; rather, the essence of a trade secret is its relative secrecy. Additionally, unlike patent law, trade secret law draws less from property principles, and more from the equitable principles surrounding confidential relationships." Mark A. Rothstein et al., *Employment Law* § 8.18, at 516 (1994).

> "The difficulty with defining 'trade secrets' in the abstract is that there are so many ways to go about it. In large part, this is a reflection of the fact that the law of trade secrets, unlike the law of patents or copyright, is a creature of the common law rather than of statute. In trying to impose a moral solution on cases of apparent breach of confidence, judges have juggled competing policy interests while trying to draw a line of protection that would lead to the result that they believed was right. . . . In other words, the development of trade secret law has been a bit chaotic . . . ." James Pooley, *Trade Secrets* § 1.01, at 1-1 to 1-3 (1997).

trade slander. See SLANDER.

tradesman (**traydz**-mən), *n.* (16c) **1.** Someone who buys and sells things for profit; esp., a shopkeeper. **2.** A shopkeeper's employee. **3.** A mechanic or artisan whose livelihood depends on manual labor; one who is skilled in a trade. — Also termed *tradesperson.*

trade surplus. See SURPLUS.

trade union. See UNION.

trade-unionism. (1867) The system, principles, or practices of trade unions. — Also termed *labor-unionism.* — Also written *trades-unionism.*

> "Another sign of the times is trades-unionism. Trades-unionism is essential in the cause of labor. One man as a laborer is in a position where it is utterly impossible for him to deal on an equality with his employer. The employer

has capital and can get along without his services, but he cannot get along without the wages which the employer pays him. Therefore, laborers unite and contribute to a fund which enables them to withdraw together and say to the employer: 'Here, we propose to deal with you on a level. We have great force.'" William Howard Taft, *Ethics in Service* 97 (1915).

trade usage. See USAGE (1).

trading. (16c) The business of buying and selling, esp. of commodities and securities.

▸ **day trading.** (1954) The act or practice of buying and selling stock shares or other securities on the same day, esp. over the Internet, usu. for the purpose of making a quick profit on the difference between the buying price and the selling price.

▸ **secondary trading.** (1947) The buying and selling of securities in the market between members of the public, involving neither the issuer nor the underwriter of the securities.

▸ **short-term trading.** (1942) Investment in securities only to hold them long enough to profit from market-price fluctuations.

trading corporation. See CORPORATION.

trading curb. (1979) A temporary restriction on trading in a particular security to curtail dramatic price movements. — Sometimes shortened to *curb.* Cf. TRADING HALT.

trading halt. (1931) A temporary suspension of trading in a particular security for a specific reason, such as an order imbalance or a pending news announcement. • Options can be exercised during a trading halt, and open orders may be canceled. — Also termed *suspended trading.* Cf. TRADING CURB.

trading partnership. See PARTNERSHIP.

trading voyage. See VOYAGE.

trading with the enemy. (17c) The federal offense of carrying on commerce with a country or with a subject or ally of a country with which the United States is at war.

"'Trading with the enemy' denotes a criminal offence, a cause of illegality and nullity in a contract or other transaction, and a ground of condemnation by the Prize Court. . . . [I]t is, at any rate to-day, equivalent to 'intercourse or contact with the enemy,' that is to say, with the enemy in the territorial sense, for we are not aware that it has ever been criminal or illegal by the common law or the law maritime to hold intercourse, otherwise lawful, with an enemy national in England. The prohibition of 'trading with the enemy' is of respectable antiquity. Lord Mansfield in *Gist* v. *Mason* refers to 2 Rolle's Abridgment, 173, *Guerre*, where mention is made of a licence granted in the thirteenth year of the reign of Edward II by the keepers of the truce (*custodes treuge*) 'to certain men to go and sell and buy their merchandise in Scotland which was then an enemy of the King,' a thing clearly illegal, if not criminal, without a licence, and also states that in the reign of William III the King's judges on being asked whether it was a crime to carry corn to the enemy in time of war replied that it was a misdemeanour. Valuable examinations of the historical aspect of the prohibition will be found in Lord Stowell's judgment in *The Hoop* in 1799, the arguments of counsel in *Potts* v. *Bell* in 1800, and the judgment of Willes J. in *Esposito* v. *Bowden* in 1857." Arnold Duncan McNair, *Legal Effects of War* 170 (2d ed. 1944).

traditio (trə-**dish**-ee-oh), *n.* [Latin] *Roman law.* The simple delivery of a piece of property by one person to another with the intention of transferring ownership. • This was the simplest form of transfer, and ultimately it was applied to land as well as movables. Constructive delivery was developed. — Also termed *traditio rei.* See BREVI MANU; CONSITUTUM POSSESSORIUM. Pl. ***traditiones*** (trə-dish-ee-**oh**-neez).

traditio brevi manu (trə-**dish**-ee-oh **bree**-vɪ **man**-yoo). [Latin] (18c) *Roman law.* The surrender of the mediate possession of a thing to the person who is already in immediate possession of it. • This is a type of constructive delivery in which a delivery to the mediate possessor and redelivery to the immediate possessor are unnecessary. See BREVI MANU. For the other two types of constructive delivery, see ATTORNMENT; CONSTITUTUM POSSESSORIUM.

"The first [type of constructive delivery] is that which the Roman lawyers termed *traditio brevi manu*, but which has no recognised name in the language of English law. . . . If, for example, I lend a book to someone, and afterwards, while he still retains it, I agree with him to sell it to him, or to make him a present of it, I can effectually deliver it to him in fulfilment of this sale or gift, by telling him that he may keep it. It is not necessary for him to go through the form of handing it back to me and receiving it a second time from my hands." John Salmond, *Jurisprudence* 306 (Glanville L. Williams ed., 10th ed. 1947).

traditio longa manu (trə-**dish**-ee-oh **long**-gə **man**-yoo). [Latin] *Roman law.* See CONSTITUTUM POSSESSORIUM.

tradition. (14c) **1.** Past customs and usages that influence or govern present acts or practices. **2.** The delivery of an item or an estate.

traditional public forum. See PUBLIC FORUM.

traditional stare decisis. See STARE DECISIS.

traditional surrogacy. See SURROGACY.

traditionary evidence. See EVIDENCE.

traditio rei. See TRADITIO.

trado tibi ecclesiam (**trad**-oh **tib**-ɪ e-**klee**-z[h]ee-əm). [Law Latin] *Hist. Eccles. law & Scots law.* I deliver this church (or living) to you. • A patron uttered this phrase when presenting an incumbent to a vacant church. Cf. ACCIPE ECCLESIAM.

traduce (trə-**d[y]oos**), *vb.* (16c) To slander; calumniate. — **traducement,** *n.*

traffic, *n.* (16c) **1.** Commerce; trade; the sale or exchange of such things as merchandise, bills, and money. **2.** The passing or exchange of goods or commodities from one person to another for an equivalent in goods or money. **3.** People or things being transported along a route. **4.** The passing to and fro of people, animals, vehicles, and vessels along a transportation route.

traffic, *vb.* (16c) To trade or deal in (goods, esp. illicit drugs or other contraband) <trafficking in heroin>.

traffic accident. See *car accident* under ACCIDENT (2).

traffic balance. (1884) The balance of moneys collected in payment for transporting passengers and freight.

traffic collision. See *car accident* under ACCIDENT (2).

traffic court. See COURT.

trafficked person. See PERSON (1).

trafficker, *n.* (16c) **1.** Someone who buys and sells illegal goods, esp. drugs. **2.** Someone who engages in human trafficking. See *human trafficking* under TRAFFICKING.

trafficking. (16c) The act of transporting, trading, or dealing, esp. in illegal goods or people. Cf. PEOPLE-SMUGGLING; SMUGGLING.

▸ **drug trafficking.** (1912) The act of illegally producing, importing, selling, or supplying significant amounts of a controlled substance.

▸ **human trafficking.** (1823) The illegal recruitment, transportation, transfer, harboring, or receipt of a person, esp. one from another country, with the intent to hold the person captive or exploit the person for labor, services, or body parts. • Human-trafficking offenses include forced prostitution, forced marriages, sweatshop labor, slavery, and harvesting organs from unwilling donors. — Also termed *trafficking in persons.* Cf. PEOPLE-SMUGGLING; TRAFFICKER; *organ trafficking.*

▸ **organ trafficking.** (1987) Illegal trafficking in human body parts, esp. transplantable organs that may be offered for sale or that have been harvested without the consent of the donor or the donor's next of kin. • In international law, organ trafficking is broadly included in the offense of human trafficking. — Also termed *trafficking in persons.* Cf. *human trafficking.*

▸ **trafficking in persons. 1.** See *human trafficking.* **2.** See *organ trafficking.*

trafficking in persons. See TRAFFICKING.

traffic regulation. (1857) A prescribed rule of conduct for traffic; a rule intended to promote the orderly and safe flow of traffic.

trailer clause. (1967) An employee's promise to assign to the employer the rights to all inventions developed while employed and for a specified time afterward. • For the covenant to be enforceable, the time restriction must be reasonable. — Also termed *holdover clause.*

traitor, *n.* (13c) **1.** Someone who commits treason against his or her country. **2.** Someone who betrays a person, a cause, or an obligation. — **traitorous,** *adj.*

tramp, *n.* (17c) **1.** Someone who roams about from place to place, begging or living without labor or visible means of support; a vagrant. **2.** TRAMP STEAMER.

tramp corporation. See CORPORATION.

tramp steamer. (1887) A ship that is not scheduled to sail between prearranged ports of call but that stops at those ports for which it has cargo. • A tramp steamer typically carries bulk cargoes such as oil, grain, coal, steel, iron ore, or lumber, and is contracted with a charterparty rather than a bill of lading. — Often shortened to *tramp.* — Also termed *tramp vessel.*

tranche (transh), *n.* [French "slice"] (1930) *Securities.* **1.** A bond issue derived from a pooling of similar debt obligations. • A tranche usu. differs from other issues by maturity date or rate of return. **2.** A block of bonds designated for sale in a foreign country. — Also spelled *tranch; trench.* See COLLATERALIZED MORTGAGE OBLIGATION.

transact, *vb.* (16c) **1.** To carry on or conduct (negotiations, business, etc.) to a conclusion <transact business>. **2.** *Civil law.* To settle (a dispute) by mutual concession. See TRANSACTION (4). **3.** To carry on or conduct negotiations or business <refuses to transact with the enemy>.

transactio (tran-**sak**-shee-oh), *n.* [Latin "compromise"] *Roman law.* The renunciation of a contested claim or defense in litigation in consideration of a quid pro quo. Pl. ***transactiones*** (tran-sak-shee-**oh**-neez).

transaction, *n.* (17c) **1.** The act or an instance of conducting business or other dealings; esp., the formation, performance, or discharge of a contract. **2.** Something performed or carried out; a business agreement or exchange. **3.** Any activity involving two or more persons. **4.** *Civil law.* An agreement that is intended by the parties to prevent or end a dispute and in which they make reciprocal concessions. La. Civ. Code art. 3071. — **transactional,** *adj.*

▸ **arm's-length transaction.** (1931) **1.** A transaction between two unrelated and unaffiliated parties. **2.** A transaction between two parties, however closely related they may be, conducted as if the parties were strangers, so that no conflict of interest arises.

▸ **closed transaction.** *Tax.* A transaction in which an amount realized on a sale or exchange can be established for the purpose of stating a gain or loss.

▸ **colorable transaction.** (18c) A sham transaction having the appearance of authenticity; a pretended transaction <the court set aside the colorable transaction>.

transactional audit. See AUDIT.

transactional immunity. See IMMUNITY (3).

transactional lawyer. 1. See LAWYER. **2.** See OFFICE PRACTITIONER.

transactional takeover defense. See TAKEOVER DEFENSE.

transaction causation. See CAUSATION.

transaction cost. See COST (1).

transaction-or-occurrence test. (1957) A test used to determine whether, under Fed. R. Civ. P. 13(a), a particular claim is a compulsory counterclaim. • Four different tests have been suggested: (1) Are the legal and factual issues raised by the claim and counterclaim largely the same? (2) Would res judicata bar a later suit on the counterclaim in the absence of the compulsory-counterclaim rule? (3) Will substantially the same evidence support or refute both the plaintiff's claim and the counterclaim? (4) Are the claim and counterclaim logically related? See *compulsory counterclaim* under COUNTERCLAIM.

transaction slip. See CONFIRMATION SLIP.

transcarceration. (1987) The movement of prisoners or institutionalized mentally ill persons from facility to facility, rather than from a prison or an institution back to the community, as when a prisoner is transferred to a halfway house or to a drug-treatment facility.

transcribe, *vb.* (16c) To make a written or typed copy of (spoken material, esp. testimony).

transcript, *n.* (14c) A handwritten, printed, or typed copy of testimony given orally; esp., the official record of proceedings in a trial or hearing, as taken down by a court reporter. — Also termed *report of proceedings; reporter's record.*

transcription. (16c) **1.** The act or process of transcribing. **2.** Something transcribed; a transcript.

transcript of proceedings. A compilation of all documents relating to a bond issue, typically including the notices, affidavits of notices, a bond resolution (or bond ordinance), official statement, trust indenture and loan agreements, and minutes of meetings of all authorizing bodies.

transeunt cum universitate (**tran**-see-ənt kəm yoo-ni-vər-sə-**tay**-tee). [Latin] *Hist.* They are transferred with the whole estate.

transfer, *n.* (14c) **1.** Any mode of disposing of or parting with an asset or an interest in an asset, including a gift, the payment of money, release, lease, or creation of a lien or other encumbrance. • The term embraces every method — direct or indirect, absolute or conditional, voluntary or involuntary — of disposing of or parting with property or with an interest in property, including retention of title as a security interest and foreclosure of the debtor's equity of redemption. **2.** Negotiation of an instrument according to the forms of law. • The four methods of transfer are by indorsement, by delivery, by assignment, and by operation of law. **3.** A conveyance of property or title from one person to another.

▸ **colorable transfer.** (1812) A sham transfer having the appearance of authenticity; a pretended transfer. See ILLUSORY-TRANSFER DOCTRINE.

▸ **constructive transfer.** (1852) A delivery of an item — esp. a controlled substance — by someone other than the owner but at the owner's direction.

▸ **incomplete transfer.** *Tax.* A decedent's inter vivos transfer that is not completed for federal estate-tax purposes because the decedent retains significant powers over the property's possession or enjoyment. • Because the transfer is incomplete, some or all of the property's value will be included in the transferor's gross estate. IRC (26 USCA) §§ 2036–2038.

▸ **inter vivos transfer (in**-tər **vi**-vohs *or* **vee**-vohs). (1930) A transfer of property made during the transferor's lifetime.

▸ **mobile transfer.** See MOBILE MONEY.

▸ **testamentary transfer.** (1887) A transfer made in a will. • The transfer may be of something less than absolute ownership. Cf. *testamentary gift* under GIFT.

▸ **transfer in contemplation of death.** See *gift causa mortis* under GIFT.

▸ **transfer in fraud of creditors.** (1883) A conveyance of property made in an attempt to prevent the transferor's creditors from making a claim to it.

transfer, *vb.* (14c) **1.** To convey or remove from one place or one person to another; to pass or hand over from one to another, esp. to change over the possession or control of. **2.** To sell or give.

transferable (trans-**fər**-ə-bəl), *adj.* (14c) Capable of being transferred, together with all rights of the original holder.

transferable letter of credit. See LETTER OF CREDIT.

transferable vote. See *single transferable vote* under VOTE (1).

transfer agent. See AGENT.

transfer-agent-run dividend-reinvestment plan. See DIVIDEND-REINVESTMENT PLAN.

transferee. (18c) One to whom a property interest is conveyed.

transferee liability. (1951) *Tax.* The liability of a transferee to pay taxes owed by the transferor. • This liability is limited to the value of the asset transferred. The Internal Revenue Service can, for example, force a donee to pay the gift tax when the donor who made the transfer cannot pay it. IRC (26 USCA) §§ 6901–6905.

transference. (17c) *Scots law.* The act of substituting a representative for a deceased litigant in a pending action. • This is similar to the common law's substitution of parties.

transfer hearing. See HEARING.

transfer in fraud of creditors. See TRANSFER.

transfer of a case. (1843) The removal of a case from the jurisdiction of one court or judge to another by lawful authority. — Also termed *transfer of a cause.* See REMOVAL (2).

transfer of proceedings. See CHANGE OF VENUE.

transfer of venue. See CHANGE OF VENUE.

transfer-on-death deed. See *beneficiary deed* under DEED.

transfer-on-death registration. (1987) The transfer without probate of a decedent's ownership of registered assets, such as securities, to a designated beneficiary. — Abbr. TOD registration. Cf. *pay-on-death account* under ACCOUNT.

transferor. (1875) Someone who conveys an interest in property.

transfer payment. (*usu. pl.*) (1945) A governmental payment to a person who has neither provided goods or services nor invested money in exchange for the payment. • Examples include unemployment compensation and welfare payments.

transfer price. See PRICE.

transferred intent. See INTENT (1).

transferred-intent doctrine. (1957) The rule that if one person intends to harm a second person but instead unintentionally harms a third, the first person's criminal or tortious intent toward the second applies to the third as well. • Thus, the offender may be prosecuted for an intent crime or sued by the third person for an intentional tort. See INTENT.

transferred malice. See MALICE.

transfer statute. (1961) A provision that allows or mandates the trial of a juvenile as an adult in a criminal court for a criminal act. • Every state has some form of transfer statute. The Supreme Court has held that a juvenile cannot be transferred to criminal court under a discretionary statute "without ceremony — without hearing, without effective assistance of counsel, without a statement of reasons." *Kent v. U.S.*, 383 U.S. 541, 554, 86 S.Ct. 1045, 1053–54 (1966).

▸ **automatic-transfer statute.** (1982) A law requiring the transfer from delinquency court to criminal court for certain statutorily enumerated offenses if certain statutory requirements are met.

▸ **discretionary-transfer statute.** (1978) A law that allows, but does not mandate, the transfer from delinquency court to criminal court for certain statutorily enumerated offenses if certain statutory requirements are met. • The prosecutor has discretion to request the transfer, and the judge has discretion to order the transfer.

▸ **reverse transfer statute.** (1990) A provision that allows a criminal court to return certain cases to juvenile court.

Transfers to Minors Act. See UNIFORM TRANSFERS TO MINORS ACT.

transfer tax. See *generation-skipping transfer tax* under TAX.

transfer warranty. See WARRANTY (2).

transformative use. (1990) *Copyright.* The use of copyrighted material in a manner, or for a purpose, that differs from the original use in such a way that the expression, meaning, or message is essentially new. • The term was coined by Judge Pierre N. Leval in a 1990 law-review article entitled *Toward a Fair Use Standard,* 103 Harv. L. Rev. 1105, 1111 (1990). The concept was first applied by the U.S. Supreme Court in *Campbell v. Acuff-Rose Music, Inc.,* 510 U.S. 569, 114 S.Ct. 1164 (1994). The Court held that the transformative use in that case was a fair, noninfringing use of the plaintiff's copyright.

transgenic (tranz-**jen**-ik), *adj.* (1981) *Patents.* Of, relating to, or describing a living organism that has been genetically altered by introducing recombinant DNA from another organism.

transgress, *vb.* (16c) **1.** To exceed the limits of (a law, rule, regulation, etc.); to break or violate. **2.** To pass over (limits, boundaries, etc.). — **transgressor,** *n.*

transgression. *Archaic.* See MISDEMEANOR.

transgressione, ad audiendum et terminandum (trans-gres[h]-ee-**oh**-nee, ad aw-dee-**en**-dəm et tər-mə-**nan**-dəm). See DE TRANSGRESSIONE, AD AUDIENDUM ET TERMINANDUM.

transgressive trust. See TRUST (3).

transience (tran-shənts), *n.* **1.** The quality or state of continuing for only a short time; slight duration. **2.** The act or practice of staying or working somewhere for only a short time.

transient (tran-shənt), *adj.* (16c) Temporary; impermanent; passing away after a short time.

transient, *n.* (17c) **1.** A person or thing whose presence is temporary or fleeting. **2.** TRANSIENT PERSON.

transient foreigner. (1820) Someone who visits a country without the intent to remain.

transient jurisdiction. See JURISDICTION.

transient merchant. (18c) A trader who sells merchandise at a temporary location without intending to become a permanent merchant in that place.

transient person. (18c) Someone who has no legal residence within a jurisdiction for the purpose of a state venue statute. — Also termed *transient.*

transit, *n.* (15c) **1.** The transportation of goods or persons from one place to another. **2.** Passage; the act of passing.

transit camp. A place where refugees are kept in temporary buildings or tents while the government decides whether they may stay in the region or must move on.

transitional alimony. See *rehabilitative alimony* under ALIMONY (1).

transition phrase. (1997) *Patents.* In a patent claim, the word or phrase that relates the preamble to the body. • The transition is often the term "comprising," "having," "including," "consisting of," or "consisting essentially of." Cf. PREAMBLE (2); BODY OF A CLAIM.

transitive covenant. See COVENANT (1).

transitory (tran-sə-tor-ee *or* **tran**-zə-), *adj.* (14c) Passing from place to place; capable of passing or being changed from one place to another.

transitory action. See ACTION (4).

transitory treaty. See TREATY (1).

transitory wrong. See WRONG.

transit passage. (1974) *Int'l law.* The right of a vessel or airplane to exercise freedom of navigation and overflight solely for the purpose of continuous and expeditious transit between one part of the high seas or an exclusive economic zone and another part of the high seas or an exclusive economic zone. — Also termed *right of transit passage.* Cf. INNOCENT PASSAGE.

transit terra cum onere (**tran**-sit [*or* **tran**-zit] **ter**-ə kəm **on**-ər-ee). [Law Latin] *Hist.* The land passes with its burdens.

translation, *n.* (14c) **1.** The transformation of language from one form to another; esp., the systematic rendering of the language of a book, document, or speech into another language.

> "Generally speaking, a translation need not consist of transferring from one language into another; it may apply to the expression of the same thoughts in other words of the same language." *Rasmussen v. Baker,* 50 P. 819, 826 (Wyo. 1897).

▸ **literal translation.** A translation that translates each word precisely instead of giving the general meaning in a more natural way.

2. *Archaic.* The transfer of property. **3.** *Eccles. law.* The removal of a bishop from one diocese to another.

translative (trans- *or* tranz-**lay**-tiv), *adj.* (1875) Making or causing a transfer or conveyance.

translative fact. See FACT.

translator, *n.* Someone who changes speech or esp. writing from one language to another. Cf. INTERPRETER (1).

transmission. *Civil law.* The passing of an inheritance to an heir.

transmit, *vb.* (15c) **1.** To send or transfer (a thing) from one person or place to another. **2.** To communicate.

transmittal letter. (1914) A nonsubstantive letter that establishes a record of delivery, such as a letter to a court clerk advising that a particular pleading is enclosed for filing. • Lawyers have traditionally opened transmittal letters with the phrase "Enclosed please find," even though that phrasing has been widely condemned in business-writing handbooks since the late 19th century. A transmittal letter may properly begin with a range of openers as informal as "Here is" to the more formal "Enclosed is." — Also termed *cover letter.*

transmutation. (14c) A change in the nature of something; esp., in family law, the transformation of separate property into marital property, or of marital property into separate property.

transnational, *adj.* (1921) **1.** Involving more than one country. **2.** Existing in more than one country.

transnational adoption. See *international adoption* under ADOPTION (1).

transnational commercial law. See LEX MERCATORIA.

transnational corporation. See *multinational corporation* under CORPORATION.

transnational law. (1944) **1.** The amalgam of common principles of domestic and international law dealing esp. with problems arising from agreements made between sovereign states and foreign private parties. **2.** The problems to which such principles apply. Cf. INTERNATIONAL LAW.

transparency. (1843) Openness; clarity; unobstructed access, esp. to business and governmental records; lack of guile and of any attempt to hide damaging information. • The word is used of financial disclosures, organizational policies and practices, lawmaking, and other activities where organizations interact with the public.

> "The concept of transparency has ambiguous meanings and is used differently, if not contradictorily, in different contexts. From the perspective of information recipients, markets are regarded as transparent when the information that is available is as comprehensive as possible. For the one holding the information, in contrast, transparency does not necessarily imply disclosure, but requires in the first instance refraining from deceit with regard to certain facts, and 'not dissimulating.' As far as information is provided, transparency concerns a clear and comprehensible form of presentation, i.e. primarily 'how,' not 'if' information is disclosed. For the rule-maker, transparency stands for the potential regulatory objective of 'see-through' markets, achievable by various means (including standardization in substance)." Florian Möslein & Karl Riesenhuber, "Transparency," in 2 *The Max Planck Encyclopedia of European Private Law* 1686, 1686–87 (Jürgen Basedow et al. eds., 2012).

transport, *vb.* (14c) To carry or convey (a thing) from one place to another.

transportation, *n.* (16c) **1.** The movement of goods or persons from one place to another by a carrier. **2.** *Criminal law.* A type of punishment that sends the criminal out of the country to another place (usu. a penal colony) for a specified period. Cf. DEPORTATION.

Transportation Security Administration. The federal agency charged with promoting safety and security of air, water, rail, and highway transportation. • The agency was created in the Department of Transportation after the terrorist attacks of September 11, 2001, and was transferred to the Department of Homeland Security in 2002. — Abbr. TSA.

transracial adoption. See ADOPTION (1).

transsexual. (1957) A person who was born with the physical characteristics of one sex but who has undergone, or is preparing to undergo, sex-change surgery. See SEX REASSIGNMENT.

transshipment. (18c) *Maritime law.* The act of taking cargo out of one ship and loading it on another. • Transshipment may also involve transfer of cargo to another mode of transportation, such as rail or truck. — **transship,** *vb.*

transvestitive fact. See FACT.

trap, *n.* (bef. 12c) **1.** A device for capturing living creatures, such as a pitfall, snare, or machine that shuts suddenly.

▸ **mantrap.** (18c) A booby-trap; esp., a device to catch a trespasser or burglar. • A mantrap is not illegal if it is designed merely to sound an alarm and not cause bodily harm. Illegal mantraps include manufactured devices such as spring guns, and dangerous hidden conditions (manufactured or natural) that can injure a person, such as pitfalls. — Also spelled *man-trap.*

2. Any device or contrivance by which one may be caught unawares; stratagem; snare. **3.** *Torts.* An ultrahazardous hidden peril of which the property owner or occupier, but not a licensee, has knowledge. • A trap can exist even if it was not designed or intended to catch or entrap anything.

trap-and-trace device. (1986) *Criminal law.* An electronic device that police sometimes use to record certain facts about wire and electronic communications, such as dialing, routing, and signaling information, but not the contents of the communications themselves.

trashing. DECONSTRUCTION.

trash pull. (1992) An investigator's removal of garbage from disposal receptacles placed outside a dwelling so that their contents can be examined for evidence that might be used in some way, esp. in criminal or civil litigation. — Also termed *trash run.*

trauma-pricing. See DRAMA-PRICING.

travaux préparatoires (tra-**voh** pray-par-ə-**twah**[**r**]**z**). [French "preparatory works"] (1935) Materials used in preparing the ultimate form of an agreement or statute, and esp. of an international treaty; the draft or legislative history of a treaty. — Also termed *preparatory work.* See LEGISLATIVE HISTORY.

> "One of the most controversial aspects of treaty interpretation is what use may be made of preparatory work of a treaty. The classification of such material in the Vienna rules as 'supplementary means of interpretation' has not in practical terms diminished its importance. Yet neither article 32 of the Vienna Convention nor the article containing definitions identifies the extent of material covered by this term. In its French form, the term has long been in use both in international courts and tribunals, and in national courts. Despite the use of the term 'preparatory work' in the authentic English text of the Vienna Convention, even in cases where they refer to the Vienna rules, judges in the UK seem to have retained a preference for '*travaux préparatoires*.' However, McNair (author of the classic, but now dated, work on the law of treaties) preferred 'preparatory work' in the title and text of his chapter on that subject. . . . The ILC did not think that anything would be gained by trying to define *travaux préparatoire*, taking the view that 'to do so might only lead to the possible exclusion of relevant evidence.' McNair described the term 'preparatory work' as 'an omnibus expression which is used rather loosely to indicate all documents, such as memoranda, minutes of conferences, and drafts of the treaty under negotiation.'" Richard K. Gardiner, *Treaty Interpretation* 24 (2008) (citations omitted).

travel-accident insurance. See INSURANCE.

Travel Act. A 1961 federal statute that prohibits conduct intended to promote, direct, or manage illegal business activities in interstate commerce. • This statute was enacted to create federal jurisdiction over many criminal activities traditionally handled by state and local governments to help those jurisdictions cope with increasingly complex interstate criminal activity. 18 USCA § 1952.

traveled place. (1894) A place where the public has, in some manner, acquired the legal right to travel.

traveler, *n.* (14c) Someone who passes from place to place, for any reason.

traveler's check. See CHECK.

traveler's letter of credit. See LETTER OF CREDIT.

travel expense. See EXPENSE.

traverse (**trav**-ərs), *n.* (15c) *Common-law pleading.* A formal denial of a factual allegation made in the opposing party's pleading <Smith filed a traverse to Allen's complaint, asserting that he did not knowingly provide false information>. See DENIAL. — **traverse (trav-ərs *or* trə-vərs),** *vb.*

"It is said that the technical term *traverse*, from *transverto*, to turn over, is applied to an issue taken upon an indictment for a misdemeanor, and means nothing more than turning over or putting off the trial to a following session or assize; and that thus it is that the officer of the court asks the party whether he is ready to try then, or will *traverse* to the next session; though some have referred its meaning originally to the denying or taking issue upon an indictment, without reference to the delay of trial, and which seems more correct." 1 Joseph Chitty, *A Practical Treatise on the Criminal Law* 486 (2d ed. 1826).

"Of *traverses* there are various kinds. The most ordinary kind is that which may be called a *common* traverse. This consists of a *tender of issue*; that is, of a denial, accompanied by a formal offer of the point denied, for decision; and the denial that it makes is by way of express contradiction, in terms of the allegation traversed." Franklin Fiske Heard, *The Principles of Pleading in Civil Actions* 118 (1880).

▸ **common traverse.** (1841) A traverse consisting of a tender of issue — that is, a denial accompanied by a formal offer for decision of the point denied — with a denial that expressly contradicts the terms of the allegation traversed. — Also termed *specific traverse.*

"The common or specific traverse is an express denial of a particular allegation in the opposing pleading in the terms of the allegation, accompanied by a tender of issue or formal offer of the point denied for trial." Benjamin J. Shipman, *Handbook of Common-Law Pleading* § 168, at 303 (Henry Winthrop Ballantine ed., 3d ed. 1923).

▸ **cumulative traverse.** (1848) A traverse that analyzes a proposition into its constituent parts and traverses them cumulatively. • It amounts to the same thing as traversing the one entire proposition, since the several parts traversed must all make up one entire proposition or point.

▸ **general traverse.** (17c) A denial of all the facts in an opponent's pleading.

▸ **special traverse.** (18c) A denial of one material fact in an opponent's pleading; a traverse that explains or qualifies the denial. • The essential parts of a special traverse are an inducement, a denial, and a verification.

▸ **specific traverse.** See *common traverse.*

traverse jury. See *petit jury* under JURY.

traverser, *n.* (14c) Someone who traverses or denies a pleading.

traverse the requirement, *vb.* (1941) *Patents.* To (1) respond in detail to a patent examiner's decision that the patent application claims more than one invention and (2) ask that the restriction requirement be reconsidered. • The traverse must specifically explain why restriction should not be required, not merely assert that the requirement is wrong. Failure to traverse a requirement forfeits any rights to appeal the decision.

treachery, *n.* (13c) A deliberate and willful betrayal of trust and confidence.

treason, *n.* (13c) The offense of attempting to overthrow the government of the state to which one owes allegiance, either by making war against the state or by materially supporting its enemies. — Also termed *high treason; alta proditio.* Cf. SEDITION. — **treasonable, treasonous,** *adj.*

"The judgment of *high treason* was, until very lately, an exception to the merciful tenor of our judgments. The least offensive form which is given in the books is, that the offender 'be carried back to the place from whence he came, and from thence to be drawn to the place of execution, and be there hanged by the neck, and cut down alive, and that his entrails be taken out and burned before his face, and his head cut off, and his body divided into four quarters, and his head and quarters disposed of at the king's pleasure.' Some of the precedents add other circumstances, of still more grossness and aggravation. But this horrible denunciation was very seldom executed in its more terrible niceties." 1 Joseph Chitty, *A Practical Treatise on the Criminal Law* 702 (2d ed. 1826).

"[S]everal important characteristics marked off high treason from all other crimes. For one thing, it earned a peculiarly ghastly punishment. For another, it was 'unclergyable,' while every felony was 'clergyable' unless some statute had otherwise ordained. Thirdly, while the felon's land escheated to his lord, the traitor's land was forfeited to the king. This last distinction influenced the development of the law." 2 Frederick Pollock & Frederic W. Maitland, *History of English Law Before the Time of Edward I* 500 (2d ed. 1899).

"Treason against the United States, shall consist only in levying war against them, or in adhering to their Enemies, giving them Aid and Comfort. No Person shall be convicted of Treason unless on the Testimony of two Witnesses to the same overt Act, or on Confession in open Court." U.S. Const. art. III, § 3.

▸ **constructive treason.** (17c) **1.** Speech that manifests a desire or intent to make war against the state or materially support an enemy, even though the speech is unaccompanied by acts that further the desire or intent. • There is no crime of constructive treason in U.S. law because treason requires an affirmative act, and intent alone cannot substitute for an act. Cf. SEDITION. **2.** *Hist.* Speech that is critical of the government. • This sense arose during the reign of Henry VIII of England. Critical speech remained a capital crime until the early 18th century.

▸ **high treason.** See main entry for TREASON.

▸ **petty treason.** (16c) *Archaic.* Murder of one's employer or husband. • Until 1828, this act was considered treason under English law. — Also spelled *petit treason.*

"The frequent reference to *high* treason is a carry-over from an ancient division of the offense that has long since disappeared. In the feudal stage of history the relation of lord to vassal was quite similar to the relation of king to subject. The relation of husband to wife came to be regarded in the same category, as also did the relation of master to servant, and that of prelate to clergyman. And just as it was *high* treason to kill the king, so a malicious homicide was *petit* treason if it involved a killing of (originally, lord by vassal, and later) husband by wife, master by mistress or servant, or prelate by clergyman. When the special brutality provided by the common law for the punishment of petit treason disappeared, this crime became merged with murder and only one crime of treason remained." Rollin M. Perkins & Ronald N. Boyce, *Criminal Law* 498–99 (3d ed. 1982).

treasonable misdemeanor. (18c) *English law.* An act that is likely to endanger or alarm the monarch, or disturb the public peace in the presence of the monarch. Cf. TREASON FELONY.

Treason Clause. *Constitutional law.* The constitutional provision defining treason against the United States as "levying War against them, or in adhering to their Enemies, giving them Aid and Comfort," as well as empowering Congress to declare the punishment for treason. U.S. Const. art. III, § 3.

treason felony. *English law.* **1.** An act that shows an intention of committing treason, unaccompanied by any further act to carry out that intention. • This offense usu. results in life imprisonment rather than the death penalty. **2.** *Scots law.* The devising of the overthrow of the sovereign or successors. **3.** *Scots law.* The devising of the levying of war on the sovereign to compel a change of measures or counsels, to intimidate Parliament, or to induce a foreign invasion. Cf. TREASONABLE MISDEMEANOR.

Treas. Reg. *abbr.* TREASURY REGULATION.

treasurer. (13c) An organization's chief financial officer. • The treasurer's duties typically include prudently depositing (or, if authorized, investing) and safeguarding the organization's funds and otherwise managing its finances; monitoring compliance with any applicable law relating to such finances and filing any required report; disbursing money as authorized; and reporting to the organization on the state of the treasury. — Also termed *finance officer; financial secretary; quartermaster.*

▸ **city treasurer.** (17c) A local officer who is responsible for managing municipal funds.

Treasurer, Lord High. See LORD HIGH TREASURER.

Treasurer of the United States. The officer in the U.S. Department of the Treasury responsible for overseeing the operations of the Bureau of Engraving and Printing and the U.S. Mint.

treasure trove. [Law French "treasure found"] (16c) Valuables (usu. gold or silver) found hidden in the ground or other private place, the owner of which is unknown. • At common law in the United States, the finder of a treasure trove can usu. claim good title against all except the true owner. But until 1996, any treasure trove found in the United Kingdom belonged to the Crown.

> "Treasure hid in the earth, not upon the earth, nor in the sea, and coin though not hidden, being found is the king's; we call it treasure trove." Henry Finch, *Law, or a Discourse Thereof* 177 (1759).

> "Treasure trove consists essentially of articles of gold and silver, intentionally hidden for safety in the earth or in some secret place, the owner being unknown, although it is probable that the category might include articles made from the required metals buried in the ground for other purposes, for example in connection with an ancient sepulture. In the United States, the state has never claimed title to lost property by virtue of its character as treasure trove, and it has been stated that the law relating thereto is merged with that of lost goods generally, although there is authority for the proposition that while treasure trove in the United States belongs to the finder, found goods not of that character go to the owner of the *locus in quo*." Ray Andrews Brown, *The Law of Personal Property* § 13, at 27–28 (2d ed. 1955).

Treasuries. (1922) Debt obligations of the federal government backed by the full faith and credit of the government. See TREASURY BILL; TREASURY BOND; TREASURY CERTIFICATE; TREASURY NOTE.

treasury. (13c) **1.** A place or building in which stores of wealth are kept; esp., a place where public revenues are deposited and kept and from which money is disbursed to defray government expenses. **2.** (*cap.*) DEPARTMENT OF THE TREASURY.

Treasury, First Lord. See FIRST LORD OF THE TREASURY.

Treasury Bench. In the British House of Commons, the first row of seats on the right hand of the speaker. • The Treasury Bench is occupied by the First Lord of the Treasury or principal minister of the Crown.

Treasury bill. (18c) A short-term debt security issued by the federal government, with a maturity of 13, 26, or 52 weeks. • These bills — auctioned weekly or quarterly — pay interest in the form of the difference between their discounted purchase price and their par value at maturity. — Abbr. T-bill. — Formerly also termed *certificate of indebtedness.*

Treasury bond. (1858) A long-term debt security issued by the federal government, with a maturity of 10 to 30 years. • These bonds are considered risk-free, but they usu. pay relatively little interest. — Abbr. T-bond.

▸ **TIPS bond.** (1997) A treasury bond whose face value is adjusted to keep pace with the inflation rate. • The acronym TIPS stands for *Treasury inflation-protected securities.* — Abbr. TIPS.

Treasury certificate. (18c) An obligation of the federal government maturing in one year and on which interest is paid on a coupon basis.

Treasury Department. See DEPARTMENT OF THE TREASURY.

Treasury inflation-protected securities. See *TIPS bond* under TREASURY BOND.

Treasury note. (18c) An intermediate-term debt security issued by the federal government, with a maturity of two to ten years. • These notes are considered risk-free, but they usu. pay relatively little interest. — Abbr. T-note.

> "Treasury Notes, short-term borrowings by the Federal Government, were first used in 1812–15. The term was one year except for those issued in 1815. Except for the small denominations, they bore interest. Over $36,000,000 were issued. Between 1837 and 1843 eights issues of treasury notes were put out, amounting to over $47,000,000 in all. During the Civil War, in addition to the interest-bearing issue, some noninterest-bearing demand notes were issued. Then came the Greenbacks, in 1862 and 1863, with $450,000,000 authorized. To pay for the silver bought under the Sherman Act of 1890, the Treasury Notes of 1890 were issued. They were noninterest bearing and were used as currency. During the [first] World War $51,000,000,000 of short-term issues were put out in anticipation of Liberty loans and tax receipts. Since then there have always been some outstanding, at first to give flexibility in debt repayment, and, after 1932, to get funds at low rates for deficits. On June 30, 1938, $9,147,000,000 were outstanding. Most were issued for a five-year term." James D. Magee, "Treasury Notes," in 5 *Dictionary of American History* 314 (James Truslow Adams ed., 1940).

Treasury Regulation. (1860) A regulation promulgated by the U.S. Treasury Department to explain or interpret a section of the Internal Revenue Code. • Treasury Regulations are binding on all taxpayers. — Abbr. Treas. Reg.

treasury security. See *treasury stock* under STOCK.

treasury share. See *treasury stock* under STOCK.

treasury stock. See STOCK.

treasury warrant. See WARRANT (2).

treat, *vb.* **1.** To negotiate; to consider and discuss terms <invitation to treat> <notice to treat>. **2.** To handle a subject in speech or writing; to give an exposition (followed by *of*) <how Cicero treats of rhetoric>. **3.** To deal with (a subject, topic, theme, etc.); to handle in discourse <to treat a difficult point with finesse and sophistication>. **4.** To pay someone else's expenses for a meal, drink, entertainment, etc. <my turn to treat>. **5.** To entertain, fête, or show hospitality to <to treat my friends to a meal>. **6.** To behave toward (someone or something) in a particular way <to treat coworkers as genuine colleagues>. **7.** To care for (a medical patient); to try to cure the illness or injury of (a person) by using medicine, hospital care, surgery, etc. **8.** To subject (a disease, debility, etc.) to a regimen of medicine, exercise, etc. **9.** To put a special substance on (something) in order to protect, clean, or preserve <to treat old bookbindings with leather conditioner>.

treating-physician rule. The principle that a treating physician's diagnoses and findings about the degree of a social-security claimant's impairment are binding on an administrative-law judge in the absence of substantial contrary evidence.

treatise (**tree**-tis), *n.* An extended, serious, and usu. exhaustive book on a particular subject. — Also termed *learned treatise.* See LEARNED-TREATISE RULE.

treaty. (15c) **1.** An agreement formally signed, ratified, or adhered to between two countries or sovereigns; an international agreement concluded between two or more states in written form and governed by international law. — Also termed *accord*; *convention*; *covenant*; *declaration*; *pact.* Cf. EXECUTIVE AGREEMENT.

> "Contracts between sovereign states are called by various names, none of which has a fixed meaning. *Treaty* is the generic term for an agreement formally signed, ratified, or adhered to by two or more sovereign states <Treaty of Warsaw>. An *accord* is any type of amicable arrangement between peoples or nations <Geneva Accord>. *Concord* is a more formal, slightly archaic equivalent of *accord.* A *protocol* is a treaty amending or supplementing an earlier treaty <Kyoto Protocol>. A *declaration* is ordinarily an agreement that declares or makes law <Declaration of Paris>. An *act* generally results from a formal conference involving high officials. A *compact* is typically an earnest exchange of promises between sovereigns <United Nations Global Compact>. *Pact,* a less formal equivalent, appears most often either in headlines because of its shortness or in certain set phrases such as *suicide pact.* A *paction* is a compact between two nations to be completed by the performance of a single act; the term is rare today. An *entente,* a shortened form of the French *entente cordiale,* is an amicable agreement between nations relating to some policy or course of action, especially involving foreign affairs <Anglo-Russian Entente>. A *convention* is usually a less formal or more specific type of multilateral treaty <Vienna Convention>. A *cartel* is a written agreement between opposing nations (belligerents) during wartime to regulate whatever dealings will take place between them <cartel for the exchange of prisoners of war>. A *concordat* is an agreement between a secular government and a church, especially the Vatican, for regulating church-state affairs <Concordat of 1801>. . . . In the U.S., an *executive agreement* is an agreement between the U.S. and another nation. Unlike a *treaty,* which must have the advice and consent of the Senate, an *executive agreement* is made by the President but not ratified by the Senate. Some writers loosely refer to *executive agreements* as *treaties.*" Bryan A. Garner, *Garner's Dictionary of Legal Usage* 902 (3d ed. 2011).

> "International law relating to treaties has largely been codified in the Vienna Convention on the Law of Treaties (1969) ('VCLT'). For the purposes of the VCLT, a 'treaty' is defined as 'an international agreement concluded between States in written form and governed by international law, whether embodied in a single instrument or in two or more related instruments and whatever its particular designation.' . . . An agreement between a State and a non-State entity does not constitute an international treaty, although such an agreement may be governed by international law and may regulate international law issues . . . ." Malgosia Fitzmaurice, "Treaties," in 9 *The Max Planck Encyclopedia of Public International Law* 1060, 1061 (Rüdiger Wolfrum ed., 2012) (citation omitted).

▸ **commercial treaty.** (18c) A bilateral or multilateral treaty concerning trade or other mercantile activities. • Such a treaty may be general in nature, as by supplying the framework of long-term commercial relations. Or it may be specific, as by detailing the conditions of particular branches of trade or other commercial transactions. Sometimes a treaty of this kind deals with an individual project, such as a guaranty agreement.

> "Commercial treaties are bilateral or multilateral treaties of public international law for the purpose of regulating conditions of, and establishing mutual rights to, trade and other commercial activities among the parties. They provide the relevant foundation of international economic law, which is essentially based on treaty law. Other sources of international law, in particular customary international law, are of limited relevance, arguably with the exception of procedural customary rules, State responsibility, and minimum standards for the treatment of aliens, in particular expropriation. . . . In addition to classic treaty law, commercial activities across national borders are informed by a variety of other legal sources, which need to be distinguished from commercial treaties: private international law on commercial activities — be it harmonized or not . . . — as well as domestic public law on external economic relations, which implements commercial treaty law or regulates market access to, and conditions of competition within, the domestic market autonomously." Matthias Oesch, "Commercial Treaties," in 2 *The Max Planck Encyclopedia of Public International Law* 406, 406 (Rüdiger Wolfrum ed., 2012).

▸ **defensive treaty.** (17c) A treaty in which each party agrees to come to the other's aid if one is attacked by another country. See *treaty of alliance.*

> "*Defensive treaties,* as generally understood, are made to secure the parties to them against aggression from other states. They may, also, aim at the maintenance of internal quiet, or of neutrality amid the conflicts of neighboring powers. To attempt to gain any of these objects is not necessarily contrary to the law of nations or to natural justice. Mutual aid, indeed, against the disturbers of internal quiet, may secure an absolute government against popular revolutions in favor of liberty, but if a confederation or alliance may secure to its members the enjoyment of free institutions, there is no reason, as far as international law is concerned, why institutions of an opposite kind may not support themselves in the same way." Theodore D. Woolsey, *Introduction to the Study of International Law* § 107, at 171 (5th ed. 1878).

▸ **dispositive treaty** (dis-**poz**-ə-tiv). (1918) A treaty by which a country takes over territory by impressing a special character on it, creating something analogous to a servitude or easement in private law.

▸ **guarantee treaty.** (18c) An agreement between countries directly or indirectly establishing a unilateral or reciprocal guarantee. — Also spelled *guaranty treaty.* — Also termed *treaty of guarantee*; *quasi-guarantee treaty*; *pseudo-guarantee treaty.*

> "In many instances where the term 'guarantee' is used in international treaties, the contracting parties merely intend to underline their willingness to comply with the obligation they have entered into. Obligations of this kind do not fall within the concept of guarantee in the proper sense of the term. In this particular respect, the expression 'pseudo-guarantees' or 'quasi-guarantee treaties' is used." George Ress, "Guarantee Treaties," in 2 *Encyclopedia of Public International Law* 634 (1995).

▸ **lawmaking treaty.** A treaty that creates general norms framed as legal propositions that govern the parties' conduct, not just between themselves but as to all states. • Examples include the Declaration of Paris of 1856 (on neutrality in maritime warfare), the Geneva Protocol of 1925 (on prohibited weapons), the General Treaty for the Renunciation of War of 1928, and the Genocide Convention of 1948.

▸ **mixed treaty.** (18c) A treaty with characteristics of different types of treaties, esp. contrasting types (e.g., permanent and transitory, or personal and real).

▸ **nonaggression treaty.** See NONAGGRESSION PACT.

▸ **nonproliferation treaty.** (1964) A treaty forbidding the transfer of nuclear weapons from a country with a nuclear arsenal to one that does not have nuclear-weapons capability. • The first such treaty was concluded in 1968, and now more than 100 countries have agreed to its terms. — Also termed *nuclear-nonproliferation treaty.*

▸ **offensive treaty.** (17c) A treaty in which the parties agree to declare war jointly on another country and join forces to wage the war. See *treaty of alliance.*

▸ **peace treaty.** (1850) A treaty signed by heads of state to end a war. — Also termed *treaty of peace.* Cf. TRUCE.

> "A peace differs not from a truce essentially in the length of its contemplated duration, for there may be very long armistices and a state of peace continuing only a definite number of years. The ancients often concluded treaties of peace which were to expire after a certain time . . . ." Theodore D. Woolsey, *Introduction to the Study of International Law* § 158, at 268 (5th ed. 1878).

▸ **permanent treaty.** (18c) A treaty that contemplates ongoing performance (as with a treaty of neutrality).

▸ **personal treaty.** (17c) *Hist.* A treaty relating exclusively to the contracting sovereign as a person. • Examples of personal treaties are family alliances and treaties guaranteeing the throne to a particular sovereign and his or her family. With the advent of constitutional government in Europe, personal treaties have lost their importance.

▸ **pseudo-guarantee treaty.** See *guarantee treaty.*

▸ **quasi-guarantee treaty.** See *guarantee treaty.*

▸ **real treaty.** (17c) A treaty relating solely to the subject matter of the compact, independently of the persons of the contracting sovereigns. • Real treaties continue to bind the state even when the heads of government change.

▸ **transitory treaty.** (1911) A treaty carried into effect once and for all, so that it is complete when the act has been performed (as with a treaty of cession).

▸ **treaty of alliance.** (16c) A treaty establishing mutual and reciprocal support obligations. • A treaty of alliance may be for support in defense, aggression, or both. See *defensive treaty*; *offensive treaty.*

> "A treaty of alliance can bind the parties to no injustice, nor justify either of them in being accessory to an act of bad faith on the part of another. Hence a defensive, still more an offensive alliance, can only contemplate, if lawful, the warding off of intended injustice." Theodore D. Woolsey, *Introduction to the Study of International Law* § 107, at 172 (5th ed. 1878).

▸ **treaty of guarantee.** See *guarantee treaty.*

▸ **treaty of neutrality.** (17c) A treaty in which the parties agree not to engage in any aggressive action against one another, whether individually or jointly with others, and not to interfere with the other party's affairs. • There is no commitment to aid another party in the event of war — only to refrain from becoming involved.

> "*Treaties of neutrality* are reciprocal engagements to have no part in the conflicts between other powers — to remain at peace in an apprehended or an actual war. They are suggested by, and prevent the evils of that interference of nations in each other's affairs, for the preservation of the balance of power or the safety of the parties interfering, which is so common in modern history." Theodore D. Woolsey, *Introduction to the Study of International Law* § 107, at 172 (5th ed. 1878).

▸ **treaty of peace.** See *peace treaty.*

2. A contract or agreement between insurers providing for treaty reinsurance. See *treaty reinsurance* under REINSURANCE. **3.** A negotiated contract or agreement between private persons.

▸ **private treaty.** (1858) An agreement to convey property negotiated by the buyer and seller or their agents. • This term is esp. common in the United Kingdom.

Treaty Clause. *Constitutional law.* The constitutional provision giving the President the power to make treaties, with the advice and consent of the Senate. U.S. Const. art. II, § 2.

treaty-created law. See CONVENTIONAL LAW.

treaty law. See CONVENTIONAL LAW.

treaty-made law. See CONVENTIONAL LAW.

treaty of reinsurance. See REINSURANCE TREATY.

treaty power. (1835) The President's constitutional authority to make treaties, with the advice and consent of the Senate. See TREATY CLAUSE.

treaty reinsurance. See REINSURANCE.

treaty transfer. (2005) The return of a foreign national convicted of a crime in one country to his or her home country if the countries have a transfer agreement in place and if the eligibility requirements are met. • Run by the Department of Justice, this program began in 1977 when Mexico and the United States entered into a bilateral treaty allowing these transfers. — Also termed *treaty-transfer program*; *International Prisoner Transfer Program.* Cf. REFOULEMENT.

treble damages. See DAMAGES.

trebucket (**tree**-bək-it). See CASTIGATORY.

trend. A price pattern in the stock market generally or in a particular stock.

▸ **major trend.** A long-term trend of the stock market; a general increase or decrease of stock prices over an extended period. — Also termed *fundamental trend.*

▸ **market trend.** The direction of stock-market prices over a several-month period.

trespass (**tres**-pəs *or* **tres**-pas), *n.* (13c) **1.** An unlawful act committed against the person or property of another; esp., wrongful entry on another's real property. Cf. *unlawful entry* under ENTRY (1). **2.** At common law, a lawsuit for injuries resulting from an unlawful act of this kind. • The lawsuit was instituted by a writ of trespass. **3.** *Archaic.* MISDEMEANOR. — **trespass,** *vb.* — **trespassory** (**tres**-pə-sor-ee), *adj.*

> "The familiar legend on notice-boards, 'Trespassers will be prosecuted,' implies that it is a crime, but this may usually be dismissed as 'a wooden lie.' Yet in time past the idea was correct, for trespass of any sort was punishable by

fine and imprisonment as well as redressible by an action for damages, and actually it was not until 1694 that the punitive element disappeared although it had faded into obsolescence long before that date. But nowadays trespass is never criminal except under special statutes which make it punishable . . . ." P.H. Winfield, *A Textbook of the Law of Tort* § 90, at 307 (5th ed. 1950).

"The term trespass has been used by lawyers and laymen in three senses of varying degrees of generality. (1) In its widest and original signification it includes any wrongful act — any infringement or transgression of the rule of right. This use is common in the Authorised Version of the Bible, and was presumably familiar when that version was first published. But it never obtained recognition in the technical language of the law, and is now archaic even in popular speech. (2) In a second and narrower signification — its true legal sense — the term means any legal wrong for which the appropriate remedy was a writ of trespass — *viz.* any direct and forcible injury to person, land, or chattels. (3) The third and narrowest meaning of the term is that in which, in accordance with popular speech, it is limited to one particular kind of trespass in the second sense — *viz.* the tort of trespass to land (trespass *quare clausum fregit*)." R.F.V. Heuston, *Salmond on the Law of Torts* 4 (17th ed. 1977).

"Before the word 'misdemeanor' became well established the old writers tended to use the word 'trespass' to indicate an offense below the grade of felony. And it was used at times by Blackstone for this purpose, as in the phrase 'treason, felony, or trespass.'" Rollin M. Perkins & Ronald N. Boyce, *Criminal Law* 405 (3d ed. 1982).

▸ **cattle-trespass.** *Hist.* Trespass by one's cattle or other animals on another's land, as a result of which the other might either distrain them damage feasant or sue for trespass in the local courts. • At first (from the early 13th century) this type of trespass applied only to intentional trespass by the keeper of the cattle, but in 1353 it was extended to beasts that had merely escaped. This type of trespass gave rise to strict liability.

"It has long been settled that liability for cattle-trespass is independent of negligence, and it is that which constitutes its strictness. And, in spite of some confusion in time past, it is quite distinct from the *scienter* type of liability. In *Lee v. Riley* [(1865), 18 C.B. (N.S.) 722] the defendant's mare strayed through a gap in his fence, which it was his duty to repair, to the plaintiff's land and there quarrelled with and kicked the plaintiff's horse. The defendant was held liable for cattle-trespass. A great deal of argument was expended at the trial on whether the defendant had notice of the ferocious disposition of his mare, but Erle, C.J., pointed out that, however relevant that might have been in a *scienter* action, it was beside the mark in one for cattle-trespass." P.H. Winfield, *A Textbook of the Law of Tort* § 148, at 518 (5th ed. 1950).

▸ **constructive trespass.** See *trespass to chattels.*

▸ **continuing trespass.** (1822) A trespass in the nature of a permanent invasion on another's rights, such as a sign that overhangs another's property.

▸ **criminal trespass.** (16c) **1.** A trespass on property that is clearly marked against trespass by signs or fences. **2.** A trespass in which the trespasser remains on the property after being ordered off by a person authorized to do so.

▸ **innocent trespass.** (18c) A trespass committed either unintentionally or in good faith.

▸ **joint trespass.** (17c) A trespass that two or more persons have united in committing, or that some have actually committed while others commanded, encouraged, or directed it.

▸ **permanent trespass.** (1871) A trespass consisting of a series of acts, done on consecutive days, that are of the same nature and that are renewed or continued from day to day, so that the acts in the aggregate form one indivisible harm.

▸ **simple trespass.** (17c) *Criminal law.* Trespass classified as a minor criminal offense.

▸ **trespass *ab initio*** (ab i-**nish**-ee-oh). (18c) An entry on land that, though begun innocently or with a privilege, is deemed a trespass from the beginning because of conduct that abuses the privilege.

▸ **trespass by relation.** (18c) A trespass committed when the plaintiff had a right to immediate possession of land but had not yet exercised that right. • When the plaintiff takes possession, a legal fiction treats the plaintiff as having had possession ever since the accrual of the right of entry. This is known as *trespass by relation* because the plaintiff's possession relates back to the time when the plaintiff first acquired a right to possession.

▸ **trespass *de bonis asportatis*** (dee **boh**-nis as-pər-**tay**-tis). [Latin "trespass for carrying goods away"] (17c) **1.** A wrongful taking of chattels. • This type of trespassory taking was also an element of common-law larceny. **2.** At common law, an action to recover damages for the wrongful taking of chattels. — Abbr. trespass d.b.a. — Often shortened to *trespass de bonis.* — Also termed *trespass to personal property.*

▸ **trespass on the case.** (15c) At common law, a lawsuit to recover damages that are not the immediate result of a wrongful act but rather a later consequence. • The lawsuit was instituted by a writ of trespass on the case. It was the precursor to a variety of modern-day tort claims, including negligence, nuisance, and business torts. — Often shortened to *case.* — Also termed *action on the case; breve de transgressione super casum.*

"The most important of the writs framed under the authority of the statute of Westminster 2 is that of 'trespass on the case,' to meet cases analogous to trespass in delict, but lacking the element of direct or immediate force or violence. This writ gave a form of action in which the court was enabled to render judgment of damages in cases of fraud, deceit, negligence, want of skill, defamation oral or written, and all other injurious acts or omissions resulting in harm to person or property, but wanting the *vi et armis*, the element of direct force and violence, to constitute trespass." Edwin E. Bryant, *The Law of Pleading Under the Codes of Civil Procedure* 7 (2d ed. 1899).

"Common law recognizes a distinction between the actions of trespass vi et armis (or simply trespass) and trespass on the case. This distinction has been expressed by stating that a tort committed by the direct application of force is remediable by an action for trespass, while a tort accomplished indirectly is a matter for trespass on the case. Other authority makes the distinction on the basis of the defendant's intent, stating that trespass involves a willful and deliberate act while trespass on the case contemplates an act or omission resulting from negligence." 1 Am. Jur. 2d *Actions* § 23, at 738 (1994).

▸ **trespass *quare clausum fregit*** (**kwair**-ee-**klaw**-zəm-**free**-jit). [Latin "why he broke the close"] (17c) **1.** A person's unlawful entry on another's land that is visibly enclosed. • This tort consists of doing any of the following without lawful justification: (1) entering on to land in the possession of another, (2) remaining on the land, or (3) placing or projecting any object on it. **2.** At common law, an action to recover damages resulting from another's unlawful entry on one's land that is visibly enclosed. — Abbr. trespass q.c.f. — Also termed *trespass to real property; trespass to land; quare clausum querentis fregit.* See *trespass vi et armis.*

"Every unwarrantable entry on another's soil the law entitles a trespass by *breaking his close*; the words of the writ of trespass commanding the defendant to shew cause, *quare clausum querentis fregit*. For every man's land is in the eye of the law enclosed and set apart from his neighbour's: and that either by a visible and material fence, as one field is divided from another by a hedge; or, by an ideal invisible boundary, existing only in the contemplation of law, as when one man's land adjoins to another's in the same field. And every such entry or breach of a man's close carries necessarily along with it some damage or other: for, if no other special loss can be assigned, yet still the words of the writ itself specify one general damage, viz. the treading down and bruising his herbage." 3 William Blackstone, *Commentaries on the Laws of England* 209–10 (1768).

▸ **trespass to chattels.** (1843) The act of committing, without lawful justification, any act of direct physical interference with a chattel possessed by another. • The act must amount to a direct forcible injury. — Also termed *trespass to goods; constructive trespass.*

"Trespass to goods is a wrongful interference with the possession of them. It may take innumerable forms, such as scratching the panel of a coach, removing a tire from a car, injuring or destroying goods, or in the case of animals, beating or killing them, or infecting them with disease. All that is necessary is that the harm done should be direct . . . ." P.H. Winfield, *A Textbook of the Law of Tort* § 99, at 345 (5th ed. 1950).

▸ **trespass to goods.** See *trespass to chattels.*

▸ **trespass to land.** See *trespass quare clausum fregit* (2).

▸ **trespass to personal property.** See *trespass de bonis asportatis.*

▸ **trespass to real property.** See *trespass quare clausum fregit* (2).

▸ **trespass to try title.** (1826) **1.** In some states, an action for the recovery of property unlawfully withheld from an owner who has the immediate right to possession. **2.** A procedure under which a claim to title may be adjudicated.

▸ **trespass *vi et armis*** (VI et ahr-mis). [Latin "with force and arms"] (17c) **1.** At common law, an action for damages resulting from an intentional injury to person or property, esp. if by violent means; trespass to the plaintiff's person, as in illegal assault, battery, wounding, or imprisonment, when not under color of legal process, or when the battery, wounding, or imprisonment was in the first instance lawful, but unnecessary violence was used or the imprisonment continued after the process had ceased to be lawful. • This action also lay for injury to relative rights, such as menacing tenants or servants, beating and wounding a spouse, criminal conversation with or seducing a wife, or debauching a daughter or servant. **2.** See *trespass quare clausum fregit.* • In this sense, the "force" is implied by the "breaking" of the close (that is, an enclosed area), even if no real force is used.

trespass-affidavit building. (1998) A crime-infested property whose owners or management have filed an affidavit authorizing police to question or arrest anyone who is in the building without permission.

trespass d.b.a. See *trespass de bonis asportatis* under TRESPASS.

trespasser. (14c) Someone who commits a trespass; one who intentionally and without consent or privilege enters another's property. • In tort law, a landholder owes no duty to unforeseeable trespassers. Cf. INVITEE; LICENSEE (2).

"The word 'trespasser' has an ugly sound, but it covers the wicked and the innocent. The burglar and the arrogant squatter are trespassers, but so are all sorts of comparatively innocent and respectable persons such as a walker in the countryside who unhindered strolls across an open field. Perhaps much of the trouble in this area has arisen from 'the simplistic stereotype' of the definition. The courts are therefore beginning to recognise that the duty of the occupier may vary according to the nature of the trespasser." R.F.V. Heuston, *Salmond on the Law of Torts* 278 (17th ed. 1977).

▸ **innocent trespasser.** (1888) Someone who enters another's land unlawfully, but either inadvertently or believing in a right to do so.

trespass for mesne profits. (18c) *Hist.* An action — supplementing an action for ejectment — brought against a tenant in possession to recover the profits wrongfully received during the tenant's occupation.

trespass notice. (1897) **1.** A sign warning against trespassing. **2.** A written statement given by a store owner to a known or suspected shoplifter not to return to the premises. Cf. PERSONA NON GRATA LETTER.

trespass q.c.f. See *trespass quare clausum fregit* under TRESPASS.

tret (tret), *n.* (16c) An allowance or abatement of a certain weight or quantity that a seller makes to a buyer because of water or dust that may be mixed with a commodity. Cf. TARE.

triable, *adj.* (15c) Subject or liable to judicial examination and trial <a triable offense>.

triable either way. (1977) *English law.* (Of an offense) prosecutable either in the Crown Court or in a magistrates' court.

"The criminal courts in England and Wales are the magistrates' courts and the Crown Court. Those offences considered least serious are summary offences, triable only in the magistrates' courts. Those offences considered most serious are triable only on indictment, in the Crown Court. A large number of offences, such as theft and most burglaries, are 'triable either way,' in a magistrates' court or the Crown Court. For these offences the defendant can elect to be tried at the Crown Court, where there is a judge and jury. If the defendant does not wish a Crown Court trial, the magistrates may decide (having heard representations from the prosecutor) that the case is so serious that it should be committed to the Crown Court for trial." Andrew Ashworth, *Principles of Criminal Law* 16 (1991).

trial. (15c) A formal judicial examination of evidence and determination of legal claims in an adversary proceeding.

▸ **abortive trial.** See MISTRIAL.

▸ **bellwether trial.** See BELLWETHER TRIAL.

▸ **bench trial.** (1954) A trial before a judge without a jury. • The judge decides questions of fact as well as questions of law. — Also termed *trial to the bench; nonjury trial; court trial; trial before the court* (TBC); *judge trial.*

▸ **bifurcated trial.** (1945) A trial that is divided into two stages, such as for guilt and punishment or for liability and damages. — Also termed *two-stage trial.* Cf. SEVERANCE (2).

▸ **closed trial.** (1942) A trial that is not open to the public, usu. because of some overriding concern such as a need to protect a child's anonymity or for security.

▸ **court trial.** See *bench trial.*

▸ **ex parte trial.** (1814) A trial in which only one side of the case is heard, usu. because the opposing party is not present. See *trial in absentia.*

▸ **fair trial.** See FAIR TRIAL.

▸ **joint trial.** (18c) A trial involving two or more parties; esp., a criminal trial of two or more persons for the same or similar offenses.

▸ **judge trial.** See *bench trial.*

▸ **jury trial.** (18c) A trial in which the factual issues are determined by a jury, not by the judge. — Also termed *trial by jury.*

▸ **mock trial.** See MOCK TRIAL.

▸ **new trial.** (16c) A postjudgment retrial or reexamination of some or all of the issues determined in an earlier judgment. • The trial court may order a new trial by motion of a party or on the court's own initiative. Also, when an appellate court reverses the trial court's judgment, it may remand the case to the trial court for a new trial on some or all of the issues on which the reversal is based. *See* Fed. R. Civ. P. 59; Fed. R. Crim. P. 33. See MOTION FOR NEW TRIAL; REMAND.

> "A new trial, as the term is used in law, is a retrial. Just why the less definite term 'new trial' is used, it would be difficult and, at present, without profit, to explain. The statutory definitions in the various states will be found substantially the same. Upon comparison with the common-law definition the only differences consist in differences of phraseology. The definition given in the California Code of Civil Procedure is as follows: 'A new trial is a re-examination of an issue of fact in the same court after a trial and decision by a jury or court or by referees.' The only perceptible reason for using the word 're-examination' in preference to the word 'retrial' is that the former is a more euphonious expression. In this instance exactitude and clearness have been sacrificed to rhetorical effect. New trial is the statutory, and therefore the exclusive and appropriate, method of re-examining issues of fact." 1 Thomas Carl Spelling, *A Treatise on New Trial and Appellate Practice* 2 (1903).

▸ **nonbinding minitrial.** See *summary jury trial.*

▸ **nonbinding summary jury trial.** See *summary jury trial.*

▸ **nonjury trial.** See *bench trial.*

▸ **perfect trial.** A trial free from all error.

▸ **political trial.** (18c) A trial (esp. a criminal prosecution) in which either the prosecution or the defendant (or both) uses the proceedings as a platform to espouse a particular political belief; a trial of a person for a political crime. See SHOW TRIAL.

▸ **public trial.** (16c) A trial that anyone may attend or observe.

▸ **separate trial.** (18c) **1.** *Criminal procedure.* The individual trial of each of several persons jointly accused of a crime. Fed. R. Crim. P. 14. **2.** *Civil procedure.* Within a single action, a distinct trial of a separate claim or issue — or of a group of claims or issues — ordered by the trial judge, usu. to conserve resources or avoid prejudice. Fed. R. Civ. P. 42(b). Cf. SEVERANCE (2).

▸ **short-cause trial.** See *short cause* under CAUSE (3).

▸ **show trial.** See SHOW TRIAL.

▸ **speedy trial.** See SPEEDY TRIAL.

▸ **state trial.** (17c) A trial for a political offense.

▸ **stipulated bench trial.** (1971) A nonjury trial, usu. in a criminal case, in which the judge considers only facts that are agreed to by the parties.

▸ **summary jury trial.** (1984) A settlement technique in which the parties argue before a mock jury, which then reaches a nonbinding verdict that will assist the parties in evaluating their positions. — Abbr. SJT. — Also termed *nonbinding summary jury trial; nonbinding minitrial.* Cf. MOCK TRIAL.

▸ **trial at bar.** (17c) *Hist.* A trial before all the judges of the court in which the proceedings take place. — Also termed *trial at the bar.*

▸ **trial at nisi prius** (nɪ-sɪ prɪ-əs). (17c) *Hist.* A trial before the justices of assize and nisi prius in the county where the facts are alleged to have occurred, and from which county the jurors have been summoned.

▸ **trial before the court.** See *bench trial.*

▸ **trial by battle.** See TRIAL BY COMBAT.

▸ **trial by certificate.** (16c) *Hist.* A trial in which the issue is decided on evidence in the form of witnesses' certificates of what they individually know.

▸ **trial by combat.** See TRIAL BY COMBAT.

▸ **trial by duel.** See TRIAL BY COMBAT.

▸ **trial by inspection.** (18c) *Hist.* A trial in which the judge decided the dispute by individual observation and investigation, without the benefit of a jury.

▸ **trial by jury.** See *jury trial.*

▸ **trial by ordeal.** See ORDEAL.

▸ **trial by record.** (18c) *Hist.* A trial in which, a record having been pleaded by one party and denied by the other, the record is inspected in order to decide the dispute, no other evidence being admissible. See NUL TIEL RECORD.

▸ **trial by the country.** See *trial per pais.*

▸ **trial by the record.** (17c) A trial in which one party insists that a record exists to support its claim and the opposing party denies the existence of such a record. • If the record can be produced, the court will consider it in reaching a verdict — otherwise, it will rule for the opponent.

▸ **trial by witnesses.** *Hist.* A trial in which the contesting parties are required to appear in court with witnesses assembled to give evidence before one or more judges, as opposed to a jury.

> "The *trial by witnesses* is in very few instances legally competent. It seems, however, that it is still applicable (as anciently) to an issue *arising on the death of the husband in an action of dower,* and in some other cases. In case of trial by *witnesses,* the court, upon issue joined, awards that both parties produce in court at a given day their respective witnesses. The judges examine and decide, and the judgment is pronounced accordingly. It is, however, laid down, that, if after the evidence, the judges are still unable to satisfy themselves on the fact, they have a discretion then to send the parties *to the country.*" Henry John Stephen, *A Treatise on the Principles of Pleading in Civil Actions* 102–03 (Samuel Williston ed., 8th Am. ed. 1857).

▸ **trial de novo** (dee *or* di **noh**-voh). (18c) A new trial on the entire case — that is, on both questions of fact and issues of law — conducted as if there had been no trial in the first instance.

▸ **trial in absentia.** (1946) A trial held without the accused being present. • In the United States, a trial may be held *in absentia* only if the accused has either voluntarily left after the trial has started or else so disrupted the proceedings that the judge orders the accused's removal as a last resort.

▸ **trial on the merits.** (18c) A trial on the substantive issues of a case, as opposed to a motion hearing or interlocutory matter.

▸ **trial per pais** (pər **pay** *or* **pays**). [Law French "trial by the country"] (17c) Trial by jury. — Also spelled *trial per pays.* — Also termed *trial by the country.* Cf. CONCLUSION TO THE COUNTRY; GOING TO THE COUNTRY; PATRIA (3).

▸ **trial to the bench.** See *bench trial.*

▸ **trifurcated trial.** (1959) A trial that is divided into three stages, such as for liability, general damages, and special damages.

▸ **two-stage trial.** See *bifurcated trial.*

trial brief. See BRIEF (1).

trial by combat. (16c) *Hist.* A trial that is decided by personal battle between the disputants, common in Europe and England during the Middle Ages; specif., a trial in which the person accused fought with the accuser, the idea being that God would give victory to the person in the right. • This method was introduced into England by the Normans after 1066, but it was a widely detested innovation and was little used. It became obsolete several centuries before being formally abolished in 1818, having been replaced in practice by the grand assize and indictment. — Also termed *trial by battle; trial by wager of battle; trial by duel; judicial combat; duel; duellum; wager of battle; ornest; vadiatio duelli; wehading.* See JUDICIUM DEI.

> "No tradition can tell us just when the trial by combat first came into existence. Wager of battle was a natural accompaniment of the state of society existing when men were accustomed to take the law into their own hands and test the right by the might that could back it up. Battle has always been the law among the lower animals and in the evolution of the species, before society had developed the standards of our present civilization, the males of the human species, in barbarous nations, won the females much oftener through the law of battle, than by the display of intellectual attainments." Edward J. White, *Legal Antiquities* 109 (1913).

trial by corsnaed. See *ordeal of the morsel* under ORDEAL.

trial by duel. See TRIAL BY COMBAT.

trial by oath. See COMPURGATION.

trial by ordeal. See ORDEAL.

trial by wager of battle. See TRIAL BY COMBAT.

trial by witness. See TRIAL.

trial calendar. See DOCKET (2).

trial counsel. See COUNSEL.

trial court. See COURT.

trial de novo. See TRIAL.

trial error. See ERROR (2).

trial examiner. See ADMINISTRATIVE-LAW JUDGE.

trial franchise. See FRANCHISE (4).

trial judge. See JUDGE.

trial jury. See *petit jury* under JURY.

trial of right of property. (1822) **1.** INTERVENTION (1). **2.** INTERVENTION (2).

trial per pais. See TRIAL.

trial-setting preference. See *special setting* under SETTING.

trial tax. *Criminal law. Slang.* The difference between the prosecution's last offer in a plea bargain and a harsher sentence imposed by a court. • This is alleged to be a punishment for refusing to accept a plea bargain and for taxing the judicial system's resources by forcing a case to go to trial.

trial-type hearing. See ADMINISTRATIVE PROCEEDING.

triangular merger. See MERGER (8).

tribal court. (*often cap.*) Under the Indian Child Welfare Act, a court that has child-custody jurisdiction and that is (1) a Court of Indian Offenses, (2) a court established and operated under an Indian tribe's code or custom, or (3) any other tribal administrative body that is vested with authority over child-custody proceedings. • The Tribal Court is composed of tribal members, is usu. situated on the reservation, and varies in its characteristics from tribe to tribe. It is not part of any state's judicial system, instead operating more or less as a judicial system of a foreign nation. See INDIAN CHILD WELFARE ACT.

tribal-exhaustion doctrine. (1995) The general principle that when an Indian tribal court, original or appellate, has personal and subject-matter jurisdiction, the parties must pursue all remedies available under tribal law before turning to nontribal courts. • A federal court may review a challenge to jurisdiction only after the tribal court has established it has jurisdiction and determined the case on the merits. *See National Farmer's Union Ins. Co. v. Crow Tribe*, 471 U.S. 845, 856–57, 105 S.Ct. 2447, 2454 (1985).

tribal land. A part of an Indian reservation that is not allotted to or occupied by individual Indians but is held as the tribe's common land. Cf. INDIAN LAND.

tribe. 1. Broadly, a discrete group of people characterized by sociological, cultural, and familial links <Celtic tribes of Gaul>. • A tribe is not necessarily a united and cohesive sociological group. The term is also used loosely to refer to any group, such as a family <the Kincaid tribe>. **2.** *American Indian law.* A definable group or organized band or pueblo of American Indians, esp. those residing on one reservation. *See* 25 USCA § 479.

> "By a 'tribe' we understand a body of Indians of the same or a similar race, united in a community under one leadership or government, and inhabiting a particular though sometimes ill-defined territory; by a 'band,' a company of Indians not necessarily, though often of the same race or tribe, but united under the same leadership in a common design." *Montoya v. U.S.*, 180 U.S. 261, 266, 21 S.Ct. 358, 359 (1901).

tribunal (trɪ-**byoo**-nəl). (15c) **1.** A court of justice or other adjudicatory body. **2.** The seat, bench, or place where a judge sits.

▸ **administrative tribunal.** (1811) **1.** A court-like decision-making authority that resolves disputes, esp. those in which one disputant is a government agency or department; an administrative agency exercising a quasi-judicial function. **2.** A governmental division established to implement legislative policy.

▸ **commercial tribunal.** (18c) A court or division of a court whose judges hear primarily or exclusively business-related cases because of their experience and expertise.

▸ **domestic tribunal.** (17c) A disciplinary body that has jurisdiction over the internal affairs of an organization, profession, or association with powers conferred by contract with the members or under a statute.

tributary (**trib**-yə-ter-ee), *n.* (14c) A stream flowing directly or indirectly into a river.

tribute (**trib**-yoot), *n.* (14c) **1.** An acknowledgment of gratitude or respect. **2.** A contribution that a sovereign raises from its subjects to defray the expenses of state. **3.** Money paid by an inferior sovereign or state to a superior one to secure the latter's friendship and protection.

tributum (tri-**byoo**-təm), *n.* [Latin] *Roman law.* Originally, a war tax; later, a regular tax on land or persons in the Roman provinces.

tri-chad. See CHAD.

trickery, *n.* (18c) The use of subterfuge or stratagems to deceive, esp. to induce some action or statement by another.

trier of fact. See FACT-FINDER.

trifle, *n.* **1.** The fact of being wholly unimportant or nonserious. **2.** Something that is not at all important.

trifurcated trial. See TRIAL.

trigamy (**trig**-ə-mee), *n.* (17c) The act of marrying a person while legally married to someone else and bigamously married to yet another.

> "Trigamy, literally three marriages, is often used for a special situation. 'Trigamy,' in the sense of the special problem of the third wife, stems from the premise that invalidity of the alleged prior marriage is a good defense to a charge of bigamy. Thus in a bigamy prosecution a so-called common-law marriage can be relied upon to establish either the first or second marriage, if it is recognized in the jurisdiction as giving rise to the marital status, but cannot be relied upon where it is not so recognized. A logical result is that a charge of bigamy may be defeated by showing that the alleged prior marriage, relied upon to support the charge, was itself void because of an even earlier marriage existing at the time—as was held about 1648 in Lady Madison's Case. For example, **D** marries **A**, and afterward while **A** is alive marries **B**, and still later when **A** is dead but **B** alive, marries **C**. The marriage to **C** is not bigamy because the marriage to **B** was bigamous and void." Rollin M. Perkins & Ronald N. Boyce, *Criminal Law* 458 (3d ed. 1982).

triggering condition. See CONDITION (2).

trimester, *n.* (1907) **1.** A three-month period; specif., one of the three three-month periods into which human pregnancies are traditionally divided. See PREGNANCY. **2.** One of three academic terms of nearly equal length into which the year is divided at some schools. Cf. SEMESTER.

Trinity House. *Maritime law.* A British corporation chartered in 1514 to train and license pilots and officially regulate pilotage. • Later, under Queen Elizabeth I and King James I, the corporation acquired authority for dredging ballast, establishing beacons, and building lighthouses on the coasts of Great Britain. Today the corporation continues to build and maintain navigational aids, including buoys, beacons, and lighthouses. It also trains pilots and operates a charity for the benefit of mariners. Its activities are funded in part through duties on commercial shipping.

Trinity sittings. (1816) *English law.* A term of court beginning on May 22 of each year and ending on June 12. • This was known until 1875 as *Trinity term.* Cf. EASTER SITTINGS; HILARY SITTINGS; MICHAELMAS SITTINGS.

trinoda necessitas. [Latin "threefold taxes"] *Hist.* The three services or taxes irrecusably owed to the Crown in Anglo-Saxon times, namely brigbote (for the building and maintenance of bridges), burghbote (for the building and maintenance of fortifications), and fyrdbote (for service in the militia when called). • Blackstone calls the three *pontis reparatio* (bridges), *arcis constructio* (fortifications), and *expeditio contra hostem* (militia). *See* 1 William Blackstone, *Commentaries on the Laws of England* 255 (1765). See BOTE (1).

tripartite (trɪ-**pahr**-tɪt), *adj.* (15c) Involving, composed of, or divided into three parts or elements <a tripartite agreement>.

tripartite lease. See *finance lease* under LEASE.

tripartite test. *Patents.* A judicial test for determining patent infringement by looking at whether a challenged device or process, though outside the literal scope of the patent claims, performs the function in substantially the same way. See SUBSTANTIAL EQUIVALENT.

triple damages. See *treble damages* under DAMAGES.

triple-L P. See *limited-liability limited partnership* under PARTNERSHIP.

triple net lease. See *net-net-net lease* under LEASE.

triple ordeal. See ORDEAL.

triple trigger. *Insurance.* (1981) A theory of coverage providing that all insurers on a risk must cover a loss from the day a claimant is first exposed to an injury-producing product (such as asbestos) to the date of diagnosis or death, whichever occurs first. • This term was first used in *Keene Corp. v. Insurance Co. of N. Am.*, 667 F.2d 1034 (D.C. Cir. 1981). — Also termed *continuous trigger.* Cf. ACTUAL-INJURY TRIGGER; EXPOSURE THEORY; MANIFESTATION THEORY.

triple witching session. See SESSION (3).

triplicate, *n.* (1801) Three identical copies or parts <wills prepared in triplicate> <triplicate receipts>.

triplicatio (trip-li-**kay**-shee-oh), *n.* [Latin] *Roman law.* A defendant's response to a plaintiff's *replicatio.* See REPLICATIO. Cf. QUADRUPLICATIO. Pl. ***triplicationes*** (trip-li-kay-shee-**oh**-neez).

TRIPs. *abbr.* (1988) *Intellectual property.* The Agreement on Trade-Related Aspects of Intellectual Property Rights, a treaty that harmonized and strengthened the intellectual-property laws of its signatories by linking the obligation to protect the intellectual-property rights of other members' citizens with a mechanism for settling international trade disputes. • TRIPs was negotiated at the 1994 Uruguay Round of the General Agreement on Tariffs and Trade (GATT). More than 150 countries are parties to the agreement. In the field of patents, TRIPs standardized patentable subject matter to include medicines, required testing for nonobviousness and utility, and protected patentees from infringing imports. In response to the agreement

Congress (1) changed patent terms to 20 years from the date of application, rather than 17 years from the date of issue; (2) allowed foreign filers to prove priority by inventive efforts that preceded filing; (3) widened the definition of infringement to cover offering for sale and importing; and (4) permitted provisional applications, with brief descriptions and no claims, to establish priority. 33 I.L.M. 1197. In the field of copyrights, TRIPs incorporates most of the provisions of the Berne Convention for the Protection of Literary or Artistic Works, and sets the length of copyright protection as the life of the author plus 50 years. In the field of trademarks, TRIPs sets the initial term of a trademark registration as not less than seven years, and makes it renewable indefinitely. Countries subject to TRIPs may make registrability dependent on use but may not require use as a condition for filing an application. — Also written TRIPS. — Also termed *TRIPs Agreement.*

> "Articles 1-8 of TRIPs include the basic principles of national treatment and most-favoured-nation treatment. That is, each Member must give to the nationals of other Members treatment no less favourable than that given to its own nationals, and must give to the nationals of all Members the same privileges as are given to the nationals of any Member. Thus, subject to certain exemptions, bilateral agreements between Members should no longer be permitted." Philip W. Grubb, *Patents for Chemicals, Pharmaceuticals and Biotechnology* 31 (3d ed. 1999).

tristis successio (**tris**-tis sək-**ses[h]**-ee-oh). See *hereditas luctuosa* under HEREDITAS.

triverbial days (trɪ-**vər**-bee-əl). See *dies fasti* under DIES.

trivial, *adj.* (16c) Trifling; inconsiderable; of small worth or importance.

TRO (tee-ahr-**oh**). *abbr.* (1969) TEMPORARY RESTRAINING ORDER.

Trojan-horse defense. (2004) *Criminal law. Slang.* In a computer-crime case, such as possession of child pornography, a defendant's argument that the illegal material was stored on the computer by someone else without the defendant's knowledge.

troll. 1. NONPRACTICING ENTITY. **2.** COPYRIGHT TROLL.

troubled asset. See ASSET.

trove. See TREASURE TROVE.

trover (**troh**-vər). (16c) A common-law action for the recovery of damages for the conversion of personal property, the damages generally being measured by the property's value. — Also termed *trover and conversion.* Cf. DETINUE; REPLEVIN.

> "Trover may be maintained for all kinds of personal property, including legal documents, but not where articles are severed from land by an adverse possessor, at least until recovery of possession of the land. It lies for the misappropriation of specific money, but not for breach of an obligation to pay where there is no duty to return specific money." Benjamin J. Shipman, *Handbook of Common-Law Pleading* § 43, at 99 (Henry Winthrop Ballantine ed., 3d ed. 1923).

TRP. *abbr.* **1.** Temporary-release program (for prison inmates). **2.** Treatment-readiness program — a substance-abuse and venereal-disease educational program for prison inmates.

truancy (**troo**-ən-see), *n.* (18c) The quality, state, or condition of shirking responsibility; esp., willful and unjustified failure to attend school by one who is required to attend. — **truant,** *adj.* & *n.*

truancy officer. (1912) An official responsible for enforcing laws mandating school attendance for minors of specified ages (usu. 16 and under). — Also termed *truant officer; attendance officer.*

truant, *n.* (15c) Someone who without permission is absent from work or school or who shirks a duty; esp., a minor who stays away from school without authorization — **truant,** *adj.*

truce. (13c) *Int'l law.* A suspension or temporary cessation of hostilities by agreement between belligerent powers. — Also termed *armistice; ceasefire; suspension of arms.* Cf. *peace treaty* under TREATY (1). — **trucial,** *adj.*

> "Truces are conventions, by which, even during the continuance of war, hostilities on each side cease for a time. DURING THE CONTINUANCE OF WAR; for, as Cicero says, in his eighth Philippic, between peace and war there is no medium. By war is meant a state of affairs, which may exist even while its operations are not continued. Therefore, as Gellius has said, a peace and a truce are not the same, for the war still continues, though fighting may cease. So that any agreement, deemed valid in the time of war, will be valid also during a truce, unless it evidently appears that it is not the state of affairs, which is considered, but the commission of particular acts of hostility. On the other hand, any thing, agreed to, to be done, when peace shall be made, cannot take place in consequence of a truce. There is no uniform and invariable period fixed for the continuance of a truce, it may be made for any time, even for twenty, or thirty years, of which there are many instances in ancient history. A truce, though a repose from war, does not amount to a peace, therefore historians are correct in saying that a peace has often been refused, when a truce has been granted." Hugo Grotius, *The Rights of War and Peace* 403–04 (1625; A.C. Campbell trans., 1901).

▸ **general truce.** (16c) A truce suspending hostilities in all places.

▸ **special truce.** (17c) A truce referring only to operations before a specific fortress or in a district, or between certain detachments of armies. — Also termed *partial truce.*

truck. (18c) *Hist. Scots law.* The payment of wages in scrip or goods. • Truck systems, once common where workers had to live in isolated areas and depended on company stores for food and clothing, were abolished in the 19th century.

> "Truck was payment not in money but in goods or tickets which could be exchanged for goods. . . . The principle that contractors could buy in bulk and retail to the workmen, deducting the cost from their wages, was sound but was open to abuse; in fact truck became a means of robbery. Railway contractors frequently made more profit from truck than from the contract. . . . Truck shops, frequently called tommy shops or tally shops, might be run by the contractor or let by him to an associate or a shopkeeper for a rent or on the basis that part of the shop profits would go back to the contractor. The goods were frequently inferior and sold at excessive prices. David M. Walker, 6 *A Legal History of Scotland* 820 (2001).

true admission. See *judicial admission* under ADMISSION (1).

true and correct. (17c) Authentic; accurate; unaltered <we have forwarded a true and correct copy of the expert's report>. — Also termed *true and exact.*

true bill, *n.* (18c) A grand jury's notation that a criminal charge should go before a petty jury for trial <the grand

jury returned a true bill, and the state prepared to prosecute>. — Also termed *billa vera*. Cf. NO BILL.

true-bill, *vb.* (1887) To make or deliver a true bill on <the grand jury true-billed the indictment>.

true copy. See COPY (1).

true defense. See DEFENSE (1).

true democracy. See *direct democracy* under DEMOCRACY.

true legal impossibility. See *legal impossibility* (1) under IMPOSSIBILITY.

true mark. See *technical trademark* under TRADEMARK.

true residue. See CLEAR RESIDUE.

true threat. An intentional statement that expresses a sincere intent to commit an act of unlawful violence against a particular individual or group. • Courts generally consider whether the statement was knowingly or intentionally communicated to the victim (it need not be directly), and undertake a totality-of-the-circumstances analysis of all relevant factors that might reasonably affect the statement's interpretation.

true trademark. See *technical trademark* under TRADEMARK.

true value. See *fair market value* under VALUE (2).

true-value rule. (1900) The rule requiring that one who subscribes for and receives corporate stock must pay par value for it, in either money or its equivalent, so that a corporation's real assets square with its books. • If true value is less than par value, the stock is deemed unpaid for to the full extent of the difference, and the affected shareholder is liable to creditors for the difference, notwithstanding the directors' good faith.

true verdict. See VERDICT (1).

truncate (trəng-kayt), *vb.* (15c) **1.** To cut short. **2.** To remove (an original paper check) from the check-collection or return process for the purpose of sending to the recipient in lieu of that check a substitute check or, by agreement, information relating to the original check. 12 USCA § 5002(18).

truncation. The practice, required of merchants by the Fair and Accurate Credit Transactions Act, of not printing more than the last five digits of the card number on a point-of-sale credit-card or debit-card receipt. • The term is sometimes loosely extended to the practice, required by the same statute, of not printing the card's expiration date. *See* 15 USCA § 1681c(g).

trust, *n.* (15c) **1.** The right, enforceable solely in equity, to the beneficial enjoyment of property to which another person holds the legal title; a property interest held by one person (the *trustee*) at the request of another (the *settlor*) for the benefit of a third party (the *beneficiary*). • For a trust to be valid, it must involve specific property, reflect the settlor's intent, and be created for a lawful purpose. The two primary types of trusts are *private trusts* and *charitable trusts* (see below). **2.** A fiduciary relationship regarding property and charging the person with title to the property with equitable duties to deal with it for another's benefit; the confidence placed in a trustee, together with the trustee's obligations toward the property and the beneficiary. • A trust arises as a result of a manifestation of an intention to create it. See FIDUCIARY RELATIONSHIP. **3.** The property so held; CORPUS (1).

"In its technical sense, a trust is the right, enforceable solely in equity to the beneficial enjoyment of property, the legal title of which is vested in another and implies separate coexistence of the legal and the equitable titles vested in different persons at the same time; in its more comprehensive sense the term embraces every bailment, every transaction by agent or factor, every deposit, and every matter in which the slightest trust or confidence exists. The word *trust*, however, is frequently employed to indicate duties, relations, and responsibilities which are not strictly and technically trusts." William C. Dunn, *Trusts for Business Purposes* 2 (1922).

"One must distinguish, . . . [in] countries where English is spoken, between a wide and a narrow sense of the word 'trust.' In the wide sense a trust exists when property is to be held or administered by one person on behalf of another or for some purpose other than his own benefit. . . . In the narrow or strict sense a trust exists when the creator of the trust . . . hands over or is bound to hand over the control of an asset which, or the proceeds of which, is to be administered by another (the trustee or administrator) in his capacity as such for the benefit of some person (beneficiary) other than the trustee or for some impersonal object. A trust in this sense is a species of the genus 'trust' in the wide sense." Tony Honoré, *The South African Law of Trusts* §§ 1–2, at 1–3 (3d ed. 1985).

"Some courts and legal writers have defined a trust as a certain kind of right that the beneficiary has against the trustee, or a certain kind of interest that the beneficiary has against the trustee, or a certain kind of interest that the beneficiary has in the trust property, thus looking at it from the point of view of the beneficiary. While it is true that the beneficiary has the right or interest described, the trust is something more than the right or interest of the beneficiary. The trust is the whole juridical device: the legal relationship between the parties with respect to the property that is its subject matter, including not merely the duties that the trustee owes to the beneficiary and to the rest of the world, but also the rights, privileges, powers, and immunities that the beneficiary has against the trustee and against the rest of the world. It would seem proper, therefore, to define the trust either as a relationship having certain characteristics stated in the definition or perhaps as a juridical device or legal institution involving such a relationship." 1 Austin W. Scott & William F. Fratcher, *The Law of Trusts* § 2.4, at 42 (4th ed. 1987).

"In the strict, traditional sense, a trust involves three elements: (1) a trustee, who hold the trust property and is subject to deal with it for the benefit of one or more others; (2) one or more beneficiaries, to whom and for whose benefit the trustee owes duties with respect to the trust property; and (3) trust property, which is held by the trustee for the beneficiaries. In a more comprehensive sense, the trust purpose is often included in discussions of the elements of the trusts . . . . Although all of these elements are present in a complete trust, either or both of elements (1) and (2) above may be temporarily absent without destroying the trust or preventing its creation." Restatement (Third) of Trusts § 2 cmt. f (2003).

▸ **2503(b) trust.** (1955) A trust that requires a distribution of income to the beneficiary at least annually, and provides that gifts to the trust qualifying as gifts of a present interest become eligible for the annual gift-tax exclusion. • It is named after the section of the IRS code on which it is based. *See* IRC (26 USCA) § 2503(b).

▸ **2503(c) trust.** (1954) A trust with only one beneficiary, who must be a minor and must have the power to withdraw all assets from the trust upon attaining the age of 21. • This type of trust derives its name from the requirements set forth in IRC (26 USCA) § 2503(c). Although the trust may continue after the beneficiary turns 21, gifts to the trust will no longer qualify for the annual exclusion if the beneficiary has no immediate right to withdraw the gift. — Also termed *minor's trust*.

▸ **A-B-Q trust.** See *bypass trust.*

▸ **A-B trust.** See *bypass trust.*

▸ **accumulation trust.** (1910) A trust in which the trustee must accumulate income and gains from sales of trust assets for ultimate disposition with the principal when the trust terminates. • Many states restrict the time over which accumulations may be made or the amount that may be accumulated.

▸ **active trust.** (1827) A trust in which the trustee has some affirmative duty of management or administration besides the obligation to transfer the property to the beneficiary. — Also termed *express active trust; special trust; operative trust.* Cf. *passive trust.*

▸ **Alaska trust.** See *asset-protection trust* (1).

▸ **alimony trust.** (1933) A trust in which the payor spouse transfers to the trustee property from which the payee spouse, as beneficiary, will be supported after a divorce or separation.

▸ **annuity trust.** (1826) A trust from which the trustee must pay a sum certain annually to one or more beneficiaries for their respective lives or for a term of years, and must then either transfer the remainder to or for the use of a qualified charity or retain the remainder for such a use. • The sum certain must not be less than 5% of the initial fair market value of the property transferred to the trust by the donor. A qualified annuity trust must comply with the requirements of IRC (26 USCA) § 664.

▸ **asset-protection trust.** (1989) **1.** A trust designed specifically to insulate assets from the settlor's creditors. • When the trust is created using the law of a state, it is also termed a *domestic asset-protection trust.* It may also be referred to by the name of the specific state, e.g., *Alaska trust, Delaware trust,* or *Nevada trust.* If it is created under foreign law, even though the assets are within the United States, it is also termed *offshore asset-protection trust.* **2.** See *self-settled trust.* — Abbr. APT.

▸ **bank-account trust.** See *Totten trust.*

▸ **blended trust.** (1882) A trust in which the beneficiaries are a group, with no member of the group having a separable individual interest. • Courts rarely recognize these trusts.

▸ **blind trust.** (1969) A trust in which the settlor places investments under the control of an independent trustee, usu. to avoid a conflict of interest. • The beneficiary has no knowledge of the trust's holdings and no right to participate in the trust's management.

▸ **bond trust.** (1922) A trust whose principal consists of bonds that yield interest income.

▸ **bypass trust.** (1981) A trust into which just enough of a decedent's estate passes, so that the estate can take advantage of the unified credit against federal estate taxes. *See* 26 USCA § 2010. • Designed to avoid estate taxes and probate costs, the bypass trust is created when two spouses grant to each other property with the provision that beneficiaries (usu. children) will obtain the property of the first spouse to die. The surviving spouse is given a life interest in that property and may be allowed to spend some of the principal. Upon the last spouse's death, all the trust property passes to the trust beneficiaries outside the estate-tax regime. — Also termed *credit-shelter trust; A-B trust; AB trust; A-B-Q trust; marital life-estate trust.* See *unified estate-and-gift tax credit* under TAX CREDIT.

▸ **charitable lead trust.** (1970) An irrevocable trust made in favor of a charity and allowing the charity to receive income from the trust property for a specified period, after which the property reverts to the settlor's estate. — Abbr. CLT.

▸ **charitable-remainder annuity trust.** (1970) A charitable-remainder trust in which the beneficiaries receive for a specified period a fixed payment of 5% or more of the fair market value of the original principal, after which the remaining principal passes to charity. — Abbr. CRAT. — Also termed *charitable-remainder-trust retirement fund.*

▸ **charitable-remainder trust.** (1961) A trust consisting of assets that are designated for a charitable purpose and paid over to the trust after the expiration of a life estate or intermediate estate. — Abbr. CRT. — Also termed *split-interest trust.*

▸ **charitable-remainder-trust retirement fund.** See *charitable-remainder annuity trust.*

▸ **charitable trust.** (18c) A trust created to benefit a specific charity, specific charities, or the general public rather than a private individual or entity. • Charitable trusts are often eligible for favorable tax treatment. If the trust's terms do not specify a charity or a particular charitable purpose, a court may select a charity. *See* Unif. Trust Act § 405. — Also termed *public trust; charitable use.* See *charitable deduction* under DEDUCTION; CY PRES. Cf. *private trust.*

▸ ***Claflin* trust.** See *indestructible trust.*

▸ ***Clifford* trust.** (1941) An irrevocable trust, set up for at least ten years and a day, whereby income from the trust property is paid to the beneficiary but the property itself reverts back to the settlor when the trust expires. • These trusts were often used by parents — with their children as beneficiaries — to shelter investment income, but the Tax Reform Act of 1986 eliminated the tax advantage by imposing the kiddie tax and by taxing the income of settlors with a reversionary interest that exceeds 5% of the trust's value. This term gets its name from *Helvering v. Clifford,* 309 U.S. 331, 60 S.Ct. 554 (1940). — Also termed *short-term trust.*

▸ **common-law trust.** See *business trust* under TRUST (4).

▸ **community land trust.** *Real estate.* A membership-based nonprofit organization designed to enable low- and moderate-income families to benefit from equity built through homeownership while preserving the affordability of homes so that future residents will enjoy the same opportunities. • The community land trust owns the land and residence, leasing the land to low- and moderate-income homeowners who agree to limit the profit they take when selling the residence, thereby ensuring its affordability to the next buyer.

▸ **community trust.** See COMMUNITY TRUST.

▸ **complete voluntary trust.** See *executed trust.*

▸ **complex trust.** (1832) A trust having elaborate provisions. See *discretionary trust.*

▸ **conservation land trust.** *Real estate.* A nonprofit conservation organization under 26 USCA §501(c)(3) that, as all or a substantial part of its mission, actively works to conserve land by undertaking or assisting in fee-land or conservation-easement acquisition through donation or purchase, or by stewardship of such land or easements.

▸ **conservation trust.** See *land trust* (2).

▸ **constructive trust.** (18c) An equitable remedy by which a court recognizes that a claimant has a better right to certain property than the person who has legal title to it. • This remedy is commonly used when the person holding the property acquired it by fraud, or when property obtained by fraud or theft (as with embezzled money) is exchanged for other property to which the wrongdoer gains title. The court declares a constructive trust in favor of the victim of the wrong, who is given a right to the property rather than a claim for damages. The obligation of the constructive trustee is simply to turn the property over to the constructive beneficiary; the device does not create a "trust" in any usual sense of that word. The name of the remedy came about because early cases applying it involved trustees who wrongfully appropriated funds from trusts, making it convenient to say that they remained constructive trustees of whatever they had wrongfully acquired. The term persists because the analogy between the remedy and a real trust is strong: in both cases the legal holder of title to property has no right to the enjoyment of it. — Also termed *implied trust*; *involuntary trust*; *trust de son tort*; *trust ex delicto*; *trust ex maleficio*; *remedial trust*; *trust in invitum*. See *trustee de son tort* under TRUSTEE (1). Cf. *resulting trust*.

"A constructive trust is the formula through which the conscience of equity finds expression. When property has been acquired in such circumstances that the holder of the legal title may not in good conscience retain the beneficial interest, equity converts him into a trustee." *Beatty v. Guggenheim Exploration Co.*, 122 N.E. 378, 380 (N.Y. 1919).

"It is sometimes said that when there are sufficient grounds for imposing a constructive trust, the court 'constructs a trust.' The expression is, of course, absurd. The word 'constructive' is derived from the verb 'construe,' not from the verb 'construct.' . . . The court construes the circumstances in the sense that it explains or interprets them; it does not construct them." 5 Austin W. Scott & William F. Fratcher, *The Law of Trusts* § 462.4 (4th ed. 1987).

▸ **contingent trust.** (18c) An express trust depending for its operation on a future event.

▸ **continuing trust.** (18c) **1.** A trust that does not end upon the grantor's death. **2.** A trust that does not end on a particular date or upon the occurrence of a particular event. • Such a trust must be planned so as not to violate the rule against perpetuities. **3.** A trust whose proceeds have not yet been distributed.

▸ **credit-shelter trust.** See *bypass trust*.

▸ ***Crummey* trust.** (1969) A trust in which the trustee has the power to distribute or accumulate income and to give the beneficiary the right to withdraw an amount equal to the annual gift exclusion (or a smaller sum) within a reasonable time after the transfer. • This type of trust can have multiple beneficiaries and is often used when the beneficiaries are minors. Gifts to a *Crummey* trust qualify for the annual gift exclusion regardless of the age of the beneficiaries. The trust assets are not required to be distributed to the beneficiaries at age 21. The validity of this type of trust was established in *Crummey v. Commissioner*, 397 F.2d 82 (9th Cir. 1968). — Also termed *discretionary trust*. See CRUMMEY POWER; *annual exclusion* (1) under EXCLUSION (1). Cf. *2503(c) trust*.

▸ **custodial trust.** (1967) A revocable trust for which a custodial trustee is named to manage the assets for an incapacitated or disabled beneficiary. • The beneficiary does not have to be disabled or incapacitated at the time the trust is created. An adult beneficiary who is not disabled or incapacitated may terminate the trust at any time before his or her disability, incapacity, or death.

▸ **declared trust.** See *express trust*.

▸ **defective trust.** (1845) A trust that is treated, for income-tax purposes, as if it were the same entity as the grantor, but for estate-tax purposes is treated as an entity separate from the grantor. • Typically a trust is an independent entity that is taxed separately from the settlor. Because trust income is taxed at higher rates than individual income, the settlor may intentionally create a defect in the trust terms so that the trust's income will be taxable to the grantor. This is achieved by violating the grantor-trust rules of IRC §§ 671–677 in a way that does not affect the completeness of the gift under IRC §§ 2035–2042. A violation renders the trust "defective" because the settlor must recognize the income even if the settlor does not actually receive it. The attribution of tax liability and payment of taxes on trust income do not give the grantor an ownership in the trust, which remains separate from the settlor's estate and is not subject to estate taxes.

▸ **Delaware trust.** See *asset-protection trust* (1).

▸ **destructible trust.** (1953) A trust that can be destroyed by the happening of an event or by operation of law.

▸ **directory trust.** (1837) **1.** A trust that is not completely and finally settled by the instrument creating it, but only defined in its general purpose and to be carried into detail according to later specific directions. **2.** See *fixed trust*.

▸ **direct trust.** See *express trust*.

▸ **discretionary trust.** (1837) **1.** A trust in which the settlor has delegated nearly complete or limited discretion to the trustee to decide when and how much income or property is distributed to a beneficiary. • This is perhaps the most common type of trust used in estate planning. **2.** See *Crummey trust*. Cf. *mandatory trust*; CRUMMEY POWER.

▸ **domestic asset-protection trust.** See *asset-protection trust* (1).

▸ **donative trust.** (1930) A trust that establishes a gift of a beneficial interest in property for a beneficiary. • Most trusts are donative trusts. — Also termed *gratuitous trust*.

▸ **donor-advised trust.** (2009) A trust set up by a public charity using cash or other assets donated by a person who will act as a director of the trust. IRC (26 USCA) § 4966(d)(2). — Also termed *donor-advised fund*.

▸ **dry trust.** (1806) **1.** A trust that merely vests legal title in a trustee and does not require that trustee to do anything. **2.** See *passive trust*.

▸ **dynasty trust.** (1989) A generation-skipping trust funded with the amount that is permanently exempt from generation-skipping tax and designed to last more than two generations. • In 2000, a settlor could contribute $1 million to a dynasty trust. Almost half the states allow dynasty trusts, despite their potential for lasting more than 100 years. — Also termed *GST supertrust.* Cf. *perpetual trust* (2).

▸ **educational trust.** (1868) **1.** A trust to found, endow, or support a school. **2.** A trust to support someone's education.

▸ **electing small-business trust.** (1992) A trust of which the beneficiaries are individuals, estates, certain charitable organizations, or certain governmental entities, who did not purchase an interest in the trust, and for which the trustee has elected to be taxed as an S corporation. IRC (26 USCA) § 1391(e)(1). — Abbr. ESBT.

▸ **equipment trust.** See EQUIPMENT TRUST.

▸ **estate trust.** (18c) A trust that is established to qualify a deceased spouse's property for the marital deduction. • The trustee may be given discretion to distribute principal or income to the donor's spouse if the donor also provides that, at the surviving spouse's death, any accumulated income and remaining principal must be distributed to the surviving spouse's estate. See *marital deduction* under DEDUCTION (2).

▸ **ex delicto trust** (də-**lik**-toh). (1999) A trust that is created for an illegal purpose, esp. to prevent the settlor's creditors from collecting their claims out of the trust property.

▸ **executed trust.** (1822) A trust in which the estates and interests in the subject matter of the trust are completely limited and defined by the instrument creating the trust and require no further instruments to complete them. — Also termed *complete voluntary trust.*

▸ **executory trust** (eg-**zek**-yə-tor-ee). (18c) A trust in which the instrument creating the trust is intended to be provisional only, and further conveyances are contemplated by the trust instrument before the terms of the trust can be carried out. — Also termed *imperfect trust.*

▸ **express active trust.** See *active trust.*

▸ **express private passive trust.** (1940) A trust in which land is conveyed to or held by one person in trust for another, without any power being expressly or impliedly given to the trustee to take actual possession of the land or exercise any ownership rights over it, except at the beneficiary's direction.

▸ **express trust.** (18c) A trust created with the settlor's express intent, usu. declared in writing; an ordinary trust as opposed to a resulting trust or a constructive trust. — Also termed *direct trust; declared trust.*

> "A trust is a confidence reposed in and accepted by some person or persons, and it is an *Express Trust* when it has been intentionally and deliberately created, as when any one gives away property to another but at the same time declares that such property shall be held or applied in a particular way for the benefit of some person or persons other than the formal donee, or of some other person or persons as well as of the donee." Augustine Birrell, *The Duties and Liabilities of Trustees* 6–7 (1920).

▸ **family-pot trust.** (1976) A trust in which all the assets are kept in a single fund for the trustee to use for multiple beneficiaries (usu. children). • Family-pot trusts are typically testamentary and used to administer a donor's property until the donor's minor children have completed their education.

▸ **family trust.** (1850) A trust created to benefit persons who are related to one another by blood, affinity, or law.

▸ **fixed trust.** (18c) A trust in which the trustee may not exercise any discretion over the trust's management or distributions. — Also termed *directory trust; nondiscretionary trust.*

▸ **foreign-situs trust** (sɪ-təs). (1954) A trust created under foreign law. • This type of trust usu. has no significant income-tax benefits and is subject to greater reporting requirements than a domestic trust. Because creditors cannot easily reach the foreign trust's assets, it is frequently used as a means of asset-protection. — Also termed *foreign trust; offshore trust.*

▸ **general trust.** See *passive trust.*

▸ **generation-skipping trust.** (1976) A trust that is established to transfer (usu. principal) assets to a skip person (a beneficiary more than one generation removed from the settlor). • The transfer is often accomplished by giving some control or benefits (such as trust income) of the assets to a nonskip person, often a member of the generation between the settlor and skip person. This type of trust is subject to a generation-skipping transfer tax. IRC (26 USCA) §§ 2601 et seq. See DEEMED TRANSFEROR; GENERATION-SKIPPING TRANSFER; *generation-skipping transfer tax* under TAX; SKIP PERSON. Cf. *dynasty trust.*

▸ **governmental trust. 1.** A type of charitable trust established to provide a community with facilities ordinarily supplied by the government, esp. by a municipality, and to promote purposes that are sufficiently beneficial to the community to justify permitting the property to be perpetually devoted to those purposes. • Examples of such facilities include public buildings, bridges, streets, parks, schools, and hospitals. **2.** A type of charitable trust established for general governmental or municipal purposes, such as defraying the expenses of a governmental entity or paying the public debt. Restatement (Second) of Trusts §§ 373, 374 (1959).

▸ **grantor-retained annuity trust.** (1989) An irrevocable trust into which the grantor transfers property in exchange for the right to receive fixed payments at least annually, based on original fair market value of the property transferred. • At the end of the specified time, the principal passes to a noncharitable beneficiary such as the grantor's child or grandchild. Essentially, the grantor makes to the remainderman a current gift of the right to trust assets at a specified date in the future. — Abbr. GRAT.

▸ **grantor-retained income trust.** (1986) A trust in which a gift's value can be reduced by the grantor's retaining an income interest, for a specified time, in the gifted property. • At the end of the specified time, the principal passes to a noncharitable beneficiary such as the grantor's child or grandchild. Essentially, the grantor makes to the remainderman a current gift of the right to trust assets at a specified date in the future. — Sometimes shortened to *retained income trust.* — Abbr. GRIT.

▸ **grantor-retained unitrust.** (1990) An irrevocable trust into which the grantor transfers property in exchange for the right to receive annual payments, the amount of which fluctuates based on the increase or decrease in the value of the property transferred. — Abbr. GRUT. Cf. *grantor-retained annuity trust.*

▸ **grantor trust.** (1923) A trust in which the settlor retains control over the trust property or its income to such an extent that the settlor is taxed on the trust's income. • The types of controls that result in such tax treatment are set out in IRC (26 USCA) §§ 671–677. An example is the revocable trust.

▸ **gratuitous trust.** See *donative trust.*

▸ **GST supertrust.** See *dynasty trust.*

▸ **half-secret trust.** (1943) A trust whose existence is disclosed on the face of the document creating it but whose beneficiaries are not disclosed. Cf. *secret trust*; *semi-secret trust.*

▸ **honorary trust.** (1844) A noncharitable trust that is of doubtful validity because it lacks a beneficiary capable of enforcing the trust. • Examples include trusts for the care and support of specific animals, or for the care of certain graves. The modern trend is to recognize the validity of such trusts, if the trustee is willing to accept the responsibility. If the trustee fails to carry out the duties, however, a resulting trust arises in favor of the settlor's residuary legatees or next of kin.

▸ **illegal trust.** (1822) A trust that is contrary to a statute, public policy, or morality.

▸ **Illinois land trust.** See *land trust* (1).

▸ **illusory trust.** (1939) An arrangement that looks like a trust but, because of powers retained in the settlor, has no real substance and is not a completed trust.

▸ **imperfect trust.** See *executory trust.*

▸ **implied trust.** **1.** See *constructive trust.* **2.** See *resulting trust.*

▸ **incentive trust.** (1954) A private trust that uses trust income, principal, or both as a tool for controlling beneficiary behavior. • An example is a trust that gives accumulated trust income and trust principal to a beneficiary only if he or she graduates from college or a trust that requires an income beneficiary to submit to regular drug tests and terminates the beneficiary's right to income if a test for illegal drugs is positive.

▸ **indestructible trust.** (1909) A trust that, because of the settlor's wishes, cannot be prematurely terminated by the beneficiary. — Also termed *Claflin trust.*

▸ **insurance trust.** (1893) A trust whose principal consists of insurance policies or their proceeds.

▸ **inter vivos trust** (**in**-tər **vɪ**-vohs *or* **vee**-vohs). (1921) A trust that is created and takes effect during the settlor's lifetime. — Also termed *living trust.* Cf. *testamentary trust.*

▸ **investment trust.** See *investment company* under COMPANY.

▸ **involuntary trust.** See *constructive trust.*

▸ **irrevocable trust** (i-**rev**-ə-kə-bəl). (1837) A trust that cannot be terminated by the settlor once it is created. • In most states, a trust will be deemed irrevocable unless the settlor specifies otherwise.

▸ **land trust.** (1828) **1.** A land-ownership arrangement by which a trustee holds both legal and equitable title to land while the beneficiary retains the power to direct the trustee, manage the property, and draw income from the trust. — Also termed *Illinois land trust*; *naked land trust.* **2.** A nonprofit entity that preserves land by acquiring title or conservation easements, dedicating the land to agricultural, forest, recreational, open-space, or similar nondevelopment uses. — Also termed *conservation trust.*

▸ **life-insurance trust.** (1835) A trust consisting of one or more life-insurance policies payable to the trust when the insured dies.

▸ **limited trust.** A trust created for a limited period. Cf. *perpetual trust* (1).

▸ **liquidating trust.** (1931) A trust designed to be liquidated as soon as possible. • An example is a trust into which a decedent's business is placed to safeguard the business until it can be sold.

▸ **living trust.** See *inter vivos trust.*

▸ **mandatory trust.** A trust in which the trustee must distribute all the income generated by the trust property to one or more designated beneficiaries. — Also termed *simple trust.* Cf. *discretionary trust.*

▸ **marital-deduction trust.** (1953) A testamentary trust created to take full advantage of the marital deduction; esp., a trust entitling a spouse to lifetime income from the trust and sufficient control over the trust to include the trust property in the spouse's estate at death. See *marital deduction* under DEDUCTION (2).

▸ **marital life-estate trust.** See *bypass trust.*

▸ **Massachusetts trust.** See *business trust* under TRUST (4).

▸ **Medicaid-qualifying trust.** (1989) A trust deemed to have been created in an effort to reduce someone's assets so that the person may qualify for Medicaid, and that will be included as an asset for purposes of determining the person's eligibility. • A person who wants to apply and qualify for Medicaid, but who has too many assets to qualify, will sometimes set up a trust — or have a spouse or custodian set up a trust — using the applicant's own assets, under which the applicant may be the beneficiary of all or part of the payments from the trust, which are distributed by a trustee with discretion to make trust payments to the applicant. Such a trust may be presumed to have been established for the purpose of attempting to qualify for Medicaid, and may be counted as an asset of the applicant, resulting in a denial of benefits and the imposition of a penalty period during which the applicant cannot reapply. Nonetheless, Medicaid rules allow three types of trusts that do not impair Medicaid eligibility, since the trust assets are not considered the beneficiary's property: *Miller trust*, *pooled trust*, and *under-65 trust.* — Abbr. MQT.

▸ ***Miller* trust.** (1991) An irrevocable trust funded with the income of an incompetent beneficiary who seeks to qualify for Medicaid in a state with an income cap. • Funding is strictly limited to the beneficiary's income (from any source). The assets in the trust are not included in the beneficiary's estate for Medicaid purposes if the trust assets will be used to reimburse the state after the beneficiary's death. Trust distributions are kept below the income cap in order to preserve the beneficiary's Medicaid eligibility. This type of trust was first judicially sanctioned in *Miller v. Ibarra*, 746 F.Supp.

19 (D. Colo. 1990). — Also termed *Miller's trust*; *qualified income trust.*

▸ **ministerial trust.** See *passive trust.*

▸ **minor's trust.** See *2503(c) trust.*

▸ **mixed trust.** A trust established to benefit both private individuals and charities.

▸ **naked land trust.** See *land trust* (1).

▸ **naked trust.** See *passive trust.*

▸ **Nevada trust.** See *asset-protection trust* (1).

▸ **nominal trust.** See *passive trust.*

▸ **nominee trust.** (1974) **1.** A trust in which the beneficiaries have the power to direct the trustee's actions regarding the trust property. **2.** An arrangement for holding title to real property under which one or more persons or corporations, under a written declaration of trust, declare that they will hold any property that they acquire as trustees for the benefit of one or more undisclosed beneficiaries. — Also termed (in sense 2) *realty trust.*

▸ **nondiscretionary trust.** See *fixed trust.*

▸ **nongrantor-owner trust.** (1982) A trust in which the beneficiary has an unrestricted power to vest the principal or interest in him or herself. IRC (26 USCA) § 678. — Also termed *678 trust.*

▸ **offshore asset-protection trust.** See *asset-protection trust* (1).

▸ **offshore trust.** See *foreign-situs trust.*

▸ **onerous trust.** A trust that places exceptionally heavy and time-consuming duties of responsibility and care on the trustee, often without providing for compensation. • Because of the burden and inequity of requiring the trust to be administered voluntarily, courts often grant a trustee a reasonable sum for the tasks performed.

▸ **operative trust.** See *active trust.*

▸ **oral trust.** (1853) **1.** A trust created by the settlor's spoken statements as opposed to a written agreement. • Trusts of real property must usu. be in writing (because of the statute of frauds). Trusts of personal property may be created orally but require clear and convincing evidence to show that an oral trust was created. Unif. Trust Act § 8407. — Also termed *parol trust.* **2.** A trust created by operation of law, such as a resulting trust or a constructive trust.

▸ **parol trust.** See *oral trust* (1).

▸ **passive trust.** (1835) A trust in which the trustee has no duty other than to transfer the property to the beneficiary. — Also termed *dry trust*; *general trust*; *nominal trust*; *simple trust*; *naked trust*; *ministerial trust*; *technical trust.* See *bare trustee* under TRUSTEE (1). Cf. *active trust.*

▸ **pension trust.** (1825) An employer-funded pension plan; esp., a pension plan in which the employer transfers to trustees amounts sufficient to cover the benefits payable to the employees.

▸ **perpetual trust.** (18c) **1.** A trust that is to continue as long as the need for it continues, such as for the lifetime of a beneficiary or the term of a particular charity. Cf. *limited trust.* **2.** A private trust that, under the local version of the rule against perpetuities, may last either indefinitely or for an extended time (e.g., 360 years). Cf. (in sense 2) *dynasty trust.*

▸ **personal-residence trust.** (1991) An irrevocable trust to which the settlor transfers ownership of his or her personal residence while retaining the right to live there for a specified term of years. • The trust cannot hold any assets other than the residence and proceeds resulting from damage to or destruction of the residence. — Abbr. PRT. Cf. *qualified personal-residence trust.*

▸ **personal trust.** See *private trust.*

▸ **pet trust.** An honorary trust that is established for the care and maintenance of a particular animal or group of animals. • Pet trusts are generally invalid because animals are incapable of compelling a trustee to act, and animals have no standing in law. Effectively, the trust has no beneficiary. But some states (e.g., Colorado) statutorily recognize these trusts as valid. Pet trusts are covered in the Uniform Trust Code (§ 408).

▸ **pooled-income fund.** See POOLED-INCOME FUND.

▸ **pooled trust.** (1941) An irrevocable, discretionary trust that (1) is established and managed by a nonprofit association, (2) is funded with the assets of disabled persons, and (3) maintains a separate trust account for each beneficiary, but (4) pools the trust assets for investment purposes. • If the trust provides for distribution of a deceased beneficiary's interest to the state in reimbursement of Medicaid expenditures, a pooled-trust beneficiary may be eligible for Medicaid benefits. The assets contributed to the trust for the individual's benefit are not treated as the beneficiary's property. — Also termed *pooled-assets trust.*

▸ **pourover trust.** (1981) An inter vivos trust that receives property (usu. the residual estate) from a will upon the testator's death. Cf. *pourover will* under WILL.

▸ **power-of-appointment trust.** (1848) A trust in which property is left in trust for the surviving spouse. • The trustee must distribute income to the spouse for life, and the power of appointment is given to the spouse or to his or her estate. A power-of-appointment trust is commonly used to qualify property for the marital deduction. See *marital deduction* under DEDUCTION (2).

▸ **precatory trust** (**prek**-ə-tor-ee). (1878) A trust that the law will recognize to carry out the wishes of the testator or grantor even though the statement in question is in the nature of an entreaty or recommendation rather than a command.

▸ **presumptive trust.** See *resulting trust.*

▸ **private trust.** A trust created for the financial benefit of one or more designated beneficiaries rather than for the public benefit; an ordinary trust as opposed to a charitable trust. • Three elements must be present for a private trust: (1) the demonstrated intent of the settlor, (2) trust property (as *res*), and (3) a certain beneficiary capable of enforcing the trust. — Also termed *personal trust.* Cf. *charitable trust.*

▸ **protective trust.** A trust that is designed to protect the trust property to ensure the continued support of the beneficiary.

> "In a broad sense, a spendthrift, support, or other similarly protective trust is one created to provide a fund for the maintenance of the beneficiary and at the same time to

secure it against the beneficiary's improvidence or incapacity." 76 Am. Jur. 2d *Trusts* § 121 (1992).

▸ **public trust.** See *charitable trust.*

▸ **purchase-money resulting trust.** (1927) A resulting trust that arises when one person buys property but directs the seller to transfer the property and its title to another. • Although a purchase-money resulting trust is properly understood as a court-imposed equitable remedy rather than as a true trust, the buyer is occasionally referred to as the "beneficiary" and the titleholder as the "trustee." — Abbr. PMRT.

▸ **QTIP trust** (**kyoo**-tip). (1985) A trust that is established to qualify for the marital deduction. • Under this trust, the assets are referred to as qualified-terminable-interest property, or QTIP. See *qualified-terminable-interest property* under PROPERTY. Cf. *qualified domestic trust.*

▸ **qualified domestic trust.** (1988) A trust for a noncitizen spouse qualifying for the marital deduction. *See* 26 USCA § 2056(d). — Abbr. QDOT. See *marital deduction* under DEDUCTION (2). Cf. *QTIP trust.*

▸ **qualified income trust.** See *Miller trust.*

▸ **qualified personal-residence trust.** (1991) An irrevocable trust that is funded with cash and the personal residence of the grantor, who retains the right to dwell in the residence for a specified term of years. • The trust may receive and hold additional cash to pay for trust expenses, mortgage installments, and improvements to the residence. — Abbr. QPRT. Cf. *personal-residence trust.*

▸ **qualified S-corporation trust.** (1987) A trust that (1) owns stock in one or more S corporations, (2) distributes all income to one individual (who must be a United States citizen or resident), and (3) requires only one beneficiary at a time. • If the principal is distributed, it must be distributed to the designated beneficiary. If the trust terminates during the beneficiary's life, all trust assets must be distributed to the beneficiary. Although the trust is rarely termed a *qualified subchapter-S corporation trust*, the common abbreviation is *QSST*, not *QSCT.*

▸ **rabbicular trust.** (1995) A rabbi trust that protects the trust assets against the claims of the employer's creditors by converting to a secular trust if the employer funding the trust becomes insolvent. • The term is a portmanteau word from *rabbi* and *secular.* Cf. *rabbi trust*; *secular trust.*

▸ **rabbi trust.** (1980) An irrevocable grantor trust whose assets remain subject to the claims of the grantor's general creditors, and from which benefits are paid to the grantor's employees if a stipulated event occurs. • A rabbi trust is a form of nonqualified deferred-compensation plan created by an employer to fund its obligation to executive employees under nonqualified benefit plans. Because the trust can be reached by creditors, the participants can avoid being taxed on the constructive receipt of the benefits held in the trust. Its name derives from the IRS letter ruling that approved its use by a synagogue. Priv. Ltr. Rul. 81-13-107 (31 Dec. 1980). Cf. *rabbicular trust*; *secular trust.*

▸ **real-estate investment trust.** See REAL-ESTATE INVESTMENT TRUST.

▸ **real-estate mortgage trust.** See REAL-ESTATE MORTGAGE TRUST.

▸ **realty trust.** See *nominee trust* (2).

▸ **reciprocal trust.** A trust arrangement between two parties in which one party is beneficiary of a trust established by the other party, and vice versa. • Such trusts are common between husband and wife.

▸ **remedial trust.** See *constructive trust.*

▸ **resulting trust.** (18c) A remedy imposed by equity when property is transferred under circumstances suggesting that the transferor did not intend for the transferee to have the beneficial interest in the property. — Also termed *implied trust*; *presumptive trust.* Cf. *constructive trust.*

> "The main distinction between express and resulting trusts is this: In an express trust an intention to create a trust is always expressed or declared. In a resulting trust the intention is not expressed, but is inferred by operation of law from the terms of the conveyance or will, or from the accompanying facts and circumstances." Norman Fetter, *Handbook of Equity Jurisprudence* § 124, at 191 (1895).

▸ **retained income trust.** See *grantor-retained income trust.*

▸ **revocable trust** (**rev**-ə-kə-bəl). (1827) A trust in which the settlor reserves the right to terminate the trust and recover the trust property and any undistributed income.

▸ **savings-account trust.** See *Totten trust.*

▸ **savings-bank trust.** See *Totten trust.*

▸ **secret trust.** An instrument, usu. a will, that appears to give an absolute gift to another although the donee has orally agreed with the grantor that he or she is to use the property for the benefit of some third party. • Courts admit evidence of the promise to prevent unjust enrichment and enforce it by imposing the remedy of a constructive trust on the reneging "trustee." Cf. *semi-secret trust*; *half-secret trust.*

▸ **secular trust.** An irrevocable trust, funded by an employer, that protects an employee-beneficiary's deferred compensation from the claims of creditors during an employer's bankruptcy or insolvency. • The trust provides the employee-beneficiary with exclusive rights. The employee enjoys security since the trust is funded and the funds are beyond the reach of creditors and immune from forfeiture, but the employee cannot defer income recognition. Cf. *rabbicular trust*; *rabbi trust.*

▸ **self-declared trust.** (1952) A revocable inter vivos trust in which the settlor acts as the trustee and usu. names himself or herself as the beneficiary for life, with the remainder at death to another beneficiary. • Self-declared trusts are treated as valid inter vivos arrangements even though legal title to the trust property does not transfer until the settlor's death. See *declaration of trust* (1) under DECLARATION (1).

▸ **self-settled trust.** (1969) A trust in which the settlor is also the person who is to receive the benefits from the trust, usu. set up in an attempt to protect the trust assets from creditors. • In most states, such a trust will not protect trust assets from the settlor's creditors. Restatement (Second) of Trusts § 156 (1959). — Also termed *asset-protection trust.*

▸ **semi-secret trust.** (1955) An instrument that indicates who is to serve as a trustee but fails to identify either the beneficiary or the terms of the trust, or both. • Traditionally, this trust was deemed to fail for want of an ascertainable beneficiary. But the modern view is to provide the same relief as that given for a secret trust: to receive evidence of the donor's intent, including the intended beneficiary, and impose a constructive trust in his or her favor. Cf. *secret trust*; *half-secret trust.*

▸ **shifting trust.** (1834) An express trust providing that, upon a specified contingency, it may operate in favor of an additional or substituted beneficiary.

▸ **short-term trust.** See *Clifford trust.*

▸ **simple trust. 1.** See *mandatory trust.* **2.** See *passive trust.*

▸ **678 trust.** See *nongrantor-owner trust.*

▸ **special-needs trust.** See *supplemental-needs trust.*

▸ **special trust.** See *active trust.*

▸ **spendthrift trust.** (1878) **1.** A trust that prohibits the beneficiary's interest from being assigned and also prevents a creditor from attaching that interest; a trust by the terms of which a valid restraint is imposed on the voluntary or involuntary transfer of the beneficiary's interest. **2.** A similar trust in which the restraint on alienation results from a statute rather than from the settlor's words in the trust instrument.

> "**Origin of the term 'spendthrift trust.'** The phrase 'spendthrift trust' seems to have been first used, as might be expected, in Pennsylvania. The earliest instance in which a use of the phrase has been found was in 1875, when it appeared in the syllabus of a case, though the court did not use it in its opinion. Four years later, in *Overman's Appeal* [88 Pa. 276 (1879)], the phrase is found in the auditor's report (in italics), while the opinion of the court in the same case refers to the trust in question as 'a trust for a spendthrift as it is termed' [*id.* at 278]. That the phrase had not become familiar by 1882 is indicated by *Thackara v. Mintzer* [100 Pa. 151 (1882)], where the head note refers to a 'spendthrift son trust,' but the court does not use that or any similar phrase. And in 1883, in the first edition of his Restraints on Alienation, [John Chipman] Gray used the phrase only rarely, and then spoke rather apologetically of 'spendthrift trusts so called.' In the second edition of this book, published twelve years later, the use of the phrase is frequent." Erwin N. Griswold, *Spendthrift Trusts* § 33, at 32 (2d ed. 1947).

▸ **split-interest trust.** See *charitable-remainder trust.*

▸ **spray trust.** See *sprinkle trust.*

▸ **sprinkle trust.** (1949) A trust in which the trustee has discretion to decide how much will be given to each beneficiary. — Also termed *spray trust.* See SPRINKLE POWER.

▸ **standby trust.** (1959) A trust created to manage a person's assets while he or she is out of the country or disabled.

▸ **supplemental-needs trust.** (1988) A trust established to provide supplemental income for a disabled beneficiary who is receiving or may be eligible to receive government benefits. • This type of irrevocable trust is often used by parents of disabled children to ensure the beneficiary's eligibility for government benefits by expressly prohibiting distributions that may be used for the beneficiary's food, shelter, or clothing. — Abbr. SNT.

▸ **support trust.** (1946) A discretionary trust in which the settlor authorizes the trustee to pay to the beneficiary as much income or principal as the trustee believes is needed for support, esp. for "comfortable support" or "support in accordance with the beneficiary's standard of living." • The beneficiary's interest cannot be voluntarily transferred, but creditors who provide necessaries can usu. reach it; general creditors cannot.

▸ **technical trust.** See *passive trust.*

▸ **tentative trust.** See *Totten trust.*

▸ **testamentary trust** (tes-tə-**men**-tə-ree *or* -tree). (1832) A trust that is created by a will and takes effect when the settlor (testator) dies. — Also termed *trust under will.* Cf. *inter vivos trust*; *continuing trust* (1).

> "The provisions of an enforceable testamentary trust are set forth in a valid will. At minimum, therefore, there must have been compliance with the formal execution requirements applicable to wills generally. The testator and the attesting witnesses, for example, must have signed the will. A testamentary trust arises when title to a portion or all of the decedent's probate estate is transferred from the executor or personal representative to the testamentary trustee. Thus, a testamentary trust cannot arise until after the testator dies. Only then does the probate property come into existence, because only then does the will speak." *Loring: A Trustee's Handbook* § 2.1.2, at 45 (Charles E. Rounds Jr. & Charles E. Rounds III eds., 2008).

▸ **Totten trust.** (1931) A revocable trust created by one's deposit of money, typically in a savings account, in the depositor's name as trustee for another. • A Totten trust is an early form of "pay on death" account, since it creates no interest in the beneficiary unless the account remained at the depositor's death. Its name derives from the earliest decision in which the court approved the concept, even though the formalities of will execution were not satisfied: *In re Totten*, 71 N.E. 748 (N.Y. 1904). A Totten trust is commonly used to indicate a successor to the account without having to create a will, and thus it is a will substitute. — Also termed *tentative trust*; *bank-account trust*; *savings-account trust*; *savings-bank trust*; *trustee bank account.*

> "A deposit by one person of his own money, in his own name as trustee for another, standing alone, does not establish an irrevocable trust during the lifetime of the depositor. It is a tentative trust merely, revocable at will, until the depositor dies or completes the gift in his lifetime by some unequivocal act or declaration, such as delivery of the pass book or notice to the beneficiary. In case the depositor dies before the beneficiary without revocation, or some decisive act or declaration of disaffirmance, the presumption arises that an absolute trust was created as to the balance on hand at the death of the depositor." *In re Totten*, 179 N.Y. 112, 125–26 (1904).

▸ **transgressive trust.** (1849) A trust that violates the rule against perpetuities. See RULE AGAINST PERPETUITIES.

▸ **trust de son tort** (də sawn [*or* son] **tor**[**t**]). See *constructive trust.*

▸ **trust ex delicto.** See *constructive trust.*

▸ ***trust ex maleficio.*** See *constructive trust.*

▸ **trust for support.** A trust that, by its terms, provides that the trustee must pay or apply only as much of the income and principal as is necessary for the education and support of the beneficiary.

▸ **trust in invitum.** See *constructive trust.*

▸ **trust under will.** See *testamentary trust.*

▸ **under-65 trust.** (2004) A discretionary trust established for the sole benefit of a Medicaid recipient who is under the age of 65. • This type of trust may be established by anyone except the beneficiary, who must be less than 65 years old at the time of creation. The assets in trust will not be included in the beneficiary's estate for purposes of determining Medicaid eligibility. The beneficiary may receive distributions from the trust during life, but any balance remaining in the trust must be used to reimburse the state for the beneficiary's Medicaid expenditures.

▸ **unit-investment trust.** (1941) **1.** A trust in which funds are pooled and invested in income-producing securities. • Units of the trust are sold to investors, who maintain an interest in the trust in proportion to their investment. **2.** An investment company that gives a shareholder an undivided interest in a fixed pool of securities held by the trustee. • This type of company can be organized in several ways (as by trust indenture, contract of custodianship or agency, or similar instrument), but is most commonly organized with a trust indenture. Such a company does not have a board of directors and issues only redeemable securities, each of which represents an undivided interest in a unit of specified securities. 15 USCA § 80a-4. — Abbr. UIT. See *investment company* under COMPANY.

▸ **unitrust.** (1971) A trust from which a fixed percentage of the fair market value of the trust's assets, valued annually, is paid each year to the beneficiary.

▸ **voluntary trust.** (18c) **1.** A trust that is not founded on consideration. • One having legal title to property may create a voluntary trust by (1) declaring that the property is to be held in trust for another, and (2) transferring the legal title to a third person who acts as trustee. **2.** An obligation arising out of a personal confidence reposed in, and voluntarily accepted by, one for the benefit of another.

▸ **voting trust.** (1885) A trust used to hold shares of voting stock in a closely held corporation, usu. transferred from a parent to a child, and empowering the trustee to exercise the right to vote. • The trust acts as custodian of the shares but is not a stockholder. Cf. VOTING GROUP.

▸ **wasting trust.** (1936) A trust in which the trust property is gradually depleted by periodic payments to the beneficiary.

4. *Archaic.* A business combination that aims at monopoly. See ANTITRUST LAW.

> "The term 'trust,' in its more confined sense, embraces only a peculiar form of business association effected by stockholders of different corporations transferring their stocks to trustees. The Standard Oil Trust was formed in this way, and originated the name 'trust' as applied to industrial associations. . . . The term 'trust,' although derived as stated, has obtained a wider signification, and embraces every act, agreement, or combination of persons or capital believed to be done, made, or formed with the intent, effect, power, or tendency to monopolize business, to restrain or interfere with competitive trade, or to fix, influence, or increase the prices of commodities." S.C.T. Dodd, *The Present Legal Status of Trusts*, 7 Harv. L. Rev. 157, 157–58 (1893).

▸ **business trust.** A form of business organization, similar to a corporation, in which investors receive transferable certificates of beneficial interest instead of stock shares. — Also termed *Massachusetts trust*; *common-law trust.*

> "The business trust was developed in Massachusetts from 1910 to 1925 to achieve limited liability and to avoid restrictions then existing there on a corporation's acquiring and developing real estate, by adoption of the trust device . . . ." Henry G. Henn & John R. Alexander, *Laws of Corporations* § 58, at 117 (3d ed. 1983).

▸ **common-law trust.** See *business trust.*

▸ **Massachusetts trust.** See *business trust.*

trust account. See CLIENT TRUST ACCOUNT.

trust agreement. See *declaration of trust* (2) under DECLARATION (1).

trustbuster, *n.* (1903) A person — esp. a federal officer — who seeks the dissolution of business trusts under the antitrust laws. See *business trust* under TRUST (4).

trust certificate. See EQUIPMENT TRUST CERTIFICATE.

trust company. See COMPANY.

trust corporation. See *trust company* under COMPANY.

trust corpus. The body of the trust and the principal of the trust, referring to all funds and other real and personal property transferred to the trust.

trust deed. 1. See *declaration of trust* (2) under DECLARATION (1). **2.** See *deed of trust* under DEED.

trust de son tort (də sawn [*or* son] **tor**[**t**]). See *constructive trust* under TRUST (3).

trust distribution. See DISTRIBUTION.

trustee (trəs-**tee**), *n.* (17c) **1.** Someone who stands in a fiduciary or confidential relation to another; esp., one who, having legal title to property, holds it in trust for the benefit of another and owes a fiduciary duty to that beneficiary. • Generally, a trustee's duties are to convert to cash all debts and securities that are not qualified legal investments, to reinvest the cash in proper securities, to protect and preserve the trust property, and to ensure that it is employed solely for the beneficiary, in accordance with the directions contained in the trust instrument. See *trustee-agent* under AGENT.

> "A trustee is bound to perform all acts which are necessary for the proper execution of his trust. But by the English rule, as he is not allowed compensation for his services, he would stand in the position of a gratuitous bailee, and be responsible only for losses or improper execution of his trust, in cases of gross negligence. The rule denying him compensation does not, however, obtain generally in America, and it is the general practice in America to allow commissions to trustees in cases of open and admitted trusts, where the trustee has not forfeited them by gross misconduct. It would seem, that in all the States where a compensation is given, he would be a bailee for hire of labor and services, and bound to exercise ordinary diligence. And he engages that he has sufficient skill to execute the duties of his office properly. And, indeed, a trustee seems generally to be bound to take the same care of the trust fund as a prudent and discreet man would take of his own property, to manage it for the best interest of the *cestui que trust*, and to make no profit or advantage out of it for himself personally." 1 William W. Story, *A Treatise on the Law of Contracts* § 374, at 328–30 (1874).

▸ **bare trustee.** (18c) A trustee of a passive trust. • A bare trustee has no duty other than to transfer the property to the beneficiary. See *passive trust* under TRUST (3).

▸ **constructive trustee.** (1818) One whom the law makes liable to hold property for the use or benefit of another, usu. on account of his or her own wrongful conduct; one who benefits from a breach of a trust to a great enough degree to become liable as a trustee. — Also termed *quasi-trustee*; *trustee de son tort.*

▸ **corporate trustee.** (1852) A corporation that is empowered by its charter to act as a trustee, such as a bank or trust company.

▸ **indenture trustee.** (1933) A trustee named in a trust indenture and charged with holding legal title to the trust property; a trustee under an indenture.

▸ **joint trustee.** See COTRUSTEE.

▸ **judicial trustee.** (18c) A trustee appointed by a court to execute a trust.

▸ **quasi-trustee.** (1830) See *constructive trustee.*

▸ **successor trustee.** (1866) A trustee who succeeds an earlier trustee, usu. as provided in the trust agreement.

▸ **testamentary trustee** (tes-tə-**men**-tə-ree *or* -tree). (1811) A trustee appointed by or acting under a will; one appointed to carry out a trust created by a will.

▸ **township trustee.** (1834) One of a board of officers to whom, in some states, a township's affairs are entrusted.

▸ **trustee ad litem** (ad lɪ-tem *or* -təm). (1921) A trustee appointed by the court.

▸ **trustee de son tort** (də sawn [*or* son] **tor**[**t**]). (1857) Someone who, without legal authority, administers a living person's property to the detriment of the property owner. See *constructive trustee*; *constructive trust* under TRUST (3); DE SON TORT.

▸ **trustee ex maleficio** (eks mal-ə-**fish**-ee-oh). (1837) Someone who is guilty of wrongful or fraudulent conduct and is held by equity to the duty of a trustee, in relation to the subject matter, to prevent him or her from profiting from the wrongdoing.

2. *Bankruptcy.* A person appointed by the U.S. Trustee or elected by creditors or appointed by a judge to administer the bankruptcy estate during a bankruptcy case. • The trustee's duties include (1) collecting and reducing to cash the assets of the estate, (2) operating the debtor's business with court approval if appropriate to preserve the value of business assets, (3) examining the debtor at a meeting of creditors, (4) filing inventories and making periodic reports to the court on the financial condition of the estate, (5) investigating the debtor's financial affairs, (6) examining proofs of claims and objecting to improper claims, (7) furnishing information relating to the bankruptcy to interested parties, and (8) opposing discharge through bankruptcy, if advisable. A trustee is appointed or elected in every Chapter 7 case, and is appointed in every Chapter 12 and Chapter 13 case under the Bankruptcy Code. A trustee is not appointed or elected in a Chapter 11 case unless the court finds that a trustee is needed and appoints one. In most Chapter 11 cases, the bankruptcy estate is administered by the debtor in possession, rather than by a trustee. The role of a bankruptcy trustee varies depending on the type of bankruptcy case. 11 USCA §§ 701–703, 1104, 1202. — Also termed (in sense 2) *bankruptcy trustee*; *trustee in bankruptcy.* See UNITED STATES TRUSTEE.

▸ **Chapter 7 trustee.** *Bankruptcy.* A representative appointed by the court in a Chapter 7 bankruptcy case to represent the interests of the bankruptcy estate and the creditors. • The trustee is responsible for reviewing the debtor's petition and schedules, liquidating the property of the estate, suing creditors or the debtor to recover property of the estate, and making distributions to creditors.

▸ **Chapter 13 trustee.** *Bankruptcy.* A representative appointed by the court to administer a Chapter 13 bankruptcy case, review the debtor's petition and schedules, liquidate property of the estate, sue creditors or the debtor to recover property of the estate, oversee the debtor's plan, receive payments from debtors, and disburse plan payments to creditors.

▸ **interim trustee.** (1847) A bankruptcy trustee appointed to perform all the functions and duties of a trustee until the regular trustee is selected and qualified. • Before the meeting of creditors, the interim trustee often preliminarily investigates the debtor's assets and financial affairs.

3. DIRECTOR (2). **4.** *Parliamentary law.* An officer who audits an organization's finances.

trustee, *vb.* (1818) **1.** To serve as trustee. **2.** To place (a person or property) in the hands of one or more trustees. **3.** To appoint (a person) as trustee, often of a bankrupt's estate in order to restrain a creditor from collecting moneys due. **4.** To attach (the effects of a debtor) in the hands of a third person.

trustee, U.S. See UNITED STATES TRUSTEE.

trustee-agent. See AGENT.

trustee bank account. See *Totten trust* under TRUST (3).

trustee in bankruptcy. See TRUSTEE (2).

trustee process. See FACTORIZING PROCESS.

trusteeship. (18c) **1.** The office, status, or function of a trustee. **2.** *Int'l law.* The administration or supervision of a territory by one or more countries, esp. under a U.N. trusteeship council. Cf. MANDATE (6).

trust endorsement. See *trust indorsement* under INDORSEMENT.

trust estate. See CORPUS (1).

trust ex delicto. See *constructive trust* under TRUST (3).

trust ex maleficio. See *constructive trust* under TRUST (3).

trust fund. (18c) The property held in a trust by a trustee; CORPUS (1).

▸ **common trust fund.** (1852) A trust fund set up within a trust department to combine the assets of numerous small trusts to achieve greater investment diversification. • Common trust funds are regulated by state law. — Abbr. CTF.

▸ **pooled-income fund.** See POOLED-INCOME FUND.

trust-fund doctrine. (1892) The principle that the assets of an insolvent company, including paid and unpaid subscriptions to the capital stock, are held as a trust fund to which the company's creditors may look for payment of their claims. • The creditors may follow the property constituting this fund, and may use it to reduce the debts, unless it has passed into the hands of a bona fide purchaser without notice. — Also termed *trust-fund theory.*

trust-fund-recovery penalty. *Tax.* A means provided by 26 USCA §6672 to facilitate the collection of unpaid trust-fund taxes when taxes are not fully collectible from the company or business that failed to pay them, and thereby enhance voluntary compliance. • A TFRP can be applied to any person required to collect, account for, and pay over taxes held in trust who willfully fails to perform these acts. — Abbr. TFRP.

trust indenture. See INDENTURE (2).

Trust Indenture Act. A 1939 federal statute designed to protect investors of certain types of bonds by requiring that (1) the SEC approve the trust indenture, (2) the indenture include certain protective clauses and exclude certain exculpatory clauses, and (3) the trustees be independent of the issuing company. 15 USCA §§ 77aaa et seq. • The Act is administered by the U.S. Securities and Exchange Commission.

trust indorsement. See INDORSEMENT.

trust in invitum (in in-VI-təm). See *constructive trust* under TRUST (3).

trust instrument. See *declaration of trust* (2) under DECLARATION (1).

trust legacy. See LEGACY (1).

trust officer. See OFFICER (1).

trustor. (1855) Someone who creates a trust; SETTLOR (1).

trust ownership. See OWNERSHIP.

trust power. See *beneficial power* under POWER (5).

trust process. See PROCESS (2).

trust property. See CORPUS (1).

trust receipt. (1873) **1.** A pre-UCC security device — now governed by Article 9 of the Code — consisting of a receipt stating that the wholesale buyer has possession of the goods for the benefit of the financier. • Today there must usu. be a security agreement coupled with a filed financing statement. **2.** A method of financing commercial transactions by which title passes directly from the manufacturer or seller to a banker or lender, who as owner delivers the goods to the dealer on whose behalf the banker or lender is acting, and to whom title ultimately goes when the banker's or lender's primary right has been satisfied.

trust relationship. See RELATIONSHIP.

trust res (reez *or* rays). See CORPUS (1).

trust territory. See TERRITORY (1).

trust under will. See *testamentary trust* under TRUST (3).

trusty, *n.* (1855) A convict or prisoner who is considered trustworthy by prison authorities and therefore given special privileges.

truth. (bef. 12c) **1.** Accuracy in the recounting of events; conformity with actuality; factuality. **2.** *Defamation.* An affirmative defense by which the defendant asserts that an alleged defamatory statement is substantially accurate. — **truthful,** *adj.* — **truthfulness,** *n.*

Truth in Lending Act. A 1968 federal statute enacted as the first subchapter of the Consumer Credit Protection Act to safeguard consumers in the use of credit by (1) requiring full disclosure of the terms of loan agreements, including finance charges, (2) restricting the garnishment of wages, and (3) regulating the use of credit cards. — Abbr. TILA. See CONSUMER CREDIT PROTECTION ACT.

truth-seeker. (1864) Someone who strives to reveal the truth <the trial lawyer should be a truth-seeker>.

truth, the whole truth, and nothing but the truth. (16c) The words used in the common oath administered to a witness who is about to testify <do you swear or affirm that you shall tell the truth, the whole truth and nothing but the truth?>. • The purpose of the second part of the oath is to preclude the possibility of *supressio veri*; the purpose of the third part is to preclude the possibility of *suggestio falsi*. See SUPPRESSIO VERI; SUGGESTIO FALSI.

try, *vb.* (13c) To examine judicially; to examine and resolve (a dispute) by means of a trial.

try title. The judicial examination of a title. See TRESPASS TO TRY TITLE; *action to quiet title* under ACTION (4).

TSA. *abbr.* TRANSPORTATION SECURITY ADMINISTRATION.

tsar. See CZAR.

TSCA. *abbr.* Toxic Substances Control Act. 42 USCA §§ 2601 et seq.

TTB. *abbr.* ALCOHOL AND TOBACCO TAX AND TRADE BUREAU.

TTTS. *abbr.* Time, interest, title, and seisin (possession). See FOUR UNITIES.

tubman (təb-mən). (18c) *Hist.* A junior barrister in the Court of Exchequer who made motions that were second in precedence to those of the postman. • The tubman was so called because he stood by a tub anciently used as a measure of capacity. Cf. POSTMAN.

Tucker Act. An 1887 federal statute enacted to ameliorate the inadequacies of the original authority of the Court of Claims by extending that court's jurisdiction to include (1) claims founded on the Constitution, a federal statute, or a federal regulation, and (2) damage claims in cases not arising in tort.

tuition voucher. See VOUCHER.

tumocracy. See PLUTOCRACY.

turncoat witness. See WITNESS.

turnkey, *adj.* (1927) **1.** (Of a product) provided in a state of readiness for immediate use <a turnkey computer network>. **2.** Of, relating to, or involving a product provided in this manner <a turnkey contract>.

turnkey, *n.* (17c) A jailer; esp., one charged with keeping the keys to a jail or prison.

turnkey contract. See *engineering, procurement, and construction contract* under CONTRACT.

turnkey drilling contract. See DRILLING CONTRACT.

turnover arrest. See ARREST (2).

turnover duty. (1988) *Maritime law.* A shipowner's obligation to provide safe working conditions and to give notice of any nonobvious hazards regarding instruments and areas that the shipowner turns over to the stevedore and longshoremen while the ship is being loaded or unloaded. Cf. ACTIVE-OPERATIONS DUTY; INTERVENTION DUTY.

turnover order. See ORDER (2).

turn state's evidence, *vb.* (1846) To cooperate with prosecutors and testify against other criminal defendants <after hours of intense negotiations, the suspect accepted a plea bargain and agreed to turn state's evidence>.

turntable doctrine. See ATTRACTIVE-NUISANCE DOCTRINE.

turpis causa (tər-pis kaw-zə). [Latin "immoral consideration"] See *immoral consideration* under CONSIDERATION (1); *condictio ob turpem vel injustam causam* under CONDICTIO.

turpitude (tər-pə-t[y]ood). See MORAL TURPITUDE.

tutela (t[y]oo-**tee**-lə), *n.* [Latin "tutelage"] *Roman law.* A type of guardianship either for those not having reached puberty (*tutela impuberum*) or for women (*tutela mulierum*). • The guardian was called the *tutor*, the ward the *pupillus*. Guardians for women no longer existed in Justinian's time. Cf. CURA.

tutelage (**t[y]oo**-tə-lij), *n.* (17c) **1.** The act of protecting or guiding; guardianship. Cf. TUTORY. **2.** *Int'l law.* The quality, state, or condition of being under the care and management of an international organization such as the League of Nations or United Nations. • This term applies, for example, to the status of a people who do not yet benefit from a fully operational government of their own — such as people displaced by war and living in a territory that will in the future be given its autonomy.

tutor, *n.* (14c) **1.** Someone who teaches; esp., a private instructor. Pl. **tutors. 2.** *Roman & civil law.* A guardian of a minor; a person appointed to have the care of the minor's person and estate. • The guardian of a minor past the age of puberty is called a *curator* and has duties somewhat different from those of a tutor. Pl. ***tutores.***

▸ ***tutor dativus*** (**t[y]oo**-tor [*or* -ər] də-**tɪ**-vəs). [Latin] *Roman law.* A tutor appointed by the court upon application. Pl. ***tutores dativi.***

▸ ***tutor gerens*** (**t[y]oo**-tor [*or* -tər] **jeer**-enz). [Latin] *Roman law.* A tutor who, though not sole tutor, actually administered the ward's affairs. Pl. ***tutores gerentes.***

▸ ***tutor legitimus*** (**t[y]oo**-tor [*or* -ər] lə-**jit**-i-məs). [Latin] (17c) *Roman law.* A tutor-at-law; a tutor by virtue of the relationship with the pupil, such as a paternal uncle. Pl. ***tutores legitimi.***

▸ ***tutor testamentarius*** (**t[y]oo**-tor [*or* -ər] tes-tə-men-**tair**-ee-əs). [Latin] (17c) *Roman law.* A tutor appointed by will to have the guardianship over the testator's children. Pl. ***tutores testamentarii.***

▸ **undertutor.** (17c) *Civil law.* A person appointed by a court to represent a minor under the care of a tutor when the interests of the minor conflict with that of the tutor. See TUTORSHIP.

tutorio nomine (t[y]oo-**tor**-ee-oh **nahm**-ə-nee). [Latin] *Hist.* In the name and character of tutor.

tutor legitimus. See TUTOR.

tutorship. (16c) *Civil law.* The office and power of a tutor; the power that an individual has, *sui juris*, to take care of one who cannot care for himself or herself. • The four types of tutorship are (1) tutorship by nature, (2) tutorship by will, (3) tutorship by the effect of the law, and (4) tutorship by judicial appointment. La. Civ. Code art. 247.

▸ **dative tutorship.** (1835) *Civil law.* Tutorship that arises from a court's appointment, usu. on the advice of the family. — Also termed *dative curatorship; tutorship by judicial appointment.*

▸ **legal tutorship.** (1843) *Civil law.* Tutorship that is bestowed by statute and does not require a court's or family's approval. • For example, a spouse has the legal tutorship of the incompetent spouse. — Also termed *tutorship by the effect of the law.*

▸ **tutorship by judicial appointment.** *Civil law.* See *dative tutorship.*

▸ **tutorship by nature.** (1829) **1.** Tutorship of a minor child that belongs by right to a surviving parent. **2.** Tutorship of a minor child that belongs to the parent under whose care the child has been placed following divorce or judicial separation. • If the parents are awarded joint custody, both have cotutorship and equal authority, privileges, and responsibilities. La. Civ. Code art. 250.

▸ **tutorship by the effect of the law.** *Civil law.* See *legal tutorship.*

▸ **tutorship by will.** (1856) Tutorship that is created (1) by the will of the parent who dies last, or (2) by any declaration of the surviving father or mother (or the parent who is the curator of the other spouse), executed before a notary and two witnesses. La. Civ. Code art. 257.

tutor testamentarius. See TUTOR.

tutory (**t[y]oo**-tər-ee). (14c) **1.** Guardianship; charge. **2.** Tutorage; tutelage. — Also spelled *tutry; tutoury.* Cf. TUTELAGE (1).

tutrix. (16c) *Archaic.* A female tutor. See TUTOR (2).

tutus accessus non fuit (**t[y]oo**-təs ak-**ses**-əs non **fyoo**-it). [Latin] *Hist.* There was no safe access.

TVA. *abbr.* (1935) TENNESSEE VALLEY AUTHORITY.

T visa. See VISA.

Twelfth Amendment. The constitutional amendment, ratified in 1804, that altered the electoral-college system by separating the balloting for presidential and vice-presidential candidates. • In 1800, members of the Electoral College could cast votes only for the office of President, and Thomas Jefferson and his running mate Aaron Burr each received the same number of votes. The House of Representatives had to break the tie.

12(b)(6) motion. See *Rule 12(b)(6) motion* under MOTION (1).

twelve-day rule. *Criminal procedure.* A rule in some jurisdictions requiring that a person charged with a felony be given a preliminary examination no later than 12 days after the arraignment on the original warrant.

twelve-month liquidation. See LIQUIDATION (3).

Twelve Tables. *Roman law.* The earliest surviving legislation enacted by the Romans, written on 12 tablets in the 5th century B.C. • The Tables set out many rights and duties of Roman citizens, including debtors' rights, family law, wills, torts, civil procedure, and some public law. They substituted a written body of laws, easily accessible and binding on all citizens of Rome, for an unwritten usage accessible to only a few. The law of the Twelve Tables was also known as the *Lex Duodecim Tabularum.*

> "The Twelve Tables continued to be recognized for many centuries as the fundamental law of the Romans; they did not formally lose this character until it was taken from them by the legislation of Justinian." James Hadley, *Introduction to Roman Law* 74–75 (1881).

> "The Twelve Tables no longer exist in complete form, but many fragments have been found, as quoted in the writings of Cicero, for example, and in the Pandects, and have been arranged by the cheerful zeal of students and commentators. They seem to have been written in very concise form and in a rude rhythm. They have been arranged by modern scholars in different ways. In Mr. Tissot's Compilation (1811), they are edited in the order of the Pandects. In the work of Messrs. Dirksen & Zell, adopted by Professor Ortolan (1844), they are arranged in a somewhat different method. Of course this order is to a large extent conjectural. If we

followed Ortolan we should find that the first, second, and third Tables concerned procedure in civil cases; the fourth concerned the paternal power; the fifth treated of inheritance and tutorship; the sixth concerned property, possession, and prescription; the seventh treated of buildings, fields, and roads, and the rights of neighboring proprietors; the eighth laid down rules *de delictis*, respecting what we may call torts, as well as certain crimes; the ninth proclaimed rules of public law, forbade special legislation in favor of an individual, punished with death the judge or arbiter who should receive a bribe; and denounced the same penalty against treason; the tenth regulated burials, prohibited intramural interments or cremations, made sumptuary regulations in regard to funerals, and forbade a tomb to be placed less than sixty feet from the property of another without his permission; the eleventh seems to have forbidden marriage between a patrician and a plebian; and, finally, the twelfth lays down rules concerning certain pledges, gives an action against masters for the torts of their slaves, makes special provisions for damages against a possessor of property in bad faith, prohibits the consecration to religious purposes of a thing in litigation, and ends by declaring the principle that a law repeals, by implication, prior laws in conflict with its provisions." William Wirt Howe, *Studies in The Civil Law, and Its Relations to the Law of England and America* 9–10 (1896).

Twentieth Amendment. The constitutional amendment, ratified in 1933, that changed the date of the presidential and vice-presidential inaugurations from March 4 to January 20, and the date for congressional convention from March 4 to January 3, thereby eliminating the short session of Congress, during which a number of members sat who had not been reelected to office. — Also termed *lame-duck amendment*.

Twenty-fifth Amendment. The constitutional amendment, ratified in 1967, that established rules of succession for the presidency and vice presidency in the event of death, resignation, or incapacity. • Article II, § 1 of the Constitution provides for the Vice President to assume the President's powers and duties but does not clearly state that the Vice President also assumes the title of President.

Twenty-first Amendment. The constitutional amendment, ratified in 1933, that repealed the 18th Amendment (which established national Prohibition) and returned the power to regulate alcohol to the states.

2503(b) trust. See TRUST (3).

2503(c) trust. See TRUST (3).

Twenty-fourth Amendment. The constitutional amendment, ratified in 1964, that prohibits the federal and state governments from restricting the right to vote in a federal election because of one's failure to pay a poll tax or other tax.

Twenty-second Amendment. The constitutional amendment, ratified in 1951, that prohibits a person from being elected President more than twice (or, if the person succeeded to the office with more than half the predecessor's term remaining, more than once).

Twenty-seventh Amendment. The constitutional amendment, ratified in 1992, that prevents a pay raise for senators and representatives from taking effect until a new Congress convenes. • This amendment was proposed as part of the original Bill of Rights in 1789, but it took 203 years for the required three-fourths of the states to ratify it. — Also termed *Madison Amendment*.

Twenty-sixth Amendment. The constitutional amendment, ratified in 1971, that sets the minimum voting age at 18 for all state and federal elections.

Twenty-third Amendment. The constitutional amendment, ratified in 1961, that allows District of Columbia residents to vote in presidential elections.

twin-count indictment. See INDICTMENT.

Twiqbal. [portmanteau fr. *Twombly* + *Iqbal*] (2009) *Slang. Civil procedure.* Collectively, the two decisions of the U.S. Supreme Court that, beginning 2007–2009, made it more difficult for plaintiffs to bring suit in federal court by requiring them to demonstrate the plausibility of their claims as opposed to merely describing the facts with enough detail to put the defendant on notice. *Bell Atl. Corp. v. Twombly*, 550 U.S. 544, 127 S.Ct. 1955 (2007); *Ashcroft v. Iqbal*, 556 U.S. 662, 129 S.Ct. 1937 (2009).

twist, *n. Slang.* An informant who provides testimony in exchange for leniency in sentencing, rather than for money. See INFORMANT.

twisting, *n.* An intentional distortion of one or more facts; esp., an insurance agent's or company's misrepresenting or misstating facts, or giving an incomplete comparison of policies, to induce an insured to give up a policy in one company and buy another company's policy.

two-controlled-studies standard. (2004) The requirement by the Federal Trade Commission that before the maker of an over-the-counter painkiller can advertise that it is better or has fewer side effects than another brand, the maker must verify the claim in two scientifically controlled studies.

two-dismissal rule. (1944) The rule that a notice of voluntary dismissal operates as an adjudication on the merits — not merely as a dismissal without prejudice — when filed by a plaintiff who has already dismissed the same claim in another court.

245(i) waiver. (2002) *Immigration law.* An Immigration and Nationality Act provision that allows certain qualified aliens who are otherwise ineligible for adjustment of their status to pay a penalty for the convenience of having their status adjusted to permanent-resident status without having to leave the United States. 8 USCA § 1255(i). Cf. ADJUSTMENT OF STATUS.

two-issue rule. (1929) The rule that if multiple issues were submitted to a trial jury and at least one of them is error-free, the appellate court should presume that the jury based its verdict on the proper issue — not on an erroneous one — and should therefore affirm the judgment.

***Twombly* test.** (2007) A heightened pleading standard requiring that a plaintiff, in order to survive a motion to dismiss for failure to state a claim on which relief can be granted, must (1) state facts that, if taken as true, make a plausible (rather than conceivable) claim, and (2) not rely solely on conclusions of law, which are not entitled to the same assumption of truth as factual allegations. — Also termed *Twombly standard; plausibility test. Bell Atl. Corp. v. Twombly*, 550 U.S. 544, 127 S.Ct. 1955 (2007).

two-party-consent state. (1979) *Criminal law.* A state in which the law makes it lawful to record a wire, oral, or electronic conversation only if all persons in the conversation have consented to the reading. Cf. ONE-PARTY-CONSENT STATE.

two-party payment. See PAYMENT (2).

two-round voting. See VOTING.

two-stage trial. See *bifurcated trial* under TRIAL.

two-tier offer. (1982) A two-step technique by which a bidder tries to acquire a target corporation, the first step involving a cash tender offer and the second usu. a merger in which the target company's remaining shareholders receive securities from the bidder (these securities ordinarily being less favorable than the cash given in the first step).

two-track system. See APPELLATE TRIAGE.

two-witness rule. (1900) **1.** The rule that, to support a perjury conviction, two independent witnesses (or one witness along with corroborating evidence) must establish that the alleged perjurer gave false testimony. **2.** *Constitutional law.* The rule, as stated in the U.S. Constitution, that no person may be convicted of treason without two witnesses to the same overt act — or unless the accused confesses in open court. U.S. Const. art. IV, § 2, cl. 2. **3.** *Criminal law.* The doctrine that a federal prosecution requires proof either by two witnesses or by one witness whose testimony is corroborated by other evidence.

tying, *adj.* (1922) *Antitrust.* Of, relating to, or involving an arrangement whereby a seller sells a product to a buyer only if the buyer purchases another product from the seller <tying agreement>.

tying arrangement. *Antitrust.* (1953) A seller's agreement to sell one product or service only if the buyer also buys a different product or service; a seller's refusal to sell one product or service unless the buyer also buys a different product or service. • The product or service that the buyer wants to buy is known as the *tying product* or *tying service*; the different product or service that the seller insists on selling is known as the *tied product* or *tied service.* Tying arrangements may be illegal under the Sherman or Clayton Act if their effect is too anticompetitive. — Also termed *tying agreement*; *tie-in*; *tie-in arrangement.* See BUNDLING (1). Cf. RECIPROCAL DEALING.

> "The courts have developed an easily articulated text for so-called *per se* illegal tying arrangements, although the test varies from one circuit court to another. . . . In operation, the tests are similar, and the three-part test combines elements that are separated in the tests of other circuits. For purpose of analysis we use this five-part test: (1) There must be separate tying and tied products; (2) there must be 'evidence of actual coercion by the seller that in fact forced the buyer to accept the tied product . . .'; (3) the seller must possess 'sufficient economic power in the tying product market to coerce purchaser acceptance of the tied product . . .'; (4) there must be 'anticompetitive effects in the tied market . . .'; and (5) there must be 'involvement of a "not insubstantial" amount of interstate commerce in the tied product market . . . .'" Herbert Hovenkamp, *Federal Antitrust Policy* 392 (2d ed. 1999) (quoting *Yetsch v. Texaco, Inc.*, 630 F.2d 46, 56, 57 (2d Cir. 1980)).

> "The traditional objection to tying arrangements is that they enable a firm having a monopoly in one market to obtain a monopoly in a second one. Thus, a firm having monopoly power in the market for business machines could obtain a monopoly on punch cards as well simply by refusing to sell or lease its machines unless the purchaser or lessee agreed to use only its punch cards in the machines." Richard A. Posner, *Antitrust Law* 197 (2d ed. 2001).

tying product. See TYING ARRANGEMENT.

tying service. See TYING ARRANGEMENT.

typed drawing. See DRAWING.

typed-form drawing. See *typed drawing* under DRAWING.

Typhoid Mary. [fr. the historical figure who spread typhoid fever in early-20th-century New York] *Slang.* A lawyer who moves from one firm to another carrying all the disqualifications that afflicted every lawyer in the previous firm.

typographum (tɪ-**pog**-rə-fəm). [Latin] *Hist.* A typeset document, as distinguished from *chirographum* ("written by hand"). Cf. CHIROGRAPHUM.

typosquatting. Registering domain names that are close misspellings of a frequently used domain name in order to catch and exploit traffic intended for the other website. • Typosquatting is a variation of cybersquatting, an illegal practice in which a domain name is acquired in bad faith. See CYBERSQUATTING.

tyranny. (14c) **1.** The severe deprivation of a natural right. **2.** The accumulation of all powers — the legislative, executive, and judicial — in the same hands (whether few or many). • Sense 2 expresses the Madisonian view of tyranny, to be found in *The Federalist*, No. 47. **3.** Arbitrary or despotic government; the severe and autocratic exercise of sovereign power, whether vested constitutionally in one ruler or usurped by that ruler by breaking down the division and distribution of governmental powers. — **tyrannical, tyrannous,** *adj.*

tyrant, *n.* (13c) A sovereign or ruler, legitimate or not, who wields power unjustly and arbitrarily to oppress the citizenry; a despot.

U

U3C. *abbr.* UNIFORM CONSUMER CREDIT CODE.

UAA. *abbr.* **1.** UNIFORM ADOPTION ACT. **2.** UNIFORM ARBITRATION ACT.

UAGA. *abbr.* UNIFORM ANATOMICAL GIFT ACT.

U.B. *abbr.* Upper Bench. See *bancus superior* under BANCUS.

uberior titulus (yoo-**beer**-ee-or **tich**-ə-ləs). [Latin] (1851) *Hist.* The fuller title.

uberrimae fidei (yoo-**ber**-ə-mee **fi**-dee-ɪ). [Latin] (1850) See *utmost good faith* under GOOD FAITH; *contract uberrimae fidei* under CONTRACT.

uberrima fides (yoo-**ber**-ə-mə **fɪ**-deez), *n.* [Latin] (18c) See *utmost good faith* under GOOD FAITH.

UBI. *abbr.* See *unrelated-business income* under INCOME.

ubi (**yoo**-bɪ *or* **oo**-bee). [Latin] Where.

ubi aberat animus foenerandi (**yoo**-bɪ ə-**ber**-at **an**-ə-məs fee-nə-**ran**-dɪ). [Latin] *Hist.* Where the intention of taking of a usurious interest was wanting. • A lender was not liable for usurious provisions in a contract unless the lender had the requisite intention of exacting the money. Cf. USURA VELATA.

ubi defunctus habuit domicilium (**yoo**-bɪ di-**fəngk**-təs **hay**-byoo-it dom-ə-**sil**-ee-əm). [Law Latin] *Scots law.* Where the decedent had his domicile.

ubi dies cessit, licet nondum venerit (**yoo**-bɪ **dɪ**-eez **ses**-it, **lɪ**-set **non**-dəm və-**neer**-it). [Latin] *Hist.* In the case where the time has arrived at which money is due, although that time has not arrived at which it may be exacted. See DEBITUM IN DIEM.

ubi dolus dedit causam contractui (**yoo**-bɪ **doh**-ləs **dee**-dit **kaw**-zəm kən-**trak**-choo-ɪ). [Latin] *Hist.* Where fraud gave rise to the contract.

ubi re vera (**yoo**-bɪ ree **veer**-ə). [Latin] Where in reality; when in truth or in point of fact.

ubi supra (**yoo**-bɪ **s[y]oo**-prə). [Latin] Where stated above.

UBIT. *abbr.* See *unrelated-business-income tax* under TAX.

UC. *abbr.* An undercover police officer or other person acting as an undercover agent.

UCAPA. *abbr.* UNIFORM CHILD ABDUCTION PREVENTION ACT.

UCC. *abbr.* **1.** UNIFORM COMMERCIAL CODE. **2.** UNIVERSAL COPYRIGHT CONVENTION.

UCC-1. An abbreviation for the required filing under the Uniform Commercial Code used to provide notice that a creditor has a security interest in a debtor's personal property. • Under the Code, the debtor must not dispose of the property without repaying the debt in full because the loan provides the creditor a security interest in the property.

UCC battle of the forms. See BATTLE OF THE FORMS.

UCCC. *abbr.* UNIFORM CONSUMER CREDIT CODE.

UCCJA. *abbr.* UNIFORM CHILD CUSTODY JURISDICTION ACT.

UCCJEA. *abbr.* UNIFORM CHILD CUSTODY JURISDICTION AND ENFORCEMENT ACT.

UCE. *abbr.* Unsolicited commercial e-mail. See SPAM.

UCEA. *abbr.* UNIFORM CONSERVATION EASEMENT ACT.

UCITA. *abbr.* UNIFORM COMPUTER INFORMATION TRANSACTIONS ACT.

UCMJ. *abbr.* UNIFORM CODE OF MILITARY JUSTICE.

UCP. *abbr.* UNIFORM CUSTOMS AND PRACTICE FOR COMMERCIAL DOCUMENTARY CREDITS.

UCR. *abbr.* UNIFORM CRIME REPORTS.

UCSA. *abbr.* UNIFORM CONTROLLED SUBSTANCES ACT.

UDDA. *abbr.* UNIFORM DETERMINATION OF DEATH ACT.

UDHR. *abbr.* UNIVERSAL DECLARATION OF HUMAN RIGHTS.

UDITPA. *abbr.* UNIFORM DIVISION OF INCOME FOR TAX PURPOSES ACT.

UDPAA. *abbr.* UNIFORM DURABLE POWER OF ATTORNEY ACT.

UDRA. *abbr.* UNIFORM DIVORCE RECOGNITION ACT.

UDRP. *abbr.* UNIFORM DOMAIN-NAME DISPUTE-RESOLUTION POLICY.

UDTPA. *abbr.* UNIFORM DECEPTIVE TRADE PRACTICES ACT.

UEFJA. *abbr.* UNIFORM ENFORCEMENT OF FOREIGN JUDGMENTS ACT.

UETA. *abbr.* UNIFORM ELECTRONIC TRANSACTIONS ACT.

UFCA. *abbr.* UNIFORM FRAUDULENT CONVEYANCES ACT.

UFTA. *abbr.* UNIFORM FRAUDULENT TRANSFER ACT.

UGMA. *abbr.* Uniform Gifts to Minors Act. See UNIFORM TRANSFERS TO MINORS ACT.

UHCDA. *abbr.* UNIFORM HEALTH-CARE DECISIONS ACT.

UIFSA. *abbr.* UNIFORM INTERSTATE FAMILY SUPPORT ACT.

UIJC. *abbr.* UNIFORM INTERSTATE JUVENILE COMPACT.

UIT. *abbr.* See *unit-investment trust* under TRUST (3).

UJCA. *abbr.* UNIFORM JUVENILE COURT ACT.

U.K. *abbr.* (1892) UNITED KINGDOM.

ukase (yoo-**kays** *or* **yoo**-kays). (18c) A proclamation or decree, esp. of a final or arbitrary nature. • This term originally referred to a decree issued by a Russian czar.

ULC. *abbr.* **1.** UNIFORM LAW COMMISSION. **2.** UNIFORM LAW COMMISSIONER.

ullage (**əl**-ij), *n.* (15c) The degree to which a container of liquid falls short of being full.

ullage, *vb.* (18c) To determine the amount of ullage in a container holding liquid.

ulna ferrea (**əl**-nə **fer**-ee-ə). [Law Latin "iron ell"] *Hist.* An iron measuring device, approximately a yard in length, kept in the Exchequer as a standard measure.

ulnage (**əl**-nij). Alnage. See ALNAGER.

ULP. *abbr.* UNFAIR LABOR PRACTICE.

ULPA. *abbr.* UNIFORM LIMITED PARTNERSHIP ACT.

ulterior intent. See INTENT (1).

ulterior remainderman. See REMAINDERMAN.

ultima ratio (əl-ti-mə **ray**-shee-oh). [Latin] (1848) **1.** The final argument; the last resort; the means last to be resorted to. **2.** A final sanction.

ultimate fact. See FACT.

ultimate issue. See ISSUE (1).

ultimate question. See *ultimate issue* under ISSUE (1).

ultimate species. See SPECIES (3).

ultimatum (əl-tə-**may**-təm), *n.* (18c) The final and categorical proposal made in negotiating a treaty, contract, or the like. • An ultimatum implies that a rejection might lead to a break-off in negotiations or, in international law, to a cessation of diplomatic relations or even to war. Pl. **ultimatums.**

ultimatum supplicum. [Law Latin "final or extreme punishment"] Capital punishment.

ultimogeniture. See BOROUGH ENGLISH.

ultimo loco (əl-ti-moh **loh**-koh). [Latin] *Hist.* In the last place. • The phrase usu. referred to the position of a claimant who takes only after all other claims have been satisfied.

ultimum tempus pariendi (əl-ti-məm **tem**-pəs par-ee-**en**-dɪ). [Law Latin "last date for giving birth"] (1819) *Hist.* A time beyond or after which a child may not be born. • The phrase was used, for example, in determining legitimacy or paternity.

ultimus heres (əl-ti-məs **heer**-eez). See HERES.

ultra fines compromissi (əl-trə **fɪ**-neez kom-prə-**mis**-ɪ). [Law Latin] *Hist.* Beyond the limits of the submission to arbitration. See ULTRA VIRES COMPROMISSI.

ultra fines decreti (əl-trə **fɪ**-neez di-**kree**-tɪ). [Law Latin] *Hist.* Beyond the limits of the decree.

ultra fines mandati (əl-trə **fɪ**-neez man-**day**-tɪ). [Law Latin] *Hist.* Beyond the limits of the mandate.

ultrahazardous, *adj.* See EXTRAHAZARDOUS.

ultrahazardous activity. (1932) An activity with a risk of serious harm that cannot be eliminated by the exercise even of the utmost care. • The Restatement (First) of Torts used this term, but it was replaced by *abnormally dangerous activity* in Restatement (Second) of Torts. Cf. ABNORMALLY DANGEROUS ACTIVITY.

ultra licitum (əl-trə **lis**-i-təm). [Law Latin] *Hist.* Beyond what is permissible or legal.

ultra mare (əl-trə **mair**-ee *or* **mahr**-ee). [Latin] See BEYOND SEAS.

ultra petita (əl-trə pə-**tɪ**-tə). [Law Latin] *Hist.* Beyond that which was sought.

> "A judgment or decision is said to be *ultra petita* when it awards more than was sought or sued for in the petition or summons; and the same thing is said of a sentence when it [does] not conform to its grounds and warrants. This affords a good ground for the reversal or reduction of such a decree." John Trayner, *Trayner's Latin Maxims* 609–10 (4th ed. 1894).

ultra reprises (əl-trə ri-**prɪz**-iz). After deduction of expenses; net.

ultra valorem (əl-trə və-**lor**-əm). [Law Latin] *Hist.* Beyond the value.

ultra vires (əl-trə **vɪ**-reez *also* **veer**-eez), *adj.* [Latin "beyond the powers (of)"] (18c) Unauthorized; beyond the scope of power allowed or granted by a corporate charter or by law <the officer was liable for the firm's ultra vires actions>. — Also termed *extra vires.* Cf. INTRA VIRES. — **ultra vires,** *adv.*

▸ **broad ultra vires.** (1926) A decision-maker's abuse of power after the legislature has granted the decision-maker broad discretion, as when the decision-maker exercises statutory discretion for some purpose other than that granted, fails to take account of relevant considerations, takes account of irrelevant considerations, or exercises power unreasonably. — Also termed *extended ultra vires.*

▸ **extended ultra vires.** See *broad ultra vires.*

▸ **narrow ultra vires.** (1976) A decision-maker's excess of power occurring when the proper exercise of that power is uncertain or when the decision-maker fails to comply with statutory procedures. — Also termed *simple ultra vires.*

▸ **procedural ultra vires.** (1951) A type of narrow ultra vires in which the decision-maker fails to follow statutorily specified procedures.

▸ **simple ultra vires.** See *narrow ultra vires.*

▸ ***ultra vires compromissi*** (əl-trə **vɪ**-reez [*also* **veer**-eez] kom-prə-**mis**-ɪ). [Law Latin] *Hist.* Beyond the force of the submission to arbitration; beyond the authority of the submission. • An arbitration award, for example, could be reduced if the award was greater than the submission warranted.

▸ ***ultra vires inventarii*** (əl-trə **vɪ**-reez [*also* **veer**-eez] in-ven-**tair**-ee-ɪ). [Law Latin] *Hist.* Beyond the value of the inventory. • An executor was not liable for the decedent's debts *ultra vires inventarii.*

ultroneous witness. See WITNESS.

umbrella insurance. See INSURANCE.

umbrella limited partnership. See PARTNERSHIP.

umbrella order. See BLANKET ORDER (1).

umbrella-partnership real-estate investment trust. See REAL-ESTATE INVESTMENT TRUST.

umbrella policy. See INSURANCE POLICY.

umbrella protective order. See *blanket protective order* under PROTECTIVE ORDER.

UM coverage. *abbr.* **1.** UNDERINSURED-MOTORIST COVERAGE. **2.** UNINSURED-MOTORIST COVERAGE.

UMDA. *abbr.* UNIFORM MARRIAGE AND DIVORCE ACT.

UMDDA. *abbr.* UNIFORM MANDATORY DISPOSITION OF DETAINERS ACT.

umpirage (əm-pɪr-ij). (16c) **1.** The office or authority of an umpire. **2.** The decision (such as an arbitral award) of an umpire.

umpire. (15c) An impartial person appointed to make an award or a final decision, usu. when a matter has been submitted to arbitrators who have failed to agree. • An arbitral submission may provide for the appointment of an umpire. — Also termed (in Scots law) *oversman.* — **umpire,** *vb.*

UMTA. See FEDERAL TRANSIT ADMINISTRATION.

un-, *prefix.* (bef. 12c) **1.** Not <unassignable>. **2.** Contrary to; against <unconstitutional>.

U.N. *abbr.* (1946) UNITED NATIONS.

unaccrued, *adj.* (1813) Not due, as rent on a lease.

una cum. [Latin] Together with.

unalienable, *adj.* See INALIENABLE.

unanimous (yoo-**nan**-ə-məs), *adj.* (17c) **1.** Agreeing in opinion; being in complete accord <the judges were unanimous in their approval of the recommendation>. **2.** Arrived at by the consent of all <a unanimous verdict>. See *unanimous consent* under CONSENT (2); *unanimous vote* under VOTE (3). Cf. WITHOUT OBJECTION.

unanimous consent. See CONSENT (2).

unanimous-consent agenda. See *consent calendar* under CALENDAR (4).

unanimous-consent agreement. (1895) *Parliamentary law.* An agreement, negotiated between opposing sides debating a motion, regarding the procedure under which the assembly will consider the motion. • The unanimous-consent agreement is a common practice in the U.S. Senate. — Also termed *time agreement.* See *unanimous consent* under CONSENT (2).

unanimous-consent calendar. See *consent calendar* under CALENDAR (4).

unanimous vote. See VOTE (3).

unascertained duty. See DUTY (4).

unassessable, *adj.* (1860) **1.** Impossible to reasonably estimate the value of (income, property, etc.) as a basis for taxation. **2.** Impossible to quantify with any precision (for damages, a fine, etc.). **3.** Not subject to taxation or other charges.

unauthorized, *adj.* (16c) Done without authority; specif. (of a signature or indorsement), made without actual, implied, or apparent authority, as by forgery. UCC § 1-201(b)(41).

unauthorized alien. See *illegal alien* under ALIEN.

unauthorized completion. *Commercial law.* The act of filling in missing information in a negotiable instrument either without any authority to do so or without adequate authority. • Unauthorized completion is a personal defense, so it can be raised against any later holder of the instrument who does not have the rights of a holder in due course. See *personal defense* under DEFENSE (4).

unauthorized endorsement. See *unauthorized indorsement* under INDORSEMENT.

unauthorized indorsement. See INDORSEMENT.

unauthorized practice of law. See PRACTICE OF LAW.

unauthorized signature. See SIGNATURE.

unauthorized use of a vehicle. See JOYRIDING.

unavailability, *n.* (1855) The status or condition of not being available, as when a witness is exempted by court order from testifying. • Unavailability is recognized under the Federal Rules of Evidence as an exemption to the hearsay rule. Fed. R. Evid. 804.

unavailable witness. See WITNESS.

una voce (yoo-nə **voh**-see). [Latin] (16c) With one voice; unanimously; without dissent.

unavoidable accident. See ACCIDENT.

unavoidable-accident doctrine. (1961) *Torts.* The rule holding no party liable for an accident that was not foreseeable and that could not have been prevented by the exercise of reasonable care. • The modern trend is for courts to ignore this doctrine and to rely instead on the basic concepts of duty, negligence, and proximate cause. — Also termed *inevitable-accident doctrine.*

unavoidable casualty. See *unavoidable accident* under ACCIDENT.

unavoidable cause. See CAUSE (1).

unavoidable danger. See DANGER.

unbanked, *adj.* (18c) Lacking a formal relationship with a bank or other financial institution. • Unbanked consumers are the most frequent users of money services businesses.

unborn beneficiary. See BENEFICIARY.

unborn child. See CHILD.

unborn-widow rule. (1957) The legal fiction, assumed under the rule against perpetuities, that a beneficiary's widow is not alive at the testator's death, and thus a succeeding life estate to her voids any remainders because the interest would not vest within the perpetuities period. See RULE AGAINST PERPETUITIES.

unbroken, *adj.* (14c) Not interrupted; continuous <unbroken possession by the adverse possessor>.

unbundling rules. (1995) *Telecommunications.* Regulations passed by the Federal Communications Commission to effectuate the local-competition requirements of the Telecommunications Act of 1996, which requires local-exchange carriers to provide access to elements of local-exchange networks on an unbundled (i.e., separated) basis. 47 USCA § 251; 47 CFR pt. 51. See NETWORK ELEMENT.

uncertain damages. See DAMAGES.

uncertainty. (14c) **1.** The quality, state, or condition of being in some degree of serious doubt. **2.** Anything that is indefinite, indeterminate, or dubious. Cf. CERTAINTY.

- **conceptual uncertainty.** (1976) *Trusts.* Unclarity of language that is serious enough to cause a trust to be declared invalid.
- **evidential uncertainty.** (1976) *Trusts.* Unclarity of a factual matter such as whether a specific claimant is indeed a beneficiary.

uncertificated security. See SECURITY (4).

uncertified security. See *uncertificated security* under SECURITY (4).

uncharged-crimes evidence. See *404(b) evidence* under EVIDENCE.

uncia (ən-shee-ə), *n.* [Latin] (1834) **1.** *Roman law.* One-twelfth of the *as* (a pound or, by analogy, an estate or inheritance). • The English word *ounce* is derived from this term. Cf. AS; BES. **2.** *Hist.* A measure of land used in a royal charter. • The size of an *uncia* is unclear, but it may have measured 1,200 square feet (i.e., 12 *modii*). **3.** Generally, the proportion of one-twelfth.

unciarius heres. See HERES.

uncitable. See NONCITABLE.

UNCITRAL Arbitration Rules. The arbitration rules of the United Nations Commission on International Trade Law, applicable to all arbitrations in which the parties stipulate that they govern, most commonly in ad hoc international arbitrations. • Originally adopted in 1976, the UNCITRAL Rules were significantly amended in 2010. — Often shortened to *UNCITRAL Rules.*

unclean bill of lading. See BILL OF LADING.

unclean-hands doctrine. See CLEAN-HANDS DOCTRINE.

uncollected funds. (1838) A credit, such as an increase in the balance of a checking or other deposit account in a financial institution, given on the basis of a check or other right to payment that has not yet been received from the drawee or other payor.

unconditional, *adj.* (17c) Not limited by a condition; not depending on an uncertain event or contingency; absolute.

unconditional delivery. See DELIVERY.

unconditional discharge. See DISCHARGE (5).

unconditional heir. See HEIR.

unconditional pardon. See *absolute pardon* under PARDON (1).

unconditional promise. See PROMISE.

unconditional release. See RELEASE (8).

unconscionability (ən-kon-shə-nə-**bil**-ə-tee). (16c) **1.** Extreme unfairness. • Unconscionability is normally assessed by an objective standard: (1) one party's lack of meaningful choice, and (2) contractual terms that unreasonably favor the other party. **2.** The principle that a court may refuse to enforce a contract that is unfair or oppressive because of procedural abuses during contract formation or because of overreaching contractual terms, esp. terms that are unreasonably favorable to one party while precluding meaningful choice for the other party. • Because unconscionability depends on circumstances at the time the contract is formed, a later rise in market price is irrelevant.

> "Traditionally, a bargain was said to be unconscionable in an action at law if it was 'such as no man in his senses and not under delusion would make on the one hand, and as no honest and fair man would accept on the other;' damages were then limited to those to which the aggrieved party was 'equitably' entitled. Even though a contract was fully enforceable in an action for damages, equitable remedies such as specific performance were refused where 'the sum total of its provisions drives too hard a bargain for a court of conscience to assist.' Modern procedural reforms have blurred the distinction between remedies at law and in equity. For contracts for the sale of goods, Uniform Commercial Code § 2-302 states the rule of this Section without distinction between law and equity. Comment 1 to that section adds, 'The principle is one of the prevention of oppression and unfair surprise . . . and not of disturbance of allocation of risks because of superior bargaining power.'" Restatement (Second) of Contracts § 208 cmt. b (1979) (citations omitted).

> "Nowhere among the [Uniform Commercial] Code's many definitions is there one of *unconscionability.* That the term is incapable of precise definition is a source of both strength and weakness." E. Allan Farnsworth, *Contracts* § 4.28, at 310 (3d ed. 1999)

▸ **procedural unconscionability.** (1973) Unconscionability resulting from improprieties in contract formation (such as oral misrepresentations or disparities in bargaining position) rather than from the terms of the contract itself.

> "Most cases of unconscionability involve a combination of procedural and substantive unconscionability, as it is generally agreed that if more of one is present, then less of the other is required." E. Allan Farnsworth, *Contracts* § 4.28, at 312 (3d ed. 1999).

▸ **substantive unconscionability.** (1973) Unconscionability resulting from actual contract terms that are unduly harsh, commercially unreasonable, and grossly unfair given the existing circumstances.

unconscionable (ən-**kon**-shə-nə-bəl), *adj.* (16c) **1.** (Of a person) having no conscience; unscrupulous <an unconscionable used-car salesman>. **2.** (Of an act or transaction) showing no regard for conscience; affronting the sense of justice, decency, or reasonableness <the contract is void as unconscionable>. Cf. CONSCIONABLE. **3.** Much more than is acceptable or reasonable <an unconscionable delay>. **4.** Shockingly unjust or unfair <an unconscionable offer>.

unconscionable agreement. See AGREEMENT.

unconscionable bargain. See *unconscionable agreement* under AGREEMENT.

unconscionable contract. See *unconscionable agreement* under AGREEMENT.

unconscious, *adj.* (18c) Without awareness; not conscious. • A person who commits a criminal act while unconscious may be relieved from liability for the act.

unconscious instrument. See INSTRUMENT (3).

unconsciousness defense. See AUTOMATISM.

unconstitutional, *adj.* (18c) *Constitutional law.* Contrary to or in conflict with a constitution, esp. the U.S. Constitution <the law is unconstitutional because it violates the First Amendment's free-speech guarantee>. Cf. NONCONSTITUTIONAL.

unconstitutional-conditions doctrine. (1935) *Constitutional law.* **1.** The rule that the government sometimes cannot condition a person's receipt of a governmental benefit on the waiver of a constitutionally protected right (esp. a right under the First Amendment). • For example, a television station cannot be forced to refrain from endorsing political candidates as a condition for receiving public funds. Because the government is often permitted to condition a benefit on the offeree's waiver of a constitutional right, the doctrine's precise meaning and scope are uncertain. **2.** The rule that the government cannot force a defendant to choose between two constitutionally protected rights. — Also termed *doctrine of unconstitutional conditions.* See BENEFIT (4).

> "[T]he so-called unconstitutional conditions problem . . . arises whenever the government offers to provide a gratuitous benefit conditioned on the offeree's waiver of a constitutional right. It has been recognized for well over a century and appears in dozens of doctrinal contexts. Despite early judicial assertions that such offers are, on the one hand, always permissible or, on the other, always unconstitutional, it is now universally recognized that such conditional offers are sometimes constitutionally permissible and sometimes not. Indeed, correctly understood, that is all the famed and contentious unconstitutional conditions doctrine holds." Mitchell N. Berman, *Coercion Without Baselines: Unconstitutional Conditions in Three Dimensions,* 90 Geo. L.J. 1, 3 (2001).

unconstitutionally vague. See VAGUE (1).

uncontestable clause. See INCONTESTABILITY CLAUSE.

uncontested divorce. See DIVORCE.

uncontested hearing. See HEARING.

uncontrollable, *adj.* (16c) Incapable of being controlled.

uncontrollable impulse. See IMPULSE.

uncontrolled-securities-offering distribution. See *securities-offering distribution* under DISTRIBUTION.

uncopyrightable, *adj.* (1926) (Of a work) ineligible for copyright protection either because the work lacks originality or because it is an idea, concept, process, or other abstraction that is not included in one of the eight covered classifications of copyrightable works. 17 USCA §§ 101–106.

uncore prist (ən[g]-kor **prist**). [Law French "still ready"] (17c) *Hist.* A plea by which a party alleges readiness to pay or perform what is justly demanded.

> "Yet sometimes, after tender and refusal of a debt, if the creditor harasses his debtor with an action, it then becomes necessary for the defendant to acknowledge the debt, and plead the tender; adding, that . . . he is still ready, *uncore prist*, to discharge it . . . ." 3 William Blackstone, *Commentaries on the Laws of England* 303 (1768).

uncorrectability defense. (1999) *Patents.* An affirmative defense in an infringement suit, established by showing (1) that a coinventor's name was omitted from a patent, and (2) that the patent cannot be corrected because the named coinventor acted with deceptive intent.

uncorroborated, *adj.* (18c) (Of a statement, testimony, account, or evidence) not confirmed or supported by additional evidence or authority. Cf. CORROBORATED.

uncounseled, *adj.* (1931) Without the benefit or participation of legal counsel <an uncounseled conviction> <an uncounseled defendant>.

uncovered option. See *naked option* under OPTION (5).

UNCRC. *abbr.* UNITED NATIONS CONVENTION ON THE RIGHTS OF THE CHILD.

unde nihil habet (ən-dee **nɪ**-hil **hay**-bət). [Law Latin "whereof she has nothing"] (16c) *Hist.* A writ of dower for a widow where no dower had been assigned to her within the time allowed by law. See WRIT OF DOWER. Cf. DE DOTE UNDE NIL HABET.

underbid. 1. See BID, *n.* (1). **2.** See BID, *vb.*

undercapitalization. See CAPITALIZATION.

undercover agent. See AGENT.

undercover officer. See POLICE OFFICER.

undercurrent of surface stream. (2004) Water that moves slowly through the bed of a stream or the lands under or immediately adjacent to the stream. • This water is considered part of the surface stream. — Also termed *underflow of surface stream.*

underdeveloped country. See DEVELOPING COUNTRY.

underemployed, *adj.* Working in a job in which one cannot use all one's skills or in which there is not enough work to do; esp., having less than adequate employment.

underemployment. See EMPLOYMENT.

underflow of surface stream. See UNDERCURRENT OF SURFACE STREAM.

underfunded, *adj.* (1970) (Of a project, organization, etc.) not having been given enough money to be effective; having been given insufficient financial resources.

underground economy. See SHADOW ECONOMY.

underground recording. See BOOTLEG RECORDING (1).

underhanded, *adj.* (1806) **1.** Accomplished dishonestly and secretly <underhanded dealings>. **2.** Engaged in cheating and deception; sly <an underhanded businessman>. — Also termed *underhand.*

underinsurance. (1893) An agreement to indemnify against property damage up to a certain amount but for less than the property's full value.

underinsured-motorist coverage. (1971) Insurance that pays for the insured's losses and injuries negligently caused by a driver does not have enough liability insurance to cover the damages. — Abbr. UM coverage. Cf. UNINSURED-MOTORIST COVERAGE.

underlease. See SUBLEASE.

underlessor. See SUBLESSOR.

underlying, *n.* An asset or other factor that gives rise to the rights and obligatives in a derivative contract. See DERIVATIVE.

> "The end-user of a derivative can use the derivative to decrease exposure to movements in the market for the underlying. That is, the end-user is acquiring protection from (hedging against) the risk of an unfavourable movement in the market for the underlying, whether that unfavourable movement is an increase or a decrease in the price of the underlying. This risk is usually referred to as price risk or market risk. A derivative used in this manner is used to reduce or to control market risk. The end-user pays a price for acquiring this protection." John-Peter Castagnino, *Derivatives: The Key Principles* 2 (3d ed. 2009).

under one's hand. (17c) (Of a person's signature) affixed manually, as opposed to printed or stamped. See HAND (1).

under protest. See PROTEST (3).

under seal. 1. Authenticated with an impression, stamp, or sign indicating that an instrument has legal status. See SEAL (2). **2.** Legally protected as secret.

Undersecretary of Commerce for Intellectual Property. See DIRECTOR OF THE UNITED STATES PATENT AND TRADEMARK OFFICE.

underservant. A servant of subordinate or subaltern rank; an inferior, low-ranking servant.

undersheriff. See *deputy sheriff* under SHERIFF (1).

undersigned, *n.* (17c) Someone whose name is signed on a document, esp. at the end <the undersigned agrees to the terms and conditions set forth above>.

under-65 trust. See TRUST (3).

understand, *vb.* (bef. 12c) To apprehend the meaning of; to know <the testator did not understand what he was signing>.

understanding, *n.* (bef. 12c) **1.** The quality, state, or process of comprehending; the mental state of a person who understands something. **2.** One's personal interpretation of an event or occurrence. **3.** An agreement, esp. of an implied or tacit nature.

under submission. (18c) Being considered by the court; under advisement <the case was under submission in the court of appeals for more than two years>.

undertake, *vb.* (13c) **1.** To take on an obligation or task <he has undertaken to chair the committee on legal aid for the homeless>. **2.** To give a formal promise; guarantee <the merchant undertook that the goods were waterproof>. **3.** To act as surety for (another); to make oneself responsible for (a person, fact, or the like) <her husband undertook her appearance in court>.

undertaking, *n.* (14c) **1.** A promise, pledge, or engagement. **2.** A bail bond.

> "An undertaking is the entrance of two parties into such relationship as that one party, on account of the bare relationship unaided by any agreement, has a new duty to perform toward the other; he *undertakes* a new duty. . . . [T]he violation of an undertaking is not a tort, properly so called. It is a careful and exact use of legal language to call an undertaking a consensual obligation; it is a burden into which the obligor must voluntarily enter." Joseph H. Beale Jr., *Gratuitous Undertakings*, 5 Harv. L. Rev. 222, 223–24 (1891).

undertenant. See SUBLESSEE.

under the influence. (1879) (Of a driver, pilot, etc.) deprived of clearness of mind and self-control because of drugs or alcohol. See DRIVING UNDER THE INFLUENCE.

Undertreasurer of England. *Hist.* An officer immediately subordinate to the Lord High Treasurer.

undertutor. See TUTOR.

underwrite, *vb.* (15c) **1.** To write beneath; to subscribe. **2.** (Of an insurer) to execute and deliver (an insurance policy). **3.** To undertake to pay (a pledge of money, a subscription, etc.). **4.** To engage to buy all the shares in (a new venture, company, or other enterprise), esp. when not subscribed for by the public; specif., to arrange to sell shares in (a company), while agreeing to buy any not sold to them. **5.** To support (an activity, plan, etc.) with money while taking on full financial responsibility for a failure.

underwriter. (17c) **1.** INSURER. **2.** Someone who buys stock from the issuer with an intent to resell it to the public; a person or entity, esp. an investment banker, who guarantees the sale of newly issued securities by purchasing all or part of the shares for resale to the public. See *investment bank* under BANK.

> "The term 'underwriter' derives its meaning from former British insurance practices. When insuring their cargo shippers would seek out investors to insure their property. The insurers would add their signatures and would write their names under those of the shippers; hence the term 'underwriters.' Both in terms of the insurance industry and the securities markets, the concept of underwriting has expanded significantly since its inception." 1 Thomas Lee Hazen, *Treatise on the Law of Securities Regulation* § 2.1, at 81–82 (3d ed. 1995).

▸ **chartered life underwriter.** (1932) An underwriter who has satisfied the requirements set forth by The American College (formerly The American College of Life Underwriters) to be designated a life insurance underwriter. — Abbr. CLU.

▸ **insurance underwriter.** (1916) **1.** INSURER. — Also termed *writer.* **2.** An insurance-company employee who is responsible for determining whether to issue a policy and the amount to charge for the coverage provided.

underwriting, *n.* (18c) **1.** The act of assuming a risk by insuring it; the insurance of life or property. See INSURANCE. **2.** The act of agreeing to buy all or part of a new issue of securities to be offered for public sale. — **underwrite,** *vb.*

▸ **best-efforts underwriting.** (1959) Underwriting in which an investment banker agrees to direct, but not guarantee, the public sale of the issuer's securities. • The underwriter, or underwriting group, sells the securities as agent for the issuer, and unsold securities are never issued.

▸ **firm-commitment underwriting.** (1959) Underwriting in which the underwriter agrees to buy and sell all the shares to be issued and assumes full financial responsibility for any unsold securities. • The underwriter, or underwriting group, buys the securities from the issuer and resells them as principal. In this type of underwriting, securities that are not sold to the public are owned by the underwriter, and the issuer is paid for those securities as well as the others.

▸ **standby underwriting.** (1950) Underwriting in which the underwriter agrees, for a fee, to buy from the issuer any unsold shares remaining after the public offering. — Also termed *strict underwriting.*

underwriting agreement. See AGREEMENT.

underwriting spread. See SPREAD (4).

undesirable discharge. See DISCHARGE (8).

unde vi (ən-dee VI). [Latin] (17c) *Roman law.* A praetorian interdict allowing one who was violently dispossessed of a thing to recover it.

undigested offering. See OFFERING.

undisclosed agency. See AGENCY (1).

undisclosed agent. See AGENT.

undisclosed information. See TRADE SECRET.

undisclosed principal. See PRINCIPAL (1).

undisputed, *adj.* (16c) Not questioned or challenged; uncontested.

undisputed fact. See FACT.

undistributed-earnings tax. See *accumulated-earnings tax* under TAX.

undistributed profit. See *retained earnings* under EARNINGS.

undivided, *adj.* **1.** Not separated into smaller parts <an undivided interest in property> **2.** Complete <undivided attention>.

undivided interest. See INTEREST (2).

undivided profit. See *accumulated profit* under PROFIT (1).

undivided right. See *undivided interest* under INTEREST (2).

undivided title. See *undivided interest* under INTEREST (2).

undocumented alien. See *illegal alien* under ALIEN.

undocumented immigrant. See *illegal alien* under ALIEN.

undue, *adj.* (14c) **1.** *Archaic.* Not yet owed; not currently payable <an undue debt>. **2.** Excessive or unwarranted <undue burden> <undue influence>. — **unduly,** *adv.*

undue-breadth rejection. See REJECTION.

undue burden, *n.* See BURDEN.

undue-burden test. (1992) *Constitutional law.* The Supreme Court test stating that a law regulating abortion will be struck down if it places a substantial obstacle in the path of a woman's right to obtain an abortion. • This test replaced the "trimester analysis" set forth in *Roe v. Wade*, in which the state's ability to restrict abortion increased after each trimester of pregnancy. *Planned Parenthood* *of Southeastern Pa. v. Casey*, 505 U.S. 833, 112 S.Ct. 2791 (1992).

undue experimentation. (1923) *Patents.* An unreasonable amount of research and testing that would be required for a person skilled in the appropriate art to make and work an invention from the specification in the patent application. • If undue experimentation would be required, the application fails the embodiment requirement of 35 USCA § 112. See WANDS TEST.

undue hardship. See HARDSHIP.

undue influence. (18c) **1.** The improper use of power or trust in a way that deprives a person of free will and substitutes another's objective; the exercise of enough control over another person that a questioned act by this person would not have otherwise been performed, the person's free agency having been overmastered. • Consent either to conduct or to a contract, transaction, or relationship is voidable if the consent is obtained through undue influence. — Also termed *implied coercion*; *moral coercion*. Cf. DUE INFLUENCE.

> "Undue influence is unfair persuasion of a party who is under the domination of the person exercising the persuasion or who by virtue of the relation between them is justified in assuming that the person will not act in a manner inconsistent with his welfare." Restatement (Second) of Contracts § 177(1) (1979).

> "When at the turn of the twentieth century, the common law doctrine of duress was expanded to provide relief for coercion irrespective of the means of coercion, much of the work of undue influence became unnecessary. The doctrine has a much more specialized role today, although often enough the precedents decided when the more general doctrine prevailed are cited and quoted to the general confusion of the profession. Today the gist of the doctrine is unfair persuasion rather than coercion. Euphoria rather than fear is often, but certainly not always, the state of mind of the party unduly influenced." John D. Calamari & Joseph M. Perillo, *The Law of Contracts* § 9-9, at 351–52 (3d ed. 1987).

2. *Wills & estates.* Coercion that destroys a testator's free will and substitutes another's objectives in its place. • When a beneficiary actively procures the execution of a will, a presumption of undue influence may be raised, based on the confidential relationship between the influencer and the person influenced. — Also termed *improper influence*; (formerly, in both senses) *suggestion*. See COERCION; DURESS. Cf. CAPTATION.

undue multiplicity of claims. See AGGREGATION OF CLAIMS.

undue-multiplicity-of-claims rejection. See REJECTION.

undue prejudice. See PREJUDICE (1).

unduly dangerous conduct. See *unreasonably dangerous conduct* under CONDUCT.

undutiful will. See *unnatural will* under WILL.

unearned income. See INCOME.

unearned increment. See INCREMENT.

unearned interest. See INTEREST (3).

unearned premium. See PREMIUM (1).

unearned-premium reserve. See RESERVE (1).

unearned surplus. See SURPLUS.

unemployment. (18c) **1.** The quality, state, or condition of not having a job even though available for work and perhaps seeking it.

▸ **structural unemployment.** (1931) Unemployment resulting from a shift in the demand for a particular product or service.

2. Unemployment compensation <collecting unemployment>. See COMPENSATION.

unemployment benefit. See *unemployment compensation* under COMPENSATION.

unemployment compensation. See *unemployment compensation* under COMPENSATION.

unemployment insurance. See INSURANCE.

unemployment tax. See TAX.

unenacted law. See LAW.

unencumbered (ən-in-**kəm**-bərd), *adj.* (18c) Without any burdens or impediments <unencumbered title to property>.

unenforceable, *adj.* (1804) (Of a contract) valid but incapable of being enforced. Cf. VOID, *adj.*; VOIDABLE.

unenforceable contract. See CONTRACT.

unenumerated right. **1.** See RIGHT. **2.** See *implied right* under RIGHT.

UNEP. *abbr.* UNITED NATIONS ENVIRONMENT PROGRAMME.

unequal, *adj.* (16c) Not equal in some respect; uneven <unequal treatment under the law>.

unequivocal (ən-i-**kwiv**-ə-kəl), *adj.* (18c) Unambiguous; clear; free from uncertainty.

unerring (ən-**ər**-ing *also* ən-**er**-ing), *adj.* (17c) Incapable of error; infallible.

UNESCO. *abbr.* (1946) UNITED NATIONS EDUCATIONAL, SCIENTIFIC, AND CULTURAL ORGANIZATION.

unessential mistake. See MISTAKE.

unethical, *adj.* (1871) Not in conformity with moral norms or standards of professional conduct. See LEGAL ETHICS.

unexhausted teind. See *free teind* under TEIND.

unexpected, *adj.* (16c) Happening without warning; not expected.

unexpired term. See TERM (4).

unfair, *adj.* (18c) **1.** Not honest, impartial, or candid; unjust. **2.** Inequitable in business dealings, esp. with regard to labor and employment.

unfair competition. (1876) **1.** Dishonest or fraudulent rivalry in trade and commerce; esp., the practice of endeavoring to pass off one's own goods or products in the market for those of another by means of imitating or counterfeiting the name, brand, size, shape, or other distinctive characteristic of the article or its packaging. **2.** The body of law encompassing various business and privacy torts, all generally based on deceitful trade practices, including passing off, false advertising, commercial disparagement, and misappropriation.

> "The legal doctrine of unfair competition is a development of the fundamental idea that dealings based on deceit are legally wrong." Harry D. Nims, *The Law of Unfair Competition and Trade-Marks* 6 (1929).

unfair hearing. See HEARING.

unfair labor practice. (1934) Any conduct prohibited by state or federal law governing the relations among employers, employees, and labor organizations. • Examples of unfair labor practices by an employer include (1) interfering with protected employee rights, such as the right to self-organization, (2) discriminating against employees for union-related activities, (3) retaliating against employees who have invoked their rights, and (4) refusing to engage in collective bargaining. Examples of unfair labor practices by a labor organization include causing an employer to discriminate against an employee, engaging in an illegal strike or boycott, causing an employer to pay for work not to be performed (i.e., featherbedding), and refusing to engage in collective bargaining. 29 USCA §§ 151–169. — Abbr. ULP. — Often shortened to *unfair practice.*

unfair persuasion. (1931) *Contracts.* A type of undue influence in which a stronger party achieves a result by means that seriously impair the weaker party's free and competent exercise of judgment. • Unfair persuasion is a lesser form of undue influence than duress and misrepresentation. The two primary factors to be considered are the unavailability of independent advice and the susceptibility of the person persuaded. See UNDUE INFLUENCE (1).

unfair surprise. (1815) A situation in which a party, having had no notice of some action or proffered evidence, is unprepared to answer or refute it.

unfair trade. An inequitable business practice; esp., the act or an instance of a competitor's repeating of words in a way that conveys a misrepresentation that materially injures the person who first used the words, by appropriating credit of some kind earned by the first user.

Unfair Trade Practices and Consumer Protection Law. A model statute patterned on the Federal Trade Commission Act and proposed by the FTC in 1967 for adoption by the states; a state law providing consumer-protection remedies, including private causes of action, for deceptive trade practices and false advertising. • The Act gives the state attorney general power to regulate unfair and deceptive trade practices. It also gives consumers a right to sue offenders directly. — Abbr. UTPCPL. — Also termed *Little FTC Acts.*

unfaithful, *adj.* (16c) **1.** Not honoring vows, promises, or allegiances; disloyal <an unfaithful friend>. **2.** (Of a person in a committed relationship) engaging in sexual relations with someone other than one's committed partner <he hired an investigator to see whether his wife was being unfaithful>. **3.** Inaccurate or untrustworthy <an unfaithful version>. Cf. FAITHFUL.

unfavorable witness. See *hostile witness* under WITNESS.

unfinished business. See BUSINESS (5).

unfinished business and general orders. See BUSINESS (5).

unfit, *adj.* (16c) **1.** Unsuitable; not adapted or qualified for a particular use or service <the buyer returned the unfit goods to the seller and asked for a refund>. Cf. FIT AND PROPER. **2.** *Family law.* Morally unqualified; incompetent <the judge found the mother unfit and so found that awarding custody of the child to the father was in the child's best interests>.

unfitness of a parent. (1878) *Family law.* A parent's failure to exhibit a reasonable concern for, interest in, or responsibility for a child's welfare. • Regardless of the specific ground for an allegation of unfitness, a court considers the parent's actions and the circumstances surrounding the conduct in deciding whether unfitness has been demonstrated.

unforeseen, *adj.* (17c) Not foreseen; not expected <unforeseen circumstances>.

unfree tenure. See TENURE (2).

unfriendly suitor. See CORPORATE RAIDER.

unfriendly takeover. See *hostile takeover* under TAKEOVER.

unfunded deferred-compensation plan. See *nonqualified deferred-compensation plan* under EMPLOYEE BENEFIT PLAN.

unhandsome dealing. *Archaic.* See SHARP PRACTICE.

unharmed, *adj.* (14c) Not injured or damaged.

unholy trinity. See THREE WICKED SISTERS OF THE COMMON LAW.

unica taxatio (**yoo**-nə-kə tak-**say**-shee-oh). [Law Latin "a single taxation"] (18c) *Hist.* The practice of having the jury assess damages against a defaulting defendant as well as a defendant who contests the case.

unico contextu (**yoo**-ni-koh kən-**teks**-t[y]oo). [Law Latin] *Hist.* In one connection. • The phrase appeared in reference to that which was accomplished by the same act or by different acts performed at the same time.

> "When there are more parties than one to a deed, it is not essential to the validity of its execution that they should subscribe *unico contextu* — i.e., it is not necessary for them to subscribe at the same time and place. But where (as was formerly required) two notaries subscribed for a person who could not write, it was necessary that they should subscribe *unico contextu* at the same time and place, and before the same witnesses." John Trayner, *Trayner's Latin Maxims* 611 (4th ed. 1894).

unidentified principal. See PRINCIPAL.

unifactoral obligation. See OBLIGATION.

unified bar. See *integrated bar association* under BAR ASSOCIATION.

unified bar association. See *integrated bar association* under BAR ASSOCIATION.

unified credit. See *unified estate-and-gift tax credit* under TAX CREDIT.

unified estate-and-gift tax. See *unified transfer tax* under TAX.

unified estate-and-gift tax credit. See TAX CREDIT.

unified family court. See COURT.

unified transfer tax. See TAX.

uniform, *adj.* (16c) Characterized by a lack of variation; identical or consistent.

uniform act. **1.** A model statute drafted with the intention that it will be adopted by all or most of the states; esp., a uniform law. See UNIFORM LAW. Cf. MODEL ACT. **2.** See *uniform statute* under STATUTE.

Uniform Adoption Act. A 1994 model statute aimed at achieving uniformity in adoption laws. • The current version of the Act was promulgated in 1994 by the National Conference of Commissioners on Uniform State Laws. State adoption has been largely unsuccessful. Earlier versions, in 1953 and 1971, were amended many times but were enacted in only a few states. — Abbr. UAA.

Uniform Anatomical Gift Act. A 1968 model statute that created protocols that govern the giving and receiving of anatomical gifts. • Under the Act, persons may donate their body or parts of their body for purposes of transplantation, therapy, research, or education. The original Act has been adopted in some form in all 50 states and the District of Columbia. It was revised in 1987, and the revised version has been adopted in some form in at least 22 states. — Abbr. UAGA.

Uniform Arbitration Act. A model statute that encourages and provides guidance for arbitration agreements and procedures. • The Act was originally promulgated by the National Conference of Commissioners on Uniform State Laws in 1956. NCCUSL promulgated a revised version in 2000. Most states have enacted some version of the Uniform Arbitration Act or the Uniform Arbitration Act (2000) (also known as the Revised Uniform Arbitration Act). — Abbr. UAA; RUAA (Revised Uniform Arbitration Act). Cf. FEDERAL ARBITRATION ACT.

Uniform Child Abduction Prevention Act. A 2006 model statute intended to prevent predivorce and postdivorce child abductions by a parent or guardian (or someone acting on his or her behalf), whether or not stemming from a divorce. • The Act identifies factors for a court to consider when analyzing the risk of abduction in individual cases and suggests abduction-prevention measures for a court to consider taking. — Abbr. UCAPA.

Uniform Child Custody Jurisdiction Act. A 1968 model statute that sets out a standard (based on the child's residence in and connections with the state) by which a state court determines whether it has jurisdiction over a particular child-custody matter or whether it must recognize a custody decree issued by another state's court. • The Uniform Child Custody Jurisdiction Act was replaced in 1997 by the Uniform Child Custody Jurisdiction and Enforcement Act. — Abbr. UCCJA. See HOME STATE (2). Cf. PARENTAL KIDNAPPING PREVENTION ACT; UNIFORM CHILD CUSTODY JURISDICTION AND ENFORCEMENT ACT.

Uniform Child Custody Jurisdiction and Enforcement Act. A 1997 model statute that provides uniform methods of expedited interstate custody and visitation orders. • This Act was promulgated as a successor to the Uniform Child Custody Jurisdiction Act. The UCCJEA brings the Uniform Child Custody Jurisdiction Act into conformity with the Parental Kidnapping Prevention Act and the Violence Against Women Act. The Act revises child-custody jurisdiction, giving clearer standards for original jurisdiction and a standard for continuing jurisdiction. The Act also provides a remedial process for enforcing interstate child custody and visitation. — Abbr. UCCJEA. Cf. UNIFORM CHILD CUSTODY JURISDICTION ACT.

Uniform Code of Military Justice. 1. CODE OF MILITARY JUSTICE. **2.** A model code promulgated by the National Conference of Commissioners on Uniform State Laws to govern state military forces when not in federal service. 11 ULA 335 et seq. (1974). — Abbr. UCMJ.

> "When Congress was contemplating unification of the services, it appeared that the establishment of one basic military justice law applicable to all services was a step in that direction. In April of 1950, Congress passed the Uniform Code of Military Justice . . . . This Code was based primarily on the Army's Articles of War, which had been amended in 1948 and had served to test many new concepts. The Code became law on 5 May 1950 and by 31 May 1951 was in full force and effect. Thereupon, naval law, Army law, Air Force law, and Coast Guard law, in effect died and in their places the Uniform Code of Military Justice, applicable to all the armed forces, was born." Edward M. Byrne, *Military Law* 9 (2d ed. 1976).

Uniform Commercial Code. A uniform statute that governs commercial transactions, including sales of goods, secured transactions, and negotiable instruments. • The Code has been adopted in some form by every state and the District of Columbia. — Abbr. UCC.

Uniform Computer Information Transactions Act. A model statute that regulates software licensing and computer-information transactions. • The act draws on contract law and the Uniform Commercial Code to create a regulatory scheme for licensing, rather than sales or lease, transactions. Among other things, UCITA applies to contracts for the licensing or purchase of software, contracts for software development, and contracts for access to databases through the Internet. It does not cover goods or services contracts within the scope of the UCC. — Abbr. UCITA.

Uniform Conservation Easement Act. A 1981 model statute designed to overcome two common-law impediments by enabling both durable restrictions and affirmative obligations to be attached to real property to protect natural and historic resources. — Abbr. UCEA.

Uniform Consumer Credit Code. A uniform law designed to simplify and modernize the consumer credit and usury laws, to improve consumer understanding of the terms of credit transactions, to protect consumers against unfair practices, and the like. • This Code has been adopted by only a few states. — Abbr. UCCC; U3C. — Also termed *Consumer Credit Code.* See CONSUMER CREDIT PROTECTION ACT.

Uniform Controlled Substances Act. A uniform act, adopted by many states and the federal government, governing the sale, use, and distribution of drugs. 21 USCA §§ 801 et seq. — Abbr. UCSA.

Uniform Crime Reports. A series of annual criminological studies (each entitled *Crime in the United States*) prepared by the FBI. • The reports include data on eight index offenses, statistics on arrests, and information on offenders, crime rates, and the like. — Abbr. UCR.

Uniform Customs and Practice for Commercial Documentary Credits. A publication of the International Chamber of Commerce that codifies widespread customs of bankers and merchants relating to the mechanics and operation of letters of credit. • Courts use this publication to supplement and help interpret primary sources of credit law, such as UCC Article 5. — Abbr. UCP.

Uniform Deceptive Trade Practices Act. A 1964 model state statute that codified many common-law intellectual-property torts, such as trademark infringement, passing off, trade disparagement, and false advertising, and that provided additional consumer protection against other forms of commercial deception. • The Act provides a laundry list of prohibited practices, all involving misrepresentation. — Abbr. UDTPA. See BABY FTC ACT.

Uniform Determination of Death Act. A 1978 model statute that provides a comprehensive basis for determining death. • This is a technical act that merely defines death clinically and does not deal with suicide, assisted suicide, or the right to die. The Act was revised in 1980. It has been adopted in almost all states. — Abbr. UDDA.

Uniform Disposition of Community Property at Death Act. A 1971 model statute designed for non-community-property states to preserve the rights of each spouse in property that was community property before the spouses moved to non-community-property states, unless they have severed or altered their community-property rights.

Uniform Division of Income for Tax Purposes Act. A uniform law, adopted by some states, that provides criteria to assist in assigning the total taxable income of a multistate corporation among the various states. — Abbr. UDITPA.

Uniform Divorce Recognition Act. A 1947 model code adopted by some states regarding full-faith-and-credit issues that arise in divorces. — Abbr. UDRA.

Uniform Durable Power of Attorney Act. A 1979 model statute that provides a simple way for a person to deal with his or her property by providing a power of attorney that will survive after the incompetence of the principal. • The Act was revised in 1987 and has been adopted in almost every state. — Abbr. UDPAA.

Uniformed Services Former Spouses' Protection Act. A federal statute that governs the disposition of military pension benefits to former spouses of persons in the armed services. 10 USCA §§ 1401 et seq. • The Act permits state courts to treat military-retirement pay as marital property and to order payment of up to 50% of the retirement pay directly to the former spouse if the spouses were married for at least ten years while the employee served in the military. — Abbr. USFSPA.

Uniform Electronic Transactions Act. A 1999 model law designed to support electronic commerce by providing means for legally recognizing and retaining electronic records, establishing how parties can bind themselves in an electronic transaction, and providing for the use of electronic records by governmental agencies. • UETA covers electronic records and digital signatures but applies only if all parties agree to do business electronically. — Abbr. UETA.

Uniform Enforcement of Foreign Judgments Act. A uniform state law giving the holder of a foreign judgment the right to levy and execute as if it were a domestic judgment. — Abbr. UEFJA.

Uniform Fraudulent Conveyances Act. A model act adopted in 1918 to deal with issues arising from fraudulent conveyances by insolvent persons. • This act differentiated between conduct that was presumed fraudulent and conduct that required an actual intent to commit fraud. — Abbr. UFCA.

Uniform Fraudulent Transfer Act. A model act designed to bring uniformity among the states regarding the definition of, and penalties for, fraudulent transfers. • This act was adopted in 1984 to replace the Uniform Fraudulent Conveyances Act. — Abbr. UFTA.

Uniform Gifts to Minors Act. See UNIFORM TRANSFERS TO MINORS ACT. — Abbr. UGMA.

Uniform Health-Care Decisions Act. A 1993 model statute that facilitates and encourages adults to make advance directives. — Abbr. UHCDA. See ADVANCE DIRECTIVE; LIVING WILL.

Uniform Interstate Family Support Act. A 1992 model statute establishing a one-order system by which an alimony or child-support decree issued by one state can be enforced against a former spouse who resides in another state. • This statute has been adopted in every state and is the basis of jurisdiction in child-support suits. The purpose of the Act is to make the pursuit of interstate child support and paternity more effective, consistent, and efficient by requiring all states to recognize and enforce consistently support orders issued in other states. Before its enactment, there was considerable disparity among the states in the way they handled interstate child-support proceedings, since each state had differing versions of the earlier uniform law, the Uniform Reciprocal Enforcement of Support Act. The Act was revised in 1996 and again in 2001. — Abbr. UIFSA.

Uniform Interstate Juvenile Compact. An agreement that regulates the treatment of juveniles who are not under proper supervision or control, or who have run away or escaped, and who are likely to endanger their own or others' health, morals, or welfare. • The Compact is relied on by the state to transport juvenile runaways back to their home states. It has now been universally adopted in the United States, but not always in its entirety. — Abbr. UIJC.

Uniformity Clause. (1881) *Constitutional law.* The clause of the U.S. Constitution requiring the uniform collection of federal taxes. U.S. Const. art. I, § 8, cl. 1.

Uniform Juvenile Court Act. A 1968 model statute designed to (1) provide for the care, protection, and moral, mental, and physical development of the children who come under its provisions, (2) provide juvenile delinquents with treatment, training, and rehabilitation rather than criminal punishment, (3) attempt to keep families together unless separation of parents and children is necessary for the children's welfare or is in the public interest, (4) provide a judicial procedure for a fair hearing and protection of juvenile delinquents' constitutional and other legal rights, and (5) provide simple interstate procedures to carry out cooperative measures among the juvenile courts of different states. — Abbr. UJCA.

uniform law. An unofficial law proposed as legislation for all the states to adopt exactly as written, the purpose being to promote greater consistency among the states. • All the uniform laws are promulgated by the National Conference of Commissioners on Uniform State Laws. For a complete collection, see *Uniform Laws Annotated.* See *uniform statute* under STATUTE. Cf. MODEL ACT.

Uniform Law Commission. The informal name of the National Conference of Commissioners on Uniform State Laws. • It was adopted in 2007. *See* Robert A. Stein, *Forming a More Perfect Union: A History of the Uniform Law Commission* 143 (2013). See NATIONAL CONFERENCE OF COMMISSIONERS ON UNIFORM STATE LAWS. — Abbr. UCL.

Uniform Law Commissioners. See NATIONAL CONFERENCE OF COMMISSIONERS ON UNIFORM STATE LAWS.

Uniform Limited Partnership Act. A model law promulgated in 1916 for adoption by state legislatures to govern the relationship between the partners of a limited partnership. • At one time it was adopted in all states except Louisiana. The National Conference of Commissioners on Uniform State Laws promulgated the Revised Uniform Limited Partnership Act (RULPA) in 1976, and made substantial amendments to it in 1985. The amended RULPA has been adopted by most states. — Abbr. ULPA.

Uniform Mandatory Disposition of Detainers Act. A 1958 model statute requiring a state to timely dispose of any untried charges against a prisoner in that state, on the prisoner's written request. • The Act has been adopted by several states. — Abbr. UMDDA. See INTERSTATE AGREEMENT ON DETAINERS ACT.

Uniform Marriage and Divorce Act. A 1970 model statute that defines marriage and divorce. • Extensively amended in 1973, the Act was an attempt by the National Conference of Commissioners on Uniform State Laws to make marriage and divorce laws more uniform. The Act's greatest significance is that it introduced, as the sole ground for divorce, irreconcilable differences. Although the UMDA has been enacted in part in only a handful of states, it has had an enormous impact on marriage and divorce laws in all states. — Abbr. UMDA. — Also termed *Model Marriage and Divorce Act.* See IRRECONCILABLE DIFFERENCES.

Uniform Parentage Act. A 1973 model statute that provides a means for determining parenthood for the general welfare of the child and for assigning child support. • The Act abolishes distinctions between legitimate and illegitimate status for children. Instead, it directs courts to determine rights and responsibilities based on the existence of a parent–child relationship. The Act has been adopted in all states. The Act was revised in 2000 and amended in 2002. Among other changes, the revisions provided frameworks for establishing the parentage (esp. paternity) of children born to married or unmarried couples, and set standards and rules for genetic testing. A minority of states have enacted a version of the revised Act. — Abbr. UPA.

Uniform Partnership Act. A 1914 model statute intended to bring uniformity to state laws governing general and limited partnerships. • The Act was adopted by almost all the states, but has been superseded in several of them by the Revised Uniform Partnership Act (1994). — Abbr. UPA.

Uniform Premarital Agreement Act. A 1983 model statute that governs the drafting of prenuptial contracts and provides a more certain framework for drafting complete and enforceable agreements. • Under the UPAA, a premarital agreement must be in writing and signed by the parties. It becomes effective only upon marriage. The agreement may govern the parties' assets, support, and obligations during the marriage, at death, and upon divorce. The UPAA has been adopted in some form in about one-third of the states. — Abbr. UPAA.

uniform price. See PRICE.

Uniform Principal and Income Act. A uniform code adopted by some states governing allocation of principal and income in trusts and estates. — Abbr. UPIA.

Uniform Probate Code. A 1969 model statute that modernizes the rules and doctrines governing intestate succession, probate, and the administration of estates. • It has been extensively amended many times since 1969 and has been enacted in a majority of states. — Abbr. UPC.

Uniform Prudent Investor Act. A 1994 model statute that sets a standard for the acts of a trustee, adopts a prudent-investor standard, and prefers a modern portfolio approach to investing. • Under the Uniform Prudent Investor Act, the trustee is given significant power to delegate the selection of investments. The prudent-investor standard replaces the prudent-person standard of investing. The portfolio approach provides that no investment will be viewed in isolation; rather, it will be viewed as part of the entire portfolio. Under this theory, even though an investor loses trust assets on an investment, if there is an overall positive return, the investor will not be liable to the beneficiaries. — Abbr. UPIA. See PRUDENT-INVESTOR RULE.

Uniform Putative and Unknown Fathers Act. A 1988 model statute aimed at codifying Supreme Court decisions on the rights of an unwed father in relation to his child. • The Act deals primarily with an unwed father's right to notice of a termination and adoption proceeding, to adjudication of paternity, to visitation, and to custody. — Abbr. UPUFA. — Also termed *Model Putative Fathers Act; Putative Fathers Act.*

Uniform Reciprocal Enforcement of Support Act. A 1950 model statute (now superseded) that sought to unify the way in which interstate support matters were processed and the way in which one jurisdiction's orders were given full faith and credit in another jurisdiction. • This Act, which was amended in 1958 and 1960, was replaced in 1997 with the Uniform Interstate Family Support Act. — Abbr. URESA. See UNIFORM INTERSTATE FAMILY SUPPORT ACT.

uniform resource locator. The global address of documents and other materials on the World Wide Web. • The first part indicates which protocol to use, and the second specifies the IP address or the domain name where the resource is located. The two parts are separated by a colon and two forward slashes. A "web address" is a URL that uses the HTTP/HTTPS protocol. — Abbr. URL.

Uniform Simultaneous Death Act. A 1940 model statute specifying that if two or more people die within 120 hours of each other, each is considered to have predeceased the others. • The Act simplifies estate administration by preventing an inheritance from being transferred any more times than necessary. The Act was revised in 1993 and has been adopted in some form by almost every state. — Abbr. USDA. See COMMORIENTES.

Uniform Status of Children of Assisted Conception Act. A 1988 model statute aimed at ensuring certainty of legal parentage when assisted conception has been used. • The adopting state has the option of regulating or prohibiting contracts with surrogate mothers. — Abbr. USCACA.

uniform statute. See STATUTE.

uniform summons. See SUMMONS.

Uniform Trade Secrets Act. A 1979 model statute, enacted by most states, defining *trade secret* differently from the common law by being at once broader (because there is no continuous-use requirement) and narrower (because information "readily ascertainable by proper means" cannot qualify). • The Act has three elements: (1) the information must qualify as a trade secret; (2) it must be misappropriated, either through wrongful means or by breaching a duty of confidentiality; and (3) the owner must have taken reasonable precautions to keep the information secret. — Abbr. UTSA. — Also termed *Uniform Trade Secrets Protection Act.*

Uniform Transfers to Minors Act. A 1983 model statute providing for the transfer of property to a minor and permitting a custodian who acts in a fiduciary capacity to manage investments and apply the income from the property to the minor's support. • The Act has been adopted in most states. It was revised in 1986. — Abbr. UTMA. — Also termed *Transfers to Minors Act.* — Formerly also termed *Uniform Gifts to Minors Act*; *Gifts to Minors Act.*

unify, *vb.* (16c) To cause to become one; to form into a single unit.

unigeniture (yoo-nə-**jen**-ə-chər). (1887) *Archaic.* The fact of being an only child.

unilateral (yoo-nə-**lat**-ər-əl), *adj.* (1802) One-sided; relating to only one of two or more persons or things <unilateral mistake>.

unilateral act. See ACT (2).

unilateral advance pricing agreement. See ADVANCE PRICING AGREEMENT.

unilateral contract. See CONTRACT.

unilateral mistake. See MISTAKE.

unimproved land. See LAND.

unincorporated association. See ASSOCIATION (3).

unindicted coconspirator. See COCONSPIRATOR.

unindicted conspirator. See *unindicted coconspirator* under COCONSPIRATOR.

uninstructed delegate. See DELEGATE.

uninsured-motorist coverage. (1956) Insurance that pays for the insured's injuries and losses negligently caused by a driver who has no liability insurance. — Abbr. UM coverage. Cf. UNDERINSURED-MOTORIST COVERAGE.

unintelligibility. Incomprehensibility; the quality of being incapable of being understood.

unintelligibility canon. The doctrine that an unintelligible legal instrument is inoperative.

unintelligible vote. See VOTE (1).

unintended murder. See *unintentional murder* (1) under MURDER.

unintentional act. See ACT (2).

unintentional murder. See MURDER.

uninterested, *adj.* (18c) Bored; not interested in an intellectual sense (as opposed to a financial sense). Cf. DISINTERESTED.

uninterrupted-adverse-use principle. See CONTINUOUS-ADVERSE-USE PRINCIPLE.

unio (yoo-nee-oh). *Eccles. law.* A consolidation of two churches into one.

union, *n.* (1833) An organization formed to negotiate with employers, on behalf of workers collectively, about job-related issues such as salary, benefits, hours, and working conditions. • Unions generally represent skilled workers in trades and crafts. — Also termed *labor union*; *labor organization*; *organization*; *industrial organization.* See TRADE COUNCIL; TRADE-UNIONISM. — **unionize,** *vb.* — **unionist,** *n.*

▸ **closed union.** (1905) A union with restrictive membership requirements, such as high dues and long apprenticeship periods. Cf. *closed shop* under SHOP.

▸ **company union.** (1917) **1.** A union whose membership is limited to the employees of a single company. **2.** A union under company domination.

▸ **craft union.** (1926) A union composed of workers in the same trade or craft, such as carpentry or plumbing, regardless of the industry in which they work. — Also termed *horizontal union.*

▸ **federal labor union.** A local union directly chartered by the AFL-CIO. See AMERICAN FEDERATION OF LABOR AND CONGRESS OF INDUSTRIAL ORGANIZATIONS.

▸ **horizontal union.** See *craft union.*

▸ **independent union.** A union that is not affiliated with a national or international union.

▸ **industrial union.** (1923) A union composed of workers in the same industry, such as shipbuilding or automobile manufacturing, regardless of their particular trade or craft. — Also termed *vertical union.*

▸ **international union.** A parent union with affiliates in two or more countries.

▸ **local union.** A union that serves as the local bargaining unit for a national or international union.

▸ **multicraft union.** (1947) A union composed of workers in different industries.

▸ **national union.** A parent union with locals in various parts of the United States.

▸ **open union.** A union with minimal membership requirements. Cf. *open shop* under SHOP.

▸ **trade union.** (1828) A union composed of workers of the same or of several allied trades; a craft union. • In BrE, *trade union* is the usual term for what in AmE is termed a *labor union* or simply a *union.*

▸ **vertical union.** See *industrial union.*

union certification. (1947) A determination by the National Labor Relations Board or a state agency that a particular union qualifies as the bargaining representative for a segment of a company's workers — a bargaining unit — because it has the support of a majority of the workers in the unit. — Also termed *certification of bargaining agent*; *certification of labor union.*

union contract. See COLLECTIVE-BARGAINING AGREEMENT.

union givebacks. See CONCESSION BARGAINING.

Union Jack. (17c) The common name of the national flag of the United Kingdom, combining the national flags of England, Scotland, and Northern Ireland. • The Union Jack was originally a small union flag flown from the jackstaff at the bow of a vessel. It is different from the Royal Standard, which bears the royal arms and is the Queen's personal flag.

union-loss clause. See MORTGAGE-LOSS CLAUSE.

union mortgage clause. See *standard mortgage clause* under MORTGAGE CLAUSE.

union rate. See RATE (2).

union-security clause. (1941) A provision in a union contract intended to protect the union against employers, nonunion employees, and competing unions.

union shop. See SHOP.

union steward. See STEWARD (2).

unique chattel. See CHATTEL.

unissued stock. See STOCK.

unit. The number of shares, often 100, in which a given stock is normally traded.

unital (**yoo**-nə-təl), *adj.* (1860) Of, relating to, or involving legal relations that exist between only two persons. Cf. MULTITAL.

> "The relations of the *cestui que trust* with the trustee are *in personam* or 'unital,' and the same is true of a contract beneficiary and the promisor . . . ." William R. Anson, *Principles of the Law of Contract* 326 n.1 (Arthur L. Corbin ed., 3d Am. ed. 1919).

unitary, *adj.* Of, relating to, or involving a system of government that effects a union that fuses the governmental organs, without any division between regional components and the national components of a central government. Cf. FEDERAL.

> "A striking difference between the British and the American constitutions is to be found in the fact that the British constitution is unitary, whilst that of the United State is federal. When, in 1707, the Kingdoms of England and Scotland were united, union was achieved by a complete fusion of governmental organs." G.W. Keeton, *The Elementary Principles of Jurisprudence* 277–78 (2d ed. 1949).

unitary business (**yoo**-nə-ter-ee). *Tax.* A business that has subsidiaries in other states or countries and that calculates its state income tax by determining what portion of a subsidiary's income is attributable to activities within the state, and paying taxes on that percentage.

unitary state. See STATE (1).

unitary tax. See TAX.

unitas actus (**yoo**-ni-tas **ak**-təs). [Latin] (1911) *Roman law.* Unity of action, esp. in the execution of a will, which must not be interrupted by any intervening act.

unitas juris (**yoo**-ni-tas **joor**-is). [Latin] (1804) *Hist.* Unity of right.

unit cost. See COST (1).

unit depreciation method. See DEPRECIATION METHOD.

unite, *vb.* (15c) **1.** To combine or join to form a whole. **2.** To act in concert or in a common cause.

United Kingdom. A country in Europe comprising England, Scotland, Wales, and Northern Ireland, but not the Isle of Man or the Channel Islands. — Abbr. U.K.

United Nations. An international organization established in 1945 to promote and ensure international peace and security, to promote friendly relations between countries, and to contribute in resolving international problems related to economic, social, cultural, and humanitarian conditions. — Abbr. U.N.

United Nations Convention on the Rights of the Child. An international instrument covering children's civil, political, economic, social, and cultural rights. • The Convention was adopted by the United Nations General Assembly on November 20, 1989. Only a few countries, including the United States, have not ratified the convention. — Abbr. UNCRC.

United Nations Educational, Scientific, and Cultural Organization. The arm of the United Nations charged with promoting the exchange of educational, scientific, and cultural enterprises among countries. • Its Copyright Law Division administers the Universal Copyright Convention. — Abbr. UNESCO.

United Nations Environment Programme. An organization created in 1972 to encourage education in and employment of environmentally sound practices in all countries. — Abbr. UNEP.

United Nations Treaty on Principles Governing the Activities of States in the Exploration and Use of Outer Space. See OUTER SPACE TREATY.

United States. See UNITED STATES OF AMERICA. — Abbr. U.S.

United States Agency for International Development. The independent federal agency that administers U.S. foreign-aid programs to give economic and humanitarian assistance to developing countries. • The agency became independent by the Foreign Affairs and Restructuring Act of 1998, although its administrator is under the direct authority and foreign-policy guidance of the Secretary of State. — Abbr. AID; USAID.

United States Air Force. The aviation branch of the United States armed forces, made up of the Regular Air Force (standing air force), the Air Force Reserve, and the Air National Guard. • The United States Air Force is under the authority of the U.S. Department of the Air Force. — Abbr. USAF.

United States Air Force Academy. An institution of higher learning in the United States Department of the Air Force responsible for educating and training commissioned officers for service in the United States Air Force. • Founded in 1954, the academy is located near Colorado Springs, Colorado. — Abbr. USAFA. — Occasionally also termed (informally) *Colorado Air Force School.*

United States Arbitration Act. *Archaic.* See FEDERAL ARBITRATION ACT. — Abbr. USAA.

United States Army. The land-combat and land-operations branch of the United States armed forces. • This branch includes supporting air- and water-transport services such as the Army Air Corps. The Army includes the Regular Army (the standing force), the Army Reserve, and the Army National Guard when in active federal service, as in time of war or other national emergency. The United States Army is under the authority of the U.S. Department of the Army. — Also termed *land forces.* — Abbr. USA.

United States Attorney. A lawyer appointed by the President to represent, under the direction of the Attorney General, the federal government in civil and criminal cases in a federal judicial district. • One U.S. Attorney is assigned to each of the federal judicial districts, except for the Northern Mariana Islands and Guam. — Abbr. USA. — Also termed *United States District Attorney.* Cf. DISTRICT ATTORNEY.

▸ **Assistant United States Attorney.** A lawyer appointed by the Attorney General to act under the direction of the United States Attorney and represent the federal government in civil and criminal cases filed in federal courts. — Abbr. AUSA.

▸ **Special Assistant to the United States Attorney.** An attorney appointed by the Attorney General for a limited period to assist a United States Attorney in specific cases. 28 USCA § 543. — Abbr. SAUSA.

United States Bankruptcy Court. See BANKRUPTCY COURT.

United States Botanic Garden. An enclosed garden on the U.S. Capitol grounds where plants are cultivated for ceremonial use, public display, and research. • Many rare botanical specimens are available for study by students and scientists at the Garden.

United States Citizenship and Immigration Services. The agency within the Department of Homeland Security responsible for handling foreign-citizens' applications for permanent residency in the United States and naturalization as U.S. citizens. See IMMIGRATION AND NATURALIZATION SERVICE.

United States Claims Court. See UNITED STATES COURT OF FEDERAL CLAIMS.

United States Coast Guard. A military service and armed-forces branch that enforces the federal laws applicable to waters subject to U.S. jurisdiction, administers laws and promulgates regulations for the safety of lives and property on waters under U.S. jurisdiction, carries out maritime rescue operations, performs oceanographic research, and at times serves as a specialized branch of the Navy. • The Coast Guard was established in 1915. 14 USCA § 1. It has been part of the U.S. Department of the Treasury and the U.S. Department of Transportation. Today it is part of the U.S. Department of Homeland Security during peacetime, and the U.S. Department of Defense during wartime. — Abbr. USCG.

United States Coast Guard Academy. An institution of higher learning responsible for educating and training commissioned officers for service in the United States Coast Guard. • The academy began in 1876 as the School of Instruction of the Revenue Cutter Service near New Bedford, Massachusetts. In 1915, the academy acquired its current name and, in 1932, moved to its current location in New London, Connecticut. — Abbr. USCGA.

United States Code. A multivolume published codification of federal statutory law. — Abbr. U.S.C.; USC.

United States Code Annotated. A multivolume publication of the complete text of the United States Code with historical notes, cross-references, and casenotes of federal and state decisions construing specific Code sections. — Abbr. USCA.

United States Commissioner. See COMMISSIONER.

United States Commission on Civil Rights. The agency that compiles information about discrimination based on race, color, religion, sex, age, disability, or national origin, and about the denial of equal protection of the laws in voting, education, employment, and housing. • The agency makes findings and recommendations to Congress but has no enforcement power. It was established by the Civil Rights Act of 1957. — Abbr. CCR.

United States Constitution. See CONSTITUTION (3).

United States Copyright Office. A branch of the Library of Congress that is responsible for implementing federal copyright laws. • In addition to processing applications for copyrights, the U.S. Copyright Office stores deposited copyrighted materials and issues opinions (by request) on questions of copyright protection. Materials deposited with this agency are not automatically added to the Library of Congress collection; a separate and direct submission to the Library may be required. The Office also administers various licensing provisions of the statute, including collecting and distributing royalties.

United States court. See *federal court* under COURT.

United States Court of Appeals. A federal appellate court having jurisdiction to hear cases in one of the 13 judicial circuits of the United States (the First Circuit through the Eleventh Circuit, plus the District of Columbia Circuit and the Federal Circuit). — Also termed *circuit court; federal circuit court.*

United States Court of Appeals for the Armed Forces. The primary civilian appellate tribunal responsible for reviewing court-martial convictions from all the military services. 10 USCA §§ 941–950. — Formerly also termed *Court of Military Appeals.*

United States Court of Appeals for the Federal Circuit. An intermediate-level appellate court with jurisdiction to hear appeals in patent cases, various actions against the United States to recover damages, cases from the U.S. Court of Federal Claims, the U.S. Court of International Trade, the U.S. Court of Appeals for Veterans Claims, the Merit Systems Protection Board, and some administrative agencies. • The Court originated in the 1982 merger of the Court of Customs and Patent Appeals and the U.S. Court of Claims (although the trial jurisdiction of the Court of Claims was given to a new U.S. Claims Court). Among the purposes of its creation were ending forum-shopping in patent suits, settling differences in patent-law doctrines among the circuits, and allowing a single forum to develop the expertise needed to rule on complex technological questions that arise in patent suits. — Abbr. CAFC; Fed. Cir. — Often shortened to *Federal Circuit.*

United States Court of Appeals for Veterans Claims. An Article I federal appellate court that has exclusive jurisdiction to review decisions of the Board of Veterans Appeals. • The Court was created in 1988 as the United States Court of Veterans Appeals; its name was changed in 1998. Its seven judges are appointed by the President and confirmed by the Senate; they serve 15-year terms. Appeals from its decisions are to the U.S. Court of Appeals for the Federal Circuit. 38 USCA §§ 7251 et seq. — Also termed *United States Court of Veterans Appeals.*

United States Court of Federal Claims. A specialized federal court created under Article I of the Constitution in 1982 (with the name *United States Claims Court*) as the successor to the Court of Claims, and renamed in 1992 as the United States Court of Federal Claims. • It has original, nationwide jurisdiction to render a money judgment on any claim against the United States founded on the Constitution, a federal statute, a federal regulation, an express or implied-in-fact contract with the United States, or any other claim for damages not sounding in tort. — Abbr. Cl. Ct.; (formerly) Ct. Cl. — Also termed *Court of Claims.*

United States Court of International Trade. A court with jurisdiction over any civil action against the United States arising from federal laws governing import transactions or the eligibility of workers, firms, and communities for adjustment assistance under the Trade Act of 1974 (19 USCA §§ 2101–2495). • Its exclusive jurisdiction also includes actions to recover customs duties, to recover on a customs bond, and to impose certain civil penalties for fraud or negligence. *See* 28 USCA §§ 1581–1584. — Abbr. USCIT; CIT. — Also termed *International Trade Court;*

Court of International Trade; (formerly) *U.S. Customs Court.*

United States Court of Veterans Appeals. See UNITED STATES COURT OF APPEALS FOR VETERANS CLAIMS.

United States currency. See CURRENCY.

United States Customs and Border Protection. The federal law-enforcement agency within the U.S. Department of Homeland Security responsible for enforcing U.S. trade, customs, and immigration laws, esp. capturing illegal immigrants at the borders, stopping the traffic of contraband, guarding against the introduction of harmful pests and diseases, and protecting businesses against intellectual-property theft. • Among its predecessors were the United States Customs Service and the Bureau of Customs. — Abbr. USCBP; CBP. — Also termed *Customs and Border Protection.*

United States Customs Court. A court that formerly heard cases involving customs and duties. • Abolished in 1980, its responsibilities have been taken over by the United States Court of International Trade. See UNITED STATES COURT OF INTERNATIONAL TRADE.

United States District Attorney. See UNITED STATES ATTORNEY.

United States District Court. A federal trial court having jurisdiction to hear civil and criminal cases within its judicial district. • The United States is divided into nearly 100 federal judicial districts. Each state has at least one judicial district. Also, the District of Columbia, Puerto Rico, Guam, the Virgin Islands, and the Northern Mariana Islands each have one district. — Abbr. U.S.D.C.

United States Fish and Wildlife Service. A unit in the U.S. Department of the Interior responsible for managing more than 93 million acres of land and water consisting of more than 500 national wildlife refuges and thousands of small wetlands. • It also administers or enforces laws relating to migratory birds, endangered species, certain marine mammals, and sports fisheries. — Abbr. FWS; USFWS.

United States flag vessel. 1. See *government vessel* under VESSEL. **2.** See *privately owned U.S. flag commercial vessel* under VESSEL.

United States Foreign Intelligence Surveillance Court. An 11-judge court that hears requests from the Attorney General for surveillance warrants under the Foreign Intelligence Surveillance Act. • The court's proceedings and records are normally closed to the public. Its rulings may be reviewed by the Foreign Intelligence Court of Review. — Abbr. FISC.

United States Foreign Intelligence Surveillance Court of Review. A panel comprising three federal judges appointed by the Chief Justice to review decisions of the United States Intelligence Surveillance Court. • The Court was established in 1978 by the Foreign Intelligence Surveillance Act.

United States Foreign Service. A division of the State Department responsible for maintaining diplomatic and consular offices and personnel in foreign countries. — Often shortened to *Foreign Service.*

United States Geological Survey. A unit in the U.S. Department of the Interior responsible for preparing and publishing maps, technical reports, and fact sheets, and for compiling information about energy and mineral resources and the use and quality of the country's water resources. — Abbr. USGS.

United States Institute of Peace. An independent federal institution created to develop and disseminate knowledge about international peace and conflict resolution. • The Institute was established in 1984.

United States International Trade Commission. An independent federal agency that compiles information on international trade and tariffs; reports its findings and recommendations to the President, the U.S. Trade Representative, and Congressional Committees; and conducts investigations into international-trade relief. — Abbr. USITC.

United States Magistrate Judge. A federal judicial officer who hears civil and criminal pretrial matters and who may conduct civil trials or criminal misdemeanor trials. 28 USCA §§ 631–639. • Magistrate judges are appointed to renewable eight-year terms under Article I of the U.S. Constitution. — Also termed *federal magistrate*; (before 1990) *United States Magistrate*; *parajudge.*

United States Marine Corps. The military service within the United States Navy whose forces are trained for land, sea, and air combat. • The United States Marine Corps is a separate service within the United States Navy under the authority of the U.S. Department of the Navy. — Abbr. USMC.

United States Marshal. See MARSHAL.

United States Marshals Service. The unit in the U.S. Department of Justice responsible for protecting federal courts and ensuring effective operation of the judicial system. • U.S. marshals make arrests, serve court papers, and enforce court orders. — Abbr. USMS.

United States Merchant Marine Academy. A military-affiliated institution of higher learning responsible for educating and training commissioned officers for service on civilian merchant vessels or in the armed forces. • The academy was founded in 1938, and since 1943 has been located at King's Point, New York. — Abbr. USMMA.

United States Military Academy. An institution of higher learning in the U.S. Department of the Army responsible for educating and training officers for service in the U.S. Army. • Founded in 1802, the academy is located on the Hudson River in West Point, New York. — Abbr. USMA. — Often termed *West Point.*

United States Mint. A unit in the U.S. Department of the Treasury responsible for producing coins to be used in trade and commerce, numismatic coins, gold and silver coins, and national medals. • It also operates the gold-storage facility at Fort Knox, Kentucky. It was formerly termed the Bureau of the Mint.

United States Naval Academy. An institution of higher learning in the United States Department of the Navy responsible for educating and training commissioned officers for service in the United States Navy and the United States Marine Corps. • Founded in 1845, the academy is located in Annapolis, Maryland. — Abbr. USNA. — Often also termed (informally) *Annapolis.*

United States Navy. The naval-operations branch of the United States armed forces, including naval aviation and the United States Marine Corps, and the United States

Coast Guard when operating as a service in the Navy. • The United States Navy is under the authority of the U.S. Department of the Navy. — Abbr. USN.

United States of America. A federal republic formed after the late-18th-century War of Independence and made up of 48 conterminous states, plus the state of Alaska and the District of Columbia in North America, plus the state of Hawaii in the Pacific. — Abbr. USA; U.S.

United States officer. See OFFICER (1).

United States Patent and Trademark Office. The Department of Commerce agency that examines patent and trademark applications, issues patents, registers trademarks, and furnishes patent and trademark information and services to the public. — Abbr. PTO; USPTO. — Often shortened to *Patent Office*; *Trademark Office*.

United States person. A U.S. resident or national (except a national living outside the United States who is employed by someone other than a United States person), a domestic American concern, and any foreign subsidiary or affiliate of a domestic concern with operations controlled by the domestic concern. • Under antiboycott regulatory controls, no United States person may participate in a secondary boycott or discrimination against Jews and others by members of the League of Arab States. 50 USCA app. § 2415(2).

United States Postal Service. An independent establishment in the executive branch responsible for operating post offices, safeguarding and delivering mail, and enforcing the laws affecting the integrity and security of the mail. • The Postal Reorganization Act of 1970 replaced the cabinet-level Post Office Department with the United States Postal Service. 39 USCA §§ 101 et seq. — Abbr. USPS.

United States Reports. The official printed record of U.S. Supreme Court cases. • In a citation, it is abbreviated as U.S., as in 388 U.S. 14 (1967).

United States Secret Service. A law-enforcement agency in the U.S. Department of Homeland Security responsible for providing security for the President, Vice President, certain other government officials, and visiting foreign diplomats, and for protecting U.S. currency by enforcing the laws relating to counterfeiting, forgery, and credit-card fraud. • The Service was transferred from the Department of the Treasury in 2003. — Often shortened to *Secret Service*.

United States Senate Committee on the Judiciary. See SENATE JUDICIARY COMMITTEE.

United States Sentencing Commission. An independent commission in the judicial branch of the federal government responsible for setting and regulating guidelines for criminal sentencing in federal courts and for issuing policy statements about their application. • The President appoints its members with the advice and consent of the Senate. It was created under the Sentencing Reform Act 1984. 28 USCA § 991.

United States Sentencing Guidelines. A detailed set of instructions for judges to determine appropriate sentences for federal crimes. — Abbr. USSG. — Also termed *federal sentencing guidelines*.

United States Supreme Court. See SUPREME COURT OF THE UNITED STATES.

United States Tax Court. See TAX COURT, U.S.

United States Trade and Development Agency. An independent federal agency in the executive branch responsible for promoting trade between the United States and developing countries to create jobs in the United States and to promote economic progress in poorer countries. • It was established in 1961 as the Trade and Development Program and was renamed in 1992. — Abbr. TDA; USTDA.

United States Trade Representative. The top U.S. trade negotiator and adviser to the President on foreign-trade policy. • The Cabinet-level office is responsible for making annual reports on countries that do not act diligently to stop piracy of copyrighted material. The Trade Representative holds the rank of ambassador. — Abbr. USTR. See OFFICE OF THE UNITED STATES TRADE REPRESENTATIVE; SPECIAL 301.

United States trustee. (1925) A federal official who is appointed by the Attorney General to perform administrative tasks in the bankruptcy process, such as appointing bankruptcy trustees in Chapter 7 and Chapter 11 cases. See TRUSTEE (2).

unities doctrine of marriage. See LEGAL-UNITIES DOCTRINE.

Uniting and Strengthening America by Providing Appropriate Tools Required to Intercept and Obstruct Terrorism. See USA PATRIOT ACT.

unit-investment trust. See TRUST (3).

unitization. (1930) *Oil & gas.* The collection of producing wells over a reservoir for joint operations such as enhanced-recovery techniques. • Unitization is usu. carried out after primary production has begun to fall off substantially, in order to permit efficient secondary-recovery operations. It is also done to comply with well-spacing requirements established by state law or regulation. Pooling, by contrast, is usu. associated with drilling a single well and operating that well by primary-production techniques. Cf. POOLING. — **unitize** (**yoo**-nə-tiz), *vb.*

▸ **compulsory unitization.** (1930) Unitization done by order of a regulatory agency. — Also termed *forced unitization*.

▸ **forced unitization.** See *compulsory unitization*.

▸ **voluntary unitization.** (1930) Unitization arranged by agreement of the owners of mineral interests.

unitization clause. (1940) *Oil & gas.* A provision in an oil-and-gas lease granting the lessee the right to unitize the leased premises, generally for enhanced-recovery operations.

unit-ownership act. (1962) A state law governing condominium ownership.

unit price. See PRICE.

unit pricing. (1958) A system in which contract items are priced per unit rather than on the basis of a flat contract price.

unit rule. 1. *Securities.* A method of valuing securities by multiplying the total number of shares held by the sale price of one share sold on a licensed stock exchange, ignoring all other facts about value. **2.** *Parliamentary law.* A convention's rule that lets a delegation's majority cast the entire delegation's votes. Cf. *instructed delegate* under DELEGATE.

unitrust. See TRUST (3).

units-of-output depreciation method. See DEPRECIATION METHOD.

units-of-production method. (1923) *Tax.* An accounting method in which the depreciation provision is computed at a fixed rate per product unit, based on an estimate of the total number of units that the property will produce during its service life. • This method is used in the oil-and-gas industry when the total number of units of production (i.e., barrels in a reserve) can be accurately estimated.

unity, *n.* (13c) **1.** The fact or condition of being one in number; oneness. **2.** Jointness in interest, possession, time, or title. • At common law, all four of these unities were required for the creation of a joint tenancy. See *joint tenancy* under TENANCY. — **unitary,** *adj.*

▸ **unity of interest.** (18c) The requirement that all joint tenants' interests must be identical in nature, extent, and duration. — Also termed *interest unity.*

▸ **unity of possession.** (18c) The requirement that each joint tenant must be entitled to possession of the whole property. — Also termed *possession unity.*

▸ **unity of time.** (18c) The requirement that all joint tenants' interests must vest at the same time. — Also termed *time unity.*

▸ **unity of title.** (18c) The requirement that all joint tenants must acquire their interests under the same instrument. — Also termed *title unity.*

unity of art. (1955) *Copyright.* The inseparable nature of utilitarian and functional aspects of applied art. • France uses the unity-of-art approach to applied art and industrial design, but stops short of protecting strictly utilitarian design under copyright. — Also termed *cumulative approach.* Cf. DUALITY OF ART.

unity of seisin (**see**-zin). (1800) The merging of seisin in one person, brought about when the person becomes seised of a tract of land on which he or she already has an easement.

universal agency. See *general agency* under AGENCY (1).

universal agent. See AGENT.

universal church. See CHURCH (4).

Universal Copyright Convention. A 1952 treaty binding signatories to give citizens of other member countries the same copyright protection that their own citizens receive. 25 U.S.T. 1341, T.I.A.S. No. 7868. • Administered by the United Nations Educational, Scientific, and Cultural Organization, the Convention does not apply between countries that are also signatories of the Berne Convention. The United States signed the treaty in 1955. — Abbr. UCC.

Universal Declaration of Human Rights. An international bill of rights proclaimed by the United Nations in December 1948, being that body's first general enumeration of human rights and fundamental freedoms. • The preamble states that "recognition of the inherent dignity and of the equal and inalienable rights of all members of the human family is the foundation of freedom, justice and peace in the world." The Declaration contains a lengthy list of rights and fundamental freedoms. For the full text of the Declaration, see Appendix C. — Abbr. UDHR. See RIGHTS OF MAN.

universal defense. See *real defense* under DEFENSE (4).

universal inheritance. See INHERITANCE.

universal-inheritance rule. (2004) *Wills & estates.* A doctrine holding that an intestate estate escheats to the state only if the decedent leaves no surviving relatives, no matter how distant. • Through the first half of the 20th century, this rule was broadly followed in American jurisdictions. The Uniform Probate Code abandons the universal-inheritance rule and provides that if no member of the third or a nearer parentela survives the decedent, the intestate estate escheats to the state. — Also termed *rule of universal inheritance.* See PARENTELA. Cf. *laughing heir* under HEIR; GRADUAL METHOD.

universalist movement. *Copyright.* A 19th-century campaign in Europe to recognize a worldwide copyright law based on an author's moral rights.

> "The universalist movement evolved both in and out of France, starting with an international Congress of Authors and Artists in Brussels in 1858, attended by delegates of literary societies and universities, as well as by authors, artists, journalists, librarians, and lawyers. The movement gained momentum at an 1878 international literary congress in Paris presided over by Victor Hugo." Paul Goldstein, *International Copyright: Principles, Law, and Practice* 19 (2001).

universality. (16c) **1.** Equality of applicability. **2.** *Copyright.* A country's policy or practice of protecting artists' rights in their creations irrespective of the creator's nationality or where the work was created. • Universality, the most generous approach to international intellectual-property rights, is generally favored in countries that treat copyright as a moral right. Cf. RECIPROCITY; NATIONAL TREATMENT.

universal jurisdiction. *Int'l law.* A principle allowing or requiring a country to conduct criminal proceedings for certain crimes, regardless of where the crime was committed and the nationality of the perpetrator or victim.

universal legacy. See LEGACY.

universal legatee. See LEGATEE.

universal life insurance. See LIFE INSURANCE.

universal malice. See MALICE.

universal partnership. See PARTNERSHIP.

universal succession. See SUCCESSION (2).

universal successor. See SUCCESSOR.

universal synod. See *general synod* under SYNOD.

universal title. See TITLE (2).

universitas (yoo-ni-**vər**-sə-tas), *n.* [Latin] (18c) *Roman law.* A union of persons or things considered as a whole; a corporation.

universitas facti (yoo-ni-**vər**-sə-tas **fak**-tɪ). [Law Latin] (1892) A plurality of corporeal things of the same kind regarded as a whole, such as a herd of cattle.

universitas juris (yoo-ni-**vər**-sə-tas **joor**-is). [Latin] (1832) *Roman & civil law.* The whole of a person's rights and liabilities; the totality of a person's legal relations.

> "A *universitas juris* is a collection of rights and duties united by the single circumstance of their having belonged at one time to some one person." Henry S. Maine, *Ancient Law* 148 (17th ed. 1901).

universitas personarum (yoo-ni-**vər**-sə-tas pər-sə-**nay**-rəm). [Latin] (1886) *Roman & civil law.* A group of people that are legally considered an entity, such as a college or corporation. Pl. ***universitates personarum.***

universitas rerum (yoo-ni-**vər**-sə-tas **reer**-əm). [Latin] (1869) *Roman & civil law.* A whole collection of things; a variety of individual things that are together regarded by the law as a whole. See JUS RERUM.

> "In the time of Justinian the *universitas rerum*, or *universitas iuris* (both expressions are used) is a somewhat abstract conception: it means the sum or whole of a man's legal position so far as it concerns the *ius rerum*. The conception is important in law only on the occasions, of which death is by far the most important, on which the *universitas* passes from one to another. . . . The expression *universitas rerum* is also used in another sense, to denote any collection of objects considered as a whole." W.W. Buckland, *A Manual of Roman Private Law* 172 (2d ed. 1939).

universus (yoo-ni-**vər**-səs). [Latin] The whole; all together.

unjudicial, *adj.* (16c) Not becoming of or appropriate to a judge.

unjust, *adj.* (14c) Contrary to justice; not fair or reasonable.

unjust delivery. (2007) The receipt of property as the result of a mistake that prevents title to the property from passing to the recipient and makes the recipient liable for the property's return. • Three types of mistakes prevent title to property from passing: mistakes of the property's identity, mistakes of subject matter, and mistakes of quantity.

unjust enrichment. (1897) **1.** The retention of a benefit conferred by another, who offered no compensation, in circumstances where compensation is reasonably expected. **2.** A benefit obtained from another, not intended as a gift and not legally justifiable, for which the beneficiary must make restitution or recompense. • Unjust enrichment is a basis of civil liability involving a claim for recovery that sometimes also goes by the name *restitution.* Instances of unjust enrichment typically arise when property is transferred by an act of wrongdoing (as by conversion or breach of fiduciary duty), or without the effective consent of the transferor (as in a case of mistake), or when a benefit is conferred deliberately but without a contract, and the court concludes that the absence of a contract is excusable — as when the benefit was provided in an emergency, or when the parties once seemed to have a contract but it turns out to be invalid. The resulting claim of unjust enrichment seeks to recover the defendant's gains. **3.** The area of law dealing with unjustifiable benefits of this kind.

unjustifiable, *adj.* Legally or morally unacceptable; devoid of any good reason that would provide an excuse or defense.

unlaw, *n.* (bef. 12c) **1.** A violation of law; an illegality. **2.** Lawlessness.

> "But lawlessness is often a superficial phenomenon and whenever the duke was strong enough to keep the peace then law revived. We hear the same of England: times of 'unlaw' alternate with times of law." 1 Frederick Pollock & Frederic W. Maitland, *The History of English Law Before the Time of Edward I* 68–69 (2d ed. 1898).

3. *Scots law.* An illegal act. **4.** *Scots law.* A fine; a penalty.

unlawful, *adj.* (14c) **1.** Not authorized by law; illegal <in some cities, jaywalking is unlawful>. **2.** Criminally punishable <unlawful entry>. **3.** Involving moral turpitude <the preacher spoke to the congregation about the unlawful activities of gambling and drinking>. — **unlawfully,** *adv.*

unlawful act. (16c) Conduct that is not authorized by law; a violation of a civil or criminal law.

unlawful arrest. See ARREST (2).

unlawful assembly. See ASSEMBLY (1).

unlawful condition. See CONDITION (2).

unlawful detainer. See DETAINER.

unlawful-detainer proceeding. (1879) An action to return a wrongfully held tenancy (as one held by a tenant after the lease has expired) to its owner. See *unlawful detainer* under DETAINER.

unlawful eavesdropping. See EAVESDROPPING.

unlawful entry. See ENTRY (1).

unlawful force. See FORCE.

unlawful interest. See USURY.

unlawful interference with contractual relations. See TORTIOUS INTERFERENCE WITH CONTRACTUAL RELATIONS.

unlawful noncitizen. See *illegal alien* under ALIEN.

unlawful picketing. See PICKETING.

unlawful sexual conduct with a minor. See IMPAIRING THE MORALS OF A MINOR.

unlawful sexual intercourse. See RAPE (2).

"unless" lease. See LEASE.

unlimited, *adj.* (15c) Without restriction or limitation.

unliquidated, *adj.* (18c) Not previously specified or determined <unliquidated damages>.

unliquidated claim. See CLAIM (3).

unliquidated damages. See DAMAGES.

unliquidated debt. See DEBT.

unlisted security. See SECURITY (4).

unlisted stock. See *unlisted security* under SECURITY (4).

unlivery. (1805) *Maritime law.* The unloading of cargo at its intended destination.

unmarketable title. See TITLE (2).

unmarried, *adj.* (13c) Not married; single.

unmerchantable title. See *unmarketable title* under TITLE (2).

unnamed principal. See *unidentified principal* under PRINCIPAL (1).

unnatural offense. See SODOMY.

unnatural will. See WILL.

unnavigable, *adj.* See INNAVIGABLE.

unnecessary, *adj.* (16c) Not required under the circumstances; not necessary.

unnecessary hardship. See HARDSHIP (4).

uno actu (yoo-noh **ak**-t[y]oo). [Latin] In a single act; by one and the same act.

uno animo (yoo-noh **an**-i-moh). [Latin] With one mind.

unoccupied, *adj.* (14c) **1.** (Of a building) not occupied; vacant. **2.** (Of a person) not busy; esp., unemployed.

unofficial subclass. See ALPHA SUBCLASS.

unofficious payment. See PAYMENT (2).

unofficious will. See *inofficious testament* under TESTAMENT.

uno flatu (**yoo**-noh **flay**-t[y]oo). [Latin] In one breath.

uno ictu (**yoo**-noh **ik**-t[y]oo). [Latin] With one blow.

unpaid dividend. See DIVIDEND.

unpaid leave. See *leave without pay* under LEAVE.

unpatentable over art. (1943) *Patents.* (Of an invention) ineligible for patent protection because of obviousness or the lack of novelty.

unperfected security interest. See SECURITY INTEREST.

unperson. (1949) Someone who for ideological or political reasons is so marginalized as to be removed completely from consideration or even recognition. — Also termed *nonperson.*

unprecedented (ən-**pres**-ə-den-tid), *adj.* (17c) Never before known; not having the support, justification, or sanction of an earlier example. Cf. PRECEDENTED.

unpremeditation. (1807) The lack of premeditation; the absence of planning. See PREMEDITATION.

unprofessional, *adj.* (1806) Behaving in a way that is unacceptable within a particular profession.

unprofessional conduct. See CONDUCT.

unpublished opinion. See OPINION (1).

unqualified endorsement. See *unqualified indorsement* under INDORSEMENT.

unqualified indorsement. See INDORSEMENT.

unqualified opinion. See OPINION (2).

unqualified ownership. See OWNERSHIP.

unques (ən[g]-kweez), *adv.* [Law French] Ever; always.

unques prist (**ən[g]**-kweez **prist**). [Law French] Always ready. • This is another form of *tout temps prist.* See TOUT TEMPS PRIST ET ENCORE PRIST.

unrealized loss. See *paper loss* under LOSS.

unrealized profit. See *paper profit* under PROFIT (1).

unrealized receivable. See RECEIVABLE.

unreasonable, *adj.* (14c) **1.** Not guided by reason; irrational or capricious. **2.** Not supported by a valid exception to the warrant requirement <unreasonable search and seizure>.

unreasonable compensation. See COMPENSATION.

unreasonable decision. See DECISION (1).

unreasonable deviation. See DEVIATION.

unreasonable refusal to submit to operation. (1925) *Workers' compensation.* An injured employee's refusal to submit to a necessary surgical procedure. • This refusal is grounds for terminating the employee's workers'-compensation benefits.

unreasonable restraint of trade. See RESTRAINT OF TRADE.

unreasonable restraint on alienation. See RESTRAINT ON ALIENATION (1).

unreasonable search. See SEARCH (1).

unreasonably dangerous conduct. See CONDUCT.

unreasonably dangerous product. See PRODUCT.

unrebuttable, *adj.* (1843) Not rebuttable <an unrebuttable presumption>.

unrecorded, *adj.* (16c) Not recorded; esp., not filed in the public record <unrecorded deed>.

unregistered security. See *restricted security* under SECURITY (4).

unrelated-business income. See INCOME.

unrelated-business-income tax. See TAX.

unrelated-business taxable income. See *unrelated-business income* under INCOME.

unrelated offense. See OFFENSE (2).

unrepentant, *adj.* (14c) Not ashamed of one's behavior or beliefs despite others' disapproval.

unresponsive answer. See ANSWER (2).

unrestricted indorsement. See *unrestrictive indorsement* under INDORSEMENT.

unrestrictive endorsement. See *unrestrictive indorsement* under INDORSEMENT.

unrestrictive indorsement. See INDORSEMENT.

unrestrictive interpretation. See INTERPRETATION (1).

unreviewable, *adj.* (1877) Not subject to legal or judicial review <the claim is unreviewable on appeal>.

unsafe, *adj.* (1904) (Of a verdict or judgment) likely to be overturned on appeal because of a defect.

unsatisfied-judgment fund. See FUND (1).

unsealing order. (1965) A court order that allows sealed court records to be disclosed. Cf. SEAL, *vb.* (2).

unseated, *adj.* (17c) (Of land) vacant and neither developed nor cultivated.

unseaworthy, *adj.* (1820) (Of a vessel) unable to withstand the perils of an ordinary voyage. Cf. SEAWORTHY.

unsecured bail bond. See BOND (2).

unsecured bond. See DEBENTURE (3).

unsecured claim. See CLAIM (5).

unsecured creditor. See CREDITOR.

unsecured debt. See DEBT.

unsecured note. See NOTE (1).

unskilled work. See WORK (1).

unsolemn war. See WAR (1).

unsolemn will. See WILL.

unsolicited commercial e-mail. See SPAM. — Abbr. UCE.

unsound, *adj.* (14c) **1.** Not healthy; esp., not mentally well <unsound mind>. **2.** Not firmly made; impaired <unsound foundation>. **3.** Not valid or well founded <unsound argument>.

unsound judgment. See *bad judgment* under JUDGMENT (1).

unspeakable crime. See SODOMY.

unsworn, *adj.* (16c) Not sworn <an unsworn statement>.

unsworn declaration under penalty of perjury. See DECLARATION (8).

unsworn-witness rule. (1980) **1.** The principle that testimony given by a person who is not under oath cannot be used against a defendant unless it is corroborated by evidence tending to establish that a crime was committed and connecting the defendant with the commission. **2.** The principle that an attorney, esp. a prosecutor in a criminal case, may not subtly impart his or her firsthand knowledge of or beliefs about a matter as evidence to the jury without swearing an oath or being subject to cross-examination.

untenantable (ən-ten-ən-tə-bəl), *adj.* (17c) Not capable of being occupied or lived in; not fit for occupancy <the city closed the untenantable housing project>.

unthrift. (14c) *Archaic.* A prodigal; a spendthrift.

untimely, *adj.* (16c) **1.** Happening too late <an untimely filing>. **2.** Happening too soon <an untimely death>. **3.** Not suitable for a particular occasion or time; inopportune <an untimely interruption>.

untrue, *adj.* (bef. 12c) **1.** (Of something said) not correct; inaccurate. **2.** (Of a person) not faithful or true (to a standard or belief).

unum quid (yoo-nəm **kwid**). [Latin] (17c) *Hist.* One thing. • The phrase implied that several items (such as movables) were, for whatever purpose, considered as one (e.g., a set of glasses).

***unus nullus* rule** (yoo-nəs **nəl**-əs). [Latin "one is nobody" + rule] (1883) *Civil law.* The evidentiary principle that the testimony of only one witness is given no weight. Cf. HALF-PROOF (1).

unusual, *adj.* (16c) **1.** Extraordinary; abnormal. **2.** Different from what is reasonably expected. Cf. USUAL.

unusual charge. See *special charge* under CHARGE (7).

unusual plaintiff. See *abnormal plaintiff* under PLAINTIFF.

unvalued policy. See INSURANCE POLICY.

unworthy, *adj. Civil law.* (Of an heir) not entitled to inherit from a person because of a failure in a duty to that person. La. Civ. Code art. 941. — **unworthiness,** *n.*

unwritten, *adj.* (14c) **1.** Not reduced to writing; oral. **2.** (Of a rule or understanding) so well known that everyone obeys despite the lack of any formal adoption.

unwritten constitution. See CONSTITUTION (3).

unwritten evidence. See EVIDENCE.

unwritten law. See LAW.

unwritten will. See *nuncupative will* under WILL.

UPA. *abbr.* **1.** UNIFORM PARTNERSHIP ACT. **2.** UNIFORM PARENTAGE ACT.

UPAA. *abbr.* UNIFORM PREMARITAL AGREEMENT ACT.

up before. *Informal.* In the presence of (a particular court or judge) <for the bail hearing you'll come up before Judge Franklin>.

UPC. *abbr.* UNIFORM PROBATE CODE.

up-front performance bond. See PERFORMANCE BOND.

UPIA. *abbr.* **1.** UNIFORM PRUDENT INVESTOR ACT. **2.** UNIFORM PRINCIPLE AND INCOME ACT.

***Upjohn* warning.** (1997) An admonition by a corporation's lawyer to one or more corporate employees that the lawyer represents the corporation only, and not them individually. *Upjohn Co. v. U.S.*, 449 U.S. 383 (1981).

UPL. *abbr.* Unauthorized practice of law <the state bar's UPL committee>. See *unauthorized practice of law* under PRACTICE OF LAW.

uplifted hand. (18c) A form of oath-taking in which a person raises one hand, held flat and upright. — Also termed *hand uplifted; raised hand.*

UPM. *abbr.* Unlawful possession of marijuana.

Upper Bench. See *bancus superior* under BANCUS.

upper chamber. See UPPER HOUSE.

upper court. See *court above* under COURT.

upper estate. See *dominant estate* under ESTATE (4).

upper house. (*usu. cap.*) (16c) A group of representatives in a country's legislature, often smaller and sometimes more powerful than the country's lower house, as with the British House of Lords. • Before passage of the House of Lords Act in 1999, the House of Lords traditionally had more members than the House of Commons. — Also termed *upper chamber.* Cf. LOWER HOUSE.

upper management. See *top management* under MANAGEMENT.

UPREIT (əp-rɪt). See *umbrella-partnership real-estate investment trust* under REAL-ESTATE INVESTMENT TRUST.

upset bid. See BID (1).

upset price. See PRICE.

upside, *n.* (1961) *Securities.* **1.** An upward movement in stock prices. **2.** The potential of an upward movement in stock prices. Cf. DOWNSIDE.

upstanding, *adj.* (bef. 12c) **1.** On one's feet <Be upstanding!>. **2.** Marked by probity, circumspection, and virtue <an upstanding citizen>.

upstate. *Criminal law. Slang.* In New York, a state-prison sentence.

upstream, *adj. Oil & gas.* Of, relating to, or involving the exploration and production activities of oil companies and their contractors, including the drilling of wells onshore, the use of land rigs, and onshore operations in support of offshore activities. Cf. DOWNSTREAM.

upstream guaranty. See GUARANTY (1).

upstreaming. (1970) A parent corporation's use of a subsidiary's cash flow or assets for purposes unrelated to the subsidiary.

upstream merger. See MERGER (8).

UPUFA. *abbr.* UNIFORM PUTATIVE AND UNKNOWN FATHERS ACT.

upward adjustment. See ENHANCEMENT.

upward departure. See DEPARTURE (1).

upward sentence departure. See *upward departure* under DEPARTURE (1).

u.r. *abbr.* UTI ROGAS.

urban, *adj.* (17c) **1.** Of, relating to, or involving a city or town; not rural. Cf. RURAL (1). **2.** *Civil law.* Of, relating to, or involving buildings typically found in cities or towns. Cf. RURAL (3).

urban-fear syndrome. See URBAN-SURVIVAL SYNDROME.

Urban Mass Transit Administration. See FEDERAL TRANSIT ADMINISTRATION.

urban open space. See GREENSPACE (1).

urban planning. See LAND-USE PLANNING.

urban prefect, *n. Roman law.* See PRAEFECTUS URBI.

urban-psychosis defense. See URBAN-SURVIVAL SYNDROME.

urban renewal. (1954) The process of redeveloping urban areas by demolishing or repairing existing structures or by building new facilities on areas that have been cleared in accordance with an overall plan.

urban servitude. See SERVITUDE (3).

urban-survival syndrome. (1990) A self-defense theory holding that a defendant who uses unreasonable force may be acquitted if the defendant lives in a dangerous environment that heightens the defendant's fears of injury to life or limb so much that the force used seemed reasonable and necessary to the defendant. — Also termed *urban-survival defense; urban-fear syndrome; urban-psychosis defense; inner-city post-traumatic-stress defense.*

urbs (ərbz), *n.* [Latin] (1837) *Roman law.* **1.** A city or town. **2.** The city of Rome.

ure (yoor). [fr. Old French *oeuvre*] (15c) Custom; practice; exercise.

URESA (yə-**ree**-sə). *abbr.* UNIFORM RECIPROCAL ENFORCEMENT OF SUPPORT ACT.

urgent deficiency bill. See *deficiency bill* under BILL (3).

Urheberrecht (oo-re-**bair**-rekt), *n.* [German] AUTHOR'S RIGHT.

URL. *abbr.* UNIFORM RESOURCE LOCATOR.

Uruguay Round. The 1994 negotiations of the General Agreement on Tariffs and Trade. • The negotiations resulted in the TRIPs agreement that established the World Trade Organization and made member countries' patent laws more uniform. See TRIPS.

U.S. *abbr.* (1834) **1.** United States. See UNITED STATES OF AMERICA. **2.** UNITED STATES REPORTS.

USA. *abbr.* **1.** UNITED STATES OF AMERICA. **2.** UNITED STATES ARMY. **3.** UNITED STATES ATTORNEY.

USAA. *abbr.* United States Arbitration Act. See FEDERAL ARBITRATION ACT.

USAF. *abbr.* (1947) UNITED STATES AIR FORCE.

USAFA. *abbr.* UNITED STATES AIR FORCE ACADEMY.

usage. (13c) **1.** A well-known, customary, and uniform practice, usu. in a specific profession or business. See CUSTOM (1). Cf. CONVENTION (6).

> "A 'usage' is merely a customary or habitual practice; a 'convention' is a practice that is established by general tacit consent. 'Usage' denotes something that people are accustomed to do; 'convention' indicates that they are accustomed to do it because of a general agreement that it is the proper thing to do." Herbert W. Horwill, *The Usages of the American Constitution* 22 (1925).

> "Although rules of law are often founded on usage, usage is not in itself a legal rule but merely habit or practice in fact. A particular usage may be more or less widespread. It may prevail throughout an area, and the area may be small or large — a city, a state or a larger region. A usage may prevail among all people in the area, or only in a special trade or other group. Usages change over time, and persons in close association often develop temporary usages peculiar to themselves." Restatement (Second) of Contracts § 219 cmt. a (1979).

▸ **custom and usage.** See CUSTOM AND USAGE.

▸ **general usage.** (16c) A usage that prevails throughout a country or particular trade or profession; a usage that is not restricted to a local area.

▸ **immemorial usage.** (17c) A usage that has existed for a very long time; longstanding custom. See TIME IMMEMORIAL.

▸ **local usage.** (18c) A practice or method regularly observed in a particular place, sometimes considered by a court in interpreting a document. UCC § 1-303(c)(3). See CUSTOM AND USAGE.

▸ **trade usage.** (1864) **1.** A practice or method of dealing having such regular observance in a region, vocation, or trade that it justifies an expectation that it will be observed in a given transaction; a customary practice or set of practices relied on by persons conversant in, or connected with, a trade or business. • While a course of performance or a course of dealing can be established by the parties' testimony, a trade usage is usu. established by expert testimony. — Also termed *usage of trade; course of trade.* Cf. COURSE OF DEALING; COURSE OF PERFORMANCE.

> "The existence and scope of a usage of trade are to be determined as questions of fact. If a usage is embodied in a written trade code or similar writing the interpretation of the writing is to be determined by the court as a question of law. Unless otherwise agreed, a usage of trade in the vocation or trade in which the parties are engaged or a usage of trade of which they know or have reason to know gives meaning to or supplements or qualifies their agreement." Restatement (Second) of Contracts § 222 (1979).

2. See *conventional custom* under CUSTOM (1).

USAID. *abbr.* UNITED STATES AGENCY FOR INTERNATIONAL DEVELOPMENT.

usance (**yoo**-zənts). (15c) The time allowed for the payment of a foreign bill of exchange, sometimes set by custom but now usu. by law.

usance credit. See *time letter of credit* under LETTER OF CREDIT.

USA Patriot Act. A statute enacted in response to the terrorist attacks of September 11, 2001, giving law-enforcement agencies broader authority to collect information on suspected terrorists, to share that information among domestic and foreign intelligence agencies, to make the country's borders more secure, to detain suspects on new types of criminal charges using new criminal procedures, and to give the Treasury Department more authority to investigate and regulate financial institutions that participate in foreign money-laundering. • The title is an acronym of Uniting and Strengthening America by Providing Appropriate Tools Required to Intercept and Obstruct Terrorism. — Often shortened to *Patriot Act.*

USC. *abbr.* UNITED STATES CODE.

USCA. *abbr.* UNITED STATES CODE ANNOTATED.

USCACA. *abbr.* UNIFORM STATUS OF CHILDREN OF ASSISTED CONCEPTION ACT.

USCBP. *abbr.* UNITED STATES CUSTOMS AND BORDER PROTECTION.

USCG. *abbr.* UNITED STATES COAST GUARD.

USCGA. *abbr.* UNITED STATES COAST GUARD ACADEMY.

USCIS. *abbr.* U.S. CITIZENSHIP AND IMMIGRATION SERVICE.

USCIT. *abbr.* UNITED STATES COURT OF INTERNATIONAL TRADE.

U.S. citizen. See *national of the United States* under NATIONAL.

U.S. Citizenship and Immigration Service. A unit in the U.S. Department of Homeland Security responsible for enforcing the country's immigration laws. • Its functions were transferred from the former Immigration and Naturalization Service of the U.S. Department of Justice in 2003. — Abbr. USCIS.

USDA. *abbr.* **1.** DEPARTMENT OF AGRICULTURE. **2.** UNIFORM SIMULTANEOUS DEATH ACT.

U.S.D.C. *abbr.* UNITED STATES DISTRICT COURT.

use (yoos), *n.* (bef. 12c) **1.** The application or employment of something; esp., a long-continued possession and employment of a thing for the purpose for which it is adapted, as distinguished from a possession and employment that is merely temporary or occasional <the neighbors complained to the city about the owner's use of the building as a dance club>.

▸ **accessory use.** *Zoning.* A use that is dependent on or pertains to a main use.

▸ **adverse use.** (1820) A use without license or permission. Cf. ADVERSE POSSESSION.

▸ **beneficial use.** *Property.* The right to use property and all that makes that property desirable or habitable, such as light, air, and access, even if someone else owns the legal title to the property.

▸ **collateral use.** *Intellectual property.* The legal use of a trademark by someone other than the trademark owner in a market different from the owner's, whereby the other party must clearly identify itself, the use of the trademark, and the absence of affiliation with the trademark owner.

▸ **commercial use.** A use that is connected with or furthers an ongoing profit-making activity. Cf. *noncommercial use.*

▸ **conditional use.** *Zoning.* A use of property subject to special controls and conditions. • A conditional use is one that is suitable to a zoning district, but not necessarily to every location within that district. — Also termed *special exception.* See SPECIAL EXCEPTION (2).

▸ **conforming use.** (1922) *Zoning.* The use of a structure or of the land in conformity with the uses permitted under the zoning classifications of a particular area, such as the building of a single-family dwelling in a residential zone.

▸ **double use.** *Patents.* An application of a known principle or process to a new use without leading to a new result or product.

▸ **exclusive use. 1.** *Trademarks.* The right to use a specific mark without exception, and to prevent another from using a confusingly similar mark. **2.** *Property.* The right of an adverse user to a property, exercised independently of any similar rights held by others; one of the elements of a prescriptive easement. See USER.

▸ **experimental use.** *Patents.* **1.** The use or sale of an invention by the inventor for experimental purposes. **2.** A defense to liability for patent infringement when the infringement took place only to satisfy curiosity or to complete an experiment, rather than for profit.

▸ **highest and best use.** *Real estate.* In the valuation of property, the use that will generate the most profit. • This standard is used esp. to determine the fair market value of property subject to eminent domain. — Often shortened to *best use.* — Also termed *most suitable use.*

▸ **incidental use.** *Zoning.* Land use that is dependent on or affiliated with the land's primary use.

▸ **most suitable use.** See *highest and best use.*

▸ **noncommercial use.** (1918) A use for private pleasure or business purposes that does not involve the generation of income or bestowing a reward or other compensation. Cf. *commercial use.*

▸ **nonconforming use.** (1922) *Zoning.* Land use that is impermissible under current zoning restrictions but that is allowed because the use existed lawfully before the restrictions took effect.

▸ **pious use.** The designation and actual use of property for recognized religious or charitable purposes. Cf. *superstitious use.*

▸ **popular use.** A person's imperfect right to enjoy public land. • A popular use is not legally enforceable. It is dependent on the government's will to allow access to the land.

▸ **public use.** (18c) **1.** *Property.* A legitimate public purpose for the condemnation of private property. • The Fifth Amendment provides that private property may be taken only for "public use." If property is taken for a legitimate public purpose — one that is within the scope of the government's police power — the public-use requirement is satisfied, regardless of who physically uses the property once it is taken. **2.** *Patents.* Any use of or offer to use a completed or operative invention in a nonsecret, natural, and intended manner. • A patent is invalid if the invention was in public use more than one year before the patent's application date.

> "The term '*public* use' is misleading, for any use from which the public is not excluded, even though none comes, is held to be public. Similarly, an actual public use of a machine, even though the invention feature be effectively concealed from inspection, is held to be public. It makes no difference whether the patent or other publication is that of the inventor or someone else." Roger Sherman Hoar, *Patent Tactics and Law* 48 (3d ed. 1950) (citing *Gillman v. Stern*, 114 F.2d 28, 31 (2d Cir. 1940)).

▸ **reasonable use.** Use of one's property for an appropriate purpose that does not unreasonably interfere with another's use of property. See REASONABLE-USE THEORY.

▸ **regular use.** *Insurance.* A use that is usual, normal, or customary, as opposed to an occasional, special, or incidental use. • This term often appears in automobile-insurance policies in the definition of a *nonowned automobile* — that is, an automobile not owned by or furnished for the regular use of the insured. Nonowned automobiles are excluded from coverage under most liability policies.

▸ **superstitious use.** A designation or use of property for religious purposes not legally recognized or tolerated (such as gifts either favoring an unrecognized religion or supporting the saying of prayers for the dead). Cf. *pious use.*

▸ **tolerated use.** *Copyright.* Unlicensed use of copyrighted material when the copyright owner knows of the infringing use but does not seek to stop it or to be compensated for it. • Examples tolerated use include Internet user-generated content such as fan sites and video sites, which may feature copyrighted photos and other materials.

2. A habitual or common practice <drug use>. **3.** A purpose or end served <the tool had several uses>. **4.** A benefit or profit; esp., the right to take profits from land owned and possessed by another; the equitable ownership of land to which another person holds the legal title <cestui que use>. See CESTUI QUE USE. — **use** (yooz), *vb.*

> "In tracing its embryonic history we must first notice the now established truth that the English word *use* when it is employed with a technical meaning in legal documents is derived, not from the Latin word *usus*, but from the Latin word *opus*, which in Old French becomes *os* or *oes*. True that the two words are in course of time confused, . . . nevertheless the earliest history of 'the use' is the early history of the phrase *ad opus*. Now this both in France and in England we may find in very ancient days. A man will sometimes receive money to the use (*ad opus*) of another person; in particular money is constantly being received for the king's use. . . . Further, long before the Norman Conquest we may find a man saying that he conveys land to a bishop to the use of a church, or conveys land to a church to the use of a dead saint. . . . In the thirteenth century we commonly find that where there is what to our eyes is an informal agency, this term *ad opus* is used to describe it. . . . [T]here is no current word that is equivalent to our *agent*; John does not receive money or chattels 'as agent for' Roger; he receives it to the use of Roger (*ad opus Rogeri*)." F.W. Maitland, *The Origin of Uses*, 8 Harv. L. Rev. 127, 127–28 (1894).

▸ **active use.** (1884) A use that requires a trustee to perform certain duties in addition to holding the property, such as caring for the property or collecting the income it produces and distributing the income to the beneficiary. • The Statute of Uses did not apply to active uses. Cf. *passive use.*

▸ **contingent use.** (17c) A use that would be a contingent remainder if it had not been limited by way of use. • An example is a transfer "to A, to the use of B for life, with the remainder to the use of C's heirs." — Also termed *future use.*

▸ **dry use.** See *passive use.*

▸ **entire use.** A use of property solely for the benefit of a married woman. • When used in the habendum of a trust deed for the benefit of a married woman, this phrase operates to keep her husband from taking anything under the deed. — Also termed *entire benefit; sole use; sole and separate use.*

▸ **executed use.** *Hist.* A use resulting from combining the equitable title and legal title of an estate, done to comply with the Statute of Uses' mandate that the holder of an estate be vested with legal title to ensure the holder's liability for feudal dues. See STATUTE OF USES.

▸ **executory use.** See *springing use.*

▸ **future use.** See *contingent use.*

▸ **official use.** *Hist.* A use imposing a duty on a person holding legal title to an estate on behalf of another, such as a requirement that a feoffee to uses sell the estate and apportion the proceeds among several beneficiaries. • The Statute of Uses eliminated this type of use.

▸ **passive use.** (1857) A use that places no duties on the trustee other than to simply hold the property for the beneficiary. • The Statute of Uses outlawed passive uses, which were usu. employed to avoid laws that hampered transfers to heirs other than the eldest son and to stymie creditors. — Also termed *dry use.* Cf. *active use.*

▸ **permissive use.** *Hist.* A passive use resorted to before passage of the Statute of Uses in 1535 to avoid an oppressive feudal law (such as mortmain) by naming one person as the legal owner of property while allowing another to possess the property and enjoy the benefits arising from it.

▸ **present use.** *Hist.* A use that has an immediate existence and is subject to the Statute of Uses.

▸ **resulting use.** (18c) A use created by implication and remaining with the grantor when the conveyance lacks consideration.

▸ **secondary use.** See *shifting use.*

▸ **shifting use.** (18c) A use arising from the occurrence of a certain event that terminates the preceding use. • In the following example, C has a shifting use that arises when D makes the specified payment: "to A for the use of B, but then to C when D pays $1,000 to E." This is a type of conditional limitation. — Also termed *secondary use.* See *conditional limitation* under LIMITATION.

▸ **sole and separate use.** See *entire use.*

▸ **springing use.** (17c) A use arising on the occurrence of a future event. • In the following example, B has a springing use that vests when B marries: "to A for the use of B when B marries." — Also termed *executory use.*

use (yooz), *vb.* **1.** To employ for the accomplishment of a purpose; to avail oneself of <they use formbooks>. **2.** To put into practice or employ habitually or as a usual way of doing something; to follow as a regular custom <to use diligence in research>. **3.** To do something customarily or habitually; to be wont or accustomed <I used to avoid public speaking, but no longer>. **4.** *Archaic.* To conduct oneself toward; to treat <he uses me well>. **5.** To make familiar by habit or practice; to habituate or inure <she is used to the pressure>. **6.** To take (an amount of something) from a supply <the firm uses 50 reams of paper each day>. **7.** To take advantage of (someone) for selfish purposes; to make (a person) an involuntary means to one's own ends <he uses his interns for personal errands>. **8.** To take usu. improper advantage of (a situation, position, etc.) <she uses her board membership to threaten staffers>. **9.** To regularly take; to partake of (drugs, tobacco, etc.) <he uses heroin>.

use-based license. See LICENSE.

use/derivative-use immunity. See *use immunity* under IMMUNITY (3).

usee. See USE PLAINTIFF.

useful, *adj. Patents.* (Of an invention) having a practical application; esp., capable of industrial application.

> "[M]ere curiosities of invention, which do not have any intelligent purpose, are not useful in a patentable sense." Roger Sherman Hoar, *Patent Tactics and Law* 37 (3d ed. 1950).

> "When applied to a machine, 'useful' means that the machine will accomplish its purpose practically when applied in industry. The word is given a practical and not a speculative meaning." 60 Am. Jur. 2d *Patents* § 131 (1987).

useful-article doctrine. See APPLIED-ART DOCTRINE.

useful life. (1923) The estimated length of time that depreciable property will generate income. • Useful life is used to calculate depreciation and amortization deductions. — Also termed *depreciable life*. See DEPRECIATION METHOD.

usefulness, *n.* **1.** The state of being helpful or worthwhile. **2.** The degree to which something is helpful or worthwhile.

use immunity. See IMMUNITY (3).

use in commerce. *Trademarks.* Actual use of a trademark in the advertising, marketing, promotion, sale, or distribution of goods or services. • Use of a trademark in commerce is a prerequisite to trademark registration. Regular use demonstrates that the trademark has become associated with currently available goods or services, as contrasted with a token use intended to reserve some right to use the trademark in the future. For goods, a trademark is used in commerce if it is displayed on or with goods offered for sale, or placed on documents related to the goods. For services, a mark is used in commerce if it appears in advertising or on documents related to the services. In addition, the goods must be used or the services rendered in more than one state, because use of a trademark in interstate commerce is a prerequisite to federal trademark registration.

use injunction. See INJUNCTION.

useless-gesture exception. (1970) *Criminal procedure.* An exception to the knock-and-announce rule whereby police are excused from having to announce their purpose before entering the premises to execute a warrant when it is evident from the circumstances that people inside the premises are of aware of the police officers' authority and purpose. See KNOCK-AND-ANNOUNCE RULE.

use plaintiff. *Common-law pleading.* A plaintiff for whom an action is brought in another's name. • For example, when the use plaintiff is an assignee ("A") of a chose in action and sues in the assignor's name ("B"), the assignor's name appears first on the petition's title: "B for the Use of A against C." — Also termed *usee.*

user (**yooz**-ər). (15c) **1.** The exercise or employment of a right or property <the neighbor argued that an easement arose by his continuous user over the last 15 years>. Cf. NONUSER (1).

▸ ***user de action*** (**yoo**-zər **dak**-shən). [Law French] The pursuing or bringing of an action.

2. Someone who uses a thing <the stapler's last user did not put it away>.

▸ **end user.** (1963) The ultimate consumer for whom a product is designed.

user agreement. See POINT-AND-CLICK AGREEMENT.

user confusion. See CONSUMER CONFUSION.

user fee. (1967) A charge assessed for the use of a particular item or facility.

Uses, Statute of. See STATUTE OF USES.

use tax. See TAX.

use value. See VALUE (2).

use variance. See VARIANCE (2).

use zoning. See *Euclidean zoning* under ZONING.

USFSPA. *abbr.* UNIFORMED SERVICES FORMER SPOUSE PROTECTION ACT.

USFWS. *abbr.* UNITED STATES FISH AND WILDLIFE SERVICE.

USGS. *abbr.* UNITED STATES GEOLOGICAL SURVEY.

usher, *n.* (18c) *English law.* A court officer responsible for maintaining silence and order in some English courts, swearing in jurors and witnesses, and otherwise aiding the judge. See BAILIFF (1).

USIP. *abbr.* UNITED STATES INSTITUTE OF PEACE.

USITC. *abbr.* UNITED STATES INTERNATIONAL TRADE COMMISSION.

USMA. *abbr.* UNITED STATES MILITARY ACADEMY.

U.S. Magistrate. See UNITED STATES MAGISTRATE JUDGE.

USMC. *abbr.* UNITED STATES MARINE CORPS.

USMMA. *abbr.* UNITED STATES MERCHANT MARINE ACADEMY.

USMS. *abbr.* UNITED STATES MARSHALS SERVICE.

USN. *abbr.* (1863) UNITED STATES NAVY.

USNA. *abbr.* UNITED STATES NAVAL ACADEMY.

U.S. national. See *national of the United States* under NATIONAL.

U.S. owned foreign corporation. See CORPORATION.

USPAP appraisal. See APPRAISAL.

USPS. *abbr.* UNITED STATES POSTAL SERVICE.

USPTO. *abbr.* UNITED STATES PATENT AND TRADEMARK OFFICE.

usque ad (**əs**-kwee ad). [Law Latin] As far as; up to; until.

usque ad coelum (**əs**-kwee ad **kɪ**-ləm). [Latin] Up to the sky <the owner of land also owns the space above the surface *usque ad coelum*>. Cf. AB ORCO USQUE AD COELUM.

usque ad sententiam (**əs**-kwee ad sen-**ten**-shee-əm). [Law Latin] *Hist.* Until the pronouncing of judgment. • Executors could be granted certain powers exercisable only *usque ad sententiam.*

USSG. *abbr.* UNITED STATES SENTENCING GUIDELINES.

USTDA. *abbr.* UNITED STATES TRADE AND DEVELOPMENT AGENCY.

USTR. *abbr.* UNITED STATE TRADE REPRESENTATIVE.

usual, *adj.* (14c) **1.** Ordinary; customary. **2.** Expected based on previous experience, or on a pattern or course of conduct to date.

usuary (**yoo**-zhoo-er-ee), *n.* (1871) *Civil law.* Someone who has the use (*usus*) of a thing to satisfy personal and family needs; a beneficiary. — Also termed (in Roman law) *usuarius.*

usucapio (yoo-zə-**kay**-pee-oh), *n. Roman & civil law.* The acquisition of ownership by long, continuous possession begun in good faith; esp., the acquisition of ownership by prescription. • In classical law, the minimum periods required were one year for movables and two for land. Under Justinian law , the minimum periods were three years for movables and ten years for land. See PRESCRIPTION (5). — Also termed *usus* (**yoo**-zoos); *usucaption* (yoo-zə-**kap**-shən); *usucapion* (yoo-zə-**kay**-pee-on *or* -ən). — **usucapt,** *vb.*; **usucaption,** *n.*

> "There is no principle in all law which the moderns, in spite of its beneficial character, have been so loath to adopt and to carry to its legitimate consequences as that which was known to the Romans as Usucapion, and which has descended to modern jurisprudence under the name

of Prescription." Henry S. Maine, *Ancient Law* 236 (17th ed. 1901).

usufruct (**yoo**-zə-frəkt), *n.* [fr. Latin *usufructus*] (17c) *Roman & civil law.* A right for a certain period to use and enjoy the fruits of another's property without damaging or diminishing it, but allowing for any natural deterioration in the property over time. • In Roman law, the usufruct was considered a personal servitude, resulting in a real right. In modern civil law, the owner of the usufruct is similar to a life tenant, and the owner of the property burdened is known as the *naked owner.* La. Civ. Code art. 535. — Also termed *perfect usufruct*; *usufructus*; *ususfructus*; (in Scots law) *liferent.* Cf. HABITATION (3).

"*Usufructus* is . . . the right of using and enjoying property belonging to another provided the substance of the property remained unimpaired. More exactly, a usufruct was the right granted to a man personally to use and enjoy, usually for his life . . . , the property of another which, when the usufruct ended, was to revert intact to the *dominus* or his heir. It might be for a term of years, but even here it was ended by death, and in the case of a corporation (which never dies) Justinian fixed the period at 100 years. A usufruct might be in land or buildings, a slave or beast of burden, and in fact in anything except things which were destroyed by use . . . , the reason, of course, being that it was impossible to restore such things at the end of the usufruct intact . . . ." R.W. Leage, *Roman Private Law* 181–82 (C.H. Ziegler ed., 2d ed. 1930).

▸ **legal usufruct.** (1886) A usufruct established by operation of law, such as the right of a surviving spouse to property owned by the deceased spouse. La. Civ. Code art. 890.

▸ **quasi-usufruct.** (1812) **1.** A right to use property that cannot be used without being expended or consumed, such as money or food. • Unlike an ordinary usufruct, a quasi-usufruct actually involves alteration and diminution of the property used. — Also termed *imperfect usufruct.* **2.** *Louisiana law.* A usufruct over consumable things, such as money or harvested crops, the value of which must be delivered to the naked owner at the end of the usufruct's term. La. Civ. Code art. 538. • The usufructuary has the right to consume or alienate the consumables and, at the end of the usufruct, to deliver to the naked owner either the value that the things had when the usufruct began or things of the same quantity and quality.

"The Roman jurists, therefore, would not acknowledge a usufruct of money; though, in their desire to carry out the wishes of testators, they came at length to recognize a quasi-usufruct. For testators, being seldom learned in the law, would often set forth as legacies in their wills the usufruct of a designated sum . . . . In such a case the person named as legatee was allowed to receive the amount . . . on giving security that when he died the same amount should be paid out of his own estate to the *heres*, the heir of the testator. The relation here, though bearing some resemblance to the usufruct, was really quite different; the person who received the money became absolute owner of it; the heir had no ownership, nothing but the assurance of receiving an equal amount at some future time." James Hadley, *Introduction to Roman Law* 193 (1881).

usufructuarius. See USUFRUCTUARY, *n.*

usufructuary (yoo-zə-**frək**-choo-er-ee), *adj.* (18c) *Roman & civil law.* Of, relating to, or involving a usufruct; of the nature of a usufruct.

usufructuary, *n.* (17c) *Roman & civil law.* One having the right to a usufruct; specif., a person who has the right to the benefits of another's property; a life-renter. — Also termed *usufructuarius.*

usufructus. See USUFRUCT.

usura (yoo-**s[y]oor**-ə *or* yoo-**z[y]oor**-ə). [Latin] *Civil law.* **1.** The amount paid for the use of money; interest. **2.** USURY. Pl. ***usurae*** (yoo-**s[y]oor**-ee).

usurae centesimae (yoo-**s[y]oor**-ee [*or* yoo-**z[y]oor**-ee] sen-**tes**-ə-mee). [Latin] (1818) Interest at the rate of 12% per year (1% per month), usu. the highest rate allowed by law. • The Romans calculated interest rates by dividing the principal sum into one hundred parts, with one part being payable monthly as interest.

usura manifesta (yoo-**s[y]oor**-ə [*or* yoo-**z[y]oor**-ə] man-ə-**fes**-tə). [Latin] (1809) Manifest or open usury. Cf. USURA VELATA.

usura maritima (yoo-**s[y]oor**-ə [*or* yoo-**z[y]oor**-ə] mə-**rit**-ə-mə). [Latin] (17c) Interest taken on a bottomry or respondentia bond, proportioned to the risk and so not restricted by any usury laws. See FOENUS NAUTICUM.

usurarius (yoo-s[y]ə-**rair**-ee-əs *or* yoo-z[y]ə-). [Law Latin] *Hist.* A usurer.

usura velata (yoo-s[y]**oor**-ə [*or* yoo-**z[y]oor**-ə] və-**lay**-tə). [Latin] (17c) Veiled or concealed usury. • A creditor was guilty of *usura velata* when the creditor added unlawfully high interest to the principal sum as if the interest amount were part of the original loan. Cf. UBI ABERAT ANIMUS FOENERANDII; USURA MANIFESTA.

usurious (yoo-**z[y]oor**-ee-əs *or* yoo-**zhuu**-ree-əs), *adj.* (17c) **1.** Practicing usury; charging unfairly high rates of interest <a usurious lender>. **2.** Characterized by usury; providing for an illegally high rate of interest <a usurious contract>.

usurpatio (yoo-sər-**pay**-shee-oh), *n.* [Latin] *Roman law.* The interruption of usucaption by reason of loss of physical possession or a lawsuit by the true legal owner. Pl. ***usurpationes*** (yoo-sər-pay-shee-**oh**-neez).

usurpation (yoo-sər-**pay**-shən *or* yoo-zər-**pay**-shən), *n.* (14c) The unlawful seizure and assumption of another's position, office, or authority. — **usurp** (yoo-**sərp** *or* yoo-**zərp**), *vb.*

▸ **usurpation of advowson** (ad-**vow**-zən). (1803) *Hist.* An injury consisting in the absolute ouster or dispossession of the patron from the advowson. • This happens when a stranger, without the right to do so, presents a clerk who is installed in office. See ADVOWSON.

usurper, *n.* (15c) One who takes another's power or position without any right to do so.

usury (**yoo**-zhə-ree), *n.* (14c) **1.** Historically, the lending of money with interest. **2.** Today, the charging of an illegal rate of interest as a condition to lending money. **3.** An illegally high rate of interest. — Also termed *illegal interest*; *unlawful interest.* — **usurer** (**yoo**-zhər-ər), *n.*

"Originally the word *usury* had the same meaning as that now conveyed by the word *interest*; but the meaning of *usury* has been so altered by changing customs and laws that now it merely signifies the *taking, under contract, of more than lawful interest for the loan or forbearance of money.* Accordingly, Judge Bouvier says: 'Usury is the illegal profit which is required by the lender of a sum of money, from the borrower, for its use.' [John Bouvier, 1 *Institutes of American Law* 299 (1851).] In the New York case of *Wilkie v. Roosevelt*, Thompson, J., more elaborately defines usury as follows: 'Usury consists in extorting or taking a rate of interest for money, beyond what is allowed by law. It is not necessary that money should be actually advanced, in order to constitute the offense of usury, but any pretence or contrivance whatever, to gain more than legal interest, when it is the intent of the parties to contract for a loan, will make that contract usurious.' [*Wilkie v. Roosevelt*, 3 Johns. Cas. 206, 206–07 (N.Y. Sup. 1802).] This sentence briefly states the present accepted meaning of the term." James Avery Webb, *A Treatise on the Law of Usury* 1–2 (1899).

usury law. (1822) A law prohibiting moneylenders from charging illegally high interest rates.

usus (**yoo**-səs *or* **yoo**-zəs), *n.* [Latin "use"] *Roman law.* **1.** The right to use another's property, without the right to receive or retain the benefits or fruits (*fructus*) produced by the property. • *Usus* was a personal servitude; it gave the holder a right in rem. Cf. USUFRUCT.

"It is essentially a fraction of a usufruct, *usus* without the *fructus*. In strictness, there was no right to any fruits but this was somewhat relaxed in practice. The usuary of a house might consume the fruits of the gardens in his household, but he might not sell them, as a usufructuary might." W.W. Buckland, *A Manual of Roman Private Law* 165 (2d ed. 1939).

2. The factual possession required for *usucapio*. **3.** Lapse of time by which a wife was brought into the husband's family and under his marital power. See MANUS (1). Cf. COEMPTIO; CONFARREATIO.

"*Usus* is the acquisition of [power over] a wife by *possession* and bears the same relation to *coemptio* as usucapion to a mancipation. A Roman citizen who bought some object of property and got possession of it, but not ownership, because he neglected to go through the mancipation prescribed by *jus civile*, might nevertheless become owner by usucapion, i.e. lapse of time; thus if the object was a movable, continuous possession for one year made him *dominus*. In like manner, if a man lived with a woman whom he treated as his wife, but whom he had not married by *coemptio* (or *confarreatio*), and the cohabitation lasted without interruption for a year, then at the end of that period the man acquired [power over] the woman as his wife, she passed to him *in manum* . . . ." R.W. Leage, *Roman Private Law* 100 (C.H. Ziegler ed., 2d ed. 1930).

usus bellici (**yoo**-səs [*or* -zəs] **bel**-ə-sɪ). [Latin] (1808) *Int'l law.* Warlike objects or uses. • This phrase refers to items that, while not inherently of a military nature, are considered contraband because they are used by a belligerent to support its war effort.

Usus Feudorum (**yoo**-səs [*or* -zəs] fyoo-**dor**-əm). See FEUDORUM LIBRI.

ususfructus. See USUFRUCT.

ut currere solebat (ət **kər**-ər-ee sə-**lee**-bat). [Latin] As it was wont to run. • This referred to the course of a stream.

ut de feodo (ət dee **fee**-ə-doh *or* **fyoo**-doh). [Law Latin] As of fee.

uterine (**yoo**-tər-in), *adj.* (15c) Born of the same mother but having different biological fathers.

uterine brother. See BROTHER.

uterine sister. See SISTER.

uterque (yoo-**tər**-kwee). [Latin] Each of two; both (considered separately).

uterque nostrum (yoo-**trəm**-kwee **nos**-trəm). See UTRUMQUE NOSTRUM.

uterus, *n.* (17c) The reproductive organ of female humans and animals in which conception and gestation occurs. — Also termed *womb.*

utfangthief (**ət**-fang-theef). See OUTFANGTHIEF.

ut hospites (ət **hos**-pə-teez). [Latin] As guests.

uti (**yoo**-tɪ), *vb.* [Latin] *Civil law.* To use.

uti frui (**yoo**-tɪ **froo**-ɪ). [Latin] *Civil law.* To have the full use and enjoyment of a thing, without damage to its substance.

utilis (**yoo**-tə-lis), *adj.* [Latin] *Civil law.* Useful; beneficial; equitable. • This word appeared in phrases such as *actio utilis* (**ak**-shee-oh **yoo**-tə-lis), meaning "equitable action."

utilitarian-deterrence theory. (1983) The legal theory that a person should be punished only if the punishment benefits society — that is, only if the punishment would help to deter future harmful conduct. — Also termed *deterrence theory.* See *hedonistic utilitarianism* under UTILITARIANISM. Cf. CONSEQUENTIALISM (3); RETRIBUTIVISM; MIXED THEORY OF PUNISHMENT.

utilitarianism. (1827) The philosophical and economic doctrine that the best social policy is that which does the most good for the greatest number of people; esp., an ethical theory that judges the rightness or wrongness of actions according to the pleasure they create or the pain they inflict and recommends whatever action creates the greatest good for the greatest number of people. • This is a type of consequentialism. For example, utilitarianism analyzes intellectual-property rights from the point of view of society rather than the individual inventor, author, or artist, and justifies the rights as an incentive for social and technological progress. See CONSEQUENTIALISM. Cf. LOCKEAN LABOR THEORY; PERSONALITY THEORY. — **utilitarian,** *adj.* & *n.*

▸ **hedonistic utilitarianism.** (1943) The theory that the validity of a law should be measured by determining the extent to which it promotes the greatest happiness to the greatest number of citizens. • This theory is found most prominently in the work of Jeremy Bentham, whose "Benthamite utilitarianism" greatly influenced legal reform in nineteenth-century Great Britain. Hedonistic utilitarianism generally maintains that pleasure is intrinsically good and pain intrinsically bad. Therefore, inflicting pain on an individual, as by punishing a criminal, is justified only if it results in a net increase of pleasure for society by deterring future harmful behavior. — Also termed *Benthamism.* See UTILITARIAN-DETERRENCE THEORY; BENTHAMITE. Cf. MIXED THEORY OF PUNISHMENT; RETRIBUTIVISM.

utiliter et equivalenter (yoo-**til**-ə-tər et i-kwiv-ə-**len**-tər). [Law Latin] *Hist.* Duly and with equal effect.

utiliter impensum (yoo-**til**-ə-tər im-**pen**-səm). [Latin] *Hist.* Usefully expended.

utility. (14c) **1.** The quality of serving some function that benefits society; meritoriousness. **2.** The degree to which something is useful.

▸ **functional utility.** (1901) The ability of an item or component to perform its intended task.

3. *Patents.* Capacity to perform a function or attain a result for which the patent applicant or holder claims protection as intellectual property. • In patent law, utility is one of the three basic requirements of patentability, the others being nonobviousness and novelty. In the calculation of damages for patent infringement, utility is the benefit or advantage of the patented product or process over the products or processes, if any, that previously had been used to produce similar results.

"[T]he utility requirement does not mandate that the invention be superior to existing products and processes in order to qualify for a patent. The utility standard reflects the judgment that society is better served by access to a library of issued patents describing as many inventions as possible, even if many of them do not achieve better results than public domain technology. This liberal view of utility allows subsequent inventors access to a greater variety of previous technologies, some of which may yet be judged the superior solution when employed within a different context." Roger E. Schechter & John R. Thomas, *Intellectual Property* § 15.1, at 316 (2003).

4. A business enterprise that performs an essential public service and that is subject to governmental regulation.

▸ **public utility.** (1895) **1.** A company that provides necessary services to the public, such as telephone lines and service, electricity, and water. • Most utilities operate as monopolies but are subject to governmental regulation. **2.** A person, corporation, or other association that carries on an enterprise for the accommodation of the public, the members of which are entitled as a matter of right to use the enterprise's facilities.

utility fund. See MUTUAL FUND.

utility model. (1909) *Patents.* A system of patent registration giving patent-like rights in some countries, usu. for a shorter term than a patent but with little or no search required. • Utility-model registration is not available in the United States or the United Kingdom, but it is offered in Japan and many European countries, including Germany and France. They are available for machines only, and not for chemicals. — Also termed *petty patent*; *second-tier patent*; *small invention.*

utility patent. See PATENT (3).

uti mos est in feudifirmis (**yoo**-tɪ **mahs** est in fyoo-di-**fər**-mis). [Law Latin] *Scots law.* As is the custom in feu-holdings.

ut infra (ət **in**-frə *also* uut). [Latin] *Hist.* As below.

ut inter bonos bene agier oportet. [Latin] As humane men should act when they act humanely.

"The law is not right reason, nor the means of a good life, nor the framework of society, nor the foundation of the world, nor the harmony of the spheres. It is a technique of administering a complicated social mechanism, so complicated that it reaches at some point almost any sphere of human conduct, but often only barely reaches it. The technique can dispense with neither logic nor experience. But law will not be good law by becoming a consummately perfect technique in regard either to logic or experience. That can be achieved only when just men perform the technical task of the law with the ancient formula before them — *ut inter bonos bene agier oportet* — 'as humane men should act when they act humanely.'" Max Radin, *Law as Logic and Experience* 163–64 (1940).

uti possidetis (**yoo**-tɪ pah-si-**dee**-tis). [Latin] (17c) **1.** *Roman law.* An interdict ordering each party to a lawsuit to maintain the possession of real property as it stands pending an official decision on who owns the property. Cf. UTRUBI. **2.** *Int'l law.* The doctrine that the administrative boundaries will become international boundaries when a political subdivision or colony achieves independence.

"The historic evolution of *uti possidetis* demonstrates that it is a norm of international law governing territorial delimitations. *Uti possidetis* is not a peremptory norm of international law, since States can derogate from it by common consent, as was often the case in Latin America, but also in Africa. In other words, *uti possidetis* is perceived as the basis of delimitation between newly constituted States until and unless those States decide to adopt different boundaries. In recent times international jurisprudence has debated the relevance of *uti possidetis* in maritime delimitations . . . ." Giuseppe Nesi, "*Uti possidetis* Doctrine," in 10 *The Max Planck Encyclopedia of Public International Law* 626, 627 (Rüdiger Wolfrum ed., 2012).

3. The doctrine that territory, as well as real and personal property, captured during wartime and still held by the captor when the war ends becomes the captor's legal property unless otherwise provided by treaty.

"The restoration of peace put an end . . . to all force, and then the general principle applied, that things acquired in war remain, as to title and possession, precisely as they stood when the peace took place. The uti possetidis is the basis of every treaty of peace, unless it be otherwise agreed. Peace gives a final and perfect title to captures without condemnation; and as it forbids all force, it destroys all hopes of recovery as much as if the vessel was carried infra presidia, and condemned." James Kent, 1 *Commentaries on American Law* *173 (George Comstock ed., 11th ed. 1866).

uti rogas (**yoo**-tɪ **roh**-gas *or* -gəs). [Latin] *Roman law.* As you ask. • This phrase was inscribed on a ballot to indicate a vote in favor of a bill or candidate. — Abbr. *u.r.*

utitur jure auctoris (**yoo**-ti-tər **joor**-ee awk-**tor**-is). [Latin] *Hist.* He exercises the right of his predecessor in title.

utitur jure communi (**yoo**-ti-tər **joor**-ee kə-**myoo**-nɪ). [Latin] *Hist.* He relies on the common law.

utitur jure privato (**yoo**-ti-tər **joor**-ee prɪ-**vay**-toh). [Latin] *Hist.* He relies on his own private right.

utitur jure suo (**yoo**-ti-tər **joor**-ee s[y]**oo**-oh). [Latin] *Hist.* He exercises his own right.

"The exercise of rights of property on the part of a proprietor . . . cannot be interfered with, even where they are injurious in their effects to the adjoining property. In such case the proprietor is only doing that which he has a right to do, *utitur jure suo.*" John Trayner, *Trayner's Latin Maxims* 618–19 (4th ed. 1894).

utlagare (ət-lag-ə-ree *or* ət-lə-**gair**-ee), *vb.* [Law Latin] *Hist.* To put (an offender) outside the protection of the law. Cf. INLAGARE; OUTLAWRY (2).

utlagation (ət-lə-**gay**-shən), *n.* [Law Latin] (17c) *Hist.* The act of placing an offender outside the protection of the law; outlawry. — Also termed *utlagatio.* Cf. INLAGATION; OUTLAWRY (2).

utlagatus (ət-lə-**gay**-təs), *n.* [Latin] *Hist.* An outlawed person; an outlaw.

utlage (**ət**-lahzh *or* -lij), *n.* [Law French] An outlaw.

utlagh (**ət**-law). [Old English] (17c) *Hist.* A person outside the protection of the law; an outlaw. Cf. INLAGH.

utland (**ət**-lənd) [Old English] (17c) *Hist.* The outer portion of a lord's demesne, used to support the lord's tenants. — Also termed *delantal* (di-**lan**-təl). Cf. INLAND (2).

utlesse. *Hist.* A felon's escape from prison.

UTMA. *abbr.* UNIFORM TRANSFERS TO MINORS ACT.

utmost care. See *great care* under CARE (2).

utmost good faith. See GOOD FAITH.

ut nihil illi desit (ət **nɪ**-hil **il**-ɪ **dee**-sit). [Latin] *Hist.* That nothing may be wanting to him.

UTPCPL. *abbr.* UNFAIR TRADE PRACTICES AND CONSUMER PROTECTION LAW.

ut prosint ad veritatem indagandam (ət **proh**-sint ad ver-ə-**tay**-təm in-də-**gan**-dəm). [Law Latin] *Hist.* That they be of service for investigating the truth.

ut res magis valeat quam pereat (rays [*or* reez *or* rez] **may**-jis **vay**-lee-at kwam **peer**-ee-at). [Latin "to give effect to the matter rather than having it fail"] **1.** A maxim of document construction applied when alternative readings are possible, one of which (usu. the broader reading) would achieve the manifest purpose of the document and the other of which (usu. the narrower reading) would reduce the document's purpose to futility or absurdity, whereby the interpreter chooses the construction that gives greater effect to the document's primary purpose. **2.** The interpretive doctrine that a legal text, esp. a statute or contract, should be interpreted in a way that gives the document force rather than makes it fail. See PRESUMPTION OF VALIDITY; CONSTITUTIONAL-DOUBT CANON; PRESUMPTION AGAINST INEFFECTIVENESS.

ut res valeat potius quam pereat (ət **rays** [*or* **reez** *or* **rez**] **vay**-lee-at **poh**-shee-əs kwam **peer**-ee-at). [Latin] *Hist.* That the thing may avail rather than perish; that the transaction may be valid rather than invalid.

utrubi (**ət**-rə-bɪ), *n.* [Latin] *Roman law.* An interdict for maintaining the status quo of possession of movable property pending a ruling to determine the property's rightful owner. • In Roman law, this interdict gave possession of movable property to the party who had held the property longer during the previous year. Justinian applied the rule of *uti possidetis* to movables. Cf. UTI POSSIDETIS (1).

utrumque nostrum (yoo-**trəm**-kwee **nos**-trəm). [Latin] Each of us. • This phrase usu. appeared in bonds. The accusative form is *uterque nostrum.*

UTSA. *abbr.* UNIFORM TRADE SECRETS ACT.

ut supra (ət **s[y]oo**-prə *also* uut). [Latin] *Hist.* As above.

UTT. *abbr.* Uniform traffic ticket.

utter, *adj.* (15c) Complete; absolute; total <an utter denial>.

utter, *vb.* (15c) **1.** To say, express, or publish <don't utter another word until your attorney is present>. **2.** To put or send (a document) into circulation; esp., to circulate (a forged note) as if genuine <she uttered a counterfeit $50 bill at the grocery store>. — **utterance** (in sense 1), **uttering** (in sense 2), *n.*

utter bar. See OUTER BAR.

utter barrister. See *outer barrister* under BARRISTER.

uttering. (18c) The crime of presenting a false or worthless instrument with the intent to harm or defraud. — Also termed *uttering a forged instrument.* See FORGERY.

ut voluntas testatoris sortiatur effectum (ət və-**lən**-tas tes-tə-**tor**-is sor-shee-**ay**-tər i-**fek**-təm). [Latin] *Hist.* That the will of the testator may be effectuated.

U visa. See VISA.

uxor (**ək**-sor), *n.* [Latin] Wife. — Abbr. *ux.* See ET UXOR. Cf. VIR.

uxore rapta et abducta (ək-**sor**-ee **rap**-tə et ab-**dək**-tə). See DE UXORE RAPTA ET ABDUCTA.

uxorial (ək-**sor**-ee-əl), *adj.* (18c) Of, relating to, or characteristic of a wife <uxorial property>.

uxoricide (ək-**sor**-ə-sɪd), *n.* (18c) **1.** The murder of one's wife. **2.** A man who murders his wife. Cf. MARITICIDE. — **uxoricidal,** *adj.*

V

v. *abbr.* **1.** VERSUS. — Also abbreviated *vs.* **2.** Volume. — Also abbreviated *vol.* **3.** Verb. — Also abbreviated *vb.* **4.** (*cap.*) Victoria — the Queen of England from 1837 to 1901. **5.** *Vide.* • This Latin term, meaning "see," is used in phrases such as *quod vide* ("which see," abbreviated *q.v.*). **6.** *Voce* (**voh**-see). • This Latin term means "voice."

VA. *abbr.* (1945) DEPARTMENT OF VETERANS AFFAIRS.

vacancy, *n.* (16c) **1.** The quality, state, or condition of being unoccupied, esp. in reference to an office, post, or piece of property. **2.** The time during which an office, post, or piece of property is not occupied. **3.** An unoccupied office, post, or piece of property; an empty place. • Although the term sometimes refers to an office or post that is temporarily filled, the more usual reference is to an office or post that is unfilled even temporarily. An officer's misconduct does not create a vacancy even if a suspension occurs; a vacancy, properly speaking, does not occur until the officer is officially removed. **4.** A job opening; a position that has not been filled.

vacancy clause. (1877) *Insurance.* A special indorsement allowing premises to be unoccupied beyond the period stipulated in the original insurance policy, so that the insurance remains in effect during policy extensions, often for a reduced amount.

vacant, *adj.* (13c) **1.** Empty; unoccupied <a vacant office>. • Courts have sometimes distinguished *vacant* from *unoccupied*, holding that *vacant* means completely empty while *unoccupied* means not routinely characterized by the presence of human beings. **2.** Absolutely free, unclaimed, and unoccupied <vacant land>. **3.** (Of an estate) abandoned; having no heir or claimant. — The term implies either abandonment or nonoccupancy for any purpose. **4.** (Of a job or position) unfilled and hence available for application by prospective employees.

vacantia (və-**kan**-sh[ee]-ə). See *bona vacantia* under BONA.

vacantia bona (və-**kan**-sh[ee]-ə **boh**-nə). See *bona vacantia* under BONA.

vacant succession. See SUCCESSION (2).

vacate, *vb.* (17c) **1.** To nullify or cancel; make void; invalidate <the court vacated the judgment>. Cf. OVERRULE. **2.** To surrender occupancy or possession; to move out or leave <the tenant vacated the premises>.

vacatio (və-**kay**-shee-oh). *Civil law.* Exemption; immunity; privilege; dispensation.

vacation, *n.* (15c) **1.** A worker's paid leave of absence from work, esp. for the purpose of taking an annual holiday. — Also termed *annual leave.* **2.** The act of vacating <vacation of the office> <vacation of the court's order>. **3.** The period between the end of one term of court and the beginning of the next; the space of time during which a court holds no sessions. • The traditional vacations in England were Christmas vacation, beginning December 24 and ending January 6; Easter vacation, beginning Good Friday and ending Easter Tuesday; Whitsun vacation, beginning on the Saturday immediately before and ending the Tuesday immediately after Whitsunday (i.e., Pentecost, the seventh Sunday after Easter); and the long vacation, beginning August 13 and ending October 23. **4.** Loosely, any time when a given court is not in session. **5.** *Eccles. law.* The act or process by which a church or benefice becomes vacant, as on the death or resignation of the incumbent, until a successor is appointed. — Also termed (in sense 5) *vacatura.*

vacation barrister. See BARRISTER.

vacatur (və-**kay**-tər), *n.* [Law Latin "it is vacated"] (17c) **1.** The act of annulling or setting aside. **2.** A rule or order by which a proceeding is vacated.

vacatura (vay-kə-**t[y]oor**-ə), *n.* [Latin] VACATION (5).

vacua possessio (**vak**-yoo-ə pə-**zes[h]**-ee-oh). [Latin "a vacant possession"] (17c) *Roman & civil law.* Free and unburdened possession, which a seller must convey to a purchaser.

vacuum abortion. See *aspiration abortion* under ABORTION.

vacuus (**vak**-yoo-əs), *adj.* [Latin] *Hist.* Empty; void; vacant; unoccupied.

vades. See VAS.

vadiare duellum (vad-ee-**air**-ee d[y]oo-**el**-əm), *vb.* [Law Latin "to wage the duellum"] *Hist.* To give pledges mutually for engaging in trial by combat.

vadiare legem (vad-ee-**air**-ee **lee**-jəm), *vb.* [Law Latin "to wage law"] *Hist.* (Of a defendant in a debt action) to give security to make one's law on a day assigned — that is, the defendant would pledge, upon giving the security, to do two things on the appointed day in court: (1) take an oath in open court that the debt was not owed, and (2) bring 11 compurgators who would swear that they believed what the defendant said.

vadiatio (vad-ee-**ay**-shee-oh), *n.* [Law Latin] *Hist.* Wager. Cf. INVADIATIO. Pl. ***vadiationes*** (vad-ee-ay-shee-**oh**-neez).

▸ ***vadiatio duelli*** (vad-ee-**ay**-shee-oh d[y]oo-**el**-ɪ). [Law Latin "wager of battle"] See TRIAL BY COMBAT.

▸ ***vadiatio legis*** (vad-ee-**ay**-shee-oh **lee**-jis). [Law Latin "wager of law"] See WAGER OF LAW.

vadimonium (vad-ə-**moh**-nee-əm), *n. Roman law.* **1.** A guarantee (originally backed by sureties) that a litigant would appear in court. **2.** A solemn promise to this effect. — Also termed *vadimony.*

vadium (**vay**-dee-əm), *n.* [Law Latin "pledge, bail, security"] *Hist.* **1.** Security by a pledge of property.

▸ ***vadium mortuum*** (**vay**-dee-əm **mor**-choo-əm). [Law Latin "dead pledge"] (18c) A mortgage. • This was considered a "dead pledge" because an estate was given as security by the borrower, who granted to the lender the estate in fee, on the condition that if the money were not repaid at the specified time, the pledged estate would continue as the lender's — it would be gone from, or "dead" to, the borrower (mortgagor). — Also termed *mortuum vadium.* See MORTGAGE.

▸ ***vadium vivum*** (**vay**-dee-əm **vɪ**-vəm). [Law Latin "live pledge"] (17c) A living pledge, which exists when an estate is granted by a borrower to a lender until a debt is paid out of the estate's proceeds. • The pledge was so called because neither the money nor the lands were lost; it was a "living pledge" because the profits of the land were constantly paying off the debt. — Also termed *vivum vadium; vif-gage.*

2. Wages; salary.

vadium ponere (**vay**-dee-əm **poh**-nə-ree), *vb. Hist.* To take bail for the appearance of a person in court.

vagabond (**vag**-ə-bond), *n.* (15c) *Archaic.* A homeless wanderer without any means or an honest livelihood; VAGRANT. • This term became archaic over the course of the 20th century, as vagrants won the right not to be forcibly removed from cities in such cases as *Papachristou v. City of Jacksonville,* 405 U.S. 156, 92 S.Ct. 839 (1972). In the 1980s and 1990s, vagabonds came to be known as *street people* and *homeless people,* or *the homeless.* — Also termed *vagabundus* (vag-ə-**bən**-dəs).

> "[A]ll idle persons or vagabonds [are] . . . divided into three classes, *idle* and *disorderly* persons, *rogues* and *vagabonds,* and *incorrigible rogues;* — all these are offenders against the good order, and blemishes in the government, of any kingdom. They are therefore all punished . . . rogues and vagabonds with whipping and imprisonment not exceeding six months . . . ." 4 William Blackstone, *Commentaries on the Laws of England* 170 (1769).

vagabondage (**vag**-ə-bon-dij). (1813) **1.** The condition of a vagabond. **2.** Vagabonds as a class. — Also termed (in sense 1) *vagabondism;* (in senses 1 & 2) *vagabondry.*

vagabundus (vag-ə-**bən**-dəs). [Law Latin] See VAGABOND.

vagrancy (**vay**-grən-see), *n.* (17c) **1.** The quality, state, or condition of wandering from place to place without a home, job, or means of support other than begging. • Vagrancy is generally considered a course of conduct or a manner of living, rather than a single act. But under some statutes, a single act has been held sufficient to constitute vagrancy. One court held, for example, that the act of prowling about and creeping up on parked cars and their occupants at night, under circumstances suggesting an intent to commit a crime, constitutes vagrancy. See *Smith v. Drew,* 26 P.2d 1040 (Wash. 1933). Many state laws prohibiting vagrancy have been declared unconstitutionally vague. — Also termed *vagrantism.* **2.** An instance of such wandering. Cf. LOITERING.

> "Vagrancy is a status resulting from misconduct and in the form of a socially harmful condition or mode of life which has been defined and made punishable by law. Until recently it was a misdemeanor, or group of misdemeanors, in most states." Rollin M. Perkins & Ronald N. Boyce, *Criminal Law* 494 (3d ed. 1982).

vagrant, *adj.* (15c) **1.** Of, relating to, or characteristic of a vagrant; inclined to vagrancy. **2.** Nomadically homeless.

vagrant, *n.* (15c) **1.** At common law, anyone belonging to the several classes of idle or disorderly persons, rogues, and vagabonds. **2.** Someone who, not having a settled habitation, strolls from place to place; a homeless, idle wanderer. • The term often refers to one who spends time in idleness, lacking any property and without any visible means of support. Under some statutes, a vagrant is an offender against or menace to the public peace, usu. liable to become a public burden. Cf. VAGABOND.

vagrantism. See VAGRANCY.

vague, *adj.* (16c) **1.** Imprecise or unclear by reason of abstractness; not sharply outlined; indistinct; uncertain.

▸ **unconstitutionally vague.** (1938) **1.** (Of a penal legislative provision) so unclear and indefinite as not to give a person of ordinary intelligence the opportunity to know what is prohibited, restricted, or required. **2.** (Of a statute) impermissibly delegating basic policy matters to administrators and judges so such a degree as to lead to arbitrary and discriminatory application.

2. (Of language) describing a distribution around a central norm, as opposed to a neatly bounded class; broadly indefinite; not clearly or concretely expressed. **3.** Characterized by haziness of thought.

vague-and-indefinite rejection. See REJECTION.

vagueness. (18c) **1.** Uncertain breadth of meaning; unclarity resulting from abstract expression <the phrase "within a reasonable time" is plagued by vagueness — what is reasonable?>. • Though common in writings generally, vagueness raises due-process concerns if legislation does not provide fair notice of what is required, restricted, or prohibited, because enforcement may become arbitrary. **2.** Loosely, AMBIGUITY.

> "**vagueness.** An imprecision of meaning, common on the borderline of a term's application. Within philosophy of language, it is controversial whether the experience of vagueness says something about the limits of meaning, the nature of truth (that there may be truth values other than 'true' and 'false') or the nature of knowledge, but the nature and cause of vagueness is probably not relevant to legal theory — only the fact (experience) of vagueness. The question for legal theory is whether the vagueness of terms (and categories) has implications for the determinacy of law. Vagueness should not be confused with ambiguity. Ambiguity is a general term, referring to an (or any) uncertainty in meaning, including 'latent ambiguity,' where an apparently clear phrase ('my cousin David') turns out to have multiple referents (I have two cousins named 'David'). By contrast, vagueness, in its narrowest philosophical sense, refers to terms *whose boundaries* are uncertain, but whose application at the core is usually quite certain." Brian H. Bix, *A Dictionary of Legal Theory* 217 (2004).

vagueness doctrine. (1957) *Constitutional law.* The doctrine — based on the Due Process Clause — requiring that a criminal statute state explicitly and definitely what acts are prohibited or restricted, so as to provide fair warning and preclude arbitrary enforcement. — Also termed *void-for-vagueness doctrine.* See *void for vagueness* under VOID. Cf. OVERBREADTH DOCTRINE; FAIR-NOTICE DOCTRINE.

valeat quantum (**vay**-lee-at [*or* -ət] **kwon**-təm). [Law Latin] *Hist.* For as much as it is worth.

valens agere (**vay**-lenz **aj**-ər-ee). [Law Latin] *Hist.* Able to act.

> "A person is said to be *valens agere* when, from age and position, he is able to protect his rights against the invasion of them by others: against such a person not protecting his rights prescription runs, while prescription does not run against one who is *non valens agere.*" John Trayner, *Trayner's Latin Maxims* 621 (4th ed. 1894).

valentia (və-**len**-shee-ə), *n.* [Law Latin from Latin *valere* "to be of value"] *Hist.* Value; worth. • In old indictments for larceny, this term often appeared to express the value of the things taken.

valentia agendi (və-**len**-shee-ə ə-**jen**-dɪ). [Law Latin] (1832) *Hist.* The power of acting. See VALENS AGERE.

valere seipsum (və-**leer**-ee see-**ip**-səm). [Law Latin] *Hist.* To be of its own value. • The phrase usu. referred to land.

valid, *adj.* (16c) **1.** Legally sufficient; binding <a valid contract>. **2.** Meritorious <that is a valid conclusion based on the facts presented in this case>. — **validate,** *vb.* — **validation, validity,** *n.*

valid agreement. See *valid contract* under CONTRACT.

validating statute. See STATUTE.

valid contract. See CONTRACT.

validity opinion. See OPINION (2).

validity search. (1905) An exhaustive search for prior art or any other facts that can be used to invalidate a patent. See BREAKING A PATENT. Cf. INFRINGEMENT SEARCH; PATENTABILITY SEARCH.

valid judgment. See JUDGMENT (2).

valid marriage. See MARRIAGE (1).

valid warrant. See WARRANT (1).

valise diplomatique (və-**lees** di-ploh-ma-**teek**). See DIPLOMATIC POUCH.

***Vallescura* rule.** (1950) *Maritime law.* The holding that when a maritime loss is due to more than one cause, and the carrier is exempt from liability for at least one of them, the burden is on the carrier to prove what loss is due to the exempt cause. • If the carrier fails to prove the exemption, it is liable for the entire loss. *Schnell v. The Vallescura*, 293 U.S. 296, 55 S.Ct. 194 (1934).

VA loan. See *veteran's loan* under LOAN.

valor (**val**-ər), *n.* [Latin] (14c) *Hist.* Value; worth; rate; a valuation. — Also spelled (esp. BrE) *valour.* See AD VALOREM.

valor beneficiorum (**val**-ər ben-ə-fish-ee-**or**-əm). [Law Latin] (1803) *Hist.* The value of all ecclesiastical benefices and spiritual preferments.

valor maritagii (**val**-ər mar-ə-**tay**-jee-ɪ). [Latin] (18c) *Hist.* The value of a marriage. • Under ancient tenures, this was the amount that a female ward forfeited to a guardian when the guardian had offered her a marriage without disparagement (inequality), and she refused. Likewise in feudal law, the guardian in chivalry had the right of tendering to a minor ward a suitable match, without disparagement. If the ward refused, she had to compensate the guardian for the value of the marriage (*valor maritagii*). — Also termed (in the accusative) *valorem maritagii*; (Scots law) *avail of marriage.*

> "If an infant ward of a guardian in chivalry refused a match tendered by the guardian, he or she forfeited the value of the marriage (*valorem maritagii*) to the guardian; that is, so much as a jury would assess, or any one would *bona fide* give to the guardian for such an alliance." 2 Alexander M. Burrill, *A Law Dictionary and Glossary* 572–73 (2d ed. 1867).

valuable, *adj.* (16c) Worth a good price; having financial or market value.

valuable consideration. See CONSIDERATION (1).

valuable improvement. See IMPROVEMENT.

valuable papers. (17c) Documents that, upon a person's death, are important in carrying out the decedent's wishes and in managing the estate's affairs. • Examples include a will, title documents, stock certificates, powers of attorney, letters to be opened on one's death, and the like. Some statutes require that, to be effective, a holographic will devising realty must be found among the decedent's valuable papers.

valuable-papers insurance. See INSURANCE.

valuation, *n.* (16c) **1.** The process of determining the value of a thing or entity. **2.** The estimated worth of a thing or entity. — **value, valuate,** *vb.*

▸ **assessed valuation.** (1825) The value that a taxing authority gives to property and to which the tax rate is applied.

▸ **special-use valuation.** (1976) An executor's option of valuating real property in an estate, esp. farmland, based on its current use rather than for its highest potential value.

valuation date. See ALTERNATE VALUATION DATE.

valuation list. (1834) *Hist.* An inventory of all the ratable hereditaments in a parish, each item in the inventory recording the name of the occupier, the owner, the property, the extent of the property, the gross estimated rental, and the ratable value. • The list was traditionally prepared by the overseers of each parish.

value, *n.* (14c) **1.** The significance, desirability, or utility of something.

▸ **social value.** (1825) The significance, desirability, or utility of something to the general public.

2. The monetary worth or price of something; the amount of goods, services, or money that something commands in an exchange. • With respect to negotiable instruments and bank collections, a person generally gives value for rights if he or she acquires them (1) in return for a binding commitment to extend credit or for the extension of immediately available credit, regardless of whether the credit is drawn on or whether a charge-back is provided for if collection proves difficult; (2) as security for or in total or partial satisfaction of a preexisting claim; (3) as accepting delivery under a preexisting contract for purchase; or (4) more generally, in return for any consideration sufficient to support a simple contract.

▸ **actual cash value.** (1853) *Insurance.* **1.** Replacement cost minus normal depreciation. **2.** See *fair market value.*

▸ **actual market value.** See *fair market value.*

▸ **actual value.** See *fair market value.*

▸ **actuarial value.** (1884) The expected value of a contingent cash-flow stream, such as payments from an annuity.

▸ **agreed value.** (18c) A property's value that is fixed by agreement of the parties, esp. the property's owner and the person or entity valuating the property. • An example is a list of property values contained in an insurance policy.

▸ **annual value. 1.** The net yearly income derivable from a given piece of property. **2.** One year's rental value of property, less the costs and expenses of maintaining the property. — Also termed *yearly value.*

▸ **assessed value.** (18c) The value of an asset as determined by an appraiser for tax purposes.

▸ **book value.** See BOOK VALUE.

▸ **cash surrender value.** (1869) *Insurance.* The amount of money payable when an insurance policy having cash value, such as a whole-life policy, is redeemed before maturity or death. — Abbr. CSV. — Also termed *surrender value*; *cash value.*

▸ **cash value. 1.** See *fair market value.* **2.** See *full cash value.* **3.** See *cash surrender value.*

▸ **clear annual value.** (16c) The net annual value of property, after payment of taxes, interest on mortgages, and other charges.

▸ **clear market value.** See *fair market value.*

▸ **clear value.** *Tax.* For purposes of an inheritance tax, whatever remains of an estate after all claims against it have been paid.

▸ **commercial value.** See *exchange value.*

▸ **commuted value** (kə-**myoo**-tid). (1869) **1.** In the assessment of damages, the present value of a future interest in property. **2.** The value of future payments when discounted to their present value.

▸ **double value.** See DOUBLE VALUE.

▸ **economic value.** See *exchange value.*

▸ **enterprise value.** (1939) A measure of a company's market value, calculated by aggregating the value of the company's market capitalization, debt, and preferred stock, and subtracting cash and cash equivalents.

▸ **exchange value.** (1869) The rate of worth set on property or services; specif., the amount of money for which property or services could be exchanged or procured if there is a ready market continually resorted to by traders — or, in the absence of such a market, the amount that could be obtained in the usual course of finding a purchaser or hirer of similar property or services. — Also termed *commercial value*; *economic value.*

▸ **fair market value.** (18c) The price that a seller is willing to accept and a buyer is willing to pay on the open market and in an arm's-length transaction; the point at which supply and demand intersect. — Abbr. FMV. — Also termed *actual value*; *actual cash value*; *actual market value*; *cash value*; *clear market value*; *fair and reasonable value*; *fair cash market value*; *fair market price*; *full value*; *market value*; *salable value*; *true value.* Cf. *fair value.*

▸ **fair value. 1.** An estimate of a good, service, or asset's potential price, based on a rational and unbiased assessment of the amount at which it could currently be bought and sold between willing parties. • A fair-value assessment is often used when a fair market value is unavailable, usu. because there is no active market for the item. **2.** *Business law.* The value ascribed to stock or partnership interests in a corporation or other entity when those interests are involuntarily sold because of the actions of the entity's majority or controlling owners. • Fair value is used when fair market value would be inequitable to a dissenter or involuntary seller, as in a merger or squeeze-out. The fair value of a dissenting shareholder's stock is generally determined without applying the marketability or minority discounts that would apply in a fair-market-value determination. — Also termed *fair cash value*; *just value.* Cf. *fair market value.*

> "[A] forced sale price is not fair value though it may be used as evidence on the question of fair value. Likewise, the fair value of saleable assets is not what they would sell for in the slow process of the debtor's trade as if the debtor were continuing business unhampered. The general idea of fair value is the amount of money the debtor could raise from its property in a short period of time, but not so short as to approximate a forced sale, if the debtor operated as a reasonably prudent and diligent businessman with his interests in mind, especially a proper concern for the payment of his debts." David G. Epstein et al., *Bankruptcy* § 6-18, at 307 (1993).

▸ **full cash value.** Market value for property tax purposes; estimated value derived by standard appraisal methods. — Also termed *cash value.*

▸ **full value.** See *fair market value.*

▸ **future value.** The value, at some future time, of a present sum or a series of monetary payments, calculated at a specific interest rate.

▸ **going-concern value.** (1909) The value of a commercial enterprise's assets or of the enterprise itself as an active business with future earning power, as opposed to the liquidation value of the business or of its assets. • Going-concern value includes, for example, goodwill. — Abbr. GCV. — Also termed *going value.* Cf. GOODWILL.

▸ **highest proved value.** (1867) In a trover action, the greatest value (as proved by the plaintiff) that the converted property reached from the time of the conversion until trial. • It is the highest amount that a plaintiff is entitled to recover.

▸ **insurable value.** (1851) The replacement cost or actual worth of the subject of an insurance contract, usu. expressed as a monetary amount.

▸ **intangible trade value.** (1938) *Intellectual property.* The measure of an enterprise's proprietary information, ideas, goodwill, and other nonphysical commercial assets. • The law of misappropriation provides some protection against the taking of intangible trade values to compete unfairly with their original owner. — Also termed *intangible asset*; *intangible trade property.*

▸ **intrinsic value.** (17c) **1.** The inherent value of a thing, without any special features that might alter its market value. • The intrinsic value of a silver coin, for example, is simply the value of the silver within it. **2.** Value in the open market without regard for any personal or sentimental value. **3.** The value inherent in an object, such as a $100 bill considered as a piece of printed paper and not as currency with a market value of $100.

▸ **just value.** See *fair market value.*

▸ **liquidation value.** (1908) **1.** The value of a business or of an asset when it is sold in liquidation, as opposed to being sold in the ordinary course of business. **2.** See *liquidation price* under PRICE.

▸ **market value.** See *fair market value.*

▸ **most-suitable-use value.** See *optimal-use value.*

▸ **net value. 1.** *Insurance.* The excess of a policyholder payments over the yearly cost of insurance; the part of an insured's annual premium that, according to actuarial tables, the insurer must set aside to meet the insurer's obligations to the insured. — Also termed *reserve.* **2.** The fair market value of shares of stock.

▸ **new value.** (17c) **1.** A value that is newly given or freshly calculated. **2.** The value obtained by taking a security, such as collateral, for any debt other than a preexisting one.

▸ **optimal-use value.** (1972) *Tax.* The highest and best use of a thing from an economic standpoint. • If a farm would be worth more as a shopping center than as a farm, the shopping-center value will control even if the transferee (that is, a donee or heir) continues to use the property as a farm. — Also termed *most-suitable-use value.*

▸ **par value.** See PAR VALUE.

▸ **policy value.** See POLICY VALUE.

▸ **present value.** See PRESENT VALUE.

▸ **residual value.** See *salvage value.*

▸ **salable value.** See *fair market value.*

▸ **salvage value.** (1917) The value of an asset after it has become useless to the owner; the amount expected to be obtained when a fixed asset is disposed of at the end of its useful life. • Salvage value is used, under some depreciation methods, to determine the allowable tax deduction for depreciation. And under the UCC, when a buyer of goods breaches or repudiates the contract of sale, the seller may, under certain circumstances, either complete the manufacture of any incomplete goods or cease the manufacture and sell the partial product for scrap or salvage value. UCC § 2-704(2). — Also termed *residual value; scrap value; terminal value.* See DEPRECIATION.

▸ **scrap value.** See *salvage value.*

▸ **settlement value.** (1898) The value of a claim if the claimant settles immediately as opposed to pursuing the claim further through litigation.

▸ **street value.** The price for which something, esp. drugs or other contraband, can be sold illegally.

▸ **surplus value.** (1816) The value of labor after the laborer's subsistence and that of his or her dependents is accounted for.

▸ **surrender value.** See *cash surrender value.*

▸ **terminal value.** (1882) **1.** MATURITY VALUE. **2.** See *salvage value* under VALUE (2).

▸ **true value.** See *fair market value.*

▸ **use value.** (1844) A value established by the utility of an object instead of its sale or exchange value.

▸ **value received.** See VALUE RECEIVED.

▸ **yearly value.** See *annual value.*

3. Sufficient contractual consideration. — **value,** *vb.* — **valuation,** *n.*

> "Value also includes paying or securing a preexisting debt, and in this regard value is broader than common-law consideration. Thus, a debtor receives value in satisfying an antecedent claim (as by paying an overdue account or an outstanding loan or by transferring property to vindicate a preexisting interest in it) or in providing collateral for a previously unsecured creditor. It makes no difference that the debtor got nothing new, in terms of property added to her estate, at the time of the transfer." David G. Epstein et al., *Bankruptcy* § 6-49, at 374 (1993).

value-added card. See STORED-VALUE CARD.

value-added model. See LABOR-DESERT MODEL.

value-added tax. See TAX.

value bill. See BILL (7).

value date. (1920) The date when the proceeds of a bill of exchange (e.g., a check) or of a foreign-exchange transaction (e.g., a sale of dollars for euros) become available for use. — Also termed *here and there.*

valued policy. See INSURANCE POLICY.

valued-policy law. (1882) A statute requiring insurance companies to pay the full amount of the insurance to the insured in the event of a total loss, regardless of the true value of the property at the time of loss.

value fund. See MUTUAL FUND.

value judgment. (1889) A decision or assessment about the merit or goodness of something, based not on inarguable facts but on personal opinions.

> "When an attempt is made to evaluate something, it is placed on a scale, real or imaginary, that runs from bad to good, from slow to fast, from light to heavy, or the like. 'The car was going fast'; 'the horse was sold at a high price'; the picture was very beautiful'; 'the orchestra gave an exquisite rendering' — all these are evaluations that in the terms of semantics are called *value judgments.* This is the name given to evaluations that cannot be confirmed by independent measurement. 'The car was moving at forty miles an hour' or 'the house was sold for five thousand dollars' — these also are evaluations, but since they could be confirmed from outside sources they are not value judgments. [E]valuations made in the form of quantitative statements are marks of the factual style, and . . . the emotive style is marked by the inclusion of the unverifiable evaluations that . . . [we] call value judgments." Frederick A. Philbrick, *Language and the Law* 99 (1949).

valuer. See APPRAISER.

value received. (17c) Consideration that has been delivered. • This phrase is commonly used in a bill of exchange or promissory note to show that it was supported by consideration.

> "'Value received.' These words, (though usual), are not necessary to give validity or force to the instrument, as a bill of exchange; but in some of the older cases the contrary was ruled. Consideration being *presumed* by law for the drawing and indorsing a bill, no argument or inference that it does not exist can be founded on the absence of the words 'value received': the presumption that a consideration existed, still arises. The precise meaning of these words, in reference to the parties by whom and from whom the value was received, depends upon the form of the bill. If it be payable to the drawer or his order, the words 'value received' import that the drawee has received consideration from the drawer: if it be payable to a third person, they signify that the drawer has received value from him, to the amount drawn for. The nature of the value or consideration may be stated, without prejudice to the validity of the instrument." Joseph Chitty, *A Practical Treatise on Bills of Exchange, Promissory Notes, and Bankers' Checks* § 9, at 9–9a (1834).

valuta (və-loo-tə), *n.* [Italian fr. Latin] (1802) Value; worth; esp., the value of a currency in relation to that of the currency of some other country.

valvasor (valv-ə-sor), *n.* [Law Latin] (16c) *Hist.* A principal vassal who, though not holding directly of the sovereign, held of those who did so; a vassal of the second degree or rank. — Also spelled *valvassor.* See VAVASOR.

VA mortgage. See MORTGAGE.

vandal. [fr. Latin *Vandalus,* a member of the Germanic tribe known as Vandals] (17c) Someone who deliberately or ignorantly destroys or damages things, esp. public property; specif., a malicious destroyer or defacer of works of art, monuments, buildings, or other property.

vandalism, *n.* (18c) **1.** Willful or ignorant destruction of public or private property, esp. of artistic, architectural, or literary treasures. **2.** The actions or attitudes of one who maliciously or ignorantly destroys or disfigures public or private property; active hostility to anything that is venerable or beautiful. — **vandalize,** *vb.* — **vandalistic,** *adj.*

vara (**vah**-rah). (17c) *Spanish-Am. law.* A measure of length equal to about 33 inches. • Local usage varies, so that a vara may sometimes be more and sometimes less than 33 inches. In Mexican land grants, the measure is equal to 32.9927 inches. The term is often found in old land grants in states that were formed from land governed by Spain or Mexico.

> "VARA, a measure of length in Spanish countries, answering to the yard, but generally something under 3 feet. Usually 100 *V.* are considered equal to 90 yards. The solid *V.* of Spain is 20.561 cubic feet." 2 L. De Colange, *The American Dictionary of Commerce, Manufactures, Commercial Law, and Finance* 1081 (1881).

variable annuity. See ANNUITY.

variable annuity contract. See CONTRACT.

variable cost. See COST (1).

variable life insurance. See LIFE INSURANCE.

variable obscenity. See OBSCENITY.

variable rate. See INTEREST RATE.

variable-rate mortgage. See *adjustable-rate mortgage* under MORTGAGE.

variance. (14c) **1.** A difference or disparity between two statements or documents that ought to agree; esp., in criminal procedure, a difference between the allegations in a charging instrument and the proof actually introduced at trial. — Also termed *variation.*

▸ **fatal variance.** (18c) A variance that either deprives the defendant of fair notice of the charges or exposes the defendant to the risk of double jeopardy. • A fatal variance is grounds for reversing a conviction. Cf. *constructive amendment of indictment* under AMENDMENT OF INDICTMENT.

▸ **immaterial variance.** (18c) A variance too slight to mislead or prejudice the defendant and is thus harmless error.

2. A license or official authorization to depart from a zoning law. — Also termed (in sense 2) *zoning variance.* See HARDSHIP (4). Cf. SPECIAL EXCEPTION (2); SPECIAL-USE PERMIT.

▸ **area variance.** (1950) A variance permitting deviation from zoning requirements about construction and placement, but not from requirements about use.

▸ **use variance.** (1929) A variance permitting deviation from zoning requirements about use.

variation. See VARIANCE (1).

varrantizatio (və-ran-ti-**zay**-shee-oh), *n.* [Law Latin] *Hist. Scots law.* A warranty.

vary, *vb.* (14c) **1.** To change in some usu. small way; to make somewhat different <by editing the contract, he varied its standard terms>. **2.** To cause to alter; to transmute <to vary one's routines>. **3.** To be altered in some way; to become different <stock prices vary from moment to moment>. **4.** (Of things fundamentally similar) to differ in details; to be subtly dissimilar <the facts vary with each witness's memory>. **5.** To be characteristically changeable or adaptive <his tastes vary with each new fashion>. **6.** To disagree in feeling or opinion; to be sentimentally or analytically at odds <I vary with the majority of the court>. **7.** To swerve or deviate to one side, esp. with unpleasant consequences <to vary from the law>. **8.** To change for the sake of relieving monotony; diversify <vary your connectives — as opposed to using "And" at the beginning of each sentence>.

varying acceptance. See ACCEPTANCE (1).

vas (vas), *n.* [Latin "surety"] A pledge, surety, bail; esp., in early law, security for a criminal defendant's appearance in court. • In Roman law under the *legis actio* procedure, a *vas* was a special surety for the defendant if there was an adjournment *in jure.* See IN JURE (2); LEGIS ACTIO. Pl. ***vades*** (**vay**-deez).

vassal (**vas**-əl), *n.* [fr. Law Latin *vassallus*] (14c) *Hist.* The grantee of a fief, feud, or fee; a feudal tenant. Cf. FREEMAN (5).

▸ ***arriere vassal*** (a-ree-**air vas**-əl). (1880) *Hist.* The vassal of a vassal.

vassalage (**vas**-əl-ij), *n.* (14c) *Hist.* **1.** The quality, state, or condition of being a vassal or feudatory. — Also termed *vasseleria.* **2.** The service required of a vassal. — Also termed *vassaticum; main-rent.* **3.** The territory held by a vassal; a fief or fee. **4.** Vassals collectively. **5.** The dominion or authority of a feudal superior over vassals. **6.** Political servility; subjection.

vassalli ligii (**vas**-ə-lɪ **lij**-ee-ɪ). [Law Latin] (1832) *Hist.* Vassals holding immediately of the Crown.

vassallo et quibus dederit (**vas**-ə-loh et **kwib**-əs **dee**-dər-it). [Law Latin] *Hist.* To the vassal and to whomsoever he shall have given it. • The phrase was included in feudal grants.

> "If the original grant had been destined to the vassal, 'and his heirs and assignees whomsoever,' this only bound the superior to receive the proper heirs of the vassal and not his assignee; but if the destination bore . . . [vassal] 'et quibus dederit,' this was construed as a consent on the part of the superior to alienation, and under which he was bound to receive as vassal his vassal's disponee. This distinction . . . was practically abolished by the Act 20 Geo. II. c. 50, which introduced a mode by which either an heir or disponee could force an entry from the superior." John Trayner, *Trayner's Latin Maxims* 622 (4th ed. 1894).

vassallo faciendo superiori quod de jure facere oportet (**vas**-ə-loh fay-shee-**en**-doh s[y]oo-peer-ee-**or**-ɪ kwod dee **joor**-ee **fay**-sə-ree ə-**por**-tet). [Law Latin] *Hist.* On the vassal performing that to the superior which, according to law, he ought to perform.

vassallus (**vas**-ə-ləs), *n.* [Law Latin] *Hist.* A feudal tenant. Cf. VASSUS.

vassal state. (1846) *Int'l law.* A state that possesses only those rights and privileges that have been granted to it by a more powerful state.

vassaticum (və-**sat**-ə-kəm). [Law Latin] See VASSALAGE (2).

vasseleria (vas-ə-**leer**-ee-ə). [Law Latin] See VASSALAGE (1).

vassus (**vas**-əs), *n.* [Law Latin] *Hist.* A feudal tenant who held immediately of the king. Cf. VASSALLUS.

vasto. See DE VASTO.

vastum (**vas**-təm), *n. Hist.* WASTE.

▸ ***vastum forestae vel bosci*** (**vas**-təm for-es-tee vel **bahs**-ɪ). *Hist.* Waste of a forest or wood.

VAT. See *value-added tax* under TAX.

Vatican Fragments. Parts of a summary of legal rules extracted from the writings of jurisconsults and from several imperial constitutions from AD 163 to AD 372. • They were discovered by the Vatican librarian and first published in 1823.

vauderie (**vaw**-dər-ee). *Hist.* Sorcery; witchcraft.

***Vaughn* index.** (1974) A comprehensive list of all documents that the government wants to shield from disclosure in Freedom of Information Act (FOIA) litigation, each document being accompanied by a statement of justification for nondisclosure. • Supported by one or more affidavits, a *Vaughn* index has three purposes: (1) forcing the government to scrutinize all material withheld; (2) enabling the trial court to fulfill its duty of ruling on the factual basis of each claimed FOIA exemption; and (3) enabling the adversary system to operate by giving the requester as much information as possible. 5 USCA §§ 552 et seq. The name derives from *Vaughn v. Reese*, 484 F.2d 820 (D.C. Cir. 1973).

vavasor (**vav**-ə-sor), *n.* [Law Latin] (14c) *Hist.* The vassal or tenant of a baron; one who held under a baron and also had subtenants. — Also spelled *vavasour* (**vav**-ə-suur). Cf. VALVASOR.

vavasory (**vav**-ə-sor-ee), *n.* [fr. Law Latin *vavasoria*] (17c) *Hist.* The lands held by a vavasor.

VAWA. *abbr.* VIOLENCE AGAINST WOMEN ACT.

VBA. *abbr.* VETERANS BENEFIT ADMINISTRATION.

VC. *abbr.* (18c) **1.** VICE-CHANCELLOR. **2.** See *venture capital* under CAPITAL.

VCAR. *abbr.* Violent crime in aid of racketeering.

VCC. *abbr.* VICE-CHANCELLOR'S COURT.

VDF. *abbr.* VOLUNTARY-DISCLOSURE FORM.

v.e. *abbr.* VENDITIONI EXPONAS.

veal-money. (17c) *Hist.* The annual rent paid by tenants of the manor of Bradford, in the county of Wiltshire, in lieu of veal formerly paid in kind.

vectigal (**vek**-tɪ-gəl), *n.* (16c) *Roman & civil law.* **1.** A tax, esp. an import or export duty, paid to the state. **2.** An annual ground rent paid in kind or in money. Pl. ***vectigalia*** (vek-tə-**gay**-lee-ə).

▸ ***vectigal judiciarium*** (vek-tɪ-gəl joo-dish-ee-**air**-ee-əm), *n.* A tax or fine to defray the expenses of maintaining courts of justice. Pl. ***vectigalia judiciaria.***

vectura (vek-**t[y]oor**-ə). (17c) *Hist. Maritime law.* Freight.

vegetative state. (1836) A coma-like medical condition resulting from severe brain damage, characterized by open eyes and the appearance of wakefulness although without clinical signs of awareness or cognitive functioning. • The person may be able to move, make sounds, and respond to stimuli. — Also termed *coma vigil.*

▸ **continuous vegetative state.** See *persistent vegetative state.*

▸ **permanent vegetative state.** (1969) A vegetative state that has lasted for at least one year, making it impossible, from a clinical point of view, that the affected person will regain awareness or cognitive functioning.

▸ **persistent vegetative state.** (1972) A vegetative state that has lasted more than four weeks but less than one year, making it very unlikely, from a clinical point of view, that the affected person will regain awareness or cognitive functioning. — Abbr. PVS. — Also termed *continuous vegetative state.*

veggie-libel law. *Slang.* See AGRICULTURAL-DISPARAGEMENT LAW.

vehicle (**vee**-ə-kəl), *n.* (17c) **1.** An instrument of transportation or conveyance. **2.** Any conveyance used in transporting passengers or things by land, water, or air.

▸ **motor vehicle.** (1890) A wheeled conveyance that does not run on rails and is self-propelled, esp. one powered by an internal-combustion engine, a battery or fuel-cell, or a combination of these.

vehicular (vee-**hik**-yə-lər), *adj.* (17c) Of, relating to, or caused by a vehicle or vehicles.

vehicular accident. See *car accident* under ACCIDENT (2).

vehicular homicide. See HOMICIDE.

veil-piercing. See PIERCING THE CORPORATE VEIL.

vein, *n.* (14c) *Mining law.* A continuous body of mineral or mineralized rock, filling a seam or fissure in the earth's crust, within defined boundaries that clearly separate it from surrounding rock.

▸ **discovery vein.** (1898) The primary vein for the purpose of locating a mining claim.

vejour (və-**zhoor**), *n.* [Law French fr. Law Latin *visores* "viewers"] (15c) *Hist.* **1.** One of several persons sent by the court to examine a place in question to help in the decision-making process. **2.** A person sent to visit persons who claim they are unable to appear in court on account of illness, to see whether they are actually so sick that they cannot appear or whether they are malingering. — Also spelled *veyor; veyour; vayowr; veiour; veighor.*

vel faciendo vel delinquendo (vel fay-shee-**en**-doh vel dee-ling-**kwen**-doh). [Law Latin] *Hist.* Either by doing something or by leaving something undone. • The phrase appeared in reference to what was accomplished by act or omission.

vellicate (**vel**-i-kayt), *vb.* (17c) **1.** To cause to twitch or contract spasmodically or convulsively. **2.** (Of a muscle) to twitch. **3.** *Archaic.* To defame. — **vellication,** *n.*

vel non (vel **non**). [Latin "or not"] (1895) Or the absence of it (or them) <this case turns solely on the finding of discrimination vel non>.

venal (**vee**-nəl), *adj.* (17c) **1.** (Of a person) capable of being bribed. **2.** Ready to trade one's services or influence, esp. from an official position, for money or other valuable consideration. **3.** Of, relating to, or characterized by corrupt bargaining. **4.** Broadly, purchasable; for sale. — **venality,** *n.*

vend, *vb.* (17c) **1.** To transfer to another for money or something else of value. • The term is not commonly applied to real estate, although its derivatives (*vendor* and *vendee*) are. **2.** To make an object of trade, esp. by hawking or peddling. **3.** To utter publicly; to say or state; to publish broadly.

vendee. (16c) A purchaser, usu. of real property; a buyer.

vendee's lien. See LIEN.

vendetta (ven-**det**-ə), *n.* (1855) A private blood feud in which family members seek revenge on one or more persons outside the family (often members of another family); esp., a private war in which the nearest of kin seek revenge for the slaying of a relative.

vend. ex. *abbr.* VENDITIONI EXPONAS.

vendible, *adj.* (14c) Salable; fit or suitable to be sold.

vendible, *n.* (17c) Anything displayed for sale.

venditae (ven-də-tee). [fr. Latin *vendere* "to sell"] *Hist.* A tax on things sold in markets and at public fairs.

venditio (ven-**dish**-ee-oh). [Latin] *Roman & civil law.* **1.** A sale; VENDITION. **2.** A contract of sale. • In this sense, the term is short for *emptio et venditio.* See EMPTIO. **3.** Broadly, any contract by which the ownership of something may be transferred for value. Pl. ***venditiones.***

▸ ***venditio corporis*** (ven-**dish**-ee-oh **kor**-pə-ris). A sale of a specific thing. — Also termed *venditio speciei.*

▸ ***venditio generis*** (ven-**dish**-ee-oh **jen**-ə-ris). (1873) A sale of goods of a class or general kind.

▸ ***venditio nominis*** (ven-**dish**-ee-oh **nom**-ə-nis). (1822) A sale or conveyance of a debt.

▸ ***venditio speciei*** (ven-**dish**-ee-oh **spee**-shee-ɪ). See *venditio corporis.*

vendition, *n.* (16c) The act of selling; a sale. — Also termed *venditio.*

venditioni exponas (ven-dish-ee-**oh**-nɪ eks-**poh**-nəs). [Latin "you are to expose for sale"] (17c) A writ of execution requiring a sale of particular goods to be made. • The writ is directed to a sheriff who has levied on goods under a *fieri facias* but has reported that the goods remain unsold for lack of buyers. In some jurisdictions, a *venditioni exponas* is issued to require a sale of property seized under an earlier writ, after the property has been condemned or passed on by inquisition. — Abbr. *vend. ex.; v.*

venditor (ven-də-tər), *n. Hist.* See VENDOR.

venditor regis (**ven**-də-tər **ree**-jis). [Latin] *Hist.* The king's seller; esp., the person who sold goods and chattels that had been seized or distrained to answer a debt due to the king.

venditrix (ven-də-triks), *n. Hist.* A female vendor.

vendor. (16c) A seller, usu. of real property. — Also termed *venditor.*

▸ ***itinerant vendor.*** (1845) A vendor who travels from place to place selling goods.

vendor's lien. See LIEN.

vendue (ven-**d**[y]**oo** *or* **ven**-d[y]oo). (17c) *Hist.* **1.** A sale; esp., a sale at public auction. **2.** See *execution sale* under SALE.

vendue master. *Hist.* See AUCTIONEER.

venereal disease. See SEXUALLY TRANSMITTED DISEASE.

venery (**ven**-ə-ree). (14c) *Archaic.* **1.** Hunting. **2.** Sexual intercourse; esp., excessive sexual indulgence.

Venetian patent statute. *Hist.* A law enacted in Venice in 1474, giving an inventor the exclusive right to make and use an invention for 10 years. • This was the first known patent law, with procedures for securing and enforcing the inventor's right to exclude others from working, using, or benefiting from the invention.

vengeance (**ven**-jəns), *n.* (13c) **1.** *Archaic.* Punishment inflicted as a deserved penalty, esp. by the person wronged, in the name of justice; retributive punishment. **2.** Passionate or unrestrained revenge; the wrathful or spiteful avenging of a wrong. Cf. REVENGE. — **vengeful,** *adj.*

venia (**vee**-nee-ə), *n.* [Latin] *Hist.* **1.** A penitent's kneeling or assuming a prostrate position on the ground. **2.** A pardon. **3.** The granting of a privilege. Pl. ***veniae.***

▸ ***venia aetatis*** (**vee**-nee-ə i-**tay**-tis). (1838) *Roman & civil law.* A privilege granted by a prince or sovereign by virtue of which an underage person is entitled to legally act and be treated as if he or she were of full age.

venial (**vee**-nee-əl), *adj.* (14c) (Of a transgression) forgivable; pardonable.

venire (və-**nɪ**-ree *or* -**neer**-ee *or* -**nɪr** *or* -**neer**). (1807) **1.** A panel of persons selected for jury duty and from among whom the jurors are to be chosen. — Also termed *array; jury panel; jury pool;* (redundantly) *venire panel.*

▸ ***special venire.*** (18c) A panel of citizens summoned when there is an unexpected need for a larger pool from which to select jurors, or a panel summoned for a particular (usu. capital) case.

2. VENIRE FACIAS.

venire de novo. See *venire facias de novo* under VENIRE FACIAS.

venire facias (və-**nɪ**-ree [*or* -**neer**-ee *or* -**nɪr** *or* -**neer**] **fay**-shee-əs). (15c) A writ directing a sheriff to assemble a jury. — Often shortened to *venire.* — Also termed *venire facias juratores* (joor-ə-**tor**-eez).

▸ ***venire facias ad respondendum*** (ad ree-spon-**den**-dəm). (1814) A writ requiring a sheriff to summon a person against whom an indictment for a misdemeanor has been issued. • A warrant is now more commonly used.

▸ ***venire facias de novo*** (dee *or* di **noh**-voh). (17c) A writ for summoning a jury panel anew because of some impropriety or irregularity in the original jury's return or verdict such that a judgment cannot be entered on it. • The result of a new venire is a new trial. In substance, the writ is a motion for a new trial, but when the party objects to the verdict because of a procedural error (and not an error on the merits), the form of motion was traditionally for a venire facias de novo. — Often shortened to *venire de novo.*

▸ ***venire facias tot matronas*** (tot mə-**troh**-nəs). (17c) A writ requiring a sheriff to summon a jury of matrons to execute a writ *de ventre inspiciendo.* See DE VENTRE INSPICIENDO.

veniremember (və-**nɪ**-ree-mem-bər *or* və-**neer**-ee- *or* və-**neer**-). (1966) A prospective juror; a member of a jury panel. — Also termed *venireman; venireperson; talesman.* See TALESMAN.

venit et defendit (**vee**-nit et di-**fen**-dit). [Latin] Comes and defends. • The phrase appeared in old-style defensive pleadings.

venit et dicit (**vee**-nit et **dɪ**-sit). [Latin] Comes and says. • The phrase appeared in old-style pleadings. Remnants of the phrase still occur in some American jurisdictions: *Now comes the plaintiff, and respectfully says . . . .*

vente (vawnt *or* vont). [French] *French law.* A sale; contract of sale.

▸ ***vente aléatoire*** (a-lay-ə-**twahr**). A sale subject to an uncertain event.

▸ ***vente à réméré*** (ah ray-may-**ray**). (1824) A conditional sale, in which the seller reserves the right to redeem or repurchase the property at the same price. • The term is used in Louisiana and in some parts of Canada.

▸ ***vente aux enchères*** (oh-zawn-**shair**). An auction. See AUCTION.

venter (**ven**-tər), *n.* [Latin "womb"] (16c) **1.** The womb of a wife or mother. **2.** One of two or more women who are sources of the same man's offspring.

> "VENTER . . . is a term nowadays considered objectionable, because it refers to the woman . . . merely as the possessor of a birth canal." Bryan A. Garner, *Garner's Dictionary of Legal Usage* 923 (3d ed. 2011).

ventre inspiciendo. **1.** See DE VENTRE INSPICIENDO. **2.** See *venire facias tot matronas* under VENIRE FACIAS.

venture. (16c) An undertaking that involves risk; esp., a speculative commercial enterprise. Cf. JOINT VENTURE.

venture capital. See CAPITAL.

venturer, *n.* (16c) **1.** Someone who risks something, and hopes to gain more, in a business enterprise. **2.** Someone who participates in an association of two or more parties in a business enterprise. See JOINT VENTURE.

venue (**ven**-yoo). [Law French "coming"] (16c) *Procedure.* **1.** The proper or a possible place for a lawsuit to proceed, usu. because the place has some connection either with the events that gave rise to the lawsuit or with the plaintiff or defendant. **2.** The territory, such as a country or other political subdivision, over which a trial court has jurisdiction. — Also termed (in senses 1 & 2) *proper venue.* Cf. JURISDICTION.

▸ **improper venue.** (1851) A place or court where jurisdiction is not authorized under a statute or by agreement of the parties.

3. Loosely, the place where a conference or meeting is being held. **4.** In a pleading, the statement establishing the place for trial. **5.** In an affidavit, the designation of the place where it was made.

> "Venue must be carefully distinguished from jurisdiction. Jurisdiction deals with the power of a court to hear and dispose of a given case; in the federal system, it involves questions of a constitutional dimension concerning the basic division of judicial power among the states and between state and federal courts. Venue is of a distinctly lower level of importance; it is simply a statutory device designed to facilitate and balance the objectives of optimum convenience for parties and witnesses and efficient allocation of judicial resources." Jack H. Friedenthal et al., *Civil Procedure* § 2.1, at 10 (2d ed. 1993).

> "The distinction must be clearly understood between jurisdiction, which is the power to adjudicate, and venue, which relates to the place where judicial authority may be exercised and is intended for the convenience of the litigants. It is possible for jurisdiction to exist though venue in a particular district is improper, and it is possible for a suit to be brought in the appropriate venue though it must be dismissed for lack of jurisdiction. The most important difference between venue and jurisdiction is that a party may consent to be sued in a district that otherwise would be an improper venue, and it waives its objection to venue if it fails to assert it promptly. This is in striking contrast to subject-matter jurisdiction, which cannot be conferred by the parties, if it has not been granted by Congress, whether by consent, waiver, or estoppel." Charles Alan Wright, *The Law of Federal Courts* § 42, at 257 (5th ed. 1994).

venue, change of. See CHANGE OF VENUE.

venue facts. (1936) Facts that need to be pleaded or established in a hearing to determine whether venue is proper in a given court.

venville (**ven**-vil), *n.* (14c) *Hist.* A tenure peculiar to the area of Dartmoor forest in Devonshire, whereby tenants have certain rights in the forest.

veracious (və-**ray**-shəs), *adj.* (17c) Truthful; accurate. — Also termed *veridical.*

veracity (və-**ras**-ət-ee), *n.* (17c) **1.** Habitual regard for and observance of the truth; truthful nature <the witness's fraud conviction supports the defense's challenge to his veracity>. **2.** Consistency with the truth; accuracy <you called into question the veracity of Murphy's affidavit>. — **veracious** (və-**ray**-shəs), *adj.*

verae causae (**ver**-I **kaw**-zI), *adj.* [Latin] Relevant to the case at hand.

veray (və-**ray**), *adj.* [Law French] *Hist.* True. • This word is an older form of the French *vrai.*

verba (**vər**-bə). [Latin] *n. pl.* Words — esp. oral as opposed to written words.

verba concepta. **1.** See FORMULA (1). **2.** See FORMULAE.

verba jactantia (**vər**-bə jak-**tan**-shee-ə). [Law Latin] (17c) *Hist.* Boastful words. • These words — esp. in a marriage declaration — are not usu. binding. See JACTITATION OF MARRIAGE.

verbal, *adj.* (15c) **1.** Of, relating to, or expressed in words. **2.** Loosely, of, relating to, or expressed in spoken words.

verbal, *n.* (1963) *English law. Slang.* A statement, usu. oral and often incriminating, allegedly made by a criminal defendant and offered as evidence against the defendant at trial. • The term often implies that a police officer inaccurately recorded or invented a defendant's statement <the defense counsel challenged the verbals presented by the police>.

verbal, *vb.* (1963) *English law. Slang.* To improperly pressure a person to make a statement, esp. one that is damaging or false <the defendant recanted and claimed that he had been verbaled>.

verbal abuse. See ABUSE.

verbal act. See ACT (2).

verbal-act doctrine. (1901) The rule that utterances accompanying conduct that might have legal effect are admissible when the conduct is material to the issue and is equivocal in nature, and when the words help give the conduct its legal significance.

verbal contract. See *parol contract* (1) under CONTRACT.

verbal-meaning theory. See TEXTUALISM.

verbal note. (1860) *Diplomacy.* An unsigned memorandum informally reminding an official of a pending request, an unanswered question, or the like.

verbal terrorism. See HECKLER'S VETO.

verbal will. See *nuncupative will* under WILL.

verba precaria (**vər**-bə pri-**kair**-ee-ə). [Latin] (1880) *Civil law.* **1.** Precatory words. **2.** Words of trust; words of request used in creating a trust.

verba solennia (**vər**-bə sə-**len**-ee-ə). [Latin] (17c) *Hist.* Solemn words; formal words. — Also termed *verba solemnia* (sə-**lem**-nee-ə).

verbatim (vər-**bay**-təm), *adj.* & *adv.* [fr. Latin *verbum* "word"] (16c) Word for word. • Courts have repeatedly held that, in the context of the requirement that a trial record must be "verbatim," absolute word-for-word accuracy is not necessary — and insubstantial omissions do not make a transcript "nonverbatim."

verbatim ac litteratim (vər-**bay**-tim ak lit-ə-**ray**-tim), *adv.* (vər-**bay**-tim ak li-tər-**ay**-tim). [Latin] Word for word and letter for letter. — Also spelled *verbatim ac literatim*; *verbatim et literatim*. — Also termed *verbatim et litteratim.*

verbiage. (18c) **1.** Speech or writing that is filled with superfluous words. **2.** Loosely, a wording. • Sense 2 is considered poor usage. "Please use this verbiage" is an impossible sentence unless the speaker or writer is unabashedly and even proudly verbose, or else sloppy in handling words.

verbi gratia (**vər**-bɪ **gray**-shee-ə). [Latin "for example"] (16c) Words for the sake of example. — Abbr. V.G.

verbruikleening (ver-**bruuk**-layn-ing), *n.* (1916) *Roman–Dutch law.* A loan for use; COMMODATUM.

verderer (**vər**-dər-ər), *n.* [fr. French *verdier* "caretaker of green things"] (16c) *Archaic.* A judicial officer who, being in charge of the royal forest, is sworn to preserve the vert (foliage) and venison, to keep the assizes, and to view, receive, and enroll attachments and presentments on matters involving trespass. — Also spelled *verderor.*

> "In all the forests there were a varying number of officers (usually four) elected in the county court, and styled Verderers. Manwood says that they should be 'gentlemen of good account, ability, and living, and well learned in the laws of the forest.' Their chief duty was to attend the forest courts; they served gratuitously; and they were immediately responsible to the crown. Possibly they were regarded as a check upon the Warden, as the coroner was upon the sheriff." 1 William Holdsworth, *A History of English Law* 96 (7th ed. 1956).

verdict. (15c) **1.** A jury's finding or decision on the factual issues of a case.

▸ **alternative verdict.** (1818) **1.** See *lesser included offense* under OFFENSE (2). **2.** One of two or more verdicts that a jury may reach. • For example, in some states, when a defendant asserts an insanity defense, the jury may find the defendant not guilty by reason of insanity or, alternatively, guilty but insane.

▸ **chance verdict.** (1820) A now-illegal verdict, arrived at by hazard or lot. — Also termed *gambling verdict*; *verdict by lot.*

▸ **compromise verdict.** (1851) A verdict reached when jurors, to avoid a deadlock, concede some issues so that other issues will be resolved as they want.

▸ **defective verdict.** (18c) A verdict on which a judgment cannot be based because of irregularities or legal inadequacies.

▸ **directed verdict.** (1912) A ruling by a trial judge taking a case from the jury because the evidence will permit only one reasonable verdict. — Also termed *instructed verdict.*

▸ **excessive verdict.** (1817) A verdict resulting from the jury's passion or prejudice and thereby shocks the court's conscience; a jury's award of damages that is substantially higher than the evidence of harm will support.

▸ **false verdict.** (16c) *Archaic.* A verdict so contrary to the evidence and so unjust that the judge may set it aside.

▸ **gambling verdict.** See *chance verdict.*

▸ **general verdict.** (17c) A verdict by which the jury finds in favor of one party or the other, as opposed to resolving specific fact questions. Cf. *special verdict.*

▸ **general verdict subject to a special case.** (1819) *Archaic.* A court's verdict rendered without regard to the jury's general verdict, given when a party does not want to put the legal question on the record but merely wants the court to decide on the basis of a written statement of all the facts in the case, prepared for the opinion of the court by counsel on either side.

▸ **general verdict with interrogatories.** (1878) A general verdict accompanied by answers to written interrogatories on one or more issues of fact that bear on the verdict.

▸ **guilty verdict.** (18c) A jury's finding that a defendant is guilty of the offense charged. — Also termed *verdict of guilt.*

▸ **inadequate verdict.** (1890) A jury's award of damages that is significantly lower than the amount of harm proved.

▸ **instructed verdict.** See *directed verdict.*

▸ **joint verdict.** (1825) A verdict covering two or more parties to a lawsuit.

▸ **legally inconsistent verdict.** (1975) A verdict in which the same element is found to exist and not to exist, as when a defendant is acquitted of one offense and convicted of another, even though the offenses arise from the same set of facts and an element of the second offense requires proof that the first offense has been committed. — Also termed *legal inconsistency.* Cf. *repugnant verdict.*

▸ **majority verdict.** (1858) A verdict agreed to by all but one or two jury members. • In some jurisdictions, a civil verdict supported by 10 of 12 jurors is acceptable.

▸ **not-guilty verdict. 1.** ACQUITTAL (1). **2.** NOT GUILTY (2).

▸ **partial verdict.** (1829) A jury verdict rendered on some but not all counts or issues, esp. as a result of a deadlock among the jurors.

▸ **perverse verdict.** (1870) A jury verdict so contrary to the evidence that it justifies the granting of a new trial.

▸ **privy verdict** (**priv**-ee). (17c) *Hist.* A verdict given after the judge has left or adjourned the court, and the jury, having agreed, obtains leave to give its verdict privately to the judge out of court so that the jurors can be delivered from their confinement. • Such a verdict was of no force unless afterward affirmed in open court. This practice has been superseded by that of rendering a sealed verdict. See *sealed verdict.*

▸ **public verdict.** (17c) A verdict delivered by the jury in open court.

▸ **rout verdict.** *Slang.* A jury's guilty verdict reached in a surprisingly short time, esp. if the deliberations lasted less time than the defense counsel's closing arguments.

▸ **quotient verdict.** (1867) An improper damage verdict that a jury arrives at by totaling what each juror would award and dividing by the number of jurors.

▸ **repugnant verdict.** (1883) A verdict that contradicts itself by containing jury findings that are irreconcilable or incompatible. • In *U.S. v. Powell*, 469 U.S. 57 (1984), the Court explained why a defendant cannot attack a conviction on one count because it is inconsistent with an acquittal on another count. It is incorrect to assume that the acquittal was proper. Inconsistency may be a product of the jury's leniency or of a mistake. To prove a mistake, a litigant would have to speculate about or inquire into the jury's deliberations. Appellate review for sufficiency of the evidence is adequate protection against jury irrationality or error. Sometimes the inconsistency occurs in a single verdict (*repugnant verdict*), and sometimes it occurs in two separate verdicts (*repugnant verdicts*). Both terms are used mainly in New York. Cf. *legally inconsistent verdict.*

▸ **responsive verdict.** (1880) *Civil law.* A verdict that properly answers the indictment with specific findings prescribed by statute, the possible findings being guilty, not guilty, and guilty of a lesser included offense.

▸ **sealed verdict.** (18c) A verdict reduced to writing and enclosed in a sealed envelope for delivery to the judge, usu. so that after reaching an agreement, the jury will not be detained any further until the court's next session.

> "The purpose of agreeing to a sealed verdict is to permit the judge and counsel to leave the court room, and also to permit the jury to separate upon agreeing to a verdict and attend to their business and home affairs until court re-convenes. All the jurors should be present in open court when the verdict is read or received, unless counsel agrees to waive this formality." Rolla R. Longenecker, *Some Hints on the Trial of a Lawsuit* § 422, at 241 (1927).

▸ **special verdict.** (17c) A verdict in which the jury makes findings only on factual issues submitted to them by the judge, who then decides the legal effect of the verdict. *See* Fed. R. Civ. P. 49. Cf. *general verdict.*

▸ **split verdict.** (1886) **1.** A verdict in which one party prevails on some claims, while the other party prevails on others. **2.** *Criminal law.* A verdict finding a defendant guilty on one charge but not guilty on another. **3.** *Criminal law.* A verdict of guilty for one defendant and of not guilty for a codefendant.

▸ **true verdict.** (16c) A verdict that is reached voluntarily — even if one or more jurors freely compromise their views — and not as a result of an arbitrary rule or order, whether imposed by the jurors themselves, the court, or a court officer.

▸ **verdict by lot.** See *chance verdict.*

▸ **verdict contrary to law.** (18c) A verdict that the law does not authorize a jury to render because the conclusion drawn is not justified by the evidence. — Also termed *wrong verdict.* Cf. JURY NULLIFICATION.

▸ **verdict of guilt.** See *guilty verdict.*

▸ **verdict subject to opinion of court.** (1820) A verdict that is subject to the court's determination of a legal issue reserved to the court upon the trial, so that judgment is ultimately entered depending on the court's ruling on a point of law.

▸ **wrong verdict.** See *verdict contrary to law.*

2. Loosely, in a nonjury trial, a judge's resolution of the issues of a case. **3.** *English law.* A coroner's determination about the cause of death, sometimes with the help of a jury. • The term *verdict* was originally used in reference to the official finding of a coroner's jury after an inquest; today it typically survives in contexts not involving a jury.

▸ **coroner's verdict.** (17c) A coroner's usu. written determination of the cause of death of someone whose dead body is found within the coroner's jurisdiction, the most usual categories being natural causes, accident, homicide, suicide, and undetermined causes.

▸ **narrative verdict.** A coroner's verdict setting forth a concise account of what led up to the death, together with the event of death itself, without attributing the cause to any particular person.

▸ **open verdict.** (18c) A verdict of a coroner's jury finding that the subject "came to his death by means to the jury unknown" or "came to his death at the hands of a person or persons to the jury unknown." • This verdict leaves open either the question whether any crime was committed or the identity of the criminal.

verdict sheet. (1945) A roster of all jury questions to be filled out by the presiding juror as the jury completes its deliberations.

veredicto. See NON OBSTANTE VEREDICTO.

veredictum (ver-ə-**dik**-təm), *n.* (17c) *Hist.* A verdict; a declaration of the truth of a matter in issue, submitted to a jury for trial.

verge (vərj), *n.* (15c) *Hist.* **1.** The area within 12 miles of the place where the king held his court and within which the king's peace was enforced. • This area was commonly referred to as being *in the verge.* The verge got its name from the staff (called a "verge") that the marshal bore. **2.** The compass of the royal court, within which the lord steward and marshal of the king's household had special jurisdiction. — Also termed (in senses 1 & 2) *Court of Verge.* **3.** The neighborhood of Whitehall, the section of London in which British government offices have traditionally been located. **4.** An uncertain quantity of land from 15 to 30 acres. **5.** A stick or rod by which a person, after holding the stick and swearing fealty, is admitted as a tenant to a copyhold estate. — Also spelled *virge.* For *tenant by the verge*, see COPYHOLDER.

vergens ad inopiam (vər-jenz ad in-**oh**-pee-əm), *adj.* [Latin "verging on poverty"] (18c) *Civil law.* Tending to become insolvent.

> "When a debtor is clearly *vergens ad inopiam*, a creditor may legally resort to certain measures, for the purpose of protecting his interests, which would not otherwise be competent to him. Thus if the debtor be bound under a bill, the creditor may, in consideration of his debtor's circumstances, obtain a precept of arrestment on the bill before it becomes due, on which he may arrest any funds due to his debtor. As this proceeding is only allowed, however, as a protective measure . . . he cannot . . . render the arrested funds available to himself until the bill falls due . . . . The fact of the debtor's being *vergens ad inopiam* will be inferred from different circumstances in different cases, and the proof of that fact will also, necessarily, be varied." John Trayner, *Trayner's Latin Maxims* 627 (4th ed. 1894).

verger, *n.* (15c) Someone who carries a verge (a rod) as an emblem of office; esp., an attendant on a bishop or justice. — Also spelled *virger.*

veridical (və-**rid**-ə-kəl). See VERACIOUS.

verification, *n.* (16c) **1.** A formal declaration made in the presence of an authorized officer, such as a notary public, or (in some jurisdictions) under oath but not in the presence of such an officer, whereby one swears to the truth of the statements in the document. • Traditionally, a verification is used as a conclusion for all pleadings that are required to be sworn. Cf. ACKNOWLEDGMENT (4). — Also termed *affidavit of verification.* **2.** An oath or affirmation that an authorized officer administers to an affiant or deponent. **3.** Loosely, ACKNOWLEDGMENT (5). **4.** See *certified copy* under COPY (1). **5.** CERTIFICATE OF AUTHORITY (1). **6.** Any act of notarizing. Cf. JURAT (1). — **verify,** *vb.* — **verifier,** *n.*

verified copy. See *certified copy* under COPY (1).

verified *non est factum*. See NON EST FACTUM.

verified plea. See PLEA.

verify, *vb.* (14c) **1.** To prove to be true; to confirm or establish the truth or truthfulness of; to authenticate. **2.** To confirm or substantiate by oath or affidavit; to swear to the truth of.

verily, *adv.* (14c) *Archaic.* Truly; in fact; certainly.

veritas (**ver**-i-tas *or* -tahs), *n.* [Latin] **1.** Truth. **2.** (*cap.*) An international institution of maritime underwriters for the survey and rating of vessels. • Founded in Belgium in 1828, it moved to Paris in 1832 and has long been represented all over the world. — Also termed *Bureau Veritas.*

veritas convicii (**ver**-i-tas kən-**vish**-ee-ɪ). [Law Latin] (18c) *Hist.* The truth of the accusation. • The phrase appeared in reference to a defense in a defamation action.

verity (**ver**-ə-tee). (14c) **1.** Truth; truthfulness; conformity to fact. **2.** An important principle or fact that is enduringly true.

vermenging (vər-**meng**-ing), *n.* [Dutch "mingling"] The extinction of a debt when the debtor's and the creditor's interests merge, as in a corporate merger.

verna (**vər**-nə). [Latin] *Hist.* A slave born in the slaveholder's house. Pl. **vernae.**

versans in illicito (**vər**-sanz in i-**lis**-i-toh). [Latin] *Hist.* Engaged in some unlawful occupation.

versari (vər-**sair**-ɪ), *vb.* [Latin] **1.** To be employed. **2.** To be conversant.

versari in re illicita (vər-**sair**-ɪ in ree i-**lis**-ə-tə). [Latin] To be engaged in an unlawful activity (as a bar to a claim for damages).

versus, *prep.* (15c) Against. — Abbr. v.; vs.

vert (vərt). [Old French "green"] (15c) *Hist.* **1.** Anything that grows and bears green leaves within a forest. **2.** A power, given by royal grant, to cut green wood in a forest.

vertical arrangement. See *vertical restraint* under RESTRAINT OF TRADE.

vertical coffin. (2004) *Slang.* Any doorway that a police officer is about to enter in searching premises.

vertical competition. See COMPETITION.

vertical equality. In per capita distribution of an estate, parity of distribution among children's families. See PER CAPITA. Cf. HORIZONTAL EQUALITY.

vertical integration. See INTEGRATION (5).

vertical merger. See MERGER (8).

vertical nonprivity. See NONPRIVITY.

vertical patrol. See VERTICAL SWEEP.

vertical price-fixing. See PRICE-FIXING.

vertical privity. See PRIVITY (1).

vertical prosecution. (1980) *Criminal law.* A method of handling assignments in a prosecutor's office whereby one high-level prosecutor is responsible for the prosecution from the initial stages through trial, as opposed to having different prosecutors at different stages.

vertical representation. (1975) *Criminal law.* The handling of a criminal defendant's case, esp. in a public defender's office, at all stages, from arraignment through trial — and perhaps through appeals.

vertical restraint. See RESTRAINT OF TRADE.

vertical stare decisis. See STARE DECISIS.

vertical sweep. (1994) *Jargon.* A systematic search of a building beginning on the ground floor and then extending to the upper and lower floors. — Also termed *vertical patrol.*

vertical trust. (1920) *Antitrust.* A combination that gathers together under a single ownership a number of businesses or plants engaged in successive stages of production or marketing.

vertical union. See *industrial union* under UNION.

verus (**veer**-əs), *adj.* [Latin] True; truthful; genuine; actual.

very heavy work. See WORK (1).

VESA. *abbr.* VIDEO ELECTRONICS STANDARDS ASSOCIATION.

vessel. (13c) A ship, brig, sloop, or other craft used — or capable of being used — to navigate on water. • To qualify as a vessel under the Jones Act, the structure's purpose must to some reasonable degree be to transport passengers, cargo, or equipment from place to place across navigable waters.

> "The term *vessel* is defined in 1 U.S.C. § 3 as follows: 'The word "vessel" includes every description of watercraft or other artificial contrivance used, or capable of being used, as a means of transportation on water.' This definition has not been very influential in admiralty and maritime cases. Litigants contending for vessel status often invoke its remarkable breadth. Those opposing vessel status typically respond, 'But the present context indicates otherwise.' When courts mention the definition favorably, it usually seems to be a makeweight argument." David W. Robertson, Steven F. Friedell & Michael F. Sturley, *Admiralty and Maritime Law in the United States* 59 (2001).

▸ **foreign-flag vessel.** (1941) A vessel registered in a nation other than the United States, regardless of the owner's nationality.

▸ **foreign vessel.** (17c) A vessel owned by residents of, or sailing under the flag of, a foreign country.

▸ **government vessel.** (1819) **1.** A vessel owned and operated directly by the United States government. **2.** A vessel operated for the United States government by an agent or contractor. • The vessel may be owned by the government or by a private party. — Also termed *United States flag vessel.*

▸ **Jones Act vessel.** (1967) A vessel whose crew members can qualify as seamen under the Jones Act; esp., a craft designed or used for transporting cargo or people on navigable waters, or that was being used for navigation at the time of a worker's injury. See JONES ACT.

▸ **privately owned U.S. flag commercial vessel.** (1958) **1.** A vessel registered and operated under United States law, used for commercial trade of the United States, and owned by a private party who is an American citizen. **2.** A government-owned vessel under bareboat charter to United States citizens who operate it for commercial trade. 48 CFR § 47.501. — Also termed *United States flag vessel.*

▸ **public vessel.** (18c) A vessel owned and used by a country or government for its public service, whether in its navy, its revenue service, or otherwise. See PUBLIC VESSELS ACT.

▸ **seagoing vessel.** (1844) A vessel that — considering its design, function, purpose, and capabilities — is normally expected both to carry passengers for hire and to engage in substantial operations beyond the boundary line (set by the Coast Guard) dividing inland waters from the high seas. • Typically excluded from the definition are pleasure yachts, tugs and towboats, fishing boats, and other vessels that do not carry passengers for hire.

▸ **seaworthy vessel.** (1803) A vessel that can withstand the ordinary stress of the wind, waves, and other weather that seagoing vessels might ordinarily be expected to encounter. • Under federal maritime law, a vessel's owner has the duty to provide a crew with a seaworthy vessel. In some legal contexts, the question whether a vessel is seaworthy includes the question whether it is fit to carry an intended cargo properly. See SEAWORTHY.

▸ **United States flag vessel. 1.** See *government vessel.* **2.** See *privately owned U.S. flag commercial vessel.*

vest, *vb.* (15c) **1.** To confer ownership (of property) on a person. **2.** To invest (a person) with the full title to property. **3.** To give (a person) an immediate, fixed right of present or future enjoyment. **4.** *Hist.* To put (a person) into possession of land by the ceremony of investiture. — **vesting,** *n.*

vested, *adj.* (18c) Having become a completed, consummated right for present or future enjoyment; not contingent; unconditional; absolute <a vested interest in the estate>.

> "[U]nfortunately, the word 'vested' is used in two senses. Firstly, an interest may be vested *in possession,* when there is a right to present enjoyment, e.g. when I own and occupy Blackacre. But an interest may be vested, even where it does not carry a right to immediate possession, if it does confer a fixed right of taking possession in the future." George Whitecross Paton, *A Textbook of Jurisprudence* 305 (G.W. Paton & David P. Derham eds., 4th ed. 1972).

> "A future interest is *vested* if it meets two requirements: first, that there be no *condition precedent* to the interest's becoming a present estate other than the *natural expiration* of those estates that are prior to it in possession; and second, that it be *theoretically* possible to identify who would get the right to possession if the interest should become a present estate *at any time.*" Thomas F. Bergin & Paul G. Haskell, *Preface to Estates in Land and Future Interests* 66–67 (2d ed. 1984).

▸ **vested in interest.** (18c) Consummated in a way that will result in future possession and use. • Reversions, vested remainders, and any other future use or executory devise that does not depend on an uncertain period or event are all said to be vested in interest.

▸ **vested in possession.** (18c) Consummated in a way that has resulted in present enjoyment.

vested estate. See ESTATE (1).

vested gift. See GIFT.

vested interest. See INTEREST (2).

vested legacy. See LEGACY (1).

vested ownership. See OWNERSHIP.

vested pension. See PENSION.

vested remainder. See REMAINDER.

vested remainder subject to complete defeasement. See *vested remainder subject to total divestment* under REMAINDER.

vested remainder subject to total divestment. See REMAINDER.

vested right. See RIGHT.

vested-rights doctrine. (1924) *Constitutional law.* The rule that the legislature cannot take away a right that has been vested by a social compact or by a court's judgment; esp., the principle that it is beyond the province of Congress to reopen a final judgment issued by an Article III court. — Also termed *doctrine of vested rights.*

> "The doctrine of vested rights most often found expression in the early national era by its infusion into the obligation of contracts clause in Article I, Section 10, of the Constitution. It was in this connection that the doctrine achieved its most positive and specific limitations upon legislative authority. *Vanhorne's Lessee v. Dorrance* (1795), wherein Justice Paterson condemned a Pennsylvania statute as a violation of the 'primary object of the social compact,' the protection of property, arose under the contract clause. It will be recalled that the doctrine was again identified with the contract clause in *Fletcher v Peck* (1810) and in *Dartmouth College v. Woodward* (1819). And again, in *Terrett v. Taylor* (1815), a case involving Virginia's attempt to take title to certain lands of the disestablished Episcopal Church, Justice Story discoursed at length upon the doctrine of vested rights, which he identified with the contract clause in imposing limitation upon the state's legislative authority. In brief, in the early nineteenth century the contract clause played somewhat the same role in the embodiment of the doctrine of vested rights as the due process clause was to play after 1890." Alfred H. Kelly & Winfred A. Harbison, *The American Constitution* 471 (5th ed. 1976).

vestigial words (ve-**stij**-ee-əl). (1933) Statutory words and phrases that, through a succession of amendments, have been made useless or meaningless. • Courts do not allow vestigial words to defeat the fair meaning of a statute.

vestigium (ve-**stij**-ee-əm). (17c) *Archaic.* A vestige, mark, or sign; a trace, track, or impression left by a person or a physical object.

vesting, remote. See REMOTE VESTING.

vesting order. (1873) A court order passing legal title in lieu of a legal conveyance.

vestita manus (ves-**tɪ**-tə **may**-nəs), *n.* [Latin "vested hand"] (1895) *Hist.* The right hand used in the ceremony of investiture.

vestita viro (ves-**tɪ**-tə **vɪ**-roh). [Law Latin] *Hist.* Clothed with a husband.

> "A married woman is said to be *vestita viro,* and so long as this coverture exists her person cannot be attached on civil diligence, unless that diligence proceeds upon a decree *ad factum praestandum,* for the performance of some act which she is bound to perform, and which cannot be validly performed except by herself, *ex. gr.,* to enter the heir of

her vassal, to produce or exhibit as a haver writings in her own custody, &c." John Trayner, *Trayner's Latin Maxims* 628 (4th ed. 1894).

vestitive fact (**ves**-tə-tiv). See *dispositive fact* (1) under FACT.

vestitus et mundus muliebris (ves-**tɪ**-təs et **mən**-dəs myoo-lee-**ee**-bris). [Latin] *Hist.* A woman's wearing of apparel and ornaments.

vestry (**ves**-tree). (14c) *Eccles. law.* **1.** The place in a church where the priest's robes are kept. — Also termed *sacristy.* **2.** An assembly of the minister, church wardens, and parishioners to conduct church business.

vestry clerk. (18c) *Eccles. law.* An officer appointed to attend a vestry and to take minutes of the proceedings.

vesture (**ves**-chər). (15c) *Hist.* **1.** The corn, grass, underwood, stubble, or other growth — apart from trees — that covers the land. — Also termed *vestura* (ves-**t[y]oor**-ə); *vestura terrae* (**ter**-ee); *vesture of land.* **2.** SEISIN; INVESTITURE.

veteran. (16c) Someone who has been honorably discharged from military service.

Veterans Administration. See DEPARTMENT OF VETERANS AFFAIRS.

Veterans Affairs, Department of. See DEPARTMENT OF VETERANS AFFAIRS.

Veterans Appeals, U.S. Court of. See UNITED STATES COURT OF APPEALS FOR VETERANS CLAIMS.

Veterans Benefits Administration. A unit in the U.S. Department of Veterans Affairs responsible for advising and assisting veterans and their families who apply for veterans' benefits. — Abbr. VBA.

Veterans' Employment and Training Service. A unit in the U.S. Department of Labor responsible for administering various programs relating to veterans' employment and training. • The agency protects the reemployment rights of veterans and the employment and retention rights of members of the Reserve and National Guard. Its regional administrators work with state employment-security agencies and with recipients of grants under the Job Training Partnership Act to ensure that veterans are provided the priority services required by law. — Abbr. VETS.

Veterans Health Administration. A unit in the U.S. Department of Veterans Affairs responsible for providing hospital, nursing-home, and medical care to eligible veterans of military service. — Abbr. VHA.

veteran's loan. See LOAN.

vetera statuta (**vet**-ə-rə sta-**t[y]oo**-tə), *n. pl.* [Law Latin "ancient statutes"] (17c) The statutes from Magna Carta (1215) to the end of Edward II's reign (1327). — Also termed *antiqua statuta* (an-**tɪ**-kwə stə-**t[y]oo**-tə). Cf. NOVA STATUTA.

vetitive (**vet**-ə-tiv), *adj.* (1853) Of, relating to, or having the power to veto.

vetitum namium (**vet**-ə-təm **nay**-mee-əm), *n.* [Law Latin "a prohibited taking"] *Hist.* See NAMIUM VETITUM.

veto (**vee**-toh), *n.* [Latin "I forbid"] (17c) **1.** A power of one governmental branch to prohibit an action by another branch; esp., a chief executive's refusal to sign into law a bill passed by the legislature. **2.** VETO MESSAGE. Pl. **vetoes.** — **veto,** *vb.*

▸ **absolute veto.** (1852) An unrestricted veto that is not subject to being overridden.

▸ **item veto.** See *line-item veto.*

▸ **legislative veto.** (1850) *Hist.* A veto allowing Congress to block a federal executive or agency action taken under congressionally delegated authority. • The Supreme Court held the legislative veto unconstitutional in *INS v. Chadha*, 462 U.S. 919, 103 S.Ct. 2764 (1983). See DELEGATION DOCTRINE.

▸ ***liberum veto*** (**lib**-ər-əm). (18c) *Hist.* Formerly in Poland, the right of any single member of the diet to invalidate a measure.

▸ **limited veto.** See *qualified veto.*

▸ **line-item veto.** (1858) The executive's power to veto some provisions in a legislative bill without affecting other provisions. • The U.S. Supreme Court declared the presidential line-item veto unconstitutional in 1998. *See Clinton v. City of New York*, 524 U.S. 417, 118 S.Ct. 2091 (1998). — Also termed *item veto.*

▸ **negative veto.** See *qualified veto.*

▸ **overridden veto.** (1971) A veto that the legislature has superseded by again passing the vetoed act, usu. by a supermajority of legislators. • In the federal government, a bill vetoed by the President must receive a two-thirds majority in Congress to override the veto and enact the measure into law.

▸ **pocket veto.** (1842) A veto resulting from the President's failure to sign a bill passed within the last ten days of the congressional session.

▸ **qualified veto.** (1853) A veto that is conclusive unless overridden by an extraordinary majority of the legislature. • This is the type of veto power that the President of the United States has. — Also termed *limited veto; negative veto.*

▸ **suspensory veto** (sə-**spen**-sə-ree). (1911) A veto that suspends a law until the legislature reconsiders it and then allows the law to take effect if repassed by an ordinary majority. — Also termed *suspensive veto.*

veto clause. 1. (*cap.*) A constitutional provision granting the executive power to reject a bill and return it to the legislature within a specified period. • When the legislature adjourns before the period expires and a bill is not signed into law, the clause is sometimes termed a *pocket-veto clause.* See *pocket veto* under VETO.

▸ **item-veto clause.** A clause in a constitution empowering the executive to veto select portions of a statute while leaving the rest intact.

2. A clause in any authoritative document granting a person or body the power to reject the actions or decisions of another person or body. **3.** In a mall's lease with an anchor tenant, a clause giving the tenant the right to disallow or restrict other potential tenants. • These clauses usu. violate antitrust laws.

vetoer, *n.* (1888) Someone who vetoes. — Also termed *vetoist.*

veto message. (1830) A statement communicating the reasons for the executive's refusing to sign into law a bill passed by the legislature. — Sometimes shortened to *veto.*

veto power. (1883) An executive's conditional power to prevent a bill that has passed the legislature from becoming law.

veto-proof majority. See MAJORITY.

VETS. *abbr.* VETERANS' EMPLOYMENT AND TRAINING SERVICE.

vetus jus (**vee**-təs **jəs**). [Latin "old law"] *Roman & civil law.* **1.** The law of the Twelve Tables. See TWELVE TABLES. **2.** Long-established or ancient law. **3.** A law in force before the passage of a later law.

vex, *vb.* (15c) **1.** To harass, disquiet, or annoy. **2.** To cause physical or emotional distress. — **vexatious,** *adj.* — **vexation,** *n.*

vexari (vek-**sair**-ɪ), *vb.* [Latin] To be harassed, vexed, or annoyed.

vexata quaestio (vek-**say**-tə **kwes**-chee-oh). See VEXED QUESTION.

vexation. (15c) The damage that results from trickery or malice.

vexatious (vek-**say**-shəs), *adj.* (16c) (Of conduct) without reasonable or probable cause or excuse; harassing; annoying.

vexatious delay. An insurance company's unjustifiable refusal to satisfy an insurance claim, esp. based on a mere suspicion but no hard facts that the claim is ill-founded. — Also termed *vexatious refusal to pay*; *refusal to pay.*

vexatious lawsuit. See VEXATIOUS SUIT.

vexatious litigant. See LITIGANT.

vexatious objection. See OBJECTION (1).

vexatious proceeding. See VEXATIOUS SUIT.

vexatious refusal to pay. See VEXATIOUS DELAY.

vexatious suit. (17c) A lawsuit instituted maliciously and without good grounds, meant to create trouble and expense for the party being sued. — Also termed *vexatious lawsuit*; *vexatious litigation*; *vexatious proceeding.* Cf. MALICIOUS PROSECUTION.

vexed question. (17c) **1.** A question often argued about but seemingly never settled. **2.** A question or point that has been decided differently by different tribunals and has therefore been left in doubt. — Also termed *vexata quaestio* (vek-**say**-tə **kwes**-tee-oh); *vexata questio.*

VFO. *abbr.* Violent felony offense. • On the redundancy of the phrase *felony offense*, see FELONY OFFENSE.

v.g. *abbr.* VERBI GRATIA.

VHA. *abbr.* VETERANS HEALTH ADMINISTRATION.

via (**vɪ**-ə), *n.* [Latin "way, road"] (17c) *Roman & civil law.* **1.** A road, way, or right-of-way.

▸ ***via publica*** (**vɪ**-ə **pəb**-li-kə). [Latin] (17c) *Roman & civil law.* A public way or road. • The land itself belongs to the public.

2. *Roman law.* A type of rural servitude that gave the holder the right to walk, ride, or drive over another's land; SERVITUS VIAE. • It was broader than and included the *servitus itineris* and the *servitus actus*; that is, *via* encompassed both *iter* (a footpath) and *actus* (a driveway). **3.** *Civil law.* The way in which legal procedures are followed.

▸ ***via executiva*** (**vɪ**-ə eg-zek-yə-**tɪ**-və). (1851) *Civil law.* Executory process by which the debtor's property is seized, without previous citation, for some reason specified by law, usu. because of an act or title amounting to a confession of judgment.

▸ ***via juris*** (**vɪ**-ə **joor**-is). [Latin] *Hist.* By means of law; by means of legal process.

▸ ***via ordinaria*** (**vɪ**-ə or-di-**nair**-ee-ə). (17c) *Civil law.* The ordinary way or process by which a citation is served and all the usual forms of law are followed.

via actionis (**vɪ**-ə ak-shee-**oh**-nis). [Latin] *Hist.* By way of an action.

viable (**vɪ**-ə-bəl), *adj.* (1832) **1.** Capable of living, esp. outside the womb <a viable fetus>. **2.** Capable of independent existence or standing <a viable lawsuit>. **3.** Capable of succeeding <a viable option>. — **viability** (vɪ-ə-**bil**-ə-tee), *n.*

viae servitus (**vɪ**-ee **sər**-və-təs). **1.** See SERVITUS VIAE. **2.** See VIA (2).

via executiva. See VIA (3).

via facti (**vɪ**-ə **fak**-tɪ), *adv.* [Law Latin "by way of deed"] By force; in a forcible way.

viagère rente. See RENTE VIAGÈRE.

via juris. See VIA (3).

via media (**vee**-ə **meed**-ee-ə), *n.* A middle way; a course of action intermediate between two extremes.

via ordinaria. See VIA (3).

via publica. See VIA (1).

via regia (**vɪ**-ə **ree**-jee-ə). [Latin "the king's highway"] (16c) *Hist.* The highway or common road — called the "king's highway" because the king authorized and protected it.

viatical settlement. See SETTLEMENT (3).

viatication (vɪ-at-ə-**kay**-shən). [fr. Latin *viaticus* "relating to a road or journey"] (1991) The purchase of a terminally or chronically ill policyholder's life insurance in exchange for a lump-sum payment equal to a percentage of the policy's full value. See *viatical settlement* under SETTLEMENT (3).

viator (vɪ-**ay**-tər). (18c) **1.** APPARITOR (1). **2.** A terminally or chronically ill life-insurance policyholder who sells the policy to a third party in return for a lump-sum payment equal to a percentage of the policy's face value.

viatorial privilege. See PRIVILEGE (1).

vi aut clam (**vɪ** awt **klam**), *adv.* [Latin] *Roman law.* By force or by stealth.

vi aut metu (vɪ awt **mee**-t[y]oo), *adv.* [Latin] *Hist.* By force or fear.

vicar. (14c) **1.** Someone who performs the functions of another; a substitute. **2.** The incumbent of an ecclesiastical benefice. Cf. RECTOR.

vicarage (**vik**-ər-ij). (15c) **1.** The benefice of a vicar. **2.** The house or household of a vicar. **3.** VICARSHIP.

vicar general. (15c) An ecclesiastical officer who helps the bishop or archbishop in the discharge of his office.

vicarial tithe (vɪ-**kair**-ee-əl). See TITHE.

vicarious (vɪ-**kair**-ee-əs), *adj.* (17c) Performed or suffered by one person as substitute for another; indirect; surrogate.

vicarious-admission doctrine. (1952) The rule that the statements of coconspirators are admissible as evidence against a conspirator.

vicarious disqualification. See DISQUALIFICATION (1).

vicarious exhaustion of remedies. See EXHAUSTION OF REMEDIES.

vicarious infringement. See INFRINGEMENT.

vicarious liability. See LIABILITY.

vicarious performance. See PERFORMANCE (1).

vicarious reduction to practice. See REDUCTION TO PRACTICE.

vicarius apostolicus (vɪ-**kair**-ee-əs ap-əs-**tahl**-ə-kəs), *n.* [Latin "apostolic vicar"] (17c) *Eccles. law.* An officer through whom the Pope exercises authority in remote regions. • This officer is sometimes sent with episcopal functions into provinces where there is no bishop resident or where there has long been a vacancy in the see.

vicarship. (16c) The office, function, or duty of a vicar. — Also termed *vicarage.*

vice (vɪs), *n.* (14c) **1.** A moral failing; an ethical fault. **2.** Wickedness; corruption. **3.** Broadly, any defect or failing.

▸ **inherent vice.** *Insurance.* A property or good's defect, hidden or obvious, that causes or contributes to damage suffered by the property or good.

vice (vɪ-see *or* vɪ-sə), *prep.* (18c) In the place of; in the stead of. • As a prefix, *vice-* (vɪs) denotes one who takes the place of.

vice-admiral. (17c) *Hist.* A civil officer exercising admiralty jurisdiction within a specific locale.

vice-admiralty. (17c) **1.** The office of a vice-admiral. **2.** The district over which a vice-admiral has jurisdiction.

vice-admiralty court. (18c) *Hist.* A tribunal established in British possessions beyond the seas, with jurisdiction over maritime cases, including those related to prize. • The governor of the colony, in the capacity of "vice-admiral," exercised judicial authority in this court.

vice-chamberlain. (16c) *Hist.* A great officer under the lord chamberlain. • In the lord chamberlain's absence, the vice-chamberlain would control and command the officers attached to the part of the royal household called the "chamber."

vice-chancellor. (1813) **1.** A judge appointed to act for the chancellor, esp. in a chancery court. **2.** The chief executive officer of a British university with responsibilities for its organization and operations. **3.** An academic official in an American university with responsibilities for a particular division or sector. — Abbr. VC.

vice-comes (vɪ-sə-**koh**-meez), *n.* [Law Latin] (16c) *Hist.* **1.** VISCOUNT. **2.** SHERIFF. — Also spelled *vicecomes.*

vicecomes non misit breve. (17c) *Hist.* An entry in a continued case's record noting that a sheriff has not yet returned a writ. — Also written *vice comes non misit breve*; *vice-comes non misit breve.*

vicecomital (vɪ-sə-**kom**-ə-təl). See VICONTIEL.

vice-comitissa (vɪ-sə-kom-ə-**tis**-ə). See VISCOUNTESS.

vice-commercial agent. See AGENT.

vice-consul. (17c) A consular officer subordinate to a consul; esp., one who is substituted temporarily to fill the place of a consul who is absent or has been relieved from duty.

▸ **career vice-consul.** (2007) A vice-consul who is a member of the Foreign Service. — Also termed *vice-consul of career.*

▸ **noncareer vice-consul.** (1930) A vice-consul who is not a member of the Foreign Service and who is appointed without examination.

vice crime. See CRIME.

vice-dominus episcopi (vɪ-sə-**dom**-ə-nəs ə-**pis**-kə-pɪ). **1.** A vicar general. **2.** A commissary of a bishop.

vicegerent (vɪs-**jeer**-ənt). (16c) A deputy; lieutenant.

vice-governor, *n.* (16c) A deputy or lieutenant governor.

vice-judex (vɪs-**joo**-deks). *Hist.* A deputy judge.

vice-marshal. (17c) An officer appointed to assist the earl marshal. See EARL MARSHAL OF ENGLAND.

vicem fructuum obtinere (vɪ-sem **frək**-choo-əm ob-ti-**nee**-ree). [Latin] *Hist.* To take the place of fruits. • The phrase typically referred to interest as the produce of money.

vice offense. See *vice crime* under CRIME.

vice president, *n.* (16c) **1.** An officer selected in advance to fill the presidency if the president dies, resigns, is removed from office, or cannot or will not serve. • The Vice President of the United States, who is elected at the same time as the President, serves as presiding officer of the Senate but may cast a vote only to break a tie. On the death, incapacity, resignation, or removal of the President, the Vice President succeeds to the presidency. **2.** A corporate officer of mid-level to high rank, usu. having charge of a department. — Abbr. V.P.; VP. — Also written *vice-president.* — **vice presidency,** *n.* — **vice-presidential,** *adj.*

vice principal. See FELLOW-SERVANT RULE.

viceregent, *n.* (16c) **1.** A deputy regent; esp., one who acts in the place of a ruler, governor, or sovereign. **2.** More broadly, an officer deputed by a superior or by proper authority to exercise the powers of the higher authority; one with delegated power.

viceroy, *n.* (16c) The governor of a kingdom or colony, who rules as the deputy of a monarch. — **viceroyal, viceregal,** *adj.*

vice-sheriff. See *deputy sheriff* under SHERIFF (1).

vice-treasurer, *n.* (16c) A deputy or assistant treasurer.

vice versa, *adj.* (17c) Of an assertion, the state of its reciprocal reverse also being valid <Kates distrusts Weller and vice versa>.

vicinage (vis-ə-nij). [Law French "neighborhood"] (14c) **1.** Vicinity; proximity. **2.** The place where a crime is committed or a trial is held; the place from which jurors are to be drawn for trial; esp., the locale from which the accused is entitled to have jurors selected. — Also termed *vicinetum* (vis-ə-**nee**-təm).

> "Whereas venue refers to the locality in which charges will be brought and adjudicated, vicinage refers to the locality from which jurors will be drawn. . . . The vicinage concept requires that the jurors be selected from a geographical

district that includes the locality of the commission of the crime, and it traditionally also mandates that such district not extend too far beyond the general vicinity of that locality." Wayne R. LaFave & Jerold H. Israel, *Criminal Procedure* § 16.1, at 738-39 (2d ed. 1992).

3. A right of common that neighboring tenants have in a barony or fee.

vicious animal. See ANIMAL.

vicious intromission. See *vitious intromission* under INTROMISSION (2).

vicious propensity. (1835) An animal's tendency to endanger the safety of persons or property. See *vicious animal* under ANIMAL.

vicontiel (vi-**kon**-tee-əl), *adj.* (17c) **1.** Of, relating to, or involving a viscount. **2.** Of, relating to, or involving a sheriff. — Also spelled *vicountiel.* — Also termed *vice-comital.*

vicontiel rent. (17c) *Hist.* Rent that a viscount or sheriff pays for the use of a royal farm.

vicontiels (vi-**kon**-tee-əlz). (16c) *Hist.* **1.** Money payable by a viscount or sheriff to the Crown. **2.** Vicontiel rents.

vicontiel writ. See WRIT.

victim, *n.* (15c) A person harmed by a crime, tort, or other wrong. — **victimize,** *vb.* — **victimization,** *n.*

victim allocution. (1979) A crime victim's address to the court before sentencing, usu. urging a harsher punishment.

victim compensation. Funds paid by a government to a crime victim to ameliorate some of the financial effects of the crime.

victimhood. (1862) The state of suffering that someone feels as a result of having been wronged.

victim-impact panel. (1993) A panel consisting of victims of drunk drivers or their surviving family members who make presentations about the consequences of drunk driving — and make them directly to those convicted of DWI or DUI, who must listen to the panel as a condition of probation or conditional release. — Abbr. VIP. — Also termed *VIP panel.*

victim-impact statement. (1980) A statement read into the record during sentencing to inform the judge or jury of the financial, physical, and psychological impact of the crime on the victim and the victim's family. — Abbr. VIS.

victimize, *vb.* (1830) **1.** To cheat or defraud (someone). **2.** To treat (someone) abusively or unfairly.

victimless offense. See *victimless crime* under CRIME.

victim-precipitated homicide. See HOMICIDE.

victim-related adjustment. (1988) An increase in punishment available under federal sentencing guidelines when the defendant knew or should have known that the victim bore a particular characteristic — e.g., the victim was unusually vulnerable (because of age or condition) — or was otherwise particularly susceptible to the criminal conduct. See USSG §§ 3A1.1, 1.2.

Victims of Child Abuse Laws. An organization of persons who claim to have been wrongly accused of sexually abusing children. — Abbr. VOCAL. Cf. FALSE MEMORY SYNDROME FOUNDATION.

victim's-shoes argument. An improper statement urging jurors to imagine themselves being a victim of the conduct at issue.

victualer (**vit**-əl-ər). (14c) *Hist.* **1.** A person authorized by law to keep a house of entertainment for the public; a publican. **2.** Someone who serves food or drink prepared for consumption on the premises. — Also spelled *victualler.*

victual rent (**vit**-[ə]l). (17c) *Scots law.* A rent paid in grain or its monetary equivalent.

victus (**vik**-təs). *Civil law.* Sustenance; support; a means of living.

vidame (vee-**dam**). [French] (16c) *Hist.* In French feudal law, an officer who represented the bishop. • Over time, these officers erected their offices into fiefs and became feudal nobles, such as the *vidame* of Chartres, Rheims, etc. They continued to take their titles from the seat of the bishop whom they represented, even though the lands held by virtue of their fiefs might be situated elsewhere.

vide (**vi**-dee *also* **vee**-day). [Latin] (16c) See. • This is a citation signal still seen in some texts, esp. in the abbreviated form *q.v.* (*quod vide* "which see"). *Vide ante* or *vide supra* refers to a previous passage in a text; *vide post* or *vide infra* refers to a later passage.

videlicet (vi-**del**-ə-set *or* -sit). [Latin] (15c) To wit; that is to say; namely; SCILICET. • The term is used primarily to point out, particularize, or make more specific what has been previously stated in general (or occas. obscure) language. One common function is to state the time, place, or manner when that is the essence of the matter at issue. — Abbr. *viz.* See VIZ.

Video Electronics Standards Association. A nonprofit organization established in 1989 to promote and develop industry-wide standards for computers to ensure interoperability, and to encourage innovation and market growth. — Abbr. VESA.

video piracy. See PIRACY (4).

Video Privacy Protection Act. A federal statute that bars video stores from disclosing to third parties the names of customers' rentals. 18 USCA § 2710. • The statute was passed in reaction to a newspaper's publication of the names of videos rented by Judge Robert Bork when he was an unsuccessful nominee to be a justice of the United States Supreme Court. — Abbr. VPPA.

video-surveillance warrant. See SEARCH WARRANT.

vidimus (**vid**-ə-məs), *n.* [Latin "we have seen"] (15c) **1.** An inspection of documents, etc. **2.** An abstract, syllabus, or summary. **3.** An attested copy of a document. **4.** INSPEXIMUS.

Vidi scivi et audivi (**vi**-di **si**-vi et aw-**di**-vi). *Hist.* I saw, knew, and heard. • This was formerly an essential part of the notary's docket attached to the end of an instrument of seisin, by which the notary claimed to have been personally present on the ground when seisin was given and thus to have known the facts to be true by having heard the words spoken and seen the acts done.

vidua regis (**vij**-oo-ə **ree**-jis), *n.* [Latin] (17c) **1.** The widow of the king. **2.** The widow of a tenant in capite. • In sense 2, she was so called because she was not allowed to marry a second time without the king's permission. She obtained her dower from the king, who was her patron and defender.

viduitatis professio (və-d[y]oo-ə-**tay**-tis prə-**fes[h]**-ee-oh), *n.* [Latin] (1854) *Hist.* A woman's solemn act of professing that she will live as a single, chaste woman.

viduity (vi-**d[y]oo**-ə-tee). (15c) *Archaic.* Widowhood.

vie (vee). [French] Life. • The term occurs in such Law French phrases as *cestui que vie* and *pur autre vie.*

Vienna rules. The principles of treaty interpretation set forth in the Vienna Convention on the Law of Treaties, signed at Vienna on May 23, 1969. • See http://legal.un.org/ilc/texts/instruments/english/conventions/9_1_1961.pdf.

> "No Claim is made that the Vienna rules resolve all problems of interpretation or lead directly to a necessarily correct result in every case. Nor are the rules an exclusive compilation of guidance on treaty interpretation, other skills and principles that are used to achieve a reasoned interpretation remaining admissible to the extent not in conflict with the Vienna rules. What is suggested here is that the Vienna rules, constituting a single framework for treaty interpretation, can now be identified as generally applicable and that those rules should be understood and used by all engaged in treaty interpretation. They are now an essential infrastructure, although using them in particular circumstances requires skills and techniques which go well beyond their brief prescriptions." Richard K. Gardiner, *Treaty Interpretation* 6 (2008).

vi et armis (**vɪ** et **ahr**-mis). [Latin] (17c) *Hist.* By or with force and arms. See *trespass vi et armis* under TRESPASS.

> "The words '*with force and arms,*' anciently '*vi et armis,*' were, by the common law, necessary in indictments for offences which amount to an actual disturbance of the peace, or consist, in any way, of acts of violence; but it seems to be the better opinion, that they were never necessary where the offence consisted of a cheat, or nonfeazance, or a mere consequential injury." 1 Joseph Chitty, *A Practical Treatise on the Criminal Law* 240 (2d ed. 1826).

> "*vi et armis* . . . was a necessary part of the allegation, in medieval pleading, that a trespass had been committed with force and therefore was a matter for the King's Court because it involved a breach of the peace. In England, the term survived as a formal requirement of pleading until 1852." Bryan A. Garner, *Garner's Dictionary of Legal Usage* 928 (3d ed. 2011).

view, *n.* (16c) **1.** The common-law right of prospect — that is, an outlook from the windows of one's house. **2.** An urban servitude that prohibits the obstruction of the outlook from a person's house. **3.** A jury's trip to inspect a place or thing relevant to the case it is considering; the act or proceeding by which a tribunal goes to observe an object that cannot be produced in court because it is immovable or inconvenient to remove. • The appropriate procedures are typically regulated by state statute. At common law, and today in many civil cases, the trial judge's presence is not required. The common practice has been for the jury to be escorted by "showers" who are commissioned for this purpose. Parties and counsel are generally permitted to attend, although this is a matter typically within the trial judge's discretion. Cf. VIEW OF AN INQUEST. **4.** In a real action, a defendant's observation of the thing at issue to ascertain its identity and other circumstances surrounding it. Cf. DEMAND OF VIEW.

viewer. (15c) A person, usu. one of several, appointed by a court to investigate certain matters or to examine a particular locality (such as the proposed site of a new road) and to report to the court.

view of an inquest. (1837) A jury's inspection of a place or property to which an inquiry or inquest refers. Cf. VIEW (3).

view of frankpledge. (16c) *Hist.* The twice-yearly gathering and inspection of every freeman within the district who was more than 12 years old to determine whether each one had taken the oath of allegiance and had found nine freeman pledges for his peaceable demeanor. See FRANKPLEDGE.

view ordinance. A local law adopted by some municipalities with desirable views of mountains, lakes, or oceans to protect a property owner's view from being obstructed by growing trees. • View ordinances rarely address structures that may block views.

viewpoint discrimination. See DISCRIMINATION (3).

viewpoint-neutral. See NEUTRAL.

vif-gage (veef-gayj *or* **vif-**). [Law French] See *vadium vivum* under VADIUM.

vigil. (13c) *Eccles. law.* The day before any solemn feast.

vigilance. (16c) Watchfulness; precaution; a proper degree of activity and promptness in pursuing one's rights, in guarding them from infraction, and in discovering opportunities for enforcing one's lawful claims and demands.

vigilant, *adj.* (15c) Watchful and cautious; on the alert; attentive to discover and avoid danger.

vigilante (vij-ə-**lan**-tee). (1856) Someone who seeks to avenge a crime by taking the law into his or her own hands.

vigilantism (vij-ə-**lan**-tiz-əm). (1937) The act of a citizen who takes the law into his or her own hands by apprehending and punishing suspected criminals.

viis et modis (**vɪ**-is et **moh**-dis). [Latin] *Eccles. law.* By all ways and means. • In ecclesiastical courts, service of a decree or citation *viis et modis* is equivalent to substituted service in temporal courts. It requires posting of a notice where a person is likely to be found. This type of service is contrasted with personal service.

vi laica amovenda. See DE VI LAICA AMOVENDA.

vill (vil). (17c) *Hist.* **1.** A part into which a hundred or wapentake was divided. **2.** A town or village.

village. (14c) **1.** Traditionally, a modest assemblage of houses and buildings for dwellings and businesses. **2.** In some states, a municipal corporation with a smaller population than a city. — Also termed (in sense 2) *town; borough.*

villanis regis subtractis reducendis (vi-**lay**-nis **ree**-jis səb-**trak**-tis ree-d[y]oo-**sen**-dis), *n.* [Latin "for returning the king's villeins who have been removed"] (17c) *Hist.* A writ that lay for the bringing back of the king's bondmen who had been carried away by others out of his manors, where they belonged.

villanum servitium (vi-**lay**-nəm sər-**vish**-ee-əm), *n.* [Latin] *Hist.* See VILLEINAGE.

villein (**vil**-ən). (14c) *Hist.* A person entirely subject to a lord or attached to a manor, but free in relation to all others; a serf. • At the time of the Domesday Inquest (shortly after the Norman Conquest), about 40% of households were marked as belonging to villeins: they were the most numerous element in the English population. Cf. FREEMAN (4).

▸ **villein in gross.** (17c) A villein who was annexed to the person of the lord, and transferable by deed from one owner to another.

▸ **villein regardant** (ri-**gahr**-dənt). (15c) A villein annexed to the manor of land.

villeinage (**vil**-ə-nij). (14c) *Hist.* **1.** The holding of property through servitude to a feudal lord; a servile type of tenure in which a tenant was obliged to render base services to a lord. See BONDAGE (1). **2.** A villein's status, condition, or service. Cf. *knight-service* under SERVICE (6); SOCAGE. — Also spelled *villenage*; *villainage*; *villanage*. — Also termed *villein tenure*.

> "The typical tenant in villeinage does not know in the evening what he will have to do in the morning. . . . [T]here is a large element of real uncertainty; the lord's will counts for much; when they go to bed on Sunday night they do not know what Monday's work will be; it may be threshing, ditching, carrying; they cannot tell. This seems the point that is seized by law and that general opinion of which law is the exponent: any considerable uncertainty as to the amount or kind of the agricultural services makes the tenure unfree. The tenure is unfree, not because the tenant 'holds at the will of the lord,' in the sense of being removable at a moment's notice, but because his services, though in many respects minutely defined by custom, cannot be altogether defined without frequent reference to the lord's will." 1 Frederick Pollock & Frederic W. Maitland, *History of English Law Before the Time of Edward I* 371 (2d ed. 1898).

> "At the lower level the services were not always defined. The duties of the peasant were chiefly agricultural. If they were unfixed, so that the lord might in theory demand all manner of work, the tenure was 'unfree' and was called *villeinage*." J.H. Baker, *An Introduction to English Legal History* 260 (3d ed. 1990).

▸ **privileged villeinage.** (18c) Villeinage in which the services to be performed were certain, though of a base and servile nature.

▸ **pure villeinage.** (18c) Villeinage in which the services were not certain, but the tenant was obliged to do whatever he was commanded whenever the command came.

villein in gross. See VILLEIN.

villein regardant. See VILLEIN.

villein service. (16c) *Hist.* A base service that a villein performed, such as working on the lord's land on certain days of the week (usu. two to four). • These services were not considered suitable to a man of free and honorable rank. — Also termed *villein servitium*. See WEEK-WORK.

villein socage (**sok**-ij). See SOCAGE.

villein tenure. See VILLEINAGE.

villenous judgment (**vil**-ə-nəs). (17c) *Hist.* A judgment that deprived a person of his *libera lex*, as a result of which he was discredited and disabled as a juror and witness, forfeited his goods and chattels and land, had his houses razed and trees uprooted, and went to prison. — Also spelled *villainous judgment*.

vinagium (vi-nay-**jee**-əm). (18c) A payment in kind of wine as rent for a vineyard.

vinculación (vin-koo-lah-**syohn**). (1868) *Spanish law.* A linking or encumbering; esp., an entail.

vinculo (**ving**-kyə-loh), *n.* [Latin "by bond"] *Spanish law.* **1.** A tie or bond; esp., the bond of marriage. See *divorce a vinculo matrimonii* under DIVORCE. **2.** An entail.

vinculum juris (**ving**-kyə-ləm **joor**-is). [Latin "a bond of the law"] (17c) *Roman law.* The tie that legally binds one person to another; legal bond; obligation. Cf. SOLUTIO OBLIGATIONIS.

vinculum personarum ab eodem stirpite descendentium (**ving**-kyə-ləm pər-sə-**nair**-əm ab ee-**oh**-dəm **stI**-pə-tee dee-sen-**den**-shee-əm). [Law Latin] (1803) *Hist.* The bond uniting persons descended from the same stock.

vindex (**vin**-deks), *n.* [Latin] *Civil law.* Someone who guaranteed the appearance of a defendant in court on pain of being liable for the judgment debt.

vindicare (vin-di-**kair**-ee), *vb.* [Latin "to claim or challenge"] *Roman law* & *Hist.* To demand as one's own; to assert a right in or to (a thing); to assert or claim ownership of (a thing).

vindicate, *vb.* (16c) **1.** To clear (a person or thing) from suspicion, criticism, blame, or doubt <DNA tests vindicated the suspect>. **2.** To assert, maintain, or affirm (one's interest) by action <the claimants sought to vindicate their rights through a class-action suit>. **3.** To defend (one's interest) against interference or encroachment <the borrower vindicated its interest in court when the lender tried to foreclose>. **4.** *Roman & civil law.* To assert a legal right to (a thing); to seek recovery of (a thing) by legal process <Antony Honoratus attempted to vindicate the sword he had lent his cousin>. — **vindication,** *n.* — **vindicator,** *n.*

vindicatio (vin-di-**kay**-shee-oh), *n.* [Latin "claim"] *Roman law.* **1.** An action by the owner to claim property.

▸ ***vindicatio servitutis*** (vin-di-**kay**-shee-oh sər-və-**t[y]oo**-tis). [Latin "claim of servitude"] (1869) *Roman law.* An action against the owner of land over which the plaintiff claims that a servitude exists. — Also termed *actio confessoria*.

2. The claiming of a thing as one's own; the assertion of a right in or title to a thing. Pl. ***vindicationes*** (vin-di-kay-shee-**oh**-neez).

vindicatory part (**vin**-də-kə-tor-ee). (1881) The portion of a statute setting forth the penalty for committing a wrong or neglecting a duty.

vindicta (vin-**dik**-tə), *n.* *Roman law.* **1.** A rod or wand. **2.** The assertion of freedom or ownership by symbolically touching the person or thing with a rod. See FESTUCA.

vindictive damages. See *punitive damages* under DAMAGES.

vindictive prosecution (vin-**dik**-tiv). See PROSECUTION (2).

viol (vyohl), *n.* [French] *French law.* Rape; indecent assault.

violation, *n.* (15c) **1.** An infraction or breach of the law; a transgression. See INFRACTION. **2.** The act of breaking or dishonoring the law; the contravention of a right or duty.

▸ **continuing violation.** An unlawful act that occurs as part a series of related or recurring unlawful acts over a period of time. • Each act is treated as a separate violation.

3. Rape; ravishment. **4.** Under the Model Penal Code, a public-welfare offense. • In this sense, a violation is not a crime. See Model Penal Code § 1.04(5). — **violate,** *vb.* — **violative** (**vI**-ə-lay-tiv), *adj.* — **violator,** *n.*

violation of parole. See PAROLE VIOLATION.

violation of probation. See PROBATION VIOLATION.

violation warrant. See WARRANT (1).

violence. (14c) The use of physical force, usu. accompanied by fury, vehemence, or outrage; esp., physical force unlawfully exercised with the intent to harm. • Some courts have held that violence in labor disputes is not limited to physical contact or injury, but may include picketing conducted with misleading signs, false statements, erroneous publicity, and veiled threats by words and acts.

▸ **domestic violence.** (1891) **1.** Violence between members of a household, usu. spouses; an assault or other violent act committed by one member of a household against another. See BATTERED-CHILD SYNDROME; BATTERED-WOMAN SYNDROME. **2.** The infliction of physical injury, or the creation of a reasonable fear that physical injury or harm will be inflicted, by a parent or a member or former member of a child's household, against a child or against another member of the household. — Also termed *domestic abuse*; *family violence*. **3.** *Archaic.* Insurrection or unlawful force fomented from within a country.

Violence Against Women Act. A federal statute that established a federal civil-rights action for victims of gender-motivated violence, without the need for a criminal charge. 42 USCA § 13981. • In 2000, the Supreme Court invalidated the statute, holding that neither the Commerce Clause nor the Enforcement Clause of the 14th Amendment authorized Congress to enact the civil-remedy provision of this Act. *U.S. v. Morrison*, 529 U.S. 598, 120 S.Ct. 1740 (2000). — Abbr. VAWA.

violent, *adj.* (14c) **1.** Of, relating to, or characterized by strong physical force <violent blows to the legs>. **2.** Resulting from extreme or intense force <violent death>. **3.** Vehemently or passionately threatening <violent words>.

violent crime. See CRIME.

violent death. See DEATH.

violent felony. See *violent offense* under OFFENSE (2).

violent offense. See *violent crime* under CRIME.

violent profits. (17c) *Scots law.* Penal damages imposed against a tenant who refused to surrender rented property to the landlord.

VIP. (1933) *abbr.* **1.** Very important person. **2.** VICTIM-IMPACT PANEL.

viperine interpretation. See *interpretatio viperina* under INTERPRETATIO (2).

VIP panel. See VICTIM-IMPACT PANEL.

vir (veer), *n.* [Latin] **1.** An adult male; a man. **2.** A husband. • In the Latin phrases and maxims that once pervaded English law, *vir* generally means "husband," as in the expression *vir et uxor* (husband and wife). See ET VIR. Cf. UXOR.

vires (vɪ-reez), *n.* (18c) **1.** Natural powers; forces. **2.** Granted powers, esp. when limited. See ULTRA VIRES; INTRA VIRES.

vir et uxor (**veer** et **ək**-sor). [Latin] Husband and wife.

virga (**vər**-gə). [Latin "branch, staff, wand"] *Hist.* A rod or staff; esp., a rod as an ensign of office.

virgata (vər-**gay**-tə). (17c) **1.** A quarter of an acre of land. See ACRE. **2.** A quarter of a hide of land. See HIDE (1).

virgata regia (vər-**gay**-tə **ree**-jee-ə). [Latin "king's verge"] *Hist.* The bounds of the king's household, within which the court of the steward had jurisdiction.

virga terrae (**vər**-gə **ter**-ee), *n.* [Latin "branch of land"] *Hist.* A variable measure of land ranging from 20 to 40 acres. — Also termed *virgata terrae*. See YARDLAND.

virge. See VERGE.

virger. See VERGER.

viridario eligendo (vir-ə-**dair**-ee-oh el-ə-**jen**-doh). (17c) *Hist.* A writ for choice of a verderer in the forest.

virile share. (1821) *Civil law.* An amount that an obligor owes jointly and severally with another. La. Civ. Code art. 1804. — Also termed *virile portion*.

virtual adoption. See *adoption by estoppel* under ADOPTION (1).

virtual child pornography. See PORNOGRAPHY.

virtual representation. See REPRESENTATION (3).

virtual-representation doctrine. (1945) The principle that a judgment may bind a person who is not a party to the litigation if one of the parties is so closely aligned with the nonparty's interests that the nonparty has been adequately represented by the party in court. • Under this doctrine, for instance, a judgment in a case naming only the husband as a party can be binding on his wife as well. See RES JUDICATA.

virtue, *n.* (13c) **1.** Moral goodness of character and behavior <striving after virtue>. **2.** A particular good quality in a person's character <among her many virtues are temperance and circumspection>. **3.** An advantage that makes something better or more useful than something else <one virtue of this approach is that no one's safety will be compromised>.

virtue ethics. (1983) *Ethics.* An ethical theory that focuses on the character of the actor rather than on the nature of the act or its consequences. • This approach received its first and perhaps its fullest expression in the works of Aristotle, esp. in his *Ethics*. See ETHICS. Cf. CONSEQUENTIALISM.

virtute cujus (vər-**t[y]oo**-tee **k[y]oo**-jəs), *adv.* [Latin] *Hist.* By virtue whereof. • This phrase began the clause in a pleading that attempted to justify an entry onto land by alleging that it was by virtue of an order from one entitled that the entry took place.

virtute officii (vər-**t[y]oo**-tee ə-**fish**-ee-ɪ), *adv.* [Latin] *Hist.* By virtue of one's office; by the authority invested in one as the incumbent of a particular office. • An officer acts *virtute officii* when carrying out some official authority as the incumbent of an office.

vis (vis). [Latin "power"] (17c) **1.** Any force, violence, or disturbance relating to a person or property.

> "*Vis*, as a legal term, was understood to denote the organizing and arming of tumultuous bodies of men for the purpose of obstructing the constituted authorities in the performance of their duty, and thus interrupting the ordinary administration of the laws. No such offence was recognised by the Criminal Code until the last century of the republic, when violent riots by hired mobs became so frequent, that M. Plautius Silvanus, Tribune of the Plebs, B.C. 89, [secured the passing of] the *lex Plautia de Vi*, in terms of which, those convicted of such practices were banished." William

Ramsay, *A Manual of Roman Antiquities* 347 (Rodolfo Lanciani ed., 15th ed. 1894).

2. The force of law. • Thus *vim habere* ("to have force") is to be legally valid. Pl. ***vires.***

VIS. *abbr.* VICTIM-IMPACT STATEMENT.

visa (**vee**-zə). (1831) An official indorsement made on a passport, showing that it has been examined and that the bearer is permitted to proceed; a recognition by the country in which a passport-holder wishes to travel that the holder's passport is valid. • A visa is generally required for the admission of aliens into the United States. 8 USCA §§ 1181, 1184. — Also termed (archaically) *visé* (**vee**-zay *or* vi-**zay**).

▸ **nonimmigrant visa.** (1925) A temporary visa that allows an alien who plans to return to his or her home country to remain in the United States for a defined period.

▸ **student visa.** (1931) A nonimmigrant visa granted to a noncitizen who enters the country for educational purposes.

▸ **T visa.** (2000) A nonimmigrant visa granted to a noncitizen who is a victim of human trafficking and has a well-founded fear of retribution if deported. See *trafficked person* under PERSON (1).

▸ **U visa.** (2000) A nonimmigrant visa granted to a noncitizen who is the victim of a violent crime or has information about such a crime and cooperates with law-enforcement authorities in connection with the crime. • It was first created in the Battered Immigrant Women Protection Act of 2000.

▸ **V visa.** (2000) A nonimmigrant visa under which the unmarried children under age 21 and spouse of a permanent resident may enter and remain in the United States during the processing of immigrant visas.

vis ablativa (**vis** ab-lə-**tɪ**-və), *n.* [Latin "ablative force"] (17c) *Civil law.* Force exerted in taking something away from another. Pl. ***vires ablativae.***

vis absoluta (**vis** ab-sə-**loo**-tə). (1886) Physical compulsion.

> The difference is between compulsion of the will (*vis compulsiva*) which results in an act though not of free volition, and physical compulsion (*vis absoluta*) in which the unavoidable movement is no act at all." Rollin M. Perkins & Ronald N. Boyce, *Criminal Law* 1054-55 (3d ed. 1982).

vis armata (**vis** ahr-**may**-tə). [Latin "armed force"] (16c) *Hist.* Force exerted by means of weapons. Cf. VIS INERMIS. — Also termed *armata vis.*

vis aut metus qui cadit in constantem virum (vis awt **mee**-təs kwɪ **kay**-dit [*or* **kad**-it] in kən-**stan**-təm **vɪ**-rəm). [Latin] *Hist.* A force or fear sufficient to overcome a man of firmness and resolution.

vis-à-vis (**veez**-ə-**vee**). [French "face to face"] (18c) In relation to; opposite to <the creditor established a preferred position vis-à-vis the other creditors>.

Visa Waiver Program. A U.S. State Department program that allows citizens or nationals of almost 40 participating countries to travel to the United States without a visa for stays of 90 days or less, when they meet a series of requirements. • Travelers must be eligible and have a valid Electronic System for Travel Authorization (ESTA) approval prior to travel.

Visby, laws of. See LAWS OF VISBY.

vis clandestina (**vis** klan-des-**tɪ**-nə), *n.* [Latin "clandestine force"] *Hist.* Force furtively used, esp. at night.

vis compulsiva (**vis** kom-pəl-**sɪ**-və), *n.* [Latin "compulsive force"] (16c) *Hist.* Force exerted to compel another to do something involuntarily; menacing force exerted by terror.

viscount (**vɪ**-kownt). (14c) **1.** The title of the fourth rank of European nobility. • In the British peerage, viscount is placed between the dignity of earl and baron. **2.** *Hist.* A sheriff.

viscountess (**vɪ**-kown-tis). (15c) **1.** The wife of a viscount. — Also termed *vice-comitissa.* **2.** A woman who holds the rank of viscount in her own right.

vis divina (**vis** di-**vɪ**-nə), *n.* (16c) *Civil law.* Divine or superhuman force; ACT OF GOD; VIS MAJOR.

visé. See VISA.

vis expulsiva (**vis** eks-pəl-**sɪ**-və), *n.* [Latin "expulsive force"] (16c) *Hist.* Force used to expel or dispossess another.

vis exturbativa (**vis** eks-tər-bə-**tɪ**-və), *n.* [Latin "eliminating force"] *Hist.* Force used to thrust out another, esp. when two claimants are contending for possession.

vis fluminis (**vis** **floo**-mə-nis), *n.* [Latin "the force of a river"] *Civil law.* The force exerted by a stream or river; waterpower.

visible, *adj.* (14c) **1.** Perceptible to the eye; discernible by sight. **2.** Clear, distinct, and conspicuous.

visible crime. See *street crime* under CRIME.

visible means of support. (1846) An apparent method of earning a livelihood. • Vagrancy statutes have long used this phrase to describe those who have no ostensible ability to support themselves.

visible offense. See *street crime* under CRIME.

vis illicita (**vis** il-**lis**-ə-tə). See VIS INJURIOSA.

vis impressa (**vis** im-**pres**-ə), *n.* [Latin "impressed force"] (17c) The original act of force from which an injury arises, as distinguished from the proximate (or immediate) force.

vis inermis (**vis** in-**ər**-mis), *n.* [Latin] (18c) Unarmed force. Cf. VIS ARMATA.

vis injuriosa (**vis** in-joor-ee-**oh**-sə), *n.* [Latin "injurious force"] *Hist.* Wrongful force. — Also termed *vis illicita.*

vis inquietativa (**vis** in-kwɪ-ə-tə-**tɪ**-və), *n.* [Latin "disquieting force"] (16c) *Civil law.* Force that prevents another from using his or her possession quietly and in peace.

visit, *n.* *Int'l law.* A naval officer's boarding an ostensibly neutral merchant vessel from another state to exercise the right of search. • This right is exercisable when suspicious circumstances exist, as when the vessel is suspected of involvement in piracy. — Also termed *visitation.* See RIGHT OF SEARCH.

visitation (viz-ə-**tay**-shən). (14c) **1.** Inspection; superintendence; direction; regulation. **2.** *Family law.* A relative's, esp. a noncustodial parent's, period of access to a child. — Also termed *parental access*; *access*; *parenting time*; *residential time.* **3.** A relative's or friend's period of access, often strictly limited access, to an inmate, hospital patient, or other person who is under the supervision of others. **4.** The process of inquiring into and correcting corporate irregularities. **5.** VISIT.

▸ **grandparent visitation.** (1973) A grandparent's court-approved access to a grandchild. • The Supreme Court recently limited a grandparent's right to have visitation with his or her grandchild if the parent objects, citing a parent's fundamental right to raise his or her child and to make all decisions concerning the child free from state intervention absent a threat to the child's health and safety. *Troxel v. Granville*, 530 U.S. 57, 120 S.Ct. 2054 (2000).

▸ **restricted visitation.** See *supervised visitation*.

▸ **stepped-up visitation.** (1997) Visitation, usu. for a parent who has been absent from the child's life, that begins on a very limited basis and increases as the child comes to know the parent. — Also termed *step-up visitation*.

▸ **supervised visitation.** (1981) Visitation, usu. court-ordered, in which a parent may visit with the child or children only in the presence of some other individual. • A court may order supervised visitation when the visiting parent is known or believed to be prone to physical abuse, sexual abuse, or violence. — Also termed *restricted visitation*.

visitation books. (17c) *Hist.* Books compiled by the heralds, when royal progresses were solemnly and regularly made into every part of the kingdom, to inquire into the state of families and to register whatever marriages and descents were verified to them upon oath.

visitation credit. (1991) *Family law.* A child-support reduction that reflects the amount of time the child lives with the noncustodial parent.

visitation order. (1944) *Family law.* **1.** An order establishing the visiting times for a noncustodial parent with his or her child. **2.** An order establishing the visiting times for a child and a person with a significant relationship to the child. • Such an order may allow for visitation between (1) a grandparent and a grandchild, (2) a child and another relative, (3) a child and a stepparent, or (4) occasionally, a child and the child's psychological parent. — Also termed *access order*.

visitation right. (1935) **1.** *Family law.* A noncustodial parent's or grandparent's court-ordered privilege of spending time with a child or grandchild who is living with another person, usu. the custodial parent. • The noncustodial parent with visitation rights may sometimes be a parent from whose custody the child has been removed because of abuse or neglect. **2.** *Int'l law.* A belligerent country's right to search a neutral vessel to find out whether it is carrying contraband or is otherwise engaged in nonneutral service. • If the searched vessel is doing either of these things, the searchers may seize the contraband and carry out an appropriate punishment. — Also termed (in both senses) *right of visitation*.

visitatorial (viz-ə-tə-**tor**-ee-əl), *adj.* (17c) Of, relating to, or involving on-site inspection or supervision. — Also termed *visitorial*.

> "To eleemosynary corporations, a visitatorial power is attached as a necessary incident. . . . [P]rivate and particular corporations, founded and endowed by individuals for charitable purposes, are subject to the private government of those who are the efficient patrons and founder. If there be no visitor appointed by the founder, the law appoints the founder himself, and his heirs, to be the visitors. The visitatorial power arises from the property which the founder assigned to support the charity; and as he is the author of the charity, the laws give him and his heirs a visitatorial power; that is, an authority to inspect the actions and regulate the behavior of the members that partake of the charity. This power is judicial and supreme, but not legislative." 2 James Kent, *Commentaries on American Law* *300-01 (George Comstock ed., 11th ed. 1866).

visitatorial power. See POWER (3).

visiting judge. See JUDGE.

visitor. (15c) **1.** Someone who goes or comes to a particular person or place.

▸ **business visitor.** See BUSINESS VISITOR.

▸ **nonoccupant visitor.** See NONOCCUPANT VISITOR.

2. A person appointed to visit, inspect, inquire into, and correct corporate irregularities.

visitorial. See VISITATORIAL.

visitorial power. See *visitatorial power* under POWER (3).

visitor of manners. A regarder's office in the forest.

vis laica (**vis lay**-ə-kə), *n.* [Latin "lay force"] *Hist.* An armed force used in holding possession of a church.

vis licita (**vis lis**-ə-tə), *n.* [Latin] Lawful force.

vis major (**vis may**-jər), *n.* [Latin "a superior force"] (17c) **1.** A greater or superior force; an irresistible or overwhelming force of nature; FORCE MAJEURE. Cf. ACT OF GOD. **2.** A loss resulting immediately from a natural cause without human intervention and that could not have been prevented by the exercise of prudence, diligence, and care. — Also termed *act of nature*; *act of providence*; *superior force*; *irresistible force*; *vis divina*.

vis major naturae (vis **may**-jor nə-**tyoor**-ee). [Latin] *Hist.* The superior force of nature. See FORCE MAJEURE.

visne (veen *or* **veen**-ee). [Law French fr. Latin *visnetum*] (15c) Neighborhood; at common law, the district from which juries were drawn; VICINAGE.

vis perturbativa (**vis** pər-tər-bə-**tɪ**-və), *n.* [Latin "perturbing force"] *Hist.* Force used between persons contending for possession of something.

vis proxima (**vis prahk**-sə-mə), *n.* [Latin "proximate force"] (1846) *Hist.* Immediate force.

vis simplex (**vis sim**-pleks), *n.* [Latin "simple force"] (1880) *Hist.* Mere force; sheer force.

VISTA (**vis**-tə). *abbr.* (1964) Volunteers in Service to America, a federal program established in 1964 to provide volunteers to help improve the living conditions of people in the poorest areas of the United States, its possessions, and Puerto Rico.

vi statuti (vɪ stə-t[y]**oo**-tɪ). [Law Latin] *Hist.* By force of statute.

Visual Artists Rights Act. *Copyright.* A 1990 federal law giving a visual artist nontransferable moral rights of integrity and attribution in original and limited-edition creations. • Enacted to meet Berne Convention standards, the Act protects the original artist — not the owner of the copyright — by granting some rights to prevent the work from being changed or destroyed, and by guaranteeing that the artist may claim authorship of the original work but may deny authorship if the work is modified. 17 USCA §§ 106A, 113. — Abbr. VARA.

visual body-cavity inspection. See *visual body-cavity search* under SEARCH (1).

visual body-cavity search. See SEARCH (1).

visus (**vɪ**-səs *or* **vɪ**-zəs), *n.* [Latin] *Hist.* An inspection of a place, person, or thing. See VIEW (3), (4).

vital statistics. (1837) Public records — usu. relating to matters such as births, marriages, deaths, diseases, and the like — that are statutorily mandated to be kept by a city, state, or other governmental division or subdivision. • On the admissibility of vital statistics, see Fed. R. Evid. 803(9).

vital term. See *fundamental term* under TERM (2).

vitiate (**vish**-ee-ayt), *vb.* (16c) **1.** To impair; to cause to have no force or effect <the new statute vitiates any common-law argument that the plaintiffs might have>. **2.** To make void or voidable; to invalidate either completely or in part <fraud vitiates a contract>. **3.** To corrupt morally <Mr. Lawrence complains that his children were vitiated by their governess>. — **vitiation,** *n.* — **vitiator,** *n.*

vitilitigate (vit-ə-**lit**-ə-gayt), *vb.* [fr. Latin *vitilitigare* "to quarrel disgracefully"] (17c) *Archaic.* To litigate merely from quarrelsome motives; to carry on a lawsuit in an unduly contentious, wrangling way. — **vitilitigation,** *n.* — **vitilitigious** (vit-ə-li-**tij**-əs), *adj.*

vitious intromission. See INTROMISSION (2).

vitium clerici (**vish**-ee-əm **kler**-ə-sɪ). [Latin] See *clerical error* under ERROR (2).

vitium reale (**vish**-ee-əm ree-**ay**-lee). [Latin "true error"] (17c) *Hist. & Scots law.* A defect in a title that renders the movable property nontransferable; specif., an inherent vice in the title of anyone who holds a stolen thing, even if acquired honestly, so that the true owner can reclaim it. Cf. LABES REALIS QUAE REI INHAERET.

> "A person who comes into possession of moveable property without any title to retain custody thereof is obliged to restore it to the person truly entitled to the possession thereof. . . . [P]roperty so acquired is affected by an inherent *vitium reale* which prevents the thief or fraudulent person from conferring a good title on anyone, even a taker from him in good faith, who has given value and taken without notice of the thief's defective title; such a person must return the property to the true owner, or pay compensation therefor. . . . An exception to the rule of *vitium reale* exists in the cases of money, bank-notes and negotiable instruments . . . ." 2 David M. Walker, *Principles of Scottish Private Law: Law of Obligations* 505–06 (1988).

vitium scriptoris (**vish**-ee-əm skrip-**tor**-is), *n.* [Latin "the mistake of a scribe"] (17c) *Hist.* A clerical error in writing.

vitricus (**vi**-trə-kəs), *n.* [Latin] (16c) *Hist.* A stepfather.

vitriol (**vit**-ree-ol), *n.* [Old French *vitriol*, lit. a caustic sulfate of metal] Caustic speech or criticism; cruel and angry language. — **vitriolic** (vi-tree-**ahl**-ic), *adj.*

vituperation (vɪ-tyoo-pə-**ray**-shən), *n.* The censuring of someone or something in abusive terms; revilement. — **vituperate,** *vb.* — ***vituperative,*** adj.

viva aqua (**vɪ**-və **ak**-wə), *n.* [Latin "living water"] *Hist.* Running water; water that comes from a spring or fountain.

viva pecunia (**vɪ**-və pi-**kyoo**-nee-ə), *n.* [Latin "living money"] (17c) *Hist.* Cattle, which obtained this name during the Saxon period, when they were received as money, usu. at regulated prices.

viva voce (**vɪ**-və **voh**-see *also* **vee**-və **voh**-chay), *adv.* [Law Latin "with living voice"] (16c) By word of mouth; orally. • In reference to votes, the term means a voice vote was held rather than a vote by ballot. In reference to the examination of witnesses, the term means that oral rather than written testimony was taken. See *voice vote* under VOTE (4).

viva voce vote. See *voice vote* under VOTE (4).

vivisection, *n.* (18c) **1.** Physiological or pathological experimentation on or investigation of living vertebrate animals using procedures likely to cause severe pain. **2.** By extension, questioning or criticism that is intense, minute, and merciless.

vivum vadium (**vɪ**-vəm **vay**-dee-əm). See *vadium vivum* under VADIUM.

viz. (viz). *abbr.* [Latin *videlicet*] (16c) Namely; that is to say <the defendant engaged in fraudulent activities, viz., misrepresenting his gross income, misrepresenting the value of his assets, and forging his wife's signature>. See VIDELICET.

VLI. *abbr.* See *variable life insurance* under LIFE INSURANCE.

vocabula artis (voh-**kab**-yə-lə **ahr**-tis), *n.* [Latin] (16c) Words of art. See TERM OF ART.

VOCAL. *abbr.* VICTIMS OF CHILD ABUSE LAWS.

vocare ad curiam (voh-**kair**-ee ad **kyoor**-ee-əm), *vb.* [Latin] To summon to court.

vocatio in jus (voh-**kay**-shee-oh in **jəs**). [Latin] (17c) *Roman law.* A plaintiff's oral summoning of a defendant to go before a magistrate. • The *vocatio in jus* occurred when the plaintiff would summon the defendant in formal words to accompany the plaintiff.

vocation. (15c) A person's regular calling or business; one's occupation or profession.

VOCD. *abbr.* Violation of conditional discharge.

vociferatio (voh-sif-ə-**ray**-shee-oh), *n.* [Latin] *Hist.* An outcry; HUE AND CRY.

voco (**voh**-koh). [Latin "I call"] *Hist.* I summon; I vouch. See VOCATIO IN JUS.

Voconian law (və-**koh**-nee-in). See LEX VOCONIA.

voice exemplar. (1954) A sample of a person's voice used for the purpose of comparing it with a recorded voice to determine whether the speaker is the same person. • Although voiceprint identification was formerly inadmissible, the trend in recent years has been toward admissibility. *See* Fed. R. Evid. 901.

voiceprint. (1962) A distinctive pattern of curved lines and whorls made by a machine that measures human vocal sounds for the purpose of identifying an individual speaker. • Like fingerprints, voiceprints are thought to be unique to each person.

voice-spectrogram analysis. (1975) A voice-identifying technique that involves transforming acoustical signals produced by human speech into a visual representation of speech characteristics. • Voice-spectrogram analysis, which is subject to the *Daubert* test, is often criticized as unreliable. Voice characteristics can be disguised, and may also change because of mood, health, age, and other factors. — Also termed *voice-spectrograph analysis.*

voice-stress analysis. (1977) A mechanical test that detects and measures strain or tension in a person's voice, both being characteristics thought to indicate deception. • The test has been discredited, as many studies have shown that its accuracy rate is little or no better than chance. — Abbr. VSA.

voice vote. See VOTE (4).

void, *adj.* (14c) **1.** Of no legal effect; to null. • The distinction between *void* and *voidable* is often of great practical importance. Whenever technical accuracy is required, *void* can be properly applied only to those provisions that are of no effect whatsoever — those that are an absolute nullity. — **void, avoid,** *vb.* — **voidness,** *n.*

▸ **facially void.** (1969) (Of an instrument) patently void upon an inspection of the contents. — Also termed *void on its face.*

▸ **void ab initio** (ab i-**nish**-ee-oh). (17c) Null from the beginning, as from the first moment when a contract is entered into. • A contract is void ab initio if it seriously offends law or public policy, in contrast to a contract that is merely voidable at the election of one party to the contract.

▸ **void for vagueness.** (1814) **1.** (Of a deed or other instrument affecting property) having such an insufficient property description as to be unenforceable. **2.** (Of a penal statute) establishing a requirement or punishment without specifying what is required or what conduct is punishable, and therefore void because violative of due process. — Also termed *void for indefiniteness.* See VAGUENESS DOCTRINE.

2. VOIDABLE. • Although sense 1 above is the strict meaning of *void*, the word is often used and construed as bearing the more liberal meaning of "voidable."

void, *vb.* **1.** To render of no validity or effect; to annul; NULLIFY <fraud in the factum voids a contract>. **2.** To emit or evacuate; to execute <to void urine>. **3.** To empty; to cause to have the contents of emitted or evacuated <to void the bowels>. **4.** To leave or vacate <the members soon voided the meeting hall>.

voidable, *adj.* (15c) Valid until annulled; esp., (of a contract) capable of being affirmed or rejected at the option of one of the parties. • This term describes a valid act that may be voided rather than an invalid act that may be ratified. — Also termed *avoidable.* Cf. UNENFORCEABLE. — **voidability,** *n.*

> "Most of the disputed questions in the law of infancy turn upon the legal meaning of the word 'voidable' as applied to an infant's acts. The natural meaning of the word imports a valid act which may be avoided, rather than an invalid act which may be confirmed, and the weight of authority as well as reason points in the same direction. Certainly, so far as executed transfers of property are concerned the authority of the decisions clearly supports this view." 1 Samuel Williston, *The Law Governing Sales of Goods* § 12, at 28 (3d ed. 1948).

> "The promise of an infant surety is voidable as distinguished from void. The infant may expressly disaffirm or assert the defense of infancy when sued at any time before the expiration of a reasonable time after majority." Laurence P. Simpson, *Handbook on the Law of Suretyship* 82 (1950).

voidable agreement. See *voidable contract* under CONTRACT.

voidable contract. See CONTRACT.

voidable judgment. See JUDGMENT (2).

voidable marriage. See MARRIAGE (1).

voidable preference. See PREFERENTIAL TRANSFER.

voidable process. See PROCESS (2).

voidable promise. See PROMISE.

voidable title. See TITLE.

voidable transfer. See PREFERENTIAL TRANSFER.

void agreement. See *void contract* under CONTRACT.

voidance, *n.* (14c) The act of annulling, canceling, or making void. — Also termed *avoidance.*

voidance clause. (1917) A contractual provision stipulating that the contract will be void upon the occurrence of some specified event.

void contract. See CONTRACT.

void for indefiniteness. See *void for vagueness* under VOID.

void for vagueness. See VOID.

void-for-vagueness doctrine. 1. See VAGUENESS DOCTRINE. **2.** See *void for vagueness* under VOID.

void judgment. See JUDGMENT (2).

void legacy. See LEGACY (1).

void marriage. See MARRIAGE (1).

void on its face. See *facially void* under VOID.

void process. See PROCESS (2).

voir dire (vwahr **deer** *also* vor **deer** *or* vor **dɪr**), *n.* [Law French "to speak the truth"] (17c) **1.** A preliminary examination of a prospective juror by a judge or lawyer to decide whether the prospect is qualified and suitable to serve on a jury. • Loosely, the term refers to the jury-selection phase of a trial. **2.** A preliminary examination to test the competence of a witness or evidence. **3.** *Hist.* An oath administered to a witness requiring that witness to answer truthfully in response to questions. — Also spelled *voire dire.* — Also termed *voir dire exam*; *examination on the voir dire.* — **voir dire,** *vb.*

voiture (vwah-**t[y]oor**), *n.* (17c) Carriage; transportation by carriage.

volatile stock. See STOCK.

volatility. In securities markets, the quality of having sudden and extreme price changes.

volens (**voh**-lenz), *adj.* [Latin] (1872) Willing. See NOLENS VOLENS.

volenti non fit injuria (voh-**len**-tɪ non fit in-**joor**-ee-ə). [Law Latin "to a willing person it is not a wrong," i.e., a person is not wronged by that to which he or she consents] (17c) The principle that a person who knowingly and voluntarily risks danger cannot recover for any resulting injury. • This is the type of affirmative defense that must be pleaded under Fed. R. Civ. P. 8(c). — Often shortened to *volenti.* See ASSUMPTION OF THE RISK.

> "[T]he maxim 'Volenti non fit injuria' . . . is certainly of respectable antiquity. The idea underlying it has been traced as far back as Aristotle, and it was also recognised in the works of the classical Roman jurists, and in the Canon Law. In English law, Bracton in his *De Legibus Angliae* (ca. A.D. 1250–1258) uses the maxim, though not with the technicality that attached to it later, and in a Year Book case of 1305 it appears worded exactly as it is now. So far as actual citation of the maxim goes, most of the modern cases use it in connexion with harm to the person rather than to property." P.H. Winfield, *A Textbook of the Law of Tort* § 13, at 24 (5th ed. 1950).

volition (və-**lish**-ən *or* voh-), *n.* (17c) **1.** The ability to make a choice or determine something. **2.** The act of making a choice or determining something. **3.** The choice or determination that someone makes. — **volitional,** *adj.*

volitional test. See IRRESISTIBLE-IMPULSE TEST.

Volksgerictshof. See PEOPLE'S COURT (2)

Volstead Act (**vol**-sted *or* **vohl**-sted). A 1919 federal statute that prohibited the manufacture, sale, or transportation of liquor. • Sponsored by Andrew Joseph Volstead (1860–1947) of Minnesota, a famous Prohibitionist, the statute was passed under the 18th Amendment to the U.S. Constitution. When the 21st Amendment repealed the 18th Amendment in 1933, the Volstead Act was voided.

volume discount. See DISCOUNT.

volumen (vol-**yoo**-mən), *n.* [Latin "a rolled-up thing"] (16c) *Civil law.* A volume. Pl. ***volumina.***

volumus (**vol**-ə-məs), *vb.* [Latin] *Hist.* We will; it is our will. • This was the first word of a clause in royal writs of protection and letters patent. It uses the royal *we* — the plural first person by which monarchs have traditionally spoken.

voluntariae jurisdictionis (vol-ən-**tair**-ee-ee joor-is-dik-shee-**oh**-nis). [Latin] *Hist.* Of, relating to, or involving voluntary jurisdiction. See *voluntary jurisdiction* under JURISDICTION.

voluntarily, *adv.* (14c) Intentionally; without coercion.

voluntarius daemon (vol-ən-**tair**-ee-əs **dee**-mən), *n.* [Law Latin "voluntary madman"] (17c) *Hist.* A drunkard; one who has voluntarily contracted madness by intoxication.

voluntary, *adj.* (14c) **1.** Done by design or intention <voluntary act>. **2.** Unconstrained by interference; not impelled by outside influence <voluntary statement>. **3.** Without valuable consideration or legal obligation; gratuitous <voluntary gift>. **4.** Having merely nominal consideration <voluntary deed>. — **voluntariness,** *n.*

voluntary abandonment. See ABANDONMENT (4).

voluntary act. See ACT (2).

voluntary appearance. See APPEARANCE.

voluntary arbitration. See ARBITRATION.

voluntary assignment. See *general assignment* under ASSIGNMENT (2).

voluntary association. See ASSOCIATION (3).

voluntary assumption of the risk. See ASSUMPTION OF THE RISK.

voluntary bankruptcy. See BANKRUPTCY (2).

voluntary bar. See *voluntary bar association* under BAR ASSOCIATION.

voluntary bar association. See BAR ASSOCIATION.

voluntary bond. See BOND (3).

voluntary commitment. See COMMITMENT.

voluntary confession. See CONFESSION (1).

voluntary consent. See CONSENT (1).

voluntary contract. See *gratuitous contract* (2) under CONTRACT.

voluntary conveyance. See CONVEYANCE (1).

voluntary courtesy. (17c) An act of kindness performed by one person toward another, from the free will of the doer, without any previous request or promise of reward made by the person who is the object of the act. • No promise of remuneration arises from such an act.

voluntary-departure order. See *departure order* under ORDER (2).

voluntary deposit. See DEPOSIT (5).

voluntary-disclosure form. (1975) *Criminal law.* A standardized sheet that prosecutors fill out to answer a defense lawyer's discovery requests and motions. — Abbr. VDF.

voluntary disclosure of offense. See DISCLOSURE (1).

voluntary discontinuance. See NONSUIT (1).

voluntary dismissal. See DISMISSAL (1).

voluntary dissolution. See DISSOLUTION (3).

voluntary escape. See ESCAPE (3).

voluntary euthanasia. See EUTHANASIA.

voluntary exposure to unnecessary danger. (1883) An intentional act that, from the standpoint of a reasonable person, gives rise to an undue risk of harm. • The phrase suggests that the actor was consciously willing to take the risk.

voluntary ignorance. (1836) Willful obliviousness; an unknowing or unaware state resulting from the neglect to take reasonable steps to acquire important knowledge.

voluntary improvement. See IMPROVEMENT.

voluntary intoxication. See INTOXICATION.

voluntary jurisdiction. See JURISDICTION.

voluntary lien. See LIEN.

voluntary liquidation. See LIQUIDATION (4).

voluntary manslaughter. See MANSLAUGHTER.

voluntary oath. See *nonjudicial oath* (1) under OATH.

voluntary partition. See PARTITION (2).

voluntary petition. See PETITION (1).

voluntary pilot. See PILOT.

voluntary pooling. See POOLING.

voluntary-registry law. See ADOPTION-REGISTRY STATUTE.

voluntary respite. See RESPITE.

voluntary sale. See SALE.

voluntary search. See SEARCH (1).

voluntary settlement. See SETTLEMENT (1).

voluntary statement. See STATEMENT.

voluntary stranding. See STRANDING.

voluntary surety. See SURETY (1).

voluntary suretyship. See SURETYSHIP.

voluntary surrender. See SURRENDER (1).

voluntary trust. See TRUST (3).

voluntary unitization. See UNITIZATION.

voluntary waste. See WASTE (1).

voluntary winding up. See WINDING UP.

voluntas (və-**lən**-tas), *n.* [Latin] *Hist.* **1.** Volition, purpose, or intention; a feeling or impulse that prompts the commission of an act. **2.** A will by which a testator plans to dispose of an estate; WILL.

voluntas testatoris (və-**lən**-tas tes-tə-**tor**-is). [Latin] (1831) *Hist.* The intention of a testator.

voluntatis non necessitatis (vol-ən-**tay**-tis non nə-ses-i-**tay**-tis). [Latin] (17c) *Hist.* A matter of choice, not of necessity.

volunteer. (16c) **1.** A voluntary actor or agent in a transaction; esp., a person who, without an employer's assent and without any justification from legitimate personal interest, helps an employee in the performance of the employer's business. **2.** The grantee in a voluntary conveyance; a person to whom a conveyance is made without any valuable consideration. See *voluntary conveyance* under CONVEYANCE. **3.** *Military law.* Someone who enters military service voluntarily and is then subject to the same rules as other soldiers. Cf. DRAFT, *n.* (2). **4.** Someone who gratuitously and freely confers a benefit on another; OFFICIOUS INTERMEDDLER. — Also termed *mere volunteer.* See *benefit officiously conferred* under BENEFIT (2).

▸ **third-party volunteer.** (1930) A volunteer who is not a party to the transaction, lawsuit, agreement, etc. at issue.

Volunteers in Service to America. See VISTA.

VOOP. *abbr.* Violation of order of protection.

VOP. *abbr.* Violation of probation.

vote, *n.* (15c) **1.** The expression of one's preference or opinion in a meeting or election by ballot, show of hands, or other type of communication <the Republican candidate received more votes than the Democratic candidate>.

▸ **absentee vote.** See *absentee voting* under VOTING.

▸ **bullet vote.** (1958) A vote cast for fewer nominees than are being elected. • A bullet vote slightly enhances the ballot's effect on the outcome. — Also termed *bullet ballot.*

▸ **casting vote.** (18c) A deciding vote cast by the chair of a deliberative assembly when the votes are tied. • The U.S. Constitution gives the Vice President the casting vote in the Senate. U.S. Const. art. I, § 3. — Also termed *deciding vote*; *tiebreaking vote.*

> "One is, that to secure at all times the possibility of a definite resolution of the body, it is necessary that the President should have only a casting vote. And to take the senator of any State from his seat as senator, to place him in that of President of the Senate, would be to exchange, in regard to the State from which he came, a constant for a contingent vote." The Federalist No. 68 (Alexander Hamilton).

▸ **deciding vote.** See *casting vote.*

▸ **effective vote.** A vote that counts toward a winning candidate, to the extent needed to win. • A vote that goes to a winning candidate is "effective" to the extent needed to win, and "excess" beyond that point. For example, if a candidate needs 100 votes and gets 150, then 50 votes are excess votes and each vote is two-thirds effective and one-third excess. Cf. *excess vote*; *wasted vote.*

▸ **excess vote.** (1897) A vote that counts toward a winning candidate, beyond the extent needed to win. Cf. *effective vote; wasted vote.*

▸ **exhausted vote.** (1987) A preferential vote on which all the ranked candidates have already been elected or eliminated. — Also termed *exhausted ballot.*

▸ **illegal vote.** (17c) A vote that does not count because it was cast by someone not entitled to vote or for an ineligible choice, or in a form or manner that does not comply with the applicable rules. See *spoiled ballot* under BALLOT (2).

▸ **legal vote.** (17c) A vote cast in the proper form and manner for an eligible choice by someone entitled to vote.

▸ **paired vote.** (1944) An abstention resulting from a pairing. See PAIR.

▸ **preferential vote.** (1871) A vote that ranks the choices in order of preference. • A preferential vote may be transferable or weighted. — Also termed *preferential ballot.* Cf. *single transferable vote*; *weighted vote.*

▸ **single transferable vote.** (1882) A preferential vote that will migrate or "transfer" away from a candidate whom it will no longer help. • Under transferable voting, a candidate wins if his or her first-choice votes reach the number needed to win, or the "threshold." If no candidate reaches the threshold, the least-preferred candidate is dropped and his or her votes transfer to the next-preferred candidate on each ballot. If a candidate reaches the threshold with an excess, that excess still transfers — after being discounted by the non-excess fraction needed to reach the threshold — among the surviving candidates. Each transfer preserves each vote as long as at least one candidate that the voter ranked survives. The redistribution continues until enough candidates reach the threshold or the number of surviving candidates equals the number of representatives still to be elected. See DROOP QUOTA. — Also termed *STV*; *transferable vote*; *choice voting.*

▸ **tiebreaking vote.** See *casting vote.*

▸ **transferable vote.** See *single transferable vote.*

▸ **unintelligible vote.** (1993) An otherwise legal vote cast in a form from which the tellers cannot ascertain the voter's intent. • On a secret ballot, no voter may properly claim an unintelligible vote for the purpose of explaining it since the vote may have been cast by another voter who cannot contradict the claimant without sacrificing his or her right to secrecy.

▸ **vote of no confidence.** See NO-CONFIDENCE VOTE.

▸ **wasted vote.** (1859) A vote that does not count toward any winning candidate. Cf. *effective vote*; *excess vote.*

▸ **weighted vote.** (1934) A nontransferable preferential vote whose strength is allocated among the ranked preferences either by the voter or according to a series of fixed weights.

2. The total number of votes cast in an election <the incumbent received 60% of the vote>. **3.** The majority or supermajority needed for a certain question <a two-thirds vote>.

▸ **majority vote.** See MAJORITY (2).

▸ **plurality vote.** See PLURALITY.

▸ **tie vote.** (1894) An equally divided vote. • A tie vote is not a deadlock unless the assembly is obliged to act, for example when electing an officer to an office that will otherwise be vacant. Cf. DEADLOCK (1).

▸ **unanimous vote.** (18c) A vote in which every voter concurs. See UNANIMOUS (2).

▸ **winner-take-all vote.** (1946) An election in which the majority (or sometimes the plurality) elects all the representatives. Cf. UNIT RULE (2); PROPORTIONAL REPRESENTATION; *proportional voting* under VOTING.

4. The act of voting, usu. by a deliberative assembly <the Senate postponed the vote on the gun-control bill>. — **vote,** *vb.*

▸ **counted vote.** (1844) *Parliamentary law.* A vote taken in a way that individually counts each voter. • Examples of a counted vote are a counted show of hands, a counted standing vote, a roll-call vote, or a written ballot.

▸ **division vote.** See *standing vote*; DIVISION (5).

▸ **lobby vote.** (1950) A counted vote taken by each voter passing through a lobby between tellers. — Also termed *teller vote.*

▸ **rising vote.** (1844) **1.** See *standing vote.* **2.** A vote of appreciation demonstrated by the members standing, sometimes silently but usu. with applause. — Also termed *rising vote of thanks.*

▸ **roll-call vote.** (1884) A counted vote by roll call, in which the secretary calls each member's name, in answer to which the member casts aloud his or her vote. • The U.S. Constitution provides that "the Yeas and Nays of the Members of either House on any question shall, at the Desire of one fifth of those Present, be entered on the Journal." U.S. Const. art. I, § 5, cl. 3. — Also termed *vote by yeas and nays*; *yeas and nays.* See *roll call* under CALL (1).

▸ **serpentine vote.** A standing vote in which the voters count off and sit down, with the count progressing up one row and down the next until each member on the side of the question being counted has voted.

▸ **standing vote.** (17c) A vote taken by the voters standing up when their side of the question is called and sitting down when instructed. • The vote may be counted or uncounted. — Also termed *rising vote*; *division of the assembly*; *division of the house*; *division vote*; *division*; *standing division.* See DIVISION (5).

▸ **teller vote.** See *lobby vote.*

▸ **viva voce vote.** See *voice vote.*

▸ **voice vote.** (1897) A vote taken by the voters collectively answering aloud, usu. with "aye" or "nay," when their side of the question is called. — Also termed *viva voce vote.*

▸ **vote by show of hands.** (1905) A vote taken by the voters raising their hands when their side of the question is counted. — Often shortened to *show of hands.*

▸ **vote by yeas and nays.** See *roll-call vote.*

vote counter. See CANVASSER.

vote dilution. See DILUTION (3).

vote immediately. See CLOSE DEBATE.

vote of no confidence. See NO-CONFIDENCE VOTE.

voter. (16c) **1.** Someone who engages in the act of voting. **2.** Someone who has the qualifications necessary for voting. — Also termed (in sense 2) *legal voter*; *qualified voter.*

▸ **registered voter.** (1832) Someone who is qualified to vote and whose name is recorded in the voting district where he or she resides.

voting. (16c) The casting of votes for the purpose of deciding an issue.

▸ **absentee voting.** (1932) **1.** Participation in an election by a qualified voter who is unable to appear at the polls on election day. **2.** The practice of allowing voters to participate in this way. — Also termed (in sense 1) *absentee ballot*; *absentee vote.* See *absentee ballot* under BALLOT (2). Cf. *early voting.*

▸ **choice voting.** See *single transferable vote* under VOTE (1).

▸ **class voting.** (1941) A method of shareholder voting in which different classes of shares vote separately on fundamental corporate changes that affect the rights and privileges of that class. — Also termed *voting by class*; *voting by voting group.*

▸ **cumulative voting.** (1877) A system in which each voter is entitled to a number of votes corresponding to the number of positions to be filled (as on a board or council) and may distribute them freely among the candidates, as by casting more than one for the same candidate. • Cumulative voting helps a minority elect at least one representative. It is common in shareholder elections.

▸ **early voting.** (1984) Voting before the day of an election, esp. during a period designated for that purpose. • Unlike with absentee voting, taking advantage of early voting does not require the voter to swear to the inability to come to the polling place on election day. Cf. *absentee voting.*

▸ **first-past-the-post voting.** See *plurality voting.*

▸ **Hare–Ware voting.** See *instant-runoff voting.*

▸ **instant-runoff voting.** (1996) A system of preferential voting that mimics a runoff election by using each voter's ranked preferences instead of a second round of voting. — Abbr. IRV. — Also termed *Hare–Ware voting*; *West Australian plan.* See *runoff election* under ELECTION (3).

▸ **limited voting.** A system in which each voter must cast fewer votes than the number of representatives being elected.

▸ **low-total voting.** (2004) A system of weighted preferential voting that adds up the ranked preferences — "1" for a first choice, "2" for a second choice, and so forth — so that the most-preferred candidate wins by having the lowest total. See *preferential voting*; *weighted vote* under VOTE (1).

▸ **majority voting.** (1890) A system in which each voter may cast one vote per representative being elected, and a simple majority is required for election.

▸ **noncumulative voting.** (1941) A corporate voting system in which a shareholder is limited in board elections to voting no more than the number of shares that he or she owns for a single candidate. • The result is that a majority shareholder will elect the entire board of directors. — Also termed *straight voting.*

▸ **plurality voting.** (1838) Election by plurality. See PLURALITY. — Also termed *first-past-the-post voting.*

▸ **preferential voting.** (1870) A system in which each voter ranks the choices in order of preference. • A preferential vote may be transferable or weighted. — Also termed *rank-order voting*; *ranked-choice voting* (RCV). See *single transferable vote* under VOTE (1); *weighted vote* under VOTE (1).

▸ **proportional voting.** (1865) A system of transferable preferential voting in a multi-representative election. — Also termed *proportional representation*. See *preferential vote, single transferable vote* under VOTE (1). Cf. *winner-take-all-vote* under VOTE (3).

▸ **ranked-choice voting.** See *preferential voting*.

▸ **rank-order voting.** See *preferential voting*.

▸ **straight voting.** See *noncumulative voting*.

▸ **two-round voting.** (1959) A system in which the voting occurs in two rounds, with the first round determining the candidate's eligibility for the second round. • The second round may be a runoff between the top two candidates from the first round, an election by plurality among candidates who won their political parties' nominations in the first round, or an election by plurality among the candidates from the first round who reached a certain threshold. See *runoff election* under ELECTION (3).

▸ **voting by class.** See *class voting*.

▸ **voting by voting group.** See *class voting*.

▸ **voting by yeas and nays.** See *roll-call vote* under VOTE (4).

voting agreement. See POOLING AGREEMENT.

voting booth. (1837) An enclosed place where one can vote in private.

voting by class. See *class voting* under VOTING.

voting by voting group. See *class voting* under VOTING.

voting group. (1972) **1.** A classification of shareholders by the type of stock held for voting on corporate matters. **2.** Collectively, the shareholders falling within such a classification.

voting member. See MEMBER (1).

Voting Rights Act. The federal statute that guarantees a citizen's right to vote, without discrimination based on race, color, or previous condition of servitude. 42 USCA §§ 1971–1974.

voting security. See *voting stock* under STOCK.

voting station. See POLLING PLACE.

voting stock. See STOCK.

voting-stock rights. (1964) A stockholder's right to vote stock in the affairs of the company. • Typically, holders of common stock have one vote for each share. Holders of preferred stock usu. have the right to vote when preferred dividends are in default for a specified period.

voting trust. See TRUST (3).

voting-trust certificate. (1901) A certificate issued by a voting trustee to the beneficial holders of shares held by the voting trust. • A voting-trust certificate may be as readily transferable as the underlying shares; it carries with it all the incidents of ownership except the power to vote. See *voting trust* under TRUST (3).

votum (**voh**-təm), *n.* [Latin] *Hist.* A vow; a promise. See *dies votorum* under DIES.

votum captandae mortis alienae (**voh**-təm kap-**tan**-dee **mor**-tis ay-lee-**ee**-nee *or* al-ee-). [Latin] (1891) *Hist.* An earnest desire for another's death. • An heir could not sell his or her rights to an ancestor's estate because such a transaction would likely induce *votum captandae mortis alienae*.

vouch, *vb.* (14c) **1.** To answer for (another); to personally assure <the suspect's mother vouched for him>. **2.** To call on, rely on, or cite as authority; to substantiate with evidence <counsel vouched the mathematical formula for determining the statistical probability>. **3.** (Of a lawyer before a jury) to comment favorably on the credibility of one or more witnesses based on the lawyer's personal knowledge. **4.** *Hist.* To call into court to warrant and defend, usu. in a fine and recovery. See FINE (1). **5.** *Hist.* To authenticate (a claim, etc.) by vouchers. — **vouching,** *n.*

vouchee (vow-**chee**), *n.* (15c) *Hist.* **1.** A person vouched into court; one who has been vouched over. See VOUCH OVER. **2.** A person cited as authority in support of some fact.

voucher, *n.* (17c) **1.** Confirmation of the payment or discharge of a debt; a receipt. **2.** A written or printed authorization to disburse money. **3.** *Hist.* Someone who calls on another person (the vouchee) as a witness, esp. in support of a warranty of title. **4.** *Hist.* The tenant in a writ of right.

▸ **tuition voucher.** (1934) A government-issued voucher representing public funds that parents may use to pay tuition at a private school or for homeschooling expenses as an alternative to public school. — Also termed *school voucher; education voucher*.

voucher to warranty. (17c) *Hist.* The calling into court of a person who has warranted lands, by the person warranted, to come and defend a lawsuit.

vouching-in. (1849) **1.** At common law, a procedural device by which a defendant may give notice of suit to a third party who may be liable to the defendant on the subject-matter of the suit, so that the third party will be bound by the court's decision. • Although this device has been largely replaced by third-party practice, it remains available under the Federal Rules of Civil Procedure. *Humble Oil & Refining Co. v. Philadelphia Ship Maintenance Co.*, 444 F.2d 727, 735 (3d Cir. 1971). **2.** The invitation of a person who is liable to a defendant in a lawsuit to intervene and defend so that, if the invitation is denied and the defendant later sues the person invited, the latter is bound by any determination of fact common to the two lawsuits. *See* UCC § 2-607(5). **3.** IMPLEADER.

vouch over, *vb.* (16c) To cite (a person) into court in one's stead. See VOUCHEE (1).

vox legis. [Latin] (vahks **lee**-jis) (17c) The voice of the law, i.e., a praetor (anciently) or a judge (modernly).

vox populi (vahks **pop**-yə-lɪ). [Latin] *Hist.* Voice of the people; popular opinion.

vox signata (vahks sig-**nay**-tə). [Law Latin] (1833) *Hist.* A technical word; a formal word. Pl. ***voces signatae.***

voyage. (14c) *Maritime law.* The passing of a vessel by sea from one place, port, or country to another. • Courts generally hold that the term includes the entire enterprise, not just the route.

▸ **foreign voyage.** (16c) A voyage to a port or place within the territory of a foreign country. • If the voyage is from one port in a foreign country to another port in the same country, it is considered a foreign voyage.

▸ **freighting voyage.** (1809) A voyage that involves a vessel's transporting cargo between terminal points.

▸ **trading voyage.** (17c) A voyage that contemplates a vessel's touching and stopping at various ports to traffic in, buy and sell, or exchange commodities on the owners' and shippers' account.

voyage charter. See CHARTER (8).

voyage charterparty. See *voyage charter* under CHARTER (8).

voyage insurance. See INSURANCE.

voyage policy. See INSURANCE POLICY.

voyeur (voy-**yər** *also* vwah-**yər**), *n.* (1900) Someone who observes something without participating; esp., one who gains pleasure by secretly observing another's genitals or sexual acts.

voyeurism, *n.* (1900) Gratification derived from observing the genitals or sexual acts of others, usu. secretly. — **voyeuristic,** *adj.*

V.P. *abbr.* VICE PRESIDENT.

VPPA. *abbr.* VIDEO PRIVACY PROTECTION ACT.

vs. *abbr.* (1889) VERSUS.

VSA. *abbr.* VOICE-STRESS ANALYSIS.

vulgar abuse. See *verbal abuse* under ABUSE.

vulgaris purgatio (vəl-**gair**-is pər-**gay**-shee-oh), *n.* [Law Latin] See ORDEAL (1).

vulgar purgation. See PURGATION.

vulgar substitution. See SUBSTITUTION (4).

vulgo concepti (**vəl**-goh kən-**sep**-tɪ), *n.* [Latin] (17c) *Hist.* Illegitimate children; bastards.

vulgo quaesiti (**vəl**-goh kwi-**sɪ**-tɪ), *n.* [Latin] (17c) *Hist.* Spurious children; the offspring of promiscuity, so that the true fathers are unknowable.

vulnerable adult. See ADULT.

vulnerable-adult abuse. See *adult abuse* under ABUSE.

vulnerable zone. See ZONE.

vulture fund. See MUTUAL FUND.

V visa. See VISA.

W-2 form. (18c) (1948) *Tax.* A statement of earnings and taxes withheld (including federal, state, and local income taxes and FICA tax) during a given tax year. • The W-2 is prepared by the employer, provided to each employee, and filed with the Internal Revenue Service. Cf. W-4 FORM.

W-4 form. (1955) *Tax.* A form indicating the number of personal exemptions an employee is claiming and that is used by the employer in determining the amount of income to be withheld from the employee's paycheck for federal-income tax purposes. — Also termed *Employee's Withholding Allowance Certificate.* Cf. W-2 FORM.

wacreour (wah-**kroor**), *n.* [Law French] *Hist.* A vagrant.

***Wade* hearing.** (1969) *Criminal law.* A pretrial hearing in which the defendant contests the validity of his or her out-of-court identification. • If the court finds that the identification was tainted by unconstitutional methods, the prosecution cannot use the identification and must link the defendant to the crime by other means. *U.S. v. Wade*, 388 U.S. 218, 87 S.Ct. 1926 (1967).

wadia (**way**-dee-ə), *n.* [Law Latin] *Hist.* Pledges.

wadset, *n.* (15c) *Scots law.* **1.** A mortgage. — Also termed (in Roman law) *fiducia.* **2.** A pledge or pawn.

wadset, *vb.* (14c) *Scots law.* **1.** To mortgage. **2.** To pledge.

wafer seal. See SEAL.

wafter (**waf**-tər), *n.* [Middle English "convoyer"] (15c) *Hist.* An English naval officer appointed under Edward IV to protect fishermen, esp. on the coast of Norfolk and Suffolk. — Also spelled *waftor.*

waga (**way**-gə), *n.* [Law Latin] (17c) *Hist.* A measure of weight; a measure of goods.

wage, *n.* (*usu. pl.*) (14c) Payment for labor or services, usu. based on time worked or quantity produced; specif., compensation of an employee based on time worked or output of production. • Wages include every form of remuneration payable for a given period to an individual for personal services, including salaries, commissions, vacation pay, bonuses, and the reasonable value of board, lodging, payments in kind, tips, and any similar advantage received from the employer. An employer usu. must withhold income taxes from wages. Cf. SALARY.

> "Wages are, in both common and legal language, the compensation paid or to be paid for services, whether computed by the day, week, or month, or by the piece or job. Payment for piece or job work is frequently spoken of as earnings, but it differs in no sense from payment computed by time, the words 'earnings' and 'wages' being often used together in statutes on the subject. In mining and elsewhere, much of the work is done by what is called contracting, one man being paid by the ton or other quantity, he paying a helper or helpers a fixed sum daily or at a given rate per unit used; but the sums received by the different workmen are alike wages; so also where a group of men are employed in the joint production of a designated unit, and the payment therefor is divided among them fractionally or by a percentage. The profits of contractors where agreements are made for the performance of work involving individual direction and the employment and guidance of subordinates, as in the erection of a building or the construction of public works, are not classed as wages. The word 'salary' is also said by some courts to be synonymous with wages, though in others it is held to mean a larger compensation for more important services, or payment for services other than of a manual or mechanical kind. Salaries of public officers are not exempt from garnishment under laws exempting wages." Lindley Daniel Clark, *The Law of the Employment of Labor* 45–46 (1911) (citations omitted).

> "[I]t is held that the term 'wages' does not include the salary of the president, manager, or superintendent of a business corporation; nor sums payable to attorneys at law for professional services rendered to the corporation upon occasional retainers; nor the compensation of a person who is employed by the company to sell its goods in a foreign country, at a fixed annual salary, with the addition of a commission and his traveling expenses. Again, the term 'wages' is not applicable to the compensation of the public officers of a municipal corporation, who receive annual salaries, which are not due until the end of the year, and who are entitled to be paid so long as they hold their offices without regard to the services rendered. So also, a person who takes a contract to perform a specified work, as, to build a house according to plans and specifications, to execute a cutting on a line of railway at a given sum per cubic yard, or the like, and who employs men under him to do the actual work or to assist him in doing it, is not a 'workman' or 'laborer,' although he does a portion of the work himself, and his compensation is not 'wages.' So again, where manufacturers receive raw material from another, and work it up for him into a finished or partly finished product, by the use of their machinery and the labor of their employés, under a contract specifying a fixed rate of payment, the money due them therefor is not wages." Henry Campbell Black, *A Treatise on the Law and Practice of Bankruptcy* § 105, at 259–60 (1914).

▸ **basic wage.** See MINIMUM WAGE.

▸ **covered wages.** (1938) Wages on which a person is required to pay social-security taxes.

▸ **current wages.** (18c) Wages for the current period; wages that are not past due.

▸ **front wages.** (1979) Prospective compensation paid to a victim of job discrimination until the denied position becomes available.

▸ **green-circle wage.** A wage that is lower than the usual minimum pay.

▸ **living wage.** (1888) **1.** A wage sufficient to provide for a worker and his or her family a reasonably comfortable existence.

> "[A] living wage means:
> "1. A wage by which the worker may obtain the means of subsistence (a) for himself, (b) for those legitimately dependent on him;
> "2. A wage by which the worker may provide reasonable home comforts and fit himself for the discharge of duties of citizenship; and
> "3. That the wage shall be earned under such conditions as regards sanitary regulations, physical and mental effort, and duration of working hours, and as will afford reasonable time for recreation and rest.
> "A wage which would meet the requirements set out in the three clauses of the above definition would enable the worker, in the widest economic sense, to attain the highest state of industrial efficiency. We might therefore adopt a more concise form of words and say:

"A living wage must be sufficient to maintain the worker in the highest level of industrial efficiency, with decent surroundings and sufficient leisure.
"For a simple definition, one might stop at the word 'efficiency,' because 'the highest state of industrial efficiency' involves 'decent surroundings and sufficient leisure'; but I add the last six words that we may not lose sight of decency and leisure as important factors in a worker's life."
Mark Oldroyd, *A Living Wage* 7–8 (1894).

2. MINIMUM WAGE.

▸ **lost wages.** (1829) Damages to compensate for past lost earnings or lost earning capacity calculated from the time of injury to trial.

▸ **minimum wage.** (1860) The lowest permissible hourly rate of compensation for labor, as established by federal statute and required of employers engaged in interstate commerce. 29 USCA § 206. — Also termed *basic wage; living wage; federal minimum wage; national minimum wage.*

▸ **noncovered wages.** (1938) Wages on which a person is not required to pay social-security taxes.

▸ **real wages.** (18c) Wages representing the true purchasing power of the dollar, derived by dividing a price index into money wages.

▸ **red-circle wage.** A wage that is higher than the usual maximum pay.

▸ **slave wage.** (*often pl.*) **1.** A substandard rate of pay, below the legal minimum, inadequate to live on, often associated with unpleasant or unsafe working conditions. **2.** A wage so low that a laborer's standard of living is no better than that of a slave. **3.** *Hist.* The wage paid to emancipated black slaves after the Civil War, usu. much lower than that paid to white workers.

wage, *vb.* (14c) **1.** To engage in (a war, etc.). **2.** *Archaic.* To give security for (a performance, etc.). Cf. GAGE.

Wage and Hour Division. The division of the Employment Standards Administration in the U.S. Department of Labor responsible for enforcing the Fair Labor Standards Act, the Family and Medical Leave Act, the Employee Polygraph Protection Act, and other workplace-related statutes and regulations. — Abbr. WHD. See EMPLOYMENT STANDARDS ADMINISTRATION.

wage-and-hour law. (1935) A law (such as the federal Fair Labor Standards Act) governing minimum wages and maximum working hours for employees.

Wage and Hours Act. See FAIR LABOR STANDARDS ACT.

wage-and-price controls. (1942) A system of government-mandated maximum prices that can be charged for different goods and services or paid to various workers in different jobs.

wage-and-price freeze. See FREEZE (1).

wage assignment. (1907) **1.** See *attachment of wages* under ATTACHMENT (1). **2.** INCOME-WITHHOLDING ORDER. **3.** See ASSIGNMENT (2).

wage-assignment order. See INCOME-WITHHOLDING ORDER.

wage-earner. (1885) **1.** Someone who works for wages or a salary. **2.** Someone in a family who earns money to support the family as a whole. — Also termed *wageworker*; (in sense 2) *breadwinner.*

wage-earner's plan. See CHAPTER 13.

wager, *n.* (14c) **1.** Money or other consideration risked on an uncertain event; a bet or gamble. **2.** A promise to pay money or other consideration on the occurrence of an uncertain event. **3.** See *wagering contract* under CONTRACT. — **wager,** *vb.* — **wagerer,** *n.*

wagering contract. See CONTRACT.

wager insurance. See INSURANCE.

wager of battle. See TRIAL BY COMBAT.

wager of law. (16c) *Hist.* A method of proof in which a person defends against a claim by swearing that the claim is groundless, and by enlisting others (*compurgators*) to swear to the defendant's credibility. — Also termed *gager del ley* (**gay**-jər del **lay**); *vadiatio legis* (vad-ee-**ay**-shee-oh **lee**-jis). See COMPURGATION.

wager policy. See *wager insurance* under INSURANCE.

wages. See WAGE.

wage scale. A schedule of wages paid for different jobs in an industry, company, or the like.

wage slave. *Slang.* A person who works to enrich another in exchange for less pay than the value produced.

"For most of the nineteenth century, American workers decried wage labor. They claimed that wage labor denied workers the 'full fruits' of their labor and reduced the proud American citizen-worker to a 'wage slave,' a term of derision popularized in the Jacksonian era as the incipient crisis of wage labor led to the rise of the organized labor movement. Free workers did not want to be identified with lifelong 'hirelings,' whom they condemned as emblematic of slavery. The very word 'wages,' one worker declared in the 1850s, was 'odious.' Wage work was a form of compulsion, the opposite of the free labor system that they valued. In a society that, until 1865, countenanced chattel slavery, these were serious charges." Lawrence Glickman, "Living Wage," in 1 *Encyclopedia of U.S. Labor and Working-Class History* 809, 810 (Eric Arnesen ed., 2007).

wage-withholding. See *attachment of wages* under ATTACHMENT (1).

wage-withholding order. See INCOME-WITHHOLDING ORDER.

wageworker. See WAGE-EARNER (1).

Wagner Act. See NATIONAL LABOR RELATIONS ACT.

wagonage (**wag**-ə-nij). (17c) **1.** Transportation by a wagon. **2.** The fee for carriage by wagon. **3.** A group of wagons.

waif, *n.* (14c) **1.** An abandoned article whose owner is unknown, esp. something stolen and thrown away by the thief in flight, usu. through fear of apprehension. • At common law, if a waif, whether stolen or merely abandoned, was seized before the owner reclaimed it, the title vested in the Crown. The owner was thus punished for leaving the property or for failing to pursue the thief and attempting to recover the property. Today, however, the general rule is that a waif passes to the state in trust for the true owner, who may regain it by proving ownership.

"Waifs, *bona waviata*, are goods stolen, and waived or thrown away by the thief in his flight, for fear of being apprehended. These are given to the king by the law, as a punishment upon the owner, for not himself pursuing the felon, and taking away his goods from him. And therefore if the party robbed do his diligence immediately to follow and apprehend the thief (which is called making fresh *suit*) or do convict him afterwards, or procure evidence to convict him, he shall have his goods again." 1 William Blackstone, *Commentaries on the Laws of England* 286–87 (1765).

2. *Hist.* A homeless person, esp. a woman or child; a social outcast. See WAIVERY.

"[In the thirteenth century] a woman, though she cannot be outlawed, can be 'waived,' declared a 'waif,' and 'waiver' seems to have all the effects of outlawry." 1 Frederick Pollock & Frederic W. Maitland, *History of English Law Before the Time of Edward I* 482 (2d ed. 1898).

wainable (**way**-nə-bəl), *adj.* (18c) *Archaic.* (Of land) plowable; tillable.

wainage (**way**-nij), *n.* (16c) *Hist.* **1.** The plow, team, and other implements used by a person (esp. a villein) to cultivate the soil; instruments of husbandry. **2.** Cultivated land or the profits from it. — Also termed *wainagium*; *waynagium* (way-**nay**-jee-əm); (in sense 2) *gainage.*

wainbote. See BOTE (2).

wait-and-see principle. (1989) A modification to the rule against perpetuities, under which a court may determine the validity of a contingent future interest based on whether it actually vests within the perpetuities period, rather than on whether it possibly could have vested outside the period. — Also termed *second-look doctrine.*

waiting clerk. (18c) *Hist.* An officer who waits in attendance on the court of chancery. • The office of the waiting clerk was abolished in 1842 by the Court of Chancery Act. St. 5 & 6 Vict. ch. 103.

waiting list. (1897) A roster of people who have requested something that is not currently available but either will be or might be in the future.

waiting period. (1897) A period that must expire before some legal right or remedy can be enjoyed or enforced. • For example, many states have waiting periods for the issuance of marriage licenses or the purchase of handguns.

waive (wayv), *n.* (16c) *Archaic.* A woman who has by her conduct deprived herself of the protection of the law; a female outlaw. • The term "outlaw" usu. referred only to a male. See OUTLAW (1), (2).

waive, *vb.* (14c) **1.** To abandon, renounce, or surrender (a claim, privilege, right, etc.); to give up (a right or claim) voluntarily. • Ordinarily, to waive a right one must do it knowingly — with knowledge of the relevant facts. **2.** To refrain from insisting on (a strict rule, formality, etc.); to forgo. **3.** *Hist.* To declare someone a waif. See WAIF (2). — **waivable,** *adj.* — **waivability,** *n.*

waiver (**way**-vər), *n.* (17c) **1.** The voluntary relinquishment or abandonment — express or implied — of a legal right or advantage; FORFEITURE (2) <waiver of notice>. • The party alleged to have waived a right must have had both knowledge of the existing right and the intention of forgoing it.

"The term *waiver* is one of those words of indefinite connotation in which our legal literature abounds; like a cloak, it covers a multitude of sins." William R. Anson, *Principles of the Law of Contract* 419 (Arthur L. Corbin ed., 3d Am. ed. 1919).

"'Waiver' is often inexactly defined as 'the voluntary relinquishment of a known right.' When the waiver is reinforced by reliance, enforcement is often said to rest on 'estoppel.' . . . Since the more common definition of estoppel is limited to reliance on a misrepresentation of an existing fact, reliance on a waiver or promise as to the future is sometimes said to create a 'promissory estoppel.' The common definition of waiver may lead to the incorrect inference that the promisor must know his legal rights and must intend the legal effect of the promise. But . . . it is sufficient if he has reason to know the essential facts." Restatement (Second) of Contracts § 84 cmt. b (1979).

"Although it has often been said that a waiver is 'the intentional relinquishment of a known right,' this is a misleading definition. What is involved is not the relinquishment of a right and the termination of the reciprocal duty but the excuse of the nonoccurrence of or a delay in the occurrence of a condition of a duty." E. Allan Farnsworth, *Contracts* § 8.5, at 561 (3d ed. 1999).

▸ **at-issue waiver.** (1985) An exemption from the attorney–client privilege, whereby a litigant is considered to have waived the privilege by taking a position that cannot be effectively challenged without analyzing privileged information. — Also termed *waiver by putting into issue; implied waiver.* Cf. *offensive-use waiver.*

▸ **express waiver.** (18c) A voluntary and intentional waiver.

▸ **implied waiver.** (18c) A waiver evidenced by a party's decisive, unequivocal conduct reasonably inferring the intent to waive.

"An implied waiver may arise where a person has pursued such a course of conduct as to evidence an intention to waive a right, or where his conduct is inconsistent with any other intention than to waive it. Waiver may be inferred from conduct or acts putting one off his guard and leading him to believe that a right has been waived. Mere silence, however, is no waiver unless there is an obligation to speak." 28 Am. Jur. 2d *Estoppel and Waiver* § 160, at 845–46 (1966).

▸ **limited waiver. 1.** See *selective waiver.* **2.** See *partial waiver.*

▸ **offensive-use waiver.** (1993) An exemption from the attorney–client privilege, whereby a litigant is considered to have waived the privilege by seeking affirmative relief, if the claim relies on privileged information that would be outcome-determinative and that the opposing party has no other way to obtain. Cf. *at-issue waiver.*

▸ **partial waiver.** (1877) A waiver of protection against disclosure for only particular portions of a privileged communication but not the entire communication. — Also termed *limited waiver.*

▸ **prospective waiver.** (1889) A waiver of something that has not yet occurred, such as a contractual waiver of future claims for discrimination upon settlement of a lawsuit.

▸ **selective waiver.** (1973) A waiver of a privileged communication's protection against disclosure for only a limited, specific purpose, such as responding to a governmental investigation, but maintained for all other purposes. • This waiver applies when a party discloses privileged information to another particular party for a limited purpose but maintains the nondisclosure privilege against other parties. — Also termed *limited waiver.*

▸ **subject-matter waiver.** (1975) A waiver that occurs when a party voluntarily discloses only some information or communications for an unreasonable purpose, such as to present evidence in a selective, misleading, and unfair manner, and fairness requires that the party further disclose related, privileged information. • Subject-matter waiver never results from an inadvertent disclosure.

▸ **waiver by putting into issue.** See AT-ISSUE WAIVER.

▸ **waiver by subsequent disclosure.** (1999) A person's waiver of a previously privileged communication by later actions that are inconsistent with maintaining the privilege.

▸ **waiver of notice.** *Parliamentary law.* The waiver that occurs when a defective notice for a meeting is issued but every member attends and participates without objecting to the defect.

2. The loss of a right to make a claim or argument because it was not raised at the right time or because its maker otherwise did not follow necessary rules. • A waiver in this sense can be inadvertent. Cf. ESTOPPEL.

> "'Waiver' is often used as a synonym for 'forfeiture,' as when the failure to present a ground to the district court is deemed to 'waive' the ground in the court of appeals." *Bank v. Truck Ins. Exchange*, 51 F.3d 736 (7th Cir. 1995).

3. An instrument by which a person relinquishes or abandons a legal right or advantage <the plaintiff must sign a waiver when the funds are delivered>.

▸ **jury waiver.** (1883) A form signed by a criminal defendant who relinquishes the right to have the trial conducted before a jury.

▸ **lien waiver.** A written and signed waiver of a subcontractor's mechanic's lien rights, usu. submitted to enable the owner or general contractor to receive a draw on a construction loan.

waiver by election of remedies. (1873) A defense arising when a plaintiff has sought two inconsistent remedies and by a decisive act chooses one of them, thereby waiving the other.

waiver by putting into issue. See WAIVER (2).

waiver by subsequent disclosure. See WAIVER (2).

waiver hearing. See *transfer hearing* under HEARING.

waiver of claims and defenses. (1975) **1.** The intentional relinquishment by a maker, drawer, or other obligor under a contract of the right to assert against the assignee any claims or defenses the obligor has against the assignor. **2.** The contractual clause providing for such a waiver.

waiver of counsel. (1870) A criminal defendant's intentional relinquishment of the right to legal representation. • To be valid, a waiver of counsel must be made voluntarily, knowingly, and intelligently.

waiver of defenses. *Real estate.* A document by which a mortgagor acknowledges that the mortgage is good and valid for the full amount of the mortgage note. • This document ensures that the mortgagor has no defenses to the mortgage. — Also termed *estoppel certificate*; *no-setoff certificate*; *declaration of no defenses.*

waiver of exemption. (1846) **1.** A debtor's voluntary relinquishment of the right to an exemption from a creditor's levy or sale of any part of the debtor's personal property by judicial process. **2.** The contractual clause expressly providing for such a waiver.

waiver of immunity. (1883) The act of giving up the right against self-incrimination and proceeding to testify. See IMMUNITY (3).

waiver of indictment. (1875) *Criminal law.* A criminal defendant's decision to bypass the grand jury and plead guilty, usu. to a felony.

waiver of notice. See WAIVER (2).

waiver-of-premium clause. (1930) *Insurance.* A provision for a waiver of premium payments after the insured has been disabled for a specified length of time, such as six months.

waiver of privilege. The voluntary relinquishment of a right, exemption, or immunity. See WAIVER (1); PRIVILEGE.

waiver of protest. (1833) A relinquishment by a party to a negotiable instrument of the formality of protest in case of dishonor. See PROTEST (2).

waiver of service. (1823) A defendant's voluntary submission to the jurisdiction made by signing an acknowledgment of receipt of the petition and stating that he or she waives all further service.

waiver of term. A voluntary relinquishment of a right or benefit in a contractual provision.

waiver of tort. (1815) The election to sue in quasi-contract to recover the defendant's unjust benefit, instead of suing in tort to recover damages. See *implied-in-law contract* under CONTRACT.

> "A person upon whom a tort has been committed and who brings an action for the benefits received by the tortfeasor is sometimes said to 'waive the tort.'" Restatement of Restitution § 525 (1937).

> "'Waiver of tort' is a misnomer. A party only waives a tort in the sense that he elects to sue in quasi-contract to recover the defendant's unjust benefit rather than to sue in tort to recover damages; he has a choice of alternative remedies. But the tort is not extinguished. Indeed it is said that it is a *sine qua non* of both remedies that he should establish that a tort has been committed." Lord Goff of Chieveley & Gareth Jones, *The Law of Restitution* 605 (3d ed. 1986).

waivery. (17c) *Hist.* The act of putting a woman outside the protection of the law. • At common law, a woman could not be "outlawed" because she was not considered "in law" — that is, she could not undertake legal proceedings on her own. By Bracton's day, the effect of outlawing a woman was achieved by "waiving" her — the act being called *waivery.*

wakening. (16c) *Scots law.* The revival of an action in which no steps had taken for at least a year and a day.

walk, *vb.* (1958) *Slang.* **1.** To be acquitted <though charged with three thefts, Robinson walked each time>. **2.** To escape any type of real punishment <despite the seriousness of the crime, Selvidge paid only $750: he walked>.

walk-and-turn test. See FIELD SOBRIETY TEST.

walk-a-straight-line test. See FIELD SOBRIETY TEST.

walker, *n.* (15c) *Hist.* A forester who inspects an assigned area of land.

***Walker Process* claim.** (1976) *Patents.* A counterclaim in an infringement suit, seeking a declaratory judgment that the patent is invalid because its owner defrauded the Patent Office. • The claim is based on antitrust law, alleging that the patentee wrongfully tried to monopolize a market. *Walker Process Equip., Inc. v. Food Mach. & Chem.*, 382 U.S. 172, 86 S.Ct. 347 (1965). — Also termed *Walker Process defense.*

walkout. (1881) **1.** An occasion when people stop working or leave a meeting in protest; STRIKE (1). **2.** The act of leaving a work assignment, meeting, or other event as a show of protest.

wall. (bef. 12c) An erection of stone, brick, or other material raised to varying heights, esp. inside or surrounding a building, for privacy, security, or enclosure.

▸ **ancient wall.** A party wall that has stood for at least 20 years, thus giving each party an easement right to refuse to allow the other party to remove or substantially change the wall.

▸ **party wall.** (17c) A wall that divides two adjoining, separately owned properties and that is shared by the two property owners as tenants in common. — Also termed *common wall.*

> "There appears to be no precise legal definition of the term 'party wall.' Four possible meanings are as follows: (a) *Tenancy in common*: the two adjoining owners are tenants in common of the wall. (b) *Divided*: the wall is divided longitudinally into two strips, one belonging to each of the neighbouring owners. (c) *Divided with easements*: the wall is divided as in (b), but each half is subject to an easement of support in favour of the owner of the other half. (d) *Ownership subject to easement*: the wall belongs entirely to one of the adjoining owners, but is subject to an easement or right in the other to have it maintained as a dividing wall." Robert E. Megarry & M.P. Thompson, *A Manual of the Law of Real Property* 303–04 (6th ed. 1993).

***Waller* test.** (1984) A four-part test for determining whether a courtroom should be closed to the public: (1) the party seeking closure must show imminent prejudice; (2) the closure must be as narrowly tailored as possible; (3) all alternatives must be properly considered; and (4) adequate factual findings must support the closure. *See Waller v. Georgia*, 467 U.S. 39 (1984).

wallia (**wahl**-ee-ə), *n.* [Law Latin] *Hist.* A wall (such as a mound or bank) erected in marshy areas for protection against the sea; a seawall.

Walsh Act. A 1926 federal statute giving federal courts the power to subpoena and compel the return, testimony, and (if requested) production of documents or other items of U.S. citizens or residents who are abroad. • The subpoena is available for criminal proceedings, including grand-jury proceedings. 28 USCA § 1783.

Walsh–Healey Act. A 1936 federal statute stipulating that government contractors that manufacture materials, supplies, articles, or equipment in any amount exceeding $10,000 must (1) pay their workers no less than the prevailing minimum wage; (2) observe the eight-hour day and 40-hour workweek (with time-and-a-half for work exceeding those hours); (3) employ no convict labor and no females under 18 or males under 16 years of age; and (4) maintain sanitary working conditions. 41 USCA §§ 35 et seq. — Also termed *Public Contracts Act*; *Walsh–Healey Public Contracts Act.*

wampum (**wom**-pəm), *n.* [Narragansett "white shell beads"] (17c) *Hist.* Indian money consisting of shells, beads, or animal pelts. • In 1637, it became the first medium of exchange for the New England colonies by order of the General Court of Massachusetts, because England had not provided the Colonies with a standard of exchange. The Court ordered that "wampampege should passe at 6 a penny for any sum under 12d." Wampum was used as the medium of exchange, esp. for small transactions, until 1652, when the General Court ordered the first metallic currency. The last recorded exchange in wampum was in New York in 1701.

***Wands* test.** (2002) *Patents.* A judicial test of "undue experimentation" for determining if a patent application's specification teaches one skilled in the art how to make and work the claimed invention. *In re Wands*, 858 F.2d 731 (Fed. Cir. 1988). • The test takes account of eight factors: (1) how much experimentation would be needed, (2) how much guidance is given, (3) whether there is a working example, (4) the nature of the invention, (5) the state of the prior art, (6) the level of skill of those in the art, (7) how predictable or unpredictable the art is, and (8) the breadth of the claims. The factors (often called *Wands factors*) are illustrative rather than mandatory. See UNDUE EXPERIMENTATION.

wanlass (**wahn**-ləs). (15c) *Hist.* An ancient form of tenure requiring the tenant to drive deer to a stand so that the lord could take a shot. — Also spelled *wanlace.*

wantage (**wahnt**-ij), *n.* (1832) A deficiency of something; specif., a vessel's deficiency of not being full, because of leakage.

wanted person. (1912) A person sought by a law-enforcement agency because the person has escaped from custody or an arrest warrant has been issued for the person's arrest.

want of amicable demand. (1832) *Louisiana law.* A defensive pleading by a defendant who seeks to avoid, delay, or defeat the plaintiff's petition. • A defendant may (1) refuse to participate in the suit (a *declinatory exception*), (2) seek to delay the litigation in the suit (a *dilatory exception*), or (3) seek to dismiss or defeat the suit (a *peremptory exception*). See *declinatory exception, dilatory exception, peremptory exception* under EXCEPTION (1).

want of consideration. (18c) The lack of consideration for a contract. See CONSIDERATION (1). Cf. FAILURE OF CONSIDERATION.

want of jurisdiction. (16c) A court's lack of power to act in a particular way or to give certain kinds of relief. • A court may have no power to act at all, may lack authority over a person or the subject matter of a lawsuit, or may have no power to act until the prerequisites for its jurisdiction have been satisfied. — Also termed *lack of jurisdiction.* See JURISDICTION.

want of prosecution. (17c) Failure of a litigant to pursue the case <dismissal for want of prosecution>. — Also termed *lack of prosecution*; *no progress.* — Abbr. w.o.p.

want of repair. (17c) A defective condition, such as a condition on a highway making it unsafe for ordinary travel.

wanton (**wahn**-tən), *adj.* (14c) Unreasonably or maliciously risking harm while being utterly indifferent to the consequences. • In criminal law, *wanton* usu. connotes malice (in the criminal-law sense), while *reckless* does not. Cf. RECKLESS; WILLFUL.

> "Wanton differs from reckless both as to the actual state of mind and as to the degree of culpability. One who is acting recklessly is fully aware of the unreasonable risk he is creating, but may be trying and hoping to avoid any harm. One acting wantonly may be creating no greater risk of harm, but he is not trying to avoid it and is indifferent to whether harm results or not. Wanton conduct has properly been characterized as 'vicious' and rates extreme in the degree of culpability. The two are not mutually exclusive. Wanton conduct is reckless plus, so to speak." Rollin M. Perkins & Ronald N. Boyce, *Criminal Law* 879–80 (3d ed. 1982).

wanton and reckless misconduct. See *wanton misconduct* under MISCONDUCT.

wanton misconduct. See MISCONDUCT (1).

wanton negligence. See *gross negligence* under NEGLIGENCE.

wantonness, *n.* (14c) Conduct indicating that the actor is aware of the risks but indifferent to the results. • Wantonness usu. suggests a greater degree of culpability than recklessness, and it often connotes malice in criminal-law contexts. Cf. RECKLESSNESS. — **wanton,** *adj.*

wapentake (**wahp**-ən-tayk *or* **wap**-), *n.* [fr. Saxon *waepen* "weapons" + *tac* "touch"] (bef. 12c) *Hist.* **1.** In some English counties, a division corresponding to the hundred or ward in other counties. • The term was used particularly in areas formerly under Norse control, including northern and eastern counties. It became obsolete in the early 20th century. See HUNDRED. **2.** The court within such a division. **3.** A bailiff who works in such a court.

war. (12c) **1.** Hostile conflict by means of armed forces, carried on between countries, states, or rulers, or sometimes between parties within the same country or state; a period of such conflict <the Gulf War>. • A state of war may also exist without armed conflict; for example, the treaty formally ending the World War II state of war between the United States and Japan was signed seven years after the fighting ended in 1945.

> "War is nothing but a duel on a larger scale. Countless duels go to make up war, but a picture of it as a whole can be formed by imagining a pair of wrestlers. Each tries through physical force to compel the other to do his will; his *immediate* aim is to *throw* his opponent in order to make him incapable of further resistance. *War is thus an act of force to compel our enemy* to do our will." Carl von Clausewitz, *On War* 83 (1818; trans. Michael Howard & Peter Paret, 1993).

▸ **civil war.** (16c) An internal armed conflict between people of the same country; esp. (*usu. cap.*), the war from 1861 to 1865, resulting from the Confederate states' attempted secession from the Union.

▸ **imperfect war.** (17c) An intercountry war limited in terms of places, persons, and things.

▸ **mixed war.** A war between a country and private individuals.

▸ **perfect war.** (17c) A war involving an entire country against another.

▸ **private war.** (16c) A war between private persons.

▸ **public war.** (16c) A war between two countries under authority of their respective governments.

▸ **revolutionary war.** (18c) A war that results in a change of ruler or political system, often by force or violence; esp. (*usu. cap.*), the American Revolutionary War by which the United States became independent of the British Empire.

▸ **solemn war.** (17c) A war formally declared — esp. by public declaration — by one country against another.

▸ **war of aggression.** (18c) A war that the attacking country initiates for reasons other than individual or collective self-defense. • This type of war is prohibited by the United Nations Charter and may be considered a crime against international peace under customary international law.

2. A dispute or competition between adversaries <fare wars are common in the airline industry>. See PRICE WAR. **3.** A struggle to solve a pervasive problem <America's war against drugs>.

warantizare. See WARRANTIZARE.

War Clause. (1943) *Constitutional law.* The provision in the United States Constitution giving Congress the power to declare war. U.S. Const. art. I, § 8, cl. 11. • The President has the power to repel sudden attacks against the nation without congressional approval but cannot declare or wage war. Pub. L. No. 93-148. — Also termed *War Powers Clause; Declaration of War Clause; Declare War Clause.* See WAR POWER.

war contribution. (18c) *Int'l law.* An extraordinary payment imposed by an occupying power on the population of an occupied territory during wartime. — Often shortened to *contribution.*

war crime. (1906) Cruelty that violates international laws governing the conduct of international armed conflicts. • Examples of war crimes are the killing of hostages, abuse of civilians in occupied territories, abuse of prisoners of war, and devastation that is not justified by military necessity.

war criminal. (1906) A person who commits an act violating the international rules of war. • Since the Nuremberg Trials after World War II, it is not a defense to a charge of committing a war crime to maintain that the act was done under the orders of a superior officer. See LAWS OF WAR; WAR CRIME.

ward. (15c) **1.** A person, usu. a minor, who is under a guardian's charge or protection. See GUARDIAN (1).

▸ **permanent ward.** (1927) A ward who has been assigned a permanent guardian, the rights of the natural parents having been terminated by a juvenile court.

▸ **temporary ward.** (1901) A minor who is under the supervision of a juvenile court but whose parents' parental rights have not been terminated.

▸ **ward-in-chancery.** (18c) *Hist.* An infant under the superintendence of the chancellor.

▸ **ward of admiralty.** (1894) A seaman — so called because of the legal view that a seaman, in contractual matters, should be treated as a beneficiary and the other contracting party as a fiduciary because of the perceived inequitability of their bargaining positions.

▸ **ward of the state.** (1832) Someone who is housed by, and receives protection and necessities from, the government. — Also termed *state's ward.*

2. A territorial division in a city, usu. defined for purposes of city government. **3.** The act of guarding or protecting something or someone. **4.** *Archaic.* Someone who guards. **5.** CASTLE-GUARD. — Formerly also termed *warda.*

warda (**wor**-də), *n.* [Law Latin] *Hist.* Wardship; guardianship.

wardage. See WARDPENNY.

warden. (13c) **1.** A person who is in charge of something and whose duties include ensuring that rules are obeyed <game warden> <port warden>; esp., the official in charge of a prison, jail, or park <prison warden> <game warden>. — Also termed *warder.* **2.** SERGEANT-AT-ARMS (4).

warden of the cinque ports (singk ports). (16c) *Hist.* A magistrate with jurisdiction over the five (now seven) cinque ports. • This office was created in imitation of the Roman policy of strengthening coasts against enemies. The warden, formally called the Lord Warden, presided over the Court of the Lord Warden of the Cinque Ports, which was created in the 14th century and, over time, variously exercised civil, equity, and admiralty jurisdiction. — Formerly termed *guardian of the cinque ports.* See CINQUE PORTS.

warder. See WARDEN (1).

ward holding. (17c) *Scots law.* The feudal tenure known in England as knight service. See KNIGHT SERVICE. See *knight-service* under SERVICE (6).

ward-horn. *Hist.* The duty of keeping watch and ward with a horn to blow in the event of a surprise. See WATCH AND WARD.

ward-in-chancery. See WARD.

wardite. *Hist.* A fine that a tenant was required to pay upon failing to fulfill the duty of castle-guard. See CASTLE-GUARD.

wardmote (word-moht). (14c) *Hist.* **1.** A court maintained in every London ward. — Also termed *wardmote court; inquest.* **2.** A meeting of a ward.

ward of admiralty. See WARD.

ward of the state. See WARD.

wardpenny, *n.* (bef. 12c) *Hist.* **1.** Money paid in lieu of military service. **2.** Money paid to the sheriff or castellans in exchange for watching and warding a castle. — Also termed *wardage; warth.*

wardship. (15c) **1.** Guardianship of a person, usu. a minor. **2.** The condition of being a ward. **3.** *Hist.* The right of the feudal lord to guardianship of a deceased tenant's minor heir, as well as to income from the fief, until the heir reached the age of majority. — Also termed (in senses 1 & 3) *guardage.*

wardship in chivalry. (17c) Wardship as a feudal incident to the tenure of knight-service.

wardship in copyholds. (1805) Wardship by which the lord is guardian of an infant tenant by special custom.

wardstaff, *n.* (17c) *Hist.* A staff carried by an authority; esp., a constable's or watchman's staff.

wardwit, *n.* (bef. 12c) *Hist.* **1.** An immunity or exemption from the duty of warding or contributing to warding. **2.** A fine for failing to watch and ward. — Also termed *warwit; wardwite.*

warectare (wor-ək-**tair**-ee), *vb.* [Law Latin "to let lie fallow"] *Hist.* To plow land in the spring and then let it lie fallow for a better wheat crop the next year.

warehouse. (14c) A building used to store goods and other items.

▸ **bonded warehouse.** (18c) A special type of private warehouse used to store products subject to customs duties. See WAREHOUSE SYSTEM.

warehouse book. (18c) A book used by merchants to account for quantities of goods received, shipped, and in stock.

warehouseman. See WAREHOUSER.

warehouseman's lien. See *warehouser's lien* under LIEN.

warehouser. (18c) Someone who, as a business, keeps or stores the goods of another for a fee. • The transaction in which a warehouser engages is a bailment for the benefit of both parties, and the bailee is liable for ordinary negligence. — Also termed *warehouseman.* See BAILEE.

warehouse receipt. (1831) A document evidencing title to goods stored with someone else; esp., a receipt issued by a person engaged in the business of storing goods for a fee. • A warehouse receipt, which is considered a document of title, may be a negotiable instrument and is often used for financing with inventory as security. See BAILMENT.

warehouser's lien. See LIEN.

warehouse system. (18c) A system of maintaining bonded warehouses so that importers can either store goods for reexportation without paying customs duties or store the goods without paying duties until the goods are removed for domestic consumption. See *bonded warehouse* under WAREHOUSE.

warehouse-to-warehouse cover. (2002) Insurance coverage for goods protecting against damage at any time during the shipping process, including the loading and unloading of the goods. See COMPLETE-OPERATION RULE. Cf. COMING-TO-REST DOCTRINE.

warehousing. (1971) **1.** A mortgage banker's holding of mortgages until the resale market improves. **2.** A corporation's giving of advance notice of a tender offer to institutional investors, who can then buy stock in the target company before public awareness of the takeover inflates the stock's price. See TENDER OFFER.

warfare. (15c) **1.** The act of engaging in war or military conflict. See WAR (1). **2.** Loosely, the act of engaging in any type of conflict.

▸ **asymmetric warfare.** Warfare in which the fighting parties have no parity in power, means, methods, organization, values, and time.

> "[T]he term 'asymmetric warfare' — by no means a legal term of art — is nothing but a description of a fact of life. In this context, it is, however, important to remember that warfare, especially in Western societies, is perceived as armed hostilities predominantly under State control and between combatants in which civilians and civilian objects are largely spared from violence and destruction. . . . From the outset of its development in the middle of the 19th century the modern law of armed conflict, or international humanitarian law . . . , has been based on that approach. To a certain extent the law of armed conflict recognizes, or implicitly accepts, the different forms of asymmetry. Still, its underlying concept is that of symmetric warfare insofar as the use of force is limited to lawful targets . . . and that the parties to the conflict will abide by its rules, and be it only because they expect their opponent to act accordingly . . . . The development of the law of armed conflict has resulted in abolishing the prevalence of military necessity over considerations of humanity (*Kriegsräson geht vor Kriegsmanier* . . .) by establishing an operable balance between the two, without making warfare impossible . . . ." Wolff Heintschel von Heinegg, "Asymmetric Warfare," in 1 *The Max Planck Encyclopedia of Public International Law* 725, 726 (Rüdiger Wolfrum ed., 2012).

▸ **biochemical warfare.** (1946) Warfare in which both biological and chemical weapons are used. See *biological warfare, chemical warfare.*

▸ **biological warfare.** (1933) The use of biological or infectious agents in war, usu. by delivering them via airplanes or ballistic missiles. Cf. *chemical warfare.*

▸ **chemical warfare.** (1912) Warfare in which deadly chemical agents, such as nerve gas, are used as weapons, usu. by delivering the chemicals via shells, missiles, or bombs. • Chemical weapons were first used in World War I. The first international treaty forbidding the use of both chemical and biological weapons, the Protocol for the Prohibition of the Use in War of Asphyxiating, Poisonous or Other Gases, and of Biological Methods of Warfare was signed in 1925 and came into force in 1928. The United States is a signatory but with reservations. Cf. *biological warfare.*

▸ **economic warfare.** (1888) **1.** A hostile relationship between two or more countries in which at least one tries to damage the other's economy for economic, political, or military ends. **2.** The collective measures that might be taken to achieve such ends.

> "'Economic warfare' is not a term of art in international law, and it is difficult to define the concept with precision. It can be, and has been, used to describe conduct ranging from economic methods of warfare such as belligerent blockade and the strategic bombing of factory infrastructure, to decentralized economic (counter) measures in peacetime, such as trade embargoes or even boycotts voluntarily undertaken by the citizens of one State against the products of another, and to collective sanctions imposed by the UN Security Council. The confusion surrounding the term 'economic warfare' is illustrated by the fact that while some leading textbooks on the law of armed conflict contain no separate chapter entitled 'economic warfare' . . . or even an index entry to that effect . . . , some textbooks on international economic law devote a whole chapter to the issue . . . ." Vaughan Lowe & Antonios Tzanakopoulos, "Economic Warfare," in 3 *The Max Planck Encyclopedia of Public International Law* 330, 330 (Rüdiger Wolfrum ed., 2012).

▸ **guerrilla warfare.** (1811) Hostilities that are conducted by individuals or small groups who are usu. not part of an organized army and who fight by means of surprise attacks, ambushes, and sabotage. • Formerly, it was thought that the hostilities had to be conducted in enemy-occupied territory. Typically, guerrilla warfare is carried out only when geographical conditions are favorable and when the civilian population is at least partly cooperative.

▸ **land warfare.** (1839) Hostilities conducted on the ground, as opposed to at sea or in the air.

▸ **political warfare.** The use of all methods short of physical aggression — namely, economic, psychological, cultural, ideological, and propagandistic tools, whether overt or covert — to achieve foreign-policy objectives.

> "Despite the term's gaining widespread use only in the middle of the twentieth century, the concept of political warfare has resonated throughout the ages, helping to define the contours of international conflict since antiquity. . . . Military power is not entirely redundant, fulfilling a key psychological function as a deterrent against enemies acting against one's interests. Yet the crux of political warfare is the realization of objectives through means that prevent resort to traditional tools of war. It is consistent with the dictum, expressed by the nineteenth-century Prussian military theorist Carl von Clausewitz, that war is a continuation of policy by other means — but with the crucial caveat that war is a distinctly political, rather than military, struggle. Political warfare is, in other words, to fight a war short of going to war. Accordingly, it has been a key characteristic of U.S. foreign relations since 1945." Kaeten Mistry, "Political Warfare," in 2 *The Oxford Encyclopedia of American Military and Diplomatic History* 145, 145–46 (Timothy J. Lynch ed., 2013).

war-mongering propaganda. See PROPAGANDA.

WARN Act (worn akt). *abbr.* WORKER ADJUSTMENT AND RETRAINING NOTIFICATION ACT.

warning. (bef. 12c) The pointing out of a danger, esp. to one who would not otherwise be aware of it. • State and federal laws (such as 21 USCA § 825) require warning labels to be placed on potentially dangerous materials, such as drugs and equipment.

▸ **adequate warning.** (1885) A warning that reasonably alerts a product's average user to a potential hazard, and the nature and extent of the danger. • Four elements have been articulated as comprising an adequate warning: (1) notice that a severe hazard exists, (2) a description of the hazard's nature, (3) a description of the hazard's possible consequences, and (4) instructions on how to avoid the hazard. In addition, the warning must be prominently displayed, and may have to illustrate the nature and severity of the hazard with pictographs.

warning label. A notice on a container's package about a product's known or potential hazards.

warnistura (wor-nə-**st**[**y**]**oor**-ə), *n.* [Law Latin] *Hist.* **1.** Furniture; provision. **2.** Garrison.

warnoth (**wor**-noht). (17c) *Hist.* A defunct custom by which a tenant who failed to pay rent on a set day had to pay double the amount due, and on failing a second time had to pay triple (and so on).

war of aggression. See WAR (1).

war offense. See WAR CRIME.

war power. (18c) *Constitutional law.* The constitutional authority of Congress to declare war and maintain armed forces (U.S. Const. art. I, § 8, cls. 11–14), and of the President to conduct war as commander-in-chief (U.S. Const. art. II, § 2, cl. 1).

War Powers Clause. See WAR CLAUSE.

war-powers resolution. (1954) A resolution passed by Congress in 1973 (over the President's veto) restricting the President's authority to involve the United States in foreign hostilities unless there is a declaration of war, a specific statutory authorization, or a national emergency created by an attack on the United States, its territories or possessions, or its armed forces. 50 USCA §§ 1541–1548.

warrandice (**wahr**-ən-dis *or* -dɪs). (15c) *Scots law.* An obligation to indemnify the grantee or buyer of land if another person establishes a superior title and takes possession.

▸ **absolute warrandice.** (17c) *Scots law.* A warranty that no one can or will reduce the grantee's title to land. • This warranty, usu. implied, is normally made explicit in a full-price conveyance of land.

▸ **personal warrandice.** (17c) An obligation to indemnify that binds the grantor and the grantor's heirs.

▸ **real warrandice.** (17c) An obligation by which certain lands are made over as security for lands conveyed to the grantee and will be transferred to the grantee if he or she is evicted from the conveyed lands by a third party.

warrant, *n.* (14c) **1.** A writ directing or authorizing someone to do an act, esp. one directing a law enforcer to make an arrest, a search, or a seizure.

▸ **administrative warrant.** (1951) A warrant issued by a judge at the request of an administrative agency that seeks to conduct an administrative search. See *administrative search* under SEARCH (1). — Also termed *administrative search warrant.*

▸ **anticipatory search warrant.** See SEARCH WARRANT.

▸ **arrest warrant.** (1894) A warrant issued by a disinterested magistrate after a showing of probable cause, directing a law-enforcement officer to arrest and take a person into custody. — Also termed *warrant of arrest.*

▸ **bench warrant.** (17c) A writ issued directly by a judge to a law-enforcement officer, esp. for the arrest of a person who has been held in contempt, has been indicted, has disobeyed a subpoena, or has failed to appear for a hearing or trial. • In most jurisdictions, a bench warrant is used only when the defendant has already appeared at least once. Otherwise, an arrest warrant is issued. A bench warrant is often issued for the arrest of a child-support obligor who is found in contempt of court for not having paid the support obligation.

▸ **blanket warrant.** See *general warrant* (2); *blanket search warrant* under SEARCH WARRANT.

▸ **border warrant.** (1816) *Hist. English law.* A writ of arrest or other warrant concerning debts owed, issued on one side of a national border for execution on the other side; esp., such a warrant issued on either side of the border between England and Scotland.

▸ **commitment warrant.** See *warrant of commitment.*

▸ **death warrant.** (18c) *Criminal law.* A warrant authorizing a warden or other prison official to carry out a death sentence. • A death warrant typically sets the time and place for a prisoner's execution.

▸ **distress warrant.** (18c) **1.** A warrant authorizing a court officer to distrain property. See DISTRESS. **2.** A writ allowing an officer to seize a tenant's goods for failing to pay rent due to the landlord.

▸ **emergency warrant.** A warrant whose issuance is expedited because of exigent circumstances.

▸ **escape warrant.** (18c) *Criminal law.* **1.** A warrant directing a peace officer to rearrest an escaped prisoner. **2.** *Hist.* A warrant granted to retake a prisoner who had escaped from a royal prison after being committed there. • The warrant was obtained on affidavit from the judge of the court in which the action had been brought, and was directed to all sheriffs throughout England, commanding them to retake and commit the prisoner to the nearest jail.

▸ **extradition warrant.** (1876) *Criminal law.* A warrant for the return of a fugitive from one jurisdiction to another. Cf. *rendition warrant.*

▸ **fugitive warrant.** (1900) *Criminal law.* An arrest warrant in one jurisdiction seeking the extradition of a defendant who is believed to have fled to another jurisdiction to avoid prosecution or punishment.

▸ **general warrant.** (16c) **1.** *Hist.* A warrant issued by the English Secretary of State for the arrest of the author, printer, or publisher of a seditious libel, without naming the persons to be arrested. • General warrants were banned by Parliament in 1766.

> "A practice had obtained in the secretaries office ever since the restoration, grounded on some clauses in the acts for regulating the press, of issuing *general* warrants to take up (without naming any person in particular) the authors, printers and publishers of such obscene or seditious libels, as were particularly specified in the warrant. When those acts expired in 1694, the same practice was inadvertently continued, in every reign and under every administration, except the four last years of queen Anne, down to the year 1763: when such a warrant being issued to apprehend the authors, printers and publishers of a certain seditious libel, its validity was disputed; and the warrant was adjudged by the whole court of king's bench to be void, in the case of Money v. Leach. *Trin.* 5 *Geo. III. E.R.* After which the issuing of such general warrants was declared illegal by a vote of the house of commons." 4 William Blackstone, *Commentaries on the Laws of England* 288 n.i (1769).

2. A warrant giving a law-enforcement officer broad authority to search and seize unspecified places or persons; a search or arrest warrant that lacks a sufficiently particularized description of the person or thing to be seized or the place to be searched. • General warrants are unconstitutional because they fail to meet the Fourth Amendment's specificity requirements. — Also termed *blanket warrant.*

> "But though there are precedents of general warrants to search all suspected places for stolen goods, these are not at common law legal, because it would be extremely dangerous to leave it to the discretion of a common officer to arrest what person, or search what houses he thinks fit. And in the great case of Money v. Leach, it was declared by Lord Mansfield, that a warrant to search for, and secure the person and papers of the author, printer and publisher of a libel, is not only illegal in itself, but is so improper on the face of it, that it will afford no justification to an officer acting under its sanction. And by two resolutions of the House of Commons such general warrants were declared to be invalid." 1 Joseph Chitty, *A Practical Treatise on the Criminal Law* 66 (2d ed. 1826).

▸ **governor's warrant.** (18c) A warrant issued by a state's governor's office to extradite a captured suspect to another state to stand trial. See *extradition warrant.*

▸ **John Doe warrant.** (1900) *Criminal law.* A warrant for the arrest of a person whose name is unknown. • A John Doe warrant may be issued, for example, for a person known by sight but not by name. This type of warrant is permitted in a few states, but not in federal practice.

▸ **justice's warrant.** See *peace warrant.*

▸ **landlord's warrant.** (1824) A type of distress warrant from a landlord to seize the tenant's goods, to sell them at public sale, and to compel the tenant to pay rent or observe some other lease stipulation. See DISTRAIN; DISTRESS.

▸ **no-knock search warrant.** See SEARCH WARRANT.

▸ **outstanding warrant.** (1899) An unexecuted arrest warrant.

▸ **parole warrant.** (1918) *Criminal law.* A warrant issued for the arrest of a parolee.

▸ **peace warrant.** (18c) A warrant issued by a justice of the peace for the arrest of a specified person. — Also termed *justice's warrant*; *warrant to keep the peace.*

▸ **possessory warrant.** (1850) A process, similar to a search warrant, used under certain circumstances by a plaintiff to search for and recover property wrongfully taken or held by another.

▸ **preliminary warrant.** (1859) *Criminal law.* A warrant to bring a person to court for a preliminary hearing on probable cause.

▸ **probation-violation warrant.** See *violation warrant.*

▸ **rendition warrant.** (1881) *Criminal law.* A warrant requesting the extradition of a fugitive from one jurisdiction to another. — Also termed *warrant of rendition.* Cf. *extradition warrant.*

▸ **search warrant.** See SEARCH WARRANT.

▸ **seizure warrant.** A warrant that allows a law-enforcement officer to seize certain property, usu. property believed to be the fruit of a crime or an instrument used to commit a crime. • The warrant is often combined with a search warrant.

▸ **sneak-and-peek warrant.** See *covert-entry search warrant* under SEARCH WARRANT.

▸ **surreptitious-entry warrant.** (1985) *Criminal law.* A warrant authorizing a law officer to enter and observe an ongoing criminal operation (such as an illegal drug lab).

▸ **tax warrant.** (18c) An official process issued for collecting unpaid taxes and under which property may be seized and sold.

▸ **valid warrant.** (1801) A warrant that is regular in form and is issued by a court, body, or official having both the authority to issue the warrant for the purpose stated and jurisdiction over the person named, all the requisite proceedings for its proper issuance having taken place.

▸ **violation warrant.** (1948) A warrant issued for the arrest of a convict who has violated the terms of probation, parole, or supervised release. — Also termed (narrowly) *probation-violation warrant.*

▸ **warrant of arrest.** See *arrest warrant.*

▸ **warrant of commitment.** (17c) A warrant committing a person to custody. — Also termed *commitment warrant.*

▸ **warrant of rendition.** See *rendition warrant.*

▸ **warrant to keep the peace.** See *peace warrant.*

▸ **warrant upon indictment or information.** (1903) An arrest warrant issued at the request of the prosecutor for a defendant named in an indictment or information. Fed. R. Crim. P. 9.

2. A document conferring authority, esp. to pay or receive money.

▸ **deposit warrant.** (1853) A warehouse receipt used as security for a loan.

▸ **dock warrant.** See DOCK RECEIPT.

▸ **interest warrant.** (18c) **1.** An order by a corporation directing a bank to pay the interest due on a note, bond, or other debt to a corporate creditor. **2.** A document by which a creditor, usu. a company, asks an insurer to pay all the interest due on the insurer's notes, bonds, or other debts held by the creditor.

▸ **municipal warrant.** (1872) An order to draw money from a municipality's treasury for the payment of the municipality's expenses or debts.

▸ **tax-anticipation warrant.** (1905) A warrant that is issued to raise public money and that is payable out of tax receipts when collected.

▸ **treasury warrant.** (1834) An order in the form of a check on which government disbursements are paid.

3. An order by which a drawer authorizes someone to pay a particular sum of money to another.

▸ **county warrant.** (17c) A warrant drawn by a county official, directing the county treasurer to pay a sum of money out of county funds to bearer, to a named individual, or to the named individual's order.

4. *Securities.* An instrument granting the holder a long-term (usu. a five- to ten-year) option to buy shares at a fixed price. • It is commonly attached to preferred stocks or bonds. — Also termed *stock warrant; subscription warrant; warrant for stock.*

warrant, *vb.* (14c) **1.** To guarantee the security of (realty or personalty, or a person) <the store warranted the safety of the customer's jewelry>. **2.** To give warranty of (title); to give warranty of title to (a person) <the seller warrants the property's title to the buyer>. **3.** To promise or guarantee <warrant payment>.

> "Even today lawyers use the verb 'to warrant' meaning to promise without necessarily indicating that the promise is a warranty." P.S. Atiyah, *An Introduction to the Law of Contract* 145 n.1 (3d ed. 1981).

4. To justify <the conduct warrants a presumption of negligence>. **5.** To authorize <the manager warranted the search of the premises>.

warrant arrest. See *lawful arrest* under ARREST (2).

Warrant Clause. (1962) *Constitutional law.* The clause of the Fourth Amendment to the U.S. Constitution requiring that warrants be issued only on probable cause.

warrant creditor. See CREDITOR.

warranted arrest. See ARREST (2).

warranted search. See SEARCH (1).

warrantee (wor-ən-**tee** *or* wahr-). (18c) A person to whom a warranty is given; esp., a person who receives a written warranty. • The term also sometimes applies to the beneficiary of an implied warranty.

warrant for stock. See WARRANT (4).

warrantia chartae. See DE WARRANTIA CHARTAE.

warrantia custodiae (wə-**ran**-shee-ə kə-**stoh**-dee-ee), *n.* [Law Latin] (17c) *Hist.* A writ for a purchaser of land held in knight's service against the seller (and heirs), who had warranted that the land was free of wardship when a wardship was later claimed.

warrantia diei. See DE WARRANTIA DIEI.

warrantizare (wor-ən-tə-**zair**-ee), *vb.* [Law Latin] *Hist.* To warrant by covenant (in a deed of conveyance) to defend the grantee's title and possession. — Also spelled *warantizare.*

warrantless arrest. See ARREST (2).

warrantless search. See SEARCH (1).

warrant of arrest. See *arrest warrant* under WARRANT (1).

warrant of attorney. (16c) **1.** POWER OF ATTORNEY (1). **2.** *Archaic.* Written authority given by a client to a lawyer to appear in court and to confess judgment in favor of a specified party. • It usu. instructed the attorney not to bring any action, seek a writ of error, or file a bill in equity that might delay the judgment. The warrant was typically given as security for an obligation on which judgment was authorized. Cf. CONFESSION OF JUDGMENT; COGNOVIT.

> "A warrant of attorney was not required to be under seal, though it generally was so. In order to guard against any imposition in procuring debtors to execute warrants of attorney or *cognovits* in ignorance of the effect of such instruments, it is provided that a warrant of attorney to confess judgment in any personal action, or *cognovit actionem*, given by any person, shall not be of any force, unless there is present some attorney of one of the superior courts on behalf of such person, expressly named by him and attending at his request, to inform him of the nature and effect of such warrant or cognovit, before the same is executed . . . ." Joshua Williams, *Principles of the Law of Personal Property* 125 (11th ed. 1881).

warrant of commitment. See WARRANT (1).

warrant of confession. See CONFESSION OF JUDGMENT.

warrant officer. (17c) **1.** OFFICER (2). **2.** SERGEANT-AT-ARMS (4).

warrant of rendition. See *rendition warrant* under WARRANT (1).

warrantor (**wor**-ən-tor *or* -tər *or* **wahr**-). (15c) Someone who gives a written warranty or becomes obligated under an implied warranty. *See* 15 USCA § 2301(5).

warrant recall, *n.* A procedure for removing from government computers information about canceled warrants in order to avoid repeated or mistaken arrests.

warrant to keep the peace. See *peace warrant* under WARRANT (1).

warrant to sue and defend. (18c) *Hist.* **1.** Written authority given by a client to a lawyer to authorize commencement or defense of a lawsuit. **2.** A special warrant from the Crown authorizing a party to appoint an attorney to sue or defend on the party's behalf.

warrant upon indictment or information. See WARRANT (1).

warranty (**wor**-ən-tee *or* **wahr**-), *n.* (14c) **1.** *Property.* A covenant by which the grantor in a deed promises to secure to the grantee the estate conveyed in the deed, and pledges to compensate the grantee if the grantee is evicted by someone having better title. • The covenant is binding on the grantor's heirs. Historically, a warrantor was expected to turn over land. But cash compensation could be substituted. See COVENANT (4). Cf. *quitclaim deed* under DEED.

▸ **collateral warranty.** (16c) A warranty that is made by a stranger to the title, and that consequently runs only to the covenantee and not with the land.

▸ **consumer warranty.** See *manufacturer's warranty.*

▸ **deed warranty.** See *covenant for title* under COVENANT (4).

▸ **encoding warranty.** (1991) A warranty made by encrypting information on a check or other item to ensure that the information has been correctly recorded. UCC § 4-209(a). • For example, such a warranty is imposed by the UCC on a depositary bank that encodes the dollar amount of a check on a computer-generated recognition line during the check-collection process.

▸ **general warranty.** (17c) A warranty against the claims of all persons.

▸ **lineal warranty.** (16c) *Hist.* A warranty existing when an heir derives title to land from the warrantor; a warranty from the same ancestor as the one from whom the land derived.

▸ **manufacturer's warranty.** A warranty given by a product's manufacturer against defects in the components and workmanship and promising to cure defects. • The warranty is usu. limited by time or specified usage, such as motor-vehicle mileage. — Also termed *consumer warranty.*

▸ **special warranty.** (17c) A warranty against any person's claim made by, through, or under the grantor or the grantor's heirs.

▸ **warranty against encumbrances.** See *covenant against encumbrances* under COVENANT (4).

▸ **warranty of further assurances.** See *covenant for further assurances* under COVENANT (4).

2. *Contracts.* An express or implied promise that something in furtherance of the contract is guaranteed by one of the contracting parties; esp., a seller's promise that the thing being sold is as represented or promised. • Although a court may treat a misrepresentation as an implied warranty, in general a warranty differs from a representation in four principal ways: (1) a warranty is conclusively presumed to be material, while the burden is on the party claiming breach to show that a representation is material; (2) a warranty must be strictly complied with, while substantial truth is the only requirement for a representation; (3) a warranty is an essential part of a contract, while a representation is usu. only a collateral inducement; and (4) an express warranty is usu. written on the face of the contract, while a representation may be written or oral. Cf. CONDITION (2), (3); GUARANTEE (1).

> "A warranty is a stipulation forming a part of the contract as it has been completed, and is construed as a condition precedent, which must be strictly complied with to the minutest detail, or else the contract is rendered void . . . . A representation is a verbal or written statement made before the issue of the policy, as to the existence of some fact, or state of facts, tending to induce the insurer more readily to assume the risk, or to assume it for less premium, by diminishing the estimate he would otherwise have formed of it." George Bliss, *The Law of Life Insurance* §§ 34–35, at 45–46 (2d ed. 1874).

> "[T]wo points must be borne in mind. In the first place, the words 'condition' and 'warranty' are not invariably kept as distinct as accuracy of definition demands; and in insurance law especially 'warranty' is very commonly used in the sense ascribed to 'condition' . . . . In the second place, the injured party, if he chooses to waive his right to repudiate the contract on breach of a condition, may still bring an action for such damages as he has sustained." William R. Anson, *Principles of the Law of Contract* 223 (Arthur L. Corbin ed., 3d Am. ed. 1919).

▸ **as-is warranty.** (1976) A warranty that goods are sold with all existing faults. See AS IS.

▸ **construction warranty.** (1968) A warranty from the seller or building contractor of a new home that the home is free of structural, electrical, plumbing, and other defects and is fit for its intended purpose.

▸ **deceptive warranty.** (1975) A warranty containing false or fraudulent representations or promises.

▸ **express warranty.** (17c) A warranty created by the overt words or actions of the seller. • Under the UCC, an express warranty is created by any of the following: (1) an affirmation of fact or promise made by the seller to the buyer relating to the goods that becomes the basis of the bargain; (2) a description of the goods that becomes part of the basis of the bargain; or (3) a sample or model made part of the basis of the bargain. UCC § 2-313.

> "To constitute an express warranty, there must be some expression by the seller amounting to an unequivocal affirmation, relied on by the buyer, that the goods are of some certain quality. It is not enough to prove mere expressions of opinion. But it is not necessary that the word 'warrant' should be used. Any affirmation amounting to it is sufficient. No particular phraseology is necessary. Any distinct assertion of the quality of the thing, made by the seller as an inducement to purchase, and relied on by the buyer, may be ground for finding a warranty. Evasive or equivocal language may be left to the jury, to determine whether it

was intended to be understood as a warranty or affirmative representation. Any positive affirmation, understood and relied on by the buyer, is a warranty, or, at least, evidence to go to the jury. The description of the goods, in a bought and sold note, advertisement, bill of parcels, invoice, or in an oral assurance to the buyer, is evidence of a warranty." Austin Abbott, *Trial Evidence* § 72, at 340–41 (1880).

"An *express warranty* arises from the contract itself, from the 'dickered' aspects of the individual bargain. Any affirmation or promise relating to the goods, any description of the goods, and any sample or model of the goods becomes an express warranty if it is 'part of the basis of the bargain.'" 1 Julian B. McDonnell & Elizabeth J. Coleman, *Commercial and Consumer Warranties* ¶ 1.02[1], at 1-7 (1991).

▸ **extended warranty.** (1936) An additional warranty often sold with the purchase of consumer goods (such as appliances and motor vehicles) to cover repair costs not otherwise covered by a manufacturer's standard warranty, by extending either the standard-warranty coverage period or the range of defects covered. — Also termed *extended service warranty*; *extended service contract*.

▸ **full warranty.** A warranty that fully covers labor and materials for repairs. • Under federal law, the warrantor must remedy the consumer product within a reasonable time and without charge after notice of a defect or malfunction. 15 USCA § 2304. *See* MAGNUSON–MOSS WARRANTY ACT. Cf. *limited warranty*.

▸ **implied warranty.** (18c) An obligation imposed by the law when there has been no representation or promise; esp., a warranty arising by operation of law because of the circumstances of a sale, rather than by the seller's express promise.

▸ **implied warranty of authority.** (1859) A warranty imposed by law against an agent who purports to act on behalf of a principal or against a person who falsely purports to be a principal's agent.

▸ **implied warranty of fitness for a particular purpose.** (1923) A warranty — imposed by law if the seller has reason to know of the buyer's special purposes for the item — that the item is suitable for those purposes. *See* UCC § 2-315. — Sometimes shortened to *warranty of fitness*.

"Those unfamiliar with the differences between the warranty of merchantability (fitness for the *ordinary* purposes for which such goods are used) and the warranty of fitness for a *particular* purpose often confuse the two; one can find many opinions in which the judges used the terms 'merchantability' and 'fitness for a particular purpose' interchangeably. Such confusion under the Code is inexcusable." 1 James J. White & Robert S. Summers, *Uniform Commercial Code* § 9-10, at 527 (4th ed. 1995).

▸ **implied warranty of habitability.** (1900) In a residential lease, a warranty from the landlord to the tenant that the leased property is fit to live in and that it will remain so during the term of the lease. — Also termed *covenant of habitability*. • This warranty usu. applies to residential property, but a few courts, esp. in Utah, have applied it to commercial property as well. — Often shortened to *warranty of habitability*. — Also termed *implied covenant of habitability*.

▸ **implied warranty of merchantability.** (1896) A merchant seller's warranty — implied by law — that the thing sold is fit for its ordinary purposes. • Under the UCC, an implied warranty of merchantability arises whenever a merchant sells goods unless the agreement expressly provides otherwise. UCC § 2-314. — Sometimes shortened to *warranty of merchantability*. — Also termed *warranty of quality*.

"The *implied warranty of merchantability* attaches when the seller is a merchant with respect to the goods involved in the exchange. Accordingly, the product must meet certain standards; it must pass without objection in the trade under the contract description and it must be fit for the ordinary purposes for which such goods are used. The concepts of marketability, operability, and repairability have emerged as varying criteria for merchantable goods." 1 Julian B. McDonnell & Elizabeth J. Coleman, *Commercial and Consumer Warranties* ¶ 1.02[1], at 1-7 (1991).

▸ **limited warranty.** (1871) A warranty that does not fully cover labor and materials for repairs. • Under federal law, a limited warranty must be clearly labeled as such on the face of the warranty. See MAGNUSON–MOSS WARRANTY ACT. Cf. *full warranty*.

▸ **personal warranty.** (18c) A warranty arising from an obligation to pay all or part of the debt of another.

▸ **presentment warranty.** (1965) An implied promise concerning the title and credibility of an instrument, made to a payor or acceptor upon presentment of the instrument for payment or acceptance. UCC §§ 3-417, 3-418.

▸ **transfer warranty.** (1964) **1.** An implied promise concerning the title and credibility of an instrument, made by a transferor to a transferee and, if the transfer is by indorsement, to remote transferees. UCC §§ 3-416, 4-207. **2.** A warranty made by a transferee of a document of title upon a transfer of the document for value to the immediate transferee. UCC § 7-507.

▸ **warranty ab initio** (ab i-**nish**-ee-oh). (1887) An independent subsidiary promise whose breach does not discharge the contract, but gives to the injured party a right of action for the damage sustained as a result of the breach. • *Ab initio* means that the warranty existed from the contract's inception. Cf. *warranty ex post facto*.

▸ **warranty against encumbrances.** See *covenant against encumbrances* under COVENANT (4).

▸ **warranty against infringement.** (1900) A merchant's warranty that the goods being sold or licensed do not violate any patent, copyright, trademark, or other intellectual-property claim. • The warranty does not arise if the buyer provides the seller with the specifications for the goods purchased. Under § 2-312(3) of the Uniform Commercial Code, the warranty against infringement is a part of the warranty of title unless it is explicitly disclaimed.

▸ **warranty ex post facto** (eks pohst **fak**-toh). (1961) A broken condition for which the injured party could void the contract, but decides instead to continue the contract, with a right of action for the broken condition (which amounts to a breached warranty). • The warranty is *ex post facto* because it was not originally part of the contract. It arises only after the injured party elects to continue the contract, thereby reducing the broken condition to a breached warranty. See CONDITION (2). Cf. *warranty ab initio*.

▸ **warranty of actual title.** See *warranty of title*.

▸ **warranty of assignment.** (18c) An assignor's implied warranty that he or she (1) has the rights assigned, (2) will do nothing to interfere with those rights, and (3) knows of nothing that impairs the value of the assignment.

▸ **warranty of authorship.** (1950) *Copyright.* An author's contractual warranty that the work is an original work by that author.

▸ **warranty of fitness.** See *implied warranty of fitness for a particular purpose.*

▸ **warranty of further assurances.** See *covenant for further assurances* under COVENANT (4).

▸ **warranty of habitability.** See *implied warranty of habitability.*

▸ **warranty of merchantability.** See *implied warranty of merchantability.*

▸ **warranty of quality.** See *implied warranty of merchantability.*

▸ **warranty of title.** (18c) A warranty that the seller or assignor of property has title to that property, that the transfer is rightful, and that there are no liens or other encumbrances beyond those that the buyer or assignee is aware of at the time of contracting. • This warranty arises automatically whenever anyone sells goods. — Also termed *warranty of actual title.*

▸ **written warranty.** (1807) A warranty made in writing; specif., any written affirmation or promise by a supplier of a consumer product to a buyer (for purposes other than resale), forming the basis of the bargain and providing that the material or workmanship is free of defects or will be repaired or replaced free of charge if the product fails to meet the required specifications. 15 USCA § 2301.

▸ **Y2K warranty.** See Y2K WARRANTY.

3. *Insurance.* A pledge or stipulation by the insured that the facts relating to the person insured, the thing insured, or the risk insured are as stated.

▸ **affirmative warranty.** (1807) A warranty — express or implied — that facts are as stated at the beginning of the policy period. • An affirmative warranty is usu. a condition precedent to the policy taking effect.

▸ **executory warranty.** (1815) A warranty that arises when an insured undertakes to perform some executory stipulation, such as a promise that certain acts will be done or that certain facts will continue to exist.

▸ **promissory warranty.** (1815) A warranty that facts will continue to be as stated throughout the policy period, such that a failure of the warranty provides the insurer with a defense to a claim under the policy. — Also termed *continuing warranty.*

warranty against encumbrances. See *covenant against encumbrances* under COVENANT (4).

warranty clause. (1806) **1.** A contractual clause containing a warranty. **2.** *Oil & gas.* A provision in an oil-and-gas lease by which the lessor guarantees that title is without defect and agrees to defend it. • If the warranty is breached, the lessor may be held liable to the lessee to the extent that the lessor has received payments under the lease. Presence of a warranty in an oil-and-gas lease may also cause after-acquired interests to pass from the lessor to the lessee by application of estoppel by deed.

warranty deed. See DEED.

warranty of further assurances. See *covenant for further assurances* under COVENANT (4).

warranty of habitability. See *implied warranty of habitability.* under WARRANT (1).

war rape. See RAPE (2).

warren (**wor**-ən *or* **wahr**-ən). (14c) **1.** A place for the preservation of certain wildlife (such as pheasants, partridges, or rabbits). **2.** A privilege to keep wildlife or game in a warren. **3.** The area to which the privilege extends.

▸ **free warren.** (16c) A warren privilege giving the grantee the sole right to kill the wildlife to the extent of the grantee's warren area. — Also termed *libera warrena.*

> "*Free warren* is a . . . franchise, erected for preservation or custody . . . of beasts and fowls of warren; which being *ferae naturae*, every one had a right to kill as he could; but upon the introduction of the forest laws . . . these animals being looked upon as royal game and the sole property of our savage monarchs, this franchise of free warren was invented to protect them; by giving the grantee a sole and exclusive power of killing such game . . . on condition of his preventing other persons. A man therefore that has the franchise of warren is in reality no more than a royal gamekeeper; but no man, not even a lord of a manor, could by common law justify sporting on another's soil, or even on his own, unless he had the liberty of free warren." 2 William Blackstone, *Commentaries on the Laws of England* 38–39 (1766).

war-risk insurance. See INSURANCE.

Warsaw Convention. *Int'l law.* A treaty (to which the United States is a party) negotiated in Warsaw, Poland, in 1929, consisting of uniform rules governing claims made for personal injuries arising out of international air travel. Cf. MONTREAL AGREEMENT.

> "Under the [Warsaw] Convention . . . air carriers are absolutely liable up to a preset monetary ceiling for any accident in which a passenger suffers bodily injury or death, as long as the accident took place on board the aircraft or in the process of any of the operations of embarking or disembarking. The Convention limits the liability of the carrier for each passenger to the sum of 125,000 francs, unless the carrier and passenger by special contract agree to a higher limit of liability, or unless it can be established that the carrier has been guilty of 'willful misconduct.' The Convention contains a two-year time limitation for bringing suit, and also absolves the carrier from liability upon a showing of due care on its part." 8A Am. Jur. 2d *Aviation* § 149, at 160–61 (1997).

warship. (16c) *Int'l law.* A ship commissioned by a country's military, operating with a military command and crew and displaying the country's flag or other external marks indicating its country of origin. • Under international maritime laws, warships are not subject to many of the safety and environmental regulations that apply to shipping vessels and passenger ships.

warth. See WARDPENNY.

warwit. See WARDWIT.

war zone. (1914) *Int'l law.* A designated area, on land or at sea, within which the rights of neutral countries are not respected by belligerent countries.

wash, *n.* (1976) **1.** A situation in which two effects offset each other. • For example, if an event produces gross income and also a deduction in the same amount so that taxable income is unchanged, the event creates a wash. **2.** The shallow part of a river or the arm of a sea; the sand, rocks, and gravel washed down by a mountain stream and deposited on level land near the mouth of a canyon.

wash sale. See SALE.

wash transaction. See *wash sale* under SALE.

waste, *n.* (15c) **1.** Permanent harm to real property committed by a tenant (for life or for years) to the prejudice of the heir, the reversioner, or the remainderman. • In the law of mortgages, any of the following acts by the mortgagor may constitute waste: (1) physical damage, whether intentional or negligent, (2) failure to maintain and repair, except for repair of casualty damage or damage caused by third-party acts, (3) failure to pay property taxes or governmental assessments secured by a lien having priority over the mortgage, so that the payments become delinquent, (4) the material failure to comply with mortgage covenants concerning physical care, maintenance, construction, demolition, or casualty insurance, or (5) keeping the rents to which the mortgagee has the right of possession. — Also termed *devastation*; *vastum*; *property waste.*

> "The old action of waste was a mixed action, being founded in part on the statute of Gloucester (A.D. 1278), which provided that 'he which shall be attainted of waste shall lose the thing wasted, and moreover shall recompense thrice as much as the waste shall be taxed at.' The action was to recover the land in which waste had been done and the treble damages. The statute of Gloucester was imported into this country, but many variant statutes now regulate the subject." Edwin E. Bryant, *The Law of Pleading Under the Codes of Civil Procedure* 13 (2d ed. 1899).

▸ **active waste.** See *commissive waste.*

▸ **affirmative waste.** See *commissive waste.*

▸ **ameliorating waste** (ə-**meel**-yə-ray-ting). (1927) A lessee's unauthorized change to the physical character of a lessor's property — technically constituting waste, but in fact resulting in improvement of the property. • Generally, equity will not enjoin such waste. — Also termed *ameliorative waste*; *meliorating waste*; *meliorative waste.*

▸ **commissive waste** (kə-**mis**-iv). (1868) Waste caused by the affirmative acts of the tenant. — Also termed *active waste*; *affirmative waste*; *voluntary waste.*

▸ **double waste.** *Hist.* The destruction occurring when a tenant having a duty to repair allows a house to deteriorate, and then unlawfully cuts down timber to repair it.

▸ **economic waste.** See ECONOMIC WASTE.

▸ **equitable waste.** (1842) Waste that abuses a privilege of nonimpeachability at common law, for which equity will restrain the commission of willful, destructive, malicious, or extravagant waste; esp., waste caused by a life tenant who, although ordinarily not responsible for permissive waste, flagrantly damages or destroys the property.

> "A life tenant with the benefit of an express exemption from liability for voluntary waste will nevertheless be restrained in equity from committing acts of flagrant destruction to the premises; hence the (seemingly paradoxical) term, 'equitable waste.' A life tenant who has engaged in, or who threatens to engage in, reprehensible acts of voluntary waste will not be permitted unconscientiously to shield behind his legal right to commit waste to the detriment of those next entitled to enjoyment of the property, for this would be to abuse the legal right." Peter Butt, *Land Law* 114-15 (2d ed. 1988).

▸ **permissive waste.** (17c) A tenant's failure to make normal repairs to property so as to protect it from substantial deterioration.

▸ **voluntary waste.** (16c) Waste resulting from some positive act of destruction. See *commissive waste.*

> "*Voluntary waste.* This involves some positive act of injury to the property, diminishing its value for the person next in succession; it is a deliberate and active change to the property. Examples are altering the character of premises by demolishing internal walls and fittings or opening and working a mine on the land (but not working a mine already opened, for the pre-existence of the mine shows an intention on the part of the grantor that the profits from the mine are to be enjoyed by the life tenant). A life tenant is liable for voluntary waste, unless the instrument conferring the interest expressly exempts liability for voluntary waste." Peter Butt, *Land Law* 114 (2d ed. 1988).

2. Refuse or superfluous material, esp. that remaining after a manufacturing or chemical process <toxic waste>.

▸ **hazardous waste.** (1974) Waste that — because of its quantity, concentration, or physical, chemical, or infectious characteristics — may cause or significantly contribute to an increase in mortality or otherwise harm human health or the environment. 42 USCA § 6903(5). — Also termed *hazardous substance.*

▸ **nuclear waste.** Radioactive and other extremely toxic byproducts produced by nuclear fuel as it is consumed to produce energy.

▸ **solid waste.** Insoluble material, including a gas or liquid in a container, that is discarded, usu. in large quantities.

▸ **toxic waste.** (1964) Hazardous, poisonous substances, such as dichlorodiphenyltrichloroethane (DDT). • Most states regulate the handling and disposing of toxic waste, and several federal statutes (such as the Comprehensive Environmental Response Compensation and Liability Act of 1980 (CERCLA), 42 USCA §§ 9601–9657) regulate the use, transportation, and disposal of toxic waste.

3. *Hist.* Untaxed land that is unusable or uncultivated within a holding.

waste book. (17c) A merchant's book for making rough entries of transactions before posting them into a journal. — Also termed *blotter.*

wasted vote. See VOTE (1).

waste generator. Any person or entity that produces or is responsible for an activity that results in materials for disposal.

waste material. See MATERIAL.

wastewater. See WATER.

wasting asset. See ASSET.

wasting property. See PROPERTY.

wasting trust. See TRUST (3).

wastor, *n.* (14c) *Hist.* A type of thief, classified in a statute of Edward III with marauding vagabonds and burglars who entered premises by lifting door latches. 5 Edw. 3, ch. 14.

watch, *n.* (16c) *Maritime law.* **1.** A division of a ship's crew <port or starboard watch>. **2.** The division of the day into time periods of service by officers and the crew <four-hour watch>.

watch, *vb.* (15c) *Hist.* To stand guard during the night.

watch and ward, *n.* (16c) *Hist.* A feudal duty that some tenants had to keep guard through continuous vigilance.

• The phrase denotes keeping guard by night (*watch*) and by day (*ward*). — Also termed *watching and warding.*

watchdog. (17c) **1.** See *guard dog* under DOG (1). — Also termed (slang) *attack dog.* **2.** A person or group that investigates, protects, and guards against loss, waste, theft, or unethical or illegal practices by a company, government, or other organization. See WATCHDOG JOURNALISM.

▸ **detached watchdog.** (1988) A watchdog that seeks to investigate and protect in an objective, neutral, and fair manner.

watchdog journalism. (1980) Investigative journalism that seeks to uncover facts and expose abuses of power, esp. by the government, to the public. See WATCHDOG (2).

water. (bef. 12c) **1.** The transparent liquid that is a chemical compound of hydrogen and oxygen (H_2O). **2.** A body of this liquid, as in a stream, river, lake, or ocean.

▸ **backwater.** (17c) Water in a stream that, because of a dam or obstruction, cannot flow forward and sometimes flows back.

▸ **coastal water.** (18c) Tidewater navigable by an ocean vessel; all water opening directly or indirectly into the ocean and navigable by a vessel coming in from the ocean. — Also termed *coast water.*

▸ **developed water.** (1895) Water brought to the surface and made available for use by the party claiming the water rights.

▸ **diffused surface water.** (1911) Water, such as rainfall runoff, that collects and flows on the ground but does not form a watercourse. • Surface water is usu. subject to different regulations from water flowing in a watercourse. — Often shortened to *surface water.* See COMMON-ENEMY DOCTRINE; WATERCOURSE.

▸ **excess water.** (18c) Water that is flowing in a stream in addition to what may be termed adjudicated waters; any water not needed for the reasonable beneficial uses of those having priority rights. — Also termed *surplus water.*

▸ **federal waters.** Territorial waters under the jurisdiction of the United States. — Also termed *waters of the United States.* See *territorial waters.*

▸ **floodwater.** (18c) **1.** Water that escapes from a watercourse in large volumes and flows over adjoining property in no regular channel. **2.** Water that is within the confines of a flood-control project.

▸ **foreign water.** (17c) Water belonging to another country or subject to another jurisdiction.

▸ **greywater.** Water that has been used for washing dishes, laundering clothes, bathing, etc.; specif., any water, other than toilet water, that drains from a household, esp. when used for irrigation and other noncontact purposes.

▸ **groundwater.** (1890) Water found in layers of permeable rock or soil.

▸ **inland waters.** See INTERNAL WATERS.

▸ **internal waters.** See INTERNAL WATERS.

▸ **navigable water.** See NAVIGABLE WATER.

▸ **navigable water of the United States.** See NAVIGABLE WATER.

▸ **percolating water.** (18c) Water that oozes or seeps through the soil without a defined channel (such as rainwater or other water that has lost its status as part of a stream). • Percolating water usu. constitutes part of the land on which it is found.

▸ **posted water.** (*usu. pl.*) (1895) A body of water that is reserved for the exclusive use of the person who owns the land surrounding it. • The owner secures the exclusive use by posting a notice prohibiting others from using the water.

▸ **private water.** (17c) Nonnavigable water owned and controlled by one or more individuals and not subject to public use. • If a body of water is small and of little or no practical value for general public use, it is considered private.

▸ **public water.** (17c) Water adapted for purposes of navigation or public access.

▸ **subterranean water.** (17c) Water that lies or flows beneath the earth's surface and that is not artificially confined.

▸ **surface water.** (18c) **1.** Water lying on the surface of the earth but not forming part of a watercourse or lake. • Surface water most commonly derives from rain, springs, or melting snow. **2.** See *diffused surface water.*

▸ **surplus water.** (18c) **1.** Water running off irrigated ground; water not consumed by the irrigation process. **2.** See *excess water.*

▸ **territorial waters.** (1813) The waters under a state's or country's jurisdiction; specif., the waters over which a country has jurisdiction, including both inland waters and ocean waters within 12 nautical miles of the coastline. • *Territorial waters* is a broader category than *territorial sea*: the first includes inland fresh waters, while the latter covers only ocean waters. — Also termed *marine belt; maritime belt; maritime boundary.* Cf. *territorial sea* under SEA.

▸ **tidewater.** See TIDEWATER.

▸ **wastewater.** (15c) **1.** Water that escapes from the canals, ditches, or other receptacles of the lawful claimant; water that is not used by the appropriator and is permitted to run off the appropriator's property. **2.** Water that is left over, esp. after a chemical or manufacturing process.

▸ **waters of the United States.** See *territorial waters.*

water bailiff. *Hist.* An officer whose job is to inspect ships in port.

water bayley (**bay**-lee). (17c) *Hist.* An officer (mentioned in the colony laws of New Plymouth in A.D. 1671) who primarily collects dues for fish taken out of the colony's waters.

waterboarding. (2004) A form of torture in which water is poured over the face of a supine, immobilized person whose head is pulled back so that he or she cannot avoid inhaling water and thus experiencing the sensation of drowning. • In some variations, fabric or plastic may be draped over the person's face, or the person may be gagged before the water is poured. See TORTURE.

watercourse. (16c) A body of water, usu. of natural origin, flowing in a reasonably definite channel with bed and banks. • The term includes not just rivers and creeks, but also springs, lakes, and marshes in which such flowing streams originate or through which they flow. — Also termed *waterway.*

▸ **ancient watercourse.** (17c) A watercourse in a channel that has existed from time immemorial.

▸ **artificial watercourse.** (1839) A man-made watercourse, usu. to be used only temporarily. • If the watercourse is of a permanent character and has been maintained for a sufficient length of time, it may be considered a natural watercourse to which riparian rights can attach.

> "An artificial waterway or stream may, under some circumstances, have the characteristics and incidents of a natural watercourse. In determining the question, three things seem generally to be taken into consideration by the courts: (1) whether the way or stream is temporary or permanent; (2) the circumstances under which it was created; and (3) the mode in which it has been used and enjoyed." 78 Am. Jur. 2d *Waters* § 196, at 644 (1975).

▸ **natural watercourse.** (18c) A watercourse with its origin in the forces of nature. • A *natural watercourse* does not include surface water, which often flows intermittently and in an indefinite channel. In addition, a natural stream is distinguished from an artificial ditch or canal, which is typically not the subject of riparian rights. See RIPARIAN RIGHT; WATER.

water district. See DISTRICT.

watered stock. See STOCK.

waterfront, *n.* (1856) Land or land with buildings fronting a body of water.

watergage, *n.* (17c) **1.** A seawall. **2.** An instrument used to measure the height of water.

watergavel, *n.* (13c) *Hist.* A fee paid for a benefit (such as fishing) obtained from a body of water.

watermark. (17c) **1.** A mark indicating the highest or lowest point to which water rises or falls.

▸ **high-water mark.** (16c) **1.** The shoreline of a sea reached by the water at high tide. • The high-water mark is usu. computed as a mean or average high tide and not as the extreme height of the water. **2.** In a freshwater lake created by a dam in an unnavigable stream, the highest point on the shore to which the dam can raise the water in ordinary circumstances. **3.** In a river not subject to tides, the line that the river impresses on the soil by covering it long enough to deprive it of agricultural value. — Also termed *high-water line.*

▸ **low-water mark.** (16c) **1.** The shoreline of a sea marking the edge of the water at the lowest point of the ordinary ebb tide. **2.** In a river, the point to which the water recedes at its lowest stage.

2. The transparent design or symbol seen when paper is held up to the light, usu. to indicate the genuineness of the document or the document's manufacturer.

water ordeal. See *ordeal by water* under ORDEAL.

water pollution. See POLLUTION.

waterpower. (1817) **1.** The force obtained by converting water into energy. **2.** The riparian owner's right consisting of the fall in the stream as it passes over or through the riparian owner's land; the difference of the level between the surface where the stream first touches one's land and the surface where the water leaves the land.

water right. (*often pl.*) (18c) The right to use water from a natural stream or from an artificial canal for irrigation, power, domestic use, and the like; RIPARIAN RIGHT. — Also termed *aquatic right.*

▸ **adjudicated water right.** (1905) A formerly disputed water right whose ownership is now established by statute, judicial order, or administrative certificate.

▸ **appropriative water right.** (1905) A right to take or receive a specific volume of water for a particular use at a specified place and time. • The right must be regularly exercised or it may be lost. It can also be sold or transferred separately from the land from which the water right originally derives.

waterscape, *n.* (1842) An aqueduct or passage for water.

waters of the United States. See *federal waters* under WATER.

waterway. See WATERCOURSE.

waveson (**wayv**-sən), *n.* (16c) *Hist.* Goods that float on the sea after a shipwreck. Cf. FLOTSAM; JETSAM; LAGAN (1).

wax scot (wak **skot**), *n. Hist.* A duty on wax candles used in churches, usu. paid twice a year. — Also termed *cerage* (**seer**-ij); *ceratium* (si-**ray**-shee-əm).

way. (bef. 12c) **1.** A passage or path. **2.** A right to travel over another's property. See RIGHT-OF-WAY.

▸ **private way.** (17c) **1.** The right to pass over another's land. **2.** A way provided by local authorities primarily to accommodate particular individuals (usu. at the individual's expense) but also for the public's passage.

▸ **way of necessity.** See *implied easement* under EASEMENT.

waybill. (1821) *Maritime law.* A document acknowledging the receipt of goods by a carrier or by the shipper's agent and the contract for the transportation of those goods. • Unlike a bill of lading, a waybill is not a document of title and is nonnegotiable. A waybill ordinarily records where the goods being sent, how much they are worth, and how much they weigh. — Abbr. WB. Cf. BILL OF LADING.

▸ **airbill.** See *air waybill.*

▸ **air-consignment note.** See *air waybill.*

▸ **air waybill.** (1934) A waybill for transportation of cargo by air. — Also spelled *airwaybill.* — Also termed *airbill*; *air-consignment note.* Cf. *overseas bill of lading* under BILL OF LADING.

▸ **blanket waybill.** (1910) A waybill covering more than one shipment or consignment of freight.

▸ **interline waybill.** (1919) A waybill covering the handling of a shipment by more than one carrier.

way-going crop. (17c) A grain crop, formerly sown by a tenant during a tenancy (esp. in Pennsylvania), that did not ripen until after expiration of the lease. • In the absence of an express agreement to the contrary, the tenant was entitled to the crop.

way-leave, *n.* (15c) **1.** A right-of-way (usu. created by an express grant) over or through land for the transportation of minerals from a mine or quarry. **2.** The royalty paid for such a right.

waynagium (way-**nay**-jee-əm). See WAINAGE.

way of necessity. See *implied easement* under EASEMENT.

ways-and-means committee. (1840) A legislative committee that determines how money will be raised for various governmental purposes.

WB. *abbr.* WAYBILL.

WC. *abbr.* WORKERS' COMPENSATION.

WCT. *abbr.* WIPO COPYRIGHT TREATY.

W.D. *abbr.* Western District, in reference to U.S. judicial districts.

WDDA (**wahd**-ə). *abbr.* Withdrawn and dismissed by district attorney.

weak mark. See *descriptive trademark* under TRADEMARK.

weak trademark. See *descriptive trademark* under TRADEMARK.

wealreaf (**weel**-reef), *n.* (17c) *Archaic.* The robbery of a dead person in a grave.

wealth. (13c) **1.** A large quantity of something. **2.** The state of having abundant financial resources; affluence.

wealth maximization. (1955) A situation resulting from a change in the allocation of resources if the change benefits the winner — i.e., the one who benefits from the change — more than it harms the loser. • A situation in which all possible wealth-maximizing changes have occurred is described as *Kaldor-Hicks efficient* or as being *potentially Pareto superior.* See PARETO OPTIMALITY; PARETO SUPERIORITY.

weapon. (bef. 12c) An instrument used or designed to be used to injure or kill someone.

▸ **bioweapon.** (1962) A weapon that contains bacteria or viruses intended to infect and possibly kill large numbers of people.

▸ **concealed weapon.** (1833) A weapon that is carried by a person but that is not visible by ordinary observation.

▸ **dangerous weapon.** (17c) An object or device that, because of the way it is used, is capable of causing serious bodily injury.

> "Three reasons, each independently sufficient, support the conclusion that an unloaded gun is a 'dangerous weapon.' First, a gun is an article that is typically and characteristically dangerous; the use for which it is manufactured and sold is a dangerous one, and the law reasonably may presume that such an article is always dangerous even though it may not be armed at a particular time or place. In addition, the display of a gun instills fear in the average citizen; as a consequence it creates an immediate danger that a violent response will ensue. Finally, a gun can cause harm when used as a bludgeon." *McLaughlin v. U.S.*, 476 U.S. 16, 17–18, 106 S.Ct. 1677, 1678 (1986).

▸ **deadly weapon.** (16c) Any firearm or other device, instrument, material, or substance that, from the manner in which it is used or is intended to be used, is calculated or likely to produce death. • In some states, the definition encompasses the likelihood of causing either death or serious physical injury. — Also termed *lethal weapon.* Cf. DANGEROUS INSTRUMENTALITY.

▸ **deadly weapon per se.** (1872) A weapon that is deadly in and of itself or would ordinarily result in death by its use <a gun is a deadly weapon per se>. — Also termed *per se deadly weapon.*

▸ **lethal weapon.** See *deadly weapon.*

▸ **nondeadly weapon.** See LESS-LETHAL.

▸ **nonlethal weapon.** See LESS-LETHAL.

▸ **weapon of mass destruction.** (*usu. pl.*) (1937) A weapon that is intended to kill human beings, without discriminating between combatants and noncombatants, on a massive scale. • Among the most frequently cited examples are nuclear weapons and chemical weapons. — Abbr. WMD.

> "In modern day international law and international relations, the term 'weapons of mass destruction' has simply become shorthand for nuclear, chemical, and biological weapons . . . . The common denominator of weapons classified as such is that the consequences of their use cannot be determined and controlled, and the damage they cause is indiscriminate as between combatants and civilians and disproportionately harmful to the environment. As such their use falls foul of international humanitarian law principles . . . . Moreover, because of the scientific and technological advances of the last half a century and the tactics of terrorist organizations since 9/11 . . . , the destructive and destabilizing potential of such weapons and their acquisition through illicit trade, and potential use or threat of use by rogue elements, have provided a new impetus for arguments in favour of the total banning and elimination of these weapons." Hendrik A. Strydom, "Weapons of Mass Destruction," in 10 *The Max Planck Encyclopedia of Public International Law* 821, 821 (Rüdiger Wolfrum ed., 2012).

weaponry (**wep**-ən-ree), *n.* (1844) Collectively, weapons, esp. those of a particular type or belonging to a particular country or group.

weapons inspector. (1988) An official, usu. an expert, who is sent to report on the status and condition of weaponry and weapons development; esp., a United Nations expert sent to a country to determine whether U.N. resolutions governing nuclear and biological weapons are being obeyed.

wear, *n.* [fr. Saxon *were* "a taking"] (bef. 12c) *Hist.* A dam made of stakes interlaced by twigs of willows that are placed across a river to more easily accommodate the netting of fish. — Also termed *weir.*

wear and tear. (17c) Deterioration caused by ordinary use; the depreciation of property resulting from its reasonable use <the tenant is not liable for normal wear and tear to the leased premises>. — Also termed *ordinary wear and tear; fair wear and tear; natural wear and tear.*

> "'Fair wear' is the deterioration caused by the reasonable use of the premises; 'fair tear' is the deterioration caused by the ordinary operation of natural forces. A tenant's repairing covenant commonly exempts the tenant from the obligation to repair damage characterisable as 'fair wear and tear' (sometimes called 'reasonable wear and tear'). In the absence of such an exempting provision, a covenant to repair requires the repairing of damage characterisable as fair wear and tear. Where a covenant to repair exempts the tenant from liability for 'fair wear and tear,' he is not responsible for deterioration or dilapidation caused by 'the reasonable use of the house by the tenant and the ordinary operation of natural forces.'" Peter Butt, *Land Law* 256 (2d ed. 1988).

weasel word. A word intended to emphasize another word but functionally weakening the other word or the statement or causing the meaning to be uncertain. • *Weasel word* was coined in 1900 in an article by Stewart Chaplin, published in the June issue of *Century Magazine.* It was popularized by Teddy Roosevelt in a 1916 speech in which he declared: "When a weasel sucks eggs, the meat is sucked out of the egg. If you use a 'weasel word' after another, there is nothing left of the other." Weasel words include many adverbs ending in *-ly,* such as *clearly* and *substantially,* other adverbs such as *rather* and *very,* and adjectives such as *undue* and *reasonable.* There are also weasel phrases, such as *if practicable* and *with all deliberate speed.* See DELIBERATE SPEED.

Web. See WORLD WIDE WEB.

Webb–Pomerene Act. A 1918 federal statute providing a qualified exemption for an export business against the prohibitions of the antitrust laws. 15 USCA §§ 61 et seq. — Abbr. WPA.

> "The Webb-Pomerene Act was passed to aid and encourage our manufacturers and producers to extend our foreign trade. Congress believed that American firms needed the power to form joint export associations in order to compete with foreign cartels, but while Congress was willing to create an exemption from the antitrust laws to serve this narrow purpose, the exemption created by the Webb-Pomerene Act was carefully hedged in to avoid substantial injury to domestic interests. Organization under the Webb-Pomerene Act does not give an export association the right to agree with foreign competitors to fix prices . . . or establish exclusive markets . . . ." 54 Am. Jur. 2d *Monopolies and Restraints of Trade* § 262, at 298 (1996).

website spoofing. See SPOOFING.

website-user agreement. See POINT-AND-CLICK AGREEMENT.

web-wrap agreement. See POINT-AND-CLICK AGREEMENT.

wedding. See MARRIAGE CEREMONY.

wedge principle. (1951) The argument that relaxation of a constitutionally imposed restraint under specific circumstances may justify further relaxation in broader circumstances. • This principle is most often raised in the context of legalized human euthanasia. But it has frequently been invoked in other contexts, such as the right to protection from unreasonable search and seizure. — Also termed *slippery-slope principle*; *parade-of-horrors objection*. See PARADE OF HORRIBLES; SLIPPERY SLOPE.

> "[T]here is the familiar argument from the 'wedge principle,' which is used to deny the possibility of looking at particular circumstances in applying moral rules." Glanville Williams, *The Sanctity of Life and the Criminal Law* 315 (1957).

wedlock. (bef. 12c) The quality, state, or condition of being married; matrimony.

week. (bef. 12c) **1.** A period of seven consecutive days beginning on either Sunday or Monday. **2.** Any consecutive seven-day period.

weekend sentence. See *intermittent sentence* under SENTENCE.

week-to-week tenancy. See *periodic tenancy* under TENANCY.

week-work. (bef. 12c) *Hist.* In feudal times, the obligation of a tenant to work two to four days in every week for his lord during the greater part of the year, and four or five during the summer months. See VILLEIN SERVICE.

wehading. See TRIAL BY COMBAT.

weighage (way-ij). (16c) A duty or other payment required in return for weighing merchandise.

weight. (bef. 12c) **1.** A measure of heaviness; a measure of the quantity of matter <the weight of the ingots>.

- ▸ **gross weight.** (16c) The total weight of a thing, including its contents and any packaging.
- ▸ **net weight.** (18c) The total weight of a thing, after deducting its container, its wrapping, and any other extraneous matter.— Also termed *neat weight*.

2. Figuratively, the quality of possessing due efficacy; impressiveness, importance, and preponderance <weight of the evidence in establishing proof>.

weighted vote. See VOTE (1).

weight of the evidence. (17c) The persuasiveness of some evidence in comparison with other evidence <because the verdict is against the great weight of the evidence, a new trial should be granted>. See BURDEN OF PERSUASION.

- ▸ **greater weight of the evidence.** See PREPONDERANCE OF THE EVIDENCE.
- ▸ **manifest weight of the evidence.** (1859) The very clear persuasiveness of some evidence in comparison with other evidence. • This phrase denotes a deferential standard of review under which a verdict will be reversed or disregarded only if another outcome is obviously correct and the verdict is clearly unsupported by the evidence. Cf. WEIGHT OF THE EVIDENCE.

***Weingarten* right.** (1975) *Labor law.* A union member's right to have a union representative present during an employment meeting that the member reasonably believes will result in disciplinary action. *NLRB v. J. Weingarten, Inc.*, 420 U.S. 251, 95 S.Ct. 959 (1975). • In July 2000, the NLRB extended *Weingarten* rights to nonunion employees. The right applies to public-sector employees only if provided for by statute, court decision, or state labor-board ruling.

weir. See WEAR.

welching. See WELSHING.

welfare. (14c) **1.** Well-being in any respect; prosperity.

- ▸ **general welfare.** (17c) The public's health, peace, morals, and safety.
- ▸ **public welfare.** (16c) A society's well-being in matters of health, safety, order, morality, economics, and politics.

2. A system of social insurance providing assistance to those who are financially in need, as by providing food stamps and family allowances. — Also termed (historically) *poor relief*; *state benefit*; (BrE) *income support*.

- ▸ **corporate welfare.** Governmental financial assistance given to a large company, usu. in the form of a subsidy.

Welfare Clause. See GENERAL WELFARE CLAUSE.

welfare plan. See EMPLOYEE BENEFIT PLAN.

Welfare Reform Act. See PERSONAL RESPONSIBILITY AND WORK OPPORTUNITY RECONCILIATION ACT.

welfare state. (1894) **1.** A system whereby the government undertakes various social-insurance programs, such as unemployment compensation, old-age pensions, family allowances, food stamps, and aid to the blind or deaf. **2.** A country with such a system. — Also termed *welfare-regulatory state*.

well, *adj. Marine insurance.* (Of a vessel) in good condition; safe and sound <the vessel was warranted well on January 1>.

well, *adv.* (bef. 12c) In a legally sufficient manner; unobjectionable <well-pleaded complaint>.

well, *n.* (bef. 12c) A hole or shaft sunk into the earth to obtain a fluid, such as water, oil, or natural gas.

- ▸ **limited-capacity well.** (1961) An oil or gas well that is limited to producing only a portion of its monthly allowable because of market demand.

▸ **stripper well.** (1934) An oil or gas well that produces only small quantities. • In some states, such as Kansas and Illinois, stripper wells are common.

well-completion clause. (1952) *Oil & gas.* A provision in an oil-and-gas lease specifying that a lessee who starts drilling before the lease terminates has the right to complete the well and to maintain the lease if the drilling achieves production. See OPERATIONS CLAUSE.

well-established, *adj.* (18c) Having existed for a long time and gained the respect and trust of the people. — Also spelled (after the noun) *well established.*

well-founded, *adj.* (18c) (Of a belief, feeling, suspicion, etc.) based on facts combined with good judgment. — Also spelled (after the noun) *well founded.*

well-founded fear of persecution. *Immigration law.* A subjectively genuine and objectively reasonable belief that one will be subjected to cruel, harsh, severe, and offensive acts. • An applicant for asylum must legitimately fear returning to the country of origin and also provide credible, direct, and specific factual evidence in support. See PERSECUTION.

well-knowing, *adj.* (17c) Intentional <a well-knowing act or omission>. • This term was formerly used in pleadings to allege scienter. See SCIENTER.

well-pleaded complaint. See COMPLAINT.

Wells notice. *Securities law.* A warning to a person or business by the U.S. Securities and Exchange Commission or the Financial Industry Regulatory Authority of a possible enforcement action, the proposed charges, and the primary evidence supporting the charges. • The term originated in 1972 when an SEC committee chaired by John A. Wells evaluated the Commission's enforcement policies and practices and recommended such a notice. — Also termed *Wells call.*

Wells submission. *Securities law.* The opportunity to present facts and legal arguments following a Wells notice to convince the U.S. Securities and Exchange Commission that no action should be brought. See WELLS NOTICE.

welshing. (1857) **1.** The act or an instance of evading an obligation, esp. a gambling debt. **2.** The common-law act of larceny in which one receives a deposit to be paid back with additional money depending on the outcome of an event (such as a horse race) but at the time of the deposit the depositee intends to cheat and defraud the depositor by absconding with the money. • Although this term is sometimes thought to be a slur against those hailing from Wales, etymologists have not been able to establish this connection. Authoritative dictionaries record the origin of the term as being unknown. — Also termed *welching.* — **welsh,** *vb.* — **welsher,** *n.*

Welsh mortgage. See MORTGAGE.

wend, *n. Hist.* A large section of land; a perambulation; a circuit.

wer. See BLOOD MONEY (1).

wergild (**wər**-gild). (13c) *Hist.* The fixed value of a person's life, being the amount that a homicide's kindred must pay to the kindred of the slain person so as to avoid a blood feud. — Also spelled *wergeld; weregild; wehrgeld.* — Also termed *manprice.* See EFFUSIO SANGUINIS; LEODES.

> "[O]n the eve of the Norman Conquest mere homicide can still be atoned for by the payment of the dead man's price or wergild, and if that be not paid, it is rather for the injured family than for the State to slay the slayer. Men of different ranks had different prices: the thegn was worth six ceorls, and it seems very plain that if a ceorl killed a thegn, he had to die for it, or was sold into slavery, for a thegnly wergild was quite beyond the reach of his modest means. In the twelfth century the old system perished of over-elaboration. The bill that a manslayer ran up became in the days of feudalism too complex to be summed, too heavy to be paid; for the dead man's lord, the lord of the place where the blood was shed, and it may be many other lords, would claim fines and forfeitures. He had to pay with his eyes or with his life a debt that he could not otherwise discharge." Frederic W. Maitland & Francis C. Montague, *A Sketch of English Legal History* 20–21 (James F. Colby ed., 1915).

West Australian plan. See *instant-runoff voting* under VOTING.

Westlaw. A West Group database for computer-assisted legal research, providing online access to legal resources, including federal and state caselaw, statutes, regulations, legal treatises, legal periodicals, and general and business news. — Abbr. WL.

Westminster Confession of Faith (**west**-min-stər). *Hist.* A document containing a statement of the religious doctrines of the Presbyterian Church, originating at a conference of British and continental Protestant divines at Westminster in 1643. • It was adopted by the General Assembly of the Kirk of Scotland and the Scottish Parliament, so becoming the basis of the Scottish Presbyterian Church. — Sometimes shortened to *Westminster Confession.*

Westminster the First, Statute of. *Hist.* An English statute divided into 51 chapters (later correlating to separate acts of Parliament), including provisions (1) protecting the property of the church from the violence and spoliation of the Crown and nobles; (2) providing for the freedom of popular elections; (3) enforcing the rules contained in Magna Carta against excessive fines; (4) enumerating and correcting the abuses of tenures (esp. concerning marriages of wards); (5) regulating the levying of tolls; (6) correcting and restraining the powers of the royal escheator and other officers; (7) amending the criminal law (esp. by classifying rape as a most grievous, though not capital, offense); and (8) making criminal and civil procedures more expeditious and less costly. 3 Edw. (1275).

West Point. See UNITED STATES MILITARY ACADEMY.

West-Saxon law. *Hist. English law.* A system of rules introduced by the West Saxons and one of the three principal legal systems prevailing in England in the beginning of the 11th century. • It was observed primarily in southern English counties from Kent to Devonshire. — Also termed *West-Saxon lage.* See MERCENLAGE; DANELAW.

wet conspiracy. *Criminal law. Slang.* A drug case in which the police, after investigating an alleged drug ring, successfully recover contraband. Cf. DRY CONSPIRACY.

wetlands, *n.* Areas where water covers the land or is just below the surface all year round or periodically throughout the year. • Wetlands may be freshwater, saltwater, or brackish. Types of wetlands include marshes, swamps, bogs, and other similar areas.

wet reckless. *Criminal law.* A criminal charge for reckless driving that is typically recognized as alcohol-related. • A wet reckless is often the plea bargain when a drunk-driving charge has been reduced because the amount of alcohol was borderline illegal, there was no accident, and the defendant has no prior record. On a later arrest, the wet reckless may be considered a prior drunk-driving conviction.

whaling. 1. The hunting of whales, usu. for their meat or oil. • The International Whaling Commission placed a moratorium on commercial whaling beginning in 1986 but allows for regulated, subsistence-level catches by indigenous peoples. **2.** See *spear phishing* under PHISHING.

wharf. (bef. 12c) A structure on the shores of navigable waters, to which a vessel can be brought for loading or unloading.

▸ **private wharf.** (18c) One that can be used only by its owner or lessee.

▸ **sufferance wharf.** See SUFFERANCE WHARF.

▸ **public wharf.** (18c) One that can be used by the public.

wharfage (worf-ij), *n.* (15c) *Hist.* **1.** The fee paid for landing, loading, or unloading goods on a wharf. **2.** The accommodation for loading or unloading goods on a wharf.

wharfinger (**wor**-fin-jər), *n.* (16c) *Hist.* The owner or occupier of a wharf; one who keeps a wharf to receive merchandise for forwarding or delivery to a consignee.

wharfing out, right of. See RIGHT OF WHARFING OUT.

Wharton's rule ([h]**wor**-tən). (1940) *Criminal law.* The doctrine that an agreement by two or more persons to commit a particular crime cannot be prosecuted as a conspiracy if the crime could not be committed except by the actual number of participants involved. • Classic examples include dueling and prostitution, crimes that cannot be committed alone. But if additional people participate, as duelists' seconds or a prostitute's pimp, for example, all the actors might be charged with conspiracy. The doctrine takes its name from the influential criminal-law author Francis Wharton (1820–1889). — Also termed *Wharton rule*; *concert-of-action rule.*

> "Wharton's Rule applies only to offenses that *require* concerted criminal activity, a plurality of criminal agents. In such cases, a closer relationship exists between the conspiracy and the substantive offense because *both* require collective criminal activity. The substantive offense therefore presents some of the same threats that the law of conspiracy normally is thought to guard against, and it cannot automatically be assumed that the Legislature intended the conspiracy and the substantive offense to remain as discrete crimes upon consummation of the latter. Thus, absent legislative intent to the contrary, the Rule supports a presumption that the two merge when the substantive offense is proved. . . . More important, as the Rule is essentially an aid to the determination of legislative intent, it must defer to a discernible legislative judgment." *Iannelli v. U.S.*, 420 U.S. 770, 785–86, 95 S.Ct. 1284, 1293–94 (1975).

what-might-happen test. *Property.* The contemplation of all conceivable circumstances and possibilities, however remote, to determine whether any could invalidate a contingent interest.

WHD. *abbr.* WAGE AND HOUR DIVISION.

wheel. (bef. 12c) **1.** *Criminal law.* A means by which criminal cases are randomly assigned to judges, the allusion being to a spinning wheel. **2.** A means by which criminal cases are assigned to court-appointed counsel. — Also termed (in senses 1 & 2) *criminal wheel.* **3.** *Hist.* An instrument of torture used in medieval Europe, consisting of a wheel or cross on which a criminal was bound with arms and legs extended, while the criminal's bones were broken one by one with an iron bar, usu. until death. **4.** The torture itself.

wheelage ([h]**weel**-ij), *n.* (17c) *Hist.* A duty or toll for a vehicle to pass over certain property.

wheel conspiracy. See CONSPIRACY.

whence, *adv.* (13c) From where <they alighted from the train at Cambridge, whence they journeyed by car to Ely>. • Because *whence* includes the idea of "from," the phrase *from whence* is considered a venial redundancy.

when-issued security. See SECURITY (4).

whereabouts, *n.* (17c) The general locale where a person or thing is <her whereabouts are unknown> <the Joneses' present whereabouts is a closely guarded secret>. • As the examples illustrate, this noun, though plural in form, may be construed with either a plural or a singular verb. — **whereabouts,** *adv.* & *conj.*

whereas, *conj.* (14c) **1.** While by contrast; although <McWilliams was stopped at 10:08 p.m. wearing a green hat, whereas the assailant had been identified at 10:04 p.m. wearing a black hat>. **2.** Given the fact that; since <Whereas, the parties have found that their 1994 agreement did not adequately address incidental expenses . . . ; and Whereas, the parties have now decided in an equitable sharing of those expenses . . . ; Now, Therefore, the parties agree to amend the 1994 agreement as follows . . . >. • In sense 2, *whereas* is used to introduce contractual recitals and the like, but modern drafters increasingly prefer a simple heading, such as "Recitals" or "Preamble," and in that way avoid the legalistic *whereases.* — **whereas** (recital or preamble), *n.*

whereas clause. 1. See RECITAL (2). **2.** See PREAMBLE (1).

whereat, *conj.* (14c) **1.** At or toward which <the point whereat he was aiming>. **2.** As a result of which; whereupon <Pettrucione called Bickley a scurrilous name, whereat a fistfight broke out>.

whereby, *conj.* (13c) By which; through which; in accordance with which <the treaty whereby the warring countries finally achieved peace>.

wherefore, *adv.* (12c) **1.** Why; for what reason. • *Wherefore* is often used as an interrogative word <Wherefore did you doubt?>. **2.** By reason of which; in consequence of which <Wherefore, premises considered . . .>.

wherefore, premises considered. (1867) *Archaic.* For all these reasons; for the reason or reasons mentioned above. • The phrase is often used to begin the final paragraph of a motion, judgment, contract, or agreement. One plain-English replacement is this: *Wilson (etc.) therefore asks this Court to . . . .*

wherefrom, *conj.* (14c) From which <the students sent two faxes to the president's office, wherefrom no reply ever came>.

wherein, *conj.* (14c) **1.** In which; where <the jurisdiction wherein Lynn practices>. **2.** During which <they listened intently at the concert, wherein both of them became convinced that the composer's "new" work was a fraud>. **3.** How; in what respect <Fallon demanded to know wherein she had breached any duty>. — **wherein,** *adv.*

whereof, *conj.* (13c) **1.** Of what <Judge Wald knows whereof she speaks>. **2.** Of which <citations whereof even the most responsible are far afield from the true issue>. **3.** Of whom

<judges whereof only the most glowing words might be said>.

whereon, *conj.* (13c) On which <the foundation whereon counsel bases this argument>. — Also termed *whereupon.*

wheresoever, *adv.* (14c) Wherever; in whatever place.

whereto, *conj.* (14c) To what place or time <at first, Campbell did not know whereto he was being taken>. — Also termed *whereunto.* — **whereto,** *adv.*

whereupon, *conj.* (14c) **1.** WHEREON <the precedent whereupon the defense bases its argument>. **2.** Soon after and as a result of which; and then <a not-guilty verdict was announced, whereupon a riot erupted>.

wherewith, *conj.* (14c) By means of which <the plaintiff lacked a form of action wherewith to state a compensable claim>.

wherewithal, *n.* (1809) The money, skill, and other resources needed in order to accomplish something.

whim. (17c) A passing fancy; an impulse <the jury was instructed to render a verdict based solely on the evidence, not on a whim>.

whip, *n.* (1850) A legislator appointed by a political party to ensure that members of that party attend and vote and to otherwise enforce party discipline.

▸ **majority whip.** (1902) The whip for the political party that has the most members.

▸ **minority whip.** (1909) The whip for a political party that does not constitute a majority of the members.

whiplash. A nonmedical term describing acute and sometimes chronic injuries to the neck that may be caused by or arise from the sudden extension of the neck, typically during an automobile accident.

whipping, *n.* (16c) A method of corporal punishment formerly used in England and a few American states, consisting of inflicting long welts on the skin, esp. with a whip.

whipsaw strike. See STRIKE (1).

whisper stock. See STOCK.

whistleblower, *n.* (1970) An employee who reports employer wrongdoing to a governmental or law-enforcement agency. • Federal and state laws protect whistleblowers from employer retaliation. — **whistleblowing,** *n.*

whistleblower act. (1984) A federal or state law protecting employees from retaliation for properly disclosing employer wrongdoing such as violating a law or regulation, mismanaging public funds, abusing authority, or endangering public health or safety. • Federal laws containing whistleblower provisions include the Whistleblower Protection Act (5 USCA § 1211), the Occupational Safety and Health Act (29 USCA § 660), CERCLA (42 USCA § 9610), and the Air Pollution and Control Act (42 USCA § 7622).

Whistleblower Protection Act. See WHISTLEBLOWER ACT. — Abbr. WPA.

Whiteacre. (17c) A fictitious tract of land used in legal discourse (esp. law-school hypotheticals) to discuss real-property issues. See BLACKACRE.

white bonnet. (18c) *Scots law.* A fictitious bidder at an auction; a shill. See BY-BIDDER.

white book. (15c) **1.** (*cap.*) *Hist.* ALBUS LIBER. **2.** A government report bound in white, common esp. in European and papal affairs.

whitecapping. (1900) *Criminal law.* The criminal act of threatening a person — usu. a member of a minority group — with violence in an effort to compel the person either to move away or to stop engaging in a certain business or occupation. • Whitecapping statutes were originally enacted to curtail the activities of the Ku Klux Klan.

white-collar crime. (1940) A nonviolent crime usu. involving cheating or dishonesty in commercial matters. • Examples include fraud, embezzlement, bribery, and insider trading.

white-collar offense. See WHITE-COLLAR CRIME.

white-heart–empty-head rule. *Criminal law. Slang.* The doctrine that a defendant cannot avoid complicity in a crime by willfully ignoring the probability of an associate's ongoing criminal activity. Cf. *ostrich defense* under DEFENSE (1).

whitehorse case. (1971) *Slang.* A reported case with facts virtually identical to those of the instant case, so that the disposition of the reported case should determine the outcome of the instant case. — Also termed *horse case; goose case; gray mule case; red-cow case.* Cf. ON ALL FOURS.

White House. 1. The official home in Washington, D.C., of the President of the United States. **2.** The President of the United States and his close advisers. • Sense 2 is a well-known example of the rhetorical figure of speech known as metonymy.

white knight. (1981) A person or corporation that rescues the target of an unfriendly corporate takeover, esp. by acquiring a controlling interest in the target corporation or by making a competing tender offer. — Also termed *friendly suitor.* See TAKEOVER. Cf. CORPORATE RAIDER.

Whiteley rule. See FELLOW-OFFICER RULE.

white lie. See LIE, *n.*

White model. (1994) *Labor law.* A method for determining whether a union member's state-law claim against the employer is preempted by federal law, by focusing on whether state law permits the claim to be waived by a private contract. • In *Lingle v. Norge Division of Magic Chef, Inc.*, 486 U.S. 399, 108 S.Ct. 1877 (1988), the Supreme Court held that a union member's state-law retaliatory-discharge claim was not preempted by the Labor-Management Relations Act because the claim could be resolved without interpreting the collective-bargaining agreement. There are at least two models for applying the *Lingle* test: the White model, which focuses on whether the claim is negotiable or nonnegotiable (that is, whether state law allows the claim to be waived by a private contract) and the Marcus model, which focuses on the independence of the claim in relation to the collective-bargaining agreement. Under the White model, all negotiable claims (those waivable by private contract) are necessarily preempted because their resolution will require an interpretation of the collective-bargaining agreement. A nonnegotiable claims (one that state law does not permit to be waived by private contract) will be preempted only if its resolution requires an interpretation of the collective-bargaining agreement. The White model is named for the author of the law-review article in which it was proposed. Rebecca

Homer White, *Section 301's Preemption of State Law Claims: A Model for Analysis*, 41 Ala. L. Rev. 377 (1990). See LINGLE TEST. Cf. MARCUS MODEL.

white paper. (1899) **1.** An intermediate draft of a policy statement circulated for final comments before the final draft is composed. **2.** (*usu. cap.*) *English law.* An official report from the British government explaining the plans and ideas underlying proposed legislation. Cf. GREEN PAPER.

white rent. (15c) *Hist.* A feudal rent paid in silver, rather than in work, grain, or money baser than silver. Cf. BLACK RENT.

white slavery. (1857) The practice of forcing a female (or, rarely, a male) to engage in commercial prostitution. • Trafficking in persons for prostitution is prohibited by the Mann Act (18 USCA §§ 2421–2424).

White Slave Traffic Act. See MANN ACT.

Whitsunday. See *quarter day* under DAY.

WHO. *abbr.* (1946) WORLD HEALTH ORGANIZATION.

whole-act rule. See WHOLE-TEXT CANON.

whole blood. See *full blood* under BLOOD.

whole-brain death. See DEATH.

whole law. The law applied by a forum court in a multistate or multinational case after referring to its own choice-of-law rules.

whole life insurance. See LIFE INSURANCE.

wholesale, *n.* (15c) The sale of goods or commodities usu. to a retailer for resale, and not to the ultimate consumer. Cf. RETAIL. — **wholesale,** *vb.* — **wholesale,** *adj.*

wholesale arrest. See *dragnet arrest* under ARREST (2).

wholesale dealer. (17c) Someone who sells goods in gross to retail dealers rather than selling in smaller quantities directly to consumers.

wholesale price. See PRICE.

wholesale price index. See PRODUCER PRICE INDEX.

wholesaler. (1857) Someone who buys large quantities of goods and resells them in smaller quantities to retailers or other merchants, who in turn sell to the ultimate consumer.

whole-statute rule. (1949) The principle of statutory construction that a statute should be considered in its entirety, and that the words used within it should be given their ordinary meanings unless there is a clear indication to the contrary.

whole-text canon. The doctrine that a legal text, esp. a statute, must be construed as a whole. — Also termed *textual-integrity canon; whole-act rule.*

wholly, *adv.* (13c) Not partially; fully; completely.

wholly and permanently disabled, *adj.* (1890) *Insurance.* (Of an insured) completely and continuously unable to perform work for compensation or profit.

wholly dependent, *adj. Workers' compensation.* (Of a person) deriving full support from a worker's wages.

wholly destroyed, *adj. Insurance.* (Of a building) so damaged that it is no longer capable of being classified as a building, although some parts may remain intact.

wholly disabled, *adj. Insurance.* (Of a person) unable to perform the substantial and material acts necessary to carry on a business or occupation in the customary and usual manner.

whopper. A blatant lie; a grossly exaggerated falsehood.

whorehouse. See BROTHEL.

WIC. *abbr.* SPECIAL SUPPLEMENTAL NUTRITION PROGRAM FOR WOMEN, INFANTS, AND CHILDREN.

WIC Program. See SPECIAL SUPPLEMENTAL NUTRITION PROGRAM FOR WOMEN, INFANTS, AND CHILDREN.

widow, *n.* (bef. 12c) A woman whose husband has died and who has not remarried.

widower, *n.* (14c) A man whose wife has died and who has not remarried.

widower's allowance. See *spousal allowance* under ALLOWANCE (1).

widow's allowance. See *spousal allowance* under ALLOWANCE (1).

widow's election. See RIGHT OF ELECTION.

wifa (wɪ-fə), *n.* [Old English] *Hist.* A mark or sign; esp., a landmark showing exclusive occupation or to prohibit an entry.

wife. (bef. 12c) A married woman; a woman who has a lawful spouse living.

▸ **common-law wife.** (1934) **1.** The wife in a common-law marriage; a woman who contracts an informal marriage with a spouse and then holds herself out to the community as being married to that spouse. See *common-law marriage* under MARRIAGE (1). **2.** *Archaic.* Loosely, a concubine.

▸ **plural wife.** (1872) One of two or more women married simultaneously to the same spouse in a polygamous marriage.

▸ **temporary wife.** *Islamic law.* A wife in a short, fixed term marriage.

wife beating. See *spousal abuse* under ABUSE.

wife's equity. See EQUITY TO A SETTLEMENT.

wife's settlement. See EQUITY TO A SETTLEMENT.

wiffem defense. [fr. dialectal pronunciation of "with them"] *Criminal law. Slang.* A criminal defendant's argument that he or she merely accompanied the perpetrators (i.e., was "with them") but did not take part in any criminal activity. Cf. MERE-PRESENCE DEFENSE.

wild animal. See ANIMAL.

wildcard exemption. *Bankruptcy.* An amount of property prescribed by state law up to a specific dollar amount (typically $2,000 to $5,000) that a debtor may exempt, regardless of the property's nature, from the bankruptcy. *See* 11 USCA § 522(d)(5).

wildcat strike. See STRIKE (1).

wild creature. See *wild animal* under CREATURE.

wild deed. See DEED.

Wild's Case, Rule in. See RULE IN WILD'S CASE.

wild title. See TITLE (2).

wilful. See WILLFUL.

will, *n.* (bef. 12c) **1.** Wish; desire; choice <employment at will>. — Also termed *human will.* **2.** The legal expression of an individual's wishes about the disposition of his or her property after death; esp., a document by which a person directs his or her estate to be distributed upon death <there was no mention of his estranged brother in the will>. — Also termed *testament; will and testament;* (archaically) *testamentary instrument.* — **will,** *vb.*

> "The word 'will' has two distinct meanings. The first, and strict, meaning is metaphysical, and denotes the sum of what the testator wishes, or 'wills,' to happen on his death. The second, and more common, meaning is physical, and denotes the document or documents in which that intention is expressed." Anthony R. Mellows, *The Law of Succession* 6 (3d ed. 1977).

▸ **ambulatory will.** (1909) A will that can be altered during the testator's lifetime.

▸ **antenuptial will.** See *prenuptial will.*

▸ **attested will.** (1837) A will that has been signed by a witness.

▸ **bogus will.** (1870) An unauthentic will, esp. one involving fraud or unauthorized changes. — Also termed *sham will.*

▸ **closed will.** See *mystic will.*

▸ **conditional will.** (1855) A will that depends on the occurrence of an uncertain event for the will to take effect. • Most jurisdictions hold a conditional will valid even though the testator's death does not result from or on the occasion of the condition mentioned in the will. The courts generally hold that the condition is the inducement for making the will rather than a condition precedent to its operation. *See Eaton v. Brown,* 193 U.S. 411, 24 S.Ct. 487 (1904); *In re Will of Cohen,* 491 A.2d 1292 (N.J. Super. Ct. App. Div. 1985). Cf. *contingent will.*

▸ **conjoint will.** See *joint will.*

▸ **contingent will.** (1851) A will that takes effect only if a specified event occurs. Cf. *conditional will.*

▸ **counter will.** See *mutual will.*

▸ **destroyed will.** A will that no longer exists because of intentional or accidental damage resulting in its complete loss. See *lost will.*

▸ **double will.** See *mutual will.*

▸ **duplicate will.** (1855) A will executed in duplicate originals by a testator who retains one copy and gives the second copy to another person. • The rules applicable to wills apply to both wills, and upon application for probate, both copies must be tendered into the registry of the probate court.

▸ **holographic will** (hol-ə-**graf**-ik). (1850) A will that is handwritten by the testator. • Such a will is typically unattested. Holographic wills are rooted in the civil-law tradition, having originated in Roman law and having been authorized under the Napoleonic Code. French and Spanish settlers introduced holographic wills in America, primarily in the South and West. Today they are recognized in about half the states. — Also termed *olographic will.* See HOLOGRAPH.

▸ **informal will.** (18c) **1.** A will that does not meet the legal requirements for a valid will. See *invalid will.* **2.** A will or instrument demonstrating testamentary intent drafted solely by the person making the testamentary dispositions. See *holographic will.*

▸ **inofficious will.** See *inofficious testament* under TESTAMENT.

▸ **international will.** A will that is executed according to formalities provided in an international treaty or convention, and that will be valid although it may be written in a foreign language by a testator domiciled in another country.

▸ **invalid will.** (18c) A will that fails to make an effective disposition of property.

▸ **joint and mutual will.** (1841) A single will executed by two or more people — to dispose of property they own separately, in common, or jointly — requiring the surviving testator to dispose of the property in accordance with the terms of the will. • A joint and mutual will is drafted to be contractually binding on the survivor. The word "joint" indicates the form of the will. The word "mutual" describes the substantive provisions. — Also termed *joint and reciprocal will.*

▸ **joint and reciprocal will.** See *joint and mutual will.*

▸ **joint will.** (18c) A single will executed by two or more testators, usu. disposing of their common property by transferring their separate titles to one devisee. — Also termed *conjoint will.*

▸ **last will.** (16c) The most recent will of a deceased; the instrument ultimately fixing the disposition of real and personal property at the testator's death. — Also termed *last will and testament.*

> "A will is the disposition of real and personal property to take effect after the death of the testator. When the will operates upon personal property, it is sometimes called a *testament,* and when upon real estate, a *devise;* but the more general and the more popular denomination of the instrument, embracing equally real and personal estate, is that of *last will and testament.*" 4 James Kent, *Commentaries on American Law* *501 (George Comstock ed., 11th ed. 1866).

▸ **last will and testament.** See *last will.*

▸ **living will.** See LIVING WILL.

▸ **lost will.** An executed will that cannot be found at the testator's death. • Its contents can be proved by parol evidence in many jurisdictions. But the overwhelming majority of American jurisdictions follow the common-law presumption of revocation if a will is proved to have been in the possession of the testator and has since been lost.

▸ **mancipatory will (man**-sip-i-tor-ee). (1873) *Roman law.* In early and classical law, a formal will sealed by seven witnesses and submitted to the praetor. See TESTAMENTUM.

▸ **mariner's will.** See *soldier's will.*

▸ **mutual will.** (*usu. pl.*) (1837) One of two separate wills in which two persons, usu. a husband and wife, establish identical or similar testamentary provisions disposing of their estates in favor of each other. • It is also possible (though rare) for the testators to execute a single mutual will, as opposed to separate ones. And it is possible (though, again, rare) for more than two parties to execute mutual wills. — Also termed *reciprocal will; counter will; double will; mutual testament.*

▸ **mystic will.** (1888) *Civil law.* A secret will signed by the testator, sealed and delivered to a notary in the presence of three to seven witnesses, accompanied by the testator's declaration that it is a valid will. • The notary is then required to indorse on the envelope containing the will a statement of all the facts surrounding the transaction, and this is signed by the notary and all the witnesses. — Also termed *mystic testament; secret will; secret testament; closed will; closed testament; sealed will; sealed testament.*

▸ **nonintervention will.** (1887) A will that authorizes an independent executor. See *independent executor* under EXECUTOR (2).

▸ **notarial will.** (1865) A will executed by a testator in the presence of two witnesses and a notary public.

▸ **nuncupative will** (**nəng**-kyə-pay-tiv *or* nəng-**kyoo**-pə-tiv). (18c) An oral will made in contemplation of imminent death, esp. from a recent injury. • Nuncupative wills are invalid in most states. Even in states allowing them, the amount that may be conveyed is usu. limited by statute. Traditionally, only personal property may be conveyed. — Also termed *oral will; unwritten will; verbal will.*

> "Nuncupative (i.e., oral) wills are by statute in almost all States required to be proved by two (sometimes three) witnesses, who were present and heard the testamentary words." John H. Wigmore, *A Students' Textbook of the Law of Evidence* 299 (1935).

▸ **nuncupative will by public act.** (1841) *Hist. Louisiana law.* A will dictated by the testator to a notary in the presence of a specified number of witnesses. • By law, the notary was required to recite the will to the testator, after which the testator and the witnesses signed the document. If the testator was physically unable to sign, another person could sign in the testator's presence on the testator's behalf. The number of required witnesses varied depending on the circumstances. This type of will was abolished in 1997. *See* La. Civ. Code art. 1574. — Also termed *nuncupative testament by public act.*

▸ **olographic will.** See *holographic will.*

▸ **oral will.** (1853) A will made by the spoken declaration of the testator and usu. dependent on oral testimony for proof. See *nuncupative will.*

▸ **parliamentary will.** *Slang.* The legislation that governs the distribution of an intestate's property. • The term arose because the legislature effectively makes an intestate's will by passing statutes regulating descent and distribution. The terms of the parliamentary will are gathered from the statutes in effect when the intestate died.

▸ **postnuptial will** (pohst-**nəp**-shəl). (1888) A will executed after marriage.

▸ **pourover will** (**por**-oh-vər). (1946) A will giving money or property to an existing trust. Cf. *pourover trust* under TRUST (3).

▸ **prenuptial will** (pree-**nəp**-shəl). (1914) A will executed before marriage. • At common law, marriage automatically revoked a spouse's will, but modern statutes usu. provide that marriage does not revoke a will (although divorce does). But if this marriage was not contemplated by the will and there is nothing otherwise on its face to indicate that the testator intentionally left nothing to any future spouse, the pretermitted spouse may be entitled to a special forced share of the estate. Unif. Probate Code § 2-508. — Also termed *antenuptial will.*

▸ **reciprocal will.** See *mutual will.*

▸ **sealed will.** See *mystic will.*

▸ **seaman's will.** See *soldier's will.*

▸ **secret will.** See *mystic will.*

▸ **self-authenticating will.** See *self-proved will.*

▸ **self-proved will.** (1963) A will proved by a self-proving affidavit. See *self-proving affidavit* under AFFIDAVIT. • This method of proof, recognized in a growing number of states, eliminates the practical problems of obtaining the live testimony of witnesses. — Also termed *self-authenticating will.*

▸ **sham will.** See *bogus will.*

▸ **soldier's will.** A soldier's informal oral or written will that is usu. valid despite its noncompliance with normal statutory formalities, as long as the soldier was in actual service at the time the will was made. — Also termed *seaman's will; mariner's will; military testament; soldier's and sailor's will.*

▸ **undutiful will.** *Civil law.* See *unnatural will.*

▸ **unnatural will.** (1854) A will that distributes the testator's estate to strangers rather than to the testator's relatives, without apparent reason. — Also termed (in civil law) *undutiful will.*

▸ **unofficious will.** See *inofficious testament* under TESTAMENT.

▸ **unsolemn will.** (1807) *Civil law.* A will in which an executor is not named.

▸ **unwritten will.** See *nuncupative will.*

▸ **verbal will.** See *nuncupative will.*

will and testament. See WILL.

will contest. *Wills & estates.* The litigation of a will's validity, usu. based on allegations that the testator lacked capacity or was under undue influence.

willful, *adj.* (13c) Voluntary and intentional, but not necessarily malicious. • A voluntary act becomes willful, in law, only when it involves conscious wrong or evil purpose on the part of the actor, or at least inexcusable carelessness, whether the act is right or wrong. The term *willful* is stronger than *voluntary* or *intentional;* it is traditionally the equivalent of *malicious, evil,* or *corrupt.* — Sometimes spelled *wilful.* Cf. WANTON. — **willfulness,** *n.*

> "The word 'wilful' or 'wilfully' when used in the definition of a crime, it has been said time and again, means only intentionally or purposely as distinguished from accidentally or negligently and does not require any actual impropriety; while on the other hand it has been stated with equal repetition and insistence that the requirement added by such a word is not satisfied unless there is a bad purpose or evil intent." Rollin M. Perkins & Ronald N. Boyce, *Criminal Law* 875–76 (3d ed. 1982).

> "Almost all of the cases under [Bankruptcy Code § 523(a)(6)] deal with the definition of the two words 'willful' and 'malicious.' Initially one might think that willful and malicious mean the same thing. If they did, Congress should have used one word and not both. Most courts feel compelled to find some different meaning for each of them." David G. Epstein et al., *Bankruptcy* § 7-30, at 531 (1993).

willful and malicious injury. See INJURY.

willful and wanton misconduct. See MISCONDUCT (1).

willful and wanton negligence. See *gross negligence* under NEGLIGENCE.

willful blindness. (1927) Deliberate avoidance of knowledge of a crime, esp. by failing to make a reasonable inquiry about suspected wrongdoing despite being aware that it is highly probable. • A person acts with willful blindness, for example, by deliberately refusing to look inside an unmarked package after being paid by a known drug dealer to deliver it. Willful blindness creates an inference of knowledge of the crime in question. *See* Model Penal Code § 2.

willful-blindness direction. See *willful-blindness instruction* under JURY INSTRUCTION.

willful-blindness instruction. See JURY INSTRUCTION.

willful, continued, and obstinate desertion. See *obstinate desertion* under DESERTION.

willful disobedience. See DISOBEDIENCE.

willful homicide. See HOMICIDE.

willful indifference to the safety of others. See *willful and wanton misconduct* under MISCONDUCT.

willful infringement. See INFRINGEMENT.

willful misconduct. See MISCONDUCT (1).

willful misconduct of an employee. See MISCONDUCT (1).

willful murder. See MURDER.

willful neglect. See NEGLECT.

willful negligence. 1. See *advertent negligence* under NEGLIGENCE. **2.** See *gross negligence* (2) under NEGLIGENCE.

willfulness. (13c) **1.** The quality, state, or condition of acting purposely or by design; deliberateness; intention. • Willfulness does not necessarily imply malice, but it involves more than just knowledge. **2.** The voluntary, intentional violation or disregard of a known legal duty. — Also termed *legal willfulness.*

willful tort. See *intentional tort* under TORT.

willful wrong. See *intentional wrong* under WRONG.

Williams Act. A 1968 federal statute that amended the Securities Exchange Act of 1934 by requiring investors who own more than 5% of a company's stock to furnish certain information to the SEC and to comply with certain requirements when making a tender offer.

willing and able. See READY, WILLING, AND ABLE.

Wills Act. 1. STATUTE OF WILLS (1). **2.** An 1837 English statute that allowed people to dispose of every type of property interest by will and that had an elaborate set of requirements for valid execution. • Some states today continue to adhere to these stringent requirements. Cf. Unif. Probate Code § 2-502. — Also termed (in sense 2) *Lord Langdale's Act.*

will substitute. A document or instrument that allows a person, upon death, to dispose of an estate in the same or similar manner as a will but without the formalities and expense of a probate proceeding. • The most common will substitutes are trusts, life-insurance plans, and retirement-benefits contracts. The creation of will substitutes has been one of the most important developments in the area of decedents' estates in the past 50 years. Cf. *nonprobate asset* under ASSET.

Winchester, Statute of. *Hist.* A 1285 English statute requiring every man to provide himself with armor to keep the peace, recognizing and regulating the offices of high and petty constables, organizing the police, and enforcing the old Saxon police laws. • It was repealed in 1827 by the Criminal Statutes (England) Repeal Act. St. 7 & 8 Geo. 4, ch. 27.

Winchester measure. (17c) *Hist.* The standard weights and measures of England, originally kept at Winchester.

windfall. (15c) An unanticipated benefit, usu. in the form of a profit and not caused by the recipient. Cf. LANDFALL (2).

windfall-profits tax. See TAX.

winding up, *n.* (1858) The process of settling accounts and liquidating assets in anticipation of a partnership's or a corporation's dissolution. Cf. DISSOLUTION (4). — **wind up,** *vb.* — **wind up,** *n.*

- ▸ **creditors' voluntary winding up.** See *involuntary winding up.*
- ▸ **involuntary winding up.** (1928) A court-ordered winding up, usu. because the company is insolvent. — Also termed *creditors' voluntary winding up.*
- ▸ **members' voluntary winding up.** See *voluntary winding up.*
- ▸ **voluntary winding up.** (1856) The liquidation procedure begun after a company's owners vote to dissolve the business. — Also termed *members' voluntary winding up.*

window-dressing. (1898) The deceptive arrangement of something, usu. facts or appearances, to make it appear more attractive or favorable. • The term is often used to describe the practice of some financial managers, esp. some managers of mutual funds, to sell certain positions at the end of a quarter to make an investment's quarterly performance appear better than it actually was. See PORTFOLIO PUMPING.

window tax. See TAX.

winner-take-all vote. See VOTE (3).

***Winship* error.** (1970) An erroneous jury instruction that reduces the reasonable-doubt standard. *See In re Winship,* 397 U.S. 358 (1970).

wipe. See SWIPE (3).

WIPO. *abbr.* WORLD INTELLECTUAL PROPERTY ORGANIZATION.

WIPO Copyright Treaty. A 1996 treaty that made changes in the Berne Convention in light of the TRIPs Agreement and dealt with new copyright issues raised by the emergence of the Internet and other digital technology. • The WIPO Treaty expressly protects computer software and databases and expressly excludes from protection "ideas, procedures, methods of operation or mathematical concepts as such." The WIPO Copyright Treaty was adopted simultaneously with the WIPO Performances and Phonograms Treaty. — Abbr. WCT.

WIPO digital agenda. See DIGITAL AGENDA.

WIPO Performances and Phonograms Treaty. A 1996 treaty giving performers the rights of attribution and integrity in their performances, and giving producers the rights of reproduction, distribution, rental, and availability. — Abbr. WPPT.

wire. *Slang.* See LISTENING DEVICE.

wired plea. See *connected plea* under PLEA (1).

wire fraud. See FRAUD.

wire-service defense. (1990) A shield against liability for defamation based on the reiteration by media of information from a false but apparently authentic news dispatch received from a recognized reliable news source, such as a reputable news-service agency. Cf. NEUTRAL-REPORTAGE PRIVILEGE.

wiretapping, *n.* (1904) Electronic or mechanical eavesdropping, usu. done by law-enforcement officers under court order, to listen to private conversations. • Wiretapping is regulated by federal and state law. — Often shortened to *tapping.* See LISTENING DEVICE; EAVESDROPPING. Cf. PEN REGISTER. — **wiretap,** *vb.* — **wiretap,** *n.*

▸ **roving wiretap.** (1987) A tap on any telephone that a suspect uses, movable from one telephone to another, with no particular locational target.

Wisby, laws of. See LAWS OF VISBY.

wish, *vb.* (bef. 12c) **1.** To desire; to hope. **2.** To will; to devise; to give.

wish-law. The law that a given critic or scholarly commentator thinks ought to exist, as opposed to that which actually exists. • The term was coined by Hans Kelsen.

witan (**wit**-ən). [Anglo-Saxon "wise men"] (1807) *Hist.* The members of the king's council who sat to assist the king in administrative and judicial matters. • Among the members were ealdormen, bishops, abbots, high officers, and occasionally the king's friends and relatives. See WITENAGEMOT.

witchcraft. (bef. 12c) The practices of a witch, esp. in black magic; sorcery. • Under the Witchcraft Act of 1541 (33 Hen. 8, ch. 8) and the Witchcraft Act of 1603 (1 Jac. ch. 12), witchcraft was a felony punishable by death without benefit of clergy. The last execution in England for witchcraft occurred in 1716. The Acts were repealed in 1736. In the United States, the most conspicuous (and nearly the last) persecution for witchcraft occurred in Salem, Massachusetts, where 19 people were hanged for this offense in 1692.

witch hunt. (1885) **1.** *Hist.* A group attempt to identify and obtain evidence against a witch. — Also termed *witch-finding.* **2.** By extension, a concerted attempt to identify and punish people whose opinions are regarded as wrong or dangerous; an investigation whose ostensible purpose is to uncover unlawful or unethical conduct but whose actual purpose is to persecute, harass, or suppress the person, group, or entity investigated because of differences in politics, ideology, viewpoints, etc.

wite (wɪt). (bef. 12c) *Hist.* A penal fine exacted by the Crown or other authority for a serious crime, such as murder. — Also spelled *wyte.*

witenagemot (**wit**-ə-nə-gə-moht). [Anglo-Saxon "a meeting of the wise"] (bef. 12c) *Hist.* A national assembly of noblemen, high ecclesiastics, and other great thanes of England who advised and aided the king in the general administration of the government. • Its composition depended on the will of the king. It passed out of existence with the Norman Conquest (1066). Although it was a precursor to the British Parliament, that was a separate growth — not a continuation of the witenagemot. — Also spelled *wittenagemot; witanagemote.* Cf. GEMOT.

> "[T]he ancient Anglo-Saxon general assembly of the notables [was] called the Witenagemot. . . . At first the power of the Anglo-Saxon Witenagemot appears to have been considerable, and in fact so much so that the kings were dependent on appointment to that office by the Witan in the early period before the royal succession became hereditary. With the tenth century centralization of power in the Alfredian line of kings, it appears that the power of the Witan began to decline." Charles Herman Kinnane, *A First Book on Anglo-American Law* 262 (2d ed. 1952).

> "We have not yet defined an Anglo-Saxon witenagemot of the tenth and eleventh centuries. Definitions based upon size, frequency, components, place and time of assembly, and business treated end in contradiction. This confusion is understandable when one realizes that the witenagemot was an amoebic sort of organization with no definite composition or function. It was not just a large assembly of the great men of England upon festive occasions such as the crown-wearing and Christmas, nor was it just a small council of constant and intimate officers and advisers of the king; it could be either. Whenever the king consulted with either body of men and it cooperated in the royal business of governing, that body can be considered a witenagemot. The nature of the business could be major or minor, and the king could consult at any place and at any time, though he favored certain towns like London and Winchester and preferred to consider major items of business at Christmas, Lent, and Easter when his court would have the greatest number of nobles present. In defining the nature of the witenagemot the most one can say is that it was an arbitrarily organized assembly completely undefined in composition. When any number, great or small, of the aristocrats were asked by the king to give him counsel and consent or to witness and license a royal act, this seemed to constitute a witenagemot. It is certain that on all important matters the king consulted with the witenagemot to secure its advice and consent." Bryce Lyon, *A Constitutional and Legal History of Medieval England* 45–46 (1960).

witepenny. (1895) *Hist.* In early English law, money paid in satisfaction of a wite.

with all deliberate speed. See DELIBERATE SPEED.

with all faults. See AS IS.

withdraw, *vb.* (13c) **1.** (*vt.*) To take back (something presented, granted, enjoyed, possessed, or allowed) <withdraw blame>. **2.** (*vt.*) To retract (one's words) <withdraw the objection>. **3.** (*vt.*) To refrain from prosecuting or proceeding with (an action) <withdraw the petition for divorce>. **4.** (*vi.*) (Of a lawyer) to terminate one's representation of a client before a matter is complete <withdraw from representation>. **5.** (*vt.*) To remove a juror <withdraw a biased juror>. **6.** (*vi.*) To leave or retire (from a community or society). **7.** (*vi.*) (Of a condition or immaterial thing) to vanish, depart.

withdrawal, *n.* (18c) **1.** The act of taking back or away; removal <withdrawal of consent>. **2.** The act of retreating from a place, position, or situation; esp., the act of canceling one's representation of a client <withdrawal from a client's representation in a contract dispute>. See NOISY WITHDRAWAL. **3.** The removal of money from a depository <withdrawal of funds from the checking account>. **4.** RENUNCIATION (3) <withdrawal from the conspiracy to commit arson>. **5.** RETRACTION (4). **6.** *Parliamentary law.* A motion's removal from consideration by its mover. • The mover controls a motion only until the chair states the question, after which the motion belongs to the assembly and the mover cannot withdraw it without the assembly's permission. See *request for permission to* *withdraw a motion* under REQUEST. **7.** *Parliamentary law.* DISCHARGE (9). — **withdraw,** *vb.*

withdrawal defense. (1975) *Criminal law.* A conspirator's affirmative defense that he or she has renounced participation in the conspiracy and has informed police of his or her abandonment of any further criminal intent. — Also termed *abandonment defense.*

withdrawal of charges. (1842) The removal of charges by the one bringing them, such as a prosecutor. See NOLLE PROSEQUI.

withdrawal of counsel. (1875) An attorney's termination of his or her role in representing a party in a case. • Normally, the attorney must have the court's permission to withdraw from a case. Permission is usu. sought by a written motion (1) explaining the reason for the requested withdrawal (often, a conflict between attorney and client over a matter such as strategy or fees), and (2) stating whether the client agrees. — Abbr. WOC. — Also termed *withdrawing of counsel.*

withdrawing a juror. (18c) The act or an instance of removing a juror, usu. to obtain a continuance in a case or, sometimes in English practice, to end the case, as when the case has settled, the parties are too anxious to proceed to verdict, or the judge recommends it because the action is not properly before the court.

withdrawing of record. (18c) **1.** With the court's permission, the usu. temporary removal of the actual court record or any portion of it from the office of the clerk of the court. **2.** *Hist.* A plaintiff's removal of the nisi prius or trial record to prevent the case from being tried, usu. either before the jury is sworn or afterward with the consent of defense counsel.

withdrawn land. 1. See *reserved land* under LAND. **2.** See RESERVATION (3).

withernam (wi<u>th</u>-ər-nahm), *n.* [fr. Saxon *weder* "other" + *naam* "a taking"] (13c) *Hist.* A reciprocal taking or distress in place of a previous one. See *capias in withernam* under CAPIAS.

withersake (wi<u>th</u>-ər-sayk). (bef. 12c) *Archaic.* An enemy; esp., a deliberately faithless renegade.

with full power. See *committee with power* under COMMITTEE (1).

withheld sentence. See *suspended sentence* under SENTENCE.

withholding, *n.* (1940) **1.** The practice of deducting a certain amount from a person's salary, wages, dividends, winnings, or other income, usu. for tax purposes; esp., an employer's practice of taking out a portion of an employee's gross earnings and paying that portion to the government for income-tax and social-security purposes. **2.** The money so deducted. — Also termed *income-tax withholding.* — **withhold,** *vb.*

withholding of evidence. (1848) The act or an instance of obstructing justice by stifling or suppressing evidence knowing that it is being sought in an official investigation or a judicial proceeding. See OBSTRUCTION OF JUSTICE.

withholding tax. See TAX.

without, *prep.* & *adv.* (bef. 12c) **1.** Not having something, esp. something basic or necessary <a house without running water>. **2.** In the absence of <without any warning>. **3.** *Archaic.* Outside <is this conduct within or without the guidelines?>

without day. See GO HENCE WITHOUT DAY.

without delay. (13c) **1.** Instantly; at once. **2.** Within the time reasonably allowed by law.

without dissent. See WITHOUT OBJECTION.

without impeachment of waste. (16c) (Of a tenant) not subject to an action for waste; not punishable for waste. • This clause is inserted in a lease to give a tenant the right to take certain actions (such as cutting timber) without being held liable for waste. But a tenant cannot abuse the right and will usu. be held liable for maliciously committing waste. — Also termed *absque impetitione vasti.*

without legal efficacy. Lacking in effectiveness, significance, power, or force under law; invalid.

without notice. (16c) Lacking actual or constructive knowledge. • To be a bona fide purchaser, one must buy something "without notice" of another's claim to the item or of defects in the seller's title. To be a holder in due course, one must take a bill or note "without notice" that it is overdue, has been dishonored, or is subject to a claim. UCC § 3-302(a)(2). See NOTICE; *bona fide purchaser* under PURCHASER.

without objection. (16c) With general consent. — Also termed *without dissent.* See *general consent* under CONSENT (2).

without prejudice, *adv.* (15c) Without loss of any rights; in a way that does not harm or cancel the legal rights or privileges of a party <dismissed without prejudice>. See *dismissal without prejudice* under DISMISSAL (1).

> "WITHOUT PREJUDICE. A phrase that, when incorporated in contracts, stipulations, and other written instruments, imports that the parties have agreed that, as between themselves, the receipt of the money by one, and the enjoyment by the other, shall not, because of the facts of the receipt and payment, have any legal effect upon the rights of the parties in the premises; that such rights will be as open to settlement by negotiation or legal controversy as if the money had not been turned over by the one to the other. In dismissing motions, actions, bills in equity, and appeals 'without prejudice,' no right or remedy of the parties is affected. The use of the phrase simply shows that there has been no decision of the case upon the merits, and prevents defendant from setting up the defense of *res adjudicata.* In other words it leaves the whole subject as open to litigation as if no proceeding had ever been had in the matter." 40 *Cyclopedia of Law and Procedure* 2130–31(William Mack ed., 1912).

without recourse. (18c) (In an indorsement) without liability to subsequent holders. • With this stipulation, one who indorses an instrument indicates that he or she has no further liability to any subsequent holder for payment. — Also termed *sans recours.*

without reserve. Of, relating to, or involving an auction at which an item will be sold for the highest bid price.

without this, that. See ABSQUE HOC.

with power. See *committee with power* under COMMITTEE (1).

with prejudice, *adv.* With loss of all rights; in a way that finally disposes of a party's claim and bars any future action on that claim <dismissed with prejudice>. See *dismissal with prejudice* under DISMISSAL (1).

with recourse, *adv.* (In an indorsement) with liability to subsequent holders. • With this stipulation, one who indorses an instrument indicates that he or she remains liable to the holder for payment.

with reserve. Of, relating to, or involving an auction at which an item will not be sold unless the highest bid exceeds a minimum price.

with strong hand. (15c) With force. • In common-law pleading, this term implies a degree of criminal force, esp. as used in forcible-entry statutes.

witness, *n.* (bef. 12c) **1.** Someone who sees, knows, or vouches for something <a witness to a testator's signature>. **2.** Someone who gives testimony under oath or affirmation (1) in person, (2) by oral or written deposition, or (3) by affidavit <the witness to the signature signed the affidavit.>. • A witness must be legally competent to testify. — **witness,** *vb.*

> "The term 'witness,' in its strict legal sense, means one who gives evidence in a cause before a court; and in its general sense includes all persons from whose lips testimony is extracted to be used in any judicial proceeding, and so includes deponents and affiants as well as persons delivering oral testimony before a court or jury." 97 C.J.S. *Witnesses* § 1, at 350 (1957).

> "Every witness is an editor: he tells you not everything he saw and heard, for that would be impossible, but what he saw and heard and found significant, and what he finds significant depends on his preconceptions." Patrick Devlin, *The Criminal Prosecution in England* 66 (1960).

▸ **absent witness.** A witness who does not attend the trial and testify in person.

▸ **accomplice witness.** (1853) A witness who is an accomplice in the crime that the defendant is charged with. • A codefendant cannot be convicted solely on the testimony of an accomplice witness.

▸ **adverse witness.** See *hostile witness.*

▸ **alibi witness.** (1897) A witness who testifies that the defendant was in a location other than the scene of the crime at the relevant time; a witness who supports the defendant's alibi.

▸ **attesting witness.** (18c) Someone who vouches for the authenticity of another's signature by signing an instrument that the other has signed <proof of the will requires two attesting witnesses>. — Also termed *subscribing witness.*

▸ **beneficiary witness.** (1928) A witness to the making of a will who also happens to be a beneficiary under it. • At common law, because this dual capacity destroyed the witness's disinterestedness, the effect was to invalidate the gift. But most jurisdictions have statutorily abrogated the requirement of disinterestedness.

▸ **character witness.** (1893) A witness who testifies about another person's character traits or community reputation. See *character evidence* under EVIDENCE.

> "Many lawyers are under the erroneous impression that the person called as a character witness must be personally, or even intimately, acquainted with the individual whose character is to be put in issue, when the rule and the nature of the testimony to be elicited is based, not upon what the character witness knows of his own knowledge, but upon what he has heard others say. If the witness has heard the character of such individual discussed by a substantial number of people who have to a substantial degree been in contact with such individual, the witness can qualify even though he has not even seen the person as to whose reputation he is called upon to give testimony." Charles W. Fricke, *Planning and Trying Cases* 194 (1952).

▸ **competent witness.** (17c) A witness who is legally qualified to testify. • A lay witness who has personal knowledge of the subject matter of the testimony is competent to testify. Fed. R. Evid. 601–602.

▸ **corroborating witness.** (1853) A witness who confirms or supports someone else's testimony.

▸ **court witness.** A witness called or re-called to testify by the judge. • The witness called to testify by the court usu. has expertise in the subject matter of the trial and is considered necessary to resolve a conflict in the testimony. The court's discretion to call its own witnesses exists in both civil and criminal cases.

▸ **credible witness.** (16c) A witness whose testimony is believable.

▸ **disinterested witness.** (18c) A witness who has no private interest in the matter at issue.

▸ **expert witness.** (1858) A witness qualified by knowledge, skill, experience, training, or education to provide a scientific, technical, or other specialized opinion about the evidence or a fact issue. Fed. R. Evid. 702–706. — Also termed *skilled witness.* See EXPERT; DAUBERT TEST; *expert opinion* under OPINION (3).

▸ **fact witness.** A witness who has firsthand knowledge of something based on the witness's perceptions through one of more of the five senses.

▸ **going witness.** (1848) *Archaic.* A witness who is about to leave a court's jurisdiction, but not the country. • An example is the witness who leaves one state to go to another.

▸ **grand-jury witness.** (1947) A witness who is called to testify before a grand jury.

▸ **hostile witness.** (1852) A witness who is biased against the examining party, is unwilling to testify, or is identified with an adverse party. • A hostile witness may be asked leading questions on direct examination. Fed. R. Evid. 611(c). — Also termed *adverse witness*; *unfavorable witness.* See *adverse party* under PARTY (2).

▸ **incompetent witness.** A witness who is legally disqualified from giving evidence.

> "Obviously, in order to the proper exercise of this important function, the proposed witness must possess certain qualifications, or, to speak more accurately, he must not labor under certain disqualifications, to be presently considered, or he will be rejected by the court or magistrate as an *incompetent* witness, and his testimony excluded. The chief reason for the exclusion of the testimony of such a witness is, that it would, if admitted, tend to mislead the jury; and it is clear that the propriety of the exclusion in each particular case must largely depend upon the constitution of the tribunal to which the evidence is submitted, and the mode of proceeding before it. Then, too, the difference which exists between judicial investigations and the ordinary transactions of life, must be considered more especially with regard to the space of time allowed for decision, the temptations to deceive, the facilities for deception, and the consequences of deciding incorrectly." Stewart Rapalje, *A Treatise on the Law of Witnesses* § 1, at 1–2 (1887).

▸ **interested witness.** (18c) A witness who has a direct and private interest in the matter at issue. • Most jurisdictions provide that a person witnessing a will may not be a devisee under the will. The Uniform Probate Code, however, has abrogated this rule.

▸ **lawyer-witness.** An attorney who is called as a fact witness. — Also termed *advocate-witness*; *attorney-witness*. See *fact witness*; LAWYER-WITNESS RULE.

▸ **lay witness.** (1853) A witness who does not testify as an expert and who is therefore restricted to giving an opinion or making an inference that (1) is based on first-hand knowledge, and (2) is helpful in clarifying the testimony or in determining facts. Fed. R. Evid. 701.

▸ **material witness.** (18c) A witness who can testify about matters having some logical connection with the consequential facts, esp. if few others, if any, know about those matters; a person who is capable of testifying in some relevant way in a legal proceeding. See MATERIAL-WITNESS PROCEEDING.

▸ **nonparty witness.** A witness who is not a party to the proceeding and usu. not testifying as an expert, as a law-enforcement officer, or in any capacity as a public official.

▸ **ordinary witness.** Any witness who does not qualify as an expert. See *expert witness*.

> "An 'ordinary witness' is a person called to testify, who, on the subject upon which he is examined, is not an expert." John D. Lawson, *The Law of Expert and Opinion Evidence Reduced to Rules* 4 (2d ed. 1900).

▸ **outcry witness.** (1976) A witness who listens to a victim's out-of-court statements about a crime, esp. very soon after the crime was committed. • An outcry witness's statement is often used during an investigation to corroborate the victim's statement. In some jurisdictions, esp. when the victim is a minor, the witness may testify about what the victim said.

▸ **party witness.** A witness who is a plaintiff or defendant in the proceeding.

▸ **percipient witness.** (1913) A witness who has perceived the things about which he or she testifies. See EYEWITNESS; EARWITNESS.

▸ **prosecuting witness.** (1823) Someone who files the complaint that triggers a criminal prosecution and whose testimony the prosecution usu. relies on to secure a conviction.

▸ **qualified witness.** (1845) A witness who, by explaining the manner in which a business records are made and kept, is able to lay the foundation for the admission of those records under an exception to the hearsay rule. Fed. R. Evid. 803(6).

▸ **rebuttal witness.** (1891) A witness who contradicts or attempts to contradict evidence previously presented.

▸ **res gestae witness.** (1894) A witness who, having been at the scene of an incident, can give a firsthand account of what happened. See RES GESTAE.

▸ **skilled witness.** (1843) **1.** See *expert witness*. **2.** A witness whose degree of knowledge in a particular subject or field is short of the standard for an expert but greater than the knowledge possessed by a typical layperson.

▸ **subscribing witness.** (17c) Someone who witnesses the signatures on an instrument and signs at the end of the instrument to that effect. See *attesting witness*.

▸ **supernumerary witness.** (17c) An unrequired witness, such as a third witness to a will where only two are required.

▸ **surprise witness. 1.** A witness whose identity was not discovered or disclosed or who was not deposed before the proceeding. **2.** A witness whose testimony is unexpected and unanticipated.

▸ **swift witness.** See *zealous witness*.

▸ **target witness.** (1965) **1.** The person who has the knowledge that an investigating body seeks. **2.** A witness who is called before a grand jury and against whom the government is also seeking an indictment.

▸ **turncoat witness.** (1947) A witness whose testimony was expected to be favorable but who becomes (usu. during the trial) a hostile witness.

▸ **ultroneous witness.** (18c) *Scots law.* A witness who comes forward without being summoned to appear in court.

▸ **unavailable witness.** A witness who is privileged against testifying, refuses to testify despite a court order, has died, cannot appear in court because of physical or mental illness, cannot recall the subject matter of a previous statement, or cannot be made to appear in court by process or other reasonable means. Fed. R. Evid. 804.

▸ **unfavorable witness.** See *hostile witness*.

▸ **zealous witness** (zel-əs). (1868) A witness who shows partiality toward the litigant that called him or her to testify and who seems eager to help that side in the lawsuit. — Also termed *swift witness*.

witness box. See WITNESS STAND.

witness clause. See TESTIMONIUM CLAUSE.

witnesseth, *vb.* Shows; records. • This term, usu. set in all capitals, commonly separates the preliminaries in a contract, up through the recitals, from the contractual terms themselves. Modern drafters increasingly avoid it as an antiquated relic. Traditionally, the subject of this verb was *This Agreement*: the sentence, boiled down, was *This Agreement witnesseth* [i.e., shows or records] *that, whereas* [*the parties have agreed to contract with one another*], *the parties therefore agree as follows* . . . . Many modern contracts erroneously retain the *Witnesseth* even though a new verb appears in the preamble: *This Agreement is between* [one party and the other party]. After the preamble is a period, followed by an all-capped WITNESSETH. It is an example of a form retained long after its utility, and most lawyers do not know what it means or even what purpose it once served.

witness fee. See FEE (1).

witnessing part. 1. See ATTESTATION CLAUSE. **2.** See TESTATUM (2).

witness jurat. See JURAT (1).

witness list. (1880) A roster of all the people that all the litigants in a given lawsuit may call as witnesses at trial. • The list includes information about each witness, including name, home and work addresses and phone numbers, other information that may help in locating the witness and scheduling the witness's appearance, and a brief synopsis of the witness's role (e.g., expert witness, character witness, arresting officer).

witness protection. See PROTECTION.

witness-protection program. (1970) A federal or state program in which a person who testifies against a criminal is assigned a new identity and relocated to another part of the country to avoid retaliation by anyone convicted as a result of that testimony. • The Federal Witness Protection Program was established by the Organized Crime Control Act of 1970 and is administered by the marshals of the U.S. Department of Justice. — Also termed *witness-security program.*

witness-security program. See WITNESS-PROTECTION PROGRAM.

witness stand. (1853) The space in a courtroom, usu. a boxed area, occupied by a witness while testifying. — Often shortened to *stand.* — Also termed *witness box.*

witness statement. (1825) **1.** See STATEMENT (3). **2.** A recorded account, made under oath or in preparation for a court proceeding, of a person's knowledge of facts about something. — Also termed *formal witness statement.* **3.** An oral assertion made without intent or expectation that it will be used in a legal proceeding, such as a comment or exclamation made at the time of an event. — Also termed *informal witness statement.* **4.** *Procedure.* A summary of the testimony that a witness will give.

witness-tampering. (1924) The act or an instance of obstructing justice by intimidating, influencing, or harassing a witness before or after the witness testifies. • Several state and federal laws, including the Victim and Witness Protection Act of 1982 (18 USCA § 1512), provide criminal penalties for tampering with witnesses or other persons in the context of a pending investigation or official proceeding. See OBSTRUCTION OF JUSTICE.

witword (**wit**-wərd). (bef. 12c) *Hist.* **1.** A legally allowed claim; esp., the right to vindicate ownership or possession by one's affirmation under oath. **2.** A will or testament.

W.L. *abbr.* WESTLAW.

wobbler. *Slang.* A crime that can be charged as either a felony or a misdemeanor.

WOC. *abbr.* WITHDRAWAL OF COUNSEL.

wolf's head. (13c) *Hist.* An outlaw, who was formerly often referred to as carrying a wolf's head (*caput lupinum*) and to be no more than a wild beast or wolf who could be slain and whose head could be carried to the king. — Also termed *woolferthfod.* See OUTLAW.

> "Outlawry is the last weapon of ancient law, but one that it must often use. As has been well said, it is the sentence of death pronounced by a community which has no police constables or professional hangmen. To pursue the outlaw and knock him on the head as though he were a wild beast is the right and duty of every law-abiding man. 'Let him bear the wolf's head:' this phrase is in use even in the thirteenth century." 1 Frederick Pollock & Frederic W. Maitland, *The History of English Law Before the Time of Edward I* 476 (2d ed. 1898).

womb. See UTERUS.

Women's Bureau. A unit in the U.S. Department of Labor responsible for formulating policies and standards to promote the welfare of wage-earning women.

women's shelter. See SHELTER (1).

women's suffrage. See SUFFRAGE (1).

Women's Suffrage Amendment. See NINETEENTH AMENDMENT.

wood-corn, *n.* (13c) *Hist.* A quantity of oats or grain paid by customary tenants to a lord for the privilege of picking up dead or broken wood.

wood-geld (**wuud**-geld). (13c) *Hist.* **1.** Money paid for the privilege of taking wood from a forest. **2.** Immunity from paying money for this privilege. — Also termed *pudzeld.*

wood-leave. (16c) *Hist.* A license or right to cut down, remove, and use standing timber.

wood-mote (**wuud**-moht). See COURT OF ATTACHMENTS.

Wood-Plea Court. *Hist.* A court held twice a year in Clun Forest, in Shropshire, to determine matters of wood and agistments.

woodshedding. See HORSESHEDDING.

woodward (**wuud**-word), *n.* (bef. 12c) *Hist.* A forest officer who patrols and protects the forest.

woolferthfod. See WOLF'S HEAD.

w.o.p. *abbr.* WANT OF PROSECUTION.

word of art. See TERM OF ART.

words actionable in themselves. (18c) Language that is libelous or slanderous per se. See *slander per se* under SLANDER; *libel per se* under LIBEL.

words of conveyance. (17c) Language in a deed or will that indicates the grantor's intent to transfer an interest and is required to make the transfer effective. • For example, a verb such as *grant, convey,* or *quitclaim* is necessary. — Also termed *words of grant.*

words of enactment. See ENACTING WORDS.

words of grant. See WORDS OF CONVEYANCE.

words of limitation. (16c) Language in a conveying instrument — often nonliteral language — describing the extent or quality of an estate. • For example, under long-standing principles of property law, the phrase "to A and her heirs" creates a fee simple in A but gives nothing to A's heirs. See LIMITATION (4).

> "'Words of limitation' is the phrase used to describe the words which limit (i.e., delimit or mark out) the estate to be taken. Thus in a conveyance today 'to A in fee simple,' the words 'in fee simple' are words of limitation, for they show what estate A is to have." Robert E. Megarry & M.P. Thompson, *A Manual of the Law of Real Property* 29 (6th ed. 1993).

words of negotiability. See NEGOTIABLE WORDS.

words of procreation (proh-kree-**ay**-shən). (18c) Language in a deed essential to create an estate tail, such as an estate "to A and the heirs of his body.

words of purchase. (17c) Language in a deed or will designating the persons who are to receive the grant. • For example, the phrase "to A for life with a remainder to her heirs" creates a life estate in A and a remainder in A's heirs. See PURCHASE (2).

words of severance. (18c) In a grant of lands, words showing that the tenants were each to take a distinct share in the property as opposed to undivided portions. • Typical words of severance are *share and share alike, to be divided among, equally,* and *between.*

work, *n.* (bef. 12c) **1.** Physical and mental exertion to attain an end, esp. as controlled by and for the benefit of an employer; labor.

▸ **additional work. 1.** Work that results from a change or alteration in plans concerning the work required, usu. under a construction contract; added work necessary to meet the performance goals under a contract. **2.** See *extra work.*

▸ **extra work.** In construction law, work not required under the contract; something done or furnished in addition to the contract's requirements; work entirely outside and independent of the contract and not contemplated by it. • A contractor is usu. entitled to charge for extra work consisting of labor and materials not contemplated by or subsumed within the original contract, at least to the extent that the property owner agrees to a change order. Materials and labor not contemplated by the contract, but that are required by later changes in the plans and specifications, are considered to be extra work. — Also termed *additional work.*

▸ **fixed-term work.** Work carried out under an employment contract that is due to end when a specified date is reached, a specified event does or does not occur, or a specified task has been completed.

▸ **flexible work.** Work purposefully carried out in an atypical or nontraditional way, usu. through an explicit understanding with the employer, as under an arrangement for compressed hours, flextime, job-sharing, term-time working, staggered hours, or annualized hours.

▸ **heavy work.** (16c) Work involving frequent lifting and carrying of large items. • Under the Social Security Administration regulations for describing a worker's physical limitations, heavy work involves lifting no more than 100 pounds, with frequent lifting or carrying of objects weighing up to 50 pounds. 20 CFR § 404.

▸ **inherently dangerous work.** (1893) Work that can be carried out only by the exercise of special skill and care and that involves a grave risk of serious harm if done unskillfully or carelessly.

▸ **light work.** (16c) Work involving some limited lifting and moving. • Under the Social Security Administration regulations for describing a worker's physical limitations, light work includes walking, standing, sitting while pushing or pulling arm or leg controls, and lifting no more than 20 pounds, with frequent lifting or carrying of objects that weigh up to 10 pounds. 20 CFR § 404. — Also termed *light-duty work.*

▸ **medium work.** (1914) Work involving some frequent lifting and moving. • Under the Social Security Administration regulations for describing a worker's physical limitations, medium work includes lifting up to 50 pounds, with frequent lifting or carrying of objects weighing up to 25 pounds. 20 CFR § 404.

▸ **sedentary work.** (18c) Work involving light lifting and only occasional walking or standing. • Under the Social Security Administration regulations for describing a worker's physical limitations, sedentary work involves lifting of no more than ten pounds, occasionally carrying small items such as docket files and small tools, and occasional standing or walking. 20 CFR § 404.

▸ **semi-skilled work.** (1935) Work that may require some alertness and close attention, such as inspecting items or machinery for irregularities, or guarding property or people against loss or injury. 20 CFR § 404.1568(b). — Also written *semiskilled work.*

▸ **skilled work.** (17c) Work requiring the worker to use judgment, deal with the public, analyze facts and figures, or work with abstract ideas at a high level of complexity. 20 CFR § 404.

▸ **unskilled work.** (18c) Work requiring little or no judgment, and involving simple tasks that can be learned quickly on the job. 20 CFR § 404.

▸ **very heavy work.** (18c) Work involving frequent lifting of very large objects and frequent carrying of large objects. • Under the Social Security Administration regulations for describing a worker's physical limitations, very heavy work involves lifting 100 pounds or more, and frequent lifting or carrying of objects weighing 50 pounds or more. 20 CFR § 404.1567(e).

▸ **work of necessity.** (1818) Work reasonably essential to the public's economic, social, or moral welfare as determined by the community standards at a particular time, and (formerly) excepted from the operation of blue laws. See BLUE LAW.

2. *Copyright.* An original expression, in fixed or tangible form (such as paper, audiotape, or computer disk), that may be entitled to common-law or statutory copyright protection. • A work may take many different forms, including art, sculpture, literature, music, crafts, software, and photography. — Also termed *copyrightable work.*

▸ **anonymous work.** (17c) A work that, on copies or phonorecords, does not identify any natural person as the author. 17 USCA § 101.

▸ **architectural work.** (1842) The copyrightable design of a building, as fixed in tangible media such as plans, drawings, and the building itself. 17 USCA § 102(8). • Only the overall design is protected, not each design element. This category of works was added to U.S. law by the Berne Convention Implementation Act of 1988. It is one of eight categories eligible for copyright protection.

▸ **artistic work.** (1855) Any visual representation, such as a painting, drawing, map, photograph, sculpture, engraving, or architectural plan.

▸ **audiovisual work.** (1967) A work consisting of related images that are presented in a series, usu. with the aid of a machine, and accompanied by sound. • An example of an audiovisual work is a lecture illustrated with a film strip, or a movie with a soundtrack.

▸ **collective work.** (1870) **1.** A publication (such as a periodical issue, anthology, or encyclopedia) in which several contributions, constituting separate and independent works in themselves, are assembled into a copyrightable whole. **2.** A selection and arrangement of brief portions of different movies, television shows, or radio shows into a single copyrightable work. • If the selecting and arranging involves any originality, the person who selects and arranges the clips may claim a copyright even if copyright cannot be claimed in the individual component parts. Cf. COMPILATION (1).

▸ **composite work** (kəm-**poz**-it). (1910) An original publication that relates to a variety of subjects and includes discrete selections from many authors. • Although the distinguishable parts are separately protectable, the owner of the composite work — not the individual authors — owns the renewal term, if any. 17 USCA § 304(a).

▸ **creative work.** See *work of authorship.*

▸ **derivative work.** (1965) A copyrightable creation that is based on a preexisting product; a translation, musical arrangement, fictionalization, motion-picture version, abridgment, or any other recast or adapted form of an original work. • Only the holder of the copyright on the original form can produce or permit someone else to produce a derivative work. 17 USCA § 101. — Sometimes shortened to *derivative*. Cf. COMPILATION (1).

> "[W]hile a compilation consists merely of the selection and arrangement of pre-existing material without any internal changes in such material, a derivative work involves recasting or transformation, i.e., changes in the pre-existing material, whether or not it is juxtaposed in an arrangement with other pre-existing materials. A catalog constitutes a compilation, and a translation of a pre-existing work constitutes a derivative work." 1 Melville B. Nimmer & David Nimmer, *Nimmer on Copyright* § 3.02, at 3-5 (Supp. 1997).

▸ **dramatic work.** (16c) Any form of nonliterary work created for performance and viewing. • The term includes plays, scripts, films, choreographic works, and similar creations.

▸ **joint work.** (17c) A work created or developed by two or more people whose contributions blend inseparably or interdependently into the whole work. • The cocreators have equal legal rights to register and enjoy the copyright, but this does not affect any other contractually unequal ownership arrangements. — Also termed *work of joint authorship.*

▸ **literary work.** (18c) A nonaudiovisual work that is expressed in verbal, numerical, or other symbols, such as words or musical notation, and embodied in some type of physical object. • Literary works are one of eight general categories that are eligible for copyright protection. 17 USCA § 102. Cf. LITERARY COMPOSITION.

> "Copyright protection extends to literary works which are defined as works, other than audiovisual works, expressed in words, numbers, or other verbal or numerical symbols or indicia, regardless of the nature of the material objects, such as books, periodicals, manuscripts, phonorecords, film, tapes, disks, or cards in which they are embodied. The term 'literary work' does not connote any criterion of literary merit or qualitative value and includes catalogs and directories; similar factual, reference or instructional works; compilations of data; computer data bases, and computer programs." 18 Am. Jur. 2d *Copyright and Literary Property* § 25, at 360 (1985).

▸ **pictorial, graphic, and sculptural work.** (1977) Two- or three-dimensional works of graphic, fine, or applied art that are eligible for copyright protection. • This is one of eight general classifications covered by copyright law. Examples include globes, architectural drawings, photographs, and models. 17 USCA § 102. — Abbr. PGS.

▸ **posthumous work.** (17c) The product of an author who died before publication.

▸ **pseudonymous work.** (1954) A work done by an author who uses a fictitious name.

▸ **work for hire.** (1961) A copyrightable work produced either by an employee within the scope of employment or by an independent contractor under a written agreement; esp., a work specially ordered or commissioned for use as (1) a contribution to a collective work, (2) a translation, (3) a supplementary work, (4) a part of a movie or other audiovisual work, (5) a compilation, (6) an instructional text, (7) a test, (8) answer material for a test, or (9) an atlas. • If the work is produced by an independent contractor, the parties must agree expressly in writing that the work will be a work for hire. The employer or commissioning party owns the copyright. 17 USCA § 101. — Also termed *work made for hire.*

▸ **work of authorship.** (1917) The product of creative expression, such as literature, music, art, and graphic designs. • Copyright protects a work of authorship if it meets three criteria. First, the work must be original, not a copy. Second, the work must be presented in a fixed medium, such as a computer disk, a canvas, or paper. Finally, some creativity must have been involved in the work's creation, although the amount of creativity required depends on the particular work. — Also termed *creative work.*

▸ **work of joint authorship.** See *joint work.*

▸ **work of the United States government.** (1965) A work created by a U.S. government officer or employee in the course of performing official duties. • By statute, federal-government works may not be copyrighted.

work, *vb.* (bef. 12c) **1.** To exert effort; to perform, either physically or mentally <lawyers work long hours during trial>. **2.** To function properly; to produce a desired effect <the strategy worked>. **3.** *Patents.* To develop and use (a patented invention, esp. to make it commercially available) <the patentee failed to work the patent>. • Failure to work a patent in a specified amount of time is grounds for a compulsory license in some countries. **4.** To cause (a hardship, inequity, etc.).

workable, *adj.* (1865) (Of a plan, system, strategy, etc.) practical and effective; feasible.

work and labor. (18c) *Hist.* A common count in an action of *assumpsit* for the work and labor performed and materials furnished by the plaintiff. See ASSUMPSIT.

worker. (14c) **1.** Someone who labors to attain an end; esp., a person employed to do work for another. **2.** Someone who offers to perform services for compensation in the employ of another, whether or not the person is so employed at a given time.

▸ **migrant worker.** (1923) **1.** *Int'l law.* Someone who works seasonally as an agricultural laborer in a foreign country, esp. in agricultural labor. **2.** Someone who works seasonally as a laborer in a different part of his or her own country. — Also termed *seasonal agricultural worker.*

Worker Adjustment and Retraining Notification Act. A federal statute that requires an employer to provide notice of a plant closing or mass layoff, 60 days before the closing or layoff, to the employees, the state-dislocated-workers unit, and the chief elected official of the unit of local government where the plant closing or layoff is to occur. 29 USCA §§ 2101–2109. — Abbr. WARN; WARN Act.

workers' compensation. (1901) A system of providing benefits to an employee for injuries occurring in the scope of employment. • Most workers'-compensation statutes both hold the employer strictly liable and bar the employee from suing the employer in tort. — Abbr. WC. — Also termed *workmen's compensation*; *employers' liability.*

> "Workers' compensation laws were designed to provide employees with expansive protection against the consequences of employment-related injuries. Injured workers no longer had to establish negligence attributable to their employer in order to obtain legal redress. They merely had to demonstrate that their conditions arose out of and during the course of their employment." Mark A. Rothstein et al., *Employment Law* § 7.3, at 406 (1994).

workers'-compensation act. (1910) A statute by which employers are made responsible for bodily harm to their workers arising out of and in the course of their employment, regardless of the fault of either the employee or the employer.

workers'-compensation board. (1939) An agency that reviews cases arising under workers'-compensation statutes and administers the related rules and regulations. — Also termed *workers'-compensation commission.*

> "Workers' compensation boards . . . are tribunals . . . of limited and special jurisdiction and have only such authority and power as have been conferred upon them by express grant, or by implication as necessary and incidental to the full exercise of their authority. The functions of such agencies may include the settlement of disputes with respect to the right to and the amount of compensation, the supervision of voluntary settlements or agreements, the collection and administration of compensation funds, and the supervision and regulation of matters pertaining to compensation insurance." 82 Am. Jur. 2d *Workers' Compensation* § 56, at 65 (1992).

workers'-compensation lien. See LIEN.

workers'-compensation subrogation lien. See *workers'-compensation lien* under LIEN.

work ethic. (1959) A belief in the moral value and worth of hard work.

work experience. (1975) One's history in workplaces, esp. in a particular type of job.

workfare. (1969) A system of requiring a person receiving a public-welfare benefit to earn that benefit by performing a job provided by a government agency or undergoing job training.

workflow. (1950) The way in which a particular project is organized within a company or organization, including what employees are to perform given tasks at what particular times.

workforce. (1961) **1.** Collectively, all the workers engaged in a particular activity or enterprise. **2.** Collectively, all the people who are available to work in a particular country or area.

work for hire. See WORK (2).

work furlough (fər-loh). (1960) A prison-treatment program allowing an inmate to be released during the day to work in the community. See WORK-RELEASE PROGRAM.

work-furlough program. See WORK-RELEASE PROGRAM.

workhouse. (17c) A jail for criminals who have committed minor offenses and are serving short sentences.

working capital. See CAPITAL.

working capital acceptance. See *finance bill* under BILL (6).

working control. See CONTROL.

working example. See EXAMPLE.

working interest. (1866) *Oil & gas.* The rights to the mineral interest granted by an oil-and-gas lease, so called because the lessee acquires the right to work on the leased property to search, develop, and produce oil and gas, as well as the obligation to pay all costs. — Also termed *leasehold interest; operating interest.* See ROYALTY (2).

working model. (1837) *Patents.* A sample of an invention, usu. built for testing and for displaying to potential buyers. • The building of a working model is called "actual reduction to practice." It is not required for a patent, but it can help the applicant to clarify the description and to establish a date of invention in the event of an interference.

working papers. (1904) **1.** WORK PERMIT; esp., an employment certificate or permit required of an employer in some states before a minor may be hired. **2.** *Accounting.* The records kept by an independent auditor of the procedures followed, tests performed, information obtained, and conclusions reached in an audit. • A reviewer may evaluate the quality of an audit by examining the working papers.

work-in-process. (1906) A product being manufactured or assembled but not yet completed. — Abbr. WIP. — Also termed *work-in-progress.*

work made for hire. See *work for hire* under WORK (2).

workmen's compensation. See WORKERS' COMPENSATION.

work of authorship. See WORK (2).

work of joint authorship. See *joint work* under WORK (2).

work of necessity. See WORK (1).

work of the United States government. See WORK (2).

workout, *n.* **1.** The act of restructuring or refinancing overdue loans. **2.** *Bankruptcy.* A debtor's agreement, usu. negotiated with a creditor or creditors out of court, to reduce or discharge the debt. — **work out,** *vb.*

work permit. (1965) An alien's documentary work authorization from the Immigration and Naturalization Service. • Under the Immigration Reform and Control Act of 1986, it is illegal for an employer to hire an alien who lacks a work permit. 8 USCA § 1324(a)(1). — Also termed *working papers.*

workpiece. (1912) *Patents.* The embodiment of an invention, usu. a device, as the patent claims describe how to make and use it.

workplace. (1828) A person's place of employment or work setting in general. See SAFE WORKPLACE.

work product. (1947) Tangible material or its intangible equivalent, in unwritten or oral form, that was either prepared by or for a lawyer or prepared for litigation, either planned or in progress. • Work product is generally exempt from discovery or other compelled disclosure. The term is also used to describe the products of a party's investigation or communications concerning the subject matter of a lawsuit if made (1) to assist in the prosecution or defense of a pending suit, or (2) in reasonable anticipation of litigation. Fed. R. Evid. 26. — Also termed *attorney work product.*

▸ **core work product.** See *opinion work product.*

▸ **fact work product.** (1979) A lawyer's tangible work product that includes facts but not the lawyer's mental impressions. • Fact work product is subject to a qualified privilege. It is not discoverable unless the party seeking discovery can show (1) a substantial need for the materials and (2) an inability to acquire the information by any other means without undue hardship. *See* Fed. R. Evid. 26(b)(3). — Also termed *ordinary work product.*

▸ **opinion work product.** (1974) A lawyer's opinions, mental impressions, conclusions, or legal theories regarding a client's case. • An adversary usu. cannot gain access to this work product despite showing substantial need and undue hardship. Fed. R. Evid. 26(b)(3). — Also termed *core work product.*

▸ **ordinary work product.** See *fact work product.*

work-product rule. (1954) The rule providing for qualified immunity of an attorney's work product from discovery or other compelled disclosure. Fed. R. Civ. P. 26(b)(3). • The exemption was primarily established to protect an attorney's litigation strategy. *Hickman v. Taylor,* 329 U.S. 495, 67 S.Ct. 385 (1947). — Also termed *work-product immunity; work-product privilege; work-product exemption; attorney-work-product privilege.*

> "Although the work-product rule has often been spoken of as creating a 'privilege,' it is a qualified one that does not grant full immunity from discovery. To the extent the term 'privilege' causes confusion between the work-product rule and the absolute privilege for confidential communications between attorney and client, it is important to keep in mind this distinction. . . . Rule 26(b)(3) provides that work-product material is subject to discovery 'only upon a showing that the party seeking discovery has substantial need of the materials in the preparation of the party's case and that the party is unable without undue hardship to obtain the substantial equivalent of the materials by other means.'" 8 Charles Alan Wright et al., *Federal Practice and Procedure* § 2025, at 371, 373–74 (2d ed. 1994).

work-related, *adj.* Connected with employment.

work-release program. (1964) A correctional program allowing prison inmates — primarily those being readied for discharge — to hold jobs outside prison. — Often shortened to *work-release.* — Also termed *work-furlough program.* See HALFWAY HOUSE.

works. (16c) **1.** A mill, factory, or other establishment for manufacturing or other industrial purposes; a manufacturing plant; a factory. **2.** Any building or structure on land. • Some states also include structures built in the sea, such as offshore-drilling platforms.

▸ **new works.** *Civil law.* A structure newly commenced on a particular estate. • A denunciation of new works is a remedy allowed for an adjacent landowner whose property will be injured if the structure is completed.

▸ **public works.** (16c) Structures (such as roads or dams) built by the government for public use and paid for by public funds.

work stoppage. (1940) A cessation of work; STRIKE.

work-to-rule. (1959) A situation in which people in a particular job perform their functions only according to the strictest interpretation of what is required of them, and no more, as a kind of protest.

world. (bef. 12c) **1.** The planet Earth <the world has limited natural resources>. **2.** All the Earth's inhabitants; the public generally <the world will benefit from this discovery>. **3.** All persons who have a claim or acquire an interest in a particular subject matter <a judgment *in rem* binds all the world>.

World Bank. A U.N. specialized agency established in 1945 to provide loans that aid in economic development, through economically sustainable enterprises. • Its capital derives from both U.N. member states and loans on the open market. — Also termed *International Bank for Reconstruction and Development.*

World Court. See INTERNATIONAL COURT OF JUSTICE.

world fund. See *global fund* under MUTUAL FUND.

World Health Organization. An agency of the United Nations established in 1948 to provide leadership on global health matters, harness research, set standards, and enhance international partnerships to combat worldwide diseases such as malaria and tuberculosis. — Abbr. WHO.

World Intellectual Property Organization. An agency of the United Nations Educational, Scientific, and Cultural Organization formed in 1967 to (1) promote intellectual-property protection worldwide through cooperation among countries, and (2) administer multilateral treaties dealing with legal and administrative aspects of intellectual property. • The organization's headquarters are in Geneva, Switzerland. — Abbr. WIPO.

worldly, *adj.* (bef. 12c) Of, relating to, or involving the present state of existence; temporal; earthly <worldly possessions>. See SECULAR.

World Trade Organization. The body charged with enforcing intellectual-property provisions of the GATT treaty; specif., the primary multilateral institution regulating international trade, established in 1995 and based in Geneva, Switzerland. • WTO comprises the signatories of the Uruguay Round of GATT negotiations, as well as other countries that have acceded to membership. — Abbr. WTO. See TRIPS.

worldwide military-locator service. (1994) A search service that locates the current duty station of a member of any branch of the United States military services, esp. for enforcing the service member's child-support obligations. • Each branch of the armed forces maintains a worldwide locator service that is available to military and nonmilitary persons, their counsel, and Title IV-D agencies. Use of the locator service requires the member's full name and social-security number.

World Wide Web. (1990) An Internet information-location system that allows electronic documents stored in different computers to be connected to other such documents by hypertext links so that users all over the globe may find and access the documents. — Abbr. WWW. — Often shortened to *Web.* Cf. INTERNET.

worship. (14c) **1.** Any form of religious devotion, ritual, or service showing reverence, esp. for a divine being or supernatural power <freedom of worship>.

▸ **public worship.** (16c) **1.** Worship conducted by a religious society according to the society's system of ecclesiastical authority, ritual propriety, and rules and regulations. **2.** Worship under public authority. **3.** Worship in a public place, without privacy or concealment. **4.** Worship allowed by all members of the public equally.

2. *English law.* A title of honor or dignity used in addressing certain magistrates or other high officers. • The title is always preceded by a possessive pronoun, usu. *your* <your worship>.

wort (wərt), *n. Archaic.* A country farm; a curtilage. — Also termed *worth.*

worth, *n.* (bef. 12c) **1.** The monetary value of a thing; the sum of the qualities that render a thing valuable and useful, expressed in the current medium of exchange. **2.** The emotional or sentimental value of something. **3.** The total wealth held by a person or entity.

▸ **net tangible worth.** (1920) A corporation's net physical value, calculated by subtracting the liabilities from the value of the tangible assets then dividing by the number of outstanding shares.

▸ **net worth.** (1930) A measure of one's wealth, usu. calculated as the excess of total assets over total liabilities. — Also termed *net assets.*

▸ **tangible worth.** (1916) The amount of wealth held in the form of physical, valuable assets, such as cash and equipment.

4. WORT.

worthier-title doctrine. (1935) **1.** *Hist.* The common-law doctrine that if a beneficiary of a will would receive an identical interest as an heir under the laws of intestacy, the person takes the interest as an heir rather than as a beneficiary. • The doctrine has been abolished in most states. **2.** *Property.* The doctrine that favors a grantor's intent by construing a grant as a reversion in the grantor instead of as a remainder in the grantor's heirs. — Also termed *doctrine of worthier title.* See REMAINDER; REVERSION.

worthiest of blood, *n.* (17c) *Hist.* Of, relating to, or involving males, because of the preference given them in the laws of descent. See PRIMOGENITURE.

"Thus sons shall be admitted before daughters; or, as our male lawgivers have somewhat uncomplaisantly expressed it, the worthiest blood shall be preferred. As if John Stiles hath two sons, Matthew and Gilbert, and two daughters, Margaret and Charlotte, and dies; first Matthew, and (in case of his death without issue) then Gilbert shall be admitted to the succession in preference to both the daughters." 2 William Blackstone, *Commentaries on the Laws of England* 213 (1766).

worthless, *adj.* (16c) Totally lacking worth; of no use or value.

worthless check. See *bad check* under CHECK.

worthless person. *Archaic.* Someone who owns nothing.

worthless security. See SECURITY (4).

worthy, *adj.* (13c) Having worth; possessing merit; valuable.

wounded feelings. (18c) Injuries resulting from insults, indignity, or humiliation, as distinguished from the usual mental pain and suffering consequent to physical injury.

wounding. (14c) **1.** An injury, esp. one involving a rupture of the skin. **2.** An injury to feelings or reputation. **3.** *Hist.* An aggravated type of assault and battery in which one person seriously injures another.

WPA. *abbr.* **1.** WEBB–POMERENE ACT. **2.** WHISTLEBLOWER PROTECTION ACT.

wrap account. See ACCOUNT.

wraparound mortgage. See MORTGAGE.

wrap-fee account. See *wrap account* under ACCOUNT.

wreck, *n.* (13c) **1.** SHIPWRECK. **2.** Goods cast ashore from a wrecked vessel and not claimed by the owner within a specified period (such as one year).

"Wreck of the sea, in legal understanding, is applied to such goods, as after shipwreck at sea, are by the sea cast upon the land; and therefore the jurisdiction thereof pertaineth not to the lord admiral, but to the common law." Edward Bullingbrooke, *The Duty and Authority of Justices of the Peace and Parish Officers for Ireland* 897 (rev. ed. 1788).

"Although in its ordinary and popular sense the word 'wreck' is used to signify the partial or total destruction of any object, yet in a legal sense it is strictly confined to ships, or parts thereof, or goods therefrom, wh[i]ch have been cast on shore by the sea, and is never extended to such things while afloat. Thus, goods taken from the body of a stranded ship and brought ashore are not within the definition, nor is the stranded ship itself, where it is afterwards repaired and floated." 30 *The American and English Encyclopaedia Law* 1298–99 (David S. Garland & Charles Porterfield eds., 2d ed. 1905).

wreckfree, *adj.* (13c) (Of a port, etc.) exempt from the forfeiture of shipwrecked goods and vessels to the Crown.

writ (rit). (bef. 12c) A court's written order, in the name of a state or other competent legal authority, commanding the addressee to do or refrain from doing some specified act.

"[W]rits have a long history. We can trace their formal origin to the Anglo-Saxon formulae by which the king used to communicate his pleasure to persons and courts. The Anglo-Norman writs, which we meet with after the Conquest, are substantially the Anglo-Saxon writs turned into Latin. But what is new is the much greater use made of them, owing to the increase of royal power which came with the Conquest." W.S. Holdsworth, *Sources and Literature of English Law* 20 (1925).

▸ **alias writ.** (18c) An additional writ issued after another writ of the same kind in the same case. • It derives its name from a Latin phrase that formerly appeared in alias writs: *sicut alias praecipimus*, meaning "as we at another time commanded." Cf. *alias execution* under EXECUTION.

▸ **alternative writ.** (1827) A common-law writ commanding the person against whom it is issued either to do a specific thing or to show cause why the court should not order it to be done.

▸ **close writ.** (17c) *Hist.* **1.** A royal writ sealed because the contents were not deemed appropriate for public inspection. Cf. *patent writ*; CLAUSE ROLLS. **2.** A writ directed to a sheriff instead of to a lord.

▸ **concurrent writ.** (1817) A duplicate of an original writ (esp. a summons), issued either at the same time as the original writ or at any time while the original writ is valid.

▸ **conventual writ.** *Hist.* A writ by which damages were sought to be recovered. • The prime common-law example was the writ covenant. Cf. *proprietary writ.*

▸ **counterpart writ.** (1841) A copy of an original writ, to be sent to a court in another county where the defendant is located.

▸ **extraordinary writ.** (17c) A writ issued by a court exercising unusual or discretionary power. • Examples are certiorari, habeas corpus, mandamus, and prohibition. — Also termed *prerogative writ.* Cf. *extraordinary relief* under RELIEF (3).

▸ **ground writ.** (1822) *Hist.* A writ issued in a county having venue of an action in order to allow a writ of *capias ad satisfaciendum* or of *fieri facias* to be executed in a county where the defendant or the defendant's property was found. • These two writs could not be executed in a county other than the county having venue of the action until a ground writ and then a *testatum* writ were first issued. This requirement was abolished in 1852. Cf. TESTATUM.

▸ **judicial writ.** (16c) **1.** A writ issuing from the court to which the original writ was returnable; a writ issued under the private seal of the court and not under the great seal of England. Cf. *original writ.* **2.** Any writ issued by a court.

▸ **junior writ.** (1839) A writ issued at a later time than a similar writ, such as a later writ issued by a different party or a later writ on a different claim against the same defendant.

▸ **optional writ.** (18c) At common law, an original writ issued when the plaintiff seeks specific damages, such as payment of a liquidated debt. • The writ commands the defendant either to do a specified thing or to show why the thing has not been done.

▸ **original writ.** (16c) A writ commencing an action and directing the defendant to appear and answer. • In the United States, this writ has been largely superseded by the summons. At common law, this type of writ was a mandatory letter issuing from the court of chancery under the great seal, and in the king's name, directed to the sheriff of the county where the injury was alleged to have occurred, containing a summary statement of the cause of complaint, and requiring the sheriff in most cases to command the defendant to satisfy the claim or else appear in court to account for not satisfying it. — Sometimes shortened to *original.* See SUMMONS.

▸ **patent writ** (**pay**-tənt). *Hist.* An open writ; one not closed or sealed up. Cf. *close writ* (1).

▸ **peremptory writ** (pər-**emp**-tə-ree). (18c) At common law, an original writ issued when the plaintiff seeks only general damages, as in an action for trespass. • The writ, which is issued only after the plaintiff gives security for costs, directs the sheriff to have the defendant appear in court.

▸ **pluries writ.** See PLURIES.

▸ **prerogative writ.** See *extraordinary writ.*

▸ **proprietary writ.** *Hist.* A writ by which the ownership of something is sought to be restored, whether lands, goods, or money. • Common-law examples were the writs of debt, of detinue, and of account. Cf. *conventual writ.*

▸ **testatum writ** (tes-**tay**-təm). See TESTATUM.

▸ **vicontiel writ** (vɪ-**kon**-tee-əl). (18c) *Hist.* A writ triable in the county court. • In the 13th–14th centuries, civil litigation could originate in the county court either by oral plaint or by a writ from the Chancery ordering the sheriff to do justice in a case. The writ that began such a proceeding was called *vicontiel* because it was addressed to the sheriff. See VICONTIEL (2).

> "*Vicontiel writs* were of two sorts, the one founded on *Torts*, the other on *Contracts*. The *vicontiel* writs adapted for torts, were those of *trespass, replegiari facias, nuisance*, and others of the like nature; and those of matters of contract were called writs of *justicies*, which was a command to the sheriff to do justice between the parties . . . ." 1 George Crompton, *Practice Common-Placed: Rules and Cases of Practice in the Courts of King's Bench and Common Pleas* vii–viii (3d ed. 1787).

▸ **writ of capias.** See CAPIAS.

writ *de haeretico comburendo.* See DE HAERETICO COMBURENDO (1).

write down, *vb.* (1894) *Accounting.* To transfer part of the balance (of an asset account) to an expense or loss account to reflect the asset's diminished value.

write off, *vb.* (1891) *Accounting.* To transfer the entire balance (of an asset account) to an expense or loss account to reflect the asset's total loss of value <the partnership wrote off the bad debt>. — **write-off,** *n.* See TAX WRITE-OFF. — **write-off,** *n.*

writer. 1. Someone who writes; esp., a person who engages in literary composition, as an author, columnist, reporter, or essayist. **2.** Someone who acts as an amanuensis, scribe, or scrivener. **3.** A copying clerk in a government office. **4.** *Archaic.* A law clerk; an apprentice in a law office. **5.** *Hist. Scots law.* A lawyer. See WRITER TO THE SIGNET. **6.** *Archaic.* A naval officer who keeps the conduct-book, station-bills, etc. **7.** A civil servant who finishes unskilled clerical work at a navy yard or navy station. **8.** *Hist. Slang.* A counterfeiter who conducts correspondence with prospective buyers. **9.** *Securities.* A person or institution that sells securities or futures option contracts. **10.** *Insurance.* See *insurance underwriter* (1) under UNDERWRITER.

writer of the tallies. (17c) *English law.* An officer of the Exchequer who writes on the tallies the letters of tellers' bills. See TALLY.

Writer to the Signet. *Scots law.* **1.** *Hist.* A member of the College of Justice, founded in 1532. **2.** A member of an Edinburgh society of solicitors who hold a few special privileges in the preparation of official documents. See WRITER (5).

write-up, *n.* (1885) **1.** A memorandum of a conference between an employer and an employee, usu. held to discuss the employee's poor work performance or a disciplinary action against the employee. **2.** A publication (such as a newspaper article) about a particular person, thing, or event.

write-up, *vb. Accounting.* To increase the valuation of an asset in a financial statement to reflect current value. • With a few minor exceptions, this is generally not permitted.

writ *fi fa.* See TESTATUM (1).

writing, *n.* (13c) Any intentional recording of words in a visual form, whether in handwriting, printing, typewriting, or any other tangible form that may be viewed or heard with or without mechanical aids. • This includes hard-copy documents, electronic documents on computer media, audio and videotapes, e-mails, and any other media on which words can be recorded.

▸ **signed writing.** (17c) A writing to which a person's signature has been affixed in some form. See SIGNATURE.

▸ **writing obligatory,** *n.* (16c) **1.** A written legal instrument, usu. a contract; esp., a *contract under seal.* See *contract under seal* under CONTRACT. **2.** A bond; a written obligation, as technically described in a pleading.

writ of *ad quod damnum.* See AD QUOD DAMNUM.

writ of aiel (**ay**-əl). See AIEL (2).

writ of assistance. (17c) **1.** A writ to enforce a court's decree transferring real property, the title of which has been previously adjudicated. **2.** *Hist.* A writ issued by the Court of Exchequer ordering the sheriff to assist in collecting a debt owed the Crown. **3.** *Hist.* In colonial America, a writ issued by a superior colonial court authorizing an officer of the Crown to enter and search any premises suspected of containing contraband. • The attempted use of this writ in Massachusetts in 1761 was one of the acts that led to the American Revolution.

"WRIT OF ASSISTANCE. A writ provided for by a statute of Charles II and confirmed by later statutes. In England it issued from the court of exchequer. In America during the French war (1755-1763) such writs were issued as means of enforcing the revenue law. They gave authority to board a ship in port and to search for smuggled goods, and also to enter vaults, warehouses, and other places. Directed to the 'Justices of the Peace, Sheriffs, Constables and all other our Officers and Subjects,' the writ directed them to 'be aiding, assisting, and helping' the customs officer in the execution of his duty. On application for a writ, in 1761, a great discussion arose before the Massachusetts superior court. Oxenbridge Thacher and James Otis appeared in opposition to the writ. Otis, John Adams tells us, was 'a flame of fire.' He eloquently declaimed against the legality of the writ, declaring that an act against the Constitution and natural equity was void. After some delay the writ was issued. Otis's declamation against general warrants — warrants which do not specify the place to be searched or the person or thing sought — was in part doubtless a foundation for the later constitutional provision against them." A.C. McLaughlin, "Writ of Assistance," in 3 *Cyclopedia of American Government* 702 (A.C. McLaughlin & Albert Bushnell Hart eds., 1963).

writ of association. (17c) *Hist. English law.* A writ whereby certain persons (usu. the clerk of assize and subordinate officers) were directed to associate themselves with the justices and serjeants so that there would be an adequate supply of commissioners for the assizes.

writ of attachment. See ATTACHMENT (3).

writ of *audita querela*. See AUDITA QUERELA.

writ of capias. See CAPIAS.

writ of *capias ad respondendum*. See CAPIAS.

writ of *capias ad satisfaciendum*. See CAPIAS.

writ of certiorari. See CERTIORARI.

writ of conspiracy. (16c) *Hist.* A writ against one who conspired to injure the plaintiff, esp. by indicting the plaintiff for treason or felony. • Under common law, all other circumstances of conspiracy were actions on the case.

writ of consultation. (16c) An extraordinary writ issued by an appellate court ordering a lower court to proceed in a matter that the lower court previously refused to hear. Cf. PROHIBITION (2).

writ of *coram nobis*. See CORAM NOBIS.

writ of *coram vobis*. See CORAM VOBIS.

writ of course. (17c) A writ issued as a matter of course or granted as a matter of right. — Also termed *writ of right*; *breve de cursu*.

writ of covenant. (16c) *Hist.* A writ for one claiming damages as a result of a breach of a promise under seal or other covenant. — Also termed *breve de conventione* (breev *or* **bree**-vee dee kən-ven-shee-**oh**-nee). See CONVENTIONE.

"The writ of covenant (*breve de conventione*) is not mentioned by Glanvill; but it appears within a short time after the publication of his book and already in the early years of Henry III. It can be had 'as of course,' at all events when the tenement that is in question is of small value. Before Henry's death it has become a popular writ . . . . The great majority of actions of covenant are brought merely in order that they may be compromised. We doubt whether any principle was involved in the choice; but may infer that the procedure instituted by this writ was cheap and expeditious for those who wished to get to their final concord." 2 Frederick Pollock & Frederic W. Maitland, *The History of English Law Before the Time of Edward I* 216–17 (2d ed. 1899).

writ of debt. See DEBT (4).

writ of deceit. (16c) *Hist.* A writ against one who deceives and damages another by acting in the other's name.

"DECEIT. A writ of deceit lies at the Common Law to give damages in some particular cases of fraud, and principally where one man does any thing in the name of another, by which he is deceived or injured; as if one brings an action in another's name, and the suffers a nonsuit where the plaintiff becomes liable to costs; or where one suffers a fraudulent recovery of lands or chattels, to the prejudice of him who hath the right." *Law Grammar* 360–61 (1791).

writ of deliverance. See DELIVERANCE (3).

writ of detinue. (17c) A writ in an action for detinue. See DETINUE.

writ of dower. (16c) A writ for the assignment of dower; DE DOTE UNDE NIHIL HABET. Cf. WRIT OF RIGHT OF DOWER.

writ of ejectment. (17c) The writ in an action of ejectment for the recovery of land. See EJECTMENT.

writ of elegit. See ELEGIT.

writ of entry. (16c) A writ that allows a person wrongfully dispossessed of real property to enter and retake the property.

writ of error. (15c) **1.** A writ issued by an appellate court directing a lower court to deliver the record in the case for review. Cf. ASSIGNMENT OF ERROR.

"The writ of error is the most common of all the forms of remedial process available to an unsuccessful party after a final determination of the merits of the action, and is in common use in this country at the present time, where the common-law modes of procedure are followed. Its object . . . is to obtain a reversal of the judgment, either by reason of some error in fact affecting the validity and regularity of the legal decision itself, or on account of some mistake or error in law, apparent upon the face of the record, from which the judgment appears to have been given for the wrong party." Benjamin J. Shipman, *Handbook of Common-Law Pleading* § 337, at 538 (Henry Winthrop Ballantine ed., 3d ed. 1923).

▸ **writ of error *coram nobis*.** See CORAM NOBIS.

▸ **writ of error *coram vobis*.** See CORAM VOBIS.

2. *Hist.* A writ issued by a chancery court, at the request of a party who was unsuccessful at trial, directing the trial court either to examine the record itself or to send it to another court of appellate jurisdiction to be examined, so that some alleged error in the proceedings may be corrected.

writ of escheat. (17c) *Hist.* A writ allowing a lord to take possession of lands that had escheated to him. See ESCHEAT (1).

writ of estrepement (e-**streep**-mənt). See DE ESTREPAMENTO.

writ of execution. See EXECUTION (4).

writ of exigent. See EXIGENT, *n.*

writ of *exigi facias*. See EXIGI FACIAS.

writ of extent. See EXTENT (2).

writ of false judgment. See FALSE JUDGMENT.

writ of *fieri facias*. See FIERI FACIAS.

writ of formedon. See FORMEDON.

writ of habeas corpus. See HABEAS CORPUS.

writ of *habere facias possessionem*. See HABERE FACIAS POSSESSIONEM.

writ of *habere facias seisinam*. See HABERE FACIAS SEISINAM.

writ of injunction. See INJUNCTION.

writ of inquiry. (17c) *Hist.* A writ ordering the sheriff to empanel a jury and act as judge in a trial held to determine the amount of damages suffered by a plaintiff who has won a default judgment on an unliquidated claim.

writ of *latitat*. See LATITAT.

writ of *levari facias*. See LEVARI FACIAS.

writ of mainprise. See MAINPRISE (3).

writ of mandamus. See MANDAMUS.

writ of mandate. See MANDATE (2).

writ of mesne (meen). See DE MEDIO.

writ of mesne process. See *mesne process* under PROCESS.

writ of monstraverunt. See MONSTRAVERUNT.

writ of ne exeat. See NE EXEAT.

writ of perambulation. (18c) *Hist.* A common-law writ issued by agreement of both parties when they are in doubt about the bounds of their respective properties, directing the sheriff to walk the jury around the property to set the boundaries with certainty. See PERAMBULATION.

writ of possession. (17c) A writ issued to recover the possession of land.

writ of praecipe. See PRAECIPE (1).

writ of prevention. (17c) A writ to prevent the filing of a lawsuit. See QUIA TIMET.

writ of privilege. (16c) *Hist.* An action to enforce or maintain a privilege, usu. one granted by statute or by a court. • Traditionally, the writ was used to protect legislators from arrest in civil suits during a legislative session. Parties and witnesses who did not reside within a court's jurisdiction were also privileged against service of process in civil suits while attending the court and while traveling to or from it.

> "The privilege of a suitor or witness to be exempt from service of process while without the jurisdiction of his residence for the purpose of attending court in an action to which he is a party, or in which he is to be sworn as a witness, is a very ancient one. It has always been held to extend to every proceeding of a judicial nature taken in or emanating from a duly-constituted tribunal which directly relates to the trial of the issues involved. It is not simply a personal privilege, but it is also the privilege of the court, and is deemed necessary for the maintenance of its authority and dignity and in order to promote the due and efficient administration of justice. At common law a writ of privilege or protection would be granted to the party or witness by the court in which the action was pending, which would be respected by all other courts. . . . [T]he writ may still be granted by courts possessing a common law jurisdiction; but while the granting of the writ is proper, it is not necessary for the enjoyment of the privilege, and the only office which it can is to afford convenient and authentic notice to those about to do what would be a violation of the privilege, and to set it forth and command due respect to it. The tendency has been not to restrict, but to enlarge, the right of privilege so as to afford full protection to parties and witnesses from all forms of civil process during their attendance at court , and for a reasonable time in going and returning." *Parker v. Marco* 32 N.E. 989, 989 (N.Y. 1893) (citations omitted).

writ of probable cause. See CERTIFICATE OF APPEALABILITY.

writ of *procedendo*. See PROCEDENDO.

writ of proclamation. (16c) *Hist.* A writ, issued at the time an *exigent* was issued, ordering the sheriff of the county of a defendant's residence to make three proclamations of outlawry in a public and notorious place a month before the outlawry is declared. See OUTLAW.

writ of prohibition. See PROHIBITION (2).

writ of protection. (17c) **1.** A writ to protect a witness in a judicial proceeding who is threatened with arrest. **2.** A writ exempting anyone in the Crown's service from arrest in a civil proceeding for a year and a day.

writ of *quare impedit*. See QUARE IMPEDIT.

writ of quominus. See QUOMINUS.

writ of *quo warranto*. See QUO WARRANTO (1).

writ of rebellion. See COMMISSION OF REBELLION.

writ of recaption. (17c) *Hist.* A writ allowing a plaintiff to recover goods and damages from a defendant who makes a second distress while a replevin action for a previous distress is pending. See RECAPTION.

writ of replevin. See REPLEVIN (2).

writ of restitution. (17c) **1.** The process of enforcing a civil judgment in a forcible-entry-and-detainer action or enforcing restitution on a verdict in a criminal prosecution for forcible entry and detainer.

> "In some states, following the British statutes, the prosecutor may have a writ of restitution for the premises immediately on the rendition of a verdict of guilty on an indictment for forcible entry and detainer; and the operation of such writ of restitution is not suspended by an appeal by the defendant." 35 Am. Jur. 2d *Forcible Entry and Detainer* § 61, at 931 (1967).

2. A common-law writ issued when a judgment is reversed, whereby all that was lost as a result of the judgment is restored to the prevailing party.

writ of review. (18c) A general form of process issuing from an appellate court to bring up for review the record of the proceedings in the court below; the common-law writ of certiorari.

writ of right. See WRIT OF COURSE.

writ of right of dower. A writ for the assignment of a residue of dower, esp. one in an estate providing a widow with a remainder in the dower to which she is entitled after part of it has been assigned by the tenant. Cf. WRIT OF DOWER.

writ of second deliverance. See *second deliverance* under DELIVERANCE (4).

writ of sequestration. (18c) A writ ordering that a court be given custody of something or that something not be taken from the jurisdiction, such as the collateral for a promissory note. • Such a writ is usu. issued during litigation, often so that the object sequestered will be available for attachment or execution after judgment.

writ of summons. (17c) *English law.* A writ by which, under the Judicature Acts of 1873–1875, all actions were commenced. See SUMMONS.

writ of supersedeas. See SUPERSEDEAS.

writ of supervisory control. (1901) A writ issued to correct an erroneous ruling made by a lower court either when there is no right to appeal or when an appeal cannot provide adequate relief and the ruling will result in gross injustice.

writ of testatum *fieri facias*. See TESTATUM (1).

writ of threats. See SECURITATE PACIS.

writ of tolt (tohlt). See TOLT.

writ of trespass. See TRESPASS.

writ of trespass on the case. See *trespass on the case* under TRESPASS.

writ of trial. (1833) *Hist. English law.* By the Civil Procedure Act of 1835, a writ ordering an action brought in a superior court to be tried in an inferior court or before the undersheriff. • It was superseded by the County Courts Act of 1867, ch. 142, § 6 authorizing a defendant, in certain cases, to obtain an order that an action is to be tried in a county court. St. 3 & 4 Will. 4, ch. 42.

writ of *venire facias*. See VENIRE FACIAS.

writ of waste. (16c) *Hist.* A writ to recover damages against a tenant who committed waste. See WASTE (1).

> "After waste had been actually committed, the ancient corrective remedy, in a court of common law, was by a writ of waste for the recovery of the place wasted, and treble damages as a compensation for the injury done to the inheritance." 78 Am. Jur. 2d *Waste* § 29, at 417 (1975).

writ of withernam. See *capias in withernam* under CAPIAS.

writ *pro retorno habendo* (proh ri-**tor**-noh hə-**ben**-doh), *n.* [Law Latin "for return to be had"] (1802) *Hist.* A writ ordering the return of goods to a defendant who, upon the plaintiff's default, obtained a favorable judgment in a replevin action. See DELIVERANCE (4).

writ system. (1890) The common-law procedural system under which a plaintiff commences an action by obtaining the appropriate type of original writ.

written contract. See CONTRACT.

written defamation. See LIBEL (1), (2).

written description. See DESCRIPTION (5).

written directive. See ADVANCE DIRECTIVE (2).

written law. See LAW.

written testimony. See TESTIMONY.

written warranty. See WARRANTY (2).

wrong, *n.* (bef. 12c) Breach of one's legal duty; violation of another's legal right. Cf. RIGHT (1). — **wrong,** *vb.*

> "A wrong may be described, in the largest sense, as anything done or omitted contrary to legal duty, considered in so far as it gives rise to liability." Frederick Pollock, *A First Book of Jurisprudence* 68 (1896).

> "A wrong is simply a wrong act — an act contrary to the rule of right and justice. A synonym of it is injury, in its true and primary sense of *injuria* (that which is contrary to *jus*) . . . ." John Salmond, *Jurisprudence* 227 (Glanville L. Williams ed., 10th ed. 1947).

▸ **civil wrong.** (17c) A violation of noncriminal law, such as a tort, a breach of contract or trust, a breach of statutory duty, or a defect in performing a public duty; the breach of a legal duty treated as the subject matter of a civil proceeding. See TORT (1). Cf. CRIME.

▸ **continuing wrong.** (1846) An ongoing wrong that is capable of being corrected by specific enforcement. • An example is the nonpayment of a debt.

▸ **intentional wrong.** (18c) A wrong in which the mens rea amounts to intention, purpose, or design. — Also termed *willful wrong.*

▸ **legal wrong.** (18c) An act that is a violation of the law; an act authoritatively prohibited by a rule of law.

▸ **moral wrong.** (18c) An act that is contrary to the rule of natural justice. — Also termed *natural wrong.*

▸ **personal wrong.** (16c) An invasion of a personal right.

▸ **positive wrong.** (18c) A wrongful act willfully committed.

▸ **private wrong.** (16c) An offense committed against a private person and dealt with at the instance of the person injured.

▸ **public wrong.** (16c) An offense committed against the state or the community at large, and dealt with in a proceeding to which the state is itself a party. • Not all public wrongs are crimes. For example, a person that breaches a contract with the government commits a public wrong, but the offense is a civil one, not a criminal one.

▸ **real wrong.** (17c) An injury to the freehold.

▸ **transitory wrong.** (2004) A wrong that, once committed, belongs to the irrevocable past. • An example is defamation.

▸ **willful wrong.** See *intentional wrong.*

▸ **wrong of negligence.** (1902) **1.** A criminal wrong in which the mens rea is a form of carelessness, as opposed to wrongful intent. **2.** A civil wrong involving the breach of a primary duty to exercise reasonable care, creating a secondary duty to compensate the harms proximately caused by the breach of the primary duty. See NEGLIGENCE.

▸ **wrong of strict liability.** (1986) **1.** A criminal wrong in which a mens rea is not required because neither wrongful intent nor culpable negligence is a necessary condition of responsibility. **2.** A civil wrong that does not involve the breach of a primary duty to exercise reasonable care but instead is defined wholly by a duty to compensate the harms proximately caused by the activity or behavior governed by the liability rule. See LIABILITY.

wrongdoer, *n.* (15c) Someone who violates the law <both criminals and tortfeasors are wrongdoers>.

wrongdoer rule. (1949) *Contracts.* The principle that when damages are established but the amount is uncertain, the defendant has the burden to show what the amount should be; specif., the rule that if a defendant's conduct has made it difficult or impossible to measure the plaintiff's damages, the burden rests on the defendant (as wrongdoer) to establish a more certain measure.

wrongdoing, *n.* (15c) **1.** Illegal or improper conduct. **2.** An instance of bad or immoral behavior.

wrongful, *adj.* (14c) **1.** Characterized by unfairness or injustice <wrongful military invasion>. **2.** Contrary to law; unlawful <wrongful termination>. **3.** (Of a person) not entitled to the position occupied <wrongful possessor>. — **wrongfully,** *adv.*

> "The word 'wrongful' requires little comment. To be 'wrongful,' an act need not be intentional. Whether an act is wrongful depends upon the duty or obligation which the defendant owed to the party injured. As was observed in a Minnesota case: 'In the case at bar, any act or omission violative of the obligations which the appellants as common carriers of passengers assumed towards the intestate would be a 'wrongful act or omission,' within the meaning of the statute. The word 'wrongful' in the statute is not used in the sense of 'willful' or 'malicious.'" Francis B. Tiffany, *Death by Wrongful Act* § 62, at 76 (1893).

wrongful act. 1. See ACT (2). **2.** See *wrongful conduct* under CONDUCT.

wrongful adoption. (1985) **1.** An adoption in which the adoption agency fails to provide adoptive parents with full or accurate information regarding the child's physical or psychological background. • The adoptive parents normally do not seek to nullify the adoption. Rather, they seek damages, usu. for medical care and for emotional distress. **2.** An adoptive parent's legal claim against an adoption agency for not fully or accurately disclosing the child's physical or psychological background. Cf. ABROGATION OF ADOPTION.

wrongful-birth action. (1972) A lawsuit brought by parents against a doctor for failing to advise them prospectively about the risks of their having a child with birth defects.

wrongful-conception action. See WRONGFUL-PREGNANCY ACTION.

wrongful conduct. See CONDUCT.

wrongful conviction. See CONVICTION (2).

wrongful death. See DEATH.

wrongful-death action. (1926) A lawsuit brought on behalf of a decedent's survivors for their damages resulting from a tortious injury that caused the decedent's death. — Also termed *death action*; *death case.* Cf. SURVIVAL ACTION.

wrongful-death statute. (1904) A statute authorizing a decedent's personal representative to bring a wrongful-death action for the benefit of certain beneficiaries. — Formerly also termed *death-damage statute.*

wrongful denial. See DENIAL (2).

wrongful denial of benefits. See DENIAL (4).

wrongful discharge. See DISCHARGE (7).

wrongful-discharge action. (1957) A lawsuit brought by an ex-employee against the former employer, alleging that the termination of employment violated a contract or was illegal. — Also termed *wrongful-termination action.*

wrongful dishonor, *n.* (1895) A refusal to accept or pay (a negotiable instrument) when it is properly presented and is payable. Cf. DISHONOR (1).

wrongful dismissal. See *wrongful discharge* under DISCHARGE (7).

wrongful-eviction action. (1973) A lawsuit brought by a former tenant or possessor of real property against one who has put the plaintiff out of possession, alleging that the eviction was illegal.

wrongful garnishment. See GARNISHMENT (1).

wrongful levy. See LEVY.

wrongful-life action. (1963) A lawsuit brought by or on behalf of a child with birth defects, alleging that but for the doctor-defendant's negligent advice, the parents would not have conceived the child or, if they had, would have aborted the fetus to avoid the pain and suffering resulting from the child's congenital defects. • Most jurisdictions reject these claims.

wrongfulness, *n.* **1.** The character, state, or quality of being wrongful or wrong. **2.** The absence of justice or equity.

wrongful-pregnancy action. (1979) A lawsuit brought by a parent for damages resulting from a pregnancy following a failed sterilization. — Also termed *wrongful-conception action.*

wrongful process. See ABUSE OF PROCESS.

wrongful process of law. See ABUSE OF PROCESS.

wrongful-termination action. See WRONGFUL-DISCHARGE ACTION.

wrong of negligence. See WRONG.

wrong of strict liability. See WRONG.

wrong verdict. See *verdict contrary to law* under VERDICT (1).

WTO. See WORLD TRADE ORGANIZATION.

WWW. *abbr.* (1992) WORLD WIDE WEB.

wyte (WIT). *Hist.* See WITE.

X

X. *abbr.* **1.** EX DIVIDEND. **2.** EX RIGHTS. **3.** EX DISTRIBUTION. **4.** EX WARRANTS.

X. 1. A mark serving as the signature of a person who is physically handicapped or illiterate. • The signer's name usu. appears near the mark, and if the mark is to be notarized as a signature, two signing witnesses are ordinarily required in addition to the notary public. **2.** A symbol equivalent to "by" when used in giving dimensions, as in 3 x 5 inches. **3.** A mark placed on a document (such as an application) to indicate a selection, such as "yes" or "no"; esp., a mark on a ballot to indicate a vote. **4.** A specific yet unidentified or unidentifiable thing <patient X>.

XD. *abbr.* EX DIVIDEND.

XDIS. *abbr.* EX DISTRIBUTION.

xenelasia (zen-ə-**lay**-zhə), *n. Hist. Rare.* A statute forbidding foreigners to reside in a country without governmental approval; specif., in Greek antiquity, a provision of the Spartan constitution prohibiting foreigners to live in Sparta without official permission.

xenodochium (zen-ə-də-**kɪ**-əm *or* -**dok**-ee-əm), *n.* [fr. Greek *xenos* "a guest" + *dochein* "to receive"] (17c) *Roman law.* **1** An inn. **2.** A hospital. • This was a charitable institution to which donations and legacies might validly be given. — Also termed *xenodochion*; *xenodocheum*; *xenodochy.*

xenophobia, *n.* The fear or irrational strong dislike of people from foreign countries. — **xenophobic,** *adj.* — **xenophobe,** *n.*

X-patent. *Patents.* An early U.S. patent, granted before the numbering system set up in the Patent Act of 1836 and so named because an *X* was added to the numbers of existing patents to avoid duplicate numbers.

XQ. See *cross-question* under QUESTION (1).

XR. *abbr.* EX-RIGHTS.

XW. *abbr.* EX-WARRANTS.

xylon (**zɪ**-lon), *n.* [fr. Greek *xulon* "wood"] *Archaic.* A Greek punishment apparatus similar to stocks.

XYY-chromosome defense. (1969) *Criminal law.* A defense, usu. asserted as the basis for an insanity plea, whereby a male defendant argues that his criminal behavior is due to the genetic abnormality of having an extra Y chromosome, which causes him to have uncontrollable aggressive impulses. • Most courts have rejected this defense because its scientific foundations are uncertain. — Also termed *XYY defense.* See INSANITY DEFENSE.

> "As one commentator has suggested . . . 'an attorney defending an XYY individual will be required to call upon both a geneticist and a psychiatrist to give expert testimony. The geneticist's role would be to testify with respect to the individual's genetic structure, any distinguishing characteristics which are relevant to an insanity defense, and the result of family studies designated to determine the influence of genetics and environment on the development of this individual. The psychiatrist's testimony would focus upon the defendant's mental capacity or condition.' But in the absence of sound medical support for an XYY defense, courts are understandably unsympathetic to defense efforts to obtain such expert testimony." Wayne R. LaFave & Austin W. Scott Jr., *Criminal Law* § 4.8, at 380 (2d ed. 1986) (quoting Note, 57 Geo. L.J. 892, 902–03 (1969)).

XYY syndrome. (1968) The abnormal presence of an extra Y chromosome in a male, theoretically resulting in increased aggressiveness and antisocial behavior sometimes resulting in criminal conduct. See XYY-CHROMOSOME DEFENSE.

XYZ correspondence. One or more letters (missives) in which the letters X, Y, and Z have been substituted for the names of principal actors in the descriptions of their activities, the generic pseudonyms providing some degree of anonymic protection or preserving confidences. • The phrase appears to have been first used in 1797–1798 in reference to letters between the United States Commissioners to France and the emissaries of Tallyrand, Hottinguer, Bellamy, and Hauteval. These emissaries were seeking a financial loan from the U.S. government for the government of France ("the Directory"), while suggesting that a rejection of the proposal would mean war. The letters were officially published by the U.S. government, the designations X,Y, and Z replacing the French agents' names.

XYZ document. Any of various papers, of a legal nature, in which the letters X, Y, and Z or similar spans of alphabetical designations are used to render anonymous the participants in certain activities described or depicted.

Y2K warranty. *abbr.* (1998) Year 2000 warranty; a warranty that software, hardware, or a product having computer hardware or software components will function properly on and after January 1, 2000. • These warranties were common in the late 1990s.

yank-cheating, *n.* The illegal practice of inserting paper money into a vending machine, then pulling the money out again after the machine has recognized it, thereby retaining the cash and unlawfully obtaining merchandise. • This practice was common in the 1980s and 1990s, when cash-receiving machines were still new. Modern technology has protected against the practice.

yardland, *n.* (15c) *Hist.* A variable quantity of land, often 20 acres. — Also termed *virga terrae* (**vər**-gə **ter**-ee).

yardstick theory. (1935) *Antitrust.* A method of determining damages for lost profits (and sometimes overcharges) whereby a corporate plaintiff identifies a company similar to the plaintiff but without the impact of the antitrust violation. Cf. BEFORE-AND-AFTER THEORY; MARKET-SHARE THEORY (1).

"To the extent that either the markets or firms being compared are dissimilar, the yardstick theory will not produce a trustworthy estimate of what the plaintiff would have earned but for the defendant's conduct. The method therefore works best in markets that are both local and relatively homogeneous." Herbert Hovenkamp, *Economics and Federal Antitrust Law* § 16.7, at 454 (1985).

yea, *n.* (17c) *Parliamentary law.* An affirmative vote.

yea and nay (yay / nay). (14c) Yes and no. • In old records, this was a mere assertion and denial without the necessity of an oath.

year. (bef. 12c) **1.** Twelve calendar months beginning January 1 and ending December 31. — Also termed *calendar year.* **2.** A consecutive 365-day period beginning at any point; a span of twelve months.

▸ **executor's year.** *English law.* The period of one year, beginning with the death of the testator, during which no one may compel the estate's personal representative to distribute the estate.

▸ **financial year.** See *fiscal year.*

▸ **fiscal year.** (1865) An accounting period of 12 consecutive months <the company's fiscal year is October 1 to September 30>. • A fiscal year is often different from the calendar year, esp. for tax purposes. — Abbr. FY. — Also termed *fiscal period; financial year.*

▸ **half-year.** (bef. 12c) In legal computation, a period of 182 days.

▸ **man-year.** See MAN-YEAR.

▸ **natural year.** (17c) *Hist.* The period of 365 days and about 6 hours, or the time it takes the earth to orbit the sun.

▸ **tax year.** (1861) The period used for computing federal or state income-tax liability, usu. either the calendar year or a fiscal year ending on the last day of a month other than December. — Also termed *taxable year; year of tax.*

Year 2000 warranty. See Y2K WARRANTY.

year and a day. (15c) The common-law time limit fixed for various purposes, such as claiming rights, exemptions, or property (such as rights to wreckage or estrays), or for prosecuting certain acts — so called because a year was formerly counted to include the first and last day, meaning that a year from January 1 was December 31, so a year and a day would then mean a full year from January 1 through January 1. — Also termed *year and day;* (formerly in Scots law) *zeir and day.* See YEAR-AND-A-DAY RULE; YEAR, DAY, AND WASTE.

"The phrase invariably used to describe the space of time which has legal results seems to point to an origin in judicial proceedings. It is not a year but 'year and day,' 'an et jour,' 'Jahr und Tag.' Now in German books this is glossed as meaning one year, six weeks and three days. Various explanations have been given of this, but all seem to point to the fact that the 'day' is a 'court day.' One of the best accredited explanations is that the court is adjourned from six weeks to six weeks and that it sits for three days; the claimant is bound to make his claim at latest at the next session after the lapse of the year; thus as a maximum term he has a year, six weeks and three days. Be this as it may, it is in connection with judicial proceedings that we first hear of year and day; in particular when a defendant in an action of land will not appear the land is seized into the king's hands, and if the contumacy continues for year and day the land is then adjudged to the plaintiff; during the year and day it lies under the king's ban. Now the suggestion is that in this contumacial procedure men saw the possibility of stable and effectual conveyances: — let the purchaser sue the vendor, let the land lie in the king's ban for year and day, then let it be adjudged to the purchaser, let him be put in seisin under the king's peace. According this theory the reverence paid in the later middle ages to possession prolonged for year and day has its root not in a primitive usucapio, but in the king's ban." Frederic W. Maitland, "Possession for Year and Day," in 2 *The Collected Papers of Frederic W. Maitland* 61, 65–66 (H.A.L. Fisher ed., 1911).

year-and-a-day rule. (1876) *Criminal law.* The common-law principle that an act causing death is not homicide if the death occurs more than a year and a day after the act was committed. • In Latin, the phrase *year and a day* was commonly rendered *annus et dies.*

"It has long been the rule that no one can be convicted of the murder or manslaughter of another person who does not die within a year and a day of the blow received or other cause of death. 'Day' was here added merely to indicate that the 365th day after that of the injury must be included. Such an indication was rendered necessary by an old rule (now obsolete) that, in *criminal* law, in reckoning a period 'from' the doing of any act, the period was (in favour of prisoners) to be taken as beginning on the very day when this act was done." J.W. Cecil Turner, *Kenny's Outlines of Criminal Law* 105 (16th ed. 1952).

"The phrase 'year and a day,' in this test [for proving causation of a person's death], means no more than a year. The accepted method of computing time today is by excluding the first day and including the last. Thus a year from January first is the first day of the following January. In ancient times, however, there was a tendency to include both the first day and the last day so that a year from January first was thought of as the thirty-first of the following December, and 'the day was added that there might be a whole year.' The use of this peculiar phrase to mean just a year in the homicide cases has found expression in some of the statutes. Other enactments have wisely dropped this ancient jingle." Rollin M. Perkins & Ronald N. Boyce, *Criminal Law* 778 (3d ed. 1982).

"Several centuries ago, when doctors knew very little about medicine, the judges created an absolute rule of law: one cannot be guilty of murder if the victim lives for a year and a day after the blow. The difficulty in proving that the blow caused the death after so long an interval was obviously the basis of the rule. Now that doctors know infinitely more, it seems strange that the year-and-a-day rule should survive to the present, but it has done so in most of the American states, either by judicial decision or by statute." Wayne R. LaFave & Austin W. Scott Jr., *Criminal Law* § 3.12, at 299 (2d ed. 1986).

"The year and a day rule is widely viewed as an outdated relic of the common law." *Rogers v. Tennessee*, 532 U.S. 451, 462, 121 S.Ct. 1693, 1701 (2001).

year and day. See YEAR AND A DAY.

Year Books. *Hist.* Books of cases anonymously reported covering primarily the period from the reign of Edward I to the time of Henry VIII. • The title "Year Books" derives from their being grouped under the regnal years of the sovereigns in whose reigns the reported cases were cited. The reports were probably originally prepared by law teachers and students and later by professional reporters or scribes. — Also written *Year-Books*; *year-books*; *yearbooks*. — Also termed *terms*. Cf. ABBREVIATIO PLACITORUM.

"[F]rom 1300 there is a continuous stream of reports of arguments in the common Pleas. The reports were written in Anglo-French, the language of courtly speech. Their authorship is unknown, and they are referred to by the generic name 'year-books' . . . . If we have to account for their beginning, the most likely explanation is that they arose from a case-method of instruction in the law school which served the apprentices of the Bench before the emergence of the inns of court . . . . For the same reason, the contemporary value of the earliest reports lay not in their historical authenticity as precedents but in the ideas and suggestions which they contained . . . . Once the age of experiment was over, the reports settled into a more uniform and at times apparently single series . . . . The year-books did not end at any fixed date. What has usually been taken as their end is the result of two concurrent factors: the advent of printing, and the practice of identifying reports by the name of the author." J.H. Baker, *An Introduction to English Legal History* 205–07 (3d ed. 1990).

year, day, and waste. (17c) *Hist.* A right of the Crown to the profits and waste for a year and a day of the land of persons convicted of petty treason or felony (unless the lord made redemption), after which the Crown had to restore the property to the lord of the fee. The right was abrogated by the Corruption of Blood Act of 1814. — Also termed (in Law French) *ann, jour, et wast*; (in Law Latin) *annus, dies, et vastum*.

year-end dividend. See DIVIDEND.

year in mourning. See ANNUM LUCTUS.

yearly value. See *annual value* under VALUE (2).

Year of Our Lord. See ANNO DOMINI.

year of tax. See *tax year* under YEAR.

year-to-year tenancy. See *periodic tenancy* under TENANCY.

yeas and nays. (16c) The affirmative and negative votes on a bill or resolution before a deliberative assembly. See *roll-call vote* under VOTE (4).

yellow-book appraisal. See APPRAISAL.

yellow-dog contract. (1920) An employment contract forbidding membership in a labor union. • Such a contract is generally illegal under federal and state law.

yeoman (**yoh**-mən). (14c) **1.** *Hist.* An attendant in a royal or noble household. **2.** *Hist.* A commoner; a freeholder (under the rank of gentleman) who holds land yielding 40 shillings per year.

"A *yeoman* is he that hath free land of forty shillings by the year; who was thereby qualified to serve on juries, vote for knights of the shire, and do any other act, where the law requires one that is *probus et legalis homo* [an upright and law-abiding man]." 1 William Blackstone, *Commentaries on the Laws of England* 394 (1765).

3. *English law.* Someone who owns and cultivates property. **4.** A petty officer performing clerical work in the U.S. Navy. — Also sometimes spelled *yoman*.

yeoman of the guard. (15c) *English law.* A member of a corps of officers whose primary duties are to ceremonially guard the English royal household. • A yeoman is usu. at least six feet tall, is of the best rank under the gentry, and is generally exempt from arrest on civil process. — Also termed *yeoman of the guard of the royal household*.

yeomanry (**yoh**-mən-ree). (15c) **1.** The collective body of yeomen. **2.** *Hist.* Volunteer cavalry units in Great Britain, later transferred to the Territorial Army.

yeven (**yev**-ən *or* **yiv**-ən). *Hist.* Given; dated. — Also spelled *yeoven* (**yoh**-vən).

***Yick Wo* doctrine** (yik **woh**). (1958) *Constitutional law.* The principle that the administration of a racially neutral law or ordinance in a discriminatory manner violates the 14th Amendment to the U.S. Constitution. *Yick Wo v. Hopkins*, 118 U.S. 356, 6 S.Ct. 1064 (1886).

yield, *n.* (bef. 12c) Profit expressed as a percentage of the investment. — Also termed *yield on investment*; *return*. See RATE OF RETURN.

▸ **coupon yield.** (1959) The annual interest paid on a security (esp. a bond) divided by the security's par value. — Also termed *nominal yield*.

▸ **current yield.** (1917) The annual interest paid on a security (esp. a bond) divided by the security's current market price.

▸ **discount yield.** (1960) The yield on a security sold at a discount.

▸ **earnings yield.** (1937) The earnings per share of a security divided by its market price. • The higher the ratio, the better the investment yield. — Also termed *earnings-price ratio*. Cf. PRICE-EARNINGS RATIO.

▸ **gross yield.** The profit or loss on an investment before deduction of taxes, expenses, and loss reserves.

▸ **net yield.** (1905) The profit or loss on an investment after deduction of taxes and all appropriate costs and loss reserves.

▸ **nominal yield.** See *coupon yield*.

yield, *vb.* (bef. 12c) **1.** To give up, relinquish, or surrender (a right, etc.) <yield the floor>. **2.** *Parliamentary law.* (Of a motion) to give way to a higher-ranking motion. Cf. PRECEDENCE (3).

"If two motions 'A' and 'B' are related under rules of parliamentary procedure in such a way that motion 'B' can be made while motion 'A' is pending and, when stated by the

> chair, can thus temporarily replace 'A' as the immediately pending question, motion 'B' *takes precedence over* (or *takes precedence of*) motion 'A,' and motion 'A' *yields to* motion 'B.' A secondary motion thus takes precedence over the main motion; and a main motion takes precedence over nothing and yields to all applicable secondary motions." Henry M. Robert, *Robert's Rules of Order Newly Revised* § 5, at 57–58 (10th ed. 2000).

3. *Hist.* To perform a service owed by a tenant to a lord <yield and pay>.

yield on investment. See YIELD.

yield spread. (1940) The differences in yield between various securities issues.

yield to maturity. (1926) The rate of return from an investment if the investment is held until it matures. — Abbr. YTM. Cf. TIME VALUE.

YO. *abbr.* YOUTHFUL OFFENDER.

yokelet (**yohk**-lit), *n.* (18c) *Hist.* A small farm requiring only one yoke of oxen to till it.

yoman. See YEOMAN.

York, custom of. *Hist.* A custom prevalent in York whereby a male intestate's effects were divided according to the doctrine of *pars rationabilis* ("a reasonable part") — that is, one-third each to the widow, children, and administrator, one-half to the administrator if the man was married but had no children or was single but had children, or all to the administrator if the man was single with no children.

York, Statute of. *Hist.* A 1322 English statute enacted to deal with attorneys, witnesses, and the taking of inquests by nisi prius.

York–Antwerp rules. *Maritime law.* A set of rules relating to the settlement of maritime losses and disputes arising from bills of lading. • Although these rules have no statutory authority, they are incorporated into almost all bills of lading. The Rules are maintained and updated by the Comité Maritime International (CMI).

***Youngblood* hearing.** See HEARING.

***Younger* abstention.** See ABSTENTION.

younger-generation devise. See DEVISE.

young offender. See *youthful offender* under OFFENDER.

your Honor. (16c) A title customarily used when directly addressing a judge or other high official. Cf. HIS HONOR.

your witness. See TAKE THE WITNESS.

Youth Correction Authority Act. A model act, promulgated by the American Law Institute in 1940, that proposed the creation of central state commissions responsible for setting up appropriate agencies that would determine the proper treatment for each youthful offender committed to the agency by the courts. • The Act is noteworthy for its emphasis on rehabilitating juvenile offenders, as opposed to punishing them.

youth court. See *teen court* under COURT.

youthful offender. (18c) **1.** See OFFENDER. **2.** JUVENILE DELINQUENT. — Abbr. YO.

youth shelter. See SHELTER (1).

yo-yo stock. See *volatile stock* under STOCK.

YTM. *abbr.* YIELD TO MATURITY.

Z

zap. See INTERSUBJECTIVE ZAP.

ZBA. *abbr.* ZERO-BRACKET AMOUNT.

Z-bond. See *accrual bond* under BOND (3).

zeal (zeel), *n.* Passionate ardor for a cause, esp. that of a client; perfervid eagerness to achieve some end, esp. the successful resolution of a client's legal needs or difficulties. — Also termed *zealousness.* See PRINCIPLE OF PARTISANSHIP.

> "Let us . . . look[] more closely at the principle of partisanship: When acting as an advocate, a lawyer must, within the established constraints on professional behavior, maximize the likelihood that the client will prevail. This principle corresponds to canon seven of the ABA Code: 'A lawyer should represent a client zealously within the bounds of the law.' Canon seven's language is borrowed in turn from canon fifteen of the 1908 ABA Canons, which asserts that '[t]he lawyer owes 'entire devotion to the interest of the client, warm zeal in the maintenance and defense of his rights and the exertion of his utmost learning and ability,' to the end that nothing be taken or be withheld from him, save by the rules of law, legally applied.' The stock expression 'zealous advocacy,' often deployed in discussions of lawyers' ethics, derives from these rules, and the doctrine of zealous advocacy is roughly equivalent to the principle of partisanship." David Luban, *Lawyers and Justice: An Ethical Study* 11 (1988).

zealot (**zel**-ət), *n.* Someone who is an immoderate, fanatical, or overzealous adherent to a cause or ideal, esp. one that is political or religious. • The noun *zealot* has derogatory connotations that are much attenuated, if not absent altogether, in the cognates *zeal* and *zealous.*

zealous (**zel**-əs), *adj.* Incited by fervor; ardently devoted to a person or cause, esp. to a legal client.

zealous advocacy. See PRINCIPLE OF PARTISANSHIP.

zealous witness. See WITNESS.

zeir and day (yeer). See YEAR AND DAY. • *Zeir* is an obsolete graphic variant of *year.*

zero-bracket amount. (1977) A tax deduction formerly available to all individual taxpayers, regardless of whether they itemized their deductions. • In 1944 this was replaced by the standard deduction. — Abbr. ZBA. See *standard deduction* under DEDUCTION.

zero-coupon bond. See BOND (3).

zero-coupon security. See SECURITY (4).

zero-rate mortgage. See MORTGAGE.

zero-sum game. (1944) A situation in which a gain for one side necessarily entails an equal and opposite loss on the other side.

zero tolerance. (1972) An outright ban. • The term came into vogue in the 1990s as a usually hyperbolic term to mean that any ascertainable incidence of a certain activity would be considered objectionable.

zero-tolerance law. (1990) A statute prohibiting even the slightest degree of a certain behavior; esp., state law making it unlawful for a motorist under the age of 21 to operate a motor vehicle after consuming even a small amount of alcohol. — Abbr. Z-T law. See *baby DWI* under DRIVING WHILE INTOXICATED.

zero-tolerance policy. (1990) An established plan or method of action stating that certain acts will not be permitted or condoned. • School districts often have a zero-tolerance policy regarding the use of drugs and alcohol on school premises or at school-sponsored functions. In 1995 Congress enacted a nationwide zero-tolerance statute to combat underage drinking.

zetetic (zi-**tet**-ik), *adj.* (17c) *Hist.* Proceeding by inquiry; investigative. — Also spelled *zetetick.*

ZIFT. *abbr.* ZYGOTE INTRAFALLOPIAN TRANSFER.

zipper clause. (1965) *Contracts.* A contractual provision that operates both as an integration clause and as a no-oral-modification clause. See INTEGRATION CLAUSE; NO-ORAL-MODIFICATION CLAUSE.

> "[A] 'zipper clause' . . . so called because the combination of the integration clause and the no-oral-modification clause is intended to foreclose claims of any representations outside the written contract . . . ." *Pace v. Honolulu Disposal Serv.*, 227 F.3d 1150, 1159 (9th Cir. 2000).

zombie, *adj. Slang.* Remaining in effect or being revived despite circumstances that should have led to extinguishment.

zombie debt. See DEBT.

zombie mortgage. See MORTGAGE.

zombie title. See TITLE (2).

zonal, *adj.* (1867) Of, relating to, or arranged into zones.

zone. (15c) **1.** An area that is different or is distinguished from surrounding areas <zone of danger>. See FREE-TRADE ZONE. **2.** An area in a city or town that, through zoning regulations, is under particular restrictions on land use, building size, and the like <the capitol is at the center of the height-restriction zone>. — Also termed (in sense 2, more specif.) *land-use zone.*

▸ **floating zone.** (1952) An amount of land assigned for a particular use but in no particular location. • An applicant who owns the specified amount of land can apply for a use permit in a specific location. See *floating zoning* under ZONING.

▸ **holding zone.** (1962) Temporary, low-density zoning used until a community determines how the area should be rezoned.

▸ **vulnerable zone.** *Environmental law.* An area of land that is likely to be adversely affected by serious environmental problems, such as flooding or soil contamination.

zone-of-danger rule. (1966) *Torts.* The doctrine allowing the recovery of damages for negligent infliction of emotional distress if the plaintiff was both located in the dangerous area created by the defendant's negligence and suffered emotional distress from the risk of physical harm.

zone of employment. (1920) *Workers' compensation.* The physical place of employment within which an employee, if injured there, can receive compensation. Cf. COURSE OF EMPLOYMENT; SCOPE OF EMPLOYMENT.

zone of interests. (1969) The class or type of interests or concerns that a statute or constitutional guarantee is intended to regulate or protect. • To have standing to challenge a ruling (esp. of an administrative agency), the plaintiff must show that the specific injury suffered comes within the zone of interests protected by the statute on which the ruling was based.

zone of peace. *Int'l law.* A place where, by multilateral or collective declaration, peace prevails for a measurable time, usu. as a result of states' attaching conditions to maritime spaces or land territories, the purpose being to halt escalating militarization or to eliminate foreign military bases and activities.

> "The so-called zones of peace were first announced by several States during the 1970s. The zones were then a novelty among the different kinds of spatial area that can occur in international relations. Of such areas, those founded under international law usually constitute arrangements based on treaties which define the status or regulate the use of a particular place or a region (eg servitudes). In contrast, the zones of peace were not established by international law, and their existence was contested or denied by various States. . . . The initiatives for the declarations relating to zones of peace arose first in South-East Asia and South Asia. The declarations were thus formulated by developing countries, including members of the Non-Aligned Movement (NAM). A few States in regions elsewhere later sought to adapt the concept to their own areas. The zones had mostly similar objectives within the context of the bipolar rivalry and confrontation prevailing between the global superpowers and between some regional powers during the Cold War (1947–91)." Peter Macalister-Smith, "Zones of Peace," in 10 *The Max Planck Encyclopedia of Public International Law* 1111, 1112 (Rüdiger Wolfrum ed., 2012).

zone of privacy. (1964) *Constitutional law.* A range of fundamental privacy rights that are implied in the express guarantees of the Bill of Rights. See PENUMBRA; RIGHT OF PRIVACY.

zone search. See SEARCH (1).

zoning, *n.* (1912) The legislative division of a region, esp. a municipality, into separate districts with different regulations within the districts for land use, building size, and the like. — **zone,** *vb.*

> "Because a zoning ordinance is adopted by a legislative body, and because zoning amendments are legislative decisions in most states, the constitutional scrutiny applied to zoning is no different from that applied to legislation at any governmental level. The courts use the due process of *Euclid* to uphold zoning if they find a reasonable relationship between the zoning and the city's police power objectives. Like other social and economic legislation, zoning comes to court clothed with a presumption of validity. A court will not question the wisdom or the motives of legislators. If a court finds any rational basis to support zoning as an implementation of the public health, safety, and welfare, the ordinance will be held valid. A court considers factors such as increased traffic and congestion, compatibility with adjacent uses, and impact on land values of neighboring properties. Courts often apply a fairly debatable rule: if reasonable minds can differ on the reasonableness of an ordinance, the municipal decision must be upheld. Some state courts are more willing than the federal courts to use theories of state constitutional law to strike down zoning regulations." Daniel R. Mandelker & Barbara Ross, "Zoning," in 4 *Encyclopedia of the American Constitution* 2088–89 (Leonard W. Levy ed., 1986).

▸ **aesthetic zoning.** (1926) Zoning designed to preserve the aesthetic features or values of an area.

▸ **bonus zoning.** See *incentive zoning.*

▸ **cluster zoning.** (1961) Zoning that permits planned-unit development by allowing a modification in lot size and frontage requirements under the condition that other land in the development be set aside for parks, schools, or other public needs. — Also termed *density zoning.* See PLANNED-UNIT DEVELOPMENT.

▸ **comprehensive zoning.** The zoning of an entire municipality, with division into districts.

▸ **conditional zoning.** (1950) Zoning in which a governmental body (without definitively committing itself) grants a zoning change subject to conditions that are usu. not imposed on similarly zoned property. — Also termed *conditional-use zoning; special-use zoning; special-permit zoning.*

> "Conditions imposed are designed to protect adjacent land from the loss of use value which might occur if the newly authorized use was permitted without restraint of any kind. Thus, conditional zoning seeks to minimize the potentially deleterious effect of a zone change on neighboring properties through reasonably conceived conditions which harmonize the landowner's need for rezoning with the public interest." 83 Am. Jur. 2d *Zoning and Planning* § 218, at 193 (1992).

▸ **contextual zoning.** (1984) An approach to zoning that considers appropriate use of a lot based on the scale and types of nearby buildings. • Contextual zoning has been used, for example, to prevent the destruction of older, smaller residences to make room for larger houses disparagingly called "monster homes" or "mc mansions." in established neighborhoods.

▸ **contract zoning.** (1960) **1.** Zoning according to an agreement, by which the landowner agrees to certain restrictions or conditions in exchange for more favorable zoning treatment. • This type of contract zoning is usu. considered an illegal abandonment of the government's police power, because by private agreement, the government has committed itself to a particular type of zoning. **2.** Rezoning of property to a less restrictive classification subject to the landowner's agreement to observe specified limitations on the use and physical development of the property that are not imposed on other property in the zone. • This device is frequently used when property is located in a more restrictive zone that borders on a less restrictive zone.

▸ **cumulative zoning.** (1960) A method of zoning in which any use permitted in a higher-use, less intensive zone is permissible in a lower-use, more intensive zone. • For example, under this method, a house could be built in an industrial zone but a factory could not be built in a residential zone.

▸ **density zoning.** See *cluster zoning.*

▸ **Euclidean zoning** (yoo-**klid**-ee-ən). (1956) Zoning by specific and uniform geographical division. • The purpose of Euclidean zoning is to ensure a municipality's orderly development by detailing what uses are permitted and where, and seeing that conflicting land uses are clearly separated. Its name comes from the Supreme Court case that approved it: *Village of Euclid v. Ambler Realty Co.,* 272 U.S. 365, 47 S.Ct. 114 (1926). — Also termed *use zoning.* Cf. *non-Euclidean zoning.*

"Operating from the premise that everything has its place, zoning is the comprehensive division of a city into different use zones. Use zoning is also known as Euclidean zoning, taking the name from the leading case of Euclid v. Ambler Realty Co., which upheld its validity. . . . In the typical zoning ordinance each zone has three varieties of uses: permitted, accessory and conditional. Ordinances may also specifically prohibit some uses." Julian Conrad Juergensmeyer & Thomas E. Roberts, *Land Use Planning and Development Regulation Law* § 4.2, at 69 (2003).

▸ **exclusionary zoning.** (1955) Zoning that excludes a specific class or type of business from a district.

▸ **floating zoning.** (1962) Zoning that allots land for particular uses but does not specify the geographic locations for those uses. • This is a type of non-Euclidean zoning. It allows a zoning board to make individual rulings on every application for a particular use and take into account the community's current feelings about where or if the use should be allowed. See *non-Euclidean zoning.*

▸ **incentive zoning.** (1970) A relaxation in zoning restrictions (such as density limits) that offers an incentive to a developer to provide certain public benefits (such as building low-income housing units). — Also termed *bonus zoning.*

▸ **interim zoning.** (1924) Temporary emergency zoning pending revisions to existing ordinances or the development of a final zoning plan. — Also termed *stopgap zoning.*

▸ **inverse zoning.** (1975) Zoning that attempts to disperse particular types of property use rather than concentrate them.

▸ **non-Euclidean zoning.** (1961) Zoning that allows a mix of land uses in the same area if the uses are or can be made nonconflicting • For example, a business might be permitted to operate in a residential area if the business adopts a certain architecture to blend in with other structures and has sufficient landscaping and setback to guarantee that nearby residents will not suffer excessive noise, pollution, or other nuisances. Cf. *Euclidean zoning.*

▸ **partial zoning.** (1925) Zoning that affects only a portion of a municipality's territory, and that is usu. invalid because it contradicts the comprehensive zoning plan. — Also termed *piecemeal zoning.*

▸ **private zoning.** (1947) The use of restrictive covenants in private agreements to restrict the use and occupancy of real property. • Private zoning often covers such things as lot size, building lines, architectural specifications, and property uses.

▸ **reverse spot zoning.** (1966) Zoning of a large area of land without regard for the zoning of a small piece of land within that area.

"When parcels around a given property are rezoned to allow for higher uses leaving an island of less intensive use, reverse spot zoning is the result." Donald G. Hagman & Julian Conrad Juergensmeyer, *Urban Planning and Land Development Control Law* § 5.4, at 136 (2d ed. 1986).

▸ **special-permit zoning.** See *conditional zoning.*

▸ **special-use zoning.** See *conditional zoning.*

▸ **spot zoning.** (1934) Zoning of a particular piece of land without regard for the zoning of the larger area surrounding the land. • Spot zoning can be illegal if it is inconsistent with a comprehensive zoning plan, the zoning surrounding the area, or the public health, safety, or general welfare.

"To the popular mind, spot zoning means the improper permission to use an 'island' of land for a more intensive use than permitted on adjacent properties. The popular definition needs several qualifications . . . . The set of facts usually involves an 'island' of more intensive use than surrounding property . . . . Usually the 'island' is small . . . . Furthermore, the term is not properly applied to development permission that comes about by variance or special exception. Rather, the term refers to a legislative act, such as a rezoning, or to a situation in which the 'island' is created by the original ordinance." Donald G. Hagman & Julian Conrad Juergensmeyer, *Urban Planning and Land Development Control Law* § 5.4, at 136 (2d ed. 1986).

▸ **stopgap zoning.** See *interim zoning.*

▸ **use zoning.** See *Euclidean zoning.*

zoning map. (1923) The map that is created by a zoning ordinance and shows the various zoning districts.

zoning ordinance. (1919) A city ordinance that regulates the use to which land within various parts of the city may be put. • It allocates uses to the various districts of a municipality, as by allocating residences to certain parts and businesses to other parts. A comprehensive zoning ordinance usu. regulates the height of buildings and the proportion of the lot area that must be kept free from buildings.

zoning variance. See VARIANCE (2).

Z-T law. *abbr.* ZERO-TOLERANCE LAW.

zygnomic (zig-**noh**-mik), *adj.* (1924) Of, relating to, or involving an act whose evolution directly abridges the freedom of a person who bears a duty in the enjoyment of a legal advantage. • This rather abstract term was coined by the philosopher Albert Kocourek in his book *Jural Relations* (1927). Cf. MESONOMIC.

zygocephalum (zɪ-gə-**sef**-ə-ləm), *n.* [Greek fr. *zygo-* "yoke, pair" + *kephalos* "head"] *Hist.* A measure of land, esp. the amount that can be plowed in one day.

zygostates (zɪ-goh-**stay**-teez), *n.* [Greek] (17c) *Roman law.* An officer who resolved controversies over weight; a public weigher.

zygote. (1891) A two-celled organism formed by the joining of egg and sperm before undergoing cleavage. — Also termed *blastocyst*; *preembryo*; *proembryo.* Cf. EMBRYO; FETUS.

zygote intrafallopian transfer. (1989) A procedure in which mature eggs are fertilized in a test tube or petri dish and then injected into a woman's fallopian tubes. — Abbr. ZIFT. — Also termed *zygote intrafallopian-tube transfer.* Cf. ARTIFICIAL INSEMINATION; GAMETE INTRAFALLOPIAN TRANSFER; IN VITRO FERTILIZATION; IN VIVO FERTILIZATION.

Appendix A

Table of Legal Abbreviations

L. Kurt Adamson*

This table is a working list of abbreviations cited in American cases, books, articles, and texts. It is not restricted to standard abbreviations found in legal citation manuals. The table includes the names of common federal and state primary sources, legal periodicals, treatises, and organizations, as well as selected words or phrases commonly found in American publications from the 19th century forward. There are also selected abbreviations for English, Canadian, Australian, and international sources.

The table has unique features in its two-part format. The main table lists fuller publication titles than may be found in similar compilations. The second part lists the full names of individual authors referred to in the main abbreviation table. These fuller titles and author names may help in finding publications through a library catalog.

Although not every variation for a publication's abbreviation is listed, the table can help you interpret abbreviations not listed. First, the same publication or organization may be abbreviated with or without periods, as with "UPA" or "U.P.A." This table lists only one version. Second, standardized citations and abbreviations were not adopted until the 20th century. For example, Willard Phillips's *Treatise on the Law of Evidence* is cited in various sources in any of these ways:

Phillips, Law of Evidence

Phillips on Evidence

Phillips, Evidence

Phillips, Ev.

Phil. Ev.

So you might use this table's information to interpret other variations of a publication's abbreviation. Because many 19th-century treatises were published in numerous editions, other parts of the citation are essential to identify which edition of a work is being cited. Further, the format "author on ____" (such as *Phillips on Evidence*) was a common citation practice throughout the 19th and early 20th centuries, even though it was only a common shorthand for the work or perhaps the title that appeared on the book's spine, but not the formal title of the work as found on the title page. Hence this table provides at least the beginning portion of titles to treatises.

The table is arranged in alphabetical order as if each abbreviation were one word without punctuation or spacing. Organizations are commonly cited without periods in the abbreviation. If an author's name is abbreviated, the full last name precedes the listed title. An author's initials are also included if there is more than one author with the same last name in the table. Finally, the ampersand (&) is treated, for purposes of order, as the word "and" in the abbreviation.

---

*Associate Director for Collection Development (ret'd), Underwood Law Library, Southern Methodist University Dedman School of Law.

This table is not intended to be comprehensive. Other abbreviations may be found in the following sources, Mary M. Prince, *Bieber's Dictionary of Legal Abbreviations: A Reference Guide for Attorneys, Legal Secretaries, Paralegals and Law Students*, 5th ed. (2001), Donald Raistrick, *Index to Legal Citations and Abbreviations*, 2d ed. (1993), Charles C. Soule, *The Lawyer's Reference Manual* (1884), or John G. Marvin, *Legal Bibliography, or A Thesaurus of American, English, Irish and Scotch Law Books* (1847). For non-English language abbreviations, see Bieber and Raistrick, as well as Igor I. Kavass and Mary M. Prince, *A World Dictionary of Legal Abbreviations* (1991–) or Arturo L. Torres and Francisco Avalos, *Latin American Legal Abbreviations: A Comprehensive Spanish/Portuguese Dictionary with English Translations* (1989).

A

A. – Atlantic Reporter
A.2d – Atlantic Reporter, Second Series
AALS – American Association of Law Schools
A. & E. Ann. Cas. – American & English Annotated Cases
A. & E. Enc. L. – American & English Encyclopedia of Law
A. & E. Enc. L. & Prac. – American & English Encyclopedia of Law and Practice
A. &. E. Ency. – American & English Encyclopedia of Law
A.B.A. – American Bar Association
A.B.A. J. – American Bar Association Journal
A.B.A. Rep. – American Bar Association Reports
Abb. N. Cas. – Abbott's New Cases (N.Y.)
Abb. Pr. – Abbott's Practice Reports (N.Y.)
Abb. Pr. (n.s.) – Abbott's Practice Reports, New Series (N.Y.)
A.B.F. Res. J. – American Bar Foundation Research Journal
A.B.F. Research Rep. – American Bar Foundation Research Reporter
ACCA Docket – ACCA Docket: the Journal of American Corporate Counsel Association
Accountancy L. Rep. (CCH) – Accountancy Law Reporter
acq. – Acquiescence
acq. in result – Acquiescence in result
A.D. – Appellate Division Reports (N.Y.)
A.D.2d – Appellate Divisions Reports, Second Series (N.Y.)
Adams, Eq. – The Doctrine of Equity: A Commentary on the Law as Administered by the Court of Chancery
Adams, Equity – The Doctrine of Equity: A Commentary on the Law as Administered by the Court of Chancery
Adams L.J. – Adams County Law Journal (Pa.)
AD Cas. (BNA) – Americans with Disabilities Cases
Addison on Contracts – Addison on Contracts: Being a Treatise on the Law of Contracts
Add. Torts – Addison, A Treatise on the Law of Torts
Adel. L. Rev. – Adelaide Law Review
Adelphia L.J. – Adelphia Law Journal
Ad. L.B. – Administrative Law Bulletin
Ad. L. Bull. – Administrative Law Bulletin
Ad. L. News – Administrative Law News
Admin. & Reg. L. News – Administrative and Regulatory Law News
Admin. L. 3d – Pike & Fischer Administrative Law, Third Series
Admin. L.J. – Administrative Law Journal
Admin. L.J. Am. U. – Administrative Law Journal of American University
Admin. L. Rev. – Administrative Law Review
Adm. L. Rev. – Administrative Law Review
Advoc. – Advocate (Idaho)
Advoc. Q. – Advocates' Quarterly
Advocates' Q. – Advocates' Quarterly
Adv. Sh. – Advance Sheet
A.E.C. – Atomic Energy Commission Reports
A.E.L.R. – All England Law Reports
Aff. Action Compl. Man. (BNA) – Affirmative Action Compliance Manual for Federal Contractors
aff'd – affirmed
aff'g – affirming
A.F. JAG L. Rev. – Air Force JAG Law Review
A.F. L. Rev. – Air Force Law Review
Afr.-Am. L. & Pol'y Rep. – African-American Law and Policy Report
Afr. L. Stud. – African Law Studies
A.F.T.R. (P-H) – American Federal Tax Reports
A.F.T.R.2d (RIA) – American Federal Tax Reports, Second Series
Agric. Dec. – Agriculture Decisions
AICPA Prof. Stand. (CCH) – AICPA Professional Standards
AID – Agency for International Development
AIDS L. & Litig. Rep. – AIDS Law and Litigation Reporter (Univ. Pub. Group)
Aik. – Aikens (Vt.)
AIPLA – American Intellectual Property Law Association
AIPLA Q.J. – AIPLA Quarterly Journal
Air & Space L. – Air and Space Law
Air & Space Law. – Air and Space Lawyer
Air. L. – Air Law
Air L. Rev. – Air Law Review
A.K. Marsh. – A.K. Marshall (Ky.)
Akron L. Rev. – Akron Law Review
Akron Tax. J. – Akron Tax Journal
Ala. – Alabama Reports
Ala. Acts – Acts of Alabama
Ala. Admin. Code – Alabama Administrative Code
Ala. App. – Alabama Appellate Courts Reports
Ala. Code – Code of Alabama
Ala. Law. – Alabama Lawyer
Ala. L.J. – Alabama Law Journal
Ala. L. Rev. – Alabama Law Review
Alaska – Alaska Reports
Alaska Admin. Code – Alaska Administrative Code
Alaska Fed. – Alaska Federal Reports
Alaska L. Rev. – Alaska Law Review
Alaska Sess. Laws – Alaska Session Laws
Alaska Stat. – Alaska Statutes
Ala. St. B. Found. Bull. – Alabama State Bar Foundation Bulletin
Alberta L. Rev. – Alberta Law Review
Alb. L. Envtl. Outlook – Albany Law Environmental Outlook
Alb. L.J. Sci. & Tech. – Albany Law Journal of Science & Technology
Alb. L. Rev. – Albany Law Review
Aldrich, Eq. Pl. & Pr. – Equity Pleadings and Practice in the Courts of Massachusetts
A.L.I. – American Law Institute
ALI-ABA Bus. L. Course Mat. J. – ALI-ABA Business Law Course Materials Journal
ALI-ABA Course Mat. J. – ALI-ABA Course Materials Journal
Allen – Allen (Mass.)
All E.R. – All England Law Reports
Allnat on Partition – A Practical Treatise on the Law of Partition
All St. Tax Guide (CCH) – All States Tax Guide
A.L.R. – American Law Reports
A.L.R.2d – American Law Reports, Second Series
A.L.R.3d – American Law Reports, Third Series
A.L.R.4th – American Law Reports, Fourth Series
A.L.R.5th – American Law Reports, Fifth Series
A.L.R.Fed. – American Law Reports, Federal
ALSA – American Legal Studies Association
ALSA F. – ALSA Forum
Alta. L. Rev. – Alberta Law Review
Alternative L.J. – Alternative Law Journal
ALWD – Association of Legal Writing Directors
Am. Acad. Psych. & L. Bull. – American Academy of Psychiatry and Law Bulletin
Am. Bankr. Inst. J. – American Bankruptcy Institute Journal
Am. Bankr. Inst. L. Rev. – American Bankruptcy Institute Law Review
Am. Bankr. L.J. – American Bankruptcy Law Journal
Am. Bankr. Rep. – American Bankruptcy Reports

Am. Bankr. Rep. N.S. – American Bankruptcy Reports, New Series
Am. B. Found. Res J. – American Bar Foundation Research Journal
Am. Bus. L.J. – American Business Law Journal
A.M.C. – American Maritime Cases
Am. Crim L. Rev. – American Criminal Law Review
Am. Dec. – American Decisions
Am. Dig. – American Digest
Amer. Rep. – American Reports
Amer. St. Rep. – American State Reports
Amer. State Reps. – American State Reports
Ames & Smith, Cases on Torts – A Selection of Cases on the Law of Torts
Ames, Cas. on B. & N. – Selection of Cases on the Law of Bills and Notes and Other Negotiable Paper
Ames, Cas. on Bills & Notes – Selection of Cases on the Law of Bills and Notes and Other Negotiable Paper
Ames, Cas. on Trusts – A Selection of Cases on the Law of Trusts
Ames, Cas. Par. – A Selection of Cases on the Law of Partnership
Ames, Cas. Pl. – A Selection of Cases on Pleading at Common Law
Ames, Cas. Sur. – A Selection of Cases on the Law of Suretyship
Ames on Trusts – A Selection of Cases on the Law of Trusts
Am. Indian J. – American Indian Journal
Am. Indian L. Rev. – American Indian Law Review
Am. Ins. Rep. – American Insolvency Reports
Am. J. Comp. L. – American Journal of Comparative Law
Am. J. Crim. L. – American Journal of Criminal Law
Am. J. Fam. L. – American Journal of Family Law
Am. J. Int'l. Arb. – American Journal of International Arbitration
Am. J. Int'l L. – American Journal of International Law
Am. J. Juris. – American Journal of Jurisprudence
Am. J.L. & Med. – American Journal of Law & Medicine
Am. J. Legal Hist. – American Journal of Legal History
Am. J. Tax Pol'y – American Journal of Tax Policy
Am. J. Trial Advoc. – American Journal of Trial Advocacy
Am. Jur. – American Jurisprudence
Am. Jur. 2d – American Jurisprudence, Second Edition
Am. L. & Econ. Rev. – American Law and Economics Review
Am. Law. – American Lawyer
Am. Law Inst. – American Law Institute
Am. Law J. – American Law Journal
Am. Law Mag. – American Law Magazine
Am. Law Rev. – American Law Review
Am. Lead. Cas. – Hare & Wallace, American Leading Cases
Am. L. Mag. – American Law Magazine
Am. L. Register – American Law Register
Am. L. Register & Rev. – American Law Register and Review
Am. L. Rev. – American Law Review
Amos & F. – The Law of Fixtures and Other Property
Amos & F. Fixt. – The Law of Fixtures and Other Property
Am. R. – American Reports
Am. Rep. – American Reports
Am. Rev. Int'l Arb. – American Review of International Arbitration
Am. Rev. Pub. Admin. – American Review of Public Administration
Am. Samoa – American Samoa Reports
Am. Samoa 2d – American Samoa Reports, Second Series
Am. Samoa Admin. Code – American Samoa Administrative Code
Am. Samoa Code Ann. – American Samoa Code Annotated
Am. Soc'y Int'l L. Proc. – American Society of International Law Proceedings
Am. Stock Ex. Guide (CCH) – American Stock Exchange Guide
Am. St. Papers – American State Papers
Am. St. R. – American State Reports
Am. St. Rep. – American State Reports
Am. U. Int'l L. Rev. – American University International Law Review
Am. U. Int. L. Rev. – American University Intramural Law Review
Am. U. Intra. L. Rev. – American University Intramural Law Review
Am. U. J. Gender & L. – American University Journal of Gender and the Law
Am. U. J. Gender Soc. Pol'y & L. – American University Journal of Gender, Social Policy & the Law
Am. U. J. Int'l L. & Pol'y – American University Journal of International Law and Policy
Am. U. L. Rev. – American University Law Review
Angell & Ames on Corps. – Treatise on the Law of Private Corporations Aggregate
Angell, Lim. – A Treatise on the Law of Limitation of Actions
Angell on Limitations – A Treatise on the Law of Limitations of Actions
Angell on Tide Waters – A Treatise in the Right of Property in Tide Waters
Angell on Watercourses – A Treatise on the Common Law of Watercourses *or* A Treatise on the Law of Watercourses
Anglo-Am. L. Rev. – Anglo-American Law Review
Animal L. – Animal Law
Annals Air & Space L. – Annals of Air and Space Law
Annals Am. Acad. Pol. & Soc. Sci. – Annals of the American Academy of – Political & Social Science
Annals Health L. – Annals of Health Law
Ann. Cas. – American and English Annotated Cases
Ann. Code – Annotated Code
Ann. Inst. on Sec. Reg. – Annual Institute on Securities Regulation
Ann. Inst. Sec. Reg. – Annual Institute on Securities Regulation
Ann. Indus. Prop. L. – Annual of Industrial Property Law
Ann. Law Reg. – Annual Law Register of the United States
Ann. Rev. Banking L. – Annual Review of Banking Law
Ann. Rev. L. Sch. N.Y.U. – Annual Review of the Law School of New York University
Ann. St. – Annotated Statutes
Ann. Surv. Am. L. – Annual Survey of American Law
Ann. Surv. Commonw. L. – Annual Survey of Commonwealth Law
Ann. Surv. Int'l & Comp. L. – Annual Survey of International and Comparative Law
Ann. Surv. Mass. L. – Annual Survey of Massachusetts Law
Anson, Contracts – Principles of the English Law of Contract and of Agency in its Relation to Contract
Antioch L.J. – Antioch Law Journal
Antitrust & Trade Reg. Rep. (BNA) – Antitrust and Trade Regulation Report
Antitrust Bull. – The Antitrust Bulletin
Antitrust L. & Econ. Rev. – Antitrust Law and Economics Review
Antitrust L.J. – Antitrust Law Journal
Antitrust Newsl. – Antitrust Newsletter (ABA)
Ant. N.P. Cas. – Anthon's Nisi Prius Cases (N.Y.)
APLA Q. – American Patent Law Association Quarterly
APLA Q. J. – American Patent Law Quarterly Journal

app. — appendix
Appalachian J. L. — Appalachian Journal of Law
App. Ct. Admin. Rev. — Appellate Court Administration Review
App. D.C. — Appeal Cases, District of Columbia
Arab L.Q. — Arab Law Quarterly
Arb. Int'l — Arbitration International
Arb. J. — Arbitration Journal (ABA)
Ariz. — Arizona Reports
Ariz. Admin. Code — Arizona Administrative Code
Ariz. Admin. Reg. — Arizona Administrative Register
Ariz. App. — Arizona Appeals Reports
Ariz. Att'y — Arizona Attorney
Ariz. B.J. — Arizona Bar Journal
Ariz. J. Int'l & Comp. L. — Arizona Journal of International and Comparative Law
Ariz. Legis. Serv. — Arizona Legislative Service
Ariz. L. Rev. — Arizona Law Review
Ariz. B.J. — Arizona Bar Journal
Ariz. Rev. Stat. — Arizona Revised Statutes
Ariz. Rev. Stat. Ann. — Arizona Revised Statutes Annotated
Ariz. Sess. Laws — Arizona Session Laws
Ariz. St. L.F. — Arizona State Law Forum
Ariz. St. L.J. — Arizona State Law Journal
Ark. — Arkansas Reports
Ark. Acts — General Acts of Arkansas
Ark. Adv. Legis. Serv. — Arkansas Advance Legislative Service
Ark. App. — Arkansas Appellate Reports
Ark. Code Ann. — Arkansas Code of 1987 Annotated
Ark. Law. — Arkansas Lawyer
Ark. Law. Q. — Arkansas Lawyer Quarterly
Ark. L. Notes — Arkansas Law Notes
Ark. L. Rev. — Arkansas Law Review
Ark. L. Rev. & B. Assn. J. — Arkansas Law Review and Bar Association Journal
Ark. Reg. — Arkansas Register
Ark. Stats. — Arkansas Statutes
Army Law. — Army Lawyer
Arn. Ins. — Maclachlan, Arnould on the Law of Marine Insurance
A.R.S. — Arizona Revised Statutes
Art & L. — Art and the Law
Artificial Intelligence & L. — Artificial Intelligence and Law
A.S. — Alaska Statutes
ASCAP — American Society of Composers, Authors, and Publishers
A.S.C.A.P. Copyright L. Symp. — ASCAP Copyright Law Symposium
Asia Bus. L. Rev. — Asia Business Law Review
Asia L. — Asia Law
Asia L. & Prac. — Asia Law and Practice
Asia-Pac. Const. Y.B. — Asia-Pacific Constitutional Yearbook
Asian Am. Pac. Is. L.J. — Asian American Pacific Islands Law Journal
Asian L.J. — Asian Law Journal
Asian Pac. Am. L.J. — Asian Pacific American Law Journal
Asian-Pac. L. & Pol'y J. — Asian-Pacific Law & Policy Journal
Asian-Pac. Tax & Investment Bull. — Asian-Pacific Tax and Investment Bulletin
Asia Pac. J. Envtl. L. — Asia Pacific Journal of Environmental Law
Asia-Pac. J. Hum. Rts. & L. — Asia-Pacific Journal of Human Rights and the Law
Asia-Pac. J. Pub. Health — Asia-Pacific Journal of Public Health
Asia Pac. L. Rev. — Asia Pacific Law Review
Asia-Pac. Tax Bull. — Asia-Pacific Tax Bulletin
ASIL Proc. — American Society of International Law Proceedings
ASILS — Association of Student International Law Societies
ASILS Int'l L.J. — ASILS International Law Journal
ASIR L. Rev. — Association for the Study of International Relations Law Review
A.S.R. — American State Reports
Atherly on Marriage Settlements — A Practical Treatise on the Law of Marriage and Other Family Settlements
ATLA — Association of Trial Lawyers of America
A.T.L.A. J. — American Trial Lawyers Association Journal
Atl. Rep. — Atlantic Reporter
Atom. Energy L.J. — Atomic Energy Law Journal
Atom. En. L. Rep. (CCH) — Atomic Energy Law Reporter
Att'y Gen. Rep. — United States Attorneys General's Reports
Auckland U. L. Rev. — Auckland University Law Review
Austin's Jurisprudence — Austin, Lectures on Jurisprudence, or, The Philosophy of Positive Law
Austl. B. Rev. — Australian Bar Review
Austl. Bus. L. Rev. — Australian Business Law Review
Austl. Disp. Resol. J. — Australian Dispute Resolution Journal
Austl. J. Asian L. — Australian Journal of Asian Law
Austl. J. Corp. L. — Australian Journal of Corporate Law
Austl. J. For. Sci. — Australian Journal of Forensic Sciences
Austl. J. Hum. Rts. — Australian Journal of Human Rights
Austl. J. Int'l Aff. — Australian Journal of International Affairs
Austl. J. Lab. L. — Australian Journal of Labour Law
Austl. J.L. & Soc'y — Australian Journal of Law and Society
Austl. J. Legal Hist. — Australian Journal of Legal History
Austl. L.J. — Australian Law Journal
Austl. Tax F. — Australian Tax Forum
Austl. Tax Rev. — Australian Tax Review
Austl. Y.B. Int'l L. — Australian Yearbook of International Law
Australasian Gay & Lesbian L.J. — Australasian Gay and Lesbian Law Journal
Auto. Cas. (CCH) — Automobile Cases
Auto. Cas. 2d (CCH) — Automobile Cases, Second Series
Auto. Ins. Cas. (CCH) — Automobile Insurance Cases
Auto. Ins. Rep. (CCH) — Automobile Insurance Reporter
Av. Cases (CCH) — Aviation Cases
Ave Maria L. Rev. — Ave Maria Law Review
Av. Ins. Rep. — Aviation Insurance Reports
Av. L. Rep. (CCH) — Aviation Law Reporter / Aviation Law Reports

B

Babington on Auctions — A Treatise on the Law of Auctions
Babington on Set-Off — A Treatise on the Law of Set-Off and Mutual Credit
Bail. — Bailey (S.C.)
Bail. Eq. — Bailey's Equity Reports (S.C.)
Baker, Quar. — The Laws Relating to Quarantine of Her Majesty's Dominions at Home and Abroad, and of the Principle Foreign States
Ballantine on Limitations — A Treatise on the Statute of Limitations
Banking L.J. — Banking Law Journal
Banking Pol'y Rep. — Banking Policy Report
Banking Rep. (BNA) — Banking Report
Bankr. — Bankruptcy Reporter

Bankr. Code – Bankruptcy Code
Bankr. Ct. Dec. (CRR) – Bankruptcy Court Decisions
Bankr. Dev. J. – Bankruptcy Developments Journal
Bankr. Form – Bankruptcy Form
Bankr. L. Rep. (CCH) – Bankruptcy Law Reports
Bankr. Rule – Bankruptcy Rule
Barb. – Barbour's Supreme Court Reports (N.Y.)
Barb. Ch. – Barbour's Chancery Reports (N.Y.)
Bates' Dig. – Bates' Digest, Ohio
BATF – Bureau of Alcohol, Tobacco, and Firearms
Bay – Bay (S.C.)
Bayley, Bills – Summary of the Law of Bills of Exchange, Cash Bills, and Promissory Notes
Baylor L. Rev. – Baylor Law Review
B.B.J. – Boston Bar Journal
B.C.A. (CCH) – Board of Contract Appeals Decisions
B.C. Envtl. Aff. L. Rev. – Boston College Environmental Affairs Law Review
B.C. Ind. & Com. L. Rev. – Boston College Industrial and Commercial Law Review
B.C. Int'l & Com. L.J. – Boston College International and Comparative Law Journal
B.C. Int'l & Comp. L. Rev. – Boston College International and Comparative Law Review
B.C. L. Rev. – Boston College Law Review
B.C. Tax Rep. (CCH) – British Columbia Tax Reporter
B.C. Third World L.J. – Boston College Third World Law Journal
Beach, Priv. Corp. – Commentaries on the Law of Private Corporations
Beach, Pub. Corp. – Commentaries on the Law of Public Corporations, with Municipal Corporations and Political or Government Corporations of Every Class
Beale, Cas. Crim. Law – A Selection of Cases and Other Authorities on Criminal Law
Beaver – Beaver County Legal Journal (Pa.)
Behav. Sci. & L. – Behavioral Sciences and the Law
Belli's Mod. Trials – Belli, Modern Trials
Bench & Bar – Bench and Bar of Minnesota
Bench & B. Minn. – Bench and Bar of Minnesota
Benefits L.J. – Benefits Law Journal
Ben. Rev. Bd. Serv. (MB) – Benefits Review Board Service
Berkeley J. Emp. & Lab. L. – Berkeley Journal of Employment and Labor Law
Berkeley J. Health Care L. – Berkeley Journal of Health Care Law
Berkeley J. Int'l L. – Berkeley Journal of International Law
Berkeley La Raza L.J. – Berkeley La Raza Law Journal
Berkeley Tech. L.J. – Berkeley Technology Law Journal
Berkeley Women's L.J. – Berkeley Women's Law Journal
Berks – Berks County Law Journal (Pa.)
Best, Ev. – The Principles of the Law of Evidence with Elementary Rules for Conducting the Examination and Cross-examination of Witnesses
Best Jur. Tr. – An Exposition of the Practice Relative to the Right to Begin and Reply in Trials by Jury
Best, Pres. – A Treatise on Presumptions of Law and Fact, with the Theory and Rules of Presumptive or Circumstantial Proof in Criminal Cases
Bevans – Treaties and Other International Agreements of the United States of America, 1776-1949
Beven, Negligence – Negligence in Law
Beverly Hills B.A. J. – Beverly Hills Bar Association Journal
BIA – Bureau of Indian Affairs
Bibb – Bibb (Ky.)
Bigelow, Estop. – A Treatise on the Law of Estoppel and Its Application in Practice
Big. Torts – Bigelow, The Law of Torts
Bill Rts. J. – Bill of Rights Journal (ABA)
Binn. – Binney (Pa.)
Bish. Cont. – Bishop, Commentaries on the Law of Contracts upon a New and Condensed Method
Bish. Crim. Law – Bishop, Commentaries on the Criminal Law
Bish. Crim. Proc. – Bishop, New Criminal Procedure, or, New Commentaries on the Law of Pleading and Practice in Criminal Cases
Bishop, Non-Contract Law – Commentaries on the Non-contract Law and Especially as to Common Affairs Not of Contract or the Every-day Rights and Torts
Bishop on Marriage & Divorce – Commentaries on the Law of Marriage and Divorce
Black – Black, U.S. Supreme Court Reports
Blackburn on Sales – A Treatise on the Effect of the Contract of Sale on the Legal Rights of Property and Possession of Goods, Wares and Merchandise
Black. Com. – Blackstone, Commentaries on the Laws of England
Blackf. – Blackford's Reports (Ind.)
Black, Interp. Laws – Handbook on the Construction and Interpretation of the Laws
Black, Judg. – A Treatise on the Law of Judgments, Including the Doctrine of Res Judicata
Black, Law. Dict. – Black, Law Dictionary
Black L.J. – Black Law Journal
Blackst. Com. – Blackstone, Commentaries on the Laws of England
Black, Tax Titles – A Treatise on the Law of Tax Titles
Blanshard on Limitations – A Treatise on the Statute of Limitations
Bl. Comm. – Blackstone, Commentaries on the Laws of England
B. Leader – Bar Leader (ABA)
Bliss, Ins. – The Law of Life Insurance, with a Chapter on Accident Insurance
BLM – Bureau of Land Management
BLS – Bureau of Labor Statistics
Blue Sky L. Rep. (CCH) – Blue Sky Law Reporter / Blue Sky Law Reports
Blume Unrep. Op. – Blume's Unreported Opinions (Mich.)
Blume Sup. Ct. Trans. – Blume's Supreme Court Transactions
B. Mon. – Ben Monroe (Ky.)
BNA – Bureau of National Affairs
Bond L. Rev. – Bond Law Review
Booth, Real Act. – The Nature and Practice of Real Actions in Their Writs and Process
Boston B.J. – Boston Bar Journal
Boston L.R. – Boston Law Reporter
Bouvier, Law Dictionary – A Law Dictionary, Adapted to the Constitution and Laws of the United States
Bouv. Inst. – Bouvier, Institutes of American Law
Bowstead – Digest of the Law of Agency
Bowstead on Agency – Digest of the Law of Agency
Boyce – Boyce (Del.)
B.R. – West's Bankruptcy Reporter
Bradf. – Bradford (Iowa)
Bract. – Bracton
Bracton's Note Book – Bracton's Note Book: A Collection of Cases Decided in the King's Court During the Reign of Henry the Third
Brandeis J. Fam. L. – Brandeis Journal of Family Law
Brandeis L.J. – Brandeis Law Journal
Brayt. – Brayton (Vt.)
BRBS – Benefits Review Board Service (MB)
Breese – Breese (Ill.)
Brev. – Brevard (S.C.)

Brice, Ultra Vires – Brice, A Treatise on the Doctrine of Ultra Vires
Brick. Dig. – Brickell, Digest of the Decisions of the Supreme Court of the State of Alabama
Bridgeport L. Rev. – Bridgeport Law Review
Brief Times Rptr. – Brief Times Reporter (Colo.)
Bright. Dig. – Brightly, An Analytical Digest of the Laws of the United States
Brit. J.L. & Soc'y – British Journal of Law and Society
Brit. Tax Rev. – British Tax Review
Brit. Y.B. Int'l L. – British Yearbook of International Law
Brook. L. Rev. – Brooklyn Law Review
Brooklyn B. – Brooklyn Bar
Brooklyn Barr. – Brooklyn Barrister
Brooklyn Daily Rec. – Brooklyn Daily Record
Brooklyn J. Int'l L. – Brooklyn Journal of International Law
Brooklyn L. Rev. – Brooklyn Law Review
Brown, Adm. – Cases on the Law of Admiralty
Browne, Div. – G. Browne, A Treatise on the Principles and Practice of the Court for Divorce & Matrimonial Causes
Browne on Statute of Frauds – A Treatise on the Construction of the Statute of Frauds
Browne, Prob. – G. Browne, A Treatise on the Principles and Practice of the Court of Probate in Contentious and Non-contentious Business
Bryce's Am. Com. – Bryce, American Commonwealth
B.T.A. – Reports of the United States Board of Tax Appeals
B.T.A. (CCH) – Board of Tax Appeals Decisions
B.T.A.M. (P-H) – Board of Tax Appeals Memorandum Decisions
Bucks – Bucks County Law Reporter (Pa.)
Buffalo L. Rev. – Buffalo Law Review
Buff. Crim. L. Rev. – Buffalo Criminal Law Review
Buff. Envtl. L.J. – Buffalo Environmental Law Journal
Buff. Hum. Rts. L. Rev. – Buffalo Human Rights Law Review
Buff. J. Int'l L. – Buffalo Journal of International Law
Buff. J. Pub. Int. L. – Buffalo Journal of Public Interest Law
Buff. L. Rev. – Buffalo Law Review
Buff. Pub. Int. L.J. – Buffalo Public Interest Law Journal: In the Public Interest
Buff. Women's L.J. – Buffalo Women's Law Journal
B.U. Int'l. L.J. – Boston University International Law Journal
B.U. J. Sci. & Tech. L. – Boston University Journal of Science & Technology Law
B.U. J. Tax Law – Boston University Journal of Tax Law
Bull. Am. Acad. Psych. & L. – Bulletin of the American Academy of Psychiatry and Law
Bull. Copy. Soc'y – Bulletin of the Copyright Society of the U.S.A.
Bull. Copyright Soc'y – Bulletin of the Copyright Society of the U.S.A.
Bull. Copyright Soc'y U.S.A. – Bulletin of the Copyright Society of the U.S.A.
Bull. L. Sci. & Tech. – Bulletin of Law, Science and Technology (ABA)
Bull. L. Sec. St. B. Tex. – Bulletin of the Business Law Section State Bar of Texas
B.U. L. Rev. – Boston University Law Review
Bump, B'k'cy – Law and Practice of Bankruptcy
Bump, Comp. – Composition in Bankruptcy
Bump, Const. Dec. – Notes of Constitutional Decisions: Being a Digest of the Judicial Interpretations of the Constitution of the United States...
Bump, Fed. Pr. – Federal Procedure: The Title Judiciary in the Revised Statutes of the United States, and the Rules Promulgated by the Supreme Court...
Bump, Fraud. Conv. – Fraudulent Conveyances: A Treatise upon Conveyances Made By Debtors to Defraud Creditors
Bump, Int. Rev. – Internal Revenue Laws
Bump, Pat. – The Law of Patents, Trade-Marks, and Copy-Rights: Consisting of Sections of the Revised Statutes of the United States with Notes under Each Section...
B.U. Pub. Int. L.J. – Boston University Public Interest Law Journal
Bur. – Burnett (Wis.)
Burns' Ann. St. – Burns' Annotated Statutes (Ind.)
Burns' Rev. St. – Burns' Revised Statues (Ind.)
Burrill, Assignm. – A Treatise on the Law and Practice of Voluntary Assignments for the Benefit of Creditors
Burrill, Circ. Ev. – A Treatise on the Nature, Principles and Rules of Circumstantial Evidence
Burrill, Pr. – A Treatise on the Practice of the Supreme Court of the State of New York in Personal Actions: with an Appendix Practical Forms
Busb. – Busbee's Law Reports (N.C.)
Busb. Eq. – Busbee's Equity Reports (N.C.)
Busb. Law – Busbee's Law Reports (N.C.)
Bus. Franchise Guide (CCH) – Business Franchise Guide
Bush – Bush (Ky.)
Bus. Law. – Business Lawyer
Bus. L.J. – Business Law Journal
Bus. L. Rev. – Business Law Review
Bus. L. Today – Business Law Today
Buswell on Personal Injuries – The Civil Liability for Personal Injuries Arising Out of Negligence
Bus. Wk. – Business Week
Bx. County Adv. – Bronx Bar Association Advocate
Byles, Bills – A Treatise on the Law of Bills of Exchange, Promissory Notes, Bank-Notes and Checks
BYU Educ. & L.J. – Brigham Young University Education and Law Journal
BYU J. Pub. L. – Brigham Young University Journal of Public Law
BYU L. Rev. – Brigham Young University Law Review

C

C.A. – California Appellate Reports
C.A.A.F. – United State Court of Appeals for the Armed Forces
CAB – Civil Aeronautics Board Reports
Cai. Cas. – Caines' Cases (N.Y.)
Cai. R. – Caines' Reports (N.Y.)
Cal. – California Reports (Supreme Court)
Cal. 2d – California Reports, Second Series
Cal. 3d – California Reports, Third Series
Cal. 4th – California Reports, Fourth Series
Cal. Adv. Legis. Serv. – California Advance Legislative Service
Cal. App. – California Appellate Reports
Cal. App. Dec. – California Appellate Decisions
Cal. App. Supp. – California Appellate Reports Supplement
Cal. App. 2d – California Appellate Reports, Second Series
Cal. App. 2d Supp. – California Appellate Reports Supplement, Second Series
Cal. App. 3d – California Appellate Reports, Third Series
Cal. App. 3d Supp. – California Appellate Reports, Fourth Series
Cal. App. 4th – California Appellate Reports Supplement, Fourth Series
Cal. Bankr. J. – California Bankruptcy Journal
Cal. Code – California Code
Cal. Code Regs. – California Code of Regulations
Cal. Crim. L. Rev. – California Criminal Law Review
Cal. Dec. – California Decisions

Calif. L. Rev. – California Law Review
Cal. Jur. – California Jurisprudence
Cal. Jur. 2d – California Jurisprudence 2d
Cal. Jur. 3d – California Jurisprudence 3d
Call – Call (Va.)
Cal. Law. – California Lawyer
Cal. Legis. Serv. – California Legislative Service
Cal. Leg. Rec. – California Legal Record
Cal. L.J. – California Law Journal (San Francisco)
Cal. L. Rev. – California Law Review
Cal. Real Prop. J. – California Real Property Journal
Cal. Reg. L. Rep. – California Regulatory Law Reporter
Cal. Regulatory Notice Reg. – California Regulatory Notice Register
Cal. Rptr. – West's California Reporter
Cal. Rptr. 2d – West's California Reporter, Second Series
Cal. Stat. – Statutes of California
Cal. St. B.J. – California State Bar Journal
Cal. Unrep. – California Unreported Cases
Cal. W. Int'l L.J. – California Western International Law Journal
Cal. W. L. Rev. – California Western Law Review
Cam. & Nor. – Conference by Cameron & Norwood (N.C.)
Cambridge L.J. – Cambridge Law Journal
Campbell L. Rev. – Campbell Law Review
Can. B. Rev. – Canadian Bar Review
Can. Bus. L.J. – Canadian Business Law Journal
Can. Com. L. Guide (CCH) – Canadian Commercial Law Guide
Can. Fam. L.Q. – Canadian Family Law Quarterly
Can. Intell. Prop. Rev. – Canadian Intellectual Property Review
Can. J. Fam. L. – Canadian Journal of Family Law
Can. J.L. & Juris. – Canadian Journal of Law and Jurisprudence
Can. J.L. & Soc'y – Canadian Journal of Law and Society
Can. J. Women & L. – Canadian Journal of Women and the Law
Can. Tax J. – Canadian Tax Journal
Can. Tax Rep. (CCH) – Canadian Tax Reporter
Can.-U.S. L.J. – Canada-United States Law Journal
Can. Y.B. Int'l L. – Canadian Yearbook of International Law
CAP – Civil Air Patrol
Cap. Def. Dig. – Capital Defense Digest
Cap. Def. J. – Capital Defense Journal
Cap. U. L. Rev. – Capital University Law Review
Cardozo Arts & Ent. L.J. – Cardozo Arts and Entertainment Law Journal
Cardozo J. Int'l & Comp. L. – Cardozo Journal of International and Comparative Law
Cardozo L. Rev. – Cardozo Law Review
Cardozo Online J. Conflict Resol. – Cardozo Online Journal of Conflict Resolution
Cardozo Stud. L. & Lit. – Cardozo Studies in Law and Literature
Cardozo Women's L.J. – Cardozo Women's Law Journal
Car. L. Rep. – Carolina Law Repository (N.C.)
Carv. Carr. – Carver, A Treatise on the Law Relating to the Carriage of Goods by Sea
Case & Com. – Case and Comment
Case W. Res. J. Int'l L. – Case Western Reserve Journal of International Law
Case W. Res. L. Rev. – Case Western Reserve Law Review
Cas. On Trusts – Ames, A Selection of Cases on the Law of Trusts
Cath. Law. – Catholic Lawyer
Cath. U. Am. L. Rev. – Catholic University of America Law Review
Cath. U. L. Rev. – Catholic University Law Review
C.B. – Cumulative Bulletin
CBA Rec. – Chicago Bar Association Record
CBC – Clark Boardman Callaghan
C.B.C. – Collier's Bankruptcy Cases (MB)
CBO – Congressional Budget Office
C.C.A. – Circuit Court of Appeals
CCC – Commodity Credit Corporation
CCH – Commerce Clearing House
C.C.L.J. – Centre County Legal Journal (Pa.)
C.C.N. – Chief Counsel Notice (IRS)
C.C.P. – Code of Civil Procedure / Code of Criminal Procedure
C.C.P.A. – Court of Customs and Patent Appeals Reports
CCR – Commission on Civil Rights
CDC – Centers for Disease Control and Prevention
CEB – California Continuing Education of the Bar
CEC (CCH) – European Community Cases
Cent. Dig. – Century Digest
Cent. Law J. – Century Law Journal
CEQ – Council on Environmental Quality
cert. – certiorari
cert. denied – certiorari denied
C.F.R. – Code of Federal Regulations
CFTC – Commodity Futures Trading Commission
C.G.S.A. – Connecticut General Statutes Annotated
ch. – chapter
Chamberlain's Stare Decisis – Chamberlain, The Doctrine of Stare Decisis: Its Reasons and Extent
Chand. – Chandler (Wis.)
Chandler's Criminal Trials – Chandler, American Criminal Trials
Chap. L. Rev. – Chapman Law Review
Chapman L. Rev. – Chapman Law Review
Ch. D. – Law Reports Chancery Division (Eng.)
Chem. Reg. Rep. (BNA) – Chemical Regulation Reporter
Chester Co. Rep. – Chester County Reports (Pa.)
Chev. – Cheves (S.C.)
Chev. Eq. – Cheves' Equity Reports (S.C)
Chi. B. Rec. – Chicago Bar Record
Chicago Bar Rec. – Chicago Bar Record
Chicago Bd. Options Ex. Guide (CCH) – Chicago Board of Options Exchange Guide
Chicago L.B. – Chicago Law Bulletin
Chicago L.J. – Chicago Law Journal
Chicago L. Rec. – Chicago Law Record
Chicago L.T. – Chicago Law Times
Chicano-Latino L. Rev. – Chicano-Latino Law Review
Chicano L. Rev. – Chicano Law Review
Chi. J. Int'l L. – Chicago Journal of International Law
Chi.-Kent L. Rev. – Chicago-Kent Law Review
Child. Legal Rts. J. – Children's Legal Rights Journal
Chi. Leg. N. – Chicago Legal News
China L. Rep. – China Law Reporter (ABA)
Chi. Trib. – Chicago Tribune
Chitty, Bl. Comm. – Commentaries on the Laws of England by Sir Wm. Blackstone (Chitty ed.)
Chitty, Com. Law – Treatise on the Laws of Commerce and Manufacturing and the Contracts Relating Thereto
Chitty, Contracts – A Practical Treatise on the Law of Contracts
Chitty, Criminal Law – A Practical Treatise on Criminal Law
Chitty, Pl. – A Practical Treatise on Pleading, and on the Parties to Actions
Chitty, Prerogative – A Treatise on the Law of Prerogatives of the Crown and the Relative Duties and Rights of the Subject

Christian, Bankruptcy – Practical Instructions for Suing Out and Prosecuting a Commission of Bankruptcy, With the Best Modern Precedents, and a Digest of Supplemental Cases
CIA – Central Intelligence Agency
CIC – Consumer Information Center
Cin. L. Rev. – Cincinnati Law Review
C.I.R. – Commissioner of Internal Revenue
Cir. – Circuit Court of Appeals (federal)
Circles: Buff. Women's J.L. & Soc. Pol'y. – Circles: The Buffalo Women's Journal of Law and Social Policy
Cir. Ct. Rule – Circuit Court Rule
City L. – NYLS Citylaw
Civ. App. – Civil Appeals Reports
Civ. Code – Civil Code
Civ. Code Practice – Civil Code of Practice
Civ. Prac. Act – Civil Practice Act
Civ. St. – Civil Statutes
C.J. – Corpus Juris
C.J.S. – Corpus Juris Secundum
Cl. – Clause
C.L.A.I.T. – Constitutions and Laws of the American Indian Tribes
Clay's Dig. – Clay, A Digest of the Laws of the State of Alabama
Cl. Ch. – Clarke's Chancery Reports (N.Y.)
Cl. Ct. – United States Claims Court Reporter
Clearinghouse Rev. – Clearinghouse Review
C. Leg. Rec. – California Legal Record
Clev. B.J. – Cleveland Bar Journal
Clev. Insan. – Clevenger, Medical Jurisprudence of Insanity or Forensic Psychiatry
Clev. Law Rec. – Cleveland Law Recorder
Clev. Law Rep. – Cleveland Law Reporter
Clev.-Mar. L. Rev. – Cleveland-Marshall Law Review
Clev.-Marshall L. Rev. – Cleveland-Marshall Law Review
Clev. St. L. Rev. – Cleveland State Law Review
Clinical L. Rev. – Clinical Law Review: A Journal of Lawyering and Legal Education
C.L.J. – California Law Journal
C.L.J. & Lit. Rev. – California Law Journal and Literary Review
C.L.N. – Chicago Legal News
C.L.R. – California Law Review
CLS – Christian Legal Society
CLS Q. – CLS Quarterly
C.L.U. – Chartered Life Underwriters
CLU J. – CLU Journal
C.M.A. – Decisions of the United States Court of Military Appeals
C.M.L.R. – Common Market Law Reports
C.M.R. – Court Martial Reports
Cobb, Dig. – Cobb, A Digest of the Statute Laws of the State of Georgia
Cobb, Slav. – An Inquiry into the Law of Negro Slavery in the United States of America
Code Civ. Proc. – Code of Civil Procedure
Code Cr. Proc. – Code of Criminal Procedure
Code Gen. Laws – Code of General Laws
Code Me. R. – Code of Maine Rules
Code Prac. – Code of Practice
Code Proc. – Code of Procedure
Code Pub. Gen. Laws – Code of Public General Laws
Code Supp. – Supplement to a Code
Cod. St. – Codified Statutes
Cold. – Coldwell (Tenn.)
Cole. & Cai. Cas. – Coleman and Caines' Cases (N.Y.)
Cole. Cas. – Coleman's Cases (N.Y.)
Co. Inst. – Coke, Institutes of the Laws of England (four parts)
Co. Lit. – Coke, First Part of the Institutes of the Laws of England, or A Commentary Upon Littleton
Collective Bargaining Negot. & Cont. (BNA) – Collective Bargaining Negotiations and Contracts
College L. Dig. (Nat'l Ass'n College & Univ. Att'ys) – College Law Digest
Collier Bankr. Cas. (MB) – Collier Bankruptcy Cases
Collier Bankr. Cas. 2d (MB) – Collier Bankruptcy Cases, Second Series
Collyer, Partnership – A Practical Treatise on the Law of Partnership
Colo. – Colorado Reports
Colo. App. – Colorado Court of Appeals Reports
Colo. Code Regs. – Code of Colorado Regulations
Colo. J. Int'l Envtl. L. & Pol'y – Colorado Journal of International Environmental Law and Policy
Colo. Law. – Colorado Lawyer
Colo. Law Rep. – Colorado Law Reporter
Colo. Legis. Serv. – Colorado Legislative Service
Colo. Reg. – Colorado Register
Colo. Rev. Stat. – Colorado Revised Statutes
Colo. Rev. Stat. Ann. – Colorado Revised Statutes Annotated
Colo. Sess. Laws – Session Laws of Colorado
Colum. Bus. L. Rev. – Columbia Business Law Review
Colum. Hum. Rts. L. Rev. – Columbia Human Rights Law Review
Colum. J. Asian L. – Columbia Journal of Asian Law
Colum. J. E. Eur. L. – Columbia Journal of East European Law
Colum. J. Envtl. L. – Columbia Journal of Environmental Law
Colum. J. Eur. L. – Columbia Journal of European Law
Colum. J. Gender & L. – Columbia Journal of Gender and Law
Colum. J.L. & Arts – Columbia Journal of Law & the Arts
Colum. J.L. & Soc. Probs. – Columbia Journal of Law and Social Problems
Colum. J. Transnat'l L. – Columbia Journal of Transnational Law
Colum. L. Rev. – Columbia Law Review
Colum. Sci. & Tech. L. Rev. – Columbia Science and Technology Law Review
Colum. Surv. Hum. Rts. L. Rev. – Columbia Survey of Human Rights Law Review
Colum.-VLA J.L. & Arts – Columbia-VLA Journal of Law and the Arts
Com. & L. – Communications and the Law
Com. L.B. – Commercial Law Bulletin
Com. L. J. – Commercial Law Journal
COMM/ENT – COMM/ENT: A Journal of Entertainment and Communications Law
Comm. Fut. L. Rep. (CCH) – Commodity Futures Law Reporter Commodity Futures Law Reports
Comm. Law. – **1.** Commercial Lawyer. **2.** Communications Lawyer.
CommLaw Conspectus – CommLaw Conspectus: Journal of Communications Law and Policy
Comm. L.J. – Commercial Law Journal
Common Mkt. L. Rep. (CCH) – Common Market Law Reports
Common Mkt. L. Rev. – Common Market Law Review
Communications Reg. (P & F) – Communications Regulations
Community Prop. J. – Community Property Journal
Comp. Gen. – Decisions of the Comptroller General (U.S.)
Comp. Gen. Laws – Compiled General Laws

Comp. Lab. L. – Comparative Labor Law
Comp. Lab. L. & Pol'y J. – Comparative Labor Law & Policy Journal
Comp. Lab. L.J. – Comparative Labor Law Journal
Comp. Laws – Compiled Laws
Compleat Law. – Compleat Lawyer (ABA)
Comp. St. – Compiled Statutes
Comptr. Treas. Dec. – Comptroller Treasury Decisions
Computer & Internet Law. – The Computer and Internet Lawyer
Computer Law – The Computer Lawyer
Computer L. J. – Computer Law Journal
Computer/L.J. – Computer/Law Journal
Comyn on Cont. – **1.** The Law of Contracts and Promises in Various Subjects
Cong. – Congress. **2.** Congressional.
Cong. Dig. – Congressional Digest
Cong. Globe – Congressional Globe
Cong. Index (CCH) – Congressional Index
Cong. Rec. – Congressional Record
Conn. – Connecticut Reports
Conn. Acts – Connecticut Public & Special Acts
Conn. Agencies Regs. – Regulations of Connecticut State Agencies
Conn. App. – Connecticut Appellate Reports
Conn. B.J. – Connecticut Bar Journal
Conn. Cir. Ct. – Connecticut Circuit Court Reports
Conn. Gen. Stat. – General Statutes of Connecticut
Conn. Gen. Stat. Ann. – Connecticut General Statutes Annotated
Conn. Ins. L.J. – Connecticut Insurance Law Journal
Conn. J. Int'l L. – Connecticut Journal of International Law
Conn. Legis. Serv. – Connecticut Legislative Service
Conn. L.J. – Connecticut Law Journal
Conn. L. Rev. – Connecticut Law Review
Conn. L. Rptr. – Connecticut Law Reporter
Conn. Prob. L.J. – Connecticut Probate Law Journal
Conn. Pub. Acts – Connecticut Public Acts
Conn. Spec. Acts – Connecticut Special Acts
Conn. Super. Ct. – Connecticut Superior Reports
Conn. Supp. – Connecticut Supplement
Conn. Surr. – Connecticut Surrogate
Consol. T.S. – Parry's Consolidated Treaty Series
Con. St. – Consolidated Statutes
Const. – Constitution
Const. Amend. – Amendment to Constitution
Const. Comm. – Constitutional Commentary
Const. Comment. – Constitutional Commentary
Const. F. – Constitutional Forum
Construction Law. – Construction Lawyer
Const. U.S. Amend. – Amendment to the Constitution of the United States
Consumer Cred. Guide (CCH) – Consumer Credit Guide
Consumer Fin. L.Q. Rep. – Consumer Finance Law Quarterly Report
Consumer Prod. Safety Guide (CCH) – Consumer Product Safety Guide
Cont. – Contracts
Cont. App. Dec. (CCH) – Contract Appeals Decisions
Cont. Cas. Fed. (CCH) – Contracts Cases, Federal
Cont. of Banking (P-H) – Control of Banking
Conv. & Prop. Law. – Conveyancer and Property Lawyer
Conv. & Prop. Law. (n.s.) – Conveyancer and Property Lawyer (new series)
Cooke – Cooke (Tenn.)
Cooke, Ins. – The Law of Life Insurance, Including Accident Insurance and Insurance by Mutual Benefit Societies
Cooley, Const. Law – General Principles of Constitutional Law in the United States
Cooley, Const. Lim. – Treatise on the Constitutional Limitations Which Rest Upon
the Legislative Power of the States of the American Union
Cooley L. Rev. – Cooley Law Review
Cooley, Princ. Const. Law – General Principles of Constitutional Law in the United States
Cooley's Blackstone – Commentaries on the Laws of England by Sir Wm. Blackstone (Cooley ed.)
Cooley, Tax'n – A Treatise on the Law of Taxation: Including the Law of Local Assessments
Cooley, Torts – Treatise on the Law of Torts, Or Wrongs Which Arise Independent of Contracts
Copy. Bull. – Copyright Bulletin
Copy. Dec. – Copyright Decisions
Copyright L. Dec. (CCH) – Copyright Law Decisions
Copyright L. Rep. (CCH) – **1.** Copyright Law Reporter. **2.** Copyright Law Reports.
Copyright L. Symp. (ASCAP) – Copyright Law Symposium (American Society of Composers, Authors, & Publishers)
Cornell Int'l. L.J. – Cornell International Law Journal
Cornell J.L. & Pub. Pol'y – Cornell Journal of Law and Public Policy
Cornell L.F. – Cornell Law Forum
Cornell L.J. – Cornell Law Journal
Cornell L.Q. – Cornell Law Quarterly
Cornell L. Rev. – Cornell Law Review
Corp. Couns. – Corporate Counsel
Corp. Couns. Q. – Corporate Counsel Quarterly
Corp. Couns. Wkly (BNA) – Corporate Counsel Weekly
Corp. Guide (Aspen Law & Bus.) – Corporation Guide
Corp. L. Rev. – Corporation Law Review
Corp. Tax'n – Corporate Taxation
Cost Accounting Stand. Guide (CCH) – Cost Accounting Standards Guide
Cow. – Cowen's Reports (N.Y.)
Cow. Cr. R. – Cowen's Criminal Reports (N.Y.)
C.P. – Common Pleas
C.P.A. – Certified Public Accountant
CPSC – Consumer Product Safety Commission
Cr. Act – Criminal Act
Cranch – **1.** Cranch, U.S. Supreme Court Reports. **2.** Cranch (D.C.).
Cranch, Pat. Dec. – Cranch's Patent Decisions
Cr. Code – Criminal Code
Creighton L. Rev. – Creighton Law Review
Crime & Delinq. – Crime and Delinquency
Crime & Just. – Crime and Justice
Crim. Just. – Criminal Justice (ABA)
Crim. Just. & Behav. – Criminal Justice and Behavior
Crim. Just. Ethics – Criminal Justice Ethics
Crim. Justice Q. – Criminal Justice Quarterly
Crim. Just. J. – Criminal Justice Journal
Crim. Law Bull. – Criminal Law Bulletin
Crim. L. Bull. – Criminal Law Bulletin
Crim. L.F. – Criminal Law Forum
Crim. L.J. – Criminal Law Journal
Crim. L.Q. – Criminal Law Quarterly
Crim. L. Rep. (BNA) – Criminal Law Reporter
Crim. L. Rev. – Criminal Law Review
Crim. L. Rptr. (BNA) – Criminal Law Reporter
Crim. Rpts. – Criminal Reports
Cr. Prac. Act – Criminal Practice Act
Cr. Proc. Act – Criminal Procedure Act
CRR – Corporate Reorganization Reporter, Inc.
C.R.S. – Colorado Revised Statutes

Cr. St. – Criminal Statutes
CSC – Civil Service Commission
CTBTO – Comprehensive Nuclear Test-Ban-Treaty Organization
Ct. Cl. – Court of Claims Reports
Ct. Cust. – Court of Customs Appeals Reports
Ct. Int'l Trade – Court of International Trade Reports
Ct. Rev. – Court Review (American Judges Assoc.)
C.U. – California Unreported Cases
Cumb. L.J. – Cumberland Law Journal
Cumb. L. Rev. – Cumberland Law Review
Cumb.-Sam. L. Rev. – Cumberland-Samford Law Review
Current Ct. Dec. – Current Court Decisions
Current Legal Probs. – Current Legal Problems
Current Med. for Att'ys – Current Medicine for Attorneys
Currents: Int'l Trade L.J. – Currents: The International Trade Law Journal
Curtis on History of the Constitution – Curtis, History of the Origin, Formation, and Adoption of the Constitution of the United States
Cush. – Cushing (Mass.)
Cust. B. & Dec. – Customs Bulletin and Decisions
Cust. Ct. – Customs Court Reports
C.W.L.R. – California Western Law Review
C.Z. Code – Canal Zone Code (Panama)

D

Daily Lab. Rep. (BNA) – Daily Labor Report
Dak. – Dakota Reports (Territorial)
Dakota – Dakota Reports
Dak. L. Rev. – Dakota Law Review
Dalhousie J. Legal Stud. – Dalhousie Journal of Legal Studies
Dalhousie L.J. – Dalhousie Law Journal
Dall. – **1.** Dallas, U.S. Supreme Court Reports. **2.** Dallas (Pa.).
Dallam – **1.** Digest of the Laws of Texas. **2.** Dallam's Opinions (Tex.).
Dana – Dana (Ky.)
D. & C. – Pennsylvania District & County Reports
D. & C. 2d – Pennsylvania District & County Reports, Second Series
D. & C. 3d – Pennsylvania District & County Reports, Third Series
D. & C. 4th – Pennsylvania District & County Reports, Fourth Series
Daniel, Neg. Inst. – A Treatise on the Law of Negotiable Instrument
Dart, Vend. – A Treatise on the Law and Practice Relating to Vendors and Purchasers of Real Estate
Davis, Cr. Law – A Treatise on Criminal Law, with an Exposition on the Office and Authority of Justices of the Peace in Virginia
Day – Day (Conn.)
D.C.B.J. – District of Columbia Bar Journal
D.C.C.E. – District of Columbia Code Encyclopedia
D.C. Code Ann. – District of Columbia Code Annotated
D. Chip. – D. Chipman (Vt.)
D.C. L. Rev. – District of Columbia Law Review
D.C. Mun. Regs. – District of Columbia Municipal Regulations
D.C. Reg. – District of Columbia Register
D.C. Stat. – District of Columbia Statutes
DEA – Drug Enforcement Administration
Decalogue J. – Decalogue Journal
Dec. Comm'r Pat. – Decisions of the Commissioner of Patents
Dec. Dig. – Decennial Digest
Dec. U.S. Mar. Comm'n – Decisions of the United States Maritime Commission
Def. – Defense
Def. Couns. J. – Defense Counsel Journal
Defense L.J. – Defense Law Journal
Del. – Delaware Reports
Del. Cas. – Delaware Cases
Del. Ch. – Delaware Chancery Reports
Del. Code Ann. – Delaware Code Annotated
Del. County – Delaware County Reports
Del. J. Corp. L. – Delaware Journal of Corporate Law
Del. Law. – Delaware Lawyer
Del. Laws – Laws of Delaware
Del. Term R. – Delaware Term Reports
Denio – Denio's Reports (N.Y.)
Den. J. Int'l L. & Pol'y – Denver Journal of International Law and Policy
Den. L. J. – Denver Law Journal
Den. L.N. – Denver Legal News
Denver L. N. – Denver Legal News
Denv. J. Int'l L. & Pol'y – Denver Journal of International Law and Policy
Denv. L. Ctr. J. – Denver Law Center Journal
Denv. L.J. – Denver Law Journal
Denv. U. L. Rev. – Denver University Law Review
DePaul Bus. L.J. – DePaul Business Law Journal
DePaul Dig. Int'l L. – DePaul Digest of International Law
DePaul J. Health Care L. – DePaul Journal of Health Care Law
DePaul-LCA J. Art & Ent. L. – DePaul-LCA Journal of Art and Entertainment Law
DePaul L. Rev. – DePaul Law Review
Dep't St. Bull. – Department of State Bulletin
Des. – Desausssure's Equity Reports (S.C.)
Desty, Tax'n – The American Law of Taxation as Determined in the Courts of Last Resort in the United States
Det. C.L. Mich. St. U. L. Rev. – Detroit College of Law at Michigan State University Law Review
Det. C. L. Rev. – Detroit College Law Review
Det. L.J. – Detroit Law Journal
Detroit B.Q. – Detroit Bar Quarterly
Detroit Law. – Detroit Lawyer
Detroit Leg. N. – Detroit Legal News
Detroit L. Rev. – Detroit Law Review
Dev. – Devereux's Law Reports (N.C.)
Dev. & Bat. – Devereux & Battle's Law Reports (N.C.)
Dev. & Bat. Eq. – Devereux & Battle's Equity Reports (N.C.)
Devlin, Deeds – Treatise on the Law of Deeds: Their Form, Requisites, Execution, Acknowledgement, Registration, Construction, and Effect
DHHS – Department of Health and Human Services
DIA – Defense Intelligence Agency
Dicey, Constitution – Introduction to the Study of the Law of the Constitution
Dicey, Parties – A Treatise on the Rules for the Selection of the Parties to an Action
Dick. J. Envtl. L. & Pol'y – Dickinson Journal of Environmental Law & Policy
Dick. J. Int'l L. – Dickinson Journal of International Law
Dick. L. Rev. – Dickinson Law Review
Dig. – Digest
Dig. & Dec. Empl. Comp. App. Bd. – Digest & Decisions of the Employees' Compensation Appeals Board
Dig. Int'l L. – Digest of International Law
Dillon, Mun. Corp. – Treatise on the Law of Municipal Corporations

Disp. Res. J. — Dispute Resolution Journal
Disp. Resol. J. — Dispute Resolution Journal
Dist. Law. — District Lawyer
D.L.R. — Dominion Law Reports (Can.)
D.L.R. 2d — Dominion Law Reports, Second Series
D.L.R. 3d — Dominion Law Reports, Third Series
D.L.R. 4th — Dominion Law Reports, 4th Series
DOD — Department of Defense
DOE — Department of Energy
DOJ Alert — Department of Justice Alert
Dominion Tax. Cas. (CCH) — Dominion Tax Cases
DOT — Department of Transportation
Doug. — Douglass (Mich.)
Drake J. Agric. L. — Drake Journal of Agricultural Law
Drake L. Rev. — Drake Law Review
Drone on Copyright — Drone, A Treatise on the Law of Property in Intellectual Productions in Great Britain and the United States: Embracing Copyright in Works of Literature and Art and Playright in Dramatic and Musical Compositions
Dud. — Dudley (S.C.)
Dud. Eq. — Dudley's Equity Reports (S.C.)
Duer, Mar. Ins. — The Law and Practice of Marine Insurance
Duer, Rep. — A Lecture on the Law of Representations in Marine Insurance
Duke Envtl. L. & Pol'y F. — Duke Environmental Law & Policy Forum
Duke Int'l & Comp. L. Ann. — Duke International and Comparative Law Annual
Duke J. Comp. & Int'l L. — Duke Journal of Comparative & International Law
Duke J. Gender L. & Pol'y — Duke Journal of Gender Law & Policy
Duke L.J. — Duke Law Journal
Du Ponceau, Const. — A Brief View of the Constitution of the United States
Duq. Bus. L. J. — Duquesne Business Law Journal
Duq. L. Rev. — Duquesne Law Review
Duv. — Duvall (Ky.)
DWI — Driving while intoxicated
D.W.I. — Descriptive Word Index

E

E.A.S. — Executive Agreement Series
ECA — Economic Commission for Africa
ECE — Economic Commission for Europe
ECLAC — Economic Commission for Latin America and the Caribbean
Ecology L.Q. — Ecology Law Quarterly
Ed. Law Rep. — West's Education Law Reporter
Edm. Sel. Cas. — Edmond's Selected Cases (N.Y.)
Edw. Ch. — Edward's Chancery Reports (N.Y.)
E.E.C. — European Economic Community
EEOC — Equal Employment Opportunity Commission
EEOC Compl. Man. (BNA) — EEOC Compliance Manual
EEOC Compl. Man. (CCH) — EEOC Compliance Manual
E. Eur. Const. Rev. — East European Constitutional Review
EIPR — European Intellectual Property Review
Elder L.J. — Elder Law Journal
Elder's Advisor — Elder's Advisor: The Journal of Elder Law and Post-Retirement Planning
ELI — Environmental Law Institute
Ell. Deb. — Elliot's Debates: The Debates in the Several State Conventions on the Adoption of the Federal Constitution: As Recommended by the General Convention at Philadelphia in 1787.
Elm. Dig. — Elmer, A Digest of the Laws of New Jersey
Elmer, Lun. — J. Elmer, The Practice of Lunacy Under Commissions and Inquisitions
Emerging Issues St. Const. L. — Emerging Issues in State Constitutional Law
E. Min. L. Inst. — Eastern Mineral Law Institute
Emory Int'l L. Rev. — Emory International Law Review
Emory J. Int'l Disp. Resol. — Emory Journal of International Dispute Resolution
Emory L.J. — Emory Law Journal
Empl. & Training Rep. (BNA) — Employment and Training Reporter
Empl. Comp. App. Bd. — Decisions of the Employees' Compensation Appeals Board
Empl. Coord. (RIA) — Employment Coordinator
Empl. Coordinator (RIA) — Employment Coordinator
Employee Benefits Cas. (BNA) — Employee Benefits Cases
Employee Rel. L.J. — Employee Relations Law Journal
Employee Rts. & Emp. Pol'y J. — Employee Rights & Employment Policy Journal
Empl. Prac. Dec. (CCH) — Employment Practices Decisions
Empl. Prac. Guide (CCH) — Employment Practices Guide
Empl. Safety & Health Guide (CCH) — Employment Safety and Health Guide
Emp. Rel. L.J. — Employee Relations Law Journal
Energy & Min. L. Inst. — Energy & Mineral Law Institute
Energy L.J. — Energy Law Journal
Energy Mgmt. (CCH) — Energy Management
Eng. Rep. — English Reports-Full Reprint
Ent. & Sp. L.J. — Entertainment & Sports Law Journal
Ent. & Sports Law — Entertainment & Sports Lawyer (ABA)
Ent. L. J. — Entertainment Law Journal
Environs Envtl. L. & Pol'y J. — Environs Environmental Law & Policy Journal
Env. L. Rep. (ELI) — Environmental Law Reporter
Envtl. Aff. — Environmental Affairs
Envtl. & Plan. L.J. — Environmental and Planning Law Journal
Envtl. Claims J. — Environmental Claims Journal
Envtl. F. — Environmental Forum
Envtl. L. — Environmental Law
Envtl. L. & Litig. — Environmental Law and Litigation
Envtl. Law. — Environmental Lawyer
Envtl. L.Q. Newsl. — Environmental Law Quarterly Newsletter (ABA)
Envtl. L. Rep. (Envtl. L. Inst.) — Environmental Law Reporter (Environmental Law Institute)
Envtl. Prac. News — Environmental Practice News
Env't Rep. (BNA) — Environment Reporter
Env't Rep. Cas. (BNA) — Environment Reporter Cases
EO — Executive Order
EPA — Environmental Protection Agency
Eq. Empl. Compl. Man. (CBC) — Equal Employment Compliance Manual
Eq. Jur. — **1.** Equitable Jurisdiction. **2.** Equity Jurisprudence.
Eq. Pl. — Equity Pleading
ERDA — Energy Research and Development Administration
Erie — Erie County Legal Journal, Pa.
ERISA — Employee Retirement Income Security Act
ERISA Litig. Rep. — ERISA Litigation Reporter
ESCAP — Economic and Social Commission for Asia and the Pacific
ESCOR — Economic and Social Council Official Record (UN)
ESCWA — Economic and Social Commission for Western Asia
ESOP — Employee Stock Ownership Plan
Est. Plan. — Estate Planning
EU — European Union
EURATOM — European Atomic Energy Commission

Eur. Bus. L. Rev. – European Business Law Review
Eur. Ct. H.R. – European Court on Human Rights
Eur. H.R. Rep. – European Human Rights Reports
Eur. L. Rev. – European Law Review
Ex. D. – Law Reports, Exchequer Division (Eng.)
Exec. Disclosure Guide (CCH) – Executive Disclosure Guide
Exec. Ord. – Executive Order
Exempt Org. Rep. (CCH) – Exempt Organizations Reports
EXIMBANK – Export-Import Bank of the United States

F

F. – Federal Reporter
F.2d. – Federal Reporter, Second Series
F.3d. – Federal Reporter, Third Series
FAA – Federal Aviation Administration
Fair Empl. Prac. Cas. (BNA) – Fair Employment Practice Cases
Fam. Advoc. – Family Advocate (ABA)
Fam. Advocate – Family Advocate (ABA)
Fam. & Conciliation Cts. Rev. – Family and Conciliation Courts Review
Fam. Ct. Rev. – Family Court Review
Fam. L. Newsl. – Family Law Newsletter (ABA)
Fam. L.Q. – Family Law Quarterly (ABA)
Fam. L. Rep. (BNA) – Family Law Reporter
Fam. L. Tax. Guide (CCH) – Family Law Tax Guide
FAO – Food and Agriculture Organization of the United Nations
F.App. – Federal Appendix
F.Appx. – Federal Appendix
F.App'x – Federal Appendix
Farwell, Powers – A Concise Treatise on Powers
FASB – Financial Accounting Standards Board
FBI – Federal Bureau of Investigation
F.B.I.S. – Foreign Broadcast Information Service
FCA – Farm Credit Administration
F. Cas. – Federal Cases
F.C.C. – **1.** Federal Communications Commission. **2.** Federal Communications Commission Reports.
F.C.C.2d – Federal Communications Commission Reports, 2d Series
F.C.C.R. – Federal Communications Commission Record
F.C.C. Rec. – Federal Communications Commission Record
FCIA – Foreign Credit Insurance Associatoin
FCIC – Federal Crop Insurance Corporation
FDA – Food and Drug Administration
FDAA – Federal Disaster Assistance Administration
FDIC – Federal Deposit Insurance Corporation
FEA – Federal Energy Administration
FEC – Federal Election Commission
Fed. Audit Guide (CCH) – Federal Audit Guide
Fed. Banking L. Rep. (CCH) – **1.** Federal Banking Law Reporter. **2.** Federal Banking Law Reports.
Fed. B.A. Sec. Tax'n Rep. – Federal Bar Association Section of Taxation Report
Fed. B.J. – Federal Bar Journal
Fed. B. News. – Federal Bar News
Fed. B. News & J. – Federal Bar News and Journal
Fed. Carr. Cas. (CCH) – Federal Carriers Cases
Fed. Carr. Rep. (CCH) – Federal Carriers Reports
Fed. Cas. – Federal Cases (U.S.)
Fed. Cas. No. – Federal Cases Number
Fed. Cir. B.J. – Federal Circuit Bar Journal
Fed. Cl. – Federal Claims Reporter
Fed. Com. L.J. – Federal Communications Law Journal
Fed. Comm. L.J. – Federal Communications Law Journal
Fed. Cont. Rep. (BNA) – Federal Contracts Report
Fed. Cts. L. Rev. – Federal Courts Law Review (Internet)
Fed. Election Camp. Fin. Guide (CCH) – Federal Election Campaign Financing Guide
Fed. Energy Reg. Comm'n Rep. (CCH) – Federal Energy Regulatory Commission Reports
Fed. Est. & Gift Tax Rep. (CCH) – **1.** Federal Estate and Gift Tax Reporter. **2.** Federal Estate and Gift Tax Reports.
Fed. Ex. Tax Rep. (CCH) – Federal Excise Tax Reporter
Fed. Home Loan Bank Bd. J. – Federal Home Loan Bank Board Journal
Fed. Inc. Gift & Est. Tax'n (MB) – Federal Income, Gift and Estate Taxation
Fed. Law. – Federal Lawyer
Fed. L. Rev. – Federal Law Review
Fed'n Ins. & Corp. Couns. Q. – Federation of Insurance and Corporate Counsel Quarterly
Fed'n Ins. Counsel Q. – Federation of Insurance Counsel Quarterly
Fed'n Ins. Couns. Q. – Federation of Insurance Counsel Quarterly
Fed. Probation – Federal Probation
Fed. R. App. P. – Federal Rules of Appellate Procedure
Fed. R. Civ. P. – Federal Rules of Civil Procedure
Fed. R. Crim. P. – Federal Rules of Criminal Procedure
Fed. Reg. – Federal Register
Fed. Rep. – Federal Reporter
Fed. Res. Bull. – Federal Reserve Bulletin
Fed. R. Evid. – Federal Rules of Evidence
Fed. R. Serv. (CBC) – Federal Rules Service
Fed. R. Serv. 2d (CBC) – Federal Rules Service, 2d Series
Fed. R. Serv. 3d (CBC) – Federal Rules Service, 3d Series
Fed. Sec. L. Rep. (CCH) – Federal Securities Law Reporter
Fed. Sec. L. Serv. (CCH) – Federal Securities Law Service
Fed. Serv. Imp. Pan. Rels. – Federal Service Impasses Panel Releases
Fed. Tax Coord. 2d (RIA) – Federal Tax Coordinator, Second Edition
Fed. Taxes (P-H) – Federal Taxes
Fed. Tax Guide Rep. (CCH) – Federal Tax Guide Reports
Fell, Guar. – A Treatise on the Law of Mercantile Guaranties, and of Principal and Surety in General
FEP (BNA) – Fair Employment Practice Cases
FEP Cas. (BNA) – Fair Employment Practice Cases
F.E.R.C. – Federal Energy Guidelines: FERC Reports
FET – Federal Estate Tax
Fett. Carr. – Fetter, A Treatise on the Law of Carriers of Passengers
FHA – Federal Housing Administration
FHLB – Federal Home Loan Bank
FHLBB – Federal Home Loan Bank Board
FHLMC – Federal Home Loan Mortgage Corporation (Freddie Mac)
FHWA – Federal Highway Administration
FIA – Federal Insurance Administration
FICA – Federal Insurance Contribution Act
Fiduciary – Fiduciary Reporter (Pa.)
Field, Corp. – A Treatise on the Law of Private Corporations
Fire & Casualty Cas. (CCH) – Fire and Casualty Cases
Fisher, Mort. – The Law of Mortgage and Other Securities upon Property
Fla. – Florida Reports
Fla. Admin. Code Ann. – Florida Administrative Code Annotated
Fla. Admin. Weekly – Florida Administrative Weekly
Fla. B.J. – Florida Bar Journal

Fla. Coastal L.J. – Florida Coastal Law Journal
Fla. Ent. Art & Sport L.J. – Florida Entertainment, Art & Sport Law Journal
Fla. Int'l L.J. – Florida International Law Journal
Fla. J. Int'l L. – Florida Journal of International Law
Fla. Jur. – Florida Jurisprudence
Fla. Jur. 2d – Florida Jurisprudence 2d
Fla. Laws – Laws of Florida
Fla. L.J. – Florida Law Journal
Fla. L. Rev. – Florida Law Review
Fla. L. Weekly – Florida Law Weekly
Fla. L. Weekly Supp. – Florida Law Weekly Supplement
Fland. Const. – Flanders, An Exposition on the Constitution of the United States
Flanders, Fire Ins. – A Treatise on the Law of Fire Insurance
Fla. Sess. Law Serv. – Florida Session Law Service
Fla. Stat. – Florida Statutes
Fla. Stat. Ann. – Florida Statutes Annotated
Fla. St. U.J. Land Use & Envtl. L. – Florida State University Journal of Land Use and Environmental Law
Fla. St. U. J. Transnat'l L. & Pol 'y – Florida State University Journal of Transnational Law and Policy
Fla. St. U. L. Rev. – Florida State University Law Review
Fla. Supp. – Florida Supplement
Fla. Supp. 2d. – Florida Supplement, Second Series
Fla. Tax Rev. – Florida Tax Review
Fletcher F. – Fletcher Forum
Fletcher F. World Aff. – Fletcher Forum of World Affairs
Flood, Lib. – A Treatise on the Law Concerning Libel and Slander
Flood, Wills – An Elementary Treatise on the Law Relating to Wills of Personal Property
F.L.R.A. – Decisions of the Federal Labor Relations Authority
F.M.C. – Federal Maritime Commission Reports
FMCS – Federal Mediation and Conciliation Service
FmHA – Farmers Home Administration
F.M.S.H.R.C. – Federal Mine Safety & Health Review Commission Reports
FNMA – Federal National Mortgage Association (Fannie Mae)
FOIA – Freedom of Information Act
Food & Drug L.J. – Food & Drug Law Journal
Food Drug Cosm. L.J. – Food Drug Cosmetic Law Journal
Food Drug Cosm. L. Rep. (CCH) – 1. Food Drug Cosmetic Law Reporter. 2. Food Drug Cosmetic Law Reports.
Foote, Priv. Int. Jur. – Foreign and Domestic Law: A Concise Treatise on Private International Jurisprudence
For. Def. – For the Defense
Fordham Ent. Media & Intell. Prop. L. F. – Fordham Entertainment, Media and Intellectual Property Law Forum
Fordham Envtl. L.J. – Fordham Environmental Law Journal
Fordham Envtl. L. Rep. – Florida Environmental Law Report
Fordham Fin. Sec. & Tax L.F. – Fordham Finance, Securities & Tax Law Forum
Fordham Intell. Prop. Media & Ent. L.J. – Fordham Intellectual Property, Media & Entertainment Law Journal
Fordham Int'l L.F. – Fordham International Law Forum
Fordham Int'l L.J. – Fordham International Law Journal
Fordham J. Corp. & Fin. L. – Fordham Journal of Corporate and Financial Law
Fordham L. Rev. – Fordham Law Review
Fordham Urb. L.J. – Fordham Urban Law Journal
For the Def. – For the Defense
Forum – The Forum
Foster, Fed. Prac. – A Treatise on Federal Practice, Civil and Criminal...
F.P.C. – Federal Power Commission Reports
F.R. – Federal Register
Franchise L.J. – Franchise Law Journal (ABA)
FRB – Federal Reserve Board
F.R.D. – Federal Rules Decisions
"Freddie Mae" – Federal National Mortgage Association
"Freddie Mac" – Federal Home Loan Mortgage Corporation
Freeman, Judgments – A Treatise on the Law of Judgments: including All Final Determinations of the Rights of Parties in Actions or Proceedings in Law or in Equity
FRS – Federal Reserve System
Fry, Sp. Perf. – A Treatise on the Specific Performance of Contracts
F.S.A. – Florida Statues Annotated
FSLIC – Federal Savings and Loan Insurance Corporation
FSIS – Food Safety and Inspection Service
F. Supp. – Federal Supplement
F. Supp.2d. – Federal Supplement, Second Series
F.T.C. – Federal Trade Commission Reports
FUTA – Federal Unemployment Tax Act
FWS – Fish and Wildlife Service

G

Ga. – Georgia Reports
GAAP – Generally accepted accounting principles
Ga. App. – Georgia Appeals Reports
Ga. B.J. – Georgia Bar Journal
Ga. Bus. Law. – Georgia Business Lawyer
Ga. Code Ann. – Code of Georgia Annotated
Ga. Comp. R. & Regs. – Official Compilation of Rules & Regulations of the State of Georgia
Ga. Dec. – Georgia Decisions
Ga. J. Int'l & Comp. L. – Georgian Journal of International and Comparative Law
Ga. J. S. Legal Hist. – Georgia Journal of Southern Legal History
Ga. Laws – Georgia Laws
Gale, Eas. – A Treatise on the Law of Easements
Ga. L.J. – Georgia Law Journal
Gall. – Gallison (U.S. Circuit Court)
Ga. L. Rep. – Georgia Law Reporter
Ga. L. Rev. – Georgia Law Review
G.& J. – Gill and Johnson (Md.)
GAO – General Accounting Office
GAOR – General Assembly Official Record (U.N.)
Ga. St. B.J. – Georgia State Bar Journal
Ga. St. U. L. Rev. – Georgia State University Law Review
Ga. Supp. – Georgia Supplement
GATT – General Agreement on Tariffs and Trade
GATS – General Agreement on Trade in Services
Gavel – Gavel-Milwaukee Bar Assoc.
Gaz. – Weekly Law Gazette (U.S.)
Gaz. Bankr. – Gazette of Bankruptcy
Gaz. L.R. – Gazette Law Reports
G.C.M. – General Counsel Memorandum (IRS)
Gen. Couns. Mem. – General Counsel Memorandum (IRS)
Gen. Dig. U.S. – General Digest of the United States
Gen. Laws – General Laws
Gen. St. – General Statutes
Geo. Immigr. L.J. – Georgetown Immigration Law Journal
Geo. Int'l Envtl. L. Rev. – Georgetown International Environmental Law Review

Geo. J. Gender & L. – Georgetown Journal of Gender and the Law
Geo. J. Int'l Aff. – Georgetown Journal of International Affairs
Geo. J. Legal Ethics – Georgetown Journal of Legal Ethics
Geo. J. on Fighting Pov. – Georgetown Journal on Fighting Poverty
Geo. J. on Fighting Poverty – Georgetown Journal on Fighting Poverty
Geo. J. on Poverty L. & Pol'y – Georgetown Journal on Poverty Law and Policy
Geo. L. J. – Georgetown Law Journal
Geo. J. L. & Pub. Pol'y – Georgetown Journal of Law & Public Policy
Geo. Mason Indep. L. Rev. – George Mason Independent Law Review
Geo. Mason L. Rev. – George Mason Law Review
Geo. Mason U. Civ. Rts. L.J. – George Mason University Civil Rights Law Journal
Geo. Mason U. L. Rev. – George Mason University Law Review
Geo. Pub. Pol'y Rev. – Georgetown Public Policy Review
Geo. U.L. Ctr. Immig. Rep. – Georgetown University Law Center Immigration Reporter
Geo. Wash. J. Int'l L. & Econ. – George Washington Journal of International Law and Economics
Geo. Wash. Int'l L. Rev. – George Washington International Law Review
Geo. Wash. L. Rev. – George Washington Law Review
Gild. – Gildersleeve Reports (N.M.)
Gill – Gill (Md.)
Gilm. – Gilman (Ill.)
Gilmer – Gilmer (Va.)
"Ginnie Mae" – Government National Mortgage Association
Glasser CLE. – Glasser LegalWorks Seminars
Glendale L. Rev. – Glendale Law Review
GMU L. Rev. – George Mason University Law Review
GNMA – Government National Mortgage Association (Ginnie Mae)
GNP – Gross National Product
Godd. Easem. – Goddard, A Treatise on the Law of Easements
Golden Gate L. Rev. – Golden Gate Law Review
Golden Gate U. L. Rev. – Golden Gate University Law Review
Gonz. L. Rev. – Gonzaga Law Review
Gould on Waters – J.M. Gould, A Treatise on the Law of Waters, including Riparian Rights, and Public and Private Rights
Gould, Pl. – Jam. Gould, A Treatise on the Principles of Pleading in Civil Actions
Gould's Dig. – Jos. Gould, A Digest of the Statutes of Arkansas
Gov't Cont. Rep. (CCH) – **1.** Government Contracts Reports. **2.** Government Contracts Reporter.
Gov't Empl. Rel. Rep (WG&L) – Government Employee Relations Report
Gov't Pub. Rev. – Government Publications Review
GPO – Government Printing Office
GP Solo & Small Firm Law. – GP, Solo and Small Firm Lawyer (ABA)
Grant – Grant (Pa.)
Grant, Bank. – A Treatise on the Law Relating to Bankers and Banking
Grant on Corp. – A Practical Treatise on the Law of Corporations In General
Gratt. – Grattan (Va.)
Graven Images – Graven Images: A Journal of Culture, Law and the Sacred
Gray – Gray (Mass.)
Gray on Perpetuities – The Rule Against Perpetuities
Gray, Perp. – The Rule Against Perpetuities
Great Plains Nat. Resources J. – Great Plains Natural Resources Journal
Green Bag 2d. – Green Bag, Second Series
Greene – Greene (Iowa)
Greenl. Ev. – A Treatise on the Law of Evidence
Greenleaf on Evidence – A Treatise on the Law of Evidence
Gresley, Eq. Ev. – A Treatise on the Law of Evidence in Courts of Equity
Gross, Guild Merchant – The Gild Merchant: A Contribution to British Municipal History
GSA – General Services Administration
Guam – Guam Reports
Guam Admin. R. & Regs. – Administrative Rules & Regulations of the Government of Guam
Guam Civ. Code – Guam Civil Code
Guam Civ. P. Code – Guam Code of Civil Procedure
Guam Code Ann. – Guam Code Annotated
Guam Gov't Code – Guam Government Code
Guam Sess. Laws – Guam Session Laws
Guild Prac. – Guild Practitioner
Gunby – Gunby's Reports (La.)
Guy, Med. Jur. – Principles of Medical Jurisprudence: with So Much Anatomy, Physiology, Pathology, and the Practice of Medicine and Surgery as are Essential to be Known by Lawyers, Coroners, Magistrates, Officers of the Army and Navy, etc., etc.

H

Hale, Precedents and Proceedings – A Series of Precedents and Proceedings in Criminal Causes Extending from the Year 1475 to 1640...
Hall, Adm. Practice – J. Hall, The Practice and Jurisdiction of the Court of Admiralty
Hall, Int. Law – A Treatise on International Law
Halleck, Int. Law – International Law, or Rules Regulating the Intercourse of States in Peace and War
Halsbury – **1.** Halsbury's Laws of England. **2.** Halsbury's Statutes of England.
Halsbury's S.I.s. – Halsbury's Statutory Instruments
Ham. Cont. – Hammon, The General Principles of the Law of Contract
Ham. Fed. – Hamilton, The Federalist [Papers]
Hamline J. Pub. L. – Hamline Journal of Public Law
Hamline J. Pub. L. & Pol'y – Hamline Journal of Public Law and Policy
Hamline L. Rev. – Hamline Law Review
H. & G. – Harris and Gill (Md.)
H. & J. – Harris and Johnson (Md.)
H. & McH. – Harris and McHenry (Md.)
Hanh. Mar. Wom. – Hanhart, A Treatise on the Law Relating to the Property of Married Women
Hard. – Hardin (Ky.)
Hare, Am. Const. Law – American Constitutional Law
Hare, Disc. – A Treatise on Discovery of Evidence, By Bill and Answer in Equity
Hare, Ev. – A Treatise on Discovery of Evidence, By Bill and Answer in Equity
Hare on Discovery – A Treatise on Discovery of Evidence, By Bill and Answer in Equity
Harm. Pen. Man. – Harmon, A Manual of the Pension Laws of the United States of America
Harp. – Harper (S.C.)
Harp. Eq. – Harper's Equity Reports (S.C.)

Harr. — Harrington (Del.)
Harr. Cr. L. — Harris, Principles of the Criminal Law
Hart. Dig. — Hartley, A Digest of the Laws of Texas
Harvard L.R. — Harvard Law Review
Harv. BlackLetter J. — Harvard BlackLetter Journal
Harv. BlackLetter L.J. — Harvard BlackLetter Law Journal
Harv. Bus. Rev. — Harvard Business Review
Harv. C.R.-C.L. L. Rev. — Harvard Civil Rights-Civil Liberties Law Review
Harv. Envtl. L. Rev. — Harvard Environmental Law Review
Harv. Hum. Rts. J. — Harvard Human Rights Journal
Harv. Hum. Rts. Y.B. — Harvard Human Rights Yearbook
Harv. Int'l. L.J. — Harvard International Law Journal
Harv. J.L. & Pub. Pol'y — Harvard Journal of Law and Public Policy
Harv. J.L. & Tech. — Harvard Journal of Law & Technology
Harv. J. on Legis. — Harvard Journal on Legislation
Harv. Latino L. Rev. — Harvard Latino Law Review
Harv. L. Rev. — Harvard Law Review
Harv. L.S. Bull. — Harvard Law School Bulletin
Harv. Negot. L. Rev. — Harvard Negotiation Law Review
Harv. Women's L.J. — Harvard Women's Law Journal
Harv. W. Tax Ser. — Harvard World Tax Series
Hastings Comm. & Ent. L.J. — Hastings Communications and Entertainment Law Journal
Hastings COMM/ENT L.J. — Hastings Communications and Entertainment Law Journal
Hastings Const. L.Q. — Hastings Constitutional Law Quarterly
Hastings Int'l & Comp. L. Rev. — Hastings International and Comparative Law Review
Hastings J. — Hastings Journal
Hastings L.J. — Hastings Law Journal
Hasting W.-Nw. J. Envtl. L. & Pol'y — Hastings West-Northwest Journal of Environmental Law and Policy
Hastings W.-N.W. J. Envtl. L. & Pol'y — Hastings West-Northwest Journal of Environmental Law and Policy
Hastings Women's L.J. — Hastings Women's Law Journal
Haw. — Hawaii Reports
Haw. App. — Hawaii Appellate Reports
Haw. B.J. — Hawaii Bar Journal
Hawkins on Construction of Wills — Hawkins, A Concise Treatise on the Construction of Wills
Hawks — Hawks (N.C.)
Haw. Rev. Stat. — Hawaii Revised Statutes
Haw. Rev. Stat. Ann. — Hawaii Revised Statutes Annotated
Haw. Sess. Laws — Hawaii Session Laws
Hay & Haz. — Hayward & Hazleton (D.C.)
Hayw. — 1. Haywood (N.C.). 2. Haywood (Tenn.).
H. Bl. — Henry Blackstone's English Common Pleas Reports
HCFA — Heath Care Financing Administration
H.C.L.M. — Health Care Labor Manual
Head — Head (Tenn.)
Health Law. — Health Lawyer
Health Matrix — Health Matrix: The Journal of Law-Medicine
Heckerling Inst. on Est. Plan. — Phillip E. Heckerling Institute on Estate Planning (U. Miami)
Heisk. — Heiskell (Tenn.)
Hen. Am. Pl. — Hening, The American Pleader and Lawyer's Guide
Hen. & M. — Hening & Munford (Va.)
Hennepin Law. — Hennepin Lawyer
HEW — Department of Health, Education and Welfare
HHS — Department of Health and Human Services
High, Inj. — A Treatise on the Law of Injunctions
High, Rec. — A Treatise on the Law of Receivers
High Tech. L.J. — High Technology Law Journal
Hill — (Hill (S.C.)
Hill & Den. — Hill and Denio's Supplement (N.Y.)
Hill. Cont. — Hilliard, The Law of Contracts
Hill Eq. — Hill's Chancery Reports (S.C.)
Hill. Inj. — Hilliard, The Law of Injunctions
Hill. Mortg. — Hilliard, The Law of Mortgages of Real and Personal Property
Hill. Real Prop. — Hilliard, The American Law of Real Property
Hill. Rem. — Hilliard, The Law of Remedies for Torts, including Replevin, Real Action, Pleading, Evidence, Damages
Hill. Sales — Hilliard, The Law of Sales of Personal Property
Hill. Tax. — Hilliard, The Law of Taxation
Hill. Torts — Hilliard, The Law of Torts or Private Wrongs
Hispanic L.J. — Hispanic Law Journal
H.L.N.R. — Health Lawyers News Report
Hoff. Ch. — Hoffman's Chancery Reports (N.Y.)
Hofstra Lab. & Emp. L.J. — Hofstra Labor & Employment Law Journal
Hofstra Lab. L.F. — Hofstra Labor Law Forum
Hofstra Lab. L.J. — Hofstra Labor Law Journal
Hofstra L. & Pol'y Symp. — Hofstra Law & Policy Symposium
Hofstra L. Rev. — Hofstra Law Review
Hofstra Prop. L.J. — Hofstra Property Law Journal
Holland, Jurisprudence — The Elements of Jurisprudence
Holmes, Com. Law — Holmes, The Common Law
Holt, Shipp. — A System of the Shipping and Navigation Laws of Great Britain and...
Hong Kong L.J. — Hong Kong Law Journal
Hopk. Ch. — Hopkin's Chancery Reports (N.Y.)
Hopk. Mar. Ins. — Hopkins, A Manual of Marine Insurance
Hough, Am. Const. — American Constitutions, Comprising the Constitution of Each State in the Union, and the United States ...
Hous. & Dev. Rep. (BNA) — Housing and Development Reporter
Hous. Bus. & Tax L. J. — Houston Business and Tax Law Journal
Hous. J. Health L. & Pol'y — Houston Journal of Health Law and Policy
Hous. J. Int'l L. — Houston Journal of International Law
Hous. Law. — Houston Lawyer
Hous. L. Rev. — Houston Law Review
Houst. — Houston (Del.)
Houst. L. Rev. — Houston Law Review
How. — Howard, U.S. Supreme Court Reports
How. L.J. — Howard Law Journal
How. Pr. — Howard's Practice Reports (N.Y.)
How. Pr. (n.s.) — Howard's Practice Reports, New Series (N.Y.)
How. Scroll. — Howard Scroll: The Social Justice Review
H.R. L.J. — Human Rights Law Journal
HRS — Hawaii Revised Statutes
HSA — Health Services Administration
HUD — Department of Housing and Urban Development
Hud. Wills — Hudson, A Practical Guide to Making and Proving Wills and Obtaining Grants of Letters of Administration
Hugh. Ins. — D. Hughes, A Treatise on the Law of Insurance in Three Parts...
Hughes — Hughes (Ky.)
Hughes, Fed. Prac. — Federal Practice, Jurisdiction & Procedure, Civil and Criminal with Forms
Hum. — Humphrey's (Tenn.)
Human Reprod. & L. Rep. (Legal-Medical Studies) — Reporter on Human Reproduction and the Law
Hum. Rts. — Human Rights (ABA)

Hum. Rts. Ann. — Human Rights Annual
Hum. Rts. Q. — Human Rights Quarterly
Hum. Rts. Rev. — Human Rights Review
Hung. L. Rev. — Hungarian Law Review
Hurd's Rev. St. — Hurd's Revised Statutes, Ill.
Hybrid: J.L. & Soc. Change U. Pa. — Hybrid: Journal of Law and Social Change University of Pennsylvania

I

IAEA — International Atomic Energy Agency
I. & N. Dec. — Administrative Decisions Under Immigration and Nationality Laws
IBRD — International Bank for Reconstruction and Development
I.C. — Idaho Code; Indiana Code; Iowa Code
ICA. — Iowa Code Annotated
ICAO — International Civil Aviation Organization
ICC — **1.** Indian Claims Commission. **2.** Interstate Commerce Commission.
I.C.C. — Interstate Commerce Commission Reports
I.C.C.2d — Interstate Commerce Commission Reports, 2d Series
I.C.C. Prac. J. — I.C.C. Practitioners' Journal
I.C.C. Valuation Rep. — Interstate Commerce Commission Valuation Reports
I.C.J. — International Court of Justice Reports of Judgments, Advisory Opinions, and Orders
I.C.J. Pleadings — Pleadings, Oral Arguments, Documents
ICSID — International Centre for Settlement of Investment Disputes
ICSID Rev. — ICSID Review
I.D. — Interior Department Decisions, Public Land
IDA — International Development Association
Idaho. — Idaho Reports
Idaho Code — Idaho Official Code
Idaho L.J. — Idaho Law Journal
Idaho L. Rev. — Idaho Law Review
Idaho Sess. Laws — Idaho Session Laws
IDEA — IDEA: The Journal of Law & Technology
IER Cas. (BNA) — Individual Employment Rights Cases
IFAD — International Fund for Agricultural Development
IFC — International Finance Corporation
IHS — Indian Health Service
IIC — International Review of Industrial Property and Copyright Law
I.L.C. Newsl. — International Legal Center Newsletter
Ill. — Illinois Reports
Ill. 2d. — Illinois Reports, Second Series
Ill. Admin. Code — Illinois Administrative Code
Ill. Ann. Stat. — Smith-Hurd Illinois Annotated Statutes
Ill. App. — Illinois Appellate Court Reports
Ill. App. 2d. — Illinois Appellate Court Reports, Second Series
Ill. App. 3d. — Illinois Appellate Court Reports, Third Series
Ill. B.J. — Illinois Bar Journal
Ill. Comp. Stat. — Illinois Compiled Statutes
Ill. Comp. Stat. Ann. — Illinois Compiled Statutes Annotated
Ill. Ct. Cl. — Illinois Court of Claims Reports
Ill. Dec. — Illinois Decisions
Ill. L.B. — Illinois Law Bulletin
Ill. Legis. Serv. — Illinois Legislative Service
Ill. L.Q. — Illinois Law Quarterly
Ill. L. Rev. — Illinois Law Review
Ill. L. Rev. Nw. U. — **1.** Illinois Law Review/Northwestern University. **2.** Illinois Law Review of Northwestern University.
Ill. Reg. — Illinois Register
Ill. Rev. St. — Illinois Revised Statutes
I.L.M. — International Legal Materials
ILO — International Labour Organization
I.L.R. — International Law Reports
ILSA J. Int'l & Comp. L. — ILSA Journal of International & Comparative Law
ILSA J. Int'l L. — ILSA Journal of International Law
IMF — International Monetary Fund
Immigr. & Nat'lity L. Rev. — Immigration and Nationality Law Review
Immigr. Briefings — Immigration Briefings
Immigr. J. — Immigration Journal
Immigr. L. & Bus. News — Immigration Law & Business News
Immigr. Newsl. — Immigration Newsletter
IMO — International Maritime Organization
Inc. — Incorporated
I.N.C.L. Brief — INCL Brief (ABA)
Ind. — Indiana Reports
Ind. Acts — Acts, Indiana
Ind. Admin. Code — Indiana Administrative Code
Ind. Adv. Legis. Serv. — Burns Indiana Advance Legislative Service
Ind. Advocate — Indian Advocate
Ind. & Lab. Rel. Rev. — Industrial and Labor Relations Review
Ind. App. — Indiana Court of Appeals Reports
Ind. Code. — Indiana Code
Ind. Code Ann. — Indiana Statutes Annotated; Annotated Indiana Code
Indian Terr. — Indian Territory Reports
Ind. Int'l & Comp. L. Rev. — Indiana International & Comparative Law Review
Ind. J. Global Legal Stud. — Indiana Journal of Global Legal Studies
Ind. J. Int'l L. — Indian Journal of International Law
Ind. Leg. Forum — Indiana Legal Forum
Ind. Legis. Serv. — Indiana Legislative Service
Ind. L.J. — Indiana Law Journal
Ind. L. Reg. — Indiana Legal Register
Ind. L. Rep. — Indiana Law Reporter
Ind. L. Rev. — Indiana Law Review
Ind. Reg. — Indiana Register
Ind. Super. — Indiana Superior Court Reports
Ind. T. Ann. St. — Indian Territory Annotated Statutes
Indus. & Lab. Rel. F. — Industrial and Labor Relations Forum
Indus. & Lab. Rel. Rev. — Industrial and Labor Relations Review
Indus. L.J. — Industrial Law Journal
Indus. L. Rev. — Industrial Law Review
Indus. Prop. Q. — Industrial Property Quarterly
Indus. Rel. J. — Industrial Relations Journal
Indus. Rel. J. Econ. & Soc. — Industrial Relations: Journal of Economy and Society
Indus. Rel. L.J. — Industrial Relations Law Journal
Ind. Y.B. Int'l Aff. — Indian Yearbook of International Affairs
Inher. Est. & Gift Tax Rep. (CCH) — Inheritance, Estate, and Gift Tax Reports
In Pub. Interest — In the Public Interest
INS — Immigration and Naturalization Service
Ins. Counsel J. — Insurance Counsel Journal
Inside Litig. — Inside Litigation
Insights. — Insights
Ins. Liability Rep. — Insurance Liability Reporter
Ins. L.J. — Insurance Law Journal
Ins. L. Rep. (CCH) — Insurance Law Reports

Inst. Min. L. — Institute on Mineral Law
Inst. on Est. Plan. — Institute on Estate Planning
Inst. on Fed. Tax'n. — Institute on Federal Taxation
Inst. on Min. L. — Institute on Mineral Law
Inst. on Oil & Gas L. & Tax'n — Institute on Oil and Gas Law and Taxation
Inst. on Plan. Zoning & Eminent Domain — Institute on Planning, Zoning, and Eminent Domain
Inst. on Priv. Inv. & Inv. Abroad — Institute on Private Investments and Investors Abroad
Inst. on Sec. Reg. — Institute on Securities Regulation
INSTRAW — International Research and Training Institute for the Advancement of Women
Int. Com. Commn. — Interstate Commerce Commission
Int. Com. Rep. — Interstate Commerce Reports
Intell. Prop. L. Rev. — Intellectual Property Law Review
Inter Alia — Inter Alia (State Bar of Nevada)
Inter-Am. L. Rev. — Inter-American Law Review
Interior Dec. — Decisions of the United States Department of the Interior
Internet L. & Reg. (P & F) — Internet Law and Regulation
INTERPOL — International Criminal Police Organization
Interst. Com. R. — Interstate Commerce Reports
Int'l & Comp. L. Bull. — International and Comparative Law Bulletin
Int'l & Comp. L.Q. — International & Comparative Law Quarterly
Int'l Arb. J. — International Arbitration Journal
Int'l Arb. L. Rev. — International Arbitration Law Review
Int'l B.J. — International Bar Journal
Int'l Bus. & Trade L. Rep. — International Business & Trade Law Reporter
Int'l Bus. Law. — International Business Lawyer
Int'l Bus. Lawyer — International Business Lawyer
Int'l Bus. Ser. — International Business Service
Int'l Comm. Jurists Rev. — International Commission of Jurists Review
Int'l Dig. Health Leg. — International Digest of Health Legislation
Int'l Dimensions — International Dimensions
Int'l Encycl. Comp. L. — International Encyclopedia of Comparative Law
Int'l Envtl. Aff. — International Environmental Affairs
Int'l Env't Rep. (BNA) — International Environment Reporter
Int'l J. — International Journal
Int'l J. Comp. & Applied Crim. Just. — International Journal of Comparative and Applied Criminal Justice
Int'l J. Cultural Prop. — International Journal of Cultural Property
Int'l J.L. & Fam. — International Journal of Law and Family
Int'l J.L. & Psych. — International Journal of Law and Psychiatry
Int'l J. Legal Info. — International Journal of Legal Information
Int'l J. Legal Prof. — International Journal of the Legal Profession
Int'l J.L. Lib. — International Journal of Law Libraries
Int'l J. Marine & Coastal L. — International Journal of Marine and Coastal Law
Int'l J. Offender Therapy & Comp. Criminology — International Journal of Offender Therapy and Comparative Criminology
Int'l J. Soc. L. — International Journal of the Sociology of the Law
Int'l Lab. Rev. — International Labor Review
Int'l L. & Trade Persp. — International Law & Trade Perspective
Int'l Law. — International Lawyer (ABA)
Int'l L. Doc. — International Law Documents
Int'l Legal Persp. — International Legal Perspectives
Int'l L.N. — International Law Notes
Int'l. L. News — International Law News
Int'l L. Persp. — International Law Perspective
Int'l L. Prac. — International Law Practicum
Int'l L.Q. — International Law Quarterly
Int'l Org. — International Organization
Int'l Prop. Inv. J. — International Property Investment Journal
Int'l Q. — International Quarterly
Int'l Rev. L. & Econ. — International Review of Law and Economics
Int'l Tax & Bus. Law. — International Tax & Business Lawyer
Int'l Tax J. — International Tax Journal
Int'l Trade L.J. — International Trade Law Journal
Int'l Trade Rep. (BNA) — International Trade Reporter
Int. Rev. Bull. — Internal Revenue Bulletin
Int. Rev. Code — Internal Revenue Code
I.O.C.C. Bull. — Interstate Oil Compact Commission Bulletin
Iowa. — Iowa Reports
Iowa Acts — Acts & Joint Resolutions of the State of Iowa
Iowa Admin. Bull. — Iowa Administrative Bulletin
Iowa Admin. Code — Iowa Administrative Code
Iowa B. News Bull. — Bulletin of the Iowa State Bar Association
Iowa Code — Code of Iowa
Iowa Code Ann. — Iowa Code Annotated
Iowa L.B. — Iowa Law Bulletin
Iowa L. Bull. — Iowa Law Bulletin
Iowa Legis. Serv. — Iowa Legislative Service
Iowa L. Rev. — Iowa Law Review
IRA — Individual Retirement Account
I.R.B. — Internal Revenue Bulletin
I.R.C. — Internal Revenue Code
Ired. — Iredell's Law Reports (N.C.)
Ired. Eq. — Iredell's Equity Reports (N.C.)
I.R.M. — Internal Revenue Manual (IRS)
I.R.R. Newsl. — Individual Rights and Responsibilities Newsletter
I.R.S. — **1.** Illinois Revised Statutes. **2.** Internal Revenue Service.
IRS Pos. (CCH) — Internal Revenue Service Positions
ISL L. Rev. — ISL Law Review
Issues L. & Med. — Issues in Law & Medicine
ITA — International Trade Administration
ITC — International Trade Centre (UNCTAD)
I.T.R.D. — International Trade Reporter Decisions (BNA)
ITU — International Telecommunication Union

J

J. Accountancy — Journal of Accountancy
J. Affordable Housing & Community Dev. L. — Journal of Affordable Housing & Community Development Law
J. Afr. L. — Journal of African Law
JAG. — Judge Advocate General
JAG Bull. — JAG Bulletin (USAF)
Jagg. Torts — Jaggard, Hand-book of the Law of Torts
JAG J. — JAG Journal
JAG L. Rev. — United States Air Force JAG Law Review
J. Agric. L. — Journal of Agricultural Law
J. Agric. Tax'n & L. — Journal of Agricultural Taxation & Law
J. Air L. — Journal of Air Law
J. Air L. & Com. — Journal of Air Law and Commerce
JALC — Journal of Air Law and Commerce

JAMA. – Journal of the American Medical Association
J. Am. Acad. Matrim. Law – Journal of the American Academy of Matrimonial Lawyers
J. Am. Acad. Psych. & L. – Journal of the American Academy of Psychiatry and the Law
J. Am. Jud. Soc'y – Journal of the American Judicature Society
J. Am. Soc'y CLU – Journal of the American Society of Chartered Life Underwriters
J. Am. Soc'y CLU & ChFC – Journal of the American Society of Chartered Life Underwriters & Chartered Financial Consultants
J. App. Prac. & Process – Journal of Appellate Practice and Process
Jarm., Wills – Jarman, Treatise on Wills
J. Art. & Ent. L. – Journal of Art and Entertainment Law
J. Arts Mgmt. & L. – Journal of Arts Management and Law
J. Arts Mgmt. L. & Soc'y – Journal of Arts Management, Law and Society
J. Bankr. L. & Prac. – Journal of Bankruptcy Law and Practice
J. Bev. Hills B.A. – Journal of the Beverly Hills Bar Association
J. Biolaw & Bus. – Journal of Biolaw and Business
J. Bus. L. – Journal of Business Law
J.C. & U.L. – Journal of College and University Law
J. Chinese L. – Journal of Chinese Law
J. Church & St. – Journal of Church and State
J. Comp. Leg. & Int'l L. 3d. – Journal of Comparative Legislation and International Law, Third Series
J. Confl. Res. – Journal of Conflict Resolution
J. Cons. Affairs – Journal of Consumer Affairs
J. Const. & Parl. Stud. – Journal of Constitutional and Parliamentary Studies
J. Const. L. – Journal of Constitutional Law
J. Const. L. E. & Cent. Eur. – Journal of Constitutional Law in Eastern & Central Europe
J. Contemp. Health L. & Pol'y – Journal of Contemporary Health Law and Policy
J. Contemp. L. – Journal of Contemporary Law
J. Contemp. Legal Issues. – Journal of Contemporary Legal Issues
J. Cont. L. – Journal of Contract Law
J. Copyright Entertainment Sports L. – Journal of Copyright Entertainment and Sports Law
J. Copyright Soc'y. – Journal of the Copyright Society of the U.S.A.
J. Copyright Soc'y U.S.A. – Journal of the Copyright Society of the U.S.A.
J. Copy. Soc'y – Journal of the Copyright Society of the U.S.A.
J. Corp. L. – Journal of Corporation Law (Iowa)
J. Corp. Tax. – Journal of Corporate Taxation
J. Corp. Tax'n. – Journal of Corporate Taxation
J. Crim. Just. – Journal of Criminal Justice
J. Crim. L. & Criminology – Journal of Criminal Law & Criminology
J.D. – Juris Doctor
J. Disp. Resol. – Journal of Dispute Resolution
J. Energy & Devel. – Journal of Energy and Development
J. Energy & Nat. Resources L. – Journal of Energy & Natural Resources Law
J. Energy L. & Pol'y. – Journal of Energy Law & Policy
J. Energy Nat. Resources & Envtl. L. – Journal of Energy, Natural Resources & Environmental Law
J. Envtl. L. & Litig. – Journal of Environmental Law and Litigation
Jeremy, Eq. Jur. – A Treatise on the Equity Jurisdiction of the High Court of Chancery
Jeremy on Carriers – H. Jeremy, The Law of Carriers, Inn-keepers, Warehousemen, and Other Depositories of Goods for Hire
J. Fam. L. – Journal of Family Law
J. Fin. Serv. Prof. – Journal of Financial Service Professionals
J. Forensic Document Examination – Journal of Forensic Document Examination
J. Forensic Econ. – Journal of Forensic Economics
J. Gender Race & Just. – Journal of Gender, Race & Justice
J. Health & Hosp. L. – Journal of Health and Hospital Law
J. Health Care L. & Pol'y. – Journal of Health Care Law & Policy
J. Health L. – Journal of Health Law
J. Health Pol. Pol'y & L. – Journal of Health, Politics, Policy & Law
J. Inst. for Study Legal Ethics. – Journal of the Institute for the Study of Legal Ethics
J. Inst. Study Legal Ethics – Journal of the Institute for the Study of Legal Ethics
J. Intell. Prop. – Journal of Intellectual Property
J. Intell. Prop. L. – Journal of Intellectual Property Law
J. Int'l Aff. – Journal of International Affairs
J. Int'l & Comp. L. – Journal of International and Comparative Law
J. Int'l Arb. – Journal of International Arbitration
J. Int'l Banking L. – Journal of International Banking Law
J. Int'l Comm. Jur. – Journal of the International Commission of Jurists
J. Int'l Fin. Markets – Journal of International Financial Markets
J. Int'l L. & Com. Reg. – Journal of International Law and Commercial Regulation
J. Int'l L. & Dipl. – Journal of International Law and Diplomacy
J. Int'l L. & Econ. – Journal of International Law and Economics
J. Int'l L. & Pol. – Journal of International Law and Politics
J. Int'l L. & Prac. – Journal of International Law and Practice
J. Int'l Legal Stud. – Journal of International Legal Studies
J. Int'l Tax'n. – Journal of International Taxation
J. Int'l Wildlife L. & Pol'y – Journal of International Wildlife Law and Policy
J. John Bassett Moore Soc'y Int'l L. – Journal of the John Bassett Moore Society of International Law
J.J. Marsh. – J. J. Marshall (Ky.)
J. Juv. L. – Journal of Juvenile Law
J. Kan. B.A. – Journal of the Kansas Bar Association
J.L. & Com. – Journal of Law and Commerce
J.L. & Econ. – Journal of Law and Economics
J.L. & Econ. Dev. – Journal of Law and Economic Development
J.L. & Educ. – Journal of Law and Education
J.L. & Fam. Stud. – Journal of Law and Family Studies
J.L. & Health. – Journal of Law and Health
J.L. & Info. Sci. – Journal of Law and Information Science
J.L. & Pol. – Journal of Law and Politics
J.L. & Pol'y. – Journal of Law and Policy
J.L. & Relig. – Journal of Law and Religion
J.L. & Religion. – Journal of Law and Religion
J. Land Res. & Envtl. L. – Journal of Land, Resources and Environmental Law
J. Land Resources & Envtl. L. – Journal of Land, Resources and Environmental Law
J.L. & Social Pol'y. – Journal of Law and Social Policy
J.J. & Soc. Pol'y – Journal of Law and Social Policy
J.L. & Soc'y – Journal of Law and Society

J.L. & Tech. — Journal of Law & Technology (ceased publication)
J.L. & Trade Am. — Journal of Law and Trade in the Americas
J. Land Use & Envtl. L. — Journal of Land Use & Environmental Law
J.L. Econ. & Org. — Journal of Law, Economics & Organization
J. Legal Econ. — Journal of Legal Economics
J. Legal Educ. — Journal of Legal Education
J. Legal Hist. — Journal of Legal History
J. Legal Med. — Journal of Legal Medicine
J. Legal Prof. — Journal of the Legal Profession
J. Legal Stud. — Journal of Legal Studies
J. Legal Stud. Educ. — Journal of Legal Studies Education
J. Legis. — Journal of Legislation
J. Leg. Stud. — Journal of Legal Studies
J.L. Fam. Stud. — Journal of Law and Family Studies
J.L. Med. & Ethics — Journal of Law, Medicine & Ethics
J.L. Ref. — Journal of Law Reform
J.L. Reform — Journal of Law Reform
J.L. Soc'y — Journal of Law in Society
J. Mar. L. & Com. — Journal of Maritime Law and Commerce
J. Mar. L.R. — John Marshall Law Review
J. Mar. L. Rev. — John Marshall Law Review
J. Marshall J. Computer & Info. L. — John Marshall Journal of Computer & Information Law
J. Marshall J. Prac. & Proc. — John Marshall Journal of Practice and Procedure
J. Marshall L.Q. — John Marshall Law Quarterly
J. Marshall L. Rev. — John Marshall Law Review
J. Med. & L. — Journal of Medicine and Law
J. Min. L. & Pol'y — Journal of Mineral Law & Policy
J. Minn. Pub. L. — Journal of Minnesota Public Law
J. Mo. B. — Journal of the Missouri Bar
J. Nat'l Ass'n Admin. L. Judges — Journal of the National Association of Administrative Law Judges
J. Nat'l Sec. L. — Journal of National Security Law
J. Nat. Resources & Envtl. L . — Journal of Natural Resources & Environmental Law
J.O. — Journal Officiel des Communautés Européennes
Johns. — Johnson's Reports (N.Y.)
Johns. Cas. — Johnson's Cases (N.Y.)
Johns. Ch. — Johnson's Chancery Reports (N.Y.)
Jones — Jones' Law Reports (N.C.)
Jones, Chat. Mortg. — A Treatise on the Law of Mortgages of Personal Property
Jones, Easem. — A Treatise on the Law of Easements
Jones Eq. — Jones' Equity (N.C.)
Jones, Liens — Treatise on the Law of Liens: Common Law, Statutory, Equitable and Maritime
Jones, Mortg. — A Treatise on the Law of Mortgages of Real Property
Jones on Bailments — W. Jones, An Essay on the Law of Bailments
Jones, Pledges — A Treatise on the Law of Pledges, including Collateral Securities
J.P. — Justice of the Peace
J. Partnership Tax'n — Journal of Partnership Taxation
J. Passthrough Entities — Journal of Passthrough Entities
J. Pat. & Trademark Off. Soc'y — Journal of the Patent and Trademark Office Society
J. Pat. Off. Soc'y — Journal of the Patent Office Society
J. Pension Plan. & Compliance — Journal of Pension Planning and Compliance
J. Pharmacy & L. — Journal of Pharmacy & Law
J. Police Sci. & Ad. — Journal of Police Science and Administration
J. Prod. Liab. — Journal of Products Liability
J. Proprietary Rts. — Journal of Proprietary Rights
J. Psych. & L. — Journal of Psychiatry and Law
J. Pub. L. — Journal of Public Law
J. Real Est. Tax'n. — Journal of Real Estate Taxation
J. Sci. & Tech. L. — Journal of Science and Technology Law
J. S. Corp. Tax'n — Journal of S Corporation Taxation
J. S. Ct. Hist. — Journal of Supreme Court History
J.S. Legal Hist. — Journal of Southern Legal History
J. Small & Emerging Bus. L. — Journal of Small & Emerging Business Law
J. Space L. — Journal of Space Law
J. State Tax'n — Journal of State Taxation
J. St. Tax'n — Journal of State Taxation
J. Suffolk Acad. L. — Journal of the Suffolk Academy of Law
J. Sup. Ct. Hist. — Journal of Supreme Court History
J. Tax. — Journal of Taxation
J. Tax'n. — Journal of Taxation
J. Tax'n Inv. — Journal of Taxation of Investments
J. Tax'n Investments — Journal of Taxation of Investments
J. Tech. L. & Pol'y — Journal of Technology Law and Policy
J. Telecomms. & High Tech. L. — Journal on Telecommunications & High Technology Law
J. Tex. Ins. L. — Journal of Texas Insurance Law
J. Transnat'l L. & Pol'y — Journal of Transnational Law & Policy
J. Transp. L., Logistics & Pol'y — Journal of Transportation Law, Logistics and Policy
Jud. Conduct Rep. — Judicial Conduct Reporter
Judges. J. — Judges Journal (ABA)
J. Urb. L. — Journal of Urban Law
Jurid. Rev. — Juridical Review
Jurimetrics J. — Jurimetrics Journal
Jurimetrics J. L. Sci. & Tech. — Jurimetrics Journal of Law, Science and Technology (ABA)
Juris Dr. — Juris Doctor
Juris Mag. — Juris Magazine
Jurist — The Jurist
Jur. Rev. — Juridical Review
Just. Sys. J. — Justice System Journal
J. U. Tex. Int'l L. — Journal of the University of Texas International Law
Juv. & Fam. Ct. J. — Juvenile and Family Court Journal

K

Kan. — Kansas Reports
Kan. Admin. Regs. — Kansas Administrative Regulations
Kan. App. — Kansas Court of Appeals Reports
Kan. App. 2d. — Kansas Court of Appeals Reports, Second Series
Kan. B.A.J. — Kansas Bar Association Journal
Kan. City L. Rev. — Kansas City Law Review
Kan. C. L. Rep. — Kansas City Law Reporter
Kan. J.L. & Pub. Pol'y — Kansas Journal of Law & Public Policy
Kan. Law. — Kansas Lawyer
Kan. L.J. — Kansas Law Journal
Kan. L. Rev. — Kansas Law Review
Kan. Reg. — Kansas Register
Kan. Stat. Ann. — Kansas Statutes Annotated
Kan. Sess. Laws — Session Laws of Kansas
K.B. — King's Bench (Eng.)
K.B.J. — Kansas Bar Journal
Keener, Quasi-Contracts — A Treatise on the Law of Quasi-Contracts

Kent – Commentaries on American Law
Kent, Comm. – Commentaries on American Law
Kent's Com. – Kent, Commentaries on American Law
Kerr, Rec. – The Law and Practice as to Receivers
Kirby – Kirby (Conn.)
KRS – Kentucky Revised Statutes
K.S.A. – Kansas Statutes Annotated
Ky. – Kentucky Reports
Ky. Acts – Kentucky Acts
Ky. Admin. Reg. – Administrative Register of Kentucky
Ky. Admin. Regs. – Kentucky Administrative Regulations
Ky. App. Rptr. – Kentucky Appellate Reporter
Ky. Bench & B. – Kentucky Bench and Bar
Ky. Children's Rts. J. – Kentucky Children's Rights Journal
Kyd, Bills – A Treatise on the Law of Bills of Exchange and Promissory Notes
Kyd, Corporations – Kyd, A Treatise on the Law of Corporations
Ky. Dec. – Kentucky Decisions
Ky. Law Rep. – Kentucky Law Reporter
Ky. L.J. – Kentucky Law Journal
Ky. L. Rptr. – Kentucky Law Reporter
Ky. L. Summary – Kentucky Law Summary
Ky. Op. – Kentucky Opinions
Ky. Rev. Stat. & R. Serv. – Baldwin's Official Edition, Kentucky Revised Statutes & Rules Service
Ky. Rev. Stat. Ann. – Kentucky Revised Statutes Annotated
Ky. St. B.J. – Kentucky State Bar Journal

L

L. – Laws (of state)
La. – Louisiana Reports
La. Acts – State of Louisiana: Acts of the Legislature
La. Admin. Code – Louisiana Administrative Code
La. Ann. – Louisiana Annual Reports
La. App. – Louisiana Court of Appeals Reports
Lab. Arb. Awards (CCH) – Labor Arbitration Awards
Lab. Arb. Rep. (BNA) – Labor Arbitration Reports
L.A. Bar Bull. – Los Angeles Bar Bulletin
Lab. Cas. (CCH) – Labor Cases
La. B.J. – Louisiana Bar Journal
Lab. Law. – Labor Lawyer
Lab. L.J. – Labor Law Journal
Lab. L. Rep. (CCH) – Labor Law Reporter
Lab. L. Serv. (CCH) – Labor Law Service
Lab. Rel. & Empl. News – Labor Relations and Employment News (ABA)
Lab. Rel. Rep. (BNA) – Labor Relations Reporter
La. Civ. Code Ann. – Louisiana Civil Code Annotated
Lack. Bar – Lackawanna Bar
Lack. Jur. – Lackawanna Jurist
Lack. Jurist – Lackawanna Jurist
Lack. Legal N. – Lackawanna Legal News
Lack. Leg. News – Lackawanna Legal News
Lack. Leg. Rec. – Lackawanna Legal Record
L.A. Law. – Los Angeles Lawyer
La. L.J. – Louisiana Law Journal
La. L. Rev. – Louisiana Law Review
L. & Contemp. Probs. – Law and Contemporary Problems
L. & Critique – Law and Critique
L. & Hist. Rev. – Law and History Review
L. & Soc. Inquiry. – Law & Social Inquiry
L. & Soc. Order – Law and Social Order
L. & Soc'y Rev. – Law and Society Review
Land & Water L. Rev. – Land & Water Law Review
Land Use & Env. L. Rev. – Land Use and Environment Law Review
Langdell, Contracts – Summary of the Law of Contracts
Langdell, Eq. Pl. – A Summary of Equity Pleading
Langdell, Sel. Cas. Sales – Selection of Cases on the Sales of Personal Property
Langdell, Summary – A Summary of the Law of Contracts
Langdell, Summary of Contracts – A Summary of the Law of Contracts
Lang. Sales – Langdell, Selection of Cases on the Sales of Personal Property
Lans. – Lansing's Reports (N.Y.)
Lans. Ch. – Lansing's Chancery Reports (N.Y.)
La Raza L.J. – La Raza Law Journal
La. Reg. – Louisiana Register
La. Rev. Stat. Ann. – Louisiana Revised Statutes Annotated
La. Sess. Law Serv. – Louisiana Session Law Service
Law. Americas – Lawyer of the Americas
Law & Contemp. Probs. – Law & Contemporary Problems
Law & Hist. Rev. – Law and History Review
Law & Hum. Behav. – Law and Human Behavior
Law & Ineq. – Law and Inequality: A Journal of Theory and Practice
Law & Ineq. J. – Law & Inequality Journal
Law & Phil. – Law and Philosophy
Law & Pol'y Int'l Bus. – Law & Policy in International Business
Law & Psychol. Rev. – Law and Psychology Review
Law & Psych. Rev. – Law and Psychology Review
Law & Sex. – Law & Sexuality: A Review of Lesbian & Gay Legal Issues
Law & Sexuality – Law & Sexuality: A Review of Lesbian & Gay Legal Issues
Law & Soc. Inquiry – Law and Social Inquiry
Law & Soc'y Rev. – Law and Society Review
Law. Competitive Edge – Lawyers Competitive Edge: The Journal of Law Office Economics and Management
Law Forum – Law Forum (U. of Baltimore)
Law Inst. J. – Law Institute Journal
Law Lib. J. – Law Library Journal
Law Libr. J. – Law Library Journal
Law. Man. on Prof. Conduct (ABA/BNA) – Lawyers Manual on Professional Conduct
Law Off. Econ. & Mgt. – Law Office Economics and Management
Laws. Man. on Prof. Conduct (ABA/BNA) – Lawyers Manual on Professional Conduct
Lawson, Exp. Ev. – The Law of Expert and Opinion Evidence Reduced to Rules
Lawson, Rights, Rem. & Pr. – Rights, Remedies, and Practice, at Law, in Equity, and Under the Codes
LC – Library of Congress
LEAA – Law Enforcement Assistance Administration
Leake, Cont. – The Elements of the Law of Contracts
Lea, Sup. and Force – Superstition and Force: Essays on Wager of Law, the Wager of Battle, the Ordeal, Torture
Lebanon – Lebanon County Legal Journal (Pa.)
L. Ed. – U.S. Supreme Court Reports, Lawyer's Edition
L. Ed. 2d. – U.S. Supreme Court Reports, Lawyer's Edition, Second Series
Leg. – Acts of the Legislature
Leg. Aff. – Legal Affairs
Legal Econ. – Legal Economics (ABA)
Legal Educ. Newsl. – Legal Education Newsletter (ABA)
Legal Reference Services Q. – Legal Reference Services Quarterly
Legal Ref. Serv. Q. – Legal Reference Services Quarterly
Legal Services Bull. – Legal Services Bulletin
Legal Stud. F. – Legal Studies Forum
Leg. Gaz. R. – Legal Gazette Reports (Pa.)

Legis. Stud. Q. — Legislative Studies Quarterly
Leg. Writing — Legal Writing: The Journal of the Legal Writing Institute
Leh. L.J. — Lehigh Law Journal, Pa
Leigh — Leigh (Va.)
LERC Monograph Ser. — LERC Monograph Series
Lewis, Em. Dom. — J. Lewis, A Treatise on the Law of Eminent Domain in the United States
Lewis, Perp. — W. Lewis, A Practical Treatise on the Law of Perpetuity
Lewis U. L. Rev. — Lewis University Law Review
Liberty, Life & Fam. — Liberty, Life and Family
Life Health & Accid. Ins. Cas. (CCH) — Life Health and Accident Insurance Cases
Life Health & Accid. Ins. Cas. 2d (CCH) — Life Health and Accident Insurance Cases, Second Series
Lincoln L. Rev. — Lincoln Law Review
Lindley, Comp. — A Treatise on the Law of Companies
Lindley, Part. — A Treatise on the Law of Partnerhip
L. in Japan — Law in Japan
Liquor Cont. L. Rep. (CCH) — Liquor Control Law Reports
Litig. — Litigation (ABA)
Litigation — Litigation (ABA)
Litt. — Littell (Ky.)
Litt. Sel. Cas. — Littell Selected Cases (Ky.)
L. Lib. J. — Law Library Journal
L. Lib. News — Law Library News
L. Libr. J. — Law Library Journal
LL.B. — Legum Baccalaureus (Bachelor of Laws)
LL.D. — Legum Doctor (Doctor of Laws)
LL.M. — Legum Magister (Master of Laws)
Lloyd's Mar. & Com. L.Q. — Lloyd's Maritime and Commercial Law Quarterly
L. Med. & Health Care — Law, Medicine and Health Care
L.N.T.S. — League of Nations Treaty Series
Lock. Rev. Cas. — Lockwood's Reversed Cases (N.Y.)
Los Angeles Bar J. — Los Angeles Bar Journal
Lowell, Transfer of Stock — The Transfer of Stock in Private Corporations
Loy. Consumer L. Rep. — Loyola Consumer Law Reporter
Loy. Consumer L. Rev. — Loyola Consumer Law Review
Loy. Ent. L.J. — Loyola Entertainment Law Journal
Loy. Intell. Prop. & High Tech. J. — Loyola Intellectual Property & High Technology Journal
Loy. L.A. Ent. L.J. — Loyola of Los Angeles Entertainment Law Journal
Loy. L.A. Ent. L. Rev. — Loyola of Los Angeles Entertainment Law Review
Loy. L.A. Int'l & Comp. L. Ann. — Loyola of Los Angeles International and Comparative Law Annual
Loy. L.A. Int'l & Comp. L.J. — Loyola of Los Angeles International and Comparative Law Journal
Loy. L.A. Int'l & Comp. L. Rev. — Loyola of Los Angeles International and Comparative Law Review
Loy. L.A. L. Rev. — Loyola of Los Angeles Law Review
Loy. L. Rev. — Loyola Law Review (New Orleans)
Loy. Intell. Prop. & High Tech. L.Q. — Loyola Intellectual Property & High Technology Law Quarterly
Loy. Mar. L. J. — Loyola Maritime Law Journal
Loy. Poverty L.J. — Loyola Poverty Law Journal
Loy. U. Chi. L.J. — Loyola University of Chicago Law Journal
Loy. U. New Orleans J. Pub. Int. L. — Loyola University of New Orleans Journal of Public Interest Law
L.P.R.A. — Laws of Puerto Rico Annotated
L. Prac. Mgmt. — Law Practice Management (ABA)
LQR — Law Quarterly Review
L.R. — Law Reports, U.S
L.R.A. — Lawyers' Reports Annotated
L.R.A. N.S. — Lawyers' Reports Annotated New Series
L. Rev. Mich. St. U.-Det. C.L. — Law Review of Michigan State University-Detroit College of Law
LRP — Labor Relations Press
L.R.R.M. (BNA) — Labor Relations Reference Manual
LSA. — Louisiana Statutes Annotated
LSA-C.C. — Louisiana Statutes Annotated—Civil Code
LSA-C.C.P. — Louisiana Statutes Annotated—Code of Civil Procedure
LSA-C.J.P. — Louisiana Statutes Annotated—Code of Juvenile Procedure
LSA-R.S. — Louisiana Statutes Annotated—Revised Statutes
Ltd. — Limited

M

MA — Maritime Administration
Mackey — Mackey (D.C.)
Maine, Ancient Law — Ancient Law: Its Connection with the Early History of Society and Its Relation to Modern Ideas
Maine, Anc. Law — Ancient Law: Its Connection with the Early History of Society...
Maine B.J. — Maine Bar Journal
Maine, Early Hist. Inst. — Lectures on the Early History of Institutions
Maine, Early Law and Custom — Dissertations on Early Law and Custom
Maine L. Rev. — Maine Law Review
Maine, Village Communities — Village Communities in the East and West, Six Lectures Delivered at Oxford
Major Tax Plan. — Major Tax Planning
Malloy — Treaties, Conventions, International Acts, Protocols, and Agreements Between the United States and Other Powers
Man. L.J. — Manitoba Law Journal
Mar. — Martin (N.C.)
Markby, Elements of Law — Elements of Law Considered with Reference to Principles of General Jurisprudence
Mar. Law. — Maritime Lawyer
Marq. Intell. Prop. L. Rev. — Marquette Intellectual Property Law Review
Marq. L. Rev. — Marquette Law Review
Marq. Sports L.J. — Marquette Sports Law Journal
Marsden, Law of Collisions — A Treatise on the Law of Collisions at Sea
Marshall on Insurance — A Treatise on the Law of Insurance
Mart. & Yer. — Martin & Yerger (Tenn.)
Mart. Ex. — Martin, A Treatise on the Powers and Duties of Executors and Administrators
Mart. (n.s.) — Martin Louisiana Term Reports, New Series (La.)
Mart. (o.s.) — Martin Louisiana Term Reports, Old Series (La.)
Marv. — Marvel (Del.)
Mass. — Massachusetts Reports
Mass. Acts — Acts and Resolves of Massachusetts
Mass. Adv. Legis. Serv. — Massachusetts Advance Legislative Service
Mass. Ann. Laws — Annotated Laws of Massachusetts
Mass. App. Ct. — Massachusetts Appeals Court Reports
Mass. App. Dec. — Massachusetts Appellate Decisions
Mass. App. Div. — Massachusetts Appellate Division Reports
Mass. Gen. Laws — General Laws of the Commonwealth of Massachusetts
Mass. Gen. Laws Ann. — Massachusetts General Laws Annotated

Mass. Legal Hist. – Massachusetts Legal History: A Journal of the Supreme Judicial Court Legal History Society
Mass. Legis. Serv. – Massachusetts Legislative Service
Mass. L.Q. – Massachusetts Law Quarterly
Mass. L. Rev. – Massachusetts Law Review
Mass. Reg. – Massachusetts Register
Mass. Regs. Code – Code of Massachusetts Regulations
Mass. Supp. – Massachusetts Reports Supplement
May, Ins. – Law of Insurance, as Applied to Fire, Accident, Guarantee, and Other Non-maritime Risks
MB – Matthew Bender
M.C.A. – Mississippi Code Annotated; Montana Code Annotated
McAdam, Landl. & T. – The Rights, Duties, Remedies, and Incidents Belonging to and Growing Out of the Relation of Landlord and Tenant
M.C.C. – Interstate Commerce Commission: Motor Carrier Cases
McCahon – McCahon (Kan.)
McCord – McCord (S.C.)
McCord Eq. – McCord's Chancery Reports (S.C.)
McCrary, Elections – Treatise on the American Law of Elections
McGeorge L. Rev. – McGeorge Law Review
McGill L.J. – McGill Law Journal
McGl. – McGloin (La.)
McKelvey, Ev. – Handbook of the Law of Evidence
M.C.L.A. – Michigan Compiled Laws Annotated
McMul. – McMullen (S.C.)
McMul. Eq. – McMullen's Equity Reports (S.C.)
Md. – Maryland Reports
Md. App. – Maryland Appellate Reports
Md. B.J. – Maryland Bar Journal
Md. Ch. – Maryland Chancery
Md. Code Ann. – Annotated Code of Maryland
Md. J. Contemp. Legal Issues – Maryland Journal of Contemporary Legal Issues
Md. J. Int'l L. & Trade – Maryland Journal of International Law and Trade
Md. Laws – Laws of Maryland
Md. L.F. – Maryland Law Forum
Md. L. Rep. – Maryland Law Reporter, Baltimore
Md. L. Rev. – Maryland Law Review
Md. Reg. – Maryland Register
Me. – Maine Reports
Me. Acts – Maine Acts
Me. B.J. – Maine Bar Journal
Mechem, Ag. – Treatise on the Law of Agency Including Not Only a Discussion of the General Subject, but also Special Chapters on Attorneys, Auctioneers, Brokers and Factors
Mechem, Part. – Elements of the Law of Partnership
Med. & L. – Medicine & Law
Med. Devices Rep. (CCH) – **1.** Medical Devices Reporter. **2.** Medical Devices Reports.
Media L. & Pol'y. – Media Law & Policy
Media L. Rep. (BNA) – Media Law Reporter
Mediation Q. – Mediation Quarterly: Journal of the Academy of Family Mediators
Medicare & Medicaid Guide (CCH) – Medicare and Medicaid Guide
Med. Leg. J. – Medico-Legal Journal
Med. Trial Tech. Q. – Medical Trial Technique Quarterly
Meigs – Meigs (Tenn.)
Me. Laws – Maine Laws
Melb. J. Int'l L. – Melbourne Journal of International Law
Melb. U. L. Rev. – Melbourne University Law Review
Me. Legis. Serv. – Maine Legislative Service
Me. L. Rev. – Maine Law Review
Memphis L.J. – Memphis Law Journal, Tenn
Memphis St. U. L. Rev. – Memphis State University Law Review
Mental & Phys. Disab. L. Rep. – Mental & Physical Disability Law Reporter (ABA)
Mental Disab. L. Rep. – Mental Disability Law Reporter (ABA)
Mercer L. Rev. – Mercer Law Review
Me. Rev. Stat. Ann. – Main Revised Statutes Annotated
Merg. & Acq. – Mergers and Acquisitions
Met. – **1.** Metcalf (Ky.). **2.** Metcalf (Mass.).
M.F.P.D. – Modern Federal Practice Digest
MGIC. – Mortgage Guaranty Insurance Corporation
M.G.L.A. – Massachusetts General Laws Annotated
Miami L.Q. – Miami Law Quarterly
Mich. – Michigan Reports
Mich. Admin. Code – Michigan Administrative Code
Mich. App. – Michigan Appeals Reports
Mich. B.J. – Michigan State Bar Journal
Mich. Bus. L.J. – Michigan Business Law Journal
Mich. Comp. Laws – Michigan Compiled Laws
Mich. Comp. Laws Ann. – Michigan Compiled Laws Annotated
Mich. Ct. Cl. – Michigan Court of Claims Reports
Mich. J. Gender & L. – Michigan Journal of Gender & Law
Mich. J. Int'l L. – Michigan Journal of International Law
Mich. J.L. Ref. – University of Michigan Journal of Law Reform
Mich. J. Race & L. – Michigan Journal of Race & Law
Mich. L. & Pol'y Rev. – Michigan Law & Policy Review
Mich. Legis. Serv. – Michigan Legislative Service
Mich. L. Rev. – Michigan Law Review
Mich. Pub. Acts – Public and Local Laws of the Legislature of the State of Michigan
Mich. Reg. – Michigan Register
Mich. Stat. Ann. – Michigan Statutes Annotated
Mich. St. U. - DCL J. Int'l L. – Michigan State University-Detroit College of Law Journal of International Law
Mich. Tax Law. – Michigan Tax Lawyer
Mich. Tax L.J. – Michigan Tax Law Journal
Mich. Telecomm. & Tech. L. Rev. – Michigan Telecommunications and Technology Law Review
Mich. Y.B. Int'l Legal Stud. – Michigan Yearbook of International Legal Studies
MIGA – Multilateral Investment Guarantee Agency
Mill – Mill (Constitutional)
Miller – H. Miller, Treaties and Other International Acts of the United States
Miller, Const. – S. Miller, Lectures on the Constitution of the United States
Mill, Log. – A System of Logic, Ratiocinative and Inductive, Being a Connected View of the Principles of Evidence and the Methods of Scientific Investigation
Mil. L. Rev. – Military Law Review
Mills, Em. Dom. – A Treatise on the Law of Eminent Domain
Minn. – Minnesota Reports
Minn. Code Agency – Minnesota Code of Agency Rules
Minn. Intell. Prop. Rev. – Minnesota Intellectual Property Review
Minn. J. Global Trade – Minnesota Journal of Global Trade
Minn. Laws – Laws of Minnesota
Minn. L. Rev. – Minnesota Law Review
Minn. R. – Minnesota Rules
Minn. Reg. – Minnesota State Register
Minn. Sess. Law Serv. – Minnesota Session Law Service
Minn. Stat. – Minnesota Statutes

Minn. Stat. Ann. – Minnesota Statutes Annotated
Minn. Trial Law. – Minnesota Trial Lawyer
Minor – Minor (Ala.)
Misc. – New York Miscellaneous Reports
Misc. 2d – New York Miscellaneous Reports, Second Series
Miss. – Mississippi Reports
Miss. C. L. Rev. – Mississippi College Law Review
Miss. Code Ann. – Mississippi Code Annotated
Miss. Dec. – Mississippi Decisions
Miss. Law. – Mississippi Lawyer
Miss. Laws – General Laws of Mississippi
Miss. L.J. – Mississippi Law Journal
Miss. Reg. – Mississippi Official and Statistical Register
Miss. St. Cas. – Mississippi State Cases
Mitf. Eq. Pl. – Mitford's Equity Pleading
M.J. – Military Justice Reporter
M.L.R. – Military Law Review
MLS. – Multiple Listing Service
Mo. – Missouri Reports
Mo. Ann. Stat. – Annotated Missouri Statutes
Mo. App. – Missouri Appeals Reports
Mo. B.J. – Missouri Bar Journal
Mo. Code Regs. Ann. – Missouri Code of State Regulations Annotated
Mod. Am. Law – Modern American Law
Mod. L. Rev. – Modern Law Review
Mo. Envtl. L. & Pol'y Rev. – Missouri Environmental Law & Policy Review
Mo. J. Disp. Resol. – Missouri Journal of Dispute Resolution
Mo. Laws – Laws of Missouri
Mo. Legis. Serv. – Missouri Legislative Service
Mo. L. Rev. – Missouri Law Review
Monag. – Monaghan (Pa.)
Monash U. L. Rev. – Monash University Law Review
Mont. – Montana Reports
Mont. Admin. R. – Administrative Rules of Montana
Mont. Admin. Reg. – Montana Administrative Register
Mont. Code Ann. – Montana Code Annotated
Monthly Lab. Rev. – Monthly Labor Review
Mont. Law. – Montana Lawyer
Mont. Laws – Laws of Montana
Mont. L. Rev. – Montana Law Review
Mont. Rev. Code Ann. – Revised Codes of Montana Annotated
Morawetz, Corporations – A Treatise on the Law of Private Corporations
Mor. Corp. – Morawetz, A Treatise on the Law of Private Corporations
Mo. Reg. – Missouri Register
Mo. Rev. Stat. – Missouri Revised Statutes
Morris – Morris (Iowa)
Morse, Banks – A Treatise on the Law of Banks and Banking
Mo. St. Ann. – Missouri Statutes Annotated
Moyle, Contract of Sale – The Contract of Sale in Civil Law, with References to the Laws of England, Scotland, and France
MPC – Model Penal Code
M.P.E.P. – Manual of Patent Examining Procedure
M.R.S.A. – Model Revised Statutes Annotated
M.S.A. – **1.** Minnesota Statutes Annotated. **2.** Michigan Statutes Annotated.
MSL L. Rev. – MSL Law Review
MSL Rev. – MSL Review: A Journal for Practitioners and Judges
M.S.P.B. – Decisions of the United States Merit Systems Protection Board
M.U.L.L. – MULL: Modern Uses of Logic in Law
Mun. Att'y – Municipal Attorney
Munf. – Munford (Va.)
Mur. – Murphey (N.C.)
Mut. Funds Guide (CCH) – Mutual Funds Guide

N

NAACP – National Association for the Advancement of Colored People
NACUA – National Association of College and University Attorneys
NAFTA: L. & Bus. Rev. Am. – NAFTA: Law & Business Review of the Americas
N. Am. Rev. – North American Review
NAS – National Academy of Science
NASA – National Aeronautics and Space Administration
NASD – National Association of Securities Dealers
Nat. Gas Law. J. – Natural Gas Lawyer's Journal
Nation Code – Navajo Nation Code
Nat'l Black L.J. – National Black Law Journal
Nat'l J. Crim. Def. – National Journal of Criminal Defense
Nat'l Jewish L. Rev. – National Jewish Law Review
Nat'l Pub. Empl. Rep. (LRP) – National Public Employment Reporter
Nat'l Rep. Legal Ethics (UPA) – National Reporter on Legal Ethics
Nat'l Tax J. – National Tax Journal
NATO – North Atlantic Treaty Organization
Nat. Res. Law. – Natural Resources Lawyer
Nat. Resources & Env't. – Natural Resources & Environment (ABA)
Nat. Resources J. – Natural Resources Journal
Nat. Resources Law. – Natural Resources Lawyer
Nat. Resources L. Newsl. – Natural Resources Law Newsletter (ABA)
Navajo Rptr. – Navajo Reporter
Naval L. Rev. – Naval Law Review
NBA Nat'l B.A. Mag. – NBA National Bar Association Magazine
NBS – National Bureau of Standards
N.C. – North Carolina Reports
N.C. Admin. Code – North Carolina Administrative Code
N.C. Adv. Legis. Serv. – Advance Legislative Service to the General Statutes of North Carolina
N.C. App. – North Carolina Court of Appeals Reports
N.C.B. – North Carolina Bar
N.C. Banking Inst. – North Carolina Banking Institute
N.C. Bar – North Carolina Bar
NCCDL – National College of Criminal Defense Lawyers and Public Defenders
N.C. Cent. L.J. – North Carolina Central Law Journal
NCDA – National College of District Attorneys
N.C. Gen. Stat. – General Statutes of North Carolina
N. Chip. – N. Chipman (Vt.)
N.C. J. Int'l L. & Com. Reg. – North Carolina Journal of International Law & Commercial Regulation
N.C. J. L. & Tech. – North Carolina Journal of Law and Technology
N.C. L. Rev. – North Carolina Law Review
N.C. Reg. – North Carolina Register
N.C.S.B. Quarterly – North Carolina State Bar Quarterly
N.C. Sess. Laws – Session Laws of North Carolina
N.C. Term R. – North Carolina Term Reports
N.D. – North Dakota Reports
NDAA – National District Attorneys Association
N.D. Admin. Code – North Dakota Administrative Code
N. Dak. L. Rev. – North Dakota Law Review
N.D. B. Br. – North Dakota Bar Briefs

N.D. Cent. Code – North Dakota Century Code
N.D. Laws – Laws of North Dakota
N.D. L. Rev. – North Dakota Law Review
N.E. – North Eastern Reporter
N.E.2d. – North Eastern Reporter, Second Series
Neb. – Nebraska Reports
Neb. Admin. R. & Regs. – Nebraska Administrative Rules & Regulations
Neb. Ct. App. – Nebraska Court of Appeals Reports
Neb. Laws – Laws of Nebraska
Neb. L.B. – Nebraska Law Bulletin
Neb. L. Bull. – Nebraska Law Bulletin
Neb. L. Rev. – Nebraska Law Review
Neb. Rev. Stat. – Revised Statutes of Nebraska
Neb. Rev. Stat. Ann. – Revised Statutes of Nebraska Annotated
Neb. St. B.J. – Nebraska State Bar Journal
Negot. J. – Negotiation Journal
Nev. – Nevada Reports
Nev. Admin. Code – Nevada Administrative Code
Nev. Law. – Nevada Lawyer
Nev. Rev. Stat. – Nevada Revised Statutes
Nev. Rev. Stat. Ann. – Nevada Revised Statutes Annotated
Nev. Stat. – Statutes of Nevada
New Eng. Int'l & Comp. L. Ann. – New England International and Comparative Law Annual
New Eng. J. Med. – New England Journal of Medicine
New Eng. J. on Crim. & Civ. Confinement – New England Journal on Criminal & Civil Confinement
New. Eng. J. on Prison L. – New England Journal on Prison Law
New Eng. J. Prison L. – New England Journal on Prison Law
New Eng. L. Rev. – New England Law Review
New Eur. L. Rev. – New Europe Law Review
New L.J. – New Law Journal
Newsl. – Newsletter
News Media & L. – News Media & the Law
NEXUS – NEXUS: A Journal of Opinion
N.H. – New Hampshire Reports
N.H.B.J. – New Hampshire Bar Journal
N.H. Code Admin. R. Ann. – New Hampshire Code of Administrative Rules Annotated
N.H. Laws – Laws of the State of New Hampshire
N.H. Rev. Stat. Ann. – New Hampshire Revised Statutes Annotated
N.H. Rulemaking Reg. – New Hampshire Rulemaking Register
NHTSA – National Highway Transportation Safety Administration
N. Ill. U. L. Rev. – Northern Illinois University Law Review
N.J. – New Jersey Reports
N.J. Admin. – New Jersey Administrative Reports
N.J. Admin. 2d – New Jersey Administrative Reports, 2d Series
N.J. Admin. Code – New Jersey Administrative Code
N.J. Eq. – New Jersey Equity Reports
N.J.L. – **1.** New Jersey Law Reports. **2.** New Jersey Lawyer.
N.J. Law. – New Jersey Lawyer
N.J. Laws – Laws of New Jersey
N.J.L.J. – New Jersey Law Journal
N.J. Misc. – New Jersey Miscellaneous Reports
N.J. Reg. – New Jersey Register
N.J. Rev. Stat. – New Jersey Revised Statutes
N.J.S.A. – New Jersey Statutes Annotated
N.J. Sess. Law Serv. – New Jersey Session Law Service
N.J. Stat. Ann. – New Jersey Statutes Annotated
N.J. St. B.J. – New Jersey State Bar Journal
N.J. Super. – New Jersey Superior Court Reports
N.J. Tax – New Jersey Tax Court Reports
N. Ky. L. Rev. – Northern Kentucky Law Review
N. Ky. St. L. F. – Northern Kentucky State Law Forum
N.L.R.B. – Decisions & Orders of the National Labor Relations Board
NLRB Dec. (CCH) – NLRB Decisions
N.M. – New Mexico Reports
N.M. Admin. Code – New Mexico Administrative Code
N.M. Adv. Legis. Serv. – New Mexico Advance Legislative Service
N. Mar. I. – Northern Mariana Islands Reporter
N. Mar. I. Code – Northern Mariana Islands Commonwealth Code
N. Mar. I. Commw. Rptr. – Northern Mariana Islands Commonwealth Reporter
N. Mar. I. Reg. – Northern Mariana Islands Commonwealth Register
N.M.B. – Determinations of the National Mediation Board
N.M. Bar Bull. – New Mexico Bar Bulletin
N.M. Laws – Laws of New Mexico
N.M. L. Rev. – New Mexico Law Review
N.M. Reg. – New Mexico Register
N.M. Stat. Ann. – New Mexico Statutes Annotated
Noise Reg. Rep. – Noise Regulation Report
nonacq. – Nonacquiescence
Notre Dame Est. Plan. Inst. – Notre Dame Estate Planning Institute
Notre Dame Est. Plan. Inst. Proc. – Notre Dame Estate Planning Institute Proceedings
Notre Dame J. Legis. – Notre Dame Journal of Legislation
Notre Dame J.L. Ethics & Pub. Pol'y – Notre Dame Journal of Law, Ethics, & Public Policy
Notre Dame Law. – Notre Dame Lawyer
Notre Dame L. Rev. – Notre Dame Law Review
Nott. & McC. – Nott & McCord (S.C.)
Nova L.J. – Nova Law Journal
Nova L. Rev. – Nova Law Review
N.R.A.B. – National Railroad Adjustment Board
N.R.C. – Nuclear Regulatory Commission Issuances
N.R.S. – Nevada Revised Statutes
n.s. – New Series
NSA – National Security Agency
NSC – National Security Council
NSF – National Science Foundation
N.T.S.B. – National Transportation Safety Board Decisions
Nuclear Reg. Rep. (CCH) – Nuclear Regulation Reports
NU Forum – NU Forum: A Cooperative Law Journal of Northeastern University School of Law
N.W. – North Western Reporter
N.W.2d. – North Western Reporter, Second Series
Nw. J. Int'l L. & Bus. – Northwestern Journal of International Law & Business
Nw. U. L. Rev. – Northwestern University Law Review
N.Y. – New York Reports
N.Y.2d. – New York Reports, Second Series
N.Y. A.D. – New York Appellate Division Reports
N.Y. A.D.2d. – New York Appellate Division Reports, Second Series
N.Y. Ann. Cas. – New York Annotated Cases
N.Y. App. Div. – New York Supreme Court, Appellate Division
N.Y. Cass. Err. – New York Cases in Error, Caine's Cases
N.Y. Ch. Ann. – New York Chancery Reports Annotated
N.Y. Ch. Sent. – New York Chancery Sentinel
N.Y. City Ct. Suppl. – New York City Court Supplement
N.Y. City H. Rec. – New York City Hall Recorder

N.Y. City L. Rev. – New York City Law Review
N.Y. Civ. Proc. R., N.S. – New York Civil Procedure Reports, New Series
N.Y. Civ. Pr. Rep. – New York Civil Procedure Reports
N.Y.C. L. Rev. – New York City Law Review
N.Y. Code Rep. – New York Code Reporter
N.Y. Code Reports, N.S. – New York Code Reports, New Series
N.Y. Comp. Codes R. & Regs. – Official Compilation of Codes, Rules & Regulations of the State of New York
N.Y. Cond. – New York Condensed Reports
N.Y. Cr. R. – New York Criminal Reports
N.Y. Daily L. Gaz. – New York Daily Law Gazette
N.Y. Daily Reg. – New York Daily Register
N.Y. Elect. Cas. – New York Election Cases
N.Y. Int'l L. Rev. – New York International Law Review
N.Y. Laws – Laws of New York
N.Y. Law B. Bull. – New York Lawyer Bar Bulletin
N.Y. Law B.J. – New York Lawyer Bar Journal
N.Y. Law J. – New York Law Journal
N.Y. L.C. Ann. – New York Leading Cases Annotated
N.Y. Leg. N. – New York Legal News
N.Y. Leg. Obs. – New York Legal Observer
N.Y. Leg. Reg. – New York Legal Register
N.Y. L.F. – New York Law Forum
N.Y. L. Gaz. – New York Law Gazette
N.Y. L.J. – New York Law Journal
N.Y. L. Rec. – New York Law Record
N.Y. L. Rev. – New York Law Review
N.Y. L. Sch. Hum. Rts. Ann. – New York Law School Human Rights Annual
N.Y.L. Sch. J. Hum. Rts. – New York Law School Journal of Human Rights
N.Y.L. Sch. Int'l L. Soc'y J. – New York Law School International Law Society Journal
N.Y.L. Sch. J. Int'l & Comp. L. – New York Law School Journal of International & Comparative Law
N.Y.L. Sch. L. Rev. – New York Law School Law Review
NYLS Citylaw – New York Law School Citylaw
N.Y. Misc. – New York Miscellaneous Reports
N.Y. Misc.2d. – New York Miscellaneous Reports, Second Series
N.Y. Month. L. Bul. – New York Monthly Law Bulletin
N.Y. Month. L.R. – New York Monthly Law Reports
N.Y. Mun. Gaz. – New York Municipal Gazette
N.Y. Ops. Atty. Gen. – Opinions of the Attorney General of New York
N.Y. Pr. Rep. – New York Practice Reports
N.Y. Rec. – New York Record
N.Y.S. – New York Supplement Reporter
N.Y.S.2d. – New York Supplement Reporter, Second Series
N.Y.S.E. Guide (CCH) – New York Stock Exchange Guide
N.Y. Sea Grant L. & Pol'y – New York Sea Grant Law and Policy
N.Y. State Bar J. – New York State Bar Journal
N.Y. St. B.A. Antitrust L. Symp. – New York State Bar Association Antitrust Law Symposium
N.Y. St. B.J. – New York State Bar Journal
N.Y. St. Reg. – New York State Register
N.Y. St. Rep. – New York State Reporter
N.Y. Sup. Ct. – New York Supreme Court Reports
N.Y.U. Ann. Surv. Am. L. – New York University Annual Survey of American Law
N.Y.U. Envtl. L.J. – New York University Environmental Law Journal
N.Y.U. J. Int'l L. & Pol. – New York University Journal of International Law and Politics
N.Y.U. J. Legis. & Pub. Pol'y – New York University Journal of Legislation and Public Policy
N.Y.U. L.Q. Rev. – New York University Law Quarterly Review
N.Y.U. L. Rev. – New York University Law Review
N.Y.U. Rev. L. & Soc. Change. – New York University Review of Law and Social Change
N.Z. L.J. – New Zealand Law Journal
N.Z. U. L. Rev. – New Zealand Universities Law Review

O

OAS – Organization of American States
OASDI – Old Age, Survivors and Disability Insurance Benefits
O.C.D. – Ohio Circuit Decisions
Ocean & Coastal L.J. – Ocean & Coastal Law Journal
Ocean Dev. & Int'l L.J. – Ocean Development and International Law Journal
Odgers, Libel and Slander – The Law of Libel and Slander, and of Actions on the Case for Words Causing Damage
OECD – Organization for Economic Cooperation and Development
OFCC. – Office of Federal Contract Compliance
OFCCP Fed. Cont. Compl. Man (CCH) – OFCCP Federal Contract Compliance Manual
OFDI – Office of Foreign Direct Investment
Off. Gaz. – **1.** Official Gazette of the United States Patent Office, Patents. **2.** Official Gazette of the United States Patent Office, Trademarks.
Off. Gaz. Pat. Office – Official Gazette of the United States Patent Office
OFPP. – Office of Federal Procurement Policy
OFR – Office of the Federal Register
O.G. – Official Gazette of the United States Patent Office
OHCHR – Office of the United Nations High Commissioner for Human Rights
Ohio. – Ohio Reports
Ohio Admin. Code – Ohio Administrative Code
Ohio App. – Ohio Appellate Reports
Ohio App.2d. – Ohio Appellate Reports, Second Series
Ohio App.3d. – Ohio Appellate Reports, Third Series
Ohio App. Unrep. – Unreported Ohio Appellate Cases (Anderson)
Ohio B. – Ohio Bar Reports
Ohio C.C. – Ohio Circuit Court Reports
Ohio C.C. (n.s.) – Ohio Circuit Court Reports, New Series
Ohio Cir. Ct. R. – Ohio Circuit Court Reports
Ohio Cir. Ct. R., N.S. – Ohio Circuit Court Reports, New Series
Ohio Cir. Dec. – Ohio Circuit Decisions
Ohio Dec. – Ohio Decisions
Ohio Dec. Reprint. – Ohio Decisions, Reprint
Ohio Dep't – Ohio Department Reports
Ohio F. Dec. – Ohio Federal Decisions
Ohio Gov't – Ohio Government Reports
Ohio Jur. – Ohio Jurisprudence
Ohio Jur. 2d – Ohio Jurisprudence 2d
Ohio Law. – Ohio Lawyer
Ohio Law Abs. – Ohio Law Abstracts
Ohio Law Bul. – Ohio Law Bulletin
Ohio Law J. – Ohio Law Journal
Ohio Law Rep. – Ohio Law Reporter
Ohio Laws – State of Ohio Legislative Acts Passed and Joint Resolutions Adopted
Ohio Legis. Bull. – Page's Ohio Legislative Bulletin
Ohio Legis. Serv. – Baldwin's Ohio Legislative Service
Ohio Leg. N. – Ohio Legal News
Ohio Misc. – Ohio Miscellaneous

Ohio Misc. 2d — Ohio Miscellaneous, Second Series
Ohio Monthly Rec. — Ohio Monthly Record
Ohio N.P. — Ohio Nisi Prius
Ohio N.P., (n.s.) — Ohio Nisi Prius, New Series
Ohio N.U. L. Rev. — Ohio Northern University Law Review
Ohio O. — Ohio Opinions
Ohio O. 2d — Ohio Opinions, Second Series
Ohio Op. — Ohio Opinions
Ohio Op. 2d. — Ohio Opinions, Second Series
Ohio Op. 3d — Ohio Opinions, Third Series
Ohio Prob. — Ohio Probate
Ohio Rev. Code Ann. — Ohio Revised Code Annotated
Ohio S. & C.P. Dec. — Ohio Superior and Common Pleas Decisions
Ohio St. — Ohio State Reports
Ohio St.2d. — Ohio State Reports, Second Series
Ohio St.3d. — Ohio State Reports, Third Series
Ohio St. B.A. Rep. — Ohio State Bar Association Report
Ohio St. J. on Disp. Resol. — Ohio State Journal on Dispute Resolution
Ohio St. L.J. — Ohio State Law Journal
Ohio Supp. — Ohio Supplement
Oil & Gas Tax Q. — Oil & Gas Tax Quarterly
Oil, Gas & Energy Q. — Oil, Gas and Energy Quarterly
O.J. — Official Journal of the European Communities
Okla. — Oklahoma Reports
Okla. Admin. Code — Oklahoma Administrative Code
Okla. B.J. — Oklahoma Bar Journal
Okla. City U.L. Rev. — Oklahoma City University Law Review
Okla. Crim. — Oklahoma Criminal Reports
Okla. L.J. — Oklahoma Law Journal
Okla. L. Rev. — Oklahoma Law Review
Okla. Sess. — Oklahoma Session Laws
Okla. Sess. Law Serv. — Oklahoma Session Law Service
Okla. Stat. — Oklahoma Statutes
Okla. Stat. Ann. — Oklahoma Statutes Annotated
Oliver on Conveyancing — Practical Conveyancing, A Selection of Forms of General Utility with Notes Interspersed
OLMS — Office of Labor-Management Standards
OMB — Office of Management and Budget
O.O. — Ohio Opinions
Op. Atty. Gen. — Opinions of the Attorney General
OPCW — Organization for the Prohibition of Chemical Weapons (UN)
OPM — Office of Personnel Management
Op. Off. Legal Counsel — Opinions of Office of Legal Counsel of Department of Justice
Op. Solic. P.O. Dep't — Official Opinions of the Solicitor for the Post Office Department
Or. — Oregon Reports
Or. Admin. R. — Oregon Administrative Rules
Or. Admin. R. Bull. — Oregon Administrative Rules Bulletin
Orange County B.J. — Orange County Bar Journal
Orange County Law. — Orange County Lawyer
Or. App. — Oregon Reports, Court of Appeals
Or. Bar Bull. — Oregon Bar Bulletin
ORC. — Ohio Revised Code
Or. Laws — Oregon Laws and Resolutions
Or. Laws. Adv. Sh. — Oregon Laws and Resolutions Advance Sheet
Or. Laws Spec. Sess. — Oregon Laws and Resolutions Special Session
Orleans App. — Orleans Appeals, La.
Or. L. Rev. — Oregon Law Review
Or. Rev. Int'l L. — Oregon Review of International Law
Or. Rev. Stat. — Oregon Revised Statutes
Or. St. B. Bull. — Oregon State Bar Bulletin
Or. Tax — Oregon Tax Reports
O.S. — **1.** Oklahoma Statutes. **2.** Old Series.
OSG — Office of the Secretary-General (UN)
Osgoode Hall L.J. — Osgoode Hall Law Journal
OSHA — Occupational Safety and Health Administration
OSHA Compl. Guide (CCH) — Human Resources Management OSHA Compliance Guide
O.S.H. Cas. (BNA) — Occupational Health and Safety Cases
O.S.H. Dec. (CCH) — Occupational Safety and Health Decisions
OSHRC — Occupational Safety and Health Review Commission
O.S.H. Rep. (BNA) — Occupational Safety and Health Reporter
Otago L. Rev. — Otago Law Review
OTS — Office of Thrift Supervision
Ottawa L. Rev. — Ottawa Law Review
Overt. — Overton (Tenn.)
Oxford J. Legal Stud. — Oxford Journal of Legal Studies

P

P. — Pacific Reporter
P.2d. — Pacific Reporter, Second Series
P.3d — Pacific Reporter, Third Series
Pa. — Pennsylvania State Reports
Pa. B.A.Q. — Pennsylvania Bar Association Quarterly
Pa. Bull. — Pennsylvania Bulletin
Pa. C. — Pennsylvania County Court Reports
Pace Envtl. L. Rev. — Pace Environmental Law Review
Pace Int'l L. Rev. — Pace International Law Review
Pace L. Rev. — Pace Law Review
Pace Y.B. Int'l L. — Pace Yearbook of International Law
Pacific C. L.J. — Pacific Coast Law Journal, San Francisco
Pac. L.J. — Pacific Law Journal
Pa. Co. Ct. R. — Pennsylvania County Court Reports
Pa. Code — Pennsylvania Code
Pa. Commw. — Pennsylvania Commonwealth Court Reports
Pa. Com. Pl. — Pennsylvania Common Pleas Reporter
Pa. Cons. Stat. — Pennsylvania Consolidated Statutes
Pa. Cons. Stat. Ann. — Pennsylvania Consolidated Statutes Annotated
Pa. Corp. — Pennsylvania Corporation Reporter
Pac. Rim L. & Pol'y J. — Pacific Rim Law & Policy Journal
Pa. C.S.A. — Pennsylvania Consolidated Statutes Annotated
Pa. D. — Pennsylvania District Reports
Pa. D. & C. — Pennsylvania District and County Reports
Pa. D. & C.2d — Pennsylvania District and County Reports, Second Series
Pa. D. & C.3d — Pennsylvania District and County Reports, Third Series
Pa. D. & C.4th — Pennsylvania District and County Reports, Fourth Series
Paige Ch. — Paige's Chancery Reports (N.Y.)
Pa. Law. — Pennsylvania Lawyer
Pa. Law J. — Pennsylvania Law Journal
Pa. Laws — Laws of Pennsylvania
Pa. Law Ser. — Pennsylvania Law Series
Pa. L. Rec. — Pennsylvania Law Record
Pa. Leg. Gaz. — Legal Gazette Reports, (Campbell) Pa.
Pa. Legis. Serv. — Purdon's Pennsylvania Legislative Service
Pa. Misc. — Pennsylvania Miscellaneous Reports
Pamph. Laws — Pamphlet Laws, Acts
P & F — Pike and Fischer
Parker Sch. J. E. Eur. L. — Parker School Journal of East European Law

Pars. Bill & N. — Parsons, A Treatise on the Law of Promissory Notes and Bills of Exchange
Pars. Cont. — Parsons, The Law of Contracts
Pars. Mar. Ins. — Parsons, Treatise on the Law of Maritime Insurance and General Average
Pars. Mar. Law — Parsons, Treatise on Maritime Law
Pars. Merc. Law — Parsons, Elements of Mercantile Law
Pars. Shipp. & Adm. — Parsons, A Treatise on the Law of Shipping and the Law and Practice of Admiralty
Pa. Stat. Ann. — Pennsylvania Statutes Annotated
Pa. Super. — Pennsylvania Superior Court Reports
Pat. L. Ann. — Patent Law Annual
Pat. L. Devs. — Patent Law Developments
Pat. Procur. & Exploitation — Patent Procurement and Exploitation
Pat. Off. Gaz. — Patent Office Gazette
Pat. Off. Rep. — Patent Office Reports
Pat. Trademark & Copyright J. (BNA) — Patent Trademark and Copyright Journal
PBGC — Pension Benefit Guaranty Corporation
P.C. — Penal Code
P.C.I.J. — Permanent Court of International Justice Reports of Judgments, Advisory Opinions, and Orders
Peck — Peck (Tenn.)
Pelt. — Peltier's Decisions, Parish at Orleans (La.)
Pen. & W. — Penrose & Watts (Pa.)
Pen. Code — Penal Code
Pen. Laws. — Penal Laws
Penne. — Pennewill (Del.)
Pennyp. — Pennypacker (Pa.)
Pens. & Ben. Rep. (BNA) — Pensions and Benefits Reporter
Pens. & Profit Sharing 2d (RIA) — Pension and Profit Sharing, Second Edition
Pens. Plan Guide (CCH) — Pension Plan Guide
Pens. Rep. (BNA) — Pension Reporter
Pepp. Disp. Resol. L.J. — Pepperdine Dispute Resolution Law Journal
Pepp. L. Rev. — Pepperdine Law Review
Perf. Arts Rev. — Performing Arts Review
Perry, Trusts — A Treatise on the Law of Trusts and Trustees
Pers. Fin. L. Q. Rep. — Personal Finance Law Quarterly Report
Personal Fin. L. Q. Rep. — Personal Finance Law Quarterly Report
Personnel Mgmt. (BNA) — Personnel Management
Perspectives — Perspectives: Teaching Legal Research and Writing
Pet. — Peters, U.S. Supreme Court Reports
P-H — Prentice-Hall
Phila. Leg. Int. — Philadelphia Legal Intelligencer, Pa.
Phil. & Pub. Aff. — Philosophy & Public Affairs
Phil. Eq. — Phillip's Equity Reports (N.C.)
Phil. Ev. — Phillips, A Treatise on the Law of Evidence
Phil. Ins. — Phillips, A Treatise on the Law of Insurance
Philippine — Philippine Reports
Philippine L.J. — Philippine Law Journal
Phil. Law — Phillip's Law Reports (N.C.)
Phillimore, Int. Law — Commentaries Upon International Law
Phillip E. Heckerling Inst. on Est. Plan. — Phillip E. Heckerling Institute on Estate Planning (U. Miami)
Phil. Pat. — Phillips, The Law of Patents of Inventions Including the Remedies and Legal Proceedings in Relation to Patent Rights
PHS. — Public Health Service
Pick. — Pickering (Mass.)
Pierce L. Rev. — Pierce Law Review
Pierce, R.R. — American Railroad Law
Pin. — Pinney (Wis.)
Ping. Chat. Mortg. — Pingrey, A Treatise on the Law of Chattel Mortgages
Pitm. Prin. & Sur. — Pitman, A Treatise on the Law of Principal and Surety
Pitt. L.J. — Pittsburgh Legal Journal
Pittsb. R. — Pittsburgh Reports, Pa.
Pitts. Leg. J. — Pittsburgh Legal Journal, Pa.
Pitts. Leg. J., N.S. — Pittsburgh Legal Journal, New Series, Pa.
Phelps, Juridical Equity — Elements of Juridical Equity
P.L. — Public Law
Pl. — Pleading
Platt, Cov. — A Practical Treatise on the Law of Covenants
Platt, Leases — A Treatise on the Law of Leases, with Forms and Precedents
PLI. — Practicing Law Institute
P.L.J. — **1.** Pacific Law Journal. **2.** Pittsburgh Legal Journal, Pa.
P.L.R. — Private Letter Rulings (IRS)
Poe, Pl. — Pleading and Practice in Courts of Common Law
Pollock, Contracts — Principles of Contract, A Treatise on the General Principles Concerning the Validity of Agreements in the Law of England
Pollock, Torts — The Law of Torts, A Treatise on the Principles of Obligations Arising from Civil Wrongs in the Common Law
Pom. Const. Law — Pomeroy, Introduction to the Constitutional Law of the United States
Pom. Eq. Jur. — Pomeroy, A Treatise on Equity Jurisprudence, as Administered in the United States
Pomeroy, Code Rem. — Code Remedies: Remedies and Remedial Rights by the Civil Action
Pomeroy, Int. Law — Lectures on International Law in Time of Peace
Pomeroy, Rem. — Remedies and Remedial Rights by the Civil Action According to the Reformed American Procedure
Pom. Spec. Perf. — Pomeroy, Treatise on the Specific Performance of Contracts
Poore, Const. — Poore, Federal and State Constitutions, Colonial Charters, and Other Organic Laws of the United States
Poore's Charters and Constitutions — Poore, Federal and State Constitutions, Colonial Charters, and Other Organic Laws of the United States
Pope, Lunacy — A Treatise on the Law and Practice of Lunacy
Port. — Porter (Ala.)
Portia L.J. — Portia Law Journal
Port. Ins. — Porter, Laws of Insurance: Fire, Life, Accident and Guarantee...
Portland U. L. Rev. — Portland University Law Review
Pothier, Obligations — A Treatise on the Law of Obligations, or Contracts
Potomac L. Rev. — Potomac Law Review
Pow. Cont. — Powell, Essay on the Law of Contracts and Agreements
Pow. Mortg. — Powell, A Treatise on the Law of Mortgages
Prac. Act — Practice Act
Prac. Law. — Practical Lawyer
Prac. Litigator — Practical Litigator
Prac. Real Est. Law. — The Practical Real Estate Lawyer (ABA)
Prac. Tax Law. — The Practical Tax Lawyer (ABA)
P.R. Dec. — Decisiones de Puerto Rico
Prest. Conv. — Preston, A Treatise on Conveyancing
Prest. Est. — Preston, An Elementary Treatise on Estates

Preventive L. Rep. – Preventive Law Reporter
Preview U.S. Sup. Ct. Cas. – Preview of United States Supreme Court Cases
Priv. Ltr. Rul. – Private Letter Ruling (IRS)
P.R. Laws – Laws of Puerto Rico
P.R. Laws Ann. – Laws of Puerto Rico Annotated
Prob. – **1.** Probate. **2.** Probation.
Prob. & Prop. – Probate & Property (ABA)
Prob. Law. – Probate Lawyer
Prob. L.J. – Probate Law Journal
Proc. N.Y.U. Nat'l Conf. on Lab. – Proceedings of the New York University National Conference on Labor
Procurement Law – Procurement Lawyer
Prod. Liab. L.J. – Products Liability Law Journal
Prod. Liab. Rep. (CCH) – **1.** Products Liability Reporter. **2.** Products Liability Reports.
Prod. Safety & Liab. Rep. (BNA) – Product Safety and Liability Reporter
Prof. Law. – The Professional Lawyer (ABA)
P.R. Offic. Trans. – Official Translations of the Opinions of the Supreme Court of Puerto Rico
Prop. Treas. Reg. – Proposed Treasury Regulation
Prosecutor: J. Nat'l District Atty's Ass'n – Prosecutor: Journal of the National District Attorneys Association
Prospectus – Prospectus: A Journal of Law Reform
Prov. Rep. (CCH) – Provincial Reporter
P.R.R. – Puerto Rico Supreme Court Reports
P.R. Sent. – Sentencias del Tribunal Supremo de Puerto Rico
P.S. – **1.** Pennsylvania Statutes. **2.** Pennsylvania Unconsolidated Statutes Annotated.
PSAA – Public Sector Arbitration Awards
Psychol. Pub. Pol'y & L. – Psychology, Public Policy & Law
PTO – Patent and Trademark Office
Pub. Acts – Public Acts
Pub. Admin. Rev. – Public Administration Review
Pub. Ad. Rev. – Public Administrative Review
Pub. Cont. L.J. – Public Contract Law Journal (ABA)
Pub. Cont. Newsl. – Public Contract Newsletter (ABA)
Pub. Ent. Advert. & Allied Fields L.Q. – Publishing, Entertainment, Advertising & Allied Fields Law Quarterly
Pub. Gen. Laws – Public General Laws
Pub. Int. L. Rev. – Public Interest Law Review
Pub. L. – Public Law
Pub. Land & Resources L. Rev. – Public Land & Resources Law Review
Pub. Land L. Rev. – Public Land Law Review
Pub. Lands Dec. – Decisions of the Dept. of Interior and General Land Office in Cases Relating to Public Lands
Pub. Laws – Public Laws
Pub. L. F. – Public Law Forum
Pub. L. Forum – Public Law Forum
Pub. L. No. – Public Law Number
Pub. Util. Fort. – Public Utilities Fortnightly
Pub. Util. Rep. (PUR) – Public Utilities Reports
PUD – Planned Unit Development
Puerto Rico. – Puerto Rico Reports
Puget Sound L. Rev. – Puget Sound Law Review
PUR – Public Utilities Reports
PWA – Public Works Administration
PWBA – Pension and Welfare Benefits Administration

Q

Q.B. – Queen's Bench (Eng.)
Q.B. Div. – Queen's Bench Division (Eng.)
QLR – QLR (Quinnipiac Law Review)
Queen's L.J. – Queen's Law Journal
Quinnipiac Health L.J. – Quinnipiac Health Law Journal
Quinnipiac L. Rev. – Quinnipiac Law Review
Quinnipiac Prob. L.J. – Quinnipiac Probate Law Journal

R

Race & Ethnic Ancestry L. Dig. – Race & Ethnic Ancestry Law Digest
Rad. Reg. (P & F) – Radio Regulation
Rad. Reg. 2d (P & F) – Radio Regulation, Second Series
Rand. – Randolph (Va.)
Rap. Lar. – Rapalje, A Treatise on the Law of Larceny and Kindred Offenses
Rap. Wit. – Rapalje, A Treatise on the Law of Witnesses
Rawle – Rawle (Pa.)
Rawle, Const. U.S. – A View of the Constitution of the United States of America
Rawle, Cov. – A Practical Treatise on the Law of Covenants for Title
Ray, Med. Jur. – A Treatise on the Medical Jurisprudence of Insanity
R.C. – Revised Code
R.C.L. – Ruling Case Law
R.C.M. – Revised Code of Montana
RCWA. – Revised Code of Washington Annotated
Real Est. Fin. L.J. – Real Estate Finance Law Journal
Real Est. L.J. – Real Estate Law Journal
Real Est. L. Rep. – Real Estate Law Report
Real Est. Rev. – Real Estate Review
Real Est. Tax'n – Real Estate Taxation
Real Prop. Prob. & Tr. J. – Real Property, Probate & Trust Journal (ABA)
Rec. Ass'n Bar City of N.Y. – Record of the Association of the Bar of the City of New York
Record – Record, Association of the Bar of the City of New York
Redf. Carr. – I. Redfield, The Law of Carriers of Goods and Passengers
Reeve, Law of Baron and Femme – The Law of Baron and Femme, of Parent and Child, of Guardian and Ward, of Master and Servant, and the Powers of the Courts of Chancery
Reeve on Descents – A Treatise on the Law of Descents in the Several United States of America
Reeves, Hist. Com. Law (Finl. ed.) – Reeves' History of the English Law (Finlason edition)
Regent U. L. Rev. – Regent University Law Review
REIT – Real Estate Investment Trust
rem'g – remanding
Remington, Bankr. – A Treatise on the Bankruptcy Law of the United States
Rep. Atty. Gen. – Attorneys General's Reports
Rep. Pat. Des. & Tr. Cas. – Reports of Patents Designs and Trademark Cases
Repub. Tex. Laws – Laws of the Republic of Texas
Research in L. & Econ. – Research in Law and Economics: A Research Annual
Res Gestae – Res Gestae (Ind. State Bar Assoc.)
RESPA – Real Estate Settlement Procedures
Rev. Civ. Code. – Revised Civil Code
Rev. Civ. St. – Revised Civil Statutes
Rev. Code – Revised Code
Rev. Code Civ. Proc. – Revised Code Civil Procedure
Rev. Code Cr. Proc. – Revised Code of Criminal Procedure
Rev. Cr. Code. – Revised Criminal Code
rev'd – reversed
Rev. Der. P.R. – Revista de Derecho Puertorriqueno
Rev. Int'l Bus. L. – Review of International Business Law
Rev. Int'l Comm. Jur. – Review of the International Commission of Jurists

Rev. Jur. U.I.P.R. – Revista Juridica de la Universidad Interamericana de Puerto Rico
Rev. Jur. U.P.R. – Revista Juridica Universidad de Puerto Rico
Rev. Laws – Revised Laws
Rev. Litig. – Review of Litigation
Rev. Mun. Code – Revised Municipal Code
Rev. Ord. – Revised Ordinances
Rev. Pen. Code – Revised Penal Code
Rev. Pol. Code – Revised Political Code
Rev. Proc. – Revenue Procedure
Rev. Rul. – Revenue Ruling
Rev. St. – Revised Statutes
Rev. Stat. – Revised Statutes
R.I. – Rhode Island Reports
RIA – Research Institute of America
RIAA – Reports of International Arbitration Awards (UN)
R.I. Acts & Resolves – Acts and Resolves of Rhode Island and Providence Plantations
R.I. B.J. – Rhode Island Bar Journal
Rice – Rice (S.C.)
Rice Eq. – Rice's Equity Reports (S.C.)
Rich. – Richardson (S.C.)
Rich. Cas. – Richardson's Cases (S.C.)
Rich. Eq. – Richardson's Equity Reports (S.C.)
Rich. J. Global L. & Bus. – Richmond Journal of Global Law and Business
Rich. J.L. & Pub. Int. – Richmond Journal of Law and the Public Interest
Rich. J.L. & Tech. – Richmond Journal of Law & Technology
R.I. Code R. – Code of Rhode Island Rules
R.I. Gen. Laws – General Laws of Rhode Island
R.I. Gov't Reg. – Rhode Island Government Register
Ril. – Riley (S.C.)
Ril. Eq. – Riley's Chancery Reports (S.C.)
R.I. Pub. Laws – Public Laws of Rhode Island and Providence Plantations
RISK – RISK: Health, Safety & Environment
Risk: Health Safety & Env't. – Risk: Health, Safety & Environment
R.L. – Revised Laws
RMMLF – Rocky Mountain Mineral Law Foundation
Rob. – **1.** Robinson (La.). **2.** Robinson (Va.).
Robards – Synopses of the Decisions of the Supreme Court of Texas Arising from Restraints by Conscript & Other Military Authorities
Roberts on Frauds – A Treatise on the Statute of Frauds
Robinson, Patents – The Law of Patents for Useful Inventions
Rob. Pat. – Robinson, The Law of Patents for Useful Inventions
Rocky Mtn. L. Rev. – Rocky Mountain Law Review/ University of Colorado
Rocky Mtn. Min. L. Inst. – Rocky Mountain Mineral Law Institute
Roger Williams U. L. Rev. – Roger Williams University Law Review
Root – Root (Conn.)
Roper, Husb. & Wife – A Treatise on the Law of Property Arising from the Relation of Husband and Wife
Rose Notes – Rose's Notes on the United States Supreme Court Reports
RRB. – Railroad Retirement Board
R.S. – Revised Statutes
R.S.N. – Revised Statutes of Nebraska
RTC. – Resolution Trust Corporation
Russ. Fac. – Russell, A Treatise on the Laws Relating to Factors and Brokers
Russ. Merc. Ag. – Russell, A Treatise on Mercantile Agency
Rut.-Cam. L.J. – Rutgers-Camden Law Journal
Rutgers Computer & Tech. L.J. – Rutgers Computer and Technology Law Journal
Rutgers J. Computers & L. – Rutgers Journal of Computers and the Law
Rutgers J. Computer Tech. & L. – Rutgers Journal of Computers, Technology and the Law
Rutgers J. Computers Tech & L. – Rutgers Journal of Computers, Technology and the Law
Rutgers L.J. – Rutgers Law Journal
Rutgers L. Rev. – Rutgers Law Review
Rutgers Race & L. Rev. – Rutgers Race and the Law Review
Rutgers U. L. Rev. – Rutgers University Law Review

S

Sadler – Sadler (Pa.)
SALT – Strategic Arms Limitation Talks
Samoan Pac. L.J. – Samoan Pacific Law Journal
Sandars, Just. Inst. – The Institutes of Justinian: with English Introduction, Translation, and Notes
Sand. Ch. – Sandford's Chancery Reports (N.Y.)
Sanders, Uses – An Essay on Uses and Trusts
San Diego Int'l L.J. – San Diego International Law Journal
San Diego Just. J. – San Diego Justice Journal
San Diego L. Rev. – San Diego Law Review
S & L – Savings and Loan Association
San Fern. V.L. Rev. – San Fernando Valley Law Review
San Fran. Atty. – San Francisco Attorney
San Joaquin Agric. L. Rev. – San Joaquin Agricultural Law Review
Santa Clara Comp. & High Tech. L.J. – Santa Clara Computer & High Technology Law Journal
Santa Clara Computer & High Tech. L.J. – Santa Clara Computer & High Technology Law Journal
Santa Clara Law. – Santa Clara Lawyer
Santa Clara L. Rev. – Santa Clara Law Review
Sara. Ch. Sent. – Saratoga Chancery Sentinel (N.Y.)
Sask. L. Rev. – Saskatchewan Law Review
Saund. War. – Saunders, A Treatise on the Law of Warranties and Representations Upon the Sale of Personal Chattels
SBA – Small Business Administration
S. Bar. J. – Journal of the State Bar of California
SBIC – Small Business Investment Companies
S.C. – South Carolina Reports
S.C. Acts – Acts and Joint Resolutions, South Carolina
S. Cal. Interdisc. L.J. – Southern California Interdisciplinary Law Journal
S. Cal. L. Rev. – Southern California Law Review
S. Cal. Rev. L. & Women's Stud. – Southern California Review of Law and Women's Studies
Scam. – Scammon (Ill.)
S.C. Code Ann. – Code of Laws of South Carolina 1976 Annotated
S.C. Code Ann. Regs. – Code of Laws of South Carolina 1976 Annotated, Code of Regulations
S.C. Envtl. L.J. – South Carolina Environmental Law Journal
S.C. Eq. – South Carolina Equity Reports
Sch. L. Bull. – School Law Bulletin
Scholar – The Scholar: St. Mary's Law Review on Minority Issues
School L. Bull. – School Law Bulletin
School L. Rep. – School Law Reporter (National Organization on Legal Problems in Education)
Schouler, Bailm. – The Law of Bailments, Including Pledge, Innkeepers and Carriers

Schouler, Dom. Rel. – Law of Domestic Relations
Schouler, Pers. Prop. – A Treatise on the Law of Personal Property
Schouler, U.S. Hist. – History of the United States of America Under the Constitution
Schouler, Wills – Law of Wills, Executors and Administrators
Sci. Am. – Scientific American
S.C. L. – South Carolina Law Reports
S.C. Law. – South Carolina Lawyer
S.C. L.Q. – South Carolina Law Quarterly
S.C.L. Rev. – South California Law Review
SCOR – Security Council Official Record (U.N.)
Scots L. T. – Scots Law Times
Scots L. Times – Scots Law Times
S.C. Reg. – South Carolina State Register
Scribes J. Leg. Writing – Scribes Journal of Legal Writing
S. Ct. – U.S. Supreme Court Reporter
S. Ct. Bull. (CCH) – Supreme Court Bulletin
S. Ct. Hist. Soc'y Y.B. – Supreme Court Historical Society Yearbook
S. Ct. Rev. – Supreme Court Review
S.D. – South Dakota Reports
S.D. Admin. R. – Administrative Rules of South Dakota
S.D. Adv. Legis. Serv. – South Dakota Advance Legislative Service
S. Dak. L. Rev. – South Dakota Law Review
S.D.C.L. – South Dakota Codified Laws
S.D. Codified Laws – South Dakota Codified Laws
S.D. Codified Laws Ann. – South Dakota Codified Laws Annotated
S.D. Laws – Laws of South Dakota
S.D. L. Rev. – South Dakota Law Review
S.D. Reg. – South Dakota Register
S.E. – South Eastern Reporter
S.E.2d. – South Eastern Reporter, Second Series
Search & Seizure Bull. (Quinlan) – Search and Seizure Bulletin
SEATO – Southeast Asia Treaty Organization
Seattle J. Soc. Just. – Seattle Journal for Social Justice
Seattle U. L. Rev. – Seattle University Law Review
S.E.C. – **1.** Securities and Exchange Commission. **2.** Securities and Exchange Commission Decisions and Reports.
SEC Accounting R. (CCH) – SEC Accounting Rules
Sec. & Fed. Corp. L. Rep. (CBC) – Securities & Federal Corporate Law Report
SEC Compl. (P-H) – Securities and Exchange Commission Compliance
SEC Docket – Securities and Exchange Commission Docket
Sec. Int'l & Comp. L. Bull. – Section of International and Comparative Law Bulletin (ABA)
Sec. L. Rev. – Securities Law Review
Sec. Reg. & L. Rep. (BNA) – Securities Regulation and Law Report
Sec. Reg. Guide (P-H) – Securities Regulation Guide
Sec. Reg. L.J. – Securities Regulation Law Journal
Secured Transactions Guide (CCH) – Secured Transactions Guide
Sedg. & W. Tr.Title Land – Sedgwick & Wait, A Treatise on the Trial of Title to Law
Sedg. Dam. – Sedgwick, A Treatise on the Measure of Damages
Seld. Soc. – Selden Society
Serg. & Rawle – Sergeant & Rawle (Pa.)
Sess. Acts. – Session Acts
Sess. Laws. – Session Laws
Seton, Decrees – Forms of Decrees, Judgments, and Order
Seton Hall Const. L.J. – Seton Hall Constitutional Law Journal
Seton Hall J. Sport L. – Seton Hall Journal of Sport Law
Seton Hall L. J. – Seton Hall Law Journal
Seton Hall L. Rev. – Seton Hall Law Review
Seton Hall Leg. J. – Seton Hall Legislative Journal
Seton Hall Legis. J. – Seton Hall Legislative Journal
S.F.L.R. – San Francisco Law Review
S.H.A. – Smith-Hurd Illinois Annotated Statutes
Shearman and Redfield on Negligence – A Treatise on the Law of Negligence
Shear. R. Prop. – Shearwood, A Concise Abridgment of the Law of Real Property and an Introduction to Conveyancing
Sheld. Subr. – Sheldon, The Law of Subrogation
Shelf. Lun. – Shelford, A Practical Treatise on the Law Concerning Lunacy, Idiots, and Persons of Unsound Mind
Shelford, Mar. & Div. – A Practical Treatise on the Law of Marriage and Divorce
Shelford on Marriage – A Practical Treatise on the Law of Marriage and Divorce
Shipping Reg. (P & F) – Shipping Regulation
S.I. – Statutory Instrument
S. Ill. U. L.J. – Southern Illinois University Law Journal
S.J.D. – Scientiae Juridicae Doctor (Doctor of Juridical Science)
S. L.Q. – Southern Law Quarterly
Smith-Hurd Ann. St. – Smith-Hurd Illinois Annotated Statutes
Smith, Merc. Law – John W. Smith, A Compendium of Mercantile Law
Smith on Negligence – H. Smith, A Treatise on the Law of Negligence
Smith's Master and Servant – C. Smith, A Treatise on the Law of Master and Servant Including Therein Masters and Workmen, in Every Description of Trade or Occupation: With an Appendix of Statutes
SMU L. Rev. – Southern Methodist University Law Review
Sneed – **1.** Sneed (Ky.). **2.** Sneed (Tenn.).
Snyder, Mines & Mining – Mines and Mining: A Commentary on the Law of Mines and Mining Rights
So. – Southern Reporter
So.2d. – Southern Reporter, Second Series
So. Cal. L. Rev. – Southern California Law Review
So. Car. L.J. – Southern Carolina Law Journal, Columbia
So. Car. L. Rev. – South Carolina Law Review
Soc. Resp.: Bus., Journalism, L. Med. – Social Responsibility, Business, Journalism, Law, Medicine
Soc. Resp.: Journalism, L. Med. – Social Responsibility, Journalism, Law, Medicine
Soc. Sec. Bull. – Social Security Bulletin
Soc. Sec. Rep. Ser. – Social Security Reporting Service (West)
Soc. Serv. Rev. – Social Service Review
So. Dak. L. Rev. – South Dakota Law Review
Software L.J. – Software Law Journal
So. Ill. L.J. – Southern Illinois University Law Journal
Solar L. Rep. – Solar Law Reporter
Sol. J. – **1.** Solicitors' Journal. **2.** Solicitors' Journal & Reporter.
Solicitor's J. – Solicitor's Journal
Sol. Op. – Solicitors Opinion
So. L.Q. – Southern Law Quarterly
So. U. L. Rev. – Southern University Law Review (La.)
South Texas L. Rev. – South Texas Law Review
Southwestern L. Rev. – Southwestern University Law Review (Calif.)
Space Pol'y – Space Policy
Sp. Acts. – Special Acts

Speers – Speers (S.C.)
Speers Eq. – Speers' Equity Reports (S.C.)
Spence, Eq. Jur. – The Equitable Jurisdiction of the Court of Chancery
Sp. Laws. – Special Laws
Sports Law. J. – Sports Lawyers Journal
Sp. Sess. – Special Session
SSA – Social Security Administration
SSI – Supplementary Security Income Program
S.S.R. – Social Security Ruling
SSS – Selective Service System
Stand. Fed. Tax Rep. (CCH) – **1.** Standard Federal Tax Reporter. **2.** Standard Federal Tax Reports.
Stan. Envtl. L. Ann. – Stanford Environmental Law Annual
Stan. Envtl. L.J. – Stanford Environmental Law Journal
Stan. J. Int'l L. – Stanford Journal of International Law
Stan. J. Int'l Stud. – Stanford Journal of International Studies
Stan. J. L. Bus. & Fin. – Stanford Journal of Law, Business & Finance
Stan. L. & Pol'y Rev. – Stanford Law & Policy Review
Stan. Law. – Stanford Lawyer
Stan. L. Rev. – Stanford Law Review
Starkie, Ev. – A Practical Treatise on the Law of Evidence
Starkie, Sland. & L. – A Treatise on the Law of Slander, Libel, Scandalum Magnatum, and False Rumours
Stat. – United States Statutes at Large
Stat. At L. – United States Statutes at Large
State Court J. – State Court Journal
State Loc. & Urb. L. Newsl. – State, Local and Urban Law Newsletter (ABA)
State Rptr. – State Reporter (Mont.)
State Tax Cas. Rep. (CCH) – State Tax Cases Reporter
State Tax Guide (CCH) – State Tax Guide
State Tax Rev. (CCH) – State Tax Review
St. B. Tex. Envtl. L.J. – State Bar of Texas Environmental Law Journal
Stearns, Real Act. – A Summary of the Law and Practice of Real Actions
Stephen, Hist. Crim. Law – J. F. Stephen, A History of the Criminal Law of England
Stephen, Pleading (Tyler's ed.) – A Treatise on the Principles of Pleading in Civil Actions (Tyler's ed.)
Steph. Pl. (Tyler's ed.) – A Treatise on the Principles of Pleading in Civil Actions (Tyler's ed.)
Stetson L.F. – Stetson Law Forum
Stetson L. Rev. – Stetson Law Review
Stew. – Stewart (Ala.)
Stew. & P. – Stewart & Porter (Ala.)
S. Tex. L. J. – South Texas Law Journal
S. Tex. L. Rev. – South Texas Law Review
St. John's J. Legal Comment. – St. John's Journal of Legal Commentary
St. John's L. Rev. – St. John's Law Review
St. Louis L. Rev. – St. Louis Law Review
St. Louis U. L.J. – St. Louis University Law Journal
St. Louis U. Pub. L. Rev. – Saint Louis University Public Law Review
St. Louis-Warsaw Transatlantic L.J. – Saint Louis-Warsaw Transatlantic Law Journal
St. Mary's L.J. – St. Mary's Law Journal
Story, Agency – Commentaries on the Law of Agency as a Branch of Commercial and Maritime Jurisprudence
Story, Bailments – Commentaries on the Law of Bailments...
Story, Bills – Commentaries on the Law of Bills of Exchange, Foreign and Inland as Administered in England and America
Story, Comm. Const. – Commentaries on the Constitution of the United States
Story, Confl. Laws – Commentaries on the Conflict of Laws, Foreign and Domestic
Story, Constitution – Commentaries on the Constitution of the United States
Story, Cont. – W. Story, Treatise on the Law of Contracts
Story, Eq. Jur. – Commentaries on Equity Jurisprudence, as Administered in England and America
Story, Eq. Pl. – Commentaries on Equity Pleadings, and the Incidents Thereof...
Story, Partn. – Commentaries on the Law of Partnership
Story, Prom. Notes – Commentaries on the Law of Promissory Notes, and Guaranties of Notes, and Checks on Banks and Bankers
Story, Sales – W. Story, Treatise on the Law of Sale of Personal Property
St. Rep. – State Reporter
Strob. – Strobhart (S.C.)
Strob. Eq. – Strobhart's Equity Reports (S.C.)
St. Tax Rep. (CCH) – State Tax Reports
St. Thomas L.F. – St. Thomas Law Forum/St. Thomas University School of Law
St. Thomas L. Rev. – Saint Thomas Law Review
Stubbs, Charters – Select Charters and Other Illustrations of English Constitutional History from the Earliest Times to the Reign of Edward the First
Stubbs, Const. Hist. Eng. – Constitutional History of England in its Origins and Development
Student Law. – Student Lawyer
Stud. L. & Econ. Dev. – Studies in Law and Economic Development
Stud. L. Pol. & Soc'y – Studies in Law, Politics & Society
SuDoc – Superintendent of Documents
Suffolk J. Trial & App. Advoc. – Suffolk Journal of Trial & Appellate Advocacy
Suffolk Transnat'l L.J. – Suffolk Transnational Law Journal
Suffolk Transnat'l L. Rev. – Suffolk Transnational Law Review
Suffolk U. L. Rev. – Suffolk University Law Review
Sugden, Powers – A Practical Treatise of Powers
Sullivan, Land Titles – The History of Land Titles in Massachusetts
S.U. L. Rev. – Southern University Law Review (La.)
Summers, Oil & Gas – Treatise on the Law of Oil and Gas
Sup. Ct. Econ. Rev. – Supreme Court Economic Review
Sup. Ct. Hist. Soc'y Y.B. – Supreme Court Society Yearbook
Sup. Ct. Rev. – Supreme Court Review
Supp. Code. – Supplement to Code
Supp. Gen. St. – Supplement to the General Statutes
Supp. Rev. – Supplement to the Revision
Supp. Rev. Code. – Supplement to the Revised Code
Supp. Rev. St. – Supplement to the Revised Statutes
S.W. – South Western Reporter
S.W.2d. – South Western Reporter, Second Series
S.W.3d – South Western Reporter, Third Series
Swan – Swan (Tenn.)
Sw. J. L. & Trade Am. – Southwestern Journal of Law & Trade in the Americas
Sw. L.J. – Southwestern Law Journal
S.W.L.J. – Southwestern Law Journal
Sw. Legal Found. Inst. On Oil & Gas L. & Tax. – Southwestern Legal Foundation Institution on Oil and Gas Law and Taxation
S.W.R. – South Western Reporter
S.W. Rep. – South Western Reporter
Sw. U. L. Rev. – Southwestern University Law Review
Sydney L. Rev. – Sydney Law Review

Symp. Priv. Invest. Abroad – Symposium, Private Investment Abroad
Syracuse J. Int'l L. & Com. – Syracuse Journal of International Law and Commerce
Syracuse J. Legis. & Pol'y – Syracuse Journal of Legislation & Policy
Syracuse L. Rev. – Syracuse Law Review

T

T. – Texas Reports
TAC – Texas Administrative Code
T.A.M. – Technical Advice Memorandum (IRS)
Tax Adviser – Tax Adviser
Tax Ct. Mem. Dec. (CCH) – Tax Court Memorandum Decisions
Tax Ct. Rep. (CCH) – Tax Court Reports
Tax Ct. Rep. Dec. (RIA) – Tax Court Reported Decisions
Taxes – Taxes- The Tax Magazine
Tax-Exempt Org. (RIA) – Tax-Exempt Organizations
Tax Law. – Tax Lawyer
Tax L. Rev. – Tax Law Review
Tax Mgmt. Compensation Plan. J. – Tax Management Compensation Planning Journal
Tax Mgmt. Est., Gifts & Trusts J. – Tax Management Estates, Gifts & Trusts Journal
Tax Mgmt. Fin. Plan. J. – Tax Management Financial Planning Journal
Tax Mgmt. Int'l J. – Tax Management International Journal
Tax Mgmt. Memo. – Tax Management Memorandum
Tax Mgmt. Real Est. J. – Tax Management Real Estate Journal
Tax'n for Acct. – Taxation for Accountants
Tax Notes – Tax Notes
Tax Notes Int'l – Tax Notes International
Tax Treaties (CCH) – Tax Treaties
Tay. – Taylor (N.C.)
Tayl. Ev. – A Treatise on the Law of Evidence as Administered in England and Ireland
Taylor – Taylor's North Carolina Term Reports
T.B.M. – Advisory Tax Board Memorandum
T.B. Mon. – T.B. Monroe (Ky.)
T.C. – Reports of the United States Tax Court
T.C.A. – Tennessee Code Annotated
T.C.M. (CCH) – Tax Court Memorandum Decisions
T.C.M. (P-H) – Tax Court Memorandum Decisions
T.C.M. (RIA) – Tax Court Memorandum Decisions
TCOR – Trusteeship Council Official Record (U.N.)
T.D. – Treasury Department Decision
TDBOR – Trade and Development Board Official Record (U.N.)
TDC – Treasury Department Circular
TDO – Treasury Department Order
Tech. Ad. Mem. – Technical Advice Memorandum
Tech. Mem. – Technical Memorandum
Teiss. – Teisser's Orleans Court of Appeals (La.)
Temp. Envtl. L. & Tech. J. – Temple Environmental Law & Technology Journal
Temp. Int'l & Comp. L.J. – Temple International and Comparative Law Journal
Temp. L.Q. – Temple Law Quarterly
Temp. L. Rev. – Temple Law Review
Temp. Pol. & Civ. Rts. L. Rev. – Temple Political & Civil Rights Law Review
Temp. Treas. Reg. – Temporary Treasury Regulation
Temp. U. L.Q. – Temple University Law Quarterly
Tenn. – Tennessee Reports
Tenn. Admin. Reg. – Tennessee Administrative Register
Tenn. App. – Tennessee Appeals
Tenn. B.J. – Tennessee Bar Journal
Tenn. Cas. – Shannon's Tennessee Cases
Tenn. Ch. – Tennessee Chancery
Tenn. Ch. A. – Tennessee Chancery Appeals
Tenn. Civ. A. – Tennessee Civil Appeals
Tenn. Code Ann. – Tennessee Code Annotated
Tenn. Comp. R. & Regs. – Official Compilation of Rules & Regulations of the State of Tennessee
Tenn. Crim. App. – Tennessee Criminal Appeals Reports
Tenn. J. Prac. & Proc. – Tennessee Journal of Practice and Procedure
Tenn. Leg. Rep. – Tennessee Legal Reporter, Nashville, Tenn
Tenn. L. Rev. – Tennessee Law Review
Tenn. Priv. Acts – Private Acts of the State of Tennessee
Tenn. Pub. Acts – Public Acts of the State of Tennessee
Ter. Laws. – Territorial Laws
Terr. Sea J. – Territorial Sea Journal
Tex. – Texas Reports
Tex. Admin. Code – Texas Administrative Code
Tex. App. – Texas Appeals Reports
Tex. B.J. – Texas Bar Journal
Tex. Civ. App. – Texas Civil Appeals Reports
Tex. Code Ann. – Texas Code Annotated
Tex. Com. App. – Texas Commission of Appeals
Tex. Crim. – Texas Criminal Reports
Tex. Ct. App. – Texas Court of Appeals Reports
Tex. F. on Civ. Lib. & Civ. Rts. – Texas Forum on Civil Liberties & Civil Rights
Tex. F. on C.L. & C.R. – Texas Forum on Civil Liberties & Civil Rights
Tex. Gen. Laws – General and Special Laws of the State of Texas
Tex. Hisp. J.L. & Pol'y – Texas Hispanic Journal of Law and Policy
Tex. Intell. Prop. L.J. – Texas Intellectual Property Law Journal
Tex. Int'l L.F. – Texas International Law Forum
Tex. Int'l L.J. – Texas International Law Journal
Tex. J. Bus. L. – Texas Journal of Business Law
Tex. Jur. – Texas Jurisprudence
Tex. Jur. 2d – Texas Jurisprudence 2d
Tex. Jur. 3d – Texas Jurisprudence 3d
Tex. J. Women & L. – Texas Journal of Women & the Law
Tex. L. & Legis. – Texas Law and Legislation
Tex. L.J. – Texas Law Journal
Tex. L. Rev. – Texas Law Review
Tex. Reg. – Texas Register
Tex. Rev. Civ. Stat. Ann. – Texas Revised Civil Statutes Annotated
Tex. Rev. Ent. & Sports L. – Texas Review of Entertainment and Sports Law
Tex. Rev. L. & Pol. – Texas Review of Law & Politics
Tex. Sess. Law Serv. – Texas Session Law Service
Tex. So. U. L. Rev. – Texas Southern University Law Review
Tex. Tech J. Tex. Admin. L. – Texas Tech Journal of Texas Administrative Law
Tex. Tech L. Rev. – Texas Tech Law Review
Tex. Wesleyan L. Rev. – Texas Wesleyan Law Review
Third World Legal Stud. – Third World Legal Studies
Thomas Jefferson L. Rev. – Thomas Jefferson Law Review
Thomas M. Cooley L. Rev. – Thomas M. Cooley Law Review
Thomas, Mortg. – A Treatise on the Law of Mortgages of Real and Personal Property in the State of New York
Thomas, Negl. – E. Thomas, The Law of Negligence

Thompson, Negligence — The Law of Negligence in Relations Not Resting in Contract Illustrated by Leading Cases and Notes
Thomp. Trials — Thompson, A Treatise on the Law of Trials in Actions Civil and Criminal
Thur. Marshall L.J. — Thurgood Marshall Law Journal
T.I.A.S. — United States Treaties and Other Agreements Series
Tidd, Prac. — The Practice of the Courts of King's Bench and Common Pleas in Personal Actions and Ejectment
Tiedeman, Real Prop. — An Elementary Treatise on the American Law of Real Property
Tied. Lim. Police Power — Tiedeman, A Treatise on the Limitations of Police Power in the United States
Tied. Mun. Corp. — Tiedeman, A Treatise on the Law of Municipal Corporations in the United States
T.I.F. — Treaties in Force
Tiffany, Landl. & Ten. — The Law of Landlord and Tenant
Tiffany, Real Prop. — A Treatise on the Modern Law of Real Property and Other Interests in Law
T.I.R. — Technical Information Release
T. Jefferson L. Rev. — Thomas Jefferson Law Review
T.M. — Technical Memorandum (IRS)
T. Marshall L.J. — Thurgood Marshall Law Journal
T. Marshall L. Rev. — Thurgood Marshall Law Review
T.M. Cooley J. Prac. & Clinical L. — Thomas M. Cooley Journal of Practical & Clinical Law
T.M. Cooley J. Prac. & Clin. L. — Thomas M. Cooley Journal of Practical & Clinical Law
T.M. Cooley L. Rev. — Thomas M. Cooley Law Review
T.M.E.P. — Trademark Manual of Examining Procedure
T.M.R. — TradeMark Reports
Tol. J. Great Lakes' L. Sci. & Pol'y — Toledo Journal of Great Lakes' Law, Science & Policy
Tort & Ins. L.J. — Tort & Insurance Law Journal
Tort Trial & Ins. Prac. L.J. — Tort Trial & Insurance Practice Law Journal (ABA)
Touro Envtl. L.J. — Touro Environmental Law Journal
Touro Int'l L. Rev. — Touro International Law Review
Touro J. Transnat'l L. — Touro Journal of Transnational Law
Touro L. Rev. — Touro Law Review
Townshend, Slander & Libel — A Treatise on the Wrongs Called Slander and Libel, and on the Remedy by Civil Action
Tr. — Trial
Trade Cas. (CCH) — Trade Cases
Trademark Rep. — Trademark Reporter
Trade Reg. Rep. (CCH) — Trade Regulation Reports
Tr. & Est. — Trusts and Estates
Transnat'l L. & Contemp. Probs. — Transnational Law & Contemporary Problems
Transnat'l Law. — Transnational Lawyer
Transp. L.J. — Transportation Law Journal
Transp. Prac. J. — Transportation Practitioners Journal
Tread. — Treadway (S.C.)
Treas. Dec. — Treasury Decisions
Treas. Dec. Int. Rev. — Treasury Decisions under Internal Revenue Laws
Treas. Reg. — Treasury Regulation
Trial — Trial (ATLA)
Trial Advoc. Q. — Trial Advocate Quarterly
Trial Law. Guide — Trial Lawyer's Guide
Trial Law Q. — Trial Lawyers Quarterly
Troubat, Lim. Part. — The Law Commandatary and Limited Partnership in the United States
Trusts & Est. — Trusts & Estates
T.S. — United States Treaty Series
Tuck. & Cl. — Tucker & Clephane (D.C.)
Tucker's Blackstone — Tucker, Notes on Blackstone's Commentaries for the Use of Students
Tudor, Char. Trusts — The Law of Charitable Trusts with the Statutes, and the Orders, Regulations, and Instructions, Issued Pursuant Thereto
Tudor, Lead. Cas. Real Prop. — A Selection of Leading Cases on Real Property, Conveyancing, and the Construction of Wills and Deeds
Tul. Civ. L.F. — Tulane Civil Law Forum
Tul. Envtl. L.J. — Tulane Environmental Law Journal
Tul. Eur. & Civ. L.F. — Tulane European & Civil Law Forum
Tul. J. Int'l & Comp. L. — Tulane Journal of International & Comparative Law
Tul. J.L. & Sexuality — Tulane Journal of Law and Sexuality
Tul. J. Tech. & Intell. Prop. — Tulane Journal of Technology and Intellectual Property
Tul. L. Rev. — Tulane Law Review
Tul. Mar. L.J. — Tulane Maritime Law Journal
Tulsa J. Comp. & Int'l L. — Tulsa Journal of Comparative & International Law
Tulsa L.J. — Tulsa Law Journal
Tulsa L. Rev. — Tulsa Law Review
TVA — Tennessee Valley Authority
Tyl. — Tyler (Vt.)
Tyler, Ej. — R. Tyler, Remedy by Ejectment and the Law of Adverse Enjoyment in the United States
Tyng — Tyng (Mass.)

U

UAGA — Uniform Anatomical Gift Act
U. Ark. Little Rock L.J. — University of Arkansas at Little Rock Law Journal
U. Ark. Little Rock L. Rev. — University of Arkansas at Little Rock Law Review
U. Balt. Intell. Prop. L.J. — University of Baltimore Intellectual Property Law Journal
U. Balt. J. Envtl. L. — University of Baltimore Journal of Environmental Law
U. Balt. L.F. — University of Baltimore Law Forum
U. Balt. L. Rev. — University of Baltimore Law Review
U. Bridgeport L. Rev. — University of Bridgeport Law Review
U. Brit. Colum. L. Rev. — University of British Columbia Law Review
U.C.A. — Utah Code Annotated
U.C.C. — Uniform Commercial Code
U.C.C.J.A. — Uniform Child Custody Jurisdiction Act
U.C.C.L.J. — Uniform Commercial Code Law Journal
UCC Rep.-Dig. — Uniform Commercial Code Reporter-Digest
U.C.C. Rep. Serv. (CBC) — Uniform Commercial Code Reporting Service
U.C. Davis J. Int'l L. & Pol'y — U.C. Davis Journal of International Law & Policy
U.C. Davis L. Rev. — University of California Davis Law Review
U.C.D. L. Rev. — UCD Law Review
U. Chi. Legal F. — University of Chicago Legal Forum
U. Chi. L. Rev. — University of Chicago Law Review
U. Chi. L. Sch. Rec. — University of Chicago Law School Record
U. Chi. L. Sch. Roundtable — University of Chicago Law School Roundtable
U. Cin. L. Rev. — University of Cincinnati Law Review
UCLA — University of California Los Angeles
UCLA-Alaska L. Rev. — UCLA-Alaska Law Review
UCLA Asian Pac. Am. L. J. — UCLA Asian Pacific American Law Journal

UCLA Bull. L. & Tech. – UCLA Bulletin of Law and Technology
UCLA Ent. L. Rev. – UCLA Entertainment Law Review
UCLA J. Envtl. L. & Pol'y – UCLA Journal of Environmental Law & Policy
UCLA J. Int'l L. & Foreign Aff. – UCLA Journal of International Law & Foreign Affairs
UCLA J. Islamic & Near E. L. – UCLA Journal of Islamic and Near Eastern Law
UCLA L. Rev. – UCLA Law Review
UCLA Pac. Basin L.J. – UCLA Pacific Basin Law Journal
UCLA Women's L.J. – UCLA Women's Law Journal
U.C.M.J. – Uniform Code of Military Justice
U. Colo. L. Rev. – University of Colorado Law Review
U.C.R. – Uniform Crime Reports
U. Dayton Intra. L. Rev. – University of Dayton Intramural Law Review
U. Dayton L. Rev. – University of Dayton Law Review
UDC/DCSL L. Rev. – University of the District of Columbia David Clarke School of Law Review
U.D.C. L. Rev. – University of the District of Columbia Law Review
U. Denv. Water L. Rev. – University of Denver Water Law Review
U. Det. J. Urb. L. – University of Detroit Journal of Urban Law
U. Det. L.J. – University of Detroit Law Journal
U. Det. L. Rev. – University of Detroit Law Review
U. Det. Mercy L. Rev. – University of Detroit Mercy Law Review
UDPAA – Uniform Durable Power of Attorney Act
U. Fla. J. L. & Pub. Pol'y – University of Florida Journal of Law and Public Policy
U. Fla. L. Rev. – University of Florida Law Review
U. Haw. L. Rev. – University of Hawaii Law Review
U. Ill. J. Tech. & Pol'y – University of Illinois Journal of Law, Technology and Policy
U. Ill. L.F. – University of Illinois Law Forum
U. Ill. L. Rev. – University of Illinois Law Review
U. Kan. City L. Rev. – University of Kansas City Law Review
U. Kan. L. Rev. – University of Kansas Law Review
U.L.A. – Uniform Laws Annotated
U. Louisville J. Fam. L. – University of Louisville Journal of Family Law
U.L.P.A. – Uniform Limited Partnership Act
U. Maine L. Rev. – University of Maine Law Review
U. Mem. L. Rev. – University of Memphis Law Review
U. Miami Bus. L.J. – University of Miami Business Law Journal
U. Miami Bus. L. Rev. – University of Miami Business Law Review
U. Miami Ent. & Sports L. Rev. – University of Miami Entertainment & Sports Law Review
U. Miami Heckerling Inst. on Est. Plan. – University of Miami Phillip E. Heckerling Institute on Estate Planning
U. Miami Inter-Am. L. Rev. – University of Miami Inter-American Law Review
U. Miami Int'l & Comp. L. Rev. – University of Miami International & Comparative Law Review
U. Miami L. Rev. – University of Miami Law Review
U. Miami Y.B. Int'l L. – University of Miami Yearbook of International Law
U. Mich. J.L. Ref. – University of Michigan Journal of Law Reform
U. Mich. J.L. Reform – University of Michigan Journal of Law Reform
UMKC L. Rev. – University of Missouri-Kansas City Law Review
U. Mo. B., Law Ser. – University of Missouri Bulletin, Law Series
U. Mo. Kan. City L. Rev. – University of Missouri at Kansas City Law Review
Unauth. Prac. News – Unauthorized Practice News (ABA)
U.N.B.L.J. – University of New Brunswick Law Journal
UNCITRAL – United Nations Commission on International Trade Law
UNCTAD – United Nations Conference on Trade & Development
UNDCP – United Nations Drug Control Programme
Underhill, Ev. – H. Underhill, A Treatise on the Law of Evidence
Underh. Torts – Underhill, Principles of the Law of Torts, or Wrongs Independent of Contracts
UNDP – United Nations Development Programme
Unempl. Ins. Rep. (CCH) – Unemployment Insurance Reports
UNEP – United Nations Environment Programme
UNESCO – United Nations Educational, Scientific and Cultural Organization
U. New Brunswick L.J. – University of New Brunswick Law Journal
U. New South Wales L.J. – University of New South Wales Law Journal
U. New S. Wales L.J. – University of New South Wales Law Journal
UNFPA – United Nations Population Fund
UNHCR – Office of the United Nations High Commissioner for Refugees
UNHSP – United Nations Human Settlements Programme
UNICEF – United Nations Children's Fund
UNICRI – United Nations Interregional Crime and Justice Research Institute
UNIDIR – United Nations Institute for Disarmament Research
UNIDO – United Nations Industrial Development Organization
UNIFEM – United Nations Development Fund for Women
Union Lab. Rep. (BNA) – Union Labor Report
UNITAR – United Nations Institute for Training and Research
UN Monthly Chron. – UN Monthly Chronicle
UNOPS – United Nations Office for Project Services
UNRISD – United Nations Research Institute for Social Development
UNRWA – United Nations Relief and Works Agency for Palestine Refugees in the Near East
U.N.T.S. – United Nations Treaty Series
UNU – United Nations University
UNV – United Nations Volunteers
UPA – **1.** Uniform Partnership Act. **2.** University Press of America.
U. Pa. J. Const. L. – University of Pennsylvania Journal of Constitutional Law
U. Pa. J. Int'l Bus. L. – University of Pennsylvania Journal of International Business Law
U. Pa. J. Int'l Econ. L. – University of Pennsylvania Journal of International Economic Law
U. Pa. J. Lab. & Emp. L. – University of Pennsylvania Journal of Labor and Employment Law
U. Pa. L. Rev. – University of Pennsylvania Law Review
U. Pa. L. Rev. & Am. L. Register – University of Pennsylvania Law Review and American Law Register
UPC – Uniform Probate Code
U. Pitt. L. Rev. – University of Pittsburgh Law Review
UPU – Universal Postal Union
U. Puget Sound L. Rev. – University of Puget Sound Law Review

Urban L.J. – University of Detroit, Urban Law Journal
Urb. L. Ann. – Urban Law Annual
Urb. Law. – Urban Lawyer
Urb. L. Rev. – Urban Law Review
U. Rich. L. Notes – University of Richmond Law Notes
U. Rich. L. Rev. – University of Richmond Law Review
U.S. – United States Supreme Court Reports
U.S. A.F. Acad. J. Legal Stud. – United States Air Force Academy Journal of Legal Studies
U. San Fernando Valley L Rev. – University of San Fernando Valley Law Review
U. San Fernando V. L. Rev. – University of San Fernando Valley Law Review
U.S. App. D.C. – United States Court of Appeals Reports
U.S. Aviation Rep. – Aviation Reports, U.S
U.S.C. – United States Code
U.S.C.A. – United States Code Annotated
U.S. Cal. Sch. L. Tax Inst. – University of Southern California School of Law Tax Institute
U.S.C.C.A.N. – United States Code Congressional and Administrative News
U.S. Code Cong. & Ad. News – United States Code Congressional and Administrative News
U.S.C.S. – United States Code Service
USDA – United States Department of Agriculture
U. Seattle L. Rev. – University of Seattle Law Review
USES – United States Employment Service
U.S.F. J.L. & Soc. Challenges – University of San Francisco Journal of Law and Social Challenges
U.S.F. L. Rev. – University of San Francisco Law Review
U.S.F. Mar. L.J. – University of San Francisco Maritime Law Journal
USIA – United States Information Agency
USIS – United States Information Service
USITC. – United States International Trade Commission
U.S. L.Ed. – Supreme Court Reports, Lawyers' Ed
U.S.L.W. – United States Law Week (BNA)
U.S.-Mex. L.J. – United States-Mexico Law Journal
U.S. P.Q. (BNA) – United States Patent Quarterly
USSB – United States Shipping Board
U.S.T. – United States Treaties and Other International Agreements
U.S. Tax Cas. (CCH) – United States Tax Cases
USTC (CCH). – United States Tax Cases
Utah. – Utah Reports
Utah 2d. – Utah Reports, Second Series
Utah Admin. Code – Utah Administrative Code
Utah B.J. – Utah Bar Journal
Utah Bull. – Utah State Bulletin
Utah Code Ann. – Utah Code Annotated
Utah Laws – Laws of Utah
Utah L. Rev. – Utah Law Review
U. Tasmania L. Rev. – University of Tasmania Law Review
Util. L. Rep. (CCH) – Utilities Law Reports
Util. Sect. Newsl. – Utility Section Newsletter (ABA)
U. Toledo L. Rev. – University of Toledo Law Review
U. Tol. Intra. L. Rev. – University of Toledo Intramural Law Review '67-68
U. Tol. L. Rev. – University of Toledo Law Review
U. Tor. Fac. L. Rev. – University of Toronto Faculty Law Review
U. Toronto Fac. L. Rev. – University of Toronto Faculty Law Review
U. Toronto L.J. – University of Toronto Law Journal
U. Wash. L. Rev. – University of Washington Law Review
U. W. Austl. L. Rev. – University of Western Australia Law Review
U. Western Ont. L. Rev. – University of Western Ontario Law Review
U. West L.A. L. Rev. – University of West Los Angeles Law Review
UWLA L. Rev. – University of West Los Angeles Law Review
U. W. Ont. L. Rev. – University of Western Ontario Law Review

V

Va. – Virginia Reports
VA – Department of Veterans Affairs
Va. Acts – Acts of the General Assembly of the Commonwealth of Virginia
Va. App. – Virginia Court of Appeals Reports
Va. B. Ass'n J. – Virginia Bar Association Journal
Va. B. News – Virginia Bar News
Va. Cas. – Virginia Cases
vac'g – vacating
Va. Code Ann. – Code of Virginia Annotated
Va. Dec. – Virginia Decisions
Va. Envtl. L.J. – Virginia Environmental Law Journal
Va. J. Int'l L. – Virginia Journal of International Law
Va. J.L. & Tech. – Virginia Journal of Law and Technology
Va. J. Nat. Res. L. – Virginia Journal of Natural Resources Law
Va. J. Nat. Resources L. – Virginia Journal of Natural Resources Law
Va. J. Soc. Pol'y & L. – Virginia Journal of Social Policy & Law
Va. J. Sports & L. – Virginia Journal of Sports and the Law
Va. Law. – Virginia Lawyer
Va. L. Rev. – Virginia Law Review
Val. U. L. Rev. – Valparaiso University Law Review
V.A.M.R. – Vernon's Annotated Missouri Rules
V.A.M.S. – Vernon's Annotated Missouri Statutes
Vand. J. Ent. L. & Prac. – Vanderbilt Journal of Entertainment Law and Practice
Vand. J. Transnat'l L. – Vanderbilt Journal of Transnational Law
Vand. L. Rev. – Vanderbilt Law Review
Va. Regs. Reg. – Virginia Register of Regulations
Va. Sports & Ent. L.J. – Virginia Sports & Entertainment Law Journal
Va. Tax Rev. – Virginia Tax Review
V.A.T.S. – Vernon's Annotated Texas Statutes
Vernon's Ann. C.C.P. – Vernon's Annotated Texas Code of Criminal Procedure
Vernon's Ann. Civ. St. – Vernon's Annotated Texas Civil Statutes
Vernon's Ann. P.C. – Vernon's Annotated Texas Penal Code
Vernon's Ann. Rules Civ. Proc. – Vernon's Annotated Texas Rules of Civil Procedure
Vet. App. – Veterans Appeals Reporter
V.I. – Virgin Island Reports
V.I.C. – Virgin Islands Code
V.I. Code Ann. – Virgin Islands Code Annotated
Vict. U. Wellington L. Rev. – Victoria University of Wellington Law Review
Vict. U. Well. L. Rev. – Victoria University of Wellington Law Review
Vill. Envtl. L.J. – Villanova Environmental Law Journal
Vill. Info. L. Chron. – Villanova Information Law Chronicle
Vill. J.L. & Inv. Mgmt. – Villanova Journal of Law & Investment Management
Vill. L. Rev. – Villanova Law Review
Vill. Sports & Ent. L.F. – Villanova Sports and Entertainment Law Forum

Vill. Sports & Ent. L.J. – Villanova Sports and Entertainment Law Journal
V.I. R. & Regs. – Virgin Islands Rules and Regulations
V.I. Sess. Laws – Session Laws of the Virgin Islands
V.S. – Vermont Statutes
V.S.A. – Vermont Statutes Annotated
Vt. – Vermont Reports
Vt. Acts & Resolves – Acts of Resolves of Vermont
Vt. B.J. & L. Dig. – Vermont Bar Journal & Law Digest
V.T.C.A. – Vernon's Texas Codes Annotated
Vt. Code R. – Code of Vermont Rules
Vt. Gov't Reg. – Vermont Government Register
Vt. L. Rev. – Vermont Law Review
V.T.S.A. – Vernon's Texas Statutes Annotated
Vt. Stat. Ann. – Vermont Statutes Annotated

W

Wade, Am. Mining Law – Manual of American Mining Law as Practiced in the Western States and Territories
Wade, Attachm. – A Treatise on the Law of Attachment and Garnishment
Wage & Hour Cas. (BNA) – Wage and Hour Cases
Wake Forest L. Rev. – Wake Forest Law Review
Walk. – Walker (Pa.)
Walk. Am. Law – J. Walker, Introduction to American Law
Walker, Pat. – Text-Book of the Patent Laws of the United States of America
Walk. Int. – J. Walker, Introduction to American Law
Wall. – Wallace, U.S. Supreme Court Reports
Wall. St. J. – Wall Street Journal
Warv. Abst. – Warvelle, A Practical Treatise on Abstracts and Examinations of Title to Real Property
Wash. – Washington (Va.)
Wash. – Washington Reports
Wash.2d. – Washington Reports, Second Series
Wash. Admin. Code – Washington Administrative Code
Wash. & Lee L. Rev. – Washington and Lee Law Review
Wash. App. – Washington Appellate Reports
Washburn L.J. – Washburn Law Journal
Washburn, Real Prop. – A Treatise on the American Law of Real Property
Wash. C.C. – Washington Circuit Court, U.S
Wash. Law. – Washington Lawyer
Wash. Law Rep. – Washington Law Reporter, D.C
Wash. Laws – Laws of Washington
Wash. Legis. Serv. – Washington Legislative Service
Wash. L. Rev. – Washington Law Review
Wash. Monthly – Washington Monthly
Wash. Rev. Code. – Revised Code of Washington
Wash. Rev. Code Ann. – Revised Code of Washington Annotated
Wash. St. B. News – Washington State Bar News
Wash. Terr. – Washington Territory Reports
Wash. U. Global Stud. L. Rev. – Washington University Global Studies Law Review
Wash. U. J.L. & Pol'y – Washington University Journal of Law and Policy
Wash. U. J. Urb. & Contemp. L. – Washington University Journal of Urban & Contemporary Law
Wash. U. L.Q. – Washington University Law Quarterly (Missouri)
Watkins, Descents – An Essay Towards the Further Elucidation of the Law of Descents
Wat. Set-Off – Waterman, A Treatise on the Law of Set-Off, Recoupment, and Coumterclaim
Watts – Watts (Pa.)
Watts & Serg. – Watts and Sergeant (Pa.P
Wayne L. Rev. – Wayne Law Review
WD – Written Determination
Weeks, Attys. at Law – A Treatise on Attorneys and Counselors at Law
Wells, Repl. – A Treatise on the Law of Replevin, as Administered in the Courts of the United States and England
Wend. – Wendell's Reports (N.Y.)
Wesk. Ins. – Weskett, Complete Digest of the Theory, Laws and Practice of Insurance
Westchester B.J. – Westchester Bar Journal
Westlake, Prin. Int. Law – Chapters on the Principles of International Law
WEU – Western European Union
WFP – World Food Programme (UN)
WG&L – Warren, Gorham & Lamont
W.H. – Wage and Hour Cases (BNA)
Whart. – Wharton (Pa.)
Whart. & S. Med. Jur. – Wharton & Stille, A Treatise on Medical Jurisprudence
Wharton, Agency – A Commentary on the Law of Agency and Agents
Wharton, Am. Cr. Law – A Treatise on the Criminal Law of the United States...
Wharton, Conf. Laws – A Treatise on the Conflict of Laws
Wharton, Cr. Ev. – A Treatise on the Law of Evidence in Criminal Issues
Wharton, Cr. Pl. & Prac. – Treatise on Criminal Pleading and Practice
Wharton, Dig. Int. Law – A Digest of the International Law of the United States
Wharton, Ev. – A Commentary on the Law of Evidence in Civil Issues
Wharton, Homicide – A Treatise on the Law of Homicide in the United States
Wharton, Maxims – G. Wharton, Legal Maxims with Observations and Cases
Wharton, Negligence – A Treatise on the Law of Negligence
Wheat. – Wheaton, U.S. Supreme Court Reports
Wheaton, International Law – The Elements of International Law
Wheaton on Maritime Captures – A Digest of the Law of Maritime Captures and Prizes
Whitak. Liens – Whitaker, A Treatise Relative to the Rights of Lien and Stoppage in Transitu
White & W. – White & Willson's Reports (Tex.)
Whittier L. Rev. – Whittier Law Review
Whitt. L. Rev. – Whittier Law Review
W.H. Man. – Wage and Hour Manual (BNA)
WHO – World Health Organization
Widener J. Pub. L. – Widener Journal of Public Law
Widener L. Symp. J. – Widener Law Symposium Journal
Wigm. Ev. – **1.** A Treatise on the System of Evidence in Trials at Common Law. **2.** A Treatise on the Anglo-American System of Evidence in Trials at Common Law.
Wigmore, Evidence – **1.** A Treatise on the System of Evidence in Trials at Common Law. **2.** A Treatise on the Anglo-American System of Evidence in Trials at Common Law.
Wigram, Wills – A Treatise on Extrinsic Evidence in Aid of the Interpretation of Wills
Will. – Williams (Mass.)
Willamette Bull. Int'l L. & Pol'y – Willamette Bulletin of International Law and Policy
Willamette J. Int'l L. & Disp. Resol. – Willamette Journal of International Law and Dispute Resolution
Willamette L.J. – Willamette Law Journal
Willamette L. Rev. – Willamette Law Review
Willcock, Mun. Corp. – The Law of Municipal Corporations, together with a Brief Sketch of Their History

Will. Eq. Jur. — Willard, A Treatise on Equity Jurisprudence
Williams & B., Adm. Jur. — R. G. Williams & Bruce, The Jurisdiction and Practice of the High Court of Admiralty
Williams, Executors — E. Williams, A Treatise on the Law of Executors and Administrators
Williams, Ex'rs R. & T. ed. — E. Williams, A Treatise on the Law of Executors and Administrators, Randolph & Talcott ed.
Williams, Pers. Prop. — Jos. Williams, A Treatise on the Law of Personal Property
Williams, Real Prop. — Jos. Williams, Principles of the Law of Real Property
Williams, Seis. — Jos. Williams, Seisin of the Freehold
Willis, Trustees — A Practical Treatise on the Duties and Responsibilities of Trustees
Williston, Contracts — The Law of Contracts
Williston, Sales — The Law Governing Sales of Goods a Common Law and Under the Uniform Sales Act
Willson — Willson's Reports (Tex.)
Win. — Winston (N.C.)
WIPO — World Intellectual Property Organization
Wis. — Wisconsin Reports
Wis.2d. — Wisconsin Reports, Second Series
Wis. Admin. Code — Wisconsin Administrative Code
Wis. Admin. Reg. — Wisconsin Administrative Register
Wis. B. Bull. — Wisconsin Bar Bulletin
Wis. Envtl. L.J. — Wisconsin Environmental Law Journal
Wis. Int'l L.J. — Wisconsin International Law Journal
Wis. Law. — Wisconsin Lawyer
Wis. Laws — Laws of Wisconsin
Wis. Legis. Serv. — Wisconsin Legislative Service
Wis. L.N. — Wisconsin Legal News
Wis. L. Rev. — Wisconsin Law Review
Wis. Stat. — Wisconsin Statutes
Wis. Stat. Ann. — Wisconsin Statutes Annotated
Wis. Women's L.J. — Wisconsin Women's Law Journal
With. Corp. Cas. — Withrow, American Corporation Cases
Witthaus & Becker, Med. Jur. — Medical Jurisprudence, Forensic Medicine, and Toxicology
W. Legal Hist. — Western Legal History: the Journal of the Ninth Judicial Circuit Historical Society
Wm. & Mary Bill Rts. J. — William & Mary Bill of Rights Journal
Wm. & Mary Envtl. L. & Pol'y Rev. — William & Mary Environmental Law and Policy Review
Wm. & Mary J. Envtl. L. — William & Mary Journal of Environmental Law
Wm. & Mary J. Women & L. — William & Mary Journal of Women and the Law
Wm. & Mary L. Rev. — William & Mary Law Review
Wm. & Mary Rev. Va. L. — William & Mary Review of Virginia Law
Wm. Mitchell L. Rev. — William Mitchell Law Review
WMO — World Meteorological Organization
Wms. P.P. — J. Williams, Principles of the Law of Personal Property
Wms. R.P. — J. Williams, Principles of the Law of Real Property
W. New Eng. L. Rev. — Western New England Law Review
Woener, Adm'n — A Treatise on the American Law of Administration
Women & Crim. Just. — Women and Criminal Justice
Women Law. J. — Women Lawyers Journal
Women's L.J. — Women's Law Journal
Women's Rts. L. Rep. — Women's Rights Law Reporter
Wood, Lim. — A Treatise on the Limitation of Actions at Law and In Equity
Wood, Master & Serv. — Law of Master and Servant, Covering the Relation, Duties and Liabilities of Employers and Employees
Wood, Nuis. — A Practical Treatise on the Law of Nuisances in Their Various Forms
Wood, Ry. Law — A Treatise on the Law of Railroads
Woolr. Waters — Woolrych, A Treatise of the Law of Waters
Work. Comp. Bus. Mgmt. Guide (CCH) — Workers' Compensation Business Management Guide
Works, Pr. — Practice, Pleading and Forms Adapted to the New revised Code of Indiana
W. Res. L. Rev. — Western Reserve Law Review
Wright, Ten. — Introduction to the Law of Tenures
W.S. — Wyoming Statutes
W.S.A. — Wisconsin Statutes Annotated
W. St. L. Rev. — Western State Law Review
W.St. U. L. Rev. — Western State University Law Review
WTO — **1.** World Trade Organization. **2.** World Tourism Organization.
W. Va. — West Virginia Reports
W. Va. Acts — Acts of the Legislature of West Virginia
W. Va. B. — West Virginia Bar
W. Va. Code — West Virginia Code
W. Va. Cod. State R. — West Virginia Code of State Rules
W. Va. Law. — West Virginia Lawyer
W. Va. L. Q. & B. — West Virginia Law Quarterly and the Bar
W. Va. L. Rev. — West Virginia Law Review
WVC. — West Virginia Code
Wyo. — Wyoming Statutes, Wyoming Reports
Wyo. Law. — Wyoming Lawyer
Wyo. L. Rev. — Wyoming Law Review
Wyo. Sess. Laws — Session Laws of Wyoming
Wyo. Stat. Ann. — Wyoming Statutes Annotated

Y

Yale Hum. Rts. & Dev. L.J. — Yale Human Rights and Development Law Journal
Yale J. Int'l L. — Yale Journal of International Law
Yale J.L. & Feminism — Yale Journal of Law & Feminism
Yale J.L. & Human. — Yale Journal of Law and the Humanities
Yale J.L. & Lib. — Yale Journal of Law and Liberation
Yale J. on Reg. — Yale Journal on Regulation
Yale J. World Pub. Ord. — Yale Journal of World Public Order
Yale L. & Pol'y Rev. — Yale Law & Policy Review
Yale Law J. — Yale Law Journal
Yale L.J. — Yale Law Journal
Yale Stud. World Pub. Order — Yale Studies in World Public Order
Yates Sel. Cas. — Yates' Select Cases
Y.B. Eur. Conv. On H.R. — Yearbook of the European Convention on Human Rights
Yeates — Yeates (Pa.)
Yer. — Yerger (Tenn.)

Z

Zoning & Plan. L. Rep. — Zoning and Planning Law Report

Authors Commonly Cited in American Sources During the 19th and Early 20th Centuries

Adams . . . . John Adams
Addison . . . . Charles G. Addison
Aldrich . . . . Peleg Emory Aldrich
Allnat . . . . Charles Blake Allnat
Ames . . . . James Barr Ames
Ames . . . . Samuel Ames
Amos . . . . Andrew Amos
Angell . . . . Joseph K. Angell
Anson . . . . William Reynell Anson
Arnould . . . . Sir Joseph Arnould
Atherly . . . . Edmund Gibson Atherly
Austin . . . . John Austin
Babington . . . . . . Richard Babington
Baker . . . . Sir Sherston Baker
Ballantine . . . . . William Ballantine
Bayley . . . . Sir John Bayley
Beach . . . . Charles F. Beach
Beale . . . . Joseph Henry Beale
Becker . . . . Tracy Chatfield Becker
Belli . . . . Melvin M. Belli, Sr.
Best . . . . William M. Best
Bevans . . . . Charles I. Bevans
Beven . . . . Thomas Beven
Bigelow . . . . Melville M. Bigelow
Bishop . . . . Joel Prentiss Bishop
Black . . . . Henry Campbell Black
Blackburn . . . . . . Lord Colin Blackburn
Blackstone . . . . . Sir William Blackstone
Blanshard . . . . . . William Blanshard
Booth . . . . George Booth
Bouvier . . . . John Bouvier
Bracton . . . . Henry de Bracton
Brice . . . . Seward Brice
Brickell . . . . Robert C. Brickell
Brightly . . . . Frederick C. Brightly
Brown . . . . Henry Billings Brown
Browne . . . . Causten Browne
Browne . . . . George Browne
Bowstead . . . . . . William Bowstead
Bruce . . . . Gainsford Bruce
Bryce . . . . Viscount James Bryce
Bump . . . . Orlando F. Bump
Burrill . . . . Alexander M. Burrill
Buswell . . . . Henry Foster Buswell
Byles . . . . Sir John Barnard Byles
Carver . . . . Thomas G. Carver
Chamberlain . . . . Daniel H. Chamberlain
Chandler . . . . Peleg W. Chandler
Chitty . . . . Joseph Chitty
Christian . . . . Edward Christian
Clay . . . . Clement Comer Clay
Clevenger . . . . . . Shobal V. Clevenger
Cobb . . . . Thomas R.R. Cobb
Coke . . . . Sir Edward Coke
Collyer . . . . John Collyer
Comyn . . . . Samuel Comyn
Cooke . . . . Frederick Hale Cooke
Curtis . . . . George Ticknor Curtis
Daniel . . . . John Warwick Daniel
Dart . . . . Joseph Henry Dart
Davis . . . . John Anthony Gardner Davis
Desty . . . . Robert Desty
Devlin . . . . Robert Thomas Devlin
Dicey . . . . Albert Venn Dicey
Dillon . . . . John Forrest Dillon
Drone . . . . Eaton S. Drone
Duer . . . . John Duer
Du Ponceau . . . . Peter Stephen Du Ponceau
Elliot . . . . Jonathan Elliot
Elmer . . . . Joseph Elmer
Elmer . . . . Lucius Q.C. Elmer
Farwell . . . . Sir George Farwell
Fell . . . . Walter William Fell
Ferard . . . . Joseph Ferard
Fetter . . . . Norman Fetter
Field . . . . George W. Field
Finlason . . . . William Francis Finlason
Fisher . . . . William R. Fisher
Flanders . . . . Henry Flanders
Flood . . . . John Charles Henry Flood
Foote . . . . John Alderson Foote
Foster . . . . Roger Foster
Freeman . . . . A. C. (Abraham Clark) Freemen
Fry . . . . Sir Edward Fry
Gale . . . . Charles James Gale
Goddard . . . . John Leybourn Goddard
Gould . . . . James Gould
Gould . . . . John M. Gould
Gould . . . . Josiah Gould
Grant . . . . James Grant
Gray . . . . John Chipman Gray
Greenleaf . . . . . . Simon Greenleaf
Gresley . . . . Richard Newcombe Gresley
Gross . . . . Charles Gross
Guy . . . . William A. Guy
Hale . . . . William Hale
Hall . . . . John Elihu Hall
Hall . . . . William E. Hall
Halleck . . . . Henry Wager Halleck
Hamilton . . . . Alexander Hamilton
Hammon . . . . Louis Lougee Hammon
Hanhart . . . . Nicolas Hanhart
Harmon . . . . Henry Clay Harmon
Hare . . . . J. I. Clark Hare
Harris . . . . Seymour F. Harris
Hartley . . . . Oliver C. Hartley
Hawkins . . . . Francis V. Hawkins
Hening . . . . William W. Hening
High . . . . James L.High
Hilliard . . . . Francis Hilliard
Holland . . . . Thomas Erskine Holland
Holt . . . . Francis Ludlow Holt
Holmes . . . . Oliver Wendell Holmes
Hopkins . . . . Manley Hopkins
Hough . . . . Franklin Benjamin Hough
Hughes . . . . David Hughes
Hughes . . . . William J. Hughes
Jaggard . . . . Edwin A. Jaggard
Jarman . . . . Thomas Jarman
Jeremy . . . . George Jeremy
Jeremy . . . . Henry Jeremy
Jones . . . . Leonard A. Jones
Jones . . . . Sir William Jones
Keener . . . . William Albert Keener
Kent . . . . James Kent
Kerr . . . . William Williamson Kerr
Kyd . . . . Stewart Kyd
Langdell . . . . Christopher Columbus Langdell
Lawson . . . . John Davison Lawson
Lea . . . . Henry Charles Lea

Leake . . . . Stephen Martin Leake
Lewis . . . . John Lewis
Lewis . . . . William David Lewis
Lindley . . . . Sir Nathaniel Lindley
Lowell . . . . A. Lawrence Lowell
Maclachlan . . . . . David Maclachlan
Maine . . . . Sir Henry Sumner Maine
Malloy . . . . William M Malloy
Markby . . . . Sir William Markby
Marsden . . . . Reginald G. Marsden
Martin . . . . Francois Xavier Martin
Marshall . . . . Samuel Marshall
McAdam . . . . David McAdam
McCrary . . . . George W. McCrary
McKelvey . . . . . . John Jay McKelvey
Mechem . . . . Floyd R. Mechem
Mill . . . . John Stuart Mill
Miller . . . . Hunter Miller
Miller . . . . Samuel Freeman Miller
Mills . . . . Henry Edmund Mills
Morawetz . . . . . . Victor Morawetz
Morse . . . . John Torrey Morse, Jr.
Moyle . . . . John B. Moyle
Odgers . . . . W. Blake Odgers
Oliver . . . . Benjamin Lynde Oliver
Parsons . . . . Theophilus Parsons
Perry . . . . Jarius W. Perry
Phelps . . . . Charles Edward Phelps
Phillimore . . . . . . Sir Robert Phillimore
Phillips . . . . Willard Phillips
Pierce . . . . Edward Lillie Pierce
Pitman . . . . Edward Dix Pitman
Platt . . . . Thomas Platt
Poe . . . . John Prentiss Poe
Pollock . . . . Sir Frederick Pollock
Pomeroy . . . . John Norton Pomeroy
Poore . . . . Benjamin P. Poore
Pope . . . . Henry M. R. Pope
Porter . . . . James Biggs Porter
Pothier . . . . Robert J. Pothier
Powell . . . . John Joseph Powell
Preston . . . . Richard Preston
Randolph . . . . . . Joseph Fitz Randolph
Rapalje . . . . Stewart Rapalje
Rawle . . . . William Rawle
Ray . . . . Charles Andrew Ray
Redfield . . . . Amasa A Redfield
Redfield . . . . Isaac F. Redfield
Reeve . . . . Tapping Reeve
Reeves . . . . John Reeves
Remington . . . . . Harold Remington
Roberts . . . . William Roberts
Robinson . . . . . . William Callyhan Robinson
Roper . . . . Stote Donnison Roper
Rose . . . . Walter Malins Rose
Russell . . . . John Archibald Russell
Sandars . . . . Thomas C. Sandars
Sanders . . . . Francis Williams Sanders
Saunders . . . . . . Thomas William Saunders
Schouler . . . . James Schouler
Sedgwick . . . . . . Arthur George Sedgwick
Seton . . . . Henry Wilmot Seton
Shearman . . . . . . Thomas G. Shearman
Sheldon . . . . Henry Newton Sheldon
Shelford . . . . Leonard Shelford
Smith . . . . Charles M. Smith
Smith . . . . Horace Smith
Smith . . . . Jeremiah Smith (with Ames)
Smith . . . . John William Smith
Snyder . . . . Wilson Isaac Snyder
Spence . . . . George Spence
Starkie . . . . Thomas Starkie
Stearns . . . . Asahel Stearns
Stephen . . . . Henry John Stephen
Stephen . . . . James Fitzjames Stephen
Stille . . . . Alfred Stille
Story . . . . Joseph Story
Story . . . . William W. Story
Stubbs . . . . William Stubbs
Sugden . . . . Edward Burtenshaw Sugden
Sullivan . . . . James Sullivan
Summers . . . . Walter L. Summers
Talcott . . . . William Talcott
Taylor . . . . Pitt Taylor
Thomas . . . . Abner Charles Thomas
Thomas . . . . Edward Beers Thomas
Thompson . . . . . . Seymour D. Thompson
Tidd . . . . William Tidd
Tiedeman . . . . . . Christopher Gustavua Tiedeman
Tiffany . . . . Herbert Thorndike Tiffany
Townshend . . . . . John Townshend
Troubat . . . . Francis Joseph Troubat
Tucker . . . . Henry St. George Tucker
Tudor . . . . Owen Davies Tudor
Tyler . . . . Ransom Hebbard Tyler
Tyler . . . . Samuel Tyler
Underhill . . . . . . Arthur Underhill
Underhill . . . . . . Henry Clay Underhill
Wade . . . . William Pratt Wade
Wait . . . . Frederick Scott Wait
Walker . . . . Albert Henry Walker
Walker . . . . James Bryant Walker
Wallace . . . . Horace Binney Wallace
Warvelle . . . . George William Warvelle
Washburn . . . . . . Emory Washburn
Waterman . . . . . . Thomas Whitney Waterman
Watkins . . . . Charles Watkins
Weeks . . . . Edward P. Weeks
Wells . . . . Edward Hyde Wells
Weskett . . . . John Weskett
Westlake . . . . John Westlake
Wharton . . . . Francis Wharton
Wharton . . . . George Frederick Wharton
Wheaton . . . . Henry Wheaton
Whitaker . . . . Richard Whitaker
Wigmore . . . . John Henry Wigmore
Wigram . . . . Sir James Wigram
Willard . . . . John Willard
Willcock . . . . John William Willcock
Williams . . . . Edward Vaughan Williams
Williams . . . . Joshua Williams
Williams . . . . Robert Griffith Williams
Willis . . . . John Walpole Willis
Williston . . . . Samuel Williston
Withrow . . . . Thomas Foster Withrow
Witthaus . . . . Rudolph August Witthaus
Woerner . . . . John Gabriel Woerner
Wood . . . . Horace Gay Wood
Woolrych . . . . . . Humphry William Woolrych
Works . . . . John Downey Works
Wright . . . . Sir Martin Wright

Appendix B

Legal Maxims

In the first edition of this dictionary, published in 1891, Henry Campbell Black remarked that the book contained "a complete collection of legal maxims," adding: "These have not been grouped in one body, but distributed in their proper alphabetical order through the book. This is believed to be the more convenient arrangement" (p. iv). Although it might indeed have been more convenient for readers who knew the maxims they wanted to look up — as 19th-century readers might have been apt to — spreading Latin sentences throughout the book is decidedly inconvenient for most dictionary users today. We have therefore collected them for ease of reference. A bibliography of works cited appears on page 1969.

Of course, many scholars have long been intolerant of those who use maxims to decide cases. As James Fitzjames Stephen, one of the great 19th-century legal scholars, incisively put it before Black's work appeared:

> It seems to me that legal maxims in general are little more than pert headings of chapters. They are rather minims than maxims, for they give not a particularly great but a particularly small amount of information. As often as not, the exceptions and disqualifications to them are more important than the so-called rules.[1]

Other scholars have been equally derisive.[2]

But there is an element of fun in legal maxims: they sometimes express surprising insights — and these from ancient writers. Though they will rarely clinch arguments, they will delight many readers who have a historical bent.

—B.A.G.

---

1. 2 James Fitzjames Stephen, *History of the Criminal Law of England* 94 n.1 (1883).
2. For a collection of critical comments, see *Garner's Dictionary of Legal Usage* 567 (3d ed. 2011).

A

Ab abusu ad usum non valet consequentia. A conclusion about the use of a thing from its abuse is invalid.

Ab assuetis non fit injuria. No injury is done by things long acquiesced in.

Abbreviationum ille numerus et sensus accipiendus est ut concessio non sit inanis. Such number and sense is to be given to abbreviations that the grant may not be void.

Absentem accipere debemus eum qui non est eo loco in quo petitur. We must consider a person absent who is not in that place in which he is sought.

Absentia ejus qui reipublicae causa abest neque ei neque alii damnosa esse debet. The absence of a person who is abroad in service to the state ought to be prejudicial neither to that person nor to another. Dig. 50.17.140.

Absoluta sententia expositore non indiget. A simple proposition needs no expositor.

Abundans cautela non nocet. Abundant caution does no harm.

Accessio cedit principali. An addition to the principal thing becomes part of it.

Accessorium non ducit, sed sequitur, suum principale. An accessory does not lead, but follows, its principal.

Accessorium non trahit principale. The accessory does not carry the principal with it.

Accessorium sequitur naturam rei cui accedit. An accessory follows the nature of the thing to which it is accessory.

Accessorium sequitur principale. The accessory follows the principal.

Accessorius sequitur naturam sui principalis. An accessory follows the nature of the principal. • That is, an accessory cannot be guilty of a higher crime than his principal.

Accessorius sequitur principalem. An accessory follows (depends on) his principal. • Where there is no principal, there can be no accessory.

Accipere quid ut justitiam facias non est tam accipere quam extorquere. To accept anything as a reward for doing justice is rather extorting than accepting.

Accusare nemo se debet nisi coram deo. No one is bound to accuse himself except before God.

Accusator post rationabile tempus non est audiendus, nisi se bene de omissione excusaverit. An accuser ought not to be heard after (the expiration of) a reasonable time, unless he can account satisfactorily for his delay.

A communi observantia non est recedendum. Common observance (or usage) is not to be departed from.

A communi observantia non est recedendum et minime mutandae sunt quae certam interpretationem habent. Common observance is not to be departed from, and things that have certain meaning are to be changed as little as possible.

Acta exteriora indicant interiora secreta. Outward acts indicate the thoughts hidden within.

Acta in uno judicio non probant in alio nisi inter easdem personas. Things done in one action cannot be taken as evidence in another, unless it is between the same parties.

Actio non datur non damnificato. An action is not given to one who is not injured.

Actio non facit reum, nisi mens sit rea. An act does not make a person guilty unless the mind is guilty. • Properly, *Actus non reum* (q.v.).

Actionum genera maxime sunt servanda. The kinds of actions are especially to be preserved.

Actio personalis moritur cum persona. A personal action dies with the person.

Actio poenalis in haeredem non datur, nisi forte ex damno locupletior haeres factus sit. A penal action is not given against an heir, unless, indeed, the heir has benefited from the wrong.

Actio quaelibet it sua via. Every action proceeds in its own course.

Actore non probante, reus absolvitur. If the plaintiff does not prove his case, the defendant is acquitted.

Actori incumbit onus probandi. The burden of proof rests on the plaintiff.

Actori incumbit (onus) probationis, reus in excipiendo fit actor. The burden of proof weighs on the plaintiff but the defendant in objecting becomes the plaintiff.

Actor qui contra regulam quid adduxit non est audiendus. A pleader ought not to be heard who advances a proposition contrary to the rule (of law).

Actor sequitur forum rei. The plaintiff follows the forum of the defendant.

Actus curiae neminem gravabit. An act of the court will prejudice no one.

Actus Dei nemini est damnosus. An act of God is injurious to no one. 2 Bl. Com. 122.

Actus Dei nemini facit injuriam. An act of God does wrong to no one. • That is, no one is responsible in damages for inevitable accidents.

Actus Dei nemini nocet. An act of God does wrong to no one.

Actus Dei vel legis nemini facit injuriam. An act of God or of the law does injury to no one.

Actus inceptus cujus perfectio pendet ex voluntate partium revocari potest; si autem pendet ex voluntate tertiae personae, vel ex contingenti, revocari non potest. An act already begun whose completion depends on the will of the parties may be recalled; but if it depends on consent of a third person or on a contingency, it cannot be recalled.

Actus judiciarius coram non judice irritus habetur; de ministeriali autem a quocunque provenit ratum esto. A judicial act before one not a judge (or without jurisdiction) is void; as to a ministerial act, from whomsoever it proceeds, let it be valid.

Actus legis nemini est damnosus. An act of the law prejudices no one.

Actus legis nemini facit injuriam. An act of the law does no one wrong.

Actus legitimi non recipiunt modum. Acts required by law admit of no qualification.

Actus me invito factus non est meus actus. An act done (by me) against my will is not my act.

Actus non facit reum nisi mens sit rea. An act does not make a person guilty unless the mind is guilty; an act does not make the doer criminal unless his mind is criminal. • Coke gives the maxim in a slightly different form: Actus non reum facit nisi mens sit rea. 3 Co. Inst. 54; 107.

Actus repugnans non potest in esse produci. A repugnant act cannot be brought into being (that is, cannot be made effectual).

Actus servi, in iis quibus opera ejus communiter adhibita est, actus domini habetur. The act of a servant in those things in which he is usually employed is considered the act of his master.

Additio probat minoritatem. An addition proves inferiority. • That is, if it be said that a person has a fee tail, it is less than if the person has the fee.

Ad ea quae frequentius accidunt jura adaptantur. The laws are adapted to those cases that occur more frequently.

A digniori fieri debet denominatio et resolutio. The denomination and explanation ought to be derived from the more worthy.

Adjuvari quippe nos, non decipi, beneficio oportet. Surely we ought to be helped by a benefit, not be entrapped by it.

Admiralitas jurisdictionem non habet super iis quae communi lege dirimuntur. A court of Admiralty has no jurisdiction over those things that are determined by common law.

Ad officium justiciariorum spectat unicuique coram eis placitanti justitiam exhibere. It is the duty of justices to administer justice to everyone pleading before them.

Ad proximum antecedens fiat relatio, nisi impediatur sententia. A relative is to be referred to the nearest antecedent, unless prevented by the sense.

Ad quaestiones facti non respondent judices; ad quaestiones legis non respondent juratores. Judges do not answer questions of fact; jurors do not answer questions of law.

Ad quaestiones legis judices, et non juratores, respondent. Judges, and not jurors, answer questions of law.

Ad recte docendum oportet primum inquirere nomina, quia rerum cognitio a nominibus rerum dependet. In order rightly to comprehend a thing, it is necessary first to inquire into the names, for a right knowledge of things depends on their names.

Ad reges enim potestas omnium pertinet; ad singulos, proprietas. Kings have (political) power over all things, while individuals own them.

Ad salutem civium civitatumque incolumnitatem conditae leges sunt. Laws were made for the safety of citizens and for the security of states. (Based on Cicero, De Legibus 2.4.11.)

Ad suum quemque aequum est quaestum esse callidum. It is reasonable that everyone should be clever to his own profit. Plautus, *Truculentus* 2.416.

Adversus extraneos vitiosa possessio prodesse solet. Possession though faulty is usually sufficient against outsiders. • Prior possession is a good title of ownership against all who cannot show a better.

Adversus periculum naturalis ratio permittit se defendere. Natural reason allows one to defend himself against danger.

Ad vim majorem vel ad casus fortuitos non tenetur quis, nisi sua culpa intervenerit. No one is held to answer for the effects of superior force or accidents, unless his own fault has contributed.

Aedificare in tuo proprio solo non licet quod alteri noceat. It is not lawful to build on one's own land what may be injurious to another.

Aedificatum solo solo cedit. What is built on the land goes with the land.

Aedificia solo cedunt. Buildings go with the land.

Aequior est dispositio legis quam hominis. The law's disposition is more impartial than man's.

Aequitas agit in personam. Equity acts on the person.

Aequitas casibus medetur. Equity relieves against accidents.

Aequitas curiae cancellariae, quasi filia conscientiae, obtemperat secundum regulas curiae. The equity of the court of chancery, as if it were the daughter of conscience, conforms to the rules of court.

Aequitas defectus supplet. Equity supplements defects.

Aequitas erroribus medetur. Equity rectifies errors.

Aequitas est aequalitas. Equity is equality.

Aequitas est correctio legis generaliter latae qua parte deficit. Equity is the correction of some part of the law where by reason of its generality it is defective.

Aequitas est perfecta quaedam ratio quae jus scriptum interpretatur et emendat; nulla scriptura comprehensa, sed sola ratione consistens. Equity is a sort of perfect reason that interprets and amends written law; comprehended in no written text, but consisting of reason alone.

Aequitas est quasi equalitas. Equity is as it were equality.

Aequitas est virtus voluntatis, correctrix ejus in quo lex propter universalitatem deficit. Equity is a virtue of the will, the corrector of that wherein the law, by reason of its universality, is deficient.

Aequitas ex lege generaliter lata aliquid excipit. Equity makes exception to a law framed generally.

Aequitas ignorantiae opitulatur, oscitantiae non item. Equity assists ignorance but not complacency (or carelessness).

Aequitas in eum qui vult summo jure agere summum jus intendit. Equity directs the rigor of the law against him who wishes to act according to the rigor of the law.

Aequitas in paribus causis paria jura desiderat. Equity in like cases requires like laws.

Aequitas jurisdictiones non confundit. Equity does not confuse jurisdictions.

Aequitas naturam rei non mutat. Equity does not change the nature of a thing.

Aequitas neminem juvat cum injuria alterius. Equity aids no man to the injury of another.

Aequitas non facit jus, sed juri auxiliatur. Equity does not create a right, but aids the right.

Aequitas non medetur defectu eorum quae jure positivo requisita sunt. Equity does not make up for a deficiency of those things that are required by positive law.

Aequitas non sinit eum qui jus verum tenuit extremum jus persequi. Equity does not allow one who has obtained a true right to prosecute it to the extremity.

Aequitas non supplet ea quae in manu orantis esse possunt. Equity does not provide for those things that may be in the hand of an applicant.

Aequitas non vaga atque incerta, sed terminos habet atque limites praefinitos. Equity is not vague and uncertain, but has boundaries and prescribed limits.

Aequitas nunquam contravenit leges. Equity never contravenes the laws.

Aequitas nunquam liti ancillatur ubi remedium potest dare. Equity never fosters a quarrel, where she can give a remedy.

Aequitas rei oppignoratae redemptionibus favet. Equity favors the redemption of a thing given in pawn.

Aequitas rem ipsam intuetur de forma et circumstantiis minus anxia. Equity focuses on the thing itself and is less concerned with form and circumstance.

Aequitas sequitur legem. Equity follows the law.

Aequitas supervacua odit. Equity abhors superfluous things.

Aequitas uxoribus, liberis, creditoribus maxime favet. Equity most favors wives, children, and creditors.

Aequitas vult omnibus modis, ad veritatem pervenire. Equity wishes by every possible means to attain the truth.

Aequitas vult spoliatos, vel deceptos, vel lapsos ante omnia restitui. Equity wishes the plundered, the deceived, and the ruined, above all, to have restitution.

Aequum et bonum est lex legum. What is equitable and good is the law of laws.

Aestimatio praeteriti delicti ex postremo facto nunquam crescit. The assessment of a past offense never increases from a subsequent fact.

A facto ad jus non datur consequentia. The inference from fact to law is not allowed. • That is, a fact does not necessarily constitute a right.

Affectio tua nomen imponit operi tuo. Your motive gives a name to your act.

Affectus punitur licet non sequatur effectus. The intention is punished even if the object is not achieved.

Affinis dicitur, cum duae cognationes, inter se divisae, per nuptias copulantur, et altera ad alterius fines accidit. Persons are said to be bound by affinity when two families, divided from one another, are united by marriage, and each approaches the borders of the other.

Affinis mei affinis non est mihi affinis. A person connected by marriage to someone connected by marriage to me is no connection of mine.

Affirmanti, non neganti, incumbit probatio. The proof is incumbent on the one who affirms, not on the one who denies.

Affirmantis est probare. The person who affirms must prove.

Affirmativum negativum implicat. An affirmative implies a negative.

Agentes et consentientes pari poena plectentur. Acting and consenting parties will be liable to the same punishment.

A jure suo cadunt. They fall from their right. • That is, they lose their right.

A justitia (quasi a quodam fonte) omnia jura emanant. From justice, as from a fountain, all rights flow.

Aleator quanto in arte est melior, tanto est nequior. The more skillful the gambler is in his art, the more wicked he is. Publilius Syrus.

Aliena negotia exacto officio geruntur. The business of another is conducted with scrupulous attention.

Alienatio licet prohibeatur, consensu tamen omnium in quorum favorem prohibita est potest fieri; et quilibet potest renunciare juri pro se introducto. Even if alienation is prohibited, it may yet take place by the consent of all in whose favor it is prohibited; it is in the power of anyone to renounce a right introduced for his own benefit.

Alienatio rei praefertur juri accrescendi. Alienation of property is favored over the right to accumulate.

A l'impossible nul n'est tenu. No one is bound to do what is impossible.

Aliquid conceditur ne injuria remaneat impunita quod alias non concederetur. Something is conceded that otherwise would not be conceded, so that a wrong not remain unpunished.

Aliquis non debet esse judex in propria causa, quia non potest esse judex et pars. A person ought not to be judge in his own cause, because he cannot act both as judge and party.

Aliud est celare, aliud tacere. To conceal is one thing, to be silent another.

Aliud est distinctio, aliud separatio. Distinction is one thing, separation another.

Aliud est possidere, aliud esse in possessione. It is one thing to possess, another to be in possession.

Aliud est vendere, aliud vendenti consentire. To sell is one thing, to give consent to the seller another.

Allegans contraria non est audiendus. A person making contradictory allegations is not to be heard.

Allegans suam turpitudinem non est audiendus. A person alleging his own wrong is not to be heard.

Allegari non debuit quod probatum non relevat. What is not relevant if proved ought not to have been alleged.

Allegatio contra factum non est admittenda. An allegation contrary to the deed (or fact) is not admissible.

Alterius circumventio alii non praebet actionem. A deception practiced on one person does not give a cause of action to another.

Alternativa petitio non est audienda. An alternative petition is not to be heard.

Ambigua responsio contra proferentem est accipienda. An ambiguous answer is to be taken against the party who offers it.

Ambiguis casibus semper praesumitur pro rege. In doubtful cases the presumption is always in favor of the king.

Ambiguitas contra stipulatorem est. A dubious expression is construed against the party using it.

Ambiguitas verborum latens verificatione suppletur; nam quod ex facto oritur ambiguum verificatione facti tollitur. A latent ambiguity in wording is resolved by evidence; for whatever ambiguity arises from an extrinsic fact is resolved by extrinsic evidence.

Ambiguitas verborum patens nulla verificatione excluditur. A patent ambiguity is not removed by extrinsic evidence (or is never helped by averment).

Ambiguum pactum contra venditorem interpretandum est. An ambiguous agreement is construed against the seller.

Ambiguum placitum interpretari debet contra proferentem. An ambiguous plea ought to be interpreted against the party pleading it.

Ambulatoria est voluntas defuncti usque ad vitae supremum exitum. The will of a decedent is ambulatory (that is, can be altered) until the last moment of life.

Ancupia verborum sunt judice indigna. Quibbling over words is unworthy of a judge.

Angliae jura in omni casu libertati dant favorem. The laws of England are favorable in every case to liberty.

Animus ad se omne jus ducit. The mind brings every right unto itself. • Often explained: It is to the intention that all law applies.

Animus hominis est anima scripti. The intention of the person is the soul of the instrument.

Anniculus trecentesimo sexagesimo-quinto die dicitur, incipiente plane non exacto die, quia annum civiliter non ad momenta temporum sed ad dies numeramur. We call a child a year old on the 365th day, when the day is clearly begun but not ended, because we calculate the civil year not by moments, but by days.

Annua nec debitum judex non separat ipse. Even the judge apportions neither annuities nor debt.

Annus est mora motus quo suum planeta pervolvat circulum. A year is the duration of the motion by which a planet revolves through its orbit.

Annus inceptus pro completo habetur. A year begun is held as completed. • Said to be of very limited application.

A non posse ad non esse sequitur argumentum necessarie negative, licet non affirmative. From impossibility to nonexistence the inference follows necessarily in the negative, though not in the affirmative.

Apices juris non sunt jura. Legal niceties are not law.

A piratis aut latronibus capti liberi permanent. Those captured by pirates or robbers remain free.

A piratis et latronibus capta dominium non mutant. Things captured by pirates or robbers do not change their ownership.

Appellatione fundi omne aedificium et omnis ager continetur. The word *land* comprehends every building and every field.

Applicatio est vita regulae. The application is the life of a rule.

Aqua cedit solo. The water goes with the ground. • A grant of the land includes the water on it.

Aqua currit et debet currere ut currere solebat. Water runs and ought to run as it has been used to run.

Arbiter nihil extra compromissum facere potest. The arbitrator can do nothing beyond the agreement to arbitrate.

Arbitramentum aequum tribuit cuique suum. A just arbitration renders to each his own.

Arbitrium est judicium. An award is a judgment.

Arbitrium est judicium boni viri, secundum aequum et bonum. An award is the judgment of a good man according to equity and virtue.

Arbor dum crescit; lignum dum crescere nequit. It is a tree while it is growing; wood when it cannot grow.

A rescriptis valet argumentum. An argument from rescripts (i.e., original writs in the register) is valid.

Argumenta ignota et obscura ad lucem rationis proferunt et reddunt splendida. Arguments bring things hidden and obscure to the light of reason and render them clear.

Argumentum ab auctoritate est fortissimum in lege. An argument drawn from authority is the strongest in law.

Argumentum ab impossibili plurimum valet in lege. An argument deduced from an impossibility has the greatest validity in law.

Argumentum ab inconvenienti plurimum valet in lege. An argument drawn from what is unsuitable (or improper) has the greatest validity in law. Co. Litt. 66a.

Argumentum a communiter accidentibus in jure frequens est. An argument from things commonly happening is frequent in law.

Argumentum a divisione est fortissimum in jure. An argument based on a subdivision of the subject is most powerful in law.

Argumentum a majori ad minus negative non valet; valet e converso. An argument from the greater to the lesser is of no force in the negative; conversely (in the affirmative) it is valid.

Argumentum a simili valet in lege. An argument by analogy (from a similar case) has force in law.

Arma in armatos sumere jura sinunt. The laws permit taking up arms against the armed.

Assignatus utitur jure auctoris. An assignee is clothed with the rights of the principal.

A summo remedio ad inferiorem actionem non habetur regressus neque auxilium. From the highest remedy to an inferior action there is no recourse or assistance.

Auctoritates philosophorum, medicorum et poetarum sunt in causis allegandae et tenendae. The authoritative opinions of philosophers, physicians, and poets are to be adduced and regarded in causes.

Aucupia verborum sunt judice indigna. Quibbling over words is unworthy of a judge.

Audaces fortuna iuvat. Fortune succors the bold.

Audi alteram partem. Hear the other side. • No one should be condemned unheard.

Audiatur et altera pars. May the other side be heard.

Auxilium principali sequitur. The aid follows the principal.

A verbis legis non est recedendum. From the words of the law there is to be no departure.

B

Baratriam committit qui propter pecuniam justitiam baractat. A person is guilty of barratry who sells justice for money.

Bello pacta cedunt reipublicae. In war contracts give way to the state.

Benedicta est expositio quando res redimitur a destructione. Blessed is the exposition when a thing is saved from destruction.

Beneficium invito non datur. A privilege or benefit is not granted against a person's will.

Beneficium non datum nisi propter officium. A remuneration is not given, unless on account of a duty performed.

Beneficium non datur nisi officii causa. A benefice is not granted except on account or in consideration of duty.

Beneficium principis debet esse mansurum. The benefaction of a prince ought to be lasting.

Benigne faciendae sunt interpretationes chartarum, ut res magis valeat quam pereat; et quaelibet concessio fortissime contra donatorem interpretanda est. Deeds should be subject to liberal interpretation, so that the matter may take effect rather than fail; and every grant is to be taken most strongly against the grantor.

Benigne faciendae sunt interpretationes propter simplicitatem laicorum, ut res magis valeat quam pereat; et verba intentioni, non e contra, debent inservire. Constructions (of written instruments) are to be made liberally, for the simplicity of laymen, in order that the matter may have effect rather than fail (or become void); and words must be subject to the intention, not the intention to the words.

Benignior sententia in verbis generalibus seu dubiis est preferenda. The more favorable construction is to be preferred in general or doubtful expressions.

Benignius leges interpretandae sunt quo voluntas earum conservetur. Laws are to be more liberally interpreted so that their intent may be preserved.

Bigamus seu trigamus, etc., est qui diversis temporibus et successive duas seu tres uxores habuit. A bigamus or trigamus, etc., is one who has had two or more wives in succession, each at a different time. 3 Co. Inst. 88.

Bis dat qui cito dat. He pays twice who pays promptly.

Bis idem exigi bona fides non patitur, et in satisfactionibus non permittitur amplius fieri quam semel factum est. Good faith does not allow the same thing to be exacted twice; and in satisfying claims, it is not permitted that more should be done after satisfaction has once been rendered.w

Bonae fidei non congruit de apicibus juris disputare. It is incompatible with good faith to insist on the extreme subtleties of the law.

Bonae fidei possessor in id tantum quod ad se pervenerit tenetur. A possessor in good faith is liable only for that which he himself has obtained (literally, what has come to him). 2 Co. Inst. 285.

Bona fide possessor facit fructus consumptos suos. A possessor in good faith is entitled to the fruits (or produce) that he consumes.

Bona fides exigit ut quod convenit fiat. Good faith demands that what is agreed on shall be done.

Bona fides non patitur ut bis idem exigatur. Good faith does not allow payment to be exacted twice for the same thing.

Bona non intelligentur nisi deducto aere alieno. Assets will not be recognized unless debts have been deducted.

Boni judicis est ampliare jurisdictionem (or justitiam). It is the role of a good judge to enlarge (or use liberally) his jurisdiction (or remedial authority).

Boni judicis est ampliare justitiam. It is the role of a good judge to enlarge or extend justice.

Boni judicis est causas litium dirimere. It is the role of a good judge to remove causes of litigation.

Boni judicis est judicium sine dilatione mandare executioni. It is the role of a good judge to render judgment for execution without delay.

Boni judicis est lites dirimere, ne lis ex lite oriatur. It is the role of a good judge to dispose of lawsuits so that one suit should not grow from another. 5 Coke 31a.

Bonum defendentis ex integra causa; malum ex quolibet defectu. A good outcome for the defendant comes from a sound case; a bad outcome from some defect.

Bonum necessarium extra terminos necessitatis non est bonum. A thing good from necessity is not good beyond the limits of the necessity.

Bonus judex secundum aequum et bonum judicat, et aequitatem stricto juri praefert. A good judge decides according to fairness and the good and prefers equity to strict law.

Breve ita dicitur, quia rem de qua agitur, et intentionem petentis, paucis verbis breviter enarrat. A writ is called a "breve" because it briefly states, in few words, the matter in dispute, and the object of the party seeking relief.

Breve judiciale debet sequi suum originale, et accessorium suum principale. A judicial writ ought to follow its original, and an accessory its principal.

Breve judiciale non cadit pro defectu formae. A judicial writ does not fail for a defect of form.

Brevia, tam originalia quam judicialia, patiuntur anglica nomina. Writs, original as well as judicial, bear English names.

C

Cancellarii angliae dignitas est, ut secundus a rege in regno habetur. The dignity of the chancellor of England is (such) that he is considered second in the realm from the sovereign.

Carcer ad homines custodiendos, non ad puniendos, dari debet. Imprisonment should be imposed for keeping people in confinement, not for punishing them (further). Co. Litt. 260a.

Carcer non supplicii causa sed custodiae constitutus. A prison is established not for the sake of punishment, but for detention under guard.

Caret periculo qui etiam cum est tutus cavet. He is most free from danger who, even when safe, is on his guard.

Casus fortuitus non est sperandus, et nemo tenetur divinare. A chance event is not to be expected, and no one is bound to foresee it.

Casus fortuitus non est supponendus. A chance event is not to be presumed.

Casus omissus et oblivioni datus dispositioni communis juris relinquitur. A case omitted and forgotten (not provided for in statute) is left to the disposal of the common law.

Casus omissus pro omisso habendus est. A case omitted is to be held as (intentionally) omitted.

Catalla juste possessa amitti non possunt. Chattels rightly possessed cannot be lost.

Catalla reputantur inter minima in lege. Chattels are considered in law among things of least consequence.

Causa causae est causa causati. The cause of a cause is the cause of the effect.

Causa causantis causa est causati. The cause of the thing causing is the cause of the effect.

Causa ecclesiae publicis aequiparatur; et summa est ratio quae pro religione facit. The cause of the church is equal to public causes; and paramount is the reason that acts in favor of religion.

Causae dotis, vitae, libertatis, fisci sunt inter favorabilia in lege. Causes of dower, life, liberty, revenue are among the things favored in law.

Causae ecclesiae publicis causis aequiparantur. The causes of the church are equal to public causes.

Causa et origo est materia negotii. The cause and origin of a matter are the substance of it. • "The law regards the original act": as in the case of a man who attempts suicide in madness, but dies after regaining sanity; such is not suicide. 1 Coke 99.

Causa patet. The reason is obvious.

Causa proxima non remota spectatur. The immediate and not the remote cause is considered.

Causa vaga et incerta non est causa rationabilis. A vague and uncertain cause is not a reasonable cause.

Caveat emptor. Let the buyer beware.

Caveat emptor qui ignorare non debuit quod jus alienum emit. Let the buyer beware; for he ought not act in ignorance when he buys what another has right to.

Caveat venditor. Let the seller beware.

Caveat viator. Let the traveler beware.

Cavendum est a fragmentis. Beware of fragments.

Certa debet esse intentio et narratio et certum fundamentum et certa res quae deducitur in judicium. The design and narration ought to be certain, the foundation certain, and the matter certain that is brought into court to be tried.

Certum est quod certum reddi potest. That is certain which can be rendered certain.

Cessante causa, cessat effectus. The cause ceasing, the effect ceases.

Cessante ratione legis cessat et ipsa lex. When the reason of the law ceases, the law itself also ceases.

Cessante statu primitivo, cessat derivativus. When the original estate comes to an end, the derivative estate is also at an end.

Cessa regnare, si non vis judicare. Cease to reign if you wish not to adjudicate.

C'est le crime qui fait la honte, et non pas véchafaud. It is the crime that causes the shame, and not the scaffold.

Cestuy que doit inheriter al pére doit inheriter al fils. The person who should have inherited from the father should also inherit from the son.

Chacea est ad communem legem. A chase (or hunting ground) exists by common law.

Charta de non ente non valet. A deed of a thing not in being is not valid.

Charta non est nisi vestimentum donationis. A deed is nothing else than the vestment (or clothing) of a gift.

Chartarum super fidem, mortuis testibus, ad patriam de necessitudine recurrendum est. (A dispute) regarding the veracity of deeds, with the witnesses dead, must necessarily be referred to the country (or jury).

Chirographum apud debitorem repertum praesumitur solutum. When the evidence (or voucher) is found in the debtor's possession, the debt is presumed to be paid.

Chirographum non extans praesumitur solutum. When the evidence of a debt is not in existence, it is presumed to have been discharged.

Circuitus est evitandus. Circuity (roundabout proceeding) is to be avoided.

Circuitus est evitandus; et boni judicis est lites dirimere, ne lis ex lite oriatur. Circuity is to be avoided; and it is the role of a good judge to determine (or dispose of) litigations so that one lawsuit may not arise from another.

Citatio est de juri naturali. A summons is by natural right.

Citationes non concedantur priusquam exprimatur super qua re fieri debet citatio. Citations should not be granted before it is stated about what matter the citation is to be made.

Civitas ea autem in libertate est posita quae suis stat viribus, non ex alieno arbitrio pendet. That state enjoys freedom which relies upon its own strength and does not depend upon the authority of another.

Clam delinquens magis punitur quam palam. A person who does wrong secretly is punished more severely than one who acts openly. 8 Coke 127.

Clam factum id videtur esse, quod quisque, quum controversiam haberet, habiturumve se putaret, fecit. That is considered done secretly which someone did when he had a legal dispute or thought he would have one.

Clausulae inconsuetae semper inducunt suspicionem. Unusual clauses always arouse suspicion.

Clausula generalis de residuo non ea complectitur quae non ejusdem sint generis cum iis quae specialim dicta fuerant. A general clause of remainder does not embrace those things that are not of the same kind as those that had been specially mentioned.

Clausula generalis non refertur ad expressa. A general clause does not refer to things expressly mentioned.

Clausula quae abrogationem excludit ab initio non valet. A clause that precludes abrogation is invalid from the beginning.

Clausula vel dispositio inutilis per praesumptionem remotam vel causam ex post facto non fulcitur. A useless clause or disposition is not supported by a remote presumption or by a cause arising afterward. • A useless clause or disposition is one that expresses no more than the law by intendment would have supplied; it is not supported by a remote presumption or foreign intendment of some purpose in regard to which it might be material, or by a cause arising afterward that may induce an operation of those idle words.

Clerici non ponentur in officiis. The clergy should not be placed in temporal offices.

Cogitationis poenam nemo meretur. No one deserves punishment for his thoughts.

Cogitationis poenam nemo patitur. No one is punished for his thoughts.

Cognomen majorum est ex sanguine tractum, hoc intrinsecum est; agnomen extrinsecum ab eventu. The cognomen is derived from the blood of ancestors and is intrinsic; an agnomen (or honorary title) arises from an event, and is extrinsic.

Cohaeredes sunt quasi unum corpus aut una persona censentur, propter unitatem juris quod habent. Coheirs are deemed as one body, or one person, on account of the unity of right that they possess.

Cohaeredes una persona censentur, propter unitatem juris quod habent. Coheirs are deemed as one person, on account of the unity of right that they possess.

Coheredes sunt quasi unum corpus, propter unitatem juris quod habent. Coheirs are treated as one person because of the unity of right that they have.

Collegium est societas plurium corporum simul habitantium. A college is a society of several people dwelling together.

Collegium seu corpus corporatum nisi regiis constitutionibus non potest existere. A college or incorporated body can not exist except by charter of the sovereign.

Commenda est facultas recipiendi et retinendi beneficium contra jus positivum a suprema potestate. A commendam is the power of receiving and retaining a benefice contrary to positive law, by supreme authority.

Commercium jure gentium commune esse debet et non in monopolium et privatum paucorum quaestum convertendum. Commerce, by the law of nations, ought to be common and not converted into a monopoly and the private gain of a few.

Commodum ex injuria sua non habere debet. (The wrongdoer) should not derive any benefit from his own wrong.

Communis error facit jus. A common error (one often repeated) makes law.

Communis error non facit jus. A common error does not make law. • This maxim expresses a view directly contradictory to the view of the immediately preceding maxim. Both are attested in legal literature.

Communiter unum officium est excusatio alterius. The performance of one duty is commonly the excuse for the nonperformance of another.

Compendia sunt dispendia. Abridgments are hindrances. Shortcuts or time-saving measures are often a loss. • Coke continues, *Melius est petere fontes.* Co. Litt. 305b.

Compromissarii sunt judices. Arbitrators are judges.

Compromissum ad similitudinem judiciorum redigitur. A compromise is brought into affinity with judgments.

Conatus quid sit non definitur in jure. What an attempt is, is not defined in law.

Concessio per regem fieri debet de certitudine. A grant by the king ought to be made of a certainty. • Coke explains, "If the king grants to me that I shall not be sheriff, without showing of what county, it is void for uncertainty." 9 Coke 46b.

Concessio versus concedentem latam interpretationem habere debet. A grant ought to have a liberal interpretation against the grantor.

Concordare leges legibus est optimus interpretandi modus. To make laws agree with laws is the best mode of interpreting them.

Concordia parvae res crescunt et opulentia lites. Small means increase by concord and litigations by opulence.

Condictio rei furtivae, quia rei habet persecutionem, haeredem quoque furis obligat. Because the condictio for a stolen thing has the aim of recovering the asset, it also binds the thief's heir. Dig. 13.1.7.2.

Conditio ad liberum tenementum auferendum non nisi ex facto placitari debet. An argument for taking away a free tenure ought not be pleaded, except from the deed.

Conditio beneficialis, quae statum construit, benigne secundum verborum intentionem est interpretanda; odiosa autem quae statum destruit stricte, secundum verborum proprietatem, accipienda. A beneficial condition that creates an estate ought to be construed favorably, according to the intention of the words; but a condition that destroys an estate is odious and ought to be construed according to the strict sense of the words.

Conditio dicitur cum quid in casum incertum qui potest tendere ad esse aut non esse confertur. It is called a condition when something is given for an uncertain event that may or may not come into existence.

Conditio ex parte extincta ex toto extinguitur. An agreement extinguished in part is wholly extinguished.

Conditio illicita habetur pro non adjecta. An unlawful condition is considered unconnected.

Conditio liberum tenementum cassans non per nuda verba sine charta valebit. A condition making void a free tenement will be of no value by bare words without a deed.

Conditio neminem juvabit nisi qui pars fuerit aut privus. An agreement shall benefit no one unless he is party or privy to it.

Conditionem testium tunc inspicere debemus cum signarent, non mortis tempore. We should consider the condition of witnesses when they sign, not at the time of death. Dig. 28.1.22.

Conditiones praecedentes ad normam legis severe exigendae; aliter de subsequentibus ubi aequitati licet damnum rei infectae pensari. Conditions precedent must be rigorously exacted according to the rules of law; but it is otherwise concerning conditions subsequent, where equity is allowed to make up for the loss incurred by the failure.

Conditiones quaelibet odiosae; maxime autem contra matrimonium et commercium. Any conditions are odious, but especially those against matrimony and commerce.

Conditio praecedens adimpleri debet prius quam sequatur effectus. A condition precedent ought to be fulfilled before the effect can follow.

Confessio facta in judicio omni probatione major est. A confession made in court is of greater effect than any proof.

Confessus in judicio pro judicato habetur et quodammodo sua sententia damnatur. A person who has confessed his guilt when arraigned is considered to have been tried and is, as it were, condemned by his own sentence.

Confirmare est id quod prius infirmum fuit simul firmare. To confirm is to make firm at once what before was not firm.

Confirmare nemo potest priusquam jus ei acciderit. No one can confirm before the right accrues to him.

Confirmatio est nulla ubi donum praecedens est invalidum. A confirmation is null where the preceding gift is invalid.

Confirmatio est possessionis jure defectivo per eos quorum jus est ratihabitio. The confirmation of a possession defective in law is a ratification by means of those whose right it is.

Confirmatio omnes supplet defectus, licet id quod actum est ab initio non valuit. Confirmation supplies all defects, even if that which has been done was not valid at the beginning.

Confirmat usum qui tollit abusum. One confirms a use who removes an abuse.

Conjunctio mariti et feminae est de jure naturae. The union of husband and wife derives from the law of nature.

Conscientia dicitur a con et scio, quasi scire cum Deo. Conscience is so called from con and scio, to know, as it were, with God.

Conscientia legalis e lege fundatur. Legal conscience is founded upon the law.

Conscientia legi nunquam contravenit. Conscience never contravenes the law.

Conscientia legis ex lege pendet. The conscience of the law depends on the law.

Consecratio est periodus electionis; electio est praeambula consecrationis. Consecration is the termination of election; election is the preamble of consecration.

Consensus est voluntas plurium ad quos res pertinet, simul juncta. Consent is the conjoint will of several people to whom the thing belongs.

Consensus facit legem. Consent makes law. • A contract constitutes law between the parties agreeing to be bound by it.

Consensus, non concubitus, facit matrimonium. Consent, not coition (or sharing a bed), constitutes marriage.

Consensus, non concubitus, facit nuptias vel matrimonium, et consentire non possunt ante annos nubiles. Consent, and not coition (or sharing a bed), constitutes nuptials or marriage, and persons cannot consent before marriageable years.

Consensus tollit errorem. Consent removes an error. • A person cannot object to something he has consented to.

Consensus voluntas multorum ad quos res pertinet simul juncta. Consent is the united will of several interested in one subject matter.

Consentientes et agentes pari poena plectentur. Those consenting and those perpetrating will receive the same punishment.

Consentire est facere. To consent to a thing is to act.

Consentire matrimonio non possunt infra (ante) annos nubiles. Persons cannot consent to marriage before marriageable years.

Consequentiae non est consequentia. The consequence of a consequence does not exist.

Consilia multorum quaeruntur (requiruntur) in magnis. The advice of many is sought in great affairs.

Consilii non fraudulenti nulla obligatio est; caeterum si dolus et calliditas intercessit, de dolo actio competit. No one is liable for honest advice; but if fraud and cunning have occurred, an action for fraud is admissible. Dig. 50.17.47.

Consortio malorum me quoque malum facit. The company of wicked men makes me also wicked.

Constitutiones tempore posteriores potiores sunt his quae ipsas praecesserunt. Later laws prevail over those that preceded them.

Constitutum esse eam domum unicuique nostrum debere existimari, ubi quisque sedes et tabulas haberet, suarumque rerum constitutionem fecisset. It is a settled principle that what ought to be considered the home of each of us is where he has his dwelling, keeps his records, and has established his business.

Constructio ad principia refertur rei. Construction refers (or applies) to the principles of a thing.

Constructio legis non facit injuriam. The construction of the law does no injury.

Consuetudo contra rationem introducta potius usurpatio quam consuetudo appellari debet. A custom introduced against reason ought rather to be called a usurpation than a custom.

Consuetudo debet esse certa. Custom ought to be fixed.

Consuetudo debet esse certa, nam incerta pro nulla (nullius) habetur. Custom ought to be fixed, for if variable it is held as null (or of no account).

Consuetudo debet esse certa, nam incerta pro nullis habentur. A custom should be certain, for uncertain things are held as nothing. • This maxim is sometimes written *Consuetudo debet esse certa, nam incerta pro nulla (nullius) habetur* (meaning "custom should be certain, for if uncertain it is held as nothing").

Consuetudo est altera lex. Custom is another law.

Consuetudo est optimus interpres legum. Custom is the best expounder of the law.

Consuetudo et communis assuetudo vincit legem non scriptam, si sit specialis; et interpretatur legem scriptam, si lex sit generalis. Custom and common usage overcome the unwritten law if it is special; and interpret the written law if the law is general.

Consuetudo ex certa causa rationabili usitata privat communem legem. Custom observed by reason of a certain and reasonable cause supersedes the common law.

Consuetudo, licet sit magnae auctoritatis, nunquam tamen praejudicat manifestae veritati. A custom, even if it is of great authority, is never prejudicial to plain truth.

Consuetudo loci observanda est. The custom of the place is to be observed.

Consuetudo manerii et loci observanda est. The custom of a manor and place is to be observed.

Consuetudo neque injuria oriri neque tolli protest. A custom can neither arise nor be abolished by a wrong.

Consuetudo non habitur (trahitur) in consequentiam. Custom is not held as (or drawn into) a precedent.

Consuetudo praescripta et legitima vincit legem. A prescriptive and lawful custom overrides the law.

Consuetudo regni Angliae est lex Angliae. The custom of the kingdom of England is the law of England.

Consuetudo semel reprobata non potest amplius induci. A custom once disallowed cannot again be introduced.

Consuetudo tollit communem legem. Custom takes away the common law.

Consuetudo vincit communem legem. Custom overrules common law.

Consuetudo volentes ducit, lex nolentes trahit. Custom leads the willing; law drags the unwilling.

Contemporanea consuetudo optimus interpres. Contempory custom is the best interpreter.

Contemporanea expositio est optima et fortissima in lege. A contemporaneous exposition is the best and most powerful in the law. • A statute is best explained by following the construction put on it by judges who lived at the time it was made, or soon after.

Contestatio litis eget terminos contradictarios. An issue requires terms of contradiction. • That is, there can be no issue without an affirmative on one side and a negative on the other).

Contractus ad mentem partium verbis notatam intelligendus. A contract is to be understood according to the intention of the parties as expressed in words.

Contractus est quasi actus contra actum. A contract is, as it were, act against act.

Contractus ex turpi causa vel contra bonos mores nullus est. A contract founded on a wrongful consideration or against good morals is null.

Contractus infantis invalidus, si in damnum sui spectet. The contract of a minor is invalid if it has his or her loss in view.

Contractus legem ex conventione accipiunt. Contracts receive legal validity from the agreement of the parties.

Contra fictionem non admittitur probatio; quid enim efficeret probatio veritatis, ubi fictio adversus veritatem fingit? Nam fictio nihil aliud est, quam legis adversus veritatem in re possibili ex justa causa dispositio. Proof is not admitted against fiction, for what could the evidence of truth effect, where fiction supposes falsehood? For fiction is no other than an arrangement of the law against truth, in a possible matter, arising from a just cause. 3 Bl. Com. 43.

Contra juris civilis regulas pacta conventa rata non habentur. Agreements made contrary to the rules of civil law are not to be construed as valid.

Contra legem facit qui id facit quod lex prohibit; in fraudem vero qui, salvis verbis legis, sententiam ejus circumvenit. A person acts contrary to the law who does what the law prohibits; a person acts in fraud of the law who, without violating the wording, circumvents the intention. Dig. 1.3.29.

Contra negantem principia non est disputandum. There is no disputing against one who denies first principles.

Contra non valentem agere nulla currit praescriptio. No prescription runs against a person unable to act (or bring an action).

Contrariorum contraria est ratio. The reason of contrary things is contrary.

Contra spoliatorem omnia praesumuntur. All things are to be presumed against the plunderer.

Contra veritatem lex nunquam aliquid permittit. The law never allows anything contrary to truth.

Contraxisse unusquisque in eo loco intelligitur, in quo ut solveret se obligavit. Everyone is understood to have contracted in that place where he has bound himself to pay.

Contrectatio rei alienae animo furandi est furtum. Touching or taking another's property with an intention of stealing is theft.

Conventio omnis intelligitur clausula rebus sic stantibus. Every contract is to be understood as being based on the assumption of things remaining as they were (that is, at the time of its conclusion).

Conventio privatorum non potest publico juri derogare. An agreement of private persons cannot derogate from public right. • That is, it cannot prevent the application of general rules of law, or render valid any contravention of law.

Conventio vincit legem. The express agreement of the parties overrides the law.

Convicia si irascaris tua divulgas; spreta exolescunt. If you are moved to anger by insults, you spread them abroad; if despised, they die out.

Copulatio verborum indicat acceptationem in eodem sensu. Coupling words together shows that they ought to be understood in the same sense.

Corporalis injuria non recipit aestimationem de futuro. A personal injury does not receive satisfaction from proceedings yet in the future.

Corpus corporatum ex uno potest consistere. One person may constitute a corporation.

Corpus corporatum neque in lite sisti; neque utlagari, neque bona forisfacere, neque attinctum pati, attornatum facere; neque excommunicari potest. A corporation can neither be brought into court or outlawed, nor can it forfeit goods, suffer attainder, take power of attorney nor is it liable to excommunication.

Corpus corporatum non habet haeredes neque executores neque mori potest. A corportation has neither heirs nor executors, nor can it die.

Corpus humanum non recipit aestimationem. The person of a human being can have no price put on it.

Corruptio optimi pessima. Corruption of the best is worst.

Counsellor nest destre oye que parle enver les presidents. A counselor ought not to be heard who speaks against precedent.

Creditor qui permittit rem venire pignus dimittit. The creditor who allows property to be sold gives up the pledge.

Creditorum appellatione non hi tantum accipiuntur qui pecuniam crediderunt, sed omnes quibus ex qualibet causa debetur. Under the name of creditors are included not only those who have lent money, but also all to whom a debt is owed from any cause.

Crescente malitia crescere debet et poena. With increase of malice, punishment ought also to increase.

Crimen ex post facto non diluitur. A crime cannot be undone (or excused) by a subsequent act.

Crimen falsi dicitur, cum quis illicitus, cui non fuerit ad hoea data auctoritas, de sigillo regis rapto vel invento brevia cartasve consignaverit. It is called "crimen falsi" when anyone to whom power has not been given for such purposes has illicitly signed writs or grants with the king's seal, either stolen or found.

Crimen laesae majestatis omnia alia crimina excedit quoad poenam. The crime of treason exceeds all other crimes in its punishment.

Crimen omnia ex se nata vitiat. Crime taints everything that springs from it.

Crimen trahit personam. The crime brings with it the person. • That is, the commission of a crime gives the courts of the place where it is committed jurisdiction over the person of the offender.

Crimen vel poena paterna nullam maculam filio infligere potest. The crime or punishment of a father inflicts no stain upon his son.

Crimina morte extinguuntur. Crimes are extinguished by death.

Cruciatus legibus invisi. Tortures are odious to the laws.

Cuicunque aliquis quid concedit concedere videtur et id sine quo res ipsa esse non potuit. One who grants something to another grants also that without which the thing granted could not exist. • This maxim is also sometimes written *Cuicunque aliquid conceditur, conceditur etiam et id sine quo res ipsa non esse potuit* (meaning "To whomever anything is granted, that also is granted without which the thing itself could not exist").

Cui jurisdictio data est, ea quoque concessa esse videntur sine quibus jurisdictio explicari non potest. To whom jurisdiction is given, those things also are considered to be granted without which the jurisdiction cannot be exercised. • That is, the grant of jurisdiction implies the grant of all powers necessary to its exercise.

Cui jus est donandi eidem et vendendi et concedendi jus est. A person who has a right to give has also a right to sell and to grant.

Cuilibet in arte sua perito est credendum. Credence should be given to a person skilled in his art (that is, when speaking of matters connected with that art).

Cuilibet licet juri pro se introducto renunciare. Anyone may waive or renounce the benefit of a principle or rule of law that exists only for his protection.

Cui licet quod majus non debet quod minus est non licere. A person who has authority to do the more important act ought not to be debarred from doing what is of less importance.

Cui pater est populus non habet ille patrem. That person to whom the people is father has not a father.

Cui plus licet quam par est plus vult quam licet. One to whom more is allowed than is just wants more than is allowed.

Cuique in sua arte credendum est. Everyone is to be believed in his own area of expertise.

Cujus est commodum, ejus debet esse incommodum. The person who has the advantage should also have the disadvantage.

Cujus est commodum, ejus est onus. The person who has the benefit has also the burden.

Cujus est dare, ejus est disponere. The person who has a right to give has the right of disposition. • That is, the bestower of a gift has a right to regulate its disposal.

Cujus est divisio, alterius est electio. When one of two parties has the division (of an estate), the other has the choice (of the shares). • In partition between coparceners, where the division is made by the eldest, the rule in English law is that she shall choose her share last.

Cujus est dominium, ejus est periculum. The risk lies on the owner.

Cujus est instituere, ejus est abrogare. Whoever can institute can also abrogate.

Cujus est solum, ejus est usque ad coelum. The person who owns the soil owns up to the sky. • One who owns the surface of the ground owns, or has an exclusive right to everything that is on or above it to an indefinite height.

Cujus est solum, ejus est usque ad coelum et ad inferos. Whoever owns the soil owns everything up to the sky and down to the depths.

Cujus juris (i.e., jurisdictionis) est principale, ejusdem juris erit accessorium. An accessory matter is subject to the same jurisdiction as its principal.

Cujus per errorem dati repetitio est, ejus consulto dati donatio est. A thing given by mistake can be recovered; if given purposely, it is a gift. Dig. 50.17.53.

Cujusque rei potissima pars est principium. The principal part of everything is the beginning.

Culpa caret qui scit sed prohibere non potest. A person is free of blame who knows but cannot prevent.

Culpae poena par esto. Let the punishment be equal to the crime.

Culpa est immiscere se rei ad se non pertinenti. It is a fault for anyone to meddle in a matter not pertaining to him.

Culpa lata dolo aequiparatur. Gross negligence is equivalent to fraud.

Culpa tenet (teneat) suos auctores. A fault binds (or should bind) its own authors.

Culpa vel poena ex equitate non intenditur. Blame or punishment does not proceed from equity.

Cum actio fuerit mere criminalis, institui poterit ab initio criminaliter vel civiliter. When an action is purely criminal, it can be instituted from the beginning either criminally or civilly.

Cum adsunt testimonia rerum, quid opus est verbis? When the proofs of facts are present, what need is there of words?

Cum aliquid impeditur, propter unum, eo remoto, tollitur impedimentum. When anything is impeded by one single cause, if that be removed, the impediment is removed.

Cum aliquis renunciaverit societati, solvitur societas. When any partner has renounced the partnership, the partnership is dissolved.

Cum confitente sponte mitius est agendum. One making a voluntary confession is to be dealt with more leniently.

Cum de lucro duorum quaeritur melior est causa possidentis. When there is a question of gain between two people, the cause of the possessor is the better.

Cum duo inter se pugnantia reperiuntur in testamento, ultimum ratum est. When two clauses in a will are found to be contradictory, the last in order prevails.

Cum duo jura concurrunt in una persona, aequum est ac si essent in duobus. When two rights meet in one person, it is the same as if they were in two persons.

Cum in corpore dissentitur, apparet nullam esse acceptionem. When there is a disagreement in the substance, there is clearly no acceptance.

Cum in testamento ambigue aut etiam perperam scriptum, est benigne interpretari, et secundum id quod credible est cogitatum credendum est. When an ambiguous or even an erroneous expression occurs in a will, it should be construed liberally, and in accordance with the testator's probable meaning.

Cum legitimae nuptiae factae sunt, patrem liberi sequuntur. Children born under a legitimate marriage follow the condition of the father.

Cum licet fugere, ne quaere litem. Do not seek a lawsuit, if you can avoid it.

Cum par delictum est duorum, semper oneratur petitor, et melior habetur possessoris causa. Where two parties are equally at fault, the claimant always is at the disadvantage, and the party in possession has the better cause.

Cum quod ago non valet ut ago, valeat quantum valere potest. When that which I do is of no effect as I do it, let it have as much effect as it can (that is, in some other way).

Curatus non habet titulum. A curate has no title (to tithes).

Curia cancellariae officina justitiae. The court of chancery is the workshop of justice.

Curia ecclesiastica locum non habet super iis quae juris sunt communis. An ecclesiastical court has no jurisdiction over matters of common law.

Curia novit jura. The court knows the laws.

Curia parliamenti suis propriis legibus subsistit. The court of parliament is governed by its own laws.

Curiosa et captiosa interpretatio in lege reprobatur. An overnice and captious interpretation in the law is rejected.

Currit tempus contra desides et sui juris contemptores. Time runs against the indolent and those who are not mindful of their rights.

Cursus curiae est lex curiae. The practice of the court is the law of the court.

Custome serra prise stricte. Custom shall be construed strictly.

Custos corporis cujusque infantis haereditas nequeat pervenire. Let each child have a guardian to whom the inheritance cannot devolve.

Custos statum haeredis in custodia existentis meliorem, non deteriorem, facere potest. A guardian can make the estate of an heir living under his guardianship better, not worse.

D

Da mihi factum, dabo tibi ius. Give me the facts, I will give you the law.

Damnum absque injuria esse potest. There can be such a thing as damage without injury.

Damnum sentit dominus. The damage falls on the owner.

Damnum sine injuria esse potest. There can be damage without any act of injustice.

Dans et retinens nihil dat. One who gives and yet retains (possession) does not give effectually (literally, gives nothing).

Da tua dum tua sunt, post mortem tunc tua non sunt. Give the things which are yours while they are yours; after death they are not yours.

Datur digniori. It is given to the more worthy.

Debet esse finis litium. There ought to be a limit to litigation.

Debet quis juri subjacere ubi delinquit. Any offender should be subject to the law of the place where he offends.

Debet sua cuique domus esse perfugium tutissimum. Every person's house should be his safest refuge.

Debile fundamentum fallit opus. A weak foundation frustrates the work (built on it).

Debita sequuntur personam debitoris. Debts follow the person of the debtor. • That is, debts belong to no locality and may be collected wherever the debtor can be found.

Debitor non praesumitur donare. A debtor is not presumed to make a gift.

Debitorum pactionibus creditorum petitio nec tolli nec minui potest. The creditors' suit can be neither quashed nor diminished by the contracts of their debtors.

Debitum et contractus sunt nullius loci. Debt and contract belong to no particular place.

Deceptis, non decipientibus, jura subveniunt. The laws help persons who have been deceived, not those deceiving.

Decet (tamen) principem servare leges quibus ipse servatus est. It is proper (nonetheless) for the prince to preserve the laws by which he himself is preserved.

Decimae de decimatis solvi non debent. Tithes ought not to be paid from that which is given for tithes.

Decimae de jure divino et canonica institutione pertinent ad personam. Tithes belong to the parson by divine right and canonical institution.

Decimae non debent solvi ubi non est annua renovatio, et ex annuatis renovantibus simul semel. Tithes ought not to be paid where there is not an annual renovation, and from annual renovations once only.

Decipi quam fallere est tutius. It is safer to be deceived than to deceive.

Decreta conciliorum non ligant reges nostros. The decrees of councils do not bind our kings.

De facto jus oritur. From fact springs law; law arises from fact.

Deficiente uno sanguine, non potest esse haeres. For lack of one blood, he cannot be heir. • Coke explains, "The blood of the father and of the mother are but one inheritable blood, and both are necessary to procreation of an heir." 3 Coke 41.

De fide et officio judicis non recipitur quaestio, sed de scientia sive sit error juris sive facti. The good faith and honesty of purpose of a judge cannot be questioned, but his knowledge may be impugned if there is an error either of law or of fact.

De jure decimarum, originem ducens de jure patronatus, tunc cognitio spectat at legem civilem, i.e., communem. With regard to the right of tithes, deducing its origin from the right of the patron, then the cognizance of them belongs to the civil law, i.e., common law.

De jure judices, de facto juratores, respondent. The judges answer regarding the law, the jury on the facts.

Delegata potestas non potest delegari. A delegated authority cannot be delegated.

Delegatus non potest delegare. A delegate (or deputy) cannot appoint another.

Deliberandum est diu quod statuendum est semel. What is to be resolved once and for all should be long deliberated on.

Delicatus debitor est odiosus in lege. A luxurious debtor is hateful in the law.

Delinquens per iram provocatus puniri debet mitius. A wrongdoer provoked by anger ought to be punished less severely. 3 Co. Inst. 55.

De majori et minori non variant jura. Concerning greater and lesser, rights do not vary (or justice does vary).

De minimis non curat lex. The law does not notice or concern itself with trifling matters.

De minimis non curat praetor. The praetor does not concern himself about trifles.

De molendino de novo erecto non jacet prohibitio. A prohibition does not lie against a newly erected mill.

De morte hominis nulla est cunctatio longa. When the death of a human being is concerned, no delay is long.

Denominatio est a digniore. Denomination is from the more worthy.

Denominatio fieri debet a dignioribus. Denomination should be made from the more worthy.

De nomine proprio non est curandum cum in substantia non erretur; quia nomina mutabilia sunt, res autem immobiles. As to the proper name, it is not to be regarded when there is no error in substance; because names are changeable, but things are immutable.

De non apparentibus et non existentibus eadem est ratio. The rule is the same respecting things that do not appear and things that do not exist.

De nullo quod est sua natura indivisibile et divisionem non patitur nullam partem habebit vidua, sed satisfaciat ei ad valentiam. A widow shall have no part from that which in its own nature is indivisible and is not susceptible of division; but let (the heir) satisfy her with an equivalent.

De nullo tenemento, quod tenetur ad terminum, fit homagii; fit tamen inde fidelitatis sacramentum. For no tenement that is held for a term is there the oath of homage, but there is the oath of fealty.

Derivativa potestas non potest esse major primitiva. Power that is derived cannot be greater than that from which it is derived.

Derogatur legi cum pars detrahitur; abrogatur legi, cum prorsus tollitur. There is derogation from a law when part of it is taken away; there is abrogation of a law when it is abolished entirely.

Designatio justiciariorum est a rege; jurisdictio vero ordinaria a lege. The appointment of justices is by the king, but their ordinary jurisdiction is by the law.

Designatio unius est exclusio alterius, et expressum facit cessare tacitum. The designation of one is the exclusion of the other; and what is expressed prevails over what is implied.

Designatio unius personae est exclusio alterius. The specification of one person is (or implies) the exclusion of another.

De similibus ad similia eadem ratione procedendum est. From like things to like things we are to proceed by the same rule. • That is, we are allowed to argue from the analogy of cases.

De similibus idem est judicium. Concerning like things the judgment is the same.

Destruere, id quod prius structum, et factum fuit, penitus evertere et diruere. To destroy that which was previously built and made is utterly to overturn and wreck it; to destroy is to overturn and demolish what was built and done before. • This is a maxim cited against any type of revolutionary action.

Deus solus haeredem facere potest, non homo. God alone, and not man, can make an heir.

Dies dominicus non est juridicus. Sunday is not a judicial day.

Dies inceptus pro completo habetur. A day begun is held as complete.

Dies incertus pro conditione habetur. An uncertain day is considered as a condition.

Dies interpellat pro homine. The arrival of the day of payment is a sufficient demand from the person owing. • That is, the due date is as compelling as the creditor at the door.

Difficile est ut unus homo vicem duorum sustineat. It is difficult for one man to sustain the position of two.

Difficilem oportet aurem habere ad crimina. One should turn a deaf (or unsympathetic) ear to criminal charges.

Dignitas supponit officium et curam, et non est partibilis. Dignity supposes office and charge, and is not divisible.

Dilationes in lege sunt odiosae. Delays in law are hateful.

Discontinuare nihil aliud quam intermittere, desenescere, interrumpere. Discontinuance is nothing else than to intermit, to abate, to interrupt.

Discretio est discernere per legem quid sit justum. Discretion is to discern through law what is just.

Discretio est scire per legem quid sit justum. Discretion consists in knowing what is just in law.

Discretio judicis est per leges discernere. The discretion of a judge is to make distinctions according to the laws.

Disparata non debent jungi. Dissimilar things ought not to be joined.

Dispensatio est mali prohibiti provida relaxatio, utilitate seu necessitate pensata; et est de jure domino regi concessa, propter impossibilitatem praevidendi de omnibus particularibus. A dispensation is the provident relaxation of a malum prohibitum weighed from utility or necessity; and it is conceded by law to the king on account of the impossibility of foreknowledge concerning all particulars.

Dispensatio est vulnus, quod vulnerat jus commune. A dispensation is a wound, because it wounds a common right.

Disseisinam satis facit qui uti non permittit possessorem, vel minus commode, licet omnino non expellat. A person commits disseisin if he does not permit the possessor to enjoy, or makes the possessor's enjoyment less useful, even if the disseisor does not expel the possessor altogether. Co. Litt. 331.

Dissimilium dissimilis est ratio. Of dissimilars the rule is dissimilar.

Dissimulatione tollitur injuria. Injury is wiped out by reconciliation.

Distinguenda sunt tempora; aliud est facere, aliud perficere. Times must be distinguished; it is one thing to do a thing, another to complete it.

Distinguenda sunt tempora; distingue tempora, et concordabis leges. Times are to be distinguished; distinguish times, and you will harmonize laws.

Districtio non potest esse, nisi pro certis servitiis. Goods cannot be distrained except for certain services (or servitudes).

Divide et impera, cum radix et vertex imperii in obendientium consensu rata sunt. Divide and govern, since the root and apex of empire are established in the consent of the obedient.Divinatio, non interpretatio, est quae omnino recedit a litera. It is a guess, not interpretation, that altogether departs from the letter.

Divisibilis est semper divisibilis. A thing divisible is always divisible.

Divortium dicitur a divertendo, quia vir divertitur ab uxore. Divorce is so called from divertendo, because a man is diverted from his wife.

Dolo facit qui petit quod redditurus est. A person acts with deceit who seeks what he will have to return.

Dolo malo pactum se non servabit. A pact made with evil intent will not be upheld. • This maxim is sometimes written *Dolo malo pactum se non servaturum* (meaning "an agreement induced by fraud will not stand").

Dolosus versatur in generalibus. A deceiver deals in generalities.

Dolum ex indiciis perspicuis probari convenit. Fraud should be proved by clear proofs.

Dolus auctoris non nocet successori. The fraud of a predecessor does not prejudice the successor.

Dolus circuitu non purgatur. Fraud is not purged by circuity.

Dolus est machinatio, cum aliud dissimulat aliud agit. Deceit is an artifice, since it pretends one thing and does another.

Dolus et fraus nemini patrocinentur (patrocinari debent). Deceit and fraud should excuse or benefit no one (they themselves require some excuse).

Dolus et fraus una in parte sanari debent. Deceit and fraud should always be remedied.

Dolus latet in generalibus. Fraud lurks in generalities. • This maxim is also sometimes written *Dolus versatur in generalibus* (meaning "fraud deals in generalities").

Dolus praesumitur contra versantem in illicito. Fraud is presumed against one engaged in an illegal act or transaction.

Dominium non potest esse in pendenti. The right of property cannot be in abeyance.

Dominus aliquando non potest alienare. An owner sometimes has no power to alienate or dispose of a property (as when it is entailed).

Dominus capitalis loco haeredis habetur, quoties per defectum vel delictum extinguitur sanguis sui tenentis. The supreme lord takes the place of the heir, as often as the blood of the tenant is extinct through deficiency or crime.

Dominus non maritabit pupillum nisi semel. A lord cannot give a ward in marriage but once.

Dominus omnium in regno terrarum rex habendus; et ab eo omnes tenent ita tamen, ut suum cuique sit. The king is considered master of all lands in the kingdom, and all (subjects) hold from him, so that each has his own.

Dominus rex nullum habere potest parem, multo minus superiorem. The king cannot have an equal, much less a superior.

Domum suam unicuique reficere licet, dum non officiat invito alteri in quo jus non habet. It is lawful for everyone to repair his own house, provided he does not cause obstruction to another without his consent, over whom he has no right.

Domus sua cuique est tutissimum refugium. Everyone's house is his safest refuge.

Domus tutissimum cuique refugium atque receptaculum sit. Everyone's house should be his safest refuge and shelter.

Dona clandestina sunt semper suspiciosa. Clandestine gifts are always suspicious.

Donari videtur quod nullo jure cogente, conceditur. That is considered to be given which is granted without the obligation of any law.

Donatio non praesumitur. A gift is not presumed.

Donationum alia perfecta, alia incepta et non perfecta; ut si donatio lecta fuit et concessa, ac traditio nondum fuerit subsecuta. Some gifts are perfect, others incipient and not perfect; for example, if a gift were read and agreed to, but delivery had not then followed.

Donatio perficitur possessione accipientis. A gift is rendered complete by the possession of the receiver.

Donatio principis intelligitur sine praejudicio tertii. A gift of the prince is understood without prejudice to a third party.

Donatio quaelibet ex vi legis sortitur effectum. A donation of any sort obtains its effect by force of the law.

Donator nunquam desinit possidere antequam donatarius incipiat possidere. A donor never ceases to have possession until the donee obtains possession.

Dormiunt aliquando leges, nunquam moriuntur. Laws sometimes sleep but never die.

Dos de dote peti non debet. Dower ought not to be sought from dower.

Dos rationabilis vel legitima est cujuslibet mulieris de quocunque tenemento tertia pars omnium terrarum et tenementorum, quae vir suus tenuit in dominio suo ut de feodo, etc. Reasonable or legitimate dower belongs to every woman of a third part of all the lands and tenements of which her husband was seised in his demesne, as of fee, etc.

Doti lex favet; praemium pudoris est, ideo parcatur. The law favors dower; it is the reward of chastity; therefore let it be preserved.

Do ut des. I give that you may give.

Do ut facias. I give that you may do.

Droit ne done pluis que soit demaunde. The law gives no more than is demanded.

Droit ne poet pas morier. Right cannot die.

Duas uxores eodem tempore habere non licet. It is not lawful to have two wives at one time.

Duo non possunt in solido unam rem possidere. Two cannot possess one thing each in entirety.

Duorum in solidum dominium vel possessio esse non potest. Ownership or possession in entirety cannot belong to two persons.

Duo sunt instrumenta ad omnes res aut confirmandas aut impugnandas, ratio et auctoritas. There are two instruments for confirming or impugning everything: reason and authority.

Duplex placitum non admittitur. A double plea is not admissible. • That is, a defendant cannot offer two separate pleas on the same issue.

Duplicationem possibilitatis lex non patitur. The law does not allow a duplication of possibility.

Dura lex sed lex. Hard law, but law.

Durum est per divinationem a verbis recedere. It is harsh (or oppressive) to depart from the words by conjecture.

E

Eadem causa diversis rationibus coram judicibus ecclesiasticis et secularibus ventilatur. The same cause is argued on different principles before ecclesiastical and secular judges.

Eadem est ratio, eadem est lex. (If) the reason is the same, the law is the same.

Eadem mens praesumitur regis quae est juris et quae esse debet, praesertim in dubiis. The mind of the sovereign is presumed to be the same as that of the law, and the same as what it ought to be, especially in ambiguous matters.

Ea est accipienda interpretatio quae vitio caret. That interpretation is to be received that is free from fault.

Eam domum unicuique nostrum debere existimari, ubi quisque sedes et tabulas haberet suarumque rerum constitutionem fecisset. (It is decided that) for each of us it should be considered his home where each has his residence and records and has set up the management of his affairs. Dig. 50.16.203.

Ea quae commendandi causa in venditionibus dicuntur, si palam appareant venditorem non obligant. Those things that, by way of commendation, are stated at sales, if they are openly apparent, do not bind the seller.

Ea quae dari impossibilia sunt, vel quae in rerum natura non sunt, pro non adjectis habentur. Those things that cannot be given, or that are not in the nature of things, are considered as not added (as no part of the agreement).

Ea quae in curia nostra rite acta sunt debitae executioni demandari debent. Those things that are properly transacted in our court ought to be committed to a due execution.

Ea quae raro accidunt non temere in agendis negotiis computantur. Those things that rarely happen are not to be taken into account in the transaction of business, without sufficient reason.

Ea sola deportationis sententia aufert quae ad fiscum perveniret. A sentence of deportation only deprives the deportee of those things which come into the treasury. Dig. 50.17.97.

Ecclesia ecclesiae decima solvere non debet. A church should not pay tithes to a church.

Ecclesia est domus mansionalis omnipotentis Dei. The church is the mansion house of the omnipotent God.

Ecclesia est infra aetatem et in custodia domini regis, qui tenetur jura et haereditates ejusdem manu tenere et defendere. The church is underage and in the custody of the king, who is bound to uphold and defend its rights and inheritances.

Ecclesia fungitur vice minoris; meliorem conditionem suam facere potest, deteriorem nequaquam. The church enjoys the privilege of a minor; it can make its own condition better but not worse.

Ecclesiae magis favendum est quam personae. The church is to be more favored than the parson (or an individual).

Ecclesia meliorari non deteriorari potest. A church can (lawfully) be improved but not made worse.

Ecclesia non moritur. The church does not die.

Edicta magistratum, constitutio principis. The ordinance of the magistracy (or civil government) is the constitution (or decree) of the Emperor.

Effectus sequitur causam. The effect follows the cause.

Ei incumbit probatio qui dicit, non qui negat. The burden of the proof rests on the person who affirms, not the one who denies.

Ei nihil turpe, cui nihil satis. Nothing is immoral to the person to whom nothing is enough.

Eisdem modis dissolvitur obligatio quae nascitur ex contractu, vel quasi, quibus contrahitur. An obligation that arises from a contract or quasi contract is dissolved in the same ways in which it is contracted.

Ejus est interpretari cujus est condere. It is that person's to interpret whose it is to enact.

Ejus est nolle, qui potest velle. A person who can will (exercise volition) has a right to refuse to will (withhold consent).

Ejus est non nolle qui potest velle. A person may consent tacitly who can consent expressly.

Ejus est periculum cujus est dominium aut commodum. He who has the dominion or advantage has the risk.

Ejus nulla culpa est cui parere necesse sit. No guilt attaches to a person who is compelled to obey.

Electa una via, non datur recursus ad alteram. When one way has been chosen, no recourse is given to another.

Electio est interna libera et spontanea separatio unius rei ab alia, sine compulsione, consistens in animo et voluntate. Choice is an internal, free, and spontaneous separation of one thing from another, without compulsion, consisting in intention and will.

Electiones fiant rite et libere sine interruptione aliqua. Let choices be made in due form and freely, without any interruption.

Electio semel facta, et placitum testatum, non patitur regressum. A choice once made, and a plea witnessed (or intent shown), allows no going back.

Electio semel facta non patitur regressum. An election once made cannot be recalled.

Emptio et venditio contrahitur simul atque de pretio convenerit, quamvis nondum pretium numeratum sit ac ne arra quidem data fuerit. The buying and selling is complete as soon as the price is agreed upon, though the price has not yet been paid nor any earnest given. Just. Inst. 3.23.

Emptor emit quam minimo potest; venditor vendit quam maximo potest. The buyer buys for as little as possible; the vendor sells for as much as possible.

En eschange il covient que les estates soient egales. In an exchange it is desirable that the estates be equal.

Enitia pars semper praeferenda est propter privilegium aetatis. The part of the elder sister is always to be preferred on account of the privilege of age.

Enumeratio infirmat regulam in casibus non enumeratis. Enumeration disaffirms the rule in cases not enumerated.

Enumeratio unius est exclusio alterius. Specification of one thing is an exclusion of the other.

Eodem ligamine quo ligatum est dissolvitur. An obligation is dissolved by the same bond by which it is contracted.

Eodem modo quo oritur, eodem modo dissolvitur. It is discharged in the same way as it is created.

Eodem modo quo quid constituitur, dissolvitur. In the same way as anything is constituted, it is dissolved (or destroyed). 6 Coke 53.

Eodem modo quo quid constituitur, eodem modo destruitur. In the same way in which something is constituted, it may be destroyed.

Ephemeris annua pars legis Anglicanae. An annual diary is part of the English law (i.e., the law that takes notice of the annual calendar).

Episcopus alterius mandato quam regis non tenetur obtemperare. A bishop need not obey any mandate save the king's.

Equitas sequitur legem. Equity follows the law.

Errores ad sua principia referre est refellere. To refer errors to their origin is to refute them.

Errores scribentis nocere non debent. The mistakes of the scribe (or copyist) ought to do no harm.

Error fucatus nuda veritate in multis est probabilior; et saepenumero rationibus vincit veritatem error. Error artfully colored is in many instances more probable than naked truth; and frequently error conquers truth by argumentation.

Error juris nocet. An error of law injures.

Error nominis nunquam nocet, si de identitate rei constat. Mistake in the name never injures if the identity of the thing is certain.

Error placitandi aequitatem non tollit. An error in the plea does not take away equity.

Error qui non resistitur approbatur. An error that is not resisted is approved.

Error scribentis nocere non debet. The error of a scribe (or copyist) ought not to injure.

Erubescit lex filios castigare parentes. The law blushes when children correct their parents.

Est aliquid quod non oportet etiam si licet; quicquid vero non licet certe non oportet. There is that which is not proper, even though permitted; but whatever is not permitted is certainly not proper.

Est autem jus publicum et privatum quod ex naturalibus praeceptis aut gentium aut civilibus est collectum; et quod in jure scripto jus appellatur, id in lege Angliae rectum esse dicitur. Public and private law is that which is collected either from natural precepts of the (law of) nations or from civil precepts; and that which in the civil law is called jus is said in the law of England to be right. Co. Litt. 558.

Est autem vis legem simulans. Violence may also put on the mask of law.

Est boni judicis ampliare jurisdictionem. It is the role of a good judge to extend the jurisdiction.

Est boni judicis ampliare justitiam, non jurisdictionem. It is the role of a good judge to extend justice, not to enlarge jurisdiction.

Est ipsorum legislatorum tanquam viva vox. The voice of the legislators themselves is like a living voice. • That is, the provisions of a statute are to be understood and interpreted as practical rules for real circumstances. Coke adds, *Rebus et non verbis legem imponimus.* 10 Coke 101.

Estoveria sunt ardendi, arandi, construendi et claudendi. Estovers (tenants' rights to material at hand) are for burning, plowing, building, and fencing.

Est pactio duorum pluriumque in idem placitum consensus. A paction (*pactio*, or bargain) is the consent of two or more in the same agreement (*placitum*, as what is pleasing to the parties).

Est quiddam perfectius in rebus licitis. There is something more perfect in things that are permitted.

Est un maxime en nostre ley "parols font ple." It is a maxim in our law: "Words make the plea."

Et sicut ad quaestionem juris non respondent juratores, sed judices; sic ad quaestionem facti non respondent judices, sed juratores. Just as a question of law is not answered by the jurors but the judges, so too a question of fact is not answered by judges but jurors.

Eum qui nocentem infamat, non est aequum et bonum ob eam rem condemnari; delicta enim nocentium nota esse oportet et expedit. It is not just and proper that one who speaks ill of a bad person should be condemned on that account; for it is fitting and expedient that the wrongdoings of bad people should be known.

Eventus est qui ex causa sequitur; et dicitur eventus quia ex causis evenit. An event is what follows from a cause; and is called an event, because it results from causes.

Eventus varios res nova semper habet. A novel matter always produces various results.

Ex abusu non arguitur ad usum. No argument can be drawn from the abuse (of a thing) against its use.

Ex antecedentibus et consequentibus fit optima interpretatio. The best interpretation is made from what precedes and what follows.

Excambium naturaliter vult in se warrantium. An exchange in itself naturally intends (or creates) a warranty.

Excambium non potest esse rerum diversae qualitatis; neque excambium inter tres partes datur. An exchange cannot be of things of a different quality; nor is it granted among three parties.

Exceptio ejus rei cujus petitur dissolutio nulla est. There is no exception based on the very matter for which a solution is being sought.

Exceptio est strictissimae applicationis. An exception is of the strictest application.

Exceptio falsi est omnium ultima. The exception for falsehood is last of all.

Exceptio firmat regulam in casibus non exceptis. An exception affirms the rule in cases not excepted.

Exceptio firmat regulam in contrarium. An exception affirms a rule to the contrary.

Exceptio nulla est versus actionem quae exceptionem perimit. There is no exception against an action that extinguishes the exception.

Exceptio probat regulam de rebus non exceptis. An exception proves a rule concerning things not excepted.

Exceptio quae firmat legem exponit legem. An exception that confirms the law expounds the law.

Exceptio quoque regulam declarat. The exception also declares the rule.

Exceptio semper ultima ponenda est. An exception is always to be put last.

Excessivum in jure reprobatur. Excessus in re qualibet jure reprobatur communi. The excessive in law is rejected. Excess in anything is rejected in common law.

Excessus in jure reprobatur. Excess in law is condemned.

Excessus in re qualibet jure reprobatur communi. Excess in anything at all is condemned by common law.

Excommunicato interdicitur omnis actus legitimus, ita quod agere non potest, nec aliquem convenire; licet ipse ab aliis possit conveniri. Every legal act is forbidden an excommunicated person, so that he cannot act, nor sue any person; but he may be sued by others.

Excusat aut extenuat delictum in capitalibus, quod non operatur idem in civilibus. That excuses or extenuates a wrong in capital causes which does not have the same effect in civil suits.

Excusatio non petita accusatio manifesta fit. An excuse that is not required is an obvious accusation (i.e., he who makes excuse before he is accused manifests his own guilt).

Excusatur quis quod clameum non apposuerit, ut si toto tempore litigii fuit ultra mare quacunque occasione. One who has not brought his claim is excused if, during the whole period in which it ought to have been brought, he was beyond the sea for any reason.

Ex delicto non ex supplicio emergit infamia. Infamy arises from the crime, not from the punishment.

Ex diuturnitate temporis omnia praesumuntur solenniter esse acta. From length of time, all things are presumed to have been done in due form.

Ex dolo malo non oritur actio. An action does not arise from a fraud.

Executio est executio juris secundum judicium. Execution is the execution of the law according to the judgment.

Executio est finis et fructus legis. Execution of the law is its end and fruition.

Executio juris non habet injuriam. The execution of the law causes no injury.

Executio legis non habet injuriam. Execution of the law cannot work an injury.

Exempla illustrant, non restringunt, legem. Examples illustrate but do not narrow the scope of a rule of law.

Exempla non restringunt regulam, sed loquuntur de casibus crebrioribus. Examples do not restrict the rule; they speak of cases that more frequently occur.

Exemplo perniciosum est ut ei scripturae credatur qua unus quisquam sibi adnotatione propria debitorem constituit. It a ruinous, as a precedent, if credit is given to that writing whereby anyone, by his own note (or memorandum) makes a debtor (of another). Bl. 3.23.369, from Just. Codex 4.19.7.

Ex facto jus oritur. The law arises out of the fact.

Ex frequenti delicto augetur poena. Punishment increases with repeated offense. 2 Co. Inst. 479.

Exilium est patriae privatio, natalis soli mutatio, legum nativarum amissio. Exile is a privation of country, a change of native soil, a loss of native laws.

Ex iniuria ius non oritur. A right does not arise from wrongdoing.

Exitus acta probat; finis, non pugna, coronat. The outcome proves (or justifies) the deeds; the conclusion, not the contest, crowns the victor.

Ex judiciorum publicorum admissis, non alias transeunt adversus haeredes poenae bonorum ademptionis quam si lis contestata et condemnatio fuerit secuta; excepto majestatis judicio. On account of admissions made at public trials, the punishment of a confiscation of goods or property does not otherwise pass against the heirs than if a contested suit and condemnation followed; excepting in the case of high treason.

Ex maleficio non oritur contractus. A contract does not arise out of an illegal act.

Ex malis moribus bonae leges natae sunt. Good laws are born from evil morals.

Ex multitudine signorum colligitur identitas vera. From a great number of signs true identity is ascertained.

Ex nihilo nihil fit. From nothing nothing comes.

Ex non scripto jus venit quod usus comprobavit. Unwritten law is that which custom has sanctioned.

Ex nuda submissione non oritur actio. From a "bare" (or naked) submission (e.g., to nonbinding arbitration) no action can arise.

Ex nudo pacto non oritur actio. No action arises on a contract without a consideration.

Ex pacto illicito non oritur actio. From an illicit contract no action arises.

Ex paucis plurima concipit ingenium. From a few words or hints the understanding conceives many things.

Expedit rei publicae ne sua re quis male utatur. It is to the advantage of the state that a person should not make bad use of his own property.

Expedit rei publicae ut sit finis litium. It is to the advantage of the state that there should be a limit to litigation.

Experientia per varios actus legem facit. Experience through various acts makes law.

Expositio quae ex visceribus causae nascitur, est aptissima et fortissima in lege. An exposition that springs from the vitals of a cause is the fittest and most powerful in law.

Ex praecedentibus et consequentibus est optima interpretatio. The best interpretation takes account of what precedes and follows.

Expressa nocent, non expressa non nocent. What is expressed does injury, that which is not expressed does not injure. Dig. 50.17.195.

Expressa non prosunt quae non expressa proderunt. There is no benefit in expressing what will benefit when unexpressed.

Expressio eorum quae tacite insunt nihil operatur. The expression of those things that are tacitly implied is of no consequence.

Expressio unius est exclusio alterius. The expression of one thing is the exclusion of another. • Also termed *Inclusio unius est exclusio alterius* or *enumeratio unius est exclusio alterius.*

Expressum facit cessare tacitum. Something expressed nullifies what is unexpressed.

Expressum servitium regat vel declaret tacitum. Let service expressed rule or declare what is silent.

Ex procedentibus et consequentibus optima fit interpretatio. The best interpretation is made from things proceeding and following (i.e., the context).

Ex qua persona quis lucrum capit, ejus factum praestare debet. From whatever calling (or role, *persona*) anyone derives profit, he ought to discharge the duty of that calling.

Exterus non habet terras. An alien holds no lands.

Extincto subjecto, tollitur adjunctum. When the substance is gone, the adjunct disappears.

Extinguitur obligatio quae rite constiterit si in eum casum inciderit a quo incipere non potuit. An obligation that has been created in due form is extinguished if it falls into that state from which it could not have arisen.

Extortio est crimen quando quis colore officii extorquet quod non est debitum, vel supra debitum, vel ante tempus quod est debitum. Extortion is a crime when, by color of office, any person extorts what is not due, or more than due, or before the time when it is due.

Ex tota materia emergat resolutio. The construction or explanation should arise out of the whole subject matter.

Extra legem positus est civiliter mortuus. An outlaw is dead as a citizen.

Extraneus est subditus qui extra terram, i.e. potestam regis, natus est. A foreigner is a subject who is born out of the territory — that is, the jurisdiction — of the king.

Extra territorium jus dicenti impune non paretur. One who gives a judgment outside his jurisdiction is disobeyed with impunity. • There is no punishment for disobeying. Dig. 2.1.20.

Extra territorium jus dicenti non paretur impune. One who gives a judgment outside his jurisdiction is not obeyed with impunity. • Anyone who executes such a judgment may be punished. 10 Coke 77.

Extrema potius pati quam turpia facere. Extremities are rather to be suffered than to do disgraceful (infamous or scandalous) things.

Extremis probatis praesumuntur media. Extremes having been proved, intermediate things are presumed.

Ex turpi causa non oritur actio. No action arises out of a wrongful consideration.

Ex turpi contractu non oritur actio. No action arises from a wrongful contract.

F

Facilis est lapsus juventutis. Easy is the failing of youth (i.e., young people are likely to make mistakes).

Facinus quos inquinat aequat. Guilt makes equal those whom it stains.

Facio ut des. I do that you may give.

Facio ut facias. I do that you may do.

Facta sunt potentiora verbis. Deeds (or facts) are more powerful than words.

Facta tenent multa quae fieri prohibentur. Deeds contain many things that are prohibited to be done.

Factum a judice quod ad ejus officium non spectat, non ratum est. A judge's act that does not pertain to his office is of no force.

Factum cuique suum, non adversario, nocere debet. Anyone's act should injure himself, not his adversary.

Factum infectum fieri nequit. What is done cannot be undone.

Factum negantis nulla probatio. No proof is incumbent on a person who denies a fact.

Factum non dicitur quod non perseverat. That is not said to be done which does not last.

Factum unius alteri nocere non debet. The deed of one should not hurt the other.

Facturi quod ad justitiam pertinet secundum legem, et consuetudinem Angliae. (One is bound) to do justice according to the law and custom of England. • This was once a part of judicial oaths.

Facultas probationum non est angustanda. The capability of offering proofs is not to be narrowed.

Falsa causa non nocet. A false motive does no injury. • Generally, an erroneous motive does not invalidate.

Falsa demonstratione legatum non perimi. A legacy is not destroyed by an incorrect description. • This maxim is sometimes written *Falsa demonstratione legatum non perimitur* (same sense).

Falsa demonstratio non nocet, cum de corpore (persona) constat. False description does not injure or vitiate, provided the thing or person intended has once been sufficiently described. • Mere false description does not make an instrument inoperative.

Falsa grammatica non vitiat chartam. False grammar does not vitiate a charter.

Falsa grammatica non vitiat concessionem. False or bad grammar does not vitiate a grant. • Neither false Latin nor false English will make a deed void when the intent of the parties plainly appears.

Falsa orthographia sive falsa grammatica non vitiat concessionem. Error in spelling or grammar does not vitiate a grant.

Falsus in uno, falsus in omnibus. False in one thing, false in everything.

Fama est constans virorum bonorum de re aliqua opinio. Fame is the constant opinion of good men concerning a thing.

Fama, fides, et oculus non patiuntur ludum. Reputation, plighted faith, and eyesight do not endure deceit.

Fama, quae suspicionem inducit, oriri debet apud bonos et graves, non quidem malevolos et maledicos, sed providas et fide dignas personas, non semel sed saepius, quia clamor minuit et defamatio manifestat. Report, which induces suspicion, ought to arise from good and grave men; not, indeed, from malevolent and malicious men, but from cautious and credible persons; not only once, but frequently, for clamor diminishes, and defamation manifests.

Fatetur facinus qui judicium fugit. A person who flees judgment confesses guilt.

Fatuus, apud jurisconsultos nostros, accipitur pro non compos mentis; et fatuus dicitur, qui omnino desipit. "Fatuous," among our jurisconsults, is applied to a man not of sound mind; one is also called "fatuous" who is altogether foolish.

Fatuus praesumitur qui in proprio nomine errat. A person is presumed to be incompetent who makes a mistake in his own name (that is, does not know his own name).

Favorabilia in lege sunt fiscus, dos, vita, libertas. The treasury, dower, life, and liberty are things favored in law.

Favorabiliores rei potius quam actores habentur. Defendants are rather to be favored than plaintiffs.

Favorabiliores sunt executiones aliis processibus quibuscunque. Executions are preferred to all other processes whatever.

Favores ampliandi sunt; odia restringenda. Favorable inclinations are to be enlarged; animosities restrained.

Felix qui potuit rerum cognoscere causas. Happy is he who could apprehend the causes of things.

Felonia, ex vi termini, significat quodlibet capitale crimen felleo animo perpetratum. Felony, by force of the term, signifies any capital crime perpetrated with a malicious intent.

Felonia implicatur in quolibet proditione. Felony is implied in every treason.

Feodum est quod quis tenet ex quacunque causa, sive sit tenementum sive redditus. A fee is that which anyone holds from whatever cause, whether tenement or rent.

Feodum simplex quia feodum idem est quod haereditas, et simplex idem est quod legituum vel purum; et sic feodum simplex idem est quod haereditas legitima vel haereditas pura. "Fee simple" is so called because fee is the same as inheritance and simple is the same as lawful or pure; and thus fee simple is the same as a lawful inheritance or a pure inheritance.

Fera vagans est nullius in rebus. A wandering beast belongs to no one.

Fere secundum promissorem interpretamur. We generally interpret in favor of the promisor.

Festinatio justitiae est noverca infortunii. The hurrying of justice is the stepmother of misfortune.

Feuda ad instar patrimoniorum sunt redacta. Lands held in feudal tenure are reduced to the character of a patrimony or succession.

Fiat jus, ruat justitia. Let law prevail, though justice fail.

Fiat justitia pereat mundus. Let justice be done though the world perish.

Fiat justitia, ruat caelum. Let justice be done though the heavens fall. • The word *caelum* sometimes appears *coelum*, but the form *caelum* is considered better Latin.

Fiat prout fieri consuevit, nil temere novandum. Let it be done as it is accustomed to be done; let no innovation be made rashly.

Fictio cedit veritati; fictio juris non est ubi veritas. Fiction yields to truth; where the truth appears, there is no fiction of law.

Fictio est contra veritatem, sed pro veritate habetur. Fiction is contrary to the truth, but it is regarded as truth.

Fictio juris non est ubi veritas. Where truth is, fiction of law does not exist.

Fictio legis inique operatur alicui damnum vel injuriam. Fiction of law works unjustly if it works loss or injury to anyone.

Fictio legis neminem laedit. A fiction of law injures no one.

Fides est obligatio conscientiae alicujus ad intentionem alterius. Faith is an obligation of conscience of one to the will of another.

Fides servanda est. Faith must be observed. • An agent must not violate the confidence reposed in him or her.

Fides servanda est; simplicitas juris gentium praevaleat. Faith is to be preserved; the simplicity of the law of nations should prevail.

Fieri non debet, sed factum valet. It ought not to be done, but if done it is valid.

Filiatio non potest probari. Filiation cannot be proved. • That is, the husband is presumed to be the father of a child born during coverture.

Filius est nomen naturae, sed haeres nomen juris. "Son" is a name of nature, but "heir" a name of law.

Filius in utero matris est pars viscerum matris. A son in the mother's womb is part of the mother's vitals.

Finis est amicabilis compositio et finalis concordia ex concensu et concordia domini regis vel justiciarum. A fine is an amicable settlement and decisive agreement by consent and agreement of our lord, the king, or his justices.

Finis finem litibus imponit. A fine puts an end to litigation.

Finis rei attendendus est. The end of a thing is to be attended to.

Finis unius diei est principium alterius. The end of one day is the beginning of another.

Firmior et potentior est operatio legis quam dispositio hominis. The operation of law is firmer and more powerful than the will of man.

Fit fabricando faber. Building makes the builder. • The law presumes that a workman becomes an expert by a long continued exercise of his particular vocation.

Flumina et portus publica sunt, ideoque jus piscandi omnibus commune est. Rivers and ports are public; and therefore the right of fishing is common to all.

Foeminae ab omnibus officiis civilibus vel publicis remotae sunt. Women are excluded from all civil and public charges or offices.

Foeminae non sunt capaces de publicis officiis. Women are not qualified for public offices.

Forma dat esse. Form gives being.

Forma legalis forma essentialis. Legal form is essential form.

Forma non observata, infertur adnullatio actus. When form is not observed, a nullity of the act is inferred.

Forstellarius est pauperum depressor, et totius communitatis et patriae publicus inimicus. A forestaller is an oppressor of the poor, and a public enemy of the whole community and the country.

Fortior est custodia legis quam hominis. The custody of the law is stronger than that of man.

Fortior et potentior est dispositio legis quam hominis. The disposition of the law is stronger and more powerful than that of man.

Fortior ratio vincit. The stronger reason prevails.

Fractionem diei non recipit lex. The law does not regard a fraction of a day.

Frater fratri uterino non succedit in haereditate paterna. A brother shall not succeed a uterine brother in the paternal inheritance.

Fraudis interpretatio semper in jure civili, non ex eventu dumtaxat, sed ex consilio quoque desideratur. In civil law the interpretation of fraud is sought not only from the outcome but also from the intention. Dig. 50.17.79.

Fraus aequitati praejudicat. Fraud is prejudicial to equity.

Fraus auctoris non nocet successori. The fraud of the author (or ancestor) does not injure his successor.

Fraus enim astringit, non dissolvit perjurium. Fraud, in fact, does not undo but aggravates perjury. Cicero, *De Officiis* 3.113.

Fraus est celare fraudem. It is a fraud to conceal a fraud.

Fraus est odiosa et non praesumenda. Fraud is odious and not to be presumed.

Fraus et dolus nemini patrocinari debent. Fraud and deceit should excuse no one.

Fraus et jus nunquam cohabitant. Fraud and justice never dwell together.

Fraus latet in generalibus. Fraud lies hidden in general expressions.

Fraus legibus invisissima. Fraud is most odious to law.

Fraus meretur fraudem. Fraud deserves fraud.

Fraus omnia corrumpit. Fraud corrupts all.

Frequentia actus multum operatur. The frequency of an act has much effect. • Continual usage establishes a right.

Fructus augent haereditatem. Fruits enhance an inheritance.

Fructus pendentes pars fundi videntur. Hanging fruits are considered part of the parcel of land.

Fructus pendentes pars fundi videntur, sed non fructus percepti. Hanging fruits make part of the realty, but gathered fruits form no part of it. Dig. 6.1.44.

Fructus perceptos villae non esse constat. It is agreed that gathered fruits are not a part of the farm.

Frumenta quae sata sunt solo cedere intelliguntur. Grain that has been sown is understood to belong to the soil.

Frustra agit qui judicium prosequi nequit cum effectu. A person sues in vain who cannot prosecute his judgment with effect.

Frustra est potentia quae nunquam venit in actum. Power that never comes to be exercised is useless.

Frustra expectatur eventus cujus effectus nullus sequitur. An event is vainly awaited from which no effect follows.

Frustra feruntur leges nisi subditis et obedientibus. Laws are made to no purpose except for those who are subject and obedient.

Frustra fit per plura quod fieri potest per pauciora. That is done vainly through many measures if it can be accomplished through fewer.

Frustra legis auxilium quaerit qui in legem committit. Vainly does a person who offends against the law seek the help of the law.

Frustra petis quod mox es restiturus. Vainly you seek what you are soon to restore.

Frustra petis quod statim alteri reddere cogeris. Vainly you seek what you will immediately be compelled to give back to another.

Frustra probatur quod probatum non relevat. It is useless to prove what if proved would not aid the matter in question.

Frustra (vana) est potentia quae nunquam venit in actum. Power that never comes into action is useless (or vain).

Furiosi nulla voluntas est. An insane person has no will.

Furiosus absentis loco est. An insane person is considered as absent.

Furiosus nullum negotium contrahere (gerere) potest (quia non intelligit quod agit). An insane person cannot make a contract (because he does not understand what he is doing).

Furiosus solo furore punitur. An insane person is punished by insanity alone.

Furiosus stipulari non potest nec aliquod negotium agere, qui non intelligit quid agit. An insane person who knows not what he does cannot make a bargain or transact any business.

Furor contrahi matrimonium non sinit, quia consensu opus est. Insanity prevents marriage from being contracted, because consent is needed.

Furtum est contrectatio rei alienae fraudulenta, cum animo furandi, invito illo domino cujus res illa fuerat. Theft is the fraudulent handling of another's property, with an intention of stealing, against the will of the proprietor, whose property it had been.

Furtum non est ubi initium habet detentionis per dominium rei. There is not theft where the holder has a beginning of detention (began holding the object) through ownership of the thing.

G

Generale dictum generaliter est interpretandum. A general expression is to be construed generally.

Generale dictum generaliter est interpretandum: generalia verba sunt generaliter intelligenda. A general statement is to be construed generally: general words are to be understood generally.

Generale nihil certi implicat. A general expression implies nothing certain.

Generale tantum valet in generalibus quantum singulare in singulis. What is general has as much validity among things general as what is particular does among things particular.

Generalia praecedunt, specialia sequuntur. Things general precede; things special follow.

Generalia specialibus non derogant. Things general do not restrict (or detract from) things special.

Generalia sunt praeponenda singularibus. General things are to be put before particular things.

Generalia verba sunt generaliter intelligenda. General words are to be understood in a general sense.

Generalibus specialia derogant. Things special restrict things general.

Generalis clausula non porrigitur ad ea quae antea specialiter sunt comprehensa. A general clause does not extend to those things that have been previously provided for specifically.

Generalis gratia proditionem et homicidium non excipit poena. General favor does not exempt treason and homicide from punishment.

Generalis regula generaliter est intelligenda. A general rule is to be understood generally.

Glossa viperina est quae corrodit viscera textus. It is a poisonous gloss that gnaws away the vitals of the text.

Grammatica falsa non vitiat chartam. False grammar does not vitiate a deed.

Gravioris injuriae species est quae scripta fit quia diutius in conspectus hominum perseverat. Vocis enim facile obliviscimur, at litera scripta manet; et per manus multorum longe, lateque vagatur. The type of injury that is done in writing is more serious, because it remains longer in public view. For we easily forget the voice (or utterance), but the written letter remains, and it passes through the hands of many, far and wide.

Gravius est divinam quam temporalem laedere majestatem. It is more serious to hurt divine than temporal majesty.

H

Habemus optimum testem, confitentem reum. We have the best witness, a confessing defendant.

Habendum in charta vel auget vel restringit, sed non novum inducit. The habendum clause in a deed either increases or restricts, but does not introduce any new provision.

Habet aliquid ex iniquo omne magnum exemplum, quod contra singulos utilitate publica rependitur. There is something of injustice in every great example of punishment, which is exacted against individuals for public benefit. Tacitus *Annales* 14.44.

Haederes successoresque sui cuique liberi, et nullum testamentum; si liberi non sunt, proximus gradus in possessione, fratres, patrii, avunculi. The children of every man are his heirs and successors, and there is no will; if there are no children, next in order of succession are brothers, paternal uncles, and maternal uncles. Tacitus, *Germania* 20

Haeredem Deus facit, non homo. God, and not man, makes the heir.

Haeredem ejusdem potestatis jurisque esse cujus fuit defunctus, constat. It is agreed that an heir has the same powers and rights as the deceased. Dig. 50.17.59.

Haeredi favetur. An heir is favored.

Haeredi magis parcendum est. Much is to be forgiven (and tolerated) in an heir.

Haeredipetae suo propinquo vel extraneo, periculoso sane custodi, nullus committatur. Let no ward be entrusted to the next heir in succession, whether his own relation or a stranger, as the next heir is surely a dangerous guardian. Co. Litt. 88b.

Haereditas est successio in universum jus quod defunctus habuerat. Inheritance is the succession to every right possessed by the late possessor.

Haereditas ex dimidio sanguine non datur. Inheritance from half blood is not granted.

Haereditas nihil aliud est quam successio in universum jus, quod defunctus habuerat. The right of inheritance is nothing other than the faculty of succeeding to all the rights of the deceased.

Haereditas nunquam ascendit. An inheritance never ascends.

Haeredum appellatione veniunt haeredes haeredum in infinitum. By the title of heirs, come the heirs of heirs to infinity.

Haeres est alter ipse, et filius est pars patris. An heir is another self, and a son is a part of the father.

Haeres est aut jure proprietatis aut jure representationis. A person is an heir by either right of property or right of representation.

Haeres est eadem persona cum antecessore. The heir is the same person as the ancestor.

Haeres est nomen collectivum. "Heir" is a collective noun.

Haeres est nomen juris, filius est nomen naturae. "Heir" is a term of law; "son" is one of nature.

Haeres est pars antecessoris. An heir is a part of the ancestor.

Haeres haeredis mei est meus haeres. The heir of my heir is my heir.

Haeres legitimus est quem nuptiae demonstrant. The lawful heir is the one whom the marriage indicates (i.e., who is born in wedlock).

Haeres minor uno et viginti annis non respondebit, nisi in casu dotis. An heir under 21 years of age is not answerable, except in the matter of the dower.

Hoc servabitur quod initio convenit. That shall be preserved which is useful in the beginning.

Homagium, non per procuratores nec per literas fieri potuit, sed in propriâ personâ tam domini quam tenentis capi debit et fieri. Homage cannot be done by proxy, nor by letters, but must be accepted and rendered by lord and tenant in person.

Home ne sera puny pur suer des briefes en court le roy, soit il a droit ou a tort. A person shall not be punished for suing out writs in the king's court, whether the person is right or wrong.

Homicidium vel hominis caedium, est hominis occisio ab homine facta. Homicide or "manslaying" is the killing of a human being by a human being.

Hominum causa jus constitutum est. Law was established for the benefit of humankind.

Homo et capax et incapax esse potest in diversis temporibus. A person may be capable and incapable at different times. • This maxim is sometimes written *Homo potest esse habilis et inhabilis diversis temporibus* (same sense).

Homo potest esse habilis et inhabilis diversis temporibus. A man may be capable and incapable at different times.

Homo vocabulum est naturae; persona juris civilis. "Man" (homo) is a term of nature; "person" (persona), a term of civil law.

Hora non est multum de substantia negotii, licet in appello de ea aliquando fiat mentio. The hour is not of much consequence to the substance of business, although in appeal it is sometimes mentioned.

Hostes sunt qui nobis vel quibus nos bellum decernimus; caeteri proditores vel praedones sunt. Enemies are those on whom we declare war, or who declare it against us; all others are traitors or pirates.

I

Ibi semper debet fieri triatio ubi juratores meliorem possunt habere notitiam. A trial should always be held where the jurors can have the best information.

Id certum est quod certum reddi potest. That is certain which can be made certain.

Id certum est quod certum reddi potest, sed id magis certum est quod de semetipso est certum. That is certain which can be made certain, but that is more certain which is certain of itself.

Idem agens et patiens esse non potest. The same person cannot be both agent and patient (i.e., the doer and person to whom the thing is done).

Idem est facere et nolle prohibere cum possis. It is the same thing to commit an act and to refuse to prohibit it when you can.

Idem est facere et non prohibere cum possis; et qui non prohibit cum prohibere possit in culpa est (aut jubet). It is the same thing to commit an act and not to prohibit it when you can; and he who does not prohibit when he can prohibit is at fault (or does the same as ordering it to be done).

Idem est nihil dicere et insufficienter dicere. It is the same thing to say nothing and not to say enough. • To say a thing in an insufficient manner is the same as not to say it at all. Applied to the plea of a prisoner.

Idem est non esse et non apparere. It is the same thing not to be as not to appear. • What does not appear on the record is considered nonexistent.

Idem est non probari et non esse; non deficit jus sed probatio. It is the same thing not to be proved and not to exist; the law is not deficient but the proof.

Idem est scire aut scire debere aut potuisse. To be bound to know or to have been able to know is the same as to know.

Idem non esse et non apparere. It is the same thing not to exist and not to appear.

Idem semper antecedenti proximo refertur. Idem (the same) always refers to the nearest antecedent.

Identitas vera colligitur ex multitudine signorum. True identity is collected from a great number of signs.

Id perfectum est quod ex omnibus suis partibus constat. That is perfect which is complete in all its parts.

Id perfectum est quod ex omnibus suis partibus constat; et nihil perfectum est dum aliquid restat agendum. That is perfect which is complete in all its parts; and nothing is perfect while anything remains to be done.

Id possumus quod de jure possumus. We are able to do that which we can do lawfully.

Id quod est magis remotum non trahit ad se quod est magis junctum, sed e contrario in omni casu. That which is more removed does not draw to itself what is more closely joined, but to the contrary in every case.

Id quod nostrum est sine facto nostro ad alium transferri non potest. What belongs to us cannot be transferred to another without our act (or deed).

Id solum nostrum quod debitis deductis nostrum est. That alone is ours which is ours after debts have been deducted.

Id tantum possumus quod de jure possumus. We can do only what we can lawfully do.

Ignorantia eorum quae quis scire tenetur non excusat. Ignorance of those things that anyone is bound to know does not excuse.

Ignorantia excusatur non juris sed facti. Ignorance of fact is excused but not ignorance of law.

Ignorantia facti excusat, ignorantia juris non excusat. Ignorance of fact excuses; ignorance of law does not excuse. • Every person must be considered cognizant of the law; otherwise, there is no limit to the excuse of ignorance.

Ignorantia judicis est calamitas innocentis. The ignorance of the judge is the misfortune of the innocent.

Ignorantia juris non excusat. Ignorance of the law does not excuse.

Ignorantia juris quod quisque scire tenetur neminem excusat. Ignorance of the law, which everyone is bound to know, excuses no one.

Ignorantia juris sui non praejudicat juri. Ignorance of one's right does not prejudice the right.

Ignorantia legis neminem excusat. Ignorance of law excuses no one.

Ignorantia praesumitur ubi scientia non probatur. Ignorance is presumed where knowledge is not proved.

Ignorare legis est lata culpa. To be ignorant of the law is gross neglect of it.

Ignoratis terminis artis, ignoratur et ars. Where the terms of an art are unknown, the art is also unknown.

Ignoscitur ei qui sanguinem suum qualiter redemptum voluit. A person is forgiven who chose to purchase his own blood (or life) on any terms whatsoever. • Whatever a person may do under the fear of losing life or limb will not be held binding on him in law. 1 Bl. Com. 127.

Ille honore dignus est, qui se suae legibus patriae, et non sine magno labore et industria, reddidit versatum. He is worthy of honor (or office), who with much labor and industry has made himself familiar with the laws of his country.

Illud quod alias licitum non est, necessitas facit licitum, et necessitas inducit privilegium quod jure privatur. That which is not otherwise lawful, necessity makes lawful; and necessity brings in as a privilege what is denied by right. 10 Coke 61.

Illud quod alteri unitur extinguitur, neque amplius per se vacare licet. That which is united to another is extinguished, nor can it again be detached.

Imaginaria venditio non est pretio accedente. It is not an imaginary sale (but a real one) if a price is added (or agreed upon). Dig. 50.17.16.

Immobilia situm sequuntur. Immovables follow (the law of) their locality.

Imperii majestas est tutelae salus. The majesty of the empire is the safety of its protection.

Imperitia culpae annumeratur. Unskillfulness is reckoned as a fault (as blameworthy conduct or neglect). • Also termed *Imperitia enumeratur culpae.*

Imperitia est maxima mechanicorum poena. Unskillfulness is the greatest punishment of mechanics (i.e., from its effect in making them liable to those by whom they are employed).

Impersonalitas non concludit nec ligat. Impersonality neither concludes nor binds.

Impius et crudelis judicandus est qui libertati non favet. A person is to be judged impious and cruel who does not favor liberty.

Impossibilium nulla obligatio est. There is no obligation to perform impossible things.

Impotentia excusat legem. Powerlessness excuses (or dispenses with) law. • The impossibility of doing what is required by the law excuses nonperformance or nonenforcement. 2 Bl. Com. 127.

Improbi rumores dissipati sunt rebellionis prodromi. Wicked rumors spread abroad are the forerunners of rebellion.

Impunitas continuum affectum tribuit delinquendi. Impunity provides a constant inclination to wrongdoing. 4 Coke 45.

Impunitas semper ad deteriora invitat. Impunity invites (an offender) to ever worse offenses.

In aequali jure melior est conditio possidentis. When the parties have equal rights, the condition of the possessor is the better.

In alta proditione nullus potest esse accessorius sed principalis solummodo. In high treason no one can be an accessory but only a principal.

In alternativis electio est debitoris. The debtor has the choice among alternatives.

In ambigua voce legis ea potius accipienda est significatio quae vitio caret; praesertim cum etiam voluntas legis ex hoc colligi possit. In an ambiguous expression of the law, the meaning will be preferred that is free of defect, especially when the intent of the law can be gathered from it.

In ambiguis casibus sempter praesumitur pro rege. In doubtful cases the presumption is always in favor of the king.

In ambiguis orationibus maxime sententia spectanda est ejus qui eas protulisset. In ambiguous expressions, the opinion (or meaning) of the person who made them is chiefly to be regarded.

In ambiguo sermone non utrumque dicimus sed id duntaxat quod volumus. When the language we use is ambiguous, we do not use it in a double sense, but merely in the sense that we intend.

In Anglia non est interregnum. In England there is no interregnum. • The heir to the throne is understood to succeed from the instant of his predecessor's death or removal.

In atrocioribus delictis punitur affectus licet non sequatur effectus. In the more atrocious crimes, the intent (or attempt) is punished even if the effect does not follow.

In capitalibus sufficit generalis malitia, cum facto paris gradus. In capital cases general malice, with an act of an equal degree of guilt, is sufficient.

In casu extremae necessitatis omnia sunt communia. In a case of extreme necessity, everything is in common.

Incaute factum pro non facto habetur. An alteration done carelessly (inadvertently) will be taken as not done. Dig. 28.4.1.

Incendium aere alieno non exuit debitorem. A fire does not release a debtor from his debt.

Incerta pro nullis habentur. Things uncertain are considered as nothing.

Incerta quantitas vitiat actum. An uncertain quantity vitiates the act.

Incertum ex incerto pendens lege reprobatur. An uncertainty depending upon an uncertainty is rejected by law.

Incidentia nolunt separari. Incidents may not be separated.

Incidentia rei tacite sequuntur. The incidents of a thing follow it implicitly (though unexpressed).

Incivile est, nisi tota lege prospecta, una aliqua particula ejus proposita, judicare vel respondere. It is improper, unless the whole law has been examined, to give judgment or advice on any single clause of it.

Incivile est, nisi tota sententia inspecta, de aliqua parte judicare. It is improper to give an opinion on any part of a passage without examining the whole.

In civilibus ministerium excusat, in criminalibus non item. In civil matters, agency (or service) excuses, but not so in criminal matters.

In civilibus voluntas pro facto reputabitur. In civil cases the will (or intention) will be reckoned as the act.

In claris non est locus conjecturis. In obvious instances there is no room for conjectures.

Inclusio unius est exclusio alterius. See *Expressio unius est exclusio alterius.*

Incolas domicilium facit. Literally, the domicile makes the residents. • That is, the principal place of residence establishes legal residency. Often rendered conversely, *Incola domicilium facit* (residence creates domicile).

In commodato haec pactio, ne dolus praestetur, rata non est. In a loan for use (*commodatum*), a pact excluding liability for fraud is invalid. • Often extended to contracts for loans in general. Dig. 13.6.17.

Incommodum non solvit argumentum. An inconvenience does not solve (or demolish) an argument.

In conjunctivis oportet utramque partem esse veram. In conjunctive constructions, each part must be true.

In consimili casu consimile debet esse remedium. In a similar case, the remedy should be similar.

In consuetudinibus non diuturnitas temporis sed soliditas rationis est consideranda. In customs, not length of time but the soundness of the reason should be considered.

In contingentibus et liberis, tota ratio facti stat in voluntate facientis. In actions that are contingent and free (or unconstrained), the whole reckoning of the act depends on the will of the doer.

In contractibus, benigna; in testamentis, benignior; in restitutionibus, benignissima interpretatio facienda est. In contracts, the interpretation or construction should be liberal; in wills, more liberal; in restitutions, most liberal.

In contractibus, rei veritas potius quam scriptura perspici debet. In contracts, the truth of the matter ought to be regarded rather than the writing.

In contractibus tacite insunt quae sunt moris et consuetudinis. In contracts, matters of custom and usage are tacitly implied. • A contract is understood to contain the customary clauses, although they are not expressed.

In contrahenda venditione, ambiguum pactum contra venditorem interpretandum est. In the contract of sale, an ambiguous agreement is to be interpreted against the seller.

In conventionibus, contrahentium voluntas potius quam verba spectari placuit. In agreements, the intention of the contracting parties should be regarded more than their words.

Incorporalia bello non adquiruntur. Incorporeal things are not acquired by war.

In criminalibus non est argumentandum a pari ultra casum a lege definitum. In criminal cases it is not allowed to argue by analogy beyond the event (or offense) defined by law.

In criminalibus probationes debent esse luce clariores. In criminal cases, the proofs ought to be clearer than light.

In criminalibus silentium praesentis consensum praesumit; in civilibus nonnunquam vel absentis et ubi ejus interest etiam ignorantis. In criminal cases, consent is presumed from the silence of a person present; in civil cases, sometimes, (consent is presumed from the silence) of a person absent and even ignorant, where the matter is (or should be) of some concern to him.

In criminalibus sufficit generalis malitia intentionis cum facto paris gradus. In criminal cases, a general wickedness of intention is sufficient if combined with an act of equal or corresponding degree.

In criminalibus voluntas reputabitur pro facto. In criminal matters, the intent will be reckoned as the deed. • In criminal attempts or conspiracy, the intention is considered in place of the act. 3 Inst. 106.

Inde datae leges ne fortior omnia posset. Laws were made lest the stronger should have unlimited power.

Indefinitum aequipollet universali. The undefined is equivalent to the whole.

Indefinitum supplet locum universalis. The undefined supplies the place of the whole.

Independenter se habet assecuratio a viaggio navis. The route insured is distinct from the voyage of the ship.

Index animi sermo. Speech is the index of the mind. • This maxim is also sometimes written *Index animi sermo est* (and can also be translated as, "Speech is an indication of thought").

Indictment de felony est contra pacem domini regis, coronam et dignitatem suam, in genere et non in individuo; quia in Anglia non est interregnum. Indictment for felony is against the peace of our lord the king, his crown and dignity, in general and not in his individual person; because in England there is no interregnum.

In disjunctivis sufficit alteram partem esse veram. In disjunctive constructions, it is sufficient if either part is true.

In dubiis benigniora praeferenda sunt. In doubtful cases, the more liberal constructions are to be preferred.

In dubiis magis dignum est accipiendum. In doubtful cases, the more worthy is to be accepted.

In dubiis non praesumitur pro testamento. In doubtful cases, there is not presumption in favor of the will.

In dubio, haec legis constructio quam verba ostendunt. In a doubtful case, the construction of the law is what the words indicate.

In dubio, pars mitior est sequenda. In a doubtful case, the gentler course is to be followed.

In dubio pro dote, libertate, innocentia, possessore, debitore, reo, respondendum est. In a doubtful case one must respond in favor of dowry, liberty, or innocence, (on the side) of the possessor, of the debtor, or of the defendant.

In dubio pro innocentia respondendum est. In a doubtful case, the answer (or decision) should be in favor of innocence.

In dubio pro lege fori. In a doubtful case, the law of the forum (is to be favored).

In dubio pro natura. When in doubt, in favor of nature.

In dubio pro reo. When in doubt, in favor of the defendant.

In dubio sequendum quod tutius est. In a doubtful case, one must follow the safer course.

In eo quod plus sit semper inest et minus. The lesser is always included in the greater.

In eo quod vel is qui petit vel is a quo petitur lucrum facturus est, durior causa est petitoris. In a case where either the plaintiff or the defendant will gain, the cause of the applicant is the harder. Dig. 50.17.33.

Inesse potest donationi modus, conditio sive causa; ut modus est; si conditio; quia causa. In a gift there may be manner, condition, or cause; as (*ut*) introduces a manner; if (*si*), a condition; because (*quia*), a cause.

In executione sententiae alibi latae, servare jus loci in quo fit executio, non ubi res judicata. In the execution of a judgment rendered elsewhere (or abroad), (one must) observe the law of the place where the execution takes effect, not where the matter was adjudged.

In expositione instrumentorum, mala grammatica, quod fieri potest, vitanda est. In the construction of instruments, bad grammar is to be avoided as much as possible.

In facto quod se habet ad bonum et malum magis de bona quam de malo lex intendit. In an act (or deed) that may be considered good or bad, the law looks more to the good than to the bad.

Infans est qui, propter defectum aetatis, pro se fari nequeat. He is an infant who, on account of defect of age, cannot speak for himself.

Infans non multum a furioso distat. An infant does not differ much from a lunatic.

Infantes de damno praestare tenentur, de poena non item. Infants are obliged to make good regarding loss, but not regarding punishment.

In favorabilibus annus incoeptus pro completo habetur. In things favored the year begun is held as completed.

In favorabilibus magis attenditur quod prodest quam quod nocet. In things favored, what does good is more regarded than what does harm.

In favorem vitae, libertatis, et innocentiae omnia praesumuntur. All presumptions are in favor of life, liberty, and innocence.

In fictione juris semper aequitas existit. In a fiction of law there is always equity. • A legal fiction is always consistent with equity.

In fictione juris semper subsistit aequitas. In a legal fiction equity always abides (or prevails).

Infinitum in jure reprobatur. That which is endless is condemned in law.

In fraudem vero qui, salvis verbis legis, sententiam ejus circumvenit. Anyone who, observing the letter of the law, circumvents the law's intent, acts in fraud of the law. Dig. 1.3.29.

In generalibus latet error. Error lurks in general expressions. • This maxim is sometimes written *In generalibus versatur error* (meaning "error dwells in general expressions").

In genere quicunque aliquid dicit, sive actor sive reus, necesse est ut probat. In general, whoever alleges anything, whether plaintiff or defendant, must prove it.

In haeredes non solent transire actiones quae poenales ex maleficio sunt. Penal actions arising from anything of a criminal nature do not pass to heirs.

In his enim quae sunt favorabilia animae, quamvis sunt damnosa rebus, fiat aliquando extentio statuti. In things that are favorable to the spirit, though injurious to property, an extension of the statute should sometimes be made.

In his quae de jure communi omnibus conceduntur, consuetudo alicujus patriae vel loci non est alleganda. In those things that by common right are conceded to all, the custom of a particular country or place is not to be adduced.

In iis quae sunt merae facultatis nunquam praescribitur. Prescription does not run against a mere power or faculty to act.

Iniquissima pax est anteponenda justissimo bello. The most unjust peace is to be preferred to the justest war.

Iniquum est alios permittere, alios inhibere mercaturam. It is inequitable to permit some to trade and to prohibit others to do so.

Iniquum est aliquem rei sui esse judicem. It is unjust for anyone to be judge in his own cause.

Iniquum est ingenuis hominibus non esse liberam rerum suarum alienationem. It is unjust for freeborn individuals not to have the free disposal of their own property.

In judiciis minori aetati succurritur. In judicial proceedings, allowance is made for a minor (in age).

In judicio non creditur nisi juratis. In court no one is trusted except those sworn.

In jure non remota causa, sed proxima, spectatur. In law, the proximate, and not the remote, cause is regarded.

In jure omnis definitio periculosa est. In law every definition is dangerous.

Injuria fit ei cui convicium dictum est, vel de eo factum carmen famosum. An injury is done to the person of whom an insult was said, or concerning whom an infamous song was made.

Injuria illata judici, seu locum tenenti regis, videtur ipsi regi illata, maxime si fiat in exercente officium. An injury offered to a judge, or person representing the king, is considered as offered to the king himself, especially if it is done in the exercise of his office.

Injuria non excusat injuriam. A wrong does not excuse a wrong.

Injuria non praesumitur. A wrong is not presumed.

Injuria propria non cadet beneficium facientis. No benefit shall accrue to a person from his own wrongdoing.

Injuria servi dominum pertingit. The servant's wrongdoing reaches the master. • The master is liable for injury done by his servant.

Injustum est, nisi tota lege inspecta, de una aliqua ejus particula proposita judicare vel respondere. It is unjust to give judgment or opinion concerning any particular clause of a law without having examined the whole law.

In lege omnia semper in praesenti stare censentur. In law all things are always judged from their present status.

In loco facti imprestabilis subsit damnum et interesse. Damages and interest come in the place of an act that cannot be performed.

In majore summa continetur minor. In the greater sum is contained the less.

In maleficiis voluntas spectatur, non exitus. In criminal offenses, the intention is regarded, not the event.

In maleficio ratihabitio mandato comparatur. In delict (or tort), ratification is equivalent to authorization. Dig. 43.16.1.15.

In maxima potentia minima licentia. In the greatest power there is the least license.

In mercibus illicitis non sit commercium. Let there be no commerce in illicit goods.

In necessariis, unitas; in non necessariis, libertas; in utrisque, caritas. In those things which are essential let there be unity; in non-essentials, liberty; in both, charity.

In nostra lege una comma evertit totum placitum. In our law, one comma upsets the whole plea.

In novo casu, novum remedium apponendum est. In a new case a new remedy must be applied.

In obscuris inspici solere quod verisimilius est, aut quod plerumque fieri solet. In obscure cases it is usual to regard what is more probable or what is more often done.

In obscuris quod minimum est sequimur. In obscure cases, we follow what is least so.

In odium spoliatoris omnia praesumuntur. Everything is presumed to the prejudice of the despoiler.

In omni actione ubi duae concurrunt districtiones, videlicet in rem et in personam, illa districtio tenenda est quae magis timetur et magis ligat. In every action where two distresses (or forms of distraint) concur, that is in rem and in personam, the distraint is to be chosen that is more dreaded and that binds more firmly. Bracton 372.

In omnibus contractibus, sive nominatis sive innominatis, permutatio continetur. In all contracts, whether express or implied, there must be something given in exchange. 2 Bl. Com. 444.

In omnibus (fere) poenalibus judiciis, et aetati et imprudentiae succurritur. In almost all penal judgments, allowance is made for age (or youth) and lack of discretion. Dig. 50.17.108.

In omnibus obligationibus, in quibus dies non ponitur, praesenti die debetur. In all obligations, when no date is fixed (for performance), the thing is due the same day.

In omnibus quidem, maxime tamen in jure, aequitas spectanda sit. In all affairs indeed, but especially in those that concern the administration of justice, equity should be regarded.

In omñi re nascitur res quae ipsam rem exterminat. In everything, the thing is born that ends the thing itself.

In pari causa possessor potior haberi debet. When two parties have equal claims, the possessor should be considered the stronger. • The phrase is also translated in this way: in an equal case the possessor ought to be preferred.

In pari causa potior est conditio possidentis. When two parties have equal claims, the position of the possessor is the stronger.

In pari delicto melior est conditio possidentis. When both parties are equally at fault, the position of the possessor is the better.

In pari delicto potior est conditio defendentis. Where both parties are equally in the wrong, the position of the defendant is the stronger.

In personam actio est, qua cum eo agimus qui obligatus est nobis ad faciendum aliquid vel dandum. An action against a person (*in personam*) is one in which we sue someone who is under obligation to us to do or to give something. Dig. 44.7.25.

In poenalibus causis benignius interpretandum est. In penal cases, the more liberal interpretation is to be made.

In praeparatoriis ad judicium favetur actori. In things preparatory to trial, the plaintiff is favored.

In praesentia majoris cessat potentia minoris. In the presence of the superior, the power of the inferior ceases. • This maxim is sometimes written *In praesentia majoris potestatis, minor potestas cessat* (meaning "in the presence of the superior power, the minor power ceases").

In pretio emptionis et venditionis naturaliter licet contrahentibus se circumvenire. In setting the price for buying and selling, it is naturally allowed to the contracting parties to get the better of each other.

In propria causa nemo judex. No one can be judge in his own cause.

Inquissima pax est anteponenda iustissimo bello. The most unfair peace is preferable to the most just war.

In quo quis delinquit, in eo de jure est puniendus. In whatever matter one offends, in that the person is rightfully to be punished. • Coke refers to forfeiture of the office abused. Co. Litt. 233b.

In rebus manifestis errat qui auctoritates legum allegat; quia perspicua vera non sunt probanda. A person errs who adduces authorities on the law in matters self-evident; because obvious truths need not be proved.

In rebus novis constituendis evidens esse utilitas debet, ut recedatur ab eo jure, quod diu aequum visum est. In settling matters anew, there should be some utility (or advantage) clearly in view, to justify departing from a rule of law that has long seemed equitable. Dig. 1.4.2.

In rebus quae sunt favorabilia animae, quamvis sunt damnosa rebus, fiat aliquando extensio statuti. In things that are favorable to people, though injurious to the things, a statute should sometimes be extended.

In re communi neminem dominorum jure facere quicquam, invito altero, posse. In common property no one of the coproprietors can do (or make) anything against the will of the other. Dig. 10.3.28.

In re communi potior (melior) est conditio prohibentis. In common property (matters of joint ownership) the partner who refuses has the stronger (or better) position.

In re dubia benigniorem interpretationem sequi non minus justius est quam tutius. In a doubtful matter, to follow the more liberal interpretation is as much the more just as it is the safer course.

In re dubia magis infitiatio quam affirmatio intelligenda. In a doubtful matter, the negation is to be understood rather than the affirmation.

In re lupanari testes lupanares admittentur. In a matter concerning a brothel, prostitutes will be admitted as witnesses.

In rem actio est per quam rem nostram quae ab alio possidetur petimus, et semper adversus eum est qui rem possidet. The action *in rem* is that by which we seek our property that is possessed by another, and is always against him who possesses the property. Dig. 44.7.25.

In re obscura melius est favere repetitioni quam adventicio lucro. In an obscure case it is better to favor repetition than adventitious gain. Dig. 50.17.41.1.

In re pari, potiorem causam esse prohibentis constat. Where joint owners have equal rights, it is agreed that the cause of him prohibiting (any proposed use) is the stronger. Dig. 10.3.28.

In re propria iniquum admodum est alicui licentiam tribuere sententiae. It is extremely unjust to assign anyone the privilege of judgment in his own cause.

In republica maxime conservanda sunt jura belli. The laws of war must be especially preserved in the state.

In restitutionem, non in poenam, haeres succedit. The heir succeeds to the restitution, not the penalty.

In restitutionibus benignissima interpretatio facienda est. The most favorable construction is to be made in restitutions.

Insanus est qui, abjecta ratione, omnia cum impetu et furore facit. The person is insane who, having cast aside reason, does everything with violence and rage.

In satisfactionibus non permittitur amplius fieri quam semel factum est. In payments, it is not permitted that more be received than has been received once for all (i.e., after payment in full).

Instans est finis unius temporis et principium alterius. An instant is the end of one time and the beginning of another.

In stipulationibus cum quaeritur quid actum sit, verba contra stipulatorem interpretanda sunt. In agreements, when there is a question whether action has been taken, the terms are to be interpreted against the party offering them.

In stipulationibus id tempus spectatur quo contrahimus. In agreements, there is regard to the time at which we reach agreement.

Instrumenta domestica seu adnotatio, si non aliis quoque adminiculis adjuventur, ad probationem sola non sufficiunt. Private family documents or a memorandum, if not supported by other evidence, are not of themselves sufficient proof.

In suo hactenus facere licet quatenus nihil in alienum immittit. One may do what he likes on his own property, so long as he does not invade (or send anything into) another's property.

In suo quisque negotio hebetior est quam in alieno. Everyone is less perceptive (of flaws) in his own business than in that of another.

Intentio caeca mala. A concealed intention is an evil one.

Intentio inservire debet legibus, non leges intentioni. The intention ought to be subject to the laws, not the laws to the intention.

Intentio legitime cognita et legibus consentanea maxime habenda. An intention legitimately known and agreeable to the laws is to be especially regarded.

Intentio mea imponit nomen operi meo. My intent gives a name to my act.

Inter alias causas acquisitionis magna, celebris et famosa, est causa donationis. Among other modes of acquiring property, a great method, frequently used and well known, is that of gift.

Inter alios res gestas aliis non posse praejudicium facere saepe constitutum est. It has been often decided that matters transacted between other parties cannot cause prejudice (to those who were not involved).

Inter arma silent leges. Amid the arms of war the laws are silent.

Interdum evenit ut exceptio quae prima facie justa videtur tamen inique noceat actori. It sometimes happens that a plea of defense that seems just prima facie nevertheless injures an actor unfairly. Gaius, *Inst.* 4.126.

Interdum venit ut exceptio quae prima facie justa videtur tamen inique noceat. It sometimes happens that a plea that seems prima facie just is nevertheless injurious and unfair.

Interest reipublicae ne maleficia remaneant impunita. It is in the interest of the state that crimes not remain unpunished.

Interest reipublicae, ne quis re sua male utatur. It is in the state's interest that no one shall use his property improperly.

Interest reipublicae ne sua quis male utatur. It is in the interest of the state that no one misuse his own property.

Interest reipublicae quod homines conserventur. It is in the interest of the state that people should be protected.

Interest reipublicae res judicatas non rescindi. It is in the interest of the state that judgments already given not be rescinded.

Interest reipublicae suprema hominum testamenta rata haberi. It is in the interest of the state that a person's last will should be held valid.

Interest reipublicae ut bonis bene sit, et male malis, et suum cuique. It is in the state's interest that things go well for the good, badly for the wicked, and that each have what is his own.

Interest reipublicae ut carceres sint in tuto. It is in the interest of the state that prisons should be secure.

Interest reipublicae ut pax in regno conservetur et quaecunque paci adversentur provide declinentur. It is in the interest of the state to preserve peace in the kingdom and prudently to decline whatever is adverse to it.

Interest reipublicae ut quilibet re sua bene utatur. It is in the interest of the state that each person make good use of his own property.

Interest reipublicae ut sit finis litium. It is in the interest of the state that there be a limit to litigation.

Inter pacem et bellum nihil medium. There is no middle course between peace and war.

Interpretare et concordare leges legibus est optimus interpretandi modus. To interpret and reconcile laws so they harmonize is the best mode of construction.

Interpretatio chartarum benigne facienda est ut res magis valeat quam pereat. The construction of a deed is to be made liberally, that the thing may rather take effect than perish.

Interpretatio fienda est ut res magis valeat quam pereat. Such a construction should be made that the measure may take effect rather than fail.

Interpretatio talis in ambiguis semper fienda est ut evitetur inconveniens et absurdum. In ambiguities, a construction should always be found such that what is unsuitable and absurd may be avoided.

Interruptio multiplex non tollit praescriptionem semel obtentam. Repeated interruptions do not remove a prescription (or acquisition by long use) once it has been obtained.

In testamentis plenius testatoris intentionem scrutamur. In wills we diligently examine the testator's intention.

In testamentis plenius voluntates testantium interpretantur. In wills the intentions of the testators are more fully (or liberally) construed.

In testamentis ratio tacita non debet considerari, sed verba solum spectari debent; adeo per divinationem mentis a verbis recedere durum est. In wills an unexpressed meaning ought not to be considered, but one must look to the words alone; so troublesome is it to depart from the words by guessing at the intention.

Intestatus decedit qui aut omnino testamentum non fecit aut non jure fecit, aut id quod fecerat ruptum irritumve factum est, aut nemo ex eo haeres exstitit. A person dies intestate who either has made no will at all or has not made it legally, or when the will that he had made has been annulled or become ineffectual, or when there is no living heir.

In toto et pars continetur. In the whole the part also is included.

In traditionibus scriptorum (chartarum) non quod dictum est, sed quod gestum (factum) est, inspicitur. In the delivery of writings (deeds), not what is said but what is done is to be considered.

Intra fortunam debet quisque manere suam. Everyone is bound to live within his means (or abide by his fate). Ovid, *Tristia* III. 4. 25–26.

Inutilis labor et sine fructu non est effectus legis. Useless and fruitless labor is not the effect of law.

Inveniens libellum famosum et non corrumpens punitur. A person who discovers a libel and does not destroy it is punished.

In veram quantitatem fidejussor teneatur, nisi pro certa quantitate accessit. Let the surety be held for the true amount unless he agreed for a certain amount.

In verbis non verba sed res et ratio quaerenda est. In wording, it is not the words but the substance and the meaning that is to be sought.

Invito beneficium non datur. No benefit is given to one unwilling. • No one is obliged to accept a benefit against his consent. Dig. 50.17.69.

In vocibus videndum non a quo sed ad quid sumatur. In discourse it is not the point from which but the end to which it is drawn that should be regarded.

Ipsae leges cupiunt ut jure regantur. The laws themselves desire that they should be governed by right.

Ira furor brevis est. Anger is a short insanity.

Ira hominis non implet justitiam Dei. The wrath of a man does not fulfill the justice of God.

Is damnum dat qui jubet dare; ejus vero nulla culpa est cui parere necesse est. He causes a loss who gives orders to cause it; but no blame attaches to him who is under the necessity of obeying. Dig. 50.17.169.

Is qui actionem habet ad rem recuperandam ipsam rem habere videtur. He who has a (valid) action to recover a thing is regarded as having the thing itself.

Ita lex scripta est. So the law is written.

Ita semper fiat relatio ut valeat dispositio. Let the relation be so made that the disposition may stand.

Iter est jus eundi, ambulandi hominis; non etiam jumentum agendi vel vehiculum. A way is a right of going or walking for a human being, and does not include the right of driving a beast of burden or a carriage.

Iudex decidere debet. The judge should decide.

Iura novit curia. The court knows the laws.

Iurisdictio inhaeret, cohaeret, adhaeret imperio; par in parem non habet iudicium. Legal authority clings to sovereignty, belongs to it, and remains inherent to it; no one may pass judgment on an equal.

Ius posterioris derogat priori. The right of one who follows detracts from the right of one who precedes.

J

Jacere telum voluntatis est; ferire quem nolueris, fortunae. To throw a dart or weapon is a matter of will; but to strike a person whom you did not wish to strike, is a matter of chance. Cicero, *Topics* 17.64.

Judex aequitatem semper spectare debet. A judge ought always to regard equity.

Judex ante oculos aequitatem semper habere debet. A judge ought always to have equity before his eyes.

Judex bonus nihil ex arbitrio suo faciat nec propositione domesticae voluntatis, sed juxta leges et jura pronunciet. A good judge should do nothing from his own preference or from the prompting of his private desire; but he should pronounce according to law and justice.

Judex damnatur cum nocens absolvitur. The judge is condemned when the guilty party is acquitted.

Judex debet judicare secundum allegata et probata. The judge ought to give judgment according to the allegations and the proofs.

Judex de pace civium constituitur. A judge is appointed for the peace of the people.

Judex est lex loquens. The judge is the speaking law.

Judex habere debet duos sales, salem sapientiae, ne sit insipidus, et salem conscientiae, ne sit diabolus. A judge should have two salts: the salt of wisdom, lest he be foolish; and the salt of conscience, lest he be devilish.

Judex non potest esse testis in propria causa. A judge cannot be a witness in his own cause.

Judex non potest injuriam sibi datum punire. A judge cannot punish a wrong done to himself.

Judex non reddit plus quam quod petens ipse requirit. The judge does not give more than the plaintiff himself demands.

Judicandum est legibus non exemplis. Judgment must be given by the laws, not by examples.

Judices non tenentur exprimere causam sententiae suae. Judges are not bound to explain the reason of their judgments.

Judices recenter et subtiliter excogitatis minime favent contra communem legem. Judges favor least of all new and subtle rationales against common law.

Judicia in curia regis non adnihilentur, sed stent in robore suo quousque per errorem aut attinctam adnullentur. Let judgments in the king's court not be invalidated but remain in force until annulled by error or attaint. 2 Inst. 360.

Judicia in deliberationibus crebro maturescunt, in accelerato processu nunquam. Judgments often ripen in the course of deliberation, never in hurried proceeding. 2 Inst. 210.

Judicia posteriora sunt in lege fortiora. The later decisions are stronger in law.

Judicia sunt tanquam juris dicta, et pro veritate accipiuntur. Judgments are, as it were, the dicta (or sayings) of the law, and are received as truth.

Judiciis posterioribus fides est adhibenda. Trust should be put in the later decisions.

Judici officium suum excedenti non paretur. A judge who exceeds his office (or jurisdiction) is not obeyed.

Judici satis poena est quod Deum habet ultorem. It is punishment enough for a judge that he has God to take vengeance on him.

Judicis est in pronuntiando sequi regulam, exceptione non probata. It is the proper role of a judge in rendering his decision to follow the rule, when the exception has not been proved.

Judicis est judicare secundum allegata et probata. It is the proper role of a judge to decide according to the allegations and proofs.

Judicis est jus dicere, non dare. It is the proper role of a judge to state the right, not to endow it. • Generally interpreted, it is the duty of the judge to administer justice and not to make law.

Judicis officium est opus diei in die suo perficere. It is the duty of a judge to finish the work of each day within that day.

Judicis officium est ut res ita tempora rerum quaerere; quaesito tempore tutus eris. It is the duty of a judge to inquire into the timing of events as much as the matters themselves; by inquiring into the time, you will be safe.

Judicium a non suo judice datum nullius est momenti. A judgment given by a person who is not its proper judge (not in the proper jurisdiction) is of no consequence. 10 Coke 76.

Judicium est iis quae pro religione faciant faveri, etsi verba desint. It is a sound decision for those things that promote religion to be favored, though the words be lacking.

Judicium est juris dictum, et per judicium jus est noviter revelatum quod diu fuit velatum. Adjudication is the utterance of the law, and by it the law that was long hidden is newly revealed.

Judicium est quasi juris dictum. Judgment is, as it were, a pronouncement of the right (or a saying of the law).

Judicium non debet esse illusorium, suum effectum habere debet. A judgment ought not to be illusory (or deceptive); it ought to have its proper effect. 2 Co. Inst. 341.

Judicium redditur in invitum, in praesumptione legis. In presumption of law, a judgment is given against one's will.

Judicium semper pro veritate accipitur. A judgment is always taken for truth.

Juncta juvant. Things joined together are helpful.

Jura debet esse omni exceptione maiora. Laws should be greater than any exception.

Jura ecclesiastica limitata sunt infra limites separatos. Ecclesiastical laws are limited within separate bounds.

Jura eodem modo destituuntur quo constituuntur. Laws are abrogated or repealed by the same means by which they are made.

Juramentum est indivisibile, et non est admittendum in parte verum et in parte falsum. An oath is indivisible; it is not to be accepted as partly true and partly false.

Jura naturae sunt immutabilia. The laws of nature are unchangeable.

Jura publica anteferenda privatis. Public rights are to be preferred to private.

Jura publica ex privato promiscue decidi non debent. Public rights ought not to be determined in confusion, from private considerations. • In Coke's example, the validity of a sheriff's warrant is not affected by a dispute among the parties. Co. Litt. 181b.

Jurare est Deum in testem vocare, et est actus divini cultus. To swear is to call God to witness, and is an act of religion.

Jura regis specialia non conceduntur per generalia verba. The special rights of the king are not granted by general words.

Jura sanguinis nullo jure civili dirimi possunt. The rights of blood (or kinship) cannot be destroyed by any civil law.

Jurato creditur in judicio. In judgment credit is given to the swearer.

Juratores debent esse vicini, sufficientes et minus suspecti. Jurors ought to be neighbors, of sufficient means and free from suspicion (literally, less suspected).

Juratores sunt judices facti. The jurors are the judges of fact.

Juratus creditur in judicio. In judgment a person who has sworn an oath is believed.

Jure naturae aequum est neminem cum alterius detrimento et injuria fieri locupletiorem. By the law of nature, it is just that no one should be enriched to the detriment and injury of another.

Juri non est consonum quod aliquis accessorius in curia regis convincatur antequam aliquis de facto fuerit attinctus. It is not consonant to justice that any accessory should be convicted in the king's court before anyone has been attainted of the fact (i.e., under sentence of attainder for committing the act). • The accessory should not be convicted before the principal is proved guilty. 2 Co. Inst. 183.

Juri sanguinis nunquam praescribitur. No prescription (or statutory limit) runs against a right by blood.

Jurisdictio est potestas de publico introducta, cum necessitate juris dicendi. Jurisdiction is a power introduced for the public good, on account of the necessity of dispensing justice.

Juris effectus in executione consistit. The effect of law (or of a right) consists in the execution.

Juris ignorantia est cum jus nostrum ignoramus. It is ignorance of law when we do not know our own right.

Juris praecepta sunt haec, honeste vivere, alterum non laedere, suum cuique tribuere. These are the precepts of the law: to live honorably, not to injure another, to render to each person his due. Just. Inst. 1.1.

Jurisprudentia est divinarum atque humanarum rerum notitia, justi atque injusti scientia. Jurisprudence is the knowledge of things divine and human, the science of the just and the unjust. Just. Inst. 1.1.1.

Jurisprudentia legis communis Angliae est scientia socialis et copiosa. The jurisprudence of the common law of England is a social science comprehensive in scope.

Juris quidem ignorantiam cuique nocere, facti verum ignorantiam non nocere. Ignorance of law is prejudicial to everyone, but ignorance of fact is not.

Jus accrescendi inter mercatores locum non habet, pro beneficio commercii. For the good of commerce, the right of survivorship has no place among merchants.

Jus accrescendi inter mercatores, pro beneficio commercii locum non habet. For the benefit of commerce, there is no right of accrual among merchants.

Jus accrescendi praefertur oneribus. The right of survivorship is preferred to incumbrances.

Jus accrescendi praefertur ultimae voluntati. The right of survivorship is preferred to a last will.

Jus civile est quod sibi populus constituit. The civil law is what a people has established for itself.

Jus constitui oportet in his quae ut plurimum accidunt, non quae ex inopinato. Law ought to be made with a view to the cases that happen most frequently, and not to those that are unexpected.

Jus descendit, et non terra. A right descends, and not the land.

Jus dicere (et) non jus dare. To state the right (and) not to endow it. • Generally interpreted, to declare the law (and) not to make it.

Jus est ars boni et aequi. Law is the science of what is good and just.

Jus est norma recti; et quicquid est contra normam recti est injuria. The law is the rule of right; and whatever is contrary to the rule of right is an injury.

Jus et fraus nunquam cohabitant. Right and fraud never abide together.

Jus ex injuria non oritur. A right does not arise from a wrong.

Jus in re inhaerit ossibus usufructuarii. A right in the thing cleaves to the person (literally, the bones) of the usufructuary.

Jusjurandi forma verbis differt, re convenit; hunc enim sensum habere debet, ut Deus invocetur. The form of taking an oath differs in language, but agrees in meaning; for it ought to have this sense, that God is invoked.

Jusjurandum inter alios factum nec nocere nec prodesse debet. An oath made between third parties ought neither to hurt nor to profit.

Jus naturae proprie est dictamen rectae rationis, quo scimus quid turpe, quid honestum, quid faciendum, quid fugiendum. The law of nature is properly the dictate of right reason, by which we know what is dishonorable and what is honorable; what should be done, and what should be avoided.

Jus naturale est quod apud homines eandem habet potentiam. Natural right is that which has the same force among (all) mankind.

Jus nec inflecti gratia, nec frangi potentia, nec adulterari pecunia potest; quod si non modo oppressum, sed desertum aut negligentia asservatum fuerit, nihil est quod quisquam se habere certum, aut a patre accepturum, aut liberis esse relicturum, arbitretur. The law cannot be bent by favor, not broken by power, nor corrupted by money; for not only if it be overthrown, but even if it be neglected or carelessly preserved, there is nothing secure in what anyone may think he has, or will inherit from his father, or yet may leave to his children. Cicero, *Pro Caecina* 73.

Jus non habenti tute non paretur. It is safe not to obey a person who has no right.

Jus non patitur ut idem bis solvatur. The law does not permit that the same thing be twice paid.

Jus non scriptum tacito et illiterato hominum consensu, et moribus expressum. The unwritten law is expressed in the tacit and unwritten agreement of the people and in their customs. Bl. Com. 1.64; Gellius 11.18.4.

Jus publicum privatorum pactis mutari non potest. A public right cannot be altered by the agreements of private persons.

Jus publicum et privatum est quod ex naturalibus praeceptis, aut gentium, aut civilibus est collectum et quod in jure scripto jus appellatur, id in lege Angliae rectum esse dicitur. Public and private law is that which is collected from the precepts of nature, of peoples in general, or of particular states; and what in written law is called "*jus*" by the law of England is said to be "right."

Jus quo universitates utuntur est idem quod habent privati. The right that corporations exercise is the same as the right that individuals possess.

Jus respicit aequitatem. Law regards equity.

Jus sanguinis numquam praescribitur. A right by blood never prescribes.

Jus summum saepe summa est malitia. The height of law is often the height of mischief. • Right too rigid hardens into wrong. Terence, *Heauton Timorumenos* 796.

Jus superveniens auctori accrescit successori. An additional or enhanced right for the possessor accrues to the successor.

Jus testamentorum pertinet ordinario. The right of testaments pertains to the ordinary.

Justitia debet esse libera, quia nihil iniquius venali justitia; plena, quia justitia non debet claudicare; et celer, quia dilatio est quaedam negatio. Justice ought not to be bought, for nothing is more hateful than venal justice; full, for justice ought not to be defective; and quick, for delay is a certain denial.

Justitiae soror incorrupta fides. Faith unbroken is the sister of justice. Horace, *Carmina* 24.6.

Justitia est constans et perpetua voluntas jus suum cuique tribuendi. Justice is a steady and unceasing disposition to render to every person his due.

Justitia est duplex: severe puniens et vere praeveniens. Justice is double: punishing with severity, and truly preventing.

Justitia est libertate prior. Justice comes before liberty.

Justitia est virtus excellens et Altissimo complacens. Justice is an excellent virtue and pleasing to the Most High.

Justitia firmatur solium. By justice the throne is strengthened.

Justitia nemini neganda est. Justice is to be denied to no one.

Justitia non est neganda, non differenda. Justice is not to be denied or delayed.

Justitia non novit patrem nec matrem, solum veritatem spectat justitia. Justice knows neither father nor mother; justice looks to truth alone.

Jus triplex est: proprietatis, possessionis, et possibilitatis. Right is threefold: of property, of possession, and of possibility.

Jus vendit quod usus approbavit. The law dispenses what use has approved.

L

La conscience est la plus changeante des régles. Conscience is the most changing of rules.

La ley favour la vie d'un home. The law favors a man's life.

La ley favour l'inheritance d'un home. The law favors a man's inheritance.

La ley voit plus tost suffer un mischiefe que un inconvenience. The law will sooner suffer a mischief than an inconvenience.

Lata culpa dolo aequiparatur. Gross negligence is equivalent to fraud.

Le contrat fait la loi. The contract makes the law.

Legatos violare contra jus gentium est. It is contrary to the law of nations to do violence to ambassadors.

Legatum morte testatoris tantum confirmatur, sicut donatio inter vivos traditione sola. A legacy is confirmed by the death of the testator, in the same manner as a gift from a living person is by delivery alone.

Legatus regis vice fungitur a quo destinatur et honorandus est sicut ille cujus vicem gerit. An ambassador fills the place of the king by whom he is appointed, and is to be honored in the same way as the person whose place he fills.

Legem enim brevem esse oportet, quo facilius ab imperitis teneatur. Laws ought to be short, that they may be more readily kept by the unlearned. Seneca, *Epistles* 94.38.

Legem enim contractus dat. The contract gives the law.

Legem terrae amittentes perpetuam infamiae notam inde merito incurrunt. Those who lose the law of the land thereby justly incur an eternal stigma of infamy.

Leges Angliae sunt tripartitae: jus commune, consuetudines, ac decreta comitiorum. The laws of England are threefold: common law, customs, and decrees of parliament.

Leges autem a victoribus dicuntur, accipiuntur a victis. Laws (or conditions) are pronounced by conquerors, accepted by the conquered.

Leges et constitutiones futuris certum est dare formam negotiis non ad facta praeterita revocari; nisi nominatim et de praeterito tempore et adhuc pendentibus negotiis cautum sit. Laws and statutes are regarded as regulating future negotiations not past transactions; unless they are expressly made to apply to both past and to pending matters.

Leges figendi et refigendi consuetudo est periculosissima. The practice of adding and annulling laws is a most dangerous one. 4 Coke pref.

Leges fixit pretio atque refixit. He shaped and reshaped laws for a price; he promulgated and annulled laws at a price. • The reference is to a judge who took bribes.

Leges humanae nascuntur, vivunt, et moriuntur. Laws that humans have made are born, live, and die.

Leges naturae perfectissimae sunt et immutabiles; humani vero juris conditio semper in infinitum decurrit, et nihil est in eo quod perpetuo stare possit. The laws of nature are most perfect and immutable; but the condition of human law is an unending succession, and there is nothing in it that can stand forever.

Leges non verbis sed rebus sunt impositae. Laws are imposed on affairs, not words.

Leges posteriores priores contrarias abrogant. Subsequent laws repeal prior conflicting ones.

Leges quae retrospiciunt raro et magna cum cautione sunt adhibendae; neque enim Janus locaretur in legibus. Laws that are retrospective should be rarely regarded and (only) with great caution; for Janus should have no place among the laws.

Leges suum ligent latorem. Laws should bind their own author.

Leges vigilantibus, non dormientibus subveniunt. The laws aid those who keep watch, not those who sleep (that is, the vigilant, not the negligent).

Lege totum, si vis scire totum. Read the whole, if you would know the whole.

Legibus sumptis desinentibus, lege naturae utendum est. Where manmade laws fail, the law of nature must be used.

Legis constructio non facit injuriam. The construction of law does not do wrong.

Legis interpretatio legis vim obtinet. The interpretation of law obtains the force of law.

Legislatorum est viva vox, rebus et non verbis legem imponere. The voice of legislators is a living voice, to impose laws on (actual) affairs and not on (mere) words.

Legis minister non tenetur, in executione officii sui, fugere aut retrocedere. The minister of the law is not bound, in the execution of his office, either to flee or to retreat.

Legis virtus haec est: imperare, vetare, permittere, punire. The force of the law is this: to command, forbid, permit, and punish. Dig. 1.3.7.

Legitime imperanti parere necesse est. One who commands lawfully must be obeyed.

Legitimus haeres et filius est quem nuptiae demonstrant. A lawful son and heir is he whom the marriage declares to be lawful.

Legum omnes servi sumus, ut liberi esse possimus. We are slaves to the law, in order to be free. Cicero, *Pro Cluentio* 53.146.

Le ley de Dieu et ley de terre sont tout un, et l'un et l'autre preferre et favour le common et publique bien del terre. The law of God and the law of the land are all one; and both promote and favor the common and public good of the land.

Le ley est le plus haut enheritance que le roy ad, car par le ley, il mesme et touts ses sujets sont rules, et si le ley ne fuit, nul roy ne nul enheritance serra. The law is the highest inheritance that the king possesses; for by the law both he and all his subjects are ruled; and if there were no law, there would be neither king nor inheritance.

Le salut du peuple est la suprême loi. The safety of the people is the highest law.

Les fictions naissent de la loi, et non la loi des fictions. Fictions arise from the law, and not law from fictions.

Les lois ne se chargent de punir que les actions exterieures. Laws undertake to punish only outward actions.

Levis exceptio excusat a spolio. A slight defense excuses from the consequences of spuilzie (a taking of movables).

Lex aequitate gaudet. Law delights in equity.

Lex aequitate gaudet; appetit perfectum; est norma recti. The law delights in equity: it covets perfection; it is a rule of right.

Lex aliquando sequitur aequitatem. The law sometimes follows equity.

Lex Angliae est lex misericordiae. The law of England is a law of mercy.

Lex Angliae lex terrae est. The law of England is the law of the land.

Lex Angliae non patitur absurdum. The law of England does not allow an absurdity.

Lex Angliae nunquam matris sed semper patris conditionem imitari partum judicat. The law of England rules that the offspring always follows the condition of the father, never that of the mother.

Lex Angliae nunquam sine parliamento mutari potest. The law of England can never be changed without (act of) parliament. • This maxim is sometimes written *Lex Angliae sine Parliamento mutari non potest* (also translatable as "the law of England cannot be changed but by Parliament").

Lex beneficialis rei consimili remedium praestat. A beneficial law affords a remedy in a similar case.

Lex certa esto; poena certa, et crimini idonea, et legibus praefinita. Let the law be certain; and let the punishment be certain, adequate to the crime, and previously determined by the laws.

Lex citius tolerare vult privatum damnum quam publicum malum. The law would sooner endure a private loss than a public evil.

Lex contra id quod praesumit probationem non recipit. The law accepts no proof against that which it presumes.

Lex deficere non potest in justitia exhibenda. The law cannot fail in dispensing justice.

Lex de futuro, judex de praeterito. The law (provides) for the future, the judge for the past.

Lex dilationes semper exhorret. The law always abhors delays.

Lex est ab aeterno. The law is from eternity.

Lex est anima regis, et rex est anima legis. Law is the soul of the king, and the king is the soul of the law.

Lex est dictamen rationis. Law is the dictate of reason.

Lex est exercitus judicum tutissimus ductor. The law is the safest leader of the army of judges.

Lex est linea recti. Law is a straight line.

Lex est norma recti. Law is a rule of right.

Lex est ratio summa, quae jubet quae sunt utilia et necessaria, et contraria prohibet. Law is the highest form of reason, which commands what is useful and necessary and forbids the contrary.

Lex est sanctio sancta, jubens honesta et prohibens contraria. Law is a sacred sanction, commanding what is right and prohibiting the contrary.

Lex est summa ratio. Law is the highest reason.

Lex est tutissima cassis; sub clypeo legis nemo decipitur. Law is the safest helmet; under the shield of the law no one is deceived.

Lex facit regem. Law makes the king (i.e., makes the monarch king).

Lex favet doti. The law favors dower.

Lex fingit ubi subsistit aequitas. Law creates a fiction where equity abides.

Lex haereditates liberas esse vult non in perpetuum astrictas. The law intends inheritances to be free for those that are not strictly bound for all time.

Lex injusta non est lex. An unjust law is not a law.

Lex intendit vicinum vicini facta scire. The law presumes that one neighbor knows the actions of another.

Lex judicat de rebus necessario faciendis quasi re ipsa factis. The law judges of things that must necessarily be done as if actually done.

Lex mercatoria est lex terrae. The mercantile law is the law of the land.

Lex necessitatis est lex temporis, i.e., instantis. The law of necessity is the law of time, i.e., time present.

Lex neminem cogit ad vana seu inutilia peragenda. The law forces no one to do vain or useless things.

Lex neminem cogit ostendere quod nescire praesumitur. The law forces no one to make known what he is presumed not to know.

Lex nemini facit injuriam. The law does wrong to no one.

Lex nemini operatur iniquum, nemini facit injuriam. The law works an injustice to no one and does wrong to no one.

Lex nil facit frustra, nil jubet frustra. The law does nothing in vain and commands nothing in vain.

Lex non a rege est violanda. The law is not to be violated by the king.

Lex non cogit ad impossibilia. The law does not compel to impossible ends.

Lex non consilia nuda, sed actus apertos respicit. The law regards not mere intentions, but open acts.

Lex non curat de minimis. The law is not concerned with matters of least consequence.

Lex non debet deficere conquerentibus in justitia exhibenda. The law ought not to fail in dispensing justice to those with a grievance.

Lex non deficit in justitia exhibenda. The law does not fail in showing justice.

Lex non exacte definit, sed arbitrio boni viri permittit. The law does not define exactly, but trusts in the judgment of a good man.

Lex non favet votis delicatorum. The law does not favor the wishes of the fastidious.

Lex non intendit aliquid impossibile. The law does not intend anything impossible.

Lex non novit patrem, nec matrem; solam veritatem. The law knows neither father nor mother; only the truth.

Lex non oritur ex injuria. The law does not arise from an unlawful act.

Lex non patitur fractiones et divisiones statuum. The law does not tolerate fractions and divisions of estates. 1 Coke 87a.

Lex non praecipit inutilia, quia inutilis labor stultus. The law does not command useless things, because useless labor is foolish.

Lex non requirit verificari quod apparet curiae. The law does not require that to be proved which is apparent to the court.

Lex nostra neminem absentem damnat. Our law condemns no one in his absence.

Lex orbis, insanis, et pauperibus pro tutore atque parente est. The law is the guardian and father of orphans, the insane, and the poor.

Lex plus laudatur quando ratione probatur. The law is more praised when it is consonant with reason.

Lex posterior derogat priori. A later statute repeals an earlier one.

Lex posterior generalis non derogat priori speciali. A later, general law does not repeal an earlier specialized law.

Lex prospicit, non respicit. The law looks forward, not backward.

Lex punit mendaciam. The law punishes falsehood.

Lex pure poenalis obligat tantum ad poenam, non item ad culpam; lex poenalis mixta, et ad culpam obligat, et ad poenam. The law that is strictly penal is binding only as to penalty, not as to fault; the mixed penal law is binding as to both fault and penalty.

Lex rejicit superflua, pugnantia, incongrua. The law rejects superfluous, contradictory, and incongruous things.

Lex reprobat moram. The law disapproves of delay.

Lex respicit aequitatem. Law regards equity.

Lex scripta si cesset, id custodiri oportet quod moribus et consuetudine inductum est; et, si qua in re hoc defecerit, tunc id quod proximum et consequens ei est; et, si id non appareat, tunc jus quo urbs Romana utitur servari oportet. If the written law is silent, that which is drawn from manners and custom ought to be observed; and, if that is in any manner defective, then what is next and consistent with it; and, if that does not appear, then the law that Rome uses should be followed.

Lex semper dabit remedium. The law will always give a remedy.

Lex semper intendit quod convenit rationi. The law always intends what is agreeable to reason.

Lex specialis derogat legi generali. A special law detracts from the general law.

Lex spectat ad proximam non ad remotam causam. The law looks to the proximate not to the remote cause.

Lex spectat naturae ordinem. The law regards the order of nature.

Lex succurrit ignoranti. The law assists the ignorant.

Lex succurrit minoribus. The law assists minors.

Lex uno ore omnes alloquitur. The law speaks to all with one mouth.

Lex vigilantibus, non dormientibus, subvenit. Law aids the watchful, not the sleeping.

Liberata pecunia non liberat offerentem. The return of money does not free the party presenting it (from liability).

Libertas est cum quisque quod velit faciat modo secundum leges bonas, communi consensu latas, certas, praefinitas, apertas. Liberty is (the condition) when each may do what he choses, so long as he acts in accordance with good laws, enacted by common consent, that are certain, predetermined, and clear.

Libertas est naturalis facultas ejus quod cuique facere libet, nisi quod de jure aut vi prohibetur. Liberty is the natural power of doing whatever one pleases, except what is prevented by law or force.

Libertas est potestas faciendi id quod jure liceat. Liberty is the power of doing what is permitted by law.

Libertas est res inestimabilis. Liberty is an inestimable thing.

Libertas inaestimabilis res est. Liberty is a priceless good.

Libertas non recipit aestimationem. Freedom does not admit of valuation.

Libertas omnibus rebus favorabilior est. Liberty is more favored than all things.

Libertates regales ad coronam spectantes ex concessione regum a corona exierunt. Royal franchises relating to the Crown have emanated from the Crown by grant of kings.

Libertatis (est) sui quemque juris dimittendi ac retinendi esse dominum. It is part of liberty that everyone be master of quitting or retaining his own right. Cicero, *Pro Balbo* 31.

Libertinum ingratum leges civiles in pristinam servitutem redignunt; sed leges Angliae semel manumissum semper liberum judicant. The civil laws reduce an ungrateful freedman to his original slavery; but the laws of England regard a person once manumitted as ever after free.

Liberum corpus nullam recipit aestimationem. The body of a free person allows no price to be set on it. Dig. 9.3.7.

Liberum est cuique apud se explorare an expediat sibi consilium. Everyone is free to ascertain for himself whether advice is to his advantage.

Liberum est cuique apud se explorare an expediatur sibi consilium. It is free for every one to weigh the matter in his own mind; or to have resort to counsel.

Librorum appellatione continentur omnia volumina, sive in charta, sive in membrana sint, sive in quavis alia materia. Under the name of books are contained all volumes, whether on paper, or on parchment, or on any other material.

Licet dispositio de interesse futuro sit inutilis, tamen potest fieri declaratio praecedens quae sortiatur effectum interveniente novo actu. Even if the grant of a future interest is inoperative, yet a declaration precedent may be made that may take effect, provided a new act intervenes.

Licet eos exheredare quos et occidere licebat. It is permissible to disinherit those whom it was lawful to kill (when the Roman *paterfamilias* had that power over his sons). Dig. 28.2.11 (mentioned as an invalid objection to treating children as *filii familias*).

Licita bene miscentur, formula nisi juris obstet. Lawful acts are well joined together, unless some form of law prevents it.

Ligeantia est quasi legis essentia; est vinculum fidei. Allegiance is, as it were, the essence of the law; it is the bond of faith.

Ligeantia est vinculum fidei; ligeantia est legis essentia. Allegiance is the bond of fealty and the essence of law.

Ligeantia naturalis nullis claustris coercetur, nullis metis refraenatur, nullis finibus premitur. Natural allegiance is restrained by no barriers, curbed by no bounds, compressed by no limits.

Ligna et lapides sub armorum appellatione non continentur. Sticks and stones are not contained under the name of arms.

Linea recta est index sui et obliqui; lex est linea recta. A right line is an index of itself and of an oblique; law is a right line. Co. Litt. 158b.

Linea recta semper praefertur transversali. The right line is always preferred to the collateral.

Literae patentes regis non erunt vacuae. Letters patent of the king will not be void.

Literae scriptae manent. Written words last.

Litis nomen omnem actionem significat, sive in rem, sive in personam sit. The word "lis" (a lawsuit) signifies every action, whether it is in rem or in personam.

Litus est quousque maximus fluctus a mari pervenit. The shore is where the highest wave from the sea has reached.

L'obligation sans cause, ou sur une fausse cause, ou sur cause illicite, ne peut avoir aucun effet. An obligation without consideration, or on a false consideration, or on unlawful consideration, cannot have any effect.

Locus actum regit. The place rules the act.

Locus contractus regit actum. The place of the contract governs the act.

Locus pro solutione reditus aut pecuniae secundum conditionem dimissionis aut obligationis est stricte observandus. The place for the payment of rent or money is to be strictly observed according to the condition of the lease or obligation.

Longa patientia trahitur ad consensum. Long sufferance is construed as consent.

Longa possessio est pacis jus. Long possession is a right of peace.

Longa possessio jus parit. Long possession begets a right.

Longa possessio parit jus possidendi et tollit actionem vero domino. Long possession produces the right of possession and deprives the true owner of his action.

Longum est iter per praecepta, breve et efficax per statuta. The journey is long when prompted by precepts; it is short and efficient when guided by statutes.

Longum tempus et longus usus qui excedit memoriam hominum sufficit pro jure. Long time and long use beyond the memory of men suffice for right.

Loquendum ut vulgus, sentiendum ut docti. We should speak as the common people; we should think as the learned.

L'ou le ley done chose, la ceo done remedie a vener a ceo. Where the law gives a right, it gives a remedy to recover.

Lubricum linguae (glossae) non facile trahendum est in poenam. A slip of the tongue ought not lightly to be submitted to punishment.

Lucrum facere ex pupilli tutela tutor non debet. A guardian ought not to make money out of the guardianship of his ward.

Lunaticus, qui gaudet in lucidis intervallis. A person is (still) a lunatic who enjoys lucid intervals.

M

Magis de bono quam de malo lex intendit. The law favors a good rather than a bad construction. • When an agreement's words are susceptible of both a favorable and unfavorable meaning, the former is adopted. Thus, a bond conditioned to assign all offices will be construed to apply to assignable offices.

Magis jus nostrum quam jus alienum servemus. We should follow our own rather than a foreign law.

Magister rerum usus; magistra rerum experientia. Use is the master of things; experience is the mistress of things.

Magistratus indicat (ostendit) virum. The office shows the man.

Magna Charta et Charta de Foresta sont appelés les deux grandes charters. Magna Carta and the Charter of the Forest are called the two great charters.

Magna componere parvis. To compare great things with small things.

Magna culpa dolus est. Great fault (or gross negligence) is equivalent to fraud.

Magna fuit quondam magnae reverentia chartae. Great was the reverence formerly paid to the Great Charter.

Magna negligentia culpa est; magna culpa dolus est. Great negligence is fault; great fault is fraud.

Maihemium est homicidium inchoatum. Mayhem is incipient homicide.

Maihemium est inter crimina majora minimum, et inter minora maximum. Mayhem is the least of great crimes, and the greatest among small.

Maihemium est membri mutilatio, et dici poterit, ubi aliquis in aliqua parte sui corporis effectus sit inutilis ad pugnandum. Mayhem is the mutilation of a limb, and can be said (to occur) when a person is injured in any part of his body so as to be useless in a fight.

Major continet in se minus. The greater includes the less.

Majore poena affectus quam legibus statuta est non est infamis. A criminal afflicted with a greater punishment than is provided by law is not infamous. 4 Co. Inst. 66.

Major haereditas venit unicuique nostrum a jure et legibus quam a parentibus. A greater inheritance comes to every one of us from right and the laws than comes from parents.

Majori summae minor inest. The lesser is included in the greater sum.

Major numerus in se continet minorem. The greater number contains in itself the less.

Majus continet minus. The greater contains the less.

Majus dignum trahit ad se minus dignum. The more worthy draws to itself the less worthy.

Majus est delictum seipsum interficere quam alium. It is a greater crime to kill oneself than to kill another.

Majus est delictum seipsum occidere quam alium. It is a greater crime to kill oneself than another.

Mala grammatica non vitiat chartam; sed in expositione instrumentorum mala grammatica quoad fieri possit evitanda est. Bad grammar does not vitiate a deed; but in the construction of instruments, bad grammar, as far as possible, is to be avoided.

Male captus, bene detentus. Wrongly captured, well detained.

Maledicta expositio quae corrumpit textum. It is a cursed construction that corrupts the text.

Male enim se res habet, cum quod virtute effici debet id tentatur pecunia. It is a bad situation when what should be achieved by merit is attempted with money. Cicero, *De Officiis* 2.6.22.

Maleficia non debent remanere impunita, et impunitas continuum affectum tribuit delinquendi. Evil deeds ought not to remain unpunished, and impunity affords continual incitement to wrongdoing. 4 Coke 45.

Maleficia propositis distinguuntur. Misdeeds are distinguished from proposals; crimes are distinguished by the intention (with which they are committed).

Malitia est acida, est mali animi affectus. Malice is sour; it is the quality of a bad mind.

Malitia supplet aetatem. Malice makes up for age.

Malitiis hominum est obviandum. The malicious designs of men must be thwarted. • Also found as *Malum hominum est obviandum.*

Malitiis hominum non est indulgendum. The malicious desires of men must not be indulged (or tolerated)

Malum non habet efficientem sed deficientem causam. Evil has not an efficient but a deficient cause.

Malum non praesumitur. Evil is not presumed.

Malum quo communius eo pejus. The more common the evil, the worse.

Malus usus est abolendus. An evil custom ought to be abolished; a bad usage should be abolished.

Malus usus est abolendus, quia in consuetudinibus, non diuturnitas temporis, sed soliditas rationis est consideranda. An evil custom is to be abolished, because, in customs, not length of time, but solidity of reason, is to be considered.

Mandata licita strictam recipiunt interpretationem, sed illicita latam et extensam. Lawful commands receive a strict interpretation, but unlawful ones receive a wide and an expansive interpretation.

Mandatarius terminos sibi positos transgredi non potest. A mandatary cannot exceed the bounds of his authority.

Mandatum nisi gratuitum nullum est. Unless a mandate is gratuitous (without payment), it is not a mandate.

Mandatum non suscipere (cui libet) liberum est; susceptum autem consummandum aut quam primum renuntiandum est, ut aut per semet ipsum aut per alium eandem rem mandator exsequatur. It is an option (for anyone) to decline a mandate, but, when undertaken, it must be fulfilled or renounced as soon as possible, so that the principal may take up the same matter in his own behalf or by another agent. Just. Inst. 3.26.

Manifesta probatione non indigent. Obvious facts are not in need of proof.

Manumittere, quod idem est extra manum vel potestatem ponere. 'Manumission' means the same as putting beyond 'hand' (*manus*) and power. Co. Litt. 137.

Maritagium est aut liberum aut servitio obligatum; liberum maritagium dicitur ubi donator vult quod terra sic data quieta sit et libera ab omni seculari servitio. A marriage portion is either free or bound to service: it is called free (or frank marriage) when the giver wills that the land thus given be exempt from all secular service. Co. Litt. 21.

Matrimonia debent esse libera. Marriages ought to be free.

Matrimonium subsequens legitimos facit quoad sacerdotium non quoad successionem propter consuetudinem regni quae se habet in contrarium. Subsequent marriage legitimates as regards priesthood but not as regards succession because of the custom of the kingdom, which is to the contrary.

Matrimonium subsequens tollit peccatum praecedens. A subsequent marriage removes preceding fault.

Matter en ley ne serra mise en bouche del jurors. Matter of law shall not be put into the mouths of jurors.

Maturiora sunt vota mulierum quam virorum. The wishes of women are of quicker maturity than those of men. • That is, women arrive earlier at eligibility for marriage. 6 Coke 71.

Maxima illecebra est peccandi impunitatis spes. The greatest incitement to sin (or wrongdoing) is the hope of impunity. Cicero, *Pro Milone* 16.43.

Maxime ita dicta quia maxima est ejus dignitas et certissima auctoritas, atque quod maxime omnibus probetur. A maxim is so called because its dignity is chiefest and its authority is the most certain, and because it is most approved by all.

Maxime paci sunt contraria vis et injuria. The greatest enemies to peace are force and wrong.

Maximus erroris populus magister. The people are the greatest master of error.

Meliorem conditionem suam facere potest minor, deteriorem nequaquam. A minor can improve or make his condition better, but in no way worse. • This maxim is sometimes written *Meliorem conditionem facere potest minor, deteriorem nequaquam* (also translatable as "a minor can make his condition better, but by no means worse").

Melior est causa possidentis. The cause of the possessor is preferable.

Melior est conditio defendentis. The condition of the defendant is the better.

Melior est conditio possidentis et rei quam actoris. Better is the condition of the possessor, and that of the defendant (is better) than that of the plaintiff.

Melior est conditio possidentis, ubi neuter jus habet. Better is the condition of the possessor where neither of the two has the right.

Melior est justitia vere praeveniens quam severe puniens. Justice that truly prevents a crime is better than that which severely punishes it.

Melius est in tempore occurrere quam post causam vulneratum remedium quaerere. It is better to respond in time than to seek a remedy after the case is damaged. • Coke introduces this maxim with the phrase *ne per negligentiam damnum incurrat*: "lest he incur damage through negligence." 2 Co. Inst. 299.

Melius est jus deficiens quam jus incertum. Law that is deficient is better than law that is uncertain.

Melius est omnia mala pati quam malo consentire. It is better to suffer every wrong than to consent to wrong.

Melius est petere fontes quam sectari rivulos. It is better to seek the sources than follow the rivulets. Coke Litt. 305b.

Melius est recurrere quam male currere. It is better to run back than to run wrong (or badly). • It is better to retrace one's steps than to proceed improperly.

Melius est ut decem noxii evadant quam ut unus innocens pereat. It is better that ten guilty persons escape than that one innocent person perish.

Melius et tutius si non festines. It is better and safer not to be in haste.

Mens testatoris in testamentis spectanda est. In wills, the intention of the testator is to be regarded.

Mentiri est contra mentem ire. To lie is to go against the mind.

Mercis appellatio ad res mobiles tantum pertinet. The term "merchandise" belongs to movable things only.

Mercis appellatione homines non contineri. Under the name of merchandise human beings are not included.

Merito beneficium legis amittit qui legem ipsam subvertere intendit. A person deservedly loses the protection of the law who attempts to overturn the law itself.

Merito retribuat Rex legi quod lex attribuat ei. The king rightly repays the law what (i.e., the power that) the law ascribes to him; let the king repay to the law what the law attributes to him.

Merx est quidquid vendi potest. Merchandise is whatever can be sold.

Metus quem agnoscunt leges in excusationem criminis est talis qui cadere possit in constantem virum. The fear that the law acknowledges in the excuse of a crime is such as can fall upon a steadfast man.

Meum est promittere, non dimittere. It is mine to promise, not to discharge.

Minatur innocentibus qui parcit nocentibus. A person threatens the innocent who spares the guilty.

Minima poena corporalis est major qualibet pecuniaria. The smallest bodily punishment is greater than any pecuniary one.

Minime mutanda sunt quae certam habuerunt interpretationem. Things that have had a fixed interpretation are to be altered as little as possible.

Minimum est nihilo proximum. The least is next to nothing.

Ministeria recipiunt vicarium, sed non item pleraque judiciaria. The offices of ministers (or administrators) allow substitution, but, for the most part, judicial offices do not.

Minor ante tempus agere non potest in casu proprietatis, nec etiam convenire. A minor before majority cannot act in a case of property, not even to agree.

Minor ante tempus agere non potest in casu proprietatis, nec etiam convenire; differetur usque aetatem; sed non cadit breve. A minor before majority cannot act in a case of property, not even to agree; it will be deferred until majority; but a writ does not fail.

Minor jurare non potest. A minor cannot take an oath.

Minor minorem custodire non debet; alios enim praesumitur male regere qui seipsum regere nescit. A minor ought not be guardian of a minor, for he is presumed to govern others ill who does not know how to govern himself.

Minor non tenetur placitare super haereditate. The minor is not bound to plead on account of his inheritance.

Minor non tenetur respondere durante minori aetati, nisi in causa dotis, propter favorem. A minor is not bound to answer during his minority, except as a matter of favor in a cause of dower.

Minor qui infra aetatem 12 annorum fuerit utlagari non potest nec extra legem poni, quia ante talem aetatem, non est sub lege aliqua nec in decenna. A minor who is under 12 years of age cannot be outlawed nor placed beyond the law, because before that age he is not under any law nor in a decennary.

Minor septemdecim annis non admittitur fore executorem. A person under 17 years of age is not admitted to be an executor.

Minor tenetur in quantum locupletior factus. A minor is bound to the extent to which he has been enriched (or benefited).

Minus est actionem habere quam rem. It is less (of an asset) to have a right of action than to have the property itself. Dig. 50.17.204.

Minus solvit qui tardius solvit; nam et tempore minus solvitur. A person pays too little who pays too late; for, from the delay, the payment is less.

Misera est servitus ubi jus est vagum aut incertum. It is a miserable slavery where the law is vague or uncertain.

Misericordia domini regis est qua quis per juramentum legalium hominum de vicineto eatenus amerciandus est, ne aliquid de suo honorabili contenemento amittat. The mercy of our lord the king is such that anyone may be amerced by a jury of good men from his vicinage (or neighborhood) to this extent (only), that he not lose any part of his honorable tenement. Glanvil, *De Legibus Angliae* IX. 11.

Mitius imperanti melius paretur. The more mildly one commands, the better is he obeyed.

Mobilia non habent situm. Movables have no fixed site or locality.

Mobilia personam sequuntur, immobilia situm. Movable things follow the person; immovable ones, their locality.

Mobilia sequuntur personam. Movables follow the person.

Modica circumstantia facti jus mutat. A small circumstance attending an act alters the right.

Modus debet esse certus, rationabilis, et perantiquus. A custom ought to be reasonable, certain, and very ancient.

Modus de non decimando non valet. A prescription not to pay tithes is void.

Modus et conventio vincunt legem. Customary form and the agreement of the parties overcome the law. • One of the first principles relative to the law of contract. 2 Coke 73.

Modus legem dat donationi. Custom (or form) gives law to a gift.

Moneta est justum medium et mensura rerum commutabilium, nam per medium monetae fit omnium rerum conveniens et justa aestimatio. Money is the just medium and measure of all exchangeable things, for by the medium of money a suitable and just estimation of all things is made.

Monetandi jus comprehenditur in regalibus quae nunquam a regio sceptro abdicantur. The right of coining is included among those rights of royalty that are never relinquished by the kingly scepter.

Monopolium dicitur, cum unus solus aliquod genus mercaturae universum emit, pretium ad suum libitum statuens. It is said to be a monopoly when one person alone buys up the whole of one kind of commodity, fixing a price at his own pleasure.

Monumenta quae nos recorda vocamus sunt veritatis et vetustatis vestigia. The monuments that we call records are the vestiges of truth and antiquity.

Mora debitoris non debet esse creditori damnosa. Delay by a debtor ought not to be injurious to a creditor.

Mora reprobatur in lege. Delay is disapproved of in law.

Mors dicitur ultimum supplicium. Death is called the "extreme penalty" (most severe and last).

Mors omnia solvit. Death dissolves all things.

Morte legatarii perit legatum. By the death of the legatee (during the life of the testator) the legacy lapses.

Morte mandatoris perit mandatum. A mandate fails on the death of the mandant.

Mortgagium scuto magis quam gladio est. A mortgage is used as a shield rather than a sword.

Mortis momentum est ultimum vitae momentum. The moment of death is the last moment of life.

Mortuus exitus non est exitus. A dead issue is not issue. • That is, a child born dead is no child.

Mos retinendus est fidelissimae vetustatis. A custom of the truest antiquity is to be retained.

Mulcta damnum famae non irrogat. A fine does not impose a loss of reputation.

Multa conceduntur per obliquum quae non conceduntur de directo. Many things are conceded indirectly that are not allowed directly.

Multa fidem promissa levant. Many promises lessen confidence.

Multa ignoramus quae nobis non laterent si veterum lectio nobis fuit familiaris. We are ignorant of many things that would not be hidden from us if the reading of old authors were familiar to us.

Multa in jure communi contra rationem disputandi pro communi utilitate introducta sunt. Many things have been introduced into the common law, with a view to the public good, that are contrary to logical reasoning. Co. Litt. 70b.

Multa multo exercitatione facilius quam regulis percipies. You will perceive many things much more easily by practice than by rules.

Multa non vetat lex quae tamen tacite damnavit. The law does not forbid many things that yet it has silently condemned.

Multa transeunt cum universitate quae non per se transeunt. Many things pass with the whole that would not pass separately.

Multi multa, nemo omnia novit. Many men know many things; no one knows everything.

Multiplex et indistinctum parit confusionem; et quaestiones quo simpliciores, eo lucidiores. Multiplicity and indistinctness produce confusion: the simpler questions are, the more lucid they are.

Multiplicata transgressione crescat poenae inflictio. The infliction of punishment should increase with the repetition of the offense. • Coke continues, *Ex frequenti delicto augetur poena* (q.v.). 2 Co. Inst. 479.

Multitudinem decem faciunt. Ten make a multitude.

Multitudo errantium non parit errori patrocinium. The multitude of those who err does not produce indulgence for error.

Multitudo imperitorum perdit curiam. A multitude of ignorant practitioners destroys a court.

Multo utilius est pauca idonea effundere, quam multis inutilibus homines gravari. It is much more useful to pour forth a few suitable things than to burden mankind with many useless things.

Mutua debet esse dominii et homagii fidelitatis connexio, ita quod quantum homo debet domino ex homagio, tantum illi debet dominus ex dominio debet praeter solam reverentiam. The bond of dominion and homage should be mutual, for as much as a man owes his lord from homage, so much the lord owes to him from his lordship, except only reverence. Co. Litt. 64b.

N

Nam qui haeret in litera haeret in cortice. For he who confines himself to the letter sticks at the surface (lit. "in the bark").

Nasciturus pro jam nato habetur quamdiu agitur de ejus commodo. One about to be born is held as already born as long as the issue is to his benefit; a child conceived is treated as born to the extent that it is to his or her benefit.

Natura appetit perfectum, ita et lex. Nature aspires to perfection, and so does the law.

Naturae vis maxima; natura bis maxima. The force of nature is greatest; (and, as some say,) nature is doubly greatest. 2 Co. Inst. 564.

Natura fide jussionis sit strictissimi juris et non durat vel extendatur de re ad rem, de persona ad personam, de tempore ad tempus. The nature of the contract of suretyship is strictissimi juris, and does not endure or should not be extended from thing to thing, from person to person, or from time to time.

Naturale est quidlibet dissolvi eo modo quo ligatur. It is natural for a thing to be dissolved in the same way in which it is bound.

Natura non facit saltum, ita nec lex. Nature makes no leap, and neither does the law.

Natura non facit vacuum, nec lex supervacuum. Nature makes no vacuum, and the law nothing purposeless.

Naufragium commune omnibus est consolatio. A calamity common to all is (also) a consolation. (Or simply *Commune naufragium,* Erasmus, *Adagia* 4.3.9.)

Ne ad consilium antequam voceris. Go not to the council chamber before you are summoned.

Nec beneficium pertinet ad eum qui non debet gerere officium. No benefit belongs to him who was not obliged to perform a certain duty.

Nec curia deficeret in justitia exhibenda. Nor should the court be deficient in showing justice.

Nec enim cum sacco adire debet. One is not obliged to carry a moneybag wherever one goes (when under an obligation to pay immediately). Dig. 46.3.105.

Necessarium est quod non potest aliter se habere. That is necessary which cannot be otherwise.

Necessitas est lex temporis et loci. Necessity is the law of time and place.

Necessitas excusat aut extenuat delictum in capitalibus, quod non operatur idem in civilibus. Necessity excuses or extenuates delinquency in capital cases, but does not have the same effect in civil cases.

Necessitas facit licitum quod alias non est licitum. Necessity makes lawful what otherwise is unlawful.

Necessitas inducit privilegium quoad jura privata. Necessity creates a privilege with regard to private rights.

Necessitas non habet legem. Necessity has no law.

Necessitas publica major est quam privata. Public necessity is greater than private necessity.

Necessitas quod cogit defendit. Necessity defends what it compels.

Necessitas sub lege non continetur, quia quod alias non est licitum necessitas facit licitum. Necessity is not restrained by law; since what otherwise is not lawful necessity makes lawful.

Necessitas vincit legem. Necessity overcomes the law.

Necessitas vincit legem; legum vincula irridet. Necessity overcomes the law; it laughs at the fetters of laws.

Nec regibus infinita aut libera potestas. The power that is given to kings is neither unlimited nor free. Tacitus, *Germania* 1.7.

Nec super eum ibimus, nec super eum mittemus, nisi per legale judicium parium suorum. Nor shall we go upon him, nor send upon him, except by the lawful judgment of his peers; we will not go against him or send against him except by the lawful judgment of his peers. • This language appears in Magna Carta, ch. 39.

Nec tempus nec locus occurrit regi. Neither time nor place thwarts the king.

Nec veniam effuso sanguine casus habet. Where blood has been spilled, the case is unpardonable.

Nec veniam, laeso numine, casus habet. Where the Divinity has been insulted, the case is unpardonable.

Nefarium est per formulas legis laqueos innectere innocentibus. It is vicious to lay snares for the innocent through forms of law.

Ne fictio plus valeat in casu ficto quam veritas in casu vero. A fiction should be of no more value in a fictitious case than truth in a real case.

Negatio conclusionis est error in lege. The denial of a conclusion is error in law.

Negatio destruit negationem, et ambae faciunt affirmationem. A negative destroys a negative, and both make an affirmative.

Negatio duplex est affirmatio. A double negative is an affirmative.

Negatio non potest probari. Denial (or negation) cannot be proved.

Negligentia semper habet infortuniam comitem. Negligence always has misfortune for a companion.

Ne impediatur legatio. May the legation not be impeded.

Ne in crastinum quod possis hodie. Put not off until tomorrow what you can do today.

Ne judex ultra petita partium. May the judge not award beyond the demands of the parties.

Ne licitatorem venditor apponat. The seller should not appoint a bidder.

Neminem laedit qui jure suo utitur. A person who exercises his own rights injures no one.

Neminem oportet esse sapientiorem legibus. No one ought to be wiser than the laws.

Nemini hora est bona ut non alicui sit mala. The hour is good for no one that is not bad for someone. Publilius Syrus.

Nemini in alium plus licet quam concessum est legibus. No one is allowed more against another than is conceded by the laws.

Nemo ad litus maris accedere prohibetur. No one is prohibited from approaching the seashore. Justinian Inst. 2.1.1.

Nemo admittendus est inhabilitare seipsum. No one is allowed to incapacitate himself.

Nemo agit in seipsum. No one acts against himself.

Nemo alienae rei, sine satisdatione, defensor idoneus intelligitur. No one is considered a competent defender of another's property, without security.

Nemo alieno nomine lege agere potest. No one can sue at law in the name of another.

Nemo aliquam partem recte intelligere potest, antequam totum iterum atque iterum perlegerit. No one can properly understand any part of a thing until he has read through the whole again and again.

Nemo allegans suam turpitudinem audiendus est. No one testifying to his own wrong is to be heard as a witness.

Nemo auditur propriam turpitudinem allegans. No one is heard when alleging his own wickedness; no one can be heard whose claim is based on his own disgraceful behavior.

Nemo bis in periculum veniet pro eodem delicto. No one will come twice into danger for the same crime.

Nemo bis punitur pro eodem delicto. No one is punished twice for the same offense.

Nemo bis vexari pro (una et) eadem causa. May no one be troubled twice for (one and) the same cause.

Nemo cogitationis poenam patitur. No one suffers punishment for his thoughts.

Nemo cogitur rem suam vendere, etiam justo pretio. No one is bound to sell his property, even for a just price.

Nemo commodum capere potest de injuria sua propria. No one can derive benefit from his own wrong.

Nemo condemnari debet inauditus nec summonitus. No one should be condemned unheard or unsummoned.

Nemo contra factum suum (proprium) venire potest. No one can contradict his own deed. 2 Co. Inst. 66.

Nemo damnum facit, nisi qui id fecit quod facere jus non habet. No one does damage except the person who did what he has no right to do.

Nemo dare potest quod non habet. No one can give that which he does not have.

Nemo dat qui non habet. No one gives who does not possess.

Nemo dat quod non habet. No one gives what he does not have; no one transfers (a right) that he does not possess. • According to this maxim, no one gives a better title to property than he himself possesses. A variation of this maxim is *Nemo dat qui non habet* (no one gives who does not have).

Nemo debet aliena jactura locupletari. No one ought to be enriched by another's loss.

Nemo debet bis puniri pro uno delicto; quod Deus non agit bis in id ipsum. No one should be punished twice for one crime, as God does not act twice against that very thing. 4 Coke 118.

Nemo debet bis vexari pro eadem causa. No one should be twice troubled for the same cause.

Nemo debet bis vexari pro una et eadem causa. No one ought to be twice troubled for one and the same cause.

Nemo debet bis vexari, si constet curiae quod sit pro una et eadem causa. No one ought to be twice troubled, if it appears to the court that it is for one and the same cause of action.

Nemo debet esse judex in propria causa. No one should be judge in his own cause.

Nemo debet esse testis in sua propria causa. No one ought to be a witness in his own cause.

Nemo debet ex alieno damno lucrari. No one should be enriched out of the loss sustained by another.

Nemo debet immiscere se rei ad se nihil pertinenti. No one should involve himself in a thing that in no respect concerns him.

Nemo debet immiscere se rei alienae ad se nihil pertinenti. No one should interfere in another's business that does not at all concern him.

Nemo debet in communione invitus teneri. No one should be retained in a partnership against his will.

Nemo debet locupletari aliena jactura. No one ought to be enriched at another's expense.

Nemo debet locupletari ex alterius incommodo. No one ought to be enriched out of another's disadvantage.

Nemo debet rem suam sine factu aut defectu suo amittere. No one should lose his property without his own act or negligence.

Nemo de domo sua extrahi potest. No one can be dragged (taken by force) from his own house. Dig. 50.17.103.

Nemo duobus utatur officiis. No one should exercise two offices.

Nemo ejusdem tenementi simul potest esse haeres et dominus. No one can be both heir and owner of the same land at the same time.

Nemo enim aliquam partem recte intelligere possit antequam totum iterum atque iterum perlegerit. No one may be able rightly to understand one part before he has again and again read through the whole.

Nemo enim invitus compellitur ad communionem. For no one is ever forced into joint ownership against his will. Dig. 12.6.26.4; 2 Bl. Com. 185.

Nemo est haeres viventis. No one is an heir of someone living.

Nemo est supra leges. No one is above the laws.

Nemo ex alterius detrimento fieri debet locupletior. No one ought to be made rich out of another person's injury.

Nemo ex alterius facto praegravari debet. No one should be burdened by the act of another.

Nemo ex consilio obligatur. No one is bound for the advice he gives.

Nemo ex dolo suo proprio relevetur aut auxilium capiat. Let no one be relieved or gain advantage by his own fraud.

Nemo ex his qui negant se debere prohibitur etiam alia defensione uti nisi lex impedit. No one who denies they are indebted is prohibited from using any other defense as well, unless the law prevents it. Dig. 50.17.43.

Nemo ex proprio dolo consequitur actionem. No one acquires a right of action from his own wrong (or deception).

Nemo ex suo delicto meliorem suam conditionem facere potest. No one can improve his condition by his own wrong.

Nemo factum a se alienum tenetur scire. No one is bound to know an act or deed that is alien to him (or has nothing to do with him).

Nemo forestam habet nisi rex. Forests belong to no one but the king.

Nemo fuit repente turpissimus. No one has become utterly vile in an instant. Juvenal, *Satire* 2.83.

Nemo habetur agere dolose qui jure se utitur. No one is held to act fraudulently who acts in exercise of his rights.

Nemo inauditus condemnari debet, si non sit contumax. No one ought to be condemned unheard, unless for contempt. • This maxim is sometimes written *Nemo inauditus nec insummonitus condemnari debet, si non sit contumax* (meaning "no one should be condemned unheard and unsummoned, unless for contempt").

Nemo in communione potest invitus detineri. No one can be held (to act) in common against his will; no one can be forced to remain in common ownership against his will. • This maxim states the premise that a coowner can always insist on the division of the property owned.

Nemo in propria causa testis esse debet. No one can be a witness in his own cause.

Nemo jus sibi dicere potest. No one can give judgment for himself.

Nemo locupletari potest cum alterius iactura. Nobody can be made rich at the expense of another.

Nemo militans Deo implicetur secularibus negotiis. No one warring for God should be troubled by secular business.

Nemo mori potest pro parte testatus pro parte intestatus. No one can die partly testate and partly intestate (under Roman law).

Nemo moriturus praesumitur mentiri. No one at the point of death is presumed to lie.

Nemo nascitur artifex. No one is born an expert. • Wisdom in the law is acquired only through diligent study. Co. Litt. 97b.

Nemo patriam in qua natus est exuere, nec ligeantiae debitum ejurare possit. No one can cast off his native land or refuse the obligation of allegiance to it.

Nemo plus commodi haeredi suo relinquit quam ipse habuit. No one leaves a greater asset to his heir than he had himself.

Nemo plus juris ad alienum transferre potest quam ipse haberet. No one can transfer to another a greater right than he himself might have. Dig. 50.17.54.

Nemo potest contra recordum verificare per patriam. No one can verify by the country against a record. • Certain matters of record cannot be contested in court. 2 Co. Inst. 380.

Nemo potest episcopo mandare praeter regem. No one can give a mandate to a bishop except the king.

Nemo potest esse dominus et haeres. No one can be both owner and heir.

Nemo potest esse simul actor et judex. No one can be at the same time suitor and judge.

Nemo potest esse tenens et dominus. No one can be at the same time tenant and landlord (of the same tenement).

Nemo potest exuere patriam. No one can cast off his own country.

Nemo potest facere per alium quod per se non potest. No one can do through another what he cannot do by himself.

Nemo potest facere per obliquum quod non potest facere per directum. No one can do indirectly what he cannot do directly.

Nemo potest gladii potestam sibi datam vel cujus alterius coercitionis ad alium transferre. No one can transfer to another a power of the sword that has been given to him, or any other power to compel.

Nemo potest immittere in alienum. No one can invade (or send anything into) another's property.

Nemo potest mutare consilium suum in alterius injuriam. No one can change his purpose to the injury of another.

Nemo potest nisi quod de jure potest. No one is able to do a thing, unless he can do it lawfully.

Nemo potest plus juris ad alium transferre quam ipse habet. No one can transfer to another a greater right than he himself (actually) has. Co. Litt. 309.

Nemo potest praecise cogi ad factum. No one can be compelled to perform a specific act. • The effect of this maxim is that an order of specific performance is not available.

Nemo potest renunciare juri publico. No one can renounce a public right.

Nemo potest sibi debere. No one can owe to himself.

Nemo potest sibi mutare causam possessionis. No one can change for himself the cause of his possession.

Nemo praedo est qui pretium numeravit. No one is a robber who has paid the price.

Nemo praesens nisi intelligat. One is not present unless he understands.

Nemo praesumitur alienam posteritatem suae praetulisse. No one is presumed to have preferred another's posterity to his own.

Nemo praesumitur donare. No one is presumed to make a gift.

Nemo praesumitur donare vel suum perdere. Nobody is presumed to give a donation or to lose what is his own.

Nemo praesumitur esse immemor suae aeternae salutatis, et maxime in articulo mortis. No one is presumed to be forgetful of his eternal welfare, and especially at the point of death.

Nemo praesumitur ludere in extremis. No one is presumed to trifle at the point of death.

Nemo praesumitur malus. No one is presumed to be bad.

Nemo prohibetur plures negotiationes sive artes exercere. No one is prohibited from exercising several kinds of business or arts.

Nemo prohibetur pluribus defensionibus uti. No one is forbidden to employ several defenses.

Nemo prudens punit ut praeterita revocentur, sed ut futura praeveniantur. No one who is wise gives punishment so that past deeds may be revoked, but so that future deeds may be prevented.

Nemo punitur pro alieno delicto. No one is punished for the crime or wrong of another.

Nemo punitur sine injuria, facto, seu defalta. No one is punished unless for some wrong, act, or default.

Nemo qui condemnare potest absolvere non potest. No one who can condemn is unable to acquit.

Nemo redditum invito domino percipere et possidere potest. No one can take and enjoy the rent without consent of the owner.

Nemo rem suam amittat, nisi ex facto aut delicto suo, aut neglectu. No one should lose his own property, except by his own deed, transgression, or neglect.

Nemo sibi esse judex vel suis jus dicere debet. No one ought to be his own judge or to administer justice in cases where his relations are concerned.

Nemo sine actione experitur, et hoc non sine breve sive libello conventionali. No one goes to trial without an action, and no one can bring an action without a writ or bill.

Nemo tenetur ad impossibile. No one is bound to an impossibility.

Nemo tenetur armare adversarium contra se. No one is bound to arm his adversary against himself.

Nemo tenetur divinare. No one is bound to foretell the future.

Nemo tenetur edere instrumenta contra se. No one is bound to produce writings against himself.

Nemo tenetur informare qui nescit sed quisquis scire quod informat. No one who is ignorant of a thing is bound to give information of it, but everyone is bound to know what he gives information of.

Nemo tenetur jurare in suam turpitudinem. No one is bound to swear to his own criminality.

Nemo tenetur prodere seipsum. No one is bound to betray himself. • In other words, no one can be compelled to incriminate himself.

Nemo tenetur seipsum accusare. No one is bound to accuse himself. • This is a formulation of the privilege against self-incrimination. In good Latin, *se ipsum* appears as two words; but in law the phrase is usually combined to one (*seipsum*).

Nemo tenetur seipsum infortuniis et periculis exponere. No one is bound to expose himself to misfortune and dangers.

Nemo tenetur seipsum prodere. No one is bound to betray himself.

Nemo unquam judicet in se. Let no one ever be a judge in his own cause.

Nemo unquam vir magnus fuit sine aliquo divino afflatu. No one was ever a great man without some divine inspiration.

Nemo videtur fraudare eos qui sciunt et consentiunt. No one is considered as deceiving those who know and consent.

Ne quaere litem cum licet fugere. Don't ask for a lawsuit when you can avoid it.

Neque enim lex aequior ulla est quam necis artifices arte perire sua. There is no law more just than that those who devise death (for others), perish by their own device. Ovid, *Ars Amatoria* 1.655-6.

Neque leges neque senatus consulta ita scribi possunt ut omnes casus qui quandoque inciderint comprehendantur; sed sufficit ea quae plerumque accidunt contineri. Neither laws nor acts of senate can be so written as to include all cases that have happened at any time; it is sufficient that those things that usually occur are encompassed. Dig. 1.3.10. pr.

Ne quid in loco publico vel itinere fiat. Let nothing be done (put or erected) in a public place or way. • The title of an interdict in the Roman law.

Nescis tu quam meticulosa res sit ire ad judicem. You don't know how frightening it is to go before a judge. Plautus, *Mostellaria* 5.1.58.

Ne te ipsum praecipites in discrimen. Don't cast yourself into jeopardy. (Cleobulus: Μὴ ῥιψοκίνδυνος ἔσο)

Nigrum nunquam excedere debet rubrum. The black should never go beyond the red. • That is, the text of a statute should never be read in a sense more comprehensive than the rubric, or title.

Nihil agitur si quid agendum superest. Nothing is done if anything remains to be done.

Nihil aliud potest rex quam quod de jure potest. The king can do nothing but what he can do legally; the king can do nothing except by law.

Nihil calliditate stultius. Nothing is more foolish than cunning.

Nihil consensui tam contrarium est quam vis atque metus. Nothing is so opposite to consent as force and fear.

Nihil cuiquam expedit quod per leges non licet. That which is contrary to law cannot be profitable to any one.

Nihil dat qui non habet. A person gives nothing who has nothing.

Nihil de re accrescit ei qui nihil in re quando jus accresceret habet. Nothing from a property accrues to a person who had no interest in the property when the right accrued. Co. Litt. 188.

Nihil dictum quod non dictum prius. Nothing is said that was not said before.

Nihil est enim liberale quod non idem justum. For there is nothing generous that is not at the same time just.

Nihil est magis rationi consentaneum quam eodem modo quodque dissolvere quo conflatum est. Nothing is more consonant to reason than that everything should be dissolved in the same way as it was made.

Nihil facit error nominis cum de corpore constat. An error in the name is nothing when there is certainty as to the person.

Nihil fit a tempore, quamquam nihil non fit in tempore. Nothing is done by time, although everything is done in time. Grotius, *De Jure Belli ac Pacis* 2.4.1.

Nihil habet forum ex scena. The court has nothing to do with what is not before it.

Nihil honestum esse potest quod justitia vacat. Nothing is honest which lacks justice. Cicero, *De Officiis* 19.62.

Nihil infra regnum subditos magis conservat in tranquilitate et concordia quam debita legum administratio. Nothing better preserves the subjects of the realm in tranquillity and concord than a due administration of the laws. 2 Co. Inst. 158.

Nihil iniquius quam aequitatem nimis intendere. Nothing is more unjust than to extend equity too far.

Nihil in lege intolerabilius est (quam) eandem rem diverso jure censeri. Nothing in law is more intolerable than that the same case should be subject (in different courts) to different views of the law.

Nihil magis justum est quam quod necessarium est. Nothing is more just than what is necessary.

Nihil nequam est praesumendum. Nothing wicked is to be presumed.

Nihil perfectum est dum aliquid restat agendum. Nothing is perfect while something remains to be done.

Nihil peti potest ante id tempus quo per rerum naturam persolvi possit. Nothing can be demanded before the time when, in the nature of things, it can be paid.

Nihil possumus contra veritatem. We have no power against truth.

Nihil praescribitur nisi quod possidetur. There is no prescription for what is not possessed.

Nihil quod est contra rationem est licitum. Nothing that is against reason is lawful.

Nihil quod est inconveniens est licitum. Nothing that is improper is lawful. Co. Litt. 66a.

Nihil quod est licitum est inconveniens. Nothing that is lawful is improper.

Nihil simile est idem. Nothing similar is identical.

Nihil simul inventum est et perfectum. Nothing is invented and perfected at the same moment.

Nihil tam absurdum dici potest ut non dicatur a philosopho. There is (or can be) nothing so absurd but that it may have been uttered by a philosopher. Cicero, *De Divinatione* 2.119.

Nihil tam conveniens est naturali aequitati quam unumquodque dissolvi eo ligamine quo ligatum est. Nothing is so consonant with natural equity as that each thing should be dissolved by the same means as it was bound.

Nihil tam conveniens est naturali aequitati quam voluntatem domini volentis rem suam in alium transferre ratam haberi. Nothing is more consistent with natural equity than to confirm the will of an owner who desires to transfer his property to another.

Nihil tam naturale est quam eo genere quidque dissolvere quo colligatum est. Nothing is so natural as that an obligation should be dissolved by the same principle by which it was contracted.

Nihil tam naturale est quam eo genere quidque dissolvere quo colligatum est; ideo verborum obligatio verbis tollitur; nudi consensus obligatio contrario consensu dissolvitur. Nothing is so natural as to dissolve anything in the way in which it was bound together; therefore the obligation of words is taken away by words; the obligation of mere consent is dissolved by the contrary consent.

Nihil tam proprium imperio quam legibus vivere. Nothing is so becoming to authority as to live according to the law.

Nil agit exemplum litem quod lite resolvit. A precedent accomplishes nothing if it settles one dispute by raising another.

Nil consensui tam contrarium est, qui ac bonae fidei iudicia sustinet, quam vis atque metus. There is nothing so contrary to consent, which sustains decisions of good faith, as force or fear. Dig. 50.11.116.

Nil facit error nominis cum de corpore vel persona constat. An error in the name is immaterial when the body or person is certain.

Nil similius insano quam inebrius. Nothing more strongly resembles a madman than a drunken man.

Nil sine prudenti fecit ratione vetustas. Antiquity did nothing without a good reason.

Nil tam proprium imperii ac libertatis quam legibus vivere. Nothing is so characteristic of dominion and liberty as to live in accordance with law.

Nil temere novandum. Nothing should be rashly changed.

Nil utile aut honestum quod legibus contrarium. Nothing is useful or honorable that is contrary to law.

Nimia certitudo certitudinem ipsam destruit. Too great certainty destroys certainty itself.

Nimia subtilitas in jure reprobatur. Too much subtlety in law is condemned.

Nimia subtilitas in jure reprobatur, et talis certitudo certitudinem confundit. Too great subtlety is disapproved of in law, and such certainty confounds certainty.

Nimium altercando veritas amittitur. By too much quarreling truth is lost.

Nobiles magis plectuntur pecunia, plebes vero in corpore. The higher classes are more punished in money, but the lower in person.

Nobiles sunt qui arma gentilitia antecessorum suorum proferre possunt. The gentry are those who are able to produce the heraldic arms of their own ancestors.

Nobiliores et benigniores praesumptiones in dubiis sunt praeferendae. When in doubt, the more generous and kind presumptions are to be preferred.

Nobilitas est duplex, superior et inferior. There are two sorts of nobility, the higher and the lower.

Nomen est quasi rei notamen. A name is, as it were, the distinctive sign (or signifier) of a thing.

Nomen non sufficit si res non sit de jure aut de facto. A name does not suffice if the thing does not exist by law or by fact.

Nomina si nescis, perit cognitio rerum. If you do not know the names of things, the knowledge of things themselves perishes.

Nomina si nescis, perit cognitio rerum; et nomina si perdas, certe distinctio rerum perditur. If you do not know the names of things, the knowledge of things themselves perishes; and, if you lose the names, the distinction of the things is certainly lost.

Nomina sunt mutabilia, res autem immobiles. Names are mutable, but things immutable.

Nomina sunt notae rerum. Names are the marks of things.

Nomina sunt symbola rerum. Names are the symbols of things.

Non accipi debent verba in demonstrationem falsam, quae competunt in limitationem veram. Words ought not to be accepted to import a false description when they are consistent with a true definition.

Non adimplenti non est adimplendum. It is not necessary to fulfill one's obligation to a person who fails to fulfill his own.

Non alienat qui dumtaxat omittit possessionem. He does not alienate who merely gives up possession. Dig. 50.17.119.

Non alio modo puniatur aliquis, quam secundum quod se habet condemnatio. A person may not be punished otherwise than according to what the sentence enjoins.

Non aliter a significatione verborum recedi oportet quam cum manifestum est aliud sensisse testatorem. We must depart from the (ordinary) significance of words only when it is evident that the testator had a different understanding. Dig. 32.69. pr.

Non auditur perire volens. One who wishes to perish is not heard.

Non autem deperditae dicuntur si postea recuperantur. Things are not said to be lost that are afterwards recovered.

Non bene conducti vendunt perjuria testes. Witnesses who are engaged for no good reason put up their perjury for sale. Ovid, *Amores* 1.10.

Non bis in idem (or imperative, ne bis in idem). Not twice for the same thing. • That is, a person shall not be twice tried for the same crime. This maxim of the civil law expresses the same principle as the familiar rule against "double jeopardy.

Non capitur qui jus publicum sequitur. One who follows public law is not liable. Dig. 50.17.116.1.

Non concedantur citationes priusquam exprimatur super qua re fieri decet citatio. Summonses should not be granted before it is expressed on what ground a summons should be issued.

Non consentit qui errat. A person who errs does not consent.

Non creditur referenti, nisi constet de relato. The reference is not to be credited, unless the thing referred to is proved.

Non crimen per se neque privatum damnum, sed publicum malum, leges spectant. The laws do not regard the crime in itself or as a private loss, but as a public evil.

Non dat qui contra leges dat. He gives nothing who gives contrary to law.

Non dat qui non habet. A person who does not have does not give.

Non debeo melioris conditionis esse quam auctor meus a quo jus in me transit. I cannot be in a better condition (as to my title) than the grantor whose title comes to me. Dig. 50.17.175.

Non deberet alii nocere quod inter alios actum esset. A person ought not to be injured by what has taken place between other parties.

Non debet actori licere quod reo non permittitur. What is not permitted to the defendant ought not to be allowed to the plaintiff.

Non debet adduci exceptio ejus rei cujus petitur dissolutio. An exception (or plea) should not be made on the very matter of which a determination is sought (in the case at hand).

Non debet alii nocere quod inter alios actum est. A person ought not to be prejudiced by what has been done between others.

Non debet alteri per alterum iniqua conditio inferri. An unfair condition ought not to be brought on one person by the act of another.

Non debet cui plus licet quod minus est non licere. A person who is permitted to do the greater thing ought not to be forbidden to do the lesser.

Non debet dici tendere in praejudicium ecclesiasticae liberatatis quod pro rege et republica necessarium videtur. What seems necessary for the king and the state ought not to be said to tend to the prejudice of spiritual liberty.

Non decet homines dedere causa non cognita. It is unbecoming to surrender people when no cause has been shown.

Non decipitur qui scit se decipi. A person is not deceived who knows himself to be deceived.

Non defendere videtur qui, praesens, negat se defendere. One who refuses to defend himself, though present (in court), is regarded as having no defense.

Non definitur in jure quid sit conatus. What an attempt is, is not defined in law.

Non differunt quae concordant re, tametsi non in verbis iisdem. Those things that agree in substance, even if not in the same words, do not differ.

Non dubitatur, etsi specialiter venditor evictionem non promiserit, re evicta, ex empto competere actionem. It is certain that even if the vendor has not given a special guarantee, an action ex empto lies against him, if the purchaser is evicted.

Non efficit affectus nisi sequatur effectus. The intention amounts to nothing unless some effect follows.

Non enim tam auctoritatis in disputando quam rationis momenta quaerenda sunt. For in debate (or discussion) it is not so much the weight of authority that should be sought after as the force of reason. Cicero, *De Natura Deorum* 1.10.

Non erit alia lex Romae, alia Athaenis; alia nunc, alia posthac; sed et omnes gentes, et omni tempore, una lex, et sempiterna, et immortalis continebit. There will not be one law at Rome, another at Athens; one law now, another hereafter; but one eternal and immortal law shall bind together all nations throughout all time.

Non est arctius vinculum inter homines quam jusjurandum. There is no closer (or firmer) link among men than an oath.

Non est certandum de regulis juris. There is no disputing rules of law.

Non est cogendus quis ad substituendum. No one is compelled to substitute another in his own place.

Non est consonum rationi quod cognitio accessorii in curia christianitatis impediatur, ubi cognitio causae principalis ad forum ecclesiasticum noscitur pertinere. It is unreasonable that the cognizance of an accessory matter, should be impeded in an ecclesiastical court, when the cognizance of the principal cause is admitted to appertain to an ecclesiastical court.

Non est deleganda reipublicae cura personae non idoneae. The care (or safe keeping) of the republic must not be delegated to a person not suitable.

Non est disputandum contra principia negantem. There is no disputing against a person who denies first principles.

Non est judex qui judicat minus quam petita partium. He is not a judge who decides less than what is requested from the parties.

Non est lex sed servitus, ad ea teneri quibus non consenseris. It is not law but servitude to be bound by what you have not consented to.

Non est novum ut priores leges ad posteriores trahantur. It is not an innovation to adapt earlier laws to later ones. Dig. 1.3.26.

Non est recedendum a communi observantia. There should be no departure from a common observance.

Non est regula quin fallat. There is no rule that may not deceive (or disappoint).

Non est reus nisi mens sit rea. A person is not guilty unless his mind is guilty.

Non est singulis concedendum quod per magistratum publice possit fieri, ne occasio sit majoris tumultus faciendi. That is not to be conceded to private persons which can be publicly done by the magistrate, lest it be the occasion of greater tumult.

Non exemplis sed legibus judicandum est. Not by examples but by the laws must judgment be made.

Non ex opinionibus singulorum, sed ex communi usu, nomina exaudiri debent. Names of things ought to be understood according to common usage, not according to the opinions of individuals.

Non facias malum ut inde veniat bonum. You are not to do evil that good may come of it.

Non impedit clausula derogatoria quo minus ab eadem potestate res dissolvantur a qua constituuntur. A derogatory clause does not prevent things from being dissolved by the same power by which they were originally made.

Non in legendo sed in intelligendo leges consistunt. The laws consist not in reading but in understanding.

Non in tabulis est jus. It is not in books that the law is to be found.

Non jus ex regula, sed regula ex jure. The law does not arise from the rule (or maxim), but the rule from the law.

Non jus, sed seisina facit stipitem. Not right, but seisin, makes a stock (from which the inheritance must descend).

Non licet quod dispendio licet. That which is permitted only at a loss is not permitted.

Non nasci et natum mori paria sunt. Not to be born and to be born dead are equivalent.

Non obligat lex nisi promulgata. A law is not binding unless it has been promulgated.

Non observata forma, infertur adnullatio actus. When the form has not been observed, an annulment of the act is inferred.

Non officit affectus nisi sequatur effectus. Sed in actrocioribus delictis punitur affectus, licet non sequatur effectus. The intention is not an offense unless an effect follow. But in the most atrocious crimes the intention is punished, although no effect follow.

Non officit conatus nisi sequatur effectus. An attempt does not harm unless a consequence follows.

Non omne damnum inducit injuriam. Not every loss produces an injury (i.e., gives a right to action).

Non omne quod licet honestum est. Not everything that is lawful is honorable; not everything that is allowable is morally right.

Non omnium quae a majoribus nostris constituta sunt ratio reddi potest. Reason cannot always be given for the institutions of our ancestors.

Non pertinet ad judicem secularem cognoscere de iis quae sunt mere spiritualia annexa. It belongs not to the secular judge to take cognizance of things that are merely spiritual.

Non possessori incumbit necessitas probandi possessiones ad se pertinere. It is not incumbent on the possessor of property to prove that his possessions belong to him.

Non potest adduci exceptio ejusdem rei cujus petitur dissolutio. An exception cannot be brought on the same matter whose determination is at issue (in the action at hand).

Non potest probari quod probatum non relevat. That cannot be proved which, when proved, is irrelevant.

Non potest quis sine brevi agere. No one can sue without a writ.

Non potest rex gratiam facere cum injuria et damno aliorum. The king cannot confer a favor that occasions injury and loss to others.

Non potest rex subditum renitentem onerare impositionibus. The king cannot load a subject with impositions against his consent.

Non potest videri desisse habere qui nunquam habuit. A person cannot be considered as having ceased to have a thing who never had it.

Non praestat impedimentum quod de jure non sortitur effectum. A thing that has no effect in law is not an impediment.

Non quod dictum est, sed quod factum est, inspicitur. Not what has been said but what has been done is regarded.

Non quod voluit testator, sed quod dixit in testamento inspicitur. Not what the testator wanted, but what he said in the will, is regarded.

Non recusat ad minora dimittere lex. The law does not refuse to descend to the lesser details.

Non refert an quis assensum suum praefert verbis an rebus ipsis et factis. It is immaterial whether a person gives assent by words or by acts themselves and deeds.

Non refert quid ex aequipollentibus fiat. It does not matter which of two equivalents happens.

Non refert quid notum sit judici, si notum non sit in forma judicii. It matters not what is known to the judge if it is not known to him judicially.

Non refert verbis an factis fit revocatio. It does not matter whether a revocation is made by words or by acts.

Non respondebit minor, nisi in causa dotis, et hoc pro favore doti. A minor shall not answer except in a case of dower, and here in favor of dower.

Non solent quae abundant vitiare scripturas. Superfluous expressions do not usually vitiate writings.

Non solet deterior conditio fieri eorum qui litem contestati sunt quam si non, sed plerumque melior. The condition of those who contest a suit does not ordinarily become worse than if they had not, but for the most part better. Dig. 50.17.86.

Non solum quid licet sed quid est conveniens considerandum, quia nihil quod inconveniens est licitum. Not only what is permitted but what is proper is to be considered, because nothing improper is lawful.

Non sunt longa ubi nihil est quod demere possis. There is no prolixity where there is nothing that you can omit.

Non temere credere est nervus sapientae. Not to believe rashly is the sinew of wisdom.

Non valebit felonis generatio nec ad haereditatem paternam vel maternam; si autem ante feloniam generationem fecerit, talis generatio succedit in haereditate patris vel matris a quo non fuerit felonia perpetrata. The offspring of a felon cannot succeed either to a maternal or paternal inheritance; but if the felon had offspring before the felony, the offspring may succeed to the inheritance of the father or mother by whom no felony was committed.

Non valet confirmatio, nisi ille, qui confirmat, sit in possessione rei vel juris unde fieri debet confirmatio; et eodem modo, nisi ille cui confirmatio fit sit in possessione. Confirmation is not valid unless the person who confirms is in possession either of the thing or of the right of which confirmation is to be made, and, in like manner, unless that person to whom confirmation is made is in possession.

Non valet donatio nisi subsequatur traditio. A gift is not valid unless delivery (or transference) follows.

Non valet exceptio ejusdem rei cujus petitur dissolutio. An exception based on the very matter of which the determination is sought is not valid.

Non valet impedimentum quod de jure non sortitur effectum. An impediment that does not derive its effect from the law has no force.

Non verbis sed ipsis rebus leges imponimus. Not on words, but on affairs themselves do we impose laws.

Non videntur qui errant consentire. They who err are not considered as consenting.

Non videntur rem amittere quibus propria non fuit. They are not considered as losing a thing if it was not their own.

Non videtur cepisse qui, per exceptionem, a petitione removetur. He is not regarded as having obtained his right who is defeated by an exception.

Non videtur consensum retinuisse si quis ex praescripto minantis aliquod immutavit. If a person has changed anything at the demand of a party threatening, he is not considered to have maintained his consent.

Non videtur perfecte cujusque id esse quod ex casu auferri potest. A thing is not considered completely to belong to anyone if it can be taken from him by chance (or occasion).

Non videtur quisquam id capere quod ei necesse est alii restituere. One is not considered to acquire any property in a thing that he is bound to restore to another. Dig. 50. 17. 51.

Non videtur vim facere qui jure suo utitur et ordinaria actione experitur. A person is not judged to use force who exercises his own right and proceeds by ordinary action.

Noscitur a sociis. It is known from its associates.

Noscitur ex socio qui non cognoscitur ex se. A person who is not known for himself is known from his associate.

Nos enim non verbis sed ipsis rebus leges imponimus. Not upon words but upon the things themselves do we impose laws. Just. Codex 6.43.2.3.

Notitia dicitur a noscendo; et notitia non debet claudicare. Notice is named from knowledge; and notice ought not to limp (that is, be imperfect).

Nova constitutio futuris formam imponere debet, non praeteritis. A new enactment ought to impose form on what is to come, not on what is past. • A new regulation should not apply retroactively but from its enactment. 2 Co. Inst. 292.

Novatio non praesumitur. A novation is not presumed.

Novitas non tam utilitate prodest quam novitate perturbat. Novelty does not as much benefit by its utility as it disturbs by its novelty.

Novum judicium non dat novum jus, sed declarat antiquum. A new judgment does not make a new right, but declares the old.

Novum judicium non dat novum jus, sed declarat antiquum; quia judicium est juris dictum, et per judicium jus est noviter revelatum quod diu fuit velatum. A new judgment does not make a new right, but declares the old; because adjudication is the declaration of a right, and by adjudication the right is newly revealed which has long been hidden. 10 Coke 42.

Nuda pactio obligationem non parit. A naked agreement (i.e., without consideration) does not create an obligation. Dig. 2.14.7.4.

Nuda ratio et nuda pactio non ligant aliquem debitorem. Bare reason and naked agreement do not bind any debtor.

Nudum pactum est ubi nulla subest causa praeter conventionem; sed ubi subest causa, fit obligatio, et parit actionem. Naked agreement (nudum pactum) is where there is no consideration besides the agreement; but when there is a consideration, an obligation is created and it gives a right of action.

Nudum pactum ex quo non oritur actio. Naked agreement (nudum pactum) is that from which no action arises.

Nudum pactum inefficax ad agendum. A naked agreement is insufficient for an action.

Nugae seria ducent in mala. Trifles lead to serious mischief. Horace *Epistle ad Pisones* (*Ars Poetica*) 451-2.

Nul charter, nul vente, ne nul done vault perpetualment, si le donor n'est seise al temps de contracts de deux droits, sc. del droit de possession et del droit de properite. No grant, no sale, no gift, is valid forever unless the donor, at the time of the contract, is seised of two rights, namely, the right of possession and the right of property.

Nulla curia quae recordum non habet potest imponere finem neque aliquem mandare carceri; quia ista spectant tantummodo ad curias de recordo. No court that does not have a record can impose a fine or commit any person to prison; because those powers look only to courts of record.

Nulla emptio sine pretio esse potest. There can be no sale without a price.

Nulla falsa doctrina est quae non permisceat aliquid veritatis. No doctrine is so false but it may not be mixed up with some truth.

Nulla impossibilia aut inhonesta sunt praesumenda; vera autem et honesta et possibilia. No impossible or dishonorable things are to be presumed; but things true, honorable, and possible.

Nulla lex, nulla iniuria. No law, no wrong.

Nulla pactione effici potest ne dolus praestetur. No agreement is sufficient to effect that there be no liability for fraud. Dig. 2.14.27.3.

Nulla res vehementius rempublicam continet quam fides. Nothing sustains the republic more strongly than its credit. Cicero, *De Officiis* 2.24.84. • The maxim is often understood, "Nothing binds the republic together more . . . than loyalty of its citizens."

Nulla sasina, nulla terra. No fee (or seisin), no land.

Nulla unquam de morte hominis cunctatio longa est. No delay is ever (too) long when a man's life is at stake. Juvenal, *Satire* 6.221.

Nulla virtus, nulla scientia locum suum et dignitatem conservare potest sine modestia. Without moderation, no virtue, no knowledge can preserve its place and dignity.

Nulle régle sans faute. There is no rule without fault.

Nulle terre sans seigneur. No land without a lord.

Nulli enim res sua servit jure servitutis. No one can have a servitude over his own property.

Nullius charta legibus potest derogare. No one's written deed can derogate from the laws.

Nullius hominis auctoritas apud nos valere debet, ut meliora non sequeremur si quis attulerit. The authority of no person ought to have (such) power among us that we should not follow better (opinions) if anyone presents them.

Nulli vendemus, nulli negabimus, aut differemus rectum vel justitiam. We shall sell to no one, deny to no one, or delay to no one, equity or justice. • This language appeared in Magna Carta.

Nullum anarchia majus est malum. There is no evil greater than anarchy.

Nullum crimen majus est inobedientia. No crime is greater than disobedience.

Nullum crimen patitur is qui non prohibet cum prohibere non potest. He who fails to prevent what he cannot prevent is guilty of no crime. Dig. 50.17.109.

Nullum damnum sine remedio. There is no loss without a remedy.

Nullum exemplum est idem omnibus. No example is the same for all purposes.

Nullum iniquum est praesumendum in jure. Nothing unjust is to be presumed in law.

Nullum matrimonium, ibi nulla dos. No marriage, there no dower.

Nullum medicamentum est idem omnibus. No medicine is the same (or equally effective) for all.

Nullum simile est idem. Nothing that is like another is the same. • That is, no likeness is exactly identical.

Nullum simile est idem nisi quatuor pedibus currit. Nothing similar is identical, unless it run on all fours.

Nullum simile quatuor pedibus currit. No simile runs on four feet (on all fours). • No simile holds in every respect.

Nullum tempus aut locus occurrit regi. No time or place bars the king.

Nullum tempus occurrit regi. No period of time bars the Crown; no length of time runs against the king. • This maxim expresses the idea that the king is not bound by any statute of limitations.

Nullum tempus occurrit reipublicae. No time runs against the commonwealth (or state).

Nullus alius quam rex possit episcopo demandare inquisitionem faciendam. No other than the king can command the bishop to make an inquisition.

Nullus commodum capere potest de injuria sua propria. No one can gain advantage by his own wrong.

Nullus debet agere de dolo, ubi alia actio subest. Where another form of action is given, no one ought to sue in the action de dolo.

Nullus dicitur accessorius post feloniam sed ille qui novit principalem feloniam fecisse, et illum receptavit et comfortavit. No one is called an accessory after the fact but that person who knew the principal to have committed a felony, and received and comforted him.

Nullus dicitur felo principalis nisi actor aut qui praesens est, abettans aut auxilians actorem ad feloniam faciendam. No one is called a principal felon except the party actually committing the felony, or the party who was present aiding and abetting the perpetrator in its commission.

Nullus idoneus testis in re sua intelligitur. No one is understood to be a competent witness in his own cause.

Nullus jus alienum forisfacere potest. No one can forfeit another's right.

Nullus liber homo capiatur, aut imprisonetur. Let no free man be taken or imprisoned. • This expression derives from Magna Carta, ch. 39

Nullus liber homo disseisietur de libero tenemento suo, nisi per legale judicium parium suorum, vel per legem terrae. No freeman shall be dispossessed of his freehold, save by the lawful judgment of his peers, or by the law of the land.

Nullus recedat e curia cancellaria sine remedio. Let no one depart from the court of chancery without a remedy.

Nullus videtur dolo facere qui suo jure utitur. No one is to be regarded as acting by fraud who exercises his legal right.

Nul ne doit s'enrichir aux depens des autres. No one ought to enrich himself at the expense of others.

Nul prendra advantage de son tort demesne. No one shall take advantage of his own wrong.

Nul sans damage avera error ou attaint. No one shall have error or attaint unless there has been damage.

Numerus certus pro incerto ponitur. A certain number is substituted for one that is uncertain.

Nummus est mensura rerum commutandarum. Money is the measure of things that are to be exchanged.

Nunquam crescit ex post facto praeteriti delicti aestimatio. The valuation (or assessment of damage) for a past offense is never increased by what happens subsequently. Dig. 50.17.138.1.

Nunquam decurritur ad extraordinarium sed ubi deficit ordinarium. One never resorts to the extraordinary but when the ordinary fails.

Nunquam fictio sine lege. There is no fiction without law.

Nunquam nimis dicitur quod nunquam satis dicitur. What is never sufficiently said is never said too much.

Nunquam praescribitur in falso. There is never prescription in case of falsehood (or forgery).

Nunquam res humanae prospere succedunt ubi negliguntur divinae. Human affairs never prosper when divine ones are neglected.

Nuptias non concubitus sed consensus facit. Not sharing a bed but consent makes the marriage.

O

Obedientia est legis essentia. Obedience is the essence of the law.

Ob infamiam non solet juxta legem terrae aliquis per legem apparentem se purgare, nisi prius convictus, vel

confessus in curia. Faced with accusation (of a crime), it is not usual for a man to acquit himself by law of the land (by battle or ordeal) unless he has been previously convicted, or confessed in open court. Glanvil Book 14, ch.2.

Obtemperandum est consuetudini rationabili tanquam legi. A reasonable custom is to be obeyed like law.

Occultatio thesauri inventi fraudulosa. The concealment of discovered treasure is fraudulent.

Occupantis fiunt derelicta. Things abandoned become the property of the (first) occupant.

Occupatio non praecedit nisi in re terminata. Seizure does not proceed except in a resolved situation.

Oderunt peccare boni, virtutis amore; oderunt peccare mali, formidine poenae. Good men hate sin through love of virtue; bad men, through fear of punishment. (Extention of Horace, *Epist.* 1.16.52.)

Odio et amore judex careat. Let a judge be free from hatred and love.

Odiosa et inhonesta non sunt in lege praesumenda. Odious and dishonest acts are not to be presumed in law.

Odiosa non praesumuntur. Odious things are not presumed.

Officia judicialia non concedantur antequam vacent. Judicial offices ought not to be granted before they are vacant.

Officia magistratus non debent esse venalia. The offices of magistrates ought not to be sold.

Officit conatus si effectus sequatur. The attempt becomes of consequence if the effect follows.

Officium nemini debet esse damnosum. An office ought to be injurious to no one.

Omissio eorum quae tacite insunt nihil operatur. The omission of those things that are silently implied is of no consequence.

Omne accessorium sequitur suum principale. Every accessory follows its principal.

Omne accessum sequitur suum principale. Every increase follows its principal.

Omne actum ab intentione agentis est judicandum; a voluntate procedit causa vitii atque virtutis. Every act must be judged by the intention of the doer; the cause of vice and virtue proceeds from the will.

Omne crimen ebrietas et incendit et detegit. Drunkenness both inflames and reveals every crime.

Omne jus aut consensus fecit, aut necessitas constituit, aut firmavit consuetudo. Every right has been derived from consent, established by necessity, or confirmed by custom.

Omne jus et omnis actio injuriarum tempore finita et circumscripta sunt. Every right and every action are limited and circumscribed by the time of the injuries.

Omne magis dignum trahit ad se minus dignum, quamvis minus dignum sit antiquius. Every worthier thing draws to it the less worthy, even if the less worthy is more ancient.

Omne magnum exemplum habet aliquid ex iniquo, quod publica utilitate compensatur. Every great example has some portion of evil, which is compensated by its public utility.

Omne majus continet in se minus. Every greater thing contains in itself the less.

Omne majus dignum continet in se minus dignum. Every more worthy thing contains in itself the less worthy.

Omne majus minus in se complectitur. Every greater thing embraces in itself the lesser.

Omne majus trahit ad se quod est minus. Every greater thing attracts to itself that which is less. Co. Litt. 43b.

Omne nimium vertitur in vitium. Every excess becomes a vice.

Omne principale trahit ad se accessorium. Every principal thing draws to itself the accessory.

Omne quod solo inaedificatur solo cedit. Everything that is built on the soil belongs to the soil.

Omne sacramentum debet esse de certa scientia. Every oath ought to be founded on certain knowledge.

Omnes actiones in mundo infra certa tempora habent limitationem. All actions in the world are limited within certain periods.

Omnes bonos bonasque accurare addecet, suspicionem et culpam ut ab se segregent. It behooves all good men and good women to take care that they keep themselves free of suspicion and blame. Plautus, *Trinummus* 41-2.

Omnes in defensionem reipublicae vita bonisque omnibus cives tenentur. All subjects are bound to defend the state with their lives and all their possessions.

Omnes licentiam habere his quae pro se indulta sunt renunciare. All have liberty to renounce these things that have been granted in their favor.

Omnes prudentes illa admittere solent quae probantur iis qui in arte sua bene versati sunt. All prudent people are accustomed to admit those things that are approved by those who are skilled in their profession.

Omnes sorores sunt quasi unus haeres de una haereditate. All sisters are as it were one heir to one inheritance.

Omnes subditi sunt regis servi. All subjects are the king's servants.

Omne testamentum morte consummatum est. Every will is consummated by death.

Omne verbum de ore fideli cadit in debitum. Every word sincerely spoken constitutes an obligation.

Omnia dat qui justa negat. One who denies what is just grants (his adversary) everything. Lucan, *Pharsalia* 1.348.

Omnia delicta in aperto leviora sunt. All crimes committed openly are considered lighter.

Omnia Deo grata, hominibus utilia, reipublicae honesta, privatis justa et commoda probant leges, et pro viribus cuique imponunt. All things pleasing to God, useful to men, honorable to the State, just and advantageous to private persons, the laws approve and impose upon each person according to his powers.

Omnia honeste et ordine fiant. Let all things be done honestly and in order.

Omnia libere et legaliter facienda. All things should be done freely and legally.

Omnia mala exempla bonis principiis orta sunt. All bad precedents have their origin in good beginnings.

Omnia praesumuntur contra spoliatorem. All presumptions are against one who wrongfully dispossesses another (a despoiler).

Omnia praesumuntur in odium spoliatoris. All things are presumed in hatred of the spoliator.

Omnia praesumuntur legitime facta donec probetur in contrarium. All things are presumed to have been done lawfully until there is proof to contrary. Co. Litt. 232b.

Omnia praesumuntur pro matrimonio. All things are presumed in favor of marriage.

Omnia praesumuntur rite ac sollemniter esse acta. All things are presumed to be done in proper and regular form; all things are presumed to have been rightly and regularly done. • *Solemniter* is sometimes written *sollenniter.* — Also written *Omnia praesumuntur rite et sollemniter acta.*

Omnia praesumuntur rite et solemniter esse acta donec probetur in contrarium. All things are presumed to have been done regularly and with due formality until the contrary is proved.

Omnia prius verbis experiri quam armis sapientem decet. It is the part of wisdom to exhaust negotiation before resorting to arms. Terence, *Eunuch* 789.

Omnia, quaecunque causae cognitionem desiderant, per libellum expediri non possunt. All those causes that require detailed examination cannot be settled by petition (*libellus*). Dig. 50.17.71.

Omnia quae jure contrahuntur contrario jure pereunt. All obligations contracted under a law are destroyed by a law to the contrary.

Omnia quae movent ad mortem sunt deodanda. All things that cause death while they are in motion become deodands.

Omnia quae nunc vetustissima creduntur nova fuere; et quod hodie exemplis tuemur inter exempla erit. All that we now consider as ancient was at one time new; and what we respect as examples today, will in the future be received as precedents. Tacitus, *Annales* 11.24.

Omnia rite esse acta praesumuntur. All things are presumed to have been done in due form.

Omnibus infra regnum orantibus legis remedium patet. The remedy of the law lies open to all within (or subject to) the realm who ask for it.

Omnis actio est loquela. Every action is a complaint.

Omnis conclusio boni et veri judicii sequitur ex bonis et veris praemissis et dictis juratorum. Every conclusion of a good and true judgment follows from good and true premises and the verdicts of jurors.

Omnis consensus tollit errorem. Every consent removes an error. 2 Co. Inst. 123.

Omnis contractus turpitudinis legibus invisus. Every contract for an immoral end is odious to the laws.

Omnis definitio in jure civili periculosa est, parum est enim ut non subverti possit. Every definition in the civil law is dangerous, for there is very little that cannot be overthrown.

Omnis exceptio est ipsa quoque regula. Every exception is itself also a rule.

Omnis indemnatus pro innoxio legibus habetur. Every uncondemned person is held by the law as innocent.

Omnis innovatio plus novitate perturbat quam utilitate prodest. Every innovation disturbs by its novelty more than it benefits by its usefulness.

Omnis interpretatio si fieri potest ita fienda est in instrumentis, ut omnes contrarietates amoveantur. Every interpretation of instruments is to be made, if it can be, so that all contradictions may be removed.

Omnis interpretatio vel declarat, vel extendit, vel restringit. Every interpretation explains, or extends, or restricts.

Omnis lascivia legibus vetita. All wantonness is contrary to law.

Omnis nova constitutio futuris formam imponere debet, et non praeteritis. Every new enactment should regulate future, not past transactions; every new law must impose its form on future cases and not past ones. • This maxim states the presumption against retroactivity. The phrase is sometimes written *Omnis nova constitutio futuris (temporibus) formam imponere debet, non praeteritis.*

Omnis persona est homo, sed non vicissim. Every person is a human being, but not every human being a person.

Omnis privatio praesupponit habitum. Every privation presupposes possession. • "Every discontinuance is a privation . . . and he cannot discontinue that estate which he never had." Co. Litt. 339a.

Omnis prohibitio mandato equiparatur. Every prohibition is equivalent to a command.

Omnis querela et omnis actio injuriarum limitata est infra certa tempora. Every plaint and every action for injuries is limited within fixed times.

Omnis ratihabitio retrotrahitur et mandato priori aequiparatur. Every subsequent ratification has a retrospective effect and is equivalent to a prior command.

Omnis regula suas patitur exceptiones et omnis exceptio est regula. Every rule is subject to its own exceptions, and every exception is a rule.

Omnium contributione sarciatur quod pro omnibus datum est. What has been given for all should be compensated by the contribution of all.

Omnium rerum quarum usus est, potest esse abusus, virtute solo excepta. Of everything of which there is a use, there can be abuse, virtue alone excepted.

Opinionis commenta delet dies, naturae judicia confirmat. Time destroys the inventions of opinion but confirms the judgments of nature. Cicero, *De Natura Deorum* 2.2.5.

Opinio quae favet testamento est tenenda. That opinion is to be followed which favors the will.

Oportet etiam quod certa res deducatur in donationem, quia incertae rei nulla est donatio. It is necessary that a certain thing be brought into the gift (or conveyance), for if the thing is uncertain, there is no gift. Bracton 2.62.

Oportet quod certae personae, certae terrae, et certi status comprehendantur in declaratione usuum. It is right that certain persons, certain lands, and certain estates should be comprehended in a declaration of uses. 9 Coke 9.

Oportet quod certa res deducatur in judicium. A thing, to be brought to judgment, must be definite.

Oportet quod certa sit res quae venditur. A thing, to be sold, must be definite.

Opposita juxta se posita magis elucescunt. Things opposite when placed together appear in a clearer light. • That is, things opposite are more conspicuous when placed together.

Optandum est ut ii qui praesunt reipublicae legum similes sint, quae, ad puniendum, non iracundia, sed aequitate ducuntur. It is desirable that those set in authority over the state shall be like the laws of the state, which, in inflicting punishment, are influenced not by anger, but by justice. Cicero, *De Officiis* 1.89.

Optima enim est legium interpres consuetudo. Custom is the best interpreter of laws. Dig. 1.3.37.

Optima est legis interpres consuetudo. Custom is the best interpreter of the law.

Optima est lex quae minimum relinquit arbitrio judicis; optimus judex qui minimum sibi. It is the best law that leaves the least to the discretion of the judge; the best judge is he who leaves least to himself.

Optima evidentia rei praevalebit. The best evidence of the matter will prevail (*or* be more efficacious).

Optima legum interpres est consuetudo. Custom is the best interpreter of law.

Optimam esse legem quae minimum relinquit arbitrio judicis; id quod certitudo ejus praestat. The law is the best that leaves the least discretion to the judge; this advantage results from its certainty.

Optima statuti interpretatrix est (omnibus particulis ejusdem inspectis) ipsum statutum. The best interpreter of a statute is (when all the separate parts of it have been considered) the statute itself.

Optimi consiliarii mortui. The dead are the best counselors.

Optimus interpres rerum usus. Usage is the best interpreter of things.

Optimus interpretandi modus est sic leges interpretare ut leges legibus accordant. The best mode of interpreting laws is to make laws agree with laws.

Optimus judex qui minimum sibi. He is the best judge who (leaves) the least to his own discretion.

Optimus legum interpres consuetudo. Custom is the best interpreter of laws.

Ordine placitandi servato, servatur et jus. When order of pleading has been preserved, the law is also preserved.

Origine propria neminem posse voluntate sua eximi manifestum est. It is manifest that no one by his own will can be stripped of his origin (or be banished from his place of origin).

Origo rei inspici debet. The origin of a thing ought to be regarded.

P

Pacta conventa quae neque contra leges neque dolo malo inita sunt, omni modo observanda sunt. Contracts that have been entered neither illegally nor with fraud must in all respects be observed.

Pacta dant legem contractui. Agreements give law to the contract.

Pacta non obligant nisi gentes inter quas inita. Agreements bind only the peoples between whom they are made.

Pacta privata juri publico derogare non possunt. Private contracts cannot restrict (or take away from) public law.

Pacta quae contra leges constitutionesque vel contra bonos mores fiunt nullam vim habere, indubitati juris est. It is a matter of unquestionable law that contracts against the laws and statutes, or against moral standards, have no force.

Pacta quae turpem causam continent non sunt observanda. Contracts founded on an immoral consideration are not to be observed.

Pacta reciproca vel utrosque ligant vel neutrum. Mutual bargains bind both parties or neither.

Pacta sunt servanda. Treaties (agreements) are to be observed.

Pacta tertiis nec nocent nec prosunt. Treaties (agreements) neither harm nor benefit third parties.

Pactis privatorum juri publico non derogatur. There is no derogation from public law by private contracts.

Pacto aliquid licitum est quod sine pacto non admittitur. By agreement (or contract) something is permitted that, without agreement, is not allowed. • Coke continues, "but not in violation of public law." Co. Litt. 166.

Pactum de assedatione facienda et ipsa assedatione aequiparantur, praecipue si possessio sequatur. An agreement to grant a lease is equivalent to the lease itself, especially if possession follows.

Pannagium est pastus porcurum, in nemoribus et in silvis, de glandibus, etc. A pannagium is a pasture of hogs, in woods and forests, upon acorns, and so forth.

Parens est nomen generale ad omne genus cognationis. "Parent" is a general name for every kind of relationship.

Parentum est liberos alere etiam nothos. It is the role of parents to support their children even when illegitimate.

Paria copulantur paribus. Similar things unite with similar.

Paribus sententiis reus absolvitur. When opinions are evenly divided, the defendant is acquitted. 4 Co. Inst. 64.

Paries oneri ferundo uti nunc est ita sit. A party wall is to remain (for both tenements) intact in its present condition.

Par in parem imperium non habet. An equal has no power over an equal.

Par in parem non habet iurisdictionem. Equals have no jurisdiction over each other.

Parium eadem est ratio, idem jus. Of things equal, the reason and the law is the same.

Partem aliquam recte intelligere nemo potest, antequam totum iterum atque iterum perlegerit. No one can rightly understand any part until he has read the whole again and again.

Parte quacumque integrante sublata, tollitur totum. When any essential part has been removed, the whole is removed (or destroyed).

Participes plures sunt quasi unum corpus, in eo quod unum jus habent, et oportet quod corpus sit integrum, et quod in nulla parte sit defectus. Many parceners are as one body, inasmuch as they have but one right, and it is necessary that the body be perfect, and that there be a defect in no part. Co. Litt. 164a.

Partus ex legitimo thoro non certius noscit matrem quam genitorem suum. The offspring of a legitimate bed does not know his mother more certainly than his father.

Partus sequitur ventrem. The offspring follows the condition of the mother (literally, the womb).

Parum cavet natura. Nature takes little heed.

Parum differunt quae re concordant. Things which agree in substance differ but little.

Parum est latam esse sententiam, nisi mandetur executioni. It is not enough that judgment has been given if it is not committed to execution.

Parum proficit scire quid fieri debet si non cognoscas quomodo sit facturum. It does little good to know what ought to happen, if you do not know how it will take effect.

Pater est quem nuptiae demonstrant. The father is the man whom the marriage indicates. • This expresses the idea that a child born to a married woman is presumed begotten by her husband.

Pater et mater et puer sunt una caro. The father, mother, and son are one flesh.

Pater is est quem nuptiae demonstrant. The father is he whom the marriage indicates.

Patria laboribus et expensis non debet fatigari. A jury ought not to be wearied with labors and expenses.

Patriam decet nobis cariorem esse quam nosmet ipsos. Our country should be dearer to us than ourselves. Cicero, *De Finibus* 3.19.64.

Patria potestas in pietate debet, non in atrocitate consistere. Parental authority should consist in devotion, not dread.

Patronum faciunt dos, aedificatio, fundus. Endowment, building, and land make a patron.

Peccata contra naturam sunt gravissima. Offenses against nature are the most serious.

Peccata suos teneant auctores, nec ulterius progrediatur metus quam reperiatur delictum. Offenses should bind their own perpetrators (only), and threat (of punishment) should not proceed further than the sphere of the crime.

Peccat mens, non corpus, et unde consilium abfuit poena abest. The mind sins, not the body, and where there was no intent, there is no blame. Livy 1.58.9.

Peccatum peccato addit qui culpae quam facit patrocinium defensionis adjungit. A person adds one offense to another, who, when he commits a crime, joins to it the protection of a defense.

Pendente lite nihil innovetur. During litigation, let nothing be changed.

Per alluvionem id videtur adici, quod ita paulatim adicitur ut intelligere non possimus quantum quoque momento temporis adiciatur. That is considered "added by alluvion" which accumulates so gradually that we cannot tell how much is added at any one moment of time. Dig. 41.1.7.1.

Pereat unus ne pereant omnes. Let one perish that all not perish. 4 Coke 124b.

Perfectum est cui nihil deest secundum suae perfectionis vel naturae modum. That is perfect which lacks nothing according to the measure of its perfection or nature.

Periculosum est res novas et inusitatas inducere. It is dangerous to introduce new and unaccustomed things.

Periculosum existimo quod bonorum virorum non comprobatur exemplo. I consider that dangerous which is not approved by the example of good men.

Periculum rei venditae, nondum traditae, est emptoris. The purchaser assumes the risk for a thing sold, but not yet delivered.

Per judicium jus est noviter revelatum quod diu fuit velatum. By judgment the law that was long concealed is newly revealed.

Perjurii poena divina exitium; humana dedecus. The divine punishment of perjury is destruction; the human punishment is disgrace. Cicero, *De Legibus* 2.22.6.

Perjuri sunt qui servatis verbis juramenti decipiunt aures eorum qui accipiunt. Those who preserve the words of an oath but deceive the ears of those who accept it are perjurors. • Coke adds, "By ancient law of England, in all oathes equivocation is utterly condemned." 3 Co. Inst. 166.

Perpetua lex est nullam legem humanam ac positivam perpetuam esse; et clausula quae abrogationem excludit ab initio non valet. It is a perpetual law that no human or positive law can be perpetual; and a clause in a law that precludes abrogation is void from the outset.

Per rationes pervenitur ad legitimam rationem. By reasoning we come to legal reason.

Per regulam igitur brevis rerum narratio traditur, et quasi causae coniectio est, quae simul cum in aliquo vitiata est perdit officium suum. By a "rule" (*regula*), therefore, a brief account of events is given, and is as it were a summary of a case, which loses its force as soon as it is vitiated in any respect. Dig. 50.17.1.

Per rerum naturam factum negantis nulla probatio est. By the nature of things, a person who denies a fact is not bound to give proof.

Persona conjuncta aequiparatur interesse proprio. A personal connection is equivalent to one's own interest.

Personae regis mergitur persona ducis. The person of duke merges in that of king.

Persona est homo cum statu quodam consideratus. A person is a human being considered with reference to a certain status.

Personae vice fungitur municipium et decuria. Towns and boroughs act in the role of persons.

Personalia personam sequuntur. Personal things follow the person.

Perspicua vera non sunt probanda. Plain truths are not to be proved.

Per varios actus legem experientia facit. In the course of various acts, experience frames the law.

Pirata est hostis humani generis. A pirate is an enemy of the human race.

Pirata non mutat dominium. A pirate (i.e., piracy) does not change ownership.

Placita de transgressione contra pacem regis, in regno Angliae vi et armis facta, secundum legem et consuetudinem Angliae sine brevi regis placitari non debent. Pleas of trespass against the peace of the king in the kingdom of England, made with force and arms, ought not, by the law and custom of England, to be pleaded without the king's writ.

Placita ex directo esse debent, et nil per inductionem supponere. Pleas ought to be directly expressed and suppose nothing by way of inference.

Placita negativa duo exitum non faciunt. Two negative pleas do not form an issue.

Placitorum alia dilatoria, alia peremptoria. Some pleas admit of delay; others are peremptory.

Placitum aliud personale, aliud reale, aliud mixtum. One plea is personal, another real, (yet) another mixed.

Placitum mendax non est placitum. A lying plea is no plea ("not pleasing" or not accepted).

Plena et celeris justitia fiat partibus. Let the parties have full and speedy justice.

Pluralis numerus est duobus contentus. The plural number is satisfied with two.

Plures cohaeredes sunt quasi unum corpus, propter unitatem juris quod habent. Several coheirs are as one body, by reason of the unity of right that they possess.

Plures participes sunt quasi unum corpus in eo quod unum jus habent. Several coheirs (or parceners) are as one body in that they have one right. Co. Litt. 164.

Plus exempla quam peccata nocent. Examples hurt more than offenses.

Plus peccat auctor quam actor. The instigator of a crime is a worse offender than the perpetrator.

Plus valet consuetudo quam concessio. Custom is more powerful than grant.

Plus valet unus oculatus testis quam auriti decem. One eyewitness is better than ten earwitnesses.

Plus valet vulgaris consuetudo quam regalis concessio. Common custom is better than royal grant.

Plus vident oculi quam oculus. Several eyes see more than one.

Poena ad paucos, metus ad omnes perveniat. Let punishment be inflicted on a few, dread on all.

Poenae potius molliendae quam exasperandae sunt. Punishments should rather be softened than aggravated.

Poenae sunt restringendae. Punishments should be restrained.

Poena ex delicto defuncti haeres teneri non debet. The heir ought not to be penalized for the wrong (or crime) of the decedent.

Poena gravior ultra legem posita estimationem conservat. A heavier punishment, set beyond the law, preserves esteem (or standing of a defendant otherwise discredited). Dig. 3.2.13.7.

Poena non debet anteire crimen. Punishment ought not to precede the charge.

Poena non potest, culpa perennis erit. Punishment cannot be, guilt will be, perpetual.

Poena suos tenere debet actores et non alios. Punishment should take hold of the guilty (who commit the wrong), and not others. Bracton 380b.

Poena tolli potest, culpa perennis erit. The punishment can be removed, but the guilt will be perpetual.

Poena vel remedium ex incremento quod prius erat non tollit. Neither punishment nor remedy takes away the preceding increase.

Politiae legibus, non leges politiis, adaptandae. Politics are to be adapted to the laws, not the laws to politics.

Polygamia est plurium simul virorum uxorumve connubium. Polygamy is being married to more than one husband or wife at one time.

Ponderantur testes, non numerantur. Witnesses are weighed, not counted.

Pondere, numero, et mensura. By weight, by number, and by measure. (A rule for the valuation of evidence)

Populus Anglicanus nemini servire nisi Deo et legibus. The people of England are subject to none but to God and the laws.

Populus Anglicanus non nisi suis legibus quas ipse elegerit tenetur obtemperare. The people of England are bound to obey only their own laws, which they themselves have chosen.

Populus vult decipi–et decipiatur. The people wishes to be deceived – and let it be deceived.

Posito uno oppositorum negatur alterum. One of two opposite positions having been affirmed, the other is denied.

Positus in conditione non censetur positus in institutione. One placed (or named) in a condition is not regarded as instituted (placed in the appointment).

Possessio contra omnes valet praeter eum cui jus sit possessionis. Possession is valid against all save him who has the right of possession.

Possessio est quasi pedis positio. Possession is, as it were, the position of the foot.

Possessio fratris de feodo simplici facit sororem esse haeredem. Possession by the brother in fee simple makes the sister an heir.

Possessio pacifica facit jus. Peaceable possession gives a right (after a legally prescribed period, by adverse possession).

Possessio pacifica per annos 60 facit jus. Peaceable possession for 60 years gives a right.

Possessio terminum tenentis possessio reversionarii est habenda. Possession by the tenant of the estate (or fund) is to be reckoned the possession of the reversioner.

Possibilitas post dissolutionem executionis nunquam reviviscatur. Possibility is never revived after the dissolution of the execution.

Posteri dies testes sunt sapientissimi. The days thereafter are the wisest witnesses. • That is, we judge the deeds best by their results.

Posteriora derogant prioribus. Later things restrict (or detract from) earlier ones.

Posteriores leges ad priores pertinent, nisi contrariae sint. Later laws pertain to earlier, if they are not in conflict.

Posteriore testamento prius ipso jure rumpitur. By a later will the earlier one is broken automatically.

Post factum nullum consilium. After the deed counsel is in vain.

Posthumus pro nato habetur. A posthumous child is considered as though born (before the father's death).

Postliminium fingit eum qui captus est semper in civitate fuisse. Postliminy (restoration of rights) imagines that a person who has been captured has never left the state. • A person captured by the enemy, who later returns, is restored to all his former rights. Just. Inst. 1.12.5.

Potentia debet sequi justitiam, non antecedere. Power ought to follow, not to precede, justice.

Potentia est duplex, remota et propinqua; et potentia remotissima et vana quae nunquam venit in actum. Possibility is of two kinds, remote and near; that which never comes into action is a power the most remote and vain.

Potentia inutilis frustra est. Useless power is in vain.

Potentia non est nisi ad bonum. Power is not conferred but for the (public) good.

Poterit enim quis rem dare et partem rei retinere, vel partem de pertinentiis, et illa pars quam retinet semper cum eo est et semper fuit. For one shall be able to grant a thing, and withhold part of the thing, or part from out the appurtenances, and that part which he withholds is always with him and always was. • This maxim expresses the idea that the operation of an exception is to retain in the grantor some portion of his former estate, and whatever is thus excepted or taken out of the grant remains in him as of his former title.

Potestas regia est facere justitiam. The power of the crown consists in the power to do justice. 2 Co. Inst. 374.

Potestas stricte interpretatur. Power is interpreted narrowly.

Potestas suprema seipsum dissolvere potest, ligare non potest. Supreme power can dissolve (or release), but cannot bind, itself.

Potest quis renunciare, pro se et suis, jus quod pro se introductum est. A person may relinquish, for himself and his heirs, a right that was introduced for his own benefit.

Potior est conditio defendentis. Stronger is the condition of the defendant (than that of the plaintiff).

Potior est conditio possidentis. Stronger is the condition of the possessor.

Potius ignoratio juris litigiosa est quam scientia. Ignorance of the law leads to litigation more than knowledge of the law. Cicero, *De Legibus* 1.6.18.

Praedium servit praedio. Land is under servitude to land. • A servitude is not a personal right, but attaches to the dominant tenement.

Praeferre patriam liberis regem decet. A king should prefer his country even before his children. Seneca, *Troades* 332.

Praepropera consilia raro sunt prospera. Hasty counsels are seldom prosperous.

Praescriptio est titulus ex usu et tempore substantiam capiens ab auctoritate legis. Prescription is a title derived from usage and time, given substance by the authority of law. Co. Litt. 113.

Praescriptio et executio non pertinent ad valorem contractus, sed ad tempus et modum actionis instituendae. Prescription and execution do not affect the validity of the contract, but affect the time and manner of bringing an action.

Praescriptio in feodo non acquirit jus. Prescription in fee acquires no right.

Praesentare nihil aliud est quam praesto dare seu offerre. To present is nothing other than to give or offer on the spot.

Praesentia corporis tollit errorem nominis, et veritas nominis tollit errorem demonstrationis. The presence of the body cancels an error in the name; the truth of the name cancels an error in the description.

Praestat cautela quam medela. Prevention is better than cure.

Praesumatur pro justitia sententiae. Let there be a presumption of sentence's justice.

Praesumitur pro legitimatione. There is a presumption in favor of legitimacy.

Praesumitur rex habere omnia jura in scrinio pectoris sui. The king is presumed to have all law in the recess of his heart. Co. Litt. 99a.

Praesumptio cedit veritati. A presumption yields to the truth.

Praesumptio ex eo quod plerumque fit. A presumption arises from what generally happens.

Praesumptio juris et de jure. A presumption of right and by right (i.e, conclusive).

Praesumptiones sunt conjecturae ex signo verisimili ad probandum assumptae. Presumptions are conjectures based on indications of probable truth, assumed for the purpose of establishing proof.

Praesumptio opponitur probationi. A presumption is distinguished from proof.

Praesumptio violenta plena probatio. Forceful presumption is full proof.

Praesumptio violenta valet in lege. Forceful presumption is effective in law.

Praetextu legis injusta agens duplo puniendus. He who under the cloak of the law acts unjustly should bear a double punishment.

Praetextu liciti non debet admitti illicitum. What is illegal ought not to be admitted under pretext of legality.

Praxis judicum est interpres legum. The practice of the judges is the interpreter of the laws.

Prescriptio non datur in bona felonum, nisi per recordum. Prescription is not granted against the goods of felons, except by record.

Presenti periculo succurrendum, ne qua oriri possit injuria. We must bring relief in the present danger, lest any injury arise.

Pretium succedit in locum rei. The price takes the place of the thing sold.

Prima pars aequitatis aequalitas. The first part of equity is equality.

Primo executienda est verbi vis, ne sermonis vitio obstruatur oratio, sive lex sine argumentis. The force of a word is to be first examined, lest by the fault of diction the sentence be destroyed or the law be without arguments.

Primus in tempore potior est in iure. The first in time is the more powerful in right.

Princeps et respublica ex justa causa possunt rem meam auferre. The king and the commonwealth can take away my property for just cause.

Princeps legibus solutus est. The emperor is not bound by statutes. Dig. 1.3.31.

Principalis debet semper excuti antequam perveniatur ad fideijussores. The principal should always be exhausted before resorting to the sureties.

Principia probant, non probantur. Principles prove; they are not proved.

Principiis obsta. Oppose beginnings. • Oppose a thing in its inception in order to have any success against it.

Principiorum non est ratio. There is no reasoning of principles.

Principium est potissima pars cujusque rei. The beginning is the most powerful part of each thing.

Prior possessio cum titulo posteriore melior est priore titulo sine possessione. Prior possession, with subsequent title, is better than prior title without possession.

Prior tempore, potior jure. Earlier in time, stronger in right.

Prius vitiis laboravimus, nunc legibus. We labored first with vices, now with laws. 4 Co. Inst. 76 (based on Tacitus, *Annales* 3.25).

Privatio praesupponit habitum. Deprivation presupposes possession.

Privatis pactionibus non dubium est non laedi jus caeterorum. There is no doubt that the rights of others (not party to the agreement) cannot be prejudiced by private agreements.

Privatorum conventio juri publico non derogat. An agreement of private persons does not derogate from public law.

Privatum commodum publico cedit. Private yields to public advantage.

Privatum incommodum publico bono pensatur. Private disadvantage is made up for by public good.

Privilegium est beneficium personale et extinguitur cum persona. A privilege is a benefit belonging to a person, and it dies with the person.

Privilegium est quasi privata lex. A privilege is, as it were, a private law.

Privilegium non valet contra rempublicam. A privilege has no force against the commonwealth.

Probandi necessitas incumbit illi qui agit. The necessity of proving rests on the one who sues (or claims some right). Just. Inst. 2.20.5.

Probationes debent esse evidentes, (id est) perspicuae et faciles intelligi. Proofs ought to be evident, (that is) clear and easily understood.

Probatis extremis, praesumitur media. When the extremes have been proved, the intermediate proceedings are presumed.

Processus legis est gravis vexatio; executio legis coronat opus. The process of the law is heavy hardship; the execution of the law crowns (or rewards) the work.

Prohibetur ne quis faciat in suo quod nocere possit alieno. It is prohibited for anyone to do on his own property what may injure another's.

Prolem ante matrimonium natam, ita ut post legitimam, lex civilis succedere facit in haereditate parentum; sed prolem, quam matrimonium non parit, succedere non sinit lex Anglorum. The civil law permits the offspring born before marriage, like offspring legitimate upon marriage, to be heirs of their parents; but the law of the English does not suffer offspring not produced by marriage to succeed. Fortescue, *De Laudibus Legum Angliae*, ch. 39.

Proles sequitur sortem paternam. The offspring follows the condition of the father.

Propinquior excludit propinquum; propinquus remotum; et remotus remotiorem. A nearer relation excludes a near one; a near relation excludes one distant (or removed); a distant relative excludes one yet more removed. Co. Litt. 10.

Propositio indefinita aequipollet universali. An indefinite proposition is equal to a general one.

Pro possessione praesumitur de jure. From possession arises a presumption of right.

Pro possessore habetur qui dolo injuriave desiit possidere. A person is considered a possessor who has ceased possession through fraud or injury.

Proprietas totius navis carinae causam sequitur. The property of the whole ship follows the condition of the keel.

Proprietates verborum observandae sunt. The proprieties (i.e., proper meanings) of words are to be observed.

Prosecutio legis est gravis vexatio; executio legis coronat opus. Litigation is a heavy hardship, but execution of the law crowns (or rewards) the work.

Protectio trahit subjectionem, subjectio protectionem. Protection brings submission; submission (brings) protection.

Pro tempore, pro spe, pro commodo minuitur eorum pretium atque auget. The value of things is lessened or increased according to time, expectation, or profit.

Proviso est providere praesentia et futura, non praeterita. A proviso is to provide for things present and future, not past.

Proximus est quem nemo antecedit; supremus est quem nemo sequitur. He is next whom no one precedes; he is last whom no one follows. Dig. 50.16.92.

Prudenter agit qui praecepto legis obtemperat. A person acts prudently who obeys the precept of law.

Pueri sunt de sanguine parentum, sed pater et mater non sunt de sanguine puerorum. Children are of the blood of their parents, but the father and mother are not of the blood of their children.

Pupillus pati posse non intelligitur. A pupil is not considered able to suffer. • That is, a pupil is not competent to permit or do what would be prejudicial to him. Dig. 50.17.110.2.

Putagium haereditatem non adimit. Promiscuity does not take away the inheritance. Glanvil 7, ch. 12.

Q

Quae ab hostibus capiuntur, statim capientium fiunt. Things taken from public enemies immediately become the property of the captors.

Quae ab initio inutilis fuit institutio, ex post facto convalescere non potest. An institution void in the beginning cannot acquire validity by a subsequent act.

Quae ab initio non valent, ex post facto convalescere non possunt. Things invalid from the beginning cannot be made valid by a subsequent act.

Quae accessionum locum obtinent, extinguuntur cum principales res peremptae fuerint. When the principal is extinguished, those things that are accessory to it are also extinguished. Dig. 33.8.2.

Quae ad omnes pertinent omnes debent tractare. Those things which pertain to all should be exercised by all.

Quae ad unum finem locuta sunt, non debent ad alium detorqueri. What speaks to one purpose ought not to be twisted to another.

Quae cohaerent personae a persona separari nequeunt. Things that belong to the person cannot be separated from the person.

Quae communi legi derogant stricte interpretantur. (Statutes) that derogate from the common law should be strictly construed.

Quae contra rationem juris introducta sunt, non debent trahi in consequentiam. Things introduced contrary to the reason of the law ought not to be drawn into precedents. • "We do find divers precedents . . . which are utterly against law and reason and for that void." 12 Coke 75.

Quae cum omnibus semper una atque eadem voce loquerentur leges inventae sunt. Laws are so designed that they may always speak with one and the same voice to all.

Quaecunque intra rationem legis inveniuntur, intra legem ipsam esse judicantur. Whatever appears within the reason of the law is considered within the law itself.

Quaecunque lex vult fieri non vult frustra fieri. Whatever the law wishes done, it wishes not to be done in vain.

Quaedam etsi honeste accipiantur inhoneste tamen petuntur. Certain things can be honorably accepted but cannot honorably be asked for. Dig. 50.13 pr. 1.5.

Quaedam in majus malum vitandum permittet lex quae tamen nequaquam probet. The law will allow certain things of which it may not at all approve, in avoidance of greater evil.

Quae dubitationis causa tollendae inseruntur communem legem non laedunt. Whatever is inserted for the purpose of removing doubt does not hurt the common law.

Quae dubitationis tollendae causa contractibus inseruntur jus commune non laedunt. What is inserted in contracts for the sake of removing doubt does not offend the common law.

Quae ex hostibus capimus jure gentium statim nostra fiunt. Things that we take from an enemy belong to us immediately, by the law of nations. Just. Inst. 2.1.16.

Quae incontinenti (vel certo) fiunt inesse videntur. Things that are done immediately (or with certainty) are considered part of the same transaction. Co. Litt. 236b.

Quae in curia acta sunt rite agi praesumuntur. What is done in court is presumed to be rightly done.

Quae in curia regis acta sunt rite agi praesumuntur. Things that are done in the king's court are presumed to be rightly done.

Quae in partes dividi nequeunt solida a singulis praestantur. Things (such as services) that cannot be divided into parts are rendered entire by each severally.

Quae inter alios acta sunt nemini nocere debent, sed prodesse possunt. Transactions between others can benefit, but should not injure, anyone who is not party to them.

Quae in testamento ita sunt scripta ut intelligi non possint, perinde sunt ac si scripta non essent. Things that are so written in a will that they cannot be understood are as if they had not been written.

Quae legi communi derogant non sunt trahenda in exemplum. Things that derogate (or detract) from the common law are not to be drawn into precedent.

Quae legi communi derogant stricte interpretantur. Things that derogate (or detract) from the common law are construed strictly.

Quaelibet concessio domini regis capi debet stricte contra dominum regem, quando potest intelligi duabus viis. Every grant of our lord the king ought to be taken strictly against our lord the king, when it can be understood in two ways.

Quaelibet concessio fortissime contra donatorem interpretanda est. Every grant is to be construed most strongly against the grantor.

Quaelibet jurisdictio cancellos suos habet. Every jurisdiction has its boundaries.

Quaelibet narratio super brevi locari debet in comitatu in quo breve emanavit. Every count upon the writ ought to be laid in the county in which the writ arose.

Quaelibet pardonatio debet capi secundum intentionem regis, et non ad deceptionem regis. Every pardon ought to be taken according to the intention of the king, and not to his deception.

Quaelibet poena corporalis, quamvis minima, major est qualibet poena pecuniaria. Every corporal punishment, although the very least, is greater than any pecuniary punishment.

Quae mala sunt inchoata in principio vix bono peraguntur exitu. Things bad in the commencement seldom end well.

Quae non fieri debent, facta valent. Things that ought not to be done are held valid when they have been done.

Quae non valeant singula, juncta juvant. Things that may not avail individually have effect when united.

Quae praeter consuetudinem et morem majorum fiunt, neque placent neque recta videntur. What is done contrary to the custom and usage of our ancestors neither pleases nor is considered right.

Quae propter necessitatem recepta sunt, non debent in argumentum trahi. Things that are accepted as a matter of necessity ought not to be brought into the argument. Dig. 50.17.162.

Quaeras de dubiis, legem bene discere si vis. Inquire into doubtful points if you wish to understand the law well.

Quaere de dubiis, quia per rationes pervenitur ad legitimam rationem. Inquire into doubtful points, because through reasoning we arrive at legal reason.

Quaerere dat sapere quae sunt legitima vere. To investigate is the way to know what things are truly lawful.

Quae rerum natura prohibentur nulla lege confirmata sunt. What is prohibited by the nature of things can be confirmed by no law.

Quaeritur, ut crescant tot magna volumina legis? In promptu causa est, crescit in orbe dolus. It is asked, how so many great (law) volumes grow? The explanation is plain: because fraud grows great in the world. 3 Coke 82a.

Quae singula non prosunt, juncta juvant. Things that are of no advantage individually are helpful when taken together.

Quaestio fit de legibus, non de personis. The question is about the laws, and not about the persons.

Quae sunt minoris culpae sunt majoris infamiae. Offenses that are of lesser guilt are of greater infamy.

Quae sunt temporalia ad agendum sunt perpetua ad excipiendum. Things that afford a ground of action, if raised within a certain time, may be pleaded at any time by way of exception.

Qualitas quae inesse debet, facile praesumitur. A quality that ought to be inherent is easily presumed.

Quam legem exteri nobis posuere eandem illis ponemus. The same law that foreign nations have put upon us we will impose upon them. 1 Bl. Com. 252.

Quam longum debet esse rationabile tempus, non definitur in lege, sed pendet ex discretione justiciariorum. How long a time should be "reasonable" the law does not define; it depends on the discretion of the judges.

Quam quisque novit artem in hoc se exerceat. Let every man employ himself in the pursuit in which he is proficient.

Quam rationabilis debet esse finis, non definitur, sed omnibus circumstantiis inspectis pendet ex justiciariorum discretione. How reasonable a fine should be is not defined, but depends on the discretion of the judges, after all the circumstances have been considered.

Quamvis aliquid per se non sit malum, tamen si sit mali exempli, non est faciendum. Although in itself a thing may not be bad, yet if it serves as a bad example, it is not to be done.

Quamvis lex generaliter loquitur restringenda tamen est, ut cessante ratione et ipsa cessat. Though the law speaks generally, it must be limited (by restrictive clauses), as, where the reason (for the law) ceases to apply, the law itself ceases. 4 Inst. 330.

Quamvis quis pro contumacia et fuga utlagetur, non propter hoc convictus est de facto principali. Though a person may be outlawed for contempt and flight, he is not on that account convicted of the principal fact.

Quando abest provisio partis, adest provisio legis. When the provision of the party is wanting, the provision of the law is at hand.

Quando aliquid conceditur, conceditur id sine quo illud fieri non possit. When anything is granted, that also is granted without which it cannot take effect.

Quando aliquid mandatur, mandatur et omne per quod pervenitur ad illud. When anything is commanded, everything by which it can be accomplished is also commanded.

Quando aliquid per se non sit malum, tamen si sit mali exempli, non est faciendum. When anything by itself is not evil, and yet if it is an example for evil, it is not to be done.

Quando aliquid prohibetur ex directo, prohibetur et per obliquum. When anything is prohibited directly, it is also prohibited indirectly.

Quando aliquid prohibetur, prohibetur omne per quod devenitur ad illud. When anything is prohibited, everything by which it is arrived at is prohibited.

Quando aliquis aliquid concedit, concedere videtur et id sine quo res uti non potest. When a person grants a thing, he is supposed to grant that also without which the thing cannot be used.

Quando charta continet generalem clausulam, posteaque descendit ad verba specialia quae clausulae generali sunt consentanea, interpretanda est charta secundum verba specialia. When a deed contains a general clause, and afterwards descends to special words that are consistent with the general clause, the deed is to be construed according to the special words.

Quando de una et eadem re, duo onerabiles existunt, unus, pro insufficientia alterius, de integro onerabitur. When two persons are liable concerning one and the same thing, if one makes default, the other must bear the whole liability.

Quando dispositio referri potest ad duas res, ita quod secundum relationem unam vitiatur et secundum alteram utilis sit, tum facienda est relatio ad illam ut valeat dispositio. When a disposition can refer to two matters, so that according to one reference it would be void and by another it would be effective, reference must be made to the latter, so that the disposition may take effect.

Quando diversi desiderantur actus ad aliquem statum perficiendum, plus respicit lex actum originalem. When different acts are required to the formation of any estate, the law chiefly regards the original act.

Quando duo jura concurrunt in una persona, aequum est ac si essent in diversis. When two rights run together in one person, it is the same as if they were in separate persons.

Quando jus domini regis et subditi concurrunt, jus regis praeferri debet. When the right of the sovereign king and of the subject run together (or clash), the right of the king ought to be preferred.

Quando lex aliquid alicui concedit, concedere videtur id sine quo res ipsa esse non potest. When the law grants anything to anyone, it is considered to grant that without which the thing itself cannot be (the sine qua non). 5 Coke 47.

Quando lex aliquid alicui concedit, omnia incidentia tacite conceduntur. When the law gives anything to anyone, it gives tacitly all that is incident to it.

Quando lex est specialis, ratio autem generalis, generaliter lex est intelligenda. When the law is special, but its reason is general, the law is to be understood generally.

Quando licit id quod majus, videtur licere id quod minus. When the greater is allowed, the lesser is considered to be allowed also.

Quando plus fit quam fieri debet, videtur etiam illud fieri quod faciendum est. When more is done than ought to be done, that at least is considered as performed that should have been performed.

Quando quod ago non valet ut ago, valeat quantum valere potest. When what I do does not have effect as I do it, let it have as much effect as it can.

Quando res non valet ut ago, valeat quantum valere potest. When the thing is of no force as I do it, let it have as much as it can have.

Quando verba et mens congruunt, non est interpretationi locus. When the words and the mind agree, there is no room for interpretation.

Quando verba statuti sunt specialia, ratio autem generalis, generaliter statutum est intelligendum. When the words of a statute are special, but the reason for it general, the statute is to be construed generally.

Quanto gradu unusquisque eorum distat stirpite, eodem distat inter se. In what degree each person is removed from the stock, to the same degree are they removed each from each other.

Quemadmodum ad quaestionem facti non respondent judices, ita ad quaestionem juris non respondent juratores. In the same manner that judges do not answer questions of fact, so jurors do not answer questions of law.

Quem sequuntur commoda eundem et incommoda sequuntur. One to whom the advantages accrue, the disadvantages also follow.

Qui abjurat regnum amittit regnum, sed non regem; patriam, sed non patrem patriae. One who abjures the kingdom leaves the kingdom, but not the king, (leaves) the fatherland, but not the father of the fatherland. 7 Coke 9b.

Qui accusat integrae famae sit et non criminosus. Let the one who accuses be of honest reputation and not implicated in a crime.

Qui acquirit sibi acquirit haeredibus. A person who acquires for himself acquires for his heirs.

Qui adimit medium dirimit finem. A person who takes away the means destroys the end.

Qui alienas res negligenter perdit aut vi vel dolo malo aufert, suas amittito. Whoever negligently ruins another man's property, or takes it away by force or fraud, let him lose his own (of equal value).

Qui aliquid statuerit parte inaudita altera, aequum licet dixerit, haud aequum fecerit. One who has decided anything without hearing the other party, even though he has said what is right, has done wrong.

Qui alterius jure utitur, eodem jure uti debet. A person who uses the right of another ought to use the same right.

Qui alterum incusat ne in eodem saltem genere sit incusandus. If one man is to accuse another, at the least he must not be subject to accusations of the same kind.

Qui animo peccandi aliquid facit, videtur peccasse ab initio. He who does anything with the intention of transgressing, seems to have transgressed from the beginning.

Qui bene distinguit bene docet. One who distinguishes well teaches well.

Qui beneficium legis extra ordinem quaerit, puras manus afferto. Whosoever seeks the benefit of the law outside the ordinary course, let him bring to bear pure hands.

Qui bene interrogat bene docet. One who questions well teaches well.

Qui bonis viris pauperibus dat legibus opitulatur; qui malis et inertibus segetem malorum fovet et legum opprobrium. One who assists good poor people assists the laws; one who assists the wicked and the lazy fosters a crop of evils and disrespect of the laws.

Qui cadit a syllaba cadit a tota causa. One who fails in a syllable fails in his whole cause.

Qui causa decedit causa cadit. One who departs from his cause loses his case.

Qui concedit aliquid, concedere videtur et id sine quo res ipsa esse non potuit (sine quo concessio est irrita). A person who grants anything is considered as granting that without which the thing itself could not be (without which the grant is invalid). • More precisely, *Cuicunque aliquis quid concedit* (q.v.). 11 Coke 52. The maxim is sometimes written *Qui concedit aliquid concedere videtur et id sine quo concessio est irrita, sine quo res ipsa esse non potuit* (meaning "he who concedes anything is considered as conceding that without which his concession would be of no effect, without which the thing itself could not exist").

Qui confirmat nihil dat. A person who confirms gives nothing.

Qui contemnit praeceptum, contemnit praecipientem. A person who shows contempt for the precept shows contempt for the author (or advocate) or it.

Quicquid acquiritur servo, acquiritur domino. Whatever is acquired by the servant is acquired for the master.

Quicquid demonstratae rei additur satis demonstratae frustra est. Whatever is added to the description of a thing already sufficiently described is of no effect.

Quicquid est contra normam recti est injuria. Whatever is against the rule of right is a wrong.

Quicquid in excessu actum est, lege prohibetur. Whatever is done in excess is prohibited by law.

Quicquid judicis auctoritati subjicitur, novitati non subjicitur. Whatever is subject to the authority of a judge is not subject to innovation.

Quicquid per se malum est, id leges omnibus vetant. Whatever is bad in itself, that the law forbids to all.

Quicquid plantatur solo, solo cedit. Whatever is affixed to the soil belongs to it.

Quicquid recipitur, recipitur secundum modum recipientis. Whatever is received is received according to the direction of the recipient.

Quicquid solvitur, solvitur secundum modum solventis. Whatever is paid is paid according to the direction of the payer.

Qui cum alio contrahit, vel est vel debet esse non ignarus conditionis ejus. A party who contracts with another either is or ought to be cognizant of that party's condition. • Otherwise, he is not excusable. Dig. 50.17.19.

Quicunque aliquid statuerit parte inaudita altera, aequum licet statuerit, haud aequus fuerit. Whoever has decided anything without hearing the other side, (even) suppose the decision prove just, has hardly been just. Seneca, *Medea* 199-200.

Quicunque jussu judicis aliquid fecerit non videtur dolo malo fecisse, quia parere necesse est. Whoever does anything by command of a judge is not reckoned to have done it with evil intent, because it is necessary to obey.

Qui dat finem dat media ad finem necessaria. A person who gives an end gives the necessary means to that end.

Qui dat pauperibus Deo dat. He gives to God who gives to the poor.

Qui destruit medium destruit finem. A person who destroys the means destroys the end.

Quid leges sine moribus vanae proficiunt. What good do laws do, (if they are) empty of moral character? Horace, *Odes* 3.24.

Qui doit inheriter al pére, doit inheriter al fitz. One who ought to inherit from the father ought to inherit from the son.

Qui dolo desierit possidere pro possidente damnatur. One who has dispossessed himself by fraud is condemned (nonetheless) as possessor.

Qui dolo male desierit possidere pro possessore damnatur. One who has fraudulently ceased to possess is condemned as if he were the possessor. Dig. 50.17.131.

Qui dolo possessit pro possidente, (ei) pro possessione dolus est. One who has taken possession by fraud, in place of the possessor, has fraud in place of possession.

Quidquid ab initio vitiosus est, non potest tractu temporis convalescere. Whatever is invalid from the outset cannot become valid by the passage of time.

Quidquid a multis peccatur inultum est. The crime that is committed by a multitude passes unpunished. Lucan, *Pharsalia* 5. 260.

Quidquid enim sive dolo et culpa venditoris accidit in eo venditor securus est. For concerning anything that occurs without deceit and guilt on the part of the vendor, the vendor is secure.

Quidquid est in territorio, est etiam de territorio. Whatever is in the territory is indeed of the territory.

Quidquid iudicii placuit, habet legis vigorem. Whatever the judgment decides has the force of law.

Quid sit jus, et in quo consistit injuria, legis est definire. What constitutes right, and wherein lies the injury, it is the function of the law to declare.

Quid tibi fieri non vis, alteri ne feceris. Do not to another what you would not wish done to you.

Quid turpi ex causa promissum est non valet. A promise arising from a wrongful cause is invalid.

Quieta non movere. Not to disturb what is settled.

Qui evertit causam evertit causatum futurum. One who overthrows the cause overthrows its future effects.

Qui excessit ex ephebis est persona. One who has left youth (is no longer a minor) becomes legally a person.

Qui excusat, accusat. He who excuses, accuses.

Qui ex damnato coitu nascuntur, inter liberos non computentur. They who are born of an illicit union should not be counted among children.

Qui ex parte testamenti aliquid donatum accipit universo testamento stabit. He who takes anything by a part of a testament will stand by the whole testament.

Qui extra causam divagatur calumniando, punitur. Whoever strays from the case indulging in slander is punished (for it).

Qui facit id quod plus est, facit id quod minus est, sed non convertitur. A person who does that which is more does that which is less, but not vice versa.

Qui facit per alium facit per se. A person who acts through another acts himself. • The acts of an agent are considered the acts of the principal.

Qui habet jurisdictionem absolvendi, habet jurisdictionem ligandi. One who has jurisdiction for dissolving (an obligation) has jurisdiction to bind.

Qui haeret in litera, haeret in cortice. One who clings to the letter clings to the shell (or surface).

Qui ignorat quantum solvere debeat, non potest improbus videri. A person who does not know what he ought to pay cannot be regarded as dishonest. • Also in reverse order: *Non potest improbus videri qui ignorat quantum solvere debeat.* Dig. 50.17.99.

Qui in alterius locum succedunt, iustam habent causam ignorantiae, an id quod peteretur deberetur. fideiussores quoque non minus quam heredes iustam ignorantiam possunt allegare. Those who succeed to someone else's position have reasonable grounds for claiming ignorance as to whether what was claimed was owed. Guarantors, no less than heirs, can allege justifiable ignorance. Dig. 50.17.42.

Qui inertibus dat industrios nudat. He who gives to the indolent defrauds the industrious.

Qui in jus dominiumve alterius succedit jure ejus uti debet. One who succeeds to another's right or property ought to use that person's right. • That is, the successor has the same rights and liabilities as attached to that property or interest in the hands of the assignor.

Qui inscienter peccat, scienter emendet. One who offends unwittingly must make good knowingly.

Qui in utero est, pro jam nato habetur quoties de ejus commodo quaeritur. A child in the womb is considered as born, whenever there is a question of benefit to the child.

Qui jure suo utitur, nemini facit injuriam. A person who exercises his proper right harms no one. • This maxim is sometimes written *Qui jure suo utitur neminem laedit* (meaning "he who exercises his right injures no one").

Qui jussu judicis aliquod fecerit non videtur dolo malo fecisse, quia parere necesse est. A person who has done anything by order of a judge is not considered to have acted in fraud, because it is necessary to obey.

Qui libenter et saepe et parvula de re juramento se obstringit perjurio proximus est. He who willingly and often binds himself by oath, even concerning small details, is very close to perjury.

Quilibet potest renunciare juri pro se inducto. Anyone may renounce a right introduced for his own benefit.

Qui male agit odit lucem. A person who does wrong hates the light (of discovery).

Qui mandat ipse fecisse videtur. A person who commands (a thing to be done) is considered to have done it himself.

Qui melius probat, melius habet. The party who gives better proof has the better (right). • Often rendered, he who proves more recovers more.

Qui molitur insidias in patriam id facit quod insanus nauta perforans navem in qua vehitur. He who plots against his country acts like the insane sailor who bores a hole in the ship that carries him. 3 Inst. 36.

Qui nascitur sine legitimo matrimonio, matrem sequitur. A child who is born out of lawful matrimony follows the condition of the mother.

Qui non cadunt in constantem virum, vani timores sunt aestimandi. Those fears are considered vain (or frivolous) that do not affect a man of stable character.

Qui non habet, ille non dat. Who has not gives not.

Qui non habet in aere, luat in corpore, ne quis peccetur impune. Let him who has not (the wherewithal to pay) in money pay in his person (i.e., by corporal punishment), lest anyone be wronged with impunity.

Qui non habet in aere, luet in corpore. What a man cannot pay with his purse, he must suffer in person.

Qui non habet in crumena luat in corpore. One who does not have (payment) in his purse should pay with his person. 5 Bl. Com. 372-3.

Qui non habet potestatem alienandi habet necessitatem retinendi. A person who has not the power of alienating is obliged to retain.

Qui non improbat approbat. A person who does not disapprove approves.

Qui non libere veritatem pronuntiat proditor est veritatis. He who does not freely declare the truth is a betrayer of the truth.

Qui non negat fatetur. A person who does not deny admits.

Qui non obstat quod obstare potest, facere videtur. A person who does not prevent what he can prevent is considered to act.

Qui non peccavit poenam non feret. He that has not transgressed must not suffer punishment.

Qui non potest donare non potest confiteri. He who is not able to give cannot confirm.

Qui non prohibet cum prohibere possit, jubet. A person who does not forbid when he can forbid commands.

Qui non prohibet quod prohibere potest, assentire videtur. A person who does not forbid what he can forbid is considered to assent.

Qui non propulsat injuriam quando potest infert. A person who does not repel an injury when he can brings it on.

Qui non vetat cum debeat et possit jubet. One who does not forbid a thing, when he can and he should, orders it.

Qui obstruit aditum destruit commodum. A person who obstructs an entrance destroys a conveniency.

Qui omne dicit nihil excludit. A person who says all excludes nothing.

Qui ordine ulteriora admittit praecedentia affirmat. One who admits what comes further in sequence affirms what precedes.

Qui parcit nocentibus innocentes punit. A person who spares the guilty punishes the innocent.

Qui peccat ebrius, luat sobrius. Let him who offends while drunk be punished when sober; one who offends when drunk must pay when sober. • The phrase is sometimes taken to mean that one who sins ignorantly must correct it knowingly.

Qui per alium facit per seipsum facere videtur. A person who does anything through another is considered as doing it himself.

Qui per fraudem agit frustra agit. He who commits fraud, acts in vain.

Qui periculum amat in eo peribit. He who loves danger will perish by it.

Qui potest et debet vetare, tacens jubet. A person who can and ought to forbid a thing (as much as) orders it, if he keeps silent.

Qui primum peccat ille facit rixam. Who first offends causes the quarrel.

Qui prior est tempore potior est jure. The person who is prior in time is stronger in right.

Qui prius jus suum insinuaverit praeferetur. One who has recorded his right earlier shall be preferred.

Qui pro me aliquid facit, mihi fecisse videtur. A person who does something in my behalf is considered to have done it to me (for me). • "To do a service for a man is to do it to him." 2 Co. Inst. 500.

Qui providet sibi, providet haeredibus. A person who provides for himself provides for his heirs.

Qui rationem in omnibus quaerunt rationem subvertunt. They who seek a reason for everything subvert reason.

Qui sciens solvit indebitum donandi consilio id videtur fecisse. A person who knowingly pays what is not due is considered to have done it with the intention of making a gift.

Qui scit se decipi non decipitur. One who knows that he is being deceived is not deceived.

Qui semel actionem renunciaverit, amplius repetere non potest. A litigant who has once renounced his action cannot bring it any longer.

Qui semel malus, semper praesumitur esse malus in eodem genere. A person who is once bad is always presumed to be bad in the same kind of affair.

Qui sentit commodum, sentire debet et onus. A person who enjoys the benefit ought also to bear the burden.

Qui sentit commodum sentire debet et onus; et e contra. A person who enjoys the benefit ought also to bear the burden; and the contrary.

Qui sentit onus, sentire debet et commodum. A person who feels the burden ought also to feel the benefit.

Quis erit innocens, si clam vel palam accusare sufficiat? If mere accusation, secret or open, can convict, who will go free?

Qui serius solvit minus solvit. He who pays late pays less.

Qui sine dolo malo ad judicium provocat, non videtur moram facere. One who demands judgment without fraud is not regarding as guilty of delay. Dig. 50.17.63.

Quisquis est qui velit jurisconsultus haberi, continuet studium, velit a quocunque doceri. Whoever there is who wishes to be regarded as a jurisconsult (legal expert) should prolong his study and be willing to be taught by everyone.

Quisquis praesumitur bonus, et semper in dubiis pro reo respondendum. Everyone is presumed to be good, and in doubtful cases, the decision must always be for the accused.

Quisquis sua facta scire et presumitur et debet. Everyone is presumed to know and ought to know his own cause.

Qui suspicionem peccati inducit, peccat. He offends who occasions the suspicion of an offense.

Qui suum recipit, licet a non debitore, non tenetur restituere. He who receives his due, although not from his debtor, is not bound to restore.

Qui tacet consentire videtur. A party who is silent appears to consent.

Qui tacet consentire videtur ubi tractatur de ejus commodo. A party who is silent is considered as assenting, when his advantage is debated.

Qui tacet non utique fatetur, sed tamen verum est eum non negare. A person who is silent does not indeed confess, but yet it is true that he does not deny.

Qui tardius solvit minus solvit. A person who pays too late pays less (than he ought).

Qui tempus praetermittit causam perdit. He who is dilatory loses his cause.

Qui timent, cavent et vitant. They who are afraid are wary and risk-averse.

Qui totum dicit nihil excipit. He who says all leaves nothing out.

Qui vi rapuit, fur improbior esse videtur. One who robs by violence is a more shameless thief. 4 Bl. Com. 242.

Quivis praesumitur bonus donec probetur contrarium. Every man is presumed good until the contrary is proved.

Qui vult decipi, decipiatur. Let one who wishes to be deceived be deceived.

Quocumque modo velit; quocumque modo possit. In any way he wishes; in any way he can.

Quod ab initio non valet, (in) tractu temporis non convalescet. What is ill from the outset will not be cured by passage of time.

Quod ad jus naturale attinet, omnes homines aequales sunt. All men are equal as far as natural law is concerned.

Quod aedificatur in area legata cedit legato. Whatever is built on land given by will passes with the gift of the land.

Quod alias bonum et justum est, si per vim vel fraudem petatur, malum et injustum efficitur. What is otherwise good and just, if it is sought by force or fraud, becomes bad and unjust.

Quod alias non fuit licitum necessitas licitum facit. Necessity makes lawful what otherwise was unlawful.

Quod approbo non reprobo. What I approve I do not disapprove.

Quod a quoque poenae nomine exactum est id eidem restituere nemo cogitur. What has been exacted from someone as a penalty no one is obliged to restore to him.

Quod attinet ad jus civile, servi pro nullis habentur, non tamen et jure naturali, quia, quod ad jus naturale attinet, omnes homines aequali sunt. So far as the civil law is concerned, slaves are not reckoned as nonentities, but not so by natural law, for so far as regards natural law, all men are equal.

Quod civile jus non idem continuo gentium; quod autem gentium idem civile esse debet. The civil law is not necessarily the law of nations, but the law of nations ought to be civil law. Cicero, *De Officiis* 3.69.

Quod conscientia vult, ubi lex deficit, aequitas cogit. When the law is lacking, equity compels what conscience wishes.

Quod constat clare, non debet verificari. What is clearly agreed need not be proved.

Quod constat curiae, opere testium non indiget. What appears true to the court needs not the help of witnesses.

Quod contra juris rationem receptum est, non est producendum ad consequentias. What has been admitted against the reason of the law ought not to be drawn into precedents.

Quod contra legem fit, pro infecto habetur. What is done contrary to the law is considered as not done.

Quod contra rationem juris receptum, non est producendum ad consequentias. That which is received against the reason of the law is not to be extended to its logical consequences.

Quodcumque est lucri commune. Whatever of profit (is found) is shared. • That is, a windfall is the common property of the finders.

Quodcunque aliquis ob tutelam corporis sui fecerit jure id fecisse videtur. Whatever one does in defense of his person, he is considered to have done legally.

Quod datum est ecclesiae, datum est Deo. What has been given to the church has been given to God.

Quod decet, non quod licet, laus est. To do what is proper, not what is permitted, is worthy of praise. (Based on Seneca, *Octavia* 454).

Quod demonstrandi causa additur rei satis demonstratae, frustra fit. What is added for the sake of demonstration to a thing sufficiently demonstrated is done to no purpose.

Quod differtur non aufertur. That which is deferred is not relinquished (omittance is no quittance).

Quod dubitas, ne feceris. When in doubt, do not do it.

Quod enim nullius est id ratione naturali occupanti conceditur. For whatever belongs to no one, by natural reason becomes property of the first taker.

Quod enim semel aut bis existit, praetereunt legislatores. Legislators pass by that which happens but once or twice.

Quod est ex necessitate nunquam introducitur, nisi quando necessarium. What is introduced of necessity is never introduced except when necessary.

Quod est inconveniens aut contra rationem non permissum est in lege. What is unsuitable or contrary to reason is not allowed in law.

Quod est necessarium est licitum. What is necessary is lawful.

Quod factum est, cum in obscuro sit, ex affectione cujusque capit interpretationem. When what has been done is in doubt, it is interpreted according to each person's attitude (originally referring to the interpreter, later to the actor). Dig. 50.17.168.

Quod fato contingit cuivis diligentissimo possit contingere. What happens by fate (or accidents) may happen to even the most diligent. Dig. 4.4.11.5.

Quod fieri debet facile praesumitur. That which ought to be done is easily presumed.

Quod fieri debet infectum valet. What ought to take effect has validity even if it is not (properly) applied.

Quod fieri debuit pro facto censetur. What ought to have been done is reckoned as done.

Quod fieri non debet, factum valet. What ought not to be done, when done, is valid.

Quod fieri vetatur ex directo vetatur etiam ab obliquo. What is forbidden to be done directly is forbidden also indirectly.

Quod fraude factum est in alios infectum esto, contra fraudatorem valet. What is done in fraud, although null and void against others, is valid against the defrauder.

Quod hodie exemplis tuemur, inter exempla erit. What today we respect as examples, will be found among precedents in future. Tacitus, *Annales* 11.24.11.

Quod inconsulto fecimus, consultius revocemus. What we have done without due consideration we should revoke with better consideration.

Quod initio non valet, tractu temporis non valet. What is void in the beginning does not become valid by passage of time.

Quod initio vitiosum est non potest tractu temporis convalescere. What is defective in origin cannot be mended by passage of time.

Quod in jure scripto jus appellatur, id in lege Angliae rectum esse dicitur. What in the civil law (literally, written law) is called jus, in the law of England is said to be rectum (right).

Quod in majore non valet nec valet in minore. That which avails not in the greater avails not in the less.

Quod in minori valet, valebit in majori; et quod in majori non valet, nec valebit in minori. What avails in the less will avail in the greater; and what does not avail in the greater will not avail in the less.

Quod in se malum ubicumque factum fuerit nulla juris positivi ratione valebit. That which is bad in itself wherever it is done cannot be valid by any reckoning of positive law.

Quod in uno similium valet, valebit in altero. What avails in one of two similar things will avail in the other.

Quod ipsis, qui contraxerunt, obstat, et successoribus eorum obstabit. That which bars those who have contracted will bar their successors also.

Quod juris in toto idem in parte. That which is law as regards the whole is also law as to the part.

Quod jussu alterius solvitur pro eo est quasi ipsi solutum esset. That which is paid at the bidding of another has the same effect as if it had been paid to that person himself. • The party who has a debt paid for him is in the same position as though the money were paid to him directly. Dig. 17.180.

Quod lege tuum est amplius esse tuum non potest. What is yours by law cannot be more yours.

Quod legis constructio non facit injuriam. That the construction of law worketh no injury. Co. Litt. 183a.

Quod meum est sine facto meo vel defectu meo amitti vel in alium transferri non potest. What is mine cannot be lost or transferred to another without my act or through my forfeiture.

Quod meum est, sine facto sive defectu meo amitti seu in alium transferri non potest. What is mine cannot be lost or transferred to another without my own act or default.

Quod meum est sine me auferri non potest. What is mine cannot be taken away without me (i.e., my consent).

Quod minus est in obligationem videtur deductum. That which is the lesser is held to be imported into the contract.

Quod naturalis ratio inter omnes homines constituit, vocatur jus gentium. What natural reason has established among all men is called the law of nations.

Quod naturaliter inesse debet praesumitur. That is presumed which ought naturally to be present.

Quod necessarie intelligitur id non deest. What is necessarily understood is not lacking.

Quod necessitas cogit, defendit. What necessity compels, it justifies.

Quod non apparet non est. That which does not appear does not exist. 2 Inst. 479.

Quod non apparet non est, et non apparet judicialiter ante judicium. What appears not does not exist, and nothing appears judicially before judgment.

Quod non capit Christus, capit fiscus. What Christ (or the church) does not take, the treasury takes.

Quod non habet principium non habet finem. What has no beginning has no end.

Quod non legitur non creditur. What is not read is not believed.

Quod non valet in principali, in accessorio seu consequenti non valebit; et quod non valet in magis propinquo, non valebit in magis remoto. What is not valid in the principal will not be valid in the accessory or consequence; and what has no effect in the nearer instance will be of no effect in the more remote.

Quod nostrum est, sine facto sive defectu nostro, amitti seu in alium transferri non potest. That which is ours cannot be lost or transferred to another without our own act, our own default.

Quod nullius esse potest, id ut alicujus fieret nulla obligatio valet efficere. What can belong to no one no agreement (or obligation) can make property of anyone. Dig. 50.17.182.

Quod nullius est, est domini regis. That which belongs to nobody belongs to our lord the king.

Quod nullius est id ratione naturali occupanti conceditur. What belongs to no one, by natural reason becomes property of the first occupant. Dig. 41.1.3.

Quod nullo interno vitio laborat et objecto impedimento cessat, remoto impedimento per se emergit. That which, laboring under no internal fault, is overcome by obstacles, emerges of itself, the obstacle being removed.

Quod nullum est, nullum producit effectum. That which is null produces no effect.

Quod omnes tangit, ab omnibus debet supportari. What touches (or concerns) all ought to be supported by all.

Quod per me non possum, nec per alium. What I cannot do in person, I also cannot do through the agency of another.

Quod per recordum probatum non debet esse negatum. What is proved by the record ought not to be denied.

Quod populus postremum jussit, id jus ratum esto. What the people have last enacted, let that be the established law.

Quod primum est intentione ultimum est in operatione. That which is first in intention is last in operation.

Quod principi placuit legis habet vigorem. What has pleased the prince (i.e., what the emperor has decided) has the force of law. Dig. 1.4.1.

Quod principi placuit legis habet vigorem; utpote cum lege regia, quae de imperio ejus lata est, populus ei et in eum omne suum imperium et potestatem conferat. A decision of the emperor has the force of law; for, by the royal law that has been made concerning his authority, the people have conferred on him all their sovereignty and power. Dig. 1.4.1.

Quod prius est verius est; et quod prius est tempore potius est jure. What is prior is truer; and what comes earlier in time is stronger in right.

Quod privilegia quae re vera sunt in praejudicium reipublicae, magis tamen speciosa habent frontispicia, et boni publici praetextum, quam bonae et legales concessiones, sed praetextu liciti non debet admitti illicitum. There are privileges that are really detrimental to the state, but that have a more colorful appearance and show of public good than good and lawful concessions. But the unlawful should not be accepted as valid on the ground of a showing of legality.

Quod pro minore licitum est et pro majore licitum est. What is lawful in the lesser is also lawful in the greater.

Quod pure debetur praesenti die debetur. That which is due unconditionally is due the same day.

Quodque dissolvitur eodem modo quo ligatur. In the same manner that anything is bound, it is unbound.

Quod quis ex culpa sua damnum sentit, non intelligitur damnum sentire. The damage that any person suffers by his own fault he is not considered to suffer as damage. Dig. 50.17.203.

Quod quisquis norit, in hoc se exerceat. Let every one employ himself in what he knows.

Quod quis sciens indebitum dedit hac mente, ut postea repeteret, repetere non potest. What one has paid knowing that it is not owed, with the intention of reclaiming it afterwards, he cannot recover. Dig. 12.6.50.

Quod remedio destituitur ipsa re valet si culpa absit. What is without a remedy is by that very fact valid if there is no fault.

Quod rex contra leges jubet pro injussu reputabitur. What the king orders contrary to the law shall be considered unauthorized.

Quod semel aut bis existit praetereunt legislatores. Legislators pass over what happens (only) once or twice.

Quod semel meum est amplius meum esse non potest. What is once mine cannot be any more completely mine.

Quod semel placuit in electione, amplius displicere non potest. That which in making his election a man has once decided, he cannot afterwards disavow.

Quod solo inaedificatur solo cedit. Whatever is built on the soil goes with the soil.

Quod statuendum est semel diu deliberandum est. Time must be taken for deliberation, when we have to determine once and for all.

Quod sub certa forma concessum vel reservatum est, non trahitur ad valorem vel compensationem. That which has been granted or reserved under a certain form is not to be drawn into valuation or compensation.

Quod subintelligitur non deest. What is understood is not lacking.

Quod tacite intelligitur deesse non videtur. What is tacitly understood does not appear to be lacking.

Quod talem eligi faciat qui melius et sciat et velit, et possit officio illi intendere. That person should be chosen who best understands and is willing and able to perform the duty of the office. 1 Bl. Com. 336 (ch. 9.2).

Quod tibi fieri non vis alteri non feceris. Do not do to another what you do not wish done to yourself.

Quod vanum et inutile est, lex non requirit. The law does not require what is vain and useless.

Quod vero contra rationem juris receptum est, non est producendum ad consequentias. But what has been admitted contrary to the reason of law ought not to be drawn into precedents.

Quod vero naturalis ratio inter omnes homines constituit, id apud omnes peraeque custoditur vocaturque ius gentium. But the law that natural reason has established among all persons, that law is observed uniformly among all, and is called the law of peoples.

Quo libelli in celeberrimis locis proponuntur, huic ne perire quidem tacite conceditur. When charges against a man are published in the most crowded places, this person is not allowed even to perish quietly. • That is, the criminal arraigned in public cannot be condemned in private. Cicero, *Pro Quinctio* 50.

Quo ligatur, eo dissolvitur. As a thing is bound, so it is unbound.

Quo modo quid constituitur eodem modo dissolvitur. In whatever mode a thing is constituted, in the same manner it is dissolved.

Quorum praetextu nec auget nec minuit sententiam, sed tantum confirmat praemissa. "Quorum praetextu" neither increases nor diminishes the meaning, but only confirms what went before.

Quot homines, tot sententiae. There are as many opinions as there are people.

Quotiens dubia interpretatio libertatis est, secundum libertatem respondendum erit. Whenever there is an interpretation doubtful as to liberty (or slavery), the decision must be in favor of liberty.

Quotiens idem sermo duas sententias exprimit, ea potissimum accipiatur quae rei gerendae aptior est. Whenever the same words express two meanings, that is to be taken most strongly which is the better fitted for carrying out the proposed end.

Quoties aequitatem desiderii naturalis ratio aut dubitatio juris moratur, justis decretis res temperanda est. Whenever natural reason or doubt about the law delays an equitable request, the matter must be resolved by just decrees. Dig. 50.17.85.2.

Quoties dubia interpretatio libertatis est secundum libertatem respondendum erit. A doubtful interpretation of liberty must be answered in favor of liberty. Dig. 50.17.20.

Quoties duplici jure defertur alicui successio, repudiato novo jure, quod ante defertur supererit vetus. As often as a succession comes to a man by a double right, the new right is laid in abeyance, and the old right by which he first succeeds, survives.

Quoties in stipulationibus ambigua oratio est, commodissimum est id accipi quo res de quo agitur in tuto sit. Whenever in stipulations the expression is ambiguous, it is most proper to give it that interpretation by which the subject matter may be in safety.

Quoties in verbis nulla est ambiguitas, ibi nulla expositio contra verba expressa fienda est. Whenever there is no ambiguity in the words, then no exposition contrary to the words is to be made.

Quoties lege aliquid unum vel alterum introductum est, bona occasio est caetera quae tendunt ad eandem utilitatem vel interpretatione, vel certe jurisdictione suppleri. Whenever some rule or other is introduced by law, it is a good opportunity for other (provisions) conducive to the same purpose to be supplied, either by interpretation or indeed by judicial decision. Dig. 1.3.13.

Quo tutela redit eo haereditas pervenit, nisi cum foeminae haeredes intercedunt. An inheritance comes in the way in which guardianship goes, unless female heirs intervene.

Quum de lucro duorum quaeratur, melior est conditio possidentis. When there is a question of gain (to one) of two parties, the condition of the possessor is the better.

Quum duae inter se repugnantia reperiantur in testamento, ultima rata est. Where there are two repugnant clauses in a will, the last clause shall prevail.

Quum in testamento ambigue aut etiam perperam scriptum est, benigne interpretari et secundum id quod credible est cogitatum, credendum est. When in a will an ambiguous or even an erroneous expression occurs, it should be construed liberally and in accordance with what is thought the probable meaning (of the testator).

Quum principalis causa non consistit, ne ea quidem quae sequuntur locum habent. When the principal cause does not stand, neither do the accessories (or consequences) obtain.

R

Ratihabitio mandato aequiparatur. Ratification is equal to a command. • This maxim is sometimes written *Ratihabitio mandato comparatur* (meaning "ratification is equivalent to a command").

Ratihabitio retrotrahitur et mandato aequiparatur. Ratification relates back and is equal to a command. Co. Litt. 180b.

Ratio est formalis causa consuetudinis. Reason is the source and formal cause of custom.

Ratio est legis anima, mutata legis ratione mutatur et lex. Reason is the soul of the law; when the reason of the law has been changed, the law is also changed.

Ratio est radius divini luminis. Reason is a ray of the divine light.

Ratio et auctoritas duo clarissima mundi lumina. Reason and authority are the two brightest lights in the world.

Ratio in jure aequitas integra. Reason in law is perfect equity.

Ratio legis est anima legis; mutata legis ratione, mutatur et lex. The reason of the law is the soul of the law; the reason of law being changed, the law is also changed.

Ratione cessante, cessat ipsa lex. The reason ceasing, the law itself ceases. (That is, no law can survive the reasons on which it is founded.)

Ratio non clauditur loco. Reason is not confined to any place.

Ratio potest allegari deficiente lege, sed vera et legalis et non apparens. A reason can be adduced when the law is defective, but it must be a true and legal reason, and not specious (or apparent).

Ratum quis habere non potest, quod ipsius nomine non est gestum. One cannot hold ratified that which has not been done in his own name.

Receditur a placitis juris potius quam injuriae et delicta maneant impunita. One departs from settled rules of law, rather than let crimes and wrongs remain unpunished.

Recipitur in modum recipientis. A thing is received in the way the recipient intends.

Recorda sunt vestigia vetustatis et veritatis. Records are vestiges of antiquity and truth.

Recuperatio est alicujus rei in causam alterius adductae per judicem acquisitio. Recovery is the acquisition, by sentence of the judge, of anything adduced in the cause of another.

Recurrendum est ad extraordinarium quando non valet ordinarium. We must have recourse to what is extraordinary when what is ordinary fails.

Reddenda singula singulis. Each must be put in each separate place. • That is, the several terms or items apply distributively, or each to its proper object.

Redditus caecus est siccus. Rent that is blind (or uncertain) is dry (barren, or "rent seck").

Regia dignitas est indivisibilis, et quaelibet alia derivativa dignitas est similiter indivisibilis. The kingly power is indivisible, just as every other derivative power is indivisible.

Regis curia et curia populi sive parliamentum non ex scripto, sed ex communi lege sunt. Courts, whether of the king, or of the people, or parliament, are established not by written but by common, law.

Regnandi causa malum coram non judice. A case of royal title (or challenge to it) is an evil without (a proper) court. (The courts represent the ruler himself and he cannot decide in his own case).

Regnum non est divisibile. The kingdom is not divisible.

Regula est, juris quidem ignorantiam cuique nocere, facti vero ignorantiam non nocere. The rule is that ignorance of the law is harmful (or prejudicial) to anyone, but ignorance of a fact is not. • Ignorance of a fact may excuse a party from the legal consequences of his conduct, but not ignorance of law.

Regula est quae rem quae est breviter enarrat, non ut ex regula jus sumatur, sed ex jure quod est regula fiat. A rule (*regula*) briefly reports what the matter is, not so that law (*ius*) may be taken from the rule but that the rule be made from the law. Dig. 50.17.1.

Regula pro lege, si deficit lex. If the law is inadequate, the maxim serves in its place.

Regulariter non valet pactum de re mea non alienanda. As a rule, a contract not to alienate my property is not binding.

Rei depositae proprietas apud deponentem manet, sed et possessio. The depositor retains ownership of a thing deposited, but also possession. Dig. 16.17.1.

Reipublicae interest voluntates defunctorum effectum sortiri. It is in the interest of the state that the wills of the dead should have their (intended) effect.

Rei turpis nullum mandatum est. There is no mandate for a thing immoral (or illegal). • Hence, there is no action for failing to act on such a mandate. Dig. 17.1.6.3.

Relatio est fictio juris et intenta ad unum. Relation is a fiction of law, and intended for one thing. • Coke explains, "Relatio is a fiction of law to make a nullity of a thing ab initio"; obstacles are removed for the one purpose, *ut res magis valeat*, that the matter have effect. 3 Coke 28.

Relatio semper fiat ut valeat dispositio. Reference should always be made in such a manner that a disposition (in a will) may have effect.

Relativorum cognito uno, cognoscitur et alterum. Of things relating to each other, one being known, the other is also known.

Religio sequitur patrem. Religion follows the father. • The father's religion is prima facie the infant's religion.

Remissius imperanti melius paretur. A person commanding not too strictly is better obeyed.

Remoto impedimento, emergit actio. When the impediment has been removed, the action arises.

Repellitur a sacramento infamis. An infamous person is prevented from taking an oath.

Repellitur exceptione cedendarum actionum. (The litigant) is defeated by the plea that the actions have been assigned.

Reprobata pecunia liberat solventem. Money refused releases the person paying (or offering payment).

Reputatio est vulgaris opinio ubi non est veritas. Reputation is a common opinion where there is no certain knowledge.

Rerum ordo confunditur, si unicuique jurisdictio non servetur. The order of things is confounded if the proper jurisdiction of each is not maintained.

Rerum progressus ostendunt multa, quae in initio praecaveri seu praevideri non possunt. The course of events reveals many things that in the beginning could not be guarded against or foreseen.

Rerum suarum quilibet est moderator et arbiter. Every one is the manager and disposer of his own matters.

Res accendent lumina rebus. Matters will throw light on (other) matters.

Res accessoria sequitur rem principalem. An accessory follows its principal.

Res bona fide vendita propter minimam causam inempta fieri non debet. A thing sold in good faith should not become unsold for a trivial cause. Dig. 18.1.54.

Rescriptum principis contra jus non valet. The prince's rescript, if contrary to law, is of no avail.

Res denominatur a principaliori parte. A thing is named from its more essential (or primary) part.

Reservatio non debet esse de proficuis ipsis quia ea conceduntur, sed de redditu novo extra proficua. A reservation ought not to be of the annual increase itself, because it is granted, but of new rent apart from the annual increase.

Reservatio ut et protestatio non facit jus sed tuetur. Reservation and protest do not create a right but protect a right.

Res est misera ubi jus est vagum et incertum. It is a miserable state of things where the law is vague and uncertain.

Res generalem habet significationem, quia tam corporea, quam incorporea, cujuscunque sunt generis naturae sive speciei, comprehendit. The word "things" has a general signification, because it comprehends corporeal as well as incorporeal objects, of whatever sort, nature, or species.

Resignatio est juris proprii spontanea refutatio. Resignation is the spontaneous rejection of one's own right.

Res inter alios acta aliis non nocet. A thing done between two parties does not damage other parties; a matter transacted between parties (e.g., to a contract) does not prejudice nonparties.

Res inter alios acta alteri nocere non debet. Things done between others ought not to injure an outsider (not party to them).

Res inter alios judicatae nullum aliis praejudicium faciunt. Matters adjudged in the lawsuits of others do not prejudice those who were not parties to them.

Res judicata exceptionem parit perpetuam. A matter judicially decided begets a perpetual exception.

Res judicata facit ex albo nigrum, ex nigro album, ex curvo rectum, ex recto curvum. A matter adjudged makes white black; black white; the crooked straight; the straight crooked.

Res judicata inter alios aliis neque nocet neque prodest. A matter decided among some litigants ought neither to harm nor benefit others.

Res judicata inter partes jus facit. A question adjudicated makes law (or establishes the right) between the parties.

Res judicata pro veritate accipitur. A matter adjudged is taken for truth.

Res judicata pro veritate habetur. A thing adjudged is held as truth. Dig. 50.17.207.

Res locata perit domino. Leased property perishes to the owner. (Loss that is not the tenant's fault is at the owner's expense.)

Res nullius naturaliter fit primi occupantis. A thing that has no owner naturally belongs to the first taker.

Resoluto jure concedentis, resolvitur jus concessum. When the right of the grantor has been extinguished, the right granted is extinguished.

Resoluto jure dantis, resolvitur jus accipientis. The right of the giver having become void, the right of the receiver is void also.

Res periit domino suo. The destruction of the thing is a loss to its owner.

Res per pecuniam aestimatur, et non pecunia per res. The value of a thing is estimated by its worth in money, and the value of money is not estimated by reference to things.

Respiciendum est judicanti nequid aut durius aut remissius constituatur quam causa deposcit; nec enim aut severitatis aut clementiae gloria affectanda est. The person judging must see to it that nothing should be either more severely or more leniently construed than the cause itself demands; neither for severity nor clemency is glory to be sought after.

Respondeat raptor, qui ignorare non potuit quod pupillum alienum abduxit. Let the ravisher answer, for he could not be ignorant that he has taken away another's ward.

Respondeat superior. Let the principal answer.

Responsio unius non omnino audiatur. The answer of one witness should not be heard at all.

Res privatae sunt quae singulorum sunt. Private things are those which belong to individuals. Gaius Inst. 2.11.

Res propria est quae communis non est. A thing is private that is not common.

Res quae intra praesidia perductae nondum sunt quanquam ab hostibus occupatae, ideo postliminii non egent, quia dominum nondum mutarunt ex gentium jure. Things that have not yet been brought within the enemy's camp, although held by the enemy, do not need the fiction of postliminy on this account, because their ownership by the law of nations has not yet changed.

Res sacra non recipit aestimationem. A sacred thing does not admit of valuation.

Res stulta est nequitiae modus. A measure (or limit) on wickedness is a foolish thing. • That is, there is no mean in mischief. (Cf. Seneca, *Agamemnon* 150; 2 Inst. 507).

Res sua nemini servit. No one can have a servitude over his own property.

Res transit cum suo onere. The thing passes with its burden.

Reus excipiendo fit actor. The defendant by a plea (or exception) becomes plaintiff.

Reus laesae majestatis punitur, ut pereat unus ne pereant omnes. A traitor is punished that one may die lest all perish.

Re, verbis, scripto, consensu, traditione, junctura vestes sumere pacta solent. Compacts usually take their clothing from the thing itself, from words, from writings, from consent, from delivery, from the joining together.

Reversio terrae est tanquam terra revertens in possessione donatori sive haeredibus suis post donum finitum. A reversion of land is as it were the return of the land to the possession of the donor or his heirs after the termination of the gift.

Rex ad justitiam faciendam non cogitur. The king is not compelled to do justice.

Rex datur propter regnum, non regnum propter regem. A king is given for the sake of the kingdom, not the kingdom for the king.

Rex debet esse sub lege, quia lex facit regem. The king should be subject to the law, for the law makes the king. 1 Bl. Com. 232.

Rex est caput et salus reipublicae. The king is the head and safety of the commonwealth.

Rex est legalis et politicus. The king is (the fount of) both law and policy.

Rex est lex vivens. The king is the living law.

Rex est major singulis, minor universis. The king is greater than any single person: less than all.

Rex est pater patriae. The king is the father of his country.

Rex est persona mixta, medicus regni, pater patriae, et sponsus regni. The king is a mixed person: the physician of the state, the father of the country, and the husband of the kingdom.

Rex est persona sacra et mixta cum sacerdote. The king is a sacred person, and joined with the priesthood.

Rex est qui metuit et qui cupit nihil. He is truly a king who fears nothing and who desires nothing.

Rex in regno suo non habet parem. The king has no equal in his own kingdom. Jenkins, *Eight Centuries* 78.

Rex lege cadere non potest. The king cannot legally cease.

Rex legi subjectus est. The king is subject to the law.

Rex nihil aliud est quam lex agens. The king is nothing else than law in action.

Rex nil dat nisi per recordum. The king gives nothing except by record.

Rex nil potest jubere nisi per curiam legitime constitutam. The king can order nothing except through his regularly constituted court (parliament).

Rex non debet esse sub homine, sed sub Deo et sub lege, quia lex facit regem. The king ought to be under no man, but under God and the law, because the law makes a king. Bracton 1.8.5.

Rex non debet judicare sed secundum legem. The king ought to judge only according to law.

Rex non est ubi voluntas dominatur. He is not king when his will is lord and master.

Rex non potest fallere nec falli. The king cannot deceive or be deceived.

Rex non potest gratiam facere cum injuria et damno aliorum. The king cannot confer a favor on anyone to the injury and damage of others.

Rex non potest invitum civem regno depellere. The king cannot expel a subject against his will from the kingdom.

Rex non potest malum vel injuriam facere. The king cannot do evil or injustice.

Rex non potest peccare. The king can do no wrong.

Rex non potest subditum onerare impositionibus. The king may not oppressively levy taxes upon a subject.

Rex nunquam infra aetatem est. The king is never under age.

Rex nunquam moritur. The king never dies.

Rex prosequi in judicio potest in qua curia sibi visum fuerit. The king can proceed in whatever court he decides upon.

Rex quod injustum est facere non potest. The king cannot do what is unjust.

Rex semper praesumitur attendere ardua regni pro bono publico omnium. The king is always presumed to attend to the business of the realm, for the public good of all.

Rex summus dominus supra omnes. The king is the great lord over all. 2 Inst. 501.

Rex tuetur legem, et lex tuetur jus. The king protects the law, and the law protects the right. Co. Litt. 130a.

Riparum usus publicus est jure gentium, sicut ipsius fluminis. The use of riverbanks is by the law of nations public, like that of the stream itself.

Rogationes, quaestiones, et positiones debent esse simplices. Demands, questions, and answers ought to be simple.

Roy n'est lie per ascun statute, si il ne soit expressement nosme. The king is not bound by any statute, if he is not expressly named.

Ruunt magna in se. Great interests (or powers) are apt to clash. (Based on Lucan, *Pharsalia* 1.81.)

S

Sacramentum habet in se tres comites, veritatem justitiam et judicium: veritas habenda est in jurato; justitia et judicium in judice. An oath has in it three components — truth, justice, and judgment: truth in the party swearing, justice and judgment in the judge (administering the oath).

Sacramentum si fatuum fuerit, licet falsum, tamen non committit perjurium. A foolish oath, though false, does not make perjury.

Sacrilegii instar est rescriptum principis obviare. It is the image of sacrilege to oppose the ruler's ruling.

Sacrilegus omnium praedonum cupiditatem et scelerem superat. A sacrilegious person surpasses the greed and wickedness of all other robbers.

Saepe constitutum est res inter alios judicatas aliis non praejudicare. It has often been settled that matters adjudged between others ought not to prejudice those who were not parties.

Saepenumero ubi proprietas verborum attenditur, sensus veritatis amittitur. Frequently where propriety of words is given attention, the meaning of truth is lost.

Saepe viatorem nova, non vetus, orbita fallit. Often it is the new track, not the old one, that deceives the traveler.

Salus populi (est) suprema lex. The safety of the people is the supreme law. • The phrase is sometimes put in the imperative: *Salus populi suprema lex esto* (let the safety of the people be the supreme law).

Salus reipublicae suprema lex. The safety of the state is the supreme law.

Salus ubi multi consiliarii. Where there are many counselors, there is safety.

Sanguinis conjunctio benevolentia devincit homines et caritate. A tie of blood overcomes human beings through benevolence and family affection.

Sapiens incipit a fine, et quod primum est in intentione, ultimum est in executione. A wise person begins from the end, and what is first in intention is last in execution.

Sapiens omnia agit cum consilio. A wise man does everything advisedly.

Sapientia legis nummario pretio non est aestimanda. No price in money is to be put on the wisdom of the law.

Sapientis judicis est cogitare tantum sibi esse permissum, quantum commissum et creditum. It is the mark of a wise judge to suppose that he is permitted only so much as has been committed and entrusted to him.

Satis dotata si bene morata. A woman is well-enough dowered for a wife if possessed of good morals. (Cf. Plautus, *Aulularia* 196.)

Satius est petere fontes quam sectari rivulos. It is better to seek the sources than to follow tributaries.

Satius est prodesse etiam malis propter bonos quam bonis deesse propter malos. Better to benefit bad men for the sake of the good than to deprive good men on account of the bad. Seneca, *De Beneficiis* 4.28.

Sauve qui peut. Save (yourself) who can. (Or every man for himself, in escaping shipwreck.)

Scelus intra se tacitum qui cogitat facti crimen habet. He who secretly meditates a crime is guilty of the deed. Juvenal, *Satires* 13.209-10.

Scientia sciolorum est mixta ignorantia. The knowledge of smatterers is ignorance diluted.

Scientia utrimque par pares contrahentes facit. Equal knowledge on both sides makes the contracting parties equal.

Scienti et volenti non fit injuria. A wrong is not done to one who knows and assents to it.

Scire debes cum quo contrahis. You ought to know with whom you make an agreement.

Scire et scire debere aequiparantur in jure. To know a thing and to be bound to know it are regarded in law as equivalent.

Scire leges non hoc est verba earum tenere, sed vim et potestatem. To know the laws is to observe not their (mere) words, but their force and power.

Scire proprie est rem ratione et per causam cognoscere. To know properly is to know a thing in its reason and by its cause.

Scribere est agere. To write is to act.

Scriptae obligationes scriptis tolluntur, et nudi consensus obligatio contrario consensu dissolvitur. Written obligations are undone by writing, and the obligation of mere consent (or naked agreement) is dissolved by a bare consent to the contrary.

Scripta litera manet. The written word endures.

Secta est pugna civilis, sicut actores armantur actionibus, et quasi accinguntur gladiis, ita rei (e contra) muniuntur exceptionibus, et defenduntur quasi clypeis. A suit is a civil battle; just as the plaintiffs are armed with actions and, as it were, girded with swords, so (against them) the defendants are fortified with pleas, and defended as though by shields.

Secta quae scripto nititur a scripto variari non debet. A suit that relies on a writing ought not to vary from the writing.

Secundum naturam est commoda cujusque rei eum sequi quem sequentur incommoda. It is according to nature that the advantages in any matter should come to the person to whom the disadvantages will attend.

Securitas legatorum utilitati poenae preponderat. The safety of ambassadors outweighs the expediency of punishment. (Cf. Grotius 2.18.4.)

Securius expediuntur negotia commissa pluribus, et plus vident oculi quam oculus. Business entrusted to several people is done more reliably, and (several) eyes see more than (one) eye does.

Sed si non prosunt singula, juncta juvant. If things separately do no good, joined together they help.

Segnius irritant animos demissa per aurem quam quae sunt oculis subjecta fidelibus. What enters through the ear rouses us more sluggishly than what is presented to the trusty eyes. Horace, *Ars Poetica* (Ad Pisones) 180–82.

Seisina facit stipitem. Seisin makes the stock.

Semel baro, semper baro. Once a baron, always a baron.

Semel civis semper civis. Once a citizen, always a citizen.

Semel malus semper praesumitur esse malus in eodem genere. Whoever is once bad is presumed to be so always in the same kind of affair.

Semper in dubiis benigniora praeferenda sunt. In dubious cases, the more favorable constructions are always to be preferred.

Semper in dubiis id agendum est, ut quam tutissimo loco res sit bona fide contracta, nisi quum aperte contra leges scriptum est. Always in doubtful cases that is to be done by which a bona fide contract may be in the safest condition, except when it has been drawn up clearly contrary to law.

Semper in obscuris quod minimum est sequimur. In obscure cases we always follow what is least obscure.

Semper in stipulationibus et in caeteris contractibus id sequimur quod actum est. In stipulations and other contracts, we always follow what was done (or agreed to). Dig. 50.17.34.

Semper ita fiat relatio ut valeat dispositio. Let the reference always be so made that the disposition may avail.

Semper necessitas probandi incumbit ei qui agit. The necessity of proving always rests on the claimant.

Semper praesumitur pro legitimatione puerorum, et filiatio non potest probari. The presumption always is in favor of the legitimacy of children, and filiation cannot be proved.

Semper praesumitur pro negante. The presumption is always in favor of the one who denies.

Semper praesumitur pro sententia. The presumption is always in favor of a judgment (or sentence).

Semper pro matrimonio praesumitur. There is always a presumption in favor of marriage.

Semper qui non prohibet pro se intervenire mandare creditur. A person who does not prohibit the intervention of another in his behalf is always believed to authorize it.

Semper sexus masculinus etiam faemininum continet. The masculine gender always includes the feminine as well. Dig. 32.63.

Semper specialia generalibus insunt. Special clauses are always included in general ones.

Senatores sunt partes corporis regis. Senators are part of the body of the king.

Sensus verborum est anima legis. The meaning of words is the spirit of the law.

Sensus verborum est duplex, mitis et asper, et verba semper accipienda sunt in mitiore sensu. The meaning of words is twofold, mild and harsh; and words are always to be received in their milder sense.

Sensus verborum ex causa dicendi accipiendus est, et sermones semper accipiendi sunt secundum subjectam materiam. The sense of words is to be taken from the occasion of speaking them, and discourses are always to be interpreted according to the subject matter.

Sententia a non judice lata nemini debet nocere. A judgment pronounced by one who is not a judge should harm no one.

Sententia contra matrimonium nunquam transit in rem judicatam. A sentence against marriage never becomes a final judgment (i.e., res judicata).

Sententia facit jus, et legis interpretatio legis vim obtinet. The judgment creates the right, and the interpretation of the law obtains the force of law.

Sententia facit jus, et res judicata pro veritate accipitur. The judgment creates the right, and what is adjudicated is taken for truth.

Sententia interlocutoria revocari potest, definitiva non potest. An interlocutory judgment may be revoked, but not a final one.

Sententia non fertur de rebus non liquidis. Judgment is not given on matters that are not clear.

Sequamur vestigia patrum nostrorum. Let us follow in the footsteps of our fathers.

Sequi debet potentia justitiam, non praecedere. Power should follow justice, not precede it.

Serjeantia idem est quod servitium. Serjeantry is the same as service. Co. Litt. 105b.

Sermo index animi. Speech is an index of the mind.

Sermones semper accipiendi sunt secundum subjectam materiam et conditionum personarum. Pleadings are to be construed by reference to the subject matter of the cause and the condition of the parties making them. 4 Co. 14.

Sermo relatus ad personam intelligi debet de conditione personae. A speech relating to the person is to be understood as relating to his condition. 4 Co. 16.

Servanda est consuetudo loci ubi causa agitur. The custom of the place where the action is brought is to be observed.

Servate terminos quos patres vestri posuere. Preserve the landmarks which your fathers have set up. (Based on Proverbs 22:28.)

Servile est expilationis crimen; sola innocentia libera. The crime of plundering (or looting) is slavish; innocence alone is free.

Servitia personalia sequuntur personam. Personal services follow the person (of the lord). • Such "personal services" were those "annexed to the person of the Mesne, as homage, fealty, etc." 2 Co. Inst. 374.

Servitus est constitutio de jure gentium, qua quis domino alieno contra naturam subjicitur. Slavery is an institution by the law of nations by which a man is subjected to a foreign master, contrary to nature. Co. Litt. 116b.

Si aes pro auro veneat non valet. If bronze is sold for gold (the contract) is invalid.

Si a jure discedas, vagus eris et erunt omnia omnibus incerta. If you depart from the law, you will wander (without a guide), and everything will be in a state of uncertainty to everyone.

Si alicujus rei societas sit et finis negotio impositus est, finitur societas. If there is a partnership in any matter, and the business is ended, the partnership ceases.

Si aliquid ex solemnibus deficiat, cum aequitas poscit subveniendum est. If anything is lacking from formal requirements, when equity requires, it will be supplied.

Si assuetis mederi possis, nova non sunt tentanda. If you can be relieved by accustomed remedies, new ones should not be tried.

Sic enim debere quem meliorem agrum suum facere, ne vicini deteriorem faciat. Everyone ought so to improve his land as not to injure his neighbor's.

Sic interpretandum est ut verba accipiantur cum effectu. Such an interpretation is to be made that the words may be taken with effect.

Sicut ad quaestionem facti, non respondent judices, ita ad quastionem juris, non respondent juratores. Inasmuch as the judges do not decide on questions of fact, so the jury do not decide on questions of law.

Sicut beatius est, ita majus est, dare quam accipere. Just as it is happier (or more blessed), it is also greater to give than to receive. 6 Co. 57.

Sic utere tuo ut alienum non laedas. Use your property so as not to damage another's; so use your own as not to injure another's property.

Sicut natura nil facit per saltum, ita nec lex. Just as nature does nothing with a leap, so neither does the law.

Sicut subditus regi tenetur ad obedientiam, ita rex subdito tenetur ad protectionem. Inasmuch as a subject is bound to obey the king, so the king is bound to protect the subject. 7 Co. 5a.

Si duo in testamento pugnantia reperientur, ultimum est ratum. If two conflicting provisions are found in a will, the latter is decisive.

Sigillum est cera impressa, quia cera sine impressione non est sigillum. A seal is a piece of wax impressed, because wax without an impression is not a seal.

Si ingratum dixeris, omnia dixeris. If you declare a man ungrateful, you have said it all. (Based on Publilius Syrus, *Dixeris maledicta cuncta,* etc.)

Si judicas, cognosce. If you judge, understand.

Silentium in senatu est vitium. Silence in the senate is a fault.

Silent leges inter arma. Laws are silent amid arms.

Si meliores sunt quos ducit amor, plures sunt quos corrigit timor. If the better are those whom love leads, the greater number are those whom fear corrects.

Similitudo legalis est casuum diversorum inter se collatorum similis ratio; quod in uno similium valet, valebit in altero. Legal similarity is a similar reason that governs various cases when compared with each other, for what avails in one similar case will avail in the other.

Simonia est voluntas sive desiderium emendi vel vendendi spiritualia vel spiritualibus adhaerentia. Contractus ex turpi causa est et contra bonos mores. Simony is the will or desire of buying or selling spiritualities, or things pertaining to them. It is a contract founded on a bad cause, and against morality.

Simplex commendatio non obligat. A simple recommendation does not bind.

Simplex et pura donatio dici poterit ubi nulla est adjecta conditio nec modus. A gift is said to be pure and simple when no condition or qualification has been annexed.

Simplicitas est legibus amica, et nimia subtilitas in jure reprobatur. Simplicity is a friend to the laws, and too much subtlety in law is condemned.

Sine possessione usucapio procedere non potest. Without possession, prescription (Roman usucapio) cannot proceed.

Singuli in solidum tenentur. Each individual is bound for the whole.

Si non appareat quid actum est, erit consequens ut id sequamur quod in regione in qua actum est frequentatur. If it is not clear what was done (or agreed on), the consequence will be that we follow what is commonly done in the place where the agreement was made. Dig. 50.17.34.

Si nulla sit conjectura quae ducat alio, verba intelligenda sunt ex proprietate, non grammatica sed populari ex usu. If there is no inference that leads to a different result, words are to be understood according to their proper meaning, not in a grammatical but in a popular and ordinary sense.

Si plures conditiones ascriptae fuerunt donationi conjunctim, omnibus est parendum; et ad veritatem copulative requiritur quod utraque pars sit vera, si divisim, quilibet vel alteri eorum satis est obtemperare; et in disjunctivis, sufficit alteram partem esse veram. If several conditions are conjunctively written in a gift, the whole of them must be complied with; and with respect to their truth, it is necessary that every part be true, taken jointly: if the conditions are separate, it is sufficient to comply with either one or the other of them; and being disjunctive, that one or the other be true.

Si plures sint fidejussores, quotquot erunt numero, singuli in solidum tenentur. If there are more sureties than one, however many they will be in number, they are individually liable for the whole.

Si quidem in nomine, cognomine, praenomine, legatarii erraverit testator, cum de persona constat, nihilominus valet legatum. Although a testator may have mistaken the *nomen, cognomen,* or *praenomen* of a legatee, yet, if it be certain who is the person meant, the legacy is valid. Just. Inst. 2.20.29.

Si quid universitati debetur, singulis non debetur, nec quod debet universitas singuli debent. If anything is due to a corporation, it is not due to the individual members of it, nor do the members individually owe what the corporation owes.

Si quis cum totum petiisset partem petat, exceptio rei judicatae vocet. If anyone sues for a part when he should have sued for the whole, the judgment should constitute res judicata (against another suit).

Si quis custos fraudem pupillo fecerit, a tutela removendus est. If a guardian commits fraud against his ward, he is to be removed from the guardianship.

Si quis praegnantem uxorem reliquit, non videtur sine liberis decessisse. If anyone dies leaving his wife pregnant, he is not considered as having died childless.

Si quis quid de republica a finitimis rumore aut fama acceperit, uti ad magistratum deferat, neve cum quo alio communicet. If anyone receive from his neighbors anything affecting the republic, by rumor or report, let him lay it before the magistrate, and not convey it to another person. Caesar, *Gallic War* 6.20.

Si quis unum percusserit cum alium percutere vellet, in felonia tenetur. If a person kills one when he meant to kill another, he is held guilty of felony.

Si suggestio non sit vera, literae patentes vacuae sunt. If the suggestion is not true, the letters patent are void.

Sive tota res evincatur, sive pars, habet regressum emptor in venditorem. If the property is taken from the purchaser by eviction, whether whole or in part, he has an action against the vendor. Dig. 21.2.1.

Si vis pacem, para bellum. If you want peace, prepare for war.

Socagium idem est quod servitium socae. Socage is the same as service of the plough. Co. Litt. 86a.

Socii mei socius meus socius non est. The partner of my partner is not my partner.

Socii plures sunt quasi unum corpus, in eo quod unum jus habent, et oportet quod corpus sit integrum et quod in nulla parte sit defectus. Several partners are as one body, since they have one right, and it is necessary that the body be perfect, and that there be defect in no part.

Sodales legem quam volent, dum ne quid ex publica lege corrumpant, sibi ferunto. Let the associates (or partners) make for themselves what law they choose, so long as they do not violate any provision of the public law. 1 Bl. Com. (ch. 18) 464.

Sola ac per se senectus donationem, testamentum aut transactionem non vitiat. Old age does not alone and of itself vitiate gift, will or transaction.

Sola innocentia libera. Innocence alone is free.

Solemnitas intervenire debet in mutatione liberi tenementi, ne contingat donationem deficere pro defectu probationis. Solemnity (or formality) ought to be observed in an exchange of free tenement, lest it happen that the gift fail through want of proof. Co. Litt. 48a.

Solemnitates juris sunt observandae. The solemnities of law must be observed.

Solicita atque anxia etiam in solitudine mala conscientia est. A bad conscience even in solitude is anxious and disturbed.

Solo cedit quod solo implantatur. What is planted in the soil belongs to the soil. • This maxim is sometimes written *Solo cedit, quicquid solo plantatur* (translatable as "what is affixed to the soil belongs to the soil").

Solo cedit quod solo inaedificatur. Whatever is built on the soil belongs to the soil.

Sol sine homine generat herbam. The sun makes the grass grow without man's assistance.

Solum rex hoc non facere potest—quod non potest injuste agere. One thing alone the king cannot do—he cannot act unjustly.

Solus Deus facit haeredem, non homo. God alone, not the man, makes the heir.

Solus Deus haeredem facit. God alone makes the heir.

Solutio pretii emptionis loco habetur. The payment of the price stands in the place of a sale.

Solvendo esse nemo intelligitur nisi qui solidum potest solvere. No one is understood to be in a state of solvency except the one who can pay all that he owes. Dig. 50.16.114.

Solvitur adhuc societas etiam morte socii. A partnership is also dissolved by the death of a partner.

Solvitur eo ligamine quo ligatur. It is released by the bond with which it is bound.

Solvitur in modo solventis. A payment is made for the purpose the payer intends.

Sommonitiones aut citationes nullae liceant fieri infra palatium regis. No summonses or citations should be permitted to be served within the king's palace.

Specilia generalibus derogant. Special words derogate from general ones.

Spes est vigilantis somnium. Hope is the dream of a waking man. 4 Inst. 203.

Spes impunitatis continuum affectum tribuit delinquendi. The hope of impunity supplies a constant inclination to wrongdoing.

Spoliatus debet ante omnia restitui. A party forcibly deprived of possession ought first of all to have restitution.

Spoliatus episcopus ante omnia debet restitui. A bishop despoiled of his see ought, above all, to be restored.

Spondet peritiam artis. He promises (to use) the skill of his art. • That is, he engages to do the work in a skillful manner.

Sponsalia dicuntur futurarum nuptiarum conventio et repromissio. A betrothal is the agreement and promise of a future marriage.

Sponsalia inter minores contracta ante septem annos nulla sunt. Betrothals contracted between parties under seven years of age are void.

Sponte virum fugiens mulier et adultera facta, doti sua careat, nisi sponsi sponte retracta. A woman leaving her husband of her own accord and committing adultery should lose her dower, unless she is taken back by her husband of his own accord.

Stabit praesumptio donec probetur in contrarium. A presumption will stand until proof is given to the contrary.

Stare decisis et non quieta movere. Literally, to stand by previous decisions and not to disturb settled matters; to adhere to precedents and not to depart from established principles.

Stat pro ratione voluntas. The will stands in place of a reason.

Stat pro ratione voluntas populi. The will of the people stands in place of a reason.

Statuta ita interpretanda ut innoxiis ne obsint. Statutes are to be so interpreted that they do not hurt the innocent.

Statuta pro publico commodo late interpretantur. Statutes made for the public advantage ought to be broadly construed.

Statuta suo clauduntur territorio, nec ultra territorium disponunt. Statutes are confined to their own territory and have no extraterritorial effect.

Statutum affirmativum non derogat communi legi. An affirmative statute does not take away from the common law.

Statutum ex gratia regis dicitur quando rex dignatur cedere de jure suo regio pro commodo et quiete populi sui. A statute is said to be by the grace of the king when the king deigns to yield some portion of his royal rights for the good and quiet of his people. 2 Inst. 378.

Statutum generaliter est intelligendum quando verba statuti sunt specialia, ratio autem generalis. A statute is to be understood generally when the words of the statute are special but its reason is general.

Statutum speciale statuto speciali non derogat. One special statute does not take away from another special statute.

Sua cuique domus arx esto. Let every man's house be his castle.

Sublata causa tollitur effectus. Remove the cause and the effect ceases.

Sublata veneratione magistratuum, respublica ruit. When respect for magistrates has been destroyed, the commonwealth perishes.

Sublato fundamento, cadit opus. When the foundation has been removed (or demolished), the structure collapses.

Sublato principali, tollitur adjunctum. When the principal has been taken away, the adjunct is also taken away.

Subornare est quasi subtus in aure ipsum male ornare, unde subornatio dicitur de falsi expressione, aut de veri suppressione. To suborn, as it were, is to supply the act itself in the ear (of another) underhandly and wickedly, from which subornation describes the expression of what is false, or the suppression of what is true. 3 Inst. 167.

Subrogatio est transfusio unius creditoris in alium eadem vel mitiori conditione. Subrogation is the substituting one creditor in the place of another in the same or a better condition.

Subsequens matrimonium tollit peccatum praecedens. A subsequent marriage removes the previous sin.

Substantia prior et dignior est accidente. The substance is prior and of more worth than the accident.

Succurritur minori; facilis est lapsus juventutis. Aid is given to a minor; easy is the slip-up of youth (i.e., youth is liable to err).

Summa caritas est facere justitiam singulis et omni tempore quando necesse fuerit. The greatest charity is to do justice to each individual and at every time when it is necessary.

Summa est lex quae pro religione facit. The highest law is the one that acts on behalf of religion.

Summa ratio est quae pro religione facit. The highest reason is that which acts in favor of religion. • Also found in indirect form, *Summam esse rationem quae pro religione facit.*

Summi cujusque bonitas commune perfugium est omnium. The goodnesss of every great man is the common refuge of all. Cicero, *De Officiis* 2.18.63.

Summum jus, summa injuria. The highest right is the utmost injury. • That is, law too rigidly interpreted produces the greatest injustice.

Super falso et certo fingitur, super incerto et vero jure sumitur. A fiction assumes that the thing feigned is certainly untrue.

Superficies solo cedit. The surface goes with the land. • That is, whatever is attached to the land forms part of it.

Super fidem chartarum, mortuis testibus, erit ad patriam de necessitate recurrendum. The truth of charters is necessarily to be referred to a jury when the witnesses are dead.

Superflua non nocent. Superfluities do no injury.

Superflua obstant; defectiva perimunt. Superfluous things oppose; defective things destroy.

Suppressio veri, expressio falsi. Suppression of the truth (is equivalent to) the expression of what is false.

Suppressio veri, suggestio falsi. Suppression of the truth (is equivalent to) the suggestion of what is false.

Surplusagium non nocet. Extraneous matter does no harm. • Superfluous allegations, not proper to the case, should have no effect.

Surrogatum sapit naturam surrogati. A thing substituted partakes of the nature of the thing for which it was substituted.

Suum cuique incommodum ferendum est potius quam de alterius commodis detrahendum. Each one must bear his own burdens rather than deprive another of his advantages. Cicero, *De Officiis* 3.6.30.

T

Tacita quaedam habentur pro expressis. Certain things though unexpressed are considered as expressed.

Talis certitudo certitudinem confundit. Such (show of) certainty confounds (real) certitude.

Talis concordia finalis dicitur eo quod finem imponit negotio, adeo quod neutra pars litigantium, ab eo de caetero poterit recedere. A final concord is that by which an end is put to the business, from which moreover neither litigant can recede.

Talis interpretatio semper fienda est ut evitetur absurdum, et inconveniens, et ne judicium sit illusorium. Interpretation is always to be made in such a manner that what is absurd and improper is avoided, and so that the judgment is not a mockery.

Talis non est eadem, nam nullum simile est idem. "Such" is not "the same," for nothing similar is the same thing.

Talis res, vel tale rectum, quae vel quod non est in homine adtunc superstite sed tantummodo est et consistit in consideratione et intelligentia legis, et quod alii dixerunt talem rem vel tale rectum fore in nubibus. Such a thing or such a right as is not vested in a person then living, but merely exists in the consideration and contemplation of law [is said to be in abeyance,] and others have said that such a thing or such a right is in the clouds. Co. Litt. 342.

Tantum bona valent, quantum vendi possunt. Things are worth as much as they can be sold for.

Tantum concessum quantum scriptum. So much is granted as is written.

Tantum habent de lege, quantum habent de justitia. (Precedents) have value in the law to the extent that they represent justice.

Tantum operatur fictio in casu ficto quantum veritas in casu vero. A legal fiction operates to the same extent and effect in the supposed case as the truth does in a real case.

Tantum praescriptum quantum possessum. There is only prescription insofar as there has been possession.

Tempis regit factum. Time rules events.

Tempus enim modus tollendi obligationes et actiones, quia tempus currit contra desides et sui juris contemptores. For time is a means of destroying obligations and actions, because time runs against those who are inactive and show little respect for their own rights.

Tempus ex suapte natura vim nullam effectricem habet. Time, of its own nature, has no effectual force.

Tempus mortis inspiciendum. (One must) look to the time of death.

Tempus regit factum. Time rules events.

Tenens domino fidem praestare debita servitia tenetur, et dominus invicem tenenti protectionem et jura sua omnia. A tenant is bound to show good faith and render services owed to his landlord, and the landlord, in turn, to protect the tenant in all his rights.

Tenens nil facere potest, propter obligationem homagii, quod vertatur domino ad exhaeredationem. A tenant, by force of the obligation of homage by which he takes title, can do nothing that tends to disinherit his landlord. Co. Litt. 65.

Tenor est pactio contra communem feudi naturam ac rationem in contractu interposita. The tenure (of an agreement) is a compact contrary to the common nature and reason of the fee, put into a contract.

Tenor est qui legem dat feudo. It is the tenor that gives law to the fee. • That is, the tenor of the feudal grant regulates its effect and extent.

Tenor investiturae est inspiciendus. The tenor of an investiture is to be scrutinized.

Terminus annorum certus debet esse et determinatus. A term of years ought to be certain and definite (with a fixed end).

Terminus et (ac) feodum non possunt constare simul in una eademque persona. Term and fee cannot both be vested in one and the same person at the same time.

Terra manens vacua occupanti conceditur. Land lying unoccupied is given to the occupant.

Terra sterilis, ex vi termini, est terra infoecunda, nullum ferens fructum. Sterile land is by force of the term barren, bearing no fruit.

Terra transit cum onere. Land passes with the incumbrances.

Tertium non datur. There is no third (option).

Testamenta, cum duo inter se pugnantia reperiuntur, ultimum ratum est; sic est, cum duo inter se pugnantia reperiuntur in eodem testamento. When two conflicting wills are found, the last prevails; so it is when two conflicting clauses occur in the same will.

Testamenta latissimam interpretationem habere debent. Wills ought to have the broadest interpretation.

Testamentum est testatio mentis, facta nullo praesente metu periculi, sed cogitatione mortalitatis. A will is a witnessing of the mind, made in view of the uncertainty of human life, but in no present fear of danger. Co. Litt. 322b.

Testamentum est voluntatis nostrae justa sententia, de eo quod quis post mortem suam fieri velit. A testament is the just expression of our will concerning that which anyone wishes done after his death. • Or, as Blackstone renders it, a testament is "the legal declaration of a man's intentions which he wills to be performed after his death." 2 Bl. Com. 499.

Testamentum omne morte consummatum. Every will is completed by death.

Testatoris ultima voluntas est perimplenda secundum veram intentionem suam. The last will of a testator is to be fulfilled according to his true intention.

Testes ponderantur, non numerantur. Witnesses are weighed, not numbered.

Testes qui postulat debet dare eis sumptus competentes. Whoever demands witnesses ought to give them suitable expenses.

Testibus deponentibus in pari numero, dignioribus est credendum. When the number of witnesses giving testimony is equal on both sides, the more trustworthy are to be believed.

Testibus, non testimoniis, credendum est. The witnesses must be believed, not (simply) their testimony.

Testimonia ponderanda sunt, non numeranda. Testimonies are to be weighed, not counted.

Testis de visu praeponderat aliis. An eyewitness outweighs others.

Testis dicere debet ab imo, "non sum doctus nec instructus, nec curo de victoria, modo ministretur Justitia." A witness should be able to say from the heart, "I am not informed nor instructed, nor do I care which party be successful, provided Justice be served." 4 Inst. 279.

Testis lupanaris sufficit ad factum in lupanari. Someone from a brothel is a sufficient witness to a happening in a brothel.

Testis nemo in sua causa esse potest. No one can be a witness in his own cause.

Testis oculatus unus plus valet quam auriti decem. One eyewitness is worth more than ten earwitnesses.

Testium numerus si non adjicitur, duo sufficiunt. If the number of witnesses is not prescribed, two are sufficient. 4 Inst. 279.

Testmoignes ne poent testifier le negative, mes l'affirmative. Witnesses cannot testify to a negative; they must testify to an affirmative.

Theftbote est emenda furti capta, sine consideratione curiae domini regis. Theftbote is compensation taken for the theft, without consideration from the king's court. 3 Inst. 134.

Thesaurus competit domino regi, et non domino libertatis nisi sit per verba specialia. A treasure belongs to the king, and not to the lord of a liberty, unless it be through special words.

Thesaurus inventus est vetus dispositio pecuniae, &c., cujus non extat modo memoria, adeo ut jam dominum non habeat. Treasure trove is an ancient hiding of money, etc., of which no recollection exists, so that it now has no owner.

Thesaurus non competit regi, nisi quando nemo scit qui abscondit thesaurum. Treasure does not belong to the king, unless no one knows who hid it.

Timores vani sunt aestimandi qui non cadunt in constantem virum. Those fears must be considered vain (or frivolous) that do not affect a man of steady character.

Titius haeres esto. Let Titius be my heir. • Titius was the Roman counterpart of John Doe.

Titulus est justa causa possidendi id quod nostrum est. Title is the just cause of possessing that which is ours.

Tolle voluntatem et erit omnis actus indifferens. Take away the will, and every action will be indifferent.

Tortura legum pessima. The torture (or twisting) of laws is the worst kind of torture.

Totum praefertur unicuique parti. The whole is preferred to any single part.

Tout ce que la loi ne defend pas est permis. Everything that the law does not forbid is permitted.

Toute exception non surveillée tend à prendre la place du principe. Every exception not watched tends to assume the place of the principle.

Tractent fabrilia fabri. Let smiths perform the work of smiths.

Traditio loqui facit chartam. Delivery makes the deed (document) speak.

Traditione pacta firmantur. Agreements are confirmed by delivery.

Traditionibus et usucapionibus, non nudis pactis, transferuntur rerum dominia. Rights of property are transferred by delivery and by prescription (founded on lengthy possession), not by naked agreements.

Traditio nihil amplius transferre debet vel potest ad eum qui accipit quam est apud eum qui tradit. Delivery neither can nor should transfer anything more to the recipient than is in possession of the one who delivers.

Trado tibi ecclesiam. I deliver this church (or living) to you.

Trahi non debent in argumentum quae propter necessitatem recepta sunt. Things that are received on account of necessity ought not to be drawn into argument.

Transferuntur dominia sine titulo et traditione, per usucaptionem, scil., per longam continuam et pacificam possessionem. Rights of dominion are transferred without title or delivery, by usucaption, to wit, long and undisturbed possession. Co. Litt. 113b.

Transgressio est cum modus non servatur nec mensura, debit enim quilibet in suo facto modum habere et mensuram. Transgression is when neither mode nor measure is preserved, for every one in his act ought to have a mode and measure.

Transgressione multiplicata, crescat poenae inflictio. When transgression is repeated, let the infliction of punishment be increased. 2 Co. Inst. 479.

Transit in rem judicatam. It passes into a judgment.

Transit terra cum onere. The land passes with its burdens.

Tres faciunt collegium. Three form a corporation.

Triatio ibi semper debet fieri ubi juratores meliorem possunt habere notitiam. Trial ought always to be held where the jurors can have the better information.

Triennalis pacificus possessor beneficii est inde securus. The undisturbed possessor of a benefice for three years is thereafter secure (from challenge).

Tristibus et tacitis non fidendum. Melancholy and secretive persons must not be trusted. *Disticha Catonis.*

Turpe est viro id in quo quotidie versatur ignorare. It is shameful for a man to be ignorant of the business in which he is engaged every day.

Turpe impossibile. An impossibility is shameful.

Turpis est pars quae non convenit cum suo toto. The part is bad that does not accord with its whole.

Tuta est custodia quae sibimet creditur. The guardianship is secure that is entrusted to itself alone.

Tutius erratur ex parte mitiori. It is safer to err on the gentler side (or on the side of leniency).

Tutius est rei incumbere quam personae. It is safer to rely on a thing than on a person. • Real security is safer than personal security.

Tutius semper est errare in acquietando quam in puniendo, ex parte misericordiae quam ex parte justitiae. It is always safer to err in acquitting than in punishing, (and) on the side of mercy than of justice.

Tutor incertus dari non potest. An uncertain person cannot be given or appointed as tutor.

Tutor in rem suam auctor fieri non potest. A tutor cannot act for his own interest.

Tutor praesumitur intus habere, ante redditas rationes. A tutor is presumed to have funds in his own hands until his accounts have been rendered.

Tutor rem pupilli emere non potest. A tutor cannot purchase the property of his ward.

U

Ubi aliquid conceditur, conceditur et id sine quo res ipsa esse non potest. When anything is granted, that also is granted without which the thing itself cannot exist.

Ubi aliquid impeditur propter unum, eo remoto, tollitur impedimentum. When anything is impeded by reason of one thing, when that is removed, the impediment is removed.

Ubi cessat remedium ordinarium, ibi decurritur ad extraordinarium. When a common remedy ceases to be of service, recourse is had to an extraordinary one.

Ubi concurrent commune jus et jus scriptum, communi standum. Where common and written law clash, we must stand by the common law.

Ubi culpa est, ibi poena subesse debet. Where the fault is, there the punishment should be imposed.

Ubicunque est injuria, ibi damnum sequitur. Wherever there is a legal wrong, there damage follows.

Ubi damna dantur victus victori in expensis condemnari debet. Where damages are awarded, the party that did not succeed ought to be adjudged to pay expenses for the party that prevailed.

Ubi diverso jure in eandem rem venire quis potuit, eo jure venisse praesumitur quod fortius ac melius sit. Where one could have come to same thing by different rights, he is presumed to have arrived at it by the stronger and better right.

Ubi duo jura concurrunt in eadem persona, idem est ac si esset in diversis. Where two rights run together (or clash) in the same person, it is the same as if it were in different persons.

Ubi duo pugnantia in charta concurrunt, prius ratum esto. Where two repugnant things meet in a charter, let the first be established.

Ubi duo sensus occurrunt, mitiori standunt. Where two meanings occur, we must abide by the milder.

Ubi eadem ratio, ibi eadem lex; et de similibus idem est judicium. Where the same reason exists, there the same law prevails; and, of things similar, the judgment is the same. 7 Coke 18b.

Ubi eadem ratio, ibi idem jus. Where there is the same reason, there is the same law. — Also rendered *Ubi eadem est ratio, ibi idem est jus.*

Ubi eadem ratio, ibi idem jus; et de similibus idem est judicium. Where there is the same reason, there is the same law; and the same judgment should be rendered on comparable facts.

Ubi est forum, ibi ergo est jus. Where the forum (or place of jurisdiction) is, there accordingly is the law.

Ubi et dantis et accipientis turpitudo versatur, non posse repeti dicimus; quotiens autem accipientis turpitudo versatur, repeti posse. Where there is misconduct on the part of both giver and receiver, we say the thing cannot be recovered; but as often as the misconduct is on the side of the receiver (alone), it can be recovered.

Ubi ex jure positivo alicujus gentis reo conceditur vel prohibetur leges Angliae jus ejus gentis in judicio respiciunt ubi actio accrevit. Where a grant is given or a prohibition made to an accused person by a positive law, the laws of England regards the law of the nation where the action arose, in adjudicating the same.

Ubi factum nullum, ibi fortia nulla. Where there is no fact, there are no strong points.

Ubi jus, ibi remedium. Where there is a right, there is a remedy.

Ubi jus incertum, ibi jus nullum. Where the right is uncertain, there is no right.

Ubi lex aliquem cogit ostendere causam, necesse est quod causa sit justa et legitima. Where the law compels someone to show cause, it is necessary that the cause be just and legal.

Ubi lex communis et aequitas in eadem re versantur, aequitas alia via agit sed non aliter sentit. Where common law and equity are involved in the same case, equity takes a different path but feels no differently (or has the same attitude).

Ubi lex deest, praetor supplet. Where the law is deficient, the praetor supplies the deficiency.

Ubi lex est specialis et ratio ejus generalis, generaliter accipienda est. Where the law is special and the reason of it is general, it ought to be taken as general.

Ubi lex non distinguit, nec nos distinguere debemus. Where the law does not distinguish, we ought not to distinguish.

Ubi major pars est, ibi totum. Where the greater part is, there is the whole.

Ubi matrimonium, ibi dos. Where there is marriage, there is dower.

Ubi non adest norma legis, omnia quasi pro suspectis habenda sunt. Where there is no rule of law, everything must be held, as it were, suspect.

Ubi non apparet dominus rei, quae olim fuerunt inventoris de jure naturali, jam efficiuntur principis jure gentium. Where the owner does not appear, those things which once belonged to the finder by the law of nature are now made property of the ruler by the law of nations. 2 Inst. 167; 1 Bl. Com. 289.

Ubi non est annua renovatio, ibi decimae non debent solvi. Where there is no annual renovation, there tithes should not be paid.

Ubi non est condendi auctoritas, ibi non est parendi necessitas. Where there is no authority to establish (a rule), there is no necessity to obey.

Ubi non est directa lex, standum est arbitrio judicis, vel procedendum ad similia. Where there is not direct law, one must rely on the judgment of the judge or refer to similar cases.

Ubi non est lex, ibi non est transgressio quoad mundum. Where there is not law, there is not transgression, as far as this world is concerned.

Ubi non est manifesta injustitia, judices habentur pro bonis viris, et judicatum pro veritate. Where there is no manifest injustice, the judges are to be regarded as honest men, and their judgment as truth.

Ubi non est principalis, non potest esse accessorius. Where there is no principal, there can be no accessory.

Ubi nulla est conjectura quae ducat alio, verba intelligenda sunt ex proprietate non grammatica sed populari ex usu. Where there is no inference that would lead in another direction, the words are to be understood according to their proper meaning, not strictly according to grammar but according to popular usage.

Ubi nullum matrimonium, ibi nulla dos. Where there is no marriage, there is no dower.

Ubi nullum placitum, ibi nullum essonium. Where there is no plea, there is no essoin. Bracton 341.

Ubi onus ibi emolumentum. Where the burden is, there is the profit or advantage.

Ubi periculum, ibi et lucrum collocatur. Where the risk is, there also the profit accrues.

Ubi pugnantia inter se in testamento juberentur, neutrum ratum est. When two directions conflicting with each other were given in a will, neither is held valid.

Ubi quid generaliter conceditur, inest haec exceptio, si non aliquid sit contra jus fasque. Where a thing is granted in general terms, this exception is implied: if there is not anything contrary to law and right.

Ubi quis delinquit ibi punietur. Where anyone commits an offense, there will he be punished.

Ubi remedium, ibi ius. Where there is a remedy, there is a right.

Ubi societas, ibi ius. Wherever there is society, there is law.

Ubi sustuleris revocationem, renatum est testamentum. When you have taken away the revocation, the will is reborn.

Ubi verba conjuncta non sunt, sufficit alterutrum esse factum. Where words are not conjoined, it is enough that one or another (of the things enumerated) has been done.

Ubi vetat quid lex neque poenam statuit, poena in discretione judicis est. Where the law forbids anything and has not prescribed a punishment, the punishment is in the discretion of the judge.

Ultima voluntas esset libera. The last will should be free (or unconstrained).

Ultima voluntas testatoris est perimplenda secundum veram intentionem suam. The last will of a testator is to be fulfilled according to his true intention.

Ultimum supplicium esse mortem solam interpretamur. We consider death alone to be the extreme punishment.

Ultra posse nemo tenetur. Nobody is held beyond his ability.

Ultra posse non potest esse et vice versa. What is beyond possibility cannot exist, and the reverse (what cannot exist is not possible).

Una electa via non datur recursus ad alteram. Once one path has been chosen it allows no recourse to another.

Una persona vix potest supplere vices duarum. One person can scarcely supply the place of two.

Unaquaeque gleba servit. Every lump of earth (on the land) is subject to the servitude.

Uniuscujusque contractus initium spectandum est et causa. The beginning and cause of each and every contract must be considered.

Unius omnino testis responsio non audiatur. Let the evidence of one witness not be heard at all.

Universalia sunt notiora singularibus. Things universal are better known than things particular.

Universitas vel corporatio non dicitur aliquid facere nisi id sit collegialiter deliberatum, etiamsi major pars id faciat. A university or corporation is not said to take any action unless the action was resolved by it as a body, even if a greater part of the body should act.

Universus terminus in lege dies unus. One day is a complete term in law.

Un ne doit prise advantage de son tort demesne. One should not take advantage from his own wrong.

Uno absurdo dato, infinita sequuntur. When one absurdity has been allowed, an infinity follows.

Unumquodque dissolvitur eodem ligamine quo ligatur. Everything is dissolved by the same binding by which it is bound together.

Unumquodque eodem modo dissolvitur quo colligatur. Any obligation is discharged in the same manner as it is constituted.

Unumquodque eodem modo quo colligatum est dissolvitur, quo constituitur, destruitur. Everything is dissolved by the same means by the same means it was put together, destroyed by the same means by which it was established.

Unumquodque est id quod est principalius in ipso. That which is the principal part of a thing is the thing itself.

Unumquodque ligamen dissolvitur eodem ligamine qui et ligatur. Every obligation is dissolved in the same manner in which it is contracted.

Unumquodque principiorum est sibimet ipsi fides; et perspicua vera non sunt probanda. Each and every one of the general principles is its own pledge of trust, and plain truths need not be proved.

Unusquisque debet esse gnarus conditionis ejus cum quo contrahit. Everyone ought to be cognizant of the condition of the person with whom he makes contract.

Unusquisque paci et justitiae publicae tenetur succurrere. Every one is bound to support peace and public justice.

Usucapio constituta est ut aliquis litium finis esset. Prescription (Roman usucapio) was instituted that there might be some end to lawsuits. Dig. 41.10.5.

Usura dicitur quia datur pro usu aeris. Usury is so called because it is given for the use of money. 2 Inst. 89.

Usus est dominium fiduciarium. Use is a fiduciary ownership.

Usus fit ex iteratis actibus. Usage arises from repeated acts.

Utatur nemo duobus officiis. No one man should exercise two offices. 4 Coke Inst. 100.

Utile per inutile non vitiatur. What is useful is not vitiated by the useless.

Uti possidetis, ita possideatis. As you possess, so you should possess.

Utlagatus est quasi extra legem positus: caput gerit lupinum. An outlaw is, as it were, put out of the protection of the law: he carries the head of a wolf.

Utlagatus pro contumacia et fuga non propter hoc convictus est de facto principali. One who is outlawed for contempt and flight is not on that account convicted of the principal act.

"Ut" modus est, "si" conditio, "quia" causa, inesse potest donationi modus conditio sive causa. In a gift there may be a manner, a condition, and a cause: the word "that" introduces a manner, the word "if," a condition, and the word "because," a cause. Co. Litt. 204a.

Ut poena ad paucos, metus ad omnes perveniat. Let punishment come to few, dread to all. 4 Coke 124b.

Ut res magis valeat quam pereat. (Interpret the law, contract, etc.) so that the transaction is upheld rather than lost (or so that a matter may avail rather than perish). • The phrase can be literally translated as "that the matter may have effect rather than fail."

Ut summae potestatis regis est posse quantum velit, sic magnitudinis est velle quantum possit. As the highest power of a king is to be able to do all he wishes, so the highest greatness of him is to wish as much as he is able to do. 3 Inst. 236.

Uxor furi desponsata non tenebitur ex facto viri. The wife of a thief shall not be bound by the act of her husband. 3 Inst. 108.

V

Vagabundum nuncupamus eum qui nullibi domicilium contraxit habitationis. We call the person a vagabond who has acquired nowhere a domicile of residence.

Valeat quantum valere potest. Let it have effect as far as it can have effect.

Valet illatio ab actu ad potentiam. Logical inference from the act is valid for the possibility. (We are able to judge the future from what has happened in the past).

Valet nunquam confirmatio nisi ille qui confirmat sit in possessione rei vel juris unde fieri debet confirmatio; et eodem modo nisi ille cui confirmatio fit, sit in possessione. Confirmation is not valid unless he who confirms is either in possession of the thing itself or of the right of which confirmation is to be made, and, in like manner, unless he to whom confirmation is made is in possession. Co. Litt. 295.

Vana est illa potentia quae nunquam venit in actum. Vain is that power that never comes into action.

Vani timores sunt aestimandi, qui non cadunt in constantem virem. Those fears are to be considered groundless that do not affect a man of steady character.

Vani timoris justa excusatio non est. There is no legal excuse based on a groundless fear.

Vectigal, origine ipsa, jus caesarum et regum patrimoniale est. Tribute in its origin is the patrimonial right of kings and emperors.

Velle non creditur qui obsequitur imperio patris vel domini. A person is not presumed to act of his own will who obeys the orders of his father or his master.

Vendens eandem rem duobus falsarius est. A vendor is fraudulent if he sells the same thing to two (separate) buyers.

Venditor nominis tenetur praestare debitum subesse, non vero debitorem locupletem esse. The seller of a debt is bound to warrant that the debt is due, but not that the debtor is a person of means (able to pay).

Veniae facilitas incentivum est delinquendi. Ease of winning pardon is an incentive to committing crime.

Venire contra factum proprium non valet. To contravene one's own act is invalid.

Verba accipienda sunt secundum subjectam materiam. Words are to be interpreted according to the subject matter.

Verba accipienda ut sortiantur effectum. Words are to be taken so that they may have some effect.

Verba aequivoca ac in dubio sensu posita intelliguntur digniori et potentiori sensu. Equivocal words and those in a doubtful sense are understood in the more suitable and more effective sense.

Verba aliquid operari debent — debent intelligi ut aliquid operentur. Words ought to have some effect — words ought to be understood so as to have some effect.

Verba aliquid operari debent; verba cum effectu sunt accipienda. Words ought to have some effect; words must be taken so as to have effect.

Verba artis ex arte. Terms of art (should be explained) from the art.

Verba attendenda, non os loquitur. We must pay attention to the words, not the face (or expression) or the speaker.

Verba chartarum fortius accipiuntur contra proferentem. The words of deeds are taken most strongly against the person offering them.

Verba cum effectu accipienda sunt. Words must be taken so as to have effect.

Verba currentis monetae tempus solutionis designant. The words "current money" refer to the time of payment.

Verba debent intelligi cum effectu, ut res magis valeat quam pereat. Words ought to be understood with effect, so that the thing have force rather than fail. 2 Bl. Com. 380.

Verba debent intelligi ut aliquid operentur. Words ought to be so understood that they may have some effect.

Verba dicta de persona intelligi debent de conditione personae. Words spoken of the person are to be understood of the condition of the person.

Verba fortius accipiuntur contra proferentem. Words are interpreted more strongly against the party who puts them forward; words are most readily accepted against the one putting them forward.

Verba generalia generaliter sunt intelligenda. General words are to be understood generally.

Verba generalia restringuntur ad habilitatem rei vel aptitudinem personae. General words are limited to the capability of the subject matter or the aptitude of the person.

Verba generalia restringuntur ad habilitatem rei vel personae. General words are limited to the capability of the subject matter or of the person.

Verba homicidium non excusant. Words (of provocation) do not excuse a homicide.

Verba illata (relata) inesse videntur. Words referred to are considered as if incorporated.

Verba in differenti materia per prius, non per posterius, intelligenda sunt. Words referring to a different subject are to be understood by what goes before, not by what follows.

Verba intelligenda sunt in casu possibili. Words are to be understood in reference to a possible case.

Verba intentioni, et non e contra, debent inservire. Words should be subject to the intention, not the reverse.

Verba ita sunt intelligenda, ut res magis valeat quam pereat. Words are to be so understood that the matter may have effect rather than fail.

Verba legis non ex vulgari sensu sed ex legis sensu, neque laxam et precariam sed certam et legibus praefinitam interpretationem requirunt. The words of the law require interpretation not from popular meaning but from the legal sense, and not a lax and precarious interpretation but one that is fixed and positive (defined by statute).

Verba mere aequivoca, si per communem usum loquendi in intellectu certo sumuntur, talis intellectus praeferendus est. When words are purely equivocal, if by common usage of speech they are taken in a certain meaning, such meaning is to be preferred.

Verba nihil operari melius est quam absurde. It is better that words should have no effect than an absurd effect.

Verba non tam intuenda quam causa et natura rei, ut mens contrahentium ex eis potius quam ex verbis appareat. The words (of a contract) are not to be looked to so much as the cause and nature of the matter, so that the intention of the contracting parties may appear from these rather than from the (mere) words.

Verba offendi possunt, immo ab eis recedere licet, ut verba ad sanum intellectum reducantur. The words can be faulted — indeed, it is permitted to depart from them, in order that the words may be restored to a sensible meaning.

Verba ordinationis, quando verificari possunt in sua vera significatione, trahi ad extraneum intellectum non debent. When the words of an ordinance can be made true in their true signification, they ought not to be warped to a foreign meaning.

Verba posteriora propter certitudinem addita, ad priora quae certitudine indigent, sunt referunda. Later words added for the purpose of certainty are to be referred to preceding words in which certainty is wanting.

Verba pro re et subjecta materia accipi debent. Words should be taken most in favor of the thing and the subject matter.

Verba quae aliquid operari possunt non debent esse superflua. Words that can have some effect ought not to be (treated as) superfluous.

Verba quantumvis generalia ad aptitudinem restringuntur, etiamsi nullam aliam paterentur restrictionem. Words, howsoever general, are confined to fitness (i.e., to harmonize with the subject matter), even if they would bear no other restriction.

Verba relata hoc maxime operantur per referentiam ut in eis inesse videntur. Words to which reference is made have, by the reference, this particular effect, that they are considered to be incorporated in those (clauses). • Words to which reference is made in an instrument have the same effect and operation as if they were inserted in the clause referring to them.

Verba relata inesse videntur. Words to which reference is made are considered incorporated.

Verba secundum materiam subjectam intelligi nemo est qui nescit. There is no one who does not know that words should be understood according to the subject matter.

Verba semper accipienda sunt in mitiori sensu. Words are always to be taken in their milder sense.

Verba strictae significationis ad latam extendi possunt, si subsit ratio. Words of a strict signification can be given a wide signification if there is reason for it.

Verba sunt indices animi. Words are indications of the intention.

Verba temere prolata parum curat lex. The law pays little regard to words rashly uttered.

Verbis standum ubi nulla ambiguitas. One must abide by the words where there is no ambiguity.

Verborum obligatio verbis tollitur. An obligation verbally incurred is verbally extinguished.

Verbum imperfecti temporis rem adhuc imperfectam significat. The verb in the imperfect tense indicates a matter as yet incomplete.

Veredictum quasi dictum veritatis; ut judicium quasi juris dictum. A verdict is, as it were, the saying of the truth, in the same manner that a judgment is the saying of the law (or right).

Veritas, a quocunque dicitur, a Deo est. Truth, by whomsoever pronounced, is from God.

Veritas demonstrationis tollit errorem nominis. The truth of the description removes the error of the name.

Veritas est justitiae mater. Truth is the mother of justice.

Veritas habenda est in juratore; justitia et judicium in judice. Truth is the desideratum in a juror; justice and judgment in a judge.

Veritas nihil veretur nisi abscondi. Truth fears nothing but to be hidden.

Veritas nimium altercando amittitur. By too much quarreling the truth is lost.

Veritas nominis tollit errorem demonstrationis. The truth of the name takes away the error of the description.

Veritas quae minime defensatur opprimitur, et qui non improbat approbat. Truth that is not sufficiently defended is overpowered, and he who does not disapprove approves.

Veritatem qui non libere pronunciat, proditor est veritatis. One who does not speak the truth freely is a traitor to the truth.

Via antiqua via est tuta. The old way is the safe way.

Via trita est tutissima. The beaten road is the safest.

Via trita, via tuta. The beaten way is the safe way.

Vicarius non habet vicarium. A deputy does not have a deputy.

Vicini viciniora praesumuntur scire. Neighbors are presumed to know things of the immediate vicinity.

Victoria pax, non pactione, parienda est. Peace is to be secured by victory, not by negotiation. Cicero, *Ad Fam.* 10.6.1.

Victus victori in expensis condemnatus est. The vanquished is to be condemned in costs to the victor.

Videbis ea saepe committi quae saepe vindicantur. You will see those offenses often committed that are often punished. Seneca, *De Clementia* 1.23.1.

Videtur qui surdus et mutus ne poet faire alienation. A deaf and mute person is considered not to be able to alienate.

Vigilantibus et non dormientibus jura subveniunt. The laws aid the vigilant, not those who sleep.

Vigilantibus iura sunt scripta. Laws are written for the vigilant.

Vigilantibus non dormientibus subvenit lex. The law supports the waking, not the sleeping.

Villa est ex pluribus mansionibus vicinata, et collata ex pluribus vicinis, et sub appellatione villarum continentur burgi et civitates. Vill is a neighborhood of many mansions, a collection of many neighbors, and under the term of "vills" boroughs and cities are contained. Co. Litt. 115.

Vim vi repellere licet, modo fiat moderamine inculpatae tutelae, non ad sumendam vindictam, sed ad propulsandam injuriam. It is lawful to repel force by force; but let it be done with the self-control of blameless defense — not to take revenge, but to repel injury.

Vinco vincentem, ergo multo magis vinco te. If I conquer your conqueror, by so much more do I conquer you.

Violenta praesumptio aliquando est plena probatio. A very powerful presumption is sometimes full proof.

Viperina est expositio quae corrodit viscera textus. That is a viperine exposition that gnaws away the innards of the text.

Vir et uxor censentur in lege una persona. Husband and wife are considered one person in law.

Virginitas vel castitas corrupta restitui non potest. Virginity or chastity, once violated, cannot be restored. Just. Codex 9.13.1pr.

Vir militans Deo non implicetur secularibus negotiis. A man fighting for God must not be involved in secular business. Co. Litt. 70b.

Virum bonum nulla spes ad turpia invitat. No expectation can allure a good man to evil.

Vis legibus est inimica. Force is inimical to the laws.

Vita reipublicae pax, et animus libertas, et corpus leges. Peace is the life of the State; liberty the soul; and the laws the body.

Vitium clerici nocere non debet. A clerical error ought not to prejudice.

Vitium est quod fugi debet, ne, si rationem non invenias, mox legem sine ratione esse clames. It is a fault that ought to be avoided, that if you do not discover the reason, you quickly exclaim that the law is without reason.

Vix ulla lex fieri potest quae omnibus commoda sit, sed si majori parti prospiciat, utilis est. Scarcely any law can be made that is advantageous to all; but if it benefits the majority, it is useful.

Vocabula artium explicanda sunt secundum definitiones prudentium. Terms of art are to be explained according to the definitions of those who are experienced in that art.

Volenti non fit injuria. There is no injury to one who consents.

Voluit sed non dixit. The person willed but did not say.

Voluntas donatoris in charta doni sui manifeste expressa observetur. The will of the donor, if clearly expressed in the deed of his gift, should be observed.

Voluntas est justa sententia de eo quod post mortem suam fieri velit. A will is an exact determination concerning that which each one wishes to be done after his death.

Voluntas et propositum distinguunt maleficia. The will and the purpose distinguish crimes.

Voluntas facit quod in testamento scriptum valeat. The will (of the testator) gives validity to what is written in the will (testament).

Voluntas in delictis non exitus spectatur. In offenses, the will and not the outcome is regarded.

Voluntas regis in curia; non in camera. The will of the king in his court (of law); not in his chamber.

Voluntas reputatur pro facto. The will is to be taken for the deed.

Voluntas testatoris ambulatoria est usque ad mortem. The will of a testator is changeable right up until death. • That is, the testator may change the will at any time. This maxim is sometimes written *Voluntas testatoris est ambulatoria usque ad extremum vitae exitum* (same sense).

Voluntas testatoris habet interpretationem latam et benignam. The will of the testator should receive a broad and liberal interpretation.

Voluntas ultima testatoris est perimplenda secundum veram intentionem suam. The last will of a testator is to be fulfilled according to his true intention.

Vox emissa volat; litera scripta manet. The uttered voice flies; the written letter remains.

Vox populi vox Dei. The voice of the people is the voice of God.

Vulgaris opinio est duplex: orta inter graves et discretos, quae multum veritatis habet, et opinio orta inter leves et vulgares homines, absque specie veritatis. Common opinion is double: that proceeding from grave and discreet men, which has much truth in it, and that proceeding from foolish vulgar men, without any semblance of truth in it.

W

Warrantizare est defendere et acquietare tenentem, qui warrantum vocavit, in seisina sua; et tenens de re warranti excambium habebit ad valentiam. To warrant is to defend and ensure in peace the tenant, who calls for warranty, in his seisin; and the tenant in warranty will have an exchange in proportion to its value. Co. Litt. 365 a.

Warrantor potest excipere quod querens non tenet terram de qua petit warrantiam, et quod donum fuit insufficiens. A warrantor may object that the complainant does not hold the land of which he seeks the warranty, and that the gift was insufficient.

Maxims Bibliography

Bl. Com. = Blackstone, William. *Commentaries on the Laws of England*. 4 vols. Reprinted Chicago and London: University of Chicago Press, 1979. From the 1st ed. Oxford: Clarendon Press 1765–1769.

Bracton = Bracton, Henry de. *De Legibus et Consuetudinibus Angliae*. G.E. Woodbine ed.; S.E. Thorne transl. 4 vols. Cambridge, Mass.: Harvard University Press, 1968.

Coke = *The Reports of Sir Edward Coke*. J.H. Thomas & J.F. Fraser eds. 13 parts in 6 vols. London: Butterworth, 1826.

Co. Inst. = Coke, Sir Edward. *The Institutes of the Laws of England*. Parts 2–4, in 4 vols. Reprinted Buffalo, N.Y.: Willam S. Hein, 1986. From the edition of London: Brooke, 1797.

Co. Litt. = Coke, Sir Edward. *The First Part of the Institutes of the Laws of England, or A Commentarie upon Littleton*. 2 vols. Reprinted New York and London: Garland, 1979. From the 1st ed. London: Societe of Stationers, 1628.

Dig. = *The Digest of Justinian*. T. Mommsen et al. 4 vols. Philadelphia: University of Pennsylvania Press, 1985.

Just. Inst. = *Justinian's Institutes*. P. Kueger ed.; P. Birks & G. McLeod transl. Ithaca, N.Y.: Cornell University Press, 1987.

Appendix C

The Declaration of Independence

In Congress, July 4, 1776

The unanimous Declaration of the thirteen united States of America

When in the Course of human events it becomes necessary for one people to dissolve the political bands which have connected them with another and to assume among the powers of the earth, the separate and equal station to which the Laws of Nature and of Nature's God entitle them, a decent respect to the opinions of mankind requires that they should declare the causes which impel them to the separation.

We hold these truths to be self-evident, that all men are created equal, that they are endowed by their Creator with certain unalienable Rights, that among these are Life, Liberty and the pursuit of Happiness. — That to secure these rights, Governments are instituted among Men, deriving their just powers from the consent of the governed, — That whenever any Form of Government becomes destructive of these ends, it is the Right of the People to alter or to abolish it, and to institute new Government, laying its foundation on such principles and organizing its powers in such form, as to them shall seem most likely to effect their Safety and Happiness. Prudence, indeed, will dictate that Governments long established should not be changed for light and transient causes; and accordingly all experience hath shewn that mankind are more disposed to suffer, while evils are sufferable than to right themselves by abolishing the forms to which they are accustomed. But when a long train of abuses and usurpations, pursuing invariably the same Object evinces a design to reduce them under absolute Despotism, it is their right, it is their duty, to throw off such Government, and to provide new Guards for their future security. — Such has been the patient sufferance of these Colonies; and such is now the necessity which constrains them to alter their former Systems of Government. The history of the present King of Great Britain is a history of repeated injuries and usurpations, all having in direct object the establishment of an absolute Tyranny over these States. To prove this, let Facts be submitted to a candid world.

He has refused his Assent to Laws, the most wholesome and necessary for the public good.

He has forbidden his Governors to pass Laws of immediate and pressing importance, unless suspended in their operation till his Assent should be obtained; and when so suspended, he has utterly neglected to attend to them.

He has refused to pass other Laws for the accommodation of large districts of people, unless those people would relinquish the right of Representation in the Legislature, a right inestimable to them and formidable to tyrants only.

He has called together legislative bodies at places unusual, uncomfortable, and distant from the depository of their Public Records, for the sole purpose of fatiguing them into compliance with his measures.

He has dissolved Representative Houses repeatedly, for opposing with manly firmness his invasions on the rights of the people.

He has refused for a long time, after such dissolutions, to cause others to be elected, whereby the Legislative Powers, incapable of Annihilation, have returned to the People at large for their exercise; the State remaining in the mean time exposed to all the dangers of invasion from without, and convulsions within.

He has endeavoured to prevent the population of these States; for that purpose obstructing the Laws for Naturalization of Foreigners; refusing to pass others to encourage their migrations hither, and raising the conditions of new Appropriations of Lands.

He has obstructed the Administration of Justice by refusing his Assent to Laws for establishing Judiciary Powers.

He has made Judges dependent on his Will alone for the tenure of their offices, and the amount and payment of their salaries.

He has erected a multitude of New Offices, and sent hither swarms of Officers to harass our people and eat out their substance.

He has kept among us, in times of peace, Standing Armies without the Consent of our legislatures.

He has affected to render the Military independent of and superior to the Civil Power.

He has combined with others to subject us to a jurisdiction foreign to our constitution, and unacknowledged by our laws; giving his Assent to their Acts of pretended Legislation:

For quartering large bodies of armed troops among us:

For protecting them, by a mock Trial from punishment for any Murders which they should commit on the Inhabitants of these States:

For cutting off our Trade with all parts of the world:

For imposing Taxes on us without our Consent:

For depriving us in many cases, of the benefit of Trial by Jury:

For transporting us beyond Seas to be tried for pretended offences:

For abolishing the free System of English Laws in a neighbouring Province, establishing therein an Arbitrary government, and enlarging its Boundaries so as to render it at once an example and fit instrument for introducing the same absolute rule into these Colonies

For taking away our Charters, abolishing our most valuable Laws and altering fundamentally the Forms of our Governments:

For suspending our own Legislatures, and declaring themselves invested with power to legislate for us in all cases whatsoever.

He has abdicated Government here, by declaring us out of his Protection and waging War against us.

He has plundered our seas, ravaged our coasts, burnt our towns, and destroyed the lives of our people.

He is at this time transporting large Armies of foreign Mercenaries to compleat the works of death, desolation, and tyranny, already begun with circumstances of Cruelty & Perfidy scarcely paralleled in the most barbarous ages, and totally unworthy the Head of a civilized nation.

He has constrained our fellow Citizens taken Captive on the high Seas to bear Arms against their Country, to become the executioners of their friends and Brethren, or to fall themselves by their Hands.

He has excited domestic insurrections amongst us, and has endeavoured to bring on the inhabitants of our frontiers, the merciless Indian Savages whose known rule of warfare, is an undistinguished destruction of all ages, sexes and conditions.

In every stage of these Oppressions We have Petitioned for Redress in the most humble terms: Our repeated Petitions have been answered only by repeated injury. A Prince, whose character is thus marked by every act which may define a Tyrant, is unfit to be the ruler of a free people.

Nor have We been wanting in attentions to our British brethren. We have warned them from time to time of attempts by their legislature to extend an unwarrantable jurisdiction over us. We have reminded them of the circumstances of our emigration and settlement here. We have appealed to their native justice and magnanimity, and we have conjured them by the ties of our common kindred to disavow these usurpations, which would inevitably interrupt our connections and correspondence. They too have been deaf to the voice of justice and of consanguinity. We must, therefore, acquiesce in the necessity, which denounces our Separation, and hold them, as we hold the rest of mankind, Enemies in War, in Peace Friends.

We, therefore, the Representatives of the united States of America, in General Congress, Assembled, appealing to the Supreme Judge of the world for the rectitude of our intentions, do, in the Name, and by Authority of the good People of these Colonies, solemnly publish and declare, That these united Colonies are, and of Right ought to be Free and Independent States, that they are Absolved from all Allegiance to the British Crown, and that all political connection between them and the State of Great Britain, is and ought to be totally dissolved; and that as Free and Independent States, they have full Power to levy War, conclude Peace, contract Alliances, establish Commerce, and to do all other Acts and Things which Independent States may of right do. — And for the support of this Declaration, with a firm reliance on the protection of Divine Providence, we mutually pledge to each other our Lives, our Fortunes, and our sacred Honor.

New Hampshire:

Josiah Bartlett, William Whipple, Matthew Thornton

Massachusetts:

John Hancock, Samuel Adams, John Adams, Robert Treat Paine, Elbridge Gerry

Rhode Island:

Stephen Hopkins, William Ellery

Connecticut:

Roger Sherman, Samuel Huntington, William Williams, Oliver Wolcott

New York:

William Floyd, Philip Livingston, Francis Lewis, Lewis Morris

New Jersey:

Richard Stockton, John Witherspoon, Francis Hopkinson, John Hart, Abraham Clark

Pennsylvania:

Robert Morris, Benjamin Rush, Benjamin Franklin, John Morton, George Clymer, James Smith, George Taylor, James Wilson, George Ross

Delaware:

Caesar Rodney, George Read, Thomas McKean

Maryland:

Samuel Chase, William Paca, Thomas Stone, Charles Carroll of Carrollton

Virginia:

George Wythe, Richard Henry Lee, Thomas Jefferson, Benjamin Harrison, Thomas Nelson, Jr., Francis Lightfoot Lee, Carter Braxton

North Carolina:

William Hooper, Joseph Hewes, John Penn

South Carolina:

Edward Rutledge, Thomas Heyward, Jr., Thomas Lynch, Jr., Arthur Middleton

Georgia:

Button Gwinnett, Lyman Hall, George Walton

Appendix D

The Constitution of the United States

We the People of the United States, in Order to form a more perfect Union, establish Justice, insure domestic Tranquility, provide for the common defence, promote the general Welfare, and secure the Blessings of Liberty to ourselves and our Posterity, do ordain and establish this Constitution for the United States of America.

Article I

Section 1. All legislative Powers herein granted shall be vested in a Congress of the United States, which shall consist of a Senate and House of Representatives.

Section 2. The House of Representatives shall be composed of Members chosen every second Year by the People of the several States, and the Electors in each State shall have the Qualifications requisite for Electors of the most numerous Branch of the State Legislature.

No Person shall be a Representative who shall not have attained to the Age of twenty five Years, and been seven Years a Citizen of the United States, and who shall not, when elected, be an Inhabitant of that State in which he shall be chosen.

Representatives and direct Taxes shall be apportioned among the several States which may be included within this Union, according to their respective Numbers, which shall be determined by adding to the whole Number of free Persons, including those bound to Service for a Term of Years, and excluding Indians not taxed, three fifths of all other Persons. The actual Enumeration shall be made within three Years after the first Meeting of the Congress of the United States, and within every subsequent Term of ten Years, in such Manner as they shall by Law direct. The Number of Representatives shall not exceed one for every thirty Thousand, but each State shall have at Least one Representative; and until such enumeration shall be made, the State of New Hampshire shall be entitled to chuse three, Massachusetts eight, Rhode Island and Providence Plantations one, Connecticut five, New York six, New Jersey four, Pennsylvania eight, Delaware one, Maryland six, Virginia ten, North Carolina five, South Carolina five, and Georgia three.

When vacancies happen in the Representation from any State, the Executive Authority thereof shall issue Writs of Election to fill such Vacancies.

The House of Representatives shall chuse their Speaker and other Officers; and shall have the sole Power of Impeachment.

Section 3. The Senate of the United States shall be composed of two Senators from each State, chosen by the Legislature thereof, for six Years; and each Senator shall have one Vote.

Immediately after they shall be assembled in Consequence of the first Election, they shall be divided as equally as may be into three Classes. The Seats of the Senators of the first Class shall be vacated at the Expiration of the second Year, of the second Class at the Expiration of the fourth Year, and the third Class at the Expiration of the sixth Year, so that one third may be chosen every second Year; and if Vacancies happen by Resignation, or otherwise, during the Recess of the Legislature of any State, the Executive thereof may make temporary Appointments until the next Meeting of the Legislature, which shall then fill such Vacancies.

No Person shall be a Senator who shall not have attained to the Age of thirty Years, and been nine Years a Citizen of the United States and who shall not, when elected, be an Inhabitant of that State for which he shall be chosen.

The Vice President of the United States shall be President of the Senate, but shall have no Vote, unless they be equally divided.

The Senate shall chuse their other Officers, and also a President pro tempore, in the Absence of the Vice President, or when he shall exercise the Office of President of the United States.

The Senate shall have the sole Power to try all Impeachments. When sitting for that Purpose, they shall be on Oath or Affirmation. When the President of the United States is tried, the Chief Justice shall preside: And no Person shall be convicted without the Concurrence of two thirds of the Members present.

Judgment in Cases of Impeachment shall not extend further than to removal from Office, and disqualification to hold and enjoy any Office of Honor, Trust or Profit under the United States: but the Party convicted shall nevertheless be liable and subject to Indictment, Trial, Judgment and Punishment, according to Law.

Section 4. The Times, Places and Manner of holding Elections for Senators and Representatives, shall be prescribed in each State by the Legislature thereof; but the Congress may at any time by Law make or alter such Regulations, except as to the Places of chusing Senators.

The Congress shall assemble at least once in every Year, and such Meeting shall be on the first Monday in December, unless they shall by Law appoint a different Day.

Section 5. Each House shall be the Judge of the Elections, Returns and Qualifications of its own Members, and a Majority of each shall constitute a Quorum to do Business; but a smaller Number may adjourn from day to day, and may be authorized to compel the Attendance of absent Members, in such Manner, and under such Penalties as each House may provide.

Each House may determine the Rules of its Proceedings, punish its Members for disorderly Behavior, and, with the Concurrence of two thirds, expel a Member.

Each House shall keep a Journal of its Proceedings, and from time to time publish the same, excepting such Parts as may in their Judgment require Secrecy; and the Yeas and Nays of the Members of either House on any question shall, at the Desire of one fifth of those Present, be entered on the Journal.

Neither House, during the Session of Congress, shall, without the Consent of the other, adjourn for more than three days, nor to any other Place than that in which the two Houses shall be sitting.

Section 6. The Senators and Representatives shall receive a Compensation for their Services, to be ascertained by Law, and paid out of the Treasury of the United States. They shall in all Cases, except Treason, Felony and Breach of the Peace, be privileged from Arrest during their Attendance at the Session of their respective Houses, and in going to and returning from the same; and for any Speech or Debate in either House, they shall not be questioned in any other Place.

No Senator or Representative shall, during the Time for which he was elected, be appointed to any civil Office under the Authority of the United States, which shall have been created, or the Emoluments whereof shall have been encreased during such time; and no Person holding any Office under the United States, shall be a Member of either House during his Continuance in Office.

Section 7. All Bills for raising Revenue shall originate in the House of Representatives; but the Senate may propose or concur with Amendments as on other Bills.

Every Bill which shall have passed the House of Representatives and the Senate, shall, before it become a Law, be presented to the President of the United States; If he approve he shall sign it, but if not he shall return it, with his Objections to the House in which it shall have originated, who shall enter the Objections at large on their Journal, and proceed to reconsider it. If after such Reconsideration two thirds of that House shall agree to pass the Bill, it shall be sent, together with the Objections, to the other House, by which it shall likewise be reconsidered, and if approved by two thirds of that House, it shall become a Law. But in all such Cases the Votes of both Houses shall be determined by yeas and nays, and the Names of the Persons voting for and against the Bill shall be entered on the Journal of each House respectively. If any Bill shall not be returned by the President within ten Days (Sundays excepted) after it shall have been presented to him, the Same shall be a Law, in like Manner as if he had signed it, unless the Congress by their Adjournment prevent its Return, in which Case it shall not be a Law.

Every Order, Resolution, or Vote to which the Concurrence of the Senate and House of Representatives may be necessary (except on a question of Adjournment) shall be presented to the President of the United States; and before the Same shall take Effect, shall be approved by him, or being disapproved by him, shall be repassed by two thirds of the Senate and House of Representatives, according to the Rules and Limitations prescribed in the Case of a Bill.

Section 8. The Congress shall have Power To lay and collect Taxes, Duties, Imposts and Excises, to pay the Debts and provide for the common Defence and general Welfare of the United States; but all Duties, Imposts and Excises shall be uniform throughout the United States;

To borrow Money on the credit of the United States;

To regulate Commerce with foreign Nations, and among the several States, and with the Indian Tribes;

To establish an uniform Rule of Naturalization, and uniform Laws on the subject of Bankruptcies throughout the United States;

To coin Money, regulate the Value thereof, and of foreign Coin, and fix the Standard of Weights and Measures;

To provide for the Punishment of counterfeiting the Securities and current Coin of the United States;

To establish Post Offices and post Roads;

To promote the Progress of Science and useful Arts, by securing for limited Times to Authors and Inventors the exclusive Right to their respective Writings and Discoveries;

To constitute Tribunals inferior to the supreme Court;

To define and punish Piracies and Felonies committed on the high Seas, and Offences against the Law of Nations;

To declare War, grant Letters of Marque and Reprisal, and make Rules concerning Captures on Land and Water;

To raise and support Armies, but no Appropriation of Money to that Use shall be for a longer Term than two Years;

To provide and maintain a Navy;

To make Rules for the Government and Regulation of the land and naval Forces;

To provide for calling forth the Militia to execute the Laws of the Union, suppress Insurrections and repel Invasions;

To provide for organizing, arming, and disciplining, the Militia, and for governing such Part of them as may be employed in the Service of the United States, reserving to the States respectively, the Appointment of the Officers, and the Authority of training the Militia according to the discipline prescribed by Congress;

To exercise exclusive Legislation in all Cases whatsoever, over such District (not exceeding ten Miles square) as may, by Cession of particular States, and the Acceptance of Congress, become the Seat of the Government of the United States, and to exercise like Authority over all Places purchased by the Consent of the Legislature of the State in which the Same shall be, for the Erection of Forts, Magazines, Arsenals, dock-Yards, and other needful Buildings;—And

To make all Laws which shall be necessary and proper for carrying into Execution the foregoing Powers, and all other Powers vested by this Constitution in the Government of the United States, or in any Department or Officer thereof.

Section 9. The Migration or Importation of such Persons as any of the States now existing shall think proper to admit, shall not be prohibited by the Congress prior to the Year one thousand eight hundred and eight, but a Tax or duty may be imposed on such Importation, not exceeding ten dollars for each Person.

The Privilege of the Writ of Habeas Corpus shall not be suspended, unless when in Cases of Rebellion or Invasion the public Safety may require it.

No Bill of Attainder or ex post facto Law shall be passed.

No Capitation, or other direct, Tax shall be laid, unless in Proportion to the Census or Enumeration herein before directed to be taken.

No Tax or Duty shall be laid on Articles exported from any State.

No Preference shall be given by any Regulation of Commerce or Revenue to the Ports of one State over those of another: nor shall Vessels bound to, or from, one State, be obliged to enter, clear or pay Duties in another.

No Money shall be drawn from the Treasury, but in Consequence of Appropriations made by Law; and a regular Statement and Account of Receipts and Expenditures of all public Money shall be published from time to time.

No Title of Nobility shall be granted by the United States: And no Person holding any Office of Profit or Trust under them, shall, without the Consent of the Congress, accept of any present, Emolument, Office, or Title, of any kind whatever, from any King, Prince, or foreign State.

Section 10. No State shall enter into any Treaty, Alliance, or Confederation; grant Letters of Marque and Reprisal; coin Money; emit Bills of Credit; make any Thing but gold and silver Coin a Tender in Payment of Debts; pass any Bill of Attainder, ex post facto Law, or Law impairing the Obligation of Contracts, or grant any Title of Nobility.

No State shall, without the Consent of the Congress, lay any Imposts or Duties on Imports or Exports, except what may be absolutely necessary for executing its inspection Laws: and the net Produce of all Duties and Imposts, laid by any State on Imports or Exports, shall be for the Use of the Treasury of the United States; and all such Laws shall be subject to the Revision and Controul of the Congress.

No State shall, without the Consent of Congress, lay any Duty of Tonnage, keep Troops, or Ships of War in time of Peace, enter into any Agreement or Compact with another State, or with a foreign Power, or engage in War, unless actually invaded, or in such imminent Danger as will not admit of delay.

Article II

Section 1. The executive Power shall be vested in a President of the United States of America. He shall hold his Office during the Term of four Years, and, together with the Vice President, chosen for the same Term, be elected, as follows:

Each State shall appoint, in such Manner as the Legislature thereof may direct, a Number of Electors, equal to the whole Number of Senators and Representatives to which the State may be entitled in the Congress: but no Senator or Representative, or Person holding an Office of Trust or Profit under the United States, shall be appointed an Elector.

The Electors shall meet in their respective States, and vote by Ballot for two Persons, of whom one at least shall not be an Inhabitant of the same State with themselves. And they shall make a List of all the Persons voted for, and of the Number of Votes for each; which List they shall sign and certify, and transmit sealed to the Seat of the Government of the United States, directed to the President of the Senate. The President of the Senate shall, in the Presence of the Senate and House of Representatives, open all the Certificates, and the Votes shall then be counted. The Person having the greatest Number of Votes shall be the President, if such Number be a Majority of the whole Number of Electors appointed; and if there be more than one who have such Majority, and have an equal Number of Votes, then the House of Representatives shall immediately chuse by Ballot one of them for President; and if no Person have a Majority, then from the five highest on the List the said House shall in like Manner chuse the President. But in chusing the President, the Votes shall be taken by States, the Representation from each State having one Vote; A quorum for this Purpose shall consist of a Member or Members from two thirds of the States, and a Majority of all the States shall be necessary to a Choice. In every Case, after the Choice of the President, the Person having the greatest Number of Votes of the Electors shall be the Vice President. But if there should remain two or more who have equal Votes, the Senate shall chuse from them by Ballot the Vice President.

The Congress may determine the Time of chusing the Electors, and the Day on which they shall give their Votes; which Day shall be the same throughout the United States.

No Person except a natural born Citizen, or a Citizen of the United States, at the time of the Adoption of this Constitution, shall be eligible to the Office of President; neither shall any Person be eligible to that Office who shall not have attained to the Age of thirty five Years, and been fourteen Years a Resident within the United States.

In Case of the Removal of the President from Office, or of his Death, Resignation, or Inability to discharge the Powers and Duties of the said Office, the Same shall devolve on the Vice President, and the Congress may by Law provide for the Case of Removal, Death, Resignation or Inability, both of the President and Vice President, declaring what Officer shall then act as President, and such Officer shall act accordingly, until the Disability be removed, or a President shall be elected.

The President shall, at stated Times, receive for his Services, a Compensation, which shall neither be increased nor diminished during the Period for which he shall have been elected, and he shall not receive within that Period any other Emolument from the United States, or any of them.

Before he enter on the Execution of his Office, he shall take the following Oath or Affirmation: "I do solemnly swear (or affirm) that I will faithfully execute the Office of President of the United States, and will to the best of my Ability, preserve, protect and defend the Constitution of the United States."

Section 2. The President shall be Commander in Chief of the Army and Navy of the United States, and of the Militia of the several States, when called into the actual Service of the United States; he may require the Opinion, in writing, of the principal Officer in each of the executive Departments, upon any Subject relating to the Duties of their respective Offices, and he shall have Power to grant Reprieves and Pardons for Offences against the United States, except in Cases of Impeachment.

He shall have Power, by and with the Advice and Consent of the Senate, to make Treaties, provided two thirds of the Senators present concur; and he shall nominate, and by and with the Advice and Consent of the Senate, shall appoint Ambassadors, other public Ministers and Consuls, Judges of the supreme Court, and all other Officers of the United States, whose Appointments are not herein otherwise provided for, and which shall be established by Law: but the Congress may by Law vest the Appointment of such inferior Officers, as they think proper, in the President alone, in the Courts of Law, or in the Heads of Departments.

The President shall have Power to fill up all Vacancies that may happen during the Recess of the Senate, by granting Commissions which shall expire at the End of their next Session.

Section 3. He shall from time to time give to the Congress Information of the State of the Union, and recommend to their Consideration such Measures as he shall judge necessary and expedient; he may, on extraordinary Occasions, convene both Houses, or either of them, and in Case of Disagreement between them, with Respect to the Time of Adjournment, he may adjourn them to such Time as he shall think proper; he shall receive Ambassadors and other public Ministers; he shall take Care that the Laws be faithfully executed, and shall Commission all the Officers of the United States.

Section 4. The President, Vice President and all civil Officers of the United States, shall be removed from Office on Impeachment for, and Conviction of, Treason, Bribery, or other high Crimes and Misdemeanors.

Article III

Section 1. The judicial Power of the United States, shall be vested in one supreme Court, and in such inferior Courts as the Congress may from time to time ordain and establish. The Judges, both of the supreme and inferior Courts, shall hold their Offices during good Behaviour, and shall, at stated Times, receive for their Services a Compensation, which shall not be diminished during their Continuance in Office.

Section 2. The judicial Power shall extend to all Cases, in Law and Equity, arising under this Constitution, the Laws of the United States, and Treaties made, or which shall be made, under their Authority;—to all Cases affecting Ambassadors, other public Ministers and Consuls;—to all Cases of admiralty and maritime Jurisdiction;—to Controversies to which the United States shall be a Party;—to Controversies between two or more States;—between a State and Citizens of another State;—between Citizens of different States;—between Citizens of the same State claiming Lands under the Grants of different States, and between a State, or the Citizens thereof, and foreign States, Citizens or Subjects.

In all Cases affecting Ambassadors, other public Ministers and Consuls, and those in which a State shall be a Party, the supreme Court shall have original Jurisdiction. In all the other Cases before mentioned, the supreme Court shall have appellate Jurisdiction, both as to Law and Fact, with such Exceptions, and under such Regulations as the Congress shall make.

The Trial of all Crimes, except in Cases of Impeachment, shall be by Jury; and such Trial shall be held in the State where the said Crimes shall have been committed; but when not committed within any State, the Trial shall be at such Place or Places as the Congress may by Law have directed.

Section 3. Treason against the United States, shall consist only in levying War against them, or in adhering to their Enemies, giving them Aid and Comfort. No Person shall be convicted of Treason unless on the Testimony of two Witnesses to the same overt Act, or on Confession in open Court.

The Congress shall have Power to declare the Punishment of Treason, but no Attainder of Treason shall work Corruption of Blood, or Forfeiture except during the Life of the Person attainted.

Article IV

Section 1. Full Faith and Credit shall be given in each State to the public Acts, Records, and judicial Proceedings of every other State. And the Congress may by general Laws prescribe the Manner in which such Acts, Records and Proceedings shall be proved, and the Effect thereof.

Section 2. The Citizens of each State shall be entitled to all Privileges and Immunities of Citizens in the several States.

A Person charged in any State with Treason, Felony, or other Crime, who shall flee from Justice, and be found in another State, shall on demand of the executive Authority of the State from which he fled, be delivered up, to be removed to the State having Jurisdiction of the Crime.

No Person held to Service or Labour in one State, under the Laws thereof, escaping into another, shall, in Consequence of any Law or Regulation therein, be discharged from such Service or Labour, but shall be delivered up on Claim of the Party to whom such Service or Labour may be due.

Section 3. New States may be admitted by the Congress into this Union; but no new State shall be formed or erected within the Jurisdiction of any other State; nor any State be formed by the Junction of two or more States, or Parts of States, without the Consent of the Legislatures of the States concerned as well as of the Congress.

The Congress shall have Power to dispose of and make all needful Rules and Regulations respecting the Territory or other Property belonging to the United States; and nothing in this Constitution shall be so construed as to Prejudice any Claims of the United States, or of any particular State.

Section 4. The United States shall guarantee to every State in this Union a Republican Form of Government, and shall protect each of them against Invasion; and on Application of the Legislature, or of the Executive (when the Legislature cannot be convened) against domestic Violence.

Article V

The Congress, whenever two thirds of both Houses shall deem it necessary, shall propose Amendments to this Constitution, or, on the Application of the Legislatures of two thirds of the several States, shall call a Convention for proposing Amendments, which, in either Case, shall be valid to all Intents and Purposes, as Part of this Constitution, when ratified by the Legislatures of three fourths of the several States, or by Conventions in three fourths thereof, as the one or the other Mode of Ratification may be proposed by the Congress; Provided that no Amendment which may be made prior to the Year One thousand eight hundred and eight shall in any Manner affect the first and fourth Clauses in the Ninth Section of the first Article; and that no State, without its Consent, shall be deprived of its equal Suffrage in the Senate.

Article VI

All Debts contracted and Engagements entered into, before the Adoption of this Constitution, shall be as valid against the United States under this Constitution, as under the Confederation.

This Constitution, and the Laws of the United States which shall be made in Pursuance thereof; and all Treaties made, or which shall be made, under the Authority of the United States, shall be the supreme Law of the Land; and the Judges in every State shall be bound thereby, any Thing in the Constitution or Laws of any State to the Contrary notwithstanding.

The Senators and Representatives before mentioned, and the Members of the several State Legislatures, and all executive and judicial Officers, both of the United States and of the several States, shall be bound by Oath or Affirmation, to support this Constitution; but no religious Test shall ever be required as a Qualification to any Office or public Trust under the United States.

Article VII

The Ratification of the Conventions of nine States, shall be sufficient for the Establishment of this Constitution between the States so ratifying the Same.

Articles in addition to, and amendment of, the Constitution of the United States of America, proposed by Congress, and ratified by the Legislatures of the Several States pursuant to the Fifth Article of the original Constitution.

Amendment I [1791]

Congress shall make no law respecting an establishment of religion, or prohibiting the free exercise thereof; or abridging the freedom of speech, or of the press; or the right of the people peaceably to assemble, and to petition the Government for a redress of grievances.

Amendment II [1791]

A well regulated Militia, being necessary to the security of a free State, the right of the people to keep and bear Arms, shall not be infringed.

Amendment III [1791]

No Soldier shall, in time of peace be quartered in any house, without the consent of the Owner, nor in time of war, but in a manner to be prescribed by law.

Amendment IV [1791]

The right of the people to be secure in their persons, houses, papers, and effects, against unreasonable searches and seizures, shall not be violated, and no Warrants shall issue, but upon probable cause, supported by Oath or affirmation, and particularly describing the place to be searched, and the persons or things to be seized.

Amendment V [1791]

No person shall be held to answer for a capital, or otherwise infamous crime, unless on a presentment or indictment of a Grand Jury, except in cases arising in the land or naval forces, or in the Militia, when in actual service in time of War or public danger; nor shall any person be subject for the same offence to be twice put in jeopardy of life or limb; nor shall be compelled in any criminal case to be a witness against himself, nor be deprived of life, liberty, or property, without due process of law; nor shall private property be taken for public use, without just compensation.

Amendment VI [1791]

In all criminal prosecutions, the accused shall enjoy the right to a speedy and public trial, by an impartial jury of the State and district wherein the crime shall have been committed, which district shall have been previously ascertained by law, and to be informed of the nature and cause of the accusation; to be confronted with the witnesses against him; to have compulsory process for obtaining witnesses in his favor, and to have the Assistance of Counsel for his defence.

Amendment VII [1791]

In Suits at common law, where the value in controversy shall exceed twenty dollars, the right of trial by jury shall be preserved, and no fact tried by jury, shall be otherwise re-examined in any Court of the United States, than according to the rules of the common law.

Amendment VIII [1791]

Excessive bail shall not be required, nor excessive fines imposed, nor cruel and unusual punishments inflicted.

Amendment IX [1791]

The enumeration in the Constitution, of certain rights, shall not be construed to deny or disparage others retained by the people.

Amendment X [1791]

The powers not delegated to the United States by the Constitution, nor prohibited by it to the States, are reserved to the States respectively, or to the people.

Amendment XI [1798]

The Judicial power of the United States shall not be construed to extend to any suit in law or equity, commenced or prosecuted against one of the United States by Citizens of another State, or by Citizens or Subjects of any Foreign State.

Amendment XII [1804]

The Electors shall meet in their respective states and vote by ballot for President and Vice-President, one of whom, at least, shall not be an inhabitant of the same state with themselves; they shall name in their ballots the person voted for as President, and in distinct ballots the person voted for as Vice-President, and they shall make distinct lists of all persons voted for as President, and of all persons voted for as Vice-President, and of the number of votes for each, which lists they shall sign and certify, and transmit sealed to the seat of the government of the United States, directed to the President of the Senate;—The President of the Senate shall, in the presence of the Senate and House of Representatives, open all the certificates and the votes shall then be counted;—The person having the greatest Number of votes for President, shall be the President, if such number be a majority of the whole number of Electors appointed; and if no person have such majority, then from the persons having the highest numbers not exceeding three on the list of those voted for as President, the House of Representatives shall choose immediately, by ballot, the President. But in choosing the President, the votes shall be taken by states, the representation from each state having one vote; a quorum for this purpose shall consist of a member or members from two-thirds of the states, and a majority of all the states shall be necessary to a choice. And if the House of Representatives shall not choose a President whenever the right of choice shall devolve upon them before the fourth day of March next following, then the Vice-President shall act as President, as in the case of the death or other constitutional disability of the President.—The person having the greatest number of votes as Vice-President, shall be the Vice-President, if such number be a majority of the whole number of Electors appointed, and if no person have a majority, then from the two highest numbers on the list, the Senate shall choose the Vice-President; a quorum for the purpose shall consist of two-thirds of the whole number of Senators, and a majority of the whole number shall be necessary to a choice. But no person constitutionally ineligible to the office of President shall be eligible to that of Vice-President of the United States.

Amendment XIII [1865]

Section 1. Neither slavery nor involuntary servitude, except as a punishment for crime whereof the party shall have been duly convicted, shall exist within the United States, or any place subject to their jurisdiction.

Section 2. Congress shall have power to enforce this article by appropriate legislation.

Amendment XIV [1868]

Section 1. All persons born or naturalized in the United States, and subject to the jurisdiction thereof, are citizens of the United States and of the State wherein they reside. No State shall make or enforce any law which shall abridge the privileges or immunities of citizens of the United States; nor shall any State deprive any person of life, liberty, or property, without due process of law; nor deny to any person within its jurisdiction the equal protection of the laws.

Section 2. Representatives shall be apportioned among the several States according to their respective numbers, counting the whole number of persons in each State, excluding Indians not taxed. But when the right to vote at any election for the choice of electors for President and

Vice-President of the United States, Representatives in Congress, the Executive and Judicial officers of a State, or the members of the Legislature thereof, is denied to any of the male inhabitants of such State, being twenty-one years of age, and citizens of the United States, or in any way abridged, except for participation in rebellion, or other crime, the basis of representation therein shall be reduced in the proportion which the number of such male citizens shall bear to the whole number of male citizens twenty-one years of age in such State.

Section 3. No person shall be a Senator or Representative in Congress, or elector of President and Vice-President, or hold any office, civil or military, under the United States, or under any State, who, having previously taken an oath, as a member of Congress, or as an officer of the United States, or as a member of any State legislature, or as an executive or judicial officer of any State, to support the Constitution of the United States, shall have engaged in insurrection or rebellion against the same, or given aid or comfort to the enemies thereof. But Congress may by a vote of two-thirds of each House, remove such disability.

Section 4. The validity of the public debt of the United States, authorized by law, including debts incurred for payment of pensions and bounties for services in suppressing insurrection or rebellion, shall not be questioned. But neither the United States nor any State shall assume or pay any debt or obligation incurred in aid of insurrection or rebellion against the United States, or any claim for the loss or emancipation of any slave; but all such debts, obligations and claims shall be held illegal and void.

Section 5. The Congress shall have power to enforce, by appropriate legislation, the provisions of this article.

Amendment XV [1870]

Section 1. The right of citizens of the United States to vote shall not be denied or abridged by the United States or by any State on account of race, color, or previous condition of servitude.

Section 2. The Congress shall have power to enforce this article by appropriate legislation.

Amendment XVI [1913]

The Congress shall have power to lay and collect taxes on incomes, from whatever source derived, without apportionment among the several States, and without regard to any census or enumeration.

Amendment XVII [1913]

[1] The Senate of the United States shall be composed of two Senators from each State, elected by the people thereof, for six years; and each Senator shall have one vote. The electors in each State shall have the qualifications requisite for electors of the most numerous branch of the State legislatures.

[2] When vacancies happen in the representation of any State in the Senate, the executive authority of such State shall issue writs of election to fill such vacancies: *Provided*, That the legislature of any State may empower the executive thereof to make temporary appointments until the people fill the vacancies by election as the legislature may direct.

[3] This amendment shall not be so construed as to affect the election or term of any Senator chosen before it becomes valid as part of the Constitution.

Amendment XVIII [1919]

Section 1. After one year from the ratification of this article the manufacture, sale, or transportation of intoxicating liquors within, the importation thereof into, or the exportation thereof from the United States and all territory subject to the jurisdiction thereof for beverage purposes is hereby prohibited.

Section 2. The Congress and the several States shall have concurrent power to enforce this article by appropriate legislation.

Section 3. This article shall be inoperative unless it shall have been ratified as an amendment to the Constitution by the legislatures of the several States, as provided in the Constitution, within seven years from the date of the submission hereof to the States by the Congress.

Amendment XIX [1920]

[1] The right of citizens of the United States to vote shall not be denied or abridged by the United States or by any State on account of sex.

[2] Congress shall have power to enforce this article by appropriate legislation.

Amendment XX [1933]

Section 1. The terms of the President and Vice President shall end at noon on the 20th day of January, and the terms of Senators and Representatives at noon on the 3d day of January, of the years in which such terms would have ended if this article had not been ratified; and the terms of their successors shall then begin.

Section 2. The Congress shall assemble at least once in every year, and such meeting shall begin at noon on the 3d day of January, unless they shall by law appoint a different day.

Section 3. If, at the time fixed for the beginning of the term of the President, the President elect shall have died, the Vice President elect shall become President. If the President shall not have been chosen before the time fixed for the beginning of his term, or if the President elect shall have failed to qualify, then the Vice President elect shall act as President until a President shall have qualified; and the Congress may by law provide for the case wherein neither a President elect nor a Vice President elect shall have qualified, declaring who shall then act as President, or the manner in which one who is to act shall be selected, and such person shall act accordingly until a President or Vice President shall have qualified.

Section 4. The Congress may by law provide for the case of the death of any of the persons from whom the House of Representatives may choose a President whenever the right of choice shall have devolved upon them, and for the case of the death of any of the persons from whom the Senate may choose a Vice President whenever the right of choice shall have devolved upon them.

Section 5. Sections 1 and 2 shall take effect on the 15th day of October following the ratification of this article.

Section 6. This article shall be inoperative unless it shall have been ratified as an amendment to the Constitution by the legislatures of three-fourths of the several States within seven years from the date of its submission.

Amendment XXI [1933]

Section 1. The eighteenth article of amendment to the Constitution of the United States is hereby repealed.

Section 2. The transportation or importation into any State, Territory, or possession of the United States for delivery or use therein of intoxicating liquors, in violation of the laws thereof, is hereby prohibited.

Section 3. The article shall be inoperative unless it shall have been ratified as an amendment to the Constitution by conventions in the several States, as provided in the Constitution, within seven years from the date of the submission hereof to the States by the Congress.

Amendment XXII [1951]

Section 1. No person shall be elected to the office of the President more than twice, and no person who has held the office of President, or acted as President, for more than two years of a term to which some other person was elected President shall be elected to the office of the President more than once. But this Article shall not apply to any person holding the office of President when this Article was proposed by the Congress, and shall not prevent any person who may be holding the office of President, or acting as President, during the term within which this Article becomes operative from holding the office of President or acting as President during the remainder of such term.

Section 2. This article shall be inoperative unless it shall have been ratified as an amendment to the Constitution by the legislatures of three-fourths of the several States within seven years from the date of its submission to the States by the Congress.

Amendment XXIII [1961]

Section 1. The District constituting the seat of Government of the United States shall appoint in such manner as the Congress may direct:

A number of electors of President and Vice President equal to the whole number of Senators and Representatives in Congress to which the District would be entitled if it were a State, but in no event more than the least populous State; they shall be in addition to those appointed by the States, but they shall be considered, for the purposes of the election of President and Vice President, to be electors appointed by a State; and they shall meet in the District and perform such duties as provided by the twelfth article of amendment.

Section 2. The Congress shall have power to enforce this article by appropriate legislation.

Amendment XXIV [1964]

Section 1. The right of citizens of the United States to vote in any primary or other election for President or Vice President, for electors for President or Vice President, or for Senator or Representative in Congress, shall not be denied or abridged by the United States or any State by reason of failure to pay any poll tax or other tax.

Section 2. The Congress shall have power to enforce this article by appropriate legislation.

Amendment XXV [1967]

Section 1. In case of the removal of the President from office or of his death or resignation, the Vice President shall become President.

Section 2. Whenever there is a vacancy in the office of the Vice President, the President shall nominate a Vice President who shall take office upon confirmation by a majority vote of both Houses of Congress.

Section 3. Whenever the President transmits to the President pro tempore of the Senate and the Speaker of the House of Representatives his written declaration that he is unable to discharge the powers and duties of his office, and until he transmits to them a written declaration to the contrary, such powers and duties shall be discharged by the Vice President as Acting President.

Section 4. Whenever the Vice President and a majority of either the principal officers of the executive departments or of such other body as Congress may by law provide, transmit to the President pro tempore of the Senate and the Speaker of the House of Representatives their written declaration that the President is unable to discharge the powers and duties of his office, the Vice President shall immediately assume the powers and duties of the office as Acting President.

Thereafter, when the President transmits to the President pro tempore of the Senate and the Speaker of the House of Representatives his written declaration that no inability exists, he shall resume the powers and duties of his office unless the Vice President and a majority of either the principal officers of the executive department or of such other body as Congress may by law provide, transmit within four days to the President pro tempore of the Senate and the Speaker of the House of Representatives their written declaration that the President is unable to discharge the powers and duties of his office. Thereupon Congress shall decide the issue, assembling within forty-eight hours for that purpose if not in session. If the Congress, within twenty-one days after receipt of the latter written declaration, or, if Congress is not in session, within twenty-one days after Congress is required to assemble, determines by two-thirds vote of both Houses that the President is unable to discharge the powers and duties of his office, the Vice President shall continue to discharge the same as Acting President; otherwise, the President shall resume the powers and duties of his office.

Amendment XXVI [1971]

Section 1. The right of citizens of the United States, who are eighteen years of age or older, to vote shall not be denied or abridged by the United States or by any State on account of age.

Section 2. The Congress shall have power to enforce this article by appropriate legislation.

Amendment XXVII [1992]

No law, varying the compensation for the services of the Senators and Representatives, shall take effect, until an election of Representatives shall have intervened.

Appendix E

Universal Declaration of Human Rights

On December 10, 1948, the General Assembly of the United Nations adopted and proclaimed the Universal Declaration of Human Rights, the full text of which appears in the following pages. Following this historic act, the Assembly called upon all Member countries to publicize the text of the Declaration and "to cause it to be disseminated, displayed, read and expounded principally in schools and other educational institutions, without distinction based on the political status of countries or territories."

Preamble

Whereas recognition of the inherent dignity and of the equal and inalienable rights of all members of the human family is the foundation of freedom, justice and peace in the world,

Whereas disregard and contempt for human rights have resulted in barbarous acts which have outraged the conscience of mankind, and the advent of a world in which human beings shall enjoy freedom of speech and belief and freedom from fear and want has been proclaimed as the highest aspiration of the common people,

Whereas it is essential, if man is not to be compelled to have recourse, as a last resort, to rebellion against tyranny and oppression, that human rights should be protected by the rule of law,

Whereas it is essential to promote the development of friendly relations between nations,

Whereas the peoples of the United Nations have in the Charter reaffirmed their faith in fundamental human rights, in the dignity and worth of the human person and in the equal rights of men and women and have determined to promote social progress and better standards of life in larger freedom,

Whereas Member States have pledged themselves to achieve, in cooperation with the United Nations, the promotion of universal respect for and observance of human rights and fundamental freedoms,

Whereas a common understanding of these rights and freedoms is of the greatest importance for the full realization of this pledge,

Now, Therefore
THE GENERAL ASSEMBLY
proclaims
THIS UNIVERSAL DECLARATION OF HUMAN RIGHTS
as a common standard of achievement for all peoples and all nations, to the end that every individual and every organ of society, keeping this Declaration constantly in mind, shall strive by teaching and education to promote respect for these rights and freedoms and by progressive measures, national and international, to secure their universal and effective recognition and observance, both among the peoples of Member States themselves and among the peoples of territories under their jurisdiction.

Article 1. All human beings are born free and equal in dignity and rights. They are endowed with reason and conscience and should act towards one another in a spirit of brotherhood.

Article 2. Everyone is entitled to all the rights and freedoms set forth in this Declaration, without distinction of any kind, such as race, colour, sex, language, religion, political or other opinion, national or social origin, property, birth or other status. Furthermore, no distinction shall be made on the basis of the political, jurisdictional or international status of the country or territory to which a person belongs, whether it be independent, trust, non-self-governing or under any other limitation of sovereignty.

Article 3. Everyone has the right to life, liberty and security of person.

Article 4. No one shall be held in slavery or servitude; slavery and the slave trade shall be prohibited in all their forms.

Article 5. No one shall be subjected to torture or to cruel, inhuman or degrading treatment or punishment.

Article 6. Everyone has the right to recognition everywhere as a person before the law.

Article 7. All are equal before the law and are entitled without any discrimination to equal protection of the law. All are entitled to equal protection against any discrimination in violation of this Declaration and against any incitement to such discrimination.

Article 8. Everyone has the right to an effective remedy by the competent national tribunals for acts violating the fundamental rights granted him by the constitution or by law.

Article 9. No one shall be subjected to arbitrary arrest, detention or exile.

Article 10. Everyone is entitled in full equality to a fair and public hearing by an independent and impartial tribunal, in the determination of his rights and obligations and of any criminal charge against him.

Article 11. (1) Everyone charged with a penal offence has the right to be presumed innocent until proved guilty according to law in a public trial at which he has had all the guarantees necessary for his defence.

(2) No one shall be held guilty of any penal offence on account of any act or omission which did not constitute a penal offence, under national or international law, at the time when it was committed. Nor shall a heavier penalty be imposed than the one that was applicable at the time the penal offence was committed.

Article 12. No one shall be subjected to arbitrary interference with his privacy, family, home or correspondence, nor to attacks upon his honour and reputation. Everyone has the right to the protection of the law against such interference or attacks.

Article 13. (1) Everyone has the right to freedom of movement and residence within the borders of each State.

(2) Everyone has the right to leave any country, including his own, and to return to his country.

Article 14. (1) Everyone has the right to seek and to enjoy in other countries asylum from persecution.

(2) This right may not be invoked in the case of prosecutions genuinely arising from nonpolitical crimes or from acts contrary to the purposes and principles of the United Nations.

Article 15. (1) Everyone has the right to a nationality.

(2) No one shall be arbitrarily deprived of his nationality nor denied the right to change his nationality.

Article 16. (1) Men and women of full age, without any limitation due to race, nationality or religion, have the right to marry and to found a family. They are entitled to equal rights as to marriage, during marriage and at its dissolution.

(2) Marriage shall be entered into only with the free and full consent of the intending spouses.

(3) The family is the natural and fundamental group unit of society and is entitled to protection by society and the State.

Article 17. (1) Everyone has the right to own property alone as well as in association with others.

(2) No one shall be arbitrarily deprived of his property.

Article 18. Everyone has the right to freedom of thought, conscience and religion; this right includes freedom to change his religion or belief, and freedom, either alone or in community with others and in public or private, to manifest his religion or belief in teaching, practice, worship and observance.

Article 19. Everyone has the right to freedom of opinion and expression; this right includes freedom to hold opinions without interference and to seek, receive and impart information and ideas through any media and regardless of frontiers.

Article 20. (1) Everyone has the right to freedom of peaceful assembly and association.

(2) No one may be compelled to belong to an association.

Article 21. (1) Everyone has the right to take part in the government of his country, directly or through freely chosen representatives.

(2) Everyone has the right to equal access to public service in his country.

(3) The will of the people shall be the basis of the authority of government; this shall be expressed in periodic and genuine elections which shall be by universal and equal suffrage and shall be held by secret vote or by equivalent free voting procedures.

Article 22. Everyone, as a member of society, has the right to social security and is entitled to realization, through national effort and international cooperation and in accordance with the organization and resources of each State, of the economic, social and cultural rights indispensable for his dignity and the free development of his personality.

Article 23. (1) Everyone has the right to work, to free choice of employment, to just and favourable conditions of work and to protection against unemployment.

(2) Everyone, without any discrimination, has the right to equal pay for equal work.

(3) Everyone who works has the right to just and favourable remuneration ensuring for himself and his family an existence worthy of human dignity, and supplemented, if necessary, by other means of social protection.

(4) Everyone has the right to form and to join trade unions for the protection of his interests.

Article 24. Everyone has the right to rest and leisure, including reasonable limitation of working hours and periodic holidays with pay.

Article 25. (1) Everyone has the right to a standard of living adequate for the health and well-being of himself and of his family, including food, clothing, housing and medical care and necessary social services, and the right to security in the event of unemployment, sickness, disability, widowhood, old age or other lack of livelihood in circumstances beyond his control.

(2) Motherhood and childhood are entitled to special care and assistance. All children, whether born in or out of wedlock, shall enjoy the same social protection.

Article 26. (1) Everyone has the right to education. Education shall be free, at least in the elementary and fundamental stages. Elementary education shall be compulsory. Technical and professional education shall be made generally available and higher education shall be equally accessible to all on the basis of merit.

(2) Education shall be directed to the full development of the human personality and to the strengthening of respect for human rights and fundamental freedoms. It shall promote understanding, tolerance and friendship among all nations, racial or religious groups, and shall further the activities of the United Nations for the maintenance of peace.

(3) Parents have a prior right to choose the kind of education that shall be given to their children.

Article 27. (1) Everyone has the right freely to participate in the cultural life of the community, to enjoy the arts and to share in scientific advancement and its benefits.

(2) Everyone has the right to the protection of the moral and material interests resulting from any scientific, literary or artistic production of which he is the author.

Article 28. Everyone is entitled to a social and international order in which the rights and freedoms set forth in this Declaration can be fully realized.

Article 29. (1) Everyone has duties to the community in which alone the free and full development of his personality is possible.

(2) In the exercise of his rights and freedoms, everyone shall be subject only to such limitations as are determined by law solely for the purpose of securing due recognition and respect for the rights and freedoms of others and of meeting the just requirements of morality, public order and the general welfare in a democratic society.

(3) These rights and freedoms may in no case be exercised contrary to the purposes and principles of the United Nations.

Article 30. Nothing in this Declaration may be interpreted as implying for any State, group or person any right to engage in any activity or to perform any act aimed at the destruction of any of the rights and freedoms set forth herein.

Appendix F

Members of the United States Supreme Court

Chief Justices

Name	State	Appointed By	Tenure
Jay, John	New York	Washington	Oct. 19, 1789–June 29, 1795
Rutledge, John	South Carolina	Washington	Aug. 12, 1795–Dec. 15, 1795
Ellsworth, Oliver	Connecticut	Washington	Mar. 8, 1796–Dec. 15, 1800
Marshall, John	Virginia	Adams, John	Feb. 4, 1801–July 6, 1835
Taney, Roger Brooke	Maryland	Jackson	Mar. 28, 1836–Oct. 12, 1864
Chase, Salmon Portland	Ohio	Lincoln	Dec. 15, 1864–May 7, 1873
Waite, Morrison Remick	Ohio	Grant	Mar. 4, 1874–Mar. 23, 1888
Fuller, Melville Weston	Illinois	Cleveland	Oct. 8, 1888–July 4, 1910
White, Edward Douglass	Louisiana	Taft	Dec. 19, 1910–May 19, 1921
Taft, William Howard	Connecticut	Harding	July 11, 1921–Feb. 3, 1930
Hughes, Charles Evans	New York	Hoover	Feb. 13, 1930–June 30, 1941
Stone, Harlan Fiske	New York	Roosevelt, F.	July 3, 1941–Apr. 22, 1946
Vinson, Fred Moore	Kentucky	Truman	June 24, 1946–Sept. 8, 1953
Warren, Earl	California	Eisenhower	Oct. 5, 1953–June 23, 1969
Burger, Warren Earl	Virginia	Nixon	June 23, 1969–Sept. 26, 1986
Rehnquist, William H.	Virginia	Reagan	Sept. 26, 1986–Sept. 3, 2005
Roberts, John G., Jr.	Maryland	Bush, G.W.	Sept. 29, 2005–

Associate Justices

Name	State	Appointed By	Tenure
Rutledge, John	South Carolina	Washington	Feb. 15, 1790–Mar. 5, 1791
Cushing, William	Massachusetts	Washington	Feb. 2, 1790–Sept. 13, 1810
Wilson, James	Pennsylvania	Washington	Oct. 5, 1789–Aug. 21, 1798
Blair, John	Virginia	Washington	Feb. 2, 1790–Oct. 25, 1795
Iredell, James	North Carolina	Washington	May 12, 1790–Oct. 20, 1799
Johnson, Thomas	Maryland	Washington	Aug. 6, 1792–Jan. 16, 1793
Paterson, William	New Jersey	Washington	Mar. 11, 1793–Sept. 9, 1806
Chase, Samuel	Maryland	Washington	Feb. 4, 1796–June 19, 1811
Washington, Bushrod	Virginia	Adams, John	Feb. 4, 1799–Nov. 26, 1829
Moore, Alfred	North Carolina	Adams, John	Apr. 21, 1800–Jan. 26, 1804
Johnson, William	South Carolina	Jefferson	May 7, 1804–Aug. 4, 1834
Livingston, Henry Brockholst	New York	Jefferson	Jan. 20, 1807–Mar. 18, 1823
Todd, Thomas	Kentucky	Jefferson	May 4, 1807–Feb. 7, 1826
Duvall, Gabriel	Maryland	Madison	Nov. 23, 1811–Jan. 14, 1835
Story, Joseph	Massachusetts	Madison	Feb. 3, 1812–Sept. 10, 1845
Thompson, Smith	New York	Monroe	Sept. 1, 1823–Dec. 18, 1843
Trimble, Robert	Kentucky	Adams, J.Q.	June 16, 1826–Aug. 25, 1828
McLean, John	Ohio	Jackson	Jan. 11, 1830–Apr. 4, 1861
Baldwin, Henry	Pennsylvania	Jackson	Jan. 18, 1830–Apr. 21, 1844

Name	State	Appointed By	Tenure
Wayne, James Moore	Georgia	Jackson	Jan. 14, 1835–July 5, 1867
Barbour, Philip Pendleton	Virginia	Jackson	May 12, 1836–Feb. 25, 1841
Catron, John	Tennessee	Jackson	May 1, 1837–May 30, 1865
McKinley, John	Alabama	Van Buren	Jan. 9, 1838–July 19, 1852
Daniel, Peter Vivian	Virginia	Van Buren	Jan. 10, 1842–May 31, 1860
Nelson, Samuel	New York	Tyler	Feb. 27, 1845–Nov. 28, 1872
Woodbury, Levi	New Hampshire	Polk	Sept. 23, 1845–Sept. 4, 1851
Grier, Robert Cooper	Pennsylvania	Polk	Aug. 10, 1846–Jan. 31, 1870
Curtis, Benjamin Robbins	Massachusetts	Fillmore	Oct. 10, 1851–Sept. 30, 1857
Campbell, John Archibald	Alabama	Pierce	Apr. 11, 1853–Apr. 30, 1861
Clifford, Nathan	Maine	Buchanan	Jan. 21, 1858–July 25, 1881
Swayne, Noah Haynes	Ohio	Lincoln	Jan. 27, 1862–Jan. 24, 1881
Miller, Samuel Freeman	Iowa	Lincoln	July 21, 1862–Oct. 13, 1890
Davis, David	Illinois	Lincoln	Dec. 10, 1862–Mar. 4, 1877
Field, Stephen Johnson	California	Lincoln	May 20, 1863–Dec. 1, 1897
Strong, William	Pennsylvania	Grant	Mar. 14, 1870–Dec. 14, 1880
Bradley, Joseph P.	New Jersey	Grant	Mar. 23, 1870–Jan. 22, 1892
Hunt, Ward	New York	Grant	Jan. 9, 1873–Jan. 27, 1882
Harlan, John Marshall	Kentucky	Hayes	Dec. 10 1877–Oct. 14, 1911
Woods, William Burnham	Georgia	Hayes	Jan. 5, 1881–May 14, 1887
Matthews, Stanley	Ohio	Garfield	May 17, 1881–Mar. 22, 1889
Gray, Horace	Massachusetts	Arthur	Jan. 9, 1882–Sept. 15, 1902
Blatchford, Samuel	New York	Arthur	Apr. 3, 1882–July 7, 1893
Lamar, Lucius Quintus C.	Mississippi	Cleveland	Jan. 18, 1888–Jan. 23, 1893
Brewer, David Josiah	Kansas	Harrison	Jan. 6, 1890–Mar. 28, 1910
Brown, Henry Billings	Michigan	Harrison	Jan. 5, 1891–May 28, 1906
Shiras, George, Jr.	Pennsylvania	Harrison	Oct. 10, 1892–Feb. 23, 1903
Jackson, Howell Edmunds	Tennessee	Harrison	Mar. 4, 1893–Aug. 8, 1895
White, Edward Douglass	Louisiana	Cleveland	Mar. 12, 1894–Dec. 18, 1910*
Peckham, Rufus Wheeler	New York	Cleveland	Jan. 6, 1896–Oct. 24, 1909
McKenna, Joseph	California	McKinley	Jan. 26, 1898–Jan. 5, 1925
Holmes, Oliver Wendell	Massachusetts	Roosevelt, T.	Dec. 8, 1902–Jan. 12, 1932
Day, William Rufus	Ohio	Roosevelt, T.	Mar. 2, 1903–Nov. 13, 1922
Moody, William Henry	Massachusetts	Roosevelt, T.	Dec. 17, 1906–Nov. 20, 1910
Lurton, Horace Harmon	Tennessee	Taft	Jan. 3, 1910–July 12, 1914
Hughes, Charles Evans	New York	Taft	Oct. 10, 1910–June 10, 1916
Van Devanter, Willis	Wyoming	Taft	Jan. 3, 1911–June 2, 1937
Lamar, Joseph Rucker	Georgia	Taft	Jan. 3, 1911–Jan. 2, 1916
Pitney, Mahlon	New Jersey	Taft	Mar. 18, 1912–Dec. 31, 1922
McReynolds, James Clark	Tennessee	Wilson	Oct. 12, 1914–Jan. 31, 1941
Brandeis, Louis Dembitz	Massachusetts	Wilson	June 5,1916–Feb. 13, 1939
Clarke, John Hessin	Ohio	Wilson	Oct. 9, 1916–Sept. 18, 1922
Sutherland, George	Utah	Harding	Oct. 2, 1922–Jan. 17, 1938
Butler, Pierce	Minnesota	Harding	Jan. 2, 1923–Nov. 16, 1939
Sanford, Edward Terry	Tennessee	Harding	Feb. 19, 1923–Mar. 8, 1930
Stone, Harlan Fiske	New York	Coolidge	Mar. 2, 1925–July 2, 1941*
Roberts, Owen Josephus	Pennsylvania	Hoover	June 2, 1930–July 31, 1945
Cardozo, Benjamin Nathan	New York	Hoover	Mar. 14, 1932–July 9, 1938
Black, Hugo Lafayette	Alabama	Roosevelt, F.	Aug. 19, 1937–Sept. 17, 1971

Name	State	Appointed By	Tenure
Reed, Stanley Forman	Kentucky	Roosevelt, F.	Jan. 31, 1938–Feb. 25, 1957
Frankfurter, Felix	Massachusetts	Roosevelt, F.	Jan. 30, 1939–Aug. 28, 1962
Douglas, William Orville	Connecticut	Roosevelt, F.	Apr. 17, 1939–Nov. 12, 1975
Murphy, Frank	Michigan	Roosevelt, F.	Feb. 5, 1940–July 19, 1949
Byrnes, James Francis	South Carolina	Roosevelt, F.	July 8, 1941–Oct. 3, 1942
Jackson, Robert Houghwout	New York	Roosevelt, F.	July 11, 1941–Oct. 9, 1954
Rutledge, Wiley Blount	Iowa	Roosevelt, F.	Feb. 15, 1943–Sept. 10, 1949
Burton, Harold Hitz	Ohio	Truman	Oct. 1, 1945–Oct. 13, 1958
Clark, Tom Campbell	Texas	Truman	Aug. 24, 1949–June 12, 1967
Minton, Sherman	Indiana	Truman	Oct. 12, 1949–Oct. 15, 1956
Harlan, John Marshall	New York	Eisenhower	Mar. 28, 1955–Sept. 23, 1971
Brennan, William J., Jr.	New Jersey	Eisenhower	Oct. 16, 1956–July 20, 1990
Whittaker, Charles Evans	Missouri	Eisenhower	Mar. 25, 1957–Mar. 31, 1962
Stewart, Potter	Ohio	Eisenhower	Oct. 14, 1958–July 3, 1981
White, Byron Raymond	Colorado	Kennedy	Apr. 16, 1962–June 28, 1993
Goldberg, Arthur Joseph	Illinois	Kennedy	Oct. 1, 1962–July 25, 1965
Fortas, Abe	Tennessee	Johnson, L.	Oct. 4, 1965–May 14, 1969
Marshall, Thurgood	New York	Johnson, L.	Oct. 2, 1967–Oct. 1, 1991
Blackmun, Harry A.	Minnesota	Nixon	June 9, 1970–Aug. 3, 1994
Powell, Lewis F., Jr.	Virginia	Nixon	Jan. 7, 1972–June 26, 1987
Rehnquist, William H.	Arizona	Nixon	Jan. 7, 1972–Sept. 26, 1986*
Stevens, John Paul	Illinois	Ford	Dec. 19, 1975–June 29, 2010
O'Connor, Sandra Day	Arizona	Reagan	Sept. 25, 1981–Jan. 31, 2006
Scalia, Antonin	Virginia	Reagan	Sept. 26, 1986–
Kennedy, Anthony M.	California	Reagan	Feb. 18, 1988–
Souter, David H.	New Hampshire	Bush, G.H.W.	Oct. 9, 1990–June 29, 2009
Thomas, Clarence	Georgia	Bush, G.H.W.	Oct. 23, 1991–
Ginsburg, Ruth Bader	New York	Clinton	Aug. 10, 1993–
Breyer, Stephen G.	Massachusetts	Clinton	Aug. 3, 1994–
Alito, Samuel A., Jr.	New Jersey	Bush, G.W.	Jan. 31, 2006–
Sotomayor, Sonia	New York	Obama	Aug. 8, 2008–
Kagan, Elena	Massachusetts	Obama	Aug. 7, 2010–

*Elevated to Chief Justice

Appendix G

Federal Circuits Map

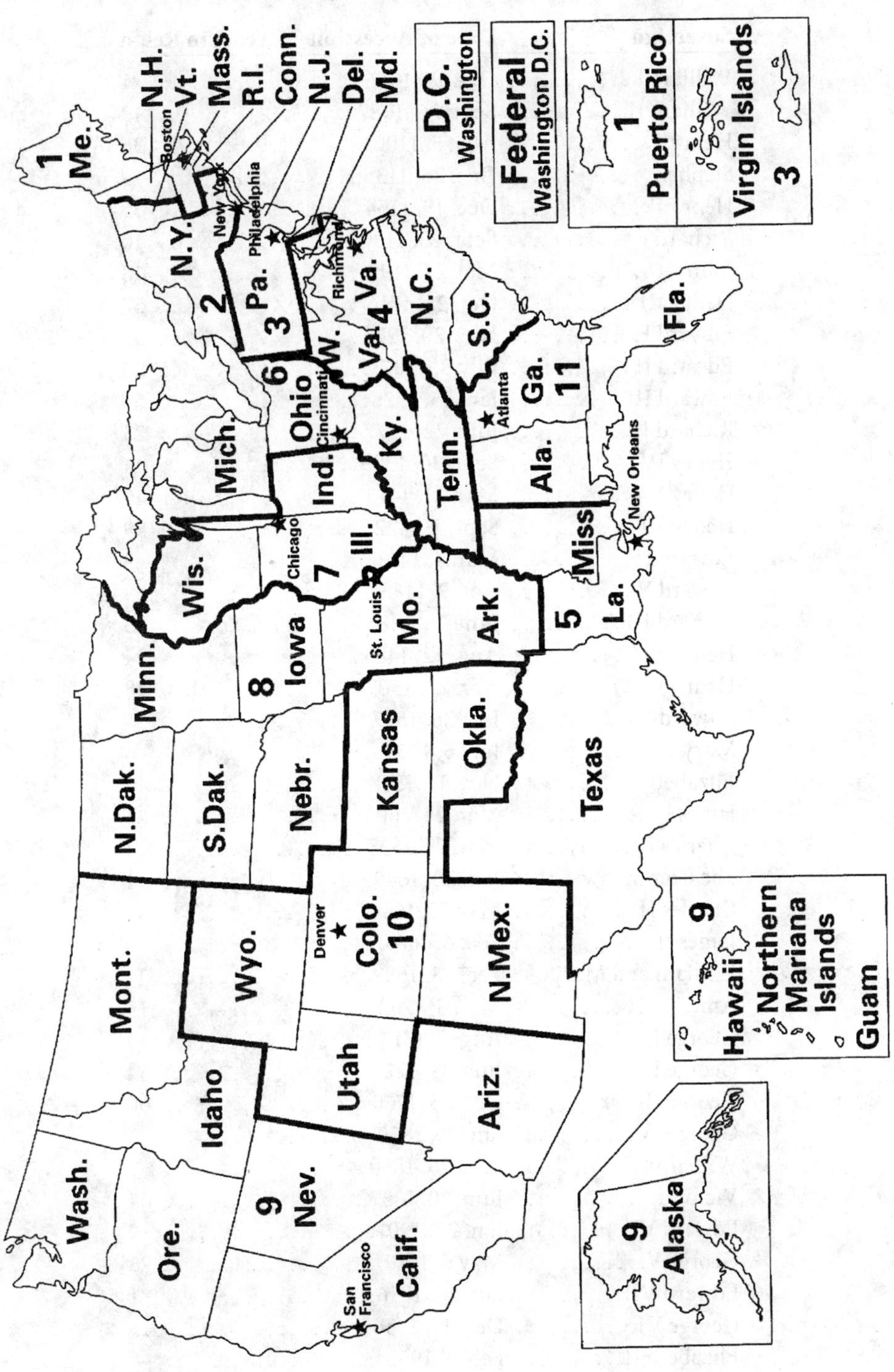

Appendix H

British Regnal Years

Sovereign	Date of Accession	Years in Reign
William I	Oct. 14, 1066	21
William II	Sept. 26, 1087	13
Henry I	Aug. 5, 1100	36
Stephen	Dec. 26, 1135	19
Henry II	Dec. 19, 1154	35
Richard I	Sept. 23, 1189	10
John	May 27, 1199	18
Henry III	Oct. 28, 1216	57
Edward I	Nov. 20, 1272	35
Edward II	July 8, 1307	20
Edward III	Jan. 25, 1326	51
Richard II	June 22, 1377	23
Henry IV	Sept. 30, 1399	14
Henry V	Mar. 21, 1413	10
Henry VI	Sept. 1, 1422	39
Edward IV	Mar. 4, 1461	23
Edward V	Apr. 9, 1483	—
Richard III	June 26, 1483	3
Henry VII	Aug. 22, 1485	24
Henry VIII	Apr. 22, 1509	38
Edward VI	Jan. 28, 1547	7
Mary	July 6, 1553	6
Elizabeth I	Nov. 17, 1558	45
James I	Mar. 24, 1603	23
Charles I	Mar. 27, 1625	24
The Commonwealth	Jan. 30, 1649	11
Charles II	May 29, 1660	37
James II	Feb. 6, 1685	4
William and Mary	Feb. 13, 1689	14
Anne	Mar. 8, 1702	13
George I	Aug. 1, 1714	13
George II	June 11, 1727	34
George III	Oct. 25, 1760	60
George IV	Jan. 29, 1820	11
William IV	June 26, 1830	7
Victoria	June 20, 1837	64
Edward VII	Jan. 22, 1901	9
George V	May 6, 1910	25
Edward VIII	Jan. 20, 1936	1
George VI	Dec. 11, 1936	15
Elizabeth II	Feb. 6, 1952	—

Appendix I

Bibliography of Books Cited

Abbott, Austin. *A Brief for the Trial of Civil Issues Before a Jury*. 2d ed. Rochester, N.Y.: Lawyers' Co-op, 1900.

Abbott, Austin. *Trial Evidence*. N.Y.: Baker Voorhis, 1880.

Abbott, Frederick M.; Thomas Cottier; and Francis Gurry. *International Intellectual Property in an Integrated World Economy*. N.Y.: Aspen, 2007.

Abbott, L.W. *Law Reporting in England*. London: Athlone, 1973.

Abraham, Kenneth S. *The Forms and Functions of Tort Law*. N.Y.: Foundation Press, 2002.

Ackerman, Bruce A. *Reconstructing American Law*. Cambridge, Mass.: Harvard Univ. Press, 1984.

Adams, Henry; et al. *Essays in Anglo-Saxon Law*. Boston: Little Brown, 1905.

Adams, Henry C. *A Juridical Glossary*. Albany, N.Y.: Weed Parsons, 1886. [Though several volumes were planned, only one appeared.]

Adams, James Truslow (ed.). *Dictionary of American History*. 5 vols. N.Y.: C. Scribner's Sons, 1940.

Alexy, Robert. *A Theory of Constitutional Rights*. Julian Rivers, trans. Oxford: Oxford Univ. Press, 2002.

Alix, Jay; and Elmer E. Heupel. *Financial Handbook for Bankruptcy Professionals*. St. Paul: West, 1991.

Allen, Carleton Kemp. *Aspects of Justice*. London: Stevens & Sons, 1958.

Allen, Carleton Kemp. *Democracy and the Individual*. London: Oxford Univ. Press, 1943.

Allen, Carleton Kemp. *Law and Orders: An Inquiry into the Nature and Scope of Delegated Legislation and Executive Powers in English Law*. 2d ed. London: Stevens, 1956.

Allen, Carleton Kemp. *Law in the Making*. 7th ed. Oxford: Clarendon Press, 1964.

Allen, Carleton Kemp. *Legal Duties and Other Essays in Jurisprudence*. Oxford: Clarendon Press, 1931.

Aman, Alfred C., Jr.; and William T. Mayton. *Administrative Law*. 2d ed. St. Paul: West, 2001.

American and English Encyclopaedia of Law, The. 32 vols. David. S. Garland & Charles Porterfield, eds. 2d ed. N.Y.: Edward Thompson, 1896–1905.

American Jurisprudence 2d. 83 vols. St. Paul.: West, 1962–present.

American Law and Procedure. 14 vols. James Parker Hall & James De Witt Andrews, eds. Chicago: La Salle Extension Univ., 1948.

American Law of Mining. 6 vols. 2d ed. N.Y.: Matthew Bender, 1984–present.

American Law of Property. 7 vols. Boston: Little Brown, 1952–1954.

American Psychiatric Ass'n. *Diagnostic and Statistical Manual of Mental Disorders*. 5th ed. Washington, D.C.: American Psychiatric Ass'n, 2013.

Anderson, Ronald A. *Uniform Commercial Code*. 8 vols. 3d ed. St. Paul: West, 1981–present.

Anderson, Roy Ryden. *Damages Under the Uniform Commercial Code*. 2 vols. Eagan, Minn.: Thomson Reuters, 2013–2014.

Anderson, William C. *A Dictionary of Law*. Chicago: T.H. Flood & Co., 1889.

Andrews, William. *Bygone Punishments*. London: William Andrews & Co., 1899.

Anson, William R. *Principles of the Law of Contract*. Arthur L. Corbin, ed. 3d Am. ed. N.Y.: Oxford Univ. Press, 1919.

Appleman, John Alan; and Jean Appleman. *Insurance Law and Practice*. 61 vols. St. Paul: West, 1941–present.

Arant, Herschel W. *Handbook of the Law of Suretyship and Guaranty*. St. Paul: West, 1931.

Archer, Gleason L. *Law Office and Court Procedure*. Boston: Little Brown, 1910.

Areeda, Phillip; and Donald F. Turner. *Antitrust Law*. 5 vols. & supp. Boston: Little Brown, 1978–1980 & 1982 (supp.).

Arnesen, Eric (ed.). *Encyclopedia of U.S. Labor and Working-Class History*. 3 vols. N.Y.: Routledge, 2007.

Ashworth, Andrew. *Principles of Criminal Law*. Oxford: Clarendon Press, 1991.

Atiyah, P.S. *An Introduction to the Law of Contract*. 3d ed. Oxford: Clarendon Press, 1981.

Atiyah, P.S. *Promises, Morals, and Law*. Oxford: Clarendon Press, 1981.

Atiyah, P.S.; and Robert S. Summers. *Form and Substance in Anglo-American Law*. Oxford: Clarendon Press, 1987.

Atkinson, Thomas E. *Handbook of the Law of Wills*. 2d ed. St. Paul: West, 1953.

Austin, Erik W. *Political Facts of the United States Since 1789*. N.Y.: Columbia Univ. Press, 1986.

Austin, John. *Lectures on Jurisprudence*. 2 vols. Robert Campbell, ed. 5th ed. London: J. Murray, 1885.

Bainbridge, David I. *Intellectual Property*. 5th ed. N.Y.: Longman, 2002.

Baird, Douglas G. *Elements of Bankruptcy*. N.Y.: Foundation Press, 2001.

Baker, J.H. *An Introduction to English Legal History.* 3d ed. London: Butterworths, 1990.

Baker, J.H. *A Manual of Law French.* Amersham, U.K.: Avebury, 1979.

Baker, J.H. *The Order of Serjeants at Law.* London: Selden Society, 1984.

Barbour, Oliver L. *A Summary of the Law of Parties to Actions at Law and Suits in Equity.* Albany, N.Y.: W.C. Little, 1864.

Barbour, Oliver L. *A Treatise on the Law of Set Off.* Albany, N.Y.: W. & A. Gould & Co., 1864.

Barclay, Hugh. *A Digest of the Law of Scotland.* 3d ed. Edinburgh: T. & T. Clark, 1865.

Barnes, Marian Quinn (ed.). *A Treatise on the Law of Crimes.* 7th ed. Mundelein, Ill.: Callaghan, 1967.

Barnouw, Erik (ed.). *International Encyclopedia of Communications.* 4 vols. N.Y.: Oxford Univ. Press, 1989.

Barton, R.T. *The Practice in the Courts of Law in Civil Cases.* 2 vols. 2d ed. Richmond, Va.: J.W. Randolph & Co., 1891–1892.

Basedow Jürgen; et al. (eds.). *The Max Planck Encyclopedia of European Private Law.* 2 vols. Oxford: Oxford Univ. Press, 2012.

Basye, Paul E. *Clearing Land Titles.* St. Paul: West, 1953.

Beale, Joseph Henry. *A Treatise on Criminal Pleading and Practice.* Boston: Little Brown, 1899.

Beale, Joseph Henry. *A Treatise on the Conflict of Laws.* 3 vols. N.Y.: Baker Voorhis, 1935.

Beard, Charles A.; and William Beard. *The American Leviathan: The Republic in the Machine Age.* N.Y.: Macmillan, 1931.

Beardsley, Arthur Sydney. *Legal Bibliography and the Use of Law Books.* Chicago: Foundation Press, 1937.

Beccaria, Cesare. *An Essay on Crimes and Punishments* [1764]. Rev. ed. Philadelphia: William Young, 1793.

Bederman, David J. *International Law Frameworks.* N.Y.: Foundation Press, 2001.

Beeton, Samuel Orchart. *Beeton's Illustrated Dictionary of Religion, Philosophy, Politics, and Law.* London: Ward, Lock & Co., 1886.

Belknap, William Worth; et al. *Proceeding of the Senate Sitting for the Trial of William W. Belknap.* Washington, D.C.: GPO, 1876.

Bell, William. *Bell's Dictionary and Digest of the Law of Scotland.* George Watson, ed. 7th ed. Edinburgh: Bell & Bradfute, 1890.

Benedict, Joseph. *Benedict's Treatise: Containing a Summary of the Jurisdiction, Powers, and Duties of Justices of the Peace in the State of New York.* 2d ed. Auburn, N.Y.: J.C. Derby & Co., 1847.

Bennett, Stephen C. *Arbitration: Essential Concepts.* N.Y.: ALM, 2002.

Bennion, F.A.R. *Statutory Interpretation.* 3d ed. London: Butterworths, 1997.

Bentham, Jeremy. *An Introduction to the Principles of Morals and Legislation.* 2 vols. London: W. Pickering, 1823.

Bentham, Jeremy. *The Works of Jeremy Bentham.* 11 vols. John Bowring, ed. Edinburgh: William Tait, 1843.

Bently, Lionel; and Brad Sherman. *Intellectual Property Law.* Oxford: Oxford Univ. Press, 2001.

Berger, Adolf. *Encyclopedic Dictionary of Roman Law.* Philadelphia: American Philosophical Society, 1953.

Bergin, Thomas F.; and Paul G. Haskell. *Preface to Estates in Land and Future Interests.* 2d ed. Mineola, N.Y.: Foundation Press, 1984.

Beven, Thomas. *Negligence in Law.* 2 vols. 3d ed. London: Stevens & Haynes, 1908.

Bigelow, Melville M. *Elements of the Law of Torts.* 6th ed. Boston: Little Brown, 1896.

Bigelow, Melville M. *The Law of Bills, Notes, and Checks.* William Minor Lile, ed. 3d ed. Boston: Little Brown, 1928.

Birks, Peter (ed.). *English Private Law.* 2 vols. Oxford: Oxford Univ. Press, 2000.

Birrell, Augustine. *The Duties and Liabilities of Trustees.* London: Macmillan, 1920.

Bishop, Joel Prentiss. *Commentaries on the Law of Contracts.* Chicago: T.H. Flood & Co., 1887.

Bishop, Joel Prentiss. *Commentaries on the Written Laws and their Interpretation.* Boston: Little Brown, 1882.

Bispham, George T. *The Principles of Equity.* Joseph D. McCoy, ed. 11th ed. N.Y.: Baker Voorhis, 1931.

Bix, Brian H. (ed.). *Analyzing Law: New Essays in Legal Theory.* Oxford: Clarendon Press, 1998.

Bix, Brian H. *A Dictionary of Legal Theory.* Oxford: Oxford Univ. Press, 2004.

Black, Henry Campbell. *Handbook of American Constitutional Law.* 4th ed. St. Paul: West, 1927.

Black, Henry Campbell. *Handbook on the Construction and Interpretation of the Laws.* 2d ed. St. Paul: West, 1911.

Black, Henry Campbell. *Handbook on the Law of Judicial Precedents.* St. Paul: West, 1912.

Black, Henry Campbell. *A Treatise on the Law and Practice of Bankruptcy.* Kansas City, Mo.: Vernon, 1914.

Black, Henry Campbell. *A Treatise on the Law of Income Taxation Under Federal and State Laws.* Kansas City, Mo.: Vernon, 1913.

Black, Henry Campbell. *A Treatise on the Law of Judgments.* 2 vols. 2d ed. St. Paul: West, 1902.

Black, Henry Campbell. *A Treatise on the Laws Regulating the Manufacture and Sale of Intoxicating Liquors.* St. Paul: West, 1892.

Blackstone, William. *Commentaries on the Laws of England.* 4 vols. Oxford: Clarendon Press, 1765–1769.

Bliss, George. *The Law of Life Insurance.* 2d ed. N.Y.: Baker Voorhis, 1874.

Block, Dennis J.; et al. *The Business Judgment Rule*. 2 vols. 5th ed. N.Y.: Aspen, 1998.

Blom-Cooper, Louis; et al. (eds.). *The Judicial House of Lords, 1876–2009*. Oxford: Oxford Univ. Press, 2009.

Blount, Thomas. *Nomo-Lexicon: A Law-Dictionary*. London: John Martin & Henry Herringman, 1670.

Boberg, P.Q.R. *The Law of Delict*. Cape Town: Juta, 1984.

Bodenheimer, Edgar. *Jurisprudence: The Philosophy and Method of the Law*. Rev. ed. Cambridge, Mass.: Harvard Univ. Press, 1974.

Bodenheimer, Edgar. *Treatise on Justice*. N.Y.: Philosophical Library, 1967.

Bonner, Robert J. *Lawyers and Litigants in Ancient Athens*. N.Y.: Barnes & Noble, 1927.

Born, Gary B. *International Commercial Arbitration*. 2 vols. Austin, Tex.: Wolters Kluwer, 2009.

Bouvier, John. *A Law Dictionary*. Philadelphia: T. & J.W. Johnson, 1839. Also: *Bouvier's Law Dictionary*. 3 vols. Francis Rawle, ed. 8th ed. Kansas City, Mo.: Vernon, 1914.

Boyer, Ralph E.; et al. *The Law of Property*. 4th ed. St. Paul: West, 1991.

Brandt, George W. *The Law of Suretyship and Guaranty*. 2 vols. 3d ed. Chicago: Callaghan & Co., 1905.

Branham, Vernon C.; and Samuel B. Kutash (eds.). *Encyclopedia of Criminology*. N.Y.: Philosophical Library, 1949.

Brierly, J.L. *The Law of Nations*. 5th ed. Oxford: Clarendon Press, 1955. (See also Clapham.)

Brittin, Burdick H. *International Law for Seagoing Officers*. 4th ed. Annapolis: Naval Inst. Press, 1981.

Bromberg, Alan R.; and Larry E. Ribstein. *Bromberg and Ribstein on Partnership*. 4 vols. Boston: Little Brown, 1988–present.

Brown, David Paul. *The Forum: Or Forty Years Full Practice at the Philadelphia Bar*. 2 vols. Philadelphia: Robert H. Small, 1856.

Brown, Harold. *Franchising: Realities and Remedies*. 2 vols. Rev. ed. N.Y.: Law Journals Seminars Press, 1993.

Brown, Ray Andrews. *The Law of Personal Property*. 2d ed. Chicago: Callaghan & Co., 1955.

Brownsword, Roger; Norma J. Hird; and Geraint Howells (eds.). *Good Faith in Contract: Concept and Context*. Brookfield, Mass.: Ashgate/Dartmouth, 1999.

Brumbaugh, Jesse Franklin. *Legal Reasoning and Briefing*. Indianapolis: Bobbs-Merrill, 1917.

Bryant, Edwin E. *The Law of Pleading Under the Codes of Civil Procedure*. 2d ed. Boston: Little Brown, 1899.

Bryce, James. *Studies in History and Jurisprudence*. 2 vols. N.Y.: Oxford Univ. Press, 1901.

Buckland, W.W. *Elementary Principles of the Roman Private Law*. Cambridge: Cambridge Univ. Press, 1912.

Buckland, W.W. *A Manual of Roman Private Law*. 2d ed. Cambridge: Cambridge Univ. Press, 1939.

Buckland, W.W. *Some Reflections on Jurisprudence*. Cambridge: Cambridge Univ. Press, 1945.

Buckland, W.W. *A Text-book of Roman Law from Augustus to Justinian*. Peter Stein, ed. 3d ed. Cambridge: Cambridge Univ. Press, 1963.

Buckland, W.W.; and Arnold D. McNair. *Roman Law and Common Law: A Comparison in Outline*. F.H. Lawson, ed. 2d ed. Cambridge: Cambridge Univ. Press, 1952.

Bullen, Edward; and Stephen Martin Leake. *Bullen and Leake's Precedents of Pleadings in Actions in the King's Bench Division of the High Court of Justice*. Alfred Thompson Denning [later Lord Denning] & Arthur Grattan-Bellew, eds. 9th ed. London: Stevens & Sons, 1935.

Bullingbrooke, Edward. *The Duty and Authority of Justices of the Peace and Parish Officers for Ireland*. Rev. ed. Dublin: G. Grierson, 1788.

Burdick, William L. *Handbook of the Law of Real Property*. St. Paul: West, 1914.

Burgess, John W. *Political Science and Comparative Constitutional Law*. 2 vols. Boston: Ginn & Co., 1890–1891.

Burn, Richard. *The Justice of the Peace and Parish Officer*. 3d ed. London: Henry Lintot, 1756.

Burn, Richard. *A New Law Dictionary*. 2 vols. London: T. Cadell, 1792.

Burnham, Scott J. *Contract Drafting Guidebook*. 2d ed. Charlottesville, Va.: Michie Co., 1992.

Burrill, Alexander M. *A Law Dictionary and Glossary*. 2 vols. 2d ed. N.Y.: Baker Voorhis, 1867.

Burrill, Alexander M. *A Treatise on the Law and Practice of Voluntary Assignments for the Benefit of Creditors*. James Avery Webb, ed. 6th ed. N.Y.: Baker Voorhis, 1894.

Burrill, Alexander M. *A Treatise on the Nature, Principles and Rules of Circumstantial Evidence*. N.Y.: J.S. Voorhies, 1868.

Burrill, Alexander M. *Treatise on the Practice of the Supreme Court of the State of New-York*. 2 vols. 2d ed. N.Y.: John S. Voorhies, 1846.

Burrows, Andrew; and Alan Rodger (eds.). *Mapping the Law: Essays in Memory of Peter Birks*. Oxford: Oxford Univ. Press, 2006.

Butt, Peter. *Land Law*. 2d ed. Sydney: Lawbook Co., 1988. Also: 3d ed. Sydney: LBC Info. Servs., 1996.

Byrne, Edward M. *Military Law*. 2d ed. Annapolis: Naval Inst. Press, 1976.

Cairns, Huntington. *The Theory of Legal Science*. Chapel Hill, N.C.: Univ. of North Carolina Press, 1941.

Calabresi, Guido. *A Common Law for the Age of Statutes*. Cambridge, Mass.: Harvard Univ. Press, 1982.

Calamandrei, Piero. *Eulogy of Judges*. John Clarke Adams & C. Abbott Phillips Jr., trans. Princeton, N.J.: Princeton Univ. Press, 1942.

Calamari, John D.; and Joseph M. Perillo. *The Law of Contracts.* 4th ed. St. Paul: West, 1998.

Callmann, Rudolf. *The Law of Unfair Competition, Trademarks and Monopolies.* 6 vols. 4th ed. St. Paul: Thomson/West, 1981–present.

Cane, Peter; and Joanne Conaghan (eds.). *The New Oxford Companion to Law.* Oxford: Oxford Univ. Press, 2008.

Caney, L.R. *A Treatise on the Law Relating to Novation.* Cape Town: Juta, 1938.

Cardozo, Benjamin N. *The Paradoxes of Legal Science.* N.Y.: Columbia Univ. Press, 1928.

Caringella, Susan. *Addressing Rape Reform in Law and Practice.* N.Y.: Columbia Univ. Press, 2009.

Carter, A.T. *A History of English Legal Institutions.* 4th ed. London: Butterworth & Co., 1910.

Castagnino, John-Peter. *Derivatives: The Key Principles.* 3d ed. Oxford: Oxford Univ. Press, 2009.

Century Dictionary and Cyclopedia, The. 10 vols. & 2-vol. supp. William Dwight Whitney, ed. N.Y.: Century Co., 1889–1897.

Chamberlayne, Charles Frederic. *A Treatise on the Modern Law of Evidence.* 5 vols. Albany, N.Y.: Matthew Bender, 1911–1916.

Chambers, Ephraim. *Cyclopaedia: Or, an Universal Dictionary of Arts and Sciences.* 2 vols. & 2 supps. 5th ed. London: D. Midwinter et al., 1747 (vol. 1), 1743 (vol. 2 & 2 supps.).

Chambers, Robert. *A Course of Lectures on the English Law: 1767–1773.* Thomas M. Curley, ed. Madison, Wis.: Univ. of Wisconsin Press, 1986.

Chance, E.W. *Principles of Mercantile Law.* Vol 1. P.W. French, ed. 13th ed. St. Albans: Donnington Press, 1950. Vol 2. P.W. French, ed. 10th ed. St. Albans: Donnington Press, 1951. [Volume 1 appears to have gone through more editions than volume 2.]

Chandler, Ralph C.; Richard A. Enslen; and Peter G. Renstrom. *The Constitutional Law Dictionary.* 2 vols. & 1-vol. supp. Santa Barbara: ABC-CLIO, 1985 (vol. 1), 1987 (vol. 2 & supp.).

Chapin, H. Gerald. *Handbook of the Law of Torts.* St. Paul: West, 1917.

Charpentier, Arthur A. (ed.). *Counsel on Appeal.* N.Y.: McGraw-Hill, 1968.

Cheshire, G.C. *Modern Law of Real Property.* 3d ed. London: Butterworth & Co., 1933.

Cheshire, G.C. *Private International Law.* 6th ed. Oxford: Clarendon Press, 1961.

Childs, Frank Hall. *Where and How to Find the Law.* Chicago: La Salle Extension Univ., 1923.

Chirelstein, Marvin A. *Concepts and Case Analysis in the Law of Contracts.* Westbury, N.Y.: Foundation Press, 1990.

Chisum, Donald S. *Patents.* 13 vols. N.Y.: Lexis, 1978–present.

Chitty, Joseph. *A Practical Treatise on Bills of Exchange, Promissory Notes, and Bankers' Checks.* Erastus Smith, ed. Springfield, Mass.: G. & C. Merriam, 1834.

Chitty, Joseph. *A Practical Treatise on the Criminal Law.* 4 vols. 2d ed. London: Samuel Brooke, 1826.

Chitty, Joseph. *A Practical Treatise on the Law of Contracts.* Boston: Wells & Lilly, 1827.

Chitty, Joseph. *A Treatise on the Parties to Actions, the Forms of Actions, and on Pleading.* 3 vols. John H. Dunlap & E.D. Ingraham, eds. 6th Am. ed. fr. 5th London ed. Springfield, Mass.: G. & C. Merriam, 1833.

Clapham, Andrew. *Brierly's Law of Nations: An Introduction to the Role of International Law in International Relations.* 7th ed. Oxford: Oxford Univ. Press, 2012. (See also Brierly.)

Clapp, James E.; et al. *Lawtalk: The Unknown Stories Behind Familiar Legal Expressions.* New Haven: Yale Univ. Press, 2011.

Clark, Barkley; and Christopher Smith. *The Law of Product Warranties.* Boston: Warren, Gorham & Lamont, 1984.

Clark, Charles E. *Handbook of the Law of Code Pleading.* 2d ed. St. Paul: West, 1947.

Clark, David G.; and Earl R. Hutchinson. *Mass Media and the Law.* N.Y.: Wiley-Interscience, 1970.

Clark, E.C. *History of Roman Private Law.* 3 vols. W.W. Buckland, ed. (vol. 3). Cambridge: Cambridge Univ. Press, 1914 (vols. 1 & 2), 1919 (vol. 3).

Clark, Elias; et al. *Gratuitous Transfers: Wills, Intestate Succession, Trusts, Gifts, Future Interests, and Estate and Gift Taxation Cases and Materials.* 4th ed. St. Paul: West, 1999.

Clark, Homer H., Jr. *The Law of Domestic Relations in the United States.* 2d ed. St. Paul: West, 1988.

Clark, Homer H., Jr.; and Ann Laquer Estin. *Domestic Relations: Cases and Problems.* 6th ed. St. Paul: West, 2000.

Clark, Lindley Daniel. *The Law of the Employment of Labor.* N.Y.: Macmillan, 1911.

Clark, William Lawrence. *Handbook of Criminal Law.* Francis B. Tiffany, ed. 2d ed. St. Paul: West, 1902.

Clark, William Lawrence. *Handbook of the Law of Contracts.* Archibald H. Throckmorton, ed. 3d ed. St. Paul: West, 1914.

Clark, William Lawrence. *A Treatise on the Law of Crimes.* Marian Quinn Barnes, ed. 7th ed. Mundelein, Ill.: Callaghan & Co., 1967.

Coates, David (ed.). *The Oxford Companion to American Politics.* 2 vols. N.Y.: Oxford Univ. Press, 2012.

Cobbey, J.E. *A Practical Treatise on the Law of Replevin.* 2d ed. Chicago: Callaghan & Co., 1900.

Coggins, George Cameron. *Public Natural Resources Law.* 3 vols. St. Paul: Thomson/West, 1990.

Coggins, George Cameron; et al. *Federal Public Land and Resources Law.* 3d ed. Westbury, N.Y.: Foundation Press, 1993.

Cohen, Morris R. *Law and the Social Order.* N.Y.: Harcourt Brace, 1933.

Cohen, Morris R. *Reason and Law.* N.Y.: Collier Macmillan, 1961.

Colebrooke, William. *A Treatise on the Law of Collateral Securities.* Chicago: Callaghan & Co., 1883.

Conte, Alba. *Attorney Fee Awards.* 2 vols. Colorado Springs: Shepard's, 1993.

Cooley, Roger W. *Handbook of the Law of Municipal Corporations.* St. Paul: West, 1914.

Cooley, Thomas M. *The Law of Taxation.* 4 vols. Clark A. Nichols, ed. 4th ed. Chicago: Callaghan & Co., 1924.

Cooley, Thomas M. *A Treatise on the Constitutional Limitations Which Rest upon the Legislative Power of the States of the American Union.* Boston: Little Brown, 1868.

Coquillette, Daniel R. *The Anglo-American Legal Heritage.* Durham, N.C.: Carolina Academic Press, 1999.

Corbin, Arthur Linton. *Corbin on Contracts.* One-vol. ed. St. Paul: West, 1952. (*See also* Anson.)

Corpus Juris Secundum (C.J.S.). 101 vols. St. Paul: West, 1936–present.

Cotterrell, Roger. *The Politics of Jurisprudence: A Critical Introduction to Legal Philosophy.* 2d ed. Oxford: Oxford Univ. Press, 2003.

Couch, George J. *Couch on Insurance.* 26 vols. 2d ed. St. Paul: West, 1959–1994.

Cowell, John. *The Interpreter.* Cambridge: John Legate, 1607.

Cowen, Zelman. *Essays on the Law of Evidence.* Oxford: Clarendon Press, 1956.

Crabb, George. *A History of English Law.* 1st Am. ed. Burlington: C. Goodrich, 1831.

Craies, William Feilden. *A Treatise on Statute Law.* 2d ed. London: Stevens & Haynes, 1911.

Craig, Laurence; et al. *International Chamber of Commerce Arbitration.* 3d ed. Dobbs Ferry, N.Y.: Oceana, 2000.

Crawford, James. *Brownlie's Principles of Public International Law.* 8th ed. Oxford: Oxford Univ. Press, 2012.

Cribbet, John E. *Principles of the Law of Property.* 2d ed. Mineola, N.Y.: Foundation Press, 1975.

Crompton, George. *Practice Common-Placed: Rules and Cases of Practice in the Courts of King's Bench and Common Pleas.* 2 vols. 3d ed. Dublin: Elizabeth Lynch, 1787.

Cross, Frank B. *The Theory and Practice of Statutory Interpretation.* Stanford, Calif.: Stanford Law Books, 2009.

Cross, Rupert. *Evidence.* 3d ed. London: Butterworths, 1967.

Cross, Rupert. *Precedent in English Law.* 1st ed. Oxford: Clarendon Press, 1961. Also: With J.W. Harris. 4th ed. Oxford: Clarendon Press, 1991.

Cross, Rupert. *Statutory Interpretation.* London: Butterworths, 1976.

Croswell, Simon Greenleaf. *Handbook on the Law of Executors and Administrators.* St. Paul: West, 1897.

Cunningham, Roger A.; et al. *The Law of Property.* 2d ed. St. Paul: West, 1993.

Curzon, L.B. *English Legal History.* 2d ed. Estover, U.K.: Macdonald & Evans, 1979.

Cyclopedia of Law and Procedure. 40 vols. & index. William Mack & H.P. Nash, eds. N.Y.: American Law Book Co., 1901–1913.

Dahl, Robert A. *A Preface to Democratic Theory.* Chicago: Chicago Univ. Press, 1956.

Dainow, Joseph (ed.). *Essays on the Civil Law of Obligations.* Baton Rouge: Louisiana State Univ. Press, 1969.

Dangel, Edward M. *Contempt.* Boston: Nat'l Lawyers' Manual Co., 1939.

Daniel, John W. *A Treatise on the Law of Negotiable Instruments.* 3 vols. Thomas H. Calvert, ed. 7th ed. N.Y.: Baker Voorhis, 1933.

Darlington, Joseph J. *A Treatise on the Law of Personal Property.* Philadelphia: T. & J.W. Johnson & Co., 1891.

Davis, George B. *The Elements of International Law.* Gordon E. Sherman, ed. 4th ed. N.Y.: Harper & Bros., 1915.

Davis, George B. *A Treatise on the Military Law of the United States.* 3d ed. N.Y.: John Wiley & Sons, 1915.

Decker, Kurt H.; and H. Thomas Felix II. *Drafting and Revising Employment Contracts.* N.Y.: Wiley Law Publications, 1991.

De Colange, L. *The American Dictionary of Commerce, Manufactures, Commercial Law, and Finance.* 2 vols. Boston: Estes & Lauriat, 1881.

De Colyar, Henry Anselm. *A Treatise on the Law of Guarantees and of Principal and Surety.* 3d ed. London: Butterworth & Co., 1897.

De Funiak, William Q. *Handbook of Modern Equity.* 2d ed. Boston: Little Brown, 1956.

Del Vecchio, Giorgio. *The Formal Bases of Law.* John Lisle, trans. N.Y.: Macmillan, 1921.

Demeter, George. *Demeter's Manual of Parliamentary Law and Procedure.* Boston: Little Brown, 1969.

Denis, Henry. *A Treatise on the Law of the Contract of Pledge as Governed by Both the Common Law and the Civil Law.* New Orleans: F.F. Hansell & Bro., 1898.

Deschler, Lewis. *Deschler's Rules of Order.* Englewood Cliffs, N.J.: Prentice-Hall, 1976.

De Tourtoulon, Pierre. *Philosophy in the Development of Law.* Martha McC. Read, trans. N.Y.: Macmillan, 1922.

De Vattel, E. *The Law of Nations or the Principles of Natural Law.* Charles G. Fenwick, trans. Washington, D.C.: Carnegie Inst. of Washington, 1916.

Devlin, Patrick [Lord Devlin]. *The Criminal Prosecution in England.* London: Oxford Univ. Press, 1960.

Devlin, Patrick [Lord Devlin]. *The Enforcement of Morals.* London: Oxford Univ. Press, 1968.

Devlin, Patrick [Lord Devlin]. *The Judge.* Oxford: Oxford Univ. Press, 1979.

De Zulueta, F. *The Roman Law of Sale.* Oxford: Clarendon Press, 1945.

Dhokalia, R.P. *The Codification of Public International Law.* Manchester: Univ. of Manchester, 1970.

Dias, R.W.M.; and B.S. Markesinis. *Tort Law.* 2d ed. Oxford: Clarendon Press, 1989.

Dicey, A.V. *Introduction to the Study of the Law of the Constitution.* E.C.S. Wade, ed. 10th ed. London: Macmillan, 1959.

Dicey, A.V.; and A. Berriedale Keith. *A Digest of the Law of England with Reference to the Conflict of Laws.* 3d ed. London: Stevens & Sons, 1922.

Dickerson, Reed. *The Interpretation and Application of Statutes.* Boston: Little Brown, 1975.

Digby, Kenelm E. *An Introduction to the History of the Law of Real Property.* 5th ed. Oxford: Clarendon Press, 1897.

Dillon, John F. *The Laws and Jurisprudence in England and America.* N.Y.: Da Capo Press, 1970.

Dobbs, Dan B. *Law of Remedies.* 3 vols. 2d ed. St. Paul: West, 1993.

Dobie, Armistead M. *Handbook on the Law of Bailments and Carriers.* St. Paul: West, 1914.

Dolan, John F. *The Law of Letters of Credit.* Boston: Warren, Gorham & Lamont, 1984.

Drake, Charles D. *A Treatise on the Law of Suits by Attachment in the United States.* 7th ed. Boston: Little Brown, 1891.

Dratler, Jay, Jr. *Cyberlaw.* N.Y.: Law Journal Press, 2001.

Dray, William. *Laws and Explanation in History.* Oxford: Clarendon Press, 1957.

Dressler, Joshua (ed.). *Encyclopedia of Crime and Justice.* 4 vols. 2d ed. N.Y.: Macmillan, 2002.

Driedger, Elmer A. *The Composition of Legislation.* Ottawa: Edmond Cloutier, 1957.

Drinker, Henry S. *Legal Ethics.* N.Y.: Columbia Univ. Press, 1953.

Drone, Eaton S. *A Treatise on the Law of Property in Intellectual Productions.* Boston: Little Brown, 1879.

Dudley, Robert J. *Think Like a Lawyer.* Chicago: Nelson-Hall, 1980.

Duhamel, Jean; and J. Dill Smith. *Some Pillars of English Law.* Reginald Hall, ed. & trans. 1st English ed. London: Sir Isaac Pitman & Sons, 1959.

Dumenil, Lynn (ed.). *The Oxford Encyclopedia of American Social History.* 2 vols. N.Y.: Oxford Univ. Press, 2012.

Dunn, William C. *Trusts for Business Purposes.* Chicago: Callaghan & Co., 1922.

Du Plessis, Paul. *Borkowski's Textbook on Roman Law.* 4th ed. Oxford: Oxford Univ. Press, 2010.

Dwight, Timothy. *Travels in New-England and New-York.* 4 vols. New Haven: For the author, 1821–1822.

Dworkin, Gerald. *Odgers' Construction of Deeds and Statutes.* 5th ed. London: Sweet & Maxwell, 1967.

Dworkin, Ronald. *Law's Empire.* Cambridge, Mass.: Belknap Press, 1986.

Easterbrook, Frank H.; and Daniel R. Fischel. *The Economic Structure of Corporate Law.* Cambridge, Mass.: Harvard Univ. Press, 1991.

Eaton, James W. *Handbook of Equity Jurisprudence.* 1st ed. St. Paul: West, 1901. Also: Archibald H. Throckmorton, ed. 2d ed. St. Paul: West, 1923.

Eddy, Jonathan A.; and Peter Winship. *Commercial Transactions.* Boston: Little Brown, 1985.

Edwards, George J., Jr. *The Grand Jury.* Philadelphia: George T. Bisel, 1906.

Eggleston, Richard. *Evidence, Proof and Probability.* London: Weidenfeld & Nicolson, 1978.

Ehrich, Manfred W. *The Law of Promoters.* Albany, N.Y.: Matthew Bender & Co., 1916.

Ehrlich, Eugen. *Fundamental Principles of the Sociology of Law.* Walter L. Moll, trans. N.Y.: Russell & Russell, 1962.

Eldredge, Lawrence H. *The Law of Defamation.* Indianapolis: Bobbs-Merrill, 1978.

Elias, Stephen. *Patent, Copyright and Trademark.* Berkeley: Nolo Press, 1996.

Elliott, Byron K.; and William F. Elliott. *A Treatise on the Law of Railroads.* 6 vols. 3d ed. Indianapolis: Bobbs-Merrill, 1921.

Ely, John Hart. *Democracy and Distrust.* Cambridge: Harvard Univ. Press, 1980.

Encyclopaedia Britannica. 24 vols. 9th ed. Akron, Ohio: Werner Co., 1907.

Encyclopaedia Britannica. 29 vols. 11th ed. N.Y.: Cambridge Univ. Press, 1910–1911.

Encyclopedia of Public International Law. 5 vols. N.Y.: North-Holland, 1992.

Endlich, G.A. *The Law of Building Associations.* Jersey City, N.J.: F.D. Linn, 1886.

Enever, F.A. *History of the Law of Distress.* London: G. Routledge & Sons, 1931.

Epstein, David G.; Steve H. Nickles; and James J. White. *Bankruptcy.* St. Paul: West, 1993.

Epstein, David M. (ed.). *Eckstrom's Licensing in Foreign and Domestic Operations.* 7 vols. 5th ed. Eagan, Minn.: Thomson/West, 2002–2011.

Erskine, John. *An Institute of the Law of Scotland.* 2 vols. James Badenach Nicolson, ed. Edinburgh: Bell & Bradfute, 1871.

Eskridge, William N., Jr.; Philip P. Frickey; and Elizabeth Garett. *Cases and Materials on Legislation.* 3d ed. St. Paul: West, 2001.

Estee, Morris M. *Estee's Pleadings, Practice, and Forms.* 3 vols. Carter P. Pomeroy, ed. 3d ed. San Francisco: L. Bancroft & Co., 1885.

Everest, Lancelot Feilding. *Everest and Strode's Law of Estoppel.* 3d ed. London: Stevens & Sons, 1923.

Ewart, John S. *An Exposition of the Principles of Estoppel by Misrepresentation.* Chicago: Callaghan & Co., 1900.

Faber, Robert C. *Landis on Mechanics of Patent Claim Drafting.* 3d ed. N.Y.: Practising Law Inst., 1990.

Farnsworth, E. Allan. *Changing Your Mind: The Law of Regretted Decision.* New Haven: Yale Univ. Press, 1998.

Farnsworth, E. Allan. *Contracts.* 2d ed. Boston: Little Brown, 1990. Also: *Farnsworth on Contracts.* 3d. ed. 3 vols. N.Y.: Aspen, 1999, 2004.

Farnsworth, Ward. *The Legal Analyst: A Toolkit for Thinking About the Law.* Chicago: Univ. of Chicago Press, 2007.

Fassbender, Bardo; and Anne Peters (eds.). *Oxford Handbook of the History of International Law.* Oxford: Oxford Univ. Press, 2012.

Fellmeth, Aaron X.; and Maurice Horwitz. *Guide to Latin in International Law.* Oxford: Oxford Univ. Press, 2009.

Fenwick, Charles G. *International Law.* N.Y.: Century Co., 1924.

Ferris, Forrest G.; and Forrest G. Ferris Jr. *The Law of Extraordinary Legal Remedies.* St. Louis: Thomas Law Book Co., 1926.

Fetter, Norman. *Handbook of Equity Jurisprudence.* St. Paul: West, 1895.

Fifoot, C.H.S. *English Law and Its Background.* London: G. Bell & Sons, 1932.

Fifoot, C.H.S. *History and Sources of the Common Law: Tort and Contract.* London: Stevens, 1949.

Finch, Henry. *Law, or a Discourse Thereof.* London: Henry Lintot, 1759.

Finlason, W.F. *Reeves' History of the English Law.* 3 vols. Rev. ed. London: Reeves & Turner, 1869.

Finnis, John. *Human Rights and Common Good.* Oxford: Oxford Univ. Press, 2011.

Finnis, John. *Intention and Identity.* Oxford: Oxford Univ. Press, 2011.

Finnis, John. *Philosophy of Law.* Oxford: Oxford Univ. Press, 2011.

Finnis, John. *Reason in Action.* Oxford: Oxford Univ. Press, 2011.

Fisch, Edith L. *The Cy Pres Doctrine in the United States.* Albany, N.Y.: Bander, 1950.

Fishback, William P. *A Manual of Elementary Law.* Arnold Bennett Hall, ed. Rev ed. Indianapolis: Bobbs-Merrill, 1896.

Flanders, Henry. *A Treatise on the Law of Shipping.* Philadelphia: T. & J.W. Johnson, 1853.

Fledman, David (ed.). *English Public Law.* Oxford: Oxford Univ. Press, 2004.

Fletcher, C. Edward. *Materials on the Law of Insider Trading.* Durham, N.C.: Carolina Academic Press, 1991.

Fletcher, George P. *Basic Concepts of Criminal Law.* N.Y.: Oxford Univ. Press, 1998.

Fletcher, George P. *Basic Concepts of Legal Thought.* N.Y.: Oxford Univ. Press, 1996.

Fletcher, George P. *The Grammar of Criminal Law: American, Comparative, and International.* Oxford: Oxford Univ. Press, 2007.

Fletcher, William Meade. *Fletcher Cyclopedia of the Law of Private Corporations.* 20 vols. St. Paul: Thomson/West, 1931–present.

Folsom, Ralph H.; and Michael W. Gordon. *International Business Transactions.* 2 vols. St. Paul: West, 1995.

Fordham, Edward Wilfrid (ed.). *Notable Cross-Examinations.* London: Constable & Co., 1951.

Forsythe, David P. (ed.). *Encyclopedia of Human Rights.* Oxford: Oxford Univ. Press, 2009.

Fox-Davies, Arthur Charles; and P.W.P. Carlyon-Britton. *A Treatise on the Law Concerning Names and Changes of Name.* London: E. Stock, 1906.

Frank, Jerome. *Courts on Trial.* Princeton, N.J.: Princeton Univ. Press, 1950.

Frank, Jerome. *Law and the Modern Mind.* N.Y.: Tudor Pub. Co., 1936.

Frederick, David C. *Supreme Court and Appellate Advocacy.* St. Paul: Thomson/West, 2003.

Freeman, A.C. *Cotenancy and Partition.* 2d ed. San Francisco: Bancroft-Whitney, 1886.

Freeman, A.C. *A Treatise of the Law of Judgments.* Edward W. Tuttle, ed. 5th ed. San Francisco: Bancroft-Whitney, 1925.

Freund, Ernst. *The Police Power.* Chicago: Callaghan & Co., 1904.

Freund, Ernst. *Standards of American Legislation.* Chicago: Univ. of Chicago Press, 1917.

Fricke, Charles W. *Planning and Trying Cases.* St. Paul: West, 1952.

Friedell, Steven F. *Benedict on Admiralty.* Vol. 1. 7th ed. N.Y.: Matthew Bender, 1996.

Friedenthal, Jack H.; et al. *Civil Procedure.* 2d ed. St. Paul: West, 1993.

Friedman, Lawrence M. *American Law in the 20th Century.* New Haven: Yale Univ. Press, 2002.

Friedman, Lawrence M. *Crime and Punishment in American History.* N.Y.: BasicBooks, 1993.

Friedman, Lawrence M. *A History of American Law.* 2d ed. N.Y.: Simon & Schuster, 1985.

Friedmann, W. *Legal Theory.* 5th ed. London: Stevens & Sons, 1967.

Frost, Thomas Gold. *A Treatise on Guaranty Insurance.* 2d ed. Boston: Little Brown, 1909.

Frost, Thomas Gold. *A Treatise on the Incorporation and Organization of Corporations.* 2d ed. Boston: Little Brown, 1906.

Froude, Thomas; and Eric V.E. White. *The Practice Relating to Debentures.* London: Pitman & Sons, 1935.

Fuller, Lon L. *Anatomy of the Law.* N.Y.: F.A. Praeger, 1968.

Fuller, Lon L. *The Morality of Law.* Rev. ed. New Haven: Yale Univ. Press, 1969.

Fullinwider, Robert K. *The Reverse Discrimination Controversy.* Totowa, N.J.: Rowman & Littlefield, 1980.

Furmston, Michael P. *Cheshire, Fifoot and Furmston's Law of Contract.* 16th ed. Oxford: Oxford Univ. Press, 2012.

Furrow, Barry R.; et al. *Health Law.* 2d ed. St. Paul: West, 2000.

Gahan, Frank. *The Law of Damages.* London: Sweet & Maxwell, 1936.

Gardiner, Richard K. *Treaty Interpretation.* Oxford: Oxford Univ. Press, 2008.

Gardner, Jane F. *Women in Roman Law and Society.* Bloomington.: Indiana Univ. Press, 1986.

Garner, Bryan A. *Garner's Dictionary of Legal Usage.* 3d ed. N.Y.: Oxford Univ. Press, 2011.

Garner, Bryan A. *Garner's Modern American Usage.* 3d ed. N.Y.: Oxford Univ. Press, 2009.

Garner, Bryan A. *The Winning Brief.* 3d ed. N.Y.: Oxford Univ. Press, 2014.

Garrie, Daniel B.; and Francis M. Allegra. *Plugged In: Guidebook to Software and the Law.* Rochester, N.Y.: Thomson Reuters, 2013–2014.

Geistfeld, Mark A. *Tort Law: The Essentials.* N.Y.: Aspen, 2008.

Geldart, William. *Introduction to English Law.* D.C.M. Yardley, ed. 9th ed. Oxford: Oxford Univ. Press, 1984.

George, William. *Handbook of the Law of Partnership.* St. Paul: West, 1897.

Gerber, Scott Douglas. *A Distinct Judicial Power: The Origins of an Independent Judiciary, 1606–1787.* Oxford: Oxford Univ. Press, 2011.

Gerhardt, Michael J. *The Power of Precedent.* Oxford: Oxford Univ. Press, 2008.

Gevurtz, Franklin A. *Corporation Law.* St. Paul: West, 2000.

Gibson, Albert; Arthur Weldon; and H. Gibson Rivington. *Gibson's Conveyancing.* 14th ed. London: Law Notes Pub. Offices, 1933.

Gifford, D.J.; and John Salter. *How to Understand an Act of Parliament.* London: Cavendish, 1996.

Gilbert, Jeffrey [Lord Chief Baron]. *A Treatise of Equity.* 3d ed. Dublin: Henry Watts, 1792.

Gillers, Stephen. *Regulation of Lawyers: Problems of Law and Ethics.* 7th ed. N.Y.: Aspen, 2005.

Gilmore, Eugene Allen. *Handbook on the Law of Partnership.* St. Paul: West, 1911.

Gilmore, Grant. *The Death of Contract.* Columbus, Ohio: Ohio State Univ. Press, 1974.

Gilmore, Grant; and Charles L. Black Jr. *The Law of Admiralty.* 2d ed. Mineola, N.Y.: Foundation Press, 1975.

Glendon, Mary Ann. *The Transformation of Family Law.* Chicago: Univ. of Chicago Press, 1989.

Glendon, Mary Ann; et al. *Comparative Legal Traditions.* 2d ed. St. Paul: West, 1994.

Glenn, Garrard. *The Law of Fraudulent Conveyances.* N.Y.: Baker Voorhis, 1931.

Goff, Robert H. [Lord Goff]; and Gareth H. Jones. *The Law of Restitution.* 3d ed. London: Sweet & Maxwell, 1986.

Golding, Martin P. *Philosophy of Law.* Englewood Cliffs, N.J.: Prentice-Hall, 1975.

Goldstein, Paul. *Copyright's Highway.* N.Y.: Hill & Wang, 1994.

Goldstein, Paul. *International Copyright: Principles, Law, and Practice.* Oxford: Oxford Univ. Press, 2001.

Golub, I.M.; et al. *COBRA Handbook.* N.Y.: Aspen, 1994.

Goodhart, Arthur L. *Essays in Jurisprudence and the Common Law.* Cambridge: Cambridge Univ. Press, 1931.

Goodin, Robert E. (ed.). *The Oxford Handbook of Political Science.* Oxford: Oxford Univ. Press, 2009.

Goodrich, Herbert F.; and Eugene F. Scoles. *Handbook of the Conflict of Laws.* 4th ed. St. Paul: West, 1964.

Gorman, Robert A. *Basic Text on Labor Law: Unionization and Collective Bargaining.* St. Paul: West, 1976.

Grange, William J. *Real Estate.* N.Y.: Ronald Press Co., 1937.

Graveson, R.H. *Conflict of Laws.* 7th ed. London: Sweet & Maxwell, 1974.

Gray, John Chipman. *The Nature and Sources of the Law.* 1st ed. N.Y.: Columbia Univ. Press, 1909. Also: 2d ed. N.Y.: Macmillan, 1921.

Gray, John Chipman. *The Rule Against Perpetuities.* Boston: Little Brown, 1886.

Gray, Tom; Martin Hinton; and David Caruso (eds.). *Essays in Advocacy.* Adelaide, Aus.: Barr Smith Press, 2012.

Green, Sanford M. *A Treatise on Townships, and the Powers and Duties of Township Officers.* 2d ed. Columbus, Ohio: For the author, 1882.

Greene, Jack P. (ed.). *Encyclopedia of American Political History.* N.Y.: Scribner, 1984.

Greene, T. Whitcombe. *Outlines of Roman Law.* 3d ed. London: Stevens & Sons, 1875.

Gregory, William A. *The Law of Agency and Partnership.* 3d ed. St. Paul: West, 2001.

Grenig, Jay E.; and Jeffrey S. Kinsler. *Handbook of Federal Civil Discovery and Disclosure.* 2d ed. St. Paul: West, 2002.

Grimes, Allen. *The City Attorney: A Practice Manual.* Washington, D.C.: Nat'l Inst. of Mun. Law Officers, 1978.

Grismore, Grover C. *Principles of the Law of Contracts.* John Edward Murray Jr., ed. Indianapolis: Bobbs-Merrill, 1965. (See also Murray.)

Griswold, Erwin N. *Law and Lawyers in the United States.* Cambridge, Mass.: Harvard Univ. Press, 1964.

Griswold, Erwin N. *Spendthrift Trusts.* 2d ed. Albany, N.Y.: Matthew Bender & Co., 1947.

Grotius, Hugo. *The Rights of War and Peace* [1625]. A.C. Campbell, trans. N.Y.: M. Walter Dunne, 1901.

Grubb, Philip W. *Patents for Chemicals, Pharmaceuticals, and Biotechnology.* 3d ed. Oxford: Clarendon Press, 1999.

Guest, A.G. (ed.). *Oxford Essays in Jurisprudence.* London: Oxford Univ. Press, 1961.

Gutteridge, H.C. *Comparative Law: An Introduction to the Comparative Method of Legal Study and Research.* Cambridge: Cambridge Univ. Press, 1946.

Hadley, James. *Introduction to Roman Law.* N.Y.: D. Appleton & Co., 1881.

Hagman, Donald G.; and Julian Conrad Juergensmeyer. *Urban Planning and Land Development Control Law.* 2d ed. St. Paul: West, 1986.

Hahlo, H.R.; and Ellison Kahn. *The South African Legal System and its Background.* Cape Town: Juta, 1968.

Hall, Kermit L. (ed.). *Oxford Companion to the Supreme Court of the United States.* N.Y.: Oxford Univ. Press, 1992.

Hall, Kermit L.; and Kevin T. McGuire (eds.). *The Judicial Branch.* Oxford: Oxford Univ. Press, 2005.

Hamilton, Alexander; James Madison; and John Jay. *The Federalist* [1788]. Clinton Rossiter, ed. N.Y.: New American Library, 1961.

Hamilton, Robert W. *Fundamentals of Modern Business.* Boston: Little Brown, 1989.

Hanbury, Harold Greville. *English Courts of Law.* London: Oxford Univ. Press, 1944.

Hanbury, Harold Greville. *Modern Equity.* 3d ed. London: Stevens & Sons, 1943.

Handelman, Jeffery A. *Guide to TTAB Practice.* 2 vols. Frederick, Md.: Aspen, 2008.

Harding, Alan. *A Social History of English Law.* Baltimore: Penguin Books, 1966.

Harris, John. *Lexicon Technicum: Or, an Universal English Dictionary of Arts and Sciences.* London: Daniel Brown et al., 1704.

Hart, H.L.A. *Punishment and Responsibility.* Oxford: Clarendon Press, 1968.

Hart, H.L.A.; and Tony Honoré. *Causation in the Law.* 2d ed. Oxford: Clarendon Press, 1985.

Hartley, T.C. *The Foundations of European Community Law.* Oxford: Clarendon Press, 1981.

Hawkland, William D. *Uniform Commercial Code Series.* 15 vols. St. Paul: West, 1982–present.

Hazard, Geoffrey C., Jr. *Ethics in the Practice of Law.* New Haven: Yale Univ. Press, 1978.

Hazard, Geoffrey C., Jr.; and Michele Taruffo. *American Civil Procedure: An Introduction* New Haven: Yale Univ. Press, 1993.

Hazen, Thomas Lee. *Treatise on the Law of Securities Regulation.* 3 vols. 3d ed. St. Paul: West, 1995.

Heard, Franklin Fiske. *The Principles of Pleading in Civil Actions.* Boston: Little Brown, 1880.

Heath, James. *Torture and English Law.* Westport, Conn.: Greenwood Press, 1982.

Helmholz, R.H. *Roman Canon Law in Reformation England.* Cambridge: Cambridge Univ. Press, 1990.

Helmholz, R.H. *The Spirit of Classical Canon Law.* Athens, Ga.: Univ. of Georgia Press, 1996.

Helmholz, R.H.; et al. *The Oxford History of the Laws of England: The Canon Law and Ecclesiastical Jurisdiction from 597 to the 1640s.* Vol. 1. Oxford: Oxford Univ. Press, 2004.

Hemingway, Richard W. *The Law of Oil and Gas.* 3d ed. St. Paul: West, 1991.

Hening, William Waller. *The Virginia Justice.* 4th ed. Richmond, Va.: For the author, 1825.

Henn, Henry G.; and John R. Alexander. *Laws of Corporations.* 3d ed. St. Paul: West, 1983.

Henson, Ray D. *Handbook on Secured Transactions Under the Uniform Commercial Code.* 2d ed. St. Paul: West, 1979. Also: 3d ed. St. Paul: West, 1983.

Heuston, R.F.V. *Salmond on the Law of Torts.* 17th ed. London: Sweet & Maxwell, 1977.

High, James L. *A Treatise on Extraordinary Legal Remedies.* Chicago: Callaghan & Co., 1884.

Hill, Mark. *Ecclesiastical Law.* 2d ed. Oxford: Oxford Univ. Press, 2001.

Hilliard, Edward. *Sheppard's Touchstone of Common Assurances.* Richard Preston, ed. London: J.W.T. Clarke, 1820.

Hinch, Frederick M. *John's American Notary and Commissioner of Deeds Manual.* 3d ed. Chicago: Callaghan & Co., 1922.

Hoar, Roger Sherman. *Patent Tactics and Law.* 3d ed. N.Y.: Ronald Press Co., 1950.

Hochheimer, Lewis. *A Treatise on the Law Relating to the Custody of Infants.* 2d ed. Baltimore: Harold B. Scrimger, 1891.

Hoffman, Leo J. *Voluntary Pooling and Unitization: Oil and Gas.* Albany, N.Y.: Matthew Bender, 1954.

Hogue, Arthur R. *Origins of the Common Law*. Bloomington, Ind.: Indiana Univ. Press, 1966.

Holdsworth, William S. *An Historical Introduction to the Land Law*. Oxford: Clarendon Press, 1927.

Holdsworth, William S. *A History of English Law*. 17 vols. [1903–1966] London: Methuen & Co., 1972.

Holdsworth, William S. *Sources and Literature of English Law*. Oxford: Clarendon Press, 1925.

Holland, Thomas E. *The Elements of Jurisprudence*. 13th ed. Oxford: Clarendon Press, 1924.

Holmes, Oliver Wendell. *Collected Legal Papers*. Harold J. Laski, ed. N.Y. Harcourt Brace, 1920.

Holmes, Oliver Wendell. *The Common Law*. Boston: Little Brown, 1881.

Holt, J.C. *Magna Carta*. Cambridge: Cambridge Univ. Press, 1965.

Honderich, Ted (ed.). *The Oxford Companion to Philosophy*. 2d ed. Oxford: Oxford Univ. Press, 2005.

Honoré, Tony. *About Law*. Oxford: Clarendon Press, 1995.

Honoré, Tony. *Law in the Crisis of Empire 379–455 AD*. Oxford: Clarendon Press, 1998.

Honoré, Tony. *Making Law Bind: Essays Legal and Philosophical*. Oxford: Clarendon Press, 1987.

Honoré, Tony. *Responsibility and Fault*. Oxford: Hart, 1999.

Honoré, Tony. *Sex Law*. London: Gerald Duckworth & Co., 1978.

Honoré, Tony. *The South African Law of Trusts*. 3d ed. Cape Town: Juta, 1985.

Hopkins, Earl P. *Handbook on the Law of Real Property*. St. Paul: West, 1896.

Horack, Frank E., Jr. *Cases and Materials on Legislation*. 2d ed. Chicago: Callaghan & Co., 1954.

Horwill, Herbert W. *The Usages of the American Constitution*. London: Oxford Univ. Press, 1925.

Horwitz, Morton J. *The Transformation of American Law, 1780–1860*. Cambridge, Mass.: Harvard Univ. Press, 1977.

Horwitz, Morton J. *The Transformation of American Law, 1870–1960*. N.Y.: Oxford Univ. Press, 1992.

Hoskins, Mark; and William Robinson (eds.). *A True European: Essays for Judge David Edward*. Oxford: Hart, 2003.

Hovenkamp, Herbert. *Economics and Federal Antitrust Law*. St. Paul: West, 1985.

Hovenkamp, Herbert. *Federal Antitrust Policy*. 2d ed. St. Paul: West, 1999.

Howard League for Penal Reform. *Counsel for the Defence: An Enquiry into the Question of Legal Aid for Poor Prisoners*. London: Howard League for Penal Reform, 1926.

Howe, William Wirt. *Studies in the Civil Law, and Its Relations to the Law of England and America*. Boston: Little Brown, 1896.

Huffcut, Ernest W. *The Law of Agency*. Boston: Little Brown, 1901.

Hughes, Charles Evans. *The Supreme Court of the United States*. Garden City, N.Y.: Garden City Pub. Co., 1936.

Hughes, T.W. *A Treatise on Criminal Law and Procedure*. Indianapolis: Bobbs-Merrill, 1919.

Hunnisett, R.F. *The Medieval Coroner*. Cambridge: Cambridge Univ. Press, 1961.

Hunter, Robert. *The Preservation of Open Spaces, and of Footpaths, and Other Rights of Way*. London: Eyre & Spottiswoode, 1896.

Hunter, William A. *Introduction to Roman Law*. F.H. Lawson, ed. 9th ed. London: Sweet & Maxwell, 1934.

Hunter, William A. *A Systematic and Historical Exposition of Roman Law*. 4th ed. London: Sweet & Maxwell, 1903.

Hurst, James Willard. *Dealing with Statutes*. N.Y.: Columbia Univ. Press, 1982.

Hurst, James Willard. *The Growth of American Law: The Law Makers*. Boston: Little Brown, 1950.

Hutchinson, Robert. *A Treatise on the Law of Carriers*. Chicago: Callaghan & Co., 1882.

Ilbert, Courtenay P. *Legislative Methods and Forms*. Oxford: Clarendon Press, 1901.

Indermaur, John. *Principles of the Common Law*. Edmund H. Bennett, ed. 1st Am. ed. San Francisco: S. Whitney & Co., 1878.

Ingersoll, Henry H. *Handbook of the Law of Public Corporations*. St. Paul: West, 1904.

Isenbergh, Joseph. *International Taxation*. N.Y.: Foundation Press, 2000.

Jackson, R.M. *The Machinery of Justice in England*. 5th ed. Cambridge: Cambridge Univ. Press, 1967.

Jacob, Giles. *A Law Grammar*. London: Henry Lintot, 1744.

Jacob, Giles. *A New Law-Dictionary*. 8th ed. London: T. Osborne, 1762. Also: John Morgan, ed. 10th ed. London: W. Strahan et al., 1782.

Jacobs, Arnold S. *Opinion Letters in Securities Matters*. Securities Law Series 8–8B. St. Paul: West, 1998.

Jacobstein, J. Myron; and Roy M. Mersky. *Fundamentals of Legal Research*. 5th ed. Westbury, N.Y.: Foundation Press, 1990.

James, Fleming; Geoffrey C. Hazard Jr.; and John Leubsdorf. *Civil Procedure*. 5th ed. N.Y.: Foundation Press, 2001.

James, Philip S. *Introduction to English Law*. 9th ed. London: Butterworths, 1976.

Janosik, Robert J. (ed.). *Encyclopedia of the American Judicial System*. 3 vols. N.Y.: Scribner, 1987.

Jefferson, Thomas. *A Manual of Parliamentary Practice*. Washington City: Samuel Harrison Smith, 1801.

Jenks, Edward. *The Book of English Law*. P.B. Fairest, ed. 6th ed. Athens, Ohio: Univ. Press, 1967.

Jenks, Edward. *Law and Politics in the Middle Ages*. N.Y.: Henry Holt, 1898.

Jensen, O.C. *The Nature of Legal Argument*. Oxford: Basil Blackwell, 1957.

Jespersen, Otto. *Growth and Structure of the English Language*. 9th ed. Garden City, N.Y.: Doubleday Anchor, 1938.

Jessup, Philip C. *A Modern Law of Nations*. N.Y.: Macmillan, 1948.

Jessup, Philip C. *The Use of International Law*. Ann Arbor: Univ. of Michigan Law School, 1959.

Johnson, James D., Jr. *Guide to Louisiana Real Actions: Ten Year and Thirty Year Prescriptions*. Baton Rouge: Claitor's Book Store, 1961.

Johnson, Samuel. *A Dictionary of the English Language*. 2 vols. London: J. &. P. Knapton, 1755.

Johnstone, Quintin; and Dan Hopson Jr. *Lawyers and Their Work*. Indianapolis: Bobbs-Merrill, 1967.

Jolowicz, H.F. *Historical Introduction to the Study of Roman Law*. Cambridge: Cambridge Univ. Press, 1952.

Jones, Eugene A. *Manual of Equity Pleading and Practice*. Washington, D.C.: J. Byrne, 1916.

Jones, Harry W. *The Efficacy of Law*. Evanston, Ill.: Northwestern Univ. Press, 1968.

Jones, Leonard A. *A Treatise on the Law of Collateral Securities and Pledges*. Edward M. White, ed. 3d ed. Indianapolis: Bobbs-Merrill, 1912.

Jones, Leonard A. *A Treatise on the Law of Mortgages*. 5th ed. Indianapolis: Bobbs-Merrill, 1908.

Jones, W.J. *The Elizabethan Court of Chancery*. Oxford: Clarendon Press, 1967.

Jowitt, William A. *The Dictionary of English Law*. 2 vols. Clifford Walsh, ed. 1st ed. London: Sweet & Maxwell, 1959. Also: 2 vols. John Burke, ed. 2d ed. London: Sweet & Maxwell, 1977. Also: 2 vols. Daniel Greenberg, ed. 3d ed. London: Sweet & Maxwell, 2010.

Joyce, Howard C. *A Treatise on the Law Relating to Injunctions*. 3 vols. Albany, N.Y.: Matthew Bender & Co., 1909.

Joyce, Joseph A.; and Howard C. Joyce. *Treatise on the Law Governing Nuisances*. Albany, N.Y.: Matthew Bender & Co., 1906.

Juergensmeyer, Julian Conrad; and Thomas E. Roberts. *Land Use Planning and Development Regulation Law*. St. Paul: Thomson/West, 2003.

Justinian. *Digest of Justinian*. 4 vols. [A.D. 533] Theodor Mommsen et al., eds. Philadelphia: Univ. of Pennsylvania Press, 1985.

Kadish, Sanford H. (ed.). *Encyclopedia of Crime and Justice*. 4 vols. N.Y.: Free Press, 1983.

Kafka, Gerald A.; and Rita A. Cavanagh. *Litigation of Federal Civil Tax Controversies*. Colorado Springs: Shepard's, 2012.

Karlen, Delmar. *Anglo-American Criminal Justice*. Oxford: Clarendon Press, 1967.

Keesey, Ray E. *Modern Parliamentary Procedure*. Rev. ed. Washington, D.C.: American Psychological Ass'n, 1994.

Keeton, G.W. *The Elementary Principles of Jurisprudence*. 2d ed. London: Pitman, 1949.

Keeton, G.W. *An Introduction to Equity*. 5th ed. London: Pitman, 1961.

Keeton, Robert E. *Judging*. St. Paul: West, 1990.

Keeton, Robert E. *Venturing to Do Justice: Reforming Private Law*. Cambridge, Mass.: Harvard Univ. Press, 1969.

Keeton, Robert E.; and Alan I. Widiss. *Insurance Law: A Guide to Fundamental Principles, Legal Doctrines, and Commercial Practices*. St. Paul: West, 1988.

Keeton, W. Page; et al. *Prosser and Keeton on the Law of Torts*. 5th ed. St. Paul: West, 1984. (See also Prosser.)

Kelly, Alfred H.; and Winfred A. Harbison. *The American Constitution*. 5th ed. N.Y. W.W. Norton & Co., 1976.

Kent, James. *Commentaries on American Law*. 4 vols. George Comstock, ed. 11th ed. Boston: Little Brown, 1866. Also: Charles M. Barnes, ed. 13th ed. Boston: Little Brown, 1884.

Kinnane, Charles Herman. *A First Book on Anglo-American Law*. 2d ed. Indianapolis: Bobbs-Merrill, 1952.

Kintner, Earl W.; and Jack L. Lahr. *An Intellectual Property Law Primer*. 2d ed. N.Y.: Clark Boardman, 1982.

Kiralfy, A.K.R. *Potter's Outlines of English Legal History*. 5th ed. London: Sweet & Maxwell, 1958. (See also Potter.)

Klein, William A.; and John C. Coffee Jr. *Business Organization and Finance*. N.Y.: Foundation Press, 2002.

Knibb, David G. *Federal Court of Appeals Manual*. 4th ed. St. Paul: West, 2000.

Koch, Charles H. *Administrative Law and Practice*. 3 vols. 2d ed. St. Paul: West, 1997.

Kocourek, Albert; and John H. Wigmore (eds.). *Formative Influences of Legal Development*. Boston: Little Brown, 1918.

Kraemer, Sandy F. *Solar Law*. Colorado Springs: Shepard's, 1978.

Kratovil, Robert. *Real Estate Law*. 6th ed. Englewood Cliffs, N.J.: Prentice-Hall, 1974.

Krause, Harry D. *Child Support in America*. Charlottesville, Va.: Michie Co., 1981.

Krieger, Joel (ed.). *The Oxford Companion to Comparative Politics*. 2 vols. N.Y.: Oxford Univ. Press, 2013.

Krieger, Joel (ed.). *The Oxford Companion to Politics of the World*. 2d ed. Oxford: Oxford Univ. Press, 2001.

Kuhn, Arthur. *Comparative Commentaries on Private International Law, or Conflict of Laws*. N.Y.: Macmillan, 1937.

Kurian, George Thomas (ed.). *A Historical Guide to the U.S. Government*. N.Y.: Oxford Univ. Press, 1998.

Kyd, Stewart. *A Treatise on the Law of Bills of Exchange and Promissory Notes*. 2d Am. ed. Albany, N.Y.: Loring Andrews, 1800.

Lacovara, Philip Allen (ed.). *Federal Appellate Practice*. Arlington, Va.: BNA Books, 2008.

LaFave, Wayne R.; and Austin W. Scott Jr. *Criminal Law*. 2d ed. St. Paul: West, 1986.

LaFave, Wayne R.; and Austin W. Scott Jr. *Substantive Criminal Law*. 2 vols. St. Paul: West, 1986–present.

LaFave, Wayne R.; and Jerold H. Israel. *Criminal Procedure*. 2d ed. St. Paul: West, 1992.

Laitos, Jan G. *Natural Resources Law*. St. Paul: West, 2002.

Lalor, John J. (ed.). *Cyclopaedia of Political Science, Political Economy, and of the Political History of the United States*. 3 vols. N.Y.: Charles E. Merrill & Co., 1893.

Larson, Lex K. *Unjust Dismissal*. 2 vols. N.Y.: Matthew Bender, 1985–present.

Laughlin, Stanley K., Jr. *The Law of United States Territories and Affiliated Jurisdictions*. Rochester, N.Y.: Lawyers Co-operative, 1995.

Law Grammar: Or, an Introduction to the Theory and Practice of English Jurisprudence. Dublin: James Moore, 1791.

Lawrence, Robert C., III. *International Tax and Estate Planning*. N.Y.: Practising Law Inst., 1989.

Lawrence, T.J. *A Handbook of Public International Law*. 10th ed. London: Macmillan & Co., 1925.

Laws of Honour: Or, A Compendious Account of the Ancient Derivation of All Titles, Dignities, Offices, Etc., The. London: R. Gosling, 1714.

Lawson, John D. *The Law of Expert and Opinion Evidence Reduced to Rules*. 2d ed. Chicago: T.H. Flood & Co., 1900.

Lawson, John D. *The Law of Presumptive Evidence*. 2d ed. St. Louis: Central Law Journal Co., 1899.

Laycock, Douglas. *The Death of the Irreparable Injury Rule*. N.Y.: Oxford Univ. Press, 1991.

Laycock, Douglas. *Modern American Remedies*. 4th ed. N.Y.: Aspen, 2010.

Leaffer, Marshall A. *Understanding Copyright Law*. 3d ed. N.Y.: Matthew Bender, 1999.

Leage, R.W. *Roman Private Law*. C.H. Ziegler, ed. 2d ed. London: Macmillan & Co., 1930.

Lee, R.W. *The Elements of Roman Law*. 4th ed. London: Sweet & Maxwell, 1956.

Leflar, Robert A. *American Conflicts Law*. 3d ed. Indianapolis: Bobbs-Merrill, 1977.

Levinson, David; and Melvin Ember (eds.). *Encyclopedia of Cultural Anthropology*. 4 vols. N.Y.: Henry Holt & Co., 1996.

Levy, Leonard W. (ed.). *Encyclopedia of the American Constitution*. 4 vols. & supp. N.Y.: Macmillan, 1986 & 1992.

Lévy-Ullmann, Henri. *The English Legal Tradition: Its Sources and History*. London: Macmillan, 1935.

Lewis, Harold S., Jr.; and Elizabeth J. Norman. *Employment Discrimination Law and Practice*. St. Paul: West, 2001.

Lieber, Francis. *Legal and Political Hermeneutics*. William G. Hammond, ed. 3d ed. St. Louis: F.H. Thomas & Co., 1880. [This posthumous edition contains Lieber's final corrections.]

Lieber, Francis. *The Miscellaneous Writings of Francis Lieber*. 2 vols. Philadelphia: J.B. Lippincott, 1880.

Lieber, Francis. *On Civil Liberty and Self-Government*. Theodore D. Woolsey, ed. 3d ed. Philadelphia: J.B. Lippincott & Co., 1883.

Lieberman, Jethro K. *The Evolving Constitution*. N.Y.: Random House, 1992.

Lile, William M.; et al. *Brief Making and the Use of Law Books*. Roger W. Cooley & Charles Lesley Ames, eds. 3d ed. St. Paul: West, 1914.

Litvinoff, Saul. *The Law of Obligations*. Louisiana Civil Law Treatise 5. 2d ed. St. Paul: West, 2001.

Llewellyn, Karl N. *The Common Law Tradition: Deciding Appeals*. Boston: Little Brown, 1960.

Lloyd, Dennis. *Introduction to Jurisprudence*. Rev. ed. N.Y.: Frederick A. Praeger, 1965.

Long, Joseph R. *A Treatise on the Law of Domestic Relations*. St. Paul: Keefe-Davidson, 1905.

Longenecker, Rolla R. *Some Hints on the Trial of a Lawsuit*. Rochester, N.Y.: Lawyers Co-operative, 1927.

Loss, Louis; and Edward M. Cowett. *Blue Sky Law*. Boston: Little Brown, 1958.

Lovell, Colin Rhys. *English Constitutional and Legal History*. N.Y.: Oxford Univ. Press, 1962.

Luce, Robert. *Legislative Problems*. Boston: Houghton Mifflin, 1935.

Luban, David. *Lawyers and Justice: An Ethical Study*. Princeton, N.J.: Princeton Univ. Press, 1988.

Lynch, Timothy J. (ed.). *The Oxford Encyclopedia of American Military and Diplomatic History*. 2 vols. Oxford: Oxford Univ. Press, 2013.

Lynn, Robert J. *The Modern Rule Against Perpetuities*. Indianapolis: Bobbs-Merrill, 1966.

Lyon, Bryce. *A Constitutional and Legal History of Medieval England*. N.Y.: Harper & Bros., 1960.

MacCormick, Neil. *Legal Reasoning and Legal Theory*. Oxford: Clarendon Press, 1978.

MacCormick, Neil. *Legal Right and Social Democracy*. Oxford: Clarendon Press, 1982.

MacCormick, Neil. *Practical Reason in Law and Morality*. Oxford: Oxford Univ. Press, 2008.

MacCormick, Neil. *Rhetoric and the Rule of Law: A Theory of Legal Reasoning*. Oxford: Oxford Univ. Press, 2005.

Mackenzie, Thomas [Lord Mackenzie]. *Studies in Roman Law*. John Kirkpatrick, ed. 7th ed. Edinburgh: William Blackwood & Sons, 1898.

Mackintosh, James. *Roman Law in Modern Practice*. Edinburgh: W. Green & Son, 1934.

Macneil, Ian R.; et al. *Federal Arbitration Law*. 5 vols. Boston: Little Brown, 1994.

Madden, Joseph W. *Handbook of the Law of Persons and Domestic Relations*. St. Paul: West, 1931.

Madden, M. Stuart. *Products Liability*. 2 vols. 2d ed. St. Paul: West, 1988.

Maine, Henry S. *Ancient Law*. 10th ed. London: John Murray, 1884. Also: 17th ed. London: John Murray, 1901.

Maitland, Frederic W. *The Collected Papers of Frederic William Maitland*. 3 vols. H.A.L. Fisher, ed. Cambridge: Cambridge Univ. Press, 1911.

Maitland, Frederic W. *The Constitutional History of England*. Cambridge: Cambridge Univ. Press, 1908; repr. 1955.

Maitland, Frederic W. *Domesday Book and Beyond*. Cambridge: Cambridge Univ. Press, 1921.

Maitland, Frederic W. *Equity*. A.H. Chaytor & W.J. Whittaker, eds. Cambridge: Cambridge Univ. Press, 1909.

Maitland, Frederic W.; and Francis C. Montague. *A Sketch of English Legal History*. James F. Colby, ed. N.Y.: G.P. Putnam's Sons, 1915.

Male, Arthur. *A Treatise on the Law and Practice of Elections*. London: J. Butterworth & Son, 1818.

Manchester, A.H. *Modern Legal History of England and Wales, 1750–1950*. London: Butterworths, 1980.

Marsden, Reginald G. *A Treatise on the Law of Collisions at Sea*. 3d ed. London: Stevens & Sons, 1891.

Martindale, W.B. *A Treatise on the Law of Conveyancing*. Lyne S. Metcalfe, ed. St. Louis: Central Law Journal Co., 1889.

Maupin, Chapman W. *Marketable Title to Real Estate*. 2d ed. N.Y.: Baker Voorhis, 1907.

May, John Wilder. *The Law of Crimes*. 3d ed. Harry Augustus Bigelow, ed. Boston: Little Brown, 1905.

McCarthy, J. Thomas. *McCarthy on Trademarks and Unfair Competition*. 5 vols. 3d ed. Deerfield, Ill.: Clark Boardman Callaghan, 1992–1996.

McCarthy, J. Thomas. *The Rights of Publicity and Privacy*. 2 vols. 2d ed. St. Paul: West, 2000.

McCormack, David R. *Racketeering Influenced Corrupt Organizations*. 2 vols. Fort Worth, Tex.: Knowles, 1988–present.

McCormick, Charles T. *Handbook on the Law of Damages*. St. Paul: West, 1935.

McCrady, Archie R. *Patent Office Practice*. 2d ed. Madison, Wis.: Pacot, 1946.

McCrary, George W. *A Treatise on the American Law of Elections*. Henry L. McCune, ed. 4th ed. Chicago: Callaghan & Co., 1897.

McCulloch, J.R. *A Dictionary, Practical, Theoretical, and Historical, of Commerce and Commercial Navigation*. 2 vols. 2d ed. London: Longman, Rees, Orme, Brown, Green & Longman, 1834.

McDonnell, Denis Lane; and John George Monroe. *Kerr on the Law of Fraud and Mistake*. 7th ed. London: Sweet & Maxwell, 1952.

McDonnell, Julian B.; and Elizabeth J. Coleman. *Commercial and Consumer Warranties*. 2 vols. N.Y.: Matthew Bender, 1991.

McIlwain, C.H. *Constitutionalism and the Changing World*. N.Y.: Macmillan, 1939.

McLaughlin, A.C.; and Albert Bushnell Hart (eds.). *Cyclopedia of American Government*. 3 vols. N.Y.: D. Appleton & Co., 1914.

McMeel, Gerard. *The Construction of Contracts*. 2d ed. Oxford: Oxford Univ. Press, 2007.

McNair, Arnold Duncan. *Legal Effects of War*. 2d ed. Cambridge: Cambridge Univ. Press, 1944.

McNair, William Lennox; Alan Abraham Mocatta; and Michael J. Mustill. *Scrutton on Charterparties and Bills of Lading*. 17th ed. London: Sweet & Maxwell, 1964.

McNeil, Bruce J. *Nonqualified Deferred Compensation Plans*. St. Paul: West, 1994.

McNeil, Kent. *Common Law Aboriginal Title*. Oxford: Clarendon Press, 1989.

McQuillin, Eugene. *A Treatise on the Law of Municipal Ordinances*. Chicago: Callaghan & Co., 1904.

Meador, Daniel John; and Jordana Simone Bernstein. *Appellate Courts in the United States*. St. Paul: West, 1994.

Mechem, Floyd R. *Elements of the Law of Partnership*. 2d ed. Chicago: Callaghan & Co., 1920.

Mechem, Floyd R. *Outlines of the Law of Agency*. Philip Mechem, ed. 4th ed. Chicago: Callaghan & Co., 1952.

Megarry, Robert E. *Lawyer and Litigant in England*. London: Stevens & Sons, 1962.

Megarry, Robert E. *Miscellany-at-Law*. London: Stevens & Sons, 1955.

Megarry, Robert E. *A Second Miscellany-at-Law*. London: Stevens, 1973.

Megarry, Robert E. *A New Miscellany-at-Law*. Bryan A. Garner, ed. Oxford: Hart, 2005.

Megarry, Robert E. (ed.). *Snell's Principles of Equity*. 23d ed. London: Sweet & Maxwell, 1947. Also: With P.V. Baker. 27th ed. London: Sweet & Maxwell, 1973.

Megarry, Robert E.; and H.W.R. Wade. *The Law of Real Property*. 5th ed. London: Stevens, 1984.

Megarry, Robert E.; and P.V. Baker. *A Manual of the Law of Real Property*. 4th ed. London: Sweet & Maxwell, 1969. Also: With M.P. Thompson. 6th ed. London: Sweet & Maxwell, 1993.

Mellows, Anthony R. *The Law of Succession*. 3d ed. London: Butterworths, 1977.

Merges, Robert P.; et al. (eds.). *Intellectual Property in the New Technological Age*. N.Y.: Aspen, 1997.

Merrill, S.S. *Law of Mandamus*. Chicago: T.H. Flood & Co., 1892.

Merwin, Elias. *Principles of Equity and Equity Pleading*. H.C. Merwin, ed. Boston: Houghton Mifflin, 1895.

Michie on Banks and Banking. 14 vols. Charlottesville, Va.: Lexis, 1931–present.

Millar, J.H. *A Handbook of Prescription*. Edinburgh: W. Green & Sons, 1893.

Millard, Christopher (ed.). *Cloud Computing Law*. Oxford: Oxford Univ. Press, 2013.

Miller, Frank W.; et al. *Cases and Materials on Criminal Justice Administration*. 3d ed. Mineola, N.Y.: Foundation Press, 1986.

Miller, Fred H.; and Alvin C. Harrell. *The Law of Modern Payment Systems*. St. Paul: Thomson/West, 2003.

Miller, Justin. *Handbook of Criminal Law*. St. Paul: West, 1934.

Millon, Theodore; et al. *Personality Disorders in Modern Life*. 2d ed. Hoboken, N.J.: John Wiley & Sons, 2004.

Milsom, S.F.C. *Historical Foundations of the Common Law*. London: Butterworths, 1969.

Milsom, S.F.C. *Studies in the History of the Common Law*. London: Hambledon Press, 1985.

Minda, Gary. *Postmodern Legal Movements*. N.Y.: NYU Press, 1995.

Moliterno, James E.; and John M. Levy. *Ethics of the Lawyer's Work*. St. Paul: West, 1993.

Moore, E. Garth; and Timothy Briden. *Moore's Introduction to English Canon Law*. 2d ed. London: Mowbray, 1985.

Moore, John Bassett. *The Collected Papers of John Bassett Moore*. 7 vols. New Haven: Yale Univ. Press, 1944.

Morgan, Edmund M. *Introduction to the Study of Law*. Chicago: Callaghan & Co., 1926.

Morton, David A., III. *Medical Proof of Social Security Disability*. St. Paul: West, 1983.

Morton, William K.; and Dale A. Whitman. *Manual of the Law of Scotland*. Edinburgh: W. Green, 1896.

Moynihan, Cornelius J. *Introduction to the Law of Real Property*. 2d ed. St. Paul: West, 1988.

Muirhead, James. *Historical Introduction to the Private Law of Rome*. Henry Goudy, ed. 2d ed. London: A. & C. Black, 1899.

Munkman, John H. *The Technique of Advocacy*. London: Stevens & Sons, 1951.

Murray, John Edward, Jr. *Cases and Materials on Contracts*. 2d ed. Indianapolis: Bobbs-Merrill, 1976.

Murray, John Edward, Jr. *Murray on Contracts*. 2d ed. Indianapolis: Bobbs-Merrill, 1974. (See also Grismore.)

Nat'l Acad. of Sciences. *Strengthening Forensic Science in the United States: A Path Forward*. Washington, D.C.: GPO, 2009.

Nat'l Conference of State Legislatures. *Mason's Manual of Legislative Procedure*. Denver: Nat'l Conference of State Legislatures, 2000.

Nelson, Caleb. *Statutory Interpretation*. N.Y.: Foundation Press, 2011.

Nelson, Grant S. *Real Estate Finance Law*. 3d ed. St. Paul: West, 1994.

Newell, Martin L. *The Law of Defamation, Libel and Slander in Civil and Criminal Cases*. Chicago: Callaghan & Co., 1890.

Newell, Martin L. *A Treatise on the Law of Malicious Prosecution, False Imprisonment, and the Abuse of Legal Process*. Chicago: Callaghan & Co., 1892.

Newman, Peter (ed.). *The New Palgrave Dictionary of Economics and the Law*. 3 vols. London: Macmillan, 1998.

New York Inst. of Finance. *How the Bond Market Works*. N.Y.: New York Inst. of Finance, 1988.

Nicholas, Barry. *An Introduction to Roman Law*. Oxford: Clarendon Press, 1962.

Nimmer, Melville B.; and David Nimmer. *Nimmer on Copyright*. 10 vols. N.Y.: Matthew Bender, 1978–1995.

Nims, Harry D. *The Law of Unfair Competition and Trade-Marks*. N.Y.: Baker Voorhis, 1929.

Noonan, John T., Jr. *Bribes*. N.Y: Macmillan, 1984.

Norris, Martin J. *The Law of Salvage*. Mount Kisco, N.Y.: Baker Voorhis, 1958.

Norton, Charles Phelps. *Handbook of the Law of Bills and Notes*. 4th ed. St. Paul: West, 1914.

Nowak, John E.; and Ronald D. Rotunda. *Constitutional Law*. 4th ed. St. Paul: West, 1991. (See also Rotunda.)

Noy, William. *A Treatise of the Principal Grounds and Maxims of the Laws of This Nation*. C. Sims, ed. 4th ed. London: T. Collins; et al., 1677.

Nussbaum, Arthur. *A Concise History of the Law of Nations*. Rev. ed. N.Y.: Macmillan, 1961.

Oakley, John Bilyeu; and Robert S. Thompson. *Law Clerks and the Judicial Process*. Berkeley: Univ. of California Press, 1980.

Odean, Kathleen. *High Steppers, Fallen Angels, and Lollipops: Wall Street Slang*. N.Y.: Dodd Mead, 1988.

O'Gallagher, Judith. *Municipal Ordinances*. 2d ed. St. Paul: West, 1998.

Oldroyd, Mark. *A Living Wage*. Leeds: McCorquodale & Co., 1894.

Oliver, David T.; and W. Nalder Williams. *Willis and Oliver's Roman Law Examination Guide*. 3d ed. London: Butterworth & Co., 1910.

O'Neill, P.T.; and J.W. Woloniecki. *The Law of Reinsurance in England and Bermuda*. London: Sweet & Maxwell, 1998.

Owen, David G. *Products Liability Law*. St. Paul: Thomson/West, 2005.

Owen, Richard B. *Patents, Trademarks, Copyrights, Departmental Practice.* Washington, D.C.: R.B. Owen, 1925.

Oxford English Dictionary. 20 vols. 2d ed. Oxford: Clarendon Press, 1989.

Page, William Herbert. *A Treatise on the Law of Wills.* 7 vols. 3d ed. Cincinnati: W.H. Anderson Co., 1941–1958.

Page, William Herbert; and Paul Jones. *A Treatise on the Law of Taxation by Local and Special Assessments.* 2 vols. Cincinnati: W.H. Anderson Co., 1909.

Pal, Radhabinod. *The History of the Law of Primogeniture.* Calcutta: Univ. of Calcutta, 1929.

Palgrave, R.H. Inglis. *Palgrave's Dictionary of Political Economy.* 3 vols. Henry Higgs, ed. 2d ed. London: Macmillan, 1925.

Palmer, Ben W. *Courtroom Strategies.* Englewood Cliffs, N.J.: Prentice-Hall, 1959.

Palmer, George E. *The Law of Restitution.* 4 vols. Boston: Little Brown, 1978.

Paton, George Whitecross. *Bailment in the Common Law.* London: Stevens, 1952.

Paton, George Whitecross. *A Textbook of Jurisprudence.* G.W. Paton & David P. Derham, eds. 4th ed. Oxford: Clarendon Press, 1972.

Patry, William F. *Copyright Law and Practice.* 3 vols. Washington, D.C.: Bureau of Nat'l Affairs, 1994.

PDM Task Force. *Psychodynamic Diagnostic Manual.* Silver Spring, Md.: Alliance of Psychoanalytic Organizations, 2006.

Perkins, Rollin M.; and Ronald N. Boyce. *Criminal Law.* 3d ed. Mineola, N.Y.: Foundation Press, 1982.

Philbrick, Frederick A. *Language and the Law.* N.Y.: Macmillan, 1949.

Phillimore, John George. *Private Law Among the Romans.* London: Macmillan, 1863.

Phillips, George L. *An Exposition of the Principles of Pleading Under the Codes of Civil Procedure.* Chicago: Callaghan & Co., 1896.

Phillips, Samuel L. *A Treatise on the Law of Mechanic's Liens on Real and Personal Property.* Boston: Little Brown, 1874.

Pierce, Richard J., Jr.; Sidney A. Shapiro; and Paul R. Verkuil. *Administrative Law and Process.* 3d ed. N.Y.: Foundation Press, 1999.

Pigeon, Louis-Philippe. *Drafting and Interpreting Legislation.* Toronto: Carswell, 1988.

Pigott, Charles. *A Political Dictionary.* N.Y.: Thomas Greenleaf, 1796.

Platt, Thomas. *A Practical Treatise on the Law of Covenants.* London: Saunders & Benning, 1829.

Player, Mack A. *Employment Discrimination Law.* St. Paul: West, 1988.

Plucknett, Theodore F.T. *A Concise History of the Common Law.* 5th ed. London: Butterworth, 1956.

Plucknett, Theodore F.T. *Edward I and Criminal Law.* Cambridge: Cambridge Univ. Press, 1960.

Pocket Lawyer and Family Conveyancer. 3d ed. Harrisburg, Pa.: G.S. Peters, 1833.

Pollock, Frederick. *Essays in Jurisprudence and Ethics.* London: Macmillan, 1882.

Pollock, Frederick. *A First Book of Jurisprudence.* London: Macmillan, 1896.

Pollock, Frederick. *An Introduction to the History of the Science of Politics.* London: Macmillan & Co., 1906.

Pollock, Frederick. *The Land Laws.* 3d ed. London: Macmillan, 1896.

Pollock, Frederick; and Frederic W. Maitland. *History of English Law Before the Time of Edward I.* 2 vols. 2d ed. Cambridge: Cambridge Univ. Press, 1898–1899.

Pollock, Frederick; and Robert Samuel Wright. *An Essay on Possession in the Common Law.* Oxford: Clarendon Press, 1888.

Polyviou, Polyvios G. *The Equal Protection of the Laws.* London: Duckworth, 1980.

Pomeroy, John Norton. *A Treatise on Equity Jurisprudence.* 6 vols. John Norton Pomeroy Jr., ed. 4th ed. San Francisco: Bancroft-Whitney, 1918–1919.

Poole, Reginald L. *The Exchequer in the Twelfth Century.* Oxford: Clarendon Press, 1912.

Pooley, James. *Trade Secrets.* N.Y.: Law Journal Seminars Press, 1997.

Posner, Richard A. *Antitrust Law.* 2d ed. Chicago: Univ. of Chicago Press, 2001.

Posner, Richard A. *Economic Analysis of Law.* 2d ed. Boston: Little Brown, 1977.

Posner, Richard A. *The Federal Courts: Crisis and Reform.* Cambridge, Mass.: Harvard Univ. Press, 1985.

Posner, Richard A. *Law and Legal Theory in England and America.* Oxford: Clarendon Press, 1996.

Posner, Richard A. *Law and Literature: A Misunderstood Relation.* Cambridge, Mass.: Harvard Univ. Press, 1988.

Posner, Richard A. *The Problems of Jurisprudence.* Cambridge, Mass.: Harvard Univ. Press, 1990.

Potter, Harold. *An Historical Introduction to English Law and Its Institutions.* 3d ed. London: Sweet & Maxwell, 1948. (See also Kiralfy.)

Potter, Harold. *The Principles and Practice of Conveyancing Under the Land Registration Act, 1925.* London: Sweet & Maxwell, 1934.

Pound, Roscoe. *Appellate Procedure in Civil Cases.* Boston: Little Brown, 1941.

Pound, Roscoe. *Contemporary Juristic Theory.* Claremont, Calif.: Claremont Colleges, 1940.

Pound, Roscoe. *The Development of Constitutional Guarantees of Liberty.* New Haven: Yale Univ. Press, 1957.

Pound, Roscoe. *The Formative Era of American Law.* Boston: Little Brown, 1938.

Pound, Roscoe. *The Ideal Element in Law* [1958]. Indianapolis: Liberty Fund, 2002.

Pound, Roscoe. *An Introduction to the Philosophy of Law*. Rev. ed. New Haven: Yale Univ. Press, 1954.

Pound, Roscoe. *Jurisprudence*. 5 vols. St. Paul: West, 1959.

Pound, Roscoe. *The Lawyer from Antiquity to Modern Times*. St. Paul: West, 1953.

Pound, Roscoe. *The Spirit of the Common Law*. Boston: Marshall Jones Co., 1921.

Powell, Richard R. *Powell on Real Property*. 17 vols. Patrick J. Rohan, ed. N.Y.: Matthew Bender, 1949–present.

Price, Griffith. *The Law of Maritime Liens*. London: Sweet & Maxwell, 1940.

Proffatt, John. *A Treatise on the Law Relating to the Office and Duties of Notaries Public*. John F. Tyler & John J. Stephens, eds. 2d ed. San Francisco: Bancroft-Whitney, 1892.

Prosser, William. *The Law of Torts*. 4th ed. St. Paul: West, 1971. (See also Keeton, W. Page.)

Pufendorf, Samuel. *Of the Law of Nature and Nations*. Basil Kennett, trans. 4th ed. London: J. Walthoe et al., 1719.

Pulling, Alexander. *The Order of the Coif*. London: William Clowes & Sons, 1884.

Purver, Jonathan M.; and Lawrence E. Taylor. *Handling Criminal Appeals*. Rochester, N.Y.: Lawyers Co-operative, 1980.

Puterbaugh, Sabin D. *Puterbaugh's Common Law Pleading and Practice*. 3d ed. Peoria, Ill.: Leslie Puterbaugh, 1873.

Putnam, Carlton B. *How to Find the Law*. 4th ed. St. Paul: West, 1949.

Quindry, Silvester E. *Bonds and Bondholders: Rights and Remedies*. 2 vols. Chicago: Burdette Smith, 1934.

Rabin, Edward H. *Fundamentals of Modern Real Property Law*. Mineola, N.Y.: Foundation Press, 1974.

Radcliffe, Cyril John [Lord Radcliffe]. *The Law and Its Compass*. Evanston, Ill.: Northwestern Univ. Press, 1960.

Radcliffe, Geoffrey; and Geoffrey Cross. *The English Legal System*. G.J. Hand & D.J. Bentley, eds. 6th ed. London: Butterworths, 1977.

Radin, Max. *Handbook of Anglo-American Legal History*. St. Paul: West, 1936.

Radin, Max. *Handbook of Roman Law*. St. Paul: West, 1927.

Radin, Max. *The Law and You*. N.Y.: New American Library, 1948.

Radin, Max. *Law as Logic and Experience*. New Haven: Yale Univ. Press, 1940.

Radin, Max; and Alexander M. Kidd (eds.). *Legal Essays in Tribute to Orrin Kip McMurray*. Berkeley: Univ. of California Press, 1935.

Radzinowicz, Leon. *A History of English Criminal Law and its Administration from 1750: The Movement for Reform, 1750–1833*. N.Y.: Macmillan, 1948.

Radzinowicz, Leon; and Marvin E. Wolfgang. *Crime and Justice*. 3 vols. N.Y.: Basic Books, 1971.

[Raithby, John.] *The Study and Practice of the Law*. London: T. Cadell Jr. & W. Davies, 1798.

Ralston, Robert. *The Principles of the Law Relating to the Discharge of Contracts*. Philadelphia: T. & J.W. Johnson & Co., 1886.

Ramsay, William. *A Manual of Roman Antiquities*. Rodolfo Lanciani, ed. 15th ed. London: Charles Griffin & Co., 1894.

Randolph, Joseph F. *A Treatise on the Law of Commercial Paper*. 3 vols. 2d ed. St. Paul: West, 1899.

Rapalje, Stewart. *A Treatise on the Law of Witnesses*. N.Y.: Banks & Bros., 1887.

Rapalje, Stewart; and Robert L. Lawrence. *A Dictionary of American and English Law*. 2 vols. Jersey City, N.J.: F.D. Linn & Co., 1883.

Rastell, John. *Les Termes de la Ley*. 26th ed. London: R. Gosling, 1721. Also: *Termes de la Ley*. 1st. Am. ed. fr. last London ed. of 1721. Portland, Me.: J. Johnson, 1812.

Rawle, William Henry. *A Practical Treatise on the Law of Covenants for Title*. 5th ed. Boston: Little Brown, 1887.

Reed, John C. *Practical Suggestions for the Management of Law-suits*. N.Y.: James Cockroft & Co., 1876.

Reeve, Tapping. *The Law of Baron and Femme*. 3d ed. Albany, N.Y.: William Gould, 1862.

Reeves, Alfred G. *A Treatise on Special Subjects of the Law of Real Property*. Boston: Little Brown, 1904.

Reilly, John W. *The Language of Real Estate*. 2d ed. Chicago: Real Estate Education Co., 1982. Also: 4th ed. Chicago: Real Estate Education Co., 1993.

Reinsch, Paul S. *American Legislatures and Legislative Methods*. N.Y.: Century Co., 1907.

Renton, Alexander Wood; and George Grenville Phillimore. *The Comparative Law of Marriage and Divorce*. London: Sweet & Maxwell, 1910.

Renton, Alexander Wood; et al. (eds.). *Encyclopaedia of the Laws of England*. 15 vols. 2d ed. London: Sweet & Maxwell, 1906–1909.

Restatement (Second) of Contracts. 10 vols. St. Paul: American Law Inst., 1981.

Restatement (Second) of Torts. 4 vols. St. Paul: American Law Inst., 1965–1979.

Restatement (Third) of Torts. 4 vols. St. Paul: American Law Inst., 1998–2012.

Restatement (Second) of Trusts. 5 vols. St. Paul: American Law Inst., 1959.

Restatement (Third) of Restitution and Unjust Enrichment. St. Paul: American Law Inst., 2011.

Restatement (Third) of the U.S. Law of International Commercial Arbitration (Tent. Draft No. 3, May 22, 2013). Philadelphia: American Law Inst., 2013.

Restatement of the Law Governing Lawyers. St. Paul: American Law Inst., 1998.

Restatement of the Law of Restitution. St. Paul: West, 1937.

Reuschlein, Harold Gill; and William A. Gregory. *The Law of Agency and Partnership.* 2d ed. St. Paul: West, 1990.

Rex, Benjamin F. *The Notaries' Manual.* J.H. McMillan, ed. 6th ed. Kansas City, Mo.: Vernon, 1913.

Reynolds, F.M.B. *Bowstead and Reynolds on Agency.* 18th ed. London: Sweet & Maxwell, 2006.

Reynolds, Osborne M., Jr. *Handbook of Local Government Law.* St. Paul: West, 1982.

Reynolds, William. *The Theory of the Law of Evidence.* 2d ed. Chicago: Callaghan & Co., 1890.

Rhode Deborah L.; and David Luban. *Legal Ethics.* Westbury, N.Y.: Foundation Press, 1992.

Rhode, Deborah L.; and Geoffrey C. Hazard. *Professional Responsibility.* N.Y.: Foundation Press, 2002.

Richardson, William P. *The Law of Evidence.* 3d ed. Brooklyn: By the author, 1928.

Richman, William M.; and William L. Reynolds. *Injustice on Appeal: The United States Courts of Appeals in Crisis.* N.Y.: Oxford Univ. Press, 2013.

Riddick, Floyd M.; and Miriam H. Butcher. *Riddick's Rules of Procedure.* N.Y.: Scribner, 1985.

Robert, Henry M. *Robert's Rules of Order Newly Revised.* 10th ed. Philadelphia: Perseus, 2000. Also: Sarah Corbin Robert et al., eds. 11th ed. Philadelphia: Da Capo, 2011.

Robertson, David W.; Steven F. Friedell; and Michael F. Sturley. *Admiralty and Maritime Law in the United States.* Durham, N.C.: Carolina Academic Press, 2001.

Robinson, Edward Stevens. *Law and the Lawyers.* N.Y.: Macmillan, 1935.

Robinson, O.F. *The Criminal Law of Ancient Rome.* Baltimore: Johns Hopkins Univ. Press, 1995.

Robinson, Paul H. *Criminal Law Defenses.* 2 vols. St. Paul: West, 1984.

Robinson, Thomas. *Robinson on Gavelkind.* Charles I. Elton & Herbert J.H. Mackay, eds. 5th ed. London: Butterworth & Co., 1897.

Roby, Henry John. *Roman Private Law in the Times of Cicero and of the Antonines.* 2 vols. Cambridge: Cambridge Univ. Press, 1902.

Roper, R.S. Donnison. *A Treatise upon the Law of Legacies.* Dublin: John Exshaw, 1800.

Rose, Michael D.; and John C. Chommie. *Federal Income Taxation.* 3d ed. St. Paul: West, 1988.

Rosenberg, Morgan D. *The Essentials of Patent Claim Drafting.* Oxford: Oxford Univ. Press, 2012.

Rosenberg, Morgan D. *Patent Application Drafting: A Practical Guide.* Oxford: Oxford Univ. Press, 2012.

Rosenfeld, Michel; and András Sajó (eds.). *The Oxford Handbook of Comparative Constitutional Law.* Oxford: Oxford Univ. Press, 2012.

Ross, Stephen F. *Principles of Antitrust Law.* Westbury, N.Y.: Foundation Press, 1993.

Rothstein, Mark A. *Occupational Safety and Health Law.* St. Paul: West, 1990.

Rothstein, Mark A.; et al. *Employment Law.* St. Paul: West, 1994.

Rothstein, Paul F. *The Federal Rules of Evidence.* 3d ed. St. Paul: West, 2003.

Rottschaefer, Henry. *Handbook of American Constitutional Law.* St. Paul: West, 1939.

Rotunda, Ronald D.; and John E. Nowak. *Treatise on Constitutional Law.* 5 vols. 3d ed. St. Paul: West, 1999. (See also Nowak.)

Rounds, Charles E., Jr.; and Charles E. Rounds III (eds.). *Loring: A Trustee's Handbook.* Austin, Tex.: Wolters Kluwer, 2008.

Rutherglen, George. *Employment Discrimination Law.* N.Y.: Foundation Press, 2001.

Sack, Robert D.; and Sandra S. Baron. *Libel, Slander, and Related Problems.* 2d ed. N.Y.: Practising Law Inst., 1994.

Safire, William. *Safire's New Political Dictionary.* N.Y.: Random House, 1993.

Salmond, John W. *Essays in Jurisprudence and Legal History.* London: Stevens & Haynes, 1891.

Salmond, John. *Jurisprudence.* Glanville L. Williams, ed. 10th ed. London: Sweet & Maxwell, 1947.

Salsich, Peter W., Jr. *Land Use Regulation.* Colorado Springs: Shepard's, 1991.

Savary des Brûlons, Jacques. *The Universal Dictionary of Trade and Commerce.* 2 vols. Malachy Postlethwayt, ed. & trans. London: John & Paul Knapton, 1751 & 1755.

Sawer, Geoffrey. *Law in Society.* Oxford: Clarendon Press, 1965.

Scalia, Antonin. *A Matter of Interpretation.* Princeton, N.J.: Princeton Univ. Press, 1997.

Scalia, Antonin; and Bryan A. Garner. *Making Your Case: The Art of Persuading Judges.* St. Paul: Thomson/West, 2008.

Scalia, Antonin; and Bryan A. Garner. *Reading Law: The Interpretation of Legal Texts.* St. Paul: Thomson/West, 2012.

Scanlan, Charles M. *The Law of Church and Grave.* N.Y.: Benziger Bros., 1909.

Scarman, Leslie. *English Law — The New Dimension.* London: Stevens, 1974.

Schacht, Joseph. *An Introduction to Islamic Law.* Oxford: Clarendon Press, 1982.

Schechter, Roger E.; and John R. Thomas. *Intellectual Property.* St. Paul: Thomson/West, 2003.

Schoenbaum, Thomas J. *Admiralty and Maritime Law.* St. Paul: West, 1987.

Schulz, Fritz. *History of Roman Legal Science.* Rev. ed. Oxford: Clarendon Press, 1967.

Schwartz, Mortimer D.; and Richard C. Wydick. *Problems in Legal Ethics.* 2d ed. St. Paul: West, 1988.

Schwarzenberger, Georg. *A Manual of International Law.* 5th ed. London: Stevens, 1967.

Schwarzenberger, Georg. *Power Politics: A Study of International Society.* 2d ed. N.Y.: F.A. Praeger, 1951.

Schweitzer, Sydney C. *Trial Guide.* 3 vols. N.Y.: Baker Voorhis, 1945–1948.

Schwing, Ann Taylor. *California Affirmative Defenses.* 2d ed. 5 vols. San Francisco: Bancroft-Whitney, 1995–1996.

Schwing, Ann Taylor. *Open Meeting Laws.* 2 vols. 3d ed. Anchorage: Fathom, 2011.

Scott, Austin W.; and William F. Fratcher. *The Law of Trusts.* 12 vols. 4th ed. Boston: Little Brown, 1987.

Scott, H.L. *Military Dictionary.* N.Y.: D. Van Nostrand, 1861.

Seagle, William. *The Quest for Law.* N.Y.: Alfred A. Knopf, 1941.

Sedgwick, Arthur George. *Elements of the Law of Damages.* 2d ed. Boston: Little Brown, 1909.

Select Essays in Anglo-American Legal History. 3 vols. Boston: Little Brown, 1907–1909.

Sender, Marta Pertegás. *Cross-Border Enforcement of Patent Rights.* Oxford: Oxford Univ. Press, 2002.

Shapiro, Scott J. *Legality.* Cambridge, Mass.: Harvard Univ. Press, 2011.

Shapo, Marshall S. *The Duty to Act.* Austin, Tex.: Univ. of Texas Press, 1977.

Shartel, Burke. *Our Legal System and How It Operates.* Ann Arbor: Univ. of Michigan Law School, 1951.

Shaw, Malcolm N. *International Law.* 4th ed. Cambridge: Cambridge Univ. Press, 1997.

Sheppard, Stephen Michael. *I Do Solemnly Swear.* Cambridge: Cambridge Univ. Press, 2009.

Shipman, Benjamin J. *Handbook of Common-Law Pleading.* Henry Winthrop Ballantine, ed. 3d ed. St. Paul: West, 1923.

Shklar, Judith N. *Legalism: Law, Morals, and Political Trials.* Cambridge, Mass.: Harvard Univ. Press, 1964.

Silbey, Joel H. (ed.). *Encyclopedia of the American Legislative System.* 3 vols. N.Y.: C. Scribner's Sons, 1994.

Simes, Lewis M.; and Allan F. Smith. *The Law of Future Interests.* 2d ed. St. Paul: West, 1956.

Simpson, A.W.B. *An Introduction to the History of the Land Law.* London: Oxford Univ. Press, 1961.

Simpson, A.W.B. *Legal Theory and Legal History.* London: Hambledon Press, 1987.

Simpson, Keith. *Forensic Medicine.* 2d ed. London: Edward Arnold & Co., 1952.

Simpson, Laurence P. *Handbook of the Law of Contracts.* St. Paul: West, 1954.

Simpson, Laurence P. *Handbook on the Law of Suretyship.* St. Paul: West, 1950.

Sims, Henry Upson. *Covenants Which Run with Land, Other Than Covenants for Title.* Chicago: Callaghan & Co., 1901.

Singer, Norman J. *Sutherland Statutes and Statutory Construction.* 8 vols. 4th ed. Chicago: Callaghan & Co., 1986.

Smith, Horace. *A Treatise on the Law of Negligence.* 1st Am. ed. fr. 2d English ed. Philadelphia: Blackstone, 1887.

Smith, Munroe. *The Development of European Law.* N.Y.: Columbia Univ. Press, 1928.

Smith, Walter Denton. *A Manual of Elementary Law.* St. Paul: West, 1896.

Soderquist, Larry D.; and Theresa A. Gabaldon. *Securities Law.* N.Y.: Foundation Press, 1998.

Soffer, Stuart B.; and Robert C. Kahrl. *Thesaurus of Claim Construction.* 2 vols. 2d ed. Oxford: Oxford Univ. Press, 2013.

Sohm, Rudolph. *The Institutes: A Textbook of the History and System of Roman Private Law.* James Crawford Ledlie, trans. 3d ed. Oxford: Clarendon Press, 1907.

Soper, John P.H. *A Treatise on the Law and Practice of Arbitrations and Awards.* David M. Lawrence, ed. 5th ed. London: Estates Gazette, 1935.

Spaht, Katherine S.; and W. Lee Hargrave. *Louisiana Civil Law Treatise: Matrimonial Regimes.* 2d ed. St. Paul: West, 1997.

Speiser, Stuart M. *The Negligence Case: Res Ipsa Loquitur.* Rochester, N.Y.: Lawyers Co-operative, 1972.

Spelling, Thomas Carl. *A Treatise on New Trial and Appellate Practice.* 2 vols. San Francisco: Bancroft-Whitney, 1903.

Standard Library Cyclopaedia of Political, Constitutional, Statistical and Forensic Knowledge, The. 4 vols. London: Henry G. Bohn, 1853.

Starkie, Thomas. *A Practical Treatise on the Law of Evidence.* 3 vols. 2d Am. ed. Boston: Wells & Lilly, 1828.

Starkie, Thomas. *A Treatise on the Law of Slander, Libel, Scandalum Magnatum, and False Rumours.* Edward D. Ingraham, ed. 1st Am. ed. N.Y.: G. Lamson, 1826.

Stearns, Arthur Aldebert. *The Law of Suretyship.* Wells M. Cook, ed. 3d ed. Cincinnati: W.H. Anderson, 1922.

Stein, Robert A. *Forming a More Perfect Union: A History of the Uniform Law Commission.* Charlottesville, Va.: LexisNexis, 2013.

Steinberg, Marc I. *Developments in Business Law and Policy.* San Diego: Cognella Academic, 2012.

Steinberg, Marc I. *Lawyering and Ethics for the Business Attorney.* 3d ed. St. Paul: West, 2011.

Steinberg, Marc I. *Understanding Securities Law.* 2d ed. N.Y.: Matthew Bender, 1996.

Stephen, Henry John. *Stephen's Commentaries on the Laws of England.* 4 vols. L. Crispin Warmington, ed. 21st ed. London: Butterworth, 1950.

Stephen, Henry John. *A Treatise on the Principles of Pleading in Civil Actions.* Samuel Williston, ed. Repr. fr. 5th English ed. Cambridge, Mass.: Harvard L. Rev. Pub. Ass'n, 1895.

Stephen, James Fitzjames. *A Digest of the Criminal Law.* 5th ed. London: Macmillan, 1894.

Stephen, James Fitzjames. *A Digest of the Law of Evidence.* George Chase, ed. Am. ed. fr. 4th English ed. N.Y.: George Chase, 1892.

Stephen, James Fitzjames. *A General View of the Criminal Law of England.* 2d ed. London: Macmillan, 1890.

Stephen, James Fitzjames. *A History of the Criminal Law of England.* 3 vols. London: Macmillan, 1883.

Stephen, James Fitzjames. *Liberty, Equality, Fraternity.* 2d ed. London: Smith, Elder & Co., 1874.

Stephenson, Andrew. *A History of Roman Law.* Boston: Little Brown, 1912.

Stephenson, Gilbert Thomas. *Wills.* N.Y.: F.S. Crofts & Co., 1934.

Stern, Robert L.; et al. *Supreme Court Practice.* 8th ed. Washington, D.C.: Bureau of Nat'l Affairs, 2002.

Stessinger, John G. *The Might of Nations.* Rev. ed. N.Y.: Random House, 1965.

Stimson, Frederic Jesup. *The Law of the Federal and State Constitutions of the United States.* Boston: Boston Book Co., 1908.

Stimson, Frederic Jesup. *Popular Law-Making.* N.Y.: Charles Scribner's Sons, 1910.

Stoebuck, William B.; and Dale A. Whitman. *The Law of Property.* 3d ed. St. Paul: West, 2000.

Stone, Ferdinand F. *Handbook of Law Study.* N.Y.: Prentice-Hall, 1952.

Story, Joseph. *Commentaries on Equity Jurisprudence.* W.E. Grigsby, ed. 1st English ed. London: Stevens & Haynes, 1884.

Story, Joseph. *Commentaries on the Constitution of the United States.* 2 vols. 3d ed. Boston: Little Brown, 1858.

Story, Joseph. *Commentaries on the Law of Agency.* Isaac R. Redfield, ed. 7th ed. Boston: Little Brown, 1869.

Story, Joseph. *Commentaries on the Law of Bailments.* Edmund H. Bennett, ed. 8th ed. Boston: Little Brown, 1870.

Story, Joseph. *Commentaries on the Law of Bills of Exchange.* Edmund Hatch Bennett, ed. 4th ed. Boston: Little Brown, 1860.

Story, Joseph. *Commentaries on the Law of Partnership.* John Chipman Gray Jr., ed. 6th ed. Boston: Little Brown, 1868.

Story, Joseph. *Commentaries on the Law of Promissory Notes.* 6th ed. Boston: Little Brown, 1868.

Story, William W. *A Treatise on the Law of Contracts.* 2 vols. Boston: Little Brown, 1874.

Story, William W. *A Treatise on the Law of Sales of Personal Property.* Boston: Little Brown, 1853.

Strong, John W.; et al. *McCormick on Evidence.* 5th ed. St. Paul: West, 1999. (See also McCormick.)

Stowell, Ellery C. *International Law: A Restatement of Principles in Conformity with Actual Practice.* N.Y.: Henry Holt & Co., 1931.

Stumberg, George Wilfred. *Principles of Conflict of Laws.* 2d ed. Brooklyn: Foundation Press, 1951.

Sturgis, Alice. *The Standard Code of Parliamentary Procedure.* 4th ed. Wilmington, Del.: American Inst. of Parliamentarians, 2001.

Sullivan, Francis Stoughton. *An Historical Treatise on the Feudal Law, and the Constitution and Laws of England.* London: J. Johnson, 1772.

Sullivan, Lawrence A. *Handbook of the Law of Antitrust.* St. Paul: West, 1977.

Sullivan, Lawrence A.; and Warren S. Grimes. *The Law of Antitrust: An Integrated Handbook.* St. Paul: West, 2000.

Summers, Robert S. (ed.). *Essays in Legal Philosophy.* Berkeley: Univ. of California Press, 1968.

Summers, Robert S. (ed.). *More Essays in Legal Philosophy.* Berkeley: Univ. of California Press, 1971.

Sumner, W.G. *Folkways.* Boston: Ginn, 1907.

Sutherland, Donald W. *The Assize of Novel Disseisin.* Oxford: Clarendon Press, 1973.

Svarlien, Oscar. *An Introduction to the Law of Nations.* N.Y.: McGraw-Hill, 1955.

Swartz, Matt; and Daniel Lee. *The Corporate, Securities, and M&A Lawyer's Job: A Survival Guide.* Chicago: ABA, 2007.

Taft, William Howard. *Ethics in Service.* New Haven: Yale Univ. Press, 1915.

Taswell-Langmead, Thomas Pitt. *English Constitutional History: From the Teutonic Conquest to the Present Time.* Theodore F.T. Plucknett, ed. 11th ed. London: Sweet & Maxwell, 1960.

Taylor, Benjamin J.; and Fred Whitney. *Labor Relations Law.* Englewood Cliffs, N.J.: Prentice-Hall, 1971.

Taylor, Hannis. *The Science of Jurisprudence.* N.Y.: Macmillan, 1908.

Tellegen-Couperus, Olga. *A Short History of Roman Law.* London: Routledge, 1993.

Thayer, James B. *A Preliminary Treatise on Evidence at the Common Law.* Boston: Little Brown, 1898.

Thomas, Ann Van Wynen; and A.J. Thomas Jr. *The Concept of Aggression in International Law.* Dallas: Southern Methodist Univ. Press, 1972.

Thompson, Seymour D. *A Treatise on the Liability of Stockholders in Corporations*. St. Louis: F.H. Thomas & Co., 1879.

Thoreau, Henry David. *Journal of Henry D. Thoreau*. 2 vols. Bradford Torrey & Francis H. Allen, eds. N.Y.: Dover, 1962.

Thornton, G.C. *Legislative Drafting*. 4th ed. London: Butterworths, 1996.

Thornton, W.W. *A Treatise on the Law Relating to Gifts and Advancements*. Philadelphia: T. & J.W. Johnson & Co., 1893.

Thorpe, Francis Newton. *The Essentials of American Constitutional Law*. N.Y.: G.P. Putnam's Sons, 1917.

Tidmarsh, Jay; and Roger H. Transgrud. *Complex Litigation*. N.Y.: Foundation Press, 2002.

Tiersma, Peter M. *Parchment, Paper, Pixels: Law and the Technologies of Communication*. Chicago: Univ. of Chicago Press, 2010.

Tiersma, Peter M.; and Lawrence B. Solan (eds.). *The Oxford Handbook of Language and Law*. Oxford: Oxford Univ. Press, 2012.

Tiffany, Francis B. *Death by Wrongful Act*. St. Paul: West, 1893.

Tiffany, Francis B. *Handbook of the Law of Banks and Banking*. St. Paul: West, 1912.

Tiffany, Francis B. *Handbook on the Law of Principal and Agent*. Richard R.B. Powell, ed. 2d ed. St. Paul: West, 1924.

Tiffany, Herbert Thorndike. *A Treatise on the Modern Law of Real Property*. Carl Zollmann, ed. Abridged ed. Chicago: Callagahan & Co., 1940.

Tiffany, Joel. *A Treatise on Government and Constitutional Law*. Albany, N.Y.: W.C. Little, 1867.

Tigar, Michael E. *Federal Appeals: Jurisdiction and Practice*. 2d ed. Colorado Springs: Shepard's, 1993.

Torcia, Charles E. *Wharton's Criminal Law*. 4 vols. 15th ed. Deerfield, Ill.: Clark Boardman Callaghan & Co., 1993.

Townes, John C. *General Principles of the Law of Torts*. Austin, Tex.: Austin Printing Co., 1907.

Townes, John C. *Studies in American Elementary Law*. Chicago: T.H. Flood & Co., 1911.

Trayner, John. *Trayner's Latin Maxims*. 4th ed. Edinburgh: William Green, 1894.

Treitel, G.H. *The Law of Contract*. 8th ed. London: Sweet & Maxwell, 1991.

Tribe, Laurence H. *American Constitutional Law*. Mineola, N.Y.: Foundation Press, 1978. Also: Vol. 1. 3d ed. N.Y.: Foundation Press, 2000.

Tribe, Laurence H. *Constitutional Choices*. Cambridge, Mass.: Harvard Univ. Press, 1985.

Turner, J.W. Cecil. *Kenny's Outlines of Criminal Law*. 16th ed. Cambridge: Cambridge Univ. Press, 1952.

Tyler, Ransom H. *A Treatise on the Remedy by Ejectment and the Law of Adverse Enjoyment in the United States*. Albany, N.Y.: William Gould & Son, 1870.

Ullmann, Walter. *The Medieval Idea of Law*. N.Y.: Barnes & Noble, 1969.

Underhill, H.C. *A Treatise on the Law of Landlord and Tenant*. 2 vols. Chicago: T.H. Flood & Co., 1909.

Underhill, H.C. *A Treatise on the Law of Wills*. 2 vols. Chicago: T.H. Flood & Co., 1900.

U.S. Office of Personnel Management. *Alternative Dispute Resolution: A Resource Guide*. Washington, D.C.: U.S. Office of Pers. Mgmt., 2001.

U.S. War Dep't. *A Manual for Courts-Martial*. Washington, D.C.: GPO, 1920.

Veasey, E. Norman; and Christine T. Di Guglielmo. *Indispensable Counsel*. Oxford: Oxford Univ. Press, 2012.

Verplanck, Gulian C. *An Essay on the Doctrine of Contracts*. N.Y.: G. & C. Carvill, 1825.

Vining, Joseph. *Legal Identity*. New Haven: Yale, 1978.

Vinogradoff, Paul. *Common Sense in Law*. H.G. Hanbury, ed. 2d ed. London: Oxford Univ. Press, 1946.

Vinogradoff, Paul. *Roman Law in Medieval Europe* [1909]. Cambridge: Speculum Historiale, 1968.

Vinogradoff, Paul. *Villainage in England*. Oxford: Clarendon Press, 1892.

Von Clausewitz, Carl. *On War* [1818]. Michael Howard & Peter Paret, trans. N.Y.: Knopf, 1993.

Voorhees, Harvey Cortlandt. *The Law of Arrest in Civil and Criminal Actions*. 2d ed. Boston: Little Brown, 1915.

Waddams, S.M. *The Law of Damages*. 3d ed. Toronto: Canada Law Book, 1997.

Wade, John. *The Cabinet Lawyer*. 14th ed. London: Simpkin, Marshall & Co., 1847.

Wade, William P. *A Treatise on the Operation and Construction of Retroactive Laws*. St. Louis: F.H. Thomas & Co., 1880.

Wadlington, Walter; and Raymond C. O'Brien. *Family Law in Perspective*. N.Y.: Foundation Press, 2001.

Walker, David M. *A Legal History of Scotland*. 7 vols. Edinburgh: W. Green/T. & T. Clark/Butterworths/LexisNexis UK, 1988–2004.

Walker, David M. *The Oxford Companion to Law*. Oxford: Clarendon Press, 1980.

Walker, David M. *Principles of Scottish Private Law*. 4 vols. 4th ed. Oxford: Clarendon Press, 1988.

Walker, David M. *The Scottish Legal System*. 6th ed. Edinburgh: W. Green/Sweet & Maxwell, 1992.

Walker, Thomas Alfred. *The Science of International Law*. London: C.J. Clay & Sons, 1893.

Walker, Timothy. *Introduction to American Law*. Clement Bates, ed. 10th ed. Boston: Little Brown, 1895.

Walsh, William F. *Outlines of the History of English and American Law*. N.Y.: New York Univ. Press, 1924.

Walsh, William F. *A Treatise on Equity*. Chicago: Callaghan & Co., 1930.

Wambaugh, Eugene. *The Study of Cases*. 2d ed. Boston: Little Brown, 1894.

Ware, Stephen J. *Alternative Dispute Resolution*. St. Paul: West, 2001.

Warren, Edward H. *The Rights of Margin Customers Against Wrongdoing Stockbrokers*. Norwood, Mass.: Plimpton Press, 1941.

Warren, Samuel. *A Popular and Practical Introduction to Law Studies*. Isaac Grant Thompson, ed. Albany, N.Y.: John D. Parsons, 1870.

Warvelle, George W. *A Treatise on the Principles and Practice of the Action of Ejectment*. Chicago: T.H. Flood & Co., 1905.

Washburn, Emory. *Lectures on the Study and Practice of the Law*. Boston: Little Brown, 1874.

Washburn, Emory. *A Treatise on the American Law of Real Property*. 3 vols. 4th ed. Boston: Little Brown, 1876.

Waterman, Thomas W. *A Treatise on the Law of Set-Off, Recoupment, and Counter Claim*. 2d ed. N.Y.: Baker Voorhis, 1872.

Waters, D.W.M. *The Constructive Trust*. London: Univ. of London, 1964.

Watson, Alan. *Ancient Law and Modern Understanding*. Athens, Ga.: Univ. of Georgia Press, 1998.

Watson, Alan. *Legal Origins and Legal Change*. London: Hambledon Press, 1991.

Watson, George. *Bell's Dictionary and Digest of the Law of Scotland*. 3d ed. Edinburgh: Bell & Bradfute, 1882.

Webb, James Avery. *A Treatise on the Law of Usury*. St. Louis: F.H. Thomas Law Book Co., 1899.

Webster, Daniel. *The Papers of Daniel Webster*. 14 vols. Charles M Wiltse, ed. Hanover, N.H.: Univ. Press of New England, 1974–1989.

Weeks, Edward P. *A Treatise on the Law of Depositions*. San Francisco: Sumner Whitney & Co., 1880.

Weintraub, Russell J. *Commentary on the Conflict of Laws*. 4th ed. N.Y.: Foundation Press, 2001.

Weiss, Samuel. *How to Try a Case*. N.Y.: Baker Voorhis, 1930.

Wentworth, Thomas. *The Office and Duty of Executors*. Henry Jeremy & E.D. Ingraham, eds. 1st Am. ed. fr. 14th London ed. Philadelphia: P.H. Nicklin & T. Johnson, 1832.

Wharton, Francis. *A Treatise on the Law of Evidence in Criminal Issues*. 2 vols. O.N. Hilton, ed. 10th ed. Rochester, N.Y.: Lawyers Co-operative, 1912.

Wharton, J.J.S. *Wharton's Law Lexicon*. Ivan Horniman, ed. 13th ed. London: Sevens & Sons, 1925.

White, Alan R. *Grounds of Liability*. Oxford: Clarendon Press, 1985.

White, Edward J. *Legal Antiquities*. St. Louis: F.H. Thomas, 1913.

White, G. Edward. *Law in American History: From the Colonial Years Through the Civil War*. Oxford: Univ. Press, 2012. [Projected to be a three-volume set.]

White, James J.; and Robert S. Summers. *Uniform Commercial Code*. 4 vols. 4th ed. St. Paul: West, 1995.

Whitebread, Charles H. *Criminal Procedure*. Mineola, N.Y.: Foundation Press, 1980.

Wiener, Frederick Bernays. *A Practical Manual of Martial Law*. Harrisburg, Pa.: Military Service Pub. Co., 1940.

Wigmore, John Henry. *Evidence in Trials at Common Law*. 11 vols. James H. Chadbourn et al., eds. 4th rev. ed. Boston: Little Brown, 1961–present.

Wigmore, John Henry. *Problems of Law*. N.Y.: Charles Scribner's Sons, 1920.

Wigmore, John Henry. *The Science of Judicial Proof*. 3d ed. Boston: Little Brown, 1937.

Wigmore, John Henry. *A Students' Textbook of the Law of Evidence*. Brooklyn: Foundation Press, 1935.

Wilhelm, Thomas. *A Military Dictionary and Gazetteer*. Rev. ed. Philadelphia: L.R. Hamersly & Co., 1881.

Willard, John. *A Treatise on Equity Jurisprudence*. 2d ed. Platt Potter, ed. N.Y.: Banks & Bros., 1879.

Williams, Glanville L. *Criminal Law: The General Part*. 2d ed. London: Stevens, 1961.

Williams, Glanville L. *Joint Obligations*. London: Butterworth & Co., 1949.

Williams, Glanville L. *Learning the Law*. 11th ed. London: Wm. Grant & Sons, 1982.

Williams, Glanville L. *The Proof of Guilt*. 3d ed. London: Stevens & Sons, 1963.

Williams, Glanville L. *The Sanctity of Life and the Criminal Law*. N.Y.: Knopf, 1957.

Williams, Glanville L. *Textbook of Criminal Law*. London: Stevens, 1978.

Williams, Joshua. *Principles of the Law of Personal Property*. 11th ed. London: Sweet, 1881.

Williams, Vergil L. *Dictionary of American Penology*. Rev. ed. Westport, Conn.: Greenwood Press, 1996.

Williston, Samuel. *The Law Governing Sales of Goods*. 4 vols. 3d ed. N.Y.: Baker Voorhis, 1948.

Williston, Samuel. *A Treatise on the Law of Contracts*. 18 vols. Walter H.E. Jaeger, ed. 3d ed. Mount Kisco, N.Y.: Baker Voorhis, 1957. Also: 31 vols. Richard A. Lord, ed. 4th ed. St. Paul: West, 2012.

Wills, William. *An Essay on the Principles of Circumstantial Evidence*. 1st Am. ed. fr. 3d London ed. Philadelphia: T. & J.W. Johnson, 1852.

Wilson, James. *Collected Works of James Wilson*. 2 vols. Kermit L. Hall & Mark David Hall, eds. Indianapolis: Liberty Fund, 2007.

Wiltsie, Charles Hastings. *A Treatise on the Law and Practice of Foreclosing Mortgages on Real Property.* Rochester, N.Y.: Williamson Law Book Co., 1893.

Windeyer, W.J.V. *Lectures on Legal History.* 2d ed. Sydney: Law Book Co., 1949.

Winfield, Percy H. *The Chief Sources of English Legal History.* Cambridge, Mass.: Harvard Univ. Press, 1925.

Winfield, Percy H. *A Textbook of the Law of Tort.* 5th ed. London: Sweet & Maxwell, 1950.

Winternitz, Ingrid. *Electronic Publishing Agreements.* Oxford: Oxford Univ. Press, 2000.

Witt, Elder (ed.). *Congressional Quarterly's Guide to the U.S. Supreme Court.* Washington, D.C.: Congressional Quarterly Inc., 1979.

Wolfe, Christopher. *The Rise of Modern Judicial Review: From Constitutional Interpretation to Judge-Made Law.* N.Y.: Basic Books, 1986.

Wolff, Hans Julius. *Roman Law: An Historical Introduction.* Norman, Okla.: Univ. of Oklahoma Press, 1951.

Wolfrum, Rüdiger (ed.). *The Max Planck Encyclopedia of Public International Law.* 10 vols. Oxford: Oxford Univ. Press, 2012.

Wood, Gordon S. *The Creation of the American Republic, 1776–1787.* Chapel Hill: Univ. of North Carolina Press, 1969.

Wood, H.G. *A Treatise on the Law of Master and Servant.* 2d ed. Albany, N.Y.: J.D. Parsons Jr., 1886.

Woodward, Frederic Campbell. *The Law of Quasi Contracts.* Boston: Little Brown, 1913.

Woolsey, Theodore D. *Introduction to the Study of International Law.* 5th ed. N.Y.: Charles Scribner's Sons, 1878.

Wright, Charles Alan. *The Law of Federal Courts.* 5th ed. St. Paul: West, 1994.

Wright, Charles Alan; et al. *Federal Practice and Procedure.* 55 vols. St. Paul: West, 1978–2014.

Yale Law School Faculty. *Two Centuries' Growth of American Law: 1701–1901.* N.Y.: Charles Scribner's Sons, 1901.

Yiannopoulos, A.N. *Property: The Law of Things — Real Rights — Real Actions.* 4th ed. St. Paul: West, 2001.

Young, Nigel J. (ed.). *The Oxford International Encyclopedia of Peace.* 4 vols. Oxford: Oxford Univ. Press, 2010.

Zander, Michael. *Lawyers and the Public Interest.* London: Weidenfeld & Nicolson, 1968.

Zelermyer, William. *Legal Reasoning.* Englewood Cliffs, N.J.: Prentice-Hall, 1960.